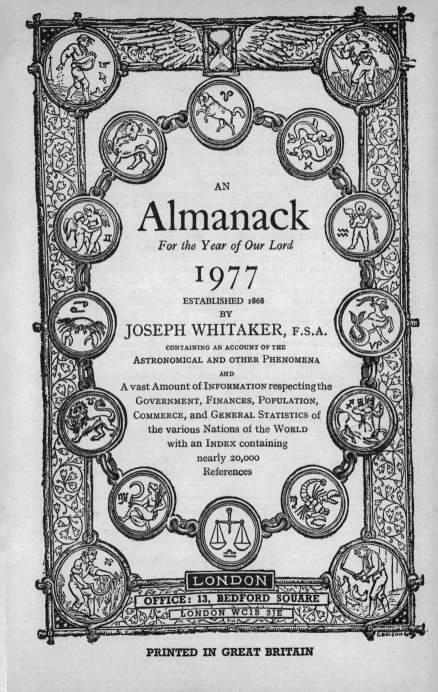

AN

Almanack

For the Year of Our Lord

1977

ESTABLISHED 1868

BY

JOSEPH WHITAKER, F.S.A.

CONTAINING AN ACCOUNT OF THE

ASTRONOMICAL AND OTHER PHENOMENA

AND

A vast Amount of INFORMATION respecting the
GOVERNMENT, FINANCES, POPULATION,
COMMERCE, and GENERAL STATISTICS of
the various Nations of the WORLD
with an INDEX containing
nearly 20,000
References

LONDON

OFFICE: 13, BEDFORD SQUARE
LONDON WC1B 3JE

PRINTED IN GREAT BRITAIN

PREFACE TO THE 109TH ANNUAL VOLUME
(1977)

In the 109th volume of " WHITAKER ", the Editor, despite increasing pressure on space, has endeavoured to preserve as many as possible of the traditional features of the Almanack, while introducing matters of particular topical interest, to which he would call attention.

The changes consequent upon Sir Harold Wilson's resignation as Prime Minister, and his succession by Mr. Callaghan, are noted, and Mr. Callaghan's subsequent reconstruction of his Ministry in September is fully recorded, with other late information, in the section of " Occurrences during Printing ".

The Queen crossed the Atlantic during the summer to attend ceremonies connected with the bicentenary of American independence and to open the Olympic Games in Montreal. Both these events are dealt with in the Almanack—the bicentenary by a special article, and the Olympic Games by a number of illustrations and a complete list of gold medallists, both at Montreal and in the winter games at Innsbruck.

Another Topic of the Year, about which an authoritative article has been supplied, has been the drought of 1976. The summer was almost unprecedented for long, dry weather, though it is interesting to observe that the very first edition of the Almanack recorded that the previous summer, 1868, had been one of almost tropical heat.

The annual article on Science, Discovery and Invention has been somewhat altered in concept, and has been renamed Science, Discovery and the Environment. The intention has been to widen the scope of topical information with which it deals, and also to give additional news of astronomy, a subject with which the Almanack has always been closely connected. The most important astronomical feature of the year has been the landings on Mars, which have been fully described, and of which there is an illustration.

As an adjunct to the section detailing the recent local government changes, a map of Scotland, showing the newly designated areas, has been supplied.

In such a wonderful summer, cricket flourished exceedingly, and large crowds were attracted to the Test Matches. The West Indies' successful retention of the Wisden Trophy is suitably marked among the illustrations.

Each year, constitutional advances in different parts of the world take place. On this occasion, within the Commonwealth, the independence of the Seychelles and Papua New Guinea is recorded, and the Gilbert and Ellice Islands have become two separate countries under the names of the Gilbert Islands and Tuvalu.

The Editor wishes yet again to express his gratitude to his many correspondents. The help and information which they continue so willingly to give is of the greatest value.

13 BEDFORD SQUARE, W.C.1.   Telephone: 01-636 4748
    October, 1976   Telegrams: " Whitmanack, London, W.C.1."

Note—" WHITAKER " for 1977 is published in three editions:

Library Edition, Leather Binding with 16 Coloured Maps, 1,220 pages—£5·75 *net*.
(SBN 85021 093 3)

Complete Edition, Red and Green Cloth Cover, 1,220 pages—£4·50 *net*.
(SBN 85021 091 7)

Shorter Edition, Orange Paper Cover, 692 pages—£2·10 *net*.
(SBN 85021 092 5)

MADE AND PRINTED IN GREAT BRITAIN BY WILLIAM CLOWES & SONS, LIMITED
LONDON, BECCLES AND COLCHESTER

TABLE OF CONTENTS

TAKE UP PELMANISM
For Courage and Clear-Thinking

The Grasshopper Mind

YOU know the people with "Grasshopper Minds" as well as you know yourself. Their minds nibble at every thing and master nothing.

At home in the evening they tune in the radio or television—tire of it—then glance through a magazine—can't get interested. Finally, unable to concentrate on anything, they either go to the pictures or fall asleep in the chair. At their work they always take up the easiest job first, put it down when it gets hard and start something else. Jump from one thing to another all the time.

There are thousands of these people with "Grasshopper Minds" in the world. In fact they are the very people who do the world's most tiresome tasks—and get but a pittance for their work. They do the world's clerical work and the routine drudgery.

If you have a "Grasshopper Mind" you know that this is true. Even the blazing sun can't burn a hole in a piece of tissue-paper unless its rays are focused and concentrated on one spot! A mind that balks at sticking to one thing for more than a few minutes surely cannot be depended upon to get you anywhere in your years of life!

What Can You Do About It?

Take up Pelmanism now! A course of Pelmanism brings out the mind's latent powers and develops them to the highest point of efficiency. It develops strong, positive, vital qualities such as Optimism, Concentration, and Reliability, all qualities of the utmost value in any walk of life.

What Pelmanism Does

Pelmanism enables you to overcome defects and failings. Amongst those most often met with are the following:

Inertia	Pessimism
Timidity	Forgetfulness
Indecision	Indefiniteness
Depression	Procrastination
Weakness of Will	Mind-Wandering

But Pelmanism does more than eliminate failings. It awakens dormant faculties. It develops powers you never thought you possessed. It strengthens mental attributes which are valuable in every career and every aspect of living. It develops:—

—Optimism	—Observation
—Perception	—Initiative
—Judgment	—Originality
—Self-Control	—Reliability
—Concentration	—Will-Power
—Mental Energy	—Personality
—Self-Confidence	—Resourcefulness
—Reliable Memory	—Presence of Mind

Pelmanists are not left to make the applications themselves. An experienced and sympathetic instructional staff shows them, in exact detail, how to apply the principles of Pelmanism to their own circumstances and aspirations. Thus every Pelman Course is an individual Course.

Remember—Everything you do is preceded by your attitude of mind

The general effect of the training is to induce an attitude of mind and a personal efficiency favourable to the happy management of life.

Send for the Free Book

Write to-day for a free copy of "*The Science of Success.*" This will give you full details of the Course, which is private, individual, to each Pelmanist, and carried out by correspondence, in your spare time, at moderate fees payable—if you like—by instalments.

PELMAN INSTITUTE
200 Tudor House
9 Chiswick High Rd.,
London W4 2ND
Founded in 1897

HOW TO LEARN LANGUAGES

The **Pelman Languages Institute** teaches **French, German, Spanish,** and **Italian** without translation. Write for particulars of the language that interests you, which will be sent to you free.

Pelman Languages Institute,
200 Tudor House, 9 Chiswick High Rd.,
London W4 2ND

AA

AI

Pages 693–1220 are omitted from the Shorter Edition

THE STAR AND GARTER HOME

for Disabled Sailors, Soldiers and Airmen
Richmond, Surrey

NEEDS HELP

by donation or legacy to maintain a true home with medical and nursing care for up to 200 disabled ex-servicemen of all ages and from all parts of the British Isles.

(The Home, founded in 1916, is an independent registered charity. Further information available from the Secretary.   Telephone 01-940 3314.)

Pages 693–1220 *are omitted from the* Shorter Edition

Pages 693–1220 are omitted from the Shorter Edition

Pages 693–1220 are omitted from the Shorter Edition

On average, people leave us £10,000 a month. This is why we feel entitled to ask for more.

We have some 250 patients of all ages, all suffering from illnesses which are as yet, incurable.

It costs us a great deal of money to run our Hospital and its residential annexe at Brighton. A lot of this comes from our patients (they all pay something), their sponsors, their relatives and our investments.

The balance must come from voluntary contributions. And that includes legacies.

This is why we feel privileged to ask you to consider leaving us some money.

Research.

We refuse to accept that disabled people cannot be helped or that illnesses at present incurable will not one day be cured.

For this reason we have made special provision for research in the Development Trust for the Young Disabled. Research to help the disabled everywhere. *Research that one day will cure the incurable.*

Today our own patients may be incurable, but they refuse just to sit around. We help them lead as full a life as possible, and with us, many make remarkable progress.

Our New Wing, which is being built for younger disabled patients, will have the sort of accommodation other, luckier, young people have.

And so, we are asking you to remember us in your will. Up to £100,000 left to a charity is free of tax. Your estate and our patients could both benefit. And your money would be used for a very *hopeful* cause.

Appeals Secretary:
Air Commodore D. F. Rixson, OBE., DFC., AFC.

**The Royal Hospital and Home for Incurables
(Putney and Brighton),
West Hill, Putney, London SW15 3SW.**

Pages 693–1220 *are omitted from the* Shorter Edition

Sharon is happy - and independent *she wasn't always*

Sharon has had malformed limbs since birth, leaving her with very little use of her arms – a daunting prospect for a young girl. She was educated at a Special School, and then – when she was sixteen – Queen Elizabeth's Foundation for the Disabled took over, trained her and gave her a job at Dorincourt, where she is an expert tile painter, holding the brush in her mouth. She operates her own specially adapted typewriter and swims every week at the Leatherhead Leisure Centre. With special aids to help her, she is now almost totally independent. And Sharon is happy – because she knows she is leading a useful life.

Dorincourt is one of four centres run by Queen Elizabeth's Foundation: the other three provide assessment and further education for school leavers; vocational training for employment in industry and commerce; and a very special holiday and convalescent home. Nearly 1,000 disabled people look to the Foundation for help each year.

The cost of our developing programme is very great, and we urgently want to be able to help even more people.

THAT IS WHY YOUR HELP WILL MEAN SO MUCH

Queen Elizabeth's Training College. Banstead Place. Dorincourt. Lulworth Court.

Queen Elizabeth's Foundation for the Disabled

6 Leatherhead Court, Leatherhead, Surrey KT22 OBN. Patron: Her Majesty Queen Elizabeth The Queen Mother.

Pages 693–1220 *are omitted from the* Shorter Edition

Pearson's Fresh Air Fund

Patron: HER MAJESTY THE QUEEN

Please help some of the thousands of needy or neglected children in Britain to be as happy as these.

£3 will ensure a week's holiday for a child in the country or at the seaside

PLEASE ALSO REMEMBER CHILDREN IN YOUR WILL

Donations to:

112 REGENCY STREET, LONDON, SW1P 4AX

We need much more than luck to save this child…

Not much wrong with him, you'd say.

A beautiful child.

But in his arms, his legs, everywhere in his body, muscular dystrophy is taking its ever-growing toll.

Last year he was unable to run.

This year he has difficulty in standing.

All too soon he will be so weakened that even the most simple of infections may prove fatal.

This is Muscular Dystrophy. As yet there is no answer. And without continuous research there never will be.

THE ANSWER MUST BE FOUND.

Please help us to help the utterly helpless.

Muscular Dystrophy Group OF GREAT BRITAIN

Nattrass House, 35 Macaulay Road, London SW4 0QP Tel: 01-720 8055

Registered Charity No. 205395

Pages 693–1220 are omitted from the Shorter Edition

Pages 693–1220 *are omitted from the* Shorter Edition

PEOPLE HAVE PROBLEMS,

and seamen aren't unique because they have problems too. But when you're away from home for nine months at a time, problems can sometimes snowball. And when they get too much to handle, that's where we come in. We can't give you case histories for obvious reasons, but our chaplains are experienced counsellors, and seamen come to us because they know we care. We care because we're Christians called to serve – do you care enough to help us?

**The Missions to Seamen,
St. Michael Paternoster Royal,
College Hill, London EC4R 2RL**

Pages 693–1220 are omitted from the Shorter Edition

Pages 693–1220 *are omitted from the* Shorter Edition

Pages 693–1220 are omitted from the Shorter Edition

Pages 693–1220 are omitted from the Shorter Edition

Pages 693–1220 are omitted from the Shorter Edition

MONEY DOES GOOD AT GUY'S

Pages 693–1220 *are omitted from the* Shorter Edition

'In gratitude for a lifetime's sight.'

GREATER LONDON FUND FOR THE BLIND

Registered in accordance with the National Assistance Act 1948 and The Charities Act 1960.

2 L WYNDHAM PLACE, LONDON, W1. Tel: 01-262 0191.
Patron: H.M. Queen Elizabeth The Queen Mother
President: The Right Hon. The Lord Mayor of London.

depends on LEGACIES to help its work. Quarterly allocations to 16 member Societies ensure that money is effectively applied to a comprehensive range of services to over 16,500 blind and partially-sighted people in the area.

Pages 693–1220 are omitted from the Shorter *Edition*

Pages 693–1220 are omitted from the Shorter Edition

CENTRAL COUNCIL FOR THE DISABLED

(Formerly Central Council for the Care of Cripples)

34 ECCLESTON SQUARE, LONDON, SWIV IPE

TEL: 01–821–1871

The Council is unique in its service to the disabled. As an organisation which is concerned with every aspect of disability rather than with the individual problems of one crippling disease, it is the national coordinating body for all those who work for disabled people.

Disablement may mean crippling pain. It certainly means loss of mobility, a special housing need, employment problems, economic hardship, fewer holidays, being shut out from cinema, church, club, pub, toilet. Disablement often means loneliness, deprivation and a loss of human dignity. There is a lot of it about.

For more than fifty years the Central Council for the Disabled has sought to improve the living conditions and environment of all physically disabled people. Dependent on voluntary contributions, your support could enable us to do so much more.

Pages 693–1220 are omitted from the Shorter Edition

Pages 693-1220 are omitted from the Shorter Edition

32

WE, THE LIMBLESS, LOOK TO YOU FOR HELP

We come from both world wars. We come from Kenya, Malaya, Aden, Cyprus . . . and from Ulster. From keeping the peace no less than from war we limbless look to you for help.
And you *can* help, by helping our Association. BLESMA (the British Limbless Ex-Service Men's Association) looks after the limbless from all the Services. It helps, with advice and encouragement, to overcome the shock of losing arms, or legs or an eye. It sees that red-tape does not stand in the way of the right entitlement to pension. And, for the severely handicapped and the elderly, it provides Residential Homes where they can live in peace and dignity.

Help BLESMA, please. We need money desperately. And, we promise you, not a penny of it will be wasted.

Donations and information:
Major The Earl of Ancaster, KCVO, TD
Midland Bank Limited, 60 West
Smithfield, London EC1A 9DX

**'GIVE TO THOSE
WHO GAVE — PLEASE'**

British Limbless Ex-Service Men's Association

THE BRITISH POLIO FELLOWSHIP

(The Infantile Paralysis Fellowship, registered as a charity in accordance with the National Assistance Act 1948)

THE NATIONAL VOLUNTARY ORGANISATION FOR THE POLIO DISABLED
(Patron: Lavinia, Duchess of Norfolk, C.B.E.)

- Founded in 1939, the Fellowship has helped thousands of polio victims to live a fuller life and to cope with their disabilities.

- Polio is no respecter of persons; it has stricken the physically strong of all age groups and from different walks of life.

- The Fellowship's work in caring for all polio victims knows no barriers and helps all who have suffered from polio.

- £215,000 spent on welfare grants, aids, residential care, etc., during the 1974/75 financial year Can you help—by donation? covenanted gift? or by legacy? Please write to:

**BELL CLOSE, WEST END ROAD, RUISLIP, MIDDX.
HA4 6LP**
Telephone: Ruislip 75515

Pages 693–1220 are omitted from the Shorter Edition

British Heart Foundation Appeal

Heart Survival Through Research

Coronary thrombosis, stroke, blood pressure and heart diseases of infants
are major subjects for research programmes receiving financial
support from the British Heart Foundation.
Over 590 important research projects have been undertaken. The cost is enormous,
but the work is vital. Can you, will you help?

● *Remember us in your will*   ● *Send a donation*   ● *Make an 'In Memoriam' gift.*

BRITISH HEART FOUNDATION APPEAL

HEAD OFFICE **Dept. WA**, 57 Gloucester Place, London W1H 4DH
SCOTTISH OFFICES 16A Chester Street, Edinburgh EH3 7RA
30 Gordon Street, Glasgow G1 3PU
WELSH OFFICE Emporium Buildings, Station Crescent, Llandrindod Wells, Powys

Pages 693–1220 *are omitted from the* Shorter Edition

Pages 693–1220 are omitted from the Shorter Edition

Pages 693–1220 *are omitted from the* Shorter Edition

APOSTLESHIP OF THE SEA

**FOUNDED IN 1920 FOR SPIRITUAL AND MATERIAL CARE OF SEA-
FARERS AND THEIR FAMILIES REGARDLESS OF RACE OR CREED**

NATIONAL HEADQUARTERS:
          ANCHOR HOUSE, 81 BARKING ROAD, LONDON E16 4HB
          TEL: 01-476 6062

FORM OF BEQUEST

I GIVE AND BEQUEATH TO THE HON. TREASURER FOR THE TIME BEING
OF THE APOSTLESHIP OF THE SEA (Episcopal Commission for England and
Wales) ANCHOR HOUSE, LONDON E16 4HB

....

....£   :   FREE OF DUTY
TO BE PAYABLE PRIMARILY OUT OF MY PERSONAL ESTATE, AND I
DECLARE THAT THE RECEIPT OF THE HON. TREASURER FOR THE TIME
BEING SHALL BE A SUFFICIENT DISCHARGE FOR THE SAME.

CODICILS AS WELL AS WILLS MUST BEAR THE SIGNATURE OF TWO
WITNESSES.

Pages 693–1220 are omitted from the Shorter Edition

Pages 693–1220 are omitted from the Shorter Edition

Pages 693–1220 are omitted from the Shorter Edition

Pages 693–1220 *are omitted from the* Shorter Edition

Pages 693–1220 *are omitted from the* Shorter Edition

Pages 693–1220 *are omitted from the* Shorter Edition

Pages 693–1220 are omitted from the Shorter Edition

Pages 693–1220 *are omitted from the* Shorter Edition

Pages 693–1220 are omitted from the Shorter Edition

Pages 693-1220 *are omitted from the* Shorter Edition

Pages 693–1220 are omitted from the Shorter Edition

Pages 693–1220 are omitted from the Shorter Edition

Pages 693–1220 *are omitted from the* Shorter Edition

Pages 693–1220 are omitted from the Shorter Edition

Pages 693–1220 are omitted from the Shorter Edition

Pages 693–1220 are omitted from the **Shorter** *Edition*

Pages 693–1220 are omitted from the Shorter Edition

Pages 693–1220 are omitted from the Shorter Edition

Pages 693–1220 *are omitted from the* Shorter Edition

Pages 693–1220 are omitted from the Shorter Edition

Pages 693–1220 are omitted from the **Shorter Edition**

Pages 693–1220 are omitted from the Shorter Edition

Pages 693–1220 are omitted from the Shorter Edition

Pages 693–1220 are omitted from the Shorter Edition

Pages 693–1220 are omitted from the Shorter Edition

Pages 693–1220 *are omitted from the* Shorter Edition

Pages 693–1220 *are omitted from the* Shorter Edition

Pages 693–1220 *are omitted from the* Shorter Edition

Pages 693–1220 *are omitted from the* Shorter Edition

Pages 693–1220 are omitted from the Shorter Edition

Pages 693–1220 are omitted from the Shorter Edition

OCCURRENCES DURING PRINTING

Home Affairs. Sept. 27. Labour Party Conference at Blackpool passed motion rejecting cuts in spending on social services and calling on all Labour-controlled councils to defy them.

Sept. 28. Mr. Healey postponed visit to Commonwealth Finance Ministers' meeting in Hong Kong as value of pound fell further. Mr. Norman Atkinson, leading left-winger, defeated Mr. Eric Varley in contest for Labour Party treasurership. At Labour Party Conference Mr. Callaghan said that Britain had lived far too long on borrowed time, borrowed money and borrowed ideas.

Sept. 29. Mr. Healey decided to apply to International Monetary Fund for loan of £2,300 million, the whole amount that might be available. Labour Party Conference passed resolutions calling for expansion of National Health Service, reversal of cuts in its spending and implementation of massive hospital-building programme, and also abolition of all prescription, ophthalmic and dental charges and nationalization of pharmaceutical industry.

Sept. 30. Labour Party Conference carried, by 3,314,000 to 526,000, proposal to nationalize leading banks and insurance companies.

Oct. 7. Bank of England raised minimum lending rate from 13 per cent. to 15 per cent. and called for further £700,000,000 of special deposits from banks. On following day, building societies raised mortgage rates to 12¼ per cent.

Oct. 8. Mr. Edward Short, deputy leader of Parliamentary Labour Party and M.P. for Newcastle Central, was appointed Chairman of Cable and Wireless (by-election pending).

Oct. 21. Mr. Michael Foot was elected deputy leader of the Labour Party with 166 votes against 128 for Mrs. Shirley Williams, the only other candidate.

Overseas. Sept. 24. Mr. Ian Smith said that Rhodesian Government accepted principle of two-year transition to Black majority rule and immediate establishment of multi-racial Council of State as interim government.

Sept. 26. Presidents of African States rejected Mr. Smith's proposals and called on Britain to convene immediate conference.

Oct. 4. Final figures in West German elections showed that Herr Schmidt's coalition Government had won 252 seats, against 244 for Christian Democrats, his majority being reduced from 46 to eight.

Oct. 6. Military *coup* in Thailand resulted in overthrow of Government and establishment of martial law.

Oct. 11. It was stated that Chiang Ching, widow of Mao Tse-Tung, had been arrested with three other radical members of Chinese Politbureau and charged with plotting a *coup d'état*: on following day it was reported that more radicals had been arrested.

Accidents. Sept. 20. Twelve men, mostly Royal Naval reservists, lost their lives when R.N.R. mine-sweeper *Fittleton* was in collision with frigate *Mermaid* during NATO exercise in North Sea.

Obituary. Sept. 21. Sir William Collins, publisher, aged 76. Oct. 6. Professor Gilbert Ryle, eminent philosopher, aged 76. Oct. 10. Most Rev. Mgr. Cyril Cowderoy, R.C. Archbishop of Southwark, aged 71. Lord Brecon, former Minister of State for Welsh affairs, aged 71. Oct. 14. Dame Edith Evans, D.B.E., distinguished actress, aged 88.

(Formed April 1976 and reconstructed Sept. 1976.)

THE CABINET

Prime Minister and First Lord of the Treasury, THE RT. HON. LEONARD JAMES CALLAGHAN, M.P., *born* March 27, 1912.

Secretary of State for Foreign and Commonwealth Affairs, The Rt. Hon. Charles Anthony Raven Crosland, M.P., *born* Aug. 29, 1918.

Chancellor of the Exchequer, The Rt. Hon. Denis Winston Healey, M.P., *born* Aug. 30, 1917.

Lord High Chancellor, The Rt. Hon. Lord Elwyn-Jones, C.H., *born* Oct. 24, 1909.

Secretary of State for the Home Department, The Rt. Hon. Merlyn Rees, M.P., *born* Dec. 18, 1920.

Secretary of State for Social Services, The Rt. Hon. David Hedley Ennals, M.P., *born* Aug. 19, 1922.

Secretary of State for Defence, The Rt. Hon. Frederick William Mulley, M.P., *born* July 3, 1918.

Secretary of State for Scotland, The Rt. Hon. Bruce Millan, M.P., *born* Oct. 5, 1927.

Secretary of State for Employment, The Rt. Hon. Albert Edward Booth, M.P., *born* May 28, 1928.

Secretary of State for Education and Science, The Rt. Hon. Shirley Vivien Teresa Brittain Williams, M.P., *born* July 27, 1930.

Secretary of State for Wales, The Rt. Hon. John Morris, M.P., *born* 1931.

Secretary of State for Trade, The Rt. Hon. Edmund Emanuel Dell, M.P., *born* Aug. 15, 1921.

Secretary of State for Industry, The Rt. Hon. Eric Graham Varley, M.P., *born* Aug. 11, 1932.

Secretary of State for the Environment, The Rt. Hon. Peter David Shore, M.P., *born* May 20, 1924.

Secretary of State for Northern Ireland, The Rt. Hon. Roy Mason, M.P., *born* April 18, 1924.

Secretary of State for Energy, The Rt. Hon. Anthony Neil Wedgwood Benn, M.P., *born* April 3, 1925.

Secretary of State for Prices and Consumer Protection and Paymaster-General, The Rt. Hon. Roy Sydney George Hattersley, *born* Dec. 28, 1932.

Secretary of State for Transport, The Rt. Hon. William Thomas Rodgers, M.P., *born* Oct. 28, 1928.

Lord President of the Council and Leader of the House of Commons, The Rt. Hon. Michael Mackintosh Foot, M.P. *born* July 23, 1913.

Lord Privy Seal and Leader of the House of Lords, The Rt. Hon. Lord Peart, *born* April 30, 1914.

Chancellor of the Duchy of Lancaster, The Rt. Hon. Norman Harold Lever, *born* Jan. 15, 1914.

Minister of Agriculture and Fisheries, The Rt. Hon. John Ernest Silkin, M.P., *born* March 18, 1923.

Minister for Overseas Development, The Rt. Hon. Reginald Ernest Prentice, M.P., *born* July 16, 1923.

Minister for Social Security, The Rt. Hon. Stanley Orme, M.P., *born* April 5, 1923.

MINISTERS NOT IN THE CABINET

Minister for Housing and Construction, The Rt. Hon. Reginald Yarnitz Freeson, M.P., *born* 1926.

Attorney-General, The Rt. Hon. Samuel Charles Silkin, Q.C., M.P., *born* 1918.

Lord Advocate, The Rt. Hon. Ronald King Murray, Q.C., M.P., *born* 1922.

Solicitor-General, Peter Kingsley Archer, Q.C., M.P., *born* 1926.

Solicitor-General for Scotland, The Lord McCluskey, Q.C., *born* 1929.

Chief Secretary to the Treasury, The Rt. Hon. Joel Barnett, M.P., *born* 1922.

Parliamentary Secretary to the Treasury, The Rt. Hon. Michael Francis Lovell Cocks, M.P., *born* 1929.

Financial Secretary to the Treasury, Robert Edward Sheldon, M.P., *born* 1923.

Ministers of State (Foreign and Commonwealth Office), The Lord Goronwy-Roberts, P.C., *born* 1913; Edward Rowlands, M.P., *born* 1940; David Anthony Llewelyn Owen, *born* 1938.

Ministers of State (Home Office), The Lord Harris of Greenwich, *born* 1930; Brynmor Thomas John, M.P., *born* 1934.

Ministers of State (Scottish Office), The Lord Kirkhill, *born* 1930; (James) Gregor Mackenzie, M.P., *born* 1916.

Minister of State (Health and Social Security), Roland Dunstan Moyle, M.P., *born* 1928.

Minister of State (Employment), Harold Walker, M.P., *born* 1927.

Minister of State (Defence), John William Gilbert, Ph.D., M.P., *born* 1927.

Ministers of State (Northern Ireland), John Dennis Concannon, M.P., *born* 1930; The Lord Melchett, *born* 1948.

Minister of State (Agriculture and Fisheries), Edward Stanley Bishop, M.P., *born* 1920.

Minister of State (Treasury), (David John) Denzil Davies, *born* 1938.

Minister of State (Privy Council Office), John Smith, M.P., *born* 1938.

Minister of State (Energy), (Jesse) Dickson Mabon, M.P., *born* 1925.

Minister of State (Environment), The Rt. Hon. Denis Herbert Howell, M.P., *born* 1923 (*Sport*).

Minister of State (Industry), Gerald Bernard Kaufman, M.P., *born* 1930; Alan John Williams, M.P., *born* 1930.

Minister of State (Civil Service Department), Charles Richard Morris, M.P., *born* 1926.

Ministers of State (Education and Science), The Lord Donaldson of Kingsbridge, *born* 1007; Gordon James Oakes, M.P., *born* 1931.

Minister of State (Prices and Consumer Protection), John Denis Fraser, M.P., *born* 1934.

PARLIAMENTARY UNDER SECRETARIES, ETC.

Agriculture and Fisheries, G. S. Strang, M.P.

Civil Service Department, J. D. Grant, M.P.

Defence, A. E. P. Duffy, M.P. (*Royal Navy*); R. C. Brown, M.P. (*Army*); A. J. Wellbeloved, M.P. (*Royal Air Force*).

Education and Science, Miss M. M. Jackson, M.P.

Employment, J. Golding, M.P.; J. Grant, M.P.

Energy, A. Eadie, M.P.; J. Cunningham, M.P.

Environment, The Baroness Birk; E. Armstrong, M.P.; K. Marks, M.P.; N. G. Barnett, M.P.

Foreign and Commonwealth Affairs, J. E. Armstrong, M.P.; D. E. T. Luard, M.P.

Health and Social Security, E. P. Deakins, M.P. (*Social Security*); A. Morris, M.P. (*Disabled*).

Home, The Hon. Shirley Summerskill, M.P.

Industry, L. J. Huckfield, M.P.,; G. R. Cryer, M.P.

Law Officers' Dept., A. Davidson, M.P.

Northern Ireland, J. A. Dunn, M.P.; R. J. Carter, M.P.

Overseas Development, F. A. Judd, M.P.

Prices and Consumer Protection, R. A. R. MacLennan, M.P.

Privy Council Office, W. G. Price, M.P.

Scottish Office, H. D. Brown, M.P.; H. Ewing, M.P.

Trade, M. H. Meacher, M.P.; S. C. Davis, M.P.

Transport, J. R. Horam, M.P.

Treasury, Junior Lords, D. R. Coleman, M.P.; T. Pendry, M.P.; J. D. Dormand, M.P.; D. L. Stoddart, M.P.; T. E. Graham, M.P.

Asst. Whips, T. M. Cox, M.P.; L. A. Pavitt, M.P.; E. G. Perry, M.P.; J. Ellis, M.P.; P. C. Snape, M.P.; A. W. Stallard, M.P.; A. Bates, M.P.; F. R. White, M.P.; J. Tinn, M.P.

Welsh Office, S. B. Jones, M.P.; T. A. Jones, M.P.

FOREIGN EXCHANGE RATES

A. London Market Rates

Country	Denomination	1939 Average Rate to £ (approx.)	30 September, 1976 Middle Rates
Austria	*Schilling*	—	28·72½
Belgium	*Franc*	26·49 *Belgas*	62·50†
Canada	*Dollar*	4·545	1·616½
Denmark	*Krone*	22·26	9·75½
Finland	*Markka*	217¼	6·42
France	*Franc*	176·10	8·20
Germany (Federal Republic of)	*D. Mark*	—	4·04
Greece	*Drachma*	545	61·60
Italy	*Lira*	85	1436¼
Japan	*Yen*	1/2d‡	476¾
Netherlands	*Guilder*	8·34	4·25½
Netherlands Antilles	*Antillian Guilder*	8·34	2·84
Norway	*Krone*	19·45	8·83½
Portugal	*Escudo*	110·07	51·80
Spain	*Peseta*	42·45	112·67½†
Sweden	*Krona*	18·59	7·08½
Switzerland	*Franc*	19·87	4·08½
U.S.A.	*Dollar*	4·485	1·6610
B. Former Scheduled Territories			
Australia	*Australian $*	A£1·2525	1·3554
Bahamas	*Bahamas $*	—	1·67
Barbados	*Barbados $*	—	3·3824
Belize	*Belize $*	—	3·33
Bermuda	*Bermuda $*	—	1·6610
Cyprus	*Cyprus $*	—	·69469½
Ghana	*New Cedi*	—	1·8858*
Hong Kong	*Hong Kong $*	—	8·0910
Iceland	*Krona*	—	337·70
India	*Rupee*	13·38	14·65
Jamaica	*Jamaica $*	—	1·5356
Jordan	*Dinar*	PAR	·540*
Kenya	*Shilling*	—	13·988¾
Kuwait	*Dinar*	—	·486½
Libya	*Dinar*	—	·4976**
Malawi	*Kwacha*	—	1·5189½
Malaysia	*Ringitt*	8·571	4·18½
Malta	*Maltese $*	—	·724743
New Zealand	*New Zealand $*	£1·2425	1·7172
Nigeria	*Naira*	—	1·137*
Pakistan	*Rupee*	—	16·54
South Africa	*Rand*	S.A.£1	1·44½
Sri Lanka	*Rupee*	13·38 (Ceylon Rs.)	14·75
Tanzania	*Shilling*	—	13·87
Trinidad	*Trinidad and Tobago $*	—	4·0653½
Uganda	*Shilling*	—	13·94½
Yemen	*Ryal*	—	7·55*
Zambia	*Kwacha*	—	1·35½
C. Other Rates			
Algeria	*Dinar*	—	7·09½
Argentina	*Peso*	19	235·40†
Bolivia	*Bolivian Peso*	141·50	33·60*
Brazil	*Cruzeiro*	82	19·04
Bulgaria	*Lev*	375	1·7266†*
Burma	*Kyat*	13·38	11·90**
Chile	*Peso*	116½	24·60*†
China	*Renmimbi Yuan*	4⅛	3·1869
Colombia	*Peso*	7·59	59·37*
Costa Rica	*Colon*	25·16	14·45
Cuba	*Peso*	4·386	1·38505
Czechoslovakia	*Koruna*	—	10·25†
Ecuador	*Sucre*	66	43·35*†
Ethiopia	*Ethiopian $*	—	3·44½
Germany (East)	*Ostmark*	—	4·25**

* Selling rate.
† Indicates that other rates are obtainable, varying according to the nature of the transaction.
‡ One shilling and two pence.

Country	Denomination	1939 Average Rate to £ (approx.)	30 September, 1976 Middle Rates
Guatemala	Quetzal	4·386	1·6610
Guinea Republic	Sily	—	36·56
Haiti	Gourde	22·4	8·40
Honduras Republic	Lempira	8⅜	3·37
Hungary	Forint	20¾	77·15†
Indonesia	Rupiah	—	680★★
Iran	Rial	80·50 (Persian)	119
Iraq	Dinar	PAR	·4803★
Israel	Israel £	PAR	14·05
Lebanon	Lebanese £	9·65	N/A
Malagasy Republic	M G Franc	175 (F. Fr.)	412·50
Mexico	Peso	—	33·26
Morocco	Dirham	176·10 (F. Fr.)	7·12½
Nicaragua	Cordoba	24	11·80
Paraguay	Guarani	—	209
Peru	Sol	24½	109★†
Philippines	Peso	—	12·19★
Poland	Zloty	23½	34·26†
Romania	Leu	655	8·25★†
Salvador, El	Colon	11·20	4·19½
Saudi Arabia	Ryal	—	5·95
Sudan	Sudan £	97½ (per £100 London)	·57½
Syria	Syrian £	—	6·78★★
Thailand	Baht	10·91	33·95
Tunisia	Tunisian Dinar	—	·721
Turkey	Turkish Lira	—	27·42
United Arab Republic (Egypt)	Egyptian £	97½ (per £100 London)	·705★
Uruguay	New Peso	9	6·50
U.S.S.R.	Rouble	23·75	1·33
Venezuela	Bolivar	14·15	7·19
Vietnam	Dong	—	N/A
Yugoslavia	New Yugoslav Dinar	197½ (Y.D.)	30·4345½†
Zaire Republic	Zaire	—	1·4797★

★ Selling rate.
★★ Approximate selling rate.
† Indicates that other rates are obtainable, varying according to the nature of the transaction.
†† One shilling and two pence.

BRITISH TRANSPORT DOCKS BOARD, 1975

Traffic

Traffic through the Board's ports in 1975 totalled 77,252,000 tonnes (1974, 84,785,000), consisting of ('000 tonnes): ores 9,037; timber, 906; coal, 6,006; petroleum 41,277; foodstuffs 4,019; manufactured goods and other commodities, 16,007. Net registered tonnage of shipping entering and leaving the ports in 1975 totalled 131,012,000 tons (1974, 136,256,000). Passengers in transit through the Board's ports in 1975 numbered 3,169,000 (1974 2,872,000).

Finance.—Gross revenue totalled £77,487,000 (1974, £64,082,000) and working expenses £64,994,000 (1974, £51,963,000). Surplus, after historic cost depreciation, before interest, £12,493,000 (1974, £12,119,000); Interest charges £6,668,000 (1974 £7,018,000); Reserve for additional depreciation, £4,419,000 (1974, £2,901,000); Net surplus, 1975. £1,689,000 (1974, £1,501,000).

HISTORIC ATLANTIC PASSAGES

Year	Days	Ship	Tons	Year	Days	Ship	Tons
1862a	9	Scotia	3,871	1932c	4d. 15h. 56m.	Europa	51,656
1869a	8	City of Brussels	3,081	1933c	4d. 17h. 43m.	Bremen	51,650
1882a	7	Alaska	6,400	1934d	4d. 6h. 58m.	Emp. of Britain	42,348
1889a	6	City of Paris	10,669	1935f	4d. 3h. 2m.	Normandie	80,000
1894a	5⅓	Lucania	12,950	1936f	4d. 0h. 27m.	Queen Mary	81,237
1897b	6	Kaiser Wilhelm	14,349	1936g	3d. 23h. 57m.	Queen Mary	81,237
1903c	5½	Deutschland	16,502	1937f	3d. 23h. 2m.	Normandie	80,000
1909a	4d. 10h. 41m.	Mauretania	30,696	1938f	3d. 21h. 45m.	Queen Mary	81,237
1924e	5d. 1h. 49m.	Mauretania	30,696	1938g	3d. 20h. 42m.	Queen Mary	81,237
1929c	4d. 18h. 17m.	Bremen	51,650	1952f	3d. 12h. 12m.	United States	51,500
1930c	4d. 17h. 6m.	Europa	51,656	1952g	3d. 10h. 40m.	United States	51,500

a From Queenstown;   *b* from Southampton;   *c* from Cherbourg;   *d* Quebec to Cherbourg;   *e* to Cherbourg;
f Bishop Rock to Ambrose Light (2,907 miles); *g* Ambrose Light to Bishop Rock (2,938 miles).

ABBREVIATIONS IN COMMON USE

Ψ = Seaport.

A

A.A., Automobile Association; Anti-Aircraft.

A.A.A., Amateur Athletic Association.

A. and M., (Hymns) Ancient and Modern.

A.B., Able-bodied Seaman.

A.B.C., Alphabet (also Aerated Bread Company).

a.c., alternating current.

a/c., accounts.

A.C.A., *Associate* of Inst of Chartered Accountants (of England and Wales)

A.C.C.A.—of the Association of Certified Accountants.

A.C.I.S.—of the Chartered Institute of Secretaries and Administrators.

A.C.M.A.—of the Institute of Cost and Management Accountants.

A.D. (*Anno Domini*), In the year of our Lord.

A.D.C., Aide-de-Camp.

Ad lib. (*ad libitum*), At pleasure.

A.F.C., Air Force Cross.

A.F.M., Air Force Medal.

A.H. (*Anno Hegirae*), In the year of the Hejira.

A.I.A., *Associate* of the Institute of Actuaries.

A.I.B.—of Bankers.

A.I.C.S.—of Chartered Shipbrokers.

A.I.M.T.A.—of Munic. Treas. and Accountants.

A.I.Q.S.—of Quantity Surveyors.

A.K.C.—of King's College.

A.L. (*Anno Lucis*), in the year of Light.

A.L.A., *Associate* of the Library Association.

A.L.C.D.—of London College of Divinity.

A.M. (*Ante meridiem*), Before noon.

A.M. (*Anno mundi*), In the year of the world.

A.M.D.G. (*Ad majorem Dei Gloriam*), To the greater glory of God.

A.N.A.R.E., Australian National Antarctic Research Expeditions.

A.N.Z.A.C., Australian and New Zealand Army Corps.

A.O.C., Air Officer Commanding.

A.R.A., *Associate* of Royal Academy.

A.R.A.M.—of Royal Academy of Music.

A.R.B.S.—of the Royal Society of British Sculptors.

A.R.C.A.—of Royal Coll. of Art.

A.R.C.M.—of Royal College of Music.

A.R.C.O.—of Organists.

A.R.I.B.A.—of Royal Institute of British Architects.

A.R.I.C.—of Royal Institute of Chemistry.

A.R.I.C.S.—of Royal Institution of Chartered Surveyors.

A.R.P.S.—of Royal Photographic Society.

A.R.R.C.—of Royal Red Cross.

A.R.W.S.—of Royal Society of Painters in Water Colours.

A.S.V.A.—of Inc. Society of Valuers and Auctioneers.

A.S.A., Amateur Swimming Association.

A.S.D.I.C., Anti-Submarine Detector Indicator Committee.

A.S.L.I.B., Association of Special Libraries and Information Bureaux.

A.T.A., Air Transport Auxiliary.

A.T.C., Air Training Corps.

A.U.C. (*Ab urbe condita*). In the year from the foundation of Rome.

A.W.O.L., Absent Without Leave.

B

B.A., *Bachelor* of Arts.

B.Arch.—of Architecture.

B.Ch. (or Ch.B.)—of Surgery.

B.C.L.—of Civil Law.

B.Com.—of Commerce.

B.D.—of Divinity.

B.D.S. (or B.Ch.D.)—of Dental Surgery.

B.Ed.—of Education.

B.Eng.—of Engineering.

B.Litt.—of Literature *or* of Letters.

B.Pharm.—of Pharmacy.

B.Phil.—of Philosophy.

B.Sc.—of Science.

B.V.M.S.—of Veterinary Medicine and Surgery.

B.A.O.R., British Army of the Rhine.

B.B., Boy's Brigade.

B.B.C., British Broadcasting Corporation.

B.C., Before Christ.

B.D.A., British Dental Assocn.

B.E.A., British European Airways.

B.E.M., British Empire Medal.

B.M.A., British Medical Assocn.

B.N.C., Brasenose College (Oxon.).

B.O.A.C., British Overseas Airways.

B.R.C.S., British Red Cross Society.

B.S.T., British Standard Time.

Bt., Baronet.

B.Th.U., British Thermal Unit.

B.V.M., Blessed Virgin Mary.

C

C.—Conservative.

ca. (*circa*), about.

C.A., Chartered Accountant (*Scottish Institute*).

Cantab., Cambridge.

Cantuar., Canterbury.

C.B., Companion of the Bath.

C.B.E., Commander of Order of British Empire.

C.B.I., Confederation of British Industry.

c.c., cubic centimetres.

C.C., County Council.

C.C.F., Combined Cadet Force.

C.E., Civil Engineer.

C.E.N.T.O., Central Treaty Organization.

C.E.T., Central European Time.

C. of E., Church of England.

cf. (confer), Compare.

C.F., Chaplain to the Forces.

C.G.M., Conspicuous Gallantry Medal.

C.G.S., Centimetre - gramme - second (system).

C.H., Companion of Honour.

Ch. Ch., Christ Church.

C.I., Lady of Imperial Order of the Crown of India.

C.I., Channel Islands.

C.I.A., Central Intelligence Agency.

C.I.D., Criminal Investigation Department.

C.I.E., Companion, Order of Indian Empire.

C.I.F. (usually cif.), Cost, Insurance and Freight.

C.I.G.S., Chief of Imperial General staff.

C.-in-C., Commander-in-Chief.

C.I.O., Congress of Industrial Organizations (U.S.A.).

C.L.B., Church Lads' Brigade.

C.M.,(*Chirurgiæ Magister*),Master of Surgery.

C.M.G., Companion, Order of St. Michael and St. George.

C.M.S., Church Missionary Society.

C.N.A.A., Council for National Academic Awards.

C.O., Commanding Officer.

C.O.D., Cash on delivery.

C.O.I.—Central Office of Information.

C.P.R.E.—Council for Protection of Rural England.

C.S.I., Companion, Order of Star of India.

C.T.C., Cyclists' Touring Club.

C.V.O., Commander, Royal Victorian Order.

cwt., Hundredweight.

D

D.B.E., Dame Commander of Order of British Empire.

d.c., direct current.

D.C., District of Columbia.

D.C.B., Dame Commander of the Order of the Bath.

D.C.L., *Doctor* of Civil Law.

D.D.—of Divinity.

D.D.S.—of Dental Surgery.

D.Litt.—of Letters, *or* of Literature.

D.Phil.—of Philosophy.

D.Sc.—of Science.

D.Th.—of Theology.

D.C.M., Distinguished Conduct Medal.

D.C.M.G.—Dame Commander, Order of St. Michael and St. George.

D.C.V.O.—Dame Commander of the Royal Victorian Order.

D.D.T., dichlorodiphenyltrichloroethane (insecticide).

del. (*delineavit*), He (she) drew it.

D.F.C., Distinguished Flying Cross.

D.F.M., Distinguished Flying Medal.

D.G. (*Dei gratia*), By the Grace of God.

D.I.C., *Diploma* of the Imperial College.

D.P.H.—in Public Health.

D.P.M.—in Psychological Medicine.

D.T.M.—in Tropical Medicine.

D.L., Deputy-Lieutenant.

D.N.B., Dictionary of National Biography.

Do. (ditto), The same. (Italian, *detto*.)

D.O.M., *Dominus Omnium Magister* (God the Master of All).

D.S.C., Distinguished Service Cross.

D.S.M., Do. Medal.

D.S.O., Companion of Distinguished Service Order.

D.V. (*Deo volente*), God willing.

dwt., Pennyweight.

E

E. and O.E., Errors and omissions excepted.

E.C., East Central District.

E.C.S.C., European Coal and Steel Community.

E.D., Efficiency Decoration.

E.E.C., European Economic Community.

E.F.T.A., European Free Trade Association.

e.g. (*exempli gratia*), for the sake of example.

E.M.A., European Monetary Agreement.

E.R., Elizabetha Regina, or Edwardus Rex.

E.R.D., Emergency Reserve Decoration.

etc. (*et cetera*). And the other things.

et seq. (*et sequentia*). And the following.

ex lib. (*ex libris*), from the books of.

F

F.A., Football Association.

F.B.A., *Fellow* of the British Academy.

F.C.A.—of Institute of Chartered Accountants (of England and Wales).

F.C.C.A.—of Association of Certified Accountants.

F.C.G.I.—of City and Guilds Institute.

F.C.I.A.—of Corporation of Insurance Agents.

F.C.I.B.—of Corporation of Insurance Brokers.

F.C.I.I.—of the Chartered Insurance Institute.

F.C.I.S.—of the Chartered Institute of Secretaries and Administrators.

F.C.I.T.—of the Chartered Institute of Transport.

F.C.M.A.—of the Institute of Cost and Management Accountants.

F.C.P.—of the College of Preceptors.

F.G.S.—of the Geological Society.

F.H.S.—of the Heraldry Society.

F.I.A.—of the Institute of Actuaries.

F.I.Arb.—of Arbitrators.

F.I.B.—of Bankers.

F.I.C.E.—of Institution of Civil Engineers.

F.I.C.S.—of Chartered Shipbrokers.

F.I.E.E.—of Electrical Engineers.

F.Inst.P.—of Physics.

F.I.Q.S.—of Quantity Surveyors.

F.J.I.—of Journalists.

F.L.A.—of Library Association.

F.L.S.—of the Linnean Society.

F.P.S.—of the Pharmaceutical Society.

F.R.A.I.—of Royal Anthropological Institute.

F.R.A.M.—of Royal Academy of Music.

F.R.A.S.—of the Royal Astronomical Society

F.R.Ae.S.—of Royal Aeronautical Society.

F.R.B.S.—of the Royal Society of British Sculptors.

F.R.C.M.—of the Royal College of Music.

F.R.C.O.—of Royal College of Organists.

F.R.C.O.G.—of Royal College of Obstetricians and Gynaecologists.

F.R.C.P., F.R.C.P.Ed., and F.R.C.P.I.—of the Royal College of Physicians of London, of Edinburgh, and in Ireland respectively.

F.R.C.P.S.G.—of the Royal Faculty of Physicians and Surgeons of Glasgow.

F.R.C.S.—of Royal College of Surgeons of England.

F.R.C.S.Ed., ditto of Edinburgh; F.R.C.S.I., of Ireland.

F.R.C.V.S.—of Royal College of Veterinary Surgeons.

F.R.G.S.—of the Royal Geographical Society.

F.R.H.S.—of the Royal Horticultural Society.

F.R.Hist.Soc., ditto Historical.

F.R.I.B.A.—of the Royal Institute of British Architects.

F.R.I.C.—of the Royal Institute of Chemistry.

F.R.I.C.S.—of the Royal Institution of Chartered Surveyors.

F.R.M.S.—of Royal Microscopical Society.

F.R. Met. S.—of Royal Meteorological Society.

F.R.N.S.—of Royal Numismatic Society.

F.R.P.S.—of Royal Photographic Society.

F.R.S.—of the Royal Society.

F.R.S.E., ditto of Edinburgh.

F.R.S.A.—of the Royal Society of Arts.

F.R.S.L.—Do. Literature.

F.S.A.—of the Society of Antiquaries.

F.S.S.—Do. Statistical Society.

F.S.V.A.—Do. Valuers and Auctioneers.

F.Z.S.—of the Zoological Society.

F.A.N.Y., First Aid Nursing Yeomanry.

F.A.O., Food and Agriculture Organization.

fcp., Foolscap.

F.D. (*Fidei Defensor*) Defender of the Faith.

Fec. (*fecit*), He did it (or made it).

F.H., Fire Hydrant.

F.I.D.O., Fog Investigation Dispersal Operations.

fl. (*floruit*), he, or she, flourished.

F.O., Flying Officer; Foreign Office.

FOB (*usually* f.o.b.), Free on board.

G

G.A.T.T., General Agreement on Tariffs and Trade.

G.B.E., Knight or Dame Grand Cross of British Empire.

G.C., George Cross.

G.C.B., Knight (or Dame) Grand Cross of the Bath.

G.C.I.E., Knight Grand Commander of Indian Empire.

G.C.M.G., Knight (or Dame) Grand Cross of St. Michael and St. George.

G.C.S.I., Knight Grand Commander of Star of India.

G.C.V.O., Knight or Dame Grand Cross of Royal Victorian Order.

G.H.Q., General Headquarters.

G.L.C., Greater London Council.

G.M., George Medal.

G.M.T., Greenwich Mean Time.

G.O.C., General Officer Commanding.

G.P.O., General Post Office.

G.R. (*Georgius Rex*),￼King George.

G.R.C.M., Graduate of the Royal College of Music.

G.R.S.M., Graduate of the Royal Schools of Music (Royal Academy and Royal College).

G.S.O., General Staff Officer.

H

H.A.C., Honble. Artillery Coy.

H.C.F., Highest Common Factor.

H.E., His Excellency; His Eminence.

H.E.H., His [Her] Exalted Highness.

H.H., His [Her] Highness.

H.I.H., His [Her] Imperial Highness.

H.I.M., His [Her] Imperial Majesty.

H.J.S., (*Hic jacet sepultus*), Here lies buried. *cf.* H.S.E.

H.M., His, or Her, Majesty.

H.M.A.S., Her Majesty's Australian Ship.

H.M.L., Her Majesty's Lieutenant.

H.M.S., Her Majesty's Ship.

H.M.S.O., Her Majesty's Stationery Office.

h.p., horse power.

H.Q., Headquarters.

H.R.H., His[Her]Royal Highness.

H.S.E. (*Hic sepultus est*), Here lies buried. *cf.* H.J.S.

H.S.H., His [Her] Serene Highness.

I

I.A., Indian Army.

Ibid. (*ibidem*), In the same place.

IBRD., Internat. Bank for Reconstruction and Development.

I.C.B.M., Inter-Continental ballistic missile.

I.C.S., Indian Civil Service.

Id. (*idem*), The same.

I.C.A.O., International Civil Aviation Organization.

i.d.c., Graduate of Imperial Defence College.

i.e. (*id est*), That is.

IFC, International Finance Corporation.

I.H.S. (*Iesus Hominum Salvator*), Jesus the Saviour of Mankind; originally, these were the Greek Capital letters, IHΣ.

I.L.O., International Labour Organization.

I.L.P., Independent Labour Party.

IMCO., Inter-Governmental Maritime Consultative Organization.

IMF, International Monetary Fund.

I.M.S., Indian Medical Service.

Incog. (*incognito*), Unknown.

In loc (*in loco*), In its place.

I.N.R.I. (*Iesus Nazarenus Rex Iudaeorum*), Jesus of Nazareth King of the Jews.

Inst. (instant), current month.

I.O.M., Isle of Man.

I.O.U., I owe you.

I.O.W., Isle of Wight.

I.P.F.A., Institute of Public Finance and Accountancy.

I.Q., Intelligence Quotient.

IRBM., Intermediate - range ballistic missile.

I.S.O., Imperial Service Order.

I.T.A., Independent Television Authority.

I.T.O., International Trade Organization.

I.T.U., International Telecommunication Union.

J

J., Judge.

J.P., Justice of the Peace.

K

K.B.E. Knight Commander of Order of British Empire.

K.C.B.—Do. the Bath.

K.C.I.E.—Do. Indian Empire.

K.C.M.G.—Do. of St. Michael and St. George.

K.C.S.I.—Do. the Star of India.

K.C.V.O.—Do. Royal Victorian Order.

K.G., Knight of the Garter.

k.o., knock out (boxing).

K.P., Knight of St. Patrick.

K.T., Knight of the Thistle.

Kt., Knight Bachelor.

L

L., Liberal.

Lab., Labour.

L.A.C., London Athletic Club; Leading Aircraftman.

L.A.H., *Licentiate* of Apothecaries' Hall, Dublin.

L.C.P., Do. of College of Preceptors.

L.D.S., Do. in Dental Surgery.

L.M., Do. in Midwifery.

L.M.S.S.A. Do. in Medicine and Surgery, Soc. of Apothecaries.

L.R.A.M., Do. of Royal Acad. of Music.

L.R.C.P., Do. of the Roy. Coll. of Physicians.

L.R.C.P.Ed., ditto Edinburgh.

L.R.C.S.Ed.—of Roy. Coll. Surg., Edinburgh.

L.R.F.P.S.G., Do. of the Royal Faculty of Physicians and Surgeons of Glasgow.

L.S.A., Do. of Society of Apothecaries.

L.Th., Licenciate in Theology.

L.T.M., Do. of Tropical Medicine.

Lat., Latitude.

lb. (*libra*). Pound weight.

L.C.C., London County Council.

L.C.J., Lord Chief Justice.

L.C.M., Least Common Multiple.

Lit., Literary.

Litt.D., Doctor of Letters.

L.J., Lord Justice.

LL.B., Bachelor of Laws.

LL.D., Doctor of Laws.

LL.M., Master of Laws.

L.S. (*loco sigilli*), Place of the Seal.

L. s. d. (*Librae, solidi, denarii*). Pounds, shillings, pence.

L.T.A., Lawn Tennis Association.

Ltd., Limited Liability.

LXX., Septuagint.

M

M., Monsieur.

M.A., *Master* of Arts.

M.Ch.—of Surgery.

M.Ch.D.—of Dental Surgery.

M.S.—of Surgery.

M.Sc.—of Science.

M.Th.—of Theology.

M.B., Bachelor of Medicine.

M.D., Doctor of ditto.

M.B.E., *Member* of British Empire Order.

M.E.C.—of Executive Council.

M.I.Chem.E.—of Institution of Chemical Engineers.

M.I.C.E.—of Institution of Civil Engineers.

M.I.E.E.—of Institution of Electrical Engineers.

M.I.Mar.E.—of Institute of Marine Engineers.

M.I.Mech.E.—of Institution of Mechanical Engineers.

M.Inst.Met.—of Institute of Metals.

M.J.I.—of Journalists.

M.L.A., *Member* of Legislative Assembly.

M.L.C., ditto Council.

M.N., Merchant Navy.

M.P., Member of Parliament (also Military Police).

M.P.S. — of Pharmaceutical Society.

M.R.C.P.—of Royal College of Physicians.

M.R.C.S.—of Royal College of Surgeons.

M.R.C.V.S.—of Royal College of Veterinary Surgeons.

M.V.O.—of Royal Victorian Order.

M.C., Military Cross.

M.C.C., Marylebone Cricket Club.

M.F.H., Master of Fox Hounds.

Mgr., Monsignor.

Min. Plenip., Minister Plenipotentiary.

Mlle., Mademoiselle.

M.M., Military Medal (also MM., Messieurs).

Mme., Madame.

M.O.H., Medical Officer of Health.

m.p.h., Miles per hour.

MS., manuscript (pl. MSS.).

Mus. D.[B.].] Doctor, [Bachelor], of Music.

N

N.A.A.F.I., Navy, Army and Air Force Institutes.

N.A.T.O., North Atlantic Treaty Organization.

N.B. (*Nota bene*). Note well; New Brunswick.

N.C.B., National Coal Board.

N.C.O., Non - commissioned Officer.

n.d., no date (of books).

N.D.P.S., National Data Processing Service.

Nem. con. (*Nemine contradicente*), No one contradicting.

N.F.U. — National Farmers' Union.

No. (*Numero*), Number.

N.P., Notary Public.

Non seq. (*non sequitur*), It does not follow.

N.R.A., National Rifle Association.

N.S., Nova Scotia.

N.S.P.C.C., National Society for the prevention of Cruelty to Children.

N.S.W., New South Wales.

N.T., New Testament.

N.U.J., *National Union of Journalists*.

N.U.R.—of Railwaymen.

N.U.S.—of Students.

N.W.P.[T.], Northwest Provinces [Territory].

N.Y., New York.

N.Z., New Zealand.

O

O.B.E., Officer of British Empire Order.

ob., or *obiit.* died.

O.C., Officer Commanding.

O.E.C.D., Organization for Economic Co-operation and Development.

O.E.D., Oxford English Dictionary.

O.H.M.S., On Her Majesty's Service.

O.M., Order of Merit (and member of).

O.P., Opposite Prompt side (of Theatre), Out of Print (of books).

op. cit. (*opere citato*), in the work cited.

O.S., Old Style.

O.S.B., Order of St. Benedict.

O.T., Old Testament.

O.U.D.S., Oxford University Dramatic Society.

Oxon., Oxford; Oxfordshire.

Oz., Ounce.

P

P.A., Press Association.

P.C., Privy Councillor.

P.E.N. (*Club*), Poets Essayists, Novelists.

p.f.c., Passed Flying College.

Ph.D., Doctor of Philosophy.

pinx(*it*), he (or she) painted it.

P.L.A., Port of London Authority.

P.M. (*post meridiem*), Afternoon (also *post mortem*).

P.M.G., Postmaster-General.

P.N.E.U., Parents' National Educational Union.

p.p., or per pro. (*per procurationem*)—by proxy.

Pro tem. (*pro tempore*), For the time being.

Prox. (*proximo*), Next Month.

P.S. (*Post scriptum*), Postscript.

p.s.c., Passed Staff College.

P.T., Physical Training.

P.T.O., Please turn over.

Q

Q.C., Queen's Counsel.

Q.e.d. (*quod erat demonstrandum*), which was to be proved.

Q.G.M., Queen's Gallantry Medal

Q.H.C., Honorary Chaplain to the Queen; Q.H.P., ditto Physician; Q.H S , ditto Surgeon; Q.H.D.S., ditto Dental Surgeon; Q.H.N.S., ditto Nursing Sister.

Q.M.G., Quartermaster-General.

Q.S., Quarter Sessions.

Q.S.O., Quasi-stellar object (quasar).

q.v. (*quod vide*), "which see".

R

R.A., *Royal* Artillery or Royal Academy (or Academician).

R.A.C.—Armoured Corps (also Royal Automobile Club).

R.A.D.C.—Army Dental Corps.

R.A.E.C.—Army Educational Corps.

R.Ae.S., Royal Aeronautical Society.

R.A.F.—Air Force.

R.A.M.—Academy of Music.

R.A.M.C.— Army Medical Corps.

R.A.N.—Australian Navy.

R.A.P.C.—Army Pay Corps.

R.A.O.C.—Army Ordnance Corps.

R.A.V.C.—Army Veterinary Corps.

R.B.A.—Society of British Artists.

R.B.S.—Society of British Sculptors.

R.C.N.—Canadian Navy.

R.C.N.C.—Corps of Naval Constructors.

R.C.T.—Corps of Transport.

R.D.—Naval Reserve Decoration.

R.E.—Engineers.

R.E.M.E.—Electrical and Mechanical do.

R.H.A.—Horse Artillery or— Hibernian Academy.

R.I.B.A.—Royal Institute of British Architects (also Member of the Institute).

R.M.—Marines.

R.M.A.—Military Academy.

R.M.S.—Mail Steamer.

R.N.—Navy; R.N.R. Naval Reserve; R.N.V.R., Naval Volunteer Reserve.

R.O.C.—Observer Corps.

R.O.I.—Institute of Oil Painters.

R.P.—Society of Portrait Painters.

R.P.C.—Pioneer Corps.

R.Sigs.—Signals.

R.S.A.—Scottish Academician.

R.S.P.C.A.—Society for the Prevention of Cruelty to Animals.

R.W.S.—Water Colour Society.

R.Y.S.—Yacht Squadron.

R.C., Roman Catholic.

R.D., Rural Dean; Refer to drawer (banking).

R.D.I., Designer for Industry of the Royal Society of Arts.

R.I.P. (*Requiescat in pace*), May he (she) rest in peace.

Ro. (*recto*), On the right-hand page. (*See* Vo.)

r.p.m., revolutions per minute.

R.R.C., Lady of Royal Red Cross.

R.S.V.P. (*Répondez s'il vous plait*), Answer, if you please.

R.V., Revised Version (of Bible).

S

Sc.D., Doctor of Science.

S.E.A.T.O.—South East Asia Treaty Organization.

S.E.T., Selective Employment Tax.

S.H.A.P.E.—Supreme Headquarters, Allied Powers, Europe.

Sic, So written.

S.J., Society of Jesus.

S.O.S. ("Save Our Souls") Distress Signal.

s.p.(*sine prole*), Without issue.

S.P.C.K., Society for Promoting Christian Knowledge.

S.P.Q.R. (*Senatus Populusque Romanus*), The Senate and People of Rome

S.R.N., State Registered Nurse.

S.S.A.F.A., Soldiers', Sailors', and Airmen's Families Assocn.

S.S.C., Solicitor in the Supreme Court (Scotland).

Stet, Let it stand.

S.T.P. (=D.D.), *Sacrae Theologiae Professor*.

T

T.A.N., Twilight all night.

t.b., Tuberculosis.

T.D., Territorial Decoration.

T.C.D., Trinity College, Dublin.

T.N.T., Trinitrotoluene (explosive).

Toc. H., Talbot House.

T.U.C., Trades Union Congress.

U

Ult. (*ultimo*), in the preceding month.

U.K., United Kingdom.

U.N.A.C., United Nations Appeal for Children.

U.N.E.S.C.O., United Nations Educational, Scientific and Cultural Organization.

U.N.O., United Nations Organization.

U.P.U., Universal Postal Union.

U.S.A. or U.S., United States of America.

U.S.C.L., United Society for Christian Literature.

U.S.S.R., Union of Soviet Socialist Republics.

V

v. (*versus*), Against.

V.A., Victoria and Albert Order or Vicar Apostolic.

V.A.D., Voluntary Aid Detachment.

V.A.T., Value Added Tax.

Ɣℭ, Victoria Cross.

V.D., Vol. Officers' Decoration.

Ven., Venerable.

Verb. sap. (*Verbum sapienti satis est*), A word to the wise is enough.

V.I.P., Very Important Person.

Viz. (*videlicet*), Namely.

Vo. (*verso*), On the left-hand page! (*See* Ro.)

V.R., Victoria Regina.

V.R.D.—Volunteer Reserve Decoration.

W

W.A.A.F., now W.R.A.F., Women's Auxiliary Air Force.

W.H.O., World Health Organization,

W.M.O. World Meteorological Organization.

W.O., Warrant Officer.

W.R.A.C., Women's Royal Army Corps.

W.R.A.F., Women's Royal Air Force.

W.R.N.S., Women's Royal Naval Service.

W.R.V.S., Women's Royal Voluntary Service.

W.S., Writer to the Signet.

Y

Y.M.C.A., Young Men's Christian Association.

Y.W.C.A., Young Women's do.

BEING THE FIRST YEAR AFTER BISSEXTILE OR LEAP YEAR

Golden Number	.. .. ..	II
Epact	.. .. ..	10
Dominical Letter	.. .. ..	B
Solar Cycle	.. .. ..	26
Roman Indiction	.. .. ..	15
Julian Period (begins at noon)	.. ..	6690
Julian Day	.. .. ..	2,443,145
New Year's Day (Saturday)	.. ..	Jan. 1
Australia Day	.. .. ..	,, 26
Accession of Queen Elizabeth II	..	Feb. 6
Septuagesima Sunday	.. ..	,, 6
New Zealand Day	.. ..	,, 6
Prince Andrew's Birthday (1960)	..	,, 19
Ash Wednesday	.. .. ..	,, 23
St. David's Day	.. .. ..	Mar. 1
Prince Edward's Birthday (1964)	..	,, 10
St. Patrick's Day	.. .. ..	,, 17
Good Friday	.. .. ..	Apr. 8
Easter Day	.. .. ..	,, 10

Birthday of Queen Elizabeth II	..	Apr. 21
St. George's Day	.. .. ..	,, 23
Ascension Day	.. .. ..	May 19
Whit Sunday	.. .. ..	,, 29
Trinity Sunday	.. .. ..	June 5
Corpus Christi	.. .. ..	,, 9
Duke of Edinburgh's Birthday (1921)	..	,, 10
Queen's Official Birthday	..	,, 14
Dominion Day Canada (1867)	..	July 1
The Queen Mother's Birthday (1900)		Aug. 4
Princess Anne's Birthday (1950)	..	,, 15
Jewish New Year (5738)	..	Sept. 13
Remembrance Sunday	.. ..	Nov. 13
Prince of Wales's Birthday (1948)	..	,, 14
First Sunday in Advent	.. ..	,, 27
St. Andrew's Day	.. .. ..	,, 30
Moslem New Year (1398)	..	Dec. 12
Christmas Day	.. .. ..	,, 25

Spring Equinox..................	Sun enters Sign Aries........March	20d 18h	⎫
Summer Solstice.................	,, ,, ,, Cancer..June	21d 12h	⎪
Autumn Equinox.................	,, ,, ,, Libra.......Sept.	23d 04h	⎬ G.M.T.
Winter Solstice.................	,, ,, ,, Capricornus..Dec.	21d 23h	⎭

CALENDAR FOR THE YEAR 1977

January
Su.	—	2	9	16	23	30
M.	—	3	10	17	24	31
Tu.	—	4	11	18	25	—
W.	—	5	12	19	26	—
Th.	—	6	13	20	27	—
F.	—	7	14	21	28	—
S.	1	8	15	22	29	—

April
Su.	..	—	3	10	17	24
M.	..	—	4	11	18	25
Tu.	..	—	5	12	19	26
W.	..	—	6	13	20	27
Th.	..	—	7	14	21	28
F.	..	1	8	15	22	29
S.	..	2	9	16	23	30

July
Su.	—	3	10	17	24	31
M.	—	4	11	18	25	—
Tu.	—	5	12	19	26	—
W.	—	6	13	20	27	—
Th.	—	7	14	21	28	—
F.	1	8	15	22	29	—
S.	2	9	16	23	30	—

October
Su.	—	2	9	16	23	30
M.	—	3	10	17	24	31
Tu.	—	4	11	18	25	—
W.	—	5	12	19	26	—
Th.	—	6	13	20	27	—
F.	—	7	14	21	28	—
S.	1	8	15	22	29	—

February
Su.	..	—	6	13	20	27
M.	..	—	7	14	21	28
Tu.	1	8	15	22	—	
W.	..	2	9	16	23	—
Th.	..	3	10	17	24	—
F.	..	4	11	18	25	—
S.	..	5	12	19	26	—

May
Su.	..	1	8	15	22	29
M.	..	2	9	16	23	30
Tu.	..	3	10	17	24	31
W.	..	4	11	18	25	—
Th.	..	5	12	19	26	—
F.	..	6	13	20	27	—
S.	..	7	14	21	28	—

August
Su.	..	—	7	14	21	28
M.	1	8	15	22	29	
Tu.	..	2	9	16	23	30
W.	..	3	10	17	24	31
Th.	..	4	11	18	25	—
F.	..	5	12	19	26	—
S.	..	6	13	20	27	—

November
Su.	..	—	6	13	20	27
M.	..	—	7	14	21	28
Tu.	1	8	15	22	29	
W.	..	2	9	16	23	30
Th.	..	3	10	17	24	—
F.	..	4	11	18	25	—
S.	..	5	12	19	26	—

March
Su.	..	—	6	13	20	27
M.	..	—	7	14	21	28
Tu.	..	1	8	15	22	29
W.	..	2	9	16	23	30
Th.	..	3	10	17	24	31
F.	..	4	11	18	25	—
S.	..	5	12	19	26	—

June
Su.	..	—	5	12	19	26
M.	..	—	6	13	20	27
Tu.	..	—	7	14	21	28
W.	..	1	8	15	22	29
Th.	..	2	9	16	23	30
F.	..	3	10	17	24	—
S.	..	4	11	18	25	—

September
Su.	..	—	4	11	18	25
M.	..	—	5	12	19	26
Tu.	..	—	6	13	20	27
W.	..	—	7	14	21	28
Th.	1	8	15	22	29	
F.	..	2	9	16	23	30
S.	..	3	10	17	24	—

December
Su.	..	—	4	11	18	25
M.	..	—	5	12	19	26
Tu.	..	—	6	13	20	27
W.	..	—	7	14	21	28
Th.	1	8	15	22	29	
F.	..	2	9	16	23	30
S.	..	3	10	17	24	31

CALENDAR FOR THE YEAR 1978

January
Su.	..	1	8	15	22	29
M.	..	2	9	16	23	30
Tu.	..	3	10	17	24	31
W.	..	4	11	18	25	—
Th.	..	5	12	19	26	—
F.	..	6	13	20	27	—
S.	..	7	14	21	28	—

April
Su.	..	—	2	9	16	23	30
M.	..	—	3	10	17	24
Tu.	..	—	4	11	18	25
W.	..	—	5	12	19	26
Th.	..	—	6	13	20	27
F.	..	—	7	14	21	28
S.	..	1	8	15	22	29

July
Su.	..	—	2	9	16	23	30
M.	..	—	3	10	17	24	31
Tu.	..	—	4	11	18	25
W.	..	—	5	12	19	26
Th.	..	—	6	13	20	27
F.	..	—	7	14	21	28
S.	..	1	8	15	22	29

October
Su.	..	1	8	15	22	29
M.	..	2	9	16	23	30
Tu.	..	3	10	17	24	31
W.	..	4	11	18	25	—
Th.	..	5	12	19	26	—
F.	..	6	13	20	27	—
S.	..	7	14	21	28	—

February
Su.	..	—	5	12	19	26
M.	..	—	6	13	20	27
Tu.	..	—	7	14	21	28
W.	..	1	8	15	22	—
Th.	..	2	9	16	23	—
F.	..	3	10	17	24	—
S.	..	4	11	18	25	—

May
Su.	..	—	7	14	21	28
M.	..	1	8	15	22	29
Tu.	..	2	9	16	23	30
W.	..	3	10	17	24	31
Th.	..	4	11	18	25	—
F.	..	5	12	19	26	—
S.	..	6	13	20	27	—

August
Su.	..	—	6	13	20	27
M.	..	—	7	14	21	28
Tu.	..	1	8	15	22	29
W.	..	2	9	16	23	30
Th.	..	3	10	17	24	31
F.	..	4	11	18	25	—
S.	..	5	12	19	26	—

November
Su.	..	—	5	12	19	26
M.	..	—	6	13	20	27
Tu.	..	—	7	14	21	28
W.	..	1	8	15	22	29
Th.	..	2	9	16	23	30
F.	..	3	10	17	24	—
S.	..	4	11	18	25	—

March
Su.	..	—	5	12	19	26
M.	..	—	6	13	20	27
Tu.	..	—	7	14	21	28
W.	..	1	8	15	22	—
Th.	..	2	9	16	23	30
F.	..	3	10	17	24	31
S.	..	4	11	18	25	—

June
Su.	..	—	4	11	18	25
M.	..	—	5	12	19	26
Tu.	..	—	6	13	20	27
W.	..	—	7	14	21	28
Th.	..	1	8	15	22	29
F.	..	2	9	16	23	30
S.	..	3	10	17	24	—

September
Su.	..	—	3	10	17	24
M.	..	—	4	11	18	25
Tu.	..	—	5	12	19	26
W.	..	—	6	13	20	27
Th.	..	—	7	14	21	28
F.	..	1	8	15	22	29
S.	..	2	9	16	23	30

December
Su.	..	—	3	10	17	24	31
M.	..	—	4	11	18	25
Tu.	..	—	5	12	19	26
W.	..	—	6	13	20	27
Th.	..	—	7	14	21	28
F.	..	1	8	15	22	29	—
S.	..	2	9	16	23	30	—

Month	Week		
		Janus, god of the portal, facing two ways, past and future. Sun's Longitude 300° ♒ 20ᵈ 22ʰ	
1	S.	**Circumcision.** A. H. Clough b. 1819	
2	⑨.	**2nd ⑨. after Christmas.** James Wolfe b. 1727	
3	M.	Josiah Wedgwood d. 1795	
4	Tu.	Augustus John b. 1879. T. S. Eliot d. 1965	
5	W.	Catherine de Medici d. 1589	
6	Th.	**Epiphany.** Twelfth Day. Joan of Arc b. 1412	
7	F.	Sir Thomas Monnington d. 1976	
8	S.	Galileo d. 1642. Chou En-lai d. 1976	
9	⑨.	**1st ⑨. after Epiphany.** Napoleon III d. 1873	
10	M.	Samuel Colt d. 1862. Col. Cody d. 1917	
11	Tu.	HILARY LAW SITTINGS BEGIN. Thomas Hardy d.	
12	W.	Dame Agatha Christie d. 1976 [1928	
13	Th.	James Joyce d. 1941	
14	F.	Edmund Halley d. 1742. Jean Ingres d. 1867	
15	S.	Emma, Lady Hamilton d. 1815	
16	⑨.	**2nd ⑨. after Epiphany.** Edward Gibbon d. 1794	
17	M.	Earl Lloyd George b. 1863	
18	Tu.	A. A. Milne b. 1882. Rudyard Kipling d. 1936	
19	W.	Edgar Allan Poe b. 1809. Cézanne b. 1839	
20	Th.	George V d. 1936. John Ruskin d. 1900	
21	F.	Lenin d. 1924. George Orwell d. 1950	
22	S.	Queen Victoria d. 1901. Byron b. 1788	
23	⑨.	**3rd ⑨. after Epiphany.** Paul Robeson d. 1976	
24	M.	Lord Randolph Churchill d. 1895. Sir W. Churchill [d. 1965	
25	Tu.	**Conversion of St. Paul.** Robert Burns b. 1759	
26	W.	AUSTRALIA DAY. Gen. Gordon d. 1885	
27	Th.	Mozart b. 1756. Verdi d. 1901	
28	F.	Charlemagne d. 814. Sir Francis Drake b. 1596	
29	S.	George III d. 1820. Earl Haig d. 1928	
30	⑨.	**4th ⑨. after Epiphany.** Charles I d. 1649	
31	M.	Schubert b. 1797. John Galsworthy d. 1933	

PHENOMENA

January 1ᵈ 02ʰ Jupiter in conjunction with the Moon. Jupiter 0°·8 N.

3ᵈ 10ʰ Perihelion 147,000,000 kilometres).

6ᵈ 08ʰ Mercury in inferior conjunction.

8ᵈ 00ʰ Saturn in conjunction with the Moon. Saturn 6° N.

12ᵈ 12ʰ Mercury in conjunction with Mars. Mercury 4° N.

18ᵈ 01ʰ Mercury in conjunction with the Moon. Mercury 2° S.

18ᵈ 12ʰ Mars in conjunction with the Moon. Mars 6° S.

23ᵈ 11ʰ Venus in conjunction with the Moon. Venus 3° S.

24ᵈ 12ʰ Venus at greatest eastern elongation (47°).

28ᵈ 10ʰ Jupiter in conjunction with the Moon. Jupiter 1° N.

29ᵈ 00ʰ Mercury at greatest western elongation (25°).

CONSTELLATIONS

The following constellations are near the meridian at

	d h		d h
Dec. 1	24	Dec. 16	23
Jan. 1	22	Jan. 16	21
Feb. 1	20	Feb. 15	19

Draco (below the Pole), Ursa Minor (below the Pole), Camelopardus, Perseus, Auriga, Taurus, Orion, Eridanus and Lepus.

MINIMA OF ALGOL

d	h	d	h
3	11	17	19
6	7	20	15
9	4	23	12
12	1	26	9
14	22	29	6

PHASES OF THE MOON

	d	m	h
○ Full Moon	5	12	10
☾ Last Quarter	12	19	55
● New Moon	19	14	11
☽ First Quarter	27	05	11

Perigee (366,450 kilometres) 16 10
Apogee (404, 370 ,,) 28 06
Mean Longitude of Ascending Node on January 1, 210°

MONTHLY NOTES

Jan. 3. Bank Holiday in England, Scotland, Wales and Northern Ireland.

4. Bank Holiday, Scotland.

6. Dividends on Consols, etc., due.

26. Republic Day, India.

Day	Right Ascension	Dec. —	Equation of Time	Rise 52°	Rise 56°	Transit	Set 52°	Set 56°	Sidereal Time	Transit of First Point of Aries
	h m s	° '	m s	h m	h m	h m	h m	h m	h m s	h m s
1	18 45 31	23 02	− 3 24	8 08	8 32	12 04	15 59	15 36	6 42 08	17 15 02
2	18 49 56	22 57	− 3 52	8 08	8 31	12 04	16 00	15 37	6 46 04	17 11 06
3	18 54 20	22 51	− 4 20	8 08	8 31	12 05	16 01	15 38	6 50 11	17 07 10
4	18 58 44	22 45	− 4 47	8 08	8 31	12 05	16 02	15 40	6 53 57	17 03 15
5	19 03 08	22 39	− 5 14	8 07	8 30	12 05	16 04	15 41	6 57 54	16 59 19
6	19 07 31	22 32	− 5 41	8 07	8 30	12 06	16 05	15 42	7 01 50	16 55 23
7	19 11 54	22 25	− 6 07	8 06	8 29	12 06	16 06	15 44	7 05 47	16 51 27
8	19 16 16	22 17	− 6 33	8 06	8 28	12 07	16 08	15 46	7 09 44	16 47 31
9	19 20 38	22 09	− 6 58	8 05	8 28	12 07	16 09	15 48	7 13 40	16 43 35
10	19 24 59	22 00	− 7 23	8 05	8 27	12 08	16 10	15 49	7 17 37	16 39 39
11	19 29 20	21 51	− 7 47	8 04	8 26	12 08	16 12	15 51	7 21 33	16 35 43
12	19 33 40	21 42	− 8 10	8 03	8 25	12 08	16 13	15 53	7 25 30	16 31 47
13	19 38 00	21 32	− 8 33	8 03	8 24	12 09	16 14	15 54	7 29 26	16 27 51
14	19 42 19	21 22	− 8 56	8 02	8 23	12 09	16 16	15 56	7 33 23	16 23 55
15	19 46 37	21 11	− 9 18	8 01	8 22	12 09	16 18	15 58	7 37 19	16 20 00
16	19 50 55	21 00	− 9 39	8 00	8 21	12 10	16 19	16 00	7 41 16	16 16 04
17	19 55 12	20 48	− 9 59	7 59	8 19	12 10	16 21	16 02	7 45 13	16 12 08
18	19 59 28	20 36	−10 19	7 58	8 17	12 10	16 22	16 04	7 49 09	16 08 12
19	20 03 43	20 24	−10 38	7 57	8 16	12 11	16 24	16 05	7 53 06	16 04 16
20	20 07 58	20 11	−10 56	7 56	8 15	12 11	16 26	16 07	7 57 02	16 00 20
21	20 12 13	19 58	−11 14	7 55	8 14	12 11	16 27	16 09	8 00 59	15 56 24
22	20 16 26	19 45	−11 31	7 54	8 13	12 12	16 29	16 11	8 04 55	15 52 28
23	20 20 38	19 31	−11 47	7 53	8 11	12 12	16 31	16 13	8 08 52	15 48 32
24	20 24 50	19 17	−12 02	7 51	8 09	12 12	16 33	16 15	8 12 48	15 44 36
25	20 29 01	19 02	−12 16	7 50	8 07	12 12	16 35	16 17	8 16 45	15 40 40
26	20 33 11	18 47	−12 30	7 49	8 06	12 13	16 37	16 20	8 20 42	15 36 45
27	20 37 21	18 32	−12 43	7 47	8 04	12 13	16 39	16 22	8 24 38	15 32 49
28	20 41 29	18 17	−12 55	7 46	8 03	12 13	16 40	16 24	8 28 35	15 28 53
29	20 45 37	18 01	−13 06	7 45	8 01	12 13	16 42	16 26	8 32 31	15 24 57
30	20 49 44	17 45	−13 16	7 44	8 00	12 13	16 43	16 28	8 36 28	15 21 01
31	20 53 50	17 28	−13 26	7 42	7 58	12 14	16 45	16 30	8 40 24	15 17 05

THE SUN   s.d. 16′·3

Duration of Civil (C), Nautical (N), and Astronomical (A), Twilight (in minutes)

Lat. °	Jan. 1 C	N	A	Jan. 11 C	N	A	Jan. 21 C	N	A	Jan. 31 C	N	A
52	41	84	125	40	82	123	38	80	120	37	78	117
56	47	96	141	45	93	138	43	90	134	41	87	130

ASTRONOMICAL NOTES

MERCURY is unsuitably placed for observation at first, inferior conjunction occurring on the 6th. For the second half of the month it may be glimpsed as a morning star, magnitude +1·0 to +0·1, low above the south eastern horizon at about the time of beginning of morning civil twilight. Despite the fact that it is at greatest western elongation on the 29th it is not very well placed for observation because of its declination (−22°).

VENUS is a brilliant evening star, magnitude −3·9, visible in the western sky for several hours after sunset.

MARS is unsuitably placed for observation.

JUPITER is a brilliant evening star, magnitude −2·1, in the eastern part of the constellation of Aries. The gibbous Moon is near Jupiter on the 1st and again on the 27th–28th.

SATURN is a bright morning star, magnitude +0·1, moving slowly westwards in the eastern part of Cancer. By the end of the month it is visible for most of the night. The gibbous Moon passes 6° S. of the planet on the night of the 7th–8th.

THE MOON

Day	R.A.	Dec.	Hor. Par.	Semi-diam.	Sun's Co-long.	P.A. of Bright Limb	Phase	Age	Rise 52°	Rise 56°	Transit	Set 52°	Set 56°
	h m	°	′	′	°	°		d	h m	h m	h m	h m	h m
1	3 13	+16·2	54·2	14·8	40	253	82	10·9	13 23	13 06	21 11	4 08	4 23
2	4 02	+18·0	54·3	14·8	52	255	89	11·9	14 01	13 43	21 59	5 06	5 24
3	4 53	+19·1	54·6	14·9	64	257	94	12·9	14 46	14 27	22 48	6 00	6 19
4	5 44	+19·2	54·9	15·0	76	255	98	13·9	15 39	15 20	23 38	6 49	7 08
5	6 37	+18·5	55·4	15·1	88	235	100	14·9	16 38	16 21	··	7 32	7 49
6	7 29	+16·9	55·8	15·2	100	139	100	15·9	17 43	17 29	0 28	8 09	8 24
7	8 21	+14·4	56·3	15·3	112	119	97	16·9	18 51	18 40	1 18	8 42	8 54
8	9 12	+11·1	56·8	15·5	125	116	93	17·9	20 02	19 55	2 07	9 11	9 19
9	10 03	+ 7·3	57·2	15·6	137	115	87	18·9	21 14	21 11	2 56	9 37	9 41
10	10 54	+ 3·1	57·7	15·7	149	115	79	19·9	22 28	22 29	3 44	10 02	10 03
11	11 46	− 1·4	58·2	15·9	161	115	70	20·9	23 43	23 48	4 33	10 27	10 24
12	12 38	− 5·8	58·6	16·0	173	113	59	21·9	··	··	5 23	10 54	10 47
13	13 32	−10·0	59·0	16·1	185	111	48	22·9	0 58	1 08	6 16	11 23	11 13
14	14 27	−13·7	59·4	16·2	197	109	37	23·9	2 15	2 28	7 10	11 58	11 44
15	15 25	−16·6	59·7	16·3	210	106	26	24·9	3 29	3 46	8 07	12 40	12 22
16	16 25	−18·5	59·8	16·3	222	102	17	25·9	4 40	4 58	9 06	13 30	13 11
17	17 27	−19·2	59·8	16·3	234	99	9	26·9	5 42	6 02	10 06	14 30	14 11
18	18 28	−18·7	59·6	16·2	246	99	4	27·9	6 35	6 53	11 05	15 38	15 21
19	19 28	−16·9	59·2	16·1	258	114	1	28·9	7 19	7 34	12 02	16 51	16 36
20	20 25	−14·1	58·7	16·0	271	214	0	0·4	7 55	8 07	12 56	18 05	17 54
21	21 20	−10·7	58·0	15·8	283	238	3	1·4	8 25	8 33	13 47	19 18	19 11
22	22 12	− 6·7	57·2	15·6	295	242	7	2·4	8 52	8 56	14 35	20 29	20 26
23	23 02	− 2·5	56·4	15·4	307	244	13	3·4	9 15	9 16	15 21	21 38	21 39
24	23 50	+ 1·6	55·7	15·2	319	245	21	4·4	9 38	9 36	16 06	22 45	22 49
25	0 37	+ 5·6	55·1	15·0	331	246	29	5·4	10 01	9 55	16 50	23 50	23 58
26	1 23	+ 9·3	54·7	14·9	344	248	39	6·4	10 26	10 16	17 34	··	··
27	2 10	+12·5	54·4	14·8	356	250	48	7·4	10 52	10 40	18 19	0 53	1 04
28	2 58	+15·2	54·2	14·8	8	253	57	8·4	11 23	11 08	19 04	1 55	2 09
29	3 46	+17·3	54·3	14·8	20	256	66	9·4	11 59	11 41	19 52	2 54	3 10
30	4 36	+18·6	54·5	14·8	32	260	75	10·4	12 40	12 22	20 40	3 49	4 08
31	5 27	+19·1	54·8	14·9	44	263	83	11·4	13 29	13 11	21 29	4 40	4 59

MERCURY ☿

Day	R.A.	Dec. −	Diam.	Phase	Transit	Day	R.A.	Dec. −	Diam.	Phase	5° high E. 52°	5° high E. 56°	Transit
	h m	°	″		h m		h m	°	″		h m	h m	h m
1	19 34	20·4	9	12	12 48	16	18 31	20·2	9	27	7 22	7 49	10 47
4	19 21	20·0	10	4	12 22	19	18 31	20·5	8	36	7 14	7 42	10 37
7	19 04	19·7	10	1	11 53	22	18 36	21·0	8	46	7 11	7 40	10 31
10	18 48	19·7	10	7	11 26	25	18 45	21·3	7	54	7 11	7 41	10 28
13	18 36	19·8	9	16	11 04	28	18 56	21·6	7	60	7 13	7 44	10 28
16	18 31	20·2	9	27	10 47	31	19 10	21·8	6	66	7 16	7 48	10 30

Mercury is too close to the Sun for observation

VENUS ♀

Day	R.A.	Dec. −	Diam.	Phase	Transit	5° high W. 52°	5° high W. 56°
	h m	°	″		h m	h m	h. m
1	21 55	14·4	20	62	15 13	19 23	19 05
6	22 16	12·1	20	60	15 15	19 38	19 23
11	22 37	9·8	21	58	15 15	19 52	19 41
16	22 56	7·4	22	55	15.15	20 05	19 57
21	23 15	4·9	23	53	15 14	20 18	20 11
26	23 33	2·5	25	50	15 12	20 29	20 24
31	23 51	0·0	26	48	15 10	20 39	20 36

MARS ♂

Day	R.A.	Dec. −	Diam.	Phase	Transit
	h m	°	″		h m
1	18 00	24·1	4	100	11 17
6	18 16	24·1	4	100	11 14
11	18 33	23·9	4	99	11 11
16	18 49	23·7	4	99	11 08
21	19 06	23·4	4	99	11 05
26	19 22	22·9	4	99	11 01
31	19 39	22·4	4	99	10 58

Mars is too close to the Sun for observation

SUNRISE AND SUNSET (G.M.T.)

Day	London a.m. h m	London p.m. h m	Bristol a.m. h m	Bristol p.m. h m	Birmingham a.m. h m	Birmingham p.m. h m	Manchester a.m. h m	Manchester p.m. h m	Newcastle a.m. h m	Newcastle p.m. h m	Glasgow a.m. h m	Glasgow p.m. h m	Belfast a.m. h m	Belfast p.m. h m
1	8 06	4 02	8 16	4 12	8 18	4 03	8 25	4 00	8 31	3 48	8 48	3 54	8 47	4 08
2	8 06	4 03	8 16	4 13	8 18	4 04	8 25	4 01	8 31	3 49	8 47	3 55	8 47	4 09
3	8 06	4 04	8 16	4 14	8 18	4 05	8 25	4 02	8 31	3 50	8 47	3 56	8 47	4 10
4	8 06	4 05	8 15	4 15	8 18	4 07	8 25	4 04	8 31	3 52	8 47	3 58	8 47	4 12
5	8 06	4 06	8 15	4 16	8 17	4 08	8 24	4 05	8 30	3 53	8 46	3 59	8 46	4 13
6	8 06	4 07	8 15	4 17	8 17	4 09	8 24	4 06	8 30	3 54	8 46	4 00	8 46	4 14
7	8 05	4 08	8 15	4 19	8 16	4 11	8 23	4 08	8 29	3 56	8 45	4 02	8 45	4 16
8	8 04	4 09	8 14	4 20	8 16	4 12	8 23	4 09	8 28	3 57	8 44	4 03	8 44	4 17
9	8 04	4 11	8 14	4 22	8 15	4 14	8 22	4 11	8 28	3 59	8 44	4 05	8 44	4 19
10	8 04	4 12	8 13	4 23	8 15	4 15	8 22	4 12	8 27	4 01	8 43	4 07	8 43	4 21
11	8 03	4 14	8 13	4 24	8 14	4 17	8 21	4 14	8 26	4 02	8 42	4 08	8 42	4 22
12	8 02	4 15	8 12	4 26	8 13	4 18	8 20	4 15	8 25	4 04	8 41	4 10	8 41	4 24
13	8 02	4 16	8 12	4 27	8 13	4 19	8 20	4 16	8 24	4 06	8 40	4 12	8 40	4 26
14	8 01	4 18	8 11	4 29	8 12	4 21	8 19	4 18	8 23	4 07	8 39	4 14	8 39	4 27
15	8 00	4 19	8 10	4 30	8 11	4 23	8 18	4 20	8 22	4 09	8 38	4 15	8 38	4 29
16	7 59	4 21	8 09	4 32	8 10	4 24	8 17	4 21	8 21	4 11	8 37	4 17	8 37	4 31
17	7 58	4 23	8 08	4 33	8 09	4 26	8 16	4 23	8 20	4 13	8 36	4 19	8 36	4 33
18	7 57	4 24	8 07	4 35	8 08	4 27	8 15	4 24	8 19	4 14	8 35	4 21	8 35	4 34
19	7 56	4 26	8 06	4 36	8 07	4 29	8 14	4 26	8 18	4 16	8 33	4 23	8 34	4 36
20	7 55	4 28	8 05	4 38	8 06	4 31	8 13	4 28	8 17	4 18	8 32	4 25	8 33	4 38
21	7 54	4 29	8 04	4 39	8 05	4 32	8 12	4 30	8 16	4 20	8 31	4 27	8 32	4 40
22	7 53	4 31	8 03	4 41	8 04	4 34	8 10	4 32	8 14	4 22	8 29	4 29	8 30	4 42
23	7 52	4 33	8 02	4 43	8 03	4 36	8 09	4 33	8 13	4 24	8 28	4 31	8 29	4 43
24	7 50	4 35	8 00	4 45	8 01	4 38	8 08	4 35	8 11	4 26	8 26	4 33	8 28	4 45
25	7 49	4 36	7 59	4 46	8 00	4 39	8 06	4 37	8 09	4 28	8 24	4 35	8 26	4 47
26	7 48	4 38	7 58	4 48	7 59	4 41	8 05	4 39	8 08	4 30	8 23	4 37	8 25	4 49
27	7 46	4 40	7 56	4 50	7 57	4 43	8 03	4 41	8 06	4 32	8 21	4 39	8 23	4 51
28	7 45	4 42	7 55	4 52	7 56	4 45	8 02	4 43	8 05	4 34	8 20	4 42	8 22	4 54
29	7 44	4 44	7 54	4 54	7 55	4 47	8 00	4 45	8 03	4 36	8 18	4 44	8 20	4 56
30	7 42	4 45	7 52	4 55	7 53	4 48	7 59	4 47	8 02	4 38	8 16	4 46	8 18	4 58
31	7 41	4 47	7 51	4 57	7 52	4 50	7 57	4 49	8 00	4 40	8 14	4 48	8 16	5 00

JUPITER ♃   SATURN ♄

Day	R.A. h m	Dec. + °	Transit h m	5° high W. 52° h m	5° high W. 56° h m	R.A. h m	Dec. + °	5° high E. 52° h m	5° high E. 56° h m	Transit h m
1	3 18	17·2	20 32	3 32	3 44	9 14	16·9	19 33	19 22	2 32
11	3 16	17·2	19 51	2 51	3 03	9 12	17·1	18 49	18 38	1 50
21	3 16	17·2	19 12	2 13	2 24	9 09	17·4	18 05	17 54	1 08
31	3 18	17·3	18 34	1 36	1 47	9 06	17·6	17 22	17 10	0 25

Equatorial diameter of Jupiter 44"; of Saturn 20". Diameters of Saturn's rings 46" and 13".

URANUS ♅   NEPTUNE ♆

Day	R.A. h m	Dec. − ° '	10° high E. 52° h m	10° high E. 56° h m	Transit h m	R.A. h m	Dec. − ° '	Transit h m	
1	14 34·4	14 40	4 27	4 52	7 51	16 54·1	21 07	10 10	Neptune is too
11	14 35·8	14 47	3 49	4 14	7 13	16 55·5	21 09	9 32	close to the
21	14 36·9	14 52	3 12	3 37	6 35	16 56·8	21 10	8 54	Sun for
31	14 37·6	14 55	2 34	3 00	5 56	16 58·0	21 12	8 16	observation

Diameter 4"   Diameter 2"

DAY OF		
Month	Week	*Februa*, Roman festival of Purification Sun's Longitude 330° ♓ 19ᵈ 13ʰ

1	Tu.	Sir Stanley Matthews b. 1915
2	W.	**Purification.** Candlemas. James Joyce b. 1882
3	Th.	Mendelssohn b. 1809
4	F.	Carlyle d. 1881. Roger Livesey d. 1976
5	S.	Sir Robert Peel b. 1788
6	S.	**Septuagesima.** QUEEN'S ACCESSION, 1952
7	M.	Sir Thomas More b. 1478. Charles Dickens b. 1812
8	Tu.	Robert Burton b. 1577★★ Ruskin b. 1819
9	W.	Lord Darnley d. 1567. Marquess of Exeter b. 1905
10	Th.	Harold Macmillan b. 1894
11	F.	Descartes d. 1650. John Buchan d. 1940
12	S.	Charles Darwin b. 1809. Abraham Lincoln b. 1809
13	S.	**Sexagesima.** Georges Simenon b. 1903
14	M.	VALENTINE'S DAY. Sir P. G. Wodehouse d. 1975
15	Tu.	Gen. Lew Wallace d. 1905
16	W.	G. M. Trevelyan b. 1876
17	Th.	Heine d. 1856. Sir Donald Wolfit d. 1968
18	F.	Queen Mary I b. 1516. Martin Luther d. 1546
19	S.	PRINCE ANDREW BORN, 1960. Garrick b. 1717
20	S.	**Quinquagesima.** Spinoza d. 1677★★
21	M.	Mary Shelley d. 1851. Gogol d. 1852
22	Tu.	George Washington b. 1732. Angela Baddeley d.
23	W.	**Ash Wednesday.** L. S. Lowry d. 1976 [1976
24	Th.	**St. Matthias.** Thomas Bowdler b. 1825
25	F.	Princess Alice, Countess of Athlone b. 1883
26	S.	Sir Christopher Wren d. 1723. Victor Hugo b. 1802
27	S.	**1st S. in Lent. Quadragesima**
28	M.	Sir Neville Cardus d. 1975

PHENOMENA

February 2ᵈ 10ʰ Saturn at opposition.

4ᵈ 04ʰ Saturn in conjunction with the Moon. Saturn 6° N.

12ᵈ 19ʰ Mercury in conjunction with Mars. Mercury 0°·1 S.

16ᵈ 12ʰ Mars in conjunction with the Moon. Mars 6° S.

16ᵈ 17ʰ Mercury in conjunction with the Moon. Mercury 7° S.

21ᵈ 17ʰ Venus in conjunction with the Moon. Venus 3° N.

24ᵈ 22ʰ Jupiter in conjunction with the Moon. Jupiter 2° N.

CONSTELLATIONS

The following constellations are near the meridian at

	d h		d h
Jan. 1 24		Jan. 16 23	
Feb. 1 22		Feb. 15 21	
Mar. 1 20		Mar. 16 19	

Draco (below the Pole), Camelopardus, Auriga, Taurus, Gemini, Orion, Canis Minor, Monoceros, Lepus, Canis Major and Puppis (Argo).

MINIMA OF ALGOL

d	h		d	h
1	3		15	11
4	00		18	8
6	20		21	4
9	17		24	1
12	14		26	22

MONTHLY NOTES

Feb. 1. Pheasant and partridge shooting ends.
4. Independence Commemoration Day, Sri Lanka.
6. National Day, New Zealand.
23. Lent begins (ends midnight April 9).

PHASES OF THE MOON

	d	h	m
○ Full Moon	4	03	56
☽ Last Quarter	11	04	07
● New Moon	18	03	37
☽ First Quarter	26	02	50

	d	h
Perigee (370,290 kilometres)	11	04
Apogee (404,360 „)	25	03

Mean Longitude of Ascending Node on February 1, 208°

QUARTER DAYS (England, Wales and Northern Ireland)

Lady Day	March 25	*Michaelmas* September 29
Midsummer	June 24	*Christmas* December 25

SCOTTISH TERM DAYS

Candlemas	February 2	*Lammas* August 1
Whitsunday	May 15	*Martinmas* November 11

Removal Terms are May 28 and November 28.

★★ Centenary.

| Day | THE SUN | | | | | | | | Sidereal Time | Transit of First Point of Aries |
| | Right Ascension | Dec. — | Equation of Time | Rise | | Transit | Set | | | |
				52°	56°		52°	56°		
	h m s	° ′	m s	h m	h m	h m	h m	h m	h m s	h m s
1	20 57 55	17 11	−13 34	7 40	7 55	12 14	16 48	16 33	8 44 21	15 13 09
2	21 02 00	16 54	−13 42	7 39	7 53	12 14	16 50	16 35	8 48 17	15 09 13
3	21 06 03	16 37	−13 49	7 37	7 51	12 14	16 51	16 37	8 52 14	15 05 17
4	21 10 06	16 19	−13 55	7 36	7 49	12 14	16 53	16 39	8 56 11	15 01 21
5	21 14 08	16 01	−14 01	7 34	7 47	12 14	16 55	16 41	9 00 07	14 57 25
6	21 18 09	15 43	−14 05	7 32	7 45	12 14	16 57	16 43	9 04 04	14 53 30
7	21 22 09	15 24	−14 09	7 30	7 43	12 14	16 59	16 46	9 08 00	14 49 34
8	21 26 09	15 06	−14 12	7 28	7 41	12 14	17 00	16 48	9 11 57	14 45 38
9	21 30 07	14 47	−14 14	7 26	7 39	12 14	17 02	16 50	9 15 53	14 41 42
10	21 34 05	14 27	−14 16	7 25	7 37	12 14	17 04	16 52	9 19 50	14 37 46
11	21 38 03	14 08	−14 16	7 23	7 35	12 14	17 06	16 54	9 23 46	14 33 50
12	21 41 59	13 48	−14 16	7 21	7 33	12 14	17 08	16 56	9 27 43	14 29 54
13	21 45 55	13 28	−14 16	7 19	7 30	12 14	17 10	16 59	9 31 40	14 25 58
14	21 49 50	13 08	−14 14	7 17	7 28	12 14	17 12	17 01	9 35 36	14 22 02
15	21 53 44	12 47	−14 12	7 15	7 26	12 14	17 14	17 04	9 39 33	14 18 06
16	21 57 38	12 27	−14 09	7 14	7 24	12 14	17 15	17 06	9 43 29	14 14 10
17	22 01 31	12 06	−14 05	7 12	7 22	12 14	17 17	17 08	9 47 26	14 10 15
18	22 05 23	11 45	−14 01	7 10	7 19	12 14	17 19	17 10	9 51 22	14 06 19
19	22 09 14	11 23	−13 55	7 08	7 17	12 14	17 21	17 12	9 55 19	14 02 23
20	22 13 05	11 02	−13 50	7 06	7 14	12 14	17 23	17 14	9 59 15	13 58 27
21	22 16 55	10 40	−13 43	7 03	7 12	12 14	17 25	17 16	10 03 12	13 54 31
22	22 20 45	10 19	−13 36	7 01	7 09	12 14	17 27	17 19	10 07 09	13 50 35
23	22 24 33	9 57	−13 28	6 59	7 06	12 13	17 29	17 21	10 11 05	13 46 39
24	22 28 22	9 35	−13 20	6 57	7 04	12 13	17 31	17 23	10 15 02	13 42 43
25	22 32 09	9 13	−13 11	6 55	7 02	12 13	17 32	17 25	10 18 58	13 38 47
26	22 35 56	8 50	−13 02	6 53	7 00	12 13	17 34	17 27	10 22 55	13 34 51
27	22 39 43	8 28	−12 51	6 51	6 58	12 13	17 36	17 29	10 26 51	13 30 55
28	22 43 28	8 05	−12 41	6 49	6 55	12 13	17 37	17 32	10 30 48	13 27 00

Duration of Civil (C), Nautical (N), and Astronomical (A), Twilight (in minutes)

| Lat. ° | Feb. 1 | | | Feb. 11 | | | Feb. 21 | | | Feb. 28 | | |
	C	N	A	C	N	A	C	N	A	C	N	A
52	37	77	117	35	75	114	34	74	113	34	73	112
56	41	86	130	39	83	126	38	81	125	38	81	124

ASTRONOMICAL NOTES

MERCURY is unsuitably placed for observation throughout the month.

VENUS is a brilliant evening star, magnitude −4·2, dominating the western sky for several hours after sunset. On the early evening of the 21st the crescent Moon passes 3° S. of Venus.

MARS is unsuitably placed for observation.

JUPITER is a brilliant evening star, magnitude −1·9, moving slowly from Aries into Taurus. On the evening of the 24th the crescent Moon passes 2° S. of Jupiter. The four Galilean satellites are readily observable with almost any small telescope or good pair of binoculars, providing that they are held rigid.

SATURN is at opposition on the 2nd and thus visible throughout the hours of darkness. Its magnitude is +0·1. Saturn is in Cancer and on the morning of the 4th the Full Moon passes 6°S. of it. Titan, Saturn's largest satellite, is of magnitude +8½, and thus visible in small telescopes.

ZODIACAL LIGHT. The evening cone may be observed in the western sky after the end of twilight, from the 5th to the 19th. This faint phenomenon is only visible under good conditions and in the absence of both moonlight and artificial lighting.

THE MOON

Day	R.A.	Dec.	Hor. Par.	Semi-diam.	Sun's Co-long.	P.A. of Bright Limb	Phase	Age	Rise 52°	Rise 56°	Transit	Set 52°	Set 56°
	h m	°	′	′	°	°		d	h m	h m	h m	h m	h m
1	6 19	+18·7	55·3	15·1	57	266	90	12·4	14 26	14 08	22 20	5 26	5 44
2	7 11	+17·5	55·9	15·2	69	267	95	13·4	15 28	15 13	23 10	6 07	6 22
3	8 04	+15·3	56·5	15·4	81	263	98	14·4	16 36	16 24	..	6 42	6 55
4	8 56	+12·3	57·1	15·6	93	219	100	15·4	17 47	17 39	0 00	7 13	7 22
5	9 49	+ 8·6	75·6	15·7	105	132	99	16·4	19 00	18 56	0 50	7 41	7 47
6	10 41	+ 4·4	58·1	15·8	117	121	96	17·4	20 15	20 15	1 40	8 07	8 09
7	11 33	− 0·1	58·5	15·9	129	117	91	18·4	21 31	21 35	2 30	8 33	8 31
8	12 26	− 4·6	58·8	16·0	141	115	83	19·4	22 47	22 55	3 21	8 59	8 54
9	13 20	− 8·9	59·0	16·1	154	112	74	20·4	..	..	4 13	9 28	9 19
10	14 15	−12·7	59·2	16·1	166	109	63	21·4	0 04	0 15	5 06	10 01	9 48
11	15 12	−15·8	59·2	16·1	178	105	52	22·4	1 18	1 33	6 02	10 40	10 24
12	16 10	−17·9	59·2	16·1	190	101	41	23·4	2 28	2 46	6 59	11 26	11 08
13	17 10	−18·9	59·1	16·1	202	97	30	24·4	3 32	3 51	7 57	12 21	12 02
14	18 09	−18·8	58·9	16·1	214	93	20	25·4	4 27	4 46	8 54	13 24	13 06
15	19 08	−17·5	58·6	16·0	227	89	12	26·4	5 14	5 30	9 50	14 32	14 17
16	20 05	−15·2	58·3	15·9	239	88	6	27·4	5 52	6 05	10 44	15 44	15 32
17	21 00	−12·0	57·8	15·8	251	92	2	28·4	6 24	6 34	11 36	16 57	16 48
18	21 52	− 8·3	57·3	15·6	263	137	0	29·4	6 52	6 58	12 25	18 08	18 04
19	22 43	− 4·3	56·7	15·4	275	229	1	0·8	7 17	7 20	13 12	19 18	19 18
20	23 32	− 0·1	56·1	15·3	288	240	4	1·8	7 41	7 40	13 58	20 27	20 29
21	0 20	+ 4·0	55·5	15·1	300	244	8	2·8	8 04	8 00	14 43	21 33	21 39
22	1 07	+ 7·8	55·0	15·0	312	247	15	3·8	8 29	8 21	15 28	22 38	22 47
23	1 54	+11·2	54·6	14·9	324	250	22	4·8	8 55	8 44	16 12	23 40	23 53
24	2 42	+14·1	54·3	14·8	336	253	31	5·8	9 24	9 10	16 58	..	..
25	3 30	+16·4	54·2	14·8	349	256	40	6·8	9 57	9 41	17 44	0 40	0 56
26	4 19	+18·0	54·3	14·8	1	260	49	7·8	10 36	10 18	18 32	1 37	1 55
27	5 09	+18·8	54·5	14·9	13	264	58	8·8	11 21	11 02	19 20	2 30	2 48
28	6 00	+18·8	55·0	15·0	25	268	68	9·8	12 13	11 55	20 09	3 18	3 36

MERCURY ☿

Day	R.A.	Dec. −	Diam.	Phase	Transit		Day	R.A.	Dec. −	Diam.	Phase	Transit	
	h m	°	″		h m			h m	°	″		h m	
1	19 15	21·8	6	68	10 31	Mercury is	16	20 40	19·8	5	84	10 57	Mercury is
4	19 30	21·8	6	72	10 34	too close to	19	20 58	18·9	5	87	11 04	too close to
7	19 46	21·6	6	76	10 39	the Sun	22	21 17	17·7	5	89	11 11	the Sun
10	20 04	21·2	6	79	10 45	for	25	21 37	16·4	5	92	11 19	for
13	20 21	20·6	6	82	10 51	observation	28	21 56	14·8	5	93	11 27	observation
16	20 40	19·8	5	84	10 57		31	22 16	13·1	5	95	11 34	

VENUS ♀   MARS ♂

Day	R.A.	Dec. +	Diam.	Phase	Transit	5° high W. 52°	5° high W. 56°	Day	R.A.	Dec. −	Diam.	Phase	Transit	
	h m	°	″		h m	h m	h m		h m	°	″		h m	
1	23 54	0·5	27	47	15 09	20 41	20 39	1	19 42	22·3	4	99	10 57	Mars is
6	0 10	2·9	28	44	15 06	20 49	20 49	6	19 58	21·6	4	99	10 54	too close
11	0 25	5·2	30	41	15 01	20 56	20 58	11	20 14	20·8	4	98	10 50	to the
16	0 39	7·5	32	38	14 55	21 01	21 05	16	20 31	20·0	4	98	10 47	Sun for
21	0 52	9·6	35	34	14 47	21 05	21 10	21	20 46	19·0	4	98	10 43	observation
26	1 02	11·5	37	30	14 38	21 06	21 12	26	21 02	18·0	4	98	10 39	
31	1 11	13·2	40	26	14 27	21 05	21 12	31	21 18	16·9	4	98	10 35	

SUNRISE AND SUNSET (G.M.T.)

Day	London a.m. h m	London p.m. h m	Bristol a.m. h m	Bristol p.m. h m	Birmingham a.m. h m	Birmingham p.m. h m	Manchester a.m. h m	Manchester p.m. h m	Newcastle a.m. h m	Newcastle p.m. h m	Glasgow a.m. h m	Glasgow p.m. h m	Belfast a.m. h m	Belfast p.m. h m
1	7 40	4 49	7 49	4 59	7 50	4 52	7 55	4 51	7 58	4 42	8 12	4 50	8 14	5 02
2	7 38	4 51	7 48	5 01	7 48	4 54	7 53	4 53	7 56	4 44	8 10	4 52	8 12	5 04
3	7 37	4 53	7 46	5 03	7 47	4 56	7 52	4 55	7 54	4 46	8 08	4 54	8 11	5 06
4	7 35	4 55	7 44	5 05	7 45	4 58	7 50	4 57	7 52	4 49	8 06	4 57	8 09	5 08
5	7 34	4 56	7 43	5 06	7 43	5 00	7 48	4 59	7 50	4 51	8 04	4 59	8 07	5 10
6	7 32	4 58	7 41	5 08	7 41	5 02	7 46	5 01	7 48	4 53	8 02	5 01	8 05	5 12
7	7 30	5 00	7 40	5 10	7 39	5 04	7 44	5 03	7 46	4 55	8 00	5 03	8 03	5 14
8	7 29	5 01	7 38	5 11	7 38	5 06	7 43	5 05	7 45	4 57	7 59	5 05	8 02	5 16
9	7 27	5 03	7 36	5 13	7 36	5 08	7 41	5 07	7 43	4 59	7 57	5 07	8 00	5 18
10	7 25	5 05	7 35	5 15	7 34	5 10	7 39	5 09	7 41	5 01	7 55	5 09	7 58	5 20
11	7 23	5 07	7 33	5 17	7 32	5 12	7 37	5 11	7 39	5 03	7 53	5 11	7 56	5 22
12	7 21	5 09	7 31	5 19	7 30	5 14	7 35	5 13	7 37	5 05	7 51	5 13	7 54	5 24
13	7 19	5 10	7 29	5 21	7 28	5 15	7 33	5 14	7 34	5 07	7 48	5 15	7 52	5 26
14	7 17	5 12	7 27	5 22	7 26	5 17	7 31	5 16	7 32	5 09	7 46	5 17	7 50	5 28
15	7 15	5 14	7 25	5 24	7 24	5 19	7 29	5 18	7 30	5 12	7 44	5 20	7 47	5 30
16	7 13	5 16	7 23	5 26	7 22	5 21	7 27	5 20	7 28	5 14	7 42	5 22	7 45	5 32
17	7 11	5 18	7 21	5 28	7 20	5 23	7 25	5 22	7 25	5 16	7 39	5 24	7 43	5 34
18	7 09	5 20	7 19	5 30	7 18	5 25	7 23	5 24	7 23	5 18	7 37	5 26	7 41	5 36
19	7 07	5 21	7 17	5 31	7 16	5 26	7 21	5 26	7 21	5 20	7 35	5 28	7 39	5 38
20	7 05	5 23	7 15	5 33	7 14	5 28	7 19	5 28	7 19	5 22	7 32	5 31	7 36	5 41
21	7 03	5 25	7 13	5 35	7 12	5 30	7 16	5 30	7 17	5 24	7 30	5 33	7 34	5 43
22	7 01	5 27	7 11	5 37	7 10	5 32	7 14	5 32	7 14	5 26	7 27	5 35	7 31	5 45
23	6 59	5 29	7 09	5 39	7 08	5 34	7 12	5 34	7 12	5 28	7 25	5 37	7 29	5 47
24	6 57	5 31	7 07	5 41	7 06	5 36	7 10	5 36	7 10	5 30	7 23	5 39	7 27	5 49
25	6 55	5 33	7 05	5 43	7 04	5 38	7 07	5 38	7 07	5 32	7 20	5 41	7 24	5 51
26	6 53	5 34	7 03	5 44	7 02	5 39	7 05	5 40	7 05	5 35	7 18	5 44	7 22	5 53
27	6 51	5 36	7 01	5 46	7 00	5 41	7 03	5 42	7 02	5 37	7 15	5 46	7 20	5 55
28	6 49	5 38	6 59	5 48	6 57	5 43	7 00	5 44	7 00	5 39	7 13	5 48	7 17	5 57

JUPITER ♃   SATURN ♄

Day	R.A. h m	Dec. + °	Transit h m	5° high W. 52° h m	5° high W. 56° h m	R.A. h m	Dec. + °	Transit h m	5° high W. 52° h m	5° high W. 56° h m
1	3 18	17·4	18 31	1 32	1 43	9 05	17·7	0 21	7 20	7 32
11	3 21	17·6	17 54	0 56	1 07	9 02	17·9	23 34	6 39	6 51
21	3 25	17·9	17 19	0 22	0 33	8 59	18·1	22 52	5 58	6 10
31	3 30	18·2	16 45	23 46	23 58	8 56	18·3	22 10	5 17	5 29

Equatorial diameter of Jupiter 40″; of Saturn 20″. Diameters of Saturn's rings 46″ and 14″.

URANUS ♅   NEPTUNE ♆

Day	R.A. h m	Dec. ° ′	10° high E. 52° h m	10° high E. 56° h m	Transit h m	R.A. h m	Dec. ° ′	10° high E. 52° h m	10° high E. 56° h m	Transit h m
1	14 37·6	14 55	2 30	2 56	5 52	16 58·1	21 12	5 44	6 33	8 12
11	14 37·9	14 56	1 51	2 17	5 13	16 59·0	21 13	5 06	5 56	7 34
21	14 37·9	14 56	1 12	1 38	4 34	16 59·7	21 14	4 28	5 18	6 55
31	14 37·5	14 54	0 32	0 58	3 54	17 00·2	21 14	3 51	4 40	6 17

Diameter 4″   Diameter 2″

Mars, Roman god of battle

Sun's Longitude 0° ♈ 20^{d} 12^{h}

Day of Month	Day of Week	
1	Tu.	St. David's Day. Lytton Strachey b. 1880
2	W.	Horace Walpole d. 1797. D. H. Lawrence d. 1930
3	Th.	Van Gogh b. 1853. Sir Henry Wood b. 1869
4	F.	R.N.L.I. founded 1824. Patrick Moore b. 1923
5	S.	James I d. 1625. Stalin d. 1953
6	S.	**2nd S. in Lent.** Adm. von Tirpitz d. 1930
7	M.	Sir Edwin Landseer b. 1802. Maurice Ravel b. 1875
8	Tu.	William III d. 1702. Kenneth Grahame b. 1859
9	W.	Amerigo Vespucci b. 1451. V. M. Molotov b. 1890
10	Th.	Prince Edward Born, 1964. Diaghilev b. 1872
11	F.	Sir Alexander Fleming d. 1955
12	S.	John Bull d. 1628. John Aubrey b. 1626
13	S.	**3rd S. in Lent.** Sir Frank Worrell d. 1967
14	M.	Admiral Byng shot 1757. Karl Marx d. 1883
15	Tu.	Julius Caesar d. B.C. 44. Visct. Chandos b. 1893
16	W.	Matthew Flinders b. 1774
17	Th.	St. Patrick's Day. Edmund Kean b. 1787
18	F.	Sir Robert Walpole d. 1745. Laurence Sterne d. [1768
19	S.	Sir Richard Burton b. 1821
20	S.	**4th S. in Lent.** Ibsen b. 1828
21	M.	Aboukir 1801. Robert Southey d. 1843
22	Tu.	Stendhal d. 1842. Nicholas Monsarrat b. 1910
23	W.	Sir Roger Bannister b. 1929
24	Th.	E. H. Shepard d. 1976. Visct. Montgomery of [Alamein d. 1976
25	F.	**Annunciation.** Bartok b. 1881
26	S.	Beethoven d. 1827. Walt Whitman d. 1892
27	S.	**5th S. in Lent.** James Callaghan b. 1912
28	M.	Rachmaninoff d. 1943
29	Tu.	Sir William Walton b. 1902. Joyce Cary d. 1957
30	W.	Goya b. 1746. Beau Brummell d. 1840
31	Th.	John Donne d. 1631. John Constable d. 1837

PHENOMENA

March 1^{d} 02^{h} Venus at greatest brilliancy.

3^{d} 09^{h} Saturn in conjunction with the Moon. Saturn 6° N.

16^{d} 05^{h} Mercury in superior conjunction.

17^{d} 12^{h} Mars in conjunction with the Moon. Mars 6° S.

20^{d} 05^{h} Mercury in conjunction with the Moon. Mercury 3° S.

20^{d} 18^{h} Vernal Equinox.

21^{d} 13^{h} Venus in conjunction with the Moon. Venus 8° N.

24^{d} 15^{h} Jupiter in conjunction with the Moon. Jupiter 2° N.

27^{d} 19^{h} Mercury in conjunction with Venus. Mercury 8° S.

30^{d} 17^{h} Saturn in conjunction with the Moon. Saturn 6° N.

CONSTELLATIONS

The following constellations are near the meridian at

	d	h		d	h
Feb.	1	24	Feb.	15	23
Mar.	1	22	Mar.	16	21
Apr.	1	20	Apr.	15	19

Cepheus (below the Pole), Camelopardus, Lynx, Gemini, Cancer, Leo, Canis Minor, Hydra, Monoceros, Canis Major and Puppis (Argo).

MINIMA OF ALGOL

d	h	d	h
1	19	19	00
4	16	21	21
7	12	24	17
10	9	27	14
13	6	30	11
16	3		

PHASES OF THE MOON

	d	h	m
○ Full Moon	5	17	13
☾ Last Quarter	12	11	35
● New Moon	19	18	33
☽ First Quarter	27	22	27

	d	h
Perigee (366,420 kilometres)	8	23
Apogee (405,090 ,,)	24	22

Mean Longitude of Ascending Node on March 1, 207

Summer Time in 1977 (*see* p. 142).—Begins: March 20 at 2 a.m. G.M.T. Ends: October 23 at 2 a.m. G.M.T.

MONTHLY NOTES

Mar. 12. Independence Day, Mauritius.

17. Bank Holiday in Northern Ireland.

25. Lady Day. Quarter Day.

31. Financial Year 1976–77 ends.

THE SUN   s.d. 16'·1

Day	Right Ascension	Dec.	Equation of Time	Rise 52°	Rise 56°	Transit	Set 52°	Set 56°	Sidereal Time	Transit of First Point of Aries
	h m s	° '	m s	h m	h m	h m	h m	h m	h m s	h m s
1	22 47 14	−7 43	−12 29	6 46	6 52	12 12	17 39	17 34	10 34 44	13 23 04
2	22 50 58	−7 20	−12 18	6 44	6 49	12 12	17 41	17 36	10 38 41	13 19 08
3	22 54 43	−6 57	−12 05	6 42	6 47	12 12	17 43	17 38	10 42 38	13 15 12
4	22 58 26	−6 34	−11 52	6 40	6 44	12 12	17 45	17 40	10 46 34	13 11 16
5	23 02 10	−6 11	−11 39	6 37	6 41	12 12	17 46	17 42	10 50 31	13 07 20
6	23 05 53	−5 48	−11 25	6 35	6 39	12 11	17 48	17 44	10 54 27	13 03 24
7	23 09 35	−5 24	−11 11	6 33	6 36	12 11	17 50	17 46	10 58 24	12 59 28
8	23 13 17	−5 01	−10 57	6 31	6 34	12 11	17 52	17 48	11 02 20	12 55 32
9	23 16 59	−4 38	−10 42	6 29	6 32	12 11	17 54	17 51	11 06 17	12 51 36
10	23 20 40	−4 14	−10 27	6 27	6 29	12 10	17 56	17 53	11 10 13	12 47 40
11	23 24 21	−3 51	−10 11	6 25	6 27	12 10	17 58	17 55	11 14 10	12 43 45
12	23 28 02	−3 27	− 9 55	6 22	6 24	12 10	17 59	17 57	11 18 07	12 39 49
13	23 31 42	−3 03	− 9 39	6 20	6 21	12 10	18 01	17 59	11 22 03	12 35 53
14	23 35 22	−2 40	− 9 23	6 18	6 19	12 09	18 03	18 01	11 26 00	12 31 57
15	23 39 02	−2 16	− 9 06	6 15	6 16	12 09	18 04	18 03	11 29 56	12 28 01
16	23 42 42	−1 52	− 8 49	6 12	6 14	12 09	18 06	18 05	11 33 53	12 24 05
17	23 46 21	−1 29	− 8 32	6 10	6 11	12 08	18 08	18 07	11 37 49	12 20 09
18	23 50 00	−1 05	− 8 15	6 08	6 08	12 08	18 09	18 09	11 41 46	12 16 13
19	23 53 40	−0 41	− 7 57	6 06	6 05	12 08	18 11	18 11	11 45 42	12 12 17
20	23 57 18	−0 18	− 7 40	6 03	6 03	12 08	18 13	18 13	11 49 39	12 08 21
21	0 00 57	+0 06	− 7 22	6 01	6 00	12 07	18 15	18 15	11 53 35	12 04 26
22	0 04 36	+0 30	− 7 04	5 59	5 57	12 07	18 17	18 17	11 57 32	12 00 30
23	0 08 15	+0 54	− 6 46	5 56	5 55	12 07	18 19	18 19	12 01 29	11 56 34
24	0 11 53	+1 17	− 6 28	5 54	5 52	12 06	18 20	18 22	12 05 25	11 52 38
25	0 15 31	+1 41	− 6 10	5 52	5 50	12 06	18 22	18 24	12 09 22	11 48 42
26	0 19 10	+2 04	− 5 52	5 50	5 48	12 06	18 24	18 26	12 13 18	11 44 46
27	0 22 48	+2 28	− 5 33	5 47	5 45	12 05	18 25	18 28	12 17 15	11 40 50
28	0 26 26	+2 51	− 5 15	5 45	5 42	12 05	18 27	18 30	12 21 11	11 36 54
29	0 30 05	+3 15	− 4 57	5 43	5 40	12 05	18 29	18 32	12 25 08	11 32 58
30	0 33 43	+3 38	− 4 39	5 40	5 37	12 04	18 30	18 34	12 29 04	11 29 02
31	0 37 22	+4 01	− 4 21	5 38	5 35	12 04	18 32	18 36	12 33 01	11 25 06

Duration of Civil (C), Nautical (N), and Astronomical (A), Twilight (in minutes)

Lat. °	Mar. 1 C	N	A	Mar. 11 C	N	A	Mar. 21 C	N	A	Mar. 31 C	N	A
52	34	73	112	34	73	113	34	74	116	34	76	120
56	38	81	124	37	80	124	37	82	129	38	84	136

ASTRONOMICAL NOTES

MERCURY is unsuitably placed for observation for almost the whole month, superior conjunction occurring on the 16th. However during the last few days of March it becomes visible as an evening star, magnitude −1·2 to −0·9, low above the western horizon at the time of end of evening civil twilight. On the evening of the 27th, probably the first evening on which it may be glimpsed, Mercury passes 8° S. of Venus.

VENUS is a magnificent evening star, magnitude −4·2, attaining its greatest brilliancy on the 1st. However the period available for observation is shortening and by the end of the month the planet sets only about an hour after the Sun.

MARS is unsuitably placed for observation.

JUPITER is a brilliant evening star, magnitude −1·7, moving slowly eastwards in the constellation of Taurus. The five day old crescent Moon is near Jupiter on the evening of the 24th.

SATURN is a bright evening star, magnitude +0·3, visible for most of the night. Saturn is in Cancer.

ZODIACAL LIGHT. The evening cone may be observed in the western sky after the end of twilight, from the 7th to the 20th.

THE MOON

Day	R.A.	Dec.	Hor. Par.	Semi-diam.	Sun's Co-long.	P.A. of Bright Limb	Phase	Age	Rise 52°	Rise 56°	Transit	Set 52°	Set 56°
	h m	°	'	'	°	°		d	h m	h m	h m	h m	h m
1	6 52	+17·9	55·5	15·1	37	272	76	10·8	13 12	12 56	20 59	4 00	4 17
2	7 44	+16·1	56·2	15·3	49	275	84	11·8	14 17	14 03	21 49	4 37	4 52
3	8 36	+13·4	56·9	15·5	62	277	91	12·8	15 26	15 16	22 39	5 10	5 22
4	9 29	+10·0	57·7	15·7	74	277	96	13·8	16 39	16 33	23 30	5 40	5 48
5	10 22	+ 6·0	58·4	15·9	86	268	99	14·8	17 55	17 53	··	6 08	6 12
6	11 15	+ 1·6	59·0	16·1	98	152	100	15·8	19 12	19 14	0 21	6 35	6 35
7	12 09	− 3·0	59·5	16·2	110	120	98	16·8	20 31	20 37	1 13	7 02	6 58
8	13 04	− 7·5	59·8	16·3	122	114	93	17·8	21 49	21 59	2 06	7 31	7 23
9	14 00	−11·6	59·8	16·3	134	109	86	18·8	23 06	23 20	3 01	8 03	7 52
10	14 58	−14·9	59·8	16·3	147	105	77	19·8	··	··	3 57	8 41	8 26
11	15 57	−17·3	59·5	16·2	159	101	67	20·8	0 19	0 36	4 54	9 26	9 08
12	16 57	−18·6	59·2	16·1	171	96	55	21·8	1 25	1 44	5 52	10 18	9 59
13	17 56	−18·7	58·8	16·0	183	91	44	22·8	2 23	2 42	6 49	11 18	10 59
14	18 54	−17·7	58·4	15·9	195	87	33	23·8	3 12	3 28	7 45	12 23	12 07
15	19 50	−15·7	57·9	15·8	207	83	23	24·8	3 52	4 06	8 39	13 33	13 19
16	20 45	−12·9	57·4	15·6	220	80	15	25·8	4 25	4 36	9 30	14 43	14 33
17	21 37	− 9·4	56·9	15·5	232	78	8	26·8	4 54	5 02	10 19	15 54	15 48
18	22 27	− 5·5	56·5	15·4	244	79	3	27·8	5 20	5 24	11 06	17 03	17 01
19	23 16	− 1·5	56·0	15·2	256	85	1	28·8	5 44	5 44	11 52	18 11	18 12
20	0 04	+ 2·6	55·5	15·1	269	209	0	0·2	6 07	6 04	12 37	19 18	19 23
21	0 51	+ 6·5	55·1	15·0	281	243	1	1·2	6 31	6 25	13 22	20 23	20 31
22	1 38	+10·0	54·7	14·9	293	249	5	2·2	6 57	6 47	14 06	21 27	21 38
23	2 26	+13·1	54·4	14·8	305	253	10	3·2	7 25	7 12	14 52	22 28	22 43
24	3 14	+15·6	54·2	14·8	317	257	16	4·2	7 56	7 41	15 38	23 26	23 43
25	4 03	+17·4	54·1	14·7	330	261	23	5·2	8 33	8 16	16 25	··	··
26	4 52	+18·5	54·2	14·8	342	265	32	6·2	9 15	8 57	17 12	0 21	0 39
27	5 43	+18·7	54·5	14·8	354	269	41	7·2	10 04	9 45	18 00	1 10	1 28
28	6 33	+18·2	54·9	15·0	6	273	51	8·2	10 58	10 42	18 49	1 54	2 11
29	7 24	+16·7	55·5	15·1	18	277	60	9·2	11 59	11 45	19 38	2 33	2 48
30	8 16	+14·4	56·2	15·3	30	281	70	10·2	13 05	12 54	20 27	3 07	3 19
31	9 07	+11·4	57·1	15·5	43	283	79	11·2	14 15	14 07	21 17	3 37	3 47

MERCURY ☿

Day	R.A.	Dec. −	Diam.	Phase	Transit		Day	R.A.	Dec.	Diam.	Phase	Transit	
	h m	°	''		h m			h m	°	''		h m	
1	22 03	14·3	5	93	11 29	Mercury is too close to the Sun for observation	16	23 44	− 3·3	5	100	12 12	Mercury is too close to the Sun for observation
4	22 22	12·5	5	95	11 37		19	0 05	− 0·7	5	99	12 21	
7	22 42	10·5	5	97	11 45		22	0 27	+ 2·1	5	97	12 31	
10	23 03	8·3	5	98	11 54		25	0 48	+ 5·0	5	93	12 41	
13	23 23	5·9	5	99	12 03		28	1 09	+ 7·8	6	88	12 50	
16	23 44	3·3	5	100	12 12		31	1 30	+10·4	6	79	12 58	

VENUS ♀

Day	R.A.	Dec. +	Diam.	Phase	Transit	5° high W. 52°	5° high W. 56°
	h m	°	''		h m	h m	h m
1	1 08	12·6	39	27	14 32	21 05	21 12
6	1 15	14·1	42	23	14 19	21 00	21 08
11	1 19	15·3	46	18	14 03	20 50	20 59
16	1 20	16·1	49	14	13 44	20 35	20 45
21	1 17	16·4	53	9	13 21	20 13	20 24
26	1 11	16·2	56	5	12 55	19 45	19 55
31	1 02	15·3	58	3	12 26	19 10	19 19

MARS ♂

Day	R.A.	Dec. −	Diam.	Phase	Transit	
	h m	°	''		h m	
1	21 12	17·3	4	98	10 37	Mars is too close to the Sun for observation
6	21 27	16·2	4	98	10 32	
11	21 43	15·0	4	97	10 28	
16	21 58	13·7	4	97	10 23	
21	22 13	12·3	4	97	10 19	
26	22 28	10·9	4	97	10 14	
31	22 42	9·5	4	96	10 09	

SUNRISE AND SUNSET (G.M.T.)

Day	London a.m. h m	London p.m. h m	Bristol a.m. h m	Bristol p.m. h m	Birmingham a.m. h.m	Birmingham p.m. h m	Manchester a.m. h m	Manchester p.m. h m	Newcastle a.m. h m	Newcastle p.m. h m	Glasgow a.m. h m	Glasgow p.m. h m	Belfast a.m. h m	Belfast p.m. h m
1	6 47	5 40	6 56	5 50	6 55	5 45	6 58	5 46	6 57	5 41	7 10	5 50	7 15	5 59
2	6 45	5 42	6 54	5 52	6 53	5 47	6 56	5 48	6 55	5 43	7 08	5 52	7 13	6 01
3	6 43	5 43	6 52	5 53	6 50	5 49	6 53	5 50	6 52	5 45	7 05	5 54	7 10	6 03
4	6 41	5 45	6 50	5 55	6 48	5 51	6 51	5 52	6 50	5 47	7 03	5 56	7 08	6 05
5	6 38	5 47	6 48	5 57	6 46	5 53	6 49	5 54	6 48	5 49	7 00	5 59	7 06	6 07
6	6 36	5 48	6 45	5 58	6 43	5 55	6 46	5 56	6 45	5 51	6 57	6 01	7 03	6 09
7	6 34	5 50	6 43	6 00	6 41	5 57	6 44	5 58	6 43	5 53	6 55	6 03	7 01	6 11
8	6 32	5 52	6 41	6 02	6 39	5 58	6 42	5 59	6 40	5 55	6 52	6 05	6 58	6 13
9	6 29	5 53	6 39	6 03	6 36	6 00	6 39	6 01	6 38	5 57	6 50	6 07	6 56	6 15
10	6 27	5 55	6 37	6 05	6 34	6 02	6 37	6 03	6 35	5 59	6 47	6 09	6 53	6 17
11	6 25	5 57	6 35	6 07	6 32	6 03	6 35	6 04	6 33	6 01	6 45	6 11	6 51	6 19
12	6 23	5 58	6 33	6 08	6 30	6 05	6 33	6 06	6 30	6 03	6 42	6 13	6 48	6 21
13	6 20	6 00	6 30	6 10	6 27	6 07	6 30	6 08	6 27	6 05	6 39	6 15	6 45	6 23
14	6 18	6 02	6 28	6 12	6 25	6 09	6 28	6 10	6 25	6 07	6 37	6 17	6 43	6 25
15	6 16	6 04	6 26	6 14	6 23	6 11	6 25	6 12	6 22	6 09	6 34	6 19	6 40	6 27
16	6 13	6 05	6 23	6 15	6 20	6 12	6 23	6 14	6 20	6 11	6 31	6 21	6 38	6 29
17	6 11	6 07	6 21	6 17	6 18	6 14	6 21	6 16	6 18	6 13	6 29	6 23	6 36	6 31
18	6 09	6 09	6 19	6 19	6 16	6 16	6 18	6 18	6 15	6 15	6 26	6 25	6 33	6 33
19	6 06	6 10	6 16	6 20	6 13	6 17	6 15	6 19	6 12	6 16	6 24	6 27	6 30	6 34
20	6 04	6 12	6 14	6 22	6 11	6 19	6 13	6 21	6 10	6 18	6 21	6 29	6 28	6 36
21	6 02	6 14	6 12	6 24	6 09	6 21	6 11	6 23	6 08	6 20	6 18	6 31	6 25	6 38
22	6 00	6 16	6 10	6 26	6 07	6 23	6 08	6 25	6 05	6 22	6 16	6 34	6 23	6 40
23	5 58	6 17	6 08	6 27	6 05	6 24	6 06	6 27	6 03	6 24	6 13	6 36	6 20	6 42
24	5 55	6 19	6 05	6 29	6 02	6 26	6 03	6 29	6 00	6 26	6 10	6 38	6 17	6 44
25	5 53	6 21	6 03	6 31	6 00	6 28	6 01	6 31	5 58	6 28	6 08	6 40	6 15	6 46
26	5 50	6 22	6 00	6 32	5 57	6 29	5 58	6 32	5 55	6 30	6 05	6 42	6 12	6 48
27	5 48	6 24	5 58	6 34	5 55	6 31	5 56	6 34	5 52	6 32	6 02	6 44	6 09	6 50
28	5 46	6 26	5 56	6 36	5 53	6 33	5 54	6 36	5 50	6 34	6 00	6 46	6 06	6 52
29	5 44	6 28	5 54	6 37	5 50	6 35	5 51	6 38	5 47	6 36	5 57	6 48	6 03	6 54
30	5 42	6 29	5 52	6 39	5 48	6 36	5 49	6 39	5 45	6 38	5 55	6 50	6 01	6 56
31	5 39	6 31	5 49	6 40	5 46	6 38	5 47	6 41	5 42	6 40	5 52	6 52	5 58	6 58

JUPITER ♃   SATURN ♄

Day	R.A. h m	Dec. + °	Transit h m	5° high W. 52° h m	5° high W. 56° h m	R.A. h m	Dec. + °	Transit h m	5° high W. 52° h m	5° high W. 56° h m
1	3 29	18·2	16 52	23 54	0 10	8 57	18·3	22 18	5 25	5 37
11	3 35	18·5	16 18	23 24	23 37	8 54	18·5	21 36	4 45	4 57
21	3 41	19·0	15 46	22 53	23 06	8 52	18·6	20 55	4 04	4 16
31	3 49	19·4	15 14	22 23	22 37	8 51	18·7	20 15	3 24	3 36

Equatorial diameter of Jupiter 36″; of Saturn 20″. Diameters of Saturn's rings 45″ and 14″.

URANUS ♅   NEPTUNE ♆

Day	R.A. h m	Dec. − ° ′	10° high E. 52° h m	10° high E. 56° h m	Transit h m	R.A. h m	Dec. − ° ′	10° high E. 52° h m	10° high E. 56° h m	Transit h m
1	14 37·6	14 55	0 40	1 06	4 02	17 00·1	21 14	3 57	4 46	6 24
11	14 37·0	14 51	23 59	0 25	3 22	17 00·4	21 14	3 18	4 07	5 45
21	14 36·0	14 47	23 14	23 40	2 42	17 00·5	21 13	2 39	3 28	5 06
31	14 34·8	14 41	22 33	22 59	2 01	17 00·3	21 13	1 59	2 48	4 27

Diameter 4″.   Diameter 2″.

Day of			

♈ *Aperire*, to open. Earth opens to receive seed.

Sun's Longitude 30° ♉ 20^d 05^h

Month	Week		
1	F.	Edgar Wallace b. 1875. R.A.F. formed 1918
2	S.	Sir J. C. Squire b. 1884. Sir Alec Guinness b. 1914
3	**S.**	**6th S. in Lent.** Palm Sunday
4	M.	Sir Cuthbert Whitaker d. 1950
5	Tu.	Swinburne b. 1837. John Wisden d. 1884
6	W.	HILARY LAW SITTINGS END. Raphael d. 1520
7	Th.	MAUNDY THURSDAY. Wordsworth b. 1770
8	F.	**Good Friday.** Picasso d. 1973
9	S.	Edward IV d. 1483. I. K. Brunel b. 1806
10	**S.**	**Easter Day.** Hazlitt b. 1778
11	M.	Easter Monday. Treaty of Utrecht 1713
12	Tu.	Franklin D. Roosevelt d. 1945
13	W.	F. W. Woolworth b. 1852
14	Th.	Handel d. 1759. Sir John Gielgud b. 1904
15	F.	Loss of *Titanic* 1912. J. S. Sargent d. 1925
16	S.	Goya d. 1828. Sir Charles Chaplin b. 1889
17	**S.**	**1st S. after Easter.** John Ford b. 1586
18	M.	Judge Jeffreys d. 1689. Albert Einstein d. 1955
19	Tu.	EASTER LAW SITTINGS BEGIN. Byron d. 1824
20	W.	W. H. Davies b. 1871. Adolf Hitler b. 1889
21	Th.	QUEEN ELIZABETH II BORN, 1926
22	F.	Henry Fielding b. 1707. Yehudi Menuhin b. 1916
23	S.	ST. GEORGE'S DAY. Shakespeare d. 1616
24	**S.**	**2nd S. after Easter.** Anthony Trollope b. 1815
25	M.	**St. Mark.** ANZAC DAY
26	Tu.	Daniel Defoe d. 1730. J. J. Audubon b. 1785
27	W.	Edward Gibbon b. 1737. Samuel Morse b. 1791
28	Th.	Mussolini d. 1945. Richard Hughes d. 1976
29	F.	Sir Thomas Beecham b. 1879
30	S.	Queen Juliana b. 1909. A. E. Housman d. 1936

PHENOMENA

April 4^d 04^h Partial eclipse of the Moon. See p. 148 for details.

6^d 06^h Venus in inferior conjunction

10^d 16^h Mercury at greatest eastern elongation (19°).

15^d 12^h Mars in conjunction with the Moon. Mars 4° S.

16^d 20^h Venus in conjunction with the Moon. Venus 5° N.

18^d 11^h Annular eclipse of the Sun. See p. 148 for details.

19^d 16^h Mercury in conjunction with the Moon. Mercury 5° N.

21^d 09^h Jupiter in conjunction with the Moon. Jupiter 3° N.

27^d 01^h Saturn in conjunction with the Moon. Saturn 6° N.

30^d 06^h Uranus at opposition.

30^d 17^h Mercury in inferior conjunction.

CONSTELLATIONS

The following constellations are near the meridian at

	d h		d h
Mar. 1	24	Mar. 16	23
Apr. 1	22	Apr. 15	21
May 1	20	May 16	19

Cepheus (below the Pole), Cassiopeia (below the Pole), Ursa Major, Leo Minor, Leo, Sextant, Hydra and Crater.

MINIMA OF ALGOL

d	h	d	h
2	8	16	16
5	5	19	13
8	1	22	10
10	22	25	6
13	19	28	3

PHASES OF THE MOON

		d	h	m
○	Full Moon	4	04	09
☽	Last Quarter	10	19	15
●	New Moon	18	10	35
☽	First Quarter	26	14	42

	d	h
Perigee (361,160 kilometres)	5	21
Apogee (406,020 ,,)	21	12

Mean Longitude of Ascending Node on April 1, 205°.

See note on *Summer Time*, p. 98.

MONTHLY NOTES

April 1. Refreshment House Licences to be renewed.

3. First day of Passover.

5. Income Tax Year (1976–77) ends.

8. Bank Holiday, Scotland.

9. Lent ends at midnight.

11. Bank and General Holiday, England, Wales and N. Ireland.

Day	Right Ascension	Dec. +	Equation of Time	Rise 52°	Rise 56°	Transit	Set 52°	Set 56°	Sidereal Time	Transit of First Point of Aries
	h m s	° ′	m s	h m	h m	h m	h m	h m	h m s	h m s
1	0 41 00	4 25	− 4 03	5 35	5 32	12 04	18 34	18 38	12 36 58	11 21 11
2	0 44 39	4 48	− 3 45	5 33	5 29	12 04	18 35	18 40	12 40 54	11 17 15
3	0 48 17	5 11	− 3 27	5 31	5 27	12 03	18 37	18 42	12 44 51	11 13 19
4	0 51 56	5 34	− 3 09	5 28	5 24	12 03	18 39	18 44	12 48 47	11 09 23
5	0 55 35	5 57	− 2 51	5 26	5 21	12 03	18 40	18 46	12 52 44	11 05 27
6	0 59 14	6 19	− 2 34	5 24	5 19	12 02	18 42	18 48	12 56 40	11 01 31
7	1 02 54	6 42	− 2 17	5 22	5 16	12 02	18 44	18 50	13 00 37	10 57 35
8	1 06 33	7 05	− 2 00	5 20	5 13	12 02	18 45	18 52	13 04 33	10 53 39
9	1 10 13	7 27	− 1 43	5 17	5 10	12 02	18 47	18 54	13 08 30	10 49 43
10	1 13 53	7 49	− 1 27	5 15	5 08	12 01	18 49	18 56	13 12 27	10 45 47
11	1 17 33	8 11	− 1 10	5 13	5 05	12 01	18 50	18 58	13 16 23	10 41 51
12	1 21 14	8 33	− 0 55	5 10	5 03	12 01	18 52	19 00	13 20 20	10 37 56
13	1 24 55	8 55	− 0 39	5 08	5 01	12 01	18 54	19 02	13 24 16	10 34 00
14	1 28 36	9 17	− 0 24	5 06	4 58	12 00	18 56	19 04	13 28 13	10 30 04
15	1 32 18	9 39	− 0 09	5 04	4 56	12 00	18 58	19 06	13 32 09	10 26 08
16	1 36 00	10 00	+ 0 06	5 02	4 53	12 00	19 00	19 08	13 36 06	10 22 12
17	1 39 43	10 21	+ 0 20	5 00	4 50	12 00	19 01	19 10	13 40 02	10 18 16
18	1 43 25	10 42	+ 0 33	4 57	4 47	11 59	19 03	19 12	13 43 59	10 14 20
19	1 47 09	11 03	+ 0 47	4 55	4 45	11 59	19 04	19 14	13 47 55	10 10 24
20	1 50 52	11 24	+ 1 00	4 53	4 43	11 59	19 06	19 17	13 51 52	10 06 28
21	1 54 36	11 45	+ 1 12	4 51	4 40	11 59	19 08	19 19	13 55 49	10 02 32
22	1 58 21	12 05	+ 1 24	4 49	4 38	11 58	19 09	19 21	13 59 45	9 58 37
23	2 02 06	12 25	+ 1 36	4 47	4 35	11 58	19 11	19 23	14 03 42	9 54 41
24	2 05 51	12 45	+ 1 47	4 45	4 32	11 58	19 13	19 25	14 07 38	9 50 45
25	2 09 37	13 05	+ 1 58	4 43	4 30	11 58	19 14	19 27	14 11 35	9 46 49
26	2 13 23	13 24	+ 2 09	4 41	4 28	11 58	19 16	19 29	14 15 31	9 42 53
27	2 17 10	13 44	+ 2 18	4 39	4 26	11 58	19 18	19 31	14 19 28	9 38 57
28	2 20 57	14 03	+ 2 28	4 37	4 23	11 57	19 19	19 33	14 23 24	9 35 01
29	2 24 44	14 21	+ 2 37	4 35	4 21	11 57	19 21	19 35	14 27 21	9 31 05
30	2 28 33	14 40	+ 2 45	4 33	4 19	11 57	19 23	19 37	14 31 18	9 27 09

Duration of Civil (C), Nautical (N), and Astronomical (A), Twilight (in minutes)

Lat. °	Apr. 1 C	N	A	Apr. 11 C	N	A	Apr. 21 C	N	A	Apr. 30 C	N	A
52	34	76	121	35	79	128	37	84	138	39	89	152
56	38	85	137	40	90	148	42	96	167	44	105	200

ASTRONOMICAL NOTES

MERCURY is an evening star, magnitude −0·9 to +2·0, for the first three weeks of the month, low above the W.N.W. horizon at the time of end of evening civil twilight. For observers in the northern hemisphere this is the best evening apparition of Mercury during 1977. On the 19th, before sunset, the crescent Moon will have passed 5° S. of Mercury. Observers may be interested in locating the two bodies shortly after sunset, since the Moon will then be only 33 hours old.

VENUS is a brilliant morning star, visible low above the E.N.E. horizon just before sunrise. During the month its magnitude varies from −3·4 on the 1st, to −3·1 on the 7th, brightening again to −4·2 by the 30th. Although inferior conjunction occurs on the 6th it is an interesting fact that Venus is 5° high at sunrise in England on the 1st and this gives the assiduous observer the rare opportunity of seeing Venus in the mornings *before* inferior conjunction, provided he has a good clear eastern horizon. Venus will be seen near the old crescent Moon on the mornings of the 16th and 17th.

MARS is unsuitably placed for observation.

JUPITER is a brilliant evening star, magnitude −1·6.

SATURN is a bright evening star, magnitude +0·4.

URANUS is at opposition on the 30th, in Libra. It is barely visible to the naked eye as its magnitude is +5·7 but it is easily located with only small optical aid. Telescopically it shows a slightly greenish disk 4″ in diameter.

ECLIPSE. A partial eclipse of the Moon occurs on the 4th, visible from the British Isles. See p. 148 for details.

ECLIPSE. An annular eclipse of the Sun occurs on the 18th. See p. 148 for details.

THE MOON

Day	R.A.	Dec.	Hor. Par.	Semi-diam.	Sun's Co-long.	P.A. of Bright Limb	Phase	Age	Rise 52°	Rise 56°	Transit	Set 52°	Set 56°
	h m	°	′	′	°	°		d	h m	h m	h m	h m	h m
1	9 59	+ 7·7	58·0	15·8	55	285	87	12·2	15 29	15 25	22 07	4 06	4 12
2	10 52	+ 3·4	58·8	16·0	67	286	94	13·2	16 45	16 45	22 59	4 33	4 35
3	11 46	− 1·1	59·6	16·2	79	285	98	14·2	18 04	18 08	23 52	5 00	4 58
4	12 41	− 5·7	60·2	16·4	91	267	100	15·2	19 25	19 33	..	5 29	5 23
5	13 39	−10·0	60·6	16·5	103	110	99	16·2	20 45	20 58	0 48	6 01	5 51
6	14 38	−13·8	60·7	16·5	116	105	95	17·2	22 03	22 19	1 45	6 37	6 24
7	15 38	−16·6	60·5	16·5	128	100	89	18·2	23 14	23 33	2 44	7 21	7 04
8	16 40	−18·3	60·2	16·4	140	95	80	19·2	..	..	3 44	8 12	7 53
9	17 41	−18·7	59·6	16·2	152	90	70	20·2	0 17	0 36	4 43	9 11	8 52
10	18 40	−18·0	58·9	16·1	164	85	59	21·2	1 09	1 27	5 41	10 16	9 59
11	19 38	−16·2	58·3	15·9	177	81	48	22·2	1 53	2 08	6 36	11 25	11 11
12	20 33	−13·5	57·6	15·7	189	77	37	23·2	2 28	2 40	7 28	12 35	12 24
13	21 25	−10·2	56·9	15·5	201	74	27	24·2	2 58	3 06	8 17	13 45	13 37
14	22 15	− 6·4	56·3	15·4	213	72	18	25·2	3 24	3 29	9 04	14 53	14 50
15	23 03	− 2·5	55·8	15·2	225	71	11	26·2	3 48	3 50	9 49	16 01	16 01
16	23 51	+ 1·5	55·3	15·1	238	71	6	27·2	4 12	4 10	10 34	17 07	17 11
17	0 38	+ 5·4	54·9	15·0	250	71	2	28·2	4 35	4 30	11 18	18 12	18 19
18	1 25	+ 9·0	54·6	14·9	262	70	0	29·2	5 00	4 51	12 02	19 16	19 27
19	2 12	+12·3	54·3	14·8	274	260	0	0·6	5 26	5 15	12 48	20 18	20 32
20	3 00	+14·9	54·1	14·7	286	260	2	1·6	5 57	5 43	13 33	21 18	21 34
21	3 49	+17·0	54·0	14·7	299	263	6	2·6	6 31	6 15	14 20	22 14	22 31
22	4 38	+18·2	54·0	14·7	311	267	11	3·6	7 11	6 53	15 07	23 05	23 23
23	5 28	+18·7	54·1	14·8	323	271	18	4·6	7 57	7 39	15 55	23 50	..
24	6 18	+18·4	54·4	14·8	335	275	26	5·6	8 49	8 32	16 43	..	0 08
25	7 08	+17·2	54·8	14·9	348	279	34	6·6	9 47	9 31	17 30	0 30	0 47
26	7 58	+15·3	55·4	15·1	0	282	44	7·6	10 49	10 36	18 18	1 05	1 19
27	8 49	+12·6	56·1	15·3	12	285	54	8·6	11 56	11 46	19 06	1 37	1 47
28	9 39	+ 9·2	57·0	15·5	24	288	64	9·6	13 06	13 00	19 55	2 05	2 12
29	10 30	+ 5·2	57·9	15·8	36	290	74	10·6	14 19	14 17	20 45	2 32	2 36
30	11 23	+ 0·9	58·9	16·0	49	291	83	11·6	15 35	15 37	21 36	2 58	2 58

MERCURY ☿

Day	R.A.	Dec. +	Diam.	Phase	Transit	5° high W. 52°	5° high W. 56°	Day	R.A.	Dec. +	Diam.	Phase	Transit	
	h m	°	″		h m	h m	h m		h m	°	″		h m	
1	1 36	11·3	6	75	13 01	19 30	19 37	16	2 41	18·8	9	23	13 04	Mercury is
4	1 55	13·6	6	65	13 07	19 48	19 57	19	2 44	19·0	10	15	12 54	too close to
7	2 11	15·5	7	54	13 11	20 02	20 12	22	2 44	18·7	10	8	12 42	the Sun
10	2 24	17·1	7	42	13 12	20 10	20 22	25	2 41	17·9	11	4	12 27	for
13	2 34	18·2	8	32	13 09	20 13	20 26	28	2 36	16·8	11	1	12 09	observation
16	2 41	18·8	9	23	13 04	20 10	20 23	31	2 30	15·5	12	0	11 51	

VENUS ♀   MARS ♂

Day	R.A.	Dec. +	Diam.	Phase	5° high E. 52°	5° high E. 56°	Transit	Day	R.A.	Dec. −	Diam.	Phase	Transit	
	h m	°	″		h m	h m	h m		h m	°	″		h m	
1	1 00	15·0	59	2	5 37	5 27	12 20	1	22 45	9·2	4	96	10 08	
6	0 49	13·5	59	1	5 16	5 06	11 49	6	23 00	7·7	4	96	10 03	Mars is
11	0 39	11·6	59	1	4 55	4 47	11 20	11	23 14	6·2	4	96	9 58	too close
16	0 31	9·6	57	4	4 38	4 32	10 52	16	23 29	4·7	5	95	9 52	to the
21	0 26	7·9	53	8	4 22	4 18	10 28	21	23 43	3·2	5	95	9 47	Sun for
26	0 25	6·5	50	12	4 09	4 06	10 08	26	23 57	1·6	5	95	9 41	observation
31	0 27	5·5	46	16	3 56	3 55	9 51	31	0 11	0·1	5	95	9 36	

SUNRISE AND SUNSET (G.M.T.)

Day	London a.m. h m	p.m. h m	Bristol a.m. h m	p.m. h m	Birmingham a.m. h m	p.m. h m	Manchester a.m. h m	p.m. h m	Newcastle a.m. h m	p.m. h m	Glasgow a.m. h m	p.m. h m	Belfast a.m. h m	p.m. h m
1	5 37	6 33	5 47	6 42	5 43	6 40	5 44	6 43	5 39	6 42	5 49	6 54	5 57	7 00
2	5 35	6 34	5 45	6 43	5 41	6 42	5 42	6 45	5 37	6 44	5 47	6 56	5 55	7 02
3	5 33	6 36	5 43	6 45	5 39	6 43	5 40	6 46	5 35	6 45	5 44	6 58	5 53	7 03
4	5 31	6 38	5 41	6 47	5 36	6 45	5 37	6 48	5 32	6 47	5 41	7 00	5 50	7 05
5	5 28	6 39	5 38	6 49	5 34	6 47	5 35	6 50	5 30	6 49	5 39	7 02	5 48	7 07
6	5 26	6 41	5 36	6 50	5 31	6 49	5 32	6 52	5 27	6 51	5 36	7 04	5 45	7 09
7	5 24	6 42	5 34	6 52	5 29	6 51	5 30	6 54	5 24	6 53	5 33	7 06	5 43	7 11
8	5 21	6 44	5 31	6 54	5 26	6 53	5 27	6 56	5 22	6 55	5 31	7 08	5 40	7 13
9	5 19	6 45	5 29	6 55	5 24	6 54	5 25	6 58	5 19	6 57	5 28	7 10	5 38	7 15
10	5 17	6 47	5 27	6 57	5 22	6 56	5 22	6 59	5 17	6 59	5 26	7 12	5 35	7 16
11	5 15	6 49	5 25	6 59	5 20	6 58	5 20	7 01	5 14	7 01	5 23	7 14	5 33	7 18
12	5 12	6 50	5 22	7 00	5 17	6 59	5 18	7 03	5 12	7 03	5 21	7 16	5 31	7 20
13	5 10	6 52	5 20	7 02	5 15	7 01	5 15	7 05	5 09	7 05	5 18	7 18	5 28	7 22
14	5 08	6 54	5 18	7 04	5 13	7 03	5 13	7 07	5 07	7 07	5 16	7 20	5 26	7 24
15	5 06	6 56	5 16	7 06	5 11	7 05	5 11	7 09	5 05	7 09	5 13	7 22	5 23	7 26
16	5 03	6 57	5 13	7 07	5 08	7 06	5 08	7 11	5 02	7 11	5 11	7 24	5 21	7 28
17	5 01	6 59	5 11	7 09	5 06	7 08	5 06	7 12	5 00	7 13	5 08	7 26	5 18	7 30
18	4 59	7 01	5 09	7 11	5 04	7 10	5 04	7 14	4 57	7 15	5 05	7 29	5 16	7 32
19	4 57	7 02	5 07	7 12	5 02	7 11	5 01	7 16	4 55	7 17	5 03	7 31	5 13	7 34
20	4 55	7 04	5 05	7 14	5 00	7 13	4 59	7 18	4 53	7 19	5 01	7 33	5 11	7 36
21	4 53	7 06	5 03	7 16	4 58	7 15	4 57	7 20	4 50	7 21	4 58	7 35	5 09	7 38
22	4 51	7 07	5 01	7 17	4 56	7 16	4 55	7 21	4 48	7 23	4 56	7 37	5 06	7 40
23	4 49	7 09	4 59	7 19	4 54	7 18	4 53	7 23	4 45	7 25	4 53	7 39	5 04	7 42
24	4 47	7 11	4 57	7 21	4 52	7 20	4 51	7 25	4 43	7 27	4 51	7 41	5 02	7 44
25	4 45	7 13	4 55	7 22	4 49	7 22	4 48	7 27	4 41	7 28	4 49	7 42	5 00	7 45
26	4 43	7 14	4 53	7 24	4 47	7 23	4 46	7 28	4 38	7 30	4 46	7 44	4 57	7 47
27	4 41	7 16	4 51	7 25	4 45	7 25	4 44	7 30	4 36	7 32	4 44	7 46	4 55	7 49
28	4 39	7 18	4 49	7 27	4 43	7 27	4 42	7 32	4 34	7 34	4 42	7 48	4 53	7 51
29	4 37	7 19	4 47	7 28	4 41	7 29	4 40	7 34	4 32	7 36	4 40	7 50	4 51	7 53
30	4 35	7 21	4 45	7 30	4 39	7 31	4 38	7 36	4 30	7 38	4 38	7 52	4 48	7 55

JUPITER ♃   SATURN ♄

Day	R.A. h m	Dec. + °	Transit h m	5° high W. 52° h m	56° h m	R.A. h m	Dec. + °	Transit h m	5° high W. 52° h m	56° h m
1	3 50	19·4	15 11	22 20	22 34	8 51	18·7	20 11	3 19	3 32
11	3 58	19·9	14 40	21 52	22 06	8 51	18·7	19 31	2 39	2 52
21	4 07	20·3	14 09	21 24	21 39	8 51	18·7	18 52	2 00	2 13
31	4 16	20·7	13 39	20 56	21 11	8 52	18·6	18 14	1 22	1 35

Equatorial diameter of Jupiter 34″; of Saturn 19″. Diameters of Saturn's rings 42″ and 13″.

URANUS ♅   NEPTUNE ♆

Day	R.A. h m	Dec. − ° ′	10° high E. 52° h m	56° h m	Transit h m	R.A. h m	Dec. − ° ′	10° high E. 52° h m	56° h m	Transit h m
1	14 34·6	14 40	22 29	22 55	1 57	17 00·3	21 13	1 55	2 44	4 23
11	14 33·2	14 33	21 48	22 13	1 17	16 59·9	21 12	1 15	2 03	3 43
21	14 31·6	14 26	21 06	21 31	0 36	16 59·2	21 10	0 35	1 23	3 03
31	14 29·9	14 18	20 24	20 49	23 51	16 58·4	21 09	23 51	0 42	2 23

Diameter 4″   Diameter 2″

Maia, goddess of growth and increase.

Sun's Longitude 60° Ⅱ 21ᵈ 04ʰ

Month	Week	
1	☉.	**3rd ☉. after Easter. St. Philip and St. James**
2	M.	Leonardo da Vinci d. 1519
3	Tu.	Thomas Hood d. 1845. R. d'Oyly Carte b. 1844.
4	W.	Joseph Whitaker b. 1820. T. H. Huxley b. 1825
5	Th.	Napoleon d. 1821. Metternich d. 1859
6	F.	Sigmund Freud b. 1856. Edward VII d. 1910
7	S.	Tschaikovsky b. 1840. *Lusitania* torpedoed 1915
8	☉.	**4th ☉. after Easter.** J. S. Mill d. 1873
9	M.	OFFICIAL END OF WAR IN EUROPE (1945)
10	Tu.	Sir H. M. Stanley d. 1904
11	W.	Fontenoy 1745. Irving Berlin b. 1888
12	Th.	Edward Lear b. 1812. D. G. Rossetti b. 1828
13	F.	Sir Frank Brangwyn b. 1867. Gary Cooper d. 1961
14	S.	Strindberg d. 1912. Sir Rider Haggard d. 1925
15	☉.	**5th ☉. after Easter.** ROGATION SUNDAY
16	M.	Albuera 1811. H. E. Bates b. 1905
17	Tu.	Edward Jenner b. 1749. Talleyrand d. 1838
18	W.	Dame Margot Fonteyn b. 1919
19	Th.	**Ascension Day.** T. E. Lawrence d. 1935
20	F.	Columbus d. 1506. Dame Barbara Hepworth d. [1975
21	S.	Alexander Pope b. 1688. Elizabeth Fry b. 1780
22	☉.	**☉. after Ascension.** Lord Olivier b. 1907
23	M.	Sir Hugh Casson b. 1910
24	Tu.	Queen Victoria b. 1819. H.M.S. *Hood* lost, 1941
25	W.	Lord Maybray-King b. 1901
26	Th.	Samuel Pepys d. 1703. Queen Mary b. 1867
27	F.	EASTER LAW SITTINGS END. Henry Kissinger b. [1923
28	S.	Henrik Ibsen d. 1906. Duke of Windsor d. 1972
29	☉.	**Whit Sunday. Pentecost.** Charles II b. 1630
30	M.	Joan of Arc d. 1431. Voltaire d. 1778
31	Tu.	Heath Robinson b. 1872. Jutland 1916

PHENOMENA

May 11ᵈ 23ʰ Venus at greatest brilliancy.

13ᵈ 18ʰ Venus in conjunction with Mars. Venus 1°·3 N.

14ᵈ 11ʰ Venus in conjunction with the Moon. Venus 1° S.

14ᵈ 12ʰ Mars in conjunction with the Moon. Mars 2° S.

16ᵈ 07ʰ Mercury in conjunction with the Moon. Mercury 2° S.

24ᵈ 11ʰ Saturn in conjunction with the Moon. Saturn 6° N.

27ᵈ 23ʰ Mercury at greatest western elongation (25°).

CONSTELLATIONS

The following constellations are near the meridian at

	d	h		d	h
Apr.	1	24	Apr.	15	23
May	1	22	May	16	21
June	1	20	June	15	19

Cephus (below the Pole), Cassiopeia (below the Pole), Ursa Minor, Ursa Major, Canes Venatici, Coma Berenices, Bootes, Leo, Virgo, Crater, Corvus, and Hydra.

ALGOL

ALGOL is inconveniently situated for observation during May.

PHASES OF THE MOON

	d	h	m
○ Full Moon	3	13	03
☽ Last Quarter	10	04	08
● New Moon	18	02	51
☽ First Quarter	26	03	20

	d	h
Perigee (357,740 kilometres)	4	05
Apogee (406,540 ,,)	18	18

Mean Longitude of Ascending Node on May 1, 204°.

See note on *Summer Time*, p. 98

MONTHLY NOTES

May 2. Bank Holiday, Scotland.
    9. Bank and General Holiday, Channel Islands.
  15. Whitsunday (Scotland). Scottish Term Day.
  17. Norway's National Day.
  23. Feast of Weeks begins.
  28. Removal Day, Scotland.

Day	Right Ascension	Dec. +	Equation of Time	Rise 52°	Rise 56°	Transit	Set 52°	Set 56°	Sidereal Time	Transit of First Point of Aries
	h m s	° ′	m s	h m	h m	h m	h m	h m	h m s	h m s
1	2 32 21	14 58	+ 2 53	4 31	4 16	11 57	19 25	19 39	14 35 14	9 23 13
2	2 36 10	15 17	+ 3 00	4 29	4 14	11 57	19 26	19 41	14 39 11	9 19 17
3	2 40 00	15 34	+ 3 07	4 27	4 12	11 57	19 28	19 43	14 43 07	9 15 22
4	2 43 50	15 52	+ 3 13	4 25	4 10	11 57	19 29	19 45	14 47 04	9 11 26
5	2 47 41	16 09	+ 3 19	4 23	4 08	11 57	19 31	19 47	14 51 00	9 07 30
6	2 51 33	16 26	+ 3 24	4 21	4 06	11 57	19 33	19 49	14 54 57	9 03 34
7	2 55 25	16 43	+ 3 29	4 20	4 04	11 56	19 35	19 51	14 58 53	8 59 38
8	2 59 17	17 00	+ 3 33	4 18	4 01	11 56	19 36	19 53	15 02 50	8 55 42
9	3 03 10	17 16	+ 3 36	4 16	3 59	11 56	19 38	19 55	15 06 47	8 51 46
10	3 07 04	17 32	+ 3 39	4 14	3 57	11 56	19 40	19 57	15 10 43	8 47 50
11	3 10 59	17 47	+ 3 41	4 13	3 55	11 56	19 41	19 59	15 14 40	8 43 54
12	3 14 53	18 03	+ 3 43	4 11	3 53	11 56	19 43	20 01	15 18 36	8 39 58
13	3 18 49	18 18	+ 3 44	4 09	3 51	11 56	19 44	20 02	15 22 33	8 36 02
14	3 22 45	18 33	+ 3 44	4 08	3 49	11 56	19 45	20 04	15 26 29	8 32 07
15	3 26 42	18 47	+ 3 44	4 06	3 48	11 56	19 47	20 06	15 30 26	8 28 11
16	3 30 39	19 01	+ 3 43	4 05	3 46	11 56	19 49	20 08	15 34 22	8 24 15
17	3 34 37	19 15	+ 3 42	4 04	3 44	11 56	19 50	20 10	15 38 19	8 20 19
18	3 38 35	19 28	+ 3 40	4 02	3 42	11 56	19 52	20 12	15 42 16	8 16 23
19	3 42 34	19 42	+ 3 38	4 01	3 40	11 56	19 54	20 13	15 46 12	8 12 27
20	3 46 34	19 54	+ 3 35	3 59	3 39	11 56	19 55	20 15	15 50 09	8 08 31
21	3 50 34	20 07	+ 3 31	3 58	3 37	11 57	19 56	20 17	15 54 05	8 04 35
22	3 54 34	20 19	+ 3 27	3 57	3 35	11 57	19 58	20 18	15 58 02	8 00 39
23	3 58 36	20 31	+ 3 23	3 55	3 34	11 57	19 59	20 20	16 01 58	7 56 43
24	4 02 37	20 42	+ 3 18	3 54	3 32	11 57	20 00	20 21	16 05 55	7 52 47
25	4 06 39	20 53	+ 3 12	3 53	3 31	11 57	20 02	20 23	16 09 51	7 48 52
26	4 10 42	21 04	+ 3 06	3 52	3 30	11 57	20 03	20 25	16 13 48	7 44 56
27	4 14 45	21 14	+ 3 00	3 51	3 29	11 57	20 04	20 27	16 17 43	7 41 00
28	4 18 48	21 24	+ 2 53	3 50	3 27	11 57	20 05	20 29	16 21 41	7 37 04
29	4 22 52	21 34	+ 2 45	3 49	3 26	11 57	20 06	20 30	16 25 38	7 33 08
30	4 26 57	21 43	+ 2 37	3 48	3 25	11 57	20 07	20 31	16 29 34	7 29 12
31	4 31 02	21 52	+ 2 29	3 47	3 24	11 58	20 08	20 33	16 33 31	7 25 16

Duration of Civil (C), Nautical (N), and Astronomical (A), Twilight (in minutes)

Lat. °	May 1 C	N	A	May 11 C	N	A	May 21 C	N	A	May 31 C	N	A
52	39	90	154	41	97	179	44	106	T.A.N.	46	116	T.A.N.
56	45	106	209	49	121	T.A.N.	53	143	T.A.N.	57	T.A.N.	T.A.N.

ASTRONOMICAL NOTES

MERCURY is unsuitably placed for observation despite the fact that it is at greatest western elongation on the 27th.

VENUS is a magnificent morning star, attaining its greatest brilliancy, magnitude −4·2, on the 11th. However it is never visible for more than an hour before sunrise. As seen through a telescope the apparent diameter shrinks from 46″ to 29″ as the distance from the Earth increases. At the same time the phase increases from a thin crescent to a 41% illuminated disk by the end of the month.

MARS is unsuitably placed for observation but may be detected telescopically within a few degrees of Venus for most of May and into June.

JUPITER is a brilliant evening star, magnitude −1·5, in the constellation of Taurus, but only visible for a short while after sunset for the first week of the month. For the remainder of the month Jupiter is too close to the Sun for observation.

SATURN is a bright evening star, magnitude +0·6, moving very slowly eastwards in the eastern part of Cancer. The crescent Moon is near Saturn on the evenings of the 23rd and 24th.

THE MOON

Day	R.A.	Dec.	Hor. Par.	Semi-diam.	Sun's Co-long.	P.A. of Bright Limb	Phase	Age	Rise 52°	Rise 56°	Transit	Set 52°	Set 56°
	h m	°	°	°	°	°		d	h m	h m	h m	h m	h m
1	12 16	− 3·7	59·8	16·3	61	291	91	12·6	16 54	17 00	22 30	3 25	3 22
2	13 13	− 8·1	60·5	16·5	73	291	96	13·6	18 15	18 26	23 27	3 55	3 47
3	14 11	−12·2	61·1	16·6	85	297	100	14·6	19 36	19 50	..	4 29	4 18
4	15 12	−15·5	61·3	16·7	97	86	100	15·6	20 53	21 11	0 26	5 10	4 55
5	16 15	−17·8	61·2	16·7	109	91	97	16·6	22 03	22 21	1 28	5 59	5 41
6	17 18	−18·7	60·8	16·6	122	88	91	17·6	23 02	23 20	2 30	6 56	6 37
7	18 21	−18·4	60·2	16·4	134	84	83	18·6	23 50	..	3 30	8 02	7 44
8	19 21	−16·9	59·4	16·2	146	79	73	19·6	..	0 06	4 28	9 12	8 56
9	20 18	−14·3	58·5	15·9	158	76	63	20·6	0 29	0 42	5 23	10 24	10 12
10	21 12	−11·1	57·6	15·7	170	73	52	21·6	1 02	1 11	6 14	11 35	11 27
11	22 03	− 7·4	56·8	15·5	183	70	41	22·6	1 29	1 36	7 02	12 45	12 40
12	22 52	− 3·4	56·1	15·3	195	69	31	23·6	1 54	1 57	7 48	13 53	13 52
13	23 40	+ 0·6	55·5	15·1	207	68	22	24·6	2 17	2 17	8 33	14 59	15 02
14	0 27	+ 4·5	55·0	15·0	219	68	15	25·6	2 40	2 36	9 17	16 04	16 10
15	1 13	+ 8·2	54·6	14·9	232	68	9	26·6	3 04	2 57	10 01	17 08	17 17
16	2 00	+11·5	54·3	14·8	244	68	4	27·6	3 30	3 20	10 45	18 11	18 23
17	2 48	+14·3	54·1	14·7	256	65	1	28·6	3 59	3 45	11 30	19 11	19 26
18	3 36	+16·5	54·0	14·7	268	12	0	29·6	4 32	4 16	12 17	20 08	20 25
19	4 25	+18·0	53·9	14·7	280	281	1	0·9	5 10	4 52	13 04	21 01	21 19
20	5 15	+18·8	54·0	14·7	293	277	3	1·9	5 53	5 35	13 51	21 49	22 07
21	6 05	+18·7	54·2	14·8	305	278	7	2·9	6 43	6 25	14 39	22 31	22 48
22	6 55	+17·7	54·5	14·8	317	281	13	3·9	7 39	7 22	15 27	23 07	23 22
23	7 45	+16·0	54·9	14·9	329	284	20	4·9	8 39	8 25	16 14	23 39	23 51
24	8 35	+13·5	55·4	15·1	342	287	29	5·9	9 43	9 32	17 01	..	..
25	9 24	+10·4	56·0	15·3	354	289	38	6·9	10 50	10 43	17 48	0 08	0 17
26	10 14	+ 6·7	56·8	15·5	6	291	49	7·9	12 00	11 56	18 36	0 34	0 40
27	11 04	+ 2·6	57·7	15·7	18	292	59	8·9	13 12	13 10	19 25	1 00	1 02
28	11 56	− 1·8	58·6	16·0	31	293	70	9·9	14 28	14 32	20 16	1 25	1 23
29	12 49	− 6·2	59·5	16·2	43	292	80	10·9	15 46	15 54	21 09	1 53	1 47
30	13 45	−10·4	60·3	16·4	55	291	88	11·9	17 05	17 18	22 07	2 23	2 14
31	14 44	−14·1	61·0	16·6	67	291	95	12·9	18 25	18 41	23 07	2 59	2 46

MERCURY ☿

Day	R.A.	Dec. +	Diam.	Phase	Transit		Day	R.A.	Dec. +	Diam.	Phase	Transit	
	h m	°	″		h m			h m	°	″		h m	
1	2 30	15·5	12	0	11 51	Mercury is	16	2 14	10·4	10	17	10 39	Mercury is
4	2 23	14·0	12	2	11 33	too close to	19	2 18	10·3	10	22	10 31	too close to
7	2 18	12·7	12	4	11 16	the Sun	22	2 24	10·6	9	28	10 25	the Sun
10	2 14	11·6	11	8	11 02	for	25	2 32	11·2	9	33	10 22	for
13	2 13	10·8	11	12	10 49	observation	28	2 42	12·0	8	38	10 20	observation
16	2 14	10·4	10	17	10 39		31	2 54	13·1	8	44	10 21	

VENUS ♀

Day	R.A.	Dec. +	Diam.	Phase	5° high E. 52°	5° high E. 56°	Transit
	h m	°	″		h m	h m	h m
1	0 27	5·5	46	16	3 56	3 55	9 51
6	0 33	5·0	42	21	3 44	3 43	9 37
11	0 42	5·0	39	25	3 33	3 32	9 26
16	0 52	5·3	36	29	3 22	3 21	9 17
21	1 05	5·9	33	33	3 12	3 10	9 10
26	1 19	6·7	31	37	3 02	3 00	9 05
31	1 34	7·8	29	40	2 52	2 49	9 01

MARS ♂

Day	R.A.	Dec.	Diam.	Phase	Transit	
	h m	°	″		h m	
1	0 11	−0·1	5	95	9 36	Mars is
6	0 25	+1·5	5	94	9 30	too close
11	0 40	+3·0	5	94	9 24	to the
16	0 54	+4·5	5	94	9 18	Sun for
21	1 08	+6·0	5	94	9 13	observation
26	1 22	+7·4	5	93	9 08	
31	1 36	+8·8	5	93	9 02	

SUNRISE AND SUNSET (G.M.T.)

Day	London a.m. h m	London p.m. h m	Bristol a.m. h m	Bristol p.m. h m	Birmingham a.m. h m	Birmingham p.m. h m	Manchester a.m. h m	Manchester p.m. h m	Newcastle a.m. h m	Newcastle p.m. h m	Glasgow a.m. h m	Glasgow p.m. h m	Belfast a.m. h m	Belfast p.m. h m
1	4 33	7 23	4 43	7 32	4 37	7 32	4 36	7 37	4 27	7 40	4 35	7 54	4 47	7 56
2	4 32	7 25	4 42	7 33	4 35	7 34	4 34	7 39	4 25	7 42	4 33	7 56	4 45	7 58
3	4 30	7 26	4 40	7 35	4 33	7 36	4 32	7 41	4 23	7 44	4 31	7 58	4 43	8 00
4	4 28	7 27	4 38	7 37	4 31	7 38	4 30	7 43	4 21	7 46	4 29	8 00	4 41	8 02
5	4 26	7 29	4 36	7 38	4 29	7 39	4 28	7 45	4 19	7 48	4 26	8 02	4 38	8 04
6	4 24	7 30	4 34	7 40	4 27	7 41	4 26	7 47	4 17	7 50	4 24	8 04	4 36	8 06
7	4 22	7 32	4 32	7 42	4 25	7 43	4 24	7 48	4 15	7 51	4 22	8 06	4 34	8 08
8	4 20	7 33	4 30	7 43	4 23	7 44	4 22	7 50	4 13	7 53	4 20	8 08	4 32	8 10
9	4 19	7 35	4 29	7 45	4 22	7 46	4 20	7 52	4 11	7 55	4 18	8 10	4 30	8 12
10	4 17	7 36	4 27	7 46	4 20	7 47	4 18	7 54	4 09	7 57	4 16	8 12	4 28	8 14
11	4 16	7 38	4 26	7 48	4 18	7 49	4 16	7 55	4 07	7 59	4 14	8 14	4 26	8 15
12	4 14	7 40	4 24	7 50	4 17	7 51	4 14	7 57	4 05	8 01	4 12	8 16	4 24	8 17
13	4 12	7 41	4 22	7 51	4 15	7 52	4 13	7 59	4 03	8 03	4 10	8 18	4 23	8 19
14	4 10	7 43	4 20	7 53	4 13	7 54	4 11	8 01	4 01	8 04	4 08	8 19	4 21	8 21
15	4 09	7 44	4 19	7 54	4 12	7 55	4 09	8 02	3 59	8 06	4 06	8 21	4 19	8 22
16	4 07	7 46	4 17	7 56	4 10	7 57	4 07	8 04	3 57	8 08	4 04	8 23	4 17	8 24
17	4 06	7 47	4 16	7 57	4 09	7 58	4 06	8 05	3 56	8 09	4 02	8 25	4 16	8 25
18	4 04	7 49	4 15	7 59	4 07	8 00	4 04	8 07	3 54	8 11	4 01	8 27	4 14	8 27
19	4 03	7 50	4 14	8 00	4 06	8 02	4 03	8 08	3 53	8 13	3 59	8 29	4 13	8 29
20	4 02	7 52	4 12	8 02	4 05	8 03	4 02	8 10	3 51	8 14	3 57	8 30	4 11	8 30
21	4 00	7 53	4 11	8 03	4 03	8 05	4 00	8 11	3 50	8 16	3 56	8 32	4 10	8 32
22	3 59	7 55	4 10	8 05	4 02	8 06	3 59	8 13	3 48	8 18	3 54	8 34	4 08	8 34
23	3 58	7 56	4 09	8 06	4 01	8 08	3 58	8 14	3 46	8 20	3 52	8 36	4 06	8 36
24	3 57	7 57	4 07	8 07	3 59	8 09	3 56	8 16	3 45	8 21	3 51	8 37	4 05	8 37
25	3 55	7 59	4 06	8 09	3 58	8 10	3 55	8 17	3 43	8 23	3 49	8 39	4 03	8 39
26	3 54	8 00	4 05	8 10	3 57	8 11	3 54	8 18	3 42	8 24	3 48	8 40	4 02	8 40
27	3 53	8 01	4 04	8 11	3 56	8 13	3 53	8 20	3 41	8 26	3 46	8 42	4 01	8 42
28	3 53	8 03	4 03	8 12	3 55	8 14	3 52	8 21	3 40	8 27	3 45	8 44	4 00	8 43
29	3 52	8 04	4 02	8 13	3 53	8 16	3 50	8 23	3 38	8 29	3 44	8 45	3 58	8 45
30	3 51	8 05	4 01	8 14	3 52	8 17	3 49	8 24	3 37	8 30	3 43	8 47	3 57	8 46
31	3 50	8 06	4 00	8 15	3 51	8 18	3 48	8 25	3 36	8 31	3 42	8 48	3 56	8 47

JUPITER ♃

Day	R.A. h m	Dec. + °	Transit h m	
1	4 16	20·7	13 39	Jupiter is
11	4 25	21·1	13 09	too close to
21	4 35	21·5	12 39	the Sun for
31	4 45	21·8	12 10	observation

SATURN ♄

Day	R.A. h m	Dec. + °	Transit h m	5° high W. 52° h m	5° high W. 56° h m
1	8 52	18·6	18 14	1 22	1 35
11	8 54	18·5	17 36	0 44	0 57
21	8 56	18·3	17 00	0 06	0 19
31	8 59	18·1	16 23	23 25	23 37

Equatorial diameter of Jupiter 33"; of Saturn 18". Diameters of Saturn's rings 40" and 12".

URANUS ⛢

Day	R.A. h m	Dec. − ° '	Transit h m	10° high W. 52° h m	10° high W. 56° h m
1	14 29·9	14 18	23 51	3 22	2 57
11	14 28·3	14 10	23 10	2 42	2 17
21	14 26·7	14 02	22 29	2 02	1 37
31	14 25·3	13 55	21 48	1 22	0 58

Diameter 4"

NEPTUNE ♆

R.A. h m	Dec. − ° '	10° high E. 52° h m	10° high E. 56° h m	Transit h m
16 58·4	21 09	23 51	0 42	2 23
16 57·5	21 07	23 11	23 58	1 43
16 56·4	21 06	22 30	23 17	1 02
16 55·3	21 04	21 49	22 37	0 22

Diameter 2"

JUNE XXX DAYS [1977

Day of Month	Week		

Junius, Roman *gens* (family).

♊

Sun's Longitude 90° ♋ 21^d 12^h

1	W.	Glorious First of June, 1794
2	Th.	CORONATION DAY, 1953. Thomas Hardy b. 1840
3	F.	George V b. 1865. Samuel Plimsoll d. 1898
4	S.	George III b. 1738. Casanova d. 1798
5	♋.	**Trinity Sunday.** Stephen Crane d. 1900
6	M.	Sir Henry Newbolt b. 1862. " D " Day, 1944
7	Tu.	TRINITY LAW SITTINGS BEGIN. Gauguin b. 1848
8	W.	Sir John Millais b. 1829
9	Th.	George Stephenson b. 1781. Charles Dickens d. 1870
10	F.	DUKE OF EDINBURGH BORN, 1921
11	S.	**St. Barnabas.** Constable b. 1776
12	♋.	**1st Sunday after Trinity.** Earl of Avon b. 1897
13	M.	Thomas Arnold b. 1795. W. B. Yeats b. 1865
14	Tu.	Naseby 1645. J. L. Baird d. 1946
15	W.	Magna Carta 1215. E. H. Grieg b. 1843
16	Th.	Duke of Marlborough d. 1722
17	F.	Sir E. Burne-Jones d. 1898
18	S.	Waterloo, 1815. Samuel Butler d. 1902
19	♋.	**2nd S. after Trinity.** James I. b. 1566
20	M.	Machiavelli d. 1527. William IV d. 1837
21	Tu.	Edward III d. 1377★★
22	W.	Puccini b. 1858. Lord Hunt b. 1910
23	Th.	Plassey 1757. Sir Leonard Hutton b. 1916
24	F.	**St. John Baptist.** Bannockburn 1314
25	S.	Earl Mountbatten of Burma b. 1900
26	♋.	**3rd S. after Trinity.** George IV d. 1830
27	M.	Cherbourg captured 1944
28	Tu.	Victor Trumper d. 1915. Treaty of Versailles 1919
29	W.	**St. Peter.** Rubens b. 1577★★
30	Th.	Elizabeth Barrett Browning d. 1861

PHENOMENA

June 3^d 13^h Venus in conjunction with Mars. Venus 1°·2 S.

4^d 10^h Jupiter in conjunction with the Sun.

5^d 14^h Neptune at opposition.

12^d 11^h Mars in conjunction with the Moon. Mars 0°·1 N.

12^d 15^h Venus in conjunction with the Moon. Venus 2°S.

15^d 05^h Mercury in conjunction with the Moon. Mercury 2° N.

15^d 07^h Venus at greatest western elongation (46°).

20^d 07^h Mercury in conjunction with Jupiter. Mercury 0°·1 N.

20^d 21^h Saturn in conjunction with the Moon. Saturn 6° N.

21^d 12^h Summer solstice.

30^d 00^h Mercury in superior conjunction.

CONSTELLATIONS

The following constellations are near the meridian at

d	h		d	h
May 1	24		May 16	23
June 1	22		June 25	21
July 1	20		July 16	19

Cassiopeia (below the Pole), Ursa Minor, Draco, Ursa Major, Canes Venatici, Bootes, Corona, Serpens, Virgo and Libra.

ALGOL

ALGOL is inconveniently situated for observation during June.

PHASES OF THE MOON

		d	h	m
○	Full Moon.......	1	20	31
☾	Last Quarter......	8	15	07
●	New Moon......	16	18	23
☽	First Quarter.....	24	12	44

	d	h
Perigee (357,060 kilometres)	1	15
Apogee (406,390 ,,)	14	21
Perigee (359,180 ,,)	30	00

Mean Longitude of Ascending Node on June 1, 202°.

See note on *Summer Time*, p. 98.

MONTHLY NOTES

June 5. Constitution Day, Denmark.

6. Spring bank holiday in England, Wales and N. Ireland.

7. Bank holiday (Queen's Silver Jubilee).

9. Corpus Christi.

11. Queen's Official Birthday.

21. Longest day.

24. Midsummer Day. Quarter Day.

★★ Centenary.

Day	Right Ascension	Dec. +	Equation of Time	Rise 52°	Rise 56°	Transit	Set 52°	Set 56°	Sidereal Time	Transit of First Point of Aries
	h m s	° '	m s	h m	h m	h m	h m	h m	h m s	h m s
1	4 35 07	22 00	+ 2 20	3 46	3 22	11 58	20 10	20 34	16 37 27	7 21 20
2	4 39 12	22 08	+ 2 11	3 45	3 21	11 58	20 11	20 35	16 41 24	7 17 24
3	4 43 18	22 16	+ 2 02	3 45	3 20	11 58	20 12	20 36	16 45 20	7 13 28
4	4 47 25	22 23	+ 1 52	3 44	3 19	11 58	20 13	20 38	16 49 17	7 09 32
5	4 51 31	22 30	+ 1 42	3 44	3 18	11 58	20 14	20 39	16 53 14	7 05 37
6	4 55 39	22 37	+ 1 31	3 43	3 18	11 59	20 15	20 40	16 57 10	7 01 41
7	4 59 46	22 43	+ 1 21	3 42	3 17	11 59	20 16	20 41	17 01 07	6 57 45
8	5 03 54	22 49	+ 1 09	3 42	3 16	11 59	20 17	20 42	17 05 03	6 53 49
9	5 08 02	22 54	+ 0 58	3 41	3 16	11 59	20 17	20 43	17 09 00	6 49 53
10	5 12 10	22 59	+ 0 46	3 41	3 15	11 59	20 18	20 44	17 12 56	6 45 57
11	5 16 19	23 04	+ 0 34	3 41	3 15	12 00	20 18	20 45	17 16 53	6 42 01
12	5 20 27	23 08	+ 0 22	3 40	3 14	12 00	20 19	20 46	17 20 49	6 38 05
13	5 24 36	23 11	+ 0 10	3 40	3 14	12 00	20 20	20 47	17 24 46	6 34 09
14	5 28 46	23 15	− 0 03	3 40	3 14	12 00	20 20	20 47	17 28 43	6 30 13
15	5 32 55	23 18	− 0 16	3 39	3 13	12 00	20 21	20 48	17 32 39	6 26 17
16	5 37 04	23 20	− 0 29	3 39	3 13	12 01	20 22	20 48	17 36 36	6 22 21
17	5 41 14	23 22	− 0 42	3 39	3 13	12 01	20 22	20 49	17 40 32	6 18 26
18	5 45 24	23 24	− 0 55	3 39	3 13	12 01	20 23	20 49	17 44 29	6 14 30
19	5 49 33	23 25	− 1 08	3 39	3 13	12 01	20 23	20 50	17 48 25	6 10 34
20	5 53 43	23 26	− 1 21	3 39	3 13	12 01	20 23	20 50	17 52 22	6 06 38
21	5 57 53	23 26	− 1 34	3 40	3 13	12 02	20 24	20 50	17 56 18	6 02 42
22	6 02 02	23 26	− 1 47	3 40	3 13	12 02	20 24	20 50	18 00 15	5 58 46
23	6 06 12	23 26	− 2 00	3 40	3 13	12 02	20 24	20 50	18 04 12	5 54 50
24	6 10 21	23 25	− 2 13	3 40	3 14	12 02	20 24	20 51	18 08 08	5 50 54
25	6 14 31	23 24	− 2 26	3 41	3 14	12 03	20 24	20 51	18 12 05	5 46 58
26	6 18 40	23 22	− 2 39	3 41	3 14	12 03	20 24	20 50	18 16 01	5 43 02
27	6 22 49	23 20	− 2 52	3 41	3 15	12 03	20 24	20 50	18 19 58	5 39 06
28	6 26 58	23 18	− 3 04	3 42	3 16	12 03	20 24	20 50	18 23 54	5 35 11
29	6 31 07	23 15	− 3 16	3 42	3 16	12 03	20 24	20 50	18 27 51	5 31 15
30	6 35 15	23 12	− 3 28	3 43	3 17	12 04	20 23	20 49	18 31 47	5 27 19

Duration of Civil (C), Nautical (N), and Astronomical (A), Twilight (in minutes)

Lat. °	June 1 C	N	A	June 11 C	N	A	June 21 C	N	A	June 30 C	N	A
52	47	117	T.A.N.	48	125	T.A.N.	49	128	T.A.N.	49	125	T.A.N.
56	58	T.A.N.	T.A.N.	61	T.A.N.	T.A.N.	63	T.A.N.	T.A.N.	62	T.A.N.	T.A.N.

ASTRONOMICAL NOTES

MERCURY is unsuitably placed for observation, superior conjunction occurring on the 30th.

VENUS is a brilliant morning star, magnitude −3·9, reaching greatest western elongation on the 15th. At the beginning of the month Venus is less than 2° from Mars: by the end of the month Venus is about 6° east of Mars. The old crescent Moon will be seen near Venus on the mornings of the 12th and 13th.

MARS gradually becomes a morning star, magnitude +1·3, during the month, visible low above the eastern horizon during morning twilight. Venus will be a useful aid to locating Mars (see above).

JUPITER is unsuitably placed for observation, conjunction occurring on the 4th.

SATURN is an evening star, magnitude +0·6 but gradually becomes too difficult to locate as it gets nearer to the Sun and it is lost in the long evening twilight before the end of the month.

NEPTUNE is at opposition on the 5th, in the constellation of Ophiuchus. The angular diameter of Neptune is only 2½″. It is not visible to the naked eye since its magnitude is about +7·7.

THE MOON

Day	R.A.	Dec.	Hor. Par.	Semi-diam.	Sun's Co-long.	P.A. of Bright Limb	Phase	Age	Rise 52°	Rise 56°	Transit	Set 52°	Set 56°
	h m	°	′	′	°	°		d	h m	h m	h m	h m	h m
1	15 46	−16·9	61·3	16·7	79	296	99	13·9	19 39	19 58	...	3 43	3 27
2	16 50	−18·5	61·4	16·7	91	35	100	14·9	20 46	21 05	0 09	4 37	4 18
3	17 54	−18·8	61·1	16·6	104	75	98	15·9	21 41	21 59	1 12	5 40	5 21
4	18 57	−17·7	60·5	16·5	116	76	93	16·9	22 26	22 41	2 13	6 50	6 33
5	19 58	−15·5	59·7	16·3	128	74	86	17·9	23 03	23 14	3 12	8 04	7 50
6	20 55	−12·4	58·8	16·0	140	71	77	18·9	23 33	23 40	4 06	9 18	9 08
7	21 48	− 8·7	57·8	15·8	152	69	67	19·9	23 59	...	4 57	10 31	10 25
8	22 39	− 4·7	56·9	15·5	165	68	57	20·9	...	0 03	5 45	11 41	11 39
9	23 28	− 0·6	56·1	15·3	177	67	46	21·9	0 23	0 24	6 31	12 49	12 51
10	0 15	+ 3·4	55·4	15·1	189	67	36	22·9	0 46	0 44	7 15	13 56	14 00
11	1 02	+ 7·2	54·8	14·9	201	68	27	23·9	1 10	1 04	7 59	15 00	15 08
12	1 49	+10·6	54·4	14·8	214	69	19	24·9	1 35	1 25	8 44	16 03	16 14
13	2 36	+13·6	54·1	14·8	226	70	12	25·9	2 02	1 50	9 28	17 04	17 18
14	3 24	+16·0	54·0	14·7	238	71	7	26·9	2 33	2 18	10 14	18 03	18 19
15	4 13	+17·7	54·0	14·7	250	70	3	27·9	3 09	2 52	11 01	18 57	19 15
16	5 02	+18·7	54·0	14·7	263	58	1	28·9	3 51	3 33	11 49	19 47	20 05
17	5 53	+18·8	54·2	14·8	275	330	0	0·2	4 39	4 21	12 37	20 31	20 49
18	6 43	+18·1	54·4	14·8	287	294	2	1·2	5 33	5 16	13 25	21 10	21 26
19	7 33	+16·6	54·7	14·9	299	290	5	2·2	6 32	6 17	14 12	21 43	21 57
20	8 23	+14·3	55·1	15·0	312	290	10	3·2	7 35	7 22	14 59	22 13	22 23
21	9 13	+11·4	55·6	15·1	324	291	16	4·2	8 40	8 32	15 46	22 40	22 47
22	10 02	+ 7·8	56·2	15·3	336	293	25	5·2	9 48	9 43	16 33	23 05	23 08
23	10 51	+ 3·9	56·8	15·5	348	293	34	6·2	10 58	10 57	17 20	23 30	23 29
24	11 41	− 0·3	57·6	15·7	0	294	44	7·2	12 11	12 13	18 09	23 55	23 51
25	12 32	− 4·6	58·4	15·9	13	293	55	8·2	13 25	13 31	18 59	...	...
26	13 26	− 8·8	59·1	16·1	25	292	66	9·2	14 41	14 52	19 53	0 23	0 16
27	14 22	−12·6	59·9	16·3	37	290	77	10·2	15 59	16 13	20 49	0 55	0 44
28	15 21	−15·8	60·5	16·5	49	287	86	11·2	17 14	17 31	21 49	1 34	1 19
29	16 23	−17·9	60·9	16·6	62	286	93	12·2	18 24	18 43	22 51	2 21	2 03
30	17 26	−18·8	61·1	16·6	74	288	98	13·2	19 26	19 44	23 54	3 18	2 59

MERCURY ☿

Day	R.A.	Dec. +	Diam.	Phase	Transit		Day	R.A.	Dec. +	Diam.	Phase	Transit	
	h m	°	″		h m			h m	°	″		h m	
1	2 58	13·5	8	46	10 21	Mercury is	16	4 30	20·7	6	79	10 55	Mercury is
4	3 13	14·8	7	52	10 24	too close to	19	4 54	22·0	5	86	11 08	too close to
7	3 29	16·2	7	58	10 29	the Sun	22	5 20	23·1	5	92	11 22	the Sun
10	3 47	17·7	6	65	10 36	for observation	25	5 48	23·9	5	96	11 38	for observation
13	4 08	19·2	6	72	10 44		28	6 16	24·4	5	98	11 55	
16	4 30	20·7	6	79	10 55		31	6 45	24·4	5	100	12 12	

VENUS ♀

Day	R.A.	Dec. +	Diam.	Phase	5° high E. 52°	56°	Transit
	h m	°	″		h m	h m	h m
1	1 38	8·0	29	41	2 51	2 48	9 00
6	1 54	9·2	27	44	2 42	2 37	8 57
11	2 12	10·5	25	47	2 33	2 27	8 55
16	2 30	11·9	24	50	2 25	2 18	8 53
21	2 49	13·3	23	53	2 17	2 09	8 53
26	3 09	14·6	21	55	2 10	2 01	8 53
31	3 30	16·0	20	58	2 03	1 53	8 54

MARS ♂

Day	R.A.	Dec. +	Diam.	Phase	5° high E. 52°	56°	Transit
	h m	°	″		h m	h m	h m
1	1 39	9·1	5	93	02 47	02 43	9 01
6	1 53	10·5	5	93	02 34	02 29	8 55
11	2 07	11·8	5	92	02 22	02 16	8 50
16	2 21	13·0	5	92	02 10	02 02	8 44
21	2 35	14·2	5	92	01 58	01 49	8 39
26	2 50	15·4	5	92	01 46	01 36	8 33
31	3 04	16·5	5	91	01 35	01 24	8 28

SUNRISE AND SUNSET (G.M.T.)

Day	London a.m. h m	London p.m. h m	Bristol a.m. h m	Bristol p.m. h m	Birmingham a.m. h m	Birmingham p.m. h m	Manchester a.m. h m	Manchester p.m. h m	Newcastle a.m. h m	Newcastle p.m. h m	Glasgow a.m. h m	Glasgow p.m. h m	Belfast a.m. h m	Belfast p.m. h m
1	3 49	8 07	3 59	8 16	3 50	8 19	3 47	8 26	3 35	8 33	3 40	8 50	3 55	8 48
2	3 48	8 08	3 58	8 17	3 49	8 20	3 46	8 28	3 34	8 34	3 39	8 51	3 54	8 50
3	3 48	8 09	3 58	8 19	3 49	8 22	3 45	8 29	3 33	8 35	3 38	8 52	3 53	8 51
4	3 47	8 10	3 57	8 20	3 48	8 23	3 44	8 30	3 32	8 36	3 37	8 53	3 52	8 52
5	3 46	8 11	3 56	8 21	3 47	8 24	3 44	8 31	3 31	8 38	3 36	8 55	3 52	8 53
6	3 45	8 12	3 55	8 22	3 46	8 25	3 43	8 32	3 31	8 39	3 36	8 56	3 51	8 54
7	3 45	8 13	3 55	8 23	3 46	8 26	3 42	8 33	3 30	8 40	3 35	8 57	3 50	8 55
8	3 44	8 14	3 54	8 23	3 45	8 26	3 42	8 34	3 29	8 41	3 34	8 58	3 50	8 56
9	3 44	8 15	3 54	8 24	3 45	8 27	3 41	8 35	3 28	8 42	3 33	8 59	3 49	8 57
10	3 43	8 15	3 53	8 25	3 44	8 28	3 41	8 36	3 28	8 43	3 33	9 00	3 49	8 58
11	3 43	8 16	3 53	8 26	3 44	8 29	3 40	8 37	3 27	8 44	3 32	9 01	3 48	8 59
12	3 43	8 17	3 53	8 26	3 44	8 29	3 40	8 38	3 27	8 45	3 32	9 02	3 48	9 00
13	3 43	8 17	3 53	8 27	3 44	8 30	3 39	8 38	3 26	8 45	3 31	9 02	3 47	9 00
14	3 42	8 18	3 52	8 28	3 43	8 31	3 39	8 39	3 26	8 46	3 31	9 03	3 47	9 01
15	3 42	8 18	3 52	8 28	3 43	8 31	3 39	8 40	3 26	8 47	3 31	9 04	3 47	9 02
16	3 42	8 19	3 52	8 29	3 43	8 32	3 39	8 40	3 26	8 47	3 31	9 04	3 47	9 02
17	3 42	8 19	3 52	8 29	3 43	8 32	3 39	8 40	3 26	8 47	3 30	9 05	3 47	9 02
18	3 42	8 20	3 52	8 30	3 43	8 33	3 39	8 41	3 26	8 48	3 30	9 05	3 47	9 03
19	3 42	8 20	3 52	8 30	3 43	8 33	3 39	8 41	3 26	8 48	3 30	9 06	3 47	9 03
20	3 42	8 20	3 52	8 30	3 43	8 33	3 39	8 42	3 26	8 49	3 30	9 06	3 47	9 04
21	3 42	8 21	3 52	8 31	3 43	8 34	3 39	8 42	3 26	8 49	3 31	9 06	3 47	9 04
22	3 43	8 21	3 53	8 31	3 44	8 34	3 39	8 42	3 26	8 49	3 31	9 06	3 47	9 04
23	3 43	8 21	3 53	8 31	3 44	8 34	3 39	8 42	3 26	8 49	3 31	9 07	3 47	9 04
24	3 43	8 21	3 53	8 31	3 44	8 34	3 40	8 42	3 27	8 49	3 32	9 07	3 48	9 04
25	3 43	8 21	3 53	8 31	3 44	8 34	3 40	8 42	3 27	8 49	3 32	9 07	3 48	9 04
26	3 44	8 21	3 54	8 31	3 45	8 34	3 41	8 42	3 28	8 49	3 32	9 07	3 49	9 04
27	3 44	8 21	3 54	8 31	3 45	8 34	3 41	8 42	3 28	8 49	3 33	9 06	3 49	9 04
28	3 45	8 21	3 55	8 31	3 46	8 34	3 42	8 42	3 29	8 49	3 33	9 06	3 50	9 04
29	3 45	8 21	3 55	8 31	3 46	8 34	3 42	8 42	3 29	8 49	3 34	9 06	3 50	9 04
30	3 46	8 21	3 56	8 31	3 47	8 34	3 43	8 42	3 30	8 49	3 35	9 06	3 51	9 04

JUPITER ♃   SATURN ♄

Day	R.A. h m	Dec. + °	Transit h m		R.A. h m	Dec. + °	Transit h m	5° high W. 52° h m	5° high W. 56° h m
1	4 46	21·9	12 07	Jupiter is too	9 00	18·1	16 20	23 21	23 33
11	4 56	22·1	11 38	close to the	9 03	17·8	15 44	22 44	22 56
21	5 06	22·4	11 08	Sun for	9 07	17·6	15 09	22 07	22 19
31	5 16	22·6	10 39	observation	9 11	17·2	14 34	21 30	21 42

Equatorial diameter of Jupiter 32"; of Saturn 17". Diameteres of Saturn's rings 38" and 11".

URANUS ♅   NEPTUNE ♆

Day	R.A. h m	Dec. − ° '	Transit h m	10° high W. 52° h m	10° high W. 56° h m	R.A. h m	Dec. − ° '	Transit h m	10° high W. 52° h m	10° high W. 56° h m
1	14 25·1	13 55	21 44	1 18	0 54	16 55·2	21 04	0 18	2 47	1 59
11	14 23·9	13 49	21 03	0 38	0 14	16 54·0	21 02	23 33	2 06	1 18
21	14 23·0	13 45	20 23	23 55	23 31	16 52·9	21 00	22 53	1 26	0 38
31	14 22·3	13 42	19 43	23 15	22 51	16 51·8	20 59	22 12	0 45	23 54

Diameter 4"   Diameter 2"

Julius Caesar, formerly *Quintilis*, 5th month (from March).

Sun's Longitude 120° ♌ 23^d 23^h

Day of Month	Day of Week	
1	F.	DOMINION DAY, CANADA. Gettysburg 1863
2	S.	Marston Moor, 1644. Lord Home b. 1903
3	S.	**4th S. after Trinity.** Earl Beauchamp b. 1903
4	M.	INDEPENDENCE DAY, U.S.A. (1776)
5	Tu.	Georgette Heyer d. 1974
6	W.	Edward VI. d. 1553. Sedgemoor 1685
7	Th.	Edward I d. 1307. Sir A. Conan-Doyle d. 1930
8	F.	Shelley d. 1822. Sir Arthur Evans b. 1851
9	S.	Edward Heath b. 1916
10	S.	**5th S. after Trinity.** Marcel Proust b. 1871
11	M.	Erasmus d. 1536. Oudenarde 1708
12	Tu.	Titus Oates d. 1705. H. D. Thoreau b. 1817
13	W.	John Clare b. 1793. Treaty of Berlin 1878
14	Th.	FÊTE NATIONALE, FRANCE (Bastille, 1789)
15	F.	St. Swithin's Day. Rembrandt b. 1606
16	S.	Sir Joshua Reynolds b. 1723
17	S.	**6th S. after Trinity.** Whistler d. 1903
18	M.	Dr. W. G. Grace b. 1848. Sir Garfield Sobers b. 1936
19	Tu.	Degas b. 1834. A. J. Cronin b. 1896
20	W.	Sir Edmund Hillary b. 1919. Marconi d. 1937
21	Th.	Hemingway b. 1898. First Men on Moon, 1969
22	F.	St. Mary Magdalen. Falkirk 1298
23	S.	Gen U. S. Grant d. 1885. Michael Foot b. 1913
24	S.	**7th S. after Trinity.** Lord Widgery b. 1911
25	M.	**St. James.** S. T. Coleridge d. 1834
26	Tu.	Aldous Huxley b. 1894. Robert Graves b. 1895
27	W.	Killiecrankie 1689. Hilaire Beloc b. 1870
28	Th.	J. S. Bach d. 1750. Robespierre d. 1794
29	F.	Mussolini b. 1883. Joseph Grimond b. 1913
30	S.	TRINITY LAW SITTINGS END. Henry Moore b. 1898
31	S.	**8th S. after Trinity.** Franz Liszt d. 1886

PHENOMENA

July 5^d 20^h Aphelion (152,000,000 kilometres).

11^d 11^h Mars in conjunction with the Moon. Mars 2° N.

12^d 10^h Venus in conjunction with the Moon. Venus 1° N.

13^d 19^h Jupiter in conjunction with the Moon. Jupiter 4° N.

18^d 03^h Mercury in conjunction with the Moon. Mercury 6° N.

18^d 09^h Saturn in conjunction with the Moon. Saturn 6° N.

20^d 01^h Mercury in conjunction with Saturn. Mercury 0°·4 N.

30^d 06^h Venus in conjunction with Jupiter. Venus 1°·6 S.

CONSTELLATIONS

The following constellations are near the meridian at

	d	h		d	h
June	1	24	June	15	23
July	1	22	July	16	21
Aug.	1	20	Aug.	16	19

Ursa Minor, Draco, Corona, Hercules, Lyra, Serpens, Ophiuchus, Libra, Scorpius and Sagittarius.

MINIMA OF ALGOL

d	h	d	h
3	2	20	7
5	23	23	4
8	20	26	0
11	16	28	21
14	13	31	18
17	10		

PHASES OF THE MOON

	d	h	m
○ Full Moon.......	1	03	24
☾ Last Quarter......	8	04	39
● New Moon......	16	08	37
☽ First Quarter.....	23	19	38
○ Full Moon.......	30	10	52

	d	h
Apogee(405,600 kilometres)	12	08
Perigee (363,470 ,,)	28	02

Mean Longitude of Ascending Node on July 1, 200°

See note on *Summer Time*, p. 98.

MONTHLY NOTES

July 1. Special Sessions for Licences to deal in Game to be held this month.

3. Dog Days begin (end Aug. 15).

5. Tynwald Day, Isle of Man.

21. National Day, Belgium.

Day	Right Ascension	Dec. +	Equation of Time	Rise 52°	Rise 56°	Transit	Set 52°	Set 56°	Sidereal Time	Transit of First Point of Aries
	h m s	° '	m s	h m	h m	h m	h m	h m	h m s	h m s
1	6 39 24	23 08	− 3 40	3 44	3 18	12 04	20 23	20 49	18 35 44	5 23 23
2	6 43 32	23 04	− 3 51	3 44	3 19	12 04	20 23	20 48	18 39 41	5 19 27
3	6 47 40	22 59	− 4 02	3 45	3 20	12 04	20 22	20 48	18 43 37	5 15 31
4	6 51 47	22 54	− 4 14	3 46	3 21	12 04	20 21	20 47	18 47 34	5 11 35
5	6 55 54	22 49	− 4 24	3 47	3 22	12 04	20 21	20 47	18 51 30	5 07 39
6	7 00 01	22 43	− 4 34	3 48	3 23	12 05	20 21	20 46	18 55 27	5 03 43
7	7 04 08	22 37	− 4 44	3 49	3 24	12 05	20 20	20 45	18 59 23	4 59 47
8	7 08 14	22 31	− 4 54	3 50	3 25	12 05	20 19	20 44	19 03 20	4 55 51
9	7 12 20	22 24	− 5 03	3 51	3 26	12 05	20 18	20 43	19 07 16	4 51 56
10	7 16 25	22 17	− 5 12	3 52	3 27	12 05	20 18	20 42	19 11 13	4 48 00
11	7 20 30	22 09	− 5 21	3 53	3 28	12 05	20 17	20 41	19 15 10	4 44 04
12	7 24 35	22 01	− 5 29	3 54	3 29	12 06	20 16	20 40	19 19 06	4 40 08
13	7 28 39	21 53	− 5 36	3 55	3 31	12 06	20 15	20 39	19 23 03	4 36 12
14	7 32 43	21 44	− 5 44	3 56	3 32	12 06	20 14	20 38	19 26 59	4 32 16
15	7 36 46	21 35	− 5 50	3 57	3 34	12 06	20 13	20 37	19 30 56	4 28 20
16	7 40 49	21 25	− 5 56	3 59	3 36	12 06	20 12	20 35	19 34 52	4 24 24
17	7 44 51	21 15	− 6 02	4 00	3 37	12 06	20 11	20 34	19 38 49	4 20 28
18	7 48 53	21 05	− 6 07	4 01	3 39	12 06	20 10	20 33	19 42 46	4 16 32
19	7 52 54	20 54	− 6 12	4 03	3 40	12 06	20 09	20 31	19 46 42	4 12 36
20	7 56 54	20 43	− 6 16	4 05	3 42	12 06	20 08	20 30	19 50 39	4 08 41
21	8 00 54	20 32	− 6 19	4 06	3 44	12 06	20 07	20 28	19 54 35	4 04 45
22	8 04 54	20 21	− 6 22	4 07	3 45	12 06	20 05	20 26	19 58 32	4 00 49
23	8 08 53	20 09	− 6 25	4 08	3 47	12 06	20 04	20 24	20 02 28	3 56 53
24	8 12 51	19 56	− 6 26	4 09	3 49	12 06	20 02	20 22	20 06 25	3 52 57
25	8 16 49	19 44	− 6 27	4 11	3 50	12 06	20 01	20 21	20 10 21	3 49 01
26	8 20 46	19 31	− 6 28	4 12	3 52	12 06	20 00	20 19	20 14 18	3 45 05
27	8 24 42	19 17	− 6 28	4 14	3 54	12 06	19 59	20 17	20 18 15	3 41 09
28	8 28 38	19 04	− 6 27	4 15	3 56	12 06	19 57	20 16	20 22 11	3 37 13
29	8 32 33	18 50	− 6 26	4 17	3 58	12 06	19 56	20 14	20 26 08	3 33 17
30	8 36 28	18 36	− 6 24	4 19	4 00	12 06	19 54	20 12	20 30 04	3 29 21
31	8 40 22	18 21	− 6 21	4 20	4 01	12 06	19 52	20 10	20 34 01	3 25 26

THE SUN   s.d. 15′·8

Duration of Civil (C), Nautical (N), and Astronomical (A), Twilight (in minutes)

Lat. °	July 1 C	N	A	July 11 C	N	A	July 21 C	N	A	July 31 C	N	A
52	48	124	T.A.N.	46	116	T.A.N.	44	107	T.A.N.	41	98	180
56	61	T.A.N.	T.A.N.	58	T.A.N.	T.A.N.	53	144	T.A.N.	49	122	T.A.N.

ASTRONOMICAL NOTES

MERCURY is unsuitably placed for observation.

VENUS is a brilliant morning star, magnitude −3·7. During the second half of the month observers with good E.N.E. horizons should be able to see it shortly before 02ʰ. On the morning of the 12th the old crescent Moon will be seen approaching Venus, passing 1°·6 S. of it during daylight. On the morning of the 30th Venus passes 1°·6 S. of Jupiter. During the second week of July Venus will be seen passing between the Hyades and the Pleiades: in particular it will pass within 0°·1 of the third magnitude star epsilon Tauri (between it and Aldebaran) on the morning of the 14th.

MARS is a morning star, magnitude +1·2, and by the end of the month is visible low in the east before 01ʰ. Mars moves from Aries into Taurus, passing between the Pleiades and the Hyades during the second half of the month. On the morning of the 11th the old crescent Moon will be seen near the planet.

JUPITER becomes a brilliant morning star early in the month, magnitude −1·5, visible for a short while before sunrise, above the eastern horizon.

SATURN is unsuitably placed for observation.

THE MOON

Day	R.A.	Dec.	Hor. Par.	Semi-diam.	Sun's Co-long.	P.A. of Bright Limb	Phase	Age	Rise 52°	Rise 56°	Transit	Set 52°	Set 56°
	h m	° ′	′	′	°	°		d	h m	h m	h m	h m	h m
1	18 30	−18.4	60.9	16.6	86	335	100	14.2	20 17	20 33	..	4 24	4 06
2	19 32	−16.7	60.4	16.5	98	59	99	15.2	20 58	21 12	0 54	5 37	5 22
3	20 31	−13.9	59.8	16.3	110	66	95	16.2	21 33	21 42	1 52	6 54	6 42
4	21 28	−10.4	58.9	16.1	122	66	89	17.2	22 02	22 07	2 46	8 09	8 01
5	22 21	− 6.4	58.0	15.8	135	66	81	18.2	22 27	22 29	3 37	9 23	9 19
6	23 12	− 2.2	57.1	15.5	147	66	72	19.2	22 51	22 50	4 25	10 34	10 34
7	0 01	+ 1.9	56.2	15.3	159	66	62	20.2	23 15	23 10	5 11	11 42	11 46
8	0 49	+ 5.9	55.5	15.1	171	67	52	21.2	23 40	23 32	5 56	12 49	12 55
9	1 36	+ 9.5	54.9	15.0	184	69	42	22.2	..	23 55	6 41	13 53	14 03
10	2 23	+12.6	54.5	14.8	196	71	33	23.2	0 06	..	7 26	14 55	15 08
11	3 11	+15.2	54.2	14.8	208	73	24	24.2	0 36	0 22	8 11	15 55	16 10
12	4 00	+17.2	54.1	14.7	220	76	17	25.2	1 10	0 54	8 58	16 51	17 08
13	4 49	+18.4	54.1	14.7	232	78	10	26.2	1 49	1 31	9 45	17 43	18 01
14	5 39	+18.8	54.2	14.8	245	79	5	27.2	2 35	2 16	10 33	18 29	18 47
15	6 30	+18.4	54.5	14.8	257	76	2	28.2	3 27	3 09	11 21	19 10	19 27
16	7 21	+17.1	54.8	14.9	269	47	0	29.2	4 24	4 08	12 09	19 46	20 00
17	8 11	+15.0	55.2	15.0	281	316	1	0.6	5 26	5 13	12 57	20 18	20 29
18	9 01	+12.2	55.6	15.2	294	299	3	1.6	6 32	6 22	13 44	20 46	20 54
19	9 51	+ 8.9	56.1	15.3	306	296	7	2.6	7 40	7 33	14 32	21 12	21 16
20	10 40	+ 5.0	56.6	15.4	318	295	13	3.6	8 49	8 46	15 19	21 36	21 37
21	11 30	+ 0.9	57.2	15.6	330	295	21	4.6	10 00	10 01	16 06	22 01	21 59
22	12 20	− 3.4	57.7	15.7	343	294	30	5.6	11 13	11 17	16 56	22 28	22 22
23	13 12	− 7.6	58.3	15.9	355	292	41	6.6	12 27	12 35	17 47	22 58	22 48
24	14 06	−11.4	58.9	16.0	7	290	52	7.6	13 41	13 54	18 40	23 32	23 19
25	15 03	−14.7	59.4	16.2	19	287	63	8.6	14 55	15 11	19 37	..	23 57
26	16 02	−17.1	59.9	16.3	32	283	74	9.6	16 06	16 24	20 36	0 14	..
27	17 02	−18.5	60.2	16.4	44	280	84	10.6	17 10	17 29	21 37	1 04	0 46
28	18 05	−18.6	60.3	16.4	56	277	91	11.6	18 05	18 22	22 37	2 04	1 46
29	19 06	−17.5	60.2	16.4	68	277	97	12.6	18 51	19 06	23 36	3 13	2 56
30	20 07	−15.2	59.9	16.3	80	296	100	13.6	19 29	19 40	..	4 27	4 13
31	21 05	−12.0	59.4	16.2	93	42	99	14.6	20 01	20 08	0 32	5 44	5 33

MERCURY ☿

Day	R.A.	Dec. +	Diam.	Phase	Transit		Day	R.A.	Dec. +	Diam.	Phase	Transit	
	h m	°	″		h m			h m	°	″		h m	
1	6 45	24.4	5	100	12 12	Mercury is too close to the Sun for observation	16	8 53	19.3	5	82	13 20	Mercury is too close to the Sun for observation
4	7 13	24.0	5	98	12 29		19	9 14	17.6	6	78	13 28	
7	7 41	23.3	5	97	12 44		22	9 33	15.8	6	74	13 35	
10	8 06	22.2	5	91	12 57		25	9 50	13.9	6	70	13 41	
13	8 30	20.8	5	87	13 09		28	10 07	12.0	6	66	13 45	
16	8 53	19.3	5	82	13 20		31	10 21	10.1	7	62	13 48	

VENUS ♀

Day	R.A.	Dec. +	Diam.	Phase	5° high E. 52°	5° high E. 56°	Transit
	h m	°	″		h m	h m	h m
1	3 30	16.0	20	58	2 03	1 53	8 54
6	3 51	17.2	19	60	1 57	1 46	8 56
11	4 13	18.4	19	62	1 53	1 41	8 58
16	4 36	19.4	18	64	1 50	1 37	9 01
21	4 59	20.3	17	66	1 48	1 34	9 04
26	5 22	21.0	16	68	1 49	1 33	9 08
31	5 46	21.5	16	70	1 50	1 34	9 13

MARS ♂

Day	R.A.	Dec. +	Diam.	Phase	5° high E. 52°	5° high E. 56°	Transit
	h m	°	″		h m	h m	h m
1	3 04	16.5	5	91	01 35	01 24	8 28
6	3 18	17.5	5	91	01 24	01 12	8 23
11	3 33	18.4	5	91	01 13	01 01	8 17
16	3 47	19.3	5	91	01 03	00 50	8 12
21	4 02	20.0	5	90	00 53	00 39	8 07
26	4 16	20.7	6	90	00 44	00 29	8 01
31	4 30	21.4	6	90	00 35	00 19	7 56

SUNRISE AND SUNSET (G.M.T.)

Day	London a.m. h m	London p.m. h m	Bristol a.m. h m	Bristol p.m. h m	Birmingham a.m. h m	Birmingham p.m. h m	Manchester a.m. h m	Manchester p.m. h m	Newcastle a.m. h m	Newcastle p.m. h m	Glasgow a.m. h m	Glasgow p.m. h m	Belfast a.m. h m	Belfast p.m. h m
1	3 47	8 21	3 57	8 30	3 48	8 33	3 44	8 41	3 31	8 48	3 36	9 05	3 52	9 03
2	3 47	8 20	3 57	8 30	3 48	8 33	3 44	8 41	3 31	8 48	3 36	9 05	3 52	9 03
3	3 48	8 20	3 58	8 29	3 49	8 32	3 45	8 40	3 32	8 47	3 37	9 04	3 53	9 02
4	3 49	8 20	3 59	8 29	3 50	8 32	3 46	8 40	3 33	8 47	3 38	9 04	3 54	9 02
5	3 50	8 19	4 00	8 29	3 51	8 32	3 47	8 39	3 34	8 46	3 39	9 03	3 55	9 01
6	3 50	8 19	4 00	8 28	3 51	8 31	3 48	8 39	3 35	8 45	3 40	9 02	3 56	9 01
7	3 51	8 18	4 01	8 27	3 52	8 30	3 49	8 38	3 36	8 45	3 41	9 02	3 57	9 00
8	3 52	8 18	4 02	8 27	3 53	8 30	3 50	8 37	3 37	8 44	3 42	9 01	3 58	8 59
9	3 53	8 17	4 03	8 26	3 54	8 29	3 51	8 36	3 39	8 43	3 44	9 00	3 59	8 58
10	3 54	8 16	4 04	8 25	3 55	8 28	3 52	8 36	3 40	8 42	3 45	8 59	4 00	8 58
11	3 55	8 16	4 05	8 25	3 56	8 28	3 53	8 35	3 41	8 41	3 46	8 58	4 01	8 57
12	3 56	8 15	4 06	8 24	3 57	8 27	3 54	8 34	3 42	8 40	3 48	8 57	4 02	8 56
13	3 57	8 14	4 08	8 23	3 59	8 26	3 56	8 33	3 44	8 39	3 49	8 55	4 04	8 55
14	3 58	8 13	4 09	8 22	4 00	8 25	3 57	8 32	3 45	8 38	3 50	8 54	4 05	8 54
15	3 59	8 12	4 10	8 21	4 01	8 24	3 58	8 31	3 46	8 37	3 52	8 53	4 06	8 53
16	4 01	8 11	4 11	8 20	4 02	8 23	3 59	8 30	3 47	8 36	3 53	8 52	4 07	8 52
17	4 02	8 10	4 12	8 19	4 04	8 21	4 01	8 28	3 49	8 34	3 55	8 50	4 09	8 50
18	4 03	8 09	4 13	8 18	4 05	8 20	4 02	8 27	3 50	8 33	3 56	8 49	4 10	8 49
19	4 04	8 08	4 15	8 17	4 07	8 19	4 04	8 26	3 52	8 32	3 58	8 48	4 12	8 48
20	4 05	8 06	4 16	8 16	4 08	8 17	4 05	8 24	3 53	8 30	3 59	8 46	4 13	8 46
21	4 07	8 05	4 17	8 15	4 09	8 16	4 06	8 23	3 55	8 28	4 01	8 44	4 15	8 44
22	4 08	8 04	4 19	8 14	4 11	8 15	4 08	8 22	3 57	8 27	4 03	8 43	4 17	8 43
23	4 09	8 03	4 20	8 13	4 12	8 14	4 09	8 21	3 58	8 25	4 04	8 41	4 18	8 41
24	4 11	8 01	4 21	8 11	4 14	8 12	4 11	8 19	4 00	8 24	4 06	8 40	4 20	8 40
25	4 12	8 00	4 23	8 10	4 15	8 11	4 12	8 18	4 02	8 22	4 08	8 38	4 22	8 38
26	4 14	7 58	4 24	8 08	4 17	8 09	4 14	8 16	4 03	8 21	4 10	8 36	4 23	8 37
27	4 15	7 57	4 25	8 07	4 18	8 08	4 15	8 15	4 05	8 19	4 11	8 34	4 25	8 35
28	4 16	7 55	4 26	8 05	4 19	8 06	4 16	8 13	4 06	8 17	4 13	8 33	4 26	8 33
29	4 18	7 54	4 28	8 04	4 21	8 05	4 18	8 12	4 08	8 16	4 15	8 31	4 28	8 32
30	4 19	7 52	4 29	8 02	4 22	8 03	4 20	8 10	4 10	8 14	4 16	8 29	4 30	8 30
31	4 21	7 51	4 31	8 01	4 24	8 02	4 21	8 08	4 11	8 12	4 18	8 27	4 31	8 28

JUPITER ♃   SATURN ♄

Day	R.A. h m	Dec. + °	5° high E. 52° h m	5° high E. 56° h m	Transit h m	R.A. h m	Dec. + °	Transit h m	
1	5 16	22·6	3 10	2 52	10 39	9 11	17·2	14 34	Saturn is too
11	5 25	22·8	2 40	2 22	10 09	9 16	16·9	13 59	close to the
21	5 35	22·9	2 09	1 51	9 39	9 21	16·5	13 24	Sun for
31	5 43	23·0	1 38	1 20	9 08	9 26	16·2	12 50	observation

Equal diameter of Jupiter 33″; of Saturn 17″. Diameters of Saturn's rings 37″ and 10″.

URANUS ♅   NEPTUNE ♆

Day	R.A. h m	Dec. − ° ′	Transit h m	10° high W. 52° h m	10° high W. 56° h m	R.A. h m	Dec. − ° ′	Transit h m	10° high W. 52° h m	10° high W. 56° h m
1	14 22·3	13 42	19 43	23 15	22 51	16 51·8	20 59	22 12	0 45	23 54
11	14 21·9	13 40	19 04	22 35	22 12	16 50·9	20 57	21 32	0 05	23 14
21	14 21·9	13 40	18 24	21 56	21 32	16 50·1	20 56	20 52	23 22	22 35
31	14 22·2	13 42	17 45	21 16	20 53	16 49·4	20 56	20 12	22 42	21 55

Diameter 4″   Diameter 2″

Julius Caesar *Augustus*, formerly *Sextilis*, 6th month (from March).

Sun's Longitude 150° ♍ 23^{d} 06^{h}

Day of Month	Day of Week	
1	M.	Queen Anne d. 1714. Battle of the Nile 1798
2	Tu.	Alexander Graham Bell d. 1922
3	W.	Rupert Brooke b. 1887. Joseph Conrad d. 1924
4	Th.	QUEEN ELIZABETH THE QUEEN MOTHER b. 1900
5	F.	Guy de Maupassant b. 1850
6	S.	**Transfiguration.** Ben Jonson d. 1637
7	**S.**	**9th S. after Trinity.** Dornford Yates b. 1885
8	M.	George Canning d. 1827. Visct. Cobham b. 1909
9	Tu.	Capt. Marryat d. 1848. Léonide Massine b. 1896
10	W.	Herbert C. Hoover b. 1874. Treaty of Trianon 1921
11	Th.	Cardinal Newman d. 1890
12	F.	William Blake d. 1827. George Stephenson d. 1848
13	S.	Florence Nightingale d. 1910. H. G. Wells d. 1946
14	**S.**	**10th S. after Trinity.** John Galsworthy b. 1867
15	M.	PRINCESS ANNE b. 1950. Napoleon b. 1769
16	Tu.	Andrew Marvell d. 1678
17	W.	Frederick the Great d. 1786. Balzac d. 1850
18	Th.	W. H. Hudson d. 1922
19	F.	James Watt d. 1819. Serge Diaghilev d. 1929
20	S.	Trotsky assassinated 1940
21	**S.**	**11th S. after Trinity.** PRINCESS MARGARET b.
22	M.	Battle of Bosworth; Richard III d. 1485 [1930
23	Tu.	William Wallace d. 1305
24	W.	**St. Bartholomew** Aubrey Beardsley b. 1872
25	Th.	Michael Faraday d. 1867. Paris Liberated, 1944
26	F.	Crecy 1346. Duke of Gloucester b. 1944
27	S.	Titian d. 1576. Sir Donald Bradman b. 1908
28	**S.**	**12th S. after Trinity.** Leigh Hunt d. 1859
29	M.	Brigham Young d. 1877** Jean Ingres b. 1780
30	Tu.	Lord Rutherford b. 1871
31	W.	John Bunyan d. 1688. Sir Bernard Lovell b. 1913

PHENOMENA

August 8^{d} 20^{h} Mercury at greatest eastern elongation (27°).

9^{d} 11^{h} Mars in conjunction with the Moon. Mars 4° N.

10^{d} 13^{h} Jupiter in conjunction with the Moon. Jupiter 4° N.

11^{d} 14^{h} Venus in conjunction with the Moon. Venus 4° N.

13^{d} 06^{h} Saturn in conjunction with the Sun.

16^{d} 23^{h} Mercury in conjunction with the Moon. Mercury 0°·9 S.

CONSTELLATIONS

The following constellations are near the meridian at

	d	h		d	h
July	1	24	July	16	23
Aug.	1	22	Aug.	16	21
Sept.	1	20	Sept.	15	19

Draco, Hercules, Lyra, Cygnus, Sagitta, Ophiuchus, Serpens, Aquila and Sagittarius.

MINIMA OF ALGOL

d	h	d	h
3	15	17	23
6	12	20	20
9	9	23	17
12	5	26	13
15	2	29	10

PHASES OF THE MOON

	d	h	m
☾ Last Quarter......	6	20	40
● New Moon......	14	21	31
☽ First Quarter.....	22	01	04
○ Full Moon.......	28	20	10

	d	h
Apogee (404,660 kilometres)	9	00
Perigee (368,400 ,,)	24	09

Mean Longitude of Ascending Node on August 1, 199°.

See note on *Summer Time*, p. 98.

MONTHLY NOTES

Aug. 1. Bank Holiday, Scotland. Lammas. Scottish Term Day.

5. Oyster season opens.

12. Grouse shooting begins.

16. First day of Ramadân.

29. Bank and General Holiday, England, Wales and N. Ireland.

** Centenary.

Day	Right Ascension	Dec. +	Equation of Time	Rise 52°	Rise 56°	Transit	Set 52°	Set 56°	Sidereal Time	Transit of First Point of Aries
	h m s	° ′	m s	h m	h m	h m	h m	h m	h m s	h m s
1	8 44 15	18 06	− 6 18	4 21	4 03	12 06	19 50	20 08	20 37 57	3 21 30
2	8 48 08	17 51	− 6 14	4 23	4 05	12 06	19 48	20 06	20 41 54	3 17 34
3	8 52 00	17 36	− 6 10	4 24	4 07	12 06	19 47	20 04	20 45 50	3 13 38
4	8 55 52	17 20	− 6 05	4 25	4 09	12 06	19 46	20 02	20 49 47	3 09 42
5	8 59 43	17 04	− 6 00	4 27	4 11	12 06	19 44	20 00	20 53 43	3 05 46
6	9 03 33	16 48	− 5 53	4 29	4 13	12 06	19 42	19 58	20 57 40	3 01 50
7	9 07 23	16 31	− 5 47	4 31	4 14	12 06	19 40	19 56	21 01 37	2 57 54
8	9 11 12	16 14	− 5 40	4 33	4 16	12 06	19 38	19 54	21 05 33	2 53 58
9	9 15 01	15 57	− 5 32	4 34	4 18	12 05	19 36	19 51	21 09 30	2 50 02
10	9 18 49	15 40	− 5 23	4 36	4 20	12 05	19 34	19 49	21 13 26	2 46 06
11	9 22 37	15 22	− 5 14	4 38	4 22	12 05	19 32	19 47	21 17 23	2 42 11
12	9 26 24	15 04	− 5 05	4 39	4 24	12 05	19 30	19 44	21 21 19	2 38 15
13	9 30 10	14 46	− 4 55	4 41	4 26	12 05	19 28	19 41	21 25 16	2 34 19
14	9 33 56	14 28	− 4 44	4 42	4 28	12 05	19 26	19 39	21 29 12	2 30 23
15	9 37 42	14 09	− 4 33	4 43	4 30	12 04	19 24	19 37	21 33 09	2 26 27
16	9 41 26	13 51	− 4 21	4 45	4 32	12 04	19 22	19 35	21 37 06	2 22 31
17	9 45 11	13 32	− 4 09	4 47	4 34	12 04	19 20	19 33	21 41 02	2 18 35
18	9 48 55	13 12	− 3 56	4 48	4 36	12 04	19 18	19 30	21 44 59	2 14 39
19	9 52 38	12 53	− 3 43	4 50	4 38	12 04	19 16	19 28	21 48 55	2 10 43
20	9 56 21	12 33	− 3 29	4 51	4 40	12 03	19 14	19 26	21 52 52	2 06 47
21	10 00 03	12 14	− 3 15	4 53	4 42	12 03	19 12	19 23	21 56 48	2 02 51
22	10 03 45	11 54	− 3 00	4 55	4 44	12 03	19 10	19 20	22 00 45	1 58 56
23	10 07 26	11 33	− 2 45	4 57	4 46	12 03	19 08	19 18	22 04 41	1 55 00
24	10 11 07	11 13	− 2 29	4 58	4 48	12 02	19 05	19 15	22 08 38	1 51 04
25	10 14 47	10 53	− 2 13	4 59	4 50	12 02	19 03	19 12	22 12 35	1 47 08
26	10 18 27	10 32	− 1 56	5 01	4 52	12 02	19 01	19 10	22 16 31	1 43 12
27	10 22 07	10 11	− 1 39	5 03	4 54	12 02	18 59	19 08	22 20 28	1 39 16
28	10 25 46	9 50	− 1 22	5 05	4 56	12 01	18 57	19 05	22 24 24	1 35 20
29	10 29 25	9 29	− 1 04	5 07	4 58	12 01	18 55	19 03	22 28 21	1 31 24
30	10 33 03	9 07	− 1 46	5 08	5 00	12 01	18 52	19 00	22 32 17	1 27 28
31	10 36 41	8 46	− 0 28	5 09	5 02	12 00	18 50	18 58	22 36 14	1 23 32

Duration of Civil (C), Nautical (N), and Astronomical (A), Twilight (in minutes)

Lat. °	Aug. 1			Aug. 11			Aug. 21			Aug. 31		
	C	N	A	C	N	A	C	N	A	C	N	A
52	41	97	177	39	89	153	37	83	138	35	79	127
56	48	120	T.A.N.	45	106	205	42	96	166	40	89	147

ASTRONOMICAL NOTES

MERCURY is not suitably placed for observation despite the fact that it is at greatest eastern elongation on the 8th.

VENUS is a brilliant morning star, magnitude − 3·5, visible in the east for several hours before sunrise. It passes south of the Twins, Castor and Pollux, on the 22nd–24th.

MARS is a morning star, magnitude + 1·1, moving eastwards in the constellation of Taurus, passing 5° N. of Aldebaran on the 1st. The old crescent Moon is near Mars on the morning of the 9th.

JUPITER is a brilliant morning star, magnitude − 1·7, moving slowly eastwards from Taurus into Gemini. The old crescent Moon is near the planet on the morning of the 10th.

SATURN is unsuitably placed for observation, conjunction occurring on the 13th.

METEORS. The maximum of the famous Perseid meteor shower occurs on the 12th. Observers will see most meteors on the nights of the 11th–12th and 12th–13th, more meteors being seen after midnight than before. Since the Moon is New on the 14th there will be no noticeable effect on the number of meteors visible.

THE MOON

Day	R.A.	Dec.	Hor. Par.	Semi-diam.	Sun's Co-long.	P.A. of Bright Limb	Phase	Age	Rise 52°	Rise 56°	Transit	Set 52°	Set 56°
	h m	°	′	′	°	°		d	h m	h m	h m	h m	h m
1	22 00	− 8·2	58·7	16·0	105	60	97	15·6	20 29	20 33	1 25	6 59	6 53
2	22 53	− 4·0	57·9	15·8	117	63	92	16·6	20 54	20 55	2 15	8 13	8 11
3	23 43	+ 0·2	57·0	15·5	129	65	85	17·6	21 19	21 16	3 03	9 24	9 25
4	0 32	+ 4·3	56·2	15·3	141	66	77	18·6	21 43	21 37	3 50	10 32	10 38
5	1 21	+ 8·1	55·5	15·1	153	68	68	19·6	22 09	22 00	4 35	11 39	11 47
6	2 09	+11·5	54·9	15·0	166	71	58	20·6	22 38	22 25	5 21	12 42	12 54
7	2 57	+14·3	54·5	14·9	178	73	49	21·6	23 10	22 55	6 06	13 44	13 58
8	3 45	+16·4	54·3	14·8	190	76	39	22·6	23 47	23 30	6 53	14 41	14 58
9	4 34	+17·9	54·2	14·8	202	80	30	23·6	··	··	7 39	15 35	15 53
10	5 24	+18·6	54·3	14·8	215	83	22	24·6	0 30	0 12	8 27	16 24	16 42
11	6 15	+18·5	54·8	14·8	227	86	15	25·6	1 20	1 02	9 15	17 07	17 24
12	7 05	+17·5	54·8	14·9	239	89	9	26·6	2 15	1 58	10 04	17 45	18 00
13	7 56	+15·7	55·3	15·1	251	89	4	27·6	3 15	3 01	10 52	18 19	18 31
14	8 47	+13·1	55·8	15·2	264	82	1	28·6	4 20	4 09	11 40	18 49	18 58
15	9 37	+ 9·9	56·3	15·3	276	2	0	0·1	5 28	5 20	12 28	19 16	19 22
16	10 27	+ 6·1	56·8	15·5	288	305	1	1·1	6 38	6 34	13 16	19 42	19 44
17	11 18	+ 2·0	57·3	15·6	300	298	5	2·1	7 50	7 49	14 04	20 07	20 06
18	12 09	− 2·2	57·8	15·8	313	295	11	3·1	9 02	9 06	14 53	20 34	20 29
19	13 01	− 6·5	58·2	15·9	325	293	18	4·1	10 16	10 24	15 44	21 02	20 54
20	13 54	−10·4	58·6	16·0	337	290	28	5·1	11 31	11 42	16 37	21 35	21 23
21	14 50	−13·8	59·0	16·1	349	287	38	6·1	12 44	12 59	17 32	22 14	21 58
22	15 47	−16·4	59·2	16·1	1	283	49	7·1	13 54	14 11	18 29	23 00	22 42
23	16 46	−18·0	59·4	16·2	14	278	61	8·1	14 59	15 17	19 27	23 54	23 36
24	17 46	−18·5	59·5	16·2	26	274	72	9·1	15 56	16 14	20 25	··	··
25	18 46	−17·9	59·5	16·2	38	270	82	10·1	16 44	17 00	21 23	0 58	0 40
26	19 46	−16·1	59·3	16·2	50	266	90	11·1	17 25	17 37	22 19	2 08	1 52
27	20 43	−13·3	59·0	16·1	62	265	96	12·1	17 59	18 08	23 13	3 21	3 10
28	21 39	− 9·8	58·6	16·0	75	271	99	13·1	18 28	18 34	··	4 36	4 28
29	22 32	− 5·8	58·0	15·8	87	11	100	14·1	18 55	18 57	0 04	5 50	5 46
30	23 24	− 1·6	57·4	15·6	99	59	98	15·1	19 20	19 19	0 53	7 03	7 02
31	0 14	+ 2·6	56·7	15·4	111	65	95	16·1	19 45	19 40	1 41	8 13	8 17

MERCURY ☿

Day	R.A.	Dec. +	Diam.	Phase	Transit	Day	R.A.	Dec.	Diam.	Phase	Transit
	h m	°	″		h m		h m	°	″		h m
1	10 26	9·5	7	60	13 48	16	11 15	+1·6	8	37	13 36
4	10 39	7·7	7	56	13 49	19	11 18	+0·7	9	31	13 28
7	10 50	6·0	7	52	13 49	22	11 20	0·0	9	24	13 17
10	11 00	4·4	8	47	13 46	25	11 18	−0·2	10	18	13 03
13	11 08	2·9	8	42	13 42	28	11 14	+0·1	10	12	12 46
16	11 15	1·6	8	37	13 36	31	11 07	+0·9	11	6	12 27

Mercury is too close to the Sun for observation (left)

Mercury is too close to the Sun for observation (right)

VENUS ♀

Day	R.A.	Dec. +	Diam.	Phase	5° high E. 52°	56°	Transit
	h m	°	″		h m	h m	h m
1	5 51	21·5	16	70	1 51	1 35	9 14
6	6 16	21·8	15	72	1 54	1 38	9 18
11	6 40	21·8	15	74	1 59	1 44	9 23
16	7 05	21·5	14	76	2 07	1 51	9 29
21	7 30	21·0	14	77	2 15	1 59	9 34
26	7 55	20·3	14	79	2 24	2 10	9 39
31	8 20	19·3	13	80	2 35	2 22	9 44

MARS ♂

Day	R.A.	Dec. +	Diam.	Phase	5° high E. 52°	56°	Transit
	h m	°	″		h m	h m	h m
1	4 33	21·5	6	90	00 33	00 17	7 55
6	4 47	22·0	6	90	00 24	00 08	7 49
11	5 02	22·5	6	89	00 16	00 00	7 44
16	5 16	22·8	6	89	00 08	23 49	7 38
21	5 30	23·1	6	89	00 01	23 41	7 33
26	5 44	23·3	6	89	23 50	23 34	7 27
31	5 57	23·3	6	89	23 44	23 27	7 21

SUNRISE AND SUNSET (G.M.T.)

Day	London a.m. h m	London p.m. h m	Bristol a.m. h m	Bristol p.m. h m	Birmingham a.m. h m	Birmingham p.m. h m	Manchester a.m. h m	Manchester p.m. h m	Newcastle a.m. h m	Newcastle p.m. h m	Glasgow a.m. h m	Glasgow p.m. h m	Belfast a.m. h m	Belfast p.m. h m
1	4 22	7 49	4 32	7 59	4 25	8 00	4 23	8 06	4 13	8 10	4 20	8 25	4 33	8 26
2	4 24	7 47	4 34	7 57	4 27	7 58	4 25	8 05	4 15	8 08	4 22	8 23	4 35	8 25
3	4 26	7 46	4 36	7 56	4 29	7 57	4 26	8 03	4 17	8 06	4 24	8 21	4 36	8 23
4	4 27	7 44	4 37	7 54	4 30	7 55	4 28	8 01	4 19	8 04	4 26	8 19	4 38	8 21
5	4 29	7 42	4 39	7 52	4 32	7 53	4 30	7 59	4 21	8 02	4 28	8 17	4 40	8 19
6	4 30	7 41	4 40	7 50	4 33	7 51	4 31	7 57	4 22	8 00	4 30	8 15	4 42	8 17
7	4 32	7 39	4 42	7 48	4 35	7 49	4 33	7 55	4 24	7 58	4 32	8 12	4 44	8 14
8	4 33	7 37	4 43	7 47	4 36	7 48	4 35	7 53	4 26	7 56	4 34	8 10	4 46	8 12
9	4 35	7 35	4 45	7 45	4 38	7 46	4 37	7 51	4 28	7 54	4 36	8 08	4 48	8 10
10	4 37	7 33	4 47	7 43	4 40	7 44	4 39	7 49	4 30	7 52	4 38	8 06	4 50	8 08
11	4 38	7 32	4 48	7 41	4 41	7 42	4 40	7 47	4 32	7 50	4 40	8 04	4 51	8 06
12	4 40	7 30	4 50	7 39	4 43	7 40	4 42	7 45	4 34	7 47	4 42	8 01	4 53	8 04
13	4 41	7 28	4 51	7 37	4 45	7 38	4 44	7 43	4 36	7 45	4 44	7 59	4 55	8 02
14	4 43	7 26	4 53	7 35	4 47	7 36	4 46	7 41	4 37	7 43	4 45	7 57	4 57	8 00
15	4 44	7 24	4 54	7 34	4 48	7 33	4 47	7 38	4 39	7 40	4 47	7 54	4 58	7 57
16	4 46	7 22	4 56	7 32	4 50	7 31	4 49	7 36	4 41	7 38	4 49	7 52	5 00	7 55
17	4 47	7 20	4 57	7 30	4 52	7 29	4 51	7 34	4 43	7 36	4 51	7 50	5 02	7 53
18	4 49	7 18	4 59	7 28	4 54	7 27	4 53	7 32	4 45	7 34	4 53	7 48	5 04	7 51
19	4 50	7 16	5 00	7 26	4 55	7 25	4 54	7 30	4 47	7 32	4 55	7 46	5 06	7 49
20	4 52	7 14	5 02	7 24	4 57	7 23	4 56	7 28	4 48	7 29	4 56	7 43	5 07	7 46
21	4 53	7 12	5 03	7 22	4 58	7 21	4 57	7 26	4 50	7 27	4 58	7 41	5 09	7 44
22	4 55	7 10	5 05	7 20	5 00	7 19	4 59	7 24	4 52	7 25	5 00	7 39	5 11	7 42
23	4 57	7 07	5 07	7 17	5 02	7 16	5 01	7 21	4 54	7 22	5 02	7 36	5 13	7 40
24	4 58	7 05	5 08	7 15	5 03	7 14	5 02	7 19	4 56	7 19	5 04	7 33	5 14	7 37
25	5 00	7 03	5 10	7 13	5 05	7 12	5 04	7 17	4 58	7 17	5 06	7 31	5 16	7 35
26	5 02	7 01	5 12	7 11	5 07	7 10	5 06	7 14	5 00	7 15	5 08	7 29	5 18	7 32
27	5 03	6 59	5 13	7 09	5 08	7 08	5 08	7 12	5 02	7 12	5 10	7 26	5 20	7 30
28	5 05	6 57	5 15	7 07	5 10	7 06	5 10	7 10	5 04	7 10	5 12	7 23	5 22	7 27
29	5 07	6 54	5 17	7 04	5 12	7 03	5 11	7 07	5 05	7 07	5 14	7 21	5 24	7 25
30	5 08	6 52	5 18	7 02	5 13	7 01	5 13	7 05	5 07	7 05	5 16	7 18	5 26	7 22
31	5 10	6 50	5 20	7 00	5 15	6 59	5 15	7 03	5 09	7 03	5 18	7 16	5 28	7 20

JUPITER ♃   SATURN ♄

Day	R.A. h m	Dec. + °	5° high E. 52° h m	5° high E. 56° h m	Transit h m	R.A. h m	Dec. + °	Transit h m	
1	5 44	23·0	1 35	1 17	9 05	9 26	16·1	12 47	Saturn is too
11	5 53	23·0	1 04	0 46	8 34	9 31	15·7	12 12	close to the
21	6 00	23·0	0 32	0 14	8 02	9 36	15·3	11 38	Sun for
31	6 07	23·0	23 56	23 38	7 30	9 41	14·9	11 04	observation

Equatorial diameter of Jupiter 35"; of Saturn 16". Diameters of Saturn's rings 37" and 9".

URANUS ♅   NEPTUNE ♆

Day	R.A. h m	Dec. ° '	Transit h m		R.A. h m	Dec. - ° '	Transit h m	10° high W. 52° h m	10° high W. 56° h m
1	14 22·3	13 43	17 41	Uranus is too	16 49·3	20 56	20 08	22 38	21 51
11	14 23·0	13 46	17 03	close to the	16 48·9	20 56	19 28	21 59	21 12
21	14 24·0	13 52	16 25	Sun for	16 48·7	20 56	18 49	21 19	20 32
31	14 25·3	13 58	15 47	observation	16 48·7	20 56	18 09	20 40	19 52

Diameter 4"   Diameter 2"

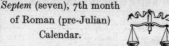

DAY OF		
Month	Week	

Septem (seven), 7th month
of Roman (pre-Julian)
Calendar.

Sun's Longitude 180° ♎ 22ᵈ 22ʰ

1	Th.	Jacques Cartier d. 1557. Louis XIV d. 1715
2	F.	Fire of London 1666. J. R. R. Tolkien d. 1973
3	S.	Britain at War, 1939. Oliver Cromwell d. 1658
4	☙.	**13th ☙. after Trinity.** E. H. Greig d. 1907
5	M.	John Wisden b. 1826
6	Tu.	Battle of the Marne 1914. Arthur Rackham d. 1939
7	W.	Queen Elizabeth I b. 1533. C. B. Fry d. 1956
8	Th.	Richard Strauss d. 1949
9	F.	Flodden 1513. F. R. Spofforth b. 1853
10	S.	Treaty of St. Germain 1919
11	☙.	**14th ☙. after Trinity.** Malplaquet 1709
12	M.	Sack of Drogheda 1649
13	Tu.	Quebec 1759. Heath Robinson d. 1944
14	W.	Dante d. 1321. Wellington d. 1852
15	Th.	Battle of Britain Day. I. K. Brunel d. 1859
16	F.	Fire of Moscow, 1812. Bonar Law b. 1858
17	S.	James II d. 1701. Smollett d. 1771
18	☙.	**15th ☙. after Trinity.** Dr. Johnson b. 1709
19	M.	Poitiers 1356. William Golding b. 1911
20	Tu.	Battle of the Alma, 1854. Sibelius d. 1957
21	W.	**St. Matthew.** H. G. Wells b. 1866
22	Th.	Boulogne reoccupied 1944
23	F.	Wilkie Collins d. 1889. Sigmund Freud d. 1939
24	S.	Horace Walpole b. 1717. Sir Alan Herbert b. 1890
25	☙.	**16th ☙. after Trinity.** William Faulkner b. 1897
26	M.	John Buchan b. 1875. Pope Paul VI b. 1897
27	Tu.	Edward II d. 1327. Degas d. 1917
28	W.	Louis Pasteur d. 1895
29	Th.	**St. Michael and All Angels.** Nelson b. 1758
30	F.	Lord Raglan b. 1788. Calais reoccupied 1944

PHENOMENA

September 4ᵈ 22ʰ Mars in conjunction with Jupiter. Mars 0°·5 N.

5ᵈ 06ʰ Mercury in inferior conjunction.

7ᵈ 07ʰ Jupiter in conjunction with the Moon. Jupiter 5° N.

7ᵈ 09ʰ Mars in conjunction with the Moon. Mars 5° N.

10ᵈ 21ʰ Venus in conjunction with the Moon. Venus 5° N.

11ᵈ 13ʰ Saturn in conjunction with the Moon. Saturn 5° N.

18ᵈ 13ʰ Venus in conjunction with Saturn. Venus 0°·4 S.

21ᵈ 08ʰ Mercury at greatest western elongation (18°).

23ᵈ 04ʰ Autumnal Equinox.

CONSTELLATIONS

The following constellations are near the meridian at

	d	h		d	h
Aug. 1	24		Aug. 16	23	
Sept. 1	22		Sept. 15	21	
Oct. 1	20		Oct. 16	19	

Draco, Cepheus, Lyra, Cygnus, Vulpecula, Sagitta, Delphinus, Equuleus, Aquila, Aquarius and Capricornus.

MINIMA OF ALGOL

d	h	d	h
1	7	18	12
4	4	21	9
7	1	24	6
9	21	27	2
12	18	29	23
15	15		

PHASES OF THE MOON

	d	h	m
☽ Last Quarter	5	14	33
● New Moon	13	09	23
☽ First Quarter	20	06	18
○ Full Moon	27	08	17

Apogee(404,230 kilometres) 5 18
Perigee (369,110 ,,) 18 09

Mean Longitude of Ascending Node on September 1, 197°.

See note on *Summer Time*, p. 98.

MONTHLY NOTES

Sept. 1. Partridge shooting begins.
    13. Jewish New Year (A.M. 5738).
    22. Day of Atonement (Yom Kippur).
    27. First day of Tabernacles. Harvest Moon.
    29. Michaelmas. Quarter day.

Day	THE SUN								Sidereal Time	Transit of First Point of Aries
	Right Ascension	Dec.	Equation of Time	Rise 52°	Rise 56°	Transit	Set 52°	Set 56°		
	h m s	° ′	m s	h m	h m	h m	h m	h m	h m s	h m s
1	10 40 19	+8 24	− 0 09	5 11	5 04	12 00	18 48	18 55	22 40 10	1 19 36
2	10 43 57	+8 02	+ 0 10	5 13	5 06	12 00	18 46	18 53	22 44 07	1 15 41
3	10 47 34	+7 40	+ 0 29	5 15	5 08	11 59	18 43	18 50	22 48 04	1 11 45
4	10 51 11	+7 18	+ 0 49	5 17	5 10	11 59	18 41	18 48	22 52 00	1 07 49
5	10 54 48	+6 56	+ 1 09	5 18	5 11	11 59	18 39	18 45	22 55 57	1 03 53
6	10 58 24	+6 34	+ 1 29	5 20	5 13	11 58	18 37	18 43	22 59 53	0 59 57
7	11 02 01	+6 12	+ 1 49	5 21	5 15	11 58	18 35	18 40	23 03 50	0 56 01
8	11 05 37	+5 49	+ 2 09	5 22	5 17	11 58	18 32	18 37	23 07 46	0 52 05
9	11 09 13	+5 27	+ 2 30	5 24	5 19	11 57	18 30	18 34	23 11 43	0 48 09
10	11 12 49	+5 04	+ 2 51	5 26	5 21	11 57	18 28	18 32	23 15 39	0 44 13
11	11 16 24	+4 41	+ 3 12	5 27	5 23	11 57	18 25	18 29	23 19 36	0 40 17
12	11 20 00	+4 18	+ 3 33	5 29	5 25	11 56	18 23	18 27	23 23 33	0 36 22
13	11 23 35	+3 55	+ 3 54	5 31	5 27	11 56	18 20	18 24	23 27 29	0 32 26
14	11 27 11	+3 32	+ 4 15	5 32	5 29	11 56	18 18	18 21	23 31 26	0 28 30
15	11 30 46	+3 09	+ 4 36	5 34	5 31	11 55	18 16	18 18	23 35 22	0 24 34
16	11 34 21	+2 46	+ 4 57	5 36	5 33	11 55	18 13	18 15	23 39 19	0 20 38
17	11 37 57	+2 23	+ 5 19	5 37	5 35	11 55	18 11	18 13	23 43 15	0 16 42
18	11 41 32	+2 00	+ 5 40	5 39	5 37	11 54	18 09	18 10	23 47 12	0 12 46
19	11 45 07	+1 37	+ 6 01	5 41	5 39	11 54	18 07	18 08	23 51 08	0 08 50
20	11 48 42	+1 13	+ 6 22	5 42	5 41	11 53	18 04	18 05	23 55 05	0 04 54
21	11 52 18	+0 50	+ 6 44	5 43	5 43	11 53	18 02	18 02	23 59 01	} 0 00 58 / 23 57 02
22	11 55 53	+0 27	+ 7 05	5 45	5 44	11 53	18 00	18 00	0 02 58	23 53 07
23	11 59 29	+0 03	+ 7 26	5 47	5 46	11 52	17 57	17 57	0 06 55	23 49 11
24	12 03 04	−0 20	+ 7 47	5 49	5 48	11 52	17 55	17 55	0 10 51	23 45 15
25	12 06 40	−0 43	+ 8 08	5 51	5 50	11 52	17 53	17 52	0 14 48	23 41 19
26	12 10 16	−1 07	+ 8 28	5 52	5 52	11 51	17 50	17 49	0 18 44	23 37 23
27	12 13 52	−1 30	+ 8 49	5 54	5 54	11 51	17 48	17 46	0 22 41	23 33 27
28	12 17 28	−1 53	+ 9 09	5 56	5 56	11 51	17 45	17 44	0 26 37	23 29 31
29	12 21 04	−2 17	+ 9 30	5 57	5 58	11 50	17 43	17 41	0 30 34	23 25 35
30	12 24 41	−2 40	+ 9 50	5 59	6 00	11 50	17 41	17 39	0 34 30	23 21 39

THE SUN s.d. 15′·9

Duration of Civil (C), Nautical (N), and Astronomical (A), Twilight (in minutes)

Lat. °	Sept. 1			Sept. 11			Sept. 21			Sept. 30		
	C	N	A	C	N	A	C	N	A	C	N	A
52	35	79	127	34	76	120	34	74	115	34	73	113
56	39	89	146	38	84	135	37	82	129	37	80	126

ASTRONOMICAL NOTES

MERCURY is visible as a morning star, magnitude +1·1 to −1·0, during the second half of the month, visible low above the eastern horizon around the time of beginning of morning civil twilight. This is the most suitable morning apparition of the year for observers in the northern hemisphere.

VENUS is a brilliant morning star, magnitude −3·4. It passes close to Saturn on the 18th and only 0°·4 N. of Regulus when they rise together on the morning of the 22nd.

MARS is a morning star, magnitude +0·9, moving eastwards in the constellation of Gemini. During the night of the 4th–5th Mars passes 0°·5 N. of Jupiter. On the morning of the 7th the old crescent Moon will be seen near Mars.

JUPITER is a brilliant morning star, magnitude −1·8 and now visible low in the east before midnight. On the morning of the 7th the Moon passes 5° S. of the planet.

SATURN gradually becomes visible as a morning star, magnitude +0·8, during the first part of the month. Saturn is in Leo, moving slowly eastwards towards Regulus.

ZODIACAL LIGHT. The morning cone may be seen in the eastern sky before twilight commences, from the 12th to the 25th. This faint phenomenon may only be detected under good conditions and in the absence of both moonlight and artificial lighting.

THE MOON

Day	R.A.	Dec.	Hor. Par.	Semi-diam.	Sun's Co-long.	P.A. of Bright Limb	Phase	Age	Rise 52°	Rise 56°	Transit	Set 52°	Set 56°
	h m	°	′	′	°	°		d	h m	h m	h m	h m	h m
1	1 03	+ 6.6	56.0	15.3	123	68	89	17.1	20 11	20 03	2 28	9 21	9 28
2	1 52	+10.1	55.4	15.1	135	71	82	18.1	20 39	20 28	3 14	10 27	10 37
3	2.40	+13.2	54.9	15.0	148	74	74	19.1	21 10	20 56	4 00	11 30	11 43
4	3 29	+15.6	54.5	14.9	160	77	65	20.1	21 45	21 29	4 46	12 30	12 45
5	4 18	+17.3	54.3	14.8	172	81	56	21.1	22 26	22 08	5 33	13 25	13 42
6	5 08	+18.3	54.3	14.8	184	85	46	22.1	23 12	22 54	6 20	14 16	14 34
7	5 58	+18.4	54.4	14.8	196	88	37	23.1	..	23 47	7 08	15 01	15 19
8	6 48	+17.8	54.7	14.9	209	92	28	24.1	0 04	..	7 56	15 41	15 57
9	7 39	+16.3	55.1	15.0	221	96	20	25.1	1 02	0 47	8 44	16 17	16 30
10	8 29	+14.0	55.7	15.2	233	98	12	26.1	2 05	1 53	9 32	16 48	16 59
11	9 20	+11.0	56.3	15.3	245	100	7	27.1	3 12	3 02	10 20	17 17	17 24
12	10 10	+ 7.4	57.0	15.5	258	99	2	28.1	4 21	4 16	11 09	17 44	17 47
13	11 01	+ 3.4	57.6	15.7	270	84	0	29.1	5 33	5 31	11 58	18 10	18 10
14	11 53	− 0.9	58.2	15.9	282	304	0	0.6	6 47	6 49	12 48	18 37	18 33
15	12 46	− 5.2	58.7	16.0	294	294	3	1.6	8 02	8 08	13 39	19 05	18 58
16	13 40	− 9.3	59.1	16.1	307	290	8	2.6	9 18	9 28	14 32	19 38	19 27
17	14 36	−12.9	59.3	16.2	319	286	16	3.6	10 33	10 47	15 27	20 15	20 00
18	15 34	−15.7	59.4	16.2	331	282	25	4.6	11 46	12 02	16 24	20 59	20 42
19	16 33	−17.6	59.4	16.2	343	277	36	5.6	12 52	13 10	17 22	21 51	21 32
20	17 32	−18.4	59.3	16.2	355	272	47	6.6	13 51	14 09	18 20	22 50	22 33
21	18 32	−18.0	59.1	16.1	8	268	58	7.6	14 41	14 58	19 17	23 57	23 41
22	19 30	−16.5	58.8	16.0	20	263	69	8.6	15 23	15 37	20 12	..	..
23	20 27	−14.1	58.5	15.9	32	260	79	9.6	15 58	16 09	21 05	1 08	0 55
24	21 22	−10.8	58.1	15.8	44	257	87	10.6	16 29	16 36	21 56	2 20	2 11
25	22 15	− 7.1	57.7	15.7	56	256	94	11.6	16 56	17 00	22 45	3 33	3 27
26	23 06	− 3.0	57.2	15.6	69	256	98	12.6	17 22	17 22	23 33	4 45	4 43
27	23 56	+ 1.2	56.7	15.4	81	265	100	13.6	17 47	17 43	..	5 55	5 57
28	0 46	+ 5.2	56.1	15.3	93	65	100	14.6	18 12	18 06	0 20	7 04	7 09
29	1 35	+ 8.9	55.6	15.1	105	71	97	15.6	18 39	18 30	1 06	8 11	8 20
30	2 23	+12.1	55.1	15.0	117	74	93	16.6	19 09	18 57	1 52	9 16	9 27

MERCURY ☿

Day	R.A.	Dec. +	Diam.	Phase	Transit		Day	R.A.	Dec. +	Diam.	Phase	5° high E. 52°	56°	Transit
	h m	°	″		h m			h m	°	″		h m	h m	h m
1	11 04	1.2	11	4	12 20	Mercury is	16	10 34	8.4	8	24	4 45	4 41	10 54
4	10 54	2.7	11	1	11 58	too close to	19	10 41	8.7	8	38	4 38	4 34	10 49
7	10 44	4.4	10	2	11 37	the Sun	22	10 52	8.3	7	52	4 39	4 36	10 49
10	10 37	6.1	10	6	11 18	for	25	11 06	7.3	6	64	4 47	4 44	10 52
13	10 33	7.5	9	14	11 04	observation	28	11 23	5.9	6	75	5 00	4 58	10 57
16	10 34	8.4	8	24	10 54		31	11 41	4.1	6	85	5 16	5 16	11 04

VENUS ♀

Day	R.A.	Dec. +	Diam.	Phase	5° high E. 52°	56°	Transit
	h m	°	″		h m	h m	h m
1	8 25	19.1	13	80	2 37	2 24	9 45
6	8 50	17.9	13	82	2 49	2 37	9 50
11	9 14	16.4	13	83	3 02	2 51	9 55
16	9 38	14.8	12	85	3 15	3 06	9 59
21	10 02	12.9	12	86	3 29	3 21	10 03
26	10 25	10.9	12	87	3 43	3 37	10 07
31	10 49	8.8	12	88	3 58	3 54	10 11

MARS ♂

Day	R.A.	Dec. +	Diam.	Phase	5° high E. 52°	56°	Transit
	h m	°	″		h m	h m	h m
1	6 00	23.5	6	88	23 43	23 25	7 19
6	6 13	23.5	6	88	23 37	23 18	7 13
11	6 26	23.5	6	88	23 31	23 12	7 07
16	6 39	23.4	7	88	23 34	23 05	7 00
21	6 52	23.3	7	88	23 18	22 59	6 52
26	7 04	23.1	7	88	23 11	22 53	6 45
31	7 16	22.0	7	88	23 05	22 47	6 37

SUNRISE AND SUNSET (G.M.T.)

Day	London a.m. h m	London p.m. h m	Bristol a.m. h m	Bristol p.m. h m	Birmingham a.m. h m	Birmingham p.m. h m	Manchester a.m. h m	Manchester p.m. h m	Newcastle a.m. h m	Newcastle p.m. h m	Glasgow a.m. h m	Glasgow p.m. h m	Belfast a.m. h m	Belfast p.m. h m
1	5 11	6 48	5 21	6 58	5 16	6 57	5 17	7 00	5 11	7 00	5 20	7 13	5 30	7 17
2	5 13	6 45	5 23	6 55	5 18	6 54	5 18	6 58	5 13	6 58	5 22	7 11	5 31	7 15
3	5 15	6 43	5 25	6 53	5 20	6 52	5 20	6 55	5 15	6 55	5 24	7 08	5 33	7 12
4	5 16	6 41	5 26	6 51	5 21	6 50	5 22	6 53	5 17	6 52	5 26	7 05	5 35	7 10
5	5 18	6 39	5 28	6 49	5 23	6 48	5 24	6 51	5 18	6 50	5 27	7 03	5 37	7 08
6	5 20	6 37	5 30	6 46	5 25	6 45	5 26	6 48	5 20	6 47	5 29	7 00	5 39	7 05
7	5 21	6 34	5 31	6 44	5 27	6 43	5 28	6 46	5 22	6 45	5 31	6 58	5 41	7 03
8	5 23	6 32	5 33	6 42	5 28	6 41	5 29	6 43	5 24	6 42	5 33	6 55	5 42	7 00
9	5 25	6 30	5 35	6 39	5 30	6 38	5 31	6 41	5 26	6 40	5 35	6 52	5 44	6 58
10	5 26	6 28	5 36	6 37	5 32	6 36	5 33	6 38	5 28	6 37	5 37	6 50	5 46	6 55
11	5 28	6 26	5 38	6 35	5 34	6 34	5 35	6 36	5 30	6 35	5 39	6 47	5 48	6 53
12	5 29	6 23	5 39	6 33	5 35	6 33	5 36	6 33	5 31	6 32	5 41	6 44	5 49	6 50
13	5 31	6 21	5 41	6 31	5 37	6 29	5 38	6 31	5 33	6 30	5 43	6 42	5 51	6 48
14	5 33	6 19	5 43	6 28	5 39	6 26	5 40	6 29	5 35	6 27	5 45	6 39	5 53	6 45
15	5 34	6 16	5 44	6 26	5 40	6 24	5 41	6 26	5 37	6 24	5 47	6 36	5 55	6 42
16	5 35	6 14	5 45	6 23	5 42	6 21	5 43	6 24	5 39	6 22	5 49	6 34	5 57	6 40
17	5 37	6 12	5 47	6 21	5 44	6 19	5 45	6 22	5 41	6 19	5 51	6 31	5 59	6 37
18	5 38	6 09	5 48	6 18	5 45	6 16	5 46	6 19	5 43	6 16	5 53	6 28	6 01	6 35
19	5 40	6 07	5 50	6 16	5 47	6 14	5 48	6 17	5 45	6 14	5 55	6 26	6 03	6 32
20	5 42	6 05	5 52	6 14	5 49	6 12	5 50	6 14	5 47	6 11	5 57	6 23	6 05	6 29
21	5 43	6 02	5 53	6 12	5 50	6 09	5 51	6 12	5 48	6 09	5 59	6 20	6 06	6 27
22	5 45	6 00	5 55	6 10	5 52	6 07	5 53	6 09	5 50	6 06	6 01	6 18	6 08	6 24
23	5 46	5 58	5 56	6 07	5 53	6 05	5 55	6 07	5 52	6 04	6 03	6 15	6 10	6 22
24	5 48	5 55	5 58	6 05	5 55	6 02	5 57	6 04	5 54	6 01	6 05	6 12	6 12	6 19
25	5 50	5 53	6 00	6 03	5 57	6 00	5 59	6 02	5 56	5 59	6 07	6 10	6 14	6 17
26	5 51	5 51	6 01	6 01	5 58	5 58	6 01	5 59	5 58	5 56	6 09	6 07	6 16	6 14
27	5 53	5 48	6 03	5 58	6 00	5 55	6 02	5 57	5 59	5 54	6 11	6 04	6 17	6 12
28	5 54	5 46	6 04	5 56	6 01	5 53	6 04	5 54	6 01	5 51	6 13	6 02	6 19	6 09
29	5 56	5 44	6 06	5 54	6 03	5 51	6 06	5 52	6 03	5 49	6 15	5 59	6 21	6 07
30	5 58	5 41	6 08	5 51	6 05	5 48	6 08	5 49	6 05	5 46	6 17	5 57	6 23	6 04

JUPITER ♃   SATURN ♄

Day	R.A. h m	Dec. + °	5° high E. 52° h m	5° high E. 56° h m	Transit h m	R.A. h m	Dec. + °	5° high E. 52° h m	5° high E. 56° h m	Transit h m
1	6 08	23·0	23 53	23 35	7 27	9 42	14·9	4 16	4 07	11 00
11	6 14	23·0	23 20	23 02	6 53	9 47	14·5	3 43	3 34	10 26
21	6 19	23·0	22 46	22 28	6 19	9 51	14·1	3 10	3 02	9 51
31	6 23	23·0	22 10	21 52	5 43	9 56	13·8	2 38	2 30	9 16

Equatorial diameter of Jupiter 38″; of Saturn 17″. Diameters of Saturn's rings 37″ and 8″.

URANUS ♅   NEPTUNE ♆

Day	R.A. h m	Dec. − ° ′	Transit h m		R.A. h m	Dec. − ° ′	Transit h m	10° high W. 52° h m	10° high W. 56° h m
1	14 25·5	13 59	15 43	Uranus is too	16 48·7	20 56	18 06	20 36	19 47
11	14 27·1	14 07	15 05	close to the	16 49·0	20 57	17 27	19 57	19 08
21	14 28·9	14 17	14 28	Sun for	16 49·5	20 59	16 48	19 18	18 30
31	14 31·0	14 27	13 50	observation	16 50·2	21 00	16 09	18 39	17 51

Diameter 4″   Diameter 2″

Day of Month	Week	

Octo (eight), 8th month
of Roman (pre-Julian)
Calendar.

Sun's Longitude 210° ♏ 23^d 07^h

1	S.	MICHAELMAS LAW SITTINGS BEGIN
2	♋.	**17th ♋. after Trinity.**　Graham Greene b. 1904
3	M.	William Morris d. 1896
4	Tu.	Rembrandt d. 1669.　John Rennie d. 1821
5	W.	Offenbach d. 1880.　R101 Disaster 1930
6	Th.	Tennyson d. 1892.　Ford Madox Brown d. 1893
7	F.	Edgar Allan Poe d. 1849.　Marie Lloyd d. 1922
8	S.	Henry Fielding d. 1754.　Kathleen Ferrier d. 1953
9	♋.	**18th ♋. after Trinity.**　Lord Hailsham b. 1907
10	M.	Verdi b. 1813.　Sir Wilfred Grenfell d. 1940
11	Tu.	Camperdown 1797
12	W.	Edward VI b. 1537.　Ramsay MacDonald b. 1866
13	Th.	Mrs Margaret Thatcher b. 1925
14	F.	Hastings 1066.　James II b. 1633
15	S.	Oscar Wilde b. 1856.　Lord Snow b. 1905
16	♋.	**19th ♋. after Trinity.**　Eugene O'Neill b. 1888
17	M.	Sir Philip Sydney d. 1586.　Chopin d. 1849
18	Tu.	**St. Luke.**　Lord Shinwell b. 1884
19	W.	Swift d. 1745.　Lord Rutherford d. 1937
20	Th.	Sir Christopher Wren b. 1632
21	F.	Trafalgar Day, 1805.　Alfred Nobel b. 1833
22	S.	Professor Arnold Toynbee d. 1975
23	♋.	**20th ♋. after Trinity.**　W. G. Grace d. 1915
24	M.	David Oistrakh d. 1974
25	Tu.	Chaucer d. 1400.　Agincourt 1415
26	W.	Hogarth d. 1764
27	Th.	Georges Carpentier d. 1975
28	F.	**St. Simon and St. Jude.**　John Locke d. 1704
29	S.	Wilfrid Rhodes b. 1877**
30	♋.	**21st ♋. after Trinity.**　R. B. Sheridan b. 1632
31	M.	Hallowmas Eve.　Vermeer b. 1632

PHENOMENA

October 4^d 21^h Jupiter in conjunction with the Moon. Jupiter 5° N.

6^d 03^h Mars in conjunction with the Moon.　Mars 6° N.

9^d 04^h Saturn in conjunction with the Moon. Saturn 5° N.

11^d 01^h Venus in conjunction with the Moon. Venus 4° N.

12^d 21^h Total eclipse of the Sun. See p. 148 for details.

18^d 23^h Mercury in superior conjunction.

CONSTELLATIONS

The following constellations are near the meridian at

	d	h		d	h
Sept. 1	24		Sept. 15	23
Oct. 1	22		Oct. 16	21
Nov. 1	20		Nov. 15	19

Ursa Major (below the Pole), Cepheus, Cassiopeia, Cygnus, Lacerta, Andromeda, Pegasus, Capricornus, Aquarius and Piscis Austrinus.

MINIMA OF ALGOL

d	h		d	h
2	20		20	1
5	17		22	22
8	14		25	19
11	10		28	15
14	7		31	12
17	4			

PHASES OF THE MOON

		d	h	m
☾ Last Quarter		5	09	21
● New Moon		12	20	31
☽ First Quarter		19	12	46
○ Full Moon		26	23	35

			d	h
Apogee(404,660 kilometres)			3	14
Perigee (364,220　　,,		)	15	09
Apogee(405,620　　,,		)	31	08

Mean Longitude of Ascending Node on October 1, 195°.

MONTHLY NOTES

Oct.　1. Pheasant shooting begins.

14. Michaelmas Fire Insurances must be paid.

23. *Summer Time* ends at 2 a.m. G.M.T.

26. Hunter's Moon.

NATIONAL DAYS.—Oct. 1, China, Nigeria; 4, Lesotho; 9, Uganda; 26, Austria, Iran.

** Centenary.

Day	Right Ascension	Dec. —	Equation of Time	Rise 52°	Rise 56°	Transit	Set 52°	Set 56°	Sidereal Time	Transit of First Point of Aries
	h m s	° ′	m s	h m	h m	h m	h m	h m	h m s	h m s
1	12 28 18	3 03	+10 09	6 01	6 02	11 50	17 38	17 37	0 38 27	23 17 43
2	12 31 55	3 27	+10 29	6 02	6 04	11 49	17 36	17 34	0 42 24	23 13 47
3	12 35 32	3 50	+10 48	6 04	6 06	11 49	17 33	17 32	0 46 20	23 09 52
4	12 39 10	4 13	+11 06	6 06	6 08	11 49	17 31	17 29	0 50 17	23 05 56
5	12 42 48	4 36	+11 25	6 07	6 10	11 48	17 29	17 26	0 54 13	23 02 00
6	12 46 27	4 59	+11 43	6 09	6 12	11 48	17 26	17 23	0 58 10	22 58 04
7	12 50 06	5 22	+12 00	6 11	6 14	11 48	17 24	17 20	1 02 06	22 54 08
8	12 53 45	5 45	+12 17	6 12	6 16	11 48	17 22	17 18	1 06 03	22 50 12
9	12 57 25	6 08	+12 34	6 14	6 18	11 47	17 19	17 16	1 09 59	22 46 16
10	13 01 06	6 31	+12 50	6 16	6 20	11 47	17 17	17 13	1 13 56	22 42 20
11	13 04 46	6 54	+13 06	6 17	6 22	11 47	17 15	17 10	1 17 53	22 38 24
12	13 08 28	7 16	+13 21	6 19	6 24	11 47	17 13	17 07	1 21 49	22 34 28
13	13 12 09	7 39	+13 36	6 21	6 27	11 46	17 11	17 04	1 25 46	22 30 31
14	13 15 52	8 01	+13 50	6 23	6 29	11 46	17 09	17 02	1 29 42	22 26 37
15	13 19 35	8 24	+14 04	6 25	6 31	11 46	17 06	16 59	1 33 39	22 22 41
16	13 23 18	8 46	+14 17	6 27	6 33	11 46	17 04	16 57	1 37 35	22 18 45
17	13 27 02	9 08	+14 30	6 28	6 35	11 45	17 02	16 55	1 41 32	22 14 49
18	13 30 46	9 30	+14 42	6 30	6 37	11 45	17 00	16 53	1 45 28	22 10 53
19	13 34 31	9 52	+14 53	6 31	6 39	11 45	16 58	16 51	1 49 25	22 06 57
20	13 38 17	10 13	+15 04	6 33	6 41	11 45	16 56	16 48	1 53 22	22 03 01
21	13 42 03	10 35	+15 15	6 35	6 43	11 45	16 54	16 46	1 57 18	21 59 05
22	13 45 50	10 56	+15 24	6 37	6 45	11 45	16 52	16 43	2 01 15	21 55 09
23	13 49 38	11 17	+15 33	6 38	6 47	11 44	16 50	16 41	2 05 11	21 51 13
24	13 53 26	11 38	+15 41	6 40	6 49	11 44	16 48	16 39	2 09 08	21 47 18
25	13 57 15	11 59	+15 49	6 42	6 51	11 44	16 46	16 36	2 13 04	21 43 22
26	14 01 05	12 20	+15 56	6 44	6 54	11 44	16 44	16 33	2 17 01	21 39 26
27	14 04 55	12 40	+16 02	6 46	6 56	11 44	16 42	16 31	2 20 57	21 35 30
28	14 08 46	13 00	+16 08	6 48	6 58	11 44	16 40	16 29	2 24 54	21 31 34
29	14 12 38	13 20	+16 12	6 49	7 00	11 44	16 38	16 27	2 28 50	21 27 38
30	14 16 31	13 40	+16 16	6 50	7 02	11 44	16 36	16 25	2 32 47	21 23 42
31	14 20 24	14 00	+16 20	6 52	7 04	11 44	16 34	16 23	2 36 44	21 19 46

THE SUN   s.d. 16′·1

Duration of Civil (C), Nautical (N), and Astronomical (A), Twilight (in minutes)

Lat. °	Oct. 1 C	N	A	Oct. 11 C	N	A	Oct. 21 C	N	A	Oct. 31 C	N	A
52	34	73	113	34	73	112	34	74	113	36	75	114
56	37	80	125	37	80	124	38	81	124	40	83	126

ASTRONOMICAL NOTES

MERCURY may be glimpsed as a difficult morning star, magnitude −1·0, low above the eastern horizon at the time of beginning of morning civil twilight, but only for the first few days of the month. Thereafter it is unsuitably placed for observation, superior conjunction occurring on the 18th.

VENUS is a brilliant morning star, magnitude −3·4. On the morning of the 11th the old crescent Moon passes 4° S. of the planet.

MARS is a morning star, magnitude +0·7, steadily moving eastwards from Gemini into Cancer. On the early morning of the 6th the Moon, one day after Last Quarter, passes 6° S. of the planet. Towards the middle of the month Mars will be seen passing south of the Twins.

JUPITER is a brilliant morning star, magnitude −2·0, almost stationary in the western part of Gemini. On the late evening of the 4th the gibbous Moon will be seen passing 5° S. of the planet.

SATURN is a morning star, magnitude +0·8, in the western part of Leo.

ECLIPSE. A total eclipse of the Sun occurs on the 12th. See p. 148 for details.

THE MOON

Day	R.A.	Dec.	Hor. Par.	Semi-diam.	Sun's Co-Long.	P.A. of Bright Limb	Phase	Age	Rise 52°	Rise 56°	Transit	Set 52°	Set 56°
	h m	°	'	'	°	°		d	h m	h m	h m	h m	h m
1	3 12	+14·8	54·7	14·9	129	78	87	17·6	19 43	19 28	2 39	10 17	10 32
2	4 02	+16·7	54·4	14·8	142	81	80	18·6	20 21	20 04	3 26	11 15	11 31
3	4 51	+18·0	54·2	14·8	154	85	72	19·6	21 05	20 47	4 13	12 07	12 25
4	5 41	+18·4	54·2	14·8	166	89	63	20·6	21 55	21 37	5 00	12 55	13 12
5	6 31	+18·0	54·4	14·8	178	93	54	21·6	22 50	22 33	5 48	13 37	13 53
6	7 21	+16·8	54·7	14·9	190	97	44	22·6	23 49	23 36	6 35	14 14	14 28
7	8 11	+14·9	55·2	15·0	202	101	35	23·6			7 23	14 46	14 58
8	9 00	+12·2	55·8	15·2	215	104	26	24·6	0 53	0 43	8 10	15 16	15 24
9	9 50	+ 8·9	56·6	15·4	227	106	17	25·6	2 01	1 53	8 58	15 43	15 48
10	10 41	+ 5·0	57·4	15·6	239	108	10	26·6	3 11	3 08	9 46	16 10	16 11
11	11 33	+ 0·8	58·2	15·9	251	109	4	27·6	4 25	4 25	10 36	16 36	16 34
12	12 26	− 3·6	59·0	16·1	264	110	1	28·6	5 40	5 44	11 28	17 04	16 59
13	13 20	− 7·8	59·6	16·2	276	275	0	0·1	6 58	7 06	12 21	17 36	17 26
14	14 17	−11·7	60·0	16·3	288	282	2	1·1	8 15	8 28	13 17	18 12	17 59
15	15 16	−14·9	60·2	16·4	300	280	6	2·1	9 31	9 47	14 16	18 54	18 38
16	16 16	−17·2	60·2	16·4	312	276	13	3·1	10 43	11 00	15 15	19 45	19 27
17	17 17	−18·3	59·9	16·3	325	271	22	4·1	11 46	12 04	16 14	20 44	20 26
18	18 18	−18·2	59·6	16·2	337	266	33	5·1	12 39	12 56	17 12	21 49	21 32
19	19 17	−16·9	59·1	16·1	349	262	44	6·1	13 24	13 39	18 08	22 59	22 45
20	20 15	−14·7	58·6	16·0	1	258	55	7·1	14 01	14 13	19 02	..	..
21	21 09	−11·6	58·0	15·8	13	255	66	8·1	14 32	14 40	19 53	0 11	0 00
22	22 02	− 8·0	57·5	15·7	25	252	76	9·1	15 00	15 05	20 41	1 22	1 15
23	22 53	− 4·1	56·9	15·5	38	250	84	10·1	15 25	15 27	21 28	2 33	2 30
24	23 42	0·0	56·4	15·4	50	249	91	11·1	15 50	15 48	22 15	3 43	3 43
25	0 31	+ 4·0	55·9	15·2	62	248	96	12·1	16 15	16 09	23 01	4 51	4 55
26	1 19	+ 7·8	55·5	15·1	74	245	99	13·1	16 41	16 32	23 47	5 58	6 05
27	2 08	+11·2	55·1	15·0	86	154	100	14·1	17 09	16 58	..	7 03	7 14
28	2 57	+14·0	54·7	14·9	98	87	99	15·1	17 41	17 27	0 33	8 06	8 19
29	3 46	+16·2	54·4	14·8	111	86	99	16·1	18 18	18 01	1 20	9 05	9 21
30	4 36	+17·7	54·2	14·8	123	88	92	17·1	19 00	18 42	2 07	10 00	10 18
31	5 25	+18·4	54·1	14·7	135	91	86	18·1	19 47	19 29	2 54	10 50	11 08

MERCURY ☿

Day	R.A.	Dec.	Diam.	Phase	Transit		Day	R.A.	Dec. −	Diam.	Phase	Transit	
	h m	°	"		h m			h m	°	"		h m	
1	11 41	+4·1	6	85	11 04	Mercury is too close to the Sun for observation	16	13 17	6·9	5	100	11 41	Mercury is too close to the Sun for observation
4	12 01	+2·0	5	91	11 11		19	13 36	9·1	5	100	11 47	
7	12 20	−0·2	5	94	11 19		22	13 54	11·2	5	100	11 54	
10	12 39	−2·4	5	97	11 26		25	14 13	13·2	5	99	12 01	
13	12 58	−4·7	5	99	11 34		28	14 31	15·1	5	98	12 07	
16	13 17	−6·9	5	100	11 41		31	14 50	16·9	5	98	12 14	

VENUS ♀

Day	R.A.	Dec.	Diam.	Phase	5° high E. 52°	5° high E. 56°	Transit
	h m	°	"		h m	h m	h m
1	10 49	+8·5	12	88	3 58	3 54	10 11
6	11 12	+6·6	12	89	4 13	4 10	10 14
11	11 35	+4·3	11	90	4 28	4 27	10 17
16	11 58	+1·9	11	91	4 43	4 44	10 20
21	12 20	−0·5	11	92	4 58	5 02	10 23
26	12 43	−2·9	11	93	5 15	5 21	10 26
31	13 06	−5·4	11	94	5 31	5 39	10 30

MARS ♂

Day	R.A.	Dec. +	Diam.	Phase	5° high E. 52°	5° high E. 56°	Transit
	h m	°	"		h m	h m	h m
1	7 16	22·9	7	88	23 05	22 47	6 37
6	7 27	22·7	7	88	22 59	22 41	6 29
11	7 38	22·4	8	88	22 52	22 34	6 20
16	7 49	22·1	8	88	22 44	22 27	6 11
21	7 59	21·8	8	88	22 36	22 20	6 01
28	8 08	21·5	8	88	22 27	22 12	5 51
31	8 17	21·2	9	89	22 18	22 03	5 40

SUNRISE AND SUNSET (G.M.T.)

Day	London a.m. h m	London p.m. h m	Bristol a.m. h m	Bristol p.m. h m	Birmingham a.m. h m	Birmingham p.m. h m	Manchester a.m. h m	Manchester p.m. h m	Newcastle a.m. h m	Newcastle p.m. h m	Glasgow a.m. h m	Glasgow p.m. h m	Belfast a.m. h m	Belfast p.m. h m
1	6 00	5 39	6 10	5 49	6 07	5 46	6 10	5 47	6 07	5 44	6 19	5 54	6 25	6 02
2	6 01	5 37	6 11	5 47	6 08	5 44	6 11	5 45	6 09	5 41	6 21	5 51	6 27	5 59
3	6 03	5 34	6 13	5 44	6 10	5 41	6 13	5 42	6 11	5 39	6 23	5 49	6 29	5 57
4	6 05	5 32	6 15	5 42	6 12	5 39	6 15	5 40	6 13	5 36	6 25	5 46	6 31	5 54
5	6 06	5 30	6 16	5 40	6 13	5 37	6 16	5 38	6 15	5 33	6 27	5 43	6 33	5 51
6	6 08	5 28	6 18	5 38	6 15	5 35	6 18	5 36	6 17	5 31	6 29	5 41	6 35	5 49
7	6 10	5 26	6 19	5 36	6 17	5 32	6 20	5 33	6 19	5 28	6 31	5 38	6 37	5 46
8	6 12	5 24	6 21	5 34	6 19	5 30	6 22	5 31	6 21	5 26	6 33	5 36	6 39	5 44
9	6 13	5 22	6 22	5 32	6 20	5 27	6 23	5 28	6 22	5 23	6 35	5 33	6 40	5 41
10	6 15	5 19	6 24	5 29	6 22	5 25	6 25	5 26	6 24	5 21	6 37	5 31	6 42	5 39
11	6 16	5 17	6 26	5 27	6 24	5 23	6 27	5 24	6 26	5 19	6 39	5 28	6 44	5 37
12	6 18	5 15	6 27	5 25	6 26	5 20	6 29	5 21	6 28	5 16	6 41	5 25	6 46	5 34
13	6 20	5 13	6 29	5 23	6 28	5 18	6 31	5 19	6 30	5 14	6 43	5 23	6 48	5 32
14	6 21	5 11	6 31	5 21	6 30	5 16	6 33	5 17	6 32	5 11	6 45	5 20	6 50	5 30
15	6 23	5 08	6 33	5 18	6 32	5 13	6 35	5 14	6 34	5 09	6 47	5 18	6 52	5 27
16	6 25	5 06	6 35	5 16	6 33	5 11	6 36	5 12	6 36	5 06	6 49	5 15	6 53	5 25
17	6 26	5 04	6 36	5 14	6 35	5 09	6 38	5 10	6 38	5 04	6 51	5 13	6 55	5 23
18	6 28	5 02	6 38	5 12	6 37	5 07	6 40	5 07	6 40	5 01	6 53	5 10	6 57	5 20
19	6 30	5 00	6 40	5 10	6 39	5 05	6 42	5 05	6 42	4 59	6 55	5 08	6 59	5 18
20	6 31	4 58	6 41	5 08	6 40	5 03	6 44	5 03	6 44	4 57	6 57	5 05	7 01	5 15
21	6 33	4 55	6 43	5 05	6 42	5 00	6 46	5 00	6 46	4 54	6 59	5 03	7 03	5 13
22	6 35	4 53	6 45	5 03	6 44	4 58	6 48	4 58	6 48	4 52	7 01	5 01	7 05	5 11
23	6 37	4 51	6 47	5 01	6 46	4 56	6 50	4 56	6 50	4 50	7 04	4 58	7 08	5 08
24	6 38	4 49	6 48	4 59	6 47	4 54	6 52	4 54	6 52	4 48	7 06	4 56	7 10	5 06
25	6 40	4 47	6 50	4 57	6 49	4 52	6 54	4 52	6 54	4 46	7 08	4 54	7 12	5 04
26	6 42	4 45	6 52	4 55	6 51	4 50	6 56	4 50	6 56	4 43	7 10	4 51	7 14	5 02
27	6 44	4 43	6 54	4 53	6 53	4 48	6 58	4 47	6 58	4 41	7 12	4 49	7 16	4 59
28	6 46	4 41	6 56	4 51	6 55	4 46	7 00	4 45	7 00	4 39	7 14	4 47	7 18	4 57
29	6 47	4 39	6 57	4 49	6 56	4 44	7 01	4 43	7 02	4 36	7 16	4 44	7 20	4 55
30	6 49	4 38	6 59	4 47	6 58	4 43	7 03	4 42	7 04	4 34	7 18	4 42	7 22	4 53
31	6 51	4 36	7 01	4 46	7 00	4 41	7 05	4 40	7 06	4 32	7 20	4 40	7 24	4 51

JUPITER ♃   SATURN ♄

Day	R.A. h m	Dec. + °	5° high E. 52° h m	5° high E. 56° h m	Transit h m	R.A. h m	Dec. + °	5° high E. 52° h m	5° high E. 56° h m	Transit h m
1	6 23	23·0	22 10	21 52	5 43	9 56	13·8	2 38	2 30	9 16
11	6 25	22·9	21 33	21 15	5 07	10 00	13·5	2 05	1 57	8 40
21	6 27	22·9	20 55	20 37	4 29	10 03	13·2	1 31	1 23	8 05
31	6 26	23·0	20 15	19 57	3 49	10 06	12·9	0 55	0 47	7 28

Equatorial diameter of Jupiter 41″; of Saturn 17″   Diameters of Saturn's rings 38″ and 7″

URANUS ♅   NEPTUNE ♆

Day	R.A. h m	Dec. − ° ′	Transit h m		R.A. h m	Dec. − ° ′	Transit h m	
1	14 31·0	14 27	13 50	Uranus is too	16 50·2	21 00	16 09	Neptune is
11	14 33·2	14 38	13 13	close to the	16 51·1	21 02	15 31	too close to
21	14 35·6	14 49	12 36	Sun for	16 52·2	21 05	14 53′	the Sun for
31	14 38·0	15 01	11 59	observation	16 53·4	21 07	14 14	observation

Diameter 4″   Diameter 2″

DAY OF		Novem (nine), 9th month of Roman (pre-Julian) Calendar.

Sun's Longitude 240° ♐ 22ᵈ 10ʰ

Month	Week	
1	Tu.	All Saints. Ezra Pound d. 1972
2	W.	All Souls' Day. Victor Trumper b. 1877★★
3	Th.	Baedeker b. 1801. Ludovic Kennedy b. 1919
4	F.	Mendelssohn d. 1847. Wilfred Owen d. 1918
5	S.	Guy Fawkes Day (1605). Inkerman 1854
6	☉.	22nd ☉. after Trinity. Tschaikovsky d. 1893
7	M.	Madame Curie b. 1867. Cardinal Heenan d. 1975
8	Tu.	Milton d. 1674. Tolstoy d. 1910
9	W.	Edward VII b. 1841. Dylan Thomas d. 1953
10	Th.	Luther b. 1483. Catherine the Great d. 1796
11	F.	ARMISTICE DAY (1918)
12	S.	Mrs. Gaskell d. 1865. Baroness Orczy d. 1947
13	☉.	23rd ☉. after Trinity. R. C. Sherriff d. 1975
14	M.	PRINCE OF WALES BORN, 1948
15	Tu.	Aneurin Bevan b. 1897. Sir Hugh Greene b. 1910
16	W.	Gustavus Adolphus d. 1632. Clark Gable d. 1960
17	Th.	Mary I d. 1558. Mervyn Peake d. 1968
18	F.	Sir W. S. Gilbert b. 1836. Proust d. 1922
19	S.	Charles I b. 1600. Schubert d. 1828
20	☉.	24th ☉. after Trinity. QUEEN'S WEDDING DAY
21	M.	Sir Arthur Quiller Couch b. 1863 [(1947)
22	Tu.	George Eliot b. 1819. J. F. Kennedy d. 1963
23	W.	Perkin Warbeck d. 1499. Richard Hakluyt d. 1616
24	Th.	John Knox d. 1572. Laurence Sterne b. 1713
25	F.	Harley Granville-Barker b. 1877★★
26	S.	William Cowper b. 1731
27	☉.	1st ☉. in Advent. Ross McWhirter d. 1975
28	M.	William Blake b. 1757
29	Tu.	Prince Rupert d. 1682. Graham Hill d. 1975
30	W.	St. Andrew. Sir Winston Churchill b. 1874

PHENOMENA

November 1ᵈ 05ʰ Jupiter in conjunction with the Moon. Jupiter 5° N.

3ᵈ 14ʰ Mars in conjunction with the Moon. Mars 7° N.

4ᵈ 16ʰ Uranus in conjunction with the Sun.

5ᵈ 18ʰ Saturn in conjunction with the Moon. Saturn 5° N.

10ᵈ 00ʰ Venus in conjunction with the Moon. Venus 0°·1 N.

28ᵈ 08ʰ Jupiter in conjunction with the Moon. Jupiter 5° N.

CONSTELLATIONS

The following constellations are near the meridian at

d h	d h
Oct. 1 24	Oct. 16 23
Nov. 1 22	Nov. 15 21
Dec. 1 20	Dec. 16 19

Ursa Major (below the Pole), Cepheus Cassiopeia, Andromeda, Pegasus, Pisces, Aquarius and Cetus.

MINIMA OF ALGOL

d	h	d	h
3	9	17	17
6	6	20	14
9	3	23	11
11	23	26	7
14	20	29	4

PHASES OF THE MOON

	d	h	m
☾ Last Quarter	4	03	58
● New Moon	11	07	09
☽ First Quarter	17	21	52
○ Full Moon	25	17	31

	d	h
Perigee (359,300 kilometres)	12	12
Apogee(406,370 ,,)	27	21

Mean Longitude of Ascending Node on November 1, 194°.

MONTHLY NOTES

Nov. 1. Hallowmas. Fox-hunting begins.

11. Martinmas. Scottish Term Day.

12. Lord Mayor's Day.

13. Remembrance Sunday.

28. Removal Day, Scotland.

★★ Centenary.

| | THE SUN | | | | | | | s.d. 16'·2 | Sidereal Time | Transit of First Point of Aries |
Day	Right Ascension	Dec. —	Equation of Time	Rise 52°	Rise 56°	Transit	Set 52°	Set 56°		
	h m s	° ′	m s	h m	h m	h m	h m	h m	h m s	h m s
1	14 24 18	14 19	+16 22	6 54	7 06	11 44	16 32	16 20	2 40 40	21 15 50
2	14 28 13	14 39	+16 23	6 56	7 08	11 44	16 30	16 18	2 44 37	21 11 54
3	14 32 09	14 57	+16 24	6 58	7 10	11 44	16 29	16 16	2 48 33	21 07 58
4	14 36 06	15 16	+16 24	7 00	7 13	11 44	16 27	16 14	2 52 30	21 04 03
5	14 40 03	15 35	+16 23	7 02	7 15	11 44	16 25	16 12	2 56 26	21 00 07
6	14 44 02	15 53	+16 21	7 04	7 17	11 44	16 23	16 09	3 00 23	20 56 11
7	14 48 01	16 11	+16 19	7 05	7 19	11 44	16 22	16 07	3 04 19	20 52 15
8	14 52 01	16 28	+16 15	7 07	7 22	11 44	16 20	16 05	3 08 16	20 48 19
9	14 56 02	16 46	+16 11	7 09	7 24	11 44	16 19	16 03	3 12 13	20 44 23
10	15 00 04	17 03	+16 05	7 11	7 26	11 44	16 17	16 02	3 16 09	20 40 27
11	15 04 06	17 20	+15 59	7 13	7 28	11 44	16 16	16 00	3 20 06	20 36 31
12	15 08 10	17 36	+15 52	7 14	7 30	11 44	16 14	15 58	3 24 02	20 32 35
13	15 12 14	17 52	+15 45	7 16	7 32	11 44	16 12	15 56	3 27 59	20 28 39
14	15 16 19	18 08	+15 36	7 18	7 34	11 44	16 10	15 54	3 31 55	20 24 43
15	15 20 25	18 24	+15 27	7 20	7 36	11 45	16 09	15 52	3 35 52	20 20 48
16	15 24 32	18 39	+15 16	7 21	7 38	11 45	16 08	15 51	3 39 48	20 16 52
17	15 28 40	18 54	+15 05	7 23	7 40	11 45	16 07	15 49	3 43 45	20 12 56
18	15 32 48	19 09	+14 53	7 25	7 42	11 45	16 05	15 48	3 47 42	20 09 00
19	15 36 57	19 23	+14 41	7 26	7 44	11 45	16 04	15 46	3 51 38	20 05 04
20	15 41 07	19 37	+14 27	7 28	7 46	11 46	16 03	15 45	3 55 35	20 01 08
21	15 45 18	19 50	+14 13	7 29	7 48	11 46	16 02	15 44	3 59 31	19 57 12
22	15 49 30	20 04	+13 58	7 31	7 50	11 46	16 00	15 42	4 03 28	19 53 16
23	15 53 42	20 16	+13 42	7 33	7 52	11 46	15 59	15 40	4 07 24	19 49 20
24	15 57 56	20 29	+13 25	7 35	7 54	11 47	15 58	15 39	4 11 21	19 45 24
25	16 02 10	20 41	+13 08	7 36	7 56	11 47	15 57	15 38	4 15 17	19 41 28
26	16 06 24	20 53	+12 50	7 38	7 58	11 47	15 56	15 37	4 19 14	19 37 33
27	16 10 40	21 04	+12 31	7 40	8 00	11 48	15 56	15 36	4 23 11	19 33 37
28	16 14 56	21 15	+12 11	7 41	8 01	11 48	15 55	15 34	4 27 07	19 29 41
29	16 19 13	21 25	+11 51	7 42	8 02	11 48	15 54	15 33	4 31 04	19 25 45
30	16 23 31	21 35	+11 29	7 44	8 04	11 49	15 54	15 32	4 35 00	19 21 49

Duration of Civil (C), Nautical (N), and Astronomical (A), Twilight (in minutes)

| Lat. ° | Nov. 1 | | | Nov. 11 | | | Nov. 21 | | | Nov. 30 | | |
	C	N	A	C	N	A	C	N	A	C	N	A
52	36	75	115	37	78	117	38	80	120	39	82	123
56	40	84	127	41	87	130	43	90	134	45	93	137

ASTRONOMICAL NOTES

MERCURY is unsuitably placed for observation.

VENUS is a conspicuous morning star, magnitude −3·4. It is drawing towards the Sun, the period available for observation shortening noticeably during the month. Venus is near Spica on the mornings of the 3rd and 4th, whilst on the morning of the 10th Venus will rise only slightly earlier than the Moon.

MARS is a bright morning star, magnitude +0·2, moving eastwards in the constellation of Cancer, passing just north of the naked-eye cluster Praesepe around the middle of the month.

JUPITER is a brilliant morning star, magnitude −2·2. It is now visible for most of the night, opposition occurring in December. The gibbous Moon passes 5° S. of the planet on the morning of the 1st and again on the morning of the 28th. Details of the eclipses and shadow transits of Jupiter's satellites are given on p. 150 for the convenience of observers with telescopes.

SATURN is a morning star, magnitude +0·8, in the constellation of Leo. At the beginning of the month it passes within a degree of Regulus. By the end of the month Saturn is visible in the eastern sky before midnight.

THE MOON

Day	R.A.	Dec.	Hor. Par.	Semi-diam.	Sun's Co-Long.	P.A. of Bright Limb	Phase	Age	Rise 52°	Rise 56°	Transit	Set 52°	Set 56°
	h m	°	'	'	°	°		d	h m	h m	h m	h m	h m
1	6 15	+18.3	54.1	14.7	147	95	78	19.1	20 39	20 22	3 42	11 34	11 51
2	7 05	+17.3	54.3	14.8	159	99	70	20.1	21 36	21 21	4 29	12 12	12 28
3	7 54	+15.7	54.6	14.9	171	102	61	21.1	22 37	22 25	5 15	12 46	12 59
4	8 43	+13.3	55.1	15.0	184	105	52	22.1	23 42	23 33	6 02	13 16	13 26
5	9 32	+10.2	55.8	15.2	196	108	42	23.1	..	..	6 48	13 43	13 50
6	10 21	+ 6.6	56.6	15.4	208	110	32	24.1	0 49	0 44	7 35	14 09	14 13
7	11 11	+ 2.6	57.5	15.7	220	111	23	25.1	2 00	1 58	8 23	14 35	14 35
8	12 02	− 1.6	58.4	15.9	232	112	14	26.1	3 13	3 15	9 13	15 02	14 58
9	12 56	− 6.0	59.3	16.2	244	113	7	27.1	4 29	4 35	10 05	15 31	15 23
10	13 52	−10.1	60.1	16.4	257	115	2	28.1	5 48	5 58	11 01	16 05	15 53
11	14 51	−13.7	60.7	16.5	269	139	0	29.1	7 06	7 20	11 59	16 44	16 30
12	15 52	−16.5	61.0	16.6	281	262	1	0.7	8 23	8 39	13 00	17 33	17 15
13	16 55	−18.1	61.0	16.6	293	266	4	1.7	9 32	9 51	14 01	18 30	18 11
14	17 58	−18.4	60.7	16.5	306	264	11	2.7	10 32	10 50	15 02	19 35	19 18
15	19 00	−17.5	60.2	16.4	318	260	19	3.7	11 22	11 38	16 01	20 46	20 31
16	19 59	−15.5	59.5	16.2	330	256	29	4.7	12 03	12 16	16 57	21 59	21 48
17	20 56	−12.6	58.7	16.0	342	253	40	5.7	12 36	12 46	17 50	23 12	23 04
18	21 50	− 9.0	57.9	15.8	354	250	51	6.7	13 05	13 11	18 40	..	..
19	22 42	− 5.1	57.2	15.6	6	249	62	7.7	13 31	13 34	19 27	0 24	0 20
20	23 31	− 1.0	56.5	15.4	19	248	71	8.7	13 55	13 54	20 13	1 34	1 33
21	0 20	+ 3.0	55.9	15.2	31	247	80	9.7	14 20	14 15	20 58	2 42	2 45
22	1 07	+ 6.8	55.4	15.1	43	247	87	10.7	14 45	14 37	21 44	3 48	3 55
23	1 55	+10.3	55.0	15.0	55	247	93	11.7	15 12	15 01	22 29	4 54	5 03
24	2 44	+13.3	54.6	14.9	67	245	97	12.7	15 42	15 29	23 16	5 57	6 10
25	3 32	+15.7	54.3	14.8	79	234	99	13.7	16 17	16 01	..	6 57	7 13
26	4 22	+17.4	54.1	14.7	91	134	100	14.7	16 56	16 39	0 03	7 54	8 11
27	5 11	+18.4	54.0	14.7	104	103	98	15.7	17 41	17 23	0 50	8 46	9 04
28	6 01	+18.5	54.0	14.7	116	101	95	16.7	18 32	18 14	1 37	9 32	9 50
29	6 51	+17.8	54.0	14.7	128	102	91	17.7	19 27	19 11	2 25	10 13	10 29
30	7 40	+16.4	54.2	14.8	140	104	84	18.7	20 26	20 13	3 11	10 48	11 02

MERCURY ☿

Day	R.A.	Dec. −	Diam.	Phase	Transit		Day	R.A.	Dec. −	Diam.	Phase	Transit	
	h m	°	"		h m			h m	°	"		h m	
1	14 56	17.4	5	97	12 16	Mercury is	16	16 29	23.9	5	90	12 51	Mercury is
4	15 14	19.0	5	96	12 23	too close to	19	16 48	24.7	5	87	12 58	too close to
7	15 33	20.5	5	95	12 30	the Sun	22	17 07	25.3	5	84	13 04	the Sun
10	15 52	21.8	5	94	12 37	for observation	25	17 25	25.7	6	80	13 11	for observation
13	16 10	22.9	5	92	12 44		28	17 42	25.8	6	75	13 16	
16	16 29	23.9	5	90	12 51		31	17 59	25.8	6	68	13 20	

VENUS ♀ / MARS ♂

Day	R.A.	Dec. −	Diam.	Phase	5° high E. 52°	56°	Transit	Day	R.A.	Dec. +	Diam.	Phase	5° high E. 52°	56°	Transit
	h m	°	"		h m	h m	h m		h m	°	"		h m	h m	h m
1	13 11	5.8	11	94	5 34	5 42	10 30	1	8 19	21.1	9	89	22 16	22 01	5 38
6	13 34	8.2	11	95	5 50	6 01	10 34	6	8 27	20.8	9	89	22 06	21 51	5 26
11	13 58	10.5	11	96	6 07	6 20	10 38	11	8 35	20.5	9	89	21 56	21 41	5 14
16	14 22	12.7	10	96	6 26	6 41	10 42	16	8 41	20.3	10	90	21 45	21 30	5 01
21	14 46	14.8	10	97	6 43	7 01	10 47	21	8 47	20.1	10	90	21 32	21 17	4 47
26	15 11	16.7	10	97	7 01	7 22	10 52	26	8 52	20.0	10	90	21 17	20 02	4 32
31	15 36	18.4	10	98	7 19	7 43	10 58	31	8 55	20.0	11	91	21 00	20 44	4 16

SUNRISE AND SUNSET (G.M.T.)

Day	London a.m. h m	London p.m. h m	Bristol a.m. h m	Bristol p.m. h m	Birmingham a.m. h m	Birmingham p.m. h m	Manchester a.m. h m	Manchester p.m. h m	Newcastle a.m. h m	Newcastle p.m. h m	Glasgow a.m. h m	Glasgow p.m. h m	Belfast a.m. h m	Belfast p.m. h m
1	6 53	4 34	7 03	4 44	7 02	4 39	7 07	4 38	7 08	4 30	7 22	4 38	7 25	4 49
2	6 55	4 32	7 04	4 42	7 04	4 37	7 09	4 36	7 10	4 28	7 24	4 36	7 27	4 47
3	6 56	4 30	7 06	4 40	7 05	4 35	7 10	4 34	7 12	4 26	7 26	4 34	7 29	4 45
4	6 58	4 29	7 08	4 39	7 07	4 33	7 12	4 32	7 14	4 24	7 28	4 32	7 31	4 43
5	7 00	4 27	7 09	4 37	7 09	4 31	7 14	4 30	7 16	4 22	7 30	4 30	7 33	4 41
6	7 02	4 26	7 11	4 36	7 11	4 29	7 16	4 28	7 18	4 20	7 32	4 28	7 35	4 39
7	7 03	4 24	7 13	4 34	7 13	4 28	7 18	4 27	7 20	4 18	7 34	4 26	7 37	4 38
8	7 05	4 22	7 14	4 32	7 15	4 26	7 20	4 25	7 22	4 16	7 36	4 24	7 39	4 36
9	7 07	4 21	7 16	4 31	7 17	4 24	7 22	4 23	7 25	4 14	7 39	4 22	7 41	4 34
10	7 09	4 19	7 18	4 29	7 19	4 22	7 24	4 21	7 27	4 12	7 41	4 20	7 43	4 32
11	7 10	4 18	7 20	4 28	7 21	4 21	7 26	4 19	7 29	4 10	7 43	4 18	7 45	4 30
12	7 12	4 16	7 22	4 26	7 23	4 19	7 28	4 18	7 31	4 09	7 45	4 16	7 47	4 28
13	7 14	4 15	7 23	4 25	7 24	4 18	7 30	4 16	7 33	4 07	7 47	4 15	7 49	4 27
14	7 15	4 13	7 25	4 23	7 26	4 16	7 32	4 15	7 35	4 06	7 49	4 13	7 51	4 25
15	7 17	4 12	7 27	4 22	7 28	4 15	7 33	4 13	7 36	4 04	7 51	4 11	7 53	4 23
16	7 19	4 10	7 29	4 20	7 30	4 13	7 35	4 11	7 38	4 02	7 53	4 10	7 55	4 22
17	7 20	4 09	7 30	4 19	7 31	4 12	7 37	4 10	7 40	4 01	7 55	4 08	7 57	4 20
18	7 22	4 08	7 32	4 18	7 33	4 11	7 39	4 08	7 43	3 59	7 58	4 06	7 59	4 18
19	7 24	4 06	7 34	4 16	7 35	4 09	7 41	4 07	7 45	3 58	8 00	4 05	8 01	4 17
20	7 26	4 05	7 36	4 15	7 37	4 08	7 43	4 06	7 47	3 56	8 02	4 03	8 03	4 16
21	7 27	4 04	7 37	4 14	7 38	4 07	7 45	4 04	7 49	3 55	8 04	4 02	8 05	4 14
22	7 29	4 03	7 39	4 13	7 40	4 06	7 47	4 03	7 50	3 53	8 05	4 00	8 07	4 13
23	7 31	4 02	7 41	4 12	7 42	4 05	7 48	4 02	7 52	3 52	8 07	3 59	8 08	4 12
24	7 32	4 01	7 42	4 11	7 43	4 03	7 50	4 01	7 54	3 51	8 09	3 57	8 10	4 11
25	7 34	4 00	7 44	4 10	7 45	4 04	7 52	4 00	7 56	3 49	8 11	3 56	8 12	4 09
26	7 35	3 59	7 45	4 09	7 46	4 02	7 53	3 59	7 58	3 48	8 13	3 55	8 14	4 08
27	7 37	3 58	7 47	4 08	7 48	4 01	7 55	3 58	7 59	3 47	8 15	3 54	8 15	4 07
28	7 38	3 57	7 48	4 08	7 49	4 00	7 56	3 57	8 01	3 46	8 17	3 53	8 17	4 06
29	7 40	3 56	7 50	4 07	7 51	3 59	7 58	3 56	8 03	3 45	8 18	3 52	8 19	4 05
30	7 41	3 55	7 51	4 06	7 52	3 58	7 59	3 55	8 04	3 45	8 20	3 51	8 20	4 05

JUPITER ♃   SATURN ♄

Day	R.A. h m	Dec. + °	5° high E. 52° h m	5° high E. 56° h m	Transit h m	R.A. h m	Dec. + °	5° high E. 52° h m	5° high E. 56° h m	Transit h m
1	6 26	23·0	20 11	19 53	3 45	10 07	12·9	0 52	0 44	7 25
11	6 24	23·0	19 29	19 11	3 04	10 09	12·7	0 16	0 08	6 48
21	6 21	23·0	18 46	18 28	2 21	10 11	12·6	23 35	23 28	6 10
31	6 17	23·1	18 02	17 44	1 38	10 12	12·5	22 57	22 50	5 32

Equatorial diameter of Jupiter 45″; of Saturn 18″   Diameters of Saturn's rings 40″ and 7″

URANUS ⛢   NEPTUNE ♆

Day	R.A. h m	Dec. ° ′	Transit h m		R.A. h m	Dec. ° ′	Transit h m	
1	14 38·3	15 02	11 56	Uranus is too	16 53·6	21 07	14 11	Neptune is too
11	14 40·7	15 13	11 19	close to the	16 55·0	21 10	13 33	close to the
21	14 43·2	15 25	10 42	Sun for	16 56·5	21 12	12 55	Sun for
31	14 45·5	15 35	10 05	observation	16 58·1	21 15	12 17	observation

Diameter 4″   Diameter 2″

DAY OF		*Decem* (ten), 10th month of Roman (pre-Julian) Calendar. *Sun's Longitude* 270° ♑ 21ᵈ 23ʰ ♑
Month	Week	

1	Th.	Henry I. d. 1135. Queen Alexandra b. 1844
2	F.	Austerlitz 1805. Marquis de Sade d. 1814
3	S.	Robert Louis Stevenson d. 1894
4	☉.	2nd S. in Advent. Samuel Butler b. 1835
5	M.	Walt Disney b. 1901. Claude Monet d. 1926
6	Tu.	Trollope d. 1882. Jefferson Davis d. 1889
7	W.	Pearl Harbour 1941
8	Th.	De Quincey d. 1859. Sibelius b. 1865
9	F.	Milton b. 1608. Lord Butler b. 1902
10	S.	Earl Alexander of Tunis b. 1891
11	☉.	3rd S. in Advent. A. Solzhenitsyn b. 1918
12	M.	Flaubert b. 1821. Robert Browning d. 1889
13	Tu.	Dr. Johnson d. 1784. John Piper b. 1903
14	W.	George VI b. 1895. Maurice Edelman d. 1975
15	Th.	Jan Vermeer d. 1675. Rasputin d. 1916
16	F.	Beethoven b. 1770. Jane Austen b. 1775
17	S.	Prince Rupert b. 1619. Simon Bolivar d. 1830
18	☉.	4th S. in Advent. Christopher Fry b. 1907
19	M.	J. M. W. Turner d. 1851
20	Tu.	Sir Robert Menzies b. 1894
21	W.	St. Thomas. MICHAELMAS LAW SITTINGS END
22	Th.	George Eliot d. 1880
23	F.	Roger Ascham d. 1568
24	S.	Christmas Eve. M. C. Cowdrey b. 1932
25	☉.	Christmas Day. Sir Isaac Newton b. 1642
26	M.	St. Stephen. Thomas Gray b. 1716
27	Tu.	St. John. Jack Benny d. 1974
28	W.	Holy Innocents'. Maurice Ravel d. 1937
29	Th.	W. E. Gladstone b. 1809. Christina Rossetti d. 1894
30	F.	Rudyard Kipling b. 1865. Pablo Casals b. 1876
31	S.	John Wycliffe d. 1384. Matisse b. 1869

PHENOMENA

December 1ᵈ 13ʰ Mars in conjunction with the Moon. Mars 7° N.

3ᵈ 03ʰ Saturn in conjunction with the Moon. Saturn 5° N.

3ᵈ 08ʰ Mercury at greatest eastern elongation (21°).

8ᵈ 02ʰ Neptune in conjunction with the Sun.

12ᵈ 00ʰ Mercury in conjunction with the Moon. Mercury 6° S.

21ᵈ 14ʰ Mercury in inferior conjunction.

21ᵈ 23ʰ Winter solstice.

23ᵈ 01ʰ Jupiter at opposition.

25ᵈ 07ʰ Jupiter in conjunction with the Moon. Jupiter 5° N.

28ᵈ 18ʰ Mars in conjunction with the Moon. Mars 8° N.

30ᵈ 09ʰ Saturn in conjunction with the Moon. Saturn 5° N.

CONSTELLATIONS

The following constellations are near the meridian at

	d h		d h
Nov. 1	24	Nov. 15	23
Dec. 1	22	Dec. 16	21
Jan. 1	20	Jan. 16	19

Ursa Major (below the Pole), Ursa Minor (below the Pole), Cassiopeia, Andromeda, Perseus, Triangulum, Aries, Taurus, Cetus and Eridanus.

MINIMA OF ALGOL

d	h	d	h
2	1	19	6
4	22	22	3
7	19	25	0
10	16	27	20
13	12	30	17
16	9		

PHASES OF THE MOON

		d	h	m
☾	Last Quarter	3	21	16
●	New Moon	10	17	33
☽	First Quarter	17	10	37
○	Full Moon	25	12	49

		d	h
Perigee (356,720 kilometres)		10	23
Apogee (406,510 ,,)		24	21

Mean Longitude of Ascending Node on December 1, 192°.

MONTHLY NOTES

Dec. 10. Grouse and Black Game Shooting ends.

12. Moslem New Year (A.H. 1398).

21. Shortest day.

25. Quarter day.

26 and 27. Bank Holiday, England, Wales and Northern Ireland.

31. Various licences expire.

Day	THE SUN									Sidereal Time	Transit of First Point of Aries
	Right Ascension	Dec. —	Equation of Time	Rise		Transit	Set				
				52°	56°		52°	56°			
	h m s	° ′	m s	h m	h m	h m	h m	h m		h m s	h m s
1	16 27 49	21 45	+ 11 08	7 45	8 06	11 49	15 53	15 31		4 38 57	19 17 53
2	16 32 08	21 54	+ 10 45	7 47	8 08	11 49	15 53	15 30		4 42 53	19 13 57
3	16 36 28	22 03	+ 10 22	7 48	8 09	11 50	15 52	15 30		4 46 50	19 10 01
4	16 40 48	22 12	+ 9 58	7 49	8 11	11 50	15 51	15 29		4 50 46	19 06 05
5	16 45 09	22 19	+ 9 34	7 50	8 12	11 51	15 50	15 29		4 54 43	19 02 09
6	16 49 30	22 27	+ 9 09	7 51	8 14	11 51	15 50	15 28		4 58 40	18 58 13
7	16 53 52	22 34	+ 8 44	7 53	8 16	11 51	15 50	15 27		5 02 36	18 54 18
8	16 58 15	22 41	+ 8 18	7 54	8 17	11 52	15 49	15 27		5 06 33	18 50 22
9	17 02 38	22 47	+ 7 51	7 55	8 19	11 52	15 49	15 26		5 10 29	18 46 26
10	17 07 01	22 53	+ 7 24	7 56	8 20	11 53	15 49	15 26		5 14 26	18 42 30
11	17 11 25	22 58	+ 6 57	7 58	8 21	11 53	15 49	15 26		5 18 22	18 38 34
12	17 15 50	23 03	+ 6 29	7 59	8 22	11 54	15 48	15 25		5 22 19	18 34 38
13	17 20 14	23 07	+ 6 01	8 00	8 23	11 54	15 48	15 25		5 26 15	18 30 42
14	17 24 39	23 11	+ 5 33	8 00	8 24	11 55	15 48	15 25		5 30 12	18 26 46
15	17 29 05	23 15	+ 5 04	8 01	8 25	11 55	15 48	15 25		5 34 09	18 22 50
16	17 33 30	23 18	+ 4 35	8 02	8 26	11 56	15 49	15 25		5 38 05	18 18 54
17	17 37 56	23 21	+ 4 06	8 02	8 27	11 56	15 49	15 25		5 42 02	18 14 58
18	17 42 22	23 23	+ 3 36	8 03	8 27	11 57	15 49	15 26		5 45 58	18 11 03
19	17 46 28	23 24	+ 3 07	8 04	8 28	11 57	15 50	15 26		5 49 55	18 07 07
20	17 51 14	23 25	+ 2 37	8 04	8 28	11 58	15 50	15 26		5 53 51	18 03 11
21	17 55 40	23 26	+ 2 07	8 05	8 29	11 58	15 51	15 26		5 57 48	17 59 15
22	18 00 07	23 26	+ 1 38	8 06	8 30	11 59	15 51	15 27		6 01 44	17 55 19
23	18 04 33	23 26	+ 1 08	8 06	8 30	11 59	15 52	15 27		6 05 41	17 51 23
24	18 08 59	23 25	+ 0 38	8 07	8 31	12 00	15 52	15 28		6 09 38	17 47 27
25	18 13 26	23 24	+ 0 08	8 07	8 31	12 00	15 53	15 29		6 13 34	17 43 31
26	18 17 52	23 23	− 0 21	8 07	8 31	12 01	15 53	15 30		6 17 31	17 39 35
27	18 22 18	23 20	− 0 51	8 08	8 32	12 01	15 54	15 31		6 21 27	17 35 39
28	18 26 44	23 18	− 1 20	8 08	8 32	12 02	15 55	15 32		6 25 24	17 31 43
29	18 31 10	23 15	− 1 50	8 08	8 32	12 02	15 56	15 33		6 29 20	17 27 47
30	18 35 35	23 11	− 2 19	8 08	8 32	12 03	15 57	15 34		6 33 17	17 23 52
31	18 40 01	23 07	− 2 47	8 08	8 32	12 03	15 58	15 35		6 37 14	17 19 56

Duration of Civil (C), Nautical (N), and Astronomical (A), Twilight (in minutes)

Lat. °	Dec. 1			Dec. 11			Dec. 21			Dec. 31		
	C	N	A	C	N	A	C	N	A	C	N	A
52	40	82	123	41	84	125	41	85	126	41	84	125
56	45	93	138	47	96	141	47	97	142	47	96	141

ASTRONOMICAL NOTES

MERCURY is unsuitably placed for observation for almost the whole of the month, inferior conjunction occurring on the 21st. However it may be glimpsed as a difficult morning star, magnitude, + 1·0, low above the south-eastern horizon, around the time of beginning of morning civil twilight, for the last few days of the month.

VENUS is a morning star, magnitude − 3·4, during the first two weeks of the month, visible low in the south-east for a short while before sunrise. Thereafter it is lost in the morning twilight. Venus is near Antares on the 10th–11th.

MARS is a bright morning star, its magnitude increasing during the month from − 0·1 to − 0·8. Mars is almost stationary in the constellation of Cancer. The gibbous Moon will be seen near the planet on the 1st and 2nd and again on the 28th and 29th.

JUPITER is at opposition on the 23rd and thus visible throughout the hours of darkness. Its magnitude is − 2·3. On the morning of the 25th the Moon passes 5° S. of Jupiter.

SATURN is a morning star, magnitude + 0·7, almost stationary in Leo, not much more than one degree E.N.E. of Regulus.

METEORS. The maximum of the well known Geminid meteor shower occurs on the 14th. Observers will see most meteors on the night of the 13th–14th. The crescent Moon sets early in the evening and will not interfere with observation.

THE MOON

Day	R.A.	Dec.	Hor. Par.	Semi-diam.	Sun's Co-Long.	P.A. of Bright Limb	Phase	Age	Rise 52°	Rise 56°	Transit	Set 52°	Set 56°
	h m	°	′	′	°	°		d	h m	h m	h m	h m	h m
1	8 29	+14.2	54.5	14.9	152	107	77	19.7	21 29	21 18	3 57	11 19	11 30
2	9 17	+11.4	55.0	15.0	164	109	68	20.7	22 34	22 26	4 43	11 46	11 55
3	10 05	+ 8.1	55.6	15.2	176	111	59	21.7	23 41	23 37	5 28	12 12	12 17
4	10 54	+ 4.3	56.4	15.4	189	112	49	22.7	..	..	6 14	12 37	12 38
5	11 43	+ 0.2	57.2	15.6	201	113	39	23.7	0 50	0 50	7 02	13 02	13 00
6	12 34	− 4.0	58.2	15.9	213	113	28	24.7	2 03	2 07	7 51	13 29	13 23
7	13 27	− 8.2	59.2	16.1	225	112	19	25.7	3 18	3 26	8 43	13 59	13 49
8	14 23	−12.0	60.1	16.4	237	112	11	26.7	4 35	4 47	9 39	14 34	14 21
9	15 23	−15.2	60.8	16.6	249	112	5	27.7	5 53	6 08	10 38	15 17	15 01
10	16 25	−17.5	61.3	16.7	262	120	1	28.7	7 08	7 25	11 40	16 09	15 51
11	17 29	−18.5	61.5	16.7	274	222	0	0.3	8 15	8 33	12 43	17 12	16 54
12	18 34	−18.2	61.3	16.7	286	252	3	1.3	9 12	9 29	13 45	18 23	18 06
13	19 37	−16.6	60.8	16.6	298	253	8	2.3	9 59	10 13	14 45	19 39	19 25
14	20 37	−13.9	60.1	16.4	310	251	15	3.3	10 37	10 48	15 42	20 55	20 45
15	21 34	−10.4	59.2	16.1	323	249	25	4.3	11 09	11 16	16 34	22 10	22 04
16	22 27	− 6.5	58.2	15.8	335	248	35	5.3	11 36	11 40	17 24	23 22	23 20
17	23 19	− 2.3	57.3	15.6	347	247	45	6.3	12 02	12 02	18 11	..	..
18	0 08	+ 1.8	56.5	15.4	359	247	56	7.3	12 26	12 23	18 57	0 32	0 34
19	0 56	+ 5.7	55.7	15.2	11	247	66	8.3	12 51	12 44	19 42	1 40	1 45
20	1 44	+ 9.3	55.1	15.0	23	248	75	9.3	13 17	13 07	20 28	2 45	2 54
21	2 32	+12.5	54.7	14.9	36	250	83	10.3	13 45	13 33	21 13	3 49	4 01
22	3 20	+15.1	54.3	14.8	48	251	89	11.3	14 18	14 03	22 00	4 50	5 05
23	4 09	+17.0	54.1	14.7	60	252	94	12.3	14 55	14 38	22 47	5 48	6 05
24	4 59	+18.2	54.0	14.7	72	249	98	13.3	15 38	15 20	23 34	6 42	7 00
25	5 49	+18.6	53.9	14.7	84	229	100	14.3	16 27	16 09	..	7 30	7 48
26	6 38	+18.1	54.0	14.7	96	138	100	15.3	17 20	17 04	0 22	8 13	8 30
27	7 28	+16.9	54.1	14.7	108	115	98	16.3	18 19	18 04	1 09	8 50	9 06
28	8 17	+15.0	54.4	14.8	120	112	94	17.3	19 20	19 08	1 55	9 23	9 35
29	9 05	+12.3	54.7	14.9	133	112	89	18.3	20 24	20 15	2 41	9 52	10 01
30	9 53	+ 9.2	55.1	15.0	145	113	83	19.3	21 29	21 24	3 26	10 18	10 24
31	10 41	+ 5.6	55.6	15.2	157	114	75	20.3	22 37	22 35	4 11	10 42	10 45

MERCURY ☿

Day	R.A.	Dec.−	Diam.	Phase	Transit		Day	R.A.	Dec.−	Diam.	Phase	Transit	
	h m	°	″		h m			h m	°	″		h m	
1	17 59	25.8	6	68	13 20	Mercury is too close to the Sun for observation	16	18 26	23.0	9	14	12 44	Mercury is too close to the Sun for observation
4	18 13	25.6	7	61	13 22		19	18 13	22.1	10	2	12 18	
7	18 24	25.1	7	51	13 21		22	17 56	21.2	10	0	11 49	
10	18 31	24.5	8	39	13 15		25	17 39	20.5	10	7	11 22	
13	18 32	23.8	8	26	13 03		28	17 28	20.1	9	16	10 59	
16	18 26	23.0	9	14	12 44		31	17 23	20.1	9	28	10 43	

VENUS ♀

Day	R.A.	Dec.−	Diam.	Phase	5° high E. 52°	56°	Transit
	h m	°	″		h m	h m	h m
1	15 36	18.4	10	98	7 19	7 43	10 58
6	16 02	19.9	10	98	7 36	8 03	11 04
11	16 28	21.2	10	99	7 53	8 23	11 11
16	16 55	22.3	10	99	8 08	8 40	11 18
21	17 22	23.0	10	99	8 22	8 57	11 25
26	17 49	23.5	10	99	8 34	9 10	11 33
31	18 17	23.6	10	100	8 43	9 20	11 40

MARS ♂

Day	R.A.	Dec.+	Diam.	Phase	5° high E. 52°	56°	Transit
	h m	°	″		h m	h m	h m
1	8 55	20.0	11	92	21 00	20 44	4 16
6	8 58	20.0	11	93	20 41	20 25	3 59
11	8 59	20.2	12	94	20 21	20 05	3 41
16	9 00	20.4	12	95	20 00	19 45	3 21
21	8 58	20.7	13	96	19 39	19 24	3 00
26	8 55	21.1	13	97	19 18	19 03	2 37
31	8 51	21.6	14	98	18 56	18 41	2 14

SUNRISE AND SUNSET (G.M.T.)

Day	London a.m. h m	London p.m. h m	Bristol a.m. h m	Bristol p.m. h m	Birmingham a.m. h m	Birmingham p.m. h m	Manchester a.m. h m	Manchester p.m. h m	Newcastle a.m. h m	Newcastle p.m. h m	Glasgow a.m. h m	Glasgow p.m. h m	Belfast a.m. h m	Belfast p.m. h m
1	7 43	3 55	7 53	4 06	7 54	3 58	8 01	3 55	8 06	3 44	8 22	3 50	8 22	4 04
2	7 44	3 54	7 54	4 05	7 55	3 57	8 02	3 54	8 08	3 43	8 24	3 49	8 24	4 03
3	7 46	3 53	7 56	4 04	7 57	3 56	8 04	3 53	8 09	3 42	8 25	3 48	8 25	4 02
4	7 47	3 53	7 57	4 04	7 58	3 56	8 05	3 53	8 11	3 41	8 27	3 47	8 27	4 01
5	7 48	3 53	7 58	4 04	8 00	3 55	8 07	3 52	8 12	3 40	8 28	3 46	8 28	4 00
6	7 50	3 52	7 59	4 03	8 01	3 55	8 08	3 52	8 14	3 40	8 30	3 46	8 30	4 00
7	7 51	3 52	8 01	4 03	8 02	3 54	8 09	3 51	8 15	3 39	8 31	3 45	8 31	3 59
8	7 52	3 51	8 02	4 02	8 04	3 54	8 11	3 51	8 17	3 39	8 33	3 44	8 33	3 59
9	7 53	3 51	8 03	4 02	8 05	3 53	8 12	3 50	8 18	3 38	8 34	3 43	8 34	3 58
10	7 54	3 51	8 04	4 02	8 06	3 53	8 13	3 50	8 19	3 38	8 35	3 43	8 35	3 58
11	7 56	3 51	8 05	4 01	8 07	3 53	8 14	3 50	8 20	3 38	8 36	3 43	8 36	3 58
12	7 57	3 51	8 06	4 01	8 08	3 53	8 15	3 50	8 21	3 38	8 38	3 43	8 37	3 58
13	7 58	3 51	8 07	4 01	8 09	3 53	8 16	3 50	8 22	3 38	8 39	3 43	8 38	3 58
14	7 58	3 51	8 08	4 01	8 10	3 53	8 17	3 50	8 23	3 38	8 40	3 43	8 39	3 58
15	7 59	3 51	8 09	4 01	8 11	3 53	8 18	3 50	8 24	3 38	8 41	3 43	8 40	3 58
16	8 00	3 51	8 09	4 02	8 12	3 53	8 19	3 50	8 25	3 38	8 42	3 43	8 41	3 58
17	8 01	3 52	8 10	4 02	8 13	3 53	8 20	3 50	8 26	3 38	8 43	3 43	8 42	3 58
18	8 02	3 52	8 11	4 02	8 14	3 53	8 21	3 50	8 27	3 38	8 44	3 43	8 43	3 58
19	8 03	3 52	8 12	4 02	8 15	3 53	8 22	3 50	8 28	3 38	8 44	3 44	8 44	3 58
20	8 03	3 53	8 12	4 03	8 15	3 54	8 22	3 50	8 28	3 38	8 45	3 44	8 44	3 58
21	8 04	3 53	8 13	4 03	8 16	3 54	8 23	3 51	8 29	3 39	8 46	3 44	8 45	3 59
22	8 04	3 54	8 13	4 04	8 16	3 55	8 24	3 52	8 30	3 40	8 46	3 45	8 46	4 00
23	8 05	3 54	8 14	4 04	8 17	3 55	8 24	3 52	8 30	3 40	8 47	3 45	8 46	4 00
24	8 05	3 55	8 14	4 05	8 17	3 56	8 24	3 53	8 30	3 41	8 47	3 46	8 46	4 01
25	8 06	3 55	8 15	4 05	8 18	3 57	8 25	3 54	8 31	3 42	8 47	3 47	8 47	4 02
26	8 06	3 56	8 15	4 06	8 18	3 57	8 25	3 54	8 31	3 42	8 48	3 48	8 47	4 02
27	8 06	3 57	8 15	4 07	8 18	3 58	8 25	3 55	8 31	3 43	8 48	3 48	8 47	4 03
28	8 06	3 58	8 15	4 08	8 18	3 59	8 25	3 56	8 31	3 44	8 48	3 49	8 47	4 04
29	8 06	3 59	8 16	4 09	8 18	4 00	8 25	3 57	8 31	3 45	8 48	3 50	8 47	4 05
30	8 06	3 59	8 16	4 10	8 18	4 01	8 25	3 58	8 31	3 46	8 48	3 51	8 47	4 06
31	8 06	4 00	8 16	4 11	8 18	4 02	8 25	3 59	8 31	3 47	8 48	3 52	8 47	4 07

JUPITER ♃   SATURN ♄

Day	R.A. h m	Dec. + °	Transit h m	5° high W. 52° h m	5° high W. 56° h m	R.A. h m	Dec. + °	5° high E. 52° h m	5° high E. 56° h m	Transit h m
1	6 17	23·1	1 38	9 08	9 26	10 12	12·5	22 57	22 50	5 32
11	6 12	23·1	0 53	8 23	8 41	10 12	12·5	22 18	22 11	4 53
21	6 06	23·2	0 08	7 38	7 56	10 12	12·6	21 38	21 31	4 14
31	6 00	23·2	23 18	6 54	7 12	10 11	12·7	20 57	20 50	3 33

Equatorial diameter of Jupiter 47″; of Saturn 19″   Diameters of Saturn's rings 43″ and 7″

URANUS ♅   NEPTUNE ♆

Day	R.A. h m	Dec. − ° ′	Transit h m		R.A. h m	Dec − ° ′	Transit h m	
1	14 45·5	15 35	10 05	Uranus is too	16 58·1	21 15	12 17	Neptune is too
11	14 47·8	15 45	9 28	close to the	16 59·7	21 17	11 39	close to the
21	14 49·8	15 55	8 51	Sun for	17 01·3	21 20	11 02	Sun for
31	14 51·7	16 03	8 13	observation	17 02·8	21 22	10 24	observation

Diameter 4″   Diameter 2″

INTRODUCTION TO ASTRONOMICAL SECTION
GENERAL

The astronomical data are given in a form suitable for those who practise naked-eye astronomy or use small telescopes. No attempt has been made to replace the *Astronomical Ephemeris* for professional astronomers. Positions of the heavenly bodies are given only to the degree of accuracy required by amateur astronomers for setting telescopes, or for plotting on celestial globes or star atlases. Where intermediate positions are required, linear interpolation may be employed.

All data are, unless otherwise stated, for 0^h G.M.T., or the midnight at the beginning of the day named.

(*See notes on British Summer Time, p. 142*).

Definitions of the terms used cannot be given in an ephemeris of this nature. They must be sought in astronomical literature and text-books. Probably the best source for the amateur is Norton's *Star Atlas* (Gall and Inglis, 15th edition, 1964; £1.05), which contains an excellent introduction to observational astronomy, and the finest series of star maps yet produced for showing stars visible to the naked eye. Certain more extended ephemerides are available in the British Astronomical Association Handbook, an annual very popular among amateur astronomers. (Secretary: Burlington House, Piccadilly, London, W.1.)

A special feature has been made of the times when the various heavenly bodies are visible in the British Isles. Since two columns, calculated for latitudes 52° and 56°, are devoted to risings and settings, the range 50° to 58° can be covered by interpolation and extrapolation. The times given in these columns are G.M.T.'s for the meridian of Greenwich. An observer west of this meridian must add his longitude (in time) and vice versa.

In accordance with the usual convention in astronomy, + and − indicate respectively north and south latitudes or declinations.

PAGE I OF EACH MONTH

The Zodiacal signs through which the Sun is passing during each month are illustrated. The date of transition from one sign to the next, to the nearest hour, is also given.

The FASTS AND FESTIVALS in black-letter type are those so given in the Prayer Book. The line immediately to the right of the Day of Week is shown heavy when the Law Courts are sitting in London.

Under the heading PHENOMENA will be found particulars of the more important conjunctions of the Sun, Moon and planets with each other, and also the dates of eclipses and other astronomical phenomena of special interest.

The CONSTELLATIONS listed each month are those that are near the meridian at the beginning of the month at 22^h local mean time. Allowance must be made for Summer Time if necessary. The fact that any star crosses the meridian 4^m earlier each night or 2^h earlier each month may be used, in conjunction with the lists given each month, to find what constellations are favourably placed at any moment. The table preceding the list of

constellations may be extended indefinitely at the rate just quoted.

Times of MINIMA OF ALGOL are approximate times of the middle of the period of diminished light (*see* p. 153).

The Principal PHASES OF THE MOON are the G.M.T.'s when the difference between the longitude of the Moon and that of the Sun is 0°, 90°, 180° or 270°. The times of perigee and apogee are those when the Moon is nearest to, and farthest from, the Earth, respectively. The nodes or points of intersection of the Moon's orbit and the ecliptic make a complete retrograde circuit of the ecliptic in about 19 years. From a knowledge of the longitude of the ascending node and the inclination, whose value does not vary much from 5°, the path of the Moon among the stars may be plotted on a celestial globe or star atlas.

The MONTHLY NOTES are self-explanatory.

PAGE II OF EACH MONTH

The Sun's semi-diameter, in arc, is given once a month.

The right ascension given is that of the true Sun. The right ascension of the mean Sun is obtained by applying the equation of time, with the sign given, to the right ascension of the true Sun, or, more easily, by applying 12^h to the column Sidereal Time. The direction in which the equation of time has to be applied in different problems is a frequent source of confusion and error. Apparent Solar Time is equal to the Mean Solar Time plus the Equation of Time. For example at noon on Aug. 8 the Equation of Time is $-5^m 36^s$ and thus at 12^h Mean Time on that day the Apparent Time is $12^h - 5^m 36^s = 11^h 54^m 24^s$.

The Greenwich Sidereal Time at 0^h and the Transit of the First Point of Aries (which is really the mean time when the sidereal time is 0^h) are used for converting mean time to sidereal time and vice versa.

The G.M.T. of transit of the Sun at Greenwich may also be taken as the L.M.T. of transit in any longitude. It is independent of latitude. The G.M.T. of transit in any longitude is obtained by adding the longitude to the time given if west, and vice versa.

The legal importance of SUNRISE and SUNSET is that the Road Traffic Act, 1956, defines Lighting-up Time for vehicles as being from half an hour after sunset to half an hour before sunrise throughout the year. In all laws and regulations " sunset " refers to the local sunset, i.e. the time at which the Sun sets at the place in question. This common-sense interpretation has been upheld by legal tribunals. Thus the necessity for providing for different latitudes and longitudes, as already described, is evident.

The times of SUNRISE and SUNSET are those when the Sun's upper limb, as affected by refraction, is on the true horizon of an observer at sea-level. Assuming the mean refraction to be 34′, and the Sun's semi-diameter to be 16′, the time given is that when the true zenith distance of the Sun's centre is 90° + 34′ + 16′ or 90° 50′, or, in other words, when the depression of the Sun's

centre below the true horizon is 50'. The upper limb is then 34' below the true horizon, but is brought there by refraction. It is true, of course, that an observer on a ship might see the Sun for a minute or so longer, because of the dip of the horizon, while another viewing the sunset over hills or mountains would record an earlier time. Nevertheless, the moment when the true zenith distance of the Sun's centre is 90° 50' is a precise time dependent only on the latitude and longitude of the place, and independent of its altitude above sea-level, the contour of its horizon, the vagaries of refraction or the small seasonal change in the Sun's semi-diameter; this moment is suitable in every way as a definition of sunset (or sunrise) for all statutory purposes.

It is well known that light reaches us before sunrise and also continues to reach us for some time after sunset. The interval between darkness and sunrise or sunset and darkness is called twilight. Astronomically speaking, twilight is considered to begin or end when the Sun's centre is 18° below the horizon, as no light from the Sun can then reach the observer. As thus defined twilight may last several hours; in high latitudes at the solstices the depression of 18° is not reached, and twilight lasts from sunset to sunrise.

The need for some sub-division of twilight was met some years ago by dividing the gathering darkness into four steps.

(1) *Sunrise or Sunset*, defined as above.
(2) *Civil twilight*, which begins or ends when the Sun's centre is 6° below the horizon. This marks the time when operations requiring daylight may commence or must cease. In England it varies from about 30 to 60 minutes after sunset.
(3) *Nautical twilight*, which begins or ends when the Sun's centre is 12° below the horizon This marks the time when it is, to all intent and purposes, completely dark.
(4) *Astronomical twilight*, which begins or ends when the Sun's centre is 18° below the horizon. This marks theoretical perfect darkness. It is not of practical importance, especially if nautical twilight is tabulated.

To assist observers the durations of civil, nautical and astronomical twilights are given at intervals of ten days. The beginning of a particular twilight is found by subtracting the duration from the time of sunrise, while the end is found by adding the duration to the time of sunset. Thus the beginning of astronomical twilight in latitude 52°, on the Greenwich meridian, on March 11 is found as $06^h 25^m - 113^m = 04^h 32^m$ and similarly the end of civil twilight as $17^h 58^m + 34^m = 18^h 32^m$.

The letters T.A.N. are printed when twilight lasts all night.

Lighting-up time is a crude attempt to approximate to civil twilight over the British Isles.

Under the heading ASTRONOMICAL NOTES will be found notes describing the position and visibility of all the planets and also of other phenomena; these are intended to guide naked-eye observers, or those using small telescopes.

PAGE III OF EACH MONTH

The Moon moves so rapidly among the stars that its position is given only to the degree of accuracy that permits linear interpolation. The right ascension and declination are geocentric, i.e. for an imaginary observer at the centre of the Earth. To an observer on the surface of the Earth the position is always different, as the altitude is always less on account of parallax which may reach 1°.

The lunar terminator is the line separating the bright from the dark part of the Moon's disk. Apart from irregularities of the lunar surface, the terminator is elliptical, because it is a circle seen in projection. It becomes the full circle forming the limb, or edge, of the Moon at New and Full Moon. The selenographic longitude of the terminator is measured from the mean centre of the visible disk, which may differ from the visible centre by as much as 8°, because of libration.

Instead of the longitude of the terminator the Sun's selenographic colongitude is tabulated. It is numerically equal to the selenographic longitude of the morning terminator, measured eastward from the mean centre of the disk. Thus its value is approximately 270° at New Moon, 360° at First Quarter, 90° at Full Moon and 180° at Last Quarter.

The Position Angle of the Bright Limb is the position angle of the midpoint of the illuminated limb, measured eastward from the north point on the disk. The column PHASE shows the percentage of the area of the Moon's disk illuminated; this is also the illuminated percentage of the diameter at right angles to the line of cusps. The terminator is a semi-ellipse whose major axis is the line of cusps, and whose semi-minor axis is determined by the tabulated percentage; from New Moon to Full Moon the east limb is dark, and vice versa.

The times given as moonrise and moonset are those when the upper limb of the Moon is on the horizon of an observer at sea-level. The Sun's horizontal parallax is about 9", and is negligible when considering sunrise and sunset, but that of the Moon averages about 57'. Hence the computed time represents the moment when the true zenith distance of the Moon is 90° 50' (as for the Sun) minus the horizontal parallax. The time required for the Sun or Moon to rise or set is about four minutes (except in high latitudes).

The tables have been constructed for the meridian of Greenwich, and for latitudes 52° and 56°. They give Greenwich Mean Time (G.M.T.) throughout the year. To obtain the G.M.T. of the phenomenon as seen from any other latitude and longitude, first interpolate or extrapolate for latitude by the usual rules of proportion. To the time thus found the longitude (expressed in time) is to be *added* if west (as it usually is in Great Britain) or *subtracted* if east. If the longitude is expressed in degrees and minutes of arc, it must be converted to time at the rate of $1° = 4^m$ and $15' = 1^m$.

The G.M.T. of transit of the Moon over the meridian of Greenwich is given: these times are independent of latitude, but must be corrected for longitude. For places in the British Isles it suffices to add the longitude if west, and vice versa. For more remote places a further correction is necessary

because of the rapid movement of the Moon relative to the stars. The entire correction is conveniently determined by first finding the west longitude λ of the place. If the place is in west longitude, λ is the ordinary west longitude; if the place is in east longitude λ is the complement to 24^h (or $360°$) of the longitude, and will be greater than 12^h (or $180°$). The correction then consists of two positive portions, namely λ and the fraction $\lambda/24$ (or $\lambda°/360$) multiplied by the difference between consecutive transits. Thus for Sydney, N.S.W., the longitude is 10^h 05^m east, so $\lambda = 13^h$ 55^m and the fraction $\lambda/24$ is 0.58. The transit on the local date 1976 Oct. 11 is found as follows:

	d	h	m
G.M.T. of transit at Greenwich....Oct.	10	09	46
λ....................................		13	55
$0.58 \times (10^h \ 36^m - 09^h \ 46^m)$.........			29
G.M.T. of transit at Sydney........	11	00	10
Corr. to N.S.W. Standard Time....		10	00
Local standard time of transit.......	11	10	10

It is evident of course, that for any given place the quantities λ and the correction to local standard time may be combined permanently, being here 23^h 55^m.

Positions of Mercury are given for every third day, and those of Venus and Mars for every fifth day; they may be interpolated linearly. The column PHASE shows the illuminated percentage of the disk. In the case of the inner planets this approaches 100 at superior conjunction and 0 at inferior conjunction. When the phase is less than 50 the planet is crescent-shaped or horned; for greater phases it is gibbous. In the case of the exterior planet Mars, the phase approaches 100 at conjunction and opposition, and is a minimum at the quadratures.

Since the planets cannot be seen when on the horizon, the actual times of rising and setting are not given; instead, the time when the planet has an apparent altitude of $5°$ has been tabulated. The phenomenon tabulated is the one that occurs between sunset and sunrise; unimportant exceptions to this rule may occur because changes are not made during a month, except in the case of Mercury. The times given may be interpolated for latitude and corrected for longitude as in the case of the Sun and Moon.

The G.M.T. at which the planet transits the Greenwich meridian is also given. The times of transit are to be corrected to local meridians in the usual way, as already described.

PAGE IV OF EACH MONTH

The G.M.T.'s of Sunrise and Sunset may be used not only for these phenomena, but also for Lighting-up Times, which, under the Road Traffic Act, 1956, are from half an hour after sunset to half an hour before sunrise throughout the year.

The particulars for the four outer planets resemble those for the planets on Page III of each

month, except that, under Uranus and Neptune, times when the planet is $10°$ high instead of $5°$ high are given; this is because of the inferior brightness of these planets. The polar diameter of Jupiter is about $3''$ less than the equatorial diameter, while that of Saturn is about $2''$ less. The diameters given for the rings of Saturn are those of the major axis (in the plane of the planet's equator) and the minor axis respectively. The former has a small seasonal change due to the slightly varying distance of the Earth from Saturn, but the latter varies from zero when the Earth passes through the ring plane every 15 years to its maximum opening half-way between these periods. The rings were completely closed on three occasions in 1966 and were open at their widest extent in the middle of 1973.

TIME

From the earliest ages, the natural division of time into recurring periods of day and night has provided the practical time scale for the everyday activities of mankind. Indeed, if any alternative means of time measurement is adopted, it must be capable of adjustment so as to remain in general agreement with the natural time scale defined by the diurnal rotation of the Earth on its axis. Ideally the rotation should be measured against a fixed frame of reference; in practice it must be measured against the background provided by the celestial bodies. If the Sun is chosen as the reference point, we obtain Apparent Solar Time, which is the time indicated by a sundial. It is not a uniform time, but is subject to variations which amount to as much as a quarter of an hour in each direction. Such wide variations cannot be tolerated in a practical time scale, and this has led to the concept of Mean Solar Time in which all the days are exactly the same length and equal to the average length of the Apparent Solar Day.

The positions of the stars in the sky are specified in relation to a fictitious reference point in the sky known as the First Point of Aries (or the Vernal Equinox). It is therefore convenient to adopt this same reference point when considering the rotation of the Earth against the background of the stars. The time scale so obtained is known as Apparent Sidereal Time.

Greenwich Mean Time

The daily rotation of the Earth on its axis causes the Sun and the other heavenly bodies to appear to cross the sky fron East to West. It is convenient to represent this relative motion as if the Sun really performed a daily circuit around a fixed Earth. Noon in Apparent Solar Time may then be defined as the time at which the Sun transits across the observer's meridian. In Mean Solar Time, noon is similarly defined by the meridian transit of a fictitious Mean Sun moving uniformly in the sky with the same average speed as the true Sun. Mean Solar Time observed on the meridian of the transit circle telescope of the Royal Observatory at Greenwich is called Greenwich Mean Time (G.M.T.) The mean solar day is divided into 24 hours and, for astronomical and other scientific purposes, these are numbered 0

to 23, commencing at midnight. Civil time is usually reckoned in two periods of 12 hours, designated a.m. (before noon) and p.m. (after noon).

Universal Time

Before 1925 January 1 G.M.T. was reckoned in 24 hours commencing at noon: since that date it has been reckoned from midnight. In view of the risk of confusion in the use of the designation G.M.T. before and after 1925, the International Astronomical Union recommended in 1928 that astronomers should, for the present, employ the term Universal Time, U.T. (or Weltzeit, W.Z.) to denote G.M.T. measured from Greenwich Mean Midnight.

In precision work it has now become necessary to take account of small variations, hitherto negligible, in Universal Time. These arise from small irregularities in the rotation of the Earth. Observed astronomical time is designated U.T.o. Observed time corrected for the effects of the motion of the poles (giving rise to a " wandering " in longitude) is designated U.T.1. There is also a seasonal fluctuation in the rate of rotation of the Earth arising from meteorological causes, often called the annual fluctuation. U.T.1 corrected for this effect is designated U.T.2 and provides a time scale free from short-period fluctuations. It is still subject to small secular and irregular changes.

Apparent Solar Time

As has been mentioned, the time shown by a sundial is called Apparent Solar Time. It differs from Mean Solar Time by an amount known as the Equation of Time, which is the total effect of two causes which make the length of the apparent solar day non-uniform. One cause of variation is that the orbit of the Earth is not a circle, but an ellipse, having the Sun at one focus. As a consequence, the angular speed of the Earth in its orbit is not constant; it is greatest at the beginning of January when the Earth is nearest the Sun. The other cause is due to the obliquity of the ecliptic; the plane of the equator (which is at right-angles to the axis of rotation of the Earth) does not coincide with the ecliptic (the plane defined by the apparent annual motion of the Sun around the celestial sphere) but is inclined to it at an angle of 23° 27′. As a result, the apparent solar day is shorter than average at the equinoxes and longer at the solstices. From the combined effects of the components due to obliquity and eccentricity, the equation of time reaches its maximum values in February (−14 mins.) and early November (+16 mins.). It has a zero value on four dates during the year, and it is only on these dates (approx. April 15, June 14, Sept. 1, and Dec. 25) that a sundial shows Mean Solar Time.

Sidereal Time

A sidereal day is the duration of a complete rotation of the Earth with reference to the First Point of Aries. The term sidereal (or " star ") time is perhaps a little misleading since the time scale so defined is not exactly the same as that which would be defined by successive transits of a selected star, as there is a small progressive motion between the stars and the First Point of Aries due to the precession of the Earth's axis. This makes the length

of the sidereal day shorter than the true period of rotation by 0·008 seconds. Superimposed on this steady precessional motion are small oscillations called nutation, giving rise to fluctuations in apparent sidereal time amounting to as much as 1·2 seconds. It is therefore customary to employ Mean Sidereal Time, from which these fluctuations have been removed. The conversion of G.M.T. to Greenwich sidereal time (G.S.T.) may be performed by adding the value of the G.S.T. at 0^h on the day in question (page II of each month) to the G.M.T. converted to sidereal time using the table on p. 146.

Example. To find the G.S.T. at August $8^d 02^h 41^m 11^s$

						h m s
G.M.T.						
G.S.T. at 0^h	..			..	..	21 05 33
G.M.T.	..	..	..	..	..	2 41 11
Acceleration for 2^h		..	..	..		20
,, ,, $41^m 11^s$		..	..			7
Sum = G.S.T. =	..	..		..	..	23 47 11

If the observer is not on the Greenwich meridian then his longitude, measured positively westwards from Greenwich, must be subtracted from the G.S.T. to obtain Local Sidereal Time (L.S.T.). Thus, in the above example, an observer 5^h east of Greenwich, or 19^h west, would find his L.S.T. as $4^h 47^m 11^s$.

Ephemeris Time

In the study of the motions of the Sun, Moon and planets, observations taken over an extended period are used in the preparation of tables giving the apparent position of the body each day. A table of this sort is known as an ephemeris, and may be used in the comparison of current observations with tabulated positions. A detailed examination of the observations made over the past 300 years shows that the Sun, Moon and planets appear to depart from their predicted positions by amounts proportional to their mean motions. The only satisfactory explanation is that the time scale to which the observations were referred was not uniform as had been supposed. Since the time scale was based on the rotation of the Earth, it follows that this rotation is subject to irregularities. The fact that the discrepancies between the observed and ephemeris positions were proportional to the mean motions of the bodies made it possible to secure agreement by substituting a revised time scale and recomputing the ephemeris positions. The time scale which brings the ephemeris into agreement with the observations has been named Ephemeris Time (E.T.).

The new unit of time has been defined in terms of the apparent annual motion of the Sun. Thus the second is now defined in terms of the annual motion of the Earth in its orbit around the Sun (1/31556925·9747 of the Tropical Year for 1900 January $0^d 12^h$, E.T.) instead of in terms of the diurnal rotation of the Earth on its axis (1/86 400 of the Mean Solar Day). In many branches of scientific work other than astronomy there has been a demand for a unit of time that is invariable, and the second of Ephemeris time was adopted by the Comité International des Poids et Mésures in 1956. The length of the unit has been

chosen to provide general agreement with U.T. throughout the 19th and 20th centuries. During 1977 the estimated difference E.T. – U.T. is 47 seconds. The precise determination of E.T. from astronomical observations is a lengthy process, as the accuracy with which a single observation of the Sun can be made is far less than that obtainable in, for instance, a comparison between clocks. It is therefore necessary to average the observations over an extended period. Largely on account of its faster motion, the position of the Moon may be observed with greater accuracy, and a close approximation to Ephemeris Time may be obtained by comparing observations of the Moon with its ephemeris position. Even in this case, however, the requisite standard of accuracy can only be achieved by averaging over a number of years.

Atomic Time

The fundamental standards of time and frequency must be defined in terms of a periodic motion adequately uniform, enduring and susceptible of measurement. This has led in the past to the adoption of standards based on the observed motions in the Solar System. Recent progress has made it possible to consider the use of other natural standards, such as atomic or molecular oscillations. The oscillations so far employed are not in fact continuous periodic motions such as the revolution of the electrons in their orbits around the nuclei. The continuous oscillations are generated in an electrical circuit, the frequency of which is then compared or brought into coincidence with the frequency characteristic of the absorption or emission by the atoms or molecules when they change between two selected energy levels. At the National Physical Laboratory regular comparisons have been made since the middle of 1955 between quartz clocks of high stability and a frequency defined by atoms of caesium. The standard has proved of great value in the precise calibration of frequencies and time intervals: it has also been possible to build up a scale of " atomic time " by using continuously-running quartz clocks calibrated in terms of the caesium frequency standard.

Radio Time Signals

The establishment of a uniform time system by the assessment of the performance of standard clocks in terms of astronomical observations is the work of a national observatory, and standard time is then made generally available by means of radio time signals. In the United Kingdom, the Royal Greenwich Observatory is responsible for the legal standard of time, and controls the " 6-pips " radio signals emitted by the British Broadcasting Corporation. Signals by land line from the Observatory correct the Post Office Speaking Clock, TIM.

For survey and scientific purposes in which the highest accuracy is required, special signals are transmitted from the Post Office Radio Station at Rugby. The International Signals, consisting of a five-minute series of pips, one-tenth of a second long, with the pips at the minutes lengthened for identification, are radiated at 02.54–03.00, 08.54–09.00, 14.54–15.00, 20.54–21.00 from GBR (16 kHz) and associated H.F. transmitters. The seconds

pulses superposed on the MSF standard frequency transmissions, which consists of five cycles of a 1,000 c.p.s. tone, are derived from the same master control at the transmitting station, and are radiated for ten minutes in each quarter-hour on $2\frac{1}{2}$, 5, and 10 MHz for 24 hours per day, and continuously on 60 kHz. The carrier frequencies of all the MSF transmissions, and of GBR, are closely controlled, and measured regularly at the National Physical Laboratory in terms of the caesium atomic resonance.

The new Coordinated Universal Time (U.T.C.) system standard frequency emissions and radio time signals are broadcast on MSF, GBR, and by other national transmitters, eg. by WWV and WWVH in the U.S.A. in conformity with the International Atomic Time Scale in which the time intervals between pips correspond exactly to the seconds defined as follows: " The second is the duration of 9 192 631 770 periods of the radiation corresponding to the transition between the 2 hyperfine levels of the ground state of the caesium 133 atom."

As the rate of rotation of the Earth is variable the time signals will be adjusted by the introduction of a leap second when necessary in order that UTC shall not depart from UT by more than $0^s \cdot 9$. For convenience it has been decided to introduce leap seconds, when necessary, on the last second of a month preferably on 31 Dec. and/or 30 June. In the case of a positive leap second $23^h\ 59^m\ 60^s$ will be followed one second later by $0^h\ 00^m\ 00^s$ of the first day of the month. In the case of a negative leap second (required if the Earth were to have a sudden change of rate and begin to gain relative to UTC) $23^h\ 59^m\ 58^s$ will be followed one second later by $0^h\ 00^m\ 00^s$ of the first day of the month.

From 1972 Jan. 1 the six pips on the BBC have consisted of 5 short pips from second 55 to second 59 followed by one lengthened pip, the start of which indicates the exact minute.

SUMMER TIME

In the United Kingdom, Summer Time, one hour in advance of G.M.T. will be kept between 02^h G.M.T. on the day following the third Saturday in March and 02^h G.M.T. on the day following the fourth Saturday in October. Thus, in 1977, Summer Time will be in force between March 20 and October 23.

Variations from the standard time of some countries occurs during part of the year: they are decided annually and are usually referred to as Summer Time or Daylight Saving Time. These variations occur in:

British Commonwealth.—Parts of Australia; Bahamas; Canada; Channel Islands; Hong Kong; New Zealand.

Foreign Countries.—Albania; Argentina; Brazil; Chile; parts of China; Costa Rica; Cuba; Egypt; Formosa; France; Greece; Iceland; Israel; Italy; Macau; Malta; Morocco; Norway; Pescadores Is.; Poland; Sicily; Sudan; Syria; Tunisia; Turkey. parts of U.S.A.;

In the Dominican Republic, the Irish Republic, and Paraguay, the variation occurs in winter and is called Winter Time.

STANDARD TIME

In the year 1880 it was enacted by statute that the word "time", when it occurred in any legal document relating to Great Britain, was to be interpreted, unless otherwise specifically stated, as the Mean Time of the Greenwich meridian.* Since the year 1883 the system of Standard Time by Zones has been gradually accepted, and now almost throughout the world a Standard Time which differs from that of Greenwich by an integral number of hours, either fast or slow, is used.

The large territories of the United States, Canada and U.S.S.R. are divided into zones approximately 7½° on either side of central meridians. The important ones are given below; there are in addition zones from 5 to 13 hours fast in the U.S.S.R. centred at 60°E. to 180°E.

Fast on Greenwich Time

12 hrs. F...Fiji, Gilbert and Ellice Is., New Zealand, Marshall Is., Caroline Is. (east of 160° E.), New Hebrides.

11½ ,, F...Norfolk I., Nauru I.

11 ,, F...New Caledonia, Santa Cruz and Solomon Is., Truk, Ponape, Sakhalin.

10 ,, F...Victoria, N.S.W. (except Broken Hill Area), Queenland, Tasmania, British New Guinea, Admiralty Islds., Caroline Islds. (west of 160°E.), Australian Capital Territory, Mariana Islds.

9½ ,, F...South Australia, Northern Territory of Australia, N.S.W. (Broken Hill Area).

9 ,, F...Japan, Schouten Islds., Kurile Islds., Manchuria, Korea, West Irian (Indonesia).

8½ ,, F...Molucca Islds.

8 ,, F...China (coast), Hong Kong, Philippine Is., Macau, Timor, Western Australia, Sulawesi (Celebes), Kalimantan†, Formosa, Pescadores Islds., Malaysia, Vietnam (south).

7½ ,, F...Singapore.

7 ,, F...Sumatra, Java, Christmas I. (Indian Ocean), Thailand, Khmer Republic, Laos, Vietnam (north).

6½ ,, F...Burma, Cocos-Keeling Islds.

6 ,, F...Bangladesh.

5½ ,, F...India, Sri Lanka, Laccadive Islds., Andaman and Nicobar Islds.

5 ,, F...Chagos Archipelago, Pakistan.

4 ,, F...Mauritius, Seychelles, Réunion, U.S.S.R., 40° E. to 52° 30′ E.

3½ ,, F...Iran.

3 ,, F...U.S.S.R. west of 40° E., Iraq, Ethiopia, Yemen (Dem. Repub.), Socotra I., Somali Republic, Comoro Islds., Madagascar, Uganda, Kenya, Tanzania.

2 ,, F...Turkey, Greece, Bulgaria, Rumania, Finland, Israel, Jordan, U.A.R., Syria, Cyprus, Rhodesia, Malawi, E. European South Africa, Mozambique, Sudan, Burundi, Rwanda, Crete, Lebanon, Libya, Zambia, Botswana, Lesotho.

1 hr. F...Sweden, Norway, Denmark, Netherlands, Belgium, Germany, France, Luxemburg, Spain, Monaco, Balearic Islds., Poland, Austria.

Central-European Hungary, Switzerland, Italy, Czechoslovakia, Yugoslavia, Albania, Tunisia, Nigeria, Malta, Sicily, Central African Republic, Cameroon Republic, Zaire, Angola, Spitsbergen, Algeria, Dahomey, Corsica, Sardinia, Portugal, Niger, Irish Republic, Gibraltar.

Greenwich Time The United Kingdom, Faroe, Channel Is., Algeria, Morocco, Iceland, Mauritania, Sierra Leone, Ivory Coast, Ifni, Ghana, Principe I., St. Helena, Gambia, Canary Is., Ascension I., Tangier, São Tomé, Rio de Oro, Madeira, Mali, Senegal, Liberia.

Slow on Greenwich time

1 hr. S...Azores, Cape Verde Is., Guinea Bissau.

2 hrs. S...Fernando Noronha I., Scoresby Sound, South Georgia.

3 ,, S...Greenland (excluding Scoresby Sound and Thule), Eastern Brazil, Argentina, Uruguay, French Guiana.

3½ ,, S...Newfoundland, Dutch Guiana.

3¾ ,, S...Guyana.

4 ,, S...Canada east of 68° W., Greenland (Thule Area), Puerto Rico, Lesser Atlantic. Antilles, Central Brazil, Falkland Islds., Paraguay, Bermuda, Bolivia, Chile, Curaçao I., Venezuela, Labrador.

5 hrs. S...Canada from 68° W. to 85° W. (north) or 90° W. (south), Eastern States of Eastern. U.S.A., Jamaica, Bahama Islds., Haiti, Peru, Panama, W. Brazil, Colombia, Cayman Is., Ecuador, Dominican Republic, Cuba.

6 hrs. S...Central parts of U.S.A., Canada from 85° W. to 102°W., Costa Rica, Central. Salvador, Honduras, part of Mexico, Guatemala, Nicaragua.

7 hrs. S...Canada from 102° W. to 120° W., Mountain. Mountain States of U.S.A., part of Mexico.

8 hrs. S...Canada west of 120° W., Alaska, Pacific. (south-east coast), Western States of U.S.A., part of Mexico, Yukon (east of 138° W.).

9 hrs. S...Alaska 137° W. to 141° W., Yukon (west of 138° W.).

10 ,, S...Alaska from 141° W. to 161° W., Low Archipelago, Austral and Society Islds., Hawaii, Fanning I., Christmas Islds. (Pacific Ocean).

11 ,, S...Aleutian Islds., Alaska (west coast), Samoa, Midway Islds.

In the Tonga Islands the time 13h fast and in Chatham Is. 12h 45m fast on Greenwich is used, as the Date line is to the East of them.

THE DATE OR CALENDAR LINE

The line where the change of date occurs is a modification of the 180th meridian, and is drawn so as to include islands of any one group on the same side of the line, or for political reasons. It is indicated by joining up the following nine points:

Lat.	Long.	Lat.	Long.	Lat.	Long.
60° S.	180°	15° S.	172½° W.	53° N.	170° E.
51° S.	180°	5° S.	180°	65½° N.	169° W.
45° S.	172½° W.	48° N.	180°	75° N.	180°

* Summer Time is the "legal" time during the period in which its use is ordained. † Formerly Indonesian Borneo.

RISING AND SETTING TIMES
Table 1. Hour Angle

Dec.	Latitude and Declination of Opposite Signs						0°	Latitude and Declination of Same Signs					
	50°	45°	40°	30°	20°	10°		10°	20°	30°	40°	45°	50°
	h m	h m	h m	h m	h m	h m	h m	h m	h m	h m	h m	h m	h m
0	6 00	6 00	6 00	6 00	6 00	6 00	6 00	6 00	6 00	6 00	6 00	6 00	6 00
1	5 55	5 56	5 57	5 58	5 59	5 59	6 00	6 01	6 01	6 02	6 03	6 04	6 05
2	5 50	5 52	5 53	5 55	5 57	5 58	6 00	6 02	6 03	6 05	6 07	6 08	6 10
3	5 45	5 48	5 50	5 53	5 56	5 58	6 00	6 02	6 04	6 07	6 10	6 12	6 15
4	5 40	5 44	5 46	5 51	5 54	5 57	6 00	6 03	6 06	6 09	6 14	6 16	6 20
5	5 36	5 40	5 43	5 48	5 52	5 56	6 00	6 04	6 08	6 12	6 17	6 20	6 24
6	5 31	5 36	5 39	5 46	5 51	5 56	6 00	6 04	6 09	6 14	6 21	6 24	6 29
7	5 26	5 32	5 36	5 44	5 50	5 55	6 00	6 05	6 10	6 16	6 24	6 28	6 34
8	5 21	5 27	5 33	5 41	5 48	5 54	6 00	6 06	6 12	6 19	6 27	6 33	6 39
9	5 16	5 23	5 29	5 39	5 47	5 53	6 00	6 07	6 13	6 21	6 31	6 37	6 44
10	5 11	5 19	5 26	5 37	5 45	5 53	6 00	6 07	6 15	6 23	6 34	6 41	6 49
11	5 06	5 15	5 22	5 34	5 44	5 52	6 00	6 08	6 16	6 26	6 38	6 45	6 54
12	5 01	5 11	5 19	5 32	5 42	5 51	6 00	6 09	6 18	6 28	6 41	6 49	6 59
13	4 56	5 06	5 15	5 29	5 40	5 51	6 00	6 09	6 20	6 31	6 45	6 54	7 04
14	4 51	5 02	5 12	5 27	5 39	5 50	6 00	6 10	6 21	6 33	6 48	6 58	7 09
15	4 46	4 58	5 08	5 24	5 38	5 49	6 00	6 11	6 22	6 36	6 52	7 02	7 14
16	4 40	4 53	5 04	5 22	5 36	5 48	6 00	6 12	6 24	6 38	6 56	7 07	7 20
17	4 35	4 49	5 00	5 19	5 35	5 48	6 00	6 12	6 25	6 41	7 00	7 11	7 25
18	4 29	4 44	4 57	5 17	5 33	5 47	6 00	6 13	6 27	6 43	7 03	7 16	7 31
19	4 23	4 39	4 53	5 14	5 31	5 46	6 00	6 14	6 29	6 46	7 07	7 21	7 37
20	4 17	4 35	4 49	5 11	5 30	5 45	6 00	6 15	6 30	6 49	7 11	7 25	7 43
21	4 11	4 30	4 44	5 09	5 28	5 44	6 00	6 16	6 32	6 51	7 16	7 30	7 49
22	4 04	4 25	4 40	5 06	5 26	5 44	6 00	6 16	6 34	6 54	7 20	7 35	7 56
23	3 58	4 19	4 36	5 03	5 24	5 43	6 00	6 17	6 36	6 57	7 24	7 41	8 02
24	3 52	4 14	4 32	5 00	5 23	5 42	6 00	6 18	6 37	7 00	7 28	7 46	8 08
25	3 45	4 09	4 28	4 58	5 21	5 41	6 00	6 19	6 39	7 02	7 32	7 51	8 15
26	3 38	4 03	4 24	4 55	5 19	5 40	6 00	6 20	6 41	7 05	7 36	7 57	8 22
27	3 30	3 57	4 19	4 52	5 17	5 39	6 00	6 21	6 43	7 08	7 41	8 03	8 30
28	3 23	3 51	4 14	4 48	5 15	5 38	6 00	6 22	6 45	7 12	7 46	8 09	8 37
29	3 15	3 45	4 09	4 45	5 14	5 38	6 00	6 22	6 46	7 15	7 51	8 15	8 45

SUNRISE AND SUNSET

The local mean time of sunrise or sunset (as defined on page 138) may be found by determining the appropriate hour angle from the table above and applying it to the time of transit given in the ephemeris for each month. The hour angle is negative for sunrise and positive for sunset. A small correction to the hour angle, which always has the effect of increasing it numerically, is necessary to allow for the Sun's semi-diameter (16') and for refraction (34'). This correction may be obtained from Table 2. The resulting local mean time may be converted into the standard time of the country by taking the difference between the longitude of the standard meridian of the country and that of the place, and adding it to the local mean time if the place is west of the standard meridian, and subtracting it if the place is east of the standard meridian.

Example.—Required the N.Z. Mean Time (12^h fast on G.M.T.) of sunset on May 24 at Auckland. The latitude is 36° 50′ south (or minus) and the longitude 11^h 39^m east. Taking the declination as +20°·7, we find

	h m
Tabular entry for 30° Lat. and Dec. 20°, opposite signs	+ 5 11
Proportional part for 6° 50′ of Lat	− 15
Proportional part for 0°·7 of Dec	− 3
Correction (Table 2)	+ 6
Hour angle	4 59
Sun transits	11 57
Longitudinal correction	+ 21
N.Z. Mean Time	17 17

Table 2. Correction for Refraction and Semi-Diameter

Latitude	Declination			
	0°	10°	20°	29°
°	m	m	m	m
0	4	4	4	5
20	4	4	5	5
30	5	5	5	6
40	5	6	6	7
50	6	6	7	9

MOONRISE AND MOONSET

It is possible to calculate the times of moonrise and moonset using Table 1 though the method is more complicated because the apparent motion of the Moon is much more rapid than that of the Sun.

Table 3. Longitude Correction

X \\ A	40^m	45^m	50^m	55^m	60^m	65^m	70^m
h	m	m	m	m	m	m	m
1	2	2	2	2	3	3	3
2	3	4	4	5	5	5	6
3	5	6	6	7	8	8	9
4	7	8	8	9	10	11	12
5	8	9	10	11	13	14	15
6	10	11	13	14	15	16	18
7	12	13	15	16	18	19	20
8	13	15	17	18	20	22	23
9	15	17	19	21	23	24	26
10	17	19	21	23	25	27	29
11	18	21	23	25	28	30	32
12	20	23	25	28	30	33	35
13	22	24	27	30	33	35	38
14	23	26	29	32	35	38	41
15	25	28	31	34	38	41	44
16	27	30	33	37	40	43	47
17	28	32	35	39	43	46	50
18	30	34	38	41	45	49	53
19	32	36	40	44	48	51	55
20	33	38	42	46	50	54	58
21	35	39	44	48	53	57	61
22	37	41	46	50	55	60	64
23	38	43	48	53	58	62	67
24	40	45	50	55	60	65	70

Notation

φ = latitude of observer
λ = longitude of observer (measured positively towards the west)
T_{-1} = time of transit of Moon on previous day
T_0 = time of transit of Moon on day in question
T_1 = time of transit of Moon on following day
δ_0 = approximate declination of Moon
δ_R = declination of Moon at moonrise
δ_S = declination of Moon at moonset
h_0 = approximate hour angle of Moon
h_R = hour angle of Moon at moonrise
h_S = hour angle of moon at moonset
t_R = time of moonrise
t_S = time of moonset

The parallax of the Moon, about $57'$, is near to the sum of the semi-diameter and refraction but has the opposite effect on these times. It is thus convenient to neglect all three quantities in the method outlined below.

METHOD

1. With arguments φ, δ_0 enter Table 1 on p. 144 to determine h_0 where h_0 is negative for moonrise and positive for moonset.

2. Form approximate times from
$$t_R = T_0 + \lambda + h_0$$
$$t_S = T_0 + \lambda + h_0$$

3. Determine δ_R, δ_S for times t_R, t_S respectively.

4. Re-enter Table 1 on p. 144 with—
   (a) arguments φ, δ_R to determine h_R
   (b) arguments φ, δ_S to determine h_S

5. Form $t_R = T_0 + \lambda + h_R + AX$
   $$t_S = T_0 + \lambda + h_S + AX$$

   where $A = (\lambda + h)$

   $X = (T_0 - T_{-1})$ if $(\lambda + h)$ is negative
   and $X = (T_1 - T_0)$ if $(\lambda + h)$ is positive

AX is the respondent in Table 3.

Example.—To find the times of moonrise and moonset at Vancouver ($\varphi = +49°$, $\lambda = +8^h\,12^m$) on 1977 October 10. The starting data (from p. 128) are

	h	m
T_{-1} =	8	58
T_0 =	9	46
T_1 =	10	36
δ =	$+3°$	

1. $h_0 = 6^h\,14^m$

2. Approximate values
$$t_R = 10^d\,09^h\,46^m + 8^h\,12^m + (-6^h\,14^m)$$
$$= 10^d\,11^h\,44^m$$
$$t_S = 10^d\,09^h\,46^m + 8^h\,12^m + (+6^h\,14^m)$$
$$= 11^d\,00^h\,12^m$$
$$\delta_R = +2°.9$$
$$\delta_S = +0°.8$$
$$h_R = -6^h\,14^m$$
$$h_S = +6^h\,04^m$$
$$t_R = 10^d\,09^h\,46^m + 8^h\,12^m - 6^h\,14^m + 4^m$$
$$= 10^d\,11^h\,48^m$$
$$t_S = 10^d\,09^h\,46^m + 8^h\,12^m + 6^h\,04^m + 30^m$$
$$= 11^d\,00^h\,32^m$$

To get the L.M.T. of the phenomenon the longitude is subtracted from the G.M.T. thus
$$\text{Moonrise} = 10^d\,11^h\,48^m - 8^h\,12^m = 10^d\,03^h\,36^m$$
$$\text{Moonset} = 11^d\,00^h\,32^m - 8^h\,12^m = 10^d\,16^h\,20^m$$

ASTRONOMICAL CONSTANTS

Solar Parallax .... $8''\cdot794$
Precession for the year 1977 .... $50''\cdot273$
    ,,   in R.A. .... $3^s\cdot074$
    ,,   in Declination .... $20''\cdot040$
Constant of Nutation .... $9''\cdot21$
Constant of Aberration .... $20''\cdot496$
Mean Obliquity of Ecliptic (1977) ..... $23°\,26'\,32''$
Moon's Equatorial Hor. Parallax ...... $57'\,02''\cdot70$
Velocity of Light in vacu *per sec.* ..... $299792\cdot5$ km.
Solar motion *per sec.* .... $20\cdot0$ km.
Equatorial radius of the Earth .... $6378\cdot160$ km.
Polar radius of the Earth .... $6356\cdot775$ km.

North Galactic Pole ⎫ R.A. $12^h\,49^m$. (1950·0).
(I.A.U. *Standard*). ⎰ Dec. $27°\cdot4$ N.
Solar Apex .... R.A. $18^h\,06^m$ Dec. $+30°$
Length of Year .. Tropical ..... $365\cdot24220$
(*In Mean*   Sidereal ...... $365\cdot25636$
 Solar Days)   Anomalistic .... $365\cdot25964$
    (*Perihelion to Perihelion*)
    Eclipse .... $346\cdot6200$

	d	h	m	s
Length of Month New Moon to New	29	12	44	02·9

(*Mean Values*)   Sidereal .... $27\,07\,43\,11\cdot5$
    Anomalistic ...... $27\,13\,18\,33\cdot2$
    (*Perigee to Perigee*)

MEAN AND SIDEREAL TIME

	Acceleration						Retardation					MEAN REFRACTION	
h	m s	h	m s	m s	s	h	m s	h	m s	m s	s	Alt. Ref.	Alt. Ref.
												° ′	° ′
1	0 10	13	2 08	0 00	0	1	0 10	13	2 08	0 00	0	1 20 21	4 30 10
2	0 20	14	2 18	3 02	1	2	0 20	14	2 18	3 03	1	1 30 20	5 06 9
3	0 30	15	2 28	9 07	2	3	0 29	15	2 27	9 09	2	1 41 19	5 50 8
4	0 39	16	2 38	15 13	3	4	0 39	16	2 37	15 15	3	1 52 18	6 44 7
5	0 49	17	2 48	21 18		5	0 49	17	2 47	21 21		2 05 17	7 54 6
6	0 59	18	2 57	27 23	4	6	0 59	18	2 57	27 28	4	2 19 16	9 27 5
				33 28	5					33 34	5	2 35 15	11 39 4
7	1 09	19	3 07	39 34	6	7	1 09	19	3 07	39 40	6	2 52 14	15 00 3
8	1 19	20	3 17	45 39	7	8	1 19	20	3 17	45 46	7	3 12 13	20 42 2
9	1 29	21	3 27	51 44	8	9	1 28	21	3 26	51 53	8	3 34 12	32 20 1
10	1 39	22	3 37	57 49	9	10	1 38	22	3 36	57 59	9	4 00 11	62 17 0
11	1 48	23	3 47	60 00	10	11	1 48	23	3 46	60 00	10	4 30	90 00
12	1 58	24	3 57			12	1 58	24	3 56				

The length of a sidereal day in mean time is $23^h 56^m 04^s \cdot 09$. Hence 1^h M.T. $= 1^h + 9^s \cdot 86$ S.T. and 1^h S.T. $= 1^h - 9^s \cdot 83$ M.T.

To convert an interval of mean time to the corresponding interval of sidereal time, enter the acceleration table with the given mean time (taking the hours and the minutes and seconds separately) and add the acceleration obtained to the given mean time. To convert an interval of sidereal time to the corresponding interval of mean time, take out the retardation for the given sidereal time and subtract.

The columns for the minutes and seconds of the argument are in the form known as Critical Tables. To use these tables, find in the appropriate left-hand column the two entries between which the given number of minutes and seconds lies; the quantity in the right-hand column between these two entries is the required acceleration or retardation. Thus the acceleration for $11^m 26^s$ (which lies between the entries $9^m 07^s$ and $15^m 13^s$) is 2^s. If the given number of minutes and seconds is a tabular entry, the required acceleration or retardation is the entry in the right-hand column *above* the given tabular entry; e.g. the retardation for $45^m 46^s$ is 7^s.

Example.—Convert $14^h 27^m 35^s$ from S.T. to M.T.

	h	m	s
Given S.T.	14	27	35
Retardation for 14^h		2	18
Retardation for $27^m 35^s$			5
Corresponding M.T.	14	25	12

For further explanation, see p. 141.
The refraction table is also in the form of a critical table.

THE SUMMER TIME ACTS

In 1916 an Act ordained that during a defined period of that year the legal time for general purposes in Great Britain should be one hour in advance of Greenwich Mean Time. The practice was stabilized (until the war) by the *Summer Time Acts,* 1922 to 1925, which enacted that "For the purposes of this Act, the period of summer time shall be taken to be the period beginning at two o'clock, Greenwich Mean Time, in the morning of the day next following the third Saturday in April, or, if that day is Easter Day, the day next following the second Saturday in April and ending at two o'clock, Greenwich Mean Time, in the morning of the day next following the first Saturday in October."

During the Second World War the duration of Summer Time was extended and in the years 1941–45 and in 1947, Double Summer Time (2 hrs. in advance of Greenwich Mean Time) was in force. Summer Time was extended in each year from 1948 to 1952 and again in 1961–1964, by Order in Council.

The duration of Summer Time during the last few years is given in the following table.

1953 Apr. 19—Oct. 4		1961 Mar. 26—Oct. 29
1954 Apr. 11—Oct. 3		1962 Mar. 25—Oct. 28
1955 Apr. 17—Oct. 2		1963 Mar. 31—Oct. 27
1956 Apr. 22—Oct. 7		1964 Mar. 22—Oct. 25
1957 Apr. 14—Oct. 6		1965 Mar. 21—Oct. 24
1958 Apr. 20—Oct. 5		1966 Mar. 20—Oct. 23
1959 Apr. 19—Oct. 4		1967 Mar. 19—Oct. 29
1960 Apr. 10—Oct. 2		1968 Feb. 18—Oct. 27
1972 Mar. 19—Oct. 29		1973 Mar. 18—Oct. 28
1974 Mar. 17—Oct. 27		1975 Mar. 16—Oct. 26
1976 Mar. 21—Oct. 24		

(British Standard Time, also one hour ahead of G.M.T., was kept between 1968 Oct. 27–1971 Oct. 31.) In 1977 Summer Time will be in force from March 20 to October 23.

ASTRONOMERS ROYAL

John Flamsteed, first Astronomer Royal . 1675–1719	Sir George Biddell Airy 1835–1881
Edmund Halley 1720–1742	Sir William Henry Mahoney Christie ... 1881–1910
James Bradley 1742–1762	Sir Frank Watson Dyson 1910–1933
Nathaniel Bliss 1762–1762	Sir Harold Spencer Jones 1933–1955
Nevil Maskelyne 1765–1811	Sir Richard van der Riet Woolley 1955–1971
John Pond 1811–1835	Sir Martin Ryle 1972–

PHENOMENA OF JUPITER'S SATELLITES, 1977

G.M.T. d	h	m	Sat.	Phen.
January				
1	21	57	I	Ec.R.
2	19	05	I	Sh.E.
5	01	50	II	Ec.R.
6	00	37	III	Ec.D.
6	02	53	III	Ec.R.
6	18	26	II	Sh.I.
6	20	56	II	Sh.E.
8	00	21	I	Sh.I.
8	02	31	I	Sh.E.
8	23	53	I	Ec.R.
9	18	50	I	Sh.I.
9	21	00	I	Sh.E.
10	18	21	I	Ec.R.
13	21	03	II	Sh.I.
13	23	33	II	Sh.E.
16	01	48	I	Ec.R.
16	18	32	III	Sh.I.
16	20	46	I	Sh.I.
16	20	46	III	Sh.E.
16	22	56	I	Sh.E.
17	20	17	I	Ec.R.
20	23	39	II	Sh.I.
21	02	09	II	Sh.E.
22	20	25	II	Ec.R.
23	22	33	III	Sh.I.
23	22	41	I	Sh.I.
24	00	48	III	Sh.E.
24	00	51	I	Sh.E.
24	22	12	I	Ec.R.
25	19	20	I	Sh.E.
29	20	29	II	Ec.D.
29	23	03	II	Ec.R.
31	00	37	I	Sh.I.
31	18	03	II	Sh.E.
February				
1	19	06	I	Sh.I.
1	21	16	I	Sh.E.
2	18	36	I	Ec.R.
3	19	01	III	Ec.R.
5	23	07	II	Ec.D.
7	18	11	II	Sh.I.
7	20	40	II	Sh.E.
8	21	02	I	Sh.I.
8	23	12	I	Sh.E.
9	20	32	I	Ec.R.
10	20	44	III	Ec.D.
10	23	03	III	Ec.R.
14	20	47	II	Sh.I.
14	23	16	II	Sh.E.
15	22	58	I	Sh.I.
16	22	27	I	Ec.R.
17	19	37	I	Sh.E.

G.M.T. d	h	m	Sat.	Phen.
February				
21	23	23	II	Sh.I.
23	20	18	II	Ec.R.
24	00	23	I	Ec.R.
24	19	23	I	Sh.I.
24	21	33	I	Sh.E.
25	18	51	I	Ec.R.
28	18	41	III	Sh.I.
28	20	59	III	Sh.E.
March				
2	22	57	II	Ec.R.
3	21	18	I	Sh.I.
3	23	29	I	Sh.E.
4	20	47	I	Ec.R.
7	22	42	III	Sh.I.
10	23	14	I	Sh.I.
11	20	22	II	Sh.E.
11	22	42	I	Ec.R.
12	19	54	I	Sh.E.
18	19	12	III	Ec.R.
18	20	29	II	Sh.I.
18	22	58	II	Sh.E.
19	19	39	I	Sh.I.
19	21	50	I	Sh.E.
20	19	06	I	Ec.R.
25	20	51	III	Ec.D.
26	21	35	I	Sh.I.
27	20	12	II	Ec.R.
27	21	01	I	Ec.R.
April				
4	20	11	I	Sh.E.
11	19	55	I	Sh.I.
12	19	20	I	Ec.R.
12	20	03	II	Sh.E.
12	21	11	III	Sh.E.
19	20	08	II	Sh.I.
19	21	15	I	Ec.R.
28	20	06	II	Ec.R.
October				
2	02	43	II	Ec.D.
2	05	17	II	Ec.R.
3	23	42	II	Sh.E.
8	22	41	III	Sh.I.
9	01	27	III	Sh.E.
9	05	17	II	Ec.D.
10	23	41	II	Sh.I.
12	23	39	I	Sh.E.
19	21	07	II	Ec.D.
19	23	22	I	Sh.I.
20	01	33	I	Sh.E.
25	04	53	II	Sh.I.

G.M.T. d	h	m	Sat.	Phen.
October				
26	03	57	I	Ec.D.
26	20	41	III	Ec.D.
26	23	31	III	Ec.R.
26	23	41	II	Ec.D.
27	01	15	I	Sh.I.
27	22	26	I	Ec.D.
28	20	51	II	Sh.E.
28	21	54	I	Sh.E.
November				
2	05	51	I	Ec.D.
3	00	40	III	Ec.D.
3	02	15	II	Ec.D.
3	03	08	I	Sh.I.
3	03	31	III	Ec.R.
3	05	19	I	Sh.E.
4	00	20	I	Ec.D.
4	20	49	II	Sh.I.
4	21	36	I	Sh.I.
4	23	28	II	Sh.E.
4	23	48	I	Sh.E.
10	04	39	III	Ec.D.
10	04	48	II	Ec.D.
10	05	01	I	Sh.I.
11	02	14	I	Ec.D.
11	23	25	II	Sh.I.
11	23	30	I	Sh.I.
12	01	41	I	Sh.E.
12	02	05	II	Sh.E.
12	20	42	I	Ec.D.
13	20	10	I	Sh.E.
13	21	26	III	Sh.E.
17	06	55	I	Sh.I.
18	04	08	I	Ec.D.
19	01	23	I	Sh.I.
19	02	02	II	Sh.I.
19	03	35	I	Sh.E.
19	04	42	II	Sh.E.
19	22	37	I	Ec.D.
20	19	51	I	Sh.I.
20	20	39	II	Ec.D.
20	22	03	I	Sh.E.
20	22	33	III	Sh.I.
21	01	25	III	Sh.E.
25	06	02	I	Ec.D.
26	03	17	I	Sh.I.
20	04	39	II	Sh.I.
26	05	29	I	Sh.E.
27	00	31	I	Ec.D.
27	21	45	I	Sh.I.
27	23	13	II	Ec.D.
27	23	57	I	Sh.E.
28	19	00	I	Ec.D.

G.M.T. d	h	m	Sat.	Phen.
December				
1	16	38	III	Ec.D.
3	05	10	I	Sh.I.
3	07	15	II	Sh.I.
3	07	23	I	Sh.E.
4	02	25	I	Ec.D.
4	23	39	I	Sh.I.
5	01	47	II	Ec.D.
5	01	51	I	Sh.E.
5	06	30	III	Sh.I.
5	20	54	I	Ec.D.
6	18	07	I	Sh.I.
6	20	20	I	Sh.E.
6	20	34	II	Sh.I.
6	23	15	II	Sh.E.
8	20	38	III	Ec.D.
10	07	04	I	Sh.I.
12	01	32	I	Sh.I.
12	03	45	I	Sh.E.
12	04	21	II	Ec.D.
12	22	49	I	Ec.D.
13	20	01	I	Sh.I.
13	22	14	I	Sh.E.
13	23	11	II	Sh.I.
14	01	52	II	Sh.E.
14	17	17	I	Ec.D.
15	16	42	I	Sh.E.
15	17	38	II	Ec.D.
16	00	37	III	Ec.D.
18	06	15	I	Ec.D.
19	03	26	I	Sh.I.
19	05	39	I	Sh.E.
19	06	56	II	Ec.D.
19	17	25	III	Sh.E.
20	00	43	I	Ec.D.
20	21	55	I	Sh.I.
21	00	08	I	Sh.E.
21	01	48	II	Sh.I.
21	04	29	II	Sh.E.
21	19	12	I	Ec.D.
22	16	23	I	Sh.I.
22	18	36	I	Sh.E.
22	20	13	II	Ec.D.
24	17	48	II	Sh.E.
26	18	28	III	Sh.I.
26	21	26	III	Sh.E.
27	23	49	I	Sh.I.
28	02	02	I	Sh.E.
28	23	22	I	Ec.R.
29	18	18	I	Sh.I.
29	20	31	I	Sh.E.
30	17	50	I	Ec.R.
31	17	44	II	Sh.I.
31	20	25	II	Sh.E.

Jupiter's satellites transit across the disk from east to west, and pass behind the disk from west to east. The shadows that they cast also transit across the disk. With the exception at times of Satellite IV, the satellites also pass through the shadow of the planet, i.e. they are eclipsed. Just before opposition the satellite disappears in the shadow to the west of the planet, and reappears from occultation on the east limb. Immediately after opposition the satellite is occulted at the west limb, and reappears from eclipse to the east of the planet. At times approximately two to four months before and after opposition, both phases of eclipses of Satellite III may be seen. When Satellite IV is eclipsed, both phases may be seen.

The list of phenomena gives most of the eclipses and shadow transits visible in the British Isles under favourable conditions.

Ec. = Eclipse	R = Reappearance
Sh. = Shadow transit	I = Ingress
D = Disappearance	E = Egress

The times given in these predictions are strictly for the centre of the satellite. Observers will appreciate that as the satellite is of considerable size the immersion and emersion phases are not instantaneous. Even when the satellite enters or leaves the shadow along a radius of the shadow the phase can last for several minutes. With satellite IV grazing phenomena can occur so that the light from the satellite may fade and brighten again without a complete eclipse taking place.

CELESTIAL PHENOMENA FOR OBSERVATION IN 1977

ECLIPSES, 1977

There will be three eclipses during 1977, two of the Sun and one of the Moon. *Penumbral eclipses are not mentioned in this section as they are difficult to observe.*

1. A partial eclipse of the Moon on April 4, visible from western Africa, western Europe (including the British Isles), the Atlantic Ocean, South America, part of Antarctica, North America except the north-western part, and the eastern part of the Pacific Ocean. The eclipse begins at $03^h 30^m$ and ends at $05^h 06^m$. At the time of maximum eclipse 0.20 of the Moon's diameter is obscured.

2. An annular eclipse of the Sun on April 18, visible as a partial eclipse from the north-eastern part of South America, part of Antarctica, South Atlantic Ocean, Africa except the north-western part, the extreme southern part of Asia and the Indian Ocean. The eclipse begins at $07^h 33^m$ and ends at $13^h 29^m$. The annular phase begins in the South Atlantic Ocean, crosses the southern part of Africa and ends in the Indian Ocean.

3. A total eclipse of the Sun on October 12. The path of totality begins in the North Pacific Ocean and crosses the northern part of South America. The partial phase is visible from the extreme north-eastern part of Asia, the North Pacific Ocean, North America except the north-eastern part, and the north-western part of South America. The eclipse begins at $17^h 48^m$ and ends at $23^h 06^m$; the total phase begins at $18^h 49^m$ and ends at $22^h 05^m$. The maximum duration of totality is $2^m 37^s$.

OCCULTATION BY URANUS

Uranus will occult a ninth magnitude star on March 10. It will be difficult to observe the actual phases of the occultation since the star is so much fainter than the planet. The event will be of considerable interest to astronomers since, if it is observed successfully, it will be the first occultation by Uranus to be observed. Photoelectric observations should enable us to gain more accurate information about the size of Uranus, and its upper atmosphere. The occultation will be visible from western Australia, Indonesia, Asia (except the eastern part), and Africa and will occur between $20^h \cdot 4$ and $21^h \cdot 6$ G.M.T., approximately.

OCCULTATIONS OF STARS

The list on the opposite page includes most of the occultations visible under favourable conditions in the British Isles. No occultation is included unless the star is at least 10° above the horizon and the Sun sufficiently far below the horizon to permit the star to be seen with the naked eye or in a small telescope. The altitude limit is reduced from 10° to 2° for stars and planets brighter than magnitude 2·0 and such occultations are also predicted in daylight. The column Phase shows whether a disappearance (1) or reappearance (2) is to be observed. The column headed " El. of Moon " gives the elongation of the Moon from the Sun, in de-

grees. The elongation increases from 0° at New Moon to 180° at Full Moon and on to 360° (or 0°) at New Moon again. Times and position angles (*P*), reckoned from the north point in the direction north, east, south, west, are given for Greenwich (Lat. 51° 30′, Long. 0°) and Edinburgh (Lat. 56° 00′, Long. 3° 12′ west). The coefficients *a* and *b* are the variations in the G.M.T. for each degree of longitude (positive to the west) and latitude (positive to the north) respectively: they enable approximate times (to within about 1^m generally) to be found for any point in the British Isles. If the point of observation is $\Delta\lambda$ degrees west and $\Delta\phi$ degrees north, the approximate time is found by adding $a.\Delta\lambda + b.\Delta\phi$ to the given G.M.T.

As an illustration the disappearance of Z.C. 577 on January 1 at Liverpool will be found from both Greenwich and Edinburgh.

	Greenwich	Edinburgh
	°	°
Longitude................	0·0	+3·2
Long. of Liverpool........	+3·0	+3·0
$\Delta\lambda$............	+3·0	−0·2
Latitude.................	+51·5	+56·0
Lat. of Liverpool.........	+53·4	+53·4
$\Delta\phi$....................	+1·9	−2·6
	h m	h m
G.M.T....................	17 46·2	17 59·8
$a.\Delta\lambda$....................	−1·2	0·0
$b.\Delta\phi$....................	+5·3	−9·4
	17 50·3	17 50·4

If the occultation is given for one station but not the other, the reason for the suppression is given by the following code.

N = star not occulted.

A = star's altitude less than 10° (2° for bright stars and planets).

S = Sun not sufficiently below the horizon.

G = occultation is of very short duration.

It will be noticed that in some cases the coefficients *a* and *b* are not given: this is because the occultation is so short that prediction for other places by means of these coefficients would not be reliable.

OCCULTATION OBSERVATIONS

Observations of the times of these occultations are made by both professional and amateur astronomers throughout the world. Such observations are later analysed at the Royal Greenwich Observatory to yield accurate positions of the Moon: this is one method of determining the difference between ephemeris time and universal time. Occultations of stars by the Moon occur almost instantaneously and many of the observations made by amateurs are obtained with the use of a stopwatch which is compared with a time signal immediately after the observation. Thus an accuracy of about one-fifth of a second is obtainable, though the observer's personal equation may amount to one-third or one-half of a second.

Date	Star No.	Mag.	Phase	El. of Moon	GREENWICH				EDINBURGH			
					U.T.	a	b	P	U.T.	a	b	P
				°	h m	m	m	°	h m	m	m	°
Jan. 1	577	6·0	1	138	17 46·2	−0·4	+2·8	37	17 59·8	0·0	+3·6	19
1	590	6·3	1	139	22 39·8	..	..	142	22 22·0	−1·5	−1·9	121
2	610	6·2	1	141	..	N	..	..	2 55·5	..	..	159
3	832	4·7	1	159	..	S	..	..	16 16·6	+0·2	+1·6	83
3	836	5·5	1	160	16 47·7	−0·2	+1·1	112	16 52·8	−0·1	+1·4	101
7	1359	5·1	2	208	20 29·5	0·0	+3·4	227	20 41·8	−0·1	+2·3	247
28	527	6·3	1	108	19 43·7	−1·7	−0·2	87	19 39·3	−1·4	+0·4	72
29	658	4·2	1	118	17 09·8	−1·0	+1·9	66	17 16·7	−0·7	+2·3	53
29	684	6·2	1	120	22 24·2	−1·2	−1·6	101	22 14·4	−1·2	−1·0	89
31	823	6·6	1	132	1 10·3	−0·1	−2·8	135	0 57·7	−0·4	−2·4	125
31	832	4·7	1	132	2 31·3	−0·3	−1·0	63	2 25·8	−0·4	−0·9	56
31	836	5·5	1	133	3 06·8	−0·1	−1·1	70	3 01·4	−0·2	−1·1	63
31	934	6·4	1	141	18 55·4	..	..	155	18 45·4	−1·2	−0·2	132
Feb. 2	1106	3·6	1	156	3 04·7	−0·5	−1·5	91	2 56·2	−0·6	−1·5	85
21	132	6·9	1	44	20 02·1	−0·4	+1·1	21	..	N	..	..
21	136	6·3	1	44	..	N	..	..	20 27·8	−0·1	−3·2	126
25	620	6·3	1	88	20 32·5	−1·1	−1·8	103	20 22·3	−1·1	−1·2	91
28	1029	5·1	1	121	18 05·9	−1·3	+1·2	85	18 08·7	−1·1	+1·8	70
Mar. 3	1397	5·5	1	159	..	G	..	..	23 23·7	−0·4	−3·1	170
8	1886	5·7	2	213	1 43·1	..	..	226	1 43·8	−1·9	+1·4	236
10	2159	5·3	2	240	3 12·0	−1·4	+0·2	276	3 09·1	−1·2	+0·3	281
24	581	6·9	1	57	19 43·7	−0·7	−1·6	92	19 34·7	−0·8	−1·3	82
28	1104	6·8	1	102	..	N	..	..	19 56·9	..	..	161
28	1106	3·6	1	102	20 36·8	−2·0	+0·9	52	20 37·7	..	..	34
29	1237	6·4	1	114	22 06·5	−1·3	−1·1	87	21 58·2	−1·3	−0·8	80
31	1359	5·1	1	127	0 08·7	−0·9	−1·3	81	0 00·2	−1·0	−1·1	76
Apr. 23	944	5·7	1	61	22 26·1	−0·2	−0·8	54	22 21·9	−0·3	−0·7	47
24	1073	6·0	1	71	21 16·1	−0·4	−2·0	113	21 05·9	−0·5	−1·9	107
30	1649	6·3	1	133	0 24·1	..	..	36	..	N	..	..
May 25	1489	6·8	1	88	21 42·5	−0·7	−1·8	108	21 32·5	−0·7	−1·7	104
June 23	1685	4·5	1	82	22 06·2	−0·5	−1·4	80	21 58·0	−0·6	−1·4	76
26	2053	4·6	1	121	22 34·1	−1·1	−1·0	83	22 26·2	−1·1	−0·9	78
July 9	257	4·5	1	280	2 49·6	..	..	139	..	S	..	..
26	2436	6·3	1	130	21 10·6	−1·4	−0·8	129	..	S	..	..
Aug. 2	3362	5·9	2	212	23 57·4	..	..	173	0 10·1	−0·5	+2·4	190
12	1106	3·6	1	327	3 48·6	+0·1	+1·5	87	..	S	..	..
Sept. 5	650	5·7	2	262	1 23·1	−0·5	+1·9	251	1 29·8	−0·5	+1·8	262
11	1410	5·3	2	331	4 33·5	−0·2	+0·6	304	..	A	..	..
20	2658	5·4 −6·2	1	95	19 10·9	−1·1	+0·9	29	19 13·1	..	..	15
21	2826	4·0	1	108	19 26·2	−1·6	−0·4	109	19 20·4	−1·4	−0·1	102
25	3269	4·3	1	149	0 32·8	−1·6	−2·2	115	0 20·7	−1·2	−1·3	98
29	257	4·5	1	199	5 17·7	−0·7	−1·0	73	5 11·9	−0·7	−0·6	59
Oct. 4	878	5·5	2	254	2 09·1	−0·9	+2·3	240	2 15·3	−0·9	+1·8	254
16	2448	6·4	1	50	17 39·8	−0·9	−0·3	52	..	S	..	..
20	3070	6·6	1	104	18 40·4	−1·4	+0·6	67	18 39·1	−1·2	+0·7	60
30	814	5·3	2	222	23 52·8	−1·3	+0·5	295	23 49·7	−1·3	−0·1	313
Nov. 2	1106	3·6	1	247	5 48·0	−1·8	+0·3	65	5 45·5	−1·8	+1·2	52
2	1106	3·6	1	247	..	S	..	..	6 36·2	−0·6	−3·2	332
4	1341	4·3	1	269	..	S	..	..	6 42·2	−1·8	+0·8	64
17	3169	6·2	1	86	18 14·7	−1·4	+0·2	72	18 11·9	−1·2	+0·4	62
18	3308	6·2	1	99	18 08·8	−1·0	+1·5	33	18 13·1	−0·7	+1·7	21
19	3459	6·6	1	113	23 00·8	−0·9	−1·2	81	22 54·0	−0·8	−0·7	66
Dec. 15	3269	4·3	1	68	19 01·1	−0·6	+0·6	31	19 03·9	−0·2	+1·4	12
15	3278	5·4	1	69	20 40·0	−1·0	−2·6	116	20 27·9	−0·8	−1·7	97
19	247	6·7	1	117	22 03·9	−1·0	+1·3	30	22 10·8	..	..	5
20	257	4·5	1	118	1 04·4	−0·5	+1·6	16	..	N	..	..
30	1468	4·9	2	230	3 20·1	−1·5	−0·6	289	3 13·0	−1·3	−0·6	298

MEAN PLACES OF STARS, 1977·0

NAME	Mag.	R.A.	Dec.	Spectrum
		h m	° '	
α Andromedæ Alpheratz.......	2·1	0 07·2	+28 58	Aop
β Cassiopeiæ Caph............	2·4	0 07·9	+59 01	F5
γ Pegasi Algenib...............	2·9	0 12·0	+15 03	B2
α Phœnicis..................	2·4	0 25·1	−42 26	Ko
α Cassiopeiæ Schedar..........	2·3	0 39·2	+56 25	Ko
β Ceti Diphda...............	2·2	0 42·4	−18 07	Ko
γ Cassiopeiæ★...............	Var.	0 55·3	+60 36	Bop
β Andromedæ Mirach.........	2·4	1 08·4	+35 30	Mo
δ Cassiopeiæ.................	2·8	1 24·3	+60 07	A5
α Eridani Achernar...........	0·6	1 36·9	−57 21	B5
β Arietis Sheratan.............	2·7	1 53·4	+20 42	A5
γ Andromedæ Almak.........	2·3	2 02·5	+42 13	Ko
α Arietis Hamal.............	2·2	2 05·9	+23 21	K2
α Ursæ Minoris Polaris........	2·1	2 09·2	+89 10	F8
β Persei Algol★...............	Var.	3 06·7	+40 52	B8
α Persei Mirfak..............	1·9	3 22·7	+49 47	F5
η Tauri Alcyone.............	3·0	3 46·1	+24 02	B5p
α Tauri Aldebaran............	1·1	4 34·6	+16 28	K5
β Orionis Rigel..............	0·3	5 13·4	− 8 14	B8p
α Aurigæ Capella.............	0·2	5 15·0	+45 59	Go
γ Orionis Bellatrix...........	1·7	5 23·9	+ 6 20	B2
β Tauri Elnath..............	1·8	5 24·8	+28 35	B8
δ Orionis...................	2·5	5 30·8	− 0 19	Bo
α Leporis...................	2·7	5 31·7	−17 50	Fo
ε Orionis...................	1·7	5 35·0	− 1 13	Bo
ζ Orionis...................	2·0	5 39·6	− 1 57	Bo
κ Orionis...................	2·2	5 46·7	− 9 41	Bo
α Orionis Betelgeuse★..........	Var.	5 53·9	+ 7 24	Mo
β Aurigæ Menkalinan.........	2·1	5 57·8	+44 57	Aop
β Canis Majoris Mirzam.......	2·0	6 21·7	−17 57	B1
α Carinæ Canopus............	−0·9	6 23·4	−52 41	Fo
γ Geminorum Alhena.........	1·9	6 36·4	+16 25	Ao
α Canis Majoris Sirius.........	−1·6	6 44·1	−16 41	Ao
ε Canis Majoris..............	1·6	6 57·7	−28 56	B1
δ Canis Majoris..............	2·0	7 07·5	−26 21	F8p
α Geminorum Castor.........	1·6	7 33·1	+31 56	Ao
α Canis Minoris Procyon........	0·5	7 38·1	+ 5 17	F5
β Geminorum Pollux.........	1·2	7 43·9	+28 05	Ko
ζ Puppis....................	2·3	8 02·8	−39 56	Od
γ Velorum...................	1·9	8 08·8	−47 16	Oap
ε Carinæ...................	1·7	8 22·0	−59 26	Ko
δ Velorum..................	2·0	8 44·1	−54 37	Ao
λ Velorum Suhail............	2·2	9 07·1	−43 20	K5
β Carinæ...................	1·8	9 13·0	−69 37	Ao
ι Carinæ...................	2·2	9 16·5	−59 11	Fo
α Hydræ Alphard.............	2·2	9 26·5	− 8 33	K2
α Leonis Regulus.............	1·3	10 07·1	+12 05	B8
γ Leonis Algeiba.............	2·6	10 18·7	+19 58	Ko
β Ursæ Majoris Merak........	2·4	11 00·5	+56 30	Ao
α Ursæ Majoris Dubhe........	1·9	11 02·3	+61 53	Ko

★ γ Cassiopeiæ, 1976 mag. 2·4.   β Persei, mag. 2·2 to 3·5.
α Orionis, mag. 0·1 to 1·2.

The positions of heavenly bodies on the celestial sphere are defined by two co-ordinates, right ascension and declination, which are analogous to longitude and latitude on the surface of the Earth. If we imagine the plane of the terrestrial equator extended indefinitely, it will cut the celestial sphere in a great circle known as the celestial equator. Similarly the plane of the Earth's orbit, when extended, cuts in the great circle called the ecliptic. The two intersections of these circles are known as the First Point of Aries and the First Point of Libra. If from any star a perpendicular be drawn to the celestial equator, the length of this perpendicular is the star's declination. The arc, measured eastwards along the equator from the First Point of Aries to the foot of this perpendicular, is the right ascension. An alternative definition of right ascension is that it is the angle at the celestial pole (where the Earth's axis, if prolonged, would meet the sphere) between the great circles to the First Point of Aries and to the star.

The plane of the Earth's equator has a slow movement, so that our reference system for right ascension and declination is not fixed. The consequent alteration in these quantities from year to year is called precession. In right ascension it is an increase of about 3^s a year for equatorial stars, and larger or smaller amounts for stars near the pole. In declination it varies between $+20''$ and $−20''$ according to the right ascension of the star.

A star or other body crosses the meridian when the sidereal time is equal to its right ascension. The altitude is then a maximum, and may be deduced by remembering that the altitude of the elevated pole is numerically equal to the latitude, while that of the equator at its intersection with the meridian is equal to the co-latitude, or complement of the latitude.

NAME	Mag.	R.A.	Dec.	Spectrum
		h　m	°　′	
δ Leonis	2·6	11 12·9	+20 39	A3
β Leonis *Denebola*	2·2	11 47·9	+14 42	A2
γ Ursæ Majoris *Phecda*	2·5	11 52·6	+53 49	Ao
γ Corvi	2·8	12 14·6	−17 25	B8
α Crucis	1·0	12 25·3	−62 58	B1
γ Crucis	1·6	12 29·9	−56 59	M3
γ Centauri	2·4	12 40·2	−48 50	Ao
γ Virginis	2·9	12 40·5	− 1 19	Fo
β Crucis	1·5	12 46·4	−59 34	B1
ε Ursæ Majoris *Alioth*	1·7	12 53·0	+56 05	Ao*p*
α Canum Venaticorum	2·9	12 55·0	+38 27	Ao*p*
ζ Ursæ Majoris *Mizar*	2·4	13 23·0	+55 03	A2*p*
α Virginis *Spica*	1·2	13 24·0	−11 02	B2
η Ursæ Majoris *Alkaid*	1·9	13 46·6	+49 26	B3
β Centauri *Hadar*	0·9	14 02·2	−60 16	B1
θ Centauri	2·3	14 05·3	−36 15	Ko
α Bootis *Arcturus*	0·2	14 14·6	+19 18	Ko
α Centauri *Rigil Kent*	0·1	14 38·0	−60 44	Go
ε Bootis	2·7	14 44·0	+27 10	Ko
β Ursæ Minoris *Kochab*	2·2	14 50·8	+74 15	K5
α Coronæ Borealis *Alphecca*	2·3	15 33·7	+26 47	Ao
δ Scorpii	2·5	15 59·0	−22 33	Bo
β Scorpii	2·9	16 04·1	−19 45	B1
α Scorpii *Antares*	1·2	16 28·0	−26 23	Mo
α Trianguli Australis	1·9	16 46·2	−68 59	K2
ε Scorpii	2·4	16 48·7	−34 15	Ko
α Herculis*	Var.	17 13·6	+14 25	M3
λ Scorpii	1·7	17 32·0	−37 05	B2
α Ophiuchi *Rasalhague*	2·1	17 33·9	+12 35	A5
θ Scorpii	2·0	17 35·7	−42 59	Fo
κ Scorpii	2·5	17 40·9	−39 01	B2
γ Draconis	2·4	17 56·1	+51 29	K5
ε Sagittarii *Kaus Australis*	1·9	18 22·6	−34 24	Ao
α Lyræ *Vega*	0·1	18 36·2	+38 46	Ao
σ Sagittarii	2·1	18 53·8	−26 20	B3
β Cygni *Albireo*	3·2	19 29·8	+27 55	Ko
α Aquilæ *Altair*	0·9	19 49·7	+ 8 48	A5
β Capricorni	3·2	20 19·7	−14 51	Go
γ Cygni	2·3	20 21·4	+40 11	F8*p*
α Pavonis	2·1	20 23·8	−56 49	B3
α Cygni *Deneb*	1·3	20 40·6	+45 12	A2*p*
α Cephei *Alderamin*	2·6	21 18·0	+62 29	A5
ε Pegasi	2·5	21 43·1	+ 9 46	Ko
δ Capricorni	3·0	21 45·8	−16 14	A5
α Gruis	2·2	22 06·8	−47 04	B5
δ Cephei*	Var.	22 28·3	+58 18	*
β Gruis	2·2	22 41·3	−47 00	M3
α Piscis Austrini *Fomalhaut*	1·3	22 56·4	−29 45	A3
β Pegasi *Scheat*	2.6	23 02·7	+27 57	Mo
α Pegasi *Markab*	2·6	23 03·6	+15 05	Ao

*αHerculis, mag. 3·1 to 3·9.

δCephei, mag. 3·7 to 4·4, Spectrum F5 to Go

Thus in London (Lat. 51° 30′) the meridian altitude of *Sirius* is found as follows:

	°	′
Altitude of equator	38	30
Declination south	16	41
Difference	21	49

The altitude of *Capella* (Dec. +45° 59′) at lower transit is:

	°	′
Altitude of pole	51	30
Polar distance of star	44	01
Difference	7	29

The brightness of a heavenly body is denoted by its magnitude. Omitting the exceptionally bright stars *Sirius* and *Canopus*, the twenty brightest stars are of the first magnitude, while the faintest stars visible to the naked eye are of the sixth magnitude. The magnitude scale is a precise one, as a difference of five magnitudes represents a ratio of 100 to 1 in brightness, Typical second magnitude stars are *Polaris* and the stars in the Belt of Orion. The scale is most easily fixed in memory by comparing the stars with Norton's *Star Atlas* (see page 138). The stars *Sirius* and *Canopus* and the planets Venus and Jupiter are so bright that their magnitudes are expressed by negative numbers. A small telescope will show stars down to the ninth or tenth magnitude, while stars fainter than the twentieth magnitude may be photographed by long exposures with the largest telescopes.

Some of the astronomical information in this ALMANACK has been taken from the *Astronomical Ephemeris*, and is published here by arrangement with, and with the permission of, the Controller of H.M. Stationery Office.

THE STRUCTURE OF THE UNIVERSE

The Solar System, although occupying a volume of space large by terrestrial standards, is only a very tiny fraction of the whole Universe. The Sun itself is just one of the millions of stars which make up our Galaxy, and our Galaxy is just one of the millions of galaxies which are distributed through the visible Universe. All these stars and galaxies are in motion, many of them with enormous velocities; yet they are so remote that to the naked eye they present almost the same configurations for a period of many thousands of years, and even with telescopic aid the measurement of their motions is a delicate matter. The nearest star is about 250,000 times as far away as the Sun, the Great Galaxy in Andromeda, one of the few galaxies visible to the naked eye, is over 500,000 times as far away as the nearest star, and the largest telescopes can penetrate to a distance of at least 500 times that of the Andromeda Galaxy. It is convenient to express astronomical distances in terms of the time that light takes to accomplish the journey. Light travels at the rate of 300,000 kilometres a second; it takes $1\frac{1}{4}$ seconds to reach us from the Moon, our nearest neighbour in space; just over 8 minutes to reach us from the Sun; four years from the nearest star; two million years from the Andromeda Galaxy, and over 1000 million years from the most distant bodies yet photographed. We therefore talk about a star as being so many light years distant. Astronomers also use another unit of distance, the parsec. 1 parsec equals 3·26 light years.

THE STARS

The stars are classed according to their apparent brightness in magnitudes. A few of the brightest stars are brighter than the first magnitude. Stars as faint as the sixth magnitude can be seen by the naked eye. The 5 metre (200-inch) telescope, the world's largest, on Mount Palomar in California, can photograph stars of the 23rd magnitude, which is about 650 million times fainter than the first magnitude. This large range in the apparent brightness of the stars is due to a combination of two factors. The first of these is distance. According to a standard law of optics, the apparent brightness of any given luminous object is inversely proportional to the square of its distance away. Thus, if two similar stars are at distances one of which is 10 times the other, the more distant star will appear to be 100 times fainter than the nearer star. The second factor affecting the apparent brightness of a star is its real intrinsic brightness. There are many different kinds of stars; some are very large luminous objects, others are small and faint.

The distances of the stars can be determined in a variety of ways. The direct trigonometric method consists in measuring the minute difference of direction of the star as seen from opposite sides of the Earth's orbit; this is always done photographically. The distances of about 15,000 stars have been measured in this way, but the method has very little accuracy for distances greater than about 250 light years. For more distant stars, distances may be estimated from a study of their spectra. The distances of some double and variable stars can

be found from their special characteristics. A star is said to be at a distance of one parsec if the radius of the Earth's orbit round the Sun subtends an angle of one second of arc at the star.

When the distance of any star has been determined and its apparent magnitude measured, the real intrinsic brightness of the star may be determined. As a convenient convention, astronomers adopt as the "absolute magnitude" of a star (or other object) that apparent magnitude which the star would have if it were moved from its real position to a distance of ten parsecs. Conversely, if the absolute magnitude of a star is known by spectroscopic or other methods, and its apparent magnitude is observed, its distance may be calculated.

STELLAR SPECTRA

A large number of stars have been examined spectroscopically, and it is found that their spectra fall, with very few exceptions, into a sequence of types, denoted by the letters O, B, A, F, G, K, M; the types merge imperceptibly one into the next. O and B stars, exemplified by the three stars which form Orion's belt, have spectra showing helium and hydrogen lines. A stars, like Sirius, are characterized by very strong hydrogen lines. F, G and K stars, like Procyon, our Sun, and Arcturus, respectively, have spectra showing large numbers of metallic lines, and hydrogen lines much weaker than in A stars. Finally, the M stars, like Betelgeuse, show very complex molecular spectra, chiefly of titanium oxide. This sequence of spectral types O to M is essentially a temperature sequence, the O stars being the hottest and the M stars the coolest. Approximate values of the surface temperatures of the stars are, a value for the middle of each type being quoted in degrees Centigrade: O, 30,000°; B, 18,000°; A, 10,000°; F, 7000°; G, 5500°; K, 4500°; M, 3000°. This sequence is also one of colour, the O stars being the bluest and the M stars the reddest. The colour of a star is capable of precise definition and measurement; there is a very close correlation between colour and surface temperature, and between colour and spectral type. The latter correlation is so good that for many astrophysical purposes colour measurements are used instead of spectral types.

When the spectral types (or colours) of a large number of stars are correlated with their absolute magnitudes, a surprising result emerges. The sequence O to M is one of decreasing absolute brightness. Approximate values of the absolute magnitudes of the stars are, a value for the middle of each type being quoted: O,−4; B, −2; A, +1; F, +3; G, +5; K, +7; M, +11. A graphical illustration of this relation between spectral type and absolute magnitude is known as the Hertzsprung-Russell Diagram (or, when colours are used instead of spectral types, as a colour-magnitude diagram). The relationship represented by this diagram is one of the corner stones of modern astrophysics. The above series of stars of types O to M and absolute magnitude decreasing from − 4 to +11, or fainter, is known as the "main se-

quence", and a large proportion of all known stars are members of this sequence. A relatively small proportion of the stars of spectral types O to M do not belong to the main sequence. Closer examination of the spectra of these stars reveals slight differences between their spectra and ordinary stars of nominally the same type on the main sequence. These differences are sufficiently characteristic to enable the two types of stars to be segregated spectroscopically without independent knowledge of their absolute magnitudes. These stars are found to be brighter than the corresponding main sequence stars of the same types. Most of those of types G, K and M have absolute magnitudes about 0; many of those types O to F and few of types G to M are still brighter, with absolute magnitudes ranging from −4 to −7. The exceptional brightness of these stars is believed to be due to their sizes: those with absolute magnitudes about 0 are called giants, those of −4 to −7 are called supergiants.

The sizes of the stars have been determined mostly by theoretical calculation. In very few cases direct determinations have been made by means of an interferometer, and sizes can also be inferred from observations of some eclipsing binary stars. The Sun is 1,392,000 kilometres in diameter. The main sequence is found to be a sequence of diminishing radii; an O star has a radius of about 20 times that of the Sun, while an average M star has a radius of one-third of the Sun. The giant stars of types G to M have radii between 10 and 100 times the Sun; supergiants have radii between 30 and 1000 times the Sun.

It is possible to determine the chemical composition of a star from a study of its spectrum. This has been done for main sequence stars and for giants and supergiants. All these stars appear to be of similar chemical composition, about 80 per cent by numbers of atoms being hydrogen, most of the remainder helium, heavier elements being less than one per cent of the total. All the differences between types O to M and main sequence, giant and supergiant stars can be accounted for by variations of surface temperature and of size (affecting the spectrum through the surface gravity).

A few stars cannot be classified according to the standard sequence O to M. Among these those classified as R and N stars show strong bands of carbon compounds instead of the titanium oxide of M stars, and the S stars show zirconium oxide instead of titanium oxide. A number of still less common types of stars show anomalous lines of strontium, barium, manganese, silicon, europium, lanthanum and other elements. The reasons for all these peculiarities are not known; it is probable that many of them are genuine differences from the standard chemical composition of the majority of the stars.

DOUBLE STARS

Many stars which appear single to the naked eye are found to be double in the telescope. These are frequently found to be in orbital motion round one another in periods varying from about one year to many thousands of years. Some binary stars are so close together that they cannot be seen separately even in large telescopes; their binary nature is revealed by the spectroscope. The varying motions of the stars in their orbits can be detected by the Doppler shifts of lines in their spectra. Some spectroscopic binaries, as they are called, are of special interest in that during their orbital motion the two components periodically eclipse each other, and the combined light of the two stars will vary. This happens when the Earth is nearly in the plane of the binary star orbits. Such binaries are called eclipsing variables, of which the best known is *Algol*, or β Persei.

VARIABLE STARS

We have already referred to the eclipsing variables, whose light variation is due to a geometrical cause. Some single stars vary in light. These include Cepheid variables, with periods of from a few hours up to about fifty days, long-period variables with periods of from a hundred to a thousand days, and numerous types of variable stars in which the periods and light fluctuations are entirely irregular. Many of these variations are attributed to pulsation of the stars by alternate expansion and contraction. The Cepheids are of particular interest because of the period-luminosity relation: the longer the period of a Cepheid the brighter is its mean absolute magnitude. An observation of the period of variation of the star immediately tells us its absolute magnitude and thence its distance.

Novæ are stars whose light increases by 10 to 15 magnitudes in a few days, and then fades gradually to normal brightness, reached a year or two later. The cause of the brightening is the sudden expansion of the star, but the reason for this is unknown. Supernovæ are stars whose brightness increases by up to 20 magnitudes; they are believed to be caused by the explosion of the whole star.

STAR CLUSTERS

Stars frequently occur in clusters; two types of clusters are known. The first, called open (or galactic) clusters, are groups of up to two or three hundred stars; the second, globular clusters, contain over one hundred thousand stars. The open clusters are found mainly in the neighbourhood of the Milky Way, the globular clusters avoid the Milky Way. Several open clusters are visible to the naked eye: the Pleiades, the Hyades and Praesepe are the best known of these. The colour-magnitude diagrams of open clusters are generally similar to those of nearby single stars; the most important difference is that when a cluster contains blue O and B stars it does not also contain red giant stars. The colour-magnitude diagrams of globular clusters are very similar among themselves, but differ greatly from the diagrams of galactic clusters and nearby stars. The main sequence does not exist in any globular cluster for stars of types O, B and A; red giants are present in all the clusters, and they range up to absolute magnitude −3. There is an additional sequence of stars with absolute magnitudes about 0 which is quite unlike any sequence in the diagrams for nearby stars.

INTERSTELLAR MATTER

The space between the stars is not empty; it contains a mixture of gas and dust which serves to

dim the light of distant objects and tends to make them appear redder than normal. Very distant objects may be obscured completely if they lie in or near the plane of the Milky Way. The density of interstellar gas averages one atom in each cubic centimetre; this may be compared with a density 26 million million million times as great in ordinary air at normal pressure and temperature. As is the case for cosmic material in general, hydrogen predominates in interstellar gas. In addition to this widely distributed matter, there are denser clouds of gas and dust existing locally. These are frequently in evidence as dark clouds in front of a brighter stellar background. Some clouds have hot stars embedded, and the interstellar gas may then shine either by reflection of the starlight or it may be heated until it glows and emits its own characteristic light. Such dense glowing clouds are termed galactic nebulæ. Sometimes the cloud is more regular in shape and is excited by one star; such clouds are termed planetary nebulæ, and the Ring Nebula in Lyra is an excellent example of these objects. Planetary nebulæ are among the denser interstellar formations; their densities range up to 20,000 atoms per cubic centimetre. Hot stars can make ordinary interstellar gas glow even when the density is low; the spherical region of glowing gas surrounding a hot star is termed an ionized-hydrogen region. These regions are of particular interest for the study of the Galaxy and of extragalactic nebulæ because they are relatively bright and can be seen at large distances.

THE GALAXY

A cursory glance at the sky is sufficient to show that the fainter stars are concentrated towards the region of the Milky Way. This implies that the stars form a flattened system which extends farther in the direction of the Milky Way than it does at right angles to it. It is now known that this system called the Galaxy, is about 100,000 light years in diameter, and has a thickness of less than 5000 light years. The Milky Way is the centre plane of the system. We in the Solar System are situated at about 27,000 light years from the centre, and not far from the central plane. All the objects mentioned earlier, single and multiple stars, variable stars, novæ and supernovæ, galactic and globular clusters, interstellar gas, dust and galactic and planetary nebulæ, form part of the Galaxy. The distribution of these various objects in the Galaxy is not all alike. The hot O and B stars, galactic clusters and interstellar matter are closely concentrated towards the Milky Way plane, mostly lying within 300 light years on either side of the plane. The stars of types A to M tend to be less closely concentrated to the plane; globular clusters show hardly any concentration, forming a nearly spherical distribution stretching to over 30,000 light years from the plane. Most Cepheid variables with periods of more than a day are closely concentrated to the galactic plane; those with periods of less than a day have a distribution similar to that of globular clusters.

The Galaxy has a spiral structure similar to that of some external galaxies. This structure was first shown by studying the positions of O and B stars; these trace out spiral arms. Radio astronomers subsequently found that interstellar neutral hydrogen gas emits radio waves on 21 centimetres wavelength. Studies of this radio radiation have enabled the density and distribution of interstellar hydrogen to be determined. The hydrogen gas is found to be situated along the same spiral arms as the O and B stars. Indeed, there is a remarkably close correlation between O and B stars and interstellar matter.

Observations by both optical and radio methods have proved that the whole Galaxy is rotating about an axis through its centre perpendicular to the galactic plane. The period of rotation varies with distance from the centre, an average value being 200 million years. The total mass of the Galaxy is about 100 thousand million times the mass of the Sun.

STELLAR POPULATIONS

The two different types of colour-magnitude (or Hertzsprung-Russell) diagram mentioned above appear to apply not only to star clusters but to other objects in our Galaxy and in other galaxies. There seems little doubt that there are two fundamentally different types of stellar population: Population I has a colour-magnitude diagram similar to that of nearby stars and open clusters, Population II has a diagram similar to that for globular clusters. Population I includes both open clusters, longer-period Cepheid variables and supergiant stars, and is intimately associated with interstellar matter; it occurs prominently in the spiral structure of our Galaxy, and is generally concentrated towards the galactic plane. Population II includes the globular clusters, short-period Cepheids and other objects, tends to avoid the spiral structure of the Galaxy, has little or no interstellar dust associated with it, but may be associated with interstellar hydrogen gas, and is not concentrated towards the galactic plane. All the available evidence suggests that Population II stars are old objects, with ages averaging 5000 million years, while Population I stars are much younger, with ages in a few cases of only a few million years. Population II stars have lower content of metals relative to hydrogen than Population I stars.

EXTERNAL GALAXIES

Outside our own Galaxy there are large numbers of objects having a more or less hazy appearance on photographs. These are known as external galaxies. Some show a well-defined spiral structure, some are elliptical in form with no marked structural features, and some are irregular in form. The spiral galaxies consist of a central bulge surrounded by spiral arms embedded in a disk-shaped structure. The elliptical galaxies and the central bulges of the spiral galaxies are believed to be composed of stars of Population II. The spiral arms are composed of Population I and some Population II, together with large quantities of gas and dust. The presence of dust is evident because of the dark patches of absorption which are a feature of the photographs of spiral galaxies; the presence of hydrogen gas has been proved by the observation of regions of glowing gas and by the

NEBULAE, CLUSTERS AND GALAXIES

Designation	Name	Type	Mag.	R.A.	Dec.	Angular Size
				(1950·0)		
				h m	°	′ ′
N.G.C. 104	47 Tucanae	GC	4	0 22	−72·4	42×42
M.31	Andromeda (Galaxy)	G	4	0 40	+41·0	160×40
Nubecula Minor		—	—	0 50	−73·9	(10 sq. deg.)
M.33		G	7	1 31	+30·4	60×40
H. VI. 33, 34	Double Cluster	OC	4	2 18	+56·9	2(36×36)
M.45	Pleiades	OC	—	3 45	+23·9	90×60
	Hyades	OC	—	4 26	+15·8	180×180
Nubecula Major		—	—	5 25	−69·3	(42 sq. deg.)
M.1	"Crab" nebula	PN	10	5 32	+22·0	6×4
M.42	"Great" nebula	N	6	5 33	− 5·4	66×60
N.G.C. 2070	30 Doradus	OC+N	—	5 39	−69·1	—
M.44	"Praesepe" or "Beehive"	OC	4	8 37	+20·2	90×90
N.G.C. 3372	η Carinae	N	—	10 43	−59·4	80×80
N.G.C. 4755	κ Crucis	OC	—	12 51	−60·1	10×10
	ω Centauri	GC	3	13 24	−47·1	45×45
M.3		GC	6	13 40	+28·6	19×19
M.13		GC	6	16 40	+36·6	23×23
M.7		OC	5	17 51	−34·8	50×50
M.20	"Trifid" nebula	N	8	17 59	−23·0	29×27
M.8	"Lagoon" nebula	N	8	18 01	−24·4	90×40
M.57	"Ring" nebula	PN	9	18 52	+33·0	1×1
M.55		GC	5	19 37	−31·0	15×15
M.27	"Dumb-bell" nebula	PN	8	19 57	+22·6	8×4

Types: N—Nebula.   PN—Planetary Nebula.   OC—Open Cluster.   GC—Globular Cluster.   G—Galaxy.

reception of radio waves on 21 centimetres wavelength. In a few of the nearer galaxies individual stars have been observed, and comparison with stars in our own Galaxy provides estimates of the distances and sizes of the galaxies. Many of them are found to be comparable with our own Galaxy—with diameters of 100,000 light years and masses 100 thousand million times the Sun. The two Magellanic Clouds are the nearest galaxies to our own, their distances being about 140,000 light years. The best known external galaxy is the Great Galaxy in Andromeda, at a distance of 2,000,000 light years; this spiral galaxy is believed to be similar to our own Galaxy in size and stellar content. External galaxies frequently occur in large clusters, each containing hundreds of galaxies. Many galaxies are in rotation in a manner similar to our own Galaxy and with comparable periods.

RADIO SOURCES

In addition to the 21 centimetre hydrogen radiation received from interstellar gas, radio noise is received on other wavelengths. Some of this originates in well-known objects; one important source of radio noise is the Crab Nebula, which is known to be the remains of the supernova of A.D. 1054. Some extragalactic nebulæ are also sources of radio noise, but many of the apparently isolated sources, "radio stars", do not seem to coincide with any visible stars or nebulæ. Recently several sources have been discovered which exhibit extremely regular variations in radio "brightness", with incredibly short periods (of the order of 1 second). These sources are now called "pulsars".

QUASARS

The observation of occultations of radio sources by the Moon has led to the accurate determination of the positions of these radio sources. Thus it has been possible to use large optical telescopes with small angular fields of view and high magnifications to photograph these positions. This has led to the discovery of a new type of object called a quasar (or quasi-stellar object or QSO). On a photographic plate such objects appear almost stellar, so they are not readily identified without the help of information from the radio astronomers. Spectroscopic examination of four of them shows that, like external galaxies, they have enormous velocities of recession. Such velocities imply great distances, yet no ordinary star (or even supergiant) would be detectable at even a fraction of these distances. The answer to the question ' what are quasars ? ' is not yet known with any certainty but the current explanation is that they are radio sources with the shape of a star but many millions of times larger, with unusually high ultra-violet radiation and sometimes with large red shifts. Already several dozen quasars are known.

COSMOLOGY

The large scale problems of the Universe are concerned with the motions and distribution of the extragalactic nebulæ through the observable region of space. It has been found that in spite of the tendency of galaxies to cluster together, on a still larger scale the galaxies are distributed remarkably uniformly. Observations have shown that distant galaxies have spectra showing " red-shifts ", which have been interpreted as Doppler shifts due to velocities of recession; all the distant galaxies appear to be moving away from us with velocities proportional to their distance. This suggests that the whole Universe is in expansion. One theory postulates a gigantic initial explosion some 5,000 million years ago. Another postulates a steady state, with continuous creation of matter producing new galaxies which eventually force the existing ones to continually increasing distances. Some recent observations suggest that the latter theory is no longer tenable.

THE SOLAR SYSTEM

The Sun is one of the millions of stars that make up the Universe. The energy that it radiates in the form of light and heat is maintained by nuclear reactions among the atoms in its interior. It is surrounded by an immense number of comparatively cold planets and comets, together with smaller particles that give rise to meteors and the zodiacal light.

The planets are solid bodies revolving about the Sun in elliptical orbits with the Sun at one focus, and at distances related to the periodic times in accordance with Kepler's third law: the squares of the periodic times vary as the cubes of the semi-major axes. All revolve in the same direction, the orbits being only slightly inclined to the plane of the ecliptic in which the Earth moves round the Sun. As seen from the Earth, therefore, the planets are always near the ecliptic, moving in general from west to east round the sky. Once in every such revolution the planet appears to become stationary and then retrograde, forming a looped path which is a consequence of the Earth's own orbital movement.

The nine major planets, of which the Earth is one, are of special interest, the five that are visible to the naked eye having been known from the earliest times. Six have satellites or moons revolving round them. These, like the planets themselves, are not self-luminous, but shine by the reflected light of the Sun. Notes on these bodies are given in the following pages. The thousands of minor planets that are also known, although of less interest to the observer, afford many problems to the mathematical astronomer. Comets are also members of the solar system; their orbits are inclined at all angles to the ecliptic, and are generally highly eccentric, reaching out to immense distances in space. The light of a comet is not due entirely to reflected sunlight, but partly to fluorescence caused by selective absorption of solar radiation. The return of a comet of short period may be predicted with some accuracy, but most comets appear quite unexpectedly. Meteoric dust appears to have a common origin with the comets, since some meteor showers have been shown to follow the orbits of certain comets.

THE SUN

The Sun is the ultimate source of most of the chemical energy available on the Earth. Hence the origin of that energy, which reaches the Earth in the form of light and heat from within the Sun, is of particular interest. The spectral distribution of the light from the Sun's surface indicates a temperature of about 5,700° C., but a relatively short distance inside the surface the temperature reaches 1,000,000° and deeper in the interior, near the centre, it is believed to be in the region of 14,000,000°. Now the constitution of the Sun is similar to that of the Earth, as shown by similarities in the chemical spectra of solar and terrestrial sources; but at these high temperatures the atoms become stripped of their outer layers of electrons. In this highly " ionized " state the substance of the Sun acts in much the same way as a " perfect gas "

does on the Earth, even though the density is high. Furthermore, the thermal velocities are sufficiently great for nuclear collisions to take place. Nuclear energy can be released in the Sun by a variety of collision-processes, in each of which the light atoms of hydrogen, by far the most abundant element, are ultimately combined into heavier atoms of helium. This energy, released almost entirely in the central regions, is transmitted by radiation and convection to the cooler outer layers of the Sun and thence to outer space, a very small proportion of it falling on the Earth. It is possible to infer with some certainty, by considering the Sun as a typical star, that this process has been going on for about three thousand million years and that it may be expected to continue similarly for perhaps a further ten thousand million years.

As viewed by projection through a low-power telescope the Sun presents various interesting features. Over most of its surface a fine mottling can be seen under good observing conditions. This " granulation " is visible evidence of a turbulent convective layer near the surface. Much more noticeable surface-markings called sunspots appear sporadically in the equatorial zones of the Sun and up to latitudes of 40°–50° north and south. These sunspots, which are sometimes visible to the naked eye, provide direct evidence of the rotation of the Sun on an axis which is inclined about 7° to the line joining the poles of the ecliptic. They also indicate that the Sun does not rotate as a solid body but somewhat faster in equatorial regions than at higher latitudes. Its mean sidereal rotation-period is about 25 days but the motion of the Earth in its orbit around the Sun results in an apparent rotation-period, as viewed from the Earth, of approximately 27 days. Associated with sunspots are bright regions called faculae but these can not be seen when the spot is near the centre of the disk.

Sunspots vary in size from small dark specks, barely visible in a telescope, but actually with an area of about a million square km., to large dark markings several thousand times as great. The largest spot ever measured (April 1947) covered 18,000 million square kilometres at its greatest, or approximately 0·7 per cent of the Sun's visible surface. Correspondingly, sunspots have lifetimes ranging from a few hours in the case of some of the smallest, to many weeks in the case of the most persistent spots, which are often regular in shape but not as a rule particularly large. The frequency of spots varies in a definite eleven-year cycle, though the number of spots may vary considerably in a haphazard way from week to week in a particular year. One of the observed properties of spots during the 11-year cycle is that high latitudes, north and south, are predominant towards the beginning of a cycle, while later on there is a gradual drift of the most densely occupied zones towards the equator. In addition, a strong magnetic-field is found to be associated with sunspots, as well as certain systematic drifts in the solar layers there. These and other observed properties, such as concern the detailed structure and movements of spots,

ELEMENTS OF THE SOLAR SYSTEM

Orb	Mean Distance from Sun		Sidereal Period	Synodic Period	Inclination of Orbit to Ecliptic	Diameter	Mass compared with Earth	Period of Rotation on Axis
	Radii of Earth's Orbit	Millions of kilometres						
			y d	Days	° ′	km.		d h m
Sun............	...	...	...	...	...	1,392,000	333,434	25 09
Mercury........	0·39	58	88	116	7 00	4,840	0·04	59
Venus.........	0·72	108	225	584	3 24	12,100	0·83	244
Earth..........	1·00	150	1 0	...	...	12,756eq.	1·00	23 56
Mars..........	1·52	228	1 322	780	1 51	6,790	0·11	24 37
Jupiter.........	5·20	778	11 315	399	1 18	{143,200eq. / 134,700p.}	318	{ 9 50 / 9 56 }
Saturn.........	9·54	1427	29 167	378	2 29	{119,300eq. / 107,700p.}	95	{ 10 14 / 10 38 }
Uranus........	19·19	2870	84 6	370	0 46	47,100	15	10 49
Neptune.......	30·07	4497	164 288	367	1 46	51,000	17	15 48
Pluto..........	39·46	5950	247 255	367	17 09	5,900?	0·06?	6 09 17?

must be explained by any comprehensive physical theory of sunspots. At present no generally accepted theory exists, though it seems clear that the magnetic field of the spot inhibits convection in the turbulent layers near the Sun's surface and so produces local cooling.

The Table below gives dates of recent maxima and minima of the sunspot cycles. It will be seen that the intervals between successive maxima (or minima) vary considerably from the average value of 11·1 years.

Maxima		Minima	
1837·2	1907·0	1843·5	1913·6
1848·1	1917·6	1856·0	1923·6
1860·1	1928·4	1867·2	1933·8
1870·6	1937·4	1878·9	1944·2
1883·9	1947·5	1889·6	1954·3
1894·1	1957·9	1901·7	1964·7
	1968·9		

The 1957 sunspot maximum was unusual in its absence of giant spots, the intense activity being due to a very large number of smaller spots.

Other features of the Sun may be detected in light of wavelengths other than those of normal integrated visual light. With the light from the centre of strong spectral absorption lines such as Hα, the C-line of hydrogen, or the H and K lines of calcium, bright regions can almost always be seen around sunspots and these regions occasionally become exceptionally bright for periods of an hour, or thereabouts. This is the phenomenon of the " solar flare ", and its occurrence may be otherwise detected upon the Earth by immediate changes in propagation-conditions for long-distance radio-communication (changes in the ionosphere caused by a sudden increase in ionizing radiation) or, in the case of large flares, by the subsequent occurrence a day or two later, of a magnetic storm. A very few large flares have had associated with them, increases, occurring a few minutes later, of the high-energy cosmic-ray flux detected at the earth's surface.

Also visible in monochromatic wavelengths are the prominences, which extend outwards from the Sun's surface into its tenuous outer regions, called the corona. At the limb prominences appear as bright forms, often arched or branching, while against the Sun's disk they appear as dark filaments. The corona itself can normally only be observed in its brightest regions by using light from certain bright spectral lines in special instruments at a high altitude on the Earth. At lower altitudes, and in the outer corona at high altitudes, scattered sky-light is too great. However, when the Sun is obscured by the Moon at a total solar eclipse, the whole corona becomes easily seen. As well as the bright lines, it shows a weak continuous spectrum. It is also found that the corona has characteristically different appearances at sunspot maximum and sunspot minimum and that it frequently shows streamers extending outwards for several million kilometres. When observed with radio wave-lengths in the range 10 cm. to 5 m. the corona is normally detected, as well as short-lived emissions from disturbed regions around sunspots.

MERCURY

Mercury is the smallest planet and the nearest to the Sun. Because it moves in an orbit between the Sun and the Earth, it is never far west or east of the Sun. If east, it appears as an evening star; if west as a morning star. The extremes of these apparent excursions are known as Greatest Elongations; their times and extent, measured by the angular distance from the Sun, are given on the first page of each month under the heading PHENOMENA. The great ellipticity of the orbit of Mercury causes the amount of these elongations to vary from 18° to 28°. The planet is best placed for naked-eye observation some days before eastern elongation on spring evenings, or after western elongation on autumn mornings, though in Great Britain at these times its actual distance from the Sun is near its minimum.

In a telescope, Mercury shows phases to the Earth like the Moon, resembling it at first quarter when at eastern elongation, and at last quarter when at western elongation. The planet is exceedingly difficult to observe telescopically and is best scrutin-

THE SATELLITES

Name	Star Mag.	Mean distance from Primary	Sidereal Period of Revolution	Name	Star Mag.	Mean distance from Primary	Sidereal Period of Revolution
		km.	d h m			km.	d h m
Earth				*Saturn*			
Moon...........	—	384,400	27 07 43	Janus...........	14	159,000	17 58
				Mimas.........	12	186,000	22 37
Mars				Enceladus.......	12	238,000	1 08 53
Phobos..........	11	9,400	7 39	Tethys..........	11	295,000	1 21 18
Deimos..........	12	23,500	1 06 18	Dione...........	11	378,000	2 17 41
Jupiter				Rhea...........	10	527,000	4 12 25
V. Unnamed....	13	181,000	11 57	Titan...........	8½	1,222,000	15 22 42
I. Io...........	5½	422,000	1 18 28	Hyperion........	15	1,483,000	21 06 38
II. Europa.......	5½	671,000	3 13 14	Iapetus.........	11	3,560,000	79 07 56
III. Ganymede....	5	1,070,000	7 03 43	Phoebe.........	14	12,950,000	550
IV. Callisto......	6	1,883,000	16 16 32	*Uranus*			
XIII. Unnamed....	—	11,000,000	240	Miranda.........	17	130,000	1 10 00
VI. ,, ...	15	11,480,000	251	Ariel...........	14	192,000	2 12 29
X. ,, ...	19	11,720,000	254	Umbriel.........	14½	267,000	4 03 28
VII. ,, ...	18	11,740,000	260	Titania.........	14	438,000	8 16 56
XII. ,, ...	18	21,200,000	620	Oberon.........	14	586,000	13 11 07
XI. ,, ...	19	22,600,000	692	*Neptune*			
VIII. ,, ...	17	23,500,000	739	Triton..........	13½	355,000	5 21 03
IX. ,, ...	18½	23,600,000	745	Nereid..........	19½	5,562,000	359 10 00

ized with large apertures in full daylight. Recent radar observations, which are supported by theoretical investigations, give a rotation period of 59 days. Close-up photographs from space probes show that its surface has many craters.

VENUS

Venus, next from the Sun, has a diameter only about six hundred kilometres less than that of the Earth. Its apparent movement with regard to the Sun is similar to that of Mercury, but, owing to the greater size of its orbit, its elongations extend as far as 47°. Venus is the brightest planet and is several times brighter than any star; it can often be seen in full daylight with the naked eye.

Apart from the beauty of its phases, Venus is a disappointing object in the telescope, its extensive atmosphere being so highly reflective, owing to dense clouds, that its true surface can never be observed. Vague dusky shadings may be seen or imagined, but conspicuous markings are both rare and evanescent.

Photographs of Venus in violet light were taken by Kuiper in 1950 and 1954 with the 2-metre reflector of the McDonald Observatory in Texas, and show that the surface of the planet is banded, three or more dark and bright bands being noted lying in a direction perpendicular to the terminator. These bands have been attributed to zones of ascending and descending currents in the atmosphere of Venus. Assuming that the bands are parallel to the equator, Kuiper deduced the position of the pole of Venus at $3^h 32^m$, $+81°$, which is in Cepheus. The equator of Venus is therefore tilted at an angle of about 32° to its orbit. Recent radar observations have provided the unexpected value for the period of rotation given on p. 157.

The spectrum of the atmosphere above the reflecting layer reveals a considerable amount of carbon dioxide, but no oxygen; such might also be the conditions on the Earth, were it not for the constant absorption of carbon dioxide by vegetation and its replacement by oxygen. A remarkable feature of the upper atmosphere is the absence of all trace of water vapour. A Russian space probe has revealed that the lower layers are extremely dense.

MARS

Mars, the first planet whose orbit is exterior to that of the Earth, is a little larger than Mercury. Oppositions occur at intervals of about 2 years 2 months, but owing to the eccentricity of the orbit the opposition distance varies between 56 and 100 million kilometres. The most favourable approaches unfortunately take place when the planet is low in the sky for northern observers; but when, as in 1956, one occurs early in September the distance may be less than 65 million kilometres and the planet just north of the equator. It is only within two or three months of opposition that Mars is near enough for its surface to be successfully studied with a telescope; even at these times only the coarser details are likely to be recognized with instruments of less than 15 cm. aperture.

Except for Mercury, Mars is the only planet whose true surface we are able to see. This exhibits many well-defined markings, most of which are permanent, and from these the rotation period has been well determined; it is about 41½ minutes longer than that of the Earth. The axis of rotation is inclined at about 24° to the plane of the orbit. There are white spots at the poles which are deposited during the winter of each hemisphere and melt or evaporate during the summer. Recent observations by a spacecraft orbiting the planet indicate that these polar caps contain solid carbon dioxide. The major portion of the surface is of a featureless orange hue, which gives rise to the ruddy appearance of Mars. But there abound large areas, often with sharp boundaries, of a blue-grey colour. The latter were once thought to be seas but it is now known that there are no large sheets of open water, and some regard areas of vegetation

as their most likely interpretation, especially as they undergo change of tint. It has been claimed that these changes follow the Martian seasons; but as 15 or 17 years must elapse between the times when we can study Mars under similar conditions, it cannot yet be confirmed that there are any changes of a truly seasonal character apart from the waxing and waning of the polar caps.

The controversy over the canal-like markings on Mars has ended with the successful close range photography of the surface by Mariner 4. The photographs show a surface covered with craters, but no " canals ".

Mars has an atmosphere which is considerably less dense than our own. The spectroscope has been unable to establish that it contains either oxygen or water vapour, which can therefore be present only in minute proportions. Recently, however, about the same amount of carbon dioxide has been detected as is found in our own atmosphere.

Mars has two faint satellites, Phobos and Deimos, which were discovered by Asaph Hall in 1877.

THE MINOR PLANETS

Moving in orbits which in general lie between those of Mars and Jupiter, are a large number of small bodies called minor planets or asteroids. It is estimated that at least 50,000 come within reach of present instruments. Scores of them are now found every year by photographing the sky. Their orbits are calculated as observations accrue, and when the results are reliable enough the new planets are given permanent numbers, and usually also names, by a central authority—now at the Cincinnati Observatory, U.S.A. At present there are over 1600 on the permanent list, and several dozen are likely to be added each year; and always there are many still under investigation. All are faint—none has ever been seen by an unaided eye except, just possibly, Vesta.

These celestial bodies are probably little more than masses of rock revolving round the Sun. The first four, found early in the 19th century, are also the largest. Recent radiometric measures of their diameters, in kilometres, are: Ceres 1000; Pallas 530; Juno 240; Vesta 530.

The periodic times of the revolutions about the Sun vary considerably around an average of $4\frac{1}{2}$ years, but interesting groups and gaps occur among the values for these times owing to disturbances of the orbits caused by the attraction on these bodies of the massive planet Jupiter. Although some of the orbits are nearly circular, others are very elongated ovals (ellipses); and though the inclinations of their planes to the ecliptic are mostly less than 20°, several exceed 30°, including Pallas 35°. The highest known, 43°, is that of Hidalgo. This planet has also the longest period, 14 years, and travels out as far as Saturn's orbit. On the other hand Icarus, discovered in 1949, comes within the orbit of Mercury, and three others Apollo, Adonis and Hermes, within that of Venus. Another, Eros, is of importance because in some circumstances it can be within 21 million kilometres of the Earth. This happened in 1931 when carefully planned photographic recording of the planet and the surrounding

stars enabled measurements of its distance to be made, and hence a new value of the distance of the Sun from the Earth to be deduced.

Similarly, certain other minor planets with suitable orbits can be used for special purposes, as in the precise measurement of the equinox and equator, or in finding the masses of Mercury or Venus.

JUPITER

Jupiter, the largest planet, has a volume over 1000 times that of the Earth, but a density only one-quarter of ours. Its oblate shape is so marked, owing to its great size and rapid rotation, as to be obvious in quite small telescopes.

The characteristic surface features of Jupiter are bright zones separated by dusky belts, running practically parallel to the planet's equator. With telescopes of moderate size some of these may be resolved into finer detail, consisting of spots, wisps, streaks, etc., but the general banded appearance still remains. When the period of rotation is determined by timing objects such as these as they cross the planet's central meridian, it is found that spots within about 10° of the equator indicate a period of approximately $9^h\ 50\frac{1}{2}^m$, while most of those in higher latitudes give periods between $9^h\ 55^m$ and $9^h\ 56^m$, the transition from the shorter to the longer being usually quite abrupt. When the rotation periods are examined in greater detail, it is found that the surface may be divided into many zones, each having a particular period characteristic of its latitude, but that the distribution in latitude of the various periods is quite haphazard. This differs from the Sun, whose rotation is also fastest at the equator, for whereas a definite formula connects the periods of solar spots with their latitude, no such law can be found for Jupiter. Actually the fastest moving spots are confined to a narrow strip in latitude about $+25°$; the last outbreak of such spots occurred in 1939.

Few Jovian markings have any degree of permanence, having generally lost their individuality after a few months. Two objects, however, form notable exceptions. The well-known " Bay " or " Hollow " in the South Equatorial Belt, which is so closely associated with the Great Red Spot, made famous in 1878–80 by its darkness and colour, is known to have existed from 1831 and the Red Spot itself may be identical with a similar object first depicted in the 17th century and followed for many years. The physical nature of the Red Spot is a mystery; its long duration suggests some connection with the solid surface, but the non-uniformity of its period of rotation seems to rule out this explanation. The other feature displaying considerable permanence is known as the South Tropical Disturbance, which has the same latitude as the Red Spot. Its rotation period is somewhat shorter than that of the latter; since its first detection in 1901 it has overtaken and passed the Red Spot eight times.

The spectroscope shows that Jupiter's atmosphere contains ammonia and considerable quantities of methane (marsh gas). The main constituents are unknown, but it is probable that hydrogen and helium abound and that the light clouds of the surface are due to minute droplets or crystals of

ammonia, the surface temperature having been found by measurement to be of the order — 120° C., which is not far from the calculated value. It has been suggested that this atmosphere is very deep; but if so, the pressure at depths below 100 kilometres or so must be such as to give it the properties of a liquid rather than a gas. A recent theory is that it may be dense enough to support in flotation a light solid body at some depth below the surface, and that what we see as the Red Spot may be a manifestation in the atmosphere above it of thermal changes in such a solid.

Jupiter has four principal satellites—the first celestial objects discovered by telescope by Galileo. The two inner major satellites are about the size of our Moon, while the two outer are about as large as Mercury. A fifth, very much smaller and fainter and nearer to Jupiter, was discovered visually by Barnard in 1892; this satellite has the most rapid motion of any in the solar system. Eight other satellites have been discovered photographically but all are minute objects; the four outermost of these have retrograde motion and are so greatly disturbed by the solar attractions that their orbits are not even approximately elliptical.

Satellite I (Io) occulted a fifth magnitude star on 1971 May 14, and from the accurate photoelectric observations of this event its equatorial diameter has been determined as 3660±4 km. From a similar event in 1972 the diameter of Satellite III (Ganymede) was found to be 5,270 km.

Intense but irregular bursts of radio noise were detected at the Carnegie Institute at Washington in January 1955, on wavelengths of 13·5 and 10 metres; these signals were received only during the few minutes while Jupiter was crossing the aerial beam. Some evidence indicates that there is a connection between the positions of the satellite Io and these radio bursts.

SATURN

This planet is unique because of its encircling ring system, which makes it a very beautiful object in even a small telescope. There are two bright rings and an inner dusky one, which is transparent enough for the body of the planet to be seen through it. The dark line separating the two outer rings is known as Cassini's division in honour of its discoverer. The rings lie almost exactly in one plane, which is inclined at 27° to the planet's orbit and is sensibly that of its equator. It has been proved theoretically, and confirmed by spectroscopic observations, that the rings consist of a vast swarm of small individual particles, each pursuing its own orbit like a satellite around Saturn. The extreme thinness of the rings is illustrated every 15 years when the plane of the rings passes through the Earth; they then become almost completely invisible even in the greatest telescopes. Thus they cannot present when edgewise a width of more than a very few kilometres.

From the few spots that have been observed on Saturn's surface, the rotation period at the equator is about 10^h 15^m, in higher latitudes 10^h 38^m has been found in the northern hemisphere and 10^h 37^m in the southern. There is thus some analogy with

Jupiter, but we are ignorant of the behaviour of intermediate zones.

The density of Saturn is less than three-quarters that of water; the oblateness is even more marked than is Jupiter's, the equatorial diameter exceeding the polar by about one part in nine. The general appearance of the disk is banded, but the dusky belts are fewer and wider than those on Jupiter and present less contrast with the brighter zones. The atmosphere is known to contain methane and ammonia.

Among the more interesting results obtained from measurements of infra-red absorption spectra with the 2-metre reflector of the McDonald Observatory in Texas are those of the constitution of Saturn's rings and the five inner satellites. The only substance which gives similar absorption bands to those observed would appear to be frost deposited on a material at very low temperatures. Estimates of the masses of Saturn's rings and of the five inner satellites show that their densities cannot be far from unity, and it is provisionally suggested that they are all composed of ice. Evaporation will be negligible at the low temperatures prevailing, and the small particles of which the ring is composed will suffer little or no loss.

Saturn has ten satellites, of which the largest, Titan, is easily seen with a small telescope. Titan is the largest satellite in the solar system, and the only one which shows definite evidence of possessing an atmosphere. The seven innermost satellites revolve nearly in the plane of the rings. When the rings are seen edgewise, these inner satellites may transit the planet or be eclipsed in the same manner as those of Jupiter. The faint outermost satellite, Phœbe, has a retrograde motion.

URANUS

This planet was discovered by William Herschel at Bath in 1781, and so has completed only two revolutions since its discovery. It is only just visible to the naked eye, but in a telescope is distinguishable by its disk, which is quite obvious, though less than 4″ in diameter, and by the different quality of its light. The two outer and brighter of its four main satellites were found by Herschel in 1787; the two inner by Lassell in 1851. Their movement is retrograde in a plane inclined 82° to the plane of the ecliptic. A fifth satellite was discovered by Kuiper in 1948. The period of rotation of Uranus has been determined spectroscopically to be 10 hours; the direction is the same as that of the satellites.

NEPTUNE

This planet is a telescopic object of about the 8th magnitude, presenting a disk of well over 2″ in diameter. A rotation period of 15·8 hours, inferred spectroscopically, is now generally accepted.

The planet was found in 1846 as a result of calculations made independently by J. C. Adams and Le Verrier, which gave the position of an unknown planet which was responsible for perturbations of the motion of Uranus. The planet was found near the indicated place by Galle of the Berlin Observatory. Neptune has two satellites, of which the inner, Triton, revolves about Neptune in a retro-

grade direction at a distance a little less than that of the Moon from the Earth.

The other satellite revolves in the normal direction in a period of about a year. Its orbit is remarkably eccentric, and the satellite's distance from Neptune varies from 1,300,000 to over 10 million kilometres.

PLUTO

The outermost planet of the solar system was discovered photographically at the Lowell Observatory in March 1930, as a result of a systematic search for a trans-Neptunian planet. The existence of such a planet had been suggested many years before, and although the predicted elements of the orbit differ in some respect from the facts, yet these predictions were undoubtedly responsible for the ultimate discovery. The planet was called Pluto, and would appear to be small, with a mass possibly much less than that of the Earth. It would also appear to be a poor reflector of the Sun's light, since it shines only as a star of the 14th–15th magnitude.

THE MOON

The Moon is the Earth's satellite, and although its motion is highly complicated, it may be considered to revolve about the Earth in an elliptical orbit inclined about 5° to the plane of the ecliptic. Owing to perturbations, the ellipse is continually varying in shape, and the whole orbit twists round in space so that the nodes, or points where the orbit intersects the ecliptic, move in a retrograde direction, making one complete revolution in 18·6 years.

The Moon, whose diameter is 3,476 kilometres, rotates in the same time that it revolves ($27^d\ 7^h\ 43^m$) so that the same face is always presented to the Earth. The tilt of its axis, and the variable speed in the orbit, cause it to undergo an apparent swaying motion called libration, which enables us, in the long run, to see rather more than an exact half of the lunar surface. In a telescope this surface shows many objects of great beauty and interest, the rugged ranges of mountains, the craters and plains forming an impressive picture of jet-black shadows and bright highlights. Recent photographs obtained from the successful *Ranger* series of lunar probes show craters as small as a metre in diameter. On 1969 July 21, the first men (Americans) landed on the Moon and returned with samples of lunar rock and dust for subsequent laboratory analysis.

The revolution of the Moon about the Earth with reference to the Sun takes rather longer than a sidereal revolution, so that the phases of the Moon repeat themselves in a period that varies slightly about a mean of $29\frac{1}{2}$ days. Each month the Moon passes in front of all stars in its path. Such an *occultation* causes the light of the star to be extinguished instantly. This, together with the sharpness and intensity of the shadows on the Moon, indicates a complete lack of atmosphere. Eclipses occur at two " seasons " of the year, when the Moon is near one of its nodes and in line with the Earth and the Sun. A lunar eclipse takes place when the Full Moon passes through the Earth's shadow, and is visible over half the Earth at any one time. A solar eclipse takes place when the New Moon passes in front of the Sun, and is visible only from a rather small area of the Earth.

As a result of its eastward movement among the stars the Moon rises later each day by a variable amount that depends on the inclination of its apparent path to the observer's horizon. When this angle is small, the Moon rises at much the same time for several days in succession. Although this occurs each month, it is most noticeable in high latitudes at the Full Moon nearest to the Autumnal Equinox. This is the Harvest Moon.

THE AURORA BOREALIS (AND AUSTRALIS)

An aurora is the visible counterpart of a marked disturbance of the Earth's magnetic field (a " magnetic storm ") apparently due to the action of a stream of electrified particles shot earthward from localized regions of the Sun, such as that of a big sunspot. The glow of auroral patches, arches or streamers results from the action of this solar stream upon the constituent gases of the Earth's upper atmosphere. The usual height of the lower limit of the auroral luminescence is about 100 kilometres; upward, it may extend to 500 kilometres or higher. Aurorae are very frequent in the so-called auroral zones (magnetic latitude about 67°); they are most frequent for the Earth as a whole near sunspot maximum. Although the solar origin of great displays (e.g. 1938 January 25, and 1949 January 24–26), can be traced to particular sunspots with solar flares, many lesser auroral displays cannot be thus associated. However, their solar origin is evidenced by their tendency to recur at intervals of 27 days, the time required for the Sun to turn once on its axis with respect to the Earth.

THE ZODIACAL LIGHT

This faint phenomenon of the late evening or early morning sky can be seen only when the air is sufficiently clear, the sky quite dark, and the ecliptic making a fairly steep angle with the horizon. It then appears as a cone of faint light stretching up from the position of the Sun (below the horizon) in the direction of the ecliptic, with its apex anything from 60° to 110° from the Sun. In our latitudes it is best seen after sunset in spring and before sunrise in the autumn, when its brightest parts may appear brighter than the Galaxy.

Occasionally, under very good conditions, an extension of the Cone may be traced right round the ecliptic. This is known as the Zodiacal Band. The Gegenschein or " Counter-glow " may also be detected as a widening of the band at the anti-solar point.

Recent work shows that the zodiacal cloud is a continuation of the Sun's corona, and that much of this fine dust must fall on the earth every day. The particles are much too small, however, to become visible (by incandescence) as they fall through the atmosphere, and there is evidence to show that they settle in the form of micro-meteorites. These probably act as centres of condensation in the formation of rain.

METEORS

The scattered particles which move in streams about the Sun give rise to occasional showers of meteors (" shooting-stars ") or fireballs—bodies that differ only in size. They are visible in varying numbers every night, being sometimes so abundant

as to be quite spectacular. Often on a particular date or dates, meteors radiate from the same part of the heavens every year. This is because a stream of particles more or less dense, is moving in an orbit that intersects that of the Earth. The orbits of some of these streams, Lyrids, Pons-Winneckeids, Perseids, Giacobinids, Leonids, are known to be closely similar to those of certain comets, but modern work on the measurement of meteor velocities by photographic and radar methods has given very different results for the other streams. Thus the Geminids and the November Taurids have been shown by Whipple (from photographic results) to have small but eccentric orbits, more like those of minor planets. The radar methods of studying meteors have the advantage of being equally useful in daylight, and unaffected by cloud. Besides making measurements of the major showers noted above, the radar technique has shown the presence of a number of extensive showers in daylight hours, particularly in the summer months. These also show the same type of small eccentric orbit as those determined by Whipple.

METEOR SHOWERS

Date	Radiant		Name
	R.A.	Dec.	
	°	°	
January 3.........	232	+52	Quadrantids
April 20–22.......	271	+33	Lyrids★
May 2–6.........	336	0	ηAquarids★
June 27–30........	213	+53	Pons-Winneckeids★
August 10–13.....	46	+58	Perseids
October 9........	262	+54	Giacobinids★
October 18–23....	96	+15	Orionids★
November 14–15..	152	+22	Leonids★
December 10–13...	112	+32	Geminids
December 22.....	217	+76	Bečvár's Stream★

★ Not plentiful each year.

The real paths of a great number of meteors have been computed, and the average heights found to be about 110 kilometres at the beginning and about 75 kilometres at the end. The speeds vary from 15 to 80 km. per second. Fireballs, or very bright meteors, appear at all times of the year unexpectedly so that they are often imperfectly noted and computation of their flight is not practicable.

Fireballs would seem to have a different origin from the ordinary shooting star, and probably arise from the belt of minor planets. The largest fireballs, when not completely consumed, land on the earth as meteorites. The largest meteorite found weighs 30 tons, and considerable collections are to be seen in our museums. Very large falls were recorded in Siberia in 1908 and 1947, while craters (formed presumably by large meteorites) are found in Arizona, Ungava and elsewhere. A number of meteorites have been found at Barwell, Leicestershire, as the result of two exploding fireballs on 1965 December 24. At the other end of the scale are the micro-meteorites which are too

small to become incandescent in the atmosphere and which drift slowly down to the earth's surface.

Above is a list of the nights when meteor showers may be expected, with the radiant points from which the meteors diverge. The dates given are those when the meteors are likely to be most abundant. In some cases, e.g. the Perseids, the apparition lasts beyond these limiting dates, and the position of the radiant, which changes from night to night, is given for the date of maximum.

COMETS

A comet is distinguished from other bodies in the solar system by its appearance: a hazy luminous patch moving in the sky, more or less round and usually brighter in the centre, sometimes with a star-like nucleus there; and from it not infrequently extends a tail which may, in bright comets, reach a length of as much as 150 million kilometres—a fine spectacle. Most comets are found accidentally and few observers search for these objects. One of the few is G. E. D. Alcock of Peterborough, Northants, who, after seaching unsuccessfully for six years, found two new comets in August, 1959, within the space of 5 days. Two naked-eye comets which appeared in 1957 (Comet Arend-Roland in April, and Comet Mrkos in August) aroused considerable interest.

Although generally large in volume, a comet is small in mass, probably less than one-millionth that of the Earth even in the largest comets—the centre being composed mainly of an aggregation of pieces of matter mostly of sizes between that of pebbles and fine dust, but probably containing also a solid core a few kilometres in diameter. According to a recent theory, the earthy material is held together by various " ices "—masses of frozen gases such as ammonia, carbon dioxide and methane —which, on approaching the Sun, begin to evaporate. The pressure of the Sun's radiation is great enough to repel these gases, together with fine dust, and thus form a tail. As the comet approaches the Sun, it grows brighter and as it recedes it grows fainter again, the tail now preceding it in its journey away from the Sun.

Most comets follow paths which are very elongated ovals (ellipses) and return to the Sun, if at all, only after hundreds or thousands of years. The arrival of such comets cannot therefore be predicted. A few dozen comets, however, mostly too faint ever to be seen with the unaided eye, move in smaller ellipses which are sufficiently accurately known to enable predictions to be made of their returns. The most famous and brightest of these periodic comets is Halley's comet whose spectacular appearances about every 75 years have been traced back over more than 2000 years— it is next due early in 1986. Two very faint comets are known which travel in nearly circular orbits and, on this account come within reach for photographic observation every year: Schwassmann-Wachmann (1), designated 1925 II, and Oterma. The former is of special interest, not only because its orbit is the only known one lying wholly between Jupiter and Saturn, but on account of the unexpected outbursts in brightness it occasionally manifests.

The shape of the Earth is that of an oblate spheroid or solid of revolution whose meridian sections are ellipses not differing much from circles, whilst the sections at right angles are circles. The length of the equatorial axis is about 12,756 kilometres, and that of the polar axis 12,714 kilometres. The mean density of the Earth is 5·5 times that of water, although that of the surface layer is less. The Earth and Moon revolve about their common centre of gravity in a lunar month; this centre in turn revolves round the Sun in a plane known as the ecliptic, that passes through the Sun's centre. The Earth's equator is inclined to this plane at an angle of 23½°. This tilt is the cause of the seasons. In mid-latitudes, and when the Sun is high above the Equator, not only does the high noon altitude make the days longer, but the Sun's rays fall more directly on the Earth's surface; these effects combine to produce summer. In equatorial regions the noon altitude is large throughout the year, and there is little variation in the length of the day. In higher latitudes the noon altitude is lower, and the days in summer are appreciably longer than those in winter.

The average velocity of the Earth in its orbit is 30 kilometres a second. It makes a complete rotation on its axis in about 23^h 56^m of mean time, which is the sidereal day. Because of its annual revolution round the Sun, the rotation with respect to the Sun, or the solar day, is more than this by about four minutes (see p. 140). The extremity of the axis of rotation, or the North Pole of the Earth, is not rigidly fixed, but wanders over an area roughly 20 metres in diameter.

THE TIDES

The tides are caused by the attraction of the Moon for the waters of the Earth, while a similar but smaller effect is due to the Sun. Normally there are two high tides every day, about 12½ hours apart. They thus occur about 50 minutes later than those of the previous day, corresponding to the 24^h 50^m interval between consecutive meridian passages of the Moon. Briefly, a high tide occurs when the Moon is near the meridian because the attraction on the water is greater than on the solid earth. On the other side of the Earth the water is farther from the Moon than the solid earth and thus is less strongly attracted to the Moon and a second high tide occurs at this point. The height of the tide varies considerably. The highest, called Spring Tides, always occur about the time of New or Full Moon, when the lunar and solar attractions act together. At Neap Tides, which occur about First and Last Quarter, the rise and fall is only about half as much as at Spring Tide.

The tidal flow of water across the Earth is greatly modified by the shape of the coastline and other geographical conditions. The complicated motion of the Moon, its changing position north or south of the equator, and its varying distance from the Earth, all add small variations; it is thus impossible to predict tides theoretically. Tide-tables for any place are always constructed from an analysis of past observations of times and heights. It is found that the height can be expressed as the sum of a series of periodic terms, which can be carried forward. (See pages 170–184.)

High water does not necessarily occur at the same time as the meridian passage of the Moon, nor do springs and neaps necessarily occur on the same day as the phases stated. Thus at London Bridge the tide is high when the Moon is somewhat west of the meridian, while Spring Tides occur about 2½ days after New or Full Moon.

The shape and depth of a channel or estuary very greatly modify the nature of the tides. At some places one of the daily tides becomes so small as to be negligible, while in other channels (e.g. Southampton Water) the high tides are doubled. The difference between high and low water, or range of the tide, may vary from a small amount, as in the land-locked Mediterranean, up to 13 metres in the Severn Estuary and 16 metres in the Bay of Fundy.

As the energy involved in this tidal flow is considerable, various schemes for harnessing tidal energy have been evolved. As a consequence of the friction caused by tidal flow, the Earth's period of rotation is increasing by about a thousandth of a second every century. Although very small at present, this effect was greater in the past, and has played a considerable part in the history of the Earth–Moon system.

High Water in the Thames, 1977

Occasions when a predicted height at London Bridge is 7·7 metres or more

March........6–9	October......13–16
April.........4–7	November....11–14
May..........4–6	December.......13
September....15,16	

TERRESTRIAL MAGNETISM

The discovery that a piece of the commonly occurring iron ore, magnetite or lodestone, is subject to a directing force causing it to take up a definite direction when freed from other restraint seems to have been made in China during the first century A.D., if not somewhat earlier. Steel needles, magnetized by rubbing with a piece of lodestone and floated on water, were being used as navigational aids by Chinese sailors before A.D. 1000. From this primitive device the Mariner's compass subsequently developed. That the direction, though roughly north to south, is by no means accurately so, was also known to the Chinese before A.D. 1000.

William Gilbert, in 1600, demonstrated that in the proximity of the Earth magnetized needles behave much as if the Earth itself were a large magnetized sphere. It was soon found that the direction of the force in a particular locality slowly changed. Henry Gellibrand, observing near Greenwich in 1634, found the direction to be about 4° east of north, whereas there was undoubted evidence that in 1580 it had been about 11° east in the same neighbourhood. In 1722, Graham, the clockmaker, found that the direction oscillated slowly through a small angle every day. In the

British Isles the movement is eastwards till about 08^h U.T., then rather quickly westwards till about 14^h U.T., after which there is a gradual return eastwards. The amplitude may be as much as 15' in the summer.

A magnetic compass points along the horizontal component of a magnetic line of force. These directions converge on the " magnetic dip-poles ". At these poles a freely suspended magnetized needle would become vertical. Not only do the positions of these poles change with time, but their exact location is ill-defined, particularly so in the case of the north dip-pole where the lines of force, on the north side of it, instead of converging radially, tend to bunch into a channel. Although it is therefore unrealistic to attempt to specify the locations of the dip-poles exactly, the present adopted positions are 76°·2 N., 100°·2 W. and 65°·8 S., 139°·5 E. The two magnetic dip-poles are thus not antipodal, the line joining them passing the centre of the Earth at a distance of about 1,100 kilometres. The distances of the magnetic dip-poles from the north and south geographic poles are about 1,600 and 2,700 kilometres respectively.

There is also a " magnetic equator ", at all points of which the vertical force is zero and a magnetized needle remains horizontal. This line runs between 2° and 10° north of the geographical equator in the eastern hemisphere, turns sharply south off the West African coast, and crosses South America through Brazil, Bolivia and Peru; it recrosses the geographical equator in mid-Pacific.

Reference has already been made to secular changes in the Earth's field. The following table indicates the changes in magnetic declination (or variation of the compass). Similar, though much smaller, changes have occurred in " dip " or magnetic inclination. Secular changes differ throughout the world. Although the London observations strongly suggest a cycle of several hundred years, an exact repetition is unlikely.

London		Greenwich	
1580	11° 15' E.	1850	22° 24' W.
1622	5 56 E.	1900	16 29 W.
1665	1 22 W.	1925	13 10 W.
1730	13 00 W.	1950	9 07 W.
1773	21 09 W.	1975	6 47 W.

In order that up-to-date information on the variation of the compass may be available, many governments publish magnetic charts on which there are lines (called isogonic) passing through all places at which specified values of declination will be found at the date of the chart.

In the British Isles, isogonic lines now run approximately north-east to south-west. Though there are considerable local deviations due to geological causes, a rough value of magnetic declination may be obtained by assuming that at 50° N. on the meridian of Greenwich, the value in 1977 is 6° 20' west and allowing an increase of 18' for each degree of latitude northwards and one of 28' for each degree of longitude westwards. For example, at 53° N., 5° W., declination will be about 6° 20' +54' +140', i.e. 9° 34' west. The average annual change at the present time is about 6'·5 decrease.

The number of magnetic observatories now approaches 200—widely scattered over the globe. In Great Britain three are maintained by the Government: at Hartland, North Devon, at Eskdalemuir in Dumfriesshire, Scotland, and at Lerwick, Shetland Islands, while a fourth is maintained by Stonyhurst College, Lancashire. Some recent annual mean values of the magnetic elements for Hartland are given below.

The normal worldwide terrestrial magnetic field corresponds approximately to that of a very strong small bar magnet near the centre of the Earth but with appreciable smooth spatial departures. The origin and slow secular change of the normal field is not yet fully understood but is generally ascribed to electric currents associated with fluid motions within the Earth's core. Superposed on the normal field are local and regional anomalies whose magnitudes may in places exceed that of the normal field; these are due to the influence of mineral deposits in the Earth's crust. A small proportion of the field is of external origin, mostly associated with electric currents in the ionosphere. The configuration of the external field and the ionization of the atmosphere depend on the incident particle and radiation flux. There are, therefore, short-term and non-periodic as well as diurnal, 27-day, seasonal and 11-year periodic changes in the magnetic field, dependent upon the position of the Sun and the degree of solar activity.

Year	Declination West	Dip or Inclination	Horizontal Force	Vertical Force
	° '	° '	oersted	oersted
1945	11 46	66 55	0·1843	0·4326
1950	11 06	66 54	0·1848	0·4334
1955	10 30	66 49	0·1859	0·4340
1960	9 59	66 44	0·1871	0·4350
1965	9 30	66 34	0·1887	0·4354
1970	9 06	66 26	0·1903	0·4364
1975	8 32	66 17	0·1921	0·4373

Magnetic Storms. Occasionally—sometimes with great suddenness—the Earth's magnetic field is subject for several hours to marked disturbance. In extreme cases, departures in field intensity as much as one tenth the normal value are experienced. In many instances, such disturbances are accompanied by widespread displays of aurorae, marked changes in the incidence of cosmic rays, an increase in the reception of ' noise ' from the Sun at radio frequencies together with rapid changes in the ionosphere and induced electric currents within the earth which adversely affect radio and telegraphic communications. The disturbances are generally ascribed to flux changes in the stream of neutral and ionized particles which emanates from the Sun and through which the Earth is continuously passing. Some of these changes are associated with visible eruptions on the Sun, usually in the region of sunspots. There is a marked tendency for disturbances to recur after intervals of about 27 days, the apparent period of rotation of the Sun on its axis, which is consistent with the sources being located on particular areas of the Sun.

ARTIFICIAL SATELLITES AND SPACE PROBES

The progress of rocket research during the last war led to the development by the Germans in 1944 of the V.2 rocket which, if fired vertically, attained a height of 180 km. Before the end of the decade the U.S. rocket engineers had increased this maximum height to 400 km by using a two-stage rocket, the first stage being a V.2 and the second a WAC Corporal. Plans for using multi-stage rockets to put artificial satellites into orbit around the earth during the International Geophysical Year (July 1957–December 1958) were announced by both the U.S. and the U.S.S.R. Such projects also called for an immense effort in establishing optical, radio, and radar tracking facilities around the world.

The historic event which heralded the Space Age occurred on 1957 October 4 when the U.S.S.R. successfully injected a " sputnik " into an orbit inclined at 65° to the earth's equator. One month later " Sputnik 2 " was also put into orbit, carrying a dog that survived the ascent trajectory and lived for several days orbiting the earth. The rate of satellite launching has increased since 1957 and by the end of 1960 the number of artificial satellites in orbit around the Earth exceeded the number of natural satellites known to be in the Solar System. All the satellites launched up to the end of 1960 have been sent up in the same direction as the rotation of the Earth, i.e., eastwards. Thus they are able to start with the benefit of the Earth's rotational velocity at the particular launching site. This is why these satellites always appear to move in an easterly direction. However, the first satellite launching of 1961 (*Samos 2*) achieved a retrograde orbit.

Satellite Orbits

To consider the orbit of an artificial satellite it is best to imagine that one is looking at the Earth from a distant point in space. The Earth would then be seen to be rotating about its axis inside the orbit described by the rapidly revolving satellite. The inclination of a satellite orbit to the Earth's equator (which generally remains almost constant throughout the satellite's lifetime) gives at once the maximum range of latitudes over which the satellite passes. Thus a satellite whose orbit has an inclination of 53° will pass overhead all latitudes between S. 53° and N. 53°, but would never be seen in the zenith of any place nearer the poles than these latitudes. If we consider a particular place on the earth, whose latitude is less than the inclination of the satellite's orbit then the Earth's rotation carries this place under first the northbound part of the orbit and then, later on, under the southbound position of the orbit, these two occurrences being always less than 12 hours apart for satellites moving in direct orbits (i.e. to the east). For satellites in retrograde orbits the words " northbound " and " southbound " should be interchanged in the preceding statement. As the value of the latitude of the observer increases and approaches the value of the inclination of the orbit, so this interval gets shorter until (when the latitude is equal to the inclination) only one overhead passage occurs each day.

Orbital Variations

The relatively simple picture described above is unfortunately complicated by the considerable variations in the shape, orientation and size of the orbit during a satellite's lifetime. The major variations are due to the Earth's oblateness and to air-drag. A third cause, radiation pressure from the Sun, is noticeable only on large satellites of extremely low density.

The oblate shape of the Earth—the equatorial diameter is 43 km longer than the polar diameter—has two marked effects on a satellite orbit. It causes a regression of the nodes, amounting to several degrees a day for close satellites. Thus from a point in space, the whole orbit is seen to twist around the Earth, making a complete turn of 360° within a few months. This regression, which may also be described as the rotation of the orbital plane around the Earth's axis, is in the opposite direction to the satellite's motion, i.e. the orbit of a satellite with a direct motion regresses to the west. The actual amount of the regression depends, first, on the inclination of the orbit to the equator, being greatest at low inclinations and zero for a true polar orbit (inclination 90°). It is also dependent on the distance of the satellite from the Earth, being greatest for small orbits. At the distance of the Moon the regression is only 19° a year.

The orbit of *Samos 2* was extremely interesting from this point of view as its regression to the east was at an almost identical rate as the movement of the Sun. Thus there was hardly any change in the area of visibility over a long period of time.

The other effect the Earth's oblateness has on a satellite orbit is to cause a rotation of the line of apsides (i.e. the line joining the perigee and apogee points of the orbit). The rate of the rotation is dependent on the inclination of the orbit, and also on the distance of the satellite, again being greater for close satellites than for more distant ones. The value of this rotation has its greatest positive value (i.e. it moves forward along the orbit in the same direction as the satellite) at the equator and becomes zero at an inclination of 63°·4. As the inclination moves from 63°·4 to 90° the value increases again numerically, but with the opposite sign, the motion of the line of apsides being backwards along the orbit.

Even at heights of several hundred kilometres there is still sufficient atmosphere to cause a retarding effect on satellites. Although air-drag will have most effect around the perigee point the actual result is to reduce the height of the apogee point with hardly any change in perigee height and thus to decrease the eccentricity of the orbit until, in the final stage of a satellite's life-time, the orbit is almost circular. Unfortunately the air density at perigee height is not constant. It alters as the perigee moves from daylight into darkness and from darkness into daylight, and also as the latitude of perigee changes

SATELLITE HEIGHTS AND VELOCITIES

Period		Height, kilometres	Velocity, km per hour	Period		Height, kilometres	Velocity, km per hour
h	m			h	m		
1	28	182	28,077	3	40	5,700	20,686
1	32	380	27,663	3	50	6,064	20,382
1	36	575	27,274	4	00	6,428	20,096
1	40	766	26,905	5	00	8,473	18,655
1	44	954	26,556	6	00	10,393	17,555
1	48	1,141	26,224	7	00	12,207	16,676
1	52	1,326	25,907	8	00	13,937	15,950
1	56	1,508	25,606	9	00	15,596	15,335
2	00	1,688	25,318	10	00	17,194	14,806
2	04	1,867	25,043	11	00	18,739	14,344
2	08	2,042	24,779	12	00	20,529	13,934
2	12	2,216	24,526	13	00	21,699	13,567
2	16	2,390	24,283	14	00	23,120	13,235
2	20	2,560	24,050	15	00	24,509	12,934
2	24	2,729	23,826	16	00	25,865	12,659
2	28	2,897	23,609	17	00	27,195	12,406
2	32	3,064	23,400	18	00	28,498	12,171
2	36	3,228	23,199	19	00	29,779	11,954
2	40	3,392	23,004	20	00	31,036	11,751
2	50	3,795	22,544	21	00	32,272	11,562
3	00	4,189	22,117	22	00	33,490	11,384
3	10	4,577	21,723	23	00	34,689	11,217
3	20	4,958	21,354	24	00	35,871	11,059
3	30	5,332	21,010				

due to the rotation of the line of apsides. There is already some evidence that the atmospheric density varies with the sunspot cycle. In addition unpredictable short-period variations in the output of solar radiation may also occur and these have the effect of increasing the air density at any given height. Thus the air-drag on a satellite is by no means a constant factor and this is the reason why it is not possible to forecast accurately the position of a satellite for any considerable period of time. There is also some retardation due to electrified particles but this effect may be included with the air-drag.

Radiation pressure from the Sun only has any appreciable effect on large satellites of extremely low density such as the 30 metre diameter balloon, *Echo* 1. For such satellites, however, this effect can be severe, and for heights greater than a few hundred kilometres, it can equal or even surpass that due to air-drag. The effect on the orbit is very much more complicated than that due to air-drag, and even the signs of the variations can change periodically with time. Thus it is possible for the eccentricity to increase rather than decrease, with an increase in apogee height and a decrease in perigee height.

For close artificial satellites the gravitational attractions of the Sun and Moon are many thousand times weaker than that of the Earth's equatorial bulge and need only be considered in an extremely precise analysis of observational material.

Height and Velocity

The mean height of a satellite above the Earth's surface, which is determined by its orbital velocity, is related to its period of revolution around the Earth as is shown by the table above.

As the orbit shrinks due to air-drag, both the mean height and the period decrease so that the retarding effect of air-drag actually causes the satellite to move faster, though in a smaller orbit.

Satellite Launchings, 1957–75

Many different types of orbit have been achieved though the vast majority have had a direct motion. The majority of the Russian satellite orbits have had inclinations of 65° or 49° and orbits entirely below 2000 kilometres in height. An important exception was Lunik 3 whose original inclination was 75° and initial apogee height 470,000 km. This satellite orbited the Moon on its first revolution, returning with the first photographs of the other side of the Moon, which were transmitted back to the Earth when near perigee.

The American satellites have been injected into orbits of various inclinations. The early Explorers and Vanguards are in orbits of inclination about 28–35° while near-polar orbits were achieved with the Discoverers. Other series of launchings such as the Transit, Tiros and Echo put satellites in orbits of intermediate inclinations. In contrast to the heavy, but short-lived, Russian satellites, a number of those launched by the U.S. have been very small and have been put in larger orbits which have given them considerably longer life-times.

A third Anglo-American satellite, Ariel 3, was launched on May 5, 1967, and has been of great interest to visual observers. Sets of mirrors and highly reflective solar cells on its sides cause the observer to see a series of flashes and the observations are used to determine the direction of the axis of rotation of the satellite.

In order to monitor the Arab–Israeli war, and in particular the Egyptian battlefield, the Russians launched a number of Cosmos satellites in the first half of October 1973. The orbits were very care-

[continued on p. 169

Desig-nation	Satellite	Launch date	i	P	e	Perigee height (km)
1975-		1975	°	m		
16	Cosmos 711-718, rocket	February 28	74·0	115·5	0·002	1462
17	SDSI, rocket	March 10	63·5	702·0	0·745	295
18	Cosmos 719, rocket, capsule	March 12	65·0	88·7	0·007	164
19	Cosmos 720, rocket, capsule	March 21	62·8	89·3	0·005	212
20	Cosmos 721, rocket, capsule	March 26	81·3	88·9	0·002	208
21	Cosmos 722, rocket, capsule	March 27	71·3	89·9	0·010	204
22	Intercosmos 13, rocket	March 27	82·9	104·9	0·095	284
23	Meteor 21, rocket	April 1	81·2	102·6	0·002	867
24	Cosmos 723	April 2	65·0	89·6	0·001	249
25	Cosmos 724	April 7	65·0	89·6	0·001	248
26	Cosmos 725, rocket	April 8	71·0	92·1	0·016	270
27	Explorer 53, rocket	April 10	115·0	101·7	0·001	833
28	Cosmos 726, rocket	April 11	83·0	104·6	0·003	956
29	Molniya 3B, launcher rocket, launcher, rocket	April 14	62·9	736·3	0·741	608
30	Cosmos 727, rocket, capsule	April 16	65·0	89·3	0·001	168
31	Cosmos 728, rocket, capsule	April 18	72·8	89·7	0·009	200
32	?	April 18	110·5	80·9	0·020	134
33	Aryabhata, rocket	April 19	50·7	96·4	0·003	569
34	Cosmos 729, rocket	April 22	83·0	105·0	0·002	980
35	Cosmos 730, rocket, capsule	April 24	81·3	89·0	0·002	210
36	Molniya 1AE, launcher rocket, launcher, rocket	April 29	62·8	736·5	0·748	430
37	Explorer 52, rocket	May 7	3·0	94·5	0·001	499
38	Telesat 3	May 7	0·0	1,424·8	0·008	35,222
39	Pollux D5B, Castor D5A	May 17	30·0	100·2	0·071	269
40	DSC5-6	May 20	28·6	88·3	0·008	150
41	Cosmos 731, rocket, capsule	May 21	65·0	89·5	0·007	203
42	Intelsat 4G, rocket	May 22	0·4	1,436·2	0·000	35,780
43	DMSP	May 24	98·9	102·0	0·005	813
44	Soyuz 18★, rocket	May 24	51·7	88·6	0·003	186
45	Cosmos 732-739, rocket	May 28	74·0	114·6	0·004	1,405
46	Cosmos 740, rocket	May 28	65·0	89.5	0·012	173
47	Cosmos 741, rocket	May 30	81·3	88·9	0·002	210
48	Cosmos 742, rocket, capsule	June 3	62·8	89·8	0·013	178
49	Molniya 1AF, SRET 2, launcher, launcher rocket, rocket	June 5	62·8	736·8	0·748	435
50	Venus 9, launcher rocket, launcher	June 8	(space	probe)		
51	?	June 8	96·4	88·8	0·009	154
52	Nimbus 6	June 12	100·0	107·3	0·001	1,092
53	Cosmos 74-, rocket, capsule	June 12	62·8	89·6	0·011	181
54	Venus 10, launcher rocket, launcher	June 14	(space	probe)		
55	?	June 18	0·2	1,435·1	0·002	35,680
56	Cosmos 744, rocket	June 20	81·2	97·1	0·002	602
57	OSO-8	June 21	32·9	95·5	0·001	544
58	Cosmos 745, rocket	June 24	71·0	92·3	0·018	264
59	Cosmos 746, rocket, capsule	June 25	62·8	89·5	0·011	180
60	Cosmos 747, rocket	June 27	62·8	89·3	0·007	193
61	Cosmos 748, rocket	July 3	62·8	89·4	0·011	178
62	Cosmos 749, rocket	July 4	74·0	95·2	0·003	509
63	Molniya 2N, launcher rocket, launcher, rocket	July 8	62·9	736·9	0·748	432
64	Meteor 2-01, rocket	July 11	81·3	102·5	0·002	858
65	Soyuz 19★, rocket	July 15	51·8	88·5	0·003	186
66	Apollo 18★, rocket	July 15	51·8	88·4	0·004	170
67	Cosmos 750, rocket	July 17	71·0	95·4	0·038	272
68	Cosmos 751, rocket	July 23	62·8	89·6	0·009	197
69	Cosmos 752, rocket	July 24	65·8	94·6	0·002	481
70	China 3, rocket	July 26	69·0	91·0	0·021	181

ARTIFICIAL SATELLITES LAUNCHED IN 1975

Desig-nation	Satellite	Launch date	i	P	e	Perigee height (km)
1975-		1975	°	m		
71	*Cosmos 753, rocket, capsule*	July 31	62·8	89·6	0·011	181
72	COS-B	August 9	90·1	2,226·7	0·881	342
73	*Cosmos 754, rocket, capsule*	August 13	71·4	89·8	0·009	204
74	Cosmos 755, rocket	August 14	82·9	105·0	0·003	974
75	Viking 1, rocket		(space	probe)		
76	Cosmos 756, rocket	August 22	81·2	97·3	0·001	622
77	Symphonie 2	August 27	0·0	1,427·4	0·006	35,364
78	*Cosmos 757, rocket, capsule*	August 27	62·8	89·5	0·010	182
79	Molniya 1AG, launcher rocket, launcher, rocket	September 2	62·9	736·8	0·741	623
80	*Cosmos 758, rocket*	September 5	67·1	89·5	0·011	174
81	Molniya 2P, *launcher rocket, launcher, rocket*	September 9	62·8	90·8	0·015	213
82	Kiku, rocket	September 9	47·0	105·9	0·009	975
83	Viking 2, rocket	September 9		(space	probe)	
84	*Cosmos 759, rocket, capsule*	September 12	62·8	89·5	0·003	231
85	*Cosmos 760, rocket, capsule*	September 16	65·0	89·6	0·012	174
86	Cosmos 761–768, rocket	September 17	74·0	114·7	0·005	1,402
87	Meteor 22, rocket	September 18	81·3	102·4	0·004	838
88	*Cosmos 769, rocket*	September 23	72·8	89·6	0·008	203
89	Cosmos 770, rocket	September 24	82·9	109·2	0·003	1,169
90	*Cosmos 771, rocket, capsule*	September 25	81·3	88·7	0·001	203
91	Intelsat 4FI, rocket	September 26	0·5	1426·1	0·006	35·358
92	Aura, rocket	September 27	21·8	655·2	0·722	566
93	*Cosmos 772, rocket*	September 29	51·8	89·4	0·008	195
94	Cosmos 773, rocket	September 30	74·1	100·9	0·001	791
95	*Cosmos 774, rocket, capsule*	October 1	71·3	89·7	0·008	204
96	Explorer 54	October 6	90·1	126·9	0·219	155
97	Cosmos 775, *launcher, launcher rocket, rocket*	October 8	0·1	1,442	0	35,900
98	?	October 9	96·4	89·3	0·017	125
99	Trial 2, rocket	October 12	90·7	95·3	0·025	362
100	GOES 1	October 16	1·0	1,435·9	0	35,770
101	*Cosmos 776, rocket, capsule*	October 17	62·8	89·4	0·007	200
102	*Cosmos 777, rocket*	October 29	65·0	89·8	0·022	123
103	Cosmos 778, rocket	November 4	83·0	104·9	0·002	978
104	*Cosmos 779, rocket*	November 4	62·8	89·7	0·012	182
105	Molniya 3C, *launcher rocket, launcher, rocket*	November 14	62·9	737·3	0·745	523
106	*Soyuz 20, rocket*	November 17	51·6	88·7	0·006	177
107	Explorer 55, rocket	November 20	19·7	117·3	0·178	157
108	*Cosmos 780, rocket*	November 21	65·0	89·3	0·006	201
109	Cosmos 781, rocket	November 21	74·0	95·2	0·003	505
110	*Cosmos 782, rocket*	November 25	62·8	90·5	0·012	218
111	*China 4, rocket*	November 26	62·9	91·1	0·022	179
112	Cosmos 783, rocket	November 28	74·1	101·0	0·001	795
113	*Cosmos 784, rocket, capsule*	December 3	81·3	89·0	0·001	215
114	? , capsule, *rocket*	December 4	96·3	88·4	0·006	157
115	Intercosmos 14, rocket	December 11	74·0	105·3	0·091	335
116	*Cosmos 785, rocket, platform*	December 12	65·0	89·6	0·001	251
117	RCA Satcom 1	December 13	1·0	1,436·0	0·000	35,770
118	IMEWS 5	December 14	0·5	1,433·3	0·003	35,620
119	China 5, rocket	December 16	69·0	90·3	0·015	186
120	*Cosmos 786, rocket, capsule*	December 16	65·0	89·5	0·011	174
121	Molniya 2Q, *launcher rocket, launcher, rocket*	December 17	62·8	736·0	0·748	431
122	Prognoz 4, *launcher rocket, launcher, rocket*	December 22	65·0	91·5	0·018	229
123	Statsionar 1, *launcher, launcher rocket, rocket*	December 22	0·1	1,434	0	35,800
124	Meteor 23, rocket	December 25	81·3	102·4	0·004	842
125	Molniya 3D, *launcher rocket, launcher, rocket*	December 27	62·8	735·1	0·747	443

fully chosen to take the satellites, at low heights, directly over the battlefield during daylight.

The space war is hotting up—two American D.O.D. satellites were blinded by powerful infra-red emissions from west Russia on October 18 1975 and November 17/18 1975. Recently the number of satellites in orbit increased markedly due to the break-up of a number of American and Russian satellites. It seems likely that 5 American and 4 Russian satellites were targets for rockets (fired from the ground) designed to prove their capabilities of destroying satellites in orbit. One of the satellites involved was the naked-eye balloon satellite Pageos A (1966-56A).

Apart from their names, *e.g.* Cosmos 6 Rocket or Injun 3, the satellites are also classified according to their date of launch. Thus 1961 α refers to the launching of Samos 2. The next satellite launching was 1961 β and so on. A number following the Greek letter is intended to indicate the relative brightness of the satellites put in orbit. From the beginning of 1963 the Greek letters are replaced by numbers and the numbers by roman letters e.g. 1963-01A. In this table are given the designation and names of the main objects in orbit (in the order A, B, C ... etc.), the launch date and some initial orbital data. These are the inclination to the equator (i), the nodal period of revolution (P), the eccentricity, e, and the perigee height. The names of those satellites which have already disintegrated in the Earth's atmosphere or returned to the Earth's surface are printed in *italics*. A satellite which carried a human being is indicated by an asterisk.

Since the last edition of *Whitaker's Almanack* the following satellites launched in the years 1964-75 have disintegrated in the Earth's atmosphere:—

1962·01	1968-109A	1970-49A	1970-49D
1970-77A	1970-101A	1970-101D	1971-18B
1971-58B	1971-76B	1972-95A	1973-99A
1974-09A	1974-47B	1974-60D	1974-102C
1975-03A	1975-06A		

Observation of Satellites

The regression of the orbit around the Earth causes alternate periods of visibility and invisibility, though this is of little concern to the radio or radar observer. To the visual observer the following cycle of events normally occurs (though the cycle may start in any position): invisibility, morning observations before dawn, invisibility, evening observations after dusk, invisibility, morning observations before dawn, and so on. With reasonably high satellites and for observers in high latitudes around the summer solstice the evening observations follow the morning observations without interruption as sunlight passing over the polar regions can still illuminate satellites which are passing over temperate latitudes at local midnight. At the moment all satellites rely on sunlight to make them visible though a satellite with a flashing light has been suggested for a future launching. The observer must be in darkness or twilight in order to make any useful observations and the durations of twilight and the sunrise, sunset times given on page II of each month will be a useful guide.

Some of the satellites are visible to the naked eye and much interest has been aroused by the spectacle of a bright satellite disappearing into the Earth's shadow. The event is even more fascinating telescopically as the disappearance occurs gradually as the satellite traverses the Earth's penumbral shadow, and during the last few seconds before the eclipse is complete the satellite may change colour (under suitable atmospheric conditions) from yellow to red. This is because the last rays of sunlight are reflected through the denser layers of our atmosphere before striking the satellite.

Some satellites rotate about one or more axes so that a periodic variation in brightness is observed. This was particularly noticeable in several of the U.S.S.R. satellites.

Satellite research has already provided some interesting results. Among them may be mentioned a revised value of the Earth's oblateness. 1/298·2, and the discovery of the Van Allen radiation belts.

ROYAL OBSERVATORIES

Royal Greenwich Observatory
Herstmonceux, Sussex

The Royal Observatory was established at Greenwich in 1675 by Charles II for improving methods of navigation. Latterly the growth of London, with its smoke and bright lights, seriously hampered astronomical observations there, and it was decided in 1946 to move the telescopes to Herstmonceux Castle in Sussex. The removal was completed by 1958. The meridian of zero longitude still passes through the old site, which now houses the Department of Navigation and Astronomy of the National Maritime Museum.

At the Observatory astronomical measurements are made of the positions, motions and distances of the heavenly bodies, and of such physical characteristics as their luminosities, masses and temperatures. Two meridian instruments and six equatorially-mounted telescopes are devoted to this work, and the Isaac Newton telescope, a 2.5 metre reflector for the use of any qualified British astronomer, was completed in 1967. The Observatory is responsible for the time service of the United Kingdom and the time zones of the world are based on Greenwich Mean Time.

H.M. Nautical Almanac Office

The *Nautical Almanac* was first published for 1767 by the Board of Longitude. The Office is now a department of the Royal Greenwich Observatory. Annual publications—Astronomical Ephemeris, Nautical Almanac, Air Almanac, Star Almanac.

Royal Observatory
Blackford Hill, Edinburgh 9

The Observatory, founded by the Astronomical Institution in 1818 on Calton Hill, was moved to its present site in 1896. Its work, which is closely linked with that of the Astronomy Department of Edinburgh University, is concerned with the physics of stars and interstellar matter and the structure and evolution of our galaxy and external galaxies. Observational data are secured with various telescopes in Edinburgh and in Monte Porzio, Italy, where the Observatory operates an outstation. The Observatory has specialized in the design and construction of advanced data processing equipment.

Astronomer Royal for Scotland and Regius Professor of Astronomy in the University of Edinburgh, Prof. V. C. Reddish O.B.E., Ph.D., D.Sc.

TIDAL CONSTANTS

THE TIME OF HIGH WATER *at the undermentioned Ports and Places may be* approximately *found by taking the appropriate Time of High Water at the* Standard Port *(as shown on pp. 172, 173, etc.) and adding thereto the quantities annexed. The columns headed " Springs " and " Neaps " show the height of the tide above datum for Mean High Water Springs and Mean High Water Neaps respectively.*

Tidal data is no longer available for a number of places which formerly appeared in the list below. These places (with the name of the substitute now recorded) are: *Air Point* (Mostyn Quay); *Ardrishaig* (East Loch Tarbert); *Arisaig* (Loch Moidart); *Ayr Pt., I.o.M.* (Peel); *Beachy Head* (Eastbourne); *Beaumaris* (Menai Bridge); *Brieile* (Scheveningen); *Broughty Ferry* (Newburgh); *Burryport* (Whiteford Lighthouse); *Caen* (Cayeux); *Caernarvon* (Llanddwyn Isld.); *Dumbarton* (Bowling); *Dumfries* (Port Carlisle); *Fareham* (Itchenor); *Fifeness* (Anstruther Easter); *Glasson Dock* (Tarn Pt.); *Gravesend* (Tilbury Dock); *Greenwich* (R. Albert Dock); *Hythe* (Totland Bay); *Lancaster* (Duddon Bar); *Lynmouth* (Porlock Bay); *Nash Pt.* (Chepstow); *Needles Pt.* (Freshwater Bay); *Neath* (Porthcawl); *Nore Lt.* (Chatham); *Port Harrington* (Heston Islet); *Portishead* (Avonmouth); *St. Agnes* (Coverack); *St. Mary's* (Sennen Cove); *Start Pt.* (Lulworth Cove); *Stockton* (Seaham); *Sutton Bridge* (Blacktoft); *Torbay* (Torquay); *Woolwich* (Hammersmith Br.); *Worms Head* (Ferryside); *Honfleur Harbour* (Duclair).

Port		Diff.	Springs	Neaps	Port		Diff.	Springs	Neaps
		h.m.	metres	metres			h.m.	metres	metres
Aberdeen	Leith	−1 16	4·3	3·4	Coverack	Bristol	−1 59	5·3	4·2
Aberdovey	Liverpool	−3 16	4·8	3·8	*Cowes (West)	London	−2 28	4·2	3·5
Aberystwyth	Liverpool	−3 34	4·8	3·7	Cromarty	Leith	−2 51	4·2	3·4
Aldeburgh	London	−3 6	2·8	2·7	Cromer	Hull	+0 37	5·3	4·2
Alderney	London	+5 32	6·3	4·7	Dartmouth	London	+4 28	4·8	3·6
Alloa	Leith	+0 46	5·6	4·2	Deal	London	−2 27	6·1	5·0
Amlwch	Liverpool	−0 47	6·3	5·7	Devonport	London	+4 00	5·5	4·4
Anstruther Easter	Leith	−0 22	5·5	4·4	Dieppe	London	−3 8	9·1	7·1
Antwerp	London	+1 20	5·4	4·5	Dingle Harbour	Liverpool	+5 30	3·5	2·6
Appledore	Bristol	−1 24	7·5	5·2	Donegal Hbr.	Liverpool	−5 26	3·6	2·7
Arbroath	Leith	−0 30	5·0	4·1	Douglas	Liverpool	−0 4	6·9	5·4
Ardrossan	Greenock	−0 20	3·2	2·7	Dover	London	−2 42	6·7	5·3
*Arundel	Leith	−1 8	3·1	2·2	Duclair	London	−0 42	7·8	6·4
Avonmouth	Bristol	0 0	13·2	10·0	Duddon Bar	Liverpool	+0 3	8·5	6·6
Ayr	Greenock	−0 20	3·0	2·6	Dunbar	Leith	−0 8	5·2	4·2
Ballycotton	Bristol	−1 41	3·8	3·0	Dundalk (Sldr's Pt.)	L'pool	+0 19	4·8	3·9
Banff	Leith	−2 41	3·2	2·5	Dundee	Leith	+0 15	5·3	4·3
Bantry Harbour	Liverpool	+6 51	3·3	2·4	Dungeness	London	−2 56	8·0	6·3
Bardsey Island	Liverpool	−3 23	4·4	3·4	Dunkirk	London	−1 57	5·8	4·7
Barmouth	Liverpool	−3 9	4·9	3·9	Eastbourne	London	−2 52	7·3	5·6
Barnstaple Bridge	Bristol	−1 7	4·1	1·4	East Loch Tarbert	G'nock	−0 5	3·2	2·8
Barrow	Liverpool	+0 15	9·2	7·1	Exmouth Dock	London	+4 50	4·0	2·8
Barry Island	Bristol	−0 25	11·6	8·9	Eyemouth	Leith	−0 20	4·7	3·7
Belfast	London	−2 48	3·5	3·0	Falmouth	London	+3 30	5·3	4·2
Berwick	Leith	0 1	4·7	3·8	Ferryside	Bristol	−1 00	6·7	4·5
Bideford	Bristol	−1 24	5·9	3·6	Filey Bay	Leith	+1 51	5·8	4·9
Blacktoft	Hull	+0 24	5·6	3·3	Fishguard	Liverpool	−4 9	4·7	3·4
Blakeney	Hull	+0 31	3·1	2·1	Flushing	London	−0 37	4·7	3·9
Blyth	Leith	+0 51	5·0	3·9	Folkestone	London	−2 54	7·1	5·7
Boscastle	Bristol	−1 39	7·3	5·6	Formby Pt.	Liverpool	−0 21	9·0	7·3
Boulogne	London	−2 48	8·9	7·1	Fowey	London	+3 48	5·4	4·3
Bowling	Greenock	+0 24	4·0	3·4	Fraserburgh	Leith	−2 16	3·9	3·1
Brest	London	+2 25	7·4	5·8	†*Freshwater Bay	London	−4 33	2·6	2·3
Bridgewater Bar	Bristol	−0 22	4·6	1·9	Galway Bay	Liverpool	−6 10	4·7	3·5
Bridlington	Leith	+2 4	6·0	4·7	Glasgow	Greenock	+0 27	4·8	4·0
Bridport	London	+4 32	4·1	3·0	Goole	Hull	+1 12	5·6	3·6
Brighton	London	−2 52	6·5	5·1	Granton Pier	Leith	0 0	5·6	4·5
Buckie	Leith	−2 54	3·6	3·0	Granville	London	+4 32	12·8	9·5
Bude Haven	Bristol	−1 34	7·7	5·8	Grimsby	Hull	−0 26	7·0	5·6
Burntisland	Leith	0 0	5·6	4·5	Hartlepool	Leith	+0 59	5·1	4·0
Calais	London	−2 25	6·9	5·6	Harwich	London	−2 18	4·0	3·4
Campbeltown	Greenock	−0 32	3·0	2·5	Hastings	London	−2 47	7·5	5·8
Cape Cornwall	Bristol	−2 26	6·0	4·3	Haverfordwest	Liverpool	−4 36	2·2	0·3
Cardiff	Bristol	−0 7	12·3	9·4	Havre, Le	London	−4 0	7·8	6·4
Cardigan	Liverpool	−4 7	4·7	3·5	Hestan Islet	Liverpool	+0 25	8·3	6·3
Carmarthen Bar	Bristol	−0 39	2·6	0·4	Hilbre Island	Liverpool	−0 16	9·0	7·2
Cayeux	London	−3 00	10·1	7·7	Holyhead	Liverpool	−0 54	5·7	4·5
Chatham (N.Lock)	London	−1 4	6·0	4·9	Hook of Holland	London	+0 19	2·0	1·7
Chepstow	Bristol	+0 20	—	—	†*Hurst Point	London	−3 43	2·7	2·3
Cherbourg	London	−6 4	6·2	4·8	Ilfracombe	Bristol	−1 9	9·2	6·9
Chester	Liverpool	+1 5	4·2	1·7	Inveraray	Greenock	+0 11	3·3	3·0
Chichester Hbr.	London	−2 30	4·9	4·0	Invergordon	Leith	−2 41	4·3	3·3
†*Christchrch Hbr.	London	−4 58	1·8	1·4	Ipswich	London	−1 58	4·7	3·4
Cobh	Liverpool	−5 59	3·7	2·8					

* Approximate figures only, owing to abnormality of tides in the area.
† 1st H.W. (Springs).

Port	Diff.	Springs	Neaps
	h.m.	metres	metres
Itchenor.........*London*	−2 21	5·1	4·0
Kinsale Harbour.*Liverpool*	−6 11	4·0	3·2
Kirkcudbright..*Liverpool*	+0 15	7·5	5·9
Kirkwall.........*Leith*	−4 11	2·6	1·9
Lamlash.......*Greenock*	−0 26	3·2	2·7
Lerwick Harbour.....*Leith*	−3 46	1·8	1·3
Limerick......*Liverpool*	−4 40	5·9	4·5
‡Littlehampton...*London*	−2 38	5·7	4·6
Lizard.............*Bristol*	−2 14	5·3	4·2
Llanddwyn Islnd.*Liverpool*	−1 47	4·3	3·4
Llanelly Bar......*Bristol*	−0 52	7·8	5·8
Loch Long.....*Greenock*	−0 5.	3·4	2·9
Loch Moidart....*Greenock*	+6 0	4·3	3·1
Londonderry.....*London*	−5 41	2·5	1·8
Looe (East)......*London*	+3 50	5·4	4·2
Lossiemouth......*Leith*	−2 58	3·7	2·9
Lowestoft........*London*	−4 26	2·4	2·1
*Lulworth Cove...*London*	+4 55	2·3	1·5
Lundy Island......*Bristol*	−1 19	8·0	5·9
Lyme Regis......*London*	+4 50	4·3	3·1
†*Lymington....*London*	−3 23	3·0	2·6
Lynn Road........*Hull*	+0 7	—	—
Margate Pier....*London*	−1 50	4·8	3·9
Maryport......*Liverpool*	+0 24	8·6	6·6
Menai Bridge...*Liverpool*	−0 25	7·4	5·8
Mevagissey....*London*	+3 48	5·4	4·3
Middlesbrough.....*Leith*	+1 10	5·6	4·5
Milford Haven..*Liverpool*	−5 12	7·0	5·2
Minehead Pier.....*Bristol*	—	10·7	8·0
Montrose..........*Leith*	−0 16	4·8	3·9
Morecambe.....*Liverpool*	+0 1	9·5	7·6
Mostyn Quay...*Liverpool*	−0 10	8·7	6·9
Newburgh......*Leith*	+0 51	4·1	3·0
Newcastle on Tyne.*Leith*	+0 55	5·3	4·1
Newhaven......*London*	−2 57	6·6	5·2
Newport (Mon.)..*Bristol*	−0 10	12·1	9·0
Newquay......*Bristol*	−1 59	6·9	5·4
New Quay (Card.).*L'pool*	−3 41	4·7	3·6
North Shields......*Leith*	+0 52	5·0	3·9
North Sunderland..*Leith*	+0 6	4·8	3·7
Oban..........*Greenock*	+5 45	4·0	2·9
Orfordness......*London*	−2 51	2·8	2·7
Ostend..........*London*	−1 33	5·6	4·7
Padstow.......*Bristol*	−1 49	7·3	5·6
Peel (I.O.M.)...*Liverpool*	−0 2	5·3	4·2
Pembroke Dock.*Liverpool*	−5 5	7·0	5·2
Penzance......*Bristol*	−2 16	5·6	4·4
Peterhead......*Leith*	−1 56	3·8	3·1
Plymouth B'water.*London*	+3 54	5·5	4·4
†*Poole(Entrance).*London*	−5 8	2·0	1·6
Porlock Bay.....*Bristol*	−0 52	10·3	8·0
Portmadoc.....*Liverpool*	−3 8	5·1	4·0
Port Patrick....*Liverpool*	+0 22	3·8	3·0
Port Talbot......*Bristol*	−0 54	9·7	7·5
Porthcawl.......*Bristol*	−0 49	9·9	7·5
Portland B'water..*London*	+5 5	2·1	1·4
Portsmouth.....*London*	−2 28	4·7	3·8
Preston.......*Liverpool*	0 0	5·4	3·5
Pwllheli........*Liverpool*	−3 18	4·9	3·7
Ramsey(I.O.M.)..*Liverpool*	+0 4	7·3	5·8
Ramsgate Harbour*London*	−2 22	4·9	3·8

Port	Diff.	Springs	Neaps
	h.m.	metres	metres
Ribble Lt.House.*Liverpool*	−0 4	—	—
Rosslare Hbr...*Liverpool*	−5 29	1·7	1·3
Rosyth............*Leith*	+0 6	5·8	4·7
R.A. Dock.......*London*	−0 25	7·1	5·8
Ryde...........*London*	−2 28	4·5	3·7
St. Helier......*London*	+4 47	11·1	8·1
St. Ives........*Bristol*	−2 9	6·6	4·9
St. Malo.......*London*	+4 26	12·0	9·0
St. Peter Port..*London*	+4 53	9·0	6·7
Salcombe.......*London*	+4 5	5·3	4·1
Saltash.........*London*	+4 9	5·6	4·4
Scarborough.....*Leith*	+1 49	5·7	4·6
Scheveningen.....*London*	+0 28	2·1	1·7
Scrabster.......*Leith*	+6 07	5·0	3·7
Seaham.........*Leith*	+0 54	5·2	4·1
Selsey Bill......*London*	−2 33	5·3	4·4
Sennen Cove.....*Bristol*	−2 26	6·1	4·8
Sharpness.......*Bristol*	+0 42	9·3	5·8
Sheerness......*London*	−1 19	5·7	4·8
Shoreham Hbr....*London*	−2 45	6·2	5·0
Silloth.........*Liverpool*	+0 35	9·2	6·9
††Southampton...*London*	−2 55	4·5	3·7
Southend......*London*	−1 24	5·7	4·8
Southwold.....*London*	−3 51	2·5	2·2
Spurn Head........*Hull*	−0 34	6·8	5·4
Stirling............*Leith*	−1 12	2·9	1·6
Stonehaven......*Leith*	−1 6	4·5	3·6
Stornoway.....*Liverpool*	−4 17	4·3	3·2
Stranraer.......*Greenock*	−0 20	3·0	2·5
Stromness.....*Leith*	−5 22	3·1	2·3
Sunderland....*Leith*	+0 52	5·2	4·2
†*Swanage....*London*	−5 18	2·0	1·6
Swansea Bay......*Bristol*	−0 43	9·6	7·3
Tarn Point.....*Liverpool*	+0 5	8·3	6·4
Tay River Bar....*Leith*	−0 18	5·2	4·2
Tees R. (Entrance).*Leith*	−1 9	5·5	4·3
Teignmouth....*London*	+4 32	4·8	3·6
Tenby............*Bristol*	−1 3	8·4	6·3
Tilbury Docks....*London*	−0 59	6·5	5·4
Tobermory....*Liverpool*	−5 14	4·5	3·4
Torquay.........*London*	+4 35	4·9	3·7
†*Totland Bay...*London*	−3 58	2·7	2·3
Troon.........*Greenock*	−0 20	3·1	2·6
Truro.........*London*	+3 38	5·3	4·2
‡Tynemouth.......*Leith*	+0 57	5·1	3·9
Ushant........*London*	+2 20	7·5	5·8
Valentia Hbr....*Liverpool*	+5 28	3·5	2·7
Walton on Naze....*London*	−2 9	4·2	3·4
Waterford Hbr...*L'pool*	−5 46	4·2	3·4
Weston S. Mare...*Bristol*	−0 25	12·0	9·1
*Wexford......*Liverpool*	−5 6	1·7	1·4
Whitby..........*Leith*	+1 32	5·4	4·3
Whiteford Lt. Hse.*Bristol*	−0 55	8·7	6·7
Whitehaven....*Liverpool*	+0 2	8·2	6·3
Wick............*Leith*	−3 23	3·4	2·7
Wisbech...........*Hull*	+0 10	7·4	5·5
Workington....*Liverpool*	+0 9	8·4	6·4
Worthing......*London*	−2 38	6·1	4·8
Yarmouth Roads...*Lond*	−5 1	2·4	2·0
††*Yarmth(I.O.W.).*Lond*	−3 33	3·1	2·5
Ymuiden......*London*	+1 13	2·1	1·7
Youghal......*Liverpool*	−5 53	3·9	3·2

* Approximate figures only, owing to abnormality of tides in area.
† 1st H.W. (Springs) — No data available
†† 1st H.W.
‡ Entrance.

The Standard Ports referred to in the heading are given in italic.

EXAMPLE.—Required times of high water at Stranraer on *January* 10, 1977:—

(a) Morning Tide.

Appropriate time of high water at *Greenock*..... 0324 hrs. (*Jan.* 10)
Tidal difference......... − 0020 hrs

H.W. at *Stranraer*... 0304 hrs.

(b) Afternoon Tide.

Appropriate time of high water at *Greenock*..... 1517 hrs. (*Jan.* 10).
Tidal difference......... − 0020 hrs.

H.W. at *Stranraer*... 1497 hrs.

JANUARY, 1977

High Water at the undermentioned Places (G.M.T.*)—

Day of Month	Day of Week	London Bridge †Datum 3·20 m. below				Liverpool †Datum 4·93 m. below				Avonmouth †Datum 6·50 m. below				Hull (Sal'end) †Datum 3·90 m. below				Greenock †Datum 1·62 m. below				Leith and Granton †Datum 2·90 m. below				Dun Laoghaire †Datum 0·20 m. above			
		Mn h.m.	Ht m.	Aft h.m.	Ht m.	Mn h.m.	Ht m.	Aft h.m.	Ht m.	Mn h.m.	Ht m.	Aft h.m.	Ht m.	Mn h.m.	Ht m.	Aft h.m.	Ht m.	Mn h.m.	Ht m.	Aft h.m.	Ht m.	Mn h.m.	Ht m.	Aft h.m.	Ht m.	Mn h.m.	Ht m.	Aft h.m.	Ht m.
1	S	1052	6·2	2329	6·4	823	7·6	2044	7·7	338	10·1	1615	10·5	240	5·8	1524	6·1	915	3·1	2157	3·0	1149	4·7	—	—	857	3·5	21 9	3·4
2	S	1156	6·3	—	—	913	7·9	2132	8·0	440	10·7	1711	11·0	342	6·0	1613	6·4	10 6	3·2	2246	3·1	0 7	4·7	1239	4·8	937	3·6	2151	3·5
3	M	019	6·6	1241	6·5	955	8·3	2214	8·6	532	11·4	18 0	11·6	434	6·3	1657	6·7	1049	3·3	2331	3·2	055	4·8	1324	5·0	1012	3·7	2226	3·6
4	Tu	1 0	6·7	1319	6·6	1033	8·6	2250	8·8	618	11·9	1842	12·0	520	6·6	1736	6·9	1126	3·4	—	—	140	5·0	14 4	5·2	1047	3·8	23 2	3·7
5	W	135	6·8	1354	6·7	11 9	8·9	2327	8·8	656	12·4	1922	12·5	6 3	6·8	1812	7·1	011	3·2	1159	3·5	221	5·2	1441	5·3	1121	3·9	2337	3·7
6	Th	211	6·9	1430	6·9	1143	9·1	—	—	734	13·0	1959	13·0	643	6·9	1848	7·2	050	3·2	1239	3·5	257	5·3	1517	5·4	1157	4·0	—	—
7	F	247	7·1	15 7	7·2	0 4	8·9	1217	9·2	810	13·0	2037	13·0	721	6·9	1923	7·3	127	3·2	1316	3·6	333	5·4	1551	5·5	013	3·8	1232	4·1
8	S	322	7·2	1545	7·3	040	9·0	1253	9·3	847	13·1	2115	13·1	758	6·9	1958	7·3	2 5	3·2	1354	3·7	4 8	5·4	1628	5·5	051	3·8	1310	4·1
9	S	357	7·2	1621	7·3	119	8·8	1330	9·2	926	13·0	2152	13·0	834	6·8	2033	7·3	244	3·2	1435	3·8	446	5·4	1710	5·5	133	3·8	1355	4·1
10	M	431	7·2	1659	7·2	158	8·8	1410	9·0	10 5	13·0	2229	12·6	911	6·7	2111	7·3	324	3·3	1517	3·8	529	5·2	1753	5·3	217	3·7	1430	4·1
11	Tu	5 8	7·1	1740	7·1	240	8·6	1454	8·9	1042	12·0	23 7	11·9	952	6·6	2155	7·0	4 4	3·3	16 1	3·8	616	5·1	1842	5·2	3 4	3·7	1524	4·1
12	W	549	6·9	1827	6·8	328	8·4	1545	8·5	1123	11·9	2351	11·6	1040	6·4	2247	6·7	445	3·3	1649	3·7	7 6	4·9	1934	5·0	359	3·6	1621	3·8
13	Th	638	6·7	1926	6·6	425	8·1	1646	8·2	1210	10·9	—	—	1136	6·2	2351	6·5	530	3·4	1743	3·5	8 7	4·8	2034	4·9	5 2	3·5	1728	3·7
14	F	745	6·5	2040	6·5	531	7·9	1759	8·0	052	10·5	1324	10·6	112	6·3	1250	6·3	630	3·4	1849	3·4	9 7	4·8	2142	4·9	613	3·5	1845	3·6
15	S	910	6·4	2159	6·5	646	8·0	1920	8·0	211	10·8	1451	10·8	234	6·4	1517	6·5	754	3·3	2011	3·3	1019	4·8	2255	4·9	725	3·5	1958	3·7
16	S	1031	6·6	2315	6·7	8 1	8·3	2036	8·3	339	10·8	1616	11·3	349	6·7	1624	6·8	917	3·2	2131	3·3	1129	4·9	—	—	828	3·7	21 1	3·7
17	M	1146	6·6	—	—	9 7	8·7	2137	8·7	457	11·6	1728	12·0	452	7·0	1721	7·0	1020	3·4	2237	3·4	0 4	5·1	1233	5·2	924	3·8	2158	3·8
18	Tu	019	6·8	1249	6·7	10 3	9·1	2231	9·0	5 6	12·6	1828	13·1	547	7·2	18 2	7·2	1113	3·5	2336	3·4	1 6	5·3	1330	5·5	1012	4·1	2247	3·9
19	W	114	6·8	1341	6·9	1051	9·5	2319	9·2	656	13·4	20 1	13·4	636	7·3	1849	7·4	1159	3·6	—	—	2 1	5·5	1420	5·7	1059	4·1	2333	4·0
20	Th	2 2	7·0	1427	7·0	1137	9·7	—	—	741	13·9	2119	13·5	8 2	7·3	1934	7·6	029	3·4	1249	3·9	249	5·7	15 6	5·8	1144	4·2	—	—
21	F	244	7·0	15 10	7·3	0 3	9·3	1220	9·8	822	14·0	2230	13·5	839	7·1	2039	7·5	118	3·5	1335	3·9	334	5·7	1549	5·8	018	4·0	1228	4·3
22	S	324	7·2	1550	7·4	046	9·3	13 2	9·6	939	13·5	23 1	12·2	914	6·8	2112	7·3	2 3	3·5	1417	3·9	416	5·7	1631	5·7	1 1	3·9	1313	4·2
23	S	4 2	7·3	1628	7·4	126	9·1	1341	9·4	1016	12·2	2330	12·2	948	6·5	2146	6·7	244	3·4	1456	3·8	457	5·5	1713	5·5	146	3·8	1357	4·1
24	M	440	7·2	17 6	7·2	2 4	8·8	1419	9·1	1049	12·2	2332	11·4	1024	6·2	2226	6·2	322	3·4	1534	3·7	538	5·3	1756	5·3	229	3·7	1443	4·0
25	Tu	515	7·0	1744	7·0	242	8·4	1457	8·6	1123	11·4	—	—	11 8	5·9	2315	5·9	357	3·4	1612	3·6	621	4·9	1839	4·9	317	3·5	1529	3·7
26	W	553	6·8	1825	6·6	322	8·0	1538	8·0	1157	10·5	—	—	—	—	1246	6·0	432	3·4	1652	3·4	7 5	4·7	1922	4·7	4 7	3·4	1618	3·5
27	Th	638	6·5	1914	6·3	4 6	7·5	1628	7·6	1 8	10·1	1243	9·8	022	5·6	1249	5·6	510	3·1	1739	3·1	752	4·5	2010	4·5	5 4	3·2	1717	3·3
28	F	734	6·1	2013	6·1	5 1	7·1	1730	7·2	022	9·5	1350	9·6	151	5·5	1420	5·5	557	3·1	1819	2·9	846	4·4	21 6	4·4	611	3·1	1827	3·2
29	S	843	5·8	2121	5·9	610	7·0	1845	7·1	151	9·4	1516	9·4	310	5·7	1539	5·6	654	3·0	1919	2·9	950	4·3	2217	4·3	719	3·1	1936	3·1
30	S	956	5·7	2235	5·9	728	7·1	20 1	7·3	310	9·9	1629	10·4	—	—	—	—	8 8	3·0	2117	2·9	1125	4·4	2337	4·5	816	3·3	2035	3·2
31	M	1115	5·8	2342	6·0	836	7·5	21 2	7·7	345	9·9	—	—	—	—	—	—	924	3·0	2221	3·0	12 5	4·6	—	—	9 4	3·4	2122	3·4

All times shown are Greenwich Mean Time.   † Difference of height in metres from Ordnance Datum (Newlyn).
‡ Difference of height in metres from Ordnance Datum (Dublin).

FEBRUARY, 1977

High Water at the undermentioned Places (G.M.T.*)—

Day of Week	Day of Month	London Bridge † Datum 3·20 m. below Mn. h.m.	Ht.	Aft. h.m.	Ht.	Liverpool † Datum 4·93 m. below Mn. h.m.	Ht.	Aft. h.m.	Ht.	Avonmouth † Datum 6·50 m. below Mn. h.m.	Ht.	Aft. h.m.	Ht.	Hull (Salend) † Datum 3·90 m. below Mn. h.m.	Ht.	Aft. h.m.	Ht.	Greenock † Datum 1·62 m. below Mn. h.m.	Ht.	Aft. h.m.	Ht.	Leith and Granton † Datum 2·90 m. below Mn. h.m.	Ht.	Aft. h.m.	Ht.	Dun Laoghaire ‡ Datum 0·20 m. above Mn. h.m.	Ht.	Aft. h.m.	Ht.
Tu	1			1210	6·0	927	8·0	2148	8·1	454	10·8	1730	11·2	412	6·1	1630	6·4	1018	3·2	2211	3·1	027	4·6	1258	4·8	945	3·6	22 3	3·5
W	2	029	6·2	1252	6·2	10 4	8·4	2228	8·5	550	11·7	1819	12·0	5 1	6·4	1712	6·7	11 2	3·4	2252	3·1	117	4·8	1342	5·0	1023	3·8	2240	3·7
Th	3	1 9	6·6	1330	6·6	1047	8·9	23 6	8·8	635	12·4	19 1	13·1	544	6·7	1751	7·0	1142	3·4			2 1	5·1	1421	5·3	1059	3·9	2316	3·8
F	4	148	6·9	1419	7·1	1122	9·2	2344	9·1	715	13·0	1941	13·1	625	7·0	1829	7·3	031	3·1	1221	3·5	239	5·3	15 1	5·5	1134	4·1	2352	3·9
S	5	2 3	7·3	1447	7·6	1159	9·5			754	13·3	2020	13·6	7 3	7·1	19 6	7·4	111	3·2	13 1	3·7	313	5·5	1532	5·6			1212	4·1
S	6	3 3	7·5	1527	7·6	022	9·3	1237	9·6	834	13·6	21 1	13·6	740	7·2	1942	7·5	150	3·2	1341	3·7	348	5·6	16 9	5·7	030	3·9	1250	4·2
M	7	339	7·6	16 3	7·1	1 1	9·4	1315	9·6	913	13·7	2138	13·5	815	7·1	2019	7·5	229	3·3	1422	3·8	426	5·5	1650	5·6	110	3·9	1330	4·2
Tu	8	414	7·5	1641	7·5	139	9·3	1352	9·5	953	13·5	2214	13·1	851	7·1	2057	7·5	3 6	3·4	15 2	3·9	5 8	5·4	1734	5·5	153	3·9	1414	4·1
W	9	452	7·3	1722	7·2	220	9·1	1434	9·4	1028	13·0	2249	12·3	931	6·9	2139	7·2	344	3·4	1545	3·9	553	5·3	1821	5·4	239	3·8	15 3	4·0
Th	10	533	7·1	18 7	6·9	3 3	8·7	1522	8·7	11 5	12·1	2327	11·1	1014	6·6	2228	6·9	423	3·4	1651	3·9	643	5·1	1912	5·2	332	3·7	1559	3·8
F	11	622	6·8	19 2	6·6	357	8·3	1621	8·2	1152	11·1			11 6	6·3	2330	6·5	5 5	3·4	1722	3·5	738	4·9	2012	4·9	432	3·5	17 6	3·6
S	12	847	6·4	2013	6·3	5 3	7·9	1736	7·8	024	10·5	1259	10·3	053	6·2	1340	6·0	557	3·0	1824	3·3	843	4·8	2123	4·8	543	3·4	1827	3·5
S	13	1013	6·2	2132	6·2	622	7·7	19 6	7·7	145	10·0	1431	10·1	226	6·2	15 0	6·0	713	3·0	1948	3·1	959	4·7	2244	4·8	813	3·5	2057	3·6
M	14	1133	6·4	2254	6·3	746	8·1	2028	8·4	322	10·6	16 6	10·7	343	6·4	1620	6·6	9 2	3·0	2127	3·1	1118	4·8			915	3·7	2153	3·7
Tu	15	1 0	6·5	1238	6·7	857	8·4	2132	8·8	447	11·4	1720	11·7	445	6·8	17 1	7·0	10 4	3·2	2237	3·1	1 0	5·2	1226	5·1	10 5	3·9	2242	3·8
W	16	147	7·1	1413	7·1	954	8·9	2223	8·8	552	12·4	1817	12·6	537	7·1	1749	7·3	1154	3·6	2331	3·2	152	5·4	1323	5·4	1133	4·1	2334	3·9
Th	17	227	7·1	1453	7·3	1040	9·3	23 6	9·1	643	13·3	19 3	13·1	622	7·3	1829	7·5	019	3·3	1239	3·8	238	5·6	1411	5·5			1213	4·1
F	18	3 4	7·3	1529	7·4	1122	9·5			726	13·7	1944	13·6	7 2	7·3	19 6	7·6	1 2	3·4	1320	3·8	318	5·6	1452	5·7	0 4	3·9	1251	4·1
S	19	339	7·3	16 4	7·4	024	9·2	1238	9·6	8 4	13·9	2021	13·5	737	7·3	1940	7·4	143	3·4	14 0	3·8	354	5·5	1530	5·7	040	3·9	1332	4·1
S	20	413	7·1	1637	7·0	1 0	9·1	1313	9·4	841	13·9	2058	13·5	8 9	7·1	2011	7·3	220	3·4	1435	3·7	430	5·5	16 7	5·6	118	3·8	1410	3·9
M	21	445	7·1	1711	7·0	133	8·9	1346	9·1	918	13·6	2129	13·2	840	6·9	2042	7·1	252	3·4	15 8	3·7	5 6	5·2	1644	5·5	157	3·7	1450	3·7
Tu	22	413	7·1	1637	7·0	2 5	8·6	1418	8·7	948	13·2	2157	12·7	910	6·7	2148	6·8	324	3·3	1541	3·5	544	4·9	1722	5·2	236	3·6	1533	3·5
W	23	445	7·1	1711	7·0	237	8·2	1454	8·2	1015	12·5	2221	12·1	941	6·4	2230	6·5	354	3·4	1617	3·3	623	4·7	18 0	5·0	3 7	3·4	1621	3·3
Th	24	520	6·9	1746	6·8	314	7·7	1536	7·7	1039	11·7	2246	11·2	1016	6·2	2230	6·2	428	3·3	1658	3·0	7 4	4·5	1839	4·8	4 4	3·2	1723	3·1
F	25	6 1	6·6	1829	6·4	4 1	7·3	1633	7·2	11 2	10·8	2318	10·4	11 2	6·1	2329	5·6	5 0	3·2	1748	3·0	750	4·3	1922	4·5	5 2	3·1	1841	3·0
S	26	650	6·2	1920	6·0	5 6	7·0	1746	6·9	1142	9·9			11 2	5·7			510	3·2	1748	4·3	851	4·2	2015	4·3	613	2·0	725	3·1
S	27	751	5·7	2023	5·6	625	6·9	1910	7·0	0 3	9·7	1241	9·4	057	5·3	1341	5·4	559	3·1	1850	2·8	851	4·2	2123	4·2	725	3·1		
M	28	9 1	5·4	2134	5·4					114	9·3	14 7	9·3					7 1	3·0	2022	2·8	108	4·2	2243	4·3	954	3·1		

All times shown are Greenwich Mean Time.   † Difference of height in metres from Ordnance Datum (Newlyn).
‡ Difference of height in metres from Ordnance Datum (Dublin).

MARCH, 1977

High Water at the undermentioned Places (G.M.T.*)—

| Day of month | Day of week | LONDON BRIDGE † Datum of Predictions 3·20 m. below | | | | LIVERPOOL † Datum of Predictions 4·93 m. below | | | | AVONMOUTH † Datum of Predictions 6·50 m. below | | | | HULL (Salterd) † Datum of Predictions 3·90 m. below | | | | GREENOCK † Datum of Predictions 1·62 m. below | | | | LEITH AND GRANTON † Datum of Predictions 2·90 m. below | | | | DUN LAOGHAIRE ‡ Datum of Predictions 0·20 m. above | | | |
		Mn. h.m.	Ht. m.	Aft. h.m.	Ht. m.	Mn. h.m.	Ht. m.	Aft. h.m.	Ht. m.	Mn. h.m.	Ht. m.	Aft. h.m.	Ht. m.	Mn. h.m.	Ht. m.	Aft. h.m.	Ht. m.	Mn. h.m.	Ht. m.	Aft. h.m.	Ht. m.	Mn. h.m.	Ht. m.	Aft. h.m.	Ht. m.	Mn. h.m.	Ht. m.	Aft. h.m.	Ht. m.
1	Tu	1016	5·4	2248	5·5	749	7·2	2025	7·4	247	9·5	1542	10·0	232	5·5	1457	5·7	823	3·0	2152	2·9	1124	4·4	2353	4·5	824	3·3	2050	3·3
2	W	1126	5·7	2350	5·9	853	7·9	2120	8·0	414	10·5	1655	11·1	341	5·9	1555	6·6	942	3·1	2246	3·0			1225	4·6	912	3·5	2135	3·5
3	Th			1217	6·2	939	8·3	2202	8·5	519	11·5	1752	12·1	434	6·3	1642	6·6	1033	3·3	2338	3·1	048	4·8	1314	4·9	955	3·7	2215	3·7
4	F	036	6·4	1302	6·7	1018	8·9	2241	9·0	610	12·4	1839	12·8	518	6·7	1725	7·0	1117	3·3			134	5·1	1356	5·3	1033	3·9	2253	3·9
5	S	120	6·9	1344	7·3	1056	9·3	2320	9·4	653	13·1	1922	13·4	558	7·1	1805	7·4	047	3·5	1159	3·5	213	5·4	1433	5·5	1114	4·1	2328	4·0
6	Su	201	7·3	1425	7·7	1135	9·7			736	13·6	2004	13·7	638	7·4	1843	7·6	127	3·7	1242	3·8	248	5·6	1509	5·7	1147	4·2		
7	M	240	7·7	1504	7·8	000	9·6	1216	9·8	817	14·0	2043	13·9	714	7·4	1923	7·7	206	3·7	1324	3·9	325	5·7	1546	5·8	006	4·1	1228	4·3
8	Tu	318	7·8	1542	7·8	040	9·7	1255	9·8	857	14·0	2122	13·8	752	7·4	2001	7·7	244	3·7	1407	3·9	404	5·7	1628	5·8	046	4·1	1308	4·3
9	W	356	7·6	1623	7·6	120	9·6	1336	9·7	936	13·7	2157	13·3	829	7·3	2042	7·6	321	3·5	1447	3·9	447	5·6	1714	5·7	129	4·0	1354	4·2
10	Th	437	7·3	1704	7·2	201	9·3	1418	9·3	1013	13·1	2234	12·5	908	7·1	2125	7·3	400	3·5	1616	3·7	534	5·4	1803	5·5	215	3·8	1446	4·1
11	F	520	7·2	1750	6·8	244	8·9	1506	8·7	1052	12·1	2314	11·5	952	6·8	2216	6·9	443	3·4	1706	3·4	625	5·2	1857	5·5	307	3·8	1543	4·1
12	S	612	6·7	1843	6·4	338	8·4	1605	8·1	1139	11·1			1042	6·4	2319	6·4	533	3·2	1807	3·1	720	4·9	1958	4·9	409	3·6	1650	3·6
13	Su	716	6·4	1949	6·1	443	7·9	1724	7·6	009	10·6	1246	10·6	1150	6·0			642	3·0	1933	2·9	826	4·7	2111	4·9	520	3·4	1814	3·4
14	M	832	6·1	2115	6·0	605	7·5	1856	7·5	131	10·4	1420	10·6	043	6·0	1317	5·9	847	3·0	2138	2·9	1116	4·8	2347	4·8	800	3·5	1939	3·4
15	Tu	955	6·1	2228	6·1	733	7·8	2010	8·1	310	10·4	1556	10·6	218	6·0	1443	6·0	1005	3·1	2233	3·1	944	4·6	2234	4·8	902	3·7	2144	3·5
16	W	1116	6·4	2343	6·4	845	8·3	2210	8·7	438	11·4	1709	11·6	334	6·3	1550	6·4	1055	3·3	2319	3·1			1214	5·0	955	3·8	2230	3·7
17	Th			1219	6·7	940	8·7	2248	9·0	539	12·4	1803	12·5	431	6·7	1644	6·8	1139	3·4			047	5·2	1310	5·3	1039	4·0	2309	3·8
18	F	041	6·7	1310	7·0	1024	9·1	2324	9·1	625	13·1	1845	13·0	519	6·9	1727	7·1	000	3·2	1220	3·5	137	5·3	1355	5·4	1117	4·1	2344	3·9
19	S	127	6·9	1354	7·1	1103	9·3	2359	9·4	705	13·4	1923	13·2	600	7·1	1807	7·3	002	3·3	1300	3·6	220	5·5	1434	5·6	1154	4·1		
20	Su	206	7·1	1432	7·4	137	9·4	1213	9·4	742	13·6	1958	13·3	636	7·2	1842	7·3	039	3·3	1338	3·6	256	5·5	1507	5·6	016	4·0	1229	4·0
21	M	243	7·3	1505	7·4	031	9·1	1245	9·2	818	13·4	2031	13·3	709	7·2	1913	7·3	116	3·4	1411	3·6	330	5·4	1541	5·5	050	3·8	1340	3·9
22	Tu	317	7·3	1538	7·3	103	9·2	1316	9·2	852	13·4	2101	13·2	738	7·1	1944	7·2	149	3·5	1444	3·5	402	5·3	1614	5·4	123	3·7	1340	3·8
23	W	348	7·1	1607	7·0	131	9·0	1345	8·6	920	13·1	2126	12·8	806	7·0	2013	7·0	220	3·5	1510	3·5	435	5·0	1650	5·2	159	3·6	1456	3·6
24	Th	419	7·1	1638	7·0	158	8·7	1419	8·6	944	12·6	2148	12·3	834	6·8	2044	6·8	247	3·5	1545	3·5	509	5·0	1726	5·0	238	3·5	1542	3·5
25	F	452	6·9	1711	6·8	235	8·0	1459	7·8	1006	11·9	2211	11·6	903	6·6	2118	6·5	316	3·4	1623	3·1	544	4·8	1802	4·8	318	3·4	1638	3·4
26	S	530	6·6	1749	6·5	318	8·6	1552	7·3	1030	11·1	2241	10·8	935	6·3	2159	6·1	350	3·4	1710	3·1	623	4·6	1844	4·6	410	3·2	1749	3·0
27	Su	612	6·1	1831	6·1	417	7·2	1711	7·1	1104	10·3	2324	10·1	1016	5·9	2251	5·7	430	3·3	1804	2·8	708	4·4	1936	4·4	513	3·1	1906	3·1
28	M	702	5·8	1919	5·7	532	7·0	1821	7·0	1156	9·7			1112	5·6			519	3·1	1915	2·8	805	4·3	2041	4·2	627	3·1	2012	3·3
29	Tu	759	5·5	2022	5·4	655	7·2	1940	7·3	028	9·6	1316	9·5	010	5·4	1234	5·4	613	3·0	1915	2·7	918	4·2	2158	4·2	736	3·3	2021	3·3
30	W	914	5·4	2143	5·5	811	7·7	2041	7·9	156	9·7	1454	10·0	144	5·4	1414	5·6	614	3·0	2212	3·0	1036	4·3	2312	4·4	832	3·5	2121	3·5
31	Th	1031	5·7	2259	5·8	808	7·7	2041	7·9	328	10·4	1616	11·0	300	5·8	1512	6·0	853	3·0	2212	3·0	1143	4·6						

*All times shown are Greenwich Mean Time.   † Difference of height in metres from Ordnance Datum (Newlyn).   ‡ Difference of height in metres from Ordnance Datum (Dublin).

APRIL, 1977

High Water at the undermentioned places (G.M.T.*)—

Day of Month	Day of Week	London Bridge †Datum 3·20 m. below — Mn. h.m.	Ht. m.	Aft. h.m.	Ht. m.	Liverpool †Datum 4·93 m. below — Mn. h.m.	Ht. m.	Aft. h.m.	Ht. m.	Avonmouth †Datum 6·50 m. below — Mn. h.m.	Ht. m.	Aft. h.m.	Ht. m.	Hull (Saltend) †Datum 3·90 m. below — Mn. h.m.	Ht. m.	Aft. h.m.	Ht. m.	Greenock †Datum 1·62 m. below — Mn. h.m.	Ht. m.	Aft. h.m.	Ht. m.	Leith and Granton †Datum 2·90 m. below — Mn. h.m.	Ht. m.	Aft. h.m.	Ht. m.	Dun Laoghaire †Datum 0·20 m. below — Mn. h.m.	Ht. m.	Aft. h.m.	Ht. m.
1	F	1136	6·2	2358	6·4	9 1	8·1	2129	8·5	440	11·5	1719	12·0	357	6·2	16 6	6·6	957	3·2	2254	3·0	011	4·7	1238	4·9	921	3·7	2145	3·7
2	S	—	—	1228	6·9	945	8·3	2211	9·1	538	12·4	1810	12·6	445	6·7	1652	7·0	1046	3·4	2335	3·1	1 0	5·1	1322	5·2	10 2	3·9	2223	3·9
3	S	048	7·5	1316	7·4	1028	9·4	2252	9·5	628	13·2	1858	13·5	527	7·1	1737	7·4	1132	3·5	—	—	141	5·4	14 3	5·5	1042	4·1	23 2	4·1
4	M	133	7·7	1358	7·7	1110	9·7	2336	9·8	715	13·7	1943	13·9	6 8	7·4	1821	7·7	017	3·3	1218	3·7	220	5·6	1441	5·8	1121	4·2	2340	4·1
5	Tu	215	7·7	1440	7·9	1153	9·9	—	—	759	14·1	2024	14·0	649	7·6	19 4	7·8	058	3·3	13 3	3·7	258	5·8	1523	5·9	—	—	12 4	4·3
6	W	256	7·7	1521	7·8	018	9·8	1236	9·9	841	14·1	21 3	13·9	728	7·4	1942	7·8	140	3·4	1347	3·8	340	5·8	16 9	5·9	022	4·2	1249	4·2
7	Th	338	7·8	16 4	7·6	1 1	9·8	1320	9·6	922	13·7	2140	13·4	8 8	7·5	2027	7·6	219	3·6	1430	3·8	427	5·7	1657	5·8	1 6	4·1	1337	4·1
8	F	423	7·6	1648	7·3	144	9·5	14 6	9·2	10 1	13·0	2221	12·6	849	7·3	2117	7·2	257	3·6	1515	3·8	516	5·5	1749	5·5	156	4·1	1432	4·0
9	S	512	7·2	1736	6·8	232	9·1	1458	8·7	1043	12·1	23 6	11·7	934	6·9	2217	6·9	338	3·6	16 3	3·6	6 9	5·3	1844	5·2	249	3·9	1531	3·8
10	S	6 5	6·8	1829	6·4	324	8·4	1554	8·1	1133	11·4	—	—	1024	6·5	2312	6·4	423	3·5	1654	3·3	7 6	5·0	1945	4·8	350	3·6	1639	3·6
11	M	7 6	6·4	1930	6·1	430	7·7	17 4	7·6	—	—	1239	10·4	1130	6·1	—	—	513	3·3	1754	3·0	811	4·8	2057	4·8	5 2	3·6	18 2	3·4
12	Tu	8 16	6·1	2037	5·9	548	7·8	1642	7·5	032	10·6	14 6	10·2	032	6·5	1253	6·0	620	3·1	1918	2·8	927	4·8	2215	4·8	623	3·5	1923	3·4
13	W	929	6·1	2156	6·0	713	7·8	1811	7·7	257	10·6	1530	10·8	158	6·1	1416	6·0	817	2·9	2112	2·8	1046	4·8	2327	4·9	740	3·5	2031	3·5
14	Th	1049	6·3	2315	6·2	824	8·2	1912	8·2	418	11·4	1646	11·6	311	6·5	1524	6·3	940	3·0	2212	2·9	1153	4·9	—	—	844	3·7	2126	3·7
15	F	1154	6·8	—	—	9 18	8·5	2147	8·8	516	12·2	1738	12·3	4 7	6·5	1617	6·6	1114	3·1	2332	3·0	025	5·1	1248	5·1	935	3·8	22 9	3·8
16	S	015	6·7	1246	7·1	10 1	8·8	2225	8·8	6 0	12·7	1820	12·8	452	6·7	17 1	6·8	025	3·1	1248	3·1	113	5·2	1332	5·3	1019	3·9	2247	3·8
17	S	1 3	7·0	1330	7·3	1039	8·9	2259	8·9	638	13·0	1856	12·8	532	6·9	1739	7·0	113	3·3	1332	3·3	154	5·3	14 2	5·4	1056	3·9	2351	3·8
18	M	144	7·2	14 8	7·4	1114	9·1	2333	9·0	716	13·0	1930	12·6	6 7	7·0	1818	7·0	154	3·4	14 2	3·4	230	5·3	1443	5·4	1131	3·9	—	—
19	Tu	220	7·2	1442	7·3	1146	9·1	—	—	751	13·0	20 3	13·0	639	7·1	1848	7·0	230	3·4	1443	3·3	3 2	5·3	1513	5·4	022	3·8	12 4	3·8
20	W	253	7·1	1511	7·2	0 5	9·1	1218	9·0	824	13·0	2032	12·9	7 9	7·0	1919	7·0	3 2	3·4	1513	3·3	334	5·2	1547	5·3	053	3·7	1237	3·7
21	Th	322	7·1	1539	7·1	035	9·0	1250	8·9	854	12·9	2056	12·7	737	7·0	1951	6·9	334	3·4	1547	3·1	4 4	5·2	1621	5·2	129	3·7	1317	3·7
22	F	353	6·8	16 9	6·9	1 4	8·7	1320	8·5	918	12·5	2121	12·3	8 4	6·7	2023	6·7	4 4	3·3	1621	3·0	438	5·0	1657	5·1	2 6	3·6	1347	3·5
23	S	427	6·6	1641	6·6	133	7·9	1354	7·9	941	12·0	2147	11·8	834	6·7	2058	6·4	438	3·3	1657	2·9	513	4·9	1734	4·9	247	3·5	1427	3·4
24	S	5 4	6·4	1716	6·1	2 8	7·6	1434	7·6	10 7	11·4	2220	11·2	9 5	6·2	2136	6·2	513	3·1	1734	2·9	552	4·7	1816	4·7	333	3·4	1516	3·2
25	M	543	6·1	1754	5·8	251	7·3	1524	7·3	1041	10·8	23 3	10·7	945	6·2	2227	5·8	552	3·1	1816	2·8	636	4·5	19 7	4·5	421	3·3	16 4	3·1
26	Tu	627	6·1	1836	6·0	344	7·4	1626	7·3	1130	10·3	2358	10·0	1034	5·9	2332	5·5	636	3·0	19 7	2·9	731	4·4	20 7	4·3	536	3·3	1721	3·2
27	W	716	5·9	1928	5·7	450	7·4	1739	7·5	—	—	1239	10·0	1143	5·7	—	—	757	3·0	20 6	3·0	836	4·4	2115	4·4	647	3·4	1821	3·3
28	Th	820	5·8	2043	5·7	6 4	7·7	1853	7·5	115	10·1	14 7	10·2	055	5·8	13 7	5·8	914	3·2	2112	3·0	947	4·5	2224	4·5	750	3·5	2025	3·3
29	F	941	6·0	2218	6·0	717	7·8	1958	8·0	241	10·6	1530	10·9	213	6·1	1443	6·1	—	—	2127	2·9	1055	4·6	2328	4·8	844	3·7	2112	3·8
30	S	1054	6·5	2318	6·5	819	8·1	2052	8·5	355	11·4	1638	11·6	315	6·5	1525	6·5	914	3·2	2215	3·0	1155	4·9	—	—	844	3·7	2112	3·8

* All times shown are Greenwich Mean Time.   † Difference of height in metres from Ordnance Datum (Newlyn).

‡ Difference of height in metres from Ordnance Datum (Dublin).

MAY, 1977

High Water at the undermentioned Places (G.M.T.*)—

Day of Month	Day of Week	LONDON BRIDGE †Datum of Predictions 3·20 m. below Mn. h.m.	Ht. m.	Aft. h.m.	Ht. m.	LIVERPOOL †Datum of Predictions 4·93 m. below Mn. h.m.	Ht. m.	Aft. h.m.	Ht. m.	AVONMOUTH †Datum of Predictions 6·50 m. below Mn. h.m.	Ht. m.	Aft. h.m.	Ht. m.	HULL (Saltend) †Datum of Predictions 3·90 m. below Mn. h.m.	Ht. m.	Aft. h.m.	Ht. m.	GREENOCK †Datum of Predictions 1·62 m. below Mn. h.m.	Ht. m.	Aft. h.m.	Ht. m.	LEITH AND GRANTON †Datum of Predictions 2·90 m. below Mn. h.m.	Ht. m.	Aft. h.m.	Ht. m.	DUN LAOGHAIRE †Datum of Predictions 0·20 m. above Mn. h.m.	Ht. m.	Aft. h.m.	Ht. m.
1	S	1154	7·0	—	—	910	8·8	2139	9·1	459	12·3	1728	12·7	4 9	6·6	1619	7·0	10 9	3·4	23 0	3·2	020	5·1	1245	5·2	931	3·9	2155	4·0
2	M	015	7·0	1248	7·4	959	9·3	2226	9·5	556	13·6	1830	13·3	455	7·0	17 8	7·6	11 1	3·5	2343	3·3	1 7	5·5	1339	5·5	1015	4·1	2235	4·1
3	Tu	1 6	7·6	1334	7·6	1046	9·6	2312	9·8	651	13·9	1921	13·8	540	7·4	1756	7·7	1151	3·6	1240	3·7	150	5·6	1415	5·7	1058	4·1	2316	4·2
4	W	151	7·6	1419	7·7	1133	9·8	2359	9·9	740	13·9	20 3	13·9	624	7·5	1842	7·7	028	3·4	1328	3·7	233	5·8	15 1	5·9	1144	4·2	2359	4·2
5	Th	237	7·6	15 3	7·7	044	9·8	13 8	9·5	825	13·9	2044	13·9	7 6	7·5	1928	7·6	112	3·5	1415	3·6	319	5·8	1549	5·8	046	4·2	1323	4·1
6	F	324	7·6	1548	7·5	131	9·6	1358	9·0	9 7	13·6	2126	13·5	749	7·5	2016	7·5	154	3·7	1551	3·4	4 7	5·8	1640	5·8	139	4·1	1418	4·1
7	S	412	7·6	1635	7·3	220	9·2	1450	8·7	949	13·0	22 1	13·1	833	7·3	21 7	7·1	237	3·7	1643	3·6	459	5·6	1734	5·3	233	4·0	1518	3·9
8	S	5 2	7·3	1723	6·9	314	8·7	1558	8·4	1034	12·0	23 0	12·2	919	7·0	22 0	6·9	3 1	3·7	1739	3·4	553	5·4	1830	5·2	333	3·9	1626	3·7
9	M	556	6·9	1814	6·5	415	8·3	1558	8·0	1126	11·4	2359	11·3	1010	6·7	23 1	6·4	4 2	3·6	1851	2·9	650	4·9	1929	4·8	442	3·7	1742	3·4
10	Tu	650	6·6	19 7	6·2	526	7·9	1651	7·8	—	—	1128	10·6	010	6·3	1221	6·1	457	3·4	2029	2·8	752	4·9	2034	4·8	557	3·6	1858	3·4
11	W	749	6·3	20 6	6·0	641	8·3	1858	7·7	1 7	10·9	1342	10·8	126	5·9	1338	6·0	559	3·1	2135	2·8	9 1	4·8	2145	4·8	712	3·6	20 4	3·5
12	Th	856	6·3	2117	6·0	750	8·5	1929	8·0	226	10·9	1518	11·3	234	6·2	1447	6·0	730	2·9	2219	3·0	1013	4·8	2254	5·0	817	3·7	2058	3·7
13	F	1013	6·3	2238	6·6	847	8·6	2029	8·5	340	11·8	1659	11·7	332	6·4	1543	6·3	858	2·9	2335	3·0	1120	5·1	2352	5·1	9 9	3·7	2144	3·7
14	S	1122	6·6	2344	—	932	8·7	2157	8·5	438	11·8	1744	12·3	420	6·5	1630	6·5	955	3·0	—	—	041	5·1	1216	5·2	955	3·7	2253	3·8
15	S	—	—	1227	7·2	1011	8·8	2233	8·8	525	12·2	18 5	12·4	5 1	6·6	1711	6·7	1041	3·3	1124	2·4	123	5·2	13 1	5·2	1033	3·7	2324	3·8
16	M	035	6·9	13 2	7·2	1122	8·7	2340	8·8	6 6	12·3	1859	12·6	537	6·8	1749	6·8	1123	3·5	12 4	2·9	2 1	5·2	1340	5·2	1140	3·7	2355	3·8
17	Tu	119	7·0	1341	7·2	1156	8·8	—	—	644	12·4	1934	12·6	611	6·9	1824	6·8	010	3·2	1317	3·1	235	5·2	1417	5·1	028	3·7	1212	3·6
18	W	157	7·1	1416	7·2	011	8·7	1228	8·7	721	12·6	20 4	12·4	643	6·9	1858	6·8	044	3·3	1350	3·0	3 7	5·2	1451	5·0	1 3	3·7	1247	3·5
19	Th	230	7·1	1446	7·0	042	8·6	13 2	8·5	757	12·5	21 0	12·3	713	6·9	1935	6·9	114	3·4	1423	3·4	412	5·2	1525	4·9	140	3·6	1325	3·4
20	F	3 0	6·9	1515	6·9	114	8·6	1337	8·2	829	12·6	2132	11·9	744	6·8	20 9	6·8	143	3·4	1458	3·4	449	5·0	16 0	4·8	221	3·6	14 4	3·4
21	S	332	6·8	1545	6·8	150	8·4	1417	8·1	856	12·4	2152	11·7	813	6·6	2046	6·6	215	3·4	1536	3·4	529	4·9	1636	4·7	3 6	3·5	1447	3·3
22	S	442	6·7	1619	6·8	230	8·3	15 3	7·9	925	11·9	2230	11·3	847	6·5	2125	6·3	250	3·4	1619	3·0	613	4·6	1713	4·6	356	3·5	1538	3·3
23	M	520	6·5	1654	6·6	319	8·0	1559	7·7	954	11·5	2337	10·9	925	6·5	23 4	5·9	331	3·4	17 5	2·9	6 3	4·7	1754	4·6	455	3·5	1635	3·3
24	Tu	5 6	6·5	18 8	6·3	416	7·8	1559	7·6	103.	11·5	2337	10·5	11 9	5·8	1219	6·1	415	3·4	1756	2·8	8 0	4·7	1842	4·8	6 0	3·5	1739	3·3
25	W	646	6·3	1729	6·3	522	7·8	15 3	7·9	111.	11·3	2341	11·5	124	5·9	1337	6·5	5 4	3·3	1756	2·9	8 0	4·6	1936	4·6	7 8	3·5	1848	3·4
26	Th	745	6·3	1856	6·3	631	8·0	1915	8·0	039	10·7	153	10·8	233	6·2	1446	6·8	559	3·2	2033	3·0	613	4·6	2035	4·5	8 9	3·5	1950	3·5
27	F	9 0	6·3	2124	6·0	738	8·3	2015	8·5	153	10·8	1554	11·5	332	6·6	1548	7·0	710	3·1	2135	3·3	710	4·7	2242	4·8	8 9	3·5	2042	3·7
28	S	1016	7·0	2240	6·6	838	8·7	2110	9·0	310	11·2	17 0	12·3	426	6·9	1644	7·2	828	3·2	2135	3·0	1112	4·9	2341	5·0	9 2	3·8	2127	3·9
29	S	1123	7·0	2346	6·9	933	9·1	22 1	9·4	421	11·9	17 0	12·3	426	6·9	1644	7·2	934	3·3	2225	3·3	1112	4·9	2341	5·0	952	4·0	2211	4·1
30	M	—	—	1222	7·3	—	—	22 1	9·4	526	12·6	1644	13·0	1031	3·4	—	—	1031	3·4	—	—	034	5·3	13 3	5·4	—	—	—	—
31	Tu	—	—	—	—	—	—	—	—	—	—	—	—	—	—	—	—	—	—	—	—	—	—	—	—	—	—	—	—

* All times shown are Greenwich Mean Time.   † Difference of height in metres from Ordnance Datum (Newlyn).
‡ Difference of height in metres from Ordnance Datum (Dublin).

JUNE, 1977

High Water at the undermentioned Places (G.M.T.*)—

Day of Month	Day of Week	London Bridge Mn h.m.	Ht m.	Aft h.m.	Ht m.	Liverpool Mn h.m.	Ht m.	Aft h.m.	Ht m.	Avonmouth Mn h.m.	Ht m.	Aft h.m.	Ht m.	Hull (Salend) Mn h.m.	Ht m.	Aft h.m.	Ht m.	Greenock Mn h.m.	Ht m.	Aft h.m.	Ht m.	Leith and Granton Mn h.m.	Ht m.	Aft h.m.	Ht m.	Dun Laoghaire Mn h.m.	Ht m.	Aft h.m.	Ht m.
		Datum of Predictions 3·20 m. below				*Datum of Predictions 4·93 m. below*				*Datum of Predictions 6·50 m. below*				*Datum of Predictions 3·90 m. below*				*†Datum of Predictions 1·62 m. below*				*†Datum of Predictions 2·90 m. below*				*†Datum of Predictions 0·20 m. above*			
1	W	043	7·2	1314	7·3	1026	9·4	2252	9·7	626	13·2	1856	13·6	515	7·3	1736	7·4	1126	3·5	—	—	124	5·5	1355	5·6	1039	4·1	2255	4·1
2	Th	134	7·3	1421	7·3	1117	9·6	2341	9·8	721	13·5	1944	13·9	6 3	7·5	1828	7·6	0 2	3·6	1220	3·5	213	5·7	1456	5·8	1127	4·1	2341	4·2
3	F	223	7·3	1449	7·3	—	—	12 7	9·6	8 8	13·7	2028	13·9	649	7·6	1920	7·6	050	3·7	1312	3·4	3 2	5·8	1537	5·8	—	—	1218	4·1
4	S	312	7·3	1535	7·3	030	9·8	1257	9·4	854	13·5	21 8	13·6	735	7·6	20 9	7·5	136	3·7	1402	3·5	352	5·8	1627	5·8	030	4·2	1310	4·0
5	S	4 2	7·5	1637	7·2	118	9·6	1348	9·1	938	13·5	2158	13·2	820	7·4	2058	7·3	222	3·7	1452	3·4	443	5·7	1719	5·6	123	4·3	14 6	3·9
6	M	451	7·4	1718	7·0	2 7	9·3	1438	8·8	1023	12·5	2247	12·4	9 7	7·2	2149	6·9	3 7	3·7	1541	3·4	536	5·5	1812	5·4	218	4·1	15 3	3·8
7	Tu	540	7·1	1754	6·8	259	8·9	1533	8·4	11 3	11·9	2342	11·8	953	6·9	2240	6·5	352	3·4	1629	3·4	631	5·2	19 2	5·2	315	4·0	1556	3·6
8	W	629	6·8	1842	6·5	353	8·5	1631	8·0	—	—	12 5	11·3	1045	6·6	2336	6·2	440	3·2	1719	3·2	727	5·0	2012	5·1	417	3·8	17 3	3·6
9	Th	720	6·5	1933	6·2	453	8·1	1735	7·7	039	11·3	13 4	11·0	—	—	1149	5·9	533	2·8	1815	3·0	826	4·8	2113	5·0	524	3·7	1824	3·5
10	F	818	6·3	2034	6·1	558	7·8	1842	7·6	141	10·9	14 6	10·7	039	5·8	1249	6·0	641	2·8	1926	2·9	930	4·7	2212	4·8	635	3·5	1930	3·4
11	S	925	6·2	2149	6·1	7 5	7·7	1946	7·7	245	10·9	1511	10·8	147	5·9	1359	6·0	8 3	2·9	2040	2·9	1036	4·8	2313	4·7	743	3·5	2025	3·4
12	S	1044	6·4	23 8	6·3	8 7	7·9	2040	7·9	347	11·1	16 8	11·0	249	6·1	15 3	6·2	910	2·9	2136	2·9	0 6	4·8	1136	4·8	840	3·5	2112	3·5
13	M	1144	6·6	—	—	859	8·1	2123	8·4	441	11·3	1659	11·4	342	6·4	1556	6·4	1036	3·0	2223	3·0	052	4·9	1227	—	926	3·6	2153	3·5
14	Tu	0 7	6·6	1234	6·8	943	8·3	2215	8·6	528	11·8	1745	11·7	427	6·6	1644	6·6	1052	3·0	23 3	—	133	5·0	13 8	4·8	1043	3·6	23 0	3·6
15	W	053	6·8	1316	7·0	1011	8·5	23 8	8·7	611	11·9	1826	12·0	5 6	6·8	1726	6·7	1137	3·3	2341	3·3	2 9	5·1	1430	4·9	1116	3·6	—	—
16	Th	134	6·8	1352	7·0	11 1	8·6	2338	8·7	651	11·9	19 3	12·3	546	6·8	18 7	6·7	016	3·3	1256	3·2	245	5·2	15 7	5·1	1150	3·6	1225	3·5
17	F	2 8	6·7	1423	6·9	1136	8·6	—	—	730	12·1	1939	12·4	621	6·9	1846	6·7	049	3·4	1332	3·4	319	5·1	1543	5·2	0 6	3·8	13 1	3·5
18	S	242	6·7	1456	6·9	024	8·8	12 7	8·8	8 5	12·3	2011	12·5	655	6·9	1923	6·8	121	3·4	14 8	3·4	353	5·1	1618	5·1	042	3·8	1342	3·4
19	S	315	6·8	1529	6·9	057	8·8	1246	8·7	839	12·4	2046	12·5	727	6·9	19 9	6·6	154	3·4	1442	3·4	429	5·0	1655	5·1	118	3·8	1424	3·4
20	M	350	6·9	16 3	6·9	133	8·7	1321	8·6	913	12·4	2121	12·4	759	6·6	2034	6·5	231	3·5	1520	3·4	5 9	4·9	1734	5·0	159	3·8	15 3	3·4
21	Tu	426	6·9	1635	6·8	2 6	8·7	14 0	8·4	947	12·3	2156	12·3	833	6·6	2112	6·5	311	3·5	16 1	3·4	551	4·8	18 9	4·8	240	3·7	1554	3·4
22	W	5 2	6·9	17 9	6·8	256	8·6	1444	8·4	1021	12·1	2236	12·0	9 2	6·5	2152	6·3	353	3·4	1642	3·4	639	4·8	1845	4·8	328	3·7	16 3	3·4
23	Th	540	6·8	1746	6·7	347	8·4	1530	8·3	11 0	11·6	2318	11·6	952	6·5	2238	6·0	438	3·2	1728	3·4	730	4·8	1924	4·7	421	3·7	17 2	3·4
24	F	622	6·7	1831	6·6	444	8·3	1627	8·2	1145	11·1	—	—	1042	6·5	2333	6·0	530	3·2	1829	3·4	827	4·8	20 2	4·7	523	3·6	18 9	3·4
25	S	716	6·6	1930	6·5	551	8·1	1728	8·1	0 8	11·1	1243	10·7	1144	6·3	—	—	633	3·2	1939	3·4	930	4·8	2043	4·8	631	3·6	1925	3·5
26	S	825	6·5	2049	6·5	7 2	8·0	1836	8·3	112	10·8	1355	10·6	041	6·3	1257	6·4	747	3·2	2057	3·2	1037	4·9	2230	4·8	740	3·6	2013	3·6
27	M	942	6·6	22 1	6·6	813	8·2	1944	8·5	230	10·9	1513	11·1	154	6·2	1413	6·4	9 2	3·3	2159	3·3	1144	5·1	2310	5·0	841	3·7	2155	3·8
28	Tu	1055	6·8	23 2	6·8	915	8·5	2047	8·8	347	11·4	1629	11·8	3 1	6·5	1524	6·7	10 8	3·3	2253	3·4	0 1	5·2	1246	5·0	935	3·7	2242	3·8
29	W	—	—	12 2	6·9	1013	8·8	2144	9·2	5 0	12·1	1736	12·6	4 0	6·8	1627	7·0	11 8	3·4	2345	3·4	1 7	5·4	1343	5·5	1026	3·9	23 5	4·0
30	Th	027	6·9	1259	6·9	11 1	9·1	2237	9·5	6 7	12·7	1836	13·3	455	7·1	1726	7·3	—	—	1246	3·4	2 4	5·4	1432	5·6	11 5	4·1	2342	4·1

* All times shown are Greenwich Mean Time.   † Difference of height in metres from Ordnance Datum (Newlyn).   ‡ Difference of height in metres from Ordnance Datum (Dublin).

JULY, 1977

High Water at the undermentioned Places (G.M.T.*)—

Datums below (difference from datum of predictions): London Bridge 3·20 m. below; Liverpool 4·93 m. below; Avonmouth 6·50 m. below; Hull (Salend) 3·90 m. below; Greenock 1·62 m. below; Leith and Granton 2·90 m. below; Dun Laoghaire 0·20 m. above.

Each place is given as: Mn. (morning, h.m.) · Ht. (m.) · Aft. (afternoon, h.m.) · Ht. (m.)

Day	DoW	LB Mn	Ht	LB Aft	Ht	Liv Mn	Ht	Liv Aft	Ht	Avon Mn	Ht	Avon Aft	Ht	Hull Mn	Ht	Hull Aft	Ht	Green Mn	Ht	Green Aft	Ht	Leith Mn	Ht	Leith Aft	Ht	Dun Mn	Ht	Dun Aft	Ht
1	F	123	6·9	1349	6·9	11 5	9·4	2328	9·7	7 4	13·2	1927	13·8	547	7·4	1821	7·4	—	—	12 6	3·3	159	5·6	1436	5·7	1116	4·0	2328	4·2
2	S	213	7·0	1436	7·0	1156	9·4	—		754	13·5	2024	14·0	636	7·6	1912	7·5	035	3·6	13 1	3·3	249	5·8	1526	5·8	—	—	12 6	4·2
3	s	3 11	7·2	1521	7·1	016	9·8	1245	9·4	839	13·5	2058	13·8	723	7·6	1959	7·5	124	3·7	1353	3·3	339	5·8	1614	5·8	018	4·3	1257	4·0
4	M	348	7·4	1648	7·4	1 3	9·7	1333	9·2	922	13·3	2142	13·4	8 6	7·6	2044	7·3	210	3·8	1442	3·3	427	5·7	17 2	5·7	1 8	4·3	1349	3·9
5	Tu	434	7·4	1730	7·3	149	9·5	1419	8·9	10 7	12·9	2224	12·7	849	7·4	2128	7·0	254	3·8	1526	3·3	516	5·5	1750	5·4	2 0	4·2	1442	3·8
6	W	518	7·3	1811	7·0	235	9·1	15 6	8·5	1049	12·3	2314	12·2	931	7·1	2210	6·6	337	3·7	16 9	3·2	6 7	5·3	1840	5·1	253	4·1	1536	3·7
7	Th	6 1	6·9	1857	6·7	322	8·7	1554	8·1	1132	11·7	2359	11·7	1013	6·8	2257	6·2	419	3·5	1651	3·3	657	5·1	1932	4·9	347	3·9	1635	3·5
8	F	646	6·6	1954	6·4	412	8·2	1647	7·7	047	10·9	13 6	10·5	1059	6·4	2347	5·9	5 5	3·3	1735	3·0	750	4·8	2026	4·7	447	3·7	1741	3·4
9	S	736	6·4	2116	6·2	5 7	7·8	1747	7·5	141	10·4	14 5	10·2	1154	6·0	—		558	3·0	1826	2·9	844	4·7	2125	4·6	553	3·5	1847	3·3
10	s	836	6·2	2220	6·1	611	7·5	1852	7·4	244	10·2	15 8	10·2	049	5·7	13 3	5·8	7 3	2·8	1931	2·8	945	4·5	2226	4·5	7 2	3·4	1947	3·4
11	M	946	6·2	2330	6·2	719	7·5	1958	7·6	350	10·4	16 7	11·2	158	5·7	1418	5·8	820	2·7	2044	2·8	1049	4·5	2327	4·6	8 3	3·3	2040	3·4
12	Tu	11 5	6·3	—		822	7·7	2054	7·8	449	10·8	17 1	11·6	3 1	5·9	1524	5·9	929	2·8	2145	2·9	1151	4·5	—		855	3·4	2124	3·5
13	W	029	6·4	1249	6·6	916	7·9	2140	8·2	541	11·3	1756	11·7	355	6·1	1619	6·2	1026	2·9	2234	3·0	016	4·7	1244	4·7	939	3·4	22 0	3·7
14	Th	110	6·5	1327	6·6	10 4	8·4	2225	8·4	625	11·7	1838	12·1	441	6·4	1705	6·6	1115	2·9	2315	3·2	057	4·8	1325	4·8	1018	3·5	2236	3·7
15	F	147	6·6	14 2	6·7	1040	8·4	2257	8·7	7 5	12·1	1916	12·4	522	6·7	1750	6·8	1159	3·0	2353	3·2	138	5·0	14 6	4·9	1053	3·5	23 9	3·8
16	s	220	6·7	1436	6·9	1117	8·7	2331	8·9	744	12·4	1953	12·6	6 0	7·0	1831	6·8	—	—	1238	2·9	219	5·1	1446	5·0	1127	3·6	2344	3·9
17	s	256	6·9	1511	7·0	1153	8·7	—		821	12·6	2031	12·8	635	7·0	19 9	6·9	028	3·3	1316	2·9	301	5·2	1527	5·1	—	—	12 2	3·7
18	M	332	7·1	1545	7·1	0 6	9·0	1228	8·8	859	12·8	21 9	12·9	710	7·1	1944	6·9	1 3	3·3	1352	2·9	342	5·2	1609	5·2	019	3·9	1239	3·7
19	Tu	4 7	7·2	1619	7·1	040	9·1	13 4	8·8	936	12·8	2146	12·8	744	7·2	2019	6·9	138	3·4	1428	2·9	424	5·3	1652	5·2	056	4·0	1317	3·7
20	W	442	7·2	1651	7·0	115	9·1	1342	8·7	1010	12·6	2222	12·6	818	7·2	2054	6·8	216	3·5	15 4	3·0	508	5·2	1737	5·2	135	4·2	1359	3·7
21	Th	519	7·0	1727	6·9	153	9·0	1421	8·7	1044	12·1	2259	12·0	854	7·1	2131	6·6	254	3·5	1542	3·0	556	5·1	1827	5·1	215	4·0	1443	3·7
22	F	6 0	6·9	1810	6·8	233	8·8	15 4	8·5	1122	11·4	2343	11·4	934	6·9	2213	6·5	335	3·6	1621	3·1	648	5·0	1923	5·0	3 1	3·9	1533	3·6
23	s	649	6·7	19 4	6·6	318	8·6	1555	8·5	—		1322	10·5	1020	6·8	23 2	6·3	419	3·5	17 3	3·1	745	4·9	2024	4·8	353	3·8	1629	3·6
24	s	754	6·5	2020	6·4	413	8·3	1655	8·0	041	10·7	1447	10·5	1116	6·5	—		5 8	3·4	1752	3·0	849	4·8	2130	4·8	453	3·7	1735	3·5
25	M	912	6·5	2145	6·4	520	8·1	18 5	8·0	2 11	10·4	1610	11·3	0 5	6·1	1228	6·3	6 6	3·3	1857	3·0	958	4·8	2244	4·9	6 4	3·7	1844	3·5
26	Tu	1031	6·6	23 6	6·6	638	8·0	1921	8·2	329	10·8	1723	12·3	121	6·1	1352	6·3	717	3·1	2026	3·0	1014	4·9	2357	5·1	719	3·6	1951	3·6
27	W	1144	6·7	—		757	8·2	2034	8·6	447	11·6	1823	13·1	237	6·3	1511	6·5	841	3·0	2143	3·1	1129	4·9	—		827	3·7	2050	3·8
28	Th	017	6·7	1246	6·7	9 6	8·6	2134	9·0	552	12·5	1915	13·7	343	6·7	1620	6·9	957	3·1	2243	3·2	—	—	1237	5·2	927	3·8	2142	4·0
29	F	114	6·8	1338	6·8	10 3	9·0	2226	9·4	652	13·1	1959	14·0	442	7·1	1719	7·2	11 1	3·2	2336	3·4	057	5·3	1335	5·4	1019	3·9	2232	4·1
30	S	2 5	6·9	1423	6·9	1056	9·3	2314	9·7	740	13·5	1959	14·0	534	7·4	1811	7·4	1159	3·2	—		152	5·5	1429	5·6	11 7	4·0	2317	4·2
31	s					1142	9·4	—		740	13·5	1959	14·0	622	7·6	1859	7·5	027	3·6	1251	3·2	240	5·7	1516	5·8	1155	4·0	—	

* All times shown are Greenwich Mean Time. † Difference of height in metres from Ordnance Datum (Newlyn). ‡ Difference of height in metres from Ordnance Datum (Dublin).

AUGUST, 1977

High Water at the undermentioned Places (G.M.T.*)—

Day of Month	Day of Week	LONDON BRIDGE † Datum of Predictions 3·20 m. below				LIVERPOOL † Datum of Predictions 4·93 m. below				AVONMOUTH † Datum of Predictions 6·50 m. below				HULL (Saltend) † Datum of Predictions 3·90 m. below				GREENOCK † Datum of Predictions 1·62 m. below				LEITH AND GRANTON ‡ Datum of Predictions 2·90 m. below				DUN LAOGHAIRE ‡ Datum of Predictions 0·20 m. below			
		Mn. h.m.	Ht. m.	Aft. h.m.	Ht. m.	Mn. h.m.	Ht. m.	Aft. h.m.	Ht. m.	Mn. h.m.	Ht. m.	Aft. h.m.	Ht. m.	Mn. h.m.	Ht. m.	Aft. h.m.	Ht. m.	Mn. h.m.	Ht. m.	Aft. h.m.	Ht. m.	Mn. h.m.	Ht. m.	Aft. h.m.	Ht. m.	Mn. h.m.	Ht. m.	Aft. h.m.	Ht. m.
1	M	249	7·2	515	7·1	0 0	9·8	1227	9·4	824	13·6	2041	14·0	7 7	7·7	1942	7·5	114	3·7	1340	3·2	324	5·8	1559	5·8	0 4	4·3	1240	4·0
2	Tu	332	7·3	546	7·3	044	9·8	1311	9·3	9 5	35	2124	13·7	748	7·5	2022	7·3	159	3·7	1425	3·3	4 8	5·6	1642	5·6	050	4·3	1326	3·9
3	W	413	7·4	1024	7·3	126	9·5	1351	9·0	944	13·2	224	13·2	826	7·5	21 0	7·1	239	3·7	15 5	3·3	453	5·6	1726	5·6	139	4·2	1413	3·8
4	Th	452	7·3	1712	7·2	2 7	9·2	1432	8·7	1021	12·6	2216	12·5	9 1	7·3	2136	6·7	318	3·7	1541	3·3	538	5·4	1811	5·1	225	4·1	15 1	3·7
5	F	530	7·0	1740	6·9	240	8·8	1512	8·2	1054	11·9	2316	11·6	938	6·9	2212	6·4	355	3·5	1617	3·2	314	3·9	1552	3·6	314	3·9	1552	3·6
6	S	610	6·7	1821	6·6	329	8·3	1555	7·8	1127	11·1	352	10·7	1016	6·5	2254	6·0	434	3·3	1655	3·1	4 6	3·7	1649	3·5	4 6	3·7	1649	3·5
7	S	655	6·4	1913	6·3	418	7·7	1647	7·4	—		1256	9·7	1016	6·1	12 5	5·7	518	3·0	1738	3·0	5 4	3·4	1753	3·3	5 4	3·4	1753	3·3
8	M	749	6·1	2018	6·0	516	7·3	1752	7·2	037	10·0	1256	9·7	059	5·5	1330	5·5	613	2·8	1831	2·8	613	3·3	1859	3·3	613	3·3	1859	3·3
9	Tu	856	5·9	2131	5·8	627	7·2	19 8	7·2	138	9·5	14 5	9·5	215	5·6	1450	5·6	724	2·7	1939	2·8	723	3·2	20 0	3·3	723	3·2	20 0	3·3
10	W	1012	5·9	2258	5·9	744	7·3	2018	7·5	254	9·6	1524	9·9	350	5·6	1617	5·9	850	2·7	2051	2·9	823	3·3	2048	3·5	823	3·3	2048	3·5
11	Th	1129	6·0	—		857	7·6	2136	8·4	410	10·2	1633	10·7	419	5·9	1553	6·0	10 2	2·8	23 0	2·9	952	3·5	2131	3·7	952	3·5	2131	3·7
12	F	0 1	6·0	1221	6·2	937	8·0	2156	8·4	5 1	11·5	1730	11·5	457	6·7	1729	6·7	1054	2·9	2251	3·1	11 3	3·7	2239	3·8	11 3	3·7	2239	3·8
13	S	043	6·3	1300	6·4	1017	8·4	2233	8·7	6 1	11·8	1815	12·4	536	6·7	17 8	7·0	1138	2·9	2330	3·2	26	5·2	1430	5·0	11 38	3·8	2239	3·8
14	S	120	6·5	1335	6·7	1120	8·7	2313	9·0	645	12·3	1855	12·6	612	7·2	1846	7·1	1138	2·9	2330	3·2	240	5·3	15 5	5·3	—		13 0	3·8
15	M	155	6·8	1412	7·0	1129	9·0	2343	9·2	723	12·7	1934	13·0	649	7·2	1957	7·1	0 8	3·3	1254	2·9	314	5·5	1538	5·5	030	4·1	1251	3·9
16	Tu	232	7·1	1447	7·3	12 6	9·4	—		8 3	13·0	2013	13·2	649	7·4	1957	7·2	045	3·2	14 8	3·0	348	5·5	1612	5·5	110	4·2	1332	3·9
17	W	3 8	7·4	1525	7·4	018	9·4	1242	9·2	842	13·2	2053	13·3	724	7·5	1957	7·1	123	3·5	1444	3·0	427	5·5	1652	5·4	152	4·1	1415	3·9
18	Th	345	7·5	1557	7·6	132	9·1	1357	8·8	920	13·2	2131	13·1	759	7·5	2032	7·1	2 1	3·5	1444	3·0	510	5·5	1734	5·3	110	4·1	1332	3·9
19	F	421	7·4	1631	7·3	218	8·8	1439	8·4	954	13·0	22 7	12·9	836	7·4	21 8	6·9	239	3·6	1520	3·2	555	5·3	1821	5·1	331	3·9	15 6	3·7
20	S	458	7·2	1709	7·1	256	8·5	1528	8·4	1027	12·4	2243	12·1	915	7·2	2148	6·7	3 8	3·6	1558	3·0	644	5·3	1913	5·0	432	3·7	17 6	3·6
21	S	539	6·6	1753	6·6	350	8·1	1629	7·9	1052	11·6	2324	11·3	10 0	6·9	2235	6·5	4 2	3·6	1640	3·2	739	5·0	2010	4·8	546	3·6	1821	3·5
22	M	627	6·6	1848	6·6	459	7·9	1743	7·6	1158	10·7	—		1057	6·6	2336	6·2	451	3·4	1727	3·1	846	4·8	2121	4·7	7 8	3·6	1936	3·5
23	Tu	728	6·3	2002	6·3	625	8·0	1919	7·7	140	10·3	1437	10·3	056	6·1	1342	6·1	548	3·4	1827	3·0	10 2	4·8	2238	4·9	821	3·6	2040	3·8
24	W	849	6·2	2254	6·4	751	8·0	2023	8·4	323	10·5	16 7	11·2	219	6·1	1613	6·6	658	3·0	20 2	2·9	1123	4·9	2350	5·0	7 8	3·6	2040	3·8
25	Th	1010	6·3	2350	6·4	9 1	8·3	2124	8·9	444	11·8	1718	12·3	331	6·6	1613	6·8	835	2·9	2239	3·0	11 23	4·9	2350	5·0	922	3·8	2134	4·1
26	F	1129	6·5	—		1044	9·0	2259	9·6	549	12·4	1813	13·2	430	7·0	17 0	7·4	959	3·0	2339	3·4	—		1232	5·2	922	3·8	2134	4·1
27	S	0 5	6·7	1232	6·7	958	8·9	2215	9·6	640	13·1	19 0	13·7	520	7·4	1757	7·4	1059	3·1	2339	3·4	052	5·3	1339	5·4	1014	3·9	2223	4·1
28	S	1 3	6·9	1323	6·9	1044	9·6	23 6	9·7	724	13·5	1943	14·0	6 5	7·7	1841	7·4	016	3·1	1237	3·1	143	5·5	1417	5·5	236	4·0	2223	4·1
29	M	151	7·1	1446	7·0	1125	9·4	2342	9·4	724	13·5	1943	14·0	520	7·7	1757	7·4	1 1	3·6	1320	3·1	2 8	5·7	1417	5·7	236	4·0	2350	4·3
30	Tu	233	7·2	1447	7·2	021	9·7	1244	9·3	8 5	13·6	2023	14·0	646	7·7	1919	7·4	1 1	3·6	1320	3·2	3 8	5·8	1540	5·7	1221	4·1	—	
31	W	311	7·4	1524	7·4	021	9·7	1244	9·3	843	13·5	21 2	13·7	723	7·7	1954	7·3	143	3·7	14 0	3·2	347	5·7	1618	5·6	13 0	4·3		

* All times shown are Greenwich Mean Time.   † Difference of height in metres from Ordnance Datum (Newlyn).   ‡ Difference of height in metres from Ordnance Datum (Dublin).

SEPTEMBER, 1977

High Water at the undermentioned Places (G.M.T.*)—

Day of Month	Day of Week	London Bridge † 3·20 m. below Mn. h.m.	Ht. m.	Aft. h.m.	Ht. m.	Liverpool † 4·93 m. below Mn. h.m.	Ht. m.	Aft. h.m.	Ht. m.	Avonmouth † 6·50 m. below Mn. h.m.	Ht. m.	Aft. h.m.	Ht. m.	Hull (Salend) † 3·90 m. below Mn. h.m.	Ht. m.	Aft. h.m.	Ht. m.	Greenock † 1·62 m. below Mn. h.m.	Ht. m.	Aft. h.m.	Ht. m.	Leith and Granton † 2·90 m. below Mn. h.m.	Ht. m.	Aft. h.m.	Ht. m.	Dun Laoghaire † 0·20 m. below Mn. h.m.	Ht. m.	Aft. h.m.	Ht. m.
1	Th	349	7·4	1559	7·4	058	9·1	1320	9·1	910	13·3	2137	13·3	758	7·5	2027	7·1	220	3·7	1437	3·3	427	5·6	1657	5·4	113	4·2	1342	3·9
2	F	423	7·3	1634	7·2	135	9·2	1355	8·7	949	12·8	22 7	12·6	830	7·3	2058	6·9	254	3·6	15 9	3·3	5 7	5·4	1738	5·1	156	4·1	1422	3·8
3	S	457	7·0	17 8	7·0	2 9	8·7	1429	8·4	1016	12·1	2235	11·7	9 3	6·9	2132	6·6	328	3·5	1541	3·3	549	5·1	1818	4·8	239	3·9	15 7	3·6
4	S	532	6·7	1747	6·7	247	8·3	15 7	7·9	1042	11·2	23 4	10·8	938	6·6	22 4	6·2	4 3	3·3	1616	3·3	630	4·8	19 0	4·6	323	3·7	1556	3·5
5	M	612	6·4	1834	6·3	330	7·7	1554	7·5	1115	10·4	2341	9·9	1018	6·1	2255	5·9	444	3·1	1658	3·1	714	4·6	1946	4·4	414	3·4	1653	3·3
6	Tu	7 2	6·1	1933	5·9	425	7·3	1655	7·1	1159	9·7			1115	5·7	2333	5·6	533	2·9	1745	3·0	8 6	4·4	2043	4·3	516	3·2	18 2	3·3
7	W	8 5	5·7	2044	5·6	536	7·0	1813	7·0	036	9·3	13 6	9·3			1220	5·5	633	2·7	1845	2·8	911	4·4	2152	4·3	633	3·1	1912	3·3
8	Th	918	5·5	22 4	5·5	7 0	7·0	1935	7·3	158	9·2	1434	9·5	120	5·5	1412	5·5	8 2	2·7	20 0	2·8	10 2	4·3	23 7	4·4	744	3·2	2010	3·4
9	F	1040	5·6	2319	5·8	814	7·4	2040	7·7	328	9·8	1558	10·4	237	5·8	1522	5·9	936	2·7	2124	2·9	1139	4·5			838	3·6	2057	3·6
10	S	1142	5·9			9 8	7·9	2127	8·3	441	10·9	17 0	11·4	336	6·2	1616	6·5	1030	2·9	2220	3·1			1235	4·7	922	3·6	2138	3·8
11	S	0 7	6·1	1225	6·3	950	8·4	22 4	8·7	536	11·8	1751	12·2	424	6·6	1659	6·7	1112	3·1	23 2	3·2	058	4·9	1323	5·0	10 0	3·8	2215	4·0
12	M	048	6·6	13 4	6·8	1028	8·9	2246	9·1	621	12·5	1833	12·8	506	7·0	1740	7·0	1149	3·0	2343	3·0	138	5·2	14 1	5·2	1036	3·9	2252	4·2
13	Tu	120	7·0	1342	7·2	11 2	9·2	2316	9·4	7 3	13·0	1913	13·3	546	7·4	1818	7·3	023	3·4	1225	3·1	214	5·4	1438	5·5	1110	4·1	2327	4·3
14	W	2 5	7·4	1420	7·6	1140	9·5	2354	9·6	744	13·3	1956	13·7	624	7·7	1855	7·4	1 3	3·5	13 5	3·0	249	5·6	1512	5·6	1147	4·1		
15	Th	243	7·7	1457	7·7			1216	9·6	824	13·6	2036	13·7	7 0	7·7	1936	7·4	143	3·4	1343	3·1	324	5·7	1549	5·7	0 4	4·3	1223	4·2
16	F	321	7·7	1535	7·8	032	9·7	1257	9·6	9 2	13·5	2115	13·6	738	7·6	2013	7·4	223	3·7	1419	3·4	4 4	5·7	1627	5·6	044	4·3	13 4	4·1
17	S	359	7·6	1613	7·6	1 2	9·6	1336	9·4	939	13·2	2152	13·0	816	7·6	2044	7·2	3 3	3·7	1457	3·4	448	5·5	17 6	5·4	129	4·3	1350	4·1
18	S	438	7·3	1654	7·3	153	9·3	1419	9·0	1016	12·6	2230	12·2	858	7·3	2125	7·0	349	3·6	1536	3·4	536	5·3	1756	5·2	217	4·1	1440	4·0
19	M	520	6·9	1742	6·9	239	8·8	15 9	8·6	1051	11·7	2314	11·2	946	7·2	2213	6·7	439	3·4	1620	3·4	628	5·0	1856	5·0	311	4·0	1538	3·8
20	Tu	610	6·5	1839	6·5	336	8·3	1612	8·1	1143	10·8			1050	6·6	2324	6·2	536	3·2	18 7	3·0	727	5·0	1956	4·8	416	3·8	1643	3·7
21	W	712	6·2	1952	6·2	449	7·8	1728	7·9	015	10·3	1258	10·2	1210	6·1			647	2·9	1945	2·9	837	4·9	2114	4·8	533	3·6	18 2	3·6
22	Th	827	6·0	2114	6·2	617	7·9	1855	7·9	143	10·0	1436	10·4	050	5·8	1345	6·0	838	2·8	2130	3·0	957	4·8	2229	5·0	659	3·6	1920	3·7
23	F	949	6·1	2237	6·4	745	8·2	2013	8·4	332	10·5	16 6	11·3	230	6·0	1510	6·5	958	2·9	2229	3·2	1129	4·9	2342	5·2	814	3·7	2028	3·8
24	S	11 9	6·4	2349	6·7	854	8·4	2114	8·8	441	11·5	1711	12·3	348	6·5	16 9	7·0	1050	3·0	2316	3·4	1220	5·4			915	3·8	2125	4·0
25	S			1212	6·7	945	8·8	22 0	9·2	539	12·5	18 2	13·1	446	7·0	17 0	7·3	1133	3·1	2358	3·4	041	5·3	1315	5·4	10 3	3·9	2211	4·2
26	M	045	7·1	13 3	7·0	1028	9·2	2241	9·5	626	13·1	1845	13·6	532	7·3	1745	7·5			1211	3·2	129	5·5	14 1	5·6	1026	4·1	2253	4·3
27	Tu	131	7·3	1347	7·2	11 5	9·3	2320	9·5	7 6	13·3	1924	13·7	612	7·5	1824	7·5	041	3·5	1253	3·2	210	5·6	1441	5·6	11 2	4·1	2331	4·3
28	W	212	7·4	1425	7·3	1142	9·4	2356	9·5	744	13·4	20 2	13·7	650	7·4	19 2	7·4	121	3·6	1330	3·3	247	5·7	1517	5·6	1158	4·1		
29	Th	249	7·4	15 0	7·4			1216	9·3	819	13·4	2038	13·5	727	7·3	1939	7·3	157	3·5	14 4	3·4	322	5·6	1552	5·6	0 9	4·2	1233	4·2
30	F	322	7·4	1534	7·4	030	9·3	1249	9·1	850	13·2	21 9	13·1	8 3	7·2	2015	7·1	233	3·4	14 34	3·4	359	5·5	1627	5·5	046	4·1	13 8	4·0

* All times shown are Greenwich Mean Time. † Difference of height in metres from Ordnance Datum (Newlyn). ‡ Difference of height in metres from Ordnance Datum (Dublin).

OCTOBER, 1977

High Water at the undermentioned Places (G.M.T.)*—

Day of Month	Day of Week	LONDON BRIDGE †Datum of Predictions 3·20 m. below				LIVERPOOL †Datum of Predictions 4·93 m. below				AVONMOUTH †Datum of Predictions 6·50 m. below				HULL (Saltend) †Datum of Predictions 3·90 m. below				GREENOCK †Datum of Predictions 1·62 m. below				LEITH AND GRANTON †Datum of Predictions 2·90 m. below				DUN LAOGHAIRE ‡Datum of Predictions 0·20 m. above			
		Mn. h.m.	Ht.	Aft. h.m.	Ht.	Mn. h.m.	Ht.	Aft. h.m.	Ht.	Mn. h.m.	Ht.	Aft. h.m.	Ht.	Mn. h.m.	Ht.	Aft. h.m.	Ht.	Mn. h.m.	Ht.	Aft. h.m.	Ht.	Mn. h.m.	Ht.	Aft. h.m.	Ht.	Mn. h.m.	Ht.	Aft. h.m.	Ht.
1	S	355	7·2	16 6	7·2	1 4	9·1	1320	8·8	917	12·9	2137	12·6	8 1	7·2	2022	6·9	229	3·5	1435	3·4	436	5·3	1745	5·1	125	4·0	1347	3·9
2	S	426	7·0	1640	7·0	136	8·7	1351	8·5	942	12·1	2211	11·8	832	6·6	2051	6·7	3 4	3·4	15 6	3·4	514	5·1	1740	4·9	2 4	3·8	1427	3·7
3	M	458	6·8	1716	6·7	210	8·3	1425	8·1	10 7	11·5	2226	11·0	9 5	6·6	2123	6·1	334	3·3	1540	3·4	554	4·9	1820	4·7	246	3·6	1510	3·6
4	Tu	534	6·5	1758	6·4	250	7·8	15 6	7·7	1037	10·8	2259	10·2	945	6·2	22 2	6·1	413	3·1	1620	3·3	636	4·6	19 3	4·5	332	3·4	16 0	3·4
5	W	617	6·1	1849	6·0	343	7·0	16 6	7·3	1117	10·0	2349	9·6	1037	5·5	2255	5·8	459	2·8	17 2	3·1	725	4·4	1958	4·1	428	3·3	17 2	3·4
6	Th	7 9	5·7	1954	5·6	450	7·0	1718	7·2	—		1219	9·5	—		12 2	5·5	553	2·8	18 2	3·0	829	4·3	21 4	4·3	538	3·4	1813	3·4
7	F	815	5·4	21 5	5·5	6 9	7·0	1840	7·2	1 5	9·3	1344	9·5	117	5·5	14 6	5·7	7 3	2·7	1924	3·0	943	4·3	2219	4·6	655	3·2	1920	3·5
8	S	935	5·4	2229	5·6	728	7·3	1954	7·6	241	9·7	1514	10·2	247	5·7	1535	6·2	854	2·7	2032	3·0	1056	4·4	2335	4·6	758	3·4	2016	3·7
9	S	1047	5·8	2320	6·1	830	7·9	2047	8·5	4 1	10·7	1624	11·1	354	6·3	16 4	6·6	955	2·9	2139	3·3	1156	4·7	—		848	3·7	21 2	3·9
10	M	1142	6·3	—		915	8·4	2129	8·7	5 1	11·7	1724	12·2	447	6·7	17 4	6·9	1036	3·0	2229	3·3	018	4·9	1246	5·0	928	3·9	2144	4·1
11	Tu	015	6·7	1228	6·9	954	9·0	22 9	9·2	553	12·6	18 6	13·0	433	7·1	17 8	7·1	1113	3·3	2312	3·4	1 4	5·2	1327	5·3	10 5	4·1	2222	4·2
12	W	055	7·2	1312	7·3	1034	9·4	2248	9·5	639	12·2	1852	13·5	515	7·4	1747	7·6	1152	3·4	2356	3·5	142	5·5	14 7	5·5	1043	4·3	2259	4·3
13	Th	137	7·6	1352	7·7	1114	9·7	2330	9·8	721	13·6	1937	13·8	556	7·7	1825	7·6	—		1233	3·4	219	5·7	1444	5·7	1119	4·3	2340	4·4
14	F	216	7·8	1433	7·9	1155	9·8	—		8 3	13·8	2019	13·9	636	7·8	19 4	7·6	041	3·6	1314	3·3	259	5·9	1523	5·8	1158	4·3	—	
15	S	258	7·8	1514	7·9	012	9·8	1236	9·8	841	13·8	2059	13·7	719	7·8	1942	7·6	123	3·7	1354	3·6	342	5·9	16 8	5·8	022	4·4	1240	4·3
16	S	339	7·7	1557	7·7	054	9·7	1319	9·6	920	13·4	2139	13·1	8 1	7·7	2023	7·4	2 7	3·7	1434	3·6	429	5·8	1655	5·6	1 0	4·3	1328	4·3
17	M	421	7·3	1644	7·4	139	9·3	14 5	9·2	959	12·7	2201	12·3	847	7·4	21 7	7·2	251	3·7	1526	3·6	521	5·6	1740	5·4	2 0	4·2	1420	4·1
18	Tu	5 8	6·8	1734	6·6	230	8·8	1456	8·6	1044	11·9	23 9	11·3	938	6·9	2156	6·8	338	3·6	16 2	3·6	615	5·4	1841	5·2	257	4·0	1518	4·0
19	W	558	6·5	1834	6·6	329	8·3	1559	8·3	1140	11·1	—		1040	6·6	2257	6·3	430	3·4	1653	3·4	716	5·1	1944	5·1	4 3	3·8	1626	3·8
20	Th	656	6·2	1941	6·3	440	7·8	1713	8·0	0 2	10·5	1255	10·6	1156	6·3	—		527	3·2	1752	3·2	824	4·9	2054	4·8	521	3·6	1743	3·7
21	F	8 6	6·0	2054	6·2	6 5	7·6	1837	8·0	136	10·2	1426	10·6	014	6·2	1321	6·2	638	2·9	1924	3·0	940	4·9	2211	4·8	645	3·6	19 2	3·8
22	S	922	6·3	2213	6·3	730	7·9	1953	8·3	3 10	10·6	1552	11·4	140	6·4	1439	6·4	830	2·8	20 9	3·1	1055	5·0	2322	5·0	8 0	3·7	2011	3·9
23	S	1042	6·3	2335	6·7	837	8·3	2053	8·7	421	11·5	1654	12·3	253	6·5	1539	6·7	942	3·0	22 7	3·2	1159	5·2	—		858	3·8	21 8	4·0
24	M	1149	6·7	—		926	8·7	2140	9·0	520	12·3	1742	12·9	350	6·9	1628	6·9	1028	3·1	2252	3·3	020	5·2	1336	5·5	946	4·0	2155	4·1
25	Tu	021	7·1	1241	7·0	10 7	9·0	2220	9·2	6 5	12·8	1825	13·2	438	7·1	1711	7·2	11 5	3·1	2335	3·4	1 7	5·4	1416	5·5	1026	4·1	2231	4·1
26	W	1 9	7·3	1334	7·3	1042	9·1	2257	9·3	642	13·0	19 0	13·3	519	7·2	1749	7·3	1145	3·2	—		147	5·5	1452	5·5	11 2	4·0	2347	4·1
27	Th	149	7·4	14 4	7·4	1117	9·2	2331	9·2	715	13·1	1937	13·2	557	7·3	1822	7·3	016	3·4	1250	3·4	224	5·5	1523	5·4	1134	4·1	—	
28	F	226	7·4	1437	7·4	1150	9·2	—		751	13·1	2012	13·1	632	7·3	1855	7·3	055	3·5	1325	3·5	3 4	5·4	1559	5·3	—		12 6	4·1
29	S	258	7·3	1510	7·3	0 6	8·9	1222	9·1	822	13·0	2044	12·9	7 4	7·1	1923	7·2	2 4	3·4	1331	3·5	333	5·4	1633	5·1	021	4·0	1240	4·0
30	S	328	7·2	1542	7·2	038	8·7	1253	8·9	848	12·8	2111	12·5	737	7·0	1952	7·0	155	3·4	14 2	3·5	444	5·2	17 8	5·0	056	3·9	1315	3·9
31	M	356	7·0	1614	7·0	1 9	8·6	1323	8·7	913	12·4	2134	12·0	811	6·8	2020	6·9	236	3·3	1433	3·5	552	4·9	1822	5·0	133	3·7	1353	3·8

* All times shown are Greenwich Mean Time.   † Difference of height in metres from Ordnance Datum (Newlyn).
‡ Difference of height in metres from Ordnance Datum (Dublin).

NOVEMBER, 1977

High Water at the undermentioned Places (G.M.T.*)—

Day of Month	Day of Week	LONDON BRIDGE †Datum of Predictions 3·20 m. below				LIVERPOOL †Datum of Predictions 4·93 m. below				AVONMOUTH †Datum of Predictions 6·50 m. below				HULL (Salend) †Datum of Predictions 3·90 m. below				GREENOCK †Datum of Predictions 1·62 m. below				LEITH AND GRANTON †Datum of Predictions 2·90 m. below				DUN LAOGHAIRE †Datum of Predictions 0·20 m. above			
		Mn. h.m.	Ht. m.	Aft. h.m.	Ht. m.	Mn. h.m.	Ht. m.	Aft. h.m.	Ht. m.	Mn. h.m.	Ht. m.	Aft. h.m.	Ht. m.	Mn. h.m.	Ht. m.	Aft. h.m.	Ht. m.	Mn. h.m.	Ht. m.	Aft. h.m.	Ht. m.	Mn. h.m.	Ht. m.	Aft. h.m.	Ht. m.	Mn. h.m.	Ht. m.	Aft. h.m.	Ht. m.
1	Tu	428	6·8	1651	6·7	143	8·3	1355	8·3	940	11·9	2159	11·4	844	6·6	2051	6·6	3 9	3·2	15 7	3·5	523	5·0	1746	4·8	213	3·6	1435	3·7
2	W	5 4	6·6	1730	6·5	221	7·9	1436	8·0	1011	11·2	2232	10·8	924	6·3	2128	6·4	347	3·1	1548	3·4	6 3	4·8	1838	4·7	257	3·4	1520	3·6
3	Th	542	6·3	1812	6·2	310	7·5	1527	7·6	1051	10·8	2317	10·2	1010	6·0	2214	6·1	430	3·0	1634	3·3	652	4·5	1920	4·5	347	3·3	1613	3·5
4	F	624	5·9	19 2	5·9	4 9	7·3	1630	7·4	1144	10·1			1112	5·9	2319	5·8	519	2·9	1723	3·2	749	4·4	2020	4·4	449	3·3	1716	3·4
5	S	714	5·7	20 2	5·7	520	7·1	1743	7·6	021	9·8	1254	9·9	041	5·8	1232	5·7	615	2·8	1821	3·1	856	4·4	2127	4·4	6 0	3·3	1826	3·5
6	S	822	5·6	2118	5·8	633	7·3	1855	7·8	146	9·8	1418	10·2	159	6·1	1352	5·8	741	2·8	1934	3·1	10 5	4·5	2235	4·6	8 7	3·6	1929	3·7
7	M	945	5·8	2228	6·2	740	7·8	1959	8·1	310	10·5	1535	11·0	3 3	6·1	1456	6·6	0 5	2·9	2052	3·2	11 8	4·8	2333	4·9	855	3·9	2024	3·8
8	Tu	1054	6·3	2330	6·8	833	8·4	2051	8·6	418	11·4	1637	11·9	356	6·9	1548	7·1	955	3·2	2149	3·5			12 3	5·2	937	4·1	2116	4·0
9	W	1151	6·9			921	8·9	2137	9·1	517	12·3	1734	12·8	445	7·3	1718	7·4	1030	3·4	2240	3·6	024	5·2	1251	5·3	1015	4·2	2153	4·1
10	Th	022	7·3	1242	7·3	10 4	9·4	2223	9·5	610	13·1	1827	13·4	534	7·6	18 0	7·7	1118	3·3	2329	3·6	115	5·5	1335	5·8	1055	4·2	2236	4·2
11	F	110	7·6	1328	7·7	1048	9·8	23 9	9·9	659	13·6	1916	13·8	617	7·7	1842	7·7	017	3·7	1247	3·5	152	5·7	1416	5·8	1136	4·4	2319	4·3
12	S	155	7·7	1413	7·8	1134	9·9	2356	10·0	743	14·0	20 2	13·7	657	7·7	19 0	7·7	1 5	3·7	1331	3·7	237	5·8	15 2	5·9	0 4	4·4	1221	4·4
13	S	239	7·7	1458	7·8			1220	10·0	824	14·0	2045	13·7	751	7·7	1924	7·7	152	3·7	1415	3·8	323	5·9	1548	5·9	053	4·3	13 2	4·4
14	M	322	7·6	1545	7·7	043	9·7	13 5	9·8	9 5	13·7	2128	13·6	840	7·4	2053	7·3	241	3·4	15 0	3·7	414	5·7	1637	5·8	147	4·4	14 2	4·3
15	Tu	4 9	7·1	1635	7·5	130	9·4	1354	9·5	948	13·0	2211	12·6	934	7·2	2143	7·0	330	3·2	1548	3·7	5 5	5·7	1731	5·6	246	4·3	15 2	4·3
16	W	457	7·1	1727	7·2	222	8·9	1446	9·0	1037	12·3	23 3	11·8	1031	6·7	2240	6·7	421	2·9	1639	3·3	5 5	5·5	1827	5·3	349	4·3	1637	4·3
17	Th	549	6·8	1824	6·8	319	8·4	1545	8·5			1134	11·6	1139	6·4	2347	6·4	517	2·9	1736	3·2	659	5·2	1926	5·1	5 3	4·1	1720	4·0
18	F	642	6·4	1923	6·5	426	8·0	1652	8·2	0 3	11·1	1241	11·1	1 4	6·2	1253	6·2	621	3·0	1853	3·1	8 3	5·0	2032	4·9	623	4·0	1837	3·8
19	S	741	6·2	2027	6·3	541	7·8	18 7	8·0	114	10·6	1359	10·9	219	6·2	14 6	6·2	751	3·1	2134	3·3	913	4·9	2142	4·9	734	3·8	1947	3·8
20	S	849	6·1	2139	6·3	658	7·8	1920	8·1	234	10·7	1517	11·2	319	6·5	15 0	6·6	9 8	3·0	2235	3·4	1025	5·0	2251	5·0	834	3·9	2045	3·9
21	M	10 6	6·2	2254	6·6	8 5	8·0	2023	8·4	347	11·6	1620	11·8	410	6·7	1642	6·7	957	3·3	2235	3·1	1129	5·1	1225	5·1	924	4·0	2216	4·0
22	Tu	1118	6·6	2354	6·9	857	8·4	2113	8·6	445	11·7	1711	12·2	455	6·9	1722	7·0	1038	3·3	2324	3·4	039	5·2	13 9	5·3	10 5	3·9	2253	4·0
23	W			1214	6·9	940	8·8	2155	8·8	532	12·1	1753	12·6	534	6·9	1757	7·1	1117	3·4	23 8	3·2	122	5·3	1350	5·3	1040	3·9	2326	3·9
24	Th	043	7·2	13 0	7·1	1018	8·8	2234	8·9	613	12·4	1833	12·6	611	6·9	1829	7·1	1154	3·4	1230	3·4	2 3	5·3	1426	5·4	1113	3·9	2359	3·9
25	F	126	7·3	1341	7·2	1055	9·0	2310	8·9	649	12·6	1911	12·6	648	6·9	19 0	7·1	031	3·4	13 3	3·5	237	5·4	1534	5·3	1145	4·0	1216	3·9
26	S	2 2	7·1	1418	7·1	1128	9·0	2344	8·9	724	12·7	1946	12·7	723	6·9	1930	7·1	1 9	3·4	1335	3·5	312	5·3	16 7	5·3			1250	3·9
27	S	236	7·2	1450	7·0			12 0	8·9	755	12·8	2017	12·5	757	6·8	1959	7·0	143	3·3	14 7	3·6	347	5·3	1642	5·2	033	3·7	1328	3·9
28	M	3 5	7·1	1531	7·0	017	8·8	1231	8·8	824	12·7	2047	12·5	832	6·6	2032	6·6	217	3·2	1442	3·6	421	5·2	1718	5·1	1 8	3·7	14 6	3·8
29	Tu	335	6·9	1555	6·9	050	8·6	13 3	8·6	852	12·5	2115	12·3					251	3·2			458	5·1			147	3·6		
30	W	4 6	6·8	1630	6·8	124	8·4	1336	8·6	923	12·2	2143	12·0																

* All times shown are Greenwich Mean Time.   † Difference of height in metres from Ordnance Datum (Newlyn).
‡ Difference of height in metres from Ordnance Datum (Dublin).

DECEMBER, 1977

High Water at the undermentioned Places (G.M.T.★)—

Day of Month	Day of Week	London Bridge (Datum 3·20 m. below) Mn. h.m.	Ht.	Aft. h.m.	Ht.	Liverpool (Datum 4·93 m. below) Mn. h.m.	Ht.	Aft. h.m.	Ht.	Avonmouth (Datum 6·50 m. below) Mn. h.m.	Ht.	Aft. h.m.	Ht.	Hull (Saltend) (Datum 3·90 m. below) Mn. h.m.	Ht.	Aft. h.m.	Ht.	Greenock (Datum 1·62 m. below) Mn. h.m.	Ht.	Aft. h.m.	Ht.	Leith and Granton (Datum 2·90 m. below) Mn. h.m.	Ht.	Aft. h.m.	Ht.	Dun Laoghaire (Datum 0·20 m. above) Mn. h.m.	Ht.	Aft. h.m.	Ht.
1	Th	441	6·7	17 8	6·7	2 0	8·2	1412	8·4	955	11·9	2215	11·6	910	6·4	21 7	6·7	327	3·1	1521	3·5	537	4·9	18 1	4·9	228	3·5	1449	3·7
2	F	515	6·5	1746	6·5	243	7·9	1457	7·8	1033	11·5	2254	11·5	952	6·2	2149	6·5	4 7	3·1	16 4	3·4	622	4·7	1847	4·7	314	3·4	1535	3·7
3	S	553	6·3	1828	6·3	334	7·6	1549	7·8	1110	11·0	2331	10·5	1042	5·9	2241	6·2	450	3·0	1650	3·4	713	4·6	1940	4·6	4 9	3·4	1629	3·6
4	S	635	6·1	1919	6·1	433	7·5	1651	7·7	1144	10·5			1144	5·8	2347	5·9	537	3·0	1742	3·3	812	4·6	2040	4·6	511	3·4	1733	3·6
5	M	731	6·0	2026	6·1	539	7·5	18 0	7·7	051	10·1	1320	10·4			1257	5·9	637	3·0	1846	3·3	914	4·6	2143	4·7	620	3·4	1841	3·6
6	Tu	849	6·0	2143	6·4	647	7·7	19 8	8·0	127	10·9	1438	10·7	1 4	6·1	1420	6·5	8 0	3·1	20 0	3·3	1020	4·8	2246	4·8	726	3·6	1944	3·7
7	W	10 9	6·4	2252	6·8	751	8·2	2013	8·4	320	10·9	1553	11·4	2 19	6·4	1510	6·9	9 0	3·1	2110	3·4	1119	5·0	2344	5·1	821	3·7	2041	3·9
8	Th	1116	6·8	2354	7·2	848	8·7	21 9	8·9	437	11·7	17 1	12·3	16 2	6·7	16 4	7·4	10 2	3·3	22 9	3·5			1215	5·2	9 8	4·0	2130	4·1
9	F			1215	7·2	939	9·2	2 2	9·2	539	12·7	18 2	13·0	322	7·0	1651	7·6	1050	3·4	2258	3·7	039	5·3	1315	5·5	9 8	4·1	2130	4·1
10	S	049	7·4	13 9	7·4	1029	9·6	2253	9·6	634	13·4	1857	13·6	419	7·3	1739	7·8	1138	3·6	2351	3·7	131	5·6	1355	5·5	953	4·3	23 2	4·2
11	S	138	7·4	1359	7·5	1117	9·9			723	13·9	1947	13·8	5 9	7·5	1825	7·8	1226	3·7			220	5·8	1444	5·9	1036	4·3	2351	4·2
12	M	225	7·4	1447	7·6			12 5	10·0	809	14·1	2031	13·8	655	7·7	1910	7·7	050	3·7	1315	3·8	4 0	5·8	1533	5·9	1119	4·4	2351	4·2
13	Tu	311	7·6	1536	7·6	032	9·4	1254	9·7	852	14·3	2115	13·5	745	7·6	1957	7·7	142	3·7	14 1	3·9	450	5·8	1623	5·9	042	4·2	1256	4·4
14	W	357	7·6	1626	7·6	121	9·4	1342	9·7	936	13·5	2159	13·0	834	7·5	2042	7·7	233	3·6	1535	3·9	543	5·7	18 8	5·5	135	4·2	1349	4·4
15	Th	444	7·3	1715	7·4	211	9·3	1432	9·3	1025	12·9	2249	11·7	924	7·3	2129	7·3	322	3·5	1624	3·7	637	5·4	19 3	5·0	229	4·1	1445	4·2
16	F	532	7·0	18 5	7·0	3 4	8·6	1525	8·6	1117	11·6	2340	11·1	1016	6·9	2219	7·2	410	3·3	1715	3·5	736	5·1	20 3	5·0	331	3·8	1545	4·1
17	S	619	6·9	1857	6·7	4 0	8·2	1621	8·4			1213	11·1	1111	6·5	2315	6·6	458	3·3	18 8	5·5	838	4·8	2114	4·8	436	3·7	1650	3·9
18	S	712	6·4	1954	6·4	5 2	7·8	1725	7·8	037	10·6	1313	11·1	1212	6·2			550	3·0	1816	5·3	945	4·8	2210	4·8	549	3·5	1915	3·7
19	M	8 9	6·1	2057	6·1	610	7·6	1836	7·8	140	10·8	1420	11·0	019	6·2	1321	6·1	654	3·0	1934	5·1	1052	4·8	2314	4·9	7 1	3·5	2018	3·7
20	Tu	1046	6·3	2212	6·3	721	7·7	1943	7·9	242	11·1	1527	11·4	133	6·1	1427	6·2	813	3·0	2051	4·9	1151	4·9			8 3	3·6	2111	3·7
21	W	1146	6·3			822	7·9	2042	8·0	354	11·8	1659	11·2	242	6·1	1525	6·5	917	3·1	2151	4·9	011	5·0	1241	5·0	857	3·7	2156	3·7
22	Th	017	6·9	1238	6·9	913	8·1	2131	8·3	450	12·0	17 8	12·0	341	6·4	1614	6·7	10 7	3·1	2242	3·7	057	5·0	1325	5·2	941	3·8	2235	3·7
23	F	1 2	7·1	1321	7·0	956	8·4	2212	8·6	539	12·5	1805	12·6	431	6·4	1657	6·9	1050	3·2	2328	3·3	141	5·1	14 5	5·2	1019	3·8	23 7	3·7
24	S	141	7·1	1359	7·0	1033	8·7	2251	8·6	621	12·7	1845	12·7	516	6·7	1734	7·0	1130	3·4			220	5·2	1442	5·3	1053	3·9	2340	3·7
25	S	215	7·1	1432	6·9	11 9	8·8	2336	8·7	659	12·4	1921	12·5	635	6·8	18 10	7·1	050	3·3	1256	3·6	256	5·3	1547	5·3	1158	3·9		
26	M	246	7·0	15 4	6·9	1142	9·0			734	12·6	1955	12·5	712	6·8	1914	7·1	127	3·2	1349	3·5	329	5·3	1620	5·3	012	3·7	1230	3·9
27	Tu	317	7·0	1538	7·0	0 0	8·7	1214	9·0	8 4	12·7	21 0	12·2	747	6·7	1945	6·9	2 2	3·2	1348	3·5	4 2	5·3	1656	5·2	047	3·7	13 4	3·9
28	W	350	6·9	1613	7·0	033	8·7	1246	9·0	836	12·7	21 0	12·6	820	6·8	2018	6·8	236	3·1	1422	3·6	436	5·3	1735	5·1	123	3·6	1342	3·9
29	Th	423	6·9	1647	6·9	1 8	8·6	1318	8·9	9 8	12·6	2133	12·5	856	6·6	2051	6·6	310	3·1	1459	3·6	513	5·1	1818	5·0	2 3	3·6	1421	3·9
30	F	455	6·8	1723	6·8	142	8·5	1352	8·7	947	12·5	22 4	12·3	923	6·4	2129	6·4	345	3·1	1539	3·6	554	4·9	18 18	5·0	246	3·5	15 3	3·8
31	S					220	8·3	1429	8·5	1017	12·2	2237						345	3·1	1539	3·6								

★ All times shown are Greenwich Mean Time.   † Difference of height in metres from Ordnance Datum (Newlyn).
‡ Difference of height in metres from Ordnance Datum (Dublin).

NOTES ON TIDAL PREDICTIONS

Changes in Chart Datum

During recent years the Department of the Hydrographer of the Navy has been carrying out a survey of tidal levels. On the conclusion of each section of the survey the Department is taking the opportunity to regularize the sequence of chart datums so that eventually chart datums throughout the British Isles will approximate to the Lowest Astronomical Tide, *i.e.* the lowest level which can be predicted to occur under average meteorological conditions and under any combination of astronomical conditions.

In some cases the changes in chart datum will be appreciable (perhaps as much as 1 metre) and the resulting predictions will appear to give heights of tide quite different from those of previous years. These changes do not imply that a physical change has taken place in tidal conditions.

It will be found that, where such datum changes have been made, the relationship between Ordnance Datum and the datum of the predictions will also have been altered. In order to compare the predictions for one year with those of another year for which the datum has been altered, it is necessary to refer both years to the same datum. Ordnance Datum (Newlyn) is a convenient datum to which tidal heights may thus be referred.

Example.—In 1972, at Folkstone, the highest predicted high water was 22·8 feet (=6·9 metres) above chart datum; chart datum for that year was 10·06 feet (3·07 metres) below Ordnance Datum (Newlyn). In 1973 the highest predicted high water was 7·4 metres above chart datum, while chart datum for this year was altered to 3·75 metres below Ordnance Datum (Newlyn). To compare these two maximum predicted levels we must reduce both to Ordnance Datum (Newlyn) with the following results:—

1972 6·9–3·07 = 3·83 metres
1973 7·4–3·75 = 3·65 metres

Thus it will be seen that the highest prediction for 1973 is approximately 0·2 metres lower than for 1972.

———

Tidal predictions for London Bridge, Liverpool, Bristol, Hull and Leith are computed by the Institute of Oceanographic Sciences, copyright reserved. Tidal predictions for Dún Laoghaire are based upon standard Port data computed by the Institute of Oceanographic Sciences, copyright reserved. Tidal predictions for Greenock are Crown Copyright and have been supplied by the Institute of Oceanographic Sciences with the permission of the Controller of H.M. Stationery Office and the Hydrographer of the Navy.

Chronological Notes

TIME MEASURES

Kelvin (1883) estimated the age of the earth's crust at 20–400 million years. Study of radioactivity has since shown cooling to have been slower. Holmes and others gave 1,500–2,000 million years as the age of the oldest known rocks. Jeffreys suggests an age not exceeding 8,000 million years for the separate existence of the earth, which, probably with other related planets, separated from the sun after a star-collision. Very early rocks, almost without traces of fossils, are variously named in North America and Europe and account for a period down to about 5000 million years ago.

PALÆOZOIC (Old Animal Life) PERIODS include:—

Cambrian, Ordovician and Silurian rocks, all named from Wales (Cambria, Ordovices, Silures, the two latter ancient Celtic peoples). These rocks account for about 200 million years and there then followed a major phase of mountain-building, called *Caledonian* because studied early in Scotland, characterized by N.E.–S.W. lines of hills and valleys in several areas.

Devonian, including the Old Red Sandstone.

Carboniferous, including Mountain Limestone, Millstone Grit and Coal Measures.

These rocks account for about 100 million years and then there followed a major phase of mountain-building called *Hercyian* because widespread in W. Germany and adjacent areas. In Britain there are E.–W. lines of hills and valleys, and some N.–S.

MESOZOIC (Middle Forms of Life) PERIODS include:—

Permian rocks, widespread in Perm district, U.S.S.R. *Triassic,* including New Red Sandstone. *Jurassic,* important in the Jura Mts. *Cretaceous,* including the Greensands and the Chalk of England. In the Mesozoic, modern large land groups of animals, reptiles, birds and mammals first appear, but almost no modern genera or species of animals are known.

CAINOZOIC or CENOZOIC (Recent forms of Life) PERIODS include:—

Eocene. A few existing genera or species. *Oligocene.* A minority of existing forms. *Miocene.* Approach to a balance of existing and extinct forms. *Pliocene.* A majority of existing forms. *Pleistocene.* A very large majority of existing forms. *Holocene.* Existing forms only, save for a few exterminated by man. In the last 50 million years, from the Miocene through the Pliocene, the Alpine-Himalayan and the circum-Pacific phases of mountain building reached their climax.

During the Pleistocene period ice sheets repeatedly locked up masses of water as land ice, its weight depressed the land, but the locking up of water lowered sea-level by 100–200 metres. Milankovitch has worked out variations of radiation theoretically receivable from the sun and has reached conclusions not very markedly different as to dates from those of Penck who studied sediments, and both can fit into Deperet's scheme based on study of river terraces. Milankovitch gives 600,000 years for the Pleistocene.

Phases of the Pleistocene:—

(*a*) Early Glaciations (probably 2), Gunz glaciations of Penck's Alpine series. About 600 to 500 thousand years ago.

(*b*) An interglacial phase with high sea level, Milazzian terraces (of Deperet's series) around the Mediterranean. About 500,000 years ago.

(*c*) A second pair of Glaciations, the Mindel of Penck's series. About 500 to rather before 400 thousand years ago.

(*d*) A long interglacial phase with high sea level, but less high than during (*b*). Tyrrhenian terraces around the Mediterranean. From about 400 to about 200 thousand years ago.

(*e*) The penultimate series of glaciations (probably 3), the Riss of Penck's series. About 200 to 150 thousand years ago.

(*f*) An interglacial phase with fairly high sea level, less high than during (*d*). Monastirian terraces around the Mediterranean. From about 150 to about 120 thousand years ago.

(*g*) The ultimate series of glaciations (probably 3, preceded perhaps by a cool phase), the Wurm of Penck's series. From about 115 to rather more than 20 thousand years ago.

(*h*) The last glacial retreat merging into the Holocene period about 10,000 or 8,000 years ago.

MAN IN THE PLEISTOCENE

In the East African Miocene have been found by Hopwood and Leakey fragmentary remains of apes with possible human links in thigh bone characters.

In S. Africa at Taungs, Sterkfontein and Kroomdraai have been found remains of *Australopithecus*, *Plesianthropus* and *Paranthropus*, possibly linked with early man in limb characters and some features of skull and teeth though the brains are small and rather ape-like. The cave deposits in which they occur are supposed to be late Pliocene or early Pleistocene.

Java and Peking finds began with Dubois' discovery (1892) of an imperfect skull cap, some teeth and a possibly related femur indicating the erect posture. Later finds by von Koenigswald and by Weidenreich (1937–41) have emphasized the human relationship of the Java specimens, and also give evidence of gigantism (the name *Meganthropus* has been used). The specimens are usually given a Middle Pleistocene age. Oppenoorth (1932) discovered robust skulls and human Pleistocene bones on a terrace of the Solo river, Java. Twelve specimens from Chou Kou Tien near Peking studied by Black and Weidenreich and called *Sinanthropus* are broadly like the Java finds; the name *Pithecanthropus* had better be used for all.

A jaw from Mauer, Heidelberg, found 1902, and dated to the mid Pleistocene is very large but human in form. A skull cap from Neandertal near Düsseldorf, Germany, has been under discussion for 100 years. It and later found congeners belong to the onset of the 4th series of Glaciations (Penck's Wurm). The best preserved of these skulls is that of La Chapelle aux Saints (France) with very strong brow-ridges. Related skulls of rather earlier date from Steinheim, Ehringsdorf, Krapina and elsewhere are less specialized and more akin to modern man. Skulls from Sacco Pastore and Circeo in Italy are related to the Neandertal group.

Mt. Carmel has yielded to Professor Dorothy Garrod and Dr. McCown several mid- or late-Pleistocene specimens apparently related both to modern types and to the Neandertal group.

A skull from Galilee, and a skull from Kabwe (formerly Broken Hill), Zambia, are related to the Neandertal group.

Oakley has estimated the age of Pleistocene fossil bones from their fluorine content. The back part of a skull from Swanscombe, N. Kent, has in this way been dated to the mid Pleistocene. Its discoverer, Marston, has won widespread support for his view linking it with modern types.

Controversy over the Piltdown skull and jaw is ended. The skull was dated by Oakley's method as late Pleistocene, or later, so the old name *Eoanthropus* is inappropriate. The ape-like jaw was found to be modern and to have nothing to do with the skull.

With the last retreat of the ice sheets it seems that the Neandertal group, and probably the Pitecanthropus group, became extinct. Well-known specimens of man of modern type with diversity of form have been found at Combe Capelle, Cro-Magnon, Chancelade and elsewhere in the later Pleistocene in France and others in Czechoslovakia.

HUMAN CULTURAL STAGES

Until about 8 or 7 thousand years ago men lived by hunting and collecting. In the middle of the Pleistocene they already made finely shaped hand axes (Abbevillean and Acheulian) from stone cores by chipping off flakes, using flint, chert, obsidian, rhyolite, quartzite, etc. in many regions, and these cultures spread from Africa to Spain, France and Britain during some interglacial periods. Apparently the men hunted and made pitfalls for animals as Leakey has shown at Olorgesailie in Kenya, while women and children collected. Fire was used very early. In the continental interior of Eurasia rough stone flakes were long used rather than shaped stone cores and apparently in cold periods at any rate this culture spread west to Britain. In the later part of the Riss-Wurm interglacial, stone flakes became finer especially in regions where contact was made with makers of core-tools, and in some groups both cores and flakes were used.

With the last retreat of the ice-sheets stone flakes became the dominant tools, with diverse types suited to scraping, boring, sawing, etc.—Aurignacian, followed in France by Solutrian, in which long leaf-like flakes were treated as cores and shaped very skilfully by pressing off flakes. The Magdalenian stage next following used flakes but specialized in implements of bone, horn and ivory. In some areas the Aurignacian grades into the Magdalenian and this seems to be largely the case in parts of Britain. All the above cultures are often grouped as Palæolithic.

About 8 or 7 thousand years ago people in S.W. Asia began to cultivate cereals on river mud laid down by annual floods, thus keeping the soil fertile and allowing durable settlement with concomitant advances in mud brick construction, pot-making, stone grinding, which had begun earlier and gave an improved control of shape, carpentering, weaving and other inventions. In all this development the Nile valley was early concerned and its regular floods from summer rains in Abyssinia could be managed to give such an advantage that Egypt gained a unique primacy in early history. Domestication of animals was added very early to cultivation of crops, most probably as a source of milk, flesh, leather, sinews, etc. Neolithic Culture was thus characterized by stone axes shaped by grinding or rubbing, by cultivation, usually by domestic animals, often by durable settlements and a variety of arts and crafts.

Especially after the practice of castration of surplus male animals was introduced, domestic beasts were used for work, notably for pulling a modified hoe to scratch the drying surface of river-mud and so keep it from caking too hard. This is the early plough, valuable in lands where plant food in the soil is drawn up nearly to the surface as moisture rises and evaporates. Animals were also used as porters and tractors.

Heating stones in fires, probably for water-heating, led to the discovery of impure copper and the invention of bronze (standardized at about 10 per cent. tin and 90 per cent. copper) at the beginning of the Bronze Age in S.W. Asia and/or Egypt. By that time, about 5,000 years ago, cities and trade were developing and the basic arts were spreading to the Indus basin, the Mediterranean and the loess areas of Central Europe. Western Europe on the one hand and N. China on the other were affected somewhat later but more than 4,000 years ago; and China rapidly advanced to a high skill in pottery and bronze. Over 3,000 years ago in Anatolia the smelting of iron was developed, and it spread thence in the next centuries, beginning the Iron Age. Iron nails and tools made possible larger boats, houses,

furniture and especially larger ploughs, working deeper into the earth and so suited to cooler lands, where plant food was often deep in the soil because evaporation was not very strong and rain might occur at every season. So the farmer needed to bring up the deeper layers to the surface in north-west Europe. With the spread of iron, especially about 2,000 to 1,000 years ago, northwest Europe emerged from its former low status and went ahead, still more after houses were improved with more privacy, chimneys and beds.

The evolution of culture in the Americas is much discussed. Early drifts of hunters viâ Alaska may have occurred in the late Pleistocene. Probably a good deal of Neolithic culture (stone implements, pottery, etc.) spread by the same route to America about or after 5,000 years ago but did not take Asiatic cereals or domestic animals. America also received contributions to its life by maritime routes especially following the North Pacific currents.

TIME MEASUREMENT AND CALENDARS

MEASUREMENTS OF TIME

Measurements of Time.—These are based on the time taken by the earth to rotate on its axis (*Day*); by the moon to revolve round the earth (*Month*); and by the earth to revolve round the sun (*Year*). From these, which are not commensurable, certain average or mean intervals have been adopted for ordinary use. Of these the first is the *Day*, which begins at midnight and is divided into 24 hours of 60 minutes, each of 60 seconds. The hours are counted from midnight up to 12 at noon (when the sun crosses the meridian), and these hours are designated A.M. (*ante meridiem*); and again from noon up to 12 at midnight, which hours are designated P.M. (*post meridiem*), except when the *Twenty-four Hour* reckoning is employed. The 24-hour reckoning ignores A.M. and P.M., and the hours are numbered 0 to 23 from midnight to midnight.

Colloquially the 24 hours are divided into *day* and *night*, day being the time while the sun is above the horizon (including the four stages of twilight defined on p. 139), Day is subdivided further into *morning*, the early part of daytime, ending at noon; *afternoon* from noon to 6 p.m. and *evening*, which may be said to extend from 6 p.m. until midnight. *Night*, the dark period between day and day, begins at the close of Astronomical Twilight (*see* p. 139) and extends beyond midnight to sunrise the next day.

The names of the *Days*—Sunday, Monday, Tuesday (Tiw = God of War), Wednesday (Woden or Odin), Thursday (Thor), Friday (Frig = wife of Odin), and Saturday are derived from Old English translations or adaptations of the Roman titles (Sol, Luna, Mars, Mercurius, Jupiter, Venus and Saturnius).

The *Week* is a period of 7 days.

The *Month* in the ordinary calendar is approximately the twelfth part of a year, but the lengths of the different months vary from 28 (or 29) days to 31.

The Year.—The *Equinoctial or Tropical Year* is the time that the earth takes to revolve round the sun from equinox to equinox, or 365·2422 mean solar days. The *Calendar Year* consists of 365 days, but a year the date of which is divisible by 4, without remainder, is called *bissextile* (see Roman Calendar) or *Leap Year* and consists of 366 days, one day being added to the month February, so that a date "leaps over" a day of the week. The last year of a century is not a leap year unless its number is divisible by 400 (*e.g.* the years 1800 and 1900 had only 365 days).

The Historical Year.—Before the year 1752, two Calendar systems were in use in England. The Civil or Legal Year began on March 25, while the Historical Year began on January 1. Thus the Civil or Legal date 1658 March 24, was the same day as 1659 March 24 Historical; and a date in that portion of the year is written as:

March 24 165⅝, the lower figure showing the Historical year.

The Masonic Year.—Two dates are quoted in warrants, dispensations etc., issued by the United Grand Lodge of England, those for the current year being expressed as *Anno Domini* 1976—*Anno Lucis* 5976. This *Year of Light* is based on the Book of Genesis I: 3, the 4000 year difference being derived from *Ussher's Notation*, published in 1654, which placed the Creation of the World in 4,000 B.C.

Regnal Years.—These are the years of a sovereign's reign, and each begins on the anniversary of his or her accession: *e.g.* Regnal year 24 of the present Queen began on Feb. 6, 1975. The system was used for dating Acts of Parliament until 1962. The *Summer Time Act* of 1925, for example, is quoted as 15 and 16 Geo. V. c. 64, because it became law in the session which extended over part of both of these regnal years. The regnal years of Edward VII began on January 22, which was the day of Queen Victoria's death in 1901, so that Acts passed in that reign are, in general, quoted with only one year number, but year 10 of the series ended on May 6, 1910, being the day on which King Edward died, and Acts of the Parliamentary Session 1910 are headed 10 Edw. VII. and 1 Geo. V.; Acts passed in 1936 were dated 1 Edw. VIII. and 1 Geo. VI.; Acts passed in 1952 were dated 16 Geo. VI. and 1 Elizabeth II. Since 1962 Acts of Parliament have been dated by the calendar year.

New Year's Day.—In England in the seventh century, and as late as the thirteenth, the year was reckoned from Christmas Day, but in the twelfth century the Anglican Church began the year with the Feast of The Annunciation of the Blessed Virgin (Lady Day) on March 25 and this practice was adopted generally in the fourteenth century. The Civil or Legal year in the British Dominions (excusive of Scotland), as opposed to the Historical, which already began on Jan. 1, began with "Lady Day" until 1751. But in and since 1752 the civil year has begun with Jan. 1. Certain dividends are still paid by the Bank of England on dates based on Old Style. The Income Tax year begins on April 6 (the New Style equivalent of March 25, Old Style) in accordance with Act of Parliament (39 Geo. III. 1798). New Year's Day in *Scotland* was changed from March 25 to Jan. 1 in 1600. On the Continent of Europe Jan. 1 was adopted as the first day of the year by Venice in 1522, Germany in 1544, Spain, Portugal, and the Roman Catholic Netherlands in 1556, Prussia, Denmark and Sweden in 1559, France 1564, Lorraine 1579, Protestant Netherlands 1583, Russia 1725, and Tuscany 1751.

The Longest Day.—The longest day measured from sunrise to sunset at any place is the day on which the Sun attains its greatest distance from the Equator, north or south, accordingly as the place is in the northern or southern hemisphere; in other words, it is the day of the Calendar on which

a Solstice falls. If a Solstice falls on June 21 late in the day, by Greenwich Time, that day will be the longest of the year at Greenwich, though it may be by only a second of time or a fraction thereof, but it will be on June 22 (local date) in Japan, and therefore June 22 will be the longest day there and at places in Eastern longitudes.

But leaving this question of locality and confining consideration to Greenwich, the Solstices are events in the Tropical Year whose length is $365\frac{1}{4}$ days less about 11 minutes, and therefore, if a Solstice happens on June 21 in one year, it will be nearly six hours later in the next, or early on June 22, and that will be the longest day. This delay of the Solstice is not permitted to continue because the extra day in Leap Year brings it back a day in the Calendar. For the remainder of this century the longest day will fall each year on June 21.

Because of the 11 minutes above mentioned the additional day in Leap Year brings the Solstice back too far by 44 minutes, and the time of the Solstice in the calendar is earlier as the century progresses. In the year 2000 the Summer Solstice reaches its earliest date for 100 years, i.e., June 21^{d} 02^{h}.

To remedy this the last year of a century is in most cases not a Leap Year, and the omission of the extra day puts the date of the Solstice later by about six hours too much, compensation for which is made by making the fourth centennial year a Leap Year.

The Shortest Day.—Similar considerations apply to the shortest day of the year, or the day of the Winter Solstice. For the remainder of this century the shortest day will fall on Dec. 21 in two years of four and on Dec. 22 in the remaining two years. In the year 2000 the Winter Solstice reaches its earliest date, Dec. 21^{d} 13^{h}. The difference due to locality also prevails in the same sense as for the longest day.

At Greenwich the Sun sets at its earliest by the clock about ten days before the shortest day, which is a circumstance that may require explanation. The daily change in the time of sunset is due in the first place to the Sun's movement southwards at this time of year, which diminishes the interval between the Sun's southing or Apparent noon, and its setting, and, secondly, because of the daily decrease of the Equation of Time subtractive from Apparent time, which causes the time of Apparent noon to be continuously later, day by day, and so in a measure counteracts the first effect. The rates of the resulting daily acceleration and retardation are not equal, nor are they uniform, but are such that their combinations causes the date of earliest sunset to be Dec. 12 or 13 at Greenwich. In more southerly latitudes the effect of the movement of the Sun is less, and the change in the time of sunset depends on that of the Equation of Time to a greater degree, and the date of earliest sunset is earlier than it is at Greenwich.

Lord Mayor's Day.—The Lord Mayor of London was previously elected on the Feast of St. Simon and St. Jude (Oct. 28), and from the time of Edward I, at least, was presented to the King or to the Barons of the Exchequer on the following day, except that day be a Sunday.

The day of election was altered to Oct. 16 in 1346, and after some further changes was fixed for Michaelmas Day in 1546, but the ceremonies of admittance and swearing-in of the Lord Mayor continued to take place on Oct. 28 and 29 respectively until 1751. In 1752, when Sept. 3 was reckoned as Sept. 14 at the reform of the Calendar, the Lord Mayor was continued in office until Nov. 8, the " New Style " equivalent of Oct. 28. The Lord Mayor is now presented to the Lord Chief Justice at the Royal Courts of Justice, on the second Saturday in November to make the final declaration of office, having been sworn in at Guildhall on the preceding day.

Dog Days.—The days about the heliacal rising of the Dog Star, noted from ancient times as the hottest and most unwholesome period of the year in the Northern Hemisphere. Their incidence has been variously calculated as depending on the Greater or Lesser Dog Star (Sirius or Procyon) and their duration has been reckoned as from 30 to 54 days. A generally accepted period is from July 3 to August 15.

Metonic (Lunar, or Minor) *Cycle.*—In the year 432 B.C. Meton, an Athenian astronomer, found that 235 Lunations are very nearly, though not exactly equal in duration to 19 Solar Years, and, hence, after 19 years the Phases of the Moon recur on the same days of the month (nearly). The dates of Full Moon in a cycle of nineteen years were inscribed in *figures of gold* on public monuments in Athens, and the number showing the position of a year in the Cycle is called the *Golden Number* of that year.

Solar (or Major) *Cycle.*—A period of twenty-eight years, in any corresponding year of which the days of the week recur on the same day of the month.

Julian Period.—Proposed by Joseph Scaliger in 1582. The period is 7980 Julian years, and its first year coincides with the year 4713 B.C. 7980 is the product of the number of years in the Solar Cycle, the Metonic Cycle and the cycle of the Roman Indication (28 × 19 × 15).

Roman Indication.—A period of fifteen years, instituted for fiscal purposes about A.D. 300.

Epact.—The age of the calendar Moon, diminished by one day, on January 1, in the ecclesiastical lunar calendar.

THE FOUR SEASONS

SPRING, the first season of the year, is defined astronomically to begin in the *Northern Hemisphere* at the Vernal Equinox when the Sun enters the sign Aries (*i.e.* about March 21) and crosses the Equator, thus causing day and night to be of equal length all over the world; and to terminate at the Summer Solstice. In *Great Britain*, Spring in popular parlance comprises the months of February, March and April; in *North America* the months of March, April and May. In the *Southern Hemisphere* Spring corresponds with Autumn in the Northern Hemisphere.

SUMMER, the second and warmest season, begins astronomically at the Summer Solstice when the Sun enters the sign of Cancer (about June 21). The Sun then attains its greatest northern declination and appears to stand still, the times of sunrise and sunset and the consequent length of the day showing no variation for several days together, before and after the Longest Day (June 21 or 22). Summer terminates at the Autumnal Equinox. In popular parlance Summer in *Great Britain* includes the months of May, June, July and August, Midsummer Day being June 24. In *North America* the season includes the months of June, July and August.

AUTUMN, the third season, begins astronomically at the Autumnal Equinox (*i.e.*, about September 21) when the Sun enters the sign Libra, the beginning of which sign is at the intersection of the Equator and the Ecliptic, the point in the sky where the Sun crosses from N. to S. of the Equator and causes the length of day and night to be equal all over the world. In *Great Britain* it is popularly held to include the months of September and October. A warm period sometimes occurs round about St. Luke's Day (Oct. 18) and is known as " St. Luke's Summer." In *North America*,

Autumn, or " The Fall," comprises September, October and November. Autumn ends at the Winter Solstice. In the *Southern Hemisphere* it corresponds with Spring of the Northern Hemisphere.

WINTER, the fourth and coldest season, begins astronomically at the Winter Solstice (*i.e.* about Dec. 21) when the Sun enters the sign Capricornus, and ends at the Vernal Equinox. In *Great Britain*

the season is popularly held to comprise the months of November, December and January, mid-winter being marked by the Shortest Day. A warm period sometimes occurs round about Martinmas (Nov.11) and is known as " St. Martin's Summer." In *North America* the season includes the months of December, January and February. In the *Southern Hemisphere* it corresponds with Summer of the Northern Hemisphere.

THE CHRISTIAN CALENDAR

In the Christian chronological system the years are distinguished by cardinal numbers before or after the Incarnation, the period being denoted by the letters B.C. (Before Christ) or, more rarely, A.C. (*Ante Christum*), and A.D. (*Annus Domini*). The correlative dates of the epoch are the 4th year of the 194th Olympiad, the 753rd year from the Foundation of Rome, A.M. 3761 (Jewish Chronology), and the 4714th year of the Julian Period. This was introduced into Italy in the sixth century, and though first used in France in the seventh it was not universally established there until about the eighth century. It has been said that the system was introduced into England by St. Augustine (A.D. 596), but was probably not generally used until some centuries later. It was ordered to be used by the Bishops at the Council of Chelsea, A.D. 816. The actual date of the birth of Christ is somewhat uncertain. Dec. 25, 4 B.C., is supported by several lines of argument.

Old and New Style.—In the Julian Calendar all the centennial years were Leap Years, and for this reason towards the close of the sixteenth century there was a difference of 10 days between the tropical and calendar years; or, in other words, the equinox fell on March 11 of the Calendar, whereas at the time of the Council of Nicaea, A.D. 325, it had fallen on March 21. In 1582 Pope Gregory ordained that Oct. 5th should be called Oct. 15th, and that of the end-century years only the fourth should be a Leap Year (*see* p. 186). This change was adopted by Italy, France, Spain, and Portugal in 1582; by Prussia, the German Roman Catholic States, Switzerland, Holland, and Flanders on Jan. 1, 1583, Poland 1586, Hungary 1587, the German and Netherland Protestant States and Denmark 1700, Sweden (gradually) by the omission of eleven leap days, 1700–1740; Great Britain and her Dominions (including the North American Colonies) in 1752, by the omission of eleven days (Sept. 3 being reckoned as Sept. 14). This *Gregorian Calendar* was adopted by Japan in 1872, China in 1912, Bulgaria in 1915, Turkey and Soviet Russia in 1918, by Yugoslavia and Rumania in 1919, and by Greece in February, 1923. The Russian, Greek, Serbian and Rumanian Churches did not abandon the Julian Calendar until May, 1923, when the Gregorian, slightly modified, was adopted. The *difference* between the Old and New Styles was 11 days after 1752, 12 days after 1800, and has been 13 days since 1900. It happened that a change of the beginning of the year from March 25 to January 1 was made in England in 1752, the year in which the change from Julian to Gregorian Calendar was made, and for that reason the words Old and New Style have been used in a sense which is not strictly correct, but is nevertheless expressive.

The Dominical Letter is one of the letters A–G which are used to denote the Sundays in successive years. If the first day of the year is a Sunday the letter is A; if the second, B; the third, C; and so on. Leap year requires two letters, the first for Jan. 1–Feb. 29, the second for March 1–Dec. 31.

Epiphany.—The Feast of the Epiphany, commemorating the manifestation of the infant Jesus to the Gentiles, later became associated with the offering of gifts by the Magi. The day was of exceptional importance from the time of the Council of Nicaea (A.D. 325) as the primate of Alexandria was charged at every Epiphany Feast with the announcement in a letter to the Churches of the date of the forthcoming Easter. The day was of considerable importance in Britain as it influenced dates, ecclesiastical and lay, *e.g.* Plow Monday, when work was resumed in the fields, falls upon the Monday in the first full week after the Epiphany.

Lent.—The Teutonic word *Lent*, which denotes the Fast preceding Easter, originally meant no more than the Spring season; but from Anglo-Saxon times, at least, it has been used as the equivalent of the more significant Latin term *Quadragesima*, meaning the " Forty Days " or, more literally, the fortieth day. As early as the fifth century some of the Fathers of the Church put forward the view that the forty days Fast is of Apostolic origin, but this is not supported or believed by modern scholars; and it appears to some that it dates from the early years of the fourth century. There is some suggestion that the Fast was kept originally for only forty hours. *Ash Wednesday* is the first day of Lent, which ends at midnight before Easter Day.

Sexagesima and Septuagesima.—It has been suggested that the unmeaning application of the names *Sexagesima* and *Septuagesima* to the second and third Sundays before Lent was made by analogy with the names *Quadragesima* and *Quinquagesima*. Another less likely conjecture is that *Septuagesima* means the seventieth day before the Octave of Easter. It is not certain whether the name *Quinquagesima* is due to the fact that the Sunday in question is the fiftieth day before Easter (reckoned inclusive) or was simply formed on the analogy of *Quadragesima* (*New English Dictionary*).

Palm Sunday commemorates the triumphal entry of Our Lord into Jerusalem and is celebrated in Britain (when palm is not available) by branches of willow gathered for use in the decoration of churches on that day.

Maundy Thursday, the day before Good Friday, the name itself being a corruption of *dies mandati* (day of the mandate) when Christ washed the feet of the disciples and gave them the mandate to love one another.

Easter-Day is the first Sunday after the full moon which happens upon, or next after, the 21st day of March; and if the full moon happens upon a Sunday, Easter-Day is the Sunday after. This definition is contained in an Act of Parliament (24 Geo. II., cap. 23), and explanation is given in the preamble to the Act that the day of Full Moon depends on certain tables that have been prepared. These are the tables whose essential points are given in the early pages of the Book of Common Prayer. The Moon referred to is not the real Moon of the heavens, but a hypothetical Moon on whose " Full " the date of Easter depends, and the

lunations of this " Calendar " Moon consist of twenty-nine and thirty days alternately with certain necessary modifications to make the date of its Full agree as nearly as possible with that of the real Moon, which is known as the *Paschal Full Moon.*

A Fixed Easter.—As at present ordained, Easter falls on one of 35 days—(March 22–April 25). On June 15, 1928, the House of Commons agreed to a motion for the third reading of the Bill that Easter Day shall, in the Calendar year next but one after the commencement of the Act and in all subsequent years, be *the first Sunday after the second Saturday in April.* Easter would thus fall between April 9 and 15, both inclusive—that is, on the second or third Sunday in April. A clause in the Bill provided that before it shall come into operation regard shall be had to any opinion expressed officially by the various Christian Churches. Efforts have been made recently by the World Council of Churches to secure a unanimous choice of date for Easter by its 239 member Churches. Press reports suggested the second Sunday in April as their most likely choice.

Holy Days and Saints Days were the normal factors in early times for settling the dates of future and recurrent appointments, *e.g.* the *Quarter Days* in England and Wales are the Feast of the Nativity, the Feast of the Annunciation, the Feast of St. John the Baptist and the Feast of St. Michael and All the Holy Angels, while *Term Days* in Scotland are Candlemas (Feast of the Purification), Whitsunday (a fixed date), Lammas (Loaf Mass) and Martinmas (St. Martin's Day). *Law Sittings* in England and Wales commence on the Feast of St. Hilary and the term which begins on Old Michaelmas Day ends on the feast of St. Thomas the Apostle.

The number of Saints commemorated in the Calendar of the Book of Common Prayer is 73, but (with the exception of All Saint's Day) " days " are appointed only for those whose names are mentioned in Scripture. *Red Letter Days (see also* p. 225) were Holy Days and Saints Days indicated in early ecclesiastical calendars by letters printed in red ink. The days to be distinguished in this way were finally approved at the Council of Nicaea, A.D. 325,

and special services are set apart for them in the Book of Common Prayer.

Rogation Days.—These are the Monday, Tuesday and Wednesday preceding Ascension Day, " Holy Thursday ", and in the fifth century were ordered by the Church to be observed as Public Fasts with solemn processions and supplications. The processions were discontinued as religious observances at the Reformation, but survive in the ceremony known as " Beating the Parish Bounds ".

Ember Days.—The Ember Days at the Four Seasons are the Wednesday, Friday and Saturday after (1) the First Sunday in Lent, (2) the Feast of Pentecost, (3) September 14, (4) December 13.

Whit Sunday.—It is generally said that this name is a variant of White Sunday, and was so called from the albs or white robes of the newly baptized. But other derivations have been suggested.

Trinity Sunday.—The Festival in honour of the Trinity is observed on the Sunday following Whit Sunday, and subsequent Sundays are reckoned in the Church of England as " after Trinity "; in the Roman Catholic Church Sundays are reckoned " after Pentecost ".

Thomas Becket, called by his contemporaries Thomas of London (*born* 1118; *murdered* Dec. 29, 1170), was consecrated Archbishop of Canterbury on the Sunday after Whit Sunday and his first act was to ordain that the day of his consecration should be held as a new festival in honour of the Holy Trinity. The observance thus originated spread from Canterbury throughout the whole of Christendom.

Advent Sunday is the Sunday nearest to St. Andrew's Day, Nov. 30, which allows three Sundays between Advent and Christmas Day in all cases. The Sunday preceding Advent is the 27th after Trinity if Easter falls on one of the days, March 22–26 inclusive. It is the 22nd after Trinity when Easter Day is on April 24 or 25. If the date of Easter were determined as proposed (*see Fixed Easter*) there would generally be 24 Sundays after Trinity, the number being 25 only in the years when Easter fell on April 9. With a Fixed Easter there would never be a sixth Sunday after Epiphany. There would be a fifth Sunday when Easter Day fell on April 15 or April 14, the year being a leap year.

A TABLE OF THE MOVABLE FEASTS FOR 10 YEARS—1974–83

Year	Ash Wednesday	Easter	Ascension	Whit Sunday	Sundays after Trinity	Advent
1974.......	Feb. 27	April 14	May 23	June 2	xxiv	Dec. 1
1975.......	Feb. 12	March 30	May 8	May 18	xxvi	Nov. 30
1976.......	March 3	April 18	May 27	June 6	xxiii	Nov. 28
1977.......	Feb. 23	April 10	May 19	May 29	xxiv	Nov. 27
1978.......	Feb. 8	March 26	May 4	May 14	xxvii	Dec. 3
1979.......	Feb. 28	April 15	May 24	June 3	xxiv	Dec. 2
1980.......	Feb. 19	April 6	May 15	May 25	xxv	Nov. 30
1981.......	Mar. 4	April 19	May 28	June 7	xxiii	Nov. 29
1982.......	Feb. 24	April 11	May 20	May 30	xxiv	Nov. 28
1983.......	Feb. 16	April 3	May 12	May 22	xxv	Nov. 27

NOTES CONCERNING TABLE OF MOVABLE FEASTS

Ash Wednesday (first Day in Lent) can fall at earliest on February 4 and at latest on March 10.
Easter Day can fall at earliest on March 22 and at latest on April 25.
Ascension Day can fall at earliest on April 30 and at latest on June 3.
Whit Sunday can fall at earliest on May 10 and at latest on June 13.
Rogation Sunday is the Sunday next before *Holy Thursday* (Ascension Day).
Trinity Sunday is the Sunday next after *Whit Sunday.*
Corpus Christi falls on the Thursday next after *Trinity Sunday.*
There are not less than xxii and not more than xxvii *Sundays after Trinity.*
Advent Sunday is the Sunday nearest to November 30.

A TABLE OF EASTER DAYS AND SUNDAY LETTERS, 1500 TO 2000

		1500—1599	1600—1699	1700—1799	1800—1899	1900—2000		
d	Mar. 22	1573............	1668........	1761........	1818........	....	d	Mar. 22
e	,, 23	1505-16........	1600........	1788........	1845-56....	1913........	e	,, 23
f	,, 24	....	1611-95....	1706-99....	....	1940........	f	,, 24
g	,, 25	1543-54....	1627-38-49....	1722-33-44....	1883-94....	1951........	g	,, 25
A	,, 26	1559-70-81-92....	1654-65-76....	1749-58-69-80.	1815-26-37....	1967-78-89.....	A	,, 26
b	Mar. 27	1502-13-24-97.....	1608-87-92....	1785-96......	1842-53-64.....	1910-21-32.....	b	Mar. 27
c	,, 28	1529-35-40....	1619-24-30....	1703-14-25...	1869-75-80....	1937-48......	c	,, 28
d	,, 29	1551-62....	1635-46-57....	1719-30-41-52....	1807-12-91....	1959-64-70....	d	,, 29
e	,, 30	1567-78-89....	1651-62-73-84....	1746-55-66-77.	1823-34........	1902-75-86-97....	e	,, 30
f	,, 31	1510-21-32-83-94....	1605-16-78-89....	1700-71-82-93....	1839-50-61-72....	1907-18-29-91....	f	,, 31
g	April 1	1526-37-48........	1621-32....	1711-16......	1804-66-77-88....	1923-34-45-56....	g	April 1
A	,, 2	1553-64........	1643-48....	1727-38-52(NS)	1809-20-93-99....	1961-72......	A	,, 2
b	,, 3	1575-80-86......	1659-70-81....	1743-63-68-74....	1825-31-36....	1904-83-88-94....	b	,, 3
c	,, 4	1507-18-91....	1602-13-75-86-97	1708-79-90....	1847-58........	1915-20-26-99....	c	,, 4
d	,, 5	1523-34-45-56....	1607-18-29-40....	1702-13-24-95.	1801-63-74-85-96	1931-42-53.....	d	,, 5
e	April 6	1539-50-61-72....	1634-45-56.....	1729-35-40-60.	1806-17-28-90....	1947-58-69-80....	e	April 6
f	,, 7	1504-77-88....	1667-72......	1751-65-76....	1822-33-44....	1901-12-85-96....	f	,, 7
g	,, 8	1509-15-20-99....	1604-10-83-94....	1705-87-92-98.	1849-55-60....	1917-28......	g	,, 8
A	,, 9	1531-42........	1615-26-37-99....	1710-21-32....	1871-82........	1939-44-50.....	A	,, 9
b	,, 10	1547-58-69.....	1631-42-53-64....	1726-37-48-57.	1803-14-87-98....	1955-66-77.....	b	,, 10
c	April 11	1501-12-63-74-85-96	1658-69-80....	1762-73-84....	1819-30-41-52....	1909-71-82-93....	c	April 11
d	,, 12	1506-17-28....	1601-12-91-96....	1789........	1846-57-68....	1903-14-25-36-98	d	,, 12
e	,, 13	1533-44........	1623-28........	1707-18......	1800-73-79-84....	1941-52......	e	,, 13
f	,, 14	1555-60-66....	1639-50-61....	1723-34-45-54.	1805-11-16-95....	1963-68-74....	f	,, 14
g	,, 15	1571-82-93....	1655-66-77-88....	1750-59-70-81.	1827-38........	1900-06-79-90....	g	,, 15
A	April 16	1503-14-25-36-87-98	1609-20-82-93....	1704-75-86-97.	1843-54-65-76....	1911-22-33-95....	A	April 16
b	,, 17	1530-41-52....	1625-36......	1715-20......	1808-70-81-92....	1927-38-49-60....	b	,, 17
c	,, 18	1557-68........	1647-52......	1731-42-56....	1802-13-24-97....	1954-65-76....	c	,, 18
d	,, 19	1500-79-84-90....	1663-74-85....	1747-67-72-78.	1829-35-40....	1908-81-87-92....	d	,, 19
e	,, 20	1511-22-95....	1606-17-79-90....	1701-12-83-94.	1851-62........	1919-24-30....	e	,, 20
f	April 21	1527-38-49....	1622-33-44....	1717-28......	1867-78-89....	1935-46-57....	f	April 21
g	,, 22	1565-76........	1660........	1739-53-64....	1810-21-32....	1962-73-84....	g	,, 22
A	,, 23	1508........	1671........		1848........	1905-16-2000....	A	,, 23
b	,, 24	1519........	1603-14-98....	1739-91......	1859........	....	b	,, 24
c	,, 25	1546........	1641........	1736........	1886........	1943........	c	,, 25

PUBLIC HOLIDAYS

BANK HOLIDAYS IN ENGLAND, WALES, NORTHERN IRELAND AND THE CHANNEL ISLANDS ARE (1977):— New Year (January 3), Easter Monday (April 11), Spring Holiday and Silver Jubilee (June 6 and 7), August Bank Holiday (August 29); December 26 and 27; (1978) Jan. 2; March 27; May 1 and 29; Aug. 28; Dec. 26.

Liberation Day (May 9) is a bank and public holiday in the Channel Islands.

Banks are also closed on Good Friday and Christmas Day and on all Saturdays.

The Stock Exchange is closed on Bank Holidays, Good Friday, Christmas Day and New Year's Day; and on Saturdays throughout the year.

Custom House and Docks, as Banks; with the Queen's Birthday (when decreed).

Excise and Stamp Offices, as Banks; with Whit Tuesday and Coronation Day, if and when decreed.

Law Offices.—Good Friday, Easter Monday and Tuesday, Spring Bank Holiday (see col. 1), Christmas Day, and first week-day after Christmas.

BANK HOLIDAYS IN SCOTLAND ARE (1977) Jan. 3 and 4; April 8; May 2; Aug. 1; and Dec. 26; (1978) Jan. 2 and 3; Mar. 24; May 1; Aug. 7; and Dec. 25.

Banks in Scotland are also closed on Good Friday, Christmas Day and on Saturdays.

Scotland has special Term (Quarter) Days:— Candlemas, Feb. 2; Whitsunday, May 15 (Fixed date); Lammas, Aug. 1; and Martinmas, Nov. 11; the Removal Terms are May 28 and Nov. 28.

THE JEWISH CALENDAR

Origin.—The story in the Book of Genesis that the Flood began on the seventeenth day of the second month; that after the end of 150 days the waters were abated; and that on the seventeenth day of the seventh month the Ark rested on Mount Ararat, indicates a calendar of some kind and that the writers recognized 30 days as the length of a lunation. There is other mention of months by their original numbers in the Book of Genesis and in establishing the rite of the Passover Moses spoke of *Abib* as the month when the Israelites came out from Egypt and Abib was to be the first month of

the year. In the first Book of Kings three months are mentioned by name, Zif the second month, Ethanim the seventh and Bul the eighth, but these are not names now in use. After the Dispersion, Jewish communities were left in considerable doubt as to the times of Fasts and Festivals, and this led to the formation of the Jewish Calendar as used to-day, which, it is said by some, was done in A.D. 358 by Rabbi Hillel II, a descendant of Gamaliel —though some assert that it did not happen until much later. This calendar is luni-solar, and is based on the lengths of the lunation and of the

tropical year as found by Hipparchus (*Circ.* 120 B.C.) which differ little from those adopted at the present day. The year 5737 A.D. (1976–77) is the 18th year of the 302nd *Metonic* (Minor or Lunar) *Cycle* of 19 years and the 25th year of the 205th *Solar* (or Major) *Cycle* of 28 years since the Era of the Creation, which the Jews hold to have occurred at the time of the Autumnal Equinox in the year known in the Christian Calendar as 3760 B.C. (954 of the Julian Period) and the epoch or starting point of Jewish Chronology corresponds to Oct. 7, 3761 B.C. At the beginning of each Solar Cycle the *Teku ah* of Nisan (the vernal equinox) returns to the same day and to the same hour.

The hour is divided into 1080 *minims* and the month between one new moon and the next is reckoned as 29 days, 12 hours, 793 minims. The normal calendar year, called a Common Regular year, consists of 12 months of 30 days and 29 days alternately. Since 12 months such as these comprise only 354 days, in order that each of them shall not diverge greatly from an average place in the solar year, a thirteenth month is occasionally added after the fifth month of the Civil year (which commences on the first day of the month Tishri), or as the penultimate month of the Ecclesiastical (which commences on the first day of month Nisan), the years when this happens being called Embolismic. Of the 19 years that form a Metonic cycle, 7 are embolismic; they occur at places in the cycle indicated by the numbers 3, 6, 8, 11, 14, 17, 19, these places being chosen so that the accumulated excesses of the solar years should be as small as possible. The first of each month is called the day of New Moon, though it is not necessarily the day of astronomical New Moon, that being the day on which conjunction of Sun and Moon occurs, but there is generally a difference of a day or two. In practice, in a month which follows one of 30 days, the day preceding its first day is also observed as a day of New Moon. The dates in the Christian calendar of the first days of the months depend on that of the first of Tishri, which therefore controls the dates of fasts and festivals in the Jewish year. For certain ceremonial reasons connected with these, the first of Tishri must not

fall on a Sunday, Wednesday or Friday, and if this should happen as the result of the computation it is postponed to the next day in the Christian calendar. Also, if the New Moon of Tishri falls on any day of the week at noon or later than noon, then the following day is to be taken for the celebration of that New Moon and is Tishri 1, provided that it is not one of the forbidden days, in which case there is a further postponement of a day. These rules and others have been considered in detail, and finally a calendar scheme has been drawn up in which a Jewish year is of one of the following six types: Common Deficient (353 days), Common Regular (354 days), Common Abundant (355 days), Embolismic Deficient (383 days), Embolismic Regular (384 days), or Embolismic Abundant (385 days).

The Regular year has an alternation of 30 and 29 days. In an Abundant year, whether Common or Embolismic, Marcheshvan, the second month of the Civil year, has 30 days instead of 29; in Deficient years Kislev, the third month, has 29 instead of 30. The additional month in Embolismic years which is called Adar I., and precedes the month called Adar in Common years and Adar II., or Ve-Adar, in Embolismic, always has 30 days, but neither this, nor the other variations mentioned, is allowed to change the number of days in the other months which still follow the alternation of the normal twelve. In Embolismic years the month intercalated precedes Adar and usurps its name, but the usual Adar festivals are kept in Ve-Adar.

These are the main features of the Jewish Calendar which must be considered permanent, because as a Jewish law it cannot be altered except by a great Synhedrion.

The Jewish day begins between sunset and nightfall. The time used is that of the meridian of Jerusalem, which is 2h. 21m. in advance of Greenwich Mean Time. Rules for the beginning of Sabbaths and Festivals were laid down for the latitude of London in the eighteenth century and hours for nightfall are now fixed annually by the Chief Rabbi.

Jewish Calendar 5737–5739

Jewish Month			A.M. 5737			A.M. 5738			A.M. 5739	
Tishri	1	..	1976 September	25	..	1977 September	13	..	1978 October	2
Marcheshvan	1	..	October	25	..	October	13	..	November	1
Kislev	1	..	November	23	..	November	11	..	December	1
Tebet	1	..	December	22	..	December	11	..	December	31
Shebat	1	..	1977 January	20	..	1978 January	9	..	1979 January	29
Adar	1	..	February	19	..	February	8	..	February	28
Ve-Adar	1	..	..			March	10	..	..	
Nisan	1	..	March	20	..	April	8	..	March	29
Iyar	1	..	April	19	..	May	8	..	April	28
Sivan	1	..	May	18	..	June	6	..	May	27
Tammuz	1	..	June	17	..	July	6	..	June	26
Ab	1	..	July	16	..	August	4	..	July	25
Elul	1	..	August	15	..	September	3	..	August	24

A.M. 5737 (known as 737 in the short system) is a Common Deficient Year of 12 months, 51 Sabbaths and 353 days. A.M. 5378 (738) is an Embolismic Regular year of 13 months, 55 Sabbaths and 384 days. A.M. 5739 (739) is a Common Abundant year of 12 months, 50 Sabbaths and 355 days.

Jewish Fasts and Festivals

Tishri	1	Rosh Hoshanah (New Year).	Tebet	10	Fast of Tebet.
,,	3	*Fast of Gedaliah.	Adar	13	§Fast of Esther.
,,	10	Yom Kippur (Day of Atonement).	,,	14	Purim.
,,	15–22	Succoth (Feast of Tabernacles).	,,	15	Shushan Purim.
,,	21	Hoshana Rabba.	Nisan	15–21	Passover.
,,	22	Solemn Assembly.	Sivan	6 and 7	Shavuot (Pentecost or Feast of Weeks).
,,	23	Rejoicing of the Law.	Tammuz	17	*Fast of Tammuz.
Kislev	25	Dedication of the Temple.	Ab	9	*Fast of Ab.

NOTES.—* If these dates fall on the Sabbath the Fast is kept on the following day.
§ This fast is observed on Adar 11 (or Ve-Adar 11 in Embolismic years) if Adar 13 falls on a Sabbath.

THE ROMAN CALENDAR

Roman historians adopted as an epoch the Foundation of Rome, which is believed to have happened in the year 753 B.C., and the ordinal number of the years in Roman reckoning is followed by the letters A.U.C. (*Ab Urbe Condita*), so that the year 1977 is 2730 A.U.C. (MMDCCXXX). The Calendar that we know has developed from one established by Romulus, who is said to have used a year of 304 days divided into ten months, beginning with March, to which Numa added January and February, making the year consist of 12 months of 30 and 29 days alternately, with an additional day so that the total was 355. It is also said that Numa ordered an intercalary month of 22 or 23 days in alternate years, making 90 days in eight years, to be inserted after Feb. 23, but there is some doubt as to the origination and the details of the intercalation in the Roman Calendar, though it is certain that some scheme of this kind was inaugurated and not fully carried out, for in the year 46 B.C. Julius Cæsar, who was then Pontifex Maximus, found that the Calendar had been allowed to fall into some confusion. He therefore sought the help of the Egyptian astronomer Sosigenes, which led to the construction and adoption (45 B.C.) of the Julian Calendar, and, by a slight alteration, to the Gregorian now in use. The year 46 B.C. was made to consist of 445 days, and is called the *Year of Confusion*. In the Roman (Julian) Calendar the days of the month were counted backwards from three fixed points, or days, and an intervening day was said to be so many days *before* the next coming point, the first *and* last being counted. These three points were (1) the Kalends; (2) the Nones; and (3) the Ides. Their positions in the months and the method of counting from them will be seen in the table below. The year containing 366 days was called *bissextilis annus*, as it had a doubled sixth day (*bissextus dies*) before the March Kalends on Feb. 24—*ante diem sextum Kalendas Martias*, or VI Kal. Mart.

Present Days of the Month	March, May, July, October have thirty-one days	January, August, December have thirty-one days	April, June, September, November have thirty days	February has twenty-eight days, and in Leap Year twenty-nine
1	Kalendis.	Kalendis.	Kalendis.	Kalendis.
2	VI. ⎫	IV. ⎫ Ante	IV. ⎫ Ante	IV. ⎫ Ante
3	V. ⎬ Ante	III. ⎭ Nonas	III. ⎭ Nonas.	III. ⎭ Nonas.
4	IV. ⎭ Nonas.	Pridie Nonas.	Pridie Nonas.	Pridie Nonas.
5	III. ⎭	Nonis.	Nonis.	Nonis.
6	Pridie Nonas.	VIII. ⎫	VIII. ⎫	VIII. ⎫
7	Nonis.	VII. ⎬	VII. ⎬	VII. ⎬
8	VIII. ⎫	VI. ⎬ Ante	VI. ⎬ Ante	VI. ⎬ Ante
9	VII. ⎬	V. ⎭ Idus.	V. ⎭ Idus.	V. ⎭ Idus.
10	VI. ⎬ Ante	IV. ⎬	IV. ⎬	IV. ⎬
11	V. ⎭ Idus.	III. ⎭	III. ⎭	III. ⎭
12	IV. ⎬	Pridie Idus.	Pridie Idus.	Pridie Idus.
13	III. ⎭	Idibus.	Idibus.	Idibus.
14	Pridie Idus.	XIX. ⎫	XVIII. ⎫	XVI. ⎫
15	Idibus.	XVIII. ⎬	XVII. ⎬	XV. ⎬
16	XVII. ⎫	XVII. ⎬	XVI. ⎬	XIV. ⎬
17	XVI. ⎬	XVI. ⎬	XV. ⎬	XIII. ⎬
18	XV. ⎬	XV. ⎬	XIV. ⎬	XII. ⎬
19	XIV. ⎬	XIV. ⎬	XIII. ⎬	XI. ⎬
20	XIII. ⎬	XIII. ⎬	XII. ⎬	X. ⎬
21	XII. ⎬ Ante Kalendas (of the month following).	XII. ⎬ Ante Klenadas (of the month following).	XI. ⎬ Ante Kalendas (of the month following).	IX. ⎬ Ante Kalendas Martias.
22	XI. ⎬	XI. ⎬	X. ⎬	VIII. ⎬
23	X. ⎬	X. ⎬	IX. ⎬	VII. ⎬
24	IX. ⎬	IX. ⎬	VIII. ⎬	VI. ⎬
25	VIII. ⎬	VIII. ⎬	VII. ⎬	V. ⎬
26	VII. ⎬	VII. ⎬	VI. ⎬	IV. ⎬
27	VI. ⎬	VI. ⎬	V. ⎬	III. ⎭
28	V. ⎬	V. ⎬	IV. ⎭	Pridie Kalendas Martias.
29	IV. ⎬	IV. ⎬	III. ⎭	
30	III. ⎭	III. ⎭	Pridie Kalendas (of the month following).	
31	Pridie Kalendas (of the month following).	Pridie Kalendas (of the month following).		

ROMAN NUMERALS

1	I	9	IX	17	XVII	70	LXX	600	DC
2	II	10	X	18	XVIII	80	LXXX	700	DCC
3	III	11	XI	19	XIX	90	XC	800	DCCC
4	IV	12	XII	20	XX	100	C	900	CM
5	V	13	XIII	30	XXX	200	CC	1000	M
6	VI	14	XIV	40	XL	300	CCC	1500	MD
7	VII	15	XV	50	L	400	CD	1900	MCM
8	VIII	16	XVI	60	LX	500	D	2000	MM

Other Examples: 43=XLIII; 66=LXVI; 98=XCVIII.

339=CCCXXXIX; 619=DCXIX; 988=CMLXXXVIII; 996=CMXCVI.

1674=MDCLXXIV; 1962=MCMLXII.

A bar placed over a numeral has the effect of multiplying the number by 1,000, *e.g.*:

6,000=V̄I; 16,000=X̄VI; 160,000=C̄LX; 666,000=D̄CLXVI.

THE MOSLEM CALENDAR

The basic date of the Moslem Calendar is the *Hejira*, or Flight of Muhammad from Mecca to Medina, the corresponding date of which is A.D. 622, July 16, in the Julian Calendar. Hejira years are used principally in Iran, Turkey, Arabia, Egypt, in certain parts of India and in Malaya. The system was adopted about A.D. 632, commencing from the first day of the month preceding the Hejira. The years are purely lunar and consist of 12 months containing in alternate sequence 30 or 29 days, with the intercalation of one day at the end of the 12th month at stated intervals in each cycle of 30 years, the object of the intercalation being to reconcile the date of the first of the month with the date of the actual New Moon. Some adherents still take the date of the evening of the first visibility of the crescent as that of the first of the month. In each cycle of 30 years 19 are common and contain 354 days and 11 are intercalary (355 days), the latter being called *kabishah*.

The mean length of the Hejira year is 354 days, 8 hours, 48 minutes and the period of mean lunation is 29 days, 12 hours, 44 minutes.

To ascertain if a Hejira year is common or *kabishah* divide it by 30; the quotient gives the number of completed cycles and the remainder shows the place of the year in the current cycle. If the remainder is 2, 5, 7, 10, 13, 16, 18, 21, 24, 26 or 29 the year is *kabishah* and consists of 355 days.

Hejira year 1397 gives a quotient of 46 with remainder 17 and is a common year. A.H. 1398 (remainder 18) is *kabishah*. A.H. 1399 (remainder 19) is common.

Hejira Years 1397 and 1398

Name and Length of Month	A.H. 1397		A.H. 1398	
Muharram (30).....	1976	Dec. 23	1977	Dec. 12
Safar (29).........	1977	Jan. 22	1978	Jan. 11
Rabía I (30).......		Feb. 20		Feb. 9
Rabía II (29).......		Mar. 22		Mar. 11
Jumâda I (30)......		April 20		April 9
Jumâda II (29)......		May 20		May 9
Rajab (30).........		June 18		June 7
Shaabân (29).......		July 18		July 7
Ramadân (30)......		Aug. 16		Aug. 5
Shawwâl (29)......		Sept. 15		Sept. 4
Dhû 'l-Qa'da (30)...		Oct. 14		Oct. 3
Dhû 'l-Hijja (29 or 30).............		Nov. 13		Nov. 2

NOTE—A.H. 1399 (common year of 354 days) begins on December 2, 1978.

OTHER EPOCHS AND CALENDARS

China.—Until the year A.D. 1911 a Lunar Calendar was in force in China, but with the establishment of the Republic the Government adopted the Gregorian Calendar, and the new and old systems were used simultaneously by the people for several years. Since 1930 the publication and use of the old Calendar have been banned by the Government, and an official Chinese Calendar, corresponding with the European or Western system, is compiled, but the old Lunar Calendar is still in use to some extent in China. The old Chinese Calendar, with a cycle of 60 years, is still in use in Tibet, Hong Kong, Singapore, Malaysia and elsewhere in South-East Asia.

Ethiopia.—In the Coptic Calendar, which is used by part of the population of Egypt and Ethiopia, the year is made up of 12 months of 30 days each, followed, in general, by 5 complementary days. Every fourth year is an Intercalary or Leap year and in these years there are 6 complementary days.

The Intercalary year of the Coptic Calendar immediately precedes the Leap year of the Julian Calendar. The Era is that of Diocletian or the Martyrs, the origin of which is fixed at A.D. 284, Aug. 29 (Julian date).

Greece.—Ancient Greek chronology was reckoned in *Olympiads*, cycles of 4 years corresponding with the periodic Olympic Games held on the plain of Olympia in Elis once in 4 years, the intervening years being the first, second, etc., of the Olympiad which received the name of the victor at the Games. The first recorded Olympiad is that of Choroebus, 776 B.C.

India.—In addition to the Moslem reckoning there are six eras used in India. The principal astronomical system was the *Kaliyuga Era*, which appears to have been adopted in the fourth century A.D. It began on Feb. 18, 3102 B.C. The chronological system of Northern India, known as the *Vikrama Samvat Era*, prevalent in Western India, began on Feb. 23, 57 B.C. The year A.D. 1977 is, therefore, the year 2034 of the Vikrama Era.

The *Saka Era* of Southern India dating from March 3, A.D. 78, was declared the uniform national calendar of the Republic of India with effect from March 22, 1957, to be used concurrently with the Gregorian Calendar. As revised, the year of the new *Saka Era* begins at the spring equinox, with five successive months of 31 days and seven of 30 days in ordinary years; six months of each length in leap years. The year A.D. 1977 is 1899 of the revised *Saka Era*.

In the Hills, the *Saptarshi Era* dates from the moment when the Saptarshi, or saints, were translated and became the stars of the Great Bear in 3076 B.C.

The *Buddhists* reckoned from the death of Buddha in 543 B.C. (the actual date being 487 B.C.); and the epoch of the *Jains* was the death of Vardhamana, the founder of their faith, in 527 B.C.

Iran.—The chronology of Iran (Persia) is the Era of Hejira, which began on A.D. 622, July 16. The *Zoroastrian Calendar* was used in pre-Moslem days and is still employed by Zoroastrians in Iran and India (Parsees) with era beginning A.D. 632, June 16.

Japan.—The Japanese Calendar is the Gregorian, and is essentially the same as that in use by Western nations, the years, months and weeks being of the same length and beginning on the same days as those of the Western Calendar. The numeration of the years is different, for Japanese chronology is based on a system of epochs or periods, each of which begins at the accession of an Emperor or other important occurrence, the method being not unlike the former British system of Regnal years, but differing from it in the particular that each year of a period closes on Dec. 31. The Japanese scheme begins about A.D. 650 and the three latest epochs are defined by the reigns of Emperors, whose actual names are not necessarily used:—

Epoch Meiji from 1868 Oct. 13 to 1912 July 31
  „ Taishō „ 1912 Aug. 1 to 1926 Dec. 25
  „ Shōwa „ 1926 Dec. 26

Hence the year Shōwa 52 begins 1977 Jan. 1. The months are not named. They are known as First Month, Second Month, etc., first month being the equivalent to January. The days of the week are Nichiyōbi (Sun-day), Getsuyōbi (Moon-day), Kayōbi (Fire-day), Suiyōbi (Water-day), Mokuyōbi (Wood-day), Kinyōbi (Metal-day), Doyōbi (Earth-day).

EASY REFERENCE CALENDAR
for any year between 1753 and 2000 together with the dates of Easter in each of those years
TO SELECT THE CORRECT CALENDAR FOR ANY YEAR consult the INDEX below

INDEX TO CALENDARS

1753	..	C										1959	..	I
1754	..	E	1795	..	I	1836	..	L*	1877	..	C	1918	..	E	1960	..	L*
1755	..	G	1796	..	L*	1837	..	A	1878	..	E	1919	..	G	1961	..	A
1756	..	J*	1797	..	A	1838	..	C	1879	..	G	1920	..	J*	1962	..	C
1757	..	M	1798	..	C	1839	..	E	1880	..	J*	1921	..	M	1963	..	E
1758	..	A	1799	..	E	1840	..	H*	1881	..	M	1922	..	A	1964	..	H*
1759	..	C	1800	..	G	1841	..	K	1882	..	A	1923	..	C	1965	..	K
1760	..	F*	1801	..	I	1842	..	M	1883	..	C	1924	..	F*	1966	..	M
1761	..	I	1802	..	K	1843	..	A	1884	..	F*	1925	..	I	1967	..	A
1762	..	K	1803	..	M	1844	..	D*	1885	..	I	1926	..	K	1968	..	D*
1763	..	M	1804	..	B*	1845	..	G	1886	..	K	1927	..	M	1969	..	G
1764	..	B*	1805	..	E	1846	..	I	1887	..	M	1928	..	B*	1970	..	I
1765	..	E	1806	..	G	1847	..	K	1888	..	B*	1929	..	E	1971	..	K
1766	..	G	1807	..	I	1848	..	N*	1889	..	E	1930	..	G	1972	..	N*
1767	..	I	1808	..	L*	1849	..	C	1890	..	G	1931	..	I	1973	..	C
1768	..	L*	1809	..	A	1850	..	E	1891	..	I	1932	..	L*	1974	..	E
1769	..	A	1810	..	C	1851	..	G	1892	..	L*	1933	..	A	1975	..	G
1770	..	C	1811	..	E	1852	..	J*	1893	..	A	1934	..	C	1976	..	J*
1771	..	E	1812	..	H*	1853	..	M	1894	..	C	1935	..	E	1977	..	M
1772	..	H*	1813	..	K	1854	..	A	1895	..	E	1936	..	H*	1978	..	A
1773	..	K	1814	..	M	1855	..	C	1896	..	H*	1937	..	K	1979	..	C
1774	..	M	1815	..	A	1856	..	F*	1897	..	K	1938	..	M	1980	..	F*
1775	..	A	1816	..	D*	1857	..	I	1898	..	M	1939	..	A	1981	..	I
1776	..	D*	1817	..	G	1858	..	K	1899	..	A	1940	..	D*	1982	..	K
1777	..	G	1818	..	I	1859	..	M	1900	..	C	1941	..	G	1983	..	M
1778	..	I	1819	..	K	1860	..	B*	1901	..	E	1942	..	I	1984	..	B*
1779	..	K	1820	..	N*	1861	..	E	1902	..	G	1943	..	K	1985	..	E
1780	..	N*	1821	..	C	1862	..	G	1903	..	I	1944	..	N*	1986	..	G
1781	..	C	1822	..	E	1863	..	I	1904	..	L*	1945	..	C	1987	..	I
1782	..	E	1823	..	G	1864	..	L*	1905	..	A	1946	..	E	1988	..	L*
1783	..	G	1824	..	J*	1865	..	A	1906	..	C	1947	..	G	1989	..	A
1784	..	J*	1825	..	M	1866	..	C	1907	..	E	1948	..	J*	1990	..	C
1785	..	M	1826	..	A	1867	..	E	1908	..	H*	1949	..	M	1991	..	E
1786	..	A	1827	..	C	1868	..	H*	1909	..	K	1950	..	A	1992	..	H*
1787	..	C	1828	..	F*	1869	..	K	1910	..	M	1951	..	C	1993	..	K
1788	..	F*	1829	..	I	1870	..	M	1911	..	A	1952	..	F*	1994	..	M
1789	..	I	1830	..	K	1871	..	A	1912	..	D*	1953	..	I	1995	..	A
1790	..	K	1831	..	M	1872	..	D*	1913	..	G	1954	..	K	1996	..	D*
1791	..	M	1832	..	B*	1873	..	G	1914	..	I	1955	..	M	1997	..	G
1792	..	B*	1833	..	E	1874	..	I	1915	..	K	1956	..	B*	1998	..	I
1793	..	E	1834	..	G	1875	..	K	1916	..	N*	1957	..	E	1999	..	K
1794	..	G	1835	..	I	1876	..	N*	1917	..	C	1958	..	G	2000	..	N*

* Leap Year

A

January
Su.	..	1	8	15	22	29
M.	..	2	9	16	23	30
Tu.	..	3	10	17	24	31
W.	..	4	11	18	25
Th.	..	5	12	19	26
F.	..	6	13	20	27
S.	..	7	14	21	28

May
Su.	7	14	21	28
M.	1	8	15	22	29
Tu.	2	9	16	23	30
W.	3	10	17	24	31
Th.	4	11	18	25
F.	5	12	19	26
S.	6	13	20	27

September
Su.	3	10	17	24
M.	4	11	18	25
Tu.	5	12	19	26
W.	6	13	20	27
Th.	7	14	21	28
F.	1	8	15	22	29
S.	2	9	16	23	30

February
Su.	5	12	19	26
M.	6	13	20	27
Tu.	7	14	21	28
W.	1	8	15	22
Th.	2	9	16	23
F.	3	10	17	24
S.	4	11	18	25

June
Su.	4	11	18	25
M.	5	12	19	26
Tu.	6	13	20	27
W.	7	14	21	28
Th.	1	8	15	22	29
F.	2	9	16	23	30
S.	3	10	17	24

October
Su.	1	8	15	22	29
M.	2	9	16	23	30
Tu.	3	10	17	24	31
W.	4	11	18	25
Th.	5	12	19	26
F.	6	13	20	27
S.	7	14	21	28

March
Su.	5	12	19	26
M.	6	13	20	27
Tu.	7	14	21	28
W.	1	8	15	22	29
Th.	2	9	16	23	30
F.	3	10	17	24	31
S.	4	11	18	25

July
Su.	2	9	16	23	30
M.	3	10	17	24	31
Tu.	4	11	18	25
W.	5	12	19	26
Th.	6	13	20	27
F.	7	14	21	28
S.	1	8	15	22	29

November
Su.	5	12	19	26
M.	6	13	20	27
Tu.	7	14	21	28
W.	1	8	15	22	29
Th.	2	9	16	23	30
F.	3	10	17	24
S.	4	11	18	25

April
Su.	2	9	16	23	30
M.	3	10	17	24
Tu.	4	11	18	25
W.	5	12	19	26
Th.	6	13	20	27
F.	7	14	21	28
S.	1	8	15	22	29

August
Su.	6	13	20	27
M.	7	14	21	28
Tu.	1	8	15	22	29
W.	2	9	16	23	30
Th.	3	10	17	24	31
F.	4	11	18	25
S.	5	12	19	26

December
Su.	3	10	17	24	31
M.	4	11	18	25
Tu.	5	12	19	26
W.	6	13	20	27
Th.	7	14	21	28
F.	1	8	15	22	29
S.	2	9	16	23	30

B (Leap year)

January
Su.	..	1	8	15	22	29
M.	..	2	9	16	23	30
Tu.	..	3	10	17	24	31
W.	..	4	11	18	25
Th.	..	5	12	19	26
F.	..	6	13	20	27
S.	..	7	14	21	28

May
Su.	6	13	20	27
M.	7	14	21	28
Tu.	1	8	15	22	29
W.	2	9	16	23	30
Th.	3	10	17	24	31
F.	4	11	18	25
S.	5	12	19	26

September
Su.	2	9	16	23	30
M.	3	10	17	24
Tu.	4	11	18	25
W.	5	12	19	26
Th.	6	13	20	27
F.	7	14	21	28
S.	1	8	15	22	29

February
Su.	5	12	19	26
M.	6	13	20	27
Tu.	7	14	21	28
W.	1	8	15	22	29
Th.	2	9	16	23
F.	3	10	17	24
S.	4	11	18	25

June
Su.	3	10	17	24
M.	4	11	18	25
Tu.	5	12	19	26
W.	6	13	20	27
Th.	7	14	21	28
F.	1	8	15	22	29
S.	2	9	16	23	30

October
Su.	7	14	21	28
M.	1	8	15	22	29
Tu.	2	9	16	23	30
W.	3	10	17	24	31
Th.	4	11	18	25
F.	5	12	19	26
S.	6	13	20	27

March
Su.	4	11	18	25
M.	5	12	19	26
Tu.	6	13	20	27
W.	7	14	21	28
Th.	1	8	15	22	29
F.	2	9	16	23	30
S.	3	10	17	24	31

July
Su.	1	8	15	22	29
M.	2	9	16	23	30
Tu.	3	10	17	24	31
W.	4	11	18	25
Th.	5	12	19	26
F.	6	13	20	27
S.	7	14	21	28

November
Su.	4	11	18	25
M.	5	12	19	26
Tu.	6	13	20	27
W.	7	14	21	28
Th.	1	8	15	22	29
F.	2	9	16	23	30
S.	3	10	17	24

April
Su.	1	8	15	22	29
M.	2	9	16	23	30
Tu.	3	10	17	24
W.	4	11	18	25
Th.	5	12	19	26
F.	6	13	20	27
S.	7	14	21	28

August
Su.	5	12	19	26
M.	6	13	20	27
Tu.	7	14	21	28
W.	1	8	15	22	29
Th.	2	9	16	23	30
F.	3	10	17	24	31
S.	4	11	18	25

December
Su.	2	9	16	23	30
M.	3	10	17	24	31
Tu.	4	11	18	25
W.	5	12	19	26
Th.	6	13	20	27
F.	7	14	21	28
S.	1	8	15	22	29

Easter Days

March 26.	1758	1769	1815	1826	1837	1967	1978
April 2.	1809	1893	1899	1961.			[1989.
April 9.	1871	1882	1939	1950.			
April 16.	1775	1786	1797	1843	1854	1865	1911
April 23.	1905.				[1922	1933	1995.

Easter Days

April 1.	1804	1888	1956.
April 8.	1792	1860	1928.
April 22.	1764	1832	1984.

CALENDAR TABLES

C – F

C

	January	May	September
Su...	7 14 21 28	6 13 20 27	2 9 16 23 30
M... 1	8 15 22 29	7 14 21 28	3 10 17 24
Tu... 2	9 16 23 30	1 8 15 22 29	4 11 18 25
W... 3	10 17 24 31	2 9 16 23 30	5 12 19 26
Th... 4	11 18 25	3 10 17 24 31	6 13 20 27
F... 5	12 19 26	4 11 18 25	7 14 21 28
S... 6	13 20 27	5 12 19 26	1 8 15 22 29

	February	June	October
Su...	4 11 18 25	3 10 17 24	7 14 21 28
M...	5 12 19 26	4 11 18 25	1 8 15 22 29
Tu...	6 13 20 27	5 12 19 26	2 9 16 23 30
W...	7 14 21 28	6 13 20 27	3 10 17 24 31
Th... 1	8 15 22	7 14 21 28	4 11 18 25
F... 2	9 16 23	1 8 15 22 29	5 12 19 26
S... 3	10 17 24	2 9 16 23 30	6 13 20 27

	March	July	November
Su...	4 11 18 25	1 8 15 22 29	4 11 18 25
M...	5 12 19 26	2 9 16 23 30	5 12 19 26
Tu...	6 13 20 27	3 10 17 24 31	6 13 20 27
W...	7 14 21 28	4 11 18 25	7 14 21 28
Th... 1	8 15 22 29	5 12 19 26	1 8 15 22 29
F... 2	9 16 23 30	6 13 20 27	2 9 16 23 30
S... 3	10 17 24 31	7 14 21 28	3 10 17 24

	April	August	December
Su... 1	8 15 22 29	5 12 19 26	2 9 16 23 30
M... 2	9 16 23 30	6 13 20 27	3 10 17 24 31
Tu... 3	10 17 24	7 14 21 28	4 11 18 25
W... 4	11 18 25	1 8 15 22 29	5 12 19 26
Th... 5	12 19 26	2 9 16 23 30	6 13 20 27
F... 6	13 20 27	3 10 17 24 31	7 14 21 28
S... 7	14 21 28	4 11 18 25	1 8 15 22 29

Easter Days

March 25.	1883 1894 1951.
April 1.	1866 1877 1923 1934 1945.
April 8.	1787 1798 1849 1855 1917.
April 15.	1759 1770 1781 1827 1838 1900 1906 1979 1990.
April 22.	1753 1810 1821 1962 1973.

D (Leap year)

	January	May	September
Su...	7 14 21 28	5 12 19 26	1 8 15 22 29
M... 1	8 15 22 29	6 13 20 27	2 9 16 23 30
Tu... 2	9 16 23 30	7 14 21 28	3 10 17 24
W... 3	10 17 24 31	1 8 15 22 29	4 11 18 25
Th... 4	11 18 25	2 9 16 23 30	5 12 19 26
F... 5	12 19 26	3 10 17 24 31	6 13 20 27
S... 6	13 20 27	4 11 18 25	7 14 21 28

	February	June	October
Su...	4 11 18 25	2 9 16 23 30	6 13 20 27
M...	5 12 19 26	3 10 17 24	7 14 21 28
Tu...	6 13 20 27	4 11 18 25	1 8 15 22 29
W...	7 14 21 28	5 12 19 26	2 9 16 23 30
Th... 1	8 15 22 29	6 13 20 27	3 10 17 24 31
F... 2	9 16 23	7 14 21 28	4 11 18 25
S... 3	10 17 24	1 8 15 22 29	5 12 19 26

	March	July	November
Su... 3	10 17 24 31	7 14 21 28	3 10 17 24
M... 4	11 18 25	1 8 15 22 29	4 11 18 25
Tu... 5	12 19 26	2 9 16 23 30	5 12 19 26
W... 6	13 20 27	3 10 17 24 31	6 13 20 27
Th... 7	14 21 28	4 11 18 25	7 14 21 28
F... 1	8 15 22 29	5 12 19 26	1 8 15 22 29
S... 2	9 16 23 30	6 13 20 27	2 9 16 23 30

	April	August	December
Su...	7 14 21 28	4 11 18 25	1 8 15 22 29
M... 1	8 15 22 29	5 12 19 26	2 9 16 23 30
Tu... 2	9 16 23 30	6 13 20 27	3 10 17 24 31
W... 3	10 17 24	7 14 21 28	4 11 18 25
Th... 4	11 18 25	1 8 15 22 29	5 12 19 26
F... 5	12 19 26	2 9 16 23 30	6 13 20 27
S... 6	13 20 27	3 10 17 24 31	7 14 21 28

Easter Days

March 24.	1940.
March 31.	1872.
April 7.	1776 1844 1912 1996.
April 14.	1816 1968.

E

	January	May	September
Su...	6 13 20 27	5 12 19 26	1 8 15 22 29
M...	7 14 21 28	6 13 20 27	2 9 16 23 30
Tu... 1	8 15 22 29	7 14 21 28	3 10 17 24
W... 2	9 16 23 30	1 8 15 22 29	4 11 18 25
Th... 3	10 17 24 31	2 9 16 23 30	5 12 19 26
F... 4	11 18 25	3 10 17 24 31	6 13 20 27
S... 5	12 19 26	4 11 18 25	7 14 21 28

	February	June	October
Su...	3 10 17 24	2 9 16 23 30	6 13 20 27
M...	4 11 18 25	3 10 17 24	7 14 21 28
Tu...	5 12 19 26	4 11 18 25	1 8 15 22 29
W...	6 13 20 27	5 12 19 26	2 9 16 23 30
Th...	7 14 21 28	6 13 20 27	3 10 17 24 31
F... 1	8 15 22	7 14 21 28	4 11 18 25
S... 2	9 16 23	1 8 15 22 29	5 12 19 26

	March	July	November
Su... 3	10 17 24 31	7 14 21 28	3 10 17 24
M... 4	11 18 25	1 8 15 22 29	4 11 18 25
Tu... 5	12 19 26	2 9 16 23 30	5 12 19 26
W... 6	13 20 27	3 10 17 24 31	6 13 20 27
Th... 7	14 21 28	4 11 18 25	7 14 21 28
F... 1	8 15 22 29	5 12 19 26	1 8 15 22 29
S... 2	9 16 23 30	6 13 20 27	2 9 16 23 30

	April	August	December
Su...	7 14 21 28	4 11 18 25	1 8 15 22 29
M... 1	8 15 22 29	5 12 19 26	2 9 16 23 30
Tu... 2	9 16 23 30	6 13 20 27	3 10 17 24 31
W... 3	10 17 24	7 14 21 28	4 11 18 25
Th... 4	11 18 25	1 8 15 22 29	5 12 19 26
F... 5	12 19 26	2 9 16 23 30	6 13 20 27
S... 6	13 20 27	3 10 17 24 31	7 14 21 28

Easter Days

March 24.	1799. [1907 1918 1929 1991.
March 31.	1771 1782 1793 1839 1850 1861
April 7.	1765 1822 1833 1901 1985.
April 14.	1754 1805 1811 1895 1963 1974.
April 21.	1867 1878 1889 1935 1946 1957.

F (Leap year)

	January	May	September
Su...	6 13 20 27	4 11 18 25	7 14 21 28
M...	7 14 21 28	5 12 19 26	1 8 15 22 29
Tu... 1	8 15 22 29	6 13 20 27	2 9 16 23 30
W... 2	9 16 23 30	7 14 21 28	3 10 17 24
Th... 3	10 17 24 31	1 8 15 22 29	4 11 18 25
F... 4	11 18 25	2 9 16 23 30	5 12 19 26
S... 5	12 19 26	3 10 17 24 31	6 13 20 27

	February	June	October
Su...	3 10 17 24	1 8 15 22 29	5 12 19 26
M...	4 11 18 25	2 9 16 23 30	6 13 20 27
Tu...	5 12 19 26	3 10 17 24	7 14 21 28
W...	6 13 20 27	4 11 18 25	1 8 15 22 29
Th...	7 14 21 28	5 12 19 26	2 9 16 23 30
F... 1	8 15 22 29	6 13 20 27	3 10 17 24 31
S... 2	9 16 23	7 14 21 28	4 11 18 25

	March	July	November
Su... 2	9 16 23 30	6 13 20 27	2 9 16 23 30
M... 3	10 17 24 31	7 14 21 28	3 10 17 24
Tu... 4	11 18 25	1 8 15 22 29	4 11 18 25
W... 5	12 19 26	2 9 16 23 30	5 12 19 26
Th... 6	13 20 27	3 10 17 24 31	6 13 20 27
F... 7	14 21 28	4 11 18 25	7 14 21 28
S... 1	8 15 22 29	5 12 19 26	1 8 15 22 29

	April	August	December
Su...	6 13 20 27	3 10 17 24 31	7 14 21 28
M...	7 14 21 28	4 11 18 25	1 8 15 22 29
Tu... 1	8 15 22 29	5 12 19 26	2 9 16 23 30
W... 2	9 16 23 30	6 13 20 27	3 10 17 24 31
Th... 3	10 17 24	7 14 21 28	4 11 18 25
F... 4	11 18 25	1 8 15 22 29	5 12 19 26
S... 5	12 19 26	2 9 16 23 30	6 13 20 27

Easter Days

March 23.	1788 1856.
April 6.	1760 1828 1980.
April 13.	1884 1952.
April 20.	1924.

CALENDAR TABLES

G – J

G

	January	May	September
Su.	5 12 19 26	4 11 18 25	7 14 21 28
M.	6 13 20 27	5 12 19 26	1 8 15 22 29
Tu.	7 14 21 28	6 13 20 27	2 9 16 23 30
W.	1 8 15 22 29	7 14 21 28	3 10 17 24
Th.	2 9 16 23 30	1 8 15 22 29	4 11 18 25
F.	3 10 17 24 31	2 9 16 23 30	5 12 19 26
S.	4 11 18 25	3 10 17 24 31	6 13 20 27

	February	June	October
Su.	2 9 16 23	1 8 15 22 29	5 12 19 26
M.	3 10 17 24	2 9 16 23 30	6 13 20 27
Tu.	4 11 18 25	3 10 17 24	7 14 21 28
W.	5 12 19 26	4 11 18 25	1 8 15 22 29
Th.	6 13 20 27	5 12 19 26	2 9 16 23 30
F.	7 14 21 28	6 13 20 27	3 10 17 24 31
S.	1 8 15 22	7 14 21 28	4 11 18 25

	March	July	November
Su.	2 9 16 23 30	6 13 20 27	2 9 16 23 30
M.	3 10 17 24 31	7 14 21 28	3 10 17 24
Tu.	4 11 18 25	1 8 15 22 29	4 11 18 25
W.	5 12 19 26	2 9 16 23 30	5 12 19 26
Th.	6 13 20 27	3 10 17 24 31	6 13 20 27
F.	7 14 21 28	4 11 18 25	7 14 21 28
S.	1 8 15 22 29	5 12 19 26	1 8 15 22 29

	April	August	December
Su.	6 13 20 27	3 10 17 24 31	7 14 21 28
M.	7 14 21 28	4 11 18 25	1 8 15 22 29
Tu.	1 8 15 22 29	5 12 19 26	2 9 16 23 30
W.	2 9 16 23 30	6 13 20 27	3 10 17 24 31
Th.	3 10 17 24	7 14 21 28	4 11 18 25
F.	4 11 18 25	1 8 15 22 29	5 12 19 26
S.	5 12 19 26	2 9 16 23 30	6 13 20 27

Easter Days

March 23.	1845	1913.					
March 30.	1755	1766	1777	1823	1834	1902	1975
	1986	1997.					
April 6.	1806	1817	1890	1947	1958	1969.	
April 13.	1800	1873	1879	1941.			
April 20.	1783	1794	1851	1862	1919	1930.	

H (Leap year)

	January	May	September
Su.	5 12 19 26	3 10 17 24 31	6 13 20 27
M.	6 13 20 27	4 11 18 25	7 14 21 28
Tu.	7 14 21 28	5 12 19 26	1 8 15 22 29
W.	1 8 15 22 29	6 13 20 27	2 9 16 23 30
Th.	2 9 16 23 30	7 14 21 28	3 10 17 24
F.	3 10 17 24 31	1 8 15 22 29	4 11 18 25
S.	4 11 18 25	2 9 16 23 30	5 12 19 26

	February	June	October
Su.	2 9 16 23	7 14 21 28	4 11 18 25
M.	3 10 17 24	1 8 15 22 29	5 12 19 26
Tu.	4 11 18 25	2 9 16 23 30	6 13 20 27
W.	5 12 19 26	3 10 17 24	7 14 21 28
Th.	6 13 20 27	4 11 18 25	1 8 15 22 29
F.	7 14 21 28	5 12 19 26	2 9 16 23 30
S.	1 8 15 22 29	6 13 20 27	3 10 17 24 31

	March	July	November
Su.	1 8 15 22 29	5 12 19 26	1 8 15 22 29
M.	2 9 16 23 30	6 13 20 27	2 9 16 23 30
Tu.	3 10 17 24 31	7 14 21 28	3 10 17 24
W.	4 11 18 25	1 8 15 22 29	4 11 18 25
Th.	5 12 19 26	2 9 16 23 30	5 12 19 26
F.	6 13 20 27	3 10 17 24 31	6 13 20 27
S.	7 14 21 28	4 11 18 25	7 14 21 28

	April	August	December
Su.	5 12 19 26	2 9 16 23 30	6 13 20 27
M.	6 13 20 27	3 10 17 24 31	7 14 21 28
Tu.	7 14 21 28	4 11 18 25	1 8 15 22 29
W.	1 8 15 22 29	5 12 19 26	2 9 16 23 30
Th.	2 9 16 23 30	6 13 20 27	3 10 17 24 31
F.	3 10 17 24	7 14 21 28	4 11 18 25
S.	4 11 18 25	1 8 15 22 29	5 12 19 26

Easter Days

March 29.	1812	1964.
April 5.	1896.	
April 12.	1868	1936.
April 19.	1772 1840 1908 1992.	

I

	January	May	September
Su.	4 11 18 25	3 10 17 24 31	6 13 20 27
M.	5 12 19 26	4 11 18 25	7 14 21 28
Tu.	6 13 20 27	5 12 19 26	1 8 15 22 29
W.	7 14 21 28	6 13 20 27	2 9 16 23 30
Th.	1 8 15 22 29	7 14 21 28	3 10 17 24
F.	2 9 16 23 30	1 8 15 22 29	4 11 18 25
S.	3 10 17 24 31	2 9 16 23 30	5 12 19 26

	February	June	October
Su.	1 8 15 22	7 14 21 28	4 11 18 25
M.	2 9 16 23	1 8 15 22 29	5 12 19 26
Tu.	3 10 17 24	2 9 16 23 30	6 13 20 27
W.	4 11 18 25	3 10 17 24	7 14 21 28
Th.	5 12 19 26	4 11 18 25	1 8 15 22 29
F.	6 13 20 27	5 12 19 26	2 9 16 23 30
S.	7 14 21 28	6 13 20 27	3 10 17 24 31

	March	July	November
Su.	1 8 15 22 29	5 12 19 26	1 8 15 22 29
M.	2 9 16 23 30	6 13 20 27	2 9 16 23 30
Tu.	3 10 17 24 31	7 14 21 28	3 10 17 24
W.	4 11 18 25	1 8 15 22 29	4 11 18 25
Th.	5 12 19 26	2 9 16 23 30	5 12 19 26
F.	6 13 20 27	3 10 17 24 31	6 13 20 27
S.	7 14 21 28	4 11 18 25	7 14 21 28

	April	August	December
Su.	5 12 19 26	2 9 16 23 30	6 13 20 27
M.	6 13 20 27	3 10 17 24 31	7 14 21 28
Tu.	7 14 21 28	4 11 18 25	1 8 15 22 29
W.	1 8 15 22 29	5 12 19 26	2 9 16 23 30
Th.	2 9 16 23 30	6 13 20 27	3 10 17 24 31
F.	3 10 17 24	7 14 21 28	4 11 18 25
S.	4 11 18 25	1 8 15 22 29	5 12 19 26

Easter Days

March 22.	1761	1818.					
March 29.	1807	1891	1959	1970.			
April 5.	1795	1801	1863	1874	1885	1931	1942
	1953.						
April 12.	1789	1846	1857	1903	1914	1925	1998.
April 19.	1767	1778	1829	1835	1981	1987.	

J (Leap year)

	January	May	September
Su.	4 11 18 25	2 9 16 23 30	5 12 19 26
M.	5 12 19 26	3 10 17 24 31	6 13 20 27
Tu.	6 13 20 27	4 11 18 25	7 14 21 28
W.	7 14 21 28	5 12 19 26	1 8 15 22 29
Th.	1 8 15 22 29	6 13 20 27	2 9 16 23 30
F.	2 9 16 23 30	7 14 21 28	3 10 17 24
S.	3 10 17 24 31	1 8 15 22 29	4 11 18 25

	February	June	October
Su.	1 8 15 22 29	6 13 20 27	3 10 17 24 31
M.	2 9 16 23	7 14 21 28	4 11 18 25
Tu.	3 10 17 24	1 8 15 22 29	5 12 19 26
W.	4 11 18 25	2 9 16 23 30	6 13 20 27
Th.	5 12 19 26	3 10 17 24	7 14 21 28
F.	6 13 20 27	4 11 18 25	1 8 15 22 29
S.	7 14 21 28	5 12 19 26	2 9 16 23 30

	March	July	November
Su.	7 14 21 28	4 11 18 25	7 14 21 28
M.	1 8 15 22 29	5 12 19 26	1 8 15 22 29
Tu.	2 9 16 23 30	6 13 20 27	2 9 16 23 30
W.	3 10 17 24 31	7 14 21 28	3 10 17 24
Th.	4 11 18 25	1 8 15 22 29	4 11 18 25
F.	5 12 19 26	2 9 16 23 30	5 12 19 26
S.	6 13 20 27	3 10 17 24 31	6 13 20 27

	April	August	December
Su.	4 11 18 25	1 8 15 22 29	5 12 19 26
M.	5 12 19 26	2 9 16 23 30	6 13 20 27
Tu.	6 13 20 27	3 10 17 24 31	7 14 21 28
W.	7 14 21 28	4 11 18 25	1 8 15 22 29
Th.	1 8 15 22 29	5 12 19 26	2 9 16 23 30
F.	2 9 16 23 30	6 13 20 27	3 10 17 24 31
S.	3 10 17 24	7 14 21 28	4 11 18 25

Easter Days

March 28.	1880	1948.
April 4.	1920.	
April 11.	1784	1852.
April 18.	1756	1824 1976.

CALENDAR TABLES
K – N

K

	January	May	September
Su...	3 10 17 24 31	2 9 16 23 30	5 12 19 26
M...	4 11 18 25	3 10 17 24 31	6 13 20 27
Tu...	5 12 19 26	4 11 18 25	7 14 21 28
W...	6 13 20 27	5 12 19 26	1 8 15 22 29
Th...	7 14 21 28	6 13 20 27	2 9 16 23 30
F...	1 8 15 22 29	7 14 21 28	3 10 17 24
S...	2 9 16 23 30	1 8 15 22 29	4 11 18 25

	February	June	October
Su...	7 14 21 28	6 13 20 27	3 10 17 24 31
M...	1 8 15 22	7 14 21 28	4 11 18 25
Tu...	2 9 16 23	1 8 15 22 29	5 12 19 26
W...	3 10 17 24	2 9 16 23 30	6 13 20 27
Th...	4 11 18 25	3 10 17 24	7 14 21 28
F...	5 12 19 26	4 11 18 25	1 8 15 22 29
S...	6 13 20 27	5 12 19 26	2 9 16 23 30

	March	July	November
Su...	7 14 21 28	4 11 18 25	7 14 21 28
M...	1 8 15 22 29	5 12 19 26	1 8 15 22 29
Tu...	2 9 16 23 30	6 13 20 27	2 9 16 23 30
W...	3 10 17 24 31	7 14 21 28	3 10 17 24
Th...	4 11 18 25	1 8 15 22 29	4 11 18 25
F...	5 12 19 26	2 9 16 23 30	5 12 19 26
S...	6 13 20 27	3 10 17 24 31	6 13 20 27

	April	August	December
Su...	4 11 18 25	1 8 15 22 29	5 12 19 26
M...	5 12 19 26	2 9 16 23 30	6 13 20 27
Tu...	6 13 20 27	3 10 17 24 31	7 14 21 28
W...	7 14 21 28	4 11 18 25	1 8 15 22 29
Th...	1 8 15 22 29	5 12 19 26	2 9 16 23 30
F...	2 9 16 23 30	6 13 20 27	3 10 17 24 31
S...	3 10 17 24	7 14 21 28	4 11 18 25

Easter Days

March 28.	1869	1875	1937.			
April 4.	1779	1790	1847	1858	1915	1926	1999.
April 11.	1762	1773	1819	1830	1841	1909	1971
	1982	1993.				
April 18.	1802	1813	1897	1954	1965.	
April 25.	1886	1943.				

L (Leap year)

	January	May	September
Su...	3 10 17 24 31	1 8 15 22 29	4 11 18 25
M...	4 11 18 25	2 9 16 23 30	5 12 19 26
Tu...	5 12 19 26	3 10 17 24 31	6 13 20 27
W...	6 13 20 27	4 11 18 25	7 14 21 28
Th...	7 14 21 28	5 12 19 26	1 8 15 22 29
F...	1 8 15 22 29	6 13 20 27	2 9 16 23 30
S...	2 9 16 23 30	7 14 21 28	3 10 17 24

	February	June	October
Su...	7 14 21 28	5 12 19 26	2 9 16 23 30
M...	1 8 15 22	6 13 20 27	3 10 17 24 31
Tu...	2 9 16 23	7 14 21 28	4 11 18 25
W...	3 10 17 24	1 8 15 22 29	5 12 19 26
Th...	4 11 18 25	2 9 16 23 30	6 13 20 27
F...	5 12 19 26	3 10 17 24	7 14 21 28
S...	6 13 20 27	4 11 18 25	1 8 15 22 29

	March	July	November
Su...	6 13 20 27	3 10 17 24 31	6 13 20 27
M...	7 14 21 28	4 11 18 25	7 14 21 28
Tu...	1 8 15 22 29	5 12 19 26	1 8 15 22 29
W...	2 9 16 23 30	6 13 20 27	2 9 16 23 30
Th...	3 10 17 24 31	7 14 21 28	3 10 17 24
F...	4 11 18 25	1 8 15 22 29	4 11 18 25
S...	5 12 19 26	2 9 16 23 30	5 12 19 26

	April	August	December
Su...	3 10 17 24	7 14 21 28	4 11 18 25
M...	4 11 18 25	1 8 15 22 29	5 12 19 26
Tu...	5 12 19 26	2 9 16 23 30	6 13 20 27
W...	6 13 20 27	3 10 17 24 31	7 14 21 28
Th...	7 14 21 28	4 11 18 25	1 8 15 22 29
F...	1 8 15 22 29	5 12 19 26	2 9 16 23 30
S...	2 9 16 23 30	6 13 20 27	3 10 17 24 31

Easter Days

March 27.	1796	1864	1932.
April 3.	1768	1836	1904 1988.
April 17.	1808	1892	1960.

M

	January	May	September
Su...	2 9 16 23 30	1 8 15 22 29	4 11 18 25
M...	3 10 17 24 31	2 9 16 23 30	5 12 19 26
Tu...	4 11 18 25	3 10 17 24 31	6 13 20 27
W...	5 12 19 26	4 11 18 25	7 14 21 28
Th...	6 13 20 27	5 12 19 26	1 8 15 22 29
F...	7 14 21 28	6 13 20 27	2 9 16 23 30
S...	1 8 15 22 29	7 14 21 28	3 10 17 24

	February	June	October
Su...	6 13 20 27	5 12 19 26	2 9 16 23 30
M...	7 14 21 28	6 13 20 27	3 10 17 24 31
Tu...	1 8 15 22	7 14 21 28	4 11 18 25
W...	2 9 16 23	1 8 15 22 29	5 12 19 26
Th...	3 10 17 24	2 9 16 23 30	6 13 20 27
F...	4 11 18 25	3 10 17 24	7 14 21 28
S...	5 12 19 26	4 11 18 25	1 8 15 22 29

	March	July	November
Su...	6 13 20 27	3 10 17 24 31	6 13 20 27
M...	7 14 21 28	4 11 18 25	7 14 21 28
Tu...	1 8 15 22 29	5 12 19 26	1 8 15 22 29
W...	2 9 16 23 30	6 13 20 27	2 9 16 23 30
Th...	3 10 17 24 31	7 14 21 28	3 10 17 24
F...	4 11 18 25	1 8 15 22 29	4 11 18 25
S...	5 12 19 26	2 9 16 23 30	5 12 19 26

	April	August	December
Su...	3 10 17 24	7 14 21 28	4 11 18 25
M...	4 11 18 25	1 8 15 22 29	5 12 19 26
Tu...	5 12 19 26	2 9 16 23 30	6 13 20 27
W...	6 13 20 27	3 10 17 24 31	7 14 21 28
Th...	7 14 21 28	4 11 18 25	1 8 15 22 29
F...	1 8 15 22 29	5 12 19 26	2 9 16 23 30
S...	2 9 16 23 30	6 13 20 27	3 10 17 24 31

Easter Days

March 27.	1785	1842	1853	1910	1921.	
April 3.	1763	1774	1825	1831	1983	1994.
April 10.	1757	1803	1814	1887	1898	1955 1966
April 17.	1870	1881	1927	1938	1949.	[1977.
April 24.	1791	1859.				

N (Leap year)

	January	May	September
Su...	2 9 16 23 30	7 14 21 28	3 10 17 24
M...	3 10 17 24 31	1 8 15 22 29	4 11 18 25
Tu...	4 11 18 25	2 9 16 23 30	5 12 19 26
W...	5 12 19 26	3 10 17 24 31	6 13 20 27
Th...	6 13 20 27	4 11 18 25	7 14 21 28
F...	7 14 21 28	5 12 19 26	1 8 15 22 29
S...	1 8 15 22 29	6 13 20 27	2 9 16 23 30

	February	June	October
Su...	6 13 20 27	4 11 18 25	1 8 15 22 29
M...	7 14 21 28	5 12 19 26	2 9 16 23 30
Tu...	1 8 15 22 29	6 13 20 27	3 10 17 24 31
W...	2 9 16 23	7 14 21 28	4 11 18 25
Th...	3 10 17 24	1 8 15 22 29	5 12 19 26
F...	4 11 18 25	2 9 16 23 30	6 13 20 27
S...	5 12 19 26	3 10 17 24	7 14 21 28

	March	July	November
Su...	5 12 19 26	2 9 16 23 30	5 12 19 26
M...	6 13 20 27	3 10 17 24 31	6 13 20 27
Tu...	7 14 21 28	4 11 18 25	7 14 21 28
W...	1 8 15 22 29	5 12 19 26	1 8 15 22 29
Th...	2 9 16 23 30	6 13 20 27	2 9 16 23 30
F...	3 10 17 24 31	7 14 21 28	3 10 17 24
S...	4 11 18 25	1 8 15 22 29	4 11 18 25

	April	August	December
Su...	2 9 16 23 30	6 13 20 27	3 10 17 24 31
M...	3 10 17 24	7 14 21 28	4 11 18 25
Tu...	4 11 18 25	1 8 15 22 29	5 12 19 26
W...	5 12 19 26	2 9 16 23 30	6 13 20 27
Th...	6 13 20 27	3 10 17 24 31	7 14 21 28
F...	7 14 21 28	4 11 18 25	1 8 15 22 29
S...	1 8 15 22 29	5 12 19 26	2 9 16 23 30

Easter Days

March 26.	1780.		
April 2.	1820	1972.	
April 9.	1944.		
April 16.	1876.		
April 23.	1848	1916	2000.

The World

The *Superficial Area* of the Earth is estimated to be 196,836,000 square miles, of which 55,786,000 square miles are Land and 141,050,000 square miles Water. The *Diameter* of the Earth at the Equator is 7,926½ English miles, and at the Poles 7,900 English miles. The Equatorial *Circumference* is 24,901·8 English miles, divided into 360 Degrees of Longitude, each of 69·17 English (or 60 Geographical) miles; these Degrees are measured from the Meridian of Greenwich, and numbered East and West of that point to meet in the Antipodes at the 180th Degree. Distance North and South of the Equator is marked by Parallels of Latitude, which proceed from zero (at the Equator) to 90° at the Poles.

The velocity of a given point of the Earth's surface at the Equator exceeds 1,000 miles an hour (24,901·8 miles in 24 hours); the Earth's velocity in its orbit round the Sun is about 66,600 miles an hour (584,000,000 miles in 365¼ days). The Earth is distant from the Sun 93,000,000 miles, on the average.

AREA AND POPULATION

The total population of the world in June, 1972, was estimated by the *United Nations Statistical Office* at 3,782,000,000 compared with 3,003,000,000 in 1960 and 2,070,000,000 in 1930. Figures of areas in the following table are of land area and inland water, but exclude uninhabited polar regions and some uninhabited islands. Figures for Europe and Asia exclude U.S.S.R. which is shown separately. Figures for Oceania exclude Hawaii which is included with North America, being the 50th State of U.S.A.

Continent, etc.	Area		Estimated Population, 1971
	Sq. miles '000	Sq. km. '000	
Europe......	1,903	4,929	466,000,000
Asia*.......	10,661	27,611	2,104,000,000
U.S.S.R.....	8,649	22,402	245,000,000
Africa.......	11,683	30,258	354,000,000
America.....	16,241	42,063	522,000,000
Oceania.....	3,286	8,510	19,800,000
Total...	52,422	135,773	3,711,000,000

* Excludes U.S.S.R. (shown separately); includes European and Asiatic Turkey.

A United Nations report (*The Future Growth of World Population*) in 1958, pointed out that the population of the world had increased since the beginning of the 20th Century at an unprecedented rate: in 1850 it was estimated at 1,094,000,000 and in 1900 at 1,550,000,000, an increase of 42 per cent. in 50 years. By 1925 it had risen to 1,907,000,000—23 per cent. in 25 years—and by 1950 it had reached 2,500,000,000, an increase of 31 per cent. in 25 years. Levels of population and the trend in distribution of the population by continents as forecast for the years 1975 and 2000 were:—

Continent	1975		2000	
	Estimated Population	Per cent.	Estimated Population	Per cent.
Europe‡....	751	19·6	947	15·1
Asia*......	2,210	57·7	3,870	61·8
Africa.....	303	7·9	517	8·2
N. America.	240	6·3	312	5·0
Latin America†.	303	7·9	592	9·4
Oceania....	21	0·5	29	0·5
World.....	3,828	100	6,267	100

[millions]

* Excluding U.S.S.R.   † Mexico and the remainder of America south of U.S.A.   ‡ Including U.S.S.R.

THE CONTINENTS

Europe (including European Russia) forms about one-fourteenth of the land surface of the globe. Its length from the North Cape, 71° 12′ N., to Cape Matapan, in the south of Greece, 36° 23′ N., is about 2,400 miles, and its breadth from Cape St. Vincent to the Urals is about 3,300 miles. The political boundary between Europe and Asia extends some distance beyond the Urals, to include the mining regions; in the south-east it follows the valley of the Manych, north of the Caucasus.

Asia (including Asiatic Russia) extends over nearly one-third of the land surface of the globe. The distance between its extreme longitudes, the west coast of Asia Minor (26° E.) and the East Cape (170° W.), is 6,000 miles. The extreme latitudes, Cape Chelyuskin (78° 30″ N.) and Cape Bulus (76 miles north of the Equator), are 5,350 miles apart. Asia is bounded by the ocean on all sides except the west. The Isthmus of Suez connects it with Africa. The land boundary between Europe and Asia is formed on the west mainly by the Ural Mountains and the Ural River. In the south-west the valley of the Manych, which stretches from the Caspian Sea to the mouth of the Don, is now taken as the line between the two continents, although the Caucasus was formerly considered as belonging to Europe. The islands of the archipelago which lie in the south-east between the continents of Asia and Australia may be divided into two groups by a line passing east of Timor, Timor Laut, the Kei Islands and the Moluccas.

Africa is about three times the area of Europe. Its extreme longitudes are 17° W. at Cape Verde and 51° 27′ 52″ E. at Ras Hafun. The extreme latitudes are Cape Blanco in 37° N. and Cape Agulhas in 35° S., at a distance of about 5,000 miles. It is surrounded by seas on all sides, except in the narrow isthmus through which is cut the Suez Canal, and may be considered as a great peninsula of the Eurasian continent.

North America, including Mexico, is a little less than twice the size of Europe. Its extreme longitudes extend from a little west of 170° W. to 52½° W. in the east of Newfoundland, and its extreme latitudes from about 80° N. lat. to 15° N. lat. in the south of Mexico. It is surrounded by seas on all sides except in the south, where it joins the Isthmian States of *Central America*, which have an area of about 200,000 square miles. The area of the *West Indies* is about 65,000 square miles, a little more than half that of the United Kingdom. They extend from about 27° N. latitude to 10° N. latitude.

South America is a little more than 1¾ times the size of Europe. The extreme longitudes are Cape Branco 35° W. and Punta Parina 81° W., and the extreme latitudes, Punta Gallinas, 12½° N. and Cape Horn 56° S. South America is surrounded by the ocean, except where it is joined to Central America by the narrow isthmus through which is cut the Panama Canal.

Oceania extends over an area 1½ times the size of Europe, from Australia (in the West) to the most easterly islands of Polynesia, and from New Zealand (in the south) to the Sandwich Islands (Hawaii) in the north.

The appended tables of area and population are based on such information as is immediately available. With regard to areas it will be realized that no complete survey of many countries has yet been either achieved or even undertaken and that consequently accurate area figures are not available. In addition, among the results of the war of 1939–1945 is a readjustment of boundaries which have not yet been definitely settled.

The populations given hereunder are derived from various sources; some have as their basis an authenticated census; some are official and some are unofficial estimates. In certain cases where later information becomes available during printing the new figures are given in the overseas sections of the ALMANACK. What has been said about the survey of many of the world's countries applies equally to the question of census.

AFRICA
Ψ Seaport

Country	Area Sq. Miles	Population	Per Sq. Mile	Capital	Population of Capital
Afars and Issas Territory.	9,000	81,200	9	Ψ Djibouti............	62,000
Algeria................	856,000	13,547,000	16	Ψ Algiers.............	943,000
Angola................	488,000	5,673,046	12	Ψ Luanda.............	346,763
Benin.................	47,000	2,948,000	63	Ψ Porto Novo........	85,000
Botswana..............	220,000	620,000	3	Gaborone............	18,000
Burundi...............	10,700	3,475,000	323	Bujumbura..........	70,000
Cameroon.............	183,000	7,000,000	38	Yaoundé............	180,000
Cape Verde Islands.....	1,516	272,071	179	Ψ Praia..............	6,000
Central African Republic	234,000	3,200,000	14	Bangui.............	301,793
Chad..................	488,000	4,000,000	8	Ndjaména...........	126,000
Congo.................	129,960	2,100,000	16	Brazzaville.........	156,000
Egypt.................	385,000	34,000,000	88	Cairo..............	8,143,000
Equatorial Guinea......	11,000	286,000	26	Ψ Malabo...........	9,000
Ethiopia (Abyssinia).....	400,000	26,000,000	65	Addis Ababa........	912,000
Gabon................	101,400	500,000	5	Ψ Libreville.........	31,000
Gambia...............	4,000	493,499	123	Ψ Banjul............	39,476
Ghana................	92,100	8,545,561	93	Ψ Accra.............	851,614
Guinea................	97,000	3,890,000	40	Ψ Conakry..........	120,000
Guinea-Bissau	14,000	600,000	43	Ψ Bissau............	6,000
Ivory Coast............	127,000	5,400,000	43	Ψ Abidjan...........	900,000
Kenya................	225,000	12,934,000	57	Nairobi.............	509,000
Lesotho...............	11,700	1,181,300	101	Maseru.............	30,000
Liberia...............	43,000	1,481,524	34	Ψ Monrovia.........	201,600
Libya.................	810,000	2,257,037	3	Ψ Tripoli...........	551,477
Madagascar............	228,000	8,000,000	35	Tananarive.........	400,000
Malawi...............	45,747	5,175,000	113	Lilongwe...........	87,000
Mali.................	465,000	4,929,000	11	Bamako............	170,000
Mauritania............	419,000	1,200,000	3	Nouakchott.........	30,000
Mauritius, etc.........	805	894,150	1,111	Ψ Port Louis........	140,000
Morocco..............	180,000	15,379,259	85	Ψ Rabat............	565,000
Mozambique...........	298,000	8,233,034	28	Ψ Maputo...........	441,363
Niger.................	459,000	4,030,000	9	Niamey............	100,000
Nigeria...............	357,000	79,760,000	224	Ψ Lagos.............	1,000,000
Réunion..............	1,000	445,500	445	St. Denis...........	85,992
Rhodesia..............	151,000	5,780,000	40	Salisbury...........	503,000
Rwanda...............	10,169	4,000,000	393	Kigali.............	7,000
St. Helena.............	47	5,058	108	Ψ Jamestown........	1,475
Ascension..........	38	1,131	30	Ψ Georgetown......	..
Tristan da Cunha.....	45	292	6	Ψ Edinburgh........	..
São Tomé & Princípe...	372	74,500	200	Ψ São Tomé.........	3,187
Senegal...............	78,000	3,800,000	49	Ψ Dakar............	581,000
Seychelles.............	171	52,650	308	Ψ Victoria..........	13,736
Sierra Leone...........	28,000	3,002,426	108	Ψ Freetown.........	274,000
Somalia...............	246,000	2,730,000	11	Ψ Mogadishu........	220,000
South Africa...........	471,447	24,920,000	53 {	Pretoria............ Ψ Cape Town........	563,384 1,107,764
S.W. Africa...........	318,000	746,328	2	Windhoek..........	61,260
Spanish Presidios:—					
Ceuta..............	5	67,187	..	..	..
Melilla.............	72	64,942	..	..	..
Sahara.............	125,000	63,000	..	Villa Cisneros.......	250
Sudan................	967,500	16,900,000	17	Khartoum...........	194,000
Swaziland.............	6,700	493,728	74	Mbabane...........	21,500
Tanzania.............	363,000	13,968,000	38	Ψ Dar-es-Salaam......	300,000
Togo.................	21,000	2,089,900	99	Lomé..............	214,200
Tunisia...............	63,380	5,600,000	88	Ψ Tunis............	1,127,000
Uganda...............	91,000	10,400,000	114	Kampala...........	331,000
Upper Volta...........	100,000	5,514,000	55	Ouagadougou.......	125,000
Zaire.................	905,000	21,637,000	24	Kinshasa...........	1,300,000
Zambia...............	291,000	4,054,000	14	Lusaka.............	238,000

AMERICA

COUNTRY	Area Sq. Miles	Population	Per Sq. Mile	Capital	Population of Capital
North America					
Canada†	3,560,000	22,800,000	6	Ottawa	626,000
Alberta	249,000	1,768,000	7	Edmonton	451,635
British Columbia	359,000	2,457,000	7	Ψ Victoria	199,000
Manitoba	212,000	1,019,000	5	Winnipeg	553,000
New Brunswick	28,000	675,000	24	Ψ Fredericton	42,000
Newfoundland	143,000	549,000	4	Ψ St. John's	88,102
Nova Scotia	20,400	822,000	40	Ψ Halifax	225,000
Ontario	344,000	8,220,000	24	Toronto	2,741,000
Prince Edward Island	2,184	119,000	54	Ψ Charlottetown	18,500
Quebec	524,000	6,188,000	12	Ψ Quebec	187,800
Saskatchewan	220,000	918,000	4	Regina	147,000
Yukon Territory	205,000	21,000	..	Whitehorse	4,771
Northwest Territories	1,305,000	38,000	..	Yellowknife	7,000
Mexico	761,604	61,000,000	80	Mexico City	8,941,912
St. Pierre and Miquelon	93	5,000	54	Ψ St. Pierre	3,500
United States*	3,536,855	214,374,000	61	Washington, D.C.	2,909,111
Central America and the West Indies					
Anguilla	35	6,500	186	......	......
Antigua and Barbuda	170	66,000	388	Ψ St. John's	22,000
Bahamas	5,380	197,000	37	Ψ Nassau	112,000
Barbados	166	254,964	1,536	Ψ Bridgetown	18,789
Belize	8,900	140,000	16	Belmopan	3,500
Bermuda	21	53,000	2,574	Ψ Hamilton	3,000
Cayman Islands	100	10,652	107	Ψ George Town	3,000
Costa Rica	19,653	1,875,000	95	San José	215,441
Cuba	44,000	8,553,000	194	Ψ Havana	1,755,360
Dominica	290	74,000	255	Ψ Roseau	10,157
Dominican Republic	19,300	4,012,000	208	Ψ Santo Domingo	817,000
Grenada	133	104,000	782	Ψ St. George's	8,600
Guadeloupe	688	323,000	469	Ψ Pointe à Pitre	39,000
Guatemala	42,000	5,400,000	128	Guatemala	790,311
Haiti	10,700	4,768,000	446	Ψ Port au Prince	400,000
Honduras	43,000	2,646,828	61	Tegucigalpa	267,754
Jamaica	4,400	2,060,300	467	Ψ Kingston	614,000
Martinique	400	332,000	830	Ψ Fort de France	60,660
Montserrat	39	12,905	331	Ψ Plymouth	1,300
Netherlands Antilles	394	234,400	595	ΨWillemstad	154,000
Nicaragua	57,000	2,400,000	42	Managua	400,000
Panama	31,900	1,678,000	53	Ψ Panama City	418,000
Panama Canal Zone	647	51,000	79	Ψ Balboa Heights	3,950
Puerto Rico	3,400	2,913,000	848	Ψ San Juan	851,247
St. Kitts-Nevis	101	48,000	475	Ψ Basseterre	17,000
St. Lucia	238	110,780	465	Ψ Castries	47,000
St. Vincent	150	92,000	613	Ψ Kingstown	23,000
El Salvador	7,700	3,863,793	500	San Salvador	620,000
Trinidad and Tobago	1,980	1,061,850	536	Ψ Port of Spain	100,000
Turks and Caicos Islds.	193	6,000	31	Ψ Grand Turk	2,339
Virgin Islands:—					
British	59	10,030	170	Ψ Road Town	2,129
U.S.	133	90,000	677	Ψ Charlotte Amalie	11,000
South America					
Argentina	1,080,000	23,360,000	22	Ψ Buenos Aires	8,774,529
Bolivia	415,000	4,658,000	11	La Paz	553,000
Brazil	3,289,000	108,000,000	33	Brasília	544,862
Chile	290,000	10,000,000	34	Santiago	4,000,000
Colombia	440,000	23,500,000	53	Bogotá	3,200,000
Ecuador	226,000	7,000,000	31	Quito	700,000
Falkland Islands	4,700	1,905	..	Ψ Stanley	1,079
Guiana, *French*	35,000	48,000	1	Ψ Cayenne	20,000
Guyana	83,000	714,233	9	Ψ Georgetown	168,000
Paraguay	157,000	2,500,000	16	Ψ Asunción	437,000
Peru	531,000	14,121,564	27	Lima	3,600,000
Surinam	54,000	480,000	9	Ψ Paramaribo	110,000
Uruguay	72,000	2,763,964	38	Ψ Montevideo	1,229,748
Venezuela	354,000	11,992,700	34	Caracas	2,183,935

★ The 50 States and Federal *District of Columbia* at the 1970 Census; for area and population of individual States *see* main article.   Ψ Seaport.   † For total areas (including freshwater), see p. 695.

ASIA

The expressions "The Near East," "The Middle East" and "The Far East" often appear in the Press of English-speaking countries, but have no definite boundaries. The following limits have been suggested:— *Near East* (Turkey to Iran) 25°–60° E. long., *Middle East* (Baluchistan to Burma) 60°–100° E. long., *Far East* (Thailand to Japan) 100°–160° E. long.
Ψ Seaport.

Country	Area Sq. miles	Population	Per Sq. Mile	Capital	Population of Capital
Afghanistan	250,000	16,516,000	66	Kabul	500,000
Bahrain	231	216,000	935	Ψ Manama	89,608
Bangladesh	55,126	71,316,517	1,294	Dacca	1,300,000
Bhutan	18,000	1,010,000	56	Thimphu	..
Brunei	2,226	162,200	73	Ψ Bandar Seri Begawan	42,000
Burma	262,000	30,834,000	118	Ψ Rangoon	3,186,886
Cambodia	70,000	7,300,000	104	Ψ Phnom Penh	2,000,000
China	3,700,000	827,850,000	223	Peking	7,570,000
Formosa (Taiwan)	13,800	15,353,291	1,112	Taipei	1,921,736
Macau	5	248,316	..	Ψ Macau	157,175
Hong Kong	404	4,379,900	..	Ψ Victoria	767,000
India	1,262,000	606,200,000	480	Delhi	4,065,698
Indonesia	735,000	129,000,000	176	Ψ Jakarta	5,000,000
Iran (Persia)	628,000	28,448,000	45	Tehran	3,150,000
Iraq	172,000	9,498,362	55	Baghdad	2,696,000
Israel	8,000	3,230,000	404	Jerusalem	380,000
Japan	143,000	110,050,000	771	Tokyo	11,671,138
Jordan	37,700	2,660,000	71	Amman	615,000
Korea:—					
North Korea	48,000	14,500,000	302	Pyongyang	286,000
South Korea	38,500	33,459,000	870	Seoul	6,289,556
Kuwait	7,500	990,000	132	Ψ Kuwait	400,000
Laos	90,000	3,000,000	33	Vientiane	174,000
Lebanon	4,300	2,645,000	615	Ψ Beirut	600,000
Malaysia	128,000	10,434,000	82	Kuala Lumpur	770,000
Johore	7,330	1,274,000	174	Johore Bahru	..
Kedah	3,640	955,000	262	Alor Star	..
Kelantan	5,765	681,000	118	Koto Bahru	..
Malacca	640	404,000	631	Ψ Malacca	..
Negri Sembilan	2,570	479,000	186	Seremban	..
Pahang	13,900	503,000	36	Kuantan	..
Penang	400	777,000	1,942	Ψ George Town	234,930
Perak	8,100	1,563,000	193	Ipoh	125,776
Perlis	310	121,000	390	Kangar	..
Sabah	29,000	656,000	23	Kota Kinabalu	41,830
Sarawak	48,000	977,000	20	Ψ Kuching	63,491
Selangor	3,166	1,629,000	515	Kuala Lumpur	500,000
Trengganu	5,000	406,000	81	Kuala Trengganu	..
Maldive Islands	115	114,500	996	Ψ Malé	13,610
Mongolia (Outer)	600,000	1,450,000	2	Ulan Bator	334,000
Nepal	54,000	11,289,000	208	Katmandu	353,756
Oman	120,000	750,000	6	Ψ Muscat	7,000
Pakistan	310,403	72,400,000	233	Islamabad	235,000
Philippine Islds	115,000	42,517,330	370	Ψ Manila	1,438,252
Qatar	4,000	180,000	45	Doha	180,000
Saudi Arabia	927,000	7,012,642	8	Riyadh	666,840
Singapore	226	2,249,900	9,973	..	..
Sri Lanka	25,332	12,747,755	503	Ψ Colombo	563,705
Syria	71,000	6,294,000	89	Damascus	557,252
Thailand (Siam)	198,000	42,000,000	212	Ψ Bangkok	4,300,000
Timor, Eastern	7,329	610,541	83	Ψ Dili	7,000
Turkey in Asia.†	285,000	36,423,964	128	Ankara	1,698,542
United Arab Emirates	32,000	655,937	20	..	..
U.S.S.R. (Asia)					
R.S.F.S.R. (Asia)	4,887,000	See Europe			
Armenia (Hyastan)	11,000	2,785,000	246	Erevan	899,000
Azerbaijan	33,000	5,607,000	168	Ψ Baku	929,000
Georgia	27,000	4,923,000	183	Tbilisi	1,006,000
Turkmenistan	188,000	2,506,000	13	Ashkhabad	289,000
Uzbekistan	157,000	13,689,000	87	Tashkent	1,595,000
Tadjikstan	54,000	3,387,000	63	Dushanbe	436,000
Kazakhstan	1,065,000	14,168,000	13	Alma Ata	837,000
Kirghizia	77,000	3,298,000	43	Frunze	486,000
Vietnam:—					
Northern Zone	63,000	23,780,375	377	Hanoi	1,378,335
Southern Zone	66,000	20,000,000	302	Ψ Saigon	3,000,000
Yemen	75,000	6,500,000	87	Sana'a	135,000
Yemen P.D.R.	180,000	1,598,275	9	Ψ Aden	250,000

† Total, incl. European parts: Area, 294,200 sq. miles; population, 40,197,669.

EUROPE AND THE MEDITERRANEAN

Country	Area Sq. Miles	Population	Per Sq. Mile	Capital	Population of Capital
Albania	10,700	2,377,600	222	Tirana	200,000
Andorra	180	28,500	158	Andorra La Vella	11,000
Austria	32,376	7,519,900	232	Vienna	1,614,841
Belgium	11,800	9,650,944	820	Brussels	1,075,000
Bulgaria	43,000	8,594,493	200	Sofia	965,728
Cyprus	3,500	634,000	177	Nicosia	235,000
Czechoslovakia	49,400	14,686,255	297	Prague	1,091,449
Denmark	17,000	5,054,909	297	Ψ Copenhagen	1,380,118
Finland	130,000	4,720,259	36	Ψ Helsinki	505,719
France	213,000	52,590,000	247	Paris	2,317,227
Germany:—					
Federal Republic of Germany‡	95,953	61,644,600	642	Bonn	283,711
German Democratic Republic	41,768	16,890,800	404	East Berlin	1,094,147
Gibraltar	2	29,934	..	Ψ Gibraltar	20,000
Greece	51,200	8,768,641	171	Athens	2,540,241
Hungary	36,000	10,572,000	294	Budapest	2,055,646
Iceland	40,500	218,682	5	Ψ Reykjavik	84,423
Irish Republic	26,600	2,978,248	112	Ψ Dublin	567,866
Italy	131,000	56,024,000	428	Rome	2,842,616
Liechtenstein	65	23,745	365	Vaduz	4,382
Luxemburg	1,000	357,300	357	Luxemburg	78,300
Malta and Gozo	121	318,481	2,636	Ψ Valletta	14,152
Monaco	⅔	24,500	..	Monaco	2,422
Netherlands	13,500	13,700,000	1,015 {	The Hague	479,369
				Ψ Amsterdam	770,805
Norway	125,000	3,972,990	32	Ψ Oslo	464,900
Poland	121,000	34,186,000	283	Warsaw	1,436,100
Portugal§	34,500	9,260,000	268	Ψ Lisbon	783,000
Rumania	91,600	20,827,525	227	Bucharest	1,528,562
San Marino	23	21,000	913	San Marino	2,000
Spain	197,000	34,032,801	173	Madrid	3,146,071
Sweden	173,000	8,177,000	47	Ψ Stockholm	1,357,558
Switzerland	16,000	6,385,000	400	Berne	162,405
Turkey in Europe	9,200	3,772,705	410	Ankara	1,698,542
THE UNITED KINGDOM†	93,026	55,521,534	597 }	Ψ London	7,379,014
England	50,053	45,870,062	916		
Wales	7,969	2,723,596	342	Ψ Cardiff	283,680
Scotland	29,798	5,227,706	171	Ψ Edinburgh	448,682
Northern Ireland	5,206	1,536,065	295	Ψ Belfast	353,700
U.S.S.R. (Europe)					
R.S.F.S.R.★	1,707,000	133,741,000	20	Moscow	7,466,000
Ukraine	252,000	48,817,000	194	Kiev	1,947,000
Belorussia	80,000	9,331,000	116	Minsk	1,133,000
Moldavia	14,000	3,812,000	274	Kishinev	452,000
Estonia	17,400	1,429,000	82	Ψ Tallinn	399,000
Latvia	25,000	2,478,000	100	Ψ Riga	796,000
Lithuania	26,000	3,290,000	126	Vilnius	433,000
Vatican City State	109 *acres*	1,000	..	Vatican City	1,000
Yugoslavia	99,000	21,352,000	216	Belgrade	1,204,000

★ Total population, Europe and Asia.   † *Land* areas are shown for U.K. and parts (*total* area of U.K., 94,216 sq. m.); populations at 1971 Census (prelim.) except Belfast.   ‡ Data include West Berlin. § Data include Madeira (314 sq. miles) and the Azores (922 sq. miles).   Ψ Seaport.

THE SEVEN WONDERS OF THE WORLD

I. THE PYRAMIDS OF EGYPT.—From Gizeh (near Cairo) to a southern limit 60 miles distant. The oldest is that of Zoser, at Saggara, built about 2,700 B.C. The Great Pyramid of Cheops covers more than 12 acres and was originally 481 ft. in height and 756 × 756 ft. at the base.

II. THE HANGING GARDENS OF BABYLON.—Adjoining Nebuchadnezzar's palace, 60 miles south of Baghdad. Terraced gardens, ranging from 75 to 300 ft. above ground level, watered from storage tanks on the highest terrace.

III. THE TOMB OF MAUSOLUS.—At Halicarnassus, in Asia Minor. Built by the widowed Queen Artemisia about 350 B.C. The memorial originated the term mausoleum.

IV. THE TEMPLE OF DIANA AT EPHESUS.—Ionic temple erected about 350 B.C. in honour of the goddess and burned by the Goths in A.D. 262.

V. THE COLOSSUS OF RHODES.—A bronze statue of Apollo, set up about 280 B.C. According to legend it stood at the harbour entrance of the seaport of Rhodes.

VI. THE STATUE OF JUPITER OLYMPUS.—At Olympia in the plain of Ellis, constructed of marble inlaid with ivory and gold by the sculptor Phidias, about 430 B.C.

VII. THE PHAROS OF ALEXANDRIA.—A marble watch tower and lighthouse on the island of Pharos in the harbour of Alexandria.

OCEANIA

Country	Area Sq. Miles	Population	Per Sq. Mile	Capital	Population of Capital
Australia..............	2,968,000	13,601,000	5	Canberra...........	201,200
New South Wales.....	309,000	4,811,100	16	Ψ Sydney.............	2,922,760
Queensland..........	667,000	2,015,100	3	Ψ Brisbane...........	958,000
South Australia......	380,000	1,241,700	3	Adelaide...........	809,482
Tasmania............	26,000	409,000	16	Ψ Hobart.............	136,550
Victoria.............	88,000	3,688,200	42	Ψ Melbourne..........	2,394,117
Western Australia....	976,000	1,138,300	1	Perth..............	787,300
Northern Territory.....	520,280	96,300	..	Ψ Darwin.............	41,000
Norfolk Island........	13	1,870	116	Ψ Kingston...........	..
Fiji..................	7,100	560,000	79	Ψ Suva..............	60,000
French Polynesia.......	2,500	119,200	48	Ψ Papeete............	15,220
Gilbert Islands..........	264	48,000	182	Tarawa............	17,000
Guam.................	209	105,000	502	Agaña..............	..
Mariana, Caroline and Marshall Islands†....	687	101,592	148	Saipan.............	..
Nauru...............	8	6,970	871	Ψ Nauru.............	..
New Caledonia.........	7,200	100,600	14	Ψ Noumea............	12,000
New Hebrides.........	5,700	89,031	15	Ψ Vila..............	5,500
New Zealand..........	104,000	3,105,400	30	Ψ Wellington.........	354,660
Cook Islands.........⎰	⎱ 200	⎰ 18,937	..	Avarua............	..
Niue...............⎱		⎱ 3,992	..	Alofi..............	956
Ross Dependency......	175,000				
Papua New Guinea.....	178,260	2,654,509	15	Ψ Port Moresby.......	110,000
Samoa:—					
Eastern..............	76	28,000	368	Ψ Pago Pago..........	1,251
Western.............	1,097	152,000	139	Ψ Apia..............	28,800
Solomon Islands........	11,500	196,708	17	Ψ Honiara...........	14,993
Tonga, etc............	270	92,360	360	Ψ Nuku'alofa.........	20,000
Tavalu...............	10	10,000	1,000	Ψ Funafuti...........	1,000

† Trust Territory of the Pacific Islands.   Ψ Seaport

OCEAN AREAS AND DEPTHS

The greatest known Ocean Depth (in the Pacific, off the Philippines, 36,198 feet) is not much greater than the greatest land height (in the Himalayas); but the mean depth of the Ocean floor exceeds 12,000 feet, while the mean height of the surface of the land area of the Earth above sea level is only 2,300 feet. The following table gives the areas of the principal oceans and seas, with the greatest known depth of each:—

Oceans

Name	Area of Basin (sq. miles)	Greatest Depth (feet)
Pacific.........	63,986,000	Mariana Trench, 36,198
Atlantic.......	31,530,000	Puerto Rico Trench, 27,498
Indian........	28,350,000	Diamantina, 26,400
Arctic.........	5,541,600	17,850

Seas

Name	Area of Basin (sq. miles)	Greatest Depth (feet)
Malay.........	3,137,000	Kei Trench, 21,342
Caribbean.....	1,770,170	Cayman, 23,000
Mediterranean..	1,145,000	Matapan, 14,435
Bering........	878,000	Buldir Trough, 13,422
Okhotsk.......	582,000	Kurile Trough, 11,154
East China.....	480,000	about 10,500
Hudson Bay....	472,000	about 1,500
Japan.........	405,000	about 10,200
Andaman......	305,000	about 11,000
North Sea.....	221,000	Skaggerak, 1,998
Red Sea......	178,000	20° N., 7,254
Baltic.........	158,000	about 1,300

PRINCIPAL LAND AREAS OF THE WORLD BELOW SEA LEVEL

(With approx. greatest depth in feet below Mean Sea Level.)

Europe: Netherlands coastal areas (15).
Asia: Jordan Valley, Dead Sea (1290).★
  China: Sinkiang, Turfan Basin (980).
  U.S.S.R.–Iran: Caspian Sea (85).★
  Arabia: Trucial Oman–Qatar (70).
Africa: Libyan Desert Depressions:—
  Qattara (440), Faiyum (150).
  Wadi Ryan (140), Sittra (110).

Africa: Libyan Desert Depressions (*continued*)—
  Areg (80), Wadi Natrun (75).
  Melfa (60), Siwa (55), Bahrain (50).
  Eritrea: Salt Plains depression (385).
  Algeria–Tunisia: Shott Melghir and El Gharsa (90).★
America: Death Valley (275), Salton Sea (245).
Australia: Lake Eyre (40).

★Water surface

THE LARGEST CITIES OF THE WORLD

Ψ = Seaport	Population*
TOKYO, Japan (1975)	11,671,138
Ψ Shanghai, China (1972)	10,820,000
MEXICO CITY, Mexico (1976)	8,941,912
Ψ BUENOS AIRES, Argentina (1970)	8,774,529
CAIRO, Egypt (1975)	8,143,000
Ψ New York, U.S.A. (1970)	7,895,563
PEKING, China (1972)	7,570,000
MOSCOW, U.S.S.R. (1975)	7,466,000
Ψ LONDON, England (1971)	7,379,014
SEOUL, Korea (1973)	6,289,556
São Paulo, Brazil (1970)	5,901,533
Ψ Bombay, India (1971)	5,850,000
Ψ JAKARTA, Indonesia (1974)	5,000,000
Ψ BANGKOK, Thailand (1975)	4,300,000
Ψ Rio de Janeiro, Brazil (1970)	4,296,782
Tientsin, China (1971)	4,280,000
DELHI, India (1971)	4,065,698
SANTIAGO, Chile (1972)	4,000,000
Ψ Leningrad, U.S.S.R. (1975)	3,853,000
LIMA, Peru (1972)	3,600,000
Ψ Karachi, Pakistan (1972)	3,469,000
Ψ Chicago, U.S.A. (1970)	3,369,357
BOGOTA, Colombia (1975)	3,200,000
Ψ RANGOON, Burma (1973)	3,186,886
TEHRAN, Iran (1970)	3,150,000
MADRID, Spain (1970)	3,146,071
Ψ Calcutta, India (1971)	3,141,180
Berlin, Germany (1975)	3,078,984
Ψ SAIGON, S. Vietnam (1973)	3,000,000
Ψ Sydney, Australia (1975)	2,922,760
ROME, Italy (1971)	2,842,616
Ψ Montreal, Canada (1974)	2,828,795
Ψ Los Angeles, U.S.A. (1970)	2,809,813
Ψ Osaka, Japan (1971)	2,778,973
Ψ Toronto, Canada (1975)	2,741,000
BAGHDAD, Iraq (1970)	2,696,000
Ψ Yokohama, Japan (1971)	2,621,704
ATHENS, Greece (1972)	2,540,241
Ψ Istanbul, Turkey (1975)	2,534,739
Ψ Madras, India (1971)	2,470,289
Shenyang, China (1957)	2,411,000
Ψ Melbourne, Australia (1971)	2,394,117
PARIS, France (1969)	2,317,227
CARACAS, Venezuela (1971)	2,183,935
Lahore, Pakistan (1972)	2,148,000
Wuhan, China (1957)	2,146,000
Chungking, China (1957)	2,121,000

Ψ = Seaport	Population*
Ψ Nagoya, Japan (1971)	2,079,676
Ψ SINGAPORE (1970)	2,074,507
BUDAPEST, Hungary (1975)	2,055,646
Ψ Pusan, Korea (1973)	2,015,162
Ψ Nanking, China (1975)	2,000,000
Ψ PHNOM PENH, Cambodia (1973)	2,000,000
Ψ Philadelphia, U.S.A. (1970)	1,949,996
TAIPEI, Formosa (1973)	1,921,730
Ψ Alexandria, Egypt (1969)	1,900,009
Kiev, U.S.S.R. (1975)	1,947,000
Ψ Canton, China (1957)	1,840,000
Ψ HAVANA, Cuba (1970)	1,755,360
Ψ Barcelona, Spain (1969)	1,750,000
Guadalajara, Mexico (1976)	1,725,107
Milan, Italy (1971)	1,724,819
Ψ Hamburg, Germany (1975)	1,717,383
ANKARA, Turkey (1975)	1,698,542
VIENNA, Austria (1972)	1,614,841
Tashkent, U.S.S.R. (1975)	1,595,000
Harbin, China (1957)	1,552,000
BUCHAREST, Rumania (1973)	1,528,562
Ψ Detroit, U.S.A. (1970)	1,513,601
Ψ Lushun-Dairen, China (1957)	1,508,000
Ψ Casablanca, Morocco (1971)	1,506,373
Kyoto, Japan (1971)	1,461,053
Johannesburg, South Africa (1975)	1,441,335
WARSAW, Poland (1975)	1,436,100
Ψ MANILA, Philippines (1971)	1,399,583
Ψ COPENHAGEN, Denmark (1972)	1,380,118
HANOI, N. Vietnam (1974)	1,378,335
Kharkov, U.S.S.R. (1975)	1,357,000
Ψ Kobé, Japan (1971)	1,360,601
Monterrey, Mexico (1976)	1,350,000
Ψ STOCKHOLM, Sweden (1973)	1,349,892
Munich, Germany (1975)	1,314,865
Sian, China (1957)	1,310,000
Dacca, Bangladesh (1974)	1,300,000
KINSHASA, Zaire (1971)	1,300,000
Gorky, U.S.S.R. (1975)	1,283,000
Novosibirsk, U.S.S.R. (1975)	1,265,000
Ψ Naples, Italy (1971)	1,258,721
Hyderabad, India (1963)	1,251,119
Ψ Sapporo, Japan (1971)	1,240,617
Ψ Houston, U.S.A. (1970)	1,232,802
Ψ Belo Horizonte, Brazil (1970)	1,232,708
BELGRADE, Yugoslavia (1970)	1,204,000

* *See* paragraph 2, p. 199. U.S.A.—Populations of the largest cities are those of the standard metropolitan statistical areas at the Census of 1970.

THE CINQUE PORTS

As their name implies the Cinque Ports were originally 5 in number, Hastings, New Romney, Hythe, Dover and Sandwich. They were in existence before the Norman Conquest and were the Anglo-Saxon successors to the Roman system of coast defence organized from the Wash to Spithead to resist Saxon onslaughts. William the Conqueror reconstituted them and granted peculiar jurisdiction, most of which was abolished in 1855. Only jurisdiction in Admiralty still survives.

At some time after the Conquest the "antient towns" of Winchelsea and Rye were added with equal privileges. The other members of the Confederation, known as Limbs, are:—Lydd, Faversham, Folkestone, Deal, Tenterden, Margate and Ramsgate.

The Barons of the Cinque Ports have the ancient privilege of attending the Coronation Ceremony and are allotted special places in Westminster Abbey.

Lord Warden, Rt. Hon. Sir Robert Menzies, K.T., C.H., Q.C.

Judge, Court of Admiralty, Sir Henry Barnard.

Registrar, James A. Johnson, New Bridge House, Dover.

Lord Wardens since 1904

Marquess Curzon	1904
The Prince of Wales	1905
Earl Brassey	1908
Earl Beauchamp	1913
Marquess of Reading	1934
Marquess of Willingdon	1936
Sir Winston Churchill	1941
Sir Robert Menzies	1965

THE WORLD'S LAKES
The areas of some of these lakes are subject to seasonal variation.

Name	Country	Length (Miles)	Area (Sq. Miles)	Name	Country	Length (Miles)	Area (Sq. Miles)
Caspian Sea	Asia	750	170,000	Amadjuak	Baffin Land	75	4,000
Superior	North America	350	31,820	Onega	U.S.S.R.	145	3,800
Victoria Nyanza	Africa	200	26,828	Eyre	Australia	130	3,700
Aral	U.S.S.R.	265	26,000	Rudolf	Africa	185	3,500
Huron	North America	206	23,010	Titicaca	South America	110	3,200
Michigan	North America	307	22,400	Athabasca	Canada	100	3,058
Tanganyika	Africa	420	12,700	Nicaragua	Central America	100	3,000
Great Bear	Canada	175	12,200	Gairdner	Australia	100	3,000
Baikal	U.S.S.R.	330	12,150	Reindeer	Canada	160	2,444
Great Slave	Canada	300	11,170	Torrens	Australia	130	2,200
Malawi	Africa	360	11,000	Koko-Nor	Tibet	68	2,300
Erie	North America	241	9,940	Issyk-Kul	U.S.S.R.	115	2,250
Winnipeg	Canada	260	9,398	Vänern	Sweden	93	2,140
Maracaibo	South America	130	8,296	Winnipegosis	Canada	122	2,086
Ontario	North America	193	7,540	Bangweolo	Africa	150	2,000
Balkhash	U.S.S.R.	323	7,050	Nipigon	Canada	70	1,870
Ladoga	U.S.S.R.	130	7,000	Manitoba	Canada	130	1,817
Chad	Africa	175	6,000	Van	Asia Minor	80	1,450
Nettilling	Baffin Land	120	5,000				

VOLCANOES OF THE WORLD

Volcano	Locality	Height in Feet	Volcano	Locality	Height in Feet
Cotopaxi	Ecuador	19,344	Nyamuragira	Zaire	10,150
Kluchevskaya	U.S.S.R.	15,584	Villarica	Chile	9,325
Mount Wrangell	Alaska	14,000	Ruapehu	New Zealand	9,175
Mauna Loa	Hawaii	13,680	Paricutin	Mexico	9,100
Cameroon	Cameroon	13,350	Asama	Japan	8,340
Erebus	Antarctica	12,200	Ngauruhoe	New Zealand	7,515
Nyiragongo	Zaire	11,560	Hecla	Iceland	4,892
Iliamna	Aleutian Range, U.S.A.	11,000	Vesuvius	Italy	4,190
Etna	Sicily	10,958	Kilauea	Hawaii	4,090
Baker	Cascades	10,778	Stromboli	Lipari Islands, Italy	3,034
Chillan	Chile	10,500			

QUIESCENT

Volcano	Locality	Height in Feet	Volcano	Locality	Height in Feet
Llullaillaco	Chile	22,057	Tristan da Cunha	South Atlantic	6,700
Demavend	Iran	18,384	Pelée	Martinique, W. Indies	4,430
Pico de Teyde	Teneriffe	12,198	Tarawera	New Zealand	3,646
Semerou	Indonesia	12,060	Soufrière	St. Vincent Is., W.I.	3,000
Haleakala	Hawaii	10,022	Krakatoa	Sunda Strait	2,600
Tongariro	New Zealand	6,458			

BELIEVED EXTINCT

Volcano	Locality	Height in Feet	Volcano	Locality	Height in Feet
Aconcagua	Andes	22,834	Elbruz	Caucasus	18,480
Chimborazo	Ecuador	20,560	Popocatapetl	Mexico	17,887
Kilimanjaro	Tanzania	19,340	Karisimbi	Rwanda and Zaire	14,786
Antisana	Ecuador	18,713	Fujiyama	Japan	12,388
Citlaltepetl	Mexico	18,700			

THE HIGHEST MOUNTAINS
The following list contains some of the principal peaks of such ranges as the Himalayas and the Andes, and the highest mountains in other ranges.

Name	Range of Country	Height in Feet	Name	Range or Country	Height in Feet
EVEREST	Himalayas	29,028	Sajama	Andes	21,390
K 2	Karakoram	28,250	Chimborazo	Andes	20,560
Kanchenjunga	Himalayas	28,208	McKinley	Alaska	20,320
Makulu	Himalayas	27,824	Mount Logan	Yukon	19,850
Dhaulagiri	Himalayas	26,810	Cotopaxi	Andes	19,344
Nanga Parbat	Himalayas	26,660	Kilimanjaro	Tanzania	19,340
Annapurna	Himalayas	26,502	Antisana	Andes	18,713
Nanda Devi	Himalayas	25,645	Citlaltepetl	S. Madre	18,700
Kamet	Himalayas	25,447	Elbruz	Caucasus	18,480
Namcha Barwa	China	25,445	Demavend	Elburz	18,384
Minya Konka	China	24,900	Mount St. Elias	Alaska	18,008
Pik Kommunizma	Pamirs	24,590	Popocatapetl	S. Madre	17,887
Pik Pobedy	Tian Shan	24,406	Foraker	Alaska	17,395
Aconcagua	Andes	22,834	Mount Lucania	Yukon	17,150
Bonete	Andes	22,545	Tolima	Andes	17,109
Ojos del Salado	Andes	22,516	Kenya	Kenya	17,058
Huascaran	Andes	22,204	Ararat	Armenia	16,945
Llullaillaco	Andes	22,057	Vinson Massif	Antarctica	16,863

THE LONGEST RIVERS

River	Outflow	Length in Miles
Nile	Mediterranean	4,150
Amazon	Atlantic	3,900
Missouri-Mississippi–Red Rock	Gulf of Mexico	3,800
Yangtze	North Pacific	3,400
Ob-Irtysh	Arctic	3,200
Hwang-ho	North Pacific	2,900
Congo	Atlantic	2,900
Amur	,, ,,	2,800
Lena	Arctic	2,800
Mekong	China Sea	2,800
Niger	Gulf of Guinea	2,600
Mackenzie	Beaufort Sea	2,500
Paraná	Atlantic	2,450
Volga	Caspian Sea	2,300
Yenisei	Arctic	2,300
Madeira	Amazon	2,100
Yukon	Bering Sea	2,000
Arkansas	Mississippi	2,000
Colorado	Gulf of California	2,000
St. Lawrence	Gulf of St. Lawrence	1,800
Rio Grande del Norte	Gulf of Mexico	1,800
São Francisco	Atlantic	1,800
Salween	Gulf of Martaban	1,800
Danube	Black Sea	1,725
Euphrates	Persian Gulf	1,700
Indus	Arabian Sea	1,700
Brahmaputra	Bay of Bengal	1,680
Zambesi	Indian Ocean	1,630
Murray	Indian Ocean	1,600

Severn	Bristol Channel	220
Thames	North Sea (Thames Head to Nore)	215

SOME FAMOUS BRIDGES

Among the outstanding *suspension bridges* of the World are the Verrazano Narrows Bridge, New York (main span, 4,260 ft.); the Golden Gate Bridge, San Francisco (4,200 ft.); Mackinac Bridge, Michigan (3,800 ft.); Bosporus, Turkey (3,523 ft.); George Washington Bridge, New York (3,500 ft.); the Ponte Salazar (Tagus Bridge), Portugal (3,323 ft.); Forth Road Bridge, Scotland (3,300 ft.); Severn Bridge, England and Wales (3,240 ft.); Tacoma Bridge, Washington, U.S.A. (2,800 ft.); Orinoco Bridge, Venezuela (2,336 ft.) and the Kanmon Bridge, Japan (2,336 ft.). Lengths shown above are all those of the main or longest span.

The Transbay Bridge (*suspension and cantilever*), crossing San Francisco Bay from Oaklands to San Francisco is 7½ miles long, with spans of 2,310 ft. each.

Among important *steel arch* bridges are the Bayonne Bridge, from New Jersey to Staten Island, U.S.A. (1,652 ft.); Sydney Harbour Bridge, Australia (1,650 ft.); the Runcorn-Widnes Bridge, England (1,082 ft.); and the Glen Canyon Bridge over the Colorado River, U.S.A. (1,028 ft.). Major *concrete trestle* bridges include the Lake Portchartain Causeway, U.S.A. of 2,170 spans extending 24 miles and the Oosterscheldebrug, Netherlands, 3⅜ miles long. Gladesville Bridge, Sydney, Australia, is a *concrete arch* bridge of 1,000 ft. span The Tay Road Bridge in Scotland is a *steel box girder* bridge supported on twin piers (42 spans), 7,365 ft. long.

The Chesapeake Bay Bridge–Tunnel (17·6 miles long) joining Cape Charles, Virginia, to Chesapeake Beach has 12·5 miles of *concrete trestle* bridge.

PRINCIPAL HEIGHTS ABOVE SEA LEVEL

	Feet
Europe: Alps—Mont Blanc	15,782
England: Scafell Pike	3,210
Wales: Snowdon	3,560
Scotland: Ben Nevis	4,406
Ireland: Carrantuohill	3,414
Asia: Everest	29,028
Africa: Kilimanjaro	19,340
North America: McKinley	20,320
South America: Aconcagua	22,834
Australia: Kosciusko	7,316
New Zealand: Cook	12,349
Oceania: Carstenz, Indonesia	16,500
Antarctica: Vinson Massif	16,863

THE LARGEST ISLANDS

Name of Island	Ocean	Area in Sq. miles
Greenland (Danish)	Arctic	840,000
New Guinea	Pacific	305,000
Borneo (various)		290,000
Madagascar	Indian	228,000
Baffin Land (Canadian)	Arctic	190,000
Sumatra (Indonesian)	Indian	163,000
Honshū (Japanese)	Pacific	88,839
Great Britain	Atlantic	88,745
Victoria (Canadian)	Arctic	80,000
Ellesmere (Canadian)	Arctic	77,000
Sulawesi (Indonesian)	Indian	69,000
South Island, N.Z.	Pacific	58,093
Java (Indonesian)	Indian	48,800
North Island, N.Z.	Pacific	44,281
Cuba	Atlantic	44,000
Newfoundland (Canadian)	Atlantic	42,750
Luzon (Phillippine)	Pacific	40,400
Iceland	Atlantic	40,000
Mindanao (Philippine)	Pacific	36,500
Ireland	Atlantic	32,600

GREAT SHIP CANALS OF THE WORLD

Canal	Opened year	Length, miles	Depth, feet	Width,§ feet
North Sea (Netherlands)	1876	14½	40	88
Corinth (Greece)	1893	4	26	72
Elbe-Lübeck (Germany)	1900	41	10	72
Gota (Sweden)*	1832	55**	10	47
Kiel (Germany)†	1895	61	45	150
Manchester (England)	1894	35½	30	120
Panama (U.S.A.)	1914	50½	45	300
Juliana (Netherlands)	1935	20	16	52
Sault Ste. Marie (U.S.A.)#	1855	1½	22	100
Sault Ste. Marie (Canada)	1895	1½	22	150
Suez (Egypt)	1869	100	42	197
Terneuzen-Gent (Netherlands-Belgium)	1895	18½	36	100
Welland (Canada)‡	1887	27½	25	200

* Reconstructed 1916. † Reconstructed 1914. ‡ Reconstructed 1929–30. # Reconstructed 1896.
** Length, including lake sections, 240 miles. § At the bottom.

WATERFALLS OF THE WORLD

In order of height

Fall	Locality	Height in Feet	
Angel Falls	Venezuela	3,212	
Ribbon Fall	Yosemite, U.S.A.	1,612	
Upper Yosemite	Yosemite, U.S.A.	1,430	(a)
Gavarnie	Pyrenees	1,385	
Wollomombie	New South Wales	1,100	(b)
Staubbach	Switzerland	980	
Seward	Peru	887	
Vettisfoss	Norway	856	
King Edward VIII	Guyana	840	
Gersoppa	Mysore, India	830	(c)
Sutherland	New Zealand	815	(d)
Kaieteur (Köituök)	Guyana	741	
Kalambo	Tanzania	704	(e)
Maletsunyane	Lesotho	630	
Bridalveil	Yosemite, U.S.A.	620	
Nevada	Yosemite, U.S.A.	594	
Skjeggedalsfoss	Norway	525	
Eas-Coul-Aulin	Scotland	511	(f)

In order of volume

Fall	Locality	Width in Yards
Khon Cataracts (1)	Indo-China	15,840
Guayra (2)	Brazil	5,300
Victoria (3)	Rhodesia—Zambia	1,760
Niagara (4)	Canada—U.S.A.	1,200

On the basis of annual flow the Guayra Falls in Brazil are the most spectacular, with a flow of 470,000 cubic feet per second (annual average).

NOTES.—(a) Out of a total fall of 2,565 ft.;
(b) 1,700 ft.; (c) 960 ft.; (d) 1,904 ft.;
(e) 3,000 ft; (f) 658 ft.

(1) Height, 50–70 ft.; (2) 90–130 ft.
(3) 236–354 ft.; (4) 158–175 ft.

LONGEST RAILWAY TUNNELS

E.R. = Eastern Region; L.M.R. = London Midland Region;
S.R. = Southern Region; W.R. = Western Region

United Kingdom

		Miles	Yards
Severn	W.R.	4	628
Totley	L.M.R.	3	950
Standedge	E.R.	3	66
Woodhead	L.M.R.	3	66
Sodbury	W.R.	2	924
Disley	L.M.R.	2	346
Bramhope	E.R.	2	241
Ffestiniog	L.M.R.	2	338
Cowburn	L.M.R.	2	182
Sevenoaks	S.R.	1	1693
Rhondda	W.R.	1	1683
Morley	E.R.	1	1609
Box	W.R.	1	1452
Catesby	L.M.R.	1	1240
Dove Holes	L.M.R.	1	1224
Littleborough (Summit)	L.M.R.	1	1125
Vict. Waterloo (Liverpool)	L.M.R.	1	946
Ponsbourne	E.R.	1	924
Polhill	S.R.	1	851
Queensbury	E.R.	1	741
Merthyr	W.R.	1	737
Kilsby	L.M.R.	1	666
Bleamoor	L.M.R.	1	869
Shepherd's Well	S.R.	1	609
Gildersome	E.R.	1	571
Strood	S.R.	1	569
Clayton	S.R.	1	499
Oxted	S.R.	1	501
Sydenham	S.R.	1	381
Drewton	E.R.	1	354

		Miles	Yards
Merstham New (Quarry)	S.R.	1	353
Wapping	L.M.R.	1	351
Mersey	Mersey	1	350
Greenock	Scottish Region	1	351
Bradway	E.R.	1	267
Slough	L.M.R.	1	255
Watford, New	L.M.R.	1	230
Caerphilly	W.R.	1	173
Llangyfelach	W.R.	1	192
Abbot's Cliff	S.R.	1	182
Corby	L.M.R.	1	166
Halton	L.M.R.	1	176
Wenvoe	W.R.	1	107
Sapperton	W.R.	1	100
Sharnbrook	L.M.R.	1	100

(The London Underground *Northern Line* between Morden and East Finchley by the City Branch serves 25 stations and uses tunnels totalling 17½ miles in length).

The World

		Miles	Yards
Simplon	Switzerland-Italy	12	560
Apennine	Italy	11	880
St. Gotthard	Switzerland	9	550
Lötschberg	Switzerland	9	130
Mont Cenis	Italy	8	870
Cascade	United States	7	1410
Arlberg	Austria	6	650
Moffat	United States	6	200
Shimizu	Japan	6	70

DISTANCE OF THE HORIZON

The limit of distance to which one can see varies with the height of the spectator. The greatest distance at which an object on the surface of the sea, or of a level plain, can be seen by a person whose eyes are at a height of 5 feet from the same level is nearly 3 miles. At a height of 20 feet the range is increased to nearly 6 miles, and an approximate rule for finding the range of vision for small heights is to increase the square root of the number of feet that the eye is above the level surface by a third of itself, the result being the distance of the horizon in miles, but is slightly in excess of that in the table below, which is computed by a more precise formula. The table may be used conversely to show the distance of an object of given height that is just visible from a point in the surface of the earth or sea. Refraction is taken into account both in the approximate rule and in the Table.

At a height of	the range is	At a height of	the range is	At a height of	the range is
5 ft.	2·9 miles	500 ft.	29·5 miles	4,000 ft.	83·3 miles
20 „	5·9 „	1,000 „	41·6 „	5,000 „	93·1 „
50 „	9·3 „	2,000 „	58·9 „	20,000 „	186·2 „
100 „	13·2 „	3,000 „	72·1 „		

RULERS OF FOREIGN COUNTRIES

Country	Ruler	Born	Acceded
Afghanistan........	Mohammad Daoud, *President*...............	1909	July 17, 1973
Albania...........	Haxhi Lleshi, *Head of State*...........	..	July 24, 1953
Algeria...........	Col. Houari Boumedienne, *President, Council of Revolution*.............................	..	June 19, 1965
Angola...........	Dr. Agostino Neto, *President*................	..	Nov. 11, 1975
Argentine........	Lt. Gen. Jorge Rafael Videla, *President*	..	Mar. 29, 1976
Austria...........	Dr. Rudolf Kirchschläger, *President*..........	1915	June 23, 1974
Bahrain...........	Shaikh Isa bin Sulman Al Khalifah, *Amir*	1932	Dec. 16, 1961
Belgium..........	Baudouin, *King*.............................	Sept. 7, 1930	July 17, 1951
Benin............	Lt. Col. Mathieu Kerekou, *President*...........	..	Oct. 26, 1972
Bhutan...........	Jigme Singye Wangchuck, *King*.............	1955	July 24, 1972
Bolivia...........	Col. Hugo Banzer, *President*................	1928	Aug. 22, 1971
Brazil............	Gen. Ernesto Geisel, *President*.............	Aug. 3, 1908	Mar. 15, 1974
Bulgaria..........	Todor Zhivkov, *Chairman, Council of State*....	..	July 7, 1971
Burma...........	U Ne Win, *President*......................	..	Mar. 2, 1962
Burundi..........	Col. Michel Micombero, *President*.........	1940	Nov. 28, 1966
Cambodia........	Khieu Samphan, *Head of State*............	..	April 5, 1976
Cameroon........	Ahmadou Ahidjo, *President*...............	..	May 5, 1960
Cape Verde Islands.	Aristides Pereira, *President*................	1924	July 5, 1975
Cent. African Rep..	Marshal Jean Bedel Bokassa, *President*.........	..	Jan. 1, 1966
Chad............	Gen. Felix Malloum, *Head of State*...........	..	April 16, 1975
Chile............	Gen. Augusto Pinochet (Ugarte), *President*.....	Nov. 25, 1915	Sept. 11, 1973
Colombia.........	Dr. Alfonso López Michelsen, *President*......	..	Aug. 7, 1974
Congo...........	Marien Ngouabi, *President*..................	..	Jan. 1, 1969
Costa Rica........	Daniel Oduber Quirós, *President*.............	1923	May 8, 1974
Cuba............	Dr. Osvaldo Dorticos Torrado, *President*......	..	July 17, 1959
Czechoslovakia....	Gustáv Husák, *President*...................	Jan. 10, 1913	May 29, 1975
Denmark.........	Margrethe II, *Queen*......................	April 16, 1940	Jan. 14, 1972
Dominican Republic	Joaquin Balaguer, *President*...............	Sept. 1, 1907	June 1, 1966
Ecuador..........	*Military Junta*............................	..	Jan. 11, 1976
Egypt............	Anwar El Sadat, *President*..................	..	Oct. 15, 1970
Equatorial Guinea..	Francisco Macias Nguema, *President*.........	1925	Oct. 12, 1968
Ethiopia.........	Brig.-Gen. Terferi Benti, *President of Provisional Military Council*	..	Nov. 28, 1974
Finland..........	Dr. U. K. Kekkonen, *President*..............	1900	Feb. 16, 1956
Formosa..........	Yen Chia-kan.................	1905	Mar. 6, 1975
France...........	Valéry Giscard d'Estaing, *President*.........	Feb. 2, 1926	May 27, 1974
Gabon...........	Omar Bongo, *President*...................	..	Dec. 1967
Germany (Fed. Rep.)	Walter Scheel, *Federal President*...............	July 18, 1919	July 1, 1974
Germany (G.D.R.).	Willi Stoph, *Chairman, Council of State*........	1914	Oct. 3, 1973
Greece...........	Constantine Tsatsos, *President*.............	1899	June 20, 1975
Guatemala........	Gen. Kjell Eugenio Laugerud Garciá, *President* ..	..	July 1, 1974
Guinea...........	Ahmed Sékou Touré, *President*..............	..	Jan. 1961
Guinea-Bissau.....	Luis Cabral, *President of Council of State*......		
Haiti............	Jean Claude Duvalier, *President*...........	1951	April 21, 1971
Honduras.........	Brig.-Gen Juan Melgar Castro, *Head of State*...	..	April 22, 1975
Hungary..........	Pál Losonczi, *President*..................	..	April 1967
Iceland..........	Dr. Kristjan Eldjarn, *President*..............	1917	Aug. 1, 1968
Indonesia........	Gen. Soeharto, *President*..................	June 9, 1921	Mar. 28, 1968
Iran.............	Shahpoor Mohammed Reza Pahlavi, *Shah*...	Oct. 26, 1919	Sept. 16, 1941
Iraq.............	Ahmad Hasan al-Bakr, *President*.............	..	July 17, 1968
Irish Republic.....	Cearbhall O'Dálaigh, *President*.............	1911	Dec. 19, 1974
Israel...........	Prof. Ephraim Katzir, *President*.............	May 16, 1916	May 24, 1973
Italy.............	Giovanni Leone, *President*...............	1908	Dec. 24, 1971
Ivory Coast.......	Felix Houphouët-Boigny, *President*.........	..	Nov. 27, 1960
Japan...........	Hirohito, *Emperor*.......................	April 29, 1901	Dec. 25, 1926
Jordan...........	Hussein, *King*........................	Nov. 14, 1935	Aug. 11, 1952
Korea, South.....	Park, Chung Hee, *President*...............	..	Mar. 22, 1962
Kuwait...........	Sabah as-Salem as Sabah, *Amir*............	1915	Nov. 24, 1965
Laos............	Souphanouvong, *President*................	..	Dec. 2, 1975
Lebanon..........	Elias Sarkis..........................	..	..
Liberia...........	William Richard Tolbert, *President*..........	1913	July 23, 1971
Libya............	Col. Muammar al-Qadhafi, *Chairman of Revolutionary Cmd. Council*......................	..	Sept. 1, 1969
Liechtenstein......	Franz Josef II., *Prince*..................	Aug. 16, 1906	July 26, 1938
Luxemburg........	Jean, *Grand Duke*......................	Jan. 5, 1921	Nov. 1964
Madagascar.......	Capt. de F. Didier Ratsiraka, *Head of State*....	..	June 15, 1975
Maldives.........	Amir Ibrahim Nasir, *President*...............	..	..
Mali............	Col. Moussa Traore, *Chairman, Nat. Lib. Cttee*..	1937	Nov. 20, 1968
Mauritania........	Moktar Ould Daddah, *President*.............	..	Nov. 28, 1958
Mexico...........	José López Portillo, *President*...............	1916	July 4, 1976
Monaco...........	Rainier, *Prince*........................	May 31, 1923	May 9, 1949

RULERS OF FOREIGN COUNTRIES—*continued*

Country	Ruler	Born	Acceded
Mongolia (Outer)...	Yu Tsedenbal, *President*.....................	..	..
Morocco..........	Hassan II, *King*..........................	July 9, 1929	Feb. 26, 1961
Mozambique.......	Samora Machel, *President*...................	1934	June 25, 1975
Nepal.............	Birendra Bir Bikram Shah Deva, *King*........	1945	Jan. 31, 1972
Netherlands........	Juliana, *Queen*...........................	April 30, 1909	Sept. 4, 1948
Nicaragua.........	Gen. Anastasio Somoza Debayle, *President*.....	..	Dec. 1, 1974
Niger.............	Lt.-Col. Seynie Kountché, *Head of State*......	..	April 15, 1974
Norway...........	Olav V., *King*............................	July 2, 1903	Sept. 21, 1957
Oman............	Qaboos bin Said, *Sultan*....................	..	July 23, 1970
Pakistan..........	Fazal Elahi Chaudhry, *President*..............	1905	Aug. 10, 1973
Panama..........	Demetrio Lakas, *President*..................	..	Dec. 18, 1969
Paraguay.........	Gen. Alfredo Stroessner, *President*...........	..	Aug. 15, 1954
Peru.............	Gen. Francisco Morales Bermudez, *President*....	..	Aug. 29, 1975
Philippine Islands...	Ferdinand Marcos, *President*................	1917	Dec. 30, 1965
Poland............	Henryk Jablonski, *Chairman of Council of State*..	1909	Mar. 28, 1972
Portugal..........	Gen. António Ramalho Eanes, *President*......	..	July 1976
Qatar.............	Khalifa bin Hamad Al-Thani, *Amir*...........	..	Oct. 24, 1960
Rumania..........	Nicolae Ceausescu, *President*................	1918	Dec. 9, 1967
Rwanda...........	Maj.-Gen. Juvenal Habyaliman, *President*......	..	July 5, 1973
El Salvador.......	Col. Arturo Armando Molina, *President*.......	..	July 1, 1972
Saudi Arabia.......	Amir Khalid bin Abdul Aziz, *King*............	1912	Mar. 25, 1975
Senegal...........	Leopold Senghor, *President*.................	..	Sept. 5, 1960
Somalia...........	Maj.Gen. Mohamed Siad Barre (*President, Revolutionary Council*......................	..	Oct. 21, 1969
South Africa......	Dr. Nicolaas Diederichs, *President*............	..	April 10, 1975
Spain.............	Juan Carlos I, *King*.......................	Jan. 5, 1938	Nov. 22, 1975
Sudan............	Maj. Gen. Gaafar Mohamed El Nimeri (*President*)	..	May 25, 1969
Sweden...........	Carl XVI Gustaf, *King*....................	April 30, 1946	Sept. 19, 1973
Switzerland........	Rudolf Gnaegi, *President*...................	..	Jan. 1, 1976
Syria.............	Lt. Gen. Hafez al Assad, *President*............	1930	Mar. 14, 1971
Thailand..........	Bhumibol Adulyadej, *King*..................	Dec. 5, 1927	June 9, 1946
Togo.............	General Gnassingbé Eyadéma, *President*........	1937	April 14, 1967
Tunisia...........	Habib Bourguiba, *President*.................	..	July 25, 1957
Turkey...........	Fahri Korutürk, *President*..................	1903	April 6, 1973
United Arab Emirates	Shaikh Zayed bin Sultan Al Nahayyan, *President*.		
United States......	Gerald R. Ford, *President*...................	July 14, 1913	Aug. 9, 1974
Upper Volta.......	Gen. Sangoulé Lamizana, *President*...........	1928	Jan. 3, 1966
Uruguay..........	Dr. Aparicio Méndez......................	..	Sept. 1, 1976
U.S.S.R..........	Nikolai V. Podgorny, *President*...............	1903	Dec. 9, 1965
Vatican City State..	Paul VI, *Pope*............................	Sept. 26, 1897	June 21, 1963
Venezuela.........	Carlos Andrés Pérez, *President*..............	1922	Mar. 12, 1974
Vietnam..........	Ton Duc Thang, *President*..................	1889	Sept. 24, 1969
Yemen A.R.......	Col. Ibrahim Mohammed al Hamdi...........	..	June 13, 1974
Yemen P.D.R......	Salim Rubi'a Ali (*Chairman, Presidential Council*)	..	..
Yugoslavia........	Josip Broz Tito, *President*...................	May 7, 1892	Jan. 14, 1953
Zaïre.............	Gen. Mobutu Sese Seko, *President*............	Oct. 30, 1930	Nov. 25, 1965

PRESIDENTS OF THE FRENCH REPUBLIC

Acceded

Committee of Public Defence..... Sept. 4, 1870
Louis Adolphe Thiers............ Aug. 31, 1871
Maréchal MacMahon............ May 24, 1873
Jules Grévy.................... Jan. 30, 1879
Sadi Carnot (assas.: June 14, 1894).. Dec. 3, 1887
Jean Casimir Périer.............. June 27, 1894
François Felix Faure............. Jan. 17, 1895
Emile Loubet................... Feb. 18, 1899
Armand Fallières................ Jan. 18, 1906
Raymond Poincaré.............. Jan. 17, 1913
Paul Deschanel................. Feb. 18, 1920
Alexandre Millerand............ Sept. 20, 1920
Gaston Doumergue.............. June 13, 1924
Paul Doumer (assas.: May 7, 1932). June 13, 1931
Albert Lebrun (deposed 1940)..... May 10, 1932
Maréchal Pétain, " Vichy " nominee July 11, 1940

[After the liberation of Paris, General Charles de Gaulle entered the capital and formed a provisional government on Sept. 10, 1944. This was regarded as a continuation of the *Third Republic*.] Acceded
Charles de Gaulle, *born* 1890....... Sept. 10, 1944
Félix Gouin.................... Jan. 23, 1946
Georges Bidault, *born* 1899....... June 2, 1946
[A new Constitution (*Fourth Republic*), adopted on Oct. 13, 1946, and amended in 1954, was in force until 1958.] Acceded
Vincent Auriol, *born* 1884......... Jan. 16, 1947
René Coty, *born* 1882........... Jan. 17, 1954
[The *Fifth French Republic* came into being on Oct. 5, 1958, after the approval of its constitution by a national referendum in September, 1958.]
Charles de Gaulle, *born* 1890....... Jan. 8, 1959
Georges Pompidou, *born* 1911..... June 20, 1969
Valéry Giscard d'Estaing, *born* 1926. May 27, 1974

ENGLISH KINGS AND QUEENS A.D. 827 TO 1603

Name	DYNASTY	MARRIED	Access.	Died	Age	Rgnd. Yrs.
	Saxons and Danes					
EGBERT	King of Wessex and all England		827	839	—	12
ETHELWULF	Son of Egbert		839	858	—	19
ETHELBALD	Son of Ethelwulf		858	860	—	2
ETHELBERT	Son of Ethelwulf		858	866	—	8
ETHELRED	Son of Ethelwulf		866	871	—	5
ALFRED THE GREAT	Son of Ethelwulf	Ealhswith of Gaini	871	899	52	28
EDWARD THE ELDER	Son of Alfred the Great	1, Egwyn; 2, Elfled; 3, Eadgifu.	899	925	55	26
ATHELSTAN	Eldest son of Edward the Elder (by 1)		925	940	45	15
EDMUND	Third son of Edward the Elder (by 3)	1, Elgivu; 2, Ethelfled	940	946	25	6
EDRED	Fourth son of Edward the Elder (by 3)		946	955	32	9
EDWY	Son of Edmund (by 1)		955	959	18	3
EDGAR	Second son of Edmund (by 1)	1, Ethelfled; 2, Elfthryth	959	975	32	17
EDWARD THE MARTYR	Son of Edgar (by 1)		975	978	17	4
ETHELRED	Younger son of Edgar (by 2)	1, Elfgifu; 2, Emma, dau. of Richard, Duke of Normandy.	978	1016	48	37
EDMUND IRONSIDE	Eldest son of Ethelred II (by 1)		1016	1016	27	0
CANUTE THE DANE	By conquest and election	1, Elfgifu of Deira; 2, Emma, widow of Ethelred II	1017	1035	40	18
HAROLD I	Son of Canute (by 1)		1035	1040		5
HARDICANUTE	Son of Canute (by 2)		1040	1042	24	2
EDWARD THE CONFESSOR	Son of Ethelred II (by 2)	Edith, dau. of Earl Godwin.	1042	1066	62	24
HAROLD II	Son of Earl Godwin		1066	1066	44	0
	The House of Normandy					
WILLIAM I	Obtained the Crown by Conquest.	Matilda, dau. of Baldwin, Count of Flanders.	1066	1087	60	21
WILLIAM II	Third son of William I.	(Died unmarried)	1087	1100	43	13
HENRY I	Youngest son of William I.	1st Matilda, dau. of Malcolm Canmore, K. of Scotland; 2nd Adelicia, dau. of Godfrey, D. of Louvaine.	1100	1135	67	35
STEPHEN	Third son of Stephen, Count of Blois, by Adela, fourth dau. of William I.	Matilda, dau. of Eustace, Count of Boulogne.	1135	1154	50	19
	The House of Plantagenet					
HENRY II	Son of Geoffrey Plantagenet by Matilda, only dau. of Henry I; his grandmother, Matilda of Scotland, was a lineal descendant of Alfred and Egbert.	Eleanor, dau. of Guienne and divorced Queen of Louis VII of France.	1154	1189	56	35
RICHARD I	Eldest surviving son of Henry II.	Berengaria, dau. of Sancho VI, K. of Navarre.	1189	1199	42	10
JOHN	Sixth and youngest son of Henry II.	1st Avisa, dau. of E. of Gloucester, divorced upon grounds of consanguinity; 2nd Isabella dau. of Aymer, Count of Angoulême.	1199	1216	50	17
HENRY III	Elder son of John.	Eleanor, dau. of Raymond, Count of Provence.	1216	1272	65	56
EDWARD I	Eldest surviving son of Henry III	1st Eleanor, dau. of Ferdinand III, K. of Castile; 2nd Eleanor, dau. of Philip III, the Hardy, K. of France.	1272	1307	68	35
EDWARD II	Eldest surviving son of Edward I.	Isabella, dau. of Philip IV, the Fair, K. of France	1307	1327	43	20

Name	DYNASTY	MARRIED	Access.	Died	Age	Rgnd.
						Yrs.
EDWARD III............	Eldest son of Edward II............	Philippa, dau. of William, Count of Holland and Hainault.	1327	1377	65	50
RICHARD II............	Son of the Black Prince, eldest son of Edward III	1st Anne, dau. of Emp. Charles IV; 2nd Isabel, dau. of Charles VI of France.	1377	dep. 1399 (d. 1400)	34	22
	The House of Lancaster					
HENRY IV............	Son of John of Gaunt, 4th son of Edward III	1st Mary de Bohun, dau. of the E. of Hereford; 2nd Joanna of Navarre, widow of John de Montford, D. of Bretagne.	1399	1413	47	13
HENRY V............	Eldest surviving son of Henry IV............	Katherine, dau. of Charles VI, K. of France....	1413	1422	34	9
HENRY VI............	Only son of Henry V (died 1471)............	Margaret of Anjou, dau. of René, D. of Anjou.	1422	dep. 1461	49	39
	The House of York					
EDWARD IV............	Son of Richard, grandson of Edmund, fifth son of Edward III; and of Anne, great-grand-daughter of Lionel, third son of Edward III.	Elizabeth Widvile (or Woodville), dau. of Sir Richard Widvile and widow of Sir John Grey of Groby.	1461	1483	41	22
EDWARD V............	Eldest son of Edward IV............	(Died unmarried)............	1483	1483	13	75 days
RICHARD III............	Younger brother of Edward IV............	Anne, dau. of the E. of Warwick, and widow of Edward, Prince of Wales, s. of Henry VI	1483	1485	32	2
	The House of Tudor					
HENRY VII............	Son of Edmund, eldest son of Owen Tudor, by Katherine, widow of Henry V; his mother, Margaret Beaufort, was great-grand-daughter of John of Gaunt.	Elizabeth, dau. of Edward IV............	1485	1509	53	24
HENRY VIII............	Only surviving son of Henry VII............	1st Catherine of Aragon, widow of his elder brother Arthur, (divorced); 2nd Anne, dau. of Sir Thomas Boleyn, (beheaded); 3rd Jane, dau. of Sir John Seymour, (died in childbirth of a son, aft. Edward VI); 4th Anne sister of William, D. of Cleves, (divorced); 5th Catharine Howard, niece of the Duke of Norfolk, (beheaded); 6th Catherine, dau. of Sir Thomas Parr and widow of Edward Nevill, Lord Latimer.	1509	1547	56	38
EDWARD VI............	Son of Henry VIII by Jane Seymour	(Died unmarried)............	1547	1553	16	6
JANE............	Grand-daughter of Mary, younger sister of Henry VIII, (beheaded Feb. 12, 1554).	Lord Guildford Dudley............	1553	1554	17	14 days
MARY I............	Daughter of Henry VIII by Katherine of Aragon.	Philip II of Spain.	1553	1558	43	5
ELIZABETH I............	Daughter of Henry VIII by Anne Boleyn..	(Died unmarried)............	1558	1603	69	44

BRITISH KINGS AND QUEENS FROM 1603

Name	DYNASTY	MARRIED	Access.	Died	Age	Rgndr Yrs.
	The House of Stuart					
JAMES I (VI OF SCOT.)	Son of Mary, Queen of Scots, granddaughter of James IV and Margaret, daughter of Henry VII.	Anne, dau. of Frederick II of Denmark	1603	1625	59	22
CHARLES I	Only surviving son of James I	Henrietta-Maria, dau. of Henry IV of France	1625	Beh.1649	48	24
	Commonwealth declared May 19, 1649					
	Oliver Cromwell, Lord Protector, 1653-8					
	Richard Cromwell, Lord Protector, 1658-9					
CHARLES II	Eldest son of Charles I, (restored 1660)	The Infanta Catharine of Portugal, dau. of John IV and sister of Alphonso VI.	1649	1685	55	36
JAMES II (VII OF SCOT.)	Second son of Charles I (Interregnum, Dec. 11, 1688—Feb. 13, 1689)	1st Lady Anne Hyde, dau. of Edward, E. of Clarendon, who died before James ascended the throne; 2nd Mary Beatrice Eleanor d'Este, dau. of Alphonso, D. of Modena.	1685	Dep.1688 Dec.1701	68	3
WILLIAM III and	Son of William Prince of Orange and grandson of Charles I	......	1689	1702	51	13
MARY II	Eldest daughter of James II	......		1694	33	6
ANNE	Second daughter of James II	Prince George of Denmark	1702	1714	49	12
	The House of Hanover					
GEORGE I	Son of Elector of Hanover, by Sophia, daughter of Elizabeth, daughter of James I	Sophia Dorothea, dau. of George William, D. of Celle.	1714	1727	67	13
GEORGE II	Only son of George I	Wilhelmina Caroline, dau. of John Frederick, Margrave of Brandenburg-Anspach.	1727	1760	77	33
GEORGE III	Grandson of George II	Charlotte Sophia, dau. of Charles Lewis Frederick, D. of Mecklenburg-Strelitz.	1760	1820	81	59
GEORGE IV	Eldest son of George III, (Regent from February 5, 1811)	Caroline Amelia Elizabeth, dau. of Charles William Ferdinand, D. of Brunswick-Wolfenbuttel, by Augusta, eldest sister of George III.	1820	1830	67	10
WILLIAM IV	Third son of George III	Amelia Adelaide Louisa Theresa Caroline, dau. of George Frederick Charles, D. of Saxe-Meiningen.	1830	1837	71	7
VICTORIA	Daughter of Edward, 4th son of George III.	Francis Albert Augustus Charles Emmanuel, D. of Saxe, Pr. of Saxe-Cobourg and Gotha.	1837	1901	81	63
	The House of Saxe-Coburg					
EDWARD VII	Eldest son of Victoria.	Princess Alexandra of Denmark.	1901	1910	68	9
	The House of Windsor					
GEORGE V	Surviving son of Edward VII.	H.S.H. Princess Victoria Mary of Teck	1910	1936	70	25
EDWARD VIII	Eldest son of George V (abdicated 1936).	(Mrs. Wallis Warfield, June 3, 1937.)	1936	1972	77	325 days
GEORGE VI	Second son of George V	The Lady Elizabeth Angela Marguerite, dau. of 14th Earl of Strathmore and Kinghorne (HER MAJESTY QUEEN ELIZABETH THE QUEEN MOTHER).	1936	1952	56	15
ELIZABETH II	Elder daughter of George VI	Philip, son of Prince Andrew of Greece (H.R.H. THE DUKE OF EDINBURGH).	1952	WHOM GOD PRESERVE.		

SCOTTISH KINGS AND QUEENS A.D. 1057 TO 1603

SOVEREIGN		MARRIED	Access.	Died
MALCOLM III (CANMORE)	Son of Duncan I	1st Ingibiorg, widow of Thorfinn, Earl of Orkney; 2nd Margaret, sister of Edgar the Atheling.	1057	1093
DONALD BAN	Brother of Malcolm Canmore		1093	—
DUNCAN II	Son of Malcolm Canmore, by first marriage		1094	1094
DONALD BAN	(Restored)		1094	1097
EDGAR	Son of Malcolm Canmore, by second marriage	Died unmarried	1097	1107
ALEXANDER I	Son of Malcolm Canmore	Sybilla, natural daughter of Henry I of England.	1107	1124
DAVID I	Son of Malcolm Canmore	Matilda, daughter of Waltheof, Earl of Northumbria widow of Simon, Earl of Northampton.	1124	1153
MALCOLM IV (THE MAIDEN)	Son of Henry, eldest son of David I	Died unmarried	1153	1165
WILLIAM I (THE LION)	Brother of Malcolm the Maiden	Ermengarde, daughter of Richard, Viscount of Beaumont.	1165	1214
ALEXANDER II	Son of William the Lion	1st Joanna, daughter of King John; 2nd Mary, daughter of Ingelram de Coucy (Picardy).	1214	1249
ALEXANDER III	Son of Alexander II, by second marriage	1st Margaret, daughter of Henry III of England; 2nd Joleta, daughter of the Count de Dreux.	1249	1286
MARGARET, MAID OF NORWAY	Daughter of Eric II of Norway, grand-daughter of Alexander III.	Died unmarried	1286	1290
JOHN BALIOL	Grandson of eldest daughter of David, Earl of Huntingdon, brother of William the Lion.		1292	1296
ROBERT I (BRUCE)	Great-grandson of 2nd daughter of David, Earl of Huntingdon, brother of William the Lion.	1st Isabella, daughter of Donald, Earl of Mar; 2nd Elizabeth de Burgh, sister of Earl of Ulster.	1306	1329
DAVID II	Son of Robert I, by second marriage	1st Joanna, daughter of Edward II of England; 2nd Margaret, widow of Sir John Logie (divorced, 1369).	1329	1371
ROBERT II (STEWART)	Son of Marjorie, daughter of Robert I by first marriage, and Walter the Steward.	1st Elizabeth, dau., of Sir Robert Mure (or More) of Rowallan; 2nd Euphemia, dau., of Hugh, Earl of Ross, widow of John, Earl of Moray.	1371	1390
ROBERT III	(John, Earl of Carrick) son of Robert II.	Annabella, daughter of Sir John Drummond of Stobhall, niece of Margaret Logie.	1390	1406
JAMES I	Son of Robert III	Jane Beaufort, daughter of John, Earl of Somerset, 4th son of John of Gaunt and grandson of Edward III of England.	1406	1437
JAMES II	Son of James I	Mary, daughter of Arnold, Duke of Gueldres.	1437	1460
JAMES III	Eldest son of James II	Margaret, daughter of Christian I of Denmark, Norway and Sweden.	1460	1488
JAMES IV	Eldest son of James III	Margaret Tudor, daughter of Henry VII.	1488	1513
JAMES V	Son of James IV	1st Madeleine, daughter of Francis I of France; 2nd Mary of Lorraine, daughter of Duc de Guise, widow of Duc de Longueville.	1513	1542
MARY	Daughter of James V, by second marriage	1st Francis, Dauphin of France; 2nd Henry, Lord Darnley; 3rd James, Earl of Bothwell.	1542	1587
JAMES VI (Ascended the Throne of England 1603)	Son of Mary, by second marriage	Anne, daughter of Frederick II of Denmark.	1567	1625

WELSH SOVEREIGNS AND PRINCES

WALES was ruled by Sovereign Princes from the "earliest times" until the death of Llywelyn in 1282, The first English Prince of Wales was the son of Edward I, and was born in Caernarvon town on April 25, 1284. According to a discredited legend, he was presented to the Welsh chieftains as their Prince, in fulfilment of a promise that they should have a Prince who "could not speak a word of English" and should be native born. This son, who afterwards became Edward II, was created "Prince of Wales and Earl of Chester" at the famous Lincoln Parliament on February 7, 1301. The title Prince of Wales is borne after individual conferment and is not inherited at birth; it was conferred on Prince Charles by Her Majesty the Queen on July 26, 1958. He was invested at Caernarvon on July 1, 1969.

INDEPENDENT PRINCES, A.D. 844 to 1282		ENGLISH PRINCES, SINCE A.D. 1301	
Rhodri the Great	844–878	Edward, b. 1284 (Edwd. II), cr. Pr. of Wales	1301
Anarawd, son of Rhodri	878–916	Edward the Black Prince, s. of Edward III	1343
Hywel Dda (or the Good)	916–950	Richard (Richard II), s. of the Black Prince	1377
Iago ab Idwal (or Ieuaf)	950–979	Henry of Monmouth (Henry V)	1399
Hywel ab Ieuaf, the Bad	979–985	Edward of Westminster, son of Henry VI	1454
Cadwallon, his brother	985–986	Edward of Westminster (Edward V)	1472
Maredudd ab Owain ap Hywel Dda	986–999	Edward, son of Richard III (d. 1484)	1483
Cynan ap Hywel ab Ieuaf	999–1008	Arthur Tudor, son of Henry VII	1489
Llewelyn ap Sitsyhlt	1018–1023	Henry Tudor (Hen. VIII), s. of Henry VII	1503
Iago ab Idwal ap Meurig	1023–1039	Henry Stuart, son of James I (d. 1612)	1610
Gruffydd ap Llywelyn ap Seisyll	1039–1063	Charles Stuart (Charles I), s. of James I	1616
Bleddyn ap Cynfyn	1063–1075	Charles (Charles II), son of Charles I	1630
Trahaern ap Caradog	1075–1081	James Francis Edward, "The Old Pretender"	
Gruffydd ap Cynan ab Iago	1081–1137	(d. 1766)	1688
Owain Gwynedd	1137–1170	George Augustus (Geo. II), s. of George I	1714
Dafydd ab Owain Gwynedd	1170–1194	Frederick Lewis, s. of George II (d. 1751)	1727
Llwelyn Fawr, the Great	1194–1240	George William Frederick (George III)	1751
Dafydd ap Llywelyn	1240–1246	George Augustus Frederick (George IV)	1762
Llywelyn ap Gruffyddap Llywelyn	1246–1282	Albert Edward (Edward VII)	1841
		George (George V)	1901
		Edward (Edward VIII)	1910
		Charles Philip Arthur George	1958

THE FAMILY OF QUEEN VICTORIA

QUEEN VICTORIA *was born* May 24, 1819; *succeeded* to the Throne June 20, 1837; *married* Feb. 10, 1840 Albert, PRINCE CONSORT (*born* Aug. 26, 1819, *died* Dec. 14, 1861); *died* Jan. 22, 1901. Her Majesty had issue:—

1. H.R.H. Princess Victoria (*Princess Royal*), born Nov. 21, 1840, married, 1858, Frederick, German Emperor; died Aug. 5, 1901, leaving issue:—

(1) H.I.M. William II., *German Emperor* 1888–1918, born Jan. 27, 1859, died June 4, 1941, having married Princess Augusta Victoria of Schleswig-Holstein-Sonderburg-Augustenburg (born 1858, died 1921), and secondly, Princess Hermine of Reuss (born 1887, died 1947). The late German Emperor's family:—

(a) The late Prince William (*Crown Prince* 1888–1918), born May 6, 1882, married Duchess Cecilia of Mecklenburg-Schwerin (who died May 6, 1954; died July 20, 1951. (The Crown Prince's children:—Prince Wilhelm, born July 4, 1906, died 1940; Prince Louis Ferdinand, born Nov. 9, 1907, married (1938) Grand Duchess Kira (died Sept. 8, 1967), daughter of Grand Duke Cyril of Russia (and has issue four sons and two daughters); Prince Hubertus, born Sept. 30 1909, died April 8, 1950; Prince Frederick George, born Dec. 19, 1911, died April 1966; Princess Alexandrine Irene, born April 7, 1915; Princess Cecilia, born Sept. 5, 1917.)

(b) The late Prince Eitel Frederick, born July 7, 1883, married Duchess Sophie of Oldenburg (marriage dissolved 1926); died Dec. 7, 1942.

(c) The late Prince Adalbert (born July 14, 1884, died Sept. 22, 1948), married Duchess Adelaide of Saxe-Meiningen. (Prince Adalbert's children:—Princess Victoria Marina, born Sept. 11, 1917; Prince Wiliiam Victor, born Feb. 15, 1919.)

(d) The late Prince Augustus William, born Jan. 29, 1887, married Princess Alexandra of Schleswig-Glucksburg (marriage dissolved 1920); died March, 1949. (Prince Augustus's son is Prince Alexander, born Dec. 26, 1912.)

(e) The late Prince Oscar, born July 27, 1888, married Countess von Ruppin, died Jan. 27, 1958. (Prince Oscar's children:—Prince Oscar, born July 12, 1915, died 1939; Prince Burchard, born Jan. 8, 1917; Princess Herzeleida, born Dec. 25, 1918; Prince William, born Jan. 30, 1922.)

(f) The late Prince Joachim, born Dec. 17, 1890, married Princess Marie of Anhalt, died July 17, 1920 (leaving issue).

(g) Princess Victoria, born Sept. 13, 1892, married (1913) the then reigning Duke of Brunswick. (Princess Victoria's children:—Prince Ernest, born March 18, 1914, married Princess Ortrud von Glucksburg, 1951; Prince George, born March 25, 1915; Princess Frederica, born April 18, 1917, married Paul I., King of the Hellenes (*see* p. 215); Prince Christian Oskar, born Sept 1, 1919; Prince Welf Heinrich, born March 11, 1923, married Princess Alexandra of Ysemburg, 1960).

(2) The late Princess Charlotte, born July 24, 1860, married (1878) the late Duke of Saxe-Meiningen, died Oct. 1, 1919. (Princess Charlotte's daughter, Princess Feodora, born May 12, 1879, married (1898) the late Prince Henry XXX. of Reuss, died Aug. 26, 1945.)

(3) The late Prince Henry, born Aug. 14, 1862, married (1888) the late Princess Irene of Hesse, died April 20, 1929 (issue, Prince Waldemar, born March 20, 1889, died May 2, 1945; Prince Sigismund, born Nov. 27, 1896).

(4) The late Princess Victoria, born April 12, 1866, married firstly (1890) Prince Adolphus of Schaumburg-Lippe, secondly (1927) Alexander Zubkov, died Nov. 13, 1929.

(5) The late Princess Sophia, born June 14, 1870

married (1889) the late Constantine, *King of the Hellenes*, died Jan. 13, 1932 leaving issue:—

(a) The late George II., *King of the Hellenes* 1922–24 and 1935–47, born July 7, 1890, married Princess Elisabeth of Roumania (marriage dissolved 1935); died April 1, 1947.

(b) The late Alexander, *King of the Hellenes* 1917–1920, born Aug. 1, 1893, married (1919) Aspasia Manos; died Oct. 25, 1920, leaving issue Princess Alexandra (born 1921) who married, March 20, 1944, King Petar II. of Yugoslavia.

(c) Princess Helena, born May 2, 1896, married (1921) late King Carol of Roumania, (marriage dissolved 1928), having issue, King Michael, G.C.V.O., born Oct. 25, 1921, married (1948) Princess Anne of Bourbon Parma, and has issue, Princess Marguerite, born March 26, 1949, Princess Helene, born Nov. 15, 1950, and Princess Irina, born Feb. 28, 1953.

(d) The late Paul (*Paul I., King of the Hellenes*), born Dec. 4, 1901, *acceded* April 1, 1947, married Jan. 9. 1938, Princess Frederica of Brunswick (*see* p. 214), and died Mar. 6, 1964, leaving issue Constantine (*Constantine XIII.*), born June 2, 1940, married, Sept. 18, 1964, H.R.H. Princess Anne-Marie of Denmark, and has issue; Sophia, born Nov. 2, 1938, married (1962) Don Juan Carlos, Prince of Spain, and has issue; and Irene, born May 11, 1942.

(e) Princess Eirene, born Feb. 13, 1904, married (1939) the Duke of Aosta, and has issue.

(f) Princess Catherine, born May 4, 1913, married (1947) Major R. C. A. Brandram and has issue.

(6) The late Princess Margarete, born April 22 1872, married (1839) the late Prince Frederick Charles of Hesse, died Jan. 21, 1954 (issue the late Prince Frederick William, born 1893, died 1916; the late Prince Maximilian, born 1894, died 1914; Prince Philipp, born 1896, married (1925) Princess Mafalda, daughter of King Victor Emmanuel III. of Italy (and has issue, Prince Maurice, born 1926, and Prince Henry, born 1927); Prince Wolfgang, born 1896; Prince Richard, born May 14, 1901).

2. H.M. KING EDWARD VII. (*see* p. 216).

3. H.R.H. Princess Alice, born April 25, 1843, married Prince Louis (afterwards reigning Grand Duke) of Hesse; died Dec. 14, 1878. Issue:—

(i) Victoria Alberta, born April 5, 1863, married Admiral of the Fleet the late Marquess of Milford Haven, died Sept. 24, 1950, leaving issue:—

(a) Alice (*H.R.H. Princess Andrew of Greece*), born Feb. 25, 1885, married Prince Andrew of Greece; died Dec. 5, 1969, leaving issue (*see* p. 217).

(b) Lady Louise Mountbatten (*Queen of Sweden*), born July 13, 1889; married Nov. 3, 1923, H.R.H. The Crown Prince of Sweden, now King Gustaf VI. Adolf (died Sept. 15, 1973); died March 7, 1965.

(c) George, Marquess of Milford Haven, G.C.V.O., born Nov. 6, 1892, Capt. R.N., married (1916) Countess Nadejda (died Jan. 22, 1963), daughter of late Grand Duke Michael of Russia; died April 8, 1938, leaving issue:—Lady Elizabeth, born 1917; David Michael, Marquess of Milford Haven, O.B.E., D.S.C., Lieutenant, R.N. ret.), born 1919, died April 14, 1970, leaving issue, George Ivar Louis, *Marquess of Milford Haven, b.* 1961; Lord Ivar Mountbatten, *b.* 1963.

(d) Louis, Admiral of the Fleet Earl Mountbatten of Burma, K.G., P.C., G.C.B., O.M., G.C.S.I., G.C.I.E., G.C.V.O., D.S.O., born June 25, 1900, Personal A.D.C. to the Queen, Governor of the Isle of Wight; married July 18, 1922, Edwina Cynthia Annette (died Feb. 20, 1960), daughter of Lord Mount Temple, and has issue two daughters, the Lady Patricia (Lady Brabourne), born 1924 and the Lady Pamela Hicks, born 1929.

(ii) Elizabeth Fedorovna (*Grand Duchess Serius of Russia*), born Nov. 1, 1864; died July 1918.

(iii) Irene (*Princess Henry of Prussia*), born July 11, 1866, married the late Prince Henry of Prussia, and died Nov. 11, 1953 (*see* p. 214).

(iv) Ernest Ludwig, Grand Duke of Hesse, born Nov. 25, 1868, died Oct. 9, 1937, having married (1905) Princess Eleonore of Solms-Hohensolmslich, with issue (a) George, Grand Duke of Hesse, born Nov. 8, 1906, married Princess Cecilie of Greece and Denmark (*see* p. 217); *accidentally killed* (with mother, wife and two sons) Nov. 16, 1937; (b) Ludwig, Grand Duke of Hesse, born Nov. 20, 1908, married (Nov. 17, 1937) Margaret, daughter of 1st Lord Geddes; died May 30, 1968.

(v) Alix (*Tsaritsa of Russia*), born June 6, 1872, married (Nov. 25, 1894) the late Nicholas II. (*Tsar of All the Russias*), assassinated July 16, 1918, with the Tsar and their issue (Grand Duchess Olga; Grand Duchess Tatiana; Grand Duchess Marie; Grand Duchess Anastasia, and the Tsarevitch).

(vi) Mary, born May 24, 1874, died Nov. 15, 1878.

4. Admiral of the Fleet H.R.H. Prince Alfred, *Duke of Edinburgh*, born Aug. 6, 1844, married Jan. 2, 1874, Marie Alexandrovna (died Oct. 25, 1920), only daughter of Alexander II., Emperor of Russia; succeeded as *Duke of Saxe-Coburg and Gotha* Aug. 22, 1893; died July 30, 1900, leaving issue:—

(1) Alfred (*Prince of Saxe-Coburg*), born Oct. 15, 1874, died Feb. 6, 1899.

(2) Marie (*Queen of Roumania*), born Oct. 29, 1875, married (1893) the late King Ferdinand of Roumania; died July 18, 1938, having issue:—

(a) King Carol II. of Roumania, K.G., born Oct. 15, 1893, married (1921) Princess Helena of Greece (*see* col. 1), died April 4, 1953.

(b) Elisabeth (*Queen of the Hellenes*), born Oct. 11, 1894, married (1921) the late King George II of the Hellenes, died Nov. 15, 1956.

(c) Marie, born Jan. 8, 1900, married (1922) the late King Alexander of Yugoslavia, died June 22, 1961 (having issue:—Petar, King of Yugoslavia, born Sept. 6, 1923, married (1944) Princess Alexandra of Greece died Nov. 5, 1970, leaving issue, Prince Alexander, born July 17, 1945; Prince Tomislav, born Jan. 19, 1928, married (1957) Princess Margarita of Baden (*see* p. 217) and has issue, Prince Nicholas, born 1958; Prince Andrej, born 1929, married 1956, Princess Christina of Hesse).

(d) H.R.H. Prince Nicolas, born Aug. 7, 1903.

(e) H.R.H. Princess Ileana, born Jan. 5, 1909; married 1st, Archduke Anton of Austria (having issue:—Stephen, born Aug. 15, 1932): 2nd, Dr. Stefan Issarescu.

(f) Prince Mircea, born Jan. 3, 1913, died 1916.

(3) Victoria, born Nov. 25, 1876, married (1894) Grand Duke of Hesse and (1905) the late Grand Duke Cyril of Russia; died March 2. 1936, having issue:—

(a) Marie, born Feb. 2, 1907, married (1925) Prince Friedrich Carl of Leiningen, died Oct. 27, 1951.

(b) Kira Cyrillovna, born May 22, 1909, married (1938) Prince Ludwig of Germany, died Sept. 8, 1967.

(c) Vladimir Cyrillovitch, born Aug. 17, 1917, married (1948) Princess Leonide Bagration-Moukhransky, and has issue, a daughter.

(4) Alexandra, born Sept. 1, 1878, married (1896) the late Prince of Hohenlohe Langenburg: died April 16, 1942, leaving issue:—

(a) Gottfried, born March 24, 1897, died May 11, 1960.

(b) Maria (*Princess Friedrich of Holstein-Glucksburg*), born Jan. 18, 1899; died Nov. 8, 1967.

(c) Princess Alexandra, born April 2, 1901; died Oct. 26, 1963.

(d) Princess Irma, born July 4, 1902.

(5) Princess Beatrice, born April 20, 1884, married 1909) Infante Alfonso Maria of Orleans (who died 1975), died July 13, 1966, leaving issue.

5. H.R.H. Princess Helena Augusta Victoria, born May 25, 1846, married July 5, 1866, General H.R.H. *Prince Christian of Schleswig-Holstein* (died Oct. 28, 1917); died June 9, 1923. Issue:—

(i) H.H. Prince Christian Victor, born April 14, 1867, died Oct. 29, 1900.

(ii) H.H. Prince Albert, born Feb. 26, 1869, died April 27, 1931.

(iii) H.H. Princess Helena Victoria, born May 3, 1870; died March 13, 1948.

(iv) H.H. Princess Marie Louise, born Aug. 12, 1872; died Dec. 8, 1956.

(v) H.H. Prince Harold, born May 12, died May 20, 1876.

6. H.R.H. Princess Louise, born March 18, 1848, married March 21, 1871, the Marquess of Lorne, afterwards the 9th Duke of Argyll K.G.; died Dec. 3, 1939, without issue.

7. Field Marshal H.R.H. Prince Arthur, *Duke of Connaught*, born May 1, 1850, married March 13, 1879, H.R.H. Princess Louisa of Prussia (died March 14, 1917); died Jan. 16, 1942. Issue:—

(i) H.R.H. Princess Margaret, born Jan. 15, 1882, married H.R.H. the Crown Prince of Sweden, later King Gustaf VI. Adolf, K.G., G.C.B., G.C.V.O. (who died Sept. 15, 1973) died May 1, 1920, leaving issue:—

(a) Duke of Westerbotten, born April 22, 1906, married (1932) Princess Sybil of Saxe-Coburg-Gotha (who died Nov. 28 1972), died Jan. 26, 1947, leaving issue one son, now King Carl XVI Gustaf of Sweden, and 4 daughters.

(b) Duke of Upland (Count Sigvard Bernadotte), born June 7, 1907.

(c) Princess Ingrid (*Queen Mother of Denmark*), born March 28, 1910, married (1935) the late King Frederick IX of Denmark, who died Jan. 14, 1972 and has issue 3 daughters.

(d) Duke of Halland, born Feb. 28, 1912.

(e) Duke of Dalecarlia, born Oct. 31, 1916.

(ii) Major-Gen. H.R.H. Prince Arthur, born Jan. 13, 1883; married Oct. 15, 1913, H.H. the Duchess of Fife; died Sept. 12, 1938, leaving issue (see below).

(iii) H.R.H. Princess Patricia (*Lady Patricia Ramsay*) born March 17, 1886, married Feb. 27, 1919, Adm. Hon Sir Alexander Ramsay (who died Oct. 8, 1972), died Jan. 12, 1974, leaving issue Alexander Arthur Alfonso David, born Dec. 21, 1919.

8. H.R.H. Prince Leopold, *Duke of Albany*, born April 7, 1853, married Princess Helena of Waldeck (died Sept. 1, 1922); died March 28, 1884. Issue:—

(i) H.R.H. Princess Alice (*Countess of Athlone*), V.A., G.C.V.O., G.B.E., Commandant in Chief Women's Transport Service. Chancellor of the University of the West Indies, born Feb. 25, 1883, married Feb. 10, 1904, Maj.-Gen. the Earl of Athlone (who died Jan. 16, 1957), having issue—

(a) Lady May Helen Emma, born Jan. 23, 1906 married (1931) Sir Henry Abel-Smith, K.C.M.G., K.C.V.O., D.S.O., and has issue a son and 2 daughters.

(b) The late *Viscount Trematon*, born 1907, died April 15, 1928.

(ii) Charles Edward, *Duke of Saxe-Coburg-Gotha* (1900–1918), born July 19, 1884, married (1905) Princess Victoria of Schleswig-Holstein, died March 6, 1954, leaving surviving issue 2 sons and 2 daughters.

9. H.R.H. Princess Beatrice, born April 14, 1857, married July 23, 1885, H.R.H. Prince Henry of Battenberg (born Oct. 5, 1858, died Jan. 20, 1896); died Oct. 26, 1944, leaving issue:—

(i) Alexander, *Marquess of Carisbrooke*, born Nov. 23, 1886, married Lady Irene Denison (died July 15, 1956); died Feb. 23, 1960, leaving issue a daughter, Lady Iris Mountbatten, born Jan. 13, 1920.

(ii) Victoria Eugénie, V.A., born Oct. 24, 1887, married May 31, 1906. His late Majesty Alfonso XIII. (*King of Spain* 1886–1931; born 1886, died 1941), died April 15, 1969, leaving issue.

(iii) Major Lord Leopold Mountbatten, G.C.V.O., born May 21, 1889; died April 23, 1922.

(iv) Maurice, born Oct. 3, 1891; died of wounds received in action, Oct. 27, 1914.

THE FAMILY OF KING EDWARD VII

KING EDWARD VII., eldest son of Queen Victoria, *born* Nov. 9, 1841; *married* March 10, 1863, Her Royal Highness Princess Alexandra, eldest daughter of King Christian IX. of Denmark; *succeeded to the Throne* Jan. 22, 1901; *died* May 6, 1910. Issue:—

1. H.R.H. Prince Albert Victor, *Duke of Clarence and Avondale and Earl of Athlone*, born Jan. 8, 1864, died Jan. 14, 1892.

2. H.M. KING GEORGE V. (*see* p. 217). Assumed by Royal Proclamation (June 17, 1917 for his House and Family as well as for all descendants in the male line of Queen Victoria who are subjects of these Realms, the name of Windsor; died Jan. 20, 1936, having had issue (*see* p. 217).

3. H.R.H. Louise, *Princess Royal*, born Feb. 20, 1867; married July 27, 1889, 1st Duke of Fife (who died Jan. 29, 1912); died Jan. 4, 1931. Issue:—

(i) H.H. Princess Alexandra, Duchess of Fife (*H.R.H. Princess Arthur of Connaught*), born May 17, 1891; married Oct. 15, 1913, H.R.H. the late Prince Arthur; died Feb. 26, 1959. Issue:—

Alastair Arthur, Duke of Connaught, born Aug. 9, 1914; died April 26, 1943.

(ii) H.H. Princess Maud, born April 3, 1893;

married Nov. 12, 1923, 11th Earl of Southesk; died Dec. 14, 1945, leaving issue:—

The Duke of Fife, born Sept. 23, 1929; married (1956) Hon. Caroline Dewar (marriage dissolved, 1966) and has issue.

4. H.R.H. Princess Victoria, born July 6, 1868; died Dec. 3, 1935.

5. H.R.H. Princess Maud, born Nov. 26, 1869; married July 22, 1896, Haakon VII., King of Norway, who died Sept. 21, 1957; died Nov. 20, 1938. Issue:—

H.M. Olav V., K.G., K.T., G.C.B., G.C.V.O., King of Norway, born July 2, 1903, *married* March 21, 1929, H.R.H. Princess Marthe of Sweden (who died April 5, 1954). Issue:—

(a) H.R.H. Princess Ragnhild, born June 9, 1930.

(b) H.R.H. Princess Astrid, born Feb. 12, 1932.

(c) H.R.H. Harald, Crown Prince of Norway, G.C.V.O., born Feb. 21, 1937.

THE FAMILY OF PRINCE ANDREW OF GREECE

Prince Andrew of Greece, *born* Feb. 2, 1882; *married* Princess Alice of Battenberg (*H.R.H. Princess Andrew of Greece*), who *died* Dec. 5, 1969 (*see* p. 215); *died* Dec. 2, 1944, having had issue:—

(1) Princess Margarita, *born* April 17, 1905, *married* Prince Gottfried of Hohenlohe-Langenburg (*see* p. 215), and has issue, Prince Kraft, *born* 1935, Princess Beatrix, *born* 1936, Prince George, *born* 1938; Prince Ruprecht and Prince Albrecht, *born* 1944

(2) Princess Theodora, *born* May 30, 1906, *married* Prince Berthold of Baden (who *died* Oct. 27, 1963), *died* Oct. 16, 1969, leaving issue, Princess Margarita, *born* 1932 (married, 1957, Prince Tomislav of Yugoslavia (see p. 215)), Prince Max, *born* 1933, Prince Louis, *born* 1937.

(3) Princess Cecilie, *born* June 22, 1911, *married* George, Grand Duke of Hesse, accidentally killed with husband and two sons, Nov. 16, 1937 (*see* p. 215).

(4) Princess Sophie, *born* June 26, 1914, *married* (i) Prince Christopher of Hesse (who died, 1944, leaving issue, Princess Christina, *born* 1933, Princess Dorothea, *born* 1934, Prince Charles, *born* 1937, Prince Rainer, *born* 1939, Princess Clarissa, born 1944); *married* (ii) Prince George of Hanover, and has further issue.

(5) Prince Philip (*H.R.H. the Prince Philip, Duke of Edinburgh*), *born* June 10, 1921 (*see* p. 218).

THE FAMILY OF KING GEORGE V

KING GEORGE V., second son of King Edward VII., *born* June 3, 1865; *married* July 6, 1893. Her Serene Highness Princess Victoria Mary Augusta Louise Olga Pauline Claudine Agnes (Queen Mary), *succeeded* to the throne May 6, 1910; *died* Jan. 20, 1936. Queen Mary died March 24, 1953. Issue:—

H.R.H. THE DUKE OF WINDSOR (EDWARD Albert Christian George Andrew Patrick David), K.G., K.T., K.P., G.C.B., G.C.S.I., G.C.M.G., G.C.I.E., G.C.V.O., G.B.E., I.S.O., M.C., F.R.S., Royal Victorian Chain, Admiral of the Fleet, Field Marshal, Marshal of the Royal Air Force, *born* June 23, 1894, *succeeded* to the Throne as KING EDWARD VIII., Jan. 20 1936; *abdicated* Dec. 11, 1936; *married* June 3, 1937, Mrs. Wallis Warfield (The Duchess of Windsor), *died* May 28, 1972.

H.M. KING GEORGE VI. (Albert Frederick Arthur George) *born* at York Cottage, Sandringham, Dec. 14, 1895; *married* April 26, 1923, to Lady Elizabeth Angela Marguerite (HER MAJESTY QUEEN ELIZABETH THE QUEEN MOTHER), daughter of the 14th Earl of Strathmore and Kinghorne, *succeeded* to the throne Dec. 11, 1936; *crowned* in Westminster Abbey, May 12, 1937; *died* Feb. 6, 1952, having had issue (*see* p. 218).

H.R.H. THE PRINCESS ROYAL (Victoria Alexandra Alice MARY), *born* April 25, 1897, *married* Feb. 28, 1922, the 6th Earl of Harewood (*born* Sept. 9, 1882; *died* May 24, 1947), *died* at Harewood House, Yorks., March 28, 1965, leaving issue:—

(1) George Henry Hubert Lascelles, *7th Earl of Harewood*, *born* Feb. 7, 1923; *married*, firstly, Sept. 29, 1949, Maria Donata (Marion), daughter of the late Erwin Stein (marriage dissolved 1967) (she married, March 14, 1973, Rt. Hon. Jeremy Thorpe), and has issue, David Henry George, Viscount Lascelles, *born* Oct. 21, 1950; James Edward, *born* Oct. 5, 1953, married, April 4, 1973, Fredericka Duhrrson; Robert Jeremy Hugh, *born* Feb. 14, 1955; secondly, July 31, 1967, Mrs. Patricia Elizabeth Tuckwell, and has issue, Mark Hubert, *born* July 5, 1964.

(2) Gerald David Lascelles, *born* Aug. 21, 1924, *married* July 15, 1952, Miss Angela Dowding and has issue, Henry Ulick, *born* May 19, 1953.

H.R.H. THE DUKE OF GLOUCESTER (HENRY WILLIAM FREDERICK Albert), Duke of Gloucester, Earl of Ulster and Baron Culloden, *born* March 31, 1900, *married* Nov. 6, 1935, Lady Alice Montagu-Douglas-Scott, daughter of the 7th Duke of Buccleuch (H.R.H. Princess Alice, Duchess of Gloucester, C.I, G.C.V.O., G.B.E., Grand Cordon of Al Kamal, Colonel-in-Chief the Royal Hussars (Prince of Wales's Own), the King's Own Scottish Borderers, Deputy Colonel-in-Chief, Royal Anglian Regt., Air Chief Commandant W.R.A.F., *born* Dec. 25, 1901); *died* June 10, 1974. Issue; H.R.H. Prince William Henry Andrew Frederick, *born* Dec. 18, 1941; *accidentally killed* Aug. 28, 1972; H.R.H. Prince RICHARD Alexander Walter George, *Duke of Gloucester*, G.C.V.O., Colonel-in-Chief, Gloucestershire Regiment, Grand Prior of the Order of St. John of Jerusalem *born* Aug. 26, 1944, *married* July 8, 1972, Brigitte von Deurs and has issue, Alexander Patrick George Richard, Earl of Ulster, *born* Oct. 24, 1974.

H.R.H. THE DUKE OF KENT (George Edward Alexander Edmund), Duke of Kent, Earl of St. Andrews and Baron Downpatrick, *born* Dec. 20, 1902, *married* Nov. 29, 1934, H.R.H. Princess Marina of Greece and Denmark (*born* Nov. 30, O.S., 1906; *died* Aug. 27, 1968). *Killed on Active Service*, Aug. 25, 1942 eaving issue:—

(1) H.R.H. Prince EDWARD George Nicholas Paul Patrick, *Duke of Kent*, G.C.M.G., G.C.V.O., *born* Oct. 9, 1935, Lt.-Col. The Royal Scots Greys, Personal A.D.C. to the Queen, Colonel, Scots Guards, Colonel-in-Chief, Royal Regiment of Fusiliers, *married* June 8, 1961, Katharine Lucy Mary, Controller Commandant, Women's Royal Army Corps, Hon. Major-General, Colonel-in-Chief Army Catering Corps, daughter of Sir William Worsley, Bt., and has issue, George Philip Nicholas, Earl of St. Andrews, *born* June 26, 1962; Helen Marina Lucy (Lady Helen Windsor), *born* April 28, 1964; Nicholas Charles Edward Jonathan (Lord Nicholas Windsor), *born* July 25, 1970. *Residences*— Anmer Hall, Norfolk; York House, St. James's Palace, S.W.1.

(2) H.R.H. Princess ALEXANDRA Helen Elizabeth Olga Christabel, G.C.V.O., *born* Dec. 25, 1936, Colonel-in-Chief, 17th/21st Lancers, Deputy Colonel-in-Chief, The Light Infantry, Hon. Colonel North Irish Horse, Air Chief Commandant, Princess Mary's Royal Air Force Nursing Service, *married* April 24, 1963, Hon. Angus Ogilvy, son of the 12th Earl of Airlie, *born* Sept. 14, 1928. and his issue, James Robert Bruce, *born* Feb. 29, 1964 and Marina Victoria Alexandra, *born* July 31, 1966. *Residence of Princess Alexandra*—Kensington Palace, W.8.

(3) H.R.H. Prince MICHAEL George Charles Franklin, *born* July 4, 1942, Captain, Royal Hussars.

H.R.H. PRINCE JOHN, *born* July 12, 1905; *died* Jan. 18, 1919.

The House of Windsor

Her Most Excellent Majesty ELIZABETH THE SECOND (Elizabeth Alexandra Mary of Windsor) by the Grace of God, of the United Kingdom of Great Britain and Northern Ireland and of Her other Realms and Territories Queen, Head of the Commonwealth, Defender of the Faith, Sovereign of the British Orders of Knighthood and Sovereign Head of the Order of St. John, Lord High Admiral of the United Kingdom, Colonel-in-Chief of The Life Guards, The Blues and Royals (Royal Horse Guards and 1st Dragoons), The Royal Scots Dragoon Guards (Carabiniers and Greys), 16th/5th The Queen's Royal Lancers, Royal Tank Regiment, Corps of Royal Engineers, Grenadier Guards, Coldstream Guards, Scots Guards, Irish Guards, Welsh Guards, The Royal Welch Fusiliers, The Queen's Lancashire Regiment, The Argyll and Sutherland Highlanders (Princess Louise's), The Royal Green Jackets, Royal Army Ordnance Corps, The Queen's Own Mercian Yeomanry, The Duke of Lancaster's Own Yeomanry, The Corps of Royal Canadian Engineers, The King's Own Calgary Regiment, Royal 22e Regiment, Governor-General's Foot Guards, The Canadian Grenadier Guards, Le Régiment de la Chaudière, Royal New Brunswick Regt., The 48th Highlanders of Canada, The Argyll and Sutherland Highlanders of Canada (Princess Louise's), The Royal Canadian Ordnance Corps, Royal Australian Engineers, Royal Australian Infantry Corps, Royal Australian Army Ordnance Corps, Royal Australian Army Nursing Corps, Royal New Zealand Engineers, Royal New Zealand Infantry Regiment, Royal Malta Artillery, Malawi Rifles, Captain-General of the Royal Regiment of Artillery, The Honourable Artillery Company, Combined Cadet Force, Royal Canadian Artillery, Royal Regiment of Australian Artillery, Royal New Zealand Artillery, Royal New Zealand Armoured Corps, Air-Commodore-in-Chief, R. Aux.A.F., R.A.F. Regiment, Royal Observer Corps, Royal Canadian Air Force Auxiliary, Australian Citizen Air Force, Commandant-in-Chief, Royal Air Force College, Cranwell, Hon. Commissioner, Royal Canadian Mounted Police, Master of the Merchant Navy and Fishing Fleets, Head of the Civil Defence Corps, Head of the National Hospital Service Reserve.

Elder daughter of His late Majesty King George VI and of Her Majesty Queen Elizabeth the Queen Mother; *born* at 17 Bruton Street, London, W.1. April 21, 1926, *succeeded* to the throne February 6, 1952, *crowned* June 2, 1953; having *married*, November 20, 1947, in Westminster Abbey Philip, Duke of Edinburgh, Earl of Merioneth and Baron Greenwich (H.R.H. The Prince Philip, Duke of Edinburgh), K.G., P.C., K.T., O.M., G.B.E., Admiral of the Fleet, Field Marshal, Marshal of the Royal Air Force, Admiral of the Fleet, Royal Australian Navy, Field Marshal, Australian Military Forces, Marshal of the Royal Australian Air Force, Admiral of the Fleet, Royal New Zealand Navy, Captain General, Royal Marines, Colonel-in-Chief, The Queen's Royal Irish Hussars, The Duke of Edinburgh's Royal Regiment (Berkshire and Wiltshire), Queen's Own Highlanders (Seaforth and Camerons), Corps of Royal Electrical and Mechanical Engineers, Army Cadet Force, The Royal Canadian Regiment, The Seaforth Highlanders of Canada, The Cameron Highlanders of Ottawa, The Queen's Own Cameron Highlanders of Canada, The Royal Canadian Army Cadets, The Royal Australian Electrical and Mechanical Engineers, The Australian Cadet Corps, Corps of Royal New Zealand Electrical and Mechanical Engineers, Colonel of Grenadier Guards, Hon. Colonel, Edinburgh and Heriot-Watt Universities Officers' Training Corps, The Trinidad and Tobago Regiment, Admiral, Sea Cadet Corps, Royal Canadian Sea Cadets, Air Commodore-in-Chief Air Training Corps, Royal Canadian Air Cadets, Master of the Corporation of Trinity House, Ranger of Windsor Park. *See p. 217.*

CHILDREN OF HER MAJESTY

H.R.H. THE PRINCE OF WALES (CHARLES Philip Arthur George), K.G., G.C.B., Prince of Wales and Earl of Chester, Duke of Cornwall and Duke of Rothesay, Earl of Carrick and Baron Renfrew Lord of the Isles and Great Steward of Scotland, Personal A.D.C. to the Queen, Great Master of the Order of the Bath, Lieutenant Royal Navy, Colonel-in-Chief The Royal Regiment of Wales (24th/41st Foot), Colonel Welsh Guards, Flight Lieutenant Royal Air Force, *born* November 14, 1948.

H.R.H. PRINCESS ANNE ELIZABETH ALICE LOUISE, G.C.V.O. Chief Commandant Women's Royal Naval Service, Colonel-in-Chief 14th/20th King's Hussars, The Worcestershire and Sherwood Foresters Regiment, 8th Canadian Hussars (Princess Louise's), Commandant-in-Chief, Ambulance and Nursing Cadets, *born* August 15, 1950, *married* Nov. 14, 1973, Capt. Mark Anthony Peter Phillips, C.V.O., Queen's Dragoon Guards, Personal A.D.C. to the Queen.

H.R.H. PRINCE ANDREW ALBERT CHRISTIAN EDWARD, *born* Feb. 19, 1960.

H.R.H. PRINCE EDWARD ANTONY RICHARD LOUIS, *born* March 10, 1964.

MOTHER OF HER MAJESTY

H.M. QUEEN ELIZABETH THE QUEEN MOTHER (Elizabeth Angela Marguerite) (daughter of the 14th Earl of Strathmore and Kinghorne), Lady of the Garter, Lady of the Thistle, Order of the Crown of India, Grand Master of the Royal Victorian Order, Dame Grand Cross of the Order of the British Empire, Royal Victorian Chain, Doctor of Civil Law, Doctor of Literature, Colonel-in-Chief 1st the Queen's Dragoon Guards, The Queen's Own Hussars, 9th/12th Royal Lancers (Prince of Wales's), The King's Regiment, The Royal Anglian Regiment, The Light Infantry, The Black Watch (Royal Highland Regiment), Royal Army Medical Corps, The Black Watch (Royal Highland Regiment) of Canada, The Toronto Scottish Regiment, The Royal Canadian Army Medical Corps, Royal Australian Army Medical Corps, Hon. Colonel The Royal Yeomanry, The London Scottish, University of London Officers' Training Corps, Commandant-in-Chief R.A.F. Central Flying School, W.R.N.S., W.R.A.C., W.R.A.F., Air Chief Commandant, Women's Royal Australian Air Force, Patron St. Andrew's Ambulance Association, Commandant-in-Chief Nursing Corps and Divisions. *Born* August 4, 1900, *married* April 26, 1923, Prince Albert Frederick Arthur George of Windsor, Duke of York (*see* King GEORGE VI).
Residences.—Clarence House, St. James's, S.W.1.; Castle of Mey, Caithness, Scotland.

SISTER OF HER MAJESTY

H.R.H. PRINCESS MARGARET ROSE (The Princess Margaret, Countess of Snowdon), C.I., G.C.V.O., Colonel-in-Chief, 15th/19th the King's Royal Hussars, The Royal Highland Fusiliers (Princess Margaret's Own Glasgow and Ayrshire Regiment), Queen Alexandra's Royal Army Nursing Corps, Women's Royal Australian Army Corps, The Highland Fusiliers of Canada (Militia), The Princess Louise Fusiliers, Deputy

Colonel-in-Chief, The Royal Anglian Regiment, Commandant-in-Chief, St. John Ambulance Brigade Cadets, Grand President, St. John Ambulance Association and Brigade, Dame Grand Cross of the Order of St. John of Jerusalem, President of the Girl Guides Association; *born* Aug. 21, 1930; *married* May 6, 1960 Anthony Charles Robert Armstrong-Jones, G.C.V.O. (*born* March 7, 1930), son of the late Ronald Armstrong Jones, Q.C. and the Countess of Rosse, *created* Earl of Snowdon, 1961, Constable of Caernarvon Castle; and has issue, David Albert Charles, Viscount Linley, *born* Nov. 3, 1961; Sarah Frances Elizabeth (Lady Sarah Armstrong-Jones), *born* May 1, 1964.

Residence.—Kensington Palace, W.8.

ORDER OF SUCCESSION TO THE THRONE

The Queen's sons and daughter are in the order of succession to the throne, and after the Princess Margaret and her son and daughter, the Duke of Gloucester and his son; then the Duke of Kent, his sons and daughter, his brother and sister and her son and daughter, then the Earl of Harewood and his sons and the Hon. Gerald Lascelles and his son; then the Duke of Fife, son of the late Countess of Southesk, and his son and daughter; then King Olav of Norway and his children and granddaughter, the the children and grandchildren of the second daughter of the late Duke of Saxe-Coburg (his eldest daughter, the late Queen Marie of Roumania, having formally renounced on her marriage all possibility of claim to the British Throne); then the children of the third daughter (the late Princess Alexandra of Hohenlohe-Langenburg); then the children of the eldest son of the late Princess Margaret of Connaught (Crown Princess of Sweden), her other sons and her daughter (Queen Ingrid of Denmark) and her children; then the son of the younger daughter of the first Duke of Connaught and Strathearn (Lady Patricia Ramsay); then the Princess Alice (Countess of Athlone) and her daughter and grandchildren.

Precedence in England

The Sovereign
The Prince Philip, Duke of Edinburgh.
The Prince of Wales, The Prince Andrew, The Prince Edward.
Archbishop of Canterbury.
Lord High Chancellor.
Archbishop of York.
The Prime Minister.
Lord President of the Council.
Speaker of the House of Commons.
Lord Privy Seal.
High Commissioners of Commonwealth Countries and Ambassadors of Foreign States.
Dukes, according to their Patents of Creation:
(1) Of England; (2) of Scotland; (3) of Great Britain; (4) of Ireland; (5) those created since the Union.
Ministers and Envoys.
Eldest sons of Dukes of Blood Royal.
Marquesses, in same order as Dukes.
Dukes' eldest Sons.
Earls, in same order as Dukes.
Younger sons of Dukes of Blood Royal.
Marquesses' eldest Sons.
Dukes' younger Sons.
Viscounts, in same order as Dukes.
Earls' eldest Sons.
Marquesses' younger Sons.
Bishops of London, Durham and Winchester.
All other English Bishops, according to their seniority of Consecration.
Secretaries of State, if of the degree of a Baron.
Barons, in same order as Dukes.
Treasurer of H.M.'s Household.
Comptroller of H.M.'s Household.
Vice-Chamberlain of H.M.'s Household.
Secretaries of State under the degree of Baron.

Viscounts' eldest Sons.
Earls' younger Sons.
Barons' eldest Sons.
Knights of the Garter if Commoners.
Privy Councillors if of no higher rank.
Chancellor of the Exchequer.
Chancellor of the Duchy of Lancaster.
Lord Chief Justice of England.
Master of the Rolls.
President of the Probate Court.
The Lords Justices of Appeal.
Judges of the High Court.
Vice-Chancellor of County Palatine of Lancaster.
Viscounts' younger Sons.
Barons' younger Sons.
Sons of Life Peers.
Baronets of either Kingdom, according to date of Patents.
Knights of the Thistle if Commoners.
Knights Grand Cross of the Bath.
Members of the Order of Merit.
Knights Grand Commanders of the Star of India.
Knights Grand Cross of St. Michael and St. George.
Knights Grand Commanders of the Indian Empire.
Knights Grand Cross of the Royal Victorian Order.
Knights Grand Cross of Order of the British Empire.
Companions of Honour.
Knights Commanders of the above Orders.
Knights Bachelor.
Official Referees of The Supreme Court.
Judges of County Courts and judges of the Mayor's and City of London Court.
Companions and Commanders *e.g.* C.B.; C.S.I.; C.M.G.; C.I.E.; C.V.O.; C.B.E.; D.S.O.; M.V.O. (4th); O.B.E.; I.S.O.
Eldest Sons of younger Sons of Peers.
Baronets' eldest Sons.

Eldest Sons of Knights in the same order as their Fathers.
M.V.O. (5th); M.B.E.
Younger Sons of the younger Sons of Peers.
Baronets' younger Sons.
Younger Sons of Knights in the same order as their Fathers.
Naval, Military, Air, and other Esquires by Office.

WOMEN

Women take the same rank as their husbands or as their eldest brothers; but the daughter of a Peer marrying a Commoner retains her title as Lady or Honourable. Daughters of Peers rank next immediately after the wives of their elder brothers, and before their younger brothers' wives. Daughters of Peers marrying Peers of lower degree take the same order of precedency as that of their husbands; thus the daughter of a Duke marrying a Baron becomes of the rank of Baroness only while her sisters married to commoners retain their rank and take precedence of the Baroness. Merely official rank on the husband's part does not give any similar precedence to the wife.

For Dames Grand Cross, *see* pp. 300-301.

LOCAL PRECEDENCE

ENGLAND AND WALES.—No written code of county or city order of precedence has been promulgated, but in Counties the Lord Lieutenant stands first, and secondly (normally) the Sheriff, and therefore in Cities and Boroughs the Lord Lieutenant has social precedence over the Mayor; but at City or Borough functions the Lord Mayor or Mayor will preside. At Oxford and Cambridge the High Sheriff takes precedence of the Vice-Chancellor.

SCOTLAND.—*See* Index.

The Queen's Household

Lord Chamberlain, The Lord Maclean, P.C., K.T., G.C.V.O., K.B.E.
Lord Steward, The Duke of Northumberland, K.G., P.C., T.D., F.R.S.
Master of the Horse, The Duke of Beaufort, K.G., P.C., G.C.V.O.
Treasurer of the Household, W. Harrison, M.P.
Comptroller of the Household, J. Harper, M.P.
Vice-Chamberlain, J. Hamilton, M.P.
Administrative Adviser, Sir Basil Smallpeice, K.C.V.O.

Gold Sticks, Field-Marshal Sir Gerald Templer, K.G., G.C.B., G.C.M.G., K.B.E., D.S.O.; Admiral of the Fleet the Earl Mountbatten of Burma, K.G., P.C., G.C.B., O.M., G.C.S.I., G.C.I.E., G.C.V.O., D.S.O., A.D.C.
Vice-Admiral of the United Kingdom, Admiral Sir Nigel Henderson, G.B.E., K.C.B.
Rear-Admiral of the United Kingdom, Admiral Sir John Bush, G.C.B., D.S.C.
First and Principal Naval Aide-de-Camp, Admiral Sir Edward Ashmore, G.C.B., D.S.C.
Aides-de-Camp General, General Sir Harry Tuzo, G.C.B., O.B.E., M.C.; General Sir John Sharp, K.C.B., M.C.; General Sir Roland Gibbs, G.C.B., C.B.E., D.S.O., M.C.
Air Aides-de-Camp, Air Chief Marshal Sir Andrew Humphrey, G.C.B., O.B.E., D.F.C., A.F.C.; Air Chief Marshal Sir Neville Stack, K.C.B., C.V.O., C.B.E., A.F.C.

Mistress of the Robes, The Duchess of Grafton, D.C.V.O.
Ladies of the Bedchamber, The Marchioness of Abergavenny, C.V.O.; The Countess of Airlie.
Women of the Bedchamber, Hon. Mary Morrison, C.V.O.; Mrs. John Dugdale, C.V.O.; Lady Susan Hussey, C.V.O.; Lady Abel Smith, C.V.O.
Extra Women of the Bedchamber, Hon. Mrs. Andrew Elphinstone, C.V.O.; Lady Rose Baring, D.C.V.O.

THE PRIVATE SECRETARY'S OFFICE
Buckingham Palace, S.W.1.
Private Secretary to the Queen, Lt.-Col. Rt. Hon. Sir Martin Charteris, G.C.V.O., K.C.B., O.B.E.
Deputy Private Secretary, Sir Philip Moore, K.C.V.O., C.B., C.M.G.
Assistant Private Secretary, W. F. P. Heseltine, C.V.O.
Defence Services Secretary, Air Vice-Marshal B. Stanbridge, C.B.E, M.V.O., A.F.C.
Press Secretary, R. Allison.
Assistant Press Secretaries, Mrs. Michael Wall, C.V.O.; R. E. Moore (temp.).
Chief Clerk, Miss Jean Taylor, C.V.O.
Secretary to the Private Secretary, A. C. Neal, M.V.O., B.E.M.
Clerks, Miss A. Bowlby, M.B.E.; Miss O. M. Short, M.V.O.; Mrs. A. Neal, M.V.O. (Press); Miss F. M. Simpson, M.V.O. (Press); Miss S. Reid; Miss C. Bailey; Miss M. Viney (Press); Mrs. C. C. Ollivant; Miss P. Keenan; Miss R. Macmillan; Miss J. Adams.

The Queen's Archives
Norman Tower, Windsor Castle.
Keeper of the Queen's Archives, Lt.-Col. Rt. Hon. Sir Martin Charteris, G.C.V.O., K.C.B. O.B.E.
Assistant Keeper, Sir Robin Mackworth-Young, K.C.V.O., F.S.A.
Registrar, Miss Jane Langton, M.V.O.
Assistant Registrars, Miss E. Cuthbert; Miss F. Dimond.

DEPARTMENT OF THE KEEPER OF THE PRIVY PURSE AND TREASURER TO THE QUEEN
Buckingham Palace, S.W.1.
Keeper of the Privy Purse and Treasurer to the Queen, Major Sir Rennie Maudslay, K.C.V.O., M.B.E.

Privy Purse Office
Assistant Keeper of the Privy Purse, Major S. G. B. Blewitt.
Chief Accountant, Edmund F. Grove, C.V.O.
Chief Clerk, D. Waters, M.V.O.
Accountant, M. Mortimore.
Clerks, Mrs. E. de Jong; Mrs. C. Kelly.

Land Agent, Sandringham, Julian Loyd, M.V.O.
Resident Factor, Balmoral, Col. W. G. McHardy, M.V.O., M.B.E., M.C.

Farm Manager, Royal Farms, Windsor, R. Reeks.
Consulting Engineers, J. Fraser (Balmoral); Sir Ralph Freeman, C.V.O., C.B.E. (Sandringham).

Treasurer's Office
Deputy Treasurer to the Queen, R. D. Wood, M.V.O., V.R.D.
Chief Accountant and Paymaster, Charles Warner. C.V.O.
Accountant, F. R. Mintram.
Establishment Officer, Peter Wright, M.V.O.

Royal Almonry
High Almoner, The Rt. Rev. the Lord Bishop of Rochester.
Hereditary Grand Almoner, The Marquess of Exeter, K.C.M.G.
Sub-Almoner, Rev. Canon J. S. D. Mansel, M.V.O., M.A., F.S.A.
Secretary, Peter Wright, M.V.O.
Assistant Secretary, Derek Wates, M.V.O.

THE LORD CHAMBERLAIN'S OFFICE
St. James's Palace, S.W.1.
Comptroller, Lt.-Col. Sir Eric Penn, K.C.V.O., O.B.E., M.C.
Assistant Comptroller, Lt.-Col. J. F. D. Johnston, M.V.O., M.C.
Secretary, D. V. G. Buchanan, M.V.O.
Assistant Secretary, J. E. P. Titman, M.V.O.
Registrar, P. D. Hartley.
State Invitation Assistant, M. E. Bishop.
Ceremonial Assistant, I. D. Campbell.
Clerks, Mrs. G. Cousland, M.V.O.; Miss M. Greiner, M.V.O.; Miss S. Hay; Miss Z. McNeile; Miss E. Quartley-Mallett; Miss S. Wilson; Mrs. A. Wolfe; Miss J. Brown.

Permanent Lords in Waiting, Brigadier The Lord Tryon, G.C.V.O., K.C.B., D.S.O.; The Lord Cobbold, K.G., G.C.V.O.
Lords in Waiting, The Earl of Westmorland, K.C.V.O.; The Lord Hamilton of Dalzell, M.C.; The Lord Jacques; The Lord Wells-Pestell; The Lord Winterbottom; The Baroness Stedman, O.B.E. (Baroness in Waiting); The Lord Oram.
Gentlemen Ushers, H. L. Carron Greig, C.V.O.; Capt. Michael Nelville Tufnell, C.V.O., D.S.C., R.N.; Air Marshal Sir Maurice Heath, K.B.E., C.B.; Lt.-Cmdr. John Arundell Holdsworth, O.B.E., R.N.; Col. William Henry Gerard Leigh, M.V.O.; Vice-Admiral Sir Ronald Brockman, K.C.B., C.S.I., C.I.E., C.B.E.; Air Commodore the Hon. Peter

Beckford Rutgers Vanneck, C.B., O.B.E., A.F.C.;
Lt.-Col. Sir Julian Tolver Paget, Bt.

Extra Gentlemen Ushers, Capt. Andrew Yates, M.V.O.,
R.N.; Major Thomas Harvey, C.V.O., D.S.O.; Brig.
Charles Richard Britten, O.B.E., M.C.; Air Vice-
Marshal Sir Ranald Reid, K.C.B., D.S.O., M.C.;
Esmond Butler, C.V.O.; Sir Austin Strutt, K.C.V.O.,
C.B.; Maj.-Gen. Sir Cyril Harry Colquhoun,
K.C.V.O., C.B., O.B.E.; Lt.-Col. Sir John Mandeville
Hugo, K.C.V.O., O.B.E.; Air Commodore John
Wilkins Hubble, C.B.E., D.S.O., A.F.C.; General Sir
Rodney Moore, G.C.V.O., K.C.B., C.B.E., D.S.O.;
Maj.-Gen. Sir James Bowes-Lyon, K.C.V.O., C.B.,
O.B.E., M.C.

Gentleman Usher to the Sword of State, Admiral Sir
Desmond Dreyer, G.C.B., C.B.E., D.S.C.

Gentleman Usher of the Black Rod, Admiral Sir Frank
Twiss, K.C.B., D.S.C.

Serjeants at Arms, C. G. R. Warner, C.V.O.; D. V. G.
Buchanan, M.V.O.; E. F. Grove, M.V.O.

Constable & Governor of Windsor Castle, Marshal of
the Royal Air Force the Lord Elworthy, G.C.B.,
C.B.E., D.S.O., M.V.O., D.F.C., A.F.C.

Keeper of the Jewel House, Tower of London, Maj.-
Gen. W. D. M. Raeburn, C.B., D.S.O., M.B.E.

Adviser for the Queen's Pictures and Drawings, Sir
Anthony Frederick Blunt, K.C.V.O., F.S.A.

Surveyor of the Queen's Pictures, Sir Oliver Nicholas
Millar, K.C.V.O., F.S.A., F.B.A.

Librarian, Sir Robin Mackworth-Young, K.C.V.O.,
F.S.A.

Librarian Emeritus, Sir Owen Morshead, G.C.V.O.,
K.C.B., D.S.O., F.S.A.

Curator of the Print Room, The Hon. Mrs. Roberts.

Adviser for the Queen's Works of Art, Sir Francis
Watson, K.C.V.O., F.S.A.

Surveyor of the Queen's Works of Art, Geoffrey de
Bellaigue, C.V.O., F.S.A.

Master of the Queen's Music, Malcolm Williamson,
C.B.E.

Poet Laureate, Sir John Betjeman, C.B.E.

Bargemaster, H. A. Barry, M.V.O.

Keeper of the Swans, F. J. Turk.

Caretaker of St. James's Palace, H. C. Philips, M.B.E.

ASCOT OFFICE
St. James's Palace, S.W.1.

Her Majesty's Representative at Ascot, The
Marquess of Abergavenny, K.G., O.B.E.

Secretary, Miss A. Ainscough, M.V.O.

ECCLESIASTICAL HOUSEHOLD
The College of Chaplains.

Clerk of the Closet, The Bishop of Sheffield.

Deputy Clerk of the Closet, Rev. Canon J. S. D.
Mansel, M.V.O., M.A., F.S.A.

Chaplains to the Queen, Canon P. L. Gilling-
ham, M.V.O., M.A.; Rev. H. D. Anderson, M.V.O.,
M.A., B.D.; Ven. E. J. G. Ward, M.V.O., M.A.;
Canon D. H. Booth, M.B.E., M.A.; Rev. J. R. W.
Stott, M.A.; Preb. S. A. Williams, M.A.; Canon
H. C. Blackburne, M.A.; Rev. C. E. M. Roderick,
M.A.; Canon C. H. G. Hopkins, M.A.; Canon W.
Garlick, M.A., B.SC.; Rev. J. G. Downward, M.A.;
Canon E. Saxon, B.A., B.D.; Canon R. S. O.
Stevens, B.SC., M.A.; Rev. P. T. Ashton, M.V.O.,
M.A.; Rev. A. H. H. Harbottle, M.A.; Canon G.
H. G. Hewitt, M.A.; Canon E. M. Pilkington,
M.A.; Canon G. R. Sansbury, M.A.; Ven. H. John-
son, M.A.; Ven. J. R. Youens, C.B., O.B.E., M.C.;
Preb. D. M. Lynch, C.B.E., M.A.; Rev. R. L.
Roberts, C.V.O., M.A.; Canon L. L. Rees; Canon
D. M. Paton, M.A.; Canon C. E. Young; Preb.
D. W. C. Ford, B.D., M.Th.; Rev. E. Hughes,

M.Th., Ph.D.; Rev. E. E. Staples, O.B.E.; Ven. R.
B. Bradford, B.A.; Ven. F. N. Towndrow, M.A.;
Rev. T. Barfett, M.A.; Canon J. P. P. Newell,
M.A.; Prof. Canon G. R. Dunstan, M.A., D.D.,
F.S.A.

Extra Chaplains, Rev. M. F. Foxell, K.C.V.O., M.A.;
Ven. A. S. Bean, M.B.E., M.A., D.D.; Rev. E. S.
Abbott, K.C.V.O., M.A., D.D.

Chapels Royal

Dean of the Chapels Royal, The Bishop of London.

Sub-Dean of Chapels Royal, Rev. Canon J. S. D.
Mansel, M.V.O., M.A., F.S.A.

Priests in Ordinary, Rev. C. J. A. Hickling, M.A.;
Rev. S. R. Cutt, M.A.

Organist, Choirmaster and Composer, T. R. W.
Farrell, F.R.C.O., A.R.C.M.

Domestic Chaplain—Buckingham Palace, Rev. Canon
J. S. D. Mansel, M.V.O., M.A., F.S.A.

Domestic Chaplain—Windsor Castle, The Dean of
Windsor.

Domestic Chaplain—Sandringham, Rev. A. Glen-
dining.

Chaplain—Royal Chapel, Windsor Great Park,
Rev. A. H. H. Harbottle, M.A.

Chaplain—Hampton Court Palace, Rev. F. V. A.
Boyse, M.A.

Chaplain—Tower of London, Rev. J. F. M. Llewellyn,
M.A.

Organist and Choirmaster—Hampton Court Palace,
Gordon Reynolds, A.R.C.M.

MEDICAL HOUSEHOLD

Physician, Head of the Medical Household, R. J. S.
Bayliss, M.D., F.R.C.P.

Physicians, Miss M. G. Blackie, M.D.; J. C. Batten,
M.D., F.R.C.P.

Serjeant Surgeon, H. E. Lockhart-Mummery, M.D.,
M.Chir., F.R.C.S., L.R.C.P.

Surgeon Oculist, S. J. H. Miller, M.D., F.R.C.S.

Surgeon Gynaecologist, G. D. Pinker, F.R.C.S.(Ed.),
F.R.C.O.G.

Surgeon Dentist, N. A. Surridge, L.D.S., B.D.S., D.D.S.

Physician to the Household, A. M. Dawson, M.D.,
F.R.C.P.

Surgeon to the Household, J. L. Dawson, M.S., F.R.C.S.

Surgeon Oculist to the Household, P. J. Holmes-Sellors,
B.M., B.Ch., F.R.C.S.

Apothecary to the Queen and to the Household, N. R.
Southward, M.B., B.Chir., M.R.C.P.

Apothecary to the Household at Windsor, J. P. Clayton,
M.V.O., M.B., B.Chir., M.R.C.S., L.R.C.P.

Apothecary to the Household at Sandringham, H. K.
Ford, M.B., B.S., D.Obst., R.C.O.G., M.R.C.G.P.

Coroner of the Queen's Household, A. G. Davies, M.B.,
B.S., M.R.C.S., L.R.C.P.

Marshal of the Diplomatic Corps, Maj.-Gen. Lord
Michael Fitzalan Howard, K.C.V.O., C.B., C.B.E.,
M.C.

Vice-Marshal, R. W. H. du Boulay, C.M.G., C.V.O.

CENTRAL CHANCERY
OF THE ORDERS OF KNIGHTHOOD
St. James's Palace, S.W.1

Secretary, Maj.-Gen. P. B. Gillett, C.B., C.V.O., O.B.E.

Chief Clerk, G. A. Harris, M.V.O., M.B.E.

Insignia Clerk, M. G. P. Kelly, M.V.O.

Clerks, J. McGurk; Miss A. A. Hamersley, M.V.O.;
Mrs. E. Rogers, M.V.O.; Mrs. A. M. Hughes,
M.V.O.; Mrs. H. Hill; Miss H. Speed.

The Honorable Corps of Gentlemen at Arms
St. James's Palace, S.W.1.

Captain, The Baroness Llewelyn-Davies of Hastoe, P.C.; *Lieutenant*, Col. H. N. Clowes, D.S.O., O.B.E.; *Standard Bearer*, Col. S. Enderby, D.S.O., M.C.; *Clerk of the Cheque & Adjutant*, Lt.-Col. P. J. Clifton, D.S.O.; *Harbinger*, Lt.-Col., J. Chandos-Pole, O.B.E.

Gentlemen of the Corps

Brigadiers, Hon. R. G. Hamilton-Russell, D.S.O.; J. E. Swetenham, D.S.O.

Colonels, C. J. Kidston-Montgomerie, D.S.O., M.C.; P. F. I. Reid, O.B.E.; R. J. V. Crichton, M.C.; P. Pardoe; A. G. Way, M.C.; A. N. Breitmeyer.

Lieutenant-Colonels, R. S. G. Perry, D.S.O.; Hon. M. G. Edwards, M.B.E.; Sir William Lowther, Bt., O.B.E.; H. A. Hope, O.B.E., M.C.; T. C. Sinclair, O.B.E., M.C.; N. H. R. Speke, M.C.; C. E. J. Eagles, R.M.; D. A. St. G. Laurie, O.B.E., M.C.; P. Hodgson; R. Steele, M.B.E.; W. S. P. Lithgow.

Majors, D. S. Allhusen; The Marquess of Donegall; Sir Richard Carne Rasch, Bt.; D. A. Jamieson, V C.; J. D. Dillon, D.S.C., R.M.; The Lord Suffield, M.C.; T. St. Aubyn; J. E. Joicey, M.C.

The Queen's Bodyguard of the Yeoman of the Guard
St. James's Palace, S.W.1.

Captain, The Lord Strabolgi; *Lieutenant*, Lt.-Col. Sir John Hornung, K.C.V.O., O.B.E., M.C.; *Clerk of the Cheque and Adjutant*, Col. H. T. Brassey, O.B.E., M.C.; *Ensign*, Col. A. B. Pemberton, M.B.E.; *Exons.*, Capt. Sir Charles McGrigor, Bt.; Major B. M. H. Shand, M.C.

MASTER OF THE HOUSEHOLD'S DEPARTMENT
Board of Green Cloth.
Buckingham Palace, S.W.1.

Master of the Household, Vice-Admiral Sir Peter Ashmore, K.C.B., M.V.O., D.S.C.

Deputy Master of the Household, Lt.-Col. B. A. Stewart-Wilson.

Chief Clerk, G. H. Franklin, M.V.O.

Deputy Chief Clerk, A. Hancock.

Assistants to the Master of the Household, M. D. Tims, M.V.O.; R. Winship.

Senior Clerk, J. S. Cowdery.

Clerks, Miss A. Tyer; Miss S. Derry; Miss M. Bull; Miss J. Heard.

Superintendent, *Windsor Castle*, Major W. Nash, M.B.E.

Palace Steward, J. Walton.

Chief Housekeeper, Miss V. Martin.

ROYAL MEWS DEPARTMENT
Buckingham Palace, S.W.1.

Crown Equerry, Lt.-Col. Sir John Mansel Miller, K.C.V.O., D.S.O., M.C.

Equerries, Major G. R. S. Broke; Lt.-Col. B. A. Stewart-Wilson; Capt. R. de L. Cazenove (*temp.*).

Extra Equerries, Vice-Admiral Sir Conolly Abel-Smith, G.C.V.O., C.B.; Lt.-Col. the Lord Adeane, P.C., G.C.B., G.C.V.O.; Vice-Adm. Sir Peter Ashmore, K.C.B., M.V.O., D.S.C.; Cdr. Colin Buist, C.V.O., R.N.; Rear-Adm. the Earl Cairns, G.C.V.O., C.B.; Lt.-Col. Rt. Hon. Sir Martin Michael Charles Charteris, C.V.O., K.C.B., O.B.E.; Vice-Adm. Sir Peter Dawnay, K.C.V.O., C.B., D.S.C.; Major Sir Geoffrey Eastwood, K.C.V.O.; C.B.E.; Air Vice-Marshal Sir Edward Fielden, G.C.V.O., C.B., D.F.C., A.F.C.; Sir Edward William Spencer Ford, K.C.B., K.C.V.O.; Brigadier Walter Douglas Campbell Greenacre, C.B., D.S.O., M.V.O.; Brig.

Sir Geoffrey Paul Hardy-Roberts, K.C.V.O., C.B.; C.B.E.; Rear-Admiral Hugh Frederick Janion,, Lt.-Col. John Frederick Dame Johnston, M.V.O., M.C.; Rt. Hon. Sir Alan Lascelles, G.C.B., G.C.V.O., C.M.G., M.C.; Major Sir Rennie Maudslay, K.C.V.O. M.B.E.; Major Sir Mark Vane Milbank, Bt., K.C.V.O., M.C.; Air Commodore Dennis Mitchell, C.V.O. D.F.C., A.F.C.; Rear-Adm. Sir Patrick John Morgan, K.C.V.O., C.B., D.S.C.; Lt.-Col. Ririd Myddleton, M.V.O.; Lt.-Col. Sir Eric Charles William Mackenzie Penn, K.C.V.O., O.B.E., M.C.; Cdr. Sir Philip John Row, K.C.V.O., O.B.E., R.N.; Maj.-Gen. Sir Arthur Guy Salisbury-Jones, G.C.V.O., C.M.G., C.B.E., M.C.; Group Capt. Peter Wooldridge Townsend, C.V.O., D.S.O., D.F.C.; Rear-Admiral Sir Richard John Trowbridge, K.C.V.O.; Air Commodore Archie Little Winskill, C.V.O., C.B.E., D.F.C. (*Captain of the Queen's Flight*).

Veterinary Surgeon, Peter Scott Dunn, M.R.C.V.S.

Supt. Royal Mews, Buckingham Palace, Major W. Phelps, M.B.E.

Comptroller of Stores, Capt. R. E. Fletcher, M.B.E.

Chief Clerk, M. Carlisle, M.V.O.

HER MAJESTY'S HOUSEHOLD IN SCOTLAND

Hereditary Lord High Constable, The Countess of Erroll.

Hereditary Master of the Household, The Duke of Argyll.

Lyon King of Arms, Sir James Grant, K.C.V.O., W.S.

Hereditary Standard-Bearer, The Earl of Dundee, P.C.

Hereditary Keepers:—
Holyrood, The Duke of Hamilton and Brandon.
Falkland, Maj. M. D. D. Crichton-Stuart, M.C.
Stirling, The Earl of Mar and Kellie.

Keeper of Dumbarton Castle, Admiral Sir Angus Cunningham Graham of Gartmore, K.B.E., C.B.

Governor of Edinburgh Castle, Lieut.-Gen. Sir David Scott-Barrett, K.B.E., M.C.

Dean of the Order of the Thistle, The Very Rev. Prof. J. McIntyre, M.A., B.D., D.Litt., D.D.

Dean of the Chapel Royal, Very Rev. H. O. Douglas, C.B.E., M.A.

Chaplains in Ordinary, Very Rev. R. W. V. Selby Wright, C.V.O., T.D., D.D., F.R.S.E., F.S.A.(Scot.); Very Rev. W. R. Sanderson, D.D.; Rev. W. H. Rogan, D.D.; Rev. W. J. Morris, B.A., B.D., Ph.D.; Very Rev. G. T. H. Reid, M.C., M.A., D.D.; Rev. H. W. McP. Cant, M.A., B.D.; Rev. K. Macvicar, M.B.E., D.F.C., T.D., M.A.; Very Rev. J. McIntyre, M.A., B.D., D.Litt.; D.D.; Rev. Prof. R. A. S. Barbour, M.C., M.A., B.D.

Extra Chaplains, Very Rev. A. J. Fraser, M.B.E., T.D., D.D.; Very Rev. the Lord MacLeod of Fuinary, M.C., D.D.; Very Rev. Prof. J. S. Stewart, D.D.; Rev. Prof. E. P. Dickie, M.C., D.D.; Very Rev. A. N. Davidson, D.D.; Very Rev. R. L. Small, C.B.E., D.D.; Rev. R. H. G. Budge, M.V.O., M.A.

Domestic Chaplain Balmoral, Rev. T. J. T. Nicol, M.B.E., M.C., M.A., D.D.

Historiographer, J. D. Mackie, C.B.E., M.C., Ll.D.

Botanist, Harold R. Fletcher, Ph.D., D.Sc., F.R.S.E.

Painter and Limner (vacant).

Sculptor, Benno Schotz, R.S.A.

Astronomer, Prof. V. C. Reddish, B.Sc., Ph.D., D.Sc., F.R.S.E.

Physicians in Scotland, Prof. K. Lowe, M.D., F.R.C.P.;

Prof. K. W. Donald, D.S.C., M.A., M.D., D.Sc., F.R.C.P.E., F.R.C.P., F.R.S.E.

Extra Physicians in Scotland, Prof. Sir Stanley Davidson, M.D., F.R.C.P., F.R.S.E.; Prof. Sir Derrick Dunlop, M.D., F.R.C.P., F.R.C.P.E., F.R.S.E.

Surgeons in Scotland, Prof. Sir Donald Macleod Douglas, M.B.E., Ch.M., M.S., D.Sc., F.R.C.S.

Extra Surgeons in Scotland, George G. Bruce, M.D., Ch.B., M.B., F.R.C.S.Ed.; Prof. Sir Charles Illingworth, C.B.E., M.D., F.R.C.S.Ed.

Surgeon Oculist in Scotland, Prof. G. I. Scott, C.B.E., M.A., F.R.C.S.Ed., F.R.S.E., F.R.C.P.

Surgeon Dentist in Scotland, John Crawford Shiach, F.D.S.

Surgeon Apothecary to the Household at Balmoral, G. F. Lindsay, M.B., Ch.B.

Surgeon Apothecary to the Household at Holyroodhouse, D. G. Illingworth, M.D., F.R.C.P., Ch.B.

THE QUEEN'S BODYGUARD FOR SCOTLAND
The Royal Company of Archers.
Archers' Hall, Edinburgh.

Captain General and Gold Stick for Scotland, Col. the Earl of Stair, C.V.O., M.B.E.

Captains, Major Sir Hugh Rose, Bt., T.D.; Major The Lord Home of the Hirsel, P.C., K.T.; Brigadier The Lord Stratheden and Campbell, C.B.E.; The Duke of Buccleuch and Queensbury, V.A.D.

Lieutenants, Admiral Sir Angus Cunninghame-Graham, K.B.E., C.B.; Lt.-Col. Sir John Gilmour, Bt., D.S.O., T.D., M.P.; Major Sir Alastair Blair, K.C.V.O., T.D. Col.; The Lord Clydesmuir, K.T., C.B.E., M.C., T.D.

Ensigns, The Lord Maclean, P.C., K.T., G.C.V.O., K.B.E.; Major Sir Hew Hamilton-Dalrymple, Bt., C.V.O. (*Adjutant*); Major The Earl of Wemyss and March. K.T.; The Earl of Airlie.

Brigadiers, Lt.-Gen. Sir William Turner, K.B.E., C.B., D.S.O.; The Earl of Dalhousie, K.T., G.B.E., M.C.; Capt. I. M. Tennant; Maj.-Gen. The Earl Cathcart, C.B., D.S.O., M.C.; Capt. N. E. F. Dalrymple-Hamilton, C.V.O., M.B.E., D.S.C., R.N.; The Marquess of Lothian; Brigadier J. C. Monteith, M.C.; Col. the Hon. John Warrender, O.B.E., M.C.; Commodore Sir John Clerk of Penicuik, Bt., C.B.E., V.R.D., R.N.R.; The Earl of Elgin and Kincardine; Col. G. R. Simpson, D.S.O., T.D.; Major D. H. Butter, M.C.; The Earl of Mintos, M.B.E.

Adjutant, Major Sir Hew Hamilton-Dalrymple, Bt., C.V.O.

Surgeon, Lt.-Col. D. N. Nicholson, T.D., M.B., F.R.C.P.E.

Chaplain, Very Rev. R. W. V. Selby Wright, C.V.O., D.D., F.R.S.E.

President of the Council and Silver Stick for Scotland, Col. the Lord Clydesmuir, K.T., C.B., M.B.E., T.D.

Vice-President, Major Sir Hugh Rose, Bt., T.D.

Secretary, Capt. G. W. Burnet.

Treasurer, Col. G. R. Simpson, D.S.O., T.D.

HOUSEHOLD OF THE PRINCE PHILIP, DUKE OF EDINBURGH
Private Secretary and Treasurer, Lord Rupert Nevill.

Equerry, Lt.-Cdr. D. A. J. Blackburn, R.N.

Extra Equerry, J. B. V. Orr, C.V.O.

Temporary Equerries, Capt. D. R. Christie-Miller, R.M.; Major C. X. S. Fenwick, Grenadier Guards.

Chief Clerk and Accountant, R. G. Davis.

HOUSEHOLD OF QUEEN ELIZABETH THE QUEEN MOTHER
Lord Chamberlain, Major the Earl of Dalhousie, K.T., G.B.E., M.C.

Comptroller and Extra Equerry, Capt. Alastair S. Aird, M.V.O.

Private Secretary and Equerry, Lt.-Col. Sir Martin Gilliat, K.C.V.O., M.B.E.

Treasurer and Equerry, Major Sir Ralph Anstruther, Bt., K.C.V.O., M.C.

Equerry, Major the Hon. Sir Francis Legh, K.C.V.O.

Press Secretary and Extra Equerry, Major Arthur J. S. Griffin, C.V.O.

Extra Equerries, The Lord Sinclair, M.V.O.; Maj. Raymond Seymour, M.V.O.; The Lord Adam Gordon, K.C.V.O., M.B.E.

Equerry (Temp.), Capt. R. H. Grimshaw.

Apothecary to the Household, Sir Ralph Southward, K.C.V.O., M.B., Ch.B., F.R.C.P.

Surgeon-Apothecary to the Household (Royal Lodge, Windsor), J. P. Clayton, M.V.O., M.A., M.B., B.Chir., M.R.C.S., L.R.C.P.

Mistress of the Robes, The Duchess of Abercorn, D.C.V.O.

Ladies of the Bedchamber, The Dowager Viscountess Hambleden, D.C.V.O.; The Lady Grimthorpe.

Extra Ladies of the Bedchamber, The Dowager Lady Harlech, D.C.V.O.; The Dowager Countess of Scarborough, D.C.V.O.

Women of the Bedchamber, The Lady Jean Rankin, D.C.V.O.; The Hon. Mrs. John Mulholland, D.C.V.O.; Ruth, Lady Fermoy, C.V.O., O.B.E.; Mrs. Patrick Campbell-Preston.

Extra Women of the Bedchamber, The Lady Victoria Wemyss, C.V.O.; The Hon. Mrs. Geoffrey Bowlby, C.V.O.; The Lady Delia Peel, D.C.V.O.; The Lady Katharine Seymour, D.C.V.O.; The Lady Elizabeth Basset, C.V.O.

Clerk Comptroller, M. Blanch, M.V.O.

Chief Accountant, J. P. Kyle, M.V.O.

Clerks, Miss L. A. Gosling; Miss F. Fletcher.

HOUSEHOLD OF THE PRINCE OF WALES
Private Secretary and Equerry, Sqn.-Ldr. D. J. Checketts, C.V.O.

Secretary, M. M. Colborne.

Equerry, Capt. T. P. G. N. Ward.

Temporary Equerry, Capt. A. J. Davies.

HOUSEHOLD OF THE PRINCESS ANNE, MRS. MARK PHILLIPS
Private Secretary, Maj. N. Lawson.

Lady in Waiting, Mrs. Rowena Brassey, M.V.O.

Extra Ladies in Waiting, Mrs. Richard Carew Pole; Miss Victoria Legge Bourke.

Personal Secretary, Mrs. David Hodgson.

Clerk, Miss P. J. Walters.

HOUSEHOLD OF THE PRINCESS MARGARET, COUNTESS OF SNOWDON
Treasurer, Major The Hon. Sir Francis Legh, K.C.V.O.

Private Secretary and Comptroller, The Lord Napier and Ettrick.

Personal Secretary, Miss M. Murray Brown, M.V.O.

Lady in Waiting, The Hon. Davina Woodhouse.

Extra Ladies in Waiting, The Lady Elizabeth Cavendish, M.V.O.; Mrs. Alastair Aird; Mrs. Robin Benson; The Lady Juliet Townsend; The Hon. Mrs. Wills; Mrs. Jocelyn Stevens; The Lady Anne Tennant; The Hon. Mrs. Whitehead.

THE DUKE AND DUCHESS OF GLOUCESTER'S HOUSEHOLD
Comptroller, Private Secretary and Equerry, Lt.-Col. S. C. M. Bland, C.V.O.

Ladies in Waiting, Mrs. Michael Wigley; Miss Jennifer Thomson.

PRINCESS ALICE, DUCHESS OF GLOUCESTER'S HOUSEHOLD

Comptroller, Private Secretary and Equerry, Lt.-Col. S. C. M. Bland, C.V.O.

Ladies in Waiting, Miss Jean Maxwell-Scott, C.V.O.; Miss Jane Egerton-Warburton (*temp.*).

Extra Ladies in Waiting, Miss Dorothy Meynell, C.V.O.; Miss Diana Harrison; The Hon. Jane Walsh.

THE DUKE AND DUCHESS OF KENT'S HOUSEHOLD

Treasurer, Sir Philip Hay, K.C.V.O., T.D.

Private Secretary, Lieut.-Cdr. Richard Buckley, C.V.O., R.N.

Ladies in Waiting, Mrs. Alan Henderson; Miss Jane Pugh.

Extra Lady in Waiting, Mrs. Peter Wilmot-Sitwell.

HOUSEHOLD OF PRINCESS ALEXANDRA

Lady in Waiting, The Lady Mary Fitzalan-Howard, M.V.O.

Private Secretary and Extra Lady in Waiting, Miss Mona Mitchell, M.V.O.

Extra Ladies in Waiting, The Hon. Lady Rowley; The Lady Mary Colman; The Lady Caroline Waterhouse.

Extra Equerry, Maj. P. C. Clarke, C.V.O.

HONORARY PHYSICIANS TO THE QUEEN (CIVIL)

(Appointed for three years from Nov. 1, 1974)

T. T. Baird, *Chief Medical Officer, Northern Ireland Office*; R. T. Bevan, *Chief Medical Officer, Welsh Office*; D. H. D. Burbridge, O.B.E., *Senior Principal Medical Officer, Department of Health and Social Security*; D. E. Cullington, *Area Medical Officer, Berkshire Area Health Authority*; J. L. Gilloran, *Specialist in Community Medicine, Lothian Health Board*; C. W. Gordon, T.D., *Regional Medical Officer, West Midlands Regional Health Authority.*

THE QUEEN'S BIRTHDAY, 1977

The date for the observance of the Queen's Birthday in 1977 both at home and abroad will be Saturday, June 11.

ROYAL SALUTES

On the Anniversaries of the Birth, Accession and Coronation of the Sovereign a salute of 62 guns is fired on the wharf at the Tower of London.

On extraordinary and triumphal occasions, such as on the occasion of the Sovereign opening,

proroguing or dissolving Parliament in Person, or when passing through London in procession, except when otherwise ordered, 41 guns only are fired.

On the occasion of the birth of a Royal infant, a salute of 41 guns is fired from the two Saluting Stations in London, *i.e.* Hyde Park and the Tower of London.

Constable of the Royal Palace and Fortress of London, Field-Marshal Sir Geoffrey Baker, G.C.B., C.M.G., C.B.E., M.C. (1975).

Lieutenant of the Tower of London, Lieut.-Gen. Sir Napier Crookenden, K.C.B., D.S.O., O.B.E.

Major, Resident Governor and Keeper of the Jewel House, Maj.-Gen. W. D. M. Raeburn, C.B., D.S.O., M.B.E.

Master Gunner of St. James's Park, Field-Marshal Sir Geoffrey Baker, G.C.B., C.M.G., C.B.E., M.C. (1970).

Master Gunner within the Tower (vacant).

THE ROYAL ARMS

QUARTERLY.—1st and 4th *gules*, three lions passant guardant in pale *or* (*England*); 2nd *or*, a lion rampant within a double tressure flory counterflory *gules* (*Scotland*); 3rd *azure*, a harp *or*, stringed *argent* (*Ireland*); the whole encircled with the Garter.

SUPPORTERS.—*Dexter*: a lion rampant guardant *or*, imperially crowned. *Sinister*: a unicorn *argent*, armed crined and unguled *or*, gorged with a coronet composed of crosses patées and fleurs de lis, a chain affixed passing between the forelegs and reflexed over the back.

BADGES.—The red and white rose united (*England*), a thistle (*Scotland*); a harp *or*, the strings *argent*, with a shamrock leaf *vert* (*Ireland*); upon a mount *vert*, a dragon passant wings elevated *gules* (*Wales*).

THE UNION JACK

The national flag of the United Kingdom is the Union Flag, generally known as the Union Jack, the name deriving from the use of the Union Flag on the jack-staff of naval vessels. It is a combination of the cross of the patron saint of England, St. George (*cross gules in a field argent*), the cross of the patron saint of Scotland, St. Andrew (*saltire argent in a field azure*) and a cross similar to that of St. Patrick, patron saint of Ireland (*saltire gules in a field argent*). The Union Flag was first introduced in 1606 after the union of England and Scotland, the cross of St. Patrick being added in 1801

ANNUITIES TO THE ROYAL FAMILY

The annuity payable to Her Majesty is known as the Civil List, and is payable out of the Consolidated Fund under the authority of a Civil List Act following the recommendation of a Parliamentary Select Committee. The amount of the Civil List was fixed in the Civil List Act 1952 at £475,000 and was increased from January 1, 1972, under the Civil List Act 1972 to £980,000, and in 1975 to £1,400,000.

The Civil List Acts also provide separate annuities payable from the Consolidated Fund to other members of the Royal Family. The amounts payable under the Acts of 1910, 1937, 1952 and 1972 are as follows:—

Queen Elizabeth The Queen Mother	£95,000
The Duke of Edinburgh	65,000
The Princess Anne	35,000
The Princess Margaret	35,000
Princess Alice, Duchess of Gloucester	20,000

In addition a sum of £60,000 a year is payable from the Consolidated Fund to the Royal Trustees (The Prime Minister, the Chancellor of the Exchequer and the Keeper of the Privy Purse) for contributions towards expenses incurred in undertaking Royal duties by other members of the Royal Family not in receipt of an annuity.

THE FLYING OF FLAGS

Days for hoisting the Union Flag on Government and Public Buildings (from 8 A.M. to sunset).

February 6 (1952).—Her Majesty's Accession.
February 19 (1960).—Birthday of the Prince Andrew.
March 1.—St. David's Day (in Wales only).
March 10(1964).—Birthday of the Prince Edward.
April 21 (1926).—Birthday of Her Majesty the Queen.
April 23.—St. George's Day (in England only). Where a building has two or more flagstaffs the Cross of St. George may be flown in addition to the Union Jack but not in a superior position.
June 2 (1953).—Coronation Day.
June 10 (1921).—Birthday of the Duke of Edinburgh.
June 11.—Queen's Official Birthday, 1977.
Aug. 4 (1900).—Birthday of Her Majesty Queen Elizabeth the Queen Mother.
Aug. 15 (1950).—Birthday of the Princess Anne.
Aug. 21 (1930).—Birthday of the Princess Margaret.
Nov. 12.—Remembrance Sunday, 1977.
Nov. 14 (1948).—Birthday of the Prince of Wales.
Nov. 20 (1947).—Her Majesty's Wedding Day.
Nov. 30.—St. Andrew's Day (in Scotland only).

And on the occasion of the opening and closing of Parliament by the Queen, flags should be flown on public buildings in the Greater London area, whether or not Her Majesty performs the ceremony in person.

The only additions to the above list will be those notified to the Department of the Environment by Her Majesty's command and communicated by the Ministry to the other Departments. The list applies equally to Government and Public Buildings in London and elsewhere in the United Kingdom. In cases where it has been the practice to fly the Union Jack daily, *e.g.* on some Custom Houses, that practice may continue.

Flags will be flown at half-mast on the following occasions:—

(*a*) From the announcement of the death up to the funeral of the Sovereign, except on Proclamation Day, when they are hoisted right up from 11 a.m. to sunset.

(*b*) The funerals of members of the Royal Family, subject to special commands from Her Majesty in each case.

(*c*) The funerals of Foreign Rulers, subject to special commands from Her Majesty in each case.

(*d*) The funerals of Prime Ministers and ex-Prime Ministers of the United Kingdom.

(*e*) Other occasions by special command of Her Majesty.

On occasions when days for flying flags coincide with days for flying flags at half mast the following rules will be observed. Flags will be flown: (*a*) although a member of the Royal Family, or a near relative of the Royal Family, may be lying dead, unless special commands be received from Her Majesty to the contrary, and (*b*) although it may be the day of the funeral of a Foreign Ruler. If the body of a very distinguished subject is lying at a Government Office the flag may fly at half mast on that office until the body has left (provided it is a day on which the flag would fly) and then the flag is to be hoisted right up. On all other Public Buildings the flag will fly as usual.

The *Royal Standard* is only to be hoisted when the Queen is actually present in the building, and never when Her Majesty is passing in procession.

RED-LETTER DAYS

Scarlet Robes are worn by the Judges of the Queen's Bench Division on *Red-Letter Days* at the sittings of a Criminal Court or of the Court of Appeal (Criminal Divn.) and on all State Occasions.

RED-LETTER DAYS AND STATE OCCASIONS, 1976.		
Jan. 25. Conversion of St. Paul.	*May* 1. St. Philip and St. James.	*Aug.* 4. Birthday of Queen Elizabeth the Queen Mother.
Feb. 2. Purification.	,, 19. Ascension Day.	
,, 6. Queen's Accession.	*June* 2. Coronation Day.	*Oct.* 18. St. Luke.
,, 23. Ash Wednesday.	,, 10. Birthday of the Duke of Edinburgh.	,, 28. St. Simon and St. Jude.
,, 24. St. Matthias.	,, 11. St. Barnabas.	*Nov.* 1. All Saints.
,, 25. Annunciation.	,, 11. Queen's Official Birthday (1977).	,, 6. Lord Mayor's Day.
Apr. 21. Queen's Birthday.	,, 24. St. John the Baptist.	,, 14. Birthday of the Prince of Wales.
,, 25. St. Mark	,, 29. St. Peter.	,, 30. St. Andrew.
	July 25. St. James.	*Dec.* 21. St. Thomas.

THE MILITARY KNIGHTS OF WINDSOR

Founded in 1348 after the Wars in France to assist English Knights, who, having been prisoners in the hands of the French, had become impoverished by the payments of heavy ransoms. They received a pension and quarters in Windsor Castle. Edward III founded the Order of the Garter later in the same year, incorporating the Knights of Windsor and the College of St. George into its foundation and raising the number of Knights to 26 to correspond with the number of the Knights of the Garter. Known later as the Alms Knights or Poor Knights of Windsor, their establishment was reduced under the will of King Henry VIII to 13 and Statutes were drawn up by Queen Elizabeth I.

In 1833 King William IV changed their designation to The Military Knights and granted them their present uniform which consists of a scarlet tail-coat with white cross sword-belt, crimson sash and cocked hat with plume. The badges are the Shield of St. George and the Star of the Order of the Garter. The Knights receive a small stipend in addition to their Army pensions and quarters in Windsor Castle. They take part in all ceremonies of the Noble Order of the Garter and attend Sunday morning service in St. George's Chapel as representatives of the Knights of the Garter.

Applications for appointment should be made to The Military Secretary, Ministry of Defence, Army Dept.

Governor, Maj.-Gen. Sir Edmund Hakewill Smith, K.C.V.O., C.B., C.B.E., M.C.

Military Knights, Lt.-Colonel R. F. Squibb, M.C.; Brigadier W. P. A. Robinson, M.C.; Brigadier A. A. Crook, D.S.O.; Lt.-Colonel R. J. L. Penfold; Lt.-Colonel L. W. Giles, O.B.E., M.C.; Colonel H. G. Duncombe, D.S.O.; Lt.-Colonel R. W. Dobbin, O.B.E.; Major H. Smith, M.B.E.; Lt.-Colonel H. R. Clark, M.C.; Lt.-Colonel C. A. Harvey; Lt.-Col. A. J. Spratley, M.B.E., M.M.; Major A. E. Wollaston

The Peerage

THE PEERAGE AND ITS DEGREES

The rules which govern the creation and succession of Peerages are extremely complicated. There were separate Peerages of England, of Scotland, and of Ireland, until the unions of the three countries: of England and Scotland, forming Great Britain, in 1707; and of Great Britain and Ireland, forming the United Kingdom, in 1801. Some Scottish Peers received additional Peerages of Great Britain or of the United Kingdom, since 1707; and some Irish Peers additional Peerages of the United Kingdom since 1801.

All Peers of England, Scotland, Great Britain, or the United Kingdom who are of full age and of British nationality are entitled to seats in the House of Lords. But Peers of Ireland who have no additional United Kingdom Peerage are not entitled to sit, although they are eligible for election to the House of Commons and to vote (if of voting age) in Parliamentary elections (which other Peers are not). The two Archbishops and 24 of the 41 diocesan Bishops of the Church of England also have seats in the House of Lords.

Certain ancient Peerages pass on death to the nearest heir, male or female, and several are now held by women who are thus Peeresses in their own Right. They are entitled to sit in the House of Lords if they are of full age and British nationality.

Since 1876 the Crown has conferred non-hereditary or Life Peerages in the degree of Baron on eminent judges to enable them to carry out the judicial function of the House of Lords. They are known as Law Lords. Under an Act passed in 1958 the Crown may confer Life Peerages on men and women giving them, in the degree of Baron or Baroness, seats in the House of Lords.

In 1963 an Act was passed enabling Peers to disclaim their Peerages for life: living Peers, within 12 months after the passing of the Act (July 31, 1963), future Peers within 12 months (one month if an M.P.) after the date of their succession, or of attaining their majority if later.

No fees for Dignities have been payable since 1937. No hereditary Peerages have been created since 1965.

PEERAGES EXTINCT SINCE THE LAST ISSUE

BARONIES.—Cozens-Hardy (cr. 1914); Godber (cr. 1956); Lyle of Westbourne (cr. 1945); Tucker (cr. 1950) (Law Life Peerage);

DISCLAIMER OF PEERAGES

The following peers have disclaimed their peerages under the Peerage Act, 1963: Earl of Durham; Earl of Home; Earl of Sandwich; Viscount Hailsham; Viscount Stansgate; Lord Altrincham; Lord Beaverbrook; Lord Fraser of Allander; Lord Monkswell; Lord Reith; Lord Sanderson of Ayot; Lord Silkin; Lord Southampton; Lord Archibald.

PEERS WHO ARE MINORS

(As at Jan. 1, 1977)

MARQUESS (1): Milford Haven (b. 1961).
EARLS (3): Craven (b. 1957); Hardwicke (b. 1971); Woolton (b. 1958).

BARONS (2): Fairfax of Cameron (b. 1956); Londesborough (b. 1959).

CONTRACTIONS AND SYMBOLS

Contractions and Symbols.—S. or I. appended to the date of creation denotes a *Scottish* or *Irish* title, the further addition of a ★ implies that the Peer in question holds also an *Imperial* title, which is specified (after the name) by its more definite description as *Engl.*, *Brit.*, or *U.K.* When both titles are alike, as in the case of Argyll, this star is appended to the conjoined date below, and it then denotes that such date is that of the imperial creation. The mark ° signifies that there is no " of " in the Marquessate or Earldom so designated; *b.* signifies born; *s.*, succeeded; *m.*, married; *w.*, widower or widow; *M.*, minor.

NUMBERS OF THE PEERAGE

	Hereditary	Minors	No Seat	Life or Term	In House of Lords
Royal Dukes	4	—	—	—	4
Archbishops	—	—	—	2	2
Dukes	26	—	—	—	26
Marquesses	38	1	—	—	37
Earls	199	3	21	—	175
Viscounts	131	—	15	—	116
Bishops	—	—	17	24	24
Barons (and Scots Lords)	485	2	36	15	462
Peeresses in own Right	20	—	1	—	19
Life Peers (under 1958 Act)	—	—	—	243	243
Life Peeresses (under 1958 Act)	—	—	—	38	38
Totals	904	6	90	322	1,148

ROYAL DUKES

Style, His Royal Highness the Duke of ——.
Addressed as, Sir, or more formally, May it please your Royal Highness.

1947 *Edinburgh,* The Prince Philip, Duke of Edinburgh, K.G., P.C., K.T., O.M., G.B.E., *b.* 1921, *m.* (see pp. 217 and 218).

1337 *Cornwall,* Charles, Prince of Wales, Duke of Cornwall (*Scottish Duke, Rothesay,* 1398). K.G., G.C.B. *b.* 1948, (see p. 218).

1928 *Gloucester* (2nd), Richard, Duke of Gloucester, G.C.V.O., *b.* 1944, *s.* 1974, *m.* (see p. 217).

1934 *Kent* (2nd), Edward, Duke of Kent, G.C.M.G., G.C.V.O., *b.* 1935, *s.* 1942, *m.* (see p. 217).

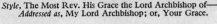

ARCHBISHOPS

Style, The Most Rev. His Grace the Lord Archbishop of——.
Addressed as, My Lord Archbishop; or, Your Grace.

Trans.
1974   Canterbury (101st), Frederick Donald Coggan, P.C., D.D., *b.* 1909, *m.*
    Consecrated Bishop of Bradford, 1956; translated to York, 1961.
1974   York (94th), Stuart Yarworth Blanch, P.C., M.A., *b.* 1918, *m. Con-*
    secrated Bishop of Liverpool, 1966.

DUKES

Style, His Grace the Duke of——. *Addressed as*, My Lord Duke; or, Your Grace. The
eldest sons of Dukes and Marquesses take, by courtesy, their father's second title.
The other sons and the daughters are styled Lord Edward, Lady Caroline. etc.

Created.	Title, Order of Succession, Name, etc.	Eldest Son or Heir.
1868I.*	*Abercorn* (4th), James Edward Hamilton (5th *Brit. Marq.*, 1790, and 13th *Scott. Earl*, 1606 both *Abercorn*), *b.* 1904, *s.* 1953, *m.*	Marquess of Hamilton, *b.* 1934.
1701S.	*Argyll*, Ian Campbell (12th *Scottish* and 5th *U.K. Duke, Argyll*), *b.* 1937, *s.* 1973, *m.*	Marquess of Lorne, *b.* 1968.
1892*		
1703 S.	*Atholl* (10th), George Iain Murray, *b.* 1931, *s.* 1957.	Arthur S. P. M. *b.* 1899.
1682	*Beaufort* (10th), Henry Hugh Arthur FitzRoy Somerset, K.G., P.C., G.C.V.O., Royal Victorian Chain, *b.* 1900, *s.* 1924, *m.* (*Master of the Horse*).	David R. S., *b.* 1928.
1694	*Bedford* (13th), John Robert Russell, *b.* 1917, *s.* 1953, *m.*	Marquess of Tavistock, *b.* 1940.
1663 S.*	*Buccleuch* (9th) & (11th) *Queensbury* (1706), Walter Francis John Montagu-Douglas-Scott, V.R.D. (8th *Engl. Earl, Doncaster*, 1662), *b.* 1923, *s.* 1973, *m.*	Earl of Dalkeith, *b.* 1954.
1694	*Devonshire* (11th), Andrew Robert Buxton Cavendish, P.C., M.C., *b.* 1920, *s.* 1950, *m.*	Marquess of Hartington, *b.* 1944.
1900	*Fife* (3rd), James George Alexander Bannerman Carnegie, *b.* 1929, *s.* 1959. (*see p. 216*).	Earl of Macduff, *b.* 1961.
1675	*Grafton* (11th), Hugh Denis Charles FitzRoy, K.G., *b.* 1919, *s.* 1970, *m.*	Earl of Euston, *b.* 1947.
1643 S.*	*Hamilton* (15th), Angus Alan Douglas Douglas-Hamilton (*Premier Peer of Scotland*; 12th *Brit. Duke, Brandon*, 1711), *b.* 1938, S. 1973, *m.*	Lord James D.-H., M.P., *b.* 1942.
1766I.*	*Leinster* (8th), Gerald FitzGerald (*Premier Duke, Marquess and Earl of Ireland*; 8th *Brit. Visct., Leinster*, 1747), *b.* 1914, *s.* 1976, *m.*	Marquess of Kildare, *b.* 1948.
1719	*Manchester* (10th), Alexander George Francis Drogo Montagu, O.B.E., *b.* 1902, *s.* 1947, *m.*	Visct. Mandeville, *b.* 1929.
1702	*Marlborough* (11th), John George Vanderbilt Henry Spencer-Churchill, *b.* 1926, *s.* 1972, *m.*	Marquess of Blandford, *b.* 1955.
1707 S.*	*Montrose* (7th), James Angus Graham (5th *Brit. Earl, Graham*, 1722), *b.* 1907, *s.* 1954, *m.*	Marquess of Graham, *b.* 1935.
1756	*Newcastle (under Lyme)* (9th), Henry Edward Hugh Pelham-Clinton-Hope, O.B.E., *b.* 1907, *s.* 1941, *m.*	Edward C. Pelham-Clinton, *b.* 1920.
1483	*Norfolk* (17th), Miles Francis Fitzalan-Howard, C.B., C.B.E., M.C. (*Premier Duke and Earl*; 12th *Eng. Baron Beaumont*, 1309; 4th *U.K. Baron Howard of Glossop*, 1869), *b.* 1915, *s.* 1975, *m.* (*Earl Marshal*).	Earl of Arundel and Surrey, *b.* 1956.
1766	*Northumberland* (10th), Hugh Algernon Percy, K.G., P.C., T.D., F.R.S., *b.* 1914, *s.* 1940, *m.* (*Lord Steward*).	Earl Percy, *b.* 1953.
1716	*Portland* (7th), William Arthur Henry Cavendish-Bentinck, K.G., T.D., (3rd *U.K. Baron, Bolsover*, 1880) *b.* 1893, *s.* 1943, *m.*	Major Sir Ferdinand W. C.-B., K.B.E., C.M.G., *b.* 1888.
1675	*Richmond* (9th) & *Gordon* (4th, 1876), Frederick Charles Gordon-Lennox (9th *Scott. Duke, Lennox*. 1675), *b.* 1904, *s.* 1935, *m.*	Earl of March and Kinrara, *b.* 1929.
1707 S.*	*Roxburghe* (10th), Guy David Innes-Ker (5th *U.K. Earl, Innes*, 1837), *b.* 1954, *s.* 1974 (*Premier Baronet of Scotland*).	Lord Robert I.-K., *b.* 1959.
1703	*Rutland* (10th), Charles John Robert Manners, C.B.E., *b.* 1919, *s.* 1940, *m.*	Marquess of Granby, *b.* 1959.
1684	*St. Albans* (13th), Charles Frederick Aubrey de Vere Beauclerk, O.B.E., *b.* 1915, *s.* 1964, *m.*	Earl of Burford, *b.* 1939.
1547	*Somerset* (18th), Percy Hamilton Seymour, *b.* 1910, *s.* 1954, *m.*	Lord Seymour, *b.* 1952.
1833	*Sutherland* (6th), John Sutherland Egerton (5th *U.K. Earl Ellesmere*, 1846), *b.* 1915, *s.* 1963, *m.*	Cyril R. E., *b.* 1905.
1814	*Wellington* (8th), Arthur Valerian Wellesley, M.V.O., O.B.E., M.C. (9th *Irish Earl, Mornington*, 1760), *b.* 1915, *s.* 1972, *m.*	Marquess of Douro, *b.* 1945.
1874	*Westminster* (5th), Robert George Grosvenor, T.D., *b.* 1910, *s.* 1967, *m.*	Earl Grosvenor, *b.* 1951.

MARQUESSES

Style, The Most Hon. the Marquess of——. *Addressed as*, My Lord Marquess.
In titles marked ° the " of " is *not* used. For the style of Marquesses' sons and
daughters, *see* under " DUKES," above.

1915   Aberdeen and Temair (5th), Archibald Victor Dudley Gordon, (11th   Lord Alastair G., *b.* 1920.
    Scott. Earl, Aberdeen, 1682), *b.* 1913, *s.* 1974.

Created.	Title, Order of Succession, Name, etc.	Eldest Son or Heir.
1876	Abergavenny (5th), John Henry Guy Larnach-Nevill, K.G., O.B.E., b. 1914, s. 1954, m.	Lord Rupert N., b. 1923.
1821	Ailesbury (8th), Michael Sidney Cedric Brudenell-Bruce, b. 1926, s. 1974, m.	Earl of Cardigan, b. 1952.
1831	Ailsa (7th), Archibald David Kennedy, O.B.E., (19th Scott. Earl, Cassillis, 1509), b. 1925, s. 1957, m.	Earl of Cassillis, b. 1956.
1815	Anglesey (7th), George Charles Henry Victor Paget, b. 1922, s. 1947, m.	Earl of Uxbridge, b. 1950.
1789	Bath (6th), Henry Frederick Thynne, E.D., b. 1905, s. 1946, m.	Viscount Weymouth, b. 1932.
1826	Bristol (6th), Victor Frederick Cochrane Hervey, b. 1915, s. 1960, m.	Earl Jermyn, b. 1954.
1796	Bute (6th), John Crichton-Stuart (11th Scott. Earl, Dumfries, 1633), b. 1933, s. 1956, m.	Earl of Dumfries, b. 1958.
1917	Cambridge (2nd), George Francis Hugh Cambridge, G.C.V.O., b. 1895, s. 1927, m.	(None.)
1812	°Camden (5th), John Charles Henry Pratt, b. 1899, s. 1943, m.	Earl of Brecknock, b. 1930.
1815	Cholmondeley (6th), George Hugh Cholmondeley, M.C. (10th Irish Viscount, Cholmondeley, 1661), b. 1919, s. 1968, m. (Lord Great Chamberlain).	Earl of Rocksavage, b. 1960.
1816I*	°Conyngham (7th), Frederick William Henry Francis Conyngham (7th U.K. Baron, Minster, U.K. 1821), b. 1924, s. 1974, m.	Earl of Mount Charles, b. 1951.
1791I.*	Donegall (7th), Dermot Richard Claude Chichester (7th Brit. Baron, Fisherwick, 1790, 6th Brit. Baron, Templemore, 1831), b. 1916, s. to Marquessate, 1975: to Templemore Barony, 1953, m.	Earl of Belfast, b. 1952.
1789I.*	Downshire (7th), Arthur Wills Percy Wellington Blundell Trumbull Sandys Hill (7th Brit. Earl, Hillsborough, 1772), b. 1894, s. 1918, m.	A. Robin I. H., b. 1929.
1888	Dufferin & Ava (5th), Sheridan Frederick Terence Hamilton-Temple-Blackwood (11th Irish Baron, Dufferin & Clandeboye, 1800), b. 1938, s. 1945, m.	(None to Marquessate), to Irish Barony, Sir Francis E. T. Blackwood, Bt., b. 1901.
1801 I.*	Ely (8th) Charles John Tottenham (8th U.K. Baron, Loftus, 1801), b. 1913, s. 1969, w.	Viscount Loftus, b. 1943.
1801	Exeter (6th), David George Brownlow Cecil, K.C.M.G., b. 1905, s. 1956, m.	Lord Martin C., b. 1909.
1800 I.*	Headfort (6th), Thomas Geoffrey Charles Michael Taylour (4th U.K. Baron, Kenlis, 1831), b. 1932, s. 1960, w.	Earl of Bective, b. 1959.
1793	Hertford (8th), Hugh Edward Conway Seymour (9th Irish Baron, Conway, 1712), b. 1930, s. 1940, m.	Earl of Yarmouth, b. 1958.
1599 S.*	Huntly (12th), Douglas Charles Lindsay Gordon (Premier Marquess of Scotland) (4th U.K. Baron, Meldrum, 1815), b. 1908, s. 1937.	Earl of Aboyne, b. 1944.
1784	Lansdowne (8th), George John Charles Mercer Nairne Petty-Fitzmaurice, P.C. (8th Irish Earl, Kerry, 1722), b. 1912, s. 1944, m.	Earl of Shelburne, b. 1941.
1902	Linlithgow (3rd), Charles William Frederick Hope, M.C. (10th Scott. Earl, Hopetoun, 1703), b. 1912, s. 1952, m.	Earl of Hopetoun, b. 1946.
1816 I.*	Londonderry (9th), Alexander Charles Robert Vane-Tempest-Stewart (6th U.K. Earl, Vane, 1823), b. 1937, s. 1955, m.	Viscount Castlereagh, b. 1972.
1701 S.*	Lothian (12th), Peter Francis Walter Kerr (6th U.K. Baron, Kerr, 1821), b. 1922, s. 1940, m.	Earl of Ancram, b. 1945.
1917	Milford Haven (4th), George Ivar Louis Mountbatten, b. 1961, s. 1970, M.	Lord Ivar M, b. 1963.
1838	Normanby (4th), Oswald Constantine John Phipps, C.B.E. (8th Irish Baron, Mulgrave, 1767), b. 1912, s. 1932, m.	Earl of Mulgrave, b. 1954.
1812	Northampton (6th), William Bingham Compton, D.S.O., b. 1885, s. 1913, w.	Earl Compton, b. 1946.
1825 I.*	Ormonde (7th), James Hubert Theobald Charles Butler, M.B.E. (7th U.K. Baron, Ormonde, 1821), b. 1899, s. 1971, w.	(None to Marquessate), to Earldoms of Ormonde and Ossory, Viscount Mountgarret (see p. 236).
1682 S.	Queensberry (12th), David Harrington Angus Douglas, b. 1929, s. 1954, m.	Viscount Drumlanrig, b. 1967.
1926	Reading (3rd), Michael Alfred Rufus Isaacs, M.B.E., M.C., T.D., b. 1916, s. 1960, m.	Viscount Erleigh, b. 1942.
1789	Salisbury (6th), Robert Edward Peter Gascoyne-Cecil, b. 1916, s. 1972, m.	Viscount Cranborne, b. 1946.
1800 I.*	Sligo (10th), Denis Edward Browne (10th U.K. Baron, Monteagle, 1806), b. 1908, s. 1952, m.	Earl of Altamont, b. 1939.
1787	°Townshend (7th), George John Patrick Dominic Townshend, b. 1916, s. 1921, m.	Viscount Raynham, b. 1945.
1694 S.*	Tweeddale (12th), David George Montagu Hay, G.C. (3rd U.K. Baron, Tweeddale, 1881), b. 1921, s. 1967, m.	Earl of Gifford, b. 1947.
1789 I.*	Waterford (8th), John Hubert de la Poer Beresford (8th Brit. Baron, Tyrone, 1786), b. 1933, s. 1934, m.	Earl of Tyrone, b. 1958.
1936	Willingdon (2nd), Inigo Brassey Freeman-Thomas, b. 1899, s. 1941, m.	(None.)
1551	Winchester (18th), Nigel George Paulet (Premier Marquess of England), b. 1941, s. 1968, m.	Earl of Wiltshire, b. 1969.
1892	Zetland (3rd), Lawrence Aldred Mervyn Dundas (5th U.K Earl of Zetland, 1838, 6th Brit. Baron Dundas, 1794), b. 1908, s. 1961, m.	Earl of Ronaldshay, b. 1937.

EARLS

Style (*see also* note, p. 257). The Right Hon. the Earl of ——. *Addressed as*, My Lord. The eldest sons of Earls take, by courtesy, their father's second title, the younger sons being styled the Hon., *e.g.* the Hon. John ——, but the daughters Lady Elizabeth ——, etc. Where marked ° the " of " is not used.

Created.	Title, Order of Succession, Name, etc.	Eldest Son or Heir.
1639 S.	*Airlie* (13th), David George Coke Patrick Ogilvy, *b.* 1926, *s.* 1968, *m.*	Lord Ogilvy, *b.* 1958.
1696	*Albemarle* (9th), Walter Egerton George Lucian Keppel, M.C., *b.* 1882, *s.* 1942, *m.*	Viscount Bury, *b.* 1965.
1952	°*Alexander of Tunis* (2nd), Shane William Desmond Alexander, *b.* 1935, *s.* 1969.	Hon. Brian J. A., *b.* 1939.
1826	°*Amherst* (5th), Jeffery John Archer Amherst, M.C., *b.* 1896, *s.* 1927.	Hon. Humphrey W. A., *b.* 1903.
1892	*Ancaster* (3rd), Gilbert James Heathcote-Drummond-Willoughby, K.C.V.O., T.D. (26th E. Baron Willoughby de Eresby, 1313), *b.* 1907, *s.* 1951, *w.*	(To Earldom, none; to Barony, Lady Nancy H.-D.-W., *b.* 1934.)
1789 I.	°*Annesley* (9th), Robert Annesley, *b.* 1900, *s.* 1957, *m.*	Viscount Glerawly, *b.* 1924.
1785 I.	*Antrim* (8th), Randal John Somerled McDonnell, K.B.E., *b.* 1911, *s.* 1932, *m.*	Viscount Dunluce, *b.* 1935.
1762 I.*	*Arran* (8th), Arthur Strange Kattendyke David Archibald Gore (4th U.K. Baron Sudley, 1884), *b.* 1910, *s.* 1958, *m.*	Viscount Sudley, *b.* 1938.
1955	°*Attlee* (2nd), Martin Richard Attlee, *b.* 1927, *s.* 1967, *m.*	Viscount Prestwood, *b.* 1956.
1961	*Avon* (1st), (Robert) Anthony Eden, K.G., P.C., M.C., *b.* 1897, *m.*	Viscount Eden, O.B.E., T.D., *b.* 1930.
1714	*Aylesford* (11th), Charles Ian Finch-Knightley, *b.* 1918, *s.* 1958, *m.*	Lord Guernsey, *b.* 1947.
1937	°*Baldwin of Bewdley* (4th), Edward Alfred Alexander Baldwin, *b.* 1938, *s.* 1976, *m.*	Viscount Corvedale, *b.* 1973.
1922	*Balfour* (4th) Gerald Arthur James Balfour, *b.* 1925, *s.* 1968, *m.*	Eustace A. G. B., *b.* 1921.
1800 I.	*Bandon* (5th), Percy Ronald Gardner Bernard, G.B.E., C.B., C.V.O., D.S.O., *b.* 1904, *s.* 1924, *m.*	Maj. Hon. Charles B. A. B., C.B.E., *b.* 1904 (Twin).
1772	°*Bathurst* (8th), Henry Allen John Bathurst, *b.* 1927, *s.* 1943, *m.*	Lord Apsley, *b.* 1961.
1919	°*Beatty* (3rd), David Beatty, *b.* 1946, *s.* 1972, *m.*	Viscount Borodale, *b.* 1973.
1815	°*Beauchamp* (8th), William Lygon, *b.* 1903, *s.* 1938, *m.*	Reginald A. L., *b.* 1904.
1797 I.	*Belmore* (8th), John Armar Lowry-Corry, *b.* 1951, *s.* 1960.	Frederick H. L.-C., *b.* 1926.
1739 I. ⎫ 1937* ⎭	*Bessborough* (2nd), Frederick Edward Neuflize Ponsonby, (10th Irish Earl Bessborough), *b.* 1913, *s.* 1956, *m.*	Arthur M. L. P., *b.* 1912 (to Irish Earldom only).
1922	*Birkenhead* (3rd), Frederick William Robin Smith, *b.* 1936, *s.* 1975.	(None.)
1815	*Bradford* (6th), Gerald Michael Orlando Bridgeman, T.D., *b.* 1911, *s.* 1957, *m.*	Viscount Newport, *b.* 1947.
1677 S.	*Breadalbane and Holland* (10th), John Romer Boreland Campbell, *b.* 1919, *s.* 1959.	(None).
1469 S.*	*Buchan* (16th), Donald Cardross Flower Erskine, (7th U.K. Baron Erskine), *b.* 1899, *s.* (to Barony), 1957, (to Earldom) 1960, *m.*	Lord Cardross, *b.* 1930.
1746	*Buckinghamshire* (9th), Vere Frederick Cecil Hobart-Hampden, *b.* 1901, *s.* 1963, *m.*	G. Miles H.-H., *b.* 1944.
1800	°*Cadogan* (7th), William Gerald Charles Cadogan, M.C., *b.* 1914, *s.* 1933, *m.*	Viscount Chelsea, *b.* 1937.
1878	°*Cairns* (5th), David Charles Cairns, G.C.V.O., C.B., *b.* 1909, *s.* 1946, *m.*	Viscount Garmoyle, *b.* 1939.
1543 S.	*Caithness* (20th), Malcolm Ian Sinclair, *b.* 1948, *s.* 1965, *m.*	Sir John R. N. B. S., Bt., *b.* 1928.
1800 I.	*Caledon* (6th), Denis James Alexander, *b.* 1920, *s.* 1968, *m.*	Viscount Alexander, *b.* 1955.
1661	*Carlisle* (12th), Charles James Ruthven Howard, M.C., *b.* 1923, *s.* 1963, *m.*	Viscount Morpeth, *b.* 1949.
1793	*Carnarvon* (6th), Henry George Alfred Marius Victor Francis Herbert, *b.* 1898, *s.* 1923.	Lord Porchester, K.B.E., *b.* 1924.
1748 I.*	*Carrick* (9th), Brian Stuart Theobald Somerset Caher Butler (3rd U.K. Baron, Butler, 1912), *b.* 1931, *s.* 1957, *m.*	Viscount Ikerrin, *b.* 1953.
1800 I.	°*Castle Stewart* (8th), Arthur Patrick Avondale Stuart, *b.* 1928, *s.* 1961, *m.*	Viscount Stuart, *b.* 1953.
1814	°*Cathcart* (6th), Alan Cathcart, C.B., D.S.O., M.C. (15th Scott. Baron, Cathcart), *b.* 1919, *s.* 1927, *m.*	Lord Greenock, *b.* 1952.
1647 I.	*Cavan* (12th), Michael Edward Oliver Lambart, T.D., *b.* 1911, *s.* 1950, *m.*	Roger C. L., *b.* 1944.
1827	°*Cawdor* (6th), Hugh John Vaughan Campbell, *b.* 1932, *s.* 1970, *m.*	Viscount Emlyn, *b.* 1962.
1801	*Chichester* (9th), John Nicholas Pelham, *b.* 1944, *s.* 1944, *m.*	Richard A. H. P., *b.* 1952.
1803 I.*	*Clancarty* (8th), William Francis Brinsley Le Poer Trench (7th U.K. Visct. Clancarty, 1823), *b.* 1911, *s.* 1975, *m.*	Hon. Power E. F. Le P. T., *b.* 1917.
1776 I.*	*Clanwilliam* (6th), John Charles Edmund Carson Meade (4th U.K. Baron Clanwilliam, 1828), *b.* 1914, *s.* 1953, *m.*	John H. M., *b.* 1919.

Created.	Title, Order of Succession, Name, etc.	Eldest Son or Heir.

1776   *Clarendon* (7th), George Frederick Laurence Villiers, *b.* 1933,   Lord Hyde, *b.* 1976.
s. 1955, *m.*

1620 I.*   *Cork & Orrery* (1660), Patrick Reginald Boyle (13th *Irish Earl* and   Hon. John W. B., D.S.C.,
9th *Brit. Baron, Boyle of Marston*, 1711), *b.* 1910, *s.* 1967, *m.*   *b.* 1916.

1850   *Cottenham* (8th), Kenelm Charles Everard Digby Pepys, *b.* 1948, *s.*   Charles D. L. P., *b.* 1909.
1968, *m.*

1762 I.*   *Courtown* (9th), James Patrick Montagu Burgoyne Stopford (8th   Hon. Jeremy N. S. *b.* 1958.
Brit. Baron, Saltersford, 1796), *b.* 1954, *s.* 1975.

1697   *Coventry* (11th), George William Coventry, *b.* 1934, *s.* 1940, *m.*   Viscount Deerhurst, *b.* 1957.

1857   °*Cowley* (7th), Garrett Graham Wellesley, *b.* 1934, *s.* 1975, *m.*   Hon. Garret G. *W.*, *b.* 1965.

1892   *Cranbrook* (4th), John David Gathorne-Hardy, C.B.E., *b.* 1900, *s.*   Lord Medway, *b.* 1933.
1915, *m.*

1801   *Craven* (7th), Thomas Robert Douglas Craven, *b.* 1957, *s.* 1965, *M.*   Hon. Simon G. C., *b.* 1961.

1398 S.*   *Crawford* (29th) *and Balcarres* (12th), Robert Alexander Lindsay, P.C.,   Lord Balniel, *b,* 1958.
(Premier Earl on Union Roll and 5th U.K. Baron, Wigan, 1826), b.
1927, *s.* 1975, *m.*

1861   *Cromartie* (4th), Roderick Grant Francis Mackenzie, M.C., T.D.,   Viscount Tarbat, *b.* 1948.
b. 1904, *s.* 1962, *m.*

1901   *Cromer* (3rd), George Rowland Stanley Baring, P.C., G.C.M.G., M.B.E.,   Viscount Errington, *b.* 1946.
b. 1918, *s.* 1953, *m.*

1633 S.*   *Dalhousie* (16th), Simon Ramsay, K.T., G.B.E., M.C. (4th *U.K. Baron,*   Lord Ramsay, *b.* 1946.
Ramsay, 1875), *b.* 1914, *s.* 1950, *m.*

1725 I.*   *Darnley* (10th), Peter Stuart Bligh (19th *English Baron, Clifton of*   Hon. Adam I. S. B., *b.* 1941.
Leighton Bromswold, 1608), *b.* 1915, *s.* 1955.

1711   *Dartmouth* (9th), Gerald Humphry Legge, *b.* 1924, *s.* 1962.   Viscount Lewisham, *b.* 1949.

1761   °*De La Warr* (10th), William Herbrand Sackville, *b.* 1921, *s.* 1976, *m.*   Lord Buckhurst, *b.* 1948.

1622   *Denbigh* (11th) *and Desmond* (10th), William Rudolph Michael   Viscount Feilding, *b.* 1970.
Feilding (10th *Irish Earl, Desmond*, 1622), *b.* 1943, *s.* 1966, *m.*

1485   *Derby* (18th), Edward John Stanley, M.C., *b.* 1918, *s.* 1948, *m.*   Hon.   Richard   S.,   *b.*
1920.

1553   *Devon* (17th), Charles Christopher Courtenay, *b.* 1916, *s.* 1935, *m.*   Lord Courtenay, *b.* 1942.

1800 I.*   *Donoughmore* (7th), John Michael Henry Hely-Hutchinson, (7th   Viscount Suirdale, *b.* 1927.
U.K. Visct. Hutchinson, 1821), *b.* 1902, *s.* 1948, *m.*

1661 I.*   *Drogheda* (11th), Charles Garrett Moore, K.G., K.B.E. (2nd *U.K*   Viscount Moore, *b.* 1937.
Baron. Moore, 1954), *b.* 1910, *s.* 1957, *m.*

1837   *Ducie* (6th), Basil Howard Moreton, *b.* 1917, *s.* 1952, *m.*   Lord Moreton, *b.* 1951.

1860   *Dudley* (4th), William Humble David Ward, *b.* 1920, *s.* 1969, *m.*   Viscount Ednam, *b.* 1947.

1660 S.*   *Dundee* (11th), Henry James Scrymgeour-Wedderburn, P.C. (1st   Lord Scrymgeour, *b.* 1949.
U.K. Baron, Glassary, 1954) *b.* 1902, *s.* 1924 *(claim admitted*, 1953),
m. (Hereditary Standard Bearer, Scotland).

1669 S.   *Dundonald* (14th), Ian Douglas Leonard Cochrane, *b.* 1918, *s.*   Lord Cochrane, *b.* 1961.
1958, *w.*

1686 S.*   *Dunmore* (9th), John Alexander Murray (4th *U.K. Baron, Dunmore,*   Reginald A. *M.*, *b.* 1911.
1831), *b.* 1939, *s.* 1962, *m.*

1822 I.   *Dunraven and Mount Earl* (7th), Thady Windham Thomas   Capt. Hon. Valentine M.
Wyndham-Quin, *b.* 1939, *s.* 1965, *m.*   *W.-Q.*, R.N., *b.* 1890.

1837   *Effingham* (6th), Mowbray Henry Gordon Howard (16th *E. Baron,*   David P. M. A. H., *b.*
Howard of Effingham, 1553), *b.* 1905, *s.* 1946, *m.*   1939.

1507 S. }   *Eglinton* (18th) *& (9th) Winton* (1600), Archibald George Montgom-   Lord Montgomerie, *b.* 1966.
1859* }   erie (6th *U.K. Earl Winton*, 1859), *b.* 1939, *s.* 1966, *m.*

1733 I.*   *Egmont* (11th), Frederick George Moore Perceval (9th *Brit. Baron,*   Viscount Perceval, *b.* 1934.
Lovel & Holland, 1762), *b.* 1914, *s.* 1932, *m.*

1821   *Eldon* (4th), John Scott, G.C.V.O., *b.* 1899, *s.* 1926, *w.*   Viscount Encombe, *b.* 1937.

1633 S.*   *Elgin* (11th), *& Kincardine* (15th) (1647), Andrew Douglas Alexander   Lord Bruce, *b.* 1961.
Thomas Bruce, (4th *U.K. Baron, Elgin*, 1849), *b.* 1924, *s.* 1968, *m.*

1789 I.*   *Enniskillen* (6th), David Lowry Cole, M.B.E., (4th *U.K. Baron, Grin-*   Viscount Cole, *b.* 1942.
stead, 1815) *b.* 1918, *s.* 1963, *m.*

1789 I.*   *Erne* (6th), Henry George Victor John Crichton (3rd *U.K. Baron,*   Viscount Crichton, *b.* 1971.
Fermanagh, 1876), *b.* 1937, *s.* 1940, *m.*

1661   *Essex* (9th), Reginald George de Vere Capell, T.D., *b.* 1906, *s.* 1966,   Robert E. de V. C., *b.* 1920.
m.

1711   °*Ferrers* (13th), Robert Washington Shirley, *b.* 1929, *s.* 1954, *m.*   Viscount   Tamworth,   *b.*
1952.

1628 I.*   *Fingall* (12th), Oliver James Horace Plunkett, M.C. (19th *I. Baron,*   (None to Earldom or U.K.
Killeen, 1449) (5th *U.K. Baron, Fingall*, 1831), *b.* 1896 *s.* 1929, *m.*   Barony), to Irish Barony
   Lord Dunsany (*see p.*
   241).

1746*   °*Fitzwilliam* (8th) William Thomas George Wentworth-Fitz-   (None.)
william (10th *Irish Earl, Fitzwilliam*, 1716), *b.* 1904, *s.* 1952, *m.*

1789   °*Fortescue* (6th), Denzil George Fortescue, M.C., T.D., *b.* 1893, *s.* 1958,   Viscount   Ebrington,   *b.*
m.   1922.

Created.	Title, Order of Succession, Name, etc.	Eldest Son or Heir.
1841	Gainsborough (5th), Anthony Gerard Edward Noel, b. 1923, s. 1927, m.	Viscount Campden, b. 1950.
1623 S.*	Galloway (12th), Randolph Algernon Ronald Stewart (5th Brit. Baron, Stewart of Garlies, 1796), b. 1892, s. 1920, w.	Lord Garlies, b. 1928.
1703 S.*	Glasgow (9th), David William Maurice Boyle, C.B. D.S.C. (3rd U.K. Baron, Fairlie, 1897), b. 1910, s. 1963, m.	Viscount of Kelburn, b. 1939.
1806 I.*	Gosford (7th), Charles David Alexander John Sparrow Acheson (5th U.K. Baron, Worlingham, 1835), b. 1942, s. 1966.	Hon. Patrick B. V. M. A., b. 1915.
1945	Gowrie (2nd), Alexander Patrick Greysteel Hore-Ruthven (3rd U.K. Baron, Ruthven of Gowrie, 1919), b. 1939, s. 1955.	Viscount Ruthven of Canberra and Dirleton, b. 1964.
1684 I.*	Granard (9th), Arthur Patrick Hastings Forbes, A.F.C. (4th U.K. Baron, Granard, 1806), b. 1915, s. 1948, m. [m.	Hon. John F., b. 1920.
1833	°Granville (5th), Granville James Leveson-Gower, M.C., b. 1918, s. 1953.	Lord Leveson, b. 1959.
1806	°Grey (6th), Richard Fleming George Charles Grey, b. 1939, s. 1963, m.	Phillip K. G., b. 1940.
1752	Guilford (9th), Edward Francis North, b. 1933, s. 1949, m.	Lord North, b. 1971.
1619 S.	Haddington (12th), George Baillie-Hamilton, K.T., M.C., T.D., b. 1894, s. 1917, m.	Lord Binning, b. 1941.
1919	°Haig (2nd), George Alexander Eugene Douglas Haig, O.B.E. b. 1918, s. 1928, m.	Viscount Dawick, b. 1961.
1944	Halifax (2nd), Charles Ingram Courtenay Wood (4th U.K. Viscount, Halifax, 1866), b. 1912, s. 1959, m.	Lord Irwin, b. 1944.
1898	Halsbury (3rd), John Anthony Hardinge Giffard, F.R.S., b. 1908, s. 1943, m.	Viscount Tiverton, b. 1934.
1754	Hardwicke (10th), Joseph Philip Sebastian Yorke, b. 1971, s. 1974, M.	Richard C. J. Y., b. 1916.
1812	Harewood (7th), George Henry Hubert Lascelles, b. 1923, s. 1947, m. (See also p. 217).	Viscount Lascelles, b. 1950.
1742	Harrington (11th), William Henry Leicester Stanhope (8th U.K. Viscount, Stanhope of Mahon, 1717), b. 1922, s. 1929, m.	Viscount Petersham, b. 1945.
1809	Harrowby (6th), Dudley Ryder, b. 1892, s. 1956, w.	Viscount Sandon, b. 1922.
1821	°Howe (6th), Edward Richard Assheton Curzon, C.B.E., b. 1908, s. 1964, m.	George C., b. 1898.
1529	Huntingdon (15th), Francis John Clarence Westenra Plantagenet Hastings, b. 1901, s. 1939, m.	David F. G. H., b. 1909.
1885	Iddesleigh (4th), Stafford Henry Northcote, b. 1932, s. 1970, m.	Viscount St. Cyres, b. 1957.
1750	Ilchester (9th), Maurice Vivian de Touffreville Fox-Strangways, b. 1920, s. 1970, m.	Hon. Raymond G. F.-S., b. 1921.
1929	Inchcape (3rd), Kenneth James William Mackay, b. 1917, s. 1939, m.	Viscount Glenapp, b. 1943.
1919	Iveagh (3rd), Arthur Francis Benjamin Guinness, b. 1937, s. 1967, m.	Viscount Elveden, b. 1969.
1925	°Jellicoe (2nd), George Patrick John Rushworth Jellicoe, P.C., D.S.O., M.C., b. 1918, s. 1935, m.	Viscount Brocas, b. 1950.
1697	Jersey (9th), George Francis Child-Villiers (12th Irish Visct., Grandison, 1620), b. 1910, s. 1923, m.	Viscount Villiers, b. 1948.
1822 I.	Kilmorey (5th), Francis Jack Richard Patrick Needham, b. 1915, s. 1961, m.	Viscount Newry and Mourne, b. 1942.
1866	Kimberley (4th), John Wodehouse, b. 1924, s. 1941, m.	Lord Wodehouse, b. 1951.
1768 I.	Kingston (11th), Barclay Robert Edwin King-Tenison, b. 1943, s. 1948, m.	Viscount Kingsborough, b. 1969.
1633 S.*	Kinnoull (15th), Arthur William George Patrick Hay (9th Brit. Baron, Hay of Pedwardine, 1711), b. 1935, s. 1938, m.	Viscount Dupplin, b. 1962.
1602 S.	Kintore (12th), (James) Ian Baird (3rd U.K. Visct., Stonehaven, 1938), b. 1908, s. to Viscountcy, 1941, to Earldom, 1974, m.	Lord Inverurie, b. 1939.
1914	°Kitchener of Khartoum (3rd), Henry Herbert Kitchener, b. 1919, s. 1937.	Hon. Charles E. K., b. 1920.
1756 I.	Lanesborough (9th), Denis Anthony Brian Butler, b. 1918, s. 1959.	Cdr. Terence B. J. D. B., b. 1913.
1624 S.	Lauderdale (17th), Patrick Francis Maitland, b. 1911, s. 1968, m.	Viscount Maitland, b. 1937.
1837	Leicester (5th), Thomas William Edward Coke, M.V.O., b. 1908, s. 1949, m.	Anthony L. C., b. 1909.
1641 S.	Leven (14th) & (13th) Melville (1690), Alexander Robert Leslie-Melville, b. 1924, s. 1947, m.	Lord Balgonie, b. 1954.
1831	Lichfield (5th), Thomas Patrick John Anson, b. 1939, s. 1960, m.	Geoffrey R. A., b. 1929.
1803 I.*	Limerick (6th), Patrick Edmund Pery (6th U.K. Baron, Foxford, 1815), b. 1930, s. 1967, m.	Viscount Glentworth, b. 1963.
1633 S.	Lindsay (14th), William Tucker Lindesay-Bethune, b. 1901, s. 1943, m.	Viscount Garnock, b. 1926.
1626	Lindsey (14th) and Abingdon (9th) (1682), Richard Henry Rupert Bertie, b. 1931, s. 1963, m.	Lord Norreys, b. 1958.
1776 I.	Lisburne (8th), John David Malet Vaughan, b. 1918, s. 1965, m.	Viscount Vaughan, b. 1945.
1822 I.*	Listowel (5th), William Francis Hare, P.C., G.C.M.G. (3rd U.K. Baron, Hare, 1806), b. 1906, s. 1931, m.	Viscount Ennismore, b. 1964.
1905	Liverpool (5th), Edward Peter Bertram Savile Foljambe, b. 1944, s. 1969, m.	Viscount Hawkesbury, b. 1972.

Created.	Title, Order of Succession, Name, etc.	Eldest Son or Heir.

1945   °*Lloyd George of Dwyfor* (3rd), Owen Lloyd George, *b.* 1924, *s.* 1968, *m.* — Viscount Gwynnedd, *b.* 1951.

1785 I.* *Longford* (7th), Francis Aungier Pakenham, K.G., P.C. (6th *U.K. Baron, Silchester,* 1821; 1st *U.K. Baron, Pakenham,* 1945). *b.* 1905, *s.* 1961, *m.* — Lord Silchester, *b.* 1933.

1807   *Lonsdale* (7th), James Hugh William Lowther, *b.* 1922, *s.* 1953, *m.* — Viscount Lowther, *b.* 1949.

1838   *Lovelace* (5th), Peter Axel William Locke King (12th *British Baron, King,* 1725), *b.* 1951, *s.* 1964. — (None.)

1795 I.* *Lucan* (7th), Richard John Bingham (3rd *U.K. Baron, Bingham,* 1934), *b.* 1934, *s.* 1964, *m.* — Lord Bingham, *b.* 1967.

1880   *Lytton* (4th), Noel Anthony Scawen Lytton (17th *English Baron, Wentworth,* 1529), *b.* 1900, *s.* 1951, *m.* — Viscount Knebworth, *b.* 1950.

1721   *Macclesfield* (8th), George Roger Alexander Thomas Parker, *b.* 1914, *s.* 1975, *m.* — Viscount Parker, *b.* 1943.

1800   *Malmesbury* (6th), William James Harris, T.D., *b.* 1907, *s.* 1950, *m.* — Viscount FitzHarris, *b.* 1946.

1776 & 1792 *Mansfield and Mansfield* (8th), William David Mungo James Murray (14th *Scott. Visct., Stormont,* 1621), *b.* 1930, *s.* 1971, *m.* — Viscount Stormont, *b.* 1956.

1565 S. *Mar* (13th) & (15th) *Kellie* (1616), John Francis Hervey Erskine, *b.* 1921, *s.* 1955, *m.* — Lord Erskine, *b.* 1949.

1785 I. *Mayo* (10th), Terence Patrick Bourke, *b.* 1929, *s.* 1962, *m.* — Lord Naas, *b.* 1953.

1627 I.* *Meath* (14th), Anthony Windham Normand Brabazon (5th *U.K. Baron, Chaworth,* 1831), *b.* 1910, *s.* 1949, *m.* — Lord Ardee, *b.* 1941.

1766 I. *Mexborough* (7th), John Raphael Wentworth Savile, *b.* 1906, *s.* 1945, *m.* — Viscount Pollington, *b.* 1931.

1920   *Midleton* (2nd), George St. John Brodrick, M.C. (10th *Irish Viscount, Midleton,* 1717), *b.* 1888, *s.* 1942, *m.* — (None to Earldom), to Irish Viscountcy, Trevor L. B., *b.* 1903.

1813   *Minto* (6th), Gilbert Edward George Lariston Garnet Elliot-Murray-Kynynmound, M.B.E., *b.* 1928, *s.* 1975, *m.* — Viscount Melgund, *b.* 1953.

1562 S.* *Moray* (20th) Douglas John Moray Stuart (12th *Brit. Baron, Stuart of Castle Stuart,* 1796), *b.* 1928, *s.* 1974, *m.* — Lord Doune, *b.* 1966.

1815   *Morley* (6th), John St. Aubyn Parker, *b.* 1923, *s.* 1962, *m.* — Visct. Boringdon, *b.* 1956.

1458 S. *Morton* (22nd), John Charles Sholto Douglas, *b.* 1927, *s.* 1976, *m.* — Lord Aberdour, *b.* 1952.

1947   °*Mountbatten of Burma* (1st), Louis Francis Albert Victor Nicholas Mountbatten, K G , P.C., G.C.B., O.M., G.C.S.I., G.C.I.E., G.C.V.O., D.S.O., *b.* 1900, *w.* (*Personal A.D.C. to the Queen*), Admiral of the Fleet. (*See also* p. 215). — Baroness Brabourne, *b.* 1924. (*see* pp. 215 and 239),

1789   *Mount Edgcumbe* (7th), Edward Piers Edgcumbe, *b.* 1903, *s.* 1965, *m.* — George A. V. E., *b.* 1907.

1831   *Munster* (6th), Edward Charles FitzClarence, *b.* 1899, *s.* 1975, *m.* — Lord Tewkesbury, *b.* 1926.

1805   °*Nelson* (8th), George Joseph Horatio Nelson, *b.* 1905, *s.* 1972, *m.* — Peter J. H. N., *b.* 1941.

1827 I. *Norbury* (6th), Noel Terence Graham-Toler, *b.* 1939, *s.* 1955, *m.* — Viscount Glandine, *b.* 1967.

1806 I.* *Normanton* (6th), Shaun James Christian Welbore Ellis Agar (9th *U.K. Baron, Mendip,* 1791) (4th *U.K. Baron, Somerton,* 1873), *b.* 1945, *s.* 1967, *m.* — Hon. Mark S. A. A., *b.* 1948.

1647 S. *Northesk* (13th), Robert Andrew Carnegie, *b.* 1926, *s.* 1975, *m.* — Lord Rosehill, *b.* 1954.

1801   *Onslow* (7th), Michael William Coplestone Onslow, *b.* 1938, *s.* 1971, *m.* — Viscount Cranley, *b.* 1967.

1925   *Oxford & Asquith* (2nd), Julian Edward George Asquith, K.C.M.G., *b.* 1916, *s.* 1928, *m.* — Viscount Asquith, *b.* 1952.

1929   °*Peel* (3rd), William James Robert Peel (4th *U.K. Viscount Peel,* 1895), *b.* 1947, *s.* 1969, *m.* — Hon. Robert M. A. P., *b.* 1950.

1551   *Pembroke* (17th) & (14th) *Montgomery* (1605), Henry George Charles Alexander Herbert, *b.* 1939, *s.* 1969, *m.* — Hon. David A. R. H., *b.* 1908.

1605 S. *Perth* (17th), John David Drummond, P.C., *b.* 1907, *s.* 1951, *m.* — Viscount Strathallan, *b.* 1935.

1905   *Plymouth* (3rd), Other Robert Ivor Windsor-Clive (15th *English Baron, Windsor,* 1529), *b.* 1923, *s.* 1943, *m.* — Viscount Windsor, *b.* 1951.

1785 I. *Portarlington* (7th), George Lionel Yuill Seymour Dawson-Damer, *b.* 1938, *s.* 1959, *m.* — Viscount Carlow, *b.* 1965.

1743   *Portsmouth* (9th), Gerard Vernon Wallop, *b.* 1898, *s.* 1943, *m.* — Viscount Lymington, *b.* 1923.

1804   *Powis* (6th), Christian Victor Charles Herbert (7th *Irish Baron, Clive,* 1762), *b.* 1904, *s.* 1974. — George W. H., *b.* 1925.

1765   *Radnor* (8th) Jacob Pleydell-Bouverie, *b.* 1927, *s.* 1968, *m.* — Viscount Folkestone, *b.* 1955.

1831 I.* *Ranfurly* (6th), Thomas Daniel Knox, K.C.M.G. (7th *U.K. Baron, Ranfurly,* 1826), *b.* 1913, *s.* 1933, *m.* — Gerald F. N. K. *b.* 1929.

1771 I. *Roden* (9th), Robert William Jocelyn, *b.* 1909, *s.* 1956, *m.* — Viscount Jocelyn. *b.* 1938.

1801   *Romney* (7th), Michael Henry Marsham, *b.* 1910, *s.* 1975. — Julian C. M, *b.* 1948.

1703 S.* *Rosebery* (7th), Neil Archibald Primrose (3rd *U.K. Earl of Midlothian,* 1911), *b.* 1929, *s.* 1974, *m.* — Lord Dalmeny, *b.* 1967.

Created.	Title, Order of Succession, Name, etc.	Eldest Son or Heir.
1806 I.	*Rosse* (6th), Laurence Michael Harvey Parsons, K.B.E., *b.* 1906, *s.* 1918, *m.*	Lord Oxmantown, *b.* 1936.
1801	*Rosslyn* (6th), Anthony Hugh Francis Harry St. Clair-Erskine, *b.* 1917, *s.* 1939.	Lord Loughborough, *b.* 1958.
1457 S.	*Rothes* (21st), Ian Lionel Malcolm Leslie, *b.* 1932, *s.* 1975, *m.*	Lord Leslie, *b.* 1958.
1861	°*Russell* (4th), John Conrad Russell, *b.* 1921, *s.* 1970.	Hon. Conrad S. R. R., *b.* 1937.
1915	°*St. Aldwyn* (2nd), Michael John Hicks-Beach, P.C., K.B.E. T.D., *b.* 1912, *s.* 1916, *m.*	Viscount Quenington, *b.* 1950.
1815	*St. Germans* (9th), Nicholas Richard Michael Eliot, *b.* 1914, *s.* 1960, *m.*	Lord Eliot, *b.* 1941.
1690	*Scarborough* (12th), Richard Aldred Lumley, (13th *Irish Visct.*, *Lumley*, 1628), *b.* 1932, *s.* 1969, *m.*	Viscount Lumley, *b.* 1973.
1701 S.	*Seafield* (13th), Ian Derek Francis Ogilvie-Grant-Studley-Herbert, *b.* 1939, *s.* 1969, *m.*	Visct. Reidhaven, *b.* 1963.
1882	*Selborne* (4th), John Roundell Palmer, *b.* 1940, *s.* 1971, *m.*	Viscount Wolmer, *b.* 1971.
1646 S.	*Selkirk* (10th) (George) Nigel Douglas-Hamilton, P.C., G.C.M.G., G.B.E., A.F.C., Q.C., *b.* 1906, *s.* 1940, *m.*	The Master of Selkirk, *b.* 1939.
1672	*Shaftesbury* (10th), Anthony Ashley-Cooper, *b.* 1938, *s.* 1961, *m.*	Hon. John P. H. N. A.-C., *b.* 1915.
1756 I.*	*Shannon* (9th), Richard Bentinck Boyle (8th *Brit. Bn.*, *Carleton* 1786), *b.* 1924, *s.* 1963, *m.*	Viscount Boyle, *b.* 1960.
1442	*Shrewsbury* (21st) & *Waterford* (I. 1446), John George Charles Henry Alton Alexander Chetwynd Chetwynd-Talbot (*Premier Earl of England and Ireland; Earl Talbot*, 1784), *b.* 1914, *s.* 1921, *m.*	Viscount Ingestre, *b.* 1952.
1961	*Snowdon* (1st), Antony Charles Robert Armstrong-Jones, G.C.V.O., *b.*, 1930, *m.* (*See also p.* 219.)	Viscount Linley *b.* 1961 (*see p.* 219).
1880	°*Sondes* (5th), Henry George Herbert Milles-Lade, *b.* 1940, *s.* 1970.	(None).
1633 S.*	*Southesk* (11th), Charles Alexander Carnegie, K.C.V.O. (3rd *U.K. Baron, Balinhard*, 1869), *b.* 1893, *s.* 1941, *m.*	The Duke of Fife, *b.* 1929 (*see pp.* 216 and 227).
1765	°*Spencer* (8th), Edward John Spencer, M.V.O., *b.* 1924, *s.* 1975, *m.*	Viscount Althorp, *b.* 1964.
1703 S.*	*Stair* (13th), John Aymer Dalrymple, C.V.O., M.B.E. (6th *U.K. Baron, Oxenfoord*, 1841), *b.* 1906, *s.* 1961, *m.*	Viscount Dalrymple, *b.* 1961.
1628	*Stamford* (10th), Roger Grey, *b.* 1896, *s.* 1910.	(None).
1821	*Stradbroke* (4th), John Anthony Alexander Rous, *b.* 1903, *s.* 1947, *m.*	Hon. Keith R., *b.* 1907.
1847	*Strafford* (7th), Robert Cecil Byng, *b.* 1904, *s.* 1951, *m.*	Viscount Enfield, *b.* 1936.
1937	*Strathmore* (4th), Fergus Michael Claude Bowes-Lyon (17th *Scottish Earl, Strathmore & Kinghorne* 1606), *b.* 1928, *s.* 1972, *m.*	Lord Glamis, *b.* 1957.
1603	*Suffolk* (21st) & (14th) *Berkshire* (1626), Michael John James George Robert Howard, *b.* 1935, *s.* 1941, *m.*	Viscount Andover, *b.* 1974.
1955	*Swinton* (2nd), David Yarburgh Cunliffe-Lister, *b.* 1937, *s.* 1972, *m.*	Hon. Nicholas J. C.-L., *b.* 1939.
1714	*Tankerville* (9th), Charles Augustus Grey Bennet, *b.* 1921, *s.* 1971, *m.*	Lord Ossulston, *b.* 1956.
1822	°*Temple of Stowe* (7th), Ronald Stephen Brydges Temple-Gore-Langton, *b.* 1910, *s.* 1966.	W. Grenville A. T.-G.-L., *b.* 1924.
1815	*Verulam* (7th), John Duncan Grimston (11th *Irish Visct.*, *Grimston*, 1719; 16th *Scott. Baron, Forrester of Corstorphine*, 1633), *b.* 1955, *s.* 1973.	Lord Grimston of Westbury, *b.* 1897 (*see p.* 242).
1729	°*Waldegrave* (12th), Geoffrey Noel Waldegrave, K.G., T.D., *b.* 1905, *s.* 1936, *m.*	Viscount Chewton, *b.* 1940.
1759	*Warwick* & °*Brooke* (1746), Charles Guy Fulke Greville (7th *Earl Brooke* and 7th *Earl of Warwick*), *b.* 1911, *s.* 1928, *m.*	Lord Brooke, *b.* 1934.
1633 S.*	*Wemyss* (12th) & (8th) *March* (1697), Francis David Charteris, K.T. (5th *U.K. Baron, Wemyss*, 1821), *b.* 1912, *s.* 1937, *m.*	Lord Neidpath, *b.* 1948.
1621 I.	*Westmeath* (13th), William Anthony Nugent, *b.* 1928, *s.* 1971, *m.*	Lord Delvin, *b.* 1965.
1624	*Westmorland* (15th), David Anthony Thomas Fane, K.C.V.O., *b.* 1924, *s.* 1948, *m.*	Lord Burghersh, *b.* 1951.
1876	*Wharncliffe* (4th), Alan James Montagu-Stuart-Wortley-Mackenzie, *b.* 1935, *s.* 1953, *m.*	Alan R. Montagu-Stuart-Wortley, *b.* 1927.
1793 I.	*Wicklow* (8th), William Cecil James Philip John Paul Forward-Howard, *b.* 1902, *s.* 1946, *m.*	Cecil A. F.-H., *b.* 1909.
1801	*Wilton* (7th), Seymour William Arthur John Egerton, *b.* 1921, *s.* 1927, *m.*	Lord Ebury, *b.* 1934 (*see p.* 241).
1628	*Winchilsea* (16th) & (11th) *Nottingham* (1681), Christopher Denys Stormont Finch-Hatton, *b.* 1936, *s.* 1950, *m.*	Viscount Maidstone, *b.* 1967.
1766 I.	°*Winterton* (7th), Robert Chad Turnour, *b.* 1915, *s.* 1962, *w.*	N. Cecil T., D.F.M., C.D., *b.* 1919.
1956	*Woolton* (2nd), Simon Frederick Marquis, *b.* 1958, *s.* 1969, *M.*	(None).
1837	*Yarborough* (7th), John Edward Pelham, *b.* 1920, *s.* 1966, *m.*	Lord Worsley, *b.* 1963.
1922	*Ypres* (3rd), John Richard Charles Lambart French, *b.* 1921, *s.* 1948, *m.*	(None.)

VISCOUNTS

Style (see also note, p. 257), The Right Hon. the Viscount——. *Addressed as*, My Lord.
The eldest sons of Viscounts and Barons have no distinctive title; they, as well as
their brothers and sisters, are styled the Hon. Robert, Hon. Mary, &c.

Created.	Title, Order of Succession, Name, etc.	Eldest Son or Heir.
1945	Addison (2nd), Christopher Addison, b. 1904, s. 1951, m.	Hon. Michael A., b. 1914.
1946	Alanbrooke (3rd), Alan Victor Harold Brooke, b. 1932, s. 1972.	(None).
1919	Allenby (2nd), Dudley Jaffray Hynman Allenby, b. 1903, s. 1936, m.	Hon. Michael A., b. 1931.
1911	Allendale (3rd), Wentworth Hubert Charles Beaumont, b. 1922, s. 1956, m.	Hon. Wentworth P. I. B., b. 1948.
1960	Amory (1st), Derick Heathcoat Amory, K.G., P.C., G.C.M.G., T.D., b. 1899.	(None).
1642 S.	Arbuthnott (16th Viscount of Arbuthnott), John Campbell Arbuthnott, D.S.C., b. 1924, s. 1966, m.	Master of Arbuthnott, b. 1950.
1751 I.	Ashbrook (10th), Desmond Llowarch Edward Flower, M.B.E., b. 1905, s. 1936, m.	Hon. Michael F., b. 1935.
1917	Astor (4th), William Waldorf Astor, b. 1951, s. 1966.	Hon. David A., b. 1912.
1781 I.	Bangor (7th), Edward Henry Harold Ward, b. 1905, s. 1950.	Hon. William M. D. W., b. 1948.
1720 I.★	Barrington (11th), Patrick William Daines Barrington (5th U.K. Baron Shute, 1880), b. 1908, s. 1960.	Eric R. W. B., b. 1904.
1925	Bearsted (3rd), Marcus Richard Samuel, T.D., b. 1909, s. 1948, m.	Hon. Peter S., M.C., T.D., b. 1911.
1963	Blakenham (1st), John Hugh Hare, P.C., O.B.E., b. 1911, m.	Hon. Michael J. H., b. 1938.
1935	Bledisloe (2nd), Benjamin Ludlow Bathurst, Q.C., b. 1899, s. 1958, m.	Hon. Christopher H. L. B., b. 1934.
1712	Bolingbroke & St. John (7th), Kenneth Oliver Musgrave St. John, b. 1927, s. 1974, m.	Hon. Henry F. St. J., b. 1957.
1960	Boyd of Merton (1st), Alan Tindal Lennox-Boyd, P.C., C.H., b. 1904, m.	Hon. Simon D. R. N. L.-B., b. 1939.
1717 S★	Boyne (10th), Gustavus Michael George Hamilton-Russell (4th U.K. Baron, Brancepeth, 1866), b. 1931, s. 1942, m.	Hon. Michael G. S. H.-R., b. 1965.
1929	Brentford (3rd), Lancelot William Joynson-Hicks, b. 1902, s. 1958, m.	Hon. Crispin W. J.-H., b. 1933.
1929	Bridgeman (2nd), Robert Clive Bridgeman, K.B.E., C.B., D.S.O., M.C., b. 1896, s. 1935, m.	Robin J. O. B. b. 1930.
1868	Bridport (4th), Alexander Nelson Hood (7th Duke of Brontë in Sicily and 6th Irish Baron, Bridport 1794), b. 1948, s. 1969, m.	Hon. Peregrine A. N. H. b. 1974.
1952	Brookeborough (2nd), John Warden Brooke, P.C. (N.I.), b. 1922, s. 1973, m.	Hon. Alan H. B., b. 1955.
1932	Buckmaster (3rd), Martin Stanley Buckmaster, b. 1921, s. 1974.	Hon. Colin J. B., b. 1923.
1939	Caldecote (2nd), Robert Andrew Inskip, D.S.C., b. 1917, s. 1947, m.	Hon. Piers J. H. I., b. 1947.
1941	Camrose (2nd), (John) Seymour Berry, T.D., b. 1909, s. 1954.	Lord Hartwell, M.B.E. T.D., b. 1911 (see p. 251).
1954	Chandos (2nd), Antony Alfred Lyttelton, b. 1920, s. 1972, m.	Hon. Thomas O. L., b. 1953.
1916	Chaplin (3rd), Anthony Freskyn Charles Hamby Chaplin, b. 1906. s. 1949, m.	(None.)
1665 I.	Charlemont (12th), Richard William St. George Caulfeild (16th Irish Baron, Caulfeild of Charlemont, 1620), b. 1887, s. 1971, w.	Charles W. C., b. 1899.
1921	Chelmsford (3rd), Frederic Jan Thesiger, b. 1931, s. 1970, m.	Hon. Frederic C. P. T., b. 1962.
1717 I.	Chetwynd (10th), Adam Richard John Casson Chetwynd, T.D., b. 1935, s. 1965.	Hon. Adam D. C., b. 1969.
1911	Chilston (3rd), Eric Alexander Akers-Douglas, b. 1910, s. 1947, w.	Alastair G. A.-D., b. 1946.
1902	Churchill (3rd), Victor George Spencer (5th U.K. Baron Churchill, 1815) b. 1934, s. 1973.	None to Viscountcy; to Barony, Richard H. R. S. b. 1926.
1718	Cobham (10th), Charles John Lyttelton, K.G., P.C., G.C.M.G., G.C.V.O. (7th Irish Baron, Westcote, 1766), b. 1909, s. 1949, m.	Hon. John W. L. L., b. 1943.
1902	Colville of Culross (4th), John Mark Alexander Colville (13th Scott. Baron, Colville of Culross, 1604), b. 1933, s. 1945, m.	Master of Colville, b. 1959.
1827	Combermere (5th), Michael Wellington Stapleton-Cotton, b. 1929, s. 1969, m.	Hon. Thomas R. W. S.-C., b. 1969.
1917	Cowdray (3rd), Weetman John Churchill Pearson (3rd U.K. Baron, Cowdray, 1910), b. 1910, s. 1933, m.	Hon. Michael P., b. 1944.
1927	Craigavon (3rd), Janric Fraser Craig, b. 1944, s. 1974.	(None.)
1886	Cross (3rd), Assheton Henry Cross, b. 1920, s. 1932, m.	(None.)
1943	Daventry (2nd), Robert Oliver FitzRoy, b. 1893, s. 1962, m.	Francis H. M. FitzRoy-Newdegate, b. 1921.
1937	Davidson (2nd), John Andrew Davidson, b. 1928, s. 1970.	Hon. Malcolm W. M. D., b. 1934.

Created.	Title, Order of Succession, Name, etc.	Eldest Son or Heir.
1956	De L'Isle (1st), William Philip Sidney, V℃., K.G., P.C., G.C.M.G., G.C.V.O., (6th *Baron De L'Isle and Dudley*, 1835), b. 1909, m.	Hon. Philip S., b. 1945.
1776 I.	De Vesci (6th), John Eustace Vesey (7th *Irish Baron, Knapton*, 1750), b. 1919, s. 1958, m.	Hon. Thomas E. V., b. 1955.
1917	Devonport (3rd), Terence Kearley, b. 1944, s. 1973, m.	
1964	Dilhorne (1st), Reginald Edward Manningham-Buller, P.C. (*Lord of Appeal*), b. 1905, m.	Hon. John M. M.-B., b. 1932.
1622 I.	Dillon (20th), Michael Eric Dillon, b. 1911, s. 1946, m.	Hon. Charles D., b 1945.
1785 I.	Doneraile (9th), Richard St. John St. Leger, b. 1923, s. 1957, m.	Hon. Richard A. St. L., b. 1946.
1680 I.*	Downe (11th), John Christian George Dawnay (4th *U.K. Baron, Dawnay*, 1897), b. 1935, s. 1965, m.	Hon. Richard D., b. 1967.
1959	Dunrossil (2nd), John William Morrison, b. 1926, s. 1961, m.	Hon. Andrew W. R. M., b. 1953.
1964	Eccles (1st), David McAdam Eccles, P.C., K.C.V.O., b. 1904, m.	Hon. John D. E., b. 1931.
1897	Esher (4th), Lionel Gordon Baliol Brett, C.B.E., b. 1913, s. 1963, m.	Hon. Christopher L. B. B., b. 1936.
1816	Exmouth (10th), Paul Edward Pellew, b. 1940, s. 1970, m.	Hon. Peter I. P., b. 1942.
1620 S.	Falkland (14th), Lucius Henry Plantagenet Cary (*Premier Scottish Viscount on the Roll*), b. 1905, s. 1961, m.	Master of Falkland, b. 1935.
1720	Falmouth (9th), George Hugh Boscawen (26th *Eng. Baron, Le Despencer*, 1264), b. 1919, s. 1962, m.	Hon. Evelyn A. H. B., b. 1955.
1918	Furness (2nd), William Anthony Furness, b. 1929, s. 1940.	(None.)
1720 I.*	Gage (6th), Henry Rainald Gage, K.C.V.O. (5th *Brit. Baron, Gage*, 1790), b. 1895, s. 1912, m.	Hon. George J. St. C. G. b. 1932.
1727 I.	Galway (10th), William Arundell Monckton, b. 1894, s. 1971, w.	Edmund S. M., b. 1900.
1478 I.*	Gormanston (17th), Jenico Nicholas Dudley Preston (*Premier Viscount of Ireland*; 5th *U.K. Baron, Gormanston*, 1868), b. 1939, s. 1940, m.	Hon. Jenico F. T. P., b. 1974.
1816 I.	Gort (8th), Colin Leopold Prendergast Vereker, b. 1916, s. 1975, m.	Hon. Foley R.S.P.V., b. 1951.
1900	Goschen (3rd), John Alexander Goschen, K.B.E., b. 1906, s. 1952, m.	Hon. Giles J. H. G., b. 1965.
1849	Gough (5th), Shane Hugh Maryon Gough, b. 1941, s. 1951.	(None.)
1937	Greenwood (2nd), David Henry Hamar Greenwood, b. 1914, s. 1948.	Hon. Michael G. H. G., b. 1923.
1946	Hall (2nd), (William George) Leonard Hall, b. 1913, s. 1965, m.	(None.)
1891	Hambleden (4th), William Herbert Smith, b. 1930, s. 1948, m.	Hon. William H. B. S., b. 1955.
1884	Hampden (6th), Anthony David Brand, b. 1937, s. 1975, m.	Hon. Francis A. B., b. 1970.
1936	Hanworth (2nd), David Bertram Pollock, b. 1916, s. 1936, m.	Hon. David P., b. 1946.
1791 I.	Harberton (9th), Henry Ralph Martyn Pomeroy, b. 1908, s. 1956.	Hon. Thomas De V. P., b. 1910.
1917	Harcourt (2nd), William Edward Harcourt, K.C.M.G., O.B.E., b. 1908, s. 1922, w.	(None.)
1846	Hardinage (4th), Caryl Nicholas Charles Hardinge, M.B.E., b. 1905, s. 1922, m.	Hon. H. Nicholas H., b. 1929.
1791 I.	Hawarden (8th), Robert Leslie Eustace Maude, b 1926, s. 1958, m.	Hon. Robert C. W. L., M., b. 1961.
1960	Head (1st), Antony Henry Head, P.C., G.C.M.G., C.B.E., M.C., b. 1906, m.	Hon. Richard A. H., b. 1937.
1550	Hereford (18th), Robert Milo Leicester Devereux (*Premier Viscount of England*), b. 1932, s. 1952, m.	Hon. Charles R. de B. D., b. 1975.
1842	Hill (8th), Antony Rowland Clegg-Hill, b. 1931, s. 1974, m.	Peter D.R.C. C.-H., b. 1945.
1796	Hood (6th), Samuel Hood, G.C.M.G. (6th *Irish Baron, Hood*, 1782), b. 1919, s. 1933.	Hon. Alexander L. H., b. 1914.
1956	Ingleby (2nd), Martin Raymond Peake, b. 1926, s. 1966, m.	(None.)
1945	Kemsley (2nd), (Geoffrey) Lionel Berry, b. 1909, s. 1968, m.	Hon. Denis G. B., T.D., b. 1911.
1911	Knollys (3rd) David Francis Dudley Knollys, b. 1931, s. 1966, m.	Hon. Patrick N. M. K., b. 1962.
1895	Knutsford (5th), Julian Thurstan Holland-Hibbert, C.B.E., b. 1920, s. 1976.	Michael H.-H., b. 1926.
1945	Lambert (2nd), George Lambert, T.D., b. 1909, s. 1958, m.	Hon. Michael J. L., b. 1912.
1954	Leathers (2nd), Frederick Alan Leathers, b. 1908, s. 1965, m.	Hon. Christopher G. L., b. 1941.
1922	Leverhulme (3rd), Philip William Bryce Lever, T.D., b. 1915, s. 1949, w.	(None.)
		[1949.
1781 I.	Lifford (8th), Alan William Wingfield Hewitt, b. 1900, s. 1954, m.	Hon. Edward J. W. H., b.
1921	Long (4th), Richard Gerard Long, b. 1929, s. 1967, m.	Hon. James R. L., b. 1960.
1957	Mackintosh of Halifax (2nd), John Mackintosh, O.B.E., b. 1921, s. 1964, m.	Hon. J. Clive M., b. 1958.

Created	Title, Order of Succession, Name, etc.	Eldest Son or Heir
1955	*Malvern* (2nd), John Godfrey Huggins, *b.* 1922, *s.* 1971, *m.*	Hon. Ashley, K. G. H., *b.* 1949.
1945	*Marchwood* (2nd), Peter George Penny, M.B.E., *b.* 1912, *s.* 1955, *m.*	Hon. David G. S. P., *b.* 1936.
1942	*Margesson* (2nd), Francis Vere Hampden Margesson, *b.* 1922, *s.* 1965, *m.*	Hon. Richard F. D. M., *b.* 1960.
1660 I.*	*Massereene* (13th) & (6th) *Ferrard* (1797), John Clotworthy Talbot Foster Whyte-Melville Skeffington (6th *U.K. Baron, Oriel,* 1821), *b.* 1914, *s.* 1956, *m.*	Hon. John D. C. W. M. S., *b.* 1940.
1939	*Maugham* (2nd), Robert Cecil Romer Maugham, *b.* 1916, *s.* 1958.	(None.)
1802	*Melville* (9th), Robert David Ross Dundas, *b.* 1937, *s.* 1971.	Hugh McK. D., *b.* 1910.
1916	*Mersey* (3rd), Edward Clive Bingham, *b.* 1906, *s.* 1956, *m.*	Master of Nairne, *b.* 1934.
1962	*Mills* (2nd), Roger Clinton Mills, *b.* 1919, *s.* 1968, *m.*	Hon. Christopher P. R. M., *b.* 1956.
1716 I.	*Molesworth* (11th), Richard Gosset Molesworth, *b.* 1907, *s.* 1961, *m.*	Hon. Robert B. K. M., *b.* 1959.
1801 I.*	*Monck* (6th), Henry Wyndham Stanley Monck, O.B.E., (3rd *U.K. Baron, Monck,* 1866), *b.* 1905, *s.* 1927, *m.*	Hon. Charles S. M., *b.* 1953.
1957	*Monckton of Brenchley* (2nd), Gilbert Walter Riversdale Monckton, C.B., O.B.E., M.C., *b.* 1915, *s.* 1965, *m.*	Hon. Christopher W. M., *b.* 1952.
1935	*Monsell* (2nd), Henry Bolton Graham Eyres-Monsell, *b.* 1905, *s.* 1969.	(None.)
1946	*Montgomery of Alamein* (2nd), David Bernard Montgomery, *b.* 1928, *s.* 1976, *m.*	Hon. Henry D. M., *b.* 1954.
1550 I.*	*Mountgarret* (17th), Richard Henry Piers Butler (4th *U.K. Baron, Mountgarret,* 1911), *b.* 1936, *s.* 1966, *m.*	Hon. Piers J. R. B., *b.* 1961.
1964	*Muirshiel* (1st), John Scott Maclay, P.C., K.T., C.H., C.M.G., *b.* 1905, *w.*	(None.)
1952	*Norwich* (2nd), John Julius Cooper, *b.* 1929, *s.* 1954, *m.*	Hon. Jason C. D. B. C., *b.* 1959.
1873	*Portman* (9th), Edward Henry Berkeley Portman, *b.* 1934, *s.* 1967, *m.*	Hon. Christopher E. B. P., *b.* 1958.
1743 I.*	*Powerscourt* (10th), Mervyn Niall Wingfield, (4th *U.K. Baron, Powerscourt,* 1885), *b.* 1935, *s.* 1973.	Hon. Mervyn A. W., *b.* 1963.
1962	*Radcliffe* (1st), Cyril John Radcliffe, P.C., G.B.E., *b.* 1899, *m.* (*Lord of Appeal,* retired).	(None.)
1900	*Ridley* (4th), Matthew White Ridley, T.D., *b.* 1925, *s.* 1964, *m.*	Hon. Matthew W. R., *b.* 1958.
1960	*Rochdale* (1st), John Durival Kemp, O.B.E., T.D. (2nd *U.K. Baron, Rochdale,* 1913), *b.* 1906, *s.* 1945, *m.*	Hon. St. John K., *b.* 1938.
1919	*Rothermere* (2nd), Edmond Cecil Harmsworth, *b.* 1898, *s.* 1940, *m.*	Hon. Vere H., *b.* 1925.
1937	*Runciman of Doxford* (2nd), Walter Leslie Runciman, O.B.E., A.F.C. (3rd *U.K. Baron, Runciman,* 1933), *b.* 1900, *s.* 1949, *m.*	Hon. Walter G. R., *b.* 1934.
1918	*St. Davids* (2nd), Jestyn Reginald Austen Plantagenet Philipps (19th English Baron, *Strange of Knokin* 1299, 7th English Baron, *Hungerford,* 1426 and *De Moleyns,* 1445), *b.* 1917, *s.* 1938, *m.*	Hon. Colwyn P., *b.* 1939.
1801	*St. Vincent* (7th), Ronald George James Jervis, *b.* 1905, *s.* 1940, *m.*	Hon. Edward R. J. J., *b.* 1951.
1937	*Samuel* (2nd), Edwin Herbert Samuel C.M.G., *b.* 1898, *s.* 1963, *m.*	Hon. David H. S., Ph.D., *b.* 1922.
1911	*Scarsdale* (2nd), Richard Nathaniel Curzon, T.D. (6th *Brit. Baron, Scarsdale,* 1761), *b.* 1898, *s.* 1925, *m.*	Francis J. N. C., *b.* 1924.
1905	*Selby* (4th), Michael Guy John Gully, *b.* 1942, *s.* 1959, *m.*	Hon. Edward T. W. G., *b.* 1967.
1805	*Sidmouth* (7th), John Tonge Anthony Pellew Addington, *b.* 1914, *s.* 1976, *m.*	Hon. Christopher J. A. *b.* 1941.
1940	*Simon* (2nd), John Gilbert Simon, C.M.G., *b.* 1902, *s.* 1954, *m.*	Hon. Jan D. S., *b.* 1940.
1960	*Slim* (2nd), John Douglas Slim, O.B.E., *b.* 1927, *s.* 1970, *m.*	Hon. Mark W. R. S., *b.* 1960.
1954	*Soulbury* (2nd), James Herwald Ramsbotham, *b.* 1915, *s.* 1971, *w.*	Hon. Sir Peter E. R., K.C.M.G., *b.* 1919.
1776 I.	*Southwell* (7th), Pryers Anthony Joseph Southwell, *b.* 1930, *s.* 1960, *m.*	Hon. Richard A. P. S., *b.* 1956.
1959	*Stuart of Findhorn* (2nd), David Randolph Moray Stuart, *b.* 1924, *s.* 1971, *m.*	Hon. James D. S., *b.* 1948.
1806 I.	*Templetown* (5th), Henry Augustus George Mountjoy Heneage Upton, *b.* 1894, *s.* 1939, *m.*	(None.)
1957	*Tenby* (2nd), David Lloyd George, *b.* 1922, *s.* 1967.	Hon. William L. G., *b.* 1927.
1952	*Thurso* (2nd), Robin Macdonald Sinclair, *b.* 1922, *s.* 1970, *m.*	Hon. John A. S., *b.* 1953.
1721	*Torrington* (11th), Timothy Howard St. George Byng, *b.* 1943, *s.* 1961.	John L. B., M.C., *b.* 1919.
1936	*Trenchard* (2nd), Thomas Trenchard, M.C., *b.* 1923, *s.* 1956, *m.*	Hon. Hugh T., *b.* 1951.
1921	*Ullswater* (2nd), Nicholas James Christopher Lowther, *b.* 1942, *s.* 1949, *m.*	Son, *born* 1975.

Created.	Title, Order of Succession, Name, etc.	Eldest Son or Heir.
1621 I.	*Valentia* (14th), Francis Dighton Annesley, M.C., *b.* 1888, *s.* 1951 (*claim established*, 1959), *m.*	Hon. Richard J. D. *A.*, *b.* 1929.
1960	*Ward of Witley* (1st), George Reginald Ward, P.C., *b.* 1907, *m.*	Hon. Anthony G. H. *W.*, *b.* 1943.
1964	*Watkinson* (1st), Harold Arthur Watkinson, P.C., C.H., *b.* 1910, *w.*	(None.)
1952	*Waverley* (2nd), David Alastair Pearson Anderson, *b.* 1911, *s.* 1958, *m.*	Hon. John D. F. *A.*, *b.* 1949.
1938	*Weir* (3rd), William Kenneth James Weir, *b.* 1933, *s.* 1975, *m.*	Hon. James W. H. *W.*, *b.* 1965.
1918	*Wimborne* (3rd), Ivor Fox-Strangways Guest (4th *U.K. Baron*, Wimborne, 1880), *b.* 1939, *s.* 1967, *m.*	Hon. Ivor M.V.G., *b.* 1968.
1923	*Younger of Leckie* (3rd), Edward George Younger, O.B.E., T.D., *b.* 1906, *s.* 1946, *m.*	Hon. George *Y.*, T.D., M.P. *b.* 1931.

BISHOPS

Style, The Right Rev. the Lord Bishop of ——. *Addressed as*, My Lord.

Apptd.		
1973	*London* (115th), Gerald Alexander Ellison, P.C., D.D., *b.* 1910, *cons.* 1950, *trans.* 1955 and 1973, *m.*
1973	*Durham* (91st), John Stapylton Habgood, M.A., Ph.D., *b.* 1927, *cons.* 1973, *m.*
1974	*Winchester* (94th), John Vernon Taylor, M.A., *b.* 1914, *cons.* 1974, *m.*
1975	*Bath and Wells* (74th), John Monier Bickersteth, M.A., *b.* 1921, *cons.* 1970, *trans.* 1975, *m.*
1969	*Birmingham* (5th), Laurence Ambrose Brown, M.A., *b.* 1907, *cons.* 1960, *m.*
1972	*Blackburn* (5th), Robert Arnold Schürhoff Martineau, M.A., *b.* 1913, *cons.* 1966, *m.*
1972	*Bradford* (5th), Ross Sydney Hook, M.C., M.A., *b.* 1917, *cons.* 1965, *m.*
1975	*Bristol* (53rd), Ernest John Tinsley, M.A., B.D., *b.* 1919, *cons.* 1975.
1972	*Carlisle* (64th), Henry David Halsey, B.A., *b.* 1919, *cons.* 1968, *trans.* 1972, *m.*
1971	*Chelmsford* (6th), Albert John Trillo, M.Th., B.D., F.K.C., *b.* 1915, *cons.* 1963, *trans.* 1968 and 1971, *m.*
1974	*Chester* (38th), Hubert Victor Whitsey, M.A., *b.* 1916, *cons.* 1971, *trans.* 1974, *m.*
1974	*Chichester* (99th), Eric Waldram Kemp, D.D., *b.* 1915, *m.*
1976	*Coventry* (5th), John Gibbs, B.A., B.D., *b.* 1917, *cons.* 1973, *trans.* 1976, *m.*
1969	*Derby* (4th), Cyril William Johnston Bowles, M.A., *b.* 1916, *cons.* 1969, *m.*
1964	*Ely* (65th), Edward James Keymer Roberts, D.D., *b.* 1908, *cons.* 1956, *trans.* 1962 and 1964, *m.*
1973	*Exeter* (68th), Eric Arthur John Mercer, *b.* 1917, *cons.* 1965, *m.*
1975	*Gloucester* (37th) John Yates, M.A., *b.* 1925, *cons.* 1972, *trans.* 1975, *m.*
1973	*Guildford* (6th), David Alan Brown, B.D., M.Th., B.A., *b.* 1922, *cons.* 1973, *m.*
1973	*Hereford* (103rd), John Richard Gordon Eastaugh, *b.* 1920, *cons.* 1973, *m.*
1953	*Leicester* (3rd), Ronald Ralph Williams, D.D., *b.* 1906, *cons.* 1953, *m.*
1974	*Lichfield* (96th), Kenneth John Fraser Skelton, C.B.E., M.A., *b.* 1918, *cons.* 1962, *m.*
1974	*Lincoln* (69th), Simon Wilton Phipps, M.C., M.A., *b.* 1921, *cons.* 1968, *trans.* 1974, *m.*
1975	*Liverpool* (6th) David Stuart Sheppard, M.A., *b.* 1929, *cons.* 1969, *m.*
1970	*Manchester* (8th), Patrick Campbell Rodger, M.A., *b.* 1920, *cons.* 1970, *m.*
1972	*Newcastle* (9th), Ronald Oliver Bowlby, M.A., *b.* 1926, *cons.* 1972, *m.*
1971	*Norwich* (69th), Maurice Arthur Ponsonby Wood, D.S.C., M.A., *b.* 1916, *cons.* 1971 *m.*
1971	*Oxford* (39th), Kenneth John Woollcombe, M.A., *b.* 1924, *cons.* 1971, *m.*
1972	*Peterborough* (35th), Douglas Russell Feaver, M.A., *b.* 1914, *cons.* 1972, *m.*
1975	*Portsmouth* (6th), Archibald Ronald McDonald Gordon, M.A., *b.* 1927, *cons.* 1975.
1976	*Ripon* (10th), Stuart Hetley Price, M.A., *b.* 1922, *cons.* 1972, *m.*
1961	*Rochester* (104th), Richard David Say, D.D., *b.* 1914, *cons.* 1961, *m.*
1970	*St. Albans* (7th), Robert Alexander Kennedy Runcie, M.C., M.A., *b.* 1921, *cons.* 1970, *m.*
1966	*St. Edmundsbury & Ipswich* (6th), Leslie Wilfred Brown, C.B.E., D.D., *b.* 1912, *cons.* 1953, *m.*
1973	*Salisbury* (75th), George Edmund Reindorp, D.D., *b.* 1911, *cons.* 1961, *trans.* 1973, *m.*
1971	*Sheffield* (4th), William Gordon Fallows, M.A., *b.* 1913, *cons.* 1968, *m.*
1966	*Sodor & Man* (77th), Vernon Sampson Nicholls, *b.* 1917, *cons.* 1974, *m.*
1959	*Southwark* (6th), Arthur Mervyn Stockwood, D.D., *b.* 1913, *cons.* 1959.
1970	*Southwell* (7th), John Denis Wakeling, M.C., M.A., *b.* 1918, *cons.* 1970, *m.*
1973	*Truro* (11th), Graham Douglas Leonard, M.A., *b.* 1921, *cons.* 1964, *m.*
	Wakefield (vacant)
1971	*Worcester* (110th), Robert Wilmer Woods, K.C.V.O., M.A., *b.* 1914, *cons.* 1971, *m.*

BARONS

Style (see *also* note, p. 257), The Right Hon. the Lord ——.
Addressed as, My Lord.

Created.	Title, Order of Succession, Name, etc	Eldest Son or Heir.
1911	*Aberconway* (3rd), Charles Melville McLaren, *b.* 1913, *s.* 1953, *m.*	Hon. Henry C. *McL.*, *b.* 1948.
1873	*Aberdare* (4th), Morys George Lyndhurst Bruce, P.C., *b.* 1919, *s.* 1957, *m.*	Hon. Alastair J. L. *B.*, *b.* 1947.
1835	*Abinger* (8th), James Richard Scarlett, *b.* 1914, *s.* 1943, *m.*	Hon. James H. *S.*, *b.* 1959.
1869	*Acton* (3rd), John Emerich Henry Lyon-Dalberg-Acton, C.M.G., M.B.E., T.D., *b.* 1907, *s.* 1924, *m.*	Hon. Richard *L.-D.-A.*, *b.* 1941.

Created.	*Title, Order of Succession, Name, etc.*	*Eldest Son or Heir.*
1887	*Addington* (5th), James Hubbard, *b.* 1930, *s.* 1971, *m.*	Hon. Dominic A. H., *b.* 1963.
1955	*Adrian* (1st), Edgar Douglas Adrian, O.M., M.D., F.R.S., *b.* 1889, *w.*	Hon. Richard H. A., *b.* 1927.
1921	*Ailwyn* (4th), Carol Arthur Fellowes, T.D., *b.* 1896, *s.* 1976, *m.*	(None.)
1907	*Airedale* (4th), Oliver James Vandeleur Kitson, *b.* 1915, *s.* 1958.	(None.)
1896	*Aldenham* (5th), and (3rd) *Hunsdon of Hunsdon* (1923), Antony Durant Gibbs, *b.* 1922, *s.* 1969, *m.*	Hon. Vicary T. G., *b.* 1948.
1962	*Aldington* (1st), Toby Austin Richard William Low, P.C., K.C.M.G., C.B.E., D.S.O., T.D., *b.* 1914, *m.*	Hon. Charles H. S. L., *b.* 1948.
1902	*Allerton* (3rd), George William Lawies Jackson, *b.* 1903, *s.* 1925. *m.*	Hon. Edward L. J., *b.* 1928.
1929	*Alvingham* (2nd), Robert Guy Eardley Yerburgh, O.B.E., *b.* 1926, *s.* 1955, *m.*	Hon. Robert R. G. Y., *b.* 1956.
1892	*Amherst of Hackney* (3rd), William Alexander Evering Cecil, C.B.E., *b.* 1912, *s.* 1919, *m.*	Hon. William C., *b.* 1940.
1881	*Ampthill* (4th), Geoffrey Denis Erskine Russell, *b.* 1921, *s.* 1973, *m.*	Hon. David W. E. R., *b.* 1947.
1929	*Amulree* (2nd), Basil William Sholto Mackenzie, M.D., *b.* 1900, *s.* 1942.	(None.)
1947	*Amwell* (2nd), Frederick Norman Montague, *b.* 1912, *s.* 1966, *m.*	Hon. Keith N. M., *b.* 1943.
1863	*Annaly* (5th), Luke Robert White, *b.* 1927, *s.* 1970.	Hon. Luke R. W., *b.* 1954.
1903	*Armstrong* (3rd), William Henry Cecil John Robin Watson-Armstrong, *b.* 1919, *s.* 1972, *m.*	(None.)
1885	*Ashbourne* (3rd), Edward Russell Gibson, C.B., D.S.O., *b.* 1901, *s.* 1942, *m.*	Hon. Edward B. G. G., *b.* 1933.
1835	*Ashburton* (6th), Alexander Francis St. Vincent Baring, K.G., K.C.V.O., *b.* 1898, *s.* 1938, *m.*	Hon. John F. H. B., *b.* 1928.
1892	*Ashcombe* (4th), Henry Edward Cubitt, *b.* 1924, *s.* 1962, *m.*	Alick J. A. C., *b.* 1927.
1911	*Ashton of Hyde* (2nd), Thomas Henry Raymond Ashton, *b.* 1901, *s.* 1933, *m.*	Hon. Thomas J. A., *b.* 1926.
1800 I.	*Ashtown* (5th), Dudley Oliver Trench, O.B.E., *b.* 1901, *s.* 1966, *m.*	Christopher O. T., *b.* 1931.
1956	*Astor of Hever* (2nd), Gavin Astor, *b.* 1918, *s.* 1971, *m.*	Hon. John J. A., *b.* 1946.
1789 I.⎫ 1793*⎭	*Auckland* (9th), Ian George Eden (9th *Brit. Baron*, *Auckland*), *b.* 1926, *s.* 1957, *m.*	Hon. Robert I. B. E., *b.* 1962.
1313	*Audley* (25th), Richard Michael Thomas Souter, *b.* 1914, *s.* 1973, *m.*	Three co-heiresses.
1900	*Avebury* (4th), Eric Reginald Lubbock, *b.* 1928, *s.* 1971, *m.*	Hon. Lyulph A. J. L., *b.* 1954.
1718 I.	*Aylmer* (12th), Hugh Yates Aylmer, *b.* 1907, *s.* 1975, *m.*	Edward A. A., D.S.C., *b.* 1892.
1929	*Baden-Powell* (3rd), Robert Crause Baden-Powell, *b.* 1936, *s.* 1962, *m.*	Hon. David M. B.-P., *b.* 1940.
1780	*Bagot* (8th), Reginald Walter Bagot, *b.* 1897, *s.* 1973, *m.*	Heneage C. B., *b.* 1914.
1953	*Baillieu* (3rd), James William Latham Baillieu, *b.* 1950, *s.* 1973, *m.*	Hon. David C. L. B., *b.* 1952.
1607 S.	*Balfour of Burleigh* (8th), Robert Bruce, *b.* 1927, *c.* 1967, *m.*	Hon. Victoria B., *b.* 1973.
1945	*Balfour of Inchrye* (1st), Harold Harington Balfour, P.C., M.C., *b.* 1897, *m.*	Hon. Ian B., *b.* 1924.
1924	*Banbury of Southam* (2nd), Charles William Banbury, *b.* 1915, *s.* 1936.	Hon. Charles W. B., *b.* 1953.
1698	*Barnard* (11th), Harry John Neville Vane, T.D., *b.* 1923, *s.* 1964, *m.*	Hon. Henry F. C. V., *b.* 1959.
1922	*Barnby* (2nd), Francis Vernon Willey, C.M.G., C.B.E., M.V.O., T.D., *b.* 1884, *s.* 1929, *m.*	(None.)
1887	*Basing* (4th), George Lutley Sclater-Booth, T.D., *b.* 1903, *s.* 1969, *m.*	Hon. Neil L. S.-B., *b.* 1939.
1647 S.	*Belhaven & Stenton* (13th), Robert Anthony Carmichael Hamilton, *b.* 1927, *s.* 1961, *m.*	Master of Belhaven, *b.* 1953.
1848 I.	*Bellew* (6th), Bryan Bertram Bellew, M.C., *b.* 1890, *s.* 1975, *m.*	Hon. James B. B., *b.* 1920.
1856	*Belper* (4th), (Alexander) Ronald George Strutt, *b.* 1912, *s.* 1956.	Hon. Richard H. S., *b.* 1941.
1938	*Belstead* (2nd), John Julian Ganzoni, *b.* 1932, *s.* 1958.	(None.)
1922	*Bethell* (4th), Nicholas William Bethell, *b.* 1938, *s.* 1967.	Hon. James N. B., *b.* 1967.
1938	*Bicester* (3rd), Angus Edward Vivian Smith, *b.* 1932, *s.* 1968.	Hugh C. V. S., *b.* 1934.
1903	*Biddulph* (4th), Robert Michael Christian Biddulph, *b.* 1931, *s.* 1972, *m.*	Hon. Anthony N. C. B., *b.* 1959.
1938	*Birdwood* (3rd), Mark William Ogilvie Birdwood, *b.* 1938, *s.* 1962, *m.*	(None.)
1958	*Birkett* (2nd), Michael Birkett, *b.* 1929, *s.* 1962, *w.*	(None.)
1935	*Blackford* (3rd), Keith Alexander Henry Mason, D.F.C., *b.* 1923, *s.* 1972.	Hon. William K. M., *b.* 1962.
1907	*Blyth* (3rd), Ian Audley James Blyth, *b.* 1905, *s.* 1943, *m.*	Hon. Anthony B., *b.* 1931.
1797	*Bolton* (7th), Richard William Algar Orde-Powlett, *b.* 1929, *s.* 1963, *m.*	Hon. Harry A. N. O.-P. *b.* 1954.
1922	*Borwick* (4th), James Hugh Myles Borwick, M.C., *b.* 1917, *s.* 1961, *m.*	Hon. George S. B., *b.* 1922.
1761	*Boston* (9th), Gerald Howard Boteler Irby, M.B.E., *b.* 1897, *s.* 1972, *m.*	Hon. Timothy G. F. B. I., *b.* 1939.
1942	*Brabazon of Tara* (3rd), Ivon Anthony Moore-Brabazon, *b.* 1946, *s.* 1974, *m.*	(None.)

Created.	Title, Order of Succession, Name, etc.	Eldest Son or Heir.
1880	*Brabourne* (7th), John Ulick Knatchbull, *b.* 1924, *s.* 1943, *m.*	Hon. Norton *K.*, *b.* 1947.
1925	*Bradbury* (2nd), John Bradbury, *b.* 1914, *s.* 1950, *m.*	Hon. John *B.*, *b.* 1940.
1962	*Brain* (2nd), Christopher Langdon Brain, *b.* 1926, *s.* 1966, *m.*	Hon. Michael C. *B.*, D.M., *b.* 1928.
1938	*Brassey of Apethorpe* (3rd), David Henry Brassey, T.D., *b.* 1932, *s.* 1967, *w.*	Hon. Edward *B.*, *b.* 1964.
1788	*Braybrooke* (9th), Henry Seymour Neville, *b.* 1897, *s.* 1943, *m.*	Hon. Robin *N.*, *b.* 1932.
1529	*Braye* (7th), Thomas Adrian Verney-Cave, *b.* 1902, *s.* 1952, *m.*	Hon. Penelope M. *V.-C.*, *b.* 1941.
1958	*Brecon* (1st), David Vivian Penrose Lewis, P.C., *b.* 1905, *m.*	(None.)
1957	*Bridges* (2nd), Thomas Edward Bridges, C.M.G., *b.* 1927, *s.* 1969, *m.*	Hon. Mark T. *B.*, *b.* 1954.
1945	*Broadbridge* (3rd), Peter Hewett Broadbridge, *b.* 1938, *s.* 1972, *m.*	Hon. Ralph G. C. *B.*, *b.* 1901.
1933	*Brocket* (3rd), Charles Ronald George Nall-Cain, *b.* 1952, *s.* 1967.	Hon. Richard P.C. *N.-C.*, *b.* 1953.
1860	*Brougham and Vaux* (5th), Michael John Brougham, *b.* 1938, *s.* 1967, *m.*	Hon. Charles *B.*, *b.* 1971.
1945	*Broughshane* (2nd), Patrick Owen Alexander Davison, *b.* 1903, *s.* 1953, *m.*	Hon. Alexander *D.*, *b.* 1936.
1776	*Brownlow* (6th), Peregrine Francis Adelbert Cust, *b.* 1899, *s.* 1927, *m.*	Hon. Edward *C.*, *b.* 1936.
1942	*Bruntisfield* (1st), Victor Alexander George Anthony Warrender, M.C., *b.* 1890, *m.*	Hon. John R. *W.*, O.B.E., M.C., T.D., *b.* 1921.
1950	*Burden* (2nd), Philip William Burden, *b.* 1916, *s.* 1970, *m.*	Hon. Andrew P. *B.*, *b.* 1959.
1529	*Burgh* (7th), Alexander Peter Willoughby Leith, *b.* 1935, *s.* 1959, *m.*	Hon. Alexander G. D. *L.*, *b.* 1958.
1903	*Burnham* (5th), William Edward Harry Lawson, *b.* 1920, *s.* 1963, *m.*	Hon. Hugh J. F. *L.*, *b.* 1931.
1897	*Burton* (3rd), Michael Evan Victor Baillie, *b.* 1924, *s.* 1962, *m.*	Hon. Evan *B.*, *b.* 1949.
1643	*Byron* (11th), Rupert Frederick George Byron, *b.* 1903, *s.* 1949, *m.*	Richard G. G. *B.*, D.S.O., *b.* 1899.
1937	*Cadman* (3rd), John Anthony Cadman, *b.* 1938, *s.* 1966.	Hon. James R. *C.*, *b.* 1944.
1796	*Calthorpe* (10th), Peter Waldo Somerset Gough-Calthorpe, *b.* 1927, *s.* 1945.	(None.)
1945	*Calverley* (3rd.), Charles Rodney Muff, *b.* 1946, *s.* 1971.	Hon. Peter R. *M.*, *b.* 1953.
1383	*Camoys* (7th), (Ralph) Thomas (Campion George Sherman) Stonor, *b.* 1940, *s.* 1976, *m.*	Hon. John E. R. *S.*, *b.* 1946.
1715 I.	*Carbery* (11th), Peter Ralfe Harrington Evans-Freke, *b.* 1920, *s.* 1970, *m.*	Hon. Michael P. *E.-F.*, *b.* 1942.
1834 I. 1838*	*Carew* (6th), William Francis Conolly-Carew, C.B.E. (6th *U.K.* Baron, *Carew*, 1838), *b.* 1905, *s.* 1927, *m.*	Hon. Patrick T. *C.-C.*, *b.* 1938.
1916	*Carnock* (3rd), Erskine Arthur Nicolson, D.S.O., *b.* 1884, *s.* 1952, *w.*	Hon. David H. A. *N.*, *b.* 1920.
1796 I. 1797*	*Carrington* (6th), Peter Alexander Rupert Carington, P.C., K.C.M.G., M.C. (6th *Brit. Baron, Carrington*, 1797), *b.* 1919, *s.* 1938, *m.*	Hon. Rupert F. J. *C.*, *b.* 1948.
1812 I.	*Castlemaine* (8th), Roland Thomas John Handcock, *b.* 1943, *s.* 1973, *m.*	Clifford F. *H.*, *b.* 1896.
1936	*Catto* (2nd), Stephen Gordon Catto, *b.* 1923, *s.* 1959, *m.*	Hon. Innes G. *C.*, *b.* 1950.
1918	*Cawley* (3rd), Frederick Lee Cawley, *b.* 1913, *s.* 1954, *m.*	Hon. John F. *C.*, *b.* 1946.
1937	*Chatfield* (2nd), Ernle David Lewis Chatfield, *b.* 1917, *s.* 1967, *m.*	(None.)
1858	*Chesham* (5th), John Charles Compton Cavendish, P.C., *b.* 1916, *s.* 1952, *m.*	Hon. Nicholas *C.*, *b.* 1941.
1945	*Chetwode* (2nd), Philip Chetwode, *b.* 1937, *s.* 1950, *m.*	Hon. Roger *C.*, *b.* 1968.
1945	*Chorley* (1st), Robert Samuel Theodore Chorley, Q.C., *b.* 1895, *m.*	Hon. Roger *C.*, *b.* 1930.
1858	*Churston* (4th), Richard Francis Roger Yarde-Buller, V.R.D., *b.* 1910, *s.* 1930, *m.*	Hon. John *Y.-B.*, *b.* 1934.
1946	*Citrine* (1st), Walter McLennan Citrine, P.C., G.B.E., *b.* 1887, *w.*	Hon. Norman *C.*, *b.* 1914.
1800 I.	*Clanmorris* (7th), John Michael Ward Bingham, *b.* 1908, *s.* 1960, *m.*	Hon. Simon J. W. *B.*, *b.* 1937.
1672	*Clifford of Chudleigh* (13th), Lewis Hugh Clifford, O.B.E., *b.* 1916, *s.* 1964, *m.*	Hon. Thomas H. *C.*, *b.* 1948.
1299	*Clinton* (22nd), Gerard Neville Mark Fane Trefusis, *b.* 1934, *title called out of abeyance* 1965, *m.*	Hon. Charles P. R. F. *T.*, *b.* 1962.
1955	*Clitheroe* (1st), Ralph Assheton, P.C., *b.* 1901, *m.*	Hon. Ralph J. *A.*, *b.* 1929.
1919	*Clwyd* (2nd), (John) Trevor Roberts, *b.* 1900, *s.* 1955, *m.*	Hon. J. Anthony *R.*, *b.* 1935.
1947	*Clydesmuir* (2nd), Ronald John Bisland Colville, K.T., C.B., M.B.E., T.D., *b.* 1917, *s.* 1954, *m.*	Hon. David R. *C.*, *b.* 1949.
1960	*Cobbold* (1st), Cameron Fromanteel Cobbold, K.G., P.C., G.C.V.O., *b.* 1904, *m.*	Hon. David A. F. *Lytton-Cobbold*, *b.* 1937.
1919	*Cochrane of Cults* (3rd), Thomas Charles Anthony Cochrane, *b.* 1922, *s.* 1968.	Hon. R. H. Vere *C.*, *b.* 1926.
1956	*Cohen of Birkenhead* (1st), Henry Cohen, C.H., M.D., D.SC., F.R.C.P., F.S.A., *b.* 1900.	(None.)
1954	*Coleraine* (1st), Richard Kidston Law, P.C., *b.* 1901, *m.*	Hon. J. Martin B. *L.*, *b.* 1931.

Created.	Title, Order of Succession, Name, etc.	Eldest Son or Heir.
1873	Coleridge (4th), Richard Duke Coleridge, K.B.E., b. 1905, s. 1955, m.	Hon. William D. C., b. 1937.
1946	Colgrain (3rd), David Colin Campbell, b. 1920, s. 1973, m.	Hon. Alastair C. L. C., b. 1951.
1917	Colwyn (3rd), (Ian) Anthony Hamilton-Smith, b. 1942, s. 1966, m.	Hon. Craig P. H.-S., b. 1968.
1956	Colyton (1st), Henry Lennox D'Aubigné Hopkinson, P.C., C.M.G., b. 1902, m.	Hon. Nicholas H. E. H., b. 1932.
1841	Congleton (8th), Christopher Patrick Parnell, b. 1930, s. 1967, m.	Hon. John P. C. P., b. 1959.
1927	Cornwallis (2nd), Wykeham Stanley Cornwallis, K.C.V.O., K.B.E., M.C., b. 1892, s. 1935, w.	Hon. Fiennes C., O.B.E., b. 1921.
1874	Cottesloe (4th), John Walgrave Halford Fremantle, G.B.E., T.D., b. 1900, s. 1956, m.	Hon. John T. F., b. 1927.
1929	Craigmyle (3rd), Thomas Donald Mackay Shaw, b. 1923, s. 1944, m.	Hon. Thomas C. S., b. 1960.
1899	Cranworth (3rd), Philip Bertram Gurdon, b. 1940, s. 1964, m.	Hon. Sacha W. R. G., b. 1970.
1959	Crathorne (1st), Thomas Lionel Dugdale, P.C., T.D., b. 1897, w.	Hon. Charles J. D., b. 1939.
1892	Crawshaw (4th), William Michael Clifton Brooks, b. 1933, s. 1946.	Hon. David B., b. 1934.
1940	Croft (2nd), Michael Henry Glendower Page Croft, b. 1916, s. 1947, w.	Hon. Bernard W. H. P. C., b. 1949.
1797 I.	Crofton (6th), Charles Edward Piers Crofton, b. 1949, s. 1974.	Hon. Guy P. G. C., b. 1951.
1375	Cromwell (6th), David Godfrey Bewicke-Copley, b. 1929, s. 1966, m.	Hon. Godfrey J. B.-C., b. 1960.
1947	Crook (1st), Reginald Douglas Crook, b. 1901, m.	Hon. Douglas C., b. 1926.
1971	Cross of Chelsea, (Arthur) Geoffrey (Neale) Cross, P.C., b. 1904, m. (Lord of Appeal, retired).	(Law Life Peerage.)
1920	Cullen of Ashbourne (2nd), Charles Borlase Marsham Cokayne, M.B.E., b. 1912, s. 1932, m.	Hon. Edmund C., b. 1916.
1914	Cunliffe (3rd), Roger Cunliffe, b. 1932, s. 1963, m.	Hon. Henry C., b. 1962.
1927	Daresbury (2nd), Edward Greenall, b. 1902, s. 1938, w.	Hon. Edward G. G., b. 1928.
1924	Darling (2nd), Robert Charles Henry Darling, b. 1919, s. 1936, m.	Hon. Robert D., b. 1944.
1946	Darwen (2nd), Cedric Percival Davies, b. 1915, s. 1950, m.	Hon. Roger M. D., b. 1938.
1923	Daryngton (2nd), Jocelyn Arthur Pike Pease, b. 1908, s. 1949.	(None.)
1932	Davies (3rd), David Davies, b. 1940, s. 1944, m.	Hon. Jonathan H. D., b. 1944.
1812 I.	Decies (6th), Arthur George Marcus Douglas de la Poer Beresford, b. 1915, s. 1944, m.	Hon. Marcus de la P.B., b. 1948.
1299	De Clifford (26th), Edward Southwell Russell, O.B.E., E.D., b. 1907, s. 1909, m.	Hon. John R., b. 1928.
1851	De Freyne (7th), Francis Arthur John French, b. 1927, s. 1935, m.	Hon. Fulke C. J. A. F., b. 1957.
1821	Delamere (4th), Thomas Pitt Hamilton Cholmondeley, b. 1900, s. 1931, m.	Hon. Hugh G. C., b. 1934.
1838	De Mauley (6th), Gerald John Ponsonby, b. 1921, s. 1962, m.	Hon. Thomas M. P., b. 1930.
1937	Denham (2nd), Bertram Stanley Mitford Bowyer, b. 1927, s. 1948, m.	Hon. Richard G. B., b. 1959.
1834	Denman (5th), Charles Spencer Denman, C.B.E., M.C., b. 1916, s. 1971, m.	Hon. Richard T. S. D., b. 1946.
1957	Denning, Alfred Thompson Denning, P.C., b. 1899, m. (Master of the Rolls).	(Law Life Peerage.)
1885	Deramore (6th), Richard Arthur de Yarburgh-Bateson, b. 1911, s. 1964, m.	(None.)
1887	De Ramsey (3rd), Ailwyn Edward Fellowes, K.B.E., T.D., b. 1910, s. 1925, m.	Hon. John A. F., b. 1942.
1881	Derwent (4th), Patrick Robin Gilbert Vanden-Bempde-Johnstone, C.B.E., b. 1901, s. 1949, m.	Hon. Robin V.-B.-J., M.V.O., b. 1930.
1831	De Saumarez (6th), James Victor Broke Saumarez, b. 1924, s. 1969, m.	Hon. Eric D. S., b. 1956.
1910	De Villiers (3rd), Arthur Percy De Villiers, b. 1911, s. 1934.	Hon. Alexander C. de V., b. 1940.
1961	Devlin, Patrick Arthur Devlin, P.C., F.B.A., b. 1905, m. (Lord of Appeal retired).	(Law Life Peerage.)
1930	Dickinson (2nd), Richard Clavering Hyett Dickinson, b. 1926, s. 1943, m.	Hon. Martin H. D., b. 1961.
1620 I.⎫ 1765⋆⎭	Digby (12th), Edward Henry Kenelm Digby, (6th Brit. Baron, Digby), b. 1924, s. 1964, m.	Hon. Henry N. K. D., b. 1954.
1968	Diplock, (William John) Kenneth Diplock, P.C., b. 1907, m. (Lord of Appeal).	(Law Life Peerage.)
1615	Dormer (16th), Joseph Spencer Philip Dormer, b. 1914, s. 1975.	Hon. Robert F. E. B. D., b. 1904.
1950	Douglas of Barloch (1st), Francis Campbell Ross Douglas, K.C.M.G., b. 1889, m.	(None.)

Created.	Title, Order of Succession, Name, etc.	Eldest Son or Heir.
1943	Dowding (2nd), Derek Hugh Tremenheere Dowding, b. 1919, s. 1970, m.	Hon. Piers H. T. D., b. 1948.
1963	Drumalbyn (1st), Niall Malcolm Stewart Macpherson, P.C., K.B.E., b. 1908, m.	(None.)
1929	Dulverton (2nd), (Frederick) Anthony Hamilton Wills, C.B.E., T.D., b. 1915, s. 1956, m.	Hon. Gilbert M. H. W., b. 1944.
1800 I.	Dunalley (6th), Henry Desmond Graham Prittie, b. 1912, s. 1948, m.	Hon. Henry P., b. 1948.
1324 I.	Dunboyne (28th), Patrick Theobald Tower Butler, b. 1917, s. 1945, m.	Hon. John F. B., b. 1951.
1802	Dunleath (4th), Charles Edward Henry John Mulholland, T.D., b. 1933, s. 1956, m.	Sir Michael H. M., Bt., b. 1915.
1439 I.	Dunsany (19th), Randal Arthur Henry Plunkett, b. 1906, s. 1957, m.	Hon. Edward P., b. 1939.
1780	Dynevor (9th), Richard Charles Uryan Rhys, b. 1935, s. 1962, m.	Hon. Hugo G. U. R., b.1966.
1928	Ebbisham (2nd), Rowland Roberts Blades, T.D., b. 1912, s. 1953, m.	(None.)
1857	Ebury (6th), Francis Egerton Grosvenor, b. 1934, s. 1957, m.	Hon. Julian F. M. G., b. 1959.
1974	Edmund-Davies (Herbert) Edmund Edmund-Davies, P.C., b. 1906, m. (Lord of Appeal).	(Law Life Peerage.)
1643 S.	Elibank (14th, Alan d'Ardis Erskine-Murray, b. 1923, s. 1973, m.	Master of Elibank, b. 1964.
1802	Ellenborough (8th), Richard Edward Cecil Law, b. 1926, s. 1945, m.	Hon. Rupert E. H. L., b. 1955.
1509 S.*	Elphinstone (18th), James Alexander Elphinstone (4th U.K. Baron Elphinstone, 1885), b. 1953, s. 1975.	(None.)
1934	Elton (2nd), Rodney Elton, T.D., b. 1930, s. 1973, m.	Hon. Edward P. E., b. 1966.
1964	Erroll of Hale (1st), Frederick James Erroll, P.C., T.D., b. 1914, m.	(None.)
1964	Erskine of Rerrick (1st), John Maxwell Erskine, G.B.E., b. 1893, m.	Hon. Iain M. E., b. 1926.
1932	Essendon (2nd), Brian Edmund Lewis, b. 1903, s. 1944, m.	(None.)
1627 S.	Fairfax of Cameron (14th), Nicholas John Albert Fairfax, b. 1956, s. 1964, M.	Hon. Hugh N. T. F., b. 1958.
1961	Fairhaven (3rd), Ailwyn Henry George Broughton, b. 1936, s. 1973, m.	Hon. James H. A. B., b. 1963.
1916	Faringdon (2nd), Alexander Gavin Henderson, b. 1902, s. 1934.	Charles M. H., b. 1937.
1756 I.	Farnham (12th), Barry Owen Somerset Maxwell, b. 1931, s. 1957, m.	Hon. Simon K. M., b. 1933.
1856 I.	Fermoy (5th), Edmund James Burke Roche, b. 1939, s. 1955, m.	Hon. Patrick M. R., b. 1967.
1826	Feversham (6th), Charles Anthony Peter Duncombe, b. 1945, s. 1963, w.	Hon. Jasper O. S. D., b. 1968.
1798 I.	ffrench (7th), Peter Martin Joseph Charles John ffrench, b. 1926, s. 1955, m.	Hon. Robuck J. P. C. M. ff., b. 1956.
1909	Fisher (3rd), John Vavasseur Fisher, D.S.C., b. 1921, s. 1955, m.	Hon. Patrick V. F., b. 1953.
1295	Fitzwalter (21st), Fitzwalter Brook Plumptre, b. 1914, called out of abeyance, 1953, m.	Hon. Julian B. P., b. 1952.
1776	Foley (8th), Adrian Gerald Foley, b. 1923, s. 1927, m.	Hon. Thomas H. F., b. 1961.
1445 S.	Forbes (22nd), Nigel Ivan Forbes, K.B.E. (Premier Baron of Scotland), b. 1918, s. 1953, m.	Master of Forbes, b. 1946.
1821	Forester (7th), Cecil George Wilfrid Weld-Forester, b. 1899, s. 1932, m.	Hon. G. C. Brooke W.-F., b. 1938.
1922	Forres (3rd), John Archibald Harford Williamson, b. 1922, s. 1954, m.	Hon. Alastair S. G. W., b. 1946.
1917	Forteviot (3rd), Henry Evelyn Alexander Dewar, M.B.E., b. 1906, s. 1947, m.	Hon. John J. E. D., b. 1938.
1946	Fraser of North Cape (1st), Bruce Austin Fraser, G.C.B., K.B.E., Admiral of the Fleet, b. 1888.	(None.)
1975	Fraser of Tullybelton, Walter Ian Reid Fraser, P.C., b. 1911, m. (Lord of Appeal).	(Law Life Peerage).
1951	Freyberg (2nd), Paul Richard Freyberg, O.B.E., M.C., b. 1923, s. 1963, m.	Hon. Valerian B. F., b. 1970.
1917	Gainford (3rd), Joseph Edward Pease, b. 1921, s. 1971, m.	Hon. George P., b. 1926.
1818 I.	Garvagh (5th), (Alexander Leopold Ivor) George Canning, b. 1920, s. 1956, m.	Hon. Spencer G. S. de R. C., b. 1953.
1942	Geddes (3rd), Euan Michael Ross Geddes, b. 1937, s. 1975, m.	Hon. James G. N. G., b. 1969.
1876	Gerard (4th), Robert William Frederick Alwyn Gerard, b. 1918, s. 1953.	Rupert C. F. G., M.B.E., b. 1916.
1824	Gifford (6th), Anthony Marice Gifford, b. 1940, s. 1961, m.	Hon. Thomas A. G., b. 1967.
1917	Gisborough (3rd), Thomas Richard John Long Chaloner, b. 1927, s. 1951, m.	Hon. Thomas P. L. C., b. 1961.
1960	Gladwyn (1st), (Hubert Miles) Gladwyn Jebb, G.C.M.G., G.C.V.O., C.B., b. 1900, m.	Hon. Miles A. J., b. 1930.
1899	Glanusk (4th), David Russell Bailey, b. 1917, s. 1948, m.	Hon. Christopher B., b. 1942.
1918	Glenarthur (4th), Simon Mark Arthur, b. 1944, s. 1976, m.	Hon. Edward A. A., b. 1973.
1921	Glenavy (3rd), Patrick Gordon Campbell, b. 1913, s. 1963, m.	Hon. Michael C., b. 1924.
1911	Glenconner (2nd), Christopher Grey Tennant, b. 1899, s. 1920, m.	Hon. Colin T., b. 1926.

Created.	Title, Order of Succession, Name, etc.	Eldest Son or Heir.
1964	Glendevon (1st), John Adrian Hope, P.C., b. 1912, m.	Hon. Julian J. S. H., b. 1950.
1922	Glendyne (3rd), Robert Nivison, b. 1926, s. 1967, m.	Hon. John N., b. 1960.
1939	Glentoran (2nd), Daniel Stewart Thomas Bingham Dixon, P.C., (N.I.), K.B.E., b. 1912, s. 1950, m.	Hon. Thomas R. V. D., M.B.E., b. 1935.
1909	Gorell (4th), Timothy John Radcliffe Barnes, b. 1927, s. 1963, m.	Hon. Ronald A. H. B., b. 1931.
1953	Grantchester (2nd), Kenneth Bent Suenson-Taylor, Q.C., b. 1921, s. 1976, m.	Hon. Christopher J. S.-T., b. 1951.
1782	Grantley (7th), John Richard Brinsley Norton, M.C., b. 1923, s. 1954, m.	Hon. Richard W. B. N., b. 1956.
1794 I.	Graves (8th), Peter George Welleslay Graves, b. 1911, s. 1963, m.	Evelyn P. G., b. 1926.
1445 S.	Gray (22nd), Angus Diarmid Ian Campbell-Gray, b. 1931, s. 1946, m.	Master of Gray, b. 1964.
1950	Greenhill (2nd), Stanley Ernest Greenhill, M.D., b. 1917, s. 1967, m.	Hon. Malcolm G., b. 1924.
1927	Greenway (4th), Ambrose Charles Drexel Greenway, b. 1941, s. 1975	Hon. Mervyn S. K. G., b. 1942.
1902	Grenfell (2nd), Pascoe Christian Victor Francis Grenfell, C.B.E., b. 1905, s. 1925, m.	Hon. Julian G., b. 1935.
1944	Gretton (2nd), John Frederic Gretton, O.B.E., b. 1902, s. 1947, m.	Hon. John H. G., b. 1941.
1869	Greville (4th), Ronald Charles Fulke Greville, b. 1912, s. 1952.	(None.)
1955	Gridley (2nd), Arnold Hudson Gridley, b. 1906, s. 1965, m.	Hon. Richard D. A. G., b. 1956.
1964	Grimston of Westbury (1st), Robert Villiers Grimston, b. 1897, m.	Hon. Robert W. S. G., b. 1925.
1880	Grimthorpe (4th), Christopher John Beckett, O.B.E., b. 1915, s. 1963, m.	Hon. Edward J. B., b. 1954.
1961	Guest, Christopher William Graham Guest, P.C., b. 1901, m. (Lord of Appeal, retired).	(Law Life Peerage.)
1945	Hacking (3rd), Douglas David Hacking, b. 1938, s. 1971, m.	Hon. Douglas F. H., b. 1968.
1950	Haden-Guest (3rd), Richard Haden Haden-Guest, b. 1904, s. 1974, m.	Hon. Peter H. H.-G., b. 1913.
1886	Hamilton of Dalzell (3rd), John D'Henin Hamilton, M.C., b. 1911, s. 1952, m.	Hon. James L. H., b. 1938.
1874	Hampton (6th), Richard Humphrey Russell Pakington, b. 1925, s. 1974, m.	Hon. John H. A. P., b 1964.
1939	Hankey (2nd), Robert Maurice Alers Hankey, K.C.M.G., K.C.V.O., b. 1905, s. 1963, m.	Hon. Donald R. A. H., b. 1938.
1958	Harding of Petherton (1st), John Harding, G.C.B., C.B.E., D.S.O., M.C., Field Marshal, b. 1896, m.	Hon. John C. H., b. 1928.
1910	Hardinge of Penshurst (3rd), George Edward Charles Hardinge, b. 1921, s. 1960, m.	Hon. Julian A. H., b. 1945.
1877	Harlech (5th), (William) David Ormsby-Gore, P.C., K.C.M.G., b. 1918, s. 1964, m.	Hon. Francis D. O.-G., b. 1954.
1939	Harmsworth (2nd), Cecil Desmond Bernard Harmsworth, b. 1903, s. 1948, m.	Hon. Eric H., b. 1905.
1815	Harris (5th), George St. Vincent Harris, C.B.E., M.C., b. 1889, s. 1932, m.	Hon. George R. H., b. 1920.
1954	Harvey of Tasburgh (2nd), Peter Charles Oliver Harvey, b. 1921, s. 1968, m.	Hon. John W. H., b 1923.
1295	Hastings (22nd), Edward Delaval Henry Astley, b. 1912, s. 1956, m.	Hon. Delaval T. H. A., b. 1960.
1835	Hatherton (7th), Thomas Charles Tasman Littleton, T.D., b. 1907, s. 1973, m.	Edward C. L., b. 1950.
1776	Hawke (9th), Bladen Wilmer Hawke, b. 1901, s. 1939, m.	Hon. Theodore H., b. 1904.
1927	Hayter (3rd), George Charles Hayter Chubb, C.B.E., b. 1911, s. 1967, m.	Hon. George W. M. C., b. 1943.
1945	Hazlerigg (2nd), Arthur Grey Hazlerigg, M.C., b. 1910, s. 1949, w.	Hon. Arthur G. H., b. 1951.
1797 I.	Headley (7th), Charles Rowland Allanson-Winn, b. 1902, s. 1969, m.	Hon. John R. A.-W., b. 1934.
1943	Hemingford (2nd), Dennis George Ruddock Herbert, b. 1904, s. 1947, m.	Hon. Dennis H., b. 1934.
1906	Hemphill (5th), Peter Patrick Fitzroy Martyn Martyn-Hemphill, b. 1928, s. 1957, m.	Hon. Charles A. M. M.-H., b. 1954.
1945	Henderson (1st), William Watson Henderson, P.C., b. 1891.	(None.)
1799 I.*	Henley (7th), Michael Francis Eden (5th U.K. Baron, Northington, 1885), b. 1914, s. 1962.	Hon. Oliver M. R. E., b. 1953.
1800 I.*	Henniker (7th), John Ernest de Grey Henniker-Major (3rd U.K. Baron, Hartismere, 1866), b. 1883, s. 1956, w.	Hon. Sir John P. E. C. H.-M., K.C.M.G., C.V.O., M.C., b. 1916.
1886	Herschell (3rd), Rognvald Richard Farrer Herschell, b. 1923, s. 1929, m.	(None.)
1935	Hesketh (3rd), Thomas Alexander Fermor-Hesketh, b. 1950, s. 1955,	Hon. Robert F.-H., b. 1951.

Created.	Title, Order of Succession, Name, etc.	Eldest Son or Heir.
1828	*Heytesbury* (6th), Francis William Holmes à Court, *b.* 1931, *s.* 1971, *m.*	Hon. James W. *H. à C.*, *b.* 1967.
1886	*Hillingdon* (4th), Charles Hedworth Mills, *b.* 1922, *s.* 1952, *m.*	Hon. Charles J. *M.*, *b.* 1951.
1886	*Hindlip* (5th), Henry Richard Allsopp, *b.* 1912, *s.* 1966, *m.*	Hon. Charles H. *A.*, *b.* 1940.
1950	*Hives* (2nd), John Warwick Hives, *b.* 1913, *s.* 1965, *m.*	Matthew *H.*, *b.* 1971.
1960	*Hodson*, Francis Lord Charlton Hodson, P.C., M.C., *b.* 1895, *w.* (*Lord of Appeal, retired*).	(Law Life Peerage.)
1912	*Hollenden* (2nd), Geoffrey Hope Hope-Morley, *b.* 1885, *s.* 1929, *m.*	Gordon H. *H.-M.*, *b.* 1914.
1897	*Holm Patrick* (3rd), James Hans Hamilton, *b.* 1928, *s.* 1942, *m.*	Hon. Hans J. D. *H.*, *b.* 1955.
1933	*Horder* (2nd), Thomas Mervyn Horder, *b.* 1911, *s.* 1955.	(None.)
1797 I.	*Hotham* (8th), Henry Durand Hotham, *b.* 1940, *s.* 1967, *m.*	Hon. William B. *H.*, *b.* 1972.
1881	*Hothfield* (4th), Thomas Sackville Tufton, *b.* 1916, *s.* 1961.	Lt.-Col. George W. A. *T.*, T.D., *b.* 1904.
1597	*Howard de Walden* (9th), John Osmael Scott-Ellis (5th *U.K. Baron, Seaford*, 1826), *b.* 1912, *s.* 1946, *w.*	Co-heiresses. To U.K. Barony, W. F. *Ellis*, *b.* 1912.
1930	*Howard of Penrith* (2nd), Francis Philip Howard, *b.* 1905, *s.* 1939, *m.*	Hon. Philip *H.*, *b.* 1945.
1960	*Howick of Glendale* (2nd), Charles Evelyn Baring, *b.* 1937, *s.* 1973, *m.*	Hon. David E. C. *B.*, *b.* 1975.
1796 I.	*Huntingfield* (6th), Gerard Charles Arcedeckne Vanneck, *b.* 1915, *s.* 1969, *m.*	Hon. Joshua C. *V.*, *b.* 1954.
1866	*Hylton* (5th), Raymond Hervey Jolliffe, *b.* 1932, *s.* 1967, *m.*	Hon. William H. M. *J.*, *b.* 1967.
1933	*Iliffe* (2nd), Edward Langton Iliffe, *b.* 1908, *s.* 1960, *m.*	Robert P. R. *I*, *b.* 1944.
1543 I.	*Inchiquin* (17th), Phaedrig Lucius Ambrose O'Brien (*O'Brien of Thomond*), *b.* 1900, *s.* 1968, *m.*	Hon. Fionn M. *O'B.*, *b.* 1903.
1962	*Inchyra* (1st), Frederick Robert Hoyer Millar, G.C.M.G., C.V.O., *b.* 1900, *m.*	Hon. Robert H. *M.*, *b.* 1935.
1964	*Inglewood* (1st), William Morgan Fletcher-Vane, T.D., *b.* 1909, *m.*	Hon. W. Richard *F.-V.*, *b.* 1951.
1946	*Inman* (1st), Philip Albert Inman, P.C., *b.* 1892, *m.*	(None.)
1919	*Inverforth* (3rd), (Andrew Charles) Roy Weir, *b.* 1932, *s.* 1975, *m.*	Hon. Andrew P. *W.*, *b.* 1966.
1941	*Ironside* (2nd), Edmund Oslac Ironside, *b.* 1924, *s.* 1959, *m.*	Hon. Charles E.G. *I.*, *b.* 1956.
1952	*Jeffreys* (2nd), Mark George Christopher Jeffreys, *b.* 1932, *s.* 1960, *m.*	Hon. Christopher H. M. *J.*, *b.* 1957.
1924	*Jessel* (2nd), Edward Herbert Jessel, C.B.E., *b.* 1904, *s.* 1950, *m.*	(None.)
1906	*Joicey* (4th), Michael Edward Joicey, *b.* 1925, *s.* 1966, *m.*	Hon. James M. *J.*, *b.* 1953.
1937	*Kenilworth* (3rd), John Tennant Davenport Siddeley, *b.* 1924, *s.* 1971, *m.*	Hon. John R. *S.*, *b.* 1954.
1935	*Kennet* (2nd), Wayland Hilton Young, *b.* 1923, *s.* 1960, *m.*	Hon. William A. *Y.*, *b.* 1957.
1776 I. ⎫ 1886* ⎬	*Kensington* (7th), William Edwardes (4th *U.K. Baron, Kensington*). *b.* 1904, *s.* 1938.	Hugh I. *E.*, *b.* 1933.
1951	*Kenswood* (2nd), John Michael Howard Whitfield, *b.* 1930, *s.* 1963, *m.*	Hon. Michael C. *W.*, *b.* 1955.
1788	*Kenyon* (5th), Lloyd Tyrell-Kenyon, C.B.E., *s.* 1927, *m.*	Hon. Lloyd *T.-K.*, *b.* 1947.
1947	*Kershaw* (4th), Edward John Kershaw, *b.* 1936, *s.* 1962, *m.*	Hon. John C. E. *K.*, *b.* 1971.
1943	*Keyes* (2nd), Roger George Bowlby Keyes, *b.* 1919, *s.* 1945, *m.*	Hon. Charles W. P. *K.*, *b.* 1951.
1909	*Kilbracken* (3rd), John Raymond Godley, D.S.C., *b.* 1920, *s.* 1950.	Hon. Christopher J. *G.*, *b.* 1945.
1971	*Kilbrandon*, Charles James Dalrymple Shaw, P.C., *b.* 1906, *m.* (*Lord of Appeal*).	(Law Life Peerage).
1900	*Killanin* (3rd), Michael Morris, M.B.E., T.D., *b.* 1914, *s.* 1927, *m.*	Hon. G. Redmond F. *M.*, *b.* 1947.
1943	*Killearn* (2nd), Graham Curtis Lampson, *b.* 1919, *s.* 1964, *m.*	Hon. Victor M. G. A. *L.*, *b.* 1941.
1789 I.	*Kilmaine* (6th), John Francis Archibald Browne, C.B.E., *b.* 1902, *s.* 1946, *m.*	Hon. John D. H. *B.*, *b.* 1948.
1831	*Kilmarnock* (7th), Alastair Ivor Gilbert Boyd, *b.* 1927, *s.* 1975.	Hon. Robin J. *B.*, *b.* 1941.
1941	*Kindersley* (2nd), Hugh Kenyon Molesworth Kindersley, C.B.E., *b.* 1899, *s.* 1954, *m.*	Hon. Robert H. M., *K.*, *b.* 1929.
1223 I.	*Kingsale* (35th), John de Courcy (*Premier Baron of Ireland*), *b.* 1941, *s.* 1969.	Nevinson R. *de C.*, *b.* 1920.
1682 S. ⎫ 1860* ⎬	*Kinnaird* (13th), Graham Charles Kinnaird (5th *U.K. Baron, Kinnaird*), *b.* 1912, *s.* 1972, *m.*	(None.)
1902	*Kinross* (4th), David Andrew Balfour, O.B.E., T.D., *b.* 1906, *s.* 1976, *m.*	Hon. Christopher P. *B.*, *b*, 1949.
1951	*Kirkwood* (3rd), David Harvie Kirkwood, Ph.D., *b.* 1931, *s.* 1970, *m.*	Hon. James S. *K.*, *b.* 1937.

Created.	Title, Order of Succession, Name, etc.	Eldest Son or Heir.

1800 I.   *Langford* (9th), Geoffrey Alexander Rowley-Conway, O.B.E., *b.* 1912, *s.* 1953, *m.* — Hon. Owen G. R.-C., *b.* 1958.

1942   *Latham* (2nd), Dominic Charles Latham, *b.* 1954, *s.* 1970. — Hon. Anthony L., *b.* 1954.

1431   *Latymer* (7th), Thomas Burdett Money-Coutts, *b.* 1901, *s.* 1949, *m.* — Hon. Hugo N. M.-C., *b.* 1926.

1869   *Lawrence* (5th), David John Downer Lawrence, *b.* 1937, *s.* 1968. — (None.)

1947   *Layton* (2nd), Michael John Layton, *b.* 1912, *s.* 1966, *m.* — Hon. Geoffrey M. L., *b.* 1947.

1859   *Leconfield* (7th), John Max Henry Scawen Wyndham (2nd U.K. Baron, Egremont, 1963), *b.* 1948, *s.* 1972. — Hon. Harry H. P. W., *b.* 1957.

1839   *Leigh* (4th), Rupert William Dudley Leigh, *b.* 1908, *s.* 1938, *m.* — Hon. John P. L., *b.* 1935.

1962   *Leighton of St. Mellons* (2nd), (John) Leighton Seager, *b.* 1922, *s.* 1963, *m.* — Hon. Robert W. H. L. S., *b.* 1955.

1797   *Lilford* (7th), George Vernon Powys, *b.* 1931, *s.* 1949, *m.* — Robert C. L. P., *b.* 1930.

1945   *Lindsay of Birker* (2nd), Michael Francis Morris Lindsay, *b.* 1909, *s.* 1952, *m.* — Hon. James F. L., *b.* 1945.

1758 I.   *Lisle* (7th), John Nicholas Horace Lysaght, *b.* 1903, *s.* 1919, *m.* — Horace L., *b.* 1908.

1925   *Lloyd* (2nd), Alexander David Frederick Lloyd, M.B.E., *b.* 1912, *s.* 1941, *m.* — (None.)

1895   *Loch* (3rd), George Henry Compton Loch, *b.* 1916, *s.* 1942, *m.* — Hon. Spencer L., M.C., *b.* 1920.

1850   *Londesborough* (9th), Richard John Denison, *b.* 1959, *s.* 1968, M. — (None.)

1541 I.   *Louth* (16th), Otway Michael James Oliver Plunkett, *b.* 1929, *s.* 1950, *m.* — Hon. Jonathan O.P., *b* 1952.

1458 S. } *Lovat* (15th), Simon Christopher Joseph Fraser, D.S.O., M.C., T.D. (4th
1837★ }   U.K. Baron, Lovat), *b.* 1911, *s.* 1933, *m.* — Master of Lovat, *b.* 1939.

1946   *Lucas of Chilworth* (2nd), Michael William George Lucas, *b.* 1926, *s.* 1967, *m.* — Hon. Simon W. L., *b.* 1957.

1929   *Luke* (2nd), Ian St. John Lawson-Johnston, K.C.V.O., T.D., *b.* 1905, *s.* 1943, *m.* — Hon. Arthur L.-J., *b.* 1933.

1839   *Lurgan* (4th), William George Edward Brownlow, *b.* 1902, *s.* 1937. — John D. C. B., O.B.E., *b.* 1911.

1914   *Lyell* (3rd), Charles Lyell, *b.* 1939, *s.* 1943. — (None.)

1859   *Lyveden* (6th), Ronald Cecil Vernon, *b.* 1915, *s.* 1973, *m.* — Hon. Jack L. V., *b.* 1938.

1959   *MacAndrew* (1st), Charles Glen MacAndrew, P.C., T.D., *b.* 1888, *m.* — Hon. Colin N. G. MacA., *b.* 1919.

1947   *MacDermott*, John Clarke MacDermott, P.C., M.C., *b.* 1896, *m.* (Lord Chief Justice of Northern Ireland, retired). — (Law Life Peerage.)

1776 I.   *Macdonald* (8th), Godfrey James Macdonald, *b.* 1947, *s.* 1970, *m.* — Hon. Alexander D. A. M., *b.* 1953.

1949   *Macdonald of Gwaenysgor* (2nd), Gordon Ramsay Macdonald, *b.* 1915, *s.* 1966, *m.* — Hon. Kenneth M., *b.* 1921.

1937   *McGowan* (3rd), Harry Duncan Cory McGowan, *b.* 1938, *s.* 1966, *m.* — Hon. Harry J. C. Mc. G., *b.* 1971.

1922   *Maclay* (3rd), Joseph Paton Maclay, *b.* 1942, *s.* 1969. — Hon. David M. M., *b.* 1944.

1955   *McNair* (2nd), (Clement) John McNair, *b.* 1915, *s.* 1975, *m.* — Hon. Duncan J. McN., *b.* 1947.

1951   *Macpherson of Drumochter* (2nd), James Gordon Macpherson, *b.* 1924, *s.* 1965, *m.* — Hon. Thomas I. M., *b.* 1948.

1937   *Mancroft* (2nd), Stormont Mancroft Samuel Mancroft, K.B.E., T.D., *b.* 1914, *s.* 1942, *m.* — Hon. Benjamin L. S. M., *b.* 1957.

1807   *Manners* (5th), John Robert Cecil Manners, *b.* 1923, *s.* 1972, *m.* — Hon. John H. R. M., *b.* 1956.

1922   *Manton* (3rd), Joseph Rupert Eric Robert Watson, *b.* 1924, *s.* 1968, *m.* — Hon. Miles R. M. W., *b.* 1958.

1908   *Marchamley* (3rd), John William Tattersall Whiteley, *b.* 1922, *s.* 1949, *m.* — Hon. William F. W., *b.* 1968.

1965   *Margadale* (1st), John Granville Morrison, T.D., *b.* 1906, *m.* — Hon. James I. M., T.D., *b.* 1930.

1961   *Marks of Broughton* (2nd), Michael Marks, *b.* 1920, *s.* 1964. — Hon. Simon R. M., *b.* 1950.

1930   *Marley* (2nd), Godfrey Pelham Leigh Aman, *b.* 1913, *s.* 1952, *m.* — (None.)

1964   *Martonmere* (1st), (John) Roland Robinson, P.C., G.B.E., K.C.M.G., *b.* 1907, *m.* — Hon. Richard A. G. R., *b.* 1935.

1776 I.   *Massy* (9th), Hugh Hamon John Somerset Massy, *b.* 1921, *s.* 1958, *m.* — Hon. David H. S. M., *b.* 1947.

1935   *May* (3rd), Michael St. John May, *b.* 1931, *s.* 1950, *m.* — Hon. Jasper B. St. J. M., *b.* 1965.

1928   *Melchett* (4th), Peter Robert Henry Mond, *b.* 1948, *s.* 1973. — (None.)

1925   *Merrivale* (3rd), Jack Henry Edmond Duke, *b.* 1917, *s.* 1951, *m.* — Hon. Derek J. P. D., *b.* 1948.

1911   *Merthyr* (3rd), William Brereton Couchman Lewis, P.C., K.B.E., T.D., *b.* 1901, *s.* 1932, *m.* — Hon. Trevor O. L., *b.* 1935.

Created.	Title, Order of Succession, Name, etc.	Eldest Son or Heir.
1919	*Meston* (2nd), Dougall Meston, *b.* 1894, *s.* 1943, *m.*	Hon. James M., *b.* 1950.
1838	*Methuen* (6th), Anthony John Methuen, *b.* 1925, *s.* 1975.	Hon. Robert A. H. M., *b.* 1931.
1905	*Michelham* (2nd), Herman Alfred Stern, *b.* 1900, *s.* 1919, *w.*	Hon. Jack *Michelham*, *b.* 1903.
1711	*Middleton* (12th), (Digby) Michael Godfrey John Willoughby, M.C., *b.* 1921, *s.* 1970, *m.*	Hon. Michael C. J. W., *b.* 1948.
1939	*Milford* (2nd), Wogan Philipps, *b.* 1902, *s.* 1962, *m.*	Hon. Hugo J. L. P., *b.* 1929.
1933	*Milne* (2nd), George Douglass Milne, *b.* 1909, *s.* 1948, *m.*	Hon. George M., *b.* 1941.
1951	*Milner of Leeds* (2nd), Michael Milner, *b.* 1923, *s.* 1967, *m.*	Hon. Richard J. M., *b.* 1959.
1947	*Milverton* (1st), Arthur Frederick Richards, G.C.M.G., *b.* 1885, *m.*	Rev. Hon. Fraser R., *b.* 1930.
1873	*Moncreiff* (5th), Harry Robert Wellwood Moncreiff, *b.* 1915, *s.* 1942, *m.*	Hon. Rhoderick H. W. M., *b.* 1954.
1884	*Monk Bretton* (3rd), John Charles Dodson, *b.* 1924, *s.* 1933, *m.*	Hon. Christopher M. D., *b.* 1958.
1728	*Monson* (11th), John Monson, *b.* 1932, *s.* 1958, *m.*	Hon. Nicholas J. M., *b.* 1955.
1885	*Montagu of Beaulieu* (3rd), Edward John Barrington Douglas-Scott-Montagu, *b.* 1926, *s.* 1929, *m.*	Hon. Ralph D-S-M., *b.* 1961.
1839	*Monteagle of Brandon* (6th), Gerald Spring Rice, *b.* 1926, *s.* 1946, *m.*	Hon. Charles J.S. R., *b.* 1953.
1943	*Moran* (1st), Charles McMoran Wilson, M.C., M.D., *b.* 1882, *m.*	Hon. R. John M. W., C.M.G., *b.* 1924.
1918	*Morris* (3rd), Michael David Morris, *b.* 1937, *s.* 1975.	Hon. Edward P. M., *b.* 1937.
1960	*Morris of Borth-y-Gest*, John William Morris, P.C., C.H., C.B.E., M.C., *b.* 1896. (*Lord of Appeal, retired*).	(Law Life Peerage).
1950	*Morris of Kenwood* (2nd), Philip Geoffry Morris, *b.* 1928, *s.* 1954, *m.*	Hon. Jonathan D. M. *b.* 1968.
1945	*Morrison* (2nd), Dennis Morrison, *b.* 1914, *s.* 1953.	(None.)
1831	*Mostyn* (5th), Roger Edward Lloyd Lloyd-Mostyn, M.C., *b.* 1920, *s.* 1965, *m.*	Hon. Llewellyn R. L.-M., *b.* 1948.
1933	*Mottistone* (4th), David Peter Seely, *b.* 1920, *s.* 1966, *m.*	Hon. Peter J. P. S., *b.* 1949.
1945	*Mountevans* (3rd), Edward Patrick Broke Evans, *b.* 1943, *s.* 1974, *m.*	Hon. Jeffrey de C. R. E., *b.* 1948.
1283	*Mowbray* (26th), *Segrave* (27th) (1283), & *Stourton* (23rd) (1448), Charles Edward Stourton (*Premier Baron of England*), *b.* 1923, *s.* 1965, *m.*	Hon. Edward W. S. S., *b.* 1953.
1932	*Moyne* (2nd), Bryan Walter Guinness, *b.* 1905, *s.* 1944, *m.*	Hon. Jonathan G., *b.* 1930.
1929	*Moynihan* (3rd), Antony Patrick Andrew Cairnes Berkeley Moynihan, *b.* 1936, *s.* 1965, *m.*	Hon. Colin B. M., *b.* 1955.
1781 I.	*Muskerry* (8th), Hastings Fitzmaurice Tilson Deane, *b.* 1907, *s.* 1966, *m.*	Hon. Robert F. D., *b.* 1948.
1627 S.*	*Napier and Ettrick* (14th), Francis Nigel Napier (5th *U.K. Baron, Ettrick*, 1872), *b.* 1930, *s.* 1954, *m.*	Master of Napier, *b.* 1962.
1868	*Napier of Magdala* (5th), (Robert) John Napier, O.B.E., *b.* 1904, *s.* 1948, *m.*	Hon. Robert N., *b.* 1940.
1940	*Nathan* (2nd), Roger Carol Michael Nathan, *b.* 1922, *s.* 1963, *m.*	Hon. Rupert H. B. N., *b.* 1957.
1960	*Nelson of Stafford* (2nd), Henry George Nelson, *b.* 1917, *s.* 1962, *m.*	Hon. Henry R. G. N., *b.* 1943.
1959	*Netherthorpe* (1st), James Turner, *b.* 1908, *m.*	Hon. James A. T., *b.* 1936.
1946	*Newall* (2nd), Francis Storer Eaton Newall, *b.* 1930, *s.* 1963, *m.*	Hon. Richard H. E. N., *b.* 1961.
1776 I.	*Newborough* (7th), Robert Charles Michael Vaughan Wynn, D.S.C., *b.* 1917, *s.* 1965, *m.*	Hon. Robert V. W., *b.* 1949.
1892	*Newton* (4th), Peter Richard Legh, *b.* 1915, *s.* 1960, *m.*	Hon. Richard T. L., *b.* 1950.
1930	*Noel-Buxton* (2nd), Rufus Alexander Buxton, *b.* 1917, *s.* 1948, *m.*	Hon. Martin C. Noel-Buxton, *b.* 1940.
1957	*Norrie* (1st), (Charles) Willoughby (Moke) Norrie, G.C.M.G., G.C.V.O., C.B., D.S.O., M.C., *b.* 1893, *m.*	Hon. George W. M. N., *b.* 1936.
1884	*Northbourne* (4th), Walter Ernest Christopher James, *b.* 1896, *s.* 1932, *m.*	Hon. Christopher G. W. J., *b.* 1926.
1866	*Northbrook* (5th), Francis John Baring, *b.* 1915, *s.* 1947, *m.*	Hon. Francis T. B., *b.* 1954.
1878	*Norton* (7th), John Arden Adderley, O.B.E., *b.* 1915, *s.* 1961, *m.*	Hon. James N. A. A., *b.* 1947.
1906	*Nunburnholme* (4th), Ben Charles Wilson, *b.* 1928, *s.* 1974, *m.*	Hon. Charles T. W., *b.* 1936.
1950	*Ogmore* (1st), David Rees Rees-Williams, P.C., T.D., *b.* 1903, *m.*	Hon. Gwilym R.-W., *b.* 1931.
1870	*O'Hagan* (4th), Charles Towneley Strachey, *b.* 1945, *s.* 1961, *m.*	Hon. Richard T. S., *b.* 1950.
1868	*O'Neill* (4th), Raymond Arthur Clanaboy O'Neill, T.D., *b.* 1933, *s.* 1944, *m.*	Hon. Shane S. O'N., *b.* 1965.
1836 I.*	*Oranmore and Browne* (4th), Dominick Geoffrey Edward Browne (2nd *U.K. Baron Mereworth*, 1926), *b.* 1901, *s.* 1927, *m.*	Hon. Dominick G. T. B., *b.* 1929.
1868	*Ormathwaite* (6th), John Arthur Charles Walsh, *b.* 1912, *s.* 1944.	(None.)

Created.	Title, Order of Succession, Name, etc.	Eldest Son or Heir.

1933   *Palmer* (3rd), Raymond Cecil Palmer, O.B.E., *b.* 1916, *s.* 1950, *m.*   Hon. Gordon W. N. P., O.B.E., T.D., *b.* 1918.

1914   *Parmoor* (2nd), Alfred Henry Seddon Cripps, *b.* 1882, *s.* 1941.   Hon. Frederick H. C., D.S.O., T.D., *b.* 1885.

1962   *Pearce*, Edward Holroyd Pearce, P.C., *b.* 1901, *m.* (*Lord of Appeal, retired.*)   (Law Life Peerage.)

1965   *Pearson*, Colin Hargreaves Pearson, P.C., C.B.E., *b.* 1899, *m.* (*Lord of Appeal, retired.*).   (Law Life Peerage.)

1937   *Pender* (3rd), John Willoughby Denison-Pender, *b.* 1933, *s.* 1965, *m.*   Hon. Henry J. R. *D.-P.*, *b.* 1968.

1866   *Penrhyn* (6th), Malcolm Frank Douglas-Pennant, D.S.O., M.B.E., *b.* 1908, *s.* 1967, *m.*   Hon. Nigel *D.-P.*, *b.* 1909.

1909   *Pentland* (2nd), Henry John Sinclair, *b.* 1907, *s.* 1925, *m.*   (None.)

1603   *Petre* (17th), Joseph William Lionel Petre, *b.* 1914, *s.* 1915, *m.*   Hon. John *P.*, *b.* 1942.

1918   *Phillimore* (3rd), Robert Godfrey Phillimore, *b.* 1939, *s.* 1947.   Hon. Claud *P.*, *b.* 1911.

1945   *Piercy* (2nd), Nicholas Pelham Piercy, *b.* 1918, *s.* 1966, *m.*   Hon. James W. *P.*, *b.* 1946.

1827   *Plunket* (8th), Robin Rathmore Plunket, *b.* 1925, *s.* 1975, *m.*   Hon. Shaun A. F. S. *P.*, *b.* 1931.

1831   *Poltimore* (6th), Hugh de Burgh Warwick Bampfylde, *b.* 1888, *s.* 1967, *m.*   Mark C. *B.*, *b.* 1957.

1690 S.   *Polwarth* (10th), Henry Alexander Hepburne-Scott, T.D., *b.* 1916, *s.* 1944, *m.*   Master of Polwarth, *b.* 1947.

1930   *Ponsonby of Shulbrede* (3rd), Thomas Arthur Ponsonby, *b.* 1930, *s.* 1976, *m.*   Hon. Frederick M. T. *P.*, *b.* 1958.

1958   *Poole* (1st), Oliver Brian Sanderson Poole, P.C., C.B.E., T.D., *b.* 1911, *m.*   Hon. David C. *P.*, *b.* 1945.

1852   *Raglan* (5th), FitzRoy John Somerset, *b.* 1927, *s.* 1964, *m.*   Hon. Geoffrey *S.*, *b.* 1932.

1932   *Rankeillour* (4th), Peter St. Thomas More Henry Hope, *b.* 1935, *s.* 1967.   Michael R. *H.*, *b.* 1940.

1953   *Rathcavan* (1st), (Robert William) Hugh O'Neill, P.C., *b.* 1883, *w.*   Rt. Hon. Phelim R. H. *O'N.*, *b.* 1909.

1916   *Rathcreedan* (2nd), Charles Patrick Norton, T.D., *b.* 1905, *s.* 1930, *m.*   Hon. Christopher J. *N.*, *b.* 1949.

1868 I.   *Rathdonnell* (5th), Thomas Benjamin McClintock Bunbury, *b.* 1938, *s.* 1959, *m.*   Hon. William L. McC *B.*, *b.* 1966.

1911   *Ravensdale* (3rd), Nicholas Mosley, M.C., *b.* 1923, *s.* 1966, *m.*   Hon. Shaun N. *M.*, *b.* 1949.

1218   *Ravensworth* (8th), Arthur Waller Liddell, *b.* 1924, *s.* 1950, *m.*   Hon. Thomas A. H. *L.*, *b.* 1954.

1821   *Rayleigh* (5th), John Arthur Strutt, *b.* 1908, *s.* 1947, *m.*   Hon. Charles *S.*, *b.* 1910.

1937   *Rea* (2nd), Philip Russell Rea, P.C., O.B.E., *b.* 1900, *s.* 1948, *m.*   John N. *R.*, M.D., *b.* 1928.

1628 S.   *Reay* (14th), Hugh William Mackay, *b.* 1937, *s.* 1963, *m.*   Master of Reay, *b.* 1965.

1902   *Redesdale* (5th), Clement Napier Bertram Freeman-Mitford, *b.* 1932, *s.* 1963, *m.*   Hon. Rupert B. *F.-M.*, *b.* 1967.

1928   *Remnant* (3rd), James Wogan Remnant, *b.* 1930, *s.* 1967, *m.*   Hon. Philip J. *R.*, *b.* 1954.

1806 I.   *Rendlesham* (8th), Charles Anthony Hugh Thellusson, *b.* 1915, *s.* 1943, *m.*   Hon. Charles W. B. *T.*, *b.* 1954.

1933   *Rennell* (2nd), Francis James Rennell Rodd, K.B.E., C.B., *b.* 1895, *s.* 1941, *m.*   J. A. Tremayne *R.*, *b.* 1935.

1964   *Renwick* (2nd), Harry Andrew Renwick, *b.* 1935, *s.* 1973, *m.*   Hon. Robert J. *R.*, *b.* 1966.

1885   *Revelstoke* (4th), Rupert Baring, *b.* 1911, *s.* 1934.   Hon. John *B.*, *b.* 1934.

1905   *Ritchie of Dundee* (4th), Colin Neville Ower Ritchie, *b.* 1908, *s.* 1975, *m.*   Hon. Harold M. *R.*, *b.* 1919.

1935   *Riverdale* (2nd), Robert Arthur Balfour, *b.* 1901, *s.* 1957, *m.*   Hon. Mark R. *B.*, *b.* 1927.

1961   *Robertson of Oakridge* (2nd), William Ronald Robertson, *b.* 1930, *s.* 1974, *m.*   Hon. William *R.*, *b.* 1975.

1938   *Roborough* (2nd), Massey Henry Edgcumbe Lopes, *b.* 1903, *s.* 1938, *m.*   Hon. Henry *L.*, *b.* 1940.

1931   *Rochester* (2nd), Foster Charles Lowry Lamb, *b.* 1916, *s.* 1955, *m.*   Hon. David C. *L.*, *b.* 1944.

1934   *Rockley* (3rd), James Hugh Cecil, *b.* 1934, *s.* 1976, *m.*   Hon. Anthony R. *C.*, *b.* 1961.

1782   *Rodney* (9th), John Francis Rodney, *b.* 1920, *s.* 1973, *m.*   Hon. George B. *R.*, *b.* 1953.

1651 S.*   *Rollo* (13th), Eric John Stapylton Rollo (4th *U.K. Baron, Dunning,* 1869), *b.* 1915, *s.* 1947, *m.*   Master of Rollo, *b.* 1943.

1866   *Romilly* (4th), William Gaspard Guy Romilly, *b.* 1899, *s.* 1905, *m.*   (None.)

1959   *Rootes* (2nd), William Geoffrey Rootes, *b.* 1917, *s.* 1964, *m.*   Hon. Nicholas G. *R.*, *b.* 1951.

1796 I.} 1838* }   *Rossmore* (7th), William Warner Westenra (6th *U.K. Baron, Rossmore*), *b.* 1931, *s.* 1958.   (None.)

1939   *Rotherwick* (2nd), (Herbert) Robin Cayzer, *b.* 1912, *s.* 1958, *m.*   Hon. H. Robin *C.*, *b.* 1954.

1885   *Rothschild* (3rd), Nathanial Mayer Victor Rothschild, G.B.E., G.M., F.R.S., *b.* 1910, *s.* 1937, *m.*   Hon. N. C. Jacob *R.*, *b.* 1936.

1911   *Rowallan* (2nd), Thomas Godfrey Polson Corbett, K.T., K.B.E., M.C., T.D., *b.* 1895, *s.* 1933, *w.*   Hon. Arthur *C.*, *b.* 1919.

1947   *Rugby* (2nd), Alan Loader Maffey, *b.* 1913, *s.* 1969, *m.*   Hon. John R. *M.*, *b.* 1949.

1945   *Rusholme* (1st), Robert Alexander Palmer, *b.* 1890.   (None.)

1975   *Russell of Killowen*, Charles Ritchie Russell, P.C., *b.* 1908, *w.* (*Lord of Appeal*).   (Law Life Peerage.)

Created.	Title, Order of Succession, Name, etc.	Eldest Son or Heir.
1919	*Russell of Liverpool* (2nd), Edward Frederick Langley Russell, C.B.E., M.C., T.D., *b.* 1895, *s.* 1920, *m.*	Simon G. J. R., *b.* 1952.
1876	*Sackville* (6th), Lionel Bertrand Sackville-West, *b.* 1913, *s.* 1965, *m.*	Hugh R. I. *S.-W.*, M.C., *b.* 1919.
1964	*St. Helens* (1st), Michael Henry Colin Hughes-Young, *b.* 1912, *w.*	Hon. Richard F. *H.-Y.*, *b.* 1945.
1559	*St. John of Bletso* (20th), Andrew Beauchamp St. John, T.D., *b.* 1918, *s.* 1976, *m.*	Hon. Anthony T. *St. J.*, *b.* 1957.
1935	*St. Just* (2nd), Peter George Grenfell, *b.* 1922, *s.* 1941, *m.*	(None.)
1852	*St. Leonards* (4th), John Gerard Sugden, *b.* 1950, *s.* 1972.	Edward C. S., *b.* 1902.
1887	*St. Levan* (3rd), Francis Cecil St. Aubyn, *b.* 1895, *s.* 1940, *m.*	Hon. John F. A. *St. A.*, D.S.C., *b.* 1919.
1885	*St. Oswald* (4th), Rowland Denys Guy Winn, M.C., *b.* 1916, *s.* 1957, *m.*	Hon. Derek E. A. *W.*, *b.* 1919.
1972	*Salmon*, Cyril Barnet Salmon, P.C., *b.* 1903, *m.* (*Lord of Appeal*).	(Law Life Peerage.)
1445 S.	*Saltoun* (19th), Alexander Arthur Fraser, M.C., *b.* 1886, *s.* 1933, *m.*	Hon. Flora M. *Ramsay*, *b.* 1930.
1945	*Sandford* (2nd), Rev. John Cyril Edmondson, D.S.C., *b.* 1920, *s.* 1959, *m.*	Hon. James J. M. *E.*, *b.* 1949.,
1871	*Sandhurst* (5th), (John Edward) Terence Mansfield, D.F.C., *b.* 1920, *s.* 1964, *m.*	Hon. Guy R. J. *M.*, *b.* 1949.
1802	*Sandys* (7th), Richard Michael Oliver Hill, *b.* 1931, *s.* 1961, *m.*	Marcus T. *H.*, *b.* 1931.
1888	*Savile* (3rd), George Halifax Lumley-Savile, *b.* 1919, *s.* 1931.	Hon. Henry L. T. *L.-S.*, *b.* 1923.
1447	*Saye and Sele* (21st), Nathaniel Thomas Allen Twisleton-Wykeham-Fiennes, *b.* 1920, *s.* 1968, *m.*	Hon. Richard I. *T.-W.-F.*, *b.* 1959.
1932	*Selsdon* (3rd), Malcolm McEacharn Mitchell-Thomson, *b.* 1937, *s.* 1963, *m.*	Hon. Callum M. M. *M.-T.*, *b.* 1969.
1916	*Shaughnessy* (3rd), William Graham Shaughnessy, *b.* 1922, *s.* 1938, *m.*	Hon. Patrick J. *S.*, *b.* 1944.
1783 I. ⎫ 1839* ⎭	*Sheffield* (8th), Thomas Henry Oliver Stanley (8th *U.K. Baron*, *Stanley of Alderley* and 7th *U.K. Baron Eddisbury*, 1848), *b.* 1927, *s.* 1971, *m.*	Hon. Richard O. *S.*, *b.* 1956.
1946	*Shepherd* (2nd), Malcolm Newton Shepherd, P.C., *b.* 1918, *s.* 1934, *m.*	Hon. Graeme G., *S*, *b.* 1949.
1784	*Sherborne* (7th), Charles Dutton, *b.* 1911, *s.* 1949, *m.*	Hon. George E. *D.*, *b.* 1912.
1964	*Sherfield* (1st), Roger Mellor Makins, G.C.B., G.C.M.G., *b.* 1904, *m.*	Hon. Christopher *M.*, *b.* 1942.
1902	*Shuttleworth* (5th), Charles Geoffrey Nicholas Kay-Shuttleworth, *b.* 1948, *s.* 1975.	Hon. Robert J. *K.-S.*, *b.* 1954.
1963	*Silsoe* (1st), (Arthur) Malcolm Trustram Eve, G.B.E., M.C., T.D., Q.C., *b.* 1894, *m.*	Hon. David M. T. *E.*, Q.C., *b.* 1930.
1971	*Simon of Glaisdale*, Jocelyn Edward Salis Simon, P.C., *b.* 1911, *m.* (*Lord of Appeal*).	(Law Life Peerage.)
1947	*Simon of Wythenshawe* (2nd), Roger Simon, *b.* 1913, *s.* 1960, *m.*	Hon. Matthew *S.*, *b.* 1955.
1449 S.	*Sinclair* (17th), Charles Murray Kennedy St. Clair, M.V.O., *b.* 1914, *s.* 1957, *m.*	Master of Sinclair, *b.* 1968.
1957	*Sinclair of Cleeve* (1st), Robert John Sinclair, K.C.B., K.B.E., *b.* 1893, *m.*	Hon. John R. K. *S.*, O.B.E., *b.* 1919.
1919	*Sinha* (3rd), Sudhindro Prosannho Sinha, *b.* 1920, *s.* 1967, *m.*	Hon. Sushanto *S.* *b.* 1953.
1828	*Skelmersdale* (7th), Roger Bootle-Wilbraham, *b.* 1945, *s.* 1973, *m.*	
1916	*Somerleyton* (3rd), Savile William Francis Crossley, *b.* 1928, *s.* 1959, *m.*	Hon. Hugh F. S. *C.*, *b.* 1971.
1784	*Somers* (8th), John Patrick Somers Cocks, *b.* 1907, *s.* 1953, *m.*	Philip S. S. *C.*, *b.* 1948.
1917	*Southborough* (3rd), Francis John Hopwood, *b.* 1897, *s.* 1960, *m.*	Hon. Francis M. *H.*, *b.* 1922.
1959	*Spens* (2nd), William George Michael Spens, *b.* 1914, *s.* 1973, *m.*	Hon. Patrick M. R. *S.*, *b.* 1942.
1640	*Stafford* (14th), Basil Francis Nicholas Fitzherbert, *b.* 1926, *s.* 1941, *m.*	Hon. Francis M. W. *F.*, *b.* 1954.
1938	*Stamp* (3rd), Trevor Charles Stamp, M.D., *b.* 1907, *s.* 1941, *m.*	Hon. Trevor *S.*, M.D., *b.* 1935.
1318	*Strabolgi* (11th), David Montague de Burgh Kenworthy, *b.* 1914, *s.* 1953.	Rev. the Hon. Jonathan M. A. *K.*, *b.* 1916.
1954	*Strang* (1st), William Strang, G.C.B., G.C.M.G., M.B.E., *b.* 1893, *w.*	Hon. Colin *S.*, *b.* 1922.
1628	*Strange* (15th), John Drummond, *b.* 1900, *title called out of abeyance* 1964, *w.*	Three co-heiresses.
1955	*Strathalmond* (2nd), William Fraser, C.M.G., O.B.E., T.D., *b.* 1916, *s.* 1970, *w.*	Hon. William R. *F.*, *b.* 1947.
1936	*Strathcarron* (2nd), David William Anthony Blyth Macpherson, *b.* 1924, *s.* 1937, *m.*	Hon. Ian D. P. *M.*, *b.* 1949.
1955	*Strathclyde* (1st), Thomas Dunlop Galbraith, P.C., *b.* 1891, *m.*	Hon. Thomas G. D. *G.*, M.P., *b.* 1917.
1900	*Strathcona and Mount Royal* (4th), Donald Euan Palmer Howard, *b.* 1923, *s.* 1959, *m.*	Hon. Donald A. *H.*, *b.* 1961.

Created.	Title, Order of Succession, Name, etc.	Eldest Son or Heir.
1836	*Stratheden & Campbell* (1841) (4th), Alastair Campbell, C.B.E., b. 1899, s. 1918, m.	Hon. Gavin C., b. 1901.
1884	*Strathspey* (5th), Donald Patrick Trevor Grant, b. 1912, s. 1948, m.	Hon. James P. G., b. 1943.
1838	*Sudeley* (7th), Nerlyn Charles Sainthill Hanbury-Tracy, b. 1939, s. 1941.	Claud E. F. *Hanbury-Tracy-Domvile*, T.D., b. 1904.
1786	*Suffield* (11th), Anthony Philip Harbord-Hamond, M.C., b. 1922, s. 1951, m.	Hon. Charles A. A. *H.-H.* b. 1953.
1893	*Swansea* (4th), John Hussey Hamilton Vivian, b. 1925, s. 1934.	Hon. Richard A. H. V., b. 1957.
1907	*Swaythling* (3rd), Stuart Albert Samuel Montagu, O.B.E., b. 1898, s. 1927, m.	Hon. David C. M., b. 1928.
1919	*Swinfen* (2nd), Charles Swinfen Eady, b. 1904, s. 1919, m.	Hon. Roger M. E., b. 1938.
1935	*Sysonby* (3rd), John Frederick Ponsonby, b. 1945, s. 1956.	(None.)
1831 I.	*Talbot of Malahide* (9th), Joseph Hubert George Talbot b. 1899, s. 1975, m.	Reginald J. R. *Arundell*, b. 1931.
1946	*Tedder* (2nd), John Michael Tedder, SC.D., Ph.D., D.SC., b. 1926, s. 1967, m.	Hon. Robin J. T., b. 1955.
1797 I.	*Teignmouth* (7th), Frederick Maxwell Aglionby Shore, D.S.C., b. 1920, s. 1964.	(None.)
1884	*Tennyson* (4th), Harold Christopher Tennyson, b. 1919, s. 1951.	Hon. Mark A. T., D.S.C., b. 1920.
1918	*Terrington* (4th), (James Allen) David Woodhouse, b. 1915, s. 1961, m.	Hon. C. Montague W., D.S.O., O.B.E., b. 1917.
1940	*Teviot* (2nd), Charles John Kerr, b. 1934, s. 1968, m.	Hon. Charles R. K., b. 1971.
1616	*Teynham* (20th), John Christopher Ingham Roper-Curzon, b. 1928, s. 1972, m.	Hon. David J. H. I. R.-C., b. 1965.
1964	*Thomson of Fleet* (2nd), Kenneth Roy Thomson, b. 1923 s.	Hon. David K. R. T., b. 1957.
1792	*Thurlow* (8th), Francis Edward Hovell-Thurlow-Cumming-Bruce, K.C.M.G., b. 1912, s. 1971, m.	Hon. Roualeyn R. *H.-T.-C.-B.*, b. 1952.
1876	*Tollemache* (5th), Timothy John Edward Tollemache, b. 1939, s. 1975.	Hon. John N. L. T., b. 1941.
1564 S.	*Torphichen* (15th), James Andrew Douglas Sandilands, b. 1946, s. 1975.	Bruce W. S., b. 1921.
1947	*Trefgarne* (2nd), David Garro Trefgarne, b. 1941, s. 1960, m.	Hon. George G. T., b. 1970.
1921	*Trevethin* (4th), *and Oaksey* (2nd), John Geoffrey Tristram Lawrence (2nd U.K. Baron, Oaksey, 1947), b. 1929, s. 1971, m.	Hon. Patrick J. T. L., b. 1960.
1880	*Trevor* (4th), Charles Edwin Hill-Trevor, b. 1928, s. 1950, m.	Hon. Mark C. *H.-T.*, b. 1970.
1461 I.	*Trimlestown* (19th), Charles Aloysius Barnewall, b. 1899, s. 1937, m.	Hon. Anthony B., b. 1928.
1940	*Tryon* (2nd), Charles George Vivian Tryon, P.C., G.C.V.O., K.C.B., D.S.O., b. 1906, s. 1940, m.	Hon. Anthony T., b. 1940.
1935	*Tweedsmuir* (2nd), John Norman Stuart Buchan, C.B.E., C.D., b. 1911, s. 1940, m.	Hon. William B., b. 1916.
1523	*Vaux of Harrowden* (9th), Rev. Peter Hugh Gordon Gilbey, b. 1914, s. 1958.	Hon. John H. P. G. b. 1915.
1800 I.	*Ventry* (7th), Arthur Frederick Daubeney Olav Eveleigh-de-Moleyns, b. 1898, s. 1936.	Andrew W. *Daubeny-De M.*, b. 1943.
1762	*Vernon* (10th), John Lawrence Venables-Vernon, b. 1923, s. 1963, m.	Visct. Harcourt (*see p.* 235).
1922	*Vestey* (3rd), Samuel George Armstrong Vestey, b. 1941, s. 1954, m.	Hon. Mark W. V., b. 1943.
1841	*Vivian* (5th), Anthony Crespigny Claude Vivian, b. 1906, s. 1940, m.	Hon. Nicholas V., b. 1935.
1963	*Wakefield of Kendal* (1st), (William) Wavell Wakefield, b. 1898, m.	(None.)
1934	*Wakehurst* (3rd), (John) Christopher Loder, b. 1925, s. 1970, m.	Hon. Timothy W. L., b. 1958.
1723	*Walpole* (9th), Robert Henry Montgomerie Walpole, b. 1913, s. 1931, m.	Hon. Robert H. W., b. 1938.
1780	*Walsingham* (9th), John de Grey, M.C., b. 1925, s. 1965, m.	Hon. Robert *de* G., b. 1669.
1936	*Wardington* (2nd), Christopher Henry Beaumont Pease, b. 1924, s. 1950, m.	Hon. William S. P., b. 1925.
1792 I.	*Waterpark* (7th), Frederick Caryll Phillip Cavendish, b. 1926, s. 1948, m.	Hon. Roderick A. C., b. 1959.
1942	*Wedgwood* (4th), Piers Anthony Weymouth Wedgwood, b. 1954, s. 1970.	John W., M.D., b. 1919.
1861	*Westbury* (5th), David Alan Bethell, M.C., b. 1922, s. 1961, m.	Hon. Richard N. B., b. 1950.
1944	*Westwood* (2nd), William Westwood, b. 1907, s. 1953, m.	Hon. William G. W., b. 1944.
1935	*Wigram* (2nd), (George) Neville (Clive) Wigram, M.C., b. 1915, s. 1960, m.	Hon. Andrew F. C. W., b. 1949.
1964	*Wilberforce*, Richard Orme Wilberforce, P.C., C.M.G., O.B.E., b. 1907, m. (*Lord of Appeal.*)	(Law Life Peerage.)

Created.	Title, Order of Succession, Name, etc.	Eldest Son or Heir.
1491	*Willoughby de Broke* (20th), John Henry Peyto Verney, M.C., A.F.C., b. 1896, s. 1923, m.	Hon. Leopold D. V., b. 1938.
1946	*Wilson* (2nd), Patrick Maitland Wilson, b. 1915, s. 1964, m.	(None.)
1937	*Windlesham* (3rd), David James George Hennessy, P.C., b. 1932, s. 1962, m.	Hon. James R. H., b. 1968.
1951	*Wise* (2nd), John Clayton Wise, b. 1923, s. 1968, m.	Hon. Christopher J. C. W. b. 1948.
1869	*Wolverton* (5th), Nigel Reginald Victor Glyn, b. 1904, s. 1932.	Jeremy C. G., b. 1930.
1928	*Wraxall* (2nd), George Richard Lawley Gibbs, b. 1928, s. 1931.	Hon. Eustace H. B. G., b. 1929.
1915	*Wrenbury* (3rd), John Burton Buckley, b. 1927, s. 1940, m.	Hon. William E. B., b. 1966.
1838	*Wrottesley* (5th), Richard John Wrottesley, M.C., b. 1918, s. 1962, m.	Clifton H. L. de V. W., b. 1968.
1919	*Wyfold* (3rd), Hermon Robert Fleming Hermon-Hodge, b. 1915, s. 1942.	(None.)
1829	*Wynford* (8th), Robert Samuel Best, M.B.E., b. 1917, s. 1943, m.	Hon. John P. R. B., b. 1950.
1308	*Zouche* (18th), James Assheton Frankland, b. 1943, s. 1965.	Hon. Roger N. F., b. 1909.

Peeresses in Their Own Right

Peerages are occasionally granted immediately to ladies of distinction or the widows of distinguished men; but frequently the instances falling under this heading are the result of regular inheritance in lines which are open to females in default of males. A Peeress in her Own Right retains her title after marriage, and if her husband's rank is the superior she is designated by the two titles jointly, the inferior one last: her hereditary claim still holds good in spite of any marriage whether higher or lower. No rank held by a woman can confer any title or even precedence upon her husband nor the rank of a Peeress in her Own Right is inherited by her eldest son (or perhaps daughter), to whomsoever she may have been married.

COUNTESSES IN THEIR OWN RIGHT.—*Style*, The Countess of ——
Addressed as, My Lady.

Created.	Title, Name, etc.	Eldest Son or Heir.
1643 S.	*Dysart*, Rosamund Agnes Greaves, b. 1914, s. 1975.	Lady Katherine Grant, b. 1918.
1452 S.	*Erroll*, Diana Denyse Hay (*Hereditary Lord High Constable and Knight Marischal of Scotland*), b. 1926, s. 1941, m.	Lord Hay, b. 1948.
1633 S.	*Loudoun*, Barbara Huddleston Abney-Hastings, b. 1919, s. 1960, m.	Lord Mauchline, b. 1942.
1404 S.	*Mar*, Margaret of Mar (*Premier Earldom of Scotland*), b. 1940, s. 1975, m.	The Mistress of Mar, b. 1963.
1660 S.	*Newburgh*, Maria Sofia Giuseppina Gravina di Ramacca (*Princess Giustiniani-Bandini*), b. 1889, s. 1941, w.	Prince Giulio Rospigliosi, b. 1907.
1235 S.	*Sutherland*, Elizabeth Millicent Sutherland, b. 1921, s. 1963, m.	Lord Strathnaver, b. 1947

BARONESSES IN THEIR OWN RIGHT.—*Style*, The Baroness ——.
Addressed as, My Lady.

Created.	Title, Name, etc.	Eldest Son or Heir.
1421	*Berkeley*, Mary Lalle Foley-Berkeley, b. 1905, *title called out of abeyance*, 1967.	Hon. Cynthia E. Gueterbock, b. 1909.
1455	*Berners*, Vera Ruby Williams, b. 1901, s. 1950, m.	Two co-heiresses.
1307	*Dacre*, Rachel Leila Douglas-Home, b. 1929, *title called out of abeyance*, 1970, m.	Hon. James T. A. D.-H., b. 1952.
1332	*Darcy de Knayth*, Davina Marcia Ingrams, b. 1938, s. 1943, w.	Hon. Caspar D. I., b. 1962.
1264	*De Ros*, Georgiana Angela Maxwell, b 1933, s. 1958, m. (*Premier Barony of England*).	Hon. Peter M., b. 1958.
1439	*Dudley*, Barbara Amy Felicity Wallace, b. 1907, s. 1972, w.	Hon. Jim A. H. W., b. 1930.
1489 S.	*Herries*, Anne Elizabeth Fitzalan-Howard, b. 1938, s. 1975.	Lady Mary F.-H., b. 1940.
1602 S.	*Kinloss*, Beatrice Mary Grenville Freeman-Grenville, b. 1922, s. 1944, m.	Master of Kinloss, b. 1953.
1663	*Lucas of Crudwell* (*Scottish Baroness, Dingwall* 1609), Anne Rosemary Palmer, b. 1919, s. 1958, m.	Hon. Ralph M. P., b. 1951.
1681 S.	*Nairne*, Katherine Evelyn Constance Bigham (*Viscountess Mersey*), b. 1912, s 1944, m.	Master of Nairne, b. 1934.
1945	*Portal of Hungerford*, Rosemary Ann Portal, b. 1923, s. 1971.	Hon. Mavis E. A. P., b. 1926.
1651 S.	*Ruthven of Freeland*, Bridget Helen Monckton, C.B.E. (*Bridget, Viscountess Monckton of Brenchley*), b. 1896, s. 1956, w.	Earl of Carlisle, M.C., b. 1923 (*see* p. 229).
1489 S.	*Sempill*, Ann Moira Sempill, b. 1920, s. 1965, m.	Master of Sempill, b. 1949.

LIFE PEERS
Created under Life Peerages Act, 1958

BARONS

1972 *Adeane*, Michael Edward Adeane, P.C., G.C.B., G.C.V.O., Royal Victorian Chain, *b.* 1910, *m.*
1974 *Alexander of Potterhill*, William Picken Alexander, Ph.D., *b.* 1905, *m.*
1973 *Allan of Kilmahew*, Robert Alexander Allan, D.S.O., O.B.E., R.D., *b.* 1914, *m.*
1976 *Allen of Abbeydale*, Philip Allen, G.C.B., *b.* 1912, *m.*
1974 *Allen of Fallowfield*, Alfred Walter Henry Allen, C.B.E., *b.* 1914, *m.*
1961 *Alport*, Cuthbert James McCall Alport, P.C., T.D., *b.* 1912, *m.*
1965 *Annan*, Noel Gilroy Annan, O.B.E., *b.* 1916, *m.*
1970 *Ardwick*, John Cowburn Beavan, *b.* 1910, *m.*
1975 *Armstrong of Sanderstead*, William Armstrong, P.C., K.C.B., M.V.O., *b.* 1915, *m.*
1975 *Ashdown*, Arnold Silverstone, *b.* 1911, *m.*
1964 *Arwyn*, Arwyn Randall Arwyn, *b.* 1897, *m.*
1973 *Ashby*, Eric Ashby, D.SC., F.R.S., *b.* 1904, *m.*
1967 *Aylestone*, Herbert William Bowden, P.C., C.H., C.B.E., *b.* 1905, *m.*
1963 *Balerno*, Alick Drummond Buchanan-Smith, C.B.E., T.D., D.SC., F.R.S.E., *b.* 1898, *w.*
1972 *Ballantrae*, Bernard Edward Fergusson, K.T., G.C.M.G., G.C.V.O., D.S.O., O.B.E., *b.* 1911, *m.*
1968 *Balogh*, Thomas Balogh. *b.* 1905.
1975 *Banks*, Desmond Anderson Harvie Banks, C.B.E., *b,* 1918.
1975 *Barber*, Anthony Perrinott Lysberg Barber, P.C., T.D., *b.* 1920, *m.*
1975 *Barnetson*, William Denholm Barnetson, *b.* 1917, *m.*
1967 *Beaumont of Whitley*, Rev. Timothy Wentworth Beaumont, *b.* 1928, *m.*
1965 *Beeching*, Richard Beeching, Ph.D., *b.* 1913, *m.*
1969 *Bernstein*, Sidney Lewis Bernstein, *b.* 1899, *m.*
1964 *Beswick*, Frank Beswick, P.C., *b.* 1912.
1968 *Black*, William Rushton Black, *b.* 1893, *m.*
1971 *Blake*, Robert Norman William Blake, F.B.A., *b.* 1916, *m.*
1964 *Blyton*, William Reid Blyton, *b.* 1899, *m.*
1958 *Boothby*, Robert John Graham Boothby, K.B.E., *b.* 1900, *m.*
1976 *Boston of Faversham*, Terence George Boston, *b.* 1930, *m.*
1964 *Bourne*, Geoffrey Kemp Bourne, G.C.B., K.B.E., C.M.G., *b.* 1902, *m.*
1964 *Bowden*, Bertram Vivian Bowden Ph.D., *b,* 1910, *m.*
1972 *Boyd-Carpenter*, John Archibald Boyd-Carpenter, P.C., *b.* 1908, *m.*
1970 *Boyle of Handsworth*, Edward Charles Gurney Boyle, P.C., *b.* 1923.
1973 *Brayley*, John Desmond Brayley, M.C., *b.* 1917.
1976 *Briggs*, Asa Briggs *b.* 1921, *m.*
1975 *Briginshaw*, Richard William Briginshaw.
1976 *Brimelow*, Thomas Brimelow, G.C.M.G., O.B.E., *b.* 1915, *m.*
1976 *Britten*, (Edward) Benjamin Britten, O.M., C.H., *b.* 1913.
1965 *Brock*, Russell Claude Brock, F.R.C.S., *b.* 1903, *m.*
1964 *Brockway*, (Archibald) Fenner Brockway, *b.* 1888, *m.*
1966 *Brooke of Cumnor*, Henry Brooke, P.C., C.H., *b.* 1903, *m.*
1976 *Brookes*, Raymond Percival Brookes, *b.* 1909, *m.*
1964 *Brown*, Wilfred Banks Duncan Brown, P.C., M.B.E., *b.* 1908, *m.*
1975 *Bruce of Donington*, Donald William Trevor Bruce, *b.* 1912, *m.*
1966 *Buckton*, Samuel Storey, *b.* 1896, *w.*
1976 *Bullock*, Alan Louis Charles Bullock, F.B.A., *b.* 1914, *m.*
1970 *Burntwood*, Julian Ward Snow, *b.* 1910, *m*
1965 *Butler of Saffron Walden*, Richard Austen Butler, K.G., P.C., C.H., *b.* 1902, *m.*
1964 *Byers*, (Charles) Frank Byers, P.C., O.B.E., *b.* 1915, *m.*
1965 *Caccia*, Harold Anthony Caccia, G.C.M.G., G.C.V.O., *b.* 1905, *m.*
1975 *Campbell of Croy*, Gordon Thomas Calthrop Campbell, P.C., M.C., *b.* 1921, *m.*
1966 *Campbell of Eskan*, John Middleton Campbell, *b.* 1912, *m.*
1964 *Caradon*, Hugh Mackintosh Foot, P.C., G.C.M.G., K.C.V.O., O.B.E., *b.* 1907, *m.*
1976 *Carr of Hadley*, (Leonard) Robert Carr, P.C., *b.* 1916, *m.*
1974 *Castle*, Edward Cyril Castle, *b.* 1907, *m.*
1964 *Chalfont*, Alun Arthur Gwynne Jones, P.C., O.B.E., M.C., *b.* 1919, *m.*
1962 *Champion*, Arthur Joseph Champion, P.C., *b.* 1897, *m.*
1963 *Chelmer*, Eric Cyril Boyd Edwards, M.C., T.D., *b.* 1914, *m.*
1974 *Chelwood*, Tufton Victor Hamilton Beamish, M.C., *b.* 1917, *m.*
1969 *Clark*, Kenneth Mackenzie Clark, O.M., C.H., K.C.B., F.B.A., *b.* 1903, *m.*
1965 *Cole*, George James Cole, G.B.E., *b.* 1906, *m.*
1964 *Collison*, Harold Francis Collison, C.B.E., *b.* 1909, *m.*
1966 *Cooper of Stockton Heath*, John Cooper, *b.* 1908.
1959 *Craigton*, Jack Nixon Browne, P.C., C.B.E., *b.* 1904.
1973 *Crowther-Hunt*, Norman Crowther Hunt, Ph.D., *b.* 1920, *m.*
1975 *Cudlipp*, Hugh Cudlipp, O.B.E., *b.* 1913, *m.*
1974 *Darling of Hillsborough*, George Darling, P.C., *b.* 1905, *m.*
1974 *Davies of Penrhys*, Gwilym Elfed Davis, *b.* 1913, *m.*
1970 *Davies of Leek*, Harold Davies, P.C., *b.* 1904, *m.*
1976 *Delfont*, Bernard Delfont, *b.* 1909, *m.*
1970 *Diamond*, John Diamond, P.C., *b.* 1907.
1967 *Donaldson of Kingsbridge*, John George Stuart Donaldson, O.B.E., *b.* 1907.
1967 *Douglass of Cleveland*, Harry Douglass, *b.* 1902, *m.*

1974 *Duncan-Sandys,* Ducan Edwin Duncan-Sandys, P.C., C.H., *b.* 1908, *m.*
1972 *Elworthy,* (Samuel) Charles Elworthy, G.C.B., C.B.E., D.S.O., M.V.O., D.F.C., A.F.C., *Marshal of the Royal Air Force, b.* 1911, *m.*
1974 *Elwyn-Jones,* Frederick Elwyn Elwyn-Jones, P.C., *b.* 1909, *m.* (*Lord High Chancellor*).
1968 *Energlyn,* William David Evans, D.Sc., Ph.D., *b.* 1912, *m.*
1967 *Evans of Hungershall,* Benjamin Ifor Evans, D.Lit., *b.* 1899, *m.*
1958 *Ferrier,* Victor Ferrier Noel-Paton, E.D., *b.* 1900, *m.*
1974 *Fisher of Camden,* Samuel Fisher, *b.* 1905, *m.*
1970 *Fletcher,* Eric George Molyneux Fletcher, P.C., Ll.D., *b.* 1903, *m.*
1967 *Foot,* John Mackintosh Foot, *b.* 1909, *m.*
1962 *Franks,* Oliver Shewell Franks, P.C., G.C.M.G., K.C.B., C.B.E., F.B.A., *b.* 1905, *m.*
1974 *Fraser of Kilmorack,* (Richard) Michael Fraser, C.B.E., *b.* 1915, *m.*
1966 *Fulton,* John Scott Fulton, *b.* 1902, *m.*
1964 *Gardiner,* Gerald Austin Gardiner, P.C., C.H., *b.* 1900, *m.*
1969 *Garner,* (Joseph John) Saville Garner, G.C.M.G., *b.* 1908, *m.*
1958 *Geddes of Epsom,* Charles John Geddes, C.B.E., *b.* 1897, *m.*
1974 *Geoffrey-Lloyd,* Geoffrey William Geoffrey-Lloyd, P.C., *b.* 1902.
1970 *George-Brown,* George Alfred George-Brown, P.C., *b.* 1914, *m.*
1975 *Gibson,* (Richard) Patrick (Tallentyre) Gibson, *b.* 1916, *m.*
1974 *Glenkinglas,* Michael Antony Cristobal Noble, P.C., *b.* 1913, *m.*
1965 *Goodman,* Arnold Abraham Goodman, C.H., *b.* 1915.
1974 *Gordon-Walker,* Patrick Chrestien Gordon-Walker, P.C., C.H., *b.* 1907, *m.*
1969 *Gore-Booth,* Paul Henry Gore-Booth, G.C.M.G., K.C.V.O., *b.* 1909, *m.*
1974 *Goronwy-Roberts,* Goronwy Owen Goronwy-Roberts, P.C., *b.* 1913, *m.*
1976 *Grade,* Lew Grade, *b.* 1906, *m.*
1967 *Granville of Eye,* Edgar Louis Granville, *b.* 1899, *m.*
1958 *Granville-West,* Daniel Granville West, *b.* 1904, *m.*
1975 *Greene of Harrow Weald,* Sidney Francis Greene, C.B.E., *b.* 1910, *m.*
1974 *Greenhill of Harrow,* Denis Arthur Greenhill, G.C.M.G., O.B.E., *b.* 1913, *m.*
1970 *Greenwood of Rossendale,* (Arthur William James) Anthony Greenwood, P.C., *b.* 1911, *m.*
1975 *Gregson,* John Gregson
1968 *Grey of Naunton,* Ralph Francis Alnwick Grey, G.C.M.G., G.C.V.O., O.B.E., *b.* 1910, *m.*
1970 *Hailsham of St. Marylebone,* Quintin McGarel Hogg, P.C., C.H., *b.* 1907, *m.*
1972 *Hale,* (Charles) Leslie Hale, *b.* 1902, *m.*
1970 *Hamnett,* Cyril Hamnett, *b.* 1906, *w.*
1975 *Harmar-Nicholls,* Harmar Harmar-Nicholls, *b.* 1912, *m.*
1974 *Harris of Greenwich,* John Henry Harris, *b.* 1930, *m.*
1968 *Hartwell,* (William) Michael Berry, M.B.E., T.D., *b.* 1911, *m.*
1971 *Harvey of Prestbury,* Arthur Vere Harvey, C.B.E., *b.* 1906, *m.*
1974 *Harvington,* Robert Grant Grant-Ferris, P.C., *b.* 1907, *m.*
1968 *Helsby,* Laurence Norman Helsby, G.C.B., K.B.E., *b.* 1908, *m.*
1972 *Hewlett,* (Thomas) Clyde Hewlett, C.B.E., *b.* 1923, *m.*
1967 *Heycock,* Llewellyn Heycock, C.B.E., *b.* 1905, *m.*
1963 *Hill of Luton,* Charles Hill, P.C., M.D., *b.* 1904, *m.*
1965 *Hilton of Upton,* Albert Victor Hilton, *b.* 1908, *m.*
1965 *Hinton of Bankside,* Christopher Hinton, O.M., K.B.E., F.R.S., *b.* 1901, *w.*
1967 *Hirshfield,* Desmond Barel Hirshfield, *b.* 1913, *m.*
1974 *Home of the Hirsel,* Alexander Frederick Douglas-Home, P.C., K.T., *b.* 1903, *m.*
1974 *Houghton of Sowerby,* (Arthur Leslie Noel) Douglas Houghton, P.C., C.H., *b.* 1898, *m.*
1961 *Hughes,* William Hughes, P.C., C.B.E., *b.* 1911, *m.*
1966 *Hunt,* (Henry Cecil) John Hunt, C.B.E., D.S.O., *b.* 1910, *m.*
1973 *Hunt of Fawley,* John Henderson Hunt, C.B.E., D.M., *b.* 1905, *m.*
1975 *Jacobson,* Sydney Jacobson, M.C., *b.* 1908, *m.*
1968 *Jacques,* John Henry Jacques, *b.* 1905, *m.*
1959 *James of Rusholme,* Eric John Francis James, *b.* 1909, *m.*
1970 *Janner,* Barnett Janner, *b.* 1892, *m.*
1976 *Kagan,* Joseph Kagan, *b.* 1915, *m.*
1965 *Kahn,* Richard Ferdinand Kahn, C.B.E., F.B.A., *b.* 1905.
1974 *Kaldor,* Nicholas Kaldor, F.B.A., *b.* 1908, *m.*
1970 *Kearton,* (Christopher) Frank Kearton, O.B.E., F.R.S., *b.* 1911, *m.*
1966 *Kilmany,* William John St. Clair Anstruther-Gray, P.C., M.C., *b.* 1905, *m.*
1965 *Kings Norton,* Harold Roxbee Cox, Ph.D., *b.* 1902, *m.*
1975 *Kirkhill,* John Farquharson Smith, *b.* 1930, *m.*
1974 *Kissin,* Harry Kissin, *b.* 1912, *m.*
1964 *Leatherland,* Charles Edward Leatherland, O.B.E., *b.* 1898.
1974 *Lee of Newton,* Frederick Lee, P.C., *b.* 1906, *m.*
1975 *Lever,* Leslie Maurice Lever, *b.* 1905, *m.*
1964 *Llewelyn-Davies,* Richard Llewelyn-Davies, *b.* 1912, *m.*
1965 *Lloyd of Hampstead,* Dennis Lloyd, Q.C., LL.D., *b.* 1915, *m.*
1973 *Lloyd of Kilgerran,* Rhys Gerran Lloyd, C.B.E., Q.C., *b.* 1907, *m.*
1974 *Lovell-Davis,* Peter Lovell-Davis, *b.* 1924, *m.*
1975 *Lyons of Brighton,* Braham Jack Dennis Lyons.
1976 *McCarthy,* William Edward John McCarthy, *b.* 1925, *m.*
1966 *McFadzean,* William Hunter McFadzean, *b.* 1903, *m.*
1974 *Mackie of Benshie,* George Yull Mackie, C.B.E., D.S.O., D.F.C., *b.* 1919, *m.*
1971 *Maclean,* Charles Hector Fitzroy Maclean, P.C., K.T., G.C.V.O., K.B.E., *b.* 1916, *m.* (*Lord Chamberlain*).

1967 *McLeavy*, Frank McLeavy, b. 1899, m.
1967 *MacLeod of Fuinary*, Very Rev. George Fielden MacLeod, M.C., D.D., b. 1895, m.
1966 *Maelor*, Thomas William Jones, b. 1898, m.
1967 *Mais*, Alan Raymond Mais, G.B.E., T.D., E.R.D., b. 1911, m.
1974 *Marples*, (Alfred) Ernest Marples, P.C., b. 1907, m.
1971 *Maybray-King*, Horace Maybray King, P.C., Ph.D., b. 1901, m.
1961 *Molson*, (Arthur) Hugh (Elsdale) Molson, P.C., b. 1903, m.
1967 *Morris of Grasmere*, Charles Richard Morris, K.C.M.G., b. 1898, m.
1971 *Moyola*, James Dawson Chichester-Clark, P.C. (N.I.), b. 1923, m.
1976 *Murray of Gravesend*, Albert James Murray, b. 1930, m.
1964 *Murray of Newhaven*, Keith Anderson Hope Murray, K.C.B., Ph.D., b. 1903.
1976 *Northfield*, (William) Donald Chapman, b. 1923.
1966 *Nugent of Guildford*, (George) Richard (Hodges) Nugent, P.C., b. 1907, m.
1973 *O'Brien of Lothbury*, Leslie Kenneth O'Brien, P.C., G.B.E., b. 1908, m.
1970 *Olivier*, Laurence Kerr Olivier, b. 1907, m.
1970 *O'Neill of the Maine*, Terence Marne O'Neill, P.C. (N.I.), b. 1914, m.
1976 *Oram*, Albert Edward Oram, b. 1913, m.
1971 *Orr-Ewing*, (Charles) Ian Orr-Ewing, O.B.E., b. 1912, m.
1975 *Paget of Northampton*, Reginald Thomas Paget, Q.C., b. 1908, m.
1974 *Pannell*, (Thomas) Charles Pannell, P.C., b. 1902, m.
1966 *Pargiter*, George Albert Pargiter, C.B.E., b. 1897, m.
1976 *Parry*, Gordon Samuel David Parry.
1961 *Peddie*, James Mortimer Peddie, M.B.E., b. 1906, m.
1967 *Penney*, William George Penney, O.M., K.B.E., Ph.D., D.SC., F.R.S., b. 1909, m.
1968 *Pilkington*, William Henry (Harry) Pilkington, b. 1905, m.
1975 *Pitt of Hampstead*, David Thomas Pitt, b. 1913, m.
1967 *Platt*, Robert Platt, M.D., b. 1900, m.
1959 *Plowden*, Edwin Noel Plowden, K.C.B., K.B.E., b. 1907, m.
1975 *Plurenden*, Rudy Sternberg, b. 1917, m.
1966 *Popplewell*, Ernest Popplewell, C.B.E., b. 1899, m.
1973 *Porritt*, Arthur Espie Porritt, G.C.M.G., G.C.V.O., C.B.E., b. 1900, m.
1975 *Pritchard*, Derek Wilbraham Pritchard, b. 1910, m.
1974 *Ramsey of Canterbury*, Rt. Rev. Arthur Michael Ramsey, P.C., D.D., Royal Victorian Chain, b. 1904, m.
1976 *Rayne*, Max Rayne, b. 1918, m.
1967 *Redcliffe-Maud*, John Primatt Redcliffe Maud, G.C.B., C.B.E., b. 1906, m.
1966 *Redmayne*, Martin Redmayne, P.C., D.S.O., T.D., b. 1910, m.
1970 *Reigate*, John Kenyon Vaughan-Morgan, P.C., b. 1905, m.
1964 *Rhodes*, Hervey Rhodes, K.G., P.C., D.F.C., b. 1895, m.
1970 *Rhyl*, (Evelyn) Nigel (Chetwoode) Birch, P.C., O.B.E., b. 1906, m.
1966 *Ritchie-Calder*, (Peter) Ritchie Calder, C.B.E., b. 1906, m.
1959 *Robbins*, Lionel Charles Robbins, C.H., C.B., F.B.A., b. 1898, m.
1961 *Robens of Woldingham*, Alfred Robens, P.C., b. 1910, m.
1969 *Roberthall*, Robert Lowe Roberthall, K.C.M.G., C.B., b. 1901, m.
1975 *Ryder of Eaton Hastings*, Sydney Thomas (Don) Ryder, b. 1916, m.
1962 *Sainsbury*, Alan John Sainsbury, b. 1902, m.
1972 *Samuel of Wych Cross*, Harold Samuel, b. 1912, m.
1976 *Schon*, Frank Schon, b. 1912, m.
1972 *Seebohm*, Frederic Seebohm, T.D., b. 1909, m.
1964 *Segal*, Samuel Segal, b. 1902, m.
1976 *Selwyn-Lloyd*, (John) Selwyn (Brooke) Lloyd, P.C., C.H., C.B.E., T.D., Q.C., b. 1904.
1958 *Shackleton*, Edward Arthur Alexander Shackleton, K.G., P.C., O.B.E., b. 1911, m.
1959 *Shawcross*, Hartley William Shawcross, P.C., G.B.E., Q.C., b. 1902, w.
1970 *Shinwell*, Emanuel Shinwell, P.C., C.H., b. 1884, m.
1970 *Slater*, Joseph Slater, B.E.M., b. 1904, m.
1964 *Snow*, Charles Percy Snow, C.B.E., b. 1905, m.
1965 *Soper*, Rev. Donald Oliver Soper, Ph.D., b. 1903, m.
1969 *Stokes*, Donald Gresham Stokes, T.D., b. 1914, m.
1976 *Stone*, Joseph Ellis Stone, b. 1903, m.
1966 *Stow Hill*, Frank Soskice, P.C., Q.C., b. 1902, m.
1971 *Tanlaw*, Simon Brooke Mackay, b. 1934, m.
1958 *Taylor*, Stephen James Lake Taylor, M.D., b. 1910, m.
1968 *Taylor of Gryfe*, Thomas Johnston Taylor, b. 1912, m.
1966 *Taylor of Mansfield*, Harry Bernard Taylor, b. 1895, m.
1971 *Thomas*, (William) Miles (Webster) Thomas, D.F.C., b. 1897, m.
1967 *Thorneycroft*, (George Edward) Peter Thorneycroft, P.C., b. 1909, m.
1962 *Todd*, Alexander Robertus Todd, D.SC., D.Phil., F.R.S., b. 1907, m.
1974 *Tranmire*, Robert Hugh Turton, P.C., K.B.E., M.C., b. 1903, m.
1974 *Trend*, Burke St. John Trend, P.C., G.C.B., C.V.O., b. 1914, m.
1968 *Trevelyan*, Humphrey Trevelyan, K.G., G.C.M.G., C.I.E., O.B.E., b. 1905, m.
1976 *Vaizey*, John Ernest Vaizey, b. 1929, m.
1964 *Wade*, Donald William Wade, b. 1904, m.
1976 *Wall*, John Edward Wall, O.B.E., b. 1911, m.
1974 *Wallace of Coslany*, George Douglas Wallace, b. 1906, m.
1961 *Walston*, Henry David Leonard George Walston, C.V.O., b. 1912, m.
1972 *Watkins*, Tudor Elwyn Watkins, b. 1903, m.

1976 Weidenfeld, (Arthur) George Weidenfeld, b. 1919, m.
1965 Wells-Pestell, Reginald Alfred Wells-Pestell, b. 1910, m.
1970 Wheatley, John Wheatley, P.C., b. 1908, m.
1971 Widgery, John Passmore Widgery, P.C., O.B.E., T.D., b. 1911, m. (Lord Chief Justice of England)
1967 Wigg, George Edward Cecil Wigg, P.C., b. 1900, m.
1974 Wigoder, Basil Thomas Wigoder, Q.C., b. 1921, m.
1962 Williamson, Thomas Williamson, C.B.E., b. 1897, m.
1964 Willis, Edward Henry Willis, b. 1918, m.
1976 Wilson of High Wray, Paul Norman Wilson, O.B.E., D.S.C., b. 1908, m.
1969 Wilson of Langside, Henry Stephen Wilson, P.C., Q.C., b. 1916, m.
1975 Wilson of Radcliffe, Alfred Wilson, b. 1909, m.
1976 Winstanley, Michael Platt Winstanley, b. 1918, m.
1965 Winterbottom, Ian Winterbottom, b. 1913, m.
1974 Wolfenden, John Frederick Wolfenden, C.B.E., b. 1906, m.
1967 Woolley, Harold Woolley, C.B.E., b. 1905, w.
1964 Wynne-Jones, William Francis Kenrick Wynne-Jones, b. 1903, w.
1971 Zuckerman, Solly Zuckerman, O.M., K.C.B., F.R.S., M.D., D.Sc., b. 1904, m.

BARONESSES

1970 Bacon, Alice Martha Bacon, P.C., C.B.E., b. 1911.
1967 Birk, Alma Birk, b. 1921, m.
1964 Brooke of Ystradfellte, Barbara Muriel Brooke, D.B.E., b. 1908, m.
1962 Burton of Coventry, Elaine Frances Burton, b. 1904.
1974 Delacourt-Smith of Alteryn, Margaret Rosalind Delacourt-Smith, w.
1972 Elles, Diana Elles, m.
1958 Elliot of Harwood, Katharine Elliot, D.B.E., b. 1903, w.
1964 Emmet of Amberley, Evelyn Violet Elizabeth Emmet, b. 1899, w.
1976 Faithfull, Lucy Faithfull, O.B.E.
1974 Falkender, Marcia Matilda Falkender, C.B.E., b. 1932.
1974 Fisher of Rednal, Doris Mary Gertrude Fisher, b. 1919, m.
1964 Gaitskell, Anna Dora Gaitskell, w.
1974 Hornsby-Smith, (Margaret) Patricia Hornsby-Smith, P.C., D.B.E., b. 1914.
1965 Hylton-Foster, Audrey Pellew Hylton-Foster, b. 1908, w.
1970 Lee of Asheridge, Janet Bevan, P.C., b. 1904, w.
1967 Llewelyn-Davies of Hastoe, Annie Patricia Llewelyn-Davies, P.C., b. 1915, m.
1971 Macleod of Borve, Evelyn Hester Macleod, b. 1915, w.
1970 Masham of Ilton, Susan Lilian Primrose Cunliffe-Lister, b. 1935, m. (Countess of Swinton).
1964 Northchurch, Frances Joan Davidson, D.B.E. (Dowager Viscountess Davidson), b. 1894, w.
1964 Phillips, Norah Mary Phillips, b. 1910, w.
=974 Pike, (Irene) Mervyn (Parnicott) Pike, b. 1918.
1974 Robson of Kiddington, Inga-Stina Robson, b. 1919, m.
1971 Seear, (Beatrice) Nancy Seear, b. 1913.
1967 Serota, Beatrice Serota, b. 1919, m.
1966 Sharp, Evelyn Adelaide Sharp, G.B.E., b. 1903.
1973 Sharples, Pamela Sharples, w.
1965 Spencer-Churchill, Clementine Ogilvy Spencer Churchill, G.B.E., b. 1885, w.
1974 Stedman, Phyllis Stedman, O.B.E., b. 1916, m.
1975 Stewart of Alvechurch, Mary Elizabeth Henderson Stewart, m.
1961 Summerskill, Edith Summerskill, P.C., C.H., b. 1901, m.
1970 Tweedsmuir of Belhelvie, Priscilla Jean Fortescue Buchan, P.C., b. 1915, m.
1975 Vickers, Joan Helen Vickers, D.B.E., b. 1907.
1975 Ward of North Tyneside, Irene Mary Bewick Ward, C.H., D.B.E., b. 1895.
1970 White, Eirene Lloyd White, b. 1909, w.
1958 Wootton of Abinger, Barbara Frances Wright, b. 1897, w.
1971 Young, Janet Mary Young, b. 1926, m.

A Life Peerage was conferred in the Birthday Honours, 1976, on Barbara, Lady Jackson, but at the time of going to press her title was not known.

Surnames of Peers and Peeresses differing from their Titles

Abney Hastings — Loudoun
Acheson—Gosford
Adderley—Norton
Addington—Sidmouth
Agar—Normanton
Akers Douglas—Chilston
Alexander—Alexander of Potterhill★
Alexander—Alexander of Tunis
Alexander—Caledon
Allan—Allan of Kilmahew★
Allen—Allen of Abbeydale★
Allen—Allen of Fallowfield★
Allanson Winn—Headley
Allsopp—Hindlip
Aman—Marley
Anderson—Waverley
Annesley—Valentia
Anson—Lichfield
Anstruther-Gray—Kilmany★
Armstrong—Armstrong of Sanderstead★
Armstrong Jones—Snowdon
Arthur—Glenarthur
Ashley Cooper—Shaftesbury
Ashton—Ashton of Hyde
Asquith—Oxford & A.
Assheton—Clitheroe
Astley—Hastings
Astor—Astor of Hever
Bailey—Glanusk
Baillie—Burton
Baille Hamilton—Haddington
Baird—Kintore
Baldwin — Baldwin of Bewdley
Balfour—Kinross
Balfour—Riverdale
Balfour — Balfour of Inchrye
Bampfylde—Poltimore
Banbury — Banbury of Southam
Baring—Ashburton
Baring—Cromer
Baring—Howick of Glendale
Baring—Northbrook
Baring—Revelstoke
Barnes—Gorell
Barnewall—Trimlestown
Bathurst—Bledisloe
Beamish—Chelwood★
Beauclerk—St. Albans

★ Life Peer created under Life Peerages Act, 1958.

★ **Life Peer created under Life Peerages Act, 1958.**

★ Life Peer created under Life Peerages Act, 1958.

★ Life Peer created under Life Peerages Act, 1958.

Wentworth Fitzwilliam—Fitzwilliam
West—Granville-West★
Westenra—Rossmore
White—Annaly
Whiteley—Marchamley
Whitfield—Kenswood
Willey—Barnby
Williams—Berners
Williams—★Falkender
Williamson—Forres

Willoughby—Middleton
Wills—Dulverton
Wilson—Moran
Wilson—Nunburnholme
Wilson—Wilson of High Wray★
Wilson—Wilson of Langside★
Wilson—Wilson of Radcliffe★
Windsor—Cornwall

Windsor—Gloucester
Windsor—Kent
Windsor Clive — Plymouth
Wingfield—Powerscourt
Winn—St. Oswald
Winn—Headley
Wodehouse—Kimberley
Wood—Halifax
Woodhouse—Terrington

Wright—Wootton of Abinger★
Wyndham—Leconfield
Wyndham Quin—Dunraven
Wynn—Newborough
Yarde Buller—Churston
Yerburgh—Alvingham
Yorke—Hardwicke
Young—Kennet
Younger—Y. of Leckie

★ Life Peers created under Life Peerages Act, 1958

Courtesy Titles (*in actual existence in* 1976)

Holders of Courtesy Titles are addressed in the same manner as holders of substantive titles.
From this list it will be seen that, for example, the "Marquess of Blandford" is heir to the Dukedom of Marlborough, and "Viscount Althorp" to the Earldom of Spencer. Titles of second heirs are also given, and the Courtesy Title of the father of a second heir is indicated by ★; e.g., Earl of Burlington, eldest son of ★Marquess of Hartington.

In addition, the heir, and sometimes the second heir, to some Scottish peerages is usually styled " The Master of——";
e.g., " The Master of Falkland " heir to Viscount Falkland; and " The Master of Lindsay " is eldest son of ★Lord Balniel, heir to the Earl of Crawford and Balcarres. Users of this style are not included here.

Marquesses.

Blandford—Marlborough
Douro—Wellington
★Graham—Montrose
Granby—Rutland
★Hamilton—Abercorn
★Hartington—Devonshire
Kildare—Leinster
Lorne—Argyll
★Tavistock—Bedford

Earls.

Aboyne—Huntly
Altamont—Sligo
Ancram—Lothian
Arundel and Surrey—Norfolk
Bective—Headfort
Belfast—Donegall
★Brecknock—Camden
★Burford—St. Albans
Burlington—★Hartington
Cardigan—Ailesbury
Cassillis—Ailsa
★Compton—Northampton
★Dalkeith—Buccleuch
Euston—Grafton
Gifford—Tweeddale
Grosvenor—Westminster
★Hopetoun—Linlithgow
Jermyn—Bristol
Macduff—Fife
★March and Kinrara—Richmond
★Mount Charles—Conyngham
Mulgrave—Normanby
Percy—Northumberland
Rocksavage — Cholmondeley
★Ronaldshay—Zetland
St. Andrews—Kent
★Shelburne—Lansdowne
Tyrone—Waterford
Ulster—Gloucester
Uxbridge—Anglesey
Wiltshire—Winchester
Yarmouth—Hertford

Viscounts.

Aithrie—★Hopetoun
Alexander—Caledon
Althorp—Spencer
Andover—Suffolk and Berkshire

Asquith—Oxford & Asquith
Bayham—★Brecknock
Boringdon—Morley
Borodale—Beatty
Boyle—Shannon
Brocas—Jellicoe
Bury—Albemarle
Calne and Calstone—★Shelburne
Campden—Gainsborough
Carlow—Portarlington
Castlereagh—Londonderry
Chelsea—Cadogan
Chewton—Waldegrave
Cole—Enniskillen
Corvedale—Baldwin of Bewdley
Cranborne—Salisbury
Cranley—Onslow
Crichton—Erne
Darymple—Stair
Dawick—Haig
Deerhurst—Coventry
Drumlanrig — Queensberry
Dunluce—Antrim
Dupplin—Kinnoull
Ebrington—Fortescue
Eden—Avon
Ednam—Dudley
Elveden—Iveagh
Emlyn—Cawdor
Encombe—Eldon
Ennismore—Listowel
Enfield—Strafford
Erleigh—Reading
Errington—Cromer
Feilding—Denbigh
FitzHarris—Malmesbury
Folkestone—Radnor
Garmoyle—Cairns
Garnock—Lindsay
Glandine—Norbury
Glenapp—Inchcape
Glentworth—Limerick
Glerawly—Annesley
Gwynnedd—Lloyd George of Dwyfor
Hawkesbury—Liverpool
Ikerrin—Carrick
Ingestre—Shrewsbury
Jocelyn—Roden
Kelburn—Glasgow

Kingsborough—Kingston
Knebworth—Lytton
Lascelles—Harewood
Lewisham—Dartmouth
Linley—Snowdon
Loftus—Ely
Lowther—Lonsdale
Lumley—Scarbrough
Lymington—Portsmouth
Maidstone — Winchilsea and Nottingham
Maitland—Lauderdale
Mandeville—Manchester
Melgund—Minto
Moore—Drogheda
Morepeth—Carlisle
Newport—Bradford
Newry and Mourne—Kilmorey
Parker—Macclesfield
Perceval—Egmont
Petersham—Harrington
Pollington—Mexborough
Prestwood—Attlee
Quenington—St. Aldwyn
Raynham—Townshend
Reidhaven—Seafield
Ruthven of Canberra and Dirleton—Gowrie
St. Cyres—Iddesleigh
Sandon—Harrowby
Slane—★Mount Charles
Stormont—Mansfield
Strabane—★Hamilton
Strathallan—Perth
Stuart—Castle Stewart
Sudley—Arran
Suirdale—Donoughmore
Tamworth—Ferrers
Tarbat—Cromartie
Tiverton—Halsbury
Vaughan—Lisburne
Villiers—Jersey
Weymouth—Bath
Windsor—Plymouth
Wolmer—Selborne

Barons (Lord—)

Aberdour—Morton
Apsley—Bathurst
Ardee—Meath
Balgonie—Leven & Melville
Bingham—Lucan
Binning—Haddington

Brooke—Warwick
Bruce—Elgin
Buckhurst—De La Warr
Burghersh—Westmorland
Cardross—Buchan
Cochrane—Dundonald
Courtenay—Devon
Dalmeny—Rosebery
Delvin—Westmeath
Doune—Moray
Dundas—★Ronaldshay
Eliot—St. Germans
Erskine—Mar & Kellie
Fintrie—★Graham
Garlies—Galloway
Glamis—Strathmore
Greenock—Cathcart
Guernsey—Aylesford
Hay—Erroll
Howland—★Tavistock
Hyde—Clarendon
Inverurie—Kintore
Irwin—Halifax
Leslie—Rothes
Leveson—Granville
Loughborough—Rosslyn
Mauchline—Loudoun
Medway—Cranbrook
Montgomerie—Eglinton and Winton
Moreton—Ducie
Naas—Mayo [March
Neidpath—Wemyss &
Norreys—Lindley & Abingdon
North—Guilford
Ogilvy—Airlie
Ossulston—Tankerville
Oxmantown—Rosse
Porchester—Carnarvon
Ramsay—Dalhousie
Rosehill—Northesk
Scrymgeour—Dundee
Settrington—★March and Kinrara
Seymour—Somerset
Silchester—Longford
Strathnaver—Sutherland
Tewkesbury—Munster
Vere of Hanworih—★Burford
Wilmington—★Compton
Wodehouse—Kimberley
Worsley—Yarborough

THE PRIVY COUNCIL

The Privy Council consists of certain eminent persons whose names are given below. Members of the Cabinet must be Privy Counsellors, and they principally form the active Privy Council. The Council is summoned as such to act " with others " upon the demise of the Crown, and many matters are referred by the Sovereign to Committees of the Council, some of which are standing Committees, and others constituted to deal with particular cases, *e.g.*, the Judicial Committee.

H.R.H. the Duke of Edinburgh	1951

Aberdare, Lord	1974
Adeane, Lord	1953
Ademola, Sir Adetokunbo	1963
Adermann, Sir Charles	1966
Aldington, Lord	1954
Alport, Lord	1960
Amery, Julian	1960
Amory, Viscount	1953
Anderson, Betty Harvie	1974
Anthony, John Douglas	1971
Armstrong of Sanderstead, Lord	1973
Atkins, Humphrey	1973
Atkinson, Sir Fenton	1968
Avon, Earl of	1934
Avonside, Lord	1962
Aylestone, Lord	1962
Azikiwe, Nnamdi	1960
Bacon, Baroness	1966
Baker, Sir George	1971
Baker, Philip J. Noel-	1945
Balfour of Inchrye, Lord	1941
Barber, Lord	1963
Barnett, Joel	1975
Barrow, Errol	1969
Barwick, Sir Garfield	1964
Beadle, Sir Hugh	1964
Beaufort, Duke of	1936
Benn, Anthony Wedgwood	1964
Beswick, Lord	1968
Bevins, John Reginald	1959
Blakenham, Viscount	1955
Booth, Albert	1976
Bottomley, Arthur George	1952
Boyd-Carpenter, Lord	1954
Boyd of Merton, Viscount	1951
Boyle of Handsworth, Lord	1962
Brecon, Lord	1960
Bridge, Sir Nigel	1975
Brooke of Cumnor, Lord	1955
Brown, Lord	1970
Browne, Sir Patrick	1974
Buckley, Sir Denys	1970
Bustamante, Sir Alexander	1964
Butler of Saffron Walden, Lord	1939
Byers, Lord	1972
Cairns, Sir David	1970
Callaghan, Leonard James	1964
Campbell, Sir Ronald Ian	1950
Campbell of Croy, Lord	1970
Canterbury, The Archbishop of	1961
Caradon, Lord	1968
Carr of Hadley, Lord	1963
Carrington, Lord	1959
Chalfont, Lord	1964
Champion, Lord	1967
Charteris, Sir Martin	1972
Chataway, Christopher	1970
Chesham, Lord	1964
Citrine, Lord	1940
Clayden, Sir John	1963
Clitheroe, Lord	1944
Cobbold, Lord	1959
Cobham, Viscount	1967
Cocks, Michael	1976
Coleraine, Lord	1943
Colyton, Lord	1952
Corfield, Sir Frederick	1970
Cousins, Frank	1964
Craigton, Lord	1961
Crathorne, Lord	1961
Crawford and Balcavres, Earl of	1972
Cromer, Earl of	1966
Crosland, Anthony	1965
Cross of Chelsea, Lord	1969
Danckwerts, Sir Harold	1961
Darling of Hillsborough, Lord	1966
Davies, John	1970
Davies, Sir Arthian	1961
Davies of Leek, Lord	1969
Deedes, William Francis	1962
de Freitas, Sir Geoffrey	1967
De L'Isle, Viscount	1951
Dell, Edmund	1970
Denning, Lord	1948
Devlin, Lord	1960
Devonshire, Duke of	1964
Diamond, Lord	1965
Diefenbaker, John	1957
Dilhorne, Viscount	1954
Diplock, Lord	1961
Drumalbyn, Lord	1962
du Cann, Edward	1964
Duncan-Sandys, Lord	1944
Dundee, Earl of	1959
Eccles, Viscount	1951
Eden, Sir John, Bt.	1972
Edmund-Davies, Lord	1966
Elwyn-Jones, Lord	1964
Emslie, Lord	1972
Ennals, David	1970
Erroll of Hale, Lord	1960
Fernyhough, Ernest	1970
Fletcher, Lord	1967
Foot, Sir Dingle	1967
Foot, Michael (*Lord President*)	1974
Forde, Francis Michael	1944
Franks, Lord	1949
Fraser of Tullybelton, Lord	1975
Fraser, Hugh	1962
Fraser, Malcolm	1976
Fraser, Thomas	1964
Freeman, John	1966
Freeson, Reginald	1976
Gardiner, Lord	1964
Geoffrey-Lloyd, Lord	1943
George-Brown, Lord	1951
Gibbs, Sir Harry	1972
Gibbs, Sir Humphrey	1969
Gibson, Sir Maurice	1975
Gilmour, Ian	1973
Glendevon, Lord	1959
Glenkinglas, Lord	1962
Godber, Joseph Bradshaw	1963
Goff, Sir Reginald	1975
Gordon-Walker, Lord	1950
Goronwy-Roberts, Lord	1968
Gorton, John Grey	1968
Greenwood of Rossendale, Lord	1964
Grimond, Joseph	1961
Guest, Lord	1961
Gunter, Raymond James	1964
Hailsham of St. Marylebone, Lord	1956
Harlech, Lord	1957
Hart, Judith	1967
Harvington, Lord	1971
Hasluck, Sir Paul	1966
Hattersley, Roy	1975
Head, Viscount	1951
Heald, Sir Lionel	1954
Healey, Denis Winston	1964
Heath, Edward	1955
Henderson, Lord	1950
Herbison, Margaret	1964
Hill of Luton, Lord	1955
Hodson, Lord	1951
Holyoake, Sir Keith Jacka	1954
Home of the Hirsel, Lord	1951
Hornsby-Smith, Baroness	1959
Houghton of Sowerby, Lord	1964
Howe, Sir Geoffrey	1972
Howell, Denis	1976
Hughes, Lord	1970
Hughes, Cledwyn	1966
Inman, Lord	1947
Irvine, Sir Arthur	1970
Irving, Sydney	1969
Isaacs, George Alfred	1945
James, Sir Morrice	1968
Jay, Douglas	1952
Jellicoe, Earl	1963
Jenkin, Patrick	1973
Jenkins, Roy Harris	1964
Jones, Aubrey	1955
Joseph, Sir Keith, Bt.	1962
Kilbrandon, Lord	1971
Kilmany, Lord	1962
Kitto, Sir Frank	1963
Kotelawala, Sir John	1954
Lane, Sir Geoffrey	1975
Lansdowne, Marquess of	1964
Lascelles, Sir Alan	1943
Lawton, Sir Frederick	1972
Lee of Asheridge, Baroness	1966
Lee of Newton, Lord	1964
Lever, Harold	1969
Listowel, Earl of	1946
Llewellyn-Davies of Hastoe, Baroness	1975
London, The Bishop of	1973
Longford, Earl of	1948
Lowry, Sir Robert	1974
MacAndrew, Lord	1952
McBride, Sir Philip	1959
McCarthy, Sir Thaddeus	1968
MacDermott, Lord	1947
MacDonald, Malcolm	1935
McEwen, Sir John	1953
McGonigal, Sir Ambrose	1975

McKell, Sir William	1948	Radcliffe, Viscount	1949	Stable, Sir Wintringham	1965
Maclean, Lord	1971	Ramgoolam, Sir Seewoosa-		Stamp, Sir Blanshard	1971
McMahon, William	1966	gur	1971	Stephenson, Sir John	1971
Macmillan, Harold	1942	Ramsden, James	1963	Stevenson, Sir Melford	1973
Macmillan, Maurice	1972	Ramsey of Canterbury,		Stewart, Michael	1964
McTiernan, Sir Edward	1963	Rt. Rev. Lord	1956	Stodart, James Anthony	1974
Mara, Sir Kamisese	1973	Rathcavan, Lord	1937	Stott, Lord	1964
Marples, Lord	1957	Rawlinson, Sir Peter	1964	Stow Hill, Lord	1948
Marsh, Sir Richard	1966	Rea, Lord	1962	Strathclyde, Lord	1953
Marshall, Sir John Ross	1966	Redmayne, Lord	1959	Strauss, George Russell	1947
Martonmere, Lord	1962	Rees, Merlyn	1974	Summerskill, Baroness	1949
Mason, Roy	1968	Reigate, Lord	1961	Thatcher, Mrs. Margaret	1970
Maudling, Reginald	1955	Renton, Sir David	1962	Thomas, George	1968
Maybray-King, Lord	1965	Rhodes, Lord	1969	Thomas, Peter	1964
Megaw, Sir John	1969	Rhyl, Lord	1955	Thomson, George Morgan	1966
Mellish, Robert	1967	Richardson, Gordon	1976	Thorneycroft, Lord	1951
Menzies, Sir Robert	1937	Richmond, Sir Clifford	1973	Thorpe, Jeremy	1967
Merthyr, Lord	1964	Rippon, Geoffrey	1962	Tranmire, Lord	1955
Millan, Bruce	1975	Robens of Woldingham,		Tredgold, Sir Robert	1957
Molson, Lord	1956	Lord	1951	Trend, Lord	1972
Morris of Borth-y-Gest,		Robinson, Kenneth	1964	Tryon, Lord	1971
Lord	1951	Rodgers, William Thomas	1975	Turner, Sir Alexander	1968
Morris, John	1970	Roskill, Sir Eustace	1971	Tweedsmuir of Belhelvie,
Mountbatten of Burma,		Ross, William	1964	Baroness	1974
Earl	1947	Rowling, Wallace	1974	Varley, Eric	1974
Muirshiel, Viscount	1952	Russell of Killowen, Lord	1962	Walker, Peter	1970
Muldoon, Robert	1976	Sachs, Sir Eric	1966	Waller, Sir George	1976
Mulley, Frederick William	1964	St. Aldwyn, Earl	1959	Wand, *Rt. Rev.* John
Murray, Lionel	1976	Salmon, Lord	1964	William Charles	1945
Murray, Ronald King	1974	Scarman, Sir Leslie	1973	Ward of Witley, Viscount	1957
Murton, Henry Oscar	1976	Selkirk, Earl of	1955	Watkinson, Viscount	1955
Noble, *Cdr.* Sir Allan	1956	Sellers, Sir Frederic	1957	Watt, David Gibson-	1974
North, Sir Alfred	1966	Selwyn-Lloyd, Lord	1962	Watt, Hugh	1974
Northumberland, Duke of	1973	Shackleton, Lord	1966	Welensky, Sir Roy	1960
Nugent of Guildford, Lord	1962	Shakespeare, Sir Geoffrey,		Wheatley, Lord	1947
Nutting, Sir Anthony, Bt.	1954	Bt.	1945	Whitelaw, William	1967
O'Brien of Lothbury, Lord	1970	Shaw, Sir Sebag	1975	Widgery, Lord	1968
Ogmore, Lord	1951	Shawcross, Lord	1946	Wigg, Lord	1964
Orme, Stanley	1974	Shearer, Hugh	1969	Wilberforce, Lord	1964
Ormrod, Sir Roger	1974	Shepherd, Lord	1965	Wild, Sir Richard	1966
Orr, Sir Alan	1971	Shinwell, Lord	1945	Willey, Frederick Thomas	1964
Owen, David	1976	Shore, Peter	1967	Williams, Eric	1964
Page, Graham	1972	Short, Edward Watson	1964	Williams, Shirley	1974
Pannell, Lord	1964	Silkin, John	1966	Willis, Eustace George	1967
Pearce, Lord	1957	Silkin, Samuel	1974	Willmer, Sir Henry Gordon	1958
Pearson, Lord	1961	Simon of Glaisdale, Lord	1961	Wilson, Sir Harold	1947
Peart, Thomas Frederick	1964	Slesser, Sir Henry	1929	Wilson of Langside, Lord	1967
Pennycuick, Sir John	1974	Smith, Sir Derek Walker-,		Windeyer, Sir Victor	1963
Perth, Earl of	1957	Bt.	1957	Windlesham, Lord	1973
Peyton, John	1970	Smith, Sir Reginald Dor-		Wood, Richard Frederick	1959
Pindling, Lynden	1976	man-	1939	Woodburn, Arthur	1947
Poole, Lord	1963	Smyth, Sir John, Bt.	1962	Woodcock, George	1967
Powell, Enoch	1960	Snedden, Billy Mackie	1972	Woodhouse, Sir Owen	1974
Prentice, Reginald Ernest	1966	Soames, Sir Christopher	1958	Wylie, Lord	1970
Prior James	1970			York, Archbishop of	1974
Pym, Francis	1970				

Clerk of the Council, N. E. Leigh, c.v.o.   *Deputy Clerk of the Council,* C. E. S. Horsford.

THE PREFIX RIGHT HONOURABLE

"Right Honourable."—By long established custom, or courtesy, members of Her Majesty's Most Honourable Privy Council are entitled to be designated "The Right Honourable," but, in practice, this prefix is sometimes absorbed in other designations; for example, a Prince of the Blood admitted a Privy Councillor remains "His Royal Highness"; a Duke remains "His Grace"; a Marquess is still styled "Most Honourable". The style of all other Peers, whether Privy Councillors or not, is "Right Honourable", although it is more usual to describe them with the prefix "The", omitting the more elaborate styles. A privy Councillor who is not a Peer should be addressed as the Right (or Rt.) Hon.——. A Peer below the rank of Marquess who is a Privy Councillor should be addressed as The Right (or Rt.) Hon. the Lord (or Earl or Viscount)——, P.C., or, less elaborately, The Lord (or Earl or Viscount)——P.C.

Orders of Chivalry

THE MOST NOBLE ORDER OF THE GARTER (1348)—K.G.

Ribbon, Garter Blue. *Motto*, Honi soit qui mal y pense (*Shame on him who thinks evil of it*).
The number of Knights Companions is limited to 24.

SOVEREIGN OF THE ORDER—THE QUEEN

Ladies of the Garter—H.M. QUEEN ELIZABETH THE QUEEN MOTHER, 1936.
H.M. THE QUEEN OF THE NETHERLANDS, 1958

ROYAL KNIGHTS

H.R.H. the Duke of Edinburgh, 1947.
H.R.H. The Prince of Wales, 1958.

EXTRA KNIGHTS

H.M. King Leopold III, 1935.
H.M. the King of Norway, 1959.
H.M. the King of the Belgians, 1963.
H.I.M. the Emperor of Japan, 1971.
H.R.H. the Grand Duke of Luxemburg, 1972.
H.R.H. Prince Paul of Yugoslavia, 1939.

KNIGHTS COMPANIONS

The Duke of Beaufort, 1937.
The Earl Mountbatten of Burma, 1946.
The Duke of Portland, 1948.
The Earl of Avon, 1954. [1959.
The Duke of Northumberland, Sir Gerald Templer, 1963.
The Viscount Cobham, 1964.
The Viscount Amory, 1968.
The Viscount De L'Isle, 1968.
The Lord Ashburton, 1969.
The Lord Cobbold, 1970.
Sir Edmund Bacon, Bt., 1970.
Sir Cennydd Traherne, 1970.
The Earl Waldegrave, 1971.
The Earl of Longford, 1971.
The Lord Butler of Saffron Walden, 1971.

The Lord Rohdes, 1972.
The Earl of Drogheda, 1972.
The Lord Shackleton, 1974.
The Lord Trevelyan, 1974.
The Marquess of Abergavenny, 1974.
Sir Harold Wilson, 1976.
The Duke of Grafton, 1976.
Prelate, The Bishop of Winchester.
Chancellor, The Viscount Cobham, K.G., P.C., G.C.M.G., G.C.V.O., T.D.
Register, The Dean of Windsor.
Garter King of Arms, Sir Anthony Richard Wagner, K.C.V.O.
Gentleman Usher of the Black Rod, Admiral Sir Frank Roddam TWISS, K.C.B., D.S.C.
Secretary, W. J. G. Verco, C.V.O.

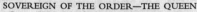

THE MOST ANCIENT AND MOST NOBLE ORDER OF THE THISTLE—K.T.

Ribbon, Green. *Motto*, Nemo me impune lacessit (*No one provokes me with impunity*)
The number of Knights is limited to 16.

SOVEREIGN OF THE ORDER—THE QUEEN

Lady of the Thistle—H.M. QUEEN ELIZABETH THE QUEEN MOTHER, 1937

ROYAL KNIGHT

H.R.H. the Duke of Edinburgh, 1952.

EXTRA KNIGHT

H.M. the King of Norway, 1962.

KNIGHTS

The Earl of Haddington, 1951.
The Lord Rowallan, 1957.
The Lord Home of the Hirsel, 1962.
Sir Robert Menzies, 1963
Sir James Robertson, 1965.

The Earl of Wemyss and March, 1966.
The Lord Maclean, 1969.
Sir Richard O'Connor, 1971.
The Earl of Dalhousie, 1971.
The Lord Clydesmuir, 1973.
The Viscount Muirshiel, 1973.
The Hon. Lord Birsay, 1973.
Sir Donald Cameron of Lochiel, 1973.
The Lord Ballantrae, 1974.

Chancellor, The Lord Home of the Hirsel.
Dean, The Very Rev. Prof. J. McIntyre, M.A., B.D., D.Litt. D.D.
Secretary and Lord Lyon King of Arms, Sir James Monteith Grant, K.C.V.O., W.S.
Usher of the Green Rod, Sir Reginald Graham of Larbert, Bt., V.C., O.B.E.

THE MOST HONOURABLE ORDER OF THE BATH (1725)

Ribbon, Crimson. *Motto*, Tria juncta in uno (*Three joined in one*). (Remodelled 1815, and enlarged many times since. The Order is divided into civil and military divisions.)

G.C.B. Mil.   G.C.B. Civ.   K.C.B. Mil.   K.C.B. Civ.   C.B. Mil.

THE SOVEREIGN; *Grand Master and First or Principal Knight Grand Cross*, H.R.H. The Prince of Wales, K.G., G.C.B.; *Dean of the Order*, The Dean of Westminster; *Bath King of Arms*, Admiral of the Fleet Sir Michael Pollock, G.C.B., M.V.O., D.S.C.; *Registrar and Secretary*, Air Marshal Sir Anthony Selway, K.C.B., D.F.C.; *Genealogist*, C. M. J. F. Swan, Ph.D.; *Gentleman Usher of the Scarlet Rod*, Rear-Admiral C. D. Madden, C.B., C.B.E., M.V.O., D.S.C.; *Deputy Secretary*, The Secretary of the Central Chancery of the Orders of Knighthood; *Chancery*, Central Chancery of the Orders of Knighthood, St. James's Palace, S.W.1.—G.C.B., Knight (or Dame) Grand Cross; K.C.B., Knight Commander; D.C.B., Dame Commander; C.B., Companion. Women became eligible for the Order from Jan. 1, 1971.

THE ORDER OF MERIT (1902)—O.M. *Ribbon*, Blue and Crimson.

This Order is designed as a special distinction for eminent men and women—without conferring a knighthood upon them. The Order is limited in numbers to 24, with the addition of foreign honorary members. Membership is of two kinds, Military and Civil, the badge of the former having crossed swords, and the latter oak leaves.
O.M.Mil. Membership is denoted by the suffix O.M., which follows the first class of the Order O.M.Civ. of the Bath and precedes the letters designating membership of the inferior classes of the Bath and all classes of the lesser Orders of Knighthood.

THE SOVEREIGN.
H.R.H. THE DUKE OF EDINBURGH (1968).

The Lord Adrian, 1942
Sir (Frank) Macfarlane Burnet, 1958.
Graham Vivian Sutherland, 1960.
Sir Basil Urwin Spence, 1962.
Henry Spencer Moore, 1963.
The Lord Britten, 1965.
Dorothy Hodgkin, 1965.

The Earl Mountbatten of Burma, 1965.
Sir William Turner Walton, 1967.
Ben Nicholson, 1968.
The Lord Zuckerman, 1968.
Malcolm MacDonald, 1969.
The Lord Penney, 1969.
Dame Veronica Wedgwood, 1969.
Sir Isaiah Berlin, 1971.

Sir George Edwards, 1971.
Sir Alan Hodgkin, 1973.
Paul Adrian Maurice Dirac, 1973.
Harold Macmillan, 1975.
The Lord Clark, 1975.
Sir Ronald Syme, 1975.
The Lord Hinton of Bankside, 1975.

Secretary and Registrar, Sir Edward Ford, K.C.B., K.C.V.O.
Chancery, Central Chancery of the Orders of Knighthood, St. James's Palace, S.W.1.

THE MOST EXALTED ORDER OF THE STAR OF INDIA (1861)

Ribbon, Light Blue, with White Edges. *Motto,* Heaven's Light our Guide.
THE SOVEREIGN; *Registrar,* The Secretary of the Central Chancery of the Orders of Knighthood; G.C.S.I. Knight Grand Commander; K.C.S.I., Knight Commander; C.S.I., Companion.
G.C.S.I. No conferments since 1947.

THE MOST DISTINGUISHED ORDER OF ST. MICHAEL AND ST. GEORGE (1818)

Ribbon Saxon Blue, with Scarlet centre. *Motto,* Auspicium melioris ævi (Token of a better age)
THE SOVEREIGN; *Grand Master,* H.R.H. The Duke of Kent, G.C.M.G., G.C.V.O., A.D.C.; *Prelate,* The Bishop of Worcester; *Chancellor,* The Viscount De L'Isle, V.C., K.G. P.C., G.C.M.G., G.C.V.O.; *Secretary,* Sir Michael Palliser, K.C.M.G.; *Registrar,* The Lord Gore-Booth, G.C.M.G., K.C.V.O.; *King of Arms,* Rt. Hon. Sir Morrice James, G.C.M.G., C.V.O., M.B.E.; *Gentleman Usher of the Blue Rod,* Sir Anthony Abell, K.C.M.G.; *Dean,* The Dean of St. Paul's; *Deputy Secretary,* Maj.-Gen. P. B. Gillett, C.B., C.V.O., O.B.E. *Chancery,* Central Chancery of the Orders of Knighthood, St. James's Palace, S.W.1.—G.C.M.G., Knight (or Dame) Grand Cross; K.C.M.G., Knight Commander; D.C.M.G., Dame Commander; C.M.G., Companion.

THE MOST EMINENT ORDER OF THE INDIAN EMPIRE (1868)

Ribbon, Imperial Purple. *Motto,* Imperatricis auspiciis (*Under the auspices of the Empress*).
THE SOVEREIGN; *Registrar,* The Secretary of the Central Chancery of the Orders of Knighthood; G.C.I.E., Knight Grand Commander; K.C.I.E., Knight Commander; C.I.E., Companion. No conferments since 1947.
G.C.I.E.

THE ROYAL VICTORIAN ORDER (1896)

Ribbon, Blue, with Red and White Edges. *Motto,* Victoria.
THE SOVEREIGN; *Grand Master,* H.M. Queen Elizabeth the Queen Mother; *Chancellor,* The Lord Chamberlain; *Secretary,* The Keeper of the Privy Purse; *Registrar,* The Secretary of the Central Chancery of the Orders of Knighthood; *Chaplain,* The Rev. Canon C. E. Young. G.C.V.O., Knight or Dame Grand Cross; K.C.V.O., Knight Commander; D.C.V.O., Dame Commander; C.V.O., Commander; M.V.O., Member, 4th or 5th Class.

THE ROYAL VICTORIAN CHAIN (1902)

Founded by King Edward VII, in 1902. It confers no precedence on its holders.
H.M. THE QUEEN

H.M. QUEEN ELIZABETH THE QUEEN MOTHER (1937).

The Duke of Beaufort (1953).
H.R.H. Prince Paul of Yugoslavia (1934).
H.M. King Leopold III (1937).
H.I.M. The Shahanshah of Iran (1948).
H.M. The Queen of the Netherlands (1950).

H.M. The King of Norway (1955).
H.M. The King of Thailand (1960).
H.I.H. The Crown Prince of Ethiopia (1965).
H.M. The King of Jordan (1966).
The Lord Adeane (1972).

H.M. King Zahir Shah of Afghanistan (1972).
Rt. Hon. Roland Michener (1973).
The Right Rev. Lord Ramsey of Canterbury, (1974).
H. M. The King of Nepal (1975).
H.M. The King of Sweden (1975).

THE MOST EXCELLENT ORDER OF THE BRITISH EMPIRE (1917)

Ribbon, Rose pink edged with pearl grey with vertical pearl stripe in centre (Military Division); without vertical pearl stripe (Civil Division). *Motto,* For God and the Empire.
G.B.E. THE SOVEREIGN; *Grand Master,* H.R.H. the Prince Philip, Duke of Edinburgh, K.G., K.B.E. P.C., K.T., O.M., G.B.E.; *Prelate,* The Bishop of London; *King of Arms,* Lieut.-Gen. Sir George Gordon Lennox, K.B.E., C.B., C.V.O., D.S.O.; *Registrar,* The Secretary of the Central Chancery of the Orders of Knighthood; *Secretary,* The Permanent Secretary to the Civil Service Department; *Dean,* The Dean of St. Paul's; *Gentleman Usher of the Purple Rod,* Sir Robert Bellinger, G.B.E.; *Chancery,* Central Chancery of the Order of Knighthood, St. James's Palace, S.W.1. G.B.E., Knight or Dame Grand Cross; K.B.E. Knight Commander; D.B.E., Dame Commander; C.B.E., Commander; O.B.E., Officer; M.B.E., Member. The Order was divided into *Military* and *Civil* divisions in Dec. 1918.

ORDER OF THE COMPANIONS OF HONOUR (June 4, 1917)—C.H.

Ribbon, Carmine, wsth Gold Edges.

This Order consists of one Class only and carries with it no title. It ranks after the 1st Class of the Order of the British Empire, *i.e.*, Knights and Dames Grand Cross (Mil. and Civ. Div.). The number of awards is limited to 65 (excluding honorary members) and the Order is open to both sexes. *Secretary and Registrar*, The Secretary of the Central Chancery of the Orders of Knighthood.

Ashley, Jack, 1975.
Ashton, Sir Frederick, 1970.
Aylestone, The Lord, 1975.
Best, Charles Herbert, 1971.
Boult, Sir Adrian, 1969.
Boyd of Merton, The Viscount, 1960.
Britten, The Lord, 1953.
Brooke of Cumnor, The Lord, 1964.
Bryant, Sir Arthur, 1967.
Butler of Saffron Walden, The Lord, 1954.
Cecil, Lord David Gascoyne, 1949.
Clark, The Lord, 1959.
Cohen of Birkenhead, The Lord, 1974.
Diefenbaker, Rt. Hon. John George, 1976.
Duncan-Sandys, The Lord, 1973.
Elwyn-Jones, The Lord, 1976.
Gardiner, The Lord, 1975.
Goodman, The Lord 1972.
Gordon-Walker, The Lord, 1968.
Gorton, Rt. Hon. John Gray, 1971.
Greene, Graham, 1966.

Hailsham of St. Marylebone, The Lord, 1974.
Hill, *Prof.* Archibald Vivian, 1946.
Holyoake, Rt. Hon. Sir Keith, 1963.
Houghton of Sowerby, The Lord, 1967.
Howells, Herbert Norman, 1972.
Kotelawala, Rt. Hon. Sir John, 1956.
Leach, Bernard Howell, 1973.
Limerick, Angela, Countess of, 1974.
McEwen, Rt. Hon. Sir John, 1969.
McMahon, Rt. Hon. William, 1972.
Marshall, Rt. Hon. Sir John Ross 1973.
Maver, Sir Robert, 1973.
Medawar, Sir Peter, 1972.
Menzies, Rt. Hon. Sir Robert, 1951.
Micklem, Rev. Nathaniel, 1974.
Moore, Henry Spencer, 1955.
Morris of Borth-y-Gest, The Lord 1975.

Muirshiel, The Viscount, 1962.
Perutz, *Prof.* Max Ferdinand, 1975.
Piper, John Egerton Christmas, 1972.
Payne, The Rev. Ernest Alexander, 1968.
Rahman, Tunku Abdul, 1960.
Richards, *Prof.* Ivor Armstrong, 1964.
Robbins, The Lord, 1968.
Selwyn-Lloyd, The Lord, 1962.
Shinwell, The Lord, 1965.
Short, Rt. Hon. Edward, 1976.
Smith, Arnold Cantwell, 1975.
Stewart, Rt. Hon. Michael, 1969.
Summerskill, The Baroness, 1966.
Ward of North Tyneside, The Baroness, 1973.
Watkinson, The Viscount, 1962.
Whitelaw, Rt. Hon. William, 1974.
Williams, Rt. Hon. Eric, 1969.
Honorary Members, M. René Massigli, 1954; Lee Kuan Yew, 1970; Dr. Joseph Luns, 1971; M. Jean Monnet, 1972.

THE ROYAL VICTORIA AND ALBERT (for Ladies)—V.A.

Instituted in 1862, and enlarged in 1864, 1865, and 1880. Badge, a medallion of Queen Victoria and the Prince Consort, surmounted by a crown, which is attached to a bow of white moiré ribbon. The honour does not confer any rank or title upon the recipient.

FIRST CLASS

H.R.H. the Princess Alice, Countess of Athlone.

THE IMPERIAL ORDER OF THE CROWN OF INDIA (for Ladies)—C.I.

Instituted Dec. 31, 1877. Badge, the royal cipher in jewels within an oval, surmounted by an Heraldic Crown and attached to a bow of light blue watered ribbon, edged white. The honour does not confer any rank or title upon the recipient. No conferments have been made since 1947.

H.M. THE QUEEN, 1947.
H.M. Queen Elizabeth the Queen Mother, 1931.
H.R.H. the Princess Margaret, Countess of Snowdon, 1947.

H.R.H. the Princess Alice, Duchess of Gloucester, 1937.
H.H. Maharani of Travancore, 1929.

Doreen Geraldine, Dowager Baroness Brabourne, 1937.
Eugenie Marie, Countess Wavell, 1943.

THE IMPERIAL SERVICE ORDER (1902)—I.S.O.

Ribbon, Crimson, with Blue Centre.

Appointment of Companion of this Order shall be open to those members of the Civil Services whose eligibility shall be determined by the grade held by such persons. The Order consists of the SOVEREIGN and Companions (not exclusively male) to a number not exceeding 1425 of whom 850 may belong to the Home Civil Services and 575 to Overseas Civil Services. *Secretary*, The Permanent Secretary to the Civil Service Department. *Registrar*, The Secretary of the Central Chancery of the Orders of Knighthood, St. James's Palace, S.W.1.

Baronets, Knights Grand Cross, Knights Grand Commanders Knights Commanders and Knights Bachelor

Badge of Baronets
of England, Great Britain, U.K.,
(and Ireland marked I.).

Badge of Baronets
of Scotland or Nova Scotia
(marked S.).

NOTES CONCERNING BARONETS

Clause II. of the Royal Warrant of February 8, 1910, ordains as follows:—" That no person whose name is not entered upon the Official Roll shall be received as a Baronet, or shall be addressed or mentioned by that title in any Civil or Military Commission, Letters Patent or other official document." When an obelisk (†) precedes a name it indicates that, *at the time of going to press*, the Baronet concerned has not been registered on the Official Roll of the Baronetage. The date of creation of the Baronetcy is given in parenthesis ( ).

Baronets are addressed as " Sir " (with Christian name) and in writing as " Sir Robert A—, Bt." Baronet's wives are addressed (formally) as " Your Ladyship " or " Lady A—," without any Christian name unless a daughter of a Duke, Marquess or Earl, in which case " The Lady Mary A—"; if daughter of a Viscount or Baron " The Hon. Lady A—."

NOTES CONCERNING KNIGHTS GRAND CROSS, ETC.

Knights Grand Cross, Knights Grand Commanders and Knights Commanders are addressed in the same manner as Baronets (*q.v.*), but in writing the appropriate initials (G.C.B., K.C.B., &c.) are appended to surname after "Bt." if they are also baronets or in place of "Bt." if they are not. Knights Bachelor are addressed as " Sir —— (first or Christian name) " and in writing as " Sir —— B——." The wife of a Knight Grand Cross, Knight Grand Commander, Knight Commander or Knight Bachelor is addressed as stated for the wife of a Baronet.

NOTES CONCERNING KNIGHTS BACHELOR

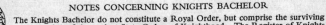

The Knights Bachelor do not constitute a Royal Order, but comprise the surviving representation of the ancient State Orders of Knighthood. The Register of Knights Bachelor, instituted by James I. in the 17th century, lapsed, and in 1908 a voluntary Association under the title of " The Society of Knights " (now " The Imperial Society of Knights Bachelor " by Royal command) was formed with the primary objects of continuing the various registers dating from 1257 and obtaining the uniform registration of every created Knight Bachelor. In 1926 a design for a badge to be worn by Knights Bachelor was approved and adopted, a miniature reproduction being shown above; in 1974 a neck badge and miniature were added. The Officers of the Society are:— *Knight Principal*, Sir Anthony Wagner, K.C.V.O., *Deputy Knight Principal*, Sir Gilbert Inglefield, G.B.E., T.D.; *Prelate*, The Bishop of London; *Hon. Registrar*, Sir John Weir Russell; *Hon. Treasurer*, Sir John Howard; *Registry and Library*, 21 Old Buildings, Lincoln's Inn, W.C.2.

BARONETAGE AND KNIGHTAGE
(Revised to Aug. 17, 1976)
Peers are not included in this list.

A full entry in italic type indicates that the recipient of a Knighthood died during the year in which the honour was conferred. The name is included for purposes of record.

Aarons, Sir Daniel Sidney, Kt., O.B.E., M.C.

Aarvold, *His Hon.* Sir Carl Douglas, Kt., O.B.E., T.D

Abal, Sir Tei, Kt.

Abayomi, Sir Kofo Adekunle, Kt.

Abbott, *Very Rev.* Eric Symes, K.C.V.O., D.D.

Abbott, *Hon.* Sir Myles John, Kt.

Abdy, Sir Robert Henry Edward, Bt. (1850).

Abeles, Sir (Emil Herbert) Peter, Kt.

Abell, Sir Anthony Foster, K.C.M.G.

Abell, Sir George Edmond Brackenbury, K.C.I.E., O.B.E.

Abercromby, Sir Ian George, Bt. (s. 1636).

Abrahams, Sir Charles, K.C.V.O.

Ackner, *Hon.* Sir Desmond James Conrad, Kt.

Ackroyd, Sir John Robert Whyte, Bt. (1956).

Acland, *Capt.* Sir Hubert Guy Dyke, Bt., D.S.O., R.N. (1890).

Acland, Sir (Hugh) John (Dyke), K.B.E.

Acland, Sir Richard Thomas Dyke, Bt. (1644).

Acton, Sir Harold Mario Mitchell, Kt., C.B.E.

Acutt, Sir Keith Courtney, K.B.E.

Adair, *Maj.-Gen.* Sir Allan Henry Shafto, Bt., G.C.V.O., C.B., D.S.O., M.C. (1838).

Adam, *Hon.* Sir Alistair Duncan Grant, Kt.

Adam, *General* Sir Ronald Forbes, Bt., G.C.B., D.S.O., O.B.E. (1917).

Adams, Sir Maurice Edward, K.B.E.

Adams, Sir Philip George Doyne, K.C.M.G.

Adamson, Sir Kenneth Thomas, Kt., C.M.G.

Adamson, Sir (William Owen) Campbell, Kt.

Adcock, Sir Robert Henry, Kt., C.B.E.

Addis, Sir John Mansfield, K.C.M.G.

Addis, Sir William, K.B.E., C.M.G.

Addison, Sir William Wilkinson, Kt.

Adeane, *Col.* Sir Robert Philip Wyndham, Kt., O.B.E.

Ademola, *Rt. Hon.* Sir Adetokunbo Adegboyega, K.B.E.

Adermann, *Rt. Hon.* Sir Charles Frederick, K.B.E.

Adrien, *Hon.* Sir Maurice Latour-, Kt.

Agnew, Sir Crispin Hamlyn, Bt. (s 1629).

Agnew, Sir Geoffrey William Gerald, Kt.

Agnew, Sir (John) Anthony Stuart, Bt. (1895).

Agnew, *Cdr.* Sir Peter Garnett, Bt. (1957).

Agnew, Sir (William) Godfrey, K.C.V.O., C.B.

Aiken, *Air Chief Marshal* Sir John Alexander Carlisle, K.C.B.

Ainley, Sir (Alfred) John, Kt., M.C.

Ainscough, Sir Thomas Martland, Kt., C.B.E.

Ainsworth, Sir John Francis, Bt. (1917).

Aird, Sir (George) John, Bt. (1902).

Airey, *Lt.-Gen.* Sir Terence Sydney, K.C.M.G., C.B., C.B.E.

Aitchison, Sir Charles Walter de Lancey, Bt. (1938).

Aitken, Sir Arthur Percival Hay, Kt.

Aitken, Sir (John William) Maxwell, Bt., D.S.O., D.F.C. (1916).

Aitken, Sir Robert Stevenson, Kt., M.D., D.Phil.

Albert, Sir Alexis François, Kt., C.M.G., V.R.D.

Albu, Sir George, Bt. (1912).

Alderson, Sir Harold George, Kt., M.B.E.

Aldington, Sir Geoffrey William, K.B.E., C.M.G.

Alexander, Sir Alexander Sandor, Kt.

Alexander, Sir Charles Gundry, Bt. (1945).

Alexander, Sir Claud Hagart-, Bt. (1886).

Alexander, *Hon.* Sir Darnley Arthur Raymond, Kt., C.B.E.

Alexander, Sir Desmond William Lionel Cable, Bt. (1809).

Alexander, Sir Douglas Hamilton, Bt. (1921).

Alexander, Sir (John) Lindsay, Kt

Alexander, Sir Norman Stanley, Kt., C.B.E.

Alford, Sir Robert Edmund, K.B.E., C.M.G.

Algie, *Hon.* Sir Ronald MacMillan, Kt.

Allan, Sir Anthony James Allan Havelock-, Bt. (1858).

Allcroft, Sir Philip Magnus-, Bt., C.B.E. (1917).

Allen, Sir Donald Richard, Kt., O.B.E., M.C.

Allen, Sir Douglas Albert Vivian, G.C.B.

Allen, Sir Milton Pentonville, Kt., O.B.E.

Allen, Sir Peter Christopher, Kt.

Allen, Sir Richard Hugh Sedley, K.C.M.G.

Allen, *Prof.* Sir Roy George Douglas, Kt., C.B.E., D.S.C., F.B.A.

Allen, Sir (William) Denis, G.C.M.G., C.B.

Allen, Sir William Guildford, Kt., C.B.E.

Allen, Sir William Kenneth Gwynne, Kt.

Alleyne, *Capt.* Sir John Meynell, Bt., D.S.O., D.S.C., R.N. (1769).

Aluwihare, Sir Richard, K.C.M.G., C.B.E.

Ameer Ali, Sir Torick, Kt.

Ames, Sir Cyril Geraint, Kt.

Amies, *Prof.* Sir Arthur Barton Pilgrim, Kt., C.M.G.

Anderson, Sir Colin Skelton, K.B.E.

Anderson, Sir David Stirling, Kt., Ph.D.

Anderson, Sir Duncan Law, K.B.E., T.D.

Anderson, Sir Edward Arthur, Kt.

Anderson, Sir Gilmour Menzies, Kt., C.B.E.

Anderson, *Prof.* Sir (James) Norman (Dalrymple), Kt., O.B.E., Q.C., F.B.A.

Anderson, *General* Sir John D'Arcy, G.B.E., K.C.B., D.S.O.

Anderson, *Maj.-Gen.* Sir John Evelyn, K.B.E.

Anderson, Sir John Muir Kt., C.M.G.

Anderson, Sir Kenneth, K.B.E., C.B.

Anderson, *Hon.* Sir Kenneth McColl, K.B.E.

Anderson, *Lt.-Gen.* Sir Richard Neville, K.C.B., C.B.E., D.S.O.

Anderson, *Prof.* Sir William Ferguson, Kt., O.B.E.

Andrew, *Rev.* Sir (George) Herbert, K.C.M.G., C.B.

Andrewes, Sir Christopher Howard, Kt., M.D., F.R.S.

Andrews, Sir Edwin Arthur Chapman-, K.C.M.G., O.B.E.

Andrews, *Rt. Hon.* Sir John Lawson Ormrod, K.B.E.

Angas, Sir John Keith, Kt.

Ankole, The Omugabe of, Kt.

Annamunthodo, *Prof.* Sir Harry, Kt., F.R.C.S.

Ansell, *Col.* Sir Michael Picton, Kt., C.B.E., D.S.O.

Ansett, Sir Reginald Myles, K.B.E.

Anson, *Rear-Admiral* Sir Peter, Bt., C.B. (1831).

Ansorge, Sir Eric Cecil. Kt., C.S.I., C.I.E.

Anstey, *Brig.* Sir John, Kt., C.B.E., T.D.

Anstice, *Vice-Adm.* Sir Edmund Walter, K.C.B.

Anstruther, Sir Ralph Hugo, Bt. K.C.V.O., M.C. (s 1694).

Anstruther, Sir Windham Eric Francis Carmichael-, Bt. (s. 1700; G.B. 1798).

Anthony, Sir (Michael) Mobolaji Bank-, K.B.E.

Antico, Sir Tristan Venus, Kt.

Antrobus, Sir Philip Coutts, Bt. (1815).

Arbuthnot, Sir Hugh Fitzgerald, Bt. (1823).

Arbuthnot, Sir John Sinclair-Wemyss, Bt., M.B.E., T.D. (1964).

Archdale, *Comdr.* Sir Edward Folmer, Bt., D.S.C., R.N. (1928).

Archer, *Lt. Gen.* Sir (Arthur) John, K.C.B., O.B.E.

Archer, Sir Clyde Vernon Harcourt, Kt.

Archey, Sir Gilbert Edward, Kt., C.B.E.

Arkell, *Capt.* Sir (Thomas) Noel, Kt.

Armer, Sir (Isaac) Frederick, K.B.E., C.B., M.C.

Armitage, Sir Arthur Llewellyn, Kt.

Armitage, Sir Robert Perceval, K.C.M.G., M.B.E.

Armstrong, Sir Andrew St. Clare, Bt. (1841).

Armstrong, Sir Thomas Henry Wait, Kt., D.MUS.

Armytage, *Capt.* Sir (John) Lionel Bt. (1738).

Arnold, *Hon.* Sir John Lewis, Kt.

Arnott, Sir John Robert Alexander, Bt. (1896).

Arnott, *Prof.* Sir (William) Melville, Kt., T.D., M.D.

Arrowsmith, Sir Edwin Porter, K.C.M.G.

Arthur, Sir Basil Malcolm, Bt. (1841).

Arthur, Sir Geoffrey George, K.C.M.G.

Arundell, *Brig.* Sir Robert Duncan Harris, K.C.M.G., O.B.E.

Arup, Sir Ove Nyquist, Kt., C.B.E.

Ashburnham, Sir Denny Reginald, Bt. (1661).

Ashenheim, Sir Neville Noel, Kt., C.B.E.

Ashmore, *Admiral* Sir Edward Beckwith, G.C.B., D.S.C.

Ashmore, *Vice-Adm.* Sir Peter William Beckwith, K.C.B., M.V.O., D.S.C.

Ashton, Sir (Arthur) Leigh (Bolland), Kt.

Ashton, Sir Frederick William Mallandaine, Kt., C.H., C.B.E.

Ashton, Sir Hubert, K.B.E., M.C.

Ashwin, Sir Bernard Carl, K.B.E., C.M.G.

Ashworth, Sir Herbert, Kt.

Aske, *Rev.* Sir Conan, Bt. (1922).

Askin, *Hon.* Sir Robert William, G.C.M.G.

Astbury, Sir George, Kt.

Astley, Sir Francis Jacob Dugdale, Bt. (1821).

Aston, *Hon.* Sir William John, K.C.M.G.

Astwood, *Lt.-Col.* Sir Jeffrey Carlton, Kt., C.B.E., E.D.

Atkins, *Prof.* Sir Hedley John Barnard, K.B.E., D.M., F.R.C.S.

Atkins, Sir William Sydney Albert, Kt., C.B.E.

Atkinson, *Rt. Hon.* Sir Fenton, Kt.

Atkinson, Sir (John) Kenneth, Kt.

Atkinson, *Maj.-Gen.* Sir Leonard Henry, K.B.E.

Attenborough, Sir Richard Samuel, Kt.

Atwell, Sir John William, Kt., C.B.E., F.R.S.E.

Auchinleck, *Field Marshal* Sir Claude John Eyre, G.C.B., G.C.I.E., C.S.I., D.S.O., O.B.E.

Austin, Sir John (Byron Fraser), Bt. (1894).

Austin, Sir John Worroker, Kt.

Austin, *Vice-Admiral* Sir Peter Murray, K.C.B.

Auswild, Sir James Frederick John, Kt., C.B.E.

Ayer, *Prof.* Sir Alfred Jules, Kt., F.B.A.

Aykroyd, Sir William Miles, Bt., M.C. (1920).

Aykroyd, Sir Cecil William, Bt. (1929).

Aylmer, Sir Felix, Kt., O.B.E.

Aylmer, Sir Fenton Gerald, Bt. (I 1622).

Backhouse, Sir Jonathan Roger, Bt. (1901).

Bacon, Sir Edmund Castell, Bt. K.G., K.B.E., T.D. *Premier Baronet of England* (1611 and 1627).

Bacon, Sir Ranulph Robert Maunsell, Kt.

Baddeley, Sir John Beresford, Bt. (1922).

Bader, *Group Capt.* Sir Douglas Robert Stewart, Kt., C.B.E., D.S.O., D.F.C.

Bagge, Sir John Alfred Picton, Bt. (1867).

Bagnall, *Hon.* Sir William Arthur, Kt., M.B.E.

Bagrit, Sir Leon, Kt.

Bailey, Sir Derrick Thomas Louis, Bt., D.F.C. (1919).

Bailey, Sir Donald Coleman, Kt., O.B.E.

Bailey, *Prof.* Sir Harold Walter, Kt., D.Phil., F.B.A.

Baillie, Sir Gawaine George Hope, Bt. (1823).

Bairamian, *Hon.* Sir Vahe Robert, Kt.

Baird, Sir David Charles, Bt. (1809).

Baird, *Prof.* Sir Dugald, Kt., M.D.

Baird, *Lt.-Gen.* Sir James Parlane, K.B.E., M.D.

Baird, Sir James Richard Gardiner, Bt., M.C. (s. 1695).

Baker, Sir (Allan) Ivor, Kt., C.B.E.

Baker, *Air Marshal* Sir Brian Edmund, K.B.E., C.B., D.S.O., M.C., A.F.C.

Baker, *Field-Marshal* Sir Geoffrey Harding, G.C.B., C.M.G., C.B.E., M.C.

Baker, *Rt. Hon.* Sir George Gillespie, Kt., O.B.E.

Baker, Sir Humphrey Dodington Benedict Sherston-, Bt. (1796).

Baker, *Prof.* Sir John Fleetwood, Kt., O.B.E., SC.D., F.R.S.

Baker, *Air Chief Marshal* Sir John Wakeling, G.B.E., K.C.B., M.C., D.F.C.

Baker, Sir Rowland, Kt., O.B.E.

Baker, Sir (Stanislaus) Josaph, Kt., C.B.

Baker, Sir (William) Stanley, Kt.

Balcon, Sir Michael, Kt.

Balfour, Sir John, G.C.M.G., G.B.E.

Balfour, *Lt.-Gen.* Sir Philip Maxwell, K.B.E., C.B., M.C.

Balfour, *General* Sir (Robert George) Victor FitzGeorge-, K.C.B., C.B.E., D.S.O., M.C.

Ball, *Air Marshal* Sir Alfred Henry Wynne, K.C.B., D.S.O., D.F.C.

Ball, *Air Vice-Marshal* Sir Benjamin, K.B.E., C.B.

Ball, Sir Nigel Gresley, Bt. (1911).

Balmer, Sir Joseph Reginald, Kt.

Bancroft, Sir Ian Powell, K.C.B.

Banks, Sir Maurice Alfred Lister, Kt.

Banner, Sir George Knowles Harmood-, Bt. (1924).

Bannerman, *Lt.-Col.* Sir Donald Arthur Gordon, Bt. (s 1682).

Bannister, Sir Roger Gilbert, Kt., D.M., F.R.C.P.

Banwell, Sir (George) Harold, Kt.

Barber, *Hon.* Sir Edward Hamilton Esler, Kt.

Barber, Sir Herbert William, Kt.

Barber, *Lt.-Col.* Sir William Francis, Bt., T.D. (1960).

Barclay, Sir Colville Herbert Sanford, Bt. (s 1668).

Barclay, Sir Roderick Edward, G.C.V.O., K.C.M.G.

Barford, Sir Leonard, Kt.

Baring, Sir Charles Christian, Bt. (1911).

Barker, Sir Alwyn Bowman, Kt., C.M.G.

Barker, Sir (Charles Frederic) James, Kt., M.B.E.

Barker, *General* Sir Evelyn Hugh, K.C.B., K.B.E., D.S.O., M.C.

Barker, Sir William, K.C.M.G., O.B.E.

Barlow, Sir Christopher Hilaro, Bt. (1803).

Barlow, Sir John Denman, Bt. (1907).

Barlow, Sir Robert, Kt.

Barlow, Sir Thomas Erasmus, Bt., D.S.C. (1902).

Barnard, Sir (Arthur) Thomas, Kt., C.B., O.B.E.

Barnard, *Capt.* Sir George Edward, Kt.

Barnard, Sir Henry William, Kt.

Barnes, Sir Denis Charles, K.C.B.

Barnes, Sir (Ernest) John (Ward), K.C.M.G., M.B.E.

Barnes, Sir James George, Kt., M.B.E.

Barnes, Sir William Lethbridge Gorell-, K.C.M.G., C.B.

Barnett, Sir Ben Lewis, K.B.E., C.B., M.C.

Barnett, *Air Chief Marshal* Sir Denis Hensley Fulton, G.C.B., C.B.E., D.F.C.

Barnett, Sir Oliver Charles, Kt., C.B.E., Q.C.

Barnewall, Sir Reginald Robert, Bt. (I 1623).

Barraclough, *Air Chief Marshal* Sir John, K.C.B., C.B.E., D.F.C., A.F.C.

Barraclough, *Brig.* Sir John Ashworth, Kt., C.M.G., D.S.O., O.B.E., M.C.

Barran, Sir David Haven, Kt.

Barran, Sir John Napoleon Ruthven, Bt. (1895).

Barrett, Sir Arthur George, Kt.

Barrett, *Lt.-Gen.* Sir David William Scott-, K.B.E., M.C.

Barrie, Sir Walter, Kt.

Barrington, Sir Charles Bacon, Bt. (1831).

Barrington, Sir Kenneth Charles Peto, Kt.

Barritt, Sir David Thurlow, Kt.

Barron, Sir Donald James, Kt.

Barrow, Sir Richard John Uniacke, Bt. (1835).

Barry, Sir (Philip) Stuart Milner-, K.C.V.O., C.B., O.B.E.

Barry, Sir Rupert Rodney Francis Tress, Bt., M.B.E. (1809).

Bartlett, *Lt.-Col.* Sir Basil Hardington, Bt. (1913).

Barton, Sir Charles Newton, Kt., O.B.E., E.D.

Barton, *Prof.* Sir Derek Harold Richard, Kt., F.R.S., F.R.S.E.

Barttelot, Sir Brian Walter de Stopham, Bt. (1875).

Barwick, *Rt. Hon.* Sir Garfield Edward John, G.C.M.G.

Barwick, Sir Richard Llewellyn, Bt. (1912).

Bassett, Sir Walter Eric, K.B.E., M.C.

Basten, Sir Henry Bolton, Kt., C.M.G.

Bastyan, *Lt.-Gen.* Sir Edric Montague, K.C.M.G., K.C.V.O., K.B.E., C.B.

Bate, Sir William Edwin, Kt. O.B.E.

Bateman, Sir Cecil Joseph, K.B.E.

Bateman, Sir Charles Harold, K.C.M.G., M.C.

Bateman, Sir Geoffrey Hirst, Kt., F.R.C.S.

Bateman, Sir Ralph Merton, K.B.E.

Bates, Sir Alfred, Kt., M.C.

Bates, *Maj.-Gen.* Sir (Edward) John (Hunter), K.B.E., C.B., M.C.

Bates, Sir Geoffrey Voltelin, Bt., M.C. (1880).

Bates, Sir John David, Kt., C.B.E., V.R.D.

Bates, Sir (John) Dawson, Bt. (1937).

Bates, Sir (Julian) Darrell, Kt., C.M.G., C.V.O.

Batho, Sir Maurice Benjamin, Bt. (1928).

Bathurst, Sir Frederick Peter Methuen Hervey-, Bt. (1818).

Batsford, Sir Brian Caldwell Cook, Kt.

Batterbee, Sir Harry Fagg, G.C.M.G., K.C.V.O.

Batty, Sir William Bradshaw, Kt., T.D.

Baxter, *Prof.* Sir (John) Philip, K.B.E., C.M.G.

Bayly, *Vice-Adm.* Sir Patrick Uniacke, K.B.E., C.B., D.S.C.

Baynes, *Lt.-Col.* Sir Rory Malcolm Stuart, Bt. (1801).

Bazley, Sir Thomas Stafford, Bt. (1869).

Bazl-ul-lah, *Sahib Bahadur* K. B., Sir Muhammad, Kt., C.I.E., O.B.E.

Beach, *Lt.-Gen.* Sir (William Gerald) Hugh, K.C.B., O.B.E., M.C.

Beadle, Sir Gerald Clayton, Kt., C.B.E.

Beadle, *Rt. Hon.* Sir (Thomas) Hugh (William), Kt., C.M.G., O.B.E.

Beale, *Hon.* Sir (Oliver) Howard, K.B.E., Q.C.

Beale, Sir William Francis, Kt., O.B.E.

Bean, Sir Edgar Layton, Kt., C.M.G.

Beaton, Sir Cecil Walter Hardy, Kt., C.B.E.

Beattie, *Hon.* Sir Alexander Craig, Kt.

Beauchamp, Sir Brograve Campbell, Bt. (1911).

Beauchamp, Sir Christopher Radstock Proctor-, Bt. (1745).

Beauchamp, Sir Douglas Clifford, Bt. (1918).

Beaumont, Sir George (Howland Francis), Bt. (1661).

Beaumont, Sir Richard Ashton, K.C.M.G., O.B.E.

Becher, Sir William Fane Wrixon, Bt., M.C. (1831).

Beck, Sir Edgar Charles, Kt., C.B.E.

Becker, Sir Jack Ellerton, Kt.

Beckett, *Capt.* Sir (Martyn) Gervase, Bt., M.C. (1921).

Bedingfeld, *Capt.* Sir Edmund George Felix Paston-, Bt. (1661).

Bednall, *Maj.-Gen.* Sir Peter, K.B.E., C.B., M.C.

Beecham, Sir Adrian Welles, Bt. (1914).

Beeley, Sir Harold, K.C.M.G., C.B.E.

Beetham, Sir Edward Betham, K.C.M.G., C.V.O., O.B.E.

Beetham, *Air Marshal* Sir Michael James, K.C.B., C.B.E., D.F.C., A.F.C.

Beevor, Sir Thomas Agnew, Bt. (1784).

Begg, *Admiral of the Fleet* Sir Varyl Cargill, G.C.B., D.S.O., D.S.C.

Behrens, Sir Leonard Frederick, Kt., C.B.E.

Beit, Sir Alfred Lane, Bt. (1924).

Beith, Sir John Greville Stanley, K.C.M.G.

Bell, Sir Arthur Capel Herbert, Kt.

Bell, Sir Gawain Westray, K.C.M.G., C.B.E.

Bell, Sir (George) Raymond, K.C.M.G., C.B.

Bell, Sir John Lowthian, Bt. (1885).

Bell, Sir William Hollin Dayrell Morrison-, Bt. (1905).

Bellew, Sir Arthur John Grattan-, Kt., C.M.G., Q.C.

Bellew, Hon. Sir George Rothe, K.C.B., K.C.V.O., F.S.A.

Bellew, Sir Henry Charles Gratton-, Bt. (1838).

Bellinger, Sir Robert Ian, G.B.E.

Bellingham, Sir Noel Peter Roger, Bt. (1796).

Bemrose, Sir (John) Maxwell, Kt.

Benn, *Capt.* Sir (Patrick Ion) Hamilton, Bt. (1920).

Benn, Sir John Andrews, Bt. (1914).

Bennett, Sir Arnold Lucas, Kt., Q.C.

Bennett, Sir Charles Mothi Te Arawaka, Kt., D.S.O.

Bennett, Sir Frederic Mackarness, Kt., M.P.

Bennett, Sir Hubert, Kt.

Bennett, Sir Ronald Wilfrid Murdoch, Bt. (1929).

Bennett, Sir Thomas Penberthy, K.B.E.

Bennett, Sir William Gordon, Kt.

Benson, Sir Arthur Edward Trevor, G.C.M.G.

Benson, *Rev.* Sir (Clarence) Irving, Kt., C.B.E.

Benson, Sir Henry Alexander, G.B.E.

Benstead, Sir John, Kt., C.B.E.

Benthall, Sir (Arthur) Paul, K.B.E.

Bentinck, *Maj.* Sir Ferdinand William Cavendish-, K.B.E., C.M.G.

Berkeley, Sir Lennox Randal Francis, Kt., C.B.E.

Berlin, Sir Isaiah, Kt., O.M., C.B.E.

Bernard, Sir Dallas Edmund Bt. (1954).

Berney, Sir Julian Reedham Stuart, Bt., (1620).

Berrill, Sir Kenneth Ernest, K.C.B.

Berry, Sir (Henry) Vaughan, Kt.

Berryman, *General* Sir Frank Horton, K.C.V.O., C.B., C.B.E., D.S.O.

Berthoud, Sir Eric Alfred, K.C.M.G.

Bethune, Sir Alexander Maitland Sharp, Bt. (s 1683).

Betjeman, Sir John, Kt., C.B.E.

Bevan, Sir Martyn Evan Evans, Bt. (1958).

Beverley, *Vice-Adm.* Sir (William) York (La Roche), K.B.E., C.B.

Bevir, Sir Anthony, K.C.V.O., C.B.E.

Beynon, *Prof.* Sir William John Granville, Kt., C.B.E., Ph.D., D.Sc., F.R.S.

Bibby, *Maj.* Sir (Arthur) Harold, Bt., D.S.O. (1959).

Biddulph, Sir Francis Henry, Bt. (1664).

Biggart, *Prof.* Sir (John) Henry, Kt., C.B.E., D.Sc., M.D., F.R.C.P.

Biggs, Sir Lionel William, Kt.

Bing, Sir Rudolf Franz Josef, K.B.E.

Bird, *Lt.-Gen.* Sir Clarence August, K.C.I.E., C.B., D.S.O.

Bird, Sir Cyril Pangbourne, Kt.

Bird, Sir Richard Geoffrey Chapman, Bt. (1922).

Bird, *Col.* Sir Richard Dawnay Martin-, Kt., C.B.E., T.D.

Birkin, Sir Charles Lloyd, Bt. (1905).

Birkmyre, Sir Henry, Bt. (1921).

Birley, Sir Robert, K.C.M.G., F.S.A.

Birsay, Lord, *see* Leslie, Sir Harald.

Bishop, Sir Frederick Arthur, Kt., C.B., C.V.O.

Bishop, Sir George Sidney, Kt., C.B., O.B.E.

Bishop, Sir Harold, Kt., C.B.E.

Bishop, *Instructor Rear-Adm.*, Sir William Alfred, K.B.E., C.B.

Bishop, *Maj.-Gen.* Sir William Henry Alexander, K.C.M.G., C.B., C.V.O., O.B.E.

Bishop, Sir William Poole, Kt., C.M.G.

Black, Sir Cyril Wilson, Kt.

Black, *Prof.* Sir Douglas Andrew Kilgour, Kt., M.D., F.R.C.P.

Black, Sir Harold, Kt.

Black, Sir Hermann David, Kt.

Black, *Prof.* Sir Misha, Kt., O.B.E.

Black, Sir Robert Andrew Stransham, Bt. (1922).

Black, Sir Robert Brown, G.C.M.G., O.B.E.

Blackall, Sir Henry William Butler, Kt., Q.C.

Blackburne, Sir Kenneth William, G.C.M.G., G.B.E.

Blacker, *General* Sir Cecil Hugh, G.C.B., O.B.E., M.C.

Blackett, Sir George William, Bt. (1673).

Blackwell, Sir Basil Henry, Kt.

Blackwood, Sir Francis Elliot Temple, Bt. (1819).

Blackwood, Sir Robert Rutherford, Kt.

Blagden, Sir John Ramsay, Kt., O.B.E., T.D.

Blair, *Maj.* Sir Alastair Campbell, K.C.V.O., D.S.O.

Blair, *Lt.-Gen.* Sir Chandos, K.C.V.O., O.B.E., M.C.

Blair, Sir James Hunter-, Bt. (1786).

Blake, Sir (Francis) Michael, Bt. (1907).

Blake, Sir Thomas Richard Valentine, Bt. (I 1622).

Blaker, Sir John, Bt. (1919).

Blakiston, Sir Arthur Norman Hunter, Bt. (1763).

Bland, Sir Henry Armand, Kt., C.B.E.

Blennerhassett, Sir Marmaduke Adrian Francis William, Bt. (1809).

Bligh, Sir Edward Clare, Kt.

Blois, Sir Charles Nicholas Gervase, Bt. (1686).

Blomefield, Sir Thomas Edward Peregrine, Bt. (1807).

Bloomfield, *Hon.* Sir John Stoughton, Kt., Q.C.

Blosse, Sir Richard Hely Lynch-, Bt. (1622).

Blount, Sir Edward Robert, Bt. (1642).

Blundell, Sir (Edward) Denis, G.C.M.G., G.C.V.O., K.B.E.

Blundell, Sir Michael, K.B.E.

Blunden, Sir William, Bt. (I 1766).

Blunt, *Prof.* Sir Anthony Frederick, K.C.V.O., F.B.A.

Blunt, Sir David Richard Reginald, Bt. (1720).

Blyde, Sir Henry Ernest, K.B.E.

Bodilly, *Hon.* Sir Jocelyn, Kt., V.R.D.

Boevey, Sir Thomas Michael Blake Crawley-, Bt. (1784).

Boileau, Sir Gilbert George Benson, Bt. (1838).

Boles, Sir Jeremy John Fortescue, Bt. (1922).

Bollers, *Hon.* Sir Harold Brodie Smith, Kt.

Bolte, *Hon.* Sir Henry Edward, G.C.M.G.

Bolton, Sir Frederic Bernard, Kt., M.C.

Bolton, Sir George Lewis French, K.C.M.G.

Bolton, Sir Ian Frederick Cheney, Bt., K.B.E. (1927).

Bonallack, Sir Richard Frank, Kt., C.B.E.

Bonar, Sir Herbert Vernon, Kt., C.B.E.

Bondi, *Prof.* Sir Hermann, K.C.B., F.R.S.

Bonham, *Maj.* Sir Antony Lionel Thomas, Bt. (1852).

Bonsor, Sir Bryan Cosmo, Bt., M.C., T.D. (1925).

Boord, Sir Nicolas John Charles, Bt. (1896).

Booth, Sir Douglas Allen, Bt. (1916).

Booth, Sir Michael Savile Gore-, Bt. (I 1760).

Boothby, Sir Hugo Robert Brooke, Bt. (1660).

Boreel, Sir Francis David, Bt. (1645).

Boreham, *Hon.* Sir Leslie Kenneth Edward, Kt.

Bornu, The Waziri of, K.C.M.G., C.B.E.

Borthwick, Sir John Thomas, Bt. M.B.E. (1908).

Borwick, *Lt.-Col.* Sir Thomas Faulkner, Kt., C.I.E., D.S.O.

Bossom, *Maj.* Hon. Sir Clive, Bt. (1953).

Boswall, Sir Thomas Houstoun-, Bt. (1836).

Bottomley, Sir James Reginald Alfred, K.C.M.G.

Bouchier, *Air Vice-Marshal* Sir Cecil Arthur, K.B.E., C.B., D.F.C.

Boughey, Sir Richard James, Bt. (1798).

Boult, Sir Adrian Cedric, Kt., C.H., D.Mus.

Boulton, Sir Edward John, Bt. (1944).

Boulton, Sir Harold Hugh Christian, Bt. (1905).

Boulton, Sir William Whytehead, Kt., C.B.E., T.D.

Bourke, *Hon.* Sir Paget John, Kt.

Bourne, Sir Frederick Chalmers, K.C.S.I., C.I.E.

Boustead, *Col.* (Sir John Edmund) Hugh, K.B.E., C.M.G., D.S.O., M.C.

Bovell, *Hon.* Sir (William) Stewart, Kt.

Bovenschen, Sir Frederick Carl, K.C.B., K.B.E.

Bowater, *Lt. Col.* Sir Ian Frank, G.B.E., D.S.O., T.D.

Bowater, Sir (John) Vansittart, Bt. (1914).

Bowater, Sir Noel Vansittart, Bt., G.B.E., M.C. (1939).

Bowden, Sir Frank, Bt. (1915).

Bowen, *Hon.* Sir Nigel Hubert, K.B.E.

Bowen, Sir Thomas Frederic Charles, Bt. (1921).

Bower, Sir John Dykes, Kt., C.V.O.

Bower, Sir Frank, Kt., C.B.E.

Bower, *Air Marshal* Sir Leslie William Clement, K.C.B., D.S.O., D.F.C.

Bower, *Lt.-Gen.* Sir Roger Herbert, K.C.B., K.B.E.

Bower, Sir (William) Guy Nott-, K.B.E., C.B.

Bowes, Sir (Harold) Leslie K.C.M.G., C.B.E.

Bowker, Sir (Reginald) James, G.B.E., K.C.M.G.

Bowlby, Sir Anthony Hugh Mostyn, Bt. (1923).

Bowman, Sir James, Bt., K.B.E. (1961).

Bowman, Sir John Paget, Bt. (1884).

Boxer, *Air Vice-Marshal* Sir Alan Hunter Cachemaille, K.C.V.O., C.B., D.S.O., D.F.C.

Boyce, Sir Robert Charles Leslie, Bt. (1916).

Boyd, Sir Alexander Walter, Bt. (1916).

Boyd, Sir John Francis, Kt.

Boyd, *Brig.* Sir John Smith Knox, Kt., O.B.E., M.D., F.R.S.

Boyes, Sir Brian Gerald Barratt-, K.B.E.

Boyle, *Marshal of the Royal Air Force* Sir Dermot Alexander, G.C.B., K.C.V.O., K.B.E., A.F.C.

Boyne, Sir Henry Brian, Kt., C.B.E.

Bradbury, *Surgeon Vice-Adm.* Sir Eric Blackburn, K.B.E., C.B.

Bradford, Sir Edward Alexander Slade, Bt. (1902).

Bradlaw, *Prof.* Sir Robert Vivian, Kt., C.B.E.

Bradley, *Air Marshal* Sir John Stanley Travers, K.C.B., C.B.E.

Bradley, Sir Kenneth Granville, Kt., C.M.G.

Bradman, Sir Donald George, Kt.

Brain, Sir (Henry) Norman, K.B.E., C.M.G.

Brain, Sir Hugh Gerner, Kt., C.B.E., M.S.M.

Braine, Sir Bernard Richard, Kt., M.P.

Bramall, *General* Sir Edwin Noel Westby, K.C.B., O.B.E., M.C.

Bramall, Sir (Ernest) Ashley, Kt.

Brancker, *His Hon.* Sir (John Eustace) Theodore, Kt., Q.C.

Brand, *Hon.* Sir David, K.C.M.G.

Brand, Sir (William) Alfred, Kt., C.B.E.

Brandon, *Hon.* Sir Henry Vivian, Kt., M.C.

Branigan, Sir Patrick Francis, Kt., Q.C.

Branson, Col. Sir Douglas Stephenson, K.B.E., C.B., D.S.O., M.C., T.D.

Bray, *General* Sir Robert Napier Hubert Campbell, G.B.E., K.C.B., D.S.O.

Bray, Sir Theodore Charles, Kt., C.B.E.

Braynen, Sir Alvin Rudolph, Kt.

Brearley, Sir Norman, Kt., C.B.E., D.S.O., M.C., A.F.C.

Brebner, Sir Alexander, Kt., C.I.E.

Brechin, Sir (Herbert) Archbold, K.B.E.

Brett, *Hon.* Sir Lionel, Kt.

Brickwood, Sir Basil Greame, Bt. (1927).

Bridge, *Rt. Hon.* Sir Nigel Cyprian, Kt.

Bridgeman, *Hon.* Sir Maurice Richard, K.B.E.

Bridges, *Hon.* Sir Phillip Rodney, Kt., C.M.G.

Briggs, Sir (Alfred) George (Ernest), Kt.

Briggs, *Hon.* Sir Francis Arthur, Kt.

Briggs, *Hon.* Sir Geoffrey Gould, Kt.

Brightman, *Hon.* Sir John Anson, Kt.

Brinckman, *Col.* Sir Roderick Napoleon, Bt. D.S.O., M.C. (1831).

Brinton, *Maj.* Sir (Esme) Tatton (Cecil), Kt.

Brisco, Sir Donald Gilfrid, Bt. (1782).

Briscoe, Sir John Leigh Charlton, Bt., D.F.C. (1910).

Brise, Sir John Archibald Ruggles-, Bt., C.B., O.B.E., T.D. (1935).

Bristow, *Hon.* Sir Peter Henry Rowley, Kt.

Britton, Sir Edward Louis, Kt., C.B.E.

Broadbent, Sir William Francis Bt. (1893).

Broadhurst, *Air Chief Marshal* Sir Harry, G.C.B., K.B.E., D.S.O., D.F.C., A.F.C.

Broadley, Sir Herbert, K.B.E.

Broadmead, Sir Philip Mainwaring, K.C.M.G., M.C.

Brocklebank, Sir Aubrey Thomas, Bt. (1885).

Brocklehurst, Sir John Ogilvy, Bt. (1903).

Brockman, *Vice-Adm.* Sir Ronald Vernon, K.C.B., C.S.I., C.I.E., C.B.E.

Brodie, Sir Benjamin David Ross, Bt. (1834).

Brodie, *Very Rev.* Sir Israel, K.B.E.

Brogan, *Lt.-Gen.* Sir Mervyn Francis, K.B.E., C.B.

Bromet, *Air Vice-Marshal* Sir Geoffrey Rhodes, K.B.E., C.B., D.S.O.

Bromhead, *Lt.-Col.* Sir Benjamin Denis Gonville, Bt., O.B.E. (1806).

Bromley, Sir Rupert Charles, Bt. (1757).

Bromley, Sir Thomas Eardley, K.C.M.G.

Brook, Sir Robin, Kt., C.M.G.

Brooke, *Maj.* Sir George Cecil Francis, Bt. (1903).

Brooke, *Maj.* Sir John Weston, Bt. (1919).

Brooke, Sir (Norman) Richard (Rowley), Kt., C.B.E.

Brooke, Sir Richard Christopher, Bt. (1662).

Brooksbank, Sir (Edward) William, Bt. (1919).

Broom, *Air Marshal* Sir Ivor Gordon, K.C.B., C.B.E., D.S.O., D.F.C., A.F.C.

Brotherston, Sir John Howie Flint, Kt., M.D., F.R.S.E.

Broughton, Sir Alfred Davies Devonsher, Kt., M.P.

Broughton, *Air Marshal* Sir Charles, K.B.E., C.B.

Broughton, Sir Evelyn Delves, Bt. (1661).

Broun, Sir Lionel John Law, Bt. (s 1686).

Brown, Sir Allen Stanley, Kt., C.B.E.

Brown, Sir (Arthur James) Stephen, K.B.E.

Brown, *Lt.-Col.* Sir (Charles Frederick) Richmond, Bt. (1863).

Brown, Sir Charles James Officer, Kt., M.D.

Brown, Sir (Cyril) Maxwell (Palmer), K.C.B., C.M.G.

Brown, Sir David, Kt.

Brown, Sir Edward Joseph, Kt., M.B.E., M.P.

Brown, *Prof.* Sir (Ernest) Henry Phelps, Kt., M.B.E., F.B.A.

Brown, Sir (Frederick Herbert) Stanley, Kt., C.B.E.

Brown, Sir James Raitt, Kt.

Brown, Sir John Douglas Keith, Kt.

Brown, Sir John Gilbert Newton, Kt., C.B.E.

Brown, Sir Kenneth Alfred Leader, Kt.

Brown, *Air Vice-Marshal* Sir Leslie Oswald, K.C.B., C.B.E., D.S.C., A.F.C.

Brown, *Hon.* Sir Ralph Kilner, Kt., O.B.E., T.D.

Brown, Sir Raymond Frederick, Kt., O.B.E.

Brown, Sir Robert Crichton-, Kt., C.B.E.

Brown, *Hon.* Sir Stephen, Kt.

Brown, Sir Thomas, Kt.

Brown, *Air Commodore* Sir Vernon Sydney, Kt., C.B., O.B.E.

Brown, Sir William Brian Pigott-, Bt. (1903).

Browne, Sir (Edward) Humphrey, Kt., C.B.E.

Browne, *Rt. Hon.* Sir Patrick Reginald Evelyn, Kt., O.B.E., T.D.

Brownrigg, Sir Nicholas (Gawen), Bt. (1816).

Bruce, Sir Arthur Atkinson, K.B.E., M.C.

Bruce, Sir (Francis) Michael Ian, Bt. (s 1628).

Bruce, Sir Hervey James Hugh, Bt. (1804).

Bruce, *Hon.* Sir (James) Roualeyn Hovell - Thurlow - Cumming -, Kt.

Brune, Sir Humphrey Ingelram Prideaux, K.B.E., C.M.G.

Brunner, Sir Felix John Morgan, Bt. (1895).

Brunton, Sir (Edward Francis) Lauder, Bt. (1908).

Bryan, Sir Andrew Meikle, Kt.

Bryan, Sir Arthur, Kt.

Bryan, Sir Paul Elmore Oliver, Kt., D.S.O., M.C., M.P.

Bryant, Sir Arthur Wynne Morgan, Kt., C.H., C.B.E.

Bryce, *Hon.* Sir (William) Gordon, Kt., C.B.E.

Buchan, Sir John, Kt., C.M.G.

Buchanan, Sir Charles Alexander James Leith-, Bt. (1775).

Buchanan, Sir Charles James, Bt. (1878).

Buchanan, *Prof.* Sir Colin Douglas, Kt., C.B.E.

Buchanan, *Maj.* Sir Reginald Narcissus Macdonald-, K.C.V.O., M.B.E., M.C.

Bucher, *General* Sir Roy, K.B.E., C.B., M.C.

Buckley, *Rt. Hon.* Sir Denys Burton, Kt., M.B.E.

Buckley, *Rear-Adm.* Sir Kenneth Robertson, K.B.E.

Budd, *Hon.* Sir Harry Vincent, Kt.

Bulkeley, Sir Richard Harry David Williams-, Bt. (1661).

Bull, Sir George, Bt. (1922).

Bull, Sir Graham MacGregor, Kt., M.D., F.R.C.P.

Bullard, Sir Edward Crisp, Kt., Ph.D., Sc.D., F.R.S.

Bullock, Sir Ernest, Kt., C.V.O., Mus.D.

Bullus, Sir Eric Edward, Kt.

Bulmer, Sir William Peter, Kt.

Bunbury, Sir (John) William Napier, Bt. (1681).

Bunbury, Sir (Richard David) Michael Richardson-, Bt. (I 1787).

Bunting, Sir (Edward) John, Kt., C.B.E.

Burbidge, Sir Herbert Dudley, Bt. (1916).

Burbury, *Hon.* Sir Stanley Charles, K.B.E.

Burder, Sir John Henry, Kt.

Burdett, Sir Savile Aylmer, Bt. (1665).

Burgen, Sir Arnold Stanley Vincent, Kt., F.R.S.

Burgess, Sir John Lawie, Kt., O.B.E., T.D.

Burgess, Sir Thomas Arthur Collier, Kt.

Burke, Sir Aubrey Francis, Kt., O.B.E.

Burke, Sir Thomas Stanley, Bt. (I 1797).

Burman, Sir (John) Charles, Kt.

Burman, Sir Stephen France, Kt., C.B.E.

Burne, Sir Lewis Charles, Kt., C.B.E., A.F.C.

Burnet, Sir (Frank) Macfarlane, O.M., K.B.E., M.D., F.R.S.

Burnett, *Air Chief Marshal* Sir Brian Kenyon, G.C.B., D.F.C., A.F.C.

Burnett, *Maj.* Sir David Humphery, Bt., M.B.E., T.D. (1913).

Burney, Sir Anthony George Bernard, Kt., O.B.E.

Burney, Sir Cecil Denniston, Bt. (1921).

Burns, Sir Alan Cuthbert, G.C.M.G.

Burns, Sir Charles Ritchie, K.B.E., M.D.

Burns, Sir John Crawford, Kt.

Burns, Sir Malcolm McRae, K.B.E.

Burns, *Maj.-Gen.* Sir (Walter Arthur) George, K.C.V.O., C.B., D.S.O., O.B.E., M.C.

Burrell, *Vice-Adm.* Sir Henry Mackay, K.B.E., C.B.

Burrell, Sir Walter Raymond, Bt., C.B.E., T.D. (1774).

Burrough, *Admiral* Sir Harold Martin, G.C.B., K.B.E., D.S.O.

Burrows, Sir Bernard Alexander Brocas, G.C.M.G.

Burrows, Sir (Robert) John (Formby), Kt.

Burton, *Air Marshal* Sir Harry, K.C.B., C.B.E., D.S.O.

Busby, Sir Matthew, Kt., C.B.E.

Bush, *Admiral* Sir John Fitzroy Duyland, G.C.B., D.S.C.

Busk, Sir Douglas Laird, K.C.M.G.

Bustamante, *Rt. Hon.* Sir (William) Alexander, Kt.

Butland, Sir Jack Richard, K.B.E.

Butler, *Hon.* Sir Milo Boughton, G.C.M.G., G.C.V.O.

Butler, Sir (Reginald) Michael (Thomas), Bt. (1922).

Butler, *Lt.-Col.* Sir Thomas Pierce, Bt., C.V.O., D.S.O., O.B.E. (1628).

Butlin, Sir William Edmund, Kt., M.B.E.

Butt, Sir (Alfred) Kenneth Dudley, Bt. (1929).

Butterfield, *Prof.* Sir Herbert, Kt., F.B.A.

Butterworth, Sir (George) Neville, Kt.

Buxton, Sir Thomas Fowell Victor, Bt. (1840).

Buzzard, Sir Anthony Farquhar, Bt. (1929).

Byass, *Col.* Sir Geoffrey Robert Sidney, Bt., T.D. (1926).

Byrne, Sir Clarence Askew, Kt., O.B.E., D.S.C.

Cable, Sir James Eric, K.C.V.O., C.M.G.

Cader, Sir Hussein Hassanaly Abdool, Kt., C.B.E.

Cadwallader, Sir John, Kt.

Cadzow, Sir Norman James Kerr, Kt., V.R.D.

Caffyn, *Brig.* Sir Edward Roy, K.B.E., C.B., T.D.

Caffyn, Sir Sydney Morris, Kt., C.B.E.

Cahn, Sir Albert Jonas, Bt. (1934).

Cain, Sir Edward Thomas, Kt., C.B.E.

Caine, Sir Sydney, K.C.M.G.

Cairncross, Sir Alexander Kirkland, K.C.M.G.

Cairns, *Rt. Hon.* Sir David Arnold Scott, Kt.

Cairns, Sir Joseph Foster, Kt.

Cakobau, *Ratu* Sir George, G.C.M.G., O.B.E.

Caldicott, *Hon.* Sir John Moore, K.B.E., C.M.G.

Caldwell, *Surgeon Vice-Adm.* Sir Eric Dick, K.B.E., C.B.

Callaghan, Sir Allan Robert, Kt., C.M.G.

Callaghan, Sir Bede Bertrand, Kt., C.B.E.

Callander, *Lt.-Gen.* Sir Colin Bishop, K.C.B., K.B.E., M.C.

Callard, Sir Eric John, Kt.

Calley, Sir Henry Algernon, Kt., D.S.O., D.F.C.

Calthorpe, *Brig.* Sir Richard Hamilton Anstruther-Gough-, Bt., C.B.E. (1929).

Cameron, *Lt.-Gen.* Sir Alexander Maurice, K.B.E., C.B., M.C.

Cameron of Lochiel, Sir Donald Hamish, K.T., C.V.O., T.D.

Cameron, *Hon.* Sir John, Kt., D.S.C., Q.C. (Lord Cameron).

Cameron, *Air Chief Marshal* Sir Neil, G.C.B., C.B.E., D.S.O., D.F.C.

Camilleri, *His Hon.* Sir Luigi Antonio, Kt, Ll.D.

Campbell, Sir Alan Hugh, K.C.M.G.

Campbell, *Maj.-Gen.* Sir (Alexander) Douglas, K.B.E., C.B., D.S.O., M.C.

†Campbell, Sir Bruce Colin Patrick, Bt. (s 1804).

Campbell, Sir Clifford Clarence, G.C.M.G., G.C.V.O.

Campbell, Sir Colin, Kt., O.B.E.

Campbell, Sir Colin Moffat, Bt., M.C. (s 1668).

Campbell, *Prof.* Sir David, Kt., M.C., M.D., Ll.D., F.R.S.E.

Campbell, *Col.* Sir Guy Theophilus Halswell, Bt., O.B.E., M.C. (1815).

Campbell, *Maj.-Gen.* Sir Hamish Manus, K.B.E., C.B.

Campbell, *Vice-Adm.* Sir Ian Murray Robertson, K.B.E., C.B., D.S.O.

Campbell, Sir Ian Vincent Hamilton, Bt., C.B. (1831).

Campbell, Sir Ilay Mark, Bt. (1808).

Campbell, Sir John Johnston, Kt.

Campbell, Sir Matthew, K.B.E., C.B., F.R.S.E.

Campbell, Sir Ralph Abercromby, Kt.

Campbell, Sir Robin Auchinbreck, Bt. (S. 1628).

Campbell, *Rt. Hon.* Sir Ronald Ian, G.C.M.G., C.B.

Campbell, Sir Thomas Cockburn-, Bt. (1821).

Campion, Sir Harry, Kt., C.B., C.B.E.

Cantley, *Hon.* Sir Joseph Donaldson, Kt., O.B.E.

Cantlie, Sir Keith, Kt., C.I.E.

Capper, Sir (William) Derrick, Kt.

Carberry, Sir John Edward Doston, Kt.

Carden, *Lt.-Col.* Sir Henry Christopher, Bt., O.B.E. (1887).

Carden, Sir John Craven, Bt. (I 1787).

Carew, Sir Thomas Palk, Bt. (1661).

Carey, Sir Peter Willoughby, K.C.B.

Carlill, *Vice-Adm.* Sir Stephen Hope, K.B.E., C.B., D.S.O.

Carmichael, Sir David Peter William Gibson-Craig-, Bt. (s 1702 and 1831).

Carmichael, Sir John, K.B.E.

Carnac, *Rev.* Sir Thomas Nicholas Rivett-, Bt. (1836).

Carnwath, Sir Andrew Hunter, K.C.V.O.

Caröe, Sir (Einar) Athelstan (Gordon), Kt., C.B.E.

Caroe, Sir Olaf Kirkpatrick, K.C.S.I., K.C.I.E.

Carr, Sir (Frederick) Bernard, Kt., C.M.G.

Carr, *Air Marshal* Sir John Darcy Baker-, K.B.E., C.B., A.F.C.

Carr, Sir William Emsley, Kt.

Carreras, *Lt.-Col.* Sir James, Kt., M.B.E.

Carroll, Sir Alfred Thomas, K.B.E.

Carter, Sir (Arthur) Desmond Bonham-, Kt., T.D.

Carter, Sir Derrick Hunton, Kt., T.D.

Carter, Sir John, Kt., Q.C.

Carter, *His Hon.* Sir Walker Kelly, Kt., Q.C.

Carter, Sir William Oscar, Kt.

Cartland, Sir George Barrington, Kt., C.M.G.

Carver, *Field-Marshal* Sir (Richard) Michael (Power), G.C.B., C.B.E., D.S.O., M.C.

Cary, Sir Robert Archibald, Bt. (1955).

Cash, Sir Thomas James, K.B.E., C.B.

Cassel, Sir Harold Felix, Bt., Q.C. (1920).

Cassels, *Field Marshal* Sir (Archibald) James Halkett, G.C.B., K.B.E., D.S.O.

Cassidy, Sir Jack Evelyn, Kt.

Casson, Sir Hugh Maxwell, Kt., P.R.A., F.R.I.B.A.

Catherwood, Sir (Henry) Frederick (Ross), Kt.

Catlin, *Prof.* Sir George Edward Gordon, Kt., Ph.D.

Catling, Sir Richard Charles, Kt., C.M.G., O.B.E.

Caughey, Sir (Thomas) Herbert Clarke, K.B.E.

Caulfield, *Hon.* Sir Bernard, Kt.

Cave, Sir Charles Edward Coleridge, Bt. (1896).

Cave, Sir Richard Guy, Kt., M.C.

Cave, Sir Robert Cave-Browne-, Bt. (1641).

Cawley, Sir Charles Mills, Kt., C.B.E., Ph.D.

Cayley, Sir Digby William David, Bt. (1661).

Cayzer, Sir James Arthur, Bt. (1904).

Cayzer, Sir (William) Nicholas, Bt. (1921).

Cazalet, *Vice-Adm.* Sir Peter Grenville Lyon, K.B.E., C.B., D.S.O., D.S.C.

Chacksfield, *Air Vice-Marshal* Sir Bernard Albert, K.B.E., C.B.

Chadwick, Sir Albert Edward, Kt., C.M.G., M.S.M.

Chadwick, Sir John Edward, K.C.M.G.

Chadwick, Sir Robert Burton Burton-, Bt. (1935).

Chain, *Prof.* Sir Ernest Boris, Kt., F.R.S., Ph.D., D.Phil.

Chalk, *Hon.* Sir Gordon William Wesley, K.B.E.

Chamberlain, Sir Henry Wilmot, Bt. (1828).

Chamberlain, *Hon.* Sir Reginald Roderic St. Clair, Kt.

Chambers, Sir (Stanley) Paul, K.B.E., C.B., C.I.E.

Champion, *Prof.* Sir Harry George, Kt., C.I.E., D.Sc.

Champion, *Rev.* Sir Reginald Stuart, K.C.M.G., O.B.E.

Champneys, *Capt.* Sir Weldon Dalrymple-, Bt., C.B. (1910).

Chance, Sir Roger James Ferguson, Bt., M.C. (1900).

Chance, Sir (William) Hugh (Stobart), Kt., C.B.E.

Chancellor, Sir Christopher John, Kt., C.M.G.

Chaplin, Sir Charles Spencer, K.B.E.

Chapman, Sir Robert Macgowan, Bt., C.B.E., T.D. (1958).

Chapman, *Air Chief Marshal* Sir Ronald Ivelaw-, G.C.B., K.B.E., D.F.C., A.F.C.

Chapman, *Hon.* Sir Stephen, Kt.

Charles, Sir John Pendrill, K.C.V.O., M.C.

Charley, Sir Philip Belmont, Kt.

Charlton, *Commodore* Sir William Arthur, Kt., D.S.C.

Charrington, Sir John, Kt.

Charteris, *Lt.-Col. Rt. Hon.* Sir Martin Michael Charles, G.C.V.O., K.C.B., O.B.E.

Chau, Sir Sik-nin, Kt., C.B.E.

Chaytor, Sir William Henry Clervaux, Bt. (1831).

Cheetham, Sir Nicolas John Alexander, K.C.M.G.

Chegwidden, Sir Thomas Sidney, Kt., C.B., C.V.O.

Cheshire, *Air Chief Marshal* Sir Walter Graemes, G.B.E., K.C.B.

Chester, Sir (Daniel) Norman, Kt., C.B.E.

Chesterman, Sir Clement Clapton, Kt., O.B.E.

Chesterman, Sir (Dudley) Ross, Kt., Ph.D.

Chesterton, Sir Oliver Sidney, Kt., M.C.

Chetwynd, Sir Arthur Ralph Talbot, Bt. (1795).

Cheyne, Sir Joseph Lister Watson, Bt., O.B.E. (1908).

Chichester, Sir (Edward) John, Bt. (1641).

Child, Sir (Coles John) Jeremy, Bt. (1919).

Chilton, *Air Marshal* Sir (Charles) Edward, K.B.E., C.B.

Chilton, *Brig.* Sir Frederick Oliver, Kt., C.B.E., D.S.O.

Chinoy, Sir Sultan Meherally, Kt.

Chisholm, Sir Henry, Kt., C.B.E.

Chitty, Sir Thomas Willes, Bt. (1924).

Cholmeley, Sir Montague John, Bt. (1896).

Christie, *Hon.* Sir Vernon Howard Colville, Kt.

Christie, Sir William, K.C.I.E., C.S.I., M.C.

Christie, Sir William, Kt., M.B.E.

Christison, *Gen.* Sir (Alexander Frank) Philip, Bt., G.B.E., C.B., D.S.O., M.C. (1871).

Christopher, Sir George Perrin, Kt.

Christophers, *Col.* Sir Samuel Rickard, Kt., C.I.E., O.B.E., F.R.S.

Christopherson, Sir Derman Guy, Kt., O.B.E., D.Phil., F.R.S.

Church, *Brig.* Sir Geoffrey Selby, Bt., C.B.E., M.C., T.D. (1901).

Cilento, Sir Raphael West, Kt., M.D.

Clague, *Col. Hon.* Sir (John) Douglas, Kt., C.B.E., M.C., T.D.

Clapham, Sir Michael John Sinclair, K.B.E.

Claribull, Sir (Gordon) Frank, Kt., Ph.D.

Clark, Sir Andrew Edmund James, Bt., M.B.E., M.C., Q.C. (1883).

Clark, *Capt.* Sir George Anthony, Bt. (1917).

Clark, Sir George Norman, Kt., D.Litt.

Clark, Sir (Gordon) Colvin Lindesay, K.B.E., C.M.G., M.C.

Clark, Sir John Allen, Kt.

Clark, Sir John Stewart-, Bt. (1918).

Clark, Sir Robert Anthony, Kt., D.S.C.

Clark, Sir Robin Chichester-, Kt.

Clark, Sir Thomas, Bt. (1886).

Clark, Sir (Thomas) Fife, Kt., C.B.E.

Clarke, Sir (Charles Mansfield) Tobias, Bt. (1831).

Clarke, *Prof.* Sir Cyril Astley, K.B.E., M.D., Sc.D., F.R.S., F.R.C.P.

Clarke, Sir Ellis Emmanuel Innocent, G.C.M.G.

Clarke, Sir Frederick Joseph, Kt.

Clarke, Sir (Henry) Ashley, G.C.M.G., G.C.V.O.

Clarke, Sir Henry Osmond Osmond-, K.C.V.O., C.B.E.

Clarke, Sir Rupert William John, Bt., M.B.E. (1882).

Clay, Sir Charles Travis, Kt., C.B.

Clay, Sir Henry Felix, Bt. (1841).

Clayden, *Rt. Hon.* Sir (Henry) John, Kt.

Claye, *Prof.* Sir Andrew Moynihan, Kt., M.D.

Clayson, Sir Eric Maurice, Kt.

Clayton, Sir Arthur Harold, Bt., D.S.C. (1732).

Clayton, *Air Marshal* Sir Gareth Thomas Butler, K.C.B., D.F.C.

Clayton, *Col. Hon.* Sir Hector Joseph Richard, Kt., E.D.

Clayton, *Prof.* Sir Stanley George, Kt., M.D.

Cleary, Sir Joseph Jackson, Kt.

Clee, Sir (Charles) Beaupré Bell, Kt., C.S.I., C.I.E.

Clegg, Sir Alexander Bradshaw, Kt.

Clegg, Sir Cuthbert Barwick, Kt.

Clements, Sir John Selby, Kt., C.B.E.

Clerk, Sir John Dutton, Bt., C.B.E., V.R.D. (s 1679).

Clerke, Sir John Edward Longueville, Bt. (1660).

Clifford, Sir (Geoffrey) Miles, K.B.E., C.M.G., E.D.

Clifford, Sir Roger Charles Joseph Gerrard, Bt. (1887).

Clore, Sir Charles, Kt.

Clucas, Sir Kenneth Henry, K.C.B.

Clutterbuck, *Vice-Adm.* Sir David Granville, K.B.E., C.B.

Coate, *Maj.-Gen.* Sir Raymond Douglas, K.B.E., C.B.

Coates, Sir Albert Ernest, Kt., O.B.E., M.D.

Coates, Sir Ernest William, Kt., C.M.G.

Coates, Sir Frederick Gregory Lindsay, Bt. (1921).

Coates, Sir James Robert Edward Clive Milnes-, Bt. (1911).

Coats, Sir Alastair Francis Stuart, Bt. (1905).

Cobb, *Hon.* Sir John Francis Scott, Kt.

Cochrane, Sir Desmond Oriel Alastair George Weston, Bt. (1903).

Cochrane, *Air Chief Marshal Hon.* Sir Ralph Alexander, G.B.E., K.C.B., A.F.C.

Cockburn, Sir John Elliot, Bt. (s 1671).

Cockburn, Sir Robert, K.B.E., C.B., Ph.D.

Cocker, Sir William Wiggins, Kt., O.B.E.

Cockerell, Sir Christopher Sydney, Kt., C.B.E., F.R.S.

Cockfield, Sir (Francis) Arthur, Kt.

Cockram, Sir John, Kt.

Cocks, Sir (Thomas George) Barnett, K.C.B., O.B.E.

Codrington, Sir Christopher William Gerald Henry, Bt. (1876).

Codrington, Sir William Alexander, Bt. (1721).

Coghill, *Capt.* Sir (Marmaduke Nevill) Patrick (Somerville), Bt. (1778).

Cohen, Sir Bernard Nathaniel Waley-, Bt. (1961).

Cohen, Sir Edward, Kt.

Cohen, Sir Jack, Kt., O.B.E.

Cohen, Sir John Edward, Kt.

Cohen, Sir Rex Arthur Louis, K.B.E.

Coldstream, Sir George Phillips, K.C.B., K.C.V.O., Q.C.

Coldstream, *Prof.* Sir William Menzies, Kt., C.B.E.

Cole, Sir David Lee, K.C.M.G., M.C.

Cole, Sir Noel, Kt.

Coles, Sir Arthur William, Kt.

Coles, Sir Edgar Barton, Kt.

Coles, Sir George James, Kt., C.B.E.

Coles, Sir Kenneth Frank, Kt.

Coles, *Air Marshal* Sir William Edward, K.B.E., C.B., D.S.O., D.F.C., A.F.C.

Colfox, Sir (William) John, Bt. (1939).

Collett, Sir Ian Seymour, Bt. (1934).

Collett, Sir (Thomas) Kingsley, Kt., C.B.E.

Collier, *Air Vice-Marshal* Sir (Alfred) Conrad, K.C.B., C.B.E.

Collier, Sir Laurence, K.C.M.G.

Collingwood, *Lt.-Gen.* Sir (Richard) George, K.B.E., C.B., D.S.O.

Collins, Sir Charles Henry, Kt., C.M.G.

Collins, Sir David Charles, Kt., C.B.E.

Collins, Sir Geoffrey Abdy, Kt.

Collins, *Vice-Adm.* Sir John Augustine, K.B.E., C.B.

Collins, Sir William Alexander Roy, Kt., C.B.E.

Colman, Sir Michael Jeremiah, Bt. (1907).

Colquhoun, *Maj.-Gen.* Sir Cyril Harry, K.C.V.O., C.B., O.B.E.

Colquhoun of Luss, Sir Ivar Iain, Bt. (1786).

Colt, Sir Edward William Dutton Bt. (1694).

Colthurst, Sir Richard La Touche, Bt. (1744).

Colville, Sir (Henry) Cecil, Kt.

Colville, Sir John Rupert, Kt., C.B., C.V.O.

Combs, Sir Willis Ide, K.C.V.O., C.M.G.

Compston, *Vice-Adm.* Sir Peter Maxwell, K.C.B.

Compton, Sir Edmund Gerald, G.C.B., K.B.E.

Conant, Sir John Ernest Michael, Bt. (1954).

Connell, Sir Charles Gibson, Kt.

Connolly, Sir Willis Henry, Kt., C.B.E.

Conroy, Sir Diarmaid William, Kt., C.M.G., O.B.E., T.D., Q.C.

Constable, Sir Robert Frederick Strickland-. Bt. (1641).

Constantine, *Air Chief Marshal* Sir Hugh Alex, K.B.E., C.B., D.S.O.

Constantine, Sir Theodore, Kt., C.B.E., T.D.

Cook, Sir Francis Ferdinand Maurice, Bt. (1886).

Cook, Sir Philip Halford, Kt., O.B.E.

Cook, Sir William Richard Joseph, K.C.B., F.R.S.

Cooke, Sir Charles Arthur John, Bt. (1661).

Cooke, Sir John Fletcher-, Kt., C.M.G.

Cooke, *Hon.* Sir Samuel Burgess Ridgway, Kt.

Cooley, Sir Alan Sydenham, Kt., C.B.E.

Coop, Sir Maurice Fletcher, Kt.

Cooper, *Maj.* Sir Charles Eric Daniel, Bt. (1863).

Cooper, Sir Francis Ashmole, Bt., Ph.D. (1905).

Cooper, Sir Frank, K.C.B., C.M.G.

Cooper, *Hon.* Sir Gilbert Alexander, Kt., C.B.E., E.D.

Cooper, Sir (Harold) Stanford, Kt.

Cooper, Sir Patrick Graham Astley, Bt. (1821).

Cooper, *Prof.* Sir (William) Mansfield, Kt.

Coote, *Capt.* Sir Colin Reith, Kt., D.S.O.

Coote, *Rear-Adm.* (E.) Sir John Ralph, Bt., C.B., C.B.E., D.S.C., *Premier Baronet of Ireland* (I 1621).

Coppleson, Sir Lionel Wolfe, Kt.

Corah, Sir John Harold, Kt.

Corbet, Sir John Vincent, Bt., M.B.E. (1808).

Cordingley, *Air Vice-Marshal* Sir John Walter, K.C.B., K.C.V.O., C.B.E.

Corfield, Sir Conrad Laurence, K.C.I.E., C.S.I., M.C.

Corfield, *Rt. Hon.* Sir Frederick Vernon, Kt., Q.C.

Corley, Sir Kenneth Sholl Ferrand, Kt.

Cormack, Sir Magnus Cameron, K.B.E.

Cornwall, *General* Sir James Handyside Marshall-, K.C.B., C.B.E., D.S.O., M.C.

Corry, Sir James Perowne Ivo Myles, Bt. (1885).

Cory, Sir Clinton James Donald, Bt. (1919).

Coryton, *Air Chief Marshal* Sir (William) Alec, K.C.B., K.B.E., M.V.O., D.F.C.

Coslett, *Air Marshal* Sir (Thomas) Norman, K.C.B., O.B.E.

Costar, Sir Norman Edgar, K.C.M.G.

Cotter, *Lt.-Col.* Sir Delaval James Alfred, Bt., D.S.O. (I. 1763).

Cotterell, Sir Richard Charles Geers, Bt., C.B.E., T.D. (1805).

Cotton, Sir John Richard, K.C.M.G., O.B.E.

Cottrell, Sir Alan Howard, Kt., Ph.D., F.R.S.

Cotts, Sir (Robert) Crichton Mitchell, Bt. (1921).

Couchman, *Admiral* Sir Walter Thomas, K.C.B., C.V.O., D.S.O., O.B.E.

Coulson, Sir John Eltringham, K.C.M.G.

Couper, Sir Robert Nicholas Oliver, Bt. (1841).

Court, *Hon.* Sir Charles Walter Michael, Kt., O.B.E.

Courtenay, *Hon.* Sir (Woldrich) Harrison, K.B.E.

Courtenay, *Air Chief Marshal* Sir Christopher Lloyd, G.B.E., K.C.B., D.S.O.

Coutts, Sir Walter Fleming, G.C.M.G., M.B.E.

Cowan, Sir Christopher George Armstrong, Kt.

Cowen, *Prof.* Sir Zelman, Kt., Q.C.

Cowley, *Lt.-Gen.* Sir John Guise, K.B.E., C.B.

Cowper, Sir Norman Lethbridge, Kt., C.B.E.

Cowperthwaite, Sir John James, K.B.E., C.M.G.

Cox, Sir Christopher William Machell, G.C.M.G.

Cox, Sir (Ernest) Gordon, K.B.E., T.D., D.Sc., F.R.S.

Cox, Sir Geoffrey Sandford, Kt., C.B.E.

Cox, Sir (George) Trenchard, Kt., C.B.E., F.S.A.

Cox, Sir John William, Kt., C.B.E.

Cox, Sir William Robert, K.C.B.

Craddock, Sir (George) Beresford, Kt.

Craddock, *Lt.-Gen.* Sir Richard Walter, K.B.E., C.B., D.S.O.

Craig, Sir John Herbert Mc-Cutcheon, K.C.V.O., C.B.

Cramer, *Hon.* Sir John Oscar, Kt.

Crane, Sir Harry Walter Victor, Kt., O.B.E.

Craufurd, Sir Robert James, Bt. (1781).

Craven, *Air Marshal* Sir Robert Edward, K.B.E., C.B., D.F.C.

Crawford, Sir (Archibald James) Dirom, Kt.

Crawford, *Brig.* Sir Douglas Inglis, Kt., C.B., D.S.O., T.D.

Crawford, Sir Frederick, G.C.M.G., O.B.E.

Crawford, *Hon.* Sir George Hunter, Kt.

Crawford, Sir John Grenfell, Kt., C.B.E.

Crawford, Sir (Robert) Stewart, G.C.M.G., C.V.O.

Crawford, *Prof.* Sir Theodore, Kt.

Crawford, Sir (Walter) Ferguson, K.B.E., C.M.G.

Crawford, *Vice-Adm.* Sir William Godfrey, K.B.E., C.B., D.S.C.

Crawshaw, *Hon.* Sir (Edward) Daniel (Weston), Kt.

Crawshay, *Col.* Sir William Robert, Kt., D.S.O., E.R.D., T.D.

Creagh, *Maj.-Gen.* Sir (Kilner) Rupert Brazier-, K.B.E., C.B., D.S.O.

Creasy, Sir Gerald Hallen, K.C.M.G., K.C.V.O., O.B.E.

Creswell, Sir Michel Justin, K.C.M.G.

Creswick, Sir Alexander Reid, Kt.

Crichton, Sir Andrew James Maitland-Makgill-, Kt.

Crichton, *Hon.* Sir (John) Robertson (Dunn), Kt.

Crichton, Sir Robert, C.B.E.

Cripps, Sir Cyril Thomas, Kt., M.B.E.

Crisp, Sir (John) Peter, Bt. (1913).

Crisp, *Hon.* Sir Malcolm Peter, Kt.

Critchett, Sir Ian (George Lorraine), Bt. (1908).

Croft, Sir Bernard Hugh Denman, Bt. (1671).

Croft, Sir John William Graham, Bt. (1818).

Crofton, Sir (Hugh) Patrick Simon, Bt. (1801).

Crofton, Sir Malby Sturges, Bt. (1828).

Crookenden, *Lt.-Gen.* Sir Napier, K.C.B., D.S.O., O.B.E.

Croom, Sir John Halliday, Kt., T.D.

Croot, Sir (Horace) John, Kt., C.B.E.

Cross, *Prof.* Sir (Alfred) Rupert (Neale), Kt., F.B.A.

Cross, *Air Chief Marshal* Sir Kenneth Brian Boyd, K.C.B., C.B.E., D.S.O., D.F.C.

Crossland, Sir Leonard, Kt.

Crossley, Sir Christopher John, Bt. (1909).

Crosthwaite, Sir (Ponsonby) Moore, K.C.M.G.

Crowe, Sir Colin Tradescant, G.C.M.G.

Crowley, Sir Brian Hurtle, Kt., M.M.

Crowther, Sir William Edward Lodewyk Hamilton, Kt., C.B.E., D.S.O., V.D.

Crutchley, *Admiral* Sir Victor Alexander Charles, ♈♋, K.C.B., D.S.C.

Cumings, Sir Charles Cecil George, K.B.E.

Cumming, Sir Duncan Cameron, K.B.E., C.B.

Cumming, Sir Ronald Stuart, Kt., T.D.

Cumming, Sir William Gordon Gordon-, Bt. (1804).

Cunard, Sir Guy Alick, Bt. (1859).

Cuninghame, Sir John Christopher Foggo Montgomery-, Bt. (N.S. 1672).

Cuninghame, Sir William Alan Fairlie-, Bt., M.C. (S. 1630).

Cunliffe, Sir David Ellis, Bt. (1750).

Cunningham, *General* Sir Alan Gordon, G.C.M.G., K.C.B., D.S.O., M.C.

Cunningham, Sir Charles Craik G.C.B., K.B.E., C.V.O.

Cunningham, Sir Graham, K.B.E.

Cunningham, *Lt.-Gen.* Sir Hugh Patrick, K.B.E.

Cunynghame, Sir (Henry) David St. Leger Brooke Selwyn, Bt. (S. 1702).

Cunynghame, Sir James Ogilvy Blair-, Kt., O.B.E.

Curle, Sir John Noel Ormiston, K.C.V.O., C.M.G.

Curlewis, *His Hon.* Sir Adrian Herbert, Kt., C.V.O., C.B.E.

Curran, Sir Charles John, Kt.

Curran, *Rt. Hon.* Sir Lancelot Ernest, Kt.

Curran, Sir Samuel Crowe, Kt., D.Sc., Ph.D., F.R.S., F.R.S.E.

Currie, Sir George Alexander, Kt.

Currie, Sir James, K.B.E., C.M.G.

Currie, Sir Walter Mordaunt Cyril, Bt. (1847).

Curtis, Sir Edward Leo, Kt.

Curtis, Sir Peter, Bt. (1802).

Cusack, *Hon.* Sir Ralph Vincent, Kt.

Cushion, *Air Vice-Marshal* Sir William Boston, K.B.E., C.B.

Cutforth, *Maj.-Gen.* Sir Lancelot Eric, K.B.E., C.B.

Cuthbert, *Vice-Adm.* Sir John Wilson, K.B.E., C.B.

Cuthbertson, Sir David Paton, Kt., C.B.E., M.D., D.Sc.

Cutler, Sir (Arthur) Roden, ♈♋, K.C.M.G., K.C.V.O., C.B.E.

Cutler, Sir Charles Benjamin, K.B.E., E.D.

Dacie, *Prof.* Sir John Vivian, M.D., F.R.S.

Dainton, *Prof.* Sir Frederick Sydney, Kt., Ph.D., D.Sc., F.R.S.

Daldry, Sir Leonard Charles, K.B.E.

Dale, Sir William Leonard, K.C.M.G.

Dalling, Sir Thomas, Kt.

Dalrymple, Sir Hew Fleetwood Hamilton-, Bt., C.V.O. (S. 1697).

Dalton, *Maj.-Gen.* Sir Charles James George, Kt., C.B., C.B.E.

Dalton, *Vice-Adm.* Sir Norman Eric, K.C.B., O.B.E.

Daly, *Lt.-Gen.* Sir Thomas Joseph, K.B.E., C.B., D.S.O.

Dalyell, Sir Tam, Bt., M.P. (N.S. 1685).

Danckwerts, *Rt. Hon.* Sir Harold Otto, Kt.

Dowse, *Maj.-Gen.* Sir Maurice Brian, K.C.V.O., C.B., C.B.E.

Doyle, *Capt.* Sir John Francis Reginald William Hastings, Bt. (1828).

D'Oyly, *Cdr.* Sir John Rochfort, Bt., R.N. (1663).

Drake, Sir (Arthur) Eric (Courtney), Kt., C.B.E.

Drake, Sir James, Kt., C.B.E.

Drew, Sir Arthur Charles Walter, K.C.B.

Drew, Sir Ferdinand Caire, Kt., C.M.G.

Drew, *Lt.-Gen.* Sir (William) Robert (Macfarlane), K.C.B., C.B.E., Q.H.P.

Dreyer, *Admiral* Sir Desmond Parry, G.C.B., C.B.E., D.S.C.

Dring, *Lt.-Col.* Sir Arthur John, K.B.E., C.I.E.

Driver, Sir Arthur John, Kt.

Drummond, *Lieut.-Gen.* Sir (William) Alexander (Duncan), K.B.E., C.B.

Drury, Sir Alan Nigel, Kt., C.B.E., M.D., F.R.S.

Dryden, Sir John Stephen Gyles, Bt. (1733 and 1795).

Drysdale, Sir (George) Russell, Kt.

Duckworth, *Maj.* Sir Richard Dyce, Bt. (1909).

Du Cros, Sir Claude Philip Arthur Mallet, Bt. (1916).

Dudding, Sir John Scarborough, Kt.

Duff, Sir Arthur Antony, K.C.M.G., C.V.O., D.S.O., D.S.C.

Duff, Sir (Charles) Michael (Robert Vivian), Bt. (1911).

Duffus, *Hon.* Sir Herbert George Holwell, Kt.

Duffus, *Hon.* Sir William Algernon Holwell, Kt.

Dugdale, Sir William Stratford, Bt., M.C. (1936).

du Heaume, Sir Francis Herbert, Kt., C.I.E., O.B.E.

Duke, Sir Charles Beresford, K.C.M.G., C.I.E., O.B.E.

Duke, *Maj.-Gen.* Sir Gerald William, K.B.E., C.B., D.S.O.

Dumas, Sir Russell John, K.B.E., C.M.G.

Dunbar, Sir Adrian Ivor, Bt., (S 1694).

Dunbar, Sir Archibald Ranulph, Bt. (S 1700).

Dunbar, Sir David Hope-, Bt. (S 1664).

Dunbar, Sir Drummond Cospatrick Ninian, Bt., M.G. (S 1698).

Dunbar, Sir John Greig, Kt.

Dunbar of Hempriggs, Dame Maureen Daisy Helen, Bt. (S 1706).

Duncan, Sir Arthur Bryce, Kt.

Duncombe, Sir Philip Digby Pauncefort-, Bt. (1859).

Dundas, Sir Robert Whyte Melville, Bt. (1821).

Dungarpur, H.H. the Maharawal of, G.C.I.E., K.C.S.I.

Dunham, *Prof.* Sir Kingsley Charles, Kt., Ph.D., F.R.S., F.R.S.E.

Dunk, Sir William Ernest, Kt., C.B.E.

Dunkley, Sir Herbert Francis, Kt.

Dunlop, *Prof.* Sir Derrick Melville, Kt., M.D.

Dunlop, Sir Ernest Edward, Kt., C.M.G., O.B.E.

Dunlop, Sir John Wallace, K.B.E.

Dunlop, Sir Thomas, Bt. (1916).

Dunlop, Sir William Norman Gough, Kt.

Dunn, *Lt.-Col.* Sir Francis Vivian, K.C.V.O., O.B.E.

Dunn, *Air Marshal* Sir Patrick Hunter, K.B.E., C.B., D.F.C.

Dunn, *Hon.* Sir Robin Horace Walford, Kt., M.C.

Dunnett, Sir George Sangster, K.B.E., C.B.

Dunnett, Sir (Ludovic) James, G.C.B., C.M.G.

Dunning, Sir Simon William Patrick, Bt. (1930).

Dunphie, *Maj.-Gen.* Sir Charles Anderson Lane, Kt., C.B., C.B.E., D.S.O.

Duntze, Sir George Edwin Douglas, Bt., C.M.G. (1774).

Dupree, Sir Peter, Bt. (1921).

Dupuch, Sir (Alfred) Etienne (Jerome), Kt., O.B.E.

Durand, *Rev.* Sir (Henry Mortimer) Dickon, Bt. (1892).

Durkin, *Air Marshal* Sir Herbert, K.B.E., C.B.

Durlacher, Sir Esmond Otho, Kt.

Durlacher, *Admiral* Sir Laurence George, K.C.B., O.B.E., D.S.C.

Durrant, Sir William Henry Estridge, Bt. (1784).

Duthie, Sir William Smith, Kt., O.B.E.

Dyer, *Prof.* Sir (Henry) Peter (Francis) Swinnerton, Bt., F.R.S. (1678).

Dyke, Sir Derek William Hart, Bt. (1677).

Earle, *Air Chief Marshal* Sir Alfred, G.B.E., C.B.

Earle, Sir Hardman Alexander Mort, Bt. (1869).

East, Sir (Lewis) Ronald, Kt., C.B.E.

Eastick, *Brig.* Sir Thomas Charles, Kt., C.M.G., D.S.O., E.D.

Easton, *Admiral* Sir Ian, K.C.B., D.S.C.

Eastwood, Sir Eric, Kt., C.B.E., F.R.S.

Eastwood, *Maj.* Sir Geoffrey Hugh, K.C.V.O., C.B.E.

Eastwood, Sir John Bealby, Kt.

Easton, *Air Commodore* Sir James Alfred, K.C.M.G., C.B., C.B.E.

Eaton, *Vice-Adm.* Sir John Willson Musgrave, K.B.E., C.B., D.S.O., D.S.C.

Ebrahim, Sir (Mahomed) Currimbhoy, Bt. (1910).

Eccles, *Prof.* Sir John Carew, Kt., D.Phil., F.R.S.

Echlin, Sir Norman David Fenton, Bt. (I 1721).

Edden, *Vice-Adm.* Sir (William) Kaye, K.B.E., C.B.

Eddie, Sir George Brand, Kt., O.B.E.

Eden, *Rt. Hon.* Sir John Benedict, Bt., M.P. (1672 and 1776).

Edge, Sir Knowles, Bt. (1937).

Edmenson, Sir Walter Alexander, Kt., C.B.E.

Edmonstone, Sir Archibald Bruce Charles, Bt. (1774).

Edwards, *Lt.-Col.* Sir Bartle Mordaunt Marsham, Kt., C.V.O., M.C.

Edwards, Sir Christopher John Churchill, Bt. (1866).

Edwards, Sir George Robert, Kt., O.M., C.B.E., F.R.S.

Edwards, *Air Commodore* Sir Hughie Idwal, VC, K.C.M.G., C.B., D.S.O., O.B.E., D.F.C.

Edwards, Sir John Arthur, Kt., C.B.E.

Edwards, Sir John Clive Leighton, Bt. (1921).

Edwards, Sir Martin Llewellyn, Kt.

Edwards, *Prof.* Sir Samuel Frederick, Kt., F.R.S.

Egerton, Sir John Alfred Roy, Kt.

Egerton, Sir (Philip) John (Caledon) Grey-, Bt. (1617).

Egerton, Sir Seymour John Louis, K.C.V.O.

Eggleston, *Hon.* Sir Richard Moulton, Kt.

Elder, Sir Stewart Duke-, G.C.V.O., M.D., F.R.S.

Eldridge, *Lt.-Gen.* Sir (William) John, K.B.E., C.B., D.S.O., M.C.

Eley, Sir Geoffrey Cecil Ryves, Kt., C.B.E.

Eliott, Sir Arthur Francis Augustus Boswell, Bt. (S 1666).

Elkins, Sir Anthony Joseph, Kt., C.B.E.

Elkins, *Vice-Adm.* Sir Robert Francis, K.C.B., C.V.O., O.B.E.

Elliot, Sir John Blumenfeld, Kt.

Elliott, Sir Hugh Francis Ivo, Bt., O.B.E. (1917).

Elliott, Sir Norman Randall, Kt., M.P.

Elliott, Sir (Robert) William, Kt., M.P.

Ellis, Sir (Bertram) Clough Williams-, Kt., C.B.E., M.C., F.R.I.B.A.

Ellis, Sir Charles Drummond, Kt., Ph.D., F.R.S.

Ellis, *Hon.* Sir Kevin, K.B.E.

Ellis, Sir Thomas Hobart, Kt.

Ellison, *Col.* Sir Ralph Harry Carr-, Kt., T.D.

Ellwood, *Air Marshal* Sir Aubrey Beauclerk, K.C.B., D.S.O.

Elmhirst, *Air Marshal* Sir Thomas Walker, K.B.E., C.B., A.F.C.

Elphinstone, Sir John, Bt. (S 1701).

Elphinstone, Sir (Maurice) Douglas (Warburton), Bt., T.D. (1816).

Elstub, Sir St. John de Holt, Kt., C.B.E.

Elton, Sir Charles Abraham Grierson, Bt. (1717).

Elyan, Sir (Isadore) Victor, Kt.

Embry, *Air Chief Marshal* Sir Basil Edward, G.C.B., K.B.E., D.S.O., D.F.C., A.F.C.

Emery, Sir (James) Frederick, Kt.

Emmerson, Sir Harold Corti, G.C.B., K.C.V.O.

Empson, Sir Charles, K.C.M.G.

Empson, *Admiral* Sir (Leslie) Derek, G.B.E., K.C.B.

Emson, *Air Marshal* Sir Reginald Herbert, K.B.E., C.B., A.F.C.

Engholm, Sir Basil Charles, K.C.B.

Engineer, Sir Noshirwan Phiroz-shah, Kt.

Engledow, *Prof.* Sir Frank Leonard, Kt., C.M.G., F.R.S.

English, Sir Cyril Rupert, Kt.

Ennor, *Prof.* Sir Hugh (Arnold Hughes), Kt., C.B.E.

Entwistle, Sir (John Nuttall) Max-well, Kt.

Ereaut, Sir Herbert Frank Cob-bold, Kt.

Errington, *Col.* Sir Geoffrey Frederick, Bt. (1963).

Errington, Sir Lancelot, K.C.B.

Erskine, Sir Derek Quicke, Kt.

Erskine, Sir (Robert) George, Kt., C.B.E.

Erskine, Sir (Thomas) David, Bt. (1821).

Esmonde, Sir Anthony Charles, Bt. (I 1629).

Esplen, Sir William Graham, Bt. (1921).

Eugster, *General* Sir Basil Oscar Paul, K.C.B., K.C.V.O., O.B.E., D.S.O., M.C.

Evans, Sir Anthony Adney, Bt. (1920).

Evans, Sir Arthur Trevor, Kt.

Evans, Sir Athol Donald, K.B.E.

Evans, Sir Bernard, Kt., D.S.O., E.D.

Evans, *Vice-Adm.* Sir Charles Leo Glandore, K.C.B., C.B.E., D.S.O., D.S.C.

Evans, Sir David Lewis, Kt., O.B.E., D.Litt.

Evans, Sir Francis Edward, G.B.E., K.C.M.G.

Evans, *Lt.-Gen.* Sir Geoffrey Charles, K.B.E., C.B., D.S.O.

Evans, Sir Geraint Llewellyn, Kt., C.B.E.

Evans, *Hon.* Sir Haydn Tudor, Kt.

Evans, Sir Hywel Wynn, K.C.B.

Evans, Sir Ian William Gwynne-, Bt. (1913).

Evans, Sir (Robert) Charles, Kt.

Evans, Sir (Sidney) Harold, Bt., C.M.G., O.B.E. (1963).

Evans, Sir Trevor Maldwyn, Kt., C.B.E.

Evans, Sir (William) Vincent (John), G.C.M.G., M.B.E., Q.C.

Eveleigh, *Hon.* Sir Edward Walter, Kt., E.R.D.

Everard, *Maj.-Gen.* Sir Christo-pher Earle Welby-, K.B.E., C.B.

Everard, Sir Nugent Henry, Bt. (1911).

Everson, Sir Frederick Charles, K.C.M.G.

Every, Sir John Simon, Bt. (1641).

Evetts, *Lt.-Gen.* Sir John Fuller-ton, Kt., C.B., C.B.E., M.C.

Ewart, Sir (William) Ivan (Cecil), Bt., D.S.C. (1887).

Ewbank, *Maj.-Gen.* Sir Robert Withers, K.B.E., C.B., D.S.O.

Ewin, Sir (David) Ernest Thomas Floyd, Kt., O.B.E., M.V.O.

Ewing, *Prof.* Sir Alexander William Gordon, Kt., Ph.D.

Ewing *Vice-Adm.* Sir (Robert) Alastair, K.B.E., C.B., D.S.C.

Ewing, Sir Ronald Archibald Orr-, Bt. (1886).

Eyre, *Lt.-Col.* Sir Oliver Eyre Crosthwaite-, Kt.

Ezra, Sir Alwyn, Kt.

Ezra, Sir Derek, Kt., M.B.E.

Fadahunsi, Sir Joseph Odeleye, K.C.M.G.

Fagge, Sir John William Frederick, Bt. (1660).

Fairbairn, Sir (James) Brooke, Bt. (1869).

Fairbairn, Sir Robert Duncan, Kt.

Fairfax, Sir Vincent Charles, Kt., C.M.G.

Fairfax, Sir Warwick Oswald, Kt.

Fairhall, *Hon.* Sir Allen, K.B.E.

Falconer, *Lt.-Col.* Sir George Arthur, K.B.E., C.I.E.

Falconer, Sir James Fyfe, Kt., M.B.E.

Falk, Sir Roger Salis, Kt., O.B.E.

Falkiner, *Lt.-Col.* Sir Terence Edmond Patrick, Bt. (I 1778).

Falkner, Sir (Donald) Keith, Kt.

Falla, Sir Robert Alexander, K.B.E., C.M.G.

Falle, Sir Samuel, K.C.V.O., C.M.G., D.S.C.

Falshaw, Sir Donald, Kt.

Falvey, *Hon.* Sir John Neil, Kt., O.B.E., Q.C.

Fanshawe, *Maj.-Gen.* Sir Evelyn Dairymple, Kt., C.B., C.B.E.

Faridkot, *Col.* H.H. the Raja of, K.C.S.I.

Farmer, Sir Lovedin George Thomas, Kt.

Farquhar, *Lt.-Col.* Sir Peter (Walter), Bt., D.S.O. (1796).

Farquharson, Sir James Robbie, K.B.E.

Farrer, Sir (Walter) Leslie, K.C.V.O.

Farrington, *Maj.* Sir Henry Francis Colden, Bt. (1818).

Faulkner, Sir Eric Odin, Kt., M.B.E.

Faulkner, Sir Percy, K.B.E., C.B.

Faulks, *Hon.* Sir Neville Major Ginner, Kt., M.B.E., T.D.

Fawcus, Sir (Robert) Peter, K.B.E., C.M.G.

Fayrer, Sir John Lang Macpher-son. Bt., (1896).

Feilden, Sir Henry Wemyss, Bt., (1846).

Feilden, *Maj.-Gen.* Sir Randle Guy, K.C.V.O., C.B., C.B.E.

Feiling, Sir Keith Grahame, Kt., O.B.E., D.Litt.

Fell, *Vice-Adm.* Sir Michael Frampton, K.C.B., D.S.O., D.S.C.

Fellowes, Sir William Albemarle, K.C.V.O.

Fenner, Sir Claude Harry, K.B.E., C.M.G.

Fennessy, Sir Edward, Kt., C.B.E.

Ferens, Sir Thomas Robinson, Kt., C.B.E.

Ferguson, *Lt.-Col.* Sir Neil Edward Johnson-, Bt., T.D. (1906).

Fergusson of Kilkerran, Sir Charles, Bt. (S. 1703).

Fergusson, Sir James Herbert Hamilton Colyer-, Bt. (1866).

Ferranti, Sir Vincent Ziani de, Kt., M.C.

Ferrier, Sir Harold Grant, Kt., C.M.G.

ffolkes, Sir Robert Francis Alex-ander, Bt. (1774).

fforde, Sir Arthur Frederic Brownlow, G.B.E.

Fidge, Sir (Harold) Roy, Kt.

Field, Sir John Osbaldiston, K.B.E., C.M.G.

Fielden, *Air Vice-Marshal* Sir Edward Hedley, G.C.V.O., C.B., D.F.C., A.F.C.

Fieldhouse, Sir Harold, K.B.E., C.B.

Fiennes, Sir John Saye Wingfield Twisleton-Wykeham-, K.C.B., Q.C.

Fiennes, Sir Maurice Alberic Twisleton-Wykeham-, Kt.

Fiennes, Sir Ranulph Twisleton-Wykeham-, Bt. (1916).

Figgers, *Col.* Sir John George, K.B.E., C.M.G.

Figgures, Sir Frank Edward, K.C.B., C.M.G.

Finch, Sir Harold Josiah, Kt.

Findlay, *Lt.-Col.* Sir Roland Lewis, Bt. (1925).

Finlay, Sir Graeme Bell, Bt., E.R.D. (1964).

Finniston, Sir (Harold) Montague, Kt., Ph.D., F.R.S.

Firth, *Prof.* Sir Raymond William, Kt., Ph.D., F.B.A.

Fisher, Sir George Read, Kt., C.M.G.

Fisher, *Hon.* Sir Henry Arthur Peers, Kt.

Fisher, Sir John, Kt.

Fisher, Sir Nigel Thomas Love-ridge, Kt., M.C., M.P.

Fison, Sir (Frank Guy) Clavering, Kt.

Fison, Sir Richard Guy, Bt., D.S.C. (1905).

Fitts, Sir Clive Hamilton, Kt., M.D.

Fitzgerald, *Rev.* Sir Edward Thomas, Bt. (1903).

FitzGerald, Sir George Peter Maurice, Bt., M.C., *The Knight of Kerry* (1880).

Fitz-Gerald, Sir Patrick Herbert, Kt., O.B.E.

Fitzgerald, Sir William James, Kt., M.C., Q.C.

FitzHerbert, Sir John Richard Frederick, Bt. (1784).

Fitzmaurice, *Lt.-Col.* Sir Desmond FitzJohn. Kt., C.I.E.

Fitzmaurice, Sir Gerald Gray, G.C.M.G., Q.C.

Fitzpatrick, *General* Sir (Geoffrey Richard) Desmond, G.C.B., D.S.O., M.B.E., M.C.

Flanagan, Sir James Bernard, Kt., C.B.E.

Flavelle, Sir (Joseph) Ellsworth, Bt. (1917).

Fleming, *Instr. Rear-Adm.* Sir John, K.B.E., D.S.C.

Fleming, *Rt. Rev.* William Launcelot Scott, K.C.V.O., D.D.

Flemming, Sir Gilbert Nicolson, K.C.B.

Fletcher, *Hon.* Sir Alan Roy, Kt.

Fletcher, Sir John Henry Lancelot Aubrey-, Bt. (1782).

Fletcher, *Hon.* Sir Patrick Bisset, K.B.E., C.M.G.

Fletcher, *Air Chief Marshal* Sir Peter Carteret, K.C.B., O.B.E., D.F.C., A.F.C.

Flett, Sir Martin Teall, K.C.B.

Flowers, *Prof.* Sir Brian Hilton, Kt., F.R.S.

Floyd, Sir Giles Henry Charles, Bt. (1816).

Follett, Sir David Henry, Kt., Ph.D.

Follows, Sir (Charles) Geoffry (Shield), Kt., C.M.G.

Fooks, Sir Raymond Hatherell, Kt., C.B.E.

Foot, *Rt. Hon.* Sir Dingle Mackintosh, Kt., Q.C.

Foots, Sir James William, Kt.

Forbes, *Hon.* Sir Alastair Granville, Kt.

Forbes, Sir Archibald Finlayson, G.B.E.

Forbes of Pitsligo, Sir Charles Edward Stuart-, Bt. (S 1626).

Forbes of Brux, *Hon.* Sir Ewan, Bt. (S 1630).

Forbes, *Hon.* Sir Hugh Henry Valentine, Kt.

Forbes, *Col.* Sir John Stewart, Bt., D.S.O. (1823).

Ford, *Capt.* Sir Aubrey St. Clair-, Bt., D.S.O., R.N. (1793).

Ford, *Prof.* Sir Edward, Kt., O.B.E., M.D.

Ford, *Maj.* Sir Edward William Spencer, K.C.B., K.C.V.O.

Ford, Sir Henry Russell, Bt. (1929).

Ford, *Prof.* Sir Hugh, Kt., F.R.S.

Ford, Sir Leslie Ewart, Kt., O.B.E.

Ford, *Maj.-Gen.* Sir Peter St. Clair-, K.B.E., C.B., D.S.O.

Ford, Sir Sidney William George, Kt., M.B.E.

Fordham, Sir (Alfred) Stanley, K.B.E., C.M.G.

Forman, Sir John Denis, Kt., O.B.E.

Forrest, Sir James Alexander, Kt.

Forrest, *Rear Adm.* Sir Ronald Stephen, K.C.V.O.

Forsdyke, Sir (Edgar) John, K.C.B.

Forte, Sir Charles, Kt.

Forwood, Sir Dudley Richard, Bt. (1895).

Foster, Sir John Galway, K.B.E., Q.C.

Foster, Sir John Gregory, Bt. (1930).

Foster, *Hon.* Sir Peter Harry Batson Woodroffe, Kt., M.B.E., T.D.

Foster, Sir Robert Sidney, G.C.M.G., K.C.V.O.

Foulis, Sir Ian Primrose Liston-, Bt. (S 1634).

Fowke, Sir Frederick (Woollaston Rawdon), Bt. (1814).

Fowler, Sir Robert William Doughty, K.C.M.G.

Fox, Sir (Henry) Murray, G.B.E.

Fox, *Hon.* Sir Michael John, Kt.

Fox, Sir (Robert) David (John) Scott, K.C.M.G.

Fox, Sir Theodore Fortescue, Kt., M.D., Ll.D.

Foxell, *Rev.* Maurice Frederic, K.C.V.O.

France, Sir Arnold William, G.C.B.

Francis, Sir Frank Charlton, K.C.B., F.S.A.

Frank, Sir Douglas George Horace, Kt., Q.C.

Frank, Sir Robert John, Bt. (1920).

Frankel, Sir Otto Herzberg, Kt., D.Sc., F.R.S.

Franklin, Sir Eric Alexander, Kt., C.B.E.

Fraser, Sir Basil Malcolm, Bt. (1921).

Fraser, Sir Bruce Donald, K.C.B.

Fraser, *General* Sir David William, K.C.B., O.B.E.

Fraser, Sir Douglas Were, Kt., I.S.O.

Fraser, *Air Marshal* Sir (Henry) Paterson, K.B.E., C.B., A.F.C.

Fraser, Sir Hugh, Bt. (1961).

Fraser, Sir Ian, Kt., D.S.O., O.B.E.

Fraser, Sir James David, Bt. (1943).

Fraser, Sir Keith Charles Adolphus, Bt. (1806).

Fraser, Sir Robert Brown, Kt., O.B.E.

Fraser, Sir (William) Robert, K.C.B., K.B.E.

Frederick, *Maj.* Sir Charles Boscawen, Bt. (1723).

Freeland, *Lt.-Gen.* Sir Ian Henry, G.B.E., K.C.B., D.S.O.

Freeman, Sir John Keith Noel, Bt. (1945).

Freeman, Sir (Nathaniel) Bernard, Kt., C.B.E.

Freeman, Sir Ralph, Kt., C.V.O., C.B.E.

Fretwell, Sir George Herbert, K.B.E., C.B.

Freund, Sir Otto Kahn-, Kt., Q.C., F.B.A.

Frith, *Brig.* Sir Eric Herbert Cokayne, Kt., C.B.E.

Frome, Sir Norman Frederick, Kt., C.I.E., D.F.C.

Frost, *Hon.* Sir Sydney Thomas, Kt.

Fry, Sir John Nicholas Pease, Bt. (1894).

Fry, Sir Leslie Alfred Charles, K.C.M.G., O.B.E.

Fryars, Sir Robert Furness, Kt.

Fryberg, Sir Abraham, Kt., M.B.E.

Fuchs, Sir Vivian Ernest, Kt., Ph.D.

Fuller, *Hon.* Sir John Bryan Munro, Kt.

Fuller, *Maj.* Sir (John) Gerard (Henry Fleetwood), Bt. (1910).

Fung Ping-Fan, *Hon.* Sir Kenneth Kt., C.B.E.

Furlonge, Sir Geoffrey Warren, K.B.E., C.M.G.

Furness, Sir Stephen Roberts, Bt. (1913).

Gadsdon, Sir Lawrence Percival, Kt.

Gage, Sir Berkeley Everard Foley, K.C.M.G.

Gaggero, Sir George, Kt., O.B.E.

Gairdner, *General* Sir Charles Henry, G.B.E., K.C.M.G., K.C.V.O., C.B.

Gaitskell, Sir Arthur, Kt., C.M.G.

Gale, *General* Sir Richard Nelson, G.C.B., K.B.E., D.S.O., M.C.

Gallwey, Sir Philip Frankland-Payne-, Bt. (1812).

Galpern, Sir Myer, Kt., M.P.

Galpin, Sir Albert James, K.C.V.O., C.B.E.

Galsworthy, Sir Arthur Norman, K.C.M.G.

Galsworthy, Sir John Edgar, K.C.V.O., C.M.G.

Gamble, Sir David Arthur Josias, Bt. (1897).

Gamble, Sir (Frederick) Herbert K.B.E., C.M.G.

Ganilau, *Ratu* Sir Penaia Kanatabatu, K.B.E., C.M.G., C.V.O., D.S.O.

Gardener, Sir Alfred John, K.C.M.G., C.B.E.

Gardner, Sir Douglas Bruce Bruce-, Bt. (1945).

Garlick, Sir John, K.C.B.

Garner, Sir Harry Mason, K.B.E., C.B.

Garran, Sir (Isham) Peter, K.C.M.G.

Garrett, *Lt.-Gen.* Sir (Alwyn) Ragnar, K.B.E., C.B.

Garrett, Sir (Joseph) Hugh, K.C.I.E., C.S.I.

Garrett, *Hon.* Sir Raymond William, Kt., A.F.C.

Garrett, Sir William Herbert, Kt., M.B.E.

Garrow, Sir Nicholas, Kt., O.B.E.

Garthwaite, Sir William Francis Cuthbert, Bt., D.S.C. (1910).

Garvey, Sir Ronald Herbert, K.C.M.G., K.C.V.O., M.B.E.

Garvey, Sir Terence Willcocks, K.C.M.G.

Gascoigne, *Maj.-Gen.* Sir Julian Alvery, K.C.M.G., K.C.V.O., C.B., D.S.O.

Gass, Sir Michael David Irving, K.C.M.G.

Gasson, Sir Lionel Bell, Kt.

Gault, *Brig.* Sir James Frederick, K.C.M.G., M.V.O., O.B.E.

Geddes, Sir (Anthony) Reay (Mackay), K.B.E.

Gentry, *Maj.-Gen.* Sir William George, K.B.E., C.B., D.S.O.

George, Sir Arthur Thomas, Kt.

Georges, Sir (James) Olva, Kt., O.B.E.

Geraghty, Sir William, K.C.B.

Gerahty, Sir Charles Cyril, Kt., Q.C.

German, Sir Ronald Ernest, K.C.B., C.M.G.

Gethin, *Lt.-Col.* Sir Richard Patrick St. Lawrence, Bt. (I 1665).

Gibberd, Sir Frederick, Kt., C.B.E., R.A.

Gibbon, *General* Sir John Houghton, K.C.B., O.B.E.

Gibbons, Sir John Edward, Bt. (1752).

Gibbs, Sir Frank Stannard, K.B.E., C.M.G.

Gibbs, *Air Marshal* Sir Gerald Ernest, K.B.E., C.I.E., M.C.

Gibbs, *Rt. Hon.* Sir Harry Talbot, K.B.E.

Gibbs, *Rt. Hon.* Sir Humphrey Vicary, G.C.V.O., K.C.M.G., O.B.E.

Gibbs, *General* Sir Roland Christopher, G.C.B., C.B.E., D.S.O., M.C

Gibson, Sir Christopher Herbert, Bt. (1931).

Gibson, *Rev.* Sir David, Bt. (1926).

Gibson, *Vice-Adm.* Sir Donald Cameron Ernest Forbes, K.C.B., D.S.C.

Gibson, Sir Donald Edward Evelyn, Kt., C.B.E.

Gibson, Sir John Hinshelwood, Kt., C.B., T.D., Q.C.

Gibson, *Hon.* Sir Marcus George, Kt.

Gibson, *Rt. Hon.* Sir Maurice White, Kt.

Gibson, Sir Ronald George, Kt., C.B.E., F.R.C.P.

Giddings, *Air Marshal* Sir (Kenneth Charles) Michael, K.C.B., O.B.E., D.F.C., A.F.C.

Gielgud, Sir (Arthur) John, Kt.

Gilbert, *Brig.* Sir Herbert Ellery, K.B.E., D.S.O.

Gilbey, Sir (Walter) Derek, Bt. (1893).

Gilchrist, Sir Andrew Graham, K.C.M.G.

Giles, Sir Alexander Falconer, K.B.E., C.M.G.

Giles, Sir Henry Norman, Kt., O.B.E.

Gillan, Sir (James) Angus, K.B.E., C.M.G.

Gillard, *Hon.* Sir Oliver James, Kt.

Gillett, Sir Edward Bailey, Kt.

Gillett, Sir (Sydney) Harold, Bt., M.C. (1959).

Gilliat, *Lt.-Col.* Sir Martin John, K.C.V.O., M.B.E.

Gillies, Sir Alexander, Kt.

Gilmour, Sir John Edward, Bt., D.S.O., T.D., M.P. (1897).

Gilmour, Sir John Little, Bt. (1926).

Gilroy, *His Eminence Cardinal* Norman Thomas, K.B.E.

Gladstone, Sir (Erskine) William, Bt. (1846).

Gladstone, *Admiral* Sir Gerald Vaughan, G.B.E., K.C.B.

Glass, Sir Leslie Charles, K.C.M.G.

Glen, Sir Alexander Richard, K.B.E., D.S.O.

Glenn, Sir Joseph Robert Archibald, Kt., O.B.E.

Glennie, *Admiral* Sir Irvine Gordon, K.C.B.

Glock, Sir William Frederick, Kt., C.B.E.

Glover, Sir Charles John, Kt.

Glover, *Col.* Sir Douglas, Kt., T.D.

Glover, Sir Gerald Alfred, Kt.

Glubb, *Lt.-Gen.* Sir John Bagot, K.C.B., C.M.G., D.S.O., O.B.E., M.C.

Gluckstein, Sir Louis Halle, G.B.E., T.D., Q.C.

Glyn, Sir Anthony Geoffrey Leo Simon, Bt. (1927).

Glyn, *Col.* Sir Richard Hamilton, Bt., O.B.E., T.D. (1759 and 1800).

Goad, Sir (Edward) Colin (Viner), K.C.M.G.

Godber, Sir George Edward, G.C.B., D.M.

Goddard, *Air Marshal* Sir (Robert) Victor, K.C.B., C.B.E.

Godfrey, Sir Walter, K.B.E.

Godwin, *Prof.* Sir Harry, Kt., F.R.S.

Goff, Sir Ernest (William) Davis-, Bt. (1905).

Goff, *Rt. Hon.* Sir Reginald William, Kt.

Goff, *Hon.* Sir Robert Lionel Archibald, Kt.

Goldman, Sir Samuel, K.C.B.

Goldsmid, Sir Henry Joseph d'Avigdor-, Bt., D.S.O., M.C. (1934).

Goldsmith, Sir Allen John Bridson, K.C.V.O., F.R.C.S.

Goldsmith, Sir James Michael, Kt.

Gombrich, *Prof.* Sir Ernst Hans Josef, Kt., C.B.E., Ph.D., F.B.A., F.S.A.

Gomes, Sir Stanley Eugene, Kt.

Gonzi, *Most Rev. Monsignor* Michael, K.B.E., D.D. (*Archbishop of Malta*).

Gooch, Sir Robert Douglas, Bt. (1866).

Gooch, *Col.* Sir Robert Eric Sherlock, Bt., K.C.V.O., D.S.O. (1746).

Goodale, Sir Ernest William, Kt., C.B.E., M.C.

Goodbody, *General* Sir Richard Wakefield, G.C.B., K.B.E., D.S.O.

Goode, Sir William Allmond Codrington, G.C.M.G.

Goodenough, Sir Richard Edmund, Bt. (1943).

Goodeve, Sir Charles Frederick, Kt., O.B.E., V.D., F.R.S.

Goodhart, Sir John Gordon, Bt. (1911).

Goodsell, Sir John William, Kt., C.M.G.

Goodson, *Lt.-Col.* Sir Alfred Lassam, Bt. (1922).

Goodwin, Sir Reginald Eustace, Kt., C.B.E.

Goodwin, *Lt.-Gen.* Sir Richard Elton, K.C.B., C.B.E., D.S.O.

Goold, Sir George Leonard, Bt. (1801).

Goonetilleke, Sir Oliver Ernest, G.C.M.G., K.C.V.O., K.B.E.

Gordon, Lord Adam Granville, K.C.V.O., M.B.E.

Gordon, Sir Andrew Cosmo Lewis Duff-, Bt. (1813).

Gordon, Sir John Charles, Bt. (S 1706).

Gordon, Sir Lionel Eldred Pottinger Smith-, Bt. (1838).

Gordon, *Hon.* Sir Sidney Samuel, Kt., C.B.E.

Gore, Sir Richard Ralph St. George, Bt. (I 1622).

Goring, Sir William Burton Nigel, Bt. (1627).

Goschen, Sir Edward Christian Bt., D.S.O. (1916).

Gosling, Sir Arthur Hulin, K.B.E., C.B., F.R.S.E.

Gosling, Sir Frederick Donald, Kt.

Gothard, Sir Clifford Frederic, Kt., O.B.E.

Gotz, *Hon.* Sir (Frank) Léon (Aroho), K.C.V.O.

Gough, Sir Arthur Ernest, Kt.

Gould, Sir Ronald, Kt.

Gould, *Hon.* Sir Trevor Jack, Kt.

Goulding, *Hon.* Sir (Ernest) Irvine, Kt.

Goulding, Sir William Basil, Bt. (1904).

Gourlay, *General* Sir (Basil) Ian (Spencer), K.C.B., O.B.E., M.C., R.M.

Gowans, *Hon.* Sir (Urban) Gregory, Kt.

Gower, Sir (Herbert) Raymond, Kt., M.P.

Graaff, Sir de Villiers, Bt., M.B.E. (1911).

Grace, Sir John te Herekiekie, Kt., M.V.O.

Grace, Sir Raymond Eustace, Bt. (1795).

Graesser, *Col.* Sir Alastair Stewart Durward, Kt., D.S.O., O.B.E., M.C., T.D.

Graham, *Admiral* Sir Angus Edward Malise Bontine Cunninghame, K.B.E., C.B.

Graham, Sir (Frederick) Fergus, Bt., K.B.E., T.D. (1783).

Graham, Sir John Moodie, Bt. (1964).

Graham, *Hon.* Sir (John) Patrick, Kt.

Graham, Sir John Reginald Noble, Bt., $\mathcal{VC}$, O.B.E. (1906).

Graham, Sir Montrose Stuart, Bt. (1629).

Graham, Sir Norman William, Kt., C.B.

Graham, Sir Richard Bellingham, Bt., O.B.E. (1662).

Grandy, *Marshal of the Royal Air Force* Sir John, G.C.B., K.B.E., D.S.O.

Grant, Sir Archibald, Bt. (S 1705).

Grant, *Maj.* Sir Ewan George Macpherson-, Bt. (1838).

Grant, Sir James Monteith, K.C.V.O.

Grant, Sir Kenneth Lindsay, Kt., O.B.E.

Grant, Sir Patrick Alexander Benedict, Bt. (S 1688).

Grantham, Sir Alexander William George Herder, G.C.M.G.

Grantham, *Admiral* Sir Guy, G.C.B., C.B.E., D.S.O.

Granville, Sir Keith, Kt., C.B.E.

Gray, Sir John Archibald Browne, Kt., G.D., F.R.S.

Gray, *Vice-Adm.* Sir John Michael Dudgeon, K.B.E., C.B.

Gray, Sir William, Bt. (1917).

Gray, Sir William Stevenson, Kt.

Grayson, Sir Ronald Henry Rudyard, Bt. (1922).

Greatbatch, Sir Bruce, Kt., K.C.V.O., C.M.G., M.B.E.

Greaves, Sir John Bewley, Kt., C.M.G., O.B.E.

Greaves, Sir (William) Walter, K.B.E.

Green, Sir (Edward) Stephen (Lycett), Bt., C.B.E. (1886).

Green, Sir George Edward, Kt.

Green, Sir John, Kt.

Green, *Lt.-Gen.* Sir (William) Wyndham, K.B.E., C.B., D.S.O., M.C.

Greenaway, Sir Derek Burdick, Bt., C.B.E. (1933).

Greenaway, Sir Thomas Moore, Kt.

Greene, Sir Hugh Carleton, K.C.M.G., O.B.E.

Greene, Sir (John) Brian Massy-, Kt.

Greenfield, Sir Cornelius Ewen Maclean, K.B.E., C.M.G.

Greenfield, Sir Harry, K.B.E., C.I.E.

Greenwell, Sir Peter McClinbock, Bt. (1906).

Greeson, *Surgeon Vice-Adm.* Sir Clarence Edward, K.B.E., C.B., Q.H.P.

Greeves, *Maj.-Gen.* Sir Stuart, K.B.E., C.B., D.S.O., M.C.

Gretton, *Vice-Adm.* Sir Peter William, K.C.B., D.S.O., O.B.E., D.S.C.

Grey, Sir Anthony Dysart, Bt. (1814).

Grey, Sir Paul Francis, K.C.M.G.

Grierson, Sir Richard Douglas, Bt. (s 1685).

Grieve, Sir (Herbert) Ronald (Robinson), Kt.

Grieve, *Prof.* Sir Robert, Kt.

Griffin, *Admiral* Sir Anthony Templer Frederick Griffith, G.C.B.

Griffin, Sir Charles David, Kt., C.B.E.

Griffin, Sir Elton Reginald, Kt., C.B.E.

Griffin, Sir Francis Frederick, Kt.

Griffin, Sir John Bowes, Kt., Q.C.

Griffiths, Sir Percival Joseph, K.B.E., C.I.E.

Griffiths, Sir Peter Norton-, Bt. (1922).

Griffiths, Sir Reginald Ernest, Kt.

Griffiths, *Hon.* Sir (William) Hugh, Kt., M.C.

Grime, Sir Harold Riley, Kt.

Groom, Sir Thomas Reginald, Kt.

Groom, *Air Marshal* Sir Victor Emmanuel, K.C.V.O., K.B.E., C.B., D.F.C.

Grotrian, Sir John (Appelbe) Brent, Bt. (1934).

Grounds, Sir Roy Burman, Kt.

Grove, Sir Charles Gerald, Bt. (1874).

Grover, Sir Anthony Charles, Kt.

Groves, Sir Charles Barnard, Kt., C.B.E.

Grubb, Sir Kenneth George, K.C.M.G.

Grundy, *Air Marshal* Sir Edouard Michael Fitzfrederick, K.B.E., C.B.

Guest, *Air Marshal* Sir Charles Edward Neville, K.B.E., C.B.

Guinness, Sir Alec, Kt., C.B.E.

Guinness, Sir Kenelm Ernest Lee, Bt. (1867).

Guise, Sir John, G.C.M.G., K.B.E.

Guise, Sir John Grant, Bt. (1783).

Gujadhur, Sir Radhamohun, Kt., C.M.G.

Gull, Sir Michael Swinnerton Cameron, Bt. (1872).

Gunn, Sir William Archer, K.B.E., C.M.G.

Gunning, Sir Robert Charles, Bt. (1778).

Gunston, *Maj.* Sir Derrick Wellesley, Bt., M.C. (1938).

Gunter, Sir Ronald Vernon, Bt. (1901).

Gunther, Sir John Thomson, Kt., C.M.G., O.B.E.

Gutch, Sir John, K.C.M.G., O.B.E.

Guthrie, Sir Giles Connop McEacharn, Bt., O.B.E., D.S.C. (1936).

Guthrie, *Hon.* Sir Rutherford Campbell, Kt., C.M.G.

Guttmann, Sir Ludwig, Kt., C.B.E., M.D., F.R.S.

Habakkuk, Sir Hrothgur John, Kt., F.B.A.

Hackett, *General* Sir John Winthrop, G.C.B., C.B.E., D.S.O., M.C.

Hackett, Sir Maurice Frederick, Kt., O.B.E.

Haddow, Sir (Thomas) Douglas, K.C.B.

Hadley, Sir Leonard Albert, Kt.

Hadow, Sir Gordon, Kt., C.M.G., O.B.E.

Hadow, Sir Reginald Michael, K.C.M.G.

Haines, Sir Cyril Henry, K.B.E.

Hale, Sir Edward, K.B.E., C.B.

Haley, Sir William John, K.C.M.G.

Hall, Sir Arnold Alexander, Kt., F.R.S.

Hall, Sir Douglas Basil, K.C.M.G.

Hall, Sir (Frederick) John (Frank), Bt. (1923).

Hall, Sir John, Kt., O.B.E., M.P.

Hall, Sir John Bernard, Bt. (1919).

Hall, Sir John Hathorn, G.C.M.G., D.S.O., O.B.E., M.C.

Hall, Sir Neville Reynolds, Bt. (s 1687)

Hall, Sir Noel Frederick, Kt.

Hall, Sir Robert de Zouche, K.C.M.G.

Hall, *Brig.* Sir William Henry, Kt., C.B.E., D.S.O., E.D.

Hallett, *Vice-Adm.* Sir Cecil Charles Hughes-, K.C.B., C.B.E.

Halliday, Sir George Clifton, Kt.

Hallinan, Sir (Adrian) Lincoln, Kt.

Hallinan, Sir Charles Stuart, Kt., C.B.E.

Hallinan, Sir Eric, Kt.

Halsey, *Rev.* Sir John Walter Brooke, Bt. (1920).

Hambling, Sir (Herbert) Hugh, Bt. (1924).

Hamilton, Sir (Charles) Denis, Kt., D.S.O.

Hamilton, Sir (Charles) William (Feilden), Kt., O.B.E.

Hamilton, Sir Edward Sydney, Bt. (1776 and 1819).

Hamilton, *Admiral* Sir John Graham, G.B.E., C.B.

Hamilton, Sir Patrick George, Bt. (1937).

Hamilton, Sir (Robert Charles) Richard Caradoc, Bt. (s 1646).

Hamilton, *Capt.* Sir Robert William Stirling-, Bt., R.N. (s 1673).

Hammett, *Hon.* Sir Clifford James, Kt.

Hammick, Sir Stephen George, Bt. (1834).

Hampshire, Sir (George) Peter, K.C.M.G.

Hanbury, Sir John Capel, Kt., C.B.E.

Hancock, *Lt.-Col.* Sir Cyril Percy, K.C.I.E., O.B.E., M.C.

Hancock, Sir Patrick Francis, G.C.M.G.

Hancock, *Air Marshal* Sir Valston Eldridge, K.B.E., C.B., D.F.C.

Hancock, *Prof.* Sir (William) Keith, K.B.E., F.B.A.

Hanger, *Hon.* Sir Mostyn, K.B.E.

Hanham, Sir Michael William, Bt., D.F.C. (1667).

Hankinson, Sir Walter Crossfield, K.C.M.G., O.B.E., M.C.

Hanley, Sir Michael Bowen, K.C.B.

Hanmer, Sir (Griffin Wyndham) Edward, Bt. (1774).

Hannah, *Air Marshal* Sir Colin Thomas, K.C.M.G., K.B.E., C.B.

Hanson, Sir Anthony Leslie Oswald, Bt. (1887).

Hanson, Sir James Edward, Kt.

Hanson, Sir (Charles) John, Bt. (1918).

Hardie, Sir Charles Edgar Mathewes, Kt., C.B.E.

Harding, Sir Harold John Boyer, Kt.

Hardinge, Sir Robert Arnold, Bt. (1801).

Hardingham, Sir Robert Ernest, Kt., C.M.G., O.B.E.

Hardman, Sir Henry, K.C.B.

Hardman, *Air Chief Marshal* Sir (James) Donald (Innes), G.B.E., K.C.B., D.F.C.

Hardy, *Prof.* Sir Alister Clavering, Kt., D.Sc., F.R.S.

Hardy, *General* Sir Campbell Richard, K.C.B., C.B.E., D.S.O., R.M.

Hardy, Sir Harry, Kt.

Hardy, Sir James Douglas, Kt., C.B.E.

Hardy, Sir Rupert John, Bt., (1876).

Hare, Sir Ralph Leigh, Bt. (1818).

Harford, Sir James Dundas, K.B.E., C.M.G.

Harford, Sir (John) Timothy, Bt. (1934).

Har Govind Misra, Sir, Kt., O.B.E.

Harington, *General* Sir Charles Henry Pepys, G.C.B., C.B.E., D.S.O., M.C.

Harland, *Air Marshal* Sir Reginald Edward Wynyard, K.B.E., C.B.

Harington, Sir Richard Dundas, Bt. (1611).

Harkness, Sir Douglas Alexander Earsman, K.B.E.

Harley, Sir Stanley Jaffa, Kt.

Harley, Sir Thomas Winlack, Kt., M.B.E., M.C.

Harman, Sir Cecil William Francis Stafford-King-, Bt. (1914).

Harman, *General* Sir Jack Wentworth, K.C.B., O.B.E., M.C.

Harmer, Sir Frederic Evelyn, Kt., C.M.G.

Harmer, Sir (John) Dudley, Kt., O.B.E.

Harmsworth, Sir (Arthur) Geoffrey (Annesley), Bt. (1918).

Harmsworth, Sir Hildebrand Alfred Beresford, Bt. (1922).

Harper, Sir Arthur Grant, K.C.V.O., C.B.E.

Harpham, Sir William, K.B.E., C.M.G.

Harris, *Marshal of the Royal Air Force* Sir Arthur Travers, Bt., G.C.B., O.B.E., A.F.C. (1953).

Harris, *Prof.* Sir Charles Herbert Stuart-, Kt., C.B.E., M.D.

Harris, Sir Charles Joseph William, K.B.E.

Harris, *Lt.-Gen.* Sir Frederick, K.B.E., C.B., M.C.

Harris, *Lt.-Gen.* Sir Ian Cecil, K.B.E., C.B., D.S.O.

Harris, *Maj.-Gen.* Sir Jack Alexander Sutherland-, K.C.V.O., C.B.

Harris, Sir Jack Wolfred Ashford, Bt. (1932).

Harris, Sir Percy Wyn, K.C.M.G., M.B.E.

Harris, Sir Ronald Montague Joseph, K.C.V.O., C.B.

Harris, Sir William Gordon, K.B.E., C.B.

Harris, Sir William Woolf, Kt., O.B.E.

Harrison, Sir Archibald Frederick, Kt., C.B.E.

Harrison, Sir (Bernard) Guy, Kt.

Harrison, Sir Cyril Ernest, Kt.

Harrison, Sir Geoffrey Wedgwood, G.C.M.G., K.C.V.O.

Harrison, *Col.* Sir (James) Harwood, Bt., T.D., M.P. (1961).

Harrison, Sir Robert Colin, Bt. (1922).

Harrod, Sir (Henry) Roy Forbes, Kt., F.B.A.

Hart, Sir Byrne, Kt., C.B.E., M.C.

Hart, Sir Francis Edmund Turton-, K.B.E.

Hart, Sir George Charles, K.B.E., B.E.M.

Hart, Sir William Ogden, Kt., C.M.G.

Hartley, *Air Marshal* Sir Christopher Harold, K.C.B., C.B.E., D.F.C., A.F.C.

Hartnett, Sir Laurence John, Kt., C.B.E.

Hartopp, Sir John Edmund Cradock-, Bt. (1796).

Hartwell, Sir Brodrick William Charles Elwin, Bt. (1805).

Hartwell, Sir Charles Herbert, Kt., C.M.G.

Harvey, Sir Richard Musgrave, Bt. (1933).

Haskard, Sir Cosmo Dugal Patrick Thomas, K.C.M.G., M.B.E.

Haslam, *Hon.* Sir Alec Leslie, Kt.

Hasluck, *Rt. Hon.* Sir Paul Meernaa Caedwalla, G.C.M.G., G.C.V.O.

Hassan, Sir Joshua Abraham, Kt., C.B.E., M.V.O., Q.C.

Hassett, *General* Sir Francis George, K.B.E., C.B., D.S.O., M.V.O.

Hatty, Sir Cyril James, Kt.

Haughton, Sir James, Kt., C.B.E., Q.P.M.

Havelock, Sir Wilfred Bowen, Kt.

Havers, Cecil Robert, Kt.

Havers, *Air Vice-Marshal* Sir (Ephraim) William, K.B.E., C.B.

Havers, Sir (Robert) Michael (Oldfield), Kt., Q.C., M.P.

Hawker, Sir (Frank) Cyril, Kt.

Hawker, Sir Richard George, Kt.

Hawkins, Sir Arthur Ernest, Kt.

Hawkins, *Admiral* Sir Geoffrey Alan Brooke, K.B.E., C.B., M.V.O., D.S.C.

Hawkins, Sir Humphry Villiers Caesar, Bt. (1778).

Hawkins, *Maj.* Sir Michael Babington Charles, K.C.V.O., M.B.E.

Hawkins, *Vice-Adm.* Sir Raymond Shayle, K.C.B.

Hawley, *Maj.* Sir David Henry, Bt. (1795).

Haworth, Sir (Arthur) Geoffrey, Bt. (1911).

Haworth, *Hon.* Sir William Crawford, Kt.

Hawthorne, *Prof.* Sir William Rede, Kt., C.B.E., Sc.D., F.R.S.

Hawton, Sir John Malcolm Kenneth, K.C.B.

Hay, Sir (Alan) Philip, K.C.V.O., T.D.

Hay, Sir Arthur Thomas Erroll, Bt., I.S.O. (S 1663)

Hay, Sir Frederick Baden-Powell, Bt. (S 1703)

Hay, Sir James Brian Dalrymple-, Bt. (1798).

Hay, *Lt.-Gen.* Sir Robert, K.C.I.E.

Hayday, Sir Frederick, Kt., C.B.E.

Hayes, Sir Claude James, K.C.M.G.

Hayes, *Vice-Adm.* Sir John Osier Chattock, K.C.B., O.B.E.

Hayman, Sir Peter Telford, K.C.M.G., C.V.O., M.B.E.

Haynes, Sir George Ernest, Kt., C.B.E.

Hayter, Sir William Goodenough, K.C.M.G.

Hayward, Sir Alfred, K.B.E.

Hayward, Sir Charles William, Kt., C.B.E.

Hayward, Sir Edward Waterfield, Kt.

Hayward, Sir Richard Arthur, Kt., C.B.E.

Head, Sir Francis David Somerville, Bt. (1838).

Heald, *Rt. Hon.* Sir Lionel Frederick, Kt., Q.C.

Healey, *Maj.* Sir Edward Randal Chadwyck-, Bt., M.C. (1919).

Heap, Sir Desmond, Kt.

Heath, *Air Marshal* Sir Maurice Lionel, K.B.E., C.B.

Heathcote, Sir Michael Perryman, Bt. (1733).

Heaton, Sir Yvo Robert Henniker-, Bt. (1912).

Hedges, Sir John Francis, Kt., C.B.E.

Heinze, *Prof.* Sir Bernard Thomas, Kt., LL.D.

Hellings, *General* Sir Peter William Cradock, K.C.B., D.S.C., M.C., R.M.

Helpmann, Sir Robert Murray, Kt., C.B.E.

Henderson, Sir Guy Wilmot McLintock, Kt., Q.C.

Henderson, Sir James Thyne, K.B.E., C.M.G.

Henderson, Sir John, Kt.

Henderson, Sir (John) Nicholas, K.C.M.G.

Henderson, Sir Malcolm Siborne, K.C.M.G.

Henderson, Sir Neville Vicars, Kt., C.B.E.

Henderson, *Admiral* Sir Nigel Stuart, G.B.E., K.C.B.

Henderson, Sir Peter Gordon, K.C.B.

Henderson, Sir William MacGregor, Kt., D.S.C., F.R.S.

Hendy, Sir Philip, Kt.

Henig, Sir Mark, Kt.

Henley, Sir Douglas Owen, K.C.B.

Henley, *Rear-Adm.* Sir Joseph Charles Cameron, K.C.V.O., C.B.

Hennessy, Sir John Wyndham Pope-, Kt., C.B.E., F.B.A., F.S.A.

Hennessy, Sir Patrick, Kt.

Henniker, *Brig.* Sir Mark Chandos Auberton, Bt., C.B.E., D.S.O., M.C. (1813).

Henriques, *Hon.* Sir Cyril George Xavier, Kt.

Henry, *Hon.* Sir Albert Royle, K.B.E.

Harry, Sir Denis Aynsley, Kt., O.B.E., Q.C.

Henry, Sir James Holmes, Bt., C.M.G., M.C., T.D., Q.C. (1923).

Henry, *Hon.* Sir Trevor Ernest, Kt.

Henty, *Hon.* Sir Norman Henry Denham, K.B.E.

Hepburn, Sir Ninian Buchan Archibald John Buchan-, Bt. (1815).

Herbert, *Lt.-Gen.* Sir (Edwin) Otway, K.B.E., C.B., D.S.O.

Herchenroder, Sir (Marie Joseph Barnabe) Francis, Kt., Q.C.

Heron, Sir Conrad Frederick, K.C.B., O.B.E.

Herries, Sir Michael Alexander Robert Young-, Kt., O.B.E., M.C.

Herring, *Lt.-Gen. Hon.* Sir Edmund Francis, K.C.M.G., K.B.E., D.S.O., M.C., E.D., Q.C.

Hetherington, Sir Arthur Ford, Kt., D.S.C.

Heward, *Air Chief Marshal* Sir Anthony Williamson, K.C.B., O.B.E., D.F.C., A.F.C.

Hewetson, *General* Sir Reginald Hackett, G.C.B., C.B.E., D.S.O.

Hewett, Sir John George, Bt., M.C. (1813).

Hewitt, Sir (Cyrus) Lenox (Simson), Kt., O.B.E.

Hewitt, Sir Nicholas Charles Joseph, Bt. (1921).

Hewitt, Sir John Francis, K.C.V.O., C.B.E.

Hewitt, Sir Nicholas Charles Joseph, Bt. (1921).

Heyes, Sir Tasman Hudson Eastwood, Kt., C.B.E.

Heygate, Sir George Lloyd, Bt. (1831).

Heyman, Sir Horace William, Kt.

Heymanson, Sir (Sydney Henry) Randal, Kt., C.B.E.

Heywood, Sir Oliver Kerr, Bt. (1838).

Hezlet, *Vice-Adm.* Sir Arthur Richard, K.B.E., C.B., D.S.O., D.S.C.

Hickinbotham, Sir Tom, K.C.M.G., K.C.V.O., C.I.E., O.B.E.

Hickman, Sir (Alfred) Howard (Whitby), Bt. (1903).

Hicks, Sir (Cedric) Stanton, Kt., M.D., Ph.D.

Hicks, *Col.* Sir Denys Theodore, Kt., O.B.E., T.D.

Hicks, Sir Edwin William, Kt., C.B.E.

Hicks, *Prof.* Sir John Richard, Kt., F.B.A.

Higgs, Sir (John) Michael (Clifford), Kt.

Hildred, Sir William Percival, Kt., C.B., O.B.E.

Hildreth, *Maj.-Gen.* Sir (Harold) John (Crossley), K.B.E.

Hildyard, Sir David Henry Thoroton, K.C.M.G., D.F.C.

Hiley, *Hon.* Sir Thomas Alfred, K.B.E.

Hill, *Prof.* Sir Austin Bradford, Kt., C.B.E., Ph.D., D.SC., F.R.S.

Hill, Sir (George) Cyril Rowley, Bt. (1 1779).

Hill, *Prof.* Sir Ian George Wilson, Kt., C.B.E., T.D., F.R.S.E.

Hill, Sir James Frederick, Bt. (1917).

Hill, Sir (James William) Francis, Kt., C.B.E.

Hill, *Prof.* Sir (John) Denis (Nelson), Kt.

Hill, Sir John McGregor, Kt., Ph.D.

Hill, Sir John Maxwell, Kt., C.B.E., D.F.C.

Hill, Sir Robert Erskine-, Bt. (1945).

Hillary, Sir Edmund, K.B.E.

Hilton, Sir Derek Percy, Kt., M.B.E.

Himsworth, Sir Harold Percival, K.C.B., M.D., F.R.S.

Hinchliffe, Sir (Albert) Henry (Stanley), Kt.

Hinde, *Maj.-Gen.* Sir (William) Robert (Norris), K.B.E., C.B., D.S.O.

Hines, Sir Colin Joseph, Kt., O.B.E.

Hirsch, *Prof.* Sir Peter Bernhard, Kt., Ph.D., F.R.S.

Hitchman, Sir (Edwin) Alan, K.C.B.

Hoare, Sir Frederick Alfred, Bt. (1962).

Hoare, Sir Peter Richard David, Bt. (1785).

Hoare, Sir Timothy Edward Charles, Bt. (1 1784).

Hobart, *Lt.-Cdr.* Sir Robert Hampden, Bt., R.N. (1914).

Hobhouse, Sir Charles Chisholm, Bt., T.D. (1812).

Hochoy, Sir Solomon, G.C.M.G., G.C.V.O., O.B.E.

Hodge, Sir John Rowland, Bt., M.B.E. (1921).

Hodge, Sir Julian Stephen Alfred, Kt.

Hodges, *Air Chief Marshal* Sir Lewis MacDonald, K.C.B., C.B.E., D.S.O., D.F.C.

Hodgkin, *Prof.* Sir Alan Lloyd, O.M., K.B.E., F.R.S., SC.D.

Hodgkinson, *Air Chief Marshal* Sir (William) Derek, K.C.B., C.B.E., D.F.C., A.F.C.

Hodson, Sir Michael Robin Adderley, Bt. (1 1789).

Hogan, Sir Michael Joseph Patrick, Kt., C.M.G.

Hogg, *Vice-Adm.* Sir Ian Leslie Trower, K.C.B., D.S.C.

Hogg, Sir John Nicholson, Kt., T.D.

Hogg, *Lieut.-Col.* Sir Kenneth Weir, Bt., O.B.E. (1846).

Hogg, Sir William Lindsay Lindsay-, Bt. (1905).

Holbrook, *Col.* Sir Claude Vivian, Kt., C.B.E.

Holcroft, Sir Reginald Culcheth, Bt. (1921).

Holden, Sir David Charles Beresford, K.B.E., C.B., E.R.D.

Holden, Sir Edward, Bt. (1893).

Holden, Sir George, Bt. (1919).

Holden, Sir James Robert, Kt.

Holden, *Hon.* Sir Michael Herbert Frank, Kt., C.B.E., E.D.

Holder, Sir John Eric Duncan, Bt. (1898).

Holder, *Air Marshal* Sir Paul Davie, K.B.E., C.B., D.S.O., D.F.C., Ph.D.

Holderness, Sir Richard William, Bt. (1920).

Holland, Sir Clifton Vaughan, Kt.

Holland, Sir Jim Sothern, Bt. (1917).

Hollings, *Hon.* Sir (Alfred) Kenneth, Kt., M.C.

Hollom, Sir Jasper Quintus, K.B.E.

Holmes, *Hon.* Sir (David) Ronald Kt., C.M.G., C.B.E., M.C., E.D.

Holmes, *Prof.* Sir Frank Wakefield Kt.

Holmes, Sir Maurice Andrew, Kt.

Holmes, *Maj.-Gen.* Sir Noel Galway, K.B.E., C.B., M.C.

Holmes, Sir Stanley, Kt.

Holmes, Sir Stephen Lewis, K.C.M.G., M.C.

Holt, Sir James Arthur, Kt.

Holt, Sir John Anthony Langford-, Kt., M.P.

Holyoake, *Rt. Hon.* Sir Keith Jacka, G.C.M.G., C.H.

Home, Sir David George, Bt. (S 1671)

Hone, Sir Brian William, Kt., O.B.E.

Hone, Sir Evelyn Denison, G.C.M.G., C.V.O., O.B.E.

Hone, *Maj.-Gen.* Sir (Herbert) Ralph, K.C.M.G., K.B.E., M.C., T.D., Q.C.

Honywood, *Col.* Sir William Wynne, Bt., M.C. (1660).

Hood, *Lt.-Gen.* Sir Alexander, G.B.E., K.C.B., K.C.V.O., M.D.

Hood, Sir Alexander William Fuller-Acland-, Bt. (1806).

Hood, Sir Harold Joseph, Bt., T.D. (1922).

Hood, *Col.* Sir Tom Fielden, K.B.E., C.B., T.D.

Hooker, Sir Leslie Joseph, Kt.

Hooker, Sir Stanley George, Kt., C.B.E., D.SC., D.Phil, F.R.S.

Hooper, Sir Stanley Robin Maurice, Bt. (1962).

Hooper, Sir Leonard James, K.C.M.G., C.B.E.

Hooper, Sir Robin William John, K.C.M.G., D.S.O., D.F.C.

Hope, Sir Archibald Philip, Bt., O.B.E., D.F.C. (S 1628).

Hope, Sir (Charles) Peter, K.C.M.G., T.D.

Hope, Sir James, Bt., M.M. (1932).

Hopkin, Sir (William Aylsham) Bryan, Kt., C.B.E.

Hopkins, *Admiral* Sir Frank Henry Edward, K.C.B., D.S.O., D.S.C.

Horlick, Sir John James Macdonald, Bt. (1914).

Hornby, Sir (Roger) Antony, Kt.

Horne, Sir Alan Edgar, Bt., M.C. (1929).

Hornibrook, Sir Manuel Richard, Kt., O.B.E.

Hornung, *Lt.-Col.* Sir John Derek, K.C.V.O., O.B.E., M.C.

Horrocks, *Lt.-Gen.* Sir Brian Gwynne, K.C.B., K.B.E., D.S.O., M.C.

Horsfall, Sir John Musgrave, Bt., M.C., T.D. (1909).

Horsley, *Air Marshal* Sir (Beresford) Peter (Torrington), K.C.B., C.B.E., M.V.O., A.F.C.

Hort, Sir James Fenton, Bt. (1767).

Hoskyns, Sir Benedict Leigh, Bt. (1676).

Hotchin, Sir Claude, Kt., O.B.E.

Houldsworth, Sir (Harold) Basil, Bt. (1956).

Houldsworth, Sir Reginald Douglas Henry, Bt., O.B.E., T.D. (1887).

House, *Lt.-Gen.* Sir David George, K.C.B., C.B.E., M.C.

How, Sir Friston Charles, Kt., C.B.

Howard, Sir Douglas Frederick, K.C.M.G., M.C.

Howard, Sir (Hamilton) Edward de Coucey, Bt., G.B.E. (1955).

Howard, Sir John Alfred Golding, Kt.

Howard, *Maj.-Gen.* Lord Michael Fitzalan-, K.C.V.O., C.B., C.B.E., M.C.

Howard, Sir Walter Stewart, Kt., M.B.E.

Howe, *Rt. Hon.* Sir (Richard Edward) Geoffrey, Kt., Q.C., M.P.

Howe, Sir Robert George, G.B.E., K.C.M.G.

Howe, Sir Ronald Martin, Kt., C.V.O., M.C.

Howie, Sir James William, Kt., M.D.

Hoyle, *Prof.* Sir Fred, Kt., F.R.S.

Hubble, *Prof.* Sir Douglas Vernon K.B.E., M.D.

Huddie, Sir David Patrick, Kt.

Hudleston, *Air Chief Marshal* Sir Edmund Cuthbert, G.C.B., C.B.E.

Hudson, Sir Edmund Peder, Kt., F.R.S.E.

Hudson, Sir William, K.B.E., F.R.S.

Hughes, Sir David Collingwood, Bt. (1773).

Hughes, *Air Marshal* Sir (Sidney Weetman) Rochford, K.C.B., C.B.E., A.F.C.

Hughes, Sir Trevor Denby Lloyd-, Kt.

Hugo, *Lt.-Col.* Sir John Mandeville, K.C.V.O., O.B.E.

Hull, *Field Marshal* Sir Richard Amyatt, G.C.B., D.S.O.

Hulme, *Hon.* Sir Alan Shallcross, K.B.E.

Hulse, Sir (Hamilton) Westrow, Bt. (1739).

Hulton, Sir Edward George Warris, Kt.

Hulton, Sir Geoffrey Alan, Bt. (1905).

Hume, Sir Alan Blyth, Kt., C.B.

Humphrey, *Marshal of the Royal Air Force* Sir Andrew Henry, G.C.B., O.B.E., D.F.C., A.F.C.

Humphreys, Sir Kenneth Owens, Kt.

Humphreys, Sir Olliver William, Kt., C.B.E.

Hunn, Sir Jack Kent, Kt., C.M.G.

Hunt, Sir David Wathen Stather, K.C.M.G., O.B.E.

Hunt, Sir John Joseph Benedict, K.C.B.

Hunt, Sir Joseph Anthony, Kt., M.B.E.

Hunt, *General* Sir Peter Mervyn, G.C.B., D.S.O., O.B.E.

Hunter, *Hon.* Sir Alexander Albert, K.B.E.

Hunter, Sir (Ernest) John, Kt., C.B.E.

Hurley, Sir John Garling, Kt., C.B.E.

Hurley, Sir Wilfred Hugh, Kt.

Hurst, *His Hon.* Sir (James Henry) Donald, Kt.

Husband, Sir (Henry) Charles, Kt., C.B.E.

Hutchinson, Sir Arthur Sydney, K.B.E., C.B., C.V.O.

Hutchinson, Sir Joseph Burtt, Kt., C.M.G., SC.D., F.R.S.

Hutchison, *Lt.-Cdr.* Sir (George) Ian Clark, Kt., R.N.

Hutchison, *Hon.* Sir James Douglas, Kt.

Hutchison, Sir James Riley Holt, Bt., D.S.O., T.D. (1956).

Hutchison, Sir Peter, Bt. (1939).

Hutchison, Sir (William) Kenneth, Kt., C.B.E., F.R.S.

Hutson, Sir Francis Challenor, Kt., C.B.E.

Hutt, Sir (Alexander McDonald) Bruce, K.B.E., C.M.G.

Hutton, Sir Leonard, Kt.

Hutton, Sir Noel Kilpatrick, K.C.B., Q.C.

Hutton, *Lt.-Gen.* Sir Thomas, G.C.I.E., C.B., M.C.

Huxley, *Prof.* Sir Andrew Fielding, Kt., F.R.S.

Huxley, Sir Leonard George Holden, K.B.E., D.Phil., Ph.D.

Hyatali, *Hon.* Sir Isaac Emanuel, Kt.

Hynes, Sir Lincoln Carruthers, Kt., O.B.E.

Ibadan, The Olubadan of, Kt., O.B.E.

Ife, The Oni of, K.C.M.G., K.B.E.

Iggulden, Sir Douglas Percy, Kt., C.B.E., D.S.O., T.D.

Illingworth, *Prof.* Sir Charles Frederick William, Kt., C.B.E.

Ilott, Sir John Moody Albert, Kt.

Imrie, Sir John Dunlop, Kt., C.B.E.

Inch, Sir John Ritchie, Kt., C.V.O., C.B.E.

Indore, H.H. *ex-*Maharaja Holkar of, G.C.I.E.

Ingilby, Sir Thomas Colvin William, Bt. (1866).

Inglefield, Sir Gilbert Samuel, G.B.E., T.D.

Inglefield, *Col.* Sir John Frederick Crompton-, Kt., T.D.

Inglis, *Maj.-Gen.* Sir Drummond, K.B.E., C.B., M.C.

Inglis of Glencorse, Sir Roderick John, Bt. (S 1703).

Ingram, Sir Herbert, Bt. (1893).

Innes, Sir Charles Kenneth Gordon, Bt. (N.S. 1686).

Innes, Sir Walter James, Bt. (S 1628).

Inniss, *Hon.* Sir Clifford de Lisle, Kt.

Inmiss, Sir Probyn Ellsworth, Kt.

Irish, Sir Ronald Arthur, Kt., O.B.E.

Ironmonger, Sir (Charles) Ronald, Kt.

Irvine, *Rt. Hon.* Sir Arthur James, Kt., Q.C., M.P.

Irving, *Rear-Adm.* Sir Edmund George, K.B.E., C.B.

Irwin, Sir James Campbell, Kt., O.B.E., E.D.

Isham, Sir Ivan Vere Gyles, Bt. (1627).

Issigonis, Sir Alec Arnold Constantine, Kt., C.B.E., F.R.S.

Ismay, Sir George, K.B.E., C.B.

Jack, *Hon.* Sir Alieu Sulayman, Kt.

Jack, Sir Daniel Thomson, Kt., C.B.E.

Jack, *Hon.* Sir Roy Emile, Kt.

Jackling, Sir Roger William, G.C.M.G.

Jackman, *Air Marshal* Sir (Harold) Douglas, K.B.E., C.B.

Jackson, Sir Donald Edward, Kt.

Jackson, *Col.* Sir Francis James Gidlow, Kt., M.C., T.D.

Jackson, Sir Geoffrey Holt Seymour, K.C.M.G.

Jackson, Sir George Christopher Mather-, Bt. (1869).

Jackson, Sir Hugh Nicolas, Bt. (1913).

Jackson, Sir John Montrésor, Bt. (1815).

Jackson, *Hon.* Sir Lawrence Walter, K.C.M.G.

Jackson, Sir Michael Roland, Bt. (1902).

Jackson, *Air Vice-Marshal* Sir Ralph Coburn, K.B.E., C.B.

Jackson, Sir Robert Gillman Allen, K.C.V.O., C.M.G., O.B.E.

Jackson, *General* Sir William Godfrey Fothergill, G.B.E., K.C.B., M.C.

Jacob, *Lt.-Gen.* Sir (Edward) Ian (Claud), G.B.E., C.B.

Jacobs, Sir Roland Ellis, Kt.

Jacobs, Sir Wilfred Ebenezer, Kt., O.B.E., Q.C.

Jaffray, Sir William Otho, Bt. (1892).

Jakeway, Sir (Francis) Derek, K.C.M.G., O.B.E.

James, *Wing-Cdr.* Sir Archibald William Henry, K.B.E., M.C.

James, Sir Gerard Bowes Kingston, Bt. (1823).

James, Sir John Hastings, K.C.V.O., C.B.

James, *Rt. Hon.* Sir (John) Morrice (Cairns), G.C.M.G., C.V.O., M.B.E.

Janes, Sir Herbert Charles, Kt.

Jansz, Sir Herbert Eric, Kt., C.M.G.

Janvrin, *Vice-Adm.* Sir (Hugh) Richard (Benest), K.C.B., D.S.C.

Jardine, *Maj.* Sir (Andrew) Rupert (John) Buchanan-, Bt., M.C. (1885).

Jardine, *Brig.* Sir Ian Liddell, Bt., O.B.E., M.C. (1916).

Jardine, Sir William Edward, Bt., O.B.E., T.D. (S 1672).

Jarrett, Sir Clifford George, K.B.E., C.B.

Jawara, *Hon.* Sir Dawda Kairaba, Kt.

Jayetileke, *Hon.* Sir Edward George Perera, Kt., Q.C.

Jeffcoate, *Prof.* Sir (Thomas) Norman (Arthur), Kt., F.R.C.S.

Jefferson, *Lt.-Col.* Sir John Alexander Dunnington-, Bt., D.S.O. (1958).

Jeffreys, *Prof.* Sir Harold, Kt., D.SC., F.R.S.

Jehanghir, Sir Hirjee Cowasjee, Bt. (1908).

Jejeebhoy, Sir Rustom, Bt. (1857).

Jenkin, Sir William Norman Prentice, Kt., C.S.I., C.I.E.

Jenkins, Sir Evan Meredith, G.C.I.E., K.C.S.I.

Jenkins, Sir Owain Trevor, Kt.

Jenkins, Sir (Thomas) Gilmour, K.C.B., K.B.E., M.C.

Jenkins, Sir William, Kt.

Jenkinson, Sir Anthony Banks, Bt. (1661).

Jenks, Sir Richard Atherley, Bt. (1932).

Jennings, Sir Albert Victor, Kt.

Jennings, Sir Raymond Winter, Kt., Q.C.

Jenour, Sir (Arthur) Maynard (Chesterfield), Kt., T.D.

Jephcott, Sir Harry, Bt. (1962).

Jerram, *Rear-Adm.* (S.) Sir Rowland Christopher, K.B.E., D.S.O.

Jessel, Sir George, Bt., M.C. (1883).

Jessel, Sir Richard Hugh, Kt.

Joel, *Hon.* Sir Asher Alexander, K.B.E.

John, *Admiral of the Fleet* Sir Caspar, G.C.B.

John, Sir Rupert Godfrey, Kt.

Johnson, *Hon.* Sir David Powell Croom-, Kt., D.S.C., V.R.D.

Johnson, *Maj.-Gen.* Sir George Frederick, K.C.V.O., C.B., C.B.E., D.S.O.

Johnson, Sir Henry Cecil, K.B.E.

Johnson, Sir Peter Colpoys Paley, Bt. (1755).

Johnson, Sir Ronald Ernest Charles, Kt., C.B.

Johnson, Sir Victor Philipse Hill, Bt. (1818).

Johnson, Sir William Clarence, Kt., C.M.G., C.B.E.

Johnston, Sir Alexander, G.C.B., K.B.E.

Johnston, Sir Charles Collier, Kt., T.D.

Johnston, Sir Charles Hepburn, G.C.M.G.

Johnston, Sir John Baines, K.C.M.G., K.C.V.O.

Johnston, Sir Thomas Alexander, Bt. (S 1626).

Johnstone, Sir Frederic Allan George, Bt. (S 1700).

Joint, Sir (Edgar) James, K.C.M.G., O.B.E.

Jolly, *General* Sir Alan, G.C.B., C.B.E., D.S.O.

Jones, *Maj.-Gen.* Sir (Arthur) Guy Salisbury-. G.C.V.O., C.M.G., C.B.E., M.C.

Jones, Sir Arthur Hope-, K.B.E., C.M.G.

Jones, Sir Brynmor, Kt., Ph.D., Sc.D.

Jones, *General* Sir Charles Phibbs, G.C.B., C.B.E., M.C.

Jones, Sir Christopher Lawrence-, Bt. (1831).

Jones, Sir (David) Fletcher, Kt., O.B.E.

Jones, *Air Marshal* Sir Edward Gordon, K.C.B., C.B.E., D.S.O., D.F.C.

Jones, *Rt. Rev.* Edward Michael Gresford, K.C.V.O., D.D.

Jones, *Rt. Hon.* Sir Edward Warburton, Kt.

Jones, Sir Edwin Martin Furnival, Kt., C.B.E.

Jones, Sir Eric Malcolm, K.C.M.G., C.B., C.B.E.

Jones, Sir Eric Newton Griffith-, K.B.E., C.M.G., Q.C.

Jones, *Prof.* Sir Ewart Ray Herbert, Kt., D.SC., Ph.D., F.R.S.

Jones, Sir Francis Avery, Kt., C.B.E., F.R.C.P.

Jones, *Air Marshal* Sir George, K.B.E., C.B., D.F.C.

Jones, Sir (George) Basil Todd-, Kt.

Jones, Sir Glyn Smallwood, G.C.M.G., M.B.E.

Jones, Sir Harry Ernest, Kt., C.B.E.

Jones, Sir Harry Vincent Lloyd-, Kt.

Jones, Sir Henry Frank Harding, G.B.E.

Jones, Sir Hildreth Glyn-, Kt., T.D.

Jones, Sir James Duncan, K.C.B.

Jones, *Air Marshal* Sir (John) Humphrey Edwardes, K.C.B., C.B.E., D.F.C., A.F.C.

Jones, Sir (John) Kenneth (Trevor), Kt., C.B.E., Q.C.

Jones, Sir John Prichard-, Bt. (1910).

Jones, *Air Chief Marshal* Sir John Whitworth, G.B.E., K.C.B.

Jones, *Hon.* Sir Kenneth George Illtyd, Kt.

Jones, Sir Owen Haddon Wansbrough-, K.B.E., C.B., Ph.D.

Jones, Sir Philip Frederick, Kt.

Jones, Sir Samuel Bankole, Kt.

Jones, Sir Samuel Owen, Kt.

Jones, Sir Simon Warley Frederick Benton, Bt. (1910).

Jones, Sir (William) Emrys, Kt.

Jones, *Hon.* Sir William Lloyd Mars-, Kt., M.B.E.

Jordan, *Air Marshal* Sir Richard Bowen, K.C.B., D.F.C.

Joseph, *Maj.* Sir (Herbert) Leslie, Kt.

Joseph, *Rt. Hon.* Sir Keith Sinjohn, Bt., M.P. (1943).

Jungwirth, Sir William John, Kt., C.M.G.

Jupp, *Hon.* Sir Kenneth Graham, Kt., M.C.

Kaberry, Sir Donald, Bt., T.D., M.P. (1960).

Kadoorie, *Hon.* Sir Leonard, Kt., G.C.I.E.

Kalat, *Maj.* H.H. the Khan of, G.C.I.E.

Kan Yuet-Keung, *Hon.* Sir, Kt., C.B.E.

Karimjee, Sir Tayabali Hassanali Alibhoy, Kt.

Kater, Sir Gregory Blaxland, Kt.

Katsina, The Emir of, K.B.E., C.M.G.

Katz, *Prof.* Sir Bernard, Kt., F.R.S.

Kay, *Prof.* Sir Andrew Watt, Kt.

Kaye, Sir Emmanuel, Kt., C.B.E.

Kaye, Sir John Christopher Lister Lister-, Bt. (1812).

Kay, Sir Stephen Henry Gordon, Bt. (1923).

Keane, Sir Richard Michael, Bt., (1801).

Kearns, Sir Fred Matthias, K.C.B., M.C.

Keatinge, Sir Edgar Mayne, Kt., C.B.E.

Keeling, Sir John Henry, Kt.

Keen, Sir Bernard Augustus, Kt., D.SC., F.R.S.

Keene, Sir Charles Robert, Kt., C.B.E.

Keith, Sir Kenneth Alexander, Kt.

Kellett, Sir Stanley Everard, Bt. (1801).

Kelliher, Sir Henry Joseph, Kt.

Kelly, Sir Arthur John, Kt., C.B.E.

Kelly, Sir William Theodore, Kt., O.B.E.

Kemp, Sir Leslie Charles, K.B.E.

Kemsley, *Col.* Sir Colin Norman Thornton-, Kt., O.B.E., T.D.

Kendall, Sir Maurice George, Kt., SC.D., F.B.A.

Kendrew, *Maj.-Gen.* Sir Douglas Anthony, K.C.M.G., C.B., C.B.E., D.S.O.

Kendrew, Sir John Cowdrey, Kt., C.B.E., SC.D., F.R.S.

Kendrick, Sir Thomas Downing, K.C.B., F.B.A., F.S.A.

Kennard, *Lt.-Col.* Sir George Arnold Ford, Bt. (1891).

Kennaway, Sir John Lawrence, Bt. (1791).

Kennedy, Sir Albert Henry, Kt.

Kennedy, Sir Clyde David Allen, Kt.

Kennedy, Sir George Ronald Derrick, Bt. (1836).

Kenny, Sir Patrick John, Kt.

Kent, Sir Harold Simcox, G.C.B., Q.C.

Kent, Sir Percy Edward (Peter) Kt., D.SC., Ph.D., F.R.S.

Kenyon, Sir Bernard, Kt.

Kenyon, Sir George Henry, Kt.

Kerley, Sir Peter James, K.C.V.O., C.B.E., M.D., F.R.C.P.

Kerr, *Lt.-Col.* Sir Howard, K.C.V.O., C.M.G., O.B.E.

Kerr, *Hon.* Sir John Robert, G.C.M.G.

Kerr, *Hon.* Sir Michael Robert Emanuel, Kt.

Kerr, *Hon.* Sir William Alexander Blair-, Kt.

Kerridge, Sir Robert James, Kt.

Keswick, Sir John Henry, K.C.M.G.

Keswick, Sir William Johnston, Kt.

Keville, Sir (William) Errington, Kt., C.B.E.

Key, Sir Neill Cooper-, Kt.

Keynes, Sir Geoffrey Langdon, Kt., M.D.

Khama, Sir Seretse, K.B.E.

Kiki, *Hon.* Sir Albert Maori, K.B.E.

Killick, Sir John Edward, K.C.M.G.

Kilpatrick, Sir William John, K.B.E.

Kimber, Sir Charles Dixon, Bt. (1904).

Kimmins, *Lt.-Gen.* Sir Brian Charles Hannam, K.B.E., C.B.

Kinahan, *Admiral* Sir Harold Richard George, K.B.E., C.B.

Kinahan, Sir Robert George Caldwell, Kt., E.R.D.

King, Sir Albert, Kt., O.B.E.

King, Sir Anthony Highmore, Kt., C.B.E.

King, Sir (Clifford) Robertson, K.B.E.

King, *General* Sir Frank Douglas, G.C.B., M.B.E.

King, Sir Geoffrey Stuart, K.C.B., K.B.E., M.C.

King, Sir James Granville Le Neve, Bt., T.D. (1888).

King, Sir Richard Brian Meredith, K.C.B., M.C.

King, Sir Sydney Percy, Kt., O.B.E.

King, Sir Wayne Alexander, Bt. (1815).

Kingsley, Sir Patrick Graham Toler, K.C.V.O.

Kininmonth, Sir William Hardie, P.R.S.A., F.R.I.B.A.

Kinloch, Sir Alexander Davenport, Bt. (S 1686).

Kinloch, Sir John, Bt. (1873).

Kipping, Sir Norman Victor, G.C.M.G., K.B.E.

Kirby, Sir Arthur Frank, G.B.E., C.M.G.

Kirby, *Hon.* Sir Richard Clarence, Kt.

Kirk, Sir Peter Michael, Kt., M.P.

Kirkbride, Sir Alec Seath, K.C.M.G., O.B.E., M.C.

Kirkman, *General* Sir Sidney Chevalier, G.C.B., K.B.E., M.G.

Kirkpatrick, Sir Ivone Elliott, Bt. (S 1685).

Kirkwood, Sir Robert Lucien Morrison, K.C.M.G.

Kirwan, Sir (Archibald) Laurence Patrick, K.C.M.G., T.D.

Kitchen, Sir Geoffrey, Kt., T.D.

Kitson, Sir George Vernon, K.B.E.

Kitson, Sir Timothy Peter Geoffrey, Kt., M.P.

Kitto, *Rt. Hon.* Sir Frank Walters, K.B.E.

Kitts, Sir Francis Joseph, Kt.

Kleinwort, Sir Alexander Santiago, Bt. (1909).

Kleinwort, Sir Cyril Hugh, Kt.

Knight, Sir Allan Walton, Kt., C.M.G.

Knight, Sir Arthur William, Kt.

Knott, Sir John Laurence, Kt., C.B.E.

Knowles, Sir Charles Francis, Bt. (1765).

Knowles, Sir Leonard Joseph, Kt., C.B.E.

Knox, Sir (Thomas) Malcolm, Kt.

Koelle, *Vice-Adm.* Sir Harry Philpot, K.C.B.

Kolhapur, *Maj.* H.H. Maharaja of, G.C.S.I.

Kotalawala, *Col. Rt. Hon.* Sir John Lionel, C.H., K.B.E.

Krebs, *Prof.* Sir Hans Adolf, Kt., M.D., F.R.S.

Krusin, Sir Stanley Marks, Kt., C.B.

Kyle, *Air Chief Marshal* Sir Wallace Hart, G.C.B., C.B.E., D.S.O., D.F.C.

Labouchere, Sir George Peter, G.B.E., K.C.M.G.

Lacon, Sir George Vere Francis, Bt. (1818).

Lacy, Sir Hugh Maurice Pierce, Bt. (1921).

Laing, Sir (John) Maurice, Kt.

Laing, Sir John William, Kt., C.B.E.

Laing, Sir (William) Kirby, Kt.

Laithwaite, Sir (John) Gilbert, G.C.M.G., K.C.B., K.C.I.E., C.S.I.

Lake, Sir (Atwell) Graham, Bt. (1711).

Lakin, Sir Henry, Bt. (1909).

Lakshmanaswami Mudaliar, *Diwan Bahadur* Sir Arcot, Kt.

Lala Gujjar Mal, *Rai Bahadur* Sir, Kt.

Lamb, Sir Lionel Henry, K.C.M.G., O.B.E.

Lambart, Sir Oliver Francis, Bt. (1911).

Lambert, Sir Anthony Edward, K.C.M.G.

Lambert, Sir Edward Thomas, K.B.E., C.V.O.

†Lambert, Sir Greville Foley, Bt. (1711).

Lancaster, *Vice-Adm.* Sir John Strike, K.B.E., C.B.

Lancaster, Sir Osbert, Kt., C.B.E.

Lane, *Rt. Hon.* Sir Geoffrey Dawson, Kt., A.F.C.

Lang, *Lt.-Gen.* Sir Derek Boileau, K.C.B., D.S.O., M.C.

Lang, Sir John Gerald, G.C.B.

Langham, Sir James Michael, Bt. (1660).

Langker, Sir Erik, Kt., O.B.E.

Langman, Sir John Lyell, Bt. (1906).

Langrishe, Sir Hercules Ralph Hume, Bt. (I 1777).

Lapsley, *Air Marshal* Sir John Hugh, K.B.E., C.B., D.F.C., A.F.C.

Lapun, Sir Paul, Kt.

Larcom, Sir (Charles) Christopher Royden, Bt. (1868).

Larking, *Lt.-Col.* Sir (Charles) Gordon, Kt., C.B.E.

Lartigue, Sir Louis Cools-, Kt., O.B.E.

Lascelles, *Rt. Hon.* Sir Alan Frederick, G.C.B., G.C.V.O., C.M.G., M.C.

Lascelles, Sir Francis William, K.C.B., M.C.

Lasdun, Sir Denys Louis, Kt., C.B.E., F.R.I.B.A.

Laskey, Sir Denis Seward, K.C.M.G., C.V.O.

Latey, *Hon.* Sir John Brinsmead, Kt., M.B.E.

Latham, Sir Joseph, Kt., C.B.E.

Latham, Sir Richard Thomas Paul, Bt. (1919).

Lathbury, *General* Sir Gerald William, G.C.B., D.S.O., M.B.E.

Latimer, Sir Courtenay Robert, Kt., C.B.E.

Lauder, *Maj.* Sir George Andrew Dick-, Bt. (S 1690).

Laurie, *Maj.-Gen.* Sir John Emilius, Bt., C.B.E., D.S.O. (1834).

Law, *Admiral* Sir Horace Rochfort, G.C.B., O.B.E., D.S.C.

Lawes, Sir John Claud Bennet, Bt. (1882).

Lawrence, Sir David Roland Walter, Bt. (1906).

Lawrence, Sir Frederick, Kt., O.B.E.

Lawrence, Sir Guy Kempton, Kt., D.S.O., O.B.E., D.F.C.

Lawrence, Sir John Waldemar, Bt., O.B.E. (1858).

Lawrence, Sir William, Bt. (1867).

Lawson, Sir Henry Brailsford, Kt., M.C.

Lawson, *Lt.-Col.* Sir John Charles Arthur Digby, Bt., D.S.O., M.C. (1900).

Lawson, *Hon.* Sir Neil, Kt.

Lawson, Sir William Howard, Bt. (1841).

Lawton, *Rt. Hon.* Sir Frederick Horace, Kt.

Laycock, Sir Leslie Ernest, Kt., C.B.E.

Layfield, Sir Frank Henry Burland Willoughby, Kt., Q.C.

Lea, Sir Frederick Meacham, Kt., C.B., C.B.E., D.SC.

Lea, *Lt.-Gen.* Sir George Harris, K.C.B., D.S.O., M.B.E.

Lea, Sir Thomas Claude Harris, Bt. (1892).

Leach, *Prof.* Sir Edmund Ronald, Kt., Ph.D., F.B.A.

Leach, Sir Ronald George, G.B.E.

Leask, *Lt.-Gen.* Sir Henry Lowther Ewart Clark, K.C.B., D.S.O., O.B.E.

Leather, Sir Edwin Hartley Cameron, K.C.M.G., K.C.V.O.

Le Bailly, *Vice-Adm.* Sir Louis Edward Stewart Holland, K.B.E., C.B.

Le Cheminant, *Air Chief Marshal* Sir Peter de Lacey, K.C.B., D.F.C.

Lechmere, Sir Berwick Hungerford, Bt. (1818).

Ledger, Sir Joseph Francis, Kt.

Ledwidge, Sir (William) Bernard (John), K.C.M.G.

Lee, Sir Arthur James, K.B.E., M.C.

Lee, *Air Chief Marshal* Sir David John Pryer, G.B.E., C.B.

Lee, Sir (George) Wilton, Kt.

Lee Hau Shik, *Col.* Sir, K.B.E.

Lee, Sir (Henry) Desmond (Pritchard), Kt.

Lee, *Col.* Sir William Allison, Kt., O.B.E., T.D.

Leeds, Sir George Graham Mortimer, Bt. (1812).

Lees, *Air Marshal* Sir (Ronald) Beresford, K.C.B., C.B.E., D.F.C.

Lees, Sir Thomas Edward, Bt. (1897).

Lees, Sir Thomas Harcourt Ivor, Bt. (1804).

Lees, Sir William Antony Clare, Bt. (1937).

Leese, *Lt.-Gen.* Sir Oliver William Hargreaves, Bt., K.C.B., C.B.E., D.S.O. (1908).

Le Fleming, Sir William Kelland, Bt. (1705).

Le Gallais, *Hon.* Sir Richard Lyle, Kt.

Legard, Sir Thomas Digby, Bt. (1660).

Leggett, Sir Frederick William, K.B.E., C.B.

Legh, *Major Hon.* Sir Francis Michael, K.C.V.O.

Leigh, Sir John, Bt. (1918).

Leighton, Sir Michael John Bryan, Bt. (1693).

Leitch, Sir George, K.C.B., C.B.E.

Leith, Sir Andrew George Forbes-, Bt. (1923).

Le Marchant, Sir Denis, Bt. (1841).

Le Masurier, Sir Robert Hugh, Kt., D.S.C.

Lemon, Sir (Richard) Dawnay, Kt., C.B.E.

Lennard, *Lt.-Col.* Sir Stephen Arthur Hallam Farnaby, Bt. (1880).

Lennard, Sir Thomas Richard Fiennes Barrett-, Bt., O.B.E. (1801).

Lennox, *Rear Adm.* Sir Alexander Henry Charles, K.C.V.O., C.B., D.S.O.

Lennox, *Lt.-Gen.* Sir George Charles Gordon, K.B.E., C.B., C.V.O., D.S.O.

Leon, Sir John Ronald, Bt. (1911).

Le Quesne, Sir (Charles) Martin, K.C.M.G.

Leslie, Sir Harald Robert, K.T., C.B.E., T.D. (Lord Birsay).

Leslie, Sir John Norman Ide, Bt. (1876).

†Leslie, Sir Percy Theodore, Bt. (S 1625).

Lethbridge, *Capt.* Sir Hector Wroth, Bt. (1804).

Lever, Sir (Tresham) Christopher Arthur Lindsay, Bt. (1911).

Levinge, *Maj.* Sir Richard Vere Henry, Bt., M.B.E. (I 1704).

Levy, Sir (Enoch) Bruce, Kt., O.B.E.

Levy, Sir Ewart Maurice, Bt. (1913).

Lewando, Sir Jan Alfred, Kt., C.B.E.

Lewin, *Admiral* Sir Terence Thornton, G.C.B., M.V.O., D.S.C.

Lewis, Sir Allen Montgomery, Kt., Q.C.

Lewis, *Admiral* Sir Andrew Mackenzie, K.C.B.

Lewis, Sir Anthony Carey, Kt., C.B.E.

Lewis, *Brig.* Sir Clinton Gresham, Kt., O.B.E.

Lewis, Sir Edward Roberts, Kt.

Lewis, Sir Ian Malcolm, Kt.

Lewis, Sir (John) Duncan Orr-, Bt. (1920).

Lewis, Sir John Todd, Kt., O.B.E.

Lewis, Sir William Arthur, Kt.

Lewthwaite, Sir William Anthony, Bt. (1927).

Ley, Sir Gerald Gordon, Bt., T.D. (1905).

Leyland, Sir Vivyan Edward Naylor-, Bt. (1805).

Lidbury, Sir Charles, Kt.

Lidbury, Sir John Towersey, Kt.

Lidderdale, Sir David William Shuckburgh, K.C.B.

Liddle, Sir Donald Ross, Kt.

Liggins, Sir Edmund Naylor, Kt., T.D.

Lighthill, *Prof.* Sir (Michael) James, Kt., F.R.S.

Lighton, Sir Christopher Robert, Bt., M.B.E. (I 1791).

Liley, *Prof.* Sir Albert William, K.C.M.G.

Lim, Sir Han Hoe, Kt., C.B.E.

Lincoln, Sir Anthony Handley, K.C.M.G., C.V.O.

Lindley, Sir Arnold Lewis George, Kt.

Lindo, Sir (Henry) Laurence, G.C.M.G.

Lindon, Sir Leonard Charles Edward, Kt.

Lindop, Sir Norman, Kt.

Lindsay, Sir Ernest Daryl, Kt.

Lindsay, Sir Harvey Kincaid Stewart, Kt.

Lindsay, Sir Martin Alexander, Bt., C.B.E., D.S.O. (1962).

Lindsay, Sir William, Kt., C.B.E.

Linstead, Sir Hugh Nicholas, Kt., O.B.E.

Lintott, Sir Henry John Bevis, K.C.M.G.

Lister, Sir (Charles) Percy, Kt.

Lithgow, Sir William James, Bt., (1925).

Little, *Hon.* Sir Douglas Macfarlane, Kt.

Little, Sir (Rudolf) Alexander, K.C.B.

Littler, Sir Emile, Kt.

Livermore, Sir Harry, Kt.

Livingston, *Air Marshal* Sir Philip Clermont, K.B.E., C.B., A.F.C.

Llewellyn, Sir David Treharne, Kt.

Llewellyn, Sir (Frederick) John, K.C.M.G.

Llewellyn, *Lt.-Col.* Sir Rhys, Bt. (1922).

Llewellyn, *Col.* Sir (Robert) Godfrey, Bt., C.B., C.B.E., M.C., T.D. (1959).

Llewelyn, Sir John Michael Dillwyn-Venables-, Bt. (1890).

Lloyd, *Maj.* Sir (Ernest) Guy (Richard), Bt., D.S.O. (1960).

Lloyd, *Air Chief Marshal* Sir Hugh Pughe, G.B.E., K.C.B., M.C., D.F.C.

Lloyd, Sir (John) Peter (Daniel), Kt.

Loane, *Most Rev.* Marcus Lawrence, K.B.E.

Lockhart, Sir Allan Robert Eliot, Kt., C.I.E.

Lockhart, Sir Muir Edward Sinclair-, Bt. (S 1636).

Lockhart, *General* Sir Rob (McGregor Macdonald), K.C.B., C.I.E., M.C.

Lockspeiser, Sir Ben, K.C.B., F.R.S.

Lockwood, Sir Joseph Flawith, Kt.

Loder, Sir Giles Rolls, Bt. (1887).

Lodge, Sir Thomas, Kt.

Loehnis, Sir Clive, K.C.M.G.

Loewen, *General* Sir Charles Falkland, G.C.B., K.B.E., D.S.O.

Logan, Sir Douglas William, Kt., D.Phil.

Lomax, Sir John Garnett, K.B.E., C.M.G., M.C.

Long, Sir Ronald, Kt.

Longden, Sir Gilbert James Morley, M.B.E.

Longland, Sir John Laurence, Kt.

Longley, Sir Norman, Kt., C.B.E.

Longworth, Sir Fred, Kt.

Looker, Sir Cecil Thomas, Kt.

Lord, Sir Ackland Archibald, Kt., O.B.E.

Lorimer, Sir Thomas Desmond, Kt.

Loring, Sir (John) Nigel, K.C.V.O.

Lousada, Sir Anthony Baruh, Kt.

Lovell, *Prof.* Sir (Alfred Charles) Bernard, Kt., O.B.E., F.R.S.

Loveridge, Sir John Henry, Kt., C.B.E.

Low, Sir James Richard Morrison-, Bt. (1908).

Lowe, Sir David, Kt., C.B.E.

Lowe, *Air Chief Marshal* Sir Douglas Charles, K.C.B., D.F.C., A.F.C.

Lowe, *Air Vice-Marshal* Sir Edgar Noel, K.B.E., C.B.

Lowe, Sir Francis Reginald Gordon, Bt. (1918).

Lowry, *Rt. Hon.* Sir Robert Lynd Erskine, Kt.

Lowson, Sir Ian Patrick, Bt. (1951).

Lowther, *Lt.-Col.* Sir (William) Guy, Bt., O.B.E. (1824).

Loyd, Sir Francis Alfred, K.C.M.G., O.B.E.

Lubbock, Sir Alan, Kt., F.S.A.

Lucas, Sir Cyril Edward, Kt., C.M.G., F.R.S.

Lucas, *Maj.* Sir Jocelyn Morton, Bt., K.B.E., M.C. (1887).

Luce, Sir William Henry Tucker, G.B.E., K.C.M.G.

Luckhoo, *Hon.* Sir Joseph Alexander, Kt.

Luckhoo, Sir Lionel Alfred, K.C.M.G., C.B.E., Q.C.

Lucy, Sir Edmund John William Hugh Cameron- Ramsay-Fairfax-, Bt. (1836).

Luddington, Sir Donald Collin Cumyn, K.B.E., C.M.G., C.V.O.

Luke, *Hon.* Sir Emile Fashole, K.B.E.

Luke, Sir Stephen Elliot Vyvyan, K.C.M.G.

Lumby, Sir Henry, Kt., C.B.E.

Lund, Sir Thomas George, Kt., C.B.E.

Lushington, Sir Henry Edmund Castleman, Bt. (1791).

Lusty, Sir Robert Frith, Kt.

Luyt, Sir Richard Edward, G.C.V.O., K.C.M.G., D.C.M.

Lydford, *Air Marshal* Sir Harold Thomas, K.B.E., C.B., A.F.C.

Lyle, Sir Gavin Archibald, Bt. (1929).

Lyle, Sir Ian Duff, Kt., D.S.C.

Lyon, *Maj.-Gen.* Sir (Francis) James (Cecil) Bowes-, K.C.V.O., C.B., O.B.E., M.C.

Lyons, Sir (Isidore) Jack, Kt., C.B.E.

Lyons, Sir James Reginald, Kt.

Lyons, *His Hon.* Sir Rudolph, Kt., Q.C.

Lyons, Sir William, Kt.

McAdam, Sir Ian William James, Kt., O.B.E.

McAdden, Sir Stephen James, Kt., C.B.E., M.P.

McAllister, Sir Reginald Basil, Kt., C.M.G., C.V.O.

McAlpine, Sir Robert Edwin, Kt.

McAlpine, Sir Robin, Kt., C.B.E.

McAlpine, Sir Thomas George Bishop, Bt. (1918).

Macara, Sir (Charles) Douglas, Bt. (1911).

Macartney, Sir John Barrington, Bt. (1 1799).

Macaulay, Sir Hamilton, Kt., C.B.E.

McAvoy, Sir Francis Joseph, Kt., C.B.E.

McBride, *Rt. Hon.* Sir Philip Albert Martin, K.C.M.G.

McCall, Sir Charles Patrick Home, Kt., M.B.E., T.D.

McCall, *Admiral* Sir Henry William Urquhart, K.C.V.O., K.B.E., C.B., D.S.O.

McCance, Sir Andrew, Kt., D.Sc., F.R.S.

McCarthy, Sir Edwin, Kt., C.B.E.

McCarthy, *Rt. Hon.* Sir Thaddeus Pearcey, K.B.E.

McCauley, *Air Marshal* Sir John Patrick Joseph, K.B.E., C.B.

McCaw, *Hon.* Sir Kenneth Malcolm, Kt., Q.C.

McCombs, *Hon.* Sir Terence Henderson, Kt., O.B.E., E.D.

McConnell, *Cdr.* Sir Robert Melville Terence, Bt., V.R.D. (1900).

McCowan, Sir Hew Cargill, Bt. (1934).

McCutcheon, Sir Walter Osborn, Kt.

McDavid, Sir Edwin Frank, Kt., C.M.G., C.B.E.

MacDermot, Sir Dermot Francis, K.C.M.G., C.B.E.

McDermott, Sir (Lawrence) Emmet, K.B.E.

McDonald, Sir Alexander Fortes, Kt.

McDonald, *Air Chief Marshal* Sir Arthur William Baynes, K.C.B., A.F.C.

Macdonald, Sir Herbert George de Lome, K.B.E.

Macdonald of Sleat, Sir Ian Godfrey Bosville, Bt. (s 1625).

McDonald, Sir James, K.B.E.

McDonald, *Hon.* Sir John Gladstone Black, Kt.

Macdonald, Sir John Ronald Maxwell-, Bt. (s 1682 and s 1707).

Macdonald, Sir Peter George, Kt.

Macdonald, *Hon.* Sir Thomas Lachlan, K.C.M.G.

McDonald, *Hon.* Sir William John Farquhar, Kt.

MacDonald, *Air Chief Marshal* Sir William Laurence Mary, G.C.B., C.B.E., D.F.C.

MacDougall, Sir (George) Donald (Alastair), Kt., C.B.E., F.B.A.

McDowell, Sir Frank Schofield, Kt.

McDowell, Sir Henry McLorinan, K.B.E.

McEvoy, *Air Chief Marshal* Sir Theodore Newman, K.C.B., C.B.E.

McEwen, *Rt. Hon.* Sir John, G.C.M.G., C.H.

McEwen, Sir Robert Lindley, Bt. (1953).

McEwin, *Hon.* Sir (Alexander) Lyell, K.B.E.

McFadzean, Sir Francis Scott, Kt.

McFarland, Sir Basil (Alexander Talbot), Bt., C.B.E. (1914).

Macfarlane, Sir George Gray, Kt., C.B.

Macfarlane, Sir James Wright, Kt.

Macfarlane, Sir Robert Mafeking, K.C.M.G.

MacFarquhar, Sir Alexander, K.B.E., C.I.E.

McGeoch, *Vice-Adm.* Sir Ian Lachlan Mackay, K.C.B., D.S.O., D.S.C.

McGonigal, *Rt. Hon.* Sir Ambrose Joseph, Kt., M.C.

McGovern, Sir Patrick Silvesta, Kt., C.B.E.

McGrath, Sir Charles Gullan, Kt., O.B.E.

MacGregor, Sir Colin Malcolm, Kt.

Macgregor, Sir Edwin Robert, Bt. (1828).

McGregor, *Hon.* Sir George Innes, Kt.

MacGregor of MacGregor, Sir Gregor, Bt. (1795).

McGrigor, *Capt.* Sir Charles Edward, Bt. (1831).

McIlrath, Sir Martin, Kt.

McIlveen, *Brig.* Sir Arthur William, Kt., M.B.E.

McIntosh, Sir Alister Donald, K.C.M.G.

McIntosh, *Vice-Adm.* Sir Ian Stewart, K.B.E., C.B., D.S.O., D.S.C.

Macintosh, *Prof.* Sir Robert Reynolds, Kt., M.D.

McIntosh, Sir Ronald Robert Duncan, K.C.B.

Macintyre, Sir Donald, Kt., C.B.E.

McIntyre, Sir Laurence Rupert, Kt., C.B.E.

Mack, *Hon.* Sir William George Albert, K.B.E.

McKaig, *Admiral* Sir (John) Rae, K.C.B., C.B.E.

Mackay, Sir George Patrick Gordon, Kt., C.B.E.

Mackay, Sir James Mackerron, K.B.E., C.B.

McKay, Sir James Wilson, Kt.

McKay, Sir John Andrew, Kt., C.B.E.

Mackay, Sir William Calder, Kt., O.B.E., M.C.

McKee, *Air Marshal* Sir Andrew, K.C.B., C.B.E., D.S.O., D.F.C., A.F.C.

McKee, *His Hon.* Sir Dermot St. Oswald, Kt.

McKee, *Maj.* Sir William Cecil, Kt., E.R.D.

McKell, *Rt. Hon.* Sir William John, G.C.M.G., Q.C.

MacKenna, *Hon.* Sir Bernard Joseph Maxwell, Kt.

McKenzie, Sir Alexander, K.B.E.

Mackenzie, Sir Alexander Alwyne Brinton Muir-, Bt. (1805).

Mackenzie, Sir (Alexander George Anthony) Allan, Bt. (1890).

Mackenzie, *Vice-Adm.* Sir Hugh Stirling, K.C.B., D.S.O., D.S.C.

Mackenzie, Sir (Lewis) Roderick Kenneth, Bt. (s 1703).

Mackenzie, Sir Robert Evelyn, Bt. (s 1673).

Mackeson, Sir Rupert Henry, Bt. (1954).

McKie, Sir William Neil, Kt., M.V.O., D.MUS.

McKinney, Sir William, Kt., C.B.E.

MacKintosh, Sir Angus Mackay, K.C.V.O., C.M.G.

Mackintosh, *Capt.* Sir Kenneth Lachlan, K.C.V.O., R.N. (*ret.*).

McKissock, Sir Wylie, Kt., O.B.E., F.R.C.S.

Macklin, Sir Albert Sortain Romer, Kt.

Mackworth, *Cdr.* Sir David Arthur Geoffrey, Bt. (1776).

Maclaren, Sir Hamish Duncan, K.B.E., C.B., D.F.C.

Maclean, Sir Fitzroy Hew Royle, Bt., C.B.E. (1957).

McLean, Sir Francis Charles, Kt., C.B.E.

MacLean, *Vice-Adm.* Sir Hector Charles Donald, K.B.E., C.B. D.S.C.

McLean, *Lt.-Gen.* Sir Kenneth Graeme, K.C.B., K.B.E.

Maclean, Sir Robert Alexander, K.B.E.

McLeay, *Hon.* Sir John, K.C.M.G., M.M.

MacLehose, Sir (Crawford) Murray, G.B.E., K.C.M.G.

MacLennan, Sir Hector Ross, Kt., M.D.

Maclennan, Sir Ian Morrison Ross, K.C.M.G.

McLennan, Sir Ian Munro, K.B.E.

MacLennan, Sir Robert Laing, Kt., C.I.E.

McLeod, Sir Alan Cumbrae Rose, K.C.V.O.

McLeod, Sir Charles Henry, Bt. (1925).

MacLeod, Sir John, Kt., T.D.

McLeod, *General* Sir Roderick William, G.B.E., K.C.B.

McLintock, Sir William Traven, Bt. (1934).

Maclure, *Lt.-Col.* Sir John William Spencer, Bt., O.B.E. (1898).

McMahon, Sir (William) Patrick, Bt. (1817).

McMeekin, *Lt.-Gen.* Sir Terence Douglas Herbert, K.C.B., O.B.E.

McMichael, *Prof.* Sir John, Kt., M.D., F.R.S.

MacMillan, *General* Sir Gordon Holmes Alexander, K.C.B., K.C.V.O., C.B.E., D.S.O., M.C.

Macmillan, Sir James Wilson, K.B.E.

McMullin, *Hon.* Sir Alister Maxwell, K.C.M.G.

Macnab, *Brig.* Sir Geoffrey Alex Colin, K.C.M.G., C.B.

Macnaghten, Sir Patrick Alexander, Bt. (1836).

McNair, Sir William Lennox, Kt.

McNee, Sir John William, Kt., D.S.O., M.D., D.SC.

McNeice, Sir (Thomas) Percy (Fergus), Kt., C.M.G., O.B.E.

McNeil, Sir Hector, Kt., C.B.E.

McNicoll, *Vice-Adm.* Sir Alan Wedel Ramsay, K.B.E., C.B., G.M.

McPetrie, Sir James Carnegie, K.C.M.G., O.B.E.

Macready, Sir Nevil John Wilfrid, Bt. (1923).

Macrory, Sir Patrick Arthur, Kt.

McShine, *Hon.* Sir Arthur Hugh, Kt.

MacTaggart, Sir Andrew McCormick, Kt.

Mactaggart, Sir Ian Auld, Bt. (1938).

MacTaggart, Sir William, Kt., R.A., R.S.A.

MacTier, Sir (Reginald) Stewart, Kt., C.B.E.

McTiernan, *Rt. Hon.* Sir Edward Aloysius, K.B.E.

McVeigh, *Rt. Hon.* Sir Herbert Andrew, Kt.

Madden, *Admiral* Sir Charles Edward, Bt., G.C.B. (1919).

Maddex, Sir George Henry, K.B.E.

Maddock, Sir Ieuan, Kt., C.B., O.B.E., F.R.S.

Maddocks, Sir Kenneth Phipson, K.C.M.G., K.C.V.O.

Maddox, Sir John Kempson, Kt., V.R.D., M.D.

Madgwick, Sir Robert Bowden, Kt., O.B.E.

Madhorao Genesh Deshpande *Rao Bahadur* Sir, K.B.E.

Magill, Sir Ivan Whiteside, K.C.V.O.

Maguire, *Air Marshal* Sir Harold John, K.C.B., D.S.O., O.B.E.

Mahon, Sir George Edward John, Bt. (1819).

Mahon, Sir Gerald MacMahon, Kt.

Maihar, The Maharaja of, K.C.I.E.

Maini, Sir Amar Nath, Kt., C.B.E.

Mais, *Hon.* Sir Robert Hugh, Bt.

Maitland, Sir Donald James Dundas, Kt., C.M.G., O.B.E.

Maitland, *Cdr.* Sir John Francis Whitaker, Kt

Maitland, Sir Richard John, Bt. (1818).

Major, *Hon.* Sir John Patrick Edward Chandos Henniker-, K.C.M.G., C.V.O., M.C.

Makgill, *Maj.* Sir (John) Donald (Alexander Arthur), Bt. (s 1627).

Makins, Sir Paul Vivian, Bt. (1903).

Malcolm, Sir David Peter Michael, Bt. (s. 1665).

Malet, *Col.* Sir Edward William St. Lo, Bt., O.B.E. (1791).

Mallabar, Sir John Frederick, Kt.

Mallaby, Sir (Howard) George (Charles), K.C.M.G., O.B.E.

Mallalieu, Sir (Edward) Lancelot, Kt.

Mallen, Sir Leonard Ross, Kt., O.B.E.

Mallet, Sir (William) Ivo, G.B.E., K.C.M.G.

Mallinson, *Col.* Sir Stuart Sidney, Kt., C.B.E., D.S.O., M.C.

Mallinson, Sir (William) Paul, Bt. (1935).

Mallowan, Sir Max Edgar Lucien, Kt., C.B.E., D.Lit., F.B.A., F.S.A.

Maltby, Sir Thomas Karran, Kt.

Mamo, Sir Anthony Joseph, Kt., O.B.E.

Mance, Sir Henry Stenhouse, Kt.

Mander, Sir Charles Marcus, Bt. (1911).

Mandi, *Col.* H.H. the Raja of, K.C.S.I.

Manifold, *Hon.* Sir (Thomas) Chester, K.B.E.

Manktelow, Sir (Arthur) Richard, K.B.E., C.B.

Mann, Sir Rupert Edward, Bt. (1905).

Manning, Sir George, Kt., C.M.G.

Manning, *Hon.* Sir James Kenneth, Kt.

Mansel, Sir Philip, Bt. (1622).

Mansergh, *Vice-Adm.* Sir (Cecil) Aubrey (Lawson), K.B.E., C.B., D.S.C.

Mansfield, *Hon.* Sir Alan James, K.C.M.G., K.C.V.O.

Mansfield, *Vice-Adm.* Sir (Edward) Gerard (Napier), K.B.E.

Mant, Sir Cecil George, Kt., C.B.E.

Mara, *Rt. Hon. Ratu* Sir Kamisese Kapaiwa Tuimacilai, K.B.E.

Marchant, Sir Herbert Stanley, K.C.M.G., O.B.E.

Marett, Sir Robert Hugh Kirk, K.C.M.G., O.B.E.

Margai, *Hon.* Sir Albert Michael, Kt.

Margetson, *Maj.* Sir Philip Reginald, K.C.V.O., M.C.

Marjoribanks, Sir James Alexander Milne, K.C.M.G.

Mark, Sir Robert, Kt.

Markham, Sir Charles John, Bt. (1911).

Marks, Sir John Hedley Douglas, Kt., C.B.E.

Marling, *Lt.-Col.* Sir John Stanley Vincent, Bt., O.B.E. (1882).

Marnham, Sir Ralph, K.C.V.O.

Marr, Sir Leslie Lynn, Bt. (1919).

Marre, Sir Alan Samuel, K.C.B.

Marriott, *Maj.-Gen.* Sir John Charles Oakes, K.C.V.O., C.B., D.S.O., M.C.

Marriott, Sir Ralph George Cavendish Smith-, Bt. (1774).

Marriott, Sir Robert Ecklin, Kt., V.D.

Marsden, Sir John Denton, Bt., (1924).

Marsh, *Rt. Hon.* Sir Richard William, Kt.

Marshall, Sir Arthur Gregory George, Kt., O.B.E.

Marshall, Sir Douglas, Kt.

Marshall, Sir Frank Shaw, Kt.

Marshall, Sir Geoffrey, K.C.V.O., C.B.E., M.D.

Marshall, Sir Hugo Frank, K.B.E., C.M.G.

Marshall, Sir James, Kt.

Marshall, *Rt. Hon.* Sir John Ross, G.B.E., C.H.

Marshall, *Prof.* Sir (Oshley) Roy, Kt., C.B.E.

Marshall, Sir Robert Braithwaite, K.C.B., M.B.E.

Marshall, Sir Stirrat Andrew William Johnson-, Kt., C.B.E., F.R.I.B.A.

Martell, *Vice-Adm.* Sir Hugo Colenso, K.B.E., C.B.

Martin, Sir David Christie, Kt., C.B.E., Ph.D., F.R.S.E.

Martin, *Admiral* Sir Deric Holland-, G.C.B., D.S.O., D.S.C.

Martin, Sir George William, K.B.E.

Martin, *Air Marshal* Sir Harold Brownlow, K.C.B., D.S.O., D.F.C., A.F.C.

Martin, Sir James, Kt., C.B.E.

Martin, *Vice-Adm.* Sir John Edward Ludgate, K.C.B., D.S.C.

Martin, *Prof.* Sir (John) Leslie, Kt., Ph.D.

Martin, Sir John Miller, K.C.M.G., C.B., C.V.O.

Martin, *Prof.* Sir Leslie Harold, Kt., C.B.E.

Martin, *Hon.* Sir Norman (Angus), Kt.

Marwick, Sir Brian Allan, K.B.E., C.M.G.

Masefield, Sir Peter Gordon, Kt.

Mason, *Hon.* Sir Anthony Frank, K.B.E.

Mason, Sir Dan Hurdis, Kt., O.B.E., E.R.D.

Mason, *Vice-Adm.* (E) Sir Frank Trowbridge, K.C.B.

Mason, Sir Frederick Cecil, K.C.V.O., C.M.G.

Mason, Sir Paul, K.C.M.G., K.C.V.O.

Massey, Sir Arthur, Kt., C.B.E.

Massey, *Prof.* Sir Harrie Stewart Wilson, Kt., Ph.D., F.R.S.

Massiah, Sir (Hallum) Grey, K.B.E., M.D.

Masterman, Sir Christopher Hughes, Kt., C.S.I., C.I.E.

Masterman, Sir John Cecil, Kt., O.B.E.

Mather, Sir William Loris, Kt., O.B.E., M.C., T.D.

Matheson, Sir James Adam Louis, K.B.E., C.M.G.

Matheson, *Major* Sir Torquhil Alexander, Bt. (1882).

Mathias, Sir Richard Hughes, Bt. (1917).

Mathys, Sir (Herbert) Reginald, Kt., T.D.

Matters, Sir (Reginald) Francis, Kt., V.R.D., M.D.

Matthews, Sir Bryan Harold Cabot, Kt., C.B.E., SC.D., F.R.S.

Matthews, Sir (Harold Lancelot) Roy, Kt., C.B.E.

Matthews, Sir James Henry John, Kt.

Matthews, Sir Peter Alec, Kt.

Matthews, Sir Stanley, Kt., C.B.E.

Maudslay, *Major* Sir (James) Rennie, K.C.V.O., M.B.E.

Mavor, *Air Marshal* Sir Leslie Deane, K.C.B., A.F.C.

Mawby, Sir Maurice Alan Edgar, Kt., C.B.E.

Maxwell, Sir Aymer, Bt. (s 1681).

Maxwell, Sir Patrick Ivor Heron-, Bt. (s 1683).

Maxwell, Sir Robert Hugh, K.B.E.

May, *Hon.* Sir John Douglas, Kt.

May, *Surg. Vice-Adm.* Sir (Robert) Cyril, K.B.E., C.B., M.C.

Mayall, Sir (Alexander) Lees, K.C.V.O., C.M.G.

Mayer, Sir Robert, Kt., C.H.

Maynard, *Air Chief Marshal* Sir Nigel Martin, K.C.B., C.B.E., D.F.C., A.F.C.   [Kt.

Mbanefo, Sir Louis Nwachukwu, Mead, Sir Cecil, Kt.

Meade, Sir (Richard) Geoffrey (Austin), K.B.E., C.M.G., C.V.O.

Meagher, Sir Thomas, Kt.

Medawar, Sir Peter Brian, Kt., C.H., C.B.E., D.SC., F.R.S.

Medlycott, Sir (James) Christopher, Bt. (1808).

Meech, Sir John Valentine, K.C.V.O.

Meere, Sir Francis Anthony, Kt., C.B.E.

Megarry, *Hon.* Sir Robert Edgar, Kt., F.B.A.

Megaw, *Rt. Hon.* Sir John, Kt., C.B.E., T.D.

Mellor, Sir John Serocold Paget, Bt. (1924).

Melville, Sir Eugene, K.C.M.G.

Melville, Sir Harry Work, K.C.B., Ph.D., D.SC., F.R.S.

Melville, Sir Leslie Galfreid, K.B.E.

Melville, Sir Ronald Henry, K.C.B.

Mensforth, Sir Eric, Kt., C.B.E.

Menter, Sir James Woodham, Kt., Ph.D., SC.D., F.R.S.

Menteth, Sir James Wallace Stuart-, Bt. (1838).

Menzies, Sir Laurence James, Kt.

Menzies, Sir Peter Thomson, Kt.

Menzies, *Rt. Hon.* Sir Robert Gordon, K.T., C.H., Q.C., F.R.S.

Meredith, *Air Vice-Marshal* Sir Charles Warburton, K.B.E., C.B., A.F.C.

Merrison, Sir Alexander Walter, Kt., F.R.S.

Merton, *Air Chief Marshal* Sir Walter Hugh, G.B.E., K.C.B.

Messent, Sir Philip Santo, Kt.

Metcalfe, Sir Ralph Ismay, Kt.

Metcalfe, Sir Theophilus John, Bt. (1802).

Meyer, Sir Anthony John Charles, Bt., M.P. (1910).

Meyjes, Sir Richard Anthony, Kt.

Meyrick, *Lt.-Col.* Sir George David Elliott Tapps-Gervis-, Bt., M.C. (1791).

Meyrick, *Maj.* Sir Thomas Frederick, Bt. (1880).

Michelmore, Sir Walter Harold Strachan, Kt., M.B.E.

Michelmore, *Maj.-Gen.* Sir (William) Godwin, K.B.E., C.B., D.S.O., M.C., T.D.

Micklethwait, Sir Robert Gore, Kt., Q.C.

Middlemore, Sir William Hawkslow, Bt. (1919).

Middleton, Sir George Humphrey, K.C.M.G.

Middleton, Sir George Proctor, K.C.V.O.

Middleton, Sir Stephen Hugh, Bt. (1662).

Miers, *Rear-Adm.* Sir Anthony Cecil Capel, V℃, K.B.E., C.B., D.S.O.

Milbank, *Maj.* Sir Mark Vane, Bt., K.C.V.O., M.C. (1882).

Milburn, Sir John Nigel, Bt. (1905).

Miles, *Prof.* Sir (Arnold) Ashley, Kt., C.B.E., M.D., F.R.S.

Miles, Sir Bernard, Kt., C.B.E.

Miles, *Admiral* Sir Geoffrey John Audley, K.C.B., K.C.S.I.

Miles, Sir William Napier Maurice, Bt. (1859).

Millais, Sir Ralph Regnault, Bt. (1885).

Millar, Sir Oliver Nicholas, K.C.V.O., F.B.A.

Millard, Sir Guy Elwin, K.C.M.G., C.V.O.

Millbourn, Sir (Philip) Eric, Kt., C.M.G.

Miller, Sir Douglas Sinclair, K.C.V.O., C.B.E.

Miller, Sir Eric Merton, Kt.

Miller, *Lt.-Gen.* Sir Euan Alfred Bews, K.C.B., K.B.E., D.S.O., M.C.

Miller, Sir (Ian) Douglas, Kt.

Miller, Sir James, G.B.E.

Miller, *Col.* Sir James MacBride, Kt., M.C., T.D.

Miller, Sir John Francis Compton, Kt., M.B.E., T.D.

Miller, Sir John Holmes, Bt. (1705).

Miller, *Lt.-Col.* Sir John Mansel, K.C.V.O., D.S.O., M.C.

Miller, Sir (Oswald) Bernard, Kt.

Miller, Sir Richard Hope, Kt.

Miller of Glenlee, Sir Frederick William Macdonald, Bt. (1788).

Milling, *Air Marshal* Sir Denis Crowley-, K.C.B., C.B.E., D.S.O., D.F.C.

Mills, *Vice-Adm.* Sir Charles Piercy, K.C.B., C.B.E., D.S.C.

Mills, Sir John Lewis Ernest Watts, Kt., C.B.E.

Mills, Sir Peter Frederick Leighton, Bt. (1921).

Milman, Sir Dermot Lionel Kennedy, Bt. (1800).

Milmo, *Hon.* Sir Helenus Patrick Joseph, Kt.

Milner, Sir (George Edward) Mordaunt, Bt. (1717).

Milward, Sir Anthony Horace, Kt., C.B.E.

Minhinnick, Sir Gordon Edward George, Kt.

Minogue, *Hon.* Sir John Patrick, Kt.

Mitchell, Sir Derek Jack, K.C.B., C.V.O.

Mitchell, Sir George Irvine, Kt., C.B., Q.C.

Mitchell, Sir Godfrey Way, Kt.

Mitchell, Sir Hamilton, K.B.E.

Mitchell, *Col.* Sir Harold Paton, Bt. (1945).

Mitchell, *Prof.* Sir Mark Ledingham, Kt.

Mitchell, Sir (Seton) Steuart Crichton, K.B.E., C.B.

Mocatta, *Hon.* Sir Alan Abraham, Kt., O.B.E.

Mockett, Sir Vere, Kt., M.B.E.

Moffat, Sir John Smith, Kt., O.B.E.

Mogg, *General* Sir (Herbert) John, G.C.B., C.B.E., D.S.O.

Mohamed, Sir Abdool Razack, Kt.

Moir, Sir Ernest Ian Royds, Bt. (1916).

Molony, Sir Hugh Francis, Bt. (1925).

Molony, Sir Joseph Thomas, K.C.V.O., Q.C.

Monahan, Sir Robert Vincent, Kt.

Moncrieff, *Admiral* Sir Alan Kenneth Scott-, K.C.B., C.B.E., D.S.O.

Moncreiffe, Sir (Rupert) Iain (Kay), Bt. (s 1685).

Monson, Sir (William Bonnar) Leslie, K.C.M.G., C.B.

Montgomery, Sir (Basil Henry) David, Bt. (1801).

Mookerjee, Sir Birendra Nath, Kt.

Moon, Sir Edward Penderel, Kt., O.B.E.

Moon, Sir John Arthur, Bt. (1887).

Moon, Sir (Peter) Wilfred Giles, Bt. (1855).

Moore, Sir Edward Stanton, Bt., O.B.E. (1923.)

Moore, Sir Harold (John de Courcy), Kt.

Moore, *Admiral* Sir Henry Ruthven, G.C.B., C.V.O., D.S.O.

Moore, *General* Sir (James Newton) Rodney, G.C.V.O., K.C.B., C.B.E., D.S.O.

Moore, *Hon.* Sir John Cochrane, Kt.

Moore, Sir Norman Winfrid, Bt. (1919).

Moore, Sir Philip Brian Cecil, K.C.V.O., C.B., C.M.G.

Moore, Sir William Samson, Bt. (1932).

Mootham, Sir Orby Howell, Kt.

Mordaunt, Sir Nigel John, Bt., M.B.E. (1611).

Mordecai, Sir John Stanley, Kt., C.M.G.

Moreton, Sir John Oscar, K.C.V.O., C.M.G., M.C.

Morgan, Sir (Clifford) Naunton, Kt.

Morgan, Sir David John Hughes-Bt., C.B.E. (1925).

Morgan, *Hon.* Sir Edward James Ranembe, Kt.

Morgan, Sir Ernest Dunstan, K.B.E.

Morgan, Sir Morien Bedford, Kt., C.B., F.R.S.

Morgan, *Rear-Adm.* Sir Patrick John, K.C.V.O., C.B., D.S.C.

Morgan, *General* Sir William Duthie, G.C.B., D.S.O., M.C.

Morland, Sir Oscar Charles, G.B.E., K.C.M.G.

Morley, Sir Godfrey William Rowland, Kt., O.B.E., T.D.

Morris, Sir Cedric Lockwood, Bt. (1806).

Morris, *Air Marshal* Sir Douglas Griffith, K.C.B., C.B.E., D.S.O., D.F.C.

Morris, Sir Geoffrey Newman-, Kt., E.D.

Morris, *Hon.* Sir Kenneth James, K.B.E., C.M.G.

Morris, *Air Marshal* Sir Leslie Dalton-, K.B.E., C.B.

Morris, *His Hon.* Sir Owen Temple Temple-, Kt., Q.C.

Morris, Sir Philip Robert, K.C.M.G., C.B.E.

Morris, *His Hon.* Sir William Gerard, Kt.

Morrison, Sir Nicholas Godfrey, K.C.B.

Morrow, Sir Arthur William, Kt., D.S.O., E.D.

Morrow, Sir Ian Thomas, Kt.

Morse, Sir Christopher Jeremy, K.C.M.G.

Morshead, Sir Owen Frederick, G.C.V.O., K.C.B., D.S.O., M.C.

Morton, Sir Brian, Kt.

Morton, Sir Ralph John, Kt., C.M.G., O.B.E., M.C.

Morton, Sir (William) Wilfred, K.C.B.

Moser, *Prof.* Sir Claus Adolf, K.C.B., C.B.E., F.B.A.

Moses, Sir Charles Joseph Alfred, Kt., C.B.E.

Mosley, Sir Oswald Ernald, Bt. (1781).

Moss, Sir Eric de Vere, Kt., C.I.E.

Moss, Sir John Herbert Theodore Edwards-, Bt. (1868).

Mostyn, Sir Jeremy John Antony, Bt. (1670).

Mott, Sir John Harmer, Bt. (1930).

Mott, *Prof.* Sir Nevill Francis, Kt., F.R.S.

Mount, Sir William Malcolm, Bt. (1921).

Mountain, Sir Brian Edward Stanley, Bt. (1922).

Mountford, Sir James Frederick, Kt., D.Litt.

Mowbray, Sir John Robert, Bt. (1880).

Mudie, Sir (Robert) Francis, K.C.S.I., K.C.I.E., O.B.E.

Muhamad Noor, *Khan Bahadur* Sir Khaja, Kt., C.B.E.

Muhammad Ahmad Sa'id Khan *Nawab* Sir, G.B.E., K.C.S.I., K.C.I.E.

Muir, Sir David John, Kt., C.M.G.

Muir, Sir Edward Francis, K.C.B.

Muir, Sir John Harling, Bt. (1892).

Muirhead, Sir David Francis, K.C.M.G., C.V.O.

Mulholland, Sir Michael Henry, Bt. (1945).

Mullens, Sir Harold Hill, Kt.

Mumford, Sir Albert Henry, K.B.E.

Munro, Sir Ian Talbot, Bt. (s. 1634).

Munro, Sir (Thomas) Torquil (Alfonso), Bt. (1825).

Murdoch, *Air Marshal* Sir Alister Murray, K.B.E., C.B.

Murphy, Sir Alexander Paterson, Kt.

Murphy, Sir (Oswald) Ellis (Joseph), Kt.

Murray, Sir Alan John Digby, Bt. (s 1628).

Murray, Sir Andrew Hunter Arbuthnot, Kt., O.B.E.

Murray, Sir (Francis) Ralph (Hay), K.C.M.G., C.B.

Murray, *General* Sir Horatius, G.C.B., K.B.E., D.S.O.

Murray, *Hon.* Sir John Murray, Kt.

Murray, Sir Kenneth, Kt.

Murray, Sir Rowland William Patrick, Bt. (s 1630).

Murray, Sir William Patrick Keith, Bt. (s 1673).

Murrie, Sir William Stuart, G.C.B., K.B.E.

Mursell, Sir Peter, Kt., M.B.E.

Musgrave, Sir Christopher Patrick Charles, Bt. (1611).

Musgrave, Sir (Frank) Cyril, K.C.B.

Musgrave, Sir Richard James, Bt. (I 1782).

Musker, Sir John, Kt.

Musson, *General* Sir Geoffrey Randolph Dixon, G.C.B., C.B.E., D.S.O.

Musto, Sir Arnold Albert, Kt., C.I.E.

Mya Bu, Sir, Kt.

Mynors, Sir Humphrey Charles Baskerville, Bt. (1964).

Mynors, *Prof.* Sir Roger Aubrey Baskerville, Kt., F.B.A.

Nairac, *Hon.* Sir André Laurence, Kt., C.B.E., Q.C.

Nairn, Sir (Michael) George, Bt. (1904).

Nairn, Sir Robert Arnold Spencer-, Bt. (1933).

Nairne, Sir Patrick Dalmahoy, K.C.B., M.C.

Nalder, *Hon.* Sir Crawford David, Kt.

Nall, *Lt.-Cdr.* Sir Michael Joseph, Bt., R.N. (1954).

Nan Kivell, Sir Rex de Charembac, Kt., C.M.G.

Napier, *Hon.* Sir John Mellis, K.C.M.G.

Napier, Sir Joseph William Lennox, Bt., O.B.E. (1867).

Napier, Sir William Archibald, Bt. (s 1627).

Nathan, Sir Maurice Arnold, K.B.E.

Nayudu, *Sri Diwan Bahadur* Sir Madura Balasundram, Kt., C.I.E.

Neal, Sir Leonard Francis, Kt., C.B.E.

Neale, Sir Alan Derrett, K.C.B., M.B.E.

Neame, *Lt.-Gen.* Sir Philip, *V.C.*, K.B.E., C.B., D.S.O.

Neave, Sir Arundell Thomas Clifton, Bt. (1795).

Neden, Sir Wilfred John, Kt., C.B., C.B.E.

Neill, *Rt. Hon.* Sir Ivan, Kt.

Nelson, *Maj.-Gen.* Sir (Eustace) John (Blois), K.C.V.O., C.B., D.S.O., O.B.E., M.C.

Nelson, *Air Marshal* Sir (Sidney) Richard (Carlyle), K.C.B., O.B.E., M.D.

Nelson, *Maj.* Sir William Vernon Hope, Bt., O.B.E. (1912).

Nepean, *Lt.-Col.* Sir Evan Yorke, Bt. (1802).

Nevill, *Air Vice-Marshal* Sir Arthur de Terrotte, K.B.E., C.B.

Neville, *Lt.-Col.* Sir (James) Edmund (Henderson), Bt., M.C. (1927).

Neville, *Maj.-Gen.* Sir Robert Arthur Ross, K.C.M.G., C.B.E., R.M.

Newbold, Sir Charles Demorée, K.B.E., C.M.G., Q.C.

Newman, Sir Geoffrey Robert, Bt. (1836).

Newman, Sir Gerard Robert Henry Sigismund, Bt. (1912).

Newns, Sir (Alfred) Foley (Francis Polden), K.C.M.G., C.V.O.

Newton, Sir (Harry) Michael (Rex), Bt. (1900).

Newton, Sir Hubert, Kt.

Newton, Sir Kenneth Garner, Bt., O.B.E., T.D. (1924).

Newton, Sir (Leslie) Gordon, Kt.

Niall, Sir Horace Lionel Richard, Kt., C.B.E.

Nicholas, Sir Alfred James, Kt., C.B.E.

Nicholas, Sir Herbert Richard, Kt., O.B.E.

Nicholetts, *Air Marshal* Sir Gilbert Edward, K.B.E., C.B., A.F.C.

Nicholls, Sir Douglas Ralph, Kt., O.B.E.

Nichols, Sir Edward Henry, Kt., T.D.

Nicholson, Sir Arthur William, Kt., O.B.E.

Nicholson, *General* Sir Cameron Gordon Graham, G.C.B., K.B.E., D.S.O., M.C.

Nicholson, *Hon.* Sir David Eric, Kt.

Nicholson, Sir Godfrey, Bt. (1958).

Nicholson, Sir John Charles, Bt. (1859).

Nicholson, Sir John Norris, Bt., K.B.E., C.I.E. (1912).

Nicklin, *Hon.* Sir (George) Francis (Reuben), K.C.M.G., M.M.

Nicoll, Sir John Fearns, K.C.M.G.

Nicolson, Sir David Lancaster, Kt.

Nield, *Hon.* Sir Basil Edward, Kt., C.B.E., Q.C.

Nield, Sir William Alan, G.C.M.G., K.C.B.

Nightingale, Sir Charles Athelstan, Bt. (1628).

Nightingale, Sir John Cyprian, Kt., C.B.E., B.E.M., Q.P.M.

Nimmo, *Hon.* Sir John Angus, Kt., C.B.E.

Nimmo, Sir Robert, Kt.

Niven, Sir (Cecil) Rex, Kt., C.M.G., M.C.

Nixon, Sir (Charles) Norman, Kt.

Nixon, *Maj.* Sir Christopher John Louis Joseph, Bt., M.C. (1906).

Noad, Sir Kenneth Beeson, Kt., M.D.

Noble, *Cmdr. Rt. Hon.* Sir Allan Herbert Percy, K.C.M.G., D.S.O., D.S.C., R.N.

Noble, Sir Andrew Napier, Bt., K.C.M.G. (1923).

Noble, *Col.* Sir Arthur, K.B.E., C.B., D.S.O., T.D.

Noble, Sir Marc Brunel, Bt. (1902).

Noble, Sir Peter Scott, Kt.

Noble, Sir (Thomas Alexander) Fraser, Kt., M.B.E.

Nock, Sir Norman Lindfield, Kt.

Noel, Sir Claude, Kt., C.M.G.

Nordmeyer, *Hon.* Sir Arnold Henry, K.C.M.G.

Norman, Sir Arthur Gordon, K.B.E., D.F.C.

Norman, Sir Charles, Kt., C.B.E.

Norman, Sir Edward James, Kt.

Norman, *Vice-Adm.* Sir (Horace) Geoffrey, K.C.V.O., C.B., C.B.E.

Norman, Sir Mark Annesley, Bt. (1915).

Norman, Sir Robert Wentworth, Kt.

Normand, Sir Charles William Blyth, Kt., C.I.E., D.Sc.

Norrington, Sir Arthur Lionel Pugh, Kt.

Norris, Sir Alfred Henry, K.B.E.

Norris, *Vice-Adm.* Sir Charles Fred Wivell, K.B.E., C.B., D.S.O.

Norris, *Air Chief Marshal* Sir Christopher Neil Foxley-, G.C.B., D.S.O., O.B.E.

Norris, Sir Eric George, K.C.M.G.

Norris, *Maj.-Gen.* Sir Frank Kingsley, K.B.E., C.B., D.S.O., E.D.

North, *Rt. Hon.* Sir Alfred Kingsley, K.B.E.

North, Sir (William) Jonathan (Frederick), Bt. (1920).

Norton, Sir Clifford John, K.C.M.G., C.V.O.

Norton, *Admiral of the Fleet* Sir Peter John Hill-, G.C.B.

Norwood, Sir Walter Neville, Kt.

Nugent, Sir Hugh Charles, Bt. (1 1795).

Nugent, *Maj.* Sir Peter Walter James, Bt. (1831).

Nugent, Sir Robin George Colborne, Bt. (1806).

Nuttall, Sir Nicholas Keith Lillington, Bt. (1922).

Nutting, *Rt. Hon.* Sir (Harold) Anthony, Bt. (1903).

Oakeley, Sir (Edward) Atholl, Bt. (1790).

Oakes, Sir Christopher, Bt. (1939).

Oakshott, *Hon.* Sir Anthony Hendrie, Bt. (1959).

Oates, Sir Thomas, Kt., C.M.G., O.B.E.

Oatley, Sir Charles William, Kt., O.B.E., F.R.S.

O'Brien, Sir David Edmond, Bt. (1849).

O'Brien, *Admiral* Sir William Donough, K.C.B., D.S.C.

O'Bryan, *Hon.* Sir Norman, Kt.

O'Connell, Sir Bernard Thomas, Kt.

O'Connell, Sir Morgan Donal Conail, Bt. (1869).

O'Connor, *Lt.-Gen.* Sir Denis Stuart Scott, K.B.E., C.B.

O'Connor, Sir Kenneth Kennedy, K.B.E., M.C., Q.C.

O'Connor, *Hon.* Sir Patrick McCarthy, Kt.

O'Connor, *General* Sir Richard Nugent, K.T., G.C.B., D.S.O., M.C.

O'Dea, Sir Patrick Jerad, K.C.V.O.

Ogden, Sir Alwyne George Neville, K.B.E., C.M.G.

Ogden, Sir George Chester, Kt., C.B.E.

Ogg, Sir William Gammie, Kt.

Ogilvie, Sir Alec Drummond, Kt.

Ogilvy, Sir David John Wilfrid, Bt. (s 1626).

Ohlson, Sir Eric James, Bt. (1920).

Okeover, *Lieut.-Col.* Sir Ian Peter Andrew Monro Walker-, Bt., D.S.O., T.D. (1886).

Oliver, *Hon.* Sir Peter Raymond, Kt.

Oldfield, Sir Maurice, K.C.M.G., C.B.E.

Oldman, *Col.* Sir Hugh Richard Deare, K.B.E., M.C.

Oliphant, Sir Mark Laurence Elwin, K.B.E., F.R.S.

Oliver, Sir (Frederick) Ernest, Kt., C.B.E., T.D.

Oliver, *Admiral* Sir Geoffrey Nigel, G.B.E., K.C.B., D.S.O.

Oliver, *Lt.-Gen.* Sir William Pasfield, G.B.E., K.C.B., K.C.M.G.

O'Loghlen, Sir Coleman Michael, Bt. (1838).

Olver, Sir Stephen John Linley, K.B.E., C.M.G.

O'Neill, *Hon.* Sir Con Douglas Walter, G.C.M.G.

O'Neill, Sir (Matthew) John, Kt., C.B.E.

Onslow, *Maj.-Gen.* Sir Denzil Macarthur-, Kt., C.B.E., D.S.O., E.D.

Onslow, Sir John Roger Wilmot, Bt. (1797).

Oppenheim, Sir Alexander, Kt., O.B.E., D.Sc., F.R.S.E.

Oppenheim, Sir Duncan Morris, Kt.

Oppenheimer, Sir Michael Bernard Grenville, Bt. (1921).

Oppenheimer, Sir Philip Jack, Kt.

Opperman, *Hon.* Sir Hubert Ferdinand, Kt., O.B.E.

Orde, Sir Charles William, K.C.M.G.

Orde, Sir John Alexander Campbell-, Bt. (1790).

Organe, *Prof.* Sir Geoffrey Stephen William, Kt., M.D.

Ormerod, *Maj.* Sir Cyril Berkeley, K.B.E.

Ormond, Sir John Davies Wilder, Kt., B.E.M.

Ormrod, *Rt. Hon.* Sir Roger Fray Greenwood, Kt.

Orr, *Rt. Hon.* Sir Alan Stewart, Kt., O.B.E.

Ortcheson, Sir John, Kt., C.B.E.

Osborn, Sir Danvers Lionel Rouse, Bt. (1662).

Osborn, Sir Frederic James, Kt.

Osborne, Sir Basil, Kt., C.B.E.

Osborne, Sir Peter George, Bt. (1 1629).

Osman, Sir Abdul Raman Mahomed, G.C.M.G., C.B.E.

Osmond, Sir Douglas, Kt., C.B.E.

Outerbridge, *Col. Hon.* Sir Leonard Cecil, Kt., C.B.E., D.S.O.

Outram, Sir Alan James, Bt. (1859).

Overall, Sir John Wallace, Kt., C.B.E., M.C.

Owen, Sir (Arthur) Douglas, K.B.E., C.B.

Owen, Sir Dudley Herbert Cunliffe-, Bt. (1920).

Owen, Sir Hugh Bernard Pilkington, Bt. (1813).

Owo, The Olowo of,. Kt.

Packard, *Lieut.-Gen.* Sir (Charles) Douglas, K.B.E., C.B., D.S.O.

Padmore, Sir Thomas, G.C.B.

Pagan, *Brig.* Sir John Ernest, Kt., C.M.G., M.B.E., E.D.

Page, *Prof.* Sir Denys Lionel, Kt., F.B.A.

Page, Sir Harry Robertson, Kt.

Paget, Sir John Starr, Bt. (1886).

Paget, Sir Julian Tolver, Bt. (1871).

Pain, *Lt.-Gen.* Sir (Horace) Rollo (Squarey), K.C.B., M.C.

Pain, *Hon.* Sir Peter Richard, Kt.

Palliser, Sir (Arthur) Michael, K.C.M.G.

Palmer, Sir Charles Mark, Bt. (1886).

Palmer, Sir Geoffrey Christopher John, Bt. (1669).

Palmer, Sir John Edward Somerset, Bt. (1791).

Palmer, *Brig.* Sir Otho Leslie Prior-, Kt., D.S.O.

Panckridge, *Surgeon Vice-Adm.* Sir (William) Robert (Silvester), K.B.E., C.B.

Pape, *Hon.* Sir George Augustus, Kt.

Pararajasingam, Sir Sangarapillai, Kt.

Parham, *Admiral* Sir Frederick Robertson, G.B.E., K.C.B., D.S.O.

Paris, Sir Edward Talbot, Kt., C.B., D.Sc.

Park, *Hon.* Sir Hugh Eames, Kt.

Parker, Sir (Arthur) Douglas Dodds-, Kt.

Parker, Sir Douglas William Leigh, Kt., O.B.E.

Parker, Sir Harold, K.C.B., K.B.E., M.C.

Parker, Sir John Edward, Kt.

Parker, Sir Karl Theodore, Kt., C.B.E., Ph.D., F.B.A.

Parker, Sir Richard (William) Hyde, Bt. (1681).

Parker, Sir (Walter) Edmund, Kt., C.B.E.

Parker, *Vice-Adm.* Sir (Wilfred) John, K.B.E., C.B., D.S.C.

Parker, Sir (William) Alan, Bt. (1844).

Parkes, Sir Alan Sterling, Kt., C.B.E., Ph.D., D.SC., SC.D., F.R.S.

Parkes, Sir Basil Arthur, Kt., O.B.E.

Parkinson, Sir Kenneth Wade, Kt.

Parr, Sir Robert, K.B.E., C.M.G.

Parrott, Sir Cecil Cuthbert, K.C.M.G., O.B.E.

Parry, Sir (Frank) Hugh (Nigel), Kt., C.B E.

Parsons, Sir Anthony Derrick, K.C.M.G., M.V.O., M.C.

Parsons, Sir (John) Michael, Kt.

Parsons, Sir Maurice Henry, K.C.M.G.

Part, Sir Antony Alexander, Kt., G.C.B., M.B.E.

Partabgarh, H.H. the Maharawab of, K.C.S.I.

Partridge, Sir (Ernest) John, K.B.E.

Pasley, Sir Rodney Marshall Sabine, Bt. (1794).

Patch, *Air Chief Marshal* Sir Hubert Leonard, K.C.B., C.B.E.

Paterson, Sir (Alexander) Swinton, K.B.E., C.M.G.

Paterson, Sir Dennis Craig, Kt.

Paterson, Sir George Mutlow, Kt., O.B.E., Q.C.

Paterson, Sir John Valentine Jardine, Kt.

Paton, *Prof.* Sir George Whitecross, Kt.

Paton, Sir Leonard Cecil, Kt., C.B.E., M.C.

Paton, *Capt.* Sir Stuart Henry, K.C.V.O., C.B.E., R.N. (*ret.*).

Paton, Sir (Thomas) Angus (Lyall), Kt., C.M.G., F.R.S.

Patron, Sir Joseph, Kt., O.B.E., M.C.

Patterson, Sir John Robert, K.B.E., C.M.G.

Pattinson, *Hon.* Sir Baden, K.B.E.

Paul, Sir John Warburton, G.C.M.G., O.B.E., M.C.

Paull, Sir Gilbert James, Kt.

Pavlides, Sir Paul George, Kt., C.B.E.

Payne, *Hon.* Sir Reginald Withers, Kt.

Payne, Sir Robert Frederick, Kt.

Peake, Sir Francis Harold, Kt.

Peake, Sir Harold, Kt.

Peard, *Rear-Adm.* Sir Kenyon Harry Terrell, K.B.E.

Pearman, *Hon.* Sir James Eugene, Kt., C.B.E.

Pearson, Sir Francis Fenwick, Bt., M.B.E. (1964).

Pearson, *Hon.* Sir Glen Gardner, Kt.

Pearson, Sir (James) Denning, Kt.

Pearson, Sir (James) Reginald, Kt., O.B.E.

Pearson, Sir Neville, Bt. (1916).

Pearson, *General* Sir Thomas Cecil Hook, K.C.B., C.B.E., D.S.O.

Pease, Sir (Alfred) Vincent, Bt. (1882).

Pease, Sir Richard Thorn, Bt. (1920).

Pechell, Sir Ronald Horace, Bt. (1797).

Peck, Sir Edward Heywood, G.C.M.G.

Peck, Sir John Howard, K.C.M.G.

Pedder, *Vice-Adm.* Sir Arthur Reid, K.B.E., C.B.

Pedler, Sir Frederick Johnson, Kt.

Peek, Sir Francis Henry Grenville, Bt. (1874).

Peek, *Vice-Adm.* Sir Richard Innes, K.B.E., C.B., D.S.C.

Peel, *Capt.* Sir (Francis Richard) Jonathan, Kt., C.B.E., M.C.

Peel, Sir John Harold, K.C.V.O.

Peel, Sir (William) John, Kt.

Peierls, Sir Rudolf Ernst, Kt., C.B.E., D.SC., D.Phil., F.R.S

Peile, *Vice-Adm.* Sir Lancelot Arthur Babington, K.B.E., C.B., D.S.O., M.V.O.

Peirse, Sir Henry Grant de la Poer Beresford-, Bt. (1814).

Pelham, Sir (George) Clinton, K.B.E., C.M.G.

Pelly, Sir Harold Alwyne, Bt., M.C. (1840).

Pemberton, Sir Francis Wingate William, Kt., C.B.E.

Pendred, *Air Marshal* Sir Lawrence Fleming, K.B.E., C.B., D.F.C.

Penn, *Lt.-Col.* Sir Eric Charles William Mackenzie, K.C.V.O., O.B.E., M.C.

Penny, Sir James Downing, K.C.I.E., C.S.I.

Pennycuick, *Rt. Hon.* Sir John, Kt.

Penrose, Sir Roland Algernon, Kt., C.B.E.

Penruddock, Sir Clement Frederick, Kt., C.B.E.

Peppiatt, Sir Kenneth Oswald, K.B.E., M.C.

Percival, Sir Anthony Edward, Kt., C.B.

Peren, *Prof.* Sir Geoffrey Sylvester, K.B.E.

Perkins, Sir (Albert) Edward, K.C.V.O.

Perkins, *Surgeon Vice-Adm.* Sir Derek Duncombe Steele-, K.C.B., K.C.V.O.

Perkins, Sir (Walter) Robert Dempster, Kt.

Perks, Sir (Robert) Malcolm Mewburn, Bt. (1908).

Perrin, Sir Michael Willcox, Kt., C.B.E.

Perring, Sir Ralph Edgar, Bt. (1963).

Perrott, Sir Donald Cyril Vincent, K.B.E.

Perry, *Hon.* Sir Alan Clifford, Kt.

Perry, Sir Walter Laing Macdonald, Kt., O.B.E., F.R.S.E.

Pestell, Sir John Richard, K.C.V.O.

Petch, Sir Louis, K.C.B.

Peters, *Admiral* Sir Arthur Malcolm, K.C.B., D.S.C.

Peters, *Prof.* Sir Rudolph Albert, Kt., M.C., F.R.S.

Peterson, Sir Arthur William, K.C.B., M.V.O.

Petit, Sir Dinshaw Manockjee, Bt. (1890).

Peto, *Brig.* Sir Christopher Henry Maxwell, Bt., D.S.O. (1927).

Peto, *Cdr.* Sir (Henry) Francis (Morton) Bt., R.N. (1855).

Petrie, Sir Charles Alexander, Bt., C.B.E. (1918).

Pettingel, Sir William Walter, Kt., C.B.E.

Pettit, Sir Daniel Eric Arthur, Kt.

Petty, *Hon.* Sir Horace Rostill, Kt.

Pevsner, *Prof.* Sir Nikolaus Bernhard Leon, Kt., C.B.E., Ph.D., F.B.A., F.S.A.

Phaltan, *Maj.* the Raja of, K.C.I.E.

Philip, Sir William Shearer, Kt., C.M.G., M.C.

Philips, *Prof.* Sir Cyril Henry, Kt.

Philipson, Sir Robert James, Kt., P.R.S.A., A.R.A.

Phillips, Sir Fred Albert, Kt., C.V.O.

Phillips, Sir Henry Ellis Isidore, Kt., C.M.G., M.B.E.

Phillips, Sir Horace, K.C.M.G.

Phillips, Sir John Grant, K.B.E.

Phillips, *Hon.* Sir (John) Raymond, Kt., M.C.

Phillips, Sir Leslie Walter, Kt., C.B.E.

Phillips, Sir Robin Francis, Bt. (1912).

Phillips, *Hon.* Sir Rowland Ricketts, Kt.

Phipps, *Rear-Adm.* Sir Peter, K.B.E., D.S.C., V.R.D.

Pickard, Sir Cyril Stanley, K.C.M.G.

Pickering, *Prof.* Sir George White, Kt., F.R.S.

Pickthorn, Sir Charles William Richards, Bt. (1959).

Pierre, Sir Joseph Henry, Kt.

Piers, Sir Charles Robert Fitzmaurice, Bt. (1 1661).

Pigot, *Brig.-Gen.* Sir Robert, Bt., D.S.O., M.C. (1764).

Pigott, *Maj.* Sir Berkeley, Bt. (1808).

Pike, Sir Philip Ernest Housden, Kt., Q.C.

Pike, Sir Theodore Ouseley, K.C.M.G.

Pike, *Marshal of the Royal Air Force* Sir Thomas Geoffrey, G.C.B., C.B.E., D.F.C.

Pike, *Lt.-Gen.* Sir William Gregory Huddleston, K.C.B., C.B.E., D.S.O.

Pilcher, Sir (Charlie) Dennis, Kt., C.B.E.

Pilcher, Sir John Arthur, G.C.M.G.

Pilditch, Sir Richard Edward, Bt. (1929).

Pile, *General* Sir Frederick Alfred, Bt., G.C.B., D.S.O., M.C. (1900).

Pile, Sir William Denis, K.C.B., M.B.E.

Pilkington, Sir Lionel Alexander Bethune (Alastair), Kt.

Pilkington, *Capt.* Sir Richard Antony, K.B.E., M.C.

Pilkington, Sir Thomas Henry Milborne - Swinnerton-, Bt. (s 1635).

Pim, *Capt.* Sir Richard Pike, K.B.E., V.R.D., R.N.V.R.

Pinsent, Sir Roy, Bt. (1938).

Piper, *Air Marshal* Sir Thomas William, K.B.E., C.B., A.F.C.

Pippard, *Prof.* Sir (Alfred) Brian, Kt., F.R.S.

Pirbhai, Sir Eboo, Kt., O.B.E.

Pirie, *Air Chief Marshal* Sir George Clark, K.C.B., K.B.E., M.C., D.F.C.

Pitblado, Sir David Bruce, K.C.B., C.V.O.

Pitman, Sir Hubert Percival Lancaster, Kt., O.B.E.

Pitman, Sir (Isaac) James, K.B.E.

Pitts, Sir Cyril Alfred, Kt.

Pixley, Sir Neville Drake, Kt., M.B.E., V.R.D.

Pizey, *Admiral* Sir (Charles Thomas) Mark, G.B.E., C.B., D.S.O.

Plant, *Prof.* Sir Arnold, Kt.

Platt, Sir Harry, Bt., M.D. (1958).

Playfair, Sir Edward Wilder, K.C.B.

Playford, *Hon.* Sir Thomas, G.C.M.G.

Pleass, Sir Clement John, K.C.M.G., K.C.V.O., K.B.E.

Plimmer, Sir Clifford Ulric, K.B.E.

Plimsoll, Sir James, Kt., C.B.E.

Plowman, Sir (John) Anthony, Kt.

Plumb, Sir (Charles) Henry, Kt.

Plummer, Sir (Arthur) Desmond (Herne), Kt., T.D.

Pochin, Sir Edward Eric, Kt., C.B.E., M.D., F.R.C.P.

Poett, *General* Sir (Joseph Howard) Nigel, K.C.B., D.S.O.

Pole, *Col.* Sir John Gawen Carew, Bt., D.S.O., T.D. (1628).

Pole, Sir Peter Van Notten-, Bt. (1791).

Pollard, Sir Charles Herbert, Kt., C.B.E.

Pollard, *Lt.-Gen.* Sir Reginald George, K.C.V.O., K.B.E., C.B., D.S.O.

Pollen, Sir John Michael Hungerford, Bt. (1795).

Pollock, Sir George, Kt., Q.C.

Pollock, Sir George Frederick, Bt. (1866).

Pollock, Sir George Seymour Montagu-, Bt. (1872).

Pollock, *Admiral of the Fleet* Sir Michael Patrick, G.C.B., M.V.O., D.S.C.

Pollock, Sir William Horace Montagu-, K.C.M.G.

Ponsonby, Sir Ashley Charles Gibbs, Bt., M.C. (1956).

Pontin, Sir Frederick William, Kt.

Poore, Sir Herbert Edward, Bt. (1795).

Pope, Sir George Reginald, Kt.

Pope, *Vice-Adm.* Sir (John) Ernle, K.C.B.

Pope, Sir Sidney Barton, Kt.

Popper, *Prof.* Sir Karl Raimund, Kt., Ph.D., F.R.S.

Porbandar, *Lt.-Col.* H.H. Maharaja of, K.C.S.I.

Portal, Sir Francis Spencer, Bt. (1901).

Portal, *Admiral* Sir Reginald Henry, K.C.B., D.S.C.

Porter, Sir Andrew Marshall Horsbrugh-, Bt., D.S.O. (1902).

Porter, *Prof.* Sir George, Kt., F.R.S., Ph.D., Sc.D.

Porter, *Air Marshal* Sir (Melvin) Kenneth (Drowley), K.C.B., C.B.E.

Porter, *Hon.* Sir Murray Victor, Kt.

Porter, *Rt. Hon.* Sir Robert Wilson, Kt., Q.C.

Pott, Sir Leslie, K.B.E.

Potter, Sir Henry Steven, K.C.M.G.

Potter, *Air Marshal* Sir Patrick Brunton Lee, K.B.E., M.D.

Potter, *Maj.-Gen.* Sir (Wilfrid) John, K.B.E., C.B.

Potter, Sir (William) Ian, Kt.

Pound, Sir Derek Allen, Bt. (1905).

Powell, Sir (Arnold Joseph) Philip, Kt., O.B.E., A.R.A., F.R.I.B.A.

Powell, *Maj.* Sir Richard George Douglas, Bt., M.C. (1897).

Powell, Sir Richard Royle, G.C.B., K.B.E., C.M.G.

Power, *Vice-Adm.* Sir Arthur Mackenzie, K.C.B., M.B.E.

Power, Sir John Patrick McLannahan, Bt. (1924).

Power, *Admiral* Sir Manley Laurence, K.C.B., C.B.E., D.S.O.

Powles, Sir Guy Richardson, K.B.E., C.M.G., E.D.

Powlett, *Vice-Adm.* Sir Peveril Barton Reibey Wallop William-, K.C.B., K.C.M.G., C.B.E., D.S.O.

Poynton, Sir (Arthur) Hilton, G.C.M.G.

Prain, Sir Ronald Lindsay, Kt., O.B.E.

Prescott, Sir Mark, Bt. (1938).

Prescott, Sir Stanley Lewis, Kt., O.B.E.

Preston, Sir Kenneth Huson, Kt.

Preston, Sir Thomas Hildebrand, Bt., O.B.E. (1815).

Pretyman, Sir Walter Frederick, K.B.E.

Prevost, *Capt.* Sir George James Augustine, Bt. (1805).

Price, Sir (Archibald) Grenfell, Kt., C.M.G.

Price, Sir Charles Keith Napier Rugge-, Bt. (1804).

Price, Sir (Charles) Roy, K.C.M.G.

Price, Sir Frank Leslie, Kt.

Price, Sir James Robert, K.B.E.

Price, Sir Leslie Victor, Kt., O.B.E.

Price, Sir Norman Charles, K.C.B.

Price, Sir Robert John Green-, Bt. (1874).

Price, Sir Rose Francis, Bt. (1815).

Prichard, Sir Montague Illtyd, Kt., C.B.E., M.C.

Prickett, *Air Chief Marshal* Sir Thomas Other, K.C.B., D.S.O., D.F.C.

Prideaux, Sir Humphrey Povah Treverbian, Kt., O.B.E.

Prideaux, Sir John Francis, Kt., O.B.E.

Pridie, Sir Eric Denholm, K.C.M.G., D.S.O., O.B.E.

Priestley, Sir Gerald William, K.C.I.E.

Primrose, Sir John Ure, Bt. (1903).

Pringle, *Air Marshal* Sir Charles Norman Seton, Kt.

Pringle, Sir Stuart Robert, Bt. (s 1683).

Pritchard, Sir Asa Hubert, Kt.

Pritchard, Sir Fred Eills, Kt., M.B.E.

Pritchard, Sir Neil, K.C.M.G.

Pritchett, Sir Victor Sawden, Kt., C.B.E.

Proby, *Maj.* Sir Richard George, Bt., M.C. (1952).

Proctor, Sir (George) Philip, K.B.E.

Proctor, Sir (Philip) Dennis, K.C.B.

Proud, Sir George, Kt.

Pryke, Sir David Dudley, Bt. (1926).

Puckey, Sir Walter Charles, Kt.

Pugh, Sir Idwal Vaughan, K.C.B.

Pugsley, *Prof.* Sir Alfred Grenvile, Kt., O.B.E., D.Sc., F.R.S.

Pumphrey, Sir (John) Laurence, K.C.M.G.

Purchas, *Hon.* Sir Francis Brooks, Kt.

Quartermaine, Sir Allan Stephen, Kt., C.B.E., M.C.

Quénet, Sir Vincent Ernest, Kt.

Quilter, Sir Anthony Raymond Leopold Cuthbert, Bt. (1897).

Raby, Sir Victor Harry, K.B.E., C.B., M.C.

Radcliffe, Sir Sebastian Everard, Bt. (1813).

Radclyffe, Sir Charles Edward Mott-, Kt.

Radford, Sir Ronald Walter, K.C.B., M.B.E.

Radzinowicz, *Prof.* Sir Leon, Kt., Ll.D.

Rae, Sir Alexander Montgomery Wilson, K.C.M.G., M.D.

Rae, *Hon.* Sir Wallace Alexander Ramsay, Kt.

Raeburn, Sir Edward Alfred, Bt. (1923).

Rahimtoola, Sir Fazil Ibrahim, Kt., C.I.E.

Raikes, Sir (Henry) Victor (Alpin MacKinnon), K.B.E.

Raikes, *Vice-Adm.* Sir Iwan Geoffrey, K.C.B., C.B.E., D.S.C.

Raisman, Sir (Abraham) Jeremy, G.C.M.G., G.C.I.E., K.C.S.I.

Rajapakse, Sir Lalita Abhaya, Kt., Q.C.

Ralli, Sir Godfrey Victor, Bt., T.D. (1912).

Ralphs, Sir (Frederick) Lincoln, Kt.

Ram Chandra Mardarai Deo, *Raja Bahadur*, Sir, Kt.

Ramgoolam, *Rt. Hon.* Sir Seewoosagur, Kt.

Rampton, Sir Jack Leslie, K.C.B.

Ramsay, *Maj.-Gen.* Sir Alan Hollick, Kt., C.B., C.B.E., D.S.O.

Ramsay, Sir Alexander William Burnett, Bt. (1806).

Ramsay, Sir James Maxwell, Kt., C.B.E., D.S.C.

Ramsay, Sir Neis Alexander, Bt. (s 1666).

Ramsay, Sir Thomas Meek, Kt., C.M.G.

Ramsbotham, *Hon.* Sir Peter Edward, G.C.V.O., K.C.M.G.

Ramsden, Sir Geoffrey Charles Frescheville, Kt., C.I.E.

Ramsden, Sir (Geoffrey) William Pennington-, Bt. (1689).

Ramsey, Sir Alfred Ernest, Kt.

Ranasinha, Sir Arthur Godwin, Kt., C.M.G., C.B.E.

Randall, Sir Alec Walter George, K.C.M.G., O.B.E.

Randall, *Prof.* Sir John Turton, Kt., D.SC., F.R.S.

Randall, Sir Richard John, Kt.

Rank, Sir Benjamin Keith, Kt., C.M.G.

Rankin, Sir Hugh (Charles Rhys), Bt. (1898).

Rankine, Sir John Dalziel, K.C.M.G., K.C.V.O.

Ransome, Sir Gordon Arthur, K.B.E.

Raper, *Vice-Adm.* Sir (Robert) George, K.C.B.

Rapp, Sir Thomas Cecil, K.B.E., C.M.G., M.C.

Rasch, *Maj.* Sir Richard Guy Carne, Bt. (1903).

Rashleigh, Sir Harry Evelyn Battie, Bt. (1831).

Ratteray, *Hon.* Sir George Oswald, Kt., C.B.E.

Rattigan, Sir Terence Mervyn, Kt., C.B.E.

Rawlinson, Sir Anthony Henry John, Bt. (1891).

Rawlinson, *Rt. Hon.* Sir Peter Anthony Grayson, Q.C., M.P.

Raymond, Sir Stanley Edward, Kt.

Rayner, Sir Derek George, Kt.

Rayner, *Brig.* Sir Ralph Herbert, Kt.

Read, *Air Marshal* Sir Charles Frederick, K.B.E., C.B., D.F.C., A.F.C.

Read, *General* Sir (John) Antony (Jervis), G.C.B., C.B.E., D.S.O., M.C.

Read, Sir John Emms, Kt.

Read, *Lt.-Gen.* Sir John Hugh Sherlock, K.C.B., O.B.E.

Reade, Sir Clyde Nixon, Bt. (1661).

Readhead, Sir James Templeman, Bt. (1922).

Rebbeck, *Rear-Adm.* Sir (Leopold) Edward, K.B.E., C.B.

Reddish, Sir Halford Walter Lupton, Kt.

Redfearn, Sir Herbert, Kt.

Redfern, Sir (Arthur) Shuldham, K.C.V.O., C.M.G.

Redgrave, Sir Michael Scudamore, Kt., C.B.E.

Redman, *Lt.-Gen.* Sir Harold, K.C.B., C.B.E.

Redshaw, Sir Leonard, Kt., T.D.

Redwood, Sir Peter Boverton, Bt. (1911).

Reece, Sir Gerald, K.C.M.G., C.B.E.

Reece, Sir (Louis) Alan, Kt., C.M.G.

Reed, *Hon.* Sir Nigel Vernon, Kt., C.B.E.

Reed, Sir Reginald Charles, Kt., C.B.E.

Rees, *Hon.* Sir (Charles William) Stanley, Kt., T.D.

Reeve, *Hon.* Sir (Charles) Trevor, Kt.

Refshauge, *Maj.-Gen.* Sir William Dudley, Kt., C.B.E.

Reid, Sir Alexander James, Bt. (1897).

Reid, *Hon.* Sir George Oswald, Kt., Q.C.

Reid, *Air Vice-Marshal* Sir (George) Ranald Macfarlane, K.C.B., D.S.O., M.C.

Reid, Sir Hugh, Bt. (1922).

Reid, Sir John Thyne, Kt., C.M.G.

Reid, Sir Norman Robert, Kt.

Reid, Sir William, Kt., C.B.E., Ph.D.

Reilly, Sir (D'Arcy) Patrick, G.C.M.G., O.B.E.

Reilly, Sir Paul, Kt.

Reiss, Sir John Anthony Ewart, Kt., B.E.M.

Renals, Sir Stanley, Bt. (1895).

Rendel, Sir George William, K.C.M.G.

Rendall, Sir William, Kt.

Rennie, *Hon.* Sir Alfred Baillie, Kt.

Rennie, Sir Gilbert (McCall), G.B.E., K.C.M.G., M.C.

Rennie, Sir John Ogilvy, K.C.M.G.

Rennie, Sir John Shaw, G.C.M.G., O.B.E.

Renshaw, Sir (Charles) Stephen (Bine), Bt. (1903).

Renton, *Rt. Hon.* Sir David Lockhart-Mure, K.B.E., T.D., Q.C., M.P.

Renwick, Sir John, Kt.

Renwick, Sir Richard Eustace, Bt. (1921).

Reporter, Sir Shapoor Ardeshirji, K.B.E.

Reynolds, Sir David James, Bt. (1923).

Rhodes, Sir John Christopher Douglas, Bt. (1919).

Rich, Sir Almeric Frederic Conness, Bt. (1791).

Richards, *Hon.* Sir Edward Trenton, Kt., C.B.E.

Richards, Sir Francis Brooks, K.C.M.G., D.S.C.

Richards, Sir Gordon, Kt.

Richards, Sir James Maude, Kt., C.B.E.

Richardson, *General* Sir Charles Leslie, G.C.B., C.B.E., D.S.O.

Richardson, Sir Egerton Rudolf, Kt., C.M.G.

Richardson, Sir George Wigham, Bt. (1929).

Richardson, Sir (Horace) Frank, Kt.

Richardson, Sir (John) Eric, Kt.

Richardson, Sir (John) Henry (Swain), Kt.

Richardson, Sir John Samuel, Bt., M.V.O., M.D. (1963).

Richardson, Sir Leslie Lewis, Bt. (1924).

Richardson, Sir Ralph David, Kt.

Richardson, Sir Simon Alasdair Stewart-, Bt. (s 1630).

Richardson, Sir William Robert, Kt.

Riches, Sir Derek Martin Hurry, K.C.M.G.

Riches, Sir Eric William, Kt., M.C.

Riches, *General* Sir Ian Hurry, K.C.B., D.S.O.

Richmond, Sir Alan James, Kt.

Richmond, *Rt. Hon.* Sir Clifford Parris, Kt.

Richmond, Sir John Christopher Blake, K.C.M.G.

Richmond, Sir John Frederick, Bt. (1929).

Richmond, *Vice-Adm.* Sir Maxwell, K.B.E., C.B., D.S.O.

Richter, *Hon.* Sir Harold, Kt.

Rickett, Sir Denis Hubert Fletcher, K.C.M.G., C.B.

Ricketts, Sir Robert Cornwallis Gerald St. Leger, Bt. (1828).

Ricks, Sir John Plowman, Kt.

Riddell, Sir John Charles Buchanan-, Bt. (s 1628).

Ride, Sir Lindsay Tasman, Kt., C.B.E., E.D.

Ridley, Sir Sydney, Kt.

Rieger, Sir Clarence Oscar Ferrego, Kt., C.B.E.

Rigby, *Lt.-Col.* Sir (Hugh) John (Macbeth), Bt. (1920).

Rigby, *Hon.* Sir Ivo Charles Clayton, Kt.

Ring, Sir Lindsay Roberts, G.B.E.

Ringadoo, *Hon.* Sir Veerasamy, Kt.

Ripley, Sir Hugh, Bt. (1880).

Risson, *Maj.-Gen.* Sir Robert Joseph Henry, Kt., C.B., C.B.E., D.S.O., E.D.

Ritchie, Sir James Edward Thomson, Bt. (1918).

Ritchie, Sir (John) Douglas, Kt., M.C.

Ritchie, Sir John Neish, Kt., C.B.

Ritchie, *General* Sir Neil Methuen, G.B.E., K.C.B., D.S.O., M.C.

Ritson, Sir Edward Herbert, K.B.E., C.B.

Roberts, Sir Bryan Clieve, K.C.M.G., Q.C.

Roberts, *Hon.* Sir Denys Tudor Emil, K.B.E., Q.C.

Roberts, Sir Frank Kenyon, G.C.M.G., G.C.V.O.

Roberts, Sir Geoffrey Newland, Kt., C.B.E., A.F.C.

Roberts, *Brig.* Sir Geoffrey Paul Hardy-, K.C.V.O., C.B., C.B.E.

Roberts, Sir Gilbert, Kt., F.R.S.

Roberts, Sir Harold Charles West, Kt., C.B.E., M.C.

Roberts, *General* Sir Ouvry Lindfield, G.C.B., K.B.E., D.S.O.

Roberts, Sir Peter Geoffrey, Bt. (1919).

Roberts, *Col.* Sir Thomas Langdon Howland, Bt., C.B.E. (1809).

Roberts, Sir Walter St. Clair Howland, K.C.M.G., M.C.

Roberts, Sir William James Denby, Bt. (1909).

Robertson, *Prof.* Sir Alexander, Kt., C.B.E.

Robertson, Sir James Anderson, Kt., C.B.E.

Robertson, Sir James Wilson, K.T., G.C.M.G., G.C.V.O., K.B.E.

Robertson, *Prof.* Sir Rutherford Ness, Kt., C.M.G.

Robieson, Sir William Dunkeld, Kt., LL.D.

Scamp, Sir (Athelstan) Jack, Kt.

Scarlett, Sir Peter William Shelley Yorke, K.C.M.G., K.C.V.O.

Scarman, *Rt. Hon.* Sir Leslie George, Kt., O.B.E.

Scherger, *Air Chief Marshal* Sir Frederick Rudolph William, K.B.E., C.B., D.S.O., A.F.C.

Schultz, Sir (Joseph) Leopold, Kt., O.B.E.

Schuster, Sir (Felix) James Moncrieff, Bt., O.B.E. (1906).

Schuster, Sir George Ernest K.C.S.I., K.C.M.G., C.B.E., M.C.

Scicluna, Sir Hannibal Publius, Kt., M.B.E.

Scoones, *Maj.-Gen.* Sir Reginald Laurence, K.B.E., C.B., D.S.O.

Scopes, Sir Frederick, Kt.

Scopes, Sir Leonard Arthur, K.C.V.O., C.M.G., O.B.E.

Scott, Sir (Arleigh) Winston, G.C.M.G, G.C.V.O.

Scott, Sir (Arthur John) Guillum, Kt., T.D.

Scott, Sir (Charles) Hilary, Kt.

Scott, Sir David Aubrey, K.C.M.G.

Scott, Sir David John Montagu-Douglas-, K.C.M.G., O.B.E.

Scott, *Lt.-Col.* Sir Douglas Winchester, Bt. (1913).

Scott, Sir Edward Arthur Dolman. Bt. (1806).

Scott, Sir Eric, Kt., O.B.E.

Scott, Sir George Edward, Kt., C.B.E.

Scott, Sir (Henry) Maurice, Kt., C.B.E., D.F.C.

Scott, Sir Ian Dixon, K.C.M.G., K.C.V.O., C.I.E.

Scott, *Lt.-Col.* Sir James Walter, Bt. (1962).

Scott, Sir Michael Fergus Maxwell, Bt. (F 1642).

Scott, Sir Oliver Christopher Anderson, Bt. (1909).

Scott, Sir Peter Markham, Kt., C.B.E., D.S.C.

Scott, Sir Robert Heatlie, G.C.M.G., C.B.E.

Scott, Sir (Ronald) Bodley, G.C.V.O., D.M.

Scott, Sir Ronald Stewart, Kt.

Scott, Sir Terence Charles Stuart Morrison-, Kt., D.S.C., D.SC.

Scott, Sir Walter, Bt. (1907).

Scott, Sir Walter, Kt., C.M.G.

Scott, *Maj.-Gen.* Sir William Arthur, K.C.M.G., C.B., C.B.E.

Scotter, *Lt.-Gen.* Sir William Norman Roy, K.C.B., O.B.E., M.C.

Scowen, *Prof.* Sir Eric Frank, Kt., M.D., D.SC.

Scragg, *Air Vice-Marshal* Sir Colin, K.B.E., C.B., A.F.C.

Scrivenor, Sir Thomas Vaisey, Kt., C.M.G.

Seale, Sir John Henry, Bt. (1838).

Sebright, Sir Hugo Giles Edmund, Bt. (1626).

Seddon, Sir Herbert John, Kt., C.M.G., D.M.

Seel, Sir George Frederick, K.C.M.G.

Seely, Sir Victor Basil John, Bt. (1896).

Selby, Sir Kenneth, Kt.

Selleck, Sir Francis Palmer, K.B.E., M.C.

Sellers, *Rt. Hon.* Sir Frederic Aked, Kt., M.C.

Sellors, Sir Thomas Holmes, Kt., D.M.

Selway, *Air Marshal* Sir Anthony Dunkerton, K.C.B., D.F.C.

Senior, Sir Edward Walters, Kt., C.M.G.

Serpell, Sir David Radford, K.C.B., C.M.G., O.B.E.

Seton, Sir (Christopher) Bruce, Bt. (S 1663).

Seton, Sir Claud Ramsay Wilmot, Kt., M.C.

Seton, Sir Robert James, Bt. (S 1683).

Seward, Sir Eric John, K.B.E.

Seward, Sir Samuel Conrad, Kt., O.B.E.

Seymour, Sir Horace James, G.C.M.G., C.V.O.

Seymour, *Cdr.* Sir Michael Culme-, Bt., R.N. (1809).

Shakerley, Sir Geoffrey Adam, Bt. (1838).

Shakerley, *Col.* Sir Geoffrey Peter, Kt., C.B.E., M.C., T.D.

Shakespeare, *Rt. Hon.* Sir Geoffrey Hithersay, Bt. (1942).

Shankland, Sir Thomas Murray, Kt., C.M.G.

Sharp, Sir Edward Harold Wilfred, Bt. (1922).

Sharp, Sir George, Kt., O.B.E.

Sharp, *General* Sir John Aubrey Taylor, K.C.B., M.C.

Sharp, Sir Milton Reginald, Bt. (1920).

Sharpe, Sir Reginald Taaffe, Kt., Q.C.

Shaw, Sir Bernard Vidal, Kt.

Shaw, *Cdr.* Sir John James Kenward Best-, Bt., R.N. (1665).

Shaw, Sir John Valentine Wistar, K.C.M.G.

Shaw, Sir Robert, Bt. (1821).

Shaw, *Rt. Hon.* Sir Sebag, Kt.

Shearman, Sir Harold Charles, Kt.

Sheehy, *Hon.* Sir Joseph Aloysius, K.B.E.

Sheffield, Sir Robert Arthur, Bt. (1755).

Shehadie, Sir Nicholas Michael, Kt., O.B.E.

Sheldon, Sir Wilfrid Percy Henry, K.C.V.O.

Shelley, Sir John Richard, Bt. (1611).

Shepheard, Sir Victor George, K.C.B.

Shepherd, Sir Peter Malcolm, Kt., C.B.E.

Sheridan, *Hon.* Sir Dermot Joseph, Kt., C.M.G.

Sherlock, Sir Philip Manderson, Kt., C.B.E.

Sherman, Sir Louis, Kt., O.B.E.

Shields, Sir Neil Stanley, Kt., M.C.

Shiffner, Sir Henry David, Bt. (1818).

Shillington, Sir (Robert Edward) Graham, Kt., C.B.E.

Shires, Sir Frank, Kt.

Shirley, *Air Vice-Marshal* Sir Thomas Ulric Curzon, K.B.E., C.B.

Sholl, *Hon.* Sir Reginald Richard, Kt.

Shone, Sir Robert Minshull, Kt., C.B.E.

Shuckburgh, Sir (Charles Arthur) Evelyn, G.C.M.G., C.B.

Shuckburgh, Sir Charles Gerald Stewkley, Bt. (1660).

Sich, Sir Rupert Leigh, Kt., C.B.

Sidey, *Air Marshal* Sir Ernest Shaw, K.B.E., C.B., M.D.

Sie, Sir Banja Tejan-, G.C.M.G.

Sieff, *Hon.* Sir Marcus Joseph, Kt., O.B.E.

Sim, Sir (George) Alexander (Strachan), Kt.

Sim, Sir Wilfred Joseph, K.B.E., Q.C.

Simeon, Sir John Edmund Barrington, Bt. (1815).

Simmonds, Sir Oliver Edwin, Kt.

Simpson, *General* Sir Frank Ernest Wallace, G.B.E., K.C.B., D.S.O.

Simpson, Sir James Dyer, Kt.

Simpson, Sir (John) Cyril Finucane, Bt (1935).

Simpson, Sir John Roughton, Kt., C.B.

Sims, Sir Alfred John, K.C.B., O.B.E.

Sinclair, Sir George Evelyn, Kt., C.M.G., O.B.E., M.P.

Sinclair, *Maj.-Gen.* Sir John Alexander, K.C.M.G., C.B., O.B.E.

Sinclair, Sir John Rollo Norman Blair, Bt. (S 1704).

Sinclair, *Air Vice-Marshal* Sir Laurence Frank, K.C.B., G.C., C.B.E., D.S.O.

Sinclair, Sir Leonard, Kt.

Sinclair, Sir Ronald Ormiston, K.B.E.

Sinclair, Sir William, Kt., C.B.E.

Singh, *Hon.* Sir Vijay Raghubir, Kt.

Singhania, Sir Padampat, Kt.

Singhateh, *Alhaj'i* Sir Farimang, G.C.M.G.

Singleton, Sir Edward Henry Sibbald, Kt.

Sinker, Sir (Algernon) Paul K.C.M.G., C.B.

Sitwell, Sir Sacheverell, Bt. (1808).

Skelhorn, Sir Norman John, K.B.E., Q.C.

Skinner, Sir Thomas Edward, K.B.E.

Skinner, Sir (Thomas) Keith (Hewitt), Bt. (1912).

Skipwith, Sir Patrick Alexander D'Estoteville, Bt. (1622).

Skyrme, Sir William Thomas Charles, K.C.V.O., C.B., C.B.E., T.D.

Slade, Sir Benjamin Julian Alfred, Bt. (1831).

Slade, *Hon.* Sir Christopher John, Kt.

Slater, *Admiral* Sir Robin (Leonard Francis) Durnford-, K.C.B.

Slattery, *Rear-Adm.* Sir Matthew Sausse, K.B.E., C.B.

Sleigh, Sir Hamilton Morton Howard, Kt.

Sleight, Sir John Frederick, Bt. (1920).

Slesser, *Rt. Hon.* Sir Henry, Kt.

Slessor, *Marshal of the Royal Air Force* Sir John Cotesworth, G.C.B., D.S.O., M.C.

Slimmings, Sir William Kenneth Macleod, Kt., C.B.E.

Slynn, *Hon.* Sir Gordon, Kt.

Small, Sir Andrew Bruce, Kt.

Smallpeice, Sir Basil, K.C.V.O.

Smallwood, *Air Chief Marshal* Sir Denis Graham, G.B.E. K.C.B., D.S.O., D.F.C.

Smeeton, *Vice-Adm.* Sir Richard Michael, K.C.B., M.B.E.

Smiley, Sir Hugh Houston, Bt. (1903).

Smirk, *Prof.* Sir Frederick Horace, K.B.E., M.D.

Smith, Sir Alexander Abel, Kt., T.D.

Smith, Sir Alexander Mair, Kt., Ph.D.

Smith, Sir (Alexander) Rowland, Kt.

Smith, Sir Allan Chalmers, Kt., M.C.

Smith, *Lieut-Gen.* Sir Arthur Francis, K.C.B., K.B.E., D.S.O., M.C.

Smith Sir Arthur Henry, Kt.

Smith, Sir Bryan Evers Sharwood-, K.C.M.G., K.C.V.O., K.B.E.

Smith, Sir Carl Victor, Kt., C.B.E.

Smith, *Maj.-Gen.* Sir Cecil Miller, K.B.E., C.B., M.C.

Smith, Sir Christopher Sydney Winwood, Bt. (1809).

Smith, *Rt. Hon.* Sir Dereck Colclough Walker-, Bt., T.D., Q.C., M.P. (1960).

Smith, *Maj.-Gen.* Sir Edmund Hakewill, K.C.V.O., C.B., C.B.E., M.C.

Smith, *Vice-Adm.* Sir (Edward Michael) Conolly Abel, G.C.V.O., C.B.

Smith, Sir (Edwin) Rodney, K.B.E.

Smith, Sir (Frank) Ewart, Kt.

Smith, *Vice-Adm.* Sir Geoffrey Thistleton-, K.B.E., C.B., G.M.

Smith, Sir (George) Guy Bracewell, Bt., M.B.E. (1947).

Smith, Sir (Harold) Gengoult, Kt., V.D.

Smith, *Col.* Sir Henry Abe K.C.M.G., K.C.V.O., D.S.O.

Smith, Sir Henry Martin, Kt., C.B.E.

Smith, Sir Henry Thompson, K.B.E., C.B.

Smith, Sir Henry Wilson, K.C.B., K.B.E.

Smith, Sir Howard Frank Trayton, K.C.M.G.

Smith, Sir Hubert Shirley-, Kt., C.B.E.

Smith, Sir John Hamilton-Spencer-, Bt. (1804).

Smith, Sir John Kenneth Newson-, Bt. (1944).

Smith, Sir Laurence Barton Grafftey-, K.C.M.G., K.B.E.

Smith, Sir Raymond Horace, K.B.E.

Smith, *Col. Rt. Hon.* Sir Reginald Hugh Dorman-, G.B.E.

Smith, Sir Richard Rathbone Vassar-, Bt., T.D. (1917).

Smith, Sir Thomas Gilbert, Bt. (1897).

Smith, *Vice-Adm.* Sir Victor Alfred Trumper, K.B.E., C.B., D.S.C.

Smith, Sir (William) Gordon, Bt., V.R.D. (1945).

Smith, Sir William Reardon Reardon-, Bt. (1920).

Smith, Sir (William) Reginald Verdon, Kt.

Smith, Sir (William) Richard Prince-, Bt. (1911).

Smithers, *Prof.* Sir David Waldron, Kt., M.D.

Smithers, Sir Peter Henry Berry Otway, Kt., V.R.D., D.Phil.

Smyth, *Brig. Rt. Hon.* Sir John George, Bt., VC, M.C. (1955).

Smyth, *Capt.* Sir Philip Weyland Bowyer-, Bt., R.N. (1661).

Smythe, Sir Reginald Harry, K.B.E.

Snelling, Sir Arthur Wendell, K.C.M.G., K.C.V.O.

Snelson, Sir Edward Alec Abbott, K.B.E.

Soame, Sir Charles Burnett Buckworth-Herne-, Bt. (1697).

Soames, *Rt. Hon.* Sir (Arthur) Christopher (John), G.C.M.G., G.C.V.O., C.B.E.

Sobell, Sir Michael, Kt.

Sobers, Sir Garfield St. Auburn, Kt.

Solomon, Sir David Arnold, Kt., M.B.E.

Somerset, Sir Henry Beaufort, Kt., C.B.E.

Somerville, Sir Robert, K.C.V.O.

Sopwith, Sir Charles Ronald, Kt.

Sopwith, Sir Thomas Octave Murdoch, Kt., C.B.E.

Sorsbir, Sir Malin, Kt., C.B.E.

South, Sir Arthur, Kt.

Southby, *Lt. Col.* Sir (Archibald) Richard (Charles), Bt., O.B.E. (1937).

Southern, Sir Richard William, Kt., F.B.A.

Southern, Sir Robert, Kt., C.B.E.

Southey, Sir Robert John, Kt., C.M.G.

Southward, Sir Ralph, K.C.V.O., F.R.C.P.

Southwell, Sir (Charles Archibald) Philip, Kt., C.B.E., M.C.

Southworth, *Hon.* Sir Frederick, Kt.

Souyave, *Hon.* Sir (Louis) Georges, Kt.

Soysa, Sir Warusahennedige Abraham Bastian, Kt., C.B.E.

Spearman, Sir Alexander Bowyer, Bt. (1840).

Spearman, Sir Alexander (Cadwallader) Mainwaring, Kt.

Speed, Sir Robert William Arney, Kt., C.B., Q.C.

Speelman, *Jonkheer* Sir Cornelis Jacob, Bt. (1686).

Speir, Sir Rupert Malise, Kt.

Spence, Sir Basil Urwin, Kt., O.M., O.B.E., T.D., R.A.

Spencer, Sir Kelvin Tallent, Kt., C.B.E., M.C.

Spender, *Hon.* Sir Percy Claude, K.C.V.O., K.B.E., Q.C.

Spicer, *Hon.* Sir John Armstrong, Kt.

Spicer, Sir Peter James, Bt. (1906).

Spotswood, *Marshal of the Royal Air Force* Sir Denis Frank, G.C.B., C.B.E., D.S.O., D.F.C.

Springer, Sir Hugh Worrell, K.C.M.G., C.B.E.

Spry, *Brig.* Sir Charles Chambers Fowell, Kt., C.B.E., D.S.O.

Spry, Sir John Farley, Kt.

Spurling, *Hon.* Sir (Arthur) Dudley, Kt., C.B.E.

Stable, *Rt. Hon.* Sir Wintringham Norton, Kt., M.C.

Stack, *Air Chief Marshal* Sir (Thomas) Neville, K.C.B., C.V.O., C.B.E., A.F.C.

Stainton, Sir Anthony Nathaniel, K.C.B., Q.C.

Stallard, Sir Peter Hyla Gawne, K.C.M.G., C.V.O., M.B.E.

Stallworthy, *Prof.* Sir John Arthur, Kt., F.R.C.S.

Stamer, Sir (Lovelace) Anthony, Bt. (1809).

Stamp, *Rt. Hon.* Sir (Edward) Blanshard, Kt.

Stainer, *Brig.* Sir Alexander Beville Gibbons, Bt., D.S.O., M.C. (1917).

Stanley, Sir Robert Christopher Stafford, K.B.E., C.M.G.

Staples, Sir John Richard, Bt. (I. 1628).

Stapleton, Sir Miles Talbot, Bt. (1679).

Stark, Sir Andrew Alexander Steel, K.C.M.G., C.V.O.

Starke, *Hon.* Sir John Erskine, Kt.

Starkey, *Lt.-Col.* Sir William Randle, Bt. (1935).

Starr, Sir Kenneth William, Kt., C.M.G., O.B.E., E.D.

Starritt, Sir James, K.C.V.O.

Stedman, Sir George Foster, K.B.E., C.B., M.C.

Steedman, *Air Marshal* Sir Alexander McKay Sinclair, K.C.B., C.B.E., D.F.C.

Steel, *Maj.* Sir (Fiennes) William Strang, Bt. (1938).

Steel, Sir James, Kt., C.B.E.

Steel, Sir (Joseph) Lincoln (Spedding), Kt.

Stenhouse, Sir Nicol, Kt.

Stening, *Col.* Sir George Grafton Lees, Kt., E.D.

Stephen, Sir Alastair Eward, Kt.

Stephen, Sir Andrew, Kt.

Stephen, Sir James Alexander, Bt. (1891).

Stephen, *Hon.* Sir Ninian Martin, K.C.B.

Stephens, Sir David, K.C.B., C.V.O.

Stephens, Sir (Leon) Edgar, Kt., C.B.E.

Stephenson, *Lt.-Col.* Sir (Henry) Francis (Blake), Bt., O.B.E., T.D. (1936).

Stephenson, *Rt. Hon.* Sir John Frederick Eustace, Kt.

Stephenson, Sir Percy, Kt.

Stephenson, Sir William Samuel, Kt., M.C., D.F.C.

Sternberg, Sir Sigmund, Kt.

Stevens, *Air Marshal* Sir Alick Charles, K.B.E., C.B.

Stevens, *Vice-Adm.* Sir John Felgate, K.B.E., C.B.

Stevens, Sir Roger Bentham, G.C.M.G.

Stevenson, *Rt. Hon.* Sir (Aubrey) Melford (Sted), Kt.

Stevenson, Sir Matthew, K.C.B., C.M.G.

Stevenson, Sir Ralph (Clarmont) Skrine, G.C.M.G.

Stevenson, Sir Simpson, Kt.

Stevenson, Sir William Alfred, K.B.E.

Steward, Sir Harold MacDonald, Kt.

Steward, Sir William Arthur, Kt.

Stewart, Sir Bruce Fraser, Bt. (1920).

Stewart, Sir David Brodribb, Bt., T.D. (1960).

Stewart, Sir David James Henderson-, Bt. (1957).

Stewart, Sir Dugald Leslie Lorn, K.C.V.O., C.M.G.

Stewart, Sir Euan Guy Shaw-, Kt., (s. 1667).

Stewart, *Prof.* Sir Frederick Henry, Kt., Ph.D., F.R.S., F.R.S.E.

Stewart, Sir Hector Hamilton, K.B.E.

Stewart, Sir Herbert Kay, Kt., C.I.E.

Stewart, Sir Hugh Charlie Godfray, Bt. (1803).

Stewart, Sir Iain Maxwell, Kt.

Stewart, Sir James Watson, Bt. (1920).

Stewart, Sir Jocelyn Harry, Bt. (1 1623).

Stewart, Sir Michael Norman Francis, K.C.M.G., O.B.E.

Stewart, Sir Ronald Compton, Bt. (1937).

Stirling, Sir Charles Norman, K.C.M.G., K.C.V.O.

Stoby, Sir Kenneth Sievewright, Kt.

Stockdale, Sir Edmund Villiers Minshull, Bt. (1960).

Stocker, *Hon.* Sir John Dexter, Kt., M.C., T.D.

Stockil, Sir Raymond Osbourne, K.B.E.

Stockwell, *General* Sir Hugh Charles G.C.B., K.B.E., D.S.O.

Stokes, Sir Harold Frederick, Kt., C.B.E.

Stone, Sir (John) Leonard, Kt., O.B.E., Q.C.

†Stonhouse, Sir Philip Allan, Bt. (1628).

Stooke, Sir George Beresford-, K.C.M.G.

Storrar, Sir John, Kt., C.B.E., M.C.

Stott, Sir Philip Sidney, Bt., (1920).

Stourton, Sir Ivo Herbert Evelyn Joseph, Kt., C.M.G., O.B.E.

Stout, Sir (Thomas) Duncan (Macgregor), Kt., C.B.E., D.S.O., E.D.

Stow, Sir Edmond Cecil Philipson-, Bt., M.B.E. (1907).

Stow, Sir John Montague, G.C.M.G., K.C.V.O.

Stracey, Sir John Simon, Bt. (1818).

Strachan, Sir Andrew Henry, Kt., C.B.E.

Strachey, Sir Charles, Bt. (1801).

Strasser, Sir Paul, Kt.

Stratton, Sir (Francis) John, Kt., C.B.E.

Stratton, *Lt.-Gen.* Sir William Henry, K.C.B., C.V.O., C.B.E., D.S.O.

Streat, Sir (Edward) Raymond, K.B.E.

Streatfeild, Sir Geoffrey Hugh Benbow, Kt., M.C.

Street, *Hon.* Sir Laurence Whistler, K.C.M.G.

Strong, Sir Charles Lorz, K.C.V.O.

Strong, *Maj.-Gen.* Sir Kenneth William Dobson, K.B.E., C.B.

Strong, *Most Rev.* Philip Nigel Warrington, K.B.E., C.M.G., D.D.

Stronge, *Capt. Rt. Hon.* Sir (Charles) Norman (Lockhart), Bt., M.C. (1803).

Strutt, Sir (Henry) Austin, K.C.V.O., C.B.

Strutt, Sir Nigel Edward, Kt., T.D.

†Stuart, Sir Philip Luttrell, Bt. (1660).

Stubblefield, Sir (Cyril) James, Kt., D.SC., Ph.D., F.R.S.

Stucley, Sir Dennis Frederic Bankes, Bt. (1859).

Studd, Sir Peter Malden, G.B.E.

Studd, Sir (Robert) Kynaston, Bt. (1929).

Studholme, Sir Henry Gray, Bt., C.V.O. (1956).

Style, *Lt. Cdr.* Sir Godfrey William, Kt., C.B.E., D.S.C., R.N.

Style, Sir William Montague, Bt. (1627).

Suffield, Sir (Henry John) Lester, Kt.

Sugden, *Maj.-Gen.* Sir Henry Haskins Clapham, K.B.E., C.B., D.S.O.

Sugerman, *Hon.* Sir Bernard, Kt.

Sullivan, Sir Richard Benjamin Magniac, Bt. (1804).

Summerfield, *Hon.* Sir John Crampton, Kt., C.B.E.

Summerhayes, Sir Christopher Henry, K.B.E., C.M.G.

Summers, Sir Felix Roland Bratten, Bt. (1952).

Summers, Sir Richard Felix, Kt.

Summerscale, Sir John Percival, K.B.E.

Summerson, Sir John Newenham, Kt., C.B.E., F.B.A., F.S.A.

Summerville, Sir (William) Alan (Thompson), Kt., D.SC.

Sunderland, *Prof.* Sir Sydney, Kt., C.M.G., M.D.

Surridge, Sir (Ernest) Rex (Edward), Kt., C.M.G.

Sutherland, Sir Benjamin Ivan, Bt. (1921).

Sutherland, Sir (Frederick) Neil, Kt., C.B.E.

Sutherland, Sir Gordon Brims Black McIvor, Kt., F.R.S.

Sutherland, Sir Maurice, Kt.

Suttie, Sir George Philip Grant-, Bt. (S 1702).

Sutton, Sir Frederick Walter, Kt., O.B.E.

Sutton, Sir (Oliver) Graham, Kt., C.B.E., D.SC., F.R.S.

Sutton, Sir Robert Lexington, Bt. (1772).

Sutton, Sir Stafford William Powell Foster-, K.B.E., C.M.G., Q.C.

Swaffield, Sir James Chesebrough, Kt., C.B.E., R.D.

Swallow, Sir William, Kt.

Swann, Sir Anthony Charles Christopher, Bt., C.M.G., O.B.E., (1906).

Swann, *Prof.* Sir Michael Meredith, Kt., Ph.D., F.R.S., F.R.S.E.

Swanwick, *Hon.* Sir Graham Russell, Kt., M.B.E.

Swartz, *Hon.* Sir Reginald William Colin, K.B.E., E.D.

Swaziland, The Ngwenyama of, K.B.E.

Swiss, Sir Rodney Geoffrey, Kt., O.B.E.

Swynnerton, Sir Roger John Massy, Kt., C.M.G., O.B.E., M.C.

Syers, Sir Cecil George Lewis, K.C.M.G., C.V.O.

Sykes, Sir Charles, Kt., C.B.E., D.SC., Ph.D., F.R.S.

Sykes, Sir Francis Godfrey, Bt. (1781).

Sykes, Sir John Charles Anthony Le Gallais, Bt. (1921).

Sykes, Sir (Mark Tatton) Richard, Bt. (1783).

Syme, Sir Colin York, Kt.

Syme, *Prof.* Sir Ronald, Kt., O.M., E.B.A.

Symonds, *Air Vice-Marshal* Sir Charles, Putnam, K.B.E., C.B.

Symonette, Sir Roland Theodore, Kt.

Synge, Sir Robert Carson, Bt. (1801).

Tailyour, *General* Sir Norman Hastings, K.C.B., D.S.O., R.M.

Tait, Sir James Blair, Kt., Q.C.

Tait, Sir James Sharp, Kt., Ph.D.

Tait, Sir Peter, K.B.E.

Tait, *Air Vice-Marshal* Sir Victor Hubert, K.B.E., C.B.

Talbot, *Vice-Adm.* Sir (Arthur Allison) FitzRoy, K.B.E., C.B., D.S.O.

Talbot, *Hon.* Sir Hilary Gwynne, Kt.

Talbot, *Lt.-Gen.* Sir Norman Graham Guy, K.B.E., T.D.

Tallack, Sir Hugh Mackay, Kt.

Tancred, Sir Henry Lawson-, Bt. (1662).

Tang, Sir Shiu-Kin, Kt., C.B.E.

Tange, Sir Arthur Harold, Kt., C.B.E.

Tanner, Sir Edgar Stephen, Kt., C.B.E., E.D.

Tansley, Sir Eric Crawford, Kt., C.M.G.

Tapp, *Maj.-Gen.* Sir Nigel Prior Hanson, K.B.E., C.B., D.S.O.

Tarbat, Sir John Allan, Kt.

Tasker, Sir Theodore James, Kt., C.I.E., O.B.E.

Tate, *Lt.-Col.* Sir Henry, Bt. (1898).

Taylor, *Lt.-Gen.* Sir Allan Macnab, K.B.E., M.C.

Taylor, Sir Alvin Burton, Kt.

Taylor, Sir Charles Stuart, Kt., T.D.

Taylor, Sir (Eric) Stuart, Bt., O.B.E., M.D. (1917).

Taylor, Sir Frank, Kt.

Taylor, Sir George, Kt., D.SC., F.R.S., F.R.S.E.

Taylor, Sir James, Kt., M.B.E., D.SC.

Taylor, Sir John Aked, Kt., O.B.E., T.D.

Taylor, Sir Robert Mackinlay, Kt., C.B.E.

Tebbit, Sir Donald Claude, K.C.M.G.

Teelock, Sir Leckraz, Kt., C.B.E.

Temple, *Maj.* Sir Richard Anthony Purbeck, Bt., M.C. (1876).

Templeman, *Hon.* Sir Sydney William, Kt., M.B.E.

Templer, *Field Marshal* Sir Gerald Walter Robert, K.G., G.C.B., G.C.M.G., K.B.E., D.S.O.

Tennant, Sir Mark Dalcour, K.C.M.G., C.B.

Tennant, Sir Peter Frank Dalrymple, Kt., C.M.G., O.B.E.

Tennyson, Sir Charles Bruce Locker, Kt., C.M.G.

Terrell, *Capt.* Sir Thomas Antonio Reginald, Kt.

Terry, *Maj.* Sir Edward Henry Bouhier Imbert-, Bt., M.C. (1917).

Terry, Sir John Elliott, Kt.

Tetley, Sir Herbert, K.B.E., C.B.

Tett, Sir Hugh Charles, Kt.

Tewson, Sir (Harold) Vincent, Kt., C.B.E., M.C.

Thesiger, *Hon.* Sir Gerald Alfred, Kt., M.B.E.

Thiess, Sir Leslie Charles, Kt., C.B.E.

Thomas, Sir Ben Bowen, Kt.

Thomas, Sir Frederick William, Kt.

Thomas, Sir (Godfrey) Michael (David) Bt. (1694).

Thomas, *General* Sir (John) Noel, K.C.B., D.S.O., M.C.

Thomas, Sir Patrick Muirhead, Kt., D.S.O.

Thomas, Sir Robert Evan, Kt.

Thomas, Sir William James Cooper, Bt. (1929).

Thomas, Sir (William) Michael (Marsh), Bt. (1918).

Thompson, Sir Edward Hugh Dudley, Kt., M.B.E., T.D.

Thompson, Sir Edward Walter, Kt.

Thompson, *Lt.-Gen.* Sir Geoffrey Stuart, K.B.E., C.B., D.S.O.

Thompson, *Prof.* Sir Harold Warris, Kt., C.B.E., D.SC., F.R.S.

Thompson, Sir (Humphrey) Simon Mersey-, Bt. (1874).

Thompson, *Hon.* Sir John, Kt.

Thompson, Sir (Joseph) Herbert, Kt., C.I.E.

Thompson, Sir Kenneth Pugh, Bt. (1963).

Thompson, Sir (Louis) Lionel (Harry), Kt., C.B.E.

Thompson, *Lt.-Col.* Sir Peile Beaumont, Bt., O.B.E. (1890).

Thompson, Sir Richard Hilton Marler, Bt. (1963).

Thompson, Sir Robert Grainger Ker, K.B.E., C.M.G., D.S.O., M.C.

Thompson, Sir (Thomas) Lionel Tennyson, Bt. (1806).

Thompson, *Lt.-Gen.* Sir Treffry Owen, K.C.S.I., C.B., C.B.E.

Thomson, Sir (Arthur) Landsborough, Kt., C.B., O.B.E., D.SC.

Thomson, *Prof.* Sir Arthur Peregrine, Kt., M.C., M.D.

Thomson, Sir Daniel, Kt., C.B., M.D., F.R.C.P.

Thomson, Sir (Frederick) Douglas David, Bt. (1929).

Thomson, Sir Ivo Wilfrid Home, Bt. (1925).

Thomson, *Hon.* Sir James Beveridge, K.B.E.

Thomson, *Lt.-Col.* Sir John, K.B.E., T.D.

Thomson, Sir Ronald (Jordan), Kt.

Thorley, Sir Gerald Bowers, Kt., T.D.

Thorn, Sir Jules, Kt.

Thornley, Sir Colin Hardwick, K.C.M.G., C.V.O.

Thornton, Sir (Henry) Gerard, Kt., D.SC., F.R.S.

Thornton, *Lt.-Gen.* Sir Leonard Whitmore, K.C.B., C.B.E.

Thornton, Sir Peter Eustace, K.C.B.

Thornton, Sir Ronald George, Kt.

Thorold, Sir Anthony Henry, Bt., O.B.E., D.S.C. (1642).

Thouron, Sir John Rupert Hunt, K.B.E.

Throckmorton, Sir Robert George Maxwell, Bt. (1642).

Thumboo Chetty, Sir Bernard, Kt., O.B.E.

Thuraisingham, Sir Ernest Emmanuel Clough, Kt., C.B.E.

Thwin, Sir U, Kt.

Tibbits, *Capt.* Sir David Stanley, Kt., D.S.C., R.N.(ret).

Tilney, Sir John Dudley Richard Tarleton, Kt., T.D., M.P.

Tippett, Sir Michael Kemp, Kt., C.B.E.

Titman, Sir George Alfred, Kt., C.B.E., M.V.O.

Titterton, *Prof.* Sir Ernest William, Kt., C.M.G.

Tivey, Sir John Proctor, Kt.

Tod, *Air Marshal* Sir John Hunter Hunter-, K.B.E., C.B.

Todd, Sir Bryan James, Kt.

Todd, Sir Geoffrey Sydney, K.C.V.O., O.B.E.

Todd, Sir Herbert John, Kt., C.I.E.

Tollemache, *Maj.-Gen.* Sir Humphry Thomas, Bt., C.B., C.B.E., R.M. (1793).

Tomkins, Sir Alfred George, Kt., C.B.E.

Tomkins, Sir Edward Emile, G.C.M.G., C.V.O.

Tomlinson, Sir Frank Stanley, K.C.M.G.

Tong, Sir Walter Wharton, Kt.

Tooth, Sir Hugh Vere Huntly Duff Munro-Lucas-, Bt. (1920).

Tooth, *Hon.* Sir Seymour Douglas, Kt.

Toothill, Sir John Norman, Kt., C.B.E.

Tory, Sir Geofroy William, K.C.M.G.

Tottenham, Sir (George) Richard (Frederick), Kt., K.C.I.E., C.S.I.

Touche, Sir Norman George, Bt. (1920).

Touche, Sir Rodney Gordon, Bt. (1962).

Townley, Sir John Barton, Kt.

Townsend, *Prof.* Sir (Sydney) Lance, Kt., V.R.D., M.D., F.R.C.S.

Traherne, *Col.* Sir Cennydd George, K.G., T.D.

Travancore, *Maj.-Gen.* H.H. the Maharajah of, G.C.S.I., G.C.I.E.

Travers, Sir Thomas A'Beckett, Kt.

Treacher, *Admiral* Sir John Devereux, K.C.B.

Treatt, *Hon.* Sir Vernon Haddon, K.B.E., M.M., Q.C.

Tredgold, *Rt. Hon.* Sir Robert Clarkson, K.C.M.G., Q.C.

Trehane, Sir Walter Richard, Kt.

Trelawny, Sir John Barry Salusbury-, Bt. (1628).

Tremayne, *Air Marshal* Sir John Tremayne, K.C.B., C.B.E., D.S.O.

Trench, Sir David Clive Crosbie, G.C.M.G., M.C.

Trench, Sir Nigel Clive Cosby, K.C.M.G.

Trevaskis, Sir (Gerald) Kennedy (Nicholas), K.C.M.G.

Trevelyan, Sir George Lowthian, Bt. (1874).

Trevelyan, Sir Willoughby John, Bt. (1662).

Trewby, *Vice-Adm.* Sir (George Francis) Allan, K.C.B.

Trinder, Sir (Arnold) Charles, C.B.E.

Tritton, *Maj.* Sir Geoffrey Ernest, Bt., C.B.E. (1905).

Trivedi, Sir Chandulal Madhavlal, K.C.S.I., C.I.E., O.B.E.

Trollope, Sir Anthony Owen Clavering, Bt. (1642).

Troubridge, *Lt.-Cdr.* Sir Peter, Bt., R.N. (1799).

Troup, *Vice-Adm.* Sir (John) Anthony (Rose), K.C.B., D.S.C.

Trout, Sir Herbert Leon, Kt.

Trowbridge, *Rear-Adm.* Sir Richard John, K.C.V.O.

Truscott, Sir Denis Henry, G.B.E., T.D.

Truscott, Sir George James Irving, Bt. (1909).

Trusted, Sir Harry Herbert, Kt., Q.C.

Tuck, Sir Bruce Adolph Reginald, Bt. (1910).

Tucker, Sir Henry James, K.B.E.

Tuckwell, Sir Edward George, K.C.V.O., F.R.C.S.

Tuite, *Maj.* Sir Dennis George, Harmsworth, Bt M.B.E. (1622).

Tunbridge, *Prof.* Sir Ronald Ernest, Kt., O.B.E., M.D., F.R.C.P.

Tupper, Sir Charles, Hibbert, Bt. (1888).

Turbott, Sir Ian Graham, Kt., C.M.G., C.V.O.

Turing, Sir John Leslie, Bt., M.C. (S 1638).

Turnbull, Sir Francis Fearon, K.B.E., C.B., C.I.E.

Turnbull, Sir Richard Gordon, G.C.M.G.

Turnbull, Sir Winton George, Kt., C.B.E.

Turner, Sir Alan George, Kt., C.B.E.

Turner, *Rt. Hon.* Sir Alexander Kingcome, K.B.E.

Turner, *Admiral* Sir (Arthur) Francis, K.C.B., D.S.C.

Turner, Sir Cedric Oban, Kt., C.B.E.

Turner, Sir Harvey, Kt., C.B.E.

Turner, Sir Henry Samuel Edwin, Kt.

Turner, Sir Michael William, Kt., C.B.E.

Turner, *Prof.* Sir Ralph Lilley, Kt., M.C., F.B.A.

Turner, *Vice-Adm.* Sir Robert Ross, K.B.E., C.B., D.S.O.

Turner, Sir (Ronald) Mark (Cunliffe), Kt.

Turner, *Lt.-Gen.* Sir William Francis Robert, K.B.E., C.B., D.S.O.

Tuttle, *Air Marshal* Sir Geoffrey William, K.B.E., C.B., D.F.C.

Tuzo, *General* Sir Harry Craufurd, G.C.B., O.B.E., M.C.

Twiss, *Admiral* Sir Frank Roddam, K.C.B., D.S.C.

Tyler, *Maj.-Gen.* Sir Leslie Norman, K.B.E., C.B.

Tymms, Sir Frederick, K.C.I.E., M.C.

Tyndall, *Hon.* Sir Arthur, Kt., C.M.G.

Tyree, Sir (Alfred) William, Kt., O.B.E.

Tyrrell, Sir Murray Louis, K.C.V.O., C.B.E.

Tyrwhitt, Sir Reginald Thomas Newman, Bt. (1919).

Udoma, Sir Ethelbert Udo, Kt.

Uhr, Sir Clive Wentworth, Kt., C.B.E.

Unsworth, Hon. Sir Edgar Ignatius Godfrey, Kt., C.M.G.

Unwin, Sir Keith, K.B.E., C.M.G.

Upjohn, Sir William George Dismore, Kt., O.B.E., M.D.

Urquhart, Sir Andrew, K.C.M.G., M.B.E.

Urquhart, Sir Robert William, K.B.E., C.M.G.

Urton, Sir William Holmes Lister, Kt., M.B.E., T.D.

Usher, Sir Peter Lionel, Bt. (1899).

Vaghjee, Sir Harilall Ranchhordas, Kt.

Valentine, Sir Alexander Balmain Bruce, Kt.

Vallat, Sir Francis Aimé, K.C.M.G., Q.C.

Vanderfelt, Sir Robin Victor, K.B.E.

Vasey, Sir Ernest Albert, K.B.E., C.M.G.

Vaughan, Sir (George) Edgar, K.B.E.

Vavasour, *Cdr.* Sir Geoffrey William, Bt., D.S.C., R.N. (1828).

Venables, Sir Peter, Kt., Ph.D.

Verdin, *Lt.-Col.* Sir Richard Bertram, Kt., O.B.E., T.D.

Verney, Sir John, Bt., M.C. (1946).

Verney, Sir Ralph Bruce, Bt., K.B.E. (1818).

Vernon, Sir James, Kt., C.B.E.

Vernon, Sir Nigel John Douglas, Bt. (1914).

Vesey, Sir (Nathaniel) Henry (Peniston), Kt., C.B.E.

Vestey, Sir (John) Derek, Bt. (1921).

Vick, Sir (Francis) Arthur, Kt., O.B.E., D.SC., Ph.D.

Vickers, Sir (Charles) Geoffrey, Kt., V℃.

Vickery, Sir Philip Crawford, Kt., C.I.E., O.B.E.

Victoria, Sir (Joseph Aloysius) Donatus, Kt., C.B.E.

Villiers, Sir Charles Hyde, Kt., M.C.

Villiers, *Vice-Adm.* Sir (John) Michael, K.C.B., O.B.E.

Vincent, Sir (Harold) Graham, K.C.M.G., C.B., C.V.O.

Vincent, Sir William Percy Maxwell, Bt. (1936).

Virtue, *Hon.* Sir John Evenden, K.B.E.

Vyse, *Lt.-Gen.* Sir Edward Dacre Howard-, K.B.E., C.B., M.C.

Vyvyan, Sir Richard Philip, Bt. (1645).

Wackett, Sir Lawrence James, Kt., D.F.C., A.F.C.

Waddell, Sir Alexander Nicol Anton, K.C.M.G., D.S.C.

Waddell, Sir James Henderson, Kt., C.B.

Wade, *Col.* Sir George Albert, Kt., M.C.

Wade, *Air Chief Marshal* Sir Ruthven Lowry, K.C.B., D.F.C.

Wadham, *Prof.* Sir Samuel McMahon, Kt.

Wadley, Sir Douglas, Kt.

Waechter, Sir Harry Leonard D'Arcy, Bt. (1911).

Wagner, Sir Anthony Richard, K.C.V.O.

Wake, Sir Hereward, Bt., M.C. (1621).

Wakefield, Sir (Edward) Humphry (Tyrell), Bt. (1962).

Wakeford, *Air Marshal* Sir Richard Gordon, K.C.B., M.V.D., O.B.E., A.F.C.

Wakeley, Sir Cecil Pembrey Grey, Bt., K.B.E., C.B., D.SC. (1952).

Wakeman, Sir (Offley) David, Bt. (1828).

Waldock, *Prof.* Sir (Claud) Humphrey (Meredith), Kt., C.M.G., O.B.E., Q.C., D.C.L.

Walker, Sir Allan Grierson, Kt., Q.C.

Walker, Sir Baldwin Patrick, Bt. (1856).

Walker, Sir (Charles) Michael, G.C.M.G.

Walker, *Vice-Adm.* Sir (Charles) Peter (Graham), K.B.E., C.B., D.S.C.

Walker, Sir Edward Ronald, Kt., C.B.E.

Walker, *Air Chief Marshal* Sir (George) Augustus, G.C.B., C.B.E., D.S.O., D.F.C., A.F.C.

Walker, *Maj.* Sir George Ferdinand Forestier-, Bt. (1835).

Walker, Sir (Horace) Alan, Kt.

Walker, *Maj.* Sir Hugh Ronald, Bt. (1906).

Walker, Sir Hugh Selby Norman-, K.C.M.G., O.B.E.

Walker, Sir James Graham, Kt., M.B.E.

Walker, Sir James Heron, Bt. (1868).

Walker, Sir John, K.C.M.G., O.B.E.

Walker, *General* Sir Walter Colyear, K.C.B., C.B.E., D.S.O.

Walker, Sir William Giles Newsom, Kt., T.D.

Wallace, *Hon.* Sir Gordon, Kt.

Wallace, Sir Martin Kelso, Kt.

Waller, *Rt. Hon.* Sir George Stanley, Kt., O.B.E.

Waller, Sir (John) Keith, Kt., C.B.E.

Waller, Sir John Stainer, Bt. (1815).

Waller, Sir Robert William, Bt. (1 1780).

Walley, Sir John, K.B.E., C.B.

Wallinger, Sir Geoffrey Arnold, G.B.E., K.C.M.G.

Wallis, Sir Barnes Neville, Kt., C.B.E., F.R.S.

Walmsley, *Air Marshal* Sir Hugh Sydney Porter, K.C.B., K.C.I.E., C.B.E., M.C., D.F.C.

Walsh, Sir David Philip, K.B.E., C.B.

Walsh, Prof. Sir John Patrick, K.B.E.

Walsham, *Rear-Adm.* Sir John Scarlett, Warren, Bt., C.B., O.B.E. (1831).

Walter, Sir Harold Edward, Kt.

Walters, Sir Roger Talbot, K.B.E., F.R.I.B.A.

Walton, *Brig.* Sir George Hands, K.B.E., C.B., T.D.

Walton, Sir John Robert, Kt.

Walton, *Hon.* Sir Raymond Henry, Kt.

Walton, Sir William Turner, Kt., O.M., MUS., DOC.

Wand, *Rt. Rev.* John William Charles, P.C., K.C.V.O., D.D.

Wanstall, *Hon.* Sir Charles Gray, Kt.

Warburg, Sir Siegmund George, Kt.

Ward, *General* Sir (Alfred) Dudley, G.C.B., K.B.E., D.S.O.

Ward, Sir Aubrey Ernest, Kt.

Ward, Sir John Guthrie, G.C.M.G.

Ward, Sir Joseph James Laffey, Bt. (1911).

Ward, *General* Sir Richard Erskine, G.B.E., K.C.B., D.S.O., M.C.

Ward, Sir Terence George, Kt., C.B.E.

Wardlaw, Sir Henry, Bt. (S 1631).

Wardle, Sir Thomas Edward Jewell, Kt.

Ware, Sir Henry Gabriel, K.C.B.

Waring, Sir Alfred Harold, Bt. (1935).

Waring, Sir Douglas Tremayne, Kt., C.B.E.

Wark, Sir Ian William, Kt., C.M.G., C.B.E., Ph.D., D.Sc.

Warmington, *Lt.-Cdr.* Sir Marshall George Clitheroe, Bt., R.N. (1908).

Warner, Sir Edward Courtenay Henry, Bt. (1910).

Warner, Sir Edward Redston, K.C.M.G., O.B.E.

Warner, Sir Frederick Archibald, K.C.M.G.

Warner, Sir Frederick Edward, Kt., F.R.S.

Warner, Sir George Redston, K.C.V.O., C.M.G.

Warren, Sir Alfred Henry, Kt., C.B.E.

Warren, Sir (Harold) Brian (Seymour), Kt.

Warren, Sir Brian Charles Pennefather, Bt. (1784).

Warren, *Hon.* Sir Edward Emerton, K.C.M.G., K.B.E.

Wass, Sir Douglas William Gretton, K.C.B.

Waterhouse, Sir Ellis Kirkham, Kt., C.B.E.

Waterlow, Sir Christopher Rupert, Bt. (1873).

Waterlow, Sir Thomas Gordon, Bt., C.B.E. (1930).

Waterman, Sir Ewen McIntyre, Kt.

Waters, *Maj.* Sir Arnold Horace Santo, Kt., *V.C.*, C.B.E., D.S.O., M.C.

Wates, Sir Ronald Wallace, Kt.

Watherston, Sir David Charles, K.B.E., C.M.G.

Watkins, *Hon.* Sir Tasker, Kt., *V.C.*

Watson, Sir (David) Ronald Milne-, Bt. (1937).

Watson, *Capt.* Sir Derrick William Inglefield Inglefield-, Bt., T.D. (1895).

Watson, Sir Francis John Bagot, K.C.V.O., F.B.A., F.S.A.

Watson, Sir James Andrew, Bt. (1866).

Watson, Sir Michael Milne-, Kt., C.B.E.

Watson, Sir Noel Duncan, K.C.M.G.

Watson, Sir Norman James, Bt. (1912).

Watson, *Vice-Admiral* Sir Philip Alexander, K.B.E., M.V.O.

Watson, *Vice-Adm.* Sir (Robert) Dymock, K.C.B., C.B.E.

Watson, Sir William, Kt.

Watt, Sir Alan Stewart, Kt., C.B.E.

Watt, *Brig.* Sir George Steven Harvie-, Bt., T.D., Q.C. (1945).

Watt, *Surgeon Vice-Adm.* Sir James, K.B.E., F.R.C.S.

Wauchope, Sir Patrick George Don-, Bt. (S 1667).

Way, Sir Richard George Kitchener, K.C.B., C.B.E.

Wayne, *Prof.* Sir Edward Johnson, Kt., M.D., Ph.D.

Weatherhead, Sir Arthur Trenham, Kt., C.M.G.

Weaver, Sir Tobias Rushton, Kt., C.B.

Webb, *Lt.-Gen.* Sir Richard James Holden, K.B.E., C.B.

Webb, Sir Thomas Langley, Kt.

Webber, Sir William James Percival, Kt., C.B.E.

Webster, Sir Richard James, Kt., D.S.O.

Webster, Sir Robert Joseph, Kt., C.M.G., C.B.E., M.C.

Wedderburn, *Cdr.* Sir John Peter Ogilvy-, Bt., R.N. (1803).

Wedderspoon, Sir Thomas Adam, Kt.

Wedgwood, Sir John Hamilton, Bt., T.D. (1942).

Weeks, Sir Hugh Thomas, Kt., C.M.G.

Weinstock, Sir Arnold, Kt.

Weipers, *Prof.* Sir William Lee, Kt.

Welby, Sir Oliver Charles Earle, Bt. (1801).

Welch, *Lt.-Col.* Sir (George James) Cullum, Bt., O.B.E., M.C. (1957).

Weld, *Col.* Sir Joseph William, Kt., O.B.E., T.D.

Weldon, Sir Thomas Brian, Bt. (I. 1723).

Welensky, *Rt. Hon.* Sir Roy (Roland), K.C.M.G.

Wellings, Sir Jack Alfred, Kt., C.B.E.

Wellington, Sir (Reginald Everard) Lindsay, Kt., C.B.E.

Wells, Sir Charles Maltby, Bt. (1944).

West, *General* Sir Michael Montgomerie Alston Roberts, G.C.B., D.S.O.

Westall, *General* Sir John Chaddesley, K.C.B., C.B.E., R.M.

Westerman, Sir (Wilfred) Alan, Kt., C.B.E.

Weston, Sir Eric, Kt.

Weston, *Air Vice-Marshal* Sir John Gerard Willsley, K.B.E., C.B.

Wetherall, *Lt.-Gen.* Sir (Harry) Edward de Robillard, K.B.E., C.B., D.S.O., M.C.

Wheare, Sir Kenneth Clinton, Kt., C.M.G., F.B.A., D.Litt.

Wheatley, Sir (George) Andrew, Kt., C.B.E.

Wheeler, Sir Frederick Henry, Kt., C.B.E.

Wheeler, *Air Chief Marshal* Sir (Henry) Neil (George), G.C.B., C.B.E., D.S.O., D.F.C., A.F.C.

Wheeler, Sir John Hieron, Bt. (1920).

Wheeler, *Hon.* Sir Kenneth Henry, Kt.

Wheldon, Sir Huw Pyrs, Kt., O.B.E., M.C.

Wheler, *Capt.* Sir Trevor Wood, Bt. (1660).

Whishaw, Sir Charles Percival Law, Kt.

Whishaw, Sir Ralph, Kt., C.B.E.

Whitaker, *Maj.* Sir James Herbert Ingham, Bt. (1936).

White, *Hon.* Sir Alfred John, Kt., C.B.

White, *Brig.* Sir Bruce Gordon, K.B.E.

White, Sir Christopher Robert Meadows, Bt. (1937).

White, Sir Dennis Charles, K.B.E., C.M.G.

White, Sir Dick Goldsmith, K.C.M.G., K.B.E.

White, Sir (Eric Henry) Wyndham, K.C.M.G.

White, Sir Ernest Keith, Kt., C.B.E., M.C.

White, Sir Frederick William George, K.B.E., Ph.D., F.R.S.

White, Sir George Stanley Midelton, Bt. (1904).

White, Sir Harold Leslie, Kt., C.B.E.

White, *Wing-Cdr.* Sir Henry Arthur Dalrymple-, Bt., D.F.C. (1926).

White, Sir John Woolmer, Bt. (1922).

White, *Admiral* Sir Peter, K.B.E.

White, Sir Thomas Astley Woollaston, Bt. (1802).

Whitehead, Sir Rowland John Rathbone, Bt. (1889).

Whitehead, *Hon.* Sir Stanley Austin, Kt.

Whiteley, Sir Hugo Baldwin Huntington-, Bt. (1918).

Whiteley, *Lt.-Gen.* Sir Peter John Frederick, K.C.B., O.B.E., R.M.

Whitford, *Hon.* Sir John Norman Keates, Kt.

Whitley, *Air Marshal* Sir John René, K.B.E., C.B., D.S.O., A.F.C.

Whitmore, Sir John Henry Douglas, Bt. (1954).

Whittaker, (Sir) Joseph Meredith, Kt., T.D.

Whitteridge, Sir Gordon Coligny, K.C.M.G., O.B.E.

Whittingham, *Air Marshal* Sir Harold Edward, K.C.B., K.B.E.

Whittle, *Air Commodore* Sir Frank, K.B.E., C.B.

Whyatt, Sir John, Kt., Q.C.

Wicks, *Hon.* Sir James, Kt.

Wien, *Hon.* Sir Philip, Kt.

Wigan, Sir Frederick Adair, Bt. (1898).

Wiggin, Sir Charles Douglas, K.C.M.G., D.F.C., A.F.C.

Wiggin, Sir John Henry, Bt., M.C. (1892).

Wigglesworth, *Prof.* Sir Vincent Brian, Kt., C.B.E., M.D., F.R.S.

Wigley, Sir Henry Rodolph, K.B.E.

Wigram, *Rev. Canon* Sir Clifford Woolmore, Bt. (1805).

Wilbraham, Sir Randle John Baker, Bt. (1776).

Wild, *Rt. Hon.* Sir (Herbert) Richard (Churton), K.C.M.G., E.D.

Wilford, Sir (Kenneth) Michael, K.C.M.G.

Wilkinson, Sir (David) Graham (Brook) Bt. (1941).

Wilkinson, *Prof.* Sir Denys Haigh, Kt., F.R.S.

Williamson, *Prof.* Sir Geoffrey, Kt., F.R.S.

Wilkinson, Sir Harold, Kt., C.M.G.

Wilkinson, Sir Peter Allix, K.C.M.G., D.S.O., O.B.E.

Wilkinson, Sir (Robert Frances) Martin, Kt.

Wilkinson, Sir Thomas Crowe Spenser-, Kt.

Willatt, Sir (Robert) Hugh, Kt.

Williams, Sir Alexander Thomas, K.C.M.G., M.B.E.

Williams, Sir Brandon Meredith Rhys-, Bt., M.P. (1918).

Williams, Sir Charles Henry Trelease, Kt., C.B.E.

Williams, *Admiral* Sir David, K.C.B.

Williams, Sir Edgar Trevor, Kt., C.B., C.B.E., D.S.O.

Williams, Sir Francis John Watkin, Bt., Q.C. (1798).

Williams, Sir Gwilym Tecwyn, Kt., C.B.E.

Williams, Sir Henry Morton Leech, Kt., M.B.E.

Williams, Sir John Francis, Kt.

Williams, Sir (John) Leslie, Kt., C.B.E.

Williams, *Capt.* Sir John Protheroe, Kt., C.M.G., O.B.E.

Williams, Sir Michael Sanigear, K.C.M.G.

Williams, Sir Osmond, Bt., M.C. (1909).

Williams, Sir Peter Watkin, Kt.

Williams, *Air Marshal* Sir Richard, K.B.E., C.B., D.S.O.

Williams, Sir Robert Ernest, Bt. (1866).

Williams, *Prof.* Sir Robert Evan Owen, Kt., M.D., F.R.C.P.

Williams, Sir (Robert) Philip (Nathaniel), Bt. (1915).

Williams, Sir Robin Philip, Bt. (1953).

Williams, Sir Rolf Dudley-, Bt. (1964).

Williams, Sir Roy Ellis Hume-, Bt. (1922).

Williams, Sir William Emrys, Kt., C.B.E.

Williams, *Lt.-Col.* Sir William Jones, K.C.V.O., O.B.E.

Williams, Sir (William) Thomas, Q.C., M.P.

Williamson, Sir (Nicholas Frederick) Hedworth, Bt. (1642).

Willink, Sir Charles William, Bt. (1957).

Willis, *Hon.* Sir Eric Archibald, K.B.E., C.M.G.

Willis, *Hon,* Sir John Ramsay, Kt.

Willison, *Lt.-Gen.* Sir David John, K.C.B., O.B.E., M.C.

Willison, Sir John Alexander, Kt., O.B.E.

Willmer, *Rt. Hon.* Sir (Henry) Gordon, Kt., O.B.E., T.D.

Willmott, Sir Maurice Gordon, Kt., M.C.

Willoughby, *Maj.-Gen.* Sir John Edward Francis, K.B.E., C.B.

Wills, *Lt.-Col.* Sir (Ernest) Edward de Winton, Bt. (1904).

Wells, Sir John Spencer, Kt.

Wills, Sir John Vernon, Bt. (1923).

Wills, *Brig.* Sir Kenneth Agnew, K.B.E., M.C., E.D.

Wilmot, Sir Henry Robert, Bt. (1759).

Wilmot, *Cdr.* Sir John Assheton Eardley-, Bt., M.V.O., D.S.C., R.N. (1821).

Wilson, Sir Alan Herries, Kt., F.R.S.

Wilson, *Lt.-Gen.* Sir (Alexander) James, K.B.E., M.C.

Wilson, Sir (Archibald) Duncan, G.C.M.G.

Wilson, Sir Arton, K.B.E., C.B.

Wilson, Sir Charles Haynes, Kt.

Wilson, Sir David, Bt. (1920).

Wilson, Sir Geoffrey Masterman, K.C.B., C.M.G.

Wilson, Sir George, K.B.E.

Wilson, *Prof.* Sir Graham Selby, Kt., M.D.

Wilson, Sir Hubert Guy Maryon, Bt. (1661).

Wilson, *Rt. Hon.* Sir (James) Harold, K.G., O.B.E., M.P.

Wilson, Sir John Foster, Kt., C.B.E.

Wilson, Sir John Martindale, K.C.B.

Wilson, Sir Keith Cameron, Kt.

Wilson, Sir Leonard, K.C.I.E.

Wilson, Sir (Leslie) Hugh, Kt., O.B.E.

Wilson, Sir Mathew Martin, Bt. (1874).

Wilson, Sir Michael Thomond, Kt., M.B.E.

Wilson, Sir Reginald Holmes, Kt.

Wilson, *Hon.* Sir Robert Christian, Kt., C.M.G.

Wilson, *Rt. Rev.* Roger Plumpton, K.C.V.O., D.D.

Wilson, Sir Roland, K.B.E.

Wilson, Sir Roy Mickel, Kt., Q.C.

Wilson, Sir Thomas Douglas, Bt., M.C. (1906).

Wilton, *Lt.-Gen.* Sir John Gordon Noel, K.B.E., C.B., D.S.O.

Wiltshire, Sir Frederick Munro, Kt., C.B.E.

Windeyer, *Prof.* Sir Brian Wellingham, Kt.

Windeyer, *Rt. Hon.* Sir (William John) Victor, K.B.E., C.B., D.S.O., E.D.

Windham, *Hon.* Sir Ralph, Kt.

Wingate, *Col.* Sir Roland Evelyn Leslie, Bt., C.B., C.M.G., C.I.E., O.B.E. (1920).

Winneke, *Hon.* Sir Henry Arthur, K.C.M.G., O.B.E.

Winnifrith, Sir (Alfred) John (Digby), K.C.B.

Winnington, Sir Francis Salwey William, Bt. (1755).

Winterton, *Maj.-Gen.* Sir (Thomas) John (Willoughby), K.C.B., K.C.M.G., C.B.E.

Wise, Sir John Humphrey, K.C.M.G., C.B.E.

Wiseman, Sir John William, Bt. (1628).

Witt, Sir John Clermont, Kt.

Wolff, *Hon.* Sir Albert Asher, K.C.M.G.

Wolfson, Sir Isaac, Bt., F.R.S. (1962).

Wollen, Sir (Ernest) Russell (Storey), K.B.E.

Wolseley, Sir Charles Garnet Mark Richard, Bt. (1628).

Wolseley, Sir Garnet, Bt. (I 1745).

Wolstenholme, Sir Gordon Ethelbert Ward, Kt., O.B.E.

Wombwell, Sir (Frederick) Philip (Alfred William), Bt., M.B.E. (1778).

Womersley, Sir Peter John Walter, Bt. (1945).

Wontner, Sir Hugh Walter Kingwell, G.B.E., C.V.O.

Wood, Sir Anthony John Page, Bt. (1837).

Wood, Sir David Basil Hill-, Bt. (1921).

Wood, Sir George Ernest Francis, K.C.M.G., I.S.O.

Wood, Sir Henry Peart, Kt., C.B.E.

Wood, Sir Ian Jeffreys, Kt., M.B.E.

Wood, Sir Kenneth Millns, Kt.

Wood, Sir Wilfred William Hill-, K.C.V.O., C.B.E.

Woodall, *Lt.-Gen.* Sir John Dane, K.C.M.G., K.B.E., C.B., M.C.

Woodhouse, *Rt. Hon.* Sir (Arthur) Owen, Kt., D.S.C.

Woodhouse, *Admiral* Sir Charles Henry Lawrence, K.C.B.

Woodroofe, Sir Ernest George, Kt., Ph.D.

Woodruff, *Prof.* Sir Michael Francis Addison, Kt., D.Sc.

Woods, *Most Rev.* Frank, K.B.E., D.D.

Woods, *Rt. Rev.* Robert Wilmer, K.C.V.O.

Woolf, Sir John, Kt.

Woolley, Sir Charles Campbell, G.B.E., K.C.M.G., M.C.

Woolley, Sir Richard van der Riet, Kt., O.B.E., F.R.S.

Worsley, *Lt.-Gen.* Sir John Francis, K.B.E., C.B., M.C.

Worsley, *Lt.-Gen.* Sir Richard Edward, K.C.B., O.B.E.

Worsley, Sir (William) Marcus (John), Bt. (1838).

Worthington, *Air Vice Marshal* Sir Geoffrey Luis, K.B.E., C.B.

Wraight, Sir John Richard, K.B.E., C.M.G.

Wrangham, Sir Geoffrey Walter, Kt.

Wraxall, Sir Morville William Lascelles, Bt. (1813).

Wray, Sir Kenneth Owen Roberts-, G.C.M.G., Q.C.

Wrey, Sir (Castel) Richard Bourchier, Bt. (1628).

Wright, Sir Denis Arthur Hepworth, G.C.M.G.

Wright, Sir (John) Oliver, K.C.M.G., D.S.C.

Wright, Sir Paul Hervé Giraud, K.C.M.G.

Wright, Sir Richard Michael Cory-, Bt. (1903).

Wright, Sir Robert Brash, Kt.

Wright, Sir Rowland Sydney, Kt., C.B.E.

Wright, *Admiral* Sir Royston Hollis, G.B.E., K.C.B., D.S.O.

Wrightson, Sir John Garmondsway, Bt. (1900).

Wrigley, Sir John Crompton, K.B.E., C.B.

Wrisberg, *Lt.-Gen.* Sir Frederick George, K.B.E., C.B.

Wyatt, *Vice-Adm.* Sir (Arthur) Guy (Norris), K.B.E., C.B.

Wykeham, *Air Marshal* Sir Peter Guy, K.C.B., D.S.O., O.B.E., D.F.C., A.F.C.

Wylie, Sir Campbell, Kt., E.D., Q.C.

Wyndham, Sir Harold Stanley, Kt., C.B.E.

Wynn, *Lt.-Col.* Sir Owen Watkin Williams-, Bt., C.B.E. (1688).

Yapp, Sir Stanley Graham, Kt.

Yarrow, Sir Eric Grant, Bt., M.B.E. (1916).

Yates, *Lt.-Gen.* Sir David Peel-, K.C.B., C.V.O., D.S.O., O.B.E.

Yates, Sir Thomas, Kt., C.B.E.

Yeabsley, Sir Richard Ernest, Kt., C.B.E.

Yeaman, Sir Ian David, Kt.

Yellowlees, Sir Henry, K.C.B.

Yocklunn, Sir Soong Chung, Kt.

Yonge, Sir (Charles) Maurice, Kt., C.B.E., D.SC., F.R.S., F.R.S.E.

Yorston, Sir (Robert) Keith, Kt., C.B.E.

Youens, Sir Peter William, Kt., C.M.G., O.B.E.

Young, *Col.* Sir Arthur Edwin, K.B.E., C.M.G., C.V.O.

Young, Sir Brian Walter Mark, Kt.

Young, *Prof.* Sir Frank George, Kt., D.SC., Ph.D., F.R.S.

Young, Sir George Samuel Knatchbull, Bt. (1813).

Young, *Hon.* Sir John McIntosh, K.C.M.G.

Young, Sir John William Roe, Bt. (1821).

Young, Sir Norman Smith, Kt.

Young, Sir Richard Dilworth, Kt.

Young, Sir Robert Christopher Mackworth-, K.C.V.O.

Young, Sir Stephen Stewart Templeton, Bt. (1945).

Young, Sir William, Kt., C.B.E.

Young, Sir William Neil, Bt. (1769).

Younger, *Maj.-Gen.* Sir John William, Bt., C.B.E. (1911).

Younger, Sir William McEwan, Bt., D.S.O. (1964).

Baronetcies Extinct (Since last issue).—Charles (U.K., 1928); Cunningham (U.K., 1963); Dixie (E., 1660); Dunn (U.K., 1921); Hawkey (U.K., 1945); Williams-Drummond (U.K., 1828).

Dames Grand Cross and Dames Commanders of the Order of the Bath, the Order of St. Michael and St. George, the Royal Victorian Order and the Order of the British Empire

NOTE.—Dames Grand Cross (G.C.B., G.C.M.G., G.C.V.O. or G.B.E.) and Dames Commanders (D.C.B., D.C.M.G., D.C.V.O. or D.B.E.) are addressed in a manner similar to that of Knights Grand Cross or Knights Commanders, *e.g.* "Miss Florence Smith" after receiving the honour would be addressed as "Dame Florence", and in writing as "Dame Florence Smith, G. (or D.) C.B., G. (or D.) C.M.G., G. (or D.) C.V.O., or G. (or D.) B.E." Where such award is made to a lady already in enjoyment of a higher title the appropriate letters are appended to her name, *e.g.* "The Countess of —— G.C.V.O." Peeresses in their own right, and Life Peeresses, are not included in this list. Dames Grand Cross rank after wives of Baronets and before wives of Knights Grand Cross. Dames Commanders rank after the wives of Knights Grand Cross and before the wives of Knights Commanders.

Peeresses are not included in this list.

DAMES GRAND CROSS AND DAMES COMMANDERS

H.M. Queen Elizabeth The Queen Mother, K.G., K.T., C.I., G.M.V.O.

H.R.H. The Princess Margaret, Countess of Snowdon, C.I., G.C.V.O.

H.R.H. The Princess Alice, Duchess of Gloucester, G.C.B., C.I., G.C.V.O., G.B.E.

H.R.H. The Princess Alice, Countess of Athlone, V.A., G.C.V.O., G.B.E.

H.R.H. The Princess Alexandra of Kent, G.C.V.O.

H.R.H. The Princess Anne, G.C.V.O.

Abbot, Dame Elsie Myrtle, D.B.E.

Abercorn, The Duchess of, D.C.V.O.

Ackroyd, Dame (Dorothy) Elizabeth, D.B.E.

Albemarle, The Countess of, D.B.E.

Alexander of Tunis, Margaret Diane, Countess, G.B.E.

Anderson, Dame Judith, D.B.E.

Anderson, Dame Kitty, D.B.E., Ph.D.

Anderson, *Brig.* Hon. Dame Mary Mackenzie (Mrs. Pihl), D.B.E.

Angliss, Jacobena Victoria, Lady, D.B.E.

Ashby, Dame Margery Irene Corbett, D.B.E.

Ashcroft, Dame Peggy (Mrs. Hutchinson), D.B.E.

Ashworth, *Air Commandant* Dame Veronica Margaret, D.B.E., R.R.C.

Baden-Powell, Olave St. Clair, Baroness, G.B.E.

Baker, Dame Janet Abbott, D.B.E.

Baring, Lady Rose Gwendolen Louisa, D.C.V.O.

Barnes, Dame (Alice) Josephine (Mary Taylor) (Mrs. Warren), D.B.E., F.R.C.P., F.R.C.S.

Barnett, *Air Commandant* Dame (Mary) Henrietta, D.B.E.

Bate, Dame Zara Kate, D.B.E.

Berry, Dame Alice Miriam, D.B.E.

Bishop, Dame (Margaret) Joyce, D.B.E.

Blaxland, Dame Helen Frances, D.B.E.

Bolte, Edith Lilian, Lady, D.B.E.

Bottomley, Dame Bessie Ellen, D.B.E.

Brecknock, The Countess of, D.B.E.

Brown, Dame Beryl Paston, D.B.E.

Bryans, Dame Anne Margaret, D.B.E.

Bryce, Dame Isabel Graham, D.B.E.

Buckley, Hon. Dame Ruth Burton, D.B.E.

Burnside, Dame Edith, D.B.E.

Buttfield, Dame Nancy Eileen, D.B.E.

Buxton, Dame Rita Mary, D.B.E.

Bynoe, Dame Hilda Louisa, D.B.E.

Campbell, Dame Kate Isabel, D.B.E., M.D.

Carte, Dame Bridget D'Oyly, D.B.E.

Cartwright, Dame Mary Lucy, D.B.E., SC.D., D.Phil., F.R.S.

Cavan, Joan, Countess of, D.B.E.

Turner, Dame Eva, D.B.E.

Turner, *Brig.* Dame Margot, D.B.E., R.R.C.

Tylecote, Dame Mabel, D.B.E.

Tyrwhitt, *Brigadier* Dame Mary Joan Caroline, D.B.E.

Van Praagh, Dame Margaret (Peggy), D.B.E.

Vaughan, Dame Janet Maria, (Mrs. Gourlay), D.B.E.

Wakehurst, Margaret, Lady, D.B.E.

Walker, Dame Susan Armour, D.B.E.

Wedgwood, Dame (Cicely) Veronica, O.M., D.B.E.

Wedgwood, Dame Ivy Evelyn, D.B.E.

Welsh, *Air Chief Commandant* Ruth Mary, Lady, D.B.E.

West, Dame Rebecca (Mrs. Andrews), D.B.E.

Whateley, *Chief Controller* Dame Leslie Violet, D.B.E.

Whyte, *Air Commandant* Dame Roberta Mary, D.B.E., R.R.C.

Williamson, *Air Commandant* Dame Alice Mary, D.B.E., R.R.C., Q.H.N.S.

Williamson, Dame (Elsie) Marjorie, D.B.E., Ph.D.

Winner, Dame Albertine Louise, D.B.E., M.D.

Woollcombe, Dame Jocelyn May, D.B.E.

Wormald, Dame Ethel May, D.B.E.

Yarwood, Dame Elizabeth Ann, D.B.E.

Younghusband, Dame Eileen Louise, D.B.E.

THE VICTORIA CROSS, $\mathcal{VC}$
For Conspicuous Bravery.

The ribbon *is Crimson* for all Services (until 1918 it was *Blue* for Royal Navy).

Instituted on January 29, 1856, the Victoria Cross was awarded retrospectively to 1854, the first being held by Lieut. C. D. Lucas, R.N. for bravery in the Baltic Sea on June 21, 1854 (gazetted Feb. 24, 1857). The first 62 Crosses were presented by Queen Victoria in Hyde Park, London, on June 26, 1857.

The $\mathcal{VC}$ is worn before all other decorations, on the left breast, and consists of a cross-pattée of bronze, 1½ inches in diameter, with the Royal Crown surmounted by a lion in the centre, and beneath there is the inscription "For Valour." Holders of the $\mathcal{VC}$ receive a tax-free annuity of £100, irrespective of need or other conditions. In 1911, the right to receive the Cross was extended to Indian soldiers, and in 1920 a Royal Warrant extended the right to Matrons, Sisters and Nurses, and the Staff of the Nursing Services and other services pertaining to Hospitals and Nursing, and to Civilians of either sex regularly or temporarily under the orders, direction or supervision of the Naval, Military, or Air Forces of the Crown.

Surviving Recipients of the Victoria Cross

Agansing Rai, *Havildar* (Gurkha Rifles),*World War*............ 1944

Ali Haidar, *Sepoy* (Frontier Force Rifles), *World War*........... 1945

Anderson, *Lt.-Col.* C. G. W., M.C.(Australian M.F.), *World War*........... 1944

Annand, *Capt.* R. W. (Durham L.I.), *World War*........... 1940

Axford, *Corpl.* T. L., M.M. (A.I.F.), *Gt. War*.. 1918

Barrett, *Col.* John C. (R. Leic. R.), *Gt. War*.. 1918

Bassett, *Col.* Cyril R. G. (N.Z.), *Gt. War*.... 1915

Bent, *R.-S.-M.* S. J. (East Lancs. R.), *Gt. War* 1914

Bhanbhagta Gurung, *Lance-Naik* (2nd Gurkha Rifles), *World War*................... 1945

Bhandari Ram,*Lance-Naik*(Baluch R.),*World War*.................. 1944

Brereton, *C.-S.-M.* A. (Manitoba R.), *Gt. War*.................. 1918

Burton, *Corpl.* R. H. (Duke of Wellington's R.), *World War*................. 1944

Campbell, *Brigadier* L. M., D.S.O., O.B.E., T.D. (A. & S. Highrs.), *World War*........... 1943

Carmichael, *Sergt.* J. (N. Staff. R.), *Gt. War*.. 1917

Carne, *Col.* J. P., D.S.O. (Glos. R.), *Korea*... 1951

Carroll, *Pte.* John (Aus. Inf.), *Gt. War*...... 1917

Cartwright, *Pte.* George (Aust.), *Gt. War*.... 1918

Chapman, *Sergt.* E. T. (Monmouthshire R.), *World War*.................... 1945

Cheshire, *Group Capt.* G. L., D.S.O., D.F.C. (R.A.F.), *World War*................. 1944

Cooper,*Lt.* E. (K.R.R.C.), *Gt. War*.......... 1917

Cruickshank, *Fl. Lt.* J. A. (R.A.F.V.R.), *World War*.................... 1944

Crutchley, *Admiral* Sir Victor Alexander, K.C.B., D.S.C. (R.N.), *Gt. War*......... 1918

Currie, *Maj.* D. V., C.B.E. (S. Alberta R., Canada), *World War*................. 1944

Cutler, Sir A. R., K.C.M.G., K.C.V.O., C.B.E. (Australia), *World War*.................. 1941

Dean, *Col.* D. J., O.B.E. (R. W. Kent R.), *Gt. War*.......................... 1918

De L'Isle, *Maj.* The Viscount, K.G., P.C., G.C.M.G., G.C.V.O.(*Hon.*W.P. Sidney)(Gren. Gds.), *World War*...................... 1944

Dinesen, *Lt.* T. (Royal Highlanders of Canada), *Gt. War*...................... 1918

Dresser, *Pte.* T. (Green Howards), *Gt. War*.. 1917

Eardley, *Sergt.* G. H., M.M. (K.S.L.I.), *World War*........................... 1944

Edwards, *Air Commodore* Sir Hughie, K.C.M.G. C.B., D.S.O., O.B.E., D.F.C. (R.A.F.), *World War*.......................... 1941

Elliott, *Lt.* the Rev. K. (N.Z.M.F.), *World War* 1942

Ervine-Andrews, *Lt.-Col.* H. M. (E. Lancs. R.), *World War*...................... 1940

Foote, *Maj.-Gen.* H. R. B., C.B., D.S.O. (R. Tank R.), *World War*............... 1942

Foote, *Rev.* J. W. (Canada), *World War*... 1942

Fraser, *Cdr.* I. E., D.S.C. (R.N.R.), *World War* 1945

Ganju Lama, *Jemadar*, M.M. (Gurkha Rifles), *World War*........................ 1944

Gardner, *Capt.* P. J., M.C. (R.T.R.), *World War*............................ 1941

Ghale, *Subedar* Gaje (Gurkha Rif.), *Wld. War* 1943

Gian Singh, *Jemadar* (Punjab R.), *World War*. 1945

Gordon, *W.O. II* J. H. (Australia), *World War* 1941

Gould, *Lt.* T. W. (R.N.), *World War*....... 1942

Gourley, *2nd Lt.* C.E., M.M. (R.F.A.), *Gt. War*............................. 1917

Graham, *Lt.-Col.* Sir Reginald, Bt., O.B.E. (M.G.C.), *Gt. War*................... 1917

Gregg, *Brig.* Hon. Milton F., C.B.E., M.C. (Nova Scotia R.), *Gt. War*............. 1918

Grimshaw, *Lt.-Col.* John (Lanc. Fus.), *Gt. War*........................... 1915

Haine,*Lt.-Col.* R. L., M.C.(H.A.C.), *Gt. War*. 1917

Hall, *Sergt.* Arthur (Australia), *Gt. War*..... 1918

Harvey, *Brig.* F. M. W., M.C. (Can. Inf.), *Gt. War*........................... 1917

Hinton, *Sergt.* J. D. (N.Z.M.F.), *World War*.. 1941

Hulme, *Sergt.* A. C. (N.Z.M.F.), *World War* 1941

Jackson, *W.O.* N.C. (R.A.F.V.R.), *Wld. War* 1944

THE GEORGE CROSS, G.C.—For Gallantry

The ribbon is *dark blue* threaded through a bar adorned with laurel leaves.

INSTITUTED *September 24th,* 1940 (with amendments, *November 3rd,* 1942).

The George Cross is worn before all other decorations (except the VC) on the left breast § and consists of a plain silver cross with four equal limbs, the cross having in the centre a circular medallion bearing a design showing St. George and the Dragon. The inscription "For Gallantry" appears round the medallion and in the angle of each limb of the cross is the Royal cypher "G VI" forming a circle concentric with the medallion. The reverse is plain and bears the name of the recipient and the date of the award. The cross is suspended by a ring from a bar adorned with laurel leaves on dark blue ribbon 1½ inches wide.

The cross is intended primarily for civilians and awards to the fighting services are confined to actions for which purely military honours are not normally granted. It is awarded only for acts of the greatest heroism or of the most conspicuous courage in circumstances of extreme danger. From April 1, 1965, holders of the Cross have received a tax-free annuity of £100.

§ When worn by a woman it may be worn on the left shoulder from a ribbon of the same width and colour fashioned into a bow.

Empire Gallantry Medal.—The Royal Warrant which ordained that the grant of the Empire Gallantry Medal should cease authorized holders of that medal to return it to the Central Chancery of the Orders of Knighthood and to receive in exchange the George Cross. A similar provision applied to posthumous awards of the Empire Gallantry Medal made after the outbreak of war in 1939.

In October 1971 all surviving holders of the Albert Medal and the Edward Medal exchanged those decorations for the George Cross.

THE DISTINGUISHED SERVICE ORDER (1886)—D.S.O.

Ribbon, Red, with Blue Edges.

Bestowed in recognition of especial services in action of commissioned officers in the Navy, Army and Royal Air Force and (1942) Mercantile Marine. The members are Companions only and rank immediately before the 4th Class of the Royal Victorian Order. A Bar may be awarded for any additional act of service.

PRINCIPAL DECORATIONS AND MEDALS (in order of Precedence)

Victoria Cross.—1856.—*V C*
George Cross.—1940.—G.C.
British Orders of Knighthood.
Royal Red Cross.—1883—R.R.C. (Class I.).—For ladies.
Distinguished Service Cross.—1914.—D.S.C.—In substitution for the Conspicuous Service Cross, 1901; is for officers of R.N. below the rank of Captain, and Warrant Officers.
Military Cross.—Dec. 1914.—M.C.—Awarded to Captains, Lieutenants, and Warrant Officers (Cl I. and II.) in the Army and Indian and Colonial Forces.
Distinguished Flying Cross.—1918.—D.F.C.—For bestowal upon Officers and Warrant Officers in the Royal Air Force (and Fleet Air Arm from April 9, 1941) for acts of gallantry when flying in active operations against the enemy.
Air Force Cross.—1918.—A.F.C.—Instituted as preceding but for acts of courage or devotion to duty when flying, although not in active operations against the enemy (extended to Fleet Air Arm since April 9, 1941).
Royal Red Cross (Class II—A.R.R.C.).
Order of British India.
Kaisar-i-Hind Medal.
Order of St. John.
Albert Medal.—1866—A.M.—" For Gallantry in Saving Life at Sea " or " on Land." (Holders receive £100 tax-free annuity).
Union of South Africa Queen's Medal for Bravery, in Gold.
Medal for Distinguished Conduct in the Field.—1854.—D.C.M.—Awarded to warrant officers, non-commissioned officers and men of the Army and R.A.F.
Conspicuous Gallantry Medal.—1874.—C.G.M.—Is bestowed upon warrant officers and men of the R.N. and since 1942 of Mercantile Marine and R.A.F.
The George Medal.—G.M.—Established by King George VI in 1940 is a recognition of acts of gallantry.
The Edward Medal.—1907.—In recognition of heroic acts by miners or quarrymen, or of others who have endangered their lives in rescuing those so employed. (Holders receive £100 tax-free annuity).
Royal West African Frontier Force Distinguished Conduct Medal.
King's African Rifles Distinguished Conduct Medal.
Union of South Africa Queen's Medal for Bravery in Silver.
Distinguished Service Medal.—1914.—D.S.M.—For chief petty officers, petty officers, men, and boys of all branches of the Royal Navy, and since 1942 of Mercantile Marine, to non-commissioned officers and men of the Royal Marines, and to all other persons holding corresponding positions in Her Majesty's Service afloat.
Military Medal.—1916.—M.M.—For warrant and non-commissioned officers and men and serving women.
Distinguished Flying Medal.—1918.—D.F.M.—and the Air Force Medal.—A.F.M.—For warrant and non-commissioned officers and men for equivalent services as for D.F.C. and A.F.C. (extended to Fleet Air Arm, April 9, 1941).
Constabulary Medal (Ireland).
Medal for Saving Life at Sea.
Colonial Police Medal for Gallantry.
Queen's Gallantry Medal—1974.
British Empire Medal.—B.E.M.—(formerly the Medal of the Order of the British Empire, for Meritorious Service; also includes the Medal of the Order awarded before Dec. 29, 1922).
Queen's Police (Q.P.M.) and Fire Services Medals for Distinguished Service, (Q.F.S.M.).

Queen's Medal for Chiefs.
War Medals and Stars (in order of date).
Polar Medals (in order of date).
Royal Victorian Medal (Gold, Silver and Bronze).
Imperial Service Medal.
Police Medals for Valuable Service.
Badge of Honour.
Jubilee, Coronation and Durbar Medals.
King George V, King George VI and Queen Elizabeth II Long and Faithful Service Medals.
Long Service and Good Conduct Medal.
Naval Long Service and Good Conduct Medal.
Medal for Meritorious Service.
Royal Marine Meritorious Service Medal.
Royal Air Force Meritorious Service Medal.
Royal Air Force Long Service and Good Conduct Medal.
Royal West African Frontier Force Long Service and Good Conduct Medal.
King's African Rifles Long Service and Good Conduct Medal.
Police and Fire Brigade Long Service and Good Conduct Medal.
Colonial Police and Fire Brigades Long Service Medal.
Colonial Prison Service Medal.
Army Emergency Reserve Decoration.—E.R.D.
Volunteer Officer's Decoration.—V.D.
Volunteer Long Service Medal.
Volunteer Officers' Decoration (for India and the Colonies).
Volunteer Long Service Medal (for India and the Colonies).
Colonial Auxiliary Forces Long Service Medal.
Medal for Good Shooting (Naval).
Militia Long Service Medal.
Imperial Yeomanry Long Service Medal.
Territorial Decoration.—1908.—T.D.
Efficiency Decoration.—E.D.
Territorial Efficiency Medal.
Efficiency Medal.
Special Reserve Long Service and Good Conduct Medal.
Decoration for Officers, Royal Navy Reserve.—1910.—R.D.
Decoration for Officers, R.N.V.R.—V.R.D.
Royal Naval Reserve Long Service and Good Conduct Medal.
R.N.V.R. Long Service and Good Conduct Medal.
Royal Naval Auxiliary Sick Berth Reserve Long Service and Good Conduct Medal.
Royal Fleet Reserve Long Service and Good Conduct Medal.
Royal Naval Wireless Auxiliary Reserve Long Service and Good Conduct Medal.
Air Efficiency Award.—1942—A.E.
The Queen's Medal.—(For Champion Shots in the Army T.A.V.R. and R.A.F.).
Cadet Forces Medal.—1950.
Coast Life Saving Corps Long Service Medal.—1911.
Special Constabulary Long Service Medal.
Royal Observer Corps Medal.
Civil Defence Long Service Medal.
Service Medal of the Order of St. John.
Badge of the Order of the League of Mercy.
Voluntary Medical Service Medal.—1932.
Women's Royal Voluntary Service Medal.
Colonial Special Constabulary Medal.
Foreign Orders, Decorations and Medals (in order of date).

THE ORDER OF ST. JOHN

The Most Venerable Order of the Hospital of St. John of Jerusalem

St. John's Gate, Clerkenwell, E.C.1

Grand Prior, H.R.H. The Duke of Gloucester, G.C.V.O.

Lord Prior. The Lord Caccia, G.C.M.G., G.C.V.O. *Chancellor,* Sir Gilbert Inglefield, G.B.E., T.D.

The British Constitution

THE EXECUTIVE

The Crown (the Queen in Council) "makes peace and war, issues charters, increases the peerage, is the fountain of honour, of office, and of justice." The Sovereign entrusts the executive power to Ministers of the Crown, appointed on the advice of the accredited leader of the party in Parliament which enjoys, or can secure, a majority of votes in the House of Commons.

The Cabinet

The Cabinet has no corporate existence, but under the *Ministers of the Crown Act* (1937), provision was made for 17 Ministers of the first rank (Cabinet Ministers) and this number has been increased by later legislation. The *Ministers of the Crown (Parliamentary Secretaries) Act* (1960) laid down an aggregate limit of 33 Parliamentary Secretaries. Parts of these Acts were repealed by the *Ministers of the Crown Act* (1964) which varied the number of Parliamentary Secretaries (other than Treasury Secretaries) to 36.

The Prime Minister

The Prime Minister is appointed by the Sovereign. When a party is in opposition and its leadership becomes vacant it makes its free choice among the various personalities available; but if the party is in office, the Sovereign's choice may anticipate, and in a certain sense forestall, the decision of the party. In 1905 the office of Prime Minister, which had been in existence for nearly 200 years, was officially recognized and its holder was granted a place in the Table of Precedence.

The Leader of the Opposition

In 1937 the office of Leader of the Opposition was similarly recognized and a salary of £2,000 per annum was assigned to the post, thus following a practice which had prevailed in the Dominion of Canada since 1906. In 1957 the salary was increased to £3,000, in 1965 to £4,500, and in 1972 to £9,500. The present Leader of the Opposition is the Right Hon. Margaret Thatcher.

LEGISLATION

Legislation is initiated in the Houses of Parliament in the form of Bills. Public Bills are of two kinds, those introduced by the Government of the day, and those introduced by a private member. A Bill (except a Money Bill, which must originate in the House of Commons) can be introduced in either House and when presented receives its *First Reading*, after which it is printed and circulated to members. The next stage is the *Second Reading*, in the debate on which the broad issues raised are discussed. If passed it reaches the *Committee Stage* and is referred to a Committee (of the whole House, Select, or Standing—*see* "Committees," p. 311). Bills of major importance are usually sent to a Committee of the whole House. In committee, a Bill is discussed clause by clause, and is returned to the House with or without amendment. A *Private Bill*, which is introduced to enable an individual or a body corporate to acquire or vary certain powers, is referred to a *Select Committee*, and if opposed, witnesses may be called and counsel heard by the Committee. The next step is the, *Report Stage*, when the Bill is accepted by the House, or sent back to the same, or sent back to another, Committee for further consideration. Finally the Bill receives its *Third Reading* (during which, in the House of Commons, only verbal amendments are permissible) and is sent to the other House. When a Bill has been passed by both Houses it becomes an *Act of Parliament*, on receiving the *Royal Assent*, which is signified by the Sovereign on the Throne, or by Commissioners (normally three Peers), in the Chamber of the House of Lords. The power to withhold assent (colloquially known as the *Royal Veto*) resides in the Sovereign, but has not been exercised in the United Kingdom since, 1707, in the reign of Queen Anne.

COUNCILLORS OF STATE

On every occasion that the Sovereign leaves the realm for distant parts of the Commonwealth or a foreign country, it is necessary to appoint Councillors of State under Letters Patent to carry out the chief functions of the Monarch, including the holding of Privy Councils and the signature of Acts passed by Parliament. The normal procedure is to appoint as Councillors three or four members of the Royal Family among those remaining in the United Kingdom. For instance, during the Queen's visit to Canada in 1967, the Councillors of State were the Prince of Wales, Queen Elizabeth the Queen Mother, Princess Margaret and the Duke of Gloucester.

In the event of the Sovereign on accession being under the age of eighteen years or at any time unavailable or incapacitated by infirmity of mind or body for the performance of the royal functions, provision is made for a Regency. Since the Prince of Wales attained the age of 18 in November 1966, the provisions of the Regency Act as to age no longer apply in the event of his accession to the throne.

SPEAKERS OF THE COMMONS SINCE 1660

PARLIAMENT OF ENGLAND

1660	Sir H. Grimston.	1685	Sir John Trevor.
1661	Sir E. Turner.	1688	H. Powle.
1673	Sir J. Charlton.	1694	Paul Foley.
1673	Edwd. Seymour.	1698	Sir T. Lyttelton.
1678	Sir Robt. Sawyer.	1700	Robert Harley
1679	Serjeant William Gregory.		(*Earl of Oxford and Mortimer*).
1680	W. Williams.	1702	John Smith.

PARLIAMENT OF GREAT BRITAIN

1708	Sir Richard Onslow (*Lord Onslow*).	1761	Sir John Cust.
		1770	Sir F. Norton.
		1780	C.W. Cornwall.
1710	Wm. Bromley.	1788	Hon. W. Grenville.
1713	Sir Th. Hanmer.		(*Lord Grenville*).
1715	Spencer Compton (*Earl of Wilmington*).	1789	Henry Addington (*Viscount Sidmouth*).
1727	Arthur Onslow.		

PARLIAMENT OF UNITED KINGDOM

1801	Sir John Mitford (*Lord Redesdale*).
1802	Charles Abbot (*Lord Colchester*).
1817	Charles M. Sutton (*Viscount Canterbury*).
1835	James Abercromby (*Lord Dunfermline*).
1839	Charles Shaw-Lefevre (*Viscount Eversley*).
1857	J. Evelyn Denison (*Viscount Ossington*).
1872	Sir Henry Brand (*Viscount Hampden*).
1884	Arthur Wellesley Peel (*Viscount Peel*).
1895	William Court Gully (*Viscount Selby*).
1905	James W. Lowther (*Viscount Ullswater*).
1921	John Henry Whitley.
1928	Hon. Edward Algernon FitzRoy.
1943	Col. D. Clifton Brown (*Viscount Ruffside*).
1951	William Shepherd Morrison (*Viscount Dunrossil*).
1959	Sir Harry Hylton-Foster.
1965	Horace Maybray King, PH.D. (*Lord Maybray-King*).
1971	(John) Selwyn (Brooke) Lloyd (*Lord Selwyn-Lloyd*).
1976	(Thomas) George Thomas.

THE HOUSES OF PARLIAMENT

Parliament emerged during the late thirteenth and early fourteenth centuries as a result of diverse forces including the general need for a superior court to deal with legal and administrative problems on a national basis, the financial needs of the Crown, ambition of the baronage to influence the King's government, and the King's desire to make his government more effective by involving in it all important sections of the community. The nucleus of early Parliaments were the officers of the King's household and the King's judges, who were joined by such ecclesiastical and lay magnates as the King might summon and occasionally by the knights of the shire, burgesses and proctors of the lower clergy. The Commons were summoned to all the Parliaments of Edward III and by the end of the reign a " House of Commons " was beginning to appear. The first known Speaker was elected in 1377. The House of Lords is the ultimate Court of Appeal for all Courts in Great Britain and Northern Ireland, except for criminal cases in Scotland. The Lords surrendered the ancient right of peers to be tried for treason or felony by their peers in 1948. Each House has the right to control its own internal proceedings and to commit for contempt.

The Commons claim exclusive control in respect of national taxation and expenditure and in respect of local rates and charges upon them. Bills such as the Finance Bill, which imposes taxation, and the Consolidated Fund Bills, which authorize expenditure, and are commonly known as Supply Bills, must begin in the Commons and have not been amended by the Lords in any respect in modern times. A bill of which the financial provisions are subsidiary may begin in the Lords; and the Commons may waive their rights in regard to Lords amendments affecting finance.

Normally a bill must be agreed to by both Houses before it receives the Royal Assent, but under the Parliament Acts, 1911 and 1949—(a) a bill which the Speaker has certified as a Money Bill, *i.e.* as concerned solely with national taxation, expenditure or borrowing, if not agreed to by the Lords within one month of its being sent to them, receives the Royal Assent and becomes law without their concurrence; (b) any other public bill (except one to extend the life of a Parliament) which has been passed by the Commons in two successive sessions and twice rejected by the Lords, receives the Royal Assent and becomes law, provided that one year has elapsed between its Second Reading in the first session and its Third Reading in the second session in the Commons.

The Parliament Act of 1911 also limited the duration of Parliament, if not previously dissolved, to 5 years. The term is reckoned from the date given on the writs for the new Parliament. During the War of 1914–18 the duration of Parliament was extended by successive Acts from 5 to 8 years, but a General Election was held before the end of the term finally prescribed and the Parliament which first met on Jan. 31, 1911, was dissolved on Nov. 25, 1918, fourteen days after the Armistice. At the outbreak of war in 1939 a similar course was followed and Parliament which first met on Nov. 26, 1935, was not dissolved until June 15, 1945.

Since 1803 reports of the proceedings of Parliament in open session have been published. From 1803–1888 these were known as *Hansard's Parliamentary Debates*, and in 1943 the word " Hansard " was restored to the title page. Copies are obtainable from H.M. Stationery Office and periodical issues are on sale throughout the country.

Payment of Members—Members of the House of Lords are unpaid. They are entitled to reimbursement of travelling expenses from their residence to the House in respect of regular attendance and repayment of expenses within a maximum of £8·50 for each day of such attendance.

Since 1911 Members of the House of Commons have received payments and travelling facilities. Their salary of £400 was increased to £600 in 1937, to £1,000 in 1947, to £1,750 in 1957, to £3,250 in 1964, to £4,500 in January 1972 and £5,750 from June 1975; they are entitled to claim income tax relief on expenses incurred in the course of their Parliamentary duties. In October 1969 Members were allowed to claim up to £500 a year for secretarial expenses; the allowance was increased to £1,000 a year from January 1972, to £1,750 a year from August 1, 1974 and to £3,200 a year from June 1975. Also since January 1972, Members can claim reimbursement, within a limit of £750 a year for the additional cost of staying overnight away from their main residence while on Parliamentary business. This limit was increased to £1,050 a year in August 1974 and to £1,814 a year from July 1975. The cost of travel allowances for 1975–76 was stated in May 1976 to be £1,006,000 (car mileage claims £682,000, rail travel £217,000 and air travel £107,000). The Members' Pension Act, 1965, introduced the first comprehensive pension scheme providing Members of Parliament and their dependants with a legal right to a pension. Under the Parliamentary and Other Pensions Act 1972 the pension scheme was modified to include provision for Ministers and other office holders. The pension scheme is funded by an Exchequer contribution of approximately three times the contribution of a participant which is 5 per cent. of salary per annum (currently 5 per cent. of £5,750, or £287·50 per annum). Members receive pensions from age 65, or on ceasing to be a Member if later, provided they have served for 4 years or more. Pensions are based on one sixtieth of salary for each year of reckonable service. Members also continue to contribute £24 per annum and the Treasury up to £22,000 a year towards a Fund to provide annual or lump sum grants to ex-Members, their widows and children whose incomes are below certain limits. The income of the Fund in 1974–75 was £45,629 and expenditure on grants £32,735. The capital account stood in 1975 at £239,083.

THE HOUSE OF LORDS

The House of Lords consists of Lords Spiritual and Temporal. The Lords Spiritual are the two Archbishops, the Bishops of London, Durham and Winchester, and the 21 senior Bishops from the remaining English sees. The Lords Temporal are: Peers and Peeresses in their own right by descent of England, Scotland, Great Britain or the United Kingdom, hereditary peers of new creation, Lords of Appeal in Ordinary and retired Lords of Appeal in Ordinary (who are life peers), and Life Peers and Life Peeresses created under the Life Peerages Act, 1958. Under the Peerage Act, 1963, a person inheriting a peerage may within one year (or one month in the case of a Member of the House of Commons) disclaim the peerage for life. The subsequent descent of the peerage after his death is not affected.

THE HOUSE OF COMMONS

By the *Representation of the People Act* (1885) membership was increased from 658 (at which it had stood since 1801 through the *Act of Union with Ireland*) to 670, and by a similar Act (1918) it was increased to 707. By the *Government of Ireland Act* (1920) and the *Irish Free State Agreement Act* (1922) membership was decreased to 615. Irish

representation being reduced from 105 to 13 members. By the *Representation of the People Act* of 1945 25 new constituencies were created, making the total 640; and by a similar Act of 1948 the total membership was reduced to 625. As the result of Orders in Council made in 1955 under the *House of Commons (Redistribution of Seats) Act*, 1949, the total membership was increased to 630 and under the same Act provision was made in 1970 for further increase to 635.

THE PALACE OF WESTMINSTER

An ordinance issued in the reign of Richard II stated that "Parliament shall be holden or kepid wheresoever it pleaseth the King" and at the present day the Sovereign summons parliament to meet and prescribes the time and place of meeting. The royal palace at Westminster, originally built by Edward the Confessor (Westminster Hall being added by William Rufus) was the normal place of Parliament from about 1340. St. Stephen's Chapel (first mentioned in the reign of John) was used from about 1550 for the meetings of the House of Commons, which had previously been held in the Chapter House or Refectory of Westminster Abbey. The House of Lords met in an apartment of the royal palace.

The disastrous fire of 1834 destroyed the whole palace, except Westminster Hall, and the present Houses of Parliament were erected on the site from the designs of Sir Charles Barry and Augustus Pugin, between the years 1840 and 1867, at a cost of £2,198,000.

The Chamber of the House of Commons was destroyed by enemy action in 1941 and the foundation stone of a new building, from the designs of Sir Giles Gilbert Scott, was laid by the Speaker on May 26, 1948. The new Chamber was used for the first time on Oct. 26, 1950.

The Victoria Tower of the House of Lords is 330 feet high and when Parliament is sitting the Union Jack flies from sunrise to sunset from its flagstaff. The clock tower of the House of Commons is 316 feet high and contains "Big Ben," the 13½-ton hour bell named after Sir Benjamin Hall, First Commissioner of Works when the original bell was cast in 1856. The dials of the clock are 23 feet in diameter, the hands being 9 feet and 14 feet long (including balance piece). The chimes and strike of "Big Ben" have achieved world-wide fame from broadcasting.

A light is displayed in the clock tower from sundown to sunrise during the hours the House is in session.

THE LORD CHANCELLOR

The Lord High Chancellor of Great Britain is (although not addressed as such) the Speaker of the House of Lords. Unlike the Speaker of the House of Commons, he takes part in debates and votes in divisions. He sits on one of the *Woolsacks*, couches covered with red cloth and stuffed with wool. If the Lord Chancellor wishes to address the House in any way except formally as Speaker, he leaves the Woolsack and steps towards his proper place as a peer, below the Royal Dukes.

PRIME MINISTER'S RESIDENCE

Number 10, Downing Street, S.W.1, is the official town residence of the Prime Minister, No. 11 of the Chancellor of the Exchequer and No. 12 is the office of the Government Whips. The street was named after Sir George Downing, Bt., soldier and diplomatist, who was M.P. for Morpeth from 1660 to 1684.

Chequers, a Tudor mansion in the Chilterns, about 3 miles from Princes Risborough, was presented together with a maintenance endowment by Lord and Lady Lee of Fareham in 1917 to serve, from Jan. 1, 1921, as a country residence for the Prime Minister of the day, the Chequers estate of 700 acres being added to the gift by Lord Lee in 1921. The mansion contains a famous collection of Cromwellian portraits and relics.

PRIME MINISTERS

Sir Robert Walpole, *Whig*, April 3, 1721.
Earl of Wilmington, *Whig*, Feb. 16, 1742.
Henry Pelham, *Whig*, Aug. 25, 1743.
Duke of Newcastle, *Whig*, May 18, 1754.
Duke of Devonshire, *Whig*, Nov. 16, 1756.
Duke of Newcastle, *Whig*, July 2, 1757.
Earl of Bute, *Tory*, May 28, 1762.
George Grenville, *Whig*, April 15, 1763.
Marquess of Rockingham, *Whig*, July 10, 1765.
Earl of Chatham, *Whig*, Aug. 2, 1766.
Duke of Grafton, *Whig*, Dec. 1767.
Lord North, *Tory*, Feb. 6, 1770.
Marquess of Rockingham, *Whig*, March 27, 1782.
Earl of Shelburne, *Whig*, July 13, 1782.
Duke of Portland, *Coalition*, April 4, 1783.
William Pitt, *Tory*, Dec. 7, 1783.
Henry Addington, *Tory*, March 21, 1801.
William Pitt, *Tory*, May 16, 1804.
Lord Grenville, *Whig*, Feb. 10, 1806.
Duke of Portland, *Tory*, March 31, 1807.
Spencer Perceval, *Tory*, Dec. 6, 1809.
Earl of Liverpool, *Tory*, June 16, 1812.
George Canning, *Tory*, April 30, 1827.
Viscount Goderich, *Tory*, Sept. 8, 1827.
Duke of Wellington, *Tory*, Jan. 26, 1828.
Earl Grey, *Whig*, Nov. 24, 1830.
Viscount Melbourne, *Whig*, July 13, 1834.
Sir Robert Peel, *Tory*, Dec. 26, 1834.
Viscount Melbourne, *Whig*, March 18, 1835.
Sir Robert Peel, *Tory*, Sept. 6, 1841.
Lord John Russell, *Whig*, July 6, 1846.
Earl of Derby, *Tory*, Feb. 28, 1852.
Earl of Aberdeen, *Peelite*, Dec. 28, 1852.
Viscount Palmerston, *Liberal*, Feb. 10, 1855.
Earl of Derby, *Conservative*, Feb. 25, 1858.
Viscount Palmerston, *Liberal*, June 18, 1859.
Earl Russell, *Liberal*, Nov. 6, 1865.
Earl of Derby, *Conservative*, July 6, 1866.
Benjamin Disraeli, *Conservative*, Feb. 27, 1868.
W. E. Gladstone, *Liberal*, Dec. 9, 1868.
Benjamin Disraeli, *Conservative*, Feb. 21, 1874.
W. E. Gladstone, *Liberal*, April 28, 1880.
Marquess of Salisbury, *Conservative*, June 24, 1885.
W. E. Gladstone, *Liberal*, Feb. 6, 1886.
Marquess of Salisbury, *Conservative*, Aug. 3, 1886.
W. E. Gladstone, *Liberal*, Aug. 18, 1892.
Earl of Rosebery, *Liberal*, March 3, 1894.
Marquess of Salisbury, *Conservative*, July 2, 1895.
A. J. Balfour, *Conservative*, July 12, 1902.
Sir H. Campbell-Bannerman, *Liberal*, Dec. 5, 1905.
H. H. Asquith, *Liberal*, April 8, 1908.
H. H. Asquith, *Coalition*, May 26, 1915.
D. Lloyd-George, *Coalition*, Dec. 7, 1916.
A. Bonar Law, *Conservative*, Oct. 23, 1922.
S. Baldwin, *Conservative*, May 22, 1923.
J. R. MacDonald, *Labour*, Jan. 22, 1924.
S. Baldwin, *Conservative*, Nov. 4, 1924.
J. R. MacDonald, *Labour*, June 8, 1929.
J. R. MacDonald, *Coalition*, Aug. 25, 1931.
S. Baldwin, *Coalition*, June 7, 1935.
N. Chamberlain, *Coalition*, May 28, 1937.
W. S. Churchill, *Coalition*, May 11, 1940.
W. S. Churchill, *Conservative*, May 23, 1945.
C. R. Attlee, *Labour*, July 26, 1945.
Sir W. S. Churchill, *Conservative*, Oct. 26, 1951.
Sir A. Eden, *Conservative*, April 6, 1955.
H. Macmillan, *Conservative*, Jan. 13, 1957.
Sir A. Douglas-Home, *Conservative*, Oct. 19, 1963.
J. H. Wilson, *Labour*, Oct. 16, 1964.
E. R. G. Heath, *Conservative*, June 19, 1970.
J. H. Wilson, *Labour*, March 4, 1974.
L. J. Callaghan, *Labour*, April 5, 1976.

OFFICERS OF THE HOUSE OF LORDS

Speaker, The Rt.Hon. Frederick Elwyn-Jones, C.H., Lord Elwyn-Jones,(+ £17,500 as *Lord Chancellor*) £2,500
    Private Secretary to the Lord Chancellor, J. A. C. Watherston.
Chairman of Committees, The Lord Aberdare, P.C... £6,750
Deputy Principal Chairman of Committees, The Baroness Tweedsmuir of Belhelvie, P.C............ £5,500

Clerk of the Parliaments, Sir Peter Henderson, K.C.B............................ £18,675
Clerk Assistant, J. E. Grey.............. £14,000
Reading Clerk and Clerk of the Journals, J. C. Sainty......................... £12,465
Counsel to Chairman of Committees, T. G. Talbot, C.B., Q.C.; D. Rippengall; Sir Charles Sopwith.................. £12,465
Principal Clerks, R. P. Cave, C.B., M.V.O. (*Judicial Office and Fourth Clerk at the Table*); E. D. Graham (*Private Bills and Committees*); M. F. Bond, M.V.O., O.B.E., F.S.A. (*Information Services and Clerk of the Records*)................. £12,465
Chief Clerks, J. V. D. Webb; M. A. J. Wheeler-Booth; J. A. Vallance-White; J. M. Davies............ £9,115 to £11,465
Senior Clerks, P. D. G. Hayter (*seconded as Secretary to the Leader of the House and the Chief Whip*); C. A. J. Mitchell; M. G. Pownall.................. £6,145 to £6,715
Deputy Clerk of the Records, H. S. Cobb, F.S.A............. £7,616 to £9,215

Assistant Clerk of the Records, D. J. Johnson £4,869 to £7,574
Accountant, E. W. Field....... £6,145 to £7,915
Assistant Accountant, R. A. Devin £5,365 to £6,365
Librarian, C. S. A. Dobson, C.B.E., F.S.A. £9,115 to £11,465
Asst. Librarian, R. H. V. C. Morgan £7,616 to £9,215
Examiners of Petitions for Private Bills, E. D. Graham; D. Scott.
Judicial Taxing Clerk, C. G. Osborne £5,365 to £6,365
Gentleman-Usher of the Black Rod and Serjeant-at-Arms, Admiral Sir Frank Twiss, K.C.B., D.S.C............... £12,465
Yeoman Usher of the Black Rod and Deputy Serjeant-at-Arms, Grp.-Capt. R. M. B. Duke-Woolley, D.S.O., D.F.C.. £5,680 to £7,003
Staff Superintendent, Lt.-Cdr. D. E. Brock,
Shorthand Writer, A. P. W. Brewin   *fees*
Editor, Official Report (Hansard), C. W. H. Blogg.......................... £8,965
Asst. do. C. R. Stanton................ £6,965

OFFICERS OF THE HOUSE OF COMMONS

Speaker, The Rt. Hon. (Thomas) George Thomas, M.P. for Cardiff, West..................... £13,000
Chairman of Ways and Means, The Rt. Hon. (Henry) Oscar Murton, O.B.E., T.D., M.P. for Poole... £6,750
First Deputy Chairman of Ways and Means, Sir Myer Galpern, M.P. for Glasgow, Shettleston...... £5,500
Second Deputy Chairman of Ways and Means, (Bryant) Godman Irvine, M.P. for Rye.............. £5,500

DEPT. OF THE CLERK OF THE HOUSE
Clerk of the House of Commons, R. D. Barlas, C.B., O.B.E................. £18,675
Clerk Asst., C. A. S. S. Gordon......... £14,000
Clerk of Committees, D. A. M. Pring, M.C.. £14,000
Principal Clerks—
  Public Bills, A. A. Birley............. £12,465
  Committee Records, E. S. Taylor, Ph.D.... £12,465
  Services, M. H. Lawrence, C.M.G....... £12,465
  Journals, F. G. Allen.................. £12,465
  Table Office, K. A. Bradshaw......... £12,465
  Expenditure Committees, R. S. Lankester. £12,465
  Overseas Offices, J. H. Willcox......... £12,465
  Private Bills, D. Scott................. £11,965
  Select Committees, C. A. James......... £11,965
  Standing Committees, H. M. Barclay.... £11,965
Special Adviser (Expenditure Committee), D. F. Hubback, C.B. (*acting*)........... £12,465
Deputy Principal Clerks, M. T. Ryle; C. J. Boulton; J. F. Sweetman, T.D.; D. W. Limon; J. R. Rose, C. B. Winnifrith; A. J. Hastings; W. R. McKay (*acting*); R. J. Willoughby (*acting*); D. J. Chapman (*acting*)............... £9,115 to £11,465
Senior Clerks, S. A. L. Panton; R. B. Sands; G. Cubie; M. R. Jack, Ph.D; D. G. Millar; Mrs. J. Sharpe; Miss A. Milner-Barry; R. W. G. Wilson; W. A. Proctor; F. A. Cranmer; C. R. M. Ward, Ph.D.; C. B. B. Heathcote-Smith, C.B.E. (*acting*); G. C. O. Key, O.B.E., D.F.C. (*acting*); P. D. Brittain (*acting*); E. James (*acting*); F. W. Clark (*acting*).................. £6,145 to £7,915
Examiners of Private Bills, E. D. Graham; D. Scott.
Taxing Officer, D. Scott.

DEPT. OF THE SPEAKER
Speaker's Secretary, Brig. N. E. V. Short, M.B.E., M.C................ £9,115 to £11,465
Speaker's Counsel, Sir Robert Speed, C.B., Q.C............................. £12,465
Speaker's Second Counsel, Sir Charles Davis, C.B............................. £12,465
Chaplain to the Speaker, The Rev. Canon D. L. Edwards.
Editor, Official Report (Hansard), R. P. Dring.................. £10,865 to £11,465
Deputy Editor, R. E. G. Slade.......... £8,715
Shorthand Writer, A. P. W. Brewin.......*fees*
Deliverer of the Vote, P. K. Marsden, O.B.E. £7,340 to £9,815
Deputy Deliverer of the Vote, G. R. Russell £5,365 to £6,590

DEPT. OF THE SERJEANT AT ARMS
Serjeant at Arms, Lt.-Cdr. P. F. Thorne, C.B.E................................ £12,465
Deputy do., Cdr. D. Swanston, D.S.O., D.S.C., R.N. (*ret.*)........... £9,115 to £11,465
Assistant do., Major G. V. S. Le Fanu..... £7,915 to £9,115
Deputy Assistant do., (vacant)

DEPT. OF THE LIBRARY
Librarian, D. Menhennet, D.Phil.......... £12,465
Deputy Librarian, D. J. T. Englefield £9,115 to £11,465
Assistant Librarians, E. C. Thompson; H. J. Palmer.................. £9,115 to £10,263
Deputy Assistant Librarians, G. F .Lock; M. A. Griffith-Jones; J. B. Poole, Ph.D.; Miss J. B. Tanfield; S. Z. Young; Mrs. H. R. Coates............ £7,616 to £9,215
Senior Library Clerks, Miss P. J. Baines; Miss E. K. Andrews; P. M. Hart; K. G. Cuninghame; Mrs. B. L. Miller; Mrs. S. Hastings; Mrs. J. M. Lourie; Mrs. F.

Poole; Miss C. B. Mann; Mrs. J. M.
Fiddick................... £4,869 to £7,746

ADMINISTRATION DEPT.
Clerk Administrator, M. H. Lawrence,
C.M.G.
Accountant, F. J. Wilkin, O.B.E., D.F.M.
£9,115 to £11,465

Deputy Accountant, J. L. G. Dobson
£7,340 to £9,215
Assistant Accountants, A. J. Lewis; G. P.
Brown; F. W. Brewer....... £5,365 to £7,090
Head of Establishments Section, H. McE.
Allen................... £9,115 to £10,865
Deputy Head of Establishments Section, D. J.
Mouat................... £5,345 to £6,840

NOTES ON PARLIAMENTARY PROCEDURE

WRITS FOR A NEW PARLIAMENT, ETC.— Writs for a new Parliament are issued, on the Sovereign's warrant, by the Lord Chancellor to Peers individually, but in the case of the Commons to the returning officers of the various constituencies. A Writ of Summons to the House of Lords, before the time when baronies were created by Letters Patent, is held (should the writ be good and the Parliament legally summoned) to create a barony for the recipient and his heirs. The oldest English peerages, the baronies of De Ros and Mowbray, are founded on writs of summons issued in 1264 and 1283 respectively. A newly-created Peer may not sit or speak in the House of Lords until he has been introduced by two sponsors of his own degree in the Peerage.

VACANT SEATS.—When a vacancy occurs in the House of Commons the Writ for a New Election is generally moved, during a session of Parliament, by the Chief Whip of the party to whom the member whose seat has been vacated belonged. If the House is in recess, the Speaker can issue a writ, should two members certify to him that a seat is vacant. He cannot, however, issue such a writ if the seat has been vacated through the former member's lunacy or his acceptance of the office of Bailiff of the *Chiltern Hundreds,* or Steward of the *Manor of Northstead,* a legal fiction which enables a member to retire from the House, for it has long been established that a member cannot, by his own volition, relieve himself of the responsibilities which his constituents which his membership involves. Until 1926, however, it was necessary for a member to retire from the House on accepting an office of profit under the Crown, which, it may be noted, subjected a private member who accepted ministerial office to the trouble and expense of seeking re-election in his constituency. The Act of 1926, which removed this necessity, retained the Chiltern Hundreds and the Manor of Northstead as offices of profit and thus perpetuated the fiction.

HOURS OF MEETING, ETC.—The House of Lords normally meets during the Session at 2.30 p.m. on Tuesday and Wednesday, and at 3 p.m. on Thursday. In the latter part of the Session, the House usually sits also on Mondays at 2.30 p.m., and occasionally on Fridays at 11 a.m. The House of Commons meets on Monday, Tuesday, Wednesday and Thursday at 2.30, and on Friday at 11. Morning sittings on Monday and Wednesday were held from February–July, 1967 and occasionally during 1968 and 1969. *Strangers* are present during the debates of both Houses on sufferance, and may be excluded at any time; this applies equally to the *Press Gallery.* Time has modified what was once a rigid exclusion and strangers have in recent years generally been admitted except during the secret sessions of war time. The proceedings are opened by Prayers in both Houses. The *Quorum* of the House of Commons is forty members, including the Speaker, and should a member point out to the Speaker at any time fewer than forty members are present, the division bells are rung, and if forty members have not appeared within four minutes, the House is said to be *Counted Out,* and the sitting is adjourned. The *Quorum* of the Lords is three.

PROROGATION AND DISSOLUTION.—A session of Parliament is brought to an end by its Prorogation to a certain date, while Parliament itself comes to an end either by Dissolution by the Sovereign or the expiration of the term of 5 years for which it was elected (*see* p. 307).

ELECTION PETITIONS.—The right of a member of the House of Commons to sit in Parliament can be challenged by petition on several grounds, *e.g.* ineligibility to sit owing to his bribery or corruption of the electors. Such petitions were originally decided by the House itself, but as party feeling was too much inclined to dictate the decision, their trial was in 1868 referred to the High Court of Justice.

STANDING ORDERS.—These are rules, which have from time to time been established by both Houses of Parliament, to regulate the conduct of business. These orders are not irrevocable, and like the Statutory Laws of England they can be easily revised, amended or repealed, and are frequently suspended or dispensed with. The custom and precedents of Parliament, which dictate the bulk of Parliamentary procedure, have acquired, in seven centuries, prescriptive rights of obedience as firmly seated as the Common Law. *Sessional Orders* are applicable only to the session in which they are passed.

GENERAL PROCEDURE.—There are differences in the rules which govern the conduct of debates in the House of Lords and in the House of Commons. The Speaker in the Commons is responsible for the preservation of order and discipline in the House, but the only duty of the Lord Chancellor or the presiding Peer is to put the question. A Peer prefaces his remarks with " My Lords," whereas a member of the House of Commons addresses himself to Mr. Speaker. A member of the House of Commons wishing to speak " rises in his place uncovered." When several members rise together the one whom the Speaker calls to continue the debate is described as *having caught the Speaker's eye.* In the House of Lords in similar circumstances, the House itself decides who shall speak. Broadly speaking, a member may not, except in Committee, speak more than once to a question except in explanation or reply, and this privilege is granted only to the mover of a motion, or to the Minister or Member in charge of a bill. A member may address the House from notes but must not read his speech, a distinction sometimes without a difference. In the Commons members must not be mentioned by name; the proceedings of the other House and matters *sub judice* must not be discussed; offensive words or epithets must not be used; a member may not speak after a question has been put, except on a point of order, and then he must address the Speaker " *seated and covered.*" He must bow to the Speaker on entering and leaving the House.

QUESTION TIME.—After Prayers the first business of importance in the House of Commons is Question Time, which lasts from 2.45 until 3.30. Two days' notice of questions must be given to the *Clerk of the House of Commons,* the senior official of the House, who presides over it in the brief interval between the first assembly of a new

Parliament and the election of a Speaker, and whose counterpart in the House of Lords is the *Clerk of the Parliaments*. Members of the House may put an unlimited number of questions to Ministers, but not more than two demanding an oral answer may be made in any one day to the same Minister. Supplementary questions may be put either by the member asking the original question, or by other members, to obtain clarification of a Minister's answer. In the House of Lords up to four questions for oral answer may be asked on each sitting day.

COMMITTEES.—On the Assembly of a new Parliament, after the election of the Speaker, the House of Commons deals with the subject of Committees, which are of three kinds:—*Committees of the Whole House*, *Select Committees* (appointed for a specific purpose) and the *Standing Committees* which consider public bills and whose composition, though laid down by Standing Orders, is frequently modified by Sessional Orders. When a bill dealing *exclusively* with Scotland or with Wales and Monmouthshire is referred to a Standing Committee, in the first place all Scottish, and in the second, all Welsh members are automatically members thereof.

CLOSURE AND THE GUILLOTINE.—To prevent deliberate waste of Parliamentary time, a procedure known as the *Closure* (colloquially known as "The Gag") was brought into effect on Nov. 10, 1882. A motion may be made *that the question be now put*. If the Speaker decides that the rights of a minority are not being prejudiced and 100 members support the motion, it is put to the vote, and, if carried, the original motion is put to the House, without further debate. The *Guillotine* represents a more rigorous and systematic application of the Closure. Under this system, a bill proceeds in accordance with a rigid time table and discussion is limited to the time allotted to each group of clauses. If the number of amendments put down appears likely to require more time than has been allotted for their discussion, the Speaker selects those which he considers are most important. The guillotine was first put into use on June 17, 1887, after prolonged debates on the Crimes Bill.

THE PREVIOUS QUESTION.—When the House is disinclined to give a decision on a particular question it is possible to avoid the issue by moving the Previous Question, which is done by one of several motions, *e.g.* "That the Question be not now put" or "That the House do now proceed to the Orders of the Day." In the House of Lords the Previous Question has been replaced by the Next Business Motion—"That the House do proceed to the next business."

MOTION FOR ADJOURNMENT.—Adjournment ends the sitting of either House and takes place either under the provisions of a Standing Order or through an *ad hoc* resolution. In the Commons a method of obtaining immediate discussion of a matter of urgency is by moving the adjournment for the purpose of discussing a specific and important matter that should have urgent consideration. A member may ask leave to make this motion by giving written notice to the Speaker after Question Time and if it obtains the support of 40 members and the Speaker considers the matter of sufficient importance, it is discussed at 7 p.m. on that day. A Committee of the Whole House cannot adjourn but its proceedings may be interrupted by a motion *That the Chairman report Progress*. This brings the Speaker back to the House and the Committee seeks permission to sit on a future date.

PRIVILEGES OF PARLIAMENT.—There are certain rights and jurisdictions peculiar to each House of Parliament, but privileges in their accepted meaning are common to both Houses. The right of imprisoning persons who commit what are in the opinion of the House breaches of privilege is beyond question, and such persons cannot be admitted to bail nor is any Court competent to investigate the causes of commitment. Each House is the sole and absolute judge of its own privileges and where law and privilege have seemed to clash a conflict of jurisdiction has arisen between Parliament and the Courts. Breaches of privilege may be described briefly as disobedience to the orders of either House; assaults or insults to Members or libels on them; and interference with the officers of the House in the carrying out of their duties. The House of Lords may imprison for a period, or may inflict a fine, but the House of Commons only commits generally and the commitment ceases on the prorogation of Parliament. The Bill of Rights established the principle that "freedom of speech and debates and proceedings in Parliament should not be impeached or questioned in any court or place out of parliament." Consequently the House itself is the only authority which can punish a member for intemperance in debate. Freedom from arrest was a much prized privilege, but it applied only to civil arrest for debt (now abolished) and arbitrary arrest by the Government; members are amenable to all other processes of the Law. Freedom from arrest, in the case of members of the House of Commons, applies to the forty days after the prorogation and the forty days before the next meeting of Parliament.

THE SPEAKER.—The *Speaker of the House of Commons* is the spokesman and president of the Chamber. He is elected by the House at the beginning of each Parliament. He was originally a partisan but throughout a century of development between Speaker Onslow (1728) and Speaker Shaw-Lefevre (1839), the theory of the non-partisan Speaker was perfected, and he now neither speaks in debates, nor votes in divisions, except when the voting is equal. His order in the precedence of the Kingdom is high, only the Prime Minister and the Lord President of the Council going before him. He takes precedence of all Peers, except the two Archbishops, and Speakers are almost invariably raised to the Peerage on vacating their office, though Speaker Whitley is believed to have declined the offer of a Viscountcy. The Speaker's most severe disciplinary measure against a member is to *Name* him. When a member has been named, *i.e.* contrary to the practice of the House called by surname and not addressed as the "Hon. Member for . . ." (his constituency), the Leader of the House moves that he " be suspended from the service of the House " for (in the case of a first offence) a period of a week. The period of suspension is increased, should the member offend again. Speaker Denison has left it on record that " The House is always kind and indulgent, but it expects its Speakers to be right. If he should be found tripping, his authority must soon be at an end." The Speaker's Deputy is the *Chairman of Committees*, officially the *Chairman of Ways and Means*, who presides in the absence of the Speaker and when the House has resolved itself into Committee by the passage of the motion *that the Speaker do now leave the Chair*. He, like the Speaker, is elected at the beginning of each Parliament, and when he is presiding as chairman of a committee neither speaks in debate nor votes (except when the voting is equal). A *Deputy Chairman of Ways and Means* is also appointed, and several temporary chairmen, who frequently preside either over a Committee of the Whole House or over Standing Committees.

The Lord Chancellor is *Speaker of the House of Lords*. Being a member of the Government, he has none of the powers to maintain order that the Speaker of the House of Commons has. (These powers, in the Lords, are exercised by the House as a whole.) A panel of Deputy Speakers is appointed by Royal Commission. The Chairman of Committees is a salaried officer of the House who takes the chair in Committee of the Whole House and in some Select Committees. He is assisted by a panel of Deputy Chairmen, headed by the salaried Principal Deputy Chairman of Committees, who is also Chairman of the European Communities Committee of the House.

GOVERNMENT BY PARTY

Before the reign of William and Mary the principal Officers of State were chosen by and were responsible to the Sovereign alone and not to Parliament or the nation at large. Such officers acted sometimes in concert with one another, but more often independently, and the fall of one did not, of necessity, involve that of others, although all were liable to be dismissed at any moment.

In 1693 the Earl of Sunderland recommended to William III the advisability of selecting a Ministry from the political party which enjoyed a majority in the House of Commons and the first united Ministry was drawn in 1696 from the Whigs, to which party the King owed his throne, the principal members being Russell (the Admiral), Somers (the Advocate), Lord Wharton and Charles Montague (afterwards Chancellor of the Exchequer). This group became known as the *Junto* and was regarded with suspicion as a novelty in the political life of the nation, being a small section meeting in secret apart from the main body of Ministers. It may be regarded as the forerunner of the *Cabinet* and in course of time it led to the establishment of the principle of joint responsibility of Ministers, so that internal disagreement caused a change of *personnel* or resignation of the whole body of Ministers.

The accession of George I, who was unfamiliar with the English language, led to a disinclination on the part of the Sovereign to preside at meetings of his Ministers and caused the appearance of a *Prime Minister*, a position first acquired by Robert Walpole in 1721 and retained without interruption for 20 years and 326 days.

In 1828 the old party of the Whigs became known as *Liberals*, a name originally given to it by its opponents to imply laxity of principles, but gradually accepted by the party to indicate its claim to be pioneers and champions of political reform and progressive legislation. In 1861 a Liberal Registration Association was founded and Liberal Associations became widespread. As the outcome of a conference at Birmingham in 1877 a National Liberal Federation was formed, with headquarters in London. The Liberal Party was in power for long periods during the second half of the nineteenth century in spite of the set-back during the Home Rule crisis of 1886, which resulted in the secession of the Liberal Unionists, and for several years during the first quarter of the twentieth century, but after a further split into National and Independent Liberals it numbered only 59 in all after the General Election of 1929, with a further fall to 12 (excluding National Liberals) after the 1945 Election. The number is now 13.

Soon after the change from Whig to Liberal the Tory Party became known as *Conservative*, a name traditionally believed to have been invented by John Wilson Croker in 1830 and to have been generally adopted about the time of the passing of the Reform Act of 1832 to indicate that the preservation of national institutions was the leading principle of the party. After the Home Rule crisis of 1886 the dissentient Liberals entered into a compact with the Conservatives, under which the latter undertook not to contest their seats, but a separate *Liberal Unionist* organization was maintained until 1912, when it was united with the Conservatives under the title of National Unionist Association of Conservative and Liberal Unionist Organizations, the members of which became known as *Unionists*.

The Labour Party.—Labour candidates for Parliament made their first appearance at the General Election of 1892, when there were 27 standing as "Labour" or "Liberal-Labour." At the General Election of 1895 the number of successful candidates fell to 12, with a further fall to 11 at the election of 1900.

In 1900 the *Labour Representative Committee* was set up in order to establish a distinct Labour Group in Parliament, with its own whips, its own policy, and a readiness to co-operate with any party which might be engaged in promoting legislation in the direct interest of labour. In 1906 the L.R.C. became known as *The Labour Party*.

Parliamentary Whips

In order to secure the attendance of Members of a particular party in Parliament on all occasions, and particularly on the occasion of an important division, *Whips* (originally known as "Whippers-in") are appointed for the purpose. The written appeal or circular letter issued by them is also known as a "whip", its urgency being denoted by the number of times it is underlined. Neglect to respond to a three-lined whip, headed "Most Important," is tantamount to secession (at any rate temporarily) from the party. Whips are officially recognized by Parliament and are provided with office accommodation in both Houses. Government Whips receive salaries from public funds, the Parliamentary (Patronage) Secretary to the Treasury (*Chief Whip in the Commons*) receiving £5,625; the Captain of the Gentlemen-at-Arms (*Chief Whip in the Lords*), the Captain of the Yeomen of the Guard (*Assistant do.*) and the first of the Junior Lords of the Treasury (*Deputy Chief Whip in the Commons*), each £3,000; the (Political) Lords in Waiting and the remaining Junior Lords of the Treasury, each £2,000.

The House of Lords

The *Government Whips* are: The Captain of the Honourable Corps of the Gentlemen at Arms (The Baroness Llewelyn-Davies of Hastoe), the Captain of the Queen's Bodyguard of the Yeomen of the Guard (Lord Strabolgi) and the (Political) Lords in Waiting.

The *Conservative Whips* are: Earl St. Aldwyn (*Chief Whip*); Lord Mowbray and Stourton; Lord Sandys; Lord Lyell; Viscount Long; Lord Redesdale; Lord Newell.

The *Liberal Whip* is Lord Amulree.

The House of Commons

The *Government Whips* are: The Parliamentary (Patronage) Secretary to the Treasury (*Chief Whip*) and the Junior Lords of the Treasury. *Assistant Whips* are also usually appointed.

The *Conservative Whips* are: The Rt. Hon. H. E. Atkins (*Chief Whip*); B. B. Weatherill (*Deputy Chief Whip*); J. S. Thomas; C. E. Parkinson; S. Le Marchant; M. H. A. Roberts; W. R. Benyon; F. J. Silvester; Hon. Anthony Berry; D. C. M. Mather; J. T. Lester; J. A. Corrie.

The *Liberal Whip* is A. J. Beith.

(Formed April 1976)

THE CABINET

Prime Minister and First Lord of the Treasury, The Rt. Hon. Leonard James Callaghan, M.P., *born* March 27, 1912.

Secretary of State for Foreign and Commonwealth Affairs, The Rt. Hon. Charles Anthony Raven Crosland, M.P., *born* Aug. 29, 1918.

Chancellor of the Exchequer, The Rt. Hon. Denis Winston Healey, M.P., *born* Aug. 30, 1917.

Lord High Chancellor, The Rt. Hon. Lord Elwyn-Jones, C.H., *born* Oct. 24, 1909.

Secretary of State for the Home Department, The Rt. Hon. Roy Harris Jenkins, M.P., *born* Nov. 11, 1920.

Secretary of State for Social Services, The Rt. Hon. David Hedley Ennals, M.P., *born* Aug. 19, 1922.

Secretary of State for Defence, The Rt. Hon. Roy Mason, M.P., *born* April 18, 1924.

Secretary of State for Scotland, The Rt. Hon. Bruce Millan, M.P., *born* Oct. 5, 1927.

Secretary of State for Employment, The Rt. Hon. Albert Edward Booth, M.P., *born* May 28, 1928.

Secretary of State for Education and Science, The Rt. Hon. Frederick William Mulley, M.P., *born*, July 3, 1918.

Secretary of State for Wales, The Rt. Hon. John Morris, M.P., *born* 1931.

Secretary of State for Trade, The Rt. Hon. Edmund Emanuel Dell, M.P., *born* Aug. 15, 1921.

Secretary of State for Industry, The Rt. Hon. Eric Graham Varley, M.P., *born* Aug. 11, 1932.

Secretary of State for the Environment, The Rt. Hon. Peter David Shore, M.P., *born* May 20, 1924.

Secretary of State for Northern Ireland, The Rt. Hon. Merlyn Rees, M.P., *born* Dec. 18, 1920.

Secretary of State for Energy, The Rt. Hon. Anthony Neil Wedgwood Benn, M.P., *born* April 3, 1925.

Secretary of State for Prices and Consumer Protection and Paymaster-General, The Rt. Hon. Shirley Vivien Teresa Brittain Williams, M.P., *born* July 27, 1930.

Lord President of the Council and Leader of the House of Commons, The Rt. Hon. Michael Mackintosh Foot, M.P., *born* July 23, 1913.

Lord Privy Seal and Leader of the House of Lords, The Rt. Hon. Lord Shepherd, *born* Sept. 27, 1918.

Chancellor of the Duchy of Lancaster, The Rt. Hon. Norman Harold Lever, *born* Jan. 15, 1914.

Minister of Agriculture and Fisheries, The Rt. Hon. Thomas Frederick Peart, M.P., *born* April 30, 1914.

Minister for Overseas Development, The Rt. Hon. Reginald Ernest Prentice, M.P., *born* July 16, 1923.

MINISTERS NOT IN THE CABINET

Minister for Housing and Construction, The Rt. Hon. Reginald Yarnitz Freeson, M.P., *born* 1926.

Minister for Transport, John William Gilbert, Ph.D., M.P., *born* 1927.

Minister for Planning and Local Government, The Rt. Hon. John Ernest Silkin, M.P., *born* 1923.

Attorney-General, The Rt. Hon. Samuel Charles Silkin, Q.C., M.P., *born* 1918.

Lord Advocate, The Rt. Hon. Ronald King Murray, Q.C., M.P., *born* 1922.

Solicitor-General, Peter Kingsley Archer, Q.C., M.P., *born* 1926.

Solicitor-General for Scotland, John Herbert McCluskey, Q.C., *born* 1929.

Chief Secretary to the Treasury, The Rt. Hon. Joel Barnett, M.P., *born* 1922.

Parliamentary Secretary to the Treasury, The Rt. Hon. Michael Francis Lovell Cocks, M.P., *born* 1929.

Financial Secretary to the Treasury, Robert Edward Sheldon, M.P., *born* 1923.

Ministers of State (Foreign and Commonwealth Office), The Rt. Hon. Roy Sydney George Hattersley, M.P., *born* 1932; The Lord Goronwy-Roberts, P.C., *born* 1913; Edward Rowlands, M.P., *born* 1940.

Ministers of State (Home Office), The Lord Harris of Greenwich, *born* 1930; Brynmor Thomas John, M.P., *born* 1934.

Ministers of State (Scottish Office), The Lord Kirkhill, *born* 1930; (James) Gregor Mackenzie, M.P., *born* 1916.

Ministers of State (Health and Social Security), The Rt. Hon. Stanley Orme, M.P., *born* 1923; The Rt. Hon. David Anthony Llewelyn Owen, *born* 1938.

Minister of State (Employment), Harold Walker, M.P., *born* 1927.

Minister of State (Defence), The Rt. Hon. William Thomas Rodgers, M.P., *born* 1928.

Ministers of State (Northern Ireland), Roland Dunstan Moyle, M.P., *born* 1928; John Dennis Concannon, M.P., *born* 1930.

Minister of State (Agriculture and Fisheries), Edward Stanley Bishop, M.P., *born* 1920.

Minister of State (Treasury), (David John) Denzil Davies, *born* 1938.

Minister of State (Privy Council Office), John Smith, M.P., *born* 1938.

Minister of State (Energy), (Jesse) Dickson Mabon, M.P., *born* 1925.

Minister of State (Environment), The Rt. Hon. Denis Herbert Howell, M.P., *born* 1923 *(Sport)*.

Ministers of State (Industry), Gerald Bernard Kaufman, M.P., *born* 1930; Alan John Williams, M.P., *born* 1930.

Minister of State (Civil Service Department), Charles Richard Morris, M.P., *born* 1926.

Ministers of State (Education and Science), Gerald Teasdale Fowler, M.P., *born* 1935; The Lord Donaldson of Kingsbridge, *born* 1907.

Minister of State (Prices and Consumer Protection), John Denis Fraser, M.P., *born* 1934.

PARLIAMENTARY UNDER SECRETARIES, ETC.

Agriculture and Fisheries, G. S. Strang, M.P.

Civil Service Department, J. D. Grant, M.P.

Defence, A. E. P. Duffy, M.P. (*Royal Navy*); R. C. Brown, M.P. (*Army*); A. J. Wellbeloved, M.P. (*Royal Air Force*).

Education and Science, Miss M. M. Jackson, M.P.

Employment, J. Golding, M.P.; J. Grant, M.P.

Energy, A. Eadie, M.P.; G. J. Oakes, M.P.

Environment, The Baroness Birk; E. Armstrong, M.P.; K. Marks, M.P.; N. G. Barnett, M.P.

Foreign and Commonwealth Affairs, J. E. Armstrong, M.P.; D. E. T. Luard, M.P.

Health and Social Security, E. P. Deakins, M.P. (*Social Security*); A. Morris, M.P. (*Disabled*).

Home, The Hon. Shirley Summerskill, M.P.

Industry, The Lord Melchett; L. J. Huckfield, M.P.

Law Officers' Dept., A. Davidson, M.P.

Northern Ireland, J. A. Dunn, M.P.; R. J. Carter, M.P.

Overseas Development, F. A. Judd, M.P.

Prices and Consumer Protection, R. A. R. MacLennan, M.P.

Privy Council Office, W. G. Price, M.P.

Scottish Office, H. D. Brown, M.P.; H. Ewing, M.P.

Trade, M. H. Meacher, M.P.; S. C. Davis, M.P.

Treasury, Junior Lords, D. R. Coleman, M.P.; T. Pendry, M.P.; J. D. Dormand, M.P.; D. L. Stoddart, M.P.; T. E. Graham, M.P.

Asst. Whips, T. M. Cox, M.P.; L. A. Pavitt, M.P.; E. G. Perry, M.P.; J. Ellis, M.P.; P. C. Snape, M.P.; A. W. Stallard, M.P.; A. Bates, M.P.; F. R. White, M.P.; J. Tinn, M.P.

Welsh Office, S. B. Jones, M.P.; T. A. Jones, M.P.

THE PRINCIPAL PARTIES IN PARLIAMENT (1929-1974)

General Election	Conservative	Liberal	Labour
1929	260	59	287
1931	471	72 (a)	65 (b)
1935	387	54 (c)	166 (d)
1945	189	25 (e)	396 (f)
1950	298 (g)	9	315 (h)
1951	320 (i)	6	296 (h)
1955	344 (i)	6	277 (j)
1959	365 (i)	6	258 (k)
1964	303 (i)	9	317
1966	253 (i)	12	363 (l)
1970	330 (m)	6	287 (n)
1974 (February)	296	14	301 (o)
1974 (October)	276	13	319 (p)

NOTES.—(a) Liberal National 35 (Simon); Liberal 33 (Samuel); 4 (Lloyd George). (b) National Labour 13 (MacDonald); Labour 52 (Henderson). (c) Liberal National 33; Liberal 21. (d) National Labour 8; Labour 154; I.L.P. 4. (e) Liberal National 13. Liberal 12. (f) Labour 393; I.L.P. 3. (g) Incl. Nat. Liberal. (h) Irish Nationalists (2) and Speaker make total of 625. (i) Including associates. (j) Sinn Fein (2) and Speaker make total of 630. (k) Independent (1) makes total of 630. (l) Republican Labour (1) makes total of 630. (m) Including Ulster Unionists. (n) Scottish Nationalist (1); Independent (5) and Speaker make total of 630. (o) United Ulster Unionist Council (11), Scottish Nationalists (7), Plaid Cymru (2); Social Democratic and Labour Party (1); Social Democrat (1); Independent Labour (1); and Speaker make total of 635. (p) Scottish Nationalists (11); United Ulster Unionist (10); Plaid Cymru (3); Social Democratic and Labour Party (1); Independent (1) and Speaker make a total of 635. Since the October 1974 election Conservatives have gained one seat (Woolwich, West) from Labour.

PARLIAMENTS SINCE 1852

Assembled	Dissolved	Duration yrs. m. d.
Victoria		
1852 Nov. 4	1857 March 21	4 4 17
1857 April 30	1859 April 23	1 11 23
1859 May 31	1865 July 6	6 1 6
1866 Feb. 1	1868 Nov. 11	2 9 10
1868 Dec. 10	1874 Jan. 26	5 1 16
1874 March 5	1880 March 25	6 0 20
1880 April 29	1885 Nov. 18	5 6 20
1886 Jan. 12	1886 June 26	0 5 14
1886 Aug. 5	1892 June 28	5 10 24
1892 Aug. 4	1895 July 9	2 11 5
1895 Aug. 12	1900 Sept. 25	5 1 14
Victoria and Edward VII		
1900 Dec. 3	1906 Jan. 8	5 1 6
Edward VII		
1906 Feb. 13	1910 Jan. 15	3 11 2
Edward VII and George V		
1910 Feb. 15	1910 Nov. 28	0 9 13

Assembled	Dissolved	Duration yrs. m. d.
George V		
1911 Jan. 31	1918 Nov. 25	7 9 25
1919 Feb. 4	1922 Oct. 26	3 8 22
1922 Nov. 20	1923 Nov. 16	0 11 27
1924 Jan. 8	1924 Oct. 9	0 9 1
1924 Dec. 2	1929 May 10	4 5 7
1929 June 25	1931 Oct. 6	2 3 11
1931 Nov. 3	1935 Oct. 25	3 11 22
George V, Edward VIII and George VI		
1935 Nov. 16	1945 June 15	9 6 25
George VI		
1945 Aug. 1	1950 Feb. 3	4 6 3
1950 March 1	1951 Oct. 5	1 7 4
George VI and Elizabeth II		
1951 Oct. 31	1955 May 6	3 6 6
Elizabeth II		
1955 June 9	1959 Sept. 18	4 3 9
1959 Oct. 27	1964 Sept. 25	4 10 29
1964 Nov. 3	1966 March 10	1 4 7
1966 April 21	1970 May 29	4 1 8
1970 July 2	1974 Feb. 8	3 7 6
1974 March 13	1974 Sept. 19	0 6 6
1974 Oct. 29		

MAJORITIES IN THE HOUSE OF COMMONS
(Since the Reform Bill, 1832).

Year	Party	Majority	Year	Party	Majority
1833	*Whig*	307	1910 (Jan.)	*Liberal*	124
1835	*Whig*	107	1910 (Dec.)	*Liberal*	126
1837	*Whig*	51	1918	*Coalition*	263
1841	*Conservative*	81	1922	*Conservative*	79
1847	*Whig*	1	1923	No Majority.	
1852	*Liberal*	13	1924	*Conservative*	225
1857	*Liberal*	79	1929	No Majority.	
1859	*Liberal*	43	1931	*National Government*	425
1865	*Liberal*	67	1935	*National Government*	247
1868	*Liberal*	128	1945	*Labour*	146
1874	*Conservative*	46	1950	*Labour*	8
1880	*Liberal*	62	1951	*Conservative*	16
1885	*Liberal* (84) and *Irish Nationalist* (82).	166	1955	*Conservative*	59
1886	*Unionist*	114	1959	*Conservative*	100
1892	*Liberal*	40	1964	*Labour*	5
1895	*Unionist*	152	1966	*Labour*	99
1900	*Unionist*	134	1970	*Conservative*	31
1906	*Liberal*	356	1974 (Feb.)	No Majority.	
			1974 (Oct.)	*Labour*	5

FORFEITED DEPOSITS AT THE GENERAL ELECTION, 1974

Candidates at parliamentary elections who fail to obtain one-eighth of the total votes cast in their constituencies forfeit the deposit of £150 which all candidates must lodge.

Deposits forfeited at the 1974 October election totalled 453, 132 more than in Feb. 1974. Deposits were lost by 15 Labour candidates, 130 Liberals, 30 Conservatives, 29 Communists, 26 Plaid Cymru, 90 National Front and 133 others. In 1950 the previous record number of 443 deposits was lost.

VOTES CAST AT THE GENERAL ELECTIONS, 1959–74
AND AT BY-ELECTIONS SINCE 1966

General Election, 1959

Conservative and Associate	13,750,965
Labour	12,195,765
Liberal	1,661,262
Welsh Nationalist	77,571
Sinn Fein	63,915
Communist	30,897
Scottish Nationalist	21,738
Others	61,225
Total	27,863,338

General Election, 1964

Labour	12,205,581
Conservative and Associate	11,980,783
Liberal	3,101,103
Irish Republican	101,628
Welsh Nationalist	68,517
Scottish Nationalist	63,053
Communist	44,576
Others	90,908
Total	27,656,149

General Election, 1966

Labour	13,064,951
Conservative and Associate	11,418,433
Liberal	2,327,533
Scottish Nationalist	128,474
Communist	62,112
Plaid Cymru	61,071
Others	201,032
Total	27,263,606

By-elections 1966–70

At 38 by-elections between the General Elections of 1966 and 1970, the following votes were cast:

Conservative and Ulster Unionist	629,970
Labour	439,358
Liberal	26,3011
Independent	57,527
Scottish Nationalist	40,737
Plaid Cymru	40,518
Communist	4,807

General Election, 1970

Conservative and Ulster Unionist	13,144,692
Labour	12,179,166
Liberal	2,117,638
Scottish Nationalist	306,796
Plaid Cymru	175,016
Communist	38,431
Others	383,068
Total	28,344,087

By-elections 1970–74

At 30 by-elections between the General Elections of 1970 and 1974, the following votes were cast:—

Labour	415,798
Conservative	351,781
Liberal	156,744
Independent	53,673
Scottish Nationalist	36,204
Plaid Cymru	11,852
Communist	1,647

General Election, February 1974*

Conservative	11,868,906
Labour	11,639,243
Liberal	6,063,470
Scottish Nationalist	632,032
Plaid Cymru	171,634
Communist	32,741
Others	207,884

General Election, October, 1974*

Labour	11,456,597
Conservative	10,464,675
Liberal	5,346,800
Scottish Nationalist	839,628
Plaid Cymru	166,321
Others	195,065

By-elections, 1974–6

At six by-elections since the General Election of October 1974. The following votes have been cast:

Conservative	113,308
Labour	85,615
Liberal	26,079
National Front	8,644
Others	2,543

* Excluding Northern Ireland

PARLIAMENTARY ASSOCIATIONS

COMMONWEALTH PARLIAMENTARY ASSOCIATION (1911)

The Commonwealth Parliamentary Association consists of 30 main branches in Parliaments of the self-governing countries of the Commonwealth and 26 auxiliary branches in countries or territories which are not yet self-governing. There are also branches in State and Provincial Legislatures, in Australia, Canada, India and Malaysia making a total of 102 branches. Commonwealth Parliamentary conferences and general meetings are held every year in different countries of the Commonwealth.
President, Hon. Sir Radhamahun Gujadhur, C.M.G. (Mauritius).
Secretary-General, Sir Robin Vanderfelt, K.B.E., Houses of Parliament, S.W.1.
Secretary, *United Kingdom Branch*, P. G. Molloy, O.B.E., M.C., Westminster Hall, Houses of Parliament, S.W.1.

THE INTER-PARLIAMENTARY UNION

Place du Petit-Saconnex 1209, Geneva, Switzerland. The Inter-Parliamentary Union has been in existence since 1889; originally started to popularize the idea of International Arbitration, it achieved its object very substantially in helping to create the Permanent Court of Arbitration by the First Hague Conference and to bring about the convocation of the Second Conference of The Hague. In 1945, the Union resumed work on all questions connected with peace and reconstruction, which have been studied under various aspects.

BRITISH GROUP.

Hon. Presidents, The Lord Chancellor; Mr. Speaker.
President, The Rt. Hon. L. J. Callaghan, M.P.
Vice-Presidents, The Lord Home of the Hirsel, P.C., K.T.; The Lord Butler of Saffron Walden. K.G., P.C., C.H.; The Rt. Hon. R. M. M. Stewart, C.H., M.P.; The Rt. Hon. E. R. G. Heath, M.B.E., M.P.; The Rt. Hon. Margaret Thatcher, M.P.; The Rt. Hon. Sir Harold Wilson, K.G., O.B.E., M.P.
Chairman, Sir Thomas Williams, Q.C., M.P.
Secretary, Brigadier P. S. Ward, C.B.E.

ALPHABETICAL LIST OF MEMBERS OF THE HOUSE OF COMMONS
(Elected October 10, 1974)

For abbreviations, *see* page 322. The number before the name of each constituency is for easy reference and corresponds to the number of that constituency given on pp. 322-45.

Maj.

*Abse, L. (*b.* 1917), *Lab.,* 470*Pontypool* 18,695
*Adley, R. J. (*b.* 1935), *C.,* 149*Christchurch and Lymington* 13,890
*Aitken, J. W. P. (*b.* 1942), *C.,* 569*Thanet, E.* 4,503
*Alison, M. J. H. (*b.* 1926), *C.,* 33*Barkston Ash* 9,941
*Allaun, F. J. (*b.* 1913), *Lab.,* 511*Salford, E.* 7,836
*Amery, Rt. Hon. J. (*b.* 1919), *C.,* 106 *Brighton, Pavilion* 7,417
*Anderson, Rt. Hon. Betty Harvie- (*b.* 1915), *C.,* 484*Renfrewshire, E.* 8,710
Anderson, D..(*b.* 1939), *Lab.,* 565*Swansea, E.* 20,721
*Archer, P. K. (*b.* 1926), *Lab.,* 596*Warley, W.* 14,857
*Armstrong, E. (*b.* 1915), *Lab.,* 207*Durham, N.W.* 18,756
Arnold, T. R. (*b.* 1947), *C.,* 299*Hazel Grove* 2,831
*Ashley, J. (*b.* 1922), *Lab.,* 551*Stoke, S.* 16,495
*Ashton, J. W. (*b.* 1933), *Lab.,* 39*Bassetlaw.* 12,169
*Atkins, Rt. Hon. H. E. (*b.* 1922), *C.,* 538 *Spelthorne* 5,948
*Atkins, R. H. (*b.* 1916), *Lab.* 475*Preston, N.* 1,784
*Atkinson, N. (*b.* 1923), *Lab.,* 579*Tottenham* 9,216
*Awdry, D.E. (*b.* 1924), *C.,* 145*Chippenham* 1,749
*Bagier, G. A. T. (*b.* 1924), *Lab.,* 558 *Sunderland, S.* 13,030
Bain, Mrs. M. A. (*b.* 1945), *Scot. Nat.,* 201 *Dunbartonshire, E.* 22
*Baker, K. W. (*b.* 1934), *C.,* 509*St. Marylebone* 6,503
*Banks, R. G. (*b.* 1937), *C.,* 290*Harrogate.* 13,314
*Barnett, Rt. Hon. J. (*b.* 1923), *Lab.,* 311 *Heywood and Royton* 7,899
*Barnett, N. G. (*b.* 1928), *Lab.,* 276*Greenwich* 9,906
*Bates, A. (*b.* 1944), *Lab.,* 45*Bebington and Ellesmere Port* 6,491
Bean, R. E. (*b.* 1935), *Lab.,* 491*Rochester and Chatham* 2,418
*Beith, A. J. (*b.* 1943), *L.,* 59*Berwick upon Tweed* 73
*Bell, R. M. (*b.* 1914), *C.,* 44*Beaconsfield.* . 10,626
*Benn, Rt. Hon. A. N. Wedgwood (*b.* 1925), *Lab.,* 110*Bristol, S.E.* 9,373
*Bennett, A. F. (*b.* 1929), *Lab.,* 546*Stockport, N.* 1,824
*Bennett Sir F. M. (*b.* 1918), *C.,* 577*Torbay* 12,438
*Bennett, R. F. B. (*b.* 1911), *C.,* 234*Fareham* 4,448
*Benyon, W. R. (*b.* 1930), *C.,* 113*Buckingham* 2,918
*Berry, Hon. A. G. (*b.* 1925), *C.,* 534*Southgate* 14,922
*Bidwell, S. J. (*b.* 1917), *Lab.,* 529*Southall.* 9,983
*Biffen, W. J. (*b.* 1930), *C.,*454 *Oswestry* . . 8,414
*Bishop, E. S. (*b.* 1920), *Lab.,* 420*Newark* . . 5,771
*Blaker, P. A. R. (*b.* 1922), *C.,* 79*Blackpool, S.* 5,221
*Blenkinsop, A. (*b.* 1911), *Lab.,* 536*South Shields* 14,825
*Boardman, H. (*b.* 1907), *Lab.,* 367*Leigh.* . 14,635
*Body, R. (*b.* 1927), *C.,* 315*Holland with Boston* 8,684
*Booth, Rt. Hon. A. E. (*b.* 1928), *Lab.,* 35 *Barrow in Furness* 7,354
*Boothroyd, Miss B. (*b.* 1930), *Lab.,* 604 *West Bromwich, W.* 14,799
*Boscawen, Hon. R. T. (*b.* 1923), *C.,* 601 *Wells* 7,701

Maj.

*Bottomley, Rt. Hon. A. G. (*b.* 1907), *Lab., Middlesbrough.* 13,807
Bottomley, P. J. (*b.* 1944). *C.,* 625 *Woolwich, W.* 2,382
*Bowden, A. (*b.* 1930), *C.,* 105*Brighton, Kemptown.* 2,605
*Bowman, Mrs. M. E. Kellett- (*b.* 1924), *C.,* 356*Lancaster* 1,421
*Boyden, H. J. (*b.* 1910), *Lab.,* 75*Bishop Auckland* 11,095
*Boyson, R. R. (*b.* 1925), *C.,* 97*Brent, N.* . . 7,312
*Bradford, Rev. R. J. (*b.* 1941), *U.U.U.,* 54*Belfast, S.* 18,401
*Bradley, T. G. (*b.* 1926), *Lab.,* 364*Leicester, E.* 3,811
*Braine, Sir B. R. (*b.* 1914), *C.,* 229*Essex, S.E.* 8,710
Bray, J. W. (*b.* 1930), *Lab.,* 416*Motherwell and Wishaw* 4,962
*Brittan, L. (*b.* 1939), *C.,* 152*Cleveland and Whitby* 1,528
Brotherton, M. L. (*b.* 1931), *C.,* 386*Louth* 2,880
*Broughton, Sir A. D. D. (*b.* 1902), *Lab.,* 41*Batley and Morley* 8,248
*Brown, Sir E. J. (*b.* 1913), *C.,* 40*Bath* 2,122
*Brown, H. D. (*b.* 1919), *Lab.,* 263*Provan.* . 9,974
*Brown, R. C. (*b.* 1921), *Lab.,* 426*Newcastle, W.* 15,074
*Brown, R. W. (*b.* 1921), *Lab.,* 281*S. Hackney and Shoreditch* 13,295
*Bryan, Sir P. E. O. (*b.* 1913), *C.,* 323 *Howden.* 4,780
*Buchan, N. F. (*b.* 1922), *Lab.,* 485*Renfrewshire, E.* 5,300
*Buchanan, R. (*b.* 1912), *Lab.,* 266*Springburn* 8,395
*Buck, P. A. F. (*b.* 1928), *C.,* 155*Colchester* 5,500
*Budgen, N. W. (*b.* 1937), *C.,* 622*Wolverhampton, S.W.* 5,300
*Bulmer, J. E. (*b.* 1935), *C.,* 346*Kidderminster.* 6,769
*Burden, F. F. A. (*b.* 1905), *C.,* 253*Gillingham.* 3,996
*Butler, Hon. A. C. (*b.* 1931), *C.,* 87 *Bosworth.* 302
*Butler, Mrs. J. S. (*b.* 1910), *Lab.,* 623*Wood Green.* 8,211
*Callaghan, J. (*b.* 1927), *Lab.,* 408*Middleton and Prestwich* 3,714
*Callaghan, Rt. Hon. L. J. (*b.* 1912), *Lab.,* 127*Cardiff, S.E.* 10,718
*Campbell, I. (*b.* 1926), *Lab.,* 202*Dunbartonshire, W.* 1,814
Canavan, D. A. (*b.* 1942), *Lab.,* 545*Stirlingshire, W.* 367
*Cant, R. B. (*b.* 1915), *Lab.,* 549*Stoke, Central* 14,653
*Carlisle, M. (*b.* 1929), *C.,* 500*Runcorn* . . . 5,468
*Carmichael, N. G. (*b.* 1921), *Lab.,* 260 *Kelvingrove* 4,118
*Carson, J. (*b.* 1930), *U.U.U.,* 53*Belfast, N.* 18,222
*Carter, R. J. (*b.* 1935), *Lab.,* 68*Northfield.* 10,597
Cartwright, J. C. (*b.* 1933), *Lab.,* 624 *Woolwich, E.* 12,425
*Castle, Rt. Hon. Barbara (*b.* 1911), *Lab.,* 77*Blackburn* 7,652
*Chalker, Mrs. L. (*b.* 1942), *C.,* 589 *Wallasey* 1,970
*Channon, H. P. G. (*b.* 1935), *C.,* 533*Southend, W.* 7.071
*Churchill, W. S. (*b.* 1940), *C.,* 550*Stretford* 1,237

Maj.

*Pink, R. B. (*b.* 1912), C., 474*Portsmouth, S.*................................. 8,071

Powell, Rt. Hon. J. E. (*b.* 1912), U.U.U., 195*Down, S.*..................... 3,567

*Prentice, Rt. Hon. R. E. (*b.* 1923), *Lab.*, 428*Newham, N.E.*................. 13,541

*Prescott, J. L. (*b.* 1938), *Lab.*, 327*Hull, E.* 25,793

*Price, C. (*b.* 1932), *Lab.*, 371*Lewisham, W.* 5,529

*Price, D. E. C. (*b.* 1924), C., 213*Eastleigh.* 7,815

*Price, W. G. (*b.* 1934), *Lab.*, 498*Rugby*... 5,204

*Prior, Rt. Hon. J. M. L. (*b.* 1927), C., 387 *Lowestoft*............................ 2,062

*Pym, Rt. Hon. F. L. (*b.* 1922), C., 122 *Cambridgeshire*..................... 12,655

*Radice, G. H. (*b.* 1936), *Lab.*, 142*Chester-le-Street*............................ 24,278

*Raison, T. H. F. (*b.* 1929), C., 25*Aylesbury* 8,973

*Rathbone, J. R. (*b.* 1933), C., 369*Lewes.*. 13,847

*Rawlinson, Rt. Hon. Sir P. A. G. (*b.* 1919), C., 226*Epsom and Ewell*...... 16,290

*Rees, Rt. Hon. M. (*b.* 1920), *Lab.*, 360 *Leeds, S.*........................... 15,265

*Rees, P. W. I. (*b.* 1926), C., 193*Dover and Deal*.............................. 2,294

*Reid, G. N. (*b.* 1940), *Scot. Nat.*, 544 *Stirlingshire E., and Clackmannan*...... 7,341

*Renton, Rt. Hon. Sir D. L. M. (*b.* 1908), C., 329*Huntingdonshire*............... 9,244

*Renton, R. T. (*b.* 1932), C., 562*Mid Sussex*............................. 11,997

*Richardson, Miss J. (*b.* 1923), *Lab.*, 32 *Barking*............................ 16,290

*Ridley, Hon. N. (*b.* 1929), C., 150*Cirencester and Tewkesbury*................. 10,160

*Ridsdale, J. E. (*b.* 1915), C., 295*Harwich.* 10,828

*Rifkind, M. L. (*b.* 1946), C., 220*Pentlands* 1,257

*Rippon, Rt. Hon. A. G. F. (*b.* 1924), C., 310*Hexham*......................... 4,641

*Roberts, A. (*b.* 1908), *Lab.*, 437*Normanton* 14,633

*Roberts, G. E. (*b.* 1928), *Lab.*, 123*Cannock* 12,222

*Roberts, I. W. P. (*b.* 1930), C., 158*Conway* 2,806

*Roberts, M. H. A. (*b.* 1927), C., 126 *Cardiff, N.W.*....................... 4,333

*Robertson, J. (*b.* 1913), *Lab.*, 458*Paisley*.. 5,590

Robinson, G. *Lab.*, 161*Coventry, N.W.*.... 3,694

*Roderick, C. E. (*b.* 1927), *Lab.*, 95*Brecon and Radnor*........................ 3,012

*Rodgers, G. (*b.* 1925), *Lab.*, 148*Chorley*.. 2,713

*Rodgers, Sir J. C., Bt. (*b.* 1906), C., 515 *Sevenoaks*......................... 11,605

*Rodgers, Rt. Hon. W. T. (*b.* 1928), *Lab.*, 548*Stockton*........................ 14,474

*Rooker, J. W. (*b.* 1941), *Lab.*, 69*Perry Bar*............................... 3,204

*Roper, J. F. H. (*b.* 1935), *Lab.*, 236*Farnworth*............................ 14,695

*Rose, P. B. (*b.* 1935), *Lab.*, 395*Blackley*... 7,119

*Ross, S. S. (*b.* 1926), L., 338*Isle of Wight.* 2,040

*Ross, Rt. Hon. W. (*b.* 1911), *Lab.*, 347 *Kilmarnock*........................ 7,529

*Ross, W. (*b.* 1936), U.U.U., 384*Londonderry*............................. 9,020

*Rossi, H. A. L. (*b.* 1927), C., 319*Hornsey* 782

*Rost, P. L. (*b.* 1930), C., 181*Derbyshire, S.E.*.............................. 1,005

*Rowlands, E. (*b.* 1940), *Lab.*, 406*Merthyr Tydfil*............................. 16,805

*Royle, Sir A. H. F. (*b.* 1927), C., 487 *Richmond upon Thames*.............. 4,215

Ryman, J. (*b.* 1931), *Lab.*, 81*Blyth*....... 78

*Sainsbury, Hon. T. A. D. (*b.* 1932), C., 322*Hove*............................. 14,876

*Sandelson, N. D. (*b.* 1923), *Lab.*, 298*Hayes and Harlington*..................... 9,420

Maj.

Scott, N. P. (*b.* 1933), C., 136*Chelsea*.... 13,167

*Sedgemore, B. C. J. (*b.* 1937), *Lab.*, 390 *Luton, W.*.......................... 6,439

*Selby, H. (*b.* 1914), *Lab.*, 258*Govan*...... 1,952

*Shaw, A. J. (*b.* 1909), *Lab.*, 332*Ilford, S.*... 1,749

*Shaw, J. G. D. (*b.* 1931), C., 477*Pudsey*... 4,581

*Shaw, M. N. (*b.* 1920), C., 514*Scarborough* 9,708

*Sheldon, R. E. (*b.* 1923), *Lab.*, 24*Ashton-under-Lyne*........................ 10,72

*Shelton, W. J. M. (*b.* 1929), C., 553 *Streatham*.......................... 2,867

Shepherd, C. R. (*b.* 1938), C., 305*Hereford* 1,112

*Shersby, J. M. (*b.* 1933), C., 586*Uxbridge.* 2,153

*Shore, Rt. Hon. P. D. (*b.* 1924), *Lab.*, 542 *Stepney and Poplar*................. 20,976

*Short, Rt. Hon. E. W. (*b.* 1912), *Lab.*, 423 *Newcastle, Central*................. 8,114

*Short, Mrs. R. (*b.* 1919), *Lab.*, 620*Wolverhampton, N.E.*..................... 14,653

*Silk, K. Kilroy- (*b.* 1942), *Lab.*, 452*Ormskirk*............................. 8,851

*Silkin, Rt. Hon. J. E. (*b.* 1923), *Lab.*, 177 *Deptford*........................... 13,034

*Silkin, Rt. Hon. S. C. (*b.* 1918), *Lab.*, 198 *Dulwich*........................... 7,459

*Sillars, J. (*b.* 1937), *Lab.*, 29*Ayrshire, S.*... 14,478

*Silverman, J. (*b.* 1905), *Lab.*, 64*Erdington.* 8,777

*Silvester, F. J. (*b.* 1933), C., 400*Withington* 2,001

*Sims, R. E. (*b.* 1930), C., 147*Chislehurst*.. 3,894

*Sinclair, Sir G. E. (*b.* 1912), C., 189 *Dorking*............................ 10,305

*Skeet, T. H. H. (*b.* 1918), C., 47*Bedford*.. 4,088

*Skinner, D. E. (*b.* 1932), *Lab.*, 83*Bolsover.* 21,066

*Small, W. W. (*b.* 1909), *Lab.*, 257*Garscadden*............................ 7,626

*Smith, Hon. A. L. Buchanan- (*b.* 1932), C., 15*North Angus and Mearns*........ 2,551

*Smith, C. (*b.* 1928), L., 490*Rochdale*..... 2,753

*Smith, Rt. Hon. Sir D. C. Walker-. Bt. (*b.* 1910), C., 307*Herts., E.*.............. 8,335

*Smith, D. G. (*b.* 1926), C., 598*Warwick and Leamington*..................... 8,245

*Smith, G. Johnson (*b.* 1924), C., 211*East Grinstead*......................... 9,280

*Smith, J. (*b.* 1938), *Lab.*, 355*Lanarkshire, N.* 8,341

*Snape, P. C. (*b.* 1942), *Lab.*, 603*West Bromwich, E.*...................... 1,529

*Spearing, N. J. (*b.* 1930), *Lab.*, 430*Newham, S.*............................... 17,721

Speed, H. K. (*b.* 1934), C., 23*Ashford*.... 6,025

*Spence, J. D. (*b.* 1920), C., 571*Thirsk and Malton*............................ 13,862

*Spicer, J. W. (*b.* 1925), C., 192*Dorset, W.* 8,685

*Spicer, W. M. H. (*b.* 1943), C., 627*Worcs., S.*............................... 9,052

*Spriggs, L. (*b.* 1910), *Lab.*, 507*St. Helens.*. 22,066

*Sproat, I. M. (*b.* 1938), C., 4*Aberdeen, S.*. 365

*Stainton, K. M. (*b.* 1921), C., 556*Sudbury and Woodbridge*................... 12,063

*Stallard, A. W. (*b.* 1921), *Lab.*, 510*St. Pancras, N.*........................ 7,553

*Stanbrook, I. R. (*b.* 1924), C., 453 *Orpington*.......................... 5,010

*Stanley, J. P. (*b.* 1942), C., 575*Tonbridge and Malling*........................ 8,609

*Steel, D. M. S. (*b.* 1938), L., 497*Roxburgh, Selkirk and Peebles*.................. 7,433

*Steen, A. D. (*b.* 1939), C., 381*Wavertree.*. 2,755

*Stevas, N. A. F. St. John- (*b.* 1929), C., 135 *Chelmsford*........................ 4,002

*Stewart, B. H. I. H. (*b.* 1935), C., 313 *Hitchin*............................ 3,186

*Stewart, D. J. (*b.* 1920), *Scot. Nat.*, 606 *Western Isles*....................... 5,232

*Stewart, Rt. Hon. R. M. M. (*b.* 1906), *Lab.*, 246*Fulham*..................... 5,321

*Stoddart, D. L. (*b.* 1926), *Lab.*, 567*Swindon* 10,270

Maj.

★Stokes, J. H. R. (*b.* 1917), *C.,* 282*Halesowen
   and Stourbridge*...................... 850
★Stott, R. W. (*b.* 1943), *Lab.,* 607*West-
   houghton*.......................... 13,575
★Strang, G. S. (*b.* 1943), *Lab.,* 217*Edinburgh,
   E.*................................ 8,456
★Strauss, Rt. Hon. G. R. (*b.* 1901), *Lab.,*
   587*Vauxhall*....................... 9,766
★Summerskill, Hon. Shirley (*b.* 1931), *Lab.,*
   283*Halifax*......................... 4,178
★Swain, T. H. (*b.* 1912), *Lab.,* 180*Derby-
   shire, N.E.*......................... 10,237
★Tapsell, P. H. B. (*b.* 1930), *C.,* 317*Horn-
   castle*.............................. 5,244
★Taylor, E. M. (*b.* 1937), *C.,* 254*Cathcart*.. 1,757
★Taylor, R. G. (*b.* 1932), *C.,* 168*Croydon,
   N.W.*.............................. 1,479
Taylor, Mrs. W. A. (*b.* 1947), *Lab.,* 85
   Bolton, W.......................... 906
★Tebbit, N. B. (*b.* 1941), *C.,* 144*Chingford*. 4,645
★Thatcher, Rt. Hon. Mrs. M. H. (*b.* 1925),
   C., 242*Finchley*.................... 3,911
★Thomas, D. E. (*b.* 1946), *P.C.,* 405
   Merioneth.......................... 2,592
★Thomas, J. (*b.* 1933), *Lab.,* 7*Abertillery*... 18,355
★Thomas, J. S. (*b.* 1925), *C.,* 411*Monmouth* 2,342
Thomas, M. S. (*b.* 1944), *Lab.,* 424*New-
   castle, E.*.......................... 6,249
★Thomas, Rt. Hon. P. J. M. (*b.* 1920), *C.,*
   303*Hendon, S.*...................... 4,963
Thomas, R. R. (*b.* 1929), *Lab.,* 108*Bristol,
   N.W.*.............................. 633
★Thomas, Rt. Hon. T. G. (*b.* 1909), *Lab.
   (now The Speaker),* 128*Cardiff, W.* 6,672
Thompson, G. H. (*b.* 1928), *Scot. Nat.,* 250
   Galloway........................... 30
★Thorne, S. G. (*b.* 1918), *Lab.,* 476*Preston,
   S.*................................. 3,749
★Thorpe, Rt. Hon. J. J. (*b.* 1929), *L.,* 179
   Devon, N........................... 6,721
★Tierney, S. (*b.* 1923), *Lab.,* 74*Yardley*.... 4,170
★Tinn, J. (*b.* 1922), *Lab.,* 482*Redcar*....... 10,430
★Tomlinson, J. E. (*b.* 1939), *Lab.,* 404
   Meriden............................ 8,966
★Tomney, F. (*b.* 1908), *Lab.,* 286*Hammer-
   smith, N.*........................... 8,122
★Torney, T. W. (*b.* 1915), *Lab.,* 92*Bradford,
   S.*................................. 8,255
★Townsend, C. D. (*b.* 1937), *C.,* 61*Bexley-
   heath*.............................. 1,987
★Trotter, N. G. (*b.* 1932), *C.,* 583*Tyne-
   mouth*.............................. 3,121
★Tuck, R. H. (*b.* 1910), *Lab.,* 594*Watford*. 3,957
★Tugendhat, C. S. (*b.* 1937), *C.,* 151*Cities
   of London and Westminster*............ 5,761
★Urwin, T. W. (*b.* 1912), *Lab.,* 321
   Houghton-le-Spring................. 20,401
★Van Straubenzee, W. R. (*b.* 1924), *C.,* 615
   Wokingham......................... 7,705
★Varley, Rt. Hon. E. G. (*b.* 1932), *Lab.,*
   141*Chesterfield*..................... 17,560
★Vaughan, G. F. (*b.* 1923), *C.,* 481*Reading,
   S.*................................. 6,666
★Viggers, P. J. (*b.* 1938), *C.,* 271*Gosport*... 6,866
★Wainwright, E. (*b.* 1908), *Lab.,* 175*Dearne
   Valley*............................. 27,269
★Wainwright, R. S. (*b.* 1918), *L.,* 156*Colne
   Valley*............................. 1,666
★Wakeham, J. (*b.* 1932), *C.,* 393*Maldon*... 6,387
★Walden, A. B. (*b.* 1932), *Lab.,* 67*Ladywood* 9,739
★Walder, A. D. (*b.* 1928), *C.,* 153*Clitheroe*. 6,868

Maj.

★Walker, Rt. Hon. P. E. (*b.* 1931), *C.,* 626
   Worcester.......................... 4,989
★Walker, T. W. (*b.* 1935), *Lab.,* 349*Kings-
   wood*.............................. 2,566
★Wall, P. H. B. (*b.* 1916), *C.,* 284
   Haltemprice........................ 11,661
★Walters, D. M. (*b.* 1928), *C.,* 605*Westbury* 6,143
Ward, M. J. (*b.* 1931), *Lab.,* 464*Peterborough* 1,848
★Warren, K. R. (*b.* 1926), *C.,* 296*Hastings*. 4,652
★Watkins, D. J. (*b.* 1925), *Lab.,* 157*Consett* 19,446
Watkinson, J. T. (*b.* 1941), *Lab.,* 269*Glos.,
   W.*................................ 409
★Watt, I. H. (*b.* 1926), *Scot. Nat.,* 31*Banff*. 1,851
★Weatherill, B. B. (*b.* 1930), *C.,* 167
   Croydon, N.E....................... 2,151
★Weetch, K. T. (*b.* 1933), *Lab.,* 336*Ipswich* 1,733
★Weitzman, D. (*b.* 1898), *Lab.,* 280*N.
   Hackney and Stoke Newington*......... 10,553
★Wellbeloved, A. J. (*b.* 1926), *Lab.,* 227
   Erith and Crayford................. 8,467
★Wells, J. J. (*b.* 1925), *C.,* 392*Maidstone* ... 10,271
Welsh, A. (*b.* 1944), *Scot. Nat.,* 16*Angus, S.* 1,824
White, F. R. (*b.* 1939), *Lab.,* 116*Bury and
   Radcliffe*........................... 442
★White, J. (*b.* 1922), *Lab.,* 262*Pollok*....... 7,091
★Whitehead, P. (*b.* 1937), *Lab.,* 178*Derby,
   N.*................................ 4,193
★Whitelaw, Rt. Hon. W. S. I. (*b.* 1918),
   462*Penrith and the Border*............ 13,756
★Whitlock, W. C. (*b.* 1918), *Lab.,* 445
   Nottingham, N..................... 6,841
★Wiggin, A. W. (*b.* 1937), *C.,* 610*Weston-
   super-Mare*......................... 12,859
★Wigley, D. (*b.* 1944), *P.C.,* 118*Caernarvon* 2,894
★Willey, Rt. Hon. F. T. (*b.* 1910), *Lab.,* 557
   Sunderland, N...................... 15,671
★Williams, A. J. (*b.* 1930), *Lab.,* 566*Swansea,
   W.*................................ 4,836
★Williams, A. L. (*b.* 1930), *Lab.,* 318*Horn-
   church*............................. 6,801
★Williams, Sir B. M. Rhys-, Bt. (*b.* 1927),
   C., 344*Kensington*................. 1,917
★Williams, Rt. Hon. Shirley (*b.* 1930),
   Lab., 306*Hertford and Stevenage*...... 9,046
★Williams, Sir W. T. (*b.* 1915), *Lab.,* 597
   Warrington........................ 12,261
★Wilson, A. (*b.* 1917), *Lab.,* 285*Hamilton*.. 3,332
★Wilson, Rt. Hon. Sir J. H. (*b.* 1916), *Lab.,*
   330*Huyton*......................... 16,233
★Wilson, P. M. E. D. McNair- (*b.* 1929),
   C., 427*New Forest*................. 13,423
★Wilson, R. G. (*b.* 1938), *Scot. Nat.,* 203
   Dundee, E.......................... 6,983
★Wilson, R. M. C. McNair- (*b.* 1930), *C.,*
   421*Newbury*........................ 1,022
★Wilson, W. (*b.* 1913), *Lab.,* 102*Coventry,
   S.E.*.............................. 12,131
★Winterton, N. R. (*b.* 1938), *C.,* 391
   Macclesfield........................ 13,093
★Wise, Mrs. A. (*b.* 1935), *Lab.,* 163*Coventry,
   S.W.*.............................. 2,118
★Wood, Rt. Hon. R. F. (*b.* 1920), *C.,* 102
   Bridlington......................... 10,106
★Woodall, A. (*b.* 1918), *Lab.,* 301*Hems-
   worth*.............................. 31,572
★Woof, R. E. (*b.* 1911), *Lab.,* 80*Blaydon*... 13,466
★Wrigglesworth, I. W. (*b.* 1939), *Lab.,*
   572*Thornaby*....................... 4,648
★Young, D. W. (*b.* 1930), *Lab.,* 84*Bolton,
   E.*................................. 4,065
★Young, Sir G. S. K., Bt. (*b.* 1941), *C.,* 10
   Acton.............................. 808
★Younger, Hon. G. K. H. (*b.* 1931), *C.,*

THE HOUSE OF COMMONS BY CONSTITUENCIES, OCTOBER 1974

The figures following the name of the Constituency denote the total number of *Electors* in the Parliamentary Division at the General Election of October 1974.

ABBREVIATIONS.—*C.* = Conservative; *Comm.* = Communist; *N.I. Lab* = Northern Ireland Labour; *Ind.* = Independent; *L.* = Liberal; *Lab.* = Labour; *P.C.* = Plaid Cymru; *Scot. Nat.* = Scottish Nationalist; *S.D.L.P.* = Social Democratic and Labour Party; *Repub.* = Republican; *U.P.N.I.* = Unionist Party of Northern Ireland; *U.U.U.* = United Ulster Unionist.

An asterisk ★ denotes membership of the last House for the same division; † for a different division.

Aberavon
E. 64,687
1★Rt. Hon. J. Morris, Q.C.,
  Lab.................. 29,683
  N. K. Hammond, C.... 7,931
  Mrs. S. Cutts, L........ 5,178
  G. Thomas, P.C....... 4,032
  J. Bevan, Ind............ 427
  Lab. maj. 21,752
  (Feb. '74, Lab. maj. 20,688)

Aberdare
E. 48,380
2★I. L. Evans, Lab....... 24,197
  G. R. Owen, P.C...... 8,133
  B. G. C. Webb, C...... 2,775
  G. Hill, L.............. 2,118
  A. T. M. Wilson,
    Comm.............. 1,028
  Lab. maj. 16,064
  (Feb. '74, Lab. maj. 11,832)

Aberdeen
NORTH E. 65,230
3★R. Hughes, Lab......... 23,130
  J. A. McGugan, Scot.
    Nat................. 13,509
  P. Fraser, C........... 5,125
  F. McCallum, L........ 3,700
  Lab. maj............ 9,621
  (Feb. '74, Lab. maj. 11,856)

SOUTH E. 68,241
4★I. M. Sproat, C......... 18,475
  R. Middleton, Lab...... 18,110
  A. Stronach, Scot. Nat... 10,481
  A. A. Robbie, L........ 5,018
  C. maj.............. 365
  (Feb. '74, C. maj. 3,558)

Aberdeenshire
EAST E. 47,736
5★D. Henderson, Scot. Nat.. 16,304
  K. W. T. Raffan, C.... 11,933
  Mrs. S. B. Sissons, Lab.. 3,173
  A. Dow, L.............. 2,232
  Scot. Nat. maj....... 4,371
  (Feb. '74, Scot. Nat. maj. 5,699)

WEST E. 55,341
6★T. R. Fairgrieve, C...... 15,111
  D. C. P. Gracie, L...... 12,643
  N. Suttar, Scot. Nat.... 9,409
  C. W. Ellis, Lab....... 5,185
  C. maj.............. 2,468
  (Feb. '74, C. maj. 1,640)

Abertillery
E. 36,561
7★J. Thomas, Lab......... 20,835
  W. A. Richards, P.C... 2,480
  Mrs. P. J. E. Larney, C... 2,364
  H. W. Clark, L........ 1,779
  Lab. maj. 18,355
  (Feb. '74, Lab. maj. 16,949)

Abingdon
E. 90,451
8★A. M. S. Neave, D.S.O.,
    O.B.E., M.C., T.D., C... 31,956
  D. E. H. Moriarty, Lab.. 21,319
  M. P. Fogarty, L....... 15,239
  C. maj.............. 10,637
  (Feb. '74, C. maj. 13,743)

Accrington
E. 50,820
9★A. Davidson, Lab....... 19,838
  J. McLaughlin, C....... 13,618
  W. I. Cooper, L........ 5,704
  D. Riley, Nat. Front.... 1,176
  Lab. maj............ 6,220
  (Feb. '74, Lab. maj. 5,032)

Acton
E. 56,689
10★Sir G. S. K. Young, Bt., C 17,669
  G. A. Barnham, Lab... 16,861
  M. R. Uziell-Hamilton,
    L.................. 4,569
  C. maj.............. 808
  (Feb. '74, C. maj. 1,451)

Aldershot
E. 80,522
11★J. M. G. Critchley, C... 26,463
  A. Burton, L.......... 16,104
  Mrs. E. P. Sudworth,
    Lab................ 14,936
  A. Greenslade, Nat.
    Front.............. 1,120
  C. maj............. 10,359
  (Feb. '74, C. maj. 10,658)

Aldridge-Brownhills
E. 61,731
12★G. Edge, Lab.......... 21,403
  A. J. M. Teacher, C.... 18,884
  J. A. Crofton, L....... 8,693
  T. Keen, Ind.......... 210
  Lab. maj............ 2,519
  (Feb. '74, Lab. maj. 366)

Altrincham and Sale
E. 73,296
13 W. F. Montgomery, C.. 23,910
  E. Wood, Lab........ 16,998
  D. Blackburn, L....... 14,980
  C. maj.............. 6,912
  (Feb. '74, C. maj. 8,696)

Anglesey
E. 44,026
14★Rt. Hon. C. Hughes,
    Lab................ 13,947
  T. V. Lewis, C........ 7,975
  D. Iwan, P.C......... 6,410
  W. D. M. Ankers, L... 5,182
  Lab. maj............ 5,972
  (Feb. '74, Lab. maj. 5,754)

Angus North and Mearns
E. 37,604
15★Hon. A. L. Buchanan-
    Smith, C........... 11,835
  I. Murray, Scot. Nat.... 9,284
  J. M. S. McEwan, Lab.. 3,344
  M. Bruce, L.......... 2,700
  C. maj.............. 2,551
  (Feb. '74, C. maj. 7,451)

Angus South
E. 52,275
16 A. Welsh, Scot. Nat.... 17,073
  *J. Bruce-Gardyne, C... 15,249
  N. L. Geaughan, Lab... 4,103
  H. Will, L............ 2,529
  Scot. Nat. maj....... 1,824
  (Feb. '74, C. maj. 5,343)

Antrim
NORTH E. 103,737
17★I. R. K. Paisley, U.U.U. 43,186
  H. Wilson, Alliance.... 8,689
  Miss M. McAllister,
    S.D.L.P............ 7,616
  U.U.U. maj......... 34,497
  (Feb. '74, Prot. U. maj. 27,631)

SOUTH E. 117,834
18★J. H. Molyneaux,
    U.U.U............. 48,892
  C. H. G. Kinahan,
    Alliance........... 10,460
  P. J. Rowan, S.D.L.P... 9,061
  U.U.U. maj......... 38,432
  (Feb. '74, U.U.U. maj. 35,644)

Argyll
E. 41,814
19★I. S. M. MacCormick,
    Scot. Nat.......... 14,967
  J. J. Mackay, C....... 11,036
  M. J. N. MacGregor,
    Lab................ 4,103
  Scot. Nat. maj....... 3,931
  (Feb. '74, Scot. Nat. maj. 3,288)

Armagh
E. 91,060
20★J. H. McCusker, U.U.U. 37,518
  S. Mallon, S.D.L.P.... 19,855
  M. McGurran, Rep.... 5,138
  U.U.U. maj......... 17,663
  (Feb. '74, U.U.U. maj. 15,104)

Arundel
E. 83,464
21★R. M. Marshall, C..... 34,215
  J. R. Kingsbury, L..... 15,404
  M. E. Stedman, Lab.... 11,286
  C. maj.............. 18,811
  (Feb. '74, C. maj. 19,943)

Ashfield
E. 74,701
22*D. I. Marquand, Lab.... 35,367
R. N. Kemm, C....... 12,452
H. C. Flint, L......... 7,959
Lab. maj............ 22,915
(Feb. '74, Lab. maj. 21,788)

Ashford
E. 58,419
23 H. K. Speed, C....... 19,294
M. B. Jackson, Lab.... 13,269
C. G. Dennis, L....... 10,983
C. maj............. 6,025
(Feb. '74, C. maj. 8,459)

Ashton-under-Lyne
E. 60,393
24*R. E. Sheldon, Lab.... 23,490
M. H. Litchfield, C..... 12,763
T. G. Jones, L....... 7,356
Lab. maj............ 10,727
(Feb. '74, Lab. maj. 8,301)

Aylesbury
E. 67,729
25*T. H. F. Raison, C..... 23,565
R. Groves, Lab....... 14,592
M. J. Cook, L......... 12,219
C. maj............. 8,973
(Feb. '74, C. maj. 11,183)

Ayr
E. 51,975
26*Hon. G. K. H. Younger,
  T.D., C............ 17,487
R. S. Stewart, Lab..... 14,268
Miss E. Robinson, Scot.
  Nat............... 6,902
M. Tosh, L.......... 2,611
C. maj............. 3,219
(Feb. '74, C. maj. 5,098)

Ayrshire
CENTRAL E. 59,273
27*D. Lambie, Lab....... 21,188
Miss M. Carse, C...... 11,633
L. Anderson, Scot. Nat. 11,533
J. Watts, L........... 2,640
Lab. maj............ 9,555
(Feb. '74, Lab. maj. 6,277)

NORTH AND BUTE E. 49,071
28*J. A. Corrie, C........ 13,599
J. N. Carson, Lab...... 10,093
J. A. Murphy, Scot. Nat. 9,055
R. Stevenson, L....... 2,224
C. maj............. 3,506
(Feb. '74, C. maj. 6,730)

SOUTH E. 51,330
29*J. Sillars, Lab......... 22,329
R. Mullin, Scot. Nat... 7,851
Mrs. J. Armstrong, C.. 7,402
R. Mabon, L.......... 2,130
Lab. maj............ 14,478
(Feb. '74, Lab. maj. 12,450)

Banbury
E. 67,530
30*H. N. Marten, C...... 24,210
A. C. Booth, Lab...... 18,019
D. Charlton, L........ 8,352
J. Barbour, Ind....... 547
C. maj............. 6,191
(Feb. '74, C. maj. 6,878)

Banff
E. 31,992
31*I. H. Watt, Scot. Nat.... 10,638
J. S. Gordon, C....... 8,787
C. Macleod, L........ 2,059
Mrs. A. W. M.
  Porteous, Lab....... 1,700
Scot. Nat. maj...... 1,851
(Feb. '74, Scot. Nat. maj. 2,785)

Barking
E. 50,039
32*Miss J. Richardson, Lab. 21,546
E. Forth, C.......... 5,256
M. F. Taylor, L....... 5,245
C. W. Bond, Nat. Front 1,661
Lab. maj............ 16,290
(Feb. '74, Lab. maj. 14,834)

Barkston Ash
E. 83,803
33*M. J. H. Alison, C..... 30,498
J. H. Muir, Lab....... 20,557
D. R. O. Paige, L....... 12,483
C. maj............. 9,941
(Feb. '74, C. maj. 13,197)

Barnsley
E. 76,572
34*Rt. Hon. R. Mason, Lab. 34,212
G. England, C........ 9,400
P. Tomlinson, L....... 8,753
Lab. maj............ 24,812
(Feb. '74, Lab. maj. 24,626)

Barrow-in-Furness
E. 54,541
35*Rt. Hon. A. E. Booth,
  Lab.............. 21,607
Lord Richard Cecil, C. 14,253
M. A. Benjamin, L..... 5,788
V. Moore, Ind........ 384
Lab. maj............ 7,354
(Feb. '74, Lab. maj. 5,107)

Barry
E. 69,992
36*Sir H. R. Gower, C..... 23,360
J. E. Brooks, Lab...... 20,457
Miss J. Lloyd, L....... 8,764
Mrs. V. Wynne-Wil-
  liams, P.C......... 1,793
C. maj............. 2,903
(Feb. '74, C. maj. 5,547)

Basildon
E. 91,416
37*E. Moonman, Lab...... 32,298
D. A. Atkinson, C..... 21,747
E. Fortune, L........ 12,816
R. Chaplin, Ind....... 599
Lab. maj............ 10,551
(Feb. '74, Lab. maj. 10,667)

Basingstoke
E. 86,782
38*D. B. Mitchell, C...... 29,038
T. E. Hunt, Lab....... 22,826
N. A. L. Whitbread, L. 14,636
G. Goodall, Nat. Front. 763
C. maj............. 6,212
(Feb. '74, C. maj. 7,797)

Bassetlaw
E. 71,724
39*J. W. Ashton, Lab...... 28,663
D. K. Harris, C....... 16,494
A. Wilkinson, L....... 7,821
A. Storkey, Ind....... 408
Lab. maj............ 12,169
(Feb. '74, Lab. maj. 11,234)

Bath
E. 62,304
40*Sir E. J. Brown, M.B.E.,
  C............... 18,470
†C. P. Mayhew, L...... 16,348
M. L. Bishop, Lab..... 14,011
J. Kemp, Ind......... 150
C. maj............. 2,122
(Feb. '74, C. maj. 5,182)

Batley and Morley
E. 61,894
41*Sir A. D. D. Broughton,
  Lab.............. 21,179
G. N. A. Crone, C..... 12,931
I. H. Lester, L........ 8,928
Lab. maj............ 8,248
(Feb. '74, Lab. maj. 7,091)

Battersea
NORTH E. 44,799
42*Rt. Hon. D. P. T. Jay,
  Lab.............. 17,161
S. J. C. Randall, C..... 6,019
C. R. Williams, L...... 3,048
R. Friend, Nat. Front.. 1,250
Miss C. Reakes, Ind.... 102
Lab. maj............ 11,142
(Feb. '74, Lab. maj. 10,423)

SOUTH E. 46,724
43*E. G. Perry, Lab....... 14,284
W. T. O. Wallace, C... 11,433
Mrs. J. Ware, L....... 4,021
T. Keen, Ind......... 170
Lab. maj............ 2,851
(Feb. '74, Lab. maj. 1,653)

Beaconsfield
E. 68,541
44*R. M. Bell, Q.C., C..... 23,234
W. H. Eastwell, L...... 12,606
Mrs. M. Johnson, Lab.. 12,253
C. maj............. 10,628
(Feb. '74, C. maj. 11,248)

Bebington and Ellesmere Port
E. 86,641
45*A. Bates, Lab......... 32,310
E. P. Cockeram, C..... 25,819
N. R. L. Thomas, L.... 9,947
Lab. maj............ 6,491
(Feb. '74, Lab. maj. 4,462)

Beckenham
E. 59,512
46*P. C. Goodhart, C...... 19,798
N. J. Sharp, Lab....... 11,140
G. D. Mitchell, L...... 10,578
C. maj............. 8,658
(Feb. '74, C. maj. 10,155)

Bedford
E. 74,143
47*T. H. H. Skeet, C...... 24,834
B. S. Parkyn, Lab...... 20,746
J. C. Griffiths, L...... 11,360
C. maj............. 4,088
(Feb. '74, C. maj. 6,221)

Bedfordshire
MID E. 75,171
48*S. L. E. Hastings, M.C.
  C............... 26,885
Mrs. J. E. Crow, Lab... 17,559
P. W. Meyer, L....... 14,388
C. maj............. 9,326
(Feb. '74, C. maj. 11,111)

SOUTH *E.* 64,329
49**W. D. Madel, C.* 20,794
R. A. Little, *Lab.* 16,351
D. J. H. Penwarden, *L.* 13,194
C. maj. 4,443
(Feb. '74, C. maj. 4,758)

Bedwellty
E. 50,183
50**N. G. Kinnock, Lab.* ... 27,418
P. L. Brooke, *C.* 4,556
R. G. Morgan, *L.* 3,621
D. Mogford, *P.C.* 3,086
Lab. maj. 22,862
(Feb. '74, Lab. maj. 21,637)

Beeston
E. 74,172
51**J. T. Lester, C.* 25,095
A. J. Gardner, *Lab.* 24,974
S. C. Reddish, *L.* 9,658
C. maj. 121
(Feb. '74, C. maj. 2,544)

Belfast
EAST *E.* 79,591
52**Rt. Hon. W. Craig,*
U.U.U. 31,594
P. J. McLachlan,
U.P.N.I. 14,417
Rt. Hon. D. W. Bleak-
ley, *N.I.Lab.* 7,415
U.U.U. maj. 17,177
(Feb. '74, U.U.U. maj. 7,740)

NORTH *E.* 71,779
53**J. Carson, U.U.U.* 29,622
T. Donnelly, *S.D.L.P.* .. 11,400
J. Ferguson, *Alliance* .. 3,807
W. R. Boyd, *N.I. Lab.* 2,481
U.U.U. maj. 18,222
(Feb. '74, U.U.U. maj. 8,776)

SOUTH *E.* 75,112
54**Rev. R. J. Bradford,*
U.U.U. 30,116
J. B. C. Glass, *Alliance* .. 11,715
S. R. McMaster, *U.U.* 4,982
B. J. Caraher, *S.D.L.P.* 2,390
J. E. Holmes, *N.I. Lab.* 1,643
U.U.U. maj. 18,401
(Feb. '74, U.U.U. maj. 3,998)

WEST *E.* 66,279
55**G. Fitt, S.D.L.P.* 21,821
J. McQuade, *S.D.L.P.* .. 16,265
Mrs. K. O'Kane, *Rep.* .. 3,547
S. M. Gibson, *Ind.* 2,690
P. Kerins, *Ind.* 203
S.D.L.P. maj. 5,556
(Feb. '74, S.D.L.P. maj. 2,180)

Belper
E. 71,197
56**R. L. MacFarquhar, Lab.* 27,365
S. D. Newall, *C.* 21,681
J. J. Wates, *L.* 9,017
Lab. maj. 5,684
(Feb. '74, Lab. maj. 2,034)

Bermondsey
E. 55,254
57**Rt. Hon. R. J. Mellish,*
Lab. 22,875
H. E. Flight, *C.* 4,294
J. Taylor, *L.* 2,520
G. Davey, *Nat. Front* . . 1,488
Lab. maj. 18,581
(Feb. '74, Lab. maj. 18,721)

Berwick and East Lothian
E. 57,503
58 *J. P. Mackintosh, Lab.* ... 20,682
**M. A. F. J. Ancram*
(Earl of Ancram), *C.* 17,942
R. Macleod, *Scot. Nat.* 6,323
C. F. Lawson, *L.* 2,811
Lab. maj. 2,740
(Feb. '74, C. maj. 540)

Berwick-on-Tweed
E. 41,861
59**A. J. Beith, L.* 14,684
C. A. E. Baker-Cress-
well, *C.* 14,611
G. T. P. Spain, *Lab.* ... 4,768
L. maj. 73
(Feb. '74, L. maj. 443)

Bethnal Green and Bow
E. 53,763
60**I. Mikardo, Lab.* 19,649
T. D. Gates, *L.* 3,700
C. P. Y. Murphy, *C.* ... 2,995
W. E. Castleton, *Nat.*
Front. 2,172
Lab. maj. 15,949
(Feb. '74, Lab. maj. 14,954)

Bexleyheath
E. 51,022
61**C. D. Townsend, C.* 17,399
J. Stanyer, *Lab.* 15,412
W. E. H. Pickard, *L.* .. 6,882
C. maj. 1,987
(Feb. '74, C. maj. 3,866)

Birkenhead
E. 60,400
62**E. E. Dell, Lab.* 21,748
E. Gearing, *C.* 12,264
G. C. Lindsay, *L.* 8,380
Lab. maj. 9,484
(Feb. '74, Lab. maj. 6,994)

Birmingham
EDGBASTON *E.* 70,078
63**Mrs. J. C. J. Knight,*
M.B.E., C. 19,483
J. G. Hannah, *Lab.* 17,073
P. Davies, *L.* 7,770
C. maj. 2,410
(Feb. '74, C. maj. 5,920)

ERDINGTON *E.* 65,764
64**J. Silverman, Lab.* 22,160
J. Alden, *C.* 13,383
Mrs. J. Mills, *L.* 6,119
T. M. Finnegan, *Nat.*
Front. 1,413
Lab. maj. 8,777
(Feb. '74, Lab. maj. 6,928)

HALL GREEN *E.* 67,043
65**R. E. Eyre, C.* 20,569
Mrs. T. J. Stewart, *Lab.* 17,945
I. G. Powney, *L.* 8,532
C. maj. 2,624
(Feb. '74, C. maj. 6,244)

HANDSWORTH *E.* 45,676
66**J. M. H. Lee, Lab.* 15,011
R. Tyler, *C.* 11,115
D. I. Grant-Smith, *L.* .. 3,205
J. Finnegan, *Nat. Front.* 838
T. L. Keen, *Ind.* 105
J. L. Hutchinson, *Ind.* .. 103
Lab. maj. 3,896
(Feb. '74, Lab. maj. 1,623)

LADYWOOD *E.* 40,394
67**A. B. Walden, Lab.* 14,818
R. Lawn, *C.* 5,079
K. G. Hardeman, *L.* ... 3,086
Lab. maj. 9,739
(Feb. '74, Lab. maj. 8,962)

NORTHFIELD *E.* 77,593
68**R. J. Carter, Lab.* 27,435
J. B. L. Cadbury, *C.* ... 16,838
D. Hains, *L.* 7,851
Mrs. E. A. Davenport,
Ind. 359
D. W. Robinson,
Comm. 180
Lab. maj. 10,597
(Feb. '74, Lab. maj. 8,529)

PERRY BAR *E.* 52,509
69**J. W. Rooker, Lab.* 18,291
J. R. Kinsey, *C.* 15,087
K. J. Hovers, *L.* 4,231
R. J. Warren, *Nat.*
Front. 826
T. L. Keen, *Ind.* 86
Lab. maj. 3,204
(Feb. '74, Lab. maj. 2,023)

SELLY OAK *E.* 62,757
70 *T. Litterick, Lab.* 17,320
**H. E. Gurden, C.* 16,994
R. A. Grant, *L.* 7,850
Lab. maj. 326
(Feb. '74, C. maj. 2,882)

SMALL HEATH *E.* 51,405
71**Rt. Hon. D. H. Howell,*
Lab. 19,703
R. O'Connor, *C.* 5,648
D. Caney, *L.* 4,260
Lab. maj. 14,055
(Feb. '74, Lab. maj. 11,878)

SPARKBROOK *E.* 49,683
72**Rt. Hon. R. S. G. Hat-*
tersley, Lab. 17,476
D. J. Savage, *C.* 8,955
C. Williams, *L.* 2,920
J. Molloy, *Ind.* 548
Lab. maj. 8,521
(Feb. '74, Lab. maj. 7,405)

STECHFORD *E.* 62,516
73**Rt. Hon. R. H. Jenkins,*
Lab. 23,075
D. J. Wedgwood, *C.* ... 11,152
G. A. Gopsill, *L.* 5,860
Lab. maj. 11,923
(Feb. '74, Lab. maj. 10,232)

YARDLEY *E.* 59,052
74**S. Tierney, Lab.* 20,834
D. M. Coombs, *C.* 16,664
J. Aldridge, *L.* 4,518
H. Challendar, *Nat.*
Front. 1,034
T. L. Keen, *Ind.* 111
Lab. maj. 4,170
(Feb. '74, Lab. maj. 1,947)

Bishop Auckland
E. 72,581
75**H. J. Boyden, Lab.* 27,181
D. W. Etheridge, *C.* .. 16,086
D. L. Cobbold, *L.* 8,168
Lab. maj. 11,095
(Feb. '74, Lab. maj. 7,875)

Brighouse and Spenborough
E. 63,645
104*G. C. *Jackson, Lab.*... 21,964
G. W. Proudfoot, *C.*.. 19,787
J. R. Smithson, *L*...... 8,265
Lab. maj........... 2,177
(Feb. '74, Lab. maj. 1,546)

Brighton
KEMPTOWN E. 65,443
105*A. *Bowden, M.B.E., C.*.. 21,725
D. H. Hobden, *Lab.*.. 19,060
S. Osborne, *L*....... 6,214
R. Beaumont, *Ind.*... 155
J. Buckle, *Ind.*...... 125
B. Ralfe, *Ind.*....... 47
C. maj............ 2,665
(Feb. '74, C. maj. 4,020)
PAVILION E. 57,351
106*Rt. Hon. J. *Amery, C.* 19,041
G. W. Humphrey, *Lab.*11,624
Mrs. D. Venables, *L.* 8,648
C. maj............ 7,417
(Feb. '74, C. maj. 10,618)

Bristol
NORTH EAST E. 51,970
107*A. M. F. *Palmer, Lab.*.. 19,647
P. Hills, *C.*.......... 11,056
W. Watts-Miller, *L*... 6,303
Lab. maj........... 8,591
(Feb. '74, Lab. maj. 6,087)
NORTH WEST E. 66,381
108 R. R. *Thomas, Lab.*... 22,156
*M. J. McLaren, *C*.... 21,523
E. David, *L*......... 8,914
Lab. maj........... 633
(Feb. '74, C. maj. 650)
SOUTH E. 61,040
109*Rt. Hon. M. F. L.
Cocks, Lab......... 25,108
R. J. Kelleway, *C*.... 10,124
D. Burrows, *L*....... 6,289
P. H. Gannaway, *Nat.
Front*............ 798
Lab. maj........... 14,984
(Feb. '74, Lab. maj. 13,167)
SOUTH EAST E. 69,427
110*Rt. Hon. A. N. *Wedg-
wood Benn, Lab.*... 25,978
J. P. Godwin, *C*...... 16,605
R. Wardle, *L*........ 8,987
R. J. Bale, *Nat. Front.* 775
R. Goding, *Ind.*...... 457
P. Rowe, *Ind.*....... 79
Lab. maj........... 9,373
(Feb. '74, Lab. maj. 7,912)
WEST E. 60,447
111*R. G. *Cooke, C.*...... 18,555
R. G. R. Stacey, *L*... 11,598
J. Malos, *Lab.*....... 9,372
C. maj............ 6,957
(Feb. '74, C. maj. 8,064)

Bromsgrove and Redditch
E. 87,849
112*H. D. *Miller, C.*...... 31,153
T. A. G. Davis, *Lab.*... 29,085
P. Kelway, *L.*........ 9,679
C. maj............ 2,068
(Feb. '74, C. maj. 3,589)

Buckingham
E. 79,077
113*W. R. *Benyon, C.*..... 26,597
I. R. Maxwell, *Lab.*... 23,679
S. B. Crooks, *L*..... 12,707
C. maj............ 2,918
(Feb. '74, C. maj. 3,123)

Burnley
E. 52,930
114*D. *Jones, B.E.M., Lab.*.. 21,642
A. Pickup, *C.*........ 9,766
S. P. Mews, *L*....... 8,119
Lab. maj........... 11,876
(Feb. '74, Lab. maj. 9,840)

Burton
E. 67,801
115*I. J. *Lawrence, C.*..... 23,496
D. R. Hill, *Lab.*..... 21,398
K. Stevens, *L*....... 7,969
C. maj............ 2,098
(Feb. '74, C. maj. 3,303)

Bury and Radcliffe
E. 77,798
116 F. R. *White, Lab.*.... 26,430
*M. M. Fidler, *C*..... 25,988
A. Benson, *L*........ 10,463
Lab. maj........... 442
(Feb. '74, C. maj. 345)

Bury St. Edmunds
E. 87,321
117*E. W. *Griffiths, C.*.... 32,179
J. K. Stephenson, *Lab.* 21,097
Mrs. S. M. Hobday, *L.* 10,631
C. maj............ 11,082
(Feb. '74, C. maj, 13,253)

Caernarvon
E. 42,508
118*D. *Wigley, P.C.*...... 14,624
E. J. Sherrington, *Lab.* 11,730
R. L. Harvey, *C*..... 4,325
D. Williams, *L*...... 3,690
P.C. maj........... 2,894
(Feb. '74, P.C. maj. 1,728)

Caerphilly
E. 56,462
119*A. T. *Evans, Lab.*..... 24,161
P. J. S. Williams, *P.C.* 10,452
D. R. Dover, *C*...... 4,897
N. H. Lewis, *L*...... 3,184
Lab. maj........... 13,709
(Feb. '74, Lab. maj. 12,882)

Caithness and Sutherland
E. 28,837
120*R. A. R. *MacLennan,
Lab.*............. 7,941
E. A. C. Sutherland,
Scot. Nat........ 5,381
M. R. Burnett, *L*.... 4,949
A. McQuarrie, *C*..... 4,240
Lab. maj........... 2,560
(Feb. '74, Lab. maj. 2,352)

Cambridge
E. 75,947
121*D. W. S. S. *Lane, C.*.. 21,790
J. P. Curran, *Lab.*.... 19,017
M. W. B. O'Loughlin,
L............... 11,129
C. J. Curry, *Ind.*..... 885
C. maj............ 2,773
(Feb. '74, C. maj. 4,676)

Cambridgeshire
E. 84,434
122*Rt. Hon. F. L. *Pym,
M.C., C.*......... 30,508
M. P. Farley, *Lab.*... 17,853
S. R. Jakobi, *L*...... 15,841
C. maj............ 12,655
(Feb. '74, C. maj. 13,812)

Cannock
E. 56,572
123*G. E. *Roberts, Lab.*.... 23,887
E. G. Hill, *C*........ 11,665
E. Freeman, *L*....... 7,459
Lab. maj........... 12,222
(Feb. '74, Lab. maj. 11,064)

Canterbury
E. 85,718
124*D. L. *Crouch, C.*..... 31,002
M. F. Fuller, *Lab.*.... 16,247
Mrs. S. E. Goulden, *L.* 13,898
K. R. McKilliam,
Nat. Front........ 1,096
C. maj............ 14,755
(Feb. '74, C. maj. 17,041)

Cardiff
NORTH E. 43,858
125*I. *Grist, C.*......... 13,480
J. Collins, *Lab.*...... 11,479
M. E. German, *L*..... 5,728
P. Richards, *P.C.*.... 1,464
C. maj............ 2001
(Feb. '74, C. maj. 3,853)
NORTH WEST E. 43,787
126*M. H. A. *Roberts, C.*.. 15,652
C. A. Blewett, *Lab.*... 11,319
H. J. O'Brien, *L*..... 6,322
C. P. Palfrey, *P.C.*... 1,278
C. maj............ 4,333
(Feb. '74, C. maj. 6,013)
SOUTH EAST E. 57,299
127*Rt. Hon. L. J. *Calla-
ghan, Lab.*........ 21,074
S. Terlezki, *C*....... 10,356
C. Bailey, *L*........ 8,006
K. Bush, *P.C.*....... 983
B. C. D. Harris, *Ind.*. 75
Lab. maj........... 10,718
(Feb. '74, Lab. maj. 7,146)
WEST E. 52,083
128*Rt. Hon. T. G. *Thomas,
Lab.* (now The
Speaker)*......... 18,153
W. F. N. Dunn, *C*... 11,481
R. M. James, *L*..... 4,669
D. Hughes, *P.C*..... 2,008
Lab. maj........... 6,672
(Feb. '74, Lab. maj. 3,346)

Cardigan
E. 43,052
129*G. W. *Howells, L*.... 14,612
D. E. Morgan, *Lab.*... 12,202
C. G. Davies, *P.C.*... 4,583
D. J. D. Williams *C.* 3,275
L. maj............ 2,410
(Feb. '74, L. maj. 2,476)

Carlisle
E. 52,319
130*R. H. *Lewis, Lab.*.... 21,079
D. G. P. Bloomer, *C.* 14,825
F. Phillips, *L*....... 5,306
Lab. maj........... 6,254
(Feb. '74, Lab. maj. 4,980)

Carlton
E. 71,779
131*P. W. *Holland, C.*.... 24,638
D. Pettitt, *Lab.*...... 20,019
D. L. Lange, *L*...... 9,859
C. Marriott, *Nat.
Front*............ 1,273
C. maj............ 4,619
(Feb. '74, C. maj. 7,158)

Carmarthen
E. 60,402

132	G. R. Evans, P.C.	23,325
*G. G. Jones, Lab.		19,685
D. R. Owen-Jones, L.		5,393
R. A. Hayward, C.		2,962
E. B. Jones, Ind.		342
	P.C. maj.	3,640

(Feb. '74, Lab. maj. 3)

Carshalton
E. 66,856

133	*Rt. Hon. L. R. Carr, C.	22,538
B. F. Atherton, Lab.		18,840
Mrs. H. M. G. Small-bone, L.		8,272
	C. maj.	3,698

(By-election, March 11, 1976)

F. N. Forman, C.		20,753
C. J. Blau, Lab.		11,021
J. Hatherley, L.		6,028
T. Denville-Faulkner, Nat. Front		1,851
R. E. G. Simmerson, Ind.		251
W. S. Dunmore, Ind.		133
W. G. Boakes, Ind.		115
	C. maj.	9,732

(Feb. '74, C. maj. 5,690)

Cheadle
E. 65,558

134	*T. Normanton, T.D., C.	25,863
C. F. Green, L.		18,687
P. D. Castle, Lab.		8,048
	C. maj.	7,176

(Feb. '74, C. maj. 6,224)

Chelmsford
E. 80,042

135	*N. A. F. St. John-Stevas, C.	26,334
S. G. Mole, L.		22,332
J. T. Acklaw, Lab.		14,711
	C. maj.	4,002

(Feb. '74, C. maj. 6,631)

Chelsea
E. 64,554

136	N. P. Scott, M.B.E., C.	19,674
G. A. Colerick, Lab.		6,507
N. L. Clarke, L.		5,758
R. E. Byron, Ind.		321
	C. maj.	13,167

(Feb. '74, C. maj. 15,308)

Cheltenham
E. 62,746

137	C. G. Irving, C.	21,691
F. C. Rodger, L.		13,237
F. C. Inglis, Lab.		12,134
	C. maj.	8,454

(Feb. '74, C. maj. 5,912)

Chertsey and Walton
E. 67,527

138	*G. E. Pattie, C.	25,151
N. J. Brady, Lab.		14,847
T. W. Robinson, L.		9,194
H. J. Redgrave, Ind.		424
	C. maj.	10,304

(Feb. '74, C. maj. 11,963)

Chesham and Amersham
E. 63,385

139	*I. H. J. L. Gilmour, C.	25,078
D. A. Stoddart, L.		14,091
J. R. Poston, Lab.		10,325
	C. maj.	10,987

(Feb. '74, C. maj. 10,416)

Chester
E. 69,605

140	*Hon. P. H. Morrison, C.	23,095
J. Crawford, Lab.		18,477
R. M. Green, L.		10,907
	C. maj.	4,618

(Feb. '74, C. maj. 6,768)

Chesterfield
E. 71,210

141	*Rt. Hon. E. G. Varley, Lab.	30,953
J. D. Taylor, C.		13,393
M. W. Brown, L.		7,349
	Lab. maj.	17,560

(Feb. '74, Lab. maj. 15,396)

Chester-le-Street
E. 68,350

142	*G. H. Radice, Lab.	33,511
D. McCourt, L.		9,233
R. L. Ditchburn, C.		8,268
	Lab. maj.	24,278

(Feb. '74, Lab. maj. 18,726)

Chichester
E. 69,768

143	R. A. Nelson, C.	26,942
G. A. Jeffs, L.		15,601
N. J. M. Smith, Lab.		8,767
	C. maj.	11,341

(Feb. '74, C. maj. 11,413)

Chingford
E. 56,984

144	*N. B. Tebbit, C.	19,022
P. F. Tinnion, Lab.		14,377
D. A. Nicholson, L.		8,438
	C. maj.	4,645

(Feb. '74, C. maj. 5,683)

Chippenham
E. 67,852

145	*D. E. Awdry, T.D., C.	22,721
R. E. J. Banks, L.		20,972
J. Whiles, Lab.		9,396
E. J. John, Ind.		278
	C. maj.	1,749

(Feb. '74, C. maj. 3,092)

Chipping Barnet
E. 56,487

146	*Rt. Hon. R. Maudling, C.	19,661
J. A. D. Mills, Lab.		11,795
Miss N. M. Wyn-Ellis, L.		8,884
R. Cole, Nat. Front		1,207
	C. maj.	7,866

(Feb. '74, C. maj. 9,911)

Chislehurst
E. 53,699

147	*R. E. Sims, C.	18,926
A. H. MacDonald, Lab.		15,032
J. M. Crowley, L.		6,900
	C. maj.	3,894

(Feb. '74, C. maj. 5,493)

Chorley
E. 76,218

148	*G. Rodgers, Lab.	27,290
G. B. Porter, C.		24,577
Mrs. N. Orrell, L.		9,831
H. Smith, Ind.		185
	Lab. maj.	2,713

(Feb. '74, Lab. maj. 405)

Christchurch and Lymington
E. 55,299

149	*R. J. Adley, C.	23,728
J. Madeley, L.		9,838
L. K. Hatts, Lab.		7,759
	C. maj.	13,890

(Feb. '74, C. maj. 14,634)

Cirencester and Tewkesbury
E. 80,408

150	*Hon. N. Ridley, C.	28,930
R. G. Otter, L.		18,770
J. R. Booth, Lab.		13,973
	C. maj.	10,160

(Feb. '74, C. maj. 10,201)

City of London and Westminster South
E. 52,170

151	*C. S. Tugendhat, C.	14,350
P. J. Turner, Lab.		8,589
T. G. Underwood, L.		4,122
D. Baxter, Nat. Front.		686
	C. maj.	5,761

(Feb. '74, C. maj. 8,247)

Cleveland and Whitby
E. 60,674

152	*L. Brittan, C.	19,973
B. J. Pimlott, Lab.		18,445
G. G. Watson, L.		7,795
	C. maj.	1,528

(Feb. '74, C. maj. 3,642)

Clitheroe
E. 52,086

153	*A. D. Walder, E.R.D., C.	19,643
B. W. McColgan, Lab.		12,775
C. W. Roberts, L.		8,503
	C. maj.	6,868

(Feb. '74, C. maj. 8,528)

Coatbridge and Airdrie
E. 59,903

154	*J. Dempsey, Lab.	23,034
D. R. M. Hill, Scot. Nat.		12,466
J. Love, C.		7,683
A. Smith, L.		1,446
	Lab. maj.	10,568

(Feb. '74, Lab. maj. 11,783)

Colchester
E. 81,836

155	*P. A. F. Buck, Q.C., C.	27,693
D. Whytock, Lab.		22,193
D. Christian, L.		12,421
	C. maj.	5,500

(Feb. '74, C. maj. 6,862)

Colne Valley
E. 60,774

156	*R. S. Wainwright, L.	21,997
D. G. Clark, Lab.		20,331
K. E. Davy, C.		7,337
	L. maj.	1,666

(Feb. '74, L. maj. 719)

Consett
E. 59,014

157	*D. J. Watkins, Lab.	27,123
M. Lycett, C.		7,677
J. Gillinder, L.		5,695
	Lab. maj.	19,446

(Feb. '74, Lab. maj. 18,343)

Conway
E. 51,730
158*I. W. P. Roberts, C... 15,614
Rev. D. B. Rees, Lab. 12,808
D. T. Jones, L........ 6,344
M. Farmer, P.C...... 4,668
C. maj............ 2,806
(Feb '74, C. maj. 4,549)

Cornwall North
E. 51,779
159*J. W. Pardoe, L....... 21,368
G. A. Neale, C........ 17,512
R. Tremlett, Lab..... 2,663
R. J. Bridgwater, Ind... 148
L. maj............ 3,856
(Feb. '74, L. maj. 8,729)

Coventry
NORTH EAST E. 63,605
160*G. M. Park, Lab...... 26,489
I. Clarke, C........ 10,520
R. Dredge, L........ 6,846
A. Wilkins, Ind...... 352
J. Hosey, Comm...... 309
Lab. maj......... 15,969
(Feb. '74, Lab. maj. 15,427)
NORTH WEST E. 49,247
161*M. Edelman, Lab.... 19,205
Hon. J. B. Guinness,
C................. 11,717
Mrs. P. Newnham, L. 5,798
Mrs. A. L. Whittaker,
Ind.............. 313
Lab. maj......... 7,488
(By-election, March 4, 1976)
G. Robinson, Lab..... 17,118
Hon. J. B. Guinness, C. 13,424
A. Leighton, L....... 4,062
A. Fountaine, Nat.
Front............. 986
J. K. Read, Ind...... 208
T. L. Keen, Ind...... 40
W. S. Dunsmore, Ind.. 33
Lab. maj......... 3,694
(Feb. '74, Lab. maj. 6,658)
SOUTH EAST E. 50,818
162*W. Wilson, Lab...... 20,771
C. Hannington, C.... 8,640
D. Woodcock, L..... 4,952
Lab. maj......... 12,131
(Feb. '74, Lab. maj. 10,751)
SOUTH WEST E. 67,841
163*Mrs. A. Wise, Lab... 23,225
J. R. Jeffrey, C....... 21,107
N. B. Chapple, L..... 8,579
R. Rickard, Nat. Front 822
T. L. Keen, Ind...... 144
Lab. maj......... 2,118
(Feb. '74, Lab. maj. 513)

Crewe
E. 59,227
164*Hon. Mrs. G. P. Dun-
woody, Lab........ 21,534
J. G. Park, C........ 14,279
E. Richardson, L..... 7,559
Lab. maj......... 7,255
(Feb. '74, Lab. maj. 5,123)

Crosby
E. 78,605
165*Rt. Hon. R. G. Page,
M.B.E., C........ 29,764
Miss M. J. Hignett,
Lab.............. 17,589
A. Hill, L.......... 10,429
C. maj............ 12,175
(Feb. '74, C. maj. 15,570)

Croydon
CENTRAL E. 66,746
166*J. E. M. Moore, C.... 20,390
D. Winnick, Lab.... 20,226
I. H. Maxwell, L..... 7,834
C. maj............ 164
(Feb. '74, C. maj. 1,314)
NORTH EAST E. 58,306
167*B. B. Weatherill, C.... 17,938
D. H. Simpson, Lab.. 15,787
P. T. Streeter, L...... 7,228
W. Stringer, Ind...... 451
C. maj............ 2,151
(Feb. '74, C. maj. 3,820)
NORTH WEST E. 55,176
168*R. G. Taylor, C...... 16,035
S. J. Boden, Lab..... 14,556
W. H. Pitt, L........ 6,563
P. Holland, Nat. Front. 1,049
C. maj............ 1,479
(Feb. '74, C. maj. 3,071)
SOUTH E. 60,090
169*W. G. Clark, C...... 25,703
D. Nunneley, L...... 11,514
D. W. Keene, Lab.... 7,203
C. maj............ 14,189
(Feb. '74, C. maj. 15,867)

Dagenham
E. 70,004
170*J. Parker, C.B.E., Lab... 29,678
A. G. Hamilton, C.... 7,684
G. Poole, L......... 7,564
G. C. Wake, Comm... 569
Lab. maj......... 21,994
(Feb. '74, Lab. maj. 23,490)

Darlington
E. 62,955
171*E. J. Fletcher, Lab. ... 21,334
B. H. Hord, C....... 17,620
P. Freitag, L........ 7,882
Lab. maj......... 3,714
(Feb. '74, Lab. maj. 2,069)

Dartford
E. 57,038
172*Rt. Hon. S. Irving, Lab. 20,817
G. F. J. Bright, C.... 15,331
G. Dunk, L......... 6,606
R. H. Aldous, Nat.
Front............. 939
Lab. maj......... 5,486
(Feb. '74, Lab. maj. 3,654)

Darwen
E. 70,611
173*C. Fletcher-Cooke, Q.C.,
C................. 23,577
D. N. Campbell-
Savours, Lab....... 17,926
A. Cooper, L....... 12,572
C. maj............ 5,651
(Feb. '74, C. maj. 9,310)

Daventry
E. 83,253
174*A. A. Jones, C...... 29,801
D. Forwood, Lab.... 20,739
D. Cassidy, L....... 13,640
C. maj............ 9,062
(Feb. '74, C. maj. 9,749)

Dearne Valley
E. 63,265
175*E. Wainwright, Lab. .. 33,315
Lord Irwin, C....... 6,046
P. Hargreaves, L..... 5,588
Lab. maj......... 27,269
(Feb. '74, Lab. maj. 26,854)

Denbigh
E. 63,506
176*W. G. O. Morgan,
Q.C., C.......... 18,751
D. L. Williams, L.... 14,200
P. P. Flynn, Lab..... 9,824
I. W. Jones, P.C..... 5,754
C. maj............ 4,551
(Feb. '74, C. maj. 6,015)

Deptford
E. 61,210
177*Rt. Hon. J. E. Silkin,
Lab.............. 21,145
C. H. Cross, C....... 8,111
M. M. Steele, L...... 4,931
R. Edmonds, Nat.
Front............. 1,731
Lab. maj......... 13,034
(Feb. '74, Lab. maj. 11,629)

Derby
NORTH E. 82,697
178*P. Whitehead, Lab..... 26,960
D. J. Penfold, C...... 22,767
M. D. Peel, L....... 10,595
H. Smith, Ind........ 242
Lab. maj......... 4,193
(Feb. '74, Lab. maj. 1,293)
SOUTH E. 74,342
179*W. H. Johnson, Lab.... 26,342
A. J. Bussell, C...... 17,010
R. Palmer, L........ 7,520
A. S. Ashby, Ind..... 793
Lab. maj......... 9,332
(Feb. '74, Lab. maj. 7,143)

Derbyshire
NORTH EAST E. 68,869
180*T. H. Swain, Lab..... 25,234
J. C. Ramsden, C.... 14,997
C. Cook, L......... 10,336
Lab. maj......... 10,237
(Feb. '74, Lab. maj. 7,282)
SOUTH EAST E. 53,739
181*P. L. Rost, C........ 18,856
R. J. Madeley, Lab... 17,851
H. Warschauer, L.... 6,404
C. maj............ 1,005
(Feb. '74, C. maj. 3,035)
WEST E. 49,142
182*J. S. R. Scott-Hopkins,
C................. 18,468
P. M. Worboys, L.... 10,622
D. A. Townsend, Lab. 9,456
C. maj............ 7,846
(Feb. '74, C. maj. 8,460)

Devizes
E. 77,793
183*Hon. C. A. Morrison,
C................. 24,842
V. E. Finlayson, Lab.. 17,821
J. B. Ainslie, L....... 15,851
C. maj............ 7,021
(Feb. '74, C. maj. 9,898)

Devon
NORTH E. 73,598
184*Rt. Hon. J. J. Thorpe,
L................. 28,209
A. Speller, C........ 21,488
Mrs. A. J. Golant, Lab. 8,356
F. Hansford-Miller,
Ind.............. 568
L. maj............ 6,721
(Feb. '74, L. maj. 11,072)

WEST E. 57,431
185*P. M. Mills, C....... 22,594
M. A. Pinney, L..... 16,665
J. B. H. Duffin, Lab... 5,899
C. maj............ 5,929
(Feb. '74, C. maj. 5,268)

Dewsbury
E. 61,508
186*D. Ginsburg, Lab..... 20,378
Mrs. M. Wood, C.... 13,477
A. Allsop, L......... 10,991
Lab. maj.......... 6,901
(Feb. '74, Lab. maj. 5,412)

Doncaster
E. 59,464
187*H. Walker, Lab....... 22,177
T. Wilkinson, C..... 14,747
W. J. Davison, L..... 6,336
Lab. maj.......... 7,430
(Feb. '74, Lab. maj. 5,476)

Don Valley
E. 88,777
188*R. Kelley, Lab........ 41,187
P. J. Le Bosquet, C... 13,767
E. Simpson, L......... 10,161
Lab. maj.......... 27,420
(Feb. '74, Lab. maj. 27,945)

Dorking
E. 58,955
189*Sir G. E. Sinclair,
C.M.G., O.B.E., C.... 22,403
G. S. A. Andrews, L... 12,098
Miss J. Chapman, Lab. 9,714
C. maj............ 10,305
(Feb. '74, C. maj. 10,313)

Dorset
NORTH E. 71,325
190*D. P. James, M.B.E.,
D.S.C., C........... 28,891
P. G. Watkins, L...... 20,350
T. G. Jones, Lab...... 7,245
C. maj............ 8,541
(Feb. '74, C. maj. 6,883)
SOUTH E. 70,416
191*E. M. King, C....... 24,351
A. Chedzoy, Lab...... 17,652
C. Sandy, L.......... 11,075
C. maj............ 6,699
(Feb. '74, C. maj. 8,615)
WEST E. 53,569
192*J. W. Spicer, C....... 20,517
R. M. Angus, L....... 11,832
P. J. Dawe, Lab...... 9,350
C. maj............ 8,685
(Feb. '74, C. maj. 7,451)

Dover and Deal
E. 74,704
193*P. W. I. Rees, Q.C., C.. 25,647
L. J. A. Bishop, Lab... 23,353
R. S. Young, L...... 9,767
C. maj............ 2,294
(Feb. '74, C. maj. 4,850)

Down
NORTH E. 93,604
194*J. A. Kilfedder, U.U.U. 40,996
K. Jones, Alliance..... 9,973
Maj. W. Brownlow,
U.P.N.I........... 6,037
U.U.U. maj...... 31,023
(Feb. '74, U.U.U. maj. 16,226)

SOUTH E. 91,354
195 Rt. Hon. J. E. Powell,
M.B.E., U.U.U.... 33,614
S. Hollywood,
S.D.L.P......... 30,047
G. O'Hanlon, Rep.... 2,327
D. Vipond, Ind....... 152
U.U.U. maj....... 3,567
(Feb. '74, U.U.U. maj. 5,602)

Dudley
EAST E. 60,381
196*J. W. Gilbert, Lab.... 23,621
J. M. Taylor, C...... 11,430
G. Hopkins, L....... 5,003
C. Knott, Nat. Front.. 1,171
Lab. maj.......... 12,191
(Feb. '74, Lab. maj. 11,622)
WEST E. 74,746
197*C. B. Phipps, Lab..... 28,740
L. E. Smith, C...... 20,215
A. Martin, L......... 7,259
Lab. maj.......... 8,525
(Feb. '74, Lab. maj. 4,669)

Dulwich
E. 67,542
198*Rt. Hon. S. C. Silkin,
Q.C., Lab.......... 21,790
E. Morley, C........ 14,331
W. H. Pearson, L.... 7,866
Lab. maj.......... 7,459
(Feb. '74, Lab. maj. 5,341)

Dumfries
E. 61,856
199*H. S. P. Monro, C.... 18,386
J. F. Wheatley, Lab.... 12,558
L. A. B. Whitley, Scot.
Nat............ 12,542
A. Sinclair, L........ 3,961
C. maj............ 5,828
(Feb. '74, C. maj. 8,968)

Dunbartonshire
CENTRAL E. 49,357
200*H. McCartney, Lab.... 15,837
A. C. W. Aitken, Scot.
Nat............ 11,452
M. W. Hirst, C....... 6,792
J. Reid, Comm....... 3,417
J. E. Cameron, L...... 1,895
Lab. maj.......... 4,385
(Feb. 74, Lab. maj. 6,664)
EAST E. 61,788
201 Mrs. M. A. Bain, Scot.
Nat............ 15,551
*J. S. B. Henderson, C.. 15,529
E. F.McGarry, Lab.... 15,122
J. A. Thompson, C.... 3,636
Scot. Nat. maj..... 22
(Feb. '74, C. maj. 3,676)
WEST E. 51,943
202*I. Campbell, Lab...... 15,511
A. Murray, Scot. Nat. 13,697
R. R. MacDonald, C. 9,421
J. D. Murricane, L..... 2,029
Lab. maj.......... 1,814
(Feb. '74, Lab. maj. 2,609)

Dundee
EAST E. 63,152
203*R. G. Wilson, Scot.
Nat............ 22,120
G. Machin, Lab...... 15,137
W. L. Walker, C..... 7,784
C. Brodie, L........ 1,302
Scot. Nat. maj..... 6,983
(Feb. '74, Scot. Nat. maj. 2,966)

WEST E. 63,916
204*P. M. Doig, Lab...... 19,480
J. Fairlie, Scot. Nat.... 16,678
C. G. Findlay, C...... 8,769
R. Hewett, L....... 2,195
H. McLevy, Comm... 381
Lab. maj.......... 2,802
(Feb. '74, Lab. maj. 6,448)

Dunfermline
E. 60,679
205*A. Hunter, Lab....... 18,470
Miss A. C. Cameron,
Scot. Nat........ 13,179
K. MacLeod, C...... 10,611
M. D. H. Valentine, L. 3,800
Lab. maj.......... 5,291
(Feb. '74, Lab. maj. 4,410)

Durham
E. 74,711
206*W. M. Hughes, Lab... 31,305
D. L. Conway, C.... 13,189
P. A. J. Heesom, L.... 9,011
Lab. maj.......... 18,116
(Feb. '74, Lab. maj. 15,203)

Durham North West
E. 61,283
207*E. Armstrong, Lab..... 27,953
M. J. B. Cookson, C. 9,197
J. K. Forster, L....... 6,418
Lab. maj.......... 18,756
(Feb. '74, Lab. maj. 17,461)

Ealing North
E. 73,898
208*W. J. Molloy, Lab..... 24,574
G. K. Dickens, C...... 21,652
C. S. Phillips, L....... 8,351
Lab. maj.......... 2,922
(Feb. '74, Lab. maj. 2,448)

Easington
E. 63,815
209*J. D. Dormand, Lab... 28,984
J. S. Smailes, C....... 8,047
N. J. Scaggs, L....... 7,005
Lab. maj.......... 20,937
(Feb. '74, Lab. maj. 20,530)

Eastbourne
E. 74,697
210*I. R. E. Gow, C....... 30,442
G. H. Millar, L...... 14,417
L. Caine, Lab........ 10,830
C. maj............ 16,025
(Feb. '74, C. maj. 7,475)

East Grinstead
E. 55,602
211*G. Johnson Smith, C... 22,035
P. Hayden, L....... 12,755
D. W. J. Blake, Lab... 6,648
C. maj............ 9,280
(Feb. '74, C. maj. 8,577)

East Kilbride
E. 65,799
212*M. S. Miller, Lab..... 21,810
G. S. Murray, Scot.
Nat............ 19,106
G. W. Parvin, C..... 8,513
D. Miller, L......... 2,644
Lab. maj.......... 2,704
(Feb. '74, Lab. maj. 7,968)

Eastleigh
E. 75,826
213*D. E. C. Price, C..... 26,869
E. A. Presman, *Lab*.. 19,054
G. D. Johnson, *L*..... 13,832
C. maj............ 7,815
(Feb. '74, C. maj. 10,110)

Ebbw Vale
E. 37,640
214*Rt. Hon. M. M. Foot,
Lab.............. 21,226
A. Donaldson, *L*..... 3,167
J. P. Evans, *C*........ 2,153
G. ap Robert, *P.C*.... 2,101
Lab. maj......... 18,059
(Feb. '74, Lab. maj. 15,664)

Eccles
E. 57,549
215*L. Carter-Jones, *Lab*.. 22,328
R. J. Dunn, *C*........ 13,062
Mrs. A. M. Collier, *L*. 6,170
T. E. Keenan, *Comm*. 348
Lab. maj......... 9,266
(Feb. '74, Lab. maj. 7,786)

Edinburgh
CENTRAL E. 64,956
216*R. F. Cook, *Lab*..... 11,129
P. Jones, *C*.......... 7,176
A. W. S. Rae, *Scot.
Nat*.............. 6,866
C. B. H. Scott, *L*..... 2,463
Lab. maj......... 3,953
(Feb. '74, Lab. maj. 961)

EAST E. 57,460
217*G. S. Strang, *Lab*..... 19,669
G. C. MacDougall,
Scot. Nat...... 11,213
A. M. Hogg, *C*...... 10,111
G. N. Dalzell, *L*...... 2,578
Mrs. I. Swann, *Comm*. 213
Lab. maj......... 8,456
(Feb. '74, Lab. maj. 5,549)

LEITH E. 39,407
218*Rt. Hon. R. K. Murray,
Q.C., *Lab*........ 11,708
W. R. V. Percy, *C*.. 8,263
R. Scott, *Scot. Nat*.... 7,688
A. J. H. Squair, *L*..... 1,836
Lab. maj......... 3,445
(Feb. '74, Lab. maj. 721)

NORTH E. 47,215
219*A. M. Fletcher, *C*.... 12,856
M. J. O'Neill, *Lab*.... 8,465
J. Lynch, *Scot. Nat*.... 7,681
M. MacDonald, *L*.... 3,677
C. maj............ 4,391
(Feb. '74, C. maj. 7,013)

PENTLANDS E. 54,955
220*M. L. Rifkind, *C*..... 14,083
G. Foulkes, *Lab*...... 12,826
J. Hutchison, *Scot.
Nat*.............. 10,189
S. P. Ross-Smith, *L*. 4,411
C. maj............ 1,257
(Feb. '74, C. maj. 4,602)

SOUTH E. 56,154
221*A. M. C. Hutchison, *C*.. 14,962
Mrs. C. Haddow, *Lab*. 11,736
R. J. Shirley, *Scot.
Nat*.............. 9,034
N. L. Gordon, *L*.... 5,921
C. maj............ 3,226
(Feb. '74, C. maj. 6,381)

Edmonton
E. 61,476
223*T. E. Graham, *Lab*... 20,229
J. Attwood, *C*....... 13,401
J. Dawnay, *L*........ 5,699
D. J. Bruce, *Nat. Front* 1,895
Lab. maj......... 6,828
(Feb. '74, Lab. maj. 5,723)

WEST E. 52,569
222 Lord James Douglas-
Hamilton, *C*....... 15,354
W. J. Taylor, *Lab*.... 10,152
Mrs. C. M. Moore,
Scot. Nat........ 8,135
D. C. E. Gorrie, *L*.... 6,666
C. maj............ 5,202
(Feb. '74, C. maj. 8,477)

Enfield North
E. 67,818
224*B. Davies, *Lab*........ 20,880
C. de H. Parkinson, *C*. 16,087
Mrs. S. Curtis, *L*..... 9,526
R. Burton, *Nat. Front* 1,330
Lab. maj......... 4,793
(Feb. '74, Lab. maj. 3,416)

Epping Forest
E. 64,055
225*J. A. Biggs-Davison, *C*. 22,392
S. J. Palfreman, *Lab*... 15,618
D. F. J. Wood, *L*..... 8,952
C. maj............ 6,774
(Feb. '74, C. maj. 8,167)

Epsom and Ewell
E. 80,597
226*Rt. Hon. Sir P. A. G.
Rawlinson, Q.C., *C*.. 32,109
D. J. H. Griffiths, *L*.... 15,819
N. J. Kearney, *Lab*.... 11,471
C. maj............ 16,290
(Feb. '74, C. maj. 16,924)

Erith and Crayford
E. 60,595
227*A. J. Wellbeloved, *Lab*.. 22,670
M. MacDonald, *C*.... 14,203
T. Hibbert, *L*....... 7,423
Lab. maj......... 8,467
(Feb. '74, Lab. maj. 7,081)

Esher
E. 47,572
228*D. C. M. Mather, *C*. .. 19,741
C. Welchman, *L*..... 8,881
A. G. Hudson, *Lab*.... 6,729
C. maj............ 10,860
(Feb. '74, C. maj. 10,715)

Essex South East
E. 76,013
229*Sir B. R. Braine, *C*...... 27,348
D. B. Jones, *Lab*...... 18,638
A. Morris, *L*........ 10,049
C. maj............ 8,710
(Feb. '74, C. maj. 9,265)

Eton and Slough
E. 63,813
230*Miss J. Lestor, *Lab*...... 22,238
S. Dolland, *C*....... 14,575
P. Goldenberg, *L*..... 8,213
A. P. Coniam, *Nat.
Front*............ 1,241
J. Renton, *Ind*....... 120
Lab. maj......... 7,663
(Feb. '74, Lab. maj. 6,891)

Exeter
E. 67,184
231*J. G. Hannam, *C*...... 21,970
F. K. Taylor, *Lab*.... 19,622
D. J. Morrish, *L*..... 12,342
C. maj............ 2,348
(Feb. '74, C. maj. 5,076)

Eye
E. 65,710
232*Sir J. H. Harrison, Bt.,
T.D., *C*......... 22,387
D. Robinson, *L*...... 14,530
R. Bushby, *Lab*...... 13,948
C. maj............ 7,857
(Feb. '74, C. maj. 7,675)

Falmouth and Camborne
E. 66,921
233*W. D. Mudd, *C*...... 23,950
M. G. Dalling, *Lab*... 18,094
E. Sara, *L*.......... 6,428
A. G. S. T. Davey, *Ind.
L*............... 2,246
C. maj............ 5,856
(Feb. '74, C. maj. 4,264)

Fareham
E. 57,330
234*R. F. B. Bennett, V.R.D.,
C............... 19,053
P. Smith, *L*......... 14,605
B. R. Townsend, *Lab*. 8,153
W. P. Boulden, *Ind*... 1,727
R. M. Doughty, *Nat.
Front*............ 617
C. maj............ 4,448
(Feb. '74, C. maj. 7,877)

Farnham
E. 62,738
235*Rt. Hon. M. V. Mac-
millan, *C*....... 23,885
P. Davies, *L*........ 15,626
Miss H. C. Hodge,
Lab.............. 8,305
C. maj............ 8,259
(Feb. '74, C. maj. 6,462)

Farnworth
E. 70,565
236*J. F. H. Roper, *Lab*.... 28,184
R. H. Shepherd, *C*... 13,489
Mrs. M. P. Rothwell,
L............... 11,059
Lab. maj......... 14,695
(Feb. '74, Lab. maj. 12,637)

Faversham
E. 76,000
237*R. D. Moate, *C*...... 25,087
M. Freedman, *Lab*.... 22,210
P. J. Morgan, *L*...... 10,979
C. maj............ 2,877
(Feb. '74, C. maj. 5,407)

Feltham and Heston
E. 78,983
238*R. W. Kerr, *Lab*...... 26,611
R. P. Ground, *C*..... 17,464
J. A. Quinn, *L*...... 7,554
Mrs. J. M. Reid, *Nat.
Front*............ 1,984
Lab. maj......... 9,147
(Feb. '74, Lab. maj. 8,055)

Fermanagh and S. Tyrone
E. 71,343
239 M. F. Maguire, Ind.... 32,795
*Rt. Hon. H. W. West,
   U.U.U............. 30,285
A. J. Evans. Ind...... 185
   Ind. maj........... 2,510
(Feb. '74, U.U.U. maj. 10,629)

Fife
CENTRAL E. 58,402
240*W. W. Hamilton, Lab. 22,400
D. V. Livingstone,
   Scot. Nat......... 14,414
P. Clarke, C....... 5,308
A. Maxwell, Comm... 1,040
   Lab. maj........ 7,986
(Feb. '74, Lab. maj. 14,094)

EAST E. 56,453
241*Sir J. E. Gilmour, Bt.,
   D.S.O., T.D., C...... 16,116
J. Braid, Scot. Nat. ... 13,202
Mrs. H. Liddell, Lab.. 7,040
D. Docherty, L...... 5,247
   C. maj............ 2,914
(Feb. '74, C. maj. 12,579)

Finchley
E. 53,933
242*Rt. Hon. Mrs. M. H.
   Thatcher, C........ 16,498
M. J. O'Connor, Lab. 12,587
L. S. Brass, L........ 7,384
Mrs. J. Godfrey, Nat.
   Front............. 993
   C. maj............ 3,911
(Feb. '74, C. maj. 5,978)

Flint
EAST E. 69,273
243*S. B. Jones, Lab....... 27,002
M. J. A. Penston, C. 17,416
R. Fairley, L......... 8,986
F. Evans, P.C........ 1,779
   Lab. maj.......... 9,586
(Feb. '74, Lab. maj. 8,852)

WEST E. 64,302
244*Sir A. J. C. Meyer, Bt.,
   C............... 20,054
N. B. Harries, Lab... 15,234
P. J. Brighton, L..... 10,881
N. Taylor, P.C....... 2,306
   C. maj............ 4,820
(Feb. '74, C. maj. 7,142)

Folkestone and Hythe
E. 64,714
245*A. P. Costain, C. 20,930
B. W. Budd, Q.C., L.. 12,488
M. J. S. Butler, Lab... 11,639
H. Button, Ind....... 265
   C. maj............ 8,442
(Feb. '74, C. maj. 8,510)

Fulham
E. 58,303
246*Rt. Hon. R. M. M.
   Stewart, C.H., Lab.. 20,616
M. Stevens, C....... 15,295
G. A. Dowden, L..... 4,577
J. Cordrey, Nat. Front. 855
   Lab. maj.......... 5,321
(Feb. '74, Lab. maj. 3,549)

Fylde
NORTH E. 74,799
247*W. Clegg, C......... 29,661
H. J. Berkeley, Lab... 12,522
A. Perry, L.......... 11,254
   C. maj............ 17,139
(Feb. '74, C. maj. 19,658)

SOUTH E. 90,861
248*E. L. Gardner, Q.C., C.. 37,193
A. Lawson, L........ 14,527
T. A. Dillon, Lab..... 13,724
   C. maj............ 22,666
(Feb. '74, C. maj. 25,379)

Gainsborough
E. 61,749
249*M. R. Kimball, C...... 19,163
R. B. Blackmore, L. .. 15,195
T. J. Lansbury, Lab... 11,797
   C. maj............ 3,968
(Feb. '74, C. maj. 6,210)

Galloway
E. 39,407
250 G. H. Thompson, Scot.
   Nat.............. 12,242
K. A. Ross, C........ 12,212
D. R. Hannay, L..... 3,181
T. G. Fulton, Lab.... 2,742
   Scot. Nat. maj...... 30
(Feb. '74, C. maj. 4,008)

Gateshead
EAST E. 63,496
251*B. Conlan, Lab....... 27,620
R. A. Ryder, C....... 10,021
K. A. Buckingham, L. 6,998
   Lab. maj.......... 17,599
(Feb. '74, Lab. maj. 15,299)

WEST E. 30,768
252*J. R. Horam, Lab..... 13,859
P. Brown, C......... 4,432
Mrs. K. Stoddart, L... 1,909
   Lab. maj.......... 9,427
(Feb. '74, Lab. maj. 8,467)

Gillingham
E. 62,099
253*F. F. A. Burden, C..... 19,042
H. G. N. Clother, Lab. 15,046
T. Jones, L.......... 12,131
S. Campbell, Nat.
   Front............. 922
   C. maj............ 3,996
(Feb. '74, C. maj. 5,882)

Glasgow
CATHCART E. 49,826
254*E. M. Taylor, C...... 16,301
Mrs. J. E. Carnegie,
   Lab............. 14,544
A. Ewing, Scot. Nat... 6,292
H. Wills, L.......... 1,058
   C. maj............ 1,757
(Feb. '74, C. maj. 2,095)

CENTRAL E. 25,516
255*T. M. McMillan, Lab.. 9,231
B. Nugent, Scot. Nat.. 2,790
N. Woolfson, C...... 1,880
E. Bennett, L........ 605
   Lab. maj.......... 6,441
(Feb. '74, Lab. maj. 5,965)

CRAIGTON E. 44,333
256*B. Millan, Lab....... 16,952
B. G. Houston, Scot.
   Nat.............. 8,171
G. F. Belton, C...... 6,734
R. McIntyre, L....... 1,728
   Lab. maj.......... 8,781
(Feb. '74, Lab. maj. 7,238)

GARSCADDEN E. 54,700
257*W. W. Small, Lab.... 19,737
K. S. Bovey, Scot. Nat. 12,111
J. Corbett, C........ 5,004
M. R. Kibby, L...... 1,915
   Lab. maj.......... 7,626
(Feb. '74, Lab. maj. 11,264)

GOVAN E. 32,094
258*H. Selby, Lab........ 11,392
Mrs. M. MacDonald,
   Scot. Nat........ 9,440
Miss M. Todd, C..... 1,623
E. Mason, L......... 444
M. A. Brooks, Nat.
   Front............. 86
T. Clyde, Ind....... 27
   Lab. maj.......... 1,952
(Feb. '74, Lab. maj. 543)

HILLHEAD E. 41,726
259*Hon. T. G. D. Gal-
   braith, C.......... 11,203
D. Welsh, Lab....... 8,507
G. Borthwick, Scot.
   Nat.............. 6,897
A. Rennie, L........ 3,596
   C. maj............ 2,696
(Feb. '74, C. maj. 6,381)

KELVINGROVE E. 42,654
260*N. G. Carmichael, Lab. 11,567
J. G. Rennie, C...... 7,448
C. D. Calman, Scot.
   Nat.............. 6,274
S. Glasgow, L........ 1,735
   Lab. maj.......... 4,119
(Feb. '74, Lab. maj. 2,398)

MARYHILL E. 51,545
261*J. M. Craigen, Lab.... 19,589
A. McIntosh, Scot.
   Nat.............. 10,171
J. S. Younger, C..... 3,160
Mrs. E. Attwooll, L. . 1,063
   Lab. maj.......... 9,418
(Feb. '74, Lab. maj. 11,383)

POLLOK E. 59,451
262*J. White, Lab........ 18,695
G. Malone, C........ 11,604
D. P. Macquarrie,
   Scot. Nat........ 10,441
M. C. Todd, L....... 2,274
   Lab. maj.......... 7,091
(Feb. '74, Lab. maj. 3,406)

PROVAN E. 54,975
263*H. D. Brown, Lab..... 20,602
R. Edwards, Scot. Nat. 10,628
R. McKay, C........ 3,448
J. Jackson, Comm..... 503
   Lab. maj.......... 9,974
(Feb. '74, Lab. maj. 15,787)

QUEENS PARK E. 38,776
264*F. P. McElhone, Lab... 14,574
D. G. MacKellar, Scot.
   Nat.............. 5,660
I. D. Mackinnon, C. . 4,421
Miss M. Aitchison, L. 966
J. R. Kay, Comm..... 354
   Lab. maj.......... 8,914
(Feb. '74, Lab. maj. 8,366)

SHETTLESTON E. 38,324
265*Sir M. Galpern, Lab. .. 13,391
R. Hamilton, Scot.
   Nat.............. 7,042
J. Cran, C.......... 3,543
R. J. Brodie, L........ 690
   Lab. maj.......... 6,349
(Feb. '74, Lab. maj. 7,736)

SPRINGBURN E. 48,066
266*R. Buchanan, Lab..... 17,444
W. J. Morton, *Scot.*
  Nat............... 9,049
S. Taylor, C........ 4,245
T. Marshall, L....... 865
N. McLellan, *Comm.*. 352
  Lab. maj.......... *8,395*
  (Feb. '74, Lab. maj. 10,395)

Gloucester
E. 62,503
267*Mrs. S. Oppenheim, C. 22,664
Mrs. A. C. Roberts,
  Lab................ 19,136
D. G. Halford, L..... 7,357
C. *maj.*............. *3,528*
  (Feb. '74, C. maj. 4,837)

Gloucestershire
SOUTH E. 79,439
268*J. Cope, C........... 26,581
Miss O. A. McDonald,
  Lab................ 22,235
D. C. Short, L....... 14,412
  C. *maj.*........... *4,346*
  (Feb. '74, C. maj. 6,459)
WEST E. 67,255
269 J. T. Watkinson, Lab.. 22,481
P. Marland, C........ 22,072
A. I. MacGregor, L... 9,353
  Lab. maj.......... *409*
  (Feb. '74, Lab. maj. 1,624)

Goole
E. 64,631
270*E. I. Marshall, Ph.D.,
  Lab................ 26,804
N. P. Kemp, C........ 12,707
J. T. Clarkson, L..... 5,285
  Lab. maj.......... *14,097*
  (Feb. '74, Lab. maj. 13,225)

Gosport
E. 48,871
271*P. J. Viggers, C....... 17,487
P. M. Tebbutt, Lab... 10,621
P. D. Clark, L....... 8,701
  C. *maj.*........... *6,866*
  (Feb. '74, C. maj. 7,228)

Gower
E. 56,867
272*I. Davies, Lab........ 25,067
D. F. R. George, C... 8,863
R. Owen, L.......... 5,453
M. Powell, P.C...... 4,369
  Lab. maj.......... *16,204*
  (Feb. '74, Lab. maj. 15,076)

Grantham
E. 78,404
273*Rt. Hon. J. B. Godber,
  C................... 27,738
Mrs. S. M. Smedley,
  Lab................ 19,708
W. T. Bailey, L...... 10,752
  C. *maj.*........... *8,030*
  (Feb. '74, C. maj. 11,343)

Gravesend
E. 87,269
274*J. F. Ovenden, Lab.... 29,569
R. F. Needham, C.... 27,264
L. Cartier, L........ 10,244
J. D. Turner, *Nat.*
  Front............. 1,304
T. L. Keen, *Ind.*...... 239
  Lab. maj.......... *2,305*
  (Feb. '74, Lab. maj. 1,582)

Greenock and Port Glasgow
E. 62,126
275*J. D. Mabon, Lab..... 21,279
J. K. Wright, *Scot.*
  Nat............... 9,324
W. M. Campbell, L.. 8,580
A. Foote, C......... 4,969
  Lab. maj.......... *11,955*
  (Feb. '74, Lab. maj. 11,776)

Greenwich
E. 52,847
276*N. G. Barnett, Lab..... 19,155
Mrs. S. M. T. Harold,
  C................... 9,249
A. J. D. Wilson, L.... 5,838
D. Green, *Ind.*....... 254
  Lab. maj.......... *9,906*
  (Feb. '74, Lab. maj. 8,870)

Grimsby
E. 66,302
277*Rt. Hon. C. A. R.
  Crosland, Lab....... 21,657
K. C. Brown, C...... 14,675
D. M. Rigby, L....... 9,487
J. McElrea, *Ind.*...... 166
  Lab. maj.......... *6,982*
  (Feb. '74, Lab. maj. 5,671)

Guildford
E. 72,302
278*D. A. R. Howell, C.... 25,564
C. J. Fox, L......... 14,660
R. W. Harris, Lab.... 11,727
  C. *maj.*........... *10,904*
  (Feb. '74, C. maj. 9,891)

Hackney
CENTRAL E. 48,524
279*S. C. Davis, Lab...... 17,650
K. S. Lightwood, C... 4,797
Mrs. M. G. Snow. L.. 3,174
  Lab. maj.......... *12,853*
  (Feb. '74, Lab. maj. 12,403)

NORTH AND STOKE NEWINGTON
E. 52,870
280*D. Weitzman, Q.C.,
  Lab................ 16,525
A. J.Wylson, C...... 5,972
S. J. Lyons, L....... 3,796
H. C. Lord, *Nat. Front*. 1,044
M. Goldman, *Comm.*. 418
M. Van der Poorten,
  Ind............... 159
  Lab. maj.......... *10,553*
  (Feb. '74, Lab. maj. 9,334)

SOUTH AND SHOREDITCH
E. 49,540
281*R. W. Brown, Lab.... 17,333
K. H. Proctor, C..... 4,038
C. Bone, L.......... 3,173
R. May, *Nat. Front*... 2,544
  Lab. maj.......... *13,295*
  (Feb. '74, Lab. maj. 12,018)

Halesowen and Stourbridge
E. 82,189
282*J. H. R. Stokes, C..... 24,387
D. Turner, Lab....... 23,537
L. T. Eden, L........ 14,672
  C. *maj.*........... *850*
  (Feb. '74, C. maj. 4,049)

Halifax
E. 63,562
283*Hon. Shirley Summerskill,
  Lab................ 20,976
S. R. Lyons, C....... 16,798
A. Clegg, L......... 8,693
R. S. Pearson, *Ind.*.... 919
  Lab. maj.......... *4,178*
  (Feb. '74, Lab. maj. 3,003)

Haltemprice
E. 76,257
284*P. H. B. Wall, M.C.,
  V.R.D., C.......... 28,206
R.Walker, L......... 16,545
L. Cross, Lab........ 12,362
  C. *maj.*........... *11,661*
  (Feb. '74, C. maj. 11,824)

Hamilton
E. 50,346
285*A. Wilson, Lab....... 18,487
I. C. H. Macdonald,
  Scot. Nat.......... 15,155
G. Warner, C........ 3,682
J. M. Calder, L...... 1,559
  Lab. maj.......... *3,332*
  (Feb. '74, Lab. maj. 6,378)

Hammersmith North
E. 52,371
286*F. Tomney, Lab....... 18,061
R. G. Beckett, C..... 9,939
S. H. J. A. Knott, L... 5,200
J. P. McFadden, *Ind.*... 633
  Lab. maj.......... *8,122*
  (Feb. '74, Lab. maj. 7,041)

Hampstead
E. 64,085
287*G. Finsberg, M.B.E., C. 18,139
A. J. Clarke, Lab..... 16,414
R. H. Longland, L.... 5,566
Mrs. M. Maguire, *Ind.* 146
R. O. Critchfield, *Ind.* 118
C. Rao, *Ind.*....... 31
  C. *maj.*........... *1,725*
  (Feb. '74, C. maj. 2,257)

Harborough
E. 65,855
288*J. A. Farr, C......... 25,776
N. G. Reynolds, L... 12,567
R. L. W. Briant, Lab. 11,934
  C. *maj.*........... *13,209*
  (Feb. '74, C. maj. 12,473)

Harlow
E. 62,964
289*A. S. Newens, Lab.... 24,961
J. E. Smith, C........ 11,510
B. E. Goldstone, L.... 10,869
  Lab. maj.......... *13,451*
  (Feb. '74, Lab. maj. 12,534)

Harrogate
E. 64,759
290*R. G. Banks, C....... 24,583
I. de C. Bayley, L..... 11,269
B. H. Seal, Lab....... 8,047
A. H. W. Brons, *Nat.*
  Front............. 1,030
C. Margolis, *Ind.*..... 719
  C. *maj.*........... *13,314*
  (Feb. '74, C. maj. 11,789)

Harrow

CENTRAL E. 45,260
291**J. A. Grant*, C........ 14,356
   D. M. Offenbach, *Lab.* 12,288
   R. S. Montgomerie, *L.* 5,566
   C. Byrne, *Nat. Front.*. 813
   C. maj............. 2,068
   (Feb. '74, C. maj. 2,917)

EAST E. 49,315
292**H. J. M. Dykes*, C.... 17,073
   R.W. Lewis, *Lab.*..... 13,595
   J. McDonnell, *L.*...... 6,268
   C. maj............. 3,478
   (Feb. '74, C. maj. 4,493)

WEST E. 56,641
293**A. J. Page*, C........ 21,924
   M. P. Reynolds, *Lab.*.. 10,342
   R. E. Bell, *L.*........ 9,903
   C. maj............. 11,582
   (Feb. '74, C. maj. 11,869)

Hartlepool

E. 65,345
294**E. L. Leadbitter*, *Lab.*... 24,440
   N. H. Freeman, C..... 16,546
   L. Tostevin, *L.*....... 6,314
   Lab. maj.......... 7,894
   (Feb. '74, Lab. maj. 4,288)

Harwich

E. 88,710
295**J. E. Ridsdale*, C..... 29,963
   J. B. Fryer, *Lab.*...... 19,135
   T. O. Kellock, Q.C., *L.* 15,048
   C. maj............. 10,828
   (Feb. '74, C. maj. 12,463)

Hastings

E. 57,023
296**K. R. Warren*, C..... 18,337
   M. J. Foster, *Lab.*..... 13,685
   A. Leggett, *L.*........ 8,793
   C. maj............. 4,652
   (Feb. '74, C. maj. 7,083)

Havant and Waterloo

E. 75,472
297**I. S. Lloyd*, C........ 24,880
   S. Brewin, *L.*........ 16,148
   T. King, *Lab.*........ 14,615
   C. maj............. 8,732
   (Feb. '74, C. maj. 9,188)

Hayes and Harlington

E. 55,960
298**N. D. Sandelson*, *Lab.*.. 20,291
   N. R. Balfour, C..... 10,871
   C. Lyon, *L.*......... 6,336
   J. S. Fairhurst, *Nat.*
    Front............. 1,189
   R. Bull, *Ind.*........ 198
   Lab. maj.......... 9,420
   (Feb. '74, Lab. maj. 10,048)

Hazel Grove

E. 67,648
299 T. R. Arnold, C...... 25,012
*M. P. Winstanley, *L.*.. 22,181
   A. Roberts, *Lab.*..... 8,527
   C. maj............. 2,831
   (Feb. '74, L. maj. 1,998)

Hemel Hempstead

E. 83,795
300 R. Corbett, *Lab.*..... 29,223
*J. H. Allason, O.B.E., C. 28,738
   Miss C. A. M. Baron,
    L................. 10,497
   Lab. maj.......... 485
   (Feb. '74, C. maj. 187)

Hemsworth

E. 69,810
301**A. Woodall*, *Lab.*..... 37,467
   P. Carvis, C......... 5,895
   R. F. Taylor, *L.*...... 5,607
   Lab. maj.......... 31,572
   (Feb. '74, Lab. maj. 34,941)

Hendon

NORTH E. 50,762
302**J. M. Gorst*, C. 16,299
   J. S. Champion, *Lab.*... 14,549
   I. Senior, *L.*......... 5,822
   C. maj............. 1,750
   (Feb. '74, C. maj. 2,612)

SOUTH E. 51,889
303**Rt. Hon. P. J. M.*
   Thomas, Q.C., C.... 16,866
   R. M. Hadley, *Lab.*... 11,903
   M. D. Colne, *L.*...... 7,404
   C. maj............. 4,963
   (Feb. '74, C. maj. 6,597)

Henley

E. 62,475
304**M. R. D. Heseltine*, C. 22,504
   S. R. C. Evans, *L.*.... 12,288
   I. M. Haig, *Lab.*..... 11,141
   C. maj............. 10,216
   (Feb. '74, C. maj. 8,900)

Hereford

E. 57,830
305 C. R. Shepherd, C.... 17,060
   C. B. T. Nash, *L.*.... 15,948
   M. K. Prendergast,
    Lab............... 10,820
   C. maj............. 1,112
   (Feb. '74, C. maj. 3,438)

Hertford and Stevenage

E. 82,218
306**Rt. Hon. Shirley*
   Williams, *Lab.*...... 29,548
   V. W. H. Bendall, C... 20,502
   T. N. Willis, *L.*...... 11,419
   K. Taylor, *Nat. Front.*. 1,232
   Lab. maj.......... 9,046
   (Feb. '74, Lab. maj. 8,176)

Hertfordshire

EAST E. 88,848
307**Rt. Hon. Sir D. C.*
   Walker-Smith, Bt.,
   T.D., Q.C., C...... 29,334
   M. M. Keir, *Lab.*..... 20,999
   P. C. Clark, *L.*...... 15,446
   C. maj............. 8,335
   (Feb. '74, C. maj. 11,358)

SOUTH E. 64,666
308**C. E. Parkinson*, C.... 21,018
   A. Dubs, *Lab.*....... 18,790
   J. D. O. Henchley, *L.* 9,393
   C. maj............. 2,228
   (Feb. '74, C. maj. 3,086)

SOUTH WEST E. 75,992
309**G. H. Dodsworth*, C.... 24,939
   A. L. C. Cohen, *Lab.*.. 19,098
   J. E. S. Jarrett, *L.*.... 14,470
   C. maj............. 5,841
   (Feb. '74, C. maj. 8,098)

Hexham

E. 65,088
310**Rt. Hon. A. G. F.*
   Rippon, Q.C., C..... 21,352
   E. Wade, *Lab.*....... 16,711
   R. Cairncross, *L.*..... 10,991
   C. maj............. 4,641
   (Feb. '74, C. maj. 7,930)

Heywood and Royton

E. 77,705
311**Rt. Hon. J. Barnett*, *Lab.* 27,206
   P. Morgan, C....... 19,307
   V. N. Bingham, *L.*... 12,969
   Lab. maj.......... 7,899
   (Feb. '74, Lab. maj. 7,162)

High Peak

E. 57,095
312**S. Le Marchant*, C.... 19,043
   D. Bookbinder, *Lab.*... 17,041
   C.Walmsley, *L.*....... 9,875
   C. maj............. 2,002
   (Feb. '74, C. maj. 2,275)

Hitchin

E. 72,815
313**B. H. I. H. Stewart*, C.. 25,842
   Miss A. Mallalieu, *Lab.* 22,656
   E. Dix, *L.*.......... 9,454
   C. maj............. 3,186
   (Feb. '74, C. maj. 4,018)

Holborn and St. Pancras South

E. 39,171
314**Mrs. L. M. Jeger*, *Lab.* 11,790
   R. F. J. Parsons, C.... 6,349
   F. M. J. Lee, *L.*...... 2,938
   Lab. maj.......... 5,441
   (Feb. '74, Lab. maj. 4,191)

Holland with Boston

E. 80,454
315**R. Body*, C......... 28,145
   M. D. Cornish, *Lab.*... 19,461
   G. R. Stephenson, *L.*.. 10,476
   C. maj............. 8,684
   (Feb. '74, C. maj. 12,381)

Honiton

E. 73,070
316**P. F. H. Emery*, C..... 29,720
   V. T. Howell, *L.*..... 16,500
   R. L. Spiller, *Lab.*.... 9,048
   C. maj............. 13,220
   (Feb. '74, C. maj. 14,123)

Horncastle

E. 49,627
317**P. H. B. Tapsell*, C... 16,750
   M. J. C. Starky, *L.*.... 11,506
   K. Bratton, *Lab.*...... 6,849
   C. maj............. 5,244
   (Feb. '74, C. maj. 6,789)

Hornchurch

E. 60,423
318**A. L. Williams*, *Lab.*... 21,336
   R. C. Squire, C...... 14,535
   B. G. McCarthy, *L.*... 7,284
   B. Percy-Davis, *Ind.*... 797
   Lab. maj.......... 6,801
   (Feb. '74, Lab. maj. 6,196)

Hornsey

E. 58,278
319**H. A. L. Rossi*, C..... 17,226
   I. H. Kuczynski, *Lab.*.. 16,444
   P. Smulian, *L.*....... 5,283
   Mrs. J. Stubbs, *Nat.*
    Front............. 973
   C. maj............. 782
   (Feb. '74, C. maj. 2,208)

Horsham and Crawley
E. 90,944
320*P. M. Hordern, C..... 29,867
M. A. Oakeshott, Lab. 26,168
Mrs. P. Greenwood, L. 13,848
A. Brewer, Nat. Front 1,101
C. maj............ 3,699
(Feb. '74, C. maj. 6,774)

Houghton-le-Spring
E. 59,905
321*T. W. Urwin, Lab.... 29,699
W. Robson, C....... 9,298
R. C. Ritchie, C....... 4,399
Lab. maj............ 20,401
(Feb. '74 Lab. maj. 23,963)

Hove
E. 73,034
322*Hon. T. A. D. Sains-
bury, C............. 27,345
J. M. Walsh, L....... 12,469
L. E. Hamilton, Lab... 11,179
C. maj............ 14,876
(Feb. '74, C. maj. 11,509)

Howden
E. 57,512
323*Sir P. E. O. Bryan,
D.S.O., M.C., C..... 19,583
S. C. Haywood, L..... 14,803
F. H. V. Lewis, Lab.. 7,291
C. maj............ 4,780
(Feb. '74, C. maj. 6,211)

Huddersfield
EAST E. 53,515
324*J. P. W. Mallalieu, Lab. 19,522
A. F. J. Povey, C..... 11,108
G. M. Lee, Lab....... 7,326
J. Robertshaw, Nat.
Front............. 764
Lab. maj............ 8,414
(Feb. '74, Lab. maj. 7,304)
WEST E. 53,510
325*K. Lomas, Lab....... 16,882
J. M. Stansfield, C.... 15,518
Mrs. K. J. L. Hasler, L. 7,503
D. Ford, Nat. Front... 760
H. Smith, Ind....... 136
Lab. maj............ 1,364
(Feb. '74, Lab. maj. 630)

Hull
CENTRAL E. 63,278
326*J. K. McNamara, Lab... 22,417
P. W. J. Carver, C..... 12,596
N. W. Turner, L....... 7,810
Lab. maj............ 9,821
(Feb. '74, Lab. maj. 7,619)
EAST E. 81,624
327*J. L. Prescott, Lab..... 34,190
S. Dorrell, C....... 10,397
J. Adamson, L....... 10,196
Lab. maj............ 23,793
(Feb. '74, Lab. maj. 23,593)
WEST E. 57,592
328*J. Johnson, Lab....... 20,393
C. M. K. Taylor, C.... 10,272
A. Michell, L....... 6,508
Lab. maj............ 10,121
(Feb. '74, Lab. maj. 7,931)

Huntingdonshire
E. 79,724
329*Rt. Hon. Sir D. L. M.
Renton, K.B.E., T.D.,
Q.C., C............. 26,989
A. G. Dowson, Lab... 17,745
D. G. Rowe, L....... 15,152
C. maj............ 9,244
(Feb. '74, C. maj. 10,002)

Huyton
E. 73,485
330*Rt. Hon. Sir J. H. Wilson,
K.G., O.B.E., Lab.... 31,750
W. Peters, C....... 15,517
M. P. Braham, L..... 4,956
Lab. maj............ 16,233
(Feb. '74, Lab. maj. 15,305)

Ilford
NORTH E. 65,195
331 Mrs. M. Miller, Lab... 20,621
*T. L. Iremonger, C... 19,843
G. L. P. Wilson, L.... 8,080
Lab. maj............ 778
(Feb. '74, C. maj. 285)
SOUTH E. 56,257
332*A. J. Shaw, Lab....... 17,538
N. Thorne, C....... 15,789
Miss E. Yates, L..... 5,734
T. L. Keen, Ind....... 169
Lab. maj............ 1,749
(Feb. '74, Lab. maj. 1,143)

Ilkeston
E. 74,980
333*L. R. Fletcher, Lab... 31,153
A. N. R. Hamilton, C. 15,295
G. F. Pool, L......... 9,671
Lab. maj............ 15,858
(Feb. '74, Lab. maj. 14,180)

Ince
E. 77,113
334*M. T. F. McGuire,
Lab.............. 35,453
J. R. Dyson, C....... 11,923
J. Gibb, L.......... 8,436
Lab. maj............ 23,530
(Feb. '74, Lab. maj. 22,759)

Inverness
E. 57,527
335*D. R. Johnston, L..... 13,128
D. G. Barr, Scot. Nat.. 11,994
R. E. Henderson, C... 8,922
J. W. L. Cumming,
Lab.............. 6,332
U. Bell, Ind.......... 155
L. maj............ 1,134
(Feb. '74, L. maj. 5,223)

Ipswich
E. 87,675
336 K. T. Weetch, Lab.... 31,566
*E. D. D. Money, C... 29,833
R. B. Salt, L......... 8,295
Lab. maj............ 1,733
(Feb. '74, C. maj. 259)

Isle of Ely
E. 68,491
337*C. R. Freud, L....... 22,040
I. T. Stuttaford, C.... 19,355
M. B. Ferris, Lab..... 11,420
L. maj............ 2,685
(Feb. '74, L. maj. 8,347)

Isle of Wight
E. 85,897
338*S. S. Ross, L......... 29,697
J. D. Fishburn, C..... 27,657
L. D. Brooke, Lab.... 8,562
L. maj............ 2,040
(Feb. '74, L. maj. 7,766)

Islington
CENTRAL E. 45,347
339*J. D. Grant, Lab...... 14,689
C. Stanbrook, C..... 5,296
P. W. Murphy, C..... 3,786
R. Score, Nat. Front.. 1,335
Lab. maj............ 9,393
(Feb. '74, Lab. maj. 8,691)
NORTH E. 41,390
340*M. J. O'Halloran, Lab. 12,973
Marquess Douro, C... 6,155
M. W. S. Davenport,
L.............. 2,736
D. Fallon, Ind........ 558
Lab. maj............ 6,818
(Feb. '74, Lab. maj. 6,628)
SOUTH AND FINSBURY E. 42,251
341*G. Cunningham, Lab... 14,544
Miss P. Hodgson, C.. 4,951
R. G. Adams, L....... 3,661
Mrs. M. Betteridge,
Comm............. 512
Lab. maj............ 9,593
(Feb. '74, Lab. maj. 8,591)

Jarrow
E. 54,735
342*Rt. Hon. E. Fernyhough,
Lab.............. 24,558
Mrs. B. Bolam, C..... 8,707
L. Ormston, L....... 5,818
Lab. maj............ 15,851
(Feb. '74, Lab. maj. 13,892)

Keighley
E. 51,741
343*G. R. Cryer, Lab..... 19,569
C. J. H. Taylor, C.... 16,488
Miss M. Holmstedt, L. 5,839
G. Wright, Nat. Front. 859
C. W. Deakin, Ind..... 179
Lab. maj............ 3,081
(Feb. '74, Lab. maj. 878)

Kensington
E. 61,105
344*Sir B. M. Rhys-
Williams, Bt., C... 15,562
J. V. Tilley, Lab..... 13,645
R. Cohen, L......... 5,236
C. maj............ 1,917
(Feb. '74, C. maj. 5,132)

Kettering
E. 85,802
345*Rt. Hon. Sir G. S. de
Freitas, K.C.M.G., Lab. 30,970
G. D. Reed, C....... 19,800
A. J. W. Haigh, L..... 12,038
Lab. maj............ 11,170
(Feb. '74, Lab. maj. 9,787)

Kidderminster
E. 78,965
346*J. E. Bulmer, C....... 25,602
R. H. Jones, Lab..... 18,833
A. J. Batchelor, L..... 14,733
C. maj............ 6,769
(Feb. '74, C. maj. 8,685)

Kilmarnock
E. 60,380
347*Rt. Hon. W. Ross,
M.B.E., Lab........ 22,184
A. MacInnes, Scot. Nat 14,655
W. Adams, C........ 9,203
K. Purcell, L........ 2,508
Lab. maj............ 7,529
(Feb. '74, Lab. maj. 9,727)

Kingston on Thames
E. 59,251
348*N. S. H. Lamont, C... 20,680
A. Quicke, Lab...... 12,266
S. J. E. Wells, L...... 9,580
   C. maj............ *8,414*
(Feb. '74, C. maj. 10,307)

Kingswood
E. 55,967
349*T. W. Walker, Lab... 20,703
D. F. J. Hunt, C...... 18,137
J. H. Aspinwall, L.... 8,216
   Lab. maj.......... *2,566*
(Feb. '74, Lab. maj. 1,641)

Kinross and West Perthshire
E. 35,237
350 N. H. Fairbairn, Q.C.,
   C................ 11,034
D. Cameron, Scot. Nat. 10,981
D. A. Barrie, L....... 2,427
D. G. Skene, Lab..... 2,028
   C. maj............ *53*
(Feb. '74, C. maj. 8,082)

Kirkcaldy
E. 60,824
351*H. P. H. Gourlay, Lab.. 20,688
R. T. Knox, Scot. Nat. 14,587
R. B. Jones, C....... 7,539
F. Young, L........ 2,788
   Lab. maj.......... *6,101*
(Feb. '74, Lab. maj. 9,382)

Knutsford
E. 55,238
352*Rt. Hon. J. E. H.
   Davies, M.B.E., C... 21,636
B. M. Lomax, L...... 11,210
D. L. Swain, Lab..... 9,565
   C. maj............ *10,426*
(Feb. '74, C. maj. 11,090)

Lambeth Central
E. 48,722
353*M. Lipton, C.B.E., Lab.. 15,381
N. Lyell, C.......... 6,704
P. Easton, L......... 3,211
S. Smart, Ind. 233
P. Bratton, Ind....... 88
   Lab. maj.......... *8,677*
(Feb. '74, Lab. maj. 7,369)

Lanark
E. 48,408
354*Rt. Hon. Judith Hart,
   Lab.............. 14,948
T. McAlpine, Scot.
   Nat............... 14,250
A. Bell, C........... 9,222
F. McDermid, L...... 1,374
   Lab. maj.......... *698*
(Feb. '74, Lab. maj. 2,100)

Lanarkshire North
E. 54,147
355*J. Smith, Lab.......... 19,902
Mrs. P. Watt, Scot.
   Nat............... 11,561
J. Crichton, C........ 9,665
A. P. Brodie, L....... 1,899
   Lab. maj.......... *8,341*
(Feb. '74, Lab. maj. 6,784)

Lancaster
E. 49,643
356*Mrs. M. E. Kellett-
   Bowman, C........ 16,540
D. Owen, Lab........ 15,119
M. Mumford, L...... 7,161
   C. maj............ *1,421*
(Feb. '74, C. maj. 2,469)

Leeds

EAST E. 67,736
357*Rt. Hon. D. W. Healey,
   M.B.E., Lab........ 24,745
J. W. Dawson, C..... 12,434
S. Marsh, L.......... 6,970
Mrs. N. Russell, Ind.. 327
   Lab. maj.......... *12,311*
(Feb. '74, Lab. maj. 10,514)

NORTH EAST E. 58,968
358*Rt. Hon. Sir K. S.
   Joseph, Bt., C....... 18,749
W. J. Gunnell, Lab... 13,121
C. J. Greenfield, L.... 6,737
   C. maj............ *5,628*
(Feb. '74, C. maj. 7,260)

NORTH WEST E. 65,062
359*Sir D. Kaberry, Bt, T.D.
   C................ 19,243
L. G. K. Fenwick, Lab. 15,216
D. Rolfe, L.......... 8,663
   C. maj............ *4,027*
(Feb. '74, C. maj. 6,671)

SOUTH E. 52,709
360*Rt. Hon. M. Rees, Lab. 21,653
T. N. M. Stow, C... 6,388
J. Adams, L.......... 5,563
   Lab. maj.......... *15,265*
(Feb. '74, Lab. maj. 11,860)

SOUTH EAST E. 49,797
361*S. Cohen, Lab........ 17,160
Mrs. M. Sexton, C... 6,144
Miss M. G. Clay, L... 4,429
W. H. Innes, Comm. . 317
   Lab. maj.......... *11,016*
(Feb. '74, Lab. maj. 9,454)

WEST E. 60,402
362*J. J. Dean, Lab....... 20,669
M. J. Meadowcroft, L. 13,062
R. D. Hall, C........ 7,907
   Lab. maj.......... *7,607*
(Feb. '74, Lab. maj. 3,985)

Leek
E. 83,930
363*D. L. Knox, C....... 30,796
B. Whittam, Lab..... 26,472
M. Holden, L........ 8,615
   C. maj............ *4,324*
(Feb. '74, C. maj. 5,732)

Leicester

EAST E. 63,899
364*T. G. Bradley, Lab.... 20,688
K. G. Reeves, C...... 16,877
W. Capstick, L....... 5,668
A. Reed-Herbert, Nat.
   Front.............. 2,967
   Lab. maj.......... *3,811*
(Feb. '74, Lab. maj. 1,413)

SOUTH E. 72,558
365 J. Marshall, Lab....... 21,588
*T. G. Boardman, C... 20,455
H. Young, L.......... 5,709
A. R. Cartwright, Nat.
   Front.............. 2,072
G. H. Rousseau, Ind.. 136
   Lab. maj.......... *1,133*
(Feb. '74, Lab. maj. 1,766)

WEST E. 64,650
366*Hon. G. E. Janner, Q.C.,
   Lab.............. 23,406
A. Simpson, C........ 13,446
J. Windram, L........ 5,135
W. J. Newcombe,
   Nat. Front......... 2,253
   Lab. maj.......... *9,960*
(Feb. '74, Lab. maj. 8,652)

Leigh
E. 65,053
367*H. Boardman, Lab.... 27,036
Mrs. M. Williams, C. 12,401
R. D. Pemberton, L.. 8,640
   Lab. maj.......... *14,635*
(Feb. '74, Lab. maj. 13,647)

Leominster
E. 44,055
368*P. Temple-Morris, C.... 15,741
R. J. Pincham, L..... 15,162
S. Allen, Lab........ 3,264
   C. maj............ *579*
(Feb. '74, C. maj. 1,619)

Lewes
E. 72,060
369*J. R. Rathbone, C..... 27,588
G. Hook, L.......... 13,741
J. F. Little, Lab...... 11,857
   C. maj............ *13,847*
(Feb. '74, C. maj. 14,257)

Lewisham

EAST E. 69,540
370*Hon. R. D. Moyle, Lab. 24,350
D. Mahony, C....... 15,398
M. A. Minter, L...... 8,069
   Lab. maj.......... *8,952*
(Feb. '74, Lab. maj. 6,306)

WEST E. 62,435
371*C. Price, Lab........ 21,102
Miss M. Marshall, C. 15,573
J. D. Eagle, L........ 5,952
P. Williams, Nat. Front 1,114
   Lab. maj.......... *5,529*
(Feb. '74, Lab. maj. 2,402)

Leyton
E. 64,341
372*B. Magee, Lab....... 22,130
B. S. Dare, C........ 10,617
R. Scott, L.......... 5,408
Mrs. S. M. Bothwell,
   Nat. Front......... 2,168
   Lab. maj.......... *11,513*
(Feb. '74, Lab. maj. 9,937)

Lichfield and Tamworth
E. 89,752
373 B. J. Grocott, Lab..... 29,872
*Maj-Gen. J. A. d'Avig-
   dor-Goldsmid,
   C.B., O.B.E., M.C., C.. 29,541
P. Rule, L.......... 10,714
   Lab. maj.......... *331*
(Feb. '74, C. maj. 1,807)

Lincoln
E. 53,022
374 Miss M. M. Jackson,
   Lab.............. 14,698
*D. Taverne, Q.C. Soc.
   Dem.............. 13,714
P. M. Moran, C...... 11,223
   Lab. maj.......... *984*
(Feb. '74, Soc. Dem. maj. 1,293)

Liverpool

EDGE HILL E. 40,970
375*Rt. Hon. Sir A. J.
   Irvine, Q.C., Lab.... 13,023
D. Alton, L.......... 6,852
S. N. Perry, C....... 5,208
   Lab. maj.......... *6,171*
(Feb. '74, Lab. maj. 5,750)

GARSTON E. 81,030
376*E. Loyden, Lab........ 27,857
D. C. Stanley, C..... 24,557
G. H. Black, L........ 5,865
Lab. maj........... 3,300
(Feb. '74, Lab. maj. 681)

KIRKDALE E. 45,344
377*J. A. Dunn, Lab...... 17,686
M. J. Jones, C........ 8,205
M. J. Storey, L....... 2,908
Lab. maj........... 9,481
(Feb. '74, Lab. maj. 6,525)

SCOTLAND EXCHANGE E. 35,146
378*R. Parry, Lab......... 15,154
P. Rankin, C......... 2,234
Mrs. P. Crockett, L... 944
R. O'Hara, Comm.. 556
Lab. maj........... 12,920
(Feb. '74, Lab. maj. 12,332)

TOXTETH E. 45,883
379*R. Crawshaw, O.B.E.,
Lab.............. 15,312
H. L. J. Malins, C.... 8,062
D. L. Mahon, L.......3,176
J. Dillon, Ind....... 365
Lab. maj........... 7,250
(Feb. '74, Lab. maj. 5,557)

WALTON E. 51,967
380*E. S. Heffer, Lab...... 20,568
R. Gould, C.......... 10,706
J. R. Watton, L....... 4,221
Lab. maj........... 9,862
(Feb. '74, Lab. maj. 8,216)

WAVERTREE E. 59,720
381*A. D. Steen, C...... 18,971
R. E. Morris, Lab.... 16,216
W. A. Limont, L..... 6,193
C. maj............. 2,755
(Feb. '74, Lab. maj. 5,275)

WEST DERBY E. 58,890
382*E. Ogden, Lab........ 23,964
J. W. Last, C......... 11,445
R. Ousby, L.......... 4,215
Lab. maj........... 12,519
(Feb. '74, Lab. maj. 9,973)

Llanelli
E. 64,495
383*D. J. D. Davies, Lab.. 29,474
M. M. Gimblett, L... 7,173
R. Williams, P.C..... 6,797
G. D. J. Richards, C.. 6,141
Lab. maj........... 22,301
(Feb. '74, Lab. maj. 21,445)

Londonderry
E. 93,141
384*W. Ross, U.U.U.... 35,138
J. Hume, S.D.L.P.... 26,118
M. Montgomery, Rep. 2,530
R. Foster, Ind........ 846
U.U.U. maj........ 9,020
(Feb. '74, U.U.U. maj. 9,390)

Loughborough
E. 70,244
385*J. D. Cronin, Lab.... 22,869
R. M. Yorke, Q.C., C. 20,521
M. Bennett, L........ 10,409
K. Sanders, Nat. Front. 1,215
H. Smith, Ind....... 125
Lab. maj........... 2,348
(Feb. '74, Lab. maj. 697)

Louth
E. 70,498
386 M. L. Brotherton, C.... 19,819
J. C. L. Sellick, L..... 16,939
R. Mitchell, Lab...... 14,747
C. maj............. 2,880
(Feb. '74, C. maj. 9,718)

Lowestoft
E. 76,936
387*Rt. Hon. J. M. L. Prior,
C................ 25,510
D. A. Baker, Lab..... 23,448
P. J. Hancock, L...... 11,165
C. maj............. 2,062
(Feb. '74, C. maj. 3,604)

Ludlow
E. 48,625
388*J. E. More, C......... 17,124
E. Robinson, L....... 10,888
J. Marek, Lab........ 8,353
C. maj............. 6,236
(Feb. '74, C. maj. 7,987)

Luton
EAST E. 53,549
389*I. M. Clemitson, Lab... 17,877
A. Johnston, C....... 14,200
E. J. Fisher, L........ 6,947
L. Byrne, Ind........ 299
Lab. maj........... 3,677
(Feb. '74, Lab. maj. 1,425)

WEST E. 58,272
390*B. C. J. Sedgemore, Lab. 20,402
R. J. Atkins, C........ 13,963
M. J. Dolling, L....... 9,289
Lab. maj........... 6,439
(Feb. '74, Lab. maj. 5,042)

Macclesfield
E. 80,150
391*N. R. Winterton, C.... 31,685
K. W. Little, Lab...... 18,592
A. J. Berry, L........ 12,764
C. maj............. 13,093
(Feb. '74, C. maj. 14,286)

Maidstone
E. 88,130
392*J. J. Wells, C......... 28,852
E. J. Burnett, L....... 18,581
K. M. Graham, Lab... 17,828
C. maj............. 10,271
(Feb. '74, C. maj. 7,656)

Maldon
E. 61,725
393*J. Wakeham, C........ 20,485
A. J. Shaw, Lab...... 14,098
J. R. C. Beale, L..... 12,473
C. maj............. 6,387
(Feb. '74, C. maj. 7,222)

Manchester
E. 47,937
394*G. B. Kaufman, Lab... 15,632
R. H. Hargreaves, C. 8,849
G. Wilmott, L....... 3,675
Lab. maj........... 6,783
(Feb. '74, Lab. maj. 4,895)

BLACKLEY E. 54,860
395*P. B. Rose, Lab....... 19,720
A. S. Lea, C........ 12,601
D. Jackson, L........ 5,517
H. Andrews, Nat.
Front............ 914
Lab. maj........... 7,119
(Feb. '74, Lab. maj. 5,506)

CENTRAL E. 39,857
396*Rt. Hon. N. H. Lever,
Lab.............. 14,753
R. Jackson, C........ 4,142
P. Coleman, L........ 2,382
Lab. maj........... 10,611
(Feb. '74 Lab. maj. 10,004)

GORTON E. 55,955
397*K. Marks, Lab....... 21,287
S. H. Waley-Cohen,
C................ 12,423
A. Cottam, L........ 5,984
Lab. maj........... 8,864
(Feb. '74, Lab. maj. 8,976)

MOSS SIDE E. 51,444
398*F. Hatton, Lab........ 15,212
J. R. L. Lee, C....... 11,101
W. J. L. Wallace, L... 5,686
N. Boyle, Ind....... 238
H. Smith, Ind....... 96
Lab. maj........... 4,111
(Feb. '74, Lab. maj. 2,392)

OPENSHAW E. 42,554
399*C. R. Morris, Lab..... 16,109
G. Green, C......... 7,596
A. R. Wood, L....... 3,980
P. Widdall, Comm... 300
Lab. maj........... 8,513
(Feb. '74, Lab. maj. 7,457)

WITHINGTON E. 58,200
400*F. J. Silvester, C..... 16,937
P. J. Hildrew, Lab.... 14,936
Mrs. A. B. Davies, L.. 7,555
C. maj............. 2,001
(Feb. '74, C. maj. 4,413)

WYTHENSHAWE E. 65,123
401*A. R. Morris, Lab..... 26,448
Mrs. J. D. W. Hill, C. 12,269
R. N. Scott, L....... 6,071
Lab. maj........... 14,179
(Feb. '74, Lab. maj. 12,438)

Mansfield
E. 69,555
402*J. D. Concannon, Lab.. 28,964
J. R. Wood, C........ 11,685
D. J. Chambers, L.... 9,358
F. C. Westacott,
Comm............. 448
Lab. maj........... 17,279
(Feb. '74, Lab. maj. 16,142)

Melton
E. 82,139
403*M. A. Latham, C..... 30,943
D. J. Knaggs, Lab.... 16,747
J. B. Pick, L........ 15,567
C. maj............. 14,196
(Feb. '74, C. maj. 12,749)

Meriden
E. 97,364
404*J. E. Tomlinson, Lab... 34,641
C. F. Horne, C....... 25,675
D. G. Minnis, L...... 12,782
Lab. maj........... 8,966
(Feb. '74, Lab. maj. 4,485)

Merioneth
E. 26,728
405*D. E. Thomas, P.C..... 9,543
W. H. Edwards, Lab.. 6,951
R. O. Jones, L....... 3,454
R. R. Owen, C....... 2,509
P.C. maj........... 2,592
(Feb. '74, P.C. maj. 588)

Merthyr Tydfil
E. 39,714
406*E. Rowlands, *Lab.*.... 21,260
E. Roberts, *P.C.*.... 4,455
L. J. Walters, *C.*...... 2,587
D. Bettall-Higgins, *L.* 1,300
T. Roberts, *Comm.*.... 509
Lab. maj........... 16,805
(Feb. '74, Lab. maj. 13,150)

Middlesbrough
E. 60,259
407*Rt. Hon. A. G. Bot-
tomley, O.B.E., *Lab.*.. 22,791
E. Leigh, *C.*......... 8,984
C. Wood, *L.*........ 5,080
Lab. maj........... 13,807
(Feb. '74, Lab. maj. 13,409)

Middleton and Prestwich
E. 76,737
408*J. Callaghan, *Lab.*...... 26,639
A. D'A. Fearn, *C.*...... 22,925
J. Clarney, *L.*......... 8,340
H. Smith, *Ind.*........ 234
Lab. maj........... 3,714
(Feb. '74, Lab. maj. 517)

Midlothian
E. 89,191
409*A. Eadie, B.E.M., *Lab.*.. 28,652
J. G. McKinlay, *Scot.
Nat.*.......... 24,568
A. Ballantyne, *C.*...... 11,046
P. Wheeler, *L.*........ 4,793
Lab. maj........... 4,084
(Feb. '74, Lab. maj. 11,742)

Mitcham and Morden
E. 65,398
410*B. L. H. Douglas-Mann,
Lab........... 22,384
D. Samuel, *C.*........ 16,193
M. Simpson, *L.*....... 7,429
S. E. French, *Comm.*.. 281
Miss G. Giddins, *Ind.*.. 106
W. G. Boaks, *Ind.*..... 68
Lab. maj........... 6,191
(Feb. '74, Lab. maj. 3,225)

Monmouth
E. 74,838
411*J. S. Thomas, *C.*...... 25,460
R. O. Faulkner, *Lab.*.. 23,118
D. M. Hando, *L.*...... 10,076
T. Brimmacombe,
P.C............... 839
C. maj............. 2,342
(Feb. '74, C. maj. 4,562)

Montgomery
E. 33,583
412*H. E. Hooson, Q.C., *L.* 11,280
W. R. C. Williams-
Wynne, *C.*........ 7,421
P. W. Harries, *Lab.*... 5,031
A. P. Jones, *P.C.*..... 2,440
L. maj............. 3,859
(Feb. '74, L. maj. 4,651)

Moray and Nairn
E. 41,174
413*Mrs. W. M. Ewing,
Scot. Nat....... 12,667
A. Pollock, *C.*........ 12,300
E. G. Smith, *Lab.*...... 2,985
K. Schellenberg, *L.*.... 2,814
Scot. Nat. maj...... 367
(Feb '74, Scot. Nat. maj. 1,817)

Morecambe and Lonsdale
E. 68,473
414*A. G. F. Hall-Davis, *C.* 24,877
E. Garbutt, *Lab.*...... 12,633
A. R. D. Stuttard, *L.*.. 12,404
C. maj............. 12,244
(Feb. '74, C. maj. 14,756)

Morpeth
E. 48,518
415*G. Grant, *Lab.*........ 22,696
D. M. Curry, *C.*..... 8,009
B. Rogers, *L.*......... 4,866
Lab. maj........... 14,687
(Feb. '74, Lab. maj. 13,034)

Motherwell and Wishaw
E. 51,506
416 J. W. Bray, *Lab.*..... 17,319
J. MacKay, *Scot. Nat.*.. 12,357
G. Rae, *C.*.......... 7,069
D. P. Young, *L.*...... 1,126
J. W. Sneddon, *Comm.* 946
Lab. maj........... 4,962
(Feb. '74, Lab. maj. 6,313)

Nantwich
E. 61,196
417*J. H. Cockcroft, *C.*..... 20,395
A. E. Bailey, *Lab.*..... 17,021
Mrs. H. Glidewell, *L.* 9,209
C. maj............. 3,374
(Feb. '74, C. maj. 5,168)

Neath
E. 52,257
418*D. R. Coleman, *Lab.*... 25,028
H. G. Evans, *P.C.*.... 7,305
M. J. Harris, *C.*...... 4,641
D. Owen, *L.*........ 3,759
Lab. maj........... 17,723
(Feb. '74, Lab. maj. 16,593)

Nelson and Colne
E. 48,356
419 E. D. H. Hoyle, *Lab.*.. 17,505
*D. C. Waddington,
Q.C., *C.*........ 16,836
A. R. Greaves, *L.*..... 4,850
Lab. maj........... 669
(Feb. '74, C. maj. 177)

Newark
E. 71,346
420*E. S. Bishop, *Lab.*..... 26,598
D. H. Cargill, *C.*..... 20,827
I. G. M. Jones, *L.*..... 8,116
Lab. maj........... 5,771
(Feb. '74, Lab. maj. 4,497)

Newbury
E. 72,587
421*R. M. C. McNair-
Wilson, *C.*........ 23,499
D. S. C. Clouston, *L.* 22,477
Mrs. C. A. Fletcher,
Lab............... 9,390
C. maj............. 1,022
(Feb. '74, C. maj. 1,201)

Newcastle-under-Lyme
E. 72,781
422*J. Golding, *Lab.*..... 28,154
N. C. Bonsor, *C.*..... 20,784
R. C. M. Fyson, *L.*.. 7,604
S. Rowe, *Ind.*....... 256
Lab. maj........... 7,370
(Feb. '74, Lab. maj. 5,648)

Newcastle-upon-Tyne
CENTRAL E. 25,156
423*Rt. Hon. E. W. Short,
C.H., *Lab*.......... 10,546
Mrs. S. Faith, *C.*...... 2,432
A. Ellis, *C.*.......... 1,716
Lab. maj........... 8,114
(Feb. '74, Lab. maj. 8,002)

EAST E. 45,651
424 M. S. Thomas, *Lab.*... 17,312
M. A. Hill, *C.*........ 11,063
T. Symonds, *L.*...... 4,391
Lab. maj........... 6,249
(Feb. '74, Lab. maj. 6,092)

NORTH E. 40,238
425*Sir R. W. Elliott, *C.*... 11,217
A. L. Banks, *Lab.*..... 10,748
D. J. Herd, *L.*....... 4,189
C. maj............. 469
(Feb. '74, C. maj. 2,980)

WEST E. 76,966
426*R. C. Brown, *Lab.*.... 30,057
R. M. Stewart, *C.*.... 14,983
R. H. B. Devereux, *L.* 7,945
Lab. maj........... 15,074
(Feb. '74, Lab. maj. 11,396)

New Forest
E. 78,109
427*P. M. E. D. McNair-
Wilson, *C.*........ 28,778
A. J. Hayes, *L.*....... 15,355
P. J. Brushett, *Lab.*... 13,825
C. maj............. 13,423
(Feb. '74, C. maj. 11,382)

Newham
NORTH EAST E. 65,975
428*Rt. Hon. R. E. Prentice,
Lab............... 22,205
T. J. Stroud, *C.*...... 8,664
L. H. Cohen, *L.*..... 4,880
J. Newham, *Nat. Front* 2,715
Miss V. Redgrave, *Ind.* 572
Lab. maj........... 13,541
(Feb. '74, Lab. maj. 13,331)

NORTH WEST E. 53,489
429*A. W. J. Lewis, *Lab.*... 18,388
Mrs. R. Brown, *C.*... 5,007
A. Hetherington, *L.*.. 4,201
Lab. maj........... 13,381
(Feb. '74, Lab. maj. 12,548)

SOUTH E. 57,695
430*N. J. Spearing, *Lab.*... 21,332
I. W. I. Shipley, *L.*... 3,611
A. D. C. Gemmill, *C.* 3,440
E. O. Bayly, *Nat. Front* 2,412
Lab. maj........... 17,721
(May '74, by-election, Lab. maj.
7,459)
(Feb. '74, Lab. maj. 18,583)

Newport
E. 75,061
431*R. J. Hughes, *Lab.*.... 30,069
G. A. L. Price, *C.*.... 16,253
J. H. Morgan, *L.*.... 9,207
G. Lee, *P.C.*......... 1,816
Lab. maj........... 13,816
(Feb. '74, Lab. maj. 11,382)

Newton
E. 95,268
432*J. Evans, *Lab.*........ 38,956
R. M. Baldwin, *C.*.... 22,484
W. N. Leather, *L.*.... 11,738
Lab. maj........... 16,472
(Feb. '74, Lab. maj. 14,770)

Norfolk
NORTH E. 90,526
433*R. F. Howell, C...... 33,312
Rev. D. M. Mason,
  Lab............. 22,191
R. G. Moore, L...... 13,776
  C. maj............ 11,121
  (Feb. '74, C. maj. 14,290)
NORTH WEST E. 79,743
434*C. Brocklebank-Fowler,
  C................ 27,513
R. L. Williams, Lab.. 26,170
R. A. Walker, L...... 8,862
  C. maj............ 1,343
  (Feb. '74, C. maj. 803)
SOUTH E. 90,810
435*J. R. R. MacGregor,
  O.B.E., C.......... 31,478
H. Gray, Lab........ 22,713
M. J. Scott, L........ 14,687
C. C. Fairhead, Ind... 317
  C. maj............ 8,765
  (Feb. '74, C. maj. 11,019)
SOUTH WEST E. 53,719
436*P. L. Hawkins, T.D., C. 19,778
H. Toch, Lab........ 14,850
B. Baxter, L......... 6,658
  C. maj............ 4,928
  (Feb. '74, C. maj. 6,043)

Normanton
E. 58,936
437*A Roberts, Lab....... 24,372
J. Makin, C......... 9,739
W. K. Whitaker, L... 7,384
  Lab. maj.......... 14,633
  (Feb. '74, Lab. maj. 15,174)

Northampton
NORTH E. 49,030
438*Mrs. M. M. Colquhoun,
  Lab............. 16,314
R. Tracey, C........ 14,776
R. B. Baker, L....... 6,160
  Lab. maj.......... 1,538
  (Feb. '74, Lab. maj. 1,033)
SOUTH E. 44,343
439*M. W. L. Morris, C.... 14,393
J. Dilks, Lab........ 14,252
R. F. Miller, L....... 4,842
  C. maj............ 141
  (Feb. '74, C. maj. 179)

Northwich
E. 52,626
440*A. R. Goodlad, C.... 18,663
P. A. Kent, Lab...... 14,053
D. Reaper, L........ 8,645
  C. maj............ 4,610
  (Feb. '74, C. maj. 6,293)

Norwich
NORTH E, 45,079
441*Rt. Hon. D. H. Ennals,
  Lab............. 17,958
T. P. C. Doe, C...... 8,754
E. M. Wheeler, L.... 5,378
  Lab. maj.......... 9,204
  (Feb. '74, Lab. maj. 7,294)
SOUTH E. 44,862
442*J. L. Garrett, Lab...... 16,590
Miss M. Tomison, C. 13,185
P. G. Smith, L....... 5,429
  Lab. maj.......... 3,405
  (Feb. '74, Lab. maj. 652)

Norwood
E. 52,893
443*J. D. Fraser, Lab...... 16,449
Miss D. B. Hancock,
  C................ 11,678
E. Hawthorne, L..... 4,377
M. J. Greatbanks, Ind. 223
  Lab. maj.......... 4,771
  (Feb. '74, Lab. maj. 4,022)

Nottingham
EAST E. 53,786
444*J. J. Dunnett, Lab...... 16,530
S. M. Swerling, C.... 10,574
E. J. Rowan, L....... 4,442
D. W. Peetz, Ind..... 736
  Lab. maj.......... 5,956
  (Feb. '74, Lab. maj. 3,978)
NORTH E. 76,490
445*W. C. Whitlock, Lab.. 24,694
M. F. Spungin, C.... 17,853
M. Crew-Gee, L..... 7,470
D. Caine, Nat. Front.. 792
J. H. Peck, Comm..... 525
  Lab. maj.......... 6,841
  (Feb. '74, Lab. maj. 4,445)
WEST E. 77,711
446*M. English, Lab....... 27,373
P. R. C. Lloyd, C.... 18,108
A. Johnson, L....... 9,598
  Lab. maj.......... 9,265
  (Feb. '74, Lab. maj. 5,797)

Nuneaton
E. 77,892
447*L. J. Huckfield, Lab.... 32,308
R. Freeman, C....... 14,547
N. Hawkins, L....... 10,729
  Lab. maj.......... 17,761
  (Feb. '74, Lab. maj. 17,493)

Ogmore
E. 67,927
448*W. E. Padley, Lab..... 30,453
R. K. Jones, C....... 8,249
Mrs. J. T. Gibbs, L... 8,203
D. I. Jones, P.C...... 4,290
  Lab. maj.......... 22,204
  (Feb. '74, Lab. maj. 17,553)

Oldham
EAST E. 50,737
449*J. A. Lamond, Lab..... 19,054
L. McGrandle, C..... 10,917
C. G. Hilyer, L....... 6,142
  Lab. maj.......... 8,137
  (Feb. '74, Lab. maj. 6,302)
WEST E. 48,062
450*M. H. Meacher, Lab.. 18,444
D. A. Trippier, C.... 10,407
K. Stocks, L......... 5,838
  Lab. maj.......... 8,037
  (Feb. '74, Lab. maj. 6,305)

Orkney and Shetland
E. 26,289
451*Rt. Hon. J. Grimond,
  T.D., L............ 9,877
H. N. Firth, Scot. Nat. 3,025
R. Fraser, C......... 2,495
W. J. G. Wills, Lab... 2,175
  L. maj............ 6,852
  (Feb. '74, L. maj. 7,305)

Ormskirk
E. 96,593
452*R. Kilroy-Silk, Lab... 35,392
B. M. Keefe, C....... 26,541
D. Parry, L......... 8,387
  Lab. maj.......... 8,851
  (Feb. '74, Lab. maj. 7,803)

Orpington
E. 65,686
453*I. R. Stanbrook, C.... 24,394
Lady Avebury, L..... 19,384
Mrs. C. Spillane, Lab. 8,121
  C. maj............ 5,010
  (Feb. '74, C. maj. 3,664)

Oswestry
E. 56,429
454*W. J. Biffen, C....... 19,165
J. Bishton, Lab...... 10,751
D. J. Evans, L....... 10,623
  C. maj............ 8,414
  (Feb. '74, C. maj. 7,010)

Oxford
E. 77,270
455 D. E. T. Luard, Lab.. 23,359
*Hon. C. M. Wood-
house, D.S.O., O.B.E.,
  C................ 22,323
Mrs. M. S. Butler, L... 8,374
I. H. M. Anderson,
  Nat. Front......... 572
Mrs. B. O. Smith, Ind. 64
  Lab. maj.......... 1,036
  (Feb. '74, C. maj. 821)

Oxon, Mid
E. 59,697
456*Hon. D. R. Hurd, C.B.E.
  C................ 20,944
M. J. Saunders, Lab.. 13,641
Miss M. E. Burton, L. 11,006
  C. maj............ 7,303
  (Feb. '74, C. maj. 7,973)

Paddington
E. 58,499
457*A. C. Latham, Lab..... 17,155
G. M. Wolfson, C.... 14,844
N. J. S. Lewis, L..... 3,742
C. D. Wertheim, Ind. 192
S. Allman, Ind...... 135
  Lab. maj.......... 2,311
  (Feb. '74, Lab. maj. 872)

Paisley
E. 66,059
458*J. Robertson, Lab...... 21,368
D. R. Rollo, Scot. Nat. 15,778
I. Robertson, C...... 7,440
D. Thompson, L..... 3,116
  Lab. maj.......... 5,590
  (Feb. '74, Lab. maj. 8,897)

Peckham
E. 63,349
459*H. G. Lamborn, Lab.. 24,587
N. B. Baker, C...... 5,760
S. W. F. Saltmarsh, L. 3,971
  Lab. maj.......... 18,827
  (Feb. '74, Lab. maj. 18,071)

Pembroke
E. 72,053
460*R. N. Edwards, C...... 23,190
G. S. D. Parry, Lab... 22,418
P. E. C. Jones, L..... 9,116
R. B. Davies, P.C..... 2,580
  C. maj............ 772
  (Feb. '74, C. maj. 1,479)

Penistone
E. 67,060
461*J. J. Mendelson, Lab... 27,146
G. C. W. Harris, C... 12,011
D. Chadwick, L...... 10,900
  Lab. maj.......... 15,135
  (Feb. '74, Lab. maj. 13,713)

Penrith and the Border
E. 55,602
462*Rt. Hon. W. S. I.
  Whitelaw, C.H., M.C.,
  C............... 23,547
J. N. D. Weedall, *Lab.* 9,791
J. G. Pease, *L*........ 7,215
  C. maj............ 13,756
  (Feb. '74, C. maj. 17,338)

Perth and East Perthshire
E. 57,646
463 G. D. Crawford, *Scot.*
  Nat............... 17,337
*I. MacArthur, *C*...... 16,544
J. White, *Lab.*........ 5,805
R. Duncan, *L*........ 2,851
  Scot. Nat. maj...... 793
  (Feb. '74, C. maj. 8,975)

Peterborough
E. 63,044
464 M. J. Ward, *Lab*..... 21,820
*Sir H. Nicholls, Bt., C. 19,972
P. J. Boizot, *L*........ 7,302
  Lab. maj........... 1,848
  (Feb. '74, C. maj. 22)

Petersfield
E. 74,260
465 M. J. Mates, *C*...... 28,689
T. W. Slack, *L*....... 19,702
J. M. Bloom, *Lab*..... 8,301
P. H. H. Bishop, *Ind*.. 117
  C. maj............. 8,987
  (Feb. '74, C. maj. 9,580)

Plymouth
DEVONPORT E. 50,105
466*Rt. Hon. D. A. L.
  Owen, *Lab*........ 17,398
Dame Joan Vickers,
  D.B.E., *C*........ 15,139
N. E. Westbrook, *L*.. 3,953
J. N. Hill, *Ind*........ 312
  Lab. maj........... 2,259
  (Feb. '74, Lab. maj. 437)

DRAKE E. 55,556
467*Miss J. E. Fookes, *C*.. 17,287
B. W. Fletcher, *Lab*... 17,253
Miss M. E. Castle, *L*.. 7,354
  C. maj............. 34
  (Feb. '74, C. maj. 2,611)

SUTTON E. 61,007
468*Hon. A. K. M. Clark,
  C................ 20,457
J. G. Priestley, *Lab*... 15,269
S. G. Banks, *L*....... 10,131
  C. maj............. 5,188
  (Feb. '74, C. maj. 8,104)

Pontefract and Castleford
E. 66,288
469*J. Harper, *Lab*....... 30,208
I. R. Bloomer, *C*..... 6,966
S. F. Galloway, *L*.... 5,259
T. Parsons, *Ind*...... 457
  Lab. maj........... 23,242
  (Feb. '74, Lab. maj. 23,804)

Pontypool
E. 55,112
470*L. Abse, *Lab*.......... 25,381
R. J. Moreland, *C*.... 6,686
E. A. R. Mathias, *L*.. 5,744
R. D. Tanner, *P.C*.... 2,223
  Lab. maj........... 18,695
  (Feb. '74, Lab. maj. 17,465)

Pontypridd
E. 70,200
471*B. T. John, *Lab*...... 29,302
I. A. S. Jones, *C*...... 10,528
Mrs. M. G. Murphy,
  L................ 8,050
R. A. Kemp, *P.C*.... 3,917
  Lab. maj........... 18,774
  (Feb. '74, Lab. maj. 16,622)

Poole
E. 83,403
472*Rt. Hon. H. O. Mur-
  ton, O.B.E., T.D., *C*... 28,982
G. M. Goode, *L*...... 17,557
G. W. Hobbs, *Lab*... 16,262
  C. maj............. 11,425
  (Feb. '74, C. maj. 10,068)

Portsmouth
NORTH E. 69,089
473*F. A. Judd, *Lab*...... 24,352
J. Ward, *C*.......... 23,007
Mrs. E. Brooks, *L*.... 5,208
T. L. Keen, *Ind*...... 527
  Lab. maj........... 1,345
  (Feb. '74, Lab. maj. 320)

SOUTH E. 70,773
474*R. B. Pink, C.B.E.,
  V.R.D., *C*......... 23,379
A. M. Halmos, *Lab*.. 15,308
M. Tribe, *L*......... 9,807
A. D. Rifkin, *Ind*.... 612
  C. maj............. 8,071
  (Feb. '74, C. maj. 10,982)

Preston
NORTH E. 51,369
475*R. H. Atkins, *Lab*.... 18,044
Miss M. Holt, *C*..... 16,260
G. Payne, *L*........ 4,948
H. Smith, *Ind*........ 138
  Lab. maj........... 1,784
  (Feb. '74, Lab. maj. 255)

SOUTH E. 51,522
476*S. G. Thorne, *Lab*.... 18,449
A. Green, C.B.E., *C*... 14,700
R. P. Marshall, *L*.... 5,456
E. Harrison, *Nat. Front* 663
H. Smith, *Ind*........ 87
  Lab. maj........... 3,749
  (Feb. '74, Lab. maj. 1,887)

Pudsey
E. 65,354
477*J. G. D. Shaw, *C*..... 20,180
S. J. Cooksey, *L*..... 15,599
K. Targett, *Lab*...... 15,293
  C. maj............. 4,581
  (Feb. '74, C. maj. 3,739)

Putney
E. 66,515
478*H. G. Jenkins, *Lab*.... 21,611
G. A. Wade, *C*...... 18,836
A. C. Slade, *L*....... 7,159
T. L. Keen, *Ind*...... 125
  Lab. maj........... 2,775
  (Feb. '74, Lab. maj. 1,439)

Ravensbourne
E. 48,541
479*J. L. Hunt, *C*........ 18,318
D. E. A. Crowe, *L*.... 9,813
C. Howes, *Lab*...... 7,204
I. Stevens, *Nat. Front*. 574
  C. maj............. 8,505
  (Feb. '74, C. maj. 8,897)

Reading
NORTH E. 64,484
480*R. A. B. Durant, *C*.... 18,734
Miss M. J. Denby,
  Lab............... 18,266
K. E. V. Watts, *L*.... 9,064
P. Baker, *Nat. Front*.. 594
  C. maj............. 468
  (Feb. '74, C. maj. 2,369)

SOUTH E. 69,124
481*G. F. Vaughan, *C*..... 21,959
P. R. Burall, *L*....... 15,293
L. Silverman, *Lab*..... 14,375
  C. maj............. 6,666
  (Feb. '74, C. maj. 5,359)

Redcar
E. 62,365
482*J. Tinn, *Lab*.......... 23,204
R. Hall, *C*.......... 12,774
N. Clark, *L*......... 7,101
  Lab. maj........... 10,430
  (Feb. '74, Lab. maj. 9,254)

Reigate
E. 72,745
483*G. A. Gardiner, *C*..... 27,769
M. G. Ormerod, *Lab*.. 14,185
A. C. Bryan, *L*....... 12,554
M. Taggart, *Ind*...... 266
  C. maj............. 13,584
  (Feb. '74, C. maj. 14,060)

Renfrewshire
EAST E. 61,811
484*Rt. Hon. Betty Harvie
  Anderson, O.B.E., T.D.,
  C................ 19,847
I. Jenkins, *Scot. Nat*... 11,137
C. J. Roberts, *Lab*.... 9,997
W. G. A. Craig, *L*.... 7,015
  C. maj............. 8,710
  (Feb. '74, C. maj. 15,486)

WEST E. 67,078
485*N. F. Buchan, *Lab*.... 20,674
C. D. Cameron, *Scot.*
  Nat............... 15,374
J. Ross-Harper, *C*.... 14,399
D. O. Brown, *L*...... 3,271
  Lab. maj........... 5,300
  (Feb. '74, Lab. maj. 2,668)

Rhondda
E. 65,787
486*T. A. Jones, *Lab*...... 38,654
D. Morgan, *P.C*...... 4,173
P. Leyshon, *C*........ 3,739
D. J. Austin, *L*....... 2,142
A. True, *Comm*...... 1,404
  Lab. maj........... 34,481
  (Feb. '74, Lab. maj. 30,141)

Richmond (Surrey)
E. 53,821
487*Sir A. H. F. Royle,
  K.C.M.G., *C*...... 17,450
A. J. Watson, *L*...... 13,235
R. G. Marshall-
  Andrews, *Lab*..... 8,714
E. A. Russell, *Nat.*
  Front............. 1,000
  C. maj............. 4,215
  (Feb. '74, C. maj. 3,827)

Richmond (Yorks.)
E. 62,002
488*Sir T. P. G. Kitson, C. 23,156
Mrs. P. Waudby, *L*... 9,528
I. A. Wilkie, *Lab*..... 8,025
  C. maj............. 13,628
  (Feb. '74, C. maj. 15,267)

Ripon
E. 50,172
489*K. Hampson, C...... 20,636
D. Austick, L........ 13,632
S. P. Meyer, Lab.... 5,330
C. maj............ *7,004*
(Feb. '74, C. maj. 4,335)

Rochdale
E. 67,029
490*C. Smith, M.B.E., L.... 20,092
J. Connell, Lab....... 17,339
R. Young, C......... 7,740
M. W. Sellors, Nat.
Front............. 1,927
L. maj............ *2,753*
(Feb. '74, L. maj. 8,899)

Rochester and Chatham
E. 79,799
491 R. E. Bean, Lab....... 25,467
*Mrs. P. E. Fenner, C.. 23,049
Mrs. M. Black, L..... 9,035
G. Hazelden, Nat.
Front............. 1,150
Lab. maj.......... *2,418*
(Feb. '74, C. maj. 843)

Romford
E. 55,337
492*M. J. Neubert, C...... 17,164
D. R. O'Flynn, Lab... 14,513
T. E. Hurlstone, L..... 7,663
L. C. H. Sampson, Ind. 200
C. maj............ *2,651*
(Feb. '74, C. maj. 3,073)

Ross and Cromarty
E. 29,411
493*J. H. N. Gray, C....... 7,954
W. McRae, Scot. Nat. 7,291
B. D. H. Wilson, Lab. 3,440
T. Glen, L........... 1,747
C. maj............ *663*
(Feb. '74, C. maj. 2,871)

Rossendale
E. 50,463
494 M. A. Noble, Lab..... 16,156
*R. W. T. Bray, C.... 15,953
J. A. Hamilton, L..... 8,693
Lab. maj........... *203*
(Feb. '74, C. maj. 797)

Rotherham
E. 61,209
495*Rt. Hon. B. K. O'Malley, Lab........... 25,874
R. A. Hambro, C..... 8,840
V. Bottomley, L..... 5,350
Lab. maj.......... *17,034*
(By-election, June 24, 1976)
J. S. Crowther, Lab.... 14,351
D. Hinckley, C....... 9,824
Miss E. Graham, L.... 2,214
G. Wright, Nat. Front. 1,696
P. Bishop, Ind........ 129
R. Robinson, Ind..... 99
Lab. maj........... *4,527*
(Feb. '74, Lab. maj. 16,734)

Rother Valley
E. 91,963
496*P. Hardy, Lab........ 44,670
G. P. A. Waller, C.... 11,893
Rev. G. Reid, L..... 9,828
Lab. maj.......... *32,777*
(Feb. '74, Lab. maj. 33,474)

Roxburgh, Selkirk and Peebles
E. 57,824
497*D. M. S. Steel, L..... 20,006
Mrs. C. M. Anderson,
C............... 12,573
A. Edmonds, Scot.
Nat............. 9,178
D. A. Graham, Lab... 4,076
L. maj............ *7,433*
(Feb. '74, L. maj. 9,017)

Rugby
E. 59,590
498*W. G. Price, Lab..... 22,926
A. R. Marlow, C.... 17,722
A. Butcher, L....... 6,775
A. S. Frost, Ind...... 137
Lab. maj.......... *5,204*
(Feb. '74, Lab. maj. 6,154)

Ruislip–Northwood
E. 54,119
499*F. P. Crowder, Q.C., C. 20,779
D. A. G. Race, Lab... 10,490
Miss J. M. Arram, L. 8,621
Mrs. W. Hobday, Ind. 458
C. maj............ *10,289*
(Feb. '74, C. maj. 11,421)

Runcorn
E. 69,929
500*M. Carlisle, Q.C., C... 25,047
A. J. Eccles, Lab..... 19,579
Rev. D. Sanders, L... 9,188
N. Dobson, Ind...... 464
C. maj............ *5,468*
(Feb. '74, C. maj. 7,268)

Rushcliffe
E. 63,976
501*K. H. Clarke, C...... 27,074
Mrs. V. Bell, Lab..... 12,131
J. E. Hamilton, L..... 10,300
C. maj............ *14,943*
(Feb. '74, C. maj. 17,709)

Rutherglen
E. 48,824
502*J. G. Mackenzie, Lab... 17,088
I. O. Bayne, Scot. Nat. 9,732
J. Thomson, C....... 9,248
R. E. Brown, L...... 2,424
Lab. maj.......... *7,356*
(Feb. '74, Lab. maj. 4,153)

Rutland and Stamford
E. 54,656
503*K. Lewis, C......... 19,101
M. R. C. Withers,
Lab............. 12,111
D. C. Howie, L...... 10,131
C. maj............ *6,990*
(Feb. '74, C. maj. 8,885)

Rye
E. 72,261
504*B. G. Irvine, C....... 30,511
D. R. S. Moore, L.... 14,828
D. W. Threlfall, Lab.. 8,303
C. maj............ *15,683*
(Feb. '74, C. maj. 16,135)

Saffron Walden
E. 62,397
505*Sir P. M. Kirk, C.... 21,291
F. P. D. Moore, L.... 14,770
H. Green, Lab....... 12,652
C. maj............ *6,521*
(Feb. '74, C. maj. 7,545)

St. Albans
E. 69,693
506*V. H. Goodhew, C.... 24,436
E. Hudson, Lab....... 15,301
A. C. Shaw, L....... 14,614
C. maj............ *9,135*
(Feb. '74, C. maj. 8,421)

St. Helens
E. 76,067
507*L. Spriggs, Lab....... 32,620
K. J. Bridgeman, C... 10,554
A. E. Lycett, L....... 7,689
Lab. maj.......... *22,066*
(Feb. '74, Lab. maj. 21,716)

St. Ives
E. 51,440
508*J. W. F. Nott, C...... 17,198
G. E. T. Tonkin, L... 11,330
B. M. Tidy, Lab...... 9,388
C. maj............ *5,868*
(Feb. '74, C. maj. 5,425)

St. Marylebone
E. 43,633
509*K. W. Baker, C...... 13,660
Mrs. P. J. Moberly,
Lab............. 7,157
B. Silver, L......... 4,067
C. maj............ *6,503*
(Feb. '74, C. maj. 8,717)

St. Pancras North
E. 41,629
510*A. W. Stallard, Lab... 14,155
J. R. Major, C....... 6,602
P. J. W. Medlicott, L. 3,428
Lab. maj.......... *7,553*
(Feb. '74, Lab. maj. 6,835)

Salford
EAST E. 40,144
511*F. J. Allaun, Lab...... 14,276
S. Latimer, C........ 6,440
A. F. Bell, L........ 3,160
Lab. maj.......... *7,836*
(Feb. '74, Lab. maj. 6,931)

WEST E. 45,833
512*Rt. Hon. S. Orme,
Lab............. 17,112
J. N. L. Tillett, C..... 8,540
A. E. Arstall, L...... 4,237
Lab. maj.......... *8,572*
(Feb. '74, Lab. maj. 6,462)

Salisbury
E. 62,817
513*M. A. Hamilton, C... 20,478
J. F. Lakeman, L..... 16,298
C. J. Connor, Lab.... 10,140
C. maj............ *4,180*
(Feb. '74, C. maj. 6,217)

Scarborough
E. 58,553
514*M. N. Shaw, C....... 19,831
M. J. L. Brook, L.... 10,123
D. J. Taylor-Goodby,
Lab............. 9,923
C. maj............ *9,708*
(Feb. '74, C. maj. 5,107)

Sevenoaks
E. 74,969
515*Sir J. C. Rodgers, Bt.,
C............... 26,670
J. Scanlan, Lab....... 15,065
R. F. Webster, L..... 15,024
C. maj............ *11,605*
(Feb. '74, C. maj. 13,713)

Sheffield

Attercliffe E. 63,917
516*A. E. P. Duffy, Lab... 29,601
Miss P. M. Santhouse,
   C............... 8,043
G. P. Broadhead, L.... 5,282
Lab. maj........... 21,558
(Feb. '74, Lab. maj. 21,176)

Brightside E. 54,095
517 Miss V. J. Maynard,
   Lab............... 18,108
E. Griffiths, Ind. Lab.. 10,182
R. E. Walker, C..... 4,905
W. T. W. Blades, L... 3,271
Lab. maj........... 7,926
(Feb. '74, Lab. maj. 20,567)

Hallam E. 77,400
518*J. H. Osborn, C....... 26,083
C. J. C. Betts, Lab.... 15,419
M. A. K. Johnson, L.. 11,724
C. maj............. 10,664
(Feb. '74, C. maj. 12,913)

Heeley E. 65,244
519*F. O. Hooley, Lab..... 24,728
A. E. Page, C........ 15,322
R. J. Fairfax, L....... 7,151
P. Revell, Nat. Front.. 723
Lab. maj........... 9,406
(Feb. '74, Lab. maj. 6,585)

Hillsborough E. 52,032
520*M. H. Flannery, Lab... 21,026
R. B. Williamson, C.. 8,718
R. C. Osner, L........ 4,912
Lab. maj........... 12,308
(Feb. '74, Lab. maj. 11,280)

Park E. 67,425
521*Rt. Hon. F. W. Mulley,
   Lab............... 30,057
F. R. Butler, C....... 6,093
R. Trench, L........ 5,539
G. Ashberry, Comm... 403
Lab. maj........... 23,964
(Feb. '74, Lab. maj. 22,677)

Shipley E. 52,006
522*J. M. Fox, C........ 18,518
Rev. M. J. Wedge-
   worth, Lab........ 15,482
G. G. Roberts, L..... 8,094
C. maj............. 3,036
(Feb. '74, C. maj. 4,155)

Shoreham E. 68,498
523*R. N. Luce, C....... 26,170
P. F. Bartram, L..... 14,797
Q. Barry, Lab........ 10,200
C. maj............. 11,373
(Feb. '74, C. maj. 9,758)

Shrewsbury E. 60,228
524*Sir J. A. Langford-Holt,
   C............... 19,064
W. Marsh, L......... 13,642
D. W. Woodvine, Lab. 11,504
C. maj............. 5,422
(Feb. '74, C. maj. 6,181)

Sidcup
E. 49,564
525*Rt. Hon. E. R. G.
   Heath, M.B.E., C.... 18,991
W. J. Jennings, Lab... 11,448
I. R. P. Josephs, L.... 6,954
D. H. Jones, Ind...... 174
M. J. Norton, Ind.... 61
C. maj............. 7,543
(Feb. '74, C. maj. 9,698)

Skipton E. 52,562
526*G. B. Drayson, T.D., C. 17,822
Mrs. K. C. Brooks, L. 17,232
C. G. Burks, Lab.... 8,109
C. maj............. 590
(Feb. '74, C. maj. 2,116)

Solihull E. 79,992
527*W. P. Grieve, Q.C., C. 31,707
J. A. Windmill, L..... 15,848
D. McShane, Lab.... 12,640
C. maj............. 15,859
(Feb. '74, C. maj. 17,363)

Somerset North E. 89,056
528*A. P. Dean, C........ 32,146
W. R. White, Lab.... 22,671
Mrs. J. M. Bourne, L. 16,428
J. K. Polling, Ind.... 387
C. maj............. 9,475
(Feb. '74, C. maj. 12,155)

Southall E. 70,832
529*S. J. Bidwell, Lab..... 24,218
R. C. Patten, C...... 14,235
C. I. M. Arnold, L.... 6,557
Lab. maj........... 9,983
(Feb. '74, Lab. maj. 8,812)

Southampton
Itchen E. 82,009
530*R. C. Mitchell, Lab.... 28,168
P. T. James, C...... 20,373
J. Cherryson, L....... 9,071
Lab. maj........... 7,795
(Feb. '74, Lab. maj. 5,590)

Test E. 73,895
531 B. C. Gould, Lab..... 22,780
*S. J. A. Hill, C...... 22,250
J. R. Wallis, L....... 8,994
Lab. maj........... 530
(Feb. '74, C. maj. 1,403)

Southend
East E. 57,295
532*Sir S. J. McAdden,
   C.B.E., C......... 18,083
Mrs. S. K. Ward, Lab. 13,480
J. W. J. Curry, L...... 7,856
C. maj............. 4,603
(Feb. '74, C. maj. 4,952)

West E. 67,438
533*H. P. G. Channon, C.. 23,480
W. Greaves, L....... 16,409
A. N. Wright, Lab.... 9,451
C. maj............. 7,071
(Feb. '74, C. maj. 5,155)

Southgate E. 70,935
534*Hon. A. G. Berry, C... 25,888
J. P. Sheppard, Lab... 10,966
G. J. Bridge, L....... 9,922
B. W. Pell, Nat. Front 1,255
C. maj............. 14,922
(Feb. '74, C. maj. 14,454)

Southport
E. 66,109
535*W. I. Percival, Q.C., C. 23,014
R. C. Fearn, L....... 17,387
I. G. James, Lab..... 8,323
C. maj............. 5,627
(Feb. '74, C. maj. 3,882)

South Shields E. 72,584
536*A. Blenkinsop, Lab.... 26,492
N. S. Smith, C....... 11,667
L. Garbutt, L........ 8,106
W. Owen, Nat. Front. 711
Lab. maj........... 14,825
(Feb. '74, Lab. maj. 11,986)

Sowerby E. 48,747
537*M. O. F. Madden,
   Lab............... 14,971
D. Thompson, C...... 14,325
D. T. Shutt, L....... 9,136
H. Smith, Ind........ 157
Lab. maj........... 646
(Feb. '74, Lab. maj. 115)

Spelthorne E. 69,411
538*Rt. Hon. H. E. Atkins,
   C............... 23,125
C. H. Dodwell, Lab.. 17,177
P. E. Winner, L....... 10,212
J. Clifton, Nat. Front. 1,180
C. maj............. 5,948
(Feb. '74, C. maj. 8,059)

Stafford and Stone E. 78,817
539*Rt. Hon. H. C. P. J.
   Fraser, M.B.E., C.... 27,173
T. E. Cowlishaw, Lab. 20,845
H. S. Martin, L....... 11,491
D. E. Sutch, Ind...... 351
C. maj............. 6,328
(Feb. '74, C. maj. 8,983)

Staffordshire South West E. 61,042
540*P. T. Cormack, C..... 2 ,604
I. K. Wymer, Lab.... 1 ,065
A. Lambert, L........ 3,355
C. maj............. 7,539
(Feb. '74, C. maj. 9,758)

Stalybridge and Hyde E. 66,389
541*T. Pendry, Lab....... 25,161
S. Burgoyne, C....... 15,404
D. F. Burden, L....... 7,725
G. Tetler, Ind........ 318
Lab. maj........... 9,757
(Feb. '74, Lab. maj. 8,068)

Stepney and Poplar E. 60,458
542*Rt. Hon. P. D. Shore,
   Lab............... 24,159
H. Greenway, C..... 3,183
Mrs. F. W. Alexander,
   L............... 3,181
K. Halpin, Comm..... 617
Lab. maj........... 20,976
(Feb. '74, Lab. maj. 23,330)

Stirling, Falkirk and Grangemouth
E. 64,362
543*H. Ewing, Lab....... 22,090
Dr. R. D. McIntyre,
  Scot. Nat.......... 20,324
G. A. Campbell, C... 7,186
J. Angles, L........... 1,477
  Lab. maj........... 1,766
(Feb. '74, Lab. maj. 3,849)

Stirlingshire
EAST AND CLACKMANNAN
E. 62,693
544*G. N. Reid, Scot. Nat. 25,998
R. G. Douglas, Lab.. 18,657
T. N. A. Begg, C.... 5,269
D. Shields, L......... 1,268
  Scot. Nat. maj...... 7,341
(Feb. '74, Scot. Nat. maj. 3,610)

WEST E. 52,989
545 D. A. Canavan, Lab... 16,698
Mrs. J. T. Jones, Scot.
  Nat.............. 16,331
D. W. Mitchell, C.... 7,875
I. MacFarlane, L....... 1,865
  Lab. maj........... 367
(Feb. '74, Lab. maj. 4,844)

Stockport
NORTH E. 52,842
546*A. F. Bennett, Lab..... 17,979
I. W. Owen, C..... 16,155
P. J. Arnold, L....... 7,085
  Lab. maj........... 1,824
(Feb. '74, Lab. maj. 203)

SOUTH E. 47,795
547*M. Orbach, Lab....... 16,281
Viscount Lewisham,
  C.............. 12,061
C. J. Carter, L...... 7,160
  Lab. maj........... 4,220
(Feb. '74, Lab. maj. 3,098)

Stockton
E. 85,519
548*W. T. Rodgers, Lab... 32,962
B. S. Mawhinney, C.. 18,488
Mrs. N. Long, L...... 6,906
Mrs. V. Fletcher, Ind.. 750
  Lab. maj........... 14,474
(Feb. '74, Lab. maj. 12,371)

Stoke-on-Trent
CENTRAL E. 61,217
549*R. B. Cant, Lab...... 24,146
W. Williams, C...... 9,493
A. Thomas, L........ 6,313
  Lab. maj........... 14,653
(Feb. '74, Lab. maj. 11,748)

NORTH E. 59,899
550*J. S. Forrester, Lab... 25,264
J. W. D. Davies, C... 10,192
M. Smith, L........ 6,239
  Lab. maj........... 15,072
(Feb. '74, Lab. maj. 12,459)

SOUTH E. 72,629
551*J. Ashley, C.H., Lab ... 30,699
J. S. Heath, C........ 14,204
Mrs. E. Johnson, L.... 5,278
  Lab. maj........... 16,495
(Feb. '74, Lab. maj. 15,669)

Stratford-on-Avon
E. 71,895
552*A. E. U. Maude, T.D.,
  C................ 27,123
M. J. W. Wright, L... 14,555
D. V. Hunt, Lab...... 11,551
  C. maj............ 12,568
(Feb. '74, C. maj. 13,221)

Streatham
E. 56,453
553*W. J. M. Shelton, C...16,515
Mrs. J. Gaffin, Lab.... 13,648
R. G. O. Silver, L.... 4,987
T. Lamb, Nat. Front .. 817
Mrs. T. Moore, Ind... 210
  C. maj............ 2,867
(Feb. '74, C. maj. 4,475)

Stretford
E. 68,766
554*W. S. Churchill, C.... 22,114
P. N. Scott, Lab...... 20,877
D. I. Wrigley, L..... 9,629
  C. maj............ 1,237
(Feb. '74, C. maj. 3,989)

Stroud
E. 69,398
555*J. A. Kershaw, M.C., C. 24,406
W. H. Maddocks, Lab. 17,352
Mrs. S. A. Ritchie, L. 13,756
J. S. Churchill, Ind... 241
  C. maj............ 7,054
(Feb. '74, C. maj. 8,471)

Sudbury and Woodbridge
E. 84,286
556*K. M. Stainton, C..... 30,049
R. E. Russell, Lab.... 17,986
N. S. Lewis, L....... 15,206
  C. maj............ 12,063
(Feb. '74, C. maj. 13,701)

Sunderland
NORTH E. 75,577
557*Rt. Hon. F. T. Willey,
  Lab.............. 29,618
J. D. S. Brown, C.... 13,947
J. A. Lennox, L....... 7,077
  Lab. maj........... 15,671
(Feb. '74, Lab. maj. 11,400)

SOUTH E. 76,479
558*G. A. T. Bagier, Lab.. 28,623
Sir J. C. Buchanan-
  Riddell, Bt., C..... 15,593
W. J. Nicholson, L... 7,828
  Lab. maj........... 13,030
(Feb. '74, Lab. maj. 8,596)

Surbiton
E. 46,073
559*Sir N. T. L. Fisher,
  M.C., C........... 15,330
A. S. Mackinlay, Lab. 9,309
D. A. S. Brooke, L... 8,931
  C. maj............ 6,021
(Feb. '74, C. maj. 6,500)

Surrey
EAST E. 55,673
560*Rt. Hon. Sir R. E. G.
  Howe, Q.C., C...... 22,227
K. S. Vaus, L....... 12,382
D. L. Allonby, Lab... 7,797
  C. maj............ 9,845
(Feb. '74, C. maj. 8,019)

NORTH WEST E. 68,928
561*W. M. J. Grylls, C... 25,524
P. F. Whiteley, Lab... 11,943
L. E. Sims, L........ 11,356
  C. maj............ 13,581
(Feb. '74, C. maj. 14,949)

Sussex, Mid
E. 61,074
562*R. T. Renton, C...... 25,126
R. A. Symes-
  Schutzman, L...... 13,129
Miss M. R. Fraser,
  Lab.............. 8,404
  C. maj............ 11,997
(Feb. '74, C. maj. 12,155)

Sutton and Cheam
E. 60,559
563*D. N. MacFarlane, C.. 22,156
G. N. Tope, L....... 16,995
J. K. Rhodes, Lab.... 7,118
Dr. Una Kroll, Ind... 298
  C. maj............ 5,161
(Feb. '74, C. maj. 1,719)

Sutton Coldfield
E. 60,491
564*P. N. Fowler, C...... 25,729
Sir J. A. Watson, Bt.,
  L................ 12,373
G. W. Wells, Lab.... 6,955
  C. maj............ 13,356
(Feb. '74, C. maj. 13,426)

Swansea
EAST E. 58,780
565 D. Anderson, Lab...... 26,735
D. J. Mercer, C...... 6,014
R. H. Anstey, L...... 5,173
J. G. Ball, P.C....... 3,978
  Lab. maj........... 20,721
(Feb. '74, Lab. maj. 19,687)

WEST. E, 65,225
566*A. J. Williams, Lab... 22,565
A. P. Thomas, C..... 17,729
B. E. Keal, L........ 6,842
G. ap Gwent, P.C.... 1,778
  Lab. maj........... 4,836
(Feb. '74, Lab. maj. 3,338)

Swindon
E. 62,900
567*D. L. Stoddart, Lab.... 24,124
J. N. Gripper, C...... 13,854
R. Hubbard, L....... 8,349
Mrs. K. B. Blakeney,
  Ind.............. 206
  Lab. maj........... 10,270
(Feb. '74, Lab. maj. 8,709)

Taunton
E. 63,654
568*Rt. Hon. E. D. L. du
  Cann, C........... 22,542
B. J. Sheerman, Lab... 15,721
M. E. Mann, L....... 11,984
L. D. Bradford, Ind... 283
  C. maj............ 6,821
(Feb. '74, C. maj. 8,440)

Thanet
EAST E. 47,941
569*J. W. P. Aitken, C..... 15,813
Mrs. S. M. Bartlett,
  Lab.............. 11,310
C. Hogarth, L....... 6,472
K. Munson, Nat. Front 708
  C. maj............ 4,503
(Feb. '74, C. maj. 6,597)

WEST E. 43,901
570*W. R. Rees-Davies,
  Q.C., C............ 13,763
  C. J. Smith, *Lab.*..... 8,655
  I. G. Tiltman, *L*..... 7,935
  C. maj............. 5,108
  (Feb. '74, C. maj. 7,660)

Thirsk and Malton
E. 63,856
571*J. D. Spence, C........ 24,779
  R. Kent, *L*......... 10,917
  R. K. Illingworth,
    Lab.............. 10,842
  C. maj............ 13,862
  (Feb. '74, C. maj. 14,408)

Thornaby
E. 62,330
572*I. W. Wrigglesworth,
  Lab............... 22,130
  J. H. V. Sutcliffe, C.... 17,482
  R. F. Tennant, *L*..... 5,442
  Lab. maj.......... 4,648
  (Feb. '74, Lab. maj. 1,718)

Thurrock
E. 89,448
573*H. J. Delargy, *Lab.*... 34,066
  P. W. C. Lomax, C... 14,986
  A. Charlton, *L*...... 12,255
  Lab. maj.......... 19,080
  (By-election, July 15, 1976)
  Miss O. A. McDonald,
    Ph.D., *Lab.*..... 22,191
  P. W. C. Lomax, C... 17,352
  A. Charlton, *L*...... 5,977
  J. Roberts, *Nat. Front* . 3,255
  F. Hansford-Miller,
    Ind.............. 187
  P. Bishop, *Ind*....... 72
  Lab. maj......... 4,839
  (Feb. '74, Lab. maj. 18,518)

Tiverton
E. 69,884
574*R. J. Maxwell-
  Hyslop, C.......... 25,265
  F. J. Suter, *L*....... 19,911
  M. Phillips, *Lab.*..... 8,946
  C. maj........... 5,354
  (Feb. '74, C. maj. 5,541)

Tonbridge and Malling
E. 65,589
575*J. P. Stanley, C....... 23,188
  Mrs. P. Knight, *Lab.*.. 14,579
  M. J. B. Vann, *L*..... 11,767
  C. maj........... 8,609
  (Feb. '74, C. maj. 10,108)

Tooting
E. 53,793
576*T. M. Cox, *Lab.*..... 18,530
  A. C. Elliot, C....... 10,675
  R. F. J. Heron, *L*..... 4,644
  R. E. Lewis, *Comm*.... 268
  Lab. maj.......... 7,855
  (Feb. '74, Lab. maj. 6,108)

Torbay
E. 85,575
577*Sir F. M. Bennett, C... 30,208
  J. M. Goss, *L*....... 17,770
  J. R. W. Tench, *Lab.*.. 14,441
  C. maj........... 12,438
  (Feb. '74, C. maj. 12,408)

Totnes
E. 80,715
578*R. L. Mawby, C...... 27,987
  A. H. Rogers, *Lab.*... 21,586
  Mrs. S. M. Spence,
    Lab............... 12,366
  C. maj............ 6,401
  (Feb. '74, C. maj. 9,643)

Tottenham
E. 47,530
579*N. Atkinson, *Lab.*..... 15,708
  P. Lilley, C......... 6,492
  Miss K. Alexander, *L*. 2,288
  R. W. Painter, *Nat.*
    Front............ 2,211
  Lab. maj.......... 9,216
  (Feb. '74, Lab. maj. 9,126)

Truro
E. 71,992
580 D. C. Penhaligon, *L*... 22,549
  P. J. S. Dixon, C..... 22,085
  A. F. Long, *Lab.*..... 11,606
  J. C. A. Whetter, *Ind.* 384
  L. maj............ 464
  (Feb. '74, C. maj. 2,561)

Tunbridge Wells
E. 69,138
581*P. B. B. Mayhew, Q.C.,
  C................. 24,829
  D. C. Owens, *L*...... 12,802
  R. C. Blackwell, *Lab.* 12,499
  C. maj........... 12,027
  (Feb. '74, C. maj. 11,028)

Twickenham
E. 72,210
582*T. F. H. Jessel, C...... 24,959
  Mrs. M. Cunningham,
    Lab.............. 15,452
  S. E. Kramer, *L*..... 13,021
  W. Burgess, *Ind*..... 287
  C. maj............ 9,507
  (Feb. '74, C. maj. 11,503)

Tynemouth
E. 76,449
583*N. G. Trotter, C...... 24,510
  J. E. Miller, *Lab.*.... 21,389
  R. S. Turner, *L*...... 10,895
  C. maj............ 3,121
  (Feb. '74, C. maj. 6,387)

Ulster, Mid
E. 81,689
584*J. Dunlop, U.U.U..... 30,552
  I. A. Cooper, S.D.L.P. 25,885
  F. Donnelly, *Rep*..... 8,091
  U.U.U. maj........ 4,667
  (Feb. '74, U.U.U. maj. 6,632)

Upminster
E. 64,429
585*J. W. Loveridge, C.... 20,966
  J. E. D. Whysall, *Lab.* 20,272
  A. Merton, *L*....... 7,844
  C. maj............ 694
  (Feb. '74, C. maj. 1,008)

Uxbridge
E. 59,746
586*J. M. Shersby, C...... 19,969
  G. E. Pringle, *Lab.*.. 17,816
  J. S. Pincham, *L*..... 7,081
  C. maj............ 2,153
  (Feb. '74, C. maj. 2,415)

Vauxhall
E. 46,502
587*Rt. Hon. G. R. Strauss,
  Lab.............. 15,493
  V. J. MacColl, C..... 5,727
  E. F. Cousins, *L*..... 3,300
  Lab. maj.......... 9,766
  (Feb. '74, Lab. maj. 8,641)

Wakefield
E. 66,535
588*W. Harrison, *Lab.*.... 25,616
  E. J. L. Koops, C.... 12,810
  A. Fussey, *L*........ 8,304
  Lab. maj......... 12,806
  (Feb. '74, Lab. maj. 11,418)

Wallasey
E. 70,095
589*Mrs. L. Chalker, C.... 23,499
  G. McNamara, *Lab.*.. 21,529
  P. E. Tyrer, *L*....... 7,643
  J. Fishwick, *Nat. Front* 787
  C. maj............ 1,970
  (Feb. '74, C. maj. 2,492)

Wallsend
E. 90,300
590*W. E. Garrett, *Lab.*... 37,180
  Miss J. F. Chambers,
    C................. 15,911
  P. Hampton, *L*...... 10,453
  K. Flynn, *Ind*...... 435
  Lab. maj......... 21,269
  (Feb. '74, Lab. maj. 17,247)

Walsall
NORTH E. 71,525
591*Rt. Hon. J. T. Stone-
  house, *Lab*......... 28,340
  R. G. Hodgson, C.... 12,455
  W. Gill, *L*......... 6,377
  J. Richards, *Comm*.... 465
  Lab. maj.......... 15,885
  (Feb. '74, Lab. maj. 14,704)
  (By-election pending)

SOUTH E. 59,241
592*B. T. George, *Lab*..... 20,917
  H. Smith, O.B.E., C... 16,255
  G. F. A. Hooper, *L*... 5,031
  J. C. Parker, *Nat.*
    Front............ 1,226
  T. L. Keen, *Ind*..... 150
  Lab. maj.......... 4,662
  (Feb. '74, Lab. maj. 1,580)

Walthamstow
E. 52,280
593*E. P. Deakins, *Lab.*... 19,088
  D. Arnold, C........ 8,424
  M. P. O'Flanagan, *L*.. 5,199
  R. Adde, *Nat. Front*.. 1,911
  Lab. maj.......... 10,664
  (Feb. '74, Lab. maj. 8,734)

Wanstead and Woodford
E. 58,378
594*Rt. Hon. C. P. F.
  Jenkin, C.......... 21,209
  R. Darlington, *Lab.*.. 10,369
  D. J. Gilby, *L*....... 8,272
  C. maj............ 10,840
  (Feb. '74, C. maj. 11,901)

Warley
EAST E. 57,530
595*A. M. W. Faulds, *Lab.* 21,065
  P. Holliday, C....... 12,888
  R. Smith, *L*........ 4,664
  Lab. maj.......... 8,177
  (Feb. '74, Lab. maj. 7,571)

WEST E. 61,274
596*P. K. Archer, Q.C., *Lab.* 24,761
R. Evans, *C.* 9,904
D. Owen, *L.* 6,363
Lab. maj. 14,857
(Feb. '74, Lab. maj. 14,624)

Warrington
E. 46,549
597*Sir W. T. Williams,
Q.C., *Lab.* 19,882
J. W. Hayton, *C.* 7,621
F. J. Deakin, *L.* 4,158
Lab. maj 12,261
(Feb. '74, Lab. maj. 11,106)

Warwick and Leamington
E. 78,666
598*D. G. Smith, *C.* 27,721
J. W. England, *Lab.* .. 19,476
T. A. Jones, *L.* 11,625
C. maj. 8,245
(Feb. '74, C. maj. 11,293)

Watford
E. 56,010
599*R. H. Tuck, *Lab.* 19,177
T. W. A. Garel-Jones,
C. 15,220
D. A. Jacobs, *L.* 8,243
J. E. Wotherspoon,
Nat. Front 671
Lab. maj. 3,957
(Feb. '74, Lab. maj. 2,795)

Wellingborough
E. 85,288
600*P. D. Fry, *C.* 29,078
J. H. Mann, *Lab.* 27,320
Mrs. P. Jessel, *L.* 11,500
C. maj. 1,758
(Feb. '74, C. maj. 2,270)

Wells
E. 69,658
601*Hon. R. T. Boscawen,
M.C., *C.* 23,979
A. A. S. Butt-Philip,
L. 16,278
G. Mortimer, *Lab.* 13,909
Miss P. Howard, *Ind.* .. 778
C. maj. 7,701
(Feb. '74, C. maj. 7,785)

Welwyn and Hatfield
E. 67,149
602 Mrs. H. V. H. Hayman,
Lab. 23,339
*Rt. Hon. Lord
Balniel, *C.* 22,819
P. H. Robinson, *L.* 8,418
Lab. maj. 520
(Feb. '74, Lab. maj. 1,415)

West Bromwich
EAST E. 58,400
603*P. C. Snape, *Lab.* 19,942
D. Mellor, *C.* 12,413
J. P. T. Hunt, *L.* 5,442
G. Bowen, *Nat. Front* 1,692
Lab. maj. 7,529
(Feb. '74, Lab. maj. 5,209)
WEST E. 59,749
604*Miss B. Boothroyd, *Lab.* 23,336
J. N. W. Bridges-
Adams, *C.* 8,537
D. J. Corney, *L.* 3,619
R. Churms, *Nat. Front* 2,022
Lab. maj. 14,799
(Feb. '74, Lab. maj. 13,431)

Westbury
E. 73,592
605*D. M. Walters, M.B.E.,
C. 24,172
A. W. G. Court, *L.* .. 18,129
A. J. Smith, *Lab.* 15,613
C. maj. 6,043
(Feb. '74, C. maj. 8,419)

Western Isles
E. 22,477
606*D. J. Stewart, *Scot.*
Nat. 8,758
Mrs. M. Doig, *Lab.* .. 3,526
N. K. Wilson, *C.* 1,180
N. MacMillan, *L.* 789
Scot. Nat. maj. 5,232
(Feb. '74, Scot. Nat. maj. 7,200)

Westhoughton
E. 72,055
607*R. W. Stott, *Lab.* 30,373
B. H. Tetlow, *C.* 16,798
R. S. Hale, *L.* 8,926
Lab. maj. 13,575
(Feb. '74, Lab. maj. 12,665)

West Lothian
E. 77,526
608*T. Dalyell, *Lab.* 27,687
W. C. Wolfe, *Scot.*
Nat. 24,997
A. H. Lester, *C.* 6,086
H. MacAulay, *L.* 2,083
C. Bett, *Comm.* 247
Lab. maj. 2,690
(Feb. '74, Lab. maj. 6,422)

Westmorland
E. 55,880
609*T. M. Jopling, *C.* 20,559
B. N. Wates, *L.* 12,844
M. Taylor, *Lab.* 7,028
C. maj. 7,715
(Feb. '74, C. maj. 6,534)

Weston-super-Mare
E. 84,988
610*A. W. Wiggin, *C.* 31,028
R. S. Miller, *L.* 18,169
P. H. Owen, *Lab.* 14,057
E. P. Iszatt, *Ind.* 296
C. maj. 12,859
(Feb. '74, C. maj. 13,601)

Whitehaven
E. 50,964
611*J. A. Cunningham, *Lab.* 21,832
P. B. Vose, *C.* 11,899
M. Gilbert, *L.* 5,563
Lab. maj. 9,933
(Feb. '74, Lab. maj. 7,362)

Widnes
E. 75,141
612*G. J. Oakes, *Lab.* 31,532
A. H. K. Maynard, *C.* 14,661
A. Turner, *L.* 7,067
Lab. maj. 16,871
(Feb. '74, Lab. maj. 16,499)

Wigan
E. 56,915
613*E. A. Fitch, *Lab.* 27,692
P. M. Beard, *C.* 8,865
J. Campbell, *L.* 5,548
Lab. maj. 18,827
(Feb. '74, Lab. maj. 18,202)

Wimbledon
E. 70,726
614*Sir R. M. O. Havers,
Q.C., *C.* 23,615
K. Bill, *Lab.* 14,909
K. N. Searby, *L.* 10,133
C. maj. 8,706
(Feb. '74, C. maj. 12,213)

Winchester
E. 82,790
615*Rear Adm. M. C. M.
Giles, D.S.O., O.B.E.,
G.M., *C.* 27,671
J. W. Matthew, *L.* ... 18,451
W. H. Allchin, *Lab.* .. 16,153
C. maj. 9,220
(Feb. '74, C. maj. 10,504)

Windsor and Maidenhead
E. 79,703
616*A. J. Glyn, E.R.D., *C.* .. 28,013
M. D. Golder, *Lab.* ... 15,172
G. H. Kahan, *L.* 14,022
C. maj. 12,841
(Feb. '74, C. maj. 14,995)

Wirral
E. 93,135
617*Rt. Hon. J. S. B. Lloyd,
C.H., C.B.E., T.D.,
Q.C., *The Speaker* ... 35,705
P. R. Thomas, *Lab.* ... 22,217
M. R. D. Gayford, *L.* 12,345
The Speaker's maj. ... 13,488
(By-election, March 11, 1976)
D. J. F. Hunt, *C.* 34,675
A. E. Bailey, *Lab.* 10,563
M. R. D. Gayford, *L.* 5,914
F. Hansford-Miller,
Ind. 466
H. Jones, *Ind.* 307
C. maj. 24,112
(Feb. '74, The Speaker's maj. 15,847)

Woking
E. 67,916
618*C. G. D. Onslow, *C.* .. 22,804
P. Wade, *L.* 14,069
J. W. Tattersall, *Lab.* .. 11,737
R. Vaughan-Smith,
Nat. Front 921
C. maj. 8,735
(Feb. '74, C. maj. 7,583)

Wokingham
E. 73,598
619*W. R. van Straubenzee,
M.B.E., *C.* 24,009
R. W. Crew, *Lab.* ... 16,304
T. Blyth, *L.* 15,329
C. maj. 7,705
(Feb. '74, C. maj. 10,432)

Wolverhampton
NORTH EAST E. 69,513
620*Mrs. R. Short, *Lab.* ... 25,788
P. W. Hawksley, *C.* .. 11,135
J. F. Porter, *L.* 7,156
A. D. C. Webber, *Nat.*
Front 1,928
Lab. maj. 14,653
(Feb. '74, Lab. maj. 12,617)

SOUTH EAST E. 55,382
621*R. J. Edwards, Lab... 21,466
  Mrs. E. J. Holt, C.... 9,768
  B. Norcott, L....... 3,636
  G. Oldland, Nat. Front 1,703
   Lab. maj........... 11,698
  (Feb. '74, Lab. maj. 10,905)
SOUTH WEST E. 64,075
622*N. W. Budgen, C..... 20,854
  I. E. Geffen, Lab..... 15,554
  J. Wernick, L....... 9,215
  G. A. Cooper, Nat.
   Front............. 1,573
   C. maj.......... 5,300
  (Feb. '74, C. maj. 6,901)

Wood Green
E. 52,019
623*Mrs. J. S. Butler, Lab.. 16,605
  T. Benyon, C...... 8,394
  M. J. Walton, L..... 4,782
  K. Squires, Nat. Front. 2,603
   Lab. maj......... 8,211
  (Feb. '74, Lab. maj. 7,644)

Woolwich
EAST E. 50,998
624 J. C. Cartwright, Lab.. 19,812
  B. H. Watson, C..... 7,387
  D. J. Woodhead, L... 4,638
  M. Skeggs, Nat. Front 1,000
   Lab. maj.......... 12,425
  (Feb. '74, Lab. maj. 11,977)
WEST E. 56,368
625*W. Hamling, Lab..... 19,614
  P. J. Bottomley, C... 16,073
  J. P. Johnson, L...... 5,962
   Lab. maj........... 3,541
  (By-election, June 26,
   1975)
  P. J. Bottomley, C.... 17,280
  J. Stanyer, Lab..... 14,898
  Mrs. S. M. Hobday, L. 1,884
  Mrs. R. Robinson,
   Nat. Front.........   856
  R. Mallone, Ind......   218
  F. Hansford-Miller,
   Ind...............   140
  R. Simmerson, Ind...   104
  P. Bishop, Ind......   41
   C. maj............ 2,382
  (Feb. '74, Lab. maj. 2,436)

Worcester
E. 74,844
626*Rt. Hon. P. E. Walker,
   M.B.E., C........ 25,183
  Rev. W. B. Morgan,
   Lab............. 20,194
  Mrs. D. Elliott, L..... 9,888
   C. maj.......... 4,989
  (Feb. '74, C. maj. 7,467)

Worcestershire South
E. 73,695
627*W. M. H. Spicer, C... 26,790
  J. P. Birch, L........ 17,738
  S. J. Randall, Lab..... 10,838
   C. maj........... 9,052
  (Feb. '74, C. maj. 7,165)

Workington
E. 53,114
628*Rt. Hon. T. F. Peart,
   Lab.............. 22,539
  R. L. Page, C........ 12,988
  Mrs. J. Burns, L...... 4,728
   Lab. maj......... 9,551
  (Feb. '74, Lab. maj. 7,770)

Worthing
E. 72,594
629*T. L. Higgins, C...... 30,036
  M. H. C. Foley, L..... 12,691
  M. W. J. Neves, Lab.. 8,890
   C. maj........... 17,345
  (Feb. '74, C. maj. 18,930)

Wrekin, The
E. 82,659
630*G. T. Fowler, Lab.... 30,385
  P. Banks, C........ 23,547
  W. Dewsnip, L....... 8,442
   Lab. maj.......... 6,838
  (Feb. '74, Lab. maj. 6,521)

Wrexham
E. 76,106
631*R. T. Ellis, Lab...... 28,885
  D. M. Thomas, L.... 12,519
  J. L. Pritchard, C..... 12,251
  H. W. Roberts, P.C.. 2,859
   Lab. maj.......... 16,366
  (Feb. '74, Lab. maj. 13,083)

Wycombe
E. 78,832
632*Sir J. Hall, O.B.E., T.D.,
   C............... 27,131
  W. F. Back, Lab...... 18,052
  M. T. James, L...... 11,333
  D. H. Smith, Nat.
   Front............. 2,049
   C. maj........... 9,079
  (Feb. '74, C. maj. 10,699)

Yarmouth
E. 70,802
633*A. Fell, C......... 22,573
  Mrs. P. L. Hollis, Lab. 20,313
  P. R. Coleby, L...... 9,250
   C. maj........... 2,260
  (Feb. '74, C. maj. 4,937)

Yeovil
E. 75,159
634*Rt. Hon. J. W. W.
   Peyton, C........ 24,709
  M. T. McVicar, Lab.. 17,330
  G. F. Taylor, L...... 17,298
  J. E. Tippett, Ind.....   332
   C. maj........... 7,379
  (Feb. '74, C. maj. 7,490)

York
E. 77,172
635*A. W. Lyon, Lab...... 26,983
  J. G. B. Watson, C... 23,294
  Miss E. Graham, L.... 7,370
  H. Smith, Ind.......   304
  H. L. Stratton, Ind....   171
   Lab. maj.......... 3,689
  (Feb. '74, Lab. maj. 831)

SMALL MAJORITIES

The smallest majorities at the election of October 1974 were as follows:

Mrs. M. A. Bain (Scot. Nat.), Dunbartonshire East	22
G. H. Thompson (Scot. Nat.), Galloway	30
Miss J. E. Fookes (C.), Plymouth, Drake	34
N. H. Fairbairn (C.), Kinross and West Perthshire	53
A. J. Beith (L.), Berwick on Tweed	73
J. Ryman (Lab.), Blyth	78
J. T. Lester (C.), Beeston	121
M. W. L. Morris (C.), Northampton, South	141
J. E. M. Moore (C.), Croydon, Central	164
M. A. Noble (Lab.), Rossendale	203
B. J. Hayhoe (C.), Brentford and Chiswick	232
Hon. A. C. Butler (C.), Bosworth	302
T. Litterick (Lab.), Selly Oak	326
B. J. Grocott (Lab.), Litchfield and Tamworth	331
I. M. Sproat (C.), Aberdeen, South	365
D. A. Canavan (Lab.), Stirlingshire, West	367
Mrs. W. M. Ewing (Scot. Nat.), Moray and Nairn	367
J. T. Watkinson (Lab.), Gloucestershire, West	409
F. R. White (Lab.), Bury and Radcliffe	442
D. C. Penhaligon (L.), Truro	464
R. A. B. Durant (C.), Reading North	468
Sir R. W. Elliott (C.), Newcastle, North	469
R. Corbett (Lab.), Hemel Hempstead	485

WOMEN MEMBERS OF PARLIAMENT

Six new Women Members of Parliament were elected in October 1974. Five were Labour Candidates (Miss M. M. Jackson, Lincoln; Mrs. H. V. H. Hayman, Welwyn and Hatfield; Miss V. J. Maynard, Sheffield, Brightside; Mrs. M. Miller, Ilford, North; Mrs. W. A. Taylor, Bolton, West). The sixth was a Scottish Nationalist, Mrs. M. A. Bain, Dunbartonshire, E.

PARLIAMENTARY SUMMARY, LORDS AND COMMONS, 1975–76

A backlog of business compelled the Government to extend the last session of Parliament which resumed on October 19, 1975, after the summer recess for four weeks and this overspill period enabled all priority legislative work to be cleared for Prorogation on November 12 in readiness for the Royal opening of the new session on November 19.

END OF 1975 SESSION.—The Government's Community Land Bill was given a third reading in the Commons on October 14 by a 15 vote majority. Voting for the Bill, which enabled local authorities to take over and manage development land, was 279 to 264. The Conservative spokesman (Mr. Hugh Rossi) warned that the Tories would ultimately " do away with " the Bill. Moving the third reading Mr. John Silkin attacked the Opposition for party political scaremongering intended not to assist but only to destroy. This kind of propaganda had been used " without any justification."

On October 15, MPs rejected peers' proposals on press freedom under the Trades Union and Labour Relations (Amendment) Bill. In successive votes the Government had substantial majorities for changes to the " Goodman amendment " to the Government's " closed shop " measure. The charter proposals put forward by Lord Goodman were rejected by the Government, who wanted a charter for journalists and editors—but without legal back up powers.

Five days later, on October 20, the issue was again joined over the closed shop and its effect on the news media, with two Government defeats in the Lords. One Labour minister forecast a " ping-pong " match when Mr. Foot's own plan for a code of practice on a voluntary basis was rejected by a vote of 188 to 77, a majority of 111 against the Government. Lord Goodman introduced his revised version of the " Goodman amendment " retaining the idea of a voluntary charter to give practical guidance. Despite Government objections, this was approved by a massive 120 majority —188 to 68.

On October 22, the Commons threw back at the Lords their rejection of part of the Industry Bill which allowed the National Enterprise Board to establish industrial undertakings. By a majority of 12 votes—265 to 253—the Commons disagreed with the Lords' amendment. On another amendment the Government's majority fell to seven. This change to the Bill, made by the Lords, aimed to prevent the National Enterprise Board from extending public ownership into profitable areas of manufacturing.

The Lords agreed to drop their insistence on surcharges and disqualification from office for councillors who defied the Tory Housing Finance Act by refusing to raise rents. As peers debated Commons reasons for rejecting their amendments to the Housing Finance Special Provisions Bill, which indemnified 400 " rebel " councillors, there were warnings about the threat to democracy contained in such legislation. The 400 councillors were not criminals who sought financial gain, but people who, technically, had not observed the law, said the Leader of the House (Lord Shepherd). He said the Lords' new clause could be looked upon as exacting punishment, but the Government's approach was to give a local community a second chance. Unlike the Clay Cross councillors these 400 had eventually complied with the law. Lord Hailsham declared that the Bill passed responsibility for the financial consequences of councillors' misdeeds to the ratepayers instead of the rent payers who had gained by those misdeeds. That struck at the very roots of democracy and the rule of law. Lord Wigoder, Liberal spokesman on

Home Affairs, said, in the circumstances it might be well to write finis to " this unhappy Bill and to one of the sorrier chapters in British Parliamentary history." The Leader of the Opposition (Lord Carrington) warned that if a feeling grew up in the country that Acts of Parliament could be disregarded because they had been passed by one's political opponents and one did not like them, the consequence would be that no orderly Government would be possible in Britain.

An Opposition move to overturn government regulations ending direct grants to grammar schools was defeated in the Commons on October 27 by 292 votes to 249—government majority 43. The abolition of direct grant schools would mean some sort of political victory for the government, but a major defeat for education, the shadow education secretary (Mr. Norman St. John-Stevas) declared. He warned that the Government's policy would be a major setback to the cause of maintaining and raising the quality of education at a time when there had never been greater anxiety among parents and teachers about what the educational system was achieving, and where it was heading. Mr. St. John-Stevas said that the next Conservative government would re-open the direct grant school list, and restore these schools on a statutory basis so that they were safeguarded. Mr. Mulley said that when a system of non-selective education for secondary education was being devised it was not sensible to provide for the direct grant schools, which were a particular form of grammar school.

On October 27, in an acrimonious debate, the Government fought off an Opposition attack on the social services secretary (Mrs. Castle) by a move to cut her £13,000 salary in half. This was defeated by 287 votes to 267. The shadow social services secretary (Mr. Norman Fowler) pin-pointed Mrs. Castle's pay beds policy as being at the heart of the dispute with the medical profession. He was accused by Mrs. Castle of being a " contemptible coward " for not condemning the doctors' action as a breach of the £6 pay limit. After protests about unparliamentary language, Mrs. Castle substituted the term " unattractive timidity." Mrs. Castle attacked an " orchestrated " press campaign about the collapse of the health service. Winding up for the Opposition, Dr. Gerard Vaughan (C), said that there was outstanding evidence of mismanagement in the health service, but the Minister of State, Health and Social Services (Dr. David Owen) accused the Opposition spokesman of having " led a petty, personalised propagandising attack on Mrs. Castle."

The Lords rose shortly before 8 a.m. on October 29 after nearly 17 hours detailed consideration of the controversial Community Land Bill. The sitting was the longest since May, 1971. Peers were faced with more than 270 amendments to the Bill which empowered council take-over of development land. Most of the sitting dealt with technical changes, but of the series of Government defeats during the night several restricted take-over powers or forced concessions. A series of Government amendments made clear that owners of plots of land up to one acre in areas scheduled for development need not notify the local authority of an intention to sell.

Both Houses of Parliament approved on October 31 the continuation of sanctions against Rhodesia for another year—the 11th since they were first imposed. The official Opposition, though critical of both the principle and effectiveness of sanctions did not oppose the decision, arguing that to do so would disrupt the present delicate balance in southern Africa which it was felt could lead to a peaceful settlement.

Peers challenged the Government on November 3 by carrying an amendment putting the power of the courts behind a Press freedom Charter. The amendment, carried by 162 votes to 73, a government defeat by 89 votes, was moved by Lord Hailsham and laid down that any decision should be enforceable in the same way as an award resulting from an arbitration agreement under the Arbitration Act. Opposing, Lord Elwyn-Jones said: " The Government are concerned with setting up a body within the newspaper industry which will overlook the terms of the charter and see it is lived with in the industry". The amendment could " wreck the running of Fleet Street and would damage the Press itself by its implications and consequences." The report of the Royal Commission on the Press, which would have the opportunity to study all the factors affecting Press freedom far more fully than had been possible within the context of this Bill, should be awaited. The Government was again defeated on an amendment by Lord Goodman that any breach of the charter should be deemed contrary to public policy, and that nothing in the charter should be taken as restricting any right in statute or common law. This was approved by 138 to 58, a majority against the Government of 80. It was moved as an addition to a Commons amendment which had made the charter admissible in evidence, before tribunals or courts in which its provisions were relevant. The Commons amendment in the changed form was then approved. The Lords' vote meant the Bill was dead in that session of Parliament.

On November 4 peers forced a further major exemption for charity land from the provisions of the Government's Community Land Bill. They carried by 154 votes to 55—majority against the Government 99—an amendment which would remove the duty of a local authority to take over development land acquired by churches and charities. The exemption was already extended for such land owned before September 12, 1974. Moving the amendment, the Bishop of London, Dr. Gerald Ellison, had described Government concessions to the churches and charities as " meagre and dry crumbs ". Dr. Ellison said the amendment meant that, although local authorities would still have a power to acquire such land as was necessary in the exercise of their ordinary statutory powers, they would not be under a duty to do so. Dr. Ellison rejected the Government's contention at an earlier stage of the Bill that this amendment would lead to the establishment of a particularly privileged class of landowners. The Bill was taking away from the churches and charities the means of doing their work. For four centuries charity land had been protected by law. There were two Government defeats over further concessions to churches and charities. A Government amendment setting out the conditions on which the cessation of prevailing use value would apply after the appointed day was defeated by 128 votes to 60 (majority 68 votes). Then an amendment moved by the Bishop of London which set out alternative conditions for compensation for the sale of charity land was carried by 127 votes to 59 (majority 68). The fourth Government defeat of the day came when an amendment from Lord Colville, to

exclude a development consisting of a single house, was approved by 118 votes to 50 (majority 68). Lord Colville said that because of changes in the Bill such a plot came within its ambit. The Government was also defeated on an Opposition amendment which sought to define land which Councils could acquire under the Bill as " development land ". Voting was 47 to 18—a majority against the Government of 29.

Government regulations compelling motorists to use headlights at night in town and country were withdrawn in the Commons on November 5 by Transport Minister, Dr. John Gilbert, who had been under fire on the count that there had been insufficient consultations before the change making head lamp use mandatory would have come into force, and use of head lamps in built-up, well lit towns and cities could prove a safety hazard and could lead to dazzle accidents to motorists and pedestrians. Dr. Gilbert, in the late night Commons debate, still favoured the dipped head lights scheme and told MPs that the Transport Road Research Laboratory supported the adoption of mandatory dipped headlights everywhere, in advance of a better system. But he said that he recognised that MPs would prefer further discussions. He promised further talks with interested parties and said that he hoped to bring the regulations back early in the next session.

The Commons on November 5 rejected a Lords bid to prevent the Government using its North Sea oil licensing powers to achieve a State stake in oil operations. They reversed a Lords amendment to the Petroleum and Sub-marine Pipelines Bill by 272 votes to 228, a Government majority of 44. Mr. Anthony Wedgwood Benn had said that the amendment would have prevented the Government implementing a policy which lay at the heart of its objectives. But his Opposition "shadow", Mr. Patrick Jenkin, alleged: " The suspicion has grown up that the Government is using its powers to blackmail the firms into surrendering 51 per cent. to the BNOC. It is absolute nonsense to regard these as voluntary negotiations." Mr. Jenkin protested: " No single act of the Government is doing greater damage to our offshore prospects than this continuing demand for 51 per cent. participation."

On November 10, the Northern Ireland Secretary, Mr. Merlyn Rees, told MPs that he had received the report of the Northern Ireland Constitutional Convention. He did not elaborate on details of the report, but he stressed: " The British Army is under the control of this Parliament only, and the sovereignty of the Queen in the Parliament of the U.K. rests also at Westminster." During questions following his statement, Mr. Rees said that the Government and Parliament would examine the report carefully, and added: " Meanwhile Northern Ireland will continue to be governed by and from this Parliament." Mr. Rees said that until Parliament decided otherwise, all functions of Government would be exercised by him (Mr. Rees) with the help of other Ministers. The report would be published as soon as possible in the new session of Parliament. " I wish to make it clear again that the Convention is not—cannot be —an advisory body to me," he said. No decision had been taken whether or not to recall it for its constitutional purposes. The report dealt with a number of fundamental issues affecting the future government of Northern Ireland, including the form of that government, its powers and functions, its legal authority, questions of constitutional rights, and its relationship with Parliament. It also covered financial assistance and taxation and responsibility for law and order and the use of the

Army. The Opposition front bench spokesman on Northern Ireland, Mr. Airey Neave, welcomed Mr. Rees's comments on the control of the Army and the sovereignty of the Queen, adding " this is undeniable, and has full support on this side of the House." Mr. James Molyneux (U.U.U.,) said that the future structure of the Government in Northern Ireland could not meaningfully be considered in isolation from forthcoming discussions on devolution in the U.K. as a whole. Amid cheers, Mr. Alan Beith (L.) declared that anyone who thought the Commons would be intimidated by violence against its members, or the British public in general, was sadly mistaken.

Peers opposed to the Government on the " press freedom " issue were told by the Leader of the House, Lord Shepherd, on November 11, that the Government would invoke the Parliament Act to get its proposals through. Despite a last minute bid by Lord Goodman for agreement in overnight talks, the warning came as peers debated the Commons rejection of changes to the Trade Union and Labour Relations (Amendment) Bill. Lord Shepherd said that it was a time for reconciliation not confrontation. " To force a clash between the two Houses of Parliament could place the growing cooperation which has developed between us in the gravest jeopardy." Describing his late night talks with the Government Lord Goodman (Ind.) said that the breakdown of negotiations had stemmed from the Government's refusal to accept that the charter should include provisions setting out rights of journalists not to be arbitrarily or unreasonably excluded or expelled from a trade union. " If the Government decide to make a constitutional issue on this matter, the fault is theirs." The Liberal leader, Lord Byers advised peers not to be put off by threats from the House of Commons. " These are not wrecking tactics. It is a sincere attempt to uphold the protection of a fundamental freedom by bringing it within the law." Peers voted 186 to 86—a majority of 100 against the Government—to reject the Commons alternative proposals on the charter and to retain Lord Goodman's formula. The Opposition did not press its amendment in the name of Lord Hailsham, which would have given the supervisory body the power to award compensation for breaches of the charter. But it insisted by 168 votes to 80, a majority against the Government of 88, on retaining legal backing for the charter.

But the next day, November 12, both Houses of Parliament were informed that the Bill which allowed the closed shop and failed to become law because of the Lords' insistence on a legally backed press charter was to be reintroduced in the next session. There were Commons protests from Conservative and Liberal spokesmen that the peers were not acting undemocratically, although Mr. Michael Foot urged M.P.s to condemn the peers for challenging democracy over their treatment of the Bill. There were Labour cheers when Mr. Foot told M.P.s: " The Lords have intervened and used their residual power to prevent us placing on the Statute Book a measure for which we have a good majority in this House and a mandate at two elections. The Government has every intention of reintroducing this Bill in the next session." Mr. James Prior said that Mr. Foot's statement was " a classic example of misrepresentation and hypocrisy." Expressing similar views in the Lords, the Leader of the Opposition (Lord Carrington) stressed that peers were using rights given them under the 1949 Parliament Act. That made it plain that after a stated period the will of the Commons would prevail.

Parliament finished its session on November 12 on a low key with a Commons debate on Wales before prorogation.

THE QUEEN'S SPEECH

The Queen opened the new session on November 19 and in her speech, setting out the Labour Government's legislative programme, said:

" My Government will maintain their firm support for the United Nations and the principles of its Charter, and for the Commonwealth with its tradition of concern for the equitable distribution of the world's resources and the promotion of mutual international understanding and co-operation. They will vigorously pursue their initiative for better order in world trade in commodities which they launched at the recent meeting of Commonwealth Heads of Government, and which has made an important contribution to subsequent international discussion. They recognize the special needs of the poorest developing countries, and will in particular seek to assist rural development and food production.

" My Government will play] their full part in the European Economic Community, devoting particular attention to the achievement of a common approach to the world's political and economic problems. My Government will also maintain their full support of international efforts to restore economic activity, and to reduce inflation and imbalances of payments. They intend to ratify the Organization for Economic Co-operation and Development Financial Support Fund Agreement.

" My Government will continue to work for international agreement on general disarmament and on preventing the spread of nuclear weapons. They will sustain their support for the North Atlantic Alliance as an instrument of *détente* as well as defence, fostering the fullest possible co-operation amongst its members, not least in the procurement of defence equipment. They will continue to play their full part in the negotiations on force reductions in Central Europe.

" My Ministers will continue also to place great value on further *détente* between East and West, including the strengthening of economic links, and on full implementation of the Final Act of the Conference on Security and Co-operation in Europe. My Ministers will continue to support the search for a comprehensive peace settlement in the Middle East, and to develop our ties with the countries of the area. They will continue to co-operate in seeking a lasting settlement in Cyprus.

" My Government will actively protect the interests of the fishing industry and will play their full part in international conservation measures and in the development of the Common Fisheries Policy. They are seeking renewed arrangements for British fishing with the Government of Iceland to replace those which have just expired.

" My Government will continue to strive for a constitutional solution to the problems of Northern Ireland. They will maintain determined efforts to eliminate terrorism, and attach particular importance to dealing through the courts with all those responsible for violence. A Bill to promote equality of opportunity in employment between people of different religious beliefs will be reintroduced, and legislative provision will be made to assist industrial development by enlarging the role of the Northern Ireland Finance Corporation.

" My Government will continue to give the highest priority to the attack on inflation and unemployment. Success for the wide range of anti-

inflation measures introduced in July is essential for the future health of our economy and our society. In particular, success in these measures is required for the achievement of a satisfactory level of productive investment and to assist in the reduction of the present unacceptable level of unemployment. It is also a necessary condition for the fulfilment of many of My Government's other economic and social objectives. The present price controls will continue to be vigorously enforced, and the programme of price display and unit pricing will be accelerated. A programme of price stabilization of more essential goods will be introduced once cost increases decline. My Ministers will continue to work closely with the Trades Union Congress, the Confederation of British Industry and with the British people as a whole on a continuing programme to control domestic inflation and to prevent its resurgence.

" The National Enterprise Board and the Scottish and Welsh Development Agencies will be major instruments in My Government's policy of industrial regeneration. My Government will also embark on a series of Planning Agreements with large companies in selected key sectors of industry, as an important step towards the identification and achievement of agreed national objectives. The Bill to bring the aircraft and shipbuilding industries into public ownership will be reintroduced early in the Session.

" Following their review of civil aviation, My Government will present proposals to implement the necessary policy changes. My Government will reintroduce legislation to remove the remaining unsatisfactory features of the Industrial Relations Act 1971.

" My Ministers will continue to encourage the development of industrial democracy in both public and private sectors. Both sides of industry will have full opportunity to express their views to the inquiry, which My Government have announced their intention to establish, to consider how industrial democracy in the private sector can best be extended. A Bill will be introduced to ensure comprehensive employment safeguards for dockworkers.

" My Government will play their full part in the development and improvement of the Common Agricultural Policy and will continue to encourage the maximum economic production of food at home in the interests of producers and consumers. Legislation will be introduced to meet the United Kingdom's obligations under the Agreement on an International Energy Programme; to control energy supplies during any shortage; and to implement energy conservation policies. My Government will continue to seek to secure the orderly development of the United Kingdom's off-shore oil and gas resources in the interests of the nation. They intend to invite applications for further licences for the exploration and development of off-shore oil and gas.

" My Government will bring forward legislative proposals for the establishment of Scottish and Welsh Assemblies to exercise wide governmental responsibilities within the framework of the United Kingdom. Proposals will be put forward for a major review of the practice and procedure of Parliament. An opportunity will be provided to decide on a permanent system for the sound broadcasting of the proceedings of Parliament.

" My Ministers will pursue vigorously their programmes of social reform by legislative and other means, within available resources. They will take energetic action to encourage the provision of more houses in both public and private sectors;

and following from a comprehensive review they will bring forward recommendations for future housing finance policy. Legislation will be brought forward to enable housing to be transferred from New Town Development Corporations and the New Towns Commission to elected local authorities. Legislation for the abolition of the agricultural tied cottage system in England and Wales will be laid before you.

" In furtherance of My Government's comprehensive policy for development land, legislation will be introduced for a development land tax. Legislation will be introduced in the course of the session to phase out private practice from National Health Service hospitals. Consultations will continue on My Government's proposals to strengthen and extend existing powers to regulate nursing homes and hospitals outside the National Health Service. Pensions and other social security benefits will be increased to protect the living standards of the most vulnerable members of the community.

" In education, My Government will seek to consolidate the improvements they have made to statutory school system. Within available resources, they will give priority to children with special needs and to the vocational preparation of young people aged 16 to 19. A Bill will be introduced to require local education authorities in England and Wales who have not already done so to make plans for the abolition of selection in secondary education, and to deal with certain other matters.

" Legislation will be laid before you to extend and improve Post Office banking services, and to reform the Trustee Savings Banks and enable them to offer a wider range of personal banking services, including personal loans to depositors. A Bill will be introduced to strengthen the law on racial discrimination. Proposals will be prepared to amend the Official Secrets Acts and to liberalise the practice relating to official information. A Bill will be introduced to provide an effective independent element in the procedure for handling complaints by members of the public against the police. My Government will give early consideration to the report, when received, of the Law Commission on the law of conspiracy in England and Wales, with a view to preparing legislation for the comprehensive reform of this branch of the law.

" My Government will persevere with efforts to improve the law and the administration of justice, and will pay continued attention to the need to reduce the number of persons in prison, especially those awaiting trial or sentence. Proposals will be placed before you to provide a Public Lending Right for authors.

Measures will be introduced relating to Scotland, including reforms in the law on crofting and on liquor licensing, and proposals for improving public access to freshwater fishing. A Bill will be introduced to establish a Development Board for Rural Wales."

M.P.s began the new session to warnings from Mr. Wilson of a challenging time for them and a difficult winter for the nation. " Our debates will be dominated by economic realities," he warned. This was the first of five days of debate on the Queen's speech. Dealing with devolution, one of the central issues in a heavy workload, Mr. Wilson promised M.P.s two Bills: one as soon as possible after the White Paper, and if that was not completed, another at the beginning of the next session. Mr. Wilson believed that the House and the country understood that Parliament needed to make the Government's policies effective in human terms, in family terms, in terms of prices in the shops and

household budgets. "To secure success in the anti-inflation policy it is a necessary pre-condition to bring down the present unacceptable level of unemployment, and move towards full employment,' he added. "I believe the nation, which in the previous session has given the Government backing in its policies to master the problems, will continue to look to this House to sustain the Government in its endeavours." Mrs. Margaret Thatcher warned that devolution must not come to mean more government but a dispersal of some powers to areas which should be less remote. On unemployment she hoped government estimates were right that figures would reach a peak of 1·2 million and then level out and reduce. But she wondered whether it was advisable to raise people's hopes falsely, for, with present levels of inflation and our difficulties in borrowing finance for public spending, she feared that the future year would be worse than that one. Attacking "out of control" public spending she said "our record borrowing is now bequeathing to posterity an interest repayment level that will bedevil national finance quite apart from the enormous burden of debt repayment it will put on fnture generations." Mrs. Thatcher also urged "moderate" Labour M.P.s to stand up and be counted "and make sure their will prevails." Mr. Jeremy Thorpe welcomed the Government's encouragement of further discussions on advancing industrial democracy. Mr. Thorpe urged the Government to consider giving grants to local authorities for "certain projects in the national interest." He called for the setting up of a "pre-legislation select committee" to consider devolution. Mr. Douglas Crawford (S.N.P.) described the Government's "backsliding" on the Scottish and Welsh Assemblies as "shocking". "The only way we can stop the appalling economic slide in Scotland is to establish a Scottish assembly with full economic powers," he declared, amid jeers from Labour backbenchers. Mr. Dafydd Wigley (Plaid Cymru) said the news that the Government's constitutional proposals were going to be delayed yet further had shocked the people of Wales. "There will be a day of reckoning when the next general election comes" he warned, and said they would welcome a referendum on the issue, giving all the options.

The five day debate on the Queen's Speech ended on November 25 with a Government majority of 14 on an Opposition amendment attacking the Government's economic policies. The Government's majority dropped to 6 on a Liberal amendment criticizing the inclusion of proposals to extend the areas covered by the National Dock Labour Scheme which, it was claimed, would lead to further unemployment and strangulation of the ports, the vote being 294–288 in favour of the Government. Then Scottish Nationalist M.P.s forced a vote as a protest over what they claimed to be Government delay in setting up an elected Scottish assembly, although technically they voted against a motion to allow a separate vote at the end of the debate on the Liberal amendment. This challenge was peremptorily rejected by 377 votes to 11, a Government majority of 326.

On November 26, the Home Secretary (Mr. Roy Jenkins) rejected any new tough action against I.R.A. terrorism in Britain or security measures which he said could tie up much of the life of the country. In introducing the Government's Prevention of Terrorism (Temporary Provision) Bill which continued the law to combat the bombers and gunmen, by exclusion orders and other methods, Mr. Jenkins did not refer to hanging.

Against the background of strong pressures from Tory M.P.s for the reintroduction of the death sentence for killer terrorists, the Home secretary said: "I understand the strong feelings about penalties." He warned: "The object of the bombers is to panic the British Government, if not into a change of policy, at least into an ill-judged response which would provide them with further opportunities for violence." However, Mr. Jenkins promised that he would not hesitate to introduce any measures in future which would make a practical and significant contribution to defeating the terrorists.

The Opposition backed the second reading of the Bill, but a number of Conservatives felt strongly that hanging should be a weapon in the Government's armoury.

From the Tory front bench, Mr. Ian Gilmour made clear that he personally was against the death penalty; It would do more harm than good.

The Trade Union and Labour Relations (Amendment) Bill, rejected by the Lords at the end of the last Parliamentary session, was reintroduced in the Commons on November 26 and given a formal first reading. The Bill's main purpose was to repeal or amend the Conservative Industrial Relations Act. It failed last session when the Lords refused to back down on proposals for a Press charter. The Government was now using the provisions of the Parliament Act to get the Bill re-introduced.

On December 2, the Industry Secretary (Mr. Eric Varley) introduced into the Commons the first major item of nationalization—the State take-over of most of Britain's aircraft and shipbuilding industries. Moving the second reading of the Aircraft and Shipbuilding Industries Bill, Mr. Varley declared: "We are taking these industries into public ownership at a time when they both face very considerable difficulties." The Shadow Industry Secretary (Mr. Michael Heseltine) condemned the measure and said that nationalized industries had shown historically that far from solving problems, the transferring of ownership to the State actually worsened the situation. The Liberal industry spokesman (Mr. Richard Wainwright) said that Liberals would vote against the Bill, which was an insult to democracy. The Bill received a second reading by 280 votes to 275, a Government majority of 5.

Sixteen M.P.s on December 4 opposed new arrangements for paying the Royal Household bill in a vote forced by Mr. William Hamilton (Lab.). However 247 ministers and M.P.s supported the second reading of the Civil List Bill to give the Government a 231 majority for the measure which introduced for the first time an annual review of the Queen's salary bill. Under the Bill, the Civil List provided only for the Sovereign, the Consort, the Children of the Sovereign, and for the widows of those children. Mr. Wilson, moving the second reading, emphasized that it involved no changes or additions to public expenditure and announced that the Queen had agreed to make an annual contribution to pay the allowances of the Duke of Kent, Princess Alexandra, the Duke of Gloucester, and Princess Alice which would initially save about £120,000, and which he described as "a generous gesture." Mr. Hamilton however thought the intention was clear—"protection for every member of the Royal Household against inflation." Mr. Enoch Powell (U.U.U.) objected to the Bill for a different reason; he supported those who objected to the annual involvement of Parliament and the exposure of the Royal Family to political debate. The Prime Minister declared that Mr. Hamilton's anti-monarchist views were "burned into his soul."

On December 5, Mr. Jenkins sought approval in

the Commons for his proposal to set up a new independent board to investigate complaints against police in England and Wales, but provoked considerable criticism with protests headed by the Shadow Home Secretary (Mr. Ian Gilmour) who considered the new legislation " grotesquely ill-timed " when the police were fighting a desperate battle to maintain law and order. Moving the second reading of the Police Bill, Mr. Jenkins said there was general agreement that a change was necessary because the handling of complaints against the police was largely in the hands of the police themselves. The police could be seen to be judge and jury in their own courts. Mr. Eldon Griffiths (C.) complained that the House was devoting its time to a Bill " to increase the ability of malicious defamers of the police service to complain against them." Dr. Shirley Summerskill said that fairness and balance must be seen to exist in the handling of complaints. The Bill was given an unopposed second reading.

An Opposition attack on the Government's off-shore oil policy was defeated in the Commons on December 8 by 293–275 votes, a Government majority of 18. Mr. Patrick Jenkin blamed the " sadly deteriorating oil scene " on what he said was the misbegotten and doctrinal nationalizing of 51 per cent. of offshore oil licences, and claimed the Government saw offshore oil as a magic to transform their future. Mr. Anthony Wedgwood Benn denied that he had seen offshore oil as solving all their problems although it could help to transform their prospects. Every country except the U.S. had adopted the objective of a national oil company.

The Government had a majority of 30 in the Commons on December 9 on the second reading of the Trade Union and Labour Relations (Amendment) Bill to permit closed shops, the voting figures being 306–276. Mr. Michael Foot said that the Bill repealed that part of the Conservative's Trade Union and Labour Relations Act which gave legal backing to complaints against unions alleged arbitrarily or unreasonably to have expelled or excluded workers. The Shadow Employment Secretary (Mr. James Prior) warned that there would be no easy passage for it and said that Conservative opposition had hardened.

M.P.s were told on December 9 that people who took out overlapping TV licences to beat the increase in fee and then had to pay the extra £6 after all were to receive back their money. The Home Secretary (Mr. Jenkins) said that he had decided not to appeal against the recent Appeal Court decision which resulted in a victory for the holders of overlapping licences, remarking " it is time this unhappy affair, for some aspects of which I have already apologized, was ended." Licence holders would be asked to ignore the revocation letters they had received and arrangements would be made to refund the extra £6 paid. The Shadow Home Secretary (Mr. Gilmour) said it was entirely fitting that the Government, which had shown such contempt for the law and the rights of the individual, should now fall foul of the courts.

THE DEATH PENALTY.—On December 4, the Prime Minister rejected a request by Mr. Michael McNair-Wilson (C) for a referendum on capital punishment. Answering Commons questions, he said the use of the referendum on continued membership of the Common Market was "a wholly exceptional process for a unique occasion." He considered M.P.s were quite capable of either representing their constituents in this matter or of representing fully in debates and in the division lobbies their own considered judgment. Mr. McNair-Wilson said he himself was opposed to

hanging but would like to see the public express their view.

On a free vote on December 11, M.P.s opposed a demand to restore the death penalty by 361 votes to 232, a majority against of 129. But the number of abolitionists fell from the total of a year before when in the wake of the Birmingham pub bombings M.P.s voted by 369–217, a majority against of 152, against the reintroduction of capital punishment. Mr. Jenkins said that there could be few things more humiliating and counter-productive than to introduce a much proclaimed deterrent which promptly proceeded to break in their hands and warned: " There will be no amnesty. I recognize no political excuses for cold-blooded crimes of murder or maiming. Those who have committed them will serve for decades; in some cases until the end of their lives." The Commons was debating a motion by Mr. Ivan Lawrence (C.) calling for capital punishment for terrorist offences causing death. Mr. Hugh Fraser (C.), who had been the target of a terrorist bomb, said that the State should take back the power of the penalty of death.

DEAL WITH CHRYSLER.—A £162·5 million deal with the Chrysler Corporation to prevent 25,000 sackings was announced in the Commons on December 16 by the Industry Secretary (Mr. Varley) who said however that there would be thousands of redundancies. The key element in the proposals was the transfer of Avenger cars from Ryton to Linwood in Scotland, a "streamlining" operation as Mr. Varley described it. Mr. Varley said that the Government had been faced with a fearsome choice: to lose all 25,000 jobs or keep 17,000 by making the transfer. He stated the £100 million deal with Iran would be safeguarded. Detailing the agreement, Mr. Varley said that £72·5 million had been committed over the next four years, there would be a Government loan of £55 million for capital expenditure, London and Scottish clearing banks had agreed in principle to provide a medium term loan of up to £35 million, making a total of £162·5 million. The Opposition spokesman (Mr. Heseltine) observed: " Having heard of the enormity of the commitment, the whole House will understand why Mr. Varley threatened to resign. He would have been well-advised to do so." He said that the Minister had abandoned the whole of the recommendations of the Central Policy Review Staff report which made it clear he should have gone in a totally different direction to the one announced. Mr. Varley replied that the announcement was in no way contrary to the Government's overall policy towards the car industry and did not detract from industrial strategy. Mr. Richard Wainwright (L.) wondered how the Government reconciled the deal with Chrysler's declaration of intent particularly concerning expansion. Mr. Varley said that funds for capital investment would be provided as a loan to Chrysler from the Government. This was secured on the assets of the Chrysler Corporation and not on Chrysler U.K. The Government had a majority of 25 at the end of the debate on the motor industry which followed later the same day. M.P.s voted 285 to 260 on a procedural motion after discussing the Chrysler rescue, British Leyland, and various reports on the industry. Mr. Varley said that the Chrysler deal represented a new starting point and the Government was prepared to make sure of success for the motor industry as a whole. Mr. Patrick Duffy, chairman of the influential Trade and Industry Sub-Committee and Labour M.P. for Attercliffe, Sheffield, gave notice that they wanted to conduct a thorough investigation, particularly to see if there was value for money in the Chrysler agreement. Next day,

December 17, the Government was given approval for the Chrysler rescue by a majority of 21 votes, M.P.s voting 287-266 for the formal order authorizing payment, on guarantee, of up to £162·5 million, the total commitment estimated by the Industry Secretary. The Tory spokesman (Mr. Heseltine) claimed that the plan would cost £218 million over the next four years and both he and the Liberal spokesman (Mr. Wainwright) forecast that Chrysler would be back for more money in the next 18 months or two years. Eight Labour back-benchers abstained but 10 Scottish Nationalists and three Plaid Cymru M.P.s voted with the Government.

When Parliament reassembled after the Christmas Recess on January 12, there was a fullscale debate on the Northern Ireland Convention which ended without a division after the Minister of State, Northern Ireland (Mr. Stanley Orme) challenged those who did not agree with the Government's policy to vote against it, otherwise it indicated " tacit support for it." Mr. Edward Heath, the former Tory prime minister, called for ruthless steps to deal with terrorism in South Armagh and along the border, and advocated the use of rockets by the Army to counter terrorist rockets and the possible mining of border roads, with suitable warnings to the general public. The Northern Ireland Secretary (Mr. Merlyn Rees) said that the Convention, which had been seeking a form of government for Ulster, should meet again on February 3, and try once more to agree proposals which would command widespread support in the community. Rejecting the Convention's original report, which opposed power-sharing with the Catholic minority, Mr. Rees demanded proposals which would give opportunities to both communities for " partnership and participation." Ways must be found of involving both communities. When the Minister of State (Mr. Orme) asked Mr. Molyneux, leader of the Ulster Unionists, if he would recommend his colleagues to attend the recalled Convention, Mr. Molyneux replied that he would urge them to " operate the democratic process and make full use of it."

DEVOLUTION.—On January 13 there began a four-day debate on the Government proposals for devolution to Scotland and Wales which Mrs. Thatcher saw as likely to lead to the maximum conflict, friction and argument between assemblies, Government and Parliament. She doubted if the Government scheme was based on elected Scottish and Welsh assemblies with wide-ranging powers, would stand the test of time. The Conservatives' test of a devolutionary system was that it should genuinely improve the machinery of government and lead to a devolution and not a confusion of power. Mr. Wilson said that the legislative proposals would embody the most fundamental constitutional development of this century. There was no go-slow by the Government; it was Parliament's duty to get the proposals right and to get the widest possible acceptance North and South of the border and East and West of the Dyke. The Scottish National party and Plaid Cymru wanted independence for Scotland and Wales. The Kilbrandon report rejected that approach and so did the Government. They also rejected the separation into independent political units of the countries that made up the U.K. The legislation they were preparing would confer power over a very wide area but the ultimate responsibility and sovereignty must remain with the U.K. as a whole. Mr. Thorpe supported a federal system and believed Britain should have a federal Parliament of 200-300 members. The Labour Party's attitude indicated that a degree of

reserved cynicism over the Government's intentions was not misplaced. Mr. Donald Stewart, leader of the Scottish Nationalists, said that S.N.P. recognized that no nation could benefit by isolation, and they intended no break up of the U.K. Their aim was to be part of the Commonwealth. Mr. Gwynfor Evans (Plaid Cymru) said that Parliament would ignore the resurgence of Welsh nationhood at its peril. The Welsh were in a position of servitude and could not make a single decision in the life of Wales.

On January 14, on the resumed debate, Mr. Edward Short, Leader of the House, declared that rejection in Parliament of the devolution proposals would be the death warrant of the U.K. Public opinion in Scotland and Wales meant that sensible devolution could not be withheld. The Government visualized the first assembly elections being held possibly at the end of 1977 but more realistically in the following spring. Mr. Buchanan-Smith, Shadow Scottish Secretary, objected to the single-chamber system of the type proposed; it was better to have an assembly working within the U.K. legislative framework and with only one executive. On January 15 Mr. John Morris, Secretary of State, Wales, said that those who asked for a referendum tended not to recognise the practical difficulties. The Labour Party in Wales had made it clear there was no going back. The *status quo* was not an alternative. The basic case for the Assembly was the need for more democracy in Wales. The Assembly would have real and effective powers of policy making and execution. The debate concluded on January 19 with three divisions. The first vote was on an Opposition amendment affirming the need for an assembly in Scotland but claiming the Government's proposals for Scotland and Wales would lead to confusion and conflict and would threaten the unity of the U.K., but it was defeated by 315-244, a Government majority of 71. In the second division, a Nationalist amendment regretting the Government's plans gave the assemblies no meaningful control over Scottish and Welsh economies was rejected by 304-27, a Government majority of 277. The third vote was on a Government motion to " take note " of the White Paper on devolution and was carried by 295-37, Government majority of 258. Mr. William Ross, Secretary of State, Scotland, accused the Scottish Nationalist Party of " a propaganda of greed over oil " and said the commitment to devolution had been there for a long time. Mr. Edward Heath said that the growth of national feeling in Scotland was deeply-rooted and substantial. Parliament could only ignore it at its peril. The Union was in danger. It was not because of the Government putting forward proposals. He believed the proposals were tardy. The House must put at the top of their priorities the problems of devolution. Mr. William Whitelaw, Deputy Leader of the Opposition and the Conservatives' spokesman on devolution, said that he was very unhappy about the proposals for Scotland and believed that those for Wales were wrong and unnecessary. The weakening of the U.K. would be very serious for their standing and bargaining power in international affairs and that would certainly happen if they were to split up into two or three smaller nations.

THE CLOSED SHOP.—The Government successfully beat off new efforts to put teeth into a Press Charter to protect editors from closed shop provisions permitted in the Trade Union and Labour Relations (Amendment) Bill on January 21. A Tory amendment for rights for journalists not to be unreasonably excluded or expelled from unions, the right to choice of union, and freedom for

editors not to join was defeated by 299–240 votes, a Government majority of 59. A Liberal amendment to make decisions on complaints binding was also defeated by 294–240 votes, Government majority of 54, while another Conservative amendment that anything contrary to the charter should be deemed contrary to public policy and that nothing in it should restrict or abridge statute or common law rights was rejected by 298–253 votes, a Government majority of 45. Mr. Foot's proposals for a voluntary Press freedom charter were approved. These proposals meant that if 12 months after the Bill became law the newspaper industry had not been able to agree on a charter the Minister would produce his own scheme to be approved by Parliament.

On January 27, the Trade Union and Labour Relations (Amendment) Bill received a third reading in the Commons by 285–249 votes, a Government majority of 36, after M.P.s had spent two lengthy days discussing " suggested amendments " from the Opposition parties. These amendments, all of which were rejected, were " suggested " because under the Parliament Act the Bill had to be sent to the Lords in the same form as at the beginning of last year.

ANTI-TERROR MEASURES.—Tougher anti-terror measures were approved in the Commons on January 28 when M.P.s debated changes to the law which had already introduced exclusion orders, and other anti-terrorism measures. The Commons approved:

An increase in penalties for publicly supporting proscribed organizations; the exclusion of U.K. citizens from Northern Ireland—as well as Great Britain—when they are suspected of terrorism; the banning of fund raising for acts of terrorism in Northern Ireland; the creation of an offence of failing to disclose information which would help to prevent terrorist activity or help in arrests or convictions. These were among changes made to the Prevention of Terrorism (Temporary Provisions) Bill which continued and altered existing anti-terror measures, including the banning of the I.R.A. On a vote the Government's disclosure proposals were carried, with Opposition support, by 196 to 24, Government majority 172. The proposal to increase penalties for support for proscribed organizations increased fines from a maximum of £200 to £400 and prison from three months to six. The Government resisted, with Opposition support, a Labour back-bench demand to delete the section giving the Home Secretary power to make exclusion orders. Voting was 140 to 21, Government majority 119. Left wing M.P.s forced a vote on the Bill's third reading, but this was approved by 118 votes to 11, a Government majority of 107.

UNEMPLOYMENT AND INDUSTRY.—On January 29 a sizeable group of Labour Leftwingers remained seated during the vote in the Commons on a Government motion expressing deep concern at the continuing rise in unemployment. The motion additionally expressed the Government's determination to take all possible effective measures to reduce unemployment, and it was approved by 234 votes to 25, a Government majority of 209. An Opposition amendment regretting that unemployment would be higher and would last longer because of the Government's failure to take early and decisive action against inflation was defeated by 299 votes to 250, a Government majority of 49. Mr. Healey said that the signs were multiplying that Britain's recession might be coming to an end and he indicated that further steps would soon be taken to help to preserve or create jobs.

The Government sustained its first defeat in the Commons on February 11 by 5 votes after a censure debate on Industry Secretary (Mr. Varley) over handling of the motor industry. M.P.s voted 214–209 to reduce Mr. Varley's salary by £1,000 which is the traditional parliamentary method of stricturing a minister. This shock result occurred after an earlier division muddle in which there was a miscount and immediately the Government Chief Whip (Mr. Bob Mellish) declared to angered Tories that the Government did not accept the decision. This provoked a general rumpus which was resolved when the Speaker called the next business. Six days later on February 17 a Government motion to disregard the expression of opinion that the Industry Secretary's salary should be reduced was carried by 296 votes to 280, a Government majority of 16.

On February 12, Mr. Healey announced in a Commons statement that the Government would provide a further sum of £55 million for modernization schemes under section 8 of the Industry Act. Some £15–£20 million would be spent in the next fiscal year and there would be £1 million more allocated for the building of small factories in rural areas. The National Enterprise Board would discuss finance for stock piling of machine tools with the industry and the Government would provide £50 million for public sector housing improvement. The maximum period of entitlement to temporary employment subsidy was to be extended from 6 to 12 months, and the minimum size of firms qualifying for redundancy was to be reduced from 25 to 10 workers. The Chancellor said that the school-leaver recruitment subsidy would be extended to those who left at Christmas, 1975, and that the job creation scheme would receive a further allocation of £30 million, his estimation being that between 20,000 to 25,000 extra temporary jobs would be created. Proposals to provide from next August 30,000–35,000 extra training places in industry would cost about £55 million and the total estimated cost of all these measures was about £220 million of which less than £140 million would be spent during 1976–77. Altogether the measures were likely to provide about 140,000 jobs or training places though not all these would last as long as a year and some might be at the expense of other jobs. The Shadow Chancellor (Sir Geoffrey Howe) commended Mr. Healey for having resisted demands to move towards a general reflation of the economy and hoped he would sustain his will in this respect through the long and testing times still to come. Mr. Norman Atkinson (Lab.), a prominent Left-winger, described the Chancellor's statement as " puff-like, will-o-the-wisp " and claimed that it would go no way towards the job " you are misleading the House you have undertaken."

SEAT BELTS.—On a free vote, a second reading was given to the Road Traffic (Seat Belts) Bill in the Commons on March 3 when the figures were 249–139. Dr. John Gilbert, Minister of Transport, moving the second reading of the Bill, which would enable the Environment Secretary to make regulations for the compulsory wearing of prescribed types of seat belts for drivers and front-seat passengers, said that vehicles covered would be cars registered since January 1965, light vans up to 30-cwt registered since April, 1967, and certain three-wheelers first used on or after September, 1970. The offence of not wearing a seatbelt would not mean licence endorsement and was not subject to disqualification from driving. But on the outcome of the vote the lives of thousands of citizens would depend. The bill would save 1,000 lives and 11,000 serious injuries each year and save £60

million in health service costs, police time and production costs.

NORTHERN IRELAND.—The Northern Ireland Secretary (Mr. Rees) announced to the Commons on March 3 that the Northern Ireland Convention would be dissolved from midnight that night, adding that it was clearly not possible " at this time to make progress towards a devolved system of government for Northern Ireland." That still remained the Government's aim but it did not contemplate any major new initiative for some time. Direct rule would be positive and would provide a firm, fair and resolute government for Northern Ireland. The shadow Ulster spokesman, Mr. Airey Neave, said that the Opposition shared the Government's profound regret that there had been no agreement, but warned of the " very great danger " that by dissolving the Convention the Secretary of State was creating a political vacuum. Mr. Gerry Fitt (S.D.L.P.) declared that the man responsible for the downfall of this Convention was none other than " a member of this House, the Rev. Ian Paisley."

MR. WILSON'S RESIGNATION.—Left-wing abstentions led to an embarrassing Government defeat in the Commons on March 10 by 28 votes over Mr. Healey's plans to curb public spending by £3,000 million. The voting was 284–256 against a Government motion supporting the " levelling off " of total public expenditure from April, 1977. An earlier vote on the Conservative attack on the proposals resulted in a victory for the Government by 304–274 votes, a Government majority of 30. But on the substantive motion to support the proposals, the Labour Left-wingers stayed in their seats while Liberals, the Nationalists, and the Tories joined forces in opposing the Government on the second vote. Mrs. Thatcher demanded that the Government should resign or seek a vote of confidence, declaring that such a defeat was unprecedented in modern times. Mr. Edward Short, Leader of the House, promised that the Prime Minister would consider the situation and announce his intention in due course. Pandemonium ensued but the Speaker insisted that the House was then on the motion to adjourn. It transpired that 37 Left-wing Labour M.P.s abstained, causing the heaviest Government defeat within living memory. The following day, March 11, a debate on a vote of confidence after the disastrous Government defeat ended in scenes of uproar but the Government won the day by 297 votes to 280, a majority of 17. Earlier Mr. Wilson, on his 60th birthday, attacked the " unholy alliance " the night before between his Left-wing and the Tories.

On March 16 the Prime Minister announced his resignation in a bombshell statement which took nearly every politician of all parties by total surprise, but the Chamber was buzzing to greet Mr. Wilson who was due to answer his usual Tuesday round of oral questions. When the Prime Minister appeared amid a flurry of cheers and counter-cheers, Mrs. Thatcher graciously observed: " In spite of the political battles we wish you well personally in your retirement," and significantly added: " The best way to resolve the uncertainty and give the new Prime Minister the authority required would be to put the matter to the people for their vote." With appropriate aplomb, Mr. Wilson acknowledged but added that he was not so sure that Mrs. Thatcher was all that keen on a general election either ! Mr. Jeremy Thorpe said that every prime minister worth his salt generated controversy and Mr. Wilson had been no exception. Mr. Edward Heath commented: " Any man who has been able to lead his Party as successfully as you have for 13 years, to be prime minister for 8

years, having won 4 elections, deserves the fullest tributes for his achievements."

A Conservative attempt to censure the Government for its defence cuts failed in the Commons on April 4 when their attack was defeated by 309 votes to 263, a Government majority of 46. The Tory amendment to the Government's motion to approve its own policy declared that the U.K.'s defences had already been reduced to " absolute bedrock." In view of the growth of the Soviet military strength and unfavourable balance between NATO and the Warsaw Pact, the Tories condemned the proposals to reduce the U.K.'s defences for the third time in a year. The Government's motion, approved by 305 votes to 275, called for support for its cuts on support services rather than front line forces, thus maintaining Britain's contribution to NATO, the security and territorial integrity of the U.K. and Northern Ireland. The Shadow Foreign Secretary (Mr. Reginald Maudling) said that the uncalled amendment signed by more than 80 Left-wing Labour M.P.s was a formidable roll-call of political support against the Government. The Minister of State, Defence (Mr. William Rodgers) replied that while the cuts were acceptable, he did not see any room for further similar cuts in the foreseeable future, and that " for me, at least, enough is enough."

The new Prime Minister (Mr. James Callaghan) made his début at the Commons despatch box on April 4 to a crescendo of cheers and friendly partisanship and less than 24 hours in office confronted M.P.s for the twice-weekly performance of questions to the Prime Minister. He received a kindly and warm welcome from Mrs. Thatcher and commented that he expected his " honeymoon " to last " at least 10 days." Congratulations emanated from the other minority party leaders and Mr. Callaghan in most diplomatic terms replied that the Government had a long-term economic policy and however long that parliament might continue the country would benefit from its policies if they could be carried on with general agreement.

THE BUDGET.—The Chancellor of the Exchequer (Mr. Denis Healey) presented his Budget on April 6 and described it as " likely to prove the most crucial of the present Parliament ". The aim was to consolidate and extend the gains made in the last year, and to prescribe the course for the fastest possible return of Britain to full employment and external balance, in a period of acknowledged world recovery. He observed: " This is above all a Budget about jobs and about inflation, which is the *main threat to jobs* in Britain today."

In his economic review, the Chancellor said world recession had been very deep, but recovery developed strongly in the second half of 1975, and should be sustained through 1976. The U.K. recession had also been very severe, the fall in exports and destocking being prominent in the decline. Unemployment rose rapidly in consequence, reaching 1·2 millions at the beginning of 1976. Towards the end of 1975, however, a moderate recovery started, with exports doing well and destocking falling back. But the outlook for unemployment seemed distinctly brighter, with marked deceleration in the monthly rate of increase. The lags between recovery in output and a fall in unemployment were long. " If we judge solely by the movement of GDP in the last few months, it may still be too soon to expect the trend in unemployment to be reversed but some of the indicators suggest that a rapid improvement may be under way." But it was wise to wait some months longer before reaching a firm conclusion on the basic trend.

The current account deficit on the balance of

payments in 1975 was £1,700 million, under half the total for 1974. The improvement was due, in part, to the fact that import volume fell more than export volume, and in part to an improvement in the terms of trade, which now seemed to have levelled out. "I believe that we will be able to hold on to this improvement in 1976, despite the upswing in home demand." On the capital account of the balance of payments there should be no difficulty in meeting external financing needs this year. But that depended upon success in fighting inflation and in maintaining confidence in our ability to pay our way.

The public sector borrowing requirement for 1975–76 was estimated to have been about £10¾ billion; this was significantly below the figures put forward by many commentators, the difference reflecting in part the unexpected depth of recession, but mainly an under-estimate of the effect of inflation on public expenditure. Growth in money supply had been firmly contained.

For the future the stance of monetary policy remained unchanged. Industrial requirements for finance must not be crowded out by demands of other sectors, nor must money supply be allowed to fuel inflation. The aim was that growth of money supply should be consistent with plans for the growth of demand expressed in current prices. If that aim were not being achieved then the Chancellor would " be ready to use the appropriate mix of policies—not just monetary policy—to redress the situation ". The most encouraging developments had been on inflation. The £6 policy represented " an act of great responsibility by the whole trade union movement, sustained with impressive unanimity ". Everyone had benefited. The rate of inflation through the second half of 1975 was 14 per cent annual rate compared to 38 per cent. in the first half. But the U.K. was still well out of line with other countries. " We cannot relax our efforts. Further progress depends crucially on the pay limit for the next pay round."

The balance of payments constraint had only one answer, expansion based on exports and import substitution and not a general reflation of domestic demand. The constraint could only reliably be removed by better performance in manufacturing industry. Recent trends of exports and imports had been encouraging and they must be competitive in the widest sense as well as in terms of prices. Some people had argued that manufactured imports would rise rapidly, much more rapidly than exports in the recovery. That, despite the contrary opinion of some economists, was unlikely to happen so long as the economy was not run at too high a pressure of demand. General import controls were rejected on domestic and international grounds. They were no answer to the nation's problems: such controls would conflict with their international obligations and could lead to a trade war from which all would lose.

Selective import controls on the other hand might have a valuable role in protecting industries whose survival was threatened by excessive imports. Several had been introduced recently, and the Government remained alert for other cases where they might be appropriate.

Mr. Healey declared: " The key to correcting the balance of payments, however, lies in making industry more efficient in the widest sense. The depreciation of sterling in recent weeks has reflected our high inflation rate relative to our competitors. But depreciation of sterling adds to prices and is not the answer to our problems. It is only by reducing industrial costs through higher productivity and a lower growth of incomes that

we can find a lasting solution to the balance of payments constraint on economic growth."

Before setting out the Budget measures, a view of the economy on the assumption of present tax rates, present expenditure plans, and present rate of pay increases would be useful. On that basis total output would grow about 3½ per cent. in the next 12 months with exports of goods and services rising 9 per cent. and private fixed investment 6–7 per cent. Private consumption would rise 1½ per cent., public expenditure on goods and services would be approximately unchanged. That was the pattern needed; there was no intention in the Budget to alter it materially. In particular because the growth was beginning to approach the rate set as the objective for 1977–1979 it was not right to add much to aggregate demand. They needed a steady and gentle acceleration, not a sudden spurt. The Budget therefore had two overriding objectives: to create the conditions in which output and productivity were most likely to recovery, and secondly in which wages and costs could be kept as low as possible without unnecessarily reducing the real value of the workers' take-home pay.

The Chancellor said: " Recent achievements have been encouraging, but this Budget must also tackle the problems of the medium-term and lay the foundations for a strategy which will enable Britain to enter the 80s with full employment, stable prices and an economy in balance both at home and abroad ". There were important differences between the coming recovery in world trade and previous upswings. Inflation was worse and many countries faced balance of payments deficits as domestic demand rose. The industrialized world generally would find it more difficult to reconcile the objectives of full employment, stable prices and external balance. Britain was not immune from those trends and could only solve its problems if our trading partners solved theirs. " Beggar my neighbour " policies risked a slump like the 1930s. That was why the U.K. had taken the lead, in the EEC, the Commonwealth and elsewhere, in organizing collective international discussion of their common problems. Britain's problems were of the same kind as other countries, but they were far bigger in scale. We had high inflation and a large balance of payments deficit even before the oil price rise cut real national income by 5 per cent. To achieve full employment and external balance, Britain needed a big shift in the use of her resources away from private and public consumption towards exports and investment.

In the longer run that meant, above all, reversing the decline of manufacturing industry. That was the aim of the industrial policies, and of public expenditure policy. In the last analysis, however, the problem could only be solved at the level of the individual company and plant.

" The target which the Government has set itself is to get unemployment down to 3 per cent. in 1979. This requires 5½ per cent. a year GDP growth, and 8½ per cent. growth of manufacturing output, between 1976 and 1979. Given the present low level of capacity use such growth rates are not impossible. But they require a rapid improvement in industrial performance in every field and at every level. Britain has the qualities needed to do this. There are two constraints on growth—temporary shortages (bottlenecks) and the balance of payments. The Government has acted on the former by selective assistance to industries like ferrous foundries; by doubling spending on industrial training; and by the NEDC studies of key sectors under the industrial strategy. Various measures in the industrial field will help with the first; on the second two sets of measures are proposed. One to

take effect immediately, and the other to take effect when the TUC has made its recommendation on the new pay limit."

Mr. Healey continued: " The Budget proposals for industry are intended to help efficiency in manufacturing industry and its ability to meet the coming upturn in demand. The Government is pledged to provide " an appropriate fiscal and economic environment for manufacturing industry so that it can finance the necessary increase in investment and obtain the manpower it will need during the recovery ".

CORPORATION TAX.—The maintenance of a stable framework for business was necessary if industrial planning was not to be disrupted. Action was accordingly being taken to strengthen stability of the tax environment.

There were three areas for action on Corporation Tax:—

(1) Stock Relief: Stock relief would continue and become permanent. There would be consultations about the best form for a permanent change in the tax system covering stock relief. Meanwhile the present system would continue in substantially its present form for 1975-76 and 1976-77. However, to help firms investing in fixed assets, calculation of profits would for stock relief purposes be net of capital allowances. To meet the full year cost of £65 million involved in that, the profits deduction would rise from 10 to 15 per cent.

(2) Capital Allowances: The main structure of the present system of capital allowances for fixed investment would continue in its existing form (excluding any necessary minor changes). On grounds of cost there would be no extension to commercial buildings.

(3) Corporation Tax: No change was proposed in the structure or in rate of corporation tax, excepting an increase in the profit level at which smaller companies qualify for preferential rate. But " the continuation of stock relief and the present system of capital allowances means that substantially the whole of any profits which a manufacturing company re-invests in its business, whether in fixed or in working capital, will effectively be relieved from corporation tax ".

FINANCE FOR INVESTMENT.—The Government were also concerned to ensure a sufficient and appropriate supply of investment finance for the recovery. There were five principal areas in which action was proposed:—

(1) Stamp Duty: The debenture market might again become a source of new finance as interest rates fell, following a successful second stage counter-inflation policy, but transfer stamp duty might inhibit the revival. Stamp duty on transfers of fixed interest stocks, excluding convertible stocks, would be abolished from 1 May, at a full year cost of £10 million.

(2) Medium-Term Bank Finance: The clearing banks still had medium-term funds available for commitment, but conceivably in the longer term their availability might be limited by prudential considerations. The Bank of England and the London and Scottish Clearing Banks were to explore that prospect, how much of a problem it was likely to be, and possible means of alleviating it such as by providing refinancing facilities.

(3) Counter-cyclical Investment: Studies of the feasibility of counter-cyclical schemes would be undertaken immediately by the new NEDC Committee on Finance for Investment. Counter-cyclical schemes had their difficulties, and finance was in any case not the most important factor in investment; but if an effective counter-

cyclical scheme could be devised then it could be an important element in the longer term strategy.

(4) Investment Schemes: A total of £285 million had been allocated to accelerated projects and industry schemes under Section 8 of the Industry Act. A further £40 million would now be allocated for industry schemes, with drawings likely to start early in 1977.

(5) Price Code: The existing Price Code would expire at the end of July. Discussions would take place on changes in the Code. The Government would take full account of the needs of industry, and in particular, of the need to allow a sufficient recovery of profits to encourage the new investment and related new jobs.

MANPOWER POLICIES.—The Government had already taken action in that field, but two further measures were proposed:—

(i) Temporary Employment Subsidy: To save more jobs for the upturn, the Temporary Employment Subsidy of £10 a week per head, would be doubled, as proposed by the T.U.C. in their Economic Review, with immediate effect for new applications, and with effect from the next 3-monthly renewal for existing cases. The scheme would be open for new applications to the end of 1976. Another 60,000 jobs should be preserved, at a gross cost of £95 million (£30 million net).

(ii) Community Industry: The extra places made available last December would be continued, if needed, beyond March. The scheme would be brought more closely in line with the Job Creation Scheme. Total cost, £2·3 million in full year.

TAXATION AFFECTING PARTICULAR INDUSTRIAL SECTORS.—There were a number of tax instruments which affected particular sectors of industry. Giving priority to manufacturing industry might involve forgoing changes which might otherwise have been desirable, if they were likely to damage the prospects of big sectors.

(i) Vehicle Excise Duty: The idea of abolishing Vehicle Excise Duty on passenger cars and raising petrol tax correspondingly, had looked increasingly attractive. But the switch to smaller cars that that would encourage would create problems for the domestic car industry, and would further stimulate imports, with consequential loss of jobs. Vehicle Excise Duty would therefore be retained.

(ii) Hire Purchase restrictions on cars: Dropping the hire purchase restrictions on cars would also stimulate imports. Restrictions would remain in force; for motor caravans in particular those objections did not hold, and hire purchase restrictions were accordingly abolished.

(iii) Higher rate VAT: Under existing circumstances the 25 per cent. rate was too high. But big revenue loss which would result from complete abolition of the higher rate would have to be covered by a rise in standard rate, which would put up prices of many everyday items purchased by ordinary working people and pensioners. The higher rate would be reduced to 12½ per cent., at full year cost of £175 million (excluding petrol). This would give help to some hard pressed sectors of industry including many small businesses, e.g., those servicing electrical appliances. The arithmetic for retailers would be based on a simple fraction, one-ninth of the tax-inclusive price.

(iv) Petrol Tax: Since petrol bore higher rate VAT its price to the motorist would drop with the reduction in the rate. To prevent that, and to increase further the incentive for fuel economy,

hydrocarbon oil duty on road fuel would rise by 7½p a gallon, implying about 1p more on a gallon of petrol. The tax on derv would also rise 7½p a gallon. These changes brought in a net £265 million in a full year.

The Chancellor said: " In recent years the emphasis of the tax system has tilted away from indirect tax. Some measures are now needed which lean in the other direction, and help to raise revenue." There would therefore be modest increases in excise duties on alcoholic drink and tobacco; because of the inflation the impact of these specific duties had been falling as a proportion of selling price. With the consequential VAT, beer would rise about 1p a pint, spirits would go up 32p on a standard bottle of whisky or gin, fortified wine up to 12p a bottle, 6p a bottle of table wine and for bottles of most made-wine. Cider and perry would be taxed for the first time, at 22p a gallon, equivalent (with VAT) to 3p a pint. Small farm producers would be exempt from the new duty. The combined revenue effect of these measures, including 8 per cent. VAT, was £165 million in a full year. The case for increases in taxation of tobacco was strong both on revenue and health grounds. There would be some increase in the level of taxation, and a first step in restructuring the duty system to fit in with EEC obligations. As a result the total tax burden on most popular sizes of cigarettes would rise 3p or 3½p a packet of 20. Tax on cigars and hand-rolling tobacco would rise in line with cigarettes. There would be no increase in the average tax burden on pipe tobacco. These changes were effective from May 10. The yield, including VAT, would be £115 million in a full year. The combined price effect of the increased tax on drink and tobacco would be about ⅜ per cent. on R.P.I.

A number of miscellaneous tax changes would also be introduced:—The Inland Revenue would be given additional powers to enable them to uncover evasion more effectively. Powers to require production of documents for inspection would be strengthened. Where artificial leasing arrangements were entered into for tax avoidance purposes by certain kinds of partnership the 100 per cent. first year allowance for capital investment would not apply. Relief would be allowable only against the rental income. Following a review of legislation on fringe benefits a number of changes would be made, applying for the time being only to directors and to employers earning over £5,000 a year. A new scale system of assessing the benefit derived by use of company cars for non-business purposes would be introduced from 1977-78, and be phased in over two years. The benefit of low interest, or interest free, loans would be taxable, except where the interest would be eligible for tax relief. For example, loans for share purchases, or for school fees, would be taxable to the full extent of remission of interest. These, and other changes, would in general take effect from 1977-78.

Three minor tax changes would be made: Firstly the aggregation of the income of a newly-married couple would not occur until the first full tax year of marriage (yield, £60 million). Secondly new administrative arrangements would be made for allowing tax relief on life assurance premiums, beginning 1979-80. Thirdly the limit of relief on premia for self-employed persons' retirement annuities would be raised from £1,500 to £2,250.

Capital transfer tax was becoming accepted as a fair tax. It had been reviewed, as promised last year. A number of changes would be made, many with retrospective effect. Amongst them would be a new business relief, applying from that day, reducing the value transferred by 30 per cent. for transfer of a sole proprietor or partnership business, or controlling shareholding in an unquoted company. Dealers in land and shares would be excluded; farmers were included, but a full-time working farmer would still be able to claim instead the special relief in respect of his land, if that was advantageous. The new business relief would substantially lighten the burden on transfer of businesses, particularly for small firms, and help to generate confidence for expansion. The present multiplier relief for full-time working farmers would be changed to an equivalent 50 per cent. reduction analogous to the new business relief. The annual amount which could be given away in life tax free after using up other exemptions would be increased from £1,000 to £2,000.

The exemption on death for works of art, historic houses and other property of national heritage value would be extended, subject to conditions, to lifetime gifts and to property held on discretionary trusts. New provisions would be introduced governing the treatment of property passing under survivorship clauses in wills.

Indexation of capital gains tax would provide an insulation against inflation for people facing capital gains tax which had not been enjoyed by income tax payers. There would, therefore, be no change in the structure of the tax, but the total disposals which could be made annually without charge would rise by £500 to £1,000, with effect from 1975-76, at a cost of £¾ million in a full year. There had been suggestions that company exchange losses on foreign currency loans should rank for tax relief. A decision would be announced in the 1977 Budget, after consultations.

On public expenditure, Mr. Healey stated: " The need to leave room in the economy for export and investment growth means limiting the demands of the public sector. The public expenditure White Paper showed that over the medium term the Government aims to stabilize total public expenditure at about the level reached in this financial year. This means painful decisions but the Government is determined to stick to them; the extension of cash limits will help it do so." The cost of the new industrial measures and of the social security provisions would be met within the planned public expenditure White Paper totals for 1976-77 and subsequent years. Social security benefits would be raised in November: pensions by over 15 per cent.—by £3·20 to £24·50 a week for married couples and by £2 to £15·30 for a single pensioner. Short-term benefits would also be raised. Income limits for Family Income Supplement would also go up in July by £7·50 for a one-child family and £4·50 for each subsequent child. The full year cost of these increases was over £1,360 million in total, including pensions, £1,070 million. From April 1977 family allowances and child tax allowances would be replaced by the Child Benefit Scheme. The rates of benefit under this would be announced separately after Easter.

Dealing with his proposals for carrying forward the attack on inflation and for encouraging the greatest possible reduction in the growth of wage costs, the Chancellor said that he hoped to achieve them through relating tax concessions to a lower limit on earnings during the next pay round. The experience of the last twelve months had brought it home to all sections of the community that inflation was the great enemy of full employment. If wages had continued to rise at the rate they were rising in the summer of 1975, the collapse of

foreign confidence in Britain would have brought the collapse of our economy. The agreement with the unions saved the situation. "The progress we can expect to make this year in the fight against inflation depends above all on the pay limit devised last summer by the trade union movement itself in full knowledge and acceptance of the nation's economic needs. We need a similar voluntary policy for incomes when the £6 limit expires at the end of July. In their Economic Review for 1976, the T.U.C. have suggested a target which the Government fully endorses. It is to reduce the rate of inflation next year to a figure well below 10 per cent. A major contribution must also be made through policies for prices, taxation and public finance. But in my view, the key to achieving a rate of inflation which is well below 10 per cent. by the end of 1977 is to relate our tax policy in the coming year to the next policy for incomes.

"I am prepared to use my powers as Chancellor of the Exchequer to help the T.U.C. to get the next pay limit as low as possible by reducing the amount of income tax which is taken from the pay packet. I intend to guarantee that the working population as a whole does not suffer by accepting a lower pay limit rather than a higher one; indeed, I would ensure that a lower pay limit leaves those who most need help—families with children—a good deal better off.

"It is clear that the next pay limit will need to be well below this year's limit of £6 a week. If we want to end next year with an inflation rate at least in line with our foreign competitors we must aim at a further halving of our inflation rate by December 1977. Since we are likely to face higher import prices, partly because our earlier inflation has caused our exchange rate to depreciate, this would require that in the next pay round the nation's money wage bill should rise by under half as much as it is likely to rise in this pay round. The proposals for income tax reliefs which I will now set out show how this result could be achieved. Part of the reliefs would have to be conditional on a low pay limit. If in the end the T.U.C. found they were unable to agree to a figure as low as that on which these tax reliefs are based I would have to reduce the amount of the reliefs accordingly. If, on the other hand, they could go lower still, I would more than compensate with still greater tax reliefs and the nation as a whole would benefit still more. I have based the tax reliefs on the assumption that the pay limit in the next wage round will be in the area of *3 per cent.* My proposals are in two parts: it is intended primarily to help sections of the population, like the old and children, who are not going to be involved in the coming negotiations on incomes policy. The second part must be conditional upon agreeing—I hope at the latest by early June—a pay limit which is consistent with a further halving of our inflation rate in the coming year. Besides the increase in pensions I have announced, I propose to increase the age allowance for single people by £60 to £1,010 and for married people by £130 to £1,555 and also to raise the ceiling for the allowance by £250 to £3,250. These increased allowances will be substantially above the rates of retirement pension which will be payable after the uprating in November and this will enable old people to continue to supplement their pension without paying tax.

"I propose to increase child tax allowances by £60 so that they will become £300 for children under 11, £335 for children between 11 and 16 and £365 for children over 16. This improvement will cost £300 million in a full year. In the confidence that we shall achieve a low limit I

propose to include it in the first part of the package and give effect to it immediately. I propose to improve the personal allowances for single and married people and as part of my policy to give as much relief as possible to families, I propose to give a greater increase this year to the married than to single persons. Among the married for this purpose I include single parents. I propose, once the low pay limit is agreed, to increase the single person's allowance and the allowance for wives' earnings by £60 to £735, the married persons allowance by £130 to £1,085 and the additional personal allowance by £70 to £350. These increases in allowances, if the pay limit enabled me to implement them, would keep 670,000 out of tax altogether and would help to reduce the administrative cost of collecting taxes. The single allowance is given to widows as well as single women pensioners under the age of 65."

Coming to the higher rate tax structure, Mr. Healey explained: "The threshold for higher rate tax has been eroded by inflation so that it now lies between 1½ times and twice average earnings. Unless I adjust it this year, the numbers subject to higher rate tax will rise from 1·3 million in 1975/76 to 1·9 million in 1976/77, including very large numbers of skilled workers.

"The counterpart of action on fringe benefits must be some reduction in the income tax burden, particularly on middle managers in industry who have seen their net pay severely reduced in real terms over recent years by inflation and the incomes policy of successive Governments. I have decided that the second, conditional, stage of the income tax package should also include an increase of £500 in the higher rate threshold and a similar increase of £500 in the next four thresholds up to a taxable income of £8,500 a year. The starting point for the higher rate at 40 per cent. would therefore be £5,000 instead of £4,500 and so on; but the 65 per cent rate would continue to start at £10,000. The total cost of these income tax reliefs, if both stages are fully implemented, would be about £1,300 million in a full year. Of this, £370 million is included unconditionally in the first part and the balance will be held over to the second part, since it is conditional on the low pay limit. The revenue from the increased duties on alcoholic drink, tobacco and petrol will broadly cover the cost of the unconditional £370 million which is concentrated on the old and children.

"In addition to the direct advantage in real take-home pay produced by the lower pay limit, it would also generate more jobs by improving the ability of our industry to compete, by stimulating investment and by improving confidence in Britain both at home and abroad."

The Chancellor said: "The Budget is an almost neutral one. Given implementation of the conditional part of the tax measures the outlook is for GDP to grow about 4 per cent. and manufacturing output over 8 per cent. in the year to mid-1977. Manufacturing investment could rise around 15 per cent. over the same period, with private investment half as fast.

"It is, however, too soon to say whether we have already reached the peak of unemployment, hence the further selective labour market measures. Given the low pay limit the additional tax reliefs are estimated to provide about 100,000 jobs over the next 18 months. On prices I believe that we can still achieve our target of under 10 per cent. next winter. The prospect for 1977 depends crucially on achieving the low pay limit. We have already halved our rate of inflation, and if we can achieve the low limit for the next round we can halve it again by the end of 1977."

The prompt reaction of Mrs. Thatcher was that this was a big borrowers' budget from a soft options Chancellor and that Mr. Healey's unprecedented proposal of offering tax relief in return for pay restraint was " putting the decision about taxation levels of the majority of the people over to a body which consisted of the minority of the people." This was taxation without representation. Until the Chancellor brought down the underlying rate of expenditure he could not do very much more than shuffle the taxes around from one taxpayer to another and one set of goods to another. He was treating the economy as if it was a patient suffering from two diseases. The current recession could be compared with an attack of influenza while the underlying deficit was like a cancer. The Chancellor was treating the influenza but ignoring the cancer by not doing anything about the structural growth which if left untouched would destroy them. Mr. Jeremy Thorpe thought that the budget was a gamble to get agreement and if it did not succeed Parliament would have to introduce some very tough measures.

Next day, April 7, increases totalling nearly £1,400 million in pensions and social security benefits, with more help towards heating costs for people on supplementary pensions and allowances, were announced in Parliament by Mrs. Barbara Castle, the increases being paid from the week beginning 15 November, 1976. Long-term benefits went up by over 15 per cent., which meant that retired couples would get £24·50 a week, an increase of £3·30, and single pensioners would get £15·30 a week, a rise of £2. Single people drawing sickness and unemployment benefit would receive increases of £1·80 a week—16 per cent. more. People receiving supplementary benefit received similar increases. There was to be an increase of over 25 per cent. in heating additions paid with supplementary benefit, and from July the limits for family income supplement were to be greatly increased. Mrs. Castle said that the increases for pensioners would more than compensate for the expected movement in earnings and prices between the last uprating and the date of implementing this one. The proportionately larger increases in short-term benefits for sickness and unemployment would more than take account of the expected movement in prices over the same period and also would narrow the gap between short-term and long-term rates. Speaking about pensions, she said: " We are confident that the proposed increases of 15 per cent. will be considerably larger than the actual and likely movement of earnings and prices from the time of the last uprating to November." Turning to short-term benefits, Mrs. Castle said that they " will be increased to take account of the actual and likely movement in prices from last November to this November, again with a comfortable margin to spare, but on this occasion we have decided in addition to make a proportionately bigger improvement in the short-term rates—compared with the long-term ones—thus narrowing the gap between them."

On April 8, the third day of the debate, the Industry Secretary (Mr. Varley) announced that he planned to introduce a scheme under which a Government guarantee could be given that stage payments would be refunded to an owner ordering a vessel at a British yard which was to be nationalized if that yard should fail before nationalization. After nationalization, the contract would be honoured by British Shipbuilders, He also intended to extend the cost escalation insurance scheme, now available only for ships built for export, to vessels ordered by British shipowners, and also announced

that he had decided that projects up to 12,500 square feet in the South East planning region and 15,000 square feet in the rest of the non-assisted areas should be free from the need to get industrial development certificates.

On the final day's debate, on April 12, Mr. Healey's 3 per cent. pay rise and tax concessions proposals linked to T.U.C. support received approval by 295 votes to 274, a Government majority of 21, while the main motion covering the budget proposals was similarly supported. A division forced by Scottish Nationalists against the proposal to increase duty on spirits by 32p per bottle was defeated by 295 votes to 19, Government majority 276, and another division pressed by the S.N.P. on the motion to raise petrol duty was also defeated by 284 votes to 22, Government majority 262. The remaining Budget resolutions were approved without a vote.

The Chancellor of the Exchequer told the Commons on May 5 that the full conditional tax reliefs promised in his Budget would be given as a result of that day's agreement between himself and the T.U.C. over a 4½ per cent. average voluntary pay rise limit. He reported the details of the agreement and said that the 5p increase in school meal charges proposed for September, 1976, would be scrapped at a cost of £35 million. Additionally, he announced that the Government would allocate an extra £15 million for training and job creation. Mr. Healey explained that there was no question of consolidating pay increases under the £6 policy into basic rates; this alone could have added as much as 2 per cent. to the total pay bill, and no special exemptions were proposed for productivity bargains. Any increase would take the form of a supplement to an individual's pay subject to a floor of £2·50 and a ceiling of £4 which would apply to incomes at all levels above £80 a week. Price controls on both profits and costs must continue but the price control régime must be so modified as to encourage investment and jobs in the economy. The Shadow Chancellor (Sir Geoffrey Howe) said that these figures introduced a far greater sense of realism than prevailed in the disastrous year of the social contract when the entire nation was taken for a ride, and Labour backbenchers reacted noisily when Sir Geoffrey asked for " a candid assurance that you have entered into no kind of undisclosed or secret undertakings with the T.U.C., which might restrict your freedom and your duty to the country to take whatever steps may be necessary still further to reduce public spending in the year ahead." Mr. Healey retorted that he had made no undisclosed commitments with anybody; the limits set provided for negotiation, not entitlement. The effect on demand of the total package, including tax reliefs, as outlined in the Budget, would be to add about one-third of 1 per cent. on the Gross Domestic Product. The Liberal economic affairs spokesman (Mr. John Pardoe) urged the Chancellor to state clearly that however satisfactory 4½ per cent. might be, it was unfortunately 4½ per cent. more than the country could actually affordr Mr. Healey replied that the effect on the rate of inflation was that the increases would add to the RPI by the end of next year about 2 per cent.

PAY BEDS.—The Government bill to phase out National Health " pay beds " was given a second reading in the Commons on April 27 by 289 votes to 269, Government majority 20, after the Social Services Secretary (Mr. Ennals), during the debate on the Health Service Bill, appealed to doctors and others to " stop tilting at windmills " by threatening industrial action. He insisted that it was not Government policy to abolish private medicine but

to separate it and declared it was time to recognize that a fair compromise had been reached. The Conservatives, on the other hand, maintained their outright opposition to the measure and the Shadow Social Services Secretary (Mr. Patrick Jenkin) said that it failed to put patients before politics and was a nasty, misbegotten piece of socialist legislation. The Liberals also opposed the second reading because of the " extreme bureaucracy " involved.

HOUSING.—On May 18, the Commons rejected by 287 votes to 257, a Government majority of 30, a Conservative motion to encourage local authorities to let council tenants buy their own homes and decided that sales policy should be fixed by each council after considering the particular area's needs. The approved Government motion stated that they encouraged the widest possible housing choice, including owner-occupation, equity sharing, cooperative ventures, and renting. The Opposition also called for an end to the ban on New Town authorities selling their houses, but the Local Government and Planning Minister (Mr. John Silkin) said that he would be having talks on that matter with the New Towns chairman. The Shadow Environment Secretary (Mr. Timothy Raison) said that in adding to the stock of human happiness the sale of council houses did not diminish the overall housing stock and another Conservative spokesman (Mr. Hugh Rossi) commented that it was wrong that there should be a monopoly ownership of other people's homes, whether it were in the hands of private individuals or the State.

DEVOLUTION AGAIN.—The Leader of the Commons (Mr. Michael Foot) made it clear on May 25 that the Government's aim was to pass the devolution measure for Scotland and Wales in the next Parliamentary session and said that there would be a single combined bill and that the Government had ruled out holding a referendum on the proposals. There would be a major change in the U.K. reserve powers but their form would be subject to direct and specific control of Parliament. Mr. Whitelaw described the decision not to have separate bills for Scotland and Wales as wrong; it did not make sense as each country had its own problems. Mr. Foot answered that the proposals would not add to the financial burden on Scotland and Wales and defended the single bill on the grounds that devolution meant that there could be different developments in Scotland, Wales, and England. Mr. Enoch Powell considered that that might be a suitable opportunity for increasing the number of Northern Ireland M.P.s, as there was no reduction in representation for Scotland and Wales at Westminster and Mr. Neil Kinnock (Lab.) remarked: " A great debate without a referendum at the end of it is like a horse race without a winning post." Mr. Foot did not accept that the proposals constituted a substantial degree of separatism of which there was not the slightest element and said there would be great difficulty in putting proposals in the form of a referendum. Mr. Eric Heffer (Lab.) called the statement a further retreat in the face of nationalist pressure and considered the tail was now wagging the dog. Mr. George Reid (S.N.P.) complained that the new Scottish Assembly would not have sufficient power to re-generate the Scottish economy or end the cycle of deprivation, but Mr. Foot said that Scottish Nationalists believed in separatism, which the Government repudiated. Mr. Jim Sillars (Lab.) said that the Labour Party had failed to fulfil pledges given in the election of October, 1974, to provide industrial power to the Assembly and Mr. Gwynfor Evans (Plaid Cymru) said that injustice was being

done to Wales, as it would not have equal powers with Scotland to deal with unemployment, depopulation and emigration. But Mr. Iain Sproat (C.) believed that most people would see the statement as nothing but " shameful appeasement." Mr. Foot agreed that people had a right to express their views and doubtless would continue to do so through their M.P.s. The Commons was the best place to pass final judgment.

CHILD BENEFIT SCHEME.—There was a major Government back-bench rebellion in the Commons on May 25 after the Social Services Secretary (Mr. Ennals) announced postponement of the planned child benefit scheme. Labour M.P.s severely criticized the proposal to implement only part of the scheme as an " insult " and an abandonment of one of the Party's main reforms. Mr. Ennals denied that there had been any abandonment and assured the House that the whole scheme would be introduced in its entirety in time but said that its application immediately would have imposed excessive strain on the pay policy and cut workers' take-home pay. Instead he announced a new system of child allowances, including the first child, to operate from April, 1977, and said that the Government had decided that the new increased child tax allowances given in the budget would remain unchanged, the new benefit being £1 for the first child and £1·50 for other children. The Opposition Social Security spokesman (Mr. Patrick Jenkin) considered the statement was " a final collapse of the Government's strategy for family support." Mrs. Barbara Castle, former Social Services Secretary, said that the announcement would be greeted with dismay by Labour M.P.s and that it looked like the abandonment of one of the Party's major reforms.

NATIONALIZATION PLANS.—There was a storm in the Commons on May 26 when the Government announced plans to press on with its nationalization of the shipbuilding and aircraft industries and shouts of " cheat," " Fascist," and " Leader of the Reichstag " were hurled against the Leader of the House (Mr. Foot), who defended the decision to hasten the passage of the nationalization measure provided the Commons' vote next day gave the " green light." Mrs. Thatcher angrily declared that if Mr. Foot was proposing to set aside the rules of the House at 24 hours' notice, he was signalling the end of Parliamentary democracy and the beginning of arbitrary government. The Speaker had ruled that Mr. Robin Maxwell-Hyslop (C.) had produced a *prima facie* case that the Shipbuilding and Aircraft Industries Bill was a hybrid measure whereupon Mr. Foot informed M.P.s of the Government move to circumvent this dilemma by tabling a special motion, which unleashed 1½ hours of nonstop fury. The Liberal Party acting Leader (Mr. Jo Grimond) told Mr. Foot: " You have been posturing around this place for years and years as a champion of this House but you are now introducing a motion to get around the Speaker's ruling." Next day, May 27, the issue was rejoined when the Commons debated the motion—in the eyes of the Opposition parties—to set aside rules which at least could delay the Bill. There was an electric atmosphere throughout the long debate which ended with charges and counter-charges and highly emotional scenes when the Opposition motion on the rules change resulted in a dead heat of 303–303. The Speaker in accord with the rules of the House gave his casting vote for the Government and the House then divided on the Government's own motion which was carried by 304–303 without the need for the Speaker to intervene. It was immediately following the second division that almost unprecedented chaos ensued. Labour

M.P.s in their jubilation sang "The Red Flag," shouted, and waved order papers in the air when suddenly the Conservative shadow industry spokesman (Mr. Heseltine) seized the Mace, the symbol of parliamentary authority, from its place on the Clerks' table and advanced towards the Government benches, holding it aloft. His Tory front-bench colleague, Mr. James Prior, restrained him and replaced the Mace while simultaneously other M.P.s were involved in bitterly angry exchanges, punches being thrown as they milled around the Bar to the Chamber, pushing and shoving, until the Speaker suspended the sitting for 20 minutes. When the Speaker returned, he gravely said: "There have been scenes of great disorder here tonight and I adjourn the House until tomorrow." M.P.s on all sides were stunned into silence and gradually dispersed but not without some taunts. On May 28, the episodes of the previous night had had an apparent cooling and sobering effect on all M.P.s and straight way Mr. Heseltine made an unreserved apology for removing the Mace and when exchanges again began to raise the temperature, the Speaker expressed the hope that "M.P.s will remember that anything that undermines the dignity of this House, undermines its authority both here and outside." Mrs. Thatcher proposed peace talks through the "usual channels" over the dispute over pairing in the Government's one-vote majority division. But she insisted that any talks should involve the Prime Minister and herself personally, to which Mr Foot agreed. After disposing of the day's business, the House seemed to heave a sign of all-round relief and adjourned for the Whitsun Recess.

On June 29 the Government won the "replay" vote on the shipbuilding and aircraft industries nationalization bill in the Commons with 311 votes to 297, a majority of 14, the margin difference being provided by the abstention of the Scottish National Party. The Tories had sought to send the bill to a select committee, and were supported by Liberals and Ulster Unionists. But Mr. Gordon Wilson (S.N.P.) warned that if the Government did not bring in the goods by providing a shipbuilding organization in Scotland his Party would vote against it on third reading.

THE POSITION OF STERLING.—Mr. Healey announced in the Commons on June 7 that the Government had obtained 5,000 million dollars of standby credit from America, the Central Banks, and the Bank for International Settlement which, he declared, showed unprecedented support for sterling against unjustified market pressure. Mr. Healey, in his statement, said: "There is no economic justification for the fall in the value of the pound. This is not a situation in which any responsible British Government can allow itself to be pushed into hasty and ill-considered changes of policy on public expenditure." There was no economic case for changing public expenditure plans for the current year but they were determined to ensure that the planned total of expenditure was not exceeded. The Government had made it clear to local authorities that they must bring their spending estimates for the current year within the figures given in the White Paper on Public Expenditure. The Bank of England was that day announcing the issue of £800 million worth of new long-dated 13¼ per cent. Exchequer Stock 1996 which would yield over 14 per cent. on redemption. The Chancellor said that any drawings on the standby credit would be only temporary though the Government would seek further drawings from the I.M.F. if it was thought necessary. The Opposition Shadow Chancellor (Sir Geoffrey Howe) was concerned that the only significant new announcements

involved significant additions to the Government's borrowing requirements both at home and overseas. The Chancellor should announce clear financial targets; the country wanted a Government which would take the difficult decisions in the interests of the nation as a whole. But Mr. Healey replied that this was a massive international endorsement of sterling. The Liberal spokesman (Mr. John Pardoe) said that all who were not totally overcome by party political passion would welcome the Chancellor's determination not to indulge in panic cuts in public expenditure. Later, the Chancellor said that he expected inflation to be halved again by the end of 1977.

On June 9 Mrs. Thatcher moved a motion of "no confidence in the Government", but despite the summoning of Tory M.P.s from the four points of the world in an all-out effort to defeat it, the Government won the division by 309 votes to 290, a Government majority of 19. Mrs. Thatcher accused the Government of drift, debt, and decay and declared that the people had the will and courage to do anything required of them so long as they believed it would lead to the rebirth of Britain. The Prime Minister (Mr. Callaghan) suggested that "all this clamour and clangour" had been to satisfy an impatient and imperious vanity.

The Opposition Shadow Chancellor (Sir Geoffrey Howe) opined that "we have ended up with a pattern of half-baked socialism. We have found socialist governments destroying the dynamic of a free society and not putting in its place the discipline of Marxist control, giving us the worst of both worlds." The Chancellor himself however suspected that Mrs. Thatcher had been committed to this "folly" of a no-confidence vote by an overexcited Chief Whip who thought there might be a chance of exploiting a national difficulty for party advantage. The 4½ per cent. pay limit was recognized throughout the world as likely to give the U.K. the lowest rate of wage settlements of any industrialized country over the next pay round.

The same day the Lords also discussed the economic situation and Lord Aldington declared that public expenditure cuts would not be "a sadistic act to satisfy heathen gods" but measures needed to strengthen the British economy. Such cuts were urgently necessary. The Leader of the House (Lord Shepherd) said that public expenditure was expected to fall back to about 53 per cent. of the gross national product by 1979 but hasty cuts in this direction would have had serious consequences for employment and would have affected the poorest people. For the Liberals, Baroness Seear congratulated the Government on keeping its nerve during the sterling crisis and agreed that it would have been unwise to take ill-thought out action by slashing public expenditure. Lord Cromer, former Governor of the Bank of England, reminded them that the pound in the pocket today was worth 35p compared with its 1963 value and said that the level of Government expenditure was almost certainly the most dangerous element in the debasement of the pound at home and abroad because of the inflationary manner of part of the financing of Government requirements. Lord Thorneycroft, former Tory Chancellor of the Exchequer, remarked that the point had come where they had faltered to a level where some of the old disciplines would have to be reintroduced, and another Tory ex-Chancellor, Viscount Amory, took the view that further cuts in public expenditure were bound to come and when they did it was only by re-sorting priorities that it would be possible to safeguard the more essential public services from danger. Lord Cobbold, another former Bank of England Governor, said

that they must fairly soon reach a more stable international monetary arrangement with sensible policies being followed by countries in deficit and in surplus. Lord Balogh, one-time economic adviser to the Government, congratulated the Chancellor for his steadfastness in the face of the " gambling excesses " with the pound and stock exchange prices and called for an immediate re-consideration of exchange regulations.

CABINET DOCUMENTS.—On June 28 the Government had a majority of 27 in the Commons after a debate on the " leak " of Cabinet documents on the decision to postpone payment of child benefits to mothers, voting being 294 to 267. The Conservatives initiated the debate after the Government had refused to make an interim statement on the inquiry into the leak conducted by Sir Douglas Allen, Head of the Civil Service. The Leader of the House (Mr. Foot) criticized the Official Secrets Act, saying that it was like an unruly eiderdown which flopped over everything. The leak was not only a conflict between right and wrong but between the need for ministers to talk in confidence and newspapers' pressure for open government. A way to reconcile these points was to ensure the Official Secrets Act was reformed. Mr. Edward Heath said that the whole machinery of government was too secretive and he called for government to be " on the record." But on July 1, Mr. Callaghan told M.P.s that the police were to investigate the leak and reported that Sir Douglas Allen had been unable to discover its source, adding that the author of the article concerned which disclosed the Cabinet documents was not to be prosecuted.

USE OF WATER.—On July 2, the Local Government and Planning Minister (Mr. John Silkin) announced legislation to give new powers of control over water use to be applied for limited periods in specific areas where the water supply situation warranted it. He added: " I do not want to exaggerate the problems. Over much of the country water supplies should be adequate to see us through without difficulty until the winter rains come but the Bill should be introduced urgently. The existing shortage and the abnormally hot and dry summer in the southern half of the country presented potentially severe problems in a number of areas." The new powers would strengthen existing powers to make drought orders. Welcoming the statement, the Opposition spokesman (Mr. Arthur Jones) promised cooperation from the Opposition. Sir Geoffrey de Freitas (Lab.) suggested a national water grid to take supplies to dry areas and for the Liberals Mr. Clement Freud, also pledging support, said that it was clear any action would be cosmetic rather than fundamental. The Minister replied that they must give precedence to production in agriculture and industry and described the drought in the south of England at least as the worst for 250 years.

PAY AND PRICES.—The Chancellor of the Exchequer (Mr. Healey) said in the Commons on July 6, at the start of a two-day debate on pay and prices policy, that the increase in gross domestic product over the coming year was likely to be 5 per cent. compared with the 4 per cent. forecast in the budget. The increase in industrial output should be 9 per cent. against the 8 per cent. in the budget. He also said that the rate of inflation in other countries might move past Britain's in the coming winter. The most important aspect of the agreement with the unions was that the U.K. would be one of the few countries in the world which could look forward to a rapid rate of economic recovery over the next 18 months. Without a pay agreement, their problems would be insoluble. Exports

were also growing faster than expected and unemployment should be lower while the public sector borrowing requirement should be less than forecast in the budget. It was unlikely that the rate of inflation would be brought down to the previous year's target of under 10 per cent., but the rate of growth was faster and consistent with getting unemployment down to 3 per cent. in 1979.

The Shadow Chancellor (Sir Geoffrey Howe) declared that Mr. Healey had told them " precisely nothing " and suggested that some Labour Left-wingers wanted to go beyond the iron curtain for an economic system. While accepting the need for a pay policy, he said that it would not cure inflation and in the end would make the cure far harder and divert attention from the essential policies. Mr. Richard Wainwright, for the Liberals, accused the Chancellor of dangerous complacency and said that while they might achieve single digit inflation by the end of 1977, he believed that it would rise again to about 12 per cent. early in 1978. Mr. Douglas Crawford, for the S.N.P., said that the U.K. ship of state was awash with borrowed money and there was no reason why a thrifty Scotland should suffer from the excesses of a spendthrift England. On the second day's debate, Mrs. Shirley Williams said that the private sector of industry might not survive if rates of return on capital continued to fall. The country was placed on yet another tightrope, that of achieving the short-term aim of defeating inflation without jeopardizing the medium term aim —the need for industrial recovery and much higher levels of industrial investment. There would have to be a rate of return to the public and private sectors to enable them to survive, invest and expand and that was one reason they had decided that a limited relaxation of the price code was necessary. For the Opposition, Mrs. Sally Oppenheim said that the Government's options had almost all run out and they were faced with the double irony of restraining pay and relaxing price controls at the same time. Mr. Edward Heath fully supported the agreement reached with the trade unions on pay restraint but said that the real test was whether the Government would say that the unions should behave in the same way towards any democratically-elected government. Winding-up, the Employment Secretary (Mr. Albert Booth) described the unemployment forecast as " bleak ", but stressed that the Government was considering new proposals to cushion the effects, particularly on young people. Industrial strategy called for a far greater readiness to change jobs. The Government had a majority of 35 on an Opposition motion deploring the absence of a convincing strategy for economic recovery based on a prosperous private sector and the reduction of State spending and borrowing, the figures being 286 votes to 251. When Scottish Nationalists forced a division on the inflation and price code White Papers, they were defeated by 279 votes to 13, a Government majority of 266, and Government Orders giving effect to pay limits and extending existing prices legislation were approved without a vote.

An all-party backbench revolt in the Commons on July 14 reduced the tax on widows' pensions when M.P.s voted 190 to 170, a majority against the Government of 20, to free the first 50 per cent. of their pensions from tax. The Government defeat occurred during the report stage of the Finance Bill when the successful amendment was moved by Mr. Robert Kilroy-Silk (Lab.), who said that the concession would help 25,000 widows from the first world war and 65,000 from the second, the cost of this exemption amounting to £3½ million a year at the most. Mr. John Nott,

Conservative spokesman on Treasury affairs, pointed out that the tax threshold had fallen so dramatically that war widows, who received one third of the average national wage, were having to pay tax. The Financial Secretary (Mr. Robert Sheldon) admitted that the " emotional case " for the war widows was justifiable but said that the way to help them was by increasing benefits rather than adjusting tax allowances and exemptions. He estimated this concession would cost up to £10 million.

There was further uproar in the Commons on July 15 when the Leader of the House (Mr. Foot) announced Government intentions to " guillotine " debate on five major controversial bills in one day, with frequent calls of " Cheat " from the Tory benches in an hour-long verbal fracas. Mrs. Thatcher accused Mr. Foot of unprecedented contempt for Parliament and declared that Conservative M.P.s would not want to pair to allow ministers to represent " such a dictatorial Government overseas." The measures to be " guillotined " were the Aircraft & Shipbuilding Industries Bill, Dock Work Regulation Bill, Education Bill, Health Services Bill, and Rent (Agriculture) Bill. Mr Foot repudiated the Opposition charges and denied that free speech was being curtailed, but Mr. John Peyton, shadow Leader of the House, angrily said that Mr. Foot had blown to pieces the last shreds of his reputation as a parliamentarian. Mr. Foot insisted that there had been previous occasions when governments had used five time-table (guillotine) motions in a single session although he conceded not on a single day. Tories stood in their places and shouted " Resign " at Mr. Foot, who however declined to accept any charge from the Opposition about his side being opposed to the proper operation of Parliament because of the introduction of guillotine motions. On July 20, after 10 hours of non-stop debate, the Government secured their motions to time-table debates on these bills in six divisions by majorities ranging from 6 to 23.

MR. HEALEY'S STATEMENT.—On July 22, the Chancellor of the Exchequer, Mr. Healey, made a statement in the Commons about measures which the Government had decided to take to secure its social and economic objectives. The Chancellor declared: " Our overriding priority is to restore the prosperity of the British economy through the regeneration of our industry and to provide the essential conditions to bring down, and to keep down, the intolerable level of unemployment. To do this we must ensure that manufacturing industry has sufficient resources available to take advantage of the exceptional opportunities open to us in the export field; we have to get our rate of inflation down to the level of our competitors' and hold it there; and we have got to do both in a way which will protect the poorest and weakest of our people and retain the social consensus on which the success of all our policies depends.

" In my Budget speech last April I said that I expected our gross domestic product, which fell during 1975, to grow by about 4 per cent., and manufacturing output to grow by about 8 per cent., in the year to mid 1977. The increase in demand would come largely from exports and stock-building: little from consumption. In fact, the recovery has proceeded faster than I then expected, led by a vigorous growth in exports. On present policies I would expect GDP to increase over the 18 months from the first half of 1976 to an annual rate of 5 per cent. and exports of goods and services by 11 per cent. This could imply a very rapid rate of increase in manufacturing production, perhaps as much as 9 per cent. We must as usual expect a lag before these developments affect the present unacceptable figures of unemployment; but on current prospects I would expect unemployment to start falling before the end of the year. Money supply has grown well within the guidelines I set at the time of the Budget.

" The balance of payments on current account, however, remains in substantial deficit. The 12 per cent. depreciation of sterling since March will inevitably worsen the balance of payments in the short term, and make it more necessary than ever for us to maintain the confidence of those from whom we may have to borrow to finance our external deficit. On the other hand the increase in our exports and in import substitution deriving from our increased competitiveness will later bring a massive improvement. In fact we have a unique opportunity for export-led growth, something we have sought in vain ever since the Second World War.

" The Prime Minister and I have said many times that the Government stands ready to take whatever action may be necessary to make room for the growth in exports and productive investment on which this country's future depends. It remains my considered judgment that there is no call for major action in the current financial year. Firm action to break into the tendency for public expenditure to exceed planned levels has already been taken. In particular, our new techniques of control, notably cash limits, will ensure that expenditure in 1976/77 is strictly contained within the limits which the Government have published. But there is no economic or financial case for further reduction in public expenditure or the PSBR this year, which I now estimate will be about £11½ billion, about £½ billion less than the Budget estimate.

" It has been right for us, like other countries, to run a large fiscal deficit in the depths of the recession so as to keep unemployment lower than it would otherwise have been. It would however be wrong to do this through the period of recovery which is now beginning. Unless the deficit falls steadily over the next 3 years as expansion proceeds, the financing of the public sector will pre-empt private savings which productive industry is likely to require on a substantial scale to finance stockbuilding and investment; or it will lead to an excessive growth of the money supply which would refuel inflation. Given the economic prospect as we now see it, we intend that the PSBR for 1977/78 shall be reduced to £9 billion or less. Next year the recovery of the economy is likely by itself to reduce the PSBR only by something like £1 billion to about £10½ billion. This alone will not be enough. Fiscal action is needed in addition to achieve the objective which the Government set. I believe that it would be wrong in present conditions to load on to taxation anything approaching the whole burden of adjustment. In particular, a major increase in the burden of personal taxation would have unacceptable consequences for take home pay. It could wreck our counter inflation policy in the coming year.

" I must therefore look to public expenditure for a major contribution and I am announcing now, public expenditure reductions of £1 billion at 1976 Survey prices for 1977/78, which will be the crucial year for recovery. In deciding where the reductions of £1 billion should fall the Government have avoided mechanical cuts across the board. We have deliberately decided to maintain the main social security benefits like pensions so as to provide the maximum support to those in need here at home. We have also decided to maintain, untouched, our aid programme to the Third World.

The main purpose of our measures is to allow manufacturing industry to take the maximum advantage of the opportunities now presented to it. Because of the priority which the Government are giving to the industrial strategy, we have been concerned to avoid damaging the trade, industry and employment programmes. We intend to move towards putting emphasis on selective, as against general, assistance to industry. We plan therefore to increase significantly the resources available for selective assistance to industry through the N.E.B. and the Scottish and Welsh Development Agencies, as well as from the Government direct, so as to support the work on the industrial strategy now under way in N.E.D.C. Our experience shows that this is the most cost-effective way of helping to achieve the reversal of our post-war industrial decline. As part of this policy of selective support for industry, the Government will also watch vigilantly the need for any extension of its existing selective import restraints to provide temporary protection to viable industries faced with unfair foreign competition. We have already taken action and we are anxious to discuss with both sides of industry the need for further action of this kind. In some areas we have already increased provision for public expenditure, especially for the Department of Employment's programme, including funds provided to the Manpower Services Commission for training. In addition, we are prepared to make provision, within the revised programme, for a possible Government contribution in 1977/78 to the collective funding of any scheme of apprentice training which may emerge from the public discussion of our recent Consultative Document on that subject. This shift of emphasis towards selective assistance to industry will require savings in expenditure of three kinds. First, Regional Employment Premium is at present £3 for men and £1·50 for women: in future it will be at a single rate of £2 for both. Second, we will introduce legislation to reduce the employer's rebate from the Redundancy Fund from 50 per cent. to 40 per cent. Third, savings will be obtained on regional development grants by imposing a delay of some 3 months in payment of approved claims. We also propose to concentrate these grants in future on manufacturing investment by withdrawing eligibility from the construction and private mining industries. Apart from further selective action still to be decided, the net effect of all these measures will be to reduce the trade, industry and employment programmes in 1977/78 by £105 million.

" Net savings of £157 million will be made on the capital investment programmes of the nationalized industries other than B.N.O.C. These savings are spread between the industries and should not affect the main industrial objectives of any of them. We believe the time has come to review the treatment of the nationalized industry programmes generally in our public expenditure figures so as to bring our practice more closely into line with that of other countries. There will be net savings of £87 million on roads and related expenditure. Net savings of £25 million will be obtained on existing agricultural and forestry programmes, largely by deferring the payment of capital grants, and ending the lime subsidy.

" Our existing plans envisaged that food subsidies would be largely phased out by 1978–79. This process will be accelerated, to save £80 million in 1977/78. The effect of this acceleration on the RPI will be only about 0·1 per cent. The Government have decided to save £5 million on overseas services other than aid in 1977/78. The planned Defence Budget for 1977/78 will be cut by

£100 million. This will be achieved by rephasing the works programme and some deferrals.

" Approvals for new housebuilding by local authorities are running at a substantially higher level than allowed for in the estimates in the last Public Expenditure White Paper. It is therefore necessary to reintroduce control over this programme and to limit the rate of approvals so that over-spending is avoided. Reductions will not be imposed in areas where housing needs are greatest. In addition, net savings of £146 million will be achieved, principally by reductions in local authority mortgage lending. The building societies have expressed their willingness to help fill this gap in mortgage lending. Net savings of £81 million will be obtained on existing programmes for other environmental services. For 1976–77 we have agreed to postpone the 5p increase in the charge for school meals that was due this September, but if the charge were kept at 15p in 1977–78, that would add £43 million to net expenditure on school meals in that year. We propose to limit this addition to £15 million by raising the charge by 10p in the autumn of 1977. We shall save £45 million on the rest of the education programme, mainly by curtailing capital expenditure on the universities and other educational building and reducing the budgets for science and the arts. The total net saving on this programme will therefore be £30 million."

The Chancellor continued: " We have given high priority to the poorer members of our society and particularly to old age pensioners. We shall continue to honour our commitments to uprate the main social security benefits regularly and we shall maintain general social security expenditure in 1977/78. Furthermore, we propose to increase the rate of the new mobility allowance in November 1977. But we shall be introducing legislation to restrict the unemployment benefit entitlement of those with substantial occupational pensions; and non-contributory invalidity benefit for housewives will now be introduced in November 1977. Taking into account the increase in mobility allowance, these measures will save about £21 million net in 1977/78. Reductions of £70 million will be made in 1977/78 in the health and personal social services programme as a whole but there will be no cuts in services for patients in the N.H.S. This will consist of £20 million on capital expenditure on the N.H.S. and on local authority personal social services; £20 million by way of extra receipts from increases in dental and ophthalmic charges and £10 million from savings on overheads and measures to curb the drugs bill; and it is proposed to save a further £20 million in 1977/78 (£40 million in a full year) by legislation to recoup mainly from insurance companies the full cost to the N.H.S. of treating road accident cases.

" A reduction of £10 million will be made mainly in expenditure on Government accommodation. A reduction of £35 million will be made in Northern Ireland. Some £3 million of this is the result of the new equalized rate of regional employment premium. The remainder of the cuts will be spread widely over the different Northern Ireland programmes.

" Together with the saving of £60 million on debt interest which results in 1977/78 from the measures I am announcing, the total public expenditure saving will be £1,012 million. This will reduce the PSBR in 1977/78 by about £80 million."

Turning to taxation, the Chancellor explained: " In addition to the public expenditure measures which I have announced, further action in the tax

field is needed to reduce the P.S.B.R. to £9 billion. A massive increase in income tax or indirect taxation would be disastrous for our counter-inflation policy, particularly since the effects would be felt immediately in the middle of the next pay round. The Government have therefore decided instead to make an addition of 2 percentage points to the employers' national insurance contribution. The Government will be introducing legislation early in the new Session, so that the addition can take effect from 6 April 1977. It will yield about £910 million in 1977/78 and about £1,030 million in a full year. Less than half of this will come from manufacturing industry. This sum will further reduce the P.S.B.R. in 1977/78 by about £700 million. The addition, like the existing contributions, will be an allowable cost for purposes of the Price Code and corporation tax. The Government's decision on the Price Code to come into effect on 1 August will include a rate of 50 per cent for investment instead of 35 per cent. proposed in the consultative document and an adjustment factor of 1·4 for depreciation instead of the earlier proposal of 1·3. These further changes should contribute to industrial expansion and in themselves make little difference to prices. The total estimated effect of the public expenditure and tax measures I have announced is to increase the price level by about 1 per cent. by March 1978, nearly 2 years from now. On current forecasts these measures will suffice to achieve the Government's objective of getting P.S.B.R. down to £9 billion in 1977/78. The measures will reduce the General Government Deficit from just under 6 per cent. of G.D.P. this year to 3 per cent. G.D.P. next year—a reduction of nearly half. If inflation and output move as forecast I would expect the growth in money supply to be lower next year than this. There remains a risk that, even after the reduction in the P.S.B.R., the necessary restraint in the growth of the money supply might result in industry being denied essential finance. I intend to ensure that that does not happen. It is essential that any increase in bank lending should be directed to priority borrowing in particular for exports, import saving, and investment and working capital for productive industry.

" As a result of these measures I expect G.D.P. to increase over the 18 months from the first half of 1976 at an annual rate of about 4½ per cent. and manufacturing production at a rate of about 8½ per cent. Unemployment in early 1978 will still be lower than expected, even though the measures may by then have reduced the fall in unemployment by about 60,000.

" The measures I have announced have one overriding purpose—to make certain that this recovery can be sustained until full employment is achieved. I believe these measures will enable both sides of industry to work closely together with the Government to achieve our common aim with full confidence that the remaining obstacles to our success are removed," Mr. Healey concluded.

The Shadow Chancellor (Sir Geoffrey Howe) welcomed the significant step in the right direction although the announcement was simply the first step along the long, hard stony road which would have to be followed to restore the balance and health of the economy. Mr. Norman Atkinson (Lab.) said that the cuts might mean some 60,000–70,000 men and women in the non-manufacturing workforce losing their jobs by the end of 1977 and if that was the case the Chancellor might have the confidence of the international creditors but he would have certainly lost the confidence of the Labour movement. Mr. Healey regretted that it had been necessary to take measures which would affect employment but a failure to do so would have consequences for sterling, the balance of payments and in the paralysis of the economy which would have completely excluded the chance of a steady and sustained return to full employment.

The Commons sat until 10.45 p.m. on July 23, a total of 11 hours 45 minutes, the longest Friday sitting since the war and probably this century. Normally Friday business terminates at 4.30 p.m. starting at 11 a.m. but on this occasion Northern Ireland M.P.s staged a full and time-exempted debate on the affairs of Ulster when the Appropriation (Northern Ireland) Order was discussed.

DEVOLUTION PROPOSALS.—Also on August 3, the Leader of the House (Mr. Foot) announced a series of changes in plans for devolved assemblies in Scotland and Wales which Mr. William Whitelaw described as welcome but of limited value. He added that the opportunity for conflict and the inevitable increase in bureaucracy contained in the original proposals remained and they were as objectionable as ever. Mr. Foot said that far from proposing to increase bureaucracy they were proposing to increase democracy. His view was that the best way of proceeding with proposals for devolution of the English regions would be to publish a document on the subject about the same time as the Government introduced its devolution bill. Mr. David Steel welcomed the improvements, particularly those which Liberals had requested in removing the so-called " Governor-General " powers of the Scottish Secretary. Mr. George Reid (S.N.P.) said that access to Scotland's own natural resources was needed, and power in fiscal areas and trade, but Mr. Foot replied that what S.N.P. wanted was separatism and there was no element of that in their proposals. Mr. Donald Anderson (Lab.) remarked that Mr. Foot was building constitutional castles in the air and said that the people of Wales and Scotland should be given a chance to express their view in a referendum. Mr. Iain Sproat (C.) described the Devolution Bill as " a dead duck even before you start." Appeasement would lend even greater strength to the opinion that a Scottish parliament would be " a start down the slippery slope to separatism." But Mr Foot answered that far from being injurious to the U.K., the way the Government proposed to proceed was the only way the U.K. could effectively be kept together. Mr. William Hamilton (Lab.) said that the more powers given to the assembly, the less defensible it became to have 71 Scottish M.P.s at Westminster.

Three more days of less controversial business elapsed before an overworked and weary House of Commons rose for the summer recess on August 6, the House of Lords having adjourned a week earlier on July 29. The Lords however reassembled on September 27 to get to grips with the highly-contentious legislation completed with considerable difficulty by the Commons, which itself decided to return on October 11 to cope with the overspill of unfinished work.

PUBLIC ACTS OF PARLIAMENT 1975-1976

This list of Public Acts commences with 17 Public Acts which received the Royal Assent before September 1975. Those Public Acts which follow received the Royal Assent after August 1975. The date stated after each Act is the date on which it came into operation.

HEARING AID COUNCIL (EXTENSION) ACT 1975 (December 29, 1975) extends the Hearing Aid Council Act 1968 to Northern Ireland.

NEW TOWNS ACT 1975 (July 3, 1975) raises the limits imposed on amounts which may be borrowed by development corporations and the Commission for the New Towns and provides for the payment of pensions to chairmen of development corporations and remuneration and allowances to members of committees conducting business for the Commission.

BRITISH LEYLAND ACT 1975 (July 3, 1975) authorises the acquisition of shares by the Secretary of State in British Leyland Motor Corporation Ltd. and provides for expenditure incurred.

APPROPRIATION ACT 1975 (August 1, 1975) applies a sum out of the Consolidated Fund to the service of the year ending on March 31, 1976 and appropriates supplies granted in this Session of Parliament and repeals certain Consolidated Fund and Appropriation Acts.

FINANCE (No. 2) ACT 1975 (August 1, 1975) grants certain duties alters others and amends the law relating to the National Debt and the Public Revenue, and makes further provision in connection with Finance.

CONSERVATION OF WILD CREATURES AND WILD PLANTS ACT 1975 (August 1, 1975) provides for the protection and conservation of wild creatures and wild plants and amends the Badgers Act 1973; for example it makes it an offence to uproot any wild plant save in the circumstances provided by the Act.

GUARD DOGS ACT 1975 (various dates) regulates the keeping and use of guard dogs; and for connected purposes.

SALMON AND FRESHWATER FISHERIES ACT 1975 (August 1, 1975) consolidates the Salmon and Freshwater Fisheries Act 1923 and certain other enactments relating to salmon and freshwater fisheries, and repeals obsolete enactments.

LIMITATION ACT 1975 (September 1, 1975) amends the law about the limitation of actions and other proceedings. The Act implements the recommendations of the Law Reform Committee's Interim Report on Limitation of Actions: Personal Injury Claims (Cmnd. 5630).

STATUTORY CORPORATIONS (FINANCIAL PROVISIONS) ACT 1975 (August 1, 1975) makes further provision for compensating nationalised industries for losses due to price restraint; and provides with respect to finance and administration in the public sector.

COAL INDUSTRY ACT 1975 (September 1, 1975) provides for grants to the NCB to meet expenditure under a scheme providing for compensation for pneumoconiosis; enables the Board to withdraw support to enable coal to be worked and to work coal in former copyhold land; provides further for opencast operations; and for connected purposes.

REMUNERATION, CHARGES AND GRANTS ACT 1975 (August 1, 1975) provides for the counter-inflationary policy set out in the White Paper ("The Attack on Inflation" Cmnd. 6151); including provision for reduction of grants to local authorities and for increases in housing subsidies.

LOTTERIES ACT 1975 (various dates) makes further provision with regard to lotteries promoted on behalf of societies or as incidents of entertainments and authorises local authorities to promote lotteries; and for connected purposes.

CRIMINAL JURISDICTION ACT 1975 (various dates) creates extra-territorial offences under the law of Northern Ireland, amends the criminal law of Northern Ireland, provides for obtaining evidence in Northern Ireland for the trial of offences in the Republic of Ireland. The Act implements the recommendations contained in the Report of the Law Enforcement Commission (Cmnd. 5627).

SOCIAL SECURITY PENSIONS ACT 1975 (various dates) provides for social security pensions and other related benefits to consist of a basic element and an additional component related to higher earnings; and makes various other provisions in relation to pensions.

CHILD BENEFIT ACT 1975 (August 7, 1975) replaces family allowances with child benefit and, pending introduction of that benefit, provides for an interim benefit for unmarried or separated parents with children; and provides for connected purposes.

NORTHERN IRELAND (EMERGENCY PROVISIONS) (AMENDMENT) ACT 1975 (August 21, 1975) amends the Act of 1973 and makes further provision with respect to criminal proceedings in Northern Ireland; and for connected purposes.

INHERITANCE (PROVISION FOR FAMILY AND DEPENDANTS) ACT 1975 (April 1, 1976) makes fresh provision for empowering the court to make orders for the making out of the estate of a deceased person of provision for the spouse former spouse, child, child of the family or dependant of that person; and for connected purposes.

IRON AND STEEL ACT 1975 (December 12, 1975) consolidates certain enactments relating to the British Steel Corporation and the iron and steel industry.

SEX DISCRIMINATION ACT 1975 (various dates) makes unlawful certain kinds of sex discrimination and discrimination on the ground of marriage, and establishes a Commission with the function of working towards the elimination of such discrimination and promoting equality of opportunity between men and women generally; and for related purposes.

RECESS ELECTIONS ACT 1975 (December 12, 1975) consolidates the enactments relating to the issue of warrants for by-elections when the House of Commons is in recess and repeals section 106(2) of the Bankruptcy Act 1914.

HOUSING FINANCE (SPECIAL PROVISIONS) ACT 1975 (November 12, 1975) prevents surcharges under the Local Government Act 1933 arising out of the Housing Finance Act 1972 and substitutes other means of making good losses or deficiencies in respect of which such surcharges would fall to be made; and for connected purposes.

INDUSTRY ACT 1975 (November 20, 1975) establishes a National Enterprise Board; confers powers on the Secretary of State to prohibit the passing to persons not resident in the U.K. of control of undertakings engaged in manufacturing industry and to acquire compulsorily the capital or assets of such undertakings where control has passed to such persons and makes various other provisions with respect to industry.

SCOTTISH DEVELOPMENT AGENCY ACT 1975 (day to be appointed) establishes a Scottish Development Agency; provides for the appointment of a Scottish

Industrial Development Advisory Board; makes provision for assistance in connection with air services serving the Highlands and Islands; and for connected purposes.

WELSH DEVELOPMENT AGENCY ACT 1975 (January 1, 1976) establishes a Welsh Development Agency and a Welsh Industrial Development Advisory Board; and for connected purposes.

EMPLOYMENT PROTECTION ACT 1975 (various dates) establishes machinery for promoting the improvement of industrial relations; amends the law relating to workers, employers, trade unions and employers' associations; provides for the establishment of a Maternity Pay Fund and for the extension of the jurisdiction of industrial tribunals; and provides for many other matters connected with employment.

CHILDREN ACT 1975 (various dates) makes further provision for children with particular reference to adoption, fostering, custody and care.

CINEMATOGRAPH FILMS ACT 1975 (November 12, 1975) provides for payments by the British Film Fund Agency to the National Film Finance Corporation and for the application of those payments by that Corporation.

PETROLEUM AND SUBMARINE PIPE-LINES ACT 1975 (January 1, 1976) establishes the British National Oil Corporation and provides for its functions; provides for licences to search for and get petroleum and for submarine pipe-lines and refineries; authorises loans and guarantees in connection with development of petroleum resources of the U.K.; and for connected purposes.

POLICYHOLDERS PROTECTION ACT 1975 (November 12, 1975) provides for the indemnification (in whole or in part) of policyholders and others who have been or may be prejudiced in consequence of the inability of authorised insurance companies carrying on business in the U.K. to meet their liabilities, and for the imposition of levies on the insurance industry to finance the protection; and for connected purposes.

LOCAL LAND CHARGES ACT 1975 (various dates) makes new provision for the keeping of local land charges registers and the registration of matters therein.

COMMUNITY LAND ACT 1975 (various dates) enables local authorities and certain other authorities to acquire, manage and deal with land suitable for development and makes provision for and in connection with the public ownership of land; amends planning law and the rules for assessing the value of land where compensation is payable; provides for the acquisition of unoccupied office premises and establishes a Land Authority for Wales.

AIRPORTS AUTHORITY ACT 1975 (December 12, 1975) consolidates the 1965 Act and certain related enactments.

CONSOLIDATED FUND (No. 3) ACT 1975 (December 19, 1975) applies certain sums out of the Consolidated Fund to the service of the years ending on March 31, 1976 and 1977.

OECD SUPPORT FUND ACT 1975 (December 19, 1975) establishes a financial support fund for the Organization for Economic Co-operation and Development.

MONEYLENDERS (CROWN AGENTS) ACT 1975 (December 19, 1975) makes provision as to the application to the Crown Agents for Overseas Governments and Administrations of the Moneylenders Acts 1900 to 1927 and the Moneylenders Acts (Northern Ireland) 1900 to 1969.

CIVIL LIST ACT 1975 (December 19, 1975) provides for supplementing out of moneys provided by Parliament the sums mentioned in the Civil List Act 1972.

NORTHERN IRELAND (LOANS) ACT 1975 (December 19, 1975) makes further provision with regard to making loans to the Northern Ireland Consolidated Fund.

NATIONAL COAL BOARD (FINANCE) ACT 1976 (March 4, 1976) increases the limit on the borrowing powers of the NCB; provides for payment to the Board out of public money towards mineworkers' pension scheme deficiency and provides for the costs of stock-piling coal and coke.

CONSOLIDATED FUND ACT 1976 (March 25, 1976) applies certain sums out of the Consolidated Fund to the service of the years ending on March 31, 1975 and 1976.

ROAD TRAFFIC (DRIVERS' AGES AND HOURS OF WORK) ACT 1976 (various dates) amends the Road Traffic Act 1972 insofar as it relates to drivers' licences and the minimum age for driving certain classes of vehicles; amends Part VI of the Transport Act 1968 relating to drivers' hours; and for connected purposes.

TRUSTEE SAVINGS BANKS ACT 1976 (various dates) establishes a Trustee Savings Banks Central Board; confers wider powers on trustee savings banks and provides for miscellaneous other connected provisions.

EDUCATION (SCHOOL-LEAVING DATES) ACT 1976 (part on March 25, 1976 the remainder on April 6, 1976) makes further provision with respect to school-leaving dates (by altering the summer leaving date); and for connected purposes.

SOLICITORS (SCOTLAND) ACT 1976 (March 25, 1976) makes provision as to the powers of the Law Society of Scotland to intervene in the professional practice and conduct of solicitors; provides for the appointment of a lay observer to examine the Society's treatment of complaints about solicitors and of lay members to the Scottish Solicitors Discipline Tribunal; provides for the indemnity of solicitors against professional liability; and for connected matters.

TRADE UNION AND LABOUR RELATIONS (AMENDMENT) ACT 1976 (March 25, 1976) repeals replaces or amends part of the Act of 1974 and provides for a charter on freedom of the Press.

PREVENTION OF TERRORISM (TEMPORARY PROVISIONS) ACT 1976 (March 25, 1976) repeals and re-enacts with amendments the provisions of the Act of 1974.

WATER CHARGES ACT 1976 (March 25, 1976) provides for the refund by water authorities in England and Wales of charges imposed on properties not connected to public sewers which were levied in 1974-75 and 1975-76.

POST OFFICE (BANKING SERVICES) ACT 1976 (March 25, 1976) extends the banking services provided by the Post Office and provides capital for those services; reduces the capital debt of the Post Office; and for connected purposes.

HOUSING (AMENDMENT) (SCOTLAND) ACT 1976 (April 13, 1976) increases the limit on the amount of advances to the Scottish Special Housing Association.

STATUTE LAW REVISION (NORTHERN IRELAND) ACT 1976 (April 13, 1976) revises the statute law of Northern Ireland by repealing obsolete enactments.

DAMAGES (SCOTLAND) ACT 1976 (May 13, 1976) amends the law of Scotland relating to the damages recoverable in respect of deaths caused by personal injuries and for patrimonial loss caused by personal injuries which reduce expectation of life; abolishes the right of assythment and provides for various connected purposes.

FATAL ACCIDENTS AND SUDDEN DEATHS INQUIRY (SCOTLAND) ACT 1976 (day to be appointed) provides in Scotland for the holding of public inquiries in respect of fatal accidents, deaths of

persons in legal custody, sudden, suspicious and unexplained deaths and deaths occurring in circumstances giving rise to serious public concern.

RATING (CARAVAN SITES) ACT 1976 (April 13, 1976) allows for the valuation and rating of caravan sites or portions of caravan sites inclusive of parts separately occupied by caravanners and of their caravans; and for connected purposes.

STATUTE LAW (REPEALS) ACT 1976 (May 27, 1976) promotes the reform of the statute law by the repeal of certain enactments which (except in so far as their effect is preserved) are no longer of practical utility and makes other provision in connection therewith.

LAND DRAINAGE (AMENDMENT) ACT 1976 (day to be appointed) amends the Acts of 1930 and 1961, the Agriculture (Miscellaneous Provisions) Act 1968 and related enactments.

LICENSING (AMENDMENT) ACT 1976 (May 27, 1976) amends the law relating to premises for which special hours certificates may be granted under the Act of 1964.

SEYCHELLES ACT 1976 (May 27, 1976) makes provision for and in connection with the attainment by Seychelles of fully responsible status as a Republic within the Commonwealth.

EDUCATION (SCOTLAND) ACT 1976 (various dates) makes provision with respect to school commencement and leaving dates and the supply of milk in schools; provides for the remuneration of members of Independent Schools Tribunals; provides as to the construction of educational endowment schemes and for connected purposes.

CROFTING REFORM (SCOTLAND) ACT 1976 (June 10, 1976) confers new rights on crofters and cottars to acquire subjects tenanted or occupied by them; confers rights on crofters to share in the value of land resumed by landlords or taken possession of compulsorily; protects the interests of crofters and cottars from planning blight; provides financial assistance for crofters, cottars and certain owner-occupiers; amends the law with respect to common grazings and provides for miscellaneous other connected purposes.

FRESHWATER AND SALMON FISHERIES (SCOTLAND) ACT 1976 (June 10, 1976) makes new provision with respect to freshwater and salmon fisheries in Scotland and for connected purposes.

ATOMIC ENERGY AUTHORITY (SPECIAL CONSTABLES) ACT 1976 (June 10, 1976) extends the powers relating to firearms of special constables appointed on the nomination of the United Kingdom Atomic Energy Authority; extends the property in respect of which, and the places where, they may exercise those and their other powers; and provides for connected purposes.

DEVELOPMENT LAND TAX ACT 1976 (August 1, 1976) imposes a new tax on the realization of the development value of land; provides for the termination of the charges on capital gains from land imposed by Chapters I and II of Part III of the Finance Act 1974; and for connected purposes. The rate of tax is 80 per cent. although there are provisions for reduced rates and exemptions.

FAIR EMPLOYMENT (NORTHERN IRELAND) ACT 1976 (part on September 1, 1976, the remainder on December 1, 1976) establishes an agency with the duties of promoting equality of opportunity in employments and occupations in Northern Ireland between people of different religious beliefs and of the working for the elimination of discrimination which is unlawful by virtue of the Act; makes unlawful in connection with such employments and occupations certain kinds of discrimination on the ground of religious belief or political opinion; and for connected purposes.

EXPLOSIVES (AGE OF PURCHASE etc.) ACT 1976 (July 22, 1976) restricts the sale to young persons of explosive substances, including fireworks, who are apparently under the age of sixteen, and increases the penalties provided by sections 31 and 80 of the Explosives Act 1875 to £200.

THEATRES TRUST ACT 1976 (day or days to be appointed but no later than January 22, 1977) establishes a Theatres Trust for the better protection of theatres; and for connected purposes.

CONGENITAL DISABILITIES (CIVIL LIABILITY) ACT 1976 (July 22, 1976) makes provision (which binds the Crown) as to civil liability in the case of children born disabled in consequence of some person's fault; and extends the Nuclear Installations Act 1965, so that children so born in consequence of a breach of duty under that Act may claim compensation. *Inter alia* the Act imposes a duty of care for the safety of her unborn child on a pregnant woman who knows she is pregnant whilst she is driving a motor vehicle.

REPRESENTATION OF THE PEOPLE (ARMED FORCES) ACT 1976 (day to be appointed) makes provision for the registration for electoral purposes of members of the armed forces and the wives and husbands of such members.

FATAL ACCIDENTS ACT 1976 (September 1, 1976) consolidates the Fatal Accidents Acts.

LEGITIMACY ACT 1976 (August 22, 1976) consolidates certain enactments relating to legitimacy.

RESTRICTIVE PRACTICES COURT ACT 1976 (day to be appointed) consolidates certain enactments relating to the Restrictive Practices Court.

POLICE PENSIONS ACT 1976 (July 22, 1976) consolidates the Police Pensions Act 1948 and certain other enactments relating to the pensions to be paid to and in respect of members of police forces.

ADOPTION ACT 1976 (day or days to be appointed) consolidates the enactments having effect in England and Wales in relation to adoption.

FOOD AND DRUGS (CONTROL OF FOOD PREMISES) ACT 1976 (September 22, 1976) amends the Food and Drugs Act 1955 by prohibiting the sale, etc., of food in certain circumstances.

DANGEROUS WILD ANIMALS ACT 1976 (October 22, 1976) regulates the keeping of certain kinds of dangerous wild animals. Under normal circumstances a licence will now be required to keep a dangerous wild animal, the licence being obtainable from the local authority—this does not apply, *inter alia*, to zoos, circuses and pet shops.

DIVORCE (SCOTLAND) ACT 1976 (section 8 on September 1, 1976 the rest on January 1, 1977) amends the law of Scotland relating to divorce and separation; facilitates reconciliation of the parties in consistorial causes; amends the court's powers to make orders relating to financial provision and aliment; abolishes the oath of calumny; and for connected purposes.

FINANCE ACT 1976 (July 29, 1976) grants certain duties, alters other duties and amends the law relating to the National Debt and the Public Revenue and makes further provision in connection with Finance: for example, it reduces the higher rate of VAT to 12½ per cent. and brings in new rules relating to the taxation of benefits derived from employment by company directors and others in higher paid employment.

PROTECTION OF BIRDS (AMENDMENT) ACT 1976 (July 29, 1976) amends further the Act of 1954.

LOTTERIES AND AMUSEMENTS ACT 1976

RESTRICTIVE TRADE PRACTICES ACT 1976.

IRON AND STEEL (AMENDMENT) ACT 1976.

BRITISH RAILWAYS ACT 1976.

APPROPRIATION ACT 1976.

DROUGHT ACT 1976.

RATING (CHARITY SHOPS) ACT 1976.

POLICE ACT 1976.

Government and Public Offices

CERTAIN APPOINTMENTS NOTED IN THE FOLLOWING PAGES HAVE BEEN SUPER-SEDED BY THE MINISTERIAL CHANGES MADE IN SEPT. 1976. A FULL LIST OF THE RECONSTRUCTED MINISTRY WILL BE FOUND ON PAGE 82.

NOTE—The salaries shown are in most cases those actually received. In certain instances, however, the National Scale without corresponding London weighting is given.

MINISTRY OF AGRICULTURE, FISHERIES AND FOOD
Whitehall Place, London, S.W.1†
[01–839 7711]

The Ministry of Agriculture, Fisheries and Food is responsible in England and Wales for administering government policy for agriculture, horticulture and fishing industries. In association with the Intervention Board for Agricultural Produce and the other Agricultural Departments in the United Kingdom it is responsible for the administration of the EEC common agricultural and fisheries policy and for various national support schemes. It also administers schemes for the control and eradication of animal and plant diseases and the improvement and drainage of agricultural land. The Ministry sponsors the food and drink manufacturing industries and distribution trades. It is concerned with the quality of food, food compositional standards, hygiene and labelling and advertising. It acts as agent for the Department of Prices and Consumer Protection in administering and operating food subsidies. It has certain responsibilities for ensuring public health standards in the manufacture, preparation and distribution of basic foods. Some functions relating to agriculture and fisheries in Wales are the joint responsibility of the Minister and the Secretary of State for Wales, and some of the Ministry's responsibilities for animal health extend to Scotland. The Ministry maintains relations with overseas countries and participates in some activities of certain international organizations concerned with agriculture, fisheries and food. The Ministry is also responsible for the Royal Botanic Gardens, Kew.

†Unless otherwise stated, this is the main address of Divisions of the Ministry.

Salary List
Minister....................	£13,000
Minister of State.............	£ 7,500
Parliamentary Secretary.......	£ 5,500
Permanent Secretary..........	£18,675
Second Permanent Secretary....	£17,175
Deputy Secretary.............	£14,000
Under Secretary.............	£12,000
Assistant Secretary...........	£ 8,650 to £11,000
Senior Principal.............	£ 7,750 to £ 9,350
Principal...................	£ 5,680 to £ 7,450
Senior Executive Officer.......	£ 4,900 to £ 5,900
(HEO-A)...........	£ 3,900 to £ 4,700
Assistant Solicitor.............	£ 9,033 to £11,000
Chief Scientific Officer........	£11,670
Deputy Chief Scientific Officer.	£10,180 to £11,190
Senior Principal Scientific Officer	£ 8,650 to £ 9,798
Chief Statistician.............	£ 8,650 to £11,000
Chief Engineer.............	£11,440

Minister, THE RT. HON. (THOMAS) FREDERICK PEART, M.P.
 Private Secretary (Principal), G. J. L. Avery.
 Assistant Private Secretary, R. C. Gurd.
 Parliamentary Private Secretary, G. Grant, M.P.
Minister of State, EDWARD STANLEY BISHOP, M.P.
 Private Secretary, Mrs. K. J. A. Brown.
Parliamentary Secretary, G. S. Strang, M.P.
 Private Secretary, F. J. H. Scollen.
Parliamentary Clerk (Senior Executive Officer), A. P. Woodhouse, T.D.
Permanent Secretary, Sir Alan Neale, K.C.B., M.B.E.
 Private Secretary, P. M. Boyling.
Second Permanent Secretary, Sir Frederick Kearns, K.C.B., M.C.
 Private Secretary, A. H. Abbott.

ESTABLISHMENT DEPARTMENT
Director of Establishments (Under Secretary), D. H. Andrews, C.B.E.

Personnel Division I
Victory House, 30–34 Kingsway, W.C.2
[01–405 4310]
Assistant Secretary, D. W. M. Herbert.

Personnel Division II
Victory House, 30–34 Kingsway, W.C.2
[01–405 4310]
Assistant Secretary, P. Pooley.

Staff Training Branch,
Government Buildings, Tolcarne Drive, Pinner, Middlesex
[01–868 7161]
Principal, Mrs. M. D. White.

Office Services Division★
Assistant Secretary, H. W. Foot.

Welfare Branch
Victory House, 30–34 Kingsway, W.C.2
[01–405 4310]
Chief Welfare Officer (Senior Executive Officer), Miss D. C. Dixson.

FINANCE DEPARTMENT
Principal Finance Officer (Under Secretary), J. M. Grant.

Finance Division I★
Assistant Secretary, Mrs. H. I. Pinkerton.

Finance Division II★
Assistant Secretary, A. Jeffrey-Smith.

Appropriation Accounts and Data Processing Division
Government Buildings, 98–122 Epsom Road, Guildford, Surrey
[0483 68121]
Assistant Secretary, D. Kimber.

Audit and Costings Division
29 Bressenden Place, S.W.1
[01–828 4366]
Assistant Secretary, S. T. K. Hester.

INFORMATION DIVISION
Chief Information Officer–A (Assistant Secretary), L. E. E. Jeanes.
Chief Press Officer, T. J. B. Dawes.
Principal Librarian, F. C. Hirst.

LEGAL DEPARTMENT
55 Whitehall, S.W.1
[01–839 7711]
Legal Adviser and Solicitor (Deputy Secretary), G. F. Aronson.
Principal Assistant Solicitors (Under Secretaries), R. W. Brown; H. R. Reade.

Legal Division A
Assistant Solicitor, G. R. J. Robertson.

Legal Division B
Assistant Solicitor, L. Neville.

Legal Division C
Assistant Solicitor, A. E. Munir.

Legal Division D
Assistant Solicitor, D. B. McGilligan.

Legal Division E
Assistant Solicitor, H. G. Roberts.

Legal Division F
Assistant Solicitor, F. A. Richards.

Legal Division G
Assistant Solicitor, A. Hall-Brown.

MANAGEMENT SERVICES
Under Secretary, G. R. Woodward.

Management Services Division I
Victory House, 30–34 Kingsway, W.C.2
[01–405 4310]
Assistant Secretary, G. Seymour.

★ At Great Westminster House, Horseferry Road. S.W.1 [01–216 6311].

Management Services Division II*
Assistant Secretary, M. Madden.
Management Services Division III
Victory House, 30–34 Kingsway, W.C.2
[01-405-4310]
Assistant Secretary, J. Stopforth.
CHIEF SCIENTIST'S GROUP
Chief Scientist (Deputy Secretary), Dr H. C. Pereira,
F.R.S.
*Chief Scientific Adviser, Food, and Deputy Chief
Scientist,* G. A. H. Elton (*Under Secretary*).*
Deputy Chief Scientist (Chief Scientific Officer),
W. F. Raymond.*

RESEARCH AND DEVELOPMENT
REQUIREMENTS DIVISION*
Assistant Secretary, M. M. A. Gray.
FOOD SCIENCE DIVISION*
Deputy Chief Scientific Officer, A. W. Hubbard.

ROYAL BOTANIC GARDENS, KEW
Kew, Richmond, Surrey
[01-940 1171]
Director (Under Secretary), J. P. M. Brenan.
Deputy Director (Deputy Chief Scientific Officer),
(vacant).
EUROPEAN ECONOMIC COMMUNITY
Under Secretary, D. F. Williamson.
European Economic Community Division I
Assistant Secretary, D. F. Roberts.
European Economic Community Division II
Assistant Secretary, D. H. Griffiths.
EXTERNAL RELATIONS,
AND TROPICAL FOODS
Under Secretary, J. H. V. Davies.
External Relations Division I
Assistant Secretary, J. C. Edwards.
External Relations Division II
Assistant Secretary, J. A. Anderson.
Tropical Foods Division
29 Bressenden Place, S.W.1
[01-828 4366]
Assistant Secretary, G. W. Ford.

AGRICULTURE
Deputy Secretary, B. D. Hayes, C.B.
GENERAL AGRICULTURAL POLICY
Under Secretary, D. Evans.
General Agricultural Policy Division I
Assistant Secretary, Mrs. A. M. Pickering.
General Agricultural Policy Division II
49/53 Parliament Street, S.W.1
[01-233-3000]
Assistant Secretary, G. Stapleton.
CEREALS AND SUGAR
Under Secretary, J. E. Dixon.
Cereals Division
49/53 Parliament Street, S.W.1
[01-2333 000]
Assistant Secretary, T. R. M. Sewell.
Sugar Division
Assistant Secretary, A. V. Vickery.

MEAT, POULTRY AND EGGS
Under Secretary, G. Wilson.
Pig and Poultry Products Division
Assistant Secretary, R. W. Holmwood.
Beef Division
Assistant Secretary, J. H. Holroyd.
Sheep and Livestock Subsidies Division
Assistant Secretary, D. R. Dow.
MILK, POTATOES AND
AGRICULTURAL MARKETING
Under Secretary, Mrs. J. Archer.
Milk and Milk Products Division
Senior Economic Adviser. (Head of Division) C. W.
Capstick, C.M.G.
Marketing Policy and Potatoes Division*
Assistant Secretary, Mrs. E. A. Attridge.

* At Great Westminster House, Horseferry Road,
S.W.1 [01-216 6311].

FISHERIES AND FOOD
Deputy Secretary, J. R. Moss, C.B.

FISHERIES DEPARTMENT*
Fisheries Secretary (Under Secretary), J. G. Kelsey.
Fisheries Division I
Assistant Secretary, W. R. Small.
Fisheries Division II
Assistant Secretary, K. W. Wilkes.
Fisheries Division III
Assistant Secretary, G. P. Jupe.
Fisheries Division IV
Assistant Secretary, C. R. Cann.
Sea Fisheries Inspectorate
Chief Inspector, P. G. Jeffery..............£9,350
Fisheries Research
Director of Fisheries Research (Chief Scientific Officer),
A. J. Lee, D.S.C.
*Deputy Directors of Fisheries Research (Deputy Chief
Scientific Officers),* Dr. D. H. Cushing; A. Preston.
Fisheries Research Laboratory
Pakefield Road, Lowestoft, Suffolk
[0502 62244]
Fisheries Radiobiological Laboratory
Hamilton Dock, Lowestoft, Suffolk
[0502 4381]
Fisheries Laboratory
Remembrance Avenue, Burnham-on-Crouch,
Essex
[0621 782658]
Fisheries Experiment Station
Benarth Road, Cònwy, Gwynedd
[049 263 2419]
Salmon and Freshwater Fisheries
Laboratory
Whitehall Place, S.W.1
[01-839 7711]
*Chief Salmon and Freshwater Fisheries Officer (Senior
Principal Scientific Officer),* I. R. H. Allan.
Fish Diseases Laboratory
The Nothe, Weymouth, Dorset
[03057 72137]
Officer-in-charge (Senior Principal Scientific Officer),
Dr. J. P. Stevenson.
Torry Research Station
P.O. Box 31, 135 Abbey Road,
Aberdeen
[0224 54171]
Director (Deputy Chief Scientific Officer), Dr. G. H. O.
Burgess, F.R.S.E.
Humber Laboratory
Wassand Street, Hull
[0482 27879]
Officer-in-charge (Senior Principal Scientific Officer),
J. R. Burt.

FOOD POLICY
Under Secretary, W. E. Mason.
Food and Drink Industries Division
Assistant Secretary, J. R. Catford.
Food Policy Division I
Assistant Secretary, J. W. Hepburn.
Food Policy Division II
Assistant Secretary, L. W. Tolladay.

FOOD STANDARDS AND SUBSIDIES*
Under Secretary, R. F. Giles.
Food Standards Division*
Assistant Secretary, H. M. Goodall.
Food Subsidies Division
Assistant Secretary, E. S. Virgo.

HORTICULTURE
Under Secretary, E. J. G. Smith.
Horticulture Division I*
Assistant Secretary, N. J. P. Hutchison.
Horticulture Division II*
Assistant Secretary, V. T. Humphreys.

*At Great Westminster House, Horseferry Road,
S.W.1 [01-216 6311]

**Emergencies, Fertilisers and
Feedingstuffs Standards Division**
Assistant Secretary, L. G. Hanson.

LAND AND SERVICES
Deputy Secretary, E. W. Maude, C.B.

LAND
Under Secretary, Miss I. O. H. Lepper.
Land Improvement Division★
Assistant Secretary, J. S. W. Henshaw.
Land Use and Tenure Division★
Assistant Secretary, H. J. B. Rice.
Land Drainage and Water Supply Division★
Assistant Secretary, A. F. Longworth.

POLLUTION, SEEDS, SAFETY AND LABOUR
Under Secretary, J. B. Foxlee.

**Environmental Pollution, Pesticides and
Infestation Control Division★**
Assistant Secretary, R. E. Melville.

Plant Variety Rights Office and Seeds Division
White House Lane, Huntingdon Road,
Cambridge
[0223 77151]
Assistant Secretary and Controller, H. A. S. Doughty.

**Agricultural Safety, Training and
Wages Division**

Eagle House, 90–96 Cannon Street, E.C.4
[01-626 1575]
Assistant Secretary, O. A. Robertson.

ANIMAL HEALTH
Under Secretary, C. H. Shillito.

Animal Health Division I
Government Buildings, Hook Rise South,
Tolworth, Surbiton, Surrey
[01–337 6611]
Assistant Secretary, H. Pease.

Animal Health Division II
Government Buildings, Hook Rise South,
Tolworth, Surbiton, Surrey.
[01–397-9121]
Assistant Secretary, I. P. M. Macdonald.

Animal Health Division III
Government Buildings, Garrison Lane,
Chessington, Surrey
[01–397 9121]
Assistant Secretary, W. T. Barker.

Animal Health Division IV
Tolworth Tower, Surbiton, Surrey
[01–337 6611]
Assistant Secretary, K. A. Bird.

ECONOMICS AND STATISTICS
Director of Economics and Statistics (Under Secretary),
L. Napolitan, C.B.
Economics Division I
Senior Economic Adviser, J. A. Evans
£8,650 to £11,000
Economics Division II
Senior Economic Adviser, G. Sharp

Economics Division III
49–53 Parliament Street, S.W.1
01-233-3000
Senior Economic Adviser, P. J. Lund
£8,650 to £11,000
Statistics Division I★
Chief Statistician, Miss J. R. Weatherburn.

Statistics Division II
Government Buildings, Tolcarne Drive,
Pinner, Middlesex
[01–868 7161]

★ At Great Westminster House, Horseferry Road,
S.W.1 [01-216 6311].

Government Buildings, 98–122 Epsom Road,
Guildford, Surrey
[0483 68121]
Whitehall Place, S.W.1
[01–839 7711]
Chief Statistician, A. H. J. Baines.

Food Economics Unit
Senior Economic Adviser, Dr. A. P. Power
£8,650 to £11,000

REGIONAL ORGANIZATION
Deputy Secretary, E. W. Maude, C.B.

Eastern Region
Block C, Government Buildings,
Brooklands Avenue, Cambridge
[0223 58911]
Chief Regional Officer, T. W. Nicol
£8,650 to £11,000

East Midland Region
Block 2, Government Buildings, Chalfont Drive,
Nottingham
[0602 292251]
Chief Regional Officer, B. J. Marshall
£8,650 to £11,000

Northern Region
Government Buildings, Kenton Bar,
Newcastle-upon-Tyne
[0632 869811]
Chief Regional Officer, F. H. Goodwin
£8,650 to £11,000

South Eastern Region
Block A, Government Offices,
Coley Park, Reading
[0734 581222]
Chief Regional Officer, R. M. Loosmore
£8,650 to £11,000

South Western Region
Block 3, Government Bldgs., Burghill Road,
Westbury-on-Trym, Bristol
[0272 500000]
Chief Regional Officer, K. Harrison Jones
£8,650 to £11,000

West Midland Region
Woodthorne, Wolverhampton
[0902 754190]
Chief Regional Officer, E. G. Griffiths
£8,650 to £11,000

Yorkshire/Lancashire Region
Block 2, Government Buildings,
Lawnswood, Leeds
[0532 674411]
Chief Regional Officer, J. A. Brown
£8,650 to £11,000

WELSH DEPARTMENT
Plas Crug, Aberystwyth, Dyfed
[0970 3162]
Welsh Secretary (Under Secretary), W. R. Smith, C.B.
Assistant Secretary (Policy), J. Medway.
Assistant Secretary (Administration), A. W. Bridges.
Senior A. D. A. S. Officer, R. W. Soden, T.D.

AGRICULTURAL DEVELOPMENT AND ADVISORY SERVICE (A.D.A.S.)
Director General (Deputy Secretary), Dr. K. Dexter.
Deputy Director General, E. S. Carter £13,230

AGRICULTURE★
Chief Agricultural Officer (Under Secretary), A. J.
Davies.
Senior Agricultural Officers, M. Barker; J. J. North
£11,000
Senior Horticultural Officer, G. C. Williams £11,000
Superintending Horticultural Marketing Inspector,
A. F. Gardner . . . . £7,750 to £9,350

AGRICULTURAL SCIENCE
Head of Service (Under Secretary), W. Dermott.★

★ At Great Westminster House, Horseferry Road,
S.W.1 [01-216 6311].

Pest Infestation Control Laboratory
London Road, Slough, Berks.
[75 34626]
Director (Chief Scientific Officer), F. H. Jacob.
Deputy Director (Deputy Chief Scientific Officer),
J. A. Freeman, O.B.E.

Plant Pathology Laboratory and Plant Health and
Seeds Inspectorate
Hatching Green, Harpenden, Herts.
[0582 75241/46]
Director (Deputy Chief Scientific Officer), A. H.
Strickland *(acting)*.★
Superintending Plant Health and Seeds Inspector, J. P.
Cleary.....................£7,750 to £9,350
Chief Science Specialist, Dr. H. C. Gough. £11,000

LAND DRAINAGE★
Chief Engineer (Directing Grade), G. Cole.

LANDS★
Chief Surveyor (Under Secretary), R. B. Sayce

VETERINARY
Government Buildings, Hook Rise South,
Tolworth, Surbiton, Surrey
[01–337 6611]
Chief Veterinary Officer, A. C. L. Brown... £13,230
Deputy Chief Veterinary Officer (Under Secretary),
A. J. Stevens.
Central Veterinary Laboratory, New Haw,
Weybridge, Surrey
[91 41111]
Deputy Chief Veterinary Officer and Director of
Veterinary Laboratories (Under Secretary), Dr.
A. B. Paterson.
Lasswade Veterinary Laboratory, Eskgrove,
Lasswade, Midlothian.
[031–663 6525]
Cattle Breeding Centre, Shinfield, Reading,
Berks.
[0734 883157]

ADAS ADMINISTRATION★
Chief Administrator (Under Secretary), B. Peart.
Agricultural Development and Advice Division
Assistant Secretary, Miss M. Hooley.
ADAS Technical Services Division
Assistant Secretary, P. A. Naylor.

ADVISORY COUNCIL FOR AGRICULTURE
AND HORTICULTURE IN
ENGLAND AND WALES
Whitehall Place, S.W.1
[01–216 7333]
Chairman, Sir Nigel Strutt, T.D.
Vice-Chairman, K. Dexter, Ph.D.
Members, Sir Richard Boughey, Bt.; Prof. D. K.
Britton; The Lord Collison, C.B.E.; Prof. G. R.
Dickson; H. A. Fell; Sir Emrys Jones; Prof.
I. A. M. Lucas; D. H. Phillips, D.F.C.; D. G.
Stevens; Sir Gwilym Williams, C.B.E.
Secretary, S. Hampson.

AGRICULTURAL RESEARCH COUNCIL
160 Great Portland Street, W.1
The Agricultural Research Council was incorporated by Royal Charter on July 23, 1931.
The *Science and Technology Act*, 1965, transferred
responsibility for the Research Council to the Secretary of State for Education and Science and a new
Charter received Royal approval in 1967. The
Council is charged with the organization and development of agricultural and food research and
may, in particular, establish or develop institutions
or departments of institutions and make grants for
investigation and research relating to the advance
of agriculture. The Council is financed jointly
from the Parliamentary vote of the Department of
Education and Science and the Ministry of Agriculture, Fisheries and Food.

★ At Great Westminster House, Horseferry, Road
S.W.1 [01–216 6311].

Council, The Hon. J. J. Astor, M.B.E. *(Chairman)*;
W. A. Biggar, O.B.E., M.C.; Prof. P. W. Brian,
C.B.E., Ph.D., SC.D., F.R.S.; A. C. L. Brown; K.
Dexter, Ph.D.; W. W. Gauld; E. M. W. Griffith;
Prof. J. L. Harley, D.Phil., F.R.S.; Prof. H. Harris,
D.Phil., F.R.S.; Prof. D. L. Hughes, Ph.D.; J. D.
Hutchison, C.B.E., M.C., T.D., D.SC., F.R.S.; Prof. Sir
Bernard Katz, M.D., Ph.D., D.SC., F.R.S.; C. Mac-
kay; Prof. J. Mandelstam, M.C., Ph.D., F.R.S.; J. S.
Martin; Prof. K. S. Mather, C.B.E., Ph.D., D.SC.,
F.R.S.; E. W. Maude, C.B.; Prof. A. Neuberger,
C.B.E., M.D., Ph.D., F.R.S.; H. C. Pereira, Ph.D., D.SC.,
F.R.S.; The Earl of Selborne; The Visct. Tren-
chard, M.C.
Secretary, Sir William Henderson, D.SC., F.R.S.
Chief Scientific Officer, G. W. Cooke, Ph.D., F.R.S.
Under Secretary, G. M. P. Myers.
Assistant Secretaries, F. V. Bird, O.B.E.; R. J. Harris;
J. L. Lake, Ph.D.
Scientific Advisers to the Secretary, K. N. Burns;
J. K. R. Gasser; R. Scarisbrick, Ph.D.; K. L.
Robinson, D.SC.; H. Fore, Ph.D.; A. J. Pritchard,
Ph.D.; D. C. Corbett; T. L. V. Ulbricht, Ph.D.,
D.SC.
Programmes Section, W. S. Wise.
Clerk to the Council, L. S. Porter, O.B.E.
Information Officer, M. F. Goodwin.
For the Research Institutes under the control of
the Council, *see* Index.

EXECUTIVE COUNCIL OF THE
COMMONWEALTH
AGRICULTURAL BUREAUX
Farnham House, Farnham Royal, Slough, Berks.
[Farnham Common: 2281]
The Commonwealth Agricultural Bureaux,
founded in 1929, consist of four Institutes and ten
Bureaux, under the control of an Executive Council,
comprising representatives of the Commonwealth
countries which contribute to its funds. Each
Institute and Bureau is concerned with its own
particular branch of agricultural science and acts as
a clearing house for the dissemination of information of value to research workers throughout the
world. They deal respectively with entomology,
mycology, helminthology and nematology, biological control, agricultural economics, animal
breeding and genetics, animal health, nutrition,
dairy science and technology, forestry, horticulture
and plantation crops, pastures and field crops, plant
breeding and genetics, and soils and fertilizers.
The information is published in journals which
have a monthly circulation of 32,000 in 150 countries. The abstract journals are produced by
computer-assisted processes, and the whole data
base is being consolidated and made available in
machine-readable form. Review articles, books,
maps, monographs and annotated bibliographies on
particular subjects are also issued.
Chairman, J. W. Greenwood *(Canada)*.
Vice-Chairman, Mrs. J. George *(Trinidad & Tobago)*.
Secretary, E. A. Runacres.

Institutes
Commonwealth Institute of Entomology, 56 Queen's
Gate, S.W.7. *Director*, A. H. Parker, Ph.D.
(acting).
Commonwealth Mycological Institute, Ferry Lane,
Kew, Surrey. *Director*, A. Johnston.
Commonwealth Institute of Biological Control, Gordon
Street, Curepe, Trinidad. *Director*, F. J. Sim-
monds, Ph.D., D.SC.
Commonwealth Institute of Helminthology, The White
House, 103 St. Peter's Street, St. Albans, Herts.—
Director, Miss S. M. Willmott, Ph.D.

Bureaux
Agricultural Economics, Dartington House, Little
Clarendon Street, Oxford.—*Director*, J. O.
Jones.
Animal Breeding and Genetics, Animal Breeding
Research Organization, The King's Buildings,
West Mains Road, Edinburgh, Scotland.—
Director, J. D. Turton.

Animal Health, Central Veterinary Laboratory, New Haw, Weybridge, Surrey.—*Director,* R. Mack.

Dairy Science and Technology, Lane End House, Shinfield, Reading.—*Director,* E. J. Mann.

Forestry, Commonwealth Forestry Institute, South Parks Road, Oxford.—*Director,* P. G. Beak, M.B.E.

Horticulture and Plantation Crops, East Malling Research Station, Maidstone, Kent.—*Director,* G. E. Tidbury.

Nutrition, Rowett Research Institute, Bucksburn, Aberdeen, Scotland.—*Director,* Miss D. L. Duncan, Ph.D.

Pastures and Field Crops, Hurley, Maidenhead, Berks.—*Director,* P. J. Boyle.

Plant Breeding and Genetics, Department of Applied Biology, Downing Street, Cambridge.—*Director,* R. H. Richens, Ph.D.

Soils, Rothamsted Experimental Station, Harpenden, Herts.—*Director,* B. Butters.

COLLEGE OF ARMS OR HERALDS COLLEGE

Queen Victoria Street, E.C.4
[01-248 2762]

The College of Arms is open daily from 10–4 (Saturdays, 10–1, by appointment) when an Officer of Arms is in attendance to deal with enquiries by the public, though such enquiries may also be directed to any of the Officers of Arms, either personally or by letter.

There are 13 officers of the College, 3 Kings of Arms, 6 Heralds and 4 Pursuivants, who specialize in genealogical and heraldic work for their respective clients. The College possesses the finest records on these subjects in the world. It is the official repository of the Arms and pedigrees of English, Northern Irish, and Commonwealth families and their descendants, and its records include official copies of the records of Ulster King of Arms, the originals of which remain in Dublin.

Arms have been and still are granted by Letters Patent from the Kings of Arms under Authority delegated to them by the Sovereign, such authority having been expressly conferred on them since at least the fifteenth century. A right to Arms can only be established by the registration in the official records of the College of Arms of a pedigree showing direct male line descent from an ancestor already appearing therein as being entitled to Arms, or by making application to the College of Arms for a Grant of Arms.

Earl Marshal, His Grace the Duke of Norfolk, C.B., C.B.E., M.C.

Kings of Arms

Garter, Sir Anthony Richard Wagner, K.C.V.O., D.Litt., F.S.A.

Clarenceux, John Riddell Bromhead Walker, M.V.O. M.C.

Norroy and Ulster, Walter John George Verco, C.V.O. (*Earl Marshal's Secretary*).

Heralds

Windsor, Alexander Colin Cole, F.S.A.

Richmond (and Registrar), John Philip Brooke Brooke-Little, M.V.O. F.S.A.

Somerset, Rodney Onslow Dennys, M.V.O., O.B.E., F.S.A.

York, Conrad Marshall John Fisher Swan, Ph.D.

Lancaster, Francis Sedley Andrus.

Chester (vacant).

Pursuivants

Portcullis, Michael Maclagan, F.S.A.

Rouge Croix, David Hubert Boothby Chesshyre.

Rouge Dragon, Theobald David Mathew.

Bluemantle, Peter Llewellyn Gwynn-Jones.

COURT OF THE LORD LYON

H.M. New Register House, Edinburgh
[031-556 7255]

The Scottish Court of Chivalry, including the genealogical jurisdiction of the *Ri-Sennachie* of Scotland's Celtic Kings, adjudicates rights to arms and administration of *The Scottish Public Register of All Arms and Bearings* (under 1672 cap. 47) and *Public Register of All Genealogies.* The Lord Lyon presides and judicially establishes rights to existing arms or succession to Chiefship, or for cadets with scientific " differences " showing position in clan or family. Pedigrees are also established by decrees of Lyon Court, and by Letters Patent. As *Royal Commissioner in Armory,* he grants Patents of Arms (which constitute the grantee and heirs noble in the Noblesse of Scotland) to "virtuous and well-deserving" Scotsmen, and petitioners (personal or corporate) in Her Majesty's overseas realms of Scottish connection, and issues birth-brieves. In Scots Law, Arms are protected by Statute; their usurpation is punishable, and the Registration Fees of Honour on patents and matriculations are payable to H.M. Exchequer.

Lord Lyon King of Arms, Sir James Monteith Grant, K.C.V.O., W.S., F.S.A. *Scot.*

Heralds

Rothesay, Lt.-Col. Harold Andrew Balvaird Lawson, C.V.O.

Albany, Sir Iain Moncreiffe of that Ilk, Bt., Ph.D., Advocate.

Marchmont, Malcolm Rognvald Innes of Edingight, W.S., F.S.A. *Scot.*

Pursuivants

Unicorn, John Inglis Drever Pottinger.

Ormond, Major David Maitland Maitland-Titterton T.D., F.S.A. *Scot.*

Carrick, John A. Spens, R.D.

Lyon Clerk and Keeper of Records, Malcolm Rognvald Innes of Edingight, W.S., F.S.A. *Scot.*

Procurator-Fiscal, Ivor Reginald Guild, W.S.

Herald Painter, Miss J. M. Mitchell.

Macer, Thomas C. Gray.

ART GALLERIES, ETC.

ROYAL FINE ART COMMISSION

2 Carlton Gardens, S.W.1
[01-930 3935]

Appointed in May, 1924, " to enquire into such questions of public amenity or of artistic importance as may be referred to them from time to time by any of our Departments of State, and to report thereon to such Department; and, furthermore, to give advice on similar questions when so requested by public or quasi-public bodies, where it appears to the said Commission that their assistance would be advantageous." In August, 1933, a Royal Warrant extended the Terms of Reference of the Commission—" so that it shall also be open to the said Commission, if they so desire, to call the attention of any of Our Departments of State, or of the appropriate public or quasi-public bodies, to any project or development which in the opinion of the said Commission may appear to affect amenities of a national or public character "; in May, 1946, a Royal Warrant further extended the Terms of Reference of the Commission as follows:—

We Do give and grant unto you, or any three or more of you, full power to call before you such persons as you shall judge likely to afford you any information upon the subject of this Our Commission; and also to call for, have access to and examine all such books, documents, registers and records as may afford you the fullest information on the subject, and to inquire of and concerning the premises by all other lawful ways and means whatsoever: We Do authorize and empower you, or any three or more of you, to visit and personally inspect such places as you may deem it expedient so to inspect for the more effectual carrying out of the purposes aforesaid:

Chairman, The Lord James of Rusholme.

Commissioners, The Countess of Airlie; Sir Hugh Casson, R.A.; Miss Elizabeth Chesterton; A. W. Cox, C.B.E.; P. M. Dowson, C.B.E.; Sir Ralph

Freeman, C.V.O., C.B.E.; Miss Elizabeth Frink.; Mark Girouard, Ph.D.; A. J. Gordon, C.B.E.; The Duke of Grafton, K.G.; Prof. Bernard Meadows; David Piper, C.B.E., F.S.A.; John Piper, C.H.; Sir Philip Powell, O.B.E., A.R.A.; Sir Paul Reilly; E. F. Ward, C.B.E.; W. Whitfield, C.B.E.; Sir Hugh Wilson, O.B.E.
Secretary, Prof. F. Fielden.

ROYAL FINE ART COMMISSION FOR SCOTLAND
22 Melville Street,
Edinburgh 3
[031-225 5434]

Commissioners, The Lord Johnston, T.D. (*Chairman*); J. A. Coia, C.B.E., R.S.A., F.R.I.B.A.; C. L. Matthew, F.R.I.B.A.; Prof. F. N. Morcos-Asãad, Ph.D.; R. Philipson, P.R.S.A.; A. Reiach, O.B.E., A.R.S.A., F.R.I.B.A.; J. D. Richards, A.R.S.A.; Prof. A. E. Thompson, Ph.D., F.R.S.A.; Mrs. Murray Usher of Cally; H. A. Wheeler, O.B.E., R.S.A.
Secretary, L. C. Prosser.

NATIONAL GALLERY
Trafalgar Square, W.C.2
[01-839 3321]

Hours of opening.—Weekdays 10 to 6 (June–Sept. Tuesdays and Thursdays 10 to 9), Sundays 2 to 6. Closed on Good Friday, Christmas Eve, Christmas Day, Boxing Day and New Year's Day.

The National Gallery is the result of a Parliamentary grant of £60,000 in 1824 for the purchase and exhibition of the Angerstein collection of pictures. The present site was first occupied in 1838 and enlarged and improved at various times throughout the years. A substantial extension to the north of the building with a public entrance in Orange Street was opened in 1975. Expenses for 1975–76 were estimated at £1,083,000.

TRUSTEES

Prof. J. Hale, F.S.A. (*Chairman*); John Piper; Sir Gordon Sutherland, F.R.S.; Prof. M. Froy; The Lord Poole, P.C., C.B.E., T.D.; H. Hodgkin; Prof. B. Yamey, C.B.E.; Sir Isaiah Berlin, O.M., C.B.E., F.B.A.; Mrs. Heather Brigstocke; The Hon. J. D. Sainsbury.

OFFICERS

Director, M. V. Levey, M.V.O.............£12,465
Keeper, C. H. M. Gould......£9,115 to £10,263
Deputy Keepers, A. Braham; A. Smith
                                            £7,616 to £9,215
Scientific Adviser to the Trustees, R. H. G. Thompson
                                            £9,115 to £10,263
Chief Restorer, A. W. Lucas, O.B.E.
                                            £9,115 to £10,263
Building and Security, G. Fox.....£6,145 to £7,915
Finance and Establishments, R. H. Mitchem
                                            £5,365 to £6,365

NATIONAL PORTRAIT GALLERY
St. Martin's Place, Charing Cross Road, W.C.2
[01-930 8511]
Open Monday to Friday 10 to 5. Saturday 10 to 6. Sunday 2 to 6.

The first grant was made in 1856 to form a gallery of the portraits of the most eminent persons in British history, the collections being successively housed in Great George Street, Westminster, in South Kensington, and in Bethnal Green. The present building was opened in 1896, £80,000 being contributed to its cost by Mr. W. H Alexander; an extension erected at the expense of Lord Duveen was opened in 1933.
Chairman, The Lord Kenyon, C.B.E., F.S.A.
Trustees, The Lord President of the Council; The President of the Royal Academy of Arts; Prof. Lawrence Gowing, C.B.E.; The Duke of Grafton, K.G., F.S.A.; Prof. J. H. Plumb, Ph.D., Litt.D., F.B.A., F.S.A.; Prof. Dame Helen Gardner, D.B.E., F.B.A.; Sir Christopher Cockerell, C.B.E., F.R.S.; The Countess of Longford, C.B.E.; Sir Philip Magnus-Allcroft, Bt., C.B.E.; Rev. Prof. J. McManners; J. P. Ehrman, F.B.A., F.S.A.; The Viscount Cobham, K.G., P.C., G.C.M.G., G.C.V.O.; Sir Oliver

Millar, K.C.V.O., F.S.A., F.B.A.; Sir Anthony Wagner, K.C.V.O., F.S.A.; Sir Huw Wheldon.
Director, Keeper, and Secretary, J. T. Hayes, Ph.D., F.S.A................................£11,000
Deputy Keeper, R. L. Ormond..£7,151 to £8,750
Assistant Keepers, C. J. Ford; J. F. Kerslake, F.S.A.; R. W. Gibson; M. Rogers...£4,404 to £7,109

TATE GALLERY
Millbank, S.W.1
[01-828 1212]
Hours of opening.—Weekdays 10 to 6. Sundays 2 to 6. Closed on New Year's Day, Good Friday, Christmas Eve, Christmas Day and Boxing Day.

The Tate Gallery comprises two national art collections: (*a*) British painting, from the 16th century to the present day, including works by Turner, Blake, Constable and the Pre-Raphaelites; (*b*) Modern Foreign Painting, from the Impressionists, and Modern Sculpture, British and foreign. There is an almost continuous programme of temporary exhibitions within the field of the collection. The Gallery was opened in 1897, the cost of erection (£80,000) being defrayed by Sir Henry Tate, who also contributed the nucleus of the present collection. The Turner Wing, built at the expense of Sir Joseph Duveen was opened in 1910. Lord Duveen defrayed the cost of galleries to contain the collection of modern foreign painting, completed in 1926, and a new sculpture hall, completed in 1937. Expenses for 1975–76 are estimated at £1,714,000
Director, Sir Norman Reid...............£12,000
Trustees, The Lord Bullock, F.B.A. (*Chairman*); Sir Richard Attenborough, C.B.E.; S. De Ferranti; Prof. M. Froy; F. L. T. Graham-Harrison, C.B.; The Lord Harlech, P.C., K.C.M.G.; H. Hodgkin; P. Huxley; N. MacDermot, O.B.E., Q.C.; Prof. C. St. J. Wilson, F.R.I.B.A.
Keeper of the British Collection, M. R. F. Butlin
                                            £8,650 to £9,798
Keeper of the Modern Collection, R. E. Alley
                                            £8,650 to £9,798
Keeper of Exhibitions and Education, M. G. Compton
                                            £8,650 to £9,798
Keeper of Conservation, The Viscount Dunluce
                                            £8,650 to £9,798
Keeper and Assistant Director, Mrs. J. Jeffreys
                                            £8,650 to £9,798
Deputy Keepers, R. E. Morphet; L. A. Parris
                                            £7,151 to £8,750
Assistant Keepers (*Class I*), Miss E. Koslovska-Einberg; T. Measham; Miss R. Rattenbury; Miss A. Seymour; R. Parkinson; D. Brown; Mrs. P. Gilmour................£4,404 to £7,109
Establishment Officer, P. G. O'Donohoe
                                            £4,900 to £5,900

WALLACE COLLECTION
Hertford House, Manchester Square, W.1
[01-935 0687]
Admission free. Open on weekdays 10 a.m. to 5 p.m.: Sundays 2 p.m. to 5 p.m. Closed on Good Friday, December 24–26, and January 1.

The Wallace Collection was bequeathed to the nation by the widow of Sir Richard Wallace, Bt., K.C.B., M.P., on her death in 1897, and Hertford House was subsequently acquired by the Government. The collection includes pictures, drawings and miniatures, French furniture, sculpture, bronzes porcelain, armour and miscellaneous *objets d'art*. The total net expenses were estimated at £340,000 in 1976–77.
Director, T. W. I. Hodgkinson, C.B.E......£9,798
Assistant Directors, R. A. Cecil; A. V. B. Norman, F.S.A.....................£4,404 to £7,109
Establishment and Finance Officer, E. Evans
                                            £3,900 to £4,700

NATIONAL GALLERIES OF SCOTLAND
17 Ainslie Place, Edinburgh
[031-556 8921]
Director, T. H. Scrutton, C.B.E..........£11,000

Trustees, J. Kane, O.B.E. (*Chairman*); R. W. Begg; E. Blackadder; H. A. D. Miles; G. Robertson; A. S. Roger; The Duke of Sutherland.
Restorer, J. P. Dick............£4,404 to £7,109
Assistant Keeper of Education and Information, C. J. M. Johnstone.................£4,404 to £7,109
Secretary, R. J. Johnston........£4,900 to £5,900
Comprising:

National Gallery of Scotland
The Mound, Edinburgh
[031-556 8921]

Open: Monday to Saturday 10 to 5 (until 8 during the Festival); Sunday 2 to 5; Closed 25, 26, 31 December; 1, 2 January.
Keeper, C. E. Thompson........£7,151 to £8,750
Assistant Keeper, H. N. A. Brigstocke
                £4,404 to £7,109
Keeper of Prints and Drawings, K. K. Andrews
                £7,151 to £8,750

Scottish National Portrait Gallery
1 Queen Street, Edinburgh
Hours—as for National Gallery of Scotland.
Keeper, R. E. Hutchison.......£7,151 to £8,750
Assistant Keepers, D. Thomson, Ph.D.; R. K. Marshall, ph.D..............£4,404 to £7,109

Scottish National Gallery of Modern Art
Inverleith House, Royal Botanic Garden, Edinburgh
[031-332 3754]
Open: Monday to Saturday 10 to 6 (or dusk, if earlier); Sunday 2 to 6; Closed 25, 26, 31 December, 1, 2 January.
Keeper, W. D. Hall..........£7,151 to £8,750

(For other British Art Galleries, *see* Index.)

UNITED KINGDOM ATOMIC ENERGY AUTHORITY
11 Charles II Street, S.W.1
[01-930 6262]
Established by the *Atomic Energy Authority Act*, 1954, the Authority took over, on August 1, 1954, the control of atomic energy research and development. The Secretary of State for Energy is responsible to Parliament for general atomic energy policy and for money provided for the Authority.
Chairman, Sir John Hill, Ph.D............£19,600
Deputy Chairman, Dr. W. Marshall, C.B., F.R.S.
                £15,600
Member (*Full-time*), A. M. Allen
         £10,100 to £14,100
(*Part-time*) The Lord Kearton, O.B.E., F.R.S.; Sir Leslie Williams, C.B.E.; Prof. Sir Brian Flowers, F.R.S.; Dr. N. L. Franklin, C.B.E.; W. B. S. Walker; *each* £1,000; C. Allday, C.B.E.; R. A. Peddie; B. G. Tucker, C.B., O.B.E. (*unpaid*).
Secretary, P. J. Searby.

BRITISH AIRPORTS AUTHORITY
2 Buckingham Gate, S.W.1
Set up under the *Airports Authority Act*, 1965, the Authority owns and manages seven major airports—Heathrow, Gatwick, Stansted, Glasgow, Prestwick, Edinburgh and Aberdeen.
Chairman, N. G. Foulkes......(*part-time*) £10,600
Chief Executive, N. G. Payne, C.B.E.

BRITISH AIRWAYS
Airways Terminal, Victoria, S.W.1
[01-828 6822]
Established in 1972 by the Civil Aviation Act of 1971 to control all the activities of B.E.A. and B.O.A.C. The group now trades under the name of British Airways. It has seven operating divisions: British Airways European Division, British Airways Overseas Division, British Airways Regional Division, British Airways Helicopters, British Airways Associated Companies, British Airways Engine Overhaul and International Aeradio. A British Airways Travel division has been set up to handle selling in the United Kingdom for the operating divisions and British Airways Cargo U.K. has been established to control cargo

handling at 18 airports in the United Kingdom. Since April, 1974, B.E.A. and B.O.A.C. have been dissolved. The British Airways Group have about 200 aircraft, total assets of over £500 millions and annual revenues of nearly £500 millions.
Chairman, Sir Frank McFadzean.........£23,330
Deputy Chairman and Managing Director, H. E. Marking, C.B.E., M.C.
Deputy Managing Directors, S. F. Wheatcroft, O.B.E.; J. R. Stainton, C.B.E.
Secretary, B. Wood.

BRITISH BROADCASTING CORPORATION
Broadcasting House, W.1
[01-580 4468]
The BBC was incorporated under Royal Charter as successor to the British Broadcasting Company, Ltd., whose licence expired Dec. 31, 1926. Its present Charter came into force July 30, 1964, for 12 years. In 1976 it was extended for three years to July 1979. The Chairman, Vice-Chairman and other Governors are appointed by the Crown. The BBC is financed by revenue from receiving licences for the Home services and by a Grant in Aid from Parliament for the External services. The total number of television licences in force in March 1976 was 17,787,984, of which 9,148,732 were for monochrome receivers and 8,639,252 for colour receivers.
Chairman, Sir Michael Swann, F.R.S......£10,000
Vice-Chairman, The Hon. Mark Bonham Carter
                £2,000
Governors, Prof. A. E. Thompson (*Scotland*) £2,000; Dr. G. T. Hughes (*Wales*), £2,000; W. O'Hara (*N. Ireland*); R. B. Fuller, C.B.E.; A. W. C. Morgan; G. Howard; The Lord Greenhill of Harrow, G.C.M.G., O.B.E.; Mrs. Stella Clarke; E. P. Chappell..................(*each*) £1,000
Director-General, Sir Charles Curran.
Special Adviser to the Director-General, Sir Huw Wheldon, O.B.E., M.C.
Managing Directors, I. Trethowan (*Television*); G. E. H. Mansell (*External Broadcasting*); P. H. Newby, C.B.E. (*Radio*).
Directors, J. Redmond, (*Engineering*); Hon. K. H. L. Lamb (*Public Affairs*); M. O. Tinniswood (*Personnel*); H. P. Hughes (*Finance*); D. Muggeridge (*Programmes, Radio*); A. D. G. Milne (*Programmes, Television*).
Deputy Director of Engineering, B. McCrirrick.
General Manager, Publications, J. G. Holmes.
Legal Adviser, R. J. Marshall.
Chief Assistant to Director-General, P. H. Scott.
Chief Secretary, C. D. Shaw.
Controller, Information Services, D. Webster.
Head of Publicity and Information, P. W. Woon.
Assistant Secretary and Head of Secretariat, J. A. Norris.

Controllers of Regional Offices
English Regions, J. F. Grist, Broadcasting Centre, Pebble Mill Road, Birmingham.
Scotland, H. A. Hetherington, Broadcasting House, Queen Margaret Drive, Glasgow, W.2.
Wales, O. Edwards, Broadcasting House, Llandaff, Cardiff.
Northern Ireland, R. T. L. Francis, Broadcasting House, 25–27 Ormeau Avenue, Belfast.

BRITISH RAILWAYS BOARD
222 Marylebone Road, N.W.1
[01-262 3232]
Chairman, P. Parker, M.V.O..............£23,100
Vice-Chairman, J. M. W. Bosworth, C.B.E. £19,100
Full-time Members, H. L. Farrimond; D. Fowler; varying sums between £12,600 and £17,600.
Part-time Members, Sir Alistair Pilkington; Sir David Serpell, K.C.B., C.M.G., O.B.E.; The Lord Taylor of Gryfe; Sir Alan Walker
              from £1,000 to £3,000
Chief Secretary, G. R. Burt.

BRITISH STEEL CORPORATION
33 Grosvenor Place, S.W.1
[01-235 1212]
The British Steel Corporation was established

under the Iron and Steel Act 1967 which vested in the Corporation the shares of the fourteen major steel companies. The Corporation's main duty is to supply such iron and steel products as it thinks fit in sufficient quantities and at such prices as will meet reasonable demand.

Chairman, Sir Charles Villiers, M.C........£28,330
Deputy Chairmen, M. Littman, Q.C.; Sir Peter Matthews *(part-time).*
Members (full-time), The Lord Layton; L. R. P. Pugh, C.B.E., V.R.D.; R. Scholey; R. Smith, C.B.E.; D. G. S. Waterstone; Executive Deputy Chairman and full-time members in salary range £16,830 to £21,830.
Members (part-time), J. Diamond; The Lord Gregson; W. D. Griffiths; Sir James Menter, F.R.S.; Sir Melvyn Rosser; A. Silberston; Sir Matthew Stevenson, K.C.B., C.M.G.; The Viscount Weir; J. B. Woodeson, C.B.E.
                          from £1,000 to £4,000
Secretary, R. W. Roseveare.

BRITISH TOURIST AUTHORITY

Queen's House, 64 St. James's Street, S.W.1
[01–629 9191]

Under the Development of Tourism Act, 1969, four co-equal statutory Tourist Boards were established: the British Tourist Authority, the English Tourist Board, the Scottish Tourist Board and the Wales Tourist Board. Each is financed mainly by direct grant-in-aid from Government and is an independent statutory body. The British Tourist Authority has specific responsibility for promoting tourism to Great Britain from overseas. It also has a general responsibility for tourism within Great Britain as a whole.
Chairman (vacant).
Director General, L. J. Lickorish, C.B.E.

BRITISH TRANSPORT DOCKS BOARD

Melbury House, Melbury Terrace, N.W.1
Constituted under the *Transport Act,* 1962. The Board owns and operates 19 active ports.
Chairman, Sir Humphrey Browne, C.B.E.
Director and General Manager, J. K. Stuart.

BRITISH WATERWAYS BOARD

Melbury House, Melbury Terrace, N.W.1
[01–262 6711]
Chairman, Sir Frank Price *(part-time)*......£6,665
Vice-Chairman, (vacant)   £2,307
Members (all part-time), The Rt. Hon. Sir Frederick Corfield, Q.C.; B. C. Gillinson; G. C. Godber, C.B.E.; I. Harrington; E. S. J. Standen; F. Welsh; The Baroness White *(each £1,000).*
General Manager, D. G. McCance.
Secretary, T. T. Luckcuck.

CABINET OFFICE

Whitehall, S.W.1
[01–233 3000]
Secretary of the Cabinet, Sir John Hunt, K.C.B.
                                      £20,175
Second Permanent Secretaries, Sir John Garlick, K.C.B.; Sir Leonard Hooper, K.C.M.G., C.B.E.; G. R. Denman, C.B., C.M.G..............£17,175
Deputy Secretaries, T. F. Brenchley, C.M.G.; D. Le B. Jones, C.B.; W. I. McIndoe; D. L. Pearson.;
                                      £14,000
Under Secretaries, A. K. H. Atkinson; J. D. Bryars; G. E. Gammie; J. W. Gibson; A. D. Gordon-Brown; J. A. Marshall; P. A. Rhodes, C.M.G.; J. S. Scott-Whyte..............£12,000
Assistant Secretaries, H. J. Blanks; D. L. Bryars; D. McI. Christie; D. Cunningham; J. S. Elliott, O.B.E.; R. A. Gomme; R. P. S. Hughes; Mrs. A. K. Jackson; J. M. Mackintosh, C.M.G.; D. A. Nicholls ; J. A. Patterson ; D. C. Thomas; W. R. Tomkys; M. W. Townley; B. O. White; C. Wilson; G. S. Wishart *(Establishment Officer)*.............£6,700 to £8,850

Senior Principals, Dr. D. C. Wilson; J. L. Wright, M.B.E......................£6,000 to £7,050
Senior Principal Scientific Officers, Dr. A. V. Cohen; Dr. J. Swaffield............£6,750 to £7,750
Deputy Establishment Officer, G. S. Royston
                                  £5,680 to £7,450
Chief Clerk and Departmental Record Officer, R. W. Smith...................£5,680 to £7,450
Central Policy Review Staff, Head, Sir Kenneth Berrill, K.C.B.....................£18,675
Deputy Secretary, C. R. Ross, C.B........£14,000
Under Secretaries, A. G. Hurrell; W. J. L. Plowden
                                          £12,000
Assistant Secretaries, A. M. W. Battishall; M. I. Goulding; D. E. Young.......£6,700 to £8,850
Senior Economic Adviser, H. C. G. Hawkins.
Special Appointments, Dr. M. Hart; Miss K. M. H. Mortimer.
Central Statistical Office:
Director and Head of the Government Statistical Service, Prof. Sir Claus Moser, K.C.B., C.B.E., F.B.A......................£17,175
Deputy Secretary, A. J. Boreham, C.B....£14,000
Under Secretaries, O. Nankivell; A. A. Sorrell; W. B. Wakefield; J. W. S. Walton......£12,000
Chief Statisticians, Miss S. P. Carter; G. A. Dean; D. W. Flaxen; J. Hibbert; P. B. Kenny; M. J. G. M. Lockyer; J. A. Rushbrook; E. J. Thompson; D. C. L. Wroe...........£6,700 to £8,850
Deputy Chief Scientific Officers, Dr. J. H. Ludley
                                   £8,100 to £9,440
Historical Section:
H. L. Theobald, O.B.E. *(Departmental Records Adviser)*..................£6,700 to £8,850

CABLE AND WIRELESS LIMITED

Head Office—Mercury House, Theobald's Road, W.C.1
[01–242 4433]
Chairman, H. G. Lillicrap, C.B.E. *(part-time).* £9,080
Managing Director, A. A. Willett........£12,830
Directors, W. H. Davies; P. A. McCunn; R. A. Rice; R. W. Cannon............£10,330
Directors (part-time), W. R. R. Haines; A. J. Kirkwood; D. Berriman.................£1,000
J. Hodgson *(unpaid).*
Secretary, A. Cooke.

CHARITY COMMISSION

Ryder Street, St. James's, S.W.1
[01–214 6000]
Graeme House, Derby Square, Liverpool
[051–27 3191]
Central Register of Charities,
St. Albans House, Haymarket, S.W.1
[01–214 6000]
The Charity Commission was constituted under Act of Parliament in 1853 and reconstituted under the Charities Act, 1900, with the general function of promoting the effective use of charitable monies and a duty to keep a register of charities in England and Wales. The Official Custodian for Charities holds investments for charities and remits the income, free of income tax, to trustees.
Chief Commissioner, T. Fitzgerald........£13,460
Commissioners, T. Keith; C. A. H. Parsons
                                          £12,000
Deputy Commissioners, C. A. Weston, D.F.C., G.M.; M. B. Tripp; Miss A. M. E. Jacobsen; F. W. Trinder; R. W. Groves; B. T. Dixon.
                                  £9,033 to £11,000
Asst. Commissioners, G. J. Morgan; A. B. Rabagliati; M. A. Rao; Miss B. K. Searle; J. Farquharson; J. F. Claricoat; J. W. M. Caine; B. B. Davies; M. G. Sayer; D. P. F. Giles; H. B. C. Horrell; G. S. Goodchild; H. K. Udvadia; Mrs. J. F. R. Quint; Mrs. H. M. Phillips. .£5,443 to £8,750
Secretary and Asst. Commissioner, R. S. Morgan
                                  £8,650 to £11,000
Principals, R. Booth *(Asst. Commissioner)*; Miss E. M. M. Thornton *(Asst. Commissioner)*; S. H. Way; W. P. Richards.............£5,680 to £7,450

Official Custodian for Charities, L. A. Jimenez
£7,750 to £9,350
Deputy Official Custodian, G. C. Robertson
£5,680 to £7,450
Establishment Officer, Miss C. M. Clark
£5,680 to £7,450
Deputy Establishment Officer, J. Macmillan
£4,900 to £5,900
Senior Executive Officers, D. McNaught; Miss S. M. St. C. Smith; J. Samuels; J. O. Nichols; Mrs. J. E. Smith; D. Forrest; R. J. Crick; K. C. Norman; P. C. A. Pyman; J. P. Beacall
£4,900 to £5,900

CHURCH COMMISSIONERS
1 Millbank, Westminster, S.W.1
[01–930 5444]

The Church Commissioners were established on April 1, 1948, by the amalgamation of *Queen Anne's Bounty* (established 1704) and the *Ecclesiastical Commissioners* (established 1836). The Commissioners have three main tasks:—

(1) the management of their capital assets so that they may earn income;
(2) the proper distribution of that income; and
(3) the discharge of a large number of administrative duties conferred on them by Acts of Parliament and Measures of the General Synod (former Church Assembly).

The Commissioners' income for the year ended March 31, 1976, was derived from the following sources:—

Stock exchange investments	£15,665,000
Land and property	14,468,000
Mortgages and loans	3,490,000
Money received for particular beneficiaries	3,852,000
	£37,475,000

This income was used as follows:—

Clergy stipends and pensions	£29,015,000
Clergy houses (maintenance, out-goings, provision and improvements)	3,975,000
Other church property	654,000
Added to capital to improve future income	68,000
Professional fees	277,000
Administrative costs of Commissioners' office	2,511,000
Administrative costs of Church of England Pensions Board and Advisory Board for Redundant Churches	255,000
For allocation after April 1, 1976	720,000
	£37,475,000

Constitution
The 2 Archbishops, the 41 diocesan Bishops, 5 deans, 10 other clerks and 10 laymen appointed by the General Synod; 4 laymen nominated by the Queen; 4 persons nominated by the Archbishop of Canterbury; The Lord Chancellor; The Lord President of the Council; the First Lord of the Treasury; The Chancellor of the Exchequer; The Secretary of State for the Home Dept.; The Speaker of the House of Commons; The Lord Chief Justice; The Master of the Rolls; The Attorney-General; The Solicitor-General; The Lord Mayor and two Aldermen of the City of London; The Lord Mayor of York and one representative from each of the Universities of Oxford and Cambridge.

Church Estates Commissioners:—
First, Sir Ronald Harris, K.C.V.O., C.B.
Second, T. W. Walker, M.P.
Third, Dame Betty Ridley, D.B.E.
Secretary, S. P. Osmond, C.B.
Under Secretary General, J. E. Shelley.
Financial Secretary, H. M. G. Pryor.

Investments Secretary, A. I. McDonald.
Estates Secretary, P. Locke.
Assistant Secretaries, D. I. Archer (*Accountant*); K. A. L. Argent (*Pastoral*); D. J. Day (*Stipends*); R. K. Pears, D.F.C. (*Houses*); D. G. Ward (*Redundant Churches*).
See Houses Officer, P. T. Rafferty.
Deputy Investments Secretary, I. D. Adam.
Deputy Accountant and Trust Officer, G. C. Baines.
Principals, J. R. Beard; J. M. Davies; M. D. Elengorn; D. N. Goodwin; W. J. Pennel; T. M. Robinson; E. E. Turner.
Senior Executive Officers, A. W. Atkins; Mrs. B. A. Bartlett; T. Batchelor; C. P. Canton; J. Cheesman; G. Duckworth; A. R. Gibson; S. E. Gray; W. R. Herbert; D. W. H. Lewis; L. C. Marshall; G. A. Modell; F. R. Neale; F. A. Norman; G. A. Pincott; J. C. A. Radley; E. J. Robinson; Miss W. M. Rossiter; M. J. Symon; N. M. Waring.

Legal Department
Official Solicitor, R. H. Rogers.
Deputy Solicitor, J. W. Cook.
Assistant Solicitor, P. Leslie.
Senior Legal Assistants, A. J. L. Campbell; B. G. Hall; B. J. T. Hanson; R. A. G. Lees; R. D. C. Murray.

Architect's Department
Official Architect, N. Riley.
Deputy Architect, V. A. Brown.

Surveyor's Department
Official Surveyor, J. M. N. Barnes.
Deputy Surveyor, R. N. May.

Agents
Messrs. Clutton, 5 Great College Street, Westminster, S.W.1; Messrs. Smiths Gore, Dean's Court, Minster Precincts, Peterborough; Messrs. Chesterton & Sons, 116 Kensington High Street, W.8.

CIVIL AVIATION AUTHORITY
Space House, 43–59 Kingsway, W.C.2
[01–379 7311]

The Civil Aviation Authority is a statutory body established by the *Civil Aviation Act* 1971, responsible for economic, technical and safety regulation, and for the operation of the National Air Traffic Services. It is the government's adviser on civil aviation matters, including airport planning; and it is responsible for general aviation, civil aviation statistics, research, consumer interest, and the running of the Scottish Highlands and Islands airports.
Chairman, The Lord Boyd-Carpenter, P.C.
Deputy Chairman, R. R. Goodison, C.B.
Secretary, A. W. G. Kean.

CIVIL SERVICE DEPARTMENT
Whitehall, S.W.1 (01–276 3000)

The Civil Service Department is under the control of the Prime Minister as Minister for the Civil Service, with responsibility for the day-to-day work of the Department delegated to the Lord Privy Seal. The Permanent Secretary is also the official head of the Home Civil Service. The Department's primary functions are recruitment and selection for permanent appointments; the pay and management of the Civil Service and the co-ordination of government policy on pay and pensions throughout the public sector. It also has central responsibility for personnel management, including recruitment planning and policy, training and career management; manpower requirements and the development and dissemination of administrative and managerial techniques including computing, and is concerned with the organization of the machinery of government.
The Prime Minister.
The Lord Privy Seal.
Minister of State in the Civil Service Department, CHARLES RICHARD MORRIS, M.P........£7,500
Head of the Home Civil Service and Permanent Secretary to the Civil Service Department, Sir Douglas Allen, G.C.B..............£20,175

Second Permanent Secretary, J. E. Herbecq..£17,175
Ceremonial Officer, Sir Stuart Milner-Barry, K.C.V.O.,
C.B., O.B.E. .... £8,650 to £11,000
Deputy Secretaries, Dr. F. H. Allen, C.B. (also First
Civil Service Commissioner); F. G. Burrett, C.B.;
E. Grebenik, C.B.; J. M. Moore, C.B., D.S.C.;
K. R. Stowe. £14,000

Central Group

Under Secretary, B. M. Thimont (Principal Establishment Officer and Principal Finance Officer) £12,000

Central Division

Assistant Secretary, B. T. Gilmore
£8,650 to £11,000

Information

Head of Division, S. T. Cursley..£8,650 to £11,000
Information Adviser to Civil Service Commission, J. T.
Hughes, O.B.E. .... £8,650 to £11,000

Personnel Services

Senior Principal, A. T. Wisbey...£7,750 to £9,350

Finance

Senior Principal, R. D. H. Baker (Finance Officer)
£7,750 to £9,350

Office Services

Senior Principal, W. J. Derbyshire, I.S.O.
£7,750 to £9,350

Chessington Computer Centre

Senior Principal, L. J. Jenkins...£7,750 to £9,350

Behavioural Sciences Research Division

Director, Dr. E. Anstey......£10,180 to £11,190

Recruitment and Selection

First Commissioner, Dr. F. H. Allen........£14,000
Commissioners (Under Secretaries), D. G. Daymond;
G. R. R. East; K. A. G. Murray (Director of Civil
Service Selection Board)................ £12,000

General Recruitment Divisions

Assistant Secretary, E. J. Morgan
£8,650 to £11,000

Civil Service Selection Board

Director, K. A. G. Murray.............. £12,000
Deputy Director, J. A. Howard £8,650 to £11,000

Management Services

Under Secretary, J. B. Pearce.............. £12,000
General: Assistant Secretary, G. W. Watters
£8,650 to £11,000
Special Assignments: Assistant Secretaries, R. N.
Burton; C. Priestley; S. D. Walker
£8,650 to £11,000
Operational Research: Chief Scientific Officer, E. K. G.
James................................ £11,670
Accountancy: Assistant Secretary, E. Walker
£8,650 to £11,000

Manpower

Under Secretary, N. E. A. Moore.........£12,000
Assistant Secretaries, B. Traynor; G. W. Watson;
G. H. Wollen .... £8,650 to £11,000

Machinery of Government

Under Secretary, W. F. Mumford £12,000
Assistant Secretaries, B. C. Bishop; A. W. Russell
£8,650 to £11,000

Pay

Under Secretary, R. W. L. Wilding.....£12,000
Assistant Secretaries, W. E. Dowling; F. N. Swales;
W. O. Wightman; R. W. Williams
£8,650 to £11,000

Statistics

Under Secretary (vacant)................. £12,000
Chief Statisticians, R. F. A. Hopes; D. B. Manwaring
£8,650 to £11,000
Assistant Secretary, C. P. H. Marks
£8,650 to £11,000

Superannuation and Home and Overseas Allowances

Under Secretary, S. D. Light............. £12,000
Assistant Secretaries, P. F. Clifton; K. H. McNeill
£8,650 to £11,000

Personnel Management

Under Secretaries, C. Bamfield; K. C. Lawrence
£12,000
Assistant Secretaries, P. R. Coster; J. D. Culverwell;
A. Duke; T. A. A. Hart; G. T. Morgan; D.
Renshaw................ £8,650 to £11,000

Central Computer Agency

Director, W. R. Atkinson............... £12,000
Assistant Secretaries, R. D. Aylward; Brig. R. H.
Borthwick; D. Eldridge; P. Hearson; R. E.
Pysden.................... £8,650 to £11,000
Deputy Chief Scientific Officer, G. H. Perry
£10,180 to £11,190
Assistant Director Engineer, (vacant)
£8,650 to £9,798

Civil Service Catering Organization

Chief Executive, H. A. Guest............£12,000
Director of Personnel and Administration, D. A. J.
Tratner.................... £7,750 to £9,350

Medical Advisory Service

Medical Adviser, Sir Daniel Thomson, C.B., M.D.,
F.R.C.P.............................. £13,230
Principal Medical Officer, A. M. Semmence, M.D.
£11,460

Civil Service College

Principal Civil Service College, E. Grebenik, C.B.
£14,000
Deputy Principal, Mrs. M. B. Sloman £12,000
Secretary, P. A. Smith........£7,750 to £9,350
Assistant Secretary (Head of Edinburgh Centre), K. J.
Shanahan.................. £8,650 to £11,000
Directors of Programmes, Mrs. A. C. Ellis; A. W.
Wyatt.................... £8,650 to £11,000
Directors of Studies, Dr. P. U. de Berker; Dr. S.
Rosenbaum; P. L. Towers; Dr. K. J. Wigley
£8,650 to £11,000

COMMONWEALTH DEVELOPMENT CORPORATION

33 Hill Street, W.1
[01-629 8484]

The Corporation was formerly known as the
Colonial Development Corporation. The change
of name was effected by the Commonwealth
Development Act, 1963, which also restored the
Corporation's full powers of operation in all
those countries which had achieved independence
within the Commonwealth since 1948. The Overseas Resources Development Act, 1969, empowered
the Corporation, with Ministerial approval, to
engage in operations in any developing country in
or out of the Commonwealth. The Corporation
is authorized to borrow up to £260,000,000 on
long or medium term and £10,000,000 on short
term.
Chairman (part-time), Sir Eric Griffith-Jones, K.B.E.,
C.M.G., Q.C.
Deputy Chairman (part-time), The Lord Grey of
Naunton, G.C.M.G., G.C.V.O., O.B.E.
Members (part-time), W. J. M. Borthwick, D.S.C;
The Lord Campbell of Eskan; J. M. Clay;
J. K. Dick, C.B.E.; The Lord Greenwood of
Rossendale, P.C.; J. M. H. Millington-Drake;
Prof. Edith Penrose; G. F. Smith, C.B.E.; The
Lord Walston.
General Manager, P. Meinertzhagen, C.M.G.

COMMONWEALTH OFFICE
see FOREIGN AND COMMONWEALTH OFFICE

COMMONWEALTH SECRETARIAT
Marlborough House,
Pall Mall, S.W.1
[01-839 3411]
Secretary-General, S. S. Ramphal.

COUNTRYSIDE COMMISSION
John Dower House, Crescent Place,
Cheltenham, Glos.
[0242 21381]
The Countryside Commission was set up under
the Countryside Act, 1968. It has absorbed the
National Parks Commission, taking over the duties

of that body under the National Parks and Access to the Countryside Act, 1949, and having in addition a wider range of advisory and executive functions relating to the whole of the countryside and coast. Members of the Commission are appointed by the Secretary of State for the Environment and the Secretary of State for Wales acting jointly.

Chairman, J. S. Cripps, C.B.E. £5,400
Deputy Chairman, R. A. E. Herbert £2,750
Members, Prof. G. W, Ashworth; T. J. A. Colman; J. Cousins; J. Disley; Mrs. E. M. C. Foulkes; R. Hoyle; B. F. Hubbard; J. Kegie, O.B.E.; B. S. Langton; Hon. Trevor Lewis; Miss J. V. Lipson; Prof. O. R. McGregor; Mrs. J. Riley
unpaid
Director, R. J. S. Hookway £12,000
Assistant Director (Executive), R. G. Brown
£8,650 to £11,000
Assistant Director (Advisory), J. M. Davidson
£11,000
Secretary, O. M. Davies .... £7,750 to £9,350
Principal Information Officer, B. Sluman
£5,680 to £7,450
Office for Wales
8 Broad Street, Newtown, Powys
[0686 26799]
Chairman, The Hon. Trevor Lewis, ... £2,750
Principal Officer, J. N. G. Davies
£5,680 to £7,450

COUNTRYSIDE COMMISSION FOR SCOTLAND
Battleby, Redgorton, Perth
[0738 27921]
Established under the Countryside (Scotland) Act, 1967, with functions for the provision, development and improvement of facilities for the enjoyment of the Scottish countryside, and for the conservation and enhancement of the natural beauty and amenity thereof.

Chairman, Mrs. Jean Balfour.
Vice-Chairman, A. B. Campbell, O.B.E.
Commissioners, Mrs. F. Ballantyne; Mrs. M. Barclay, O.B.E.; The Marquess of Bute; Dr. W. J. Eggeling, C.B.E., F.R.S.E.; Prof. P. G. Jarvis; D. N. Lowe, O.B.E.; J. Maxwell-Macdonald; W. H. Murray, O.B.E.; B. K. Parnell; D. Ross.
Director, J. Foster.
Deputy Director, T. Huxley.
Secretary, W. B. Prior.
Asst. Directors. D. Aldridge (*Conservation Education*); J. D. Fladmark (*Research and Development*); J. R. Turner (*Planning*).

COVENT GARDEN MARKET AUTHORITY
Market Towers, New Covent Garden Market,
1 Nine Elms Lane, S.W.8
[01-720 2211]
The Covent Garden Market Authority is constituted under the Covent Garden Market Acts, 1961 to 1969, the members being appointed by the Ministry of Agriculture, Fisheries and Food. The Authority owns a 68-acre site comprising a fruit and vegetable market, a flower market and an administration building. The Authority is empowered to borrow capital up to £45,000,000.
Chairman, Sir Samuel Goldman, K.C.B.
Members, G. A. H. Cadbury; J. K. Dick, C.B.E.; P. J. Hunt; E. I. Kingston; P. A. Land; Hon. J. A. Turner.
General Manager, C. M. G. Allen.
Secretary, C. H. Bates.

CROWN AGENTS FOR OVERSEA GOVERNMENTS AND ADMINISTRATIONS
4 Millbank, S.W.1
[01-222 7730]
The Crown Agents act as financial, commercial and professional agents for almost 100 governments and over 200 public authorities and international bodies. Their services are available to any govern-

ment and to any organisation in the public sector, they are a public service and do not act for individuals or for commercial concerns in the private sector.
The Crown Agents also act for the United Nations and as authorised agents for projects financed by the International Bank for Reconstruction and Development (The World Bank), the International Development Association and the Asian Development Bank.
Chairman, J. G. Cuckney.

CROWN ESTATE COMMISSIONERS
13/15 Carlton House Terrace, S.W.1
[01-214 6000]
Mount Lane, Bracknell, Berks.
[0344 20321]
THE CROWN ESTATE (formerly The Crown Lands).—The Land Revenues of the Crown in *England and Wales* have been collected on the public account since 1760, when George III surrendered them and received a fixed annual payment or *Civil List.* At the time of the surrender the gross revenues amounted to about £89,000 and the net return to about £11,000.
In the year ended March 31, 1976, the total Receipts by the Commissioners were £10,350,000. The Expenditure was £5,150,000. The sum of £5,300,000 was paid to the Exchequer in 1975–76 as *Surplus Revenue,* being a net sum from which no deductions have been made for administration.
The Land Revenues in *Ireland* have been carried to the Consolidated Fund since 1820; from April 1, 1923, as regards Southern Ireland, they have been collected and administered by the Irish Free State (Republic of Ireland).
The Land Revenues in *Scotland* were transferred to the Commissioners in 1833.
First Commissioner and Chairman (part-time), The Earl of Perth, P.C.
Second Commissioner (and Secretary), W. A. Wood, C.B. £14,000
Commissioners (part-time), The Lord Allen of Fallowfield, C.B.E.; R. B. Caws; Sir Oliver Chesterton, M.C.; O. H. Colburn; G. D. Lillington; Capt. I. M. Tennant; The Lord Walston.
Deputy Commissioner, P. S. Bolshaw, C.B.E.
£8,650 to £11,000
Assistant Commissioner and Clerk to the Board, J. Griffiths, O.B.E. .... £7,750 to £9,350
Crown Estate Surveyor, F. A. Burgess
£8,650 to £9,798
Deputy Crown Estate Surveyor, A. R. Roper
£6,280 to £7,450
Establishment Officer, E. F. Richards
£5,680 to £7,450
Crown Estate Receiver for Scotland, D. T. Hunt
£5,680 to £7,450
Accountant and Receiver-General, A. Barker
£4,900 to £5,900
Senior Executive Officers, S. A. Allwood; D. W. Broughton; G. R. Clark; J. L. Isom; Miss J. Phillips; C. R. Smith; J. Stumbke
£4,900 to £5,900
Legal Advisor and Solicitor, H. P. Hall, £12,000
Senior Legal Assistants, M. A. Jaffe; J. B. Postgate
£6,625 to £8,750
Civil Engineer (Marine Survey), J. G. Edwards, M.B.E. .... £6,468 to £8,833
Solicitor, Scotland, D. F. Stewart.

Windsor Estate
Surveyor and Deputy Ranger, A. R. Wiseman.

BOARD OF CUSTOMS AND EXCISE
King's Beam House, Mark Lane, E.C.3
[01-626 1515]
Commissioners of Customs were first appointed in 1671 and housed by the King in London, the present "Long Room" in the Custom House,

Lower Thames Street, E.C.3, replacing that built by Charles II and rebuilt after destruction by fire in 1718 and 1814. The Excise Department was formerly under the Inland Revenue Department, and was amalgamated with the Customs Department on April 1, 1909.

The Board

Chairman, Sir Ronald Radford, K.C.B., M.B.E.
                                                    £18,675
Private Sec., Mrs. F. R. Boardman.
Deputy Chairmen, J. M. Woolf, C.B.; A. J. Phelps,
  C.B. £14,000
Commissioners, H. E. Christopherson; C. T. Cross;
  A. M. Fraser, T.D.; C. Freedman; L. D. Hawken;
  E. A. Knight; B. H. Knox; J. C. Leeming; H.
  Tennant. £12,000

Headquarters Offices

Assistant Secretaries, A. S. Ball; J. Barber; M. K.
  Barford; W. A. Bassett; A. R. Beach; O. A.
  Brown, M.M., B.E.M.; N. J. Collings; Miss D. R.
  A. Cooper; R. Coote; J. E. Donald; G. Duncan;
  J. D. Farmer; D. J. Fellingham; R.A. Fowkes; R.
  E. Grimstead; W. J. Haswell; W. K. Herbert;
  S. J. House; D. J. Howard; G. F. Howell; P.
  Jefferson-Smith; T. M. Jenkins; A. Jones; P. B.
  Kent; P. J. Little; M. M. McLaren; J. Midgley;
  T. R. Moore, M.M.; W. A. R. Phillips; K. C.
  Piper; G. Porter; G. M. A. Smith, O.B.E.; Mrs.
  V. P. M. Strachan; E. N. Taylor; K. Taylor;
  J. H. Tee; D. Tidy; J. E. Tipton, D.F.C.; J. E.
  Turnbull; G. H. Tyson; F. Veasey; R. C. R.
  Vincent; H. A. Ward; A. Watson; H. J. Webb;
  C. J. Wilcox; R. H. Yates
                                £8,650 to £11,000
Head of Press and Information Division, C. M. Huntly
                                £5,993 to £7,763
Chief Statistician, B. F. Middleton
                                £8,650 to £11,000

V.A.T. Central Unit
Alexander House, 21 Victoria Avenue,
Southend-on-Sea, Essex
[Southend: 48944]
Controller, D. G. Pitt. . . . . £8,650 to £11,000
Deputy Controller, C. A. Pilgrim. £7,750 to £9,350

Solicitor's Office

Solicitor, G. Krikorian, C.B. £14,000
Principal Assistant Solicitors, G. F. Gloak; R. K. F.
  Hutchings; P. J. Sutton. £12,000
Assistant Solicitors, R. G. R. Cross; V. E. Eaton;
  P. J. C. Ellis; J. A. D. Heal; W. S. Hill; A. J.
  Jeddere-Fisher; V. E. Jenvey; R. G. C. King;
  W. Rawlinson; P. V. H. Smith; Miss E. S.
  Thomas; F. Townley. . . . . . . £9,033 to £11,000

Accountant and Comptroller-General's Office
Accountant and Comptroller-General, G. G. Leighton
  Boyce. £12,000
Deputy Accountant-General, B. Halliwell
                                £8,650 to £11,000

Statistical Office
Controller, R. Ash. . . . . £8,650 to £11,000

Investigation Division
14 New Fetter Lane, E.C.4
[01-353 6500]
Chief Investigation Officer, D. A. Jordan
                                £8,650 to £11,000

Collectors of Customs and Excise
England and Wales
Birmingham: F. Humphreys.
Brighton: R. F. Mountjoy.
Bristol: W. H. Leach.
Chester: J. A. H. Bracken.
Douglas: (*Collector-Surveyor*), D. J. Broughton (*c*).
Dover: R. Colling.
Harwich: H. C. Kenway, T.D.
Hull: F. W. Jones.
Leeds: J. E. Tate.
Liverpool: W. J. Campbell, M.B.E. (*b*)

London Airports: J. F. Blunt (*b*).
London Central: G. G. Lawrance.
London North: D. C. Restorick.
London Port: B. M. Field.
London South: D. S. Frampton.
London West: J. E. Ruberry.
Manchester: E. Kellett.
Newcastle: H. Peart.
Northampton: G. B. Diamond.
Nottingham: W. S. Williams.
Plymouth: J. E. Buckland.
Preston: R. A. Overin.
Reading: A. H. Barrett.
Southampton: J. Hall.
South Wales and the Borders: J. R. Allsopp.
  Scotland
Aberdeen: J. M. Kerrigan.
Edinburgh: W. Surtees.
Glasgow: R. L. Mitchell.
Greenock: A. A. Robinson.
  Northern Ireland
Belfast: D. R. Inglis.
Salaries:
  All £8,650 to £11,000 except (*a*) £11,670; (*b*)
  £11,320; (*c*) £4,900 to £5,900.

MINISTRY OF DEFENCE
See Armed Forces Section.

DEVELOPMENT COMMISSION
11 Cowley Street, S.W.1
[01-222 9134]
Chairman, The Lord Northfield.
Other Commissioners, The Marquess of Bute; B.
  Davies; J. P. R. Glyn, C.B.E.; Sir Jack Longland;
  Mrs. F. M. Reed; Dr. R. C. Tress, C.B.E.
  (one vacancy)
Secretary, K. J. Reeves. . . . . £8,650 to £11,000

THE DUCHY OF CORNWALL
10 Buckingham Gate, S.W.1
[Telephone: 01-834 7346]
The Duchy of Cornwall was instituted by
Edward III in 1337 for the support of his eldest
son, Edward, the Black Prince, and since that
date the eldest son of the Sovereign has succeeded
to the Dukedom by inheritance.

The Council
The Earl Waldegrave, K.G., T.D. (*Lord Warden of the
  Stannaries*); The Hon. John Baring (*Receiver
  General*); The Lord Clinton; Major Sir Rennie
  Maudslay, K.C.V.O., M.B.E.; The Lord Franks,
  P.C., G.C.M.G., K.C.B., C.B.E., F.B.A.; A. J. L. Lloyd,
  Q.C. (*Attorney-General to the Prince of Wales*);
  F. J. Williams; F. A. Gray (*Secretary*).

Other Officers of the Duchy of Cornwall
Auditor, J. H. Bowman.
Solicitor. M. H. Boyd-Carpenter.
Asst. Secretary, M. R. E. Ruffer, M.V.O., T.D.
Deputy Receiver, G. A. Briggs, M.V.O.
Sheriff (1976–77), Lt.-Cdr. J. D. Tetley, R.N.

THE DUCHY OF LANCASTER
Lancaster Place, Strand, W.C.2
[01-836 8277]
The estates and jurisdiction known as the Duchy
and County Palatine of Lancaster have been
attached to the Crown since 1399, when John of
Gaunt's son came to the throne as Henry IV.
As the Lancaster inheritance it goes back to 1265.
Edward III erected Lancashire into a County
Palatine in 1351.
Chancellor of the Duchy of Lancaster, THE RT. HON.
  HAROLD LEVER, M.P. £9,750
Private Secretary, H. G. Walsh.
*Attorney-General and Attorney and Serjeant within the
  County Palatine of Lancaster*, M. C. Nourse, Q.C.
Receiver-General, Major Sir Rennie Maudslay,
  K.C.V.O., M.B.E.
Vice-Chancellor, His Hon. A. J. Blackett-Ord.
Clerk of the Council and Keeper of Records, E. R.
  Wheeler, C.V.O., M.B.E.
Solicitor, H. G. Southern.
Asst. Solicitor, K. E. P. J. Harding.
Chief Clerk, P. C. Clarke, C.V.O.

DEPARTMENT OF EDUCATION AND SCIENCE
Elizabeth House, York Road, S.E.1
[01-928 9222]

The Government Department of Education was, until the establishment of a separate office, a Committee of the Privy Council appointed in 1839 to supervise the distribution of certain grants which had been made by Parliament since 1834. The Act of 1899 established the Board of Education, with a President and Parliamentary Secretary, and created a Consultative Committee. The Education Act of 1944 established the Ministry of Education. In April 1964 the office of the Minister of Science was combined with the Ministry to form the Department of Education and Science. The cost of administration for the financial year 1976–77 was estimated at £15,989,000.

Secretary of State for Education and Science, THE RT. HON. FREDERICK WILLIAM MULLEY, M.P.
£13,000

Private Sec., C. Booth.
Parliamentary Private Secretary, Mrs. W. A. Taylor, M.P.
Minister of State, GERALD TEASDALE FOWLER, M.P.
£9,500
Minister for the Arts, THE LORD DONALDSON OF KINGSBRIDGE....................... £9,500
Parliamentary Under Secretary of State, Miss M. M. Jackson, M.P........................ £5,500
Permanent Secretary, J. A. Hamilton, C.B., M.B.E.
£18,675
Deputy Secretaries, J. A. Hudson, C.B.; A. Thompson; E. H. Simpson, C.B.; C. W. Wright, C.B.; G. E. Dudman, C.B. (*Legal Adviser*); Miss S. J. Browne (*Senior Chief Inspector*)........ £14,000
Secretary for Welsh Education (*Under-Secretary*), L. Jones........................ £12,000
Under Secretary for Finance and Accountant General, W. K. Reid.................... £12,000
Under Secretaries, R. H. Bird; J. D. Brierley; G. F. Cockerill; K. G. Forecast (*Director of Statistics*); H. A. Harding, C.M.G.; N. T. Hardyman; F. A. Harper, M.B.E. (*Director of Establishments*); J. R. Jameson; D. F. E. King; J. L. H. Kitchin (*Chief Architect*); D.E. Lloyd Jones, M.C.; J. A. Richards; G. J. Spence; R. Toomey............ £12,000

Architects and Building Branch
Assistant Secretary, D. W. Tanner
£8,650 to £11,000
Principals, D. M. Forrester; M. McBride; G. H. Osborne; D. R. Pollard.... £5,680 to £7,450
Directing Architects, K. E. Foster; J. D. Kay; D. L. Medd, O.B.E....................... £11,000
Superintending Architects, R. Clynes; W. A. Fletcher; D. H. Griffin; M. S. Hacker; G. E. Hughes; R. L. Thompson............ £8,650 to £9,798
Superintending Quantity Surveyor, R. C. King
£8,650 to £9,798
Superintending Engineer (*Mechanical and Electrical*), L. E. J. Piper................ £8,650 to £9,798
Principal Architects, R. W. U. Alcock; G. W. Ballard; J. N. Boon; A. J. Branton; J. S. B. Coatman; A. G. Davidson; Miss C. G. Edwards; R. L. Fitzwilliam; L. J. P. Halstead, O.B.E.; F. Jackson; D. S. Nightingale; G. J. Parker; D. H. W. Poole; T. W. Prosser; O. M. Stepan £6,280 to £7,450
Principal Quantity Surveyors, G. C. Battersby; P. F. Bottle; D. W. Carden; B. A. Staples; B. G. Whitehouse............ £6,280 to £7,450
Principal Engineers (*Mechanical and Electrical*), A Grimshaw; G. R. Hammond £6,280 to £7,450
Architects, Grade I, E. C. Bissell; J. R. C. Brooke; A. M. Cutler; J. C. Greves; H. F. Kendall; Mrs. K. M. S. Livingston; Miss E. J. Lloyd-Jones; P. Marriott; R. R. Oak; D. S. Pearce; R. D. Post; K. F. Routledge; Mrs. J. Sachs; J. J. Wilson
£4,720 to £5,930
Quantity Surveyors, Grade I, R. B. Boosey; E. E. N. Fry; M. J. Lawton.......... £4,720 to £5,930
Senior Executive Officers, G. A. Dinmore; G. L. Emmett.................... £4,900 to £5,900

Arts and Libraries Branch
38, Belgrave Square, S.W.1
[01-235 4801]
Assistant Secretaries, C. Graham; H. C. Rackham
£8,650 to £11,000
Principals, Miss O. R. Arnold; P. F. Curran; W. Gamble; D. R. Jones; Miss M. Nicholls
£5,680 to £7,450
Library Advisers, E. M. Broome; A. C. Jones; P. H. Sewell, O.B.E.; G. W. J. Wheatley
£5,680 to £7,450
Senior Executive Officer, G. W. Dickerson
£4,900 to £5,900

Establishments and Organization Branch
Assistant Secretaries, D. J. Brazier, D.S.M.; J. V. Cowen .... £8,650 to £11,000
Senior Principals, W. G. Easeman, T.D.; Miss V. G. Ford; R. E. Judd.......... £7,750 to £9,350
Principals, C. G. Benjamin; M. M. Capey; Miss D. C. Fordham; E. W. Grogan; F. Sussex; A. K. Usher; R. S. Young.... £5,680 to £7,450
Senior Executive Officers, Miss J. Y. Alexander; A. Allison; Miss P. I. Cartwright; K. L. R. English; Miss J. C. Esnouf; G. H. Evans; V. H. Froggett; Miss T. Gale; D. C. Hobbs; K. R. Knapp; Miss M. J. Smith; I. J. Wade...... £4,900 to £5,900

Information and Library
Information Department
Chief Information Officer, Miss J. Price
£8,650 to £11,000
Principal Information Officers, A. G. Campbell; J. G. Millwood; T. J. Perks....... £5,680 to £7,450
Senior Information Officers, M. H. L. Clemans; H. L. Cook; Mrs. S. M. Ellingford; B. H. Hill; Mrs. P. A. O'Brien; D. J. O'Reilly; I. M. Paterson.................... £4,900 to £5,900
Library
Librarian, Miss D. M. Jepson..... £4,900 to £5,900

Finance Branch
Deputy Accountant General (*Assistant Secretary*), N. B. W. Thompson...... £8,650 to £11,000
Director of Financial Services, V. J. Delany
£8,650 to £11,000
Senior Economic Adviser, B. E. Rodmell
£8,650 to £11,000
Senior Principals, E. Ll. Evans; D. H. Grattidge
£7,750 to £9,350
Principals, P. W. Fulford-Jones; M. D. Phipps; G. R. E. Stewart; D. F. H. Taylor; A. W. Thompson.................. £5,680 to £7,450
Economic Advisers, J. M. Bateson; S. T. Cook
£5,680 to £7,450
Senior Executive Officers, J. A. E. Blackburn; E. B. Robson; R. J. Taylor
£4,900 to £5,900

Higher and Further Education Branch I
Assistant Secretaries, R. E. Duff; M. L. Herzig; B. C. Peatey................... £8,650 to £11,000
Principals, W. J. Archibald; Mrs. C. M. Chattaway; W. H. Miller; M. J. G. Smith
£5,680 to £7,450
Senior Executive Officers, R. S. Darawulla; Miss B. S. Gilbert; F. C. Street....... £4,900 to £5,900
Senior Catering Adviser, Miss F. M. Cowell
£5,680 to £7,450

Higher and Further Education Branch II
Assistant Secretaries, C. A. Clark; Miss D. J. Dawson; R. H. Stone................ £8,650 to £11,000
Principals, R. W. Chattaway; K. R. Coppinger; G. Dickson; Mrs. Z. M. Dovey; Mrs. M. E. Granshaw; R. Klein; E. R. Morgan; M. J. F. Rabarts.................... £5,680 to £7,450
Senior Executive Officers, P. A. Clarke; L. A. Hendry; A. A. J. Howling; J. D. Searle
£4,900 to £5,900

Higher and Further Education Branch III
Assistant Secretaries, M. B. Baker; D. G. Libby; J. W. Nisbet............. £8,650 to £11,000

Senior Principal, K. W. Morris..£7,750 to £9,350
Principals, G. J. Aylett; R. Carpenter, D.S.C.; L. G. Cook; E. R. Gibbs; J. C. Hedger; W. J. Huntingford; R. P. Norton; A. H. Prosser; S. M. Smith; D. K. Timms.......£5,680 to £7,450
Senior Executive Officer, Miss V. D. Steer
£4,900 to £5,900

Higher and Further Education Branch IV
Assistant Secretaries, L. J. Melhuish; D. F. Robinson; J. H. Thompson...........£8,650 to £11,000
Senior Principal Scientific Officer, H. J. Norton
£8,650 to £9,798
Principals, Miss V. D. M. Chapman; G. Etheridge; J. C. Walne...............£5,680 to £7,450
Principal Scientific Officers, G. R. Field; F. P. Verdon
£5,514 to £7,205
Senior Executive Officers, C. H. Boxall; J. K. Bushnell; G. E. Huggins; F. M. Scott; J. Walmsley; G. M. Weaver; J. Wilde......£4,900 to £5,900

Legal Branch
Assistant Legal Adviser, S. A. Williams
£9,033 to £11,000
Senior Legal Assistant, Mrs. R. E. Durkin
£6,625 to £8,750
Senior Executive Officer, Miss M. J. Bryant
£4,900 to £5,900

Pensions Branch
Mowden Hall, Staindrop Road,
Darlington, Co. Durham
[Darlington: 60155]
Assistant Secretary, S. B. Hallett, C.B.E.
£8,650 to £11,000
Principals, R. K. Bradley; K. H. R. Maynard, O.B.E.;
£5,680 to £7,450
Senior Executive Officers, Miss M. D. Bishop; Miss B. Hyman; J. F. Price; J. N. Thomason.
£4,900 to £5,900

Planning and Programmes
Assistant Secretary, E. C. Appleyard
£8,650 to £11,000
Principals, B. Bekhradnia; Miss J. A. Gilbey; D. McLaughlin...............£5,680 to £7,450

Schools Branch I
Assistant Secretaries, A. S. Gann; M. W. Hodges; E. E. H. Jenkins...........£8,650 to £11,000
Senior Principal, J. R. Middleton
£7,750 to £9,350
Principals, E. B. Granshaw; G. F. Hawker; J. I. Langtry; R. W. J. Mitchell; R. P. Ritzrema; Miss S. L. Scales; D. V. Stafford; W. J. Stewart; N. D. Wolf; A. G. B. Woollard
£5,680 to £7,450
Senior Executive Officer, J. K. Sawtell
£4,900 to £5,900

Schools Branch II
Assistant Secretaries, J. I. Jones; P. S. Litton; Mrs. D. M. White...........£8,650 to £11,000
Principals, J. A. Reeve; H. C. Riddett, O.B.E.; N. J. Sanders...............£5,680 to £7,450
Senior Executive Officer, H. G. Rutherford
£4,900 to £5,900
Senior Catering Adviser, Miss M. J. Warrington
£5,680 to £7,450
Catering Advisers, Mrs. M. I. Graham; Mrs. H. J. E. Robertson...............£4,900 to £5,900

Schools Branch III
Assistant Secretaries, A. E. D. Chamier; H. O. Dovey...............£8,650 to £11,000
Staff Inspector, B. W. Kay...........£10,508
Principals, J. G. Bagley; B. L. Baish; D. L. Corder, O.B.E.; Miss M. S. Hardwick; J. C. Hedger; Miss N. E. Jones; Miss I. Luxton; M. J. G. Smith
£5,680 to £7,450
Senior Executive Officers, Miss J. Reynolds; Mrs. C. K. Saville...............£4,900 to £5,900

Science Branch
Assistant Secretaries, D. E. Morgan; J. A. G. Banks (*Sec. Council for Scientific Policy*)
£8,650 to £11,000

Principals, K. E. G. Barber; Miss H. F. Graham; M. D. Phipps...............£5,680 to £7,450
Senior Executive Officer, A. J. Kirk, M.M.
£4,900 to £5,900

Statistics Branch
Assistant Secretary, W. H. G. Harvey
£8,650 to £11,000
Senior Principal, F. C. Heward..£7,750 to £9,350
Chief Statisticians, H. Collings; Mrs. C. M. Firth
£8,650 to £11,000
Principals, R. Griffiths; P. Ramsden; S. G. Reed; L. R. F. Wiggins...........£5,680 to £7,450
Statisticians, C. J. Bellis; A. R. Hammond; Mrs. S. Keith; N. Lescure; B. O. Longman; C. A. McIntyre; Mrs. A. E. Mellor; J. R. Watkins
£5,680 to £7,450
Senior Research Officer, D. J. Hodges
£5,680 to £7,450
Senior Executive Officers, Mrs. P. Adames; K. Baxter; Miss M. A. Bellamy; J. S. Blackmore; D. L. Coglan; I. A. C. Cooke; K. Coombs; R. S. Evans; T. H. Hunt; Miss D. E. Lorenz; R. C. Martin; J. Melbourne; D. G. Smith; C. J. Wood; R. Woodward......£4,900 to £5,900

Teachers Branch (Supply Salaries and Qualification)
Assistant Secretaries, N. Summers; I. R. M. Thom
£8,650 to £11,000
Senior Principal, H. G. Jenkins...£7,750 to £9,350
Principals, Miss N. Bartman; J. Blatcher; G. L. Macey, I.S.O.; L. C. Smith...£5,680 to £7,450
Senior Executive Officers, B. Lowe; H. V. Pines
£4,900 to £5,900

Welsh Education Office
Assistant Secretary, R. Dellar...£8,650 to £11,000
Principal, D. M. Basey...£5,680 to £7,450

H.M. Inspectorate (England)
Chief Inspectors, F. Makin; Miss M. J. Marshall; E. J. Sidebottom; N. Thomas...............£11,440
Divisional Inspectors, M. J. Beaver; J. K. Brierley; P. M. Burns; J. T. G. Chung; J. Dalglish; W. S. Fowler; W. G. Hamflett; F. C. Ruffett .£10,508
Staff Inspectors, Miss P. M. Ash; N. Booth; Miss K. M. P. Burton; I. B. Butterworth; E. C. Cordell; P. D. Dudley; M. Edmundson; G. W. Elsmore; D. W. Emery; J. R. Fish; T. J. Fletcher; H. E. Gardiner; R. P. Greenwood; D. Hilton; D. Hollingsworth; W. T. John; H. C. H. Jones; H. R. Jones; B. W. Kay; D. G. Lambert; J. G. Lavender; Eric Lord; Miss E. McDougall; Miss E. McKaig; J. Maitland-Edwards; D. T. E. Marjoram; G. W. Milburn; R. F. Mildon; C. A. Norman; W. H. Parry; Mrs. P. Perry; P. Phillips; Miss E. G. Pollard; Miss M. Rayment; C. W. Rowland; P. Samuel; E. Sims; J. G. Slater; J. L. Smedley; G. Snowball; L. Speak; M. E. Sprinks; E. W. Sudale; D. F. Symes; G. R. A. Titcomb; Miss K. M. Tobin; D. G. Toose; W. H. Wainwright; R. A. Wake; W. M. White; E. Whiteley; M. R. Wigram; R. C. Williams; P. G. Willmore...........£10,508
H.M. Inspectors, Miss K. Addison; O. P. Alexander; T. W. F. Allan; D. J. Allen; T. I. Ambrose; H. M. Archer; P. T. Armistead; A. Arnison; R. Arnold; B. C. Arthur; A. Ashbrook; Miss J. L. Atkin; D. Baillie; R. C. Baker; D. Bamber; A. M. Barnes; G. Barratt; D. A. Barton Wood; E. A. Bassett; A. Bell; Mrs. J. Bell; G. Benfield; T. H. Bennetts; Miss P. Biggs; S. G. L. Bignell; D. B. F. Billimore; Miss G. M. Bishop; R. W. Blake; E. J. Bolton, T.D.; Mrs. G. A. Bolton; Mrs. J. W. Bonnard; P. R. Booth; Mrs. B. K. Bottomley; D. M. W. Boulton; R. J. Brake; W. H. Briggs; E. F. H. Brittain; J. Broadbent; Miss M. I. Brogden; P. Brown; D. G. Buckland; T. A. Burdett; K. R. Burford; J. M. Burgess; P. J. Burn; Miss A. Burns; J. W. Butler; I. B. Butterworth; P. Cadenhead; Mrs. D. M. Caffery; Miss M. E. Caistor; W. F. Campbell; C. B. Carr; T. Carroll; Mrs. E. Cave; R. B. Chalmers; M. G. C. Channon; B. A. Chaplin;

Miss J. Chreseson; Miss G. D. Clark; A. G. Clegg; Miss M. I. Clough; E. W. Clubb; Miss M. Corlett; A. T. Cox; G. Cranmer; J. Creedy; Mrs. M. E. Crisp; Miss S. Crisp; J. D. Dale; Mrs. R. D. Dale; R. Daniels; D. M. Davies; Miss I. E. Davies; J. A. Davies, D.F.C.; Miss M. B. Davison; J. E. B. Dawson; M.B.E., J. R. Deans; Mrs. E. V. de Bray; D. A. Denegri; T. Dickinson; Mrs. G. Dolden; J. A. S. Dossett; R. C. Dove; F. J. Downs; S. R. G. Downs; W. Drabble; K. T. Elsdon; P. Enticknap; J. M. Evans; Miss V. J. Evans; J. A. Everson; J. H. Fairhurst; E. Fanthorpe; V. A. Farthing; Miss P. E. Fassom; J. Featherstone; Miss R. R. Feldmeier; B. P. Fitzgerald; D. Flanagan; P. H. Forrest; R. S. Fowler; R. C. Fox; J. P. A. Frain; Miss J. M. Francis; W. H. Francis; G. R. Frater; J. A. Fuller; P. Gannon; Mrs. M. Gaskell; B. Gay; G. D. Gibbs; A. Gibson; M. D. Gill; C. R. Gillings; M. S. Girling; D. J. Gold; G. Goldstein; Mrs. K. W. Gosling; J. G. Goulding; Miss S. Gracey; J. Graham; W. Graham; Miss S. E. Grant; F. H. Green; V. Green; R. P. Greenwood; N. M. Griffiths; R. M. Griffiths; L. S. Grimsdale; P. C. Haeffner; Miss D. Haigh; D. S. Hale; B. J. Hall; J. Hampson; B. R. Harris; K. N. Hastings; B. W. V. Hawes; F. W. Hawkins; G. H. Haworth; B. P. Hayes; G. M. Hearnshaw; R. A. S. Hennessey; P. M. Hesketh; G. A. Hicks; P. Highfield; R. Hiley; Miss B. E. Hill; J. A. Hill; M. W. Himsworth; Mrs. M. I. Holmes; J. R. de S. Honey; T. Howarth; B. W. Howes; Miss A. M. Hughes; R. A. J. Hughes; J. B. Hurn; W. E. Husband; J. B. Huskins; K. B. Hutton; A. J. Hymans; E. S. Ingledew; A. R. Ivatts; K. M. Jack; L. Jackson; K. Jary; R. A. Jeffery; J. C. Jennings; D. W. John; Miss S. H. Johns; Miss D. M. Jones; H. Jones; J. L. Kay; Miss V. M. Keating; Miss M. Kellett; L. P. Kelly; R. A. Kelly; F. R. Kitchen; J. Kitching; Miss A. A. Knowles; Miss M. Knox-Johnston; G. N. E. Lageard; B. M. Lane; E. H. Leaton; M. Le Guillou; J. P. Leigh; D. F. Lewis; D. J. Lewis; Miss M. K. Lightowler; Miss B. M. Lockwood; Mrs. R. Lockwood; A. G. Loosemore; W. G. Lowe; G. A. Lucas, T.D.; J. A. Mabey; D. W. McAllister; F. McDonald; Mrs. J. E. McDonald; J. McGinn; Mrs. J. C. McGinty; G. W. S. Mackay; Miss J. L. Maltby; W. J. A. Mann; D. J. Marjoram; Miss R. J. Marlor; P. F. Marlow; A. R. Marshall; Mrs. G. D. Marshall; T. W. Martin; C. H. Maude; J. H. Mayhew; Miss B. E. Megson; T. P. Melia; T. G. Melling; D. Mills; A. R. H. Monk; J. O'C. Morgan; D. A. Morris; Miss N. R. Mulcahy; R. W. Mycock; H. Myers; Miss P. W. Myers; G. J. Neal; G. F. Neesham; R. Nicholls; P. M. Nixon; E. Norris; J. P. O'Connor; Miss K. M. O'Leary; P. J. Oliver; P. I. Orr; Miss M. Osborn; J. Ounsted; A. Owen; I. P. Owen; Miss P. Park; K. Parker; J. B. Parnaby; F. Parrott; C. P. Parsons; E. H. Parsons; Miss J. Paterson; Mrs. R. W. Peacocke; G. T. Peaker; Miss I. Perlmutter; K. Pinder; B. J. Pitchers; P. B. Pitman; Miss S. A. Polak; Miss E. M. Potts; D. R. Prestwich; H. A. Price; B. H. Proctor; P. B. Rattenbury; D. Raymond; D. Ll. Rees; Mrs. B. Rees-Davies; J. Reynolds; J. D. Richards; C. D. Roberts; J. R. Roberts; I. A. Robertson, D.F.C.; C. M. Robinson; N. H. Roche; G. R. Romans; A. J. Rose; R. Roundhill; C. K. Rowland; D. H. Rutt; I. P. Salisbury; M. V. Salter; K. J. Sargent; Miss H. M. Sebestyen; C. H. Selby; E. L. Sewell; D. R. Shannon; D. T. V. Sharman; B. E. Shaw; J. R. Shirtcliff; B. D. Short; T. A. G. Silk; P. J. Silvester; R. H. D. Sinclair; P. Singh; Mrs. M. M. Smart; P. F. Smart; P. R. Smith; R. T. Smith; W. H. Snowdon; Mrs. M. H. Somers; D. E. Soulsby; J. F. Spencer; M. E. Sprakes; J. W. Steel; Mrs. E. M. Stenton; J. W. Stephens; L. W. Stewart, T.D.; R. W. Stockdale; R. Summersby; Miss J. Sumner Smith; E. F. A. Suttle; G. H. Swinden; D. W. Sylvester; C. J. Symonds; B. Taylor; Miss P. M. M. Taylor; W. W. Taylor; J. D. Thomas; R. V. Thomas; Miss A. D. Thompson; W. H. Thomson, D.S.C.; J. E. Trickey; T. N. Tunnard; A. F. Turberfield; M. J. Tyerman; J. R. Ungoed-Thomas; D. G. Vallis; G. W. Verow; D. E. Walker; A. Walmsley; Miss P. Walters; R.E. Ward; Miss J. R. Warner; R. K. Warren; E. R. Wastnedge; R. G. Watson; D. H. Watts; Miss O. C. Weilenbeck; D. J. Wells; P. E. Weston; J. B. Whinnerah; C. G. White; Miss S. Whitworth; J. B. Willcock; I. G. E. Wilding; A. J. Wiles; J. Wilkinson; G. M. Willan, D.F.C.; D. G. Williams; H. G. Williams; Miss D. E. Wiseman; D. C. Wollman; Miss M. S. Wood; J. A. Woodrow; J. T. Woodend; Miss B. M. Wright; E. H. Wright; J. L. Wright; M. Wylie; E. P. Young; R. E. Young; T. R. Young. . . . . . . £6,625 to £9,415

H.M. Inspectorate Support Services

Senior Executive Officer, N. J. Bennett
£4,900 to £5,900

H.M. Inspectorate (Wales)

Chief Inspector, E. O. Davies. £11,440
Staff Inspectors, Miss E. C. Edwards; G. L. Jones; I. R. Lloyd; P. E. Owen; C. Reid; T. H. Thomas; P. C. Webb £10,508
H.M. Inspectors, S. J. Adams; Miss M. Anthony; H. W. Davies; Mrs. J. E. Davies; T. R. Edwards; G. Evans; K. M. Evans; L. M. Evans; N. B. Evans; J. Garrett, O.B.E.; Mrs. K. P. Godfrey; A. Higgins; G. E. Humphreys; E. H. Hutton; R. L. James; W. R. Jenkins; T. W. John; A. H. Jones; D. B. Jones; G. D. Jones; L. Jones; O. E. Jones; R. E. Jones; I. M. Lewis; Miss N. O. Lloyd-Jones; R. A. Lowe; J. K. Millington; I. G. Morgan; J. Nicholas; Miss P. A. Nicholas; T. G. Prosser; Miss D. Selleck; M. W. Stone; D. A. Thomas; Glyndwr Thomas; P. Thomas; W. E. Thomas; G. Warren; Miss E. N. Williams; M. J. F. Wynn. . . . . £6,625 to £9,415

ELECTRICITY AUTHORITIES

THE ELECTRICITY COUNCIL
30 Millbank, S.W.1

Chairman, Sir Peter Menzies. £23,100
Members, R. W. Orson; W. J. Prior
(each) £12,600 to £17,600
Members from the Central Electricity Generating Board, Sir Arthur Hawkins; F.E. Bonner, C.B.E.; R. A. Peddie.
Secretary, B. C. O. Murphy.

CENTRAL ELECTRICITY GENERATING BOARD
Sudbury House, 15 Newgate Street, E.C.1
[01-248 1202]

Chairman, Sir Arthur Hawkins. £21,100
Deputy Chairman, F. E. Bonner, C.B.E. £18,100
Members, R. A. Peddie; D. R. R. Fair, O.B.E. each. £13,600
Part-time Members, A. G. Derbyshire, F.R.I.B.A.; The Lord Kearton, O.B.E., F.R.S.; G. England; A. G. Frame. . . . . each £1,000
Secretary and Solicitor, A. L. Wright.

ELECTRICITY BOARDS
The 12 Area Electricity Boards
(The Chairmen of Area Boards receive a salary o £12,600 to £17,600).

London, 46 New Broad Street, E.C.2. *Chairman,* O. Francis, C.B. *Sec.,* D. G. Rees.
South Eastern, Queen's Gardens, Hove, Sussex. *Chairman,* T. Rutherford. *Sec.,* D. A. Green.
Southern, Southern Electricity House, Littlewick Green, Maidenhead, Berks. *Chairman,* A. W. Bunch. *Sec.,* C. M. de L. Byrde, M.B.E.
South Western, Electricity House, Colston Avenue, Bristol 1. *Chairman,* G. England. *Sec.,* S. G. Marshall.

Eastern, P.O. Box 40, Wherstead, Ipswich, Suffolk. *Chairman*, H. D. B. Wood, C.B.E. *Sec.*, W. L. M. French.

East Midlands, P.O. Box 4, North P.D.O., 398 Coppice Road, Arnold, Nottingham. *Chairman*, P. A. Lingard. *Secs.*, T. F. C. Walker.

Midlands, P. O. Box 8 Mucklow Hill, Halesowen, West Midlands. *Chairman*, G. T. Shepherd. *Sec.* P. Cuthill.

South Wales, St. Mellons, Cardiff. *Chairman*, W. E. Richardson. *Sec.*, R. G. Williams.

Merseyside and North Wales, Sealand Road, Chester. *Chairman*, D. G. Dodds. *Sec.*, M. M. Parker.

Yorkshire, Wetherby Road, Scarcroft, Leeds. *Chairman*, E. S. Booth, C.B.E. *Sec.*, E. K. Richmond, T.D.

North Eastern, Carliol House, Newcastle upon Tyne 1. *Chairman*, A. H. Norris. *Sec.*, J. Millar.

North Western, Cheetwood Road, Manchester 8. *Chairman*, J. D. M. Bell *Sec.*, B. Benson.

NORTH OF SCOTLAND HYDRO-ELECTRIC BOARD

16 Rothesay Terrace, Edinburgh 3

[031–225 1361]

Chairman, Sir Douglas Haddow, K.C.B. (*part-time*) £8,415

Deputy Chairman and Chief Executive, K. R. Vernon. *Members* (*part-time*), D. D. S. Craib, C.B.E. (*Chairman of Consultative Council*) (£2,100); F.L. Tombs (*unpaid*); A. Wallace; W. Kemp, M.B.E.; I. S. Campbell; Mrs. A. G. Keay; C. A. MacLeod each £1,000

Secretary and Solicitor, D. A. S. MacLaren.

SOUTH OF SCOTLAND ELECTRICITY BOARD

Inverlair Avenue, Glasgow

[041–637 7177]

Chairman, F. L. Tombs................£16,600
Deputy-Chairman, D. R. Berridge.......£13,100
Part-time Members, W. D. Coats; W. G. P. Fraser; J. Kane, O.B.E.; E. McCulloch; C. H. Martineau (*Chairman of Consultative Council*) (£2,100); W. Ure, M.B.E. (£1,000); Sir Douglas Haddow, K.C.B., F.R.S.E. (*unpaid*).
Secretary, D. M. McGrouther.

DEPARTMENT OF EMPLOYMENT

8 St. James's Square. S.W.1

[01–214 6000]

The Department of Employment is responsible for Government policies affecting the working life of the country's population and the needs of potential workers.

These policies include the promotion of good industrial relations, pay, measures to deal with unemployment and redundancy and regional employment problems.

The Department is also responsible for producing and publishing a wide range of statistics, including the figures for retail prices, earnings, employment and unemployment and industrial disputes.

Many of the Department's executive functions and services have been transferred to a number of new bodies, operating independently, but reporting to the Secretary of State for Employment.

Secretary of State for Employment, THE RT. HON. ALBERT EDWARD BOOTH, M.P..........£13,000
Private Secretary, M. Emmott.
Assistant Private Secretaries, Miss W. A. C. Harris; Miss K. M. Hegarty.
Parliamentary Private Secretary, C. R. Roderick, M.P.
Minister of State, HAROLD WALKER, M.P.....£7,500
Under-Secretaries of State, J. D. Grant, M.P.; J. Golding, M.P..................£5,500
Permanent Secretary, K. Barnes, C.B.......£21,000
Deputy Secretaries, D. J. Derx, C.B.; A. R. Thatcher, C.B.; I. F. Hudson, C.B................£15,000
Solicitor, J. B. H. Billam, D.F.C.........£15,000

Industrial Relations

Under Secretaries, J. H. Galbraith; D. B. Smith £12,000
Assistant Secretaries, N. Covington; A. F. Hatfull; G. W. Robertson; A. Burridge £8,650 to £11,000
Chief Conciliation Officer, A. S. Kerr......£11,670

Incomes Division

Under Secretaries, G. A. Brand; D. J. Hodgkins £12,000
Assistant Secretaries, R. J. Dawe, O.B.E.; D. R. Bower; A. Burridge........£8,650 to £11,000
Chief Wages Inspector, I. Prost...£7,750 to £9,350
Secretary of Wages Councils, Miss Y. M. Simmons £5,680 to £7,450

Economic Policy (Manpower) Division

Under Secretary, C. A. Larsen............£12,000
Assistant Secretaries, Mrs. J. M. Collingridge; T. G. T. Taylor; R. S. Allison......£8,650 to £11,000

Manpower General

Under Secretary, Mrs. D. M. Kent........£12,000
Assistant Secretaries, B. D. Winkett; B. A. Smith; Miss M. E. Green; D. J. Sullivan £8,650 to £11,000

Overseas Division

Under-Secretary, N. S. Forward..........£12,000
Assistant Secretary, C. M. J. Hess £8,650 to £11,000

Research and Planning Division

Under Secretary, N. S. Forward..........£12,000
Assistant Secretary, J. L. B. Garcia £8,650 to £11,000
Chief Psychologist, G. Jessup.....£8,650 to £9,798
Senior Economic Adviser, E. G. Whybrew £8,650 to £11,000

Establishments Division

Director of Establishments, A. F. A. Sutherland £12,000
Assistant Secretaries, D. Shipton; L. J. Goss, C.B.E.; G. A. E. Laming, O.B.E......£8,650 to £11,000
Director of Information, K. D. McDowell..£11,670
Deputy Director of Information, M. Butcher £7,750 to £9,350
Chief Inspector, E. W. Fawcett..£7,750 to £9,350

Finance Division

Accountant-General, E. A. Ferguson.......£12,000
Director of Accounts and Audit, S. H. N. Hinton £8,650 to £11,000
Assistant Accountant General, G. S. Day £7,750 to £9,350
Regional Finance Officers, F. O. Lewis (*Wales and South Western*); T. R. Muncie (*Midlands*); T. H. G. Symons (*South East*) (£5,680 to £7,450); F. Collier (*North Western*); Mrs. H. D. Bradley (*Scotland*); L. V. Higgins (*Yorkshire and Humberside and Northern*)..£4,976 to £6,159

Solicitor's Division

Solicitor, J. B. H. Billam, D.F.C.........£15,000
Principal Assistant Solicitor, D. E. Belham, C.B. £12,000
Assistant Solicitors, G. E. McClelland; D. M. D.D. Grazebrook; Miss V. Rice-Pyle £8,650 to £11,000
Senior Legal Assistants, K. Halil; M. Harris; Miss G. S. Johnson; Miss B. R. Heitzman; H. R. L. Purse; C. N. L. Angellier.....£6,625 to £8,750

Statistics Division

Director of Statistics, A. R. Thatcher, C.B...£15,000
Deputy Director, A. G. Carruthers........£12,000
Assistant Secretary, Miss M. A. Barkess £8,650 to £11,000
Chief Statisticians, F. G. Forsyth; R. Turner; D. W. Flaxen...................£8,650 to £11,000

Regional Offices

Northern Region

Regional Director, R. M. Walker £8,650 to £11,000

Deputy Regional Director, A. R. Hill
£7,750 to £9,350

Yorkshire and Humberside Region
Regional Director, A. A. G. McNaughton
£8,650 to £11,000
Regional Benefit Manager, S. Duncalf
£7,750 to £9,350

South East Region
Regional Director, G. Morgan............£11,670
Deputy Regional Directors, G. C. Breden; E. Reeves
£7,750 to £9,350

South West Region
Regional Director, W. D. Scott.£8,650 to £11,000

Wales
Director, A. E. L. Winter......£8,650 to £11,000

Midland Region
Regional Director, M. J. Porter. £8,650 to £11,000
Deputy Regional Director, E. H. Thomas
£7,750 to £9,350

North West Region
Regional Director, D. A. Savage £8,650 to £11,000

Scotland
Director, A. Y. W. Cowie..............£11,670
Deputy Director, A. P. D. Ross..£7,750 to £9,350

Health and Safety Commission
Chairman, W. Simpson..................£16,580
Members of the Commission, E. M. Jukes, C.B.E., Q.C. (*Deputy Chairman*); J. Anderson; F. D. Bushell; M. Cobb, M.B.E.; P. Jacques; G. Lloyd; T. Parry; R. Richards;
Secretary, V. G. Munns........£7,750 to £9,350

Health and Safety Executive
Director General, J. H. Locke............£14,670
Deputy Director General (Director of Nuclear Safety), H. J. Dunster........................£14,000

Hazardous Substances Group
Director, Miss L. A. Pittom.............£12,000

Safety and General Group
Director, D. Richardson................£12,000

HM Alkali Inspectorate
H.M. Chief Alkali Inspector, F. E. Ireland. £12,000

HM Mines and Quarries Inspectorate
H.M. Chief Inspector of Mines and Quarries, J. Carver
£13,230

Employment Medical Advisory Service
Director of Medical Services, Dr. K. P. Duncan
£13,230

HM Factory Inspectorate
H.M. Chief Inspector of Factories, J. D. G. Hammer
£12,000

HM Nuclear Installations Inspectorate
H.M. Chief Nuclear Inspector, R. Gausden £12,000

Research and Scientific Support Division
Director of Research and Laboratories and Head of Safety in Mines Research Establishment, Dr. B. P. Mullins.............................£12,000

DEPARTMENT OF ENERGY
Thames House, South,
Millbank, S.W.1 (unless otherwise stated)
[01-211 3000]

The Department of Energy is responsible within the Government for the development of policies in relation to all forms of energy. It also discharges governmental functions connected with the publicly-owned coal, gas and electricity industries. It is responsible for the Atomic Energy Authority; is the sponsoring Department for the nuclear power industry and is responsible for the development of oil and gas resources on the British sector of the Continental Shelf. It is the sponsoring Department for the oil industry and is responsible for international aspects of energy problems, including relations and co-operation with oil producing countries. The Department is the co-ordinating body for energy conservation policy and for encouraging the development of new sources of energy.

Secretary of State for Energy, THE RT. HON ANTHONY WEDGWOOD BENN, M.P................£13,000
Principal Private Secretary, B. D. Emmett.
Parliamentary Private Secretary, J. W. Ashton, M.P.
Assistant Private Secretaries, A. R. Phillips; C. L. Ambrose; R. W. Proud.
Minister of State for Energy, J. DICKSON MABON, M.P...........................£9,500
Private Secretary, Dr. C. M. Palmer.
Assistant Private Secretary, Miss S. McMaster.
Parliamentary Under-Secretaries of State, A. Eadie, B.E.M., M.P.; G. J. Oakes, M.P...........£5,500
Permanent Under Secretary of State, Sir Jack Rampton, K.C.B.........................£17,175
Private Secretary, A. J. T. Steele.
Deputy Secretaries, P. le Cheminant, C.B.; J. G. Liverman, C.B., O.B.E.; B. G. Tucker, C.B., O.B.E.; T. P. Jones.........................£14,000
Chief Scientist, Dr. W. Marshall, C.B.E., F.R.S.
Chief Economic Adviser, F. J. Atkinson, C.B.
Director of Information, B. Ingham.
Parliamentary Clerk, P. E. R. Cohen.

Establishment Division
Principal Establishment Officer (Under Secretary), I. T. Manley...........................£12,000
Assistant Secretaries, D. E. R. Scarr; P. J. Walker
£8,650 to £11,000
Senior Principal, A. D. Hampson. £7,750 to £9,350

Electricity Division
Under Secretary, G. W. Monger.........£12,000
Assistant Secretaries, J. I. Morphet; Miss J. A. M. Oliver; J. Whaley; B. Hampton
£8,650 to £11,000
Chief Electrical Engineering Inspector, A. T. Baldock

Coal Division
Under Secretary, J. R. Cross, C.M.G.......£12,000
Assistant Secretaries, C. N. Tebay; G. W. Thyme
£8,650 to £11,000

Atomic Energy Division
Under Secretary, C. Herzig..............£12,000
Assistant Secretaries, W. C. F. Butler; W. E. Fitzsimmons..................£8,650 to £11,000
Senior Principal, J. L. Cohen....£7,750 to £9,350

Energy Technology Division
Under Secretary, L. H. Leighton.........£12,000
Deputy Chief Scientific Officers, D. C. Gore; Dr. R. G. S. Skipper.............£8,650 to £11,000
Offshore Technology Unit
Senior Principal Scientific Officer, M. S. Igglesden.

Energy Policy and Conservation Division
Under Secretary, G. G. Campbell.........£12,000
Assistant Secretaries, Miss S. M. Cohen; R. H. Ellingworth; W. K Pryke; R. Wakefield
£8,650 to £11,000

Economics and Statistics Division
Under Secretary, T. A. Kennedy..........£12,000
Chief Statisticians, F. W. Hutber; W. N. T. Roberts
£8,650 to £11,000
Senior Economic Advisers, N. J. Cunningham; B. D. Cullen; J. M. Barber.......£8,650 to £11,000

Community and International Policy Division
Under Secretary, Miss G. Brown.........£12,000
Assistant Secretaries, P. T. Harding; R. Custis; A. R. M. Watts, O.B.E.......£8,650 to £11,000

Oil Policy (Home) Division
Under Secretary, R. H. Wilmott, C.M.G. ..£12,000
Assistant Secretaries, L. F. Barclay; Mrs. D. E. F. Carter; C. L. Jones.......£8,650 to £11,000
Senior Principal, D. W. Hills....£7,750 to £9,350

Gas Division
Under Secretary, J. A. Roberts.........£12,000
Assistant Secretaries, S. W. Fremantle; S. W. T. Mitchelmore..............£8,650 to £11,000

Gas Standards Branch
Government Buildings, Saffron Road, Wigston, Leicester
[Wigston: 5354]
Controller, G. R. Boreham.

Petroleum Production Division
Under Secretary, G. F. Kear............£12,000
Assistant Secretaries, J. A. Molyneux; A. R. D. Murray; P. H. Agrell.....£8,650 to £11,000
Petroleum Specialist, H. R. George.......£11,670

Offshore Supplies Office
Headquarters Office:
Alhambra House, 45 Waterloo Street, Glasgow
[041–221 8777]
Director General, J. P. Gibson...........£13,000
Deputy Director General, A. Blackshaw...£12,000
Assistant Secretaries, J. E. W. d'Ancona; A. Wilson
£8,650 to £11,000
Deputy Chief Scientific Officer, Dr. J. E. P. Miles
£10,180 to £11,190
London Office
Assistant Secretary, R. Beasley..£8,650 to £11,000
Director/Engineer, C. H. Hunt..........£11,000
Assistant Director/Engineer, S. C. Bridges
£8,680 to £9,798

Corporate Planning and Finance Division
Under Secretary, S. W. Spain...........£12,000
Assistant Secretaries, P. S. Ross; M. H. Cadman; R. Walker...................£8,560 to £11,000

Continental Shelf Policy Division
Under Secretary, C. E. H. Tuck.........£12,000
Assistant Secretaries, G. Corti; C. E. Henderson; R. Priddle..................£8,650 to £11,000

DEPARTMENT OF THE ENVIRONMENT
2 Marsham Street, S.W.1
[01–212 3434]
The Department of the Environment is responsible for the range of functions affecting the physical environment. These include housing, construction, transport, planning and local government. The Department is also concerned with the co-ordination of work on the prevention of environmental pollution, with special responsibility for clean air and anti-noise functions, and for research into roads, buildings, hydraulics, water pollution, fire prevention and use of timber. The Property Services Agency is an integral part of the Department responsible for government property management services, building construction, maintenance and supplies.
Secretary of State for the Environment, THE RT. HON. PETER DAVID SHORE, M.P..............£13,00
Private Secretary, J. W. S. Dempster
Special Assistant, J. Straw.
Parliamentary Private Secretary, B. C. Gould, M.P.
Minister for Planning and Local Government, THE RT. HON. JOHN ERNEST SILKIN, M.P.
£9,500
Private Secretary, K. E. C. Sorenson.
Special Assistant, Mrs. A. Carlton.
Parliamentary Private Secretary, B. J. Grocott, M.P.
Minister for Transport, JOHN WILLIAM GILBERT, Ph.D., M.P...............................£9,500
Private Secretary, A. J. Goldman.
Parliamentary Private Secretary, G. M. Park, M.P.
Minister for Housing and Construction, THE RT. HON. REGINALD FREESON, M.P..............£9,500
Private Secretary, G. N. Benden
Parliamentary Private Secretary, R. E. Bean, M.P.
Minister of State, THE RT. HON. DENIS HERBERT HOWELL, M.P.. ....£7,500
Private Secretary, J. J. Rendell.
Parliamentary Under-Secretaries of State:—
G. M. Barnett, M.P.; K. Marks, M.P.; The Baroness Birk; E. Armstrong, M.P.......£5,500
Permanent Secretary, Sir Ian Bancroft, K.C.B. £18,675
Private Secretary, D. A. Edmonds.
Second Permanent Secretaries, P. R. Baldwin, C.B.; Si r Robert Marshall, K.C.B., M.B.E......£17,175

Private Secretaries(to Mr. Baldwin), W. Sutherland; *(to Sir Robert Marshall)*, I. McBrayne.
Chief Executive, Property Services Agency, Sir Robert Cox, K.C.B...................£17,175
Private Secretary, P. J. J. Britton.
Industrial Adviser on Construction, R. W. Evans.

PLANNING
Deputy Secretary and Chief Planner, W. Burns, C.B., C.B.E..................................£14,000

Development Plans and Regional Strategies
Under Secretary, Mrs. J. Toohey.........£12,000
Assistant Secretaries, R. A. Isaacson; G. M. Wedd
£8,650 to £11,000
Assistant Chief Planners, A. Buchanan; R. T. White
£11,000

Planning Land Use Policy
Under Secretary, Mrs. J. Bridgeman.....£12,000
Assistant Secretaries, J. H. H. Baxter; R. Lloyd-Thomas; A. G. Lyall, C.M.G.; B. S. Quilter
Director "B", T. O'Toole...........£11,000

Planning Urban and Passenger Transport
Under Secretary, D. Holmes............£12,000
Assistant Secretaries, F. W. Girling; G. Hopkinson; M. W. Jackson; D. C. Milefanti.
£8,650 to £11,000

Local Transportation and Roads
Under Secretary, D. Bishop, M.C.........£12,000
Assistant Secretaries, W. H. Alexander; Mrs. E. F. Hitchins............£8,650 to £11,000
Deputy Chief Scientific Officer, R. Spence
£8,100 to £9,440
Assistant Chief Engineer, D. Greenwood...£11,000

Urban Affairs and Commercial Property
Under Secretary, (vacant)..............£12,000
Assistant Secretaries, E. W. Bryant; S. T. Garrish; R. C. Lawrance...........£8,650 to £11,000
Assistant Chief Planner, J. Peake........£11,000
Chief Estate Officer, P. G. Burnett........£11,000

Planning Intelligence
Duputy Chief Planner, D. E. Johnson......£10,240
Assistant Chief Planner, Miss K. B. Pailing.

CONSTRUCTION, NEW TOWNS, SPORT AND COUNTRYSIDE
Deputy Secretary, C. P. Scott-Malden, C.B..£14,000

Sport and Countryside
Under Secretary, A. Leavett............£12,000
Assistant Secretaries, J. E. Morton; D. O'Connell; J. B. W. Robins; D. A. S. Sharp
£8,650 to £11,000

New Towns
Under Secretary, J. A. L. Barber.........£12,000
Assistant Secretaries, A. Flexman; J. C. H. Marlow; H. W. Pryce; M. L. Woods £8,650 to £11,000

Construction Industry Home
Under Secretary, P. N. Gerosa..........£12,000
Assistant Secretary, B. Taylor....£8,650 to £11,000

Construction Industry Overseas
Under Secretary, J. H. Burgess...........£12,000
Assistant Secretary, D. P. Walley
£8,650 to £11,000

PLANNING REGIONAL INCLUDING LONDON AND CONSERVATION
Deputy Secretary, T. H. Shearer, C.B......£14,000

Regional and Minerals
Under Secretary, J. Crocker............£12,000
Assistant Secretaries, L. M. Dunston; O. H. Lawn; R. T. Scowen............£8,650 to £11,000

Planning London
Under Secretary, J. A. L. Gunn...........£12,000
Assistant Secretary, P. L. Daniel. £8,650 to £11,000
Assistant Chief Planner, M. Richardson....£11,000
Assistant Chief Engineer, G. E. Rowland ...£11,000

Ancient Monuments and Historic Buildings
Under Secretary, V. D. Lipman..........£12,000
Assistant Secretaries, R. G. Clubley; R. Ditchfield;
  H. L. Warburton ....£8,650 to £11,000
Assistant Director, J. C. Ellis.............£11,000

ENVIRONMENTAL PROTECTION
Deputy Secretary, T. P. Hughes, C.B.......£14,000

Water
Under Secretary, A. G. Semple £12,000
Director "A", D. C. Musgrave...........£11,440
Assistant Secretaries, R. J. Dorrington; R. J. Green;
  W. C. Knox...........£8,650 to £11,000
Directors "B", A. J. Herlihy; R. E. Smith.£11,000

Noise, Clean Air and Wastes
Under Secretary, J. R. Niven...........£12,000
Assistant Secretaries, W. J. S. Batho; Miss E. P.
  Kruse....................£8,650 to £11,000

Central Unit on Environmental Pollution
Under Secretary, A. J. Fairclough.........£12,000
Assistant Secretaries, T. W. Hall; D. R. Lewis
  £8,650 to £11,000

Water Engineering
Directors, O. Gibb; A. W. Kenny; S. F. White
  £11,440
Assistant Directors, R. Best; T. A. Dick; L. E. Ellis;
  D. H. Newsome; J. Sumner, O.B.E.; L. E. Taylor;
  R. J. White....................£11,000

TRANSPORT INDUSTRIES
Deputy Secretary, T. L. Beagley, C.B......£14,000

Ports
Under Secretary, J. E. Sanderson.........£12,000
Assistant Secretaries, J. M. Hope; F. A. Osborn
  £8,650 to £11,000

Railways
Under Secretary, J. Palmer £12,000
Assistant Secretaries, R. G. S. Johnston; K. Peter
  £8,650 to £11,000
Chief Inspecting Officer, Lt.-Col. I. K. A.
  McNaughton......................£11,440

International Transport and Nationalized Industries (General)
Under Secretary, S. M. A. Banister.......£12,000
Assistant Secretaries, D. G. Fagan; C. K. Spinks
  £8,650 to £11,000

Freight
Under Secretary, J. A. Dole.............£12,000
Assistant Secretaries, R. J. E. Dawson; G. Flanagan
  £8,650 to £11,000

Traffic Area Offices
Chairmen of Traffic Commissioners and Licensing

Authorities
East Midlands (Nottingham), C. M. Sheridan, C.M.G.
Eastern (Cambridge), H. E. Robson.
Metropolitan (Acton), A. S. Robertson.
Northern (Newcastle upon Tyne), B. J. Foster, O.B.E.
North West (Manchester), R. D. Hutchings.
Scotland, A. B. Birnie.
South East (Eastbourne), R. S. Thornton.
West Midlands (Birmingham), A. A. Crabtree.
Western (Bristol), Maj.-Gen. Sir John Potter, K.B.E.,
  C.B.
Yorkshire (Leeds), Maj.-Gen. V. H. J. Carpenter,
  C.B., M.B.E.
South Wales (Cardiff), R. R. Jackson. *(each)* £11,000

HIGHWAYS
Director General, J. A. Jukes, C.B.........£14,000

Road Construction Units
Eastern (Bedford)
Director, J. Tiplady....................£11,440
North East (Harrogate)
Director, K. C. Westhorp...............£11,440

North West (Preston)
Director, D. F. Dean...................£11,440
Midland (Leamington Spa)
Director, A. N. Brant..................£11,440
South East (Dorking)
Director, B. F. Edbrooke...............£11,440
South West (Taunton)
Director, N. Dean.....................£11,440

Highways Engineering
Chief Highway Engineer, R. J. Bridle.....£13,230
Deputy Chief Highway Engineers, K. Sriskandan;
  H. Williams.......................£11,440
Assistant Chief Engineers, B. M. Cobbe, O.B.E.;
  K. L. Duncan; P. Elliott; J. R. Lake; P.
  M. Lee.........................£11,000

Highways Programming, Contracts and Lands
Under Secretary, J. Lane...............£12,000
Assistant Secretaries, G. Cockerham; L. E. Hender-
  son; G. D. Miles.........£8,650 to £11,000
Senior Economic Adviser, G. A. C. Searle
  £8,650 to £11,000

Highways Planning and Management
Under Secretary, G. D. Spearing.........£12,000
Assistant Secretary, K. P. Leary.£8,650 to £11,000
Assistant Chief Engineers, J. L. Hammond; R. P.
  Sleep...........................£11,000

Road Safety
Under Secretary, H. F. Ellis-Rees.........£12,000
Assistant Secretaries, V. G. Curtis; N. S. Despicht;
  A. B. Saunders; P. A. Waller
  £8,650 to £11,000

Vehicle Engineering and Inspection
Chief Mechanical Engineer, J. W. Furness..£11,440
Assistant Chief Engineers, G. Donald; C. C. Toyne
  £11,000

HOUSING
Deputy Secretary, P. E. Lazarus, C.B.......£14,000

Housing "A"
Under Secretary, K. T. Barnett...........£12,000
Assistant Secretaries, P. F. Owen; P. W. Rumble
  £8,650 to £11,000

Housing "B"
Under Secretary, J. E. Hannigan..........£12,000
Assistant Secretaries, R. E. K. Holmes; W. P.
  Jackson; R. J. A. Sharp.....£8,650 to £11,000

Housing "C"
Under Secretary, S. W. Gilbert...........£12,000
Assistant Secretaries, M. S. Albu; D. R. Smith
  £8,650 to £11,000
Director " B ", A. D. H. Embling........£11,000

Housing "D"
Under Secretary, T. L. Jones............£12,000
Assistant Secretaries, D. J. Crouch; J. Pealer;
  G. J. Skinner...........£8,650 to £11,000
Director " B ", I. C. MacPherson........£11,000

Housing Development
Director, Miss P. R. Tindale.............£12,000
Assistant Directors, D. T. I. G. Davies; A. G.
  Rayner...........................£11,000

RESEARCH
Director General of Research, M. W. Holdgate.
  £14,000

Research Requirements
Director, W. J. Reiners.................£12,000
Deputy Chief Scientific Officers, F. Gale; A. J. M.
  Hitchcock; D. A. Senior, O.B.E.; A. F. E. Wise
  £8,100 to £9,440

Research Management
Deputy Chief Scientific Officer, R. E. Jeanes
  £8,650 to £11,000

Systems Analysis Research Unit
Deputy Chief Scientific Officer, P. C. Roberts
£8,650 to £11,000

Secretariat
Assistant Secretary, W. Deakin..£8,650 to £11,000

Building Research Establishment
Director, J. B. Dick.....................£13,230
Deputy Director, M. E. Burt...........£11,670
Deputy Chief Scientific Officers, P. L. Bakke; S. C. C. Bate; D. F. Cornelius; E. J. Gibson; T. J. Griffiths; G. R. Nice; W. H. Ward; R. H. Wood
£8,650 to £11,000

Hydraulics Research Station
Director, R. C. H. Russell..............£11,670

Transport and Road Research Laboratory
Director, A. Silverleaf.................£13,230
Deputy Director, L. B. Mullett..........£11,670
Assistant Director, W. A. Lewis £8,650 to £11,000
Deputy Chief Scientific Officers, J. W. Fitchie; L. J. Griffin; A. P. Goode; G. Margason; J. H. Nicholas; H. Taylor; F. V. Webster
£8,650 to £11,000

PROPERTY SERVICES AGENCY
Chief Executive, Sir Robert Cox, K.C.B....£17,175

Secretariat and Planning Unit
Assistant Secretary, P. Critchley £8,650 to £11,000

DEPUTY CHIEF EXECUTIVE I
Deputy Secretary, A. Sylvester-Evans, C.B..£14,000

Civil Accommodation
Director, J. Delafons...................£12,000
Assistant Secretaries, D. W. Cain; J. R. Coates; F. G. Rickard...................£8,650 to £11,000
Assistant Directors, M. J. Baggott; A. W. Loten
£11,000

Estate Surveying Services
Director, A. R. J. Baldwin.............£12,000
Deputy Director (vacant)................£11,440
Assistant Directors, D. L. Bowyer; B. E. Hodgson; N. P. Lawrence.....................£11,000

Estate Management Overseas
Director, B. Roberts....................£11,670

DEPUTY CHIEF EXECUTIVE II
Deputy Secretary, E. H. A. Stretton, C.B....£14,000

Scottish Services
Director, G. M. Patrick, C.M.G., D.S.C......£12,000
Assistant Secretary, M. D. King. £8,650 to £11,000
Assistant Director, R. W. Leeper.........£11,000

Home Regional Services
Director, N. P. Walsh..................£12,000
Assistant Secretaries, J. C. Goldsmith; S. J. Vincent
£8,650 to £11,000
Director "B", C. J. N. Lowe £11,000

Property Services Agency Regions (Home)
Regional Works Directors:
London, A. MacInnes..................£12,000
Eastern, H. J. Giles....................£11,320
Midland, A. G. Gosling................£11,320
North East, J. F. Hill, O.B.E., T.D........£11,320
North West, S. J. Heritage..............£11,320
South East, J. M. Rex, T.D...............£11,320
South West, F. S. Butler................£11,320
Southern, M. J. Hislop..................£11,320
Central Office for Wales, M. M. Davis..£11,320

Establishments, Property Services Agency
Principal Establishment Officer, P. D. Davies..£12,000
Assistant Secretaries, F. C. Argent; P. S. Draper; Miss J. M. Foster.......£8,650 to £11,000
Director "B", R. MacNeil..............£11,000

Finance, Property Services Agency
Principal Finance Officer, G. May.........£12,000
Assistant Secretaries, A. E. Coules; B. Strong
£8,650 to £11,000
Comptroller of Accounts, P. H. Elsley
£8,650 to £11,000

Contracts
Director, I. C. Fletcher, C.B.E.............£11,670

Assistant Secretaries, R. F. Halse; J. H. Lewis
£8,650 to £11,000
Director Accountant, P. L. Jones. £8,650 to £11,000

DEPUTY CHIEF EXECUTIVE III
Deputy Secretary, H. P. Johnston.........£14,000

Defence Services I
Director, E. Vickers....................£12,000
Assistant Secretaries, P. C. Aggleton; D. Wright
£8,650 to £11,000
Directors "B", K. W. Dando; G. T. Richards
£11,000

Defence Services II
Director, F. R. Martin..................£12,000
Assistant Secretaries, P. J. M. Butter; J. P. G. Rowcliffe..................£8,650 to £11,000
Directors "B", J. I. Dawson; A. Levy; G. V. Rose
£11,000

Post Office Services
Director, I. T. Lawman.................£12,000
Assistant Secretary, J. M. Entwistle
£8,650 to £11,000
Director "B", B. G. Skeates.............£11,000

DIRECTOR GENERAL OF DESIGN SERVICES
Deputy Secretary, W. D. Lacey, C.B.E.....£14,000

Design Office
Director "B", G. F. Woodward..........£11,000

Building Developments
Director, W. I. Appleton...............£12,000
Directors "B", M. F. Chaplin; A. K. W. Morgan
£11,000

Civil Engineering Developments
Director, F. Walley....................£12,000
Assistant Directors, D. F. Evans; R. S. C. Stewart
£11,000

Engineering Developments
Director, A. C. Gronhaug...............£12,000
Assistant Directors, H. Dixon; E. G. Mallalieu
£11,000

Quantity Surveying Developments
Director, K. Linsdell...................£12,000
Assistant Directors, D. W. Azzaro; R. Neil. £11,000

SUPPLIES
Controller, W. J. Sharp.................£12,000
Assistant Controllers, L. A. Baldwin; D. Castle; A. E. Davies; F. J. Garvey; A. D. Ormond
£8,650 to £11,000

CENTRAL SERVICES

AUDIT INSPECTORATE
Chief Inspector of Audit, S. V. Collins, C.B...£12,000
Deputy Chief Inspector, L. Tovell.........£11,440

PLANNING INSPECTORATE
Chief Planning Inspector C. F. Allen, C.B.. £12,000
Deputy Chief Planning Inspectors, W. Orbell, M.B.E.; R. F. F. Williams, G.M.......£8,650 to £11,000

LEGAL
Solicitor and Legal Adviser, K. A. T. Davey, C.B.
£14,000
Principal Assistant Solicitors, J. S. Ryan; H. Woodhouse, C.B. £12,000

RESOURCE ALLOCATION AND CENTRAL ECONOMICS AND STATISTICS
Director General, Economics and Resources, H. J. D. Cole...................................£14,000

Central Policy Planning Unit
Under Secretary, P. J. Harrop.............£12,000
Assistant Secretary, E. B. C. Osmotherly
£8,650 to £11,000

Economics, Statistics, Housing

Under Secretary, D. J. Ovens............£12,000
Senior Economic Advisers, A. E. Holmans; R. M.
Kirwan.................£8,650 to £11,000
Chief Statisticians, Miss G. P. Ford; R. F. Sellwood
£8,650 to £11,000

Economics and Statistics, Environmental and General

Under Secretary, E. H. M. Price.........£12,000
Senior Economic Advisers, P. T. McIntosh; J. F.
Smith...................£8,650 to £11,000
Chief Statistician, P. S. MacCormack
£8,650 to £11,000

Statistics

Under Secretary, G. Penrice..............£12,000
Chief Statisticians, H. Palca; W. H. Stott
£8,650 to £11,000

Economics and Statistics, Transport

Under Secretary, R. Fry................£12,000
Senior Economic Advisers, D. F. Hagger; G. A. C.
Searle; J. K. Welsby.......£8,650 to £11,000
Chief Statisticians, B. J. Billington; F. D. Sando
£8,650 to £11,000

FINANCE AND LOCAL GOVERNMENT

Deputy Secretary (Principal Finance Officer), G. C.
Wardale, C.B........................£14,000

Finance, Housing, Transport Industries and Central Services

Finance Officer, A. J. Rosenfeld...........£12,000
Assistant Secretaries, D. J. Burr; D. J. Lyness
£8,650 to £11,000

Local Government Finance Policy

Finance Officer, G. H. Chipperfield.......£12,000
Assistant Secretaries, H. H. Browne; D. J. Chapman;
T. R. Hornsby; A. A. Pelling
£8,650 to £11,000
Senior Economic Adviser, P. R. Smethurst
£8,650 to £11,000
Chief Statistician, B. J. Buckingham
£8,650 to £11,000

Local Authority Expenditure

Finance Officer, A. G. Rayner...........£12,000
Assistant Secretaries, C. D. Packett; C. E. Seward;
I. Yass....................£8,650 to £11,000

Local Government

Under Secretary, K. F. J. Ennals.........£12,000
Assistant Secretaries, E. S. Foster; D. T. Routh;
D. J. Wilbin
£8,650 to £11,000

ESTABLISHMENT AND MANAGEMENT SERVICES

Director General, Organization and Establishments,
G. W. Moseley.....................£14,000

Organization and Development

Assistant Secretary (vacant)

Senior Staff Management

Under Secretary, N. H. Calvert.........£12,000
Assistant Secretaries, G. T. Bright; Miss I. M. Davis
£8,650 to £11,000

Personnel, Manpower and Training

Under Secretary, A. R. Atherton.........£12,000
Assistant Secretaries, G. D. Crane; Miss A. R. Head;
D. C. Pickup; R. A. Stead; J. G. Thompson
£8,650 to £11,000

Management Services

Under Secretary, M. Mendoza...........£12,000
Assistant Secretaries, R. C. Geall; D. W. Royle
£8,650 to £11,000
Chief Librarian, W. Pearson, M.B.E.
£5,680 to £7,450

Information

Director, N. Taylor....................£12,000
Deputy Director, P. G. Broderick
£8,650 to £11,000

Driver and Vehicle Licensing

Under Secretary, W. Dawson...........£12,000
Assistant Secretaries, J. A. Fowles; N. H. Kelly;
F. Kendall................£8,650 to £11,000

REGIONAL OFFICES
West Midlands (Birmingham)
*Regional Director and Economic Planning Board Chair-
man*, Miss S. W. Fogarty.............£12,000
Regional Controllers, S. Jones; R. D. Law; W. W.
Morris...................£8,650 to £11,000

Yorkshire and Humberside (Leeds)
*Regional Director and Economic Planning Board Chair-
man*, R. G. Wilson, M.B.E.............£12,000
Regional Controllers, J. W. Blows; P. I. Wolf
£8,650 to £11,000

North West (Manchester)
*Regional Director and Economic Planning Board Chair-
man*, W. R. Corrie.................£12,000
Regional Controllers, D. M. Beaton; P. W. Peck;
R. W. Porteous..........£8,650 to £11,000

Northern (Newcastle upon Tyne)
*Regional Director and Economic Planning Board Chair-
man*, D. J. King.....................£12,000
Regional Controllers, S. D. Olley; R. Williams
£8,650 to £11,000

South West (Bristol)
*Regional Director and Economic Planning Board Chair-
man*, P. R. Sheaf....................£12,000
Regional Controllers, S. H. Godsell; A. W. Wright
£8,650 to £11,000

East Midlands (Nottingham)
*Regional Director and Economic Planning Board Chair-
man*, A. E. A. Brain.................£12,000
Regional Controllers, W. Johnson; N. Thompson
£8,650 to £11,000

South East
*Regional Director and Economic Planning Board Chair-
man*, (vacant) £12,000
Regional Controllers, P. A. Bays; N. Hamilton; L.
Mann....................£8,650 to £11,000

Eastern
*Regional Director and Economic Planning Board
Chairman for East Anglia*, H. W. Marshall
£12,000
Regional Controllers, F. P. Davis; J. R. Fells; A. H.
Pollington
£8,650 to £11,000

EQUAL OPPORTUNITIES COMMISSION

Overseas House, Quay Street, Manchester
[061-833 9244]

Established on December 29, 1975 under the Sex
Discrimination Act 1975, the duties of the Commission are (a) to work towards the elimination of
discrimination; (b) to promote equality of opportunity between men and women generally; and
(c) to keep under review the working of the Sex
Discrimination Act and the Equal Pay Act. In
addition, the Commission has a specific duty to
keep under review, in consultation with the Health
and Safety Commission, those provisions in legislation dealing with health and safety at work, which
requires different treatment for men and women.
Chairman, Miss Betty Lockwood.
Deputy Chairman, Lady Howe.
Members, Miss M. Allen; The Lord Allen of
Fallowfield, C.B.E.; J. Beale; Miss E. Chipchase,
M.B.E.; Mrs. S. Denman; Miss A. Mackie; A.
Nicol, C.B.E.; Miss A. Patrick; Mrs. M. Patter-
son; E. Robinson; Mrs. C. Woodroffe; P. Jones.
Chief Officer, D. Dolton...............£12,000

EXCHEQUER AND AUDIT DEPARTMENT
Audit House, Victoria Embankment, E.C.4
[01-353-8901]

This is the Department of the Comptroller and
Auditor General, an office created by the Act 29
& 30 Vict. c. 39 (1866) to replace, with extended
powers, the separate offices of Comptroller
General of the Receipt and Issue of the Exchequer

and of the Commissioners for Auditing the Public Accounts. This officer is appointed by Letters Patent under the Great Seal, and is irremovable except upon an address from the two Houses of Parliament. In his capacity of Comptroller General of the Receipt and Issue of the Exchequer, he authorizes all issues from the Consolidated and National Loans Funds after satisfying himself that Parliament has given authority for them. He examines the accounts of the Consolidated and National Loans Funds and makes an annual report on them to Parliament. In his capacity of Auditor General of Public Accounts, he is charged with the duty of examining on behalf of the House of Commons the accounts of expenditure out of funds provided by Parliament, the accounts of the receipt of revenue, and generally all other public accounts, including the accounts of Government stores and of trading services conducted by Government Departments. The results of this examination of those accounts are reported to the House of Commons. He is also the auditor by agreement of the accounts of many bodies, generally in receipt of public moneys, and of certain international organizations; he reports, when required to do so, to the governing bodies concerned.

Comptroller and Auditor General, Sir Douglas Henley, K.C.B....................£18,675
Secretary, J. F. T. Cheetham...........£13,460
Deputy Secretary, P. R. Billett..........£11,670
Director of Establishments and Accounts, G. N. Debenham.
Directors of Audit, R. C. Hooper; J. French; D. F. Smith; F. T. Womack; R. A. Best; F. W. Eele; R. Stewart; R. Thomas; P. M. Jefford
£8,650 to £11,000
Deputy Directors of Audit, T. N. Finch; P. G. Spary; J. C. McDowell; M. F. Hughes; H. Solomon; F, J. E. Blanks; D. K. Clark; H. D. Myland; G. W. Garside; J. A. Collens; C. J. Stacey; P. J. C. Keemer; D. A. Dewar; M. J. R. Paul; D. T. Lipscombe; D. G. Lusmore; A. S. Woodward; P. J. Beck; A.E. Grove; T. Dobson; V. W. Merrett; I. M. Ross.........£7,750 to £9,350

EXPORT CREDITS GUARANTEE DEPARTMENT

P.O. Box 272, Aldermanbury House, Aldermanbury, E.C.2
[01–606–6699

The Export Credits Guarantee Department is responsible to the Secretary of State for Trade. The export Guarantees Act, 1975, enables E.G.C.D. to encourage U.K. exports by making available export credit insurance to British firms engaged in selling overseas, to guarantee repayment to British banks providing finance for export credit and, in clearly defined circumstances, to refinance a proportion of banks' medium and long-term export credit advances. Guarantees under Section 1 of the 1975 Act are given after consultation with an Advisory Council of businessmen.

The Overseas Investment and Export Guarantees Act 1972 empowers E.C.G.D. to insure British private investment overseas against political risks, such as war, expropriation and restrictions on remittances.

Secretary, K. Taylor, C.B................£14,000
Under Secretaries, K. W. Cotterill, C.M.G.; J. Gill; R. T. Kemp; D. C. Smith............£12,000
Assistant Secretaries, C. C. Birch, M.B.E.; M. S. Bremner; V. I. Chapman; J. A. Dyer; L. Elmes; R. A. Freeman (*Finance Officer*); M. W. Gentle; J. H. Hall; W. H. Johnson, D.F.C., D.F.M.; E. G. Lowton; E. Panton; W. H. Paxman; M. G. Stephens; E. T. Walton (*Establishment Officer*)
£8,650 to £11,000
Senior Principals, L. M. Broad; J. A. Crossen; J. Cunningham; Mrs. E. Davidson; K. C. Harrison; R. G. Jack; E. J. Jackson; F. C. Mann; R. K. Pearson; J. G. Sorbie; G. P. Stay; D. H. Twyford; V. E. Young.........£7,750 to £9,350

Principal Information Officer, C. F. A. Salaman
£5,680 to £7,650
Principals, A. E. J. Berry; G. C. Bird; G. Blackburn; J. Bolsover; A. J. Bray; G. E. J. Breach; G. Bromley; F. J. Chapman; J. G. M. Cochrane; J. W. Coggins; T. H. Collinson; D. R. Coombe; A. J. Croft; M. C. Cunningham; B. J. Davison; A. Dawson; T. W. Denyer; K. Dixey; P. C. B. Duncan; J. E. Elliott; A. C. Elston; P. A. F. Field; R. D. Foister; W. Ford; J. M. Foster; A. P. Fowell; C. Foxall; D. H. J. Furbank; C. W. Gentry; D. A. Green; L. M. Haines; D. G. Hake; L. C. Harmer; G. A. Harvey; T. W. Hawes; P. Henley; N. J. A. Hooker; R. H. K. Hughes; K. I. Humphrey; Miss S. J. Hunt; I. Jennings; F. Jones; H. K. Jones; J. Lake; F. H. Light; G. J. A. Link; J. R. Llewelyn; K. G. Lockwood; M. J. Long; W. A. Mann; R. C. Milsted; R. A. Napier-Andrews; B. Oattes; J. W. Pannell; W. J. C. Pinnell; P. G. Plows; A. C. Polti; R. A. Ranson; E. A. F. Rides; A. J. Saunders; J. K. Sedman; D. W. Shannon; B. M. Sidwell, T.D.; A. J. Somerville; H. L. H. Stevens, M.B.E.; C. R. Stickland; C. H. Thorogood; F. W. Vernau; J. F. Vose; R. Wild; F. Wilmot; T. D. Wright; J. R. G. Wythers, B.E.M......£6,680 to £7,450
Statistician, M. J. Le Good......£5,680 to £7,450
Chief Accountant, J. S. Hurst......£5,680 to £7,450
Senior Executive Officers, H. E. Allen; J. S. Anderson; P. Armstrong; C. F. Bailey; J. V. Baker; A. W. Balcombe; H. R. Barber; T. L. Barry; R. H. Bayliffe; J. A. H. Bayliss; A. E. Beedle; Miss D. Bell; A. B. Bennett; R. Bennett; B. Blades; R. Blunt; C. M. Bossom; R. A. Bounds; Miss D. E. Brandel; A. J. Brander; F. Burge; A. R. Burrows; J. D. Cameron; A. P. C. Carcas; L. D. N. Charman; P. G. Coles; J. A. Collin; P. Connolly; W. H. Cosslett; Miss P. A. Currin; R. A. Dew; B. J. Duffield; Miss I. E. Dunlop; C. L. W. Durning; R. X. Fear; J. L. Fielding; L. C. Ford; G. M Foster; R. R. Fryatt; P. C. Gaudoin; J. F. Gaynor; A. R. J. Gibbs; W. J. Gouch; C. Haddy; P. Handovsky; C. W. Hanny; H. Harris; S. B. Harris; Miss V. M. Harvey; J. Hawkins; Miss O. K. R. Hender; H. E. Higgs; G. H. Hill; W. F. G. Hills; W. F. Hinshelwood; R. C. Hirschfield; R. Holloway; Miss B. M. Howard; V. D. Hunt; R. E. Johnson; A. L. Jolley; G. G. Jones; L. Jones; R. Jones; N. A. Lambert; R. W. Lane; B. H. Lewis; Mrs. M. J. Linter; E. S. Lowe; K. A. Marshall; Miss R. M. Martin; G. E. Milan; P. L. Neal; C. C. Ostle; E. R. Packer; A. E. Paice; C. H. G. Pearce; E. J. Perkin; O. H. Pettafor; R. A. Phelps; C. W. Pither; R. J. Pomeroy; C. F. Proctor; C. G. Purdy; H. J. Quilter; A. A. Rand; R. F. Reville; Miss J. A. Roffey; S. Rosenthal; F. Rossington; H. Ryden; T. Sanderson; J. R. Savage; R. Scott; R. W. Smeatham; R. M. Sutton; L. T. Syrett; D. P. Taylor; C. D. M. Thomas; R. J. Thomas; Miss E. Thornhill; D. L. Townley; E. J. Walsby; J. A. Walsh; H. Watson; D. S. Webb; R. S. Wheaton; R. A. Wilson; D. E. Wiltshire; R. J. Wise; C. R. Wright; G. A. Young.......£4,900 to £5,900
Senior Information Officer, J. W. Pilbeam
£4,900 to £5,900

Regional Offices

Belfast: River House, High Street, Belfast (0232-31743); *Birmingham:* Colmore Centre, 115 Colmore Row, Birmingham (021-233-1771); *Bristol:* Robinson Building, 1 Redcliff Street, Bristol 1 (0272-299971); *Cambridge:* 72–80 Hills Road, Cambridge (0223-68801/7); *Central London:* Waverley House, 7–12 Noel Street, W.1 (01-437-2292); *Glasgow:* Fleming House, 134 Renfrew Street, Glasgow (041-332-8707); *Leeds:* West Riding House, 67 Albion Street, Leeds (0532-450631); *London (North):* 593–599 High Road, Tottenham, N.17 (01-808-4570); *London (South):* 320 Purley Way, Croydon (01-686-9921); *Manchester:* Elisabeth House, St. Peter's Square, Manchester (061-228-3621).

Export Guarantees Advisory Council
Chairman, Sir Michael Wilson, M.B.E.
Deputy Chairman, J. A. R. Staniforth, C.B.E.
Other Members, Hon. Robin D. Campbell; Dr.
W. H. Darlington, M.B.E.; H. W. A. Francis,
C.B.E.; D. W. Hardy; Hon. Hugo Kindersley;
R. A. S. Lane, M.C.; Sir Peter Matthews; J. N. S.
Ridgers; J. R. Steele.

Investment Insurance Advisory Committee
Chairman, Sir Michael Wilson, M.B.E.
Members, Sir George Bishop, C.B., C.B.E.; R. J. Blair,
O.B.E.; G. V. K. Burton, C.B.E.; E. J. Symons.

FOREIGN AND COMMONWEALTH OFFICE

On the recommendations of the Committee on
Representational Services Overseas appointed by
the Prime Minister under the Chairmanship of
Lord Plowden in 1962, H.M. Diplomatic Service
was created on Jan. 1, 1965, by the amalgamation of
the Foreign Service, the Commonwealth Service,
and the Trade Commission Service, and is now
responsible for the manning of the overseas posts of
these three former services. On Aug. 1, 1966, the
Colonial Office was merged into the Commonwealth Relations Office to form the Commonwealth Office. The Foreign Office and
Commonwealth Office combined on Oct. 1, 1968.

In November 1970 overseas development became
the ultimate responsibility of the Secretary of State
for Foreign and Commonwealth Affairs, although
it remained in the day-to-day charge of the
Minister for Overseas Development, except for the
period from March 1974 to June 1975 when the
Ministry of Overseas Development reverted to its
independent status.

Downing Street, S.W.1
[01-233-3000]
Secretary of State, THE RT. HON. (CHARLES) AN-
THONY (RAVEN) CROSLAND, M.P........£13,000
Private Secretary, E. A. J. Fergusson
£9,465 to £11,115
Assistant Private Secretaries, R. N. Dales; Miss M.
Turner; P. J. Weston....£6,145 to £7,915
Political Adviser, D. Lipsey....£6,700 to £7,110
Parliamentary Private Secretary, P. Hardy, M.P.
Social Secretary, Mrs. G. A. Fawcett.
Ministers of State, THE RT. HON. ROY SYDNEY
GEORGE HATTERSLEY, M.P.; THE LORD GORONWY-
ROBERTS, P.C. £9,500; EDWARD ROWLANDS, M.P.
£7,500
Parliamentary Under Secretaries of State, J. E. Tom-
linson, M.P.; D. E. T. Luard, M.P.......£5,500
*Permanent Under Secretary of State and Head of the
Diplomatic Service,* Sir Michael Palliser, K.C.M.G.
£20,175
Private Secretary, J. O. Kerr.
Deputy Under Secretaries, M. D. Butler, C.M.G.
H. A. H. Cortazzi, C.M.G.; Sir Antony Duff,
K.C.M.G., C.V.O., D.S.O., D.S.C. (*Deputy to the Perm-
anent Under Secretary of State*); R. A. Hibbert,
C.M.G., H. B. C. Keeble, C.M.G. (*Chief Clerk*);
E. N. Larmour, C.M.G.; R. A. Sykes, C.M.G., M.C.
£14,000
Assistant Under Secretaries, N. Aspin, C.M.G.; R. A.
Burrows, C.M.G.; R. W. H. du Boulay, C.M.G.,
C.V.O. (*Vice Marshal of the Diplomatic Corps*);
R. H. G. Edmonds, C.M.G..., MB.E.; R. S. Faber;
O. G. Forster, C.M.G., M.V.O. (*Deputy Chief Clerk*);
M. J. E. Fretwell, C.M.G.; D. F. Hawley, C.M.G.
M.B.E.; J. P. Hayes (*Chief Economic Adviser*); J. D.
Hennings, C.M.G.; P. H. Laurence, C.M.G., M.C.
(*Chief Inspector*); P. J. E. Male, C.M.G., M.C.; J. C. M.
Mason, C.M.G.; K. R. C. Pridham, C.M.G. (*Director
of Communications*); R. S. Scrivener, C.M.G.; H. S.
Stanley, C.M.G.; I. J. M. Sutherland, C.M.G. J. A.
Thomson, C.M.G.; M. S. Weir, C.M.G. £12,465
Inspectors, G. L. Bullard; The Hon. E. H. B. Gibbs;
O. G. Griffiths, M.V.O., O.B.E.; P. McKearney; C.
McLean, M.B.E.; M. H. Morgan
£9,115 to £11,465
Legal Adviser, I. M. Sinclair, C.M.G.......£15,100
Second Legal Adviser, J. R. Freeland, C.M.G..£14,000

Deputy Legal Advisers, H. G. Darwin, C.M.G.;
A. R. Rushford, C.M.G...............£12,465
Legal Counsellors, D. H. Anderson; R. K. Batstone;
F. D. Berman; F. Burrows; Mrs. E. M. Denza;
H.Steel,C.M.G., O.B.E........£9,498 to £11,465
Historical Adviser, R. d'O. Butler, C.M.G....£6,879
Senior Economic Advisers, Miss P. I. J. Harvey;
A. Smith.
Overseas Labour Adviser (vacant).........£12,135
Overseas Police Adviser, M. J. Macoun, C.M.G., O.B.E.,
Q.P.M...................£9,115 to £10,263

*Signals Department (Government Communications
Headquarters)*
Priors Road, Cheltenham, Gloucestershire
[0242-21491]
Director, A. W. Bonsall, C.B.E...........£14,000
Principal Establishment Officer, J. A. F. Somerville,
C.B.E...........................£12,000

Heads of Departments

(£9,115 to £11,465. Assistant Heads of Dept.,
£6,090 to £7,860; except where stated)
Accommodation and Services Dept., K. C. Thom;
Assts., R. W. Hopcroft; R. S. Ford.
Arms Control and Disarmament Dept., J. C. Edmonds,
C.V.O.; *Assts.,* D. A. Burns; Miss B. Richards; D.
Thomas; M. J. Wilmshurst.
Caribbean Dept., M. P. Preston.
Central and Southern African Dept., H. M. S. Reid;
Assts., A. Ibbott; M. Reith.
Claims Dept., D. F. Burdon; *Asst.,* J. Lee, D.F.C.
Commonwealth Co-ordination Dept., Mrs. M. B.
Chitty; *Asst.,* J. C. E. Hyde.
Communications Administration Dept., N. Walton
O.B.E.; *Deputy Head of Dept.,* W. F. Walker.
Communications Engineering Dept., H. S. Rowe,
M.B.E.; *Deputy Head of Dept.,* B. V. Harris.
Communications Operations Dept., J. M. Brown;
Deputy Heads of Dept., W. J. Mundy; I. S. Zetter.
Communications Planning Staff, A. Routledge; *Asst.,*
B. B. Bushell.
Communications Technical Services Dept., A. B. P.
Smart; *Assts.,* J. P. Allen; R. W. Read.
Consular Dept., F. C. Hensby, O.B.E.; *Assts.,* T. T.
Gaffy, O.B.E.; D. R. Avery, O.B.E.
Cultural Exchange Dept., C. F. Hill; *Asst.,* W. T.
Hull, M.B.E.
Cultural Relations Dept., J. A. L. Morgan; *Asst.,*
M. F. Daly.
Defence Dept., W. J. A. Wilberforce; *Assts.,* A. E.
Palmer; T. C. Wood.
East African Dept., M. K. Ewans; *Asst.,* P. E. Ros-
ling, M.V.O.
Eastern European and Soviet Dept., B. G. Cartledge.
Energy Dept., S. L. Egerton; *Assts.,* H. D. A. C.
Miers; M. J. Wilmshurst.
European Integration (External) Dept., H. J. Arbuth-
nott; *Asst.,* N. H. R. A. Broomfield.
European Integration (Internal) Dept., (vacant)
Deputy Head of Dept., Miss J. J. D'A. Collings;
Asst., T. J. B. George.
Far Eastern Dept., W. Bentley; *Asst.,* P. J. L.
Popplewell.
Finance Dept., G. W. Jewkes; *Deputy Head of Dept.,*
E. G. White, O.B.E.; *Assts.,* T. W. Sharp; T. H.
Steggle.
Financial Relations Dept., The Hon. H. J. H. Maud;
Assts., P. E. Hall; R. Thomas.
Gibraltar and General Dept., E. G. Lewis, C.M.G.,
O.B.E.
Guidance and Information Policy Dept., N. J. Barring-
ton, C.V.O.; *Deputy Head of Dept.,* P. R. Metcalfe;
Assts., M. Kendall, M.V.O.; A. R. Sinclair.
Hong Kong J. A. B. Stewart, O.B.E. *Asst.,* D. F.
Milton.
India Office Library and Records: Director, Miss J. C.
Lancaster, F.S.A.; *Deputy Librarian,* R. G. C.
Desmond; *Deputy Archivist,* M. I. Moir.
Library: Assistant Keepers, Miss O. M. Lloyd; Mrs.
M. Archer; M. J. C. O'Keefe; Mrs. U. Sims-
Williams; Mrs. U. Tripathi; *Records: Assistan*

Keepers, A. J. Farrington; R. J. Bingle, D.Phil.; J. M. Sims; Mrs. P. J. Tuson.

Information Administration Depts., C. G. Mays; *Asst.*, (vacant)

Information Research Dept., R. W. Whitney, O.B.E.; *Deputy Head of Department and Assistant*, J. G. McMinnies, O.B.E.; *Assts.*, P. Joy, O.B.E.; Mrs. J. M. O'Connor-Howe.

Latin American Dept., H. M. Carless, C.M.G.; *Asst.*, A. J. Collins, O.B.E.

Library and Records Dept., B. Cheeseman, O.B.E.; *Assts.*, Miss E. C. Blayney; Miss M. D. Croft; H. G. F. Harcombe.

Marine and Transport Dept., A. C. Buxton; *Asst.*, M. W. Atkinson, M.B.E.

Middle East Dept., Hon. I. T. M. Lucas; *Asst.*, S. P. Day.

Migration and Visa Dept., H. E. Rigney; *Assts.*, J. H. Mallett, M.M.; A. Shepherd.

Nationality and Treaty Dept., A. J. Brown; *Asst.*, R. R. G. B. Smedley.

Near East and North Africa Dept., A. B. Urwick; *Asst.*, F. B. Wheeler.

News Dept., W. E. H. Whyte; *Deputy Head*, Miss E. M. Booker, O.B.E.; *Asst.*, J. Bourgoin, O.B.E.

North America Dept., M. R. Melhuish; *Asst.*, G. N. Smith.

Pacific Dependent Territories Dept., E. A. W. Bullock; *Assts.*, R. S. Pettitt; F. S. E. Trew.

Permanent Under Secretary's Dept., J. M. Edes; *Deputy Head*, D. Tonkin; *Asst.*, P. H. C. Eyers, M.V.O.

Personnel Operations Dept., H. B. Walker; *Deputy Head*, R. J. Carrick, M.V.O.; *Assts.*, A. J. Beamish; G. A. Fletcher; J. B. Weymes, O.B.E.

Personnel Policy Dept., P. H. Moberly; *Asst.*, R. A. Neilson, M.V.O.

Personnel Services Dept., A. J. Hunter; *Assts.*, D. L. Benest, O.B.E.; A. S. Donkin; B. T. Holmes.

Planning Staff, B. L. Crowe.

Protocol and Conference ,Dept., R. W. H. du Boulay, C.M.G., C.V.O. (*H.M. Vice-Marshal of the Diplomatic Corps*); S. W. F. Martin; G. G. Collins (*Assistant Marshals of the Diplomatic Corps*). £6,090 to £7,860. *Asst.*, Miss P. T. Metcalfe, O.B.E.

Republic of Ireland Dept., G. W. Harding, C.V.O.; *Asst.*, J. D. N. Hartland-Swann.

Research Dept., E. E. Orchard, C.B.E. (*Director*).

Rhodesia Dept., P. M. Laver; *Asst.*, P. J. Barlow.

Science and Technology Dept., S. J. Barrett; *Asst.*, P. R. Fearn.

Security Dept., C. J. Howells; *Assts.*, A. E. Furness; K. Kirby, O.B.E.

South Asian Dept., R. J. O'Neill; *Asst.*, C. H. Seaward.

South-East Asian Dept., A. M. Simons; *Asst.*, A. K. Goldsmith.

Southern-European Dept., (vacant).; *Assts.*, R. H. Baker; R. L. B. Cormack.

South-West Pacific Dept., R. G. Britten, C.M.G.

Trade Relations and Exports Dept., J. C. Cloake; *Assts.*, B. W. Gordon, O.B.E.; P. J. L. Popplewell.

Training Dept. Head of Dept. and Director of Language Centre (P. G. de Courcy Ireland; *Assts.*, H. Gilmartin; C. W. M. Wilson.

United Nations Dept., P. M. Maxey; *Asst. and Deputy Head*, M. L. Tait, M.V.O.; *Asst.*, J. H. Symons.

West African Dept., M. E. Heath; *Asst.*, M. A. Holding.

West Indian and Atlantic Dept., P. C. Duff; *Asst.*, J. M. Willson.

Western European Dept., A. D. S. Goodall; *Assts.*, D. Beattie, A. C. McCarthy.

Passport Office
Clive House, Petty France, S.W.1
[01-222-8010]

Chief Passport Officer, M. G. Dixon, O.B.E.
£8,650 to £11,000

Deputy Chief Passport Officer, R. P. B. Cave, O.B.E.
£7,750 to £9,350

Liverpool Office
India Buildings, Water Street, Liverpool 2
[051-227-3461]

Officer in Charge, Miss V. M. Brady
£5,680 to £7,450

Glasgow Office
Empire House, 131 West Nile Street, Glasgow, C.1
[041-332-0271]

Officer in Charge, J. T. Robertson
£5,680 to £7,450

Newport Office
Olympia House, Upper Dock Street, Newport, Gwent
[0633-52431]

Officer in Charge, Mrs. T. M. Godfrey
£5,680 to £7,450

Peterborough Office
55 Westfield Road, Peterborough
[0733-263636]

Officer in Charge, R. W. Dennis. £5,680 to £7,450

Belfast Agency
30 Victoria Street, Belfast 1
[0232-32371]

Officer in Charge, Mrs. M. T. Haughey.

Corps of Queen's Messengers
Superintendent of the Queen's Messenger Service, Capt J. G. Canning, O.B.E.

Queen's Diplomatic Service Messengers, R. A. Perryman, M.B.E.; T. D. Nettleton; Lt.-Col. A. F. Rowe; Lt.-Col. C. F. V. Bagot, O.B.E.; Lt.-Col. J. M. B. Poyntz, O.B.E.; Maj. M. P. D. Cruickshank; Sq.-Ldr. A. P. Hollick; A. P. H. Lousada; Wing-Cdr. T. Stevenson, A.F.C.; Sq.-Ldr. S. G. R. White; Capt. D. V. Walmesley; Maj. W. R. A. Catcheside; J. H. Kidner; R. C. H. Risley; J. O. Hollis; Flt.-Lt. P. C. Stevens, D.F.C.; Lt.-Col. B. A. A. Plummer; Maj. P. Sherston-Baker, M.C.; Maj. C. M. Tuffill; Maj. J. K. Nairne; Lt.-Col. B. A. Hannaford; F. N. Cory-Wright; Group Capt. S. P. Coulson, D.S.O., D.F.C.; Sqn.-Ldr. L. V. Davies, D.F.M.; E. W. J. Eyers; Maj. A. W. Gay; J. A. Golding, C.V.O.; Maj. L. A. Smeeton, M.M.; Maj. K. H. M. O'Kelly; Lt.-Col. H. Forwood; Maj. D. B. Metcalfe; Lt.-Col. C. R. Simms-Reeve; Maj. R. J. Angel; Sqn.-Ldr. L. C. Bazalgette; Maj. C. T. H. Campbell; Maj. G. M. Benson; Lt.-Cdr. B. R. Bezance; Maj. M. J. Fuller; G. F. Miller; Maj. A. M. Farmer; Lt.-Col. B. C. F. Arkle, M.B.E.; Lt.-Col. E. M. T. Crump; J. W. Hannah, M.B.E.; P. L. Burkinshaw, O.B.E.; Maj. L. M. Phillips; Maj. P. T. Dunn; Wing-Cdr. R. A. Nash; Capt. D. F. A. Bloom, G.M.; C. J. d'E. Willoughby; C. Page, C.P.M.; Lt.-Cdr. R. N. J. Wright.

India Office Library and Records
Orbit House, 197 Blackfriars Road, S.E.1
The Record Office has the custody of the archives of the East India Company (1600–1858), the Board of Control (1784–1858), the India Office (1858–1947) and the Burma Office (1937–1947).
Director, Miss J. C. Lancaster, F.S.A.

FORESTRY COMMISSION
231 Corstorphine Road, Edinburgh
[031-334-0303]
The Forestry Commissioners are charged with the general duty of promoting the interests of forestry, the development of afforestation, the production and supply of timber and the maintenance of reserves of growing trees in Great Britain. Including the former Crown Woods, transferred to it in 1924, the Commission has acquired about 3,000,000 acres of land (75 per cent. being plant-

able), of which about 2,000,000 acres are under plantations. Under various grant schemes, financial assistance is given to private owners and local authorities in respect of approved works of afforestation.

Chairman J. Mackie, (*part-time*)	£6,200
Director-General and Deputy Chairman, J. A. Dickson, C.B.	£14,000
Head of Forest and Estate Management, G. G. Stewart, M.C.	£12,000
Head of Administration and Finance, J. M. Hunter, M.C.	£12,000
Head of Harvesting and Marketing, G. D. Holmes	£12,000
Senior Officer, Wales (Churchill House, Cardiff), J. W. L. Zehetmayr, V.R.D.	£11,000

NATIONAL FREIGHT CORPORATION
Argosy House, 215 Great Portland Street, W.1
[01-636-8688]

The National Freight Corporation is a statutory corporation set up under the Transport Act, 1968, to provide integrated road and rail freight services in Great Britain and in so doing to make the maximum economic use of rail, with due regard to the needs of the person for whom the goods are being carried, and the requirements of the goods themselves. On January 1, 1969, it inherited the securities, rights and liabilities of the Road Haulage and Shipping Subsidiaries of the Transport Holding Company. It also acquired from the British Railways Board, National Carriers Ltd. and a 51 per cent. interest in Freightliners Ltd. (formerly the "Sundries" and "Freightliner" Divisions respectively of the Railways Board).

Chairman, Sir Daniel Pettit	£19,863
Members, The Lord Allen of Abbeydale, G.C.B.;	

Members, The Lord Allen of Abbeydale, G.C.B.; Prof. R. J. Ball; Sir Sidney Greene, C.B.E.; F. S. Law (£2,000); R. L. E. Lawrence, O.B.E., E.R.D.; D. G. MacDonald; D. D. Sieff; R. O. C. Swayne, M.C.; C. H. Urwin; L. G. Whyte, C.B.E. each (*part-time*) £1,000
Vice-Chairman, Executive Board, V. G. Paige.
Chief Secretary and Legal Adviser, P. A. Mayo.

REGISTRY OF FRIENDLY SOCIETIES (CENTRAL OFFICE) AND OFFICE OF THE INDUSTRIAL ASSURANCE COMMISSIONER
17 North Audley Street, W.1
[01-629-7001]

A Barrister was appointed in 1828 to certify the Rules of Savings Banks, and in 1829 to certify those of Friendly Societies. In 1846 he was constituted Registrar of Friendly Societies. By the Friendly Societies Act, 1875, the Central Office of the Registry of Friendly Societies was created consisting of the Chief Registrar and the Assistant Registrars for England. It exercises numerous and important functions under the Friendly Societies Acts, the Industrial and Provident Societies Acts, the Building Societies Acts, the Trustee Savings Banks and National Savings Bank Acts, the Loan Societies Act, the Shop Clubs Acts and the Superannuation and other Trust Funds (Validation) Act. Under the Industrial Assurance Acts and the Insurance Companies Acts, the Chief Registrar is charged with various powers and duties in relation to Industrial Assurance Companies and Collecting Societies, and in that capacity is styled the Industrial Assurance Commissioner.

Chief Registrar and Industrial Assurance Commissioner, K. Brading, C.B., M.B.E.	£13,230
Private Sec., Mrs. W. Hughes.	
Asst. Registrar and Deputy Head of Department, A. Vollmar	£11,440
Asst. Registrar, J. E. Gower, O.B.E., M.C.	£9,033 to £11,000
Executive Registrar and Establishment Officer, J. A. Walter	£8,650 to £11,000
Senior Legal Assistant, M. J. Pearce	£6,625 to £8,750
Legal Assistant, C. B. E. White.	£3,424 to £6,125

egistration and Disputes Branch (Head), J. W. D. Goss, £5,680 to £7,450; (Asst. Head), M. F. G. Howell. : .... £4,900 to £5,900
Returns and Statistics Branch (Head), E. S. Burgess, £5,680 to £5,450; (Asst. Head) I. D. Christie
£4,900 to £5,900
Establishment and Records Branch (Head), L. G. Hill
£4,900 to £5,900
Investigations Branch (Head), R. E. Kilbey
£4,900 to £5,900

Registry of Friendly Societies, Scotland
19 Heriot Row, Edinburgh, 3
[031-556-4371]
Assistant Registrar, J. Craig, O.B.E., W.S.

GAMING BOARD FOR GREAT BRITAIN
Berkshire House, 168-173 High Holborn, W.C.1
[01-240-0821]

Established on October 25, 1968, to maintain a broad oversight of developments in gaming in Great Britain, to check prospective gaming licensees management and staff, and to advise the Home Secretary on making regulations which may be needed for the further control of gaming.
Chairman, Sir Stanley Raymond.
Members, The Lord Allen of Abbeydale, G.C.B.; R. T. M. McPhail; Hon. R. O. Stanley; Sir James Starrit, C.V.O.
Secretary, W. J. Stephens.

BRITISH GAS CORPORATION
59 Bryanston Street W1.
[01-723-7030]

Chairman, Sir D. E. Rooke, C.B.E.	
(plus allowances £1,000)	£20,000
Deputy Chairman, J. H. Smith	
(plus allowances £500)	£16,000
Secretary, W. Burnstone.	

THE GOVERNMENT ACTUARY
Steel House, Tothill Street, S.W.1
[01-273-3000]

Government Actuary, E. A. Johnston, C.B.	£15,100
Under-Secretaries (Directing Actuaries), L. V. Martin; G. G. Newton; C. M. Stewart	£12,000
Principal Actuaries, C. L. Cannon; J. L. Field; R. T. Foster; R. C. Gilder; D. H. Loades; J. R. Watts	£8,650 to £11,000
Actuaries, D. G. Ballantine; C. D. Daykin; A. H. Gould; C. A. Harris; M. D. May; A. P. Pavelin; M. A. Pickford; D. F. Renn.	£7,150 to £9,350

THE GOVERNMENT CHEMIST
See under DEPARTMENT OF TRADE AND INDUSTRY

GOVERNMENT HOSPITALITY FUND
2 Carlton Gardens, S.W.1
[01-214-6000]

Instituted in 1908 for the purpose of organizing official hospitality on a regular basis, with a view to the promotion of international goodwill.
Minister in Charge, C. R. Morris, M.P.
Secretary, C. F. R. Barclay, C.M.G.

GOVERNMENT SOCIAL SURVEY DEPARTMENT
See OFFICE OF POPULATION CENSUSES AND SURVEYS.

DEPARTMENT OF HEALTH AND SOCIAL SECURITY
Alexander Fleming House, Elephant and Castle, S.E.1
[01-407-5522]

The Department of Health and Social Security was created on November 1, 1968, from the Ministry of Health and Ministry of Social Security. The new Department performs the functions of the two former Ministries.

The Department is responsible for the administration of the National Health Service in England and for the personal social services run by local authorities in England for children, the elderly, in-

firm, handicapped and other persons in need. It has functions relating to food hygiene and welfare foods. The Department is also concerned with the medical and surgical treatment of war pensioners in England, the Channel Isles, Isle of Man or living in the Irish Republic, and is responsible for the ambulance and first aid services in emergency, under the Civil Defence Act, 1948. The Department represents the United Kingdom on the World Health Organization of the United Nations. Responsibility for the administration of the Health Services in Wales was transferred to the Welsh Office on April 1, 1969. The Department is responsible for the social security services in England, Scotland and Wales. These services comprise schemes for war pensions, national insurance, family allowances and supplementary benefits. Within the Department, the Supplementary Benefits Commission is responsible, subject to regulations made by the Secretary of State for Social Services, for guiding the scheme of supplementary benefits.

Secretary of State for Social Services, THE RT. HON. DAVID HADLEY ENNALS, M.P. £13,000
Private Secretary, M. C. Malone-Lee
£8,650 to £11,000
Assistant Private Secretaries, G. A. Johnson; Mrs. P. A. Folger.
Parliamentary Private Secretary, R. L. MacFarquhar, M.P.
Ministers of State, THE RT. HON. STANLEY ORME, M.P. (Social Security); THE RT. HON. DAVID ANTHONY LLEWELLYN OWEN, M.P. (Health)
£7,500
Parliamentary Under Secretary of State, E. P. Deakins, M.P. (Social Security); A Morris, M.P. (Disablement)
Chairman, Supplementary Benefits Commission, Prof. D. V. Donnison £7,180
Deputy Chairman, Mrs. C. M. Carmichael. . £2,000
Members, E. P. Brown; Miss B. Dean; K. J. Griffin, O.B.E.; Mrs. C. G. Holtham; A. F. Stabler; Dr. B. A. Tanner.
Permanent Secretary, Sir Patrick Nairne, K.C.B., M.C.
£18,675
Private Secretary, W. Healey.
Second Permanent Secretary, Sir Lance Errington, K.C.B. £17,175
Private Secretary, D. J. Russell.
Deputy Secretaries, J. A. Atkinson, C.B., D.F.C.; P. Benner, C.B.; C. L. Bourton; A. J. Collier; R. Gedling, C.B.; R. A. Matthews; G. J. Otton
£14,000
Chief Medical Officer, Sir Henry Yellowlees, K.C.B.
£17,175
Librarian, Miss A. M. C. Kahn. . £5,680 to £7,450

Establishment and Personnel Division I
Director of Establishments and Personnel (Departmental)
Under Secretary, R. S. Swift. £12,000
Assistant Secretaries, Miss J. A. Bates; D. V. Chislett; H. T. Elsworth; R. Graham, D.S.O.
£8,650 to £11,000

Establishment and Personnel Division II
Director of Establishments and Personnel (Headquarters)
Under Secretary, N. E. Clarke. £12,000
Assistant Secretaries, G. A. Hart; V. H. Hemming, O.B.E. £8,650 to £11,000

Regional Directorate
Under Secretary, E. L. Trew £12,000
Assistant Secretaries, N. Hanson; J. H. C. Nightingall; E. T. Randall. . . . . . £8,650 to £11,000

Insurance Division L
Under Secretary, A. J. G. Crocker, C.B. £12,000
Assistant Secretaries, Mrs. A. E. Bowtell; D. W. Polley; F. Sutton. . . . . £8,650 to £11,000

Statistics and Research Division
Director of Statistics and Research, A. R. Smith
£12,000
Assistant Secretary, M. E. H. Platt
£8,650 to £11,000
Chief Statisticians, J. B. Dearman; D. S. S. Hutton, O.B.E.; Mrs. C. Palmer; J. A. Rowntree; F. E. Whitehead. . . . . £8,650 to £11,000

International Relations Division
Under Secretary, F. B. Hindmarsh. £12,000
Assistant Secretaries, H. S. McPherson; L. G. Refell; H. W. Seabourn. . . . . £8,650 to £11,000

Information Division
Director of Information, A. P. G. Brown. . . £11,670
Deputy Directors and Chief Information Officers, J. M. Bolitho; I. M. Gillis. . . . . . . £7,750 to £11,000

Economic Advisers Office
Chief Economic Adviser, Prof. J. L. Nicholson
£12,000
Senior Economic Advisers, J. D. Pole; C. H. Smee; R. Van Slooten. . . . . £8,650 to £11,000

Solicitors Office
Solicitor, M. W. M. Osmond. £14,000
Principal Assistant Solicitors, H. Knorpel; R. F. N. Thoyts; R. N. Williams £12,000

Insurance Division A
Under Secretary, D. C. Ward. £12,000
Assistant Secretaries, I. G. Gilbert; B. W. Taylor
£8,650 to £11,000

Insurance Division B
Under Secretary, C. M. Regan. £12,000
Assistant Secretaries, B. J. Ellis; E. D. McGinnis; R. D. F. Whitelaw. . . . . £8,650 to £11,000

Insurance Division C
Under Secretary, S. B. Kibbey. £12,000
Assistant Secretaries, M. E. Caines; T. A. Howell; J. D. H. Long; J. M. Nicholson £8,650 to £11,000

Insurance Division K
Under Secretary, E. W. Whittemore, M.M. . £12,000
Assistant Secretaries, T. S. Heppell; S. M. Nicholson
£8,650 to £11,000

Registrar of Non-Participating Employments
Registrar, J. D. Hiscocks. . . . . £5,680 to £7,450

Supplementary Benefits—Division 1
Under Secretary, M. J. A. Partridge. £12,000
Assistant Secretaries, Miss J. I. Barnes; A. C. Palmer
£8,650 to £11,000

Supplementary Benefits—Division II
Under Secretary (vacant) £12,000
Assistant Secretaries, J. S. Campbell-Dick; G. W. Woodman. . . . . £8,650 to £11,000

Finance Divisions
(Health & Personal Social Services)
Under Secretaries, R. E. Radford; P. J. Kitcatt
£12,000
Assistant Secretaries, Mrs. G. T. Banks; S. Bayfield; B. H. Betts; R. L. Gordon; K. A. Sidford; C. G. Taylor; J. E. Vaughan. . . . . £8,650 to £11,000
(Social Security)
Under Secretary, P. R. Oglesby. £12,000
Assistant Secretaries, B. Bridges; L. J. Hayward; J. L. Oxlade; J. H. Ward. . . £8,650 to £11,000

Medical Divisions (Health)
Deputy Chief Medical Officers, H. M. Archibald, M.B.E.; F. D. Beddard, C.B.; J. J. A. Reid, C.B.; R. M. Shaw, C.B. £14,000
Senior Principal Medical Officers, J. Brothwood; D. H. D. Burbidge, O.B.E.; D. A. Cahal; E. F. Carr; N. D. B. Evans; F. A. Fairweather; Gillian Ford; T. J. Geffen; A. B. Harrington; E. L. Harris; J. L. Kilgour; Elizabeth C. Shore; Esther E. Simpson; J. M. G. Wilson; W. Wintersgill. £12,000
Consultant Advisor, Prof. I. D. P. Wootton.
Chief Scientific Officer, J. C. A. Raison.
Principal Medical Officers, R. St. J. Buxton; M. F. Cuthbert; F. J. Darby, T.D.; Sylvia Darke; J. A. Holgate; J. L. Hunt; W. H. Inman; Marjorie Kuck; W. Lees, C.B.E.; M. J. MacCulloch; D. S. McKenzie; G. K. Matthew; D. Ower; Eileen M. Ring; P. Seelig; M. Vitali; R. Wilkins. £10,240

N.H.S. PERSONNEL DIVISIONS

Division P1
Under Secretary, J. P. Cashman.........£12,000
Assistant Secretaries, R. A. Birch; Miss J. M. Firth;
W. F. Lake; W. O. Roberts; S. Smith
£8,650 to £11,000

Division P2
Under Secretary, P. G. Perry............£12,000
Assistant Secretaries, B. H. Goodale; V. J. Harley;
B. M. Street; D. White.....£8,650 to £11,000

Division P3
Under Secretary, R. B. Hodgetts.........£12,000
Assistant Secretaries, J. B. Brown; Mrs. P. G. Lee;
A. L. Parrott; S. I. Smith; Miss E. M. Walker
£8,650 to £11,000

Division P4
Under Secretary, E. B. S. Alton, M.B.E., M.C. £12,000
Assistant Secretaries, M. W. Draper; W. F. Farrant;
R. J. Petch.................£8,650 to £11,000

Supply Division
Controller of Supply, A. G. Beard........£12,000
Directors of Supply, N. Hollens; G. E. John; D. S.
Monks.................£8,650 to £11,000
Director of Scientific and Technical Branch, P. M.
Harms.

Industry and Exports Division
Under Secretary, S. M. Davies, C.M.G......£12,000
Assistant Secretaries, A. J. Merifield; R. Wright
£8,650 to £11,000

Socially Handicapped Division
Under Secretary, J. T. Woodlock..........£12,000
Assistant Secretaries, G. M. Bebb; R. Cattran; Mrs.
M. A. J. Pearson; Mrs. V. J. M. Poole.
£8,650 to £11,000

Mental Health Division
Under Secretary, K. Moyes..............£12,000
Assistant Secretaries, J. R. Brough; C. Emerson;
Mrs. P. M. Williamson.....£8,650 to £11,000

Regional Liaison Division
Under Secretary, G. Beltram.............£12,000
Assistant Secretaries, L. Devine; J. Hallowell; F. D.
K. Williams, C.B.E.; P. J. Wormald
£8,650 to £11,000

Regional Planning Division
Under Secretary, J. C. C. Smith..........£12,000
Assistant Secretaries, C. Graham; R. S. King; M.
Nelson...................£8,650 to £11,000

Central Planning and Services Division
Under Secretary, G. G. Hulme...........£12,000
Assistant Secretaries, P. J. Fletcher; T. R. H. Luce
£8,650 to £11,000

Computers and Research Division
Under Secretary, B. R. Rayner..........£12,000
Assistant Secretaries, J. W. E. Clutterbuck; E. J. C.
Fowell; W. T. Hartland; T. J. Maddison; R.
Toulmin..................£8,650 to £11,000

Children's Division
Under Secretary, J. W. Stacpoole.........£12,000
Assistant Secretaries, A. C. Clarke; P. V. Foster;
A. F. Taggart.............£8,650 to £11,000

Local Authority—Social Services Division
Under Secretary, G. G. Hulme...........£12,000
Assistant Secretaries, P. D. Watson; C. H. Wilson
£8,650 to £11,000

Social Work Service
Chief Social Work Officer, W. B. Utting..£14,000
Deputy Director of Social Work Service, Miss A. M.
Sheridan..........................£11,320
Assistant Directors, R. I. L. Guthrie; Miss P. E. Harwood; Mrs. B. J. Kahan; Mrs. D. Ottley
£8,650 to £11,000

Principal Social Work Service Officers, Miss G.
Browne-Williamson; J. K. Corcoran; Miss M. I.
Denham; J. Hodder; Miss M. A. L. Howard;
Mrs. I. Midforth; Dr. N. S. Tutt; Miss J. M.
Vann........(+ allce. £312) £6,000 to £7,750

Medicines and Environmental Health Division
Under Secretary, Dr. E. L. Harris.........£12,000
Assistant Secretaries, E. W. L. Keymer, M.C.; R. E.
Tringham..................£8,650 to £11,000

Superannuation Division
Under Secretary, E. B. S. Alton, M.B.E., M.C.. £12,000
Assistant Secretary, R. P. Pole..£8,650 to £11,000

Health Service—Division 1
Under Secretary, N. M. Hale............£12,000
Assistant Secretaries, J. B. Cornish; E. L. Mayston
£8,650 to £11,000

Health Service—Division 2
Under Secretary, N. E. Nodder..........£12,000
Assistant Secretaries, M. W. Draper; N. Illingworth;
R. B. Mayoh...............£8,650 to £11,000

Public and Environmental Health Division
Under Secretary, N. M. Hale............£12,000
Assistant Secretaries, R. P. Pole; J. B. Sharp
£8,650 to £11,000

Hospital Building Division
Under Secretary, D. Somerville, C.B......£12,000
Assistant Secretaries, W. J. Littlewood; W. D. Paget;
B. A. R. Smith; E. L. Wallis
£8,650 to £11,000

Catering and Dietetics Branch
Chief Officer on Catering and Dietetics, A. R. Horton
£7,074 to £8,250
Deputy Chief Officer, P. C. Pillow
£5,600 to £6,981

Domestic Services Management Branch
Chief Officer, I. W. Little, M.B.E. £7,750 to £9,350

Architectural Division
Chief Architect, R. H. Goodman.........£12,000
Assistant Chief Architects, M. J. Bench; C. Davies;
M. A. Meager; P. L. Ward...........£11,000

Surveying Division
Chief Surveyor, B. E. Drake.............£12,000
Assistant Chief Surveyors, R. T. V. Amery; A. P. R.
Pell-Hiley................£11,000
Superintending Surveyors, N. G. M. Barton; W. V. F.
Buckle; D. A. Butler; D. B. James; D. A. Turner
£8,650 to £9,798

Engineering Division
Chief Engineer, J. Bolton..............£12,000
Assistant Chief Engineers, E. R. Haynes; R. Manser;
Dr. K. I. Murray; T. R. Nicholls......£11,000

Medical Division (Social Security)
Chief Medical Adviser, Dr. J. A. G. Carmichael.
Deputy Chief Medical Adviser, G. O. Mayne.
Principal Medical Officers, S. Conlan; M. R. Hayes;
R. M. McGowan; E. G. Wright, O.B.E.

Dental Division
Chief Dental Officer, G. D. Gibb.........£12,000
Deputy Chief Dental Officer, G. B. Roberts. £9,440
Senior Dental Officers, H. A. Dixey; I. C. S. Fraser;
F. D. R. Geldard; H. M. Hughes; V. D. Lees;
R. Middleton; W. N. McNiven; J. Rodgers,
D.F.M.; J. B. Woodward.

Nursing Division
Chief Nursing Officer, Miss P. M. Friend, C.B.E.
£12,000
Deputy Chief Nursing Officer, Miss A. M. Lamb;
O.B.E.; Miss M. H. McLeod; Miss J. G. Whitehead................................£9,818

Pharmaceutical Division
Chief Pharmacist, T. D. Whittet.........£10,950

Deputy Chief Pharmacists, Dr. J. M. Calderwood;
A. G. Fishburn .... £8,650 to £9,798
Pharmacists, Superintending Grade, R. Baker; S. F.
Hall .... £8,650 to £9,798
Pharmacists, Senior Grade, Mrs. H. E. Bailey; Miss
N. C. Cone; J. Flint; B. H. Hartley; Miss J. P.
Kirby; Mrs. M. R. Pratt; Dr. M. Rogers; J. R.
Sharp; R. Smith; Miss R. J. Smith; A. G.
Stewart .... £6,280 to £7,450
Senior Principal Scientific Officers, C. A. Johnson;
G. R. Kitteringham, O.B.E. .... £8,650 to £9,798

Blackpool Central Office
Controller, K. Shuttleworth .... £8,650 to £11,000

Newcastle upon Tyne Central Office
Controller, C. K. Whitaker £12,000

Scotland
Argyll House, 3 Lady Lawson Street, Edinburgh
Controller, J. C. Moy £11,670

Wales
Government Buildings, Gabalfa, Cardiff.
Controller, R. K. Meatyard .... £8,650 to £11,000

Regional Organisation [England]
Northern, Arden House, Regent Farm Road, Gos-
forth, Newcastle upon Tyne. *Regional Con-
troller,* S. Watson, D.F.C.
Yorkshire and Humberside, Government Buildings,
Otley Road, Lawnswood, Leeds. *Regional
Controller,* J. M. Tones.
East Midlands and East Anglia, Block 1, Government
Buildings, Chalfont Drive, Nottingham. *Reg-
ional Controller,* R. A. E. Tow.
London North, Olympic House, Olympic Way,
Wembley, Middx. *Regional Controller,* S. H.
Bate.
London South, Sutherland House, 29–37 Brighton
Road, Sutton, Surrey. *Regional Controller,*
B. C. James.
London West, Grosvenor House, Basing View,
Basingstoke, Hants. *Regional Controller,* L. C. H.
Stadames.
South Western, Government Buildings, Flowers
Hill, Bristol. *Regional Controller,* J. C. Lewis.
West Midlands, Cumberland House, 200 Broad
Street, Birmingham 15. *Regional Controller,*
V. M. Thompson.
North Western (Manchester), Albert Bridge House
East, Bridge Street, Manchester. *Regional Con-
troller,* G. Collins.
North Western (Merseyside), St. Martin's House,
Stanley Precinct, Bootle. *Regional Controller,*
D. J. Francis.

NATIONAL INSURANCE ADVISORY COMMITTEE
Keysign House, 429 Oxford Street, W.1
[01–499–4040]
The National Insurance Advisory Committee
is constituted under the Social Security Act 1975 to
give advice and assistance to the Secretary of
State in connection with the discharge of his (or her)
functions under the Act, and to perform any other
duties allotted to it under the Act. These other duties
include the consideration of preliminary drafts of
regulations to be made under the Social Security
Act, and of representations received thereon. When
the regulations are laid before Parliament, the
Committee's Report on the preliminary draft is
laid with them, together with a statement by the
Secretary of State showing what amendments to
the preliminary draft have been made, what effect
has been given to the Committee's recommendations, and, if effect has not been given to any
recommendation, the reasons for not adopting it.
The Secretary of State may also refer to the Committee for consideration and advice any questions
relating to the operation of the Act (including
questions as to the advisability of amending it).
Chairman, Prof. D. S. Lees.

Members, Dr. R. J. Donaldson, O.B.E.; Prof. J. A.
Faris; Dr. G. Harry; P. R. A. Jacques; P. M.
Madders; H. K. Mitchell; Miss A. M. Patrick.
Secretary, K. Edwards.

INDUSTRIAL INJURIES ADVISORY COUNCIL
Keysign House, 421–429 Oxford Street, W.1.
[01–499–4040]
The Industrial Injuries Advisory Council is a statu-
tory body under the Social Security Act, 1975, which
considers and advises the Secretary of State for
Social Services on Regulations and other questions,
as the Secretary of State thinks fit, relating to in-
dustrial injuries benefit or its administration.
Chairman, Prof. D. S. Lees.
Members, Prof. T. Anderson, C.B.E.; Dr. P. L.
Bidstrup; R. W. Buckton; Dr. R. J. Donaldson,
O.B.E.; R. G. Hitchcock; P. R. A. Jacques; Prof.
C. R. Lowe; J. L. I. McQuitty, Q.C.; J. C. Mil-
ligan, O.B.E.; T. Parry, O.B.E.; Mrs. C. M. Patter-
son, O.B.E.; D. M. Rea; I. G. Reid; S. J. Stan-
brook; Dr. Alice M. Stewart; Dr. J. Watkins-
Pitchford, C.B.
Secretary, D. M. Woolley.

NATIONAL INSURANCE AND INDUSTRIAL INJURIES JOINT AUTHORITIES
10 John Adam Street, W.C.2
[01–217–3000]
Members, The Secretary of State for Social Services;
the Head of the Department of Health and Social
Services for Northern Ireland.
Deputies for the Secretary of State for Social Ser-
vices, Sir Patrick Nairne, K.C.B., M.C., F. B.
Hindmarsh; for the Head of the Department of
Health and Social Security for Northern Ireland,
N. Dugdale; C. G. Oakes.
Joint Financial Advisers, E. A. Johnston; P. R.
Oglesby; F. A. Elliott.
Secretary, D. S. Beaumont.

PNEUMOCONIOSIS, BYSSINOSIS AND MIS-CELLANEOUS DISEASES BENEFIT SCHEME (1966) AND WORKMEN'S COMPENSATION (SUPPLEMENTATION) SCHEME (1966)
Norcross, Blackpool, Lancs.
[Blackpool: 52311]
Chairman, D. M. Campbell, Q.C.
Deputy Chairman, Sir Lionel Brett.
Members, D. W. Boydell; A. J. Collins; A. J. Lewis,
G. H. Lowthian, C.B.E.; W. Malt; B. W. Taylor.
Secretary, H. V. Hutson.

NATIONAL INSURANCE: OFFICE OF THE CHIEF INSURANCE OFFICER
Cumberland House,
15/17 Cumberland Place, Southampton
[0703–34541]
Chief Insurance Officer, R. Dronfield.
Deputy Chief Insurance Officer, P. G. H. Ewer.

OFFICE OF THE REGISTRAR OF NON-PARTICIPATING EMPLOYMENTS
Apex Tower, High Street,
New Malden, Surrey
[01–942–8949]
Registrar, J. D. Hiscocks.
Deputy Registrar, Miss R. Shipley.

NATIONAL HEALTH SERVICE REGIONAL HEALTH AUTHORITIES

England is divided between 14 Regional Health
Authorities, each with at least one university medical school within its boundaries. Each Region
contains a number of Area Health Authorities
(which are the operational NHS authorities, responsible for assessing needs in their areas, for
planning, organising and administering area health
services to meet them). The Area Health Authorities
are generally coterminous with the local authorities
which provide complementary personal social

services. At the moment the 12 post-graduate teaching hospitals in London continue to be administered by Boards of Governors. The Chairmen, and members of Regional Health Authorities and Boards of Governors, and the Chairmen of Area Health Authorities are appointed by the Secretary of State for Social Services.

Regions

Northern, Benfield Road, Walker Gate, Newcastle upon Tyne. *Chairman*, Colonel Sir William Lee, O.B.E., T.D. *Regional Administrator*, A. B. Baker.

Yorkshire, Park Parade, Harrogate. *Chairman*, W. Tweedle, C.B.E., T.D. *Regional Administrator*, H. Inman.

Trent, Fulwood House, Old Fulwood Road, Sheffield. *Chairman*, Sir Sydney King, O.B.E. *Regional Administrator*, W. M. Naylor, C.B.E.

East Anglia, Union Lane, Chesterton, Cambridge. *Chairman*, The Hon. Leo Russell, C.B.E., T.D. *Regional Administrator*, S. W. Smith.

North East Thames, 40 Eastbourne Terrace, W2 *Chairman*, H. R. Moore, C.B.E. *Regional Administrator*, M. J. Fairey.

North West Thames, 40 Eastbourne Terrace, W2. *Chairman*, Mrs. B. F. R. Paterson, C.B.E. *Regional Administrator*, G. H. Weston, C.B.E.

South East Thames, Randolph House, 46/48 Wellesley Road, Croydon, Surrey. *Chairman*, J. C. Donne. *Regional Administrator*, H. N. Lamb.

South West Thames, 40 Eastbourne Terrace, W2. *Chairman*, The Baroness Robson of Kiddington. *Regional Administrator*, M. W. Southern.

Wessex, Highcroft, Romsey Road, Winchester, Hants. *Chairman*, K. Williams. *Regional Administrator*, J. Hoare.

Oxford, Old Road, Headington, Oxford. *Chairman*, D. Woodrow. *Regional Administrator*, D. Norton.

South Western, 27 Tyndalls Park Road, Bristol. *Chairman*, B. H. Bailey. *Regional Administrator*, A. J. Brooking.

West Midlands, Arthur Thomson House, 146–150 Hagley Road, Birmingham. *Chairman*, D. A. Perris, M.B.E. *Regional Administrator*, K. F. Bales.

Mersey, Wilberforce House, The Strand, Liverpool. *Chairman*, E. W. Driver. *Regional Administrator*, J. D. Shepherd.

North Western, Gateway House, Piccadilly South, Manchester. *Chairman*, S. C. Hamburger, C.B.E. *Regional Administrator*, F. Pethybridge.

SCOTTISH HOME AND HEALTH DEPARTMENT
and
NATIONAL HEALTH SERVICE, SCOTLAND
See Scottish Office

HERRING INDUSTRY BOARD
10 Young Street, Edinburgh 2
[031–225–2515]

Chairman and Chief Executive, W. J. Lyon Dean, O.B.E. (*part-time*) £5,575 *in respect of this and other appointments in White Fish Authority.*

Members, E. H. M. Clutterbuck; Admiral Sir Deric Holland-Martin, G.C.B., D.S.O., D.S.C. (*part-time*) £1,000

HIGHLANDS AND ISLANDS DEVELOP-MENT BOARD
Bridge House, Bank Street, Inverness.

The Board, a grant-aided body, responsible to the Secretary of State for Scotland, has two broad objectives. These are (1) to assist the people of the Highlands and Islands to improve their economic

and social conditions; (2) to enable the Highlands and Islands to play a more effective part in the economic and social development of the nation. To this end the Board will concert, promote, assist or undertake measures for economic and social development.

Secretary, J. A. Mackaskill.

HISTORIC BUILDINGS COUNCILS
Under the *Historic Buildings and Ancient Monuments Act*, 1953, as since amended, these councils advise the Secretary of State for the Environment and the Secretaries of State for Scotland and Wales on the exercise of the powers contained in the Act to make grants and loans towards the repair or maintenance of buildings of outstanding historic or architectural interest, their contents and adjoining land, and, where necessary, to acquire such buildings or to assist the National Trusts or local authorities to acquire them.

Also under the *Town and Country Planning (Amendment) Act* 1972, to advise the Secretaries of State on their powers to make grants or loans towards the cost incurred in the promotion, preservation or enhancement of the character or appearance of outstanding conservation areas. In 1975–76 £2,250,000 is available for repair grants in England, £107,500 in Wales and £225,000 in Scotland. In addition, the amounts available for conservation grants are £1,250,000 in England, £50,000 in Wales and £100,000 in Scotland, where there is a further allocation of £100,000 for the Edinburgh New Town Conservation Area.

England
25 Savile Row, W.1

Chairman, Mrs. Jennifer Jenkins.

Members, J. H. Benson, F.R.I.B.A.; J. M. Brandon-Jones; Miss Elizabeth Chesterton; H. M. Colvin, C.B.E., F.B.A.; R. G. Cooke, M.P.; J. Cornforth; Dr. J. M. Crook; T. E. N. Driberg; The Duke of Grafton, F.S.A.; The Lord Holford, R.A., F.R.I.B.A.; E. Hollamby, O.B.E., F.R.I.B.A.; D. W. Insall, F.R.I.B.A.; J. Parker, C.B.E., M.P.; Sir Nikolaus Pevsner, C.B.E., Ph.D., F.B.A., F.S.A.; J. Smith, C.B.E.; Miss Dorothy Stroud, M.B.E.; Sir John Summerson, C.B.E., F.S.A., F.B.A.; A. A. Wood.

Secretary, I. M. Glennie.

Wales
Welsh Office, St. David's House,
Wood Street, Cardiff

Chairman, Maj. H. J. Lloyd-Johnes, O.B.E., T.D., F.S.A.

Members, The Marquess of Anglesey, F.S.A.; J. Eynon, F.R.I.B.A., F.S.A.; Rt. Hon. J. D. Gibson-Watt, M.C.; The Earl Lloyd George of Dwyfor; J. B. Hilling; Prof. Glanmor Williams, D.Litt.

Secretary, W. G. M. Jones.

Scotland
25 Drumsheugh Gardens, Edinburgh.

Chairman, The Earl of Crawford and Balcarres.

Members, Rt. Hon. Betty Harvie Anderson, O.B.E., T.D., M.P.; R. G. Cant; The Lady Mary Cumming, O.B.E.; Mrs. K. Dalyell; J. D. Dunbar-Nasmith; J. F. A. Gibson, T.D.; W. A. P. Jack, C.B.E., F.R.I.B.A.; C. E. Jauncey, Q.C.; J. Liddell, M.B.E.; Rt. Hon. A. Woodburn.

Secretary, H. J. Graham.

HISTORICAL MANUSCRIPTS COMMISSION
See Record Office

ROYAL COMMISSION ON HISTORICAL MONUMENTS [ENGLAND]

Fortress House, 23 Savile Row, W.1
[01-734-6010]

The Royal Commission on Historical Monuments (England) was appointed in 1908 to survey and publish in inventory form an account of every building, earthwork or stone construction up to the year 1714. A new Royal Warrant in 1943 abolished the date limit and the Commissioners then set themselves a limit of 1850, but with discretion to record later buildings of outstanding significance The Commission has published up to present date inventories covering in whole or in part eleven counties, four cities, Roman York and Roman London. It is a purely recording body and though the Commissioners may recommend that certain structures should be preserved, they have no power to implement their recommendations. The Commission is also responsible for the direction of the National Monuments Record, created in 1964, which includes the National Buildings Record begun in 1941, of which the Commissioners are the managing trustees.

Chairman, The Lord Adeane, P.C., G.C.B., G.C.V.O.
Commissioners, H. M. Colvin, C.B.E., F.S.A.; A. J. Taylor, C.B.E., F.S.A.; Prof. W. F. Grimes, C.B.E., D.Litt., F.S.A.; Prof. S. S. Frere, C.B.E.; Prof. R. J. C. Atkinson, F.S.A.; Prof. H. C. Darby, O.B.E., Litt.D., F.B.A.; Prof. G. Zarnecki, C.B.E., F.B.A., F.S.A.; H. M. Taylor, C.B.E., T.D., F.S.A.; Prof. J. K. S. St. Joseph, O.B.E., Ph.D., F.S.A.; A. R. Dufty, C.B.E., F.S.A.; P. Ashbee, F.S.A.; M. Girouard, Ph.D. and the Lords Lieutenant of the counties at the time of survey.
Secretary, R. W. McDowall, O.B.E., F.S.A.

ROYAL COMMISSION ON ANCIENT AND HISTORICAL MONUMENTS IN WALES

Edleston House, Queens Road, Aberystwyth
[Aberystwyth: 4381]

The Commission was appointed in 1908 to make an inventory of the Ancient and Historical Monuments in Wales and Monmouthshire. The Commission now includes the National Monuments Record for Wales.

Chairman, Prof. W. F. Grimes, C.B.E., F.B.A., F.S.A.
Commissioners, Prof. R. J. C. Atkinson, F.S.A.; Prof. I. Ll. Foster, F.S.A.; Prof. E. M. Jope, F.S.A.; D. M. Rees, O.B.E., F.S.A.; H. N. Savory, D.Phil., F.S.A.; A. J. Taylor, C.B.E., F.S.A.; Prof. Dewi-Prys Thomas; Prof. Glanmor Williams, Litt. D.; Prof. J. G. Williams; R. B. Wood-Jones, D.Phil., F.S.A.
Secretary, P. Smith, F.S.A.

ROYAL COMMISSION ON ANCIENT AND HISTORICAL MONUMENTS OF SCOTLAND

54 Melville Street, Edinburgh 3
[031-225-5994]

The Commission was appointed in 1908 to make an inventory of the Ancient and Historical Monuments of Scotland from the earliest times to 1707, and to specify those that seem most worthy of preservation. The terms of reference were extended by Royal Warrant dated Jan. 1, 1948, to cover the period since 1707 at the Commissioners' discretion. The National Monument Records of Scotland, a branch of the Commission housed in the same premises, contains an extensive collection of photographs, drawings and printed books relating to Scottish architecture, which may be consulted by members of the public.

Chairman, The Earl of Wemyss and March, K.T.
Commissioners, Prof. S. Piggott, C.B.E., F.B.A., F.S.A., F.R.S.E.; Prof. K. H. Jackson, F.B.A.; Prof. G. Donaldson, Ph.D.; Prof. A. A. M. Duncan; J. D. Dunbar-Nasmith, R.I.B.A.; Prof. Rosemary Cramp, F.S.A.Scot.
Secretary, K. A. Steer, Ph.D., F.S.A., F.R.S.E.

ANCIENT MONUMENTS BOARDS
England

Fortress House, 23 Savile Row, W.1.
Chairman, Sir Edward, Muir, K.C.B., F.S.A.
Members, R. L. S. Bruce-Mitford, V.P.S.A., F.S.A. Scot.; P. H. G. Chamberlin, C.B.E., A.R.A., F.R.I.B.A.; Prof. J. G. D. Clark, C.B.E., Sc.D., Ph.D., F.B.A., F.S.A.; Prof. Rosemary Cramp, F.S.A.; Prof. B. W. Cunliffe, Ph.D., F.S.A.; B. M. Feilden, C.B.E., F.R.I.B.A., F.S.A.; Sir David Follett, Ph.D.; Prof. S. S. Frere, C.B.E., F.B.A., F.S.A.; B. J. Greenhill, C.M.G., F.S.A.; Prof. W. F. Grimes, C.B.E., D.Litt., F.S.A.; R. W. McDowall, O.B.E., F.S.A.; P. J. Nuttgens, Ph.D.; Prof. A. C. Renfrew, Ph.D., F.S.A., F.S.A.Scot; Prof. J. K. S. St. Joseph, O.B.E., Ph.D., F.S.A.; A. J. Taylor, C.B.E., F.B.A., P.S.A.; Prof. D. M. Wilson, F.S.A.
Secretary, J. S. M. Vinter, M.C.

Wales

Government Buildings, Ty Glas, Llanishen, Cardiff
Chairman, J. D. K. Lloyd, O.B.E., F.S.A.
Members, Miss I. E. Anthony, Ph.D., F.S.A.; Prof. R. J. C. Atkinson, F.S.A.; Prof. W. F. Grimes, C.B.E., D.Litt., F.S.A.; C. N. Johns, F.S.A.; E. D. Jones, C.B.E., F.S.A.; L. Jones; Mrs. H. Ramage; D. M. Rees, O.B.E., F.S.A.; H. N. Savory, D.Phil., P.S.A.; P. Smith, F.S.A.; A. J. Taylor, C.B.E., F.S.A.
Secretary, G. H. Jones.

Scotland

Argyle House, Edinburgh 3
Chairman, Sir Alan Hume, C.B.
Members, Prof. L. Alcock, F.S.A., F.S.A.Scot.; J. D. Dunbar-Nasmith; G. Jobey, D.S.O., F.S.A.; Prof. S. G. E. Lythe, F.S.A.Scot.; B. R. S. Megaw, F.R.S.E., F.S.A., F.S.A.Scot.; R. M. Orr; Prof. Anne S. Robertson, D.Litt., F.S.A., F.S.A.Scot.; G. G. Simpson, Ph.D., F.S.A., F.S.A.Scot.; K. A. Steer, Ph.D., F.R.S.E., F.S.A. F.S.A.Scot.; R. B. K. Stevenson, F.S.A., F.S.A.Scot.; Prof. E. L. G. Stones, Ph.D., F.S.A.; A. S. Taylor, C.B.E., D.Litt., F.B.A., F.S.A.
Secretary, A. M. Thomson.

HOME OFFICE

Whitehall, S.W.1
[01-213-3000]

The Home Office deals with such internal affairs in England and Wales as are not assigned to other Departments. The Home Secretary is the channel of communication between the Crown and the subjects of the realm, and between the U.K. Government and the Governments of the Channel Islands and the Isle of Man. He exercises certain prerogative powers of the Crown of which the most important are the prerogative of mercy and the maintenance of the Queen's Peace. He is also concerned with the administration of justice; criminal law; the treatment of offenders; probation; the prison service; public morals and certain public safety matters; the police, fire and civil defence services; immigration and nationality; community relations and community and urban programmes.

Other Home Office responsibilities include: addresses and petitions to the Queen and the preparation of presentations to Parliament; preparation of patents of nobility for peers and formal proceedings for the granting of honours; requests for the extradition of criminals; scrutiny of local authority byelaws; grant of licences for scientific experiments on animals; game laws and the protection of wild birds; cremation and burials, exhumation and removal of bodies; firearms; dangerous drugs and poisons; general policy on liquor licensing laws, gaming and lotteries; taxis; charitable collections and Charities Act 1960; theatre and cinema licensing; co-ordination of government action in relation to the voluntary social services; and sex discrimination policy.

Secretary of State for the Home Department, THE RT. HON. ROY JENKINS, M.P. £13,000
Principal Private Secretary, R. M. Morris.
Private Secretaries, C. Farrington; W. J. A. Innes.

Special Advisers A. P. Lester, Q.C.; M. A. Oakeshott.

Parliamentary Private Secretary, I. W. Wrigglesworth, M.P.

Parliamentary Clerk (Senior Executive Officer), J. C. Dilling.

Ministers of State, THE LORD HARRIS OF GREENWICH; BRYNMOR THOMAS JOHN, M.P. £7,500

Parliamentary Under-Secretary of State, Dr. Shirley Summerskill, M.P. £5,500

Correspondence Secretary (Principal), G. E. Dunkley
£5,680 to £7,450

Permanent Under Secretary of State, Sir Arthur Peterson, K.C.B., M.V.O. . . . . £17,175 to £20,175

Deputy Under Secretaries of State, R. J. Andrew *(Principal Establishment Officer);* R. T. Armstrong, C.B., C.V.O.; N. F. Cairncross, C.B.; Sir Kenneth Jones, C.B.E., Q.C.*(Legal Adviser);* Dr. O. Simpson *(Chief Scientist);* P. J. Woodfield, C.B., C.B.E. E. D. Wright, C.B. *(Director-General of the Prison Service)* £14,000

Chief Medical Officer (at Department of Health and Social Security), Sir Henry Yellowlees, K.C.B.

Broadcasting Department

Waterloo Bridge, House, Waterloo Road, S.E.1
[01-275-3000]

Assistant Under-Secretary of State, D. J. Trevelyan
£12,000

Assistant Secretaries, A. O. Carter; A. H. Turney
£8,650 to £11,000

Principals, J. P. Jarvis; Miss S. R. Muir; R. W. Story, D.F.C.; Mrs. M. Tuck; C. J. Walters
£5,680 to £7,450

Senior Executive Officers, S. J. Baggott; E. T. Dole;
£4,900 to £5,900

Community Programmes and Equal Opportunities Department

Horseferry House, Dean Ryle Street, S.W.1
[01-211-3000]

Assistant Under-Secretary of State, J. T. H. Howard-Drake* £12,000

Assistant Secretary, G. P. Renton
£8,650 to £11,000

Principals, P. R. Burleigh; R. R. G. Watts
£5,680 to £7,450

Race Relations Adviser's Office

Assistant Secretary, Miss N. Peppard, C.B.E.
£8,650 to £11,000

Senior Executive Officer, R. M. Waye
£4,900 to £5,900

*Race Relations Legislation Unit**

Assistant Secretary, N. J. Fries . . £8,650 to £11,000

Principals, A. J. Butler; Miss B. M. Latimer
£5,680 to £7,450

Sex Discrimination Unit

Senior Principal, F. B. Warner. . . £7,750 to £9,350

Urban Deprivation Unit

Head of Unit, Senior Economic Adviser, G. J. Wasserman. . . . . £8,650 to £11,000

Principals, P. Done; F. N. Jasper; A. R. Rawsthorne; G. K. Sandiford . . . . . £5,680 to £7,450

*At Whitehall

Voluntary Services Unit

Kingsgate House, 66–74 Victoria Street, SW1
(01-828 7722)

Assistant Secretary, Miss M. A. Clayton
£8,650 to £11,000

Principal, B. G. Chaplin. . . . £5,680 to £7,450

Senior Executive Officers, T. N. Gerrish; Miss S. M. Wade. . . . . £4,900 to £5,900

Criminal Justice Department

Assistant Under-Secretary of State, D. H. J. Hilary
£12,000

Assistant Secretaries, E. R. Cowlyn; R. L. Jones; C. H. Prior, C.B.E., B.E.M. . . . £8,650 to £11,000

Senior Principal, N. F. Law. . . . . £7,750 to £9,350

Principals, Miss P. C. Drew; P. C. Edwards; Mrs. H. E. Forbes; G. T. L. Hubert; B. F. Jones; A. Marshall; Miss M. Norman; Mrs. J. E. Reisz; M. H. Rumble; E. A. Slater; D. B. Staines; F. J. A. Warne. . . . . £5,680 to £7,450

Senior Executive Officers, Miss P. L. Boxall; Miss J. E. Clarke; P. A. Drury; G. Greenall; S. D. Holdershaw; Mrs. S. Murray; W. F. Whiteing
£4,900 to £5,900

Criminal Policy Department

Assistant Under-Secretary of State, M. J. Moriarty
£12,000

Assistant Secretaries, J. C. Hindley; N. M. Johnson
£8,650 to £11,000

Principals, P. E. Bolton; J. C. Davey; Miss C. L. Jones; Miss K. A. O'Neill, O.B.E.; J. G. Pilling; N. R. Varney; Mrs. P. D. White
£5,680 to £7,450

Senior Executive Officer, Mrs. R. M. Mitev
£4,900 to £5,900

Criminal Policy Planning Unit
41–42 Parliament Street, S.W.1
[01–233–3000]

Assistant Secretary, C. J. Train . £8,650 to £11,000

Principals, R. J. Baxter; A. Harding
£5,680 to £7,450

Establishment Department

Whittington House, 19–30 Alfred Place, WC1
(01-637 2355)

Assistant Under Secretaries of State, D. A. C. Morrison *(Personnel);* R. R. Pittam *(Organisation & Management)* £12,000

Assistant Secretaries, B. O. Bubbear; Miss E. M. Chadwell; R. J. P. Hayes; T. C. Platt; E. A. Sedgley; V. H. Wallis . . . . . £8,650 to £11,000

Senior Principals, S. R. Cameron; R. F. Elliott; B. Morgan; J. R. Troop . . . . . . £7,750 to £9,350

Senior Librarian, D. B. Gibson

Principals, K. J. Bradley; D. L. Cole; A. F. Davies; M. E. Dewberry; B. H. Ford; D. J. Hardwick; J. Hay; J. T. Horrocks; R. M. Hoare; D. J. Hollis; J. H. Howard; A. D. Jackson; P. W. Jamieson; I. D. King; J. D. Lodder; L. G. Martin; R. G. Oram, I.S.O.; H. G. Pearson; A. G. Pridmore; J. Roy; L. A. Scudder; I. R. Thomas; G. W. Waring; M. L. Winspear, T.D.
£5,680 to £7,450

Senior Executive Officers, J. Barsby; C. H. Basson; A. Best; D. R. Birleson; J. Blythin; F. J. Brown; H. H. Collin; P. Cook; R. G. W. Cook; J. D. Forster; D. W. French; G. Gibson; G. N. Greening; Miss G. M. Griffiths; G. E. Guy; J. A. Hart; G. Hoyle; Mrs. E. J. Hughes; R. Hulley; D. P. King; J. W. March; D. Massey; D. Mullarky; M. J. Murphy; K. R. North; J. Norton; F. Parker; L. J. Parsons; J. Plumridge; K. M. F. Quintaba; R. J. Ridout; Miss S. K. Rooney; G. A. Rouse; E. E. Severn; H. Stead; Miss M. Symon; T. Temple; W. J. Vale; N. F. Willder.
£4,900 to £5,900

Home Office Unit at Civil Service Selection Board
Standard House, 28 Northumberland Avenue, WC2
(01-273 3529)

Assistant Secretary, P. A. McIlvenna, M.B.E.
£12,000

Principal, E. J. White. . . . . £5,680 to £7,450

Home Office Unit for Educational Methods
Fire Service Technical College,
Moreton-in-Marsh, Gloucestershire
(Moreton-in-Marsh 50831)

Head of Unit, J. F. Barton . . . . . £6,355 to £7,100

Finance Department

Kingsgate House, 66–74 Victoria Street, SW1
(01-828 7722)

Assistant Under-Secretary of State (Principal Finance Officer), D. A. Peach £12,000

Assistant Secretaries, R. W. Mott; G. P. Pratt
£8,650 to £11,000

Senior Principal, M. G. Thompson
£7,750 to £9,350

Principals, J. A. Atfield; S. W. Boys Smith; M. A. Christian; Miss J. M. F. Cousins; D. V. Horsley; Mrs. M. R. Ryan; F. Stewart; C. H. Taylor; R. E. Wiscombe............£5680 to £7450
Senior Executive Officers, H. Blackbourn; J. W. Burgess; V. B. Dixon; H. W. Gillies, M.B.E.; G. C. Jones-Evans; Miss B. Niehorster; Miss L. Noble; F. E. Turner; J. Walsh; Miss M. Wilder
£5,680 to £7,450

Fire Department
Horseferry House, Dean Ryle Street, S.W.1
[01-211-3000]
Assistant Under-Secretary of State, N. S. Ross
£12,000
Assistant Secretaries, J. McIntyre, C.B.E.; H. V. H. Marks; G. T. Rudd; D. R. Sands
£8,650 to £11,000
Principals, D. R. Dewick; J. T. Dungan; D. S. J. Evans; R. O. Lane, D.F.C.; D. Polley; C. L. Scoble; E. Soden; B. J. Valentine
£5,680 to £7,450
Principal Scientific Officer, P. L. Parsons
£5,514 to £7,205
Senior Executive Officers, Miss G. V. Cooksley; N. C. L. Hackney; E. R. Hall; R. J. Peate; Mrs. B. Simmonds; W. H. Simon. £4,900 to £5,900

Fire Service Inspectorate
Chief Inspector, K. L. Holland, C.B.E......£11,618
Inspectors (Grade I), C. Bidgood, O.B.E.; A. Bloomfield; L. O. Clarke, O.B.E.; E. T. Hayward, O.N.E.; N. F. Richards, M.B.E.; P. S. Wilson-Dickson, O.B.E......£8,999 to £9,682
Inspectors (Grade II), S. C. Baker; J. Bingley; J. L. Brock; W. J. Carvin; F. W. Harbridge, M.B.E., P. G. Robinson; H. J. Shayle; A. H. Warren, O.B.E......£6,749 to £7,262
Engineering Inspectors, F. C. A. Shirling, O.B.E.; R. M. Simpson............£6,630 to £7,800

Fire Service Staff College
Wotton House, Abinger Common, Dorking, Surrey
[Dorking: 730441]
Commandant, S. F. Crook, O.B.E.
£8,999 to £9,682

Fire Service Technical College
Moreton-in-Marsh, Gloucestershire
[Moreton-in-Marsh: 50831]
Commandant, D. Blacktop, O.B.E.
£8,999 to £9,682
Secretary (Principal), C. J. Titchener
£5,680 to £7,450

General Department
Assistant Under-Secretary of State, R. F. D. Shuffrey
£12,000
Assistant Secretaries, W. J. Bohan; Capt. N. F. Carrington, D.S.C., R.N.(ret.); J. E. Hayzelden; E. N. Kent..................£8,650 to £11,000
Principals, M. J. Addison; M. K. Brenchley; Miss M. D. Cook; J. L. Goddard; N. F. Home; E. C. Huggett; F. H. Keens; R. C. Morris; Mrs. E. A. Sandars; Miss E. J Sermon; J. Stephens; Miss A. Turner..................£5,680 to £7,450
Senior Executive Officers, J. W. Clark; N. K. Finlayson; Miss E. E. Harrison; Mrs. M. J. McFarlane; J. Reitler..................£4,900 to £5,900

Immigration and Nationality Department
Lunar House, Wellesley Road, Croydon, Surrey
[01-686-0333]
Assistant Under-Secretary of State, A. J. E. Brennan
£12,000
Assistant Secretaries, J. A. Chilcot; A. E. Corben; W. M. Lee; P. L. Taylor...£8,650 to £11,000
Senior Principals, W. Middlemass; Miss M. E. Millson, I.S.O.; R. M. Whitfield..£7,750 to £9,350
Principals, S. J. Gregory; J. A. Ingman; J. E. Johnson; R. A. McDowell; D. G. McMurray; A. Parkinson; R. K. Prescott; R. B. Prosser; J. D. Webb; R. S. Weekes; J. V. Wingfield; M. Youngs
£5,680 to £7,450

Senior Executive Officers, P. G. Bailey; P. D. Brown; Miss G. Cobbler; W. G. Chalmers; L. F. Curteis; W. G. Feakins; E. A. Gray; D. W. Greenhalgh; B. Hunter; R. B. Ingham; B. J. Jordan; E. J. Kings; Miss B. Korman; K. L. McDonald; W. R. Mann; K. B. Mitchell; Mrs. N. Needler; A. Norbury; K. V. Osborne; P. M. Pawsey; F. G. Pegg; R. S. Pepper; A. M. Pickersgill; J. Pitty; A. R. Ralf; K. E. R. Rogers; Mrs. H. M. Searle; T. J. Tuffield; D. J. H. Walker; J. L. Ward; D. A. Wrigley..................£3,756 to £4,542

Immigration Service
Chief Inspector, H. J. G. Richards
£8,650 to £11,000
Deputy Chief Inspectors, R. J. Lemon; R. E. Smith
£7,750 to £9,350
Assistant Chief Inspectors, A. A. Holton; J. A. Lomas; H. J. Pickering; P. J. Saunders; R. G. Smith; C. F. Woodiss............£5,680 to £7,450
Inspectors, F. W. Flemen; C. B. Manchip; A. A. Stevens..................£5,045 to £5,900

Legal Adviser's Branch
Legal Adviser, Sir Kenneth Jones, C.B.E., Q.C.
£14,000
Principal Assistant Legal Advisers, P. Harvey; J. D. Semken, M.C..................£12,000
Assistant Legal Advisers, A. H. Hammond; J. Nursaw; J. Pakenham-Walsh; Miss B. R. Pugh; T. H. Williams; H. W. Wollaston
£9,033 to £11,000
Senior Legal Assistants, J. R. O'Meara; A. W. D. Wilson..................£6,625 to £8,750

Police Department
Horseferry House, Dean Ryle Street, S.W.1
[01-211-3000]
Assistant Under-Secretaries of State, A. S. Baker, O.B.E., D.F.C.; D. Heaton; W. N. Hyde; R. A. James, M.C..................£12,000
Assistant Secretaries, G. L. Angel; G. H. Baker, D.S.C.; J. F. D. Buttery; K. H. Dawson; G. W. A. Duguid; D. E. R. Faulkner; Mrs. S. Littler; Miss G. M. B. Owen........£8,650 to £11,000
Principals, C. Barlow; D. J. Belfall; M. J. Butcher; J. M. Clift; Mrs. B. H. Fair; T. S. Fookes; Miss W. M. Goode; J. F. Halliday; E. Hutchings; D. McQueen; G. C. Maxted; N. L. Morgan; N. Nagler; J. A. Pemberton; D. Roberts; J. F. Rogers; L. P. M. Scott; H. S. Seaford; Miss P. I. Stacey; R. M. Whalley; Mrs. P. M. White; F. J. Woodland; A. C. Yeates...£5,680 to £7,450
Principal Scientific Officer, Dr. J. A. Harwood
£5,514 to £7,205
Senior Executive Officers, J. L. Baker; D. A. Birks; J. W. Clark; K. A. Day; J. L. Durward; J. Wake
£4,900 to £5,900

Police National Computer Unit
Charles House, 375 Kensington High Street, W.14
[01-603-3399]
Assistant Secretary, J. R. Cubberley
£8,650 to £11,000
Senior Principals, G. F. Atherton; A. G. Bailey; C. S. Duke; E. Quinney; R. G. Urquhart
£7,250 to £9,350
Principals, M. A. Button; J. Clarke; W. Clements; G. M. Cole; D. Dunin; T. Egan; R. Gregory; R. Oliver; D. Quarmby; H. Randall; T. G. Roberts..................£5,680 to £7,950
Principal Scientific Officers, J. R. Lowe; R. T. Robinson; J. Watts..........£5,514 to £7,205
Senior Executive Officers, D. Blackwood; J. Cane; C. A. Carter; D. Chapman; W. S. Cowie; Mrs. C. Cowley; G. Dorow; L. Edgar; D. H. Faulks; S. Frean; K. Gadsdon; D. H. Gannon; F. Goodsell; D. Grant; R. Harwood; J. Henderson; L. Hunt; P. Jackson; P. J. Kelly; D. Lovering; L.

McLaren; D. C. Moulton; D. Perkins; B. Pullin; R. Ritchie; A. Rouse; M. Scandrett; R. Shelvey; K. M. Shewry; G. Skinner; P. J. A. Somerville; B. G. Stocking; J. Truscorr; T. W. Wrighton
£4,900 to £5,900

Joint ADP Unit
Tintagel House, Albert Embankment, S.E.1
[01–230 1212]
Assistant Secretary, M. D. Hutton
£8,650 to £11,000
Senior Principals, H. Eccles; R. V. Robinson; K. E. Salmon...............£7,750 to £9,350
Principals, T. Clark; T. S. Diaper; F. R. Hayhurst; A. F. G. Hitchman; P. G. V. Pike; D. W. Punshon; J. K. Richards; J. Smedley
£5,680 to £7,450
Senior Executive Officers, C. A. Allison; M. J. Bloomfield; R. C. Case; T. G. Cronin; B. J. Flaherty; A. Hall; A. L. Jenkins; D. G. Jones; I. Joyce; Mrs. J. Morgan; D. J. Moss; C. Muid; H. D. Poulson; D. S. Roberts; B. Rollins; G. Sharp; A. Silver; S. D. Walsh; H. Warland; J. Waud; R. C. Weller; F. H. Wormley
£4,900 to £5,900

Directorate of Telecommunications
60 Rochester Row, S.W.1
[01–828–9848]
Director of Telecommunications, W. P. Nicol
£11,000
Deputy Directors, J. N. Hallett; R. M. Hughes; N. Morley; P. H. L. Trodden....£8,650 to £9,798
Principals, D. E. N. Boon; S. Klein
£5,680 to £7,450
Senior Executive Officers, A. O. Cambrook; Mrs. R. W. Harvey; R. F. J. Heath; K. F. Templar
£4,900 to £5,900
Chief Wireless Engineers, C. Bell; R. J. Chamberlain; H. L. Collins; E. W. Crompton; R. E. Fudge; J. R. Harris; W. R. Harris; J. J. E. Lebutt; J. C. Lucas; G. J. Mewett; D. S. Oldnall; M. J. Phillips; J. A. Portanier; P. P. H. Smith; R. S. Stoodley; J. P. Titheradge; L. T. Whitside; H. Woodmansey.................£6,280 to £7,450

H.M. Inspectorate of Constabulary
H.M. Chief Inspector of Constabulary, Sir James Haughton, C.B.E...................£15,707
H.M. Inspectors, C. Cooksley, C.B.E., Q.P.M.; J. W. D. Crane; R. G. Fenwick, C.B.E., Q.P.M.; S. E. Peck, C.B.E., B.E.M., Q.P.M.; G. Twist, C.B.E., Q.P.M.
£14,202
Assistant Chief Training Officer, Lt.-Col. G. W. Laverick...................£5,159 to £5,939

Police Scientific Development Branch
Director, G. Phillips...................£11,190
Deputy Director, A. T. Burrows, M.B.E., E.R.D.
£8,650 to £9,798
Senior Principal Scientific Officers, G. C. Duckney; A. Holt; A. N. Rapsey
Principal Scientific Officers, Dr. B. J. Blain; G. Church; Dr. A. Ganson; Dr. B. S. Luetchford; M. E. Moncaster; C. D. Payne; Dr. D. M. S. Peace; Dr. G. Turnbull; Dr. P. A. Young
£5,514 to £7,205
Principal, F. A. V. Jenkins.....£5,680 to £7,450

Police College
Bramshill House, Basingstoke, Hampshire
[Hartley Witney 2931]
Commandant, T. G. Lamford.
Deputy Commandant and Dean of Police Studies, J. C. J. Maskell.
Dean of Academic Studies, I. A. Watt
£8,037 to £8,913
Principal, J. C. Quarrell........£5,680 to £7,450

Home Defence College
The Hawkhills, Easingwold, Yorks.
[Easingwold: 21405]
Principal, Air Marshal Sir Leslie Mavor, K.C.B. A.F.C.................£9,033
Vice-Principal, Major A. I. Fennell

Home Office H.Q. Warning and Monitoring Organization
Horsefair, Banbury, Oxon.
[Banbury 56151]
Director, V. G. Barry, D.F.C.....£7,750 to £9,350
Deputy Directors, R. F. Cooke; G. A. Potter, O.B.E.
£5,680 to £7,450

Forensic Science Service
Horseferry House
Controller, Dr. A. S. Curry
Principal, W. J. Carney........£5,680 to £7,450
Principal Scientific Officer, Dr. D. A. Patterson
£5,514 to £7,205

Prison Department
89 Eccleston Square, S.W.1
[01–828–9848]
Director-General of the Prison Service, E. D. Wright, C.B....................£14,000
(Assistant Under-Secretaries of State), M. S. Gale, M.C. *(Controllers, Operational Administration)*; K. J. Neale, O.B.E. *(Planning and Development)*; T. G. Weiler *(Personnel and Services)*......£12,000
Chief Inspector of the Prison Service, G. W. Fowler
£11,670
Director of Prison Medical Services, Dr. J. H. Orr
£12,000
Assistant Secretaries, P. Beedle; R. J. Langdon; S. G. Norris; R. W. G. Smith; A. P. Wilson
£8,650 to £11,000
Assistant Controllers, W. A. Brister; E. A. Towndrow...................£11,000
Assistant Director of Prison Medical Services, Dr. R. C. Ingrey-Senn...................£11,440
Senior Principals, V. G. Gotts; P. Leyshon
£7,750 to £9,350
Governors I, S. E. Henderson Smith; D. W. Higman; C. P. Honey; R. A. B. A. Howden; Maj. P. L. James; Miss O. Parry...........£9,424
Principals, P. Canovan; I. M. Clark; C. S. Cullerne-Brown; P. A. Chadwell; R. G. Ferguson; W. O. Fortune; E. W. A. Fryer; B. R. Gange; E. Grant; A. K. Guymer; G. E. Hart; A. H. Hewins; R. W. B. Hurley; J. B. Irving; J. E. A. Mumford; Miss M. Peck; D. L. Smith; Maj. L. Snowden, M.B.E.; J. F. Theobald; Mrs. J. Thompson; G. P. Willmets; D. A. R. Wood..£5,650 to £7,450
Governors II, G. J. Dadds; I. M. Dunbar; R. L. D. Skrine.................£7,083 to £8,066
Chaplain General, Rev. Canon L. Lloyd Rees £6,609
Director of Psychological Services, G. E. Twiselton
£8,650 to £9,798
Chief Education Officer, A. S. Baxendale
£7,750 to £9,350
Chief Physical Education Officer, I. T. Copeland
£5,680 to £7,450
Governors III, N. Berry; L. C. Davies; C. B. Graves; E. Martin; F. B. O'Friel; A. G. Pearson; J. F. Richardson; G. Walker.......£5,690 to £6,717
Senior Executive Officers, L. G. Ball; C. A. Bartley; M. F. Butters; T. P. R. Crompton; J. Finn; G. P. Gee; J. A. Gibbs; J. B. Harvey; R. E. P. A. Hughes; R. James; M. J. D. Jones; J. Osborne; G. Rendell; J. Simpson; J. A. E. Taylor; M. Wann; R. J. White........£4,900 to £5,900

Chief Architect's Branch and Directorate of Works
St. Vincent House, 30 Orange Street, W.C.2
[01–930–8499]
Chief Architect and Director of Works, J. G. H. D. Cairns.....................£11,440
Deputy Chief Architect and Deputy Director of Works, A. Ball....................£11,000
Superintending Architects, R. H. Clare; N. E. Hill; G. E. F. Slatter.........£8,650 to £9,798
Superintending Engineer, T. R. Jones
£8,650 to £9,798
Superintending Quantity Surveyor, K. F. J. Kenward
£8,650 to £9,798
Principal Professional and Technology Officers, H. G. S. Banks; M. J. Bridgford; M. A. Brooks; J. A. Burrell; B. D. Charlson; G. W. Chrisp; J. H.

Cooper; H. J. Davies; R. D. Evernden; A. W. Gillman; R. A. Greaves; R. W. T. Haines; D. W. Harris; A. F. Lane; L. O. Lee; L. E. Luck; R. F. W. Malthouse; C. A. G. Poole; B. R. Redd; J. E. Sheldon; B. A. Stickley; V. A. C. Trigwell; P. A. G. Walker............£6,280 to £7,450
Senior Executive Officer, J. V. Dyer
£4,900 to £5,900

Directorate of Industries and Supply
Tolworth Tower, Tolworth, Surbiton, Surrey
[01-399-5491]
Director, J. H. J. Beck.
Managers, O. P. Allen; P. E. Baker; D. Beaton; A. Donkin; P. F. Hewett; J. Hewitson; S. Horne; H. A. Layton; C. E. Marshall; D. A. Norman; D. F. Scagell; I. E. Scarlett; P. Stephenson; P. D. Stevens; D. J. Wilkes.
Senior Executive Officers, E. H. Armstrong; H. Brooke; J. D. Cleary; B. Ferguson; J. H. Henderson; K. Shirley; E. R. Thomas; D. C. Twine; H. J. Woodbridge..........£4,900 to £5,900
Professional & Technology Officers, Grade I, C. Austin; J. E. Belcher; L. M. Cohen; C. R. Cope; G. A. Hallam; J. H. Smith; R. W. Squibb; F. Wilson
Farms & Gardens Managers (Regional), N. Carver; M. Codd; R. Cunningham; R. A. Fletcher; J. W. Fallows.

Supply and Transport Branch
Crown House, 52 Elizabeth Street,
Corby, Northants.
[Corby 2101]
Director, P. R. Wall.........£7,750 to £9,350
Senior Executive Officers, S. E. Ilett; J. W. Little; L. Moore....................£4,900 to £5,900

Regional Offices

Birmingham
Regional Director, M. D. McLeod.......£11,000
Deputy Regional Directors, W. B. Gibbs (*Administration*) (£5,680 to £7,450); A. W. Driscoll (*Operations*; J. L. Rham (*Treatment and Training*)
£7,083 to £8,066
Bristol
Regional Director, D. W. Fisher.........£11,000
Deputy Regional Directors, G. C. Woods (*Administration*) (£5,680 to £7,450); B. A. Marchant (*Operations*)................£7,083 to £8,066
Manchester
Regional Director, L. J. F. Wheeler.......£11,000
Deputy Regional Directors, D. L. Tacey (*Administration*) (£5,680 to £7,450); R. M. Dauncey; Lt.-Cdr. S. E. Hawkins (*Operations*); J. D. U. Lewis (*Young Offenders*)......£7,083 to £8,066
Tolworth
Regional Director, K. Gibson...........£11,000
Deputy Regional Directors, R. W. Hampton (*Administration*) (£5,680 to £7,450); E. S. Nash; J. A. Absolom (*Operations*); D. A. Brown (*Young Offenders*)...................£7,083 to £8,066

PRISONS
Governors
Acklington, Northumberland, R. Cooper
£5,690 to £6,717
Albany, I.O.W., G. Lister................£9,424
Appleton Thorn, Lancs., M. Langdon
£5,690 to £6,717
Ashwell, Leics., P. O. E. Randell.£7,083 to £8,066
Askham Grange, Yorks., Miss S. F. McCormick
£5,690 to £6,717
Aylesbury, D. A. Guild.........£5,690 to £6,717
Bedford, D. J. Thompson........£7,083 to £8,066
Birmingham, W. Perrie...................£9,424
Blundeston, Suffolk, J. E. Simmons
£7,083 to £8,066
Bristol, D.O'C. Grubb........£7,083 to £8,066
Brixton, S.W.2., B. D. Wigginton........£9,424
Camp Hill, I.O.W., D. A. Ward.£7,083 to £8,066
Canterbury, S. Mitchell.......£7,083 to £8,066
Cardiff, J. S. McCarthy.......£7,083 to £8,066
Channings Wood, Devon, R. Clarke
£5,690 to £6,717
Chelmsford, M. F. G. Selby.....£7,083 to £8,066

Coldingley, Surrey, J. A. Green..£7,083 to £8,066
Dartmoor, C. B. Heald.......£5,690 to £6,717
Dorchester, S. Brumby.........£5,690 to £6,717
Drake Hall, Stafford, Miss M. A. Carden
Durham, I. W. F. Steinhausen..........£9,424
Exeter, J. W. N. Brown.........£7,083 to £8,066
Featherstone, Wolverhampton, J. R. Sandy
Ford, Sussex, R. K. Lawson.....£7,083 to £8,066
Gartree, Leics., G. H. Lakes......£7,083 to £8,066
Gloucester, A. H. Rayfield........£7,083 to £8,066
Grendon and Spring Hill, Bucks., Dr. R. L. Jillet (*Medical Superintendent*)...............£11,440
Haverigg, Cumbria, W. E. Cowper-Johnson
£7,083 to £8,066
Highpoint, Newmarket, J. S. Shulman
Holloway, N.7, Dr. M. P. Bull..£7,083 to £8,066
Hull, H. Parr.................£7,083 to £8,066
Kingston, Portsmouth, E. R. E. Skelton
£5,690 to £6,717
Kirkham, Lancs., J. K. Beaumont.£7,083 to £8,066
Lancaster, R. Fall.............£5,690 to £6,717
Leeds, B. A. Emes....................£9,424
Leicester, N. F. Low...........£7,083 to £8,066
Lewes, C. T. Pratt............£7,083 to £8,066
Leyhill, Glos., D. Atkinson......£7,083 to £8,066
Lincoln, D. St. L. Simon......£7,083 to £8,066
Liverpool, D. T. Cross................£9,424
Long Lartin, Worcs., J. Williams........£9,424
Maidstone, P. Timms........£7,083 to £8,066
Manchester, A. R. Moreton.............£9,424
Moor Court, Staffs., Miss H. V. Liessner
Northallerton, A. Cruickshank....£5,690 to £6,717
Northeye, Sussex, L. Stones.....£5,690 to £6,717
Norwich, M. J. Brown.........£7,083 to £8,066
Nottingham, P. L. Harrap.......£5,690 to £6,717
Oxford, M. D. Jenkins.........£5,690 to £6,717
Parkhurst, I.O.W., M. Bryan............£9,424
Pentonville, T. R. Carnegie..............£9,424
Preston, R. E. Adams.........£7,083 to £8,066
Ranby Camp, E. A. Stratford....£5,690 to £6,717
Reading, R. A. Richards........£5,690 to £6,717
Shepton Mallet, G. J. Burford....£5,690 to £6,717
Shrewsbury, D. Shaw..........£5,690 to £6,717
Stafford, A. C. Kearns.................£9,424
Standford Hill, E. R. Cooper....£7,083 to £8,066
Styal, Cheshire, Miss M. Morgan.£7,083 to £8,066
Sudbury, W. S. Smith, D.S.C....£7,083 to £8,066
Swansea, L. Lewis............£5,690 to £6,717
Swinfen Hall, Staffs., G. W. Axe
£5,690 to £6,717
Thorp Arch, Yorks., E. Sumner...£5,690 to £6,717
The Verne, Dorset, C. J. Knight, D.S.M.
£7,083 to £8,066
Wakefield, Maj. M. Oldfield, M.C., E.R.D...£9,424
Wakefield Staff College, W. J. Booth.....£9,424
Wandsworth, S. W.18, L. A. Portch........£9,424
Winchester, F. M. Liesching.....£7,083 to £8,066
Wormwood Scrubs, W.12, N. C. Honey.....£9,424

BORSTALS
Governors
Bullwood Hall, Essex, Miss J. A. M. Kinsley
£5,690 to £6,717
Deerbolt, R. J. T. Nash........£5,690 to £6,717
Dover, P. L. Pye.............£7,083 to £8,066
East Sutton Park, Kent, Miss M. Farmery
£5,690 to £6,717
Everthorpe, Humberside, P. R. D. Meech
£7,083 to £8,066
Feltham and Finnamore Wood, E. V. H. Williams
£7,083 to £8,066
Gaynes Hall, Cambs., W. J. Cooper, M.B.E.
£5,690 to £6,717
Glen Parva, C. J. Jones........£5,690 to £6,717
Guys Marsh, Dorset, A. J. Webley
£5,690 to £6,717
Hatfield, Yorks., E. Owens......£5,690 to £6,717
Hewell Grange, Worcs., P. J. Kitteridge
£5,690 to £6,717
Hindley, Lancs, F. S. Richardson.£5,690 to £6,717
Hollesley Bay Colony, Suffolk, A. F. H. Arnold
£7,083 to £8,066
Huntercombe, Oxon., J. H. M. Anderson
£5,690 to £6,717

Lowdham Grange, Notts., F. M. Mitchell
£7,083

Onley, Warwicks., L. C. Oxford £7,083 to £8,066
Portland, Dorset, D. F. Dennis... £7,083 to £8,066
Rochester, S. A. Bester....... £7,083 to £8,066
Stoke Heath, Salop, W. B. Ritson
£7,083 to £8,066
Usk, Gwent, D. F. Campbell.... £5,690 to £6,717
Wellingborough, J. W. Green.... £7,083 to £8,066
Wetherby, Yorks., G. W. A. Ellington
£5,690 to £6,717

REMAND CENTRES
Governors

Ashford, Middx., R. A. Attrill... £7,083 to £8,066
Brockhill, Worcs., R. Sharp.... £5,690 to £6,717
Latchmere House, Surrey, J. C. Dugdale
£4,673 to £5,340
Low Newton, Co. Durham, D. M. Brooke
£4,673 to £5,340
Pucklechurch, Bristol, A. A. Fyfe.. £5,690 to £6,717
Risley, Cheshire, R. F. Owens........... £9,424
Thorp Arch, Wetherby, H. Jones
£4,673 to £5,340

DETENTION CENTRES
Wardens

Aldington, Kent, J. L. Smith..... £5,690 to £6,717
Blantyre House, Kent, D. C. Leach
£5,690 to £6,717
Buckley Hall, Lancs., R. M. Parfitt
£5,690 to £6,717
Campsfield House, Oxford, F. E. C. Jones
£4,673 to £5,340
Eastwood Park, Glos., E. K. Wheeler
£4,763 to £5,340
Erlestoke House, Wilts. (vacant)
£5,690 to £6,717
Foston Hall, Derby, W. L. Thom £4,673 to £5,340
Haslar, Hants., A. R. Parsons.... £5,690 to £6,717
Kirklevington, Cleveland, D. A. Marsden
£4,673 to £5,340
Medomsley, Co. Durham, J. M. Reid
£5,690 to £6,717
New Hall, Yorks., W. A. Martin £5,690 to £6,717
North Sea Camp, Lincs., B. E. N. Lyte
£5,690 to £6,717
Send, Surrey, Capt. P. E. Marshall, V.R.D.
£5,690 to £6,717
Werrington House, Staffs., J. M. Williams
£5,690 to £6,717
Whatton, Notts., C. B. Cogman. £5,690 to £6,717

Probation and After-Care Department
Romney House, Marsham Street, S.W.1
[01-212-7676]
Assistant Under-Secretary of State, A. W. Glanville
£12,000
Assistant Secretaries, G. I. de Deney; G. Emerson;
M. E. Head............. £8,650 to £11,000
Principals, N. W. R. Baker; S. W. Bennett; Miss
R. E. Henn; Miss S. J. Hepworth; B. Lockett;
J. A. Peacock; Miss P. M. Strong; Miss M. Wake-
field-Richmond; R. J. H. West; W. J. Wright
£5,680 to £7,450
Senior Executive Officers, Miss R. M. Glen; Miss
J. M. Jeffrey; S. R. Mann; B. G. Meilton; Mrs.
M. E. W. Pusovnik; K. W. Rowe; P. G.
Spurgeon; A. Wakefield..... £4,900 to £5,900
Chief Probation Inspector, M. H. Hogan... £11,000
Deputy Chief Probation Inspectors, R. W. Spiers;
R. S. Taylor........................ £9,861
Superintending Inspectors, G. C Orton; Miss M. D.
Samuels; C. T. Swann....... £7,750 to £9,350
Senior Inspector, D. F. Duchemin
£5,680 to £7,600

Drugs Branch
Chief Inspector, C. G. Jeffery.... £7,450 to £9,350
Deputy Chief Inspector, H. B. Spear
£5,680 to £7,450
Principals, H. R. Emery; R. Kendall; D. G. Turner
£5,680 to £7,450
Senior Executive Officer, E. A. Downham
£4,900 to £5,900

Cruelty to Animal Acts Inspectorate
Chief Inspector, D. J. Rankin, Ph.D....... £11,440
Superintending Inspectors, Group Capt. J. R. Cellars,
A.F.C.; Dr. J. D. Laws; Dr. R. L. Macpherson,
M.B.E.............................. £11,000

Public Relations Branch
Home Office, Whitehall, S.W.1
[01-213-3000]
Director of Information Offices, D. Grant.... £11,670
Chief Information Officers, P. L. Marshall; W. J.
Rawles

Radio Regulatory Department
Waterloo Bridge House, Waterloo Rd., S.E.1
[01-275-3000]
Assistant-Under-Secretary of State, J. L. Bantock
£12,000
Assistant Secretary, D. E. Baptiste
£8,650 to £11,000
Director of Radio Technology, W. H. Bellchambers
£11,000
Deputy Director, R. A. Dilworth
£8,650 to £9,798
Senior Principal, A. A. Mead.... £7,750 to £9,350
Principals, D. L. Bird; E. R. Emery; W. Goldsmith;
T. F. H. Howarth
£5,680 to £7,450
Senior Executive Officers, A. A. Reeves; Miss B. R.
West .... £4,900 to £5,900

Statistical Department
Tolworth Tower, Tolworth, Surrey
[01-399-5191]
Assistant Under-Secretary of State, Miss S. V. Cunliffe
£12,000
Chief Statisticians, Dr. C. M. Glennie; J. N. Lithgow;
J. R. Williams............. £8,650 to £11,000
Statisticians, C. J. C. Brown; P. Chandler; L. David-
off; D. E. Edwards; A. S. Greenhorn; L. B.
Lancicki; Dr. F. O'Hara; S. M. Speller; R. M.
Taylor; B. H. Ward; Mrs. E. Whitwill
£5,680 to £7,450
Senior Executive Officers, P. W. Brand; T. Chapman;
J. D. Fuller; L. C. Green; D. E. Powell
£4,900 to £5,900

Research Unit
Romney House, Marsham Street, S.W.1
[01-212-7676]
Head of Unit, I. J. Croft....... £8,650 to £11,000
Senior Principal Research Officers, Dr. R. V. G.
Clarke; Dr. M. S. Folkard
Senior Research Officers, R. J. Baxter, Ph.D.; A. F.
C. Crook; K. H. Heal; T. F. Marshall; Miss J. W.
Mott; K. G. Pease, Ph.D.; Miss M. J. Shaw; D. E.
Smith..................... £5,680 to £7,450
Principal, Miss W. M. Goode, C.B.E.
£5,680 to £7,450
Senior Executive Officer: T. F. Corbett
£4,000 to £5,000

Scientific Advisory Branch
Horseferry House, Dean Ryle Street, S.W.1
[01-211-3000]
Director, J. K. S. Clayton..... £10,180 to £11,190
Senior Principal Scientific Officer, S. F. J. Butler
£8,650 to £9,798
Principal Scientific Officers, J. C. Cotterill; J. R. Lowe;
J. A. Miles; Miss P. M. Morgan; P. L. Parsons;
F. H. Pavry; A. D. Perryman; J. E. Simes; R. C.
Stephen; Dr. Janet Thompson; F. H. Venables;
A. M. Western............. £5,514 to £7,205

Women's Royal Voluntary Service
17 Old Park Lane, W.1
[01-499-6040]
Chairman, Lady Pike.
Chief Administrator (Regions), Miss E. Hyatt.

HORSERACE TOTALISATOR BOARD
Tote House, 8-12 New Bridge Street, E.C.4.
[01-353-1066]
Established by the Betting and Gaming Act, 1960,
as successor in title to the Racecourse Betting
Control Board established by the Racecourse
Betting Act, 1928.

Its function is to operate totalisators on approved racecourses in Great Britain, and it also provides off-course cash and credit offices. Under the Horse-race Totalisator and Betting Levy Board Act, 1972, it is now further empowered to offer bets at starting price (or other bets at fixed odds) on any sporting event.

Chairman, W. L. Wyatt................£8,000
Deputy Chairman, Sir Leonard Barford.
Members, Sir Alexander Glen, K.B.E., D.S.C.; Dame Elizabeth Ackroyd, D.B.E.; G. H. C. Ardron, M.B.E., Ph.D. (Director-General).

INDEPENDENT BROADCASTING AUTHORITY
70 Brompton Road, S.W.3
[01-584-7011]

The Authority was created in July 1954 as the Independent Television Authority. In July 1972 it was renamed the Independent Broadcasting Authority and its functions extended to cover the provision of independent local radio. The Chairman and Members of the Authority are appointed by Ministers responsible for broadcasting matters. The eleven members of the Authority constitute the body which has the statutory task of providing the independent broadcasting services in television and radio. This task includes both the provision of the transmitting facilities and the general supervision of programmes and advertising. In both media, the Authority is required to obtain its normal programme supply from programme companies operating under contract to the Authority. Fifteen television programme companies hold contracts to provide programmes in the 14 independent television regions of Britain (two companies share the contract for London—one on weekdays, the other at weekends). They are financed by selling advertising time. The contractors pay a rental to the Authority to meet the I.B.A.'s own requirements, and an additional rental, which is calculated in relation to their profits, to the Exchequer to recognize their use of frequencies which are public assets. Under the terms of the Independent Broadcasting Act 1973, the I.B.A. has set up 19 independent local radio stations.

Chairman, The Lady Plowden, D.B.E......£10,000
Deputy Chairman, C. Bland...............£2,000
Members, W. C. Anderson, C.B.E.; The Marchioness of Anglesey; W. J. Blease (Northern Ireland); Dr. T. F. Carbery (Scotland); Mrs. A. M. Coulson; Prof. H. Morris-Jones (Wales); A. W. Page, M.B.E.; Prof. J. Ring; Mrs. M. Warnock.£1,000
Director-General, Sir Brian Young.
Deputy Directors General, B. C. Sendall, C.B.E. (Programme Services); A. W. Pragnell, O.B.E., D.F.C.(Administrative Services).
Director of Engineering, F. H. Steele.
Director of Internal Finance, R. D. Downham.
Director of External Finance, A. Brook.
Head of Information, B. C. L. Keelan.
Head of Programme Services, D. Glencross.
Head of Advertising Control, P. B. Woodhouse.
Director of Radio, J. B. Thompson.
Secretary, B. Rook.
Regional Officers, F. W. L. G. Bath (Midlands); J. Blair-Scott (South England); W. A. C. Collingwood, O.B.E. (South-West England, Channel Islands); R. Cordin (Yorkshire); L. J. Evans, O.B.E. (Wales and the West); A. D. Fleck (Northern Ireland); J. N. R. Hallett, M.B.E. (East of England); J. E. Harrison (North-West England); J. Lindsay (Scotland); R. J. F. Lorimer (North-East England, the Borders and the Isle of Man.).

DEPARTMENT OF INDUSTRY
1 Victoria Street, S.W.1
[01-215 7877]

The Department of Industry is responsible for general industrial policy, and for the industrial component of regional policy, including financial assistance to industry under the Industry Act (except that certain regional industrial policy functions in Scotland and Wales are now exercised by the Scottish and Welsh Offices). It sponsors individual manufacturing industries, including iron and steel, aircraft and shipbuilding; it is responsible for two nationalised industries, the British Steel Corporation and the Post Office. The Department, is responsible for technical services to industry, and for industrial research and development, including civil aerospace research and the supervision of the industrial research establishments of the former Department of Trade and Industry. The Design Council and the National Research Development Corporation also come within its sphere.

SALARY LIST

Secretary of State......................£13,000
Ministers of State......................£9,500
Parliamentary Under Secretary of State......£5,500
Permanent Secretary.....................£18,675
Second Permanent Secretary..............£17,175
Head of Government Accounting Service....£17,175
Deputy Secretary........................£14,000
Under Secretary.........................£12,000
Assistant Secretary........£8,650 to £11,000
Chief Statistician.........£8,650 to £11,000
Senior Economic Adviser....£8,650 to £11,000
Director Engineer.......................£11,000
Senior Principal...........£7,750 to £9,350
Principal.................£5,680 to £7,450
The Solicitor...........................£14,000
Under Secretary (Legal)..................£12,000
Assistant Solicitor........£9,033 to £11,000
Senior Director of Accountants...........£11,670
Director of Accountants....£8,650 to £11,000
Chief Scientific Officer.................£10,950
Deputy Chief Scientific Officer...£8,330 to £9,440
Chief Information Officer (A)..£8,650 to £11,000
(B).....£7,750 to £9,350

Research Establishments

Director, National Physical Laboratory......£14,000
Director, National Engineering Laboratory...£13,230
Government Chemist......................£12,000
Director, Warren Spring Laboratory.......£12,000
Director, Computer Aided Design Centre.....£9,440

Secretary of State for Industry, THE RT. HON. ERIC GRAHAM VARLEY, M.P.
Principal Private Secretary, M. J. Michell.
Parliamentary Private Secretary, R. W. Stott, M.P.
Special Adviser, K. J. Griffin.
Ministers of State, ALAN JOHN WILLIAMS, M.P.; GERALD BERNARD KAUFMAN, M.P.
Private Secretaries, (to Mr. Williams), R. M. D. Ure; (to Mr. Kaufman), D. H. Johnson.
Parliamentary Under Secretaries of State for Industry, The Lord Melchett; L. J. Huckfield, M.P.
Permanent Secretaries, Sir Peter Carey, K.C.B.
Private Secretary, R. Heyhoc.
Second Permanent Secretary, A. K. Rawlinson, C.B.
Head of Government Accountancy Service and Accountancy Adviser to the Department of Industry, K. J. Sharp, T.D.
Deputy Secretaries, L. S. Berman, C.B. (Director of Statistics); R. H. W. Bullock, C.B.; R. E. Dearing; M. J. Kerry, C.B. (The Solicitor); A. J. Lippitt; D. A. Lovelock, C.B. (Principal Establishment and Finance Officer); Sir Ieuan Maddock, C.B., O.B.E., F.R.S. (Chief Scientist); G. D. W. Odgers (Director, Industrial Development Unit); Professor A. T. Peacock, D.S.C. (Chief Economic Adviser); R. F. Prosser, C.B., M.C.; P. W. Ridley, C.B.E.
Industrial Adviser, P. Turner.
Parliamentary Clerk (Principal), Miss P. Davey.

Air Division
Monsanto House, 10–18 Victoria Street, S.W.1
[01-215 7877]

Under Secretary, A. Warrington.
Assistant Secretaries, D. R. Ford; D. J. Gerhard; R. Jardine; R. Mountfield.
Deputy Chief Scientific Officer, K. W. Smith

Space and Air Research Division
Monsanto House, 10–18 Victoria Street, S.W.1
[01-215 7877]
Under Secretary, H. G. R. Robinson, O.B.E.
Deputy Chief Scientific Officers, D. Cavanagh; R. A. Jeffs.

Concorde Division
Monsanto House, 10–18 Victoria Street, S.W.1
[01-215 7877]
Under Secretary, K. G. Binning, C.M.G.
Assistant Secretary, B. E. P. MacTavish.
Deputy Chief Scientific Officer, J. D. Hayhurst, O.B.E.

Research and Development Requirements Division
Abell House, John Islip Street, S.W.1
[01-211 3000]
Under Secretary, B. W. Oakley.
Assistant Secretary, C. B. Nixon.
Deputy Chief Scientific Officers, Dr. J. A. Catterall; A. C. Ladd; P. H. Stephenson.

Research and Development Contractors Division
Abell House, John Islip Street, S.W.1
Under Secretary (vacant)
Deputy Chief Scientific Officers, E. Barlow-Wright; R. J. F. Franklin; A. C. Nicholas.

National Physical Laboratory
Teddington, Middlesex
[01-977 3222]
Director, Dr. J. V. Dunworth, C.B., C.B.E.

Laboratory of the Government Chemist
Cornwall House, Stamford Street, S.E.1
[01-928 7900]
Government Chemist, Dr. H. Egan.

National Engineering Laboratory
East Kilbride, Glasgow
[East Kilbride: 20222]
Director (Chief Scientific Officer), D. H. Mallinson

Warren Spring Laboratory
Gunnels Wood Road, Stevenage, Herts.
[Stevenage: 3388]
Director, A. J. Robinson.

Computor Aided Design Centre
Madingley Road, Cambridge
[Cambridge: 63125]
Director, A. I. Llewelyn, O.B.E

Industrial and Commercial Policy Division
1 Victoria Street, S.W.1
[01-215 7877]
Under Secretary, Miss A. E. Mueller.
Assistant Secretaries, S. W. Treadgold; M. Z. Wasilewski; W. B. Willott; J. A. Woolmer.

Regional Industrial Development Division
Millbank Tower, Millbank, S.W.1
[01-211 3000]
Under Secretary, M. H. M. Reid.
Assistant Secretaries, V. F. Lane; D. Steel

Regional Industrial Finance Division
Millbank Tower, Millbank, S.W.1
[01-211 3000]
Under Secretary (vacant)
Assistant Secretaries, J. L. Judd; A. B. Powell, C.M.G.; A. C. Russell.

Regional Development Grants Division
Millbank Tower, Millbank, S.W.1
[01-211 3000]
Under Secretary, D. G. C. Lawrence, O.B.E.
Assistant Secretaries, O. E. G. Dickson; S. J. Irwin.

Small Firms Division
Abell House, John Islip Street, S.W.1
[01-211 3000]
Under Secretary, D. G. C. Lawrence, O.B.E.
Assistant Secretary, J. E. Cammell.

Industrial Planning Division
Millbank Tower, Millbank, S.W.1
[01-211 3000]
Under Secretary, H. Scholes.
Assistant Secretaries, Dr. E. B. Bates; J. A. Battersby; A. J. P. MacDonald; N. N. Walmsley.

REGIONAL ORGANISATION
Northern Regional Office
Wellbar House, Gallowgate, Newcastle upon Tyne
[Newcastle upon Tyne: 27575]
Regional Director (Under Secretary), R. L. Sutton
Regional Industrial Director (Under Secretary), H. T. Hill

North West Regional Office
Sunley Bldg., Piccadilly Plaza, Manchester
[061-236 2171]
Regional Director (Under Secretary), N. S. Belam
Regional Industrial Director (Under Secretary), G. Moore

Yorkshire and Humberside Regional Office
Priestley House, Park Row, Leeds
[Leeds: 443171]
Regional Director (Under Secretary), J. H. McEnery
Regional Industrial Director (Under Secretary), A. R. M. Graham

West Midlands Regional Office
Ladywood House, Stephenson Street, Birmingham
[021-632 4111]
Regional Director (Deputy Chief Scientific Officer), J. K. L. Thompson, M.B.E., T.D.

East Midlands Regional Office
Cranbrook House, Cranbrook Street, Nottingham
[Nottingham: 46121]
Regional Director (Assistant Secretary), N. Lott

South West Regional Office
The Pithay, Bristol
[Bristol: 291071]
Regional Director (Assistant Secretary), R. C. McVickers.

South West Industrial Development Office
Phoenix House, Notte Street, Plymouth
[Plymouth: 21891]
Regional Industrial Director (Assistant Secretary) (part time), C. E. Cannell

Eastern Regional Office
Charles House, 375 Kensington High Street, W.14
[01-603-2070]
Regional Director (Assistant Secretary), B. Feinstein.

London and South Eastern Regional Office
Charles House, 375 Kensington High Street, W.14
[01-603-2060]
Regional Director (Assistant Secretary), A. C. Coging.

Industrial Development Unit
Millbank Tower, Millbank, S.W.1
[01-211 3000]
Director, G. D. W. Odgers
Deputy Directors, D. Eastmond; M. G. M. Haines; I. F. Halliday; R. L. Hamilton.
Secretariat and General Policy:
Assistant Secretary, C. B. Benjamin

Iron and Steel Division
Thames House South, Millbank, S.W.1
[01-211 3000]
Under Secretary, S. J. Gross, C.M.G.
Assistant Secretaries, J. D. Henes; D. J. R. Huck; J. H. Pownall
Deputy Chief Scientific Officer, R. L. Long.

Paper, Timber and Miscellaneous Manufactures Branch
Millbank Tower, Millbank, S.W.1
[01-211 3000]
Under Secretary, D. G. C. Lawrence, O.B.E.
Assistant Secretary, J. E. Sellars.

Chemicals and Textiles Division
Millbank Tower, Millbank, S.W.1
[01-211-3000]
Under Secretary, P. G. Hudson.
Assistant Secretaries, D. M. Dell; D. M. J. Gwinnell; Miss L. Lowne.

Shipbuilding Policy Division
Millbank Tower, Millbank, S.W.1
[01-211 3000]
Under Secretary, M. B. Casey.
Assistant Secretaries, A. McDonald; J. G. Walmsley; T. E. Wyatt.
Deputy Chief Scientific Officer, D. Neville-Jones.

Minerals, Metals, Electrical Engineering, Process Plant and Industrial Technologies Division
Millbank Tower, Millbank, S.W.1
[01-211 3000]
Under Secretary, D. C. Clark.
Assistant Secretaries, M. D. C. Johnson; E. W. Pearcey.
Directing Engineer, A. J. Havelock.

Machine Tools and Mechanical Engineering Division
Abell House, John Islip Street, S.W.1
[01-211 3000]
Under Secretary, D. N. Byrne.
Assistant Secretary, C. M. Drukker.
Deputy Chief Scientific Officer, R. Gill.
Senior Principal, R. K. Paskins.

Vehicle Division
Abell House, John Islip Street, S.W.1
[01-211-3000]
Under Secretary, W. R. G. Bell.
Assistant Secretaries, R. M. Allott; P. J. Cooper; A. J. Suich.
Director Engineer, F. C. Munns.

Computers, Systems and Electronics Division
Dean Bradley House, 52 Horseferry Road, S.W.1
[01-212 7676]
Under Secretary, M. P. Lam.
Assistant Secretaries, M. P. Gillings; B. Murray.
Deputy Chief Scientific Officers, D. Harrison; J. H. Major.

Posts and Telecommunications Division
Waterloo Bridge House, Waterloo Road, S.E.1
[01-275 3000]
Under Secretary, R. Williams.
Assistant Secretaries, J. E. M. Beale; Miss S. P. M. Fisher; J. M. Healey; T. U. Meyer.

DEPARTMENTS OF INDUSTRY, TRADE AND PRICES AND CONSUMER PROTECTION–COMMON SERVICES
1 Victoria Street, S.W.1
[01-215 7877]
SALARY LIST

Deputy Secretary	£14,000
Under Secretary	£12,000
Assistant Secretary	£8,650 to £11,000
Chief Statistician	£8,650 to £11,000
Senior Economic Adviser	£8,650 to £11,000
Senior Principal	£7,750 to £9,350
Principal	£5,680 to £7,450
The Solicitor	£14,000
Under Secretary (Legal)	£12,000
Assistant Solicitor	£12,000
Senior Director of Accountants	£9,033 to £11,000
Director of Accountants	£11,670
Chief Scientific Officer	£8,650 to £11,000
Deputy Chief Scientific Officer	£10,950
Chief Information Officer (A)	£8,330 to £9,440
(B)	£8,650 to £11,000
	£7,750 to £9,350

Deputy Secretaries, L. S. Berman, C.B. (*Director of Statistics*); M. J. Kerry, C.B. (*The Solicitor*); D. A. Lovelock, C.B. (*Principal Establishment and Finance Officer*); Prof. A. T. Peacock, D.S.C. (*Chief Economic Adviser*)

Establishment Senior Staff Management Division
1 Victoria Street, S.W.1
[01-215 7877]
Under Secretary, G. Parker, C.B.
Assistant Secretary, J. L. Clark.

Establishment Personnel Division
Under Secretary, E. J. D. Warne.
Assistant Secretaries, K. L. Blake; J. S. H. White.
Norman Shaw South Building,
Victoria Embankment, S.W.1
[01-839 7799]
Assistant Secretary, F. A. Carter.

Establishment Management Services and Manpower Division
Sanctuary Buildings,
16-20 Great Smith Street, S.W.1
[01-215 7877]
Under Secretary, G. C. Lowe.
Assistant Secretary, H. A. Dawson.
Assistant Secretaries, D. G. Church, O.B.E.; D. L. Gatland.

Establishment General Services Division
1 Victoria Street, S.W.1
[01-215 7877]
Under Secretary, J. Fish.
Assistant Secretaries, N. E. Ablett; D. J. Minchin.

Finance and Economic Appraisal Division
Abell House, John Islip Street, S.W.1
[01-211 3000]
Under Secretary, R. H. F. Croft.
Assistant Secretaries, K. W. N. George; D. W. Hellings; Miss E. P. Marston.

Accounts Branch
24-26 Newport Road, Cardiff
[Cardiff 42611]
Senior Principal (*Director of Accounts*), J. G. P. Cater.

Internal Audit
Chapter St. House, Chapter Street, S.W.1
[01-834 7032]
Senior Principal (*Head of Internal Audit*), B. E. Elkington.

Programme Analysis Unit
Grimesdyke House, Chilton, Didcot, Oxon.
[Abingdon: 4141]
Deputy Chief Scientific Officer (*Director of Unit*), Dr. P. M. S. Jones.

Solicitor's Department
Kingsgate House, 66-74 Victoria Street, S.W.1.
[01-215 7877]
The Solicitor, M. J. Kerry, C.B.
Under Secretaries (*Legal*), J. B. Evans; G. A. Preston; T. D. Salmon; J. A. Trapnell.
Assistant Solicitors, Mrs. N. M. P. Chappell; D. A. Grant, M.C.; H. S. A. Hart; R. Higgins; A. D. Howlett; K. A. M. Johnson; J. McElheran; R. M. Malbey; D. E. Moore; T. J. G. Pratt; G. Preston; C. B. Robson; Mrs. F. A. Scarborough; F. A. Thompson; L.V. Wellard.

Economics and Statistics Division 1
1 Victoria Street, S.W.1
[01-215 7877]
Under Secretary, D. R. H. Sawers.
Senior Economic Advisers, M. S. Bradbury; M. J. Fores; N. K. A. Gardner; R. S. Howard; N. C. Owen.

Economics and Statistics Divisions 3
Dean Bradley House, 52 Horseferry Road,
[01-212 7676]
Under Secretary, P. M. Rees.
Chief Statisticians, W. E. Boyd; A. Crystal; J. R. Howe; J. D. Wells; W. A. Wessell.
Senior Economic Adviser, D. A. W. Broyd.

Economics and Statistics Divisions 4
Under Secretary, R. O. Goss.
Chief Statistician, M. L. M. Neifield.

Senior Economic Advisers, M. S. Bradbury; H. Christie; P. J. Goate; J. H. Rickard.

Economics and Statistics Division 5
Under Secretary, T. S. Pilling.
Chief Statisticians, P. D. Dworkin; B. A. Wainewright.
Senior Economic Advisers, D. R. Coates; G. P. Jefferies.

Economics and Statistics Division 6
Under Secretary, Miss R. J. Maurice.
Chief Statisticians, Mrs. J. G. Cox; M. J. M. Erritt; P. H. Richardson.

Business Statistics Office
Cardiff Road, Newport, Gwent
[Newport: 56111]
Under Secretary, M. C. Fessey.
Assistant Secretary, J. A. Tiffin.
Chief Statisticians, J. M. Simmonds; Dr. R. H. S. Phillips; Dr. B. Mitchell.
Senior Principal, R. W. Makepeace.

Accountancy Services Division
Hillgate House, 26 Old Bailey, E.C.4
[01-248 5757]
Senior Director, H. A. Parfitt, C.B.E.
Directors, N. A. Atley; W. H. Cunningham.

Information Division
1 Victoria Street, S.W.1
[01-215 7877]
Head of Information Division, R. J. J. Tuite, M.B.E.
Chief Information Officers, D. S. Evans; R. Mayes.
Gaywood House, Great Peter Street, S.W.1
[01-212 7676]
Chief Information Officer, D. M. Edwards.

CENTRAL OFFICE OF INFORMATION
Hercules Road, S.E.1
[01-928-2345]
The Central Office of Information is a common service department which produces information and publicity material, and supplies publicity services, for other Government departments which require them. In the United Kingdom it conducts Government display press, television and poster advertising (except for the National Savings Committee), produces and distributes booklets, leaflets, films, television material, exhibitions, photographs and other visual material; and distributes departmental press notices. For the overseas departments it supplies British Information posts overseas with press, radio and television material, booklets, magazines, reference services, films, exhibitions, photographs, display and reading room material; manages schemes for promoting the overseas sale of British newspapers and periodicals; arranges tours in the United Kingdom for official visitors from overseas. Administrative responsibility for the Central Office of Information rests with Civil Service Department Ministers, while the ministers whose departments it serves are responsible for the policy expressed in its work.
Director-General, H. L. James............£13,695
Private Secretary, Mrs. M. L. Evans.
Controllers, R. A. Fleming (*Overseas*); (vacant) (*Home*)..................................£12,135
Assistant Controllers, P. W. Probert (*Home*); K. W. Sutton, O.B.E. (*Overseas*)......£8,215 to £9,815
Head of Research, N. H. Phillips. £8,215 to £9,815
Principal Information Officer, Miss G. R. Hembry
£6,145 to £7,915
Senior Information Officers, Miss B. M. E. Breden, M.B.E.; C. A. Cross; K. Meadows; Mrs. P. Mills; Miss E. S. Stainforth.........£5,365 to £6,365
Advertising Division
Director, O. G. Thetford......£9,115 to £11,465
Chief Information Officer, B. C. Davies
£8,215 to £9,815
Principal Information Officers, M. J. C. Brodie; D. G. Marsh; G. W. Tavender; Miss V. E. Thorne, O.B.E......................£6,145 to £7,915

Senior Information Officers, M. F. Bowtell; E. W. Buckle; J. C. Danckwerts; A. H. C. Royou; I. F. Russell; J. C. Segrue.........£5,365 to £6,365
Senior Executive Officer, E.A.Davis. £5,365 to £6,365

Establishment and Organization Division
Atlantic House, Holborn Viaduct, E.C.1
[01-583-5744]
Director, A. Youngs (*Establishment Officer*)
£9,115 to £11,465
Senior Principal, W. F. Garnett..£8,215 to £9,815
Principals, E. Bridger; M. Collins; A. H. Robinson
£6,145 to £7,915
Senior Executive Officers, Miss G. E. A. Bargus; W. J. Colwill; D. Drake; S. G. Kerr; I. L. Margetts; D. P. Morgan; J. G. Rowbotham; M. Rowland; R. F. Stapley; K. R. Stephens
£5,365 to £6,365

Exhibitions Division
St. Christopher House Annexe,
Sumner Street, S.E.1
[01-928-2371]
Director, E. R. I. Allan, O.B.E. . £9,115 to £11,465
Principal Information Officers, D. A. Loxley; R. J. Reeves; B. H. Reynolds..... £6,145 to £7,915
Senior Information Officers, M. W. Chitty; L. J. Darnell; M. D. Dyer; A. D. Estill; R. C. Fullford; R. S. Harper; I. E. Lain; P. J. London; C. B. Seymour; R. J.Vallance; J. B. Yearsley
£5,365 to £6,365
Senior Executive Officer, J.F.Hinds. £5,365 to £6,365

Films and Television Division
Director, Miss D. V. F. Cockburn
£9,115 to £11,465
Chief Information Officers, R. J. Hall; A. C. White
£8,215 to £9,815
Principal Information Officers, Sir John Barran, Bt.; Mrs. R. Brownrigg; W. J. G. Evans; J. A. Leys; A. W. Thomson..........£6,145 to £7,915
Principal, Miss J. M. Reid......£6,145 to £7,915
Senior Information Officers, D. S. Andrews; P. S. Brawn; P. W. Coldham; Mrs. D. C. Crawshaw; L. S. Dawes; M. J. Draper; R. A. P. Duval; L. F. Eaton; Miss S. L. Y. Eley; J. B. Frankfort; B. V. Gillman; F. G. Hermges; Miss A. B. I. James; P. G. Jones; Miss E. V. Moynihan; Miss F. Nelson; J. B. Parsons; R. V. Prime; Mrs. M. G. Reynolds; R. W. Salmon; Miss R. Serlin; Miss H. P. Standage; C. S. Still; Mrs. A. A. Unsworth; G. A. Woodford..................£5,365 to £6,365

Finance and Accounts Division
Director, D. J. Etheridge.......£9,115 to £11,465
Finance Branch
Principal, G. W. M. Pearson....£6,145 to £7,915
Senior Executive Officers, D. C. Marquet; E. W. Whyman..................£5,365 to £6,365

Accounts Branch
Sutherland House, Brighton Road,
Sutton, Surrey
[01-642-6022]
Principal, R. K. Evans.........£5,955 to £7,725
Senior Executive Officer, Miss K. R. Walker
£5,175 to £6,175

Overseas Press and Radio Division
Director, H. J. Watters........£9,115 to £11,465
Chief Information Officer, J. K. Holroyd
£8,215 to £9,815
Principal Information Officers, J. Ensoll; Miss M. M. Foster; R. C. Herbert; K. G. Hicks; D. W. James; R. J. Macdonald; D. J. Payton-Smith; F. R. Pickering, M.B.E.; D. A. Smith; G. L. Stickland; E. Turnbull.....£6,145 to £7,915
Senior Information Officers, A. A. J. Arthur; Mrs. A. A. Beattie; J. D. Beaumont; N. H. Browne; R. J. Chalk; T. P. Cleaver; R. E. Collins; M. A. David; R. M. Douglas; G. L. Duffus; J. E. Everett; M. S. C. Fare; R. Gair; R. C. Gordon-Walker; R. H. Hall; O. Henry; S. Hindley; J. E. Horton; F. R. Mackenzie; H. R. Mander; J. H. Nell; M. J. Quan; P. J. Reynolds; R. W. Tindall; Miss P. J. Tyler; P. D. Wallace; J. F. Webb; Mrs. C. A. Whelan; F. Wilson; Miss M. L. Yardley
£5,365 to £6,365

Senior Executive Officer, P. Abbott
£5,365 to £6,365

Photographs Division
Director, C. H. Bourchier...... £8,215 to £9,815
Principal Information Officer, J. A. Bond
£6,145 to £7,915
Senior Information Officers, D. J. Cooper; Miss H. R.
Dunt; D. F. Eddleston; S. I. Robertson
£5,365 to £6,365
Senior Executive Officer, A. H. Kemp
£5,345 to £6,365

Publications and Design Services Division
Director, E. R. Kelly......... £9,115 to £11,465
Chief Information Officer, A. E. Bevens
£8,215 to £9,815
Principal Information Officers, J. L. Bishop; P. R.
Daniell; F. V. Ellis; D. N. Steward
£6,145 to £7,915
Senior Information Officers, T. A. Benger; P. Bowen;
R. W. Brand; R. Doughty; H. Edwards; A. E.
Gatland; M. Jacobson; Miss B. M. Kirby; Miss
M. E. J. Orna; G. R. Parsons; Miss J. Penfold;
M. F. Reid; D. M. Robarts; E. H. Sired; C. J.
Wakeling; Miss B. M. Worthing
£5,365 to £6,365
Senior Executive Officer, K. F. G. Fogwill
£5,365 to £6,365

Reference Division
Director, E. G. Farmer......... £8,215 to £9,815
Principal Information Officers, Mrs. J. Bonnor;
H. Witheford............... £6,145 to £7,915
Senior Information Officers, A. Baron; D. W. C.
Beynon; Dr. T. Kempinski; J. F. Langley; S. C.
Lyle-Smythe; C. E. F. Manning; Mrs. S.
Saunders; Miss E. D. Skinner. £5,365 to £6,365
Senior Executive Officer, R. Widdup
£5,365 to £6,365

Tours and Distribution Division
Director, N. Bicknell.......... £8,215 to £9,815
Principal Information Officer, J. B. Crompton
£6,915 to £7,915
Senior Information Officers, Mrs. B. G. E. Bryan-
Brown; L. K. Carley; D. J. T. Cooke; C. J.
Davies; C. M. Hull; M. H. Pelly
£5,365 to £6,365
Senior Executive Officers, G. W. S. Gilbert; D. Ross
£5,365 to £6,365

News Distribution Service
Duty Officer, T. P. Blakiston.

Regional Offices
Northern—Andrews House, Gallowgate,
Newcastle upon Tyne
Chief Regional Officer, H. G. Roberts
£7,750 to £9,350
Senior Information Officers, J. F. Dougray; L. W.
Mandy, M.B.E............... £4,900 to £5,900

Yorkshire and Humberside—City House,
New Station Street, Leeds
Chief Regional Officer, T. Cooban
£7,750 to £9,350
Senior Information Officers, P. M. Craven; C. E.
Dove...................... £4,900 to £5,900

East Midland—Severus House,
20 Middle Pavement, Nottingham
Chief Regional Officer, P. J. Brazier
£7,750 to £9,350
Senior Information Officers, Mrs. J. M. Beilby; A.
Waller;.................... £4,900 to £5,900

Eastern—Block D, Government Buildings,
Three Crowns House, 72-80 Hills Road
Cambridge
Chief Regional Officer, A. A. McLoughlin
£7,750 to £9,350
Senior Information Officers, O. J. B. Prince-White;
D. C. Robinson............. £4,900 to £5,900

London and South Eastern—
St. Christopher House Annexe,
Sumner Street, S.E.1
Chief Regional Officer, R. Dean, O.B.E.
£8,215 to £9,815

Senior Information Officers, A. J. Goodson; S. T.
Sharpe.................... £5,365 to £6,365

Southern—Market Place House, Reading
Chief Regional Officer, A. S. Poole
£5,680 to £7,450
Senior Information Officers, T. G. S. Crawford; J. R.
Wood..................... £4,900 to £5,900

South Western—The Pithay, Bristol, 1
Chief Regional Officer, P. D. Yorke
£5,680 to £7,450
Senior Information Officers, P. D. Breen; J. W. Coe
£4,900 to £5,900

West Midland—Five Ways House,
Islington Row Middle Way, Birmingham 15
Chief Regional Officer, D. C. Boyd
£7,750 to £9,350
Senior Information Officers, G. F. Phoenix; A.
Thompson.................. £4,900 to £5,900

North Western—Sunley Building,
Piccadily Plaza, Manchester
Chief Regional Officer, P. B. Porter
£7,750 to £9,350
Senior Information Officers, H. Booth; J. Bradbury;
R. C. Stockdale............ £4,900 to £5,900

BOARD OF INLAND REVENUE
Somerset House, W.C.2
[01-438 6622]

The Board of Inland Revenue was constituted
under the Inland Revenue Board Act, 1849, by the
consolidation of the Board of Excise and the Board
of Stamps and Taxes. In 1909 the administration
of excise duties was transferred to the Board of
Customs. The Board of Inland Revenue administers and collects direct taxes—mainly income tax,
corporation tax, capital gains tax, capital transfer tax, stamp duty and petroleum revenue tax—
and advises the Chancellor of the Exchequer on
policy questions involving them. The Head Office
is in London and there are Inspectors of Taxes
offices and Collection offices throughout the United
Kingdom. The Department's Valuation Office is
responsible for valuing property for tax purposes,
for compensation and for compulsory purchase
and (in England and Wales) for local rating
purposes. In 1974/5 Inland Revenue collected
over £14,000,000,000 tax at a cost of approximately
£250,000,000.

The Board
Chairman (Permanent Secretary), Sir William Pile
K.C.B., M.B.E.............................. £18,675
Private Secretary, Miss A. Kirkness.
Deputy Chairmen (Deputy Secretaries), J. M. Green,
C.B.; A. H. Dalton, C.B................. £14,000
Directors General (Deputy Secretaries), E. V. Symons,
C.B.; E. V. Adams.................. £14,000
Commissioners (Under Secretaries), J. Webb; Miss G.
E. M. Wolters; Mrs. A. H. Smallwood, C.M.G.;
A. J. G. Isaac; J. D. T. Thompson; J. H.
Gracey............................. £12,000

Policy Divisions
Under Secretaries, J. D. Taylor Thompson; J. Webb;
T. J. Painter; Miss G. E. M. Wolters; Mrs. A. H.
Smallwood, C.M.G.; D. B. Vernon..... £12,000
Assistant Secretaries, R. J. Bitton; J. M. Crawley;
P. Lewis; D. J. Lawday; F. B. Harrison; R. F.
Baily; G. Briddon; D. G. Draper; I. R. Spence;
L. J. H. Beighton; R. A. Blythe; J. B. Bryce;
C. W. Corlett; M. H. Collins; D. Hopkins; B.
Pollard; P. G. Heard; T. M. Holmes; F. I.
Robertson................ £8,650 to £11,000

Economic Services and Intelligence Section
Central Divisions
Under Secretary, J. H. Gracey............ £12,000
Assistant Secretaries, R. I. McConnachie; B. J.
Thomas.................. £8,650 to £11,000
Senior Economic Adviser, E. B. Butler
£8,650 to £11,000

Technical Divisions
Directors, K. C. Southall; D. H. Moorcraft; C. G.
Ware................................ £12,000
Assistant Directors, R. E. Kirby; T. J. Thompson;
N. Hannah; J. K. Ward; A. Gill; R. G. Savage;
D. B. Rogers; P. Tyrer; I. R. E. Symons; F. S.

Dodd; P. L. O'Leary; P. Tillson; D. A. Jones;
L. F. Robins; O. P. Davies, C.B.E.; J. A. Stephenson; W. A. Perry; W. M. Dermit; L. S. Stratford;
A. S. Wray; W. P. A. Winton; R. D. Rawson
£11,440
Assistant Secretaries, J. Livesey; A. I. J. Steadman;
E. Walker; L. C. L. Lavender; A. Fleming; R. M.
Ellis; W. C. Gladstone; J. N. Allen; F. H. Shea;
R. C. Murgatroyd; T. Scott; T. Bingham; D. P.
Harwood.................£8,650 to £11,000
Investigating Officer, J. T. Tudor

£5,680 to £7,450

Management Divisions
Director of Personnel, R. W. Rae.........£12,000
Assistant Directors, C. W. Adam (£11,440); E. Mc-
Givern; W. M. Stewart; F. W. Newcombe; G.
Galey; D. H. Stanton......£8,650 to £11,000
Director of Manpower/Director of Training, F. H.
Brooman..........................£12,000
Assistant Directors, J. E. Lawrance (£11,440); C. L.
Deller; H. A. White; E. J. King
£8,650 to £11,000
Assistant Secretary, T. M. Ditchfield
£8,650 to £11,000
Director of Organisation, E. W. Boyles....£12,000
Assistant Directors, J. B. Shepherd; G. E. Stoker; G.
B. Walker, I.S.O.; N. T. Shepherd; A. R. Bruns-
don; H. S. C. Webber; G. D. Wroe
£8,650 to £11,000
N. I. Behr................£9,798 to £10,563
Controller of Office Services, D. B. Willis
£7,750 to £9,350
Press Officer, J. P. O. Lewis....£5,680 to £7,450

Operations Division
Director of Operations, J. F. Boyd.........£12,000
Assistant Directors, T. W. M. Tuite (£11,440); J. H.
Roberts; E. Dowsland; J. B. Sweeting; D. F.
Pike; P. B. G. Jones.........£8,650 to £11,000
Controller Enforcement Office, C. E. Howick
£7,750 to £9,350
Assistant Director, G. D. Wroe..£8,650 to £11,000
Assistant Secretary, N. Wainwright
£8,650 to £11,000

Finance Division
Principal Finance Officer, F. H. Brooman..£12,000
Assistant Secretary, D. Y. Pitts..£8,650 to £11,000
Controller, S. G. Ash, M.B.E.....£7,750 to £9,350

Statistics Division
Director, S. F. James.................£12,000
Chief Statisticians, A. T. Dunn; N. Harvey; Dr. J.
R. L. Schneider........£8,650 to £11,000
Assistant Secretary, E. A. Rapsey
£8,650 to £11,000

Office of the Controller of Stamps
Bush House, South-West Wing, Strand, W.C.2
and Barrington Road, Worthing, Sussex
Controller, A. A. E. E. Ettinghausen, O.B.E... £9,524

Estate Duty Office
Minford House, Rockley Road,
Controller, W. J. G. Allen...............£12,000
Deputy Controllers, K. W. Chetwood; P. H. Flet-
cher; E. J. Mann......................£11,000
Asst. Controllers, H. Booth, M.B.E.; J. F. Daykin;
R. D'A. J. Dean; R. R. Greenfield; H. J. Hall;
W. Hall; R. K. Johns, I.S.O.; J. F. Johnson; P. H.
Moss; P. B. Smallwood; G. A. Spencer; C. D.
Hughes..............................£9,278
Senior Principal, R. Ellis........£7,750 to £9,350

Solicitors of Inland Revenue
Somerset House, W.C.2
Solicitor, E. G. R. Moses, C.B.............£14,000
Principal Assistant Solicitors, R. S. Boyd; J. S.
Clark, M.C.; J. W. Weston...........£12,000
Assistant Solicitors, A. L. L. Alexander; R. T.
Brand; P. Carter; J. C. Doggett; J. F. Easton;
M. C. Furey; P. D. Hall; Miss A. Hopkin; E. O.
Jackson; J. D. H. Johnstone; H. G. Kingston;
A. A. Mackeith; R. K. Miller
£9,033 to £11,000

Superannuation Funds Office
Apex Tower, High Street, New Malden, Surrey
Controller, R. C. Tebboth.....£8,650 to £11,000
Assistant Controllers, P. Beever; Miss D. Bickmore;
J. N. Gosling; W. T. Lyons..£7,750 to £9,350

Surtax Office and Office of the Inspector of Foreign Dividends
Lynwood Road, Thames Ditton, Surrey
*Controller of Surtax and Inspector of Foreign Divi-
dends*, D. S. Kirtley......£8,650 to £11,000
Assistant Inspector of Foreign Dividends, N. W. Sydee
£7,750 to £9,350

Tithe Redemption Office
Barrington Road, Worthing, West Sussex
Controller, D. H. Pooley.......£5,680 to £7,450

Office of the Chief Valuer
New Court, Carey Street, W.C.2
Chief Valuer, M. I. Prevett...............£14,000
Deputy Chief Valuers, R. A. Garner; C. H.
Tinsley...........................£12,000
Assistant Chief Valuers, H. Ab Iorwerth; E. A.
Bullock; J. A. Christopher; J. J. Claringbull; M.
Clark; J. B. Hyne; W. G. M. Williams.£11,320
Superintending Valuers, R. H. Azevedo; N. I. Behr;
P. J. Borrett; A. Crosby; W. S. Culwick; A. C.
Dolbey-Jones; P. G. Heard; A. B. Fallows; E.
Nuttall; J. S. Preston, T.D.; E. G. Rogers; R. J.
Schumacher..............£9,798 to £10,563

INLAND REVENUE (SCOTLAND)
Senior Principal Inspector of Taxes
12 Lauriston Place, Edinburgh
Senior Principal Inspector of Taxes, I. D. Thomson
£11,440

Controller of Stamps and Taxes
12 Lauriston Place, Edinburgh
Controller, D. M. Watson, I.S.O.
£5,680 to £7,450

Estate Duty Office
16 Picardy Place, Edinburgh
Registrar of Death Duties, I. W. Grant....£11,000
Deputy Registrar of Death Duties, J. W. Grant
£9,278
Chief Examiners, Miss M. M. M. Armstrong; I. S.
Beveridge; P. G. Bruce; J. B. Donald; G. T.
Graham, D.S.C.; F. F. King; J. B. M. McKean;
A. M. McPake; J. A. Taylor..£5,680 to £7,599

Solicitor's Office
16 Waterloo Place, Edinburgh
Solicitor, T. H. Scott.................£11,190
Senior Legal Assistant, (vacant)..£6,625 to £8,750

Office of the Chief Valuer, Scotland
43 Rose Street, Edinburgh
Chief Valuer, J. Beggs.................£11,440
Assistant Chief Valuers, J. Fergus; J. Gilchrist
£9,798 to £10,563

SPECIAL COMMISSIONERS OF INCOME TAX
Turnstile House, High Holborn, W.C.1
[01-438 6622]
The Special Commissioners are an independent
body appointed by the Treasury to hear appeals
concerning income tax, surtax, corporation tax,
capital gains tax, capital transfer tax and petroleum
revenue tax.
Presiding Special Commissioner, R. A. Furtado, C.B.
£12,540
Special Commissioners, J. B. Hodgson; B. James; J.
G. Lewis; H. H. Monroe, Q.C.; A. K. Tavaré
£11,440
Clerk to Special Commissioners, G. Britton
£5,680 to £7,450

INTERVENTION BOARD FOR AGRICULTURAL PRODUCE
Steel Houe, Tothill Street, S.W.1
[501-273 3696]

Fountain House, 2 West Mall, Reading
[Reading: 583626]

The Board was formed as a Government Department on November 22, 1972, and is responsible under the Agricultural Ministers for the implementation within the United Kingdom of the guarantee functions of the Common Agricultural Policy of the European Economic Community. Policy matters are the responsibility of the Agricultural Ministers of the United Kingdom.

Chairman: A. F. Shaw.
Chief Executive (Under Secretary), A. Savage★
£12,000

SECRETARIAT

Secretary and Information Officer (Senior Executive Officer), J. A. Colmer★........£4,900 to £5,000

ESTABLISHMENTS BRANCH

Establishments Officer (Principal), G. R. Holloway
£5,680 to £7,450
Senior Executive Officers, J. Bird; D. A. Maddock
£4,900 to £5,900

FINANCE AND AUDIT DIVISION

Finance Officer (Assistant Secretary), H. R. Neilson
£8,650 to £11,000

Finance Branch

Principal, J. Owen............£5,680 to £7,450
Senior Executive Officers, E. J. Kennedy; R. H. Ebsworth; M. E. Statham....£4,900 to £5,900

Audit Branch

Chief Accountant, W. McLaren...£5,680 to £7,450
Senior Accountant, G. Thomas..£4,900 to £5,000
Senior Executive Officer, D. H. Potter
£4,900 to £5,900

INTERNAL MARKET DIVISION

Assistant Secretary, J. N. Jotcham
£8,650 to £11,000
Senior Principal, J. A. Bamford..£7,750 to £9,350
Principals, J. N. Diserens; J. O. Macarthur; W. Thomson..................£5,680 to £7,450
Commodity Specialists, J. I. Payne; D. G. Griffiths
£5,680 to £7,450
Senior Executive Officers, D. L. Underwood; N. P. J. Rowe; T. U. Gamble.......£4,900 to £5,900

IMPORT AND EXPORT DIVISION

Senior Principal, D. Salton........£7,750 to £9,350
Principals, J. F. Robinson, O.B.E.; E. Prince
£5,680 to £7,450
Senior Executive Officers, A. D. Williams; P. E. Robinson; R. W. Roughley; D. J. Jones; J. H. McLean..................£4,900 to £5,900

UNITED KINGDOM SEEDS EXECUTIVE

Prof. O. G. Williams *(Chairman),*★ D. J. Alexander; J. Cormack; H. A. S. Doughty; J. Gray, O.B.E.; T.D.; Prof. J. D. Ivins; J. D. Palmer; A. F. Shaw.
Secretary, J. A. Colmer *(S.E.O.)*
★ At Steel House.

H.M. LAND REGISTRY

Lincoln's Inn Fields, W.C.2
[01-405 3488]

The registration of title to land was first introduced in England and Wales by the Land Registry Act, 1862. Many changes have been made to the original system by subsequent legislation and H.M. Land Registry operates today under the Land Registration Acts, 1925 to 1971. The object of registering title to land is for dealings with it to be made more simple and economical. This is achieved by maintaining a register of land owners whose title is guaranteed by the State and by providing simple forms for the transfer, mortgage and other dealings with real property. Under the Land Registration Act 1966, the voluntary first registration of land in non-compulsory areas was severely curtailed in order to facilitate an accelerated programme for the extension of the compulsory system to cover all the built-up areas of the country as soon as possible. The intention is that registration of title shall ultimately be universal throughout England and Wales. Nevertheless, a great deal of land was formerly registered voluntarily in non-compulsory areas and it is still possible to register building estates, upon certain conditions, throughout the country. A great deal of land in non-compulsory areas is therefore already registered. H.M. Land Registry is administered under the Lord Chancellor by th Chief Land Registrar and the work is decentr_ ized to a number of regional offices. The Chief Land Registrar is also responsible for the Land Charges Department and the Agricultural Credits Department.

Headquarters Office

Chief Land Registrar, R. B. Roper.......£14,000
Deputy Chief Land Registrar, A. G. W. James
£12,000
Chief Assistant (Establishment Officer), K. E. Aris
£11,320
Land Registrar, C. N. T. Waterer £9,033 to £11,000
Assistant Land Registrars, P. A. Meehan; C. J. West
£6,625 to £8,750
Assistant Secretaries, H. R. Goose *(Controller North);* B. M. White *(Controller South)* £8,650 to £11,000
Senior Principal (Management Services), J. L. Memory
£7,750 to £9,350
Principals, R. G. W. Brazier; T. Chipperfield; R. J. Fenn; P. Gittings, I.S.O.; J. J. Manthorpe; E. F. Martin; J. B. Plail..........£5,680 to £7,450

Establishment and Accounts

Deputy Establishment Officer, A. M. Wallace
£7,750 to £9,350
Chief Accountant, K. Batey.....£5,680 to £7,450
Finance Officer, J. H. Haynes....£5,680 to £7,450

Croydon District Land Registry

Sunley House, Bedford Park, Croydon
[01-686 8833]

District Land Registrar, M. H. Baines
£9,033 to £11,000
Land Registrar, U. Davidson...£9,033 to £11,000
Assistant Land Registrars, A. E. Farwell; R. G. Glenister; S. Jacey........£6,625 to £8,750
Area Manager, A. W. Pardey...£7,750 to £9,350

Durham District Land Registry

Aykley Heads, Durham
[Durham 61361]

District Land Registrar, E. J. Pryer
£9,033 to £11,000
Assistant Land Registrars, P. H. Curnow; J. L. Hinchliffe; H. M. Taylor
£6,625 to £8,750
Area Manager, D. R. H. Grigg..£5,680 to £7,450

Gloucester District Land Registry

Twyver House, Bruton Way, Gloucester
[Gloucester: 28666]

District Land Registrar, C. W. K. Donaldson
£9,033 to £11,000
Assistant Land Registrars, D. M. J. Moss; F. Quickfall; A. E. H. Sladen.............£6,625 to £8,750
Area Manager, H. J. Wiles......£7,750 to £9,350

Harrow District Land Registry

Lyon House, Harrow, Harrow, Middlesex
[01-427 8811]

District Land Registrar, A. O. Viney
£9,033 to £11,000
Assistant Land Registrars, Miss J. E. Bagshaw; A. D. Dewar; Miss A. M. Phillips
£6,625 to £8,750
Area Manager, A. G. Caudle....£7,750 to £9,350

Lytham District Land Registry

Birkenhead House, Lytham St. Annes, Lancs.
[Lytham: 736999]

District Land Registrar, R. E. Shorrocks
£9,033 to £11,000
Land Registrar, B. E. Berry....£9,033 to £11,000
Assistant Land Registrars, J.F.Bamber; K. L. Charles; J. B. Duckworth; L. D. Jefferies; Mrs. D. C. Palmer; J. B. Rhodes £6,625 to £8,760
Area Manager, P. J. Dix........£7,750 to £9,350

Nottingham District Land Registry
Chalfont Drive, Nottingham
[Nottingham: 291111]
District Land Registrar, D. L. Groom
£9,033 to £11,000
Land Registrar, N. U. A. Hogg. £9,033 to £11,000
Assistant Land Registrars, F. G. Adamson; Miss C.
M. Bannister; P. D. Smith... £6,625 to £8,750
Area Manager, C. Hotham...... £7,750 to £9,350

Plymouth District Land Registry
Railway Offices, North Road, Plymouth, Devon
[Plymouth 69381]
District Land Registrar, W. D. Hosking
£9,033 to £11,000
Assistant Land Registrar, E. G. Thomas
£6,625 to £8,750
Area Manager, E. W. Hannam.. £5,680 to £7,450

Land Charges and Agricultural Credit
Department,
Burrington Way, Plymouth
[Plymouth: 779 831]
Superintendent of Land Charges, D. I. Whyte
£5,680 to £7,450
Head of Computer Services Division, R. B. Parker
£7,750 to £9,350
Principal, A. A. Restorick...... £5,680 to £7,450

Stevenage District Land Registry
Brickdale House, Danestrete, Stevenage, Herts.
[Stevenage: 4488]
District Land Registrar, G. A. Weddell
£9,033 to £11,000
Assistant Land Registrars, W. W. Budden; H. S.
Early; F. G. D. Emler; D. M. T. Mullett
£6,625 to £8,750
Area Manager, A. C. Forrester.. £7,750 to £9,350

Swansea District Land Registry
37, The Kingsway, Swansea, Glam.
[Swansea 50971]
District Land Registrar, A. P. Roberts
£9,033 to £11,000
Assistant Land Registrar, J. L. Inskip
£6,625 to £8,750
Area Manager, J. O. Sheldon (acting)
£5,680 to £7,450

Tunbridge Wells District Land Registry
Curtis House, Tunbridge Wells, Kent
[Tunbridge Wells 26141]
District Land Registrar, D. P. Chivers
£9,033 to £11,000
Land Registrar, P. Kendall..... £9,033 to £11,000
Assistant Land Registrars, J. S. R. Bevington;
R. H. Ellis; A. Gould; D. G. Thomas;
£6,625 to £8,750
Area Manager, J. C. Eames, M.B.E. £7,750 to £9,350

LAW OFFICERS' DEPARTMENT
Attorney-General's Chambers,
Royal Courts of Justice, W.C.1.
The Law Officers of the Crown for England and
Wales (the Attorney-General and the Solicitor-
General) represent the Crown in courts of justice,
advise Government departments and represent
them in court. The Attorney-General has also
certain administrative functions, including super-
vision of the Director of Public Prosecutions.
Attorney General, THE RT. HON. SAMUEL CHARLES
SILKIN, Q.C., M.P.................. £14,500
Parliamentary Private Secretary, D. Anderson, M.P.
Solicitor General, PETER KINGSLEY ARCHER, Q.C.,
M.P............................... £11,000
Parliamentary Private Secretary, J. W. Rooker, M.P.
Parliamentary Secretary, A. Davidson, M.P. £5,500
Legal Secretary, W. C. Beckett........ £12,000
Asst. Legal Sec., M. G. de Winton, C.B.E., M.C.
£12,000

LIBRARIES

THE BRITISH LIBRARY
Store Street, W.C.1
[01-636 0755]
The British Library was established on July 1,

1973, under the British Library Act, 1972, to
provide, on a national scale, comprehensive reference, lending, bibliographic and other services
based on its vast collections of books, manuscripts
maps, music, periodicals and other material.
The Library was created by bringing together
under a management Board a number of national
organizations to form three main Divisions. The
Reference Division comprises the former library
departments of the British Museum including the
Newspaper Library at Colindale and Science
Reference Library. The Lending Division comprises the former National Lending Library for
Science and Technology and the former National
Central Library. The Bibliographic Services Division incorporates the British National Bibliography
and the (former British Museum) Copyright Receipt Office. There is also a Research and Development Department, and a Central Administration.
The Reference Division contains more than
9,000,000 printed books, about 80,000 Western and
35,000 Oriental manuscripts, and outstanding collections of newspapers, official papers, papyri, charters,
seals, maps, music and postage stamps. Admission
to the reading rooms for research is by ticket only.
The Science Reference Library is the principal
public reference library in the United Kingdom for
contemporary literature of science and technology,
and here no reader's ticket is necessary.
The Lending Division in Yorkshire operates a
rapid postal loan or photocopy service for organizations and currently receives about 2,500,000
requests a year. Individuals should apply through
their local libraries. The stock contains some
2,350,000 volumes of books and periodicals, about
1,500,000 documents in microfilm, and large
quantities of semi-published materials such as
reports, translations and theses.

BOARD MEMBERS
Chairman, The Viscount Eccles, P.C., K.C.V.O.
Deputy Chairman and Chief Executive, H. T. Hook-
way.
Directors General, Reference Division, D. T.
Richnell, C.B.E.; Bibliographic Services Division,
R. E. Coward; Lending Division, M. B. Line.
Part-time Members, The Lord Adeane, P.C., G.C.B.,
G.C.V.O. (appointed by Her Majesty The Queen);
J. W. Barrett, C.B.E.; Sir John Brown, C.B.E.; Sir
Denis Hamilton, D.S.O.; Mrs. Alison Munro,
C.B.E.; A. E. Ritchie; J. S. Watson; Prof. Glan-
mor Williams; A. Wilson

CENTRAL ADMINISTRATION
Secretary to the Board and Head of Central Adminis-
tration (vacant)
REFERENCE DIVISION
Reference Division, Gt. Russell St., London, W.C.1
[01-636 1544]
Science Reference Library
25 Southampton Buildings, London, W.C.2
[01-405 8721]
and
10 Porchester Gardens, London, W.2
[01-405 8721]
Newspaper Library, Colindale Avenue, N.W.9
[01-205 6039]
Keepers, Department of Printed Books, J. L. Wood;
R. J. Fulford.
Keeper, Department of Manuscripts, D. P. Waley.
Keeper, Department of Oriental Manuscripts and
Printed Books, G. E. Marrison.
Director of Science Reference Library, M. W. Hill.

LENDING DIVISION
Boston Spa, Wetherby, West Yorks.
[0937 843434]
Executive Director, K. Barr.

BIBLIOGRAPHIC SERVICES DIVISION
Store Street, W.C.1
[01-636 0755]
Director of Copyright and English Language Services,
J. Downing.

RESEARCH AND DEVELOPMENT DEPARTMENT
Sheraton House, Great Chapel Street, W.1
[01-734 6767]
Director, J. C. Gray.

PRESS AND PUBLIC RELATIONS SECTION
Store Street, W.C.1
[01-636 0755]

NATIONAL LIBRARY OF SCOTLAND
George IV Bridge, Edinburgh
[01-226 4531]
Open free. Reading Room, weekdays, 9.30 a.m.
to 8.30 p.m. Saturdays 9.30 to 1. Map Room,
weekdays, 9.30 to 5 p.m.; Saturdays, 9.30 to
1. Exhibition, weekdays, 9.30 a.m. to 5 p.m.
Saturdays, 9.30 to 1; Sundays, 2 to 5.
The Library, which had been founded as the
Advocates' Library in 1682, became the National
Library of Scotland by Act of Parliament in 1925.
It continues to share the rights conferred by succes-
sive Copyright Acts since 1710. Its collections of
printed books and MSS., augmented by purchase
and gift, are very large and it has an unrivalled
Scottish collection. The present building was
opened by H.M. the Queen in 1956.
The Reading Room is for reference and research
which cannot conveniently be pursued elsewhere.
Admission is by ticket issued to an approved
applicant.
Chairman of the Trustees, M. F. Strachan, M.B.E.
Librarian and Secretary to the Trustees, E. F. D.
Roberts, Ph.D. £11,000
Secretary of the Library, B. G. Hutton
£7,151 to £8,750
Assistant Keepers, First Class, M. A. Begg; W. B.
Jay; A. M. Marchbank, Ph.D. . £4,404 to £7,100
Keepers of Printed Books, J. R. Seaton £8,550 to
£9,798); W. H. Brown, E.R.D.; A. M. Cain,
Ph.D.; R. Donaldson, Ph.D. . . . . £7,151 to £8,750
Assistant Keepers, First Class, T. A. F. Cherry; R.
Duce; Alison A. Harvey Wood; Alexia F. Howe;
W. A. Kelly; I. D. McGowan; J. B. McKeeman;
Ann Matheson; J. Morris; I. R. M. Mowat;
Margaret Wilkes. . . . . £4,404 to £7,109
Senior Research Assistants, Margaret E. Cramb;
Ruth I. Hope; Christine E. G. Wright
£4,185 to £5,778
Keepers of Manuscripts, J. S. Ritchie; T. I. Rae, Ph.D.
£7,151 to £8,750
Assistant Keepers, First Class, A. S. Bell; P. M.
Cadell; I. C. Cunningham; P. Kelly; I. F. Mac-
Iver; S. M. Simpson; Elspeth D. Yeo
£4,404 to £7,109

THE NATIONAL LIBRARY OF WALES
LLYFRGELL GENEDLAETHOL CYMRU
Aberystwyth
Readers' room open on weekdays, 9.30 a.m. to
6 p.m. (Saturdays, 5 p.m.); closed on Sundays.
Admission by Reader's Ticket.
Founded by Royal Charter, 1907, and maintained by annual grant from the Treasury. One of
the six libraries entitled to most privileges under
Copyright Act. Contains nearly 2,000,000 printed
books, 30,000 manuscripts, 3,500,000 deeds and
documents, and numerous maps, prints and draw-
ings. Specializes in manuscripts and books relating
to Wales and the Celtic peoples. Repository for
pre-1858 Welsh probate records. Approved by the
Master of the Rolls as a repository for manorial
records and tithe documents, and by the Lord
Chancellor for certain legal records. Bureau of the
Regional Libraries Scheme for Wales.
Librarian, D. Jenkins.
Secretary, D. B. Lloyd.
Heads of Departments, G. M. Griffiths (*Manuscripts
and Records*); M. I. Williams, Ph.D. (*Printed
Books*); Mydrim L. Timothy (*Prints, Drawings
and Maps*).

LOCAL GOVERNMENT. *See* **DEPARTMENT
OF THE ENVIRONMENT**

LONDON TRANSPORT EXECUTIVE
55 Broadway, S.W.1
[01-222 5600]
The Greater London Council is responsible for
the overall policy and financial control of London
Transport, but the Executive is wholly responsible
for the day-to-day management and operation.
Chairman, The Rt. Hon. Kenneth Robinson
£19,600
Deputy Chairman and Chief Executive, R. Bennett
£15,600
Managing Director (Railways), R. M. Robbins
£14,100
Members, J. G. Glendinning, O.B.E.; W. W. Maxwell; D. A. Quarmby; J. C. F. Cameron (*each
£12,100*); S. J. Barton; Sir Peter Masefield (*part-
time*). . . . . *each* £1,000
Chief Secretary, P. E. Garbutt, M.B.E.

LORD ADVOCATE'S DEPARTMENT
Fielden House, 10 Great College Street,
Westminster, S.W.1
The Law Officers for Scotland are the Lord
Advocate and the Solicitor-General for Scotland.
The Lord Advocate's Department is responsible
for drafting Scottish legislation, for providing legal
advice to other departments on Scottish questions
and for assistance to the Law Officers for Scotland
in certain of their legal duties.
Lord Advocate, The Rt. Hon. Ronald King Murray,
Q.C., M.P. £11,000
Solicitor-General for Scotland, J. H. McCluskey, Q.C.
£7,750
Legal Secretary and First Parliamentary Draftsman,
J. M. Moran, Q.C. £14,000
Deputy Legal Secretary and Parliamentary Draftsman,
A. C. B. Reid. £12,000
Asst. Legal Secs. and Parlty. Draftsmen, N. J. Adam-
son; Sir George Mitchell, C.B., Q.C.; J. F. Wal-
lace. . . . . £9,798 to £11,440
Junior Legal Secs. and Asst. Parlty. Draftsmen, J. C.
McCluskie; G. M. Clark; Miss J. M. Daly; D. J.
S. Duncan. . . . . £6,625 to £8,750

LORD GREAT CHAMBERLAIN'S OFFICE
House of Lords, S.W.1
[01-219 3100]
The Lord Great Chamberlain is a Great
Officer of State, the office being hereditary since
the grant of Henry I to the family of De Vere,
Earls of Oxford.
Lord Great Chamberlain, The Marquess of Chol-
mondeley, M.C.
Secretary to the Lord Great Chamberlain, Admiral Sir
Frank Twiss, K.C.B., D.S.C.
Clerks to the Lord Great Chamberlain, Lady Elizabeth
Barne; Miss G. Holland

LORD PRIVY SEAL
House of Lords
Lord Privy Seal and Leader of the House of Lords, THE
LORD SHEPHERD, P.C.
Private Secretary, N. B. J. Gurney.

OFFICE OF MANPOWER ECONOMICS
22 Kingsway, W.C.2
[01-405 5944]
The Office of Manpower Economics was set up
in 1970. It is an independent non-statutory organization which is responsible for providing a common
secretariat for three review bodies which advise on
sectors of public service pay for which no negotiating machinery is appropriate: these are the Review
Body on Top Salaries which covers the Higher
Judiciary, the Chairmen and members of the
nationalized industry Boards, the senior grades of
the Higher Civil Service and senior officers of the
armed forces; Pay Review Body on Armed Forces
Pay, which advises on the pay and allowances of all
ranks up to and including Brigadier and equivalent;
and the Review Body on Doctors' and Dentists'
Remuneration, which advises on the remuneration
of doctors and dentists in the National Health

Service. It also provides the secretariat for committees of inquiry.
Director, Miss J. F. H. Orr.
Chief Statistician, R. F. Burch.

MANPOWER SERVICES COMMISSION
Selkirk House, 166 High Holborn, W.C.1
[01–836 1213]

The Manpower Services Commission was established under the Employment and Training Act 1973, and administers the employment and training services previously provided by the Department of Employment, through two executive arms; the Employment Service Agency and the Training Services Agency. The Commission also advises the Government on manpower policies, and comprises representatives of employers, unions, local government and education. The Commission's chief functions are to help people train for and obtain jobs which satisfy their aspirations and abilities, and to help employers find suitable workers.

Chairman, R. O'Brien.................£16,580
Deputy Chairman, D. A. C. Dewdney, C.B.E.
Members, M. O. Bury, O.B.E.; D. J. Docherty; K. Graham, O.B.E.; R. L. Helmore; D. McGarvey, C.B.E.; V. G. Paige; C. H. Urwin; Mrs. E. A. Yates, C.B.E.;
Director, J. Cassels.....................£14,000
Director of Manpower, Intelligence and Planning, G. Reid..............................£12,000
Finance Officer, I. M. Miller....£8,650 to £11,000
Head of Information, A. P. Dignum.......£8,500
Head of Planning, G. Holland..£8,650 to £11,000

MEDICAL RESEARCH COUNCIL
20 Park Crescent, W.1
[01–636 5422]

Members, The Duke of Northumberland, K.G., P.C., T.D., F.R.S. (*Chairman*); Sir John Gray, Sc.D., F.R.S. (*Deputy Chairman and Secretary*); Sir Douglas Black, M.D., F.R.C.P.; Sir John Brotherston, M.D., F.R.C.P.E., F.R.S.E.; Prof. A. J. Buller; Sir Arnold Burgen, M.D., F.R.C.P., F.R.S.; Prof. A. C. Dornhorst, M.D., F.R.C.P.; K. P. Duncan; Prof. A. P. M. Forrest, M.D., F.R.C.S.; The Earl of Halsbury, F.R.S.; H. Kay, Ph.D.; Helen Muir, M.A., D.Phil.; Prof. D. C. Phillips, Ph.D., F.R.S.; Cicely M. S. Saunders, O.B.E., F.R.C.P.; Prof. J.N. Walton, T.D., M.D., D.Sc., F.R.C.P.; Sir Henry Yellowlees, K.C.B., F.R.C.P.
Second Secretary, S. G. Owen, M.D.
Administrative Secretary, J. G. Duncan.

Neurobiology and Mental Health Board
Chairman, Prof. A. J. Buller

Physiological Systems and Disorders Board
Chairman, Prof. A. C. Dornhorst, M.D., F.R.C.P.

Environmental Medicine Research Policy Committee
Chairman, H. Kay, Ph.D.

HEADQUARTERS OFFICE

Research Programmes Division A
Principal Medical Officer, Katherine Lévy.
Senior Medical Officers, M. J. Fisher; D. M. G. Murphy.
Senior Principal Scientific Officers, Bronwen Loder, D.Phil.; T. Vickers, Ph.D.
Medical Officers, June R. Hill; Soraja Ramaswamy.
Principal Scientific Officers, J. Alwen, Ph.D.; J. E. Dowman, Ph.D.; K. Gibson, Ph.D.; Ann Horn; A. B. Stone, D.Phil.; J. Woodland-Galloway, Ph.D.

Research Programmes Division B
Principal Medical Officer, Sheila Howarth.
Senior Medical Officers, H. W. Bunjé, M.D.; F.R.C.P.; P. J. Chapman; Barbara Rashbass.

Medical Officers, Enid Bennett; Joan Box; A. J. G. Dickens; Helen N. Duke, Ph.D.; D. Sturrock.
Principal Scientific Officers, M. B. Kemp, Ph.D.; A. Victoria Harrison, D.Phil.

Commissioned Research Group
Senior Principal Medical Officer, R. C. Norton.
Senior Medical Officer, Joan Faulkner.

Secretariat and Universities Division
Head of Division, C. A. Kirkman.
Secretariat, J. H. Morris, Ph.D.
Universities and Grants, D. J. Cawthron.

Administrative Division
Head of Division, J. G. Duncan.
Assistant Secretaries, J. M. Jeffs; D. Noble; F. Rushton.

Establishment and Management Services
Head of Section, Norma Morris.

National Institute for Medical Research
Mill Hill, N.W.7
[01–959 3666]
Director, Sir Arnold Burgen, M.D., F.R.C.P., F.R.S.

Clinical Research Centre
Watford Road, Harrow, Middlesex
[01–864 5311]
Director, Sir Graham Bull, M.D., F.R.C.P.

Research Units

Applied Psychology Unit, 15 Chaucer Road, Cambridge. *Director*, A. D. Baddeley, Ph.D.
Biochemical Parasitology Unit, Molteno Institute, Downing Street, Cambridge. *Director*, B. A. Newton, Ph.D.
Blood Group Reference Laboratory, Gatliff Road, S.W.1. *Director*, Carolyn Giles, Ph.D. (*acting*).
Blood Group Unit, University College, London, Wolfson House, 4 Stephenson Way, N.W.1 *Director*, Ruth Sanger, Ph.D., F.R.S.
Blood Pressure Unit, Western Infirmary, Glasgow. *Director*, A. F. Lever, F.R.C.P.
Brain Metabolism Unit, University Dept. of Pharmacology, 1 George Square, Edinburgh. *Director*, G. W. Ashcroft, D.Sc., F.R.C.P.E.
Cell Biophysics Unit, Dept. of Biophysics, King's College, 26–29 Drury Lane, W.C.2. *Hon. Director*, Prof. M. H. F. Wilkins, C.B.E., Ph.D., F.R.S.
Cell Mutation Unit, University of Sussex, Falmer, Brighton. *Director*, Prof. B. A. Bridges, Ph.D.
Cellular Immunology Unit, Sir William Dunn School of Pathology, Oxford. *Director*, Prof. J. L. Gowans, C.B.E., D.Phil., F.R.C.P., F.R.S.
Clinical and Population Cytogenetics Unit, Western General Hospital, Crewe Road, Edinburgh. *Director*, Prof. H. J. Evans, Ph.D., F.R.S.E.
Clinical Genetics Unit, Institute of Child Health, 30 Guilford Street, W.C.1. *Director*, Prof. C. O. Carter, D.M., F.R.C.P.
Clinical Oncology Unit, Medical School, Hills Road, Cambridge, *Hon. Director*, Prof. N. M. Bleehen, F.R.C.P.
Clinical Pharmacology Unit, University Department of Clinical Pharmacology, Radcliffe Infirmary, Oxford. *Hon. Director*, Prof. D. G. Grahame-Smith, Ph.D., F.R.C.P.
Clinical Psychiatry Unit. Graylingwell Hospital, Chichester, Sussex. *Director*, P. Sainsbury, M.D.
Cyclotron Unit, Hammersmith Hospital, Ducane Road, W.12. *Director*, D. D. Vonberg.
Demyelinating Diseases Unit, Newcastle General Hospital, Westgate Road, Newcastle-upon-Tyne. *Director*, H. M. Wisniewski, M.D., Ph.D.
Dental Unit, Dental School, Lower Maudlin Street, Bristol. *Hon. Director*, Prof. A. I. Darling, C.B.E., D.D.Sc.
Dental Epidemiology Unit, The London Hospital. Medical College, Turner Street, E.1. *Hon. Director*, Prof. G. L. Slack, C.B.E., T.D., D.D.S.

Unit on the Development and Integration of Behaviour, Subdept. of Animal Behaviour, Madingley, Cambridge. *Hon. Director*, Prof. R. A. Hinde, Sc.D., F.R.S.

Developmental Neurobiology Unit, M.R.C. Laboratories, Woodmansterne Road, Carshalton, Surrey. *Director*, R. Balázs, Dr.Med., Dr.Phil.

Developmental Psychology Unit, Drayton House, Gordon Street, W.C.1. *Director*, N. O'Connor, Ph.D.

Dunn Nutrition Unit, Milton Road, Cambridge. *Director*, R. G. Whitehead, Ph.D.

Unit for the Study of Environmental Factors in Mental and Physical Illness, London School of Economics and Political Science, 20 Hanway Place, W.1. *Director*, J. W. B. Douglas.

Environmental Hazards Unit, St. Bartholomew's Hospital Medical College, Charterhouse Square, E.C.1. *Director*, Prof. P. J. Lawther, D.Sc., F.R.C.P.

Environmental Physiology Unit, London School of Hygiene and Tropical Medicine, Keppel Street, W.C.1. *Director*, Prof. J. S. Weiner, D.Sc.

Epidemiology and Medical Care Unit, Northwick Park Hospital, Harrow, Middx. *Director*, T. W. Meade.

Epidemiology Unit (South Wales), 4 Richmond Road, Cardiff. *Director*, P. C. Elwood, M.D.

Unit for Epidemiological Studies in Psychiatry, University of Psychiatry, Royal Edinburgh Hospital, Morningside Park, Edinburgh. *Director*, N. B. Kreitman, M.D.

Experimental Haematology Unit, St. Mary's Hospital Medical School, W.2. *Director*, Prof. P. L. Mollison, M.D., F.R.C.P., F.R.S.

Unit on the Experimental Pathology of Skin, The Medical School, The University, Birmingham. *Director*, C. N. D. Cruickshank, M.D.

Gastroenterology Unit, Central Middlesex Hospital, Park Royal, N.W.10. *Director*, E. N. Rowlands, M.D., F.R.C.P.

Hearing and Balance Unit, Institute of Neurology, National Hospital, Queen Square, W.C.1. *Director*, J. D. Hood, D.Sc.

Human Biochemical Genetics Unit, Galton Laboratory University College London, Wolfson House, 4 Stephenson Way, N.W.1. *Hon. Director*, Prof. H. Harris, M.D., F.R.C.P., F.R.S.

Immunochemistry Unit, University Department of Biochemistry, South Parks Road, Oxford. *Hon. Director*, Prof. R. R. Porter, Ph.D., F.R.S.

Industrial Injuries and Burns Unit, Birmingham Accident Hospital, Bath Row, Birmingham. *Director*, J. P. Bull, C.B.E., M.D., F.R.C.P.

M.R.C. Laboratories, The Gambia Fajara, The Gambia, W. Africa. *Director*, R. S. Bray, D.Sc.

M.R.C. Laboratories, Jamaica, University of the West Indies, Mona, Kingston, Jamaica. *Director*, G. R. Serjeant, M.D.

Laboratory Animals Centre, M.R.C. Laboratories, Woodmansterne Road, Carshalton, Surrey. *Director*, J. Bleby.

Leukaemia Unit, Royal Postgraduate Medical School, Ducane Road, W.12. *Hon. Director*, Prof. D. A. G. Galton, M.D., F.R.C.P.

Lipid Metabolism Unit, Hammersmith Hospital, Ducane Road, W.12. *Director*, N. B. Myant, D.M., F.R.C.P.

Mammalian Development Unit, University College London, Wolfson House, 4 Stephenson Way, N.W.1. *Director*, Anne McLaren, D.Phil., F.R.S.

Mammalian Genome Unit, Dept. of Zoology, University of Edinburgh, West Mains Road, Edinburgh. *Director*, Prof. P. M. B. Walker, Ph.D.

Medical Sociology Unit, Institute of Medical Sociology, Westburn Road, Aberdeen. *Director*, Prof. R. Illsley, Ph.D.

Unit for Metabolic Studies in Psychiatry, University Dept. of Psychiatry, Middlewood Hospital, P.O. Box 134, Sheffield. *Hon. Director*, Prof. F. A. Jenner, Ph.D.

Mineral Metabolism Unit, The General Infirmary, Great George Street, Leeds. *Director*, Prof. B.E.C. Nordin, M.D., D.SC., F.R.C.P.

Laboratory of Molecular Biology, University Postgraduate Medical School, Hills Road, Cambridge. *Chairman of Governing Board*, M. F. Perutz, C.H., C.B.E., Ph.D., F.R.S.

Unit on Neural Mechanisms of Behaviour, 3 Malet Place, W.C.1. *Director*, I. S. Russell, Ph.D.

Neurochemical Pharmacology Unit, University Dept. of Pharmacology, Hills Road, Cambridge. *Director*, L. L. Iversen, Ph.D.

Neurological Prostheses Unit, Institute of Psychiatry, De Crespigny Park, Denmark Hill, S.E.5. *Hon. Director*, Prof. G. S. Brindley, M.D., F.R.C.P. F.R.S.

Neuropharmacology Unit, The Medical School, Birmingham 15. *Hon. Director*, Prof. P. B. Bradley, D.Sc.

Perceptual and Cognitive Performance Unit, Experimental Psychology Laboratory, University of Sussex, Falmer, Brighton. *Director*, Prof. W. P. Colquhoun, Ph.D.

Pneumoconiosis Unit, Llandough Hospital, Penarth, Glam. *Director*, P. C. Elmes, M.D., F.R.C.P.

Radiobiology Unit, Harwell, Didcot, Oxon. *Director*, R. H. Mole, F.R.C.P.

Reproduction and Growth Unit, Princess Mary Maternity Hospital, Newcastle-upon-Tyne, *Director*, Prof. A. M. Thomson.

Reproductive Biology Unit, 2 Forrest Road, Edinburgh. *Director*, Prof. R. V. Short, Sc.D., F.R.S.

Rheumatism Unit, Canadian Red Cross Memorial Hospital, Taplow, Maidenhead, Berks. *Director*, E. J. Holborow, M.D.

Social and Applied Psychology Unit, Dept. of Psychology, University of Sheffield. *Director*, P. B. Warr, Ph.D.

Social Psychiatry Unit, Institute of Psychiatry, De Crespigny Park, Denmark Hill, S.E.5. *Director*, Prof. J. K. Wing, M.D., Ph.D.

Statistical Research and Services Unit, University College, Hospital Medical School, 115 Gower Street, W.C.1. *Director*, I. Sutherland, D.Phil.

Toxicology Unit, M.R.C. Laboratories, Woodmansterne Road, Carshalton, Surrey *Director*, T. A. Conners, D.Sc.

Unit for Laboratory Studies in Tuberculosis, Royal Postgraduate Medical School, Ducane Road, W.12. *Hon. Director*, Prof. D. A. Mitchison, F.R.C.P.

Tuberculosis and Chest Diseases Unit, Brompton Hospital, Fulham Road, S.W.3. *Director*, W. Fox, C.M.G., M.D. F.R.C.P.

Virology Unit, Institute of Virology, Church Street, Glasgow. *Hon. Director*, Prof. J. H. Subak-Sharpe, Ph.D., F.R.S.E.

Vision Unit, School of Biological Sciences, University of Sussex, Falmer, Brighton. *Director*, Prof. H. J. A. Dartnall, D.Sc.

METRICATION BOARD
22 Kingsway, W.C.2
[01–242 6828]

Chairman, The Lord Orr-Ewing, O.B.E.
Deputy Chairman, J. M. Wood, O.B.E.
Members, M. A. Abrams, Ph.D.; B. N. Baxter, Ph.D.; Miss F. K. College, M.B.E.; E. Cust; D. H. Darbishire; J. C. Dewar; J. M. Ferguson, C.B.E.; D. Hobman; Miss D. D. Hyams, O.B.E.; F. Lacey (*Director*), D. M. Landau; Prof. M. L. McGlashan; H. P. Scanlon; Mrs. A. Stanley, O.B.E.; Mrs. J. Upward.
Secretary, A. B. Clarke.

THE ROYAL MINT
Llantrisant, nr. Pontyclun,
Mid-Glamorgan
[0443–222111]

Master Works and Warden, The Chancellor of the Exchequer (*ex officio*).
Deputy Master and Comptroller, J. R. Christie*.
Secretary and Establishment Officer, E. W. Powell-Chandler . . . . £7,750 to £9,350
Director of Marketing and Sales, A. J. Dowling, O.B.E., D.F.C.* . . . . £8,650 to £11,000

Director of Production, R. A. Yates £11,000
Superintendent, E. J. Howlett ... £8,650 to £9,798
Senior Principal (Financial Controller) D. C. Snell
£7,750 to £9,350
Principals, A, R. W. Letherington*; H. L. Em-
den* ; B. Hatcher; M. J. Mansley.
£5,680 to £7,450
Principal Professional and Technology Officers, E. M.
Phillips; R. W. Gravenor; E. F. Butler
£6,280 to £7,450
Principal Scientific Officer, I. Hepburn (*Quality
Manager*).................. £5,514 to £7,205
Chief Engraver, E. Sewell ...... £5,871 to £6,463

* Stationed at Royal Mint, Tower Hill, E.C.3
[01-488-3424].

MONOPOLIES AND MERGERS COMMISSION

New Court, 48 Carey Street, W.C.2
[01-831 6111]

The Commission was established under the
Monopolies and Restrictive Practices (Inquiry and
Control) Act 1948 as the Monopolies and Restrictive Practices Commission and was reconstituted
on subsequent occasions. It became the Monopolies and Mergers Commission when the Fair
Trading Act, 1973, came into operation on November 1, 1973. The Commission has the duty of
investigating and reporting on questions referred to
it in accordance with the Act with respect to (a) the
existence or possible existence of monopoly situa-
tions not registrable under the Restrictive Trade
Practices Act, 1956, as extended by the 1973 Act,
and relating to the supply of goods or services to
the United Kingdom or part of the United Kingdom or to the supply of goods for export; (b) the
transfer of a newspaper or newspaper's assets; (c)
the creation or possible creation of a merger
situation qualifying for investigation within the
meaning of the Act.

In monopoly references (except those " limited
to the facts ") and in merger references it is the duty
of the Commission to report on the effect of the
facts which they find on the public interest and
to consider and, if they think fit, to recommend
the action to be taken to remedy or prevent adverse
effects. In addition the Fair Trading Act, 1973,
provides for references to the Commission on the
general effect on the public interest of specified
monopoly or other uncompetitive practices and of
restrictive labour practices.

Chairman, J. G. Le Quesne, Q.C.......... £16,350
Deputy Chairmen, Sir Max Brown, K.C.B., C.M.G.
(*part time*) £4,320); E. L. Richards, C.B.E., M.C.,
T.D. (*part-time*) £6,480
Members, G. F. Ashford, O.B.E.; R. G. Aspray;
Prof. T. Barna, C.B.E., Ph.D.; Sir Dallas Bernard,
Bt.; Lady Bowden; J. S. Copp; Sir Roger Falk,
O.B.E.; C. J. M. Hardie; F. E. Jones, M.B.E., Ph.D.,
D.Sc., F.R.S.; T. P. Lyons; Mrs. C. M. Miles; R.
G. Opie, C.B.E.; C. T. H. Plant, C.B.E.; S. A
Robinson; J. S. Sadler; M'ss R. Stephen, M.B.E.;
Prof. H. Street, F.B.A.; Prof. B. S. Yamey, C.B.E.
each £2,300
Secretary, Miss Y. Lovat Williams.

MUSEUMS
STANDING COMMISSION ON MUSEUMS AND GALLERIES

2 Carlton Gardens, S.W.1
[01-930 0995]

First appointed Feb. 11, 1931. The functions of
the Commission are:—(1) To advise generally on
questions relevant to the most effective development of the National Institutions as a whole and on
any specific questions which may be referred to
them from time to time; (2) to promote co-
operation between the National Institutions themselves and between the National and Provincial
Institutions; (3) to stimulate the generosity and
direct the efforts of those who aspire to become
public benefactors.

Chairman, The Earl of Rosse, K.B.E., F.S.A.
Members, Sir Frank Claringbull, Ph.D.; Sir Trench-
ard Cox, C.B.E., F.R.S.A., F.S.A.; Sir Arthur Drew,
K.C.B.; Prof. I. Ll. Foster, F.S.A.; Prof. Sir Ernst
Gombrich, C.B.E., Ph.D., F.B.A., F.S.A.; Prof. B. R.
Morris, D.Phil.; Sir Terence Morrison-Scott,
D.S.C., D.Sc.; Sir John Pilcher, K.C.M.G.; The Earl
of Plymouth; P. F. Scott; F. J. Stott, O.B.E.; Sir
Charles Wilson; Sir Duncan Wilson, G.C.M.G.
Secretary, A. D. Heskett, M.B.E.

THE BRITISH MUSEUM

Great Russell Street, W.C.1
[01-636 1555]

Antiquities Department: Egyptian, Greek and
Roman, Mediæval and Later, Oriental, Prehistoric
and Roman-British Western Asiatic; also, Coins
and Medals, Prints and Drawing, Ethnography.
Main entrance, Great Russell Street, W.C.1; *North
entrance,* Montague Place, W.C.1. Open weekdays
(including Bank Holidays) 10 to 5 and Sundays 2.30
to 6. Closed on Good Friday, Christmas Eve,
Christmas Day, Boxing Day and New Year's Day.
The ethnographical collections are displayed in
The Museum of Mankind at 6 Burlington Gardens,
W.1. Opening times as above.

The British Museum may be said to date from
1753, when Parliament granted funds to purchase
the collections of Sir Hans Sloane and the Harleian
manuscripts, and for their proper housing and
maintenance. The building (Montague House)
was opened in 1759. The present buildings were
erected between 1823 and the present day, and the
original collection has increased to its present
dimensions by gifts and purchases. The administrative expenses were estimated at £5,030,000 in
1976–77, and were met by a vote under " Museums,
Galleries and the Arts ", Class X of the Civil
Estimates. The constitution of the British Museum
was revised under the terms of the British Museum
Act, 1963.

Under the provisions of the British Library Act
1972 and the British Library Act (Appointed Day)
Order 1973, the Library Departments of the British
Museum were transferred on July 1, 1973, from the
responsibility of the Trustees of the British Museum
to that of the British Library Board and became
part of the British Library.

BOARD OF TRUSTEES

Appointed by the Sovereign: H.R.H. The Duke of
Gloucester. *Appointed by the Prime Minister:*
The Lord Trevelyan, K.G., G.C.M.G., C.I.E., O.B.E
(*Chairman*); The Lord Annan, O.B.E.; Prof. Sir
Misha Black, O.B.E.; The Viscount Boyd of
Merton, P.C., C.H.; The Lord Boyle of Hands-
worth, P.C.; Sir Arthur Drew, K.C.B.; The Lord
Fletcher, P.C., LL.D.; Prof. Sir Ernst Gombrich,
C.B.E., Ph.D., F.B.A., F.S.A.; Prof. L. C. B. Gower,
M.B.E., F.B.A.; E. T. Hall, D.Phil.; Sir Denis
Hamilton, D.S.O.; Simon Hornby; Sir Richard
Thompson, Bt.; The Lord Trend, P.C., G.C.B.,
C.V.O.
*Nominated by the Royal Society, Royal Academy,
British Academy and Society of Antiquaries of London:*
Sir John Kendrew, C.B.E. (*Royal Society*); Miss
Elizabeth Frink, C.B.E., A.R.A. (*Royal Academy*);
Sir Max Mallowan, C.B.E., D.Litt., F.B.A., F.S.A.
(*British Academy*); Prof. J. G. D. Clark, C.B.E.,
SC.D., F.B.A. (*Society of Antiquaries*).
Appointed by the Trustees of the British Museum: The
Lord Ashby, D.Sc., F.R.S.; The Earl of Drogheda,
K.G., K.B.E.; Prof. L. B. Gowing, C.B.E., D.Sc.,
F.R.S.; Dame Kathleen Kenyon, D.B.E., D.Litt.,
L.H.D., F.B.A., F.S.A.; Sir Edmund Leach, Ph.D.,
F.B.A.

OFFICERS

Director (vacant)
Deputy Director, Maysie F. Webb
£10,180 to £11,000
Secretary, G. B. Morris........ £7,151 to £8,750
Assistant Secretary, Barbara J. Youngman
£4,404 to £7,109

Administrative Assistant, Jean M. Rankine
£4,404 to £7,109
Assistant Keeper, Information Services, Marilyn R. Bruce-Mitford..............£4,404 to £7,109
Education Officer, Margaret Lyttelton
£7,151 to £8,750
Design Officer, Margaret Hall, O.B.E.
£4,404 to £7,109
Senior Principal, C. W. Berry ... £7,750 to £9,350
Principals, J. F. W. Ryde; R. A. J. French
£5,680 to £7,450
Senior Executive Officers, G. E. Cooper; F. T. Jones: D. A. Thomas..............£4,900 to £5,900
Guide Lecturer, K. P. Whitehorn
£4,185 to £5,778
Keeper of Prints and Drawings, J. A. G. Gere
£8,650 to £9,798
Deputy Keepers, P. H. Hulton; J. K. Rowlands
£7,151 to £8,750
Assistant Keepers, Frances A. Carey; N. J. L. Turner
£4,404 to £7,109
Keeper of Coins and Medals, G. K. Jenkins
£8,650 to £9,798
Deputy Keepers, R. A. G. Carson; J. P. C. Kent
£7,151 to £8,750
Assistant Keepers, M. G. Powell-Jones; Marion M. Archibald; N. M. Lowick; M. J. Price
£4,404 to £7,109
Keeper of Egyptian Antiquities, T. G. H. James
£8,650 to £9,798
Assistant Keepers, W. V. Davies; M. L. Bierbrier; A. J. Spencer..............£4,404 to £7,109
Keeper of Western Antiquities, E. Sollberger
£8,650 to £9,798
Deputy Keeper, T. C. Mitchell.. £7,151 to £9,798
Assistant Keepers, J. E. Curtis; C. B. F. Walker
£4,404 to £7,109
Keeper of Greek and Roman Antiquities, R. A. Higgins (*acting*) ....£8,650 to £9,798
Assistant Keepers, Ann Birchall; B. F. Cook
£4,404 to £7,109
Keeper of Mediæval and Later Antiquities, N. M. Stratford..................£8,650 to £9,798
Deputy Keeper, G. H. Tait...... £7,151 to £8,750
Assistant Keepers, J. Cherry; Leslie E. Webster; R. M. Camber; R. Marks; D. Kidd
£4,404 to £7,109
Keeper of Prehistoric and Romano-British Antiquities, I. H. Longworth............£8,650 to £9,798
Deputy Keeper, K. S. Painter; G. de G. Sieveking
£7,151 to £8,750
Assistant Keepers, I. M. Stead; I. A. Kinnes
£4,404 to £7,109
Keeper of Oriental Antiquities, D. E. Barrett
£8,650 to £9,798
Assistant Keepers, W. Zwalf; L. R. H. Smith; Jessica M. Rawson; R. Whitfield
£4,404 to £7,109
Keeper of Ethnography, M. D. McLeod
£8,650 to £9,798
Deputy Keeper, B. A. L. Cranstone
£7,151 to £8,750
Assistant Keepers, Elizabeth M. Carmichael; Sheila G. Weir; Dorota Starzecka; J. C. H. King
£4,404 to £7,109
Keeper of Research Laboratory, M. Tite
£8,650 to £9,798
Principal Scientific Officers, A. D. Baynes-Cope; W. A. Oddy..............£5,514 to £7,205
Keeper of Conservation, H. Barker
£8,650 to £9,798

THE BRITISH MUSEUM (NATURAL HISTORY)
Cromwell Road S.W.7
[01-589 6323]
Open free on week-days (except New Year's Day, Good Friday, Christmas Eve, Christmas Day and Boxing Day) 10 to 6, and on Sundays from 2.30 to 6.
The Natural History Museum originates from the natural history departments of the British Museum, Bloomsbury. During the 19th century the natural history collections grew so extensively

that it became necessary to find new quarters for them and in 1881 they were moved to South Kensington. The British Museum Act, 1963, made the Natural History Museum completely independent with its own body of Trustees. The Zoological Museum, Tring, bequeathed by the second Lord Rothschild, has formed part of the Museum since 1938. Research workers are admitted to the libraries and study collections by Student's Ticket, applications for which should be made in writing to the Director. There are lectures for visitors at 3 p.m. on week-days and lecturers are also available at other times for special parties by arrangement with the Department of Public Services.
The administrative expenses were estimated at £3,771,000 in 1976-77.

Board of Trustees
Chairman, Dr. A. Williams, F.R.S.
Appointed by the Prime Minister: Sir Hugh Casson, P.R.A.; Prof. Sir Frederick Dainton, F.R.S.; Prof. J. M. Dodd, F.R.S.; Sir Arthur Drew, K.C.B.; Sir Hugh Elliott, Bt., O.B.E.; Prof. T. R. E. Southwood; Prof. D. H. Valentine; The Lord Zuckerman, O.M., K.C.B., F.R.S.
Nominated by the Royal Society: Prof. J. Sutton, F.R.S.
Appointed by the Trustees of the British Museum (Natural History): Prof. G. F. Fogg, F.R.S.; Sir Michael Perrin, C.B.E.

Director, R. H. Hedley, D.SC.............£12,465
Deputy Director and Secretary to the Board of Trustees A. P. Coleman..........£10,645 to £11,655

Department of Administrative Services
Museum Secretary (*Establishment Officer*), R. Saunders
£8,215 to £9,815
Office Manager, B. Johnston.... £6,145 to £7,915

Department of Zoology
Keeper, J. G. Sheals, Ph.D...... £10,645 to £11,655
Deputy Keepers, C. R. Curds, Ph.D.; J. F. Peake
£9,115 to £10,263
Senior Principal Scientific Officers, P. H. Greenwood, D.SC.; C. A. Wright, D.SC.... £9,115 to £10,263
Principal Scientific Officers, I. R. Bishop; Miss A. M. Clark; Miss P. L. Cook; J. D. George, Ph.D.; Miss A. G. C. Grandison; Mrs. J. Jewell, Ph.D.; R. J. Lincoln, Ph.D.; R. W. Sims; J. D. Taylor, Ph.D.; P. J. P. Whitehead, Ph.D.
£5,979 to £7,670

Sub-Department of Ornithology
Park Street, Tring, Herts.
[Tring: 4181]
Senior Principal Scientific Officer, D. W. Snow, D.SC. (*Head*)...............£8,650 to £9,798
Principal Scientific Officers, P. J. K. Burton, Ph.D.; I. C. J. Galbraith; R. P. D. Goodwin
£5,514 to £7,205

Department of Entomology
Keeper, P. Freeman, D.SC...... £10,645 to £11,655
Deputy Keepers, L. A. Mound, D.SC.; D. R. Ragge, Ph.D....................£9,115 to £10,263
Senior Principal Scientific Officers, R. W. Crosskey, D.SC.; V. F. Eastop, D.SC.; P. F. Mattingly, D.SC.
£9,115 to £10,263
Principal Scientific Officers, D. S. Fletcher; P. M. Hammond; D. Hollis; W. J. Knight, Ph.D.; I. W. B. Nye, Ph.D.; R. D. Pope; K. S. O. Sattler, Ph.D. F. G. A. M. Smit; K. G. V. Smith; R. I. Vane-Wright; Miss C. M. F. von Hayek; A. Watson; P. E. S. Whalley.... £5,979 to £7,670

Department of Palaeontology
Keeper, H. W. Ball, Ph.D...... £9,115 to £10,263
Deputy Keepers, C. G. Adams, D.SC.; G. F. Elliot, D.SC....................£9,115 to £10,263
Senior Principal Scientific Officer, C. Patterson, Ph.D.
£9,115 to £10,263

Principal Scientific Officers, R. H. Bate, ph.d.;
C. H. C. Brunton, ph.d.; A. J. Charig, ph.d.;
L. R. M. Cocks, D.Phil.; R. A. Fortey, Ph.D.; A.
W. Gentry, D.phil.; M. K. Howarth, Ph.D.; R.
P. S. Jefferies, Ph.D.; C. P. Nuttall; H. G. Owen,
ph.d.; A. J. Sutcliffe, Ph.D.....£5,979 to £7,670

Sub-Department of Physical Anthropology
Principal Scientific Officer, D. Tills, D.Phil.
£5,979 to £7,670

Department of Mineralogy
Keeper, A. C. Bishop, ph.d.... £9,060 to £10,263
Deputy Keeper, D. R. C. Kempe, D.Phil.
£9,115 to £10,263
Principal Scientific Officers, R. J. Davis, D.Phil.;
P. G. Embrey; R. Hutchison, ph.d.; A. R.
Woolley, Ph.D.............£5,979 to £7,670

Department of Botany
Keeper, R. Ross............£10,645 to £11,655
Deputy Keeper, J. F. M. Cannon
£9,115 to £10,263
Principal Scientific Officers, A. Eddy; P. W. James;
A. C. Jermy; J. Lewis; J. M. Pettitt, Ph.D.; J. H.
Price; N. K. B. Robson, ph.d.
£5,979 to £7,670

Department of Library Services
Head, M. J. Rowlands.......£9,115 to £10,263

Department of Public Services
Head, R. S. Miles, D.SC........£9,115 to £10,263
Education Officer, F. H. Brightman
£5,979 to £7,670
Exhibition Development Officer, W. R. Hamilton,
Ph.D......................£5,979 to £7,670
Exhibition Production Officer, M, G. Belcher
£6,145 to £7,915

Department of Central Services
Head, G. B. Corbet, ph.d.....£9,115 to £10,263
Biometrics, M. Hills, ph.d.......£5,979 to £7,670
Electronic Data Processing, D. B. Williams, ph.d.
£5,979 to £7,670
Electron Microscope Unit, C. G. Ogden
£4,650 to £6,243
Technical Services, B. S. Martin. £4,650 to £6,243
Publications, R. S. Cross.......£6,145 to £7,915

MUSEUM OF LONDON
The Museum of London was due to open in
December 1976 in its new building at the corner of
London Wall and Aldersgate Street in the City. It
is based on the amalgamation of the former Guild-
hall Museum and London Museum, both now
closed. The Museum is controlled by a Board of
Governors, appointed (6 each) by the Government,
the Corporation of London and the Greater London
Council. The exhibition will illustrate the history
of London from prehistoric times to the present
day.
Chairman of Board of Governors, The Viscount
Harcourt, K.C.M.G., O.B.E.
Director, T. A. Hume, F.S.A.

THE SCIENCE MUSEUM
South Kensington, S.W.7
[01–589 6371]
Open on weekdays 10 to 6; Sundays 2.30 to 6.
Closed on Good Friday, Christmas Eve, Christmas Day, Boxing Day and New Year's Day.
For Science Museum Library, see below.
The Science Museum, which is the National
Museum of Science and Industry, was instituted in
1853 under the Science and Art Department as a
part of the South Kensington Museum, and opened
in 1857; to it were added in 1883 the collections of
the Patent Museum. In 1909 the administration
of the Science Collections was separated from that
of the Art Collections, which were transferred to
the Victoria and Albert Museum. The collections
in the Science Museum illustrate the development
of science and engineering and related industries.

The administrative expenses of the Museum,
Library and the National Railway Museum were
estimated at £2,729,000 for 1976–77.

Director and Secretary, Miss Margaret Weston
£12,000
Museum Superintendent, V. C. Clark
£6,458 to £8,228

Department of Physics
Keeper I, V. K. Chew........£9,115 to £10,263
Deputy Keepers, A. B. Sahiar; D. Vaughan
£5,621 to £8,326

Department of Chemistry
Keeper I, F. Greenaway.......£9,115 to £10,263
Assistant Keepers (First Class), D. A. Robinson;
R. G. W. Anderson.........£5,182 to £7,887

Department of Electrical Engineering,
Communications and Circulation
Keeper I, W. Winton ....£9,115 to £10,263
Deputy Keepers, B. P. Bowers; W. K. E. Geddes
£5,621 to £8,326
Assistant Keeper, G. C. Sneed....£5,182 to £7,887

Department of Transport
Keeper I, G. W. B. Lacey.....£9,115 to £10,236
Assistant Keepers (First Class), B. W. Bathe; Mrs.
L. A. West; P. D. Stephens.. £5,182 to £7,887

Department of Mechanical and Civil Engineering
Keeper I, J. T. van Riemsdijk.. £9,115 to £10,263
Deputy Keepers, R. J. Law; A. K. Corry
£5,621 to £8,326
Assistant Keeper, A. E. Butcher.. £5,182 to £7,887

Department of Astronomy, Mathematics and the
Earth Sciences
Keeper I, J. Wartnaby.......£9,115 to £10,263
Assistant Keepers, E. J. S. Becklake; Miss J. M. Pugh;
J. C. Robinson.............£5,182 to £7,887

Department of Museum Services
Keeper I, D. B. Thomas.......£9,115 to £10,263
Keeper II, M. R. Preston.......£7,929 to £9,215
Assistant Keepers, A. L. Rowles; I. M. Bell
£5,182 to £7,887

Library
SCIENCE MUSEUM LIBRARY, South Kensington,
S.W.7.—A national library especially devoted
to pure and applied science, 448,000 volumes,
14,400 periodicals and transactions of learned
societies, about 5,650 current. Bibliographies sup-
plied.—Open on weekdays 10 to 5.30. Closed on
Sundays and Bank Holiday weekends. Photo-
copying and microfilm service.
Keeper I, L. R. Day..........£9,115 to £10,263
Deputy Keeper, Miss H. J. Parker £7,924 to £9,215
Assistant Keepers, H. Woolfe; Mrs. E. M. Rolfe;
L. G. Sharp;...............£5,182 to £7,887

National Railway Museum
Leeman Road, York
[0904–21261]
Keeper II, J. A. Coiley.........£7,414 to £8,750
Assistant Keeper, P. W. B. Semmens
£4,717 to £7,422

THE VICTORIA AND ALBERT MUSEUM
South Kensington, S.W.7
[01–589 6371]
Hours 10 to 5.50 (weekdays and Bank Holidays);
Sundays, 2.30 to 5.50. Closed Good Friday, Christmas Eve, Christmas Day, Boxing Day, New Year's
Day and May 1. The National Art Library is open
on weekdays from 10 to 5.45 and the Print Room
from 10 to 4.35. A museum of all branches of fine
and applied art, under the Department of Education
and Science, it descends direct from the Museum
of Manufactures (later called Museum of Ornamental Art), opened in Marlborough House in 1852.
The Museum was moved in 1857 to become part of

the collective South Kensington Museum. It was renamed the Victoria and Albert Museum in 1899. The branch museum at Bethnal Green was opened in 1872 and the building is the most important surviving example of the type of glass and iron construction used by Paxton for the Great Exhibition of 1851. The Victoria and Albert Museum also administers the Wellington Museum (Apsley House), Ham House, Richmond, Osterley Park, Middlesex, and the Theatre Museum, due to open shortly. Administrative expenses of the Museum were estimated at £4,131,000 for 1976–77.

Director and Secretary, R. C. Strong, Ph.D., F.S.A.
£12,000
Assistant to the Director, J. F. Physick (*Secretary to Advisory Council*)..........£7,151 to £8,750

Department of Architecture and Sculpture
Keeper, J. G. Beckwith.........£8,650 to £9,798
Deputy Keeper, C. H. F. Avery. £4,404 to £7,109†
Assistant Keeper I, A. F. Radcliffe
£4,404 to £7,109

Department of Ceramics
Keeper, J. V. E. Mallet........£8,650 to £9,798
Deputy Keeper, D. M. Archer.. £4,404 to £7,109†
Assistant Keeper I, T. P. P. Clifford
£4,404 to £7,109

Department of Education and Regional Services
Keeper, Mrs. M. F. Mainstone.. £8,650 to £9,798
Education
Keeper (vacant)
Assistant Keeper I, G. W. Squire. £4,404 to £7,109
Regional Services
Keeper, C. Hogben (*acting*)......£7,151 to £8,750
Deputy Keeper, Mrs. B. J. Morris (*acting*)
£4,404 to £7,109†
Assistant Keeper I, M. Haworth-Booth
£4,404 to £7,109

Library
Keeper, J. P. Harthan.........£8,650 to £9,798
Deputy Keeper, R. W. Lightbown
£4,404 to £7,109†
Assistant Keepers I, R. C. Kenedy; A. P. Burton;
Miss J. I. Whalley..........£4,404 to £7,109

Department of Metalwork
Keeper, C. Blair...............£8,650 to £9,798
Deputy Keeper, Mrs. S. J. Bury.. £4,404 to £7,109†
Assistant Keeper, J. K. D. Cooper. £4,404 to £7,109

Department of Prints and Drawings and Paintings
Keeper, C. M. Kauffmann..... £8,650 to £9,798
Deputy Keepers, J. H. Mayne; P. W. Ward-Jackson
£4,404 to £7,109†
Assistant Keepers I, J. Murdoch; Miss S. B. Lambert
£4,404 to £7,109†

Department of Museum Services
Keeper, J. F. Physick...........£7,151 to £8,750
Deputy Keeper (*Publications Production*), T. M. MacRobert...............£4,404 to £7,109†
Assistant Keepers I, I. Heal (*Design*); M. D. Darby
(*Exhibitions*)...............£4,404 to £7,109

Department of Textiles
Keeper, D. King...............£8,650 to £9,798
Deputy Keeper, Miss N. K. A. Rothstein
£4,404 to £7,109†
Assistant Keeper I, Mrs. V. D. Mendes
£4,404 to £7,109

Department of Furniture and Woodwork
Keeper, P. K. Thornton.........£8,650 to £9,798
Deputy Keeper, S. S. Jervis.... £4,404 to £7,109†
Assistant Keeper I, J. J. S. L. Hardy
£4,404 to £7,109

Oriental Department
Keeper, J. C. Irwin............£8,650 to £9,798
Indian Section
Deputy Keeper, R. W. Skelton. £4,404 to £7,109†
Assistant Keeper I, J. J. Lowry... £4,404 to £7,109
Far Eastern Section
Keeper, J. G. Ayers...........£7,151 to £8,750
Assistant Keeper I, E. G. Capon.. £4,404 to £7,109

Department of Conservation
Keeper, N. S. Brommelle......£8,650 to £9,798

Secretariat
Museum Superintendent, R. Burgess, M.B.E.
£5,680 to £7,450

Theatre Museum
Curator, A. Schouvaloff........£7,151 to £8,750
† Plus *Allce.* £438.

BETHNAL GREEN MUSEUM OF CHILDHOOD
Cambridge Heath Road, Bethnal Green, E.2.

A branch of the Victoria and Albert Museum, opened in 1872. Toys, dolls, dolls' houses, model theatres, children's books and costume. Also items connected with local history, and, temporarily, wedding dresses, continental 19th century furniture, Japanese armour and sculptures by Rodin. A new gallery of children's costumes has recently opened.
Keeper, Miss E. M. Aslin.......£7,151 to £8,750

THE COMMONWEALTH INSTITUTE
Kensington High Street, W.8
[01–602 3252]

The management of the Institute is vested in a Board of Governors of which Sir David Hunt, K.C.M.G., O.B.E. is the Chairman. Membership of the Board consists of the High Commissions in London of the Commonwealth Governments and of representatives of Commonwealth, educational, cultural and commercial interests as appointed by the Minister.

Exhibition Galleries open weekdays, 10 a.m. to 5.30 p.m.; Sundays, 2.30 p.m. to 6 p.m. Admission free. Cinema. Closed Good Fridays, Christmas Eve, Christmas Day, Boxing Day and New Year's Day.
Director, J. K. Thompson, C.M.G...........£11,465
Deputy Director, F. Lightfoot, M.B.E.......£8,987
Chief Education Officer, J. F. Callander
£6,458 to £8,228
Establishment and Finance Officer, S. A. Christy, M.B.E.....................£6,458 to £8,228
Chief Exhibition Officer, C. W. Tosdevin
£6,458 to £8,228
Curator, Art Gallery, D. G. Bowen, F.R.S.A.
£5,678 to £6,678
Librarian, M. J. Foster.........£5,678 to £6,678
Senior Education Officers, C. K. Kumar; J. C. McKenzie..................£5,678 to £6,678
Theatre Manager, L. Black......£4,678 to £5,478
Publicity Officer, M. G. Evans... £4,678 to £5,478

IMPERIAL WAR MUSEUM
Lambeth Road, S.E.1
[01–735 8922]

Open daily (except Good Friday, Christmas Eve, Christmas Day, Boxing Day and New Year's Day) 10 a.m.–6 p.m. Reference Depts. open Monday–Friday (except on public holidays), 10 a.m.–5 p.m.

The Museum, which was founded in 1917 and established by Act of Parliament in 1920, illustrates and records all aspects of the two world wars and other military operations involving Britain and the Commonwealth since 1914. It was opened in its present home, formerly Bethlem Hospital or Bedlam, in 1936. Its extensive collections include aircraft, armoured fighting vehicles, artillery, uniforms, models, orders and decorations, badges and insignia, works of art, posters, photographs, films, books, documents and sound recordings.

The Museum provides regular programmes of films and talks for visiting parties from schools, colleges and the armed services. General administrative expenses of the Museum 1976–1977, £1,246,000.
Director, A. N. Frankland, C.B.E., D.F.C., D.Phil., F.S.A....................................£11,465

Deputy Director, C. H. Roads, Ph.D.
£9,115 to £10,263
Assistant Director and Keeper of Department of Art (Deputy Keeper), J. C. Darracott
£7,929 to £9,215
Deputy Keepers, G. T. C. Coultass; C. Dowling, D.Phil.; P. J. Simkins........£7,929 to £9,215
Assistant Keepers (First Class), G. M. Bayliss, Ph.D.; R. W. K. Crawford; D. G. Lance; D. J. Penn; R. W. A. Suddaby........£5,186 to £7,887
Deputy Keeper, J. J. Chadwick . £7,929 to £9,215
Establishment and Finance Officer (Senior Executive Officer), J. F. Golding........£5,678 to £6,678

NATIONAL MARITIME MUSEUM
Greenwich, S.E.10
[01–858 4422]

Open weekdays 10 till 6 (Mon.–Fri. in winter, 10–5); Sundays 2.30 to 6. Closed on Good Friday, Christmas Eve, Christmas Day, Boxing Day and New Year's Day.

Reading Room open on weekdays 10 to 5; tickets of admission on written application to the Director.

The National Maritime Museum was established by Act of Parliament in 1934, for the illustration of the maritime history, archæology and art of Great Britain. The Museum is in two groups of buildings, in Greenwich Park, the Main Buildings, centred round the Queen's House (built by Inigo Jones, 1617–35) and the Old Royal Observatory, including the Wren Flamsteed House, to the south. The collections include paintings; actual craft and ship-models; ships' lines; prints and drawings; maps, atlases and charts; navigational and astronomical instruments; uniforms and relics; books and MSS. The amount for salaries and expenses, including a Grant-in-Aid, was estimated at £1,423,000 for 1975–76.

Director and Accounting Officer, B. J. Greenhill, C.M.G.
£11,670
Deputy Director, D. W. Waters
£8,650 to £9,798
Secretary (Principal), Capt. T. L. Martin, R.N.
£5,680 to £7,450
Keeper, B. T. Carter...........£8,650 to £9,798
Deputy Keepers, P. G. W. Annis; Dr. A. P. McGowan; J. Munday; D. V. Proctor
£7,151 to £8,750
Assistant Keepers (First Class), E. H. H. Archibald; H. D. Howse, M.B.E., D.S.C.; J. F. McGrail; A. W. H. Pearsall; H. H. Preston; Dr. M. W. B. Sanderson; Mrs. A. M. Shirley; A. N. Stimson; Dr. R. J. B. Knight; C. C. W. Terrell; J. A. H. Lees, O.B.E.; N. E. Upham...£4,404 to £7,109
Restorer I, W. W. Percival-Prescott
£4,404 to £7,109

(For other Museums in England—*see* Index)

THE NATIONAL MUSEUM OF WALES
AMGUEDDFA GENEDLAETHOL CYMRU
Cardiff

Open on weekdays, 10 a.m. to 5 p.m. (April to Sept., 10 a.m. to 6 p.m.). Sundays 2.30 to 5 p.m. Bank Holidays and Tuesdays following, 10 a.m. to 6 p.m. Closed on Christmas Eve, Christmas Day, Boxing Day, New Year's Day and Good Friday.

Founded by Royal Charter, 1907, and maintained principally by annual grant from the Government and partly by Museum rate from the Cardiff City Council. The collections consist of: (Geology), Collections of geological specimens (rocks, minerals and fossils) from all parts of Wales with comparative material from other regions. Relief maps, models and photographs illustrating the structure and scenery of Wales. (Botany), the Welsh National Herbarium, illustrating especially the flora of Wales and comprising the Griffith, D. A. Jones, Vachell, Salter, Shoolbred, Wheldon and other herbaria, and display collections illustrating general and forest botany and the ecology of Welsh plants. (Zoology), Collections of skins, British mammals and birds, eggs of British birds, extensive entomological collections, Melvill-Tomlin collection of molluscs, spirit collections, chiefly of Welsh interest. (Archæology), Welsh prehistoric. Roman and mediæval antiquities, casts of pre-Norman monuments of Wales, important numismatic collection. (Industry), The history and development of industry in Wales, illustrated by models, dioramas, original objects and machines. (Art), The works of Richard Wilson, Augustus John, O.M., and Sir Frank Brangwyn, are well represented; the Gwendoline and Margaret Davies Bequests of works of the 19th-century French School, the British School and Old Masters, Pyke Thompson collection of watercolour drawings, and a general collection of paintings in oil; sculpture, including many works by Sir W. Goscombe John, R.A., Swansea and Nantgarw porcelain, the De Winton collection of Continental porcelain and the Jackson collection of silver, etc.
President, A. B. Oldfield-Davies, C.B.E.
Vice-President, Col. Sir William Crawshay, D.S.O., E.R.D., T.D.
Director, G. O. Jones, Ph.D., D.Sc.
Secretary, D. W. Dykes, F.S.A.
Keepers (Geology), D. A. Bassett, Ph.D.; *(Botany)*, S. G. Harrison; *(Zoology)*, J. A. Bateman; *(Archæology)*, H. N. Savory, D.Phil., F.S.A.; *(Industry)*, D. Morgan Rees, F.S.A.; *(Art)*, R. L. Charles, M.C.

Welsh Folk Museum
Amgueddfa Werin Cymru
St. Fagans

The museum is situated 4 miles west of Cardiff. Open weekdays July and August 10 a.m. to 6 p.m., April, May, June, Sept. 10 a.m. to 5 p.m. October to March (admission 10p). Open Sundays 12.30 p.m. to 6 p.m., April to September 2.30 to 5 p.m., Oct. to March. Closed on Christmas Eve, Christmas Day, Boxing Day and New Year's Day. The museum was made possible by the gift of St. Fagans Castle and its Grounds by the Earl of Plymouth in 1946. The rooms of the Castle contain period furniture; the gardens are maintained. A woollen factory from Brecknockshire, a tannery from Radnorshire, a 16th-century barn from Flintshire, four farmhouses, an 18th-century cockpit from Denbigh, a turnpike house, a cottage, a smithy and an 18th-century chapel have been re-erected and other typical Welsh buildings are being re-erected in an area adjoining the Castle to picture the Welsh way of life and to show the rural crafts of the past. The new museum building contains galleries of Material Culture, Costume, Agriculture and Agricultural Vehicles.
Curator, T. M. Owen, F.S.A.
Keepers (Material Culture), J. G. Jenkins, F.S.A.; *(Oral Traditions and Dialects)*, V. H. Phillips.

Legionary Museum of Caerleon
Caerleon, Gwent.

Open on weekdays (May–September), 9.30 a.m. to 7 p.m., (March, April and Oct.) 9.30 a.m. to 5.30 p.m. (Nov.–Feb.), 9.30 a.m. to 4 p.m. Sundays from 2 p.m. Closed on Christmas Eve, Christmas Day, Boxing Day and New Year's Day. Admission Free.

Contains material found on the site of the Roman fortress of Isca and its suburbs.

Turner House Art Gallery
Penarth, N. Cardiff

Open weekdays, 11 a.m.–12.45 p.m. and 2 p.m. to 5 p.m. Sundays, 2 p.m. to 5 p.m. Closed Mondays, except Bank Holidays, and on Christmas Eve, Christmas Day, Boxing Day, New Year's Day and Good Friday.

North Wales Quarrying Museum,
Llanberis, Gwynedd

Open weekdays and Sundays, 9.30–7, Easter to September. Admission 20p. Waterwheel, foundry, smithy, fitting shops, slate-sawing tables and dressing machines, items from quarry hospital, office furniture, etc.

Segontium Roman Fort Museum,
Beddgelert Road, Caernarvon, Gwynedd
Open weekdays at 9.30, Sundays at 2. Closes at
7 from May to September, at 5.30 in March, April
and October, at 4 from November to February.
Admission 10p. On the site of the fort, in the
guardianship of the Department of the Environment. Contains mostly material excavated there.

Graham Sutherland Gallery
Picton Castle, Haverfordwest
In association with the Picton Castle Trust.
Works on display include oil paintings, watercolours, works in mixed media, lithographs, etchings
and aquatints. Open 11 a.m. to 1 p.m. and 2 p.m. to
6 p.m. on Tuesday, Wednesday, Thursday,
Saturday, Sunday and Bank Holiday Monday from
April–September; 2–5 on Saturday and Sunday
from October–March. Admission free. Parking
charges for coaches and cars.

Museum of the Woollen Industry
Dre-fach Felindre
It occupies part of a working mill, the Cambrian
Mills. Its collection of textile machinery dates back
to the 18c and the exhibition traces the development of the industry from the Middle Ages to the
present day. Open 10 p.m. to 5 p.m. Monday–
Saturday from 1 April to 30 September. Admission free.

ROYAL SCOTTISH MUSEUM
Chambers Street, Edinburgh
[031–225 7534]
Open, Mon.–Sat., 10 a.m. to 5 p.m.; and Sun.,
2 to 5 p.m.
Director, N. Tebble, D.SC..............£11,000
Keeper, Department of Art and Archæology, R. Oddy
£7,195 to £8,855
Keeper, Department of Technology, A. G. Thomson,
Ph.D....................£7,195 to £8,855
Keeper, Department of Natural History, A. S. Clarke,
Ph.D....................£7,195 to £8,855
Keeper, Department of Geology, C. D. Waterston,
Ph.D....................£7,195 to £8,855
Assistant Keepers (First Class), M. C. Baker; H. O.
A. F. Fernandez; Miss D. Idiens; A. Livingstone,
Ph.D.; I. H. J. Lyster; Mrs. P. C. Macdonald,
Ph.D.; H.G. Macpherson, Ph.D.; M. J. Moore; E.
C. Pelham-Clinton; Miss J. M. Scarce; A. D.
Simpson; G. Smaldon, Ph.D.; J. D. Storer; Miss
N. E. A. Tarrant; Miss M. S. Thomson
£4,404 to £7,109

NATIONAL MUSEUM OF ANTIQUITIES OF SCOTLAND
Queen Street, Edinburgh, 2
[031–556–8921]
Founded in 1781 by the Society of Antiquaries
of Scotland, and transferred to the Nation in 1858.
Open free. Weekdays, 10 a.m. to 5 p.m.; Sundays,
2–5 p.m.
Keeper, R. B. K. Stevenson, C.B.E........£10,282
Deputy Keepers, S. Maxwell; A. Fenton.
Assistant Keeper, Miss J. Close-Brooks.
Principal Scientific Officer, Dr. H. McKerrell.

NATIONAL BUS COMPANY
25 New Street Square, E.C.4
[01–583 9177]
The National Bus Company is a statutory body
under the provisions of the Transport Act, 1968.
It controls more than 50 operating companies
covering almost every part of England and Wales
outside London and the municipal undertakings.
The N.B.C. bus and coach fleets total about 20,000
vehicles and it employs a staff of about 70,000.
Chairman, F. A. S. Wood.....(*part-time*) £8,825
Members (part-time), A. P. de Boer; The Lord
Cooper of Stockton Heath; W. F. Higgins; I. S.
Irwin; A. E. Orchard-Lisle, C.B.E. (*each* £1,000).
Chief Executive, S. J. B. Skyrme.

NATIONAL COAL BOARD
Hobart House, Grosvenor Place, S.W.1
[01–235 2020]
The National Coal Board was constituted in 1946.
It took over the mines on January 1, 1947.
Chairman, Sir Derek Ezra, M.B.E.........£23,100
Deputy Chairman, N. Siddall, C.B.E........£19,100
Members, D. M. Clement, C.B.E.; D. Davies, O.B.E.;
L. Grainger; L. J. Mills; G. C. Shephard
£12,600 to £17,600
Part-time Members, K. J. Griffin, O.B.E.; R. F.
Richardson, C.B.E.; P. H. Robinson; Sir Jack
Wellings, C.B.E....................£1,000
Secretary, D. G. Brandrick.

NATIONAL DEBT OFFICE
and Office for Payment of Government
Life Annuities
Royex House, Aldermanbury Square, E.C.2
Secretary of the National Debt Commissioners and
Comptroller-General, I. de L. Radice, C.B.
£12,000
Asst. Comptroller, F. D. Ashby, O.B.E.
£7,750 to £9,350
Chief Executive Officer, S. J. Payne
£5,680 to £7,450
Senior Executive Officers, W. G. Stevens; G. F. W.
Berry; L. A. S. Swift; E.T. Taylor
£4,900 to £5,900
Brokers, Messrs. Mullens & Co........£2,000

NATIONAL DOCK LABOUR BOARD
22–26 Albert Embankment, S.E.1
The National Dock Labour Board administers
the scheme for giving permanent employment to
dock workers under the *Dock Workers (Regulation of*
Employment) (Amendment) Scheme, 1967.
Chairman, P. G. H. Lewison.
General Manager, J. H. C. Pape.

NATIONAL ECONOMIC DEVELOPMENT OFFICE
Millbank Tower, Millbank, S.W.1
[01–211 3000]
Council
Government Members, The Chancellor of the
Exchequer (*Chairman*); the Secretaries of State
for Employment, Energy, Prices and Consumer
Production, Industry, Trade, and the Chancellor
of the Duchy of Lancaster. *Management Mem-*
bers: G. V. K. Burton, C.B.E.; J. C. Fraser; A. A.
Jarratt, C.B.; R. E. B. Lloyd; M. J. Methuen;
The Viscount Watkinson, P.C., C.H. *Trade Union*
Members: The Lord Allen of Fallowfield, C.B.E.;
D. Basnett; J. L. Jones, M.B.E.; D. McGarvey,
C.B.E.; The Right Hon. L. Murray, O.B.E.; H.
Scanlon. *Independent Members*, Sir Eric Roll,
K.C.M.G., C.B.; The Lord Ryder; M. Young.
National Economic Development Office, Sir Ronald
McIntosh, K.C.B. (*Director-General*).

Secretary, T. U. Burgner.
Industrial Director, B. Asher.
Industrial Advisers and Assistant Industrial Directors,
J. R. S. Homan; P. F. D. Wallis; H. R. Windle.
Manpower Director, J. Cousins.
Economic Director, D. Stout.

NATIONAL GALLERIES
See ART GALLERIES
NATIONAL HEALTH SERVICE
See HEALTH SERVICE
(under Ministry of Health)

OFFICE OF THE NATIONAL INSURANCE COMMISSIONER
6 Grosvenor Gardens, S.W.1
[01–730 9236]
23 Melville Street, Edinburgh 3
[031–225 2201]
Portcullis House, 21 Cowbridge Road East, Cardiff
[0222 388531, Ext. 395]

The Commissioner is the final Statutory Authority to decide claims under the Family Allowances Acts and the Social Security Acts.

Chief Commissioner, R. J. A. Temple, C.B.E., Q.C.
Commissioners, H. A. Shewan, C.B., O.B.E., Q.C. (*Edinburgh*); V. G. H. Hallett; D. Reith, Q.C. (*Edinburgh*); H. B. Magnus, Q.C.; J. S. Watson, M.B.E., Q.C.; R. S. Lazarus, Q.C.; E. R. Bowen, Q.C. (*Cardiff*); J. G. Monroe.
Secretary, A. J. Macklin, M.B.E.
Senior Legal Assistants, Mrs. C. R. Corbett; Mrs. M. V. Steel.
Legal Assistant, D. E. Buckley.

NATIONAL PORTS COUNCIL
Commonwealth House, 1-19 New Oxford St., W.C.1
Chairman, E. P. Chappell, C.B.E.
Deputy Chairman, J. L. Jones, M.B.E.
Members, J. Morris Gifford, C.B.E. (*Director General*); F. O. P. Brann; J. F. Denholm, C.B.E.; P. G. H. Lewison; Sir William Lithgow, Bt.; Sir Daniel Pettit; L. T. J. Reynolds, M.B.E.
Joint Secretaries, R. C. Livesey (*Asst.-Director General*); K. A. Heathcote.

NATIONAL RESEARCH DEVELOPMENT CORPORATION
Kingsgate House, 66-74 Victoria Street, S.W.1
[01-828 3400]
The National Research Development Corporation operates under the Development of Inventions Act 1967. Its function is to secure, "where the public interest so requires", the development and exploitation of inventions derived from publicly supported research and from other sources. The Corporation provides firms with the opportunity to take up, under licence, inventions arising from public research. It also offers financial assistance towards the development of technically new products. These may be based on a firm's own ideas or on inventions which it has acquired from the Corporation or from other sources.
Chairman, The Lord Schon.
Managing Director, W. Makinson.
Head of Public Relations, B. S. W. Mann.

DEPARTMENT FOR NATIONAL SAVINGS
Blythe Road, W.14
[01-603 2000]
The Department for National Savings was established as a Government Department when the former Post Office Savings Department became separated from the Post Office on October 1, 1969. At the same time the civil service staff supporting the National Savings Committees for England and Wales and for Scotland, were integrated with the Department, so that its scope was extended to cover the promotion as well as the operation of National Savings. The Department operates the National Savings Bank and maintains the records of holdings of National Savings Certificates, Save As You Earn contracts, Premium Savings Bonds, British Savings Bonds (and their forerunners Defence and National Development Bonds) and Government stock on the National Savings Stock Register.
Director of Savings, J. Littlewood, C.B. £15,000
Deputy Directors, P. E. Plummer (*Controller (National Savings Bank)*); Miss B. K. Billot. £12,000
Assistant Directors, J. Higson; S. A. Ingham
£8,650 to £11,000
Establishment Officer, C. W. Hand
£8,650 to £11,000
Finance Officer, R. H. Dryden. £8,650 to £11,000
Controllers, G. W. Mantle, O.B.E.; H. R. West, O.B.E.; J. P. Wilde, O.B.E.; J. H. Mackenzie (*Publicity*) . . . . £8,650 to £11,000
Senior Principals, J. A. Cuthbertson; A. Green
£7,750 to £9,350
Principals, M. Marshall, I.S.O.; B. C. Smith, M.B.E.; S. J. Allison; M. Morris, I.S.O.; D. M. Jones; J. R. Acland; C. M. Roberts; C. F. H. Taylor; Miss

J. M. J. Wedge; R. J. F. Lindsay; C. L. Dann; T. Wilson; Miss C. N. Lall, M.B.E.; J. Stamp; R. S. Robinson; G. R. Wilson; A. Hirst; L. B. Clark, M.B.E.; J. W. Richardson; S. W. Shepherd; B. White; J. G. Booth; D. J. Goodman; J. Crooks; G. E. Long; A. W. Hasmall; I. B. Arkinstall; C. J. Paul; R. S. Watts; R. H. Lee; R. A. Boyes; C. L. Sturrock . . . . £5,680 to £7,450
Principal Information Officers, P. G. Hutchings; P. N. S. Hickman-Robertson. £5,680 to £7,450

THE NATIONAL SAVINGS COMMITTEE
Alexandra House, Kingsway, W.C.2
[01-836-1599]
President and Chairman, Sir John Anstey, C.B.E., T.D.
Vice-President, Sir Athelstan Caröe, C.B.E.
Vice-Chairmen, General Sir Geoffrey Musson, G.C.B., C.B.E., D.S.O.; Rt. Hon. L. Murray, O.B.E.; J. Archbold, O.B.E.; Mrs. E. Perkins, C.B.E.; Sir Campbell Adamson.

OFFICERS
Secretary, K. T. Pinch. . . . . £8,650 to £11,000
Deputy Secretary, J. C. Timms, O.B.E.
£7,750 to £9,350
Principals, A. F. Brown; S. Burke; K. G. Burton; M. Falder; K. J. Griffin; R. J. Heathorn; F. E. Mack; K. Nicholas; R. Rees, M.B.E.; J. K. Roberts; R. T. Rowland; G. Thomas
£5,650 to £7,450

NATIONAL SAVINGS COMMITTEE FOR SCOTLAND
22 Melville Street, Edinburgh
[031-225 5486]
President, The Hon. Lord Birsay, K.T., C.B.E., T.D.
Chairman, The Earl of Elgin and Kincardine.
Vice-Chairmen, D. M. McIntosh, C.B.E., F.R.S.E.; R. M. Addison, O.B.E.
Secretary, A. K. Grant, O.B.E. . . . . £7,750 to £9,340
Deputy Secretary, Mrs. J. W. A. Reaper, M.B.E.
£5,680 to £7,450

NATURAL ENVIRONMENT RESEARCH COUNCIL
Alhambra House, 27-33 Charing Cross Road, W.C.2
[01-930 9232]
The Natural Environment Research Council was established by Royal Charter on June 1, 1965, under the Science and Technology Act, 1965, to encourage, plan and conduct research in those sciences, both physical and biological, which relate to man's natural environment.
The Council carries out research and training through its own institutes and grant-aided institutes, and by grants, fellowships and post-graduate awards to universities and other institutions of higher education.
Chairman, Sir Peter Kent, F.R.S.
Secretary, R. J. H. Beverton, C.B.E., F.R.S.

RESEARCH INSTITUTES
Institute of Geological Sciences
Exhibition Road, South Kensington, S.W.7
[01-589 3444]
The Geological Museum, Exhibition Road, South Kensington, S.W.7. Open weekdays, 10 to 6; Sundays 2.30 to 6. Closed on Good Friday, Christmas Eve, Christmas Day and Boxing Day.
Director, A. W. Woodland, C.B.E., Ph.D.

Institute of Oceanographic Science
Wormley Laboratory, Godalming, Surrey
[042879 2122]
Director, H. Charnock, F.R.S.
Bidston Observatory, Birkenhead
[051-052 2396]
Taunton Laboratory, Crossway, Taunton
[0823 82691]

Institute for Marine Environmental Research
67–69 Citadel Road, Plymouth
[0752 20681]
Director, R. S. Glover.

Institute of Marine Biochemistry
St. Fittick's Road, Aberdeen
[0224 875695]
Director, P. T. Grant, Ph.D.

Institute of Hydrology
Maclean Building, Crowmarsh Gifford,
Wallingford, Oxon.
[0491 38800]
Director, J. S. G. McCulloch, Ph.D.

Institute of Terrestrial Ecology
68 Hills Road, Cambridge
[0223–69745]
Director (vacant).
Research Stations: Merlewood, Monks Wood;
Furzebrook; Colney; Edinburgh (Bush and Hope
Terrace); Banchory (Hill of Brathens and Black-
hall); Bangor; Culture Centre of Algae and Pro-
tozoa, Cambridge.

Unit of Invertebrate Virology
5 South Parks Road, Oxford
[0865–52081]
Director, T. W. Tinsley, Ph.D.

British Antarctic Survey
Madingley Road, Cambridge
[0223 61188]
Director, R. M. Laws, Ph.D.

Research Vessel Base
No. 1 Dock, Barry, South Glamorgan
[04462 77451]
Director, Capt. D. M. H. Stobie, D.S.C., R.N.(ret.).

Experimental Cartography Unit
6A Cromwell Place, S.W.7
[01–589 0026]
Director, D. P. Bickmore.

GRANT-AIDED INSTITUTES
Marine Biological Association of the U.K.
The Laboratory, Citadel Hill, Plymouth
[0752 21761]
Director, Prof. E. J. Denton, C.B.E., F.R.S.

Scottish Marine Biological Association
Dunstaffnage Marine Research Laboratory
P.O. Box No. 3, Oban, Argyll
[0631 2244]
Director, R. I. Currie

Freshwater Biological Association
The Ferry House, Far Sawrey,
Ambleside, Cumbria
[09662 2468]
Director, E. D. Le Cren.

NATURE CONSERVANCY COUNCIL
19–20 Belgrave Square, S.W.1
[01–235 3241]
Establishes, maintains and manages National
Nature Reserves, advises generally on nature
conservation, gives advice to the Government on
nature conservation policies and on how other
policies may affect nature conservation, and sup-
ports, commissions and undertakes relevant re-
search.
Chairman, Sir David Serpell, K.C.B., C.M.G., O.B.E.
Director, R. E. Boote, C.V.O.
Country Headquarters:
England: Calthorpe House, Calthorpe Street
Banbury, Oxon.
Director, Dr. M. Gane.
Scotland: 12 Hope Terrace, Edinburgh.
[031–447 4784]
Director, Dr. J. Morton Boyd.
Wales: Penrhos Road, Bangor, Gwynedd.
[Bangor 2201]
Director, Dr. T. Pritchard.

NORTHERN IRELAND OFFICE
Great George Street, S.W.1
[01–930 4300]
Stormont Castle, Belfast
[Belfast: 63011]

The Secretary of State for Northern Ireland in
the Cabinet is responsible for Government adminis-
tration in Northern Ireland. The Northern Ireland
Act 1974 made temporary arrangements for the
government of Northern Ireland, exercised through
the Secretary of State.
Secretary of State for Northern Ireland, THE RT. HON.
MERLYN REES, M.P..................£13,000
Private Secretary, J. M. Stewart.
Assistant Private Secretaries, N. R. Cowling*; Miss
P. M. Kenneally.
Special Adviser, R. Darlington.
Parliamentary Private Secretary, Dr. E. I. Marshall,
M.P.
Parliamentary Clerk, Miss A. F. Brown.
Ministers of State, ROLAND DUNSTAN MOYLE, M.P.
(£9,500); JOHN DENNIS CONCANNON, M.P.;
£7,500
Parliamentary Under Secretaries of State, R. A. Carter,
M.P.; J. A. Dunn, M.P.................£5,500
Permanent Secretary, B. C. Cubbon, C.B.
£18,675
Permanent Secretary (NICS), M. K. Harris, C.B.*
£13,250
Deputy Secretaries, P. T. E. England*; J. D. W.
Janes, C.B.......................£14,000
Deputy Secretaries (NICS), J. V. Morrison*; J. H.
Parkes* £12,230
Under Secretaries, T. C. Barker*; J. B. Bourn*; J.
A. Cradock*; J. H. G. Leahy*; W. J. Smith, C.B.;
J. F. Waterfield (*Principal Establishment and Finance
Officer*)..........................£12,000
Senior Assistant Secretaries (NICS), D. Gilliland*;
W. G. Robinson*....................£11,610
Assistant Secretaries, J. N. Allan*; S. S. Bampton;
E. N. Barry*; I. M. Burns; P. W. J. Buxton*;
T. A. Cromey*; W. I. Davies*; A. F. Dowling,
M.V.O., M.B.E., T.D.; F. B. Hall*; S. C. Jackson*;
R. A. McDonald*; A. R. Marsh*; D. K. Middle-
ton*; A. E. Mullin*; Miss R. F. Nockolds*; P. E.
Pickering; R. G. Smartt*; R. S. Sterling*; B.
M. Webster*; A. P. D. Westhead*; W. A.
Willis*; D. J. Wyatt*......£8,650 to £11,000
Chief Information Officer, R. J. Seaman
£8,650 to £11,000
* Located in Northern Ireland.

ORDNANCE SURVEY
Romsey Road, Maybush, Southampton
[Southampton 775555]
Director-General, Maj.-Gen. B. St.G. Irwin, C.B.
£12,000
Directors:
Field Survey, Brig. G. A. Hardy, A.D.C.
Map Publication, A. G. Dalgleish.......£11,000
Establishment and Finance, W. L. W. Isdale
£8,650 to £11,000
Deputy Directors:
Field Survey, B. E. Furmston..£8,650 to £9,798
Planning and Development, Col. R. N. Atkey.
Map Production, Col. E. X. Halliday, M.B.E.
Establishments, W. Rayer.....£7,750 to £9,350
Publications, Miss B. D. Drewitt
£7,750 to £9,350
Finance, J. A. Evenett........£7,605 to £9,379
Assistant Directors:
Geodetic Services, Lt.-Col. M. R. Richards.
Topographic Surveys, Lt.-Col. T. A. Linley.
Cartography, P. MacMaster.. £7,584 to £8,345
Reproduction, A. C. Marles ....£7,584 to £8,345
Training and Information, D. T. Arnott
£7,584 to £8,345
Research and Development J. F. Bell
£7,584 to £8,345
Computer, K. Nolan.........£5,680 to £7,450
Publications, J. Chapman.....£5,680 to £7,450
Personnel, A. St. J. Perkins.... £5,680 to £7,450
Office Services, F. Judd, B.E.M. £5,680 to £7,450
Management Services, D. L. Dowds
£5,680 to £7,450

MINISTRY OF OVERSEAS DEVELOPMENT

Eland House, Stag Place, S.W.1
[01–834 2377]

The Ministry of Overseas Development deals with British development assistance to overseas countries. This includes both capital aid on concessional terms and technical assistance (mainly in the form of specialist staff abroad and training facilities in the United Kingdom), whether provided directly to developing countries or through the various multilateral aid organizations, including the United Nations and its specialized agencies.

Minister for Overseas Development, The Rt. Hon. Reginald Ernest Prentice, M.P. £13,000
Private Secretary, R. G. M. Manning.
Parliamentary Private Secretary, M. J. Ward, M.P.
Parliamentary Secretary, F. A. Judd, M.P. £5,500
Permanent Secretary, Sir Richard King, K.C.B., M.C.
£18,675

Private Secretary, Miss V. M. Read.
Deputy Secretaries, C. W. Fogarty, C.B.; R. S. Porter, C.B., O.B.E.; D. Williams, C.V.O..£14,000
Under Secretaries, R. A. Browning; J. L. F. Buist; E. C. Burr; Dr. J. L. Kilgour; D. J. Kirkness; M. P. J. Lynch; L. C. J. Martin; A. R. Melville, C.B., C.M.G.; C. R. A. Rae; H. S. Stanley, C.M.G.; J. E. C. Thornton, O.B.E.; J. K. Wright. £12,000

Economic Planning Staff

Director General of Economic Planning, R. S. Porter, C.B., O.B.E. £14,000
Deputy Director General of Economic Planning, J. K. Wright £12,000
Directors, Dr. J. M. Healey (*International Economics Division*); G. A. Bridger (*Geographical Division*); K. V. Henderson (*Statistics Division*) ...£11,440
Senior Economic Advisers, R. M. Ainscow; Dr. B. E. Cracknell; G. A. C. Houston; N. B. Hudson; P. W. Stutley, O.B.E.; J. B. Wilmshurst
£8,650 to £11,000
Economic Advisers, A. D. Adamson; G. A. Beattie; J. M. Exeter; M. J. Hebblethwaite; B. R. Ireton; D. B. Jones; J. A. Peat; J. T. Roberts; G. P. M. Sandersley; C. J. B. White; Mrs. J. M. White; J. T. Winpenny .... £5,680 to £7,450
Chief Statisticians, R. M. Allen; G. C. Greenfield
£8,650 to £11,000
Statisticians, T. L. F. Devis; J. R. B. King; M. C. Walmsley; S. J. Webster; M. V. Wilshire
£5,680 to £7,450

Information Department

Chief Information Officer (vacant).
Principal Information Officers, J. W. T. Cooper; Mrs. N. Good .... £5,680 to £7,450
Senior Information Officers, G. V. T. Church; K. J. Hanford; Mrs H. Dean ...... £4,900 to £5,900

Heads of Development Division

Caribbean (Bridgetown), Sir Bruce Greatbatch, K.C.V.O., C.M.G., M.B.E.; *Middle East* (Amman), J. C. Rowley; *East Africa* (Nairobi), M. de N. Ensor, O.B.E.; *South-East Asia* (Bangkok), N. B. Hudson; *Southern Africa* (Blantyre) W. T. A. Cox
£8,650 to £11,000

Assistant Secretaries, K. G. Ashton; R. L. Baxter; M. L. Cahill; D. E. B. Carr; R. F. R. Deare; A. J. A. Douglas, C.M.G., O.B.E.; P. C. Duff; F. P. Dunnill; J. C. Edwards; K. G. Fry; D. E. Glason; I. H. Harris; C. R. O. Jones; A. A. W. Landymore, C.B.E.; P. S. McLean, O.B.E.; W. D. Maniece; K. O. H. Osborne; A. J. Peckham; J. E. Rednall; A. K. Russell; D. F. Smith; G. W. Thom, O.B.E.; A. M. Turner; J. E. Whitelegg; K. J. Windsor, O.B.E.; R. W. Wootton; Miss E. M. Young .... £8,650 to £11,000
Senior Principals, J. H. D. Gambold; G. C. Lawrence, C.M.G., O.B.E.; L. V. Martin, O.B.E.; W. D. J. Morgan; J. L. West; T. J. Wilshire
£7,750 to £9,350
Principals, M. D. Allen; Miss A. M. Archbold; B. D. Barber; E. T. Barnes; M. G. Bawden; Miss P. M. D. Baxter; E. A. Bennett; W. T. Birrell;

J. M. B. Blair-Fish; S. A. Bunce; J. A. Burgess, O.B.E.; P. J. Burton; D. G. Camps; R. O. Carter; Miss R. M. B. Chevallier; D. J. Church; B. Cook; A. D. Cooper; D. Craxton; L. E. Dawes; J. A. L. Faint; A. S. Fair; M. J. Fairlie, O.B.E.; C. R. V. Farran; H. J. Finch; F. W. Foreman; D. S. Foster; P. D. M. Freeman; K. W. G. Frost; Hon. D. C. Geddes; C. T. Gerard; J. R. Gilbert; D. W. Goodman, M.B.E.; R. M. Graham-Harrison; S. K. Green; W. Hobman; F. J. Holloway; H. Holmes; M. H. Jay; P. H. Johnston, C.M.G.; B. T. Jordan; J. V. Kerby; R. O. Kiernan; K. D. Law, I.S.O.; A. N. MacCleary; M. C. McCulloch; Miss M. P. Maguire; R. G. M. Manning; B. A. Mitchell; H. A. Moisley; K. H. R. Mundy; Miss S. Mylroie; I. T. Nance; D. G. Osborne; K. P. O'Sullivan; P. G. Ottewill, G.M., A.F.C.; M. F. Page, C.B.E.; M. A. Pattison; S. C. Pennock; R. G. Pettit; M. A. Power; M. Prescott; R. M. Prideaux; R. S. Ridgwell; A. G. Ridley, M.V.O.; G. F. Roberts; A. K. Robertson; Mrs. M. C. Rosser; D. Sands-Smith; E. Scott; P. L. J. Scott; J. M. Scoular; A. G. Simpson; F. E. Sitch; J. A. B. Smith; D. L. Stanton; G. F. H. Stapley; I. F. Stickels; A. H. Tansley; A. M. Trick; Miss S. E. Unsworth; J. M. M. Vereker; R. J. Walsgrove; A. F. Watkins; S. Wellington; D. M. Whitecross; Mrs. P. M. Wilkinson; J. W. Willby; G. A. Williams; K. A. F. Woolverton; T. D. Wright, M.V.O............... £5,680 to £7,450
Senior Executive Officers, J. A. Anning; A. D. Appleby; Miss J. W. Balls, M.B.E.; E. H. Becraft; D. H. Braun; W. A. Brownlie; P. H. Charters; Miss D. W. Cherry; T. W. Church; G. H. Clark; B. B. Davies; E. Eames; K. C. Elkins; C. E. Eyles; Miss M. Fairlie, M.B.E.; J. A. Featherstone; Mrs. S. P. Fleming; D. I. Fletcher; C. F. G. Foss; C. T. R. Gordon; Miss P. Grosvenor; C. W. Hall; J. R. Hards; A. H. Harrison; N. E. Hoult; Miss G. V. Jackson; I. N. Jenkins; Mrs. B. M. Kelly; D. Lawless; P. S. Lindsey; B. W. Lister; J. McCarthy; J. M. McDonough; V. J. McGee; J. C. Machin; C. A. Maher; E. Martin; E. M. Minns; Miss D. Nicholls; Miss P. M. North; P. T. Perris; Miss L. H. R. Roberts; Miss E. F. Saracco; P. J. Shaw; G. H. Sinclair; B. A. Thorpe; W. J. C. Tomlinson; Miss E. M. Ware; P. J. Watson; H. C. Williams; P. M. Wilson
£4,900 to £5,900

Advisory and Specialist Staff

Chief Education Adviser, J. E. C. Thornton, O.B.E.
£12,000
Deputy Chief Education Adviser, W. A. Dodd
£10,180 to £11,190
Education Advisers, P. Collister; Dr. I. Griffiths; Dr. R. B. Ingle .... £8,650 to £9,798
Education Adviser (Technical), Dr. O. G. Pickard, C.B.E. .... £8,650 to £9,798
Principal Engineering Adviser, B. M. U. Bennell
£8,100 to £9,440
Engineering Advisers, B. G. Little; P. H. Scarlett
£8,650 to £9,798
Assistant Engineering Adviser, S. P. Kirk
£5,514 to £7,205
Architectural Advisers, E. H. Riley; M. V. S. Smith
£8,650 to £9,798
Employment Adviser, F. J. Glynn, O.B.E.
£8,650 to £9,798
Chief Medical Adviser, Dr. J. L. Kilgour (*See also Department of Health & Social Security*)
Medical Advisers, Dr. J. A. B. Nicholson, M.B.E.; Dr. A. M. Baker......................... £11,000
Nursing Adviser (part-time), Miss B. G. Schofield, O.B.E. £3,752
Chief Natural Resources Adviser, A. R. Melville, C.M.G. £12,000
Deputy Chief Natural Resources Adviser, J. Wyatt-Smith .... £10,180 to £11,190
Principal Agricultural Adviser, D. C. P. Evans
£10,180 to £11,190
Agricultural Advisers, A. W. Peers, O.B.E.; P. Tuley, M.B.E...................... £8,650 to £9,798

Assistant Agricultural Advisers, J. B. Warren; M. F. Watson; K. Wilson-Jones;..£5,514 to £7,205
Senior Agricultural Economics and Management Adviser, P. W. Stutley, O.B.E........£8,650 to £11,000
Agricultural Economics and Management Adviser, M. J. Hebblethwaite..........£5,680 to £7,450
Principal Agricultural Research Adviser, Dr. R. K. Cunningham............£10,180 to £11,190
Assistant Agricultural Research Adviser, R. W. Smith
£5,514 to £7,205
Principal Animal Health Adviser, A. L. C. Thorne, C.B.E.................£10,180 to £11,190
Animal Health Adviser, J. Davie..£8,650 to £9,798
Co-operatives Adviser, B. J. Youngjohns
£8,650 to £9,798
Environment Co-ordination Adviser, Dr D. W. Hall
£8,650 to £9,798
Principal Fisheries Adviser, Dr D. N. F. Hall
£10,180 to £11,190
Fisheries Adviser, J. Stoneman....£8,650 to £9,798
Principal Forestry Adviser, J. Wyatt-Smith
£10,180 to £11,190
Forestry Adviser, D. F. Davidson, O.B.E.
£8,650 to £9,798
Land Tenure Adviser, J. C. D. Lawrance, O.B.E.
£8,650 to £9,798
Physical (Land Use) Planning Adviser, G. H. Franklin
£8,650 to £9,798
Overseas Police Adviser, M. J. Macoun, C.M.G., O.B.E., Q.P.M. } *See also Foreign and Commonwealth Office.*
Deputy Overseas Police Adviser, E. P. Bellamy, Q.P.M.
Social Development Adviser, A. R. G. Prosser, C.M.G., M.B.E..............£8,650 to £9,798

Centre for Overseas Pest Research
College House, Wrights Lane, W.8
[01-937 8191]
Director, P. T. Haskell, C.M.G., Ph.D.......£11,670

Technical Education and Training Organisation for Overseas Countries
Grosvenor Gardens House,
35-37 Grosvenor Gardens, S.W.1
[01-828 6751]
Director-General, W. L. Bell, C.M.G., M.B.E. £11,190

Directorate of Overseas (Geodetic and Topographic) Surveys
Kingston Road, Tolworth, Surbiton, Surrey
[01-377 8661]
Director, D. E. Warren, C.M.G..£10,180 to £11,190

Inter-University Council for Higher Education Overseas
90-91 Tottenham Court Road, W.1
[01-580 6572]
Director, R. C. Griffiths...............£12,000

Land Resources Division
Tolworth Tower, Surbiton, Surrey
[01-399 5281]
Director, A. J. Smyth........£10,180 to £11,190

Overseas Services Resettlement Bureau
Eland House, Stag Place, S.W.1
[01-834 2377]
Director and Head of Bureau, Sir Edwin Arrowsmith, K.C.M.G..................£5,680 to £7,450

Population Bureau
29 Bressenden Place, S.W.1
[01-828 4366]
Director and Head of Bureau, J. D. Greig....£9,798

Tropical Products Institute
56-62 Gray's Inn Road, W.C.1
[01-242 5412]
Director, P. C. Spensley, D.Phil...........£11,670

OFFICE OF THE PARLIAMENTARY COMMISSIONER AND HEALTH SERVICE COMMISSIONER
Church House, Great Smith Street, S.W.1
[01-212 7676]
The Parliamentary Commissioner for Administration is responsible for investigating complaints referred to him by Members of the House of Commons from members of the public who claim to have sustained injustice in consequence of maladministration in connection with administrative action taken by or on behalf of Government Departments. Certain types of action by Departments are excluded from investigation. Actions taken by other public bodies (such as local authorities, the police, the Post Office and nationalised industries) are outside the Commissioner's scope.

The Health Service Commissioners for England, for Scotland and for Wales are responsible for investigating complaints against National Health Service authorities that are not dealt with by those authorities to the satisfaction of the complainant. Complaints can be referred direct by the member of the public who claims to have sustained injustice or hardship in consequence of the failure in a service provided by a relevant body, failure of that body to provide a service or in consequence of any other action by that body. Certain types of action are excluded, in particular, action taken solely in consequence of the exercise of clinical judgment. The three offices are initially held by the Parliamentary Commissioner.

Parliamentary Commissioner and Health Service Commissioner, Sir Idwal Pugh, K.C.B....£18,675
Secretaries, H. B. McK.Johnston; J. L. C. Scarlett, C.B.E................................£12,000
Directors, R. J. S. Bryant; Miss M. F. Gracey; K. H. Green; Miss J. Horsham; T. W. Jones, O.B.E.; H. T. Sowden; A. Thompson (*Establishment Officer*)..................£8,650 to £11,000
Principals, J. R. Abbott; J. P. Bannister; J. P. Carey; F. D. Chessell; A. Davies; J. H. W. Gatford; W. D. George; D. M. P. Jones; M. W. Lindsay-Smith; J. A. Mahoney; D. F. J. Mills; R. A. Pocock; B. R. Smith; W. Thain; J. Wallbank; B. W. White.................£5,680 to £7,450

PARLIAMENTARY COUNSEL
36 Whitehall, S.W.1 [01-273 3000]
First Counsel, Sir Anthony Stainton, K.C.B., Q.C.
£18,675
Second Counsel, H. P. Rowe, C.B.; T. R, F. Skemp, C.B..................................£15,100
Counsel, G. J. Carter; G. J. J. Engle, C.B.; P. Graham; F. B. Humphrey, C.B.; C. H. de Waal; D. Rippengal; J. D. M. Rennie......*up to* £14,000

PAROLE BOARD
Romney House, Marsham Street, S.W.1
[01-212 6009]
The Board was constituted under section 59 of the Criminal Justice Act, 1967 and the Members were appointed on November 7, 1967.

The function of the Board is to advise the Secretary of State for the Home Department with respect to: (1) Release on licence under section 60 (i) or 61 and recall under section 62 of the Criminal Justice Act, 1967 of persons whose cases have been referred to the Board by the Secretary of State; (2) The conditions of such licences, and the variation and cancellation of such conditions; and (3) any other matter so referred which is connected with release on licence or recall of persons to whom section 60 or 61 of the Act applies.

Chairman, Sir Louis Petch, K.C.B.
Vice-Chairman, The Hon. Mr. Justice Cusack.
Members, Dr. D. Anton-Stephens; G. W. Appleyard, O.B.E.; Miss E. E. Barnard; His Hon. C. Beaumont; J. Bliss, Q.P.M.; O. V. Briscoe; The Hon. Mr. Justice Bristow; Mrs. D. L. Butt; S. G. Clarke, C.B.E.; His Hon. Judge da Cunha; Mrs. P. M. David; A. R. Davies, C.B.E.; S. R. Elliott; A. Falla, M.D.; L. Frayne; Lady Katherine Giles; Dr. W. Gray, C.B.; His Hon. Judge Green; The Hon. Mr. Justice Griffiths, M.C.; His Hon. Judge Harrison-Hall; Sir Richard Hayward, C.B.E.; K. L. Hollingsworth; P. W. Hopson; Miss M. B. Jobling; Miss J. K. Lawrence; R. M. Lee; I. P. Llewellyn-Jones; D. M. Lowson; Mrs. D. Marlow; Mrs. A. Morris; M. A. Partridge, D.M.; P. W. Paskell, O.B.E.; Mrs. M. Richardson; Miss M. I. Roeves; Dr. M. R. P. Williams, C.B.E.
Secretary, H. L. J. Gonsalves....£6,090 to £7,860

PATENT OFFICE
(and Industrial Property and Copyright Department,
Department of Trade and Industry)
25 Southampton Buildings, W.C.2
[01–405 8721]
Sale Branch: Orpington, Kent

The duties of the Department consist in the administration of the Patent Acts, the Registered Designs Act and the Trade Marks Act and in dealing with questions relating to the Copyright Acts. The Department also provides information service about patent specifications published during the last 50 years. In 1975 the Office sealed 39,019 patents and registered 3,019 designs and 11,440 trade marks.

Comptroller-General, E. Armitage, C.B...... £13,230
Assistant Comptrollers, J. D. Fergusson (£11,670); R. Bowen; I. J. G. Davis.............. £11,440
Superintending Examiners, K. M. Smith; D. G. Gay; H. W. Brace; N. W. P. Wallace; R. E. Branton; G. O. Byfleet; K. J. Kearley; A. L. Pheasey; F. C. Strachan; D. L. T. Cadman...... £11,190
Principal Examiners, O. O. Thorp; E. A. McMillan; A. E. Bishop; W. J. Cluff; R. E. Dalley; C. W. Smith; T. H. Mobbs; G. A. C. Ashcroft; M. D. Moore; K. F. Sloman; H. F. Viney; James Harrison; A. H. W. Kennard; A. G. Edwards; D. C. Snow; J. C. Keeping; J. R. Mends; W. Anderton; D. J. H. Day; D. S. G Collins; D. A. Cowlett; J. G. Clark; B. P. Scanlan; H. C. Bailey; A. K. Jones; J. K. Sigournay; A. F. C. Miller; R. E. Bridges; C. W. Hackett; F. E. Wastell; C. G. Harrison; V. S. Dodd; A. G. Lilleker; N. A. Robertson; D. C. L. Blake; D. F. Carter; G. E. K. Askew; R. H. P. Barber; L. L. Bow; N. B. Dean; K. P. Jessop; N. G. Tarnofsky; R. M. E. Bennett; C. S. Richenberg; M. Fox; J. F. Elliott; P. E. Taylor; A. J. F. Chadwick; C. I. C. Byrne; V. Tarnofsky; J. Mather; K. E. Butterworth; M. G. Currell; R. G. Williams; J. B. Partridge; L. J. Hedge; D. Spencer; P. G. Cruickshank; J. G. Bennett; J. S. Lea-Wilson; D. O. Westrop; S. A. Goodchild; J, Winter; M. N. Walesby.... £9,415 to £10,180
Assistant Registrar, Trade Marks, R. L. Moorby £8,650 to £11,000
Senior Principals, A. R. Summers; A. F. Gilmour £7,750 to £9,350
Senior Examiner, Information Retrieval Services, P. A. Higham.............. £6,125 to £8,750

Manchester Office
Baskerville House, Browncross Street, Salford
[061–832 9571]
Keeper, F. J. McDougal................. £4,890

PAYMASTER GENERAL
H.M. Treasury, Parliament Street, S.W.1
[01–930 1234]
Paymaster General, THE RT. HON. MRS. SHIRLEY WILLIAMS, M.P..................... £13,000
Private Secretary, G. E. Rees.

Paymaster General's Office
Russell Way, Crawley, West Sussex
[Crawley 27833]
The Paymaster General's Office was formed by the consolidation in 1835 of various separate pay departments then existing, some of which dated back at least to the Restoration of 1660. Its function is that of paying agent for Government Departments, other than the Revenue Departments. Most of its payments are made through banks, to whose accounts the necessary transfers are made at the Bank of England. The payment of many types of public service pensions is an important feature of its work. The expenses of the office were estimated at £4,290,000 for 1976–77.
Assistant Paymaster General, F. J. Clay, O.B.E. £8,650 to £11,000

Dep. Asst. Paymaster Gen., D. M. Wheble, O.B.E. £7,750 to £9,350
Senior Principal, N. C. Norfolk, I.S.O. £7,750 to £9,350
Principals, L. A. Andrews; D. R. L. Breed; R. A. Heavens, M.B.E.; A. Lawrence; H. T. Reading; E. F. Webster, M.B.E........ £5,680 to £7,450
Senior Executive Officers, D. R. Alexander; J. K. Bell; O. J. Breeden; S. W. Cole; D. J. P Dutton; J. H. Edwards; T. R. George; E. D. Hatswell; A. Jones; H. C. Leng, M.B.E.; A. J. McClatchey; D. N. McNee; I. J. Pells; R. F. Russen, B.E.M.; K. Sullens; G. Thomas; G. F. Tidy; P. R. Tight; G. T. Wheway............. £4,900 to £5,900

POLITICAL HONOURS SCRUTINY COMMITTEE
Civil Service Department, Standard House, Northumberland Avenue, W.C.2
[01–373 3000]
Chairman, The Lord Crathorne, P.C., T.D.
Members, The Lord Rea, P.C., O.B.E.; The Baroness Summerskill, P.C., C.H.
Secretary, Sir Stuart Milner-Barry, K.C.V.O., C.B., O.B.E.

OFFICE OF POPULATION CENSUSES AND SURVEYS
St. Catherine's House, W C.2
[01–242 0262]
The Office of Population Censuses and Surveys was created by a merger in May 1970 of the General Register Office and the Government Social Survey Department. The Registrar General controls the local registration service in England and Wales in the exercise of its registration and marriage duties. Copies of the original registrations of births, stillbirths, marriages and deaths are kept in London. A register of adopted children is held at Titchfield. Central indexes are compiled quarterly and certified copies of entries may be obtained on payment of certain fees. Since 1841 the Registrar General has been responsible for taking the census of population. He also prepares and publishes a wide range of statistics and appropriate commentary relating to population, fertility, births, still-births, marriages, deaths and cause of death, infectious diseases, sickness and injuries. The Registrar General also maintains, at Southport, a central register of persons on doctors' lists, for the purposes of the National Health Service.
Hours of public access, Mon.–Fri., 8.30 a.m.–4.30 p.m.
Director and Registrar General, G. Paine, C.B., D.F.C. £15,000
Deputy Director, P. Redfern.............. £12,000
Deputy Registrar General, F. A. Rooke-Matthews £8,650 to £11,000
Assistant Secretaries, S. Witzenfeld, I.S.O. (*Establishment Officer*); P. H. Kenney.. £8,650 to £11,000
Chief Statisticians, A. M. Adelstein (*Medical*), £12,000; N. H. W. Davis (*Population*); D. Newman (*Census*); Miss J. H. Thompson (*Population*) £8,650 to £11,000
Senior Statisticians (*Medical*), P. M. Lambert; Mrs. J. A. C. Weatherall........... £11,000
Head of Social Survey Division, C. G. Thomas £11,320
Chief Social Survey Officer 'A', Miss R. Merton-Williams................. £8,650 to £11,000
Senior Principals, G. F. P. Boston; T. E. Broughton; A. A. Cushion; Miss A. B. Graham; J. P. Hisley; J. R. Jeffery................. £7,750 to £9,350
Chief Social Survey Officer 'B', K. Barnes; R. K. Thomas; Miss J. E. Todd.... £7,750 to £9,350
Statisticians, L. Bulusu; R. A. Campbell; J. Craig; M. P. Curwen; R. C. Everett; A. J. Fox; T. J. Orchard; D. L. Pearce; Mrs. A. E. Redwood; Miss L. V. Roberts; J. B. Werner £5,680 to £7,450
Principals, B. S. T. Alcock; G. P. Barnes; R. H. Birch; N. W. Brown; P. J. Cook; G. A. Fielden; R. K. Freeman; A. L. Gay; E. Graver; K. R.

Hedderly; I. Hutchinson; C. F. James; F. G. Johnson; E. T. Jones; G. P. Knight; M. L. Pennington; T. A. Russell; R. P. Thorby; Miss M. M. Turvey; T. B. West; T. O. Youlten

£5,680 to £7,450

Principal Social Survey Officers, Mrs. P. E. Astbury; Miss J. Atkinson; R. M. Blunden; Miss A. I. Harris; Mrs. E. A. Hunt; S. R. Parker; A. J. Pearce . . . . £5,680 to £7,450
Senior Research Officers, R. J. Beacham; C. J. Denham; S. M. Farid; G. P. Hawes

£5,680 to £7,450

Senior Social Survey Officers, N. Bateson; F. Birch; Mrs. M. R. Bone; M. J. Bradley; S. M. Brown; D. R. Cable; Mrs. K. H. Dunnell; Mrs. M. L. Durant; E. S. Finch; Mrs. E. M. Goddard; Miss J. A. Higgins; I. B. Knight; Mrs. M. Mansfield; Mrs. J. Martin; Miss E. M. McCrossan; Mrs. C. M. Pillay; Mrs. I. Rauta; R. O. Redpath; Miss J. Ritchie; K. K. Sillitoe; Mrs. A. C. Thomas

£4,900 to £5,900

Senior Executive Officers, A. G. Ammon; T. Anderson; N. E. Auckland; E. Barton; J. L. Bennett; D. E. Birch; Mrs. F. R. Bowker; T. B. Bryson; R. J. Carpenter; A. M. Clark; D. H. Cleverly; R. J. Deacon; J. Denton; G. P. S. Fitterer; H. D. Gee; F. B. Gentle; P. H. Gibson; I. M. Golds; J. E. Good; S. A. Haskell; P. Howell; W. Jenkins; G. J. A. Johnson; A. F. Jones; J. H. Kempf; Miss J. D. Kennaway; B. G. Little; J. H. Lloyd; Miss R. M. Loy; R. McLeod; J. A. McNiven, M.B.E.; M.E. M. Mumford; L. Nelson; R. M. Nicholls; D. L. Nix; Miss D. M. Pace; N. L. Perryman; Mrs. M. J. Porter; J. A. Rampton; J. V. Ribbins; C. F. Savage; A. A. Sellar; P. Shepherd; E. E. Simpson; G. W. Smith; K. J. Stalker; D. Stewart; D. F. Stobart; Mrs. D. M. Stobart; S. C. Stracey; D. Taylor; H. D. Terry; A. W. Tester; S. R. Turner; Miss M. C. C. Tyler; P. A. Wake; J. R. Watkins; R. D. Whymark; C. A. Wileman; D. W. Williams; S. E. Wright

£4,900 to £5,900

Research Officer, Mrs. C. Hakim. £4,404 to £5,433

PORT OF LONDON AUTHORITY
Head Office, World Trade Centre, E.1
[01–476 6900]

Under the Port of London Authority (Constitution) Revision Order 1975, the membership of the Board consists of a minimum of nine and a maximum of 17 members. In addition to the Chairman a minimum of seven and a maximum of 10 non-executive members are appointed by the Secretary of State for the Environment.

A minimum of one executive member and a maximum of six executive members may be appointed by the Board.

The working of the Port for the year ended Dec. 31, 1974, showed a profit of £553,000.
Chairman, The Lord Aldington, P.C., K.C.M.G. C.B.E., D.S.O., T.D.
Vice-Chairman, J. M. Meyer, C.B.E.

Managing Director, W. Bowrey.
Executive Directors, N. N. B. Ordman (*Planning and Development*); J. D. Presland (*Finance*).
Assistant Director-General, A. M. Cameron.
Director of Real Estate and Legal Adviser, I. Hughes.
Director of Manpower, J. H. Gabony.
Director of Marine Services, Capt. P. A. Leighton.
Director of Tilbury, J. N. Black.
Director of Upper Docks, J. S. McNab.
Secretary, J. C. Jenkinson.

THE POST OFFICE
23 Howland Street, W.1
[01–631 2345]

Crown services for the carriage of Government despatches were set up about 1516. The conveyance of public correspondence began in 1635 and the mail service was made a Parliamentary responsibility with the setting up of a Post Office in 1657. Telegraphs came under the Post Office control in 1870 and the Post Office Telephone

Service began in 1880. The National Data Processing Service, the Post Office's commercial computer bureau, was set up in 1967. The Giro service of the Post Office began in 1968. The Post Office ceased to be a Government Department on October 1, 1969, following the Post Office Act 1969. On that date the office of Postmaster General was abolished and responsibility for the running of the postal, telecommunications, giro, remittance and data processing services was transferred to the new public authority called the Post Office. The Chairman and members of the Post Office Board are appointed by the Secretary of State but responsibility for the running of the Post Office as a whole rests with the Board in its corporate capacity.

Post Office Board
Chairman, Sir William Ryland, C.B. £23,300
Deputy Chairman and Managing Director, Telecommunications, Sir Edward Fennessy, C.B.E.
£19,300
Managing Director, Posts, A. Currall, C.B., C.M.G.
Member for Technology, Prof. J. H. H. Merriman, C.B., O.B.E.
Member for Personnel and Industrial Relations, K. M. Young.
Managing Director, Giro and Data Processing, A. E. Singer.
Member for Finance and Corporate Planning, M. Elderfield.
Salary range of Members . . . . . . £13,800 to £16,200

PRICE COMMISSION
Neville House, Page Street, S.W.1
[01–222 8020]

The Commission is responsible for the application of the Price Code, including the " vetting " of submissions for price increases, investigation and enforcement work and the monitoring of fresh food retail prices.
Chairman, Sir Arthur Cockfield.
Deputy Chairman, K. A. Noble, C.B.E.
Secretary, C. D. E. Keeling.
Members, Miss S. P. Black; Prof. D. C. Hague; Miss M. E. Head, O.B.E.; A. W. Howitt; A. W. John, C.B.E.; B. I. Petch.

DEPARTMENT OF PRICES AND CONSUMER PROTECTION
1 Victoria Street, S.W.1
[01–215 7877]

The Department of Prices and Consumer Protection was set up in March 1974, under a Secretary of State, and took over responsibility from the former Department of Trade and Industry for policy on prices and consumer affairs, and from the Ministry of Agriculture, Fisheries and Food for policy on food prices. *Prices*. The Department is the focal point for measures to deal with the generality of prices questions. It sponsors the Price Commission and has the principal responsibility for policy over the whole range of retail prices, including food prices, except for those of the nationalised industries. It has overall responsibility for policy on food subsidies, though other Departments undertake the detailed administration. *Consumer protection*. The Department deals with consumer affairs generally and is responsible for policy on fair trading, home and consumer safety, consumer credit, standards, weights and measures, including metrication, and for monopolies, mergers and restrictive practices. The Director General of Fair Trading is appointed by the Secretary of State.

SALARY LIST
Secretary of State	£13,000
Minister of State	£7,500
Parliamentary Under Secretary of State	£5,500
Permanent Secretary	£18,675
Deputy Secretary	£14,000
Under Secretary	£12,000
Assistant Secretary . . . . £8,650 to £11,000
Principal . . . . £5,680 to £7,450
Chief Information Officer (A) . . . . £8,650 to £11,000

Director Engineer.......................£11,000
Secretary of State for Prices and Consumer Protection,
THE RT. HON. MRS. SHIRLEY WILLIAMS, M.P.
  Private Secretary, G. E. Rees
  Parliamentary Private Secretary, J. C. Cartwright,
  M.P.
  Special Advisers, J. Lyttle; Dr. J. Mitchell.
Minister of State for Prices and Consumer Protection,
JOHN DENIS FRASER, M.P.
  Private Secretary, Mrs. K. B. Elliott.
Parliamentary Under Secretary of State, R. A. R.
Maclennan, M.P.
Permanent Secretary, Sir Kenneth Clucas, C.B.
  Private Secretary, M. G. Mecham.
Deputy Secretaries, L. S. Berman, C.B. (*Director of
Statistics*); J. C. Burgh, C.B.; M. J. Kerry, C.B.
(*The Solicitor*); D. A. Lovelock, C.B. (*Principal
Establishment and Finance Officer*); Prof. A. T. Pea-
cock, D.S.C. (*Chief Economic Adviser*).
Personnel and General Co-ordinator (*Assistant Secre-
tary*), Miss J. Blow
Head of Information Division (*CIO* (*A*)), Miss S.
Jefferies.
Parliamentary Clerk (*Principal*), Miss P. A. Davey.

Prices Policy and Consumer Credit Division
Under Secretary, W. Nicoll, C.M.G.
Assistant Secretaries, D. G. Hyde; Miss E. M.
Llewellyn-Smith; J. H. M. Solomon.

Food Prices and Distribution Division
Under Secretary, I. H. Lightman.
Assistant Secretaries, B. H. B. Dickinson; A. J. Lane;
J. G. Morris.

Fair Trading Division
Under Secretary, C. E. Coffin.
Assistant Secretaries, M. B. Casey; A. Dunning;
A. J. Nieduszynski; G. Stapleton.

**Metrology, Quality Assurance and Standards
Division**
Abell House, John Islip Street, S.W.1
[01-211 3000]
Under Secretary, Dr. E. N. Eden.
Assistant Secretary, A. Fortnam.
Deputy Chief Scientific Officer, E. E. Williams, O.B.E.
26 Chapter Street, S.W.1
[01-834 7032]
Director Engineer, J. D. Platt.

PRIVY COUNCIL OFFICE
Whitehall, S.W.1
Lord President of the Council (*and Leader of the House
of Commons*), RT. HON. MICHAEL MACKINTOSH
FOOT, M.P.......................£13,000
  Private Secretary, C. H. Saville.
  Assistant Private Secretary, Miss B.Owen.
  Parliamentary Private Secretary, C. E. Roderick,
  M.P.
Minister of State, JOHN SMITH, M.P.........£9,500
Clerk to the Council, N.E. Leigh, C.V.O.....£12,000
Deputy Clerk to the Council, C. E. S. Horsford
£8,650 to £11,000
Senior Clerk, A. W. Kimberley.. £5,276 to £6,509

PUBLIC HEALTH LABORATORY SERVICE
Headquarters Office:
Lower Entrance, Colindale Hospital,
Colindale Avenue, N.W.9
[01-205 1295]
  The Service was originally set up in 1939 as an
emergency service to augment the existing public
health resources of England and Wales in combating outbreaks of infectious diseases such as might
arise from enemy action or abnormal conditions in
time of war. In 1945 the Government decided to
retain the Service on a permanent footing, and
statutory authority for doing so was included in the
National Health Service Act, 1946, the Minister of
Health being empowered to provide a Bacterio-
logical Service in England and Wales for the control of the spread of infectious diseases. The
Service was administered by the Medical Research

Council, as agents of the Ministry of Health until
August 1, 1961, when, under the provision of the
Public Health Laboratory Service Act, 1960, a new
Public Health Laboratory Service Board was
established as a statutory body capable of acting in
its own right as agent for the Department of Health
and Social Security.
Members of the Board: C. E. G. Smith, C.B., M.D.
(*Chairman*), F. A. Adams, C.B.; H. M. Archibald,
C.B.; W. G. Harding; W. C. D. Lovett, O.B.E.,
M.D.; Prof. K. McCarthy, M.D.; Prof.D. D. Reid,
M.D.; A. J. Rowland; Prof. J. A. Scott, M.D.;
The Lady Sherman; Prof. R. A. Shooter, M.D.;
C. C. Stevens, O.B.E.; G. I. Watson, O.B.E., M.D.
Director, Sir Robert Williams, M.D.
Deputy Directors, J. C. Kelsey, M.D.; J. E. M.White-
head, M.D.
Secretary, J. D. Whittaker B.E.

CENTRAL PUBLIC HEALTH LABORATORY,
LONDON, N.W.9
Director, E. R. Mitchell.

REFERENCE LABORATORIES
(*With name of Director*)
Cross-Infection Reference (*incorporating Streptococcus
and Staphylococcus Reference*) M. T. Parker. M.D.
Disinfection Reference, J. C. Kelsey, M.D.,
Enteric Reference, Prof. E. S. Anderson, M.D., F.R.S.
Leptospirosis Reference L. H. Turner, M.B.E., M.D.
Mycological Reference (London School of Hygiene
and Tropical Medicine), D. W. R. Mackenzie,
Ph.D.
Mycoplasma Reference, Public Health Laboratory,
Norwich, B. E. Andrews.
Salmonella and Shigella Reference, B. Rowe.
Tuberculosis Reference, University Hospital of
Wales, Cardiff. J. Marks, M.D.
Venereal Diseases Reference, London Hospital, E.1.
A. E. Wilkinson (*part-time*).
Virus Reference, Mrs. M. S. Pereira, M.D.

SPECIAL LABORATORIES
(*With name of Director*)
Bacterial Metabolism Research Laboratory, M. J. Hill
Computer Trials, S. P. Lapage.
Epidemiology Research Laboratory, T. M. Pollock.
Food Hygiene, R. J. Gilbert.
National Collection of Type Cultures, S. P. Lapage.
Quality Control, P. B. Crone, M.D.
Standards Laboratory for Serological Reagents, Mrs.
C. M. P. Bradstreet.

CONSTITUENT PUBLIC HEALTH LABORATORIES
(*With name of Director*)
Bath, P. G. Mann, M.D.; *Birmingham*, J. G.
P. Hutchinson, M.D.; *Brighton*, B. T. Thom; *Bristol*,
H. R. Cayton; *Cambridge*, C. E. D. Taylor, M.D.;
Cardiff, C. H. L. Howells, M.D.; *Carlisle*, D. G.
Davies, M.D.; *Carmarthen*, H. D. S. Morgan;
Chelmsford, R. Pilsworth, M.D.; *Chester*, Miss
P. M. Poole, M.D.; *Conway*, F. B. Jackson; *Coventry*,
P. J. Mortimer, M.D.; *Derby*, R. Darnell (*acting*);
Dorchester, G. H. Tee, Ph.D.; *Epsom*, D. R. Gamble;
Exeter, B. Moore, M.D.; *Gloucester*, A. E. Wright,
T.D., M.D.; *Guildford*, Miss J. M. Davies, M.D.; *Here-
ford*, D. R. Christie; *Hull*, J. H. McCoy; *Ipswich*,
P. K. Fraser, M.D.; *Leeds*, G. L. Gibson, M.D.;
Leicester, N. S. Mair; *Lincoln*, J. G. Wallace; *Liver-
pool*, G. C. Turner, M.D.; *London*, (vacant) (*Central
Middlesex Hospital*); C. Dulake (*Dulwich Hospital*);
D. G. Fleck, M.D. (*St. George's Hospital, Tooting
Grove*); B. Chattopadhay (*Whipps Cross Hospital*);
Luton, A. T. Willis, M.D.; *Maidstone*, A. L. Furniss,
M.D.; *Manchester*, D. M. Jones, M.D.; *Newcastle*, J.
H. Hale, O.B.E., M.D.; *Newport*, R. D. Gray, M.D.;
Norwich, W. Shepherd; *Nottingham*, M. J. Lewis;
Oxford, J. O'H. Tobin; *Peterborough*, E. J. G.
Glencross; *Plymouth*, P. D. Meers, M.D.; *Poole*,
W. L. Hooper; *Portsmouth*, D. J. H. Payne;
Preston, L. Robertson; *Reading*, J. V. Dadswell;
Salisbury, P. J. Wormald, M.D.; *Sheffield*, B. W.
Barton; *Shrewsbury*, G. A. Morris, M.D.; *South-
ampton*, A. M. R. Mackenzie; *Southend*, J. A.
Rycroft; *Stoke-on-Trent*, P. Cavanagh, M.D.;

Swansea, W. Kwantes; *Taunton*, J. V. S. Pether; *Truro*, G. I. Barrow, M.D.; *Watford*, B. R. Eaton; *Wolverhampton*, I. A. Harper (*Hon.*); *Worcester*, M. J. Skirrow (*acting*).

PUBLIC RECORD OFFICE
See RECORD OFFICES

PUBLIC TRUSTEE OFFICE
Kingsway, W.C.2
[01-405 4300]

Public Trustee, A. A. Creamer, D.F.C...... £14,045
Assistant Public Trustee, J. Radford....... £12,465
Chief Administrative Officers, J. A. Boland; D. A.
    Wakeford................£9,811 to £11,778
Acceptance Officer, R. A. Cunningham
                         £6,458 to £8,228
Officer in Charge of Legality of Investments, S. B. Ince
                         £7,403 to £9,528
Senior Legal Assistants, J. G. Allen; R. C. Annis;
    V. J. Burt; A. J. Dawes; S. J. Dunn; T. R.Her-
    zog; J. B. Measures; A. G. Prideaux; J. C. Rowe
                         £7,403 to £9,528
Establishment Officer, F. C. Yeomans
                         £8,528 to £10,128
Deputy Establishment Officer, G. Davison
                         £5,678 to £6,678
Training Officer, G. A. Mars.... £4,678 to £5,478
Chief Accountant, R. R. Smith. £8,528 to £10,128
Asst. Chief Accountants, F. A. Boocock; J. E. Duffy;
    R. L. Mew................£6,458 to £8,228
Accountants, A. S. Baker; R. J. Beal; M. J. Blyth;
    L. J. Cobley; D. M. Cox; J. A. Matson
                         £5,678 to £6,678
Income Tax Officer, R. V. Walsh. £5,678 to £6,678
Chief Investment Manager, F. A. Beecham
                         £8,528 to £10,128
Senior Investment Managers, I. L. Brydon; A. L.
    Childs; K. Stilliard......... £6,458 to £8,228
Investment Managers, R. J. M. Gibson; T. H.
    Nicholls................£5,678 to £6,678
Securities Officer, A. R. Smith.... £5,678 to £6,678
Chief Property Adviser, R. Myers
                         £7,058 to £8,228
Senior Property Adviser, D. E. Fewings
                         £5,498 to £6,708

PUBLIC WORKS LOAN BOARD
Royex House, Aldermanbury Square, E.C.2
[01-606 7321]

The Board is an independent statutory body, consisting of 12 unpaid Commissioners appointed by the Crown to hold office for 4 years; 3 Commissioners retire each year and may be re-appointed.

The functions of the Commissioners, derived chiefly from the Public Works Loans Act, 1875, and the National Loans Act, 1968, are to consider applications for loans by Local Authorities and other prescribed bodies, and when loans are approved, to collect the repayments.

Funds for loans are authorised from time to time by Parliament and are drawn from the National Loans Fund. Rates of interest on the Board's loans and fees to cover management expenses are fixed by the Treasury.

During the year ended March 31, 1976, gross issues from the National Loans Fund for advance by the Public Works Loan Board amounted to £2,113,000,000.

Chairman, SirBernard Waley-Cohen, Bt..... *unpaid*
Deputy Chairman, F. Haywood, C.B.E........ *unpaid*
Other Commissioners, W. Bowdell, C.B.E.; Miss F.
    M. Cook; J. E. A. R. Guinness; W. R. Harman,
    M.B.E.; E. G. Hopper; Miss D. J. Hope-Wallace,
    C.B.E.; T. N. Ritchie, T.D.; Dr. C. H. Stout; S. F.
    Tongue; C. G. Vaughan-Lee, D.S.C...... *unpaid*
Secretary, H. W. Darvill, O.B.E.. £8,650 to £11,000
Asst. Secretary and Establishment Officer (vacant)
                         £5,680 to £7,450
Senior Executive Officers, T. S. Kirk; W. H. Clarke;
    I. H. Peattie................£4,900 to £5,900

RACE RELATIONS BOARD
5 Lower Belgrave Street, S.W.1
[01-730 6291]
Chairman, Sir Geoffrey Wilson, K.C.B., C.M.G.
                         £10,600
Members, Mrs. E. Christie; Mrs. S. Denman; L.
    Freedman; M. R. Malik; Miss A. Patrick; C. T.
    H. Plant, C.B.E.; Miss S. Roberts; T. S. Roberts;
    Mota Singh; Sir Roy Wilson, Q.C...... £1,000
Chief Officer, T. Connelly.

RECORD OFFICES, ETC.
THE PUBLIC RECORD OFFICE
Chancery Lane, W.C.2
[01-405 0741]

National Records since the Norman Conquest brought together from Courts of Law and Government Departments. Search rooms open daily to holders of readers' tickets from 9.30 to 5; Saturdays, 9.30 to 1. The Museum (open Monday to Friday, 1 to 4 p.m., and to organized parties at other times by arrangement) contains *Domesday Book* (2 vols.), made by order of William the Conqueror in 1085, and *Domesday Chest*; the *Gunpowder Plot* papers (1605); bull of Pope Clement VIII, confirming Henry VIII as *Fidei Defensor* (1524); the Log Book of H.M.S. *Victory* at Trafalgar (1805); and many other documents of national interest.

Keeper of Public Records, J. R. Ede......... £12,000
Deputy Keeper, A. W. Mabbs.... £8,650 to £9,798
Records Administration Officer, E. W. Denham
                         £8,650 to £9,798
Establishment Officer, J. A. Gavin. £5,680 to £7,450
Principal Assistant Keepers, Miss P. M. Barnes;
    L. Bell; Miss D. H. Gifford; R. F. Hunnisett;
    A. A. H. Knightbridge; M. Roper; E. K.
    Timings................£7,151 to £8,750
Assistant Keepers, First Class, J. D. Cantwell; C. D.
    Chalmers; N. G. Cox; N. E. Evans; Mrs. J. M.
    Hoare; Mrs. H. E. Jones; C. J. Kitching; Mrs. A.
    N. Nicol; P. A. Penfold; J. L. Walford
                         £4,404 to £7,109
Senior Inspecting Officer, J. G. Wickham
                         £5,680 to £7,450
Inspecting Officers, D. Ashton; B. S. Freeman; P. F.
    McCaffrey; A. J. W. McDonald; N. D. Robert-
    son; C. B. Townshend...... £4,900 to £5,900
Senior Executive Officer, L. G. Seed
                         £4,900 to £5,900

ADVISORY COUNCIL ON PUBLIC RECORDS
Public Record Office, Chancery Lane, W.C.2
Created by the Public Records Act, 1958, to advise the Lord Chancellor, as minister responsible for public records, on matters concerning public records in general and, in particular, on those aspects of the work of the Public Record Office which affect members of the public who make use of its facilities.
Chairman, The Master of the Rolls.
Members, The Rt. Hon. Lord Justice Buckley,
    M.B.E.; The Lord Bullock, F.B.A.; Prof. A. G.
    Dickens, C.M.G., F.B.A.; P. C. Goodhart, M.P.;
    Prof. M. Gowing, F.B.A.; Prof. J. C. Holt, F.S.A.;
    G. D. Squibb, Q.C.; The Lord Teviot; The Lord
    Trend, G.C.B., C.V.O.; A. B. Walden, M.P.; Prof.
    Glanmor Williams; Prof. C. H. Wilson, F.B.A.
Secretary, Mrs. A. Nicol.

HOUSE OF LORDS RECORD OFFICE
House of Lords, S.W.1
[01-219 3074]
Since 1497, the records of Parliament have been kept within the Palace of Westminster. They are in the custody of the Clerk of the Parliaments, who in 1946 established a record department to supervise their preservation and their production to students. The Search Room of this office is open to the public throughout the year, Mondays to Fridays inclusive from 9.30 a.m. to 5.30 p.m. The records preserved number some 3,000,000 documents, and

include Acts of Parliament from 1497, Journals of the House of Lords from 1510. Minutes and Committee proceedings from 1610, and Papers laid before Parliament from 1531. Amongst the records are the Petition of Right, the Death Warrant of Charles I, the Declaration of Breda and the Bill of Rights. The House of Lords Record Office also has charge of the Journals of the House of Commons (from 1547), and other surviving records of the Commons (from 1572), which include plans and annexed documents relating to Private Bill legislation from 1818. Among other documents are the records of the Lord Great Chamberlain, the political papers of certain members of the two Houses (including those papers previously preserved in the Beaverbrook Library), and documents relating to Parliament acquired on behalf of the nation. All the manuscripts and other records are preserved in the Victoria Tower of the Houses of Parliament.

Clerk of the Records and Principal Clerk, Information Services, M. F. Bond, M.V.O., O.B.E., F.S.A.
                            £12,410
Deputy Clerk of the Records, H. S. Cobb, F.S.A.
                   £7,561 to £9,160
Assistant Clerk of the Records, D. J. Johnson
                 £4,814 to £7,519

ROYAL COMMISSION ON HISTORICAL MANUSCRIPTS

Quality House, Quality Court, Chancery Lane, W.C.2
[01-242 1198]

The Historical Manuscripts Commission was first appointed by Royal Warrant in 1869, and was empowered to make enquiry into the place of deposit of collections of manuscripts and papers of historical interest and with the consent of the owners to publish their contents. The Commission was reconstituted by Royal Warrant in 1959, with wider terms of reference, including the preservation of records and assistance to other bodies working in the same field. The Master of the Rolls, who is the Chairman of the Commission, exercises through it his responsibility under the Law of Property (Amendment) Act 1924, and the Tithe Act, 1936, for manorial and tithe documents. The Commission has published over 200 volumes of printed reports upon manuscripts of historical import and compiles the *National Register of Archives*, which now contains over 20,000 typed reports upon privately-owned records, with extensive indexes, and may be consulted by historical researchers. The Commission undertakes to advise owners upon the preservation and use of their manuscripts and records.

Chairman, The Master of the Rolls.
Commissioners, Prof. Sir J. G. Edwards, D.Litt, F.B.A., F.S.A.; Prof. G. R. Potter, Ph.D., F.S.A.; Dame Veronica Wedgwood, O.M., D.B.E., F.B.A.; Sir David L. Evans, O.B.E.; The Very Rev. S. J. A. Evans, C.B.E., F.S.A.; Sir John Summerson, C.B.E., F.B.A., F.S.A.; Sir Edgar Stephens, C.B.E., F.S.A.; Sir Robert Somerville, K.C.V.O., F.S.A.; Prof. J. C. Beckett; The Lord Kenyon, C.B.E., F.S.A.; The Lord Fletcher, P.C. LlD., F.S.A.; Prof. A. Goodwin; The Hon. Nicholas Ridley, M.P.; The Duke of Northumberland, K.G., F.R.S.; J. P. W. Ehrman, F.B.A., F.S.A.; The Earl of Wemyss and March, K.T.; The Lord Blake, F.B.A.; Prof. S. F. C. Milsom, F.B.A.
Secretary, G. R. C. Davis, D.Phil., F.S.A.
Assistant Secretary, H. M. G. Baillie, M.B.E., F.S.A.

SCOTTISH RECORD OFFICE

H.M. General Register House, Edinburgh 1
[031-556 6585]

The Scottish Record Office has a continuous history from the 13th century. Its present home, the General Register House, was founded in 1774 and built to designs by Robert Adam, later modified by Robert Reid. Here are preserved, in accordance with the Treaty of Union, the older public records of Scotland and many

collections of local and church records and family muniments. Search Rooms open daily from 9 to 4.45; Saturdays, 9 to 12.30 (Historical Search Room only). Certain groups of records, mainly the more modern records of courts and government departments and the plans collection, are preserved in the Scottish Record Office's auxiliary repository at the West Register House in Charlotte Square—the former St. George's Church which was designed by Robert Reid. The West Register House Search Room opens daily from 9 to 4.45 (Mondays to Fridays). Permanent and special exhibitions of documents are mounted in the Museum at the West Register House, which is open to the public on weekdays during Search Room hours. The National Register of Archives (Scotland), which is a branch of the Scottish Record Office, is based in the West Register House.
Keeper of the Records of Scotland, J. Imrie.

DEPARTMENT OF THE REGISTERS OF SCOTLAND

Register House, Edinburgh
[031-661 6111]

The Registers of Scotland consist of:—
(1) General Register of Sasines; (2) Register of Deeds in the Books of Council and Session; (3) Register of Protests; (4) Register of English and Irish Judgments; (5) Register of Service of Heirs; (6) Register of the Great Seal; (7) Register of the Quarter Seal; (8) Register of the Prince's Seal; (9) Register of Crown Grants; (10) Register of Sheriffs' Commissions; (11) Register of the Cachet Seal; (12) Register of Inhibitions and Adjudications; (13) Register of Entails; (14) Register of Hornings.

The largest of these is the General Register of Sasines, which forms the chief security in Scotland of the rights of land and other heritable (or real) property.

Keeper of the Registers of Scotland, D. Williamson
            £8,650 to £11,000
Deputy Keeper, J. D. Robertson.. £8,063 to £9,350
Assistant Keepers, A. Farquharson; W. S. Morwood; W. S. Penman; W. Russell; J. F. Stewart
           £5,993 to £7,763
Accountant, J. Carmichael ...... £5,637 to £6,637
Senior Examiners, G. I. Fraser; W. G. Lobban; J. MacDonald; J. D. Morton; T. M. Nichol; J. Spence; J. Robertson; E. B. Sanderson; D. Sharp; J. Shaw; P. G. Skea; A. A. Snowdon
           £5,213 to £6,213

CORPORATION OF LONDON RECORDS OFFICE

Guildhall, E.C.2
[01-606 3030]

Contains the municipal archives of the City of London which are regarded as the most complete collection of ancient municipal records in existence. Includes charters of William the Conqueror, Henry II, and later Kings and Queens to 1957; ancient custumals: Liber Horn, Dunthorne, Custurmarum, Ordinacionum, Memorandorum and Albus, Liber de Antiquis Legibus, and collections of Statutes; continuous series of judicial rolls and books from 1252 and Council minutes from 1275; records of the Old Bailey and Guildhall Sessions from 1603, and financial records from the 16th century, together with the records of London Bridge from the 12th century and numerous subsidiary series and miscellanea of historical interest. A Guide was published in 1951. Readers' Room open Monday to Friday, 9.30 A.M. to 5 P.M.; Saturday, by appointment only.
Keeper of the City Records, The Town Clerk.
Deputy Keeper, Miss B. R. Masters.
Assistant Keeper, J. R. Sewell.

ROYAL COMMISSION FOR THE EXHIBITION OF 1851

1 Lowther Gardens, Exhibition Road, S.W.7
[01-589 3665]

Incorporated by Supplemental Charter as a

permanent Commission after winding up the affairs of the Great Exhibition of 1851. It has for its object the promotion of scientific and artistic education by means of funds derived from its Kensington Estate, purchased with the surplus left over from the Great Exhibition.
President, H.R.H. The Duke of Edinburgh, K.G., P.C., K.T., O.M., G.B.E.
Chairman Board of Management, Marshal of the Royal Air Force Lord Elworthy, G.C.B., C.B.E., D.S.O., M.V.O., D.F.C., A.F.C.
Secretary to Commissioners, C. A. H. James.

SCIENCE RESEARCH COUNCIL
State House, High Holborn, W.C.1
[01–242 1262]
Chairman, Prof. Sir Samuel Edwards, F.R.S.
Members of the Council, Prof. Sir Hermann Bondi, K.C.B., F.R.S.; Prof. W. E. Burcham, F.R.S.; Prof. H. G. Callan, F.R.S.; Prof. H. Elliot, F.R.S.; J. M. Ferguson; J. H. Horlock; A. T. James, Ph.D.; A. J. Kennedy; Sir Norman Lindop; D. J. Lyons, F.R.S., C.B.; Sir Ieuan Maddock, C.B., C.B.E., F.R.S.; Prof. R. Mason, F.R.S.; R. W. Pringle, O.B.E., Ph.D.; Prof. D. W. N. Stibbs.
Secretary, R. St. J. Walker, C.B.E.

SCOTTISH OFFICE
Dover House, Whitehall, S.W.1
[01–930 6151]
Secretary of State for Scotland, THE RT. HON. BRUCE MILLAN, M.P. £13,000
Private Secretary, N. J. Shanks.
Assistant Private Secretaries, A. J. Bree; M. J. Hunter.
Parliamentary Private Secretary, I. Campbell, M.P.
Ministers of State, THE LORD KIRKHILL (*Development*) (£7,500); (JAMES) GREGOR MACKENZIE, M.P (*Economic Planning and Oil*) £9,500
Parliamentary Under Secretaries of State, H. D. Brown, M.P. (*Agriculture and Housing*), H. Ewing, M.P. (*Devolution, Health and Home Affairs*); F. P. McElhone, M.P. (*Education and Social Work Services*) £5,500
Permanent Under Secretary of State, Sir Nicholas Morrison, K.C.B. £18,675
Private Secretary, J. C. Judson.
Assistant Under-Secretary of State, I. M. Wilson £12,000
Liaison Staff:
Assistant Secretary, A. M. Stephen, O.B.E. £8,650 to £11,000
Principals, C. T. Hole, O.B.E.; G. A. M. McIntosh £5,680 to £7,450
Senior Executive Officer, G. A. D. Philip £4,900 to £5,900
Deputy Director, Scottish Information Office, J. Woodrow . . . . £7,750 to £9,350
Parliamentary Clerk, Miss W. M. Doonan.

New St. Andrew's House, St. James's Centre, Edinburgh
[031–556 8400]
MANAGEMENT GROUP SUPPORT STAFF
Principal, J. J. McCabe . . . . £5,680 to £7,450

CENTRAL SERVICES
Deputy Secretary (Central Services), W. K. Fraser £14,000

Devolution Division
Under Secretary, J. M. Ross £12,000
Assistant Secretary, H. H. Mills £8,650 to £11,000
Principals, R. C. Allan; Miss M. B. Farquhar £5,680 to £7,450
Senior Executive Officer, C. D. Henderson £4,900 to £5,900

Personnel Division
Under Secretary, J. A. Ford, M.C. (*Principal Establishment Officer*) £12,000
Assistant Secretary, J. Inglis . . . . . £8,650 to £11,000

Senior Principals, D. H. Bayes; J. R. Gordon; J. Smith . . . . £7,750 to £9,350
Principals, H. M. L. Batts; R. M. Bell; I. F. Hunter; A. Newbigging; D. B. D. Petrie; R. S. Reid; R. J. T. S. Walker . . . . £5,680 to £7,450
Senior Executive Officers, T. Chalmers; P. Charles; J. S. Cornwall; A. C. Darby; J. R. M. Flucker; G. H. Fox; D. W. Garland; Miss M. E. Graham; P. McLaren; C. Moir; D. Murie; D. M. Rowani; R. Tait; G. Thompson; T. J. H. Wishart; J. Wood . . . . £4,900 to £5,900

Management Services Division
Under Secretary, J. S. Gibson. £12,000
Assistant Secretary, P. Mackay. . £8,650 to £11,000
Senior Principal, W. J. A. Scott . . £7,750 to £9,350
Principals, R. W. Alexander; D. C. Anderson; W. G. Dalgleish; Miss I. W. Inglis; N. MacLeod; J. Pettigrew; Mrs. F. J. Ross . . . £5,680 to £7,450
Senior Executive Officers, S. S. Anderson; A. T. Boyle; D. Burnett; S. M. Ellis; E. D. Ewing; T. G. Gass; J. R. Grant; A. Johnston; Miss M. P. Lawrie; R. C. Lawson; J. McGhee; T. Naysmith; W. B. Ritchie; I. J. Robertson; T. M. Thomson; G. W. Tucker . . . . £4,900 to £5,900
Librarian, H. A. Colquhoun . . . . £4,900 to £5,900

Computer Service
Broomhouse Drive, Edinburgh 11
[031–443 4040]
Manager (Assistant Secretary), J. S. Robertson £8,650 to £11,000
Deputy Manager (Senior Principal), J. S. Wheeler £7,750 to £9,350
Principals, J. Duffy; F. Ibbotson; Dr. D. Wishart £5,680 to £7,450
Senior Executive Officers, R. Barrie; J. R. Brown; Mrs. S. Crearie; J. B. Currie; W. Davidson; A. R. Donaldson; I. W. Goodwin; C. B. Knox; K. A. MacDonald; R. T. McGeorge; H. Mackay; W. McMaster; A. B. Patton; G. A. Paul; C. F. Weaver; T. G. Whitehead . . . £4,900 to £5,900

Finance Division
Under-Secretary, R. A. Dingwall-Smith . . . £12,000
Assistant Secretaries, I. R. Duncan, O.B.E.; J. E. Fraser; W. A. M. Good; R. R. Hillhouse; A. H. M. Mitchell . . . . £8,650 to £11,000
Senior Principals, F. B. Drysdale; I. Nicholson; I. S. Scott . . . . £7,750 to £9,350
Principals, A. J. Crawford; P. W. Daley; R. Earle; E. E. Hancock; G. Hardie; T. E. Hartland; T. J. Kelly; J. F. Kerr; R. W. MacIntosh; P. McKinlay; T. M. MacNair; T. J. Muirhead; D. M. W. Napier; G. Paterson; J. F. Reid; A. D. Robertson; G. G. Stewart; A. Walker; R. G. B. Wilkie; Miss E. M. Wilson £5,680 to £7,450
Chief Accountants, R. G. Carter; T. W. Forsyth; T. C. Hill; H. Holden; R. Turnbull; R. K. West £5,680 to £7,450
Senior Executive Officers, P. E. Anderson; W. Anness; J. A. Boyd; J. Brown; D. Cook; D. H. F. Dee; L. P. S. Dunbar; A. B. Forrest; G. L. Kerr; W. A. Lamberton; D. A. McNiven; J. Mann; D. R. Mayer; J. F. Munro; T. A. Murray; A. Naismith; W. Pilmer; R. S. Pryor; R. R. Ross; J. R. Sinclair; J. T. Skinner; D. Stewart; W. T. Tait; B. P. Underwood; G. P. Walker; T. Winwick . . . . £4,900 to £5,900

Solicitor's Office
(*For the Scottish Departments and certain U.K. services including H.M. Treasury, in Scotland.*)
Solicitor, R. W. Deans £14,000
Deputy Solicitor, A. G. Brand, M.B.E. £12,000
Divisional Solicitors, *J. B. Allan; H. D. Glover; J. L. Jamieson; A. A. McMillan; E. S. Robertson; *A. J. Sim; J. A. Stewart; *A. J. F. Tannock, M.C.; J. E. Taylor; Miss M. Y. Walker; C. J. Workman, T.D. . . . . £9,033 to £11,000
★ Seconded to Scottish Law Commission

Scottish Information Office
*(for the Scottish Departments and certain
U.K. services)*
Director, C. MacGregor, M.B.E..£8,650 to £11,000

Statistical Services
Chief Statistician, C. M. Glennie, Ph.D.
£8,650 to £11,000

Inquiry Reporters
44 York Place, Edinburgh 1
[031-556 9191]
Chief Reporter, A. J. Hunt, O.B.E.........£12,000
Deputy Chief Reporter, A. G. Bell
£9,798 to £11,000

**DEPARTMENT OF AGRICULTURE AND
FISHERIES FOR SCOTLAND**
Chesser House, 500 Gorgie Road, Edinburgh
[031-443 4020]
Dover House, Whitehall, London, S.W.1
[01-930 6151]
Secretary, J. I. Smith, C.B................£14,000
Fisheries Secretary, J. Cormack;.........£12,000
Under Secretaries, W. W. Gauld; N. J. Steele
£12,000
Assistant Secretaries, A. T. Brooke; B. Gordon;
Miss I. F. Haddow, C.B.E.; L. P. Hamilton;
J. F. Laing; D. A. Leitch; A. I. Macdonald; H. G.
Robertson; Miss J. L. Ross; S. H. Wright
£8,650 to £11,000
Principals, J. Blaikie; T. M. Brown; Miss E. A.
Buglass; Miss M. I. Davis; W. Dinnie; E. W.
Ferguson; D. A. Flett; E. W. Frizzell; P. Gowans;
J. J. Haughney; J. N. Johnston; G. G. Lyall; J. I.
Macbeath A. Macdonald; A. J. Matheson; A. J.
Monk; Miss E. V. Ramsay; A. B. Scott; D. Stott;
D. C. Todd; B. G. S. Ward; C. Wilkinson
£5,680 to £7,450
Senior Executive Officers, H. W. Bradford; W. M.
Bremner; D. R. Dickson; G. B. Downie; Miss
A. M. Hamilton; J. L. Helm; J. G. Henderson;
G. P. S. Macarthur; K. W. McKay; Miss G. B.
Mackie; J. A. M. McLeod; W. Malcolm; Miss
I. H. Rose; Miss M. F. M. Roy; T. Spence; Miss
N. C. Telfer; A. G. Templeman; D. Watson;
I. M. Whitelaw............£4,900 to £5,900
Chief Agricultural Officer, C. Mackay.....£12,000
Deputy Chief Agricultural Officer, A. H. Boggon
£11,000
Divisional Agricultural Officers, D. C. Collie; A.
Edwards; R. Macdonald; I. L. Mackenzie
£8,650 to £9,798
Chief Agricultural Economist, J. M. Dunn, D.Phil.
£8,650 to £11,000
Chief Fatstock Officer, A. Scott, O.B.E.
£5,680 to £7,450
Chief Food and Dairy Officer, M. E. M. Anderson
£6,466 to £8,075
Chief Surveyor, J. G. Cullen....£8,650 to £9,798
Scientific Adviser, J. G. Brotherston
£10,180 to £11,190
Technical Development Officer, J. Ferguson
£8,650 to £9,798

Royal Botanic Garden
Inverleith Row, Edinburgh 3
[031-552 7171]
Regius Keeper, D. M. Henderson, F.R.S.E.
£10,180 to £11,190
Assistant Keeper, J. Cullen, Ph.D..£8,650 to £9,798

Agricultural Scientific Services
East Craigs, Corstorphine, Edinburgh 12
[031-334 0355]
Director, J. M. Todd........£10,180 to £11,190
Deputy Director, D. C. Graham, Ph.D., F.R.S.E.
£8,650 to £9,798
Assistant Director, R. D. Seaton
£8,650 to £9,798

Fisheries Research Services
Marine Laboratory, P.O. Box 101,
Victoria Road, Torry, Aberdeen
[0224 876544]
Director of Fisheries Research and Controller of Fisheries

Research and Development (U.K.), B. B. Parrish,
F.R.S.E...............................£11,670
Deputy Director, J. H. Steele, D.SC., F.R.S.E.
£10,180 to £11,190
Senior Principal Scientific Officers, J. J. Foster; A. D.
McIntyre, D.SC., Ph.D., F.R.S.E.; A. Saville; T. H.
Simpson, Ph.D., F.R.S.E.; H. J. Thomas, Ph.D.,
F.R.S.E........................£8,650 to £9,798

Freshwater Fisheries Laboratory,
Faskally, Pitlochry, Perthshire
[0796 2060]
Senior Principal Scientific Officer, A. V. Holden,
F.R.S.E......................£8,650 to £9,798

Sea Fisheries Inspectorate
Chief Inspector of Sea Fisheries, M. J. MacLeod
£9,350
Inspector of Salmon and Freshwater Fisheries, S. D.
Sedgwick.................£5,687 to £7,205
Marine Superintendent, Captain A. T. Horsburgh
£7,341 to £7,636

Crofters Commission
4/6 Castle Wynd, Inverness
[0463 37231]
Chairman, J. S. Grant, C.B.E............£9,000
Members (part-time), N. A. MacAskill (£4,467);
R. H. W. Bruce, C.B.E.; A. Fraser, Ph.D.;
J. MacDonald; D. J. MacCuish; J. M. Macmillan,
O.B.E..............................£2,236
Secretary and Solicitor, A. W. Brodie
£7,750 to £9,350
Assistant Secretary, (vacant).....£5,680 to £7,450
Chief Technical Officer, W. Macfarlane
£6,280 to £7,450

Red Deer Commission
Knowsley, 82 Fairfield Road, Inverness
[0463 31751]
Chairman, I. Miller......................£3,350
Secretary, J. Dooner..........£4,900 to £5,900

**SCOTTISH DEVELOPMENT
DEPARTMENT**
New St. Andrew's House, St. James's Centre,
Edinburgh
[031-556 8400]
Dover House, Whitehall, London, S.W.1
[01-930 6151]
Secretary, E. L. Gillett.................£14,000
Under Secretaries, R. D. Cramond; J. B. Fleming;
P. C. Rendle.......................£12,000
Assistant Secretaries, S. C. Aldridge; D. Connelly;
G. F. Hendry; H. F. G. Kelly; J. Kerr; T. L. Lister;
D. G. Mackay; J. B. More; M. H. Orde, O.B.E.;
N. E. Sharp; W. W. Scott; J. W. Sinclair; J.
Walker..................£8,650 to £11,000
Principals, J. W. Barron; N. G. Campbell; J. A.
Clare; M. P. Cunliffe; J. M. Currie; N. J. Fother-
ingham; Mrs K. S. Gillender; H. J. Graham;
J. Hamill; J. C. Henderson; A. Heyworth; J. M.
Howieson; C. K. Lambie; J. W. L. Lonie; J.
Loudfoot; Mrs. E. J. Lugton; Miss E. A. Mackay;
K. Mackay; J. R. McKechnie; A. S. Neilson;
S. G. Patterson; R. Patton; B. V. Philp; W. M.
Robertson; G. Robson; D. Stevenson; A. M.
Thomson; J. Watson; R. G. B. Wilkie
£5,680 to £7,450
Director, Road Safety Advisory Unit, Lt.-Col. D.
Birrell.....................£5,680 to £7,450
Senior Executive Officers, J. T. Brown; D. J. Chalm-
ers; M. A. Duffy; J. F. Fraser; M. A. Grant; J. M.
Haynes; F. H. Hunter W. E. Irvine; Miss M. M.
Jamieson; T. Johnston; J. B. Jolly; P. Kemp; Miss
E. M. Living stone; G. P. McConnell; E. D. F.
McGaughrin; A. Maclean; C. McLean; A. R.
Menzies; Miss M. N. Mowat; D. M. Porter;
A. W. Russell; R. S. Stewart; J. Thompson; H.
Young....................£4,900 to £5,900

Professional Staff
Chief Engineer, S. C. Agnew............£12,000
Deputy Chief Engineer, E. H. Nicoll.....£11,000
Assistant Chief Engineers, P. Martin; J. G. Munro;
J. Storry; J. O. Thorburn; A. Wotherspoon
£8,650 to £9,798

Chief Architect, B. P. Beckett............£12,000
Deputy Chief Architect, D. I. Black.......£11,000
Superintending Architects, A. R. H. Bott; Miss M. J. Blanco White, O.B.E.; J. H. Fullarton; R. W. Naismith; J. Robin; R. I. Watson; P. E. White; D. E. Whitham................£8,650 to £9,798
Chief Planning Officer, W. D. C. Lyddon...£12,000
Deputy Chief Planning Officers, H. Irving; R. G. H. Turnbull............................£11,000
Regional Planning Officers, W. Amcotts; P. D. McGovern, PH.D.; A. MacKenzie; G. R. Sloman
............................£8,650 to £9,798
Chief Research Officer, Miss B. D. Baker, O.B.E. ..
............................£8,650 to £11,000
Senior Principal Research Officers, C. P. A. Levein, PH.D.; C. C. Macdonald....£7,750 to £9,350
Chief Quantity Surveyor, A. Y. Hamilton..£11,000
Deputy Chief Quantity Surveyor, A. Duncan
............................£8,650 to £9,798
Superintending Quantity Surveyors, R. R. Armour; D. J. Campbell; D. C. Russell
............................£8,650 to £9,798
Chief Road Engineer, J. A. M. Mackenzie...£12,000
Deputy Chief Road Engineer, D. P. Gray...£11,000
Assistant Chief Road Engineer, L. Clements £11,000
Superintending Engineers, D. M. Fisher; E. G. Miller; W. G. Ross; G. F. Storey....£8,650 to £9,798
H.M. Chief Industrial Pollution Inspector, W. Mc-Camley............................£11,000
Chief Estates Officer, P. H. Miller £8,650 to £9,798

SCOTTISH ECONOMIC PLANNING DEPARTMENT
New St. Andrew's House, St. James's Centre, Edinburgh
[031–556 8400]
Dover House, Whitehall, S.W.1
[01–930 6151]
Secretary, T. R. H. Godden, C.B.........£14,000
Under Secretary (Regional Development) and Chief Economic Adviser, R. G. L. McCrone, PH.D.
............................£12,000
Under Secretary, J. A. Scott, M.V.O.......£12,000
Assistant Secretaries, R. F. Butler; D. J. Essery; J. Glendinning, M.B.E.; G. S. Murray; G. R. Wilson
............................£8,650 to £11,000
Senior Economic Adviser, W. M. McNie
............................£8,650 to £11,000
Senior Principal, J. J. Hunter, D.F.C.
............................£7,750 to £9,350
Principals, G. B. Baird; I. G. F. Gray; R. M. Laidlaw; A. Lindsay; W. R. McKie; J. G. Middlemiss; H. Morison; E. S. Wall; M. R. Wilson
............................£5,680 to £7,450
Senior Executive Officers, T. Blacklock; E. Boulton; H. G. Kelly; R. N. Shaw
............................£4,900 to £5,900

Industrial Development Division
Alhambra House, 45 Waterloo Street, Glasgow
[041–248 2855]
Under Secretaries, A. G. Manzie; W. B. Kirkpatrick
............................£12,000
Assistant Secretaries, T. M. Band; R. Burns
............................£8,650 to £11,000
Senior Principals, J. E. Milne; R. J. Pounce; O.B.E.; L. C. Roberts............£7,750 to £9,350
Principals, H. J. Henson; G. W. H. Kelly; A. D. M. Malcolm..................£5,680 to £7,450
Senior Executive Officers, L. J. Baston; L. S. Nash; Miss B. O'Callaghan; W. F. Robertson; J. Scullion; G. H. Smith; G. M. Thomson; J. S. Whitehouse.................£4,900 to £5,900

SCOTTISH EDUCATION DEPARTMENT
New St. Andrew's House, St. James's Centre, Edinburgh
[031–556 8400]
Dover House, Whitehall, London, S.W.1
[01–930 6151]
Secretary, J. A. M. Mitchell, C.V.O. M.C....£14,000
Under Secretaries, Miss P. A. Cox; J. B. Hume; I. M. Robertson, C.B., M.V.O..............£12,000
Assistant Secretaries, G. M. Fair; J. J. Farrell; B. J.

Fiddes; A. K. Forbes (*H.M. Chief Inspector of Schools*); I. D. Hamilton; J. Kidd; J. F. McClellan; A. M. Macpherson; H. Robertson, M.B.E.; R. E. Smith......£8,650 to £11,000
Senior Principals, Mrs. E. C. G. Craghill; A. J. C. Mitchell.................£7,750 to £9,350
Principals, G. E. Brewerton; Mrs. L. J. Clare; E. C. Davison; A. C. Easson; T. B. Haig; A. W. M. Heggie; S. R. Hook; D. K. C. Jeffery; L. Jobson; Miss J. M. Lawson; K. J. Mackenzie; J. McCallum; R. P. C. Macnab; J. S. B. Martin; R. Naylor; T. Rarity; Mrs. G. M. Stewart; Miss W. J. Strongman; Miss M. B. Tait; G. H. Walker; W. Weir; A. C. Wilson
............................£5,680 to £7,450
Senior Executive Officers, G. H. J. Bell; W. A. Bruce; D. A. Christie; Miss W. S. Duguid; Miss E. B. Hewitt; W. A. McGhee; H. M. McGilvray; Miss M. M. Marshall; W. E. M. Maxwell; G. T. Reed; W. H. Stein; B. V. Surridge; I. M. Watt; N. Wood.................£4,900 to £5,900

H.M. Inspectors of Schools
Senior Chief Inspector, J. F. McGarrity....£12,000
Depute Senior Chief Inspectors, A. D. Chirnside; J. A. Ferguson.................£11,440
Chief Inspectors, W. K. Ferguson; D. S. Graham; R. S. Johnston; S. E. McClelland, PH.D.; J. G. Morris; W. R. Ritchie; Miss H. J. S. Sandison; H. F. Smith; E. F. Thompkins; J. H. Thomson; T. F. Williamson.................£11,000
Inspectors, J. N. Alison; M. T. J. Axford; W. T. Beveridge; W. F. L. Bigwood; J. Boyes; Miss C. L. Boyle; T. Brown; J. Bryce; J. W. Burdin; Miss C. S. Cameron; Miss G. C. Campbell; D. G. Carter; L. Clark; C. Cleall; G. A. B. Craig; M. Q. Cramb; A. H. B. Davidson; S. A. Dell; R. F. Dick; J. C. Dignan; D. W. Duncan; Miss K. M. Fairweather; A. H. Ferguson; A. W. Finlayson; B. Fryer; T. N. Gallacher; A. R. Gallon; A. B. Giovanazzi; G. P. D. Gordon; J. Hay; Miss M. J. Hay; J. Howgego; L. A. Hunter; J. Inglis; M. Jack; A. W. Jeffrey; E. S. Kelly; J. Kiely; D. G. Kirkpatrick; I. Lawson; J. C. Leitch; J. E. F. Longman; R. E. Lygo; M. McAllan; J. McAlpine; I. M. MacAskill; D. McCalman; J. F. MacDonald; A. S. McGlynn; D. W. Mack; Miss M. C. McKellar; H. M. MacLaren; M. Macleod; D. R. McNicoll; A. A. McPherson; A. J. Macpherson; H. L. Martin; A. Maltby; A. C. T. Mascarenhas; W. M. Mein; A. Milne; S. Milne, PH.D.; J. Mitchell; H. Morris; Miss W. Morrison; Miss E. R. Mowat; G. S. Mutch; R. H. Nelson; B. Nickerson, PH.D.; W. Nicol; A. Nisbet; J. Nisbet; D. A. Osler; I. P. Pascoe; J. Picken; Miss A. H. M. Prain; R. B. Prescott; A. M. Rankin; T. A. Rankin; J. C. Rankine; D. Reid; W. M. Roach, Ph.D.; I. D. S. Robertson; J. N. Robertson; A. L. Robson; M. Roebuck; J. Rorrison; M. G. Scott; G. M. Sinclair, Ph.D.; S. T. S. Skillen; J. A. Sloggie; A. L. Small; H. Smith; A. M. Steele; W. P. Stewart; Miss E. M. W. Thomson; H. Walker; G. Wallis; R. S. Weir; D. M. Whyte; R. G. Wilson; J. G. L. Wright; D. B. Young; R. W. J. Young, Ph.D..............£6,625 to £9,415

Social Work Services Group
St. Andrew's House, Edinburgh
[031–556 8501]
The Social Work Services Group, which is attached to the Scottish Education Department, administers the provisions of the Social Work (Scotland) Act, 1968.
Under-Secretary, A. F. Reid............£12,000
Assistant Secretaries, R. J. W. Clark; G. J. Murray; A. M. Thomson........£8,650 to £11,000
Senior Principal, Mrs. E. C. G. Craghill
............................£7,750 to £9,350
Principals, D. A. Bennet; R. J. Edie; Mrs. E. M. A. McGregor; G. G. McHaffie; K. B. T. Mackenzie; W. A Smith; J. P. Wallace..£5,680 to £7,450
Senior Executive Officers, Miss M. R. M. Bald; J. Graham; R. W. Willamson..£4,900 to £5,900
Chief Adviser on Social Work in Scotland, Miss B. Jones............................£11,670

Deputy Chief Advisers on Social Work in Scotland,
D. Colvin; Miss M. M. McInnes
£8,650 to £11,000
Senior Advisers on Social Work in Scotland, A. C.
Adams; Miss D. M. Boardman; Miss B. E. Drake;
J. Gallacher; Miss P. M. Hammond; Miss C. P.
Kerr; R. Percival; W. J. McCollam; D. S,
Roulston; J. Smith . . . . £8,250 to £9,798

SCOTTISH HOME AND HEALTH
DEPARTMENT
New St. Andrew's House, St. James's Centre,
Edinburgh
[031–556 8400]
Dover House, Whitehall, London,
S.W.1
[01–930 6151]

Secretary, R. P. Fraser, C.B. £14,000
Under Secretaries, D. J. Cowperthwaite; E. U. E.
Elliott-Binns; A. L. Rennie; I. L. Sharp. £12,000
Assistant Secretaries, G. P. H. Aitken; A. H. Bishop;
F. H. Cowley; J. Keeley; W. P. Lawrie; Miss M.
K. MacDonald; T. H. McLean; H. McNamara;
Miss M. A. McPherson; A. T. F. Ogilvie; I. D.
Penman; E. Redmond; G. Robertson; J. E.
Tinkler; W. A. P. Weatherston
£8,650 to £11,000
Senior Principals, G. Aithie; J. Leithead
£7,750 to £9,350
Principals, D. A. Bennet; H. J. Boatwright; J.
Borthwick; Miss M. H. B. Brown; R. D. M.
Calder; D. H. Collier; T. Collinson; D. J. David-
son; J. N. Davison; J. S. Dick; H. C. Fraser; J. P.
Fraser; T. B. Hamilton; D. Harrison; W. W.
Howitt; S. M. Liddle; W. Liddle; J. Linn; D.
G. McCulloch; A. Macdonald; W. M. Mc-
Intyre; I. J. Mackenzie; Miss M. Maclean; I. A.
Macpherson; Miss L. R. Maddock; W. R.
Miller; K. W. Moore; R. Mowat; G. N. Munro;
G. Murray; E. C. Reavley; F. H. Roberts; R.
E. S. Robinson; J. Rodger; D. D. Rose; G.
Scott; A. Simmen; N. W. Smith; W. A. Strain;
J. A. Sutherland; J. Taylor; A. Walker
£5,680 to £7,450
Senior Executive Officers, N. Archer; M. Bunney;
J. S. Burnett; N. F. Butler; Mrs. F. M. Cruick-
shanks; D. M. Ferguson; P. G. Glynn; Miss D.
Jones; I. K. Kennedy; J. S. C. Little; Miss M.
Macdonald, M.B.E.; G. Mason; T. Melville; R.
Nurse; G. Pearson; A. W. Rhind; R. N.
Roberts; D. A. Robertson; J. S. Ross; W. H.
Ross; R. M. Russell; J. L. Sime; G. Simmons;
Miss K. J. Sinclair; Miss A. C. C. Smart; A.
Stephenson; W. H. Stewart; Miss M. B. M.
Talbot; M. T. A. Vance; B. A. F. Vincent; S. J.
B. Walker; I. T. Wallace; J. T. Watt; T. W.
Wilson; J. C. Young . . . . £4,900 to £5,900

Medical Services
Chief Medical Officer, Sir John Brotherston, M.D.,
F.R.S.E. £14,000
Deputy Chief Medical Officers, I. S. Macdonald;
G. A. Scott £12,000
Principal Medical Officers, M. Ashley-Miller; J. H.
Grant; J. H. Henderson; W. K. Henderson; J. K.
Hunter, O.B.E.; D. W. A. McCreadie; I. M. Mac-
Gregor; D. M. Pendreigh; W. T. Thom, O.B.E.
£11,440
Senior Medical Officers, A. E. Bell; Margaret Bell;
J. T. Boyd; F. B. Davidson; W. Forbes; J. W.
Gibb; K. T. Gruer; L. F. Howitt; J. H. Leckie;
A. D. McIntyre; A. M. Melville; H. Miller; A.
T. B. Moir; J. A. Morton; W. M. Prentice; R.
A. W. Ratcliff; G. W. Simpson; D. J. Sloan;
D. E. Walker £11,000
Medical Officers, P. W. Brooks; R. G. Covell; D. C.
Drummond; G. I. Forbes; G. Gilray; Margaret
Hennigan; Iole L'E. K. McLean; J. S. Patter-
son; B. C. S. Slater; J. L. Tester, O.B.E.; Elizabeth
M. Whiteside; H. W. Woolner; A. B. Young
£6,987 to £9,562
Regional Medical Officers, I. G. Conn; J. A. Fergus-
son; T. E. S. Fergusson; J. W. Logan, D.S.O.;
H. McBain; A. C. McBelane; J. B. Morris; D. N.
B. Morrison; C. Murray; R. C. Nimmo-Smith;

J. Pearson; W. M. Reid; P. I. T. Walker
£6,987 to £9,562
Chief Scientist, Prof. Sir Andrew Kay, F.R.S.E.
Chief Dental Officer, J. L. Trainer £11,440
Senior Dental Officer (vacant) £11,000
Dental Officers, J. Gall; A. B. Potts; A. Boyd
£6,987 to £9,502
Chief Nursing Officer, (vacant) £10,865
Chief Pharmacist, R. Higson . . . . £8,650 to £9,798
Senior Principal Scientific Officer, W. F. Gunn
£8,650 to £9,798

Miscellaneous Appointments
H.M. Chief Inspector of Constabulary for Scotland,
D. Gray, O.B.E. £14,955
H.M. Inspector of Constabulary, Q. C. Wilson, O.B.E.
£14,202
Commandant, Scottish Police College, Col. R. C.
Robertson-Macleod, D.S.O., M.C., T.D. . £10,697
Director of Telecommunications, A. F. Harrison
£8,650 to £9,798
H.M. Inspector of Fire Services, J. Jackson, O.B.E.
£8,799 to £9,632
Commandant, Scottish Fire Service Training School,
J. Hartil . . . . £4,900 to £5,900
Secretary, Scottish Health Service Planning Council,
T. D. Hunter.

Prisons Division
Broomhouse Drive, Edinburgh 11
[031–443 4040]
Director of Scottish Prison Service, J. Scrimgeour
£11,670
Assistant Controller (Operations), A. C. Meikle
£8,650 to £11,000
Assistant Secretary (Controller, Administration), J.
Keeley . . . . £8,650 to £11,000
Senior Principal (Personnel), G. Aithie
£7,750 to £9,350
Principal (Controller, Industries and Supplies), T.
Collinson . . . . £5,680 to £7,450
Inspector of Scottish Prison Service, J. H. Frisby
£9,424
Assistant Inspector of Scottish Prison Service, W.
McVey . . . . £5,690 to £6,717
Governor Seconded to Headquarters, A. C. Meikle
£7,083 to £8,044

Prison Governors
Aberdeen, G. B. Duncan . . . . £5,690 to £6,717
Castle Huntly Borstal Institution, J. Drummond
£5,690 to £6,717
Cornton Vale, Lady Martha Bruce, O.B.E., T.D.
£7,083 to £8,066
Dumfries Young Offenders Institution, T. McLaughlan
£5,690 to £6,717
Edinburgh, A. Gallacher . . . . £7,083 to £8,066
Edinburgh Young Offenders Institution, T. Binnie
£5,690 to £6,717
Glasgow (Barlinnie), R. F. Hendry £9,424
Glasgow (Barlinnie Special Unit), W. Geddes;
£5,690 to £6,717
Glasgow (Barlinnie Young Offenders Institution), R.
M. McLeod . . . . £4,673 to £5,340
Glenochil Detention Centre, G. N. S. Neave. £9,424
Greenock, J. P. Dow . . . . £4,673 to £5,340
Inverness, T. A. M. Davidson . . . £5,690 to £6,717
Longriggend Remand Institution, D. Robertson
£5,690 to £6,717
Low Moss, W. Gordon . . . . £5,690 to £6,717
Noranside Borstal Institution, A. J. Smith
£5,690 to £6,717
Penninghame, J. S. Bertram . . . . . £4,673 to £5,340
Perth, G. Dingwall . . . . £7,083 to £8,066
Perth (Friarton Young Offenders Institution), N. Mc-
Phail . . . . £5,690 to £6,717
Peterhead, W. Gardner £9,424
Polmont Borstal Institution, C. W. Hills
£7,083 to £8,066
Scottish Prison Service College, W. T. Finlayson
£5,690 to £6,717

Mental Welfare Commission for Scotland
22 Melville Street, Edinburgh, 3
Chairman, The Hon. Lord McDonald, M.C.; *Commissioners,* Prof. W. M. Miller, C.B.E., M.D.; Lt.-
Col. R. C. M. Monteith, M.C., T.D.; J. F. A.

Gibson, T.D.; H. F. Smith; Miss M. Megan
Browne, O.B.E.; Mrs. N. H. Mansbridge; M. M.
Whittet, O.B.E. £330
Medical Commissioners, Anne N. M. Brittain;
J. M. Loughran. £11,000
Medical Officers, Elizabeth M. Whiteside; Iole L'E.
K. Maclean; H. W. Woolner £6,987 to £9,562
Secretary, Miss M. McDonald, M.B.E.
. . . .£4,900 to £5,900
*Counsel to the Secretary of State for Scotland under
Private Legislation Procedure (Scotland) Act,* 1936
India Buildings, Victoria Street, Edinburgh 1).
Senior Counsel, G. S. Douglas, Q.C.
Junior Counsel, P. K. Vandore

NATIONAL HEALTH SERVICE, SCOTLAND
Health Boards

Argyll and Clyde, Gilmour House, Paisley. *Chairman*, W. P. Blyth, T.D. *Secretary*, W. G. Ayling.
Ayrshire and Arran, Ailsa Hospital, P.O. Box 13, Ayr. *Chairman*, J. Lockhart. *Secretary*, R. A. McCrorie.
Borders, Huntlyburn, Melrose, Roxburghshire. *Chairman*, J. Gibb. *Secretary*, A. G. Welstead.
Dumfries and Galloway, Charnwood Road, Dumfries. *Chairman*, J. Wyllie-Irving, T.D. *Secretary*, E. Errington.
Fife, 5 Comely Park, Dunfermline. *Chairman*, J. Crawford. *Secretary*, R. Mitchell.
Forth Valley, 33 Spittal Street, Stirling. *Chairman*, J. A. Macreadie. *Secretary*, J. Wallace, M.B.E.
Grampian, 1–5 Albyn Place, Aberdeen. *Chairman*, W. S. Crosby. *Secretary*, W. D. Hardie.
Greater Glasgow, 351 Sauchiehall Street, Glasgow. *Chairman*, Sir Simpson Stevenson. *Secretary*, R. D. R. Gardner.
Highland, Reay House, 17 Old Edinburgh Road, Inverness. *Chairman*, R. Wallace, C.B.E. *Secretary*, R. R. W. Stewart.
Lanarkshire, 14 Beckford Street, Hamilton, Lanarkshire. *Chairman*, A. R. Miller, C.B.E. *Secretary*, H. K. Mitchell.
Lothian, 11 Drumsheugh Gardens, Edinburgh. *Chairman*, Mrs. R. T. Nealon. *Secretary*, W. L. Douglass.
Orkney, Balfour Hospital, New Scapa Road, Kirkwall, Orkney. *Chairman*, S. P. Robertson, M.B.E. *Secretary*, F. G. Cusiter.
Shetland, 44 Commercial Street, Lerwick. *Chairman*, R. Adair. *Secretary* (vacant)
Tayside, P.O. Box 75, Vernonholme, Riverside Drive, Dundee. *Chairman*, D. K. Thomson, C.B.E., T.D. *Secretary*, G. G. Savage.
Western Isles, Newton House, Stornoway, Isle of Lewis. *Chairman*, R. Stewart. *Secretary*, J. Paterson.

Common Services Agency
Trinity Park House, South Trinity Road, Edinburgh
Secretary, A. McPhee. *Treasurer*, J. W. Morrison.

GENERAL REGISTER OFFICE (Scotland)
New Register House, Edinburgh 1
[031-556 3952]
Registrar General, W. Baird. £11,670
Deputy Registrar General, V. C. Stewart (*Establishment Officer*). . . . .£8,650 to £11,000
Assistant Secretary (*Marriage Legislation*), R. MacLeod. . . . .£8,650 to £11,000
Chief Statistician, H. B. Lawson. £8,650 to £11,000
Statisticians, R. A. De Mellow; B. N. Downie; J. Travers. . . . .£6,293 to £7,763
Principals, D. J. Baird; G. F. Baird; A. R. Clark; J. G. Dewar; J. A. Hamilton; A. R. Irons
. . . .£6,293 to £7,763
Senior Executive Officers, A. W. Auld; D. Bannatynne; I. G. Bowie; J. Bush; H. G. Cottrell; J. C. Duncan; A. Lister; J. B. Lyall; J. M. Nicol; J. Paterson; D. M. Robertson; R. R. Taylor; Mrs. J. B. Walker; J. O. Wastle; H. A. Waugh; R. T. Wilson. . . . .£5,213 to £6,213

SOCIAL SCIENCE RESEARCH COUNCIL
1 Temple Avenue, E.C.4
[01-353 5252]
The S.S.R.C. was set up by Royal Charter in 1965 for the promotion of social science research. The Council carries out its role by awarding research grants, by initiating research and research contracts, by awarding postgraduate studentships, bursaries and fellowships, and through its research units. In addition the Council provides advice and disseminates knowledge on the social sciences. A list of publications is available from the S.S.R.C. Information Section.
Chairman, D. Robinson.
Secretary, C. S. Smith.

HER MAJESTY'S STATIONERY OFFICE
Atlantic House, Holborn Viaduct, E.C.1
[01-248 9876]
Sovereign House, Botolph Street, Norwich
[0603 22211]
Bookshops in London:—
Retail.—49 High Holborn, W.C.1.
Wholesale and post orders.—P.O. Box 569, S.E.1.
Her Majesty's Stationery Office was established in 1786 and is the British Government's central organization for the supply of printing, binding, office supplies and office machinery of all kinds, and published books and periodicals, for the Public Service at home and abroad; it also undertakes duplicating and distributing for government departments. The Stationery Office is the publisher for the Government, and has bookshops for the sale of Government publications in London, Edinburgh, Cardiff, Manchester, Bristol, Birmingham and Belfast; leading booksellers in the larger towns act as agents; and there are wholesale departments in London, Edinburgh and Belfast from which booksellers may obtain supplies. It is also the agent for the sale of publications of the United Nations and its specialized agencies and for certain other international organizations. The Controller of the Stationery Office is under Letters Patent the *Queen's Printer of the Acts of Parliament* and in him is vested the Copyright in all British Government documents.
Government publications are of a wide and varied range and over 7,500 publications are produced each year. They include *London Gazette*, which has been issued since 1665, and *Hansard*, the verbatim report of the proceedings in both Houses of Parliament, available on the morning following the debate. The Stationery Office has in stock some 90,000 titles and its subscriptions and standing order lists contain about 150,000 addresses. The annual sales total about 37,000,000 copies.
The aggregate net estimate for the department for 1976–77 was £88,549,000 (an increase of £15,214,000 on the same estimate for 1975–76).
Generally the department obtains its supplies from commercial sources by competitive tender. For printing and binding, however, the Stationery Office has its own printing works and binderies which produce about one-third of the total requirement, including telephone directories, pension allowance books, national savings certificates and stamps, postal orders, premium bonds. National Insurance stamps, road fund licences, and television licences.
The staff employed on April 1, 1976, was 7,412 (an increase of 229 over the previous year), including 1,661 in warehouses and 2,442 at printing works: the total space occupied was 3,135,447 square feet, including 1,037,000 sq. ft. for warehouse space and 1,087,000 sq. ft. for the printing works.
Controller, H. Glover. £14,000
Executive Assistant, P. R. C. Gainsborough.
Personal Secretary, Mrs. M. A. Hawkins.
Assistant Controllers, J. J. Cherns; G. D. Macaulay; R. T. Walker. £11,670
Head of Printing Services, E. J. Deller
. . . .£8,650 to £11,000
Head of Finance, D. C. Dashfield, O.B.E., M.V.O.
. . . .£8,650 to £11,000

Head of Publishing, F. E. Davey. £8,650 to £11,000
Director of Supply, C. W. Blundell, O.B.E.
£8,650 to £11,000
Directors of Works, K. A. Allen; W. D. Bisset
£8,650 to £11,000
Adviser of Typography, Ruari McLean, C.B.E.

Accountants

Chief Accountants, M. C. Holgate; D. T. J. Rutherford; C. G. Wood; R. T. Wykes
£5,680 to £7,450
Senior Accountants, R. W. Chapman; D. T. Cooke; R. M. Glenn; B. J. Jackson; P. J. Macdonald; B. F. Perry; D. Silver; K. H. Staff
£4,900 to £5,900
Accountancy Executive, J. A. Wills
£5,310 to £6,310

Central Planning and Policy Co-ordination Unit

Director, B. C. E. Lee.......... £5,680 to £7,480
Assistant Directors, R. E. H. Mills; D. N. Roberts
£4,900 to £5,900

Finance Division

Director, H. V. Roe, O.B.E...... £7,750 to £9,350
Deputy Directors, P. W. Buckerfield; P. Jefford
£5,680 to £7,450
Assistant Directors, W. H. Burberry; G. F. C. Clarke; Miss F. V. Page; B. Wilson; E. J. Woods
£4,900 to £5,900
Chief Examiner, Printers' & Binders' Accounts, S. R. Hays...................... £4,900 to £5,900

Industrial Relations Division

Director, R. C. Beever......... £8,160 to £9,760
Deputy Directors, D. D. Hinnigan; R. E. Wooldridge...................... £5,680 to £7,450
Assistant Directors, W. N. Greenaway; Mrs. J. S. Muir; R. A. Myers......... £4,900 to £5,900

Management Services

Director, D. J. Balls........... £5,860 to £7,450
Assistant Directors, J. W. Rowe; M. J. M. Salt
£4,900 to £5,900
Chief Work Study Officer, D. S. Henshall
£4,900 to £5,900

Personnel Services Division

Director, R. H. Chisholm, O.B.E.. £7,750 to £9,350
Deputy Directors, A. M. Foote; T. S. Harris, M.B.E.; F. J. Wilson................. £5,680 to £7,450
Assistant Directors, J. R. Allen; M. J. Cuming; E. L. Franklin; F. G. Gibbs; H. B. Jackson; J. H. Jones; C. J. Penn; G. C. Robbie; C. N. Southgate; J. R. Wilson..... £4,900 to £5,900

Print Procurement Division

Director, A. A. Smith.......... £7,750 to £9,350
Deputy Director (Norwich), J. H. Hynes, O.B.E.
£5,680 to £7,450
Deputy Director (London), C. E. S. Robbs
£5,680 to £7,450
Assistant Directors, B. W. P. Downing; A. Hunter; K. E. Hutchings, B.E.M.; T. H. Kearsley; J. N. Palmer..................... £4,900 to £5,900

Printing Works Division

Head of Works Administration, K. P. Sandford
£5,680 to £7,450
Head of Works Production and Resource Planning, E. B. McKendrick.............. £5,680 to £7,450
Assistant Directors, R. W. Bent; R. P. Hearsey; E. C. Hudgell.............. £4,900 to £5,900
Senior Works Managers, A. R. Affolter; F. J. Beasley; D. G. Forbes; W. N. Frost
£5,680 to £7,450
Works Managers, A. J. B. Baptie; R. A. De Cleyn; C. J. Newman; E. J. Smith. . £4,900 to £5,900
Deputy Senior Works Managers, A. S. Brown; R. Buckley; R. T. Canning; R. M. Gair; A. R. Ling; A. Mackie; K. Morgan; F. L. Pymm; R. S. Roberts; G. Stewart; D. J. Wintle
£4,900 to £5,900
Head of Works Engineering Services, R. Miller
£6,280 to £7,450
Deputy Head of Works Engineering Services, C. F. Croisdale.................. £4,720 to £5,930

Publishing Group

Director of Publishing, H. W. Leader
£7,750 to £9,350
Director of Publications Distribution, J. P. Morgan
£7,750 to £9,350
Director of Publication Marketing, D. G. R. Perry
£9,760
Director of Graphic Design, J. Westwood
£5,680 to £7,450
Deputy Directors, E. S. Brooks; J. Carpenter £5,680 to (£7,450); R. Brearley.... £4,900 to £5,900
Assistant Directors, R. C. Barnard; E. Beaumont; L. C. de Brunner; G. E. Finch; Mrs. K. P. D. Griffiths; L. B. Mills; D. Newton; J. F. Phillips, M.B.E.; J. F. Saville.......... £4,900 to £5,900

Reprographic Centre

Director, G. B. Furn........... £7,750 to £9,350
Assistant Director, A. Mackenzie. £4,900 to £5,900
Manager, J. W. Brunton....... £5,680 to £7,450
Production Manager, (vacant).... £4,900 to £5,900
Administration Manager, F. J. Meads
£4,900 to £5,900
Co-ordinator of Reprographic Services, A. W. Martyn
£5,680 to £7,450
Deputy Co-ordinator, G. J. York. £4,900 to £5,900
Assistant Co-ordinators, J. S. Nash; J. A. Owen
£4,900 to £5,900

Supply Division

Director, C. W. Blundell, O.B.E.. £8,650 to £11,000
Deputy Directors, A. E. J. Brunwin; S. A. Cowie; R. F. Norris; W. S. Porter; D. W. Ray
£5,680 to £7,450
Assistant Directors, F. E. Ashman; E. G. N. Calver; J. Doherty; A. A. Gummett; C. E. Harrold; H. R. Higgs; C. G. Lloyd; S. A. Munns; F. R. Payne; D. A. Prutton; R. A. Youl
£4,900 to £5,900
Manager, Office Machinery Technical Service, D. W. Farquhar.................... £4,720 to £5,930

Technical Services Division

Director, (vacant)............. £7,750 to £9,350
Deputy Director, K. J. Lowe... £5,680 to £7,450
Assistant Directors, E. J. Cletheroe; T. J. Soutar; H. S. Todd................ £4,900 to £5,900
Head of Laboratory, S. M. Goldfarb
£6,280 to £7,450
Deputy Heads of Laboratory, F. E. Arnold; W. J. R. Howell; J. O. P. Jones....... £4,720 to £5,930

REGIONAL OFFICES AND BOOKSHOPS

Scotland

Government Buildings, Bankhead Avenue, Edinburgh
Bookshop: 13a Castle Street, Edinburgh
Director, K. J. Rhodes, M.B.E.... £5,680 to £7,450
Deputy Director, G. S. McGowan
£4,900 to £5,900

Northern Ireland

Chichester Street, Belfast
Retail and Trade Bookshop, Chichester Street, Belfast
Director, F. A. G. Lonon....... £5,680 to £7,450

Manchester

Broadway, Chadderton, Lancs.
Bookshop: Brazennose House, Brazennose Street, Manchester
Director, R. A. Dunn.......... £5,680 to £7,450
Deputy Director, Miss E. M. Coyle
£4,900 to £5,900
Assistant Director, M. D. Lynn; J. McDonald
£4,900 to £5,900

Western

66 Ty Glas Road, Llanishen, Cardiff
Ashton Vale Road, Bristol
Bookshops: 258 Broad Street, Birmingham; Southey House, Wine Street, Bristol; 41 The Hayes, Cardiff.
Director, G. L. Birch........... £5,680 to £7,450

STATUTE LAW COMMITTEE
House of Lords, S.W.1
President, The Lord Chancellor.
Vice-Chairman, Mr. Justice Cooke.
Members, The Attorney-General; the Lord Advocate; Sir Ian Bancroft, K.C.B.; R. D. Barlas, C.B., O.B.E.; Sir Dennis Dobson, K.C.B., O.B.E., Q.C.; C. Fletcher Cooke, Q.C., M.P.; H. Glover; B. B. Hall; Sir Michael Havers, Q.C., M.P.; Sir Peter Henderson, K.C.B.; J. E. Herbecq; The Hon. Lord Hunter; The Lord Kilbrandon; Rt. Hon. Sir Robert Lowry; J. Moran, Sir Nicholas Morrison, K.C.B.; Sir Arthur Peterson, K.C.B., M.V.O.; H. W. Pritchard, C.B.E.; The Lord Simon of Glaisdale, P.C.; Sir Robert Speed, C.B., Q.C.; Sir Anthony Stainton, K.C.B.; T. G. Talbot, C.B., Q.C.; The Lord Wilberforce, P.C., C.M.G., O.B.E.; Sir Thomas Williams, Q.C., M.P.
Secretary, J. M. Davies.

Statutory Publications Office
12 Buckingham Gate
Editor, P. J. A. Smith. . . . . £9,443 to £11,410
Assistant Editors, J. M. Gibson; R. N. Ogle
£7,035 to £9,160

SUGAR BOARD
52 Mark Lane, E.C.3
[01–480 6221]
The Sugar Board was constituted under the Sugar Act, 1956, on October 15, 1956. The Board buys the sugar which the United Kingdom has contracted to buy under the Commonwealth Sugar Agreement up to the end of 1974 at prices negotiated triennially by the Government and re-sells the sugar commercially at world prices. To meet the difference between the two prices, the Treaty of Accession to the E.E.C. provides for the Board to levy a charge on the importation of the sugar if the world prices are lower than the negotiated prices, or to pay a subvention in the reverse position if world prices exceed them.
Chairman, R. G. R. Wall, C.B. £10,750
Vice-Chairman, Sir Leonard Cooke, O.B.E. . £4,125
Members (part-time), P. G. Smith, C.B.E.; N. Vinson; Sir John Wall, O.B.E. £1,000
General Manager, A. V. Parsons, M.B.E.
Secretary and Finance Officer, E. G. Pearson

NATIONAL THEATRE BOARD
South Bank, S.E.1
[01–928 2033]
Appointed by the Minister with special responsibility for the Arts.
Chairman, The Lord Rayne.
Members, A. R. M. Carr; H. W. Cutler, O.B.E.; I. Harrington, O.B.E.; H. W. Hinds; Sir Ronald Leach, C.B.E.; V. Mishcon; J. C. Mortimer, Q.C.; The Lord O'Brien of Lothbury, P.C., G.B.E.; H. H. Sebag-Montefiore; Prof. T. J. B. Spencer.
Director of National Theatre, Peter Hall, C.B.E.
Secretary, D. Gosling.

DEPARTMENT OF TRADE
1 Victoria Street, S.W.1
(unless otherwise stated)
[01–215 7877]
Overseas Trade. The Department is responsible for commerical policy and relations with overseas countries and is concerned with economic policies affecting the international position of the United Kingdom. It promotes United Kingdom commercial interests overseas, negotiates on trade and commercial matters and administers U.K. protective tariffs. Under the direction of the British Overseas Trade Board, which was set up in January 1972 and has the Secretary of State for Trade as President, the Department promotes British exports, providing an export information service to industry and commerce, largely through the eight regional offices, and handling Government support for overseas trade fairs.

Shipping and civil aviation. The Department is the sponsor for the United Kingdom shipping and civil aviation industries including the conduct of international negotiations. It is also responsible for the regulation of marine safety. The Department sponsors the British Airways Board, the British Airports Authority and the Civil Aviation Authority, and approves the capital investment of these bodies. In addition, the Department issues policy guidance to the Civil Aviation Authority and administers the Authority's annual grant until such time as full recovery of costs is attained.

Commerce and Industry. The Department is responsible in general for the basic legal framework for the regulation of industrial and commercial enterprises, administering a number of statutes governing company affairs and insolvency. It also holds general responsibility for company law, patent, trade mark and copyright matters, and for all matters affecting insurance. The Department of Trade is also the sponsor Department for tourism and the hotel and travel industries; the newspaper, printing and publishing industries; the film industry and the distributive and service trades.

SALARY LIST

Secretary of State £13,000
Parliamentary Under Secretaries of State £5,500
Permanent Secretary £18,675
Deputy Secretary £14,000
Under Secretary £12,000
Assistant Secretary . . . . £8,650 to £11,000
Senior Principal . . . . £7,750 to £9,350
Principal . . . . £5,680 to £7,450
Controller, Export Licensing Branch £7,450
Chief Information Officer (A) . . . . . £8,650 to £11,000
Inspector General of the Insolvency Service . . £12,000
Deputy Inspectors General £11,320
Inspector of Companies £11,320
Accidents Investigation Branch:
Chief Inspector of Accidents £10,950
Deputy Chief Inspector of Accidents
£8,650 to £11,000
Marine Survey Service:
Surveyor General £8,950
Chief Nautical Surveyor ⎫
Engineer Surveyor in Chief ⎬ £8,850
Chief Ship Surveyor ⎭
Secretary of State for Trade and President of the Board of Trade, THE RT. HON. EDMUND EMANUEL DELL, M.P.
Principal Private Secretary, A. C. Hutton.
Parliamentary Private Secretary, A. Woodall, M.P.
Parliamentary Under Secretaries of State, M. H. Meacher, M.P. (*Trade*); S. C. Davis, M.P. (*Companies, Aviation and Shipping*)
Permanent Secretary, Sir Peter Thornton, K.C.B.
Private Secretary, M. V. Boxall.
Deputy Secretaries, L. S. Berman, C.B. (*Director of Statistics*); P. A. R. Brown; R. W. Gray; M. J. Kerry, C.B. (*The Solicitor*); D. A. Lovelock, C.B. (*Principal Establishment and Finance Officer*); Prof. A. T. Peacock, D.S.C. (*Chief Economic Adviser*); P. S. Preston, C.B.; W. P. Shovelton, C.B., C.M.G.
Industrial Advisers, S. Baker (*Co-ordinator*); B. Nicholls.

Trade
Commercial Relations and Exports
Division 1
[01–215 7877]
Under Secretary, S. Abramson
Assistant Secretaries, P. Gent; J. B. Ingram; E. Wright

Division 2
Under Secretary, W. M. Knighton
Assistant Secretaries, Mrs. E. C. Jones; M. G. Petter; M. J. Treble

Division 3
Under Secretary, D. N. Royce
Assistant Secretaries, A. H. K. Slater; P. D. Stobart, C.B.E.

Division 4
Under Secretary, L. Lightman
Assistant Secretaries, C. W. Roberts; Miss M. Z. Terry

Division 5
Under Secretary, J. Caines
Assistant Secretaries, M. W. B. Hunt; D. M. March

Export Development Division
[01-215 7877]
Under Secretary, R. N. Royce
Assistant Secretaries, Miss B. M. Eyles; J. S. Norman

Europe, Industry and Technology Division
[01-215 7877]
Under Secretary, Miss K. E. Boyes
Assistant Secretaries, P. E. Dougherty; C. L. Silver

General Division
[01-215 7877]
Under Secretary, J. R. Steele
Assistant Secretaries, G. A. Barry; P. G. M. Clark; F. R. Mingay

Export Licensing Branch
Sanctuary Bldgs., 16-20 Gt. Smith Street, S.W.1
[01-215 7877]
Controller, E. P. Ellerton.

British Overseas Trade Board
1 Victoria Street, S.W.1
[01-215 7877]
Chairman, Sir Frederick Catherwood
Vice-Chairman, H.R.H. The Duke of Kent, G.C.M.G., G.C.V.O.
Members, S. Baker; The Lord Briginshaw; J. W. Buckley, C.B.E.; R. H. W. Bullock, C.B.; Sir Derek Ezra, M.B.E.; R. W. Gray; Sir Denis Hamilton, D.S.O.; J. L. Jones, M.B.E.; Sir Jan Lewando, C.B.E.; The Earl of Limerick; Sir Peter Matthews; J. H. Neill, C.B.E., T.D.; P. S. Preston, C.B.; Sir John Read; Sir Francis Sandilands, C.B.E.; B. F. W. Scott, C.B.E., T.D.; The Lord Shackleton, K.G., P.C., O.B.E.; N. Statham, C.M.G., C.V.O.; K. Taylor, C.B.; J. Whitehorn, C.M.G.
Chief Executive, B. D. Wilks.

Hillgate House, 26 Old Bailey, E.C.4
[01-248 5757]
Special Adviser on Japanese Market, J. I. McGhie
Overseas Project Group
1 Victoria Street, S.W.1
[01-215 7877]
Assistant Secretary, P. G. F. Bryant

Export Services and Promotions Division
Export House, 50 Ludgate Hill, E.C.4
[01-248 5757]
Under Secretary, W. K. Ward
Assistant Secretaries, D. P. Dick; V. F. Kimber; W. T. Pearce, C.M.G.; A. R. Titchener
Senior Principal, G. McMahon

Patent Office and Industrial Property and Copyright Department
25 Southampton Buildings, W.C.2
[01-405 8721]
Comptroller General of Patents, Designs and Trade Marks, E. Armitage, C.B.
Assistant Comptrollers, R. Bowen; I. J. G. Davis; J. D. Fergusson
Assistant Registrar of Trade Marks(Assistant Secretary) R. L. Moorby.
Senior Principal, A. F. Gilmour.

Insurance Division
Sanctuary Bldgs., 16-20 Gt. Smith Street, S.W.1
[01-215 7877]
Under Secretary, M. S. Morris
Assistant Secretaries, R. E. Clarke; R. F. Fenn; E. J. Lindley; D. Simpson.

Companies Policy Division
Sanctuary Bldgs.,
16-20 Great Smith Street, S. W.1
[01-215-7877]
Under Secretary, R. C. M. Cooper.
Assistant Secretary, J. W. Preston.

Companies Administration Division
Sanctuary Bldgs., 16-20 Gt. Smith Street, S.W.1
[01-215 7877]
Under Secretary, D. Eagers.
Assistant Secretary, Miss C. H. Welch.

Companies House, 55-71 City Road, E.C.1
[01-253 9393]
Registrar of Companies and Registrar of Business Names (Assistant Secretary) (vacant).

2-14 Bunhill Row, E.C.1
[01-606 4071]
Companies Investigation Branch, Inspector of Companies, H. C. Gill

The Insolvency Service
2-14 Bunhill Row, E.C.1
[01-606 4071]
Inspector General of the Insolvency Service, E. G. Harper.
Deputy Inspectors General, J. B. Clemetson; A. D. Gwyther.

Accidents Investigation Branch
Shell Mex House, Strand, W.C.2
[01-217 3000]
Chief Inspector of Accidents, W. H. Tench
Deputy Chief Inspector of Accidents, G. M. Kelly

Civil Aviation Policy Division
Shell Mex House, Strand, W.C.2
[01-217 3000]
Under Secretary, G. C. Dick.
Assistant Secretaries, J. R. Gildea; N. F. Ledsome; G. R. Smith; G. R. Sunderland
Civil Aviation Safety Adviser, J. R. Neill.

Civil Aviation International Relations Division
Shell Mex House, Strand, W.C.2
[01-217 3000]
Under Secretary, G. T. Rogers
Assistant Secretaries, A. P. Gardner; O. I. Green; O. H. Kemmis; W. B. Lello.

Shipping Policy Division
The Adelphi, John Adam Street, W.C.2
[01-217 3000]
Under Secretary, G. Lanchin
Assistant Secretaries, E. Y. Bannard; J. K. T. Frost; K. W. McQueen, O.B.E.

Marine Division
Sunley House, 90-93 High Holborn, W.C.1
[01-405 6911]
Under Secretary, J. N. Archer
Assistant Secretaries, S. N. Burbridge; E. R. Hargreaves; M. J. Service; L. F. Standen
Surveyor General, D. MacIver Robinson, O.B.E.
Chief Nautical Surveyor, Capt. J. A. Hampton
Engineering Surveyor in Chief, Dr. J. Cowley.
Chief Ship Surveyor, N. Bell

Printing, Publishing, Services and Distribution Division
Cleland House, Page Street, S.W.1
[01-834 2255]
Under Secretary, Miss M. J. Lackey, O.B.E.
Assistant Secretaries, H. F. Heinemann; N. E. Pulvermacher

Information Division
Head of Division, N. S. Gaffin.
Deputy Head of Division, M. R. C. Pentreath.
Chief Press Officer, Mrs. H. Rowe.

TRAINING SERVICES AGENCY
162-168 Regent Street, W.1
[01-214-600]
Chief Executive, K. R. Cooper £12,000
Deputy Chief Executives, D. G. Storer *(Training Opportunities)*; F. C. Hayes *(Industry)* . . . £10,950
Director of Training, Dr. R. M. Johnson £9,860
Director of Corporate Services, L. R. Levy
£8,650 to £11,000
Director of Marketing Services, A. P. Dignum
£7,750 to £9,350

Director of Training Opportunities Services, D. W. J.
Orchard..................£8,650 to £11,000
Director of Training Opportunities Operations, J. R.
Shipway..................£8,650 to £11,000
Director of Training Opportunities Development, M.
W. Smart..................£8,650 to £11,000

THE TREASURY
Parliament Street, S.W.1
[01-233-3000]

The Office of the Lord High Treasurer has been continuously in commission for well over 200 years. The Lord High Commissioners of H.M. Treasury consist of the First Lord of the Treasury (who is also the Prime Minister), the Chancellor of the Exchequer and five Junior Lords. This Board of Commissioners is assisted at present by the Chief Secretary, a Parliamentary Secretary who is the Chief Whip, a Financial Secretary and Minister of State (who are also members of the Government) and by the Permanent Secretary. The Prime Minister and First Lord is not primarily concerned in the day-to-day aspects of Treasury business. The Parliamentary Secretary and the Junior Lords are Government Whips in the House of Commons. The management of the Treasury devolves upon the Chancellor of the Exchequer and, under him, the Chief Secretary, the Financial Secretary and the Minister of State. The Chief Secretary is responsible for the control of public expenditure. The Financial Secretary discharges the traditional responsibility of the Treasury for the largely formal procedure for the voting of funds by Parliament. All Treasury Ministers are concerned in tax matters.

Prime Minister and First Lord of the Treasury, THE
RT. HON. (LEONARD) JAMES CALLAGHAN, M.P.
£20,000
Parliamentary Private Secretary, J. A. Cunningham,
Ph.D., M.P.

Lord Commissioners of the Treasury
The Prime Minister (*First Lord*); The Chancellor
of the Exchequer.
Junior Lords of the Treasury
D. R. Coleman, M.P.; T. Pendry, M.P.; J. D.
Dormand, M.P.; D. L. Stoddart, M.P.; T. E.
Graham, M.P..................each £4,000

Chancellor of the Exchequer, THE RT. HON. DENIS
WINSTON HEALEY, M.B.E., M.P........£13,000
Principal Private Secretary, N. J. Monck.
Private Secretary, S. C. T. Matheson.
Parliamentary Clerk, B. O. Dyer.
Parliamentary Private Secretary, H. G. Lamborn,
M.P.
Chief Secretary to the Treasury, THE RT. HON. JOEL
BARNETT, M.P.........................£9,500
Private Secretary, B. S. Morris.
Assistant Private Secretary, I. L. Smith.
Parliamentary Private Secretary, W. M. Hughes,
Ph.D., M.P.
*Parliamentary Secretary to the Treasury and Deputy
Leader of the House of Commons*, THE RT. HON.
MICHAEL FRANCIS LOVELL COCKS, M.P..£9,500
Private Secretary, Sir Alfred Warren, C.B.E.
Financial Secretary, ROBERT EDWARD SHELDON,
M.P.................................£9,500
Private Secretary, M. Brown.
Minister of State, (DAVID JOHN) DENZIL DAVIES.
M.P.................................£9,500,
Private Secretary, Miss M. O'Mara.
Assistant Whips, A. Bates, M.P.; T. M. Cox, M.P.;
J. Ellis, M.P.; P. C. Snape, M.P.; A. W. Stallard,
M.P.; J. Tinn, M.P.; F. R. White, M.P..each £4,000
Permanent Secretary, Sir Douglas Wass, K.C.B.
£20,175
Private Secretary, M. T. Folger.
Second Permanent Secretaries, A. Lord, C.B.; Sir
Derek Mitchell, K.C.B., C.V.O.; L. Pliatzky, C.B.
£17,175
*Head of Government Economic Service and Chief
Economic Adviser to the Treasury*, Sir Bryan
Hopkin, C.B.E.......................£15,350

Deputy Secretaries, L. Airey, C.B.; F. R. Barratt,
C.B.; K. E. Couzens, C.B.; G. S. Downey; F.
Jones, C.B.E.; N. Jordan-Moss, C.B., C.M.G.
£14,000

Central Area
Establishments and Organisation Group:
Under Secretary, D. J. S. Hancock......£12,000
Assistant Secretary, P. R. Gordon
£8,650 to £11,000
Senior Economic Adviser, G. J. Mungeam
£8,650 to £11,000
Information Division:
Head of Division (Assistant Secretary), P. V. Dixon
£8,650 to £11,000
Deputy Head (Chief Information Officer(B)), E. C.
Crosfield.
Central Unit:
Under Secretary, A. J. G. Isaac..........£12,000
Economic Briefing:
Senior Economic Adviser, D. A. C. Heigham
£8,650 to £11,000

Chief Economic Adviser's Sector
Short Term Forecast and Analysis Development Group:
Under Secretary (Economics), J. R. Shepherd
£12,000
Senior Economic Advisers, H. P. Evans; Mrs. V. H.
Stamler...................£8,650 to £11,000
Medium Term and Policy Analysis Group
Under Secretary (Economics), H. H. Leisner
£12,000
Senior Economic Advisers, A. J. C. Britton; Mrs. J.
M. Marquand............ £8,000 to £11,000

Overseas Finance Sector
Overseas Finance A.:
International Finance Group:
Under Secretary, J. G. Littler............£12,000
Assistant Secretaries, G. R. Ashford; G. E. Fitchew;
C. H. W. Hodges..........£8,650 to £11,000
Finance Economic Unit:
Under Secretary (Economics), F. Cassell.....£12,000
Overseas Finance B.:
Overseas Finance General Group:
Under Secretary, Mrs. M. E. Hedley-Miller
£12,000
Assistant Secretaries, A. J. C. Edwards; D. A.
Walker...................£8,650 to £11,000
Aid and Export Group:
Under Secretary, M. Widdup..........£12,000
Assistant Secretaries, Miss J. Kelley; M. C. Scholar;
J. F. Slater, C.M.G..........£8,650 to £11,000

Domestic Economy Sector
Counter Inflation and Public Finance.
Home Finance Group:
Under Secretary, J. M. Bridgeman........£12,000
Assistant Secretaries, K. J. Jordan; H. S. Lee; P. E.
Middleton.................£8,650 to £11,000
Accounts Branch:
Assistant Secretary, L. J. Taylor. £8,650 to £11,000
Fiscal Policy Group:
Under Secretary, A. H. Lovell............£12,000
Assistant Secretary, B. T. Houghton
£8,650 to £11,000
Senior Economic Advisers, P. G. Davies; D. Todd
£8,650 to £11,000
Counter Inflation Group:
Under Secretary, L. M. Brandes..........£12,000
Assistant Secretary, A. J. Wiggins
£8,650 to £11,000

Industry
Industrial Policy Group:
Under Secretary, A. M. Bailey...........£12,000
Assistant Secretary, W. L. St. Clair
£8,650 to £11,000
Senior Economic Adviser, J. T. Caff
£8,650 to £11,000
Industry and Agriculture Group:
Under Secretary, R. G. Lavelle...........£12,000
Assistant Secretaries, D. A. Hadley; W. J. E. Norton;
J. W. Whitaker............£8,650 to £11,000

Public Enterprises Group:
Under Secretary, C. W. France..........£12,000
Assistant Secretaries, Mrs. R. E. J. Gilmore; D. J. L.
Moore; P. Mountfield......£8,650 to £11,000

Public Services Sector
Social Services Group:
Under Secretary, J. B. Unwin.........£12,000
Assistant Secretaries, M. Phillips; Miss E. Walley
£8,650 to £11,000
Home Transport and Education Group:
Under Secretary, Miss J. M. Forsyth......£12,000
Assistant Secretary, C. H. A. Judd; A. J. Perry
£8,650 to £11,000
Local Government and Devolution Group:
Under Secretary, P. Cousins..........£12,000
Assistant Secretaries, M. S. Buckley; P. H. Halsey,
M.V.O.; R. Jones..........£8,650 to £11,000
Defence Policy and Material Group:
Under Secretary, R. L. Sharp..........£12,000
Assistant Secretaries, J. S. Beastall; J. E. Hansford
£8,650 to £11,000
Public Sector Economic Group:
Under Secretary (Economics), I. C. R. Byatt
£12,000
Senior Economic Advisers, J. L. Carr; G. P. Smith
£8,650 to £11,000

General Expenditure
General Expenditure Policy Group:
Under Secretary, J. Anson..............£12,000
Assistant Secretary, Miss J. E. Court
£8,650 to £11,000
Chief Statistician, I. B. Beesley..£8,650 to £11,000
Senior Principal, Mrs. D. J. Halley
£7,750 to £9,350
General Expenditure Analysis Group:
Under Secretary (Economics), Miss M. P. Brown
£12,000
Assistant Secretary, F. E. R. Butler
£8,650 to £11,000
Chief Statistician, B. C. Brown..£8,680 to £11,000
Accounts and Purchasing Group:
Under Secretary, D. McKean..........£12,000
Assistant Secretary, E. P. Kemp..£8,650 to £11,000
Senior Principal, W. Winnard...£7,750 to £9,350

Treasury Representatives in U.S.A.
*Economic Minister, Financial Adviser and Head of U.K.
Treasury and Supply Delegation,* W. S. Ryrie.
Assistant Secretary, H. M. Griffiths.

Rating of Government Property
Jameson House, 69 Notting Hill Gate, W.11
[01–229 9841]
Treasury Valuer, W. W. Brown..........£11,320
Deputy Treasury Valuer, P. J. Dahlhoff......£9,748
Inspector of Rates, R. C. Robin..........£8,650

Queen's and Lord Treasurer's Remembrancer
See Scottish Law Courts and Offices.

THE TREASURY SOLICITOR
Department of H.M. Procurator-General and
Treasury Solicitor
Matthew Parker Street, S.W.1
[01–930–7363 and 1124]
Procurator-General and Treasury Solicitor, B. B. Hall,
C.B., M.C., T.D.....................£21,000
Deputy Treasurer Solicitor, T. C. Hetherington,
C.B.E., T.D.....................£15,000

Advisory Division
Under Secretary (Legal), J. C. Hooton, C.M.G., M.B.E.
£12,465
Assistant Solicitors, D. L. Davies; O.B.E.; G. A.
Hosker; A. D. Osborne...£9,498 to £11,465
Senior Legal Assistants, R. Armitage; Miss W. G.
Beer; R. P. Ellis; R. N. Ricks; E. W. Wills
£7,090 to £9,215

Litigation Divisions
Under Secretaries (Legal), J. B. Bailey; R. K. Price;
F. B. Stone.....................£12,465

Assistant Solicitors, W. H. Godwin; M. J. C. Hainer;
J. A. Hornsby, T.D.; N. D. Ing; M. E. Mead; R.
D. Munrow; A. J. Murray; G. S. Payne; Miss V.
M. Peto; G. F. Sills; D. A. Watson; J. H.
Wilkinson.................£9,498 to £11,465
Senior Legal Assistants, A. Bridge; J. E. Collins; I.
Hood; Mrs. D. J. Jones; N. D. Knowles; A. D.
Lawton, C. G. Leonard; Mrs. A. D. B. McFee;
A. J. Sandal; R. E. Seely; M. B. Sturdy
£7,090 to £9,215
Principals, A. Deane; E. J. King; L. V. Patterson;
E. J. Pratt; G. Roberts.......£6,145 to £7,915

Queen's Proctor Division
Queen's Proctor, B. B. Hall, C.B., M.C., T.D.
Assistant Queen's Proctor, G. S. Payne
£9,498 to £11,465

Conveyancing Division
Under Secretary (Legal), R. B. Gardner....£12,465
Assistant Solicitors, R. W. Corbett; E. J. D. Eastham;
J. Holdron; J. E. H. Jones; J. C. Leck; N. J.
Orchard; J. B. Sweetman...£9,498 to £11,465
Senior Legal Assistants, D. E. T. Bevan; E. K.
Bridges; R. W. M. Cooper; M. R. M. Davis;
R. W. Dyer; Mrs. A. M. I. Frankl; D. J. C.
Garnett; Miss G. Gilder; D. H. Godkin; J. B.
Howe; I. T. Lewis; A. P. Millar; P. Noble; G. E.
Papes; D. F. Pascho; Miss S. L. Sargant; D. A. J.
Simpson; P. M. Sprott; Mrs. J. M. Stone; S. A.
Tobin; J. Wyer..........£7,090 to £9,215
Principals, A. K. Applegate; T. W. Brigden, B.
J. Brockwell; B. A. Brown; L. H. Pountney,
I.S.O.....................£6,145 to £7,915

Accounts, Costs and Establishments Division
Legal Personnel Officer, R. D. Munrow
£9,498 to £11,465
Establishment Officer, G. J. Judge..£6,145 to £7,915
Chief Accountant, B. C. Shephard
£6,145 to £7,915
Head of Costs Branch, A. M. Niven
£6,145 to £7,915

Bona Vacantia Division
12 Buckingham Gate, S.W.1
[01–930–7363 and 1124]
Assistant Solicitor, J. D. Harries-Jones
£9,498 to £11,465
Senior Legal Assistant, C. R. Crockett
£7,090 to £9,215
Principal, R. A. Roberts.......£6,145 to £7,915

Department of Energy Branch
Kingsgate House, 66–74 Victoria Street, S.W. 1
[01–215–3910]
Legal Adviser (Under Secretary (Legal)), P. G.
Ashcroft.....................£12,465
Assistant Solicitors, A. W. Baker; G. B. Claydon; J.
E. Coleman; D. R. M. Long. £9,498 to £11,465
Senior Legal Assistants, G. Hewitt; D. H. Ingham;
R. M. C. Venables..........£7,090 to £9,215

COUNCIL ON TRIBUNALS
6 Spring Gardens, Cockspur Street, S.W.1
[01–930–8691]
The Council on Tribunals, with its Scottish
Committee, was constituted in 1958 under the
provisions of the *Tribunals and Inquiries Act* of
that year to act as an advisory body in the field of
administrative tribunals and statutory inquiries. It
now operates under the Tribunals and Inquiries Act,
1971.
Its principal functions are (*a*) to keep under review
the constitution and working of the various tribunals which have been placed under its general supervision by the Act; (*b*) to report on particular
matters relating to any tribunal which may be
referred to it by the Lord Chancellor and the
Lord Advocate; and (*c*) to report on matters relating
to statutory inquiries which may be similarly referred to it or which the Council may determine to
be of special importance. In addition, the Council

must be consulted both about rules of procedure for statutory inquiries and before rules are made for any of the tribunals under its general supervision, and it may make general recommendations about appointments to membership of such tribunals. The numerous tribunals which have been placed under the Council's supervision are concerned with a wide variety of matters varying from agriculture and road traffic to independent schools and pensions. They include the main National Health Service and National Insurance Tribunals, together with such tribunals as the Civil Aviation Authority, Industrial Tribunals, the Land Tribunal, the Mental Health Review Tribunals, Local Valuation Courts, Rent Tribunals, Rent Assessment Committees and the Transport Tribunal. There is power in the 1971 Act to extend the Council's jurisdiction to additional classes of tribunals and inquiries or hearings.

The Scottish Committee of the Council considers Scottish tribunals and matters relating only to Scotland.

The Members of the Council are appointed by the Lord Chancellor and the Lord Advocate. The Scottish Committee is composed partly of members of the Council designated by the Lord Advocate and partly of other persons appointed by him. The Parliamentary Commissioner for Administration is *ex officio* a member both of the Council and of the Scottish Committee.

The Council submits an annual report on its proceedings and those of the Scottish Committee to the Lord Chancellor and the Lord Advocate, which must be laid before Parliament.

Chairman, The Lord Tweedsmuir, C.B.E., C.D.
Members, Mrs. E. Bayliss; Prof. K. M. Bell; I. R. Guild, W.S.; Sir Desmond Heap; D. C.-H. Hirst, Q.C.; J. MacDonald; The Lord Mancroft, K.B.E., T.D.; C. Moseley; Sir William Murrie, G.C.B., K.B.E.; Sir Idwal Pugh, K.C.B. (*Parliamentary Commissioner for Administration*); J. M. Turner, O.B.E.; R. K. Will, W.S.
Secretary, J. M. Hawksworth.

Scottish Committee
22 Melville Street, Edinburgh 3
[031–225–3236]
Chairman, I. R. Guild, W.S.
Members, Mrs. B. Leburn, M.B.E.; J. MacDonald; J. A. Matheson; R. Moore, C.B.E.; Sir Idwal Pugh, K.C.B. (*Parliamentary Commissioner for Administration*); D. M. Ross, Q.C.; J. M. Turner, O.B.E.
Secretary, R. Walker.

CORPORATION OF TRINITY HOUSE
Trinity House, Tower Hill, E.C.3
[01–480–6601]
Trinity House, the first General Lighthouse and Pilotage Authority in the Kingdom, was a body of importance when Henry VIII granted the institution its first charter in 1514. The Corporation is the general lighthouse authority for England and Wales, the Channel Islands and Gibraltar, with certain statutory jurisdiction over aids to navigation maintained by local harbour authorities, etc., and by the General Lighthouse Authorities for Scotland and Ireland. It is also responsible for dealing with wrecks dangerous to navigation, except those occurring within port limits or wrecks of H.M. ships. The Lighthouse Service, including those of Scotland and Ireland, is maintained out of the General Lighthouse Fund which is provided from light dues levied on ships using the ports of the United Kingdom and Eire. The Corporation is also the principal pilotage authority in the United Kingdom and is responsible for London and 40 other districts. Certain charitable trusts are administered by the Corporation for the relief of aged or distressed mariners and their dependants. The affairs of the Corporation are managed by a Board of ten active Elder Brethren and the Secretary, assisted by Administrative, engineering and marine staff. The active Elder Brethren also act as nautical assessors in marine causes in the Admiralty Division of the High Court of Justice.

Elder Brethren
Master, H.R.H. the Duke of Edinburgh, K.G.
Deputy Master, Captain M. B. Wingate. *Elder Brethren,* H.R.H. The Prince of Wales, K.G.; Commodore T. L. Owen, O.B.E., R.D., R.N.R.(ret.); Capt. G. C. H. Noakes, R.D., R.N.R.(ret.); Admiral of the Fleet the Earl Mountbatten of Burma, K.G., P.C., G.C.B., O.M., G.C.S.I., G.C.I.E., G.C.V.O., D.S.O.; Capt. G. P. McCraith; Capt. R. J. Galpin, R.D., R.N.R.(ret.); The Earl of Avon, K.G., P.C., M.C.; Capt. Sir George Barnard; Capt. R. N. Mayo, C.B.E.; Capt. D. A. G. Dickens; Capt. J. E. Bury; Capt. J. A. N. Bezant, D.S.C., R.D., R.N.R.(ret.); Capt. D. J. Cloke; The Rt. Hon. Sir Harold Wilson, K.G., O.B.E., M.P.; The Rt. Hon. E. R. G. Heath, M.B.E., M.P.; Capt. I. R. C. Saunders; The Visct. Runciman of Doxford, O.B.E., A.F.C.; Capt. P. F. Mason; Capt. T. Woodfield; The Lord Simon of Glaisdale, P.C.; Sir Eric Drake, C.B.E.; Admiral Sir Terence Lewin, K.C.B., M.V.O., D.S.C.; Captain D. T. Smith.

Officers
Secretary, L. N. Potter.
Deputy Secretary, S. W. Heesom.
Engineer-in-Chief, I. C. Clingan.
Principal, Lights Department, J. R. Backhouse.
Chief Accountant, A. Snook.
Chief, Administration Department, N. F. Matthews.
Establishment Officer, G. Warnes.
Surveyor of Shipping, W. R. Foley.
Principal, Pilotage Department, H. E. Oliver.
Principal, Corporate Department, V. G. Stamp.
Press Officer, J. Manning.

COMMISSIONERS OF NORTHERN LIGHTHOUSES
84 George Street, Edinburgh.
[031–226–7051]
The Commissioners of Northern Lighthouses are the General Lighthouse Authority for Scotland and the Isle of Man. The present Board owes its origin to an Act of Parliament passed in 1786 which authorized the erection of 4 lighthouses; 19 Commissioners were appointed to carry out the Act. At the present time the Commissioners operate under the Merchant Shipping Act, 1894 and are 18 in number.

The Commissioners control 61 Major manned Lighthouses, 27 Major unmanned Lighthouses, 86 Minor Lights and many Lighted and Unlighted Buoys. They have a fleet of 3 Motor Vessels.

Commissioners
The Lord Advocate, the Solicitor General, the Lord Provosts of Edinburgh, Glasgow and Aberdeen; the Provost of Inverness; the Chairman of Argyll & Bute; the Sheriffs-Principal of North Strathclyde; Tayside, Central & Fife; Grampian, Highlands & Islands; South Strathclyde, Dumfries & Galloway; Lothians & Borders; and Glasgow & Strathkelvin; W. A. Robertson, D.S.C.; J. P. H. Mackay, Q.C.; W. D. H. Gregson, C.B.E.; T. Macgill; Capt. W. E. McMeiken.

Officers:
General Manager, W. Alastair Robertson, D.S.C.
Engineer-in-Chief, P. H. Hyslop, D.S.C.
Secretary, J. Robson.

CLYDE PORT AUTHORITY
16 Robertson Street, Glasgow
Chairman, A. G. McCrae, C.B.E.
Deputy Chairman and Managing Director, J. P. Davidson.
Secretary and Solicitor, J. B. Maxwell.

UNIVERSITY GRANTS COMMITTEE
14 Park Crescent, W.1
[01–636–7799]
The Committee was appointed by the Chan-

cellor of the Exchequer in July, 1919, and its present terms of reference are as follows:

" To inquire into the financial needs of university education in Great Britain; to advise the Government as to the application of any grants made by Parliament towards meeting them; to collect, examine, and make available information relating to university education throughout the United Kingdom; and to assist, in consultation with the universities and other bodies concerned, the preparation and execution of such plans for the development of the universities as may from time to time be required in order to ensure that they are fully adequate to national needs."

Chairman, Sir Frederick Dainton, F.R.S.....£17,175
Other Members, Prof. R. J. C. Atkinson; Sir Donald Barron; Prof. A. J. Brown, C.B.E., D.Phil., F.B.A.; D. P. J. Browning; Prof. Violet R. Cane; Prof. K. M. Clayton; Prof. J. Cruickshank; Prof. T. W. Goodwin, C.B.E., F.R.S.; Prof. B. G. Gowenlock, F.R.S.E.; Prof. J. C. Gunn, C.B.E., F.R.S.E.; Miss M. Hulme; Prof. N. C. Hunt, C.B.E., Ph.D.; J. Munn, O.B.E.; Prof. Barbara M. H. Strang; Prof. Sir Charles Stuart-Harris, C.B.E., M.D.; Prof. J. C. West; Dr. E. Anne Whiteman.
Secretary, J. P. Carswell..............£14,000
Under Secretary, E. H. St. G. Moss.......£12,000
Assist. Secretaries, L. P. Angell; A. P. J. Edwards; Miss M. L. Senior; N. P. Thomas

£8,650 to £11,000

Principals, A. Callaghan; Miss M. J. Darby; A. Eaves (*Statistician*); P. J. Fallon; D. H. Griffiths; K. C. Humphrey; S. R. C. Jones; Miss B. D. Naylor....................£5,680 to £7,450
Directing Architect, W. R. C. Cleary......£11,000
Superintending Quantity Surveyor, I. H. Keates
£8,650 to £9,798

VALUE ADDED TAX TRIBUNALS

Value added tax tribunals for England and Wales are established in London, Cardiff, Birmingham and Manchester, and value added tax tribunals for Scotland and Northern Ireland in Edinburgh and Belfast respectively. A person dissatisfied with a decision of the Commissioners of Customs and Excise relating to certain aspects of value added tax may appeal to a tribunal.

The tribunals are entirely independent of the Commissioners. They are under the supervision of the Council on Tribunals and are intended to determine disputes concerning value added tax speedily and with a minimum of formality, and to assist in obtaining uniformity in the application of the tax throughout the United Kingdom.

17 North Audley Street, W.1
[01–629–5542]
President, The Lord Grantchester, Q.C.
Registrar (*Senior Principal*), R. J. Powell, I.S.O.

Tribunal Centres

London: 17 North Audley Street, W.1
[01–629–5542]
Chairman, N. P. M. Elles.
Edinburgh: 44 Palmerston Place, Edinburgh
[031–226–3551]
Vice-President, Scotland, D. Y. Abbey.

Belfast: Midland Hotel, Whitla Street, Belfast [Belfast 749214]
Manchester: Warwickgate House, Warwick Road, Old Trafford, Manchester [061–872–6471]
Chairman, P. A. Ferns, T.D.

COMMONWEALTH WAR GRAVES COMMISSION

2 Marlow Road, Maidenhead, Berkshire
[Maidenhead: 34221]

The Commonwealth War Graves Commission (formerly Imperial War Graves Commission) was founded by Royal Charter in 1917. It is responsible for the commemoration of 1,695,000 members of the forces of the Commonwealth who fell in the two world wars. More than one million graves are maintained in 23,589 burial grounds throughout the

world. Nearly three-quarters of a million men and women who have no known grave or who were cremated are commemorated by name on memorials built by the Commission.

The funds of the Commission are derived from the seven Governments participating in its work— The United Kingdom, Canada, Australia, New Zealand, South Africa, India and Pakistan.
President, H.R.H. The Duke of Kent, G.C.M.G., G.C.V.O.
Chairman: The Secretary of State for Defence.
Vice-Chairman, General Sir Noel Thomas, K.C.B., D.S.O., M.C.
Members, The Minister for Housing and Construction; The High Commissioners for Canada, the Commonwealth of Australia, New Zealand, and India; the Ambassadors for the Republics of South Africa and Pakistan; Sir Robert Black, G.C.M.G., O.B.E.; Miss Joan Woodgate, C.B.E., R.R.C.; Sir John Winnifrith, K.C.B.; Admiral Sir Frank Twiss, K.C.B., D.S.C.; E. L. Gardner, Q.C., M.P.; The Lord Wallace of Coslany; Air Chief Marshal Sir John Barraclough, K.C.B., C.B.E., D.F.C., A.F.C.
Director-General, A. K. Pallot, C.M.G.
Assistant Directors-General, A. S. Laing, M.V.O. (*Secretariat*); J. Saynor (*Administration*).
Legal Adviser and Solicitor, P. R. Matthew.
Director of External Relations, P. H. M. Swan.
Director of Works, W. H. Dukes.
Director of Horticulture, W.F.W. Harding, O.B.E.
Director of Information Services, S. G. Campbell, M.C.
Establishment Officer, H.Westland.
Chief Finance Officer, P. J. Cook.
Hon. Consulting Engineer, P. A. Scott.
Hon. Botanical Adviser, Sir George Taylor, D.SC., F.R.S., F.R.S.E.

Imperial War Graves Endowment Fund
Trustees, Sir John Hogg, T.D.; E. M. P. Welman; General Sir Noel Thomas, K.C.B., D.S.O., M.C.
Hon. Secretary to the Trustees, A. K. Pallot, C.M.G.

WELSH OFFICE

Gwydyr House, Whitehall, S.W.1
[01–233–3000]
Secretary of State, THE RT. HON. JOHN MORRIS, Q.C., M.P..........................£13,000
Private Secretary, J. C. Price.
Parliamentary Private Secretary, I. L. Evans, M.P.
Parliamentary Under-Secretaries of State, S. B. Jones, M.P.; T. A. Jones, M.P.................£5,500
Permanent Secretary, Sir Hywel Evans, K.C.B.,£21,000
Private Secretary, L. Williams
Assistant Secretary, S. T. Charles, C.B.E.
£8,650 to £11,000
Principal, Mrs. M. Evans.......£5,680 to £7,450

Cathays Park, Cardiff
[0222–28066]
Deputy Secretary, O. H. Morris, C.M.G...£14,000
Under Secretaries, J. A. Annand; R. T. Bevan; J. H. Clement; I. Davey; I. S. Dewar; D. A. R. Hall; P. S. Hosegood; P. B. Hunt; L. Jones; R. A. Lloyd-Jones; A. J. Sutton; A. Owen, M.C.
£12,000
Principal Finance Officer, D. G. Jones......£12,000
Assistant Secretaries, M. E. Bevan; B. H. Evans; W. J. Griffiths; R. Hall-Williams; L. H. Hayward; H. E. O. Hughes, C.B.E.; R. W. Jarman; D. W. Jones; R. H. Jones, C.V.O.; J. W. Lloyd; L. M. Lloyd, M.B.E.; R. A. Owen; R. D. Potter; L. Pritchard; O. Rees; D. J. Tallis; H. K. Trimmell; E. K. Williams.............£8,650 to £11,000
Establishment Officer, J. E. King.£8,650 to £11,000
Finance Officer, W. B. Jones...£8,650 to £11,000
Senior Principals, M. G. Evans; A. H. H. Jones; J. C. Lewis; P. E. Loveluck; L. R. Rogers
£7,750 to £9,350
Principals, R. M. Abel; R. D. J. Barber; S. K. Bateman; W. A. Beaumont; H. R. Bollington; J. E. Booker, O.B.E.; F. E. Brewer; J. H. Brown; J. L. Caddy; J. A. Chadwick; W. L. Chapman; M. Cohen; G. C. G. Craig; J. F. Craig; I. B. Cullis;

D. J. M. Davies; G. Davies; J. B. Davies; J. I. Davies; J. N. G. Davis; G. G. Elliott; G. T. Evans; Mrs. M. Evans; Mrs. S. G. Evans; P. Finnigan; J. S. Gill; L. L. Ginn; W. J. Griffiths; S. H. Handley, M.B.E.; C. W. Harris; F. Hind; Mrs. E. O. James; G. M. Jenkins; N. S. Jones; L. Kane; A. Kitchen; H. E. Leonard, O.B.E.; D. F. Little; D. T. Marshall; G. H. Miles; B. S. Millwood; D. Morgan, O.B.E.; J. A. Morgan; D. S. Murphy; J. C. Price; J. Rhys; C. W. Robbins; T. Roberts; H. I. W. Sparkes; J. Taffinder; Miss E. E. J. Thomas; W. E. Thomas; E. A. Tredget; W. A. Vinall; A. Whitaker; R. J. E. Wilcox; A. D. Williams..............£5,680 to £7,450
Head of Road Safety Unit, G. G. Gates, M.B.E.
£3,635 to £4,908

Architectural Staff
Chief Architect, G. J. Kelly..............£11,000
Architects (Senior Grade), H. O. M. Coleman; J. R. Coward; C. Eyres; S. C. Halbritter; G. N. Harding; S. W. Voaden; E. T. Williams
£6,280 to £7,450
Quantity Surveyors (Senior Grade), R. Broad; T. A. Campden; K. G. G. Cosslett; I. Smith
£7,450

Engineering Staff
Chief Engineer, H. Cronshaw..........£11,000
Superintending Engineers, G. M. Jones; A. S. R. Mutch..................£8,650 to £9,798
Engineering Inspector, W. D. A. Waters
£6,468 to £8,833
Engineers (Senior Grade), J. Jarvis; C. A. Jenkins; H. Ruttley; J. E. Saunders.....£6,280 to £7,450

Engineering Staff (Transport and Highways Group)
Director of Highways, D. A. R. Hall......£12,000
Superintendent Engineers, J. E. Morgan; A. Orme
£8,650 to £9,798
Senior Engineers, P. I. Adams; P. C. Dunstan; J. G. Evans; M. Griffin; J. A. L. Harries; B. J. W. Martin; W. H. Prosser; A. Tait; E. G. Whitcutt
£6,280 to £7,450
Senior Quantity Surveyor, D. G. Minas
£6,280 to £7,450

Health Staff
Chief Medical Officer, R. T. Bevan, M.D...£12,000
Principal Medical Officers, P. Alwyn-Smith; W. C. D. Lovett, O.B.E...................£11,440
Senior Medical Officers, A. G. Jones; R. B. Morley-Davies; J. N. M. Parry; Miss F. M. Richards
£11,000
Chief Nursing Officer, Miss E. A. Bell......£9,818
Medical Officers, D. J. W. Anderson; R. Buntwal; R. F. Doyle; G. M. Evans; A. M. George; A. J. R. Hudson, V.R.D.; J. N. P. Hughes; D. F. Lewis; G. J. Moses; H. A. Mullen, T.D.; H. C. Nirula; L. J. Powell; T. T. Westhead; P. R. E. Williams
£6,987 to £9,562
Chief Dental Officer, D. R. Edwards........£11,000
Dental Officers, A. Cobb; G. Morris; T. A. Williams..................£6,987 to £9,562
Principal Nursing Officers, E. E. Beckerton; Miss I. John........................£8,638
Nursing Officers, Miss E. G. Bennett; Miss M. Coker; Miss P. D. Jones; Miss M. D. Wells; Miss J. P. White; Miss P. M. Yeo......£6,968 to £7,761
Scientific Adviser, R. A. Saunders £8,650 to £9,798
Pharmaceutical Adviser, D. L. Thomas
£8,650 to £9,798

Area Health Authorities
Clwyd, Pont-y-Garreg, Wrexham Street, Mold. *Chairman*, The Lord Kenyon, C.B.E. *Administrator*, D. C. Cope.
Dyfed, Starling Park House, Johnstown, Carmarthen. *Chairman*, A. D. Lewis. *Administrator*, E. C. Morris.

Mid Glamorgan, 18 Cathedral Road, Cardiff. *Chairman*, J. Warren. *Administrator*, P. V. Davies.
South Glamorgan, Temple of Peace and Health, Cathays, Cardiff. *Chairman*, C. R. Cory. *Administrator*, A. M. Evans.
West Glamorgan, 4 High Street, Swansea. *Chairman*, Prof. W. M. Williams. *Administrator*, J. Button.
Gwent, Mamhilad, Pontypool. *Chairman*, D. R. Evans. *Administrator*, G. S. Evans.
Gwynedd, Coed Mawr, Bangor. *Chairman*, J. A. Barry O.B.E. *Administrator*, R. O. Freeman.
Powys, Mansion House, Bronllys, nr. Brecon. *Chairman*, C. Roberts. *Administrator*, H. G. Argent.

Planning Staff
Chief Planner, J. A. Colley..............£11,000
Principal Planner, C. J. Curry .£8,650 to £9,798
Senior Research Officers. A. S. Dredge; C. G. Parry; W. P. Roderick; I. E. Thompson
£5,680 to £7,450
Senior Planning Officers, D. B. Courtier; G. Fairhurst; I. N. Jones; J. O. Pryce; C. W. W. Smart; B. G. Taylor; Miss M. P. Thomas
£6,280 to £7,450
Senior Estate Officer, G. K. Hoad..£6,280 to £7,450
Principal Scientific Officers, J. C. Finnigan; J. N. M. Firth...................£5,514 to £7,205
Senior Housing and Planning Inspectors, M. R. Mullins, M.B.E.; L. G. H. Pannell; E. M. Roberts; J. W. Tester...............£7,093 to £8,650

Industry Staff
Senior Principal Scientific Officers, H. F. Jones, £8,650 to £9,798; I. E. Thompson..£5,680 to £7,450
Principal Professional and Technical Officer, F. J. Davies.....................£6,280 to £7,450

Legal Staff
Legal Adviser, G. Davies.......£9,033 to £11,000
Assistant Solicitors, A. J. Beale; D. G. Lambert
£9,033 to £11,000
Senior Legal Assistants, J. D. H. Evans; P. J. Murrin; A. J. Watkins...............£6,625 to £8,750

Information Staff
Director, Information Division, J. E. B. Evans
£8,650 to £11,000

Social Work Service
Chief Social Work Service Officer, E. Glithero
£8,650 to £11,000
Principal Social Work Service Officers, R. L. Jones; Miss Z. E. Williams........£8,250 to £9,798
Social Work Service Officers, E. E. Beatty; W. F. Brian; Miss W. O. M. Copleston; G. H. Davies; D. G. Evans; Mrs. B. M. Johnson; Miss J. C. M. Jones; J. F. Mooney; Mrs. C. Owens; L. Pugh; G. W. Smith; A. W. Verney..£5,680 to £7,750
Senior Economic Adviser, O. T. Hooker
£8,650 to £11,000
Chief Statistician, D. A. Jones..£8,650 to £11,000
Statisticians, P. D. Arkell; M. J. Barker; Mrs. B. J. Wilson...............£5,680 to £7,450

WHITE FISH AUTHORITY
Sea Fisheries House,
10 Young Street, Edinburgh 2
[031–225–2515]
Chairman, C. I. Meek, C.M.G. £5,914
Deputy-Chairman, Sir Matthew Campbell, K.B.E., C.B., F.R.S.E. (*part-time*).
Members (*part-time*), Dr. W. J. L. Dean, O.B.E.; E. H. M. Clutterbuck, O.B.E.; K. L. Hall, C.B.E.; Admiral Sir Deric Holland-Martin, G.C.B., D.S.O., D.S.C.; Miss J. Stewart.
Chief Executive, C. I. Meek, C.M.G.
Secretary, J. R. D. Murray.

COMMISSIONS, ETC.

COMMISSION FOR LOCAL ADMINISTRATION IN ENGLAND

21 Queen Anne's Gate, London, S.W.1
[01-930-3333]

Three Local Commissioners are responsible for investigating complaints from members of the public in England who claim to have suffered injustice because of maladministration by a local authority, a water authority or a police authority. Certain types of action are excluded from investigation, particularly personnel matters and commercial transactions unless they relate to the purchase or sale of land. Complaints must normally be made through a member of the authority against which the complaint is made although a complaint can be put to a Local Commissioner direct if a member fails or refuses to refer it. A free booklet "Your Local Ombudsman" is available from the Commission's office.

Chairman of the Commission and Local Commissioner,
The Baroness Serota £16,581
Vice Chairman and Local Commissioner, D. B. Harrison £12,331
Local Commissioner, F. P. Cook £11,781
Commissioner, The Parliamentary Commissioner for Administration
Secretary, M. R. Hyde.

COMMUNITY RELATIONS COMMISSION

15–16 Bedford Street, W.C.2
[01-836-3545]

Established on November 26, 1968, under the Race Relations Act, 1968, to help people of different races and cultures to live and work together in harmony.
Chairman, Hon. Mark Bonham Carter.
Deputy Chairmen, The Very Rev. A. Jowett, C.B.E.; The Lord Pitt of Hampstead.
Members, The Lord Campbell of Eskan; P. C. Chitnis; Mrs. P. Crabbe, O.B.E.; C. Plant, O.B.E.; A. F. A. Sayeed; The Baroness Serota; Mrs. R. L. Wolff; P. L. B. Woodroffe.

FOREIGN COMPENSATION COMMISSION

Alexandra House, Kingsway, W.C.2

The Commission was set up by the *Foreign Compensation Act,* 1950, to distribute funds paid by foreign governments as compensation for expropriated British property and other losses sustained by British nationals. The *Foreign Compensation Act,* 1962, provided, *inter alia,* for the payment out of moneys provided by Parliament of additional compensation in respect of claims arising in connection with certain events in Egypt. The Foreign Compensation Act, 1969, provided, *inter alia,* for the payment by the Board of Trade to the Commission for distribution of moneys held by the Custodian of Enemy Property being former property of a Baltic State or ceded territory. The Commission has completed the final distribution of the funds contributed by Yugoslavia, Czechoslovakia, Bulgaria, Poland, Rumania and Hungary, and the moneys received from the Board of Trade in respect of claims under the U.S.S.R. Distribution Order. The Commission has registered certain British claims in Czechoslovakia and also in the Baltic States and territories annexed by the Soviet Union. The £27,500,000 compensation paid by the Government of the United Arab Republic under the financial agreement of Feb. 28, 1959, has been fully distributed. The Foreign Compensation (Egypt) Order in respect of British-owned property affected by Egyptian measures of nationalization between 1960 and 1964 came into operation on Feb. 1, 1972, and the Commission is engaged in determining claims thereunder. The Foreign Compensation (German Democratic Republic) (Registration) Order 1975 which came into operation on May 7, 1975,

enables certain claims relating to property in the German Democratic Republic and Berlin (East) owned by United Kingdom nationals or relating to debts owed by persons resident in the German Democratic Republic and Berlin (East) to United Kingdom nationals to be registered with, and reported upon by, the Commission.
Chairman, Sir Ralph Windham.
Commissioner, Sir James Henry, Bt., C.M.G., M.C., T.D.
Legal Officer, J. R. Whimster.
Secretary and Chief Examiner, Miss H. M. Walsh, O.B.E.
Registrar, T. W. Leopard.

ROYAL COMMISSION ON ENVIRONMENTAL POLLUTION

Church House, Great Smith Street, S.W.1
[01-212 8620]

Set up on Feb. 20, 1970, " to advise on matters, both national and international, concerning the pollution of the environment; on the adequacy of research in this field; and the future possibilities of danger to the environment."
Chairman, Prof. H. L. Kornberg, F.R.S.
Members, The Marchioness of Anglesey; D.W. Bowett; Prof. T. J. Chandler; F. J. Chapple; J. G. Collingwood; T. O. Conran; Prof. E. J. Denton, C.B.E., F.R.S.; Sir Richard Doll, O.B.E., F.R.S.; Prof. P. J. Lindop; Prof. J. M. Mitchison; Prof. R. E. Nicholl; Prof. T. R. E. Southwood; P. P. Streeten; Sir Ralph Verney, K.B.E.; Sir Frederick Warner, F.R.S.; The Baroness White.
Secretary, L. F. Rutterford.

ROYAL COMMISSION ON CIVIL LIABILITY AND COMPENSATION FOR PERSONAL INJURY

22 Kingsway, W.C.2
[01-242-6828]

Appointed on March 19, 1973, " to consider to what extent, in what circumstances and by what means compensation should be payable in respect of death or personal injury (including antenatal injury) suffered by any person—(a) in the course of employment; (b) through the use of a motor vehicle or other means of transport; (c) through the manufacture, supply or use of goods or services; (d) on premises belonging to or occupied by another; or (e) otherwise through the act or omission of another where compensation under the present law is recoverable only on proof of fault or under the rules of strict liability—having regard to the cost and other implications of the arrangements for the recovery of compensation, whether by way of compulsory insurance or otherwise."
Chairman, The Lord Pearson, P.C., C.B.E.
Members, The Lord Allen of Abbeydale, G.C.B.; W. C. Anderson, C.B.E.; Mrs. M. Brooke, O.B.E.; The Hon. Lord Cameron, D.S.C.; Prof. R. B. Duthie, F.R.C.S.; R. A. MacCrindle, Q.C.; N. S. Marsh, Q.C.; D. A. Marshall; Prof. A. R. Prest, PH.D.; A. E. Sansom; Prof. R. S. F. Schilling, C.B.E., M.D., D.SC., F.R.C.P.; R. S. Skerman, C.B.E.; Prof. Olive Stevenson; J. Stewart, W.S.; A. W. Ure, R.D.
Secretary, Mrs. M. E. Parsons.

ROYAL COMMISSION ON THE DISTRIBUTION OF INCOME AND WEALTH

Neville House, Page Street, S.W.1.
[01-222 8020]

The Commission was appointed in August 1974 to enquire into and report on such matters concerning the distribution of personal incomes, both

earned and unearned, and wealth, as may be referred to it by the Government.

Chairman, The Lord Diamond, P.C.

Members, Sir Neville Butterworth; R. A. Cox, G. H. Doughty; Prof. J. Greve; D. E. Lea; L. F. Murphy; Prof. Sir Henry Phelps-Brown, M.B.E.; Mrs. D. E. C. Wedderburn.

Secretary, F. J. Bayliss.

ROYAL COMMISSION ON THE PRESS

Standard Hse., 27 Northumberland Ave., W.C.2
[01-839 2855/8]

Set up on May 2, 1974, " to enquire into the factors affecting the maintenance of the independence, diversity and editorial standards of newspapers and periodicals, and the public's freedom of choice, of newspapers and periodicals, nationally, regionally and locally, with particular reference to—(*a*) the economics of newspaper and periodical publishing and distribution; (*b*) the interaction of the newspaper and periodical interests held by the companies concerned with their other interests and holdings, within and outside the communications industry; (*c*) management and labour practices and relations in the newspaper and periodical industry; (*d*) conditions and security of employment in the newspaper and periodical industry; (*e*) the distribution and concentration of ownership of the newspaper and periodical industry, and the adequacy of existing law in relation thereto; (*f*) the responsibilities, constitution and functioning of the Press Council; and to make recommendations."

Chairman, Prof. O. R. McGregor.

Members, Mrs. E. Anderson; D. Basnett; Sir George Bishop; The Hon. R. R. E. Chorley; G. Goodman; Prof. L. C. B. Gower; M. Horsman; The Lord Hunt, C.B.E., D.S.O.; P. Johnson; J. E. Jones, O.B.E.; I. Richardson; Miss E. Roberts, O.B.E.; Z. A. Silberston.

Secretary, P. McQuail.

CRIMINAL INJURIES COMPENSATION BOARD

10-12 Russell Square, W.C.1
[01-636-2812]

The Board was constituted in 1964 to administer the Government scheme for the compensation of victims of crimes of violence, which came into operation on August 1, 1964.

Chairman, M. Ogden, Q.C.

Members, D. A. Barker, Q.C.; I. J. Black, Q.C.; J. S. Boyle; Sir William Carter; B. W. Chedlow, Q.C.; J. Law, Q.C.; Miss J. Littlewood; D. G. A. Lowe, Q.C.; W. I. Stewart, Q.C.; D. B. Weir, Q.C.; C. H. Whitby, Q.C.

Secretary, D. H. Harrison.

THE BRITISH COUNCIL

10 Spring Gardens, S.W.1

The British Council was established in 1934. Its Royal Charter (1940) defines its aims as the promotion of a wider knowledge of Britain and English abroad, and the development of closer cultural relations with other countries. Most of its funds are provided by Parliament: the gross budget for 1976-77 is £36,603,000, and it administers a further sum, estimated for 1976-77 at £25,420,000, as agent for Government Departments and international organizations.

Chairman, The Lord Ballantrae, K.T., G.C.M.G., G.C.V.O., D.S.O., O.B.E.

Director-General, Sir John Llewellyn, K.C.M.G., Ph.D., D.SC.

THE NATIONAL TRUST

40-42 Queen Anne's Gate, Westminster, S.W.1
[01-930 0211]

The National Trust was founded in 1895 by Miss Octavia Hill, Sir Robert Hunter and Canon Rawnsley, their object being to preserve as much as possible the history and beauty of their country for its people. It became an organization incorporated by Act of Parliament (1907) to ensure the preservation of lands and buildings of historic interest or natural beauty for public access and benefit. It is independent of the State and relies on the voluntary support of private individuals for working funds. As a charity, however, it is allowed certain tax exemptions.

The Trust is now the largest private landowner in the country and third overall only to the Crown and the Forestry Commission. It protects nearly 500,000 acres, much of it superb hill country in the Lake District, Snowdonia, the Peak District and other National Parks. The Trust also owns and opens to the public some 200 country houses and gardens, and preserves villages, nature reserves, archaeological sites and many farms.

In 1965 the Trust launched a campaign to acquire as much as possible of the most beautiful stretches of coastline which were under threat from development. The Trust now protects 367 miles of coastline, the first target of £2,000,000 was reached in November 1973, and the appeal continues.

The Trust has now over 530,000 members paying an annual subscription and about 100,000 new members are joining each year. Rents, admission fees, legacies and gifts are other important sources of support and income.

The policy of the Trust is determined by the governing body, the Council. Half of its members are appointed by national institutions, such as the British Museum, the National Gallery, the Ramblers' Association and the Royal Horticultural Society; the other half are elected by Trust members at the Annual General Meeting. The Council appoints the Executive Committee, which in turn has established Regional Committees responsible for the management of the Trust's properties.

THE NATIONAL TRUST FOR SCOTLAND

5 Charlotte Square, Edinburgh 2

The National Trust for Scotland was founded in 1931, and its objects are similar to those of the National Trust. Like that organization, it is incorporated by Act of Parliament, is dependent for finance upon legacies, donations and the subscriptions of its members, is recognized as a charity for tax exemption purposes, and enjoys certain privileges under various Finance Acts regarding death duties.

The Trust administers about 80 major properties covering over 82,000 acres. Great houses in its care include:— The Binns, West Lothian; Brodick Castle, Isle of Arran; Crathes Castle, Kincardineshire; Culzean Castle, Ayrshire; Falkland Palace, Fife; Hill of Tarvit and Kellie Castle, Fife, and the Castle of Drum, Castle Fraser, Leith Hall and Craigievar Castle, Aberdeenshire.

In the Trust's care are also several noteworthy gardens. Some are associated with the great houses, others are:— Inverewe, in Wester Ross; the re-created 17th century garden of Pitmedden in Aberdeenshire; and Threave in Kirkcudbrightshire, where a School of Practical Gardening is run;

Branklyn Gardens, Perth, and Greenbank, Clarkston, Glasgow.

Among the mountainous country owned by the Trust is the Pass of Glencoe and the mountain group " The Five Sisters of Kintail " and the estate of Torridon in Wester Ross.

Islands in the Trust's care include the St. Kilda group, and Fair Isle. At Bannockburn, Killiecrankie, Glenfinnan and Culloden, the Trust owns sites associated with Scottish history.

Among smaller properties are houses associated with famous Scots:— the birthplaces of Barrie in Kirriemuir, Carlyle in Ecclefechan, and Hugh Miller in Cromarty; and Burns' Bachelors' Club, Tarbolton and Souter Johnnie's House, Kirkoswald in Ayrshire.

At Culross in Fife, and at Dunkeld, Perthshire, the restoration of attractive groups of houses led to the creation of a special fund under which such properties are brought, restored and sold. Under this scheme over 100 properties in the coastal burghs of East Fife and elsewhere have been and are being restored. This operation was one of the four pilot projects in the United Kingdom selected for special allocation during European Architectural Heritage Year, 1975 and in 1976 was awarded the European Prize for the Preservation of Ancient Monuments, given by the F.V.S. Foundation of Hamburg.

BRITISH STANDARDS INSTITUTION
British Standards House, 2 Park Street, W.1

The British Standards Institution is the recognized authority in the U.K. for the preparation and publication of national standards for industrial and consumer products. The Institution originated in 1901, when the Institutions of Civil, Mechanical and Electrical Engineers, together with the Iron and Steel Institute and the Institution of Naval Architects, formed a joint Engineering Standards Committee—which subsequently became the British Engineering Standards Association. A Royal Charter was granted in 1929 and with the extension of the scope of the organization to include the building, chemical and textile industries its title was later changed to " British Standards Institution ".

The Institution, in consultation with the interests concerned, now prepares standards relating to nearly every sector of the nation's industry and trade. There are over 7,000 British Standards covering specifications of quality, construction dimensions, performance or safety; methods of test and analysis; glossaries of terms; and codes of practice. About 500 new and revised British Standards are published each year.

The Institution represents the U.K. in the International Organization for Standardization (ISO), the International Electrotechnical Commission (IEC) and other international bodies concerned with harmonizing standards.

British Standards are issued for voluntary adoption though in a number of cases compliance with a British Standard is required by legislation. The Institution operates certification schemes under which industrial and consumer products are certified as complying with the relevant British Standard and manufacturers satisfying the requirements of such schemes may use the Institution's registered certification mark (known as the " Kitemark "). Other testing and certification services, together with information services, are available to industry, including help in meeting technical requirements in export markets.

The Institution is financed by voluntary subscriptions, an annual Government grant, the sale of its publications and fees for testing and certification. There are more than 16,000 subscribing members of B.S.I., including public authorities, trade and technical bodies, professional institutions, manufacturers, distributors and large scale purchasers.

Chairman of the Executive Board, Sir Arthur Hetherington, D.S.C.
Director General, G. B. R. Feilden, C.B.E., F.R.S.

HOUSING CORPORATION
Sloane Square House, S.W.1
[01-730-9991]

A Government agency established in 1964 which promotes, finances and supervises non-profit making housing associations. Over 40,000 new or improved homes a year are currently being approved to be let at fair rents.

Chairman, The Lord Goodman, C.H.
Deputy Chairman, The Lord Greenwood of Rossendale, P.C.
Members, Rev. P. Byrne, O.B.E.; J. R. Coward, C.B.E.; Miss B. Cooper; J. Kegie, O.B.E.; J. R. Madge, C.B. (*Chief Executive*); D. Mumford; K. Ryden, M.C.; W. L. Taylor; L. E. Waddilove, O.B.E.

DESIGN COUNCIL
28 Haymarket, S.W.1
[01-839-8000]

The Council, originally set up in 1944 as the Council of Industrial Design, is sponsored by the Department of Industry to promote the improvement of design in the products of British industry. Its name was changed in 1972 to reflect its increasing activity in the field of engineering design.

The Council's services to industry are based on teams of engineering field officers and industrial officers who visit companies throughout the United Kingdom to diagnose engineering design problems and to discuss and advise on design policy. The Council's Record of Engineering Design Expertise provides information about consultants, companies, universities and research organizations able to advise companies on engineering design problems and the Council's Designer Selection Service can recommend selected industrial designers for specific jobs.

The Council maintains permanent exhibitions of independently selected British goods from Design Index and its Design Centres in London's Haymarket and at 72 St. Vincent Street, Glasgow. Thematic exhibitions are also mounted at the Design Centres and at the Council's smaller Welsh Office in Cardiff. Design Index, the Council's unique photographic and sample record of about 10,000 current British products selected for their good design, can also be consulted at the Design Centres.

Other services include annual award schemes for consumer and contract goods, engineering products and components, and medical and motor vehicle equipment; training courses and conferences for retail staff, manufacturer's and managers; publications, including the monthly magazines *Design and Engineering*; a slide loan library; and press and information services. *Crafts* magazine is published bi-monthly by the Council as part of its services to the Crafts Advisory Committee.

Chairman, The Viscount Caldecote, D.S.C.
Director, Sir Paul Reilly.
Chairman of Scottish Committee, Sir Robert Fairbairn.
Chief Executive Scottish Committee, K. G. Clark.

SPORTS COUNCIL
70 Brompton Road, S.W.3
[01-589 3411]

The Sports Council received its Royal Charter

on April 1, 1972, formally recognizing it as an independent body, with the primary aims of promoting sport and recreation in Great Britain and of fostering the provision of facilities. For this purpose the Sports Council receives an annual grant-in-aid from the Department of the Environment.

Chairman, Sir Robin Brook, C.M.G., O.B.E.
Vice-Chairman, J. I. Disley.
Members, B. P. Atha,; H. Baxter; N. R. Collins; N. Croucher; T. Glyn Davies, C.B.E.; Mrs. M.

A. Glen Haig, M.B.E.; A. Hardaker, O.B.E.; P. Heatley, C.B.E.; F. J. Hill, C.B.E.; J. W. T. Hill; L. E. Liddell, E.R.D., T.D.; Lt.-Col. H. M. Llewellyn, C.B.E.; P. B. Lucas, D.S.O., D.F.C.; E. Major, M.B.E.; A. J. M. Miller, D.S.C., V.R.D.; K. K. Mitchell; D. D. Molyneux; Lord Rupert Nevill; A. Pascoe, M.B.E.; Miss M. Peters, M.B.E.; Prof. H. B. Rodgers; W. J. Slater; R. J. W. Struthers, M.B.E.; Lieut.-Gen. Sir James Wilson, K.B.E., M.C.
Director, W. Winterbottom, C.B.E.
Administrator, J. F. Coghlan, M.B.E., T.D.

THE BANK OF ENGLAND
Threadneedle Street, E.C.2.

The Bank of England was incorporated in 1694 under Royal Charter. It is the banker of the Government on whose behalf it manages the Note Issue, and also manages the National Debt and administers the Exchange Control regulations. As central reserve bank of the country, the Bank keeps the accounts of British banks, who maintain with it a proportion of their cash resources, and of most overseas central banks; but it has gradually withdrawn from new commercial business.
Governor, The Rt. Hon. Gordon William Humphreys Richardson, M.B.E.
Deputy Governor, Sir Jasper Quintus Hollom, K.B.E.
Directors, George Blunden; George Adrian Hayhurst Cadbury; Sir Robert Anthony Clark, D.S.C.; John Martin Clay; Leopold David de Rothschild; John Christopher Roderick Dow; John Standish Fforde; The Lord Greene of Harrow Weald, C.B.E.; Hector Laing; Sir (John)

Maurice Laing; Christopher William McMahon; The Lord Nelson of Stafford; Sir Alastair (Lionel Alexander Bethune) Pilkington, F.R.S.; The Lord Robens of Woldingham, P.C.; Sir Eric Roll, K.C.M.G., C.B.; The Lord Weir.
Chief Cashier, J. B. Page.
Chief Accountant, G. J. Costello.
Chief of the Overseas Dept., S. W. Payton, C.M.G.
Chief of the Economic Intelligence Dept., M. J. Thornton, M.C.
Chief of Administration, P. A. S. Taylor.
Chief of Establishments, K. J. S. Andrews, M.B.E.
Head of Computer Services, G. L. L. de Moubray.
Chief of Exchange Control, E. B. Bennett, D.S.C.
General Manager, Printing Works, M. J. S. Cubbage, M.B.E.
Banking Supervision, W. P. Cooke.
Adviser to the Governor, Sir Henry Benson, G.B.E.
Secretary, G. C. Gough.

THE LONDON CLEARING BANKS

COMMITTEE OF LONDON CLEARING BANKERS (1821), 10 Lombard Street, E.C.3
The Committee consists of the Chairmen of the six Clearing Banks (Barclays, Coutts, Lloyds, Midland, National Westminster, and Williams & Glyn's) and meets regularly to discuss matters of common interest. It is the body through which the Bank of England communicates official policy to the banks and through which the banks may present their views to the Bank of England and the Treasury.
Secretary-General, P. J. Nicholson.

BANKERS' AUTOMATED CLEARING SERVICES, LTD.
3 De Havilland Road, Edgware, Middlesex
Bankers' Automated Clearing Services is a company wholly owned by the London Clearing Banks. Its function is to receive money transfers recorded on magnetic tape and to distribute them to the appropriate bank. Nearly all standing orders in Great Britain are interchanged through BACS as is a substantial volume of direct debits originated by non-banking organizations for payments of rates, insurance premiums and hire purchase payments. Credits are also received on magnetic tape, mainly for payment of salaries and pensions.
Managing Director, D. J. Pyne.

BANKERS' CLEARING HOUSE
10 Lombard Street, E.C.3
This is the organization through which the Clearing Banks and the Bank of England exchange cheques drawn on each other and settle their indebtedness to one another. The clearing system

came into being in London during the second half of the eighteenth century, and has served as a pattern for the Clearing Houses that have been established since throughout the world.

To obtain payment for any cheque received from a customer for his credit, a banker must present it for payment to the bank on which it is drawn, and the Bankers' Clearing House affords a quick and efficient means of doing this. On an average day 4,000,000 cheques with a total value of £8,400 million, are exchanged and paid for by the Clearing Banks and the Bank of England on behalf of their branches throughout England and Wales which number over 10,000.

At present two cheque clearings are operated each business day. The Town Clearing, which takes place from 2.30 p.m. until 3.50 p.m., enables cheques of £5,000 and over to be cleared the same day, provided that such cheques are drawn on, and paid into, a Town Clearing branch. There are one hundred branches of the Clearing Banks so designated within a half-mile radius of the Clearing House.

The General Clearing, which takes place each morning, handles all cheques, drawn on branches of the member banks, which cannot be passed through the Town Clearing or cleared under local arrangements. Since April, 1960, a Credit Clearing has been operated through which the member banks exchange credit items in respect of monetary transfers between their customers. The daily average for this Clearing, including work passed through the Bankers' Automated Clearing Service, is 1,161,000 items with a total value of £209 million.

At the end of the day each member bank works out the net balance resulting from its transactions in that day's Town Clearing, the previous day's General Clearing and Credit Clearing and B.A.C.S. output and such differences as need to be adjusted. This net balance is either credited to or deducted from the bank's own account at the Bank of England.

Chief Inspector, S. C. Veal.
Deputy Inspector, B. L. Newitt.

BRITISH BANKERS' ASSOCIATION

10 Lombard Street, E.C.3.

The Association provides a means of communication and consultation for the commercial banking industry in this country. Membership is restricted to institutions accepted as banks or discount houses by the Bank of England—over 300. The Association is a member of the E.E.C. Banking Federation.

Secretary-General, R. K. C. Giddings, M.C.

PRINCIPAL BANKS OPERATING IN THE BRITISH COMMONWEALTH

* *Clearing Bankers.* ‡ *Army Agents.*

London Banking Hours are 9.30 a.m. to 3.30 p.m. (Saturdays, *closed*). In addition, some branches open on one evening a week from 4.30 p.m. to 6.00 p.m. *Scotland.*—Banking hours in Scotland are: Mon.-Wed., 9.30–12.30; 1.30–3.30; Thursday, 9.30–12.30; 1.30–3.30; 4.30–6 p.m.; Fri. 9.30–3.30; Saturday, *Closed*.

ALEXANDERS DISCOUNT CO., LTD. (1810), 24 Lombard St., E.C.3.—Capital, paid up, £5,055,570. Published Reserves, £4,524,911. Deposits, etc. (31 Dec. 1975) £469,804,294.

ALLIED IRISH BANKS LTD. (1966 by alliance of Munster and Leinster, Provincial and Royal Banks).Lansdowne House, Ballsbridge, Dublin, 4. London Agents, Barclays Bank Ltd., Midland Bank, National Westminster Bank. (31.3.76) Capital issued, £11,088,000; Share Premium and Reserves £60,803,000. Total Assets £1,485,682,000. Current Deposit and other accounts £1,378,327,000. Advances to Customers and other accounts, less provisions, £588,765,000.

ALLEN HARVEY & ROSS LIMITED (1888), 45 Cornhill. (1975), Issued Capital, £1,864,000; Reserves, £1,936,000; Deposit, etc., £150,431,000.

THE AMERICAN EXPRESS INTERNATIONAL BANKING CORPORATION. The Subsidiary of American Express Co., New York (1868), 65 Broadway, *New York*, U.S.A.; 52 Cannon Street, E.C.4.— Capital, $31,000,000 (Shares fully paid).

ANGLO-PORTUGUESE BANK, LTD. (1929), 7 Bishopsgate, E.C.2.—Capital, £10,000,000. Issued and fully paid, £7,500,000; Share Premium Account, £2,250,000; Reserves £5,000,000; Deposits, 31/12/75, £82,834,171.

AUSTRALIA AND NEW ZEALAND BANKING GROUP LIMITED, *Registered Office*, 71 Cornhill, E.C.3.— Capital Authorized, £50,000,000; issued and paid up, £36,720,000; Reserves, £99,523,000; Total assets, £4,618,888,000 (at 30/9/75).

AUSTRALIA AND NEW ZEALAND SAVINGS BANK LIMITED, *Head Office*, 351 Collins Street, *Melbourne*; Capital Authorized, $A14,000,000; Issued and Paid up, $A5,000,000; Reserve Fund at 30/9/75, $A24,700,000. Total Assets at 30/9/75, $A1,368,253.

A.N.Z. SAVINGS BANK (NEW ZEALAND) LIMITED, *Regd. Office*, 196 Featherston Street, *Wellington*, New Zealand. Capital Authorized, Issued and Paid up, $NZ500,000; Deposits, etc., at 30/9/75, $NZ124,895,000; Reserve Fund, $NZ2,700,000; Total Assets at 30/9/75, $NZ128,568,000.

BANCO DE BILBAO (1857), *Bilbao*, Spain (Bilbao House, 36 New Broad Street, E.C.2.; 40 King Street, W.C.2.; 74 Commercial Street, E.1.; 32 Cranbourn Street, W.C.2; 3 Sloane Street, S.W.1, New Covent Garden Market, S.W.8; 28–29 High Street, Southampton.—Capital subscribed and paid-up, Pesetas 9,413,040,500; Reserve Fund, Pesetas 11,513,492,331. Deposits, etc., Pesetas 324,592,037,338. (Over 500 Branches in Spain, France, United Kingdom and New York.) Representative offices in Milan and Frankfurt.

BANGKOK BANK LTD. (1941), *Bangkok*, Thailand (59–67 Gresham Street, E.C.2.)—(31/12/75)

Capital issued and paid-up, Baht 1,050,000,000 Reserves, Baht 1,693,900,000; Undivided Profit Baht 16,648,344; Deposits, etc., Baht 43,533,331,269.

BANKERS TRUST COMPANY, 280 Park Avenue, *New York* 10017(9 Queen Victoria Street, E.C.4 and 32–34 Grosvenor Square, W.1).—Capital stock (par value $010 per share), $105,120,000.

BANK LEUMI (U.K.) LTD. 4–7 Woodstock Street W.1.—Capital: Authorized, £2,500,000 (31/12/75); Issued and fully paid, £2,000,000, ordinary shares £1 each; Reserves £2,100,000 (31/12/75). Established in 1959 as Anglo-Israel Bank Ltd. to take over the business of Bank Leumi le-Israel B.M. London Branch. In 1973 the name was changed to Bank Leumi (U.K.) Ltd.

BANK OF ADELAIDE (1865), *Adelaide*, South Australia (11 Leadenhall St., E.C.3). Capital, Authorized $A50,000,000; issued $A31,504,687 (Shares in units of $A1 each, fully paid); Reserve Fund, $A23,894,033. (141 Offices.)

BANK OF AMERICA NATIONAL TRUST AND SAVINGS ASSOCIATION (1904), *San Francisco, California* U.S.A. (25 Cannon Street, E.C.4 and 29 Davies Street, W.1).—Capital Funds, $2,084,551,000; Total Deposits, $57,274,116,000. Over 1,000 branches in California and over 100 foreign branches plus representative offices, subsidiaries and/or affiliates in more than 80 countries.

BANK OF BERMUDA, LTD. (1889), *Hamilton*, Bermuda (*London Agents*, Bank of Bermuda (Europe, Ltd.))—Capital paid up BD$4,320,000; Reserves, BD$7,000,000; Total Deposits, BD$476,537,733. Undivided Profits, BD$1,375,320.

BANK OF ENGLAND. *See* p. 446.

BANK OF INDIA (1906), *Bombay* (Kent House, 11–16 Telegraph Street, E.C.2).—Capital paid up, *Rs.* 4,05,00,000. Reserve Fund, *Rs.* 10,75,46,822 (948 Branches).

BANK OF IRELAND (1783), Lower Baggot Street, *Dublin* (*London Agents*, Bank of England; Lloyds Bank Ltd.; Coutts & Co.; Brown, Shipley & Co. Ltd.).—Capital (Authorized), £40,000,000; (Issued and Fully Paid), £25,26,8052. Reserves, £62,523,000. Deposit, current and other accounts, £1,379,127. Dividend (31/3/76) 12.5p per £1 of Capital Stock.

BANK OF LONDON & MONTREAL, LTD. (1958), P.O. BOX N 1262, Nassau, Bahama Islands. A member of the Lloyds Bank Group. Capital (Authorized), $Bah. 30,000,000; (Paid up), $Bah. 21,450,000. (13 Branches and Agencies).

BANK OF LONDON & SOUTH AMERICA, LTD. (1862), 40–66 Queen Victoria Street, E.C.4.—*See* LLOYDS BANK INTERNATIONAL LTD.

BANK OF MONTREAL (1817), *Montreal*, Canada. (47, Threadneedle St., E.C.2, and 9, Waterloo Place, S.W.1).—Capital, authorized $100,000,000; fully paid $68,343,750. Rest, $382,000,000;

Deposits, 31/10/75, $16,550,476,748; Dividend, 1975, 96 cents per share. (Over 1,243 Branches and Agencies.)

BANK OF NEW SOUTH WALES (1871) AND BANK OF NEW SOUTH WALES SAVINGS BANK LTD. (1955), Head Office, *Sydney*, N.S.W. (29 Threadneedle St., E.C.2, 9–15 Sackville Street, W.1. and 14 Kingsway, W.C.2).—At 30/9/75: Capital, authorized and paid up, $A107,500,000; Reserve Fund, $A139,383,000; Aggregate Assets, $A8,805,583,000; Dividend, 14 p.c. (1,343 Branches and Agencies.)

BANK OF NEW ZEALAND, Incorporated in New Zealand in 1861. (1 Queen Victoria St., E.C.4.) 31/3/75: Capital Authorized and Paid up, NZ $26,500,000; Reserves, NZ $49,097,000; Deposits, NZ $1,173,731,000; Total Assets, NZ $1,333,336,000 (407 Branches and Agencies in New Zealand; also Branches in Melbourne, Sydney, Fiji and London and Representative Offices in Tokyo and Singapore).

BANK OF NOVA SCOTIA (1832). *Halifax*, N.S.; Executive Offices, *Toronto*, Ontario, Canada (Regional Office, 12 Berkeley Square, W.1.)— Capital, Authorized, $50,000,000; Paid-up $37,125,000 ($C2 Shares); Reserve Fund, $437,000,000; Total Assets, $16,005,998,218 (at Oct. 31, 1975); (1,000 Branches and Representative Offices in 41 countries.)

BANK OF SCOTLAND (1695), The Mound, *Edinburgh*; (30 Bishopsgate, E.C.2; 16/18 Piccadilly, W.1.; 57–60 Haymarket, S.W.1; 332 Oxford Street, W.1. and 140 Kensington High Street, W.8).— Capital £32,250,000; Reserve Fund and Balance carried forward, £74,532,000. Deposits and Credit Balances, 29/2/75, £1,170,517. (583 Branches and Sub-Branches.)

BANK OF VALLETTA LTD. (1974), 45 Republic Street, Valletta, *Malta*. (Merger of National Bank of Malta, Ltd. (1946), Sciclunas Bank (1830) and Tagliaferro Bank Ltd. (1812)). Authorized capital, £6,000,000. Paid up £3,000,000. Branches: 27 in Malta and Gozo.

BANQUE BELGE LTD. (1934), 16 St. Helen's Place E.C.3.—Capital Authorized £8,100,000: Issued £8,100,000; Paid up, £6,100,000.

BANQUE CANADIENNE NATIONALE, *Montreal*, Canada (Bank of Hochelaga and Banque Nationale amalgamated).—Capital (issued) $16,000,000; Reserve $97,000,000; Assets, $5,000,000,000. (476 Offices in Canada.)

BANQUE NATIONALE DE PARIS LTD. (formerly British and French Bank Ltd.), *Head Office:* (temp.) Plantation House, 10–15 Mincing Lane, E.C.3. Authorized Share Capital, £20,000,000; Issued and fully paid share capital, £10,000,000 (Subsidiary of the BANQUE NATIONALE DE PARIS.)

BARCLAYS BANK LIMITED (1896), *Head Office*, 54 Lombard St., E.C.3; *City Office*, 170 Fenchurch Street, E.C.3.—Capital Authorized, £275,000,000. Capital Issued £200,924,535; Reserves, £384,592,000; Deposits, £6,558,657,000. Dividend, 1975: Ord. Stock 13·8356 p.c., Staff stock, 21·5384 p.c. Over 3,000 branches in England and Wales. Subsidiary Companies, U.K Division: BARCLAYS BANK U.K. MANAGEMENT LTD.; MERCANTILE CREDIT COMPANY LTD.; BARCLAYS BANK FINANCE COMPANY (JERSEY) LTD.; BARCLAYS FINANCE COMPANY (GUERNSEY) LTD.; BARCLAYS FINANCE COMPANY (ISLE OF MAN) LTD. International Division: BARCLAYS BANK INTERNATIONAL LTD.; BARCLAYS NATIONAL BANK LTD.; BARCLAYS BANK OF NIGERIA LTD.; BARCLAYS BANK OF CALIFORNIA; BARCLAYS DISCOUNT BANK LTD.; BARCLAYS BANK OF UGANDA LTD.; BARCLAYS BANK OF ZAMBIA LTD.; BARCLAYS BANK S.A.; BARCLAYS BANK OF GHANA LTD.; BARCLAYS BANK OF NEW YORK; SOCIÉTÉ BANCAIRE BAR-

CLAYS (SUISSE) S.A.; BARCLAYS BANK OF SIERRA LEONE LTD.; BARCLAYS BANK S.Z.A.R.L.; BARCLAYS OVERSEAS DEVELOPMENT CORPORATION LTD.; BARCLAYS NATIONAL MERCHANT BANK LTD.; BARCLAYS BANK OF JAMAICA LTD.; BARCLAYS BANK OF TRINIDAD AND TOBAGO LTD.; BARCLAYS AUSTRALIA LTD.; BANCA BARCLAYS CASTELLINI S.p.A.; BARCLAYS KOL AND COMPANY N.V.; BARCLAYS BANK OF SWAZILAND LTD.; BARCLAYS CANADA LTD.; BANCO POPULAR ANTILIANO N.V.; BARCLAYS BANK OF BOTSWANA LTD. Financial Services Division: BARCLAYS MERCHANT BANK LTD.; BARCLAYS BANK (LONDON AND INTERNATIONAL) LTD.; BARCLAYS BANK TRUST COMPANY LTD.; BARCLAYS UNICORN LTD.; BARCLAYS UNICORN INTERNATIONAL LTD.; BARCLAYS UNICORN INTERNATIONAL (CHANNEL ISLANDS) LTD.; BARCLAYS UNICORN INTERNATIONAL (ISLE OF MAN) LTD.; BARCLAYS LIFE ASSURANCE COMPANY LTD.; BARCLAYS UNICORN (TRUSTEES) LTD.; BARCLAYTRUST CHANNEL ISLANDS LTD.; BARCLAYTRUST ISLE OF MAN LTD.; BARCLAYTRUST INTERNATIONAL LTD.; BARCLAYTRUST INTERNATIONAL (BERMUDA) LTD.; BARCLAYTRUST PROPERTY MANAGEMENT LTD.; BARCLAYS EXPORT AND FINANCE COMPANY LTD.; BARCLAYS BAIL S.A.; BARCLAYS LEASING B.V.; BARCLAYS INSURANCE SERVICES COMPANY LTD.; BARCLAYS INSURANCE BROKERS INTERNATIONAL LTD. Associated Companies: BANK OF SCOTLAND; TOZER KEMSLEY & MILLBOURN (HOLDINGS) LTD.; SOCIÉTÉ FINANCIERE EUROPÉENNE—S.F.E. LUXEMBOURG BANQUE DE LA SOCIÉTÉ FINANCIERE EUROPÉENNE; YORKSHIRE BANK LTD.; BANQUE BRUXELLES LAMBERT S.A.; BARIC COMPUTING SERVICES LTD.; BANCO DEL DESARROLLO ECONOMICO ESPANOL; ANGLO-ROMANIAN BANK LTD.; INTERNATIONAL ENERGY BANK LTD.

BARCLAYS BANK INTERNATIONAL LTD, 54 Lombard, St., E.C.3.—Authorized Capital, £130,000,000; Issued Capital, £130,000,000; Reserves, £175,000,000; Deposits, 31/3/76, £8,683,000,000. (1,743 Branches, Sub-Branches, and Agencies.)

BARING BROTHERS & CO., LTD. (1763), 88 Leadenhall Street, E.C.3, and Liverpool.—Capital, Authorized, issued and fully paid, £5,550,000; Reserve, £12,500,000; Deposits, 31/12/75, £223,796,588.

BRANDTS, LTD. see Grindlay Brandts Ltd.

BRITISH BANK FOR FOREIGN TRADE, LTD. (1911), 1 Crown Court, Cheapside, E.C.2.—Subscribed Capital, £700,000; 7,000,000 Shares of 10p each fully paid.

BRITISH BANK OF COMMERCE (1936), 4 West Regent Street, Glasgow.—Capital, fully-paid, £5,559,654; Ultimate holding company—National and Grindlays Holdings Ltd.

THE BRITISH BANK OF THE MIDDLE EAST (1889) 20 Abchurch Lane, E.C.4.— Capital; authorized £25,000,000; issued and fully paid, (£1 shares) £17,500,000: 31/12/75; Revenue Reserves, £19,041,027; Current, deposit and other accounts, £981,785,033; Dividend, 1975, 23.3p. per share.

BROWN, SHIPLEY & CO. LTD. (1810), Founders Court, Lothbury, E.C.2.—Capital, Authorized and Issued, £5,000,000; Reserves £3,655,000; Deposits, £113,546,000.

BUNGE & CO., LIMITED (1905), Bunge House, St. Mary Axe, E.C.3.—Capital subscribed and paid up £1,000,000. Reserves, £10,879,000 (1974).

CATER RYDER & CO. LTD. (1960), 1 King William Street, E.C.4.—Capital authorized, £6,000,000; issued and fully paid, £5,469,000. Reserve

£3,000,000. Deposits, etc., 30/4/75, £315,336,320; Dividend 1975-6, 24.2 p.c.

CENTRAL BANK OF INDIA (1911), *Bombay.* 31/12/75: Paid-up capital (wholly owned by Central Government of India), Rs.4,75,14,600; Reserve Fund and other reserves, Rs.11,65,93,569; Deposit and other accounts, Rs.11,80,53,43,129. (1,305 branches, etc.)

CHARTERED BANK (1853), 10 Clements Lane, E.C.4. —Capital, Authorized, £15,000,000 (divided into 15,000,000 shares of £1 each) Issued and converted into stock, £9,680,000; Reserves, £81,934,000; Deposits, 31/12/75, £1,681,253,000. A subsidiary of Standard Chartered Bank Ltd.

CHARTERHOUSE JAPHET LIMITED (1880), 1 Paternoster Row, E.C.4.—Capital, authorized and paid-up, £6,000,000.

THE CHASE MANHATTAN BANK, *N.A. New York, U.S.A.* (Woolgate House, Coleman Street, E.C.2 and 1 Mount Street, W.1.)—Capital, $400,739,475; Surplus, $501,306,738; Undivided Profits, $719,162,157; Total Deposits $33,928,000,000. (223 Branches in New York and affiliated Branches and associated Banks in over 80 overseas countries.)

CLIVE DISCOUNT COMPANY, LTD. (1946), 1 Royal Exchange Avenue, E.C.3.—Capital, Authorized, issued and fully paid, £4,100,000.

CLYDESDALE BANK, LTD (1838), St. Vincent Place, *Glasgow.* (*Edinburgh,* Chief Office, 29 George St.), Chief London Office, 30 Lombard St., E.C.3. *Affiliated to* Midland Bank, Ltd.—Authorized Capital, £10,419,000; Paid-up Capital, £6,419,000; Reserve Fund, £40,192,000; Deposits, 31/12/75, £635,082,000. (367 Branches.)

COMMERCIAL BANK OF AUSTRALIA, LTD. (1866), Collins St., *Melbourne* (12 Old Jewry, E.C.).— Paid-up Capital; $A43,864,168 ($A20 Preference, fully paid; $A1 Ordinary, fully paid); Deposits, etc., 30/6/75, $A1,736,039,000; Reserve Funds $A30,260,000. (751 Branches and Agencies.)

COMMERCIAL BANK OF THE NEAR EAST, LTD. (1922) Bankside House, 107-112 Leadenhall Street, E.C.3.—Capital, fully paid, £200,000; Reserve Fund £1,050,000. Deposits, 31/12/74, £36,064,535.

COMMERCIAL BANKING CO., OF SYDNEY, LTD. (1834), 343 George St., *Sydney,* N.S.W. (27-32 Old Jewry, E.C.2).—Authorized Capital, $A50,000,000 (Shares of $A1 each) Issued and paid-up $A40,115,000 ($A1 shares); Reserve Fund, $A26,200,000. (638 Branches in Australia.)

COMMONWEALTH SAVINGS BANK OF AUSTRALIA *Sydney,* N.S.W. (8 Old Jewry, E.C.2. and 48 Aldwych, W.C.2.) Owned and guaranteed by the Australian Government. Deposits, etc., 30/6/75, $A4,847,918,257; Reserve Fund, $A56,060,533. (7,376 Branches and Agencies.)

COMMONWEALTH TRADING BANK OF AUSTRALIA (1953), *Sydney,* N.S.W. (8 Old Jewry, E.C.2; Australia House, Strand, W.C.2.)—Owned and guaranteed by the Australian Government. 30/6/75: Deposits, etc., $A3,956,425,690; Reserve Fund, $A31,174,000. (1,258 Branches and Agencies.)

CONTINENTAL ILLINOIS NATIONAL BANK AND TRUST COMPANY OF CHICAGO, *Chicago.,* Ill., U.S.A. (58-60 Moorgate, E.C.2 and 47 Berkeley Square, W.1).—31/12/75. Capital Stock, $200,000,000; Surplus (Reserves) $488,000,000; Undivided Profits, $179,041,000; Total Deposits $15,142,639,000. (16 Branches, 16 Represen-

tative Offices, 11 Subsidiaries and 30 affiliates world-wide).

CO-OPERATIVE BANK LTD. (1872), New Century House, *Manchester*—Capital paid up, £8,000,000. (60 Branches.)

COPLEYS BANK, LTD. (1916), Ludgate House, 107-11 Fleet Street, E.C.4.—Capital authorized, £2,500,000; paid up, £1,000,000.

*COUTTS & CO. (1692), 440 Strand, W.C.2; (Temporary Head Office during rebuilding, 1 Suffolk St., S.W.1; Strand Office (temporary), 59 Strand, W.C.2); 15 Lombard St., E.C.3; 1 Old Park Lane, W.1.; 16 Cavendish Square, W.1.; 1 Cadogan Place, Sloane St., S.W.1.; 10 Mount St., W.1.; 188 Fleet St., E.C.4; 162 Brompton Road, S.W.3.; and 15 High St., Eton, *Windsor.*—Capital issued and paid up, £1,000,000; Reserves, £10,091,000; Current, Deposit and other accounts (31/12/75), £591,238,000. (*A subsidiary of* National Westminster Bank, Ltd.) *Main Subsidiary:* COUTTS FINANCE CO.

CREDIT LYONNAIS (1863), 19 Boulevard des Italiens, *Paris* (84-94 Queen Victoria St., E.C.4; 18 Regent St., S.W.1.; 19 Old Brompton Road, S.W.7.)— Capital, Frs. 480,000,000; Reserve Fund, Frs. 638,000,000. (2,500 Branches throughout the world.)

DISCOUNT BANK (OVERSEAS) LTD., 63-66 Hatton Garden, E.C.1; 89 Duke Street, W.1.

FIRST NATIONAL CITY BANK OF NEW YORK (1812), 399 Park Avenue, *New York* 10022 (Citibank House, 336 Strand, W.C.2., 34 Moorgate, E.C.2., and 17 Bruton St., Berkeley Sq., W.1). 31/12/74: Capital $638,191,000; 4 p.c. Convertible Capital; Notes $22,482,000; Deposits, $44,989,342, Surplus, Undivided Profits and unallocated Reserve for Contingencies, $1,545,604,000. (243 Branches in New York, 250 Branches in 103 countries, overseas.)

FLEMING (ROBERT) & CO. LTD. (1932), 8 Crosby Square, E.C.3.

ANTONY GIBBS HOLDINGS LTD. (1808), 23 Blomfield St., E.C.2.

GILLETT BROTHERS DISCOUNT CO., LTD. (1867), 65 Cornhill, E.C.3. Issued Capital, £2,296,066; Deposits, 1976, £181,654,039. Dividend, 1976, 13 p.c.

GRINDLAY BRANDTS LIMITED (1805). Formerly Brandts, Ltd. 36 Fenchurch St., E.C.3.—Capital Authorized, £10,000,000; Issued and Fully Paid, £7,500,000.

GRINDLAYS BANK LIMITED, P.O. Box 280, 23 Fenchurch Street, E.C.3.—(31/12/75) Capital authorized, £30,000,000; Issued and paid up £15,776,000 (Shares of £1 each); Advances £1,147,176,000; Deposits £1,825,573,000 (over 225 offices).

GUINNESS MAHON & CO. LTD. (1836), 32 St. Mary at Hill, E.C.3. (a member of the Guinness Peat Group).

GUINNESS MAHON LTD. (1836), 17 College Green, *Dublin* 2 (a member of the Guinness Peat Group).

HAMBROS BANK, LTD. (1839). *Head Office,* 41 Bishopsgate, E.C.2; *West End Office,* 67 Pall Mall, S.W.1; *Holborn Office,* 1 Charterhouse St., E.C.1.—Authorized Capital, £13,000,000. Banking Group Consolidated figures: Reserve, £30,444,000; Deposits, 31/3/76, £866,281,000. Hambros Bank Ltd. is a wholly-owned subsidiary of Hambros Ltd., the dividend of which for 1975-76 was 77·5p on £10 shares (£2·50 paid) and 7·75p on 25p fully-paid shares; 4·2p on £1 " A " shares.

HARRODS (KNIGHTSBRIDGE) LIMITED, (1889), 87-135 Brompton Rd., S.W.1.

HELBERT, WAGG & CO., LTD. See J. HENRY SCHRODER WAGG & CO. LIMITED.

HILL SAMUEL GROUP LTD. (1831), 100 Wood Street, E.C.2.—(31/3/76): Capital, authorized £17,500,000; Issued, £14,636,424 (shares of 25p each); Reserves, £50,191,000; Current, Deposit and other accounts, £644,219,000; Dividend, 1975-76, 3·8775p per share net.

C. HOARE & CO. (1672), 27 Fleet St., E.C.4, and 16 Waterloo Place, S.W.1.—Capital and Reserve Fund, £1,000,000; Deposits, 5/4/76, £62,755,793.

HONGKONG AND SHANGHAI BANKING CORPORA-TION (1865), 1 Queen's Road Central, Hong Kong (9 Gracechurch St., E.C.3).—Capital, authorized, $H1,250,000,000; Issued and fully paid $HK867,662,430 ($HK 2·50 Shares); Reserve Funds, $HK820,000,000; Deposits, etc., 31/12/75, $HK22,511,792,324.

INTERNATIONAL WESTMINSTER BANK LTD. (as from 1/1/73). Previously Westminster Foreign Bank Ltd. (1913), 41 Lothbury, E.C.2.

IONIAN BANK, LTD. (1839), 64 Coleman Street, E.C.2.—Capital, Authorized, £2,500,000; Issued and fully paid £1,925,000; Reserves, £883,000; Deposits, £15,057,000.

ISLE OF MAN BANK LTD. (1865). (A Member Bank of the National Westminster Group), Douglas, I.O.M. (London Agents, National Westminster Bank Ltd.).—Issued Capital, £2,000,000 in 2,000,000 shares of £1 each, fully paid, con-verted into stock; Reserve Fund £5,909,099; Deposits, 31/12/75, £59,216,064. (20 Branches.)

S. JAPHET & CO. LTD., see CHARTERHOUSE JAPHET LIMITED.

LEOPOLD JOSEPH & SONS LTD. (1919), 31 Gresham Street, E.C.2.—Capital, authorized, £5,000,000; Issued and paid up, £3,902,456.

JESSEL, TOYNBEE & CO. LTD. (1922), 30 Cornhill, E.C.3.—Capital authorized £3,000,000; Issued and fully paid, £2,110,390.

KEYSER ULLMANN LIMITED (1966). Amalgamation of Ullmann & Co. Ltd. (1932) and A. Keyser & Co. Ltd. (Estd. 1868, Inc. 1946). Regd. Office. 25 Milk Street, E.C.2. Capital, authorized, issued and fully paid, £50,000,000, in ordinary shares of £1. Current, Deposit and other accounts, £198,232,000.

KING & SHAXSON, LTD. (1866), 52 Cornhill E.C.3. Capital authorized £3,000,000; issued and fully paid, £2,600,000; General Reserve, £1,700,000.

KLEINWORT, BENSON LIMITED (1830), 20 Fenchurch St., E.C.3. Total Assets, £1,116,890,000. De-posits, etc., £886,118,000.

LAZARD BROTHERS & CO. LTD. (1870), 21 Moor-fields, E.C.2. Capital authorized and paid up, £15,187,500.

*‡LLOYDS BANK, LIMITED (1865), Head Office, 71 Lombard St., E.C.3; Branches Stock Office, 111 Old Broad Street, E.C.2; Overseas Department, 6 Eastcheap, E.C.3; Trust Division, 34 Thread-needle Street, E.C.2. Principal London Offices:— City Office, 72 Lombard Street, E.C.3; 39 Threadneedle Street, E.C.2.; 6 Pall Mall, S.W.1 (Cox's & King's Branch); 16 St. James' Street, S.W.1; Law Courts, 222 Strand, W.C.2.— Capital authorized, £150,000,000, increased (25/2/76) to £200,000,000, issued £129,766,000; Reserves, £327,993,000; Current Deposit and Other Accounts, 31/12/75: £4,260,908,000; Dividend 1975, interim 3.377p per share and final 4·0203p per share. 2,420 Branches. The LLOYDS BANK GROUP, in addition to LLOYDS BANK LIMITED, comprises LLOYDS BANK INTERNATIONAL LIMITED, LLOYDS ASSOCIATED BANKING COMPANY LIMITED, LEWIS'S BANK LIMITED, THE NATIONAL BANK OF NEW ZEALAND LIMITED, EXPORTERS' REFINANCE CORPORATION LIMITED, LLOYDS ASSOCIATED AIR LEASING LIMI-TED, LLOYDS BANKING & TRUST COMPANY (ISLE OF MAN) LTD.; LLOYDS BANK TRUST COMPANY (CHANNEL ISLANDS) LIMITED, LLOYDS BANK PRO-PERTY COMPANY LIMITED, LLOYDS BANK UNIT TRUST MANAGERS LIMITED, LLOYDS FIRST WESTERN CORPORATION, LLOYDS LEASING LIMI-TED AND BEEHIVE LIFE ASSURANCE COMPANY LTD. LLOYDS BANK LIMITED is closely associated with NATIONAL AND COMMERCIAL BANKING GROUP LIMITED, GRINDLAYS HOLDINGS LIMITED, YORK-SHIRE BANK LIMITED, LLOYDS & SCOTTISH LIMITED, FINANCE FOR INDUSTRY LIMITED, THE JOINT CREDIT CARD COMPANY LIMITED.

LLOYDS BANK INTERNATIONAL (1971), 40-66 Queen Victoria Street, E.C.4.—Author-ized Capital, £75,000,000; Paid-up Capital, £39,801,919. Wholly owns Bank of London & South America Limited, Lloyds Bank Inter-national (France) Limited, Bank of London & Montreal Limited, Lloyds Bank International (Belgium) S.A. and Lloyds Bank (Cannes) S.A.

MANUFACTURERS HANOVER TRUST COMPANY (1961), New York, U.S.A. (7 Princes Street, E.C.2 and 88 Brook Street, W.1).—Capital stock $210,000,000; Surplus $440,000,000.

MARTINS BANK LTD. (1838). Merged 15/12/69 with BARCLAYS BANK LIMITED, q.v.

MERCANTILE BANK LTD. (1853), 1 Queen's Road Central, Hong Kong (15 Gracechurch Street, E.C.3).—Issued Capital, £2,940,000 (2,940,000 Ordinary Shares, £1 each fully paid); Reserve Fund, £6,500,000; Deposits, £98,340,655. Share capital acquired in 1959 by Hongkong and Shanghai Banking Corporation.

*MIDLAND BANK, LTD. (1836), Head Office, Poultry, E.C.2; Principal City Branches, Poultry and Princes St., E.C.2; 5 Threadneedle St., E.C.2; Interna-tional Division, 60 Gracechurch Street, E.C.3.— Authorized Capital, £150,000,000; Issued Capi-tal, £132,473,941 (Shares of £1 each, fully paid); Reserve Fund, £285,273,000; Deposits, 31/12/75, £7,138,903,000; Dividend, 1975, 11·47802p per share. (Group operates through more than 3,600 branches and offices in British Isles and Republic of Ireland, and 160 overseas.) Principal Trading Subsidiaries: CLYDESDALE BANK LTD., CLYDESDALE BANK FINANCE CORPORATION LTD., CLYDESDALE BANK INSURANCE SERVICES LTD., SCOTTISH COMPUTER SERVICES LTD., NORTHERN BANK LTD., NORTHERN BANK DEVELOPMENT CORPORATION LTD., NORTHERN BANK EXECUTOR AND TRUSTEE COMPANY LTD., NORTHERN BANK TRUST CORPORATION LTD., MIDLAND BANK INSURANCE SERVICES LTD., MIDLAND BANK FINANCE CORPORATION LTD., FORWARD TRUST LTD., MIDLAND MONTAGU LEASING LTD., GRIFFIN FACTORS LTD., MIDLAND BANK TRUST CORPORATION (JERSEY) LTD., MIDLAND BANK TRUST CORPORATION (GUERNSEY) LTD., MIDLAND BANK TRUST COMPANY LTD., MIDLAND BANK GROUP UNIT TRUST MANAGERS LTD., THE THOMAS COOK GROUP LTD., THOMAS COOK LTD., THOMAS COOK OVERSEAS LTD., THOMAS COOK BANKERS LTD., SAMUEL MONTAGU & CO. LTD., (Incorporating DRAYTON), DRAYTON MON-TAGU PORTFOLIO MANAGEMENT LTD., GUYER-ZELLER ZURMONT BANK AG; NORTHERN BANK FINANCE CORPORATION LTD.; MIDLAND MON-TAGU INDUSTRIAL FINANCE LTD.; JERSEY INTER-NATIONAL BANK OF COMMERCE LTD.; BLAND PAYNE HOLDINGS LTD., BLAND PAYNE LTD., BLAND PAYNE REINSURANCE BROKERS LTD.;

BLAND PAYNE (U.K.) LTD., SOUTHERN MARINE & AVIATION UNDERWRITERS INC.; BLAND PAYNE AUSTRALIA LTD.; LONDON AMERICAN FINANCE CORPORATION LTD., BRITISH OVERSEAS ENGINEERING & CREDIT COMPANY LTD., DRAKE (U.K.) INTERNATIONAL LTD., DRAKE AMERICA CORPORATION; EXPORT CREDIT CORPORATION.

MIDLAND BANK TRUST CO. LTD. (1909), *Head Office*, 6 Threadneedle Street, E.C.2. *Affiliated to* Midland Bank Ltd. Subscribed Capital, £1,000,000; Paid-up Capital, £1,000,000 (200,000 shares of £5 fully paid); Reserve Fund, £885,000 (40 Offices).

SAMUEL MONTAGU & CO. LTD. (*Incorporating* Drayton) (1853), 114 Old Broad Street, E.C.2. Capital authorized and paid up, £40,000,000; Reserves, £12,410,000; Loan Capital, £9,591,000; Current Deposits, etc., £802,557,000 (31/12/75).

MORGAN GRENFELL & CO. LIMITED (1838), 23 Great Winchester St., E.C.2.; Private limited Coy. (1934).—Authorized Capital, £12,500,000; issued and fully paid, £12,500,000.

MORGAN GUARANTY TRUST COMPANY OF NEW YORK (1959), 23 Wall Street, *New York*, U.S.A. (33 Lombard Street, E.C.3 and 31 Berkeley Sq., W.1).—Capital, $228,085,000 (9,123,400 shares —$25 par); Surplus Fund, $336,500,000.

NATIONAL AND COMMERCIAL BANKING GROUP LIMITED. Registered Office: 36 St. Andrew Square, *Edinburgh*. *London Office*, 3 Bishopsgate, E.C.2.—(30/9/75): Capital authorized. £60,000,000; issued, £57,090,000; Reserves, £173,838,000; Customers' current and deposit accounts, £2,913,544,000. Ordinary dividend; interim 1·05p per share; final 1·0932p per share. (Approximately 900 offices.) Owns (*inter alia*) all capital of THE ROYAL BANK OF SCOTLAND LIMITED and WILLIAMS & GLYN'S BANK LIMITED.

NATIONAL BANK OF AUSTRALASIA, LTD., THE (1858), Collins St., *Melbourne* 3001 (6–8 Tokenhouse Yard, E.C.2, Australia House, Strand, W.C.2 and 11 Albemarle Street, W.1.—Capital, paid up $A86,221,170; Reserve fund, $A62,441,000; Deposits, 30/9/75, $A2,631,490,000. Dividend, 1975; 13·5 p.c. (910 Branches and Agencies in Australia.) THE NATIONAL BANK SAVINGS BANK LIMITED (Collins Street, Melbourne) a wholly owned subsidiary of The National Bank of Australasia Limited was incorporated on May 16, 1962, with Capital, authorized, $A20,000,000; paid-up, $A8,000,000.

NATIONAL BANK OF NEW ZEALAND, LTD. (1872), 8 Moorgate, E.C.2.—Capital (Authorized, £6,000,000), Issued and fully-paid, £3,500,000; Reserve Fund, £3,662,955. (208 Branches and Agencies.)

NATIONAL DISCOUNT CO., LTD. Merged on June 16, 1970, with GERRARD & REID, LTD., under the name of GERRARD & NATIONALDISCOUNT CO.LTD.

*NATIONAL WESTMINSTER BANK LIMITED, *Head Office*: 41 Lothbury, E.C.2. Est. 1968 to merge the businesses of National Provincial, Westminster and District Banks: Balance sheet at 31/12/75 showed Capital, Authorized, £265,000,000; Issued £197,394,252; Reserves, £552,199,102; Total Assets, £8,964,844,000. Deposit, Current and other accounts, £8,014,091. Dividend 1975, 13·15614p. (Over 3,300 branches.) Principal subsidiary companies: CENTRE-FILE LTD.; COUNTY BANK LTD.; COUTTS & CO. (*q.v.*); CREDIT FACTORING INTERNATIONAL LTD.; ISLE OF MAN BANK LTD.; LOMBARD NORTH CENTRAL LTD. and its subsidiaries; NATIONAL WESTMINSTER BANK FINANCE (C.I.) LTD.; NATIONAL WESTMINSTER GUERNSEY TRUST CO. LTD.; NATIONAL WESTMINSTER INSURANCE SERVICES LTD.; NATIONAL WESTMINSTER

JERSEY TRUST CO. LTD.; NATIONAL WESTMINSTER UNIT TRUST MANAGERS LTD.; ULSTER BANK LTD. and its subsidiaries; INTERNATIONAL WESTMINSTER BANK LTD., EUROCOM DATA (HOLDINGS) LTD., NATIONAL WESTMINSTER (HONG KONG) LTD.

NORTHERN BANK LTD. (1824), *Belfast* (*Affiliated with* Midland Bank Ltd.).—Capital, £6,000,000, (£1 Shares); Capital paid up, £6,000,000; Reserve Fund, £25,586,000; Deposits, 31/12/75, £350,623,000; Dividend, interim dividend of 7·5p per share on 1/10/75 and final dividend for the year of 7·5p per share on 1/4/76 (171 Branches and 91 Sub-Branches).

OTTOMAN BANK (1863), Bankalar Caddes, Karaköy, *Istanbul*, Turkey (23 Fenchurch Street, E.C.3), —Capital, £10,000,000 (£20 Shares, £10 paid), Statutory Reserve, £1,250,000.

PROVINCIAL BANK OF CANADA (1900) (BANQUE PROVINCIALE DU CANADA), 221 St. James St. *Montreal*.—Capital $11,700,000 ($2 Shares, fully paid); Reserve Fund, $45,000,000; Deposits, 30/4/74 $2,190,151,125. Regular dividend, 1973, 41·5 p.c.; Special, nil. (284 Branches and 34 Agencies.)

GERALD QUIN, COPE & CO. LTD. (1892), 52–54 Gracechurch Street, E.C.3.

RELIANCE BANK, LTD. (1900), 101 Queen Victoria St., E.C.4.—Capital, £60,000; Reserve Fund, £505,311; Deposits, 31/3/76, £8,433,027.

RESERVE BANK OF NEW ZEALAND (1934), *Wellington*, N.Z. Branches at *Christchurch* and *Auckland*, N.Z. (*London Agents*, Bank of England). Owned by the New Zealand Government.—Reserve Funds, $NZ24,848,585; Total Assets, 31/3/76, $NZ1,355,517,381.

N. M. ROTHSCHILD & SONS LTD. (1804), New Court, St. Swithin's Lane, E.C.4.—Capital issued and paid up £10,023,850.

ROYAL BANK OF CANADA (1869), *Montreal* (6 Lothbury, E.C.2, and 2 Cockspur St., S.W.1), —Capital, $100,000,000 ($2 Shares); Paid-up. $72,951,051; Rest Account, $569,076,616; Undivided Profits, $1,249,317; Assets, $25,211,131,473; Deposits, 31/10/75, $22,870,875,156; Dividend, 1975, $1·23 per share (1,605 Branches).

ROYAL BANK OF SCOTLAND LIMITED, THE. *Registered Office*: 42 St. Andrew Square, Edinburgh. (30/9/75).—Capital, authorized and issued, £37,500,000; Reserves, £67,617,000; Deposit and current accounts, £1,362,961,000. Approximately 590 Branches in Scotland and in London. Owns all capital of NATIONAL COMMERCIAL & GLYNS LIMITED, ROYAL BANK DEVELOPMENT LIMITED, ROYAL BANK LEASING LIMITED, ROYAL SCOT FINANCE COMPANY LIMITED (HONG KONG) and LOGANAIR LIMITED. Also owns 40·6 p.c. of the capital of LLOYDS & SCOTTISH LIMITED. A member of the NATIONAL AND COMMERCIAL BANKING GROUP LTD.

DAVID SASSOON AND CO., LIMITED (1860), 57–60 Haymarket, S.W.1.—Capital authorized, £5,000,000; Paid up, £2,000,000.

J. HENRY SCHRODER WAGG & CO. LIMITED (1804), 120 Cheapside, E.C.2.—Capital, Authorized, £10,000,000; issued and paid up, £10,000,000.

SINGER & FRIEDLANDER LTD. (1907), 20 Cannon Street, E.C.4. A member of the C. T. Bowring & Co. Ltd. Group.—Authorized Capital, £10,000,000 (Ordinary Shares of £1 each). Issued and fully paid, £7,000,000 (ordinary shares of £1 each).

SLATER, WALKER, LIMITED, 30 St. Paul's Churchyard, E.C.4. Capital Authorized, £10,000,000; issued and fully paid up, £10,000,000. Reserve, £7,873,171; Deposits, £211,013,433 (31/12/74).

SMITH ST. AUBYN & CO. LTD. (1801), White Lion Court, Cornhill, E.C.3.—Capital authorized, £2,970,000; Issued, £2,970,000; Deposits and Contingency Reserve, £14,401,248.

SOCIÉTÉ GÉNÉRALE (1864), 29 Boulevard Haussmann, *Paris* (105-108 Old Broad St., E.C.2 and 28-32 Fountain Street, Manchester).—Subscribed Capital authorized, issued and paid up, Francs 800,000,000. Reserve Funds, Francs 500,000,000. (2,600 Branches.)

STANDARD BANK, LTD., THE (1862), 10 Clements Lane E.C.4.—Authorized Capital, £40,000,000 (divided into 40,000,000 shares of £1 each); Issued Capital, £26,808,000; Reserves £114,311,000. Deposits, £2,941,938,000 (31/3/76). A subsidiary of STANDARD CHARTERED BANK LTD.

STANDARD CHARTERED BANK LTD., (1969) 10 Clements Lane, E.C.4.—Capital Authorized, £70,000,000 (divided into 70,000,000 shares of £1 each); Issued Capital, £69,110,000; Reserves, £235,123,000; Deposits £6,312,328,000 (31/3/76). More than 1,500 offices in over sixty countries. See also THE CHARTERED Bank and The Standard Bank Ltd.

STATE BANK OF INDIA (1955), *Bombay, Calcutta, Madras, New Delhi, Ahmedabad, Hyderabad, Kanpur, Bhopal* and *Patna.* (Clements House, Gresham Street, E.C.2; 10/12 Clifford Street, W.1; King's House, The Green, Southall.)—Capital, Authorized, *Rs.* 20,00,00,000; Paid up, *Rs.* 5,62,50,000; Reserve, *Rs.* 45,82,75,052.

GEORGE STEUART & CO. LTD., *Colombo,* Sri Lanka (*London Correspondents,* Coutts & Co.).

SWISS BANK CORPORATION (1872), *Basle* (99 Gresham Street, E.C.2).—Capital and Reserves, *Swiss Francs* 2,380,721,800 (31/12/75); Dividend, 1975, 10 p.c. on increased capital. (156 Branches, etc.)

TORONTO-DOMINION BANK, *Toronto,* Ontario, Canada (an amalgamation (1955) of The Bank of Toronto (1856) and The Dominion Bank (1871)) (St. Helens, 1 Undershaft, E.C.3. Regional Office Europe and Africa, 62 Cornhill, E.C.3. and 103 Mount Street, W.1.).—Capital (paid-up), $36,988,002; Rest Account, $400,000,000; Undivided Profits, $3,433,968. (900 Branches in Canada.)

ULSTER BANK, LTD. (1836, *Head Office,* Donegall Place, *Belfast.* (A member of the National Westminster Group).—Capital, £3,000,000 (£1 Shares); Issued and fully paid, £2,250,000; Reserve Fund, £16,506,000; Share Premium Account, £250,000; Deposits, 31/12/75, £452,481,000; Dividend, 1975, 14 p.c. (142 Offices and 98 Sub-Offices.)

UNION BANK OF INDIA LTD. (1919), 66-80 Bombay Sanachar Marg, *Bombay* 400 023. Acquired July 18, 1969 by the Government of India. Capital: paid-up. *Rs.* 12,500,000; Deposits, 31/12/74 *Rs.* 3,962,502,000. (644 branches.)

UNION DISCOUNT COMPANY OF LONDON, LTD. (1885), 78/80 Cornhill, E.C.3.—Capital Issued, £7,500,000 in units of £1 each fully paid; Reserves and carry forward, £6,502,676; Deposits, provisions and other liabilities £772,740,140; Dividend, 1975, 18·16 p.c.

UNITED COMMERCIAL BANK, 10 Brabourne Road, *Calcutta* (wholly owned by the Govt. of India). —Capital, paid-up *Rs.* 2,80,00,000; Reserves *Rs.* 7,00,00,000. (833 Branches.)

WALLACE BROTHERS BANK LTD. (1963); 4 Crosby Square, E.C.3. Issued Capital, £9,000,000. Combines the businesses of Wallace Bros. & Co. Ltd. (1837) and E. D. Sassoon Banking Co. Ltd. (1930).

WARBURG (S. G.) & CO. LTD. (Incorporating Seligman Brothers), 30 Gresham Street, E.C.2. —Capital, authorized, £20,000,000; issued and paid-up, £18,255,000.

★WILLIAMS & GLYNS BANK, LTD., *Registered Office,* 20 Birchin Lane, E.C.3. Established in 1970 to merge the businesses of WILLIAMS DEACON'S, GLYN, MILLS and NATIONAL BANKS. Capital authorized and issued, £33,750,000; Reserves, £69,339,000; Deposit and current accounts, £1,574,020,000. (321 branches in England and Wales.)

YORKSHIRE BANK LIMITED (1911), 2 Infirmary Street, *Leeds* (56-58 Cheapside, E.C.2). Capital, £12,000,000 (Capital, paid up £12,000,000, £1 Shares fully paid); Reserves, £23,863,336; Deposits, 31/12/75, £304,564,801, (183 branches.)

PREMIUM SAVINGS BONDS

One of the most popular forms of saving in the United Kingdom is through Premium Savings Bonds. These bonds are a United Kingdom Government security and were first introduced on November 1, 1956. Instead of earning interest, however, each bond offers to its holder the chance of winning a money prize in a prize draw. Bonds are issued in values ranging from £5 to £500 and each £1 buys one bond unit, which has one chance in the prize draw.

Prizes are paid from a fund formed by the interest, at present 5⅝ per cent. *per annum,* on each bond eligible for the draw. A bond becomes eligible for the draw three clear calendar months following the month of purchase and goes into every subsequent draw whether or not it has won a prize until the end of the month in which it is repaid. Bonds belonging to a deceased bondholder will remain eligible for all Prize Draws held in the month of death and in the following 12 calendar months, provided they have not been repaid earlier. They will then become ineligible for all further draws. These terms also apply to bonds purchased before August 1, 1960 (Series "A"). Prizes range in value from £5,000 to £25, a single prize of £100,000 and a second prize of £25,000 each month, one of £50,000 and 25 of £1,000 each week, the winning numbers being selected by the electronic random number indicator equipment—usually called "ERNIE". Winning numbers are printed monthly in the *London Gazette.*

It is estimated that by the end of June, 1976, bonds to the value of £2,014,029,527 had been sold. Of these £864,171,077 had been cashed, leaving £1,149,858,450 still invested. After the draws in July, 1976, 13,236,826 prizes, totalling £530,328,700 had been distributed since the inception of the Premium Savings Bond Scheme.

NATIONAL SAVINGS CERTIFICATES

The amount, including accrued interest, remaining to the credit of investors in National Savings Certificates on March 31,1976 was approximately £2,673,071,000. In 1975–76, £588,803,270 was subscribed and £402,826,505 (excluding interest) was repaid. Note—Certificates of the current Fourteenth Issue may be purchased in denominations of 1, 2, 3, 4, 5, 10, 20, 50, 100, 200 and 500 units and certificates of the Index-Linked Retirement Issue in denominations of 1, 2, 5, 10, 20 and 50 units.

Issue and Maximum Holding	Unit Cost s. d.	Value After Years	Value After £ p	Interest Per Unit
1st (1916–22)........	15 6	} 52	} 3·40	After 52 years, $\frac{5}{18}$p per completed month★.
2nd (1922–23)........	16 0			
3rd (1923–32) and Conversion (1932)	16 0	43	2·70	After 43 years, $\frac{5}{8}$p per completed month★.
4th (1932–33)........	16 0	42	2·36$\frac{5}{8}$	After 42 years, 1$\frac{7}{24}$p per completed 3 months★.
5th (1933–35)........	16 0	40	2·24$\frac{1}{8}$	After 40 years, 1$\frac{7}{24}$p per completed 3 months★.
6th (1935–39)........	15 0	36	2·05	After 36 years, 1$\frac{1}{4}$p per completed 3 months★.
7th (1939–47)........ (Maximum holding, 1st–7th Combined, 500 units)	15 0	27	1·62$\frac{1}{2}$	After 27 years, 1$\frac{1}{2}$p per completed 3 months plus 2$\frac{1}{2}$p bonus at end of 29th year.
		29	1·75	During 30th year, 2$\frac{1}{12}$p per completed 4 months.
		30	1·81$\frac{1}{2}$	After 30 years, 2$\frac{1}{2}$p per completed 4 months plus bonus of 1$\frac{1}{2}$p at end of 35th year.
		35	2·20	During 36th year, 4p per completed 4 months.
		37		During 37th year, 5p per completed 4 months.
		38	2·65	During 38th year, 6p per completed 4 months†.
£1 (1943–47)........ (250)	£1	28	1·57$\frac{1}{2}$	After 28 years, 1$\frac{1}{2}$p per completed 4 months plus 5p bonus at end of 29th year; 2$\frac{1}{2}$p per completed 4 months in 30th year.
		30	1·73	After 30 years, 2$\frac{1}{2}$p per completed 4 months plus 4$\frac{1}{2}$p bonus at end of 33rd year.
		33	2·00	After 33 years, 4$\frac{1}{2}$p per completed 4 months plus a bonus of 1p at end of 35th year†.
		35	2·28	
8th (1947–51)........ (1,000)	10 0	24	1·02$\frac{1}{2}$	During 25th year, 1$\frac{3}{8}$p per completed 4 months.
		25	1·07$\frac{1}{2}$	After 25th year, 1$\frac{1}{2}$p per completed 4 months plus 4$\frac{1}{2}$p bonus at end of 29th year.
		29	1·30	During 30th year, 2$\frac{1}{2}$p per completed 4 months.
		31	1·48	During 31st year, 3$\frac{1}{2}$p per completed 4 months†.
9th (1951–56)........ (1,400)	15 0	19	1·40	After 19th year, 1$\frac{3}{8}$p per completed 4 months plus 2$\frac{1}{2}$p bonus at end of 22nd year.
		22	1·57$\frac{1}{2}$	After 22nd year, 2p per completed 4 months plus 4$\frac{1}{2}$p bonus at end of 25th year.
		25	1·80	After 25th year, 4p per completed 4 months plus 1p bonus at end of 27th year.
		27	2·05	
10th (1956–63)....... (1,200)	15 0	12	1·18$\frac{3}{4}$	After 12 years, 1$\frac{1}{4}$p per completed 4 months plus 2$\frac{1}{2}$p bonus at end of 15th year.
		15	1·32$\frac{1}{2}$	During 16th year, 1$\frac{3}{4}$p per completed 4 months.
		16	1·37$\frac{1}{2}$	After 16th year, 2p per completed 4 months plus a 4$\frac{1}{2}$p bonus at end of 19th year.
		19	1·60	During 20th year, 3$\frac{1}{2}$p per completed 4 months.
		21	1·83	During 21st year 4p per completed 4 months plus $\frac{1}{2}$p bonus at year-end†.
11th (1963–66)....... (600)	£1	9	1·40	After 9 years, 1$\frac{3}{8}$p per completed 4 months plus 5p bonus at end of 12th year.
		12	1·60	During 13th year, 3$\frac{1}{2}$p per completed 4 months.
		14	1·83	During 14th year 4p per completed 4 months plus $\frac{1}{2}$p bonus at year-end.
12th (1966–70)....... (1,500)	£1	5	1·25	After 5 years, 1$\frac{1}{2}$p per completed 4 months plus 7p bonus at end of 9th year.
		9	1·50	During 10th year, 3p per completed 4 months.
		11	1·71	During 11th year 4p per completed 4 months†.
Decimal (1970–74).... (1,500)	£1	4	1·25	After 1 year, 3p is added; during 2nd year, 1$\frac{1}{2}$p per completed 4 months; during 3rd year, 2$\frac{1}{2}$p per completed 4 months; during 4th, year 3p per completed 4 months plus 1p bonus at year-end.
		6	1·43	During 5th year, 2$\frac{1}{2}$p per completed 4 months; during 6th year 3$\frac{1}{2}$p per completed 4 months†.
Fourteenth (1974–) ... (1,000)	£1	4	1·34	After 1 year, 6p is added; during 2nd year, 2$\frac{1}{2}$p per completed 4 months; during 3rd year, 3p per completed 4 months; during 4th year, 3$\frac{1}{2}$p per completed 4 months plus 1p bonus at year-end†.
Index Linked Retirement Issue (1975).. (50)	£10			Unlike conventional issues where interest is accrued periodically the repayment value of Index-Linked Certificates, subject to their being held a year, is related to the movement of the United Kingdom General Index of Retail Prices. If held for 5 years a bonus of 4 per cent. of the Purchase Price will be added to the repayment value. Any gain is free of UK income tax or capital gains tax and the precise terms of the Issue are set out in a Prospectus. NB. Certificates of the Retirement Issue are available only to men aged 65 years and over and women aged 60 years and over, maximum £500 per person.

May be held from date of issue: ★ until further notice; † as announced by the Treasury.

BRITISH SAVINGS BONDS

8½% British Savings Bonds (Jubilee Issue) are a guaranteed state security. They cost £5 each and may be held up to a maximum of £10,000. Bonds acquired by inheritance do not count towards this limit. They may be held by individuals solely or jointly; by trustees; by charitable, friendly and provident societies; by clubs and funds, by corporate bodies generally. Interest is earned at the rate of 8½% a year, provided they are held for a minimum period of 6 months. The interest which is payable half yearly is taxable but tax is not deducted at source. The value of British Savings Bonds remains constant and they may be encashed at par on one month's notice. They will be redeemable at the rate of £104 for £100 of Bonds on the next interest date after 5 years have passed from the purchase date. The £4 capital bonus is exempt from United Kingdom Tax. British Savings Bonds may be bought at any Post Office transacting Savings Bank business, Trustee Savings and other Banks.

GOVERNMENT STOCKS AND BONDS

Government Stocks and Bonds on the National Savings Stock Register can be bought and sold at low rates of commission through the Department for National Savings, Bonds and Stock Office, Lytham St. Annes, Lancashire, or a Trustee Savings Bank. Prices are those current on the Stock Exchange at the time of the transaction. Application forms and information leaflets with a list of the Stocks and Bonds are available at Post Offices transacting Savings Bank business and at Trustee Savings Banks. The amount standing to the credit of holders in the Department for National Savings section of the National Savings Stock Register as at March 31, 1976 was £891,152,000.

SAVE AS YOU EARN

The " Save As You Earn " Scheme was brought into operation on October 1, 1969. A Second Issue was introduced on July 1, 1974, and a Third Issue (" Index-linked ") was brought in on July 1, 1975. Any individual aged 16 years or over may participate by making regular monthly payments with a minimum of £4 and a maximum of £20.

Savings may be contributed by deductions from pay, by standing order on a bank or National Giro or by cash payments at most post offices.

Indexation applies only to completed savings contracts, except that contracts terminated by the death of the saver will attract indexation if repaid after the first year. At the end of five years, the repayment value of completed contracts will be the total contributions plus any increase due to the monthly linking of contributions to the Retail Price Index. Completed contracts which are not withdrawn will qualify for further index-linking and a bonus equal to two monthly contributions at the end of seven years.

Savers who wish to stop payments will be able to withdraw the total sum saved, but there cannot be partial withdrawals. Tax-free compound interest will be paid at the rate of 6 per cent. per annum on amounts withdrawn after the first year.

By the end of June 1976, 607,075 live SAYE contracts remained registered with the Department for National Savings, with a total monthly commitment to save of £6,876,810. The total payments received since October 1, 1969, amounted to £184,731,386.

SAVINGS BANKS

National Savings Bank.—On December 31, 1975, there were approximately 21,000,000 active accounts with the sum of £1,524,794,624 due to depositors in Ordinary accounts and £615,832,044 in Investment accounts. Interest on National Savings Bank Ordinary deposits is allowed at 4 per cent. per annum. A higher rate of interest is paid on deposits in National Savings Bank Investment accounts (the current rate can be ascertained at any Savings Bank Post Office). A depositor may have more than one account in either series. The total balance in the Ordinary account is subject to a limit of £10,000 with certain exceptions; there is no upper limit on the balance that may be held in an Investment account.

On December 31, 1975, the average amount held in Ordinary accounts was £72·81; in Investment accounts, approximately £757·00.

Trustee Savings Banks were started in the early years of the 19th century by public-spirited men who recognized the importance of individual thrift to the well-being of the community.

On Nov. 20, 1975, there were 14,279,750 active accounts in the Trustee Savings Banks. The total assets of the Banks amounted to £4,461,792,537 which comprised £3,852,135,661 due to depositors in the Ordinary, Current and Special Investment Departments, £438,975,109 Stocks and Bonds held for depositors, £79,828,051 in respect of Save As You Earn contributions and £90,853,716 representing the accumulated surplus of the individual Trustee Savings Banks throughout the country. Information about these banks and their offices, can be obtained from the *Trustee Savings Banks Central Board,* P.O. Box 99, 3 Gracechurch Street, E.C.3. *Chairman,* A. Rintoul, C.B.E. *Chief General Manager,* T. Bryans, M.B.E.

Law Courts and Offices

LAW SITTINGS (1976)—*Hilary*, Jan. 12 to April 14; *Easter*, April 27 to May 28; *Trinity*, June 8 to July 31; *Michaelmas*, Oct. 1 to Dec. 21.

THE JUDICIAL COMMITTEE

The Judicial Committee of the Privy Council consists of the Lord Chancellor, Lord President, ex-Lords President, the Lords of Appeal in Ordinary (*see* below) with such other members of the Privy Council as shall from time to time hold or have held " high judicial office," and certain judges from the Commonwealth.

Office—Downing Street, S.W.1.
Registrar of the Privy Council, E. R. Mills.
Chief Clerk (Judicial), J. K. Dixon.

THE HOUSE OF LORDS

The Supreme Judicial Authority for Great Britain and Northern Ireland is the House of Lords, which is the ultimate Court of Appeal from all the Courts in Great Britain and Northern Ireland (except criminal courts in Scotland).
The Lord High Chancellor—
The Rt. Hon. the Lord Elwyn-Jones, C.H. (*born* 1909, *apptd.* 1974), (£17,500 as Judge and £2,500 as Speaker of the House of Lords)
Lords of Appeal in Ordinary (each £21,175)
Apptd.

Rt. Hon. Lord Wilberforce, C.M.G., O.B.E. *born* 1907............................ 1964
Rt. Hon. Lord Diplock, *born* 1907........ 1968
Rt. Hon. Viscount Dilhorne, *born* 1905.... 1969
Rt. Hon. Lord Simon of Glaisdale, *born* 1911 1971
Rt. Hon. Lord Kilbrandon, *born* 1906..... 1971
Rt. Hon. Lord Salmon, *born* 1903........ 1972
Rt. Hon. Lord Edmund-Davies, *born* 1906................................ 1974
Rt. Hon. Lord Fraser of Tullybelton, *born* 1911................................ 1975
Rt. Hon. Lord Russell of Killowen, *born* 1908................................ 1975
Registrar: The Clerk of the Parliaments, Sir Peter Henderson, K.C.B.

SUPREME COURT OF JUDICATURE
COURT OF APPEAL

Ex officio Judges.—The Lord High Chancellor, the Lord Chief Justice of England, the Master of the Rolls, and the President of the Family Division.
The Master of the Rolls (£21,175)
The Rt. Hon. Lord Denning (*born* 1899, *apptd.* 1962).
Secretary, Miss P. B. Bergin; *Clerk* (vacant).
Lords Justices of Appeal (each £19,425)— Apptd.
Rt. Hon. Sir John Megaw, C.B.E., T.D., *born* 1909............................ 1969
Rt. Hon. Sir Denys Burton Buckley, M.B.E., *born* 1906............................ 1970
Rt. Hon. Sir David Arnold Scott Cairns, *born* 1902............................ 1970
Rt. Hon. Sir (Edward) Blanshard Stamp, *born* 1905............................ 1971
Rt. Hon. Sir John Frederick Eustace Stephenson, *born* 1910................. 1971
Rt. Hon. Sir Alan Stewart Orr, O.B.E., *born* 1911................................ 1971
Rt. Hon. Sir Eustace Wentworth Roskill, *born* 1911............................ 1971
Rt. Hon. Sir Frederick Horace Lawton, *born* 1911................................ 1972

Rt. Hon. Sir Leslie George Scarman, O.B.E., *born* 1911........................... 1973
Rt. Hon. Sir Roger Fray Greenwood Ormrod, *born* 1911...................... 1974
Rt. Hon. Sir Patrick Reginald Evelyn Browne, O.B.E., T.D., *born* 1907........ 1974
Rt. Hon. Sir Geoffrey Dawson Lane, A.F.C., *born* 1918........................ 1974
Rt. Hon. Sir Reginald William Goff, *born* 1907............................ 1975
Rt. Hon. Sir Nigel Cyprian Bridge, *born* 1917 1975
Rt. Hon. Sir Sebag Shaw, *born* 1906...... 1975
Rt. Hon. Sir George Stanley Waller, O.B.E. *born* 1911........................... 1976

HIGH COURT OF JUSTICE
Chancery Division
President, The Lord High Chancellor
Judges (each £18,675)— Apptd.
Hon. Sir Robert Edgar Megarry, *born* 1910 (*Vice-Chancellor*)...................... 1967
Hon. Sir (John) Patrick Graham, *born* 1906 1969
Hon. Sir Peter Harry Batson Woodroffe Foster, M.B.E., T.D., *born* 1912...... 1969
Hon. Sir John Norman Keates Whitford, *born* 1913............................ 1970
Hon. Sir John Anson Brightman, *born* 1911 1970
Hon. Sir (Ernest) Irvine Goulding, *born* 1910 1971
Hon. Sir Sydney William Templeman, M.B.E., *born* 1920...................... 1972
Hon. Sir Raymond Henry Walton, *born* 1915............................ 1973
Hon. Sir Peter Raymond Oliver, *born* 1921 1974
Hon. Sir Michael John Fox, *born* 1921 1975
Hon. Sir Christopher John Slade, *born* 1927.. 1975

Queen's Bench Division
The Lord Chief Justice of England (£23,050)
The Rt. Hon. The LORD WIDGERY, O.B.E., T.D. (*born* 1911, *apptd.* 1971)
Secretary, S. E. S. Bollon; *Clerk*, A. E. Shelton.
Judges (each £18,675)— Apptd.
Rt. Hon. Sir (Aubrey) Melford (Steed) Stevenson, *born* 1902.................. 1957
Hon. Sir Gerald Alfred Thesiger, M.B.E., *born* 1902............................ 1958
Hon. Sir Basil Edward Nield, C.B.E., *born* 1903............................ 1960
Hon. Sir Bernard Joseph Maxwell MacKenna, *born*, 1905.......................... 1961
Hon. Sir Alan Abraham Mocatta, O.B.E., *born* 1907............................ 1961
Hon. Sir John Thompson, *born* 1907....... 1961
Hon. Sir Helenus Patrick Joseph Milmo, *born* 1908............................ 1964
Hon. Sir Joseph Donaldson Cantley, O.B.E., *born* 1910............................ 1965
Hon. Sir Hugh Eames Park, *born* 1910..... 1965
Hon. Sir Ralph Vincent Cusack, *born* 1916. 1966
Hon. Sir Stephen Chapman, *born* 1907..... 1966
Hon. Sir John Ramsay Willis, *born* 1908... 1966
Hon. Sir Graham Russell Swanwick, M.B.E., *born* 1906............................ 1966
Hon. Sir Patrick MacCarthy O'Connor, *born* 1914............................ 1966
Hon. Sir John Francis Donaldson, *born* 1920 1966
Hon. Sir (John) Robertson (Dunn) Crichton, *born* 1912............................ 1967

Hon. Sir Samuel Burgess Ridgway Cooke, born 1912............................. 1967
Hon. Sir Bernard Caulfield, *born 1914*..... 1968
Hon. Sir Hilary Gwynne Talbot, *born 1912* 1968
Hon. Sir Edward Walter Eveleigh, E.R.D., born 1917.............................. 1968
Hon. Sir William Lloyd Mars-Jones, M.B.E., born 1915.............................. 1969
Hon. Sir Ralph Kilner Brown, O.B.E., T.D., born 1909.............................. 1970
Hon. Sir Phillip Wien, *born 1913*.......... 1970
Hon. Sir Peter Henry Rowley Bristow, *born 1913*............................... 1970
Hon. Sir Hugh Harry Valentine Forbes, *born 1917*................................. 1970
Hon. Sir Desmond James Conrad Ackner, born 1920.............................. 1971
Hon. Sir William Hugh Griffiths, M.C., *born 1923*............................... 1971
Hon. Sir Robert Hugh Mais, *born 1907*.... 1971
Hon. Sir Neil Lawson, *born 1908*.......... 1971
Hon. Sir David Powell Croom-Johnson, D.S.C., V.R.D., *born 1914*............... 1971
Hon. Sir Tasker Watkins, ⅤC̄, *born 1918* 1971
Hon. Sir (John) Raymond Phillips, M.C., *born 1915*............................... 1971
Hon. Sir Leslie Kenneth Edward Boreham, born 1918.............................. 1972
Hon. Sir John Douglas May, *born 1923*.... 1972
Hon. Sir Michael Robert Emanuel Kerr, born 1921.............................. 1972
Hon. Sir (Alfred William) Michael Davies, born 1921.............................. 1973
Hon. Sir John Dexter Stocker, M.C., T.D., born 1918.............................. 1973
Hon. Sir Kenneth George Illtyd Jones, *born 1921*............................... 1974
Hon. Sir Peter Richard Pain, *born 1913*.... 1975
Hon. Sir Kenneth Graham Jupp, M.C. *born 1917*............................... 1975
Hon. Sir John Francis Scott Cobb, *born 1922*. 1975
Hon. Sir Robert Lionel Archibald Goff, *born 1926*................................. 1975
Hon. Sir Gordon Slynn, *born 1930*......... 1976

Court of Appeal (Criminal Division)
Judges, The Lord Chief Justice of England, The Master of the Rolls, Lord Justices of Appeal and all the Judges of the Queen's Bench Division.

Family Division
President (£20,175)
Rt. Hon. Sir George Gillespie Baker, O.B.E. (*born 1910, apptd. 1971*).
Sec., Mrs. H. M. Keegan; *Clerk*, B. H. Erhard.
Judges (each £18,675)— Apptd.
Hon. Sir Charles William Stanley Rees, T.D., born 1907.............................. 1962
Hon. Sir Reginald Withers Payne, *born 1904* 1962
Hon. Sir Neville Major Ginner Faulks, M.B.E., T.D., *born 1908*...................... 1963
Hon Sir (James) Roualeyn Hovell-Thurlow-Cumming-Bruce, *born 1912*........... 1964
Hon. Sir John Brinsmead Latey, M.B.E., *born 1914*............................... 1965
Hon. Dame Elizabeth Kathleen Lane, D.B.E., born 1905.............................. 1965
Hon. Sir Henry Vivian Brandon, M.C., *born 1920*............................... 1966
Hon. Sir Robin Horace Walford Dunn, M.C., *born 1918*...................... 1969
Hon. Sir William Arthur Bagnall, M.B.E., born 1917.............................. 1970

Hon. Sir (Alfred) Kenneth Hollings, M.C., born 1918.............................. 1971
Hon. Sir John Lewis Arnold, *born 1915*.... 1972
Hon. Sir (Charles) Trevor Reeve, *born 1915*. 1973
Hon. Sir Francis Brooks Purchas, *born 1919*. 1974
Hon. Sir Haydn Tudor Evans, *born 1920*... 1974
Hon. Dame Rose Heilbron, D.B.E., *born 1914* 1974
Hon. Sir Stephen Brown, *born 1924*...... 1975

Judge Advocate of the Fleet, W. M. Howard, Q.C.
Queen's Proctor, Sir Henry Ware, K.C.B.

LORD CHANCELLOR'S OFFICE
House of Lords, S.W.1
[01-219-3000]
Permanent Secretary and Clerk of the Crown, Sir Denis Dobson, K.C.B., O.B.E., Q.C............£18,675
Private Secretary to the Lord Chancellor, J. A. C. Watherston................£6,625 to £8,750
Private Secretary to Permanent Secretary, Miss D. Dalgliesh, M.B.E............£3,900 to £4,700
Deputy Secretary, J. W. Bourne, C.B............£14,000
Secretary of Commissions, Sir Thomas Skyrme, K.C.V.O., C.B., C.B.E., T.D............£12,000
Under Secretaries, K. M. H. Newman; R. H. Widdows................£12,000
Deputy Secretary of Commissions, Sir Bryan Roberts, K.C.M.G................£9,033 to £11,000
Assistant Solicitors, M. C. Blair; D. S. Gordon; R. C. L. Gregory, C.B.E.; T. S. Legg £9,033 to £11,000
Senior Legal Assistants, M. C. Blair; W. H. Elliot; M. D. Huebner; D. H. O. Owen
£6,625 to £8,750
Legal Assistants, M. H. Collon; J. R. A. Hanratty; P. G. Harris; P. M. Harris; Miss M. McLellan
£3,424 to £6,125
Assistant Secretaries of Commissions, R. F. N. Anderson, O.B.E., M.C.; E. R. Horsman, O.B.E.; D. J. Williams................£5,680 to £7,450
Secretary for Ecclesiastical Patronage, C. V. Peterson.
Assistant Secretary for Ecclesiastical Patronage, Col. W. A. Salmon, O.B.E............£5,259 to £6,793
Crown Office
Clerk of the Crown, Sir Denis Dobson, K.C.B., O.B.E., Q.C.
Deputy Clerk of the Crown, J. W. Bourne, C.B.
Clerk of the Chamber, Miss D. M. P. Malley, M.B.E................£4,900 to £5,900

Court Business Branch
67 Tufton Street, S.W.1
[01-212 3781]
Deputy Secretary, A. D. M. Oulton........£12,000
Assistant Solicitor, A. M. F. Webb, C.M.G.
£9,033 to £11,000
Senior Legal Assistants, D. R. Wells; W. B. Scott, C.B.E................£6,625 to £8,750

Establishments and Finance Division
Romney House, Marsham Street, S.W.1
[01-212 3781]
Principal Establishment Officer, J. A. Bergin
£12,000
Assistant Secretaries, Miss J. M. Brewster; D. B. Frudd; J. A. C. Kelsey; M. D. Hobkirk
£8,650 to £11,000

SUPREME COURT OFFICES, ETC.
Conveyancing Counsel of the Supreme Court
J. Monckton; P. W. E. Taylor; E. G. Nugee, T.D.

Examiners of the Court
(Empowered to take Examination of Witnesses in all Divisions of the High Court)
M. F. Meredith-Hardy; R. Walker; K. S. Lewis; M. R. M. Nunns.

Official Referees of the Supreme Court
His Honour Norman Grantham Lewis Richards,
O.B.E., Q.C.; His Honour William Walter Stabb,
Q.C.; His Honour Edgar Stuart Fay, Q.C.

Official Solicitor's Department
48–49 Chancery Lane, W.C.2
Official Solicitor to the Supreme Court, N. H. Turner
............................£12,000
Asst. Do., T. W. Swift..... £9,033 to £11,000
Assistant Solicitor, R. S. Dhondy
............£9,033 to £11,000
Senior Legal Assts., H. D. S. Venables; D. C. Relf;
W. H. McBryde; H. J. Baker £6,625 to £8,750
Legal Assistants, Mrs C. L. Hastings; Miss W. V.
Drake; I. G. M. Wingfield.... £3,424 to £6,125
Chief Clerk, J. A. P. Morris..... £5,680 to £7,450
Principal Clerks, B. C. Harris; R. F. Dunn; J. A.
Dawson.................... £5,680 to £7,450

Court Funds Office
Royal Courts of Justice, W.C.2
Accountant General, Sir Denis Dobson, K.C.B., O.B.E.,
Q.C.
Chief Accountant, F. W. Hathaway
............£5,680 to £7,450
Senior Executive Officers, W. P. Coult; E. D. Fagg;
T. C. Weidner; B. Williams.. £4,900 to £5,900

Central Office of the Supreme Court
Royal Courts of Justice, W.C.2
*Senior Master of the Supreme Court (Q.B.D.), and
Queen's Remembrancer*, I. H. Jacob, Q.C. £12,500
Masters of the Supreme Court (Q.B.D.), I. H. Jacob;
J. Ritchie, M.B.E.; J. B. Elton; J. R. Bickford-
Smith; S. J. Waldman; I. S. Warren; C. W. S.
Lubbock; P. B. Creightmore......... £11,000
Chief Clerk (Central Office), J. F. Mason
............£5,680 to £7,450
Chief Clerk to the Q.B. Judges in Chambers, N. Sims
............£5,680 to £7,450

Action Department★
Head Clerk, C. F. Jones......... £5,348 to £5,900
Filing Department★
Chief Clerk, C. J. Harman....... £5,348 to £5,900
*Masters' Secretary's Department and Queen's
Remembrancer's Department*★
Chief Clerk (Secretary to the Masters), F. Simpson
............£5,348 to £5,900
Crown Office and Associates' Dept.
Head Clerk (Crown Office), F. Hearn
............£5,348 to £5,900
Chief Associate, B. M. Spicer, M.B.E.
............£5,348 to £5,900
Criminal Appeals Office
(Royal Courts of Justice, W.C.2)
Registrar, D. R. Thompson, C.B......... £12,500
Assistant Registrars, W. H. Greenwood; M. W.
Palmer.................... £9,033 to £11,000
Deputy Assistant Registrars, P. C. Kratz; E. G.
Blandford, C.B.E.; G. Hoffman £6,625 to £8,750
Assistant Solicitor, P. J. Morrish.
Senior Legal Assistants, Mrs. B. M. Hindley; E. M.
Kotwal; C. Jones.......... £6,625 to £8,750
Head Clerk, A. F. P. Ottway... £5,348 to £5,900
Courts-Martial Appeals Office
(Royal Courts of Justice, W.C.2)
Registrar, D. R. Thompson, C.B......... £12,500
Assistant Registrar, W. H. Greenwood.... £11,000
★ Office hours, 10 to 4.30; (1 Aug. to 31 Aug.,
10 to 2.30.) Saturdays, closed.

Supreme Court Taxing Office
Chief Master, Graham John Graham-Green, T.D.
............£12,500
Masters of the Supreme Court, Leonard Humphrey
Razzall; Edwin James Thomas Matthews, T.D.;
Frederic Thomas Horne; Michael Arthur Clews;
Frederic George Berkeley; Alan John Wright;
Charles Roger Nicholas Martyn....... £11,000

Chief Clerk, D. Hutchings...... £5,680 to £7,450
Principal Clerks, A. G. Warren; G. H. R. Scales;
J. Price; R. W. E. Ranger; E. W. Guest; C. R.
Blinks; G. P. Tandy; D. C. Dennis; A. J. Bur-
roughs; P. J. Moran; V. H. Masters
............£5,348 to £5,900

CHANCERY DIVISION
Chancery Judges' Chambers
Royal Courts of Justice, W.C.2
Chief Master (attached to all the Judges), Robert
Edward Ball, M.B.E.................. £12,500
Chief Clerk, W. E. Loveday.... £5,680 to £7,450
GROUP A
At Chambers.—Masters of the Supreme Court, A to F.
Marshal Butler Cholmondeley Clarke; *G to N*,
Robert Edward Ball, M.B.E.; *O to Z*, Edmund
Rawlings Heward.................... £11,000
GROUP B
At Chambers.—Masters of the Supreme Court, A to F,
Peter Athol Taylor; *G to N*, John Michael Dyson;
O to Z, Richard Chamberlain, T.D..... £11,000
Principal Clerks, C. A. C. Partridge; D. F. J. Emery;
W. E. Loveday; D. F. James; A. T. D. Higgs;
A. T. Cole; K. A. B. Nias; P. J. Angel
............£5,348 to £5,900

Chancery Registrars' Office
Royal Courts of Justice, W.C.2
Chief Registrar, C. M. Kidd............. £11,000
Registrars, H. J. Wilson; D. G. Leach; M. S. Ed-
wards; H. W. Nichols; A. W. Hancock; R. F.
Russell.................... £8,717 to £10,298
Senior Assistant Registrars, R. S. Stevens; D. G.
Pullen; J. T. Glover.......... £6,140 to £8,110
Assistant Registrars, W. R. Heeler; C. I. R. Wil-
liams...................... £3,659 to £5,754
Chief Clerk and Secretary to Chief Registrar, W. E.
Loveday.

Companies Court
Thomas More Building,
Royal Courts of Justice, W.C.2
Judges, The Hon. Mr. Justice Brightman; The Hon.
Mr. Justice Templeman; The Hon. Mr. Justice
Oliver; The Hon. Mr. Justice Slade.
Registrar, G. F. Dearbergh.
Chief Clerk, A. A. Clipstone..... £5,680 to £7,450
Senior Executive Officers, H. H. Stringer; J. B. Baker
............£5,348 to £5,900
Senior Official Receiver, Companies Department,
J. B. Clemetson.

Bankruptcy (High Court) Department
Thomas More Building, Royal
Courts of Justice, Strand, W.C.2
Judges, The Hon. Mr. Justice Foster; The Hon Mr.
Justice Goulding; The Hon. Mr. Justice Walton;
The Hon. Mr. Justice Fox.
Chief Registrar, G. M. Parbury.......... £12,500
Registrars, R. H. Hunt; A. J. Wheaton.... £11,000
Official Receivers' Department
Senior Official Receiver, J. B. Clemetson.
Official Receivers, J. Tye; D. A. Thorne.
Assistant do. C. G. Churcher; T. J. White; K. V.
Whiting; A. D. Davenport; D. E. Dolman.

FAMILY DIVISION
PRINCIPAL REGISTRY
Somerset House, W.C.2
Senior Registrar, R. L. Bayne-Powell...... £12,500
Registrars, W. D. S. Caird; D. R. L. Holloway; L. I.
Stranger-Jones; C. Kenworthy; B. Garland;
Mrs. A. E. O. Butler-Sloss; B. P. Tickle; C. F.
Turner; T. G. Guest; D. H. Colgate; D. E.
Morris........................... £11,000
Secretary, R. B. Rowe......... £5,680 to £7,450

Establishment Officer, Miss J. J. Learmonth
£5,680 to £7,450
Clerk of the Rules and Orders (Royal Courts of Justice), W. G. Mason....... £5,680 to £7,450
Principal, B. W. Campbell..... £5,680 to £7,450
Senior Executive Officers, Miss K. W. Simes; R. S. G. Norman; Miss I. L. Murray; Mrs. P. M. Fern; L. T. Hyder; G. A. Wood; W. I. Martyn; G. A. Goodwin; E. W. Morris; R. Conn; Miss P. M. Granger.................. £4,900 to £5,900

DISTRICT PROBATE REGISTRIES

Birmingham, F. R. E. Jones.
Brighton and *Maidstone*, E. E. Hosking.
Bristol, *Exeter* and *Bodmin*, T. B. Williams.
Ipswich, *Norwich* and *Peterborough*, R. C. Robinson.
Leeds, *Hull* and *York*, H. Wilkinson.
Liverpool and *Lancaster*, G. Wentworth.
Llandaff, *Bangor* and *Carmarthen*, A. Crawshaw.
Manchester, G. A. Terian.
Newcastle, *Carlisle* and *Middlesbrough*, J. D. Drayson.
Nottingham, *Leicester* and *Lincoln*, C. S. Fisher.
Oxford and *Gloucester*, Miss M. L. Farmborough.
Sheffield, *Chester* and *Stoke on Trent*, H. W. Jackson.
Winchester, F. G. Diddams.

Admiralty Registry and Marshal's Office
Royal Courts of Justice, W.C.2

Registrar, J. D. H. Rochford............ £11,000
Marshal and Chief Clerk, P. V. Gray
£5,680 to £7,450

COURT OF PROTECTION
25 Store Street, W.C.1

Master, J. A. Armstrong, O.B.E., T.D.
Chief Clerk, J. A. Johnston.

OFFICE OF THE LORD CHANCELLOR'S VISITORS
Staffordshire House, Store Street, W.C.1

Legal Visitor, I. G. H. Campbell, T.D., Q.C...£11,250
Medical Visitors, A. B. Monro, M.D., Ph.D., F.R.C.P.; T. M. Cuthbert; J. Harper........... £11,250

RESTRICTIVE PRACTICES COURT
Thomas More Building,
Royal Courts of Justice, W.C.2

Judicial Members, Mr. Justice Mocatta (*President*); Mr. Justice Cumming-Bruce; Mr. Justice Bagnall; Lord Kissen; Lord Justice Gibson.
Lay Members, P. A. Delafield; A. I. Mackenzie; N. C. Pearson, O.B.E., T.D.; W. R. Booth; N. L. Salmon; P. G. Walker.
Clerk of the Court, Mr. Registrar Dearbergh.
Senior Executive Officer, H. H. Stringer.

LAW COMMISSION
England and Wales
Conquest House, 37–38 John Street,
Theobalds Road, W.C.1

Set up on June 16, 1965, under the Law Commissions Act, 1965, to make proposals to the Government for the examination of the Law and for its revision where it is unsuited for modern requirements, obscure, or otherwise unsatisfactory. It recommends to the Lord Chancellor programmes for the examination of different branches of the law and suggests whether the examination should be carried out by the Commission itself or by some other body. The Commission is also responsible for the preparation of Consolidation and Statute Law Revision Bills.

Chairman, The Hon. Mr. Justice Cooke.
Members, S. B. Edell; W. D. T. Hodgson, Q.C.; N. S. Marsh, Q.C.; L. W. P. M. North
Secretary, J. M. Cartwright Sharp.

CIRCUIT JUDGES
(each £13,000)

Midland and Oxford Circuit
W. A. L. Allardice; B. D. Bush; R. M. A. Chetwynd-Talbot; F. L. Clark, Q.C.; W. N. Davison; A. R. M. Ellis; C. H. Gage; H. J. Garrard; G. Green; M. K. Harrison-Hall; T. R. Heald; C. G. Heron; R. H. Hutchinson; J. E. M. Irvine; J. G. Jones; T. O. Kellock, Q.C.; J. T. C. Lee; E. Daly Lewis; D. T. Lloyd; J. R. Macgregor; G. K. Mynett, Q.C.; P. C. Northcote; J. Perrett; J. Ross, Q.C.; W. A. Sime, M.B.E., Q.C.; H. A. Skinner, Q.C.; S. C. Sleeman; G. F. I. Sunderland; I. R. Taylor, Q.C.; R. J. Toyn; W. R. Wickham; J. Brooke Willis; B. Woods.

Northern Circuit
J. R. Arthur, D.F.C.; D. P. Bailey; R. M. Bingham, T.D., Q.C.; A. J. Blackett-Ord (*Vice Chancellor, County Palatine of Lancaster*); A. S. Booth, Q.C.; J. Booth; R. J. H. Collinson; P. Curtis; J. W. Da Cunha; J. M. Davies, Q.C.; K. W. Dewhurst; A. A. Edmondson; J. Fitzhugh, Q.C.; D. G. F. Franks; B. H. Gerrard; F. P. R. Hinchliffe, Q.C.; W. H. W. Jalland; J. E. Jones; H. A. Kershaw; P. C. S. Kershaw; K. K. F. Lawton; R. R. Leech; Sir Rudolph Lyons, Q.C. (*Recorder of Liverpool*); Sir William Morris (*Recorder of Manchester*); F. J. Nance; W. H. Openshaw; F. D. Paterson; T. H. Pigot, Q.C.; A. M. Prestt, Q.C.; J. W. Stansfield; R. Wood; J. Zigmond.

North Eastern Circuit
H. C. Beaumont, M.B.E.; H. G. Bennett, Q.C.; C. D. Chapman, Q.C.; Myrella Cohen, Q.C.; J. A. Cotton; C. R. Dean, Q.C.; D. S. Forrester-Paton, Q.C.; S. S. Gill; M. Gosnay; H. G. Hall; G. H. Hartley; V. R. Hurwitz; J. R. Johnson; A. C. Lauriston, Q.C.; G. Milner; T. R. Nevin, T.D.; H. S. Pears; J. Pickles; P. Stanley Price, Q.C.; J. H. E. Randolph; H. C. Scott, Q.C.; A. G. Sharp, M.B.E., Q.C.; R. P. Smith, Q.C.; L. B. Stephen; R. A. R. Stroyan, Q.C.; H. G. Suddards; J. D. Walker; L. Wilkes.

South Eastern Circuit
J. S. R. Abdela, T.D., Q.C.; M. J. Anwyl-Davies, Q.C.; M. V. Argyle, M.C., Q.C.; A. P. Babington; J. A. Baker; R. A. Barr; R. I. S. Bax, Q.C.; F. E. Beezley; P. M. Blomefield; J. Bolland; B. R. Braithwaite; H. T. Buckee, D.S.O.; J. H. Buzzard; C. V. Callman; K. B. Campbell, Q.C.; Sir Harold Cassel, Bt., T.D. Q.C.; F. H. Cassels, T.D.; B. R. Clapham; E. Clarke, Q.C.; R. G. Clover,T.D., Q.C.; Patricia Coles, Q.C.; J. F. Coplestone-Boughey; P. J. Corcoran; M. E. F. Corley; P. H. Counsell; P. V. Crocker; C. J. Cunliffe; N. H. Curtis-Raleigh; J. J. Dean; T. Dewar; R. G. Dow; The Lord Dunboyne; T. K. Edie; J. H. Ellison, v.R.D.; R. M. H. Everett, Q.C.; E. S. Fay, Q.C.; I. B. Fife, M.C., T.D.; A. L. Figgis; I. Finestein, Q.C.; B. Finlay, Q.C.; J. A. R. Finlay, Q.C.; R. H. Forrest, Q.C.; R. G. Freeman; A. G. Friend; E. B. Gibbens, Q.C.; F. E. H. G. Gibbens; B. B. Gillis, Q.C.; J. H. Gower, Q.C.; D. A. Grant, D.S.O., Q.C.; H. B. Grant; P. B. Greenwood; J. M. G. Griffith-Jones, M.C. (*Common Serjeant*); Jean Graham Hall; R. E. Hammerton; A. H. Head; M. R. Hickman; D. E. Hill-Smith, v.R.D.; V. G. Hines, Q.C.; J. B. Hobson; A. E. Holdsworth, Q.C.; F. Honig; W. H. Hughes; A. D. Karmel, Q.C.; W. Kee; M. A. B. King-Hamilton, Q.C.; J. F. Kingham; E. H. Laughton-Scott, Q.C.; C. Lawson, Q.C.; P. H. Layton; C. G. Lea, M.C.; J. C. B. W. Leonard; N. Lermon, Q.C.; G. F. Leslie; B. Lewis; A. C. L. Lewisohn; A. Lipfriend; J. C. Llewellyn; I. B. Lloyd, Q.C.; A. Lonsdale; G. D. Lovegrove, Q.C.; Noreen M.

Lowry; R. D. Lymbery, Q.C.; D. L. McDonnell, O.B.E.; F. D. L. McIntyre, Q.C.; N. N. McKinnon, Q.C.; J. L. E. MacManus, T.D., Q.C.; M. J. P. Macnair; J. F. Marnan, M.B.E., Q.C.; O. S. Martin, Q.C.; G. F. P. Mason, Q.C.; J. H. E. Mendl; J. W. Miskin, Q.C. (*Recorder of London*); E. F. Monier-Williams; G. R. F. Morris, Q.C.; S. A. Morton, T.D.; J. D. F. Moylan; J. I. Murchie; S. H. Noakes; Suzanne F. Norwood; C. R. Oddie; S. O. Olson; R. B. C. Parnall; D. E. Peck; J. C. Perks, M.C., T.D.; F. H. L. Petre; A. J. Phelan; J. R. Pickering; D. C. L. Potter; R. D. Ranking; R. G. Rees; E. B. B. Richards; N. G. L. Richards, O.B.E., Q.C.; Deborah M. Rowland; K. W. Rubin; H. S. J. Ruttle; C. Salmon, Q.C.; J. H. A. Scarlett; N. W. M. Sellers, V.R.D.; G. G. Slack; E. D. Smith; M. B. Smith; A. P. Solomon; W. W. Stabb, Q.C.; D. J. Stinson; E. Stockdale; F. A. Stockdale; J. S. Streeter; J. H. A. Stucley, D.S.C.; W. D. M. Sumner, O.B.E., Q.C.; E. D. Sutcliffe, Q.C.; D. A. Thomas, M.B.E.; A. S. Trapnell; J. T. Turner; L. J. Verney, T.D.; R. W. Vick; B. J. Wakley, M.B.E.; M. E. Ward; D. S. West-Russell; F. J. White; D. H. Wild; J. E. Williams; R. B. Willis, T.D.; W. G. Wingate, Q.C.; E. E. Youds.

Wales and Chester Circuit

J. G. Burrell, Q.C.; R. R. D. G. David, Q.C.; D. Meurig Evans; W. N. Francis; B. F. Griffiths, Q.C.; J. D. Seys Llewellyn; D. T. Lloyd-Jones, V.R.D. P. Hopkin Morgan, Q.C.; D. Morgan Hughes; C. N. Pitchford; D. W. Powell; J. C. Rutter; E. P. Wallis-Jones; R. G. Woolley.

Western Circuit

G. B. Best; N. R. Blaker, Q.C.; N. J. L. Brodrick, Q.C.; A. C. Bulger; R. C. Chope; P. H. F. Clarke; J. A. Cox; T. Elder-Jones; W. H. Ewart-Jones; G. A. Forrest; A. C. Goodall, M.C.; I. S. Hill, Q.C.; M. G. King; C. M. Lavington, M.B.E.; A. M. Lee, D.S.C., Q.C.; Sir Ian Lewis; H. E. L. McCreery, Q.C.; G. G. Macdonald; E. B. McLellan; J. R. Main, Q.C.; D. E. T. Pennant; M. G. Polson, Q.C.; H. S. Russell; J. G. K. Sheldon; K. C. L. Smithies; R. Stock, Q.C.; D. H. W. Vowden, Q.C.; K. M. Willcock, Q.C.

CENTRAL CRIMINAL COURT
Old Bailey, E.C.4

Judges,

The Lord Mayor,	Judges of the High Court,
The Aldermen of the City	The Recorder of London,
	The Common Serjeant of London.
	Crown Court Judges, Recorders, Deputy Crown Court Judges and Magistrates in the case of Appeals and Committals for sentence.

Courts Administrator, Leslie Balfour Boyd.
Secondary and Under-Sheriff, Ralph Mordaunt Snagge, M.B.E., T.D., 78 Cranmer Court, S.W.3.

COURTS SERVICE

First-tier centres deal with both civil and criminal cases and are served by High Court and Circuit Judges. Second-tier centres deal with criminal cases only but are served by both High Court and Circuit Judges. Third-tier centres deal with criminal cases only and are served only by Circuit Judges.

Midland and Oxford Circuit

First-tier—Birmingham, Lincoln, Nottingham, Stafford, Warwick. Second-tier—Leicester, Northampton, Oxford, Shrewsbury, Worcester. Third-tier—Coventry, Derby, Dudley, Grimsby, Hereford, Huntingdon, Stoke-on-Trent, Walsall, Warley, West Bromwich, Wolverhampton.

Circuit Administrator, C. W. Pratley, 2 Newton Street, Birmingham..................£12,000
Deputy Circuit Administrator, T. A. F. Lawler.
Courts Administrators, Birmingham Group, F. Cox; *Northampton Group,* C. A. Green; *Nottingham Group,* G. Jones; *Stafford Group,* F. H. Yendle.

North Eastern Circuit

First-tier—Leeds, Newcastle upon Tyne, Sheffield, Teesside. Second-tier—York. Third-tier Beverley, Bradford, Doncaster, Durham, Huddersfield, Kingston-upon-Hull, Wakefield.
Circuit Administrator, T. A. Whittington, National Westminster House, 4th Floor, 29 Bond Street, Leeds..................£12,000
Deputy Circuit Administrator, B. Cooke.
Courts Administrators, Leeds Group, H. L. Flower; *Newcastle upon Tyne Group,* M. McKenzie; *Sheffield Group,* C. A. White.

Northern Circuit

First-tier—Carlisle, Liverpool, Manchester (Courts of Justice), Preston. Third-tier—Barrow-in-Furness, Birkenhead, Burnley, Kendal, Lancaster, Manchester (Minshull Street).
Circuit Administrator, C. R. Seaton, Aldine House, West Riverside, New Bailey Street, Salford. £12,000
Deputy Circuit Administrator, E. T. Connolly.
Courts Administrators, Manchester Group, C. W. Wood; *Liverpool Group,* Miss M. L. Williams, O.B.E.; *Preston Group,* G. Davies.

South Eastern Circuit

First-tier—London, Norwich. Second-tier—Chelmsford, Ipswich, Lewes, Central Criminal Court (*q.v.*), Maidstone, Reading, St. Albans. Third-tier—Aylesbury, Bedford, Brighton, Bury St. Edmunds, Cambridge, Canterbury, Chichester, Guildford, King's Lynn, Kingston-on-Thames, Snaresbrook, Southend, Croydon.
Middlesex Guildhall, S.W.1. *Administrator,* F. H. B. Clough; Inner London Sessions House, S.E.1. *Administrator,* R. Grobler.
Circuit Administrator, P. D. Robinson, Thanet House, 231/2 Strand, W.C.2.........£13,460
Deputy Circuit Administrator, G. M. O. Briegel.
Courts Administrators, Chelmsford Group, K. A. Henderson; *Maidstone Group,* J. E. Greenwood, M.C., T.D.; *Norwich Group,* (vacant); *Kingston Group,* C. Dall.

Wales and Chester Circuit

First-tier—Caernarvon, Cardiff, Chester, Mold, Swansea. Second-tier—Carmarthen, Newport, Welshpool. Third-tier—Dolgellau, Haverfordwest, Knutsford, Merthyr Tydfil.
Circuit Administrator, A. Howe, Churchill House, Churchill Way, Cardiff..............£12,000
Deputy Circuit Administrator, S. W. L. James.
Courts Administrators, Cardiff Group, L. A. Gay; *Chester Group,* A. H. Howard; *Swansea Group,* E. H. Thomas.

Western Circuit

First-tier—Bodmin, Bristol, Exeter, Winchester. Second-tier—Dorchester, Gloucester, Plymouth. Third-tier—Barnstaple, Bournemouth/Poole, Devizes, Newport (I.O.W.), Portsmouth, Salisbury, Southampton, Swindon, Taunton.
Circuit Administrator, I. E. Ashworth, Bridge House, Clifton, Bristol.................£12,000
Deputy Circuit Administrator, R. Potter.
Courts Administrators, Bristol Group, B. G. R. Barratt; *Exeter Group,* R. A. J. Barker; *Winchester Group,* J. K. W. Phipps.

RECORDERS

F. J. Aglionby; J. D. Alliott, Q.C.; B. J. Appleby, Q.C.; J. F. A. Archer, Q.C.; P. Ashworth, Q.C.; T. G. F. Atkinson; P. Back, Q.C.; G. Baker, Q.C.; J. B. Baker, Q.C.; P. M. Baker, Q.C.; D. A. Barker, Q.C.; D. Barker, Q.C.; J. M. A. Barker; R. O. Barlow; A. R. Barrowclough, Q.C.; P. M. Beard; C. O. M. Bedingfield, T.D., Q.C.; A. R. A. Beldham, Q.C.; A. W. Bell; P. Bennett, Q.C.; R. H. Bernstein, D.F.C. Q.C.; J. C. Beveridge; T. H. Bingham, Q.C.; G. J. Black, D.S.O., D.F.C.; I. J. Black, Q.C.; F. A. Blennerhassett, Q.C.; J. C. C. Blofeld, Q.C.; J. F. Blythe, T.D.; Joyanne W. Bracewell; J. N. W. Bridges-Adams; S. E. Brodie, Q.C.; D. D. Brown, Q.C.; J. W. A. Butler-Sloss; N. M. Butter, Q.C.; A. C. Caffin; D. C. Calcutt, Q.C.; G. A. Carman, Q.C.; B. R. O. Carter; B. H. Cato; P. Chadd, Q.C.; M. L. M. Chavasse, Q.C.; B. W. Chedlow, Q.C.; J. D. Clarke; D. J. Clarkson, Q.C.; J. L. Clay, T.D.; C. M. Clothier, Q.C.; J. N. Coffey; G. J. K. Coles, Q.C.; J. M. Collins, Q.C.; J. P. Comyn, Q.C.; R. K. Cooke, O.B.E.; Margaret D. Cosgrave; A. G. W. Coulthard; D. M. Cowley, Q.C.; A. E. Cox; B. R. E. Cox, Q.C.; P. J. Cox, D.S.C., Q.C.; J. Crabtree; P. J. Crawford; C. J. Crespi; M. A. L. Cripps, C.B.E., D.S.O., T.D., Q.C.; F. P. Crowder, Q.C., M.P.; R. H. Curtis; G. W. Davey; I. T. R. Davidson; Sir Alun Davies, Q.C.; L. J. Davies, Q.C.; W. L. M. Davies, Q.C.; C. F. Dehn, Q.C.; W. E. Denny, Q.C.; A. C. H. de Piro, Q.C.; T. M. Dillon, Q.C.; J. M. Dodson; F. M. Drake, D.F.C., Q.C.; D. P. Draycott, Q.C.; G. A. Draycott; J. M. Drinkwater, Q.C.; B. R. Duckworth; M. Dyer.

T. M. Eastham, Q.C.; J. B. S. Edwards; Q. T. Edwards, Q.C.; A. H. M. Evans, R.D., Q.C.; J. F. Evans, Q.C.; J. K. Q. Evans; T. M. Evans, Q.C.; A. B. Ewbank, Q.C.; G. N. Eyre Q.C.; P. Fallon, Q.C.; D. H. Farquharson, Q.C.; B. A. Farrer; P. R. Faulks, M.C.; M. H. Feeny; J. D. A. Fennell, Q.C.; D. B. B. Fenwick; T. G. Field-Fisher, T.D., Q.C.; W. A. B. Forbes, Q.C.; J. R. B. Fox-Andrews, Q.C.; C. J. S. French, Q.C.; A. N. Fricker; R. H. K. Frisby, Q.C.; B. J. F. Galpin; E. L. Gardner, Q.C., M.P.; P. N. Garland, Q.C.; L. Gassman; M. Gibbon, Q.C.; R. B. Gibson, Q.C.; W. J. Glover, Q.C.; P. W. Goldstone; R. N. Gooderson; K. F. Goodfellow, Q.C.; M. B. Goodman; J. K. Gore; J. P. Gorman, Q.C.; H. G. A. Gosling; The Lord Grantchester, Q.C.; G. Gray, Q.C.; R. I. Gray, Q.C.; W. P. Grieve, Q.C., M.P.; I. O. Griffiths, Q.C.; J. C. Griffiths, Q.C.; L. Griffiths; H. Hague; J. A. S. Hall, D.F.C., Q.C.; Sir Lincoln Hallinan; A. W. Hamilton, Q.C.; G. M. Hamilton, T.D.; R. G. Hamilton; J. A. T. Hanlon; R. J. Hardy; Rosina S. A. Hare, Q.C.; R. D. Harman, Q.C.; J. P. Harris, D.S.C., Q.C.; C. S. Harvey, M.B.E., T.D.; R. J. S. Harvey, Q.C.; C. L. Hawser, Q.C.; J. B. R. Hazan, Q.C.; D. Herrod, Q.C.; H. Hewitt; B. J. Higgs, Q.C.; W. D. T. Hodgson, Q.C.; D. A. Hollis, V.R.D., Q.C.; The Hon R. B. Holroyd-Pearce, Q.C.; H. F. Hooson, Q.C., M.P.; A. C. W. Hordern; R. Houlker, Q.C.; W. M. Howard, Q.C.; D. W. Howells; J. Hugill, Q.C.; G. W. Humphries; D. S. Hunter, Q.C.; A. E. Hutchinson; M. Hutchinson, Q.C.; G. B. Hutton; B. A. Hytner, Q.C.; C. F. Ingle; J. H. Inskip, Q.C.; N. F. Irvine, Q.C.; F. C. Irwin, Q.C.; R. Ives; J. Jeffs, Q.C.; A. C. Jolly; E. S. Jones; I. H. M. Jones, Q.C.; T. G. Jones; E. F. Jowitt, Q.C.; D. Karmel, C.B.E., Q.C.; D. N. Keating, Q.C.; R. D. L. Kelly, M.C.; M. E. I. Kempster, Q.C.; I. A. Kennedy, Q.C.; P. J. M. Kennedy, Q.C.; R. I. Kidwell, Q.C.

H. L. Lachs; G. F. B. Laughland; R. B. Lauriston; L. D. Lawton, Q.C.; N. Lees; A. P. Leggatt, Q.C.; H. J. Leonard, Q.C.; J. G. Le Quesne, Q.C.; J. M. Lever; S. Levine; E. ap G. Lewis, Q.C.; Gwynedd M. Lewis; T. E. I. Lewis-Bowen; A. L. J. Lincoln, Q.C.; F. A. Lincoln, Q.C.; V. J. Lissack; I. P. Llewellyn-

Jones; J. Lloyd-Eley, Q.C.; J. H. Lord; R. J. Lowry, Q.C.; E. Lyons, Q.C., M.P.; J. R. V. McAulay; A. J. D. McCowan, Q.C.; I. C. R. McCullough, Q.C.; A. C. Macdonald; G. A. MacDonald; D. B. McNeill, Q.C.; W. A. MacPherson, T.D., Q.C.; J. G. Marriage, Q.C.; M. J. W. Marsh, M.C., T.D.; P. W. Medd, O.B.E., Q.C.; K. S. W. Mellor, Q.C.; J. C. K. Mercer; A. L. Mildon, Q.C.; Sir Joseph Molony, K.C.V.O., Q.C.; D. G. Morgan; L. J. J. Morgan; W. G. O. Morgan, Q.C., M.P.; M. Morland, Q.C.; I. H. Morris-Jones, Q.C.; A. J. H. Morrison; J. B. Mortimer, Q.C.; H. C. Muscroft; M. J. Mustill, Q.C.; A. L. Myerson, Q.C.; A. S. Myerson, Q.C.; B. T. Neill, Q.C.; F. P. Neill, Q.C.; E. G. Neville; J. H. R. Newey, Q.C.; R. M. H. Noble; M. P. Nolan, Q.C.; J. S. Oakes; E. M. Ogden, Q.C.; H. H. Ognall, Q.C.; B. R. Oliver; D. A. Orde; P. H. Otton, Q.C.; J. A. D. Owen, Q.C.; P. L. W. Owen, T.D., Q.C.; Helen E. Paling; R. H. S. Palmer; M. C. Parker, Q.C.; T. I. Payne; I. Percival, Q.C., M.P.; R. A. Percy; A. Phillips, O.B.E.; D. A. Phillips; O. B. Popplewell, Q.C.; F. M. Potter; F. H. Potts, Q.C.; H. C. Pownall; M. J. Pratt, Q.C.; A. J. Price, Q.C.; E. J. Prosser.

A. Rankin, Q.C.; A. D. Rawley; L. F. Read, Q.C.; H. C. Rigby, D.F.C.; Sir Ivo Rigby; H. E. P. Roberts, Q.C.; J. H. Robson; J. O. Roch, Q.C.; J. W. Rogers, Q.C.; G. H. Rooke, T.D.; R. G. Rougier, Q.C.; T. P. Russell, Q.C.; P. J. M. Ryan; D. M. Savill, Q.C.; H. M. Self, Q.C.; B. C. Sheen, Q.C.; M. D. Sherrard, Q.C.; L. S. Shields, Q.C.; G. J. Shindler, Q.C.; A. Simpson; J. K. E. Slack, T.D.; P. M. J. Slot; F. B. Smedley; M. S. Smith, Q.C.; D. A. L. Smout, Q.C.; Jean M. Southworth, Q.C.; G. C. H. Spafford; J. A. C. Spokes, Q.C.; R. O. C. Stable, Q.C.; S. A. Stamler, Q.C.; C. S. T. J. T. Staughton, Q.C.; J. Stephenson; N. F. Stogdon; C. S. Stuart-White; J. G. St. G. Syms, Q.C.; H. C. Tayler; J. B. Taylor, M.B.E., T.D.; K. J. Taylor; P. M. Taylor, Q.C.; E. S. Temple, M.B.E., Q.C.; K. J. Tetley; D. O. Thomas, Q.C.; J. Thomas, Q.C., M.P.; Rt. Hon. P. J. M. Thomas, Q.C., M.P.; R. N. Thomas, Q.C.; S. B. Thomas, Q.C.; R. N. Titheridge, Q.C.; H. J. M. Tucker, Q.C.; R. H. Tucker, Q.C.; M. J. Turner, Q.C.; A. R. Tyrrell, Q.C.; M. T. B. Underhill, Q.C.; A. R. Vandermeer; A. O. R. Vick; D. C. Waddington, Q.C.; D. St. J. R. Wagstaff; A. F. Waley, V.R.D., Q.C.; M. Walker; P. H. C. Walker; B. Walsh; M. B. Ward; R. L. Ward, Q.C.; J. R. Warde; R. G. Waterhouse, Q.C.; V. B. Watts; C. D. G. P. Waud; P. A. Webster; P. E. Webster, Q.C.; P. Weitzman, Q.C.; W. T. Wells, Q.C.; M. C. B. West, Q.C.; C. H. Whitby, Q.C.; G. G. A. Whitehead, D.F.C.; F. Whitworth, Q.C.; The Lord Wigoder, Q.C.; G. W. Willett; D. B. Williams, T.D., Q.C.; H. G. Williams; Sir Thomas Williams, Q.C., M.P.; J. G. Wilmers, Q.C.; J. K. Wood, M.C., Q.C.; J. Woodcock, T.D.; H. K. Woolf; G. H. Wootton; N. G. Wootton; G. N. Worthington; J. M. Wright, Q.C.; O. Wrightson; R. Wyeth; R. M. Yorke, Q.C.; C. G. Young.

METROPOLITAN STIPENDIARY MAGISTRATES

Bow Street, Covent Garden, W.C.2

Chief Metropolitan Stipendiary Magistrate, Kenneth James Priestley Barraclough, C.B.E., T.D.

£13,000

Magistrates, Evelyn Charles Sackville Russell; William Edward Charles Robins; Harold Cook
(each) £11,750

Chief Clerks, R. Hines; Mrs. J. M. Ferley. £8,970
to £9,735 or £10,005

Camberwell Green, D'Eynsford Road, S.E.5

Magistrates, Maurice Juniper Guymer; Edgar Leonard Bradley; Ralph Hamilton Lownie; David Prys Jones..............(each) £11,750

Senior Chief Clerk, I. Fowler............£10,005
Chief Clerk, P. Unwin.........£8,970 to £9,735
 Clerkenwell, Kings Cross Road, W.C.1
Magistrates, John Denis Purcell; Mark Romer;
 Christopher John Bourke........(each) £11,750
Senior Chief Clerk, W. A. W. Strachan.....£10,005
Chief Clerk, J. Patron.........£8,970 to £9,735
 Greenwich, Blackheath Road, S.E.10
Magistrates, Nigel Francis Maltby Robinson; D.
 Barr.......................(each) £11,750
Senior Chief Clerk, G. Edwards...........£10,005
 Woolwich, Market Street, S.E.18
Magistrates (as Greenwich).
Chief Clerk, I. Pepper..........£8,970 to £9,735

 Highbury Corner, Holloway Road, N.7
Magistrates, Tobias Springer; Ian Graeme McLean;
 David Armand Hopkin........(each) £11,750
Senior Chief Clerk, A. L. Gooch.........£10,005
Chief Clerk, J. Jordan...........£8,970 to £9,735
 Horseferry Road, Horseferry Road, S.W.1
Magistrates, Kenneth Douglas Evelyn Herbert
 Harington; David Fairbairn; Edmond Geoffrey
 MacDermott..................(each) £11,750
Senior Chief Clerk, S. G. Clixby.........£10,005
Chief Clerk, P. W. Johnson.....£8,970 to £9,735
Chief Clerk (Licensing), L. G. Bowerman
       £8,970 to £9,735

 Marlborough Street,
 Great Marlborough Street, W.1
Magistrates, St. John Bernard Vyvyan Harmsworth,
 Neil Martin McElligott.........(each) £11,750
Chief Clerk, E. L. Yabsley......£8,970 to £9,735
 Marylebone, 181 Marylebone Road, N.W.1
Magistrates, Rupert Rawden Smith; Peter Walter
 Goldstone; Roderick Jessel Romain; Brian John
 Canham.....................(each) £11,750
Senior Chief Clerk, D. V. Wainwright.....£10,005
 Old Street, E.C.1
Magistrates, Kenneth John Heastey Nichols; James
 Hobson Jobling................(each) £11,750
Chief Clerk, K. Anderson......£8,970 to £9,735
 South Western, Lavender Hill, S.W.11
Magistrates, Charles Richard Beddington; Albert
 William Clark; John William Cheeseman
      (each) £11,750
Senior Chief Clerk, C. E. Hollingdale.....£10,005
Chief Clerk, J. S. Pulford.......£8,970 to £9,735
 Thames, Aylward Street, E.1
Magistrates, Peter Duncan Fanner; Ronald David
 Bartle......................(each) £11,750
Senior Chief Clerk, J. A. Bradbury.......£10,005
Chief Clerk, I. J. Senior........£8,970 to £9,735
 Tower Bridge, Tooley Street, S.E.1
Magistrates, Richard Kenneth Cooke, O.B.E.;
 Ronald Knox Mawer..........(each) £11,750
Chief Clerk, J. P. S. Walker....£8,970 to £9,735
 Wells Street, 59/65 Wells Street, W.1
Magistrates, Christopher Besley; Edward James
 Branson; Mrs. Audrey Mary Frisby; Geoffrey
 Lindsay James Noel...........(each) £11,750
Senior Chief Clerk, G. D. Shaw...........£9,227
Chief Clerk, Miss I. Snatt............£8,920
 West London, Southcombe Street, W.14
Magistrates, Eric Crowther; Peter Gilmour Noto
 Badge.......................(each) £11,750
Senior Chief Clerk, K. Edwards..........£10,005

Unattached Magistrates, Sir Ivo Rigby; David Barr
      (each) £11,750

---

*Principal Chief Clerk & Clerk to the Committee of
Magistrates* (office: 3rd Floor, North West Wing,
Bush House, Aldwych, W.C.2), C. A. Reston
      £11,472
Chief Clerk (Training), R. Harbord.......£10,059

Juvenile Courts, 185 Marylebone Road, N.W.1
Senior Chief Clerk, Miss P. M. Austin....£10,197
Chief Clerk, J. A. Laing.......£8,920 to £9,927

STIPENDIARY MAGISTRATES

Birmingham, John Frederick Milward (1951).
Greater Manchester, John Nimmo Coffey (1975);
 Cecil Thomas Latham, O.B.E. (1976)
Kingston upon Hull, Ian Robertson Boyd (1972).
Leeds, Francis David Lindley Loy (1972).
Merseyside, Norman Godfrey Wootton (1976).
Merthyr Tydfil, David Powys Rowland (1961).
Mid Glamorgan, David Alan Phillips.
South Glamorgan, Sir (Adrian) Lincoln Hallinan
 (1976).
South Yorkshire, John Alfred Henham (1975).
Wolverhampton, Howard William Maitland Coley
 (1961).

CITY OF LONDON JUSTICE ROOMS
MANSION HOUSE JUSTICE ROOM.

Chief Magistrate, The Lord Mayor.
Chief Clerk, J. H. Tratt.............£10,395
Deputy Chief Clerk, C. F. Grimwood.....£7,797
   GUILDHALL JUSTICE ROOM
Chief Clerk, A. G. J. Chandler, O.B.E. £10,395
Deputy Chief Clerk, F. A. Treeby........£7,554

DIRECTOR OF PUBLIC PROSECUTIONS
4/12 Queen Anne's Gate, S.W.1

Director, Sir Norman Skelhorn, K.B.E., Q.C.
Deputy Director, M. J. Jardine, C.B.
Assistant Directors, P. R. Barnes; K. Dowling.
Assistant Solicitors, P. M. J. Palmes; J. Wood; A. G.
 Flavell; J. E. Leck; T. J. Taylor; J. M. Walker;
 K. M. Horn; D. G. Williams.

OFFICE OF THE JUDGE ADVOCATE
GENERAL OF THE FORCES
*(Lord Chancellors Establishment; Joint Service for the
Army and the Royal Air Force)*
6 Spring Gardens, Cockspur Street, S.W.1

Judge Advocate General, F. H. Dean, C.B...£14,000
Vice Judge Advocate General, J. G. Morgan-Owen,
 M.B.E................................£12,160
Assistant Judge Advocates General, B. R. Allen;
 J. Stuart-Smith; G. Ll. Chapman; C. G. Gould;
 J. E. Pullinger; G. E. Empson; G. R. Canner;
 F. L. Daly................£9,998 to £11,465
Deputy Judge Advocates, E. G. Moelwyn-Hughes;
 A. P. Pitts; S. B. Spence......£7,090 to £9,215

METROPOLITAN POLICE OFFICE
New Scotland Yard, Broadway, S.W.1
[01–230 1212]

Commissioner, Sir Robert Mark, Q.P.M....£18,675
Deputy Commissioner, C. P. J. Woods, C.B.E.
      £14,646
Receiver, R. J. Guppy, C.B..............£13,420
   "A" Department
  Administration and Operations
Assistant Commissioner, R. J. Mastel, C.B.E. £13,290
Deputy Assistant Commissioners, W. H. Gibson,
 Q.P.M.; G. J. Kelland, Q.P.M... £9,777 to £10,884
Principals, W. T. Davis; C. R. A. Messenger
     £5,680 to £7,450
Commanders, R. P. Bryan; K. G. Hannam; E. F.
 Maybanks; E. T. Matthews; R. C. Steventon
     £8,733 to £9,165
Senior Executive Officers, D. W. Brown; N. W. H.
 Fairfax; D. L. Gomez; J. R. S. Hurworth; B. A.
 Phillips..................£4,900 to £5,900
Metropolitan Special Constabulary, Chief Commandant,
 A. A. Hammond.

   "B" Department
    Traffic
Assistant Commissioner, P. B. Kavanagh, Q.P.M.
     £13,290

Deputy Assistant Commissioners, H. Hodgson, O.B.E.;
D. Powis.................£9,777 to £10,884
Senior Principal, R. V. Clark.... £7,750 to £9,350
Principals, R. S. Ainsworth; P. A. Barwood;
S. H. Carter; J. C. Cutts, O.B.E.; P. I. May;
G. H. T. Shrimpton, C.B.E., T.D.
£5,680 to £7,450
Commanders, R. A. C. Barker; G. E. H. Maggs,
Q.P.M.; J. Toogood......£8,733 to £9,165
Senior Executive Officers, D. H. Auld; A. J. Chatwin;
D. Giddings; P. J. Groom; J. S. Johnstone; P.
O'Neill; C. A. A. Roberts; H. C. Stock; K. J.
Tetley; K. H. Varney........£4,900 to £5,900

"C" Department
Criminal Investigation
Assistant Commissioner, J. S. Wilson, O.B.E.
£13,290
Deputy Assistant Commissioners, R. H. Anning,
Q.P.M.; R. A. Davis; V. S. Gilbert; J. Morrison,
Q.P.M.; H.D. Walton, Q.P.M. £9,777 to £10,884
Principal, M. J. Pratt..........£5,680 to £7,450
Commanders, R. L. J. Ashby, Q.P.M.; J. Cass; D. C.
Dilley, Q.P.M.; T. M. Edwards, Q.P.M.; R.
Habershon, M.B.E.; G. T. C. Lambourne; D.
Neesham; J. F. Nevill; K. G. Pendered; P. A.
Saunders; H. D. Walton, Q.P.M.; R. A. Watts
£8,733 to £9,165
Senior Executive Officers, J. Greenwood; K. Jones;
J. Joyce; R. D. Mearns; D. R. Pidgeon; K.
Pleant; H. J. Wyborn........£4,900 to £5,900

Metropolitan Police Laboratory
Director, R. L. Williams....£10,180 to £11,430
Deputy Director, (vacant)........£8,650 to £9,798
Assistant Directors, B. J. Culliford; D. Neylan; B. B.
Wheals....................£8,650 to £9,798
Principal Scientific Officers, R. R. Berrett; Mrs. S. J.
Butcher; K. Chaperlin; B. E. Connett; D. M.
Ellen; N. A. Fuller; J. V. Jackson; Mrs. S. M.
Keating; C. J. O. Lee; Mrs. F. R. Lewington; L.
Morse; B. H. Parkin; D. Rudram; R. A.
Stedman; M. J. Whitehouse. . £5,514 to £7,205

"D" Department
Personnel and Training
Assistant Commissioner, H. J. E. Hunt, C.B.E. £13,290
Deputy Assistant Commissioners, J. A. Dellow; S.
Leckey..................£9,777 to £10,884
Principals, M. N. Ferry, T.D.; R. G. Giddings; R. J.
Whyman.................£5,680 to £7,450
Commanders, N. Baxter; F. E. Chalkley; D. P. Hunt;
Miss K. D. Skillern..........£8,733 to £9,165
Senior Executive Officers, O. A. Collier; J. H.
Mailing; C. E. D. Reeves; R. C. Vivian
£4,900 to £5,900
Welfare Officer, Capt. A. H. Little, C.B.E., R.N. (ret.)
£4,900 to £5,900
Director of Catering, Col. R. R. Owens, O.B.E.
£7,750 to £9,350
Deputy Director, A. F. Taylor....£6,625 to £7,450
Metropolitan Police Cadet Corps
Commander, N. Baxter........£8,733 to £9,165
Director of Academic Studies, K. H. Patterson, V.R.D.
£4,900 to £6,875
Medical and Dental Branch
Chief Surgeon, R. W. Nevin, T.D.
Consulting Physician and Deputy to Chief Surgeon, Sir
John Richardson, Bt., M.V.O.
Medical Officer, E. C. A. Bott.
Dental Officer, Group Capt. H. V. Jessop.

Area Headquarters
Deputy Assistant Commissioners, S. Coates; J. S.
Crisp; J. H. Gerrard, O.B.E., M.C., Q.P.M.; P. C.
Newens, Q.P.M............£9,777 to £10,884

Commanders, J. T. R. Barnett, Q.P.M.; A. H.
Howard; T. J. O'Connell; A. S. Wickstead,
Q.P.M.....................£8,733 to £9,165

Management Services
Director, Col. J. E. Owen..............£11,000
Senior Principal Scientific Officer and Deputy Director,
N. E. Hand................£8,650 to £9,798
Principal, J. R. Hamilton.......£5,680 to £7,450
Chief Work Study Officer, J. E. Holbrow
£5,680 to £7,450
Principal Psychologist, J. H. Jones-Lloyd
£5,680 to £7,450
Principal Scientific Officer, R. P. du Parcq
£5,514 to £7,205
Senior Executive Officers, C. J. Boorman; Mrs. C.
Macleod..................£4,900 to £5,900
Senior Work Study Officers, R. C. Bright; A. Kasler
£4,900 to £5,900

DIRECTORATE OF ADMINISTRATION
AND FINANCE
Deputy Receiver, B. G. David............£11,670

"E" Department
Establishments and Secretariat
Secretary, D. Meyler, D.S.C.... £8,650 to £11,000
Senior Principals, M. Lee; G. E. Stonely
£7,750 to £9,350
Principals, F. A. W. Pilborough; J. E. Tubb
£5,680 to £7,450
Senior Executive Officers, Miss B. Arnold; T. J. Beer;
R. P. Cundy; A. Hartley, M.B.E.; A. J. Hender-
son; J. E. G. King; G. C. Nockles; M. W.
Simmons; R. W. Smith; B. W. Smyth; A. M. J.
Williams.................£4,900 to £5,900
General Registry
Senior Executive Officer, E. G. Harvey
£4,900 to £5,900

"F" Department
Finance
Director of Finance, R. H. Beaver, O.B.E.
£8,650 to £11,000
Deputy Directors of Finance, J. L. Davies; R. F.
Gridley...................£7,750 to £9,350
Assistant Directors of Finance, R. W. Barker; E. R.
Bright; J. A. Crutchlow......£5,680 to £7,450
Senior Executive Officers, J. G. Day; J. E. Geater;
Miss S. M. Goater; B. J. B. Rawlings; N. A. E.
Rex; J. A. Starling; J. C. H. Taylor
£4,900 to £5,900

"G" Department
Administration
Director of Administration, P. J. G. Buckley
£8,650 to £11,000
Deputy Directors of Administration, N. N. I. Batten;
H. E. W. Hodson; L. Joughin, M.C.
£7,750 to £9,350
Principals, H. Brothers; D. F. F. Hannaford;
R. B. Jones; M. W. Maidment; A. Morley,
M.B.E.; D. Wilson..........£5,680 to £7,450
Statistical Adviser, G. C. Reed....£5,680 to £7,450
Senior Executive Officers, D. H. Burr; D. M. Davis;
P. Emmerson, T.D.; A. Fearon; I. M. Fernie;
C. E. Ford; H. D. Moore; D. F. Poole; R. P.
Sargent; J. S. Steele; I. H. Taylor
£4,900 to £5,900
Controller of Printing and Reprographic Services, H. T.
Hudson, M.B.E..............£5,680 to £7,450

Chief Architect and Surveyor's Department
Chief Architect and Surveyor, M. L. Belchamber
£11,000

Deputy Chief Architect and Surveyor G. B. Vint
£8,650 to £9,798
Assistant Chief Architect C. A. Legerton
£8,650 to £9,798
Assistant Chief Surveyors, D. N. Fogden (*Estates*) ;
A. H. Bailey (*Building*) . . . . . . £8,650 to £9,798
Senior Architects, D. E. Chapman; C. G. Liardet:
A. E. Matcham; I. G. Mowat; J. A. A. Rainbow;
P. Silsby. . . . . £6,280 to £7,450
Senior Surveyors, J. W. Burton; J. A. Chipchase; L.
Hibbs; K. R. Sewell; R. E. Winchester
£6,280 to £7,450
Senior Public Health Engineers, M. Randall; F. A.
Rowbotham . . . . £6,280 to £7,450

Chief Engineer's Department
Chief Engineer, B. France. £11,000
Deputy Chief Engineers, D. Hale; D. E. Mosley
£8,650 to £9,798
Principal Professional and Technology Officers, E.
Blade; C. W. Cornock; D. E. Keech; L. F. Squibb;
F. H. G. Taylor; J. M. Wardle; P. J. Wright
£6,280 to £7,450
Senior Engineer, I. O. Levy . . . . . £6,280 to £7,450

"S" Department
Solicitors
Solicitor, R. E. T. Birch. £13,420
Deputy Solicitor, D. M. O'Shea. £12,000
Assistant Solicitors, G. E. Clark; J. B. Egan; R. L.
Kiley; R. G. Mays; W. H. S. Relton; A. H.
Simpson; J. M. Tuff; D. W. Warran; C. N.
Winston. . . . . £9,033 to £11,000
Senior Legal Assistants, R. P. Coupland; Miss J. M.
Craig; R. W. Davies; H. J. Drake; W. S. Frost;
I. G. F. Graham; H. B. Hargrave; S. M. How-
ard; Miss P. M. Long; J. R. McCann; R. E.
Marsh; J. O'Keeffe; C. S. Porteous; P. A.
Shawdon; R. M. D. Thorne; B. R. Vince; M. H.
Wilmott; H. A. Youngerwood
£6,625 to £8,750
Legal Assistants, Miss D. Crebbin; G. R. Edwards;
P. R. Essex; A. M. P. Falk; G. Gibb; P. S. K.
Haddock; Miss F. M. Hegarty; Miss A. M.
Hewett; J. R. P. Hyde; Miss S. M. James; A. G.
Mainds; J. P. McCooey; Miss A. M. Martin;
S. A. O'Doherty; Miss J. M. Perrigo; Miss P. J.
Phipps; R. N. Short; R. C. Wheeler
£3,424 to £6,125
Senior Principal Legal Executive, W. McCrorie
£7,750 to £9,350
Principal Legal Executives, W. E. Ball; C. W. White;
E. Worboys. . . . . £5,680 to £7,450
Senior Legal Executive Officers, A. Astill; J. Clarke;
G. Davies; A. Kirkwood; J. Niblett; P. Stenning;
K. Stokes; B. Tickner. . . . . £4,900 to £5,900

"P" Department
Public Relations
Director of Information, P. Marshall
£9,777 to £10,884
Deputy Director of Information, J. S. Courtney
£7,750 to £9,350
Head of News Branch, E. Wright
£5,680 to £7,450
Head of Publicity Branch, J. H. V. Bradley
£5,680 to £7,450
Senior Information Officers, E. Davies; M. C. John-
son; J. L. Miller; R. A. A. Moore
£4,900 to £5,900
Senior Executive Officers, M. G. Down, M.B.E.; T.
Gibson; A. J. James; J. C. Stern
£4,900 to £5,900

*General Secretary of the Association of Chief Police
Officers of England, Wales and Northern Ireland,* F.
G. Hulme, O.B.E., Q.P.M. . . . . . . £6,625 to £7,450

CITY OF LONDON POLICE
26 Old Jewry, E.C.2
Commissioner, C. J. Page, Q.P.M. £14,646
Assistant Commissioner, E. W. Bright
£10,419 to £11,244
Commanders, J. F. Stimson (*Operations*), P. Coppack
(*Crime*) . . . . £8,733 to £9,165
Chief Superintendents, G. A. Lee (*Traffic and Com-
munications*); D. W. Smith (" *B* " *Divn.*); D. B.
Sparkes (" *C* " *Divn.*); A. T. Francis (" *D* "
Divn.); S. H. Smith (*C.I.D.*); K. Taylor (*C.I.D.*);
B. A. Rowland (*Sec. of Superintendents' Association
of England & Wales & Northern Ireland*)
£7,538 to £8,135
Superintendent, K. Richiardi (*Administration*)
£6,935 to £7,298

City of London Special Constabulary
Commandant, Major S. Holmes, T.D.
Chief Staff Officer, J. Oakley.

INDUSTRIAL AND OTHER TRIBUNALS
The Industrial Tribunals
Established under the Industrial Training Act
1964.

Central Office (England and Wales)
93 Ebury Bridge Road, S.W.1
President, E. A. Seeley. £13,500
Secretary, G. R. Fisher . . . . £5,992 to £7,762
Central Office (Scotland)
St. Andrew House, 141 West Nile Street, Glasgow
President, I. MacDonald. £13,250
Chairmen, T. W. Strachan; G. V. McLaughlin; R.
C. Hay. £11,750
Secretary, B. M. Sheridan. £6,159

Lands Tribunal
5 Chancery Lane, W.C.2
[01-831-6611]
President, D. G. H. Frank, Q.C.
Members, J. R. Laird, T.D.; R. C. Walmsley;
J. S. Daniel, Q.C.; J. H. Emlyn Jones, M.B.E.;
E. C. Strathon; J. D. Russell-Davis; V. G.
Wellings, Q.C.; W. H. Rees.
Registrar, O. L. Mott.

Patents and Registered Designs Appeal Tribunal
Room 169, Royal Courts of Justice, W.C.2
Judges, The Hon. Mr. Justice Graham; The Hon.
Mr. Justice Whitford.
Registrar, D. F. James.

Performing Right Tribunal
Room 105, 25 Southampton Buildings, W.C.2
Chairman, H. E. Francis, Q.C.
Secretary, A. Holt.

Transport Tribunal
Watergate House, 15 York Buildings,
Adelphi, W.C.2
President, G. D. Squibb, Q.C.
Registrar and Secretary, Miss P. E. Kennedy.

**Parliamentary and Local Government Election
Petitions Office**
Room 120, Royal Courts of Justice, W.C.2
Prescribed Officer, I. H. Jacob, Q.C.
Clerk, F. W. Simpson.

Pensions Appeal Tribunals
Staffordshire House, Store Street, W.C.1
President, Hon. Sir Alastair Forbes.
Secretary, P. Barker.

Immigration Appeals
Head Office, Thanet House,
231 Strand, W.C.2
Chief Adjudicator, J. D. Peterkin, M.B.E.
Immigration Appeals Tribunal
President, Sir Derek Hilton, M.B.E.
Vice-Presidents, P. N. Dalton; D. L. Neve.
Secretary to the Appellate Authorities, P. G. Bailey.

SCOTTISH LAW COURTS AND OFFICES, PARLIAMENT SQUARE, EDINBURGH

COURT OF SESSION (Established 1532).
Lord President, Lord Emslie (Rt. Hon. George Carlyle Emslie, M.B.E.)

INNER HOUSE.—*First Division.*
The Lord President, Lord Emslie, Rt. Hon. George Carlyle Emslie, M.B.E. £20,425
Lord Cameron, Sir John Cameron, D.S.C... 16,675
Lord Johnston, Douglas Harold Johnston, T.D. 16,675
Lord Avonside, Rt. Hon. Ian Hamilton Shearer 16,675

Lord Kincraig, Robert Smith Johnston... 16,675
Lord Maxwell, Peter Maxwell.......... 16,675
Lord McDonald, Robert Howat McDonald, M.C. 16,675
Lord Wylie, Rt. Hon. Norman Russell Wylie, V.R.D. 16,675
Lord Stewart, Ewan Stewart, M.C........ 16,675

Second Division
Lord Justice Clerk, Lord Wheatley, Rt. Hon. John Wheatley of Shettleston £19,300
Lord Hunter, John Oswald Mair Hunter (*Seconded to Scottish Law Commission*)... 16,675
Lord Kissen, Manuel Kissen............. 16,675
Lord Leechman, James Leechman........ 16,675

OUTER HOUSE
Lord Thomson, Alexander Thomson.... £16,675
Lord Robertson, Ian Macdonald Robertson, M.B.E., T.D. 16,675
Lord Stott, Rt. Hon. George Gordon Stott 16,675
Lord Dunpark, Alastair McPherson Johnston, T.D. 16,675
Lord Keith, Henry Shanks Keith........ 16,675
Lord Grieve, William Robertson Grieve... 16,675
Lord Brand, David William Robert Brand 16,675

Principal Clerk of Session and Clerk of Justiciary, O. J. Brown............... £8,650 to £11,000
Deputy Principal Clerk, G. H. Robertson £5,680 to £7,450
Keeper of the Rolls, J. Watson... £4,900 to £5,900
Deputy Keeper of the Rolls, N. H. Reid £4,900 to £5,900
Depute Clerks, Inner House, A. Wylie; E. Smith £4,900 to £5,900
Depute Clerks, Outer House, D. Scott; A. S. D. Rodger; H. C. Macpherson; H. S. Foley; V. A. Woods; A. Brown; R. Sibbald; W. Gillon; M. Weir; J. Robertson; R. F. Grieve £4,900 to £5,900
Deputy Principal Clerk of Justiciary, W. Howard................... £5,680 to £7,450
Deputies and Assistants, G. Paton; J. F. McNish; A. A. Brown...... £4,900 to £5,900

NOTE.—The word "Lord" prefixed to the names of Judges of the Court of Session, or to titles different from their names, is strictly an official honour and may be compared with the terms "Hon. Mr. Justice" and "Lord Chief Justice" in England.

Lord Advocate's Department
See Index
Crown Office,
9 Parliament Square, Edinburgh
Crown Agent, W. G. Chalmers, M.C...... £13,230
Deputy Crown Agent, A. V. Sheehan £9,780 to £11,000
Senior Legal Assistants, Miss I. McGillivray; K. M. Maciver................... £6,625 to £8,750
Legal Assistants, J. Martin; S. R. Houston £3,424 to £6,125

Exchequer Office
102 George Street, Edinburgh
Queen's and Lord Treasurer's Remembrancer, J. B. I. McTavish, O.B.E..... £9,033 to £10,180
Chief Clerk, D. E. D. Robertson £5,680 to £7,450
Senior Executive Officers, A. J. Ware; S. P. Frater................ £4,900 to £5,900

Companies Registration Office
102 George Street, Edinburgh
Registrar (and Keeper, Edinburgh Gazette Office), J. B. I. McTavish, O.B.E.

Sheriff Court of Chancery
16 North Back Street, Edinburgh
Sheriff of Chancery, W. J. Bryden, C.B.E., Q.C.
Sheriff Clerk of Chancery, W. D. McInnes.

H.M. Commissary Office,
16 North Bank Street, Edinburgh
Commissary Clerk, W. D. McInnes.
Deputy do., A. D. Stevenson.

Crown Estate Commissioners
11 Charlotte Square, Edinburgh
Crown Estate Receiver, D. T. Hunt.

SCOTTISH LAND COURT
1 Grosvenor Crescent, Edinburgh
Members, The Hon. Lord Birsay, K.T., C.B.E., T.D. (*Chairman*); D. W. Cunningham; John McVicar; A. Gillespie; D. D. McDiarmid.
Principal Clerk, T. MacD. Wilson.
Depute Clerks of Court and Senior Legal Assessors, S. Forrest; D. H. Cameron.
Deputy Clerks of Court and Legal Assessors, J. G. Riddoch; K. H. R. Graham.
Clerk of Accounts and Establishment, R. Landels.

SCOTTISH LAW COMMISSION
Old College, South Bridge, Edinburgh
[031-668-2131]
Chairman, The Hon. Lord Hunter.
Commissioners, Prof. T. B. Smith, Q.C., Ll.D., F.B.A.; A. E. Anton, C.B.E. (*full-time*); R. B. Jack (*part-time*); J. P. H. McKay, Q.C.
Secretary, J. B. Allan.
Asst. Secretary, A. J. Sim.
Chief Clerk, R. L. Spark.

STIPENDIARY MAGISTRATES (GLASGOW)
Court Chambers
Central, Thomas Joseph McLauchlan (1966).
Marine, Martin S. Morrow (1972).
Govan, Robert Mitchell (1975).

SHERIFFS PRINCIPAL, SHERIFFS, SHERIFF CLERKS AND PROCURATORS FISCAL OF COUNTIES IN SCOTLAND

SHERIFFDOM AND SHERIFF PRINCIPAL	SHERIFFS	SHERIFF CLERKS	PROCURATORS FISCAL
Grampian, Highland and Islands.— G. S. Gimson, Q.C., 11 Royal Circus, Edinburgh.	*Aberdeen, Stonehaven,* M. J. A. Rose, D.F.C.; A. M. G. Russell, Q.C.; M. Layden	J. B. Blair....... A. Oliver.......	M. T. MacNeill. M. MacPhail.
	Banff and Peterhead, T. M. Croan (*also Aberdeen*).	C. Gordon.......	W. A. Brown. I. S. McNaughton.
	Elgin, R. A. Wilson..........	T. Fyffe.......	A. Wither.
	Wick, E. Stewart............	W. J. Burns..... B. J. Young.....	G. E. Scott. A. M. Skinner. C. S. MacKenzie.
	Inverness, Stornoway and Lochmaddy, Fort William, Portree, Nairn, W. J. Fulton; S. Scott Robinson, M.B.E., T.D.		W. A. H. Merry. D. Macmillan.
	Kirkwall, Lerwick, A. A. MacDonald.	J. M. Lynn...... L. Johnson.......	A. W. Wright. D. J. McLeay.
	Dingwall and Tain, Dornoch, Captain W. R. M. Murdoch, C.B.E., D.S.C., V.R.D., R.N.R. (ret.).	D. D. Mackay... D. MacDonald...	T. F. Aitchison. J. D. McNaughton.
Tayside, Central and Fife.— R. R. Taylor, Ph.D., Q.C., 51 Northumberland Street, Edinburgh.	*Arbroath, Forfar,* S. O. Kermack (*also Perth*).	D. M. Cameron.. R. G. Davis.....	C. D. G. Hillary. A. L. Ingram.
	Dundee, J. B. W. Christie; G. L. Cox.	J. A. C. Weir....	C. G. Hogg.
	Perth, H. F. Ford.............	A. A. Steele.....	R. L. J. Miln.
	Falkirk, R. R. Kerr...........	R. D. S. Mercer..	D. B. MacFarlane.
	Stirling, Alloa, W. C. Henderson	D. Waddell...... K. McKenzie....	K. Valentine. Miss M. W. Robertson.
	Cupar, J. C. McInnes (*also Kirkcaldy*)	P. G. Corcoran..	H. R. Annan.
	Dunfermline, G. I. W. Shiach...	J. S. Douglas.....	J. H. Douglas.
	Kirkcaldy, J. Allan............	J. G. C. Bone....	E. H. Galt.
Lothian and Borders.— W. J. Bryden, C.B.E., Q.C., Sheriff Principal's Chambers, Sheriff Court House, Lawnmarket, Edinburgh.	*Edinburgh, Peebles,* V. D. B. Skae (*except Peebles*); C. G. B. Nicholson (*except Peebles*); N. MacVicar (*except Peebles*); J. A. Dick, M.C., Q.C. (*except Peebles*); Miss I. L. Sinclair, Q.C. (*also Selkirk*); K. W. B. Middleton (*also Haddington, not Peebles*); R. D. Ireland, Q.C.★ (*Director, Scottish Courts Administration*); C. R. Macarthur, Q.C.★; J. L. M. Mitchell.★	W. D. McInnes..	E. G. Smith. C. B. Allan.
	Linlithgow, W. T. Hook.......	R. W. M. Hall...	D. R. Smith.
	Haddington, K. W. B. Middleton (*also Edinburgh*).	J. Cumming.....	R. W. McConachie.
	Jedburgh, Duns, Selkirk, J. V. Paterson (*except Selkirk*); Miss I. L. Sinclair, Q.C. (*except Jedburgh and Duns*).	Mrs.E.S.P.Smart.	C. B. Allan. J. C. Whitelaw. C. B. Allan.
North Strathclyde.— F. W. F. O'Brien, Q.C., 12 Boswall Road, Edinburgh.	*Dunoon, Campbeltown, Oban, Rothesay,* N. Milne (*except Dunoon and Rothesay*); H. Lyons (*except Oban and Campbeltown—but also Greenock*).	J. McGhie.......	W. D. Stewart. D. MacNeill. G. H. Pagan. Miss C. McNaughton.
	Dumbarton, J. C. M. Jardine; J. P. Murphy; B. Kearney.★	J. R. Cowie	I. Dean.
	Paisley, A. K. F. Hunter; H. R. MacLean; R. A. Inglis.	A. McDougall...	J. B. R. Mackinnon.
	Greenock, J. B. Patrick; H. Lyons (*also Dunoon and Rothesay*).	A. P. McPherson.	W. Macnab.
	Kilmarnock, R. N. Levitt, O.B.E., T.D.; D. B. Smith.	R. R. Dale......	J. L. McLeod.

SHERIFFDOM AND SHERIFF PRINCIPAL	SHERIFFS	SHERIFF CLERK	PROCURATORS FISCAL
Glasgow and Strathkelvin.— The Lord Wilson of Langside, P.C., Q.C., Sheriff Principal's Chambers, Sheriff Court House, 149 Ingram Street, Glasgow.	*Glasgow*, F. Middleton; J. Bayne; S. E. Bell; C. H. Johnston, Q.C.; J. I. Smith; P. G. B. McNeill; J. M. Peterson; N. D. MacLeod; A. C. Horsfall; J. J. Maguire; A. A. Bell, Q.C.; I. D. MacPhail; J. S. Mowat; M. Stone.	D. McMillan.....	J. Skeen.
South Strathclyde, Dumfries and Galloway.— R. Reid, Q.C., 33 Regent Terrace, Edinburgh.	*Hamilton*, I. A. Dickson; P. Thomson; N. E. D. Thomson. *Lanark*, M. G. Gillies, T.D., Q.C. *Ayr*, N. Gow, Q.C. *Stranraer*, *Kirkcudbright*, N. J. G. Ramsay (*also Dumfries*). *Dumfries*, K. G. Barr.......... *Airdrie*, A. R. McIlwraith; A. L. Stewart.	J. Davidson...... J. A. Watson..... J. Shaw.......... J. M. Ross....... M. Hardy .... W. B. Davidson... J. H. Thomson...	J. M. Tudhope. T. J. Cochrane. I. G. Pirie. R. F. Gibb. W. M. Morton. J. T. MacDougall. F. J. Keane.

★ Floating Sheriff

BRITISH FORCES BROADCASTING SERVICE

King's Buildings, Dean Stanley Street, London S.W.1

The Service came into existence during the early part of the Second World War to entertain, inform and to maintain the morale of the Serviceman in the field. No exact date can be given for the inception of the Service because, in answer to the need, special broadcasting for the Services overseas began in many different places almost simultaneously during 1942.

In 1960 B.F.B.S. was reorganised; a Director was appointed and a Head Office was created in London. In addition to directing the activities of the Service Head Office also produces every week some 30 hours of radio programmes featuring leading personalities in sport, music and entertainment, which the stations overseas cannot produce themselves. These programmes are recorded and dubbed in London and flown to the B.F.B.S. stations abroad, as well as to H.M. Ships in many parts of the world, and for the benefit of unaccompanied personnel serving in places such as Belize.

B.F.B.S. Television, a service combining programmes from all three channels in the U.K., started at Celle, near Hannover on September 18, 1975. When the full transmitter chain is completed, it will serve all the main concentrations of personnel and their families in West Germany.

The Combined Services Entertainment section of B.F.B.S. organises stage shows, about 45 of which are sent out every year to tour Northern Ireland and Commands overseas.

The staff of B.F.B.S. are all civilian, professional broadcasters and engineers. The Service is administered by the Army on behalf of the other two Services and is financed from Ministry of Defence funds.

Director, I. J. Woolf.

THE ARMED FORCES

MINISTRY OF DEFENCE
Main Building, Whitehall, S.W.1.
[01–218 9000]
Secretary of State for Defence, THE RT. HON. ROY MASON, M.P.......................£13,000
Private Secretary, J. F. Mayne.
Assistant Private Secretaries, A. J. Cragg; D. Spalding; E. E. Rowlands; P. A. Rotheram; R. C. Hack.
Parliamentary Private Secretary, A. L. Williams, M.P.
Minister of State for Defence, THE RT. HON. WILLIAM THOMAS RODGERS, M.P................£9,500
Private Secretary, C. T. Sandars.
Assistant Private Secretaries, S. Webb; B. J. Colver.
Parliamentary Under Secretary of State for Defence for the Royal Navy, A. E. P. Duffy, Ph.D., M.P.
£5,500
Parliamentary Under Secretary of State for Defence for the Army, R. C. Brown, M.P...........£5,500
Parliamentary Under Secretary of State for Defence for the Royal Air Force, A. J. Wellbeloved, M.P.
£5,500
Chief of Defence Staff Marshal of the Royal Air Force Sir Andrew Humphrey, G.C.B., O.B.E., D.F.C., A.F.C.
Chief of the Naval Staff and First Sea Lord, Admiral

Sir Edward Ashmore, G.C.B., D.S.C., A.D.C.
Chief of the General Staff, General Sir Roland Gibbs, G.C.B., C.B.E., D.S.O., M.C.
Chief of the Air Staff, Air Chief Marshal Sir Neil Cameron, G.C.B., C.B.E., D.S.O., D.F.C.

Permanent Under Secretary of State, Sir Frank Cooper, G.C.B., C.M.G........................£18,675
Private Secretary, J. F. Howe, O.B.E.
Second Permanent Under Secretary of State (Administration), Sir William Geraghty, K.C.B....£17,175
Vice Chief of Defence Staff, Vice-Admiral H. C. Leech.
Director-General of Intelligence (Ministry of Defence), Lt.-Gen. Sir David Willison, K.C.B., O.B.E., M.C.
£14,100
Deputy Chief of the Defence Staff (Intelligence), Air Marshal R. G. Wakeford, C.B., M.V.O., O.B.E., A.F.C.
Deputy Chief of Defence Staff (Operational Requirements), Lt.-Gen. Sir Hugh Cunningham, K.B.E.
Chief of Personnel and Logistics, Air Chief Marshal Sir Ruthven Wade, K.C.B., D.F.C.
Assist. Chief of Personnel and Logistics, Rear-Admiral F. W. Hearn.
Assistant Chiefs of Defence Staff, Rear-Admiral C.

Rusby, M.V.O. (*Operations*); Air Vice-Marshal J. Gingell, C.B.E. (*Policy*); Air Vice-Marshal S. M. Davidson, C.B.E. (*Signals*).

Chief of Naval Personnel and Second Sea Lord, Admiral Sir David Williams, K.C.B.
Chief of Fleet Support, Admiral Sir Peter White, K.B.E.
Vice-Chief of Naval Staff, Vice-Admiral R. D. Lygo.
Chief Scientist (Royal Navy), B. W. Lythall, C.B. £14,000

Adjutant-General, General Sir Jack Harman, K.C.B., O.B.E., M.C.
Quartermaster-General, General Sir William Jackson, K.C.B., O.B.E., M.C., A.D.C. (*Gen.*)
Vice-Chief of the General Staff, Lieutenant General Sir William Scotter, K.C.B., O.B.E., M.C.
Chief Scientist (Army), D. Cardwell, C.B... £14,000

Air Member for Personnel, Air Chief Marshal Sir John Aiken, K.C.B., D.F.C.
Air Member for Supply and Organization, Air Marshal Sir Alasdair Steedman, K.C.B., C.B.E., D.F.C.
Vice-Chief of the Air Staff, Air Marshal Sir D. G. Evans, C.B.E., D.F.C.
Chief Scientist (Royal Air Force), W. J. Charnley, C.B. £14,000

Defence Services Secretary, Air Vice-Marshal B. G. T. Stanbridge, C.B.E., M.V.O., A.F.C.
Naval Secretary, Rear-Admiral P. W. Buchanan.
Military Secretary, Lt.-Gen. Sir Patrick Howard-Dobson, K.C.B.
Air Secretary, Air Chief Marshal Sir Neville Stack, K.C.B., C.V.O., C.B.E., A.F.C.
Chief Scientific Adviser, Prof. Sir Hermann Bondi, K.C.B., F.R.S. £18,675
Director-General of Supply Co-ordination, Maj.-Gen. J. T. Stanyer, C.B.E. £12,000
Director, Women's Royal Naval Service, Commandant S. V. A. McBride.
Director, Women's Royal Army Corps, Brig. Eileen J. Nolan, C.B.E., Hon.A.D.C.
Director, Women's Royal Air Force, Group Captain Joy Tamblin
Chaplain of the Fleet, The Ven. B. A. O'Ferrall, Q.H.C.
Chaplain-General to the Forces, The Ven. P. Mallett, Q.H.C.
Chaplain-in-Chief, R.A.F., The Ven. J. H. Wilson, Q.H.C.
Matron-in-Chief, Queen Alexandra's Royal Naval Nursing Service, Miss P. Gould, R.R.C.
Matron-in-Chief (Army) and Director of Army Nursing Services, Brig. Helen Cattanach, C.B.E., R.R.C., Q.H.N.S.
Matron-in-Chief, Princess Mary's R.A.F. Nursing Service, Air Commandant Barbara M. Ducat-Amos, C.B., R.R.C., Q.H.N.S.
Chief Executive, Royal Dockyards, H. R. P. Chatten, C.B. £14,000
Commandant, Royal College of Defence Studies, Admiral Sir Ian Easton, K.C.B., D.S.C.
Deputy Under Secretaries of State,
(*Royal Navy*), D. R. J. Stephen, C.B. (*Civilian Management*); E. Broadbent, C.B., C.M.G.
(*Army*), R. C. Kent, C.B. (*Policy and Programmes*); A. P. Hockaday, C.B., C.M.G.
(*Air*) P. J. Hudson (*Finance and Budget*); A. R. M. Jaffray (*Personnel and Logistics*); R. Haynes, C.B. (each) £14,000
Director of Dockyard Manpower and Productivity, J. C. Allen. £12,000
Director of Dockyard Production and Support, Rear-Admiral M. H. Griffin, C.B.

Deputy Chief Adviser (Projects and Nuclear), V. H. B. Macklen, C.B. £14,000
Assistant Chief Scientific Advisers, Dr. D. H. Davies (*Projects*); Dr. I. J. Shaw, O.B.E. (*Studies*); Dr. F. H. Panton, M.B.E. (*Nuclear*) £12,000
Assistant Under Secretaries of State, G. F. Carpenter, E.R.D. (*Civilian Management (General)*); T. Cullen (*Naval Personnel*); B. M. Day (*Civilian Management (Administrators)*); J. Dromgoole (*General Staff*); H. L. Emmett (*Civilian Management (B)*); G. E. Emery (*Director-General of Defence Accounts*); D. M. Evans (*Programmes and Budget*); K. E. Glover (*Statistics*); G. T. Glue (*Director-Gen., Supplies and Transport (Naval)*); A. A. Golds (*Royal College of Defence Studies*); J. S. Goldsmith (*Fleet Support*); A. D. Harvey (*Organization (Air)*); A. M. Hastie-Smith (*Naval Staff*); T. C. G. James, C.M.G. (*Personnel (Air)*); J. H. Nelson (*Air Staff*); R. N. Noyes (*Logistics*); J. M. Parkin (*Adjutant Gen./Quartermaster Gen. (Army Dept.)*); A. A. Pritchard (*Operational Requirements*); J. Roberts (*Personnel (Defence Secretariat)*); B. E. Robson (*Supply (Air)*); J. L. Sabatini (*Management Services*); J. H. Taylor (*Central Finance*); W. I. Tupman (*Director General of Internal Audit*); C. A. Whitmore (*Defence Staff*) £12,000
General Managers of H.M. Dockyards, F. P. Skinner (*Chatham*); Capt. J. Wright, D.S.C., R.N. (ret.) (*Devonport*); W. R. Seward (*Portsmouth*); K. H. W. Thomas (*Rosyth*) £12,000
Deputy Chief Scientist (Royal Navy), Dr. J. Tunstead. £12,000
Deputy Chief Scientist (Army), Dr. E. R. R. Holmberg. £12,000
Deputy Chief Scientist (R.A.F.), E. Benn. £12,000
Director, Defence Operational Analysis Establishment, Dr. A. Stratton. £12,000

Procurement Executive

Chief Executive, E. C. Cornford, C.B. £18,675
Private Secretary, R. J. Rooks.
Deputy Under-Secretary of State (Policy), G. H. Green £14,000
Head of Defence Sales, Sir Lester Suffield, C.B. £15,100
Deputies to Head of Defence Sales, J. L. Roberts (*Assistant Under Secretary*) (£12,000); Maj.-Gen. A. J. Jackson.
Assistant Under Secretaries, J. E. D. Street (*Sales Admin.*); G. C. B. Dodds (*International and Industrial Policy*) £12,000
Director-General Defence Contracts, E. F. Hedger, O.B.E. £12,000
Deputy Under-Secretary of State (Administration), F. W. Armstrong. £14,000
Director-General Quality Assurance, P. Corner £12,000
Assistant Under Secretaries, J. G. Ashcroft (*Management Services*); E. W. Sarginson (*Personnel*); P. H. M. Brightling (*Finance*) £12,000
Master-General of the Ordnance, General Sir John Gibbon, K.C.B., O.B.E.
Deputy Master-General of the Ordnance, Maj.-Gen. G. Burch
Director-General, Guided Weapons and Electronics (Army), P. R. Wallis £13,230
Assistant Under Secretary (Ordnance), N. Craig £12,000
Director-General Fighting Vehicles and Engineer Equipment, Maj.-Gen. A. M. L. Hogge.
Director-General Weapons (Army), Maj.-Gen. D. E. Isles, O.B.E.
Managing Director Royal Ordnance Factories, S. C. Bacon, C.B. £14,100

Directors-General, Ordnance Factories, R. J. MacDonald (Production); J. S. W. Henderson (Procurement and Admin.); (vacant) (Finance); W. Meakin (Weapons and Fighting Vehicles)........£12,000

Controller of the Navy, Vice-Admiral R. P. Clayton.

Assistant Controller, Rear-Admiral G. W. Bridle, M.B.E.

Assistant Under Secretary (Material) (Naval), M. G. Power...........................£12,000

Director-General Ships, R. J. Daniel, O.B.E.

Deputy Director-General Ships, Rear-Admiral D. G. Satow.

Director of Research, Ships and Scientific Adviser to Director General Ships, F. S. Burt......£12,000

Director of Naval Ship Production, Rear-Admiral P. R. Marrack.

Director of Warships Design, L. J. Rydill, O.B.E.
£14,160

Deputy Directors, R. Hawkes (Design Constructive " A "); J. C. Lawrence (Design Constructive " B "); Capt. W. F. Moore, R.N. (Design Marine Engineering); F. W. Butler (Design Electrical); F. E. Hutchins (Engineering Electrical); C. P. Oldridge (Ship Production).......................£12,000

Director of Engineering (Ships), Rear Admiral E. J. W. Flower.

Deputy Directors, Capt. K. B. Birkett, R.N. (Engineering (Marine)); P. E. Hutchins (Engineering (Electrical)); L. J. Brooks (Engineering (Constructive)).

Director-General Weapons (Navy), Vice-Admiral Sir Philip Watson, K.B.E., M.V.O.

Director of Surface Weapons Projects (Navy), Commodore L. S. Bryson

Director Underwater Weapons Projects (Naval), J. E. Twinn.............................£12,000

Director Weapons (Production), J. I. G. Evans £12,000

Chief Polaris Executive, Rear-Admiral W. D. S. Scott, C.B.

Deputy Chief Polaris Executive, Commodore P. G. M. Herbert, O.B.E.

Controller Aircraft, Air Marshal Sir Douglas Lowe, K.C.B., D.F.C., A.F.C.

Deputy Under-Secretary of State (Air Systems) (P.E.) R. Anderson........................£14,000

Vice-Controller Aircraft, L. F. Nicholson, C.B £13,230

Deputy Controllers, Dr. W. Stewart (Aircraft " A ") (£13,230); Rear-Admiral D. J. Titford (Aircraft "B"); Air Vice-Marshal A. D. Dick, C.B.E., A.F.C. (Aircraft "C"); H. W. Pout, O.B.E. (Aircraft "D")
£13,230

Director-General, Strategic Electronic Systems, Air Vice-Marshal A. A. Morris............£12,000

Director-General, Air Electronic Systems, S. E. Shapcott..........................£12,000

Assistant Under Secretary (Aircraft), J. N. H. Blelloch
£12,000

Director-General of Equipment, F. O'Hara..£12,000

Director-General Multi-Role Combat Aircraft, H. W. Turner.............................£12,000

Director-General Engines (PE), I. M. Davidson
£12,000

Director-General Performance and Cost Analysis, D. J. Harper.............................£12,000

Controller Research and Development Establishments and Research, Dr. W. H. Penley, C.B., C.B.E.
£15,100

Deputy Controller " A " R & D Estabs. and Research and Chief Scientists (Royal Navy), B. W. Lythall, C.B................................£14,000

Director-General Establishments, Resources and Programmes " A ", Dr. D. H. Parkinson...£12,000

Director-General Research (Electronics), Dr. M. H. Oliver............................£12,000

Deputy Controller " B " R & D Estabs. and Research and Chief Scientist (Army), D. Cardwell, C.B.
£14,000

Director-General Establishments, Resources and Programmes " B ", Dr. F. H. Panton......£13,230

Director-General Research Weapons, P. R. Wallis
£12,000

Deputy Controller " C " R & D Estabs. and Research and Chief Scientist, (R.A.F.,) W. J. Charnley, C.B.
£14,000

Director-General for Research, "C", J. F. Barnes
£12,000

Assistant Under-Secretary (R & D Estabs. and Research Administration), V. H. E. Cole....£12,000

Research Establishments

Director, Admiralty Surface Weapons Establishment, J. Alvey £13,230

Director, Admiralty Underwater Weapons Establishment, I. L. Davies...................£13,230

Director, Admiralty Research Laboratory, A. B. Mitchell............................£12,000

Director, Chemical Defence Establishment, Dr. R. G. H. Watson............................£12,000

Director, Micro-Biological Research Establishment, Prof. R. J. C. Harris.......................£12,000

Director, Military Vehicles and Engineering Establishment, I. H. Johnston...............£12,000

Director, National Gas Turbine Establishment, T. H. Kerr.............................£12,000

Director, Royal Aircraft Establishment, R. P. Probert, C.B................................£14,000

Director, Royal Armament Research and Development Establishment, W. B. H. Lord..........£13,230

Director, Royal Signals and Radar Establishments, R. J. Lees..........................£13,230

Meteorological Office

London Road, Bracknell, Berks.
[Bracknell: 20242]

The Meteorological Office is the State Meteorological Service. It forms part of the Ministry of Defence, the Director General being ultimately responsible to the Secretary of State for Defence.

Except for the common services provided by other government departments as part of their normal functions, the cost of the Meteorological Office is borne by Defence Votes.

Of the expenditure chargeable to Defence Votes about £16,900,000 represents expenditure associated with staff and £8,400,000 on stores, communications and miscellaneous services. About £5,600,000 is recovered from outside bodies in respect of special services rendered, sales of meteorological equipment, etc.

Director General, B. J. Mason, C.B., D.SC., F.R.S.
£14,000

Director of Research, J. S. Sawyer, F.R.S.....£12,000

Director of Services, J. K. Bannon, I.S.O. £12,000

THE ROYAL NAVY

THE QUEEN

Admirals of the Fleet

The Lord Fraser of North Cape, G.C.B., K.B.E., *born* Feb. 5, 1888.........................Oct. 22, 1948
H.R.H. the Prince Philip, Duke of Edinburgh, K.G., P.C., K.T., O.M., G.B.E., *born* June 10, 1921...Jan. 15, 1953
The Earl Mountbatten of Burma, K.G., P.C., G.C.B., O.M., G.C.S.I., G.C.I.E., G.C.V.O., D.S.O., *born*
June 25, 1900..Oct. 22, 1956
Sir Caspar John, G.C.B., *born* March 22, 1903..May 23, 1962
Sir Varyl C. Begg, G.C.B., D.S.O., D.S.C., *born* Oct. 1, 1908...............................Aug. 12, 1968
Sir Peter Hill-Norton, G.C.B., *born* Feb. 8, 1915..March 12, 1971
Sir Michael Pollock, G.C.B., M.V.O., D.S.C., *born* Oct. 19, 1916...........................March 1, 1974

Admirals

Sir Edward Ashmore, G.C.B., D.S.C. (*Chief of Naval Staff and First Sea Lord*) (*First and Principal Naval Aide-de-Camp*).

Sir Terence Lewin, G.C.B., M.V.O., D.S.C. (*C.-in-C., Naval Home Command*).

Sir David Williams, K.C.B. (*Chief of Naval Personnel and Second Sea Lord*).

Sir John Treacher, K.C.B. (*C.-in-C., Fleet, Allied C.-in-C., Channel and C.-in-C., Eastern Atlantic Area*).

Sir Ian Easton, K.C.B., D.S.C. (*Commandant, Royal College of Defence Studies*).

Sir Peter White, K.B.E. (*Chief of Fleet Support*).

Vice-Admirals

Sir James Watt, Q.H.S. (*Medical Director-General*).

Sir Anthony Troup, K.C.B., D.S.C. (*Flag Officer, Scotland and North Ireland, Commander, Northern Sub-Area Eastern Atlantic and Commander Nore Sub-Area Channel*).

Sir Iwan Raikes, K.C.B., C.B.E., D.S.C.

Sir Philip Watson, K.B.E., M.V.O. (*Director-General Weapons and Chief Naval Engineering Officer*.

H. C. Leach (*Vice-Chief of the Defence Staff*).

J. G. Jungius (*Deputy Supreme Allied Commander, Atlantic*).

A. G. Tait, D.S.C. (*Flag Officer, Plymouth, Port Admiral Devonport, Commander Sub-Area Eastern Atlantic and Commander Plymouth Sub-Area Channel*).

R. D. Lygo (*Vice-Chief of Naval Staff*).

A. S. Morton (*Flag Officer, First Flotilla*).

R. P. Clayton (*Controller of the Navy*).

L. R. Bell-Davies (*European Representative, Supreme Allied Commander, Atlantic*).

R. D Macdonald, C.B.E. (*Chief of Staff to Commander Allied Forces, Southern Europe*).

P. E. C. Berger, M.V.O., D.S.C. (*Chief of Staff to C.-in-C., Fleet*).

Rear-Admirals

W. D. S. Scott, C.B. (*Chief Polaris Executive*).

M. H. Griffin, C.B. (*Director of Dockyard Production and Support*).

H. W. E. Hollins, C.B. (*Admiral Commanding Reserves*).

J. H. F. Eberle (*Flag Officer, Carriers and Amphibious Ships*).

A. G. Watson, C.B. (*Assistant Chief of Naval Staff (Operational Requirements)*).

J. O. Roberts, C.B. (*Flag Officer, Naval Air Command*).

D. G. Satow (*Deputy Director-General. Ships*).

H. Gardner, C.B. (*Senior Naval Member, Ordnance Board*).

D. A. Loram, M.V.O. (*Commandant National Defence College*).

S. F. Berthon (*Asst. Chief of Nava Staff (Operational Requirements)*).

A. D. Cassidi (*Director General Naval Manpower and Training*).

F. W. Hearn (*Assistant Chief of Personnel and Logistics and Chief Naval Supply and Secretariat Officer*).

W. N. Ash, M.V.O. (*Director of Service Intelligence*).

A. J. Monk, C.B.E. (*Rear Admiral Engineering to FONAC*).

P. R. Marrack (*Director of Naval Ship Production*).

S. R. Sandford, C.B.

C. Rusby, M.V.O. (*Assistant Chief of Defence Staff (Operations)*).

A.E. Cadman, C.B., O.B.E., Q.H.D.S. (*Director of Naval Dental Services*).

T. B. Homan (*Director-General Naval Personnel Services*).

J. M. Forbes.

J. D. E. Fieldhouse (*Flag Officer, Submarines*).

G. W. Bridle, M.B.E. (*Assistant Controller of the Navy*).

K. G. Ager (*Flag Officer, Admiralty Interview Board*).

C.R.P.C.Branson, C.B.E. (*Assistant Chief of Naval Staff (Operations)*).

J. G. P. Rawlins, O.B.E., Q.H.P. (*Medical Officer-in-Charge, Institute of Naval Medicine and Dean of Naval Medicine*).

J. A. Bell (*Director of Naval Education Service*).

P. D. G. Pugh, O.B.E., Q.H.S. (*Surgeon Rear-Admiral, Naval Hospitals*).

D. W. Haslam, O.B.E. (*Hydrographer of the Navy*).

O. N. A. Cecil (*Flag Officer, Malta*).

J. R. S. Gerard-Pearse.

E. J. W. Flower (*Director of Engineering (Ships)*).

R. W. Halliday, D.S.C. (*Commander British Navy Staff, Washington and UK National Representative to SACLANT*).

H. P. Janion (*Flag Officer, Royal Yachts*).

H. R. Mallows, Q.H.P. (*Surgeon Rear-Admiral, Ships and Establishments*).

J. S. C. Lea (*Assistant Chief of Fleet Support*).

M. L. Stacey (*Flag Officer and Port Admiral, Gibraltar*).

W. T. Pillar (*Port Admiral, Rosyth*).

A. J. Cooke (*Senior Naval Member, Royal College of Defence Studies*).

W. J. McClune (*Chief Staff Officer (Engineering) to C.-in-C. Fleet*).

B. C. Perowne (*Director of Management and Support Intelligence*).

W. D. M. Staveley (*Flag Officer, Second Flotilla*).

D. G. Titford (*Deputy Controller of Aircraft "B"*).

J. H. E. Baird (*Chief of Staff to C.-in-C., Naval Home Command*).

P. W. Buchanan (*Naval Secretary*).

G. I. Pritchard (*Flag Officer, Sea Training*).

C. A. W. Weston (*Admiral President, R.N.C. Greenwich*).

C. M. Bevan (*Flag Officer Medway and Port Admiral, Chatham*).

B. J. Straker (*Assistant Chief of Naval Staff (Policy)*).

W. J. Grahame (*Flag Officer and Port Admiral, Portsmouth*).

HER MAJESTY'S FLEET

Type/Class	Operational, preparing for service or engaged on trials and training	Reserve or undergoing long refit, conversion, etc.
Aircraft Carrier................	*Ark Royal*	
ASW Carriers–Commando Ships.	*Hermes*	*Bulwark*
Submarines...................	(23)	(8)
Polaris Submarines...........	*Repulse, Renown, Revenge*	*Resolution*
Fleet Submarines.............	*Valiant, Warspite, Superb,★ Churchill, Dreadnought, Swiftsure, Sovereign*	*Conqueror, Courageous*
OBERON Class...............	*Onyx, Otus, Opossum, Opportune, Ocelot, Onslaught, Odin, Otter, Osiris, Oracle, Orpheus, Oberon*	*Olympus*
PORPOISE Class..............	*Finwhale, Narwhal, Cachalot, Walrus*	*Sea Lion, Porpoise*
Assault Ships.................	*Fearless*	*Intrepid*
Cruisers.....................	*Tiger*	*Blake*
Guided-Missile Destroyers	(9)	
County Class................	*Norfolk, Kent, Devonshire, Antrim, Fife, Glamorgan, London*	
Type 82.....................		*Bristol*
Type 42.....................	*Sheffield, Birmingham★*	
General Purpose Frigates	(33)	(6)
LEANDER Class...............	*Leander, Ajax, Galatea, Juno, Danae, Andromeda, Charybdis, Jupiter, Hermione, Bacchante, Scylla, Achilles, Diomede, Apollo, Ariadne, Penelope, Naiad, Euryalus, Aurora, Cleopatra*	*Arethusa, Phoebe, Sirius, Dido, Minerva, Argonaut*
Type 21.....................	*Amazon, Antelope, Ambuscade, Arrow★, Active★*	
Tribal Class.................	*Ashanti, Gurkha, Mohawk, Nubian, Eskimo, Tartar, Zulu*	
MERMAID Class..............	*Mermaid*	
Anti-Aircraft Frigates		
Type 41.....................		*Lynx, Jaguar*
Aircraft Direction Frigates	(3)	
Type 61.....................	*Salisbury, Llandaff*	*Chichester, Lincoln*
Anti-Submarine Frigates........	(14)	
	Rothesay, Yarmouth, Plymouth, Lowestoft, Berwick, Falmouth, Brighton, Rhyl, Eastbourne, Torquay	*Londonderry*
Type 14.....................	*Exmouth, Keppel, Dundas*	*Hardy*
Mine Countermeasure Forces	(37)	(3)
Coastal Minesweepers/Mine-hunters....................	(32)	
Inshore Minesweepers........	(5)	
Fleet Maintenance Ships.......		*Triumph*
Submarine Depot Ship.........	*Forth*	
MCM Support Ship...........	*Abdiel*	
Diving Trials Ship............	*Reclaim*	
Trials Ship	*Matapan*	
Coastal Patrol Vessels.........	(5)	
Fast Training/Patrol Boats.....	(7)	
Seaward Defence Boats.........	*Droxford, Dee*	
Royal Yacht/Hospital Ship......	*Britannia*	
Ice Patrol Ship...............	*Endurance*	
Survey Ships/Vessels...........	(13)	
Submarine Tender	*Wakeful*	
Offshore Patrol Vessels.........	*Jura, Reward, Jersey,★ Guernsey★*	
Patrol Craft..................	*Alert, Vigilant*	

★Under construction on March 31, 1976, and planned to enter Service during the year.

ROYAL MARINES

The Corps of Royal Marines, about 7,000 strong, first formed in 1664, is part of the Royal Navy and provides Britain's sea soldiers, in particular a commando brigade Headquarters and four commandos, of which one is serving in Malta and one specializes in mountain and arctic warfare. They also serve at sea in H.M. Ships and provide landing craft crews, special boat sections (frogmen) and other detachments for amphibious operations. The Royal Marines Band Section provides bands for the Royal Navy and Royal Marines.

The Royal Marines Reserve of about 1,000 volunteers consists of five main centres at London, Bristol, Liverpool, Newcastle and Glasgow.

Commander-General, Royal Marines, Lieut.-General Sir Peter Whiteley, K.C.B., O.B.E.

Major-Generals, P. J. Ovens, O.B.E., M.C. (*Commandant, Joint Warfare Establishment*); D. C. Alexander, C.B.; R. J. Ephraims, O.B.E. (*Commando Forces*); R. P. W. Wall (*Chief of Staff*); J. C. C. Richards (*Training Group*).

THE ARMY

THE QUEEN

Field Marshals

Sir Claude J. E. Auchinleck, G.C.B., G.C.I.E., C.S.I., D.S.O., O.B.E., Col. 1 Punjab R. and Indian Grenadiers, *born June 21, 1884*...June 1, 1946

H.R.H. the Prince Philip, Duke of Edinburgh, K.G., P.C., K.T., O.M., G.B.E., Field-Marshal, Australian Military Forces, Col.-in-Chief, Q.R.I.H., D.E.R.R., Q. O. Hldrs., Corps of Royal Electrical and Mechanical Engineers, A.C.F., Col. W. G., *born June 10, 1921*.......Jan. 15, 1953

The Lord Harding of Petherton, G.C.B., C.B.E., D.S.O., M.C., *born Feb. 10, 1896*............July 21, 1953

Sir Gerald W. R. Templer, K.G., G.C.B., G.C.M.G., K.B.E., D.S.O., Col. R. H. G./D., *born Sept. 11, 1898*...Nov. 27, 1956

Sir Richard A. Hull, G.C.B., D.S.O., *born May 7, 1907*....................................Feb. 8, 1965

Sir A. James H. Cassels, G.C.B., K.B.E., D.S.O., *born Feb. 28, 1907*..........................Feb. 29, 1968

Sir Geoffrey H. Baker, G.C.B., C.M.G., C.B.E., M.C., Col. Comdt. R.A. and R.H.A. (*Constable of the Royal Palace and Fortress of London*) (*Master Gunner, St. James's Park*), *born June 20, 1912*
March 31, 1971

Sir Michael Carver, G.C.B., C.B.E., D.S.O., M.C., Col. Comdt., R.A.C., *born April 24, 1915*......July 18, 1973

Generals

Sir John Sharp, K.C.B., M.C., A.D.C. (*Gen.*), Col. Comdt. R.H.A., R.A. (*C.-in-C., Allied Forces, Northern Europe*).

Sir William Jackson, G.B.E., K.C.B., M.C., Col. Gurkha Engrs, Col. Comdt. R.E. and R.A.O.C. (*Quartermaster-General*).

Sir Harry Tuzo, G.C.B., O.B.E., M.C., A.D.C. (*Gen.*) Col. Comdt. R.A. (*Deputy Supreme Allied Commander, Europe*).

Sir John Gibbon, K.C.B., O.B.E., A.D.C. (*Gen.*), (*Master General of the Ordnance*).

Sir Roland Gibbs, G.C.B., C.B.E., D.S.O., M.C., A.D.C. (*Gen.*), Col. Comdt. 2 R.G.J. and Para. Regt. (*Chief of the General Staff*).

Sir David Fraser, K.C.B., O.B.E. (*U.K. Military Representive, H.Q., N.A.T.O.*).

Sir Frank King, G.C.B., M.B.E., Col. Comdt. A.A.C. (*C.-in-C., B.A.O.R.*).

Sir Jack Harman, K.C.B., O.B.E., M.C., Col. 1 Q.D.G. (*Adjutant General*).

Sir Edwin Bramell, K.C.B., O.B.E., M.C., Col. Comdt. 3 R.G.J. (*C.-in-C., United Kingdom Land Forces*).

Lieutenant-Generals

Sir James Baird, K.B.E., M.D., Q.H.P. (*Director-General, Army Medical Services*).

Sir Patrick Howard-Dobson, K.C.B.

Sir James Wilson, K.B.E., M.C., Deputy Col. (Lancs.) Royal Regt. of Fusiliers Col. Comdt. Queen's Div. and R.A.E.C. (*G.O.C., South-East District*).

Sir William Scotter, K.C.B., O.B.E., M.C., Col. King's Own Border (*Vice-Chief of the General Staff*).

Sir David Scott-Barrett, K.B.E., M.C., Col. Comdt. Scottish Div. (*G.O.C., Scotland and Governor of Edinburgh Castle*).

Sir David House, K.C.B., C.B.E., M.C., Col. Comdt. The Light Div. and S.A.S.C. (*G.O.C., and Director of Operations, Northern Ireland*).

Sir Rollo Pain, K.C.B., M.C., Col. Comdt., M.P.S.C. (*Director of Movements*).

Sir Richard Worsley, K.C.B., O.B.E. (*Commander 1, (B.R.) Corps*).

Sir John Archer, K.C.B., O.B.E. (*Commander, British Forces, Hong Kong*).

Sir John Cunningham, K.B.E. (*Deputy Chief of Defence Staff (Operational Requirements*)).

Sir Hugh Beach, K.C.B., O.B.E., M.C., Col. Comdt. R.E.M.E. and R.P.C. (*Deputy C.-in-C., United Kingdom Land Forces*).

R. C. Ford, C.B., C.B.E. (*Military Secretary*).

Major-Generals

T. A. Richardson, C.B., M.B.E. (*Defence and Military Adviser India*).

A. H. Farrar-Hockley, D.S.O., M.B.E. M.C. (*Director of Combat Development (Army*)).

H. E. Roper, C.B., Col. Comdt., R. Signals.

J. M. W. Badcock, C.B., M.B.E., Col. Comdt., R. Signals (*Head of British Defence Liaison Staff and Defence Attaché, Canberra*).

J. M. Brockbank, C.B.E., M.C. (*Vice-Adjutant-General*).

H. D. G. Butler, C.B. (*Chief of Staff, Contingency Planning, SHAPE*).

D. J. St. M. Tabor, M.C. (*G.O.C., Eastern District*).

T. M. Creasey, C.B., O.B.E. (*Director of Infantry*).

M. E. Tickell, C.B.E., M.C. (*Commandant, Royal Military College of Science*).

P. Blunt, M.B.E., G.M., Col. Comdt. R.C.T. and Hon. Col. 160 Regt. R.C.T. (T.A.V.R.).

J. G. R. Allen, C.B., Col. Comdt. R.T.R. (*Senior Army Member, Royal College of Defence Studies*).

R. Lyon, C.B., O.B.E. (*G.O.C., South-West District*).

J. M. Gow, Col. Comdt. Int. Corps (*Director of Army Training*).

P. J. H. Leng, C.B., M.B.E., M.C. (*Director of Military Operations*).

P. Hudson, C.B.E. (*Chief of Staff to C.-in-C., Allied Forces, Northern Europe*).

G. Burch (*Deputy Master-General of the Ordnances*).

P. J. N. Ward, C.B.E. (*G.O.C. London District and Commander, Household Division*).

J. W. Stanier, M.B.E. (*Commandant, Staff College, Camberley*).

W. D. Mangham (*Vice-Quartermaster General*).

R. L. C. Dixon, M.C.

A. P. Dignan, M.B.E., Q.H.S. (*Director of Army Surgery and Consultant Surgeon to the Army*).

K. G. Galloway, O.B.E., Q.H.D.S. (*Director of Army Dental Services*).

J. Kelsey, C.B.E. (*Director of Military Survey*).

J. H. Page, O.B.E., M.C. (*Director of Personal Services*).

R. M. Carnegie, O.B.E. (*Chief of Staff, H.Q., B.A.O.R.*).

G. L. C. Cooper, M.C. (*Director, Army Staff Duties*).

P. C. Shapland, M.B.E. (*Director, Volunteers, Territorials and Cadets*).

C. E. Eberhardie, M.B.E., M.C. *Assistant Chief of Staff (Intelligence) SHAPE*).

P. A. M. Tighe, M.B.E. (*Signal Officer in Chief*).

R. W. L. McAlister, O.B.E. (*Deputy Commander Land Forces, Hong Kong*).

G. H. Mills, O.B.E. (*Director of Manning(Army)*).

J. H. Foster (*Engineer-in-Chief*).

K. J. McQueen (*G.O.C., North-West District*).

H. Macdonald-Smith (*Director Electrical and Mechanical Engineering*).

D. B. Wood (*Director of Army Quartering*).

H. S. Gavourin, M.B.E., Q.H.S. (*Commandant, Royal Army Medical College*).

R. P. Bradshaw (*Director of Medical Services, B.A.O.R.*).

W. O'Brien, O.B.E., M.D., Q.H.P. (*Director of Army Medicine*).

A. M. L. Hogge (*Director-General, Fighting Vehicles and Engineering Equipment*).

K. Perkins, M.B.E., D.F.C. (*Commander, Sultan's Armed Forces*).

D. G. Milne, Q.H.S. (*Deputy Director, Army Medical Services*).

S. E. Large, M.B.E., Q.H.P. (*Director of Medical Services, U.K. Land Forces*).

D. T. Young (*Commander, Land Forces, N. Ireland*).

K. Saunders, O.B.E. (*Paymaster-in-Chief*).

D. E. Isles, O.B.E., Col. Comdt. King's Div., Col. D.W.R. (*Director-General, Weapons (Army)*).

H. E. M. L. Garrett, C.B.E. (*Vice-Adjutant-General*).

R. M. F. Redgrave, M.C. (*G.O.C. Berlin (British Sector)*).

H. A. J. Sturge (*Chief Signals Officer, B.A.O.R.*).

P. J. O'B. Minogue (*Commander, Base Organisation, R.A.O.C.*).

T. L. Morony, O.B.E. (*Director, Royal Artillery*).

J. A. Ward-Booth, O.B.E. (*Director, Army Air Corps*).

P. H. Benson, C.B.E., Hon. Col. 161 Reg., R.C.T. (*Transport Officer-in-Chief*).

A. J. Jackson (*Deputy to Military Board of Defence Sales*).

F. E. Kitson, C.B.E., M.C. (*G.O.C. 2 Div.*).

N. T. Bagnall, M.C. (*G.O.C., 4 Div.*).

D. B. Alexander-Sinclair (*G.O.C. 1 Div.*).

T. S. C. Streatfeild, O.B.E. (*Chief of Staff, Logistics*).

A. G. C. Jones, M.C. (*President, Regular Commissions Board*).

S. L. Lecky, O.B.E. (*Director, Military Assistance Office*).

F. J. Plaskett, M.B.E. (*Director of Movements*).

W. J. Macfarlane (*Chief of Staff, U.K. Land Forces*).

J. D. C. Graham, C.B.E. (*G.O.C., Wales*).

R. L. S. Green (*Vice-President, Ordnance Board*).

G. B. Wilson (*Major-Gen., Royal Artillery, B.A.O.R.*).

M. J. H. Walsh (*G.O.C., No. 3 Div.*).

D. W. R. Walker (*Commander, Support Group, R.E.M.E.*).

H. G. Woods, M.B.E., M.C. (*G.O.C., North-East District*).

L. H. Plummer, C.B.E. (*Asst., Joint Services Liaison Organization, B.A.O.R.*).

D. S. Appleby, M.C., T.D. (*Director, Army Legal Services*).

L. Howell, C.B.E. (*Director of Army Education*).

L. W. A. Gingell (*i/c Administration, U.K. Land Forces*).

P. A. Downward (*G.O.C., West Midlands District*).

M. Callan (*Director of Ordnance Services*).

C. B. Pollard (*Chief Engineer, B.A.O.R.*).

P. D. Reid (*Director Royal Armoured Corps*).

CONSTITUTION OF THE BRITISH ARMY

The Regular Forces include the following Arms, Branches and Corps. Soldiers' Records Offices are shown at the end of each group; the records of officers are maintained at the Ministry of Defence.

Household Cavalry.—The Life Guards; The Blues and Royals (Royal Horse Guards and 1st Dragoons). *Records*, Horse Guards, London, S.W.1.

Royal Armoured Corps.—Cavalry Regiments: 1st The Queen's Dragoon Guards; The Royal Scots Dragoon Guards (Carabiniers and Greys); 4th/7th Royal Dragoon Guards; 5th Royal Inniskilling Dragoon Guards; The Queen's Own Hussars; The Queen's Royal Irish Hussars; 9th/12th Royal Lancers (Prince of Wales's); The Royal Hussars (Prince of Wales's Own), 13th/18th Royal Hussars (Queen Mary's Own); 14th/20th King's Hussars; 15th/19th The King's Royal Hussars; 16th/5th The Queen's Royal Lancers; 17th/21st Lancers; Royal Tank Regiment comprising four regular regiments. *Records*, Friern Barnet Lane, Whetstone, N.20.

Artillery.—The Royal Regiment of Artillery. *Records*, Foots Cray, Sidcup, Kent.

Engineers.—The Corps of Royal Engineers. *Records*, Ditchling Road, Brighton.

Signals.—The Royal Corps of Signals. *Records*, Balmore House, Caversham, Reading.

Infantry.—The Brigades/Regiments of Infantry of the Line have now been reformed into Divisions as follows:—

The Guard's Division—Grenadier, Coldstream, Scots, Irish and Welsh Guards. Divisional HQ: HQ Household Division, Horse Guards, S.W.1. *Depot:* Pirbright Camp, Brookwood, Surrey. *Records:* Each Regiment of Foot Guards has its own Record Office. Grenadier Guards and Scots Guards at 4 Bloomsbury Court, W.C.1; Coldstream, Irish and Welsh Guards at King's Buildings, Dean Stanley Street, S.W.1.

The Scottish Division—The Royal Scots (The Royal Regiment); The Royal Highland Fusiliers (Princess Margaret's Own Glasgow and Ayrshire Regiment); The King's Own Scottish Borderers; The Black Watch (Royal Highland Regiment); Queen's Own Highlanders (Seaforth and Camerons); The Gordon Highlanders; The Argyll and Sutherland Highlanders (Princess Louise's). *Divisional HQ*, The Castle, Edinburgh. *Depots*, Scottish Divisional Depôts, Glencorse, Milton Bridge, Midlothian and Gordon Barracks, Bridge of Don, Aberdeen. *Records*, Cavalry Barracks, Fulford, York.

The Queen's Division—The Queen's Regi-

ment, The Royal Regiment of Fusiliers, The Royal Anglian Regiment. *Divisional HQ*, Bassingbourn Barracks, Royston, Herts. *Depôt*, Bassingbourn Barracks, Royston, Herts. *Records*, Higher Barracks, Exeter, Devon.

The King's Division—The King's Own Royal Border Regiment, The King's Regiment; The Prince of Wales's Own Regiment of Yorkshire; The Green Howards (Alexandra, Princess of Wales's Own Yorkshire Regiment); The Royal Irish Rangers (27th (Inniskilling) 83rd and 87th); The Queen's Lancashire Regiment; The Duke of Wellington's Regiment (West Riding). *Divisional HQ*, Imphal Barracks, York. *Depôts*, The King's Division Depôt (Lancashire) Fulwood Barracks, Preston, Lancs. The King's Division Depôt (Yorkshire), Queen Elizabeth Barracks, Strensall, Yorks. The King's Division Depôt (Royal Irish Rangers), St. Patrick's Barracks, Ballymena, Northern Ireland. *Records*, Cavalry Barracks, Fulford, York.

The Prince of Wales's Division—The Devonshire and Dorset Regiment; The Cheshire Regiment; The Royal Welch Fusiliers, The Royal Regiment of Wales; The Gloucestershire Regiment; The Worcestershire and Sherwood Foresters Regiment (29th/45th Foot); The Royal Hampshire Regiment; The Staffordshire Regiment (The Prince of Wales's); The Duke of Edinburgh's Royal Regiment (Berkshire and Wiltshire). *Divisional HQ*, Whittington Barracks, Lichfield, Staffs. *Depôts*, Wessex Depôt, The Prince of Wales's Division, Wyvern Barracks, Exeter, Devon; Mercian Depôt, The Prince of Wales's Division, Whittington Barracks, Lichfield, Staffs; Welsh Depôt, The Prince of Wales's Division, Cwrt-y-Gollen, Crickhowell, Powys. *Records*, Cavalry Barracks, Fulford, York.

The Light Division—The Light Infantry; The Royal Green Jackets, Divisional H.Q., Peninsula Barracks, Winchester, Hants. *Depôts*, The Light Infantry Depôt, Sir John Moore Barracks, Copthorne, Shrewsbury, Salop. The Rifle Depôt, Peninsula Barracks, Winchester, Hants. *Records*, Higher Barracks, Exeter.

The Parachute Regiment—*Depot*, Browning Barracks, Aldershot, Hants. *Records*, Higher Barracks, Exeter.

The Brigade of Gurkhas—2nd King Edward VII's Own Gurkha Rifles (The Sirmoor Rifles); 6th Queen Elizabeth's Own Gurkha Rifles; 7th Duke of Edinburgh's Own Gurkha Rifles; 10th Princess Mary's Own Gurkha Rifles, Gurkha Engineers, Gurkha Signals, Gurkha Transport Regt. *Brigade HQ*, Victoria Barracks, Hong Kong. *Depot*, Training Depôt, Brigade of Gurkhas, Sek Kong (South), Hong Kong, B.F.P.O. 1. *Records*, The Brigade of Gurkha Record Office, Hong Kong, B.F.P.O. 1.

The Special Air Service Regiment—*Regimental HQ*, Duke of York's Headquarters, Sloane Square, S.W.3. *Depôt*, Bradbury Lines, Hereford. *Records*, Higher Barracks, Exeter, Devon.

Royal Corps of Transport, Army Catering Corps. *Records*, Ore Place, Hastings.

Royal Army Medical Corps, Royal Army Dental Corps, Queen Alexandra's Royal Army Nursing Corps, and Women's Royal Army Corps. *Records*, Lower Barracks, Winchester.

Royal Army Ordnance Corps, Royal Electrical and Mechanical Engineers. *Records*, Glen Parva Barracks, Saffron Road, South Wigston, Leicester.

Small Arms School Corps. *Records*, Higher Barracks, Exeter.

General Service Corps. *Records*, Cavalry Barracks, Fulford Road, York.

Army Air Corps, Royal Military Police, Royal Army Pay Corps, Royal Army Veterinary Corps, Royal Army Educational Corps, Royal Pioneer Corps, Intelligence Corps, and other ancillary corps not listed above. *Records*, Higher Barracks, Exeter, Devon.

Ulster Defence Regiment *HQ*, Magheralave Road, Lisburn, Co. Antrim. *Records*, Cavalry Barracks, Fulford Road, York.

The Territorial and Army Volunteer Reserve (TAVR) came into being on April 1, 1967, replacing the Army Emergency Reserve and the Territorial Army. Its main function is to reinforce the Regular Army in times of national emergency.

The Establishment is approximately 74,000 and the TAVR is designed to provide a reserve of highly trained and well equipped units and individuals.

THE ROYAL AIR FORCE

THE QUEEN

Marshals of the Royal Air Force

Sir Arthur T. Harris, Bt., G.C.B., O.B.E., A.F.C., *born* April 13, 1892	Jan. 1, 1946
Sir John C. Slessor, G.C.B., D.S.O., M.C., *born* June 3, 1897	June 8, 1950
H.R.H. the Prince Philip, Duke of Edinburgh, K.G., P.C., K.T., O.M., G.B.E. (*Air Commodore-in-Chief, Air Training Corps, Marshal of the R.A.A.F.*) *born* June 10, 1921	Jan. 15, 1953
Sir William F. Dickson, G.C.B., K.B.E., D.S.O., A.F.C., *born* Sept. 24, 1898	June 1, 1954
Sir Dermot A. Boyle, G.C.B., K.C.V.O., K.B.E., A.F.C., *born* Oct. 2, 1904	Jan. 1, 1958
Sir Thomas G. Pike, G.C.B., C.B.E., D.F.C., *born* June 29, 1906	April 6, 1962
The Lord Elworthy, G.C.B., C.B.E., D.S.O., M.V.O., D.F.C., A.F.C. (*Governor and Constable of Windsor Castle*), *born* March 23, 1911	April 1, 1967
Sir John Grandy, G.C.B., K.B.E., D.S.O., *born* Feb. 8, 1913 (*Governor and Commander-in-Chief, Gibraltar*)	April 1, 1971
Sir Denis Spotswood, G.C.B., C.B.E., D.S.O., D.F.C., *born* Sept. 26, 1916	March 31, 1974
Sir Andrew Humphrey, G.C.B., O.B.E., D.F.C., A.F.C., *born* Jan. 10, 1921 (*Chief of the Defence Staff*)	Aug. 1976

Air Chief Marshals

Sir Neil Cameron, G.C.B., C.B.E., D.S.O., D.F.C., A.F.C., A.D.C. (*Chief of the Air Staff*).

Sir Douglas Lowe, K.C.B., D.F.C., A.F.C. (*Controller of Aircraft*).

Sir Peter le Cheminant, K.C.B., D.F.C. (*Deputy C.-in-C., Allied Forces, Central Europe*).

Sir Ruthven Wade, K.C.B., D.F.C. (*Chief of Personnel and Logistics*).

Sir Neville Stack, K.C.B., C.V.O., C.B.E., A.F.C. (*Air Secretary*).

Sir Nigel Maynard, K.C.B., C.B.E., D.F.C., A.F.C. (*A.O.C.-in-C., Strike Command and C.-in-C., U.K. Forces*).

Sir John Aitken, K.C.B. (*Air Member for Personnel*).

Air Marshals

Sir Reginald Harland, K.B.E., C.B. (*A.O.C.-in-C., Support Command*).

Sir Geoffrey Dhenin, K.B.E., A.F.C., G.M., Q.H.P. (*Director-General of Medical Services*).

Sir Ivor Broom, K.C.B., C.B.E., D.S.O., D.F.C., A.F.C. (*Controller, National Air Traffic Services*).

Sir Alfred Ball, K.C.B., D.S.O., D.F.C. (*U.K. Representative, Permanent Military Deputies Group, CENTO*).

Sir Richard Wakeford, K.C.B., M.V.O., O.B.E., A.F.C. (*Deputy Chief of Defence Staff (Intelligence)*).

Sir Michael Beetham, K.C.B., C.B.E., D.F.C., A.F.C. (*C.-in-C., R.A.F., Germany*).

Sir Alasdair Steedman, K.C.B., C.B.E., D.F.C. (*Air Member for Supply and Organization*).

D. G. Evans, C.B.E. (*Vice-Chief of the Air Staff*).

Sir Herbert Durkin, K.B.E., C.B. (*Controller of Engineering and Supply*).

R. W. G. Freer, C.B.E. (*A.O.C., No. 18 Group*).

R. D. Roe, C.B., A.F.C. (*A.O.C.-in-C., Training Command*).

W. J. Stacey, C.B.E. (*Deputy C.-in-C., Strike Command*).

Air Vice-Marshals

A. Sidney-Wilmot, O.B.E. (*Director of Legal Services*).

F. B. Sowrey, C.B., O.B.E., A.F.C. (*Director-General of R.A.F. Training*).

R. W. G. Freer, C.B.E. (*A.O.C., No. 18 Group*).

P. J. O'Connor, C.B., O.B.E., Q.H.P. (*Consultant Advisor, Central Medical Establishment*).

F. R. L. Mellersh, D.F.C. (*Air Officer, Flying and Officer Training, Training Command*).

A. Griffiths, C.B., A.F.C. (*Commandant-General, R.A.F. Regiment*).

F. S. Hazlewood, C.B., C.B.E., A.F.C.

A. C. Davies, C.B., C.B.E. (*Deputy Chief of Staff (Operations and Intelligence) NATO H.Q.*).

R. D. Austen-Smith, C.B., D.F.C. (*Commander, British Forces, Cyprus*).

P. G. K. Williamson, C.B.E., D.F.C. (*A.O.C., No. 38 Group*).

W. J. Stacey, C.B.E.

J. M. Nicholls, C.B.E., D.F.C., A.F.C. (*Assistant Chief of the Air Staff (Operational Requirements)*).

G. H. Ford, C.B. (*Director-General of Engineering and Supply Management*).

W. E. Colahan, C.B.E., D.F.C. (*A.O.C. and Commandant, Cranwell*).

P. J. Lagesen, C.B., D.F.C., A.F.C. (*A.O.C., No. 1 Group*).

N. E. Hoad, C.V.O., C.B.E., A.F.C. (*Senior R.A.F. Member, Royal College of Defence Studies*).

J. Gingell, C.B.E. (*Assistant Chief of Defence Staff (Policy)*).

P. D. G. Terry, C.B., A.F.C. (*Assistant Chief of Staff (Plans and Policy), SHAPE*).

J. I. R. Bowring, C.B.E. (*Air Officer Engineering and Supply Support Command*).

G. E. Thirlwall, C.B. (*Air Officer Engineering, Strike Command*).

D. F. G. Macleod, Q.H.D.S. (*Director of R.A.F. Dental Services*).

J. J. McNair, Q.H.P. (*P.M.O., Support Command*).

G. C. Lamb, C.B.E., A.F.C. (*Chief of Staff, No. 18 Group*).

B. G. Lock, C.B.E., A.F.C. (*Commander, North Maritime Air Region and Air Officer Scotland and Northern Ireland*).

D. L. Attlee, M.V.O. (*A.O.A., Training Command*).

K. A. Williamson, A.F.C. (*Commandant, R.A.F. College, Bracknell*).

S. M. Davidson, C.B.E. (*Assistant Chief of Defence Staff (Signals)*).

G. C. Cairns, C.B.E., A.F.C. (*Commander, Southern Maritime Air Region*).

W. Harbison, C.B.E., A.F.C. (*A.O.C., No. 11 Group*).

C. G. Maughan, C.B., C.B.E., A.F.C. (*S.A.S.O., Strike Command*).

D. B. Craig, O.B.E. (*Assistant Chief of the Air Staff (Operations)*).

P. M. S. Hedgeland, O.B.E. (*Vice-President, Ordnance Board*).

B. G. T. Stanbridge C.B.E., M.V.O., A.F.C. (*Defence Services Secretary*).

A. D. Dick, C.B.E. A.F.C. (*Deputy Controller of Aircraft C*).

M. C. S. Shepherd, C.B., O.B.E. (*A.O.A., Strike Command*).

D. C. A. Lloyd (*Deputy Commander, R.A.F., Germany*).

J. B. Curtiss (*Director-General of Organisation*).

C. E. Ness, C.B.E.

D. G. Bailey, C.B.E. (*Deputy Commander, R.A.F., Germany*).

J. A. Gilbert, C.B.E. (*Assistant Chief of Air Staff (Policy)*).

A. Maisner, C.B.E., A.F.C. (*Director-General of Personnel Management*).

P. R. Mallorie, A.F.C.

C. J. W. Soutar, Q.H.S.

A. A. Morris (*Director-General, Strategic Electronic Systems*).

P. Turner.

THE UNION JACK SERVICES CLUBS

Patron-in-Chief: Her Majesty the Queen.

President: Major-Gen. Sir Julian Gascoigne, K.C.M.G., K.C.V.O., C.B., D.S.O.

Comptroller: Col. C. A. la T. Leatham.

Club Secretary: L. F. Moulton.

THE UNION JACK CLUB

Sandell Street, S. E.1

[Tel: 01-928 6401]

The Union Jack Club has recently been rebuilt and the new premises stand on the site of the old building. It provides residential accommodation for service and ex-service men and women and their families. All serving men and women below commissioned rank are members. Ex-service membership is by election. Honorary membership is extended to the Forces of other nations visiting the United Kingdom.

The new premises provides the most modern standards of accommodation with 417 single bedrooms and 55 double bedrooms for families. The facilities include restaurant, bars, a full range of public rooms including billiards, a sauna bath and launderette. A new feature of the Union Jack Club is a separate conference area with a maximum capacity of 200 persons for meetings, or 100 for Regimental or Association dinners.

The original Union Jack Club was erected by public subscription as a National Memorial to those who had fallen in the South African War and other campaigns and was opened in 1907 by King Edward VII.

SERVICE SALARIES AND PENSIONS

The military salaries for Service men and women, effective from April 1, 1975, were increased with effect from April 1, 1976 by a pay supplement of £6 a week, subject to a limit on individual earnings of £8,500 a year, and with proportionately smaller increases for juniors and apprentices. The rates of pay shown below are those introduced on April 1, 1975 and do *not* include the pay supplement. The Review Body on Armed Forces Pay, who recommended the payment of the supplement in their Fifth Report, was concerned with ranks up to and including that of Brigadiers, whilst the salaries of Major-Generals (or equivalent rank) and above, and also the salaries of medical and dental officers, are subject to separate review. Since 1970 the determining factor of the Review Body's recommendations has been the relation of forces' salaries to civilian earnings by job evaluation. On this occasion their recommendation was made in the context of the Government's incomes policy as set out in "The Attack on Inflation." The undermentioned salaries for the Women's Services reflect equal pay for equal work and conditions but because the X-factor for women is lower than that for men, women's rates approximate to 95·45 per cent. of the rates for men.

ROYAL NAVY AND ROYAL MARINES
Normal Rates

Rank (and equivalent rank, R.M.)	Pay Daily	Pay Annual
	£	£
Midshipman	4·68	1,708
After 1 year in the rank	6·25	2,281
Sub-Lieutenant	7·33	2,675
After 2 years in the rank	9·11	3,325
After 3 years in the rank	9·83	3,588
Lieutenant R.N.	11·29	4,121
After 1 year in the rank	11·59	4,230
After 2 years in the rank	11·89	4,340
After 3 years in the rank	12·19	4,449
After 4 years in the rank	12·49	4,559
After 5 years in the rank	12·79	4,668
After 6 years in the rank	13·09	4,778
Lieutenant R.M.	9·11	3,325
After 1 year in the rank	11·29	4,121
After 2 years in the rank	11·59	4,230
After 3 years in the rank	11·89	4,340
After 4 years in the rank	12·19	4,449
After 5 years in the rank	12·49	4,559
After 6 years in the rank	12·79	4,668
After 7 years in the rank	13·09	4,778
Lieutenant-Commander/Captain R.M.	13·98	5,103
After 1 year in the rank	14·32	5,227
After 2 years in the rank	14·66	5,351
After 3 years in the rank	15·00	5,475
After 4 years in the rank	15·34	5,599
After 5 years in the rank	15·68	5,723
After 6 years in the rank	16·02	5,847
After 7 years in the rank	16·36	5,971
After 8 years in the rank	16·70	6,096
Commander R.N./Major R.M.	18·47	6,742
After 2 years in the rank or with 19 years' service	18·96	6,920
After 4 years in the rank or with 21 years' service	19·45	7,099
After 6 years in the rank or with 23 years' service	19·94	7,278
After 8 years in the rank or with 25 years' service	20·43	7,457
Captain R.N./Lieutenant-Colonel R.M.	22·38	8,169
After 2 years in the rank	22·97	8,384
After 4 years in the rank	23·56	8,599
Captain R.N. with 6 years' seniority/Colonel R.M.	27·40	10,001
Rear-Admiral/Major-General R.M.	32·87	11,998
Vice-Admiral/Lieutenant-General R.M.	38·35	13,998
Admiral/General R.M.	49·11	17,925
Admiral of the Fleet	53·90	19,674

ARMY
Normal Rates

Rank	Pay Daily	Pay Annual
	£	£
Second-Lieutenant	7·33	2,675
Lieutenant	9·11	3,325
After 1 year in the rank	9·35	3,413
After 2 years in the rank	9·59	3,500
After 3 years in the rank	9·83	3,588
After 4 years in the rank	10·07	3,676
Captain	11·29	4,121
After 1 year in the rank	11·59	4,230
After 2 years in the rank	11·89	4,340
After 3 years in the rank	12·19	4,449
After 4 years in the rank	12·49	4,559
After 5 years in the rank	12·79	4,668
After 6 years in the rank	13·09	4,778
Major	13·98	5,103
After 1 year in the rank	14·32	5,227
After 2 years in the rank	14·66	5,351
After 3 years in the rank	15·00	5,475
After 4 years in the rank	15·34	5,599
After 5 years in the rank	15·68	5,723
After 6 years in the rank	16·02	5,847
After 7 years in the rank	16·36	5,971
After 8 years in the rank	16·70	6,096
Lieutenant-Colonel—Special List	18·61	6,793
Lieutenant-Colonel	18·47	6,742
After 2 years in the rank or with 19 years' service	18·96	6,920
After 4 years in the rank or with 21 years' service	19·45	7,099
After 6 years in the rank or with 23 years' service	19·94	7,278
After 8 years in the rank or with 25 years' service	20·43	7,457
Colonel	22·38	8,169
After 2 years in the rank	22·97	8,384
After 4 years in the rank	23·56	8,599
After 6 years in the rank	24·15	8,815
After 8 years in the rank	24·74	9,030
Brigadier	27·40	10,001
Major-General	32·87	11,998
Lieutenant-General	38·35	13,998
General	49·11	17,925
Field-Marshal	53·90	19,674

ROYAL AIR FORCE
Normal Rates

Rank *In this rank	Daily	Annual	Rank *In this rank	Daily	Annual
	£	£		£	£
Acting Pilot Officer............	6·25	2,281	Squadron Leader—*contd.*		
After 6 months* (aircrew officers			After 7 years*..............	16·36	5,971
only).............................	6·42	2,343	After 8 years*..............	16·70	6,096
Pilot Officer....................	7·33	2,675	Wing Commander..............	18·47	6,742
Flying Officer...................	9·11	3,325	After 2 years* or 19 years'		
After 1 year*................	9·35	3,413	commissioned service........	18·96	6,920
After 2 years*...............	9·59	3,500	After 4 years* or 21 years'		
After 3 years*...............	9·83	3,588	commissioned service........	19·45	7,099
After 4 years*...............	10·07	3,676	After 6 years* or 23 years'		
Flight Lieutenant................	11·29	4,121	commissioned service........	19·94	7,278
After 1 year*................	11·59	4,230	After 8 years* or 25 years'		
After 2 years*...............	11·89	4,340	commissioned service........	20·43	7,457
After 3 years*...............	12·19	4,449	Group Captain................	22·38	8,169
After 4 years*...............	12·49	4,559	After 2 years*...............	22·97	8,384
After 5 years*...............	12·79	4,668	After 4 years*...............	23·56	8,599
After 6 years*...............	13·09	4,778	After 6 years*...............	24·15	8,815
Squadron Leader................	13·98	5,103	After 8 years*...............	24·74	9,030
After 1 year*................	14·32	5,227	Air Commodore...............	27·40	10,001
After 2 years*...............	14·66	5,351	Air Vice Marshal.............	32·87	11,998
After 3 years*...............	15·00	5,475	Air Marshal..................	38·35	13,998
After 4 years*...............	15·34	5,599	Air Chief Marshal.............	49·11	17,925
After 5 years*...............	15·68	5,723	Marshal of the Royal Air Force...	53·90	19,674
After 6 years*...............	16·02	5,847			

ALL SERVICES
Rates for Officers promoted from the ranks

Years of commissioned service	Years of Service in the Ranks					
	Less than 12 years		12 years but less than 15 years		15 years or more	
	Daily	Annual	Daily	Annual	Daily	Annual
	£	£	£	£	£	£
On appointment................	11·89	4,340	12·49	4,559	13·09	4,778
After 1 year..................	12·19	4,449	12·79	4,668	13·31	4,858
After 2 years.................	12·49	4,559	13·09	4,778	13·53	4,938
After 3 years.................	12·79	4,668	13·31	4,858	13·75	5,109
After 4 years.................	13·09	4,778	13·53	4,938	13·97	5,099
After 5 years.................	13·31	4,858	13·75	5,019	14·19	5,179
After 6 years.................	13·53	4,938	13·97	5,099	14·41	5,260
After 8 years.................	13·75	5,019	14·19	5,179	14·63	5,340
After 10 years................	13·97	5,099	14·41	5,260	—	—
After 12 years................	14·19	5,179	14·63	5,340	—	—
After 14 years................	14·41	5,260	—	—	—	—
After 16 years................	14·63	5,340	—	—	—	—

ROYAL NAVY SEAMAN BRANCH
Daily Rates

Rating/Rank	Less than 6 years Scale A			6 years but less than 9 years Scale B			9 years or more Scale C		
Scale	III	II	I	III	II	I	III	II	I
	£	£	£	£	£	£	£	£	£
Ordinary Rating..................	—	4·68	5·11	—	4·98	5·41	—	5·43	5·86
Able Rating......................	5·63	6·09	6·49	5·93	6·39	6·79	6·38	6·84	7·24
Leading Rating...................	—	7·52	8·03	—	7·82	8·33	—	8·26	8·78
Petty Officer.....................	—	8·70	8·86	—	9·00	9·16	—	9·45	9·61
Chief Petty Officer (incl. Artisans)....	—	9·63	9·81	—	9·93	10·11	—	10·38	10·56
Fleet Chief Petty Officer.............	—	—	10·82	—	—	11·12	—	—	11·57

ARTIFICERS AND MECHANICIANS
Daily Rates

Rating	less than 6 years	6 years but less than 9 years	9 years or more
	Scale A	Scale B	Scale C
	£	£	£
Mechanician 5th Class (Able Rating)	6·49	6·79	7·24
Artificer 3rd Class (Leading Rating) / Mechanician Acting 4th Class (Acting Leading Rating)	7·52	7·82	8·27
Mechanician 4th Class (Leading Rating)	8·03	8·33	8·78
Mechanician 3rd Class (Petty Officer) / Artificer Acting 2nd Class (Acting Petty Officer)	8·92	9·22	9·67
Petty Officer 2nd Class	9·36	9·66	10·11
Chief Petty Officer 1st Class	10·38	10·68	11·13
After 2 years	10·71	11·01	11·46
After 4 years	10·82	11·12	11·57
After 6 years	10·90	11·20	11·65
Chief Artificer/Mechanician	11·22	11·52	11·97
Fleet Chief Petty Officer	11·54	11·84	12·29

ARMY
Other Ranks — Daily Rates

Rank		Scale A★			Scale B★			Scale C★		
	Band	1	2	3	1	2	3	1	2	3
		£	£	£	£	£	£	£	£	£
Private	Class IV	4·68	—	—	4·98	—	—	5·43	—	—
	Class III	5·08	5·63	—	5·38	5·93	—	5·83	6·38	—
	Class II	5·40	5·95	—	5·70	6·25	—	6·15	6·70	—
	Class I	5·74	6·29	6·90	6·04	6·59	7·20	6·49	7·04	7·65
Lance Corporal	Class III	5·74	6·29	—	6·04	6·59	—	6·49	7·04	—
	Class II	6·10	6·65	—	6·40	6·95	—	6·85	7·40	—
	Class I	6·49	7·04	7·65	6·79	7·34	7·95	7·24	7·79	8·40
Corporal	Class II	6·97	7·52	—	7·27	7·82	—	7·72	8·27	—
	Class I	7·48	8·03	8·64	7·78	8·33	8·94	8·23	8·78	9·39

Rank		Scale A★				Scale B★				Scale C★			
	Band	4	5	6	7	4	5	6	7	4	5	6	7
		£	£	£	£	£	£	£	£	£	£	£	£
Sergeant		8·10	8·70	9·36	—	8·40	9·00	9·66	—	8·85	9·45	10·11	—
Staff Sergeant		8·56	9·16	9·82	10·54	8·86	9·46	10·12	10·84	9·31	9·91	10·57	11·29
Warrant Officer Class II		9·05	9·65	10·31	11·03	9·35	9·95	10·61	11·33	9·80	10·40	11·06	11·78
Class I		9·56	10·16	10·82	11·54	9·86	10·46	11·12	11·84	10·31	10·91	11·57	12·29

★ SCALES.—A=less than 6 years; B=6 years but less than 9 years; C=9 years or more.

LENGTH OF SERVICE INCREMENTS

R.N., R.M., Q.A.R.N.N.S. and W.R.N.S.					ARMY, Q.A.R.A.N.C. and W.R.A.C.					
	No. of years' Service					No. of years' Service				
Rating/Rank	9	12	16	22	Rank	9	12	15	18	22
	£	£	£	£		£	£	£	£	£
Able/Marine 1st Class	0·20	0·30	—	—	Private	0·20	0·30	0·30	0·30	0·30
Leading/Corporal (R.M.)	0·20	0·30	—	—	Lance-Corporal	0·20	0·30	0·30	0·30	0·30
P.O./Sergeant (R.M.)	0·25	0·35	0·55	—	Corporal	0·20	0·30	0·35	0·35	0·35
C.P.O./Colour Sergeant	0·30	0·50	0·60	—	Sergeant	0·25	0·35	0·45	0·55	0·55
Warrant Officer Class II (R.M.)	0·30	0·50	0·65	0·80	Staff-Sergeant	0·25	0·35	0·45	0·60	0·60
Fleet C.P.O./Warrant Officer Class I (R.M.)	0·30	0·50	0·65	0·85	Warrant Officer Class II	0·25	0·35	0·45	0·60	0·70
					Warrant Officer Class I	0·25	0·35	0·45	0·60	0·85

ROYAL AIR FORCE

Rank				Rank			
AIRCREW (i) Pilots, Navigators, Air Electronics Operators and Air Engineers (A)	A★	B★	C★	AIRCREW (ii) Air Signallers, Air Engineers and Air Loadmasters	A★	B★	C★
	£	£	£		£	£	£
Sergeant	9·36	9·66	10·11	Sergeant	8·70	9·00	9·45
Flight Sergeant	10·82	11·12	11·57	Flight Sergeant	10·10	10·40	10·85
Master Aircrew	11·54	11·84	12·29	Master Aircrew	10·82	11·12	11·57

★ SCALES.—A=less than 6 years; B=6 years but less than 9 years; C=9 years or more.

AIRMEN (Ground Trades)

Rank	Band	Less than 6 years Scale A			6 years but less than 9 years—Scale B			9 years or more Scale C		
		1	2	3	1	2	3	1	2	3
		£	£	£	£	£	£	£	£	£
Aircraftman		4·68	4·68	4·68	4·98	4·98	4·98	5·43	5·43	5·43
Leading Aircraftman		5·08	5·63	6·24	5·38	5·93	6·54	5·83	6·38	6·99
Senior Aircraftman		5·74	6·29	6·90	6·04	6·59	7·20	6·49	7·04	7·65
Junior Technician		6·49	7·04	7·65	6·79	7·34	7·95	7·24	7·79	8·40
Corporal		7·39	7·94	8·64	7·69	8·24	8·94	8·14	8·69	9·39

Rank	Band	4	5	6	7	4	5	6	7	4	5	6	7
		£	£	£	£	£	£	£	£	£	£	£	£
Sergeant		8·10	8·70	9·36	—	8·40	9·00	9·66	—	8·85	9·45	10·11	—
Chief Technician		8·41	9·01	9·67	—	8·71	9·31	9·97	—	9·16	9·76	10·42	—
Flight Sergeant		8·73	9·33	10·10	10·82	9·03	9·63	10·40	11·12	9·48	10·08	10·85	11·57
Warrant Officer		9·56	10·16	10·82	11·54	9·86	10·46	11·12	11·84	10·31	10·91	11·57	12·29

LENGTH OF SERVICE INCREMENTS

R.A.F. P.M.R.A.F.N.S. (N.C.E.) and W.R.A.F. Rank	No. of years' Service				
	9	12	15	18	22
	£	£	£	£	£
Leading Aircraftman, Senior Aircraftman and Junior Technician	0·20	0·30	0·30	0·30	0·30
Corporal	0·20	0·30	0·35	0·35	0·35
Sergeant	0·25	0·35	0·45	0·55	0·55
Chief Technician	0·25	0·35	0·45	0·60	0·60
Flight Sergeant	0·25	0·35	0·45	0·60	0·60
Warrant Officer	0·25	0·35	0·45	0·60	0·85

Officers of W.R.N.S.

Rank	Daily	Annual
	£	£
Probationary 3rd Officer	7·00	2,555
3rd Officer	7·57	2,763
After 2 years in the rank	8·70	3,176
After 3 years in the rank	8·92	3,256
After 4 years in the rank	9·15	3,340
After 5 years in the rank	9·38	3,424
After 6 years in the rank	9·61	3,508
2nd Officer	10·78	3,935
After 1 year in the rank	11·06	4,037
After 2 years in the rank	11·35	4,143
After 3 years in the rank	11·64	4,249
After 4 years in the rank	11·92	4,351
After 5 years in the rank	12·21	4,457
After 6 years in the rank	12·49	4,559
1st Officer	13·34	4,869
After 1 year in the rank	13·67	4,990
After 2 years in the rank	13·99	5,106
After 3 years in the rank	14·32	5,227
After 4 years in the rank	14·64	5,344
After 5 years in the rank	14·97	5,464
After 6 years in the rank	15·29	5,581
After 7 years in the rank	15·62	5,701
After 8 years in the rank	15·94	5,818
Chief Officer	17·63	6,435
After 2 years in the rank or 19 years' service	18·10	6,607
After 4 years in the rank or 21 years' service	18·57	6,778
After 6 years in the rank or 23 years' service	19·05	6,953

W.R.N.S.—*continued*

Rank	Daily	Annual
	£	£
After 8 years in the rank or 25 years' service	19·54	7,132
Superintendent	21·70	7,921
After 2 years in the rank	22·29	8,136
After 4 years in the rank	22·88	8,351
After 6 years in the rank	23·47	8,567
After 8 years in the rank	24·06	8,782
Director W.R.N.S.	26·99	9,851

Officers of W.R.A.C., and non-nursing officers of Q.A.R.A.N.C.

Rank	Daily	Annual
	£	£
Second-Lieutenant	7·00	2,555
Lieutenant	8·70	3,176
After 1 year in the rank	8·92	3,256
After 2 years in the rank	9·15	3,340
After 3 years in the rank	9·38	3,424
After 4 years in the rank	9·61	3,508
Captain	10·78	3,935
After 1 year in the rank	11·06	4,037
After 2 years in the rank	11·35	4,143
After 3 years in the rank	11·64	4,249
After 4 years in the rank	11·92	4,351
After 5 years in the rank	12·21	4,457
After 6 years in the rank	12·49	4,559
Major	13·34	4,869
After 1 year in the rank	13·67	4,990
After 2 years in the rank	13·99	5,106
After 3 years in the rank	14·32	5,227
After 4 years in the rank	14·64	5,344
After 5 years in the rank	14·97	5,464
After 6 years in the rank	15·29	5,581
After 7 years in the rank	15·62	5,701
After 8 years in the rank	15·94	5,818
Lieutenant Colonel	17·63	6,435
With 19 years' service or after 2 years in the rank	18·10	6,607
With 21 years' service or after 4 years in the rank	18·57	6,778
With 23 years' service or after 6 years in the rank	19·05	6,953
With 25 years' service or after 8 years in the rank	19·54	7,132
Colonel	21·70	7,921
After 2 years in the rank	22·29	8,136
After 4 years in the rank	22·88	8,351
After 6 years in the rank	23·47	8,567
After 8 years in the rank	24·06	8,782
Brigadier	26·99	9,851

Officers of W.R.A.F.

Rank	Daily	Annual
	£	£
Acting Pilot Officer............	5·97	2,179
Pilot Officer..................	7·00	2,555
Flying Officer.................	8·70	3,176
After 1 year in the rank.......	8·92	3,256
After 2 years in the rank......	9·15	3,340
After 3 years in the rank......	9·38	3,424
After 4 years in the rank......	9·61	3,508
Flight Lieutenant..............	10·28	3,935
After 1 year in the rank.......	11·06	4,037
After 2 years in the rank......	11·35	4,143
After 3 years in the rank......	11·64	4,249
After 4 years in the rank......	11·92	4,351
After 5 years in the rank......	12·21	4,457
After 6 years in the rank......	12·49	4,559
Squadron Leader...............	13·34	4,869
After 1 year in the rank.......	13·67	4,990
After 2 years in the rank......	13·99	5,106
After 3 years in the rank......	14·32	5,227
After 4 years in the rank......	14·64	5,344
After 5 years in the rank......	14·97	5,464
After 6 years in the rank......	15·29	5,581
After 7 years in the rank......	15·62	5,701
After 8 years in the rank......	15·94	5,818
Wing Commander...............	17·63	6,435
After 2 years★ or 19 years' commissioned service........	18·10	6,607
After 4 years★ or 21 years' commissioned service........	18·57	6,778
After 6 years★ or 23 years' commissioned service........	19·05	6,953
After 8 years★ or 25 years' commissioned service........	19·54	7,132

Officers of W.R.A.F.—contd.

Rank	Daily	Annual
	£	£
Group Captain.................	21·70	7,921
After 2 years★................	22·29	8,136
After 4 years★................	22·88	8,351
After 6 years★................	23·47	8,567
After 8 years★................	24·06	8,782
Air Commodore................	26·99	9,851

★ In the rank.

W.R.N.S. Ratings

Rating	Scale	Band 1	Band 2	Band 3
		£	£	£
Wren (Ordinary)	under 17½	3·38	3·38	3·38
	at 17½	4·47	4·47	4·47
Wren (Able).....	III	4·83	5·36	5·94
	II	5·27	5·80	6·38
	I	5·65	6·18	6·76
Leading Wren...	II	6·64	7·17	7·75
	I	7·12	7·65	8·23

	Scale	Band 4	Band 5	Band 6	Band 7
		£	£	£	£
P.O. Wren......	II	7·64	8·21	8·84	9·53
	I	7·80	8·37	9·00	9·69
Chief Wren......	II	8·21	8·78	9·41	10·10
	I	8·43	9·00	9·63	10·32
Fleet Chief Wren.	I	9·11	9·68	10·31	11·00

W.R.A.C.

Rank	Band	Less than 6 years Scale A			6 years but less than 9 years Scale B			9 years or more Scale C		
		1	2	3	1	2	3	1	2	3
		£	£	£	£	£	£	£	£	£
Private Class IV under 17½..		3·38	—	—	—	—	—	—	—	—
Class IV............		4·47	—	—	4·77	—	—	5·22	—	—
Class III...........		4·83	5·36	—	5·13	5·66	—	5·58	6·11	—
Class II............		5·14	5·67	—	5·44	5·97	—	5·89	6·42	—
Class I.............		5·46	5·99	6·57	5·76	6·29	6·87	6·21	6·74	7·32
Lance Corporal Class III....		5·46	5·99	—	5·76	6·29	—	6·21	6·74	—
Class II.....		5·80	6·33	—	6·10	6·63	—	6·55	7·08	—
Class I.....		6·18	6·71	7·29	6·48	7·01	7·59	6·93	7·46	8·04
Corporal Class II..........		6·64	7·17	—	6·94	7·47	—	7·39	7·92	★
Class I...........		7·12	7·65	8·23	7·42	7·95	8·53	7·87	8·40	8·98

Rank	Band	4	5	6	7	4	5	6	7	4	5	6	7
		£	£	£	£	£	£	£	£	£	£	£	£
Sergeant...................		7·72	8·29	8·92	—	8·02	8·59	9·22	—	8·47	9·04	9·67	—
Staff Sergeant...............		8·16	8·73	9·36	10·05	8·46	9·03	9·66	10·35	8·91	9·48	10·11	10·80
Warrant Officer Class II....		8·62	9·19	9·82	10·51	8·92	9·49	10·12	10·81	9·37	9·94	10·57	11·26
Class I....		9·11	9·68	10·31	11·00	9·41	9·98	10·61	11·30	9·86	10·43	11·06	11·75

Sergeants and above whose employment classification is Class II and Corporals whose employment classification is Class III shall be paid £0·12 or £0·06 a day respectively less than the rates shown.

W.R.A.F. AIRWOMEN

Rank	Band	Less than 6 years Scale A			6 years but less than 9 years Scale B			9 years or more Scale C		
		1	2	3	1	2	3	1	2	3
		£	£	£	£	£	£	£	£	£
Aircraftwoman under 17½.....		3·38	—	—	—	—	—	—	—	—
17½ and above.........		4·47	4·47	4·47	—	—	—	—	—	—
Leading Aircraftwoman......		4·83	5·36	5·94	5·13	5·66	6·24	5·58	6·11	6·69
Senior Aircraftwoman........		5·46	5·99	6·57	5·76	6·29	6·87	6·21	6·74	7·32
Junior Technician............		6·18	6·71	7·29	6·48	7·01	7·59	6·93	7·46	8·04
Corporal...................		7·04	7·57	8·23	7·34	7·87	8·53	7·79	8·32	8·98

Rank	Band	4	5	6	7	4	5	6	7	4	5	6	7
		£	£	£	£	£	£	£	£	£	£	£	£
Sergeant....................		7·72	8·29	8·92	—	8·02	8·59	9·22	—	8·47	9·04	9·67	—
Chief Technician.............		8·02	8·59	9·22	—	8·32	8·89	9·52	—	8·77	9·34	9·97	—
Flight Sergeant..............		8·32	8·89	9·63	10·32	8·62	9·19	9·93	10·62	9·07	9·64	10·38	11·07
Warrant Officer..............		9·11	9·68	10·31	11·00	9·41	9·98	10·61	11·30	9·86	10·43	11·06	11·75

Q.A.R.N.N.S., Q.A.R.A.N.C., P.M.R.A.F.N.S.

Rank	Daily	Annual
	£	£
Nursing Sister/Lieutenant/Flying Officer....................	8·70	3,176
After 1 year in the rank........	8·92	3,256
After 2 years in the rank.......	9·15	3,340
After 3 years in the rank.......	9·38	3,424
After 4 years in the rank.......	9·61	3,508
Senior Nursing Sister/Captain/Flight Officer..............	10·78	3,935
After 1 year in the rank........	11·06	4,037
After 2 years in the rank.......	11·35	4,143
After 3 years in the rank.......	11·64	4,249
After 4 years in the rank.......	11·92	4,351
After 5 years in the arnk.......	12·21	4,457
After 6 years in the rank.......	12·49	4,559
Superintending Sister/Major/Squadron Officer...........	13·34	4,869
After 1 year in the rank........	13·67	4,990
After 2 years in the rank.......	13·99	5,106
After 3 years in the rank.......	14·32	5,227
After 4 years in the rank.......	14·64	5,344
After 5 years in the rank.......	14·97	5,464
After 6 years in the rank.......	15·29	5,581
After 7 years in the rank.......	15·62	5,701
After 8 years in the rank.......	15·94	5,818
Matron/Lieutenant-Colonel/Wing Officer...............	17·63	6,435
After 2 years* or with 19 years' service....................	18·10	6,607
After 4 years* or with 21 years' service....................	18·57	6,778
After 6 years* or with 23 years' service....................	19·05	6,953
After 8 years* or with 25 years' service....................	19·54	7,132
Principal Matron/Colonel/Group Officer..............	21·70	7,921
After 2 years in the rank.......	22·29	8,136
After 4 years in the rank.......	22·88	8,351
After 6 years in the rank.......	23·47	8,567
After 8 years in the rank.......	24·06	8,782
Matron-in-Chief/Brigadier/Air Commandant.................	26·99	9,851

* In this rank

CHARGES FOR MARRIED QUARTERS

Type of Quarter	Weekly	Annual
Standard Accommodation	£	£
Other Ranks		
A............................	5·25	273·75
B............................	7·28	379·60
C............................	8·40	438·00
D/WO.......................	9·10	474·50
Officers		
V............................	—	609·55
IV...........................	—	722·70
III...........................	—	821·25
II............................	—	923·45
I............................	—	1,032·95
Sub-standard Accommodation		
Other Ranks		
A............................	3·50	182·50
B............................	4·83	251·85
C............................	5·60	292·00
D/WO.......................	6·09	317·55
Officers		
V............................	—	405·15
IV...........................	—	481·80
III...........................	—	547·50

CHARGES FOR SINGLE QUARTERS

Rank	Weekly	Annual
Standard Accommodation	£	£
Young servicemen receiving less than the minimum adult rate (i.e. Private IV rate).........	1·89	98·55
Corporal and below...........	2·45	127·75
Warrant Officer and Senior N.C.O......................	4·69	244·55
Captain and below............	6·65	346·75
Major........................	8·12	423·40
Lieutenant Colonel and above..	9·10	474·50
Senior Officers occupying single rooms		
Major........................	6·86	357·70
Lieutenant Colonel and above..	7·35	383·25
Sub-Standard Accommodation		
Young servicemen receiving less than the minimum adult rate (i.e. Private IV rate).........	1·26	65·70
Corporal and below...........	1·61	83·95
Warrant Officer and Senior N.C.O......................	3·15	164·25
Captain and below............	4·41	229·95
Major........................	5·39	281·05
Lieutenant Colonel and above..	6·09	317·55

SERVICE RETIREMENT BENEFITS, ETC.
(Applicable to those retiring after March 31st, 1976)

NOTE—A major change in the Armed Forces pension arrangements was made in 1975 with the introduction, from April 1, of "preserved" pensions to comply with the appropriate provisions of the Social Security Act 1973. Those who leave the Forces having served at least five years after the age of 21, but not long enough to qualify for the appropriate immediate pension, now qualify for a preserved pension and terminal grant both of which are payable at age 60. The tax-free resettlement grants shown below are payable on release to those who qualify for a preserved pension and who have completed 9 years service from age 21 (officers) or 12 years from age 18 (other ranks)

RETIREMENT BENEFITS (MEN)
Officers—All Services

No. of years' reckonable service completed	Lt. (R.N./R.M.) Capt.(Army) (incl. Q.M.) Flt. Lt., and below	Lt. Cdr., Capt.(R.M.) Major (Army) (incl. Q.M.) Sqn. Ldr.	Cdr., Maj. (R.M.) Lt.-Col. (Army) Wg. Cdr.	Lt.-Col. (Q.M.) (Army)	Capt.(R.N.) Lt.-Col., (R.M.) Col. (Army) Gp. Capt.	Capt. (R.N.) (after 6 yrs) Colonel (R.M.) Brigadier, Air Cdre.	Rear Adm. Maj.-Gen. (R.M./Army) Air Vice-Marshal	Vice-Adm., Lt.-Gen., (R.M.) Army) Air Marshal	Admiral, General, AirChief Marshal
	£ a year	£ a year	£ a year	£ a year	£ a year	£ a year	£ a year	£ a year	£ a year
16	1,451	1,685	2,061	1,867	—	—	—	—	—
17	1,515	1,764	2,156	1,946	—	—	—	—	—
18	1,579	1,843	2,251	2,025	2,640	—	—	—	—
19	1,643	1,922	2,345	2,104	2,749	—	—	—	—
20	1,707	2,001	2,440	2,183	2,858	—	—	—	—
21	1,772	2,080	2,535	2,262	2,967	—	—	—	—
22	1,836	2,159	2,630	2,341	3,075	3,517	—	—	—
23	1,900	2,238	2,725	2,420	3,184	3,628	—	—	—
24	1,964	2,317	2,820	2,499	3,293	3,739	4,487	—	—
25	2,028	2,396	2,914	2,578	3,401	3,850	4,620	—	—
26	2,092	2,476	3,009	2,658	3,510	3,961	4,754	—	—
27	2,156	2,555	3,104	2,737	3,619	4,072	4,887	6,108	—
28	2,220	2,634	3,199	2,816	3,728	4,183	5,020	6,275	—
29	2,284	2,713	3,294	2,895	3,836	4,294	5,154	6,441	—
30	2,349	2,792	3,389	2,974	3,945	4,406	5,287	6,608	9,252
31	2,413	2,871	3,483	3,053	4,054	4,517	5,420	6,775	9,485
32	2,477	2,950	3,578	3,132	4,163	4,628	5,553	6,942	9,719
33	2,541	3,029	3,673	3,211	4,271	4,739	5,687	7,108	9,952
34	2,605	3,108	3,768	3,290	4,380	4,850	5,820	7,275	10,185

Admirals of the Fleet, Field Marshals and Marshals of the Royal Air Force recieve half-pay of £11,500.

Ratings, Soldiers and Airmen

No. of years' reckonable service completed	Able Rating, Marine, Pte./L.-Cpl., Aircraftman	Leading Rating, Corporal (R.M., Army, R.A.F.)	Petty Officer, Sergeant (R.M. Army, R.A.F.)	Chief Petty Officer, Col. Sgt. (R.M.) Staff Sgt., (Army), Flight Sgt.	Warrant Officer Class II (R.M., Army)	Fleet Chief P.O. Commissioned Officer, W.O. ClassI (R.M., Army), W.O. (R.A.F.)
	£ a year	£ a year	£ a year	£ a year	£ a year	£ a year
22	952	1,160	1,261	1,386	1,416	1,514
23	985	1,201	1,305	1,434	1,467	1,570
24	1,019	1,241	1,349	1,483	1,517	1,625
25	1,052	1,282	1,393	1,531	1,568	1,681
26	1,085	1,322	1,437	1,579	1,618	1,737
27	1,118	1,363	1,481	1,628	1,669	1,793
28	1,152	1,403	1,525	1,676	1,720	1,848
29	1,185	1,444	1,569	1,724	1,770	1,904
30	1,218	1,484	1,614	1,773	1,821	1,960
31	1,251	1,525	1,658	1,821	1,871	2,016
32	1,285	1,565	1,702	1,869	1,922	2,071
33	1,318	1,606	1,746	1,918	1,973	2,127
34	1,351	1,646	1,790	1,966	2,023	2,183
35	1,384	1,687	1,834	2,014	2,074	2,239
36	1,418	1,727	1,878	2,063	2,124	2,294
37	1,451	1,768	1,922	2,111	2,175	2,350

RETIREMENT BENEFITS (WOMEN)

Q.A.R.N.N.S., W.R.N.S., Q.A.R.A.N.C., W.R.A.C., A.F.N.S., W.R.A.F. (The annual rates for W.R.A.C. are given: these apply to equivalent ranks in all Services, including the Nursing Services).

OFFICERS.—Captain, 16–34 years' service: £1,386–2,488; Major, 16–34 years': £1,609–2,968; Lt.-Col., 16–34 years': £1,968–3,598; Colonel, 18–34 years': £2561–4249; Brigadier, 22—34 years': £3,464–4,777.

SERVICEWOMEN (22–37 years' service).—Below Corporal: £909–1,386; Corporal: £1,108–1,688; Sergeant: £1,204–1,836; Staff Sergeant: £1,324–2,016; Warrant Officer Class II: £1,352–2,077; Warrant Officer Class I: £1,446–2,244.

NOTES

Terminal grants are in each case three times the rate of retired pay or pension. There are special rates of retired pay for Chaplains, Flight Lieutenants (Specialist Aircrew), and certain other ranks not shown above. Deductions may be made in cases of voluntary retirement. Gratuities may be payable instead of preserved pension in certain instances, e.g., male officers with 10 years' qualifying service would receive £3,260 with a further £650 for each additional year. The normal rates of gratuity for officers with short-service commissions are £495 (men) and £473 (women) for each year completed. Resettlement grants are: officers, £1,697 (men) and £1,621 (women); non-commissioned ranks, £1,209 (men) and £1,155 (women).

The Church of England

Province of Canterbury

CANTERBURY. £9,420

101st *Archbishop and Primate of All England*, Most Rev. and Rt. Hon. Frederick Donald Coggan, D.D. (Lambeth Palace, S.E.1), *cons.* 1956, 1961 and 1975. [Signs Donald Cantuar:]......................................1975

Bishops Suffragan (£3,650)

Dover, Rt. Rev. Anthony Paul Tremlett, M.A. (Upway, St. Martin's Hill, Canterbury)....1964
Croydon, Rt. Rev. John Taylor Hughes, C.B.E., M.A. (209 Turnpike Lane, East Croydon)..1956
Maidstone, Rt. Rev. Richard Henry McPhail Third (Bishop's House, Egerton, Ashford)..1976
Assistant Bishop, Rt. Rev. Kenneth Charles Harman Warner, D.S.O., D.D. (*cons.* 1947)...1962

Dean (£3,650)

Very Rev. Victor Alexander de Waal, M.A...1976

Canons Residentiary (£2,200)

J. Robinson, M.Th.,	Archd. Pawley....1972
B.D............1968	D. I. Hill, M.A.,
A. M. Allchin, M.A.,	F.S.A.
B.Litt..........1973	

Organist, Allan Wicks, M.A., F.R.C.O.......1961

Archdeacons

Canterbury, Ven. B. C. Pawley, M.A.........1972
Croydon, The Bishop of Croydon...........1968
Maidstone (vacant)
Beneficed Clergy, 224; *Curates*, &c., 76
Vicar-General of Province and Diocese, Sir Harold Kent, G.C.B.
Commissary of Diocese, J. H. F. Newey, Q.C., M.A., Ll.B......................1971
Registrar of the Province and Archbishop's Legal Sec., D. M. M. Carey, M.A., 1 The Sanctuary, S.W.1.
Registrar of the Diocese of Canterbury, D. M. M. Carey, M.A., 9 The Precincts, Canterbury.

LONDON. £6,820

115th *Bishop*, Rt. Rev. and Rt. Hon. Gerald Alexander Ellison, D.D., *cons.* 1950, *trs.* 1955 and 1973 (19 Cowley Street, S.W.1.) [Signs Gerald Londin:].......................1973

Bishops Suffragan

Kensington, Rt. Rev. Ronald Cedric Osbourne Goodchild, M.A. (19 Campden Hill Square, W.8)........................1964
Willesden, Rt. Rev. Geoffrey Hewlett Thompson, M.A. (173 Willesden Lane, Brondesbury, N.W.6)........................1974
Stepney, Rt. Rev. Ernest Urban Trevor Huddleston, M.A. (400 Commercial Road, E.1.) (*cons.* 1962)..........1968
Edmonton, Rt. Rev. William John Westwood, B.A. (167 Friern Barnet Lane, Whetstone, N.20)........................1975
Fulham (for North and Central Europe), Rt. Rev. John Richard Satterthwaite, B.A. (19 Brunswick Gardens, W.8)................1970
Assistant Bishops, Rt. Rev. Cecil John Patterson, C.M.G., C.B.E., D.D. (*cons.* 1942) 1969; Rt. Rev. Mark Allin Hodson, B.A. (*cons.* 1956), 1973; Rt. Rev. Edward George Knapp-Fisher, M.A. (*cons.* 1960), 1976; Rt. Rev. Kenneth Walter Howell, M.A. (*cons.* 1963)..1976

Dean of St. Paul's (£3,962)

Very Rev. Martin Gloster Sullivan, D.D., M.A., The Deanery, Dean's Court, E.C.4.......1967

Canons Residentiary (each £2,750)

L. J. Collins, M.A...1948	D. Webster, M.A.,.1969
Archd. Wood-	E. M. Pilkington,
house.........1968	M.A............1976

Organist, C. H. Dearnley, M.A., B.Mus., F.R.C.O..1968
Receiver of St. Paul's, Sir David Floyd Ewin, O.B.E., M.V.O., M.A.

Archdeacons

London, Ven. S. M. F. Woodhouse, M.A.....1967
Middlesex, Ven. J. N. Perry, B.A..........1975
Hampstead, Ven. F. Pickering, M.A........1974
Hackney, Ven. G. B. Timms, M.A..........1971
Northolt, Ven. R. Southwell, A.K.C.........1970
Beneficed Clergy, 415; *Curates*, &c., 285
Chancellor and Commissary of the Dean and Chapter G. H. Newsom, Q.C., M.A..........1971
Registrar, D. W. Faull, 1 The Sanctuary, S.W.1.1969
Chapter Clerk, R. M. Hollis.

Westminster. £3,170

The Collegiate Church of St. Peter—(A Royal Peculiar)
Dean, Very Rev. Edward Frederick Carpenter, M.A., B.D., Ph.D., F.K.C.............1974

Canons Residentiary (£2,045)

D. L. Edwards, M.A.	Bishop Knapp-
(*Sub-Dean*).....1970	Fisher.........1975
J. A. Baker, M.A.,	T. R. Beeson, M.A.,
B.Litt..........1973	A.K.C..........1976

Archdeacon, Rt. Rev. E. G. Knapp-Fisher, M.A.1975
Chapter Clerk, Registrar, and Receiver General, W. R. J. Pullen, M.V.O., Ll.B.............1959
Precentor, Rev. E. R. G. Job, M.A..........1974
Organist, D. A. Guest, C.V.O., M.A., Mus.B., F.R.C.M., F.R.C.O.................1963
Legal Secretary, C. L. Hodgetts, Ll.B.........1973

WINCHESTER. £4,530

94th *Bishop*, Rt. Rev. John Vernon Taylor, M.A. (Wolvesey, Winchester) [Signs John Winton:]......................1974

Bishops Suffragan

Southampton, Rt. Rev. John Kingsmill Cavell, M.A. (Shepherds, Shepherds Lane, Compton, Winchester)....................1972
Basingstoke, Rt. Rev. Colin Clement Walter James, M.A. (11 The Close, Winchester)....1973

Dean (£3,170)

Very Rev. Michael Staffurth Stancliffe, M.A....1969

Dean of Jersey, Very Rev. Thomas Ashworth Goss, M.A......................1971
Dean of Guernsey, Very Rev. Frederick Walter Cogman, A.K.C., B.D...................1966

Canons Residentiary (£2,045)

F. Bussby, M.B.E.,	A. G. Wedderspoon,
M.A., M.Litt., B.D.1967	M.A., B.D.......1970
	Bp. of Basingstoke.1973

Organist, Martin Neary, M.A., F.R.C.O.......1972

Archdeacons

Winchester, Ven. E. D. Cartwright, M.A......1973
Basingstoke, Ven. G. G. Finch, M.A.........1971
Beneficed Clergy, 247; *Curates*, &c., 61
Chancellor, Prof. A. Phillips, O.B.E., M.A., Ph.D.1964
Registrar and Legal Secretary, R. C. White, M.A..1975

BATH AND WELLS. £3,985

75th *Bishop*, Rt. Rev. John Monier Bickersteth, M.A. *cons.* 1970. (The Palace, Wells) [Signs John Bath & Wells]...................1975

Bishop Suffragan

Taunton, Rt. Rev. Francis Horner West, M.A. (The Old Rectory, Dinder, Wells)........1962

Dean (£3,170)
Very Rev. Patrick Reynolds Mitchell, M.A....1973
  Canons Residentiary of Wells (each £2,045)
P. M. Martin, M.A..1970 | A. L. Birbeck, M.A. 1974
Archd. Haynes....1974 | D. R. Vicary, M.A.1975
Organist, A. Crossland....................1970

Archdeacons
Bath, Ven. J. E. Burgess, B.D...............1975
Taunton, Ven. A. Hopley..................1971
Wells, Ven. P. Haynes, M.A................1974
  Beneficed Clergy, 290; Curates, &c., 50.
Chancellor, G. H. Newsom, Q.C............1970
Registrar, Sec. & Chapt. Clerk, N. M. Cavender, Wells.

BIRMINGHAM. £3,985
5th *Bishop*, Rt. Rev. Laurence Ambrose Brown, M.A.(cons. 1960,trans. 1969) (Bishop's Croft, Harborne, Birmingham 17) [Signs Laurence Birmingham]..................1969

Bishop Suffragan
Aston, Rt. Rev. Mark Green, M.C., M.A. (5 Greenhill Road, Wylde Green, Sutton Coldfield) 1972

Provost
Very Rev. Basil Stanley Moss, M.A.........1972

Archdeacons
Aston, Ven. F. F. G. Warman, M.A..........1965
Birmingham, Ven. G. Hollis, M.A...........1974
  Beneficed Clergy, 165; Curates, &c., 78
Organist, D. M. Bruce-Payne, B.MUS., F.R.C.O., A.R.C.M................................1974
Chancellor, F. J. Aglionby................1970
Registrar and Legal Secretary, R. L. Ekin, B.A. (85 Cornwall Street, Birmingham 3).

BRISTOL. £3,985
53rd *Bishop*, Rt. Rev. Ernest John Tinsley, M.A., B.D. (Bishop's House, Clifton Hill, Bristol [Signs John Bristol] 1975

Bishop Suffragan
Malmesbury, Rt. Rev. Frederick Stephen Temple, M.A. (Morwena, Mill Lane, Swindon)..............................1973

Dean
Very Rev. Alfred Hounsell Dammers, M.A.....1973

Canons Residentiary
C. H. Shells, M.A..1973 | P. E. Coleman, LL.B., A.K.C.....1971
Organist, Clifford Harker, B.MUS., F.R.C.O., A.R.C.M................................1949

Archdeacons
Bristol, Ven. L. A. Williams, M.A...........1967
Swindon, Ven. J. S. Maples, M.A............1974
  Beneficed Clergy, 138; Curates, &c., 68
Chancellor, D. C. Calcutt, ll.B., MUS.B........1971
Registrar and Sec., T. R. Urquhart..........1972

CHELMSFORD. £3,985
6th *Bishop*, Rt. Rev. Albert John Trillo, F.K.C., B.D., M.Th. (cons. 1963) (Bishopscourt, Chelmsford) [Signs John Chelmsford].....1971

Bishops Suffragan
Colchester, Rt. Rev. Roderic Norman Coote, D.D. (Bishop's House, 32 Inglis Road, Colchester) (cons. 1951)....................1966
Barking, Rt. Rev. Albert James Adams, B.A. (670 High Road, Buckhurst Hill)..........1975
Bradwell, Rt. Rev. Charles Derek Bond, A.K.C. (c/o Bishopscourt, Chelmsford)...........1976
Provost, Very Rev. Hilary Martin Connop Price, M.A...............................1967
Organist, J. W. Jordan, M.A., MUS.B., F.R.C.O...1966

Archdeacons
Southend, Ven. P. S. G. Bridges............1972

West Ham, Ven. J. B. Taylor, M.A..........1975
Colchester, (vacant)
  Beneficed Clergy, 498; Curates, &c., 142
Chancellor, Miss S. M. Cameron, M.A........1970
Diocesan Registrar, D. W. Faull, 1 The Sanctuary, S.W.1...........................1963

CHICHESTER. £3,985
99th *Bishop*, Rt. Rev. Eric Waldram Kemp, D.D. (The Palace, Chichester) [Signs Eric Cicestr:]...........................1974

Bishops Suffragan
Lewes, Rt. Rev. James Herbert Lloyd Morrell, F.K.C. (83 Davigdor Road, Hove)........1959
Horsham, Rt. Rev. Ivor Colin Docker, M.A. (The Old Rectory, Worth, nr. Crawley)...1975
Assistant Bishops, Rt. Rev. Richard Ambrose Reeves, M.A. (cons. 1949)...............1966
Rt. Rev. Albert Kenneth Cragg, M.A., D.Phil. (cons. 1970).........................1974

Dean
Very Rev. John Walter Atherton Hussey, M.A.1955

Canons Residentiary
A. K. Walker, B.SC., Ph.D..........1971 | R. T. Greenacre, M.A......1975
Organist, J. A. Birch, M.A., F.R.C.O..........1958

Archdeacons
Chichester, Ven. R. M. S. Eyre M.A.........1975
Horsham, Ven. F. G. Kerr-Dineen, M.A......1975
Lewes and Hastings, Ven. M. L. Godden, M.A..1975
  Beneficed Clergy, 309; Curates, &c., 126
Chancellor, B. T. Buckle, M.A..............1960
Legal Secretary to the Bishop, and Diocesan Registrar, C. L. Hodgetts, LL.B.

COVENTRY. £3,985
6th *Bishop*, Rt. Rev. John Gibbs, B.A., B.D. (cons. 1973) (The Bishop's House, 23 Davenport Road, Coventry.) [Signs John Coventry.]................................1976
Assistant Bishop, Rt. Rev. John David McKie, M.A. (cons. 1946).....................1960
Provost, Very Rev. Harold Claude Noel Williams, B.A............................1958
Organist, R. G. Weddle, M.A., F.R.C.O........1972

Canons Residentiary
J. W. Poole, M.A...1963 | K. E. Wright, B.A., B.SC.............1974
G. P. A. Spink....1970
P. A. Berry, M.A...1973

Archdeacons
Coventry, Ven. E. A. Buchan, B.A...........1965
Warwick, Ven. E. Taylor, A.K.C............1974
  Beneficed Clergy, 165, Curates, &c., 42
Chancellor, His Hon. Conolly Hugh Gage, M.A.1948
Registrar, S. L. Penn, Coventry............1957

DERBY. £4,285
4th *Bishop*, Rt. Rev. Cyril William Johnston Bowles, M.A. (Bishop's House, Turnditch, Derby) [Signs Cyril Derby.]..............1969

Bishop Suffragan
Repton, Rt. Rev. William Warren Hunt, M.A. (Underwood, Baslow Road, Bakewell)....1965
Assistant Bishop, Rt. Rev. Thomas Richards Parfitt, M.A. (cons. 1952)................1962
Provost, Very Rev. Ronald Alfred Beddoes, M.A...................................1953

Canons Residentiary
P. W. Miller.....1966 | D. P. Wilcox, M.A..1972

Archdeacons
Chesterfield, Ven. T. W. I. Cleasby, M.A......1963
Derby, Ven. R. S. Dell, M.A................1973
Organist, W. M. Ross, Mus. Bac., F.R.C.O.....1958

Beneficed Clergy, 198; Curates, &c., 21
Chancellor, J. A. D. Owen, Q.C., M.A.........1973
Registrar, J. R. S. Grimwood-Taylor, Derby.

ELY. £3,985
65th Bishop, Rt. Rev. Edward James Keymer
Roberts, D.D. (cons. 1956, trans. 1962 and 1964)
(The Bishop's House, Ely) [Edward Elien:]..1964

Bishop Suffragan
Huntingdon, Rt. Rev. Eric St. Quintin Wall,
M.A. (Whitgift House, Ely)...............1972

Dean (£3,170)
Very Rev. Michael Sausmarez Carey, M.A....1970

Canons Residentiary (each £2,045)
G. Youell, M.A.....1970 | B. of Huntingdon.1972
G. C. Stead, M.A....1971 | A. J. Morcom, M.A.1974
Organist, A. W. Wills, MUS. DOC., F.R.C.O....1959

Archdeacons
Ely, Ven. J. S. Long, M.A..................1970
Wisbech, Ven. B. G. B. Fox, M.C...........1965
Huntingdon, Ven. D. N. de L. Young, M.A...1975
Beneficed Clergy, 250; Curates, &c., 85
Chancellor, Rev. K. G. Routledge, LL.B., M.A..1973
Registrar, J. B. Green, M.A.
Legal Secretary, D. M. Moir Carey, M.A., 1 The
Sanctuary, S.W.1.

EXETER. £3,000
68th Bishop, Rt. Rev. Eric Arthur John Mercer
(cons. 1965) (The Palace, Exeter) [Signs Eric
Exon:]....................................1973

Bishops Suffragan
Crediton, Rt. Rev. Philip John Pasterfield, M.A.
(10 The Close, Exeter)...................1974
Plymouth, Rt. Rev. Richard Fox Cartwright,
M.A., D.D. (Bishop's Lodge, Yeoland Lane,
Yelverton)...............................1972
Assistant Bishops, Rt. Rev. John Armstrong,
C.B., O.B.E. (cons. 1963); Rt. Rev. Charles
Robert Claxton, D.D. (cons. 1946); Rt. Rev.
John Maurice Key, D.D. (cons. 1947); Rt.
Rev. Wilfrid Arthur Edmund Westall, D.D.
(cons. 1954).

Dean (£2,400)
Very Rev. Clifford Thomas Chapman, Ph.D.,
B.A., B.D., M.Th., A.K.C................1973

Canons Residentiary
Archd. Ward.....1970 | F. G. Rice........1970
                     | J. A. Thurmer, M.A.1973
Organist, L. Nethsingha, M.A., F.R.C.O........1972
Chapter Clerk, J. F. Eden, M.A.............1966

Archdeacons
Barnstaple, Ven. R. G. Herniman, B.A.......1970
Totnes, Ven. J. M. Lucas..................1976
Plymouth, Ven. F. A. J. Matthews, M.A......1962
Exeter, Ven. A. F. Ward, B.A..............1970
Beneficed Clergy, 279; Curates, &c., 112
Chancellor, D. Calcutt, M.A., LL.B., MUS.B......1971
Registrar and Secretary, J. F. G. Michelmore, 18
Cathedral Yard, Exeter.

GLOUCESTER. £3,985
37th Bishop, Rt. Rev. John Yates, M.A. (cons.
1972) (Bishopscourt, Gloucester) [Signs
John Gloucestr:].........................1975

Bishop Suffragan
Tewkesbury, Rt. Rev. Thomas Carlyle Joseph
Robert Hamish Deakin, M.A. (Green Acre,
Hempsted, Gloucester)....................1973

Dean (£3,170)
Very Rev. Alfred Gilbert Goddard Thurlow
M.A., F.S.A..............................1972

Canons Residentiary (£2,045)
W. T. Wardle, | A. J. Holloway,
M.A..........1948 | B.D., M.Th......1974
W. R. Houghton, | D. C. St. V. Welander,
M.A..........1968 | B.D..............1975
Archd. Evans, M.A. 1969 |
Organist, J. D. Sanders, M.A., MUS.B., F.R.C.O.,
A.R.C.M.....................................1967

Archdeacons
Gloucester, Ven. W. T. Wardle, M.A........1948
Cheltenham, Ven. T. E. Evans, M.A.........1975
Beneficed Clergy, 228; Curates, &c., 49
Chancellor & Vicar-Gen., Rev. E. Garth Moore,
M.A..1957
Registrar, H. A. Gibson, 34 Brunswick Road,
Gloucester.
Legal Sec., D. M. Moir Carey, M.A., 1 The
Sanctuary, Westminster, S.W.1.
Diocesan Sec., J. H. Martin, Church House,
College Green, Gloucester.

GUILDFORD. £3,985
6th Bishop, Rt. Rev. David Alan Brown,
A.L.C.D., B.D., M.Th., B.A. (Willow Grange,
Stringer's Common, Guildford) [Signs
David Guildford]........................1973

Bishop Suffragan
Dorking, Rt. Rev. Kenneth Dawson Evans,
M.A. (13 Pilgrim's Way, Guildford)........1968
Assistant Bishop, Rt. Rev. St. John Surridge
Pike, D.D. (cons. 1958)...................1963
Dean, Very Rev. Antony Cyprian Bridge....1968

Canons Residentiary
L. E. Tanner, M.A...1971 | F. S. Telfer, M.A...1973
R. W. Gibbin, M.A.1973 |
Organist, P. Moore........................1974

Archdeacons
Surrey, Ven. J. M. Evans, M.A.............1968
Dorking, Ven. W. H. S. Purcell, M.A........1968
Beneficed Clergy, 147; Curates, &c., 56
Chancellor, M. B. Goodman, M.A.
Legal Sec., R. M. Hollis, M.A.
Registrar of Diocese, R. M. Hollis, M.A.
Registrar of the Archdeaconries, R. M. Hollis, M.A.

HEREFORD. £4,897
102nd Bishop, Rt. Rev. John Richard Gordon
Eastaugh, B.A. (The Palace, Hereford) [Signs
John Hereford]...........................1973

Dean (£3,962)
Very Rev. Norman Stanley Rathbone, M.A...1968
Canons Residentiary (£2,750)
J. M. Irvine, M.A...1965 | C. A. Shaw, M.A...1975
Archd. Lewis.....1970 |
Organist, Roy Massey, B.MUS., F.R.C.O.......1974

Archdeacons
Hereford, Ven. T. Barfett, M.A............1976
Ludlow, Ven. A. H. Woodhouse, D.S.C., M.A..1970
Beneficed Clergy, 105; Curates, &c., 73
Chancellor, Rev. K. J. T. Elphinstone.......1952
Registrar, Philip Gwynne James, 5 St. Peter
Street, Hereford.

LEICESTER. £3,985
3rd Bishop, Rt. Rev. Ronald Ralph Williams,
D.D. (Bishop's Lodge, Leicester.) [Signs
Ronald Leicester]........................1953
Assistant Bishops, Rt.Rev. John Ernest Llewellyn
Mort, C.B.E., M.A. (cons. 1952)..........1972
Rt. Rev. Thomas Samuel Garrett, M.A. (cons.
1971)...................................1975
Provost, Very Rev. John Chester Hughes, M.A..1963

Canons Residentiary
D. W. Gundry, | Bp. Mort........1970
B.D., M.Th.......1963 |
Organist, Peter White, M.A., MUS.B., F.R.C.O...1968

Archdeacons

Leicester, Ven. R. B. Cole..................1963
Loughborough, Ven. H. Lockley, Ph.D........1963
Beneficed Clergy, 220; Curates, &c., 45
Chancellor, R. A. Forrester, C.V.O., M.A.......1953
Registrars, R. J. Moore and G. K. J. Moore,
  5 Bowling Green Street, Leicester.

LICHFIELD. £4,897

96th Bishop, Rt. Rev. Kenneth John Fraser
  Skelton, C.B.E., M.A. (cons. 1962) (Bishop's
  House, The Close, Lichfield) [Signs Kenneth
  Lichfield]................................1975

Bishops Suffragan

Shrewsbury, Rt. Rev. Francis William Cocks,
  C.B., M.A. (Athlone, London Road, Shrews-
  bury)....................................1970
Stafford, Rt. Rev. John Waine, B.A. (St.
  Thomas' Lodge, Radford Rise, Stafford)...1975

Dean (£3,962)

Rt. Rev. George Edward Holderness, M.A......1969

Canons Residentiary (each £2,750)

Archd. Ninis.....1974 | D. F. J. Rutt......1976
Organist, R. G. Greening, M.A., B.Mus., F.R.C.O.1959

Archdeacons

Stafford, Ven. R. B. Ninis, M.A.............1974
Salop, Ven. S. D. Austerberry..............1959
Stoke on Trent, Ven. C. W. Borrett, M.A.....1971
Beneficed Clergy, 374; Curates, &c., 105
Chancellor (vacant)
Diocesan Registrar and Bishop's Sec., M. B. S.
  Exham.

LINCOLN. £3,985

69th Bishop, Rt. Rev. Simon Wilton Phipps,
  M.C., M.A. (cons. 1968, trans. 1974) (Bishop's
  House, Eastgate, Lincoln). [Signs Simon
  Lincoln:]................................1974

Bishops Suffragan

Grimsby, Rt. Rev. Gerald Fitzmaurice Colin,
  M.A. (21 Westgate, Louth)................1966
Grantham, Rt. Rev. Dennis Gascoyne Hawker,
  M.A. (Fairacre, Barrowby High Road,
  Grantham)................................1972
Assistant Bishops, Rt. Rev. Anthony Otter, M.A.
  (cons. 1949).............................1965
  Rt. Rev. Kenneth Healey, M.A. (cons. 1958)..1965
  Rt. Rev. George William Clarkson, M.A.
  (cons. 1954).............................1968

Dean (£3,170)

Very Rev. the Hon. Oliver William Twisleton-
  Wykeham-Fiennes, M.A.....................1968

Canons Residentiary (£2,045)

P. B. G. Binnall, | D. C. Rutter, M.A..1965
M.A., F.S.A......1962 | Archd. Dudman...1971
Organist, Philip Marshall, MUS.DOC., F.R.C.O....1966

Archdeacons

Stow, Ven. D. Scott, M.A...................1975
Lincoln, Ven. A. C. Smith, V.R.D., M.A......1960
Lindsey, Ven. R. W. Dudman, B.A............1971
Beneficed Clergy, 350; Curates, &c., 110
Chancellor, M. B. Goodman, M.A............1971
Registrar, H. J. J. Griffith, 2 Bank Street,
  Lincoln.

NORWICH. £3,985

69th Bishop (and 110th of East Anglia, Rt. Rev.
  Maurice Arthur Ponsonby Wood, D.S.C.,
  M.A. (The Bishop's House, Norwich) [Signs
  Maurice Norvic]..........................1971

Bishops Suffragan

Lynn, Rt. Rev. William Aubrey Aitken, M.A.
  (Elsing, Dereham)........................1973
Thetford, (vacant)

Dean

Very Rev. Alan Brunskill Webster, M.A., B.D...1970

Canons Residentiary

H. Drury, B.A....1973 | F. Colquhoun, M.A.1973
                     | P. Bradshaw, M.A..1974
Organist, M. B. Nicholas, M.A., F.R.C.O.......1971

Archdeacons

Norfolk, The Bishop of Thetford............1962
Norwich, Ven. T. Dudley-Smith, M.A.........1973
Lynn, The Bishop of Lynn..................1973
Beneficed Clergy, 302; Curates, &c., 30
Chancellor, His Hon. J. H. Ellison, V.R.D., M.A..1955
Registrar and Sec., B. O. L. Prior, T.D.

OXFORD. £3,985

39th Bishop, Rt. Rev. Kenneth John Woollcombe, M.A. (Bishop's House, Cuddesdon,
  Oxford) [Signs Kenneth Oxon]...........1971

Bishops Suffragan

Buckingham, Rt. Rev. Simon Hedley Burrows,
  M.A. (Sheridan, Grimms Hill, Great Mis-
  senden)..................................1974
Dorchester, Rt. Rev. Peter Knight Walker, M.A.
  (Christ Church, Oxford)..................1972
Reading, Rt. Rev. Eric Wild, M.A. (The Well
  House, Upper Basildon, Reading).........1972
Assistant Bishop, Rt. Rev. David Goodwin
  Loveday, M.A. (cons. 1957)...............1971

Dean of Christ Church (£3,170)

Very Rev. Henry Chadwick, D.D.............1969

Canons Residentiary

Archd. Witton- | J. Macquarrie, D.Lit.
  Davies.....1956 | 1969
W. R. F. Brown- | M. F. Wiles, M.A......1970
  ing, M.A., B.D. | Bp. of Dorchester.1972
  (Canon of the | P. R. Baelz, M.A..1972
  Cathedral Church) | J. McManners, M.A.
  1965 | 1972
Organist, S. Preston M.A., B.Mus.............1970

Archdeacons

Oxford, Ven. C. Witton-Davies, M.A.........1956
Berks., Ven. W. R. Birt...................1973
Bucks., Ven. D. I. T. Eastman, M.C., M.A.....1970
Beneficed Clergy, 370; Curates, &c., 93
Chancellor, P. T. S. Boydell...............1958
Registrar and Legal Sec., F. E. Robson.......1969

Windsor.

(The Queen's Free Chapel of St. George within
  Her Castle of Windsor—A Royal Peculiar)
Dean, Rt. Rev. Michael Ashley Mann.......1976

Canons Residentiary

G. B. Bentley, M.A.1957 | S. E. Verney, M.A..1970
J. A. Fisher, M.A....1958 | A. O. Dyson, B.D.,
                          | M.A., D.Phil....1974
Organist, C. J. Robinson, M.A., B.Mus., F.R.C.O..1974
Chapter Clerk, H. G. M. Bass, C.M.G., M.A.

PETERBOROUGH. £3,985

35th Bishop, Rt. Rev. Douglas Russell Feaver,
  M.A. (The Palace, Peterborough) [Signs
  Douglas Petriburg].......................1972
Assistant Bishops, Rt. Rev. Archibald Rollo
  Graham-Campbell, C.B.E., M.A. (cons.
  1948)....................................1965
  Rt. Rev. Guy Marshall, M.B.E., A.K.C. (cons.
  1967)....................................1974
  Rt. Rev. Alan Francis Bright Rogers, M.A.
  (cons. 1959).............................1975

Dean (£3,120)

Very Rev. Richard Shuttleworth Wingfield-
  Digby, M.A...............................1966

Canons Residentiary (each £2,045)

Archd. Towndrow1966 | P. H. Cecil, B.D.,
A. S. Gribble, M.A..1967 | A.K.C..........1971

Master of the Music, W. S. Vann, D.MUS.,
F.R.C.O....................................1953

Archdeacons
Northampton, Ven. B. R. Marsh, B.A........1964
Oakham, Ven. F. N. Towndrow, M.A.......1967

Beneficed Clergy, 250; *Curates*, &c., 30
Chancellor, Rev. K. G. Routledge, M.A.......1976
Registrar, R. Hemingray, 37 Priestgate,
Peterborough.

PORTSMOUTH. £3,985
6th Bishop, Rt. Rev. Archibald Ronald Mc-
Donald Gordon, M.A. (Bishopswood, Fare-
ham, Hants.) [Signs Ronald Portsmouth]...1975
Provost, Very Rev. Michael John Nott, B.D.,
A.K.C....................................1972
Organist, C. Gower, M.A., F.R.C.O.

Canons Residentiary
F. C. Carpenter, | N. H. Crowder,
M.A...........1968 | M.A...........1975

Archdeacons
Portsmouth, Ven. C. Prior, C.B., M.A.......1969
I. of Wight, Ven. R. V. Scruby, M.A........1965
Beneficed Clergy, 119; *Curates*, &c., 62
Chancellor, B. T. Buckle, M.A.............1971
Registrar and Legal Sec. (vacant)

ROCHESTER. £4,397
104th Bishop, Rt. Rev. Richard David Say, D.D.
(Bishopscourt, Rochester), [Signs David
Roffen:]................................1961

Bishop Suffragan
Tonbridge, Rt. Rev. Philip Harold Ernest
Goodrich, M.A. (Bishop's Lodge, St. Bo-
tolph's Road, Sevenoaks)................1973
Assistant Bishop, Rt. Rev. John Keith Russell,
M.A. (*cons.* 1955).......................1965

Dean (£3,170)
Rt. Rev. Stanley Woodley Betts, C.B.E., M.A..1966

Canons Residentiary
P. A. Welsby, M.A., | M. J. Baddeley,
Ph.D...........1966 | M.A...........1974
| Archd. Palmer....1977
Organist, R. J. Ashfield, D.MUS., F.R.C.O......1956

Archdeacons
Tonbridge, Ven. E. E. Maples Earle, M.A.....1952
Bromley, Ven. H. W. Cragg, M.A...........1969
Rochester, Ven. D. G. Palmer, M.A..........1977
Beneficed Clergy, 220; *Curates*, &c., 124
Chancellor, M. B. Goodman, M.A...........1971
Registrar, O. R. Woodfield, Rochester.......1955
Sec. D. W. Faull, 1 The Sanctuary, S.W.1....1963

ST. ALBANS. £3,985
7th Bishop, Rt. Rev. Robert Alexander Ken-
nedy Runcie, M.C., M.A. (Abbey Gate House,
St. Albans) [Signs Robert St. Albans]......1970
Bishops Suffragan
Bedford, Rt. Rev. John Tyrell Holmes Hare,
M.A. (168 Kimbolton Road, Bedford)......1968
Hertford, Rt. Rev. Peter Mumford, M.A. (Hert-
ford House, Abbey Mill Lane, St. Albans)..1974
Dean (£3,170)
Very Rev. Peter Clement Moore, M.A., D.Phil..1973
Organist, P. Hurford, M.A., MUS.B., F.R.C.O.,
A.R.C.M..................................1958

Archdeacons
St. Albans, Ven. D. J. Farmbrough, M.A......1974
Bedford, Ven. R. S. Brown, M.A............1973
Beneficed Clergy, 265; *Curates*, &c., 154
Chancellor, G. H. Newsom, Q.C., M.A........1958
Joint Registrars and Legal Secs., D. W. Faull
(1963) and P. F. B. Beesley (1969), 1 The
Sanctuary, S.W.1.

ST. EDMUNDSBURY AND IPSWICH. £4,285
6th Bishop, Rt. Rev. Leslie Wilfrid Brown,
C.B.E., D.D. (Bishop's House, Ipswich), *cons.*
1953, *trans.* 1966 [Signs Leslie St. Edm. &
Ipswich]..................................1966

Bishop Suffragan
Dunwich (vacant)
Provost, Rt. Rev. David Rokeby Maddock,
M.A.....................................1976

Canons Residentiary
C. Rhodes, M.A....1964   D. A. Payne, M.A..1973
Archdeacons
Ipswich, Ven. G. D. J. Walsh, M.A..........1976
Suffolk, Ven. D. J. Smith................1975
Sudbury, Ven. K. Child, B.A..............1970
Organist, T. F. H. Oxley, M.A., B.MUS., F.R.C.O. 1957
Beneficed Clergy, 213; *Curates*, &c., 19
Chancellor, J. C. C. Blofeld, M.A...........1974
Registrar, J. D. Mitson, M.A., LL.B. 22-28
Museum Street, Ipswich.

SALISBURY. £3,985
75th Bishop, Rt. Rev. George Edmund Rein-
dorp, D.D. (South Canonry, The Close,
Salisbury) (*cons.* 1961, *trans.* 1973) [Signs
George Sarum]...........................1973

Bishops Suffragan
Sherborne, Rt. Rev. John Dudley Galtrey
Kirkham, M.A. (69 The Close, Salisbury)...1976
Ramsbury, Rt. Rev. John Robert Geoffrey
Neale, A.K.C. (Chittoe Vicarage, Bromham,
Chippenham)............................1974

Dean (£3,170)
Very Rev. William Fenton Morley, M.A., B.D..1971

Canons Residentiary (£2,045)
Arch. Wingfield- | I. G. D. Dunlop,
Digby.........1968 | M.A., F.S.A........1972
| C. Moxon, M.A....1975
Organist, R. G. Seal, M.A., F.R.C.O..........1968

Archdeacons
Wilts, The Bishop of Ramsbury............1975
Dorset, Ven. R. L. Sharp, M.A.............1975
Sherborne, Ven. E. J. G. Ward, M.V.O., M.A....1967
Sarum, Ven. S. B. Wingfield-Digby, M.B.E.,
M.A.....................................1968
Beneficed Clergy, 305; *Curates*, &c., 54
Chancellor of the Diocese, His Hon. J. H. Ellison,
M.A.....................................1955
Registrar and Legal Secretary, Alan M. Barker,
B.A., Bishop's Walk, The Close, Salisbury.

SOUTHWARK. £3,985
6th Bishop, Rt. Rev. Arthur Mervyn Stock-
wood, D.D. (Bishop's House, 38 Tooting Bec
Gardens, S.W.16) [Signs Mervyn South-
wark]....................................1959
Assistant Bishops, Rt. Rev. John Arthur Thomas
Robinson, M.A., Ph.D., D.D. (*cons.* 1959); Rt.
Rev. Edward George Knapp-Fisher, M.A.
(*cons.* 1960).............................1975

Bishops Suffragan
Kingston on Thames, Rt. Rev. Hugh William
Montefiore, M.A., B.D. (23 Bellevue Road,
Wandsworth Common, S.W.17).........1970
Woolwich, Rt. Rev. Michael Eric Marshall,
M.A. (4 College Gardens, Dulwich, S.E. 21).1975
Provost, Very Rev. Harold Edward Frankham.1970

Canons Residentiary
D. M. Tasker, B.A..1961 | I. G. Smith-Camer-
| on, B.A...........1972
P. H. Penwarden, | P. A. Delaney,
M.A...........1971 | A.K.C...........1973
Organist, H. Bramma.....................1976

Archdeacons

Southwark, Ven. M. H. D. Whinney, M.A.....1973
Lewisham, Ven. I. G. Davies, B.A., B.D........1972
Kingston, Ven. P. D. Robb, M.A................1953
Wandsworth, Ven. P. B. Coombs, M.A........1975
Chancellor, Rev. E. Garth Moore, M.A........1948
Secretary and Registrar, D. W. Faull, 1 The
Sanctuary, S.W.1..........................1963

TRURO. £4,548

11th Bishop, Rt. Rev. Graham Douglas
Leonard, M.A., D.D. (Lis Escop, Truro) (cons.
1964, trans. 1973) [Signs Graham Truron:]..1973

Bishop Suffragan

St. Germans, Rt. Rev. Cecil Richard Rutt,
C.B.E., M.A., D.Litt. (32 Falmouth Road,
Truro) (cons. 1966).......................1974

Dean

Very Rev. Henry Morgan Lloyd, D.S.O., O.B.E.,
M.A......................................1960

Canons Residentiary

Archd. Young....1965	P. L. Maddock,
M. S. F. Thornton,	B.A............1976
M.A., S.T.D......1975	

Organist, J. Winter.........................1971

Archdeacons

Cornwall, Ven. P. C. Young, B.Litt., M.A.....1965
Bodmin, Ven. C. J. E. Meyer, M.A............1969
Beneficed Clergy, 170; Curates, &c., 23
Chancellor, P. T. S. Boydell, Q.C............1957
Registrar and Secretary, R. W. Money, 2 Princes
Street, Truro.

WORCESTER. £3,985.

110th Bishop, Rt. Rev. Robert Wilmer Woods,
K.C.V.O., M.A. (The Bishop's House, Hartle-
bury Castle, Kidderminster) [Signs Robin
Worcester]................................1970
Assistant Bishop, Rt. Rev. David Howard
Nicholas Allenby, M.A. (cons. 1962).......1968

Bishop Suffragan

Dudley (vacant)

Dean (£3,170)

Very Rev. Thomas George Adames Baker,
M.A......................................1975

Canons Residentiary (£2,045)

G. C. B. Davies,	E. S. Turnbull, M.A.1971
D.D..............1963	Archd. Williams...1975
W.E. Purcell, M.A.1966	

Organist, D. Hunt, Mus.D., F.R.C.O..........1975

Archdeacons

Dudley, Ven. C. R. Campling, M.A............1976
Worcester, Ven. J. C. Williams, B.A..........1975
Beneficed Clergy, 130; Curates, &c., 83
Chancellor, P. T. S. Boydell Q.C............1959
Registrar, Rev. J. A. Dale, Diocesan Registry,
Worcester.

Province of York

YORK. £7,070

94th Archbishop and Primate of England Most
Rev. and Rt. Hon. Stuart Yarworth Blanch,
M.A., cons. 1966, trans. 1974 (Bishopthorpe,
York) [Signs Stuart Ebor:]................1974
Assistant Bishops, Rt. Rev. George Eyles Irwin
Cockin, B.A. (cons. 1959)...............1969
Rt. Rev. Douglas Noel Sargent, M.A. (cons.
1962)....................................1972

Bishops Suffragan

Selby, Rt. Rev. Morris Henry St. John Mad-
docks, M.A. (Tollgarth, Tadcaster Road,
Dringhouses, York).....................1972
Whitby, Rt. Rev. Clifford Conder Barker,
M.A. (60 West Green, Stokesley, Middles-
brough)..................................1975
Hull (vacant)

Dean (£3,170)

Very Rev. Ronald Claude Dudley Jasper, D.D.1975

Canons Residentiary (£2,045)

R. E. Cant, M.A....1957	A G. Widdess, M.A.1975

Organist, Francis Jackson, Mus.D., F.R.C.O.....1946

Archdeacons

York, Ven. L. C. Stanbridge, M.A............1972
East Riding, Ven. D. G. Snelgrove, M.A......1970
Cleveland, Ven. J. E. Southgate, B.A........1974
Beneficed Clergy, 297; Curates, &c., 76
Official Principal and Auditor of the Chancery
Court, Sir Harold Kent, G.C.B.
Chancellor of the Diocese, Rev. K. J. T. Elphin-
stone, M.A..............................1971
Vicar-General of the Province and Official Principal
of the Consistory Court, Rev. K. J. T. Elphin-
stone, M.A.
Registrar and Secretary, G. P. Knowles, M.A.,
LL.B....................................1968

DURHAM. £5,635

91st Bishop, Rt. Rev. John Stapylton Habgood,
M.A., Ph.D. (Auckland Castle, Bishop Auckland) [Signs John Dunelm]...............1973

Bishop Suffragan

Jarrow, Rt. Rev. Alexander Kenneth Hamilton, M.A. (Melkridge House, Gilesgate,
Durham).................................1965

Dean (£3,170)

Very Rev. Eric William Heaton, M.A........1974

Canons Residentiary (£2,045)

D. R. Jones, M.A...1964	S. W. Sykes, M.A...1974
Archd. Perry......1970	R. L. Coppin, M.A.1974
C. H. G. Hopkins,	Archd. Marchant...1974
M.A..............1970	

Organist, R. Lloyd, Mus.B., F.R.C.O..........1974

Archdeacons

Durham, Ven. M. C. Perry, M.A.............1970
Auckland, Ven. G. J. C. Marchant, B.A.......1974
Beneficed Clergy, 235; Curates, &c., 89
Chancellor, Rev. E. Garth Moore, M.A......1954
Registrar and Legal Secretary, W. K. Wills,
Ll.B.....................................1975

BLACKBURN. £3,985

5th Bishop, Rt. Rev. Robert Arnold Schurhoff
Martineau, M.A., cons. 1966, trans. 1972 (Bis-
hop's House, Blackburn) [Signs Robert
Blackburn]...............................1972

Bishops Suffragan

Lancaster Rt. Rev. Dennis Fountain Page, M.A.
(Winmarleigh Vicarage, nr. Preston).....1975
Burnley, Rt. Rev. Richard Charles Challinor
Watson, M.A. (Palace House, Burnley).....1970
Assistant Bishop, Rt. Rev. Anthony Leigh
Egerton Hoskyns-Abrahall (cons. 1955).....1975
Provost, Very Rev. Lawrence Jackson, A.K.C...1973

Canons Residentiary

G. A. Williams,	P. C. Ruffle, B.D..1974
M.A..............1965	J. M. Taylor......1975

Archdeacons

Lancaster, Ven. G. Gower-Jones, M.A........1966
Blackburn, Ven. C. W. D. Carroll, M.A.......1973
Organist, J. Bertalot, M.A., F.R.C.O., A.R.C.M....1964
Beneficed Clergy, 240; Curates, &c., 54
Chancellor, R. A. Forrester, M.A............1949
Registrar, Leslie Ranson, LL.B..............1954

BRADFORD. £3,985

5th Bishop, Rt. Rev. Ross Sydney Hook, M.C.,
M.A. (Bishopscroft, Ashwell Road, Heaton,
Bradford), cons. 1965, trans. 1972 [Signs Ross
Bradford]................................1972
Provost, Very Rev. William Hugh Alan
Cooper, M.A.............................1962

Canons Residentiary

J. W. Towell, M.A.1967   F. P. Sargeant, B.A..1973
Organist, K. V. Rhodes, B.Mus., F.R.C.O......1964

Archdeacons

Bradford, Ven. W. Johnston, M.A............1965
Craven, Ven. M. Kaye, M.A.................1972
Beneficed Clergy, 123; Curates, &c., 23
Chancellor, D. M. Savill, Q.C..............1976
Registrar and Secretary, H. Firth, Martins Bank
Chambers, Tyrrel Street, Bradford.

CARLISLE. £3,985
64th Bishop, Rt. Rev. Henry David Halsey, B.A.
(Rose Castle, Dalston, Carlisle), cons. 1968.
[Signs David Carliol]....................1972

Bishop Suffragan
Penrith, Rt. Rev. William Edward Augustus
Pugh, M.A................................1970

Dean (£3,170)
Very Rev. John Howard Churchill, M.A.......1973
Canons Residentiary (£2,045)
Archd. Bradford..1966 | R. M. Wadding-
A. H. Attwell, | ton, M.A.........1972
M.A., M.Th.....1972
Organist, R. A. Seivewright, M.A., A.R.C.O....1960

Archdeacons
Carlisle, Ven. R. B. Bradford, B.A.........1971
West Cumberland, Ven. A. G. Hardie, M.A....1971
Westmorland and Furness, Ven. W. F. Ewbank,
M.A., B.D................................1971
Beneficed Clergy, 229
Chancellor, His Hon. D. J. Stinson, M.A.....1971
Registrar and Sec., I. S. Sutcliffe, M.A., LL.B.,
Carlisle.................................1964

CHESTER. £3,985
38th Bishop, Rt. Rev. Hubert Victor Whitsey,
M.A. (Bishop's House, Chester) (cons. 1971)
[Signs Victor Cestr:]....................1973

Bishop Suffragan
Stockport, Rt. Rev. Rupert Gordon Strutt, B.D.
(Bishop's Lodge, Macclesfield Road, Alderley
Edge)...................................1965
Birkenhead, Rt. Rev. Ronald Brown, B.A.
(Trafford House, Queen's Park, Chester)...1974
Dean (£3,170)
Very Rev. George William Outram Addle-
shaw, M.A., B.D., F.S.A..................1963
Canons Residentiary (£2,045)
R. Simpson, M.V.O., | J. S. Lawton, M.A.,
M.A..............1974 | B.D., D.Phil.....1975
K. M. Maltby, M.A., | K. M. Whittam,
B.D..............1974 | M.A.............1975
Organist, R. A. Fisher, M.A., F.R.C.O.......1967

Archdeacons
Chester, Ven. H. L. Williams, B.A..........1975
Macclesfield, Ven. F. H. House, O.B.E., M.A...1967
Beneficed Clergy, 290; Curates, &c., 78
Chancellor, Rev. K. J. T. Elphinstone, M.A....1950
Legal Secretaries, Gamon & Co., 2 White Friars,
Chester.

LIVERPOOL. £3,985
6th Bishop, Rt. Rev. David Stuart Sheppard,
M.A. (cons. 1969) (Bishop's Lodge, Woolton
Park, Liverpool) [Signs David Liverpool]..1975

Bishop Suffragan
Warrington, Rt. Rev. Michael Henshall, B.A..1975
Asst. Bishop, Rt. Rev. William Scott Baker,
M.A. (cons. 1943)........................1968
Dean (£3,170)
Very Rev. Edward Henry Patey, M.A.........1964
Canons Residentiary
C. B. Naylor, M.A..1956 | Archd. Corbett....1971
L. F. Hopkins, | G. Bates..........1973
M.A., B.D......1964 |
Organist, Noel Rawsthorne, F.R.C.O.........1955

Archdeacons
Liverpool, Ven. C. E. Corbett, M.A..........1971
Warrington, Ven. J. A. Lawton, M.A.........1970
Beneficed Clergy, 227; Curates, &c., 103
Chancellor, His Hon. E. Steel, LL.B.........1957
Registrar, R. H. Arden, 1 Hanover Street,
Liverpool 1.

MANCHESTER. £4,285
8th Bishop, Rt. Rev. Patrick Campbell Rodger,
M.A. (Bishopscourt, Bury New Road, Manchester 7), [Signs Patrick Manchester]......1970

Bishops Suffragan
Hulme, Rt. Rev. David George Galliford, M.A.
(31 Bland Road, Prestwich, Manchester)....1975
Middleton, Rt. Rev. Edward Ralph Wickham,
B.D. (1 Portland Road, Eccles, Manchester)..1959
Assistant Bishops, Rt. Rev. Richard Patrick
Crosland Hanson, D.D. (cons. 1970) 1974; Rt.
Rev. Kenneth Venner Ramsey, M.A., B.D.
(cons. 1953).............................1975
Dean (£3,170) Very Rev. Alfred Jowett, C.B.E.,
M.A.....................................1964
Canons Residentiary (£2,045)
M. M. Hennell | Archd. Ballard....1972
M.A..............1970 | A. C. Hall, M.A....1974
G. O. Morgan,
B.Sc.............1971
Organist, D. E. Cantrell, M.A., B.Mus., F.R.C.O.1961

Archdeacons
Manchester, Ven. A. H. Ballard, M.A.........1972
Rochdale, Ven. H. O. Fielding, M.A.........1972
Beneficed Clergy, 300; Curates, &c., 120
Chancellor, G. C. H. Spafford, M.A., ll.B...1976
Registrar and Bishop's Secretary, J. Maloney, 90
Deansgate, Manchester..................1972

NEWCASTLE. £3,985
9th Bishop, Rt. Rev. Ronald Oliver Bowlby,
M.A. (The Bishop's House, 29 Moor Road,
South, Newcastle upon Tyne) [Signs
Ronald Newcastle:].....................1973
Assistant Bishop, Rt. Rev. Anthony George
Weaver Hunter (cons. 1968)..............1976
Provost, Very Rev. Christopher Garnett How-
sin Spafford, M.A.......................1976

Canons Residentiary
Archd. Unwin....1963 | D. E. F. Ogden,
A. Wilson, M.A....1964 | B.A............1966
Organist, Russell A. Missin, F.R.C.O.... ...1967

Archdeacons
Northumberland, Ven. C. P. Unwin, T.D., M.A..1963
Lindisfarne, Ven. M. H. Bates, M.A.........1970
Beneficed Clergy, 151; Curates, &c., 55
Chancellor, His Hon. A. J. Blackett-Ord, M.A..1971
Registrar and Sec., R. R. V. Nicholson, 46
Grainger Street, Newcastle upon Tyne.

RIPON. £4,897
10th Bishop, Rt. Rev. Stuart Hetley Price, M.A.
(Bishop Mount, Ripon.) (cons. 1972)
[Signs Hetley Ripon]....................1976

Bishop Suffragan
Knaresborough, Rt. Rev. Ralph Emmerson,
B.D., A.K.C. (76 Leadhall Lane, Harrogate)...1972
Dean (£3,962)
Very Rev. Frederick Edwin Le Grice, M.A....1968
Canons Residentiary (each £2,045)
J. G. B. Ashworth, | W. Dillam, L.Th...1973
L.Th., B.A......1965 | Archd. Burbridge.1976
Organist, Ronald Perrin, F.R.C.O..........1966
Archdeacons
Leeds, Ven. A. C. Page, M.A...............1969
Richmond, Ven. J. P. Burbridge, M.A........1976

Beneficed Clergy, 145; Curates, &c., 45
Chancellor, J. B. Mortimer, Q.C., M.A........1971
Registrar and Legal Secretary, J. R. Balmforth,
M.A., Phoenix House, South Parade, Leeds..

SHEFFIELD. £4,585
4th Bishop, Rt. Rev. William Gordon Fallows,
M.A. (Bishopscroft, Snaithing Lane, Sheffield
10) (cons. 1968) [Signs Gordon Sheffield]....1971
Bishop Suffragan
Doncaster, Rt. Rev. David Stewart Cross, M.A.
(344 Grimesthorpe Road, Sheffield 4)......1976
Provost, Very Rev. Wilfred Frank Curtis,
A.K.C..1974

Archdeacons
Sheffield, Ven. H. Johnson, M.A..............1963
Doncaster, Ven. E. J. G. Rogers, B.A.........1967
Organist, G. Matthews, B.Mus., F.R.C.O........1967
Beneficed Clergy, 161; Curates, &c., 112
Chancellor, G. B. Graham, Q.C.................1971
Registrar and Legal Sec., V. H. Sandford, M.A.,
30 Bank Street, Sheffield.

SODOR AND MAN. £4,897
77th Bishop, Rt. Rev. Vernon Sampson
Nicholls (The Bishop's House, 8 Co-
burg Road, Ramsey, Isle of Man) [Signs
Vernon Sodor and Man]...................1974
Archdeacon, Ven. E. B. Glass, M.A...........1964
Beneficed Clergy, 27; Curates, &c., 14
Vicar-General and Registrar, P. W. S. Farrant,
24 Athol Street, Douglas.
Assistant Secretary, C. Curphey.

SOUTHWELL. £3,985
7th Bishop, Rt. Rev. John Denis Wakeling,
M.C., M.A. (Bishop's Manor, Southwell)
[Signs Denis Southwell].....................1970
Bishop Suffragan
Sherwood, Rt. Rev. Harold Richard Darby,
B.A..1975

THE CHURCH IN WALES

BANGOR. £3,970
78th Bishop and 7th Archbishop of Wales, Most
Rev. Gwilym Owen Williams, D.D., b. 1913
(Ty'r Esgob, Bangor, Gwynedd), cons. 1957,
elected Archbishop of Wales, 1971.

LLANDAFF. £4,607
100th Bishop, Rt. Rev. John Richard Worthington Poole Hughes, M.A., b. 1916 (Llys
Esgob, The Cathedral Green, Llandaff, Cardiff, cons. 1962, trans. 1976................1976

MONMOUTH. £4,456
6th Bishop of Monmouth, Rt. Rev. Derrick
Greenslade Childs, B.A., b. 1918 (Bishopstow,
Stow Hill, Newport, Gwent)..............1972

BISHOPS ABROAD

CANADA
Primate
The Most Rev. Edward Walter Scott........1971
Sees.   Apptd. Clgy.
Province of Canada
The Most Rev. Archbishop
Eastern Newfoundland and Labrador,
Robert Lowder Seaborn, b. 1911 (cons.
1958), Archbishop and Metropolitan....1975 123
The Rt. Rev. Bishops
Central Newfoundland, M. Genge........1976
Eastern Newfoundland and Labrador (see
above)
Fredericton, H. L. Nutler, b. 1923......1971 180
Montreal, R. Hollis...................1975 113
Nova Scotia, G. F. Arnold, b. 1914 (cons.
1967).......................................1975

Asst. Bishop, Rt. Rev. Bernard Markham, B.A.
(cons. 1962)...............................1972
Provost, Very Rev. John Francis Isaac Pratt,
M.A...1970
Canons Residentiary
E. E. Roberts.....1969 | C. S. Bayes, B.A....1970
Organist, K. B. Beard, M.A., Mus.B., F.R.C.O...1959
Archdeacons
Newark, Ven. B. W. Woodhams, B.A........1965
Nottingham, Ven. M. R. W. Brown, M.A......1960
Beneficed Clergy, 170; Curates, &c., 45
Chancellor, B. T. Buckle, M.A..............1959
Registrar, P. H. Mellors, M.A., Ll.B..........1970

WAKEFIELD. £3,985
Bishop (vacant)
Bishop Suffragan
Pontefract, Rt. Rev. Thomas Richard Hare,
M.A. (306 Barnsley Road, Wakefield)......1971
Asst. Bishops, Rt. Rev. Kenneth Graham
Bevan (cons. 1940)....................1968
Provost, Very Rev. John Field Lister, M.A....1971
Archdeacons
Pontefract, Ven. E. C. Henderson, B.D.......1968
Halifax, Ven. J. R. Alford, M.A.............1972
Organist, J. L. Bielby, M.A., Mus.B., F.R.C.O...1971
Beneficed Clergy, 212; Curates, &c., 44
Chancellor, G. B. Graham, Q.C., Ll.B.........1959
Registrar and Sec., C. E. Coles, M.A., Burton
Street, Wakefield.........................1963

The General Synod of the Church of England,
Church House, Dean's Yard, S.W.1.—Presidents,
The Archbishop of Canterbury; The Archbishop of
York; Sec.-Gen., W. D. Pattinson. THE HOUSE
OF BISHOPS.—Chairman, The Archbishop of Can-
terbury; Vice-Chairman, The Archbishop of York.
THE HOUSE OF CLERGY.—Chairman, Canon P. A.
Welsby; Vice-Chairman, Canon Prof. D. R. Jones.
THE HOUSE OF LAITY, Chairman, Prof. Sir Norman
Anderson; Vice-Chairman, O. W. H. Clark.

ST. ASAPH. £4,607
73rd Bishop, Rt. Rev. Harold John Charles,
M.A., b. 1914 (Esgobty, St. Asaph, Clwyd)..1971

ST. DAVID'S. £4,385
123rd Bishop, Rt. Rev. Eric Matthias Roberts,
M.A., b. 1914 (Llys Esgob, Abergwili, Carmarthen, Dyfed)...........................1971

SWANSEA AND BRECON. £4,600
6th Bishop, Rt. Rev. Benjamin Noel Young
Vaughan, M.A., b. 1917 (Ely Tower, Brecon,
Powis).......................................1976

Sees   The Rt. Rev. Bishops Apptd. Clgy.
Quebec, T. J. Matthews, b. 1907........1971 50
Western Newfoundland, W. G. Legge, b.
1912 (cons. 1968)........................1975

Province of Rupert's Land
The Most Rev. Archbishop
Qu' Appelle, George Frederic Clarence
Jackson, b. 1907 (Archbishop and Metro-
politan) 1970.............................1960 63
The Rt. Rev. Bishop
Arctic, J. R. Sperry, b. 1924............1974 24
Athabasca, F. H. W. Crabb, b. 1915.....1975 19
Brandon, J. F. S. Conlin................1975 36
Calgary, M. L. Goodman, b. 1917........1967 61
Edmonton, J. A. W. Langstone, b. 1913..1976
Keewatin, H. J. P. Allan, b. 1928.......1974 19

Sees	Apptd.	Clgy.
Rupert's Land, B. Valentine, *b.* 1927 (*cons.* 1969)................................1970		63
Saskatchewan, H. V. R. Short, *b.* 1914..1970	1970	30
Saskatoon, D. A. Ford, *b.* 1917........1970	1970	28

Province of Ontario
The Most Rev. Archbishop

Moosonee, James Augustus Watton, *b.* 1915 (*cons.* 1963), Archbishop and Metropolitan................................1974		29

The Rt. Rev. Bishops

Algoma, F. F. Nock, *b.* 1916............1975		79
Huron, T. D. B. Ragg, *b.* 1919..........1974		216
Bps. Suff., M. C. Robinson (1974); G. H. Parke-Taylor................1976		
Moosonee (see above)		
Niagara, J. C. Bothwell (*cons.* 1971).....1973		148
Bp. Suff., E. K. Clarke............1976		
Ontario, H. G. Hill, *b.* 1921...........1975		61
Ottawa, W. J. Robinson, *b.* 1916.......1970		85
Toronto, L. S. Garnsworthy, *b.* 1922 (*cons.* 1968)............................1973		327
Bp. Suff., A. A. Read.		

Province of British Columbia
The Rt. Rev. Bishops

British Columbia, F. R. Gartrell, *b.* 1914.1970		55
Caledonia, D. W. Hambridge, *b.* 1927....1969		19
Cariboo, J. S. P. Snowden...........1974		15
Kootenay, R. E. F. Berry............1971		31
New Westminster, T. D. Somerville, *b.* 1915 (*cons.* 1969) (*Metropolitan*, 1975).1971		85
Yukon, J. T. Frame, *b.* 1930..........1968		14

AUSTRALIA
Primate of Australia
The Most Rev. Frank Woods, K.B.E., Archbishop of Melbourne, *b.* 1907, *cons.* 1952, *trs.* 1957. Elected Primate of Australia, 1971.

Province of New South Wales
Archbishop and Metropolitan

Sydney, The Most Rev. Marcus Lawrence Loane, K.B.E., *b.* 1911 (*cons.* 1958)...1966		302
Bps. Coadj., A. J. Dain, *b.* 1912 (1965); J. R. Reid, *b.* 1929 (1972); D. W. B. Robinson, *b.* 1922 (1973); K. H. Short, *b.* 1927 (1975); E. D. Cameron, *b.* 1926 (1975)		

The Rt. Rev. Bishops

Armidale (vacant)		43
Bathurst, E. K. Leslie, O.B.E., *b.* 1911....1958		43
Canberra and Goulburn, C. A. Warren, *b.* 1924 (*cons.* 1965)....................1971		63
Grafton, D. N. Shearman, *b.* 1926 (*cons.* 1963)............................1973		41
Newcastle, I. W. A. Shevill, *b.* 1917 (*cons.* 1953)............................1973		85
Riverina, B. R. Hunter, *b.* 1927.......1971		35

Province of Victoria
Archbishop and Metropolitan

Melbourne (see above).		319
Bps. Coadj., R. W. Dann, *b.* 1914 (1969); J. A. Grant, *b.* 1931 (1970); G. B. Muston (*b.* 1927)...........1971		

The Rt. Rev. Bishops

Ballarat, J. Hazlewood, *b.* 1924........1975		60
Bendigo, O. S. Heyward, *b.* 1926........1975		31
Gippsland, G. R. Delbridge, *b.* 1917 (*cons.* 1969)......................1974		37
St. Arnaud, D. H. W. Shand, *b.* 1921...1973		26
Wangaratta, M. McN. Thomas, *b.* 1926.1975		34

Province of Queensland
Archbishop and Metropolitan

Brisbane, The Most Rev. Felix Raymond Arnott, *b.* 1911 (*cons.* 1963)........1970		
Bp. Coadj., R. E. Wicks, *b.* 1921....1973		

Sees	Apptd.	Clgy.

The Rt. Rev. Bishops

Carpentaria, H. T. U. Jamieson, *b.* 1932..1974		14
N. Queensland, H. J. Lewis, *b.* 1926......1971		30
Northern Territory, K. B. Mason, *b.* 1927.1968		
Papua New Guinea, G. D. Hand, *b.* 1918 (*cons.* 1950).....................1963		16
Asst. Bps., G. S. Ambo (1960); B. S. Meredith, *b.* 1927 (1967); H. T. A. Kendall, *b.* 1905 (1968).		
Rockhampton, J. B. R. Grindrod, *b.* 1919 (*cons.* 1966)........................1971		

Province of Western Australia
Archbishop and Metropolitan

Perth, The Most Rev. Geoffrey Tremayne Sambell, *b.* 1914 (*cons.* 1962)..1969		125
Asst. Bps., T. B. Macdonald, O.B.E., *b.* 1911 (1964); A. C. Holland (1970).		

The Rt. Rev. Bishops

Bunbury R. G. Hawkins, *b.* 1911........1957		34
Coadj. Bp. W. S. Bastian...........1968		
N.W. Australia, H. A. J. Witt, *b.* 1920..1965		13

Province of South Australia
Archbishop and Metropolitan

Adelaide, The Most Rev. Keith Rayner, *b.* 1929 (*cons.* 1969).................1975		154

The Rt. Rev. Bishops

Murray, R. G. Porter, *b.* 1924 (*cons.* 1967)1970		
Willochra, S. B. Rosier, *b.* 1928 (*cons.* 1967)............................1970		24

Extra-Provincial Diocese

Tasmania, R. E. Davies, *b.* 1913 (*cons.* 1960)..........................1963		78

PROVINCE OF NEW ZEALAND
Archbishop and Primate

Waikato, The Most Rev. Allen Howard Johnston, *b.* 1912, *cons.* 1953, *trans.* 1969............................1972		62

The Rt. Rev. Bishops

Auckland, E. A. Gowing, *b.* 1913.......1960		164
Asst. Bp., S. N. Spence (*cons.* 1970) :.1976		
Christchurch, W. A. Pyatt, *b.* 1916......1966		118
Dunedin, P. W. Mann, *b.* 1924.........1976		
Nelson, P. E. Sutton, *b.* 1923...........1965		35
Polynesia, J. L. Bryce, *b.* 1935..........1975		24
Bp. Suff. (*Nuku' alofa*), F. T. Halapua, *b.* 1910........................1967		
Waiapu, P. A. Reeves, *b.* 1932..........1971		49
Bp. Suff. (*Aotearoa*), M. A. Bennett, *b.* 1918..........................1968		
Wellington, E. K. Norman, *b.* 1916......1973		133
Asst. Bp., M. L. Wiggins, *b.* 1915 (*cons.* 1959)............................1976		

PROVINCE OF MELANESIA
Archbishop

Central Melanesia, The Most Rev. Norman Kitchener Palmer, M.B.E., *b.* 1928.1975		

The Rt. Rev. Bishops

Malaita, L. Alufurai, O.B.E...........1963		
New Hebrides, D. A. Rawcliffe, O.B.E.....1974		
Ysabel, D. Tuti, O.B.E..............1963		

PROVINCE OF SOUTH AFRICA
Archbishop and Metropolitan

Cape Town, The Most Rev. Bill Bendyshe Burnett, *b.* 1917 (*cons.* 1957)......1974		141
Bp. Suff., G. A. Swartz, *b.* 1928.....1972		

The Rt. Rev. Bishops

Bloemfontein, F. A. Amoore, *b.* 1913....1967		
Damaraland, C. O'B. Winter, *b.* 1928..1968		23
Bp. Suff., R. Wood, *b.* 1920..........1973		
George, P. H. F. Barron, *b.* 1911 (*cons.* 1964)..........................1966		26
Grahamstown K. C. Oram, *b.* 1919......1974		
Johannesburg, T. J. Bavin, *b.* 1935......1974		140
Bp. Suff., J. S. Carter, *b.* 1921....1968		

Sees	Apptd.	Clgy.

Kimberley & Kuruman (vacant)
Lebombo (vacant)
  Bps. Suff., P. S. Litumbe, b. 1918 (1976);
  D. S. Sengulane, b. 1946...........1976
Lesotho, D. M. Tutu, b. 1931...........1976   36
  Bp. Suff., F. Makhetha, b. 1916......1967
Natal, P. W. W. R. Russell, b. 1919 *(cons.*
  1966)........................1974
  Bp. Suff., K. B. Hallowes, b. 1913....1969
Port Elizabeth, B. R. Evans, b. 1929.....1974
Pretoria, M. Nuttall, b. 1934...........1975   48
  Bp. Suff., M. Nye, b. 1909..........1973
St. Helena, G. K. Giggall, b. 1914......1973   4
St. John's, J. L. Schuster, b. 1912......1956   106
  Bp. Suff., E. A. Sobukwe, b. 1908....1969
Swaziland, B. L. N. Mkhabela, b. 1927..1975
Zululand, L. B. Zulu, b. 1937...........1975   65

PROVINCE OF THE WEST INDIES
Archbishop of West Indies
Guyana, The Most Rev. Alan John
  Knight, C.M.G., *Archbp. & Metropolitan*,
  b. 1902 *(cons, 1937)*...............1950   42
  Bp. Suff. (*Stabroek*), (vacant)
The Rt. Rev. Bishops
Antigua, O. U. Lindsay, b. 1928.........1970   28
Barbados, D. W. Gomez, b. 1937.......1972   59
Belize, E. A. Sylvester.................1972   9
Jamaica, H. D. Edmondson *(cons. 1972)*..1975
  Bps. Suff. (*Kingston*) (vacant); (*Mande-*
  ville), W. A. Murray (1976); (*Mon-*
  tego Bay), M. W. de Souza (1973)
Nassau and the Bahamas, M. H. Eldon
  (cons. 1971).....................1972   30
Trinidad, C. O. Abdulah.............1970   40
Venezuela, H. H. Jones.................1976
Windward Isles, E. C. M. Woodroffe,
  C.B.E., b. 1918....................1969   22

PROVINCE OF WEST AFRICA
Archbishop
Sierra Leone, The Most Rev. Moses
  Nathanael Christopher Omobiala
  Scott, C.B.E., b. 1911 *(cons. 1961) elected*
  Archbp. of West Africa.............1969   35
The Rt. Rev. Bishops
Aba, H. A. I. Afonya *(cons. 1957)*......1972   35
Accra, I. S. M. LeMaire *(cons. 1963)*....1968   57
  Asst. Bp., K. A. Nelson............1966
Benin, A. Iwe........................1962   80
Egba-Egbado, J. S. Adeniyi *(cons. 1970)*..1976
Ekiti, J. A. Adetiloye.................1970   77
Enugu, G. N. Otubelu, b. 1927.........1969   30
Gambia and Rio Pongas, J. R. Elisee....1972   8
Ibadan, T. O. Olufosoye, b. 1918 *(cons.*
  1965)..........................1970   94
Ijebu, I. B. O. Akintemi...............1976
Ilesha, J. A. I. Falope.................1974   8
Kumasi, J. B. Arthur *(cons. 1966)*......1973   17
Kwara, H. Haruna....................1974   37
Lagos, F. O. Segun *(cons. 1970)*........1975   128
The Niger, J. A. Onyemelukwe........1975   73
Niger Delta, Y. A. Fubara.............1971   35
Northern Nigeria, T. E. Ogbonyomi....1975   49
Ondo, E. O. Idowu...................1971   81
Owerri, B. C. Nwankiti *(cons. 1968)*.....1969   82

PROVINCE OF CENTRAL AFRICA
Archbishop
Southern Malawi, The Most Rev. Donald
  Seymour Arden, b. 1916 *(cons. 1961)*..1971
The Rt. Rev. Bishops
Botswana, C. S. Mallory, b. 1936.......1972
Central Zambia, J. Cunningham, b. 1922.1971
Lake Malawi, J. Mtekateka, b. 1903 *(cons.*
  1965)..........................1971
Lusaka, F. Mataka, b. 1909 *(cons. 1964)*..1970

Sees.	Apptd.	Clgy.

Mashonaland, J. P. Burrough, M.B.E., b.
  1916.............................1968
  Asst. Bp., P. A. Murindagomo, b. 1925.1973
Matabeleland, S. M. Wood, b. 1919....1971
Northern Zambia, J. Mabula, b. 1922....1971

PROVINCE OF KENYA
Archbishop
Nairobi, The Most Rev. Festo Habakkuk
  Olang' *(cons. 1955)*................1970   27
Asst. Bp. C. Nzano..................1975
The Rt. Rev. Bishops
Maseno North, J. Mundia..............1970
Maseno South, H. Okullu.............1974
Mombasa, P. Mwang'ombe............1964   27
Mount Kenya East, D. Gitari..........1975
Mount Kenya, South (vacant)
  Asst. Bp., E. Ngaruiya.............1972
Nakuru, M. Kuria *(cons. 1970)*.........1976   42

PROVINCE OF TANZANIA
Archbishop
Dar es Salaam, The Most Rev. John
  Sepeku, b. 1907 *(cons. 1963)*.........1965
The Rt. Rev. Bishops
Central Tanganyika, Y. Madinda, b. 1926
  (cons. 1964).....................1971
Masasi, H. G. Chisonga...............1968
Morogoro, G. Chitemo.................1965
Ruvuma, M. Ngahyoma................1971
South West Tanganyika, J. Mlele *(cons.*
  1965)..........................1974
Victoria Nyanza, J. Rusibamayila......1976
Western Tanganyika, M. Kahurananga, b.
  1921 *(cons. 1962)*................1969
Zanzibar and Tanga, Y. Jumaa.........1968

PROVINCE OF UGANDA, RWANDA,
BURUNDI AND BOGA-ZAIRE
Archbishop
Kampala, The Most Rev. Janani Luwum
  (cons. 1969).....................1974
The Rt. Rev. Bishops
Ankole, A. Betungura.................1970
Boga-Zaire, P. B. Ridsdale.............1972
  Asst. Bp., B. Ndahura..............1975
Bujumbara, S. Sindamuka.............1975
Bukedi, Y. Okoth....................1972
Bunyoro, Y. Ruhindi.................1972
Butare, J. Ndandali...................1975
Busoga, C. Bamwoze..................1972
Buye, Y. Nkunzumwami *(cons. 1965)*...1966
Karamoja, B. Herd....................1976
Kigezi, F. Kivengere...................1972
Kigulu, A. Sebununguri *(cons. 1965)*....1966
  Asst. Bp., W. Rukirande........:.....1975
Madi and West Nile, S. G. Wani *(cons.*
  1964)..........................1969
Lango, M. Otim......................1976
  Asst. Bp., R. Ringtho...............1976
Mbale, J. A. Wasikiye.................1976
Namirembe, D. K. Nsubuga *(cons. 1964)*.1965
  Asst. Bp., M. Kauda...............1975
Northern Uganda, B. Ogwal...........1974
Ruwenzori, Y. Rwakaikara *(cons. 1967)*..1972
Soroti, G. Ilukor.....................1976
West Buganda, C. Senyonjo...........1975

PROVINCE OF THE INDIAN OCEAN
Archbishop
Mauritius (vacant)
The Rt. Rev. Bishops
Antananarivo, E. Randrianovona.......1975
Diego Suarez, G. Josoa *(cons. 1957)*.....1969
Mauritius (vacant)
Seychelles, G. C. Briggs...............1973
Tamatave, S. Rafanomezana..........1975

PROVINCE OF SOUTH AMERICA
The Rt. Rev. Bishops
Argentina and E. S. America with Falkland Is., R. S. Cutts......................1975
Chile, Bolivia and Peru, G. E. D. Pytches, b. 1931 (cons. 1971)..................1975
Asst. Bps. C. F. Bazley (1969); J. W. H. Flagg......................1969
Northern Argentina, P. B. Harris, b. 1934.1973
Asst. Bp., D. Leake..................1969
Paraguay, D. Milmine................1973

UNDER THE ARCHBISHOP OF CANTERBURY
The Rt. Rev. Bishops
Bermuda, (vacant)
Gibraltar, J. R. Satterthwaite, b. 1925...1970
Asst. Bp., H. Isherwood, M.V.O., O.B.E..1974

Kuching, B. Temengong...............1968
Pusan, W. Choi......................1974
Sabah, Chhoa Heng Sze...............1971
Seoul, P. Lee.......................1965
Singapore, Chiu Ban It..............1966
Taejon, M. Pae......................1974
West Malaysia, J. G. Savarimuthu (cons. 1958)......................1973

THE EPISCOPAL CHURCH IN JERUSALEM AND THE MIDDLE EAST
Bishop President, Rt. Rev. H. B. Dehqani-Tafti.1976
Asst. Bp., A. K. Cragg...............1970
Jerusalem, F. I. Haddad (cons. 1974).........1976
Iran, H. B. Dehqani-Tafti...................1961
Egypt, I. Musaad......................1974
Cyprus and the Gulf, L. J. Ashton (cons. 1974)..1976

CHURCH OF ENGLAND ARCHBISHOPS AND BISHOPS WHO HAVE RESIGNED THEIR SEES OR SUFFRAGAN BISHOPRICS

	Cons.	Res.
G. F. Allen, b. 1902; *Derby*...........	1947	1968
D. H. N. Allenby, b. 1909; *Kuching*....	1962	1969
S. F. Allison, b. 1907; *Winchester*....	1951	1974
G. Appleton, b. 1902; *Jerusalem*.......	1961	1974
J. Armstrong, b. 1905; *Bermuda*.......	1963	1968
M. Armstrong, b. 1906; *Jarrow*.......	1958	1964
R. G. Arthur, b. 1909; *Grafton*......	1956	1973
H. E. Ashdown, b. 1904; *Newcastle*....	1957	1972
W. S. Baker, b. 1902; *Zanzibar*......	1943	1968
C. K. N. Bardsley, b. 1907; *Coventry*..	1947	1976
W. F. Barfoot, b. 1893; *Rupertsland*..	1941	1958
F. R. Barry, b. 1890; *Southwell*......	1941	1963
L. J. Beecher, b. 1906; *Nairobi*.......	1950	1970
S. W. Betts, b. 1912; *Maidstone*......	1956	1966
K. G. Bevan, b. 1898; *E. Szechwan*....	1940	1950
C. L. P. Bishop, b. 1908; *Malmesbury*..	1962	1973
J. D. Blair, b. 1906; *Dacca*.........	1951	1975
T. Bloomer, b. 1895; *Carlisle*.......	1946	1966
P. J. Brazier, b. 1903; *Ruanda-Urundi*..	1951	1964
S. C. Bulley, b. 1907; *Carlisle*.......	1959	1972
H. J. Buxton, b. 1880; *Gibraltar*.....	1933	1947
W. G. Burch, b. 1911; *Edmonton*......	1960	1976
E. M. H. Capper, b. 1905; *St. Helena*..	1967	1972
H. J. Carpenter, b. 1901; *Oxford*.....	1955	1970
T. H. Cashmore, b. 1892; *Dunwich*....	1955	1967
W. F. P. Chadwick, b. 1905; *Barking*...	1959	1975
L. M. Charles-Edwards, b. 1902; *Worcester*...........................	1956	1970
G. W. Clarkson, b. 1897; *Pontefract*....	1954	1961
C. R. Claxton, b. 1903; *Blackburn*....	1964	1971
K. J. Clements, b. 1905; *Canberra and Goulburn*...........................	1949	1971
R. G. Clitherow, b. 1919; *Stafford*....	1958	1974
G. E. I. Cockin, b. 1908; *Owerri*.....	1959	1969
W. R. Coleman, b. 1917; *Kootenay*....	1961	1968
N. E. Cornwall, b. 1903; *Borneo*......	1949	1963
G. F. Cranswick, b. 1894; *Tasmania*...	1944	1966
W. H. H. Crump, b. 1903; *Saskatchewan*...........................	1960	1971
J. H. Cruse, b. 1908; *Knaresborough*...	1965	1972
E. E. Curtis, b. 1906; *Mauritius*........	1965	1975
J. C. S. Daly, b. 1903; *Taejon*........	1935	1967
W. W. Davis, b. 1908; *Nova Scotia*....	1958	1975
R. S. Dean, b. 1915; *Cariboo*........	1957	1973
J. H. Dickinson, b. 1901; *Melanesia*...	1930	1937
C. Eastaugh, b. 1897; *Peterborough*....	1949	1972
E. L. Evans, b. 1904; *Barbados*......	1957	1972
W. L. S. Fleming, b. 1906; *Norwich*....	1949	1971
D. A. Garnsey, b. 1909; *Gippsland*....	1959	1974
G. V. Gerard, b. 1898; *Waiapu*.......	1938	1944
W. P. Gilpin, b. 1902; *Kingston upon Thames*...........................	1952	1970
H. R. Gough, b. 1905; *Sydney*........	1948	1966

	Cons.	Res.
G. P. Gower, b. 1899; *New Westminister*	1951	1971
A. R. Graham-Campbell, b. 1903; *Colombo*...........................	1948	1964
E. M. Gresford-Jones, b. 1901; *St. Albans*	1942	1969
W. A. Hardie, b. 1904; *Ballarat*......	1960	1974
M. H. Harland, b. 1896; *Durham*......	1942	1960
K. Healey, b. 1899; *Grimsby*.........	1958	1965
E. B. Henderson, b. 1910; *Bath and Wells*	1955	1975
M. A. Hodson, b. 1907; *Hereford*......	1956	1973
G. E. Holderness, b. 1913; *Burnley*....	1955	1969
J. T. Holland, b. 1912; *Polynesia*.....	1951	1975
F. T. Horan, b. 1905; *Tewkesbury*....	1960	1973
J. L. C. Horstead, b. 1898; *Sierra Leone*.	1936	1961
A. L. E. Hoskyns-Abrahall, b. 1903; *Lancaster*...........................	1955	1974
J. A. G. Housden, b. 1904; *Newcastle, N.S.W.*...........................	1958	1972
K. W. Howell, b. 1909; *Chile, Bolivia and Peru*...........................	1963	1971
W. J. Hughes, b. 1894; *Trinidad*.......	1944	1970
T. G. V. Inman, b. 1904; *Natal*......	1951	1974
A. G. W. Hunter, b. 1916; *Swaziland*..	1968	1975
L. S. Hunter, b. 1890; *Sheffield*.......	1939	1962
F. M. E. Jackson, b. 1902; *Trinidad*....	1946	1949
J. M. Key, b. 1905; *Truro*..........	1947	1973
E. G. Knapp-Fisher, b. 1915; *Pretoria*..	1960	1975
E. H. Knell, b. 1903; *Reading*........	1955	1972
D. R. Knowles, b. 1898; *Antigua*.....	1953	1969
K. E. N. Lamplugh, b. 1901; *Southampton*...........................	1951	1971
W. Q. Lash, b. 1904; *Bombay*.......	1947	1961
W. S. Llewellyn, b. 1907; *Lynn*......	1963	1972
T. Longworth, b. 1891; *Hereford*.....	1939	1961
D. G. Loveday, b. 1896; *Dorchester*....	1957	1971
F. E. Lunt, b. 1900; *Stepney*........	1957	1968
A. C. MacInnes, b. 1901; *Jerusalem*....	1953	1968
R. K. Maguire, b. 1926; *Montreal*.....	1963	1975
M. A. Mann, b. 1924; *Dudley*........	1974	1976
B. Markham, b. 1907; *Nassau*........	1962	1972
H. H. Marsh, b. 1899; *Yukon*........	1962	1968
C. A. Martin, b. 1895; *Liverpool*......	1944	1965
J. A. A. Maund, b. 1905; *Lesotho*......	1950	1976
J. A. Meaden; *Newfoundland*.........	1956	1965
R. H. Moberly, b. 1884; *Stepney*......	1936	1952
R. W. H. Moline, b. 1889; *Perth*......	1947	1962
J. R. H. Moorman, b. 1905; *Ripon*.....	1959	1975
E. R. Morgan, b. 1888; *Truro*.......	1943	1959
A. H. Morris, b. 1898; *St. E. and Ipswich*	1949	1965
J. E. L. Mort, b. 1915; *N. Nigeria*.....	1952	1969
S. C. Neill, b. 1901; *Tinnevelly*......	1939	1945
A. Otter, b. 1896; *Grantham*........	1949	1965
T. R. Parfitt, b. 1911; *Madagascar*....	1952	1961
C. G. St. M. Parker, b. 1900; *Bradford*.	1953	1971

	Cons.	Res.
W. A. Parker, *b.* 1897; *Shrewsbury*	1959	1969
C. J. Patterson, *b.* 1908; *Niger*	1942	1969
J. H. L. Phillips, *b.* 1910; *Portsmouth* ..	1960	1975
S. C. Pickard, *b.* 1910; *Lebombo*	1958	1968
H. G. Pigott, *b.* 1894; *Windward Islands*	1962	1969
St. J. S. Pike, *b.* 1909; *Gambia*	1958	1963
V. J. Pike, *b.* 1907; *Sherborne*	1960	1975
D. B. Porter, *b.* 1906; *Aston*	1962	1972
J. A. Ramsbotham, *b.* 1906; *Wakefield.*	1940	1967
A. M. Ramsey, *b.* 1904; *Canterbury*	1952	1975
K. V. Ramsey, *b.* 1909; *Hulme*	1953	1975
T. I. Reed, *b.* 1902; *Adelaide.*	1957	1975
A. S. Reeve, *b.* 1907; *Lichfield.*	1953	1974
R. A. Reeves, *b.* 1899; *Johannesburg* ...	1949	1961
R. E. Richards, *b.* 1908; *Bendigo*	1957	1974
K. Riches, *b.* 1908; *Lincoln.*	1952	1974
C. J. G. Robinson, *b.* 1903; *Bombay* ...	1947	1970
J. A. T. Robinson, *b.* 1919; *Woolwich* .	1959	1969
A. F. B. Rogers, *b.* 1907; *Edmonton*	1959	1975
J. K. Russell, *b.* 1916; *N. Uganda*	1955	1964
C. R. Rutt, *b.* 1925; *Taejon*	1967	1975
W. G. Sanderson, *b.* 1905; *Plymouth*	1962	1972
C. K. Sansbury, *b.* 1905; *Singapore*	1961	1966
D. N. Sargent, *b.* 1907; *Selby*	1962	1971
G. D. Savage, *b.* 1915; *Southwell*	1960	1970
G. Sinker, *b.* 1900; *Nagpur*	1949	1954
G. B. Snell, *b.* 1907; *Toronto*	1956	1972
G. D'O. Snow, *b.* 1903; *Whitby*	1961	1971
R. W. Stannard, *b.* 1895; *Woolwich* ...	1947	1959
A. Stanway, *b.* 1908; *Cent. Tanganyika.*	1951	1971

	Cons.	Res.
H. V. Stiff, *b.* 1916; *Keewatin*	1969	1974
L. E. Stradling, *b.* 1908; *Johannesburg* ..	1945	1974
C. E. Storrs, *b.* 1889; *Grafton*	1946	1955
C. E. Stuart, *b.* 1893; *Uganda*	1932	1952
R. S. Taylor, *b.* 1909; *Cape Town*	1941	1974
F. O. Thorne, *b.* 1892; *Nyasaland*	1936	1961
G. L. Tiarks, *b.* 1909; *Maidstone*	1969	1976
O. S. Tomkins, *b.* 1908; *Bristol*	1959	1975
G. F. Townley, *b.* 1891; *Hull*	1957	1965
E. J. Trapp, *b.* 1910; *Bermuda*	1947	1975
E. Treacy, *b.* 1907; *Wakefield*	1961	1976
C. J. Tucker, *b.* 1911; *Argentina*	1965	1975
L. C. Usher-Wilson, *b.* 1903; *Mbale* ...	1936	1961
J. C. Vockler, *b.* 1924; *Polynesia*	1959	1968
B. N. Y. Vaughan, *b.* 1917; *Honduras.* .	1961	1971
J. W. C. Wand, *b.* 1885; *London*	1934	1954
A. K. Warren, *b.* 1900; *Christchurch* ...	1951	1966
R. H. Waterman, *b.* 1897; *Nova Scotia.*	1948	1963
W. L. M. Way, *b.* 1905; *Masai*	1952	1959
G. A. West, *b.* 1893; *Rangoon*	1935	1954
W. A. E. Westall, *b.* 1900; *Crediton* ...	1954	1974
P. W. Wheeldon, *b.* 1913; *Kimberley and Kuruman*	1954	1976
R. B. White, *b.* 1896; *Tonbridge*	1959	1967
M. L. Wiggins, *b.* 1915; *Victoria Nyanza*	1959	1976
F. R. Willis, *b.* 1900; *Delhi*	1951	1966
D. J. Wilson, *b.* 1903; *Trinidad*	1938	1956
R. P. Wilson, *b.* 1905; *Chichester*	1959	1974
L. H. Woolmer, *b.* 1906; *Lahore*	1949	1968

ECCLESIASTICAL COURTS

Judge, The Rt. Worshipful Sir Harold Kent, G.C.B., Q.C.

[Judge of the Provincial Courts of Canterbury and York under " The Ecclesiastical Jurisdiction Measure, 1963."]

Court of Arches

Registry, 1 The Sanctuary, Westminster, S.W.1

Dean, The Rt. Worshipful Sir Harold Kent, G.C.B., Q.C.

Registrar, D. M. M. Carey.

Court of Faculties

[Registry and Office for Marriage Licences (Special and Ordinary). Appointment of Notaries Public, &c., 1, The Sanctuary, Westminster, S.W.1. Office hours, 10 to 4; Saturdays, 10 to 12.]

Master, The Rt. Worshipful Sir Harold Kent, G.C.B., Q.C.

Registrar, D. M. M. Carey.

Vicar General's Office

for granting Marriage Licences for Churches in the Province of Canterbury, and COURT OF PECULIARS, 1 The Sanctuary Westminster, S.W.1. Office hours, 10 to 4; Saturdays, 10 to 12.

Vicar General & Chancellor, Sir Harold Kent, G.C.B., Q.C.

Registrar, D. M. M. Carey.

Apparitor General, M. Saunders.

OFFICE OF THE VICAR GENERAL OF THE PROVINCE OF YORK.

Vicar General & Chancellor, The Worshipful Kenneth John Tristran Elphinstone.

Registrar, G. P. Knowles.

Chancery Court of York

Auditor, Sir Harold Kent, G.C.B., Q.C.

Registrar, G. P. Knowles.

THE CHURCH OF SCOTLAND

Church Office, 121 George Street, Edinburgh 2.

THE CHURCH OF SCOTLAND is Presbyterian in constitution, and is governed by Kirk Sessions, Presbyteries, Synods, and the General Assembly, which consists of both clerical and lay representatives from each of the Presbyteries. It is presided over by a Moderator (chosen annually by the Assembly), to whom Her Majesty the Queen has granted precedence in Scotland, during his term of office, next after the Lord Chancellor of Great Britain. The Sovereign, if not present in person, is represented by a Lord High Commissioner, who is appointed each year by the Crown. The country, for Church purposes, is divided into 12 Synods and 46 Presbyteries, and there are about 2,000 ministers and licentiates engaged in ministerial and other work. The figures at Dec. 31, 1975, were:—

Congregations, 1,964: total membership 1,041.772. In 21 Overseas Mission fields there are 184 European missionaries (and in addition many missionaries' wives, most of whom are doing mission work in the various fields).

LORD HIGH COMMISSIONER (1976). Sir Hector Mac-Lennan, M.D.

MODERATOR OF THE ASSEMBLY (1976–77), Right Rev. T. F. Torrance, M.B.E., B.D., D.Th.

Principal Clerk, Rev. D. F. M. Macdonald, M.A., Ll.B.

Depute Clerk, Rev. A. G. McGilvray, M.A., B.D.

Procurator, C. K. Davidson, Q.C.

Law Agent and Solicitor of the Church, R. A. Paterson, M.A., Ll.B.

Parliamentary Solicitor, Colin McCulloch (London).

General Treasurer, W. G. P. Colledge, C.A.

The Presbyterian Church in Ireland.—The largest of the Presbyterian churches in Ireland consists of 22 presbyteries, 441 ministers, 564 congregations, with 135,125 communicants, 128,407 families and 6,642 Sabbath-school teachers. During the 12 months ended Dec. 31, 1975, the branch contributed by congregational effort £616,422 for religious, charitable, and missionary purposes. The total income for the period raised by congregations for all purposes was £4,339,301—*General Sec.*, Rev. A. J. Weir, M.SC., D.D., Church House, Belfast, 1.

UNITED REFORMED CHURCH

The *United Reformed Church* was formed by the union of the Congregational Church in England and Wales and the Presbyterian Church in England on October 5, 1972. It is divided into 12 Provinces, each with a Provincial Moderator, and 65 Districts. 187,408 members, and 1,837 ministers. It carries out its overseas work through the Council for World Mission (Congregational and Reformed).

Its ministers are trained at five recognized colleges.
General Sec.: Rev. A. L. Macarthur, M.A., M.Litt., Church House, 86 Tavistock Place, W.C.1.

Those members of the Congregational Church who did not join the United Reformed Church comprise the Congregational Federation. *Sec.*, J. B. Wilcox, 12 Canal Street, Nottingham.

THE EPISCOPAL CHURCH IN SCOTLAND

Sees. THE RT. REV. BISHOPS.	Cons. Clgy.	Stipd.
Aberdeen and Orkney, Ian Forbes Begg, D.D., *b.* 1909	1972..19	£*2,472
Argyll and the Isles, Richard Knyvet Wimbush, M.A., *b.* 1909 (*Most Rev. Primus*, 1973)	1963..12	£*2,983
Brechin, Lawrence Edward Luscombe, *b.* 1925	1975..22	£*2,038
Edinburgh, Alastair Iain Macdonald Haggart, *b.* 1915	1975..74	£*2,600

Sees. THE RT. REV. BISHOPS.	Cons. Clgy.	Stipd.
Glasgow and Galloway, Frederick Goldie, M.A., *b.* 1914	1974..60	*2,970
Moray, Ross and Caithness, George Minshull Sessford, M.A., *b.* 1918	1970..19	£*2,740
St. Andrews, Dunkeld and Dunblane, Michael Geoffrey Hare-Duke, M.A., *b.* 1925	1969..31	£*2,389

* With residence.

Registrar of the Episcopal Synod, I. R. Guild, W.S., 16 Charlotte Square, Edinburgh, 2.
Churches, Mission Stations, &c., 348.   Clergy, 251;   Communicants, 45,692

THE CHURCH OF IRELAND

Sees	ARCHBISHOPS	Appointed	Clergy
*Armagh**..........	Most Rev. George Otto Simms, Ph.D., D.D., *b.* 1910 (*cons.* 1952)...	1969	 60
Dublin............	Most Rev. Alan Alexander Buchanan, M.A., D.D., *b.* 1907 (*cons.* 1958)	1970	 78
	BISHOPS		
Meath & Kildare....	(vacant)...	.. ....	29
Cashel & Waterford..	Rt. Rev. John Ward Armstrong, B.D., *b.* 1915..................	1969	 14
Clogher............	Rt. Rev. Robert William Heavener, M.A., *b.* 1905.............	1973	 37
Connor.............	Rt. Rev. Arthur Hamilton Butler, M.B.E., D.D., *b.* 1912 (*cons.* 1958)	1970	 118
Cork, Cloyne & Ross	Rt. Rev. Richard Gordon Perdue, D.D., *b.* 1910 (*cons.* 1958).......	1957	 35
Derry & Raphoe....	Rt. Rev. Robert Henry Alexander Eames, Ll.B., Ph.D., *b.* 1937....	1975	 66
Down & Dromore...	Rt. Rev. George Alderson Quin, M.A., *b.* 1914..................	1970	 114
Killaloe............	Rt. Rev. Edwin Owen, M.A., *b.* 1910	1972	 14
Kilmore, Elphin & Ardagh..........	Rt. Rev. Edward Francis Butler Moore, Ph.D., D.D., *b.* 1906.......	1958	 31
Limerick & Ardfert...	Rt. Rev. Donald Arthur Richard Caird, B.D., *b.* 1925.............	1970	 14
Ossory, Ferns & Leighlin..........	Rt. Rev. Henry Robert McAdoo, Ph.D., D.D., *b.* 1916.............	1962	 43
Tuam..............	Rt. Rev. John Coote Duggan, B.D., *b.* 1918.....................	1970	 12

**Primate.*

ST. PATRICK'S NATIONAL CATHEDRAL, DUBLIN. *Dean and Ordinary*, Very Rev. V. G. B. Griffin, Ph.D., B.A.

Chief Officer and Secretary to the REPRESENTATIVE CHURCH BODY, J. G. Briggs, Church of Ireland House, Church Avenue, Rathmines, Dublin 6.

THE METHODIST CHURCH

The Methodist Church is governed primarily by the Conference, secondarily by the District Synods (held in the autumn and the spring), consisting of all the ministers and of selected laymen in each district, over which a chairman is appointed by the Conference; and thirdly by the circuit meeting of the ministers and lay officers of each circuit. The authority of both Synods and Circuit Meetings is subordinate to the Conference, which has the supreme legislative and judicial power in Methodism.

President of the Conference (July 1976–77), Rev. C. M. Morris, B.A.

Vice-President of the Conference (July 1976–77), C. J. Bennett.

Secretary of the Conference, Rev. K. G. Greet, D.D., 1 Central Buildings, Westminster, S.W.1.

President Designate (1977–78), Rev. B. A. Shaw, B.A.

Vice-President Designate (1977–78), Dr. E. M. Waterhouse.

Statistics.—In 1975 in association with the Conference in Great Britain there were 3,865 Ministers, 16,962 Local Preachers, 557,249 Members in 734 Circuits. Statistics are published triennially.

The *World Methodist Council*, founded 1881, re-

organized 1951, associates Methodism throughout the world in 82 countries.

The Methodist Church was founded in 1739 by the two brothers Wesley and rapidly spread throughout the British Isles and to America before 1770. The Methodist Church in Great Britain was united in 1932 by the fusion of the Wesleyan Methodist Church which was the original section, the Primitive Methodist Church, which arose through the evangelists Hugh Bourne and William Clowes in 1810, and the United Methodist Church, itself a fusion in 1907 of the Methodist New Connexion which dated from 1797, the Bible Christian Methodist Church, which dated from 1815 and the United Methodist Free Churches which originated in controversies in 1828 and 1849. The United Methodist Church of America was formed by a union of United Methodist denominations with the United Evangelical Brethren.

METHODIST CHURCH IN IRELAND

The Methodist Church in Ireland has 224 Ministers, 271 Lay Preachers, 23,898 Adult and 16,978 Junior Members.

President (1976–77), Rev. R. Greenwood.

Secretary, Rev. H. Sloan, 3 Upper Malone Road, Belfast, 9.

THE UNITED CHURCH OF CANADA

The United Church of Canada is the result of the union (1925) of Methodist, Presbyterian and Congregational Churches in Canada. Subsequently several other communions have become part of the Church. *Moderator*, Rt. Rev. W. K. Howard, B.A., D.D. *Sec. of General Council*, Rev. D. G. Ray, D.F.C., B.A., D.D., The United Church House, 85 St. Clair E., Toronto.

INDEPENDENT METHODISTS

Independent Methodists.—This body is Congregational in its organization, with an unpaid Ministry. Its first Conference was held in 1805. In 1976 there were in Great Britain 183 Ministers, 5,187 Members, 130 Chapels and 4,644 Sunday scholars, *Secretary*, J. M. Day, The Old Police House, Croxton, Stafford.

WESLEYAN REFORM UNION

This Union is Methodist in doctrine, Congregational in government, with, if any church desires it, a paid ministry. It is the remnant of the original Reformers expelled from Wesleyan Methodism in 1849. The adherents are mainly in the Midland and Northern counties. In 1975 there were in Great Britain 22 Ministers, 218 Lay Preachers, 4,353 Members, 150 Chapels and 5,008 Sunday scholars.—*President (1976–7)*, L. Cook, Matlock. *General Secretary and Connexional Editor*, Rev. D. A. Morris, Wesleyan Reform Church House, 123 Queen Street, Sheffield 1.

THE PRESBYTERIAN CHURCH OF WALES

The PRESBYTERIAN OR CALVINISTIC METHODIST CHURCH OF WALES is the only Church of purely Welsh origin, and embraces a very large section of the Welsh-speaking population. Its form of government is Presbyterian, and it is a constituent of the World Alliance of Reformed Churches. It is also a member of the British Council of Churches and the World Council of Churches.

In 1975 the body numbered—chapels and other buildings, 1,228; ministers in pastoral charge, 276; elders, 5,636; communicants 94,116; Sunday scholars 37,160; Contributions for various religious purposes (including the ministry), £1,544,440.

The *Eastern Association* which includes nine of the English Presbyteries, was formed in 1947.

Moderator of General Assembly (1976–77), L. Howell, O.B.E., Cardiff.

Moderators of Associations (1976–77) South Wales, Miss M. Roberts, Amlwch; *North Wales*, Rev. E. Hughes, B.A., Ruthin, *The East*, Rev. G. D. Bowen, Aberdare.

Chief Secretary, Rev. G. Evans, B.A., 9 Camden Road, Brecon, Powys.

The BAPTISTS have over 33,000,000 members in all countries. In Britain they are for the most part grouped in associations of churches, and the majority of these belong to the Baptist Union, which was formed in 1812–13. In the British Isles there were, in 1975, 1,608 pastors. The members numbered 187,066, young people (14–20), 37,009, juveniles (under 14) 142,278. *President of the Baptist Union of Great Britain and Ireland (1976–77)*, Rev. F.

A. Goodwin. *Secretary*, Rev. D. S. Russell. *Office*, 4 Southampton Row, W.C.1.

THE JEWS

It is estimated that about 410,000 Jews are resident in the British Isles, some 280,000 being domiciled in Greater London.

The *Board of Deputies of British Jews*, established in 1760, is the representative body of British Jewry and is recognized by H.M. Government. The basis of representation is mainly synagogal, but secular organizations are also represented. It is a deliberative body and its objects are to watch over the interests of British Jewry, to protect Jews against any disability which they may suffer by reason of their creed and to take such action as may be conducive to their welfare. *President*, The Lord Fisher of Camden.

Office, Woburn House, Upper Woburn Place, W.C.1.

CHIEF RABBI—The Very Rev. I. Jakobovits, Ph.D. *Executive Director*, M. Davis. *Office*, Adler House, Tavistock Square, W.C.1.

The *Beth Din* (Court of Judgment) is a rabbinic body consisting of *Dayanim* (Assessors) and the Chief Rabbi, who is President of the Court. The Court arbitrates when requested in cases between Jew and Jew and gives decisions on religious questions. The decisions are based on Jewish Law and practice and do not conflict with the law of the land. The *Beth Din* also deals with matters concerning dietary laws and marriages and divorces, according to Jewish Law.

Dayanim, L. Grossnass; Dr. M. Lew; M. Swift.

Clerk to the Court, Marcus Carr, Adler House, Tavistock Square, W.C.1.

OTHER RELIGIOUS DENOMINATIONS

The General Assembly of Unitarian and Free Christian Churches has about 176 ministers, 272 chapels and other places of worship in Great Britain and Ireland. *Gen. Sec.*, Rev. B. L. Golland, Essex Hall, Essex Street, W.C.2.

The Salvation Army, first known as the Christian Mission, was founded by William Booth, in the East End of London in 1865. In 1878 it took its present name and adopted a quasi-military method of government. Since then it has become established in over 80 countries of the world. The head of the denomination, known as the General, is elected by a High Council, consisting of all active Commissioners and Territorial Commanders who have held the rank of Colonel for at least two years. In 1975 there were in Great Britain, 1,965 Corps (Churches) and 1,959 Officers engaged in evangelistic and social work. The latest statistics for the world (1975) are 16,262 Corps and 24,776 Officers. *General*, Clarence D. Wiseman.

International Headquarters:—101 Queen Victoria Street, E.C.4.

The Society of Friends (Quakers) consists of 19,998 members in Great Britain, and has 440 places of worship (*Recording Clerk*, Arthur J. White). The total number in the world is about 198,750

(121,232 are in U.S.A. and Canada). *Central Office* (*Great Britain*), Friends House, Euston Road, N.W.1, (*Ireland*), 6 Eustace Street, Dublin.

The First Church of Christ, Scientist, in Boston, Massachusetts, U.S.A. (District Manager, Committees on Publication for Great Britain and Ireland, 108 Palace Gardens Terrace, W.8), has about 300 branch churches and societies in Great Britain and Ireland.

The Moravian Church, 5 Muswell Hill, N.10, has in the U.K. 40 congregations and preaching stations, with 3,500 communicants.

The Free Church of England (otherwise called The Reformed Episcopal Church) has 33 churches in England. *Gen. Sec.*, Rev. A. Ward, 65 Elmfield Avenue, Teddington, Middlesex.

The Seventh Day Adventists (*Hdqrs.*, Stanborough Park, Watford, Herts.), have 149 organized churches, 45 companies and 12,680 members in the British Isles.

At Woking, Surrey, is the Shah Jehan Mosque for Moslems, the first in Great Britain, built in 1889. There are also Mosques at Southfields, S.W.18, Commercial Road, E.1, Birmingham, Manchester, Cardiff, Newcastle upon Tyne, South Shields, Coventry and Glasgow.

THE ROMAN CATHOLIC CHURCH

HIS HOLINESS POPE PAUL VI (Giovanni Battista Montini), Roman Pontiff, *born* in Concesio, Italy, September 26, 1897; *ordained priest* May 29, 1920; nominated *Archbishop* of Milan, November 1, 1954; *Cardinal*, December 15, 1958; *elected Pope* June 21, 1963; *crowned* June 30, 1963.

THE SACRED COLLEGE OF CARDINALS, when complete, consisted of six Cardinal Bishops, fifty Cardinal Priests and fourteen Cardinal Deacons. This number was fixed by Pope Sixtus V in 1586. Pope John XXIII created 52 new Cardinals. The present Pope created 27 new Cardinals on Feb. 22, 1965, 27 on June 26, 1967, 33 on Apr. 28, 1969, 30 on March 5, 1973, 20 on May 24, 1976. In July 1976 there were 137 Cardinals. The Cardinals are advisers and assistants of the Sovereign Pontiff and form the supreme council or Senate of the Church. On the death of the Pope they elect his successor. The assembly of the Cardinals at the Vatican for the election of a new Pope is known as the Conclave in which, in complete seclusion, the Cardinals elect by secret ballot; a two-thirds majority is necessary before the vote can be accepted as final. When a Cardinal receives the necessary votes the Dean of the Sacred College formally asks him if he will accept election and the name by which he wishes to be known. On his acceptance of the office the Conclave is dissolved and the First Cardinal Deacon announces the election to the assembled crowd in St. Peter's Square. On the first Sunday or Holyday following the election the new Pope is crowned with the tiara, the triple crown, the symbol of his supreme spiritual authority. A new pontificate is dated from the coronation.

FORMS OF ADDRESS: *Cardinal*, " His Eminence Cardinal . . . " (if an Archbishop, " His Eminence the Cardinal Archbishop of . . . "); *Archbishop* " The Most Rev. Archbishop of . . . "; *Bishop*, " The Rt. Rev. the Bishop of . . . "

ENGLAND AND WALES

Apostolic Delegate to Gt. Britain and Gibraltar, The Most Rev. Bruno Heim.

The Most Revd. Archbishops CONS. CLERGY★

Westminster, H.E. Cardinal Basil Hume
  (1976)...........................1976   971
  Auxil., Basil Christopher Butler.....1966
  Auxil., Victor Guazzelli............1970
  Auxil., Gerald Mahon..............1970
Birmingham, George Dwyer (1966)....1959 592
  Auxil., Joseph Cleary.............1966
Cardiff, John A. Murphy (1961).......1948 188
  Auxil., Daniel Mullins............1970
Liverpool, Derek Worlock (1976)......1965 661
  Auxil., Augustine Harris..........1966
  Auxil., Joseph Gray..............1969
Southwark, Cyril Cowderoy.........1949 578
  Auxil., Charles Henderson........1972

The Rt. Revd. Bishops
Arundel and Brighton, Michael Bowen
  (1971)...........................1970 357
Brentwood, Patrick Casey (1970)........1966 239

                               CONS. CLERGY
Clifton, Mervyn Alexander (1975).....1972 278
East Anglia, Alan Clark..............1976
Hexham and Newcastle, Hugh Lindsay
  (1975)............................1970 373
Lancaster Brian C. Foley..........1962 289
  Auxil., Thomas Pearson...........1949
Leeds, Gordon Wheeler..............1964 405
  Auxil, Gerald Moverley...........1968
Menevia (*Wales*), Langton Fox (1972)..1965 180
Middlesbrough, John McClean.........1967 247
Northampton, Charles Grant.........1961 278
Nottingham, James McGuinness (1975)..1972 318
Plymouth, Cyril Restieaux...........1955 200
Portsmouth, Anthony Emery (1976)....1968 347
Salford, Thomas Holland, D.S.C. (1964).1961 591
  Auxil., Geoffrey Burke...........1967
Shrewsbury, William Eric Grasar......1962 287
  Auxil., John Brewer.............1972

★ In addition there are 61 priests serving as regular chaplains in H.M. Forces. The Right Rev, Gerard Tickle, *Bp.* of *Bela*, was appointed Bishop-in-Ordinary to H.M. Forces in 1963.

CONS. CLERGY

SCOTLAND
The Most Revd. Archbishops

St. Andrews & Edinburgh, H.E. Cardinal
Gordon Gray.....................1951 232
   Auxil., James Monaghan..........1970
Glasgow, Thomas Winning (1974)....1972 375
The Rt. Revd. Bishops
Aberdeen (vacant).................. 78
Argyle & Isles, Colin MacPherson.....1969 33
Dunkeld, William Hart..............1955 73
Galloway, Joseph McGee............1952 80
Motherwell, Francis Thompson......1965 187
Paisley, Stephen McGill (1969)........1960 99

NORTHERN IRELAND†
The Most Revd. Archbishop

Armagh, H.E. Cardinal William Conway
(1963)..............................1958 278
   Auxil., Francis Lenny..............1974
The Rt. Revd. Bishops
Clogher, Patrick Mulligan...........1969 140
Derry, Edward Daly.................1974 151
Down & Connor, William Philbin.....1962 328
Dromore, Eugene O'Doherty........1944 64
Kilmore, Francis McKernan..........1972 126

BRITISH COMMONWEALTH
Europe CONS.
The Most Revd. Archbishop

Malta, Michael Gonzi, K.B.E.(1943)........ 1924
The Rt. Revd. Bishops
Gozo, Nicola Cauchi (1972).............. 1967
Gibraltar, Edward Rapallo............... 1973

America

Pro-Nuncio to Canada, Most Rev. Guido Del
Mestri (*Archbishop of Tuscamia*).
The Most Revd. Archbishops CONS.
Edmonton, Joseph MacNeill (1973)......... 1969
Grouard-McLennan, Henri Legare.......... 1972
Halifax, James Martin Hayes (1967)....... 1965
Kingston, Joseph L. Wilhelm (1967)...... 1963
Moncton, Donat Chiasson................ 1972
Montreal, Paul Gregoire.................. 1968
Ottawa, Joseph A. Plourde (1967)........ 1964
Port of Spain, Anthony Pantin............ 1967
Quebec, H.E. Cardinal Maurice L. Roy, O.B.E.
(1947)............................... 1946
Regina, Michael C. O'Neill.............. 1948
Rimouski, Giles Ouelett (1972)........... 1968
St. Boniface, Antony Hacault (1974)....... 1964
St. John's, Newfoundland, Patrick Skinner (1951) 1950
Sherbrooke, John Fortier (1968)......... 1962
Toronto, Philip F. Pocock (1971).......... 1951
Vancouver, B.C., James F. Carney (1969)..... 1966
Winnipeg, H.E. Cardinal George Flahiff (1961) 1961
Winnipeg (*Byzantine Rite*), Maxim Her-
maniuk (1956)........................ 1951
The Rt. Revd. Bishops
Alexandria, Eugene Larocque............. 1974
Amos, Gaston Hains (1969)............... 1964
Antigonish, William Power............... 1960
Bathurst in Canada, Edgar Godin.......... 1969
Belize, Robert Hodapp.................. 1968
Calgary, Paul J. O'Byrne................ 1968
Castries, B.W.I., Patrick Webster (1974).... 1969
Charlottetown, Francis John Spence........ 1970
Chicoutimi, Mario Paré.................. 1956
Churchill-Baie d'Hudson, Omer Robidoux.. 1970
Edmundston, Fernand Lacroix............ 1970
Edmonton (*Byzantine Rite*), Nicholas Savaryn
(1943)............................... 1956

Gaspé, Bertrand Blanchet................ 1973
Georgetown, Benedict Singh.............. 1972
Grand Falls–Harbour Grace, Alphonsus Penney 1972
Gravelbourg, Noel Delaquis.............. 1974
Hamilton, Paul, F. Reding 1973
Hamilton in Bermuda (vacant)
Hauterive (vacant)
Hearst, Roger A. Despati................. 1973
Hull, Adolphe E. Proulx (1973)........... 1967
Joilette, René Audet (1968).............. 1963
Kamloops, B.C., Adam Exner............. 1974
Keewatin-Le Pas, Paul Dumouchel........ 1955
Kingston (*Jamaica*), Samuel Carter (1970).... 1966
Labrador-Schefferville, Peter A. Sutton (1974). 1974
London, Gerald Carter (1964)............ 1962
MacKenzie—Fort Smith, Paul Piché (1967).. 1959
Mont Laurier, Joseph Ouellette (1957)...... 1965
Montego Bay, Edgerton Clarke............ 1967
Moosonee, Jules Leguerriere (1967)......... 1964
Nassau (Bahamas), Leonard Hagarty (1960). 1950
Nelson, Wilfrid Doyle................... 1958
Nicolet, Joseph Martin.................. 1950
Pembroke, Joseph Windle................ 1971
Peterboro', Anthony Marrocco (1968) 1956
Prince Albert, Lawrence Morin (1959)...... 1955
Prince George. Fergus J. O'Grady.......... 1956
Roseau (*Dominica*), Arnold Boghaert....... 1957
Rouyn-Noranda, Jean-Guy Hamelin........ 1974
St. Anne de la Pocatière, Charles Lévesque (1968) 1965
St. Catharines, Thomas J. McCarthy (1958).. 1955
St. George's, N.F., Richard McGrath...... 1970
St. George's (*Grenada*), Sidney Charles...... 1974
St. Hyacinthe, Albert Sanschagrin......... 1967
St. Jean de Ouebec, Gerard Coderre (1955).. 1951
St. Jerome, Bernard Hubert.............. 1971
St. John, New Brunswick, Canada, Arthur J.
Gilbert.............................. 1974
St. Paul in Alberta, Raymond Roy........ 1972
Saskatoon, James P. Mahoney............ 1967
Saskatoon (*Byzantine Rite*), Andrew Robo-
recki (1956)......................... 1948
Sault Ste Marie, Alexander Carter (1958)... 1957
Thunder Bay, Norman Gallagher......... 1970
Timmins, Jacques Landriault............. 1971
Toronto (*Byzantine Rite*), Isidore Borecky
(1956).............................. 1948
Trois Rivières, Georges L. Pelletier (1947).. 1943
Valleyfield, Robert Lebel................ 1976
Victoria, B.C., Remi De Roo............. 1962
Whitehorse, Hubert O'Connor............ 1971
Yarmouth, Austin Burke 1968

Africa

EAST AFRICA: Pro-Nuncio to Uganda, Most
Rev. Luigi Bellotti; Pro-Nuncio to Malawi
and Zambia, Most Rev. Luciano Angeloni;
Pro-Nuncio to Kenya, Most Rev. Pierluigi
Satorelli; Pro-Nuncio to Tanzania, Franco
Brambilla.

WEST CENTRAL AFRICA: Most Rev. Amelio
Poggio.

WEST AFRICA: Most Rev. John Mariani.
The Most Revd. Archbishops

Blantyre, James Chiona (1967)............ 1965
Cape Coast, John Kodwo Amissah (1960)... 1957
Dar-es-Salaam, H.E. Cardinal Laurence
Rugambwa (1969).................... 1952
Freetown and Bo, Thomas Brosnahan....... 1953
Kaduna, John McCarthy (1959)........... 1954
Kampala, H.E. Cardinal Emmanuel Nsubuga
(1967).............................. 1966
Kasama, Elias Mutale (1973).............. 1971
Lagos, Anthony Okogie (1973)............ 1971
Lusaka, Emmanuel Milingo............... 1969
Nairobi, H.E. Cardinal Maurice Otunga.... 1971
Onitsha, Francis Aringe (1967)............ 1965

---

† There is one hierarchy for the whole of Ireland.
Several of the Dioceses listed above have territory
partly in the Republic of Ireland and partly in
Northern Ireland.

CONS.

Salisbury, Francis Markall................ 1956
Tabora, Mark Mihayo................... 1960

The Rt. Revd. Bishops

Abakaliki, Thomas McGettrick (1973)...... 1955
Accra, Dominic Kodwo Andoh.......... 1971
Arua, Angelo Tarantino................. 1959
Arusha, Denis Durning.................. 1963
Bafia, Andrea Loucheur................. 1968
Bathurst in Gambia, Michael Molony, C.B.E.. 1959
Benin City, Patrick Ebosele Ekpu.......... 1973
Buea, Pius Awa (1973).................. 1971
Bukoba, Nestor Timanywa............... 1974
Bulawayo, Ernest Karlen (1974)........... 1968
Calabar, Brian Usanga (1970)............. 1969
Chikwawa, Franz Vroemen, S.M.M........ 1965
Chipata, Medardo Mazombwe............. 1970
Dedza, Cornelius Citsulo (1959).......... 1957
Dodoma, Matthias Isuja................. 1972
Ekiti, Michael Fagun (1972).............. 1971
Eldoret, Joseph Njenga................. 1970
Enugu, Godfrey Okoye (1970)............ 1961
Fort Portal, Serapio Magambo (1972)...... 1967
Gaborone, Urban Murphy, C.P............ 1966
Gulu, Cipriano Kihangire (1969).......... 1963
Gweio, Louis Haene (1955)............... 1950
Hoima, Edward Baharagate............... 1969
Ibadan, Felix Job (1974)................. 1971
Ijebu-Ode. Antonio Sansusi.............. 1969
Ikot Ekpene, Dominic Ekandem (1954).... 1963
Ilorin, William Mahony................. 1969
Iringa Mario Mgulunde................. 1970
Issele-Uku, Anthony Gbuji............... 1973
Jinja, Joseph Willigers.................. 1967
Jos, Gabrielle Ganaka (1974)............. 1973
Kabale, Barnabas Halem' Imana........... 1969
Kenema, Joseph Ganda.................. 1970
Keta, Francis Lodonu................... 1973
Kigoma, Alphonse Nsabi................. 1969
Kisii, Tiberio Mugendi.................. 1969
Kisumu (vacant).......................
Kitui, William Dunne................... 1964
Kumasi, Peter Sarpong.................. 1970
Lilongwe, Patrick Kalilombe............. 1972
Lira, Caesar Asili (1968)................. 1969
Livingstone, Phelim O'Shea (1959)........ 1950
Lodwar, John Mahon (Pref.-Ap.)..........
Lokoja, Alexis Makozi.................. 1972
Machakos, Urbanus Kioko............... 1973
Mahenge, Patrick Iteka.................. 1973
Maiduguri, Timothy Cotter, O.S.A......... 1966
Makeni, Augusto Azzolini 1962
Makurdi, Donald Murray, C.S.Sp........ 1968
Mansa, James Spaitia................... 1974
Mangochi, Allesandro Assolar............ 1974
Marsabit, Charles Cavellera.............. 1964
Masaka, Adrian Ddungu................. 1962
Mbala, Adolf Furstenberg (1968).......... 1959
Mbarara, John Kakubi.................. 1969
Mbeya, James Sangu.................... 1966
Mbulu, Basil Hhando................... 1971
Meru, Laurence Bessone................. 1954
Minna, Christopher Abba................ 1973
Mombasa, Eugene Butler................ 1957
Monze, James Corboy................... 1962
Morogoro, Adrian MKoba............... 1967
Moroto, Sisto Mazzildi (1967)............ 1966
Moshi, Joseph Sipendi.................. 1967
Mtwara, Maurus Libaba................. 1973
Musoma, John Rudin................... 1957
Mwanza, Renatus Lwamosa Butibubage (1966) 1960
Mzuzu, Jean Jobidon................... 1961
Nachingwea, Bernard Cotey.............. 1963
Nakuru, Raphael Ndingi................. 1971
Navrongo, Rudolph Akanlu.............. 1973
Ndola, Nicola Agnozzi O.F.M. Conv. (1966). 1962
Nyeri, Kenya, Caesar Gatimu (1964)...... 1961

CONS.

Ngong, Colin Davies (Pref.-Ap.)..........
Njombe, Raymond Mwanyika............ 1971
Ogoja, Joseph Ukpo (1973).............. 1971
Ondo, William Field.................... 1958
Oweri, Mark Unegbu................... 1970
Oyo, Julius Adelakun.................. 1973
Port Harcourt, Edmund Fitzgibbon (Adm. Ap.)
Port Louis, Jean Margéot................ 1969
Port Victoria, Gervais Aeby (Adm. Ap.)
Qacha's Nek, Joseph des Rosiers, O.M.I. (1951) 1948
Rulenge, Christopher Mwoleka........... 1969
Same, Henry Winkelmolen (Pref.-Ap.).
Sekondi-Takoradi, Amihere Essuah (1969)... 1962
Shinyanga, Edward McGurkin............ 1956
Singida, Bernard Mabula................ 1972
Sokoto, Michael Dempsey, O.P........... 1967
Solwezi Severiano Potani (Pref.-Ap.)
Songea, James Komba (1969)............. 1962
Sumbawanga, Charles Msakila (1970)...... 1958
Sunyani, James Kwadwo Owusu.......... 1973
Tamale (vacant)
Tanga, Maura Komba................... 1970
Tororo, James Odongo.................. 1969
Umtali, Daniel Lamont.................. 1957
Umuahia, Antony Nwedo, O.B.E.......... 1959
Wa, Peter P. Dery...................... 1960
Wankie, Ignatius Vega.................. 1963
Warri, Luca Nwazeapu.................. 1964
Yola, Patrick Sheehan.................. 1970
Zanzibar and Pemba, Adrian Mkoba (Ap.
  Admin.) (1969)...................... 1967
Zomba, Matthias Chimole................ 1970

Asia

Pro-Nuncio to India, Most Rev. John Gordon 1969
Pro-Nuncio to Bangladesh, Most Rev. Edward
  Cassidy............................. 1973
Apostolic Delegate to Sri Lanka, Most Rev.
  Carlo Curis......................... 1969

The Most Revd. Archbishops

Agra, Domenic Athaide.................. 1956
Bangalore, Packiam Arokiaswamy......... 1971
Bhopal, Eugene D'Souza (1963)........... 1951
Bombay, H.E. Cardinal Valerian Gracias (1950) 1946
Calcutta, H.E. Cardinal Lorenzo Picachy.... 1969
Changanacherry, Anthony Padiyara (1970) .. 1955
Colombo, H.E. Cardinal Thomas Cooray
  (1947)............................. 1946
Dacca, Theotonius Ganguly (1968)........ 1960
Delhi, Angelo Fernandes (1967).......... 1959
Ernakulam, H.E. Cardinal Joseph Parecattil
  (1956)............................. 1953
Gauhati-Shillong, Alberto D'Rosario (1969). 1964
Hyderabad, Saminini Arulappa............ 1972
Madhurai, Justin Diraviam.............. 1967
Madras and Mylapore, Rayappa Arulappa... 1965
Malac:a-Johore, James Chan.............. 1973
Nagpur (vacant)
Pondicherry, Venmani Selvanather (1973)... 1949
Ranchi, Pio, Kerketta (1961) 1961
Trivandrum (Syro-Malankara Rite), Gregorios
  Thangalathil (1955).................. 1953
Verapoly, Joseph Kelanthara............. 1971

The Rt. Revd. Bishops

Ahmedabad, Charles Gomez.............. 1974
Ajmer and Jaipur, Leo D'Mello........... 1949
Allahabad Alfred Ferrandez (1970)....... 1967
Alleppey, Michael Arattukulam........... 1954
Amravati, Joseph A. Rosario............. 1955
Balasone, Jacob Vadakevetil (Pref. Ap.)
Badulla, Leo Nanayakkara (1972).......... 1959
Banaras, Patrick D'Souza................ 1970
Baroda, Ignatius de Souza............... 1966
Belgaum, Ignazio Lobo.................. 1968
Bellary, Ambrose Yednapally, O.F.M....... 1964
Berhampur, Thomas Thiruthalil.......... 1974

	CONS.
Bhagalpur, Urban McGarry	1965
Bijnor (*Malabar Rite*), Graziona Mundadan	1972
Calicut, Aldo Patroni	1948
Chanda, Paul Palathuruthy	1968
Chikmagalur, Alphonse Matthias	1964
Chilaw, Frank M. Fernando (1972)	1965
Chittagong, Joachim Rozario	1968
Cochin, Alexander Edezhath	1952
Coimbatore, Manuel Visuvasam	1972
Cuttack-Bhubaneswar, Henry D'Souza	1973
Cyprus, Elias Farah	1954
Daltonganj, George Saupin	1971
Darjeeling, Enrico Benjamin	1962
Dibrugarh, Robert Kerketta	1970
Dinajpur, Michael Rozario	1968
Dumka, Leone Tigga	1962
Galle, Antonio De Sacrum (1965)	1963
Guntar (vacant)	
Hong Kong, John Baptist Wu	1975
Indore, George Marian Anathil	1973
Jabalpur, Leonard de Souza (1966)	1964
Jaffna, Jacob Deogupillai (1972)	1967
Jagdalpur (*Malabar Rite*), Paul Jeera Kath	1972
Jalpaiguri, James Toppa	1971
Jamshedpur, Joseph Rodericks	1970
Jhansi, Bapist Mudartha (1967)	1963
Jullundar, Symphorian Keeprath	1972
Kandy, Paul Perera	1973
Kashmir and Jammu, John Boerkamp(*Pref. Ap.*)	
Khulna, Michael D'Rozario	1970
Kohima-Imphal, Abraham Alamgrimattathil	1973
Kota Kinabalu, Peter Chung Wan Ting	1972
Kothamangalam, Matthew Potanamuzhi	1956
Kottar, Marianus Arokiasamy	1970
Kottayam, Kuriakose Kunnacherry (1947)	1968
Krishnagar, Matteo Baroi	1973
Kuala Lumpur, Dominic Vendargon	1955
Kuching, Charles Reiterer, V.A. (1968)	1967
Kumbakonam, Paul Arulswami	1955
Kurnool, Joseph Rayappa	1967
Lucknow, Cecil D'Sa	1972
Mananthavady, Jacob Toomkuzhy	1973
Mangalore, Basil D'Souza	1965
Meerut, Patrick Nair	1974
Miri, Anthony Galvin, V.A.	1960
Multan, Ernest Boland, O.P.	1966
Mysore, Matthias Fernandes	1964
Nellore, Pudhota Chinniah Balasamy	1974
Ootacamund, James Aruldas	1974
Palai, Sebastian Vayalil	1950
Palayamkottai, Sava Iruthayara	1973
Palghat, Joseph Irimpen	1974
Patna, Augustine Wildermuth	1947
Penang, Gregorio Yong Sooi Nghean	1968
Poona, William Gomes (1967)	1961
Quilon, Jerome Fernandez	1937
Raigarh-Ambikapur, Francis Ekka	1971
Raipur, John Weidner (*Ap. Admin.*)	
Sagar, Clemens Thottunkai	1968
Salem, Michael Duraisamy	1974
Sambalpur, Raphael Cheenath	1974
Satna, Abraham Mattam (1968)	1974
Silchar, Denzil de Souza	1969
Simla and Chandigarh, Gilbert Rego	1971
Tanjore, Arokiaswami R. Sundaram	1953
Tellicherry, Sebastian Valloppilly	1956
Tezpur, Joseph Mittathani	1969
Tiruchirapally, James Fernando (1970)	1953
Tiruvalla, Cheriyan Polachirakal (1955)	1954
Trichur, Joseph Kundukulam	1970
Trincomalee, Leo Anthony (1974)	1968
Trivandrum (*Latin Rite*), Peter Pereira (1966)	1955
Tura, Oreste Marengo (*Ap. Admin.*)	
Tuticorin, Mathal Ambrose	1972
Ujjain, John Perumattam	1968
Varanasi, Patrick D'Souza	1970
Vellore, Royappan Anthonimuthu	1971

	CONS.
Vijayapuram, Cornelius Elanjikal	1971
Vijayavada, Joseph S. Thumma	1971
Visakhapatnam, Ignatio Gopu (1966)	1962
Warangal, Alfonso Beretta (1951)	1953

Australia

Pro-Nuncio to Australia, Papua and New
Guinea, Most Rev. Gino Paro	1969

The Most Revd. Archbishops
Adelaide, James Gleeson (1971)	1957
Brisbane, Francis Robert Rush (1973)	1961
Canberra-Goulburn, Thomas Cahill, C.B.E. (1967)	1949
Hobart, Guilford Young (1955)	1948
Melbourne, Thomas Francis Little (1974)	1973
Perth, Lancelot Goody (1969)	1954
Sydney, H.E. Cardinal James Freeman (1971)	1957

The Rt. Revd. Bishops
Armidale, Henry Kennedy	1971
Australia (*Byzantine Rite*), John Prasko	1958
Ballarat, Ronald Mulkaearns (1971)	1968
Bathurst, Albert Thomas	1963
Broome, John Jobst (1966)	1959
Bunbury Myles McKeon (1969)	1962
Cairns, John Ahern Torple	1967
Darwin, John O'Loughlin	1949
Geraldton, Francis Thomas	1962
Lismore, John Satterthwaite (1971)	1969
Maitland, Leo Clarke	1976
Port Pirie, Bryan Gallagher	1952
Rockhampton, Bernard Wallace	1974
Sale, Arthur Francis Fox (1968)	1957
Sandhurst, Bernard Stewart (1950)	1947
Toowoomba, William Brennan	1953
Townsville, Anthony Faulkner	1967
Wagga-Wagga, Francis Patrick Carroll (1968)	1967
Wilcannia-Forbes, Douglas J. Warren (1967)	1964
Wollongong (vacant)	

New Zealand
Pro-Nuncio to New Zealand and the Pacific
Islands, Most Rev. Angelo Acerbi (1974).	

The Most Revd. Archbishop
Wellington, H.E. Cardinal Reginald John Delargey (1974)	1958

The Rt. Revd. Bishops
Auckland, John Mackey	1974
Christchurch, Brian Patrick Ashby	1964
Dunedin, John Kavanagh (1957)	1949
Rarotonga, John Rodgers (1973)	1954

Oceania
The Most Revd. Archbishops
Madang, Adolf Noser (1966)	1947
Port Moresby, Virgil Copas (1966)	1960
Rabaul, John Hohne (1966)	1963
Suva, George Pearce (1957)	1956
Tonga and Niue Islands, Patrick Punou-Ki-Hihifo Finau	1972

The Rt. Revd. Bishops
Aitape, Kevin Rowell	1969
Apia, Pio Taofinu'u	1956
Bereina, Virgil Copas (*Ap. Admin.*)	
Bougainville, Gregory Singkai	1974
Daru, Gerard Deschamps	1966
Gizo, John Crawford (1966)	1960
Goroka, John Cahill	1969
Honiara, Daniel Stuyvemberg (1966)	1957
Kavieng, Alfred Stemper (1966)	1957
Lae, Enrico van Lieshout	1966
Mendi, Firmin Schmitt	1966
Mount Hagen, George Bernarding (1966)	1960
Port Vila, Pierre Martin	1976
Sideia, Desmond Moore	1970
Taiohae, Herve-Marie Le Cleac'h (*Apost. Admin.*)	
Tarawa, Pierre Guichet (1966)	1961
Vanimo, Pascal Sweeney	1966
Wewak, Leo Arkfield (1966)	1948

LONDON CATHEDRALS, CHURCHES, ETC.

ST. PAUL'S CATHEDRAL, CITY of London, E.C.4 (1675–1710), cost £747,660. The cross on the dome is 365 ft. above the ground level, the inner cupola 218 ft. above the floor. "Great Paul," in S.W. tower weighs 17 tons. Organ by Father Smith (enlarged by Willis) in case carved by Grinling Gibbons (who also carved the choir stalls). The choir and high altar were restored in 1958 after war damage and the North Transept in 1962. The American War Memorial Chapel was consecrated in November, 1958. The Chapel of the Most Excellent Order of the British Empire in the Crypt of the Cathedral was dedicated on May 20, 1960. Nave and transepts free; Fees to the following parts (on weekdays only, 10.45 a.m. to 3.15 p.m. and—during Summer Time only—4.45 p.m. to 6 p.m.); Crypt, 30p; library, whispering gallery, stone gallery and ball, 30p: total 60p (Children half-price). Service on Sundays at 8, *10.30 and *3.15. Weekdays at 8, *10, *4.

WESTMINSTER ABBEY, S.W.1. (built A.D. 1050–1760).—Open on weekdays 8 a.m. to 6 p.m. (8 p.m., Weds.). Admission beyond the Choir Screen by fee of 40p. (children 5p) (weekdays) except on Wednesdays from 6 p.m. to 8 p.m. (open free). Transepts and Nave open on Sundays only between services.

Holy Communion at 8; matins at 10.30; Holy Communion at 11.40. Evensong at 3. Evening service with Sermon at 6.30; Daily—Holy Communion at 8 a.m; Westminster School Service at 9 a.m. (term-time only); matins 9.20 a.m. (choral Tuesdays and Fridays); evensong (choral), 5.0 p.m. (said on Wednesdays) (Saturday, 3 p.m.). Chapel of Henry VII Chapter House and Cloisters; King Edward the Confessor's shrine, A.D. 1269, tombs of kings and queens (Edward I, Edward III, Henry V, Mary Queen of Scots, Queen Elizabeth I), and many other monuments and objects of interest, including the grave of "An Unknown Warrior" and St. George's Chapel at the W. end of Nave and Poets' Corner. The Coronation Chair encloses the "Stone of Scone" brought from Scotland by Edward I in 1297.

SOUTHWARK CATHEDRAL, south side of the Thames, near London Bridge, S.E.1.—Mainly 13th century, but the nave is largely rebuilt. Open 7.30 a.m. to 6.30 p.m., free. Sunday services, Holy Communion, 9 and 11 a.m., Choral Evensong, 3.30 p.m. Weekdays: Mondays, Holy Communion, 5.30 p.m., Tuesdays, Wednesdays and Thursdays, Holy Communion, 8 a.m., Thursdays, Holy Communion, 5.30 p.m., Fridays, Holy Communion, 1.10 p.m., Saturdays, Holy Communion, 12 noon.

Evensong, Tuesdays 6 p.m. (sung), Wednesdays 5.30 p.m. (said), Fridays 5.30 p.m. (sung). The tomb of John Gower (1330–1408) is between the Bunyan and Chaucer memorial windows, in the N. aisle; Shakespeare effigy backed by view of Southwark and Globe Theatre in S. aisle; the altar screen (erected 1520) has been restored; the tomb of Bishop Andrews (died 1626) is near screen. The Early English Lady Chapel (behind the choir), restored 1930, is the scene of the Consistory Courts of the reign of Mary (Gardiner and Bonner); and is

still used for this purpose. John Harvard, after whom Harvard University is named was baptized here in 1607.

TEMPLE CHURCH, The Temple, E.C.4.—The nave formed one of five remaining round churches in England, the others being at Cambridge, Northampton, Little Maplestead (Essex), and Ludlow Castle. Rebuilding of the church was completed in 1958. Sunday morning services, open to the public, 11.15 a.m., except in August and September. *Master of the Temple,* Very Rev. R. L. P. Milburn, M.A. *Reader,* Rev. Preb. W. D. Kennedy-Bell, M.A.

Church of Scotland

CROWN COURT CHURCH, Russell Street, Covent Garden, W.C.2.—Sundays, 11.15 and 6.30. *Minister,* Rev. J. M. Scott, M.A., B.D., F.S.A.Scot.
ST. COLUMBA'S, Pont Street, S.W.1. Sundays, 11 and 6.30. *Minister,* Rev. J. F. McLuskey, M.C., D.D.

United Reformed

CITY TEMPLE, Holborn Viaduct E.C.1.—Sundays 11 and 6.30. *Minister,* Rev. B. Johanson, B.A., B.D., D.D.
WESTMINSTER CHAPEL, Buckingham Gate, S.W.1. —Sundays. 11 and 6.30. *Minister,* (vacant).

Methodist

CENTRAL HALL, Westminster, S.W.1.—Sunday Services, 11 a.m. and 6.30 p.m. *Minister,* Rev. M. Barnett, M.A., B.D., Ph.D.
KINGSWAY METHODIST CHURCH, Kingsway, W.C.2.—Sundays at 10, 11, and 6.30, *Minister,* Rev. the Lord Soper, M.A., Ph.D.

Baptist

BLOOMSBURY CENTRAL BAPTIST CHURCH, Junction of Shaftesbury Avenue and New Oxford Street, W.C.2.—Sundays, 11 and 6.30. *Minister,* Rev. H. Howard Williams, Ph.D.

Society of Friends

FRIENDS' HOUSE, Euston Road, N.W.1.

Roman Catholic

WESTMINSTER CATHEDRAL, Ashley Place, Westminster, S.W.1. (close to Victoria Station), built 1895–1903 from the designs of J. F. Bentley (the campanile is 283 feet high—open to public by lift, 15p).—*Sundays.* Masses, 7, 8, 9, 10.30 (High), 12 noon, 5.30 p.m. and 7 p.m.; Solemn Vespers and Benediction, 3.30. *Weekdays.* Masses, 7, 7.30, 8, 8.30, 9, 10.30 (High), 12.30, 5.30 and 6 p.m. Morning Office, 10.5, Vespers and Benediction, 5 p.m. *Holy days of obligation.* Low Masses, 7, 7.30, 8, 8.30, 9, 10.30 (High), 11.50, 12.30, 6 and 8 p.m. Cathedral open 6.45 a.m. to 8 p.m.

THE ORATORY, Brompton, S.W.7.—*Sundays:* Masses, 7, 8, 9, 10, 11; (High Mass); 12.30 4.30, 7; Vespers and Benediction, 3.30. *Weekdays:* Masses, 7, 7.30, 8, 10; 12.30, 6 p.m. (no 12.30 on Sats.). Service Thurs. 8 p.m. *Holy days:* Masses 6.15, 7, 8, 9, 10, 12.15, 1.15 and 8 p.m.; 6 p.m. (High Mass). On the eve, Vespers and Benediction, 5.30 p.m.

EDUCATION DIRECTORY

THE UNIVERSITY OF OXFORD

FULL TERMS, 1977

Hilary, Jan. 16 to March 12
Trinity, April 24 to June 18
Michaelmas, Oct. 9 to Dec. 3

NUMBER OF UNDERGRADUATES IN RESIDENCE

Michaelmas Term, 1975, 8,250

UNIVERSITY OFFICES, &c.

	Elect.
Chancellor, Rt. Hon. Harold Macmillan, O.M., Balliol	1960
High Steward, The Lord Wilberforce, P.C., C.M.G., O.B.E., M.A., All Souls	1967
Vice-Chancellor, Sir John Habakkuk, M.A., F.B.A., Principal of Jesus	1973
Proctors, H. A. O. Hill, M.A. Queen's; J. D. Fleeman, M.A., D.Phil., Pembroke	1976
Assessor, A. M. Hudson, M.A., D.Phil., Lady Margaret Hall	1975
Assessor of the Chancellor's Court, Sir Humphrey Waldock, C.M.G., O.B.E., Q.C., D.C.L., All Souls	1947
Public Orator, J. G. Griffith, M.A., Jesus	1973
Bodley's Librarian, R. Shackleton, M.A., D.Litt., F.B.A., Brasenose	1966
Keeper of Archives, T. H. Aston, M.A., Corpus Christi	1969
Director of the Ashmolean Museum, D. T. Piper, M.A., Worcester	1973
Keeper of the Dept. of Western Art, K. J. Garlick, M.A., Balliol	1968
Keeper of Dept. of Antiquities, H. J. Case, M.A., Balliol	1969
Keeper of Dept. of Eastern Art, J. C. Harle, M.A., D.Phil., Christ Church	1966
Keeper of Heberden Coin Room, C. M. Kraay, M.R., D.Phil.	1962
Curator of the Museum of History of Science, F. R. Maddison, M.A., Linacre	1964
Registrar of the University, G. K. Caston, M.A., Merton	1972
Surveyor to the University, J. Lankester, M.A., St. Catherine's	1956
Secretary of Faculties, H.W. Deane, M.A.	1971
Secretary of the Chest,W. T. Horsley, M.A., Hertford	1972
Deputy Registrars, A. L. Fleet, M.A., Pembroke (Administration); A. J. Dorey, M.A., D.Phil., Linacre (General)	1973
Chief Accountant, W. Hyde,	1976
Establishment Officer, D. W. Roberts, M.A. (Pembroke)	1975
Land Agent,E. M. Brookes,M.A., St. Cross	1976
Head of Data Processing and Management Services,W. A. Platts	1976
Senior Assistant Registrars, C. H. Paterson, M.A., Corpus (1971); Mrs. E. R. M. Brain, M.A., Linacre (1969); A. Ostler, B.C.L., M.A., Queen's (1970); P. Garnham, M.A., Worcester	1973
Assistant Registrars, R. A. Malyn, M.A., St. Peter's (1961); H. P. Ruglys, M.A., Hertford (1966); G. P. Collyer, M.A., St. Catherine's (1966); P. S. Crane, M.A., Jesus (1966); J. P. W. Roper, M.A., Lincoln (1967); Miss M. E. Grinyer, M.A., St. Hilda's (1968); Miss A. M. Barr (1969), I. M. Herrman, D. Phil., St. Catherine's (1970); J. D. Brown (1971); M. J. Stanley, M.A., St. Catherine's (1973); A. P. Weale, M.A. University	1973
Information Officer, E. E. Sabben-Clare, M.A., New College	1970

Registrar of the Chancellor's Court, F. R. Williamson, M.A., Pembroke	1964
University Counsel, F. H. B. W. Layfield, M.A., Corpus	1971
Clerk of the Schools, G. A. Barnes	1971
Director, Department of Educational Studies, H. G. Judge, M.A., B.N.C.	1973

SECRETARY TO DELEGATES OF:—

Examination of Schools, A. R. Davis, M.A., St. John's.
Local Exams., C. G. Hunter, M.A., St. Hilda's.
Science Area, G. E. S. Turner, M.A., St. Catherine's.
University Press, G. B. Richardson, M.A., St. John's.

SECRETARY OF:—

Accommodation Committee, A. W. Davies, M.A., Magdalen.
Committee for Appointments, T. Snow, M.A., New College.
The Rhodes Trustees, Sir Edgar Williams, C.B., C.B.E., D.S.O., M.A., Balliol.

HEBDOMADAL COUNCIL

Ex-Officio Members, the Chancellor; the Vice-Chancellor; Warden of Merton (Vice-Chancellor Elect); D. M. Stewart, M.A., Wadham (Vice Chairman of the General Board); the Proctors; the Assessor.

Elected by Congregation—

The Provost of Oriel; the Provost of Queen's; the Dean of Christ Church; the Principal of Linacre; the Principal of St. Hilda's; the Principal of St. Anne's; the Rector of Exeter; The Master of St. Catherine's; Sir Edgar Williams, C.B., C.B.E., D.S.O., M.A.; Prof. J. H. Burnett, M.A., D.Phil., St. John's; R. P. H. Gasser, M.A., D.Phil.; H. Kidd, M.A.; Miss E. A. O. Whiteman, M.A., D.Phil.; R. N. Franklin, M.A., D.Phil., Keble; A. H. Cooke, M.A., D.Phil.; Prof. R. J. Elliott, M.A., D.Phil., F.R.S.; Prof. Sir Richard Doll, D.M., F.R.S.; Prof. J. K. B. M. Nicholas, M.A.

Oxford Colleges and Halls

(With dates of foundation)

All Souls (1438), J. H. A. Sparrow, O.B.E., M.A., Warden (1952).
Balliol (1263), J. E. C. Hill, M.A., D.Litt., F.B.A., Master (1965).
Brasenose (1509) Prof. H. L. A. Hart, M.A., F.B.A., Principal (1973).
Christ Church (1546), Very Rev. H. Chadwick, D.D., F.B.A., Dean (1969).
Corpus Christi (1517), K. J. Dever, M.A., President (1976).
Exeter (1314), W. G. Barr, M.A., Rector (1972).
Hertford (1874), G. J. Warnock, M.A., Principal (1972).
Jesus (1571), Sir John Habakkuk, M.A., F.B.A., Principal (1967).
Keble (1868), Rev. D. E. Nineham, B.D., M.A., Warden (1969).
Linacre (1962), J. B. Bamborough, M.A., Principal (1962).
Lincoln (1427), The Lord Trend, P.C., G.C.B., C.V.O., M.A., Rector (1973).
Magdalen (1458), J. H. E. Griffiths, O.B.E., M.A., D.Phil., President (1968).
Merton (1264), R. E. Richards, M.A., D.Phil., D.SC., F.R.S., Warden (1969).

New College (1379), A. H. Cooke, M.A., D.Phil. (1976).

Nuffield (1937), Sir Norman Chester, M.A., *Warden* (1976).

Oriel (1326), K. C. Turpin, M.A., B.Litt., *Provost* (1957).

Pembroke (1624), Sir Geoffrey Arthur, K.C.M.G., M.A., *Master* (1974).

Queen's (1340), The Lord Blake, M.A., F.B.A., *Provost* (1969).

St. Antony's (1950), A. R. M. Carr, M.A., *Warden* (1968).

St. Catherine's (1962), The Lord Bullock, M.A., D.Litt., F.B.A., *Master* (1962).

St. Cross (1965), W. E. van Heyningen, M.A., Ph.D., D.Sc., *Master* (1965).

St. Edmund Hall (1270), Rev. Canon J. N. D. Kelly, D.D., *Principal* (1951).

St. John's (1555), Sir Richard Southern, M.A., F.B.A., *President* (1969).

St. Peter's (1929) Sir Alec Cairncross, K.C.M.G., *Master* (1968).

Trinity (1554), A. G. Ogston, M.A., D.SC., F.R.S., *President* (1970).

University (1249), The Lord Goodman, C.H., *Master* (1976).

Wadham (1612), S. N. Hampshire, M.A., F.B.A., *Warden* (1970).

Wolfson (1965), The Hon. Sir Henry Fisher, M.A., *President* (1975).

Worcester (1714), The Lord Briggs, P.C., G.C.M.G., M.A., *Provost* (1976).

Campion Hall, Rev. B. Winterborn, M.A. *Master* (1972).

St. Benet's Hall, Rev. C. L. J. Forbes, M.A., *Master* (1964).

Mansfield (1886), Rev. G. B. Caird, D.Phil., D.D., F.B.A., *Principal* (1970).

Regent's Park, Rev. B. R. White, M.A., D.Phil., *Principal* (1972).

Greyfriars Hall, Very Rev. C. J. Reel, B.Litt., M.A., *Warden* (1972).

Lady Margaret Hall (1878), Mrs. E. M. Chilver, M.A. *Principal* (1971).

St. Anne's (1952) (Originally *Society of Oxford Home-Students* (1879)), Mrs. N. K. Trenaman, M.A., *Principal* (1966).

St. Hilda's (1893), Mrs. M. L. S. Bennett, M.A., *Principal* (1965).

St. Hugh's (1886), Miss M. R. Trickett, M.A., *Principal* (1973).

Somerville (1879), Mrs. B. Craig, M.A., *Principal* (1967).

UNIVERSITY PROFESSORS   Elect.

American History (*Harmsworth*), J. Blum, M.A., *Queen's*........................... 1976

American History and Institutions (*Rhodes*), H. G. Nicholas, M.A., *New College*...... 1969

Anatomy (*Lee's*), C. G. Phillips, D.M., F.R.S., *Hertford*............................. 1975

Anæsthetics (*Nuffield*), A. C. Smith, M.A., *Pemb*................................ 1965

Anglo-Saxon, E. G. Stanley, M.A., *St. Peter's* 1977

Anthropology, Social, R. Needham, M.A., D. Litt., *All Souls*...................... 1976

Arabic (*Laudian*), A. F. L. Beeston, M.A., D.Phil., *St. John's*...................... 1955

Archæology of the Roman Empire, S. S. Frere, M.A., F.B.A., *All Souls*................ 1966

Archæology, Classical (*Lincoln*), C. M. Robertson, M.A., F.B.A., *Linc*.............. 1961

Archæology, European, B. W. Cunliffe, M.A., Ph.D., *Keble*........................ 1972

Armenian Studies (*Gulbenkian*), C. J. F. Dowsett, M.A., D.Phil., *Pembroke*......... 1965

Astronomy (*Savilian*), D. E. Blackwell, M.A., Ph.D., *New Coll.*...................... 1960

Biochemistry (*Whitley*), R. R. Porter, M.A., Ph.D., F.R.S., *Trinity*................... 1967

Biomathematics, P. Armitage, M.A., Ph.D., *St. Peter's*......................... 1976

Botany (*Sherardian*), F. R. Whatley, M.A., Ph.D., F.R.S., *Magdalen*................ 1971

Byzantine and Modern Greek Lang. and Lit. (*Bywater and Sotheby*), C. Mango, M.A., *Exeter*............................... 1973

Celtic, I. Ll. Foster, M.A., *Jesus*............ 1947

Chemical Crystallography (*Royal Society's Wolfson Research Professor*), Mrs. D. M. Hodgkin, O.M., D.SC., M.A., F.R.S., *Somerville*.............................. 1960

Chemical Microbiology (*Iveagh*), J. Mandelstam, M.A., F.R.S., *Linacre*............... 1966

Chemical Pathology, E. P. Abraham, C.B.E., M.A., D.Phil., F.R.S., *Lincoln*........... 1964

Chemistry, Inorganic, J. B. Goodenough, M.A., Ph.D., *St. Catherine's*.............. 1976

Chemistry (*Lee's*), J. S. Rowlinson, M.A., D.Phil., F.R.S., *Exeter*................... 1974

Chemistry (*Waynflete*), Sir Ewart Jones, M.A., F.R.S., *Magd*...................... 1955

Chinese, P. van der Loon, M.A., *University*... 1972

Civil Law (*Regius*), A. M. Honoré, D.C.L., *All Souls*............................. 1971

Clinical Biochemistry, P. J. Randle, M.A., D.Phil., M.D., *Hertford*.................. 1975

Clinical Neurology, W. B. Matthews, D.M., *St. Edmund Hall*...................... 1970

Clinical Pharmacology, D. G. Grahame-Smith, M.A., Ph.D., *Corpus*................... 1971

Comparative Philology, Mrs. A. E. Davies, M.A., *Somerville*...................... 1971

Comparative Slavonic Philology, R. Auty, M.A., Dr. Phil., *Brasenose*............. 1965

Divinity (*Regius*), Rev. Canon M. F. Wiles, D.D., *Ch. Ch.*...................... 1970

Divinity (*Lady Margaret*), Rev. Canon J. Macquarrie, M.A., *Ch. Ch.*............. 1970

Eastern Religions and Ethics (*Spalding*), (vacant)

Ecclesiastical History (*Regius*), Rev. Canon J. McManners, M.A., *Ch. Ch.*............ 1972

Economic History (*Chichele*), P. Mathias, M.A., *All Souls*........................ 1968

Economics, Applied, J. A. C. Brown, M.A., *Merton*............................. 1970

Economics, J. A. Mirrlees, M.A., Ph.D., *Nuffield* 1968

Economics of Underdeveloped Countries (vacant).

Egyptology, J. R. Baines, M.A., D.Phil., *Queen's*............................ 1976

Engineering, H. Motz, M.A., Dr. Ing., *St. John's*.............................. 1972

Engineering Science, D. W. Holder, M.A., D.SC., F.R.S., B.N.C.................... 1961

Engineering (*Stewarts and Lloyds*), W. S. Hemp, M.A., *Keble*..................... 1965

English Language, E. J. Dobson, M.A., D.Phil., *Jesus*.................................. 1961

English Language and Literature (*Merton*), N. Davis, M.B.E., M.A., F.B.A., *Merton*.... 1959

English Literature (*Merton*), J. Carey, M.A., D.Phil., *Merton*...................... 1975

English Literature (*Goldsmiths'*), R. Ellmann, M.A., *New Coll.*....................... 1970

English Literature (*Thomas Warton*), J. O. Bayley, M.A., *St. Catherine's*............ 1974

Elect.

Exegesis (Ireland), Rev. G. B. Caird, D.Phil., D.D., Queen's............................ 1977
Experimental Philosophy (Lee's), B. Bleaney, C.B.E., M.A., D.Phil., F.R.S., Wadham...... 1957
Fine Art (Slade), H. Hibbard, M.A., All Souls 1976
Forest Science, J. L. Harley, M.A., D.Phil., F.R.S., St. John's........................ 1969
French (Foch), J. Scherer, M.A., All Souls.... 1973
French Literature, I. D. McFarlane, M.B.E., M.A.,Wadham........................... 1971
Genetics, W. F. Bodmer, M.A., F.R.S., Keble. 1970
Geography, J. Gottmann, M.A., D. ès L., Hertford.................................. 1968
Geography (Mackinder), J. W. House, M.A., St. Peter's.............................. 1974
Geology, E. A. Vincent, M.A., Ph.D., University.................................. 1966
Geometry (Savilian), I. M. James, M.A., D.Phil., F.R.S., St. John's................ 1970
George Eastman Visiting, S. Wolin, M.A., Balliol 1976
German, P. F. Ganz, M.A., Ph.D., St. Edmund Hall................................... 1972
German Language and Literature (Taylor), S. S. Prawer, M.A., D.Litt., Queen's.......... 1969
Government and Public Administration (Gladstone), S. E. Finer, M.A., All Souls....... 1957
Greek (Regius), P. H. J. Lloyd-Jones, M.A., F.B.A., Ch. Ch......................... 1960
Hebrew (Regius), W. D. McHardy, M.A., D.Phil., Ch. Ch. 1960
History, Ancient (Camden), P. A. Brunt, M.A., F.B.A., Brasenose...................... 1970
History, Ancient Wykeham), W. G. G. Forrest, M.A., New Coll........................ 1977
History of Art, F. J. H. Haskell, M.A., Trinity 1967
History of the British Commonwealth (Beit), R. E. Robinson, M.A., Balliol............ 1971
History of Latin America, D. C. M. Platt, M.A., D.Phil., St. Antony's............... 1973
History of Philosophy, J. L. Ackrill, M.A., B.N.C................................. 1966
History of Science, Mrs. M. M. Gowing, M.A., Linacre................................ 1973
History of War (Chichele), M. E. Howard, M.A., F.B.A., All Souls.................. 1977
International Relations (Montague Burton), (vacant)
Interpretation of Holy Scripture, J. Barr, M.A., B.D., F.B.A., Oriel................... 1976
Italian (Serena), C. Grayson, M.A., Magdalen 1958
Jurisprudence, R. M. Dworkin, M.A., University.................................. 1969
Latin (Corpus), R. G. M. Nisbet, M.A., F.B.A., Corpus.............................. 1970
Law (Comparative), J. K. B. M. Nicholas, M.A., Brasenose......................... 1971
Law (English), (vacant).
Law (English) (Vinerian), Sir Rupert Cross, D.C.L., F.B.A., All Souls............... 1964
Logic (Wykeham), Sir Alfred Ayer, M.A., F.B.A., New Coll....................... 1959
Mathematical Logic, D. S. Scott, M.A., Ph.D., Merton.............................. 1972
Mathematics, J. F. C. Kingman, M.A., D.Sc., F.R.S., St. Cross....................... 1969
Mathematics (Rouse Ball), R. Penrose, M.A., Ph.D., F.R.S., Wadham.................. 1973
Mathematics (Theory of Plasma), L. C. Woods, M.A., D.Phil., D.Sc., Balliol............ 1970
Medicine (Regius), Sir Richard Doll, O.B.E., D.M., M.D., D.Sc., F.R.C.P., F.R.S., Christ Church............................... 1969
Medicine, Cardiovascular (Field Marshal Alexander), P. Sleight, D.M., Exeter...... 1973
Medicine, Clinical (Nuffield), D. J. Weatherall, M.D., F.R.C.P., Magd................... 1974

Elect.

Medicine, Social and Community, M. P. Vessey, M.A., M.D., St. Cross............. 1974
Metallurgy (Wolfson), Sir Peter Hirsch, M.A., D.Phil., F.R.S., St. Edmund Hall.......... 1966
Metallurgy, Physical, J. W. Christian, M.A., D.Phil., F.R.S., St. Edmund Hall........... 1967
Metaphysical Philosophy (Waynflete), P. F. Strawson, M.A., F.B.A., Magd............... 1968
Modern History (Chichele), J. M. Wallace-Hadrill, M.A., D.Litt., F.B.A., All Souls..... 1974
Modern History (Regius), H. R. Trevor-Roper, M.A., F.B.A., Oriel............... 1957
Modern History, R. C. Cobb, M.A., F.B.A., Worcester............................ 1973
Molecular Biophysics, D. C. Phillips, Ph.D., F.R.S., Corpus Christi................... 1966
Moral and Pastoral Thelogy (Regius), Rev. Canon P. R. Baelz, M.A., Christ Church... 1975
Moral Philosophy (White's), R. M. Hare, M.A., F.B.A., Corpus Christi................. 1966
Morbid Anatomy, J. O'D. McGee, Ph.D., Linacre................................. 1975
Music, D. M. Arnold, M.A., Wadham........ 1975
Natural Philosophy (Sedleian), A. E. Green, Ph.D., Sc.D., F.R.S., Queen's............ 1968
Numerical Analysis (and Director of Computing Laboratory), L. Fox, M.A., D.Phil., D.Sc., Balliol............................... 1964
Nuclear Structure, K. W. Allen, M.A., Ph.D., Balliol................................ 1963
Obstetrics and Gynæcology (Nuffield), A. C. Turnbull, M.D., M.A., Queen's.......... 1973
Orthopædic Surgery (Nuffield), R. B. Duthie, M.A., F.R.C.S., Worcester.................. 1966
Paediatrics, J. P. M. Tizard, M.A., F.R.C.P., Jesus................................ 1972
Pathology, H. Harris, M.A., D.Phil., F.R.S., Lincoln............................... 1963
Pathology (Royal Society's), J. L. Gowans, M.A., D.Phil., F.R.S., St. Catherine's....... 1962
Pharmacology, W. D. M. Paton, C.B.E., D.M., F.R.S., New Coll....................... 1959
Philosophy of the Christian Religion (Nolloth), B. G. Mitchell, M.A., Oriel.............. 1967
Physics (Wykeham), R. J. Elliott, M.A., D.Phil., F.R.S., New College.............. 1974
Physics, Elementary Particle, D. H. Perkins, M.A., Ph.D., F.R.S., St. Catherine's........ 1965
Physics, Experimental (vacant).
Physics, Theoretical (Royal Society's), R. H. Dalitz, M.A., Ph.D., F.R.S., All Souls...... 1963
Physiology (Waynflete), D. Whitteridge, B.Sc., D.M., F.R.S., Magd................. 1968
Poetry, J. B. Wain, M.A., B.N.C............ 1973
Political Economy (Drummond), J. E. Stiglitz, M.A., Ph.D., All Souls............... 1976
Psychiatry (Handley), M. G. Gelder, D.M., Merton............................... 1969
Psychology, L. Weiskrantz, M.A., Ph.D., Magdalen............................... 1967
Psychology (Watts), J. S. Bruner, M.A., Ph.D., Wolfson......................... 1972
Public International Law (Chichele), D. P. O'Connell, M.A., D.C.L., All Souls...... 1972
Pure Mathematics (Waynflete), G. Higman, M.A., D.Phil., F.R.S., Magdalen.......... 1960
Race Relations (Rhodes), K. Kirkwood, M.A., St. Ant............................... 1954
Romance Languages (vacant).
Rural Economy (Sibthorpian), J. H. Burnett, M.A., D.Phil., St. John's................ 1970
Russian, J. L. I. Fennell, M.A., Ph.D., New Coll. 1966
Russian and Balkan History, D. Obolensky, M.A., Ph.D., F.B.A., Ch. Ch............. 1961
Sanskrit (Boden) (vacant).

Elect.

Social and Political Theory (Chichele), C. M.
Taylor, M.A., D.Phil., *All Souls*........... 1976
Spanish Studies (King Alfonso XIII), P. E.
Russell, M.A., *Exeter*.................. 1953
Surgery (Nuffield), P. J. Morris, M.A., Ph.D.,
F.R.C.S., *Balliol*.................... 1974
Zoology (Entomology) (Hope), G. C. Varley,
M.A., Ph.D., *Jesus*................... 1948
Zoology (Linacre), J. W. S. Pringle, M.B.E.,
M.A., D.SC., F.R.S., *Merton*............. 1961

THE UNIVERSITY OF CAMBRIDGE

FULL TERMS, 1977

Lent, Jan. 7 to Mar. 11; Easter, Apr. 19 to June 10
Michaelmas, Oct. 4 to Dec. 2

NUMBER OF UNDERGRADUATES IN RESIDENCE
1975–76: Men, 7,127; Women, 1,732

Chancellor, (vacant).
Vice-Chancellor, Miss A. R. Murray, M.A.,
D.Phil., *President of New Hall*........... 1975
High Steward, The Lord Devlin, P.C., M.A.,
F.B.A., *Chr*....................... 1966
Deputy High Steward, Rt. Hon. J. S. B. Lloyd,
C.H., C.B.E., Q.C., M.P., M.A., *Magd*........ 1971
Commissary, The Lord Morris of Borth-y-
Gest, P.C., C.B.E., M.C., Q.C., *Tr. H*....... 1968
Orator, F. H. Stubbings, M.A., Ph.D.......... 1974
†Registrary, R. E. Macpherson, M.A., *King's* 1969
†Deputy Registrary, R. F. Holmes, M.A.,
Darw........................... 1972
Librarian, E. B. Ceadel, M.A., *Corp*......... 1967
Treasurer, T. C. Gardner, C.B.E., M.A., *Wolfs.* 1969
Deputy Treasurer, A. B. Shone, M.A., *Selw* .. 1969
Secretary General of the Faculties, A. D. I.
Nicol, M.A., Ph.D., *Fitzw*.............. 1972
Deputy Secretary General of the Faculties,
L. M. Harvey, M.A., *Chur*.............. 1963
Esquire Bedell, P. T. Sinker, M.A., *Cla*...... 1960
Proctors, P. A. Linchan, M.A., Ph.D., *Joh.*;
T. R. Langley, M.A., *Sid*. (for 1976–7)
Organist, G. H. Guest, M.A., Mus.B., *Joh*..... 1974
Director, Dept. of Applied Economics, Hon.
W. A. H. Godley, M.A., *King's*.......... 1970
Director of the Fitzwilliam Museum, Prof. A.
M.Jaffé, M.A., *King's*................ 1973
Director of the Museum of Zoology, K. A.
Joysey, M.A., *Fitzw*................. 1970
Director, University Computing Service, D. F.
Hartley, M.A., Ph.D., *Darw*............. 1970
Director in Industrial Co-operation, *Wolfson
Cambridge Industrial Unit*, D. B. Welbourn,
M.A., *Selw*....................... 1971
Curator of the Museum of Archæology and
Ethnology, P. W. Gathercole, M.A., *Pet*.... 1970
Curator of the Museum of Classical Archæology,
Prof. A. M. Snodgrass, M.A., D.Phil....... 1976
Curators of the Sedgwick Museum of Geology,
C. L. Forbes, M.A., Ph.D., *Cla*.......... 1967
R. B. Rickards, M.A., *Emm*............. 1968
Curator of the Whipple Museum of the History
of Science, D. Bryden, B.SC., M.A., *Caius*.. 1970
Director of the Botanic Garden, S. M. Walters,
M.A., Ph.D., *King's*................. 1973
Representative on General Medical Council,
W. S. Lewin, M.A., *Darw*.............. 1971

SECRETARY TO:—

Local Examinations Syndicate, F. Wild, M.A.,
Ph.D., *Down*...................... 1972
Board of Extra-mural Studies, J. M. Y. Andrew,
M.A., *Cath*., Madingley Hall........... 1967

† Correspondence for the *Registrary* and *Deputy
Registrary* should be sent to the *University Registry*,
The Old Schools, Cambridge.

Elect.

Highest Grade Schools Examination Syndicate,
H. F. King, M.A., M.SC., *Emm*., 10 Trump-
ington Street...................... 1969
Appointments Board, W. P. Kirkman, M.A.,
Wolfs., Stuart House, Mill Lane........ 1968
University Press, G. A. Cass, M.A., *Jes*...... 1972

COUNCIL OF THE SENATE
(Secretary, The Registrary)

Ex officio Members, The Chancellor; Vice-Chan-
cellor.
Heads of Colleges, The Master of *Jesus;* The Master
of *Fitzwilliam;* The President of *Queens'*.
Professors and Readers, Prof. A. D. Buckingham,
Ph.D., *Pemb.;* Prof. M. B. Hesse, M.A., Ph.D., F.B.A.,
Wolfs.; Miss P. M. Deane, M.A., *Newn.;* Prof.
Sir Peter Swinnerton-Dyer, Bt., M.A., F.R.S.,
Cath.
Elected as Members of the Regent House, Mrs. C. U.
Bertram, Ph.D., *L.Cav.;* S. G. Fleet, M.A., Ph.D.,
Down; C. B. Goodhart, M.A., Ph.D., *Cai.;* C. M.
P. Johnson, M.A., Ph.D., *Joh.;* J. S. Morrison, M.A.,
Wolfs.; P. O'Higgins, M.A., Ph.D., *Chr.,* G. A.
Reid, M.A., Ph.D., *Joh.;* J. F. Q. Switzer, M.A.,
Sid.

Cambridge Colleges
(With dates of foundation)

Christ's (1505), The Lord Todd, M.A., F.R.S., *Master*
(1963).
Churchill (1960), (men and women) Prof. Sir
William Hawthorne, C.B.E., M.A., F.R.S., *Master*
(1968).
Clare (1326) (men and women), R. C. O. Matthews,
M.A., F.B.A. *Master* (1975).
Clare Hall (1966) (men and women), Prof. R. W.
K. Honeycombe, Ph.D., *President* (1973).
Corpus Christi (1352), Sir Duncan Wilson, G.C.M.G.,
Master (1971).
Darwin (1964) (men and women), Prof. M. I. Finley,
Ph.D., M.A., F.B.A. *Master* (1976).
Downing (1800), Sir Morien Morgan, C.B., M.A.,
F.R.S., *Master* (1972).
Emmanuel (1584), Sir Gordon Sutherland, SC.D.,
F.R.S., *Master* (1964).
Fitzwilliam (1966), E. Miller, M.A., *Master* (1971).
Gonville & Caius (1348), H. W. R. Wade, M.A.,
D.C.L., F.B.A., *Master* (1976).
Jesus (1496), Sir Alan Cottrell, M.A., Ph.D., SC.D.,
F.R.S., *Master* (1974).
King's (1441) (men and women), Prof. Sir
Edmund Leach, M.A., Ph.D., *Provost* (1966).
Magdalene (1542), W. Hamilton, M.A., *Master* (1966).
Pembroke (1347), W. A. Camps, M.A., *Master* (1970).
Peterhouse (1284), Prof. J. G. D. Clark, C.B.E.,
SC.D., F.B.A., *Master* (1973).
Queens' (1448), D. W. Bowett, M.A., Ph.D., Ll.D.,
President (1970).
Robinson, Prof. T. Lewis, Ph.D., D.SC., M.A., F.R.S.,
Warden (1975).
St. Catharine's (1473), Prof. Sir Peter Swinnerton-
Dyer, Bt., M.A., F.R.S., *Master* (1973).
St. Edmund's House (1896), Very Rev. Canon G. D.
Sweeney, M.A., *Master* (1964).
St. John's (1511), Prof. P. N. S. Mansergh, O.B.E.,
Litt.D., F.B.A., *Master* (1969).
Selwyn (1882) (men and women from Oct. 1976),
Rev. Prof. W. O. Chadwick, D.D., F.B.A., *Master*
(1956).
Sidney Sussex (1596) (men and women), Prof. D. H.
Northcote, Ph.D., SC.D., F.R.S., *Master* (1976).
Trinity (1546), The Lord Butler of Saffron Walden,
K.G., P.C., C.H., M.A., *Master* (1965).
Trinity Hall (1350) (men and women from Oct·
1977), T. M. Sugden, SC.D., F.R.S., *Master* (1976)

Wolfson (1965) (men and women), J. S. Morrison, M.A., *President* (1966).

COLLEGES FOR WOMEN

Girton (1869), Mrs. B. E. Rymen, M.A., Ph.D., *Mistress* (1976).

New Hall (1954), Miss A. R. Murray, M.A., D.Phil., *President.*

Newnham (1871), Mrs. J. Floud, C.B.E., B.SC. (Econ.), M.A., *Principal* (1972).

APPROVED SOCIETIES

Hughes Hall (*formerly Cambridge T.C.*) (1885), (for post-graduate students and candidates for B.Ed.), Sir Desmond Lee, M.A., *President* (1974).

Lucy Cavendish Collegiate Society (1965) (for women research students and mature undergraduates), Mrs. C. K. Bertram, M.A., Ph.D., *President* (1970).

UNIVERSITY PROFESSORS

	Elect.
Aerial Photographic Studies, J. K. S. St. Joseph, M.A., Ph.D., *Selw*	1973
Aeronautical Engineering (*Francis Mond*), W. A. Mair, C.B.E., M.A., *Down*	1952
Agriculture (*Drapers*), J. W. L. Beament, SC.D., F.R.S., *Qu*	1969
American History and Institutions (*Pitt*), E. B. Genovese (for 1976–77).	
Anatomy, R. J. Harrison, M.D., F.R.S., *Down.*	1968
Ancient History, M. I. Finley, M.A., *Jes*	1970
Ancient Philosophy (*Laurence*), G. E. L. Owen, M.A., B.Phil., F.B.A., *King's*	1973
Anglo-Saxon (*Elrington and Bosworth*), P. A. M. Clemoes, Ph.D., *Emm*	1969
Animal Embryology (*Charles Darwin*), C. R. Austin, M.A., *Fitzw*	1967
Applied Mathematics, G. K. Batchelor, Ph.D., F.R.S., *Trin*	1964
Applied Numerical Analysis, M. J. D. Powell, B.A., *Pet*	1976
Applied Thermodynamics (*Hopkinson and Imperial Chemical Industries*), Sir William Hawthorne, C.B.E., M.A., SC.D., F.R.S., *Chur.*	1951
Arabic (*Sir T. Adam's*), R. B. Serjeant, Ph.D., *Trin*	1970
Archæology (*Disney*), G. E. Daniel, Litt.D., F.S.A., *Joh.*	1974
Architecture, C. A. St. J. Wilson, M.A., F.R.I.B.A., *Chur*	1975
Astronomy and Experimental Philosophy (*Plumian*), M. J. Rees, M.A., Ph.D., *King's.*	1973
Astronomy and Geometry (*Lowndean*), J. F. Adams, M.A., Ph.D., F.R.S., *Trin*	1970
Astrophysics, D. Lynden-Bell, M.A., Ph.D., *Cla.*	1972
Biochemistry (*Sir William Dunn*), H. L. Kornberg, M.A., D.SC., Ph.D., F.R.S., *Chr*	1975
Biology (*Quick*), R. R. A. Coombs, SC.D., F.R.S., *Corp*	1966
Biophysics (*John Humphrey Plummer*), Sir Alan Hodgkin, O.M., K.B.E., SC.D., F.R.S., *Trin.*	1970
Botany, P. W. Brian, SC.D., F.R.S., *Qu*	1968
Cellular Pathology, K. C. Dixon, M.D., *King's*	1973
Chemical Engineering, J. F. Davidson, SC.D., *Trin*	1975
Chemical Engineering (*Shell*), P. V. Danckwerts, G.C., M.B.E., M.A., F.R.S., *Pemb*	1959
Chemical Microbiology, E. F. Gale, SC.D., F.R.S., *Joh.*	1960
Chemistry (1968), A. D. Buckingham, Ph.D., *Pemb*	1969
Chemistry (1970), J. Lewis, M.A., F.R.S., *Sid.*	1970
Chinese, D. C. Twitchett, M.A., Ph.D., *Cath*	1968
Civil Law (*Regius*), P. G. Stein, M.A., Ll.B., *Qu*	1968

	Elect.
Classical Archæology (*Laurence*), A. M. Snodgrass, M.A., D.Phil.	1976
Clinical Biochemistry, H. Lehmann, SC.D., *Chr.*	1967
Clinical Oncology (*Career Research Campaign*), N. M. Bleehen, M.A., B.SC., B.M., B.Ch.	1975
Community Medicine, R. M. Acheson, M.A, D.M., B.Ch., SC.D., F.R.C.P.	1976
Comparative Law, J. A. Jolowicz, M.A., *Trin.*	1976
Comparative Philology, W. S. Allen, M.A., Ph.D., *Trin*	1955
Comparative Physiology, J. A. Ramsay, M.B.E., M.A., Ph.D., F.R.S., *Qu*	1969
Computer Technology, M. V. Wilkes, M.A., Ph.D., F.R.S., *Joh*	1965
Criminology (*Wolfson*), N. D. Walker, M.A., Ph.D., D.Litt., *King's*	1973
Divinity (*Ely*), Rev. G. C. Stead, M.A., *King's*	1971
,, (*Lady Margaret's*), Miss M. D. Hooker, M.A., Ph.D.	1976
,, (*Norris-Hulse*), D. M. MacKinnon, M.A., *Corp.*	1960
Divinity (*Regius*), Rev. Canon G. W. H. Lampe, M.C., D.D., *Cai.*	1971
Drama, R. H. Williams, Litt.D., *Jes.*	1974
Ecclesiastical History (*Dixie*), Rev. E. G. Rupp, D.D., F.B.A., *Emm*	1968
Economic History, D. C. Coleman, B.SC., Ph.D	1971
Economics (1970), F. H. Hahn, M.A., *Chur.*	1972
Economics (1965), R. R. Neild, M.A., *Trin.*	1971
Economics and Statistics, D. G. Champernowne, M.A., *Trin.*	1970
Education, P. H. Hirst, M.A., *Wolfs.*	1971
Egyptology (*Herbert Thompson*), Rev. J. M. Plumley, M.A., *Selw*	1957
Electrical Engineering, P. S. Brandon, M.A., *Jes*	1971
Engineering, A. H. W. Beck, M.A., *Corp.* (1966); M. F. Ashby, M.A., Ph.D., *Cl. H.* (1973); A. G. J. MacFarlane, Ph.D., D.SC., *Selw* (1974); A. N. Schofield, M.A., Ph.D., *Chur.* (1974); J. Heyman, M.A., Ph.D., *Pet.* (1971); D. E. Newland, M.A., SC.D. (1976); (*Rank*) J. E. Ffowcs-Williams, M.A., *Emm.*	1972
English, I. R. D. Jack, Litt.D., *Pemb.* (1976); C. B. Ricks, M.A., B.Litt., *Chr.*	1975
English Constitutional History, G. R. Elton, Litt.D., F.B.A., *Cla*	1967
English Law (*Rouse Ball*), G. Ll. Williams, Q.C., LL.D., F.B.A., *Jes*	1968
English Literature (*King Edward VII*), J. F. Kermode, M.A., *King's.*	1974
Experimental Psychology, O. L. Zangwill, M.A., *King's.*	1952
Finance and Accounting (*P. D. Leake*), J. R. N. Stone, C.B.E., SC.D., F.B.A., *King's.*	1955
Fine Art (*Slade*), J. H. Golding, M.A., Ph.D. (for 1976–77).	
French, Miss A. A. B. Fairlie, Ph.D., *Girton* (1972); R. A. Leigh, Litt.D., *Trin.*; Mrs. O. M. H. L. de Mourqes, L.H.D., *Girton*	1975
French (*Drapers*), Ll. J. Austin, M.A., F.B.A., *Jes*	1967
French Literature, J. B. M. Barrère, M.A., *Joh.*	1954
Genetics (*Arthur Balfour*), J. M. Thoday, SC.D., F.R.S., *Emm*	1959
Geography, M. D. I. Chisholm, M.A. *Cath.*, (1976); R. J. Chorley, SC.D., *Sid.*	1974
Geology (*Woodwardian*), H. B. Whittington, M.A., F.R.S., *Sid*	1966
Geophysics, J. A. Jacobs, M.A., Ph.D., D.SC.	1974
German (*Schröder*), L. W. Forster, M.A., *Selw.*	1961
Greek (*Regius*), G. S. Kirk, Litt.D., *Tr. H.*	1973
Hæmatological Medicine (*Leukaemia Research Fund*), F. G. J. Hayhoe, M.D., *Darw*	1968

Elect.

Hebrew (Regius), Rev. J. A. Emerton, D.D., Joh.... 1968

Histology, C. C. D. Shute, M.D., Chr... 1969

History of International Relations, F. H. Hinsley, O.B.E., M.A., Joh... 1969

History of the British Commonwealth (Smuts), E. T. Stokes, M.A., Ph.D., Cath... 1970

History of Western Art, A. M. Jaffé, M.A., King's... 1973

Imperial and Naval History (Vere Harmsworth), J. A. Gallagher, M.A., Trin... 1970

Industrial Relations (Montague Burton), H. A. F. Turner, M.A., Chur... 1964

International Law, C. Parry, Ll.D., Down... 1969

International Law (Whewell), R. Y. Jennings, Q.C., M.A., Ll.B., Jes... 1955

Italian, U. Limentani, M.A., Magd... 1962

Land Economy, D. R. Denman, M.A., Pemb... 1968

Latin (Kennedy), E. J. Kenney, M.A., F.B.A., Pet... 1974

Latin-American Studies (Simón Bolívar), F. H. Cardoso (for 1976–77).

Law, S. C. Milsom, M.A., F.B.A., Joh... 1976

Laws of England (Downing), G. H. Jones, Ll.D., Trin... 1975

Legal Science (Arthur Goodhart), X. Blanc-Jouvan, Qu. (for 1976–7).

Mathematical Physics, J. C. Polkinghorne, M.A., Ph.D., F.R.S., Trin... 1968

Mathematical Statistics, D. G. Kendall, M.A., F.R.S., Chur... 1962

Mathematics, Sir Peter Swinnerton-Dyer, Bt. M.A., F.R.S., Cath... 1971

Mathematics (Lucasian), Sir James Lighthill, B.A., F.R.S., F.B.A., Trin... 1969

Mathematics (Rouse Ball), J. G. Thompson, M.A., Chur... 1971

Mathematics for Operational Research (Churchill), P. Whittle, M.A., Chur... 1967

Mechanics, W. Johnson, B.Sc., B.Sc.Tech., D.Sc., Fitzw... 1975

Mechanics of Solids, R. Hill, Sc.D., Cai... 1972

Medicine, I. H. Mills, M.D., Chur... 1963

Medieval and Renaissance English, J. A. W. Bennett, M.A., Magd... 1964

Medieval History, W. Ullmann, Litt.D., Trin... 1972

Membrane Physiology, I. M. Glynn, M.D., Trin... 1975

Metallurgy (Goldsmiths'), R. W. K. Honeycombe, Ph.D., Tr. H... 1966

Mineralogy and Petrology, W. A. Deer, Ph.D., F.R.S., Tr. H... 1961

Modern English, J. Holloway, Litt.D., Qu... 1972

Modern History, C. H. Wilson, M.A., F.B.A., Jes... 1963

Modern History (Regius), Rev. W. O. Chadwick, D.D., F.B.A., Selw... 1968

Modern Languages, D. H. Green, M.A., Trin... 1966

Music, A. Goehr, Tr. H... 1976

Natural Philosophy (Jacksonian), A. H. Cook, Sc.D., Corp... 1972

Numismatics, P. Grierson, Litt.D., F.B.A., Cai... 1971

Obstetrics and Gynaecology, C. P. Douglas, B.A., M.B., Ch.B... 1976

Organic Chemistry (1702), R. A. Raphael, M.A., Chur... 1972

Organic Chemistry (1969), A. R. Battersby, M.A., F.R.S., Cath... 1969

Palaeoecology, R. G. West, Sc.D., Cla... 1975

Pathology, P. Wildy, M.A., M.B., B.Chir., Cai... 1975

Pharmacology (Sheild), G. V. R. Born, D.Phil., F.R.S., Cai... 1973

Philosophy, Miss G. E. M. Anscombe, M.A., New H... 1970

Philosophy (Knightbridge), B. A. O. Williams, M.A., King's... 1967

Elect.

Philosophy of Science, Miss M. B. Hesse, M.A., Ph.D., F.B.A., Wolfs... 1975

Physic (Regius), W. J. H. Butterfield, O.B.E., M.A., D.M., M.D., F.R.C.P., Down... 1975

Physical Chemistry, (vacant).

Physics, D. Shoenberg, B.A., Ph.D., Cai. (1973); D. Tabor, Sc.D., Cai. (1973); B. D. Josephson, M.A., Ph.D., Trin... 1974

Physics (Cavendish), Sir Brian Pippard, F.R.S., Cl. H... 1971

Physics (John Humphrey Plummer), Sir Samuel Edwards, M.A., Ph.D., Cai... 1972

Physiology, R. D. Keynes, Sc.D., Chur... 1973

Physiology of Reproduction (Mary Marshall and Arthur Walton), (vacant).

Plant Biochemistry, D. H. Northcote, Ph.D., Sc.D., F.R.S., Sid... 1972

Political Economy, W. B. Reddaway, M.A., Cla... 1969

Political Science, W. B. Gallie, M.A., Pet... 1967

Pure Mathematics, A. Baker, M.A., Ph.D., Trin... 1974

Pure Mathematics (Sadleirian), J. W. S. Cassels, Ph.D., F.R.S., Trin... 1967

Radio Astronomy, Sir Martin Ryle, M.A., F.R.S., Trin... 1959

Radio Astronomy (1971), A. Hewish, M.A., Ph.D., F.R.S., Chur... 1971

Sanskrit, J. Brough, M.A., F.B.A., Joh... 1967

Slavonic Studies, L. R. Lewitter, M.A., Ph.D., Christ's... 1968

Social Anthropology, E. R. Leach, M.A., Ph.D., King's... 1972

Social Anthropology (William Wyse), J. R. Goody, Sc.D., Joh... 1973

Sociology, J. A. Barnes, D.S.C., M.A., D.Phil., Chur... 1975

Spanish, C. C. Smith, M.A., Ph.D., Cath... 1975

Surgery, R. Y. Calne, M.A., F.R.S., F.R.C.S., Tr. H... 1965

Theoretical Astronomy, R. A. Lyttelton, M.A., Ph.D., F.R.S., Joh... 1969

Theoretical Physics, V. Heine, M.Sc., Ph.D., Cla... 1976

Veterinary Clinical Studies, A. T. Phillipson, M.A., Ph.D., Chur... 1963

Zoology, (vacant).

THE UNIVERSITY OF DURHAM

(Founded 1832; re-organized 1908, 1937 and 1963)
Old Shire Hall, Durham

Undergraduates (1975–76), 4,073

Chancellor, Rt. Hon. Malcolm J. MacDonald, O.M., M.A.

Vice-Chancellor and Warden, Sir Derman Christopherson, O.B.E., D.Phil., F.R.S.

Pro-Vice-Chancellor, Prof. W. K. R. Musgrave, Ph.D., D.Sc.

Second Pro-Vice-Chancellor, Prof. J. L. Brooks, M.A.

Registrar and Secretary, I. E. Graham, M.A.

Professor of Education, G. R. Batho, M.A.

Director of Institute of Education, J. J. Grant, C.B.E., M.A., Ed.B.

Colleges

University, D. W. MacDowell, M.A., D.Phil., F.S.A., Master.

Hatfield, T. Whitworth, M.A., D.Phil., Master.

Grey, S. Holgate, M.A., Ph.D., Master.

Van Mildert, P. W. Kent, M.A., Ph.D., D.Phil., D.Sc., D.Litt., Master.

Collingwood, P. C. Bayley, M.A., Master.

St. Chad's, Rev. J. C. Fenton, M.A., B.D., Principal.

St. John's, Rev. J. C. P. Cockerton, M.A., Principal.

St. Mary's, Miss F. I. Calvert, M.A., Principal.

St. Aidan's, Miss I. Hindmarsh, M.A., Principal.

Trevelyan, Joan Constance Bernard, M.A., B.D., *Principal.*

St. Hild and St. Bede, J. V. Armitage, B.SC., Ph.D., *Principal.*

★Neville's Cross, R. G. Emmett, B.SC. (Econ.), M.A., Ph.D., *Principal.*

St. Cuthbert's Society, Prof. J. L. Brooks, M.A., *Principal.*

The Graduate Society, Prof. W. B. Fisher, B.A., DOC. D'UNIV., *Principal.*

Ushaw, Rt. Rev. Mgr. P. Loftus, B.C.L., *President.*
★ Hall of Residence.

THE UNIVERSITY OF LONDON, 1836
Senate House, W.C.1

Internal Students (1974–75), 42,634, External Students, 28,430.

Visitor, H.M. the Queen in Council.

Chancellor, H.M. Queen Elizabeth the Queen Mother.

Vice-Chancellor, F. Hartley, C.B.E., B.SC., Ph.D., F.R.S.

Chairman of the Court, Rt. Hon. Sir Leslie Scarman, O.B.E., M.A.

Chairman of Convocation, Prof. J. P. Quilliam, M.SC., D.SC., F.R.C.P.

Principal, F. M. G. Willson, B.A. (Admin.), M.A., D.Phil. (1975).

THE COURT
Ex Officio, The Chancellor, The Vice-Chancellor, The Chairman of Convocation.

Appointed by the Senate, Prof. F. R. Crane, Il.B.; Prof. N. F. Morris, M.D.; Prof. Sir Cyril Philips, M.A., Ph.D.; B. Thwaites, M.A., Ph.D.; R. C. Tress, C.B.E., B.SC., D.SC.; Sir Bernard Waley-Cohen, Bt., M.A.; *By Her Majesty in Council*, Sir Michael Clapham, M.B.E., M.A.; P. Parker, M.V.O., M.A.; The Lord Shawcross, G.B.E., P.C., Q.C.; *By the I.L.E.A.*, Sir Reginald Goodwin, C.B.E.; Sir Desmond Plummer, T.D.; *Home Counties and Outer London Boroughs Member*, T. I. Smith, O.B.E., M.A.; *Co-opted Member*, Rt. Hon. A. G. F. Rippon, Q.C., M.A., M.P.

THE SENATE
Ex-Officio, The Chancellor, The Vice-Chancellor, The Chairman of Convocation, The Principal.

Heads of the following Schools—University College, King's College, Bedford College, Birkbeck College, Imperial College of Science and Technology, London School of Economics and Political Science, Queen Mary College, Royal Holloway College, School of Oriental and African Studies, Westfield College. *Appointed by Convocation*—(*Arts*) H. A. L. Cockerell, O.B.E.; A. H. Chaplin; Miss M. C. Grobel; D. D. A. Leslie; H. B. A. Wise; (*Economics*), J. B. Bonham; (*Engineering*) J. Gratwick; Dr. N. A. White; (*Laws*), Mrs. M. C. Hoare; (*Medicine*); Dr. A. J. M. Reese; N. A. Thorne; (*Music*), C. P. J. Steinitz; (*Science*), Mrs. M. F. Church; J. S. Cook; M. V. Hoare; W. C. Peck; J. H. Pryor; (*Theology*), Rev. Dr. G. Huelin. *Appointed by the Faculties*—(*Arts*), Prof. J. E. Varey; Prof. A. G. Dickens; Prof. R. Quirk; Prof. F. M. L. Thompson; (*Economics*), Prof. H. C. Edey; (*Engineering*), Prof. J. Brown; Prof. A. D. Young, O.B.E.; (*Laws*), Prof. F. R. Crane; (*Medicine*), Prof. J. N. Hunt; Prof. M. D. Milne; Prof. N. F. Morris; Prof. Sheila Sherlock; (*Music*), Prof. I. W. A. Spink; (*Science*), Prof. F. E. G. Cox; Prof. R. Howie; Prof. W. G. Overend; Prof. W. F. Widdas; (*Theology*), Rev. Prof. P. R. Ackroyd. *Appointed by General Medical Schools*, Dr. J. C. Houston; D. Ranger. *By King's College Theological Dept.*, Rev. Canon S. H. Evans. *By University College*, Sir Bernard Waley-Cohen, Bt. *Director of British Post-Graduate Medical Federation*, Prof. G. Smart. *Co-opted Members*, Dr. H. S.

Darling, C.B.E.; Dr. K. G. Denbigh; Prof. Sir Cyril Phillips; Prof. Sir Brian Windeyer.

Principal Officers
Clerk of the Court, J. R. Stewart, C.B.E., M.A.

Administration Secretary and Clerk of the Senate, H. F. Patterson, M.A.

Registrar, P. F. Vowles, M.A.

Secretary to University Entrance and School Examinations Council, A. R. Stephenson, M.A.

Director of Central Library Services, K. Garside, M.A.

Director, Careers Advisory Service, E. H. K. Dibden, B.SC., M.A.

Secretary to the Athlone Press, A. M. Wood, M.SC., M.A.

University Institutes
Courtland Institute of Art, 20 Portman Square, W.1., Prof. P. E. Lasko, B.A., F.S.A., *Dir.*

Institute of Advanced Legal Studies, 17 Russell Square, W.C.1, Prof. A. L. Diamond, Ll.M., *Dir.*

Institute of Archæology, 31–34 Gordon Square, W.C.1, Prof. J. D. Evans, M.A., Ph.D., F.S.A., *Dir.*

Institute of Classical Studies, 31–34 Gordon Square, W.C.1, Prof. E. W. Handley, M.A., F.B.A., *Dir.*

Institute of Commonwealth Studies, 27 Russell Square, W.C.1, Prof. W. H. Morris-Jones, B.SC.(Econ.), *Dir.*

Institute of Education, Malet Street, W.C.1, W. Taylor, B.SC. (Econ.), Ph.D., M.A., *Dir.*

Institute of Germanic Studies, 29 Russell Square, W.C.1, Prof. C. V. Bock, M.A., Dr.Phil., Hon. *Dir.*

Institute of Historical Research, Senate House, W.C.1 Prof. A. G. Dickens, C.M.G., M.A., D.Lit., F.B.A., F.S.A., *Dir.*

Institute of Latin American Studies, 31 Tavistock Square, W.C.1, Prof. J. Lynch, M.A., Ph.D., *Dir.*

British Institute in Paris, 9–11 Rue de Constantine, 75007, Paris, Prof. F. H. Scarfe, C.B.E., M.A., M.Litt., *Dir.*

School of Slavonic and E. European Studies, University of London, Senate House, W.C.1, A. H. Walker, M.A., *Dir.*

Institute of United States Studies, 31 Tavistock Square, W.C.1, Prof. E. Wright, M.A., *Dir.*

Warburg Institute, Woburn Square, W.C.1, Prof. J. B. Trapp, M.A., *Dir.*

Schools of the University★
Bedford College, Inner Circle, Regent's Park, N.W.1, J. N. Black, M.A., D.Phil., D.SC., F.R.S.E., *Principal* (1971).

Birkbeck College, Malet Street, W.C.1, R. C. Tress, C.B.E., B.SC.(Econ.), D.SC., *Master* (1968).

Chelsea College, Manresa Road, S.W.3, D. J. E. Ingram M.A., D.Phil., D.SC., *Principal* (1973).

Imperial College of Science and Technology, South Kensington, S.W.7, Sir Brian Flowers, M.A., M.SC., D.SC., F.R.S., *Rector* (1973).

King's College, Strand, W.C.2, Sir Richard Way, K.C.B., C.B.E., *Principal* (1975).

London School of Economics and Political Science, Houghton Street, Aldwych, W.C.2, Prof. R. G. Dahrendorf, Ph.D., Dr.Phil., *Director* (1974).

Queen Elizabeth College, Campden Hill Road, W.8, K. G. Denbigh, D.SC., F.R.S., *Principal* (1966).

Queen Mary College, Mile End Road, E.1, Sir James Menter, M.A., Ph.D., SC.D., F.R.S., *Principal* (1976).

Royal Holloway College, Egham Hill, Egham, Surrey, L. H. Butler, M.A., D.Phil., *Principal* (1973).

★ For Medical Schools, Training Colleges and Veterinary Colleges, *see under* Professional Education.

School of Oriental and African Studies, Malet Street, W.C.1, Prof. C. D. Cowan, M.A., Ph.D., *Dir.* (1976).
School of Pharmacy, 29–39 Brunswick Square, W.C.1, J. Swarbrick, D.Sc., *Dean* (1976).
University College, Gower Street, W.C.1, The Lord Annan, O.B.E., M.A., *Provost* (1966).
Westfield College, Kidderpore Avenue, Hampstead, N.W.3, B. Thwaites, M.A., Ph.D., *Principal* (1966).
Wye College, Wye nr. Ashford, Kent, H. S. Darling, C.B.E., M.Agric., Ph.D., D.Sc., B.Sc. (1968).
King's College Theological Department, Rev. Canon S. H. Evans, M.A., B.D., *Dean* (1956).
New College, 527 Finchley Road, N.W.3, Rev. C. S. Duthie, M.A., D.D., *Principal* (1964).
Heythrop College, 11 Cavendish Square, W.1, Rev. W. J. Mahoney, S.J., M.A., D.D., *Principal* (1976).
Lister Institute of Preventive Medicine, Chelsea Bridge Road, S.W.1, Prof. W. R. H. Collier, M.D., D.SC., *Director* (1976).

THE UNIVERSITY OF MANCHESTER
Oxford Road, Manchester
(Founded 1851; re-organized 1880 and 1903).
Full-time Students (1975–76), Men, 9,661; *Women*, 4,375.
Chancellor, The Duke of Devonshire, P.C., M.C. (1965).
Vice-Chancellor, Prof. Sir Arthur Armitage, M.A. (1970).
Registrar, V. Knowles, M.A. (1951).

MANCHESTER INSTITUTE OF SCIENCE AND TECHNOLOGY (1824)
Sackville Street, Manchester
Full-time Students (1974–75), (*Men*) 2,981; (*Women*), 434.
Prof. R.N. Haszeldine, M.A., Ph.D.; D.Sc.; SC.D. F.R.S.
Secretary and Registrar, D. H. McWilliam, B.A.

THE UNIVERSITY OF NEWCASTLE
(Founded 1852; re-organized 1908, 1937 and 1963)
Newcastle upon Tyne.
Students (1974–75), 6,316.
Chancellor, The Duke of Northumberland, K.G., T.D., F.R.S. (1963).
Vice-Chancellor, (vacant).
Pro-Vice-Chancellors, Prof. J. R. O'Callaghan, B.E., M.SC.; Prof. E. S. Page, M.A., Ph.D., B.SC.
Registrar, E. M. Bettenson, M.A.

THE UNIVERSITY OF BIRMINGHAM
Birmingham 15
Full-time Students (1975–76), 7,880.
Chancellor, Sir Peter Scott, C.B.E., D.S.C., M.A.
Vice-Chancellor and Principal, R. B. Hunter, M.B.E., M.B., Ch.B., F.R.C.P. (1968).
Secretary, H. Harris, B.Sc.(Econ.), Ll.B.
Registrar, W. R. G. Lewis, B.A.

THE UNIVERSITY OF LIVERPOOL, 1903
Liverpool
Students (1976), 7,446.
Chancellor, Sir Kenneth Wheare, C.M.G., F.B.A.
Vice-Chancellor, R. F. Whelan, M.D., Ph.D., D.Sc.
Treasurer, B. L. Rathbone.
Registrar, H. H. Burchnall, M.A. (1962).

THE UNIVERSITY OF LEEDS, 1904
Full-time Students (1976), 9,479.
Chancellor, H.R.H. the Duchess of Kent (1966).
Vice-Chancellor, The Lord Boyle of Handsworth, P.C., M.A., (1970).
Registrar, J. MacGregor, B.A., M.Ed., Ph.D. (1971).
Bursar, R. Head (1976).

THE UNIVERSITY OF SHEFFIELD, 1905
Sheffield
Full-time Students (1974–75)—Men, 4,558; Women, 2,397.
Chancellor, The Lord Butler of Saffron Walden, K.G., P.C., C.H., M.A. (1959).
Vice-Chancellor, Prof. G. D. Sims, O.B.E,. M.SC., Ph.D. (1974).
Registrar and Secretary, A. M. Currie, B.A., B.Litt. (1965).

THE UNIVERSITY OF BRISTOL, 1909
Full-time Students (1975)—Men, 4,005; Women 2,679.
Chancellor, Prof. Dorothy Hodgkin, O.M., M.A., Ph.D., D.SC., SC.D., F.R.C.P., F.R.S. (1971).
Vice-Chancellor, Sir Alec Merrison, B.SC., Ph.D., F.R.S. (1967).
Director of Administration, D. G. H. Cannon, M.A. (1973).
Registrar, E. C. Wright, M.A. (1973).

THE UNIVERSITY OF READING, 1926
Whiteknights, Reading
Number of Students (1975), 5,369.
Chancellor, The Lord Sherfield, G.C.B., G.C.M.G. (1970).
Vice-Chancellor, H. R. Pitt, Ph.D., F.R.S. (1964).
Registrar, J. F. Johnson, B.A. (1955).

THE UNIVERSITY OF NOTTINGHAM, 1948
University Park, Nottingham
Chancellor, Sir Francis Hill, C.B.E., M.A., Ll.M. (1972).
Vice-Chancellor, B. C. L. Weedon, C.B.E., D.SC., F.R.S.
Registrar, A. Plumb, M.A. (1958).

THE UNIVERSITY OF SOUTHAMPTON, 1952
Students (1975–76), Men, 3,591; Women, 1,786.
Chancellor, Sir Eric Roll, K.C.M.G., C.B., Ph.D. (1974).
Vice-Chancellor, L. C. B. Gower, Ll.M., F.B.A. (1971).
Secretary and Registrar, R. M. Urquhart, O.B.E., M.A. (1966).
Academic Registrar, D. A. Schofield, M.A. (1969).

THE UNIVERSITY OF HULL, 1954
Full-time Students (1975–76)—Men, 2,473; Women, 1,710.
Chancellor, The Lord Cohen of Birkenhead, C.H., M.D., F.R.C.P. (1970).
Vice-Chancellor, Prof. S. R. Dennison, C.B.E., M.A. (1972).
Registrar, F. T. Mattison, M.A., Ll.B.

THE UNIVERSITY OF EXETER, 1955
Full-time Students (1975–76), 4,169.
Chancellor, The Viscount Amory, K.G., P.C., G.C.M.G., T.D., M.A.
Vice-Chancellor, H. Kay, M.A., Ph.D.
Academic Registrar and Secretary, K. T. Nash, M.A.

THE UNIVERSITY OF LEICESTER, 1957
Full-time Students (1974–75), 3,775.
Chancellor, Prof. Sir Alan Hodgkin, K.B.E., O.M., F.R.S. (1971).
Vice-Chancellor, (vacant).
Registrar, M. A. Baatz, M.A. (1973).

THE UNIVERSITY OF SUSSEX, 1961
Brighton
Full-time Students (1975–76), 4,209.
Chancellor, The Lord Shawcross, P.C., G.B.E., Q.C.
Vice-Chancellor, Sir Deny's Williamson, Ph.D., SC.D., M.A., F.R.S.
Registrar and Secretary, G. Lockwood, B.SC.(Econ.).

THE UNIVERSITY OF KEELE, 1962
Keele, Staffordshire.

Undergraduates (1975–76), 2,659.
Chancellor, H.R.H. The Princess Margaret, Countess of Snowdon, C.I., G.C.V.O. (1962).
Vice-Chancellor, Prof. W. A. C. Stewart, M.A., Ph.D.
Registrar, J. F. N. Hodgkinson, M.A.

THE UNIVERSITY OF EAST ANGLIA, 1963
Norwich

Students (1975–76), 3,500.
Chancellor, The Lord Franks, P.C., G.C.M.G., K.C.B., C.B.E., M.A., F.B.A. (1965).
Vice-Chancellor, F. Thistlethwaite, M.A.
Registrar and Secretary, G. A. Chadwick, B.Sc.

THE UNIVERSITY OF YORK, 1963
Heslington, York

Undergraduates (1974), 2,300.
Chancellor, The Lord Clark, O.M., C.H., K.C.B., F.B.A. (1969).
Pro-Chancellors, R. S. Butterfield, O.B.E., M.C.; A. S. Rymer, O.B.E.
Vice-Chancellor, G. M. Carstairs, M.A., M.D., D.P.M., F.R.C.P. Ed.
Registrar, J. P. West-Taylor, O.B.E., M.A.

THE UNIVERSITY OF LANCASTER, 1964
Bailrigg, Lancaster

Undergraduates (1976–77), 3,600.
Chancellor, H.R.H. the Princess Alexandra, G.C.V.O.
Vice-Chancellor, C. F. Carter, M.A., D.Econ.Sc., F.B.A.
Secretary, A. S. Jeffreys, B.A., B.Litt.

THE UNIVERSITY OF ESSEX, 1964
Wivenhoe Park, Colchester

Students (1976–77), 2,550.
Chancellor, The Lord Butler of Saffron Walden, K.G., P.C., C.H., M.A.
Pro-Chancellors, Col. Sir John Ruggles-Brise, Bt., C.B., O.B.E., T.D.; J. F. Crittall, M.A.
Vice-Chancellor, A. E. Sloman, M.A., D.Phil.
Registrar, G. E. Chandler, B.A.

THE UNIVERSITY OF WARWICK, 1965
Coventry, Warwickshire

Students (1974–75), 3,375.
Chancellor, The Viscount Radcliffe, P.C., G.B.E.
Pro-Chancellor, Sir Stanley Harley, B.Sc.
Vice-Chancellor, J. B. Butterworth, M.A.
Secretary and Registrar, A. Rowe-Evans, B.A.

UNIVERSITY OF KENT AT CANTERBURY, 1965
Canterbury, Kent

Students (1976–77), 3,250.
Chancellor, Rt. Hon. J. Grimond, T.D., M.P. (1970).
Vice-Chancellor, G. Templeman, M.A., Ph.D., F.S.A.
Registrar, E. Fox, M.A.

LOUGHBOROUGH UNIVERSITY OF TECHNOLOGY, 1966

Students (1975–76), 4,022.
Chancellor, The Lord Pilkington.
Vice-Chancellor, C. C. Butler, PhD., F.R.S.
Registrar, F. L. Roberts, B.A.

THE UNIVERSITY OF ASTON IN BIRMINGHAM, 1966
Gosta Green, Birmingham 4

Full-time Students (1975–76), 4,718.
Chancellor, The Lord Nelson of Stafford, M.A.
Vice-Chancellor, J. A. Pope, D.Sc., Ph.D.
Secretary, P. R. Tebbit, B.A.
Registrar, K. N. Houghton, M.A.

THE CITY UNIVERSITY, 1966
St. John Street, E.C.1

Students (1975–76), 2,571.
Chancellor, The Lord Mayor of London.
Vice-Chancellor, E. W. Parkes, Sc.D.
Academic Registrar, L. A. Fairbairn, B.Sc., Ph.D.

BRUNEL UNIVERSITY, 1966
Uxbridge, Middlesex

Students (1975–76), 3,900.
Chancellor, The Earl of Halsbury, F.R.S.
Vice-Chancellor, S. L. Bragg.
Academic Registrar, E. R. Chandler.

UNIVERSITY OF BATH, 1966
Claverton Down, Bath, Avon.

Undergraduates (1975–76), 2,970.
Chancellor, The Lord Hinton of Bankside, O.M., K.B.E., M.A., F.R.S.
Vice-Chancellor, P. T. Matthews, C.B.E., M.A., Ph.D., F.R.S.
Registrar, G. S. Horner, M.A.

UNIVERSITY OF BRADFORD, 1966

Undergraduates (1975–76), *Men*, 2,335; *Women*, 1,074.
Chancellor, Rt. Hon. Sir Harold Wilson, K.G., O.B.E., M.P., M.A., F.R.S.
Vice-Chancellor and Principal, E. G. Edwards, Ph.D., B.Sc.
Registrar, I. M. Sanderson, M.B.E., B.Sc.

UNIVERSITY OF SURREY, 1966
Guildford, Surrey

Undergraduates (1975–76), 2,414.
Chancellor, The Lord Robens of Woldingham, P.C.
Vice-Chancellor, A. Kelly, Sc.D., F.R.S.
Academic Registrar, G. Haigh, Ph.D.

UNIVERSITY OF SALFORD, 1967

Undergraduates (1975–76), 3,455.
Chancellor, H.R.H. the Prince Philip, Duke of Edinburgh, K.G., P.C., K.T.
Vice-Chancellor, Prof. J. H. Horlock, M.A., Ph.D., Sc.D., F.R.S.
Registrar, S. R. Bosworth, B.A.

ROYAL COLLEGE OF ART, 1837
Kensington Gore, S.W.7

Under Royal Charter (1967) the Royal College of Art grants the degrees of Doctor, Doctor of Philosophy, Master of Arts and Master of Design (RCA).
Students (1976), 577 (all postgraduate).
Provost, Sir Colin Anderson, K.B.E.
Rector and Vice-Provost, The Viscount Esher, C.B.E., M.A.
Registrar, B. Cooper, B.A.

CRANFIELD INSTITUTE OF TECHNOLOGY
1969
Cranfield, Bedford

Under Royal Charter (1969) the Cranfield Institute of Technology grants the degrees of Doctor and Master in applied science, engineering, technology and management.
Students (1975), 590 (all postgraduate); 2,500 short course.
Chancellor, The Lord Kings Norton, Ph.D., D.I.C., D.Sc.
Vice-Chancellor, A. H. Chilver, D.Sc., Ph.D., M.A.
Secretary, Air Vice-Marshal P. C. Cleaver, C.B., C.B.E., M.Sc.

THE OPEN UNIVERSITY (1969)
Walton Hall, Milton Keynes, Bucks.
Students (1975), 50,000.
   Tuition by correspondence linked with special radio and television programmes, summer schools and a locally-based tutorial and counselling service. Under Royal Charter the University awards degrees of B.A., B.Phil., M.Phil., Ph.D., D.Sc. and D.Litt. There are six faculties—arts, educational studies, mathematics, science, social sciences and technology.
Chancellor, The Lord Gardiner, P.C.
Vice-Chancellor, Sir Walter Perry, O.B.E., M.D., D.SC.
Secretary, A. Christodoulou, M.A.
Deputy Secretary and Registrar, D. J. Clinch, B.A.

UNIVERSITY COLLEGE AT BUCKINGHAM
(1976)
Buckingham
Students (1976): Men 59, Women, 11
Independent of state finance.
Chairman of Council, Sir Sydney Caine, K.C.M.G.
Principal, Prof. M. Beloff, M.A., F.B.A.
Registrar and Secretary, L. Wilson, M.A.

THE UNIVERSITY OF WALES, 1893
University Registry, Cardiff
Chancellor, H.R.H. the Prince of Wales, K.G., G.C.B., (1976).
Pro-Chancellor, The Lord Edmund-Davies, P.C. (1974).
Vice-Chancellor, A. F. Trotman-Dickenson, D.SC. (1975).
Registrar, J. Gareth Thomas, M.A. (1962).

COLLEGES
(with number of undergraduates, 1975–76)
Aberystwyth (3,028).—*Princ.*, Sir Goronwy Daniel, K.C.V.O., C.B., D.Phil. (1969).
Bangor, N. Wales (2,750).—*Princ.*, Sir Charles Evans, M.A., D.SC., F.R.C.S. (1958).
Cardiff, Institute of Science and Technology (2,521).—*Princ.*, A. F. Trotman-Dickenson, M.A., Ph.D., D.SC. (1968).
Cardiff, National School of Medicine (579).—*Provost*, J. P. D. Mounsey, M.A., M.D., F.R.C.P. (1969).
Cardiff (University College) (4,604).—*Princ.* C. W. L. Bevan, C.B.E., D.SC. (1966).
Lampeter (St. David's College) (543).—*Princ.* B. R. Rees, M.A., Ph.D., (1975).
Swansea (3,156).—*Princ.* R. W. Steel, M.A. (1974).

SCOTLAND

UNIVERSITY OF ST. ANDREWS, 1411
Students (1975–76), *Men*, 1,758; *Women*, 1,525.
Chancellor, Brigadier The Lord Ballantrae, K.T., G.C.M.G., G.C.V.O., D.S.O., O.B.E. (1975).
Principal and Vice-Chancellor, J. S. Watson, M.A., D.Litt., F.R.S.E. (1966).
Registrar and Secretary, D. M. Devine, M.A., Ll.B. (1972).

UNIVERSITY OF GLASGOW, 1451
Gilmorehill, Glasgow
Students (1975–76), *Men*, 6,166; *Women*, 4,079.
Chancellor, Sir Alec Cairncross, K.C.M.G., F.B.A.
Vice-Chancellor, Prof. A. Williams, D.SC., F.R.S., (1976).
Secretary to the University Court and Registrar, J. McCargon, M.A.

UNIVERSITY OF ABERDEEN, 1495
Undergraduates (1976), 4,913.
Chancellor, The Lord Polwarth, T.D.
Principal, Sir Thomas Noble, M.B.E., M.A., (1976).
Vice-Principal, Prof. R. C. Cross, C.B.E., M.A.
Secretary, T. B. Skinner, M.A.

UNIVERSITY OF EDINBURGH, 1583
Old College, South Bridge, Edinburgh 8
Students (1975–76), 11,103.
Chancellor, H.R.H. the Prince Philip, Duke of Edinburgh, K.G., P.C., K.T. (1952).
Vice-Chancellor and Principal, Prof. Sir Hugh Robson, M.B., Ch.B., F.R.C.P., F.R.C.P.E. (1974)
Secretary, C. H. Stewart, O.B.E., M.A., Ll.B. (1948).

UNIVERSITY OF STRATHCLYDE, 1964
George Street, Glasgow
Full-time Students (1975–76), 5,926.
Chancellor, The Lord Todd, D.SC., D.Phil., P.R.S.
Principal, Sir Samuel Curran, M.A., Ph.D., D.SC., F.R.S. (1964).
Registrar, D. W. J. Morrell, M.A., Ll.B. (1973).

HERIOT-WATT UNIVERSITY, 1966
Edinburgh
Students (1975–76), 2,792.
Chancellor, The Lord Home of the Hirsel, K.T., P.C. (1966).
Principal and Vice-Chancellor, G. M. Burnett, Ph.D., D.SC., F.R.S.E. (1974).
Secretary, D. I. Cameron, B.L. (1966).

UNIVERSITY OF DUNDEE, 1967
Full-time Students (1975–76), 2,778.
Chancellor, H.M. Queen Elizabeth the Queen Mother.
Principal and Vice-Chancellor, J. Drever, M.A., F.R.S.E.
Secretary, R. Seaton, M.A., Ll.B.

UNIVERSITY OF STIRLING, 1967
Undergraduates (1975–76), 1,945.
Chancellor, The Lord Robbins, C.H., C.B., M.A., B.SC. (Econ.), A.B. (1967).
Vice-Chancellor, W. A. Cramond, O.B.E., M.D., (1975).
Secretary, R. G. Bomont, B.SC. (Econ.) (1973).

NORTHERN IRELAND

THE QUEEN'S UNIVERSITY OF BELFAST, 1908
Full-time Students (1975–76), 5,708.
Chancellor, The Lord Ashby, M.A., D.SC., F.R.S. (1970).
President and Vice-Chancellor, P. Froggatt, M.A., M.D., Ph.D.
Secretary, G. R. Cowie, M.A., Ll.B. (1948).
Secretary to the Academic Council, D. G. Neill, M.A. (1966).

NEW UNIVERSITY OF ULSTER, 1965
Coleraine, Co. Londonderry
(First students admitted, 1968)
Undergraduates (1975–76), 1,550.
Chancellor, The Duke of Abercorn.
Vice-Chancellor, W. A. Cockcroft, M.A., D.Phil. (1976).
Registrar and Secretary, W. T. Ewing, M.A., Ll.B. (1966).

THE ASSOCIATION OF COMMONWEALTH UNIVERSITIES
36 Gordon Square, W.C.1
   The Association holds quinquennial Congresses of the Universities of the Commonwealth and other meetings in the intervening years, publishes the *Commonwealth Universities Yearbook*, handbooks listing scholarships and fellowships, etc., acts as a general information centre on universities in U.K. and other Commonwealth countries and provides an advisory service for the filling of university teaching staff appointments overseas. It also supplies the secretariat for the Commonwealth

Scholarship Commission in the United Kingdom, for the Marshall Aid Commemoration Commission and for the Kennedy Memorial Trust.
Secretary General, Sir Hugh Springer, K.C.M.G., C.B.E., M.A.

REPUBLIC OF IRELAND

UNIVERSITY OF DUBLIN TRINITY COLLEGE, 1591
Undergraduates and post-graduates (1975–76), 4,882.
Chancellor, F. H. Boland (1964).
Provost, F. S. L. Lyons, M.A., Ph.D., F.B.A. (1974).
Registrar, A. Clarke, M.A., Ph.D. (1974).

NATIONAL UNIVERSITY OF IRELAND, DUBLIN, 1908
49 Merrion Square, Dublin 2
Chancellor, Dr. T. K. Whitaker (1976).
Vice-Chancellor, T. Murphy, M.D.
Registrar, J. Bourke, Ph.D., M.Comm.

CONSTITUENT COLLEGES
Univ. Coll., *Dublin,* T. Murphy, M.D. (1972).
Univ. Coll., *Cork,* M. D. McCarthy, M.A., Ph.D., D.SC., *President* (1967).
Univ. Coll., *Galway,* C. ó hEocha, Ph.D., *President* (1975).

COUNCIL FOR NATIONAL ACADEMIC AWARDS
344–354 Gray's Inn Road, W.C.1
Established in 1964 with powers to award degrees and other academic distinctions, comparable in standard with awards granted and conferred by universities to students in polytechnics and other institutions of higher education in the United Kingdom which do not have the power to award their own degrees. The Council awards degrees and honours degrees of B.A., B.Ed. and B.Sc. and has higher and research degrees and doctorates. On Sept. 1, 1974, the Council assumed responsibility for the work formerly undertaken by the National Council for Diplomas in Art and Design, and in September, 1976, for the Diploma on Management Studies.
President, H.R.H. the Prince of Wales, K.G., G.C.B.
Chairman, Sir Michael Clapham, K.B.E., M.A.
Chief Officer, E. Kerr, B.Sc., Ph.D.

POLYTECHNICS
CITY OF BIRMINGHAM POLYTECHNIC, Perry Barr, Birmingham.—*Dir.,* S. W. Smethurst.
BRIGHTON POLYTECHNIC, Moulsecoomb, Brighton. —*Dir.,* G. R. Hall.
BRISTOL POLYTECHNIC, Coldharbour Lane, Bristol. —*Dir.,* Dr. W. Birch.
HATFIELD POLYTECHNIC, Hatfield, Herts.—*Dir.,* Sir Norman Lindop.
HUDDERSFIELD POLYTECHNIC, Queensgate, Huddersfield.—*Rector,* K. J. Durrands.
KINGSTON POLYTECHNIC, Penrhyn Road, Kingston upon Thames.—*Dir.,* L. E. Lawley, Ph.D.
LANCHESTER POLYTECHNIC, Priory Street, Coventry. —*Dir.,* G. Holroyde.
LEEDS POLYTECHNIC, Calverley Street, Leeds.— *Dir.,* P. J. Nuttgens, Ph.D.
LEICESTER POLYTECHNIC, P.O. Box 143, Leicester. —*Dir.,* D. Bethel.
LIVERPOOL POLYTECHNIC, Richmond House, 1 Rumford Place, Liverpool.—*Rector,* G. Bulmer.
LONDON:
CITY OF LONDON POLYTECHNIC, 117–119 Houndsditch, E.C.3.—*Prov.,* A. Suddaby, Ph.D.

NORTH-EAST LONDON POLYTECHNIC, Romford Road, E.15.—*Dir.,* G. S. Brosan, T.D., Ph.D.
POLYTECHNIC OF CENTRAL LONDON, 309 Regent Street, W.1.—*Dir.,* C. Adamson, D.Sc.
POLYTECHNIC OF NORTH LONDON, Holloway Road, N.7.—*Dir.,* T. G. Miller, T.D.
POLYTECHNIC OF THE SOUTH BANK, Borough Road, S.E.1.—*Dir.,* V. Pereira Mendoza.
THAMES POLYTECHNIC, Wellington Street, S.E.18, —*Dir.,* D. E. R. Godfrey, Ph.D.
MANCHESTER POLYTECHNIC, Lower Ormond Street, All Saints, Manchester.—*Dir.,* Sir Alex Smith, Ph.D.
NEWCASTLE UPON TYNE POLYTECHNIC, Ellison Building Ellison Place, Newcastle upon Tyne.— *Dir.,* G. S. Bosworth, C.B.E.
NORTH STAFFORDSHIRE POLYTECHNIC, Beaconside, Stafford.—*Dir.,* J. F. Dickenson, Ph.D.
OXFORD (Oxford Polytechnic; Lady Spencer-Churchill College, Wheatley, Oxon.).—*Dir.,* B. B. Lloyd, D.SC.
PLYMOUTH POLYTECHNIC, Drake Circus, Plymouth.—*Dir.,* R. F. M. Robbins, Ph.D.
PORTSMOUTH POLYTECHNIC, Ravelin House, Museum Road, Portsmouth.—*Pres.,* W. Davey.
SHEFFIELD CITY POLYTECHNIC, Pond Street, Sheffield. —*Principal,* Rev. G. Tolley, Ph.D.
SUNDERLAND POLYTECHNIC, Chester Road, Sunderland.—*Rector,* E. A. Freeman, D.SC., Ph.D.
TEESIDE POLYTECHNIC, Borough Road, Middlesbrough, Cleveland.—*Dir.,* J. Houghton, Ph.D.
TRENT POLYTECHNIC, Burton Street, Nottingham. —*Dir.,* R. Hedley.
THE POLYTECHNIC—WOLVERHAMPTON, Wulfruna Street, Wolverhampton.—*Dir.,* R. Scott, C.B.E.
POLYTECHNIC OF WALES, Pontypridd, Mid Glamorgan.—*Dir.,* D. W. F. James, Ph.D.
Two further Polytechnics remain to be established, a proposed polytechnic in central Lancashire based on the Harris College, Preston and part of the work of Blackburn College of Technology and Design; and The Middlesex Polytechnic based on Enfield College of Technology, Hendon College of Technology and Hornsey College of Art.
In addition to these colleges, there are 7,968 Evening Institutes and similar types of establishment providing a wide variety of non-vocational classes for adults.

EDUCATIONAL TRUSTS
CARNEGIE TRUST FOR THE UNIVERSITIES OF SCOTLAND, The Merchants Hall, Hanover Street, Edinburgh.—*Sec. and Treasurer,* A. E. Ritchie.
CASSEL EDUCATIONAL TRUST, 21 Hassocks Road, Hurstpierpoint, Sussex.—*Sec.,* D. Hardman.
DARTINGTON HALL TRUST, Totnes, Devon.— *Chairman,* M. A. Ash.
EDUCATION SERVICES, 19 Norham Road, Oxford.— *Hon. Sec.,* Mrs. R. W. Bellerby.
GILCHRIST EDUCATIONAL TRUST, 1 York Street, W.1.—*Sec.,* Miss S. Salmon.
HARKNESS FELLOWSHIPS OF THE COMMONWEALTH FUND OF NEW YORK, Harkness House, 38 Upper Brook Street, W.1.
KING GEORGE'S JUBILEE TRUST, 8 Buckingham Street, W.C.2.—*Sec.* Sir Michael Hawkins, K.C.V.O., M.B.E.
LEVERHULME TRUST FUND (1925), 15–19 New Fetter Lane, E.C.4.—Annual income, about £1,500,000. Awards to institutions, at home and overseas, mainly in the form of fellowships, studentships and scholarships for research and education. Awards to individuals are also made on the recommendation of a Research Awards Advisory Committee under six specific schemes.

LORD KITCHENER NATIONAL MEMORIAL FUND, Barn Meadow, Great Warley, Brentwood, Essex. —*Sec.*, C. R. Allison. Awards annually for university courses 30 to 40 scholarships, established to reward long and distinguished service, and especially war service, in H.M. Armed Forces. Competition is open to (*a*) sons of members or ex-members (men or women) of the British Navy, Army or Air Force, aged over 17 and under 20 on 1st January of year competing, and (*b*) male applicants aged under 30, who have done regular or national service. *No awards are made in respect of post-graduate studies.* Application forms, available after Oct. 1, are returnable by Dec. 1.

MITCHELL CITY OF LONDON CHARITY AND EDUCATIONAL FOUNDATION, 24–30 Holborn, E.C.1.— *Clerk*, A. E. L. Cox.

ELIZABETH NUFFIELD EDUCATIONAL FUND (1956). Nuffield Lodge, Regent's Park, N.W.1.—*Sec.*, Miss D. Dutton.

ROYAL COMMISSION FOR THE EXHIBITION OF 1851, 1 Lowther Gardens, Exhibition Road, S.W.7.— *Sec.*, C. A. H. James.

SIR RICHARD STAPLEY EDUCATIONAL TRUST, 121 Gloucester Place, Portman Square, W.1.—*Sec.*, R. Groves.

CITY PAROCHIAL FOUNDATION (TRUSTEES OF THE LONDON PAROCHIAL CHARITIES) 10 Fleet Street, E.C.4. Gross income 1975, £1,033,629. Grants made for the maintenance of City Churches and for the welfare of the poorer classes of the Metropolitan Police District of London and the City of London.

THOMAS WALL TRUST, 1 York Street, W.1. *Sec.*, Miss B. S. Salmon.

WINSTON CHURCHILL MEMORIAL TRUST (Churchill Fellowships).—15 Queen's Gate Terrace, S.W.7. —*Dir.-Gen.*, Maj.-Gen. H. A. Lascelles, C.B., C.B.E., D.S.O.

LOCAL EDUCATION AUTHORITIES

English and Welsh Counties

AVON, Avon House North, St James Barton, Bristol.—*Chief Education Officer*, D. Williams.

BEDFORDSHIRE, County Hall, Bedford.—*Chief Education Officer*, D. P. J. Browning.

BERKSHIRE, Kennet House, 80/82 Kings Road, Reading.—*Director*, R. J. Hornsby.

BUCKINGHAMSHIRE, County Offices, Aylesbury.— *Chief Education Officer*, R. P. Harding.

CAMBRIDGESHIRE, Shire Hall, Cambridge.—*Chief Education Officer*, (vacant).

CHESHIRE, County Hall, Chester.—*Director*, J. R. G. Tomlinson.

CLEVELAND, Woodlands Road, Middlesbrough.— *Director*, A. D. Jackson.

CLWYD, Shire Hall, Mold.—*Director*, J. H. Davies.

CORNWALL, County Hall, Truro.—*Director*, K. Cruise.

CUMBRIA, 5 Portland Square, Carlisle.—*Director*, P. C. Boulter.

DERBYSHIRE, County Offices, Matlock.—*Director*, C. W. Philips.

DEVON, County Hall, Exeter.—*Chief Education Officer*, J. G. Owen.

DORSET, County Hall, Dorchester.—*Director*, R. D. Price.

DURHAM, County Hall, Durham.—*Director*, D. H. Curry.

DYFED, County Hall, Carmarthen.—*Director*, H. D. Thomas.

ESSEX, Threadneedle House, Market Road, Chelmsford.—*Chief Education Officer*, J. A. Springett.

GLOUCESTERSHIRE, Shire Hall, Gloucester.—*Chief Education Officer*, R. D. Clark.

GWENT, County Hall, Cwmbran.—*Director*, E. H. Loudon.

GWYNEDD, Castle Street, Caernarfon.—*Director*, T. Ellis.

HAMPSHIRE, The Castle, Winchester.—*County Education Officer*, J. H. Aldam, M.C.

HEREFORD and WORCESTER, Castle Street, Worcester.—*Director*, M. J. Gifford.

HERTFORDSHIRE, COUNTY HALL, Hertford.—*County Education Officer*, D. Fisher.

HUMBERSIDE, County Hall, Beverley.—*Director*, J. Bower.

ISLE OF WIGHT, County Hall, Newport.—*Director*, R. O. Burton.

KENT, Springfield, Maidstone.—*County Education Officer*, W. H. Petty.

LANCASHIRE, County Hall, Preston.—*Chief Education Officer*, J .C. D. Rainbow.

LEICESTERSHIRE, County Hall, Glenfield, Leicester. —*Director*, A. N. Fairbairn, M.C.

LINCOLNSHIRE, County Offices, Lincoln.—*County Education Officer*, G. V. Cooke.

MID GLAMORGAN, County Hall, Cathays Park, Cardiff.—*Director*, J. L. Brace.

NORFOLK, County Hall, Norwich.—*Chief Education Officer*, D. Coatesworth, M.B.E.

NORTHAMPTONSHIRE, Northampton House, Wellington Street, Northampton.—*Chief Education Officer*, M. J. Henley.

NORTHUMBERLAND, Eldon House, Regent Centre, Gosforth, Newcastle upon Tyne.—*Director*, M. H. Trollope.

NOTTINGHAMSHIRE, County Hall, West Bridgford. —*Director*, J. A. Stone.

OXFORDSHIRE, Macclesfield House, New Road, Oxford.—*Unit Education Officer*, J. Garne, M.C.

POWYS, County Hall, Llandrindod Wells.—*Director*, R. W. Bevan.

SHROPSHIRE, Shirehall, Shrewsbury.—*County Education Officer*, J. Boyers.

SOMERSET, County Hall, Taunton.—*Chief Education Officer*, B. Taylor.

SOUTH GLAMORGAN, County Offices, Kingsway, Cardiff.—*Director*, F. J. Adams.

STAFFORDSHIRE, Tipping Street, Stafford and Earl Street, Stafford.—*Director*, A. Riley.

SUFFOLK, County Hall, Ipswich.—*Chief Education Officer*, F. J. Hill, C.B.E.

SURREY, Penrhyn Road, Kingston upon Thames.— *Chief Education Officer*, J. W. Henry.

SUSSEX (East), County Hall, Lewes.—*Chief Education Officer*, J. Rendel-Jones.

SUSSEX (West), County Hall, Chichester.—*Director*, G. R. Potter.

WARWICKSHIRE, 22 Northgate Street, Warwick.— *County Education Officer.*—M. L. Ridger.

WEST GLAMORGAN, Princess House, Princes Way, Swansea.—*Director*, J. Beale.

WILTSHIRE, County Hall, Trowbridge.—*Chief Education Officer*, J. F. Everett, M.B.E., T.D.

YORKSHIRE (North), County Hall, Northallerton.— *Director*, E. E. L. Owens, Ph.D.

London

INNER LONDON EDUCATION AUTHORITY.—*Education Officer*, P. Newsam.

Education Officers

BARKING, Town Hall.—J. L. Haseldon.

BARNET, Town Hall, Friern Barnet, N.11.—J. Dawkins.

BEXLEY, Town Hall, Crayford.—P. Geen.

BRENT, Chesterfield House, Park Lane, Wembley.— Miss G. M. Rickus.

BROMLEY, Sunnymead, Bromley Lane, Chislehurst.—G. Ellerby.

CROYDON, Taberner House, Park Lane.—K. J. Revell.

EALING, 81 Uxbridge Road, W.5.—R. J. Hartles.

ENFIELD, Civic Centre, Enfield.—C. Hutchinson.

HARINGEY, Somerset Road, Tottenham, N.17.—A. G. Groves.

HARROW, Civic Centre, Harrow.—*Director*, M. Johnson.

HAVERING, Mercury House, Mercury Gardens, Romford, Essex.—B. K. Laister.

HILLINGDON, Belmont House, 38 Market Square, Uxbridge, Middx.—*Director*, A. H. R. Calderwood.

HOUNSLOW, Civic Centre.—*Director*, P. J. Lee.

KINGSTON UPON THAMES, Tolworth Tower, Surbiton, Surrey.—W. F. E. Gibbs.

MERTON, Station House, London Road, Morden, Surrey.—R. Greenwood.

NEWHAM, 29 The Broadway, Stratford, E.15.—J. S. Wilkie, PH.D.

REDBRIDGE, Lynton House, High Road, Ilford, Essex.—J. E. Fordham.

RICHMOND UPON THAMES, Regal House, Twickenham, Middx.—D. Naismith.

SUTTON, The Grove, Carshalton, Surrey.—C. Melville.

WALTHAM FOREST, Municipal Offices, High Road, Leyton, E.10.—E. A. Hartley.

Metropolitan District Councils

BARNSLEY, 50 Huddersfield Road, Barnsley.—*Education Officer*, T. Brooks.

BIRMINGHAM, Margaret Street, Birmingham 3.—*Chief Education Officer*, K. Brooksbank, D.S.C.

BOLTON, Paderborn House, Civic Centre.—*Chief Education Officer*, P. Waddington.

BRADFORD, Provincial House, Bradford.—*Director*, W. R. Knight.

BURY, Athenaeum House, Market Street.—*Director*, M. Gray.

CALDERDALE.—Alexandra Buildings, King Edward Street, Halifax.—*Chief Education Officer*, A. Pickvance.

COVENTRY, Council Offices, Earl Street.—*Director*, R. Aitken.

DONCASTER, Princegate.—*Chief Education Officer*, M. J. Pass.

DUDLEY, 2 St. James's Road, Dudley.—*Education Officer*, J. Buck.

GATESHEAD, Prince Consort Road.—*Director*, Miss M. A. Sproat.

KIRKLEES, Oldgate House, Huddersfield.—*Director*, E. T. Butcher.

KNOWSLEY, Huyton Hey Road, Huyton.—*Director*, P. M. Neafsey.

LEEDS, Municipal Buildings, Calverley Street.—*Director*, R. S. Johnson.

LIVERPOOL, 14 Sir Thomas Street.—*Education Officer*, K. A. Antcliffe.

MANCHESTER, Cumberland House, Crown Square.—*Chief Education Officer*, D. A. Fiske.

NEWCASTLE UPON TYNE, Civic Centre, Barras Bridge.—*Director*, J. F. Chadderton.

NORTH TYNESIDE, The Chase, North Shields.—*Director*, J. F. Partington.

OLDHAM, Old Town Hall, Chadderton.—*Director*, G. R. Pritchett.

ROCHDALE, Town Hall, Middleton.—*Chief Education Officer*, A. N. Naylor.

ROTHERHAM, Municipal Offices, Howard Street, —*Director*, L. G. Taylor.

ST. HELENS, Century House, Hardshaw Street.—*Director*, W. H. Cubitt.

SALFORD, Chapel Street.—*Director*, J. A. Barnes.

SANDWELL, Highfields, High Street, West Bromwich.—*Director*, G. A. Brinsdon.

SEFTON, Burlington House, Crosby, Liverpool 22.—*Director*, K. Robinson.

SHEFFIELD, Leopold Street.—*Director*, G. M. A. Harrison.

SOLIHULL, The Council House.—*Director*, C. Humphrey.

SOUTH TYNESIDE, Town Hall, Jarrow.—*Director*, K. Stringer.

STOCKPORT, Town Hall.—*Director*, B. L. Harmon.

SUNDERLAND, Town Hall.—*Director*, J. Hall.

TAMESIDE, Town Hall, Dukinfield.—*Director*, G. Mayall.

TRAFFORD, Town Hall, Sale.—*Director*, D. J. Hatfield.

WAKEFIELD, 8 Bond Street.—*Director*, R. Eyles.

WALSALL, Civic Centre, Walsall.—*Director*, R. D. Nixon.

WIGAN, Civic Centre.—*Director*, R. C. Hodgkinson.

WIRRAL, Municipal Buildings, Birkenhead.—*Director*, R. E. Price.

WOLVERHAMPTON, St. John's Square.—*Director*, D. Grayson.

Channel Islands, etc.

JERSEY, P.O. Box 142, Highlands, St. Saviour.—*Director*, J. S. Rodhouse.

GUERNSEY, La Couperderle, St. Peter Port.—*Director*, M. D. Hutchings.

ISLE OF MAN, Strand Street, Douglas.—*Director*, F. Bickerstaff.

ISLES OF SCILLY, Town Hall, St. Mary's.—*Chief Executive*, R. Phillips.

Scottish Regional and Islands Councils

BORDERS, County Offices, Newtown St. Boswells.—Director, J. McLean.

CENTRAL, Viewforth, Stirling.—*Director*, I. Collie.

DUMFRIES AND GALLOWAY, 30 Edinburgh Road, Dumfries.—*Director*, J. K. Purves.

FIFE, Wemyssfield, Kirkcaldy.—*Director*, I. S. Flett.

GRAMPIAN, Woodhill House, Ashgrove Road West, Aberdeen.—*Director*, J. A. D. Michie.

HIGHLAND, Regional Buildings, Glenurquhart Road, Inverness.—*Director*, R. MacDonald.

LOTHIAN, 40 Torphichen Street, Edinburgh.—*Director*, W. D. C. Semple.

ORKNEY, County Offices, Kirkwall, Orkney.—*Director*, A. Bain.

SHETLAND, Brentham Place, Harbour Street, Lerwick.—*Director*, R. A. B. Barnes.

STRATHCLYDE, 25 Bothwell Street, Glasgow.—*Director*, E. Miller.

TAYSIDE, 14 City Square, Dundee.—*Director*, D. G. Robertson.

WESTERN ISLES, Council Offices, Stornoway, Isle of Lewis.—*Director*, A. Macleod.

Northern Ireland

Education and Library Boards

BELFAST, Board Headquarters, 40 Academy Street, Belfast 1.—*Chief Officer*, W. C. H. Eakin.

NORTH-EASTERN, Education Office, County Hall, Galgorm Road, Ballymena, Co. Antrim.—*Chief Officer*, R. J. Dickson, PH.D.

SOUTH-EASTERN, 18 Windsor Avenue, Belfast 9.—*Chief Officer*, F. H. Ebbitt.

SOUTHERN, 3 Charlemont Place, The Mall, Armagh.—*Chief Officer*, W. J. Dickson.

WESTERN, Headquarters Offices, Omagh, Co. Tyrone.—*Chief Officer*, M. H. F. Murphy.

ADULT EDUCATION

Adult Education is carried on in the United Kingdom by universities and university colleges (pp. 501–510), local education authorities (pp. 512–513) and by a wide variety of voluntary organizations.

The Universities Council for Adult Education, consisting of one representative from each university, was constituted in 1946 for interchange of ideas and formulation of common policy on extra-mural education.—*Hon. Secretary*, N. A. Jepson, B.A., Ph.D. Department of Adult Education, The University, Leeds.

The National Institute of Adult Education (England and Wales), De Montfort House, Leicester (*Dir.* A. K. Stock), and the Scottish Institute of Adult Education, 57 Melville Street, Edinburgh (*Sec.*, F. J. Taylor), exist to provide a means of consultation and co-operation between the various forces in adult education.

UNIVERSITY DEPARTMENTS OF EXTRA-MURAL STUDIES AND ADULT EDUCATION

OXFORD, Department for External Studies, Rewley House, Wellington Square, Oxford.—*Dir.*, R. G. Smethurst.

CAMBRIDGE, Board of Extra-Mural Studies, Madingley Hall, Madingley, Cambridge.—*Dir.*, J. M. Y. Andrew.

DURHAM, Department of Extra-Mural Studies, 32 Old Elvet, Durham.—*Dir.*, J. F. Dixon.

LONDON, Department of Extra-Mural Studies, University of London, 7 Ridgmount Street, W.C.1. —*Dir.* (vacant).

BIRMINGHAM, Department of Extra-Mural Studies, P.O. Box 363, University of Birmingham, Birmingham, 15.—*Dir.*, A. M. Parker.

BRISTOL, Department of Extra-Mural Studies, The University, Bristol.—*Dir.*, Prof. G. Cunliffe.

EXETER, Department of Extra-Mural Studies, The University, Exeter.—*Head*, Prof. T. F. Daveney.

HULL, Department of Adult Education, the University, Hull.—*Dir.*, Prof. B. Jennings.

KEELE, Department of Adult Education, The University, Keele, Staffs.—*Dir.*, Prof. R. F. Dyson.

LEEDS, Department of Adult Education and Extra-Mural Studies, The University, Leeds, 2.—*Head of Dept.*, Prof. N. A. Jepson.

LEICESTER, Department of Adult Education, The University, Leicester.—*Head of Dept.*, Prof. H. A. Jones, C.B.E.

LIVERPOOL, Institute of Extension Studies, 1 Abercromby Square, Liverpool.—*Dir.*, Prof. E. Rhodes.

MANCHESTER, Department of Extra-Mural Studies, The University, Manchester, 13.—*Dir.*, Prof. O. Ashmore.

NEWCASTLE, Department of Adult Education, The University, Newcastle upon Tyne.—*Dir.* E. W. Hughes.

NOTTINGHAM, Department of Adult Education, 14–22 Shakespeare Street, Nottingham.—*Dir.* Prof. M. D. Stephens.

READING, The University, Whiteknights, Reading. *Registrar*, J. F. Johnson.

SHEFFIELD, Department of Extra-Mural Studies, The University, Sheffield.—*Dir.* Prof. G. W. Roderick.

SOUTHAMPTON, Department of Adult Education, University of Southampton.—*Dir.*, P. E. Fordham.

WALES, The University Extension Board, University Registry, Cathays Park, Cardiff.—*Sec.*, J. Gareth Thomas.

ABERYSTWYTH, University College, Aberystwyth. —*Dir.*, W. Davies.

BANGOR, University College, Bangor.—*Dir.*, Prof. A. Llywelyn-Williams.

CARDIFF, University College Cardiff, Department of Extra-Mural Studies, 38–40 Park Place, Cathays Park, Cardiff.—*Dir.* J. S. Davies.

SWANSEA, University College Swansea.—*Dir.*, I. M. Williams.

ABERDEEN, Department of Adult Education and Extra-Mural Studies, The University, Aberdeen. —*Dir.*, K. A. Wood.

DUNDEE, Department of Extra-Mural Education, The University, Dundee.—*Dir.*, A. G. Robertson.

EDINBURGH, Department of Educational Studies, 11 Buccleuch Place, Edinburgh.—*Head*, N. D. C. Grant (*acting*).

EDINBURGH, Department of Extra-Mural Studies, 11 Buccleuch Place, Edinburgh.—*Head*, B. C. Skinner (*acting*).

GLASGOW, Department of Extra-Mural and Adult Education, 57–9 Oakfield Avenue, Glasgow —*Dir.*, N. Dees.

ST. ANDREWS, Department of Adult Education and Extra-Mural Studies, University of St. Andrews, 3 St. Mary's Place.—*Dir.* J. C. Geddes.

BELFAST, Queen's University, Department of Extra-Mural Studies and Adult Education.—*Dir.* E. C. Read.

RESIDENTIAL COLLEGES FOR ADULT EDUCATION

(Offering courses for a year or longer)

England

CLIFF COLLEGE, Calver, Sheffield. Residential Methodist Lay Training College open to all denominations (Men and Women).—*Principal*, Rev. H. A. G. Belben.

CO-OPERATIVE COLLEGE, Stanford Hall, Loughborough, Leics. (Men and Women).—*Principal*, R. L. Marshall. O.B.E.

FIRCROFT COLLEGE, Selly Oak, Birmingham 29 (Men) (50).—*Warden*, A. J. Corfield.

HILLCROFT RESIDENTIAL COLLEGE FOR WOMEN, Surbiton, Surrey (75).—*Principal*, Mrs. J. Cockerill.

PLATER COLLEGE, Headington, Oxford (Men and Women) (80).—*Principal*, J. R. Kirwan.

RUSKIN COLLEGE, Oxford (Men and Women) (180). *Principal*, H. D. Hughes.

WOODBROOKE, 1046 Bristol Road, Selly Oak, Birmingham 29. Quaker centre for religious, social and international studies (Men and Women). Shorter Courses also available.— *Warden*, E. Priestman.

Wales

COLEG HARLECH, Harlech, Gwynedd (Men and Women) (120).—*Warden*, I. W. Hughes.

Scotland

NEWBATTLE ABBEY COLLEGE, Dalkeith, Midlothian (Men and Women).—*Warden*, A. D. Reid.

Residential Colleges

(Offering Shorter Courses)

BELSTEAD HOUSE, Ipswich, Suffolk.—*Warden*, D. C. Barbanell.

BURTON MANOR, Burton, Wirral, Cheshire.— *Principal*.—A. Kingsbury.

DENMAN COLLEGE, Marcham, Abingdon, Oxon. (N.F.W.I.).—*Warden*, Miss H. Anderson.

DILLINGTON HOUSE, Ilminster, Somerset.—*Director*, (vacant).

DUNFORD HOUSE, Midhurst, Sussex (Y.M.C.A. Adult Education and Training Centre).—*Principal*, Rev. P. G. Hayman.

EASTHAMPSTEAD PARK, Wokingham, Berks.—*Principal*, D. G. E. Hurd.

GRANTLEY HALL, Ripon, Yorks.—*Warden*, Dr. H. C. Strick.

HOLLY RYDE COLLEGE (Manchester University Extra-Mural Dept.), 56–64 Palatine Road, West Didsbury, Manchester 20.—*Director*, Dr. A. Wilson.

HORNCASTLE RESIDENTIAL COLLEGE, Horncastle, Lincs.—*Warden*, B. Jenkins.

KNUSTON HALL, Irchester, Wellingborough, Northants.—*Principal*, Miss E. Smith.

MISSENDEN ABBEY, Great Missenden, Bucks.—*Warden*, P. F. Hebden.

MOOR PARK COLLEGE, Farnham, Surrey.—*Warden*, J. F. Powell.

ROFFEY PARK MANAGEMENT COLLEGE, Horsham, Sussex.—*Director*, W. J. Giles.

URCHFONT MANOR, Devizes, Wilts.—*Warden*, A. T. C. Slee, Ph.D.

WEDGWOOD MEMORIAL COLLEGE, Barlaston, nr. Stoke-on-Trent.—*Warden*, D. Goodman.

WESTHAM HOUSE, Barford, nr. Warwick.—*Principal*, F. Owen, O.B.E., T.D.

PRINCIPAL UNIVERSITY SETTLEMENTS AND ADULT EDUCATION CENTRES

BERNHARD BARON ST. GEORGE'S JEWISH SETTLEMENT, 192 Hanbury Street, E.1.—*Sec.*, Mrs. I. Marks.

BIRMINGHAM SETTLEMENT, 318 Summer Lane, Birmingham; Residential Centre, 3 Tower Street, Birmingham.—*Warden and Dir.*, P. D. Houghton.

BOSTON, Department of Adult Education, University of Nottingham, Pilgrim College.—*Warden and Residential Tutor*, A. Champion.

BRADFORD, LEEDS UNIVERSITY ADULT EDUCATION CENTRE, 10 Mornington Villas, Manningham Lane, Bradford 8. (Dept. of Adult Education and Extra-Mural Studies, University of Leeds.)—*Warden*, R. K. S. Taylor.

BRISTOL, Bristol Folk House Adult Education Centre, 40 Park Street.—*Warden*, R. J. Cann.

BRISTOL (University Settlement, Bristol Community Association), 43 Ducie Road, Bristol.—*Director*, M. Sykes.

CAMBRIDGE HOUSE AND TALBOT, 131–139 Camberwell Road and 48 Addington Square, S.E.5—*Head*, T. Cook.

CITY LITERARY CENTRE for adult studies, Stukeley Street, Drury Lane, W.C.2.—*Principal*, R. J. South, Ph.D.

DOCKLAND SETTLEMENTS, branches at Isle of Dogs, E.14; Bristol; Rotherhithe, S.E.16; Dagenham, Essex; Stratford, E.15 (2 branches); Hainault Estate, Chigwell, Essex; Glasgow; School of Adventure, Ross-shire; Guest House, Herne Bay, Kent—*Office*, 24 Portland Place, W.1.

EDINBURGH UNIVERSITY SETTLEMENT, Student Centre, Bristol Street, Edinburgh.—*Dir.*, J. R. Waddington; *Adult Education Centre*, Kirk o' Field College, Wilkie House, Guthrie Street, Edinburgh, 1.—*Sec.*, Miss E. Wood.

GOLDSMITHS' COLLEGE, New Cross, S.E.14.—*Dean, School of Adult and Social Studies*, P. A. Baynes.

LEICESTER UNIVERSITY Centre, Vaughan College, St. Nicholas Circle.—*Warden*, D. J. Rice.

LIVERPOOL SETTLEMENT (SOUTH), Nile Street.—*Directors*, J. P. Warren; R. Quarless; J. B. Smith.

LOUGHBOROUGH, Quest House, Loughborough Technical College, Radmoor.—*Warden*, D. H. Bodger, Dept. of Adult Education, University of Nottingham.

MIDDLESBROUGH: NEWPORT SETTLEMENT YOUTH AND COMMUNITY CENTRE, 130–132 Newport Road, Middlesbrough.—*Warden*, A. Thompson.

MIDDLESBROUGH: UNIVERSITY ADULT EDUCATION CENTRE, 37 Harrow Road, Middlesbrough (Department of Adult Education and Extramural Studies, University of Leeds.)—*Warden*, J. W. Saunders.

MANSFIELD HOUSE, Fairbairn Hall, E.13.—*Warden*, Rev. Canon E. A. Shipman.

ROBERT BROWNING SETTLEMENT, Browning Street, Walworth, S.E.17.—*Warden*, C. R. Dunnico (*acting*).

ROLAND HOUSE SCOUT CENTRE, 29 Stepney Green, E.1.—*Warden*, H. L. Ransome.

ST. MARGARET'S HOUSE SETTLEMENT, 21 Old Ford Road, Bethnal Green, E.2.—*Warden*, R. V. Glazebrook.

SPENNYMOOR SETTLEMENT, King Street, Spennymoor, Co. Durham.

TOYNBEE HALL, THE UNIVERSITIES' SETTLEMENT IN EAST LONDON, 28 Commercial Street, Whitechapel, E.1.—*Warden*, Mrs. M. Press (*acting*).

WORKING MEN'S COLLEGE, Crowndale Road, N.W.1.—*Principal*, L. P. Thompson-McCausland, C.M.G.; *Warden*, W. J. Evans.

YORK EDUCATIONAL SETTLEMENT, 128 Holgate Hill.—*Wardens*, A. J. Peacock; M. Peacock.

PROFESSIONAL EDUCATION
(excluding *postgraduate* study)

NOTE.—References to university courses in the sections following cover first degrees; the considerable facilities available at universities for postgraduate study or research are not treated.

ACCOUNTANCY

See also Business Management and Administration).

First Degrees in *Accounting* or *Accountancy* are granted by the Universities of Birmingham, Exeter, Glasgow, Kent, Strathclyde and Wales (University of Wales Institute of Science and Technology). At several other universities one of these subjects can be combined with e.g. Financial Administration, Finance or Economics.

Courses leading to first degrees in *Accounting* granted by the Council for National Academic Awards are provided by City of Birmingham Polytechnic, Bristol, Polytechnic (*Accounting and Finance*), City of London Polytechnic, Glasgow College of Technology, Kingston Polytechnic, Leeds Polytechnic, Liverpool Polytechnic, Manchester Polytechnic, Middlesex Polytechnic (*Accounting and Finance*), North East London Polytechnic (*Finance with Accounting*), Polytechnic of North London, Portsmouth Polytechnic, Trent Polytechnic (*Accountancy and Finance*).

Professional Bodies.—The main bodies granting membership on examination after a period of practical work are:

INSTITUTE OF CHARTERED ACCOUNTANTS IN ENGLAND AND WALES, Chartered Accountants' Hall, Moorgate Place, E.C.2.

INSTITUTE OF CHARTERED ACCOUNTANTS OF SCOTLAND, 27 Queen Street, Edinburgh, and 218 St. Vincent Street, Glasgow.

ASSOCIATION OF CERTIFIED ACCOUNTANTS, 22 Bedford Square, W.C.1.

CHARTERED INSTITUTE OF PUBLIC FINANCE AND ACCOUNTANCY, 1 Buckingham Place, S.W.1.

INSTITUTE OF COST AND MANAGEMENT ACCOUNTANTS, 63 Portland Place, W.1.

ACTUARIAL SCIENCE

First Degrees in *Actuarial Science* are granted by the City University and in *Actuarial Mathematics* by Heriot-Watt University.

Two professional organizations grant qualifications after examination:

INSTITUTE OF ACTUARIES, Staple Inn Hall, High Holborn, W.C.1.

FACULTY OF ACTUARIES IN SCOTLAND, *Hall and Library*, 23 St. Andrew Square, Edinburgh.

AERONAUTICS
and Aeronautical Engineering

First Degrees in *Aeronautical Engineering* are granted by the Universities of Bath, Belfast, Bristol, Cambridge (*Aeronautics*), the City University, the Universities of Glasgow, London (Imperial College of Science and Technology; Queen Mary College), Loughborough (*Aeronautical Engineering and Design*), Manchester, Salford and (*Aeronautics and Astronautics*), Southampton; and in *Air Transport Engineering* by the City University. Courses leading to first degrees in *Aeronautical Engineering* granted by the Council for National Academic Awards are provided by Hatfield Polytechnic and Kingston Polytechnic.

CHELSEA COLLEGE OF AERONAUTICAL AND AUTOMOBILE ENGINEERING, Shoreham Airport, Sussex.

COLLEGE OF AIR TRAINING, Hamble, Southampton.

AGRICULTURE

First Degrees in *Agriculture* or *Agricultural Science(s)* are granted by the Universities of Aberdeen, Belfast, Edinburgh, Glasgow, Leeds, London (Wye College), Newcastle upon Tyne, Nottingham, Oxford (*Agricultural and Forest Sciences*), Reading and Wales (University Colleges of Aberystwyth and Bangor); and in *Horticulture* by Bath, London (Wye College), Nottingham, Reading and Strathclyde.

Other schools of agriculture are:

ABERDEEN (North of Scotland College of Agriculture, 581 King Street—*Sec.*, H. Munro.

CIRENCESTER, Royal Agricultural College.— *Principal*, Sir Emrys Jones, B.SC.

EDINBURGH SCHOOL OF AGRICULTURE, THE, West Mains Road, Edinburgh.—*Principal*, Prof. N. F. Robertson, B.SC., PH.D.

HARPER ADAMS AGRICULTURAL COLLEGE, Newport, Salop—*Principal*, R. Kenney. B.SC.

SEALE-HAYNE AGRICULTURAL COLLEGE, Newton Abbot, S. Devon.—*Principal*, G. J. Dowrick, B.SC., Ph.D.

SHUTTLEWORTH AGRICULTURAL COLLEGE, Old Warden Park, Biggleswade, Bedfordshire.— *Principal*, J. E. Scott, B.SC., M.S.

WEST OF SCOTLAND AGRICULTURAL COLLEGE, Auchincruive, Ayr.—*Principal*, Prof. J. S. Hall, C.B.E., B.SC.

There are in addition over twenty country Agricultural Institutes giving a one-year course.

ARBITRATION

THE INSTITUTE OF ARBITRATORS, 75 Cannon Street E.C.4 conducts examinations and maintains a Register of Fellows and Associates, and a panel of arbitrators.—*Sec.*, B. W. Vigrass, O.B.E., V.R.D.

ARCHÆOLOGY

First Degrees in *Archæology* (sometimes in combination with another subject) are granted by the Universities of Belfast, Birmingham, Bradford, Bristol, Cambridge, Durham, Edinburgh, Exeter, Glasgow, Lancaster, Leeds, Leicester, Liverpool, London (Institute of Archæology, Bedford, King's and University Colleges; also School of Oriental and African Studies for *Archæology of South or South-East Asia*), Manchester, Newcastle upon Tyne, Nottingham, Reading, Sheffield, Southampton, Wales (University Colleges of Bangor and Cardiff).

ARCHITECTURE

The Board of Education of THE ROYAL INSTITUTE OF BRITISH ARCHITECTS, 66 Portland Place, W.1, sets standards and guides the whole system of architectural education throughout the United Kingdom. Courses at the following Schools are recognized by the R.I.B.A. They are visited regularly by the R.I.B.A. Visiting Board to ensure that they meet the minimum standards for exemption from the R.I.B.A.'s own examinations.

UNIVERSITY SCHOOLS

(Subject to exceptions noted below, courses are full-time for five years, leading to a first degree or diploma; number of students and name of Head of School or Department of Architecture are included.)

BATH: University School of Architecture and Building Engineering, Claverton Down (228).— Prof. W. G. Gregory (6-yr. sandwich course in architecture in conjunction with 4-year sandwich course in building engineering).

BELFAST: Queen's University (151).—Prof. W. J. Kidd.

BRISTOL: University Dept. of Architecture (200).— Prof. I. Smith.

CAMBRIDGE: Department of Architecture (190).— Prof. C. St. J. Wilson.

CARDIFF: The Welsh School of Architecture, University of Wales, Institute of Science and Technology (230).—Prof. D-P. Thomas.

DUNDEE: School of Architecture, University of Dundee: Duncan of Jordanstone College of Art, Perth Road (185).—J. Paul.

EDINBURGH: University of Edinburgh, Dept. of Architecture (200).—Prof. G. B. Oddie.
—Heriot-Watt University (joint course with Edinburgh College of Art), Lauriston Place (200).—Prof. R. Cowan.

GLASGOW: Mackintosh School of Architecture, Glasgow University and Glasgow School of Art, 167 Renfrew Street (307).—Prof. A. MacMillan. University of Strathclyde, Dept. of Architecture and Building Science.—Prof. T. A. Markus; Prof. F. N. Morcos-Asaad; Prof. T. W. Maver.

LIVERPOOL: University of Liverpool School of Architecture (220).—Prof. J. N. Tarn.

LONDON: School of Environmental Studies. University College London (190).—*Bartlett Professor of Architecture*, N. Watson.

MANCHESTER: University of Manchester School of Architecture (196).—Prof. E. G. Benson.

NEWCASTLE UPON TYNE: University School of Architecture (180).—Prof. R. Crowe.

NOTTINGHAM: University Dept. of Architecture (170) Prof. C. Riley.

SHEFFIELD: University Dept. of Architecture (200). —Prof. K. H. Murta; Prof. D. Gosling.

NON-UNIVERSITY SCHOOLS

(Subject to the exceptions listed below, courses are full-time and lead to a diploma. Number of students and name of Head of School are shown.)

ABERDEEN: Scott Sutherland School of Architecture, Robert Gordon's Institute of Technology (200).—Prof. S. Wilkinson (C.N.A.A. degree (hons.)).

BIRMINGHAM: School of Architecture, Franchise Street, Perry Barr (200).—A. J. Howrie.

BRIGHTON: School of Architecture, Brighton Polytechnic, Grand Parade (156).—J. P. Lomax, Ph.D.

CANTERBURY: School of Architecture, Canterbury College of Art, New Dover Road (161).—A. Wade.

HULL: Brunswick Avenue (92).—M. S. Robinson (acting); M. R. Lloyd (*Consultant Head*)

KINGSTON UPON THAMES: Polytechnic School of Architecture, Knight's Park (230).—D. Berry.

LEEDS: School of Architecture and Landscape, Leeds Polytechnic, Brunswick Terrace (267).—W. T. Bradshaw.

LEICESTER: Polytechnic School of Architecture, P.O. Box 143, (232).—B. Farmer.

LIVERPOOL: Polytechnic (B.A. Architectural Studies).

LONDON: Architectural Association School of Architecture, 36 Bedford Square, W.C.1. (620).—A. Boyarsky.

Department of Architecture, Polytechnic of the South Bank, Wandsworth Road, S.W.8. (121).—H. Haenlein.

Unit of Architecture, School of Environment. Polytechnic of Central London, 35 Marylebone Road, N.W.1.

Dept. of Environmental Design, Polytechnic of North London, Holloway, N.7 (186).—M. Quantrill (C.N.A.A. degree).

Thames Polytechnic, School of Architecture, Vencourt House, King Street, W.6. (255)—Dr. J. Paul.

MANCHESTER: Polytechnic School of Architecture Dept. of Environmental Design, Cavendish Street (6-yr. composite course) (170).—M. H. Darke.

OXFORD: Polytechnic School of Architecture, Gypsy Lane (280).—R. A. Maguire.

PORTSMOUTH: Polytechnic School of Architecture, King Henry I Street (198).—G. H. Broadbent.

ART

First Degrees in *Art* or *History of Art* (sometimes in combination with another subject) are granted by the University of Aberdeen, Bristol, Cambridge, East Anglia, Edinburgh, Essex, Exeter, Glasgow, Leeds, London (Courtauld Institute of Art; Birkbeck, University and Westfield Colleges), Manchester, Newcastle upon Tyne, Nottingham, Reading, St. Andrews, Sussex, Wales (University College, Aberystwyth) and Warwick. The degrees in *Art*, granted by the Royal College of Art are higher degrees.

Courses leading to first degrees in *Art and Design* granted by the Council for National Academic Awards are provided by more than 40 colleges, schools of art and polytechnics.

LONDON.—Royal Academy Schools of Painting and Sculpture, Burlington Gardens, W.1. (65).—*Keeper*, Peter Greenham, R.A.; *Secretary*, S. C. Hutchison; *Curator*, W. Woodington: *Registrar*, K. J. Tanner.

LONDON.—The Slade School of Fine Art, University College, W.C.1. provides undergraduates courses in Drawing and Painting.—*Slade Professor*, Lawrence Gowing, C.B.E.; *Sec.*, M. Watson, M.A.

LONDON.—Royal Drawing Society, 17 Carlton House Terrace, S.W.1.—*Pres.*, J. Mills, F.S.A.; *Sec.*, D. Flanders.

LONDON.—Royal College of Art, *see* p. 509.

OXFORD, The Ruskin School of Drawing and Fine Art, at 74 High Street, Oxford (90 students).—*Principal*, P. Morsberger (Ruskin Master of Drawing). Courses in Drawing, Painting and Printmaking. The University awards a Certificate in Fine Art.

GLASGOW, School of Art, 167 Renfrew Street.—*Director*, H. J. Barnes, C.B.E.; *Sec. & Treas.*, F. W. Kean.

ASTRONOMY

First Degrees in *Astronomy* are granted by the University of Glasgow, Leicester (*Mathematics with Astronomy*), London (Queen Mary and University Colleges), Newcastle upon Tyne, St. Andrews and Sussex (*Physics with Astronomy*); and in *Astrophysics* by the Universities of Edinburgh, Leeds (*Physics with Astrophysics*), Leicester (*Physics with Astrophysics*), London (Queen Elizabeth College—*Physics and Astrophysics*; Queen Mary College) Newcastle upon Tyne (*Astronomy and Astrophysics*), and the University of Wales (University College, Aberystwyth (*Physics with Planetary and Space Physics*).

BANKING

First Degrees with specialization in *Banking and Finance* are granted by the Universities of Birmingham and Wales (Institute of Science and Technology; also (provisional) *Banking, Insurance and Finance* at Bangor University College), the City University (*Banking and International Finance*) and Loughborough University of Technology.

Professional organizations granting qualifications after examination:—

THE INSTITUTE OF BANKERS, 10 Lombard Street, E.C.3.

THE INSTITUTE OF BANKERS IN SCOTLAND, 20 Rutland Square, Edinburgh.

BIOLOGY, CHEMISTRY, PHYSICS

First Degrees are granted by Universities and by the Council for National Academic Awards. Many technical College courses lead to diplomas, certificates or associateships. Professional qualifications are awarded by:—

THE INSTITUTE OF BIOLOGY, 41 Queen's Gate, S.W.7.—*Gen. Sec.*, D J. B. Copp.

THE INSTITUTE OF PHYSICS, 47 Belgrave Square, S.W.1.

THE ROYAL INSTITUTE OF CHEMISTRY, 30 Russell Square, W.C.1.—*President*, C. N. Thompson, *Sec. and Registrar*, R. E. Parker, PH.D.

BREWING

FIRST Degrees in *Brewing* are granted by Heriot-Watt University.

BUILDING

(*See also* Estate Management and Surveying)

First Degrees in *Building, Building Engineering* or *Building Technology* are granted by the following Universities: Aston in Birmingham (also *Building Economics and Quantity Surveying*), Bath, Brunel, Heriot-Watt (also *Building Economics and Quantity Surveying*), Liverpool, London (University College: *Architecture, Planning, Building and Environmental Studies*), Manchester (Manchester Institute of Science and Technology), Reading (also *Quantity Surveying* and *Building Surveying*), and Salford (also *Building Surveying* and *Quantity Surveying* and *Construction Economics*). Courses leading to First degrees in Building granted by the Council for National Academic Awards are provided by Brighton Polytechnic, Polytechnic of Central London, Lanchester Polytechnic, Leeds Polytechnic, Sheffield Polytechnic (*Construction*), the Polytechnic of the South Bank, and Trent Polytechnic.

Examinations are conducted by:—

THE INSTITUTE OF BUILDING, Englemere, King's Ride, Ascot, Berks.

THE INSTITUTE OF CLERKS OF WORKS OF GREAT BRITAIN, 6 Highbury Corner, N.5.—*Sec.* A. P. Macnamara.

THE INSTITUTION OF MUNICIPAL ENGINEERS, 25 Eccleston Square, S.W.1 (Building Control Officers' Ordinary and Higher Certificates).

BUSINESS, MANAGEMENT AND ADMINISTRATION

First Degrees in *Business Studies* are granted by the Universities of Bath (*Business Administration*), Belfast (*Business Administration*), Bradford (also *Operations Management*), City (provisional), Heriot-Watt (*Business Organization*), Salford, Sheffield, Stirling, Strathclyde (*Marketing* and *Operational Research*), Wales (University College, Aberystwyth) (*Economics and Business*), Wales (Institute of Science and Technology) (*Business Administration*); in *Administration* by the Universities of Aston in Birmingham (*Managerial and Administrative Studies*) and Dundee; in *Management Sciences/Studies* by the City University (*Systems and Management*), Loughborough University of Technology, and the Universities of Kent at Canterbury (also *Public Administration and Management*), Lancaster, Leeds (*Textile Management*), Manchester (Institute of Science and Technology; also *Textile Economics and Management*) Wales (Cardiff University College), and Warwick; and in *Commerce* by the following universities: Birmingham, Edinburgh and Liverpool. These subjects also form part of degree courses in other universities.

Courses leading to first degrees in *Business Studies* or *Business Administration* granted by the Council for National Academic Awards are provided by City of Birmingham Polytechnic, Brighton Polytechnic, Bristol Polytechnic, City of London Polytechnic, Dundee College of Technology, Ealing Technical College, Glasgow College of Technology, Hatfield Polytechnic, Huddersfield Polytechnic, Kingston Polytechnic, Lanchester Polytechnic, Leeds Polytechnic, City of Leicester Polytechnic, Liverpool Polytechnic, Manchester Polytechnic, Middlesex Polytechnic (also *European Business Administration*), Napier College of Commerce and Technology, Newcastle upon Tyne Polytechnic, North East London Polytechnic, N. Staffordshire Polytechnic, Oxford Polytechnic, Plymouth Polytechnic, Polytechnic of Central London, Portsmouth Polytechnic, Preston Polytechnic, Robert Gordon's Institute of Technology, Sheffield Polytechnic, Polytechnic of the South Bank, Teeside Polytechnic, Thames Polytechnic, Trent Polytechnic, Ulster Polytechnic, Polytechnic of Wales, and Wolverhampton Polytechnic.

The Thames Polytechnic also provides courses for the C.N.A.A. first degrees in *International Marketing*; Huddersfield Polytechnic courses for C.N.A.A. degrees in *Marketing* (*Engineering*) or (*Chemicals*) and *Textile Marketing*; and City of Leicester, Manchester, Sheffield, Teeside and Trent Polytechnics and Glasgow College of Technology courses for C.N.A.A. first degrees in *Public Administration*.

Professional bodies conducting training and/or examinations in Administration and Management include:

ROYAL INSTITUTE OF PUBLIC ADMINISTRATION, Hamilton House, Mabledon Place, W.C.1.
THE INSTITUTE OF HEALTH SERVICE ADMINISTRATORS 75 Portland Place, W.1.
THE INSTITUTE OF PERSONNEL MANAGEMENT, Central House, Upper Woburn Place, W.C.1.
INSTITUTION OF WORKS MANAGERS, 45 Cardiff Road, Luton, Beds.
INSTITUTE OF HOUSING MANAGERS, Victoria House, Southampton Row, W.C.1.
INSTITUTE OF ADMINISTRATIVE MANAGEMENT, 205 High Street, Beckenham, Kent.

ADMINISTRATIVE STAFF COLLEGE, Greenlands, Henley-on-Thames, Oxon.—*Princ.*, Prof. T. Kempner (1972).

LONDON GRADUATE SCHOOL OF BUSINESS STUDIES, Sussex Place, Regent's Park, N.W.1.—*Princ.*, Prof. R. J. Ball, Ph.D.
MANCHESTER BUSINESS SCHOOL, Booth Street West, Manchester.—*Dir.*, Prof. W. G. McClelland.

Courses of advanced training in most branches of commerce, including preparation for examinations of the recognized professional organizations as well as for the National Certificates in Business Studies are available at the Polytechnics and other institutions listed by cities on p. 511.
Throughout the country commercial education at a lower level is provided at *Evening Institutes*, particulars of which may be obtained from the Local Education Authority.
There are also numbers of well-established private schools awarding certificates which are widely accepted.
Institutions awarding Professional Qualifications in Commerce:—

A. GENERAL

THE ROYAL SOCIETY OF ARTS EXAMINATIONS BOARD, 18 Adam Street, Adelphi, W.C.2.
THE LONDON CHAMBER OF COMMERCE AND INDUSTRY, Marlowe House, Station Road, Sidcup, Kent.
THE EAST MIDLAND EDUCATIONAL UNION, Robins Wood House, Robins Wood Road, Apsley, Nottingham.
THE NORTHERN COUNTIES TECHNICAL EXAMINATIONS COUNCIL, 5 Grosvenor Villas, Grosvenor Road, Newcastle upon Tyne.
THE UNION OF EDUCATIONAL INSTITUTIONS, Norfolk House, Smallbrook Queensway, Birmingham 5.
NORTH WESTERN REGIONAL ADVISORY COUNCIL FOR FURTHER EDUCATION (incorporating the Union of Lancashire and Cheshire Institutes), The Town Hall, Walkden Road, Worsby, Manchester.
THE YORKSHIRE AND HUMBERSIDE COUNCIL FOR FURTHER EDUCATION, Bowling Green Terrace, Leeds.
WELSH JOINT EDUCATION COMMITTEE, 245 Western Avenue, Cardiff.

B. SPECIALIZED

THE INSTITUTE OF CHARTERED SECRETARIES AND ADMINISTRATORS, 16 Park Crescent, W.1.
THE FACULTY OF SECRETARIES, 51 Tormead Road, Guildford, Surrey.
THE INSTITUTE OF EXPORT, World Trade Centre, E.1.
THE INSTITUTE OF CHARTERED SHIPBROKERS, 25 Bury Street, E.C.3.
INSTITUTE OF MARKETING, Moor Hall, Cookham, Maidenhead, Berks.
THE CHARTERED INSTITUTE OF TRANSPORT, 80 Portland Place, W.1.
THE ADVERTISING ASSOCIATION, Abford House, 15 Wilton Road, S.W.1.
INSTITUTE OF PRACTITIONERS IN ADVERTISING, 44 Belgrave Square, S.W.1.
INSTITUTE OF PURCHASING AND SUPPLY, York House, Westminster Bridge Road, S.E.1.
INSTITUTE OF PERSONNEL MANAGEMENT, Central House, Upper Woburn Place, W.C.1.

COMPUTER SCIENCE

First Degrees in *Computer/Computing Science(s)/ Computing, Computational Science* are granted by Brunel, City, Heriot-Watt and Loughborough Universities and by the Universities of Aberdeen, Belfast, Bradford, Cambridge, East Anglia, Edinburgh, Essex, Glasgow, Hull, Keele, Kent (also *Computers and Cybernetics*), Lancaster, Leeds, Liver-

pool, London (Imperial, Queen Mary, University and Westfield Colleges; London School of Economics and Political Science), Loughborough (also *Data Processing*), Manchester (*also* Institute of Science and Technology, Newcastle upon Tyne, Reading, Salford, St. Andrews, Stirling, Strathclyde, Sussex, Wales (University College, Aberystwyth; University College, Cardiff: *Computer Systems*; University College, Swansea: *Computer Technology*), and Warwick. These subjects also form part of degree courses, often as Mathematics/Statistics and Computer Science, at many other universities and colleges.

Courses leading to first degrees in *Computer Science* granted by the Council for National Academic Awards are provided by Brighton Polytechnic, City of London Polytechnic (*Statistics and Computing*), Hatfield Polytechnic, Kingston Polytechnic, Lanchester Polytechnic, Leeds Polytechnic (*Operational Research with Computing*), City of Leicester Polytechnic, Liverpool Polytechnic ((*Applied*) *Statistics and Computing*), Polytechnic of North London (*Statistics and Computing*), North Staffordshire Polytechnic, Paisley College of Technology (*Computing with Operational Research*), Portsmouth Polytechnic, Sheffield Polytechnic, Teeside Polytechnic (also *Computer Technology*), Thames Polytechnic, Ulster Polytechnic, Wolverhampton Polytechnic and Polytechnic of Wales; in *Computer and Control Systems* by Lanchester Polytechnic; and in *Mathematics and Computer Science/ Computing* by Polytechnic of North London, Oxford Polytechnic and the Polytechnic of the South Bank, Polytechnic of Wales.

DANCING

THE ROYAL ACADEMY OF DANCING (incorporated by Royal Charter), 48 Vicarage Crescent, S.W.11. Three years' teachers' course and professional and children's examinations.—*Director*, J. Field.

THE ROYAL BALLET SCHOOL, 155 Talgarth Road, W.14. and White Lodge, Richmond Park.— *Director*, M. Wood.

IMPERIAL SOCIETY OF TEACHERS OF DANCING (1904), 70 Gloucester Place, W.1.—*Gen. Sec.*, P. J. Pearson.

DEFENCE

First Degrees in *Peace Studies* are granted by the University of Bradford.

Royal Naval Colleges

ROYAL NAVAL COLLEGE
Greenwich, S.E.10.

Admiral President, Rear-Admiral C. A. W. Weston.
Captain of the College, Capt. D. S. Wyatt, O.B.E., R.N.
Dean of the College, Capt. T. O. K. Spraggs, R.N.
Director, R.N. War College, Capt. P. I. F. Beeson, M.V.O., R.N.
Director, R.N. Staff College, Capt. D. E. Macey, R.N.

INSTITUTE OF NAVAL MEDICINE
Alverstoke, Hants.

Medical Officer in Charge and Dean of Naval Medicine, Surgeon Rear Adm. J. S. P. Rawlins, O.B.E., Q.H.P.

BRITANNIA ROYAL NAVAL COLLEGE
Dartmouth

Captain, Capt. P. W. Greening, R.N.
Commander, Cdr. D. F. Watts, R.N.
Dir. of Studies, H. G. Stewart, M.B.E., M.A.

ROYAL NAVAL ENGINEERING COLLEGE
Officers of the Royal Navy and Royal Corps of Naval Constructors as well as officers of Commonwealth and Foreign Navies are prepared for CNAA degrees in Mechanical and Electrical Engineering.

Captain, Capt. R. G. Baylis, O.B.E.
Dean, Capt. H. E. Morgan.
Executive Officer, Cdr. A. E. Sturgeon.
Dir. of Naval Engineering, Cdr. J. M. T. Hilton.
Dir. of Electrical Engineering, Cdr. R. G. Emmons.
Dir. of Mechanical Engineering, Capt. J. E. Franklin.

Military Colleges

STAFF COLLEGE, CAMBERLEY
Officers who graduate at the college have the letters *p.s.c.* after their names in Service Lists.
Commandant, Maj.-Gen. J. W. Stanier, M.B.E.
Deputy Commandant, Brig. D. K. Neville.

ROYAL MILITARY ACADEMY SANDHURST
Camberley, Surrey.

The Royal Military Academy, Woolwich, founded in 1741, and the Royal Military College, Sandhurst, founded in 1799, were amalgamated in 1947 under the above title.

Mons Officer Cadet School, Aldershot, opened in 1942 for the training of short service officers, also became part of RMA Sandhurst in 1972.
Commandant, Maj.-Gen. P. J. N. Ward, C.B.E.

ROYAL MILITARY COLLEGE OF SCIENCE
Shrivenham, nr. Swindon, Wilts.

The College was founded at Woolwich in 1864 and transferred to Shrivenham in 1946. Officer (and some civilian) students from U.K., Commonwealth and foreign armies are prepared for first degrees in Applied Science and Engineering of the Council for National Academic Awards.
Commandant, Maj.-Gen. M. E. Tickell, C.B.E., M.C.
Dean, F. J. M. Farley, SC.D., F.R.S.
Registrar, H. E. Davies.

ARMOUR SCHOOL
R.A.C. CENTRE
Bovington Camp, nr. Wareham, Dorset.

Commanding Officer and Chief Instructor, Col. B. C. Greenwood.

WELBECK COLLEGE
Worksop, Notts.

Headmaster, M. J. Maloney.
Bursar, Col. R. Mathews.

INSTITUTE OF ARMY EDUCATION
Court Road, S.E.9 (90)

Commandant, Col. W. C. J. Naylor, D.S.C.

Royal Air Force Colleges

ROYAL AIR FORCE STAFF COLLEGE
Bracknell, Berks.

Commandant, Air Vice-Marshal, K. A. Williamson, A.F.C.

ROYAL AIR FORCE COLLEGE
Cranwell

Founded in 1920, the College provides permanent officers for the General Duties, Engineer, Supply, Secretarial and R.A.F. Regiment Branches of the Royal Air Force. It also provides initial specialist training for all officers of the Engineering Supply and Secretarial branches, and advanced training in tactics, operations, navigation and systems engineering for officers of the General Duties and Engineer branches.
Air Officer Commanding and Commandant, Air Vice-Marshal W. E. Colahan, C.B.E., D.F.C.

ROYAL AIR FORCE SCHOOL OF EDUCATION
Newton, Nottingham

Commanding Officer, Gp. Capt. A. G. Duguid.

DENTISTRY

First Degrees in Dentistry are granted by the University of Belfast, Birmingham, Bristol, Dundee, Edinburgh, Glasgow, Leeds, Liverpool, London (Guy's Hospital Dental School, King's College Hospital Medical School, London Hospital Medical College, Royal Dental Hospital School of Dental Surgery, University College Hospital Medical School), Manchester, Newcastle upon Tyne, Sheffield, Wales (University College, Cardiff, and Welsh National School of Medicine).

Any person is entitled to be registered in the Dentists Register if he holds the degree or diploma in dental surgery of a University in the United Kingdom or Republic of Ireland or the diploma of any of the Licensing Authorities (The Royal College of Surgeons of England, of Edinburgh and in Ireland, and the Royal College of Physicians and Surgeons of Glasgow).

DIETETICS

First Degrees in *Nutrition and Dietetics* are granted by Queen's University of Belfast. Courses leading to first degrees in *Dietetics* granted by the Council for National Academic Awards are provided by Queen Margaret College, Edinburgh, The Queen's College, Glasgow, Leeds Polytechnic and Robert Gordon's Institute of Technology (*Nutrition and Dietetics*). The professional association is the British Dietetic Association, 305 Daimler House, Paradise Street, Birmingham. Membership is open to dietitians holding a recognized qualification who may also become State Registered Dietitians through the Council for Professions Supplementary to Medicine (*q.v.*),

DRAMA

First Degrees in Drama are granted by the Universities of Birmingham, Bristol, Exeter, Hull, Loughborough, and Manchester. Drama also forms part of degree courses in other universities.

The chief training institutions in Drama are:—

GUILDHALL SCHOOL OF MUSIC AND DRAMA (*see* p. 526).

ROYAL ACADEMY OF DRAMATIC ART (founded by Sir Herbert Beerbohm Tree, 1904), 62–64 Gower Street, W.C.1.—*Principal*, H. P. Cruttwell; *Administrator-Registrar*, R. O'Donoghue.

BRITISH THEATRE ASSOCIATION (formerly BRITISH DRAMA LEAGUE), 9 Fitzroy Square, W.1.

CENTRAL SCHOOL OF SPEECH AND DRAMA, Embassy Theatre, Swiss Cottage, N.W.3.

ROSE BRUFORD COLLEGE OF SPEECH AND DRAMA, Lamorbey Park, Sidcup, Kent.—*Principal*, J. N. Benedetti.

ENGINEERING

First Degrees in *General Engineering* or *Engineering Science* are granted by the Universities of Aberdeen, Cambridge, Durham, Edinburgh, Exeter, Leicester, Loughborough, Oxford, Reading, Surrey, and Warwick. Courses leading to first degrees in *Engineering* granted by the Council for National Academic Awards are provided by Kingston Polytechnic, Lanchester Polytechnic, Manchester Polytechnic (*Engineering Technology*), Middlesex Polytechnic, Oxford Polytechnic, Paisley College of Technology (*Engineering with Marketing*), Sheffield Polytechnic, and Thames Polytechnic, also by the Royal Military College of Science. The fifteen member institutions of The Council of Engineering Institutes, 2 Little Smith Street, S.W.1, are the principal qualifying Societies (*see below*).

Aeronautical Engineering

See main heading:

AERONAUTICS AND AERONAUTICAL ENGINEERING

Agricultural Engineering

First Degrees in *Agricultural Engineering* and *Agricultural Mechanisation* are granted by the University of Newcastle upon Tyne. Courses in *Agricultural Engineering* leading to degrees granted by Cranfield Institute of Technology are provided by National College of Agricultural Engineering, Silsoe, Beds.

Chemical Engineering

First Degrees are granted by the Universities of Aston in Birmingham, Bath, Belfast, Birmingham, Bradford, Cambridge, Edinburgh, Exeter, Heriot-Watt, Leeds, London (Imperial College of Science and Technology; University College), Loughborough, Manchester (Manchester Institute of Science and Technology), Newcastle upon Tyne, Nottingham, Salford, Sheffield, Strathclyde, Surrey, Wales (University College, Swansea). Courses leading to first degrees granted by the Council for National Academic Awards are provided by North East London Polytechnic, the Polytechnic of the South Bank, Teeside Polytechnic and Polytechnic of Wales.

Civil, Electrical & Mechanical Engineering

Degrees in *Civil*, *Electrical and Mechanical Engineering* are granted by Aberdeen, Aston in Birmingham, Bath (*E. & M. & Structural*), Belfast, Birmingham, Bradford, Bristol, Brunel (*E. & M.*), Cambridge, City, Dundee, Edinburgh, Glasgow, Heriot-Watt, Lancaster, Leeds, Liverpool, London (Imperial College of Science and Technology, King's College, Queen Mary College, University College), Loughborough, Manchester, *also* Manchester Institute of Science and Technology, Newcastle upon Tyne, Nottingham, Reading (*E. & M.*), Salford, Sheffield, Southampton, Strathclyde, Surrey, Sussex (*E. & M. & Structural*), Wales (University Colleges at Cardiff and Swansea; Institute of Science and Technology, Cardiff; University College, Bangor E.).

Some 30 polytechnics or colleges of technology provide courses (in one or more of civil, electrical and mechanical engineering) leading to first degrees granted by the Council for National Academic Awards.

Electronic Engineering & Electronics

First Degrees in *Electronic Engineering* or *Electronics* or *Electrical and Electronic Engineering* or *Electrical Engineering* (*including Electronics*) are granted by the following universities: Aston, Bath, Belfast, Birmingham, Bradford, Bristol, City, Dundee, Edinburgh, Essex, Glasgow, Heriot-Watt, Hull, Keele, Kent at Canterbury, Leeds, Liverpool, London (Chelsea College, Imperial College of Science and Technology, King's, Queen Mary and University Colleges), Loughborough, Manchester (*also* Manchester Institute of Science and Technology), Newcastle upon Tyne, Nottingham, Salford, Sheffield, Southampton, Strathclyde, Surrey, Sussex, Wales (University Colleges of Bangor, Cardiff and Swansea, Institute of Science and Technology).

Courses leading to first degrees in *Electronic Engineering* or in *Electrical and Electronic Engineering*, granted by the Council for National Academic Awards are provided by more than 20 polytechnics or colleges of technology.

Marine Engineering and Naval Architecture

First Degrees in *Marine Engineering* and *Naval Architecture and Shipbuilding* are granted by the University of Newcastle upon Tyne; in *Naval Architecture and Ocean Engineering* by the University of London (University College); in *Naval Architecture* by Glasgow and Strathclyde; in *Ship Science* by the

University of Southampton and in *Maritime Technology* by the University of Wales (Institute of Science and Technology).

Offshore Engineering

First Degrees are granted by Heriot-Watt University.

Production Engineering

First Degrees are granted by the following Universities: Aston in Birmingham, Bath, Birmingham, Brunel, City, Liverpool (*Industrial Engineering*), Loughborough, Nottingham, Salford, Strathclyde and Wales, Institute of Science and Technology. Courses leading to first degrees granted by the Council for National Academic Awards are provided by City of Birmingham Polytechnic (*Industrial Engineering*), Dundee College of Technology (*Industrial Engineering*), Hatfield Polytechnic (*Industrial Engineering*), Lanchester Polytechnic, Leeds Polytechnic and Trent Polytechnic.

Structural Engineering

First Degrees are granted by the Universities of Bath, Bradford (*Civil and Structural Engineering*), Cambridge (*Structural and Civil Engineering*), Heriot-Watt, London (University College: *Civil, Structural and Environmental Engineering*), Sheffield (*Civil and Structural Engineering*), Sussex, and Wales (University College, Cardiff (*Civil and Structural Engineering*)).

Qualifying Engineering Institutions

Royal Aeronautical Society, 4 Hamilton Place, W.1.

Institute of Fuel, 18 Devonshire Street, W.1.

Institution of Chemical Engineers, 165/171 Railway Terrace, Rugby, Warwickshire; London Office and Library, 15 Belgrave Square, S.W.1.

Institution of Civil Engineers, Great George Street, S.W.1.

Institution of Electrical Engineers, Savoy Place, W.C.2.

Institution of Electronic and Radio Engineers, 8/9 Bedford Square, W.C.1.

Institution of Gas Engineers, 17 Grosvenor Crescent, S.W.1.

Institute of Marine Engineers, 76 Mark Lane, E.C.3.

Institution of Mechanical Engineers, 1 Birdcage Walk, S.W.1.

Institution of Mining Engineers, Hobart House, Grosvenor Place, S.W.1.

Institution of Mining and Metallurgy, 44 Portland Place, W.1.

Institution of Municipal Engineers, 25 Eccleston Square, S.W.1.

Institution of Production Engineers, 66 Little Ealing Lane, W.5.

Institution of Structural Engineers, 11 Upper Belgrave Street, S.W.1.

Royal Institution of Naval Architects, 10 Upper Belgrave Street, S.W.1.

ESTATE MANAGEMENT AND SURVEYING

First Degrees are granted by the Universities of Aberdeen (*Land Economy*), Cambridge (*Land Economy*), Heriot-Watt (*Estate Management*), and Reading (*Land Management*).

First Degrees in *Surveying Science* are granted by the University of Newcastle upon Tyne, in *Building Economics and Quantity Surveying* by the University of Aston in Birmingham and by Heriot-Watt University, in *Quantity Surveying* by the University of Reading, and in *Quantity Surveying and Construction Economics* by the University of Salford.

Courses leading to first degrees granted by the Council for National Academic Awards are provided by the following: in *General Practice Surveying* by Newcastle upon Tyne Polytechnic, in *Land Administration* by North East London Polytechnic, in *Land Surveying Sciences* by North East London Polytechnic, in *Building Surveying* by City of Leicester Polytechnic, Liverpool Polytechnic and Thames Polytechnic; in *Quantity Surveying* by Bristol Polytechnic, Polytechnic of Central London, Glasgow College of Technology with Glasgow College of Building and Printing, Leeds Polytechnic, Liverpool Polytechnic, Newcastle upon Tyne Polytechnic, Portsmouth Polytechnic, Robert Gordon's Institute of Technology, Polytechnic of the South Bank, Thames Polytechnic, Trent Polytechnic and Polytechnic of Wales; in *Housing Studies* by Sheffield Polytechnic; in *Estate Management* with courses at City of Leicester Polytechnic, Polytechnic of Central London, Oxford Polytechnic, Polytechnic of the South Bank and Thames Polytechnic, in *Land Economics* with courses at Paisley College of Technology; in *Urban Estate Management* at Liverpool Polytechnic and the Polytechnic of Wales, in *Urban Estate Surveying* by Trent Polytechnic, in *Urban Land Economics* by Sheffield Polytechnic; in *Urban Land Administration* by Portsmouth Polytechnic; and in *Valuation and Estate Management* by Bristol Polytechnic.

Qualifying professional bodies include:

The Incorporated Society of Valuers and Auctioneers, 3 Cadogan Gate, S.W.1.

Rating and Valuation Association, 115 Ebury Street, S.W.1.

The Incorporated Association of Architects and Surveyors, 29 Belgrave Square, S.W.1.

Joint Examinations Board for Building Control Surveyors, 29 Belgrave Square, S.W.1.

The Royal Institution of Chartered Surveyors, 29 Lincoln's Inn Fields, W.C.2.

The Institute of Quantity Surveyors, 98 Gloucester Place, W.1.

The Faculty of Architects and Surveyors, with which is incorporated the Institute of Registered Architects, 68 Gloucester Place, W.1.

FISHERY SCIENCE

First Degrees in *Wildlife and Fisheries Management* are granted by the University of Edinburgh.

Courses leading to first degrees in Fishery Science granted by the Council for National Academic Awards are provided by Plymouth Polytechnic.

FOOD AND NUTRITION SCIENCE
(See also Dietetics, Home Economics and Hotelkeeping)

First Degrees in *Food Science* are granted by the Universities of Belfast, Leeds, London (Queen Elizabeth College: *Food and Management Science*), Loughborough (*Food Processing Technology*), Nottingham, Reading (also *Food Technology*), and Strathclyde; and in *Nutrition* by the Universities of London (Queen Elizabeth College), Nottingham and Surrey.

Courses leading to first degrees in *Food Science* granted by the Council for National Academic Awards are provided by the Polytechnic of the South Bank; and in *Nutrition and Dietetics* by Robert Gordon's Institute of Technology.

Scientific and professional bodies include: Nutrition Society, Chandos House, 2 Queen Anne Street, W.1.

FORESTRY

First Degrees in Forestry are granted by the Universities of Aberdeen, Edinburgh, Oxford (*Agricultural and Forest Sciences*), and also (*Wood Science*) Wales (University College, Bangor).

Professional Organizations

THE COMMONWEALTH FORESTRY ASSOCIATION, 11 Keble Road, Oxford.

THE ROYAL FORESTRY SOCIETY OF ENGLAND, WALES AND NORTHERN IRELAND, 102 High Street, Tring, Herts.

THE ROYAL SCOTTISH FORESTRY SOCIETY, 18 Abercromby Place, Edinburgh.

THE INSTITUTE OF FORESTERS OF GREAT BRITAIN, 6 Rutland Square, Edinburgh.

FUEL AND ENERGY STUDIES

First Degrees in *Fuel and Combustion Science* and in *Fuel and Energy Engineering* are granted by the University of Leeds; in *Petroleum Engineering* by London (Imperial College of Science and Technology); in *Natural Gas Engineering* by the University of Salford; in *Energy Studies* by the Universities of Sheffield and Wales (University College, Swansea); and in *Fuel Technology* by the University of Sheffield.

Courses leading to certificates and qualification by professional bodies are available at many Technical Colleges.

The principal professional bodies are:—

THE INSTITUTION OF GAS ENGINEERS, 17 Grosvenor Crescent, S.W.1.

THE INSTITUTE OF FUEL, 18 Devonshire Street, Portland Place, W.1.

THE INSTITUTE OF PETROLEUM, 61 New Cavendish Street, W.1.

GEOLOGY

First Degrees in *Geology* or *Geological Sciences* or *Applied Geology* are granted by the Universities of Aberdeen, Aston in Birmingham, Belfast, Birmingham, Bristol, Cambridge, Dundee, Durham, East Anglia, Edinburgh, Exeter (*also Physical Geology*), Glasgow, Hull, Keele, Leeds, Leicester, Liverpool, London (Bedford College, Birkbeck College, Chelsea College, Goldsmiths' College, Imperial College of Science and Technology, King's College, Queen Mary College, University College), Manchester, Newcastle upon Tyne, Nottingham, Oxford, Reading, St. Andrews, Sheffield, Southampton, Strathclyde, Wales (University Colleges at Aberystwyth, Cardiff and Swansea). Courses leading to first degrees in *Geology* for external students of the University of London are provided by Derby College of Art and Technology.

Courses leading to first degrees in *Geology* granted by the Council for National Academic Awards are provided by City of London Polytechnic, Kingston Polytechnic, in *Geology and Environment* by Oxford Polytechnic, and in *Engineering Geology* by Portsmouth Polytechnic.

HOME ECONOMICS AND CATERING

(*See also* DIETETICS, FOOD, HOTELKEEPING and INSTITUTIONAL MANAGEMENT).

First Degrees are granted by the Universities of Strathclyde (*Hotel and Catering Managment*) and Surrey (*Home Economics*; and *Hotel and Catering Administration*).

Courses leading to first degrees in *Catering Studies* granted by the Council for National Academic Awards are provided by Huddersfield, Oxford and Sheffield Polytechnics.

In addition to Colleges listed below, the Colleges of Education marked with an asterisk on pp. 529-31 offer specialist courses in Home Economics:

BATH (Coll. of Higher Education, Sion Hill Place).

CARDIFF (Llandaff College of Education (Home Economics)).

EASTBOURNE, Sussex (East Science College of Higher Education, Meads Road).

EDINBURGH, Queen Margaret College, Clerwood Terrace.

LEEDS POLYTECHNIC, Department of Educational Studies.

LEICESTER (Coll. of Education (Home Economics Dept.), Knighton Fields).

LIVERPOOL (F. L. Calder College of Education, Dowsefield Lane).

LONDON (Battersea Coll. of Education, Manor House, 58 North Side, Clapham Common, S.W.4).

SHREWSBURY (Radbrook College).

HOTELKEEPING

First Degrees are granted by the Universities of Strathclyde (*Hotel and Catering Management*) and Surrey (*Hotel and Catering Administration*).

Courses leading to first degrees in *Catering Studies* granted by the Council for National Academic Awards are granted by Huddersfield, Oxford and Sheffield Polytechnics.

Three-year courses leading to a Higher National Diploma in Hotelkeeping and Catering are available at the following centres:—Barnet (Hendon Coll. of Technology); Birmingham Coll. of Food and Domestic Arts; Blackpool College of Technology and Art; Bournemouth College of Technology; Brighton Polytechnic; S. Devon Technical College; Ealing Technical College; N. Gloucestershire Technical College; Huddersfield Polytechnic; Westminster Technical College; Manchester (Hollings College); Oxford Polytechnic; and in Wales at Llandrillo Technical College.

Two-year full-time courses leading to an Ordinary National Diploma are available at all the above centres and at 48 other colleges in England and Wales.

Details of the diploma conditions are obtainable from H.M. Stationery Office. (*See also* DOMESTIC SCIENCE AND CATERING).

INSTITUTIONAL MANAGEMENT

Three-year sandwich courses leading to a Higher National Diploma in Institutional Management are available at the following centres in England and Wales:

CARDIFF.—Llandaff College of Education and Home Economics.

GLOUCESTER.—Gloucestershire College of Education.

LEEDS.—Leeds Polytechnic.

LONDON.—Polytechnic of North London.

MANCHESTER.—Elizabeth Gaskell College of Education.

NEWCASTLE UPON TYNE.—Newcastle College of Further Education.

OXFORD.—Oxford Polytechnic.

SHEFFIELD.—Sheffield Polytechnic.

SHREWSBURY.—Radbrook College.

Two-year full-time courses leading to an Ordinary National Diploma are available at the Birmingham, Leeds, Manchester and Newcastle centres mentioned above and at 28 other centres in England and Wales.

Qualifying professional bodies in the two subjects above are:

HOTEL, CATERING AND INSTITUTIONAL MANAGEMENT ASSOCIATION, 191 Trinity Road, S.W.17.

INSURANCE

First Degrees in *Banking, Insurance and Finance* are granted by the University of Wales (University College, Bangor) (provisional).

Organizations conducting examinations and awarding diplomas:—

THE CHARTERED INSURANCE INSTITUTE, 20 Aldermanbury, E.C.2.

THE ASSOCIATION OF AVERAGE ADJUSTERS, 3–6 Bury Court, St. Mary Axe, E.C.3.

THE CHARTERED INSTITUTE OF LOSS ADJUSTERS, Manfield House, 376 Strand, W.C.2.

JOURNALISM

Courses for trainee newspaper journalists are available at 10 centres. One-year full-time courses are available for selected students leaving school. Particulars of all these courses are available from the Director of the National Council for Training of Journalists, Harp House, 179 High Street, Epping, Essex.

Short courses for experienced journalists are also arranged by the National Council. For periodical journalists courses are offered at a London College through N.C.T.J. enrolment including a one-year full-time course for school leavers.

LANGUAGES

First Degrees in a very wide range of languages (including Oriental and African languages) are granted by universities. Degrees in *Linguistics* are awarded by the Universities of East Anglia, Lancaster, London (School of Oriental and African Studies and University College), Reading (also *Linguistics and Language Pathology*) and Wales (University College, Bangor), in *Language* by the University of York, and in *Languages (Interpreting and Translating)* by Heriot-Watt University. These subjects also form part of degree courses at many other universities.

Courses leading to first degrees in various *Languages* granted by the Council for National Academic Awards are provided by Bristol Polytechnic, Cambridgeshire College of Arts and Technology, City of London Polytechnic, Polytechnic of Central London, Ealing Technical College, Kingston Polytechnic, Lanchester Polytechnic, Leeds Polytechnic, Liverpool Polytechnic, Manchester Polytechnic, Newcastle upon Tyne Polytechnic, North East London Polytechnic, Sheffield Polytechnic, Polytechnic of North London, Portsmouth Polytechnic, Sheffield Polytechnic, Polytechnic of the South Bank and Wolverhampton Polytechnic.

LAW

First Degrees in Law are granted by the Universities of Aberdeen, Belfast, Birmingham, Bristol, Brunel, Cambridge, Dundee, Durham, East Anglia (provisional), Edinburgh, Exeter, Glasgow, Heriot-Watt (*Business Law*) (provisional), Hull, Keele, Kent at Canterbury, Leeds, Leicester, Liverpool, London (King's College; London School of Economics and Political Science; Queen Mary College; School of Oriental and African Studies; University College), Manchester, Newcastle upon Tyne, Nottingham, Oxford, Reading, Sheffield, Southampton, Strathclyde, Sussex, Wales (University Colleges at Aberystwyth and Cardiff, Institute of Science and Technology) and Warwick.

Courses leading to first degrees in Law granted by the Council for National Academic Awards are provided by City of Birmingham Polytechnic, Bristol Polytechnic, Polytechnic of Central London, Chelmer Institute of Higher Education, City of London Polytechnic (also *Business Law*), Ealing Technical College, Kingston Polytechnic, Lanchester Polytechnic (*Business Law*), Leeds Polytechnic, City of Leicester Polytechnic, Liverpool Polytechnic, Manchester Polytechnic, Middlesex Polytechnic, Newcastle upon Tyne Polytechnic, North East London Polytechnic, Polytechnic of North London, North Staffordshire Polytechnic, Preston Polytechnic, Polytechnic of the South Bank, Trent Polytechnic and Wolverhampton Polytechnic.

Qualifications for Barrister are obtainable only at one of the Inns of Court or Faculty of Advocates; for Solicitor, from the Law Society or its equivalent in Scotland or Ireland.

THE INNS OF COURT

THE SENATE OF THE INNS OF COURT AND THE BAR

11 South Square, Gray's Inn, W.C.1.

The governing body of the Barristers' branch of the legal profession, established in 1974 assuming the functions of the former Senate of the Four Inns of Court and the former General Council of the Bar.

President, The Rt. Hon. Lord Justice Scarman, Q.C.
Chairman, P. E. Webster, Q.C.
Vice-Chairman, D. B. McNeill, Q.C.
Treasurer, H. H. Monroe, Q.C.
Secretary, Sir Arthur Power, K.C.B., M.B.E.

THE INNER TEMPLE, E.C.4

Treasurer (1976), G. D. Squibb, Q.C.
Sub-Treasurer, Cdr. R. S. Flynn, R.N.
Deputy Sub-Treasurer, Miss J. Morris.

THE MIDDLE TEMPLE, E.C.4

Treasurer (1976) The Rt. Hon. Sir George Baker, O.B.E.
Under-Treasurer, Capt. J. B. Morison, R.N. *(ret.).*
Asst. Under-Treasurer, H. W. Challoner.

LINCOLN'S INN, W.C.2

Treasurer (1976) His Hon. Judge Gillis, Q.C.
Master of the Library, The Lord Widgery, P.C., O.B.E., T.D.
Under-Treasurer, Lt.-Col. E. R. Bridges, O.B.E., R.M.
Deputy do., E. M. T. Segar.

GRAY'S INN, W.C.1

Treasurer (till Dec. 31, 1976) The Rt. Hon. Lord Justice Megaw, C.B.E., T.D.
Master of Library, Rt. Hon. Sir Frederic Sellers, M.C.
Under-Treasurer, Oswald Terry.
Deputy do., C. R. G. Hughes.

COUNCIL OF LEGAL EDUCATION

(4 Gray's Inn Place, W.C.1.)

Established by the four Inns of Court to superintend the Education and Examination of Students for the English Bar.

Chairman, Rt. Hon. Lord Justice Scarman.
Vice-Chairmen, R. L. A. Goff, Q.C.; His Hon. Judge Monier-Williams.
Chairman, Board of Studies, R. L. A. Goff, Q.C.
Chairman of the Finance Committee, His Hon. Judge Monier-Williams
Inns of Court School of Law, Dean of Faculty, C. A. Morrison.
Sub-Dean, E. Tenenbaum.

FACULTY OF ADVOCATES

(Advocates' Library, Edinburgh)

Application for admission as an Advocate of the Scottish Bar is made by Petition to the Court of Session. The candidate is remitted for examination to the Faculty of Advocates. Enquiries should be addressed to The Clerk of Faculty.

Dean of Faculty, D. M. Ross, Q.C.
Vice-Dean, J. P. H. Mackay, Q.C.
Treasurer, D. A. O. Edward, Q.C.
Clerk of Faculty, J. M. Pinkerton.
Keeper of the Library, C. K. Davidson, Q.C.
Agent, R. K. Will.

NORTHERN IRELAND

Admission to the Bar of Northern Ireland is controlled by the Honourable Society of the Inn of Court of Northern Ireland (established Jan. 11, 1926), Royal Courts of Justice, Belfast.

Treasurer, Rt. Hon. Sir Robert Porter, Q.C.
Under-Treasurer and Librarian, J. A. L. McLean, Q.C.

THE LAW SOCIETY
(113 Chancery Lane, W.C.2)

The Society controls the education and examination of articled clerks, and the admission of solicitors in England and Wales. Number of members, over 27,000.

President of the Society (1976–77), D. Napley.
Vice-President (1976–77), R. K. Denby.
Secretary-General, J. L. Bowron.
Secretaries, J. F. Warren (*Education and Training*); P. A. Leach (*Future of the Profession*); J. R. Bonham (*Non-Contentious Business*); D. Edwards (*Legal Aid*); P. G. W. Simes (*Professional Purposes*); G. P. Sanctuary (*Professional and Public Relations*); J. A. Nicholson (*Finance and Administration*); M. T. Sennett (*Contentious Business*).

THE COLLEGE OF LAW (incorporating The Law Society's School of Law), Braboeuf Manor, St. Catherine's, Guildford, Surrey (and at 33–35 Lancaster Gate, W.2, 27 Chancery Lane, W.C.2, and Christleton Hall, Chester), provides courses for The Law Society, Bar and London, Il.b. examinations.

LAW SOCIETY OF SCOTLAND

Law Society's Hall, 26–27 Drumsheugh Gardens, Edinburgh

The Society comprises all practising solicitors in Scotland. It controls the examination of legal apprentices and the admission of solicitors in Scotland and acts as registrar of solicitors under the Solicitors (Scotland) Acts, 1933 to 1965.

The Law Society of Scotland administers the Legal Aid and Advice Scheme set up under the Legal Aid and Advice (Scotland) Acts, 1967 and 1972.

LIBRARIANSHIP AND ARCHIVE ADMINISTRATION

First Degrees are granted by the University of Belfast (*Library and Information Studies*), Loughborough University of Technology (*Library Studies and Information Science*), and the University of Wales (Aberystwyth) (*Librarianship*) (jointly with the College of Librarianship, Wales), and by the University of Strathclyde (*Librarianship* with another subject). Courses leading to first degrees in *Librarianship* or *Library Studies* granted by the Council for National Academic Awards are provided by Birmingham Polytechnic, Leeds Polytechnic, Liverpool Polytechnic, Manchester Polytechnic, Polytechnic of North London, Newcastle upon Tyne Polytechnic and Robert Gordon's Institute of Technology; in *Librarianship with Modern Languages* by Brighton Polytechnic; and in *Information Science* by Leeds Polytechnic.

The Library Association, 7 Ridgmount Street, W.C.1, maintains the professional register of Chartered Librarians (Fellows and Associates), for which examinations are held twice yearly.

Schools of Librarianship conducting full-time courses of instruction in preparation for the examinations of the Library Association: Robert Gordon's Institute of Technology, Aberdeen; College of Librarianship, Wales, Llanbadarn, Aberystwyth; Birmingham Polytechnic, Birmingham 4; Brighton Polytechnic, Brighton 7; Ealing Technical College, W.5; Leeds Polytechnic; Polytechnic of North London, N.W.5; Loughborough Tech-

nical College, Leics.; Manchester Polytechnic; The Polytechnic, Education Precinct, St. Mary's Place, Newcastle upon Tyne.

MATHEMATICS

First Degree in *Mathematics* and/or *Applied Mathematics* are granted by all universities.

Courses leading to first degrees in *Mathematics* granted by the Council for National Academic Awards are provided by City of London Polytechnic, Hatfield Polytechnic, Lanchester Polytechnic, City of Leicester Polytechnic, Middlesex Polytechnic (*Mathematics for Business*), Newcastle upon Tyne Polytechnic, Polytechnic of North London (*Mathematics and Computing*), North Staffordshire Polytechnic (*Mathematical Analysis for Business*), Oxford Polytechnic (*Mathematics and Computer Science Computing*), Portsmouth Polytechnic, Polytechnic of the South Bank (*Mathematics and Computing*), Robert Gordon's Institute of Technology, Teeside Polytechnic, Thames Polytechnic and the Polytechnic of Wales (*Mathematics and Computer Science*).

MEDICINE

First Degrees in *Medicine and Surgery* are granted by the Universities of Aberdeen, Belfast, Birmingham, Bristol, Cambridge, Dundee, Edinburgh, Glasgow, Leeds, Leicester, Liverpool, London (*see* Teaching Hospitals, *below*), Manchester, Newcastle upon Tyne, Nottingham, Oxford, Sheffield, Southampton, Wales (University College, Cardiff, and Welsh National School of Medicine).

MEDICAL SCHOOLS OF TEACHING HOSPITALS IN LONDON

Under the National Health Service (Designation of Teaching Hospitals) Order, 1957, and subsequent amendments, the following were designated Teaching Hospitals for the *University of London.*

CHARING CROSS HOSPITAL (FULHAM), Fulham Palace Road, W.6.

GUY'S HOSPITAL, St. Thomas Street, S.E.1.—Medical School, *Dean* J. C. Houston, M.D., F.R.C.P.; *Dean of Dental Studies,* Prof. R. D. Emslie, M.Sc., *Secretary,* D. G. Bompas, C.M.G.

KING'S COLLEGE HOSPITAL, Denmark Hill, S.E.5.

THE LONDON HOSPITAL, Whitechapel, E.1.— Medical College and Dental School, Turner Street, E.1. *Dean* J. R. Ellis, M.B.E., M.D., F.R.C.P. *Dean of Dental Studies,* Prof. G. R. Seward. *Secretary,* H. P. Laird.

THE MIDDLESEX HOSPITAL, Mortimer Street, W.1.—Medical School. *Dean,* D. Ranger, F.R.C.S. *Secretary,* G. Clark.

ROYAL DENTAL HOSPITAL OF LONDON, Leicester Square, W.C.2.—School of Dental Surgery: *Dean,* Prof. G. L. Howe, T.D. *Secretary,* E. G. Smith.

ROYAL FREE HOSPITAL, Pond Street, Hampstead, N.W.3.—School of Medicine, Hunter Street, W.C.1. *Dean,* B. B. MacGillivray. *Secretary,* G. W. Fenn.

ST. BARTHOLOMEW'S HOSPITAL, West Smithfield, E.C.1. Medical College. *Dean,* Prof. R. A. Shooter. *Secretary,* C. E. Morris, O.B.E.

ST. GEORGE'S HOSPITAL, Hyde Park Corner, S.W.1. Medical School. *Dean,* R. D. Lowe, M.D., Ph.D., F.R.C.P. *Secretary,* E. Fairhurst.

ST. MARY'S HOSPITAL, Norfolk Place, W.2. Medical School. *Dean,* C. H. Edwards, F.R.C.P. *Secretary,* J. E. Stevenson.

ST. THOMAS' HOSPITAL, S.E.1.—Medical School. Albert Embankment, S.E.1. *Dean,* Dr. W. D. Wylie. *Secretary,* V. H. Warren.

UNIVERSITY COLLEGE HOSPITAL, Gower Street, W.C.1.—Medical School. University Street, W.C.1. *Dean,* T. A. J. Prankerd, M.D., F.R.C.P.; *Secretary,* D. H. Lloyd Morgan.

WESTMINSTER HOSPITAL, Dean Ryle Street, S.W.1. Medical School, *Dean*, Dr. J. B. Wyman, M.B.E. *Secretary*, Capt. A. D. Robin, D.S.C., R.N. *(ret.)*.

POSTGRADUATE MEDICAL SCHOOLS OF THE UNIVERSITY OF LONDON

London School of Hygiene and Tropical Medicine, Keppel Street, W.C.1. C.E. Gordon Smith, C.B., *Dean*.

ROYAL POSTGRADUATE MEDICAL SCHOOL, Du Cane Road, Shepherd's Bush, W.12. M. P. W. Godfrey, F.R.C.P., *Dean*.

British Postgraduate Medical Federation (University of London), 33 Millman Street, W.C.1. G.A. Smart, B.SC., M.D., F.R.C.P., *Director*.
Comprises:—

INSTITUTE OF BASIC MEDICAL SCIENCES, Royal College of Surgeons, Lincoln's Inn Fields, W.C.2. H. Hanley, C.B.E., M.D., F.R.C.S., *Dean*.

INSTITUTE OF CANCER RESEARCH, Fulham Road, S.W.3. Prof. T. Symington, M.D., F.R.S.E., *Director*.

CARDIO-THORACIC INSTITUTE, Fulham Road, S.W.3. R. Balcon, M.D., *Dean*.

INSTITUTE OF CHILD HEALTH, 30 Guildford Street, W.C.1. Prof. J. A. Dudgeon, M.C., T.D., M.A., M.D., F.R.C.P., *Dean*.

INSTITUTE OF DENTAL SURGERY, Eastman Dental Hospital, Gray's Inn Road, W.C.1. Prof. I. R. H. Kramer. *Dean*.

INSTITUTE OF DERMATOLOGY, St. John's Hospital for Diseases of the Skin, Lisle Street, W.C.2. R. H. Meara, M.A., M.B., B.Chir., F.R.C.P.

INSTITUTE OF LARYNGOLOGY AND OTOLOGY, Royal National Throat, Nose and Ear Hospital, 330–336 Gray's Inn Road, W.C.1. Prof. L. Michaels, M.D., *Dean*.

INSTITUTE OF NEUROLOGY, National Hospital, Queen Square, W.C.1. P. C. Gautier-Smith, M.D., F.R.C.P., *Dean*.

INSTITUTE OF OBSTETRICS AND GYNÆCOLOGY, Chelsea Hospital for Women, Dovehouse Street, S.W.3. R. B. K. Rickford, M.D., F.R.C.S., *Dean*.

INSTITUTE OF OPHTHALMOLOGY, Judd Street, W.C.1. J. Gloster, M.D., Ph.D., *Dean*.

INSTITUTE OF ORTHOPÆDICS, Royal National Orthopædic Hospital, 234 Great Portland Street, W.1. P. D. Byers, B.SC., Ph.D., M.D., *Dean*.

INSTITUTE OF PSYCHIATRY, De Crespigny Park, Denmark Hill, S.E.5. J. L. T. Birley, B.A., B.M., F.R.C.P., *Dean*.

INSTITUTE OF UROLOGY, 172 Shaftesbury Avenue, W.C.2. D. Innes Williams, M.D., M.Chir., F.R.C.S., *Dean*.

ROYAL ARMY MEDICAL COLLEGE, Millbank, S.W.1. —*Commandant and Postgraduate Dean*, Maj.-Gen. H. S. Gavourin, M.B.E., Q.H.S.

LIVERPOOL SCHOOL OF TROPICAL MEDICINE, Pembroke Place, Liverpool 3.—*Dean*, Prof. W. Peters.

Licensing Corporations granting Diplomas
THE ROYAL COLLEGE OF PHYSICIANS OF LONDON AND THE ROYAL COLLEGE OF SURGEONS OF ENGLAND, Examining Board in England, Examination Hall, Queen Square, W.C.1.

THE SOCIETY OF APOTHECARIES, Black Friars Lane, E.C.4.

ROYAL COLLEGE OF OBSTETRICIANS AND GYNÆCOLOGISTS, 27 Sussex Place, Regent's Park, N.W.1.

THE ROYAL COLLEGE OF PHYSICIANS AND THE ROYAL COLLEGE OF SURGEONS, Edinburgh.

THE ROYAL COLLEGE OF PHYSICIANS AND SURGEONS OF GLASGOW, 242 St. Vincent Street, Glasgow.

THE SCOTTISH TRIPLE QUALIFICATION BOARD, 18 Nicolson Street, Edinburgh and 242 St. Vincent Street, Glasgow.

PROFESSIONS SUPPLEMENTARY TO MEDICINE

The standard of professional education in chiropody, dietetics, medical laboratory technology, occupational therapy, orthoptics, physiotherapy, radiography and remedial gymnastics is the responsibility of eight professional boards, which also publish an annual register of qualified practitioners. The work of the Boards is co-ordinated and supervised by The Council for Professions Supplementary to Medicine (York House, Wesminster Bridge Road, S.E.1).

CHIROPODY

Professional qualifications are granted by the Society of Chiropodists, 8 Wimpole Street, W.1, to students who have passed the qualifying examinations after attending a course of fulltime training for three years at one of the eight recognized schools in England and Wales and two in Scotland. Qualifications granted by the Society are approved by the Chiropodists Board for the purpose of State Registration, which is a condition of employment within the National Health Service.

DIETETICS
(See main heading, p. 520)

MEDICAL LABORATORY SCIENCES

Courses at higher and further education establishments and training in medical laboratories are approved for progress to the professional examinations and qualifications of the Institute of Medical Laboratory Sciences, 12 Queen Anne Street, W.1.

OCCUPATIONAL THERAPY

Professional qualifications are awarded after examination by the British Association of Occupational Therapists, 20 Rede Place, Bayswater, W.2. which recognizes 14 training schools in England, Wales, Scotland, N. Ireland and Eire.

ORTHOPTICS

Orthoptists undertake the diagnosis and treatment of all types of squint and other anomalies of binocular vision, under the direction of an ophthalmic surgeon or a recognized ophthalmic medical practitioner. The training and maintenance of professional standards are the responsibility of the Orthoptists Board of the Council for the Professions Supplementary to Medicine. The examining and qualifying body is the British Orthoptic Council. Training consists of a three-year course at one of 10 approved Orthoptic Schools in England and Wales and 1 in Scotland.

The Professional Association is the British Orthoptic Society. The registered office of the Council and Society is at the Manchester Royal Eye Hospital, Oxford Road, Manchester.

(See also under Optics.)

PHYSIOTHERAPY

Examinations leading to qualification are conducted by the Chartered Society of Physiotherapy, 14 Bedford Row, W.C.1. Full-time 3-yr. courses are available at 39 recognized schools in Great Britain.

RADIOGRAPHY AND RADIOTHERAPY

Examinations leading to qualification are conducted by The Society of Radiographers, 14 Upper Wimpole Street, W.1.

There are recognized training centres in radiography and radiotherapy at many cities and towns in England and Wales, Scotland and Northern Ireland.

In London courses are available at the London Teaching Hospitals listed on p. 524; and at Hammersmith, Lambeth and Royal Northern Hospitals, at Bromley, Oldchurch County Hospital, Romford, Essex and Woolwich.

METALLURGY

First Degrees in *Metallurgy* and/or *Metallurgical Engineering* are granted by the following universities: Aston in Birmingham, Birmingham, Brunel, Cambridge, Leeds, Liverpool, London (Imperial College of Science and Technology), Loughborough, Manchester, *also* Manchester Institute of Science and Technology, Newcastle upon Tyne, Nottingham, Oxford, Salford, Sheffield, Strathclyde, Surrey, Wales (University Colleges at Cardiff and Swansea).

Courses leading to first degrees in *Metallurgy/ Metallurgy and Materials* granted by the Council for National Academic Awards are provided by the City of London Polytechnic, and Sheffield Polytechnic.

THE INSTITUTION OF METALLURGISTS, Northway House, High Road, Whetstone, N.20, is a qualifying body.

METEOROLOGY

First Degrees in *Meteorology* are granted by the University of Reading.

MINING AND MINING ENGINEERING

First Degrees in *Mining* or *Mining Engineering* are granted by the following universities: Birmingham (*Minerals Engineering*), Leeds, London (Imperial College of Science and Technology), Newcastle upon Tyne, Nottingham, Strathclyde, Wales (University College, Cardiff: *Mineral Exploitation*). Courses leading to first degrees in *Mining Engineering* granted by the Council for National Academic Awards are provided by North Staffordshire Polytechnic and in *Mining* by Camborne School of Mines. Courses of study in preparation for certificates of competence in Mining and Mining Engineering awarded by the Board for Mining Examinations and the Institution of Mining Engineers are available at these universities together with most Technical Colleges, in mining districts.

Miscellaneous Authorities

THE INSTITUTION OF MINING ENGINEERS, Hobart House, Grosvenor Place, S.W.1.

COUNCIL OF ENGINEERING INSTITUTIONS, 2 Little Smith Street, S.W.1.

MUSIC

First Degrees in *Music* are granted by the Universities of Aberdeen, Bath (course at Bath College of Higher Education), Belfast, Birmingham, Bristol, Cambridge, City, Durham, East Anglia, Edinburgh, Exeter, Glasgow, Hull, Lancaster, Leeds, Liverpool, London (King's College, Royal Holloway College; *also* Goldsmiths' College, Royal Academy of Music, Royal College of Music, and Trinity College of Music), Manchester, Newcastle upon Tyne, Nottingham, Oxford, Reading, St. Andrews, Sheffield, Southampton, Surrey, Sussex, Wales University Colleges at Aberystwyth, Bangor and Cardiff), and York. Courses leading to first degrees in Music granted by the Council for National Academic Awards are provided by Dartington College of Arts, Huddersfield Polytechnic, Kingston Polytechnic (*Music Education*) and North East Essex Technical College.

ASSOCIATED BOARD OF THE ROYAL SCHOOLS OF MUSIC, 14 Bedford Square, W.C.1.

Conducts the local examinations in music and speech for the four Royal Schools of Music—the Royal Academy of Music and the Royal College of Music in London, the Royal Northern College of Music, Manchester and the Royal Scottish Academy of Music and Drama, Glasgow.

Secretary, P. Cranmer, M.A. B.Mus., F.R.C.O. F.R.N.C.M.

ROYAL ACADEMY OF MUSIC (1822)
Marylebone Road, N.W.1

A complete training is offered to students of both sexes intending to take up music as a profession. There is a wide range of concert and opera opportunities for performers. The G.R.S.M. Diploma confers graduate status. The L.R.A.M. Diploma is open to external candidates.

Principal, Sir Anthony Lewis, C.B.E., M.A., MUS.B., F.R.C.M.
Administrator, G. J. C. Hambling, D.S.C.
Warden, N. Cox, B.Mus., F.R.A.M.

ROYAL COLLEGE OF MUSIC (1883)
Prince Consort Road, South Kensington, S.W.7

A.R.C.M., and G.R.S.M. awarded by examination. No. of Students 700.

Director, David Willcocks, C.B.E., M.C., F.R.C.M.
Registrar, M. G. Matthews, F.R.C.M., A.R.C.O.
Bursar, Maj. D. A. Imlay.

GUILDHALL SCHOOL OF MUSIC AND DRAMA (1880)
John Carpenter Street, E.C.4
(from May 1977, Barbican, E.C.2)

Full-time and part-time courses in Music, Speech and Drama. Awards Diplomas of Graduate (G.G.S.M.), Associate (A.G.S.M.) and Licentiate (L.G.S.M.). The Diploma of Graduateship(G.G.S.M.) confers graduate addition to salary.

Principal, A. Percival, C.B.E., MUS.B.
Director of Drama, P. A. Bucknell.
Director of Music, L. East, M.Mus.
Gen. Administrator, J. Isard.

TRINITY COLLEGE OF MUSIC (1872)
Mandeville Place, W.1

Complete training in music for teachers and performers. Courses lead to the university degree of B.Mus., the Graduate Diploma in Music (approved for Graduate equivalent status), the Teacher's Diploma in Music and the Performer's Diploma in Music.

Principal, M. Foggin, C.B.E., F.R.A.M.
Dir. of Studies, C. Cork, B.Mus.
Dir. of Examinations, E. Heberden, M.A.

LONDON COLLEGE OF MUSIC
Great Marlborough Street, W.1

Comprehensive full-time musical training for performers and teachers. Graduate and School Music Courses recognised by the Dept. of Education and Science and Burnham Committee.

Director, W. S. Lloyd-Webber, D.MUS., F.R.C.M., F.R.C.O.
Secretary, K. R. Beard.

ROYAL COLLEGE OF ORGANISTS (1864)
Kensington Gore, S.W.7

For the promotion of the highest standard in organ playing and choir-training. Awards Diplomas of Associateship (A.R.C.O.) and Fellowship (F.R.C.O.); and choir-training (CHM).

Hon. Sec., Sir John Dykes Bower, C.V.O., M.A., D.MUS.

BIRMINGHAM SCHOOL OF MUSIC
Paradise Circus, Birmingham 3
Head, L. Carus, L.R.A.M.

TONIC SOLFA ASSOCIATION
108 High Street,
Battersea, S.W.11
International examining body maintaining the Tonic Solfa College (1863) and the Curwen Institute (1975)

ROYAL SCHOOL OF CHURCH MUSIC
Addington Palace, Croydon, Surrey
Founded (1927) for the advancement of good music in the Church
Director, L. Dakers, B.MUS., F.R.A.M.
Secretary, V. E. Waterhouse.

ROYAL NORTHERN COLLEGE OF MUSIC
124 Oxford Road, Manchester
Principal, J. Manduell, F.R.A.M.

ROYAL MILITARY SCHOOL OF MUSIC
Kneller Hall, Twickenham (42)
Commandant, Col. M. ff. Woodhead, O.B.E.
Director of Music and Chief Instructor, Lt.-Col. T. Le M. Sharpe, M.B.E.

ROYAL MARINES SCHOOL OF MUSIC
Deal, Kent
Commandant, Col. J. D. Shallow, M.C. (1976).
Principal Director of Music, Royal Marines, Lt.-Col. P. J. Neville, M.V.O., F.R.A.M., R.M. (Ten Bands in Commission in 1976).

ROYAL SCOTTISH ACADEMY OF MUSIC AND DRAMA
St. George's Place, Glasgow, 2 (900)
Curriculum provides for all branches of study necessary for entry into the professions of music and drama. Special Diploma Courses for those who wish to teach music and drama in schools.
Principal, D. Lumsden, M.A., D.Phil., Mus.B.

NAUTICAL STUDIES
The University of Wales grants a first degree in *Maritime Technology, Maritime Commerce, Maritime Geography* (courses at Institute of Science and Technology) and the University of Southampton grants a first degree in *Nautical Studies*. Courses leading to first degrees in *Nautical Studies* granted by the Council for National Academic Awards are provided by Liverpool Polytechnic, Plymouth Polytechnic (also *Fishery Science*) and Sunderland Polytechnic.

Merchant Navy Training Schools
For Officers
MERCHANT NAVY COLLEGE, Greenhithe, Kent.—
Principal, Capt. E. K. Ballard.
SOUTHAMPTON SCHOOL OF NAVIGATION, WARSASH, SOUTHAMPTON
Director, Capt. C. N. Phelan.
For Seamen
INDEFATIGABLE AND NATIONAL SEA TRAINING SCHOOL FOR BOYS (Direct Grant Nautical School (Residential)), Plas Llanfair, Llanfairpwll, Anglesey (140); Capt. W. Wade; *Sec.*, R. N. Hatfield, Room 22, Oriel Chambers, 14 Water Street, Liverpool, 2.
NATIONAL SEA TRAINING COLLEGE, Denton, Gravesend, Kent. *Princ.*, Capt. P. H. Adlam; *Secretary*, M. H. S. Salter, 146–150 Minories, E.C.3.

NURSING
Courses in which academic study at a University may be combined with nursing training/practical nursing in hospitals are provided by the following universities: Brunel (*mental nursing*), City, Edinburgh, Hull, Liverpool, London (Bedford College and London School of Economics), Manchester, Southampton, Surrey, Ulster and Wales (Welsh National School of Medicine).

Courses leading to first degrees in *Nursing* granted by the Council for National Academic Awards are provided by Dundee College of Technology, Leeds Polytechnic, Newcastle upon Tyne Polytechnic and Polytechnic of the South Bank.

Three-year courses for State Registration in general, sick children's mental and mental deficiency nursing. Two-year course for State enrolment. Training schools in many parts of Great Britain.

THE ROYAL COLLEGE OF NURSING
THE UNITED KINGDOM
Henrietta Place, W.1
The Royal College of Nursing, within its Institute of Advanced Nursing Education, provides education at post-basic level in hospital, occupational health and community health fields. Advanced courses are held in preparation for senior posts in administration and teaching and also preparatory courses.
Director of Education, Miss M. D. Green.

CENTRAL MIDWIVES BOARD
39 Harrington Gardens, S.W.7
Chairman, Miss M. I. Farrer, O.B.E.
Secretary, R. J. Fenney, C.B.E., B.A. (Admin.).

CENTRAL MIDWIVES BOARD
for Scotland
24 Dublin Street, Edinburgh 1
Chairman, G. D. Matthew, M.D., F.R.C.O.G., F.R.C.S.E.
Secretary, Miss D. S. Young, M.A.

OPTICS
First Degrees in *Ophthalmic Optics* are granted by the following Universities: Aston in Birmingham, Bradford, City (also *Visual Science*), Manchester (Manchester Institute of Science and Technology), and Wales (Institute of Science and Technology). Courses leading to first degrees in *Ophthalmic Optics* granted by the Council for National Academic Awards are provided by the Glasgow College of Technology.

Examining bodies granting qualifications as an ophthalmic or dispensing optician:—
THE BRITISH OPTICAL ASSOCIATION, 65 Brook Street, W.1.
THE WORSHIPFUL COMPANY OF SPECTACLE MAKERS, Apothecaries Hall, Black Friars Lane, E.C.4.

THE ASSOCIATION OF DISPENSING OPTICIANS, 22 Nottingham Place, W.1 (training institution; qualification as dispensing optician).
THE SCOTTISH ASSOCIATION OF OPTICIANS, 116 Blythswood Street, Glasgow, C.2 (qualification as ophthalmic optician).

OSTEOPATHY
LONDON COLLEGE OF OSTEOPATHY, 24–25 Dorset Square, N.W.1.

PATENT AGENCY
The Register of Patent Agents is kept, under the authority of the Department of Trade by the Chartered institute of Patent Agents. Qualification is by examination; Intermediate and Final Examinations are held each year. Details can be obtained from the Institute.
CHARTERED INSTITUTE OF PATENT AGENTS, Staple Inn Buildings, W.C.1.—*Sec. and Registrar*, P. E. Lincroft, M.B.E.

PHARMACY

First Degrees in *Pharmacy* are granted by the Universities of Aston in Birmingham, Bath, Belfast, Bradford, Heriot-Watt, London (Chelsea College and the School of Pharmacy), Manchester, Nottingham, Strathclyde, Wales (Institute of Science and Technology).

Courses leading to first degrees in Pharmacy granted by the Council for National Academic Awards are provided by Brighton Polytechnic, City of Leicester Polytechnic, Liverpool Polytechnic, Portsmouth Polytechnic, Robert Gordon's Institute of Technology, and Sunderland Polytechnic.

Further information may be obtained from The Registrar, The Pharmaceutical Society of Great Britain, 1 Lambeth High Street, S.E.1.

PHOTOGRAPHY

Courses leading to first degrees in *Photographic Arts* and in *Photographic Sciences* granted by the Council for National Academic Awards are provided by the Polytechnic of Central London.

INSTITUTE OF INCORPORATED PHOTOGRAPHERS (1901) (*formerly* BRITISH PHOTOGRAPHERS), Amwell End, Ware, Herts.—*Gen. Sec.*, E. I. N. Waughray.

Professional qualifying examinations in Commercial and Industrial, Scientific and Technical, Medical, Portrait, Illustrative, Advertising and Editorial Photography, for Associateships; general vocational examinations in photography leading to Licentiateships. Fellowships awarded for distinguished ability and experience in one or more branches of photography or photographic technology.

PHYSICAL EDUCATION AND SPORTS SCIENCE

First Degrees in *Physical Education* are granted by the University of Birmingham and by Loughborough University of Technology (*Physical Education and Sports Science*). Courses in *Sports Science* leading to first degrees granted by the Council for National Academic Awards are provided by Liverpool Polytechnic.

Physical Education also forms part of the course at many colleges leading to a B.Ed. granted by the Council for National Academic Awards.

Training Colleges

M.=For Men; *W.*=For Women

BEDFORD (College of Higher Education). *W.* (1,500).—*Director*, D. G. Lyne.

BIRMINGHAM UNIVERSITY. *M.* & *W.* (110).—*Director*, W. J. Slater.

CANTERBURY (Nonington College of Physical Education, Dover). *M.* & *W.* (470).—*Principal*, S. Beaumont.

CHESTER (Chester College) *see* p. 529.

DARTFORD, Kent (Dartford College of Education), *see* p. 529.

EASTBOURNE (Chelsea College of Physical Education, Denton Road). *W.* (520).—*Principal*, Miss A. J. Bambra.

EDINBURGH (Dunfermline College of Physical Education, Cramond). *W.* (600). *Principal*, Miss M. P. Abbott.

EXETER (St. Luke's College). *See* p. 529.

LIVERPOOL (I. M. Marsh College of Physical Education, Barkhill Road, Liverpool, 17), Liverpool Education Committee. *W.* (470).—*Principal*, Miss M. I. Jamieson.

LONDON (I.L.E.A. Coll. of Physical Education, 16 Paddington Street, W.1). Courses for serving teachers only. *M.* & *W.*—*Principal* Miss J. McLaren.

LOUGHBOROUGH, Leics. (Loughborough T.C.). *See* p. 530.

MADELEY, Staffs. (Madeley College), *see* p. 530.

SUTTON COLDFIELD, Warwickshire (Anstey Dept. of Physical Education, Chester Road). (City of Birmingham Polytechnic). *W.* (150).

WENTWORTH WOODHOUSE, Yorks. (Lady Mabel College of Education), *see* p. 532.

YORK (St. John's College). *M.* & *W.*—*see* p. 531.

PRINTING

First Degrees in *Typography and Graphic Communication* are awarded by the University of Reading.

Courses leading to first degrees in *Printing Technology* granted by the Council for National Academic Awards are provided by Watford College of Technology.

Courses in technical and general, design and administrative aspects of printing are available at technical colleges throughout the United Kingdom. Details can be obtained from the Institute of Printing and the British Federation of Master Printers (*see below*).

In addition to the examining and organizing bodies listed below, examinations are held by various independent regional examining boards in further education.

INSTITUTE OF PRINTING (1961), 10–11 Bedford Row, W.C.1.

JOINT COMMITTEE (AND SCOTTISH JOINT COMMITTEE) FOR NATIONAL CERTIFICATES IN PRINTING.

BRITISH PRINTING INDUSTRIES FEDERATION, 11 Bedford Row, W.C.1.

PSYCHIATRIC SOCIAL WORK

The main patterns of training are: (1) a degree or diploma in social studies (*see below*) followed by some social work experience and a one-year postcredential course at a university in psychiatric social work; or (2) a degree in a subject other than social studies, followed by a postgraduate social studies course and, after some social work experience, by a professional course in psychiatric social work; or (3) a degree in a subject other than social studies followed by an 18-month or two-year postgraduate course combining social studies and social work; or (4) a 4-year degree course in combined studies and social work.

SOCIAL WORK

First Degrees in *Social Studies* or in *Social Sciences* are granted by most universities. Courses leading to first degrees in *Social Science* or *Social Sciences or Sociology* granted by the Council for National Academic Awards are provided by more than 20 polytechnics and colleges.

The following are among the associations awarding professional qualifications and/or providing training:—

BRITISH ASSOCIATION OF SOCIAL WORKERS, 16 Kent Street, Birmingham, 5.

MIND (THE NATIONAL ASSOCIATION FOR MENTAL HEALTH), 22 Harley Street, W.1.—*Dir.*, A. Smythe.

THE INSTITUTE OF HOUSING MANAGERS, Victoria House, Southampton Row, W.C.1.—*Sec.*, H. Key.

JOSEPHINE BUTLER HOUSE, 34 Alexandra Drive, Liverpool, 17.

SPEECH SCIENCE

(*see also* "Languages ")

First Degrees in *Speech* are awarded by the University of Newcastle upon Tyne, in *Speech Therapy* by the University of Essex, in *Speech Science* by the University of Sheffield, in *Speech Pathology and*

Therapy by the University of Manchester and in *Speech Pathology and Therapeutics* (with courses at Jordanhill College of Education) by the University of Glasgow.

The Directory of qualified Speech Therapists is published by the College of Speech Therapists, 47 St. John's Wood High Street, N.W.8. Courses leading to the Diploma of Licentiateship of The College of Speech Therapists are available at:

THE CENTRAL SCHOOL OF SPEECH AND DRAMA (Department of Speech Therapy), Embassy Theatre, Swiss Cottage, N.W.3.

CITY OF BIRMINGHAM POLYTECHNIC SCHOOL OF SPEECH THERAPY, Perry Bar, Birmingham.

CITY OF MANCHESTER COLLEGE OF HIGHER EDUCATION (incorporating Elizabeth Gaskell, Manchester, and Mather College, of Education), Hathersage Road, Manchester.

LEEDS POLYTECHNIC, School of Speech Therapy, Calverley Street, Leeds 1.

EDINBURGH SCHOOL OF SPEECH THERAPY, Queen Margarite College, Clerwood Place, Edinburgh.

ABERDEEN SCHOOL OF SPEECH THERAPY, Robert Gordon's Institute of Technology, St. Andrew's Street, Aberdeen.

CARDIFF SCHOOL OF SPEECH THERAPY, Llandaff College of Technology, Western Avenue, Cardiff.

LEICESTER POLYTECHNIC, School of Speech Pathology, Scraptoft, Leicester.

NATIONAL HOSPITALS COLLEGE OF SPEECH-SCIENCES, 59 Portland Place, W.1.

SCHOOL FOR THE STUDY OF DISORDERS OF HUMAN COMMUNICATION, 86 Blackfriars Road, S.E.1.

SURVEYING, see ESTATE MANAGEMENT AND SURVEYING

TEACHING

First Degrees in *Education* (B.Ed.) are granted by many universities (to selected students training to become teachers at colleges of education associated with the Universities usually through their Institutes or Schools of Education). Graduates in other subjects may take at many universities a one-year course leading to a postgraduate diploma or certificate in education.

Courses leading to the degree of B.Ed. granted by the Council for National Academic Awards are provided by some 30 colleges of education.

COLLEGES OF EDUCATION

(With number of students and name of Principal, Colleges marked* below offer specialist courses in Home Economics; for Colleges of Physical Education, *see* p. 527-28.)

M.=For Men; W.=For Women; L.E.A.=Local Education Authority; C. of E.=Church of England; R.C.=Roman Catholic.

ABERDEEN (Aberdeen College, Hilton Place). *M. & W.* (1,400).—J. Scotland, C.B.E.

ABINGDON, Oxon. (Culham College). C. of E. *M. & W.* (525).—J. F. Wyatt.

AMBLESIDE, Cumbria (Charlotte Mason College). *M. & W.* (300).—S. W. Percival.

AYR (Craigie College of Education). *M. & W.* (900).—P. C. McNaught.

*BANGOR, (Normal College, Bangor). L.E.A. North Wales Counties Joint Education Committee *M. & W.* (750).—J. A. Davies.

BARNET, Barnet, Enfield, Haringey, (Joint Education Committee), Middlesex Polytechnic, Trent Park, Cockfosters.—*Dean*, Dr. Alison Grady.

BARNSLEY, Yorks. (Wentworth Castle College). L.E.A. *M. & W.* (200).—J. G. Minton, PH.D.

BARRY, S. Wales (The Polytechnic of Wales). L.E.A. *M. & W.* (650).—C. Roberts.

BATH, Avon (College of Higher Education: Newton Park and Sion Hill). L.E.A. *M. & W.* (1,050)—N. P. Payne.

BEDFORD (Bedford College of Higher Education, Bedford), L.E.A. *M. & W.* (660).—Miss P. B. Dempster.

BINGLEY, YORKS. L.E.A. *M. & W.* (750).— W. R. Stirling.

BIRMINGHAM (City of Birmingham Polytechnic Centre for Teacher Education and Training) *M. & W.* (1,200),-S. W. Smethurst.

" (Newman College, Bartley Green). R.C. *M. & W.* (610).—S. Quinlan.

" (St. Peter's College, Saltley). C. of E. *M. & W.* (400).—Rev. C. Buckmaster.

" (Westhill College, Selly Oak). Free Church. *M. & W.* (530).—A. G. Bamford.

BISHOP'S STORTFORD, Herts. (Hockerill College). *M. & W.* (280). C. of E.—Miss J. A. Hall.

BOGNOR REGIS, Sussex (Bognor Regis College, Upper Bognor Road). L.E.A. *M. & W.* (750). —J. P. Parry.

BOLTON (Bolton College of Education (Technical), Chadwick Street). L.E.A. *M. & W.* (550).— *Director*, V. J. Sparrow.

BRADFORD COLLEGE (Margaret McMillan School of Education). L.E.A. *M. & W.* (700).—E. Robinson.

BRENTWOOD, Essex (Chelmer Institute of Higher Education, Faculty of Education, Arts and Humanities, Sawyers Hall Lane, Brentwood). L.E.A. *M. & W.* (700)—*Dean*, S. G. Fisher.

BRIGHTON (Faculty of Education Studies, Brighton Polytechnic). L.E.A. *M. & W.* (1,500).—E. C. Ryman.

BRISTOL (The College of St. Matthias, Fishponds). " C. of E. *M. & W.* (801).—R. A. Adcock.

BROMSGROVE, Worcs. (North Worcestershire College). L.E.A. *M. & W.* (1,500).—D. Brailsford.

CAERLEON (Gwent College). L.E.A. *M. & W.* (600).—M. I. Harris.

CAMBRIDGE (Homerton College). *W.* (700).— Miss A. C. Shrubsole.

CANTERBURY (Christ Church College). C. of E. *M. & W.* (700).—M. Berry.

CARDIFF (City of Cardiff College, Cyncoed). *M & W.* (950).—L. G. Bewsher.

CARMARTHEN (Trinity College). Church in Wales. *Bilingual*. *M. & W.* (600).—K. M. J. Jones.

CHALFONT ST. GILES, Bucks. (Buckinghamshire College of Higher Education, Newland Park). L.E.A. *M. & W.* (526).—A. M. D. I. Oakeshott.

CHELTENHAM, Glos. (St. Mary's College). *W.* (530). C. of E.—Miss G. M. Owen, PH.D.

" (St. Paul's College). *M.* (550). C. of E.— G. D. Barnes.

CHESTER (College of Higher Education). *M. & W.* (850). C. of E.—M. V. J. Seaborne.

CHICHESTER, Sussex (Bishop Otter College). *M. & W.* (600). C. of E.—G. P. McGregor.

CHORLEY, Lancs. (Chorley College, (Preston) Polytechnic, School of Education). L.E.A. *M. & W.* (1,100).—L. Kenworthy.

CLACTON-ON-SEA, Essex* (Colchester Institute of Higher Education, Marine Parade). L.E.A. *M. & W.* (420).—A. Owen.

COVENTRY, Warwicks (Coventry College). L.E.A. *M. & W.* (1,100).—Miss J. G. Lawrence.

CREWE (Crewe and Alsager College of Higher Education). L.E.A. *M. & W.* (2,400).—Miss B. P. R. Ward.

DARLINGTON (Darlington College). Voluntary. *M. & W.* (238).—J. A. Huitson.

,, (Middleton St. George College). L.E.A. *M. & W.* (460).—E. L. Black.

DARTFORD, Kent (Thames Polytechnic, Dartford College of Education). *M. & W.* (600).— K. Challinor.

DERBY (Bishop Lonsdale College, Western Road, Mickleover). *M. & W.* (750). C. of E.— N. Evans.

DONCASTER (Doncaster Metropolitan Institute of Higher Education, Waterdale, Doncaster). Teacher Education Department at High Melton and Scawsby. *M. & W.* (900).—D. C. A. Bradshaw.

DUDLEY, West Midlands (Dudley College, Castle View). L.E.A. *M. & W.* (950).—D. Broadhurst.

DUNDEE (Dundee College, Gardyne Road). *M. & W.* (1,000).

DURHAM (Neville's Cross College). L.E.A. *M. & W.* (600).—R. Emmett.

,, (St. Hild and St. Bede), *M. & W.* (850). C. of E.—J. V. Armitage.

EASTBOURNE, Sussex (East Sussex College of Higher Education, Milnthorpe Courts, Meads Road). *M. & W.* (1,200).—G. R. Tyler.

EDINBURGH (Craiglockhart College). R.C. *M. & W.* (450).—Sister Sheila M. Hayes.

,, (Moray House College). *M. & W.* (2,800). Prof. B. T. Ruthven.

EXETER (St. Luke's College). *M. & W.* (980). C. of E.—J. C. Dancy.

EXMOUTH, Devon (Rolle College). L.E.A. *M. & W.* (900).—F. C. A. Cammaerts.

FALKIRK, Stirlingshire (Callendar Park College). *M. & W.* (550).—C. E. Brown.

GLASGOW (Jordanhill College). *M. & W.* (3,700). —T. R. Bone, Ph.D.

,, (Notre Dame College, Bearsden). R.C. *M. & W.* (1,400).

GLOUCESTER* (Gloucestershire College). L.E.A. *M. & W.* (450).—J. H. Hunter.

HAMILTON (Hamilton College, Bothwell Road). *M. & W.* (900).—G. Paton.

HEREFORD (County College). L.E.A. *M. & W.* (440).—G. R. F. Drew.

HERTFORD (Balls Park College). L.E.A. *M. & W.* (590).—P. E. Sangster.

HUDDERSFIELD (Polytechnic, Dept. of Education).

ILKLEY, Yorks.* (Ilkley College). L.E.A. *M. & W.* (530).—Miss B. M. Mayer.

KINGSTON ON THAMES, Surrey (Gipsy Hill College, Kenry House, Kingston Hill). L.E.A. *M. & W.* (785).—Miss F. D. Batstone.

KINGSTON UPON HULL (Hull College of Higher Education, Cottingham Road, Hull. *M. & W.* (1,000).—J. Stoddart.

LANCASTER (St. Martin's College). C. of E. *M. & W.* (700).—R. Clayton.

LEEDS (Leeds Polytechnic, School of Education).

,, (Trinity College). R.C. *W.* (720).—Sister Augusta Maria; *and* (All Saints' College). R.C. *M.*—A. M. Kean.

LEICESTER (Leicester Polytechnic, Faculty of Education, Humanities and Social Sciences). L.E.A. *M. & W.* (1,100).—B. A. Fisher, Ph.D.

LINCOLN (Bishop Grosseteste College). *M. & W.* (600). C. of E.—L. G. Marsh.

LIVERPOOL (City of Liverpool, C. F. Mott College, Prescot). L.E.A. *M. & W.* (1,200).—B. S. Cane.

,, (F. L. Colder College of Education, Dowsefield Lane). L.E.A. *M. & W.* (300).— F. Kenworthy.

,, (S. Katharine's College). *M. & W.* (650). C. of E.—G. L. Barnard, Ph.D.

,, (Notre Dame College, Mount Pleasant). *M. & W.* (750). R.C.—Miss K. M. Hughes.

LONDON (Avery Hill College, Eltham, S.E.9). L.E.A. *M. & W.* (1,200; Annexe, 300).— Mrs. K. E. Jones.

,, (Battersea College of Education, 58 North Side, Clapham Common, S.W.4 and Manresa House, Holybourne Avenue, S.W.15, (630).

,, *(College of All Saints, N.17). C. of E. *M. & W.* (600).—P. G. Hampton.

,, The Polytechnic of North London, Prince of Wales Road, N.W.5. L.E.A. *M. & W.* (300). Day College.—S. Jones.

,, (Philippa Fawcett and Furzedown College, Leigham Court Road, S.W.16). L.E.A. *M. & W.* (1,100).—Mrs. R. O. Brown.

,, *(Digby Stuart College of the Sacred Heart, Roehampton Institute of Higher Education, Roehampton, S.W.15). *M. & W.* (800). R.C.—Sister D. Bell.

,, (Froebel Institute College, Grove House, Roehampton Lane, S.W.15). *M. & W.* (660).—M. Morgan.

,, (Garnett College (Technical), Downshire House, Roehampton Lane, S.W.15). L.E.A. *M. & W.* (1,500).—(vacant).

,, (Goldsmiths' College, New Cross, S.E.14). London Univ. *M. & W.* (1,000).—Dr. R. Hoggart.

,, (St. Mary's College, Strawberry Hill, Twickenham). *M. & W.* (1,200). R.C.—Very Rev. T. P. Cashin.

,, Shoreditch College, Cooper's Hill, Englefield Green, Surrey). L.E.A. *M. & W.* (655). —J. N. Smith.

,, (Sidney Webb School of Educ., Polytechnic of Central London, 9–12 Barrett Street, W.1). L.E.A. *M. & W.* (450).—Miss R. Beresford.

,, (Southlands College (Roehampton College of Further Education), 65 Wimbledon Parkside, S.W.19). *M. & W.* (780). Methodist.— Miss M. P. Callard.

,, (Stockwell College, Bromley, Kent). L.E.A. *M. & W.* (700).—Miss R. F. Carr.

,, (West London Institute of Higher Education) (Borough Road, College, Isleworth, Middlesex and Maria Grey College, Twickenham, Middlesex. *M. & W.* (3,000).—J. E. Kane.

,, (Whitelands College, West Hill, Putney, S.W.15). C. of E. *M. & W.* (750).—R. F. Knight.

LOUGHBOROUGH, Leics. (Loughborough College). L.E.A. *M. & W.* (1,000).—Miss T. B. Jones.

MADELEY, Staffs. *(College, Madeley, nr. Crewe). L.E.A. *M. & W.* (1,150).—K. B. Thompson.

MANCHESTER (Manchester College of Higher Education (incorporating Elizabeth Gaskell, Manchester and Mather Colleges of Education) L.E.A. *M. & W.* (1,800).—Dr. A. Johnston.

,, (Sedgley Park College, Prestwich). *M. & W.* (500). R.C.—Sister Barbara Hughes.

MATLOCK, Derbyshire. L.E.A. *M. & W.* (730). —D. H. Udall.

MIDDLETON, Manchester (De la Salle College). *M. & W.* (900). R.C.—The Rev. Brother Augustine.

MILTON KEYNES., Bucks. L.E.A. *M. & W.* (400).— T. J. Cox.

NEWCASTLE UPON TYNE (Newcastle Polytechnic Faculty of Education). L.E.A. *M. & W.* (1,185).—G. Bosworth.
„ (St. Mary's College). *M. & W.* (700). R.C. —Sister P. M. G. Wilson.

NORTHUMBERLAND (Northumberland College, Ponteland). L.E.A. *M. & W.* (960).—Dr. D. R. Shadbolt.

NORWICH (Keswick Hall). *M. & W.* (700). C. of E.—W. Etherington.

ORMSKIRK, Lancs. (Edge Hill College of Higher Education, St. Helens Road). L.E.A. *M. & W.* (1,300).—P. K. C. Millins.

OXFORD (Westminster College, North Hinksey). *M. & W.* (550). Methodist.—D. W. Crompton. (*See also* WHEATLEY.)

PLYMOUTH, Devon (College of St. Mark and St. John, Derriford Road). C. of E. *M. & W.* (700).—J. E. Anderson.

PORTSMOUTH (Faculty of Educ., Portsmouth Polytechnic). *M. & W.* (800).—I. F. Rolls.

POULTON-LE-FYLDE, Nr. Blackpool, Lancs. (Preston Polytechnic, School of Education). L.E.A. *M. & W.* (550).—*Dean*, A. B. Butterworth.

READING, Berks. (Bulmershe College). L.E.A. *M. & W.* (1,250).—J. F. Porter.

RETFORD, Notts. (Eaton Hall College). L.E.A. *M. & W.* (550).—E. R. Morgan.

RUGBY, Warwicks. (St. Paul's College, Newbold Revel, Stretton-under-Fosse). *W.* (520). R.C. —Sister Joan Thornhill.

SALISBURY, Wilts. (College of Sarum St. Michael). C. of E. *M. & W.* (250).—C. J. R. Wilson.

SCARBOROUGH, North Yorks. (North Riding College). L.E.A. *M. & W.* (400).—F. W. Wright.

SHEFFIELD* (Totley-Thornbridge College, Totley). L.E.A. *M. & W.* (1,000).—P. G. Spinks.

SOUTHAMPTON (La Sainte Union College, The Avenue). *M. & W.* (736). R.C.—Sister Imelda Marie.

SUNDERLAND (Faculty of Education, Sunderland Polytechnic). L.E.A. *M. & W.* (900).—*Dean*, H. Webster.

SWANSEA (Swansea College, Townhill Road, Cockett). L.E.A. *M. & W.* (715).—Miss M. R. Smith.

WAKEFIELD, Yorks. (Bretton Hall College). L.E.A. *M. & W.* (740).—A. S. Davies.

WARRINGTON, Cheshire (Padgate College, Fearnhead). L.E.A. *M. & W.* (800).—J. R. Williams.

WATFORD, Herts. (Wall Hall College, Aldenham). L.E.A. *M. & W.* (700).—Miss A. K. Davies.

WENTWORTH WOODHOUSE, Yorks. (Lady Mabel College of Education). *M. & W.* (425).— J. Foster.

WEYMOUTH, Dorset. (Weymouth College, Dorset Institute of Higher Education). L.E.A. *M. & W.* (1,000).—Miss N. M. O'Sullivan.

WHEATLEY, Oxon. (Lady Spencer-Churchill College). L.E.A. *W.* Graduates (*M. & W.*), (560).—Lady Linstead, D.Phil.

WINCHESTER, Hants. (King Alfred's College). *M. & W.* (1,008). C. of E.—M. Rose.

WOLVERHAMPTON (Day College, Walsall Street). L.E.A. *M. & W.* (350).—Miss J. Garrett.
„ (Technical Teachers' College, Compton Road West). L.E.A. *M. & W.* (450).—E. A. J. Turner.

WORCESTER* (Worcester College, Henwick Grove). L.E.A. *M. & W.* (1,250).—E. G. Peirson, C.B.E.

WREXHAM (North-East Wales Institute of Higher Education, Cartrefle College). L.E.A. *M. & W.* (700).—Dr. G. O. Phillips.

YORK (College of Ripon and York St. John). *M. & W.* C. of E. (950 at York; 550 at Ripon)— J. V. Barnett.

For Teachers of the Deaf

DEPARTMENT OF AUDIOLOGY AND EDUCATION OF THE DEAF, Manchester University. *M. & W.* (130).—*Head of Dept.*, Prof. I. G. Taylor, M.D.

COURSE FOR TEACHERS OF THE DEAF, Oxford Polytechnic/Lady Spencer-Churchill College, Wheatley, Oxon. *M. & W.* (50).—*Princ.*, B. Lloyd, D.SC.

For Teachers of the Blind

THE COLLEGE OF THE TEACHERS OF THE BLIND Hon. Registrar, B. Hechle, Royal School for the Blind, Church Road North, Wavertree, Liverpool 15. Award certificates after examination to blind pianoforte tuners, school teachers and craft instructors of the blind (700).

Courses of training are also available at:

THE NORTH REGIONAL ASSOCIATION FOR THE BLIND. *M. & W.* Headingley Castle, 72 Headingley Lane, Leeds.

TECHNICAL EDUCATION

First Degrees in one or more technologies are awarded by almost all universities; and many polytechnics and colleges of technology provide courses leading to first degrees granted by the Council for National Academic Awards. Details are given under individual subject headings.

(*See also:* AERONAUTICS; BUILDING; COMPUTER SCIENCE; ENGINEERING; FUEL TECHNOLOGY; MINING; OPTICS; PATENT AGENCY; PRINTING AND TEXTILES.)

CITY AND GUILDS OF LONDON INSTITUTE
76 Portland Place, W.1

Chairman, D. E. Woodbine Parish, C.B.E.
Director General, Sir Cyril English.
Secretary, B. B. Phillips.

Regional Advisory Councils

Set up in 1947 (i) to bring education and industry together to find out the needs of young workers and advise on the provision required, and (ii) to secure reasonable economy of provision. They also have certain responsibilities in connection with the procedure for the approval by the Department of Education and Science of advanced courses, and issue handbooks, etc., giving, for the guidance of students and teachers, information about the facilities available within a region or district for various types of training (*e.g.* electrical engineering, textiles, building and chemistry). There are ten Regional Advisory Councils in England and Wales:—

REGION 1 (LONDON AND HOME COUNTIES).— Regional Advisory Council for Technological Education, Tavistock House South, Tavistock Square, W.C.1.

REGION 2 (SOUTHERN).—Regional Council for Further Education, 26 Bath Road, Reading.

3 (SOUTH-WEST).—Regional Council for Further Education, 37–38 Fore Street, Taunton.

4 (WEST MIDLANDS).—Advisory Council for Further Education, Norfolk House, Smallbrook Queensway, Birmingham.

5 (EAST MIDLANDS).—Regional Advisory Council for the Organization of Further Education, Robins Wood House, Robins Wood Road, Aspley, Nottingham.

6 (EAST ANGLIAN).—Regional Advisory Council for Further Education, County Hall, Martineau Lane, Norwich.

7 (YORKSHIRE AND HUMBERSIDE).—Council for Further Education, Bowling Green Terrace, Green Terrace, Leeds.

8 (NORTH-WESTERN).—North Western Regional Advisory Council for Further Education, (incorporating the Union of Lancashire and Cheshire Institutes), Town Hall, Walkden Road, Worsley, Manchester.

9 (NORTHERN).—Advisory Council for Further Education, 5 Grosvenor Villas, Grosvenor Road, Newcastle upon Tyne.

10 (WALES).—Welsh Joint Education Committee, 245 Western Avenue, Cardiff.

――――――

For Polytechnics, etc., *see* p. 511

Scottish Technical Colleges

Technical education is available at approximately 100 day-course schools and colleges in Scotland, including those which specialize in a particular subject. The following are among those recognized by the Scottish Education Department as " central institutions " (colleges for higher technical learning); other Scottish central institutions appear under Agriculture, Art, Domestic Science and Music.

ABERDEEN: ROBERT GORDON'S INSTITUTE OF TECHNOLOGY, Aberdeen.—*Director*, P. Clarke, Ph.D.

DUNDEE COLLEGE OF TECHNOLOGY, Bell Street, Dundee.—*Princ.*, H. G. Cuming, Ph.D.

GALASHIELS: SCOTTISH COLLEGE OF TEXTILES, Galashiels, Selkirkshire.—*Princ.*, J. C. Furniss.

LEITH NAUTICAL COLLEGE, 59 Commercial Street, Leith, Edinburgh.—*Princ.*, E. T. Morgan.

PAISLEY COLLEGE OF TECHNOLOGY, High Street, Paisley.—*Princ.*, T. M. Howie.

Northern Ireland

BELFAST (College of Technology).—*Princ.*, W. F. K. Kerr, Ph.D.

LONDONDERRY (College of Technology (with Teacher Training).—*Princ.*, T. Williams, M.B.E.

Industrial Training Boards

Established under the Industrial Training Act, 1964.

AGRICULTURAL, HORTICULTURAL AND FORESTRY, Bourne House, 32–34 Beckenham Road, Beckenham, Kent.—*Dir.*, R. S. Butler.

CARPET, Evelyn House, 32 Alderley Road, Wilmslow, Cheshire.—*Sec.*, D. Borthwick.

CERAMICS, GLASS AND MINERAL PRODUCTS, Bovis House, Northolt Road, Harrow, Middx.—*Sec.*, H. B. Chubb, O.B.E.

CHEMICAL AND ALLIED PRODUCTS, Staines House, 158–162 High Street, Staines, Middx.—*Sec.*, G. Plant.

CLOTHING AND ALLIED PRODUCTS, Tower House, Merrion Way, Leeds.—*Chief Executive*, K. F. Swinfen.

CONSTRUCTION, Radnor House, London Road, Norbury, S.W.16.—*Sec.*, G. R. Gardner.

DISTRIBUTIVE INDUSTRY, MacLaren House, Talbot Road, Stretford, Manchester.—*Sec.*, H. A. Whitehead, M.B.E.

ENGINEERING, 54 Clarendon Road, Watford, Herts. *Sec.*, H. M. Lang.

FOOD, DRINK AND TOBACCO, Barton House, Barton Street, Gloucester.—*Sec.*, J. T. Newton.

FOOTWEAR, LEATHER AND FUR SKIN, Maney Building, 29 Birmingham Road, Sutton Coldfield, West Midlands.—*Sec.*, C. J. Bailey.

FOUNDRY INDUSTRY TRAINING COMMITTEE, 50–54 Charlotte Street, W.1.—*Sec.*, L. A. Rice.

FURNITURE AND TIMBER, 31 Octagon Parade, High Wycombe, Bucks.—*Sec.*, J. M. Webber.

HOTEL AND CATERING, Ramsey House, Central Square, Wembley, Middx.—*Sec.*, H. A. Lax.

IRON AND STEEL, 4 Little Essex Street, W.C.2. —*Dir.*, R. Duncan.

KNITTING, LACE AND NET, 4 Hamilton Road, Nottingham.—*Sec.*, A B. Ross.

MAN-MADE FIBRES PRODUCING, 3 Pond Place, S.W.3.—*Chief Officer*, D. W. Ashby.

PAPER AND PAPER PRODUCTS, Star House, Potters Bar, Herts.—*Sec.*, O. T. P. Carne, M.B.E.

PETROLEUM, York House, Empire Way, Wembley, Middx.—*Sec.*, J. A. Bey.

PRINTING AND PUBLISHING, Merit House, Edgware Road, Colindale, N.W.9.—*Sec.*, G. F. Reid.

ROAD TRANSPORT, Capitol House, Empire Way, Wembley, Middx.—*Dir. Gen.*, T. E. Tindall.

RUBBER AND PLASTICS PROCESSING, Brent House, 950 Great West Road, Brentford, Middx.—*Sec.*, S. K. Hardy.

SHIPBUILDING, Raeburn House, Northolt Road, South Harrow, Middx.—*Sec.*, D. O. Savill.

WOOL, JUTE AND FLAX, Butterfield House, Otley Road, Baildon, Shipley, W. Yorks.—*Sec.*, F. Bingham.

――――――

LOCAL GOVERNMENT TRAINING BOARD, 8 The Arndale Centre, Luton, Beds.—*Dir.*, D. Lofts.

Industrial Training Foundation
18 Thurloe Place, S.W.7

Formed in 1964 with the support of the Ministry of Labour (now Department of Employment and Productivity) and the Department of Education and Science to assist in implementing the Industrial Training Act, 1964.

It provides a service for all industries and all categories of employees through its six regional offices. A Training Officer and Advisory Service assists individual firms in the development of training programmes and makes available the part-time services of qualified training officers. This service also provides assistance in maintaining training records required by Industrial Training Boards and advice on dealing with questionnaires and grant claims.

The main activities of the ITF are: assessment of training needs; provision of training for apprentices, operators, supervisors, instructors and salesmen. There is a personal tutorial service for management. The Foundation operates training schemes to the requirements of individual firms or on a group basis.

A further activity of the ITF under its training officer service is the operation of the Engineering Industries Group Apprenticeship Scheme (EIGA) formed in 1953, which serves 1,000 firms throughout the country and provides 3,000 training places.

TEXTILES

First Degrees in *Textiles* or *Fibre Science* are awarded by the Universities of Bradford, Leeds, Manchester (Manchester Institute of Science and Technology), Strathclyde. Courses leading to first degrees in *Textile Marketing* granted by the Council for National Academic Awards are provided by Huddersfield Polytechnic; and in *Textile Technology* by the City of Leicester Polytechnic.

THE TEXTILE INSTITUTE, 10 Blackfriars Street, Manchester.—*Gen. Sec.*, R. G. Denyer.

THEOLOGY

First Degrees in *Theology* or *Divinity* are granted by the Universities of Aberdeen, Belfast, Birmingham, Bristol, Cambridge (*Theological and Religious Studies*), Durham, Edinburgh, Exeter, Glasgow, Hull, Kent at Canterbury, Leeds (*Theology and Religious Studies*), London (Heythrop and King's Colleges), Manchester, Nottingham, Oxford, St.

Andrews, Southampton and Wales (Bangor, Cardiff, and St. David's University Colleges); in *Biblical Studies* by the Universities of Manchester; Sheffield and Wales (Bangor and Cardiff University College); and in *Religious Studies* by the Universities of Aberdeen, Cambridge (*Theological and Religious Studies*), Edinburgh, Lancaster, Leeds (*Theology and Religious Studies*), London (King's College), Newcastle upon Tyne, Stirling, Sussex and Wales (University College, Cardiff and St. David's University College).

Course leading to first degrees in *Theology* granted by the Council for National Academic Awards are provided by the London Bible College and Spurgeon's College.

Theological Colleges
Church of England and Church in Wales
BANGOR (University Anglican Chaplaincy) (Church Hostel) (28).—*Warden*, Rev. G. Hopley.
BIRMINGHAM (Queen's Coll., Somerset Road, Edgbaston) (75).—*Princ.*, Rev. A. P. Bird (Ecumenical College).
BRISTOL. Trinity College (110).—*Princ.*, Rev. J. A. Motyer.
CAMBRIDGE (Ridley Hall) (52).—*Princ.*, Rev. K. N. Sutton.
,, (Westcott House, Jesus Lane) (50).—*Princ.*, Rev. M. Santer.
CHICHESTER (50).—*Princ.*, Rev. Canon R. J. Halliburton, D.Phil.
CUDDESDON, Oxon. (Ripon College) (54).—*Princ.*, Rev. J. L. Houlden.
DURHAM. *See* University of Durham—St. Chad's; St. John's.
LAMPETER (St. David's College) *see* University of Wales.
LINCOLN (Theological College) (65).—*Warden*, Rev. Canon A. A. K. Graham.
LLANDAFF, Cardiff (St. Michael's) (76).—*Warden*, Rev. J. G. Hughes.
LONDON (King's College, W.C.2).—*See* University of London.
MIRFIELD (College of the Resurrection) (50).—*Princ.*, Rev. B. Green.
NOTTINGHAM (St. John's College, Bramcote)—*Princ.*, Rev. R. E. Nixon.
OAK HILL (Southgate, N.14) (72).—*Princ.*, Rev. D. H. Wheaton.
OXFORD (St. Stephen's House) (55).—*Princ.*, Rev. D. M. Hope, D.Phil.
,, (Wycliffe Hall) (60).—*Princ.*, Rev. J. P. Hickinbotham.
SALISBURY AND WELLS (100).—*Princ.*, Rev. Canon R. J. A. Askew.

Church of Scotland
ABERDEEN (Christ's Coll.).—*Master*, Rev. Prof. J. S. McEwen, D.D.
EDINBURGH (New Coll., Faculty of Divinity, Univ. of Edinburgh) (196).—*Princ.*, Rev. D. W. D. Shaw.
GLASGOW (Trinity Coll.) (70).—*Princ.*, Rev. Prof. A. D. Galloway, Ph.D.
ST. ANDREWS (College of St. Mary, University of St. Andrews).

Scottish Episcopal Church
EDINBURGH (24).—*Princ.*, Rev. Canon F. V. Weston.

Presbyterian
BELFAST (Presbyterian Coll.).—*Princ.*, Rev. Prof. J. M. Barkley, Ph.D., D.D.

CAMBRIDGE (Westminster Coll.) (36).—*Princ.*, Rev. A. G. MacLeod.

Presbyterian Church of Wales
ABERYSTWYTH (United Theological Coll.) (31).—*Princ.*, Rev. Prof. S. I. Enoch.

Methodist
BELFAST (Edgehill Coll.) (25).—*Princ.*, Rev. V. Parkin.
BRISTOL (Wesley Coll., Westbury-on-Trym) (58).—*Princ.*, Dr. J. A. Newton.
CAMBRIDGE (Wesley House) (20).—*Princ.*, Rev. M. J. Skinner.
RICHMOND.—*See* University of London.

Congregational
BANGOR (Bala-Bangor Independent Coll.)—*Princ.*, R. T. Jones, D.Phil., D.D.

United Reform
CAMBRIDGE (Cheshunt College, with Westminster College, Madingley Road, Cambridge).—*Pres.*, Rev. J. E. Newport.
EDINBURGH (Scottish Congregational College, 9 Rosebery Crescent (10).—*Princ.*, Rev. J. Wood.
MANCHESTER (Congregational College) (36).—*Princ.*, Rev. E. Jones, Ph.D.
OXFORD (Mansfield College) (105).—*Princ.*, Rev. G. B. Caird, D.Phil., D.D., F.B.A.
SWANSEA (34).—*Princ.*, Prof. W. T. Pennar Davies, Ph.D.

Roman Catholic
(Colleges for the Diocesan Clergy)
ABERYSTWYTH (St. Mary's College (for late vocations, secular and regular)) (30).—*Prior*, Very Rev. D. C. Flanagan, O. Carm.
ALLEN HALL, 28 Beaufort Street, Chelsea, S.W.3.—*Rector*, Rt. Rev. Mgr. J. O'Brien.
GLASGOW (St. Peter's Coll., Cardross, Dunbartonshire) (33).—*Rector*, Very Rev. J. McMahon.
OSCOTT COLL., Sutton Coldfield, West Midlands (110).—*Rector*, Rt. Rev. Mgr. F. G. Thomas.
OSTERLEY, Middlesex (Campion House, 112 Thornbury Road) (165).—*Superior*, Rev. J. R. Brooks, S.J.
UPHOLLAND, Skelmersdale, Lancs. (now the Upholland Northern Institute for Adult Christian Education).—*Rector*, Rt. Rev. Mgr. W. Dalton.
USHAW (Durham) (180).—*Pres.*, Rt. Rev. Mgr. P. Loftus.
WONERSH, Guildford (St. John's) (114).—*Rector*, Rt. Rev. J. P. McConnon.

Baptist
BANGOR (North Wales Baptist Coll.) (22).—*Princ.*, Rev. D. E. Morgan.
BRISTOL (40).—*Pres.*, Rev. Dr. W. M. S. West.
CARDIFF (S. Wales Baptist Coll.) (16).—*Princ.*, D. G. Davies.
GLASGOW (The Baptist Theological College of Scotland, 31 Oakfield Avenue, Glasgow, W.2) (17).—*Princ.*, Rev. R. E. O. White.
LONDON (Spurgeon's Coll., South Norwood Hill, S.E.25) (62).—*Princ.*, Rev. R. Brown, Ph.D.
MANCHESTER (Northern Baptist College, Brighton Grove, Rusholme) (affiliated to Manchester Univ.) (65).—*Princ.*, Rev. M. H. Taylor.
OXFORD (Regent's Park College) (54).—*Princ.*, Rev. B. R. White, D.Phil.

Unitarian
MANCHESTER (Unitarian College, Victoria Park) —*Princ.*, Rev. A. J. Long.

Interdenominational—Unitarian
OXFORD (Manchester Coll.).—*Princ.*, Rev. B. Findlow.

Jewish

JEWS' COLLEGE, 11 Montagu Place, W.1.—*Princ.*, Rabbi N. L. Rabinovitch, Ph.D.

LEO BAECK COLLEGE, 33 Seymour Place, W.1.— *Rabbinic Director*, Rabbi Dr. A. H. Friedlander.

TOWN AND COUNTRY PLANNING

First Degrees are granted by Heriot-Watt University (*Town Planning*), and by the Universities of Dundee (*Town and Regional Planning*), London (University College: *Architecture, Planning, Building and Environmental Studies*), Manchester (*Town and Country Planning*), Newcastle upon Tyne (*Town and Country Planning*), and Wales (Institute of Science and Technology: *Town Planning Studies*). Courses leading to first degrees in *Town Planning* granted by the Council for National Academic Awards are provided by City of Birmingham Polytechnic and Polytechnic of the South Bank; Liverpool Polytechnic and Trent Polytechnic; and in *Urban and Regional Planning* by Lanchester Polytechnic and Oxford Polytechnic.

The ROYAL TOWN PLANNING INSTITUTE, 26 Portland Place, W.1, conducts examinations in town planning.

VETERINARY STUDIES

First Degrees in *Veterinary Science/Medicine and Surgery* are granted by the Universities of Bristol, Cambridge, Edinburgh, Glasgow, Liverpool and London (Royal Veterinary College).

PUBLIC SCHOOLS

The Association of Governing Bodies of Public Schools (G.B.A.) comprises 254 schools, of which 172 are independent and 78 are direct grants, and includes schools in membership of the Headmasters' Conference (with a few exceptions) together with the following schools:—

Ackworth, Pontefract, Yorks.
Adams' Grammar Sch., Newport, Salop.
Austin Friars Sch., Carlisle.
Avonhurst School, Bristol.
Bearwood College, Wokingham.
Belmont Abbey Sch., Hereford.
Bentham Grammar Sch., Bentham, Lancs.
Bethany School, Goudhurst, Kent.
†Canon Slade Gr. Sch., Bolton.
Carmel College, Wallingford.
Cokethorpe School, Witney.
Colston's Boys' Sch., Bristol.
Dollar Academy, Clackmannan.
Duke of York's R.M. Sch., Dover.
Dundee High School.
Frensham Heights, Rowledge, Surrey.
Friends' Sch., Great Ayton, N. Yorks.
Friends' Sch., Saffron Walden.
Friends' School, Wigton, Cumbria.
Grenville Coll., Bideford, Devon.
Keil School, Dumbarton.
King's School, Gloucester.
Langley School, Norwich.
Lindisfarne College, Wrexham.
Millfield School, Somerset.
Milton Abbey School, Blandford Forum, Dorset.
Morrison's Academy, Crieff.

Newcastle High Sch., Staffs.
Oswestry School, Salop.
Pangbourne College, Berks.
Pierrepoint School, Frensham, Surrey.
Rannoch School, Perthshire.
Reading Blue Coat School, Caversham, Berks.
Redrice Sch., nr. Andover, Hants.
Rishworth Sch., nr. Halifax, Yorks.
Royal Lancaster Grammar School.
Royal Wolverhampton School.
Ruthin School, Clwyd.
Ryde School, Isle of Wight.
St. Augustine's Coll., Ramsgate, Kent.
St. Bede's Coll., Manchester.
St. Boniface's Coll., Plymouth.
St. Brendan's Coll., Bristol.
St. John's Coll., Southsea, Hants.
Seaford College, Petworth, Sussex.
Shebbear Coll., Beaworthy, Devon.
Shiplake Coll., Henley, Oxon.
†Sidcot Sch., Winscombe, Som.
Truro Cathedral School.
Wakefield Grammar School.
†Wells Cathedral School.
Woodbridge School, Suffolk.
　　　　　　† Co-educational School.

Sec., F. J. Walesby, 27 Church Road, Steep, Petershead, Hants.

HEADMASTERS' CONFERENCE SCHOOLS

THE HEADMASTERS' CONFERENCE—*Chairman* (1976), R. W. Young (George Watson's College); *Principal Sec.*, E. J. Dorrell, 29 Gordon Square, W.C.1; *Deputy Sec.*, R. F. Glover. The annual meetings are, as a rule held at the end of September.

In considering applications for election to membership the Committee will have regard to the scheme or other instrument under which the school is administered (taking particularly into consideration the degree of independence enjoyed by the Headmaster and the Governing Body); the number of boys over thirteen years of age in the school; the number of boys in proportion to the size of the school who are in the sixth form, *i.e.* engaged on studies at the Advanced Level of the General Certificate of Education.

Name of School	F'ded.	No. of Boys	Annual Fees D=Day Boys	Headmaster (*With date of Appointment*)
England and Wales				
Abbotsholme, Uttoxeter, Staffs........	1889	250†	£1,872..D £1,248	S. D. Snell (1967)
Abingdon, Oxfordshire..............	1256	570	£1,480....D £720	M. St. J. Parker (1975)
Aldenham, Elstree, Herts.........	1597	352	£1,710..D £1,044	P. W. Boorman (1974)
Alleyn's School, Dulwich, S.E.22.....	1619	800	........D £840	D. A. Fenner (1976)
Allhallows, Rousdon, Dorset.........	1515	292†	£1,620....D £936	D. J. Mathewson (1974)
Ampleforth College (R.C.), York......	1802	700	£1,620........	Rev. N. P. Barry, O.S.B. (1964)
Archbishop Holgate's Grammar, York..	1546	750	£600.......Dnil	D. A. Frith (1959)
Ardingly Coll.,Hayward's Heath,Sussex*	1858	366	£1,740..D £1,155	C. H. Bulteel, M.C. (1962)
Arnold School, Blackpool............	1870	800†	£1,194....D £612	A. J. C. Cochrane (1974)
Ashville College, Harrogate..........	1877	425	£1,101....D £570	G. R. Southam (1958)
Bablake, Coventry................	1344	862†	........D £522	E. H. Burrough, T.D. (1962)
Bancroft's, Woodford Green, Essex....	1737	620	£1,428....D £729	I. M. Richardson (1965)
Barnard Castle, Co. Durham.........	1883	490	£1,199....D £590	S. D. Woods (1965)
Bedales, Petersfield, Hants..........	1893	438†	£1,575....D £960	C. P. Nobes (1974)
Bedford School.................	1552	1050	£1,509....D £789	C. I. M. Jones (1975)
Bedford Modern School..........	1834	1050	£1,194....D £618	B. H. Kemball-Cook (1965)
Berkhamsted, Herts.............	1544	720	£1,590....D £810	J. L. Spencer, T.D. (1972)
Birkenhead, Merseyside............	1860	740	£1,416....D £660	J. A. Gwilliam (1963)
Bishop's Stortford College, Herts......	1868	320	£1,500..D £1,095	G. C. Greetham (1970)
Bloxham School, Banbury, Oxon*.....	1860	357†	£1,620....D £999	D. R. G. Seymour (1965)
Blundell's, Tiverton.............	1604	400†	£1,698....D £975	A. C. S. Gimson, M.B.E., M.C.
Bolton.....................	1524	994	........D £597	C.D.A. Baggley (1966) [(1971)
Bootham, York................	1823			J. H. Gray (1972)
Bradfield College, Berks..........	1850	450	£1,785..D £1,190	A. O. H. Quick (1971)
Bradford Grammar, Yorks..........	1662	1088	........D £588	D. A. G. Smith (1974)
Brentwood School, Essex..........	1557	900	£1,368....D £804	R. Sale (1966)
Brighton College, Sussex...........	1845	430	£1,545..D £1,020	W. S. Blackshaw (1971)
Brislington School, Bristol..........	1956	1765†	.........Dnil	J. S. Hellier (1956)
Bristol Cathedral School..........	1542	420	........D £666	D. J. Jewell (1970)
Bristol Grammar School..........	1532	1000	........D £666	J. R. Avery (1975)
Bromsgrove, Worcs................	1688	550	£1,635..D £1,152	Rev. J. N. F. Earle (1971)
Bryanston School, Blandford.........	1928	526	£1,935..D £1,290	Rev. D. I. S. Jones (1974)
Bury Grammar, Lancs............	1726	700	........D £570	W. J. H. Robson (1969)
Canford, Wimborne, Dorset..........	1923	502	£1,740..D £1,200	M. M. Marriott (1976)
Caterham, Surrey...............	1811	598	£1,234....D £654	S. R. Smith (1974)
Charterhouse, Godalming..........	1611	700†	£1,860..D £1,350	B. Rees (1973)
Cheadle Hulme..............	1855	1000†	£1,467....D £687	D. C. Firth (1977)
Cheltenham College...............	1841	449	£1,752..D £1,167	D. Ashcroft, T.D. (1959)
Chigwell, Essex................	1629	450	£1,410....D £909	B. J. Wilson (1971)
Christ College, Brecon............	1541	275	£1,350....D £999	J. B. Cook, Ph.D. (1972)
Christ's Hospital, Horsham..........	1553	840	(various).........	D. H. Newsome (1970)
City of London, E.C.4............	1442	780	........D £930	J. A. Boyes (1965)
Claysmore, Iwerne Minster, Blandford.	1896	250†	£1,500....D £990	R. McIsaac (1966)
Clifton College, Bristol...........	1862	690	£1,806..D £1,080	S. M. Andrews (1975)
Cranleigh, Surrey...............	1863	530	£2,025..D £1,410	M. van Hasselt (1970)
Culford School, Bury St. Edmunds.....	1881	720†	£1,473....D £681	D. Robson (1971)
Dame Allan's Sch., Newcastle on Tyne.	1705	450	....D £480–648	F. Wilkinson (1970)
Dauntsey's, Devizes................	1543	500	£1,494....D £690	G. E. King-Reynolds (1969)
Dean Close, Cheltenham...........	1884	400†	£1,800..D £1,185	C. G. Turner (1968)
Denstone College, Uttoxeter, Staffs.*....	1873	322†	£1,740..D £1,080	D. Maland (1969)
Douai (R.C.), Woolhampton..........	1818	262	£1,404......	Rev. P. W. Sollom, O.S.B.
Dover College, Kent...............	1871	400†	£1,815..D £1,386	D. R. Cope (1973) [(1975)
Downside (R.C.), Stratton-on-the-Fosse, Somerset........	1606	575	....	Dom R. Appleby (1975)
Dulwich College, S.E.21............	1619	1370	£1,575....D £840	D. A. Emms (*Master*) (1975)
Durham.....................	1414	300	£1,632..D £1,059	M. W. Vallance (1972)

† Pupils.   * A Woodard Corporation School.

Name of School	F'ded.	No. of Boys	Annual Fees D = Day Boys	Headmaster (With date of Appointment)
Eastbourne College, Sussex............	1867	489†	£1,492..D £1,061	S. J. B. Langdale (1973)
Ellesmere College, Salop★...........	1884	330	£1,800..D £1,100	D. J. Skipper (1969)
Eltham College, S.E.9...............	1842	570	£1,302....D £705	C. Porteous (1959)
Epsom College, Surrey..............	1855	606†	£1,575..D £1,050	O. J. T. Rowe (1970)
Eton College, Windsor..............	1440	1249	£1,800..........	M. W. McCrum (1970)
Exeter, Devon......................	1633	550	£1,281....D £636	M. R. Hone (1966)
Felsted, Dunmow, Essex............	1564	476†	£1,650..D £1,035	A. F. Eggleston, O.B.E. (1968)
Forest School, Snaresbrook, E.17.....	1834	371	£1,332....D £921	D. A. Foxall (1960)
Framlingham College, Suffolk........	1864	415	£1,404....D £819	L. I. Rimmer (1971)
Giggleswick, Settle, Yorks..........	1512	261	£1,600....D £950	R. A. C. Meredith (1970)
Gresham's, Holt, Norfolk...........	1555	460†	£1,800..D £1,149	L. Bruce-Lockhart (1955)
Haberdashers' Aske's, Elstree, Herts..	1690	1300	£1,497....D £786	B. H. McGowan (1973)
Haileybury, Herts..................	1862	633†	£1,725..D £1,191	D. M. Summerscale (*Master*)
Harrow, Middlesex.................	1571	730	£1,800....D £900	B. M. S. Hoban (1971) [(1976)
Hereford, Cathedral School.........	1381	387†	£1,155...D £630	B. B. Sutton (1975)
Highgate, N.6.....................	1565	650	£1,668....D £864	R. C. Giles (1974)
Hulme Grammar School, Oldham.....	1611	740	..........D £570	S. W. Johnson (1965)
Hurstpierpoint College, Sussex★.....	1850	383	£1,500..D £1,245	R. N. P. Griffiths (1964)
Hymers College, Hull..............	1889	572	..........D £450	J. Ashurst (1971)
Ipswich, Suffolk...................	1400	560	£1,377-1,476 D £855-900	J. M. Blatchly, Ph.D. (1972)
The John Lyon School, Harrow......	1876	450	..........D £690	G. V. Surtees (1968)
Kelly College, Tavistock...........	1877	300	£1,689..D £1,089	D. W. Ball, M.B.E. (1972)
Kent College, Canterbury...........	1885	460†	£1,074....D £600	D. E. Norfolk (1960)
Kimbolton, Cambs..................	1600	460	£1,320....D £666	D. W. Donaldson (1973)
King Edward VII School, Lytham.....	1908	556	..........D £585	C. J. Lipscomb (1966)
King Edward's, Bath, Avon..........	1552	513	..........D £621	B. H. Holbeche, C.B.E. (1961)
King Edward's, Birmingham.........	1552	700	..........D £648	F. G. R. Fisher (*Chief Master*)
King Edward's, Witley, Surrey.......	1553	420	£1,260..........	J. T. Hansford (1969) [(1974)
King Henry VIII, Coventry..........	1545	865†	..........D £435	R. Cooke (1974)
King's College, Taunton★...........	1522	419	£1,521..D £1,014	J. M. Batten (1969)
King's College, Wimbledon, S.W.19	1819	584	£1,470....D £870	C. S. C. B. Wightwick (1975)
King's School, Bruton..............	1519	300	£1,512..D £1,167	G. H. G. Doggart (1972)
King's School, Canterbury..........	600	695	£1,782..D £1,191	Rev. Canon P. Pilkington
King's School, Chester.............	1541	455	..........D £645	A. R. Munday (1964) [(1975)
King's School, Ely.................	970	384†	£1,593..D £1,002	H. Ward (1970)
King's School, Macclesfield.........	1502	1260	..........D £588	A. H. Cooper (1966)
King's School, Rochester...........	604	520	£1,524....D £816	R. A. Ford (1975)
King's School, Worcester...........	1541	620	£1,365....D £693	D. M. Annett (1959)
Kingston Grammar, Surrey..........	1561	560	..........D £744	J. A. Strover (1970)
Kingswood School, Bath............	1748	430†	£1,497....D £990	L. J. Campbell (1970)
Lancaster, Royal G. S..............	1469	800	£780......Dnil	A. M. Joyce (1972)
Lancing College, Sussex★...........	1848	471	£1,680..D £1,080	I. D. S. Beer (1969)
Latymer Upper, Hammersmith, W.6...	1624	1125	..........D £756	M. L. R. Isaac (1971)
Leeds Gr. Sch., Leeds 6............	1552	1069	..........D £651	A. C. F. Verity (1976)
Leighton Park Sch., Reading........	1890	320†	£1,485....D £990	W. H. Spray (1971)
The Leys School, Cambridge.........	1875	410	£1,785..........	B. T. Bellis (1975)
Liverpool College, Liverpool 18......	1840	710	£1,194....D £744	M. F. Robins (1970)
Llandovery College...............	1848	266†	£1,245....D £750	R. B. Jones (1976)
Lord Wandsworth Coll., Long Sutton, Hants.....................	1912	377	£1,380....D £996	C. A. N. Henderson (1968)
Loughborough Grammar............	1495	830	£1,362....D £657	J. S. Millward (1973)
Magdalen College School, Oxford....	1480	505	£1,485....D £720	W. B. Cook (*Master*) (1972)
Malvern College, Worcester........	1865	600	£1,665..D £1,065	M. J. W. Rogers (1971)
Manchester Grammar School.........	1515	1440	..........D £675	P. G. Mason, M.B.E. (*High Master*) (1962)
Manchester, Wm. Hulme's Gr.......	1881	800	......D £507-700	P. A. Filleul (1974)
(Sir Roger) Manwood's Sch., Sandwich, Kent....................	1563	420	£816........Dnil	J. F. Spalding (1960)
Marlborough College, Wilts..........	1843	879	£1,725..........	R. W. Ellis (*Master*) (1972)
Merchant Taylors', Crosby..........	1620	800	£1,464....D £699	Rev. H. M. Luft (1964)
Merchant Taylors', Northwood......	1561	680	£1,275....D £900	F. Davey (1974)
Mill Hill, N.W.7..................	1807	480	£1,614..D £1,095	A. F. Elliott (1974)
Monkton Combe, Bath..............	1868	308†	£1,443..D £1,080	R. J. Knight (1968)
Monmouth........................	1614	498	£1,200....D £657	N. R. Bomford (1977)
Mount St. Mary's Coll., Spinkhill, Derbyshire (R.C.)...............	1842	290	£1,380....D £729	Rev. A. A. Nye, S.J. (1968)
Newcastle on Tyne, Royal Gr. Sch....	1545	850	..........D £750	A. S. Cox (1972)
Norwich School....................	1250	580	£1,434....D £666	P. G. Stibbe (1975)

† Pupils.   ★ A Woodard Corporation School.

Name of School	F'ded	No. of Boys	Annual Fees D=Day Boys	Headmaster (With date of Appointment)
Nottingham High School	1513	982	D £570	D. T. Witcombe, Ph.D. (1970)
Oakham, Rutland, Leics.	1584	900†	£1,650 D £950	J. D. Buchanan, M.B.E. (1958)
The Oratory (R.C.), Woodcote, Reading	1859	340	£1,515 D £1050	A. J. Snow (1972)
Ottershaw Sch., Surrey	1948	250	£999	A. E. R. Dodds (1964)
Oundle, Peterborough, Northants	1556	728	£1,782	B. M. W. Trapnell, Ph.D. (1968)
Perse Sch., Cambridge	1615	430	£1,459 D £672	A. E. Melville (1969)
Plymouth College	1877	642	£1,260 D £630	R. H. Merrett (1975)
Pocklington Sch., York	1514	635	£1,077 D £438	G. L. Willatt (1966)
Portsmouth Gr. Sch.	1732	750	D £630	D. M. Richards (1975)
Prior Park Coll. (R.C.), Bath	1924	280	£1,470 D £996	Rev. M. P. Power (1972)
Queen Elizabeth's Gr., Blackburn	1567	940	D £600	D. J. Coulson (1965)
Queen Elizabeth Gr. Sch., Wakefield	1591	874	£1,155 D £705	J. G. Parker (1975)
Queen Elizabeth's Hospital, Bristol	1586	425	£1,250 D £660	H. G. Edwards, M.B.E. (1967)
Queen Mary's Gr., Walsall, Staffs.	1554	630	D nil	S. L. Darby (1956)
Queen's College, Taunton, Som.	1843	445	£1,332 D £846	M. Robinson (1974)
Radley Coll., Abingdon	1847	540	£1,680	D. R. W. Silk (Warden) (1968)
Ratcliffe Coll. (R.C.), Leicester	1847	298	£1,380 D £750	Rev. A. J. Baxter (1973)
Reed's, Cobham, Surrey	1813	350	£1,440 D £975	R. N. Exton (1963)
Rendcomb Coll., Cirencester, Glos.	1920	250†	£1,395	R. M. A. Medill (1970)
Repton School, Derby	1557	496	£1,875 D £1,350	J. F. Gammell, M.C. (1968)
Rossall, Fleetwood, Lancs.	1844	545	£1,716 D £1,156	J. Sharp, D.Phil. (1973)
Rugby, Warwickshire	1567	720	£1,770 D £882	J. S. Woodhouse (1967)
Rydal, Colwyn Bay, Clwyd	1885	287†	£1,485 D £855	P. F. Watkinson (1968)
St. Albans, Herts.	1570	670	D £720	F. I. Kilvington (1964)
St. Bees, Cumbria	1586	265	£1,680 D £999	G. W. Lees (1963)
St. Benedict's, Ealing, W.5. (R.C.)	1902	600	D £735	Rev. G. G. Brown, O.S.B. (1969)
St. Dunstan's, Catford, S.E.6.	1888	920	D £675	B. D. Dance (1973)
St. Edmund's, Canterbury	1749	410	£1,407 D £1,032	F. R. Rawes, M.B.E. (1964)
St. Edmund's Coll. (R.C.), Ware, Herts.	1568	530	£1,500 D £825	Rev. M. G. Garvey (1968)
St. Edward's, Oxford	1863	500	£1,764 D £1,323	C. H. Christie (Warden) (1970)
St. George's Coll., Weybridge (R.C.)	1869	560	£1,245 D £825	Rev. J. I. M. Evans (1976)
St. John's, Leatherhead	1851	421	£1,566 D £1,173	E. J. Hartwell, T.D. (1970)
St. Lawrence Coll., Ramsgate	1879	350	£1,650 D £1,110	P. H. Harris (1969)
St. Mary's College, Gt. Crosby	1919	660	D £588	Br. N. D. O'Halloran (1972)
St. Paul's, Lonsdale Rd., Barnes, S.W.13	1509	682	£1,575 D £1,050	J. W. Hele (High Master) (1973)
St. Peter's, York	627	420	£1,596 D £882	P. D. R. Gardiner (1967)
Scarborough Sixth Form College	1973	500†	D nil	P. A. Gardiner, M.C. (1973)
Sedbergh, Yorks.	1525	465	£1,680 D £1,120	P. J. Attenborough (1975)
Sevenoaks School, Kent	1418	850	£1,485 D £927	A. R. Tammadge (1971)
Sherborne, Dorset	1550	625	£1,590 D £1,200	R. D. MacNaghten (1974)
Shrewsbury School	1552	630	£1,845 D £1,170	W. E. K. Anderson (1975)
Silcoates School, Wakefield, Yorks.	1820	375	£1,200 D £798	R. J. M. Evans, Ph.D. (1960)
Solihull, Warwicks.	1560	930	£1,410 D £810	G. D. Slaughter (1973)
Stamford, Lincs.	1532	840	£1,326 D £594	H. A. Staveley (1968)
Stockport Gr. Sch.	1487	570	D £600	F. W. Scott (1962)
Stonyhurst Coll. (R.C.), nr. Whalley, Lancs.	1593	500	£1,635	Rev. M. J. F. Bossy, S.J. (1971)
Stowe, Bucks.	1923	666†	£1,890 D £1,323	R.Q. Drayson, D.S.C. (1964)
Sutton Valence, Kent	1576	356	£1,713 D £1,143	M. R. Ricketts (1967)
Taunton, Somerset	1847	600	£1,539 D £1,068	N. S. Roberts (1970)
Tettenhall College, Staffs.	1863	380	£1,392 D £861	W. J. Dale (1968)
Tiffin Sch., Kingston-upon-Thames	1638	800	D nil	A. J. V. Roberts (1972)
Tonbridge, Kent	1553	626	£1,575 D £1,116	C. H. D. Everett (1975)
Trent College, Long Eaton, Derbyshire	1868	510†	£1,581 D £1,005	A. J. Maltby (1968)
Trinity School, Croydon	1596	750	D £720	R. J. Wilson (1972)
Truro, Cornwall	1880	640	£1,200 D £600	D. W. Burrell (1959)
(Sir William) Turner's Sch., Redcar, Cleveland	1692	362†	£395 D nil	S. G. Barker (Principal) (1971)
University Coll. Sch., Frognal, N.W.3.	1830	510	D £954	W. A. Barker (1975)
Uppingham, Leics.	1584	690†	£1,690	C. MacDonald (1975)
Warwick	914	950	£1,236 D £636	P. W. Martin, T.D. (1962)
Watford Gr. Sch.	1704	1000	D nil	L. K. Turner (1963)
Wellingborough, Northants.	1595	260	£1,638 D £1,005	G. Garrett (1973)
Wellington Coll. Crowthorne, Berks.	1856	725†	£1,575 D £1,050	Hon. F. F. Fisher, M.C. (Master) (1970)
Wellington Sch., Somerset	1841	620	£1,020 D £462	J. MacG. K. Kendall-Carpenter [(1966) (1973)]
West Buckland Sch., Barnstaple	1856	426	£1,248 D £594	Rev. G. Ridding (1968)
Westminster, Dean's Yard, S.W.1.	1560	498	£1,890 D £1,290	J. M. Rae, Ph.D. (1970)
Whitgift, Croydon	1596	850	D £840	D. A. Raeburn (1970)
Winchester College	1382	600	£1,890 D £1,350	J. L. Thorn (1968)

† Pupils

Name of School	F'ded.	No. of Boys	Annual Fees D=Day Boys	Headmaster (With date of Appointment)
Woodhouse Grove Sch., Bradford.....	1812	470	£1,236....D£653	D. A. Miller (1972)
Worcester College for the Blind.......	1866	75	£2,631..........	R. C. Fletcher (1959)
Worcester, Royal Gr...............	1561	780	£705........Dnil	A. G. K. Brown (1950)
Worksop College, Notts.*..........	1895	415	£1,650..D£1,245	R. J. Roberts (1975)
Worth School, Crawley, Sussex (R.C.).	1933	455	£1,650..........	Rev. K. Taggart (1977)
Wrekin Coll., Wellington, Salop......	1880	392†	£1,725..D£1,170	G. C. L. Hadden (1971)
Wycliffe Coll., Stonehouse, Glos.....	1882	282†	£1,509....D£309	R. D. H. Roberts (1967)

Scotland

Name of School	F'ded.	No. of Boys	Annual Fees D=Day Boys	Headmaster (With date of Appointment)
Daniel Stewart's and Melville Coll., Edinburgh (amalgamated, 1973).......	1832	1415	£1,275....D£600	R. M. Morgan (1977) [(1962)
The Edinburgh Academy.............	1824	550	£1,515....D£765	H. H. Mills, M.C., Ph.D. (Rector)
Fettes College, Edinburgh...........	1870	520†	£1,680..D£1,018	A. Chenevix-Trench (1971)
George Heriot's, Edinburgh..........	1628	1500	.....D£378-441	A. S. McDonald (1970)
George Watson's Coll., Edinburgh....	1723	2370†	£1,275....D£600	R. W. Young (1958)
Glasgow Academy..................	1846	960	.........D£570	R. de C. Chapman (Rector)
Glenalmond (Trinity College), Perthshire.....................	1841	390	£1,680..........	J. N. W. Musson [(1975) (Warden) (1972)
Gordonstoun, Elgin, Morayshire......	1934	420	£1,860..........	J. W. R. Kempe (1968)
Hutchesons' Gr. Sch., Glasgow.......	1650	1720†	.....D£354-378	P. Whyte (1966)
Jordanhill College School, Glasgow...	1920	1000†	............Dnil	W. T. Branston (1956)
Kelvinside Academy, Glasgow........	1878	683	.....D£369-507	C. J. R. Mair (1958)
Loretto Sch., Musselburgh, Midlothian.	1827	246	£1,650....D£750	D. B. McMurray (1976)
Merchiston Castle, Edinburgh........	1833	325	£1,590....D£990	D. J. Forbes (1969)
Robert Gordon's Coll., Aberdeen.....	1729	869	£1,096....D£352	J. Marshall (1960)
Strathallan, Forgandenny, Perthshire....	1912	350	£1,590..........	C. D. Pighills (1975)

Northern Ireland

Name of School	F'ded.	No. of Boys	Annual Fees D=Day Boys	Headmaster (With date of Appointment)
Bangor Gr. Sch., Co. Down..........	1856	803	.........D£300	R. J. Rodgers, Ph.D. (1975)
Belfast Methodist College.............	1865	2206†	£922......D£312	J. Kincade, Ph.D. (1974)
Belfast Royal Academy..............	1785	1180†	.........D£335	J. L. Lord (1968)
Campbell Coll., Belfast..............	1894	430	£1,377...D£573	R. M. Morgan (1971)
Coleraine Academical Institution.......	1860	1150	£800....D£275	G. Humphreys, Ph.D. (1955)
Portora Royal Sch., Enniskillen........	1608	500	£1,190....D£340	T. J. Garrett (1973)
Royal Belfast Academical Instn........	1810	1030	.........D£366	S. V. Peskett (1959)

Isle of Man

Name of School	F'ded.	No. of Boys	Annual Fees D=Day Boys	Headmaster (With date of Appointment)
King William's College...............	1668	460	£1,545....D£960	G. R. Rees-Jones (Principal) (1958)

Channel Islands

Name of School	F'ded.	No. of Boys	Annual Fees D=Day Boys	Headmaster (With date of Appointment)
Elizabeth Coll., Guernsey.............	1563	550	£1,134....D£315	R. A. Wheadon (1972)
Victoria Coll., Jersey.................	1852	515	£1,212....D£252	M. H. Devenport (1967)

Republic of Ireland

Name of School	F'ded.	No. of Boys	Annual Fees D=Day Boys	Headmaster (With date of Appointment)
St. Columba's College, Rathfarnham, Dublin.....................	1843	210	£1,140 D£540–630	D. S. Gibbs, O.B.E. (Warden) (1974)

SOCIETY OF HEADMASTERS OF INDEPENDENT SCHOOLS
Hon. Secretary, S. M. Mischler, M.B.E., 8 Gwarnick Road, Truro, Cornwall

Name of School	F'ded.	No. of Boys	Annual Fees D=Day Boys	Headmaster (With date of Appointment)
Austin Friars, Carlisle (R.C.)...........	1951	305	£1,137....D£612	Rev. B. O'Rourke, O.S.A. (1973)
Bearwood Coll., Wokingham, Berks....	1827	335	£1,500..D£1,020	P. M. Cunningham (1963)
Belmont Abbey, Hereford (R.C.).......	1926	314	£1,230....D£720	J. M. Jabale, O.S.B. (1969)
Bembridge, Isle of Wight.............	1919	260	£1,290....D£780	R. L. Whitby, M.V.O. (1974)
Bentham Grammar, North Yorks......	1726	260†	£1,008....D£492	J. F. D. Hagen (1972)
Bethany Sch., Goudhurst, Kent........	1866	275	£1,362....D£909	C. A. H. Lanzer (1970)
Carmel College, Wallingford, Oxon....	1948	318†	£1,935..D£1,062	Rabbi J. Rosen (1971)

† Pupils.   * A Woodard Corporation School.

Name of School	F'ded.	No. of Boys	Annual Fees D=Day Boys	Headmaster (With date of Appointment)
Churcher's College, Petersfield, Hants...	1722	446	£894........Dnil	D. I. Brooks (1973)
Colston's, Bristol.....................	1710	290	£1,374....D£870	G. W. Searle (1975)
Cotton College, Oakamoor, Staffs.(R.C.)	1763	200	£990.....D£660	Rev. Mgr. T. J. Gavin (1967)
Fort Augustus School, Inverness-shire (R.C.)............................	1880	132†	£1,470....D£882	Rev. G. F. Davidson (1972)
Grenville College, Bideford, Devon*...	1954	331	£1,545....D£873	D. C. Powell-Price (1975)
Keil Sch., Dumbarton................	1915	200	£1,176....D£666	J. B. Widdowson (1976)
Kingham Hill School, Oxford.........	1886	220	£750...........	E. C. Cooper (1954)
King's School, Gloucester............	1541	450	£1,578....D£930	A. P. David (1969)
Milton Abbey Sch., nr. Blandford, D'set	1954	285	£1,500........	W. M. T. Holland (1969)
Oswestry, Salop.....................	1407	325†	£1,200....D£780	F. E. Gerstenberg (1974)
Pangbourne College, Berks...........	1917	340	£1,629..D£1,110	P. D. C. Points (1969)
Pierrepont School, Farnham, Surrey....	1947	280	£1,620..D£1,020	A. G. Hill (1962)
Rannoch School, Perthshire..........	1959	268	£1,275-1,395.....	P. T. MacLellan (1967)
Royal Russell Sch., Croydon, Surrey..	1853	500†	£1,626....D£945	S. Hopewell (1974)
Royal Wolverhampton Sch., Staffs....	1850	320	£1,401....D£963	P. G. C. Howard (1961)
Ruthin School, Clwyd...............	1574	250	£1,440....D£870	A. S. Hill (1967)
Ryde School, Isle of Wight..........	1921	475	£1,275....D£585	K. N. Symons (1966)
Scarborough College, Yorks..........	1896	345†	£1,590....D£882	R. W. Wilkinson (1974)
Seaford College, Petworth, Sussex.....	1884	440	£1,320........	Rev. C. E. Johnson (1944)
Shebbear College, Beaworthy, Devon..	1841	338	£1,197....D£549	G. W. Kingsnorth (1964)
Shiplake College, Henley, Oxon.......	1959	272	£1,695..D£1,230	J. D. Eggar, T.D. (1963)
Sidcot School, Winscombe, Somerset..	1808	340†	£1,470....D£960	R. N. Brayshaw (1957)
Stanbridge Earls School, Romsey......	1952	156†	£1,845..D£1,230	R. J. Gould (1959)
Truro Cathedral School, Cornwall.....	1549	233	£1,116....D£726	F. S. G. Pearson (Advocate)
Wells Cathedral Sch., Somerset.......	1180	600†	£1,320....D£747	A. K. Quilter (1964) [(1973)
Woodbridge Sch., Suffolk............	1662	480†	£1,161....D£636	A. F. Vyvyan-Robinson, R.D. (1976)

† Pupils. ★ A Woodard Corporation School. NOTE.—The Headmasters of Abbotsholme School, Bedales School, Lord Wandsworth College, Prior Park College, Rendcomb College, St. Edmund's College, St. George's College, Weybridge and Tettenhall College are also Members of the Society. Details of these schools are included in the list of Headmasters' Conference Schools.

PUBLIC SCHOOLS OVERSEAS

NOTE.—Headmasters of Schools marked (★) are Members of the *Headmasters' Conference*; marked (§) of the *Headmasters' Conference of Australia*.

Name of School	F'ded.	No. of Boys	Annual Fees D=Day Boys	Headmaster (With date of Appointment)
South America				
★Markham College, Lima, Peru.......	1046	1000	.........D£400	R. C. Pinchbeck, O.B.E. (1966)
Queen's Coll., Georgetown, Guyana..	1844	744†	...........Dnil	C. I. Trotz (1974)
★St. George's Coll., Quilmes, Argentina	1898	334	$150,000.D$75,000	C. G. Graham (1968)
India				
★Cathedral and John Connor School, Bombay........................	1860	1725	Rs.780-1,260.....	K. K. Jacob (1965)
★St. Joseph's Coll., Darjeeling........	1889	676	Rs.5,000..DRs.960	G. van Walleghem, S.J. (1973)
★St. Paul's, Darjeeling..............	1823	420	Rs.5,500.........	M. W. Cross (Rector) (1974)
★Doon Sch., Chand Bagh, Dehra Dun..	1935	513	Rs.4,000.........	E. J. Simeon (1971)
Scindia School, Gwalior.............	1897	660	Rs.3,500...DRs.75	S. P. Sahi (Principal) (1968)
Canada				
★Ashbury Coll., Ottawa.............	1891	370	$4,800....D$2,600	W. A. Joyce, D.S.O. (1966)
★Brentwood Coll., Sch., Vancouver....	1923	330	$4,750....D$1,850	W. T. Ross (1976)
Hillfield-Strathallan, Hamilton, Ont..	1901	404†	....D$2,065-2,560	M. B. Wansbrough (1969)
Lakefield Coll., Sch., Ontario..	1879	240	$5,175....D$2,300	J. J. M. Guest (1971)
Lower Canada Coll., Montreal......	1909	598	.........D$2,370	G. H. Merrill (1968)
Ridley Coll., St. Catherine's, Ont....	1889	506†	$5,250....D$2,550	R. A. Bradley (1971)
★St. Andrew's Coll., Aurora, Ont.....	1899	365	$5,500....D$3,025	T. A. Hockin, Ph.D. (1974)
Shawnigan Lake Sch., B.C..........	1916	220	$4,950....D$2,860	Rev. W. H. H. McClelland, (1976)
★Trinity Coll. Sch., Port Hope, Ont....	1865	340	$5,100....D$2,900	A. C. Scott (1962) [M.B.E. (1975)
★Upper Canada Coll., Toronto........	1829	900	$5,250....D$2,750	R. H. Sadleir (Principal) (1975)

† Pupils.

School	F'ded.	No. of Boys	Annual Fees D=Day Boys	Headmaster (*With date of appointment*)
Australia				
N.S.W.:				
*§The Armidale Sch., Armidale........	1894	385	$A2,370..D $A885	A. H. Cash (1962)
*§Barker Coll., Hornsby..............	1890	1190†	$A2,865.D $A1,425	T. J. McCaskill (1963)
*§Sydney C. of E. Gr. Sch., N. Sydney.	1889	1070	$A2,970.D $A1,485	B. H. Travers, O.B.E. (1959)
*§Cranbrook Sch., Sydney............	1918	1046	$A1,065...D $A505	M. Bishop (1962)
*§The King's School, Parramatta......	1831	876	$A3,270.D $A1,710	Rev. S. W. Kurrle (1965)
§Knox Gr. Sch., Wahroonga........	1924	1485	$A2,865.D $A1,395	I. W. Paterson, Ph.D. (1969)
§Newington Coll., Stanmore........	1863	1120	$A3,015 D $A1,515	A. J. Rae (1972)
§St. Aloysius Coll. (*R.C.*), Sydney....	1879	1017	.....D $A600–780	Rev. G. F. Jordan, S.J. (1974)
§St. Ignatius Coll. (*R.C.*), N.S.W. 2066	1880	932	$A2,439 D $A1,017	Rev. P. B. Quin, S.J. (1974)
§St. Joseph's Coll. (*R.C.*), Hunter's Hill	1881	832	$A1,920..........	Br. A. Dwyer (1970)
*Scots College, The, Sydney.........	1893	1070	$A2,802 D $A1,392	G. Wilson, M.C. (1966)
*§Sydney Gr. Sch...................	1854	1047	........D $A1,470	A. M. Mackerras (1969)
§Trinity Gr. Sch., Sydney...........	1913	709	$A3,255 D $A1,515	R. I. West (1975)
Victoria:				
§Ballarat and Clarendon College......	1864	830†	$A2,880 D $A1,530	R. M. Horner (1967)
*§Carey Baptist Gr. Sch., Kew........	1923	1240	........D $A1,755	G. L. Cramer (1965)
§Caulfield Gr. Sch..................	1881	906	$A3,099 D $A1,541	B. C. Lumsden (1965)
*§Geeling Coll., Geelong............	1861	889†	$A3,804 D $A1,794	S. P. Gebhardt (1976)
*§Geelong C. of E. Gr. Sch., Corio	1855	1650†	$A3,774 D $A1,743	Hon. C. D. Fisher (1974)
*§Haileybury Coll., E. Brighton	1892	1270	$A2,835 D $A1,635	A. M. H. Aikman (1974)
§Ivanhoe Gr. Sch..................	1915	900	$A1,620 D $A1,455	Rev. C. E. A. Sligo (1975)
*§Melbourne, C. of E. Gr. Sch........	1859	1521	$A3,960 D $A1,983	N. A. H. Creese (1970)
*Scotch Coll., Hawthorn, Melbourne	1851	1882	$A3,621 D $A1,671	P. A. V. Roff (1975)
§Trinity Gr. Sch., Kew..............	1902	990	....D $A900–1,200	J. J. Leppitt (1959)
§Wesley Coll., Melbourne............	1865	1250	$A3.465 D $A1.815	D. H. Prest (1972)
§Xavier Coll. (*R.C.*), Melbourne......	1878	810	$A1,350 D $A1,170	Rev. P. Brennan, S.J. (1974)
Queensland:				
*§All Souls' and St. Gabriel's School, Charters Towers...................	1920	583	$A1,850..D $A750	Rev. R. W. Gregory (1972)
*Brisbane C. of E. Gr. Sch...........	1912	1462	$A2,460 D $A1,035	W. Hayward (1974)
§Brisbane Grammar Sch..............	1868	1170	$A2,397 D $A1,137	M. A. Howell (1964)
St. Joseph's Coll., Brisbane.........	1875	925	.........D $A450	Br. B. M. Buckley (1973)
§Toowoomba Gr. Sch..............	1815	562	$A1,920..D $A780	W. M. Dent (1970)
South Australia:				
§Sacred Heart Coll., Somerton Park...	1902	830	$A1,575..D $A525	Br. T. Orrell (1976)
*St. Peter's College, Adelaide.........	1847	1004	$A3,195 D $A1,695	Rev. J. S. C. Miller (1961)
*Prince Alfred Coll., Adelaide........	1869	910	$A2,940 D $A1,470	G. B. Bean (1970)
§Pulteney Gr. Sch., Adelaide.........	1847	711	........D $A1,410	J. A. Mackinnon (1973)
*§Scotch College, Adelaide............	1919	819†	$A3,420 D $A1,740	W. M. Miles (1975)
Western Australia:				
*§Christ Church Gr. Sch., Claremont...	1910	831	$A2,559 D $A1,335	P. M. Moyes (1951)
*§Guildford C. of E. Gr. Sch..........	1896	681	$A2,565 D $A1,320	D. A. Lawe-Davies (1957)
*§Hale School, Wembley Downs......	1858	850	$A2,625 D $A1,380	K. G. Tregonning (1967)
*Scotch Coll., Swanbourne............	1897	864	$A2,840 D $A1,580	W. R. Dickinson (1972)
§Wesley Coll., Perth................	1923	773	$A2,580 D $A1,350	C. A. Homer (1965)
Tasmania:				
§Launceston Church Gr. Sch.........	1846	331	$A2,900 D $A1,750	R. P. Hutchings (1971)
*§Hutchins Sch., Hobart..............	1846	620	$A2,650 D $A1,350	Rev. D. B. Clarke (1971)
§Scotch College, Launceston.........	1901	300†	$A875....D $A480	J. P. Herbert (1972)
New Zealand				
Auckland Gr. Sch..................	1869	1440	$NZ930......Dnil	D. J. Graham (1973)
King's Coll., Otahuhu..............	1896	680	$NZ1,815	I. P. Campbell (1973)
			D $NZ960	
*Christchurch Boys' High..............	1881	1140	$NZ750...$NZ10	I. D. Leggat (1976

School	F'ded.	No. of Boys	Annual Fees See note (a) D=Day Boys	Headmaster (With date of appointment)
*Christ's Coll., Christchurch.........	1850	593	$NZ1,866 D$NZ873	A. M. Brough (1971)
Nelson College, Nelson.............	1856	930	$NZ1,000 D$NZ20	E. J. Brewster (1970)
New Plymouth Boys' High School....	1882	920	$NZ945......Dnil	G. R. Cramond (1972)
*St. Andrew's Coll., Christchurch......	1916	735	$NZ1,600 D$NZ750	I. T. Galloway, C.B.E., E.D. (1962)
*Timaru High Sch...............	1880	653	$NZ750......Dnil	R. J. Welch (1965)
*Waitaki Boys' High Sch., Oamaru....	1883	910	$NZ905......Dnil	J. H. Donaldson (1961)
*Wanganui Collegiate...............	1854	569	$NZ1,860 D$NZ780	T. U. Wells (1960)
Wellington Coll., Wellington........	1867	1068	$NZ900......Dnil	S. H. W. Hill (1963)
South Africa				
*St. Andrew's Coll., Grahamstown.....	1855	501	R1,995.....DR837	E. B. Norton (1972)
*Diocesan Coll., Rondebosch..........	1849	420	R1,640.....DR968	A. W. H. Mallett (1964)
St. John's Coll., Johannesburg........	1898	437	R1,950...DR1,089	J. J. Breitenbach (1971)
*Hilton College, Natal...........	1872	422	R1,850...........	R. G. Slater (1967)
*Michaelhouse, Balgowan, Natal.......	1896	425	R1,800...........	R. F. Pennington (Rector) (1969)
Rhodesia				
*Falcon College, Essexvale...........	1954	360	$1,305...........	D. E. Turner (1962)
*Peterhouse, Marandellas.............	1955	380	$1,500...........	B. R. Fieldsend (1968)
*St. George's College, Salisbury.......	1896	680	$900.......D$460	Rev. H. Wardale, S.J. (1975)
Hong Kong				
St. Stephen's College...............	1903	620	$HK5,050 D$HK600	L. J. P. Yip (1974)
Kenya				
Alliance High Sch., Kikuyu..........	1926	594	KSh.1,100/-.......	E. M. Wangai (1975)
Lenana School, Nairobi.............	1949	720	KSh.2,100/- DKSh.1,300	A. S. Maina (1973)
West Indies				
*Harrison College, Barbados..........	1729	650	.......D$BDS18	A. G. Williams (1965)
Lodge School, St. John, Barbados.....	1721	570	$BDS1,578 D$BDS18	C. E. A. Smith (1972)
*Munro College, Jamaica.............	1856	500	nil...........Dnil	R. B. Roper (1955)
Malta				
St. Edward's College, Cottonera......	1929	411	£M165...D£M40	A. Cachia-Carnana (1975)

PRINCIPAL GIRLS' SCHOOLS

NOTES:—(a) "Annual Fees" represents average amount payable annually, *exclusive* of fees for optional subjects. (b) "Headmistress." In certain schools other titles prevail, *e.g.*, St. Paul's, "High Mistress." (c) Headmaster.

Name of School	F'ded.	No. of Girls	Annual Fees See note (a) D=Day Girls	Headmistress See notes (b) and (c)
Abbey School, Malvern Wells........	1880	232	£1,710....D£885	(c) A. P. C. Pollard (1975)
Abbey School, Reading..............	1887	610	.........D£474	S. M. Hardcastle (1960)
Abbots Hill, Hemel Hempstead........	1912	207	£1,659...D£1,032	Mrs. J. E. Anderson (1966)
The Alice Ottley School, Worcester....	1883	680	£436.....D£231	E. D. Millest (1964)
All Hallows, Ditchingham, Bungay, Suffolk......................	1864	165	£403.....D£240	D. M. Forster (1968)
Ashford, Middlesex, St. David's......	1716	290	£1,257....D£840	J. M. Gardner (1973)
Ashford Sch. for Girls, Kent..........	1910	750	£1,281....D£711	S. M. Thompson (1972)
Badminton School, Bristol...........	1858	340	£1,512....D£756	M. F. C. Harvey (1969)
Bath, Royal School for Daughters of Officers of the Army...............	1864	415	£1,395....D£810	M. Campbell (1968)
Bedford High School...............	1882	718	£1,239....D£618	Mrs. M. E. A. Kaye (1976)
Bedford, Dame Alice Harpur Sch......	1882	920	£618.....D£543	S. M. Morse (1970)
Bedgebury Park, Goudhurst, Cranbrook	1920	205	£1,455..........	J. M. Nixon (1964)
Benenden, Kent....................	1923	335	£1,632..........	J. R. Allen (1976)
Berkhamsted Sch. for Girls, Herts.....	1888	600	£1,353....D£549	M. R. Bateman (1971)
Bishop's Stortford, Herts. and Essex High School....................	1909	600	.............Dnil	J. Hammersley (1965)
Blackpool, Elmslie Girls' Sch..........	1918	520	D=......D£435	E. L. Oldham (1952)
Bolton School, Lancs................	1954	650	.........D£597	M. D. Higginson (1954)
Bradford Girls' Gr. Sch............	1875	605	......D£420-531	R. M. Gleave (1976)

School	F'ded.	No. of Girls	Annual Fees (See note (a)) D=Day Girls	Headmistress See notes (b) and (c)
Bridlington High Sch.	1905	610	£612........Dnil	D. I. Matthews (1956)
Bruton Sch. for Girls, Som.	1900	585	£1,185 ..D £687	D. F. Cumberlege (1964)
Burgess Hill, Sussex	1906	324	£1,050 ...D £675	Mrs. D. E. Harford (1971)
Casterton Sch., Kirkby Lonsdale, Cumbria	1823	316	£1,320...D £723	(c) T. S. Penny (1973)
Charters Towers, Bexhill on Sea, Sussex	1929	272	£460......D £200	D. L. Howe (1971)
Chatham, Gr. Sch. for Girls	1907	550	...........Dnil	Mrs. L. A. Goulding (1975)
Chelmsford County High Sch.	1907	690	...........Dnil	P. Pattison (1961)
Cheltenham Ladies' College	1853	846	£1,617...D £990	M. G. Hampshire (*Principal*)
Christ's Hospital, Hertford	1552	295	Various.........	E. M. Tucker (1972) [(1964)
Church Schools Company (29 Euston Road, N.W.1.):				
Eothen, Caterham, Surrey	1892	300	..........D £750	D. C. Raine (1973)
Guildford High School	1887	521	....D £351–693	M. J. Harley-Mason (1969)
Southampton, Atherley Sch.	1926	450	..........D £645	A. Ward (1973)
Sunderland Church High Sch.	1884	360	..........D £200	J. L. Wisbach (1957)
Surbiton High Sch.	1884	477	..........D £645	E. M. Kobrak (1964)
York College	1908	320	....D £360–699	M. G. Drury (1967)
Clarendon School, Abergele	1898	205	£1,380...D £870	S. Haughton (1965)
Clifton High Sch. for Girls	1877	720	£1,461...D £681	P. M. Stringer (1965)
Cobham Hall, Kent	1962	290	£1,620..D £1,020	J. L. Hanson (1972)
Colston's Girls' Sch., Bristol	1891	670	..........D £198	A. M. S. Dunn (1954)
Commonweal Lodge, Purley, Surrey	1916	240	....D £121–289	J. M. Blunden (1966)
Cranborne Chase Sch., Tisbury, Wilts.	1946	160	£1,770.........	(c) M. D. Neal (1969)
Croft House Sch., Shillingstone, Dorset	1941	220	£1,422...D £948	Mr. & Mrs. E. H. Warley
Croham Hurst, South Croydon, Surrey	1899	500	....D £270–675	D. J. Seward (1970) [(1971)
Derby High School	1892	436	..........D £193	D. M. Hatch (1948)
Downe House, Cold Ash, Newbury	1907	274	£500......D £350	Mrs. P. M. Wilson (1967)
Durham High School	1884	400	..........D £350	C. I. Salter (1958)
Edgbaston C. of E. College	1886	510	....D £294–540	M. E. Joice (1967)
Edgehill Coll., Bideford, N. Devon	1884	496	£1,314...D £642	(c) J. T. Shepherd (1976)
Exeter, Maynard's Girls' Sch.	1658	584	..........D £561	J. M. Bradley (1963)
Farnborough Hill, Hants.	1889	515	£1,110...D £675	Sr. M. Dawson (1971)
Farringtons School, Chislehurst	1911	450	£1,134...D £750	Mrs. F. V. Hatton (1973)
Felixstowe College, Suffolk	1929	350	£1,530...D £930	E. M. Manners, T.D. (1967)
Girls' Public Day School Trust (26 Queen Anne's Gate, Westminster, S.W.1.):				
Bath High	1875	550	£1,152....D £624	D. J. Chapman (1969)
Birkenhead High	1901	816	..........D £624	F. Kellett (1971)
Blackheath High	1880	564	..........D £645	F. Abraham (1962)
Brighton and Hove High	1876	621	£1,233....D £624	J. P. Turner (1969)
Bromley High	1883	634	..........D £645	P. M. F. Reid (1971)
Croydon High	1874	1102	..........D £645	A. M. McMaster (1975)
Ipswich High	1878	580	..........D £624	P. M. Hayworth (1971)
Liverpool (Belvedere)	1880	569	..........D £624	S. Downs (1972)
Newcastle (Central) High	1895	776	..........D £624	C. Russell (1962)
Norwich High	1875	732	..........D £624	R. H. Standeven (1976)
Nottingham High	1875	947	..........D £624	L. L. Lewenz (1967)
Notting Hill and Ealing High	1873	626	..........D £645	M. J. Percy (1974)
Oxford High	1875	499	£1,146...D £624	E. H. Kaye (1972)
Portsmouth High	1882	585	..........D £624	M. L. Clarke (1968)
Putney High	1893	718	..........D £645	R. Smith (1963)
Sheffield High	1878	595	..........D £624	M. C. Lutz (1959)
Shrewsbury High	1885	580	..........D £624	M. Crane (1963)
South Hampstead High	1876	614	..........D £645	Mrs. D. Burgess (1975)
Streatham Hill and Clapham High	1887	517	..........D £645	Mrs. N. Silver (1973)
Sutton High	1884	917	..........D £645	I. A. Wulff (1974)
Sydenham High	1887	631	..........D £645	M. Hamilton (1966)
Wimbledon High	1880	669	..........D £645	Mrs. A. Piper (1962)
Godolphin, Salisbury	1726	300	£1,605....D £960	V. M. Fraser (1968)
Gravesend Sch. for Girls	1926	600	...........Dnil	Mrs. M. H. Dell (1971)
Gt. Crosby, Lancs., Seafield Gr. Sch., Sacred Heart of Mary (R.C.)	1908	658	..........D £339	Sr. B. Browne (1975)
Greenacre, Banstead, Surrey	1933	360	£1,335....D £705	G. W. Steele (1962)
Hampden House Sch., Gt. Missenden	1864	120	£1,320...D £705	Mrs. E. A. Scott (1973)
Harrogate College	1893	420	£1,560...D £705	Mrs. J. C. Lawrance (1974)
Haslemere, Royal Naval School	1840	300	£1,620..D £1,080	Mrs. D. M. Otter (1970)
Headington Sch., Oxford	1915	519	£468.....D £240	P. A. Dunn (1959)
Howell's, Denbigh	1857	420	£1,665..D £1,065	J. Sadler (1969)
Howell's Llandaff	1860	665	£1,463....D £650	M. Ll. Lewis (1941)

School	F'ded.	No. of Girls	Annual Fees See note (a) D=Day Girls	Headmistress See notes (b) and (c)
Hunmanby Hall, Yorks..............	1928	400	£1,323....D£870	M. Bray (1967)
King Edward VI High School, B'ham..	1883	530	.........D£546	J. R. F. Wilks (1965)
The King's High School for Girls, Warwick......................	1879	590	.........D£582	M. Leahy (1970)
Lady Eleanor Holles, Hampton, Middx.	1710	720	.....D£225-245	M. C. Smalley (1974)
Leamington, Kingsley Sch.............	1884	380	£1,050-1,185 D£480-705	N. K. Jones (1961)
Leeds, Girls' High....................	1876	550	.........D£650	E. M. Smithies (1976)
Lillesden Sch., Hawkhurst, Kent......	1901	180	£1,455...D£750	Mrs. M. Hill (1974)
Liverpool, Huyton College............	1894	420	£1,485....D£855	Mrs. E. M. Rees (1971)
Liverpool, Everton Valley, Notre Dame Collegiate (R.C.)..................	1872	570	.........D£480	Sr. R. J. Fleming, S.N.D. (1972)
London*:				
C. E. Brooke Sch., Langton Rd., S.W.9..........................	1898	360	............Dnil	C. F. A. Frazer (1970)
Camden, Sandall Rd., N.W.5.......	1870	720	............Dnil	Mrs. C. M. Handley (1971)
Channing Sch., Highgate, N.6.......	1878	390	.....D£444-606	E. M. Saunders (1964)
City of London, Barbican, E.C.2......	1894	560	.........D£786	L. E. Mackie (1972)
Godolphin and Latymer, W.6........	1905	680	............Dnil	B. F. Dean (1974)
Haberdashers' Aske's, Elstree........	1875	800	.........D£678	Mrs. S. Wiltshire (1974)
Haberdashers' Aske's, Hatcham, S.E.14	1876	600	............Dnil	J. A. Kirby (1958)
Francis Holland, Clarence Gate, N.W.1...........................	1878	265	.........D£660	A. E. Holt (1974)
Francis Holland, Graham Terr., S.W.1.	1878	300	.........D£230	R. Colvile (1965)
James Allen's Girls', Dulwich, S.E.22.	1741	560	.........D£645	I. Prissian (1969)
Lady Margaret, Parsons Green, S.W.6.	1917	404	............Dnil	A. E. Cavendish (1971)
Mary Datchelor, Camberwell Green, S.E.5...........................	1877	640	............Dnil	E. B. Godwin
North London Collegiate, Canons, Edgware......................	1850	850	.........D£675	M. M. N. McLauchlan (1965)
Queen's College, Harley St., W.1.....	1848	310	.........D£780	Mrs. S. C. P. Fierz (1964)
St. Angela's, Ursuline Convent Sch., Forest Gate, E.7. (R.C.)..........	1862	900	............Dnil	M. M. Walsh, O.S.U. (1971)
St. Paul's Girls' Sch., Brook Grn., W.6.	1904	535	.........D£870	Mrs. H. Brigstocke (1974)
Loughborough High Sch., Leics.......	1850	580	£1,059...D£594	P. J. Hadley (1963)
Loughton County High School........	1906	610	............Dnil	Mrs. W. J. Delchar (1972)
Malvern Girls' College..............	1893	500	£1,692..D£1,128	V. M. H. Owen (1968)
Manchester High School for Girls......	1874	1000	.........D£378	M. N. Blake (1975)
Merchant Taylors', Gt. Crosby........	1888	600	.........D£609	M. E. Walsh (1963)
Monmouth School for Girls..........	1892	506	£990....D£525	A. Page (1960)
Newcastle upon Tyne Church High Sch.	1885	600	.........D£540	P. E. Davies (1974)
North Foreland Lodge, Sherfield-on-Loddon, Hants....................	1909	160	£1,500.........	D. R. K. Irvine (1967)
Northwood Coll., Northwood, Middx..	1878	462	£1,089-1,215 £312-645	M. D. Hillyer-Cole (1966)
Oakdene, Beaconsfield..............	1911	490	£915.....D£600	A. J. Havard (1959)
Orme Girls' Sch., Newcastle under Lyme	1876	619	............Dnil	Mrs. W. M. G. Buxton (1969)
Overstone Sch., Northampton........	1929	170	£450....D£292	(c) Col. P. B. Clarke, C.B.E.
Pate's Gr. Sch., Cheltenham.........	1905	800	............Dnil	M. M. Moon (1971) [(1974)
Perse Sch. for Girls, Cambridge.......	1881	500	.........D£540	C. M. Bedson (1967)
Plymouth, Notre Dame High (R.C.)...	1860	410	.........D£415	Sr. V. Henderson, S.N.D. (1968)
Polam Hall, Darlington..............	1888	500	£1,311...D£639	Mrs. S. M. Owen (1975)
Preston, Winckley Sq. Convent (R.C.)..	1908	554	.........D£525	Sr. C. Walsh (1968)
Princess Helena Coll., Temple Dinsley, Hitchin, Herts...................	1820	180	£1,482....D£942	(c) D. Clarke, Ph.D. (1971)
Queen Anne's, Caversham............	1894	343	£1,380...D£750	M. J. Challis (1958)
Queen Ethelburga's, Harrogate‡......	1912	218	£1,647...D£990	(c) J. E. H. Kingdon (1973)
Queen Margaret's, Escrick Park, York‡.	1901	270	£1,545...D£900	B. D. Snape (1960)
Queen Mary, Lytham................	1930	850	.........D£585	J. Charlton (1970)
Queen's School, Chester.............	1878	425	.........D£630	M. Farra (1973)
Queenswood, Hatfield, Herts.........	1894	425	£1,722.........	M. C. Ritchie (1972)
Redland High School, Bristol.........	1882	600	.........D£579	W. M. Hume (1969)
The Red Maid's, Bristol..............	1634	400	£1,134....D£576	D. D. Dakin (1960)
Rochester Gr. Sch., Kent.............	1888	700	............Dnil	B. J. Trollope (1973)
Roedean, Brighton...................	1885	435	£1,670.........	(c) J. M. Hunt (1971)
Rosemead, Littlehampton............	1919	259	£420....D£285	Mrs. N. R. Tobenhouse (1969)
Rye St. Anthony, Oxford.............	1930	231	£1,200....D£600	P. M. Sumpter (1976)
St. Albans High School, Herts........	1889	637	.........D£540	Mrs. T. D. Lucey (1966)

★ See also: Girls' Public Day School Trust, and Church Schools Company.
‡ A Woodard Corporation School.

School	F'ded	No. of Girls	Annual Fees See note (a) D=Day Girls	Headmistress See notes (b) and (c)
St. Anne's School, Windermere........	1863	350	£1,305....D£816	(c) C. M. G. R. Jenkins (1972)
St. Clare, Polwithen, Penzance‡........	1885	200	£1,443....D£897	M. M. Coney (1969)
St. Dominic's High Sch., Stoke-on-Trent (R.C.)......................	1857	760	.........D£543	Sr. M. E. House, O.P. (1970)
St. Elphin's, Darley Dale, Matlock.....	1844	480	£1,194....D£645	A. L. Mayhew (1975)
St. Felix, Southwold, Suffolk..........	1897	415	£1,416....D£810	M. Oakeley (1958)
St. Helen's, Northwood..............	1899	723	£1,167–1,323 D£423–768	J. D. Leader (1966)
St. James's School, West Malvern......	1896	200	£588.........	R. R. Braithwaite (1969)
St. Joseph's Coll., Bradford (R.C.).....	1906	1030	£681.....D£441	Sr. W. M. Daly, C.P. (1965)
St. Margaret's, Bushey, Herts.........	1749	340	£1,410....D£840	B. Scatchard (1965)
St. Mary & St. Anne, Abbots Bromley‡	1874	563	£1,380....D£920	M. E. Roch (1953)
St. Mary Sch., Baldslow, St. Leonard's..	1913	215	£1,200....D£600	Sr. B. Allen, C.H.F. (1958)
St. Mary's, Calne, Wilts..............	1873	270	£1,410....D£771	Mrs. J. D. Bailey (1972)
St. Mary's Convent, Cambridge (R.C.).	1898	600	£350....D£185	Sr. M. D. Harris (1972)
St. Mary's Hall, Brighton.............	1836	340	£467....D£310	Mrs. E. D. Leslie (1973)
St. Mary's Sch., Wantage, Oxon.......	1873	265	£1,620.........	Mrs. E. M. Calver (1975)
St. Michael's, Burton Park, Petworth‡..	1844	290	£1,665..D£1,110	F. E. H. Davies (1973)
St. Stephen's College, Broadstairs......	1867	266	£515....D£320	B. Seymour (1974)
Salford, Adelphi House (R.C.).........	1852	750	.........D£510	Sr. N. P. Conlan, F.C.J. (1973)
Stamford High Sch., Lincs.............	1876	750	£1,422....D£594	M. L. Medcalf (1968)
Stonar, Atworth, Melksham, Wilts......	1921	390	£1,407....D£768	F. D. Denmark (1962)
Stover Sch., Newton Abbot...........	1932	220	£1,215....D£714	C. A. Smith (1969)
Talbot Heath Sch., Bournemouth......	1886	550	£1,069....D£582	C. E. Austin-Smith (1976)
Tormead, Cranley Road, Guildford....	1905	460	£1,380....D£690	M. C. Shackleton (1959)
Truro High School..................	1880	530	£1,212....D£642	E. J. Davies (1971)
Tudor Hall, Wykham Park, Banbury..	1850	196	£1,455....D£885	Mrs. M. R. Blyth (1969)
Uplands School, Sandecotes, Poole.....	1903	260	.........D£732	M. P. Poots (1971)
Upper Chine, Shanklin, I.O.W........	1799	356	£1,060....D£710	P. M. Gifford (1955)
Wadhurst College..................	1930	270	£1,194....D£789	D. Swatman (1972)
Walthamstow Hall, Sevenoaks, Kent...	1838	425	£1,257....D£624	E. B. Davies, M.B.E. (1970)
Wentworth Milton Mt., Bournemouth..	1871	300	£1,125....D£705	N. A. E. Hibbert (1961)
Westonbirt, Tetbury, Glos.............	1928	293	£1,770..D£1,170	M. Newton (1965)
Wycombe Abbey, Bucks..............	1896	460	£1,775.........	P. M. Lancaster (1974)
York, The Mount School.............	1785	178	£1,440....D£960	J. Blake (1960)
Scotland				
Craigholme, Glasgow.................	1894	640	.........D£393	I. W. McNeillie (1975)
Laurel Bank, Glasgow...............	1903	560	....D£307–463	A. J. B. Sloan (1968)
Mary Erskine, Edinburgh............	1694	1060	....D£390–600	J. Thow (1967)
Morrison's Academy, Crieff...........	1861	520	£1,125....D£465	A. D. Mackinnon (1972)
Park Sch., 25 Lynedoch St., Glasgow...	1879	525	....D£360–459	J. Rutherford (1974)
St. Bride's, Helensburgh.............	1895	370	£1,236....D£459	F. Orr (1976)
St. Columba's, Kilmacolm............	1897	500	....D£372–477	Mrs. S. M. Caldwell (1976)
St. Denis', Edinburgh...............	1858	473	£440.....D£210	Mrs. N. E. Law (1971)
St. George's, Garscube Terr., Edinburgh	1888	826	£1,170–1,299 D£360–639	Mrs. J. L. Clanchy (1976)
St. Leonard's, St. Andrews, Fife........	1877	510	£1,680....D£810	M. Hamilton (1970)
Isle of Man, Channel Islands				
Buchan Sch., Castletown, I.O.M.......	1875	225	£1,194....D£507	Mrs. J. M. Watkin (1961)
Jersey College for Girls, Jersey.........	1880	830	.........D£252	Mrs. E. M. Pullin (1974)

‡ A Woodard Corporation School.

EVENTS OF THE YEAR (SEPT. 16, 1975—SEPT. 15, 1976)

THE ROYAL HOUSE

(1975) Sept. 24. Princess Margaret visited R.A.F. Bruggen. **30.** The Duke of Edinburgh arrived back from Morocco.

Oct. 6. It was announced the Queen had approved changes to start in 1976, to the Queen's Award to Industry which would be replaced by two separate awards, the Queen's Award for Export Achievement and the Queen's Award for Technological Achievement. **11.** The Queen Mother visited Perth and opened Queen's Barracks, the new TAVR Centre. **13.** The Queen arrived at Buckingham Palace. **14.** The Queen Mother visited H.M.S. Ark Royal at sea in the Moray Firth. Princess Margaret opened the new school for physically handicapped children at New Mossford, Barkingside. **24.** The Duke of Edinburgh travelled to Amsterdam to attend the congress on the European Architecural Heritage organised by the Council of Europe. **30.** Princess Anne visted Westonbirt School, Tetbury, and opened new buildings and in the evening opened the Roses Theatre, Tewkesbury. **31.** The Queen with the Duke of Edinburgh attended dinner in the Officers' Mess at H.Q. Strike Command, R.A.F. High Wycombe, to mark the golden jubilee of the Royal Observer Corps..

Nov. 3. The Queen and the Duke of Edinburgh accompanied by Prince Andrew arrived at Aberdeen in the royal train and drove to the Dyce office of British Petroleum Development Ltd. The Queen subsequently inaugurated oil production from the B.P. Forties Field and after lunch flew back to London. The Duke flew to Germany to visit units of British Army of the Rhine and R.A.F. Germany. **4.** The Prince of Wales and Princess Anne attended the 200th anniversary dinner of the Royal Thames Yacht Club at Guildhall. **6.** The Duke of Edinburgh attended the centenary dinner of the Royal Yachting Association. **7.** The Queen drove to Bangor Cathedral and attended a thanksgiving service in celebration of the 1,450th anniversary of the first Christian settlement by St. Deiniol on the site of the present building. **9.** The Queen and the Duke of Edinburgh with the Prince of Wales laid wreaths at the Cenotaph on Remembrance Day. **10.** The Queen with the Duke of Edinburgh attended a Royal variety performance at the London Palladium. The Queen Mother visited Merchant Taylors' School at Northwood to open the new teaching block and music room. **11.** The Queen Mother laid the foundation stone of the Malcolm Gavin Hall of Residence, Chelsea College, on the Springfield site, Wandsworth. **18.** The President of Tanzania (Mr. Julius Nyerere) arrived in London on a State visit. The Queen and the Duke of Edinburgh gave a State banquet at Buckingham Palace in honour of the President, which was attended by members of the Royal family. **19.** The Queen, accompanied by the Duke of Edinburgh, the Prince of Wales, Princess Anne and Capt. Mark Phillips, went in State to open the session of Parliament. The Duke of Edinburgh attended the 60th anniversary dinner of the Gallipoli Association at the Café Royal. **20.** The Queen and the Duke of Edinburgh and the Queen Mother were entertained at a banquet by President Nyerere at Claridge's. **21.** President Nyerere left Buckingham Palace at the end of his visit to the Queen and the Duke of Edinburgh. The Queen flew to R.A.F. Bentwaters, Suffolk and drove to the new Post Office Research Centre at Martlesham, Woodbridge, to open it. **24.** The Queen and Duke of Edinburgh were present at a reception given by the

Building Societies Association at Guildhall to mark the 200th anniversary of the movement. The Prince of Wales was present at the 50th anniversary dinner of the Cambridge and Oxford University Air Squadron at the Royal Hospital, Chelsea. **25.** The Duke of Edinburgh visited Student Centre House, Edinburgh and opened the reconstructed north east wing of the Royal Scottish Museum. **26.** The Duke of Edinburgh drove to Glasgow Stock Exchange and later visited other schemes in connection with European Architectural Heritage Year. **27.** The Queen was represented by the Duke of Edinburgh at the ceremonies marking the accession of King Juan Carlos I in Madrid.

Dec. 3. The Queen and Duke of Edinburgh visited the Royal Smithfield Show at Earls Court. The Duke was present at lunch at the Punch Table and later gave a reception at Buckingham Palace for potential and newly-commissioned officers of the Grenadier Guards, being present at the 4th Bn. Grenadier Guards' dinner later at Brooks's, St. James' Street. The Prince of Wales attended the 50th anniversary dinner of the Royal Ocean Racing Club at Grosvenor House. Princess Anne named and launched H.M.A.S. *Otama* at Greenock. **4.** The Prime Minister told the Commons when giving second reading of the Civil List Bill, that the Queen's offer to take over responsibilities for payments to four members of the Royal family—Duke of Kent, Princess Alexandra, Duke of Gloucester, and Princess Alice, Countess of Athlone—from next year had been accepted by the Government. Princess Anne opened the Lion Yard Redevelopment Complex at Cambridge and later the Kelsey Kerridge sports hall. **5.** The Queen visited the Royal British Legion village at Maidstone to mark its 50th anniversary. **7.** The Duke of Edinburgh, President of the Federation Equestre Internationale, left for Brussels to attend meetings of the Bureau of the Federation and the ordinary general assembly. The Queen Mother was present at a royal variety gala at the Victoria Palace in aid of the Injured Jockeys Fund. **9.** The Queen attended a poetry reading in Skinners' Hall to celebrate 150th anniversary of Royal Society of Literature. **17.** Princess Anne and Capt. Mark Phillips were present at the opening night of the Olympic show jumping championships in aid of the British Equestrian Olympic Fund at Olympia. **18.** The Prime Minister in a Parliamentary written reply announced the programme approved by the Queen of the celebrations during the summer of 1977 to mark the 25th anniversary of her accession to the throne. **23.** The Queen and the Duke of Edinburgh arrived at Windsor Castle. **25.** The Queen delivered her usual televised Christmas Day message to the Commonwealth, which was recorded.

(1976) Jan. 1. The Duke of Edinburgh opened the International Boat Show at Earls Court. **21.** The Duke of Kent left Heathrow Airport, London, on the inaugural flight of British Airways *Concorde* to Bahrain.

Feb. 2. The Queen and Duke of Edinburgh visited the National Exhibition Centre at Birmingham, the Queen declaring it open, and both later toured the International Spring Fair. **9.** The Prince of Wales was piped aboard the mine-hunter H.M.S. *Bronington* at Rosyth when he took up his first command. **12.** The Queen visited the Union Jack Club, Waterloo, and declared open the new building. **18.** The Queen with the Duke of Edinburgh attended the annual dinner of the Inns of Court and the Bar at the Middle Temple Hall. The Duke of Edinburgh visited the Royal Veterinary College, and the College field station at Potters

Bar. **19.** The Duke of Edinburgh presided at a conference at St. James's Palace to close the European Architectural Heritage Year. **20.** The Duke of Edinburgh visited Rosyth Dockyard and H.M.S. *Bronington* where he was received by the Prince of Wales. Princess Anne visited the municipal buildings, Aberavon, and opened the new shopping centre at Port Talbot. **24.** The Queen Mother opened the biology complex at Queen Mary College, London University. **26.** The Queen and the Duke of Edinburgh visited the newspaper industry in London and lunched with the Chairman and members of the Newspaper Publishers' Association in the Press Centre. **27.** Princess Anne was admitted to the freedom of the City of London at Guildhall, being accompanied by Capt. Mark Phillips, and both were entertained at lunch by the Lord Mayor, the Lady Mayoress, and Corporation at Mansion House.

Mar. 4. The Duke of Edinburgh opened the National Playing Fields Association's new offices in Ovington Square. He also attended a festival of music, ancient and modern, in Westminster Cathedral in aid of the Cathedral appeal fund. **5.** The Queen and Duke of Edinburgh visited Oxford. At the County Hall, the Queen formally opened the building. After visiting the Radcliffe Science Library, they arrived at New College. They later visited Oriel College and in the evening dined with the Dean of Christ Church and then attended a reception. **8.** Princess Anne attended a concert given by the Boston Symphony Orchestra at Royal Festival Hall. Princess Margaret attended a special preview of the 1976 Daily Mail Ideal Home Exhibition at Olympia. The Queen Mother, recovering from influenza, cancelled two engagements for the week. **17.** The Queen Mother attended the Irish Guards' St. Patrick's Day parade at the Guards Depot, Pirbright. **18.** The Duke of Edinburgh visited the Royal Navy at Portsmouth and embarked in H.M.S. *Sheffield* and H.M.S. *Antrim* before visiting the dockyard workshops and new developments. Princess Anne visited Hall Russell's shipyard, Aberdeen, and launched H.M.S. *Jersey.* **19.** A statement issued from Kensington Palace said: " Princess Margaret and the Earl of Snowdon have mutually agreed to live apart. The Princess will carry out her public duties and functions unaccompanied by Lord Snowdon. There are no plans for divorce proceedings." Accompanied by Princess Alexandra and Mr. Angus Ogilvy, the Queen Mother was present at the royal film performance in aid of the Cinema and T.V. Benevolent Fund at the Odeon Theatre, Leicester Square. **25.** The Queen Mother opened the new wing of Brinsworth House, the Entertainment Artistes' Benevolent Fund's home at Twickenham. **26.** The Queen and the Duke of Edinburgh visited the Royal Signals and Radar Establishment at Malvern. **31.** The Queen and Duke of Edinburgh were present at the inauguration by Princess Alice, Duchess of Gloucester, of the exhibition, " Soldier Royal," at the Imperial War Museum.

Apr. I. The Queen appointed four new members of the Order of Merit—Mr. Harold Macmillan, Lord Hinton of Bankside, Lord Clark and Sir Ronald Syme. The Queen was represented by the Duke of Edinburgh at the funeral of Field Marshal Viscount Montgomery of Alamein at St. George's Chapel, Windsor Castle. **2.** The Queen Mother opened the new buildings at the Royal School for Deaf Children, Margate. **8.** The Queen inaugurated the World of Islam Festival by opening the Arts of Islam exhibition at the Hayward Gallery. **13.** The confirmation of Prince Andrew, son of the Queen and Duke of Edinburgh, and Viscount

Linley, son of Princess Margaret and Earl of Snowdon, took place in St. George's Chapel, Windsor Castle. **14.** The Queen opened the 1776 exhibition at the National Maritime Museum, Greenwich, to mark the bicentenary of the American War of Independence. **15.** Royal Maundy ceremony was held for the first time in Hereford Cathedral, where the Queen made presentations to 100 elderly men and women. **19.** Celebrations to mark the Queen's 50th birthday next day began at Windsor Castle with a dinner party for 60 members of the Royal family and close friends who were joined by 500 guests for a ball in the Queen's ballroom. **21.** Princess Anne was knocked unconscious and sustained a hairline crack of the vertebra in a fall when competing in the Portman Horse Trials near Blandford, Dorset, where she was riding the Queen's horse Candlewick. She was admitted to Poole General Hospital, Dorset, and on April 22 was transferred to King Edward VII Hospital for Officers, London. Princess Anne left hospital on April 25 and returned to her Sandhurst home. **22.** Buckingham Palace announced that Mr. Harold Wilson was made a Knight Companion of the Order of the Garter and that the Duke of Grafton was also appointed to the Order. **26.** The Queen Mother was present at a performance of Bach's B Minor Mass at the Royal Albert Hall to mark the centenary of the Bach Choir. **29.** Princess Margaret left Heathrow to visit Morocco and Tunisia.

May 3. The Queen Mother was present at the Royal Festival Hall silver jubilee celebrations. **4.** The President of Brazil and Senhora Geisel arrived in London in a 4-day State visit to the Queen and the Duke of Edinburgh at Buckingham Palace. The Queen and the Duke of Edinburgh gave a State banquet in the evening in their honour and among those also present were the Queen Mother, Princess Alice, Duchess of Gloucester, the Duke and Duchess of Gloucester, the Duke and Duchess of Kent, Prince Michael of Kent, Princess Alexandra and Mr. Angus Ogilvy, and Princess Alice, Countess of Athlone. **6.** The Queen visited Guy's Hospital to mark its 250th anniversary, and opened the new Guy's Tower. The Queen and the Duke of Edinburgh, the Queen Mother, Princess Alice, Duchess of Gloucester, the Duke and Duchess of Gloucester, the Duke of Kent and Princess Alexandra and Mr. Angus Ogilvy were entertained at a banquet by the President of Brazil and Senhora Geisel at the Brazilian Embassy. **7.** Princess Margaret arrived at Heathrow Airport on completion of her visit to Morocco and Tunisia. **13.** The Queen was present at a reception at the Tara Hotel to mark the 60th anniversary of the National Savings Committee. The Queen Mother opened Dundee College of Education. Princess Margaret was present at 75th anniversary ball of the Victoria League at Inn on the Park. **18.** The Duke of Edinburgh carried out engagements in the Isle of Man and Cumbria in connection with his Award scheme. In the evening he attended a variety club dinner at the Adelphi Hotel, Liverpool and left later in the royal train for Dumfries. **19** The Queen visited the Royal Hospital and Homes for Incurables and opened the new Chatsworth Wing. The Duke of Edinburgh carried out engagements in southern Scotland in connection with his Award scheme. **21.** The Queen and Duke of Edinburgh arrived at Wrexham and the Queen opened the Milk Marketing Board creamery. Later she opened the Theatr Clwyd and educational technology centre at Mold and with the Duke of Edinburgh heard a performance by Clwyd Youth Orchestra. They attended a gala performance at Theatr Clwyd given by BBC Welsh Symphony Orches-

tra. **24.** The Queen and the Duke of Edinburgh left London Airport for a 4-day State visit to Finland, returning on June 1. The Queen Mother, Princess Margaret, and other members of the Royal family visited the Chelsea show of the Royal Horticultural Society in the gardens of the Royal Hospital. **25.** The Queen Mother visited Queen's College, Oxford. **26.** The Queen Mother gave a reception for a delegation of U.S. Congressmen to mark the bi-centenary of American Independence. **28.** The Queen Mother visited Oundle School for its centenary celebrations.

June 1. The Duke of Edinburgh opened the new pilot station at the Royal Terrace pier, Gravesend, toured Tilbury docks, and opened Harwich pilot station. **2.** The Queen, the Duke of Edinburgh, the Queen Mother and other members of the Royal family attended Epsom races. **3.** The Queen and Duke of Edinburgh were present at a reception at London Zoo to mark the 150th anniversary of the Zoological Society of London. The Queen inaugurated the new lion terraces. The Prince of Wales took the salute at Beating Retreat by the massed bands of the Household Division on Horse Guards Parade. The Queen Mother visited the Bath and West and Southern Counties Agricultural Show at Shepton Mallet. **6.** The Duke of Edinburgh visited the centenary regatta of the Model Yacht Sailing Association in the Round Pond in Kensington Gardens. **8.** The Duke of Edinburgh toured parts of the Kennet and Avon Canal in Wiltshire and Berkshire and was entertained at luncheon by British Waterways Board at Newbury. Princess Anne visited the Dame Alice Owen School, Potters Bar, which she declared open. **9.** The Queen attended a reception at St. James's Palace to mark the centenary of the foundation of the Mothers' Union. The Duke of Edinburgh visited the new signalling installation at London Bridge station. **10.** The Queen witnessed the ceremony of Beating the Retreat by the massed bands of the Royal Marines on Horse Guards Parade at which the Duke of Edinburgh took the salute. The Queen Mother was present at a service of praise and thanksgiving in Westminster Abbey to mark the centenary of the Mothers' Union. **11.** The Queen's Birthday Honours List was published and contained a total of 701 honours including four life peers (3 barons and 1 baroness), 4 Privy Councillors, and 31 knights bachelor. The Queen and the Duke of Edinburgh gave a reception at Buckingham Palace for the Duke and Duchess of Beaufort to celebrate the Duke of Beaufort's 40 years as Master of the Horse. **14.** The Queen, accompanied by the Duke of Edinburgh and the Queen Mother, held a Chapter of the Most Noble Order of the Garter in the Throne Room of Windsor Castle. The Queen invested Sir Harold Wilson, and the Duke of Grafton with the insignia of Knights Companions of the Order. **15, 16, 17.** The Queen and the Duke of Edinburgh attended Ascot races. **15.** Princess Anne visited the Three Counties show at Malvern. Princess Margaret attended the 50th anniversary gala performance by the Ballet Rambert at Sadler's Wells Theatre. **21.** The Queen and Duke of Edinburgh were present at the Test match between England and the West Indies at Lord's. **22.** The President of the French Republic and Madame Valéry Giscard D'Estaing arrived in London on a State visit to the Queen and the Duke of Edinburgh at Buckingham Palace. Princess Margaret welcomed the President and Mme. Giscard d'Estaing on behalf of the Queen at Gatwick Airport. At Victoria Station, they were met by the Queen and the Duke of Edinburgh, who gave a State banquet in their honour attended also by the Queen Mother, Princess Anne and Capt. Mark Phillips, Princess Margaret, Princess Alice, Duchess of Gloucester, the Duke and Duchess of Gloucester, the Duke and Duchess of Kent, Prince Michael of Kent, and Princess Alexandra and Mr. Angus Ogilvy. **23.** It was announced that the Queen had bought a mansion, Gatcombe Park, Gloucestershire, for Princess Anne and Capt. Mark Phillips. The Queen and the Duke of Edinburgh entertained the French President and Mme. Valéry Giscard d'Estaing at a gala performance at the Royal Opera House, Covent Garden, the Queen Mother and Princess Margaret being among those present. **24.** The Queen and the Duke of Edinburgh, the Queen Mother, Princess Margaret and other members of the Royal family were entertained at a banquet by the French President and Mme. Giscard d'Estaing at the French Embassy. **25.** The Queen and the French President, Mme. Giscard d'Estaing and the Duke of Edinburgh left Heathrow Airport for R.A.F. Turnhouse and drove to the Royal Scottish Academy for a reception, later driving to Holyroodhouse Palace where the Queen and the Duke of Edinburgh gave a luncheon party in honour of the French President and Mme. Giscard d'Estaing before the conclusion of their visit. **28.** The Queen and the Duke of Edinburgh were present at a reception in H.M.S. *Wellington* to mark the 50th anniversary of the Honourable Company of Master Mariners. **29.** The Queen Mother visited the Royal College of Nursing of the United Kingdom to mark the diamond jubilee. **30.** The Duke of Edinburgh opened the Learning Resources Centre and Students Union buildings of Plymouth Polytechnic and was entertained at dinner by the Lord Mayor and Council of Plymouth and received the Wand of office as Lord High Steward of the City.

July 3. The Queen and the Duke of Edinburgh flew from Heathrow Airport to Bermuda en route to the U.S. to take part in the bicentennial celebrations and a six-day State visit. **6.** The Queen Mother dined with the Pilgrims at the Savoy Hotel to commemorate the bicentennial of the Declaration of American Independence. **9.** The Queen Mother inaugurated the Thames Water Reservoir at Datchet. Princess Margaret undertook engagements in Cumbria. **13.** The Queen and the Duke of Edinburgh sailed in the Royal Yacht *Britannia* into Halifax, Nova Scotia, to begin their two-week Canadian tour. **14.** The Queen Mother was present at a service of thanksgiving for the restoration of Selby Abbey. **15.** The Queen Mother was present at the 150th anniversary celebrations of the Bowes Railway at Springwell and inaugurated the Bowes Railway Presentation Scheme. Later she opened the costume gallery at Bowes Museum, Barnard Castle. **17.** The Queen, accompanied by the Duke of Edinburgh, declared open the Olympic Games in Montreal. **23.** The Prince of Wales and Prince Edward flew into Montreal to join the rest of the Royal family for the closing stages of their visit to the Olympic Games. The Prince of Wales was elected Chancellor of the University of Wales, Cardiff. **26.** The Queen with Prince Andrew and Prince Edward arrived at Heathrow Airport from Canada. The Prince of Wales also arrived at Heathrow from Canada. **27.** The Queen attended the annual service of the Order of St. Michael and St. George at St. Paul's Cathedral.

Aug. 2. The Queen opened the Queen Elizabeth Country Park at Butser, Hampshire. The Duke of Edinburgh arrived at Heathrow Airport from Canada. **8.** The Queen with Prince Andrew, Prince Edward and Princess Anne left Slough in the Royal Train for Gourock. The Prince of Wales

embarked in H.M. Yacht *Britannia*, at Greenock. **9.** The Queen and the Duke of Edinburgh with Prince Andrew, Prince Edward and Princess Anne embarked in *Britannia* at Greenock. **25.** The Duke of Edinburgh left Dyce Airport, Aberdeen, for the Netherlands where he competed in the world driving championships at Apeldoorn, and returned on August 29. **27.** The Prince of Wales was officially welcomed at a reception in Lubeck City hall after his mine-hunter, *Bronington*, arrived for a 6-day visit to the West German Baltic port. **Sept. 6.** The Duke of Edinburgh, accompanied by Prince Andrew and Prince Edward, visited Farnborough International Air Show.

BRITISH POLITICS

(1975) Sept. 20. The Tory Reform Group was launched in London as a new pressure group to the left of the Conservative Party. The Liberal Party annual assembly concluded at Scarborough with a demand for a fair voting system, devolution of power from Westminster, and reform of Parliament. **23.** Lord Winterbottom, defence spokesman, detailed to the Lords the next steps the Government had decided on the procurement of major guided weapons systems for British forces, including opening of negotiations with France, Germany and the U.S. for equipment if the terms were right and cancellation of the British missiles projects. **25.** The Government suffered three more defeats on the Employment Protection Bill during its committee stage in the Lords, making a total of seven defeats on the measure during the week in the Upper Chamber which had re-assembled for four days during the summer recess to deal with a backlog of legislation. **26.** Mrs. Thatcher, Opposition Leader, returned to London from her North American tour, and denied accusations by members of the Government that she had attacked Britain in her speeches there. **28.** At an eve-of-conference meeting the Labour Party's national executive, a motion calling on the Government to impound Chilean assets in Britain was carried by 20 votes to 7. **29.** The Labour Party Conference in Blackpool carried by a large majority on a show of hands a resolution supporting the £6-a-week voluntary restraint on incomes agreed by the Government and T.U.C. A motion calling for the abolition of private education in Britain by 1980 was carried narrowly despite the national executive's request that it should be remitted and another resolution carried against the national executive advice criticised the Government for not assisting the end of " private landlordism " and not extending the municipalization of housing. **30.** Results of the ballot for the national executive of the Labour Party included the removal from it of the Chancellor of the Exchequer (Mr. Healey) and his replacement by Mr. Eric Heffer, M.P. for Walton, Liverpool. The Party Conference carried by a large majority on a show of hands a resolution calling on the whole Labour movement to support the Government's anti-inflation fight.

Oct. 1. At the Labour Party Conference, a resolution calling for the 250 major monopolies, banks, insurance companies and land to be nationalized was massively rejected by 5,721,000–407,000 votes. On a show of hands, a motion was carried demanding an immediate substantial increase in health expenditure and opposing cuts in the National Health Service and welcoming the proposed removal of private practice from it with the long-term aim of the total abolition of private practice and the prohibition of all private patients' insurance plans. **7.** The Conservative Party conference opened in Blackpool and carried a resolution stating that some short term financial assistance to

industry might sometimes be necessary, and also another which expressed concern at falling educational standards, calling on the Conservative Party to redefine its priorities in education. Another motion approved deplored the " erosion of individual freedom, choice, and responsibility." **8.** At the Conservative Party conference, a motion " deploring the ineffectiveness of the Tory Party in opposition " was declared defeated on a show of hands, the session ending in protests as constituency delegates unsuccessfully demanded a ballot. By a substantial majority, a resolution was carried opposing any modifications of the electoral system which would make voting more complicated or increase the likelihood of ineffective minority governments. **9.** The Conservative Party conference overwhelmingly carried a motion viewing with alarm the " increasing threat to the rule of law posed by groups and individuals who resorted to direct action and intimidation." **11.** Mr. Karamanlis, the Greek Prime Minister, left London after two days of talks on the Cyprus situation and Greece's application for E.E.C. membership. **15.** The Commons rejected by 281–265 votes, a Government majority 16, the "Goodman amendments " to the Trade Union and Labour Relations (Amendment) Bill which were carried overwhelmingly in the Lords in March 1975 to protect editors and outside contributors from closed shop legislation. On October 20 the Lords rejected a Government amendment and approved an amendment proposed by Lord Goodman to safeguard the right of editors not to belong to a trade union and to commission articles from non-journalists. **20.** Mr. John Stonehouse, Labour M.P. for Walsall North, made a statement to the Commons on " the events surrounding my disappearance last November." The Prime Minister announced in the Commons the setting-up of a Royal Commission on the National Health Service. **23.** The Prime Minister announced the setting-up of a Royal Commission on gambling under the chairmanship of Lord Rothschild to inquire into the existing law and practice on betting, gaming, lotteries and prize competitions. **27.** An Opposition censure motion on the Social Services Secretary (Mrs. Castle) over her handling of the N.H.S. was defeated in the Commons by 287–267 votes, Government majority of 20. **29.** The Lords rose at 7.51 a.m. after an all-night sitting in the committee stage of the Community Land Bill which lasted 16 hours 42 minutes, the longest for more than 4 years in the Upper House.

Nov. 4. The second report from the Select Committee on Assistance to Private Members was published with a recommendation that each M.P. who wants one should be able to have a full-time personal assistant paid for by public funds. **11.** Resisting " closed shop " provisions which in their view would fetter the freedom of the Press, the Lords " killed " the Government's Trade Union and Labour Relations (Amendment) Bill for the current parliamentary session by insisting on the re-insertion of amendments embodying *inter alia* a Press Charter. Mr. Ron Hayward, Labour Party general secretary, accepted the report by Mr. Anthony Barker, Reader in Government at Essex University, that there was no overall bias by B.B.C. against Labour in its coverage of the last general election after the Labour Party itself instituted the inquiry. **12.** The Employment Secretary (Mr. Foot) confirmed that the Government intended to invoke the Parliament Act in favour of the Trade Union and Labour Relations (Amendment) Bill. Parliament was prorogued. **19.** The Queen opened the new session of Parliament, and in the Speech outlining the Government's legislative

THE QUEEN AND THE FRENCH PRESIDENT

The Queen in the grounds of Buckingham Palace with the President of France, M. Giscard d'Estaing, and Princess Margaret during President Giscard's State visit in June.

THE QUEEN AND PRESIDENT FORD

The Queen and President Ford listening to the playing of their national anthems on the lawn of the White House after Her Majesty arrived in Washington in July.

THE QUEEN IN THE U.S.A.

The Queen arrived in Philadelphia on July 7, and is seen with the Duke of Edinburgh looking at the Liberty Bell.

THE NEW PRIME MINISTER

After three ballots, Mr. James Callaghan was elected the new Labour Party leader on April 5 in succession to Mr. Harold Wilson, and was appointed Prime Minister by the Queen on the same day.

HOSTAGES RESCUED FROM UGANDA

One of the pilots being greeted in Tel Aviv on July 4 after their return from the successful commando raid to rescue hostages held at Entebbe Airport.

THE DROUGHT

A view in August of the Talybont reservoir near the Brecon Beacons which normally supplies water to populous areas of South Wales.

CONSEQUENCES OF THE DROUGHT

As a result of the dry weather, serious heath fires broke out in many parts of the British Isles. Residents are seen fighting a blaze on August 22 at Matcham in the New Forest.

THE LANDING ON MARS

A view of the landscape on Mars transmitted from the U.S. Viking spacecraft which landed on the planet on July 20.

THE FOXBAT

A Soviet Air Force jet fighter Mig 25 *Foxbat*, after it made a forced landing at Hakodate, Japan, on Sept. 6.   The pilot asked for political asylum in U.S.A., which was subsequently granted.

DIED IN 1976

Dame Sybil Thorndike (*right*), the distinguished actress, who died on June 9 at the age of 93 and Dame Agatha Christie, the author of many detective novels and plays, who died on Jan. 12, aged 85.

DEATHS OF FAMOUS MEN

Among famous men who died during the year were Cardinal John Heenan, Archbishop of Westminster (*top left*), Field-Marshal Viscount Montgomery of Alamein (*top right*), General Franco, the Spanish leader (*bottom left*) and Sir Mortimer Wheeler, the archaeologist (*bottom right*).

HONOURED IN 1976

Among those who received honours in 1976 were Benjamin Britten (*top left*), who was made a Life Peer, Janet Baker (*top right*), who became a D.B.E., Richard Attenborough (*bottom left*) and Douglas Bader (*bottom right*), who both received knighthoods.

PIGGOTT'S SEVENTH DERBY

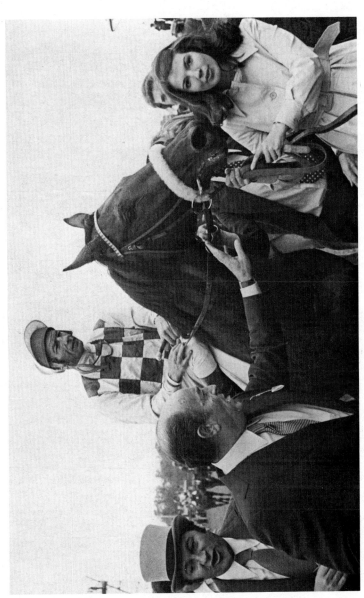

Lester Piggott became the first jockey to win the Derby seven times, when he rode the French horse, Empery, to victory at Epsom on June 2.

OLYMPIC WINNERS

The presentation to the team who became the first British Olympic winners in the modern pentathlon, at the Montreal Games, Jim Fox, Adrian Parker and Danny Nightingale.

OLYMPIC WINNERS

Two more British gold medallists, John Curry, who won the men's figure skating event in the Winter Games at Innsbruck, and David Wilkie, who won the 200 metres breast stroke at Montreal.

THE WISDEN TROPHY

The West Indies cricketers are seen at The Oval with their replicas of the Wisden Trophy, which the West Indies won by defeating England in the series 3-0.

programme were plans to nationalize the aircraft and shipbuilding industries, the phasing out of N.H.S. pay-beds and compulsory reorganization of " selective " secondary schools as comprehensives. **25.** The Government decided to send three frigates to the disputed Icelandic fishing grounds. **27.** The Government's proposals for devolution entitled " Our Changing Democracy: Devolution to Scotland and Wales," were published as a White Paper. **28.** The first register of M.P.'s interests was published following the order passed by the Commons on June 12, 1975, to establish it.

Dec. 2. The Government's major bill to nationalize the aircraft and shipbuilding industries was given a second reading in the Commons by only 5 votes, 280–275. **3.** The Committee of Privileges of the House of Commons recommended the exclusion from the precincts of the House for six months of Mr. Andrew Knight, editor of *The Economist*, and Mr. Mark Schreiber, a journalist, because on October 11 *The Economist* published an article which gave details of a confidential draft report, the Committee finding that this publication constituted a contempt of Parliament. **4.** The Prime Minister announced eight ministerial changes mainly because of the resignations of Lord Balogh (Minister of State, Energy) on reaching 70 years of age and Lord Beswick (Minister of State, Industry) in view of his impending appointment as chairman of the organizing committee for British Aerospace. **11.** In a free vote, the Commons rejected a motion for the restoration of the death penalty for terrorist killings by 361–232, a majority against restoration of 129. **17.** The Chancellor of the Exchequer announced in the Commons measures to create and save jobs with limited temporary restraint on imports, selective relaxation of hire-purchase restrictions, and steps to help industry to replenish stocks. Nine new life peers were announced from Downing Street but only one by-election was involved. A meeting in Glasgow agreed in principle to establish an independent Scottish Labour Party which would urge more powers for the Scottish Assembly than those proposed by the Labour Government. **18.** Mr. Healey announced that " in consequence of the major issues involved ", he did not feel able to introduce a wealth tax during the parliamentary session, but he had instructed the Inland Revenue to continue with their preparatory work. **30.** The British Ambassador to Chile (Mr. Reginald Secondé) was recalled in protest against the torture by Chilean security police of Dr. Sheila Cassidy, released after two months in detention for allegedly treating a wounded left-wing revolutionary.

(1976) Jan. 7. Mrs. Thatcher began a 5-day tour of the Middle East. **11.** Mr. Mick McGahey, vice-president, N.U.M., was elected chairman of the Communist Party. **14.** The Foreign Secretary (Mr. Callaghan) told the Commons that there was to be a major review headed by Sir Kenneth Berrill of Britain's requirements at home and abroad with consideration of future pattern of overseas representation. The Home Secretary (Mr. Jenkins) announced he had asked Sir Claus Moser, director of Central Statistical Office, to inquire into the " clerical error " about immigration from the new Commonwealth in 1973. **15.** Mr. John Robertson, Labour M.P. for Paisley, joined the breakaway Scottish Labour Party, following a similar decision earlier by Mr. James Sillars, Labour M.P. for Ayrshire South. There were five newcomers and five changes of duties in a list of Opposition Front-bench spokesmen announced by Mrs. Thatcher. **18.** The Scottish Labour Party was formally launched in Glasgow. **19.** U.K. agreed to withdraw her naval protection vessels from the

disputed Icelandic fishing waters and invited Iceland's Prime Minister to London for talks. The Government announced it was proposed to allocate up to £500,000 for official British contributions to the celebrations commemorating the bicentenary of the U.S. The four-day debate in the Commons on the Government's devolution proposals ended with the Government's motion to " take note " of its White Paper being carried by 295–37 votes, a Government majority of 258 after the Opposition amendment was rejected by 315–244 votes, Government majority of 71. A Scottish Nationalist amendment was defeated by 304–27 votes, Government majority 277. **22.** The Prime Minister announced the Government's acceptance of new rules concerning the publication of ministerial memoirs as recommended in a report of a committee of Privy Councillors chaired by Lord Radcliffe. Retailers agreed to give broad support to the Government's new 5 per cent. price restraint programme after concessions from the Prices and Consumer Protection Secretary (Mrs. Williams). **25.** Iceland's Prime Minister (Mr. Hallgrimsson) conferred in London with Mr. Callaghan over the cod war dispute, after he had had talks at Chequers the previous day with Mr. Wilson. **29.** Trawlermen who had started to leave the cod waters off Iceland decided to remain and resume fishing after the British Government offered about £100,000 compensation for loss of earnings. A group of at least 50 Labour M.P.s abstained during the vote in the Commons for a Government motion expressing deep concern at the continuing rise in unemployment, but the motion was approved by 234–25 votes, Government majority 209, the official Opposition also abstaining, and then the Conservative amendment critical of the Government's failure to take decisive action against inflation was defeated by 299–250, Government majority 49. Mr. Jeremy Thorpe, the Liberal leader, issued a statement that there was no truth in the " wild allegations " after a man later placed on probation in Barnstaple magistrates' court for dishonestly obtaining social security payments had declared that he was being hounded because of his relationship with Jeremy Thorpe.

Feb. 2. Mr. George Thomas, Labour M.P. for Cardiff West, and the Deputy Speaker, was elected speaker of the House of Commons to succeed Mr. Selwyn Lloyd who resigned. Mr. Oscar Murton (Con. Poole) was appointed Deputy Speaker and Chairman of Ways and Means. **4.** The Liberal Chief Whip (Mr. Cyril Smith) issued a statement after a meeting of Liberal M.P.s at the Commons which said that Mr. Jeremy Thorpe re-affirmed to his colleagues that there was no truth in the allegations made against him by " one Norman Josiffe (Scott) " and that the party re-affirmed its support for Mr. Thorpe's continued leadership. **5.** R.N. frigates were ordered back into the waters off Iceland after a gunboat cut the warps of the Hull trawler, *Loch Eriboll*. **9.** Mr. Wilson told the Commons that it appeared probable that a number of British mercenaries had been shot in Angola although he could not confirm that 14 had been executed for refusing to fight, and disclosed that a considerable number of Britons had been killed in other war operations. On Feb. 10, Mr. Wilson ordered an inquiry under Lord Diplock into the recruitment of British mercenaries for Angola as more than 40 arrived home and were questioned about the previous week's reported execution of 14 of their comrades. **10.** New pension provisions were announced by the Social Services Secretary (Mrs. Castle) to ensure that women would have the same access to occupation schemes as men from April 1978. **11.** The Conservatives secured a

surprise defeat of the Government in the Commons on a motion to reduce the salary of the Industry Secretary (Mr. Varley) in protest at Government industrial policies, the vote against the Government being 214–209, an Opposition majority of 5. The position was restored on Feb. 17 when the Government won a motion 296–280, a majority of 16. **12.** Mr. Healey announced the Government's decision to spend a further £220 million on saving and creating jobs. **17.** The Government's Green Paper "Direct elections to the European Assembly," was published. **19.** Walsall North constituency Labour Party decided unanimously not to re-adopt Mr. John Stonehouse, M.P. as candidate at the next general election. **21.** Miss Joan Lestor, Parliamentary Under-Secretary, Ministry of Education and Science, resigned in protest against the proposed cuts in education, adding that she had not been happy about the directions of " some policies for some time." **24.** Lord Greenhill, former head of the Diplomatic Service, flew to Salisbury, Rhodesia, on a " purely exploratory " Government mission to find out if Mr. Ian Smith's attitude " is now such that there is any real possibility of our helping to promote a settlement." Another frigate, H.M.S. *Andromeda*, was ordered to sail for Icelandic waters after a collision off north-east Iceland between H.M.S. *Yarmouth* and the Icelandic gunboat *Thor*. An Opposition amendment in the Lords to incorporate a " conscience " clause in the Trade Union and Labour Relations (Amendment) Bill to enable compensation to be claimed by a worker dismissed from a closed shop because he objected on grounds of conscientious conviction to belonging to the recognized trade union was carried, against Government advice, by 128–91 votes, a majority of 37 against the Government. **26.** Mr. Frank Tomney, Labour M.P. for Hammersmith North, was rejected as candidate for the constituency at the next general election by 45–31 votes at a constituency party management committee meeting.

Mar. 2. Lord George-Brown, former deputy leader of the Labour Party, resigned from it in protest at the Government's closed shop legislation. Earlier he was among 71 peers who voted against the Government's plan to provide a " Press charter " in the Trade Union and Labour Relations (Amendment) Bill on the grounds of its inadequacy to defend Press freedom under the closed shop provisions, although the Government won the division by 109–71, majority of 38. **4.** The Government won the by-election in Coventry N.W. with a majority of 3,694 over the Conservatives compared with its general election majority of 7,488. **5.** Defence Secretary (Mr. Roy Mason) announced that the U.K. had decided to proceed with Germany and Italy in the production of the Multi Role Combat Aircraft (MRCA) and that the R.A.F. would take 385 of them. **6.** Government chief whip (Mr. Robert Mellish) was re-elected chairman of Greater London regional council of the Labour Party by 687,000 votes against 443,000 for his challenger, Mr. Arthur Latham, left-wing Labour M.P. **8.** Proposed new procedure for future elections of the leader of the Liberal Party was published as a discussion paper. **9.** The Prime Minister told the Commons at question time that he had " no doubt at all that there was strong South African participation in recent activities relating to Mr. Thorpe," Mr. Wilson said there had been " very strong and heavily-financed private master-minding of certain political operations," although there was no evidence that the South African Government was involved. The controversial Trade Unions and Labour Relations (Amendment) Bill completed its

third reading stage in the Lords without discussion and no vote but with one amendment about "sincerely-held personal conscientious convictions " which was however rejected by the Commons on March 18 by 298 votes to 253, Government majority of 45. **10.** The Government was defeated in the Commons on its own motion supporting its plans for public expenditure by 284–256 votes, an Opposition majority of 28, after abstentions by 37 left-wing Labour M.P.s. Earlier the Government rejected an Opposition amendment declining to approve their White Paper on Public Expenditure by 304–274 votes, Government majority of 30. On March 11 the Government had a majority of 17 in the Commons on a vote of confidence following their major defeat on public expenditure, voting being 297–280; three Parliamentary Private Secretaries who abstained on March 10 lost their unpaid posts. **11.** Conservatives retained Carshalton and The Wirral in by-elections with majorities of 9,732 and 24,112 respectively. **16.** Mr. Wilson, in an unexpected statement, announced he was to resign the premiership as soon as the Parliamentary Labour Party had elected a new leader. On a free vote, the Commons decided by a majority of 175 that B.B.C. and independent radio should be permitted to sound broadcast their proceedings, the favourable vote being 299–124. **17.** The Parliamentary Liberal party decided that there should be no leadership election until after the Liberal Assembly in September. The Defence Secretary (Mr. Roy Mason) published the Defence White Paper. **22.** In a Commons statement on Rhodesia, Mr. Callaghan set out four pre-conditions for negotiations in a constitution for the country. Mr. Gromyko, Russia's Foreign Minister, arrived in U.K. for three days of talks. **24.** Mr. Cyril Smith, M.P. for Rochdale, resigned as Liberal Chief Whip and Mr. Alan Beith, M.P. for Berwick on Tweed, succeeded him. **25.** Result of the first ballot for the Labour Party leadership and choice of the next Prime Minister was: Mr. Michael Foot 90, Mr. James Callaghan 84, Mr. Roy Jenkins 56, Mr. Wedgwood Benn 37, Mr. Denis Healey 30, Mr. Anthony Crosland 17. Mr. Crosland automatically dropped out of the second ballot. **30.** Result of the second ballot for Labour Party leadership, Mr. Jenkins and Mr. Wedgwood Benn having previously withdrawn from the contest, was: Mr. Callaghan 141, Mr. Foot 133, Mr. Healey 38. Mr. Healey was automatically eliminated.

Apr. 5. The third and final ballot for the Labour party leadership resulted: Mr. Callaghan 176, Mr. Foot 137. Mr. Callaghan was appointed Prime Minister by the Queen two hours after the announcement. In his speech to the Parliamentary Labour Party, Mr. Callaghan declared: " My task will be to lead a united Government and a united party." **6.** Mr. Denis Healey presented his Budget proposals in the Commons and announced income tax reliefs conditional on T.U.C. agreement to a pay rise limit " in the order of 3 per cent." **7.** Mr. John Stonehouse, M.P. for Walsall North, resigned from the Parliamentary Labour Party, and decided to sit as an independent on the opposition benches, but on April 14 joined the English National Party. **8.** The Prime Minister announced his first cabinet which included four new members and excluded four members of Mr. Wilson's Cabinet. New Cabinet ministers were Mr. Bruce Millan (Scottish Secretary), Mr. Albert Booth (Employment Secretary), Mr. Edmund Dell (Trade Secretary) and Mr. David Ennals (Social Services Secretary). Departing Cabinet ministers were: Mr. Edward Short (Lord President of the Council and Leader of the Commons), Mr. William Ross

(Scottish Secretary), Mrs. Barbara Castle (Social Services Secretary), and Mr. Robert Mellish (Govt. Chief Whip). 13. Mr. John Stonehouse, Ind. M.P. Walsall North, was ordered to leave the Commons for disorderly conduct after he had clashed more than once with the Deputy Speaker (Sir Myer Galpern). 14. The Prime Minister issued the second and final list of his new administration which resulted in promotion for 10 backbench M.P.s and the dropping of 4 ministers. 29. Britain's first export cargo of North Sea crude oil from the Forties Field was carried in the B.P. tanker, *British Dragoon*, from the Firth of Forth to Wilhelmshaven.

May 3. Leader of the House (Mr. Foot) told the Commons that official travel by the 635 M.P.s cost taxpayers about £1,000,000 in 1975–76, the money being incurred by members' journeys between their homes, constituencies and the House and on attending official functions. 6. The Agriculture Minister (Mr. Peart) announced in the Commons that two more R.N. frigates were being sent to join the four protecting British trawlers off Iceland. 9. Fifteen Conservative M.P.s formed a Parliamentary committee to oppose plans for Scottish and Welsh Assemblies. 10. Mr. Jeremy Thorpe resigned as leader of the Liberal Party after 9 years in office and spoke of "a sustained witch hunt" against him, and a "campaign of denigration which has endured for over three months," declaring also that no man could effectively lead a party "if the greater part of his time has to be devoted to answering allegations as they arise and countering plots and intrigues." The Labour party's organization committee ordered that the annual general meeting of Newham North-East constituency party in February, when Mr. Reg Prentice, Overseas Development minister and the local M.P., was dropped as their candidate at the next general election, be reconvened and that all delegates' credentials be inspected to ensure they were eligible to vote. 12. Mr. Jo Grimmond, Liberal Party leader from 1956–67, agreed to resume the leadership until a special conference of the Party in June set in motion a new procedure to elect the leader by July 12. 14. Scottish Conservative and Unionist Party at their annual conference in Perth approved a compromise resolution on devolution which supported the principle of a directly-elected assembly in Edinburgh, but opposed any Government proposals based on the present White Paper on Devolution. 25. The Leader of the Commons (Mr. Foot) told M.P.s that the Government's proposals for devolution for Scotland and Wales would be covered in a single bill to be introduced in the autumn. Social Services Secretary (Mr. Ennals) announced that the Government had decided to postpone the introduction of the child benefit scheme under which benefits would be paid direct to mothers with husbands losing tax allowances for their children and instead to pay a new family allowance of £1 a week for the first child from April 1977, with £1·50 allowance, as now, for other children. 26. Sir Harold Wilson, the former Prime Minister, announced his resignation honours list, including nine new life peers. There were furious scenes in the Commons over the future of the Government's bill to nationalize the major part of the aircraft and shipbuilding industries when Mr. Foot proposed that M.P.s should debate a Government motion to dispense with delaying procedural committee work after the Speaker had ruled the measure was *prima facie* "hybrid," which meant that it would have to go before a select committee of M.P.s. On May 27 the Commons was adjourned by the Speaker because of "scenes of grave disorder" after the

Government had a one-vote majority on the motion to dispense with private standing orders and thus allow the bill to proceed, the figures being 304–305. Labour M.P.s stood to sing "The Red Flag" and Mr. Michael Heseltine, Shadow Industry Secretary, removed the mace and brandished it towards the Government benches until Mr. James Prior, Opposition spokesman on employment, returned it to the Clerks' Table. Blows were exchanged as the Speaker suspended the sitting for 20 minutes. Immediately the House resumed, the Speaker adjourned the sitting until next day when Mr. Heseltine apologized for his behaviour. A golden copy of the Magna Carta was handed over in Westminster Hall to a delegation of 25 senators and members of the House of Representatives as a gift to mark the bicentenary of U.S.A., the presentations being made by the Speaker to his American equivalent, Mr. Carl Albert. 27. The Labour Party published its economic and social programme extending into the 1980s. 28. The Conservative Opposition decided to adhere to their decision to stop pairing and other cooperation with the Government following the Commons row on May 27. The decision followed a meeting between the Prime Minister and Mrs. Thatcher. 30. The annual conference of Scottish National Party ended at Motherwell when a motion to campaign for independence rather than devolution was defeated by 564–481 votes, a majority against of 83.

June 1. The third cod war between Britain and Iceland ended when a 6-month agreement was signed by the U.K. Foreign Secretary (Mr. Crosland) and Iceland's Foreign Minister (Mr. Agustsson) to allow an average of 24 British trawlers a day to fish within the 200-mile zone claimed by Iceland. 9. An Opposition motion of no confidence in the Government was defeated by 309 votes to 290, Government majority of 19, in the Commons, the Conservatives voting their full strength were supported by 11 Scottish Nationalists, 3 Welsh Nationalists, one United Ulster Unionist, and one independent while the Liberals and the rest of the United Ulster Unionists abstained. 12. At a special assembly in Manchester, the Liberals became the first party in Britain to elect their leader by popular poll when delegates decided on a constituency system of voting with Liberal M.P.s controlling only the nomination of candidates. 17. The Prime Minister ordered an "urgent and thorough" inquiry to identify the person who leaked a set of Cabinet papers on the decision to postpone the introduction of the child benefit scheme and told M.P.s the investigation would be conducted by Sir Douglas Allen, head of the home civil service. On July 1, the Prime Minister told Parliament police were being called in to investigate the leak and said he was setting up a committee of 3 Privy Councillors to examine the present rules for handling Cabinet documents. 22. The Prime Minister appealed to the Conservatives to end their campaign of non-cooperation with the Government in Westminster and offered a re-run of the disputed one-vote majority on May 27 in procedures on the bill to nationalize the aircraft and shipbuilding industries. The Government won this vote on June 29 with a majority of 14 after the 14 Scots and Welsh Nationalist M.P.s abstained following an eleventh-hour promise by Mr. Foot to consider the demand for a separate Scottish entity within the State board which would run the industry. The first report from the House of Commons select committee on direct elections to the European Assembly was published. 23. It was announced after talks at 10 Downing Street between President Giscard d'Estaing and Mr. Callaghan that the French President and the British Prime

Minister were to hold regular annual meetings starting in the autumn. Earlier the French President addressed both Houses of Parliament in the Royal Gallery at Westminster. **24.** The Labour Party won the Rotherham by-election with a majority of 4,527 over the Conservative candidate compared with a majority of 17,034 at the last general election. **30.** Relaxations in the Prices Code, adding about one per cent. to prices over the next year, were announced in the Commons by Prices Secretary (Mrs. Williams). At the same time a Government White Paper, "The Attack on Inflation: the Second Year," was published, stating that industry had to be permitted to achieve sufficient profitability to generate funds for investment.

July 1. Mrs. Thatcher decided to resume the pairing of M.P.s with the Government after assurances from the Labour Party about stricter pairing arrangements. **7.** Mr. David Steel, M.P. for Roxburgh, Selkirk and Peebles, was elected new leader of the Liberal Party, the electoral college, representing all constituency associations, giving him 12,541 votes compared with 7,032 for Mr. John Pardoe, M.P. for North Cornwall, the only other contender. **12.** Mr. Foot announced a £6 a week increase in M.P.s salary, bringing the annual salary to £6,062, but this should only be drawn if it did not put the total earnings above the £8,500 limit for an increase under the present pay policy. M.P.s would also be able to claim up to £6-a-week increase for their secretaries. **14.** During the report stage of the Finance Bill, M.P.s voted 190–170, a majority against the Government of 20, to free the first 50 per cent. of war widows pensions from tax. **15.** Mrs. Thatcher again called off pairing with Government ministers and M.P.s after Mr. Foot announced that the Government intended to guillotine five major bills on one day, in an unprecedented use of the Parliamentary time-table motions. Labour held their seat at the Thurrock by-election with a majority over the Tories of 4,839 compared with a majority at the October 1974 general election of 19,680. **20.** The Government had a majority of 6 in the Commons on a motion to guillotine debates on bills to phase out pay beds from N.H.S. hospitals and to extend the scope of work which might be done by registered dock workers, voting being 311–305. Another motion restricting debating time on the bill to nationalize the aircraft and shipbuilding industries was carried by 311–294, a Government majority of 17, a division in which 14 Scottish and Welsh Nationalist M.P.s abstained. A third time-table motion on bills to enforce comprehensive secondary education and to give security of tenure to tenants in tied agricultural cottages was also won by the Government. **20.** Proposals of the Scottish National Party for an independent Scotland to maintain a " practical working relationship with the rest of Britain " were announced. **22.** Mr. Healey announced in the Commons cuts in public spending amounting to £1,012 million in the year beginning April 1977, and an increase of 2 per cent. in employers' national insurance contributions effective from April 6, 1977, to yield about £910 million in 1977/78 and about £1,030 million in a full year. **23.** It was announced that the London living allowance of M.P.s was to rise by £200 a year with their car allowance raised from 10·2p per mile to 11·8p backdated to April. M.P.s voted in the Commons to approve a £6 weekly rise in their Parliamentary salary. **26.** Mr. Jim Sillars, M.P. for South Ayrshire, and Mr. John Robertson, M.P. for Paisley, who formed the breakaway Scottish Labour party, said that they would no longer accept the Labour Whip because they were totally opposed to the Government's public spending cuts. **28.** Labour Party's

national executive committee endorsed the new version of the social contract by 13–7 votes and carried by similar figures a motion attacking the public expenditure cuts. Britain broke diplomatic relations with Uganda, the first time U.K. had taken the lead in cutting links with a Commonwealth nation. **29.** The Bill to nationalize the aircraft and shipbuilding industries received a third reading in the Commons by 311 votes to 308, a Government majority of 3. Seventy-eight Labour M.P.s signed a motion criticizing the Government's decision to cut public expenditure in the next financial year.

Aug. 3. Mr. Foot told M.P.s of changes and additions to the Government's plans for devolution and repeated the Government's determination to proceed with them despite warnings from Labour and Tory back-benchers. A White Paper was published dealing with these revised proposals for devolved assemblies for Scotland and Wales. The report of the Committee of Privy Councillors appointed to inquire into the recruitment of mercenaries was published with a recommendation for legislation to prohibit such recruitment. **17.** An announcement from 10 Downing Street stated that Mr. John Stonehouse, M.P. for Walsall North, had been removed from the Privy Council at his own request. **19.** The second report from the Select Committee on Direct Elections to the European Assembly was published and favoured single-member constituencies for the first elections in 1978, being against the introduction of the single transferable vote for the 81 seats allotted the U.K., the proposed basis being England 66, Scotland 8, Wales 4, Northern Ireland 3. **26.** The report of the committee chaired by Lord Houghton on financial aid to political parties was published. The majority recommendation was for annual grants to be paid from Exchequer funds to the central organizations of parties for general purposes on the basis of 5p for each vote cast for its candidates at the previous General Election. Four of the 12 members considered that no case had been made out for state assistance. **27.** Mr. John Stonehouse, M.P. for Walsall North, who was serving a 7-year sentence for forgery, fraud and false pretences, resigned his Parliamentary seat.

Sept. 10. Prime Minister carried out major ministerial reshuffle; among nine Cabinet changes announced was appointment of Mr. Merlyn Rees (formerly Secretary of State for Northern Ireland) as Home Secretary in succession to Mr. Roy Jenkins (who would be taking over as President of European Commission in 1977), Mrs. Shirley Williams (formerly Secretary of State for Prices and Consumer Protection) became Secretary of State for Education and Science, and Mr. Roy Mason (formerly Secretary of State for Defence) became Secretary of State for Northern Ireland.

IRELAND

(1975) Sept. 22. At least nine Ulster cities and towns from Londonderry to Belfast were hit by bomb and gun attacks in one of the worst days of violence since the Provisional I.R.A. announced its ceasefire in February 1975; twelve civilians and three policemen were injured. Two men were given life sentences at Belfast City Commission for the murder of a young Roman Catholic on the outskirts of Portadown on Oct. 27, the judge declaring that the real and primary reason for his death was religion. Mr. Merlyn Rees, Northern Ireland Secretary denied in a statement read on his behalf in the House of Lords, reports of a document containing a list of 12 points of a " peace deal " with the Provisionals being found when David O'Connell was arrested in Dublin and that it was

in the hands of the Dublin authorities. **29.** Mr. William Craig, Vanguard Party leader, resigned as deputy chairman of United Ulster Unionist coalition because of his statement that a voluntary coalition government between Loyalists and the S.D.L.P. was essential until the present emergency ended. A 20-year old nurse alleged to have admitted carrying bomb-making materials into an R.C. church near the centre of Belfast in January 1975 was sentenced at Belfast City Commission to six years jail.

Oct. 2. Five people died and nine were injured in a series of shootings and bomb attacks in Belfast, including three people, two sisters among them, who were shot dead at a Roman Catholic beer bottling factory. Four more deaths occurred when a bomb-carrying car with four men in it, exploded in the village of Farren Lester, near Coleraine, Co. Londonderry, while a tenth fatality was a woman killed in a bomb attack in a bar at Killylea, Co. Down, where 10 people were also reported injured. **3.** The Eire Government refused to release three leading Provisional I.R.A. prisoners or to make any major concessions in return for the life of Dr. Tiede Herrema, the Dutch managing director of the Ferenka factory near Limerick, who was kidnapped near his home in Co. Limerick in the morning, but the management of Ferenka decided to close down for 24 hours as demanded by the gang. On Oct. 22 Irish police and troops surrounded the council house in Monasterevin, Co. Kildare, where Dr. Herrema was held captive. On Oct. 26 Provisional I.R.A.'s political wing, Sinn Fein, appealed to the kidnappers to free Dr. Herrema. Late on Nov. 7 he was released unhurt and the I.R.A. pair who had been holding him hostage for a total of 36 days, Eddie Gallagher and Marian Coyle, surrendered to the Eire police. On March 11, Gallagher and Coyle were jailed for 20 years and 15 years respectively in Dublin Special Criminal Court for their part in the kidnapping and also received concurrent sentences for other offences connected with it, including the wounding of a detective. Two accomplices, Brian McGowan and John Vincent Walsh, were each jailed for 8 years. David Dunne, who pleaded guilty to kidnapping, was sentenced to 3 years' imprisonment suspended for 3 years. **11.** Mr. William Craig, leader of Ulster's Vanguard Unionist Party, was backed by his party's central council which supported a motion of confidence in him by 128–79 votes following his proposal for an emergency coalition between the Unionist majority in Northern Ireland and the Social Democratic and Labour Party. After the vote, nine Vanguard members of the N.I. Convention resigned. Eire released 84 prisoners from jail to mark the canonization next day in Rome of Blessed Oliver Plunkett, executed at Tyburn in 1681; none were guilty of politically-connected crimes. **14.** A meeting of the United Ulster Unionists Council in Belfast suspended Mr. William Craig, and three followers from membership because of their attitude to voluntary emergency power-sharing. On Oct. 24 Mr. Craig was expelled from the U.U.U. Coalition. **15.** A Provisional I.R.A. bomb smashed part of the Castlereagh barracks of the R.U.C. in Belfast's eastern suburbs, injuring slightly four police officers and three civilians. **29.** One man was shot dead and at least 14 wounded in a series of Belfast ambushes involving Republican extremists. **30.** A 6-year-old girl was shot dead when a gunman burst into her parents' home in the Republican Upper Falls Road area and sprayed the living room with bullets. **31.** Seamus McCusker, who administered Provisional Sinn Fein " incident centres " linked with the Security forces, was shot dead by teenage terrorists in the New Lodge Road district of Belfast.

Nov. 4. Mr. Merlyn Rees told the Commons that people convicted of terrorist offences in Ulster after March 1, 1976, would not be given the status of special category prisoners. **7.** The Northern Ireland Convention, set up six months earlier, ended its term with the 78 members unable to agree on recommendations to the U.K. Government about a form of future devolved government for Ulster. The Convention's formal report was submitted to the Northern Ireland Secretary on Nov. 8. **11.** Four men were killed and four others wounded as the quarrelling between the Official and Provisional wings of the I.R.A. continued. **14.** Eire's Government retained its majority when Fine Gael held by a majority of 3,000 votes the West Mayo seat in a by-election. **19.** Mr. Roy Bradford, Vanguard Unionist M.P. for South Belfast, resigned from the party and applied to join the Official Unionists. Eire Government introduced the Criminal Law Jurisdiction Bill to enable Eire courts to try fugitive offenders from Ulster and Britain. **22.** Three soldiers were killed and one was seriously injured in Ulster when Provisional I.R.A. men surrounded their observation post in South Armagh. **25.** Two policemen were killed and two others wounded when their Land-Rover was ambushed by terrorists on a lonely country road between Pomeroy and Castlecaulfield, Co. Tyrone. **29.** A man was killed and three people injured superficially when two bombs exploded at Dublin Airport, the airport being evacuated and closed for six hours.

Dec. 5. Mr. Rees ended detention without trial in Ulster when he signed release orders for the last 73 of the 1,981 men and women held at various times since internment started in August 1971. **11.** Nine people were hurt when a bomb exploded at an Army H.Q. in the centre of Belfast and a large area of shops and offices was damaged. **17.** The Prime Minister of Eire (Mr. Cosgrave) disclosed in the Dail that the total cost in compensation for damage and lost earnings from terrorism and business because of the terrorist campaign in Ulster was about £250 million while in the current year alone cost of the Army and police would be about £120 million. **21.** Terrorists unsuccessfully tried to blow up buildings at Belfast Airport after taking four workers hostage and forcing two other workmates to drive a truck loaded with explosives into the airport compound. **29.** Terrorists hijacked a goods train and blew it up on the main Dublin–Belfast line shortly before the southbound Dublin Enterprise express was due to pass.

(1976) Jan 1. Total death toll in Ulster in 1975 comprised 14 soldiers, 11 R.U.C. men, 5 part time members of U.D.R., and 216 civilians, or 33 more dead than in 1974. **2.** About 90 Provisional I.R.A. prisoners at Eire's Port Laoise maximum security prison ended a 36-hour hunger strike without any of their demands being met by the Dublin authorities. **3.** At least 42 people were injured in Ulster in bomb attacks on public houses in Camlough and Portadown. **4.** Terrorists shot dead five members of the Social Democratic and Labour Party in two separate incidents in Co. Armagh. **5.** Ten Protestant men travelling home from work at a textile factory in a mini-bus in South Armagh were ambushed and shot dead. **6.** Mr. Wilson ordered the Army's " spearhead battalion " to move immediately to South Armagh following the previous night's wave of violence. **8.** An agreement between Mr. Rees and the Irish Justice Minister (Mr. Cooney), was reached to set up a hot line to connect British Army's H.Q. in Bessbrook and the Irish Army's forward base at Dundalk as part of

closer cooperation between U.K. and Eire in the campaign against terrorists. **12.** Mr. Rees announced that the Ulster Convention would be reconvened on Feb. 3 for four weeks in the hope that it would reach agreement on " partnership and participations " in the future government of the Province. Mr. Wilson told the Commons of intensified security measures to make the whole of Co. Armagh a special emergency area. **13.** Two I.R.A. men who planted it and two other people were killed by a bomb which exploded in a Belfast shopping arcade and 20 other persons were injured. **14.** Provisional I.R.A. announced a campaign of terror against senior civil servants in Ulster, disclosing that it had begun on Jan. 5 with bomb attacks on homes of four officials. **22.** Eire police and troops discovered the largest cache of I.R.A. explosives found on either side of the Irish border, uncovering nearly 3 tons of materials and equipment in a field at Gormanstown, Co. Meath. Terrorists claimed the lives of six more people in Ulster, including two policemen killed when a booby-trapped shotgun exploded. **28.** Eire's Finance Minister (Mr. Richie Ryan), presenting his budget proposals, declared the Provisional I.R.A.s " forces of evil " were costing the country vast amounts of money and announced price rises on whiskey (up 5p to 56p a double), beer (up 5p to 30p a pint), cigarettes up 3p to 43p for 20), and petrol (up 10p a gallon to 86p).

Feb. 6. Provisional I.R.A. blew up part of the Belfast–Dublin Enterprise express over a bridge at Scarva, Co. Armagh, but only 4, including 2 children, were slightly injured. **8.** The new leader of the Provisional I.R.A. was named as Leo Martin of Belfast in succession to Seamus Twomey, ousted chief of staff. **10.** Two bombs in the centre of Belfast and 8 incendiary devices planted in shops marked the first anniversary of the " ceasefire " in Ulster. **13.** A bomb exploded at Dublin's Shelbourne Hotel. The building was cleared after a warning and no one was hurt. A series of firebombs went off almost simultaneously in seven of the City's department stores. Roman Catholic youths in western areas of the City hijacked cars, stoned soldiers and attacked police. **20.** Eight people were taken to hospital in Belfast after a bomb was thrown into a bar from a passing car following a series of incendiary attacks on shops in the City centre. **28.** Glen Barr, Leader of the Workers' Defence Council during the 1974 Ulster general strike, resigned as political adviser to Ulster Defence Association and severed all links with the para-military organizations.

Mar. 3. The Eire Parliament gave final approval by 65–61 votes to the Criminal Law Jurisdictions Bill which sought to prevent the Republic being a sanctuary for terrorists. **5.** Ulster's Convention was formally dissolved by Mr. Rees because there was " no prospect of agreement between the parties there ", but he made it clear that direct rule would be positive and not negative. **6.** Fourteen mortar rockets were fired at Belfast's Aldergrove Airport from a hijacked lorry, but no one was injured. **26.** Terrorists fired six mortar bombs at the Army base in Fort George, Londonderry, but caused only slight damage, no one being hurt. **31.** Three soldiers were killed and a fourth wounded when their Land-Rover was blown up by a land mine in a country road in South Armagh. An estimated £700,000 was stolen by Provisional I.R.A. in an armed raid on a mail train near Dublin. Patrick Joseph Thompson, unemployed coach-builder of Tullydonnell, South Armagh, was jailed for life and recommended to serve no less than 30 years when convicted at Belfast City Commission of murdering four soldiers in a booby trap explosion in South Armagh in July 1975.

April 3. Thirty-eight people were injured when a bomb exploded in the Roman Catholic Lower Falls area of Belfast in a crowded bar. **19.** An I.R.A. gunman murdered a prison officer in his Belfast home while his wife was held in another room by a second gunman. Earlier another prison officer was shot and badly wounded outside Crumlin Road jail by two teenaged terrorists. **21.** The Eire Government banned the Dublin demonstration planned for Sunday, April 25, by the Provisional I.R.A. to mark the 60th anniversary of the 1916 Easter rising, this being the first ban of its kind in Dublin since the 1930s. **22.** Two U.U.F. men, David Wallace and Thomas Lawder, both of Belfast, were each sentenced at Belfast City Commission to 20 years jail on charges of bombing a public house in the Roman Catholic Markets area of Belfast in August 1975, attempting to murder a customer, and having a gun and ammunition. **23.** Robert Welsh, aged 19, an apprentice joiner of Belfast, was sentenced to life imprisonment at Belfast City Commission and recommended to serve not less than 15 years for the murder of a Roman Catholic street cleaner in Belfast on Feb. 10. **28.** Irish Parliamentary Labour party withdrew the whip from one of its deputies, Dr. David Thornley, for appearing in the Dail with Provisional I.R.A. leaders at the previous week-end's illegal Sinn Fein parade in Dublin. Mr. Rees told Westminster M.P.s that committees had been set up in Northern Ireland to review the provisions for compensation for injury and damage to property.

May 5. About 600 troops of the Army's spearhead Battalion left Ulster, the pull-out leading to greater involvement by R.U.C. and Royal Military Police in West Belfast. Nine prisoners, two serving sentences for attempted murder, and all members of Irish Republican Socialist party, escaped from Maze Prison, Co. Antrim, by digging a tunnel with makeshift tools. **6.** Eight men of the Special Air Services unit of the British Army appeared in a Dublin special criminal court on firearms charges after being arrested about 500 yards inside Eire and were released on bail of £5,000 each, the Army Minister (Mr. Bob Brown) informing the Commons at Westminster, that the soldiers had inadvertently crossed the border due to a map-reading error. **6.** The Irish Supreme Court declared that the Criminal Law (Jurisdiction) Bill did not offend the constitution and the measure was signed by the Irish President so that the Dublin Special Criminal Court became able to try terrorists for offences committed north of the border. **15.** Ten people including four R.U.C. officers were killed in four Ulster bomb incidents, three policemen by a border booby-trap in the village of Belcoo, Co. Fermanagh, after the police station was machine-gunned, a fourth policeman being wounded; two people by an explosion in the Avenue Bar, Belfast, as customers watched the Scotland–England football match on T.V., with 27 others injured; another policeman when his car was ambushed on the Newry–Warren Point Road, with two policemen wounded; and three persons by a blast in a public house at Charlemont, Co. Armagh, where 12 people were also injured. **23.** The Protestant para-military Ulster Volunteer Force announced that it was calling off its terrorist activity in Republican areas for the next three months. The European Commission of Human Rights rejected on technical grounds petitions brought by seven men who alleged they were tortured by British troops and police in Northern Ireland in 1972. **29.** The new Protestant vigilante force, the Ulster Service Corps, claimed that the first two battalions of armed vigilantes patrolled parts of South

Armagh, and on May 30 the Corps made its debut at a church parade of 500 volunteers at Portadown, Co. Armagh.

June 3. Dublin High Court quashed a lower court's extradition order against a suspected terrorist wanted in Britain in connection with bombing of Mr. Edward Heath's home in 1974 and with other explosions on the grounds the offences were political. **6.** Ten people died in a week-end of violence in Ulster with 78 injured. **9.** A married couple, Noel and Maria Murray, were convicted of shooting a Dublin policeman after a bank robbery in September 1975 and were sentenced to death for his capital murder by Dublin's Special Criminal Court. **18.** A man was killed and 36 people were injured when bombers attacked a public house in Shore Road, North Belfast, without warning. **28.** A strike by 10,000 bank officials over a pay dispute closed all commercial banks in the Irish Republic. **29.** Four members of the Irish Republican Socialist party were jailed at Belfast City Commission for terrorist offences in Co. Armagh for between 30 months and 10 years.

July 2. Four people were killed and 5 injured when gunmen opened fire inside a crowded public house, the Ramble Inn, on the main Antrim to Ballymena road. The Attorney-General informed the Westminster Parliament that the maximum penalty for carrying a firearm in a public place was to be increased from 5 to 10 years imprisonment. **5.** Mr. Callaghan paid his first visit to Ulster as Prime Minister. **15.** The Irish Court ordered a top-level inquiry into how five captured I.R.A. Provisionals smuggled plastic explosives into the cells of Dublin Special Criminal Court and then blasted their way out in an escape operation. One Provisional was knocked unconscious and three others were recaptured wtihin half-an-hour. **21.** The British Ambassador to the Republic of Ireland (Mr. Christopher Ewart-Biggs) was assassinated when his car was wrecked by a terrorist landmine near the Ambassador's official residence south of Dublin. Miss Judith Cook, secretary to Mr. Brian Cubbon, head of the civil service at the Northern Ireland Office in Belfast, was also killed and Mr. Cubbon and Mr. Brian O'Driscoll, the Ambassador's chauffeur, were seriously injured.

Aug. 3. Holidaymakers and staff were evacuated from cafés, shops and an amusement arcade in the resort of Portrush, Co. Antrim, as eight terrorist bombs exploded causing extensive damage. **9.** Mrs. Maire Drumm, vice-president of Provisional Sinn Fein, was arrested by police and troops at her home in Belfast and was held under emergency legislation. Mr. Gerry Fitt, M.P., leader of Social Democratic and Labour Party drove a Republican mob of some 30 rioters from his house at pistolpoint after they had invaded it at dawn; his wife and his 13-year-old daughter witnessed the attack. **10.** Two children, Joanna McGuire, 8, and her brother, Andrew, six weeks old, were killed and their mother and another brother, John, 2½ years old, were seriously injured when troops pursued I.R.A. gunmen through south-western Belfast, the terrorists' hijacked vehicle ploughing into the McGuire family as its driver was shot dead. John died in hospital on Aug. 11. **14.** Some 10,000 Roman Catholic and Protestant women and children demanding an end to violence in Ulster paraded through the Roman Catholic Andersonstown area of Belfast, the peace demonstrators praying and singing hymns. **18.** Mr. Brian Faulkner, the last prime minister of Northern Ireland, announced his resignation as leader of the Unionist party two years previously, and his retirement from politics. **20.** The remains of William Joyce, "Lord Haw-Haw"

of the German wartime propaganda broadcasts, were re-interred at Galway, after the body was exhumed from the prison grave at Wandsworth where he was buried after his execution 30 years earlier. **23.** The two-month long strike by 10,000 bank workers in the Irish Republic was settled when staff voted to accept the Government recommended pay increases of between £3 and £5 plus 2 per cent. **24.** New and heavier penalties for terrorists and those who incited or assisted them with additional powers for the Irish Army or police were contained in the Emergency Powers Bill published by the Irish Government. The appointment was announced of Mr. Robin Haydon, British High Commissioner in Malta, as British Ambassador in Dublin to succeed Mr. Christopher Ewart-Biggs, who was murdered in July. A new Irish-American organization, the Ireland Fund, was announced in Dublin to raise money for Irish charities. **25.** Belfast police captured an 8-strong gang of I.R.A. bombers in the Malone district and with the aid of a priest ended a three-hour siege by three armed men holding an elderly gardener hostage in West Belfast. **27.** Mrs. Maire Drumm, vice-president of Provisional Sinn Fein, was freed by a Belfast court when the Crown decided not to proceed further against her for taking part in an illegal procession on Aug. 8. **28.** Nearly 25,000 Roman Catholics and Protestants marched along Belfast's Shankill Road in another women's demonstration for peace. In Dublin a similar crowd staged a march of support and several other towns in the Republic also marched for peace. **30.** A series of fire bombs was set off in cinemas and public houses in Dublin.

Sept. 1. A national state of emergency was formerly declared in the Irish Republic because of the "armed conflict in Northern Ireland" and was approved by both Houses of Parliament. In the Dail voting was 70–65 in favour of the motion and in the Senate it was 35–18. The Official Unionist party H.Q. in Glengall Street, Belfast, was destroyed by fire. **2.** The report of the European Commission of Human Rights on complaints of inhuman treatment and torture by the Irish Republic against the U.K. Government in Northern Ireland was published in Strasbourg.

ENVIRONMENT AND LOCAL AFFAIRS

(1975) Sept. 22. It was announced that the Prime Minister had asked Mr. Harold Lever, Chancellor of the Duchy of Lancaster, to carry out a thorough assessment of the financial problems facing the arts. **25.** The Commons Expenditure Committee published its report on Charity Commissioners and their accountability, and recommended a new system for their appointment. A discussion document, "Devolution and Regional Government in England," was published by the N.E.C. of the Labour Party. **30.** The Minister for Sport (Mr. Denis Howell) announced new regulations for coaches carrying football supporters, including limited stops and banning of alcohol, were being introduced immediately in a pilot scheme in the Newcastle upon Tyne area and that he was setting up a wider inquiry into anti-social behaviour on public transport.

8. **Oct.** The Environment Department issued a statement outlining certain relaxations to some of the provisions of the Community Land Bill which gave local authorities power to acquire land for development. **13.** The number of first-class letters dropped by over one-fifth or 20·6 per cent between August, 1974, and August, 1975, and the number of second-class letters increased by 6·6 per cent, the Minister of State for Industry (Mr. Gregor MacKenzie) told Parliament. British Tourist Authori-

ity's annual report showed that despite a 15 per cent. fall in the number of American tourists who visited Britain last year, the country was 211,000 up on overseas visitors, who totalled 7,935,000, compared with 1973. **16.** The White Paper, " Better Services for the Mentally Ill," was published and in a foreword the Social Services Secretary (Mrs. Castle) stated that at least 24 million working days were lost each year by people suffering from mental ill health. The Isles of Scilly were designated as an area of outstanding natural beauty by the Country-side Commission. **29.** Education Secretary (Mr. Fred Mulley) announced proposals to abolish the free travel concession for pupils with over three miles to go to school and to introduce instead flat rates for all schoolchildren.

Nov. 3. The Queen officially opened British Petroleum's pipeline in a control room at Dyce, Aberdeen, to bring ashore the first oil from a major British field, The Forties, in the North Sea. **4.** Proposed regulations compelling motorists to use headlights at all times at night were withdrawn in the Commons by the Transport Minister (Mr. John Gilbert) following criticism from M.P.s of all parties. Llanelli, Dinefwr and Aberconway voted for Sunday public house opening in Welsh referendum. **11.** The Parliamentary Commissioner (Ombudsman) (Sir Alan Marre) published his report into Home Office arrangements for increasing T.V. licence fees in April and for its action against people who replaced licences early to avoid fee increases, while the Home Secretary reaffirmed to the Commons his intentions announced in June 1975 to start reviewing overlapping licences taken out before April 1, 1975, unless the £6 extra fee was paid by Dec. 1. **21.** The Environment Secretary (Mr. Crosland) announced a cut of one per cent. equal to £100 million, in the proportion of local council spending which would be paid for by the Government and warned that the Government would not bail out councils which ignored the call for a standstill in providing local services. **23.** Leeds opened its first Race Relations Festival in an attempt to ease tensions among its 25,000 immigrant population. **25.** Government proposals to improve firework safety, including a ban on sale of fireworks to children under 16, were announced in the Commons.

Dec. 8. A census report, " Population Trends," published by the Office of Population Censuses and surveys, stated the number of " New Commonwealth " people living in Britain in mid-1974 was 1,744,000 or 3·2 per cent. of the population, or 258,000 more than at the time of the 1971 census. **9.** Drilling started at Troon, Cornwall, at the beginning of an experiment to discover if energy could be obtained from hot rocks deep below the earth's surface. The Government laid an order before Parliament to postpone the next Greater London Council elections from 1976 until 1977 and the London Borough elections from 1977 until 1978 with future London elections being held at 4-year intervals. A fight to preserve the public's right to use a footpath within 500 yards of the terrace at Chequers, the Prime Minister's official country home, failed in the High Court, the footpath being diverted for security reasons. **10.** According to the Government publication, " Social Trends 1975 " the U.K. had a population of 28,800,000 women and 27,300,000 men in 1974 and the birth rate continued to decline in that year to a 20th-century low figure of 13 per 1,000, the death rate for men and women remaining constant at 12 per 1,000, and the divorce rate declining from a figure of 9·5 in 1972 to 8·4 per 1,000 married population although rising by almost a fifth in Scotland and Ulster.

(1976) Jan. 1. Under new regulations driving licences issued from that day would last until the holder's 70th birthday. **2.** It was announced that the Greater London Council's policy of dispersing population and industry to areas outside London was to be reversed because of social and economic effects. **9.** Cuts in many local council services and increased charges in others were forecast following publication of a Government circular setting out the economic background to the rate support grant settlement for the next financial year. **15.** The report of the review body set up by Norfolk County Council and the Area Health Authority to look into the circumstances surrounding the death of Steven Meurs, the 16-month-old baby found dead in his cot in King's Lynn in April 13 1975, was published. **27.** The final report of the advisory committee on falsework, the temporary support used to carry the weight as the permanent structure was erected, was published following the inquiry ordered by the Court after 3 men died in the collapse of the Loddon Bridge, near Reading, in 1972. **28.** The report of the Committee of Inquiry into the structure of the electricity supply industry in England and Wales was published.

Feb. 2. Greater London Council planning committee approved a scheme, agreed with Westminster City Council, for the future of Piccadilly Circus and involving removal of Eros' statue 10-15 feet south-east of its existing position. **3.** The Office of Population Censuses issued figures showing that the total number of abortions notified in England and Wales in 1975 was 140,521 compared with 163,117 in 1974 and 167,149 in 1973. The Select Committee on Nationalized Industries published their report on the Post Office's Letter Post services. **4.** Concorde was given permission to operate Transatlantic scheduled flights to U.S. when the U.S. Transport Secretary (Mr. William Coleman) announced the decision to permit trial services to Washington and New York for 16 months, British Airways, and Air France receiving allowance for four flights a day to New York's Kennedy Airport and two to Washington's Dulles international. **11.** The Prices Secretary (Mrs. Shirley Williams) announced her selective price restraint scheme with a 5 per cent. price rise limit on certain foods and articles to begin on Feb. 16. **16.** The number of weekly newspapers in Britain fell by 51 during the year; from 1,193 in January 1975 to 1,142 in January 1976; one new evening newspaper was published bringing the number of daily and Sunday newspapers to 143. **19.** The second report of the Parliamentary Commissioner for Administration (The Ombudsman), annual report, 1975, disclosed that he had received 928 complaints through M.P.s during the year, a 70 per cent. increase on 1971. **27.** It was announced that Sunday letter collections were to end and that all post offices would close on Saturday afternoons because of further postal economies. Late collections in London and major provincial cities were to be withdrawn for a year's trial period.

Mar. 1. The Commons in a free vote, gave a second reading to the Road Traffic (Seat Belts) Bill by 249-139, a majority in favour of compulsory wearing of seat-belts of 110. **2.** A bill was published to amend the Weights and Measures Act 1963 and the Weights and Measures Act 1963 and the Weights and Measures Act (Northern Ireland) 1967 to provide powers to change over to metrication by 1980 in light of an E.E.C. directive. **3.** The Home Office stated that an estimated 27,000 dependants of Commonwealth citizens were accepted for settlement in the U.K. in 1975 compared with 20,845 in 1974 and 19,945 in 1973. **4.** A new senior citizen railcard scheme offering pensioners rail

travel anywhere and at anytime at half-fare to-gether with day return tickets at half-price was announced by British Rail starting in April. **9.** World's population topped 4,000 million mark in January, according to U.N. Demographic Year Book. **18.** The Government's consultative docu-ment on water reorganization, "Review of the Water Industry in England and Wales," was pub-lished. **23.** The Government postponed the second reading of the Weights and Measures Bill which would expedite changeover by U.K. to metrication by 1980 to allow "more time for consultation about the measure." **29.** The report of the Ombudsman (Sir Alan Mzrre) on the health hazards of the asbestos factory at Hebden Bridge, Yorkshire, closed down in 1970, was released.

April 8. The annual report of the Director-General of Fair Trading (Mr. John Methven) was published and disclosed that over 400,000 com-plaints about goods and services were made in the 12 months to Sept, 1975. **13.** The Post Office announced the suspension of Sunday collections from letter boxes from May 2. **25.** The Women's Royal Voluntary Service's annual report showed it issued 14,174,789 meals on wheels to the sick and disabled during the year ended Sept. 30, 1975. **28.** The report of the Blennerhassett Committee on drinking and driving was published. **29.** The Industry Secretary (Mr. Varley) ordered the Post Office to cut the proposed 25 per cent. increase in parcel charges to 13 per cent.

May 6. Local government elections in the metro-politan districts and district councils in England and Wales resulted in more than 1,800 net gains in seats for the Conservatives, who took over power in 70 councils. Labour lost over 1,300 seats net and the Liberals 200 net. **12.** The Government an-nounced that it would scrap immediately Britain's latest new town at Stonehouse, 18 miles outside Glasgow (3 years after its designation and after £4 million had been spent) in favour of urban renewal in Glasgow. It was disclosed that 10 for-mer councillors of Clay Cross, Derbyshire, had saved themselves from bankruptcy by paying off a surcharge of about £3,000, the money being raised by Labour parties and trade unions. **13.** A hospital administrator, a doctor, and two nursing officers were criticized in the report of an inquiry into the deaths of four patients in the psychiatric unit at Darlington Memorial Hospital. **19.** The report of the committee of inquiry into local government finance chaired by Mr. Frank Layfield, Q.C., was published. **25.** According to preliminary figures issued by Office of Population, Censuses and Sur-veys, a total of 230,700 people left Britain in 1975 compared with 188,900 new settlers.

June 10. "Free Festivals," the first report of the working group on pop festivals, was published. **16.** The number of immigrants from the "New Commonwealth" and Pakistan admitted to U.K. for settlement increased by 9,201 to 34,510 accord-ing to the annual Home Office White Paper on immigration statistics. **17.** The Government decided to grant Sikh motor-cyclists special exemption on religious grounds to allow them to wear turbans instead of crash helmets. **21.** The Education Secretary (Mr. Mulley) announced a national investigation to establish how to deal with truancy and indiscipline in schools after a private meeting with leaders of 15 organizations represent-ing teachers, local authorities and welfare workers. **24.** The Battle Abbey estate, site of the Battle of Hastings, was bought at auction by the Department of the Environment for £690,000. Most of the finance was provided by an unnamed American academic institution " with a view to the whole of this historic site being preserved in the British

national interest and as a real and tangible token of the enduring link between the U.S.A. and the U.K. in this bicentennial year of the U.S.A."

July 2. Minister for Planning and Local Govern-ment (Mr. John Silkin) told the Commons that the Government would introduce a bill urgently to give statutory water undertakings new powers of control over use of water in times of shortage, and described the present drought as Britain's worst for 250 years. **13.** Mr. Silkin announced that the Government was to lift its ban on the sale of houses in new towns to tenants. **14.** Fines of up to £400 for ignoring restrictions on the use of water during a drought were proposed in a new measure, the Drought Bill. **16.** The report of the four-month public inquiry by Mr. Robin Auld, Q.C., into conditions and standards at the William Tyndale Junior School, Islington, London, was published. **29.** The Commons Select Committee on Abortions reported and recommended tighter restrictions on abortions, abortion agencies, clinics and pregnancy testing.

Aug. 1. The National Trust acquired eight miles of Dyfed coastline at Stackpole, Pembrokeshire. **2.** The Energy Secretary (Mr. Benn) told the Commons that people too poor to pay their electricity bills were to receive a £25 million sub-sidy in the following winter. Regulations making Lassa fever and rabies notifiable diseases were brought into force at midnight when the Social Services Secretary (Mr. Ennals) signed orders under the Public Health Act. **4.** The Transport Minister announced that the necessary legislation would be introduced as soon as practicable to implement the report by the Blennerhassett Committee on strengthening the drive-drink laws with the excep-tion of the recommended new type of breath analysis device. The report of the Working Party on Dogs, which recommended an increase in dog licences to £5 a year to pay for uniformed wardens dealing with strays, was published. **5.** Coalite and Chemical Products plant at Bolsover, near Chester-field, the only plant in the U.K. making the same chemical as the "poison cloud" factory in Italy, had been shut down at the request of the Health and Safety Executive, it was stated. The Environment Secretary (Mr. Shore), in a Parliamentary statement pledged support for the strategic plan to revitalize 5,500 acres of London's dockland. **9.** One million people in south-east Wales had their water supplies cut off because of the continuing drought. On Aug. 23 these 13-hour cuts were extended to 17 hours, from 2 p.m. to 7 a.m. daily. **10.** The Post Office stated that they were to introduce a £4 million scheme to switch Britain's biggest cities—London, Leeds, Manchester, Birmingham, Liver-pool, and Bristol—to mechanical letter-sorting in the next 18 months, making use of postal codes essential. **16.** Big Ben was stopped at noon for repairs after the clock broke down 12 days before, due to a major fault in the quarter bell mechanism; it was restarted 12 hours later without the chimes. **17.** Water pressure in London was cut by 25 per cent. to help conserve supplies depleted by the drought, with the aim of saving 40 million gallons a day. **18.** A report, "Equal Status for Men and Women in Occupational Pension Schemes," by the Occupational Pensions Board, was published and recommended complete equality between the sexes. **20.** Ramblers and picnickers were asked to keep clear of tinder-dry forests until the end of the drought because of the risk of fires and the Forestry Commission announced that roads and tracks into forests in Dorset, Shropshire, Herefordshire, Cheshire, Staffordshire and Nottinghamshire were being closed. **24.** Mr. Denis Howell, Minister for Sport, was appointed to coordinate Government

action during the drought emergency. He warned householders of higher costs, inconvenience, and " possibly some discomfort," in an appeal to domestic users to cut water consumption by half all over the country.

FINANCE

(1975) Oct. 6. The First National Finance Corporation announced a loan of £73,440,000 for the six months to June, 1975, believed to be the largest loss made by a bank in Britain. The total hire purchase debt in Britain was down 3 per cent. on a year before at £2,238 million, the Industry Department reported. All the British major banks raised their interest rates by 1 per cent., the base lending rate increasing from 10 per cent. to 11 per cent. **16.** A pledge of support was given in the Commons by the Minister for Overseas Development (Mr. Reg Prentice) to the Crown Agents, the semi-official agency, for which the Government had already agreed to provide a recoverable grant of £85 millions to cover the writing down of asset values in the 1974 accounts. **17.** The September statistics published by the Employment Department showed that Britain's annual rate of inflation dropped for the first time in a year being 26·6 per cent. compared with 26·9 per cent. in the 12 months to August. **20.** Employees of the workers' co-operative newspaper, the *Scottish Daily News*, voted unanimously to appoint a provisional liquidator in an effort to prevent the paper's collapse. Barclay's Bank appointed a receiver and manager for the Norton Villiers Triumph factory at Small Heath, Birmingham. **24.** Mr. Jim Slater resigned as chairman and director of Slater Walker Securities and of its subsidiaries and associated companies. **29.** After the Chrysler Corporation in Detroit had announced a world-wide loss of $254,600,600 (about £125,400,000) for the first nine months of the year Mr. John Riccardo, the chairman, said that the British subsidiary was their biggest headache but " we have no timetable on any decision we might take." Talks on the future of Chrysler's British operations were held at Chequers on Nov. 3 between the Prime Minister, Mr. Riccardo, and Mr. Eric Varley, Industry Secretary. **30.** According to Government figures, bankruptcies and company failures were at a 15-year peak; bankruptcies in the third quarter of 1975 totalled 1,719, 24·8 per cent. up on a year earlier and company liquidations reached 1,135, nearly 37 per cent. higher than the same period the previous year.

Nov. 7. It was announced that Britain had made application to borrow almost £1,000 million from the International Monetary Fund. **12.** The Prices Secretary (Mrs. Williams) told the Commons that Hoffman–La Roche, the Swiss drug manufacturers, had agreed to repay about £3,750,000 for excessive profits made between January 1970 and April 1973 in addition to repayments of £1,600,000 for the years 1967 to 1969 in settlement of the dispute over the tranquillisers Librium and Valium, which were prescribed in the N.H.S.

Dec. 2. British Aircraft Corporation announced the signing by Persia of Britain's largest single missile export contract worth £186 million. **9.** British Leyland announced their decision to stop almost all capital spending until productivity improved; the management proposed a six-point plan to union leaders to improve productivity. **10.** The select committee on a Wealth Tax, appointed a year earlier, was unable to agree to a majority report but decided to publish the minutes of evidence and the minority reports of M.P.s or groups in the Committee. **16.** The Government announced its rescue operation for Chrysler's British subsidiary

with a financial commitment of a minimum of £72,500,000 and a potential maximum of £162,500,000 involving a job loss of 8,000. **19.** The report of the Commons sub-committee on public expenditure was published with some critical recommendations about the borrowing requirement procedures. It was announced that the Government was to provide a £275,000 loan to assist part of Norton Villiers Triumph, the motor-cycle firm, to enable stocks of motor-cycles held overseas to be disposed of in an orderly fashion, but made clear that it had undertaken no commitment to support continued manufacture by NVT of motor-cycles.

(1976) Jan. 14. Mr. Healey announced that the Government was to provide a further £30 million towards financing accelerated investment projects additional to the £90 million already allocated. **20.** Italian Government announced that it had closed the country's foreign exchange market after the underlying balance of payments position was reported to have worsened. **29.** After two Dept. of Trade inspectors investigating the collapse of London and County Securities, the secondary bank, had reported that " this venture in secondary banking must remain a cautionary tale for any leading politican," Mr. Jeremy Thorpe, the Liberal leader, who joined the board of the company as a non-executive director in 1971 and who was cleared absolutely of any responsibility for the collapse, stated that he accepted the inspectors' conclusions.

Feb. 3. World Bank approved $33 million (£16,500,000) loan to Chile for copper development. **10.** Directors of Felixstowe Dock, a privately-owned port, rejected a take-over bid from European Ferries, the cross-Channel company, in favour of that by the State-owned British Transport Docks Board. **19.** Publication of the Treasury White Paper on Public Expenditure outlined cuts in public spending of nearly £3,000 million by the 1978–79 financial year and about £5,000 million over the 1976–80 period. **23.** Receivers were appointed by Barclay's Bank, at the firm's request, to manage Brentford Nylons. **26.** A receiver was called in by Bear Brand, the Liverpool-based hosiery company. **27.** The Bank of England's minimum lending rate came down ½ per cent. to 9¼ per cent., the lowest since July 1973.

Mar. 5. The pound fell below $2 for the first time and at the close of trading in London it stood at $1·9820. **8.** M.P.s were told that the Govt. had borrowed about £343,000 million since March 1974, most of it being required to refinance maturing debt, while the net additional borrowing by the Government in that period was about £15,000 million. **16.** Shareholders of the State-controlled British Leyland were told at the annual meeting in London that the company broke even in the 5 months to the end of February after losing £123 million in the year ending September 1975.

April 2. According to Treasury figures, U.K. reserves fell by £584 million in March, the biggest loss recorded. **9.** The Department of Trade inspectors' report on the Vehicle and General Insurance Co. Ltd. was published. **13.** Shell and British Petroleum, the two British firms named in the Italian oil bribery allegations, admitted that they had made payments to Italian political parties, Shell Italiana paying over £2 million between 1969–73 and BP paying £800,000 in the same period. Both companies stated that their payments were not illegal and did not violate Italian tax laws. French Total Oil group also admitted on April 14 that it had been involved in making payments to Italian political parties " in accordance with local custom." The ceiling on the fund for loans and grants to firms under section 8 of the Industry Act was lifted from £550 million to £1,600 million

under a new bill introduced in the Commons by the Industry Secretary (Mr. Varley). Six big firms which were to enter into talks with the Government to produce "planning agreements" about their long-term development were named in the Commons. The Governments White Paper on the Crown Agents was published and contained proposals for improved financial controls. **20.** Switzerland imposed import controls on all foreign banknotes to the limit of 20,000 Swiss francs (about £4,500) per person per quarter. **23.** The Bank of England raised minimum lending rate by 1½ per cent. to 10½ per cent. in an attempt to steady the pound. **26.** The pound sank to another record low figure at $1·802, 38·2 per cent. below the 1971 parity, but later steadied. Switzerland had its biggest budget deficit in the previous year of about £290 million, it was officially announced in Berne, mainly because the economic recession reduced tax receipts. **28.** The Bank of England announced that investigations were being conducted in conjunction with the Treasury " with a view to discovering whether any official of the Bank has knowingly been involved in any breaches of the Exchange Control Act, 1947."

May 4. It was announced that Chrysler made a loss of £35½ million on its British operations in the previous year, this being more than double the £17,700,000 deficit in 1974. Mr. Healey announced that Britian was to take up the first part of $800 million from its credit with the International Monetary Fund during May. **5.** Italy imposed heavy import curbs after an emergency Cabinet meeting with a 50 per cent. import deposit scheme. **7.** The London visit of President Geisel of Brazil ended with an offer of over £300 million worth of orders for Britain. **11.** Common Market bankers agreed to grant Italy a £250 million credit line to strengthen the country's financial position. **12.** I.C.I., in the largest capital-raising operation undertaken by a single British company, asked its shareholders for about £200 million of new money through a rights issue. **13.** An equity bank to provide additional equity finance for industry was launched in London under the name of Equity Capital for Industry with the initial aim of raising £30 million to £50 million to supplement the existing facilities of the capital market. **20.** Burmah Oil sold its North American interests to the American firm, R. J. Reynolds Industries, for £290 million in cash. **21.** A new loan of £8,600,000 was made to British Gas Corporation by the Luxemburg-based European Investment Bank to help finance a pipeline across Southern England to carry North Sea natural gas to the south west.

June 7. Mr. Healey told the Commons that " recent pressures in the exchange markets carried sterling to a level which can not be justified " and that the Governor of the Bank of England had just issued a statement that " financial authorities from the Group of Ten Countries and Switzerland together with the Bank for International Settlements had agreed to make available to the Bank of England a standby credit in excess of $5 billion (about £3,000 millions)," which was a short-term facility made up of $2 billion from the U.S. authorities and of $3·3 billion from the central banks. **16.** It was disclosed that the State-owned Govan Shipbuilders lost £9,573,000 in 1975 compared with a deficit of £5,317,000 in 1974. **24.** The Government provisionally decided to advance £5 million to Lonrho to buy the bulk of Brentford Nylons assets. **28.** Port of London Authority Chairman (Lord Aldington) announced the port had made a loss of £8,400,000 in 1975 and said that a surplus of dock workers at the port would cost between £6–

£7 million in 1976 in addition to an estimated £5 million redundancy payments.

July 1. British Petroleum agreed to give British National Oil Corporation an option to buy 51 per cent. of its North Sea output. **6.** The report by two Department of Trade inspectors into the affairs of Lonrho, the international trading group, was published after an investigation lasting 3 years. Mr. Angus Ogilvy, a former Lonrho director, issued a statement that as he had been placed " in an impossible position " by the report's criticisms and was denied legal redress, he was proposing to resign his directorships. **8.** The Government announced substantial changes in its Budget plan to tax executives for the use of their company cars. **12.** The Halifax Building Society agreed to merge with the Wakefield Building Society to protect the latter, which had discovered a loss of some £500,000. **14.** Israel announced that it was to end its currency link with the American dollar and link its pound to a selected " basket" of currencies, including the pound sterling, the French franc, the Deutschemark, and the Dutch florin. **18.** The Israeli Cabinet decided that devaluations of the Israeli pound would in future take place at irregular intervals and at varying rates of up to 8 per cent. every four months. **21.** The Industry Secretary (Mr. Varley) announced that the Government had accepted the recommendation from the National Enterprise Board to advance the first £100 million instalment of planned Government loans to British Leyland. **23.** Kirkby Manufacturing and Engineering Co., a workers' cooperative, announced that it had lost £1½ million of Govt. money 18 months after being founded with a grant of £3,900,000, but a workers' meeting was told that the company had a healthy future. **26.** British Airports Authority announced a £16,800,000 trading profit last year compared with £10,100,000 in 1974–75 with net profit after interest was paid and before tax of £13,100,000 compared with £8,400,000 in the previous year. **28.** A White Paper, The British Aid Programme in 1975, disclosed that U.K.'s official development aid to poorer countries amounted to £432 million in 1975 against £352 million in 1974.

Aug. 26. British Airways annual report and accounts were published showing a net loss of £16·3 million in the year ending March 31 compared with a net loss of £9·4 million the previous year, but before paying interest on capital borrowings of £14 million, tax, and a special provision of £15·6 million to cover increased costs of repaying foreign loans due to the fall in the pound's value, the airline made a profit of £10·1 million, £4·7 million more than the previous year. **31.** The British Government agreed to pay Burmah Oil £103 million for the bulk of its remaining North Sea assets.

ACCIDENTS AND DISASTERS

(1975) Sept. 20. Thirteen miners were killed a mile below the surface of a mine shaft in Queensland by explosion and cave-in. **25.** Four Italian air force Starfighter jets crashed into a hillside on the West German border with Luxemburg near Bitburg five minutes after take-off from the American airfield at Bitburg, all four pilots being killed. **26.** All 16 American Air Force personnel aboard a Sikorsky CH-53 helicopter were killed when it crashed near Paderborn in north-west Germany. **28.** Ten territorial soldiers were drowned in the River Trent at Cromwell Lock, near Newark, when their assault craft capsized during watermanship exercises, there being only one survivor. Four men died when their Piper Cherokee plane crashed in the Galloway Hills in

south west Scotland after taking off from Prestwick. **29.** Mike Burke, 32 year-old BBC assistant cameraman, and a member of the British team which climbed Everest the previous week, was killed when attempting a second assault on the summit by the south-west face. **30.** All 60 people aboard a Russian-built Tupolev-154 airliner of Malev, the Hungarian airline, were killed when the plane crashed into the sea on approaching Beirut airport.

Oct. I. An explosive blew up and levelled a Montreal factory where it was being manufactured, killing eight workers. **14.** Five members of the crew of an R.A.F. Vulcan bomber were killed when the plane exploded and crashed near Valetta, Malta, on its approach to Luqa after a training flight from Waddington, Lincs., the pilot and co-pilot escaping with back injuries, and a girl of 16 was also killed and 20 other people were injured as parts of the wreckage crashed into a narrow street at Zabbar. **25.** Five people died and many were treated for carbon monoxide poisoning in the Dunkirk area after coal and gas heating appliances failed to function properly in heavy fog. **28.** More than 25 people died, another 25 were missing, and over 500 were treated for injuries as a result of Hurricane Olivia in the Mexican port of Mazatlan; 30,000 people were made homeless. **30.** At least 75 people were believed to have died when a Yugoslav DC9 charter plane with 115 Czechoslovak holidaymakers and 5 crew members hit a hilltop in heavy fog near Prague.

Nov. I. Three men died and three were seriously hurt in an explosion on the North Sea oil production platform, Alpha, in the Ekofisk field. **4.** Five workers were killed and 13 injured by an explosion at a British Steel Corporation plant in Scunthorpe, Lincs., the death toll later rising to eleven. **7.** Fourteen men were killed and 100 injured in a Dutch chemical plant explosion at a works owned by Dutch State Mines at Beek, southern Holland. **8.** Five young children died in fire which destroyed their home at Whelley, near Wigan. **12.** H.M.S. *Achilles*, a 2,500 tons frigate, and the Panamanian tanker, *Olympic Alliance* (97,200 tons) collided in the English Channel in fog and an oil slick was formed. **20.** A mother and five schoolgirls were killed when their car exploded in flames after being struck by a Hawker Siddeley executive jet piloted by Group Capt. John Cunningham, the wartime flying ace, whose plane hit a flock of birds on taking off from the testing ground at Dunsfold airfield near Guildford before striking the vehicle on the main road. Group Capt. Cunningham and eight passengers in the plane escaped with minor injuries. **23.** Four sailors were killed and four were missing after a collision between U.S. guided missile cruiser, *Belknap*, 7,900 tons, and U.S. aircraft carrier, *John F. Kennedy*, 87,000 tons, at sea off Sicily, during night flying operations, at least 16 others were injured, more than 50 men being rescued from the water. **25.** Twenty Israeli military personnel were killed in the country's worst air disaster when an air force Hercules transport plane crashed in Sinai after hitting the top of a mountain. **29.** Graham Hill, former racing driver, and five members of his Grand Prix team, died when his light aircraft crashed on to a Hertfordshire golf course while approaching Elstree Aerodrome. Another four people were killed when their light aircraft crashed while trying to land at Birmingham's Elmdon airport.

Dec. 2. Sixteen African passengers were killed and 70 injured near Salisbury, Rhodesia, when a swarm of bees entered the bus, causing it to crash. **14.** Sixteen people were killed and some 60 injured when two trains collided in thick fog in the station of Fornos de Algodres, Portugal. **26.** The death toll in Sydney's Christmas Day fire tragedy rose to 15 with the deaths of two more of those injured when the Savoy Hotel was burnt out. **27.** 372 Indian miners were trapped underground at the Chasnala coalfield, Bihar State, after an explosion. On Dec. 29 rescue officials announced that they had abandoned all hope of rescuing anyone alive.

(1976) Jan. I. Five Britons were among 82 people killed in a Middle East Airlines Boeing 720 which crashed in the Saudi Arabian desert. During a New Year revel in the Belgian town of La Louvière, fire roared through a room used for dancing behind a café and 15 young people were killed and 33 injured. **3.** Gales reported to be the worst for 30 years in Britain resulted in at least 23 deaths. **6.** Five people died after a fire in a five-storey seafront block of flatlets at Brighton and 20 other occupants were rescued. **7.** Four children died in a fire which swept through a three-storey house in Harlesden. **18.** An avalanche killed 12 porters crossing a pass 15,100 ft. up in the Himalayas. **24.** The tanker *Olympic Bravery* was holed when she ran aground on a rocky island west of Brest, on her maiden voyage.

Feb. 6. An explosion in an electricity transformer in a tunnel near Finsbury Park station, London, disrupted rush-hour services on the Piccadilly and Victoria lines and hundreds of homeward bound commuters were temporarily trapped underground. **20.** Thirty people were killed and 75 injured when a passenger train and a crowded bus collided on a level crossing at Pitiquito, Mexico.

March 1. Six men were drowned when a Norwegian oil rig ran aground in a storm off Feete island, north of Bergen, the remaining 44 crew members being saved by helicopters. **3.** Three children were killed and 13 injured when lightning struck a primary school at Lari, near Nairobi, the third time the school had been hit in 15 years. **8.** The pilot and 13 passengers escaped when a helicopter crashed into the North Sea, 25 miles off Spurn Point, Humberside, while returning with rig workers from Whiskey Alpha gas platform to the mainland. **9.** A mountain cable-car filled with skiers crashed in the Italian Dolomites killing 43 people, mostly West Germans and Austrians. Four men working inside a concrete unit were killed when it fell 185 ft. at the Olympic Stadium site in Montreal after supporting steel cables broke. **12.** Eleven men including three mine inspectors died after an explosion at a coal mine at Oven Fork, Kentucky, three days following a similar explosion at the same mine when 15 miners were killed. **12.** It was officially confirmed that an Il-18 aircraft flying from Moscow to Armenia had crashed the previous week, at least 120 people being killed. **13.** Storms in the western approaches to the English Channel resulted in the deaths of 4 French fishermen, with 7 missing, and 2 ships abandoned. The Greek tanker, *Olympic Bravery*, broke in two off the Brittany coast where she had been grounded since Jan. 24. **21.** Mme. Safia Tarzi, who held the women's world altitude record, and Mlle Diane de la Sabbiere died when a hot air balloon in which they were passengers, caught fire and exploded as the craft prepared to land at Fontaines Les Nonnes, near Paris, during a race. The pilot was seriously burned. **26.** Over 100 people died when fire occurred on a Caribbean ferry boat bound from Dame-Marie to Port-au-Prince, Haiti. **30.** Twelve people were killed, more than 220 injured, and hundreds left homeless by tornadoes which struck a number of small communities in Arkansas and Mississippi.

April 9. At least 10 people were killed and 50 seriously hurt by earthquake in Esmeraldas, Ecuador. **12.** John Clements, 22 year-old member of the staff of Sheppards Wood School, Welwyn Garden City, and two of his pupils died in a hotel fire at Sappada in the Italian Dolomites while on a school ski-ing holiday and after Mr. Clements had saved several children from the blaze. **12.** The Ministry of Defence stated that Capt. Terence Thompson, of HQ3 Commando Squadron, Plymouth, a Royal Marine officer with the joint British-Nepalese army expedition to Everest, had been killed in a fall on the mountain. About 39 people were killed and some 700 injured when a tornado struck villages south of Dacca. Twenty-one people were trampled to death during a faith healing service in Rio de Janeiro when panic broke out after a woman fell into a trance. **13.** Forty-five people, mainly women, were killed in an explosion at a munitions factory at Lappo, West Finland, and 30 others were taken to hospital. **14.** Forty underground workers escaped when fire occurred in a pressurized section of the new Essex-Kent tunnel at Dartford, three being taken to hospital with minor burns. **22.** The *Bild* newspaper reported that three top East German oarsmen were drowned during a pre-Olympic training session on Lake Mueggel, near East Berlin, three weeks earlier in stormy weather but that the authorities had thrown "a veil of secrecy round the fatal accident." **25.** Twenty-six people died in floods affecting 28 villages in north-east Persia. **27.** At least 47 people died when an American Airlines Boeing 727 crashed when attempting to land at St. Thomas in the Virgin Islands. **30.** Four R.A.F. pilots were killed when two Gnat jets collided in mid-air over Dolgellau on a routine training flight from R.A.F. Valley, Anglesey.

May 1. Three potholers were found drowned in Langstroth Pot, near Buckden, in the Yorkshire Dales, two others being rescued, and a sixth escaped to raise the alarm. **2.** Three ratings and a fireman were taken to hospital after being overcome by smoke from a fire in H.M.S. *Warspite*, a nuclear submarine, during a goodwill visit to Crosby, Liverpool. Twenty-four people, including children, were killed and many were hurt when two trains collided head-on at Schiedam, Holland. **6.** A major earthquake in the Udine area of Italy devastated parts of north eastern Italy and shook other countries in Central Europe. Official estimate of the death toll on May 13 was 914 with at least 300 persons missing believed dead, while it was also estimated that 1,530 people were injured and 150,000 people made homeless in 24 Alpine towns in the region. **9.** A Persian Air Force Boeing 747 Jumbo jet crashed near the town of Huete, 95 miles east of Madrid, all 17 members of the crew being reported killed. **11.** Two earth tremors shook the Ionian seabed near the Greek island of Zakinthos. Two earthquakes rocked Southern Italy, including Naples and Taranto, but no damage or casualties were reported. **14.** Four young brothers died when fire swept their home in Widnes, both parents escaping with shock and cuts. **17.** Three tremors shook N.W. Italy bringing to 76 the number of earthquakes since the disaster on May 6, but no casualties or damage was reported. Six people were killed and 14 injured when a church roof caved in during a service at Almeria, Spain. **20.** Russia disclosed that more than 10,000 people were made homeless on May 17 by an earthquake which affected a wide area of Soviet central Asia, and that there had been some deaths. Five people were killed when a car ran through a column of 25 walkers out on their first summer ramble near Rushton, Northants.

26. Five people were killed and 35 injured when a coach crashed over an embankment near Girvan, Ayr, and landed on its roof in a stream. **28.** Red Cross officials and Philippine police reported that 185 people were killed and 800,000 made homeless after 9 days of rain, wind, and floods caused by Typhoon Olga.

June 1. Peking Radio reported two severe earthquakes had hit part of Yunnan province in Southern China. **2.** All 250 passengers escaped unhurt when a Penzance–Paddington express was derailed at Reading about 100 yards short of the platform. **4.** A total of 427 fishermen and 39 vessels were stated to be missing in the last two days after a cyclonic storm struck the Bombay coast, but later 400 succeeded in getting ashore although 14 were reported drowned. **5.** Part of the 300-ft. high retaining wall of the Teton Dam, north of Idako Falls, U.S., collapsed releasing 80,000 million gallons of water, and 53 people were listed as missing with 5 others confirmed dead and 81 injured, and 30,000 made homeless. President Ford declared the entire valley a disaster area. On June 7 the death toll rose to six with 100 people still missing. **6.** At least 150 people were buried alive and six severely injured in a landslide at the village of Pahirikheti, 125 miles north-west of Kathmandu, caused by swollen rivers. **7.** The newly-elected Chief Minister of the Malaysian state of Sabah (Tun Faud Stephens), the Finance Minister (Saleh Sulong), Local Govt. Minister (Peter Mojuntin), and Communications Minister (Chong Tiam Voon) were killed when their aircraft crashed into the sea on approaching the airport at Kota Kinabalu, capital of Sabah, all 11 aboard being killed including the Chief Minister's son. **8.** Eight people at least were reported dead after flooding in Serbian regions of Yugoslavia with many thousands made homeless. **16.** Fifty-eight people were reported to have died in a cyclone which hit coastal areas of Gujarat State in Western India and in Dacca officials said that six people had died in heavy floods following monsoon rains in Bangladesh. **13.** Five French climbers were killed and a sixth gravely injured in 900 ft. fall in the French Alps near Briançon. **16.** Three Japanese climbers were reported killed in attempting the 24,105 ft. Gasherbrun II peak in Pakistan. **19.** Three American women tourists were killed and 17 injured when a coach overturned near Gatwick Airport. **25.** A passenger train from St. Pancras, London, collided with an empty passenger train backing out of Luton and 21 people, including a train-driver were treated for cuts and bruises. **27.** Eleven people died and 59 were injured when five coaches of an Amsterdam–Paris train were derailed at Neufville, six miles from Mons in southern Belgium.

July 1. Lightning killed three boys and a man in a sudden storm near northern Portuguese town of Chaves and injured seven people. **2.** Several thousand Indonesian villagers were still unaccounted for after a violent earthquake which killed some 350 people in the remote province of Irian Jaya the previous week-end. **4.** Four young girls, from Bakewell, Derbyshire, were found dead in bed at a residential youth centre at Charlesworth, near Glossop, and 10 other people, including seven teenagers, were taken to hospital with carbon monoxide poisoning. Nine people, including three children, were killed when a coach veered across the M4 motorway near Swindon in a thunderstorm and collided with four cars travelling in the opposite direction. **9.** A force of 200 firemen, forestry workers and volunteers fought a forest blaze covering an estimated 2,000,000 acres near Carrbridge, Inverness. **18.** Lightning killed nine people on the hills near Arezzo, central Italy, while

attending a celebration of partisans observing the area's resistance in the 1939–45 War. **22.** A cloud of poison gas formed over Seveso, near Milan, after a chemical plant explosion, 35 people receiving hospital treatment. **23.** The Q.E.2 returned to Southampton after an engine room fire when the liner was 80 miles west of the Isles of Scilly on her way to New York with 1,200 passengers. Five passengers and the engine-driver were killed when the Riviera Express travelling from Italy to West Germany, left the rails after coming out of the Simplon tunnel on the Swiss side. **25.** Monsoon rains in the Pakistan provinces of Baluchistan and Sind caused 31 deaths, disrupted rail and road communications and damaged crops and houses. **27.** Flame-throwing units of the Italian Army were moved to the north Italian area threatened by the cloud of poison gas which seeped on to the main road between Como and Milan. **28.** Tangshan, a coal-mining city of one million people, was reported to be " ruined totally " by an earthquake which hit north-eastern China, the Chinese Communist party stating that " great losses " were suffered in lives and property. **29.** Fire-fighting tugs rescued five employees when flames enveloped Southend pier and scores of holidaymakers reached safety by the railway which runs along the 1½ mile pier, the longest in Britain.

Aug. 1. Four people were killed when a section of the Reichsbruecke linking Vienna to the new suburbs across the Danube collapsed. At least 58 people were killed when torrential rain turned a trout stream in a Colorada canyon into a rampaging flood and on Aug 4 the official death toll was put at 100. The Royal National Lifeboat Institution reported that lifeboatmen answered 1,604 calls and rescued 786 people in 1975. **8.** Reports in Srinagar stated that floods had killed 43 people and made thousands homeless in Kashmir. **9.** Ten people died and 21 were injured when a Spanish Air Force DC-4 plane crashed near Chiclana de la Frontera, south of Cadiz, Spain, the dead including three women and two children. Forty-one people were drowned and 16 were missing after Typhoon Billie whipped up Japan's Pacific coastal waters, 17 children being among the dead. **10.** H.M.S. *Reward*, 1,600 ton oil patrol ship, sunk between the Forth rail and road bridges after being in collision with the British cargo ship, *Plainsman*, outward bound from Grangemouth. Thirteen people were drowned when a boat capsized in the flood-swollen Poonch River near Kotli, Kashmir. **12.** It was reported that floods had killed 67 people and caused widespread distress in Kashmir, mostly in Jammu province. On Aug. 18 the toll rose to 120 deaths. **13.** Several hundred people had died and over 4 million were affected by monsoon floods in Pakistan, reports disclosed. **15.** Four British explorers were reported missing and two of their companions injured after the Mount Sangay volcano they were climbing in Ecuador unexpectedly erupted on Aug. 11. On Aug. 17 it was stated officially that two explorers, Lt. Adrian Ashby-Smith, of R.A.O.C., Bicester, and Ronald Mace, photographer, had died close to the summit; the two other survivors being both seriously hurt. The Peruvian Minister of Transport and Communications, Gen. Artemio Garcia Vargas, was killed when his helicopter crashed on landing at Moquegua, near the Chilean border. **17.** Over 1,600 people were killed by earthquakes and tidal waves which destroyed parts of the Philippines, leaving about 50,000 homeless, and President Marcos declared a " state of calamity " in the southern port of Mindanao, second largest island, and the Sula Archipelago. On Aug. 18 the

death toll rose to over 4,000 with 2,000 people more missing. The official Hsinhua news agency stated that China's second major earthquake in three weeks, on Aug. 16 between Sungpan and Pingwu in the northern part of central China's Szechuan Province, caused " very slight " losses because it had been predicted but that it caused " strong shocks " in Chengtu, the provincial capital. **19.** Western Turkey was shaken by two earthquakes and four people were killed and 50 others injured, Denizli being the largest of several towns affected. **20.** Holiday families were moved from the path of a forest fire in North Wales and 10 miles of the road between Towyn and Machynlleth were closed. In France holidaymakers were rescued by sea because of a forest fire when an appeal was made to all craft in the area south of La Rochelle to head for the beaches near Royan to pick up bathers and campers. **22.** Forest fires occurred in the south of England where drought conditions made the areas like tinder-boxes and near Ringwood, Hants, 360 old people were evacuated from St. Leonard's hospital, while 200 holiday caravans were also evacuated from a site nearby, and similar action was forced on occupants of another caravan park and bungalows three miles away at Matcham's Heath. It was officially announced that the probable death toll from the recent earthquake and tidal waves in the southern Philippines was 8,000 consisting of 4,000 known dead and 4,000 missing presumed dead; over 35,000 families lost their homes. **28.** A U.S. Starlifter C141 transport aircraft crashed into a sugar beet field at Knarr Cray, near Thorney, on the outskirts of Peterborough, during a thunderstorm, all 18 on board being killed. Another U.S. Starlifter exploded when landing at Sonderstrom air base, Greenland, 21 of the 27 passengers and crew being killed. Eight British Servicemen were killed when an R.A.F. helicopter crashed shortly after take-off in Belize, on a training flight. **29.** Alf Bontoft, a power-boat race driver, died after his craft went out of control at Cowes, Isle of Wight, at the start of an international power-boat race from Cowes to Torquay and back. A hailstorm struck Mexico City over the weekend causing 12 deaths and forcing the evacuations of over 10,000 people from their homes.

Sept. 10. A British Airways Trident jet and a Yugoslav DC9 airliner collided while flying over northern Yugoslavia, killing all 176 people aboard the two planes; it was the worst ever mid-air disaster. **11.** A crashing petrol tanker exploded and devastated the heart of the Bedfordshire village of Westoning.

CRIMES, TRIALS, ETC.

(1975) Sept. 21. A bomb was exploded in the pedestrian section of Clyde tunnel, Glasgow, but there were no injuries. **22.** A bomb exploded in the entrance to the underground car park at the Portman Hotel, Portman Square, London, slightly injuring a patrolling policeman and two other people. The formation of Scotland's first special bomb squad by Strathclyde police following two bomb attacks in the Glasgow area in the past week was announced. **23.** A bomb explosion damaged a valve control unit at Kinfauns, three miles east of Perth. **25.** A bomb placed in a holdall exploded outside the Hare and Hounds public-house in Maidstone, frequented by troops from the Royal Engineers' Invicta Barracks nearby, but a young soldier had seen it and raised the alarm in time to clear the bars and adjacent terraced houses, the only

injuries being sustained by two police constables cut by flying glass. **28.** Three armed West Indians held seven Italians hostage in a basement storeroom at the Spaghetti House restaurant, Knightsbridge, London, after being trapped by police during an alleged attempted robbery. One hostage was later released. On Sept. 29 a second hostage was released. On Oct. 2 an Italian and a German were arrested and charged with conspiracy to rob the Spaghetti House restaurant. The siege ended on Oct. 3, one of the gunmen having shot himself in the stomach after all six Italian hostages had been freed unharmed, the other two gunmen coming out with their hands up. **30.** Alistair Steadman, 34 year-old ex-R.A.F. fiight lieutenant, was imprisoned for nine years at Mold Crown Court, for offering to sell secret information to the Russians.

Oct. 9. A bomb exploded outside Green Park underground station, Piccadilly, killing one young man and injuring 18 other people. Six men, three of them brothers, who at Birmingham Crown Court admitted offences of trafficking in morphine smuggled into Britain from their native Hong Kong were sentenced to prison terms ranging from 9 years to 2 years. **13.** A bomb in a black holdall planted between a window ledge and railings outside Lockets Restaurant, Marsham Court, Westminster, a restaurant used by M.P.s, was defused after it was seen by a porter. **13.** A railway guard was fined £25 at Hatfield for being drunk in charge of a train and £15 for obstructing a railway official who tried to board it. **17.** The Appeal Court ordered two youths convicted at the Central Criminal Court in November 1972, to be freed after quashing the conviction of one of them of murdering Maxwell Confait of Catford, and of arson at Confait's flat and the conviction of the other of manslaughter and arson. A third youth who had been on parole from a four year detention order on the arson charge also had his conviction quashed. **22.** Three members of the Provisional I.R.A. and an 18-year-old London girl were sentenced to Life imprisonment at the Central Criminal Court after being found guilty of murdering five people in the bombing of the Horse and Groom public house in Guildford. Two of the men were also convicted of the murders of two men in an explosion at the Kings Arms, Woolwich. **23.** A bomb placed under the car of Mr. Hugh Fraser, Conservative M.P. and ex-minister, exploded outside his Holland Park home, killing Prof. Gordon Hamilton Fairley, a world authority on leukaemia, who was walking by. **28.** The Criminal Injuries Compensation Board paid out £251,699 in compensation for death or injury resulting from terrorist acts since January, 1972, Minister of State, Home Office (Mr. Alex Lyon) told the Commons. **29.** Twenty-eight people were injured in a bomb explosion at the Trattoria Fiori, an Italian restaurant in Mayfair, 18 of the injured being taken to hospital.

Nov. 2. A security officer saved the Royal Pavilion, Brighton, from being extensively damaged by fire after the Music Room was set alight by a man later arrested. **3.** A London solicitor, Mr. Richard Charnley, escaped with a fractured leg and cuts when a terrorist bomb planted under his car exploded as he drove away from his house in Connaught Square, near Marble Arch, the vehicle being completely wrecked. **9.** A terrorist bomb was defused seconds before it was due to explode beneath a car parked next door to the London home of Mr. Edward Heath, in Wilton Street, Belgravia. **12.** One man was killed and 16 people injured when a bomb exploded at Scott's Restaurant, Mount Street, Mayfair. **14.** Mr. Justice Talbot, who said that the trial had exposed a world of "sexual vice," imprisoned Kenneth

Fromant, of Crowthorne, Berks, and Lizzie Thompson of Waterlooville, Hants, for life at Winchester Crown Court after a jury returned murder verdicts against both for a crime committed four years previously. **16.** Soldiers, Police and Customs men raided the liner *Queen Elizabeth 2* in Southampton Docks after a week-end police swoop uncovered a Provisional I.R.A. store of explosives. Forty-six men were detained under the Prevention of Terrorism Act. On Nov. 19, 18 of those held for questioning were released. Police confirmed that no explosives had been found aboard the Cunarder. Five men were arrested when an 18-year-old Greek Cypriot girl, Aloi Kaloghirou, a student, was found unharmed near her North London home where she had been kidnapped 11 days before. **18.** Two people were killed and 19 injured, five seriously, as Provisional I.R.A. terrorists resumed their campaign of violence by throwing a bomb through the window of Walton's Restaurant, Chelsea, the restaurant, which was crowded with customers, being wrecked. **21.** Patrick David Mackay, a gardener, pleaded not guilty at the Central Criminal Court to the murder of two women aged 87 and 89 and a Roman Catholic priest aged 63 but guilty to manslaughter on grounds of diminished responsibility. The pleas were accepted by Mr. Justice Milmo who described Mackay as "a highly dangerous man"; he was jailed for life. Two other murder charges were left on the court file. Mackay also pleaded guilty to two robberies and asked for 24 others to be considered. **23.** The Court of Appeal in London quashed convictions against John Bartholomew Melia and John Sylvester McCluskey of conspiring to cause explosions and substituted convictions of conspiring to commit arson. They had been sentenced on March 18, 1975, to 20 years jail for plotting a firebomb raid on stores in Uxbridge, and the new sentence resulted in 10 years imprisonment. Another Irishman, Robert John Cunningham, had his conviction of plotting explosions at Uxbridge quashed and a conviction of conspiracy to commit arson substituted, his 20 year sentence being halved. **26.** Four gunmen robbed a Midland Bank branch in Dunstable, of a reported £200,000 after holding one of its accountants hostage with his wife and son for more than 15 hours at their home four miles away. **27.** Mr. Ross McWhirter, joint compiler of the Guinness Book of Records, was shot dead by a gang of gunmen in the doorway of his home at Enfield, Middlesex.

Dec. 1. Edward Reginald Mansfield, hotel kitchen porter, was sentenced to ten terms of life imprisonment at the Old Bailey on seven charges of manslaughter and three of arson, following a fire in which seven people died at Worsley Hotel Maida Vale, London in Dec., 1974. **4.** Sentences totalling 26 years were imposed on three high-ranking Loyal Orange Lodge officers and one member of the para-military Ulster Volunteer Force at Preston Crown Court for conspiring to cause explosions in Ulster. Three men received seven years' jail each and the fourth man five years' imprisonment. **5.** Peter Mathews, farmer and sportsman, of Playden, Sussex, was jailed for 15 years at the Central Criminal Court for kidnapping Sheila, Viscountess Devonport, he being convicted of three charges. **6.** Armed police sealed off Dorset Square, Marylebone, when four I.R.A. gunmen retreated into a council flat in Balcombe Street and took a middle aged couple hostage. The hostages, Mr. & Mrs. John Matthews, were freed on Dec. 12 and the terrorists surrendered to police. **8.** The Home Secretary told the Commons that new safeguards were to be introduced over the discharge and transfer procedures for criminally insane patients

following " grave and sadistic murders " committed by three men released from mental homes in the last two years. **9.** Three Lowry paintings were taken from the Crane-Kalman Gallery in Brompton Road, Chelsea, estimated to be valued together at about £30,000. **11.** Five members of a gang of armed robbers were jailed at the Central Criminal Court for from 6 to 15 years and two other members each received 2 years' prison sentences suspended for 2 years after a trial lasting 111 days, the Judge declaring that the offences were " executed with callous indifference to the safety of others ". **20.** Five people were injured in a bomb explosion which damaged Biddy Mulligan's Irish public-house in Kilburn, North London.

(1976) Jan. 6. One of the people who damaged the Headingley wicket and wall during the Third test between England and Australia in 1975 was jailed for 18 months and three others who also admitted damaging the pitch and walls at Headingley were given suspended prison sentences at Birkenhead Crown Court. **8.** Raymond Lester, of Dumbarton, an 18-year-old Clydeside shipyard apprentice, admitted in Glasgow High Court of causing an explosion likely to endanger life and seriously damage property on the railway line near Dumbarton East station in Sept. 1975 and also pleaded guilty to two charges of placing explosives at the Bank of England, Glasgow in June 1975 and the Clyde Tunnel, Glasgow, in Sept. while acting with Robert Maldar, of Scotstounhill, Glasgow. Lester was sentenced to six years in a young offender's institution and Maldar to four years, while sentence on a 15-year-old defendant from Dumbarton, who was found guilty of the railway line charge was reserved for a year. **12.** Seven dining-car workers employed by British Rail were sentenced at the Central Criminal Court to terms ranging from 4 years to 30 months' imprisonment after pleading guilty to various charges of conspiracy to defraud, theft of money, forgery and uttering forged documents between early 1974 and 1975, involving a total of £66,704. **15.** A bank manager, his wife and their four children were held hostage in their Carshalton, Surrey, home by an armed gang, who then stole £20,000 from his branch office in New Addington, Croydon. **28.** Thomas Youdall, of Springburn, Glasgow, was sentenced at Glasgow High Court to 12 years in a young offenders' institution; Andrew Wotherspoon, of Springburn, was jailed for 12 years; and Ronald Paterson of Townhead, Glasgow, was jailed for 18 months. All three were found guilty of receiving six drums of sodium chlorate; Youdale and Wotherspoon were also found guilty of possessing explosives to enable other people to endanger life or cause serious damage to property and further of possessing two shotguns, a rifle, a pistol and more than 500 rounds of ammunition. Paterson was found guilty of possessing the six drums of sodium chlorate. **29.** Norman Scott, aged 35, described as an author, of Barnstaple, admitted two charges of dishonestly obtaining social security payments and asked for two similar offences to be considered at Barnstaple magistrates' court, and was put on probation for two years.

Feb. 2. The Home Office announced that indictable offences in England and Wales in 1974 were 1,963,360, of which 63,781 were offences of violence against the person. **10.** Sabi Nikoloff, Bulgarian-born, of Leicester, was imprisoned for life at Leicester Crown Court after his pleas of guilty to manslaughter on the grounds of diminished responsibility were accepted by the prosecution, following the killing of a police sergeant, an ambulanceman, and a housewife. Nikoloff also admitted attempting to murder a woman police

constable and a postman, and endangering the lives of his former wife, and their son, by setting fire to their house. **11.** Antony Collins, a racehorse trainer and former Stock Exchange member, of Troon, Ayrshire, and William Murphy, a builder of Cork, were found guilty by majority verdicts at Preston Crown Court and each fined £1,000 for a betting conspiracy in August 1974 and ordered to pay £500 each towards the costs of the prosecution. **12.** Frank Stagg, a Provisional I.R.A. staff officer, of Coventry, died in the hospital wing of Wakefield prison, West Yorkshire, after a 61-day hunger strike. **13.** A bomb weighing about 20 lbs, was found at Oxford Circus underground station during the rush hour and defused by Scotland Yard Bomb Squad officers after being noticed by a booking clerk. **14.** Two people were taken to hospital when a bomb explosion occurred on the first floor of a block of flats off Edgware Road. **21.** Four people were injured and another had a heart attack when a bomb exploded in a basement of Selfridge's departmental store in Oxford Street. **23.** John Stanley Hine, chairman of the Braby Leslie engineering group, of Diseworth, Leics., and Dennis Bell, chartered auctioneer and surveyor, of Brailsford, Derbyshire, admitted at Leicester Crown Court of conspiring with others unknown to flout the Custom Control Act 1947 by exporting Krugerrand gold coins without permission and were fined £10,000 each and ordered to pay £800 costs between them. **26.** Rev. Stephen Care, of Plymouth, pleaded guilty at Exeter Crown Court to robbing a bank of £1,775 and a series of other thefts and was sentenced to seven years' imprisonment. His housekeeper, Mrs. Stella Bunting, who pleaded guilty to a school burglary, was given a conditional discharge. **27.** A car bomb attack was made by terrorists in Harcourt Terrace, off the Fulham Road, Chelsea and caused extensive damage.

Mar. 1. A bomb exploded on a pavement in Stanhope Gardens, South Kensington, injuring an Irishman who had severe abdominal injuries and lost a hand. **2.** A bomb factory was found at a house in Clapham Common Northside during a series of raids by detectives investigating the South Kensington explosion. **4.** Three bomb explosions were launched in London. Hundreds of commuters escaped on the 7.49 a.m. Sevenoaks-Cannon Street train when they left it only a few minutes before a 10 lb. bomb ripped open a carriage. Other blasts occurred in King Street, Covent Garden, and at Tavistock Square, Bloomsbury, windows being shattered and cars damaged. Mrs. Annie Maguire, was jailed at the Central Criminal Court for 14 years for possessing nitroglycerine at her home in Harlesden, North London. Also sentenced on the same charge were her husband, who also received 14 years' imprisonment; their son, Vincent John, who was imprisoned for five years and another son, who was ordered to be detained for at least 4 years at a place selected by the Home Office. Three men were each jailed for 12 years for a similar offence: Patrick Joseph Conlon, uncle of the Maguire boys; William John Smyth, another uncle; and Patrick Joseph O'Neill. Mitchell Henry, of Bracknell, Berks, former chauffeur to the late Countess of Portarlington, was jailed for 2 years at Reading Crown Court after being found guilty of steaing two Canaletto paintings and was ordered to pay £40,000 compensation to the trustees of the Portarlington family estate. **7.** An A.A. patrolman removed a terrorist bomb which he spotted near a car close to the restaurant in the south-bound car park of the M.1 service station at Newport Pagnell, Bucks., minutes before it exploded damaging two vehicles. **11.**

Foreign currency, gold and gems were stolen at a British Airways store at Heathrow Airport by an armed gang who forced security guards to unlock the security cage. Leonard Richard Kirzynowski, a polytechnic art student, pleaded guilty to setting fire to the Royal Pavilion, Brighton, on Nov. 2 and was sentenced at Lewes Crown Court to 6 years' imprisonment. **15.** Julius Stephen, West Indian driver of an underground train, was shot dead as he chased a gunman after a terrorist bomb exploded in one of the train's carriages near West Ham station, injuring 9 passengers. The gunman then fired at a Post Office worker who tackled him and who was hit in a lung, but he was cornered by unarmed police, shooting himself in the chest with his own revolver. **16.** Terror bombers placed a bomb on an empty underground train at Wood Green station, which exploded while the train was at the platform waiting to leave to collect supporters at the Arsenal–Newcastle football match at Highbury; only one man was injured. An all-night siege at Maidstone jail, Kent, ended when prison officers broke into the barricaded office where a prisoner serving 10 years held one of their colleagues at knifepoint for 16 hours. **19.** Andrew Gino Newton, a pilot, of Chiswick, was sentenced at Exeter Crown Court to two years' jail after being found guilty of possessing a gun with intent to endanger life. He was also sentenced to six months' imprisonment on each of three other charges, which he had admitted, all to run concurrently with the 2 year sentence, of destroying a dog belonging to Norman Scott, possessing a Mauser automatic pistol in a public place, and not having the necessary firearm certificate for the weapon and ammunition. **24.** J. Murphy & Sons, of Highbury House, Highbury, London, the construction firm, and an associate company, J. M. Piling Ltd., and eight individual accused, who had all denied the charges, were found guilty at the Central Criminal Court of conspiring between April 1972 and June 1974 to cheat and defraud the Inland Revenue. The prosecution alleged the total involved was £1,468,356 but later stated "a more realistic sum of the tax losses" would be £956,000. On March 25 Messrs. Murphy & Sons was fined £675,000 and ordered to pay costs of £52,300; three of its directors were jailed for 3 years and fined £10,000; the associate company of J. M. Piling Ltd. was fined £75,000; other men received lesser sentences. On March 29 the fine on Murphy & Sons was reduced by £175,000 to £500,000 but other fines and sentences remained unchanged. **26.** Hurford-Jones Ltd., of Oxford, a scrap metal firm, was fined a total of £211,000, David Hurford-Jones, the managing director, of Alvescot, Oxon, was fined a total of £38,000 and ordered to pay £5,000 costs, Nigel Rupert Clarkson, of Burford, and Crispin Welby of Boars Hill, were fined £3000 and £2,250 respectively at Oxford Crown Court in a case involving illegal shipments of scrap metal contrary to an E.E.C. embargo. At Winchester Crown Court, Edward May, former railway carriage cleaner of Maidstone, was sentenced to a total of 10 years' imprisonment after pleading guilty to eight charges of stealing mailbags between 1969 and 1975 and asked for 22 other offences to be considered. He also admitted assaulting a police officer and handling and obtaining money by means of a forged instrument, and received 9 years' imprisonment concurrently on each of the mailbag charges with a further year for assaulting the police. May's wife, admitted two charges of forgery and obtaining property by deception and asked for 58 other offences to be considered; she was given a 12-month sentence suspended for 2 years. **27.**

Eighty-five people, several of them children, were injured when a bomb planted in a dustbin exploded at the Ideal Home exhibition, Olympia, London. One of the injured died in hospital on April 17. A Securicor guard was shot dead and two others were wounded when 5 gunmen attacked a security van on the A2 at Dartford, Kent. **30.** Joseph Wilkins, West End night club owner, who ran two Mayfair escort agencies, was found guilty at the Central Criminal Court of living on immoral earnings and trading while an undischarged bankrupt and was jailed for 3½ years. Also imprisoned was Walter Birch, who received 30 months for living on immoral earnings. Wilkins's wife was convicted of aiding and abetting him in the offences of living on immoral earnings and trading while an undischarged bankrupt and was conditionally discharged for 12 months and ordered to pay £150 costs. Kathleen Andon, 22, of Cadogan Square, Belgravia, was found guilty of exercising control over prostitutes and received a 15-month suspended prison sentence. Vijitha Udurawana, 32, of North Kensington, was found guilty of living on immoral earnings and received a 6-month suspended prison sentence.

April 2. Sydney McCullough, a builder of Tynemouth, was jailed for 3 years at Teesside Crown Court for his part in a corruption conspiracy and for their part in the same offence three Durham councillors were also sentenced. Robert Urwin, of Chester-le-Street, was sentenced to 30 months; Sidney Docking, of Chester-le-Street, 15 months; and Matthew Allon, of Washington, one year suspended for 18 months. **9.** Peter Hain, of Putney, was found not guilty at the Central Criminal Court of stealing £490 from a Putney bank in October, 1975.

May 3. Three gunmen escaped with £175,000 in a wages robbery at the *Daily Express* in Fleet Street, London. **5.** Brian Davis, of no settled address, was sentenced to 7 years' imprisonment at Gloucester Crown Court for demanding money from the family of the kidnapped Lesley Whittle. **6.** Thelma Crayton-White, an unemployed American model stated to be a member of an international gang of jewellery thieves, was jailed for 10 years at the Central Criminal Court after pleading guilty to thefts of a £22,000 diamond solitaire and a £56,000 emerald ring from Harrods and Garrards in London. **7.** Ronald Joseph McCarney, Belfast born, of no settled address was sentenced at Winchester Crown Court to three terms of life imprisonment for the attempted murders of three policemen, 20 years for bank conspiracy and two sentences of 14 years each for two firearms offences, all to run concurrently. Robert Relf, a concrete worker, became the first person to be committed to prison resulting from a refusal to comply with the Race Relations Act 1968 when he was jailed for contempt at Birmingham County Court for breaking an injunction granted on Nov. 21, 1975, restraining him from displaying a racially discriminatory notice outside his house in Leamington Spa, which stated that it was for sale only to an English family. He was released on June 21 after 45 days on health grounds. **11.** The Home Secretary (Mr. Jenkins) told the Commons that George Davis, a mini-cab driver, who was convicted in 1975 of robbery and wounding with intent to resist arrest, being sentenced to consecutive terms of 17 and 3 years' imprisonment, later altered by the Court of Appeal to run concurrently, would be released from gaol that day and that after considering certain evidence he had decided to recommend the exercise of the Royal

prerogative to remit the remainder of the sentence. Guilty verdicts on all counts were returned in Manchester I.R.A. trial against five defendants described by Mr. Justice Cantley as dangerous and disgusting young men. Brendan Dowd, was found guilty on 11 charges of conspiracy to cause explosions and murder, attempted murder, possessing firearms, explosives, and ammunition, and was sentenced to life imprisonment with concurrent terms totalling 20 years. Sean Kinsella was also given life imprisonment with concurrent terms of 20 years on the conspiracy charges, three attempted murders, possessing firearms and ammunition and explosives. Stephen Nordone, was convicted on 15 counts, including conspiracy and six attempted murders, and was jailed for life with concurrent terms of 20 years. Paul Norney, and Noel Gibson, were each found guilty of 9 counts of conspiracy, attempted murder, and possessing firearms and were each jailed for life and for a concurrent 20 years. **19.** Patrick Meehan was freed from prison by Scottish Secretary (Mr. Bruce Millan) with a recommendation for a Royal pardon after serving seven years of a life sentence on conviction for murdering a 72-year-old woman. **26.** Parcel bombs were defused after being posted to the Attorney-General (Mr. Sam Silkin), Lord Justice Shaw, Maj.-Gen. Robert Ford (Commandant, Royal Military Academy) and three Home Office civil servants in Coleraine and Londonderry.

June 1. A small bomb in a plastic carrier bag exploded in Pimlico underground station but the only casualty was a woman railway worker treated for shock. **4.** Maurice Cochrane, former head of Rotary Tools, was found guilty at Glasgow Sheriff Court of 8 charges involving bribery and corruption but not guilty on six other similar charges, the jury finding mitigating circumstances involving two of the bribery charges on which he was found guilty. He was jailed for 12 months. **23.** Christina Morris, aged 18, formerly of Staveley, Derbyshire, was jailed at Worcester Crown Court for 3 years after admitting taking part in 597 burglaries and thefts involving property worth more than £75,000 in two years with different gangs of men. **24.** Roy Edgeler, of Clapton, and his brother, Keith Edgeler, were jailed for life at Lewes Crown Court for the murder of Mrs. Barbara Gaul, wife of Mr. Alfred John Gaul, a property dealer now living abroad, outside a Patcham, Brighton, hotel in January. The Edgeler brothers were said to have been paid £5,000 to kill Mrs. Gaul. **28.** Two men with forged papers walked into three separate strongrooms at Heathrow Airport and signed for currency totalling about £2 million, the thefts being discovered when genuine couriers arrived to collect the cash. **30.** Three black gunmen, Franklin Peter Davies, Wesley Dick and Anthony Munroe, who held seven Italians captive for six days during the Spaghetti House siege in Knightsbridge in Sept. 1975 were jailed for 21 years, 18 years and 17 years respectively at the Central Criminal Court.

July 1. Donald Neilson, of Bradford, was found guilty at Oxford Crown Court of murdering Lesley Whittle, the 17-year-old heiress, of Highley, Shropshire. He had admitted kidnapping her and demanding a £50,000 ransom. Sentence was deferred because other charges against him had still to be considered. **5.** At Maidstone Crown Court, Mrs. Henrietta Berens, 55, wife of film producer Mr. Leslie Berens was fined £10,000 and given two 12-month suspended prison sentences on three currency charges after prosecution described her as the English limb of a Belgian-based smuggling ring.

Leslie Berens was also fined £10,000 on one charge and ordered to pay £2,000 costs. Two Belgian women, Yvonne Ceulleers, and Marianne Verstappen, her grand-daughter, said to be couriers in the operations were each sentenced to three months, imprisonment which meant their immediate release as they had been in Holloway since their arrest nine weeks previously. All four pleaded guilty to attempting to export illegally £167,740 in English banknotes. Mrs. Berens also pleaded guilty to two similar charges. **13.** Derek Deevy, of Toxteth, Liverpool, who admitted three specimen charges of obtaining £18, £16 and £22 by deception from the Department of Health and Social Security, was jailed for six years at Liverpool Crown Court. Counsel said that Deevy had lived " on the fat of the land by fiddling to the extent of something just over £36,000." Judge Pigot ordered that all documents and a transcript of evidence should be sent to the appropriate Departmental Minister. **15.** Fourteen prison warders accused of occasioning actual bodily harm and common assault on six I.R.A. bombers remanded to Winson Green prison in Nov. 1974, after bombs planted in two Birmingham public houses had killed 21 people, were found not guilty on unanimous verdicts on all 18 charges at Birmingham Crown Court. **21.** Donald Neilson was sentenced at Oxford Crown Court to five life terms of imprisonment for the murders of three sub-postmasters, the murder of the kidnapped heiress Lesley Whittle, aged 17, and for causing grievous bodily harm to a sub-postmistress, the Judge Mr. Justice Mars-Jones, telling Neilson " In your case life must mean life." Neilson also received concurrent jail sentences on other charges. **22.** Three Appeal Court judges decided unanimously that David Cooper, of Leyton, and Michael Grahame McMahon, of Islington were properly convicted in March 1970, of the murder of a Luton sub-postmaster in a gun raid, the Home Secretary having referred the case back to the court for the second time after two previous attempts by the men in the Court of Appeal had failed. In another case referred to the court by Mr. Jenkins, the same three judges rejected appeals by Patrick Colin Murphy of Dalston, William Albert Davis of Bermondsey, against their convictions in 1970 of robbing a North London sub-postmaster, for which they received 12-year sentences each.

Aug. 6. John Stonehouse, M.P. for Walsall North and a former Labour party minister, was sentenced at the Central Criminal Court to a total of seven years imprisonment. On Aug. 5 the jury unanimously decided that he was guilty of uttering a forged application for a passport in the name of Joseph Arthur Markham, stealing the proceeds of a banker's draft for $12,500, obtaining an American Express credit card in the name of Joseph Arthur Markham by forgery, and attempting to enable his wife to obtain from the Royal Insurance Co. £30,000 by fabricating evidence from which his death would be presumed. On Aug. 6, on majority verdicts, the jury decided that Stonehouse was guilty of four other charges of trying by false pretences to enable his wife to obtain £95,000 from insurance companies. He was also found guilty of five charges of false pretences and four charges of stealing cheques. He was sentenced to six years on the theft charges, six years concurrent for obtaining travellers' cheques and airline tickets, six years concurrent on the insurance charges and five years concurrent on charges relating to overdrafts. He was sentenced to six months concurrent for obtaining a credit card and one year consecutive for the passport application offence. Mrs. Sheila

Buckley, his secretary, was found guilty on five charges relating to four cheques and a banker's overdraft and was given a two-year suspended sentence. Stonehouse and Mrs. Buckley were found not guilty by unanimous verdicts of conspiring to defraud creditors of his company, Export Promotion and Consultancy Services. **9.** Richard Ingrams, editor of *Private Eye* was fined £250 in the High Court on an application by Sir James Goldsmith, the financier, to commit him to prison for contempt; fines of £250 for contempt were also imposed on the magazine's publishers, Pressdram Ltd., its main distributors, Moore-Harness Ltd., and on Michael Gillard, a contributor, and the defendants were also ordered to pay the costs of the application after being found guilty of contempt for breaking undertakings given to the court on May 21. **12.** Zulnarwarin Dom, an inspector in the Malaysian Police, was sentenced at Middlesex Crown Court to 10 years' imprisonment; Shanmugarajah Selvadurai, described by the prosecution as leader of the group, to 12 years in jail, and his secretary, Mary Irene Phillips, to 10 years imprisonment, for importing 8,122 grammes of diamorphine on April 20 and an unspecified amount on Feb. 26, the value of which according to the prosecution was not less than £1 million. **13.** Frank Saviour Mifsud, a Maltese, formerly of Camberwell, was found guilty by a jury at the Central Criminal Court of suborning Harold Stocker to commit perjury at a trial in 1967 and was jailed for five years and fined £50,000, and being ordered to pay £5,000 costs. **17.** Ten paintings valued at an estimated £305,000 were found to have been stolen from Edward Speelman, the Piccadilly art dealers. **30.** Riots occurred in Notting Hill, London, at the end of a three-day Caribbean Carnival organized by the area's West Indian community; they resulted in injuries to 325 police and 131 civilians and damage to 31 premises and 35 police vehicles and looting of three shops; 60 people were arrested.

Sept. 3. Rioting prisoners at Hull top security jail surrendered after talks from the roof of " A " wing which they had occupied for three days in protest against alleged brutality by prison officers. **6.** A gunman shot dead a newsagent at Sutton, Surrey and robbed him of his weekend takings. **10.** Shane Paul O'Doherty, Irish student, was sentenced to life imprisonment at Central Criminal Court after being convicted on charges of sending letter and parcel bombs. **14.** Maurice Henn and Khalail Wafai were convicted at Central Criminal Court of dishonestly handling private papers belonging to Sir Harold Wilson, the former Prime Minister.

LABOUR AND TRADE UNIONS

(1975) Sept. 23. The National Union of Seamen who had banned members from crewing British-registered ships to Chile as a protest against the new régime, reached a compromise agreement with shipowners. An offer of £6 a week wage increase was made to 30,000 workers on national and London evening newspapers by the Newspaper Publishers Association effective from Oct. 1 for the next 12 months. **26.** Local authorities granted 500,000 manual workers the full £6-a-week wage increase permitted under the Government's anti-inflation policy at a cost to ratepayers in a full year of £205 million, an average of 2·8p in the £. **27.** Six members of the Electricity Supply Union, not recognized by employers in a national agreement, and who worked at the Ferrybridge power station, Knottingley, West Yorkshire, were dis-

missed for refusing to join a recognized union. **29.** Vauxhall Motors announced the introduction of a closed shop agreement for production workers at Luton, Dunstable and Ellesmere Port, Cheshire.

Oct. 1. Result of a ballot of N.U.J. members on annual delegate meeting decisions on compulsory introduction of a closed shop and the position of editors rejected five of seven points adopted as policy by the conference, editors now being offered freedom of choice on membership and 100 per cent. post-entry membership not now being a provision of future national and house agreements. **3.** The Labour Party Conference ended after a resolution was carried overwhelmingly calling for widespread changes in the control and financing of the Press. **8.** Junior hospital doctors in Plymouth, Sheffield, Leicester, Exeter, Norwich and other centres decided to reject the new pay deal and working conditions accepted by the B.M.A. on their behalf the previous week, the main grievance was about overtime rates of 13p an hour. The B.B.C.'s monthly-paid staff accepted a £6-a-week pay increase costing £6,240,000 a year. **10.** Junior doctors were informed by the Health Department that the new pay and conditions contract would be suspended while talks continued. **12.** No copies of the *Daily Telegraph* were produced in London or Manchester after a dispute involving the stereo department of the National Graphical Association. **13.** Representatives of 1,500 junior hospital doctors in the North West voted to treat emergency cases only from Oct. 15, but rejected proposals for a full-scale strike. In Plymouth, hospitals in the City were brought down to an emergency service when junior staff stopped work for 24 hours. **14.** Restrictions on services continued at several northern hospitals and doctors at Blackburn, Bury, Bolton, Leigh and Salford decided to join the emergency-cases-only action. The Government rejected a demand from the A.U.E.W. for an inquiry into the affairs of Norton Villiers Triumph, the motor-cycle manufacturers, to examine whether public money staked in the industry had been used wisely. **16.** Junior doctors decided to hold a national ballot on likely industrial action after the refusal by Mrs. Castle (Social Services Secretary) to make more money available to them. The Central Electricity Generating Board announced that 28 power stations in England and Wales were to be shut down and another 20 partly closed over the next two years, affecting 4,952 jobs, but without compulsory redundancies for two years. **17.** The crew of the car ferry, *Eagle*, sold to a French company, prevented vehicles leaving the ship when she docked for the last time in Southampton and dockers blocked the loading ramp with two tractors. On Oct. 20 the blockade was called off after P. & O. made financial concessions to the crew. **20.** Doctors withdrew their threat to boycott the Royal Commission on the N.H.S. when the Prime Minister told the Commons that the inquiry would be free to consider the relationship between the N.H.S. and private medical practice. The Jockey Club agreed to form a National Joint Council for stable lads. **21.** Britain's first North Sea oil terminal of the Ekofisk pipeline at Seal Sands, Cleveland, Teesside, was inaugurated, **22.** The *Financial Times* was not published after N.G.A. members rejected management reassurances on redundancy plans and stopped work. British Steel Corporation announced the formation of a new management company, B.S.C. (Industry) to concentrate and expand the Corporation's efforts to bring new industry into steel closure areas. **23.** More junior doctors throughout the country joined the campaign of industrial action

which was affecting care in many hospitals. A further effort by British Rail to agree terms with union leaders for economies failed to progress over the issue of compulsory redundancies. **26.** North-West Thames region of the Junior Medical Staff Association, representing 1,600 doctors, decided to withdraw all but emergency services in their dispute with the Social Services Secretary. **28.** A change in the production of Northern editions of national newspapers involving editing from London by modern production methods was announced in Manchester by the Mirror Group Newspapers and led to an immediate walk-out by N.G.A. members. **31.** Unions representing 240,000 ancillary manual workers in the N.H.S. settled for a £6-a-week wage increase from second week of December.

Nov. 1. The 17-day strike by coke oven workers which threatened to close British Steel Corporation's Ravenscraig plant in Lanarkshire ended. **4.** A 10-day old strike by property men over new manning proposals at Thames Television which disrupted programme production at the Teddington studios, ended after their union refused to make the dispute official. **5.** A " closed shop " agreement whereby all new employees of British Gas Corporation must join one of the two recognized unions was negotiated in the gas industry. A £6-a-week pay rise for 90,000 building workers employed by local authorities was agreed, costing £28 million in a full year. No copies of the *Daily Mirror* were printed in Manchester because members of N.U.J. went home without working in a dispute over redundancy proposals, and on Nov. 6 *Daily Telegraph* northern editions were stopped because of a meeting of N.U.J. members protesting against delay in a management statement on production plans in Manchester. **8.** The *Scottish Daily News*, the workers' cooperative newspaper launched six months earlier, ceased publication. **11.** A joint meeting at Coventry decided to appoint joint management-union committees to save Chryslers and ensure its future in U.K. London editions of *Daily Express* were not published because of a pay dispute involving engineering union members. **14.** Normal working on London editions of national newspapers was resumed following interim settlement of an unofficial stoppage in the pay dispute involving Engineering members employed by the *Daily Express*. **17.** Forty members of the Peterborough branch of the National Union of Journalists were ordered by their national executive to pay fines of between £20 and £40 for working against union instructions during a printing workers' pay dispute and five of them received a one-year suspension from membership. A record £6 a week pay rise for farm workers was awarded by the Agricultural Wages Board for England and Wales. **18.** Moderate candidates captured control of the national executive of the Amalgamated Union of Engineering Workers when results of the postal ballots were declared. A £6-a-week pay increase for 34,000 manual workers in the water supply industry was agreed. **20.** Doctors' leaders decided to call on hospital consultants to treat only emergency cases from Dec. 1 as part of the campaign against the Government's plan to end pay beds in N.H.S. hospitals. **25.** The Government won by six votes when the Liberals' amendment objecting to the proposal to extend the National Dock Labour Scheme to all port transport work within 5 miles of the sea was defeated by 294-288 votes in the Commons. **26.** The National Union of Bank Employees was formally readmitted to the T.U.C. **28.** Effects of the junior hospital doctors' industrial action over their pay

dispute resulted in closures of some hospitals units and wards. Delegates representing 90,000 company busmen voted unanimously in London to accept the £6 flat rate increase permissible from March 1976. **30.** A dispute which closed over 470 public houses in the Midlands ended when workers at Ansells Brewery, Birmingham, agreed to return to work, following settlement over union representation of public-house managers.

Dec. 3. The meeting between the Prime Minister and doctors' leaders at 10 Downing Street produced no immediate solution to the dispute over the N.H.S. The National Union of Public Employees blacked all 158 private beds in Birmingham's 18 hospitals because of industrial action by consultants. **8.** By 32-20 votes, the engineering section national committee of the A.U.E.W. instructed the executive to " comply with the policy on wages as adopted by the 1975 T.U.C." Members of the N.U.J. employed on provincial and London suburban newspapers voted to accept a pay offer of £6 a week for seniors by the Newspaper Society against the recommendation of their own executive. Qualified agreement was announced between national newspaper publishers and leaders of four print unions for a policy of no compulsory redundancies and other measures to reduce manning levels with the introduction of new technology. **9.** The teachers' panel of the Burnham Committee agreed to accept the £6 pay rise limit for their next claim due to be effective in April 1976 although they decided to press for the whole £6. **12.** Leaders of junior hospital doctors decided to advise their colleagues to accept a new agreement in pay and contractual terms, but on Dec. 16 the doctors decided to continue their overtime ban. **19.** The strike by 800 office workers ended and averted a threatened shut-down of British Steel Corporation's Ebbw Vale works, the lay-off of 3,600 other workers being cancelled. **29.** Rolls-Royce announced that it was to close two of its factories— Dundonald in Northern Ireland, and Wellhouse Mill at Barnoldswick, Yorks.—and that it was to reduce its work force by 6,000 in 1976 by " natural wastage if possible." The B.B.C. cancelled all its main news programmes on both T.V. and radio when 700 journalists staged a one-day strike in a dispute over payments for working unsocial hours. **30.** The British Steel Corporation announced that it was proceeding with economies aimed at saving £200 million a year.

(1976) Jan. 4. Several thousand steelworkers reported for work at plants in South Wales and the Midlands in defiance of the B.S. Corporation's ban on most week-end shifts as part of its programme to reduce losses, but no steel was produced. **11.** Strikers at B.S.C.'s Port Talbot steelworks voted to continue their stoppage against economy measures. **19.** Port of London announced it was to close West India and Millwall docks general cargo handling by the end of 1976, the work being transferred to the Royal Group. **21.** Unions agreed to accept a £6-a-week increase for nearly 460,000 teachers payable from April 1. **25.** Work restarted at 3 of the 4 South Wales plants affected by strikes protesting at the British Steel Corporation costs-cutting plan and the fourth plant resumed the following day. **26.** The Civil and Public Servants' Association with 230,000 clerical members, and the Society of Civil Servants, with 97,000 members, announced proposals for a merger.

Feb. 2. A 24-hour unofficial strike by Southern Region train drivers affected 70,000 home-going commuters with at least 40 of the normal 150 rush-hour services from Waterloo being cancelled.

Pan American cancelled all its Heathrow flights for 24 hours after maintenance men staged a lightning one-day strike over three non-union workers brought in from outside. **3.** Six Ferrybridge power station workers at Knottingley, near Doncaster, won their industrial tribunal claim for unfair dismissal against the Central Electricity Generating Board which arose from a closed shop agreement with four T.U.C. unions. A settlement of the strike at Chrysler's Linwood plant was agreed after protracted negotiations, the deal giving the 50 Scottish packing worker's the £1·10 a week extra which was the cause of the dispute. **8.** Nearly a million copies of the *Sunday Times* and *Sunday People* were lost through unofficial industrial action by members of S.O.G.A.T. in a dispute over distribution of newspapers. **11.** Improved overtime payments for junior hospital doctors were recommended by the independent Doctors' Pay Review Body; these were accepted by the Government. The Industrial Secretary (Mr. Varley) told M.P.s that a group representing the major motor manufacturers and unions was to be set up to try to deal with the problems facing the British motor industry. **12.** Results of a ballot of hospital consultants over the private practice issue showed 4,438 voted to accept the compromise proposals of Lord Goodman and 2,048 voted against, and the consultants' committee then decided to suspend emergency only sanctions and resume normal working while the proposals were examined. N.U.M. decided to impose a national overtime ban from Feb. 16 in protest against the planned closure of Langwith Colliery, Derbyshire. **13.** British Steel Corporation announced proposals for a total reduction by March 1978 of about 8,000 of the work force in its Welsh plants, of which 2,300 would be white-collar employees, in its attempt to save £170 million over the next two years. Agreement was reached between publishers and leading print unions to set up a supervisory board to monitor developments in the national newspaper industry as part of a joint effort to overcome its problems. **16.** The new £65 million blast-furnace at Llanwern, South Wales, was opened one year late because of industrial disputes. **19.** Five of the six Ferrybridge power station workers lost their claim for reinstatement to their former jobs, the sixth man not applying for his job back as he had joined a textile firm. The national executive of N.U.M. at a special meeting voted to end the overtime ban imposed on Feb. 15 and decided to hold a ballot of members to endorse the return to normal working. **23.** Leaders of N.U.R. voted to seek an immediate meeting with the Prime Minister about fares and investment levels proposed for the railways and decided to seek a joint approach with the other two rail unions, A.S.L.E.F. and T.S.S.A. Redundancy payments were made to 340,215 workers in 1975 at a cost of £178,284,000 compared with 182,161 payments at a cost of £73,560,000 in 1974, the Under Secretary, Employment (Mr. John Fraser) told the Commons. **24.** Junior hospital doctors agreed to accept a new N.H.S. contract under which they would receive overtime money after 40 hours work a week instead of 80, thus ending their long dispute with the Social Services Secretary over pay and terms of service. **25.** The Social Services Department confirmed that nurses and midwives would get a £6 a week pay rise from April 1 and that lodging charges would be raised by about £1 a week. N.H.S. staff in professions complementary to medicine would receive similar rises.

Mar. 1. Six men were dismissed for refusing to rejoin the National Society of Metal Mechanics,

their employers, Haverhill, of Tetbury, Gloucestershire having a closed shop agreement with the union. A new procedure for resolving disputes in the engineering industry was signed after five years during which no formal arrangements had existed between unions and employers. **4.** A minimum wage for stable staff of £30 for a 40-hour week effective from April 1 was agreed by the National Joint Council. **7.** About 3 million copies of national Sunday newspapers were not printed or distributed in London because of unofficial industrial action by members of S.O.G.A.T. **8.** Inter-City and commuter services out of King's Cross and other Eastern Region services were disrupted by unofficial lightning strikes by A.S.L.E.F. train drivers protesting at British Rail economy cuts; thousands of passengers were stranded. In a 67 per cent. poll by N.U.M.'s 260,000 members, 61 per cent. approved their executive's action in calling-off the previous month's overtime ban over the N.C.B.'s decision to close Langwith Colliery, Derbyshire, voting being 109,410 in favour and 69,369 against. **9.** Continued unofficial strikes by train drivers affected 21 depots on the Eastern Regions as the protests over service cuts spread. On March 10 A.S.L.E.F. national executive called on unofficial strikers to return to work. On March 12, British Rail refused union demands that the *status quo* be accepted and the cuts restored but recognized that a breakdown in negotiating procedure had led to the walk-outs. A.S.L.E.F. appealed for normal working, which was fully restored by March 16. **23.** The March figures published by the Employment Department showed the first drop for 22 months in the number of wholly unemployed to 19,501 to 1,284,915 or 5·5 per cent. of the working population. **29.** Britain and France agreed in Paris to manufacture spare parts in advance of orders for the 5 *Concorde* aircraft still unsold, thus providing employment over the next 2½ years. **30.** The executive of A.U.E.W. instructed the 32 Birmingham toolmakers at the S.U. Carburettors factory, whose strike was threatening to stop all Leyland car production, to return to work. Another group of toolroom strikers at the Coventry Triumph plant was also ordered to return to work. In both cases the reason given was that their demands could not be met within the £6 pay limit. **31.** The Employment Secretary (Mr. Foot) announced the U.K. was to have a new bank holiday from 1978 to mark May Day, traditional festival of the Labour movement.

April 2. Four employees were dismissed by British Rail who issued notices of dismissal to 23 others for refusing to comply with its closed shop policy and join a trade union; it was stated that another 72 employees were awaiting a decision. Five strikes affecting British Leyland earlier in the week were reduced to two when 400 toolmakers at Solihull Rover plant and at 8 components factories in Birmingham ended their 3-week stoppage over a pay dispute, strikes in Leyland plants at Canley, Coventry and Llanelli being settled the previous day. **3.** Junior Hospital Doctors' Association agreed to merge with the Hospital Consultants' and Specialists' Association to campaign against the Government's proposals to abolish pay-beds. The 32 toolroom men on strike at British Leyland's S.U. Carburettor factory in Birmingham returned to work after failing to win a £6 a week rise backdated to December but accepting the increase from April 1. **7.** A 24-hour lightning strike by stewards and stewardesses over a manning dispute brought most of British Airways European Division to a standstill. **10.** Ten bargees and tugmen blockading two docks at Hull

were served with writs and summonses ordering them to lift their action. **11.** The week-long strike of 80 cargo riggers at Hull was called off but the blockade of King George and Queen Elizabeth docks by British Waterways crews continued. **13.** Four printing unions accepted proposals of British Printing Industries Federations and Newspaper Society for new wage agreements operating from April 24 after balloting their members. **14.** British Leyland toolmakers at Longbridge, Birmingham, voted to return to work after their shop stewards had been called before the A.U.E.W. national executive. **15.** Industrial action by 300 ambulance officers in London was called off when it was announced by their union, NALGO, that their assimilation into the national pay structure at the level they had been seeking would take place. **20.** The Scottish T.U.C. annual conference at Perth defeated a motion calling for " an end to incomes policy measures like the £6 wage limit and any similar scheme " by 1,187 votes to 632. Delegates unanimously supported a demand for old-age pensions of £30 a week or not less than 50 per cent. of adult earnings for married couples and £20 or one third of average earnings for single people. **21.** Normal working was resumed by the 157 prison officers at Risley remand centre, near Warrington, to allow discussion between the Governor and officials of the Prison Officers' Association following a work-to-rule and 3-hour strike on April 20 over overtime cuts. Scottish T.U.C. annual conference heavily rejected the Government's pay limit but also turned down another motion refusing any form of incomes policy by 1,049 votes to 717. The conference unanimously supported a proposal for a Scottish assembly with powers over the economy and industry, but opposed a referendum of Scottish people on separation. The boycott of British Leyland products imposed by Arab States because of the firm's dealings with Israel had been officially lifted after six years, it was confirmed. **23.** Hospital doctors in N.W. England voted to hold one-day strikes in protest against the Government's pay-beds bill. Rail members at 18 ports and others at British Transport Docks Board's London H.Q. received a £6 a week pay rise from April 26. The 32 British Leyland lorry drivers from Rubery Owen factory at Darlaston, Staffs. agreed to return to work on April 26 after a week-long strike over lay-offs, while at Leyland's Cowley management and union officials agreed on a formula to end the stoppage by 3,350 workers over the dismissal of two men for a clocking offence. **24.** The Welsh T.U.C. meeting in Llandudno rejected the Government's pay deal and overwhelmingly carried a motion declaring that the Chancellor had failed to reduce unemployment, control prices, or promote growth in Wales. **25.** The 900 striking craftsmen at Ebbw Vale steel plant returned to work after promises of talks on the dispute over Easter Monday night shift payment. **26.** Three thousand car assembly workers at British Leyland's Cowley plant ended their strike over dismissal of two men for " clocking " offences, and production also resumed at Longbridge, Birmingham, when 32 drivers at the Rubery Owen components firm in Darlaston went back.

May 2. Prison officers, at Swansea and at Gartree Jail, Leicestershire, began an overtime ban in protest at reduction of their working hours due to budget cuts; similar disputes at other prisons during April were settled after talks on staffing levels. **5.** Mr. Healey announced agreement with the T.U.C. negotiating team of a new pay policy giving rises of between £2·50 and £4 a week in the year beginning August 1. The T.U.C. General Council

approved the agreement by 25 votes to 5. The Chancellor later announced that if the T.U.C. special conference on June 16 approved the deal, the Government proposed to recommend to Parliament the enactment in full of the conditional tax reliefs specified in the Budget on April 6. The Institution of Professional Civil Servants decided on a card vote at their Eastbourne conference by 54,434 to 38,246 to seek immediate affiliation to T.U.C. **6.** The *Daily Telegraph* northern editions were affected by a dispute with members of the N.U.J. chapel in Manchester over office staffing in the interim rundown period to the introduction of new technology in two years' time. **11.** The Government accepted the award recommended by the independent review body, back-dated to April 1, for a £16 a week pay rise for doctors and dentists whose income was under £8,500 a year, at a cost of £12·6 million. **14.** Journalists at the *Daily Telegraph* returned to work after N.U.J. officials called off a 10-day dispute, which halted publication of the paper in London for two days and which concerned introduction of new technology. **25.** London printing of *The Times* and *The Guardian* was stopped by pay and inter-union manning disputes. **27.** British Rail issued notices of dismissal to 23 Southern region employees who refused to join a trade union.

June 7. Delegates of white collar workers in the gas industry voted at the gas group meeting at NALGO's annual conference at Eastbourne to ban regular overtime from Aug. 1 to create jobs for other workers. **16.** Another year of wage restraint from August 1 was approved at the special T.U.C. conference in London where on a card vote delegates decided to support the Government's 4½ per cent. pay deal by 9,262,000 votes to 531,000 . **24.** A Government White Paper based on a report from the Occupational Pensions Board proposed that half the seats on all bodies concerned with the general management of occupational pensions schemes should be filled by trade union nominees. **28.** A 24 hour wildcat strike by A.S.L.E.F. drivers at Waterloo rail station, the Southern Region terminal, began at midnight in protest over disciplinary action against a driver who took a crowded passenger train through a red signal. The dockers' unofficial shop stewards' committee at Hull lifted their 21 month blacking of British Inland Waterways Board, bringing to an end the dispute over the introduction of the Danish-owned BACAT (barge-aboard-catamaran) cargo service which was forced to withdraw from the Humber 6 months earlier. **30.** A plan by British Leyland management to raffle five of the new 3500 Rover saloons in a deal for higher productivity disrupted production of the new model because it was open only to assembly line workers.

July 8. At its annual conference in the Isle of Man, the National Union of Miners voted without dissent to demand retirement at 60 in January 1977, followed by a six-monthly lowering of the age to 55 by June 1980, without loss of pay or concessionary fuel up to the State retirement age. **13.** London Fire Brigade ended work-to-rule after an independent inquiry was set up to investigate their grievances. **15.** Leaders of junior hospital doctors decided to resume a ban on overtime working in a dispute over holiday and study leave pay and their decision was supported by a large majority at B.M.A.'s annual representative meeting in London. **19.** Industrial action by junior hospital doctors over holiday and study leave pay began in Birmingham where a ward was closed at the city's general hospital and other hospitals in the area postponed appointments. The Industry

Secretary (Mr. Varley) announced a further investment of £100 million for steelmaking at Port Talbot and a re-examination of the prospects for Shotton in view of changed circumstances since the closure proposal was first made. **20.** The number unemployed for this month totalled 1,478,200, the highest July figure since the end of the war, with a record 209,037 jobless school leavers. **21.** An industrial tribunal in Manchester decided that four workers at the Eaton Transmission Co., Walkden, Lancs, expelled after a strike in March 1975, were entitled to be members of the Amalgamated Union of Engineering Workers, the tribunal chairman stating the union's Bolton District Committee had taken "a plain decision" to expel four loyal trade unionists without being fully aware of the facts of their case. **28.** Executive of British Medical Association gave official approval for industrial action by junior doctors in their dispute over holiday and study pay. **29.** Under an agreement drawn up by the National Joint Council for Gas Staffs and senior officers, white-collar workers joining the gas industry must join or remain members of one of five trade unions from Oct. 1, 1976. **30.** Civil servants in the Department of Trade and Industry imposed an immediate ban on overtime in protest at the Government's plan to reduce Whitehall jobs by 26,000; the ban was backed by the Civil and Public Services Association and the Society of Civil Servants.

Aug. 3. The Employment Secretary (Mr. Booth) announced jobs, training courses or work experience schemes for 60,000 young people, who might otherwise be unemployed in the autumn, under a plan to help school-leavers. A £2,900,000 plan to add 900 jobs to the advance factory programme in the regions was announced by the Department of Industry. **6.** Strikers at the Jaguar plant in Coventry agreed to return to work, after setting up of an immediate inquiry by Advisory, Conciliation and Arbitration Service into the case of nine members of the Transport Union who had joined the Engineering Union. **11.** London Broadcasting, the commercial radio station, went back on the air when striking journalists called off their industrial action over alleged delays in negotiating a new staff house agreement. **12.** Work resumed for the first time in nearly eight weeks on a "blacked" Concorde at British Aircraft Corporation's test centre at Fairford, Glos. **13.** Journalists on the *Daily Mirror*, whose industrial dispute over allowances resulted in no London editions, voted 69–34 for a return to work pending further talks. **16.** Stage staff at the new National Theatre began an unofficial strike in a pay dispute and performances were cancelled until it ended after four days. **19.** The Hospital Junior Staffs Committee decided to strike for 24 hours on Aug. 31 if their dispute with the Government over leave and study pay was not ended. **20.** Tunnel workers on many sites in the country were recommended to return to work after their representatives agreed to end their unofficial stoppage over pay, after talks in London with T.G.W.U. leaders who decided to negotiate at national level. **23.** The Government decided not to lift its ban on the plan by Toyota G.B., the wholly British manned company which imports Toyota vehicles, to set up a storage base for Japanese cars at Bristol, the company having been refused an industrial development certificate to establish a warehousing and distributions complex in the new West Dock at Avonmouth to employ 400 workers. The National Coal Board decided to sell its entire stock of 85,000 homes at half-price with first refusal being given to sitting

tenants. **24.** Central Electricity Generating Board announced that it was to pay in full the £16,774 compensation awarded to the "Ferrybridge Six" power station workers by a Leeds industrial tribunal which ruled their dismissal was unfair. **25.** Junior doctors called-off the 24-hour strike threatened the following week after a settlement with the Social Services Secretary (Mr. Ennals) over pay during holidays and study leave. Unemployment figures of 1,501,976, the worst since the war, were announced. The Employment Secretary (Mr. Booth) signed an Order enabling workers in firms with fewer than four employees to complain to an industrial tribunal if they felt they had been unfairly dismissed. **26.** Ford workers at Halewood, Liverpool, agreed to resume work when the company agreed to increase supervisors' manning levels and to allow four sewing-machine mechanics to revert to a higher grade with more pay. **27.** National Graphical Association instructed all members employed by United Newspapers and East Midland Allied Press, two large provincial groups, to strike from 5 p.m. in a dispute over "unrecognized" print work. Discussions to reach a solution were fixed for an early date and publications of the newspapers affected resumed on Sept. 3. **30.** Some 10,000 British Leyland workers in the Midlands were idle because of a pay and recognition dispute which stopped Jaguar, Mini, Allegro and Princess production. Coventry paintshop workers struck for 24-hours in protest at plans to build a new £12 million paint shop in Birmingham. **31.** Hull dockers who unload fish resumed normal working after a 2-month work-to-rule over 50 redundancy notices, now withdrawn.

Sept. 2. Eighteen thousand workers were laid off by British Leyland after a walk-out by 2,000 maintenance men at the plant at Longbridge, Birmingham, in a dispute arising from another dispute involving tool setters. Junior hospital doctors accepted an agreement worked out between the British Medical Association and the Department of Social Services to end the dispute over pay for leave and study. **6.** On first day of Trades Union Congress in Brighton, the National Union of Seamen reported that its members had voted in favour of industrial action in support of pay claim; two days later, executive of Union voted to call national strike from midnight on Sept. 11, which was subsequently postponed for two weeks. **8.** British Leyland's plant at Longbridge was re-opened after decision by striking toolmakers to return to work. T.U.C. in Brighton rejected by large majority a return to unrestricted free collective bargaining when present wage restraint policy ended in August, 1977. **12.** Publication of the whole print of *Sunday Telegraph* was prevented because of industrial action.

LEGAL

(1975) Oct. 1. The Lord Chief Justice (Lord Widgery), in a reserved judgment in the High Court, ruled that he could see no grounds in law to stop publication of the first volume of the diaries of the late Mr. Richard Crossman relating to Cabinet affairs between 1964 and 1966 and that although the courts did have power to prevent breaches of Cabinet confidences they should intervene only in the clearest of cases "where the continuing confidentiality of the material can be demonstrated." The Attorney General (Mr. Sam Silkin) had sought an injunction to stop publication against two publishers and the literary executives of Mr. Crossman and another injunction against Times Newspapers which had published edited extracts from the memoirs in the *Sunday Times*. The Report of the

Committee on Mentally Abnormal Offenders under the chairmanship of Lord Butler was published and called for major changes in the law and practice relating to prosecutions, detentions, treatment, and after-care of mentally abnormal offenders. 2. Mr. Justice Megarry left the Law Courts for Ocean Island in the Pacific which was the subject of an action by native landowners against the British Government and British Phosphate Commissioners, this being the first time an English High Court judge had " sat " outside the U.K. 16. In the annual report on the legal aid schemes published by the Law Society, it was stated that total costs of legal aid and advice in civil cases and legal aid for criminal cases in magistrates courts rose to £28,907,691 in 1974–75 compared with £21,247,676 in the previous year. 24. The report of the committee on criminal procedure in Scotland under Lord Thomson, appointed six years earlier, was published and proposed improvements but " not radical change " with increased police powers of arrest and detention. 27. Mr. Justice Foster ruled in the High Court that the T.U.C. Disputes Committee had acted outside its powers in making an order for the Association of Professional, Executive, Clerical and Computer Staff to call off its merger with the Staff Association of General Accident Assurance Group and that the T.U.C. General Council's decision to enforce the order was similarly in excess of the Council's powers.

Nov. 5. The House of Lords relaxed its rule that English money judgments must be expressed in sterling only.

Dec. 3. The House of Lords by a majority of 3–2 held that the Water Act 1973 did not empower a water authority to require the owner or occupier of premises not connected to its main drainage to pay charges demanded for 1974 in respect of sewerage and sewage disposal services and that statutory orders made under the Act which prescribed the charges were *ultra vires*. 4. A London solicitor, Mr. Andrew Congreve, of Maida Vale, achieved victory in the Appeal Court for thousands of viewers who took out overlapping licences to beat the £6 colour licence fee increase when three judges ruled unanimously that the Home Secretary had acted illegally in revoking or threatening to revoke licences taken out before April 1 unless the extra amount was paid. On December 9 the Home Secretary told the Commons he had decided not to seek leave to appeal to the House of Lords, that the licence holders concerned would be asked to ignore the revocation letters, and that he was making arrangements to refund the additional £6 paid by those who took out overlapping licences and responded to requests for the extra money. 10. The Report of the Advisory Group on the Law of Rape under the chairmanship of Mrs. Justice Heilbron, the High Court Judge, was published with recommendations on anonymity for rape victims in court cases and new rules to curtail cross-examination about their sexual history. The House of Lords Appeal Committee ruled that it was an offence under the Trades Description Act to confirm a passenger's booking knowing that the flight might be overbooked and that a confirmation that a passenger had a seat reserved should be taken as a statement of fact and not a promise of intention.

(1976) Jan. 28. In a test case for severely handicapped people who had their houses or flats adapted to allow them to live at home, the House of Lords by a majority of 4–1 ruled that a London solicitor who had been paralysed for the past 18 years, was not entitled to rating relief on his specially-equipped flat, thus reversing a majority decision of the Court

of Appeal and a Lands Tribunal ruling that he qualified for relief.

Feb. 12. Mr. Wilson announced the setting up of a royal commission on lawyers and legal services with wide terms of reference including solicitors' monopoly of conveyancing. 23. Reforms of the conspiracy laws with new offences to deal with squatting, sex shows, public indecency, and obscene films were proposed in a report published by the Law Commission under the chairmanship of Mr. Justice Cooke. 31. A report published by the Law Commission proposed new laws to clarify the liability of occupiers of land and premises to those who were injured or suffered damage while trespassing.

April 12. The House of Lords Privileges Committee recommended that Mr. Geoffrey Russell, 54, should succeed to the Barony of Ampthill which had also been claimed by his stepbrother, Mr. John Russell, 25, whose case was rejected. 14. Three Appeal Court judges all agreed in the High Court that Greater London Council were breaking the law by allowing grossly indecent films to be shown in public cinemas and that G.L.C. was applying the wrong test when deciding that films should be banned because they had a tendency to deprave and corrupt whereas the test was whether the films were indecent in common law. 21. The Island Parliament of Sark agreed to set up a special committee to consider introducing a law on divorce. 27. The House of Lords agreed without a division to the recommendations of its Committee for Privileges that Mr. Geoffrey Russell should succeed to the barony of Ampthill.

May 4. Mr. Justice Tudor-Evans ruled in the High Court that newspapers publishing reports about children who were wards of court, risked punishment for contempt unless a judge had authorized publicity. 6. By a 2–1 majority decision, the Court of Appeal ruled that the N.S.P.C.C. could be compelled by the courts to reveal the names of informants in suspected child cruelty cases. 13. After the Court of Appeal freed Christopher Whitby, sentenced to six years' imprisonment for robbery in 1974 after new evidence was produced, Lord Justice James announced that five judges would examine a number of cases involving identification evidence so that courts could act while waiting for the Devlin report to be implemented. 26. The House of Lords ruled that three anti-Fascists who distributed pamphlets during the October 1974 general election urging voters not to support National Front candidates were guilty of offences under the election laws and in a unanimous decision the five law lords hearing the D.P.P.'s successful appeal held it was an offence for a person without an election agents' authority to incur the expense of issuing pamphlets. 27. The Attorney-General (Mr. Silkin) announced new guidelines to prevent wrongful conviction on identification evidence in prosecutions brought by the Director of Public Prosecutions.

June 4. Ministers from 18 European countries approved the draft European Convention on the Suppression of Terrorism covering the use of explosives, firearms, hijacking and kidnapping, it being approved in Brussels by member nations of the Council of Europe. 15. The Lord Chancellor (Lord Elwyn Jones) announced plans to abolish legal aid in undefended divorce cases and to extend the " divorce by post " procedure to all undefended cases. 18. The longest action in English legal history concluded its arguments in the High Court in London after 221 working days in a case in which the former inhabitants of Ocean Island in the Pacific claimed £21 million in royalties for phosphate mining by Britain. 24. By a 4–1 majority, the

Law Lords ruled in the House of Lords that it was unlawful for a tenant to receive a premium for the transfer of a protected tenancy under the Rent Act even though he had surrendered the remainder of his tenancy and the lease to the new tenant was granted by the landlord.

July 5. In the High Court, Mr. Justice Brightman ordered the London Co-operative Society to compensate its pension fund because of the low rates of interest paid for borrowings from March 1952 to July 1969. **6.** A specially-constituted five-judge Appeal Court sat in London to hear the first of five cases to lay down guidelines to judges and juries on identification evidence in criminal trials following its establishment in May after two controversial cases. On July 9 the Lord Chief Justice (Lord Widgery) sitting with 4 other judges, issued these guidelines, saying that the important aspect of identification was its quality. **7.** The Monopolies and Mergers Commission, published report recommending the abolition of the " two-counsel " rule operated by barristers in England and Wales and by advocates in Scotland under which in general a Q.C. might not appear in court without a junior and which, the Commission declared, constituted a monopoly. The House of Lords, in the first reference to reach them on points of law following the acquittal of a soldier serving in Northern Ireland on an indictment charging him with murder, decided unanimously that the form of the reference made it impossible for them to give any general guidance as to the use of force by soldiers serving in the Province. **12.** The Lord Chief Justice (Lord Widgery) in the High Court, ordered the Tameside Council, Greater Manchester, to obey the directive of the Education Secretary (Mr. Mulley) and make its schools comprehensive under section 68 of the 1944 Education Act. On July 26 three Appeal Court judges unanimously decided that the Education Secretary had acted unlawfully in issuing this directive and allowed the Council's appeal with costs against the High Court order, also refusing the Education Secretary permission to appeal to the House of Lords. On July 29 five law lords granted the Education Secretary leave to appeal. On Aug. 2 the judicial committee of the House of Lords unanimously dismissed this appeal. **26.** The High Court ruled that the decision of the Yorkshire area of the National Union of Mineworkers to suspend two former pit officials after they had given evidence on subpoena for a newspaper against which their President, Mr. Arthur Scargill, had brought a successful libel action was contempt of court and granted temporary injunction lifting the two-year suspensions on the two men until a full hearing of the men's court action challenging the validity of the union's disciplinary decision. **28.** Five law lords ruled that a motorist unlawfully arrested after being asked for a breath test could not be convicted of a drink and driving offence if his alcohol level was found later to be over the statutory limit. **29.** The Monopolies Commission published a report recommending relaxation on restrictions on advertising by solicitors and called for a new code of advertising practice to be evolved with the appropriate professional bodies. **30.** After a 10-day hearing, Mr. Justice Mocatta granted Laker Airways a declaration that the Department of Trade was not entitled at the moment to withdraw Skytrain's " designations " under an international agreement as a British air service on the American route, and ruled that the Environment Secretary acted beyond his powers in issuing " guidelines " in a White Paper last February that Skytrain's licence should be revoked.

SPORT

(1975) Sept. 22. Baroness Birk, Under-Secretary,

Environment, told the House of Lords that the Government was setting-up long-term research into football violence. **30.** *Crossbow*, a 55-feet vessel with a five-man crew and owned by Mr. Timothy Colman, became the first sailing craft to break the 30-knot barrier during the fifth World Sailing Speed Trials at Weymouth by averaging 30.8 knots (nearly 35 m.p.h.) over a half-kilometre course.

Oct. 10. Seven Rugby Union players, four from Falmouth and three from Bideford, were sent off at Falmouth in the match between the clubs. **25.** Terry Paine, Hereford player-coach and former Southampton and England forward, broke the record with his 765th Football League appearance at home to Peterborough.

Nov. 6. David Wilkie, the double world breaststroke champion and winner of three European Cup events was voted Britain's " Sportsman of the Year." The " Sportswoman of the Year " title was awarded to Lucinda Prior-Palmer, the European three-day event champion, and the Wightman Cup squad took the team award.

Dec. 6. John H. Stracey of London, became the world welterweight champion when he stopped José Napoles of Mexico, in the sixth round in Mexico City. **22.** Ladbrokes, the bookmaking firm, announced that it had concluded an agreement which guaranteed that the Grand National would be run at Aintree in 1976 and 1977 and under which they would manage Aintree for the next 7 years although the agreement could be terminated in 1977.

(1976) Jan. 14. Seven holes were dug in the Centre Court turf at the All England Lawn Tennis Club, Wimbledon, and red and white paint was daubed on the grass, some walls and windows. **15.** John Curry, of Britain, won the men's individual title in European figure skating championship in Geneva, the first British success for 37 years. **20.** Stewards of the Jockey Club decided that on Feb. 16 the Rules of Racing would be changed to allow women to ride against men not only on the flat but in hurdle races and steeplechases.

Feb. 7. Miss Diane Thorne, 22, became the first woman to win a race under National Hunt rules following the granting of permits to women jockeys, when she rode Ben Ruler to victory in the Nimrod Hunters' 'Chase at Stratford-on-Avon. **11.** John Curry won the men's figure skating gold medal at the Winter Olympic Games in Innsbruck. **19.** The University of Bath announced that it was to provide the first sports scholarships in the U.K. from October. **22.** Jean-Pierre Coopman, of Belgium, was banned for two years from European Boxing Union competitions for ignoring the E.B.U.'s decision that he should not meet Muhammad Ali, who knocked him out in the fifth round in San Juan, Puerto Rico.

March 4. John Curry became Britain's first men's figure skating champion of the world for 37 years when he won the title in Gothenburg. **20.** John H. Stracey, of Britain, defeated his American challenger, Hedgemon Lewis, at Wembley to retain his world welterweight boxing title, the fight being stopped in the 10th round. Oxford beat Cambridge in the annual university boat race in the record time of 16 min. 58 secs., 37 secs. faster than the previous best.

April 4. Jill Hammersley became England's first European woman table tennis champion when she defeated Maria Alexandru, of Rumania, in the singles final in Prague. **6.** Richard Dunn, British and Commonwealth heavyweight champion, won the European boxing title at the Royal Albert Hall when he stopped Bernd August, of Berlin, in the

third round. **11.** Wide Awake, the Badminton Horse Trials winner, died on its lap of honour immediately after its rider, Lucinda Prior-Palmer, received from the Queen the Whitbread Trophy for the three-day event. **26.** Lincoln City, Fourth Division champions, extended their Football League points record to 74 by drawing their last match of the season 1-1.

May 2. Southampton, the Second Division club, in their first visit to Wembley in their 89th year, beat Manchester United, of Division One, 1-0 in the F.A. Cup Final. **4.** The Nigerian Squash team withdrew from the world amateur championships at Cheltenham after a telephone call from the country's High Commission in London and without explanation. Liverpool won the Football League Championship for a record ninth time by winning away 3-1 to Wolverhampton Wanderers. **7.** Disciplinary committee of U.E.F.A. meeting in Brussels banned Real Madrid from all European competition matches for one year as the result of a young fan running on to the pitch after the Real Madrid-Bayern Munich semi-final European Cup and knocking the referee to the ground. **14.** The Rhodesian Ridgebacks cricket team decided not to visit Britain after being banned by the Minister for Sport (Mr. Howell), who said however team members would be allowed in as ordinary tourists and would be permitted to play cricket as individuals but not to play together as a team.

June 2. Lester Piggott won the Derby at Epsom on Empery and created a record of seven Derby victories. **9.** The European Football Union's control and disciplinary committee banned Wales from the 1978-80 European championship after considering reports of crowd misbehaviour at Ninian Park, Cardiff, during the quarter-final match against Yugoslavia in May. **14.** Britain's athletics selectors nominated a team of 55 men and women, the smallest squad since 1956, for the Olympic Games in Montreal. **22.** John H. Stracey of Britain lost his world welterweight boxing title at Wembley Pool when the referee stopped his fight against Carlos Palomino, a Californian-based Mexican, in the 12th round. **23.** Chelsea Football Club had asked chartered accountants to investigate their financial position, it was confirmed.

July 1. U.S. withdrew from the Davis Cup lawn tennis organisation after failure of a move at the competition's annual meeting in London to impose a ban on countries which refused to play matches for political reasons. Britain and France withdrew from the 1977 competition but remained in the organization. Jamaica banned the M.C.C. young cricketers team, beginning a tour of the West Indies on July 24 because some players had been on a private tour of South Africa, Guyana having already banned such cricketers. **3.** New Zealand's Minister for Recreation and Sport (Mr. Alan Highet) declared that his Government would not allow amateur sport to become an instrument of government policy after the Organisation of African Unity had condemned New Zealand for allowing the All-Blacks rugby team to tour South Africa. **4.** Princess Anne and her horse, Goodwill, were selected for the Olympic 3-day event and she became the first member of the Royal Family to be chosen for the Olympics. Her husband, Captain Mark Phillips, was selected as the team's reserve rider. **13.** The Olympic flame was lit by a magnifying glass from the sun's rays at Olympia and transferred from Greece to Canada through a space satellite. **15.** Brisbane was approved as the venue for the 1982 Commonwealth Games, the 1978 Games being planned for Edmonton, Canada. **17.**

Nineteen African and Arab countries boycotted the official opening of the Olympic Games in Montreal by the Queen in protest against the New Zealand rugby team's tour of South Africa. Taiwan withdrew from the Games after the Canadian Government refused to let it compete under the name of the Republic of China. On July 18 Guyana withdrew, Somalia, Mauritius, and Tanzania having already decided not to send teams. The Games' organizers announced that they had been notified officially of withdrawals by Congo-Brazzaville, Ethiopia, Kenya, Ghana, Nigeria, Chad, and Zambia. On July 19, it was officially stated that other nations who had withdrawn their teams were Mali, Tanzania, Cameroons, Niger, Togo, Uganda, and Swaziland. On July 20 Morocco and Egypt joined the walk-out. Tunisia withdrew on July 21, leaving 92 nations to participate, the lowest since the Melbourne Olympics of 1956. **19.** Boris Onischenko, fencing silver medallist at the Mexico City and Munich Olympics, was banned from the Olympics after an inquiry found his épée in the modern pentathlon competition had two bared electric wires which caused a short circuit when crossed with another piece of wire carried secretly in the weapon's handle. **21.** The International Cricket Conference at Lord's expressed concern about dangerous and intimidatory bowling, unanimously condemned it as unfair and required umpires in all countries to be instructed to enforce strictly the provisions of Law 46. The Conference also deplored the decline in Test over-rates and agreed a minimum of $17\frac{1}{2}$ six-ball overs an hour or 13 eight-ball overs, deciding to rely for compliance on voluntary co-operation for the time being. **28.** The Olympic flame was rekindled after it had gone out during a cloudburst.

Aug. 1. Two more Olympic athletes from Eastern Europe asked for asylum in Canada, bringing the number of political defectors at the Games to 5. **4.** To celebrate the centenary of the Women's Cricket Association, women cricketers of England and Australia played at Lords' for the first time in history. **6.** The Test and County Cricket Board, meeting at Lord's, discussed the noise at Test and other matches and expressed their concern at the din which was described as not only irritating but " sometimes intimidating to players and umpires," and they outlined plans to deal with this problem. **9.** The 38-member Polish team in third place in the Olympics for the Physically Disabled in Toronto, withdrew from the games over the issue of South African participation, four other countries—Hungary, India, Cuba, and Jamaica—having already left, while Kenya and Yugoslavia told the organizers before the games they would not compete. Clive Lloyd, the West Indian captain, scored a double century in the match against Glamorgan at Swansea in 120 minutes and equalled the world record for fast scoring. **11.** Clive Lloyd and Tony Greig, the West Indies and England cricket captains, publicly appealed for a stilling of the tom-tom beat of drums and the non-stop rhythmic clashing of drink cans during the Fifth Test beginning at The Oval on Aug. 12. **13.** Vivian Richards, the West Indian batsman, set an individual Test record for a West Indian in England, in scoring 291 runs in the Fifth Test at The Oval. **14.** West Indies supporters invaded The Oval Test pitch and the umpires had to bring off the players just after 6 p.m., play being suspended for 8 minutes. **31.** Wendy Brook, a twenty-year-old student teacher, of Ossett, Yorks, set a new record by swimming the English Channel in 8 hours 56 minutes to beat the previous record of 9 hours 3 minutes.

Sept. 12. Rugby Football Union announced that merit tables, for four divisions of the country, were

to be introduced for experimental period of not more than three years.

TRANSPORT

(1975) **Oct. 2.** It was announced that the Environment Secretary (Mr. Crosland) had called in British Rail's application for outline planning permission to build a new railway station, bus centre, hotel, offices, shops, and community facilities on 25 acres in and around Liverpool Street & Broad Street, London. **8.** London Transport announced that minimum fares were to be doubled to 10p on the Underground from Nov. 2, being part of a 26 per cent. overall increase for buses and tube trains. **26.** British Rail said no trains would be run on Christmas Day or Boxing Day. **30.** All 86 airlines operating scheduled services into and out of the U.K. were ordered by the Government to pay only the approved rates of commission to ticket agencies from Nov. 1.

Nov. 5. Collection of surcharges at airports was banned by the Association of British Travel Agents whose changed code also forbad the cancellation of holidays by tour firms after the date on which the client's full payment was due except in extreme circumstances. **10.** Western Region, British Rail, announced that from Jan. 5, 1976, from Mondays to Fridays, 11 trains a day to and from Paddington were to be cut and a further 27 services altered to save £500,000 a year. The region disclosed further cuts on Nov. 24 in West of England local services. **12.** The Minister of Transport (Dr. Gilbert) announced that the 50 m.p.h. and 60 m.p.h. fuel-saving speed limits introduced in December, 1974, were to remain for a further year. **21.** British Rail, Eastern Region, announced cuts in services from May 1976 in a plan to save £1 million a year by withdrawing some inter-city services and introducing reductions and alterations to week-end services.

(1976) **Jan. 21.** Two Concordes took-off simultaneously from Heathrow and Charles de Gaulle airport in Paris on their inaugural commercial flights, British Airways plane touching down in Bahrain and Air France's plane arriving at Rio de Janeiro. The State-owned National Freight Corporation lost £30 million in the previous year and grants of up to £8 million were approved for the early months of 1976 by the Minister of Transport (Dr. Gilbert). **Feb. 11.** The Trade Secretary (Mr. Shore), in a statement on the Government's civil aviation policy in the Commons, announced that the proposed Laker Skytrain service for the North Atlantic market would not be allowed to operate. **17.** Fare increases ranging from 10-17½ per cent. were announced by British Rail to start on March 28.

March 15. Sir Richard Marsh, chairman of British Rail, said he did not wish to be considered for re-appointment when his 5-year term of office ended in September. **April 13.** British Rail's Southern Region announced cuts from April 20 of 66 peak hour services and 38 off-peak trains. **May 19.** British Rail announced that rail fares, including season tickets, would not be increased for the rest of 1976. **24.** Concorde airliners from London and Paris made successful landings at Dulles Airport, Washington, after the first commercial supersonic flights over the North Atlantic. **28.** The Australian Government announced that it had given official permission for Concorde to start regular services to Australia after " a thorough investigation into the environmental impact of the plane."

July 7. London Transport said that there would be a year's freeze on bus and underground fares but it would not come into effect until after the next increase in Tube fares in July 18. **16.** Aeroflot, the Soviet airline, inaugurated its first Moscow-Madrid route when a TU-154 passenger jet left for Spain. Aeroflot and Iberia Spanish airline agreed a once-a-week flight between the capitals. **Aug. 10.** The Minister of Transport (Dr. Gilbert) announced a stricter and extended M.O.T. test from January 1, 1977. **18.** Air France confirmed that it was to open a regular Paris-Washington-Mexico City service with Concorde, the starting date to be announced after agreement with U.S.

BRITISH COMMONWEALTH

(1975) **Sept. 21.** The Sultan of the North East State of Kelantan, was sworn in as sixth king of Malaysia with the Sultan of Pahang as his deputy. **24.** The Royal Navy lowered the flag for the last time in Singapore when the frigate *Mermaid*, last British warship to be stationed in South East Asia, sailed for the U.K., marking the end of over 150 years of British naval presence in the area. **28.** At the end of an arms amnesty on Sept. 13, police charged over 1,000 people in Bangladesh with illegally possessing arms.

Oct. 2. New regulations were announced in Malaysia to combat Communist terrorism. **3.** The decision to return to the Parliamentary system of democracy in Bangladesh with a government elected from Parliament was announced in a broadcast by President Khondaker Mostaque Ahmed, who also announced fresh Parliamentary elections in February 1977. **4.** Bangladesh Government released over 1,000 political prisoners. **14.** Forty-six people were injured when Typhoon Elsie battered Hong Kong with 100 m.p.h. winds; seven ships were torn from their moorings and 50 international flights in and out of Kaitak airport were cancelled. Mr. Trudeau, Canadian Prime Minister, announced that a 10 per cent guideline for wage increases and controls limiting price rises to justified increases in production costs would be imposed " for a considerable time " because of the country's economic problems. Australia's Energy Minister (Mr. Rex Connor) resigned following a request by the Prime Minister (Mr. Gough Whitlam) and was the second Cabinet minister forced out by what was called the " Overseas Loan Scandal " which came to light in Parliament in July 1975. **15.** The Deputy Speaker of the Kenyan Parliament (Mr. John Seroney) and Mr. Martin Shikukku, an M.P. critical of the government, were arrested in the Parliament building in Nairobi, no reasons being given. Mr. Malcolm Fraser, leader of the Liberal and Country Party in Australia, decided to block Government finance bills in the Senate, where it had a slender majority, to try to force a general election. **22.** All airmail and surface post from U.K. to Canada was suspended indefinitely because of a Canadian postal workers' strike.

Nov. 3. The Bangladesh Army took control of the country in the second major military move in three months. **5.** Britain flew troops into its Central American dependency of Belize to reinforce the garrison of about 650 men after increased Guatemalan military activity near the frontier, and additionally a detachment of R.A.F. Harrier vertical take-off fighters was arriving to provide air cover. **7.** The Supreme Court of India upheld the appeal of the Prime Minister (Mrs. Gandhi) against the Allahabad High Court judgment that she was guilty of election malpractices. this decision automatically setting aside the order disqualifying her from holding office for six years and also validated her election to Parliament in 1971. **10.** Australia's ruling Labour Party agreed to call election on Dec. 15 for half the Senate, where opposition parties had blocked budget funds. **11.** The Governor-General

of Australia (Sir John Kerr) withdrew the commission of the Labour Prime Minister (Mr. Gough Whitlam) and appointed Mr. Malcolm Fraser, leader of the Liberal party, to form a caretaker government until a general election was held. **18.** Two people were injured by a parcel bomb which exploded in the offices of the Queensland State Premier (Mr. Bjelke Petersen) in Brisbane. **19.** A bomb package was found in the Canberra offices of Australia's caretaker Prime Minister (Mr. Fraser) and defused by police explosive experts and on Nov. 21 a letter-bomb addressed to the Australian Governor-General (Sir John Kerr) was detected in a Canberra mail room and safely defused. **26.** India's High Commissioner to Dacca (Mr. Samar Sen) was seriously injured after being shot three times at the High Commission offices by a gang of six Bangladeshis. **29.** With a 10·5 per cent. general election swing, New Zealand returned to power the National Party with a majority of at least 19 in the 87-seat House of Representatives, the Labour Government with a 23-seat majority in the last Parliament being ousted.

Dec. 8. Legislation announced in New Delhi gave the Indian Government tighter control over newspapers and publications and dissolved the Press Council of India. **12.** New Zealand placed a temporary ban on immigration from Britain while the Government worked out its immigration policy **13.** Australia's former Labour Prime Minister, Mr. Whitlam, conceded defeat in the general election which resulted in the Liberal and National Country Coalition having a majority of 55 in the House of Representatives. **29.** The working committee of the Indian Congress Party decided to recommend the term of the present Parliament, due to expire in February, be extended by a full year and that the general elections due in March be postponed for at least a year.

(1976) Jan. 15. Deputy Premier Datuk Hussein Onn was sworn in as Malaysia's prime minister following the death of Tun Abdul Razak. **14.** Australia announced a major relaxation of immigrant controls and stated it was to drop its system of re-entry visas for temporary overseas visits by foreign citizens resident in the country. **22.** Agreement on a constitution making Seychelles independent on June 28 was reached in London. Power for the Indian Government to detain political prisoners without having to disclose reasons was approved by the Indian Parliament's Lower House. **25.** A 3-month amnesty for an estimated 50,000 illegal immigrants was announced by the Australian Government. **27.** Mr. Gough Whitlam won the election for the leadership of the Australian Labour Party on the first ballot with 36 out of 63 votes. New Zealand introduced an import deposit scheme to cut demand for overseas goods and reduce the trade deficit and also pegged wages.

Feb. 2. Opposition M.P.s walked out of both houses of the Indian Parliament in protest at the dismissal by Mrs. Gandhi of the Government of Tamil Nadu (formerly Madras) State. **3.** Cuts in federal government departments, except defence, to save £225 million were announced by the Australian Prime Minister (Mr. Fraser). **6.** Indian Parliament voted to guarantee a sixth year in office for Mrs. Gandhi's government with the existing state of emergency continuing. Sir Oliver Goonetilleke, former Governor-General of Ceylon, now Sri Lanka, who lives in London, was sentenced to 4 years hard labour by the Criminal Justice Commission in Colombo after being found guilty with others of foreign exchange violations and was also fined about £60,000. **13.** The Nigerian Government claimed in Lagos it had quashed an

attempted *coup d'état* by a group of young Army officers during which President Murtala Mohammed was killed with four Nigerian soldiers. New head of state was Lt.-Gen. Olusegun Obasanjo. **19.** All commercial flights in Australia were stopped for 48 hours by a nation-wide strike of airport traffic controllers over the future of a colleague taken ill. **21.** Military aircraft evacuated nearly 1,000 people, mostly women and children, as floodwaters threatened the New South Wales town of Collarenebri after torrential rain. **22.** The city of Bundaburg, on Australia's east coast, was devastated by a storm which affected half of the 37,000 population.

March 7. A unanimous resolution passed by Australia's Labour party federal executive stated Mr. Gough Whitlam their leader and former prime minister, Dr. David Coombe, the party secretary, and Mr. Bill Hartley, Victoria executive member, had been guilty of " grave errors of judgment " in entertaining suggestions of campaign funds from Iraq. **8.** Indian Government announced the rupee had been revalued by 2·1 per cent against the pound sterling. **16.** Nicos Sampson, installed as President of Cyprus in July, 1974, by the then ruling Greek military junta, was arrested in Nicosia and accused of complicity in the *coup d'état* which led to the temporary overthrow of the President, Archbishop Makarios. **30.** New Zealand naval patrol launch *Taupo* fired a 15 mm cannon across the bows of the Formosan squid boat *Kinnan* seen fishing inside the 12-mile limit.

April 7. Mr. Glafkos Clerides resigned as Greek Cypriot negotiator in the Cyprus peace talks after his admission of a secret deal with the Turkish Cypriots. **16.** The Indian Government, announcing its new population policy, instructed States with the necessary facilities to make sterilization legally compulsory for all couples with three or more children while simultaneously raising the minimum marriageable age from 18 for boys and 14 for girls to 21 and 18 respectively. India and China agreed to exchange ambassadors after a break caused by the border troubles of 1962. **21.** Six masked bandits with sub-machine guns and pistols stole nearly £1 million from Melbourne bookmakers in Australia's biggest robbery, when they raided the Victoria Club, Melbourne. **25.** Communist terrorists blew up a stretch of Malaysia's main north-south railway line and all traffic between Kuala Lumpur, the federal capital, and northern towns was halted. **28.** The Supreme Court in New Delhi ruled that the Indian government's powers of arrest and detention under the state of emergency were absolute and the courts were powerless to intervene, the five judges holding that the suspension of all basic rights by presidential order was valid.

May 4. Australia's Prime Minister (Mr. Fraser) told the House of Representatives that " Waltzing Matilda " had been adopted as the country's national anthem but that " God save the Queen " would still be played on vice-regal occasions. **10.** The Jamaican Government imposed a curfew on the capital Kingston, after a freak outbreak of political violence in which shops were burnt and many people injured. **14.** New Zealand Government announced a 12-month freeze on wage rises and limits on dividends and on all professional fees and charges. India and Pakistan agreed to resume diplomatic relations severed at the time of their war over the secession of Bangladesh in December, 1971. **20.** The Australian Government cut A$2,600 million (about £1,700 million) from its spending programme for the next financial year. **25.** A government statement said that India's population had reached 605 million with 21 million births every

year and 9 million deaths, giving an annual population growth of 2 per cent. Australian Government announced that it would spend A$12,000 million (about £8,100 million) on defence over next five years, increasing annual defence budget by about 5·5 per cent.
June 4. The Australian Prime Minister (Mr. Fraser) reversed a ban on visits by nuclear warships to Australian ports. Canada announced that it would extend its fishing limits from 12 to 200 miles from Jan 1, 1977. **19.** The Jamaican Government declared a state of emergency following the discovery of a large arms cache in Kingston where over 70 people had been killed in acts of violence during the year. **23.** The National Unity Party of Mr. Rauf Denktash, the Turkish-Cypriot leader, won 30 of the 40 seats on election for the "Turkish Federalist State of Cyprus."
July 11. Two million workers supported Australia's first national strike, called for 24 hours, in protest at Government's plans to change Medibank, the country's health scheme. **13.** The Queen and the Duke of Edinburgh sailed into Halifax, Nova Scotia, on the Royal yacht *Britannia*, to begin their two-week tour of Canada, including the official opening of the Olympic Games in Montreal on July 17. **15.** Jamaica's state of emergency laws were extended for 100 days. Canada and the Soviet Union signed a new long-term economic agreement. **20.** Rangoon Radio stated that President Ne Win of Burma had survived an assassination plot by rebel military officers and that 14 officers had been arrested.
Aug. 16. The Indian Parliament extended for another year the Government's power to hold political prisoners without charges. **17.** The Australian budget gave incentives for business and industry without increasing direct or indirect tax and was aimed at boosting economic recovery and reducing inflation with cuts in public expenditure in all spheres except education, defence, and social security. **30.** It was announced that the New Zealand Government planned legislation restricting the right of trade unions to call political strikes after a strike by seamen and dockers in Wellington over the visit by the U.S. nuclear-powered light cruiser *Truxtun*, 9,200 tons, which had disrupted the port since Aug. 27 and stopped ferry services between North and South Islands. **31.** Nicos Sampson, onetime EOKA gunman and for eight days president of Cyprus, was jailed for 20 years by a Nicosia court after pleading guilty to usurping presidential powers after the coup of July 15, 1974, which temporarily ousted Archbishop Makarios.
Sept. 1. Opposition M.P.s walked out of Indian Parliament after attacking a bill which would make 59 changes to the constitution. Australian dockers' unions at New South Wales port of Newcastle voted to begin a campaign of industrial action against Japanese ships in protest at the award of Government shipbuilding contracts to Japan. **5.** Three Palestinians who had hijacked a Dutch airliner over France surrendered in Cyprus. **15.** Mr. Callaghan began two days of talks in Ottawa with Mr. Trudeau, Canadian Prime Minister.

MIDDLE EAST

(1975) Sept. 23. Egyptian and Israeli negotiators concluded a protocol implementing the new Sinai disengagement agreement. **26.** Eight people at least were killed and 40 wounded in renewed violence in Beirut, jeopardizing the latest ceasefire, while a number of kidnappings were reported. **28.** Israel raised taxes and devalued its currency by 10 per cent. to cut public spending and to curb a soaring deficit.
Oct. 8. Over 50 people were killed and hundreds

reported wounded when the Lebanese civil war erupted again in Beirut and Tripoli. **9.** On the day after the announcement of the sixth ceasefire in the latest round of violence in the Lebanon, renewed fighting resulted in the deaths of 65 people in Beirut and North Lebanon, and the Prime Minister (Mr. Rashid Karami) visited Damascus for urgent talks with Syrian leaders. **10.** Israel formally signed the Sinai interim agreement and transferred the Ras Sudar oil fields to American technicians as representatives of Egypt. **12.** President Sadat of Egypt confirmed the death sentences on two men condemned for plotting to overthrow his regime, but commuted the death sentence on a third man to hard labour for life. **13.** In Turkey's Senate elections, the Prime Minister's party, the Justice Party, lost five seats and the opposition Republican People's Party led by Mr. Bulent Ecevit, gained 17. **22.** First meeting of the Israeli and Egyptian military delegations supervising the Sinai interim agreements took place at a U.N. post between Baluza and Kantara, east of the Suez Canal. **24.** Six people were killed and 20 injured in a mortar bomb attack on a hospital in a Beirut suburb.
Nov. 2. The Greek cargo ship *Olympos*, carrying the first Israeli cargo permitted through the Suez Canal since the signing of the Israel-Egypt Sinai accord in September, made the 11½ hour journey from the Mediterranean to the Red Sea, transporting 8,500 tons of cement. **12.** Officials of the Arab League's Boycott Office issued orders blacklisting ships which carried Israeli cargoes through the Suez Canal. **14.** Israeli troops handed over the Ras Sudar oilfield and its township to U.N. soldiers under the terms of the interim peace agreement with Egypt to whom control was transferred on Nov. 15. **22.** The 3-week ceasefire between Moslems and Christians in Beirut, Lebanon, ended, at least 15 people being killed and 35 wounded, bringing the death toll in the 7-month civil war to 4,160. **23.** The Israeli pound was devalued by 1½ per cent. to I£7.10 to the U.S. dollar, the second devaluation in two months. **30.** U.N. Security Council approved a 6-month extension of the mandate of U.N. buffer-force in the Golan Heights.
Dec. 2. It was stated that 77 people were killed and 107 injured in Israeli raids on Palestinian refugee camps and towns and villages in the Lebanon and two Israeli border towns were reported to have come under rocket attack. **6.** A Russian diplomat was critically wounded and another injured and some 60 people killed in fresh fighting in Lebanon. **7.** Another 90 people were reported killed in Beirut's street fighting. **8.** More violence in Beirut left at least 50 people dead. **10.** Nazareth became the first town in Israel to have a Communist administration when the Rakah Arab Communist Party captured 11 of the 17 seats in a municipal election. President Giscard d'Estaing of France arrived in Egypt for a six-day visit. **13.** At the end of Beirut's worst week of the civil war, 71 were reported dead and 137 wounded, and a further 17 were killed in Tripoli and Zahle. **14.** Fire swept a tented camp of Moslem pilgrims near the Holy City of Mecca, killing 138 people and injuring 151.
(1976) Jan. 16. Lebanese Air Force fighter-bombers bombed and strafed Palestinian and Leftist positions near Damour which had been under siege for 48 hours, the jet attacks being the first of their kind in the 9-month-old civil war. **18.** Mr. Rashid Karami, Lebanon's prime minister, resigned after a week-end of widespread fighting. The Israeli Cabinet approved an order making publication of secret messages between Israeli and foreign leaders and secret meetings between Israeli leaders and countries with which Israel had no diplomatic

relations, punishable by up to 15 years' imprisonment. **26.** Final implementation of the Sinai cease-fire took place when Egyptian troops took over their first area in the north along the Mediterranean coast.

Feb. 6. The Syrian Foreign Minister (Mr. Abdel Halim Khaddam) announced that Lebanon and Syria had reached agreement on "a complete political settlement" covering all aspects of the Lebanese crisis. Syria formally undertook to guarantee "in letter and spirit" the implementation of a seven-year-old agreement between Lebanon and the Palestinians after a meeting in Damascus between President Assad of Syria and President Franjieh of Lebanon. **14.** President Franjieh proclaimed a 17-point political reform programme. **16.** First secretary at Turkish embassy in Beirut was shot dead in pin-ball parlour by a gunman using a silenced pistol. Israeli Government increased travel taxes on holidays abroad which had drained the country's foreign currency reserves. **24.** The Lebanese Prime Minister announced measures to make £50 million available to commerce, industry, and property owners to rebuild the economy after 10 months of civil war.

March 7. It was officially stated that traffic through the Suez Canal had about reached the 68 vessels a day level achieved before the 1967 war. At the end of his 4-day visit to Cairo, U.S. Treasury Secretary (Mr. William Simon) announced an American-Egyptian plan for strengthening the Egyptian economy. **8.** An Egyptian Interior Ministry official reported in Cairo the arrest of a seven-man "assassination squad" allegedly sent by Col. Gaddafi, Libyan leader, to commit "sabotage, murders, and kidnapping." **11.** President Franjieh of Lebanon rejected Army demands that he and his government should resign. **12.** Lebanese army officers set up a military command council to govern the country until the politicians established a reformed democratic government. **14.** President Sadat asked the Egyptian parliament to abrogate the 1971 treaty of friendship and cooperation with Russia. This decision was confirmed by 307–2 votes. **19.** An assassination attempt on Mr. Karami, Lebanese prime minister, and other Moslem leaders failed when their plane was struck by a rocket as it waited at Beirut airport to fly them to Damascus, but the peace talks in Syrian capital were postponed until next day. The Egyptian prime minister (Mr. Salem) named four new ministers and a number of ministry amalgamations to deal with the country's economic problems. **22.** Israel and P.L.O. sat down together for first time at the U.N. Security Council in New York after U.S. had cast a solitary vote against inviting P.L.O. to join in the debate on recent disorders and unrest on the Israeli-occupied West Bank. **26.** President Sadat unofficially confirmed in Cairo he had ended Egyptian port facilities for the Russian Navy, but confirmed the action during his Paris visit on April 4. **30.** Six Arabs were killed and 300 people arrested during rioting in villages around Nazareth in Israel, accompanied by a partly-effective strike against the expropriation of Jewish and Arab land for urban projects.

April 7. Syria began a sea-blockade of Lebanon to help to reinforce the ceasefire by stopping ammunition and supplies reaching Leftist-held areas. **9.** Syrian troops crossed into Lebanon and occupied the town of Masnaa and a clash between Syrians and men of the rebel Lebanese Arab army was reported. **18.** Israel devalued its pound by 2 per cent. from 7·52 to 7.67 to the dollar, this being the 17th devaluation since the State was established in 1948. **24.** The Lebanese President (M. Suleiman Franjieh) signed a constitutional amendment to

make possible the immediate selection of his successor. Fighting in the civil war continued in Beirut. **25.** Two-thirds of Israeli civil servants, went on strike against payment of higher wages to "a privileged class" in the civil service.

May 5. A new ceasefire stopped the shooting in the Beirut port area after 4 days and nights of heavy fighting with many casualties. **8.** Lebanon's parliament elected Mr. Elias Sarkis, a Maronite Christian, as President to succeed Mr. Suleiman Franjieh. **10.** Six Iraqi ministers were relieved of their posts in a major cabinet reshuffle. **16.** A new outbreak of fighting ended Lebanon's 30th truce in 13 months of civil war. **25.** Suitcases exploded in Tel Aviv's Ben-Gurion Airport, killing three people and injuring nine, two of the dead being Israeli security guards. **27.** Syria renewed the 6-month mandate for the U.N. observer force on the Golan Heights. **31.** Syrian soldiers supported by tanks and other armour crossed into Lebanon and advanced on positions in the north-east Akkar Valley held by the Lebanese Arab army.

June 3. Troops in Beirut enforced a general strike on most of the capital in protest against Syrian intervention in Lebanon. **4.** Syria sent more troops into Lebanon in the eastern Bekaa Valley. **5.** Egypt ordered the withdrawal of its diplomatic mission from Damascus and the closing of the Syrian embassy in Cairo after an attack on the Egyptian Embassy in Damascus by students. The Lebanese leftist leader, Kamal Jumblatt, appealed to United Nations "to put an end immediately to the invasion of Lebanon by Syrian troops." **7.** Syria ordered its invasion force in the east of Lebanon to capture guerilla strongholds in the mountains, while the militia loyal to the Damascus regime went into action against Palestinian units in Beirut. **9.** Arab nations decided to send a peacekeeping force drawn from Algeria, Libya, Saudi Arabia, Sudan, and the Palestine Liberation Organization to Lebanon despite protests from Syria and President Franjieh of Lebanon. **10.** An emergency conference of Arab foreign ministers in Cairo adopted resolutions demanding immediate withdrawal of Syrian troops from the Lebanon, and Iraq announced a partial call-up of reservists. **15.** U.N. Security Council agreed in New York to a 6-month extension of the peace-keeping force mandate in Cyprus. **16.** Mr. Francis Meloy, American Ambassador to Lebanon, was ambushed, kidnapped, and murdered by left-wing terrorists in Beirut. His economic adviser, Mr. Robert Waring, and their Moslem Lebanese chauffeur, were also killed. **20.** British and U.S. refugees totalling 263, 97 of them British, boarded a U.S. landing craft at a pier in Beirut to be ferried to a U.S. Navy ship which took them to Athens. **21.** Syrian troops handed over control of Beirut airport to Arab peace-keeping troops as part of the peace agreement announced in Damascus by Major Jalloud, Libyan prime minister and mediator in Lebanon. **22.** Syria and Egypt agreed to renew diplomatic relations. **27.** Members of the Popular Front for the Liberation of Palestine skyjacked an Air France airbus carrying 257 people, including 83 Israelis, soon after it took off from Athens on a flight from Tel Aviv to Paris and ordered the pilot to fly to Benghazi in Libya where it refuelled before heading south-east across the Sahara to land at Entebbe Airport, Uganda. On June 29 the Terrorists threatened "severe heavy penalties" if a demand for the release of 53 prisoners in jails in different countries was not met. On July 1, 100 passengers were released, including 3 Britons, and flew to Paris. On July 3 a force of Israeli commandos flew to Uganda in three Hercules transport planes, launched an attack at Entebbe Airport, stormed the building where 106 hostages, mostly

Jews, were guarded, and in a 36-minute battle rescued them, including the crew of the airbus. Twenty Ugandan soldiers and 7 skyjackers, one a German woman, were killed. Three hostages and one Israeli commando were also killed. All the surviving hostages and commandos boarded the military planes and flew to Israel. The Israeli force destroyed 11 Russian built MIGs and some civilian aircraft. **30.** The Libyan Ambassador in Cairo (Mr. Milod El-Seddik) was expelled by Egypt for distributing subversive pamphlets.

July 1. The Soviet Embassy in Beirut began evacuating its nationals from Lebanon by ship from the southern part of Sidon. **18.** A Greek ship carrying ammunition from Egypt to the Leftists and Palestinians in Lebanon was arrested by the Israeli Navy. **24.** Five hundred people were reported trapped under a collapsed bomb shelter on the outskirts of Beirut's besieged Tal Zaatar Palestinian camp. **27.** An American-organized evacuation of refugees from Beirut by sea aboard the *Coronado* of the U.S. Sixth Fleet included 150 Americans and 20 Britons.

Aug. 1. Mahmoud Ayoubi resigned as prime minister of Syria and was succeeded by Maj.-Gen. Abdel-Rahman Khleifawi, a former premier. **6.** A Turkish research ship, *Sismik I*, began a 10-day mission into the Aegean Sea to explore for oil amid a dispute over areas of control with Greece. **12.** The Palestinian camp of Tal Zaatar near Beirut fell to right wing Lebanese forces after heavy artillery bombardment. It was announced in Cairo that Egypt was moving infantry, paratroopers, and armour to its borders with Libya " in preparation for any protective measures deemed appropriate." **14.** Seven people were killed and 51 injured when a bomb exploded in a luggage rack of a crowded train in Alexandria. **23.** Three Arabs hijacked a Boeing 737 Egyptian airliner soon after it left Cairo on a tourist flight to the resorts of Luxor and Aswan in southern Egypt and demanded the release of three Libyans serving life sentences for the attempted assassination of an ex-member of Libya's Revolutionary Council now a political refugee in Egypt, and the release of a South Yemeni and a Palestinian awaiting trial for the attempted killing in Cairo of former South Yemen premier, Mohamed Aly Hathem. Egyptian commandos stormed the plane when it landed at Luxor to refuel, freed the 94 passengers and crew unharmed, and wounded three terrorists, who were captured. **27.** Leaders of the Right in the Lebanese civil war accepted in principle an Arab League peace plan to normalize the country.

Sept. 1. The Turkish submarine, *Dumlupinar*, was in collision with the Soviet merchant ship, *Fizik Vavilov*, 8,151 tons, in the Dardanelles, and was badly damaged.

U.S.A.

(1975) Sept. 22. A second assassination attempt on President Ford was made when a 45-year-old woman, later named as Mrs. Sara Jane Moore, fired a shot which missed as Mr. Ford emerged from the St. Francis Hotel in San Francisco. **30** Emperor Hirohito of Japan and Empress Nagako arrived in the U.S. for a 13-day State tour.

Oct. 2. The House of Representatives reversed their opposition and voted partly to lift Congress embargo on U.S. arms sales to Turkey, a bill releasing 185 million dollars in shipments being approved by 237-176 votes. Publication of the *Washington Post* was suspended after employees caused destruction and sabotage which put out of action all nine of the newspaper's printing presses in a strike over wages, overtime rules, and manning. **4.** U.S. and Spain reached agreement in principle on a new five-year deal for America's continued use of Spanish military bases. **6.** President Ford proposed $28,000 million (£14,000 million) in permanent tax reductions to start in 1976 on condition that the Democrats, who controlled Congress, cut public spending by a similar amount. **8.** House of Representatives approved the plan to send 200 volunteer U.S. technicians to Sinai to monitor peace agreement, voting in favour being 341-69. **9.** President Ford announced that he had no intention of cutting America's defence budget. A man released from prison in May 1975 after serving 5 years for threatening to kill former President Nixon was jailed for 5 more years for telephoning the Secret Service agents in Sacramento, California, and threatening to kill President Ford. **10.** President Ford sent Congress his plan for a $100,000 million (£49,000 million) Government corporation to help finance the development of new sources of energy and called for the establishment of an Energy Independence Authority. **14.** President Ford's car was in collision with another vehicle at a crossing in Hartford, Connecticut, but the President was unhurt. **17.** New York was saved from bankruptcy when the teachers' union agreed to lend the City $150 million (about £75 million) from its pension fund which automatically brought about additional aid from New York State and allowed the City to pay off $453 million (£226·5 million) in debts due by the banks' closing time. **20.** U.S. agreed to sell Russia 30 million metric tons of wheat and maize in the ensuing 5 years the White House announced. **21.** A 3-year plan to cut New York City's budget by $724 million (£362 million) was approved by the State's Emergency Financial Control Board. **23.** New York State Lottery was suspended because of allegations of irregularities in prize money distribution. **27.** President Sadat of Egypt arrived in Washington for talks with President Ford, including the question of arms supplies.

Nov. 3. President Ford announced three new members of his Cabinet after the Vice-President, Mr. Nelson Rockefeller, said that he was stepping aside as Mr. Ford's prospective running mate in next year's elections. **24.** Five guards held hostage for 24 hours by about 1,200 prisoners at a jail on Rikers Island, New Jersey, were released after the authorities promised to improve prison conditions. **27.** A jury of 8 women and 4 men found Lynette Fromme guilty of attempting to assassinate President Ford in Sacramento, California, on Sept. 5. On Dec. 17 she was sentenced to life imprisonment.

Dec. 1. President Ford, accompanied by Mrs. Ford, began their four-day official visit to China. **10.** A New York criminal court judge ruled that spying on customers in store dressing-rooms to catch them shoplifting was unconstitutional. **17.** The State Department rejected resolutions by the Senate and the House of Representatives urging that the exiled Russian author, Alexander Solzhenitsyn, should be granted honorary American citizenship. **19.** The Senate voted 54-22 to stop U.S. arms aid to Angola. **29.** At least 12 people were killed and many injured when two bombs exploded at a baggage-handling terminal in La Guardia Airport, New York.

(1976) Jan. 12. U.S. was alone in voting in U.N. Security Council against inviting Palestine Liberation Organization to take part in the Middle East debate as if it were a member state, U.K., France, and Italy abstaining. On Jan. 13, New York police found and dismantled a time bomb planted to coincide with the U.N. debate. **14.** Mr. John Dunlop, U.S. Labour Secretary, resigned in a dispute over union picketing rights with President Ford. **21.** President Ford, sending Congress his

budget proposals, stated that he would balance the country's books by 1979. **26.** In his annual economic message to Congress, President Ford claimed that the American economy was " steadily growing healthier " but that unemployment remained " distressingly high." **28.** The U.S. Senate voted 77–19 to declare a 200-mile fishing limit. **29.** The House of Representatives voted 246–124, a majority of 122, to block release of a Congressional report on secret operations of the Central Intelligence Agency. **30.** A 30-year-old man, Erwin Simants, who murdered six members of a next-door family was sentenced to death in Platte, Nebraska.

Feb. 4. U.S. Transport Secretary (Mr. William Coleman) announced trial services for 16 months for Concorde to fly to Washington and New York. **5.** The Lockheed Aircraft Corporation ordered a new investigation into payments concerning sales contracts after charges that the Company bribed executives of several international airlines were made in U.S. Senate sub-committee on multinational corporations. **5.** A proposal to ban Concorde permanently from the U.S. was defeated by 10–9 votes in the Senate Commerce Committee and another proposal to ban the plane until it should meet American noise standards was also defeated. **13.** Lockheed's two top executives, Mr Daniel Haughton, chairman and Mr. A. Carl Kotchian, president, resigned after disclosures that the company had paid $24·4 million (about £12 million) to foreign government officials. **16.** Hamilton National Bank of Chattanooga, Tennessee, was declared insolvent by U.S. Government, blame being attributed to mortgage defaults. **17.** President Ford announced plans for a major re-organization of the U.S.'s intelligence services. **20.** Former President Richard Nixon and his wife left Los Angeles on a private visit to China in a Boeing 707 specially sent for their flight by the Chinese. **22.** The Energy Research and Development Administration confirmed experiments on 18 men, women, and children injected with doses of radioactive plutonium 30 years ago to determine what effects it might have on workers manufacturing nuclear weapons.

March 14. Four Black Moslems, members of the " Death Angels " cult were convicted of murdering 14 Whites in San Francisco after a 12-month trial; they were also convicted of involvement in seven assaults, a rape, and the attempted kidnapping of three children. **18.** President Ford and Mr. Liam Cosgrave, Eire prime minister, after their meeting at the White House urged American-Irish people to stop supporting I.R.A. terrorism. **20.** Patricia Hearst, 22 year-old newspaper heiress, was found guilty by a jury after an eight-week trial in San Francisco, of armed bank robbery. **26.** The U.S. military bases in Turkey were to re-open under an arms aid agreement reached in Washington by Dr. Kissinger and the Turkish Foreign Minister (Mr. Caglayangil). **31.** President Ford formally announced the setting up of a Cabinet Legal Commission headed by Mr. Elliot Richardson the Commerce Secretary, to inquire into the allegations of bribery and corruption by American firms to obtain foreign orders.

April 3. Tentative settlement in the 3-day national strike by U.S. truck drivers was announced by the Secretary of Labour. **12.** Patricia Hearst was given a provisional 35-year maximum sentence for armed bank robbery and criminal use of a gun. **14.** President Ford signed a law unilaterally extending U.S. fishing limits from 12 to 200 miles on March 1, 1977. **18.** A check on valuables stolen the previous week by masked gunmen in a raid on a Florida hotel established that it was the biggest jewel robbery in U.S., the market value of the gold and precious stones taken from safe-deposit boxes being estimated at about £3·5 million plus £22,500 in cash and cheques. **19.** F.B.I. sharpshooters on a commercial jetliner shot and killed Roger Lentz, when he boarded the plane in Denver, Colorado, after he had for 7 hours previously held as hostages the pilot and mechanic of a small private plane while negotiating for the larger aircraft. **22.** A bomb thought to be linked with Boston's week of racial incidents exploded in a court building, injuring 18 persons. **24.** Dr. Kissinger left R.A.F. Waddington, England, after talks with new British Foreign Secretary (Mr. Crosland) to fly to Nairobi on the first leg of his tour of seven African countries. **26.** A New York jury awarded $1·1 million (about £600,000) damages to a Brooklyn woman, Miss Laureen Berstein, who claimed she suffered emotionally after being falsely arrested for shoplifting at a department store. **29.** Senator Hubert Humphrey announced that he would not actively seek the Democratic presidential nomination.

May 28. The City University of New York was ordered to close after it was unable to meet its $15 million dollar payroll for 18,000 faculty members. On June 1 New York City Board of Higher Education voted to impose tuition fees on the undergraduates of the City University from September, 1976.

June 14. The City University re-opened with the help of a $27 million (£15½ million) financial aid package from the State plus introduction of tuition fees next term for the first time. **18.** Mr. Wayne Hays, the Ohio Democratic Representative involved in an alleged sex scandal, tendered his resignation as chairman of the House Administration Committee of U.S. Congress and it was accepted. **23.** A Senate sub-committee which had been investigating aspects of the assassination of President Kennedy published its report and stated that it had discovered no evidence of a conspiracy. **29.** U.S. vetoed Security Council resolution which sought to affirm Palestinian right to sovereignty in Palestine.

July 1. New York's municipal trade unions agreed to new two-year contracts with the City which would result in a saving of $24 million (about £14 million) a year in its labour costs. **2.** The U.S. Supreme Court upheld the death penalty and ruled that it was not a " cruel and unusual punishment," but in a separate ruling the Court invalidated laws in North Carolina and Louisiana that made death mandatory for such crimes as premeditated murder or the killing of a policeman. Bombs destroyed an Eastern Airlines plane at Boston International Airport, damaged a courthouse in Newburyport, 40 miles away, and destroyed vehicles at a Boston National Guard armoury. **4.** The U.S. celebrated its Bicentennial with a series of spectacular events. The Queen and the Duke of Edinburgh, on board the Royal yacht, *Britannia*, sailed up the east coast of America for Philadelphia for the start on July 6 of their six-day State visit to the U.S. **14.** Mr. Jimmy Carter was voted the Democratic nominee for the Presidency at the Party's New York convention. On July 15 he chose Senator Walter Mondale, of Minnesota, as his running mate. A Washington taxi-driver who was found standing on the lawn of the White House was shot dead by a police guard after ignoring repeated orders to halt.

Aug. 4. Appointment of the first Black, Rear-Admiral Samuel Gravely, to command a U.S. Navy fleet was announced. A team of over 1,000 medical experts were investigating the mysterious " Legionnaires disease " which killed 22 men who attended an American Legion convention in Phila-

delphia 11 days before and resulted in the admission of 122 to hospital, and on Aug. 5 the death toll rose to 24 with 138 still receiving hospital treatment; a 25th man died later. On Aug. 6 medical experts stated the infection had been caused by a toxic chemical substance but its nature remained a mystery. **12.** A Mississippi court awarded $1,250,599 (about £700,000) in damages against the National Association for the Advancement of Coloured People to 12 white merchants in Port Gibson, Mississippi, to compensate for losses they suffered as a result of the Association's successful boycott of local shops in 1966. Judge George Haynes found that the Association and 132 individual defendants had "wrongfully combined and colluded a civil conspiracy." **19.** President Ford won the nomination as Republican candidate in the U.S.'s November elections by 1,187 votes to 1,070 over Mr. Ronald Reagan at his party convention in Kansas City. He named Senator Robert Dole, of Kansas, as his vice-presidential running mate. **31.** William and Betty Harris, who as members of the Symbionese Liberation Army took part in the kidnapping of Patricia Hearst, were sentenced in Los Angeles to indeterminate terms of 11 years to life imprisonment for kidnapping, robbery, and car theft.

Sept. 3. *Viking II* spacecraft landed on Mars.

COMMON MARKET

(1975) Sept. 29. A special sugar refining margin of about £6 a ton to keep Commonwealth sugar flowing to Britain's cane refineries and stop it being diverted to Continental beet-plants was set by Common Market agricultural ministers in Brussels. **Oct. 1.** The Common Market Commission decided to suspend trade negotiations with Spain in protest over the executions on Sept. 27 of five Spanish terrorists. **13.** West Germany, France, Italy and Belgium rejected a Common Market plan to provide financial aid to poor countries not formally associated with the E.E.C. **15.** The U.K. rejected a Common Market requirement that the maximum working day for lorry drivers be reduced from 10 hours to 8, the Minister of Transport (Dr. John Gilbert) saying that Britain would seek an exemption of two years from the ruling due to operate on Jan. 1, 1976. **17.** First grants—655 in number amounting to £80 million—were announced in Brussels under the Common Market regional fund, Britain's share being about £11 million.

Nov. 5. Mr. Callaghan told his E.E.C. colleagues in Brussels that Britain was still unable to endorse proposals for direct elections to the European Parliament in or after 1978. **Dec. 1.** Common Market summit opened in Rome. Mr. Wilson obtained approval in principle for his proposals for closer scrutiny of the Brussels budget and accepting also in principle the idea of direct elections to the European Parliament. **9.** The Common Market accepted a U.K. proposal allowing Britain to adopt its own system of pollution controls subject to certain safeguards concerning industrial poisons dumped by factories. **18.** Britain was granted the equivalent of about £33 million from E.E.C. regional fund, bringing the total for the U.K. for the year to £43 million.

(1976) Jan. 1. Britain made the fourth of five tariff adjustments to bring her into line with the rest of the E.E.C. **7.** M. Leo Tindemans, Belgian Prime Minister, presented his report to Common Market leaders in Brussels on the future of European Union. **8.** The E.E.C. gave permission for U.K. Government to provide up to £26,200,000 in various forms of aid for the coal industry and at same time also approved proposed grants by the

French, German, and Belgian Governments to their coal industries. **17.** The E.E.C. completed a trade agreement with Algeria following similar deals with Morocco and Tunisia which opened the European Market to set amounts of Algerian oil, olive oil, wine, and cork. **20.** The Common Market countries agreed to suspend their common external tariff on potato imports in an effort to ease the shortage. **22.** The Brussels Commission registered its " concern " at the display of trade protectionism in America after the decision by the American International Trade Commission to recommend import quotas for special steel. **27.** E.E.C. loans totalling £85 million for steel expansion projects in the U.K. were announced.

Feb. 16. Loans of £500 million and £150 million to Italy and Ireland respectively were approved by the Finance Ministers of E.E.C.

March 5. E.E.C.'s long-term finance institution, the European Investment Bank, granted two loans totalling £13 million to the National Water Council for major supply schemes in the north of England. **6.** E.E.C. agricultural ministers reached agreement on a package raising Common Market farm prices for 1976 by an average of 7·6 per cent. **14.** The French Government decided to withdraw the franc from the European joint currency float or " snake " and to float it independently from following day.

April 6. The Common Market decided to provide aid worth £13 million for countries in southern Africa affected by the Angolan war and the Rhodesian situation. **29.** The European Communities Commission announced grants to U.K. firms and local councils of £18 million to create work in the regions. An E.E.C. proposal to reduce subsidies in U.K. food imports by up to 2½ per cent. to offset the fall in the value of sterling was rejected at an emergency meeting of Common Market agriculture ministers in Luxemburg.

May 11. The E.E.C. announced allocation of aid worth £37·2 million to African countries as the first instalment from the European Development Fund. **13.** European Community announced social fund grants totalling about £16 million for retraining workers in member States. **30.** E.E.C. officials in Brussels stated that the Common Market had abandoned the proposal to create a common summer time for 1977 and had postponed any similar attempt until 1978.

June 10. The E.E.C. Commission announced that it had fined the Swiss firm Hoffman-La Roche the equivalent of £200,000 for abusing its dominant position in the vitamin market. **29.** E.E.C. foreign ministers agreed to begin formal negotiations in July on admitting Greece to the Community. E.E.C. members agreed to pool their security activities in a move to thwart international terrorism, a six-point plan being approved.

July 6. Canada became the first advanced non-European country to sign an economic co-operation agreement with the E.E.C. **12.** The Common Market countries agreed at their heads of Government meeting in Brussels to a scheme for direct elections to the European Parliament in 1978, providing for 410 members, the U.K., France, Germany and Italy having 81 seats each, Holland 25, Belgium 24, Denmark 16, Ireland 15, and Luxembourg 6. **13.** The Common Market countries in Brussels agreed to Mr. Callaghan's proposal that Mr. Roy Jenkins should become the next President of the European Commission from Jan. 1, 1977. The E.E.C. also agreed unanimously against the taking of hostages for any reason and to instruct the appropriate ministers to ensure that any terrorists caught in E.E.C. countries would face trial or extradition. **20.** It was announced that U.K. was

to receive £32,800,000 Common Market aid, including a £17,600,000 low-interest loan to the Post Office to improve north-east 'phone services. A draft declaration provisionally approved by E.E.C. Foreign Affairs Council accepted a general extension of Community fishing limits to 200 miles.

Aug. 20. The Common Market proposed to ease the effect of the drought by suspending its import duties on many fresh vegetables until Sept. 30.

AFRICA

(1975) Sept. 26. Seven people died when security forces fired on a crowd in Addis Ababa airport in retaliation for shots aimed at them, the Ethiopian Government said. **28.** Mr. Joshua Nkomo was elected president of the African National Council during a two-day congress of council branches in Salisbury, Rhodesia. **30.** Ethiopia's military government proclaimed a state of emergency because of workers' and students' unrest.

Oct. 2. Paramount Chief Kaiser Matanzima announced that South Africa's Transkei Bantustan would become fully independent on Oct. 26, it being the first of South Africa's 10 Bantustans to do so. **7.** The South African Government, employers, and the trade unions reached a new agreement to hold down prices, wages, and profits. **12.** Mr. Vorster, South African Prime Minister, said in a statement that remarks by Mr. Ian Smith, Rhodesian Prime Minister, blaming him for the collapse of the recent Rhodesian settlement talks, were " not in accord with the facts," and on Oct. 20 Mr. Smith apologised for " any embarrassment caused." **15.** The Deputy Speaker of the Kenyan Parliament, Mr. John Seromey, and Mr. Martin Shikuku, an M.P. critical of the Government, were arrested in the Parliament building in Nairobi, no reasons being given. **21.** First contingent of 20,000 volunteers set off from the eastern province of Ksar Es Souk, Morocco, towards the border of Spanish Sahara at the start of the peace march launched by King Hassan to send 350,000 unarmed people into the disputed territory. On Oct. 22 Spanish authorities in the Sahara capital of El Aaiun recommended Government employees and military personnel to send their wives and children out of the territory. On Oct. 25 Dr. Kurt Waldheim, U.N. Secretary-General, left for Rabat, the Moroccan capital, and next day held urgent talks with King Hassan. The Spanish Legion imposed a curfew and full military control over El Aaiun on Oct. 28. Prince Juan Carlos flew to Spanish Sahara on Nov. 2 to review his troops and Spain formally warned U.N. Security Council that she would use military force to " repel " the Moroccan civilians. On Nov. 3, the Moroccan Prime Minister (Mr. Ahmed Osman) flew into Madrid. On Nov. 5, King Hassan announced that his " march of conquest " would begin on Nov. 6 despite threats from Spain and Algeria. Chanting Moroccans armed only with copies of the Koran and their national flag began crossing into Spanish Sahara on Nov. 6 to claim the territory. They halted at the mine-strewn " dissuasion zone " established by the Spanish Army 8 miles inside the border. U.N. Security Council called on Morocco immediately to withdraw the marchers. King Hassan called off the march on Nov. 9 saying " we shall resolve this problem another way." On Nov. 14 Spain agreed to withdraw from the country on Feb. 28, 1976, after handing over the territory to Morocco and Mauritania. On Jan. 27, 1976, Moroccan and Algerian troops clashed near Amgala, an oasis in the Western Sahara. **23.** Britain's honorary consul in Asmara, capital of Eritrea, Mr. Basil Durwood-Taylor, was kidnapped by members of the Eritrean Liberation Front. **27.** The French Army withdrew from its

two bases in Chad as the Chad Government's ultimatum expired under agreements dating back to 1960.

Nov. 10. Portugal announced Angola's independence and withdrew from the territory while the Marxist Popular Movement for the Liberation of Angola (MPLA) raised its flag in the capital of Luanda and the National Front for the Liberation of Angola (FNLA) and National Union for Total Independence of Angola (UNITA) set up a joint revolutionary council at Novo Lisban. **19.** Mr. Paul Ngei, Minister for Local Government, was removed from office by a Kenyan High Court judgment which found him guilty of threatening to kill his opponent on nomination day in the 1974 general election, and was banned from contesting any parliamentary election for the ensuing five years. **27.** Nine African miners were killed and 48 injured in a tribal faction fight at the Witwatersrand Nigel gold mine near Heidelberg, south-east of Johannesburg. **31.** President Nyerere of Tanzania was re-elected; he was the only candidate and received 91·5 per cent support in the ballot. Lagos State authorities, Nigeria, announced the removal of 247 more officials in a fresh purge of the public service for various reasons, including malpractices and declining productivity, bringing the total of officials who had lost their jobs to 3,000.

Dec. 1. Agreement to start full constitutional negotiations on Rhodesia was signed in Salisbury by Mr. Ian Smith and Mr. Joshua Nkomo, leader of the African National Council. **17.** South Africa admitted for first time that her troops were in direct contact with M.P.L.A. forces in Angola. **23.** Col. Ignatius Acheampong, Head of State, said that a plot to overthrow the Ghana Government had been uncovered and that those involved had been arrested.

(1976) Jan. 1. France confirmed its intention of granting independence to the territory of the Afars and Issas, the former French Somaliland, the last French possession in Africa. **5.** South African Broadcasting Corporation presented its first full evening's programme of television after 8 months of test transmissions. **13.** The conference of the Organisation of African Unity ended in Addis Ababa divided over the Angolan civil war. **23.** Five ringleaders of an attempt in the summer of 1975 to replace the regime of President Nimeri of the Sudan were executed by firing squad. **26.** The Marxist M.P.L.A. spokesman in Luanda admitted for the first time that Russian T-34 tanks had been in action in Angola against the Western-backed U.N.I.T.A. forces and F.N.L.A. troops. **28.** The Defence Amendment Act published by thh Government in Cape Town enabled South Africa e forces to be sent legally into action in Africa anywhere south of the Equator. The Rhodesian Government announced that Rhodesian territorials were being called up to counter a new terrorist incursion in the operational area.

Feb. 2. Ten Sudanese soldiers were executed in Khartoum for taking part in an abortive coup in Sept. 1975 against President Nimeri. **4.** A young girl died and 5 other children were injured when French troops stormed a school bus carrying 30 schoolchildren, held by guerillas on the Djibouti-Somalia frontier. President Samora Machel of Mozambique decreed an end to private property ownership and announced his administration would in future collect all rents. The seaside capital of Lourenço Marques was re-named Maputo. **9.** Soviet tanks driven by Cubans overran Huambo, capital of the U.N.I.T.A. movement in the south of Angola, forcing the U.N.I.T.A. army to flee towards the Zaire frontier. **11.** M.P.L.A. forces captured Silva Porto, military H.Q. of U.N.I.T.A.,

who abandoned the base.   **13.** The Nigerian Government said that it had quashed an attempted *coup d'etat* by a group of young Army officers during which President Martala Mohammed was killed.   New head of state was Lt.-Gen. Olusegun Obasanjo.   Dr. Agostinho Neto, leader of M.P.L.A., announced the discovery of the bodies of 14 British mercenaries executed by firing squad by their own colleagues after capturing the F.N.L.A. stronghold of Maquela in northern Angola.   **15.** Morocco admitted that it had suffered heavy casualties when Algerian troops recaptured the desert outpost of Amgala in the former Spanish Sahara.   **18.** Officials announced in Dar Es Salaam that all privately-owned shops in the Lindi region of south-east Tanzania were to be abolished, only co-operative or State shops being permitted.   **19.** The M.P.L.A. Government in Angola was recognised by most countries including U.K. who condemned foreign intervention and demanded withdrawal of Cuban and South African troops.   **22.** A firing squad executed three more soldiers in Khartoum bringing to 19 the number executed for participating in the abortive coup of Sept. 1975 against President Nimeri.   **26.** The Zaire Foreign Secretary said that over one million Angolan refugees had escaped across the border into Zaire.   Lord Greenhill, Britain's special envoy, met Mr. Ian Smith in Salisbury.   Spain handed over her last colony, the Sahara, to Morocco and Mauritania.   **27.** An " Arab democratic republic " was proclaimed in the Western Sahara by nationalists of the Polisario Front, a guerilla movement which opposed the takeover of the territory by Morocco and Mauritania.

March 3. President Samora Machel of Mozambique closed his 800-mile frontier with Rhodesia, seized all Rhodesian assets in his country, and placed Mozambique on a war footing as a result of a " hot pursuit " attack by Rhodesian security forces the previous week in which 24 guerilas were killed inside Mozambique.   **7.** Morocco and Mauritania broke off diplomatic relations with Algeria in their dispute over former Spanish Sahara.   **10.** Miss Ohelagat Mutai, a 23-year-old Kenya M.P., was sentenced in Nairobi to 25 years' imprisonment for inciting workers on a Rift Valley sisal estate to burn down fences and uproot the sisal.   **12.** South Africa announced that its forces in southern Angola had been withdrawn to within 10 miles of the South West African frontier.   Lagos radio reported that 33 anti-Government conspirators were executed in Nigeria the previous day by firing squad for their part in an unsuccessful *coup* on Feb. 13.   The leader of the *coup*, Lt. Col. B. S. Dimka, was executed on May 15.   **15.** U.S.A. suspended diplomatic relations with Republic of Equatorial Guinea.   **19.** Rhodesia's constitutional talks collapsed, Mr. Ian Smith's Government and Mr. Joshua Nkomo's nationalists admitting that there was total impasse.   The South African Government announced that self-governing status was to be granted to the Caprivi region of South-West Africa on April. 1.   **31.** The South African Finance Minister announced increase in defence spending by 40 per cent to about £813 million to protect her borders.

April 9. Five Kenyans were killed in the border town of Kapenguria by Ugandan troops who crossed into north-west Kenya, according to Nairobi police.   **12.** Nine people were sentenced to death by a court martial for their part in an abortive *coup* in the Republic of Niger and 22 others were jailed for life.   **13.** Four people were killed and 72 wounded in N'Djamena, Chad, after hand grenades were thrown in an attempt to assassinate President Felix Malloum, who was unhurt.   **19.** African guerillas launched two separate raids in the far south of Rhodesia near the Transvaal frontier, killed three Easter holidaymakers from South Africa, and blew up a Rhodesia Railways train and part of the track on the Rutenga link to Beit Bridge, Rhodesia's only direct rail connection with South Africa.   **21.** Seven people condemned to death after an abortive *coup* against President Seyni Kountche of Niger in March were executed by firing squad at Niamey, Niger.   **26.** Rhodesian Government announced the immediate formation of a national security committee under the control of Minister of Law and Order.   **28.** Rhodesia's first Black Cabinet ministers were sworn into office after the announcement the previous day that four tribal chiefs and six other Africans would join the Government, two ministers and three deputy ministers being assigned to Mashonaland and a similar number to Matabeleland.

May 1. Rhodesian security forces announced preparations to call-up part-time territorial soldiers for the campaign against African nationalist guerillas.   **3.** The British Consul in Asmora, Ethiopia Mr. Burwood-Taylor, kidnapped in Oct. 1975 by rebels, was freed.   **5.** Rhodesian Government increased national service from 12 to 18 months.   **12.** Two members of South West African People's Organisation (S.W.A.P.O). were sentenced to death in the Supreme Court in Swakopmund, Namibia, for participating in " terroristic " activities, and two female members of the Organisation were jailed for 7 and 5 years respectively.   This was the first time anyone in South Africa or Namibia had been condemned to death under the Terrorism Act.   **24.** Rhodesian nationalist guerilas blew up the main railway from Bulawayo to South Africa.

June 7. Ethiopia halted the march of its peasant army on Eritrea and sent a peace mission to neighbouring Arab states.   The International Commission of Inquiry on Mercenaries set up by the Angolan Government held its first session in Luanda.   **11.** President Amin escaped an assassination attempt in Kampala when three grenades were thrown at a police passing-out parade.   Radio Uganda stated that one man was killed and 36 persons injured.   **13.** Defence H.Q. in Salisbury, Rhodesia, said that saboteur's had hit the main Umtali rail-line east of Macheke the previous day and that a train set off a bomb on the Bulawayo-Mafeking line near Botswana border.   **16.** Eight people including two black children and two white men stoned by rioters were killed during rioting in Soweto, near Johannesburg, after police fired on demonstrators protesting at the introduction of the Afrikaans language as a compulsory medium of education.   On June 17 rioting, burning, and looting continued and the casualty list was reported to have risen to at least 50 dead with 250 injured, as the unrest spread to Kagiso, near Krugersdorp.   On June 18, the third day of rioting, figures of dead rose to 97 with 1,000 injured.   More rioting and shooting erupted on June 21 in townships in the Transvaal with 10 dead and 10 injured, the official toll in 6 days of violence being given as 140 dead with 1,148 people injured.   **18.** Four Zambians, including an ex-opposition M.P., were sentenced to death by the High Court in Lusaka after being found guilty of treason.   **24.** Angola's application for membership of the United Nations was vetoed in the Security Council by the United States.   **25.** After 10 days of rioting, South Africa's Minister of Justice and Police said that the official death toll had risen to 176, including two whites, with 1,139 people injured of whom 22 were police officers.   President Amin was made life President of Uganda by members of his Defence Council.   **27.** Kenya Radio reported that at least seven Kenyans were killed in the pre-

vious week after a border clash with Ugandan troops. **28.** The new Republic of Seychelles emerged as an independent country with James Mancham as President and Albert Rene as Prime Minister. **28.** Three Britons, Costas Georgiou (" Col. Callan ") of King's Cross, London; Andrew MacKenzie, and John Derek Barker, both of Aldershot, and Daniel Gearhart, from Washington, D.C., were sentenced to death by firing squad when the trial of 13 mercenaries ended in Luanda, Angola. The nine others—7 Britons and 2 Americans—were sentenced to jail terms ranging from 16 to 30 years. Mr. Callaghan sent a private personal message to President Neto of Angola seeking clemency for the three British mercenaries sentenced to death. On July 5 it was disclosed that the Queen had also appealed to President Neto to show mercy to the British mercenaries. On July 10 in Luanda, an Angolan firing squad of military police executed the three British mercenaries and one U.S. mercenary sentenced to death, despite appeals for mercy from leaders all over the world.

July 2. An attempt to overthrow President Nimeri of Sudan was crushed after hours of street fighting in Khartoum between loyalist and rebel troops. On July 4 Sudan filed official complaint to U.N. Security Council and Arab League against Libya, of masterminding the abortive coup; Sudan also recalled its Ambassador to Libya. **6.** A Libyan Boeing 727 with 86 people aboard was sky-jacked on an internal flight between Tripoli and Benghazi by a passenger armed with toy pistols and flew to Majorca when the man, a Libyan, surrendered to the police. South African Minister of Bantu Education announced that compulsory teaching in the Afrikaans language in Black schools, the issue stated to have set off the Soweto riots, was to be dropped. The 13th Organisation of African Unity conference ended in Mauritius attended by only 7 Heads-of-State of the 48-nation members. President Nimeri of Sudan announced a complete break in relations with Libya involving diplomatic, communications and economic ties. **9.** President Amin of Uganda ordered an inquiry into the whereabouts of Mrs. Dora Bloch, the missing 75-year-old skyjack hostage who had dual British-Israeli nationality; this followed a statement on July 7 to the British House of Commons by Minister of State, Foreign Office (Mr. Rowlands) that the Ugandan reply about her whereabouts was " totally unacceptable." On July 10, Britain rejected President Amin's claim to know nothing about Mrs Bloch's fate. On July 12, the British High Commission official, Mr. Peter Chandley, second secretary in Kampala, who saw Mrs. Bloch in a Kampala hospital shortly before she vanished on July 4, was ordered to leave Uganda by midnight on July 13 along with Mrs. Chandley and two other Britons. The British Government stated that there was " little doubt " that Mrs. Bloch had died in Uganda and in a statement to the British House of Commons Mr. Rowlands demanded that President Amin put on trial those responsible. On July 13, the Ugandans demanded the recall of the British acting High Commissioner in Kampala, Mr. James Horrocks. **11.** The funerals took place of 13 people killed in tribal clashes on July 10 in the Afars and Issas between supporters of the National Union of Independence and the opposition African Popular League for Independence. **12.** Following increased tension between Kenya and Uganda over the Entebbe rescue of Israeli and other hostages, the U.S. sent the frigate *Beaty* to Mombasa, a Navy patrol plane to Nairobi, and a 7th Fleet task force headed by an aircraft carrier into the Indian Ocean.

13. Ethiopian military rulers announced that 18 people, including a leading general, had been shot for high treason after the discovery of a plot to overthrow the régime. **18.** Libya confirmed that it had sent French Mirage fighters to Uganda to replace the MIG 19s destroyed in the Entebbe raid, and Kenya said that Ugandans had been arrested near vital installations in Kenya. **20.** A mob of some 3,000 Black youths attacked Indians, Whites, and others in the Witbank area 70 miles east of Pretoria, one African man being reported killed and 20 injured. Guerillas threw stick grenades into a nightclub and a restaurant in Salisbury city centre, Rhodesia, seriously injuring a white man and slightly hurting a woman. **22.** It was reported that at least 115 Moroccan troops were killed the previous week at Bir Enzaran where their convoy was ambushed by the Polisario Front independence movement. **24.** Uganda, which provides a third of Kenya's electricity, cut off supplies and also announced that to save fuel all international flights by foreign carriers would be banned in Uganda.

Aug. 4. Police fired bullets and tear gas at rampaging Black mobs in Soweto, the African township near Johannesburg, during fresh violence in which unofficial reports stated that three Africans were killed and at least 18 wounded, although police denied that there were any deaths. Sudanese firing squads executed 81 people for taking part in the abortive attempt in July to overthrow the régime of President Nimeri, and on Aug. 5 executed a further 17 people. Five students were reported dead and several wounded after military police opened fire on an anti-government demonstration at Uganda's Mauerere University, and hundreds of students were stated to have been under arrest. **6.** Kenya and Uganda agreed, after three days of ministerial talks in Nairobi, to withdraw all troops from their common border, to allow free access of all supplies and to end belligerency. **8.** Rhodesian forces sustained their biggest single loss with the deaths in action of five white Territorial Army troops, believed to have occurred on the eastern border with Mozambique. **10.** Defence H.Q. in Salisbury, Rhodesia, stated that more than 300 guerillas and 30 Frelimo troops were killed in a Rhodesian security force strike against a terrorist camp in Mozambique and that 10 black civilians assisting the terrorists had also been killed in the attack, the Rhodesian forces suffering no casualties. President Nimeri of Sudan appointed a civilian, Sayed El Rashid Tahir, as Prime Minister and named other supporters to take over key functions previously part of the presidency. **11.** A 30-minute mortar bombardment of white residential suburbs of Umtali, Rhodesia, close to the Mozambique border, caused no personal injuries but six houses were destroyed and some residents were evacuated. Rhodesian security officials put the responsibility on Frelimo troops. Police sealed Cape Town's three African townships after several incidents of stone-throwing and isolated arson attempts. **12.** Twenty-seven Africans died in overnight rioting in South Africa's three black townships in the Cape Town area and two others near Johannesburg. Thousands of Africans began violence and arson in the Cape Town region and liquor stores were looted; over 70 people were reported injured. **18.** Eight Blacks were killed in renewed anti-Government riots in Port Elizabeth, South Africa, and 18 were wounded by gunfire. The White delegation to the South West Africa constitutional talks in Windhoek agreed to a multi-racial interim government before independence, the target date for which was Dec. 31, 1978. The Ministry of Overseas Development stated that Britain had agreed to lend Mozambique £5 million for development aid. **19.**

Another violent day in two Port Elizabeth townships resulted in the deaths of 18 Blacks and injuries to 28 others; three schools, a shopping centre, and a hospital were burned. **24.** Six people were killed and 100 injured in renewed Soweto clashes. **25.** Police shot three Black South Africans dead in Soweto when Zulu gangs clashed with other Blacks during a 3-day strike called by militants. **27.** Soweto was calm after 4 days of violence in which 35 people died and over 300 were hurt mainly in inter-tribal disturbances. **30.** Eight Africans were sentenced to death for acts of sabotage and terrorism in Salisbury during June and July, all of them pleading guilty to six counts under the Law and Order Maintenance Act.

Sept. 2. Police and over 3,000 coloured students clashed in Cape Town. **7.** It was reported that at least five Blacks and Coloured people were shot dead in riots across wide areas of Cape peninsula; on Sept. 9, fifteen people were shot dead by riot police as violence spread. **13.** Armed Whites were reported to have killed at least eight Coloured people in revenge attacks against rioters in townships around Cape Town. **14.** Mr. Ian Smith, the Rhodesian leader, and Mr. Vorster, Prime Minister of South Africa, had talks in Pretoria. Dr. Kissinger, U.S. Secretary of State, arrived in Tanzania at start of his African diplomatic mission. **15.** Strikes by African and Coloured workers, which had crippled much of Johannesburg, spread to Cape Town.

OTHER COUNTRIES

Sept. (1975) 21. Chairman Mao Tse-Tung received Mr. Edward Heath, former leader of the Conservative Party, for talks at his bungalow. **24.** South East Asia Treaty Organisation members agreed in New York to run it down over the next two years. It was announced that Government spending in France in 1976 was to increase by 13·1 per cent. over the initial forecast for the current year largely because of 55,000 jobs created for State employers. **25.** An unofficial Israeli political delegation, the first to visit Russia since 1973 Middle East war, arrived in Moscow to discuss prospects for restoring Israeli-Soviet relations; members of the five-man party stated that they had been invited separately by the Soviet Peace Committee. **26.** General Franco refused to commute the death sentences imposed on five Spanish terrorists for killing policemen and they were executed on Sept. 27. Portugal's Revolutionary Council announced the creation of a new " force of intervention " after 50,000 rebellious soldiers and extreme-Left civilians secured the release of two soldiers jailed in a military prison. **28.** Protests against the execution of the five Spanish guerillas spread throughout north-west Spain and across Europe. Ten ambassadors to Madrid from Britain, France, Italy, Holland, Belgium, Denmark, Sweden, Norway and West and East Germany were recalled also in protest. Six Turkish soldiers and the head of a small Kurdish clan were killed in a gun battle in Eastern Turkey. France launched a satellite from its space base in Guyana to study the sun and stars. **29.** A newly-formed terrorist movement with aims to keep Corsica French went into action for first time by blowing up an Ajaccio restaurant belonging to a separatist. **30.** Fifteen people were killed and 16 wounded in Thailand when a hand grenade was thrown into a meeting negotiating an end to a protest over foreign-owned mining companies.

Oct. 1. Portuguese Prime Minister called off military occupation of radio and television stations. Spanish terrorists killed three riot policemen and seriously wounded a fourth as they guarded suburban banks in Madrid. President Costa Gomes of Portugal arrived in Moscow for an official five-day visit. **3.** East Germany severed diplomatic relations with Spain. **5.** Official result of Austria's general election gave the Socialists 93 seats, the People's Party 80 seats, and the Freedom Party 10, the same composition as the last Parliament. Three civil guards were killed in the Basque region of Spain when their land-rover was blown up by a terrorist bomb; another two were injured in the blast. Boeing 737 of Argentine Airlines, hijacked by Left-wing guerillas after unsuccessful attack on army base in provincial capital of Formosa, landed near Santa Fe, the terrorist gang escaping. Casualties in the fighting were 15 terrorists killed, 11 army personnel killed, and 26 injured. **8.** A Spanish diplomat, Capt. Bartolome Garcia, deputy military attaché, was shot and seriously wounded in a Paris suburb. Argentine para-military sources said that at least 20 terrorist guerillas had been killed in fresh clashes with security forces in the north-western province of Tucuman, and seven soldiers lost their lives. Forty-five employees of a firm in Vaeteraas, Central Sweden, who staged an illegal 5-day strike over pay in July 1975, were ordered by the Swedish Labour Court to pay their firm damages and the firm's costs. **9.** More than 60 persons, including soldiers, were injured when rebellious Portuguese troops occupying an artillery barracks in Oporto opened fire on the military police and a reconnaissance platoon sent to disperse rival political demonstrators. The rebel soldiers withdrew a week later after a compromise. It was announced that Dr. Andrei Sakharov, the dissident Soviet scientist, had been awarded the 1975 Nobel peace prize. **10.** A group of armed Latin American refugees who held a number of U.N. officials hostage in Buenos Aires for 48 hours left the U.N. High Commission building in the Argentine capital to board a plane out of the country after protesting about delays in resettling political refugees from Chile. **14.** Emperor Hirohito and Empress Nagako of Japan arrived back in Tokyo after their visit to the United States. **15.** Iceland extended her fishing limits from 50 to 200 miles around her shores. The principle of retirement for all at 60 on full pension was adopted by the French Government which made clear that the economy would not stand the stress of carrying it out immediately for every category of workers. Ten people were killed and 50 injured when police fired tear gas to break up a political rally in Lahore, Pakistan. Icelandic gunboats attempted to enforce their new 200-mile fishing limit by harrying 20 West German trawlers. **17.** A Czech court sentenced Barry Meeker, an American helicopter pilot, to ten years' imprisonment in his absence for flying refugees to the West. **20.** Over 50 passengers were killed when a computerised train of Mexico City's underground system rammed into a stationary train, and at least 175 people were injured. **22.** Gunmen shot dead Mr. Dans Tunaligil, the Turkish Ambassador, in his Vienna Embassy. Radical Leftists stormed and occupied the radio Renascenca transmitting station in Lisbon which had been closed on the orders of President Gomes the previous week. Russia successfully landed a space probe from the spacecraft Venus 9 on the surface of the planet Venus. **24.** Mr. Ismail Erez, Turkish Ambassador in France, was shot dead in his car in a Paris street by two men who also killed his chauffeur. A Bill to grant the territory of Surinam independence on Nov. 25 after 308 years of colonial rule was approved by the Dutch Lower House. **26.** Five policemen were killed in Argentina when their two patrol cars were ambushed by two carloads of gunmen as the officers were leaving duty at the presidential palace. Jews from 15 Russian cities issued a public protest against a pending resolution in the

U.N. attacking Zionism as racist. **27.** Soldiers occupied the provincial government's H.Q. in the Southern Algarve after Communists, Socialists and Centre Popular Democrats fought a running battle in the building. A Puerto Rican terrorist group, the F.A.L.N., exploded nine bombs in New York, Washington and Chicago. **28.** West Germany's first research satellite, HEOS 1, splashed down in the Antarctic after orbiting the earth 542 times over 7 years. **30.** Prince Juan Carlos of Spain agreed to assume power " provisionally " as Head of State because of Gen. Franco's critical illness. Two former officials, accused after Lloyd's Bank International lost £31,980,000 through currency deals at its branch in Lugano, Switzerland, were given suspended sentences after a 5-man jury and 3 judges at Lugano found them guilty of mismanagement and falsification of accounting documents but cleared them of illegally obtaining personal gains through unauthorised foreign exchange operations.

Nov. 1. Two thieves broke into Cologne's 13th century cathedral and stole treasures valued at £500,000. **2.** Chile's military Government announced that it was to set up a Council of State as the first step to establishing a new constitutional order. Fighting occurred between rival nationalist forces in Bacau, second largest town in East Timor. **4.** France agreed to supply arms to Turkey. **6.** North Korea's Communist Government ordered the Australian Embassy at Pyongyang to close immediately and accused the five diplomats there of acts of sabotage and " endangering public order," a week after North Korean diplomats suddenly left their embassy in Canberra. **7.** Portuguese paratroopers following orders of the Military Council of the Revolution blew up the Lisbon transmitter station of Radio Renascenca, voice of the revolutionary Left. **9.** Official sources reported that more than 1,300 people were arrested in Argentina over the week-end in the Army's campaign against Left-wing guerillas. **11.** Entire cabinet of President Perón of Argentina resigned to allow restructuring of the Government. **12.** Russia refused permission to Andrei Sakharov, a leading campaigner for civil rights, to go to Oslo to receive the Nobel Peace Prize which he was awarded in October. **14.** Leaders of the six major industrial countries—Britain, U.S., France, West Germany, Japan, and Italy—began a three-day summit meeting at Château Rambouillet near Paris to try to coordinate their economic, monetary, energy, aid and raw materials policies. **17.** Talks in Reykjavik on a new fishery agreement between Iceland and Britain collapsed. **18.** Following a Cabinet meeting, it was announced the Argentine Government had agreed to advance the date of the next presidential election to the last quarter of 1976 instead of March, 1977. **19.** Fifty British trawlers off Iceland were shepherded into a 100-mile-long area to be protected against attacks by Icelandic gunboats; the British Ministry of Agriculture hired unarmed ships to intercept attempts to board British vessels or cut their trawl wires. An unmanned Soviet spacecraft docked automatically with the 19-ton orbiting laboratory Salyut-4. **20.** Spain started 30 days of official mourning for General Francisco Franco, who died in the early hours. Portugal's Revolutionary Council dismissed the military security chief, General Otelo de Carvalho, as Lisbon military district commander. **22.** In the Cortes, Madrid, 37-year-old Juan Carlos de Bourbon was sworn in as Spain's first king for 44 years. **25.** British frigate *Leopard* arrived in the disputed Icelandic fishing waters after British Government decided to assign three frigates to guard the U.K. fishing fleet. **25.** A state of emergency was declared in the Lisbon area where troops were placed on alert after a rebellion

by Leftist paratroopers. King Juan Carlos of Spain pronounced a general pardon for common and political prisoners. Surinam became independent. **27.** Gen. Otelo Saraiva de Carvalho resigned from command of Portugal's Copcon, the military security force, and Carlos Fabiao, Chief of Staff of the Army, also resigned. Copcon was disbanded. **28.** The Left-wing Fretilin movement unilaterally declared East Timor independent.

Dec. 2. A gang of five armed South Moluccan terrorists held some 70 hostages after seizing a Dutch train near Beilen, Holland, and killing the driver and one passenger, although six other passengers escaped. On Dec. 3, 17 hostages escaped and a field telephone was installed to enable the Moluccans to negotiate directly with the authorities. On Dec. 4, Dutch 43rd Armoured Division encircled the hijacked train after another hostage was killed and a second group of South Moluccan gunmen seized the Indonesian consulate in Amsterdam, 110 miles away, and held 17 children and at least 15 adults, wounding critically one of the staff who escaped. An explosion aboard the train on Dec. 5 seriously injured one terrorist and a male hostage, two other hostages being slightly hurt, but by that time 10 children had been released from the consulate. On Dec. 7 two octogenarians were released from the train, leaving 31 hostages aboard. The Amsterdam terrorists released another hostage on Dec. 8, having earlier released the last four teenagers but holding still 26 adults. The death toll in the two terrorist sieges rose to four when a man died in hospital after jumping from a window of the Consulate. On Dec. 11 two elderly hostages were released from the train and next day another hostage was set free, leaving behind 24 others. On Dec. 14 the Moluccans surrendered and freed their hostages after holding the train for 12 days. On Dec. 19 seven young South Moluccans laid down their guns and ended their seige of the Indonesian Consulate which lasted 15 days. **3.** King Savang Vatthana of Laos abdicated and the country was proclaimed a " People's Democratic Republic ". The Portuguese Government decided to take direct control of radio and TV services but Radio Renascenca, the Roman Catholic radio station seized by leftists, was to be returned to the church. Chinese scientists succeeded in bringing back to earth the satellite launched on Nov. 25. **4.** The strike by 870,000 members of Japan's public corporation unions ended, the eight-day stoppage to back the demand for the right to strike being the longest and biggest in the country's history. It was officially announced that 151 people had been arrested in Yugoslavia for allegedly plotting against the State. **5.** King Juan Carlos confirmed Señor Arias in his post of Spanish prime minister. **7.** Indonesian paratroopers, supported by a seaborne landing and naval bombardment, seized Portuguese Timor's capital, Dili. **11.** The Icelandic gunboat *Thor* fired the first shots of the cod war at a group of unarmed British fishery defence vessels and unsuccessfully tried to arrest one. Portuguese Timor's second largest town, Baucau, fell to pro-Indonesian forces. **12.** A leading Russian dissident, Dr. Sergi Kovalev, was sentenced to 7 years in prison and 3 years in exile for his part in publishing and distributing uncensored material in Russia. **15.** Gunter Guillaume, a close aide of Herr Brandt when German Chancellor, was sentenced at Dusseldorf to 13 years' jail for high treason and breach of official secrecy. His wife received an 8-year sentence for treason and complicity in betraying government secrets. **18.** A group of Argentine Air Force officers called on the rest of the armed forces to join them in a *coup* against President Maria Péron's Government,

seizing the Moron air base and the transport command at the Metropolitan airport. The revolt ended on Dec. 22 after failing to win support of the Army and Navy and rest of the Air Force. **20.** The last U.S. warplanes left Thailand. A volcano erupted in northern Iceland leaving a crater on Mount Leirhnukur. **22.** The Austrian Government accepted the demands of a gang of Palestinian guerillas who the previous day seized 70 hostages, including 11 ministers, at the Vienna H.Q. of the Organisation of Petroleum Exporting Countries; one terrorist was seriously wounded and a policeman and two officials were killed. A DC-9 jet airliner carrying the guerillas and some hostages, including Sheikh Yamani, Saudi Arabia's Oil Minister, later landed at Tripoli, Libya. In Algiers earlier the gang freed the non-Middle Eastern delegates to OPEC. The six terrorists were granted political asylum in Algeria, it was reported on Dec. 29. **23.** An American diplomat, Mr. Richard Welch, was shot dead as he left his car and walked to his house in an Athens suburb. **28.** H.M.S. *Andromeda* and the Icelandic gunboat *Tyr* collided off eastern Iceland in another cod war incident but no one was injured. **29.** The Chilean military government released Sheila Cassidy, a British doctor, held in detention since Nov. 1, and she was flown to London. **30.** Dmitri Ioannidis, Greece's former chief of military police, and George Papadopoulos, former dictator of the country, were convicted in connection with the incidents at Athens Polytechnic in November 1973 when at least 24 people were killed and over 1,000 injured in protests against the colonels' régime. Ioannidis was sentenced to life imprisonment and Papadopoulos to 25 years' imprisonment. Of 32 accused, 20 were found guilty and received penalties ranging from 5 months to life imprisonment, the others being acquitted.

(1976) Jan. 1. The Venezuelan Government nationalised the country's oil industry, fifth largest in the world. The Soviet authorities agreed to relax travel regulations for Western journalists based in Moscow, giving them from March 1 the same travel privileges as diplomats. **4.** A full-scale inquiry into allegations of torture of political prisoners held without trial by the Portuguese revolutionary régime was ordered by Gen. Ramalho Eanes, Army Chief of Staff. **5.** A new Cambodian constitution came into force and the country became known as Democratic Cambodia with a new national anthem and a new flag. **6.** It was officially disclosed that the 1975 inflation rate in the Argentine reached 334.8 per cent., the worst in the country's history. **7.** Italy's minority Centre Left coalition Government of Christian Democrats and Republicans resigned after the Socialists decided to withdraw their support. **11.** Icelandic seamen blocked two entrances to the Nato base at Keflavik, Iceland, because of the cod war. President Guillermo Rodriguez Lara handed over power as President of Ecuador, to a 3-man military junta. **12.** Rumania agreed to pay Britain £3,500,000 over the next 4 years to settle claims by British holders of Rumanian Bonds and the seizure in 1948 of some oil companies, assets. President Giscard d'Estaing of France moved three Cabinet ministers and created five new Government posts. **13.** Argentina demanded the withdrawal of the British Ambassador, Mr. Derrick Ashe, in the dispute over the Falkland Islands and he returned to London on Jan. 21 for consultations. **14.** Spanish Government conscripted Madrid's 4,000 striking postmen and placed the Central Post Office under military control. A bill providing heavier penalties for introducing and employing unauthorised foreign workers in France was approved by the Government. **15.** British

Cultural Institute in Cordoba, Argentina, was badly damaged by two bombs but there were no injuries. The Spanish Cabinet decided to delay for a year the elections due in March to allow electoral reforms giving wider representation. **16.** Spanish police arrested members of the Madrid strike co-ordinating committee as they planned a general stoppage. The Belgian Government banned the export of potatoes to combat an acute shortage. France had a foreign trade surplus of nearly £630 million last year compared with a deficit in 1974 of £1,780 million. **19.** Spanish Government put 72,000 railmen under military control because of sporadic walk-outs the previous week. **21.** Britain and Russia, co-chairmen of 1962 Geneva Conference which guaranteed the neutrality of Laos, agreed formally to wind-up the International Control Commission. **22.** President Maria Perón of Argentina completed a major cabinet reshuffle. **24.** Under a treaty signed by U.S.A. and Spain, U.S.A. would withdraw its 10 Polaris submarines from Spain in 1979, the treaty allowing U.S.A. three air force bases in Spain and the use of the navy base at Rota for five years. **25.** Army and air force manoeuvres in Georgia and Armenia were the first Soviet exercises to be watched by invited Nato observers, Greece and Turkey. **26** A West Berliner, Rainer Schubert, was convicted by the East Berlin court on several counts of smuggling refugees to the West including helping 97 people to escape from East Germany, and was sentenced to 15 years' imprisonment. **27.** It was announced that presidential elections would not be held in Argentina on Oct. 17. **28.** Spain's liberalisation programme was announced by the Prime Minister (Señor Carlos Arias Navarro) involving establishment of an assembly with two chambers of equal power, limited fiscal reform and amendment of the penal code outlawing opposition groups. The Portuguese Government decided to return the newspaper, *Republica*, to its editor, Senhor Paul Rego, ending a 9-month occupation by Leftists. Engravings by Picasso valued at £290,000 were stolen from a Paris gallery. **29.** Prices in France rose by 9·6 per cent. last year compared with 15·2 per cent. in 1974, it was announced in Paris. **30.** Illegal Spanish Christian Democratic parties opened a three day international conference in Madrid on Spain's future in Europe. **31.** Thieves stole 127 paintings by Picasso in a raid on the Old Papal Palace, at Avignon, Southern France, two watchmen being seriously injured.

Feb. 2. Two Marxists, members of a five-man gang found guilty of terrorist activities, were executed in Persia, the Shah commuting the death sentence of two others and the fifth being jailed for 10 years. **4.** The Argentine destroyer, *Almirante Storni*, fired shots across the bows of the unarmed British research vessel *Shackleton*, off the coast of the Falkland Islands, after she allegedly refused to stop for " inspection ". The *Shackleton* reached the safety of Port Stanley in the islands later. It was feared that 600 people were killed and over 2,000 injured in Guatemala City after an earthquake which was also felt in Honduras and El Salvador. **5.** Unofficial death toll in Guatemala's earthquake rose to 2,500 with a possible 5,000 others injured as relief supplies were flown in from neighbouring countries. On Feb. 8 the number killed was estimated at 12,804 with 30,328 injured. **6.** France used veto in U.N. to block the Security Council resolution calling on her to abandon plans for referendum in Indian Ocean island of Mayotte. The Spanish Government announced major reforms of the anti-terrorist laws. **7.** Leaders of Japan's ruling Liberal-Democratic party met in emergency session to discuss the alleged bribes in the sale to Japan of Lockheed Air-

craft Corporation's F-104 Starfighters and decided to postpone the national elections from the spring to the autumn. Gen. Antionio de Spinola, former Portuguese Head of State, was expelled from France after making an unsuccessful attempt to cross the Pyrenees border into Spain. **8.** The Dutch Government announced that it was to investigate U.S. allegations that Prince Bernhard of the Netherlands had accepted a bribe from the Lockheed Aircraft Corporation in connection with the sale of 95 Starfighter planes to Netherlands; the Government statement added that the Prince stated that " he never received or accepted any money " and that he would welcome an inquiry. Crowds clashed with police in Barcelona when thousands of demonstrating Catalans demanded home rule and a political amnesty. It was announced in Peking that Hua Kuo-feng, Minister of Public Security, had been appointed acting Chinese Premier in succession to Chou En-lai, who died on Jan. 8. **9.** Señora Maria Caride de Lanusse, daughter-in-law of ex-Argentine President Lanusse, was killed by a parcel bomb at her Buenos Aires home. Spain announced an 11 per cent. devaluation of the peseta. **10.** Signor Moro, Italy's Christian Democrat Prime Minister, informed President Leone that he was prepared to accept a mandate to form the country's 38th government in the last 32 years and his new minority Government was sworn-in on Feb. 12. **15.** Official death toll in the Guatemala earthquake on Feb. 4 was given as over 22,000. **18.** Barcelona's striking police and firemen were placed under military control to try to stop the unrest during the first royal tour of Catalonia by King Juan Carlos. **20.** Iceland formally broke off diplomatic relations with Britain over the cod war. **23.** The Argentine peso was devalued by 4·6 per cent. against the U.S. dollar, the new rate being 74·30 to the dollar. **24.** The 25th Congress of the Soviet Communist party opened in Moscow. **27.** Military sources in Bangkok said that Gen. Boonchai Bamrungphong, C-in-C, Royal Thai Army, had crushed an attempted *coup d'état*.

Mar. 4. A riot police chief inspector and a winegrower were shot dead in a gun battle near Carcassone, southern France, between police and winegrowers demanding an end to cheap imports of Italian and other foreign wines. Fourteen people were sent to jail in Florence for up to 8 years for producing and selling fake wine. **5.** The Argentine Government launched a new austerity programme to deal with the country's economic crisis, devalued the peso by about 22 per cent., and granted all workers 12 per cent. pay rise. **10.** Col. Mileta Perovich, leader of the anti-Tito Russian-backed Yugoslav Communist Party, with H.Q. in Paris since 1975, was expelled from France and his deputy was given a week to leave the country. **11.** The French Ministry of the Interior confirmed that the International Revolutionary Action Group (GARI) was behind the unsuccessful bomb attack in Toulouse the previous day on the life of the Minister of the Interior, M. Michel Poniatowski, during which two young terrorists were killed by their own bomb. **12.** Four Yugoslavs, including two former ministers, received prison sentences in Belgrade district court of up to ten years for plotting against President Tito and asking émigrés in Hungary and Russia if the Soviet would respond to an appeal to enter Yugoslavia from dissidents inside the country. **15.** One person at least was killed and 29 were seriously injured when a bomb exploded in the 20-storey Army H.Q. in Buenos Aires. **16.** President of Mexican Football Federation was freed in Guadalajara after 8 days in hands of kidnappers, a ransom of £38,000 being paid. Maj.-Gen. Dimitrios Ioannidis, member of the Greek military

régime during 1967–1974, was sentenced to 14 years' imprisonment for having been the moral instigator of an abortive Army officers' conspiracy after the restoration of the democratic régime in 1975. Retired Col. Dimitrios Papapostolou was found guilty of having been Ioannidis's successor at the head of the officers' conspiracy and was sentenced to 10 years' imprisonment. **18.** West German Parliament passed a bill extending workers' participation to nearly a 50–50 basis for all big firms and giving workers in some 600 large businesses equal representation on supervisory boards with the shareholders' delegates. **20.** Thailand ordered U.S.A. to discontinue all its military activities in the country within 4 months, only 270 American military advisers being allowed to remain. Fishermen in the Faroes accepted a 15 per cent. cut in their cod catch within Iceland's 200-mile fishing limit, West Germany, Belgium, and Norway having already agreed to cuts. **23.** Swiss and Italian police recovered 3 priceless Renaissance paintings undamaged after their theft 13 months ago from the museum in the ducal palace at Urbino, Italy. **24.** Argentine's military leaders seized power from President Maria Perón in a bloodless *coup*; Congress was dissolved, and political parties and trade unions were suspended, the Army, Navy and Air Force commanders installing themselves as the governing junta. President Perón was placed under house arrest. Eight people were killed and 10 wounded when a hand grenade was thrown into a political rally in Chaihat province, 100 miles north of Bangkok, only four days after a grenade blast killed 4 people and wounded over 80 during another Leftist demonstration in Bangkok. **26.** Spain's two main opposition groups, the Democratic Junta and the Democratic Platform, agreed in Madrid to form a united front. General Jorge Rafael Videla, Army commander-in-chief, was appointed President of Argentine. A Federation of European Liberal Parties was founded in Stuttgart, West Germany, by all Common Market countries except Eire. Seven Moluccan terrorists who occupied a Dutch train for 12 days and killed 3 men on board were each jailed for 14 years at Assen, Holland, after being found guilty of murder, manslaughter, and illegal possession of firearms. **27.** France introduced summer time, two hours ahead of Greenwich Mean Time, clocks being advanced an hour on European standard time, in the hope of saving 1 per cent. on energy bills. **28.** A new law operative from July 1 was passed by the Hungarian Parliament to make military education, including psychological and germ warfare training, a compulsory priority part of the school curriculum for all children over 12. **31.** Gunmen in Barranquilla, Columbia, shot dead the Lebanese consul. A former Indonesian Cabinet Minister, Dr. Oei Tjoe Tat, held without trial for 9 years, was sentenced to 13 years' jail for failing to condemn the abortive Communist coup in 1965, the term he had served being deducted from the sentence.

April 2. Three gunmen escaped in a speedboat through Amsterdam's canals after snatching £120,000 from a bank in the city centre. **4.** Cambodian cabinet accepted Prince Sihanouk's resignation as Head of State. In Thailand's general election the Prime Minister, Mr. Kukrit Pramoj, was defeated, the Democrats winning 114 seats out of 279 in the House of Representatives. **5.** Peking's streets were back to normal after troops of the People's Liberation Army spent the night dispersing large crowds which demonstrated against China's radical Leftists. **7.** Seventy-three passengers and crew members were held hostage in a Philippines BAC-111 airliner as three armed Moslem hijackers demanded freedom for six prisoners and a £150,000

ransom. Teng Hsiao-ping was dismissed as vice-premier of China, vice-chairman of the Communist party, and chief of staff of the People's Liberation Army and Hua Kuo-feng was confirmed as premier. The Cambodian Cabinet resigned " because the mission of the present government of Democratic Cambodia was completed." **8.** Seven young South Moluccans were each sentenced to six years in prison for holding 43 people hostage in the Indo-nesian consulate in Amsterdam in December, all pleading guilty to deprivation of liberty, threaten-ing to kill their hostages, and illegal possession of firearms. **9.** A former Polish world fencing cham-pion, Capt. Jerzy Pawlovski, was jailed for 25 years for espionage for " a Nato state ". **11.** Three Filipino separatists who skyjacked a plane from Manila to Bangkok on April 7 agreed to give up their hostages in return for a plane to Libya. Some 4,000 traders in Srinagar, Kashmir, were jailed or fined on charges of food adulteration and profiteer-ing, being among 6,000 traders sent for trial in the year ending in March. **14.** Khieu Samphan was proclaimed Chief of State in Cambodia with Tol Saut as prime minister. **16.** For the first time since 1932, the national congress of the General Workers' Union (U.G.T.) was convened openly in Madrid. **18.** Vigilante squads were organised over the week-end by over 5,000 workers at the Fiat car factories at Mirafiori and Rivalta near Turin, and Pirelli Tyre employees at Settino Torinese, to prevent fresh arson attempts against the plants. **19.** Newsprint for three newspapers was destroyed by fire in what police regarded as the latest in a series of arson attacks in Italy. **21.** Head of Chevron Oil Co. in Italy, Signor Giovanni Theodoli, was critically wounded by members of a self-styled " Communist armed formation " as he motored from his home in Rome to the suburbs. **23.** An East German military tribunal sentenced Volker Franke, a West Berliner, to 15 years' imprisonment for allegedly spying out Communist military secrets in coordination with the Christian Democratic party in West Germany and West Berlin. **25.** Portugal's first free parlia-mentary elections in 50 years took place with these results: Socialists 35·1 per cent, Popular Democrats 23·8 per cent, Centre Democrats 15·75 per cent, Communists 14·7 per cent. **26.** Nationalist China and South Africa agreed to exchange ambassadors to improve relations. **27.** North and South Viet-nam announced that their top Communist leaders had gained major victories in Sunday's general elections for a national assembly for a unified Viet-nam for which there were no opposition candidates. **28.** All 450 West German newspapers were stopped by a printers' strike for a 9 per cent. pay rise and an employers' lock-out. Spanish Prime Minister, Señor Arias, outlined the Government's plan for reform and said that it called for a referendum on Parliamentary reform in October and general elections early in 1977 if the Cortes (Parliament) approved the draft laws. **29.** An explosion dam-aged the Russian Embassy in Peking, killing two Chinese guards. **30.** Signor Aldo Moro, the Italian Christian Democratic prime minister, and his Cabinet resigned after 79 days in office. Albania announced the dismissal of the ministers of agricul-ture and education and their replacement by women, and that the " anti-Chinese group had been swept away."

May 3. West Germany's newspaper strike ended although the return to work was provisional pend-ing the result of pay negotiations, but on May 6 production was again halted. On May 13 the dis-pute was called off after agreement on a pay rise. **5.** Corsican freedom fighters claimed responsibility for 16 explosions during a series of night attacks in the island and in southern France but there were no

injuries. **7.** Former Argentine President, Maria Estela Perón, was ordered to stand trial for allegedly issuing a £400,000 cheque in the account of a State-supported charity foundation for deposit in the estate of her late husband Gen. Juan Perón; four others were also charged with misuse of funds and improper accounts of spending in a charity founda-tion. **9.** Prince Carlos Hugo, Pretender to Spanish throne, and his wife, Princess Irene, escaped unhurt when attending the annual rally of his Carlist party on Mount Montejurra in Navarre, northern Spain, after firing broke out by alleged Right-wing Carlists, during which one man was shot dead and another died of wounds. Prince Hugo withdrew over the French border. Later Prince Sixtus Enrique de Borbon Palma, younger brother of Prince Carlos Hugo, was reported as having been expelled from Spain. **11.** General Joaquin Zenteno Gnaya, Bolivian ambassador to France was assas-sinated in Paris by two men firing at point blank range and a group calling itself the Che Guevara Brigade claimed responsibility. **12.** The Icelandic gunboat, *Aegir*, sent boarding parties to arrest the British trawler, *Primella*, after firing shots across her bow and stern but the attempt was thwarted when other trawlers arrived and a Nimrod reconnaissance aircraft issued a warning. **14.** M. Jacques Chaine, president of the Crédit Lyonnais Bank, was shot dead outside the Bank's H.Q. in the Boulevard des Italiens in Paris as he stepped from his car; his assailant then killed himself. According to reports from the mainland of China, two people had been sentenced to death and 10 others given up to 30 years' hard labour for their part in the Tien An Men square disturbances in Peking, the previous month. **14.** Finland's five-party coalition government which submitted its resignation on May 13 over a clash on economic policy was requested by Presi-dent Kekkonen to continue. **21.** Six gunmen seized a Philippine airliner with 109 people aboard and demanded about £200,000 ransom, hijacking a BAC-111 jet after it had taken off from Davao City for Manila. **23.** Thirteen people were killed when a skyjacked airliner exploded and hostage passengers were caught in a gun battle at Zam-boanga Airport in the Philippines, the dead includ-ing 3 of the 6 skyjackers, believed to be Moslem rebels, who seized the BAC-111 in an internal flight on May 21; 22 people were also injured. **24.** The Spanish Government demilitarised 72,000 em-ployees of the State-run railways, R.E.N.F.E., in a move to normalise labour relations after wide-spread demonstrations and strikes. **26.** By 303–181 votes French National Assembly approved a bill which proposed annual defence spending by 1982 of 114,575 million francs (£13,639 million), a doubling of the defence budget over the next six years. It was disclosed that a Yugoslav court sent a Russian woman to prison for five years for spying for the Soviet Union, the first known case of a Russian national being sentenced for espionage in Yugoslavia. **31.** King Juan Carlos of Spain and Queen Sophia began their first overseas tour since assuming the Spanish throne when they flew to the Dominican Republic before continuing next day to U.S.A. Four Italian warships were sent to the Straits of Sicily as incidents continued between Italian fishing boats and Tunisian and Libyan vessels.

June 1. Two bombs exploded at the Frankfurt H.Q. of the American V Corps, injuring 16 people. **3.** The Argentine Government announced that General Juan José Torres, left-wing former Presi-dent of Bolivia, had been found dead under a bridge 60 miles from Buenos Aires with three bullets in the head after disappearing from his home

on June 1. **6.** For first time for 40 years, the Spanish Government authorised a conference of left-wingers when 1,500 people attended the third congress of the Popular Socialist party in Madrid. **8.** Senor Carlos Abdala, Uruguay's Ambassador to Paraguay, died in Asuncion from a gunshot wound which he received the previous day. **9.** The Spanish Parliament passed by 338–91 votes with 24 abstentions the first of two bills providing for the return of political parties which had been banned under Gen. Franco, but later the Government was defeated without a direct vote on the second bill which provided for changes in the penal code under which most types of political association could be punished by up to 20 years in jail, **13.** It was stated that Uruguayan military leaders, who ousted President Bordaberry at the week-end, planned to restore a traditional two-party political system gradually. Alberto Demichelli was sworn in as President on June 12. **18.** The Argentine Federal police chief was killed when a terrorist bomb exploded at his flat in Buenos Aires. **20.** Italians began a day and a half of polling in general and local government elections. Final results were: Chamber of Deputies —Christian Democrats 38·8 per cent (263 seats), Communists 34·5 per cent (228 seats), Socialists 9·6 per cent (57 seats), Republicans 3·1 per cent (14 seats), Social Democrats 3·4 per cent (15), Liberals 1·3 per cent (5), Italian Social Movement 6·1 per cent (35), Proletarian Democracy 1·5 per cent (6), South Tirol party 0·5 per cent (3), Radical party 1·1 per cent (4). Senate—Christian Democrats 38·9 per cent (135 seats), Communists 33·8 per cent (116), Socialists 10·2 per cent (29), Republicans 2·7 per cent (6), Social Democrats 3·1 per cent (6), Liberals 1·4 per cent (2), Italian Social Movement 6.6 per cent (15). U.S. withdrew from the U-Tapco airfield on the Gulf of Thailand and also from Ramasun in north east Thailand, used as a military intelligence monitoring station, these being the last U.S. troops in the country. **23.** Talks began in a Bavarian resort hotel between Mr. Vorster, South Africa's prime minister, and Dr. Kissinger, U.S. Secretary of State. The Argentine military junta used new powers to bar in perpetuity Señora Maria Estela Perón, the deposed President, and 35 other persons prominent in or under the Peronist Government from political, public, and trade union office. **25.** Poland decided to withdraw food price rises of up to 100 per cent. "for further consideration" after workers had gone on strike, torn up railway lines and halted the Paris-Warsaw express. Radio Warsaw announced on June 30 that at least two people died and 77 policemen were injured in these riots, all in the town of Radom. **27.** The seven-nation economic summit of heads of government, foreign and finance ministers from U.K., France, West Germany, Italy, Canada, Japan, and U.S. began in Puerto Rico. In the Portuguese presidential election, Gen. Antonio Eanes, the Army Chief of Staff, gained more than 61 per cent of the votes and his nearest rival, Major Otelo de Carvalho, the Left-wing candidate, received almost 17 per cent. The Prime Minister (Admiral José Pinheiro de Azevedo) had 14 per cent. and the official Communist candidate, Senhor Octavio Pato, obtained less than 8 per cent. **28.** Peru devalued its currency, the exchange rate being set at 65 sols to the U.S. dollar against 45 previously. **29.** The summit meeting of European Communist parties met in East Berlin for two days and was attended by leaders of 29 parties who adopted a new charter which declared all Communist parties to be equal and independent. **30.** France and Russia reached agreement to prevent the risk of either country launching an accidental nuclear attack on the other. Hundreds of homes were abandoned in

northern Philippines after a typhoon caused widespread flooding.

July 1. Peru's military government suspended constitutional rights and declared a state of emergency throughout the country after hundreds of demonstrators rampaged in Lima, the capital, protesting at increased taxes and public service charges. **2.** Vietnam National Assembly officially approved the reunification of the country with a flag and national anthem unchanged from those of North Vietnam. Ton Duc Thang, last president of North Vietnam, was elected first President of the Socialist Republic of Vietnam. **3.** Señor Adolpho Suarez was appointed Prime Minister of Spain in place of Señor Carlos Arias Navarro, who resigned on July 1. **5.** Signor Pietro Ingrao, a Communist, was elected President of the Chamber of Deputies in the Italian Parliament following a post general election agreement with the Christian Democrats. Signor Amintore Fanfani, a Christian Democrat, was named President of the Senate. **9.** Twenty-six foreign missionaries, many of them French, reached Bangkok, after being expelled by Vietnam. Two Soviet deputy agriculture ministers were relieved of their duties. **10.** Thousands of postal workers in Spain won a pay rise and returned to work after a 5-day strike in the first labour challenge to the new Suarez government. **13.** Signor Giulio Andreotti, the outgoing Christian Democrat Budget Minister, was named as Prime Minister to form Italy's 39th Government in 33 years. **14.** The Spanish Government approved changes in the penal code to give new freedom to political parties although one clause enabled the Government to maintain the ban on the Communist party. **16.** The Portuguese Socialist leader, Dr. Mario Soares, was appointed Prime Minister. **17.** Five Left-wingers were omitted from Peru's military government after the previous day's resignation of the Prime Minister, Gen. Jorge Fernandez Maldonado, and his replacement by Gen. Guillermo Arbulu Galliani. **18.** Robbers escaped with a world record haul of an estimated £6 million, after tunnelling via a sewer to the safe deposit vaults of the Société Générale Bank in central Nice. **19.** Six men involved in riots in June against proposed food price increases in Poland were sentenced to between 4 and 10 years' jail, having been convicted of taking part in group violence and damaging public property at Radom, near Warsaw. **22.** Honduras forces announced that El Salvador troops with heavy artillery had attacked five positions on the Honduras border; El Salvador had previously claimed that Honduran troops had attacked a military position, killing two soldiers. **23.** Dr. Mario Soares, Portuguese Prime Minister, announced his new Cabinet of Socialists and a few military officers representing the country's first popularly-elected government in 50 years. **27.** Mr. Kakuei Tanaka, former Prime Minister of Japan, was arrested and charged with violating the Japanese foreign exchange control law. **28.** Christian Ranucci, sentenced to death in March for the murder of an 8-year-old child, was guillotined in the Baumettes prison at Marseilles. **30.** Italy's minority Christian Democrat Government was sworn in; the new ministers included Signorina Tina Anselini, Italy's first woman Cabinet minister, as Minister of Labour. Under an amnesty granted by King Juan Carlos after a meeting of the Spanish Cabinet, political prisoners were to be freed in the following few weeks.

Aug. 4. Polisorio Front guerillas killed or wounded 300 Moroccan and Mauritanian troops in four attacks in southern Morocco and northern Mauritania. **9.** Dr. Giulio Carlo Argan accepted the candidature of Mayor of Rome, being the first

Communist to occupy the position. **10.** Ex-President Antonio Spinola, who left Portugal 18 months before, returned to Lisbon. He was taken to Caxias prison for questioning, but was released on Aug. 12. The Italian Cabinet approved an emergency fund of nearly £27 million to finance decontamination and health projects in the northern area of Brianza, near Milan, which was affected by a poison gas cloud. On Aug. 11 a special medical commission announced that pregnant women living in the Brianza district would be allowed to ask for an abortion. **11.** Four people were killed by gunfire and grenades at Istanbul Airport in an attack on passengers of an Israeli El Al airliner by terrorists with Kuwaiti passports. Fire at the Hotel d'Amérique in the Pigalle district of Paris resulted in 12 deaths. **12.** Senorita Margarita Lopez Portillo, sister of Mexico's president-elect, suffered shock after guerillas shot dead two of her bodyguards and her chauffeur in a suburban street of Mexico City, one guerilla also being killed. **13.** East German border guards turned back at the Helmstedt checkpoint busloads of young Christian Democratic demonstrators bound for West Berlin to attend a protest rally on the Berlin Wall's 15th anniversary. **15.** Thousands of people from three towns in the Caribbean island of Guadeloupe were ordered to leave their homes as the volcano, La Sonfrière, threatened eruption. **17.** It was disclosed that thieves tunnelled through sewers into the Paris branch of the Société Générale's bank at Ile Saint-Louis over the week-end and ransacked safe deposit boxes in a near identical raid on the Nice branch of the same bank a month before. **18.** Two U.S. officers, assigned to the United Nations in Seoul, were killed by North Korean border guards in the demilitarized zone between North and South Korea near Panmunjon when a detachment of U.S. and South Korean troops escorted a work party of labourers to cut back trees claimed by the North Koreans to be on land under their control. A further four Americans and five South Koreans were wounded in the clash with 30 North Korean guards armed with axes and pikes. **19.** Gen. Omar Carlos Actis, president of the organising committee for the 1978 World Cup soccer championship in Argentina, was shot dead by left-wing guerillas in a Buenos Aires suburb. The country's official news agency, Antara, reported that 1,166 political prisoners in Java had been released by Indonesia, those liberated being involved in the Communist attempt to overthrow Dr. Sukarno in 1965. **20.** Thirty young people were found dead in a field in Fatima village, 40 miles from Buenos Aires, having apparently been shot with their bodies blown by a bomb, in another wave of political violence in Argentina. It was stated that the Swiss-owned Icmesa chemical factory at Seveso where an explosion spread a cloud of TCDD poison in July would be closed. **21.** Kim Il Sung, the Communist leader in North Korea, expressed his " regrets " to U.S. over the incident on Aug. 18 when two U.S. officers in charge of a tree-cutting detail in the demilitarised zone were killed by North Korean guards. **22.** Because of a work-to-rule by air traffic controllers at Barcelona, thousands of U.K.

holiday-makers bound for Spain were stranded at airports by long delays, the go-slow also affecting airports in Majorca, Ibiza, Minorca, Valencia, and Alicante. Switzerland expelled a Russian diplomat and a member of Rumanian Embassy staff for " political espionage." It was stated that the Trade Minister in Soviet Adzharia, Georgia, and two senior policemen had been dismissed over an alleged embezzlement affair. **24.** Spanish Government issued a decree prohibiting servicemen from belonging to political parties. **25.** M. Jacques Chirac resigned as Prime Minister of France and was succeeded by M. Raymond Barre, Minister for Foreign Trade. **26.** Prince Bernhard of the Netherlands resigned from all his defence and business appointments after publication of the report of the 3-man independent commission of inquiry into his relationship with the American Lockheed Aircraft Corporation. The Dutch Prime Minister, Mr. Joop den Uyl, said the Government had decided against setting up a criminal investigation into the Prince's conduct and the commission of inquiry failed to find any proof of allegations that he had taken $1,100,000 in pay-off's, directly or indirectly, from Lockheed Corporation, the Commission stating that " he showed himself open to dishonourable requests and offers." **26.** A senior Russian foreign trade official was given a long jail sentence for revealing commercial secrets to two West German businessmen. The strike at the Paris newspaper, *France Soir*, ended after 600 journalists throughout France had demonstrated outside the building following discontent over the purchase of a half share in the paper by M. Robert Hersant, owner of the Paris daily, *Le Figaro*. **27.** Three Americans who admitted trying to smuggle 62 lbs. of heroin through Russia to Western Europe were sentenced to terms in labour camps of 8 years, 7 years, and 5 years. **29.** The ruler of Kuwait dissolved the National Assembly and after accepting the Government's resignation, re-appointed Crown Prince Jaber Al-Ahmed as Prime Minister. The Archbishop of Lille, Monsignor Marcel Lefebvre, who had been suspended from all priestly functions, defied the Vatican's decrees by holding a forbidden 16th century Latin Mass in Lille Sports Stadium attended by 6,000 people. **30.** The Dutch Parliament unanimously approved the Government's handling of the Donner Commission report on the inquiry into allegations of bribery by Lockheed involving Prince Bernhard at the end of a televised Parliamentary debate.

Sept. 1. Señor Aparicio Mendez, a lawyer, was sworn in as President of Uruguay and immediately banned hundreds of people, including leading politicians, from political activities for 15 years. **4.** Dr. Kissinger, U.S. Secretary of State, and Mr. Vorster, the South African Prime Minister, began talks in Zürich on situation in southern Africa; on Sept. 6, Dr. Kissinger flew to London for meeting with Mr. Callaghan. **6.** A Russian Air Force pilot landed his top secret *MiG* 25 fighter aircraft at airport in northern Japan and asked for political asylum in U.S.A., which was subsequently granted. **9.** Chairman Mao Tse-tung died in Peking at the age of 82.

OBITUARY, OCT. 1, 1975–SEPT. 30, 1976

Aalto, *Prof.* Hugo Alvar Henrik, Finnish architect, aged 78—*May.*

Baddeley, Angela, actress, aged 71—*Feb. 22.*

Baker, Sir Stanley, actor and producer, aged 48—*June 28.*

Barker, Ronald Ernest, O.B.E., secretary of the Publishers Association, aged 55—*May 22.*

Bennett, Sir John Wheeler Wheeler-, G.C.V.O., C.M.G., O.B.E., F.B.A., distinguished historian, aged 73—*Dec. 9, 1975.*

Berkeley, Busby, film musical director, aged 80—*March 14.*

Biggs, Christopher Thomas Ewart Ewart-, C.M.G., O.B.E., British Ambassador in Dublin (*assassinated*), aged 54—*July 21.*

Britton, Cliff, former footballer, aged 66—*Dec. 1, 1975.*

Carpentier, Georges, former world light-heavy-weight boxing champion, aged 81—*Oct. 27, 1975.*

Casey, Richard Gardiner Casey, K.G., P.C., G.C.M.G., C.H., D.S.O., M.C., Baron, Governor-General of Australia from 1965 to 1969, aged 85—*June 17.*

Chou En-lai, Premier of China, aged 77—*Jan. 8.*

Christie, Dame Agatha Mary Clarissa, D.B.E., author, aged 85—*Jan. 12.*

Cobb, Lee J., U.S. actor, aged 64—*Feb. 11.*

De La Warr, Herbrand Edward Dundonald Brassey Sackville, P.C., G.B.E., 9th Earl, former Cabinet Minister, aged 75—*Jan. 28.*

Delargy, Hugh James, Labour M.P. for Thurrock since 1950, aged 67—*May 4.*

Edelman, Maurice, Labour M.P. for Coventry North West, author and journalist, aged 64—*Dec. 14, 1975.*

Fairley, *Prof.* Gordon Hamilton, leading cancer specialist, aged 45—*Oct. 23, 1975.* (*See p. 583*).

Franco Bahamonde, *Generalissimo* Don Francisco, Head of Spanish State, aged 82—*Nov. 20, 1975.*

Gallico, Paul Williams, writer, aged 78—*July 15.*

Getty, Jean Paul, U.S. multi-millionaire, aged 83—*June 6.*

Gilligan, Arthur Edward Robert, distinguished cricketer and former President of M.C.C., aged 81—*Sept. 5.*

Gui, Vittorio, distinguished Italian conductor, aged 90—*Oct. 16, 1975.*

Heenan, *His Eminence Cardinal* John Carmel, D.D., Ph.D., Archbishop of Westminster since 1963, aged 70—*Nov. 7, 1975.*

Hill, Graham, O.B.E., former world champion racing driver, aged 46—*Nov. 29, 1975.* (*See p. 580*).

Holford, William Graham Holford, R.A., Baron, leading town planner, aged 68—*Oct. 17, 1975.*

Hughes, Howard, U.S. multi-millionaire, aged 70 *April 5.*

Hughes, Richard Arthur Warren, O.B.E., author, aged 76—*April 28.*

James, *Rt. Hon.* Sir Arthur Evan, a Lord Justice of Appeal since 1973, aged 59—*May 13.*

James, Sid, comedy actor, aged 62—*April 26.*

Kempe, Rudolf, conductor, aged 65—*May.*

Kitson Clark, George Sidney Roberts, LITT.D., historian, aged 75—*Dec. 8, 1975.*

Lang, Fritz, film director, aged 85—*Aug. 2.*

Lehmann, Lotte, noted soprano singer, aged 88—*Aug. 26.*

Leighton, Margaret, C.B.E., actress, aged 53—*Jan. 14.*

Leon, *His Honour* Henry Cecil, M.C., author and former County Court Judge, aged 73—*May 21.*

Livesey, Roger, actor, aged 69—*Feb. 4.*

Lowry, Laurence Stephen, R.A., artist, aged 88—*Feb. 23.*

Mao Tse-tung, Chinese national and Communist leader, aged 82—*Sept. 9.*

McWhirter, Ross, editor and publicist, aged 50—*Nov. 27, 1975.* (*See p. 583*).

Menges, Isolde, violinist, aged 82—*January.*

Milton, Sir Frank, former Chief Metropolitan Magistrate, aged 70—*Jan. 8.*

Mollet, Guy, former French Prime Minister, aged 69—*Oct. 3, 1975.*

Monnington, Sir Walter Thomas, President of Royal Academy since 1966, aged 73—*Jan. 7.*

Montgomery of Alamein, *Field-Marshal* Bernard Law Montgomery, K.G., G.C.B., D.S.O., 1st Visct., outstanding military commander, aged 88—*March 24.*

O'Malley, *Rt. Hon.* Brian Kevin, Minister of State, Department of Health and Social Security, and Labour M.P. for Rotherham since 1963, aged 46—*April 6.*

Naughton, Charlie, comedian and member of the Crazy Gang, aged 89—*February.*

Nervo, Jimmy, comedian and member of the Crazy Gang, aged 78—*Dec. 5, 1975.*

Oldfield, William Albert Stanley, M.B.E., noted Australian wicketkeeper, aged 81—*Aug. 10.*

Onslow, *Admiral* Sir Richard George, K.C.B., D.S.O., naval commander in Second World War, aged 71—*Dec. 16, 1975.*

Penfield, *Dr.* Wilder Graves, O.M., distinguished neurosurgeon, aged 85—*April 5.*

Pickthorn, *Rt. Hon.* Sir Kenneth William Murray, Bt., LITT.D., historian and former Conservative M.P., aged 83—*Nov. 12, 1975.*

Reed, Sir Carol film producer and director, aged 69—*April.*

Robeson, Paul Le Roy, singer and actor, aged 77—*Jan. 23.*

Shepard, Ernest Howard, O.B.E., M.C., artist and illustrator, aged 96—*March 24.*

Sherriff, Robert Cedric, F.S.A., playwright, aged 79—*Nov. 13, 1975.*

Sim, Alastair, C.B.E., actor, aged 75—*Aug. 19.*

Stopford, *Rt. Rev.* Robert Wright, P.C., K.C.V.O., C.B.E., D.D., Bishop of Bermuda and former Bishop of London, aged 75—*Aug. 13.*

Storm, Lesley, playwright, aged 71—*Oct. 19, 1975.*

Streeter, Fred, B.B.C. broadcaster on gardening, aged 98—*Nov. 1, 1975.*

Teyte, Dame Maggie, D.B.E., prima donna, aged 88—*May 26.*

Thomson of Fleet, Roy Herbert Thomson, G.B.E., 1st Baron, newspaper owner, aged 82—*Aug. 4.*

Thorndike, Dame Sybil, C.H., D.B.E., distinguished actress and manager, aged 93—*June 9.*

Toynbee, *Prof.* Arnold Joseph, C.H., eminent historian, aged 86—*Oct. 22, 1975.*

Tucker, Frederick James Tucker, P.C., Baron, former Lord of Appeal in Ordinary, aged 87—*Nov. 17, 1975.*

Warner, Oliver, distinguished naval historian, aged 73—*Aug. 14.*

Wheeler, Sir Robert Eric Mortimer, C.H., C.I.E., M.C., F.R.S., F.B.A., F.S.A., distinguished archaeologist, aged 85—*July 22.*

Wilder, Thornton Niven, American novelist and playwright, aged 78—*Dec. 7, 1975.*

Willis, *Admiral of the Fleet* Sir Algernon Usborne, G.C.B., K.B.E., D.S.O., distinguished naval career, aged 86—*April 12.*

THE CENTENARIES OF 1977

The year 1877, like its predecessor, was dominated by the Eastern Question. The conference at Constantinople, which had been convened late in 1876 in anattempt to settle the differences between Russia and Turkey, continued into the new year, but broke down in the middle of January. The demands of the Powers for administrative autonomy in the Balkan provinces were modified, but Turkey was unable to accept them even in their amended terms.

In consequence, Russia made preparations for war. She gave a secret undertaking to Austria that

the latter might, when the time came, occupy Bosnia and Herzegovina, and M. Ignatieff, the Russian Ambassador in Constantinople, was sent on a mission round the European Courts to sound out their attitudes. On March 31 a Protocol was signed in London by the major Powers, calling on Turkey to reduce its army to a peace footing and to put in hand the reforms which they had long urged; in return Russia would demobilise the forces deployed on the frontier. The Turks, however, refused to comply and on April 21 the Russian armies were ordered to begin operations.

The British Government announced its neutrality, contingent on Russian promises to respect Egypt, the Suez Canal, the Persian Gulf, Constantinople and the Bosphorus. These promises were duly given.

Mr. Gladstone, who had been drawn from semi-retirement the previous year by his indignation at the " Bulgarian Atrocities ", continued in his anti-Turkish policy, but his proposal for a declaration that Turkey had forfeited all claim to British support was defeated in the House of Commons.

There were, however, serious divisions in Lord Beaconsfield's Cabinet, aggravated by the steady Russian advance and the possible threat to Constantinople. The Prime Minister was anxious to safeguard British interests there, but Lord Derby, the Foreign Secretary, together with Lord Salisbury and Lord Carnarvon, were opposed to active measures. The fleet was again despatched to Besika Bay, as it had been in 1876, and the Mediterranean garrisons were strengthened. But Lord Beaconsfield's proposals for an expedition to hold Gallipoli and for the fleet to go to Constantinople, were not supported by his senior colleagues.

A respite was secured by the check to the Russian army at Plevna, which was defended against them for no less than four months, and did not finally fall until December 9. The threat to Constantinople was then renewed, and after prolonged Cabinet discussions, during which the Prime Minister threatened to resign, it was finally agreed that Parliament should be summoned earlier in the New Year, that the armed forces should be materially increased, and that Britain should offer to mediate between Russia and Turkey. At the end of the year Turkey did in fact ask the Powers to intervene. During the Cabinet controversy, the Queen marked her support for Lord Beaconsfield by doing him what was then considered the exceptional honour of visiting him at his home at Hughenden and lunching with him.

On January 1, at a spectacular Durbar at Delhi, presided over by Lord Lytton, the Viceroy, in state, Queen Victoria was proclaimed Kaisar-i-Hind, Empress of India. She noted in her Journal that that day she signed herself for the first time V.R. & I.

Sir Theophilus Shepstone had been sent by the British Government to investigate the situation in the Transvaal with power to annex the country if the position appeared to warrant it, and on April 12 he took this step.

Towards the end of the Parliamentary session, the Irish Nationalist M.P.s, under the leadership of Mr. Parnell, began a campaign to obstruct Government business and succeeded in delaying legislation. The measures taken at the time to thwart obstruction were not very effective, and the Nationalists' action was a foretaste of their continued subsequent policy.

The result of the Presidential election in the U.S.A. in the previous autumn had remained undecided, and an Electoral Commission had been appointed by Congress to resolve the deadlock between Mr Hayes (Republican) and Mr. Tilden (Democrat). The Commission, by a strictly party vote, decided in favour of Mr. Hayes, who took office at the beginning of March.

In France, the President, Marshal MacMahon, forced the resignation of the moderate Republican government, which had been constitutionally elected in the previous year, and replaced it by a non-elected ministry under the Monarchist Duc de Broglie. In June the President dissolved the Chamber, and with his new ministers made strenuous endeavours to secure a majority at the ensuing elections. The Republicans, under M. Gambetta, made the funeral of M. Thiers, the former President, who died on Sept. 3, the occasion for a great political demonstration. Shortly afterwards, M. Gambetta was sentenced to three months' imprisonment for libelling Marshal MacMahon. However, the elections on Oct. 14 resulted in a sweeping Republican victory, 335 Republicans being returned against 198 official candidates, and the President was eventually compelled to appoint another moderate Republican Ministry.

On January 27, when he celebrated his eighteenth birthday, the Queen conferred the Order of the Garter on her eldest grandchild Prince William of Prussia, later the Kaiser William II.

On February 28, London University resolved to admit women to degrees in medicine—an early recognition of women's rights.

Two new English dioceses were created during the year. On April 25 Dr. Edward White Benson (later Archbishop of Canterbury) was consecrated the first Bishop of Truro, and on June 12, Dr. Claughton, previously Bishop of Rochester, was enthroned as Bishop of the newly-formed see of St. Albans.

On May 1 it was announced that the Queen had extended the award of the Albert Medal to cases of gallantry in saving life on land; this was done so that the medal could be given to the rescuers of a large number of miners who had been entombed when the Troedyrhiw Colliery in the Rhondda had been flooded in the previous month.

The railway bridge over the Tay estuary—then the longest railway bridge in the world—was opened on September 25. Part of this bridge was blown into the river only two years later, with a train which was crossing it at the time, resulting in much loss of life.

The obelisk popularly known as Cleopatra's Needle was removed from its site at Alexandria during the year, and on Sept. 21 it was taken in tow by the steamship *Olga* for removal to England. The voyage was eventful, the obelisk having to be taken into Ferrol after being rescued from the Bay of Biscay; it did not finally reach England till January 1878.

During the year Mr. Andrew Barclay Walker, Mayor of Liverpool, presented the Walker Art Gallery, built at his sole cost, to the corporation of Liverpool. On Sept. 27 the foundation stone of the University College at Nottingham was laid, Mr. Gladstone speaking at the ceremony.

The only instance of a dead-heat in the history of the Oxford and Cambridge boat race occurred when the race was rowed on March 24.

A special service was held at Westminster Abbey on June 2 to commemorate the 400th anniversary of the first book known to have been printed in England, by William Caxton.

The year is not a notable one for literary anniversaries. *The American*, by Henry James, is perhaps one of the few books first published in 1877 to be still widely read, though Herbert Spencer's *Principles of Sociology* had considerable influence in its day.

THE CENTENARIES OF 1977

The following is a list of the principal centenaries which will be celebrated in 1977.

Died 1877

March 13	Charles Cowden Clarke. Man of letters.
March 24	Walter Bagehot. Author and economist.
May 21	Sir Matthew Digby Wyatt. Architect.
May 24	John Lothrop Motley. U.S. historian.
Aug. 29	Brigham Young. Mormon leader.
Sept. 5	Louis Adolphe Thiers. French statesman.
Sept. 17	William Henry Fox Talbot. Pioneer of photography.

Born 1877

Feb. 8	Sir Humphrey Milford. Publisher.
April 10	Lord Goddard. Lord Chief Justice.
May 16	Sir Bernard Spilsbury. Pathologist.
May 17	Lord Iliffe. Newspaper proprietor.
May 20	Sir Desmond MacCarthy. Critic.
Aug. 29	Sir Dudley Pound. Admiral of the Fleet.
Sept. 9	James Agate. Dramatic critic.
Sept. 11	Sir James Jeans. Astronomer.
Oct. 10	Visct. Nuffield. Motor manufacturer and philanthropist.
Oct. 17	Sir Robert Ensor. Historian.
Oct. 29	Wilfred Rhodes. Cricketer.
Nov. 1	Roger Quilter. Composer.
Nov. 2	The Aga Khan. Moslem leader and racehorse owner.
	Victor Trumper. Australian cricketer.
Nov. 25	Harley Granville-Barker. Man of the theatre.
Dec. 2	Benno Elkan. Sculptor.

Born 1777

July 9	Henry Hallam. Historian.

Died 1677

Feb. 20	Baruch Spinoza. Philosopher.

Born 1577

June 29	Peter Paul Rubens. Painter.

Died 1377

June 21	King Edward III.

THE CENTENARIES OF 1978

The following is a list of the principal centenaries which will be celebrated in 1978.

Died 1878

Jan. 9	Victor Emmanuel, first King of Italy.
Feb.	George Cruickshank. Artist.
Feb. 7	Pope Pius IX.
March 27	Sir George Gilbert Scott. Architect.
May 28	Earl Russell. Former Prime Minister.
June 24	Charles Mathews. Actor.
Oct. 5	Lord Chelmsford. Former Lord Chancellor.
Oct. 5	Sir Francis Grant. President of the Royal Academy.
Nov. 6	Samuel Phelps. Actor.
Nov. 30	George Henry Lewes. Man of letters.
Dec. 14	Princess Alice. Daughter of Queen Victoria.

Born 1878

Jan. 6	Dame Adelaide Genée. Dancer.
Jan. 23	Rutland Boughton. Composer.
Feb. 10	Jeffery Farnol. Novelist.
March 16	Emile Cammaerts. Belgian poet.
April 26	Sir A. V. Roe. Aviation pioneer.
April 28	Lionel Barrymore. Stage and screen actor.
June 1	John Masefield. Poet Laureate.
July 24	Lord Dunsany. Man of letters.
Aug. 12	Ambrose McEvoy. Painter.
Oct. 3	J. H. Thomas. Politician.
Oct. 8	Sir Alfred Munnings. Painter.
Nov. 27	Sir William Orpen. Painter.

Died 1778

Jan. 10	Carl Linnaeus. Botanist.
May 11	Earl of Chatham. Statesman.
May 30	Voltaire (François Marie Arouet).
July 2	Jean Jacques Rousseau.

Born 1778

April 10	William Hazlitt. Man of letters.
Sept. 10	Lord Brougham. Politician and Lord Chancellor.
Dec. 17	Sir Humphry Davy. Chemist.

Died 1678

Aug. 16	Andrew Marvell. Poet.

Born 1578

April 1	William Harvey. Discoverer of circulation of the blood.

POPES FROM 1800

Sovereign Pontiff	Family Name	Elected		Sovereign Pontiff	Family Name	Elected
Pius VII	Chiaramonti	1800		Pius XI	Ratti	1922
Leo XII	della Genga	1823		Pius XII	Pacelli	1939
Pius VIII	Castiglioni	1829		John XXIII	Roncalli	1958
Gregory XV	Cappellari	1831		Paul VI	Montini	1963
Pius IX	Mastaï-Ferretti	1846				
Leo XIII	Pecci	1878				
Pius X	Sarto	1903				
Benedict XV	della Chiesa	1914				

Adrian IV (Nicholas Breakspear, the only Englishman elected Pope) was born at Langley, near St. Albans; elected Pope, on the death of Anastasius IV, 1154; died 1159.

NATIONAL INSURANCE AND RELATED CASH BENEFITS

The State insurance and assistance schemes in force from July 5, 1948, comprised schemes of national insurance and industrial injuries insurance, national assistance and non-contributory old age pensions, and family allowances. The Ministry of Social Security Act, 1966, introduced a scheme of non-contributory benefits, termed supplementary allowances and pensions, in place of national assistance and non-contributory old age pensions, and provided for the establishment of a new Ministry of Social Security (now the Department of Health and Social Security), with overall responsibility for the existing insurance schemes and family allowances scheme and the new scheme of supplementary benefits, in place of the Ministry of Pensions and National Insurance and the National Assistance Board, which were abolished.

The Conservative Government's Social Security Act, 1973, which was intended to be brought into force in April, 1975, provided for the replacement of the National Insurance scheme by a basic scheme of social security, offering a range of benefits, including flat-rate basic pensions, similar to those under the existing legislation; a separate reserve pension scheme providing, in addition to the basic pension, earnings-related pensions for those employees not in recognized pensionable employment; and the assimilation of the Industrial Injuries scheme to the basic scheme. It also laid down minimum conditions for recognition of occupational pension schemes so as to exempt the employers and employees concerned from liability to contribute to the reserve pension scheme.

The new Labour Government decided that the basic scheme provisions of the 1973 Act should come into force on April 6, 1975, as planned, but it decided not to bring into effect the provisions of that Act relating to the reserve pension scheme or the recognition tests for occupational pension schemes seeking exemption from the reserve pension scheme (except the provisions relating to the preservation of benefits under occupational schemes). Effect was given to the Government's decisions by an order made in June 1974 under the 1973 Act, and by the Social Security (Amendment) Act, 1974, passed in December, 1974.

Three measures—the Social Security Act, 1975 (now the principal Act); the Social Security (Consequential Provisions) Act, 1975; and the Industrial Injuries and Diseases (Old Cases) Act, 1975—were enacted on March 20, 1975, for the purpose of consolidating the law relating to social security in Great Britain, and corresponding measures were passed for Northern Ireland.

The Labour Government published in September, 1974, in a White Paper, " Better Pensions fully protected against inflation ", its proposals for a new pensions scheme. The Social Security Pensions Bill based upon these proposals, after consultation with interested bodies, was introduced, with an explanatory memorandum, in February, 1975, and after amendment was passed as the Social Security Pensions Act, 1975, in August, 1975. Preparations are being made for the new scheme to come into force in 1978 (see p. 616).

SOCIAL SECURITY SCHEME, 1975

From April 6, 1975, the National Insurance scheme 1948–1975 was replaced by a new scheme of social security benefits and contributions under the Social Security Act, 1975, as amended, and regulations made thereunder. Like the former scheme, the new scheme is financed on a pay-as-you-go basis mainly by contributions but in part out of Exchequer funds (rates of benefit and of contributions being reviewed normally annually in accordance with statutory criteria), but the new scheme contributions, to a greater extent than national insurance contributions, are earnings-related. The graduated pension scheme 1961–1975 has been wound up (existing rights being preserved); otherwise the new scheme provides a pattern of pension and other benefits similar to that of the old scheme. The Industrial Injuries scheme continues with only minor changes, but steps have been taken to assimilate the industrial injuries legislation to the general scheme: thus the separate industrial injuries contribution and the Treasury supplement thereto under the Industrial Injuries Acts have been abolished, and the Industrial Injuries Fund has been merged with the National Insurance Fund.

CONTRIBUTIONS AND CONTRIBUTION CONDITIONS

The funds required for paying benefits payable under the Social Security Act, 1975, as amended, out of the National Insurance Fund and not out of other public money; for the making of payments towards the cost of the National Health Service and into the Redundancy Fund; and for paying benefit under the Industrial Injuries and Diseases (Old Cases) Act, 1975, are provided by means of contributions payable by earners, employers and others (such as non-employed persons paying voluntary contributions), together with the Treasury supplement.

Contributions are of four classes:

> Class 1, earnings-related:
> > (a) primary Class 1 contributions from employed earners; and
> > (b) secondary Class 1 contributions from employers and other persons paying earnings;
>
> Class 2, flat-rate, payable weekly by self-employed earners;
>
> Class 3, flat-rate, payable by earners and others voluntarily with a view to providing entitlement to benefit, or making up entitlement; and
>
> Class 4, payable by self-employed persons in respect of the profits or gains of a trade, profession or vocation, or in respect of equivalent earnings.

Particulars of current rates of contributions for each class are given on p. 619.

Regulations state the cases in which earners may be excepted from liability to pay contributions, and the conditions upon which contributions are credited to persons who are excepted.

The Secretary of State for Social Services is empowered by the Social Security Act, 1975, as amended, to alter certain rates of contributions by order approved by both Houses of Parliament, and is required by the same enactment to make annual reviews of the general level of earnings in order to determine whether such an order should be made. The Government Actuary has pointed out that with a system of mainly earnings-related contributions the income of the National Insurance Fund will rise automatically with increases in the general level of earnings and will broadly be sufficient to meet the cost of corresponding increases in the level of benefits provided the earnings limits for contribution liability and the flat-rate (Classes 2 and 3) contributions are adjusted regularly. Following the decision in the summer of 1975 to make further increases in benefits in November, 1975. provision was made by the Social Security (Contributions, Re-rating) Order, 1975, made in November, 1975,

for increases in certain rates of contributions and for changes in the various earnings limits for contribution liability for the 1976–77 tax year. The new rates and limits applied from April 6, 1976 (see p. 619). It is expected that a further order will be made later in 1976 setting out the amounts which are to apply for the tax year 1977–78.

The yearly Treasury supplement to the National Insurance Fund is equal to 18 per cent. of the contributions of the four classes paid during the year after deducting the National Health Service allocation and the allocation to the Redundancy Fund (see p. 619).

BENEFITS

The benefits payable under the Social Security Act, 1975, as amended, are as follows:

(1) Contributory Benefits:
Unemployment benefit.
Sickness benefit.
Invalidity pension and allowance.
Maternity benefit, comprising maternity grant and maternity allowance.
Widow's benefit, comprising widow's allowance, widowed mother's allowance and widow's pension.
Child's special allowance.
Retirement pensions of the following categories:
Category A.
Category B.
Death grant.

(2) Non-contributory Benefits:
Guardian's allowance (see p. 618).
Attendance allowance (see p. 618).
Non-contributory invalidity pension (see p. 618).
Mobility Allowance (see p. 618).
Invalid care allowance (see p. 618).
Retirement pensions of the following categories.
Category C (see p. 618).
Category D (see p. 618).

(3) Benefits for Industrial Injuries and Diseases.

Cash benefits provided under other enactments (supplementary benefits, family allowances and child benefit, and family income supplement) are dealt with on pp. 617–18.

The Social Security Act, 1975, empowers the Secretary of State to increase certain rates of benefit by order approved by both Houses of Parliament, and requires him to increase certain rates by such an order if an annual review shows that they have not retained their value in relation to the general level of earnings and prices obtaining in Great Britain.

The first order providing for increases in benefit rates took effect from November 17, 1975. The next increases in benefits were authorised by the Social Security Benefits Up-rating Order, 1976, made in July, 1976. These new rates are to apply from November 15, 1976.

Entitlement to the contributory benefits provided by the Act of 1975 (except invalidity benefit) depends on contribution conditions being satisfied either by the claimant or by some other person (depending on the kind of benefit). The class or classes of contribution which for this purpose are relevant to each benefit are as follows:

Short-term benefits

Unemployment benefit	Class 1
Sickness benefit	Class 1 or 2
Maternity grant	Class 1, 2 or 3
Maternity allowance	Class 1 or 2
Widow's allowance	Class 1, 2 or 3

Other benefits

Widowed mother's allowance	
Widow's pension	
Child's special allowance	Class 1, 2 or 3
Category A retirement pension	
Category B retirement pension	
Death grant	

With the change from a system of flat-rate national insurance and industrial injuries contributions and graduated pension contributions to a system of wholly earnings-related contributions for employed earners the contribution conditions for entitlement to benefit could no longer be based on the number of weekly contributions paid in a contribution year or throughout a working life. The Social Security Act, 1975, introduced a new system of contribution conditions related to yearly levels of earnings on which contributions have been paid. The contribution conditions for different benefits are set out in sections 13 to 33 of and Schedule 3 to the Act, and in summary form in leaflets on the benefits available at local Social Security offices. There are two contribution conditions for most of the benefits. The first condition must be satisfied to qualify for benefit at all; the second condition generally determines whether benefit is paid at the standard rate or at a reduced rate. Under the arrangements made for the transition from the old scheme to the new one, provision has been made for such matters as treating old-style flat-rate contributions as new-style earnings-related contributions and vice versa, and the use of modified contribution tests for short-term benefits for an initial period following the start of the new scheme.

There is one system of adjudication on all claims for benefit under the Act; with certain exceptions, questions as to the right to benefit are decided by independent statutory authorities, consisting of insurance officers, local tribunals and the Chief Commissioner and Commissioners.

The rates of benefit stated below are, unless otherwise indicated, the standard rates having effect from November 15, 1976.

UNEMPLOYMENT BENEFIT

The *standard weekly rates of flat-rate benefit payable to primary Class 1 contributors* are as follows:

	£
Man, single woman or widow	12·90
Married woman: normal rate	9·20
Increase of benefit for only child or elder or eldest child (ordinary rate)	4·05
Increase of benefit for each additional child (ordinary rate) in addition to family allowances	2·55
Increase of benefit for wife or other adult dependant (ordinary rate) where payable	8·00

Waiting Period.—Flat-rate benefit is not payable for the first three days of a period of interruption of employment.

Duration of Benefit.—Benefit is payable in a period of interruption of employment for up to 312 days (a year). Spells of unemployment and sickness not separated by more than 13 weeks count as one period of interruption of employment.

Requalification for Benefit.—A person who has exhausted benefit requalifies therefor when he has again worked as an employed earner for at least 21 hours a week for 13 weeks.

Disqualifications.—There are disqualifications for receiving benefit, e.g. for a period not exceeding six weeks if a person has lost his employment through his misconduct, or has voluntarily left his employment without just cause, or has, without

good cause, refused an offer of suitable employment or training.

Earnings-related Supplement.—This supplement is payable to claimants under minimum pension age who are entitled to flat-rate unemployment or sickness benefit. The amount of the supplement depends upon reckonable earnings in the relevant income tax year. Where based on earnings in the 1974–75 income tax year, it is one-third of the amount of reckonable weekly earnings lying between £10 and £30 and 15 per cent. of those lying between £30 and £54. Where it is based on earnings in the 1975–76 income tax year, the upper limit on the band of weekly earnings on which it is paid at 15 per cent. will be increased from £54 to £69. The total benefit, including increases for dependants, is subject to a maximum of 85 per cent. of earnings. The supplement starts from the thirteenth day of a period of interruption of employment and lasts for up to a maximum of six months. Periods of unemployment or sickness not separated by more than 13 weeks are treated as one period of interruption of employment. Where employment is suspended but not terminated by the employer, e.g. short-time working or lay-off, the supplement is not payable for the first six days (except Sundays and holidays) in any continuous period of suspension.

SICKNESS BENEFIT

Standard Rates of flat-rate Benefit payable to primary Class 1 and to Class 2 contributors while incapable of work through illness or disablement.—Same as for unemployment benefit.

Waiting Period.—Same as for unemployment benefit.

Duration of Benefit.—Sickness benefit is payable for 28 weeks of sickness and is then replaced by invalidity benefit (see below).

Disqualifications.—Regulations provide for disqualifying a person for receiving sickness or invalidity benefit for a period not exceeding six weeks if he has become incapable of work through his own misconduct or if he fails without good cause to attend for or submit himself to prescribed medical or other examination or treatment, or observe prescribed rules of behaviour.

Earnings-related Supplement.—The supplement and the rules as to duration are the same as for the supplement to unemployment benefit.

INVALIDITY BENEFIT

Normally, after 28 weeks of sickness, sickness benefit is replaced by an *invalidity pension* of £15·30 (£9·20 for a wife) unless the claimant is over pension age and has retired from regular employment. In addition an *invalidity allowance* is payable if incapacity for work begins more than five years before pension age. The allowance varies in amount from £1·00 to £3·20 a week, according to the age on falling sick, and if still in payment at pension age will continue as an addition to retirement pension. The increases of benefit for children of an invalidity pensioner are at the higher rate, viz., £7·45 for the first child and £5·95 for any other child, in addition to family allowances. Earnings-related supplement is not payable with invalidity benefit. The dependent wife of an invalidity pensioner residing with him is subject to the same tapered earnings rule as applies to retirement pensioners which begins to operate when earnings exceed £35 (after April 1977 £50). As to the age addition if the pensioner or dependant is 80 or over, and, non-contributory invalidity pensions, see p. 618).

MATERNITY BENEFITS

Maternity Grant.—A cash grant of £25 is payable on the mother's own insurance or on her husband's, or late husband's, whether she is confined at home or in hospital. Extra grants are payable, in certain circumstances, if more than one child is born.

Maternity Allowance.—A woman who has been employed or self-employed and paying contributions at the full rate receives in addition a maternity allowance of £12·90 a week normally for 18 weeks beginning eleven weeks before the expected week of confinement, provided that she abstains from work. The rate of allowance is increased where the woman has dependants. Earnings-related supplement is payable with maternity allowance if the claimant's title to the supplement has not been used up in respect of other benefits, see above.

WIDOW'S BENEFITS

Only the late husband's contributions of any class count for widow's benefit in any of its three forms.

Widow's Allowance.—A woman who at her husband's death is under 60 (or over 60, if he had not retired), receives (during the first 26 weeks of widowhood) a cash allowance usually of £21·40 a week with increases of £7·45 for the first or only child and £5·95 for each other child, in addition to family allowances. She may also be entitled to an earnings-related addition to her widow's allowance based on her late husband's earnings (reckoned in the same way as for earnings-related supplements to unemployment and sickness benefit), see above.

Widowed Mother's Allowance.—When the 26 weeks of widow's allowance have elapsed, a widow who is left with one or more dependent children receives a cash allowance usually of £22·75 a week as long as she has a child of qualifying age, and in addition £5·95 for each additional child, as well as family allowances. A widowed mother's personal allowance, usually £15·30 a week, is payable to widows who, when their widow's or widowed mother's allowance ends, have living with them a child under 19, who has left school and is not an apprentice.

Widow's Pension.—A widow receives this pension usually of £15·30 a week when widow's allowance ends, if she was over 50 at the time of her husband's death; or (ii) when her widowed mother's allowance or widowed mother's personal allowance ends, if she is then over 50 (40 if widowed before February 4, 1957).

Flat-rate widow's pensions on a graduated s ale were introduced in April 1971 for women who are widowed between the ages of 40 and 50, or who cease to be entitled to a widowed mother's allowance between those ages.

Widow's benefit of any form ceases upon remarriage.

CHILD'S SPECIAL ALLOWANCE

A woman whose marriage has been dissolved or annulled and who has not re-married is paid a special allowance on the ex-husband's death based on his contribution record. The normal condition is that she has a child to whose maintenance he was contributing, or had been liable to contribute, at least 25p a week in cash or its equivalent. The allowance is £7·45 a week for the first or only child and £5·95 for each other child, in addition to family allowances.

RETIREMENT PENSION
(CATEGORIES A AND B)

A *Category A pension* is payable for life to men or women on their own contributions if (a) they are

over pension age (65 for a man and 60 for a woman), and (b) they have retired from regular employment. Men aged 70 or over and women aged 65 or over are not required to satisfy condition (b).

The standard flat-rate pension, when the contribution conditions are fully satisfied, is £15·30, *plus* £9·20 for a dependent wife who is not herself qualified for a pension, *plus* £7·45 for the first or only child and £5·95 for each other child, in addition to family allowances. An increase for a dependent wife is reduced, under the earnings rule, below, if she earns more than a certain amount. (As to the age addition payable at 80, see p. 618.)

Where a person does not retire at 65 (60 for a woman) or later cancels retirement, and does not draw a Category A pension, the weekly rate of pension is increased, when he or she finally retires or reaches the age of 70 (65 for a woman), in respect of contributions paid when employed or self-employed during the five years after reaching minimum pension age. For periods of deferred retirement after April 5, 1975, the rate of pension (without any increases except invalidity allowance), when it is finally awarded, will normally be increased by one-eighth of one per cent. for each week of deferment except those weeks in which other benefits (such as sickness or unemployment benefit) were drawn. A married man can also earn extra pension for his wife.

A *Category B pension* is normally payable for life to a woman on her husband's contributions when he has retired, or is over 70, and has qualified for his own Category A pension, and she has reached 60 and retired from regular work or has reached 65. It is also payable on widowhood after 60 whether or not the late husband had retired and qualified for his own pension. The weekly pension is payable at the lower rate of £9·20 while the husband is alive, and at the higher rate of £15·30 on widowhood after 60. Where a woman is widowed before she reaches 60, a Category B pension is paid to her on reaching 60 at the same weekly rate as her widow's pension if she retires. If a woman qualifies for a pension of each category she receives whichever pension is the larger. For periods of deferred retirement after April 5, 1975, a Category B pension will normally be increased by one-sixteenth of one per cent. of the husband's pension rate (apart from any increase other than invalidity allowance) for each week while both husband and wife defer retirement. If the husband dies after April 5, 1975, the extra pension which he earned for his wife by not drawing his pension after she reached 60 will be doubled. She will also receive half of any extra pension he earned for any period before she reached 60. (As to the age addition payable at 80, see p. 618.)

A man aged 65 to 70, or a woman aged 60 to 65, who has qualified for pension will have it reduced if he or she earns more than a certain amount. Until April 1977 the pension will be reduced by 5p for each 10p of net earnings between £35 and £39 and by 5p for each 5p earned over £39. During the twelve months following, the "earnings rule" will start to operate when earnings exceed £50. A man's pension is not affected by his wife's earnings unless he is drawing an increase of his pension for her.

Unemployment, sickness or invalidity benefit is payable to men between 65 and 70 and women between 60 and 65 who have not retired from regular work at the same rate as the basic retirement pension they would have received had they retired. A retirement pension will be increased by the amount of any invalidity allowance the pensioner was getting within the period of 13 weeks before reaching minimum pension age. As to attendance allowance and invalid care allowance, see p. 618.

Persons who do not qualify for a Category A or B pension may qualify for a Category C or D pension (see p. 618), or for a supplementary pension (see p. 617).

GRADUATED PENSION

The graduated pension scheme under which national insurance contributions and retirement pensions were graduated within specified limits, according to earnings, was discontinued in April, 1975, under the Social Security Act, 1975. Any graduated pension which an employed person over 18 and under 70 (65 for a woman) had earned by paying graduated contributions between April 6, 1961, when the scheme started and April 5, 1975, will be paid when the contributor retires, or at 70 (65 for a woman), in addition to any retirement pension for which he or she qualifies.

Graduated pension is at the rate of 2½p a week for each "unit" of graduated contributions paid by the employee (half a unit or more counts as a whole unit). A unit of contributions is £7·50 for men, and £9·00 for women, of graduated contributions paid.

A wife can get a graduated pension in return for her own graduated contributions, but not for her husband's. A widow gets a graduated addition to her retirement pension equal to half of any graduated additions earned by her late husband, plus any additions earned by her own graduated contributions. If a person defers retirement beyond 65 (60 for a woman), half the graduated pension he or she has forgone by deferring retirement (whether before or after April 5, 1975) will be treated as extra graduated contributions paid, and will count towards further graduated pension on retirement or at 70 (65 for a woman).

DEATH GRANT

A death grant is payable on the death of a qualifying contributor or of his wife, child or widow or, if the contributor is a woman, of her husband, child or widower, and also in respect of the deaths of certain handicapped persons on the insurance of close relatives. The normal grant is for an adult £30, a child aged 6–17 £22·50, a child aged 3–5 £15, a child under 3 £9. For the deaths of people who on July 5, 1948, were between 55 and 65 (men) or between 50 and 60 (women) the grant is £15. No grant is payable for deaths of persons already over pension age on July 5, 1948.

The grant is paid to the deceased person's executors or administrators, if any; otherwise it is paid to the person who meets the funeral expenses or to the next of kin.

FINANCE

Under the National Insurance Acts before April 6, 1975, two funds were set up, viz. the National Insurance Fund, and the National Insurance (Reserve) Fund. The income from contributions, Exchequer grants and interest from both funds were paid into the National Insurance Fund, and payments were made out of the Fund to meet the cost of benefits and administration. Under the National Health Service Contributions Act, provision was made for separate National Health Service contributions to be collected in conjunction with the National Insurance contributions, in place of payments formerly made from the Fund towards the cost of the National Health Service.

Approximate receipts and payments of the National Insurance Fund for the year ended March 31, 1975, were as follows:—

Receipts	£'000
Balance, April 1, 1974	574,094
Flat-rate contributions from employers and insured persons	2,040,241
Exchequer contribution	817,000
Graduated contributions	2,828,470
Income from investments	71,465
Transfer from the Reserve Fund of income from investments, etc.	38,647
Other receipts	124
	6,370,041

Payments		
Benefit:—	£'000	£'000
Unemployment benefit	214,122	
Sickness benefit	345,320	
Invalidity benefit	319,585	
Maternity benefit	47,000	
Widow's benefit	310,000	
Guardian's allowance	1,300	
Child's special allowance	200	
Retirement pension	3,578,379	
Death grant	13,900	
Pensioners' lump sum payments	88,300	
Other payments	12,302	
		4,930,407(a)
Administration expenses		201,448
Other payments		48,352
Balance, March 31, 1975		1,189,834
		6,370,041

(a) Including estimated amounts of earnings-related supplement as follows: unemployment benefit £34·0 million; sickness benefit £84·0 million; widow's benefit £8·0 million; graduated retirement benefit £39·0 million.

Receipts exceeded payments during the year by £615·7 million. Compared with 1973–74 receipts increased by £1,515·1 million and payments by £1,138·8 million.

The balance in the Reserve Fund at March 31, 1975, was £886·7 million.

INDUSTRIAL INJURIES BENEFITS

The National Insurance (Industrial Injuries) Act, 1946, substituted for the Workmen's Compensation Acts, 1925 to 1945, a system of insurance against personal injury caused by accident arising out of and in the course of a person's employment and against prescribed diseases and injuries due to the nature of a person's employment. The scheme, which insures against personal injuries caused and prescribed diseases and injuries developed on or after July 5, 1948, now operates under the Social Security Act, 1975, and regulations made under the Act. The Social Security Benefits Up-rating Order, 1976, provided for increases in the rates of benefit with effect from November 15, 1976. Rates of benefit are now reviewed annually.

Supplementary allowances payable in certain circumstances in cases arising before the Industrial Injuries scheme started are governed by the Industrial Injuries and Diseases (Old Cases) Act, 1975, and regulations made under the Act. Statutory schemes have also been made providing for the payment of allowances supplementing workmen's compensation in certain circumstances, and for the payment of benefits in certain cases where neither workmen's compensation nor Industrial Injuries benefits are payable.

The scope of " employed earners " and their employments to which the industrial injuries scheme applies is defined in the Social Security Act, 1975, and regulations made under the Act.

Separate industrial injuries contributions were discontinued in April, 1975. The Industrial Injuries Fund was at the same time merged in the National Insurance Fund, and the separate Treasury Supplement to the Industrial Injuries Fund came to an end.

BENEFITS

Injury Benefit is payable for not more than the first 26 weeks of incapacity, but not usually for the first three days. Benefit is payable to persons over 18 and to juveniles with dependant's allowances, at the weekly rate of £15·65 (days being paid for at one-sixth of the weekly rate): with increases of £8·00 for a wife or other adult dependant, and normally £4·05 for the first or only child and £2·55 for each other child, in addition to family allowances. Other juveniles receive lower rates. Where a claimant who is entitled to sickness benefit draws injury benefit instead, any earnings-related supplement to sickness benefit to which he is entitled will be paid with the injury benefit (*see* p. 613).

Disablement Benefit is payable if at or after the end of the injury benefit period the employed earner suffers from loss of physical or mental faculty such that the resulting disablement is assessed at not less than one per cent. (In cases of pneumoconiosis and byssinosis disablement benefit is paid from the start without a period of injury benefit.) The amount of disablement benefit varies according to the degree of disablement (in the form of a percentage) assessed by a medical board or medical appeal tribunal. In cases of disablement of less than 20 per cent., except in pneumoconiosis or byssinosis cases, benefit normally takes the form of a *gratuity* paid according to a prescribed scale, but not exceeding £1,660. Where the degree of disablement is 20 per cent. or more, or if it is due to pneumoconiosis or byssinosis, the benefit is a weekly *pension* payable either for a limited period or for life, according to the following scale:

Degree of disablement	Weekly Rate £
100 per cent.	25·00
90 ,, ,,	22·50
80 ,, ,,	20·00
70 ,, ,,	17·50
60 ,, ,,	15·00
50 ,, ,,	12·50
40 ,, ,,	10·00
30 ,, ,,	7·50
20 ,, ,,	5·00

These are basic rates applicable to adults and to juveniles entitled to an increase for a child or adult dependant; other juveniles receive lower rates.

Basic rates of pension are not related to the pensioner's loss of earning power, and are payable whether he is in work or not. Upon prescribed conditions, however, pension is supplemented for unemployability and in cases of special hardship. There is provision also for increases of pension during approved hospital treatment or if the pensioner requires constant attendance or if his disablement is exceptionally severe. If the beneficiary is entitled to an unemployability supplement there are increases of £7·45 for the first or only child and £5·95 for any other child, and, subject to the earnings rule, £9·20 for an adult dependant. Subject to certain exceptions, a pensioner who is not in receipt of unemployability supplement can draw sickness or invalidity benefit as appropriate, in addition to disablement pension, during spells of incapacity for work.

Death Benefit, in the form of a pension, a gratuity or a weekly allowance for a limited period, available for widows and other dependants in fatal cases, depends in amount upon their relationship to the deceased and their circumstances at the time of death and not upon the deceased's earnings. A widow who was living with her husband at the time of his death receives a pension of £21·40 a week for the first 26 weeks *plus* any earnings-related addition she would have received if she had been entitled to national insurance widow's pension (*see* p. 613), and thereafter a pension of £15·85 or less a week according to circumstances, *plus* £7·45 for the first or only child and £5·95 for each other child, in addition to family allowances.

Regulations impose certain obligations on claimants and beneficiaries and on employers, including, in the case of claimants for injury or disablement benefit, that of submitting to medical examination and treatment.

Industrial Diseases, etc.—The scheme extends insurance to prescribed industrial diseases and prescribed personal injuries not caused by accident, which are due to the nature of an employed earner's employment and developed on or after July 5, 1948.

Determination of Questions and Claims.—Provision is made for the determination of certain questions by the Secretary of State for Social Services, and of " disablement questions " by a medical board (or a single doctor) or medical appeal tribunal or, on appeal on a point of law, by the Commissioners, subject to leave. Claims for benefit and certain questions arising in connection with a claim for or award of benefit (e.g. whether the accident arose out of and in the course of the employment) are determined by an insurance officer appointed by the Secretary of State, or a local appeal tribunal consisting of a chairman appointed by the Secretary of State and equal numbers of members representing employers and employed earners, or, on appeal, by the Commissioners.

FINANCE

Before April 6, 1975, contributions from employers, insured persons and the Exchequer were paid into, and benefits and administrative expenses were paid out of, a fund established under the Industrial Injuries Act, viz., the Industrial Injuries Fund.

Receipts, 1974–75	£'000
Balance, April 1, 1974................	400,479
Contributions from employers and insured persons.....................	154,555
Exchequer contribution...............	30,000
Income from investments..............	24,202
Other receipts.......................	967
	610,203

Payments, 1974–75		
Benefit:—	£'000	
Injury......................	34,999	
Disablement...............	110,097	
Death.....................	17,200	
Other benefits.............	4,099	
		166,395
Administration expenses...............		21,621
Balance, March 31, 1975..............		422,187
		610,203

PLANS FOR EARNINGS-RELATED PENSIONS

The Social Security Pensions Act, 1975, which became law in August 1975, embodied proposals for the future coordinated development of State and occupational pensions. When the Act comes into force in April 1978, the present flat-rate retirement and other State pensions will be replaced for employed earners by fully earnings-related pensions, but it will be twenty years after that before any pensions become payable at the full rate.

The aims of the Act will be, by providing better pensions, to reduce reliance upon means-tested supplementary benefit in old age, in widowhood and in chronic ill-health; to ensure that occupational pension schemes which are contracted out of part of the State scheme fulfil the conditions of a good scheme; that pensions are adequately protected against inflation; and that in both the State and occupational schemes men and women are treated equally.

Under the new State scheme retirement, invalidity and widow's pensions for employees will be related to the earnings on which contributions have been paid. The lower earnings limit for Class 1 contribution liability will be broadly the current level of the basic component of the retirement pension—in April 1975 terms £11·60 a week. Employees with earnings at or above this base level in any week will pay contributions on all their earnings up to a limit of about seven times the base level—in April 1975 terms about £80 a week. The standard rate of contribution set by the Act is 16½ per cent. (which includes 1 per cent. for the National Health Service and 0·2 per cent. for the Redundancy Fund), employees paying 6½ per cent. and employers 10 per cent., instead of the 1975 figures of 5½ per cent. and 8½ per cent. Provision is made for the rate to be reviewed before the new scheme comes into operation. Employees who are contracted out will pay the full rate of contribution on earnings up to the lower limit, but on higher earnings up to the upper limit the rate will be 9½ per cent. (4 per cent. for employees and 5½ per cent. for employers), the rate to be reviewed at intervals of not more than five years. The Treasury supplement will be 18 per cent. of all contributions, calculated so as to include those that would have been received if there had been no contracting out. Self-employed persons will pay contributions towards the basic pension. The non-employed and employees with earnings below the lower limit may contribute voluntarily for basic pension. Women who marry for the first time after the new scheme begins will no longer have a right to elect not to pay the full contribution rate. No primary Class 1 contributions or Class 2 or Class 4 contributions will be payable by persons who work beyond pension age (65 for men, 60 for women), but the employer's liability for secondary Class 1 contributions will continue.

The new system of earnings-related pensions for retirement, widowhood and invalidity to replace the present flat-rate schemes will provide for employees of either sex with a complete insurance record a category A pension in two parts, a basic and an additional component. The rate of the basic component set by the Act is £11·60 (the flat-rate pension payable under the present system from April 7, 1975): up to this level the pensioner will receive weekly, from the start of the new scheme, £1 for £1 of average weekly earnings on which contributions have been paid. The additional component will be 1¼ per cent. of average earnings above the level of the basic component and up to the upper earnings limit of about £80 for each year

of such earnings under the scheme, and will thus build up to 25 per cent. in twenty years. When the number of years exceeds twenty, pensions will be based on contributors' twenty best years of earnings between age 16 and pension age. Actual earnings are to be revalued in terms of the earnings level current in the last complete tax year before pension age (or death or incapacity). In April 1975 terms the total personal retirement pension at maturity under the new scheme would vary from £11·60 for average earnings of £11·60 a week to about £29·00 for average earnings of about £80 or over; a married couple's pension (on the husband's contribution record alone) from £18·50 to £35·90; and a married couple's pension (where both have contributed) from £23·20 to £58·00. The basic component of pensions in payment will be uprated annually in line with the movement of earnings or prices, whichever is increasing the faster, and the additional component in line with the movement of prices. Graduated retirement pensions in payment and rights to such pensions earned by people who are still working will be brought into the annual review of benefits. Among other steps to be taken to give women equal treatment in benefit provision the State scheme will permit years of home responsibilites to count towards satisfying the contribution conditions for retirement pension, widowed mother's allowance and widow's pension, and from April 1979 the " half-test " by which a married woman cannot qualify for a Category A retirement pension unless she has contributed on earnings at the basic level in at least half the years between marriage and pension age is to be abolished. The range of short-term social security benefits and industrial injury benefits under the Social Security Act, 1975, will continue with only minor changes: these will include the repeal of the provision which at present imposes a lower rate of sickness and unemployment benefit on married women.

Members of occupational pension schemes which meet the standards laid down by the Act can be contracted out of a part of the State retirement and widow's benefits. A contracted-out scheme will be required to provide a minimum level of pension calculated on a basis similar to that for the additional component of retirement pension under the State scheme, with a widow's pension at half this rate. The benefits payable from the State scheme will be correspondingly reduced. The State scheme will help in meeting the cost of giving pensions under contracted-out schemes the same protection against inflation as if they had not been contracted out. The Act contains provisions designed to give women the same rights as men to belong to an occupational pension scheme. The Occupational Pensions Board established under the Social Security Act, 1973, will be responsible for deciding whether an occupational scheme should be accepted as a contracted-out scheme, and for ensuring that a contracted-out scheme has adequate financial resources. The Secretary of State for Social Services is empowered to make regulations for requiring employers to inform employees and their organisations and to have consultations before making an election to contract out.

SUPPLEMENTARY BENEFITS

The Ministry of Social Security Act, 1966, as amended by later measures, enacted a scheme of non-contributory benefits termed supplementary allowances and pensions in place of national assistance and of non-contributory old age pensions, and vested responsibility for these supplementary benefits in a new Ministry of Social Security (now the Department of Health and Social Security).

A Supplementary Benefits Commission within the Department is now responsible, subject to Regulations made by the Secretary of State for Social Services, for operating the scheme of supplementary benefits.

The supplementary pension may be claimed by persons over pension age and the supplementary allowance by persons aged 16 or over but under pension age, who are not in full-time work. The benefit payable is the amount, assessed under the provisions of the Act, by which the claimant's income requirements exceed his resources. The basic weekly rates of supplementary benefit (exclusive of rent) since November 15, 1976, are as follows:

	Ordinary	Blind persons
	£	£
Married couple................	20·65	21·90 (a)
Single householder............	12·70	
Other persons:—		
Aged 18 or over............	10·15	13·95
Aged 16–17.................	7·80	8·70
Aged 13–15.................	6·50	6·50
Aged 11–12.................	5·35	5·35
Aged 5–10..................	4·35	4·35
Aged under 5...............	3·60	3·60

(a) £22·70 when both are blind.

The long-term weekly rates, which apply, with certain exceptions, to supplementary pensioners, and also to those below pension age, other than the unemployed who are required to register for work, after they have been in receipt of an allowance for two years, are as follows:

	Ordinary	Blind persons
	£	£
Married couple................	24·85	26·10 (a)
Single householder............	15·70	
Other persons aged 18 or over	12·60	16·95

(a) £26·90 when both are blind.

Where the claimant or a dependant is aged 80 or over a further 25p is added to these long-term rates. Any extra allowances on account of exceptional expenses, other than for heating and certain other items, will be set off against part of the long-term rates, viz., 50p (75p in the case of those over 80). See as to attendance allowances, p. 618.

The amount to be added for rent if the claimant (or his wife or her husband) is the householder is normally the net rent and rates in full; and, in the case of the non-householder aged 16 or over, £1·20 a week.

The rules for the computation of resources contain provisions for the treatment of capital and earnings and for certain disregards.

Individual awards of benefit are determined by the Commission; a claimant who is dissatisfied with the decision on his claim has a right of appeal to an independent Appeal Tribunal.

The Commission may vary an assessment if there are exceptional circumstances but, in the case of a claim to supplementary pension, may not reduce it. The Commission also has powers, similar to those in the national assistance scheme, to award lump-sum payments to meet non-recurring exceptional requirements, and to meet charges for appliances or services supplied under the National Health Service, e.g. for glasses, dentures or dental treatment, and prescriptions.

OLD PERSONS' PENSIONS

The Social Security Act, 1975, provides, subject to a residence test, a non-contributory retirement pension of £9·20 a week (£5·60 for a wife or other adult dependant) for persons who were over pen-

sionable age on July 5, 1948, and for women whose husbands are so entitled if they are over pension age and have retired from regular work, with increases for adult and child dependants (Category C pension); and for others when they reach 80 if they are not already getting a retirement pension of any category or if they are getting that pension at less than these rates (Category D pension). An *age addition* of 25p per week is payable if persons entitled to retirement pension or their dependants are aged 80 or over.

ATTENDANCE ALLOWANCES

The Act of 1975 provides for the payment out of Exchequer funds of a tax-free and non-means-tested attendance allowance to the severely disabled, as determined by the Attendance Allowance Board. The full rate of £12·20 a week is paid to those in need of a great deal of attention or supervision both by day and by night. The allowance is paid at the lower rate of £8·15 a week to those whose need for attention or supervision arises either by day or by night. The allowance is treated as an additional requirement under the supplementary benefits scheme.

NON-CONTRIBUTORY INVALIDITY PENSION

The Social Security Act, 1975, provides for a non-contributory invalidity pension for persons of working age, other than married women supported by their husbands, who have been incapable of work for a period of at least 28 weeks but who do not qualify for a contributory invalidity pension. The benefit has been payable since November 15, 1976, at the rate of £9·20 a week, with additions for dependants. The cost is met from the Consolidated Fund.

INVALID CARE ALLOWANCE

The Social Security Act, 1975, also provides for a non-contributory invalid care allowance for persons of working age, other than married women supported by their husbands, who are not gainfully employed because they are regularly and substantially engaged in caring for a severely disabled relative who is receiving attendance allowance. The benefit has been payable since November 15, 1976, at the rate of £9·20 a week, with additions for dependants. The cost is met from the Consolidated Fund.

MOBILITY ALLOWANCE

The Social Security Pensions Act, 1975, made provision for a new non-contributory cash benefit under the principal Act which, subject to certain conditions, is to be payable to persons over the age of 5 and under pensionable age who are suffering from such physical disablement that they are unable to walk or virtually unable to do so, and their handicap is likely to last for at least a year. The allowance which is taxable is being introduced for different age groups over a period of three years or less starting in January, 1976. The weekly rate of the allowance is initially £5·00, but provision has been made for the rate to be reviewed in each tax year.

GUARDIAN'S ALLOWANCE

Where the parents of a child are dead, the person who has the child in his family receives a guardian's allowance of £7·45 a week while the child is of qualifying age. The allowance is a non-contributory benefit under the Social Security Act, 1975, and, on certain conditions, is payable on the death of only one parent. The allowance cannot be claimed in addition to family allowance or other benefits for children.

FAMILY ALLOWANCES AND CHILD BENEFIT

Until April 4, 1977, family allowances of £1·50 a week will continue to be payable out of moneys provided by Parliament for each child in a family after the first while he or she is of school age or under, and up to 19 if he or she is undertaking full-time instruction in a school or is an apprentice. Until the same date child interim benefit, a new benefit introduced in April, 1976, under the Child Benefit Act, 1975, will be payable at £1·50 a week for the first or only child within the age limits in certain one-parent families.

From April 5, 1977, when the permanent provisions of the Child Benefit Act come into operation, family allowances and child interim benefit will be replaced by child benefit payable for all children in a family within the age limits, including the first or only child. The rates at the outset will be £1·00 for the first or only child (£1·50 in the case of certain one-parent families) and £1·50 for each child after the first. Consequential adjustments will be made in dependency benefit for first or only children under the Social Security Act, 1975.

FAMILY INCOME SUPPLEMENT

A benefit met out of Exchequer funds is payable under the Family Income Supplements Act, 1970, and regulations made thereunder, to families, including a single person, with at least one dependent child under 16 (or over 16 if still at school), whose total family income is below the "prescribed amount" if the head of the family (in the case of a couple, the man) is employed or self-employed, and normally so engaged, in remunerative full-time work (i.e., 30 or more hours work a week). The "prescribed amount" is £39·00 if there is one child in the family and rises by £4·50 for each additional child. "Total income" includes gross earnings, family allowances and a wife's earnings. The supplement is one-half of the amount by which the family's total income falls below the "prescribed amount", subject, since July 20, 1976, to a maximum payment of £8·50 for families with one child, rising by 50p for each additional child: odd amounts are rounded up to the next 10p above, and the minimum amount payable is 20p a week. Usually the supplement is awarded for 52 weeks and is not affected if the claimant's circumstances change during that time. Claim forms can be obtained at a Social Security Office or a Post Office. Claims are decided by the Supplementary Benefits Commission but there is an appeal to an independent Appeal Tribunal.

NATIONAL INSURANCE CONTRIBUTIONS

From April 6, 1975, when the National Insurance and Industrial Injuries schemes were replaced by a new scheme of social security benefits and contributions under the Social Security Act, 1975, combined weekly flat-rate Class 1 contributions ceased to be payable, and the graduated pension scheme was wound up (existing rights being preserved). Under the new scheme employees and their employers both pay wholly earnings-related contributions, based on a percentage of the employee's earnings (Class 1). Self-employed persons continue to pay flat-rate Class 2 contributions, but may also be liable to pay a contribution (Class 4) based on their profits or gains within certain limits. Class 3 contributions are voluntary, and may be paid to help qualify for certain benefits, including retirement pension. The contribution rates and earnings limits stated below apply for the tax year starting on April 6, 1976.

Class 1 contributions.—Primary Class 1 contributions are payable by employed earners and office holders over minimum school-leaving age with gross earnings at or above the lower earnings limit of £13 a week. For those with gross earnings at or above this level, contributions are payable on *all* earnings up to an upper limit of £95 a week. "Gross earnings" include overtime pay, commission, bonus, etc., without deduction of any superannuation contributions. The standard rate of primary contribution is 5·75 per cent. of reckonable earnings (National Insurance Fund 5·35 per cent.; National Health Service 0·4 per cent.). Married women and most widows who have elected not to pay contributions at the full rate pay at a reduced rate of 2 per cent. over the same earnings range: this covers industrial injuries benefits and a contribution of 0·4 per cent. to the National Health Service. An election or change of election relates to complete tax years. No primary contributions are payable by retirement pensioners when in employment, by persons over pension age with no title to pension, or by men over 70 and women over 65 who continue to work. *Secondary* Class 1 contributions are payable by employers of employed earners, and by the appropriate authorities in the case of office-holders, except in the case of persons earning less than the lower earnings limit of £13 a week. The rate is 8·75 per cent. (National Insurance Fund 7·95 per cent; National Health Service 0·6 per cent; Redundancy Fund 0·2 per cent.) over the same earnings range as primary contributions (regardless of the employed earner's contribution rate). Primary contributions are deducted from earnings by the employer, and are paid, together with the employer's contributions, to the Inland Revenue along with income tax collected under the PAYE system, so dispensing with contribution cards for employed earners.

Class 2 contributions.—These contributions are payable by self-employed earners over school-leaving age at a flat-rate normally of £2·41 a week for men and £2·20 for women. The women's rate is to be raised to the men's rate by 1980. Those with earnings below £775 a year can apply for exception from liability to pay Class 2 contributions for the tax year 1976–77. Married women and most widows can choose whether or not to pay Class 2 contributions when self-employed. An election or change of election relates to complete tax years. No Class 2 contributions are payable by retirement pensioners when self-employed, by persons over pension age with no title to pension, or by men over 70 and women over 65 who continue to work. There are special rules for those who are concurrently employed and self-employed. Class 2 contributions may be paid by direct debit of a bank or National Giro account or by stamping a contribution card. People who while self-employed are excepted from liability to pay contributions on the grounds of small earnings may pay either Class 2 or Class 3 contributions voluntarily. Self-employed earners (whether or not they pay Class 2 contributions) may also be liable to pay Class 4 contributions based on profits or gains within certain limits.

Class 3 contributions.—These are voluntary flat-rate contributions payable by persons over school-leaving age who would otherwise be unable to qualify for retirement pension and certain other benefits because they have an insufficient record of Class 1 or Class 2 contributions. The rate is £2·10 a week. Payment may be made by stamping a contribution card or by direct debit through a bank or Giro account. Married women and widows who have elected not to pay Class 1 (full rate) or Class 2 contributions cannot pay Class 3 contributions.

Class 4 contributions.—These contributions are payable by self-employed earners under 70 (65 for women), whether or not they pay class 2 contributions, on annual profits or gains from a trade, profession or vocation chargeable to income tax under Schedule D. The rate of contribution is 8 per cent. (including a contribution of 0·6 per cent. to the National Health Service) of such profits or gains falling between £1,600 and £4,900 a year. The maximum Class 4 contribution, payable on profits or gains of £4,900 or more, is £264. The contribution is based on profits or gains subject to certain allowances and relief, which differ in some respects from those for income tax. Class 4 contributions are generally assessed and collected by the Inland Revenue along with Schedule D income tax. Self-employed persons under 16, or who are over pension age and have retired from regular work or are treated as having retired, or do not qualify for a retirement pension on their own contributions, can apply for exception from liability for Class 4 contributions. There are special rules for people who have more than one job, or who pay Class 1 contributions on earnings which are chargeable to income tax under Schedule D.

The cuts in public spending announced by the Chancellor of the Exchequer in the House of Commons on July 22, 1976, were accompanied by an increase from April 6, 1977, of 2 percentage points in employers' national insurance (secondary Class 1) contributions.

Leaflets relating to each class of contribution, and an employer's guide to national insurance contributions, are obtainable from local Social Security offices.

CONFEDERATION OF BRITISH INDUSTRY
21 Tothill Street, London, S.W.1.

The Confederation of British Industry was founded in August 1965 to promote the prosperity of British industry and those elements of British business closely associated with it. It combines in a single, democratic and voluntary association the rôles previously played by the British Employers' Confederation, the Federation of British Industries and the National Association of British Manufacturers.

The C.B.I. is recognized nationally and internationally as the representative organization of the management side of industry for the United Kingdom. It acts as a national point of reference for all those who seek the views of industry and management and it advises the Government on all aspects of Government policy which affect the interests of industry and business, both at home and abroad.

Membership of the C.B.I. consists of more than 10,000 companies and over 200 trade associations and employers' organizations. In addition to these most of the nationalized industries are in membership as public sector members and thereby able to work with the C.B.I. on problems that are the concern of all management.

The governing body of the C.B.I. is the Council, which meets monthly in London. It is assisted by some 30 expert standing committees which advise on the main aspects of policy. There is a C.B.I. Regional Council and seven C.B.I. offices in the administrative regions of England and offices and Councils covering Scotland, Wales and Northern Ireland. These Regional Councils send their representatives to the governing body. The C.B.I. is represented in more than 100 centres overseas.

The C.B.I. provides its members with a wide range of services and practical advice on economic, industrial relations, commercial, technical, social and export questions. The organization is financed by the subscriptions of its members.

President, The Lord Watkinson, P.C., C.H.

Vice-Presidents, Sir Michael Clapham, K.B.E., Sir Ralph Bateman, K.B.E.

Director-General, J. Methven.

Secretary, E. M. Felgate.

NATIONAL BUILDING AGENCY
N.B.A. House, Arundel Street, W.C.2
(North St. Andrew Street, Edinburgh; Bedford House, Bedford Street, Belfast; 115 Portland Place, Manchester; Caerwys House, Windsor Place, Cardiff; Newton House, Sauchiehall Street, Charing Cross, Glasgow 2; 187A West Street, Sheffield.)

The NBA is a Government-sponsored, non-profit distributing Agency, whose aims are to encourage improved methods of design, construction and management in the building industry. Founded in 1964 it was initially concerned with the appraisal of building systems (which it now does jointly with the Agrément Board) with metrication and with demonstration housing projects. Currently it provides a wide range of technical and building management services to public authorities, housing associations, government departments and private clients. It receives a grant from the Department of the Environment for certain services to the local authorities and the Housing Corporation, but charges normal fees for its consultancy work.

Chairman (part-time), The Lord Goodman, C.H.

Managing Director, A. W. Cleeve Barr, C.B.E., F.R.I.B.A.

HOME-GROWN CEREALS AUTHORITY
Hamlyn House, Highgate Hill, N.19.

Constituted under the Cereals Marketing Act, 1965, the Authority consists of 9 members representing cereal growers, 9 representing dealers in, or processors of, grain and 5 independent members. The purpose of the Authority is to improve the marketing of home-grown cereals. Production now exceeds 15 million tons per annum; at full E.E.C. prices this is valued at over £1,200,000,000. The Authority is empowered by the Act to provide a market intelligence service; to operate schemes for the encouragement of forward sales, and the orderly phasing of supplies according to market needs; and to undertake research aimed at the expansion of the market for home-grown cereals. It has been appointed executive agent for the Intervention Board for Agricultural Produce in respect of the denaturing of wheat and intervention buying,

storage and disposal of cereals under the Common Agricultural Policy of the E.E.C. It submits advice to Ministers on matters affecting cereals marketing.

Chairman, Sir Henry Hardman, K.C.B.

Deputy Chairman, Dr. Clare Burgess, C.B.E.

Members (Independent), The Lord Collison, C.B.E.; Prof. D. K. Britton; O. G. Williams, C.B.E.

(*Cereal Growers*), R. Ankers; G. E. Daniels; K. Deighton; J. Macaulay; S. W. Passmore; E. Richards; P. Savory; S. Shaw; J. Stobo.

(*Merchants, Dealers & Processors*), K. J. Arnott; N. B. Baird; F. S. D. Brown; J. R. Crawford; J. Gray, O.B.E., T.D.; P. A. Metaxa; H. Paul, O.B.E.; B. C. Read; L. J. Wright.

General Manager and Secretary, H. Pitchforth.

PERIODS OF GESTATION AND INCUBATION
The table shows approximate periods of gestation or incubation for some common animals and birds. In some cases the periods may vary and where doubt arises professional advice should be sought.

Species	Shortest Period. Days	Usual Period. Days	Longest Period. Days	Species	Shortest Period. Days	Usual Period. Days	Longest Period. Days
Human	240	273	313	Turkey	25	28	28
Mare	305	336	340	Duck	28	28	32
Ass	365	—	374	Goose	28	30	32
Cow	273	280	294	Pigeon	17	18	19
Ewe	140	147–50	160	Canary	12	14	14
Goat	147	151	155	Guinea Pig	63	—	70
Sow	109	112	125	Mouse	18	—	19
Bitch	55	63	70	Rat	21	—	24
Cat	53	56	63	Elephant		2 years	
Rabbit	30	32	35	Camel		45 weeks	
Hen	20	21	22	Zebra		56 weeks	

THE UNITED KINGDOM

Area.—The land area of the United Kingdom (England, Wales, Scotland and N. Ireland) is 93,026 sq. miles or 59,537,000 acres. The area of inland water* in the United Kingdom is 1,190 sq. miles. Total 94,216 sq. miles.

	Land Area		Inland water*	Total
	Sq. miles	'000 acres	Sq. miles	Sq. miles
England........................	50,053	32,034	280	50,334
Wales...........................	7,969	5,100	48	8,016
Scotland........................	29,798	19,071	616	30,414
Northern Ireland................	5,206	3,332	246	5,452

*Excluding tidal water

POPULATION: CENSUS RESULTS, 1801–1971   Thousands

	United Kingdom			England and Wales			Scotland			Northern Ireland†		
	Total	Male	Female	Total	Male	Female	Total	Male	Female	Total	Male	Female
1801	11,944	5,692	6,252	8,893	4,255	4,638	1,608	739	869	1,443	698	745
1811	13,368	6,368	7,000	10,165	4,874	5,291	1,806	826	980	1,397	668	729
1821	15,472	7,498	7,974	12,000	5,850	6,150	2,092	983	1,109	1,380	665	715
1831	17,835	8,647	9,188	13,897	6,771	7,126	2,364	1,114	1,250	1,574	762	812
1841	20,183	9,819	10,364	15,914	7,778	8,137	2,620	1,242	1,378	1,649	800	849
1851	22,259	10,855	11,404	17,928	8,781	9,146	2,889	1,376	1,513	1,443	698	745
1861	24,525	11,894	12,631	20,066	9,776	10,290	3,062	1,450	1,612	1,396	668	728
1871	27,431	13,309	14,122	22,712	11,059	11,653	3,360	1,603	1,757	1,359	647	712
1881	31,015	15,060	15,955	25,974	12,640	13,335	3,736	1,799	1,936	1,305	621	684
1891	34,264	16,593	17,671	29,003	14,060	14,942	4,026	1,943	2,083	1,236	590	646
1901	38,237	18,492	19,745	32,528	15,729	16,799	4,472	2,174	2,298	1,237	590	647
1911	42,082	20,357	21,725	36,070	17,446	18,625	4,761	2,309	2,452	1,251	603	648
1921	44,027	21,033	22,994	37,887	18,075	19,811	4,882	2,348	2,535	1,258	610	648
1931	46,038	22,060	23,978	39,952	19,133	20,819	4,843	2,326	2,517	1,243	601	642
1951	50,225	24,118	26,107	43,758	21,016	22,742	5,096	2,434	2,662	1,371	668	703
1961	52,709	25,481	27,228	46,105	22,304	23,801	5,179	2,483	2,697	1,425	694	731
1971	55,515	26,952	28,562	48,750	23,683	25,067	5,229	2,515	2,714	1,536	755	781

NOTES.—1. Before 1801 there existed no official return of the population of either England or Scotland. Estimates of the population of England at various periods, calculated from the number of baptisms, burials and marriages, are: in 1570, 4,160,221; 1600, 4,811,718; 1630, 5,600,517; 1670, 5,773,646; 1700, 6,045,008; 1750, 6,517,035.

2. The last official Census of Population in respect of England and Wales, Scotland, Northern Ireland, the Isle of Man and Guernsey, was taken on the night of April 25, 1971, and in respect of Jersey on April 4, 1971. The figures for 1971 are based on the final results of the 1971 Census.

3.†All figures refer to the area which is now Northern Ireland. Figures for N. Ireland in 1921 and 1931 are estimates based on the Censuses held in 1926 and 1937.

ISLANDS.—*The figures given above do not include islands of the British seas.* Populations of these islands at census years since 1900 were:—

	ISLE OF MAN			JERSEY			GUERNSEY		
	Total	Male	Female	Total	Male	Female	Total	Male	Female
1901............	54,752	25,496	29,256	52,576	23,940	28,636	43,042	21,140	21,902
1911............	52,016	23,937	28,079	51,898	24,014	27,884	45,001	22,215	22,786
1921............	60,284	27,329	32,955	49,701	22,438	27,263	40,529	19,303	21,226
1931............	49,308	22,443	26,865	50,462	23,424	27,038	42,743	20,675	22,068
1951............	55,123	25,749	29,464	57,296	27,282	30,014	45,747	22,094	23,380
1961............	48,151	22,060	26,091	57,200	27,200	30,000	47,178	22,890	24,288
1971............	56,289	26,461	29,828	72,532	35,423	37,109	52,708	25,382	27,326

INCREASE OF THE PEOPLE

Mid-year estimates of the future total population of the United Kingdom are based on estimates by the Registrars General of the total population at mid-1973. The projections have been prepared by the Government Actuary's Department in consultation with the Registrars General. It is assumed in their projections below that, at ages under 60 for males and 70 for females, death rates will decline over the period of the projection until after 40 years, they are three-quarters of present rates. Above these ages the assumed improvement becomes proportionately smaller as age advances until they vanish at ages over 90. Annual live births implied in the projections are 751,000 in mid-1973/74, 735,000 in

1974/75 and 732,000 in 1975/76 followed by a gradual increase in birth and fertility rates until 1983/84 when the number of births reaches 914,000. The projection for 2001/02 is 845,000 and for 2012/2013 is 950,000. The ratio of male to female births is taken as 1·06 (N. Ireland 1·07) throughout and allowance has been made for a net outward migration of 19,000 in 1973/74 rising to 50,000 a year from 1978 onwards.

Estimated Future Population of the U.K.
Thousands

1973 (base) . 56,021	1991 . 57,988	2011 . . . 60,754
1981 56,302	2001 . 59,368	

LOCAL GOVERNMENT IN ENGLAND AND WALES

The Local Government Act, 1972 provided for the reorganisation of local government in England (outside Greater London whose local government was reorganised in 1965) and Wales. On April 1, 1974 the former county, county borough, and county district councils were abolished. Two tiers of new local authorities, county and district councils, covering metropolitan and non-metropolitan counties and districts, replaced them.

Structure and Areas in England

Six *metropolitan counties* cover the main conurbations outside Greater London: Tyne and Wear, West Midlands, Merseyside, Greater Manchester, West Yorkshire and South Yorkshire. They range in population from 1,200,000 (Tyne and Wear) to 2,800,000 (West Midlands). Each metropolitan county extends to the edge of the general continuously built-up area of the conurbation. Thus each of the major conurbations outside London has now one local authority to administer strategic functions over the whole conurbation.

The six metropolitan counties are divided into 36 *metropolitan districts*. These range in population from 173,000 (South Tyneside) to 1,100,000 (Birmingham). Most of them have a population of over 200,000 and most include a former county borough. They form compact areas.

There are 39 *non-metropolitan counties* ranging in population from 110,000 (Isle of Wight) and 283,000 (Northumberland) to 1,400,000 (Kent). These counties have generally been formed by combining former administrative counties and associated county boroughs, i.e. they are based on geographical counties. There are, however, three completely new non-metropolitan counties: Avon, Cleveland, and Humberside. Some former counties have been merged to form Cumbria (Cumberland, Westmorland and the Furness area of Lancashire); Hereford and Worcester; Cambridgeshire (Huntingdon and Peterborough and Cambridgeshire and Isle of Ely); and Leicestershire (Leicestershire and Rutland). Smaller boundary adjustments have been made between, e.g. Berkshire and Oxfordshire, Buckinghamshire and Berkshire, and Hampshire and Dorset.

Each of the non-metropolitan counties is divided into *non-metropolitan districts*, of which there are 296. These districts have been formed generally by the amalgamation of former county districts to cover areas with populations broadly between 60,000 and 100,000. About one third of the non-metropolitan districts, however, have populations above this range because of the need to avoid dividing large towns. Some districts, mainly in sparsely populated areas, have populations below 60,000 though only 14 have populations below 40,000 (as compared with three quarters of the 1,210 former authorities).

Permanent Local Government Boundary Commissions for England and Wales have been set up to keep the areas and electoral arrangements of the new local authorities under review.

Constitution and Elections

The new county and district councils consist of directly elected councillors. The broad range of sizes of councils are: county councils 60–100 members; metropolitan district councils 50–80 members; non-metropolitan district councils 30–60 members. The councillors elect annually one of their number as chairman. There are no aldermen under the new system, though councils may give past councillors the title "honorary alderman". The title carries no right to sit on the council.

All the new authorities were elected *en bloc* in 1973 (as "shadow" authorities until they took on their functions on April 1, 1974). After a transitional period all councillors will be elected for a term of four years. All county councils will be elected *en bloc* in 1977 and every four years thereafter. One third of the councillors for each ward of each metropolitan district will be elected from 1975 in each of the three years between county council elections. Non-metropolitan district councils can choose whether to have elections on the county council or metropolitan district council basis. Most of their electoral areas will need revision and the next elections will therefore be held in 1976 on a whole council basis. If they choose whole council elections these will be held in the mid-year between county council elections. If they choose elections by thirds, for geographical reasons it may not be practicable to arrange for elections by thirds in every ward. Local elections will normally be held on the first Thursday in May.

Greater London (See below) is not affected by reorganisation. Elections to local authorities in Greater London are, however, to be brought into line with the rest of England so that the normal term of office for councillors on the G.L.C. and the London Borough Councils will be four years instead of three. Greater London Council elections will take place in the same year as county council elections in 1977 and every fourth year thereafter. Aldermen will cease to sit as members of the G.L.C. after the 1977 elections. The next London Borough Council elections will be held in May 1978. Aldermen will cease to sit as members of London Borough Councils after the 1978 elections.

Internal Organisation and Local Government Services in England

The council are the final decision making body within any authority. They are free to a great extent to make their own internal organisational arrangements. Normally questions of major policy are settled by the full council, while the administration of the various services is the responsibility of committees of members. Day to day decisions are delegated to the council's officers, who act within the policies laid down by the members.

Many councils have set up corporate management teams of the Chief Executive and chief officers. Such teams consider the operations of their authority as a whole, rather than dealing with each service separately, as was often the case in the past.

Local authorities are empowered or required by various Acts of Parliament to carry out functions in their areas. The legislation concerned comprises public general Acts and "local" Acts which local authorities have promoted as private bills. Functions are divided everywhere between two tiers of authorities, though their allocation within the metropolitan areas is somewhat different from outside, the metropolitan district councils exercising more functions than the non-metropolitan district councils.

Responsibility for the main local government functions is allocated as follows (though responsible authorities may involve other authorities in the provision of certain of their services through agency arrangements):

County councils: Strategic planning (e.g. structure plans; major projects); traffic, transport and highways; police; fire service; consumer protection (other than hygiene); refuse disposal; smallholdings.

Non-metropolitan county and metropolitan district councils: Education; social services; libraries.

District Councils: Local planning: housing; high-

ways (maintenance of certain urban roads and off-street car parks); building regulations; environmental health; refuse collection; cemeteries and crematoria.

Concurrent (county and district councils); Recreation (e.g. parks, playing fields, swimming pools); museums: encouragement of the arts.

The sewerage and sewage disposal functions of local authorities have been transferred to 9 new water authorities and the Welsh National Water Development Authority. Water authorities, however, are expected to make agreements whereby the new district councils discharge sewerage functions on an agency basis. Apart from these functions, the water authorities are responsible for water supply and conservation; river pollution control and river management; fisheries; land drainage; and use of water space for recreation and amenity purposes.

The personal health functions of local authorities have been transferred to area health authorities, whose areas are the same as non-metropolitan and Welsh counties and metropolitan districts. The area health authorities will work within strategies formulated by regional health authorities. They will work in close collaboration with local education, social services and environmental health authorities.

London.—The Greater London Area embraces the old counties of London and Middlesex (except Potter's Bar, Staines and Sunbury-on-Thames) and parts of the neighbouring counties of Essex, Herts., Kent and Surrey and the whole of the county boroughs of Croydon, East Ham and West Ham.

For those functions which need to be considered for the whole of the Area, the Greater London Council is responsible; such functions as traffic, major roads and overall planning. All other matters are the concern of the 32 London borough councils; the City of London, besides retaining its previous functions, has the powers of a London borough.

Parishes

The existing rural parishes in England are generally not affected by local government reorganisation except that the powers of parish councils have been extended and a few of them have been divided by the boundaries of new counties and districts. 300 former small borough and urban district councils have become parish councils with the same powers as other parish councils.

Parishes with 200 or more electors must generally have parish councils, and about three-quarters of the parishes have councils. A parish council comprises at least 5 members, the number being fixed by the district council. All parishes have parish meetings, comprising the electors of the parish.

Parish council functions include; allotments; arts and crafts; community halls, recreational facilities (e.g. open spaces, swimming pools); cemeteries and crematoria; and many minor functions. They must also be given an opportunity to comment on planning applications. They may, like county and district councils, spend up to a 2p rate for the general benefit of the parish. They precept on the district councils for their rate funds. Parish councils will be elected, after a transitional period, every four years, in the year in which the local district councillor is elected.

Civic dignities

District councils may petition for a royal charter granting borough status to the district. In boroughs the chairman of the council is the mayor. The status " city " with or without the right to call the mayor " Lord Mayor " may also be granted

by letters patent. Parish councils may call themselves " town councils ", in which case their chairman is the " town mayor ".

Charter trustees are established for those former boroughs which are too large to have parish councils and are situated in districts without city or borough status. The charter trustees are the district councillors representing the former borough and they elect a mayor, continue civic tradition, and look after the charters, insignia and civic plate of the former borough.

Local Government Elections

Generally speaking, all British subjects or citizens of the Republic of Ireland of 18 years or over, resident on the qualifying date in the area for which the election is being held are entitled to vote at local government elections. A register of electors is prepared and published annually by local electoral registration officers.

A returning officer has the overall responsibility for an election. Voting takes place at polling stations, arranged by the local authority and under the supervision of a presiding officer specially appointed for the purpose. Candidates, who are subject to various statutory qualifications and disqualifications designed to secure that they are suitable persons to hold office, must be nominated by electors for the electoral area concerned.

Local Commissioners for England and Wales

There now exist Local Commissioners for England and Wales whose duty it is to investigate complaints of maladministration in many aspects of local government.

Wales

Wales, including the former Monmouthshire, has been divided into eight counties; Gwynedd; Clwyd; Powys; Dyfed; West, Mid and South Glamorgan; and Gwent. They range in population from 99,000 (Powys) to 536,000 (Mid-Glamorgan). There are 37 new districts in Wales, many of those in the less populated parts reflecting the areas of former Welsh counties. Their populations range from 18,000 (Radnor) to 285,000 (Cardiff).

The arrangements for Welsh counties and districts are generally similar to those for English non-metropolitan counties and districts. There are some differences in functions: Welsh district councils have refuse disposal as well as refuse collection functions and they may provide on-street as well as off-street car parks with the consent of the county council. A few districts have also been designated as library authorities.

In Wales parishes have been replaced by communities. Unlike England, where many areas are not in any parish, communities have been established for the whole of Wales; there is one for each Welsh parish, county borough, borough or urban district (or part where the former area is divided by a new boundary). Community meetings may be convened as and when desired. Community councils already exist where there were formerly parish councils, and also in nearly all the former boroughs and urban districts, and further councils may be established at the request of the community meeting. Community councils have broadly the same range of powers as English parish councils. Community councillors will be elected *en bloc* on the same basis as parish councillors in England, i.e. at the same time as a district council election and for a term of four years.

Local Government Finance

Local government is financed from various sources. (1) *Rates.*—Levied by district councils and in London by the City Corporation and the London

boroughs. Sums required by the Greater London Council and by county councils are included ·in the rates levied by London boroughs and district councils. Rates are levied by a poundage tax on the rateable value of property in the area of the rating authority. Under the General Rate Act, 1967, rating authorities are required to charge a lower rate in the pound on dwellings than on property generally in their area. Differentials of 13p and 18½p for England (33½p and 36p for Wales) respectively were prescribed for 1974–75 and 1975–76. New valuation lists, prepared by valuation officers of the Board of Inland Revenue, came into force on April 1, 1973. These are updated as new property enters the list, and changes to existing property necessitate amendments to the rateable value. The lists remain in force until the next general revaluation due in 1980. Certain types of property are exempt from rates, e.g. agricultural land and buildings, and churches. Some charities and other non-profit making organisations can receive partial exemption. Under the General Rate Act, 1967, as amended by the Local Government Act, 1974, local authorities can resolve to rate specified classes of empty property by an amount up to 100 per cent. of the full rates. Since April 1, 1974 rating authorities must levy a surcharge on empty commercial property at double the normal rates for the first twelve months, treble the rates for the second twelve months and so on progressively during the period of non-use. The Local Government Act, 1974, also makes provision for rate rebates for domestic ratepayers, regardless of the type of property in which they live, eligibility depending on income and family circumstances.

(2) *Government Grants.*—In addition to specific Government grants in aid of revenue expenditure on particular services, from April 1, 1974 grants known as rate support grants are payable to local authorities under the provisions of Part 2 of the Local Government Act, 1974. These grants, which replace the block grants previously paid under the Local Government Act, 1966, consist of three elements: the needs element, the resources element and the domestic element. The needs element, which is payable to non-metropolitan counties, metropolitan districts, London boroughs, the City of London, and the Isles of Scilly, is intended to compensate for variations between authorities in the amount they need to spend per head of population to provide a comparable level of service. The grant is distributed to local authorities on the basis of a distribution formula, which may vary from year to year, using various objective factors for measuring the relative needs of each authority. The resources element is payable to those rating authorities whose rateable resources per head of population fall short of a prescribed national standard for the year, and is so calculated to bring their resources effectively up to that national standard. The domestic element is payable to all rating authorities to reimburse them for the cost of giving the domestic rate relief prescribed for the year.

In order to arrive at the total amount of the rate support grants to local authorities in England and Wales for any year, the aggregate of Exchequer grants to local authorities in respect of their relevant expenditure for the year is determined in advance (housing subsidies and specific grants towards expenditure on rate rebates and mandatory awards to students and trainee teachers are outside this aggregate amount) and from this is deducted the estimated amount of specific grants for the year in aid of revenue expenditure and the supplementary grants for transport purposes and in connection with national parks; the resulting balance is the

amount of rate support grant. This amount can be subsequently increased if there is a substantial increase in the relevant expenditure of local authorities due to an increase in the level of prices, costs or remuneration, or because later legislation has created new areas of expenditure.

Forecasts of local authority relevant expenditure for 1976–77 in England and Wales adopted by the Government for rate support grant purposes were as follows. The amounts given are at November 1975 prices.

Service	£M
Education	£5,296
Libraries, Museums and Art Galleries	178
Port Health	2
Personal Social Services	874
Concessionary Fares	62
Police	837
Fire	216
Urban Programme	26
Administration of Justice	95
Other Home Office Services	20
Local Transport Finance	1078
Refuse	279
Recreation, Parks and Baths	291
Town and Country Planning	201
General Administration	264
Housing	348
Miscellaneous Services	394
Total	10,461

The aggregate amount of Exchequer grants for 1976–77 was determined at £6,852,000,000 being 65·5 per cent. of the estimated relevant expenditure. Of this, the specific revenue grants and the transport and National Parks supplementary grants were estimated at £931,000,000 giving a total for rate support grants of £5,921,000,000 of which £3,565,000,000 was in respect of the needs element, £640,000,000 the domestic element and £1,716,000,000 the resources element.

Rates and Rateable Values.—The total rateable value for England and Wales on April 1, 1975 was £6,742,000,000. The latest estimate of the amount to be raised in rates (net of rate rebates) in 1976–77 is £4,135,000,000.

Average Rates.—The estimated average rates levied in England in 1976–77 were: Inner London Boroughs, *domestic rate* 48·6p, *non-domestic rate* 69·2p; Outer London, 55·6p and 74·8p; Metropolitan Districts, 56·2p and 75·4p; Non-metropolitan districts, 51·6p and 71p. In Wales the estimated average rates levied were, *domestic rate* 50·3p, *non-domestic rate*, 87p. The average rates levied in England and Wales were estimated as 52·7p (*domestic*) and 72·4p (*non-domestic*).

SCOTLAND

Under the new structure of local government, in terms of the Local Government (Scotland) Act, 1973, which came into administrative effect on May 16, 1975, Scotland is for local government purposes divided into 9 regions, and 3 islands areas covering respectively Orkney, Shetland and the Western Isles. Within the regions there is a second independent tier of 53 districts.

Functions.—Regions and districts have separate responsibility for specific functions. In addition they share responsibility for certain concurrent functions. Islands area councils are all-purpose authorities responsible in these areas for the functions (except police and fire services) which are the separate or concurrent responsibility of regions and districts.

Regional Functions.—The new regional authorities are directly responsible for overall planning strategy and the highly technical or expensive services, e.g. the provision of major infrastructure services including transportation, roads and passenger transport, airports, water, sewerage, river purification, flood prevention, as well as education, social work, police and fire services.

District Functions.—The district authorities deal with more local matters such as local planning; development control; building control; housing; environmental health including cleansing, refuse collection and disposal, food hygiene, inspection of shops, offices and factories, clean air, markets and slaughterhouses, burial and cremation; regulation and licensing, including cinemas and theatres, betting and gaming, taxis, house to house collections; libraries.

Concurrent Functions.—These include countryside and tourism, industrial development, recreation parks, art galleries and museums.

Community Councils.—Provision is also made in the Act for setting up community councils under schemes prepared by each district and islands authority. The Act required that the schemes be submitted to the Secretary of State for approval by May 16, 1976. Such councils are not local authorities but have a statutory base. They have no statutory functions but are expected to take such action in the community as appears to their members to be desirable and practicable.

Local Government Electors.—In October 1975 there were 3,763,194 electors in Scotland. The first ordinary elections of all the new authorities took place on May 7, 1974.

Rates and Rateable Values.—In 1973–74, the latest year for which final figures were available, a total of £285,085,000 was received from the general rates of local government in Scotland and £11,939,000 from domestic water rates. The rate-

able value on which rates were leviable was £296,668,000 on the general rates and £172,869,000 on the domestic water rates. The average general rate levied was 96p and the domestic water rate levied was 7p.

Provisional figures for 1974–75 show total receipts from general rates of £331,968,000 and £14,762,000 from domestic water rates, and £434,801,000 and £18,235,000 for 1975–76. The rateable value leviable for 1974–75 was £301,127,000 (general) and £174,055,000 (domestic water rate) and £309,484,000 (general) and £174,936,000 (domestic water rate) for 1975–76. The average rate per £ levied for 1974–75 was 110p (general) and 8·5p (domestic water) and 140·5p (general) and 10·5p (domestic water) for 1975–76.

NORTHERN IRELAND

On October 1, 1973 a single-tier system of 26 district councils, based on the main centres of population, replaced the former system of two-tier county and district and the single-tier county borough councils.

The new district councils are responsible for a wide range of local services including refuse collection and disposal, the provision and maintenance of recreational and social facilities, street cleansing, environmental health, tourist development, enforcement of building regulations, miscellaneous licensing and registration matters, and gas supply.

They have in addition a consultative function, partly statutory and partly administrative, in relation to roads, housing, water and planning and also nominate representatives as members of public bodies responsible for education, health and housing.

Electors:—The register published on February 15, 1975, contained the names of 1,039,544 local government electors. Of this total, 252,992 related to the City of Belfast and 50,642 to Londonderry District.

THE NATIONAL PARKS

The ten National Parks described below in their order of designation have been established in England and Wales. These areas are not public property and visitors are not free to wander over private land within the Park boundaries. They have been marked out for special care aimed at two prime purposes: to preserve and enhance their natural beauty, and to promote their enjoyment by the public.

Peak District National Park (542 sq. miles).—Mainly in Derbyshire but extending into Staffordshire, Cheshire, South Yorkshire, West Yorkshire and Greater Manchester. In the south and east are limestone uplands, and finely wooded dales with swift, clear rivers and unspoilt stone villages. Northwards, moorlands, edged by gritstone crags, attract hill walkers and climbers. There are information centres at Bakewell, Edale, Castleton and at Buxton (just outside the Park) and an information caravan tours the Park

Lake District National Park (866 sq. miles).—In Cumbria. Spectacular mountain scenery with wooded lower slopes enhanced by lakes and tarns. The area includes England's highest mountains (Scafell Pike, Helvellyn and Skiddaw) and largest lakes. Walking and rock-climbing are the principal recreations, but there are fishing, swimming, sailing, boating and winter sports as well. There are information centres at Keswick, Ambleside and Bowness. Information vans are sited at Waterhead, Coniston, Glenridding and Hawkeshead. At Brockhole, Windermere, is a National Park centre.

Snowdonia National Park (838 sq. miles).—In Gwynedd in North Wales. A mountainous region supporting farms, forest, reservoirs and power stations and traversed by high passes, offering some of the finest rock-climbing and mountain walking for both beginner and expert. The main valleys,

often finely wooded, hold lakes and are watered by rivers with cascading falls. There are information centres at Aberdyfi, Bala, Blaenau Ffestiniog, Conwy, Harlech, Dolgellau, Llanberis and Llanrwst.

Dartmoor National Park (365 sq. miles).—In Devon, the highest area of high moorland in southern England, famous for its granite "tors" often weathered into strange shapes. Fine hanging oak woods adorn the river valleys which lead up into the Moor. The Park is rich in prehistoric relics and offers fine walking and riding. Information vans are sited at Yelverton, Haytor and New Bridge.

Pembrokeshire Coast National Park (225 sq. miles).—A spectacular section of Britain's coastline, where rock cliffs alternate with bays and sandy coves. In the north is Mynydd Preseli, abounding in prehistoric relics. The Park includes the fine Milford Haven waterway reaches, Tenby, the cathedral of St. David's, and Carew and other Norman castles. There are information centres at Tenby, St. David's, Pembroke, Fishguard, Kilgetty and Haverfordwest. A countryside unit is open at Broad Haven.

North York Moors National Park (553 sq. miles).—In North Yorkshire and Cleveland, the Park stretches from the Hambleton Hills in the west to the coastline above Scarborough. On the coast sheltered bays and sandy beaches alternate with

headlands harbouring villages such as Staithes and Robin Hood's Bay. The heart of the Park offers tracts of open moorland, intersected by beautiful wooded valleys. Mount Grace Priory and the abbeys of Rievaulx and Byland are within the Park. There are information centres at Danby Lodge and Sutton Bank.

Yorkshire Dales National Park (680 sq. miles).—An area of upland moors, cut by deep valleys, mostly in North Yorkshire but extending into Cumbria. The Park includes some of the finest limestone scenery in Britain: Kilnsey Crag in Wharfedale, Gordale Scar, and Malham Cove in Malhamdale. In the Park also are Swaledale and Wensleydale, the three peaks of Ingleborough, Whernside and Pen-y-Ghent, and many relics of the past such as the Roman fort at Bainbridge and Bolton Abbey in Wharfedale. There are information centres at Clapham, Aysgarth Falls, Malham and Settle. An information caravan is sited at Hawes.

Exmoor National Park (265 sq. miles).—Mainly in Somerset but extending into Devon, this is a moorland plateau seamed with finely wooded combes. The well-known coastline between Minehead and Combe Martin Bay is exceptionally beautiful. In the east are the Brendon Hills. There are information centres at Minehead, Lynmouth and Dulverton. An information van is sited at Combe Martin.

Northumberland National Park (398 sq. miles).—A region of hills and moorland, stretching from Hadrian's Roman Wall in the south to the Cheviot Hills on the Scottish Border. The area is rich in historic interest. There are information centres at Byrness, Ingram and Once Brewed and an information van tours the Park.

Brecon Beacons National Park (519 sq. miles).—The most recent National Park, established in 1957, is centred on " The Beacons " with its three peaks: Pen y Fan, Corn Du and Cribyn rising to nearly 3,000 feet. But it includes the Black Mountains to the east and the Black Mountain to the west, thus taking in parts of Gwent and Dyfed as well as southern Powys and a small area of mid-Glamorgan. The Upper Usk Valley, Llangorse Lake, Brecon Cathedral, Carreg Cennen Castle and Llanthony Abbey are all within the Park. There are information centres at Brecon, Abergavenny, Llandovery and a mountain centre near Libanus, Brecon.

AREAS OF OUTSTANDING NATURAL BEAUTY

Anglesey (83 sq. miles).—Except for breaks around the urban areas and in the vicinity of Wylfa, the designated area extends along the entire coastline. The varied scenery is famed for its beauty, as also are the Menai Straits, separating the island from the mainland.

Arnside and Silverdale (29 sq. miles).—Lying along the upper half of Morecambe Bay, the area embraces the Kent estuary where it adjoins the Lake District National Park and includes extensive tidal flats in the Bay. The varied coastal landscape contains several limestone hills, woodland and bog areas locally known as " mosses ". Known for its wildfowl breeding grounds, the whole area is of considerable ecological value.

Cannock Chase (26 sq. miles).—This is an area of high heathland in Staffordshire, relieved by varied scenery in which parklands adjoin farms, woodlands and pleasant villages. Deer continue to roam over the Chase.

Chichester Harbour (29 sq. miles).—Well known for its small boating and sailing facilities, the area extends from Hayling Island in the west to Apuldram in the east and contains the whole of Thorney Island.

Chilterns (309 sq. miles).—The well-known chalk downlands from Goring in South Oxfordshire northeastwards through Buckinghamshire, Hertfordshire and Bedfordshire to Dunstable and Luton, including the outlying group of hills beyond Luton. Contains several National Trust properties and Whipsnade Zoo.

Cornwall (360 sq. miles).—Comprising a number of separate areas including Bodmin Moor and some of the finest and best-known coastal scenery in Britain. Most of the Land's End peninsula; the coast between St. Michael's Mount and St. Austell with Falmouth omitted; and the Fowey Estuary are all included: in north Cornwall most of the coast to Bedruthan Steps, north of Newquay, and between Perranporth and Godrevy Towans.

Cotswold (582 sq. miles).—Contains the great limestone escarpment overlooking the Vales of Gloucester and Evesham. The remainder is high undulating country and narrow wooded valleys traversed by shallow rapid streams. Noted for its beautiful villages.

Dedham Vale (22 sq. miles).—This, the smallest area so far designated, is the flat land of water meadows with hedges and woodland, bordering Essex and Suffolk, where John Constable (1776–1837) painted during most of his life. Flatford Mill, Willy Lott's Cottage and the church of Stoke-by-Nayland still stand.

East Devon (103 sq. miles).—The area comprises the fine stretch of coastline between Orcombe Rocks, near Exmouth, and the Dorset area near Lyme Regis, with Sidmouth, Beer and Seaton omitted. Inland Gittisham Hill, East Hill and Woodbury and Aylebeare Commons are all included.

North Devon (66 sq. miles).—Comprising three sections of fine coastline—the whole of the Hartland peninsula; from Bideford Bar to the western limits of Ilfracombe, and from east of Ilfracombe to the boundary of the Exmoor National Park. Clovelly, Braunton Burrows, Woolacombe and Combe Martin are all included.

South Devon (128 sq. miles).—It includes the magnificent coast between Bolt Head and Bolt Tail. a National Trust property; Salcombe, Slapton Sands and Dartmouth, and the four estuaries and valleys of the Yealm, Erme, Avon and Dart.

Dorset (400 sq. miles).—Takes in the whole of the coastline between Lyme Regis and Poole, with the Isle of Portland and Weymouth omitted, and stretches inland to include the Purbeck Hills and the downs, heaths and wooded valleys of the Hardy country.

Forest of Bowland (310 sq. miles).—A fine tract of high open moorland running westward from near Settle and Bolton by Bowland in the Pennines, to Caton and Scorton in Central Lancashire. A small outlying area east of the River Ribble includes Pendle Hill and Pendleton Moor.

Gower (73 sq. miles).—In the county of West Glamorgan, South Wales, the area is known for its beautiful coastline, its rocky limestone cliffs, sandy bays and coves and for its wooded ravines stretching inland.

East Hampshire (151 sq. miles).—The area stretches from the outskirts of Winchester to the Hampshire/Sussex border at a distance of about 10 miles inland from the south coast.

South Hampshire Coast (30 sq. miles).—14 miles of coastline on the northern shores of the Solent, between Hurst Castle and Calshot Castle, southeast of Fawley, with the central part of the area extending inland up the Beaulieu River for about six miles, including a beautiful part of the New Forest. Along much of the coast woods of oak and

Scots pine stretch down to the water's edge, while at the western end are some attractive salt marshes.

Kent Downs (326 sq. miles).—Running from the Surrey border near Westerham (its boundary adjoining that of the Surrey Hills area), about 60 miles to the coast near Dover and Folkestone, with a coastal outlier at South Foreland and a narrow strip of the old sea cliff escarpment west of Hythe overlooking Romney Marsh. Pleasant pastoral scenery, picturesque villages, ancient churches and castles, with the Downs rising to 600 feet.

Lincolnshire Wolds (216 sq. miles).—The area extends in a south-east direction from Laceby and Caistor in the north to the region of Spilsby, about ten miles west of Skegness. Its charm is derived from the undulating terrain, sparse settlement pattern and the excellent views from the chalk escarpments. The wolds are extensively farmed and contain numerous small, attractive villages.

Lleyn (60 sq. miles).—An isolated peninsula in Gwynedd, North Wales, of unique character, still largely unspoilt by the hand of man.

Malvern Hills (40 sq. miles).—The area embodies the whole range of the Malvern Hills in the county of Hereford and Worcester, just touching Gloucestershire. Such well-known features as the Worcestershire Beacon, North Hill, the Herefordshire Beacon, and Midsummer Hill, a National Trust property, are within the area.

Mendip Hills (78 sq. miles).—Comprising over half of the Mendip Hills, the area stretches, east to west, from Bleadon Hill to the A.39 road north of Wells. Blagdon Lake and Chew Magna Lake are within the boundary which, in the south, takes in Cheddar Gorge. The plateau, rising to over 1,000 ft., commands fine views over the Bristol Channel and surrounding countryside. Noted for its caves, including Wookey Hole, the area is of great scientific and historic interest.

Norfolk Coast (174 sq. miles).—With coastal scenery ranging from salt marsh and mudflats, sand-dunes and shingle ridges to sea cliffs, this area includes six miles of the south-east coast of the Wash, an almost continuous coastal strip three to five miles in depth from Hunstanton to Bacton, with a further small strip between Sea Palling and Winterton-on-Sea. The area, which is rich in wild-life, also includes part of the Sandringham Estate.

Northumberland Coast (50 sq. miles).—Low cliffs and rocky headlands with active fishing villages comprise this area which stretches from just south of Berwick to Amble. It includes Holy Island, with the oldest monastic ruins in the country; the Farne Islands, and the great castles of Bamburgh, Dunstanburgh and Warkworth.

Quantock Hills (38 sq. miles).—The main feature of this area in Somerset is the range of red sandstone hills rising to a height of 1,260 feet at Will's Neck above Crow Combe.

Isles of Scilly.—There are about 140 islands and skerries in the Scillies group of which only five are inhabited. Geologically, the formation is similar to Land's End and other granite areas in Cornwall. The coastline is dramatically rocky, interspersed

with sheltered sandy beaches and areas of dune of bleached decomposed granite, glistening with mica and shells. There are coastal paths round the larger islands, and a number of sites of Special Scientific Interest, identified by the Nature Conservancy Council.

Shropshire Hills (300 sq. miles).—This area includes the fine landscape around Church Stretton, with Caer Caradoc, the Long Mynd, the Stiperstones, and the long ridge of Wenlock Edge from which it extends north-east to the Wrekin and the Ercall.

Soloway Coast (41 sq. miles).—A stretch of beautiful coastline in Cumbria from above Maryport to the estuaries of the Rivers Eden and Esk (with Silloth omitted) backed by the Solway Plain and noted for its historic and scientific interests.

Suffolk Coast and Heaths (151 sq. miles).—Takes in 38 miles of coastline and parts of the Stour and Orwell estuaries, while the Deben, Alde and Blyth flow through it. With heath, woodland, marsh and beaches, the scenery is attractively varied and the area important to ornithologists.

Surrey Hills (160 sq. miles).—The Hog's Back and the ridge of the North Downs from Guildford to Titsey in the east are within this area, as are Leith Hill, Hindhead Common, the Devil's Punch Bowl; the well-known villages of Abinger, Shere, Hambledon and Chiddingfold; Box Hill and Frensham Ponds.

Sussex Downs (379 sq. miles).—The area includes the chalk escarpment of the South Downs from Beachy Head to the West Sussex/Hampshire border, with such well-known features as Firle Beacon and Chanctonbury Ring, and stretches down to the coast between Eastbourne and Seaford. In the west the boundary adjoins the East Hampshire and Surrey Hills areas.

North Wessex Downs (671 sq. miles).—An upland area in Hampshire, Wiltshire, Oxfordshire and Berkshire, bounded by the Marlborough and Lambourn Downs in the west and the Chiltern Hills in the east. To the south of the downs the area is intersected by the Kennet Valley, the Vale of Pewsey and Enbourne Vale, with Savernake Forest in the midst. The southern section comprises the North Downs where they descend to the Test Valley which, together with Salisbury Plain, form the southern limit of what is so far the largest area designated.

Isle of Wight (73 sq. miles).—A number of separate areas comprising unspoiled stretches of coastline, the Yar Valley, the high downland behind Ventnor and the fine chalk downland ridge east of Newport to Culver Cliff and Foreland.

Wye Valley (125 sq. miles).—This area lies within the counties of Gwent, Gloucestershire and Hereford and Worcester. The lower Wye Valley landscape is characterised by its steeply-wooded slopes, cliffs and gorges where the river has cut through limestone outcrops. Further north the valley is broader and the river meanders through pleasant pastureland. Tintern Abbey and the well-known viewpoint from Symonds Yat are within this beautiful area. The flora include many rare species.

BRITISH ISLES

SHETLAND IS.
Lerwick

ORKNEY IS.
Kirkwall
PENTLAND FIRTH

Stornoway

MORAY FIRTH
Inverness

HEBRIDES

SCOTLAND
Aberdeen

Perth   Dundee

Oban
Stirling   *FIRTH OF FORTH*
Glasgow   Edinburgh
Ayr
FIRTH OF CLYDE

NORTH
SEA

NORTHERN
IRELAND   Belfast
SOLWAY FIRTH
Newcastle
Carlisle

ENGLAND

ISLE OF MAN
IRISH SEA
York
Bradford   Leeds   Hull

REPUBLIC OF
IRELAND
Liverpool   Manchester
Dublin   Sheffield
ANGLESEY   Stoke
Nottingham   *THE WASH*

Leicester
Birmingham   Coventry   Norwich
WALES
Stratford   Cambridge

Cork
Swansea   Oxford
Cardiff   Bristol
BRISTOL CHANNEL   LONDON
Winchester   Canterbury
Southampton   Portsmouth   Calais
Exeter   ISLE OF WIGHT
Plymouth

ENGLISH CHANNEL

SCILLY IS.

0   50   100 MILES

CHANNEL IS.   FRANCE

ATLANTIC

OCEAN

THE KINGDOM OF ENGLAND

Position and Extent.—The Kingdom of England occupies the southern position of the island of Great Britain and lies between 55° 46′ and 49° 57′ 30″ N. latitude (from the mouth of the Tweed to the Lizard), and between 1° 46′ E. and 5° 43′ W. (from Lowestoft to Land's End). England is bounded on the north by the summit of the Cheviot Hills, which form a natural boundary with the Kingdom of Scotland; on the south by the English Channel; on the east by the Straits of Dover (Pas de Calais) and the North Sea; and on the West by the Atlantic Ocean, Wales and the Irish Sea. It has a total area of 50,333 sq. miles (land 50,053; inland water 280) and a population (1971 Census) of 46,029,000.

Relief.—There is a natural orographic division into the hilly districts of the north, west and south-west, and the undulating downs and low-lying plains of the east and south-east. In the extreme north the *Cheviot Hills* run from east to west, culminating in the Cheviot, 2,676 feet above mean sea level. Divided from the Cheviots by the Tyne Gap is the *Pennine Chain*, running N. by W. to S. by E., with its highest point in Cross Fell, 2,930 feet above mean sea level. West of the Pennines are the *Cumbrian Mountains*, which contain in *Scafell Pike* (3,210 feet) the highest land in England, and east of the Pennines are the *Yorkshire Moors*, their highest point being Urra Moor (1,489 feet). South of the Pennines are the *Peak of Derbyshire* (2,088 feet) and *Dartmoor* (High Willhays, 2,039 feet). In the western county of Salop are the isolated Wrekin (1,335 feet), Longmynd (1,696 feet), and Brown Clee (1,792 feet); in Hereford the Black Mountain (2,310 feet), in Worcester the Malvern Hills (1,395 feet); the Cotswold Hills of Gloucestershire contain Cleeve Cloud (about 1,100 feet).

Hydrography.—The *Thames* is the longest and most important river of England, with a total length of 210 miles from its source in the Cotswold Hills to its outflow into the North Sea, and is navigable by ocean-going steamers to London Bridge. The Thames is tidal to Teddington (69 miles from its mouth) and forms county boundaries almost throughout its course; on its banks are situated London, the capital of the British Commonwealth; Windsor Castle, the home of the Sovereign, Eton College, the first of the public schools, and Oxford, the oldest university in the kingdom. The *Severn* is the longest river in Great Britain, rising in the north-eastern slopes of Plinlimmon (Wales) and entering England in Salop with a total length of 220 miles from its source to its outflow into the Bristol Channel, where it receives on the left the Bristol Avon, and on the right the Wye, its other tributaries being the Vrynwy, Tern, Stour, Teme and Upper (or Warwickshire) Avon. The Severn is tidal below Gloucester, and a high bore or tidal wave sometimes reverses the flow as high as Tewkesbury (13½ miles above Gloucester). The scenery of the greater part of the river is very picturesque and beautiful, and the Severn is a noted salmon river, some of its tributaries being famous for trout. Navigation is assisted by the Gloucester and Berkeley Ship Canal (16¼ miles), which admits vessels of 350 tons to Gloucester. The *Severn Tunnel*, begun in 1873 and completed in 1886 (at a cost of £2,000,000) after many difficulties from flooding, is 4 miles 628 yards in length of which 2¼ miles are under the river). A road bridge over the Severn estuary, between Haysgate,

Gwent, and Almondsbury, Glos., with a centre span of 3,240 ft. was opened by Her Majesty the Queen on September 8, 1966. Of the remaining English rivers those flowing into the North Sea are the Tyne, Wear, Tees, Ouse and Trent from the Pennine Range, the Great Ouse (160 miles) from the Central Plain, and the Orwell and Stour from the hills of East Anglia. Flowing into the English Channel are the Sussex Ouse from the Weald, the Itchen from the Hampshire Hills, and the Axe, Teign, Dart, Tamar and Exe from the Devonian Hills; and flowing into the Irish Sea are the Mersey, Ribble and Eden from the western slopes of the Pennines and the Derwent from the Cumbrian Mountains. The *English Lakes* are noteworthy rather for their picturesque scenery and poetic associations than for their size. They lie in Cumbria, the largest being Windermere (10 miles long), Ullswater and Derwentwater.

Islands.—The *Isle of Wight* is separated from Hampshire by the Solent; total area 147 sq. miles, population (estimated 1975) 112,000. The climate is mild and healthy, and many watering places have grown up during the last century. Capital, Newport, at the head of the estuary of the Medina, Cowes (at the mouth) being the chief port; other centres are Ryde, Sandown, Shanklin, Ventnor, Freshwater, Yarmouth, Totland Bay, Seaview and Bembridge. The *Scilly Islands*, 25 miles from Land's End, consist of about 40 islands, with a total area of about 4,000 acres, only St. Mary's, Tresco, St. Martin's, St. Agnes and Bryher being inhabited (population, 1971, 2,428). The capital is Hugh Town, in St. Mary's. The climate is unusually mild, and vegetation luxuriant, semi-tropical plants flourishing in the open. *Lundy* (= Island) 11 miles N.W. of Hartland Point, Devon, is about 2 miles long and about ½ mile broad (average), with a total area of about 1,050 acres (mainly picturesque), and a population of about 20; it became the property of the National Trust in 1969 and has 3 lighthouses (one disused).

Climate.—The *mean annual air temperature* reduced to sea-level varies from 11°C. in the extreme south-west to 9°C. near Berwick-on-Tweed. In January the south and west are warmer than the east, the mean temperature reduced to sea-level being less than 4.5°C. over the eastern half of the country. In July the warmest districts are more definitely in the south and inland, the range being from 17°C. around London to less than 5.9°C. in the extreme north. The decrease of mean temperature with height is about 0.6°C. per 100 metres. The coldest month of the year is January and the warmest July. Sea temperature reaches its maximum rather later than air temperature. The average annual *rainfall* decreases from west to east, owing to the preponderance of south-west winds, and also increases with altitude. The annual average, 1916–1950, varies from 20 in. (500 mm.) in the neighbourhood of the Thames Estuary and locally in Cambridgeshire to more than 100 in. (2,500 mm.) over the mountains of the Lake District. Rather more rain falls in the summer half-year in parts of the east, but in the west much more rain falls in the winter half-year. The months of least rain are March to June and the wettest months October to January. The mean annual number of hours of bright *sunshine* varies from 1,750 hours along the south-east coast to less than 1,300 hours in the neighbourhood of the Pennine range. June is the sunniest month followed by May, July and August in that order.

EARLY INHABITANTS

Prehistoric Man.—Palæolithic and Neolithic remains are abundantly found throughout England. The Neolithic period is held to have merged into the Bronze Age about 2000 to 1500 B.C., and a date between these years has been given to *Stonehenge* (10 miles N. of Salisbury, Wiltshire) which consists of two circles of menhirs (the largest monolith being 22½ feet in height). The village of *Avebury* and its surroundings were scheduled in 1937, and in 1943 about 1,000 acres of Avebury were purchased by the National Trust, thus preserving the Circle of megalithic monuments, the Avenue, Silbury Hill, etc., relics of Stone Age culture of 1900–1800 B.C., which make this one of the most important archæological sites in Europe. The *Devil's Arrows*, near Boroughbridge, Yorkshire, are regarded as the finest remaining megalithic monoliths in northern Europe; the tallest arrow is 30 ft. 6 in. high and its greatest circumference is 16 ft. In the latter part of the Bronze Age the *Goidels*, a people of Celtic race, and in the Iron Age other Celtic races of *Brythons* and *Belgae*, invaded the country and brought with them Celtic civilization and dialects, place names in England bearing witness to the spread of the invasion over the whole kingdom.

The Roman Conquest.—Julius Cæsar raided Britain in 55 B.C. and 54 B.C. The Emperor Claudius, nearly 100 years later (A.D. 42), dispatched Aulus Plautius, with a well-equipped force of 40,000, and himself followed with reinforcements in the same year.

The British leader from A.D. 48–51 was *Caratacus* (Caractacus), who was finally captured and sent to Rome. By A.D. 70 the conquest of South Britain was completed, a great revolt under *Boadicea*, Queen of the Iceni, being crushed in A.D. 61. In A.D. 122, the Emperor Hadrian visited Britain and built a continuous rampart, since known as *Hadrian's Wall*, from Wallsend to Bowness (Tyne to Solway). The work was entrusted by the Emperor Hadrian to Aulus Platorius Nepos, legate of Britain from 122 to 126, and it is now regarded as " the greatest and most impressive relic of the Roman frontier system in Europe. "

The Romans administered Britain as a Province under a Governor, with a well-defined system of local government, each Roman municipality ruling itself and the surrounding territory. Colchester, Lincoln, York, Gloucester and St. Albans stand on the sites of five Roman municipalities, while London was the centre of the road system and the seat of the financial officials of the Province of Britain. Well-preserved Roman towns have been uncovered at (or near) *Silchester* (Calleva Atrebatum), 10 miles south of Reading, *Wroxeter* (Viroconium), near Shrewsbury, and *St. Albans* (Verulamium) in Hertfordshire.

Four main groups of roads radiated from London, and a fifth (the Fosse) ran obliquely from Ermine Street (at Lincoln), through Leicester, Cirencester and Bath to Exeter. Of the four groups radiating from London one ran S.E. to Canterbury and the coast of Kent, a second to Silchester and thence to parts of Western Britain and South Wales, a third (now known as *Watling Street*) ran through Verulamium to Chester, with various branches, and the fourth reached Colchester, Lincoln, York and the eastern counties.

Christianity reached the Roman province of Britain from Gaul in the 3rd century (or possibly earlier), *Alban*, " the protomartyr of Britain,"

being put to death as a Christian during the persecution of Diocletian (June 22, 303), at his native town Verulamium. The Bishops of Londinium, Eboracum (York), and Lindum (Lincoln) attended the Council of Arles in 314.

The Roman garrison of Britain was much harassed in the 4th century by Saxon pirates, who invaded the eastern areas. A system of coast defence was organized from the Wash to Southampton Water, with forts at Brancaster, Burgh Castle (Yarmouth), Walton (Felixstowe), Bradwell, Reculver, Richborough, Dover, Stutfall, Pevensey and Porchester (Portsmouth). About A.D. 350 incursions in the north of Irish (Scoti) and Picts became most formidable, and towards the end of the 4th century many troops were removed from Britain for service in other parts of the Roman Empire. Early in the 5th century Gaul was taken from the Romans by Teutonic invaders and Britain was cut off from Rome. The last Roman garrison was withdrawn from Britain in A.D. 442 and the S.E. portion was conquered by the Saxons.

The Latin-speaking Celts of England were replaced by their heathen and Teutonic conquerors, to the submergence of the Christian religion and the loss of Latin speech. According to legend, the British King *Vortigern* called in the Saxons to defend him against the Picts, the Saxon chieftains being *Hengist* and *Horsa*, who landed at Ebbsfleet, Kent, and established themselves in the Isle of Thanet. Bede, a Northumbrian monk, author of the Ecclesiastical History at the opening of the 8th century, described these settlers as Jutes, and there are traces of differences in Kentish customs from those of other Anglo-Saxon kingdoms.

Anglo-Saxons and Normans.—What happened in Britain during the 150 years which elapsed between the final break with Rome and the coming of St. Augustine is shrouded in the deepest mystery. The Jutes, the Saxons and the Angles (whose gods Twi, Woden, Thunor and Frigg are commemorated in " Tuesday, Wednesday, Thursday and Friday ") were converted to Christianity by a mission under Augustine (dispatched by Pope Gregory in 597), which established Archbishoprics at Canterbury and York, and England appears to have been again converted by the end of the 7th century. In the 8th century Offa, King of Mercia, is stated to have built a wall and rampart, afterwards known as *Offa's Dike*, from the mouth of the Dee to that of the Wye, as a protection against the Welsh.

The greatest of the English kingdoms was *Wessex*, with its capital at Winchester, and the greatest of the Wessex kings was *Alfred the Great* (871–899), who resisted the incursions of the Northmen (Danes) and fixed a limit to their advance by the Treaty of Wedmore (878). In the 10th century the Kings of Wessex recovered the whole of England from the Danes, but subsequent rulers were unable to resist the invaders, and England paid tribute (*Danegelt*) for many years, and was ruled by Danish Kings from 1016 to 1042, when Edward the Confessor was recalled from exile. In 1066 Harold (brother-in-law of Edward and son of Earl Godwin of Wessex) was chosen King of England, but after defeating (at Stamford Bridge, Yorkshire, Sept. 25) an invading army under Harald Hadraada, King of Norway (aided by the outlawed Earl Tostig, of Northumbria, younger son of Earl Godwin), he was himself defeated at the *Battle of Hastings* on Oct. 14, 1066, and the Norman Conquest secured the throne of England for Duke William of Normandy.

AREA AND POPULATION OF ENGLISH COUNTIES

County	Administrative Headquarters	Acreage	Population (Reg. Gen's Est.)	Rateable Value 1976	Rate Levied
				£	p.
Avon.............	Avon Hse., The Haymarket, Bristol	332,596	919,600	110,419,181	53·03–59·23
Bedford..........	★Cauldwell St., Bedford	305,026	493,800	72,122,882	69·3
Berkshire.........	†Reading	310,178	658,300	106,651,090	50·6–51·6
Buckinghamshire...	★Aylesbury	465,019	501,800	80,229,035	56
Cambridgeshire....	†Castle Hill, Cambridge	842,433	540,300	69,094,556	53
Cheshire..........	★Chester	575,375	910,900	117,833,723	58
Cleveland........	Municipal Bldgs., Middlesbrough	144,086	565,400	69,909,978	61
Cornwall..........	★Truro	876,295‡	401,500‡	40,402,815	48
Cumbria..........	The Courts, Carlisle	1,682,239	473,800	42,541,507	50
Derbyshire.......	County Offices, Matlock	650,146	902,820	91,706,931	58
Devonshire.......	★Exeter	1,658,285	936,300	101,286,071	52
Dorset............	★Dorchester	655,818	572,900	74,620,194	58
Durham...........	★Durham	601,939	607,600	52,313,768	53·48–58·28
Essex.............	★Chelmsford	907,850	1,411,000	209,170,370	51
Gloucester........	†Gloucester	652,741	487,600	57,973,099	57
Greater Manchester.	★Piccadilly Gdns., Manchester	317,285	2,730,000	306,107,000	23·5
Hampshire.........	The Castle, Winchester	934,474	1,434,700	183,359,060	56
Hereford and Worcester.......	†Worcester	970,203	585,900	72,197,830	58
Hertford.........	★Hertford	403,787	938,100	153,559,625	58·5
Humberside.......	Kingston Hse S., Bond St., Kingston-upon-Hull	867,784	848,200	88,101,000	53
Kent.............	★Maidstone	922,196	1,445,400	165,667,374	52·09
Lancashire........	★Preston	751,063	1,369,200	131,211,850	54
Leicestershire.......	★Glenfield, Leicester	630,842	836,500	98,497,059	49
Lincoln..........	County Offices, Lincoln	1,454,351	521,300	51,000,000	—
Greater London....	★S.E.1.	390,302	7,111,500	1,910,000,000	—
Merseyside........	Metropolitan Hse., Old Hall St., Liverpool	159,750	1,588,400	187,098,691	28
Norfolk..........	★Martineau Lane, Nwch.	1,323,371	659,300	76,976,000	53·1–58·2
Northampton......	★Northampton	584,970	500,100	60,705,337	56
Northumberland...	★Newcastle-upon-Tyne	1,243,692	285,700	26,776,866	55
Nottinghamshire...	★West Bridgford, Nottingham	534,735	982,700	108,185,066	58
Oxfordshire.......	★New Road, Oxford	645,314	539,100	71,364,297	57
Salop.............	†Abbey Foregate, Shrewsbury	862,479	354,800	37,749,873	49
Somerset..........	★Taunton	852,434	401,700	42,956,452	54
Staffordshire.......	County Bldgs., Stafford	671,184	988,400	108,900,000	55·3
Suffolk............	★Ipswich	940,800	570,000	67,500,000	52·5
Surrey............	★Kingston upon Thames	414,922	1,000,700	159,385,608	59·37
Sussex, East........	★Pelham Hse., St. Andrew's Lane, Lewes	443,634	657,300	90,076,732	54·8–55·4
Sussex, West.......	★West St., Chichester	498,178	623,100	83,280,000	51
Tyne and Wear....	Sandyford Hse., Newcastle	133,390	1,192,600	117,611,160	29
Warwick..........	†Warwick	489,405	471,800	84,135,390	54·7
West Midlands.....	★Lancaster Circus, Birmingham	222,258	2,777,500	4,000,000	23
Wight, Isle of......	★Newport, I.O.W.	94,134	111,000	12,061,580	53
Wiltshire..........	★Trowbridge	860,109	511,600	52,670,773	52
Yorkshire, North...	★Northallerton	2,053,126	648,600	62,281,804	52
Yorkshire, South...	★Barnsley	385,605	1,317,200	123,733,809	21
Yorkshire, West....	★Wakefield	503,863	2,082,600	192,187,610	22

★ County Hall   † Shire Hall   ‡ excluding Isles of Scilly

Lords Lieutenant of Counties.—The actual words used in the Letters Patent relative to these appointments are " Her Majesty's Lieutenant of and in the County of . . ." and this is the official title whether the individual appointed be a Peer or a Commoner. In documents of the highest formality the proper term is therefore " Her Majesty's Lieutenant." In less formal and informal documents and colloquially, the style " Lord Lieutenant " has been applied to H.M. Lieutenants, Peers and Commoners alike, for a great many years. The duties of the Lord Lieutenant are to advise the Lord Chancellor as to the appointment of magistrates to the county bench, to appoint Deputy Lieutenants and to raise the militia, if need be, in time of riot or invasion. The Lord Lieutenant is often a peer or a baronet and a large landowner and is often appointed *custos rotulorum* (keeper of the records).

ENGLISH COUNTIES AND SHIRES

LORDS LIEUTENANT, HIGH SHERIFFS AND CHAIRMEN OF COUNTY COUNCILS

County or Shire	Lord Lieutenant	★High Sheriff, 1976–77	Chairman of C.C.
(1) Avon	Sir John V. Wills, Bt., T.D.	S. M. Wills	G. Walker
(2) Bedford	Maj. Simon Whitbread	D. H. C. Harland	J. W. Johnson
(3) Berks	J. L. E. Smith, C.B.E.	Cdr. J. Marriott, R.N. (*ret.*)	F. D. Pickering, C.B.E.
(4) Bucks	Maj. J. D. Young	Sir Francis Dashwood, Bt.	J. T. Ireland
(5) Cambridge	Lt.-Col. The Hon. P. E. Brassey	P. B. Taylor	J. R. Horrell, T.D.
(6) Cheshire	The Viscount Leverhulme, T.D.	C. C. Taylor	G. J. Ford
(7) Cleveland	Maj. C. Crosthwaite, M.B.E., T.D.	Col. J. A. Pounder	A. S. Seed
(8) Cornwall	Col. Sir John C. Pole, Bt., D.S.O., T.D.	Lt. Cdr. J. D. Tetley, R.N. (*ret.*)	W. T. H. Rowse
(9) Cumbria	J. C. Wade, O.B.E.	J. H. H. Harris	T. P. Naylor
(10) Derby	Col. Sir Ian P. A. M. Walker-Okeover, Bt., D.S.O., T.D.	Maj. D. B. Kenning	G. C. Coleman
(11) Devon	The Lord Roborough	Lt. Cdr. J. A. Holdsworth, R.N.	C. A. Ansell
(12) Dorset	Col. Sir Joseph Weld, O.B.E., T.D.	G. E. S. Woodhouse	Lt.-Col. G. W. Mansell, T.D.
(13) Durham	The Lord Barnard, T.D.	M. R. Ferens, M.B.E., T.D.	G. Fishburn [C.B.E.
(14) Essex	Col. Sir John Ruggles-Brise, Bt., C.B., O.B.E., T.D.	Lt.-Col. R. W. Collins-Charlton, O.B.E.	G. C. Waterer
(15) Gloucester	Col. The Duke of Beaufort, K.G., P.C.	D. F. S. Godman	Lt.-Col. W. A. McLelland, T.D.
(16) Greater Manchester	W. A. Downward [G.C.V.O.	Col. Sir Richard D. Martin-Bird, C.B.E., T.D.	D. Bennett [T.D.
(17) Hampshire	The Earl of Malmesbury, T.D.	Capt. M. P. R. Boyle	The Lord Porchester, K.B.E.
(18) Hereford & Worcester	Admiral Sir Deric Holland-Martin, G.C.B., D.S.O., D.S.C.	D. V. S. Cottrell	Sir Michael Higgs
(19) Hertford	Maj.-Gen. Sir George Burns, K.C.V.O., C.B., D.S.O., O.B.E., M.C.	P. C. Spencer-Smith	P. T. Ireton, C.B.E.
(20) Humberside	The Earl of Halifax	R. A. Bethell	F. Hall
(21) Kent	The Lord Astor of Hever	Lt.-Col. G. L. Doubleday, T.D.	J. B. D. Waite
(22) Lancashire	S. P. E. C. W. Towneley	G. P. Bowring, M.C., T.D.	L. Broughton
(23) Leicestershire	Col. R. A. St. G. Martin, O.B.E.	G. H. Boyle	The Duke of Rutland,
(24) Lincoln	H. N. Nevile	W. W. Maitland	J. H. Lewis [C.B.E.
(25) Greater London	Marshal of the Royal Air Force, The Lord Elworthy, G.C.B., C.B.E., D.S.O., M.V.O., D.F.C., A.F.C.	A. W. Ramsay	The Lord Ponsonby of Shulbrede
(26) Merseyside	Brig. Sir Douglas I. Crawford, C.B., D.S.O., T.D.	S. Minion, O.B.E.	W. H. Sefton
(27) Norfolk	Col. Sir Edmund Bacon, Bt., K.G., K.B.E., T.D.	Sir Alex Alexander	J. P. Winter
(28) Northampton	Lt.-Col. J. Chandos-Pole, O.B.E.	L. G. Stopford-Sackville	R. E. Warwick
(29) Northumberland	The Duke of Northumberland, K.G., P.C., T.D.	Maj. M. J. B. Cookson	The Viscount Ridley, T.D
(30) Nottingham	Cmdr. M. B. P. Francklin, D.S.C., R.N.(*ret.*)	A. G. Buchanan	Mrs. B. Sharrard, O.B.E.
(31) Oxford	Col. Sir John Thomson, K.B.E., T.D.	Maj. A. G. Mann, M.B.E.	R. C. Weir
(32) Salop	J. R. S. Dugdale	Lt. Col. R. C. H. Armitshead	Lt.-Col. R. C. G. Morris-Eyton, T.D.
(33) Somerset	Col. C. T. Mitford-Slade	Capt. J. S. Lloyd, M.C.	W. M. F. Knowles
(34) Stafford	Sir Arthur Bryan	Maj. J. A. Hawley, T.D.	G. W. Newman, C.B.E.
(35) Suffolk	Cdr. The Earl of Stradbroke, R.N.(*ret.*)	The Hon. C. B. A. Bernard	Sir Joshua Rowley, Bt.
(36) Surrey	The Lord Hamilton of Dalzell, M.C.	T. I. Smith, O.B.E.	Brig. D. T. Bastin, C.B.E., T.D.
(37) Sussex, East	The Marquess of Abergavenny, O.B.E.	L. C. Hardy	T. H. B. Mynors
(38) Sussex, West	Lavinia, Duchess of Norfolk, C.B.E.	D. S. W. Blacker	E. J. F. Green
(39) Tyne and Wear	Sir James Steel, C.B.E.	R. A. S. Sisterson	J. F. Richardson
(40) Warwick	C. M. T. Smith-Ryland	Maj. Sir John H. Wiggin, Bt., M.C.	F. W. H. Parrott
(41) West Midlands	The Earl of Aylesford	Lt.-Col. J. H. C. Horsfall	W. E. Jarvis
(42) Wight, Isle of	Admiral of the Fleet, The Earl Mountbatten of Burma, K.G., P.C., G.C.B., O.M., G.C.S.I., G.C.I.E., G.C.V.O., D.S.O.	F. R. J. Britten, C.B.E.	Rear Adm. J. L. Blackham, C.B.
(43) Wiltshire	The Lord Margadale, T.D.	G. J. Ward	Gp. Capt. F. A. Willan, C.B.E., D.F.C.
(44) Yorkshire, North	The Marquess of Normanby, C.B.E.	N. C. Forbes-Adam	J. T. Fletcher, C.B.E.
(45) Yorkshire, South	G. F. Young, C.B.E.	J. M. M. Jenkinson	G. H. Moores
(46) Yorkshire, West	Brig. K. Hargreaves, C.B.E., T.D.	M. E. Lyon	H. Sheldon

★ High Sheriffs are nominated by the Queen on November 12 and come into office after Hilary Term.

ENGLISH COUNTIES AND SHIRES

CHIEF EXECUTIVES OF COUNTY COUNCILS, COUNTY TREASURERS AND CHIEF CONSTABLES

County or Shire	Chief Executive	County Treasurer	Chief Constable
(1) Avon.............	W. J. Hutchinson	D. G. Morgan	K. W. L. Steele, O.B.E., K.P.M.
(2) Bedford..........	J. W. Elven	V. F. Phillips	A. Armstrong, Q.P.M.
(3) Berks.............	R. W. Gash	M. C. Beasley	}D. Holdsworth, C.B.E., Q.P.M. (a)
(4) Bucks.............	J. Stevenson	G. B. Ravens	
(5) Cambridge........	J. K. Barratt	J. E. Barton	F. D. Porter, O.B.E., Q.P.M.
(6) Cheshire..........	J. K. Boynton, M.C.	C. T. Fletcher	W. Kelsall, O.B.E., Q.P.M.
(7) Cleveland.........	J. B. Woodham	B. Stevenson	C. Payne
(8) Cornwall..........	A. L. Dennis	K. Hyde	J. C. Alderson, Q.P.M.
(9) Cumbria..........	T. J. R. Whitfield	J. R. Ford	W. T. Cavey, O.B.E., Q.P.M.
(10) Derby............	H. Crossley	E. J. Cobb	W. Stansfield, C.B.E., M.C., Q.P.M.
(11) Devon............	C. V. Lucas	O. A. Sanders	J. C. Alderson, Q.P.M.
(12) Dorset...........	K. A. Abel	D. M. Gasson	A. Hambleton, O.B.E., M.C., Q.P.M.
(13) Durham..........	J. Procter	J. M. Wright	A. G. Puckering, O.B.E., Q.P.M.
(14) Essex............	(vacant)	E. A. Twelvetree	Sir John Nightingale, C.B.E., B.E.M., [Q.P.M.
(15) Gloucester.......	J. V. Miller	T. N. Hobson	B. Weigh, Q.P.M.
(16) Greater Manchester	G. A. Harrison	K. J. Bridge	C. J. Anderton
(17) Hampshire.......	L. K. Robinson	B. Dufton	Sir Douglas Osmond, C.B.E., Q.P.M.
(18) Hereford and Worcester......	A. J. R. Ward	A. B. Turner	D. V. S. Cottrell
(19) Hertford........	F. P. Boyce	C. C. Jasper	R. N. Buxton, O.B.E., B.E.M., Q.P.M.
(20) Humberside......	J. H. W. Glen, C.B.E.	J. A. Parkes	D. Hall
(21) Kent.............	W. U. Jackson	P. E. W. Stoodley	B. N. Pain, Q.P.M.
(22) Lancashire.......	B. Hill	W. O. Jolliffe	S. Parr, C.B.E., Q.P.M.
(23) Leicestershire.....	S. Jones	J. S. Blackburn	A. Goodson, Q.P.M.
(24) Lincoln..........	D. D. Macklin	G. R. Prentice	L. Byford, Q.P.M.
(25) Greater London...	Sir James Swaffield, C.B.E., R.D.	M. F. Stonefrost	(Metropolitan Police Area)
(26) Merseyside........	Sir Stanley Holmes	P. W. Jenkins	K. G. Oxford, Q.P.M.
(27) Norfolk..........	B. J. Capon	B. Taylor, M.C.	C. G. Taylor, Q.P.M.
(28) Northampton.....	A. J. Greenwell	H. Lawson	F. A. Cutting, Q.P.M.
(29) Northumberland ..	C. W. Hurley, O.B.E., T.D.	W. H. Foakes	C. H. Cooksley, C.B.E., Q.P.M.
(30) Nottingham.......	R. F. O'Brien	G. E. Daniel	C. McLachlan
(31) Oxford...........	A. T. Brown	B. P. Harty	D. Holdsworth, C.B.E., Q.P.M. (a)
(32) Salop............	W. N. P. Jones	R. R. Renville	A. A. Rennie, Q.P.M.
(33) Somerset.........	J. E. Whittaker	B. M. Tanner	K. W. L. Steele, O.B.E., K.P.M.
(34) Stafford	J. B. Brown	G. Woodcock	A. M. Rees, C.B.E., Q.P.M.
(35) Suffolk...........	C. W. Smith	E. T. Knott	S. L. Whiteley, Q.P.M.
(36) Surrey...........	F. A. Stone	G. W. Payne-Butler	P. J. Matthews, O.B.E., Q.P.M.
(37) Sussex, East......	R. M. Beechey	J. Unsworth	}G. W. R. Terry, C.B.E., Q.P.M.
(38) Sussex, West......	J. R. Hooley	B. Fieldhouse	
(39) Tyne and Wear	J. J. Gardner	C. J. Davies	S. M. Bailey, Q.P.M.
(40) Warwick.........	E. Cust	C. G. McMillan	R. B. Matthews, C.B.E., Q.P.M.
(41) West Midlands....	J. D. Hender	K. E. Rose	P. D. Knights, C.B.E., Q.P.M.
(42) Wight, Isle of.....	J. S. Horsnell	D. A. Tuck	Sir Douglas Osmond, C.B.E., Q.P.M.
(43) Wiltshire.........	R. P. Harries	R. L. W. Moon	G. R. Glendinning, O.B.E., Q.P.M.
(44) Yorkshire, North..	H. J. Evans	K. R. Hounsome	R. P. Boyes, Q.P.M.
(45) Yorkshire, South..	F. A. Mallett	D. B. Chynoweth	R. S. Barratt
(46) Yorkshire, West...	P. J. Butcher	G. S. Pollard	R. Gregory, Q.P.M.

(a) Thames Valley Police Authority

GREATER LONDON COUNCIL

The Greater London Council and 32 London Borough Councils were constituted under the London Government Act, 1963. They replaced, on April 1, 1965, the London County Council, the Middlesex County Council, the County Borough Councils of Croydon, East Ham and West Ham, 28 metropolitan borough, 39 non-county borough and 15 urban district councils. The boundaries and constitution of the Corporation of the City of London were not affected.

Under the Act, Greater London became for the first time a clearly defined local government area including, in addition to the former counties of London and the greater part of Middlesex, parts of Metropolitan Essex, Kent, Surrey and Hertfordshire.

The Greater London Council at present consists of 92 councillors and 15 aldermen. Councillors are elected for single-member electoral divisions which are conterminous with the parliamentary constituencies. Councillors hold office for four years. Aldermen are elected by the councillors from among councillors or persons eligible to be councillors. The Local Government Act 1972 provides for the abolition of the position of alderman at the end of the current term of office. The Chairman, Vice-Chairman and Deputy Chairman are elected annually by the councillors and aldermen. The political head of the administration is the Leader of the Council, elected by the majority party. The Council meets at three-weekly intervals at 2.30 p.m. on Tuesdays except in holiday periods. Most committees and sub-committees meet at three-weekly intervals.

Greater London Council
(Elected April 12, 1973)

Greater London comprises an area of 610 sq. miles and has a population of 7,111,500 (1975 mid-year estimates).

Chairman (1976–77), The Lord Ponsonby of Shulbrede.

Vice-Chairman (1976–77), P. F. N. Russell.

Deputy-Chairman (1976–77), Mrs. L. Townsend, C.B.E.

Leader of the Council, Sir Reginald Goodwin, C.B.E.

Leader of the Opposition, H. W. Cutler, O.B.E.

*Abbot, F. (*C.*)...........*Alderman*
*Aplin, G. W. (*C.*).......*Croydon South*
 Archer, F. W. (*Lab.*).....*Erith and Crayford*
*Bains, L. A. (*C.*)........*Hornsey*
 Balfe, R. A. (*Lab.*).......*Dulwich*
*Banks, A. (*Lab.*).........*Fulham*
 Barker, D. E. R. (*Lab.*)...*Croydon North West*
 Basset, P. (*Lab.*).........*Carshalton*
*Bell, E. P., O.B.E. (*Lab.*)..*Newham South*
*Bell, W. (*C.*)............*Chelsea*
*Bennett, F., C.B.E. (*C.*)....*Alderman*
*Black, P. (*C.*)...........*Hendon South*
*Bolton, S. C. (*C.*).......*Wimbledon*
*Bondy, L. (*Lab.*).........*Islington North*
*Bonham, Mrs. I. (*Lab.*)....*Hammersmith North*
*Bramall, Sir Ashley (*Lab.*).*Bethnal Green and Bow*
*Branagan, J. (*Lab.*).......*Stepney and Poplar*
*Brew, R. M. (*C.*)........*Chingford*
*Brown, B. J. (*C.*).........*Ruislip-Northwood*
*Carr, E. G., B.E.M. (*Lab.*)..*Vauxhall*
 Carradice, D. A. (*Lab.*)....*Ilford South*
*Chalkley, D. (*Lab.*).......*Deptford*
*Chaplin, Mrs. I. (*Lab.*)....*Hackney South and Shoreditch*
*Chorley, A. F. J., M.B.E. (*Lab.*)................*Alderman*
*Clack, W. S. (*C.*).......*Harrow Central*
*Collins, R. (*Lab.*).........*Alderman*
 Cooper, F. A. (*Lab.*)......*Hendon North*
*Cutler, H., O.B.E. (*C.*).....*Harrow West*
 Daly, J. (*Lab.*)...........*Brentford and Isleworth*
*Denington, Dame Evelyn, D.B.E. (*Lab.*).........*Islington Central*
*Dimson, Mrs. G. F. C.B.E. (*Lab.*)................*Battersea North*
*Dobson, J. C. (*C.*)......*Acton*
 Eden, D. (*Lab.*)..........*Feltham and Heston*
*Edwards, A. F. G. (*Lab.*)..*Newham North-West*
*Fielding, D. M. (*C.*).......*Sidcup*
*Freeman, L., O.B.E. (*C.*)....*Alderman*
 Freeman, R. (*C.*).........*Finchley*
*Garside, Mrs. M. E. (*Lab.*) *Woolwich East*
*Geddes, Hon. Mrs. J. (*C.*)..*Streatham*
 Gillies, Mrs. L. G. (*Lab.*)..*Tooting*

*Goodwin, Sir Reginald, C.B.E. (*Lab.*)...........*Bermondsey*
*Grieves, Mrs. A. Ll. (*Lab.*).*Lambeth Central*
 Hacker, Mrs. R. (*Lab.*)...*St. Pancras North*
*Hardy, A. (*C.*)..........*Brent North*
*Harrington, I. (*Lab.*).......*Brent South*
*Harris, D. (*C.*)..........*Ravensbourne*
 Harwood, Miss M. (*Lab.*).*Alderman*
 Haseler, Dr. S. M. (*Lab.*)..*Wood Green*
 Hatch, S. (*Lab.*)..........*Battersea South*
*Henry, J. C. (*Lab.*).......*Lewisham East*
*Hichisson, A. J. (*C.*) .....*Alderman*
*Hillman, E. S. (*Lab.*).......*Hackney Central*
*Hinds, H. (*Lab.*).........*Peckham*
 Howard, N. (*Lab.*).......*Brent East*
*Jenkins, Mrs. M. (*Lab.*)..*Putney*
 Jenkinson, T. A. (*Lab.*)...*Newham North-East*
 Judge, A. (*Lab.*).........*Mitcham and Morden*
 Kay, H. (*Lab.*)...........*Dagenham*
*Kazantzis, A. (*Lab.*)......*Holborn and St. Pancras South*
*Langton, V. R. M. (*C.*)..*Bexleyheath*
 Lemkin, J. (*C.*)...........*Uxbridge*
 Livingstone, K. (*Lab.*).....*Norwood*
 Lourie, S. (*Lab.*).........*Hornchurch*
 McIntosh, A. R. (*Lab.*)...*Tottenham*
 Mansfield, Dr. W. K. (*Lab.*)..............*Alderman*
*Marks, R. (*C.*)..........*Chipping Barnet*
 Mason, B. S. (*Lab.*).......*Edmonton*
 Mason, Rev. D., O.B.E. (*Lab.*).)..............*Ealing North*
 Mayne, S. (*Lab.*).........*Alderman*
 Merriton, Mrs. J. (*Lab.*)...*Paddington*
*Mitchell, R. (*C.*).........*Wanstead and Woodford*
*Mitcheson, T. (*C.*).......*Southgate*
 Morgan, Miss G. E. (*C.*)..*Croydon North East*
*Mote, H. T. (*C.*).........*Harrow East*
*O'Connor, L. P. (*Lab.*)...*Alderman*
 Partridge, B. Brook- (*C.*)..*Romford*
*Pitt, The Lord (*Lab.*).....*Hackney North and Stoke Newington*
*Ponsonby of Shulbrede, The Lord (*Lab.*)........*Alderman*
 Rees, Mrs. M. (*Lab.*).....*Woolwich West*
 Ridoutt, T. (*Lab.*).........*Ilford North*
*Ripley, S. (*C.*)..........*Kingston upon Thames*
*Roberts, Miss S. (*C.*).....*Upminster*
 Rundle, Dr. S. (*L.*).......*Richmond*
 Russell, P. F. N. (*Lab.*)...*Hayes and Harlington*
 Sandford, H. H., O.B.E., D.F.M. (*C.*)............*St. Marylebone*
*Scorgie, M. (*C.*).........*The City of London and Westminster South*

*Seaton, G. J. D. (C.).....Surbiton
Shaw, Mrs. R. (L.)......Sutton and Cheam
Sieve, Mrs. Y. (Lab.).....Southall
Simson, W. (Lab.).......Lewisham West
*Smith, F. W. (C.)........Beckenham
Stutchbury, O. (Lab.)....Alderman
Styles, F. W., B.E.M. (Lab.) Greenwich
Tatham, Mrs. J. (C.).....Orpington
*Taylor, Dr. G. W. (C.)...Alderman
*Townsend, Mrs. L., C.B.E.
  (C.)................Alderman
*Tremlett, G. (C.)........Twickenham

*Vigars, R. (C.).........Kensington
Walsh, J. J. (Lab.)........Leyton
*Ward, J. B. (Lab.).......Barking
Warren, J. G. (Lab.)......Alderman
White, D. (Lab.).........Croydon Central
White, Dr. J. (Lab.)......Enfield North
*Wicks, A. E. (Lab.).......Islington South and
                   Finsbury
Wistrich, Mrs. E. (Lab.)...Hampstead
Wykes, Mrs. J. (C.)......Chislehurst
Young, R. (Lab.).........Walthamstow
   * Denotes members of the last Council.

Director-General and Clerk to the Council, Sir James Swaffield, C.B.E., R.D.

G.L.C. Services

The services provided by the G.L.C. include planning, roads, traffic management and control, fire services, refuse disposal, housing, parks and licensing. For certain services it shares responsibility with the London Borough Councils and the City Corporation.

Education.—The local education authority for an area corresponding with the area of the twelve inner London boroughs and the City of London is the Inner London Education Authority, a special committee of the G.L.C. consisting of the members of the Council elected for the inner London boroughs together with a representative of each inner London Borough Council and of the Common Council. The Council charges to the rating authorities in the Inner London Education Area the expenditure of the I.L.E.A., the amount being determined by the Authority. This unique arrangement preserves the continuity of the service which has developed since 1870 as a unity without regard to local boundary divisions.

The total number of pupils on the rolls of the Authority's nursery, primary and secondary schools (including special schools for handicapped children) is 412,241. There are 41 nursery, 716 county (including 1 at Children's homes), 342 voluntary and 119 special schools, staffed by the equivalent of 24,284 full-time teachers. Vocational instruction, cultural studies and recreational activities for persons over compulsory school age are arranged at the various establishments for further education. The Authority maintains 24 colleges and makes grants to 5 polytechnics and 8 other institutions. Non-vocational classes are offered at 31 evening and literary institutes, 1 recreational institute and 77 youth centres, including 2 drama centres. Nine colleges for the training of teachers are also managed by the Authority. The 20 outer London Borough Councils are the education authorities for their Boroughs.

Housing.—The Council shares with the London Borough Councils responsibility for housing in London and it accommodates about 14,000 families a year, 2,500 of them in expanding towns many miles from London. The G.L.C. has about 200,000 homes, nearly 50,000 homes having been transferred to the London Borough Councils since 1971.

Planning and Transportation.—The Council as planning authority for Greater London as a whole has prepared a strategic development plan which lays down basic planning policies and principles for the whole area. The Greater London Development Plan has recently been modified by the Secretary of State for the Environment in the light of findings of a Public Inquiry. The Secretary of State is now considering objections to the modified plan. Since the submission of the original plan, the Transport (London) Act, 1969, has given the G.L.C. responsibility for preparing more detailed transport plans, and, through a London Transport Executive appointed by the Council, for London Transport

policies and finance. It is thus now able to consider and co-ordinate priorities for investment in all forms of transport in London.

Within the framework of the Development plan, the London Borough Councils and the City Corporation will prepare their own detailed local development plans. Town planning control of private development proposals is mainly the concern of the London Boroughs but the G.L.C. has some responsibilities in this field. As planner and developer the Council is involved in many major schemes. Notable examples are the Thamesmead project and the Covent Garden area.

The Council is responsible for the construction, improvement and maintenance of principal roads. As the traffic authority for all roads in Greater London it prepares or approves schemes for one-way working, traffic signals, clearways, bus-only lanes, waiting and loading restrictions and speed limits and makes the orders which enforce them. It maintains the Thames tunnels, the Woolwich Free Ferry, and all but four of the Thames bridges (London, Tower, Blackfriars and Southwark, which are maintained by the Corporation of London).

The Transport (London) Act, 1969, gives the Council the primary responsibility for overall transport planning, including the fullest possible integration of all forms of public transport, traffic measures and the development of the most important roads, in close association with land use planning.

Expanding towns.—One aspect of the Council's policy is the provision of homes for people in housing need from London, willing to move to jobs in towns expanding under agreements with the G.L.C. made under the Town Development Act 1952. The Council has such agreements with over 20 towns.

Parks.—The Council maintains some 5,500 acres of parks and open spaces. The London Borough Councils and the City Corporation between them provide a further 26,650 acres. Up to 1,000 open-air entertainments are arranged in G.L.C. parks each summer and almost all games and sports are provided for. At Crystal Palace, in addition to the Council's 70 acre park is the Crystal Palace National Sports Centre, owned by the Council and managed by the Sports Council.

Other features of the G.L.C.'s administration include its responsibility for the Royal Festival Hall, Queen Elizabeth Hall and Purcell Room and the Hayward Gallery; the maintenance of the Iveagh Bequest, Kenwood, several other buildings of historic interest and two museums. The Greater London Record Office and Library house official records and other manuscripts, books, maps, drawings and photographs relating to London and are open to the public for reference purposes. The Research and Intelligence unit is concerned with information and research on any matters concerning

Greater London. The results of its work will be available to government departments, local authorities and the public.

Refuse disposal.—The Council is responsible for the disposal of refuse throughout Greater London—almost 3,000,000 tons being handled each year. It operates twenty-five transfer stations (where refuse is transferred into bulk road vehicles or barges) and five incinerators. Refuse is used for infilling at some twenty land reclamation sites. The Boroughs continue to be responsible for refuse collection. Well over 18,000 old vehicles and more than 150,000 tons of bulky household refuse (the latter deposited direct by members of the public but included in the total of 3,000,000 tons) are also dealt with as a means of improving the environment under the Civic Amenities Act, 1967.

Land Drainage and Flood Prevention.—The G.L.C. and the Borough Councils exercise land drainage functions on certain watercourses within a 400 sq. mile area in and adjoining Greater London known as the London Excluded Area. The G.L.C. undertakes flood prevention works and maintains unobstructed flows in main metropolitan watercourses including the Ravensbourne, Beverley Brook, Wandle, Crane and Brent rivers. The Council also has flood prevention functions along some 120 miles of riverbank of the Thames and its tidal tributaries. Work has started, and will continue over the next four years, on the construction of a barrier across the Thames at Silvertown which, with associated bank raising schemes, will provide flood protection against surge tides.

Licensing.—The Council is the licensing authority in Greater London for certain places of entertainment, greyhound race tracks and petroleum installations and, as agent for the Department of the

Environment, licenses motor vehicles and drivers.

Fire Services.—The Council runs the fire service for its whole area.

The London Fire Brigade set up on April 1, 1965, under the London Government Act, 1963, consists of the Brigades of the former counties of London and Middlesex (excluding the districts of Staines, Sunbury and Potters Bar), the former county boroughs of East Ham, West Ham and Croydon and of parts of Essex, Herts., Kent and Surrey. *Headquarters*, 8 Albert Embankment, S.E.1.

The Brigade has 114 land and 2 river stations. Wholetime authorized establishment, 6,658. There are 578 fire-fighting appliance vehicles and three fire boats in commission. In 1975, there were 93,542 calls to fires and other emergencies.

Acting Chief Officer and Deputy Chief Officer, D. R. Burrell, Q.F.S.M.

Finance.—The gross revenue expenditure of the G.L.C. (excluding London Transport) in 1976–77 is estimated in the annual budget at over £693,100,000 and that of the I.L.E.A. £453,400,000, making a total of £1,146,500,000; of this total about 60 per cent. (£695,100,000) will be met from rates, about 28 per cent. (£321,600,000) from income from rents, services, etc., and the balance of about 12 per cent. (£129,800,000) from central Government grants. The amount levied by the G.L.C. in rate precepts varies for different London Borough Councils according to the services provided.

Gross capital expenditure of the G.L.C. and the I.L.E.A., approved in the annual budget and mainly met by borrowing, amounts to about £375,000,000. Capital expenditure on housing and loans for house purchase accounts for over two-thirds of the total.

THE CORPORATION OF LONDON

The City of London is the historic centre at the heart of London known as "the square mile" around which the vast metropolis has grown over the centuries. The City's population is 4,232 (1971 Census, preliminary). The civic government is carried on by the Corporation of London through the Court of Common Council, a body consisting of the Lord Mayor, 25 other Aldermen and 150 Common Councilmen. The legal title of the Corporation is "the Mayor and Commonalty and Citizens of the City of London."

The City is the financial and business centre of London and includes the head offices of the principal banks, insurance companies and mercantile houses, in addition to buildings ranging from the historic interest of the Roman Wall and the 15th century Guildhall, to the massive splendour of St. Paul's Cathedral and the architectural beauty of Wren's spires.

The City of London was described by Tacitus in A.D. 62 as "a busy emporium for trade and traders". Under the Romans it became an important administration centre and hub of the road system. Little is known of London in Saxon times when it formed part of the kingdom of the East Saxons. In 886 Alfred recovered London from the Danes and reconstituted it a burgh under his son-in-law. In 1066 the citizens submitted to William the Conqueror who in 1067 granted them a charter, which is still preserved, establishing them in the rights and privileges they had hitherto enjoyed. The mayoralty was established on the recognition of the corporate unity of the citizens by Prince John in 1191, the first Mayor being Henry Fitz Ailwyn who filled the office for 21 years and was succeeded by Fitz Alan (1212–15). A new charter was granted by King John in 1215, directing the Mayor to be

chosen annually, which has ever since been done, though in early times the same individual often held the office more than once. A familiar instance is that of "Whittington, thrice Lord Mayor of London" (in reality four times, A.D. 1397, 1398, 1406, 1419); and many modern cases have occurred. The earliest instance of the phrase "Lord Mayor" in English is in 1414. It is used more generally in the latter part of the 15th century and becomes invariable from 1535 onwards. At Michaelmas the Liverymen in Common Hall choose two Aldermen who have served the office of Sheriff for presentation to the Court of Aldermen, and one is chosen to be Lord Mayor for the ensuing mayoral year. The Lord Mayor is presented to the Lord Chief Justice at the Royal Courts of Justice on the second Saturday in November to make the final declaration of office, having been sworn in at Guildhall on the preceding day. The procession to the Royal Courts of Justice is popularly known as the *Lord Mayor's Show*.

Aldermen are mentioned in the 11th century and their office is of Saxon origin. They were elected annually between 1377 and 1394, when a charter of Richard II directed them to be chosen for life. The *Common Council*, elected annually on December 17, was, at an early date, substituted for a popular assembly called the *Folkmote*. At first only two representatives were sent from each ward, but the number has since been greatly increased.

Sheriffs were Saxon officers: their predecessors were the *wic-reeves* and *portreeves* of London and Middlesex. At first they were officers of the Crown, and were named by the Barons of the Exchequer; but Henry I (in 1132) gave the citizens permission to choose their own Sheriffs, and the annual election of Sheriffs became fully operative

under King John's charter of 1199. The citizens lost this privilege, as far as the election of Sheriff of Middlesex is concerned, by the Local Government Act, 1888; but the Liverymen continue, as heretofore, to choose two Sheriffs of the City of London, who are appointed on Midsummer Day, and take office at Michaelmas.

Officers.—The Recorder was first appointed in 1298. The office of Chamberlain is an ancient one, the first contemporary record of which is 1276. The Town Clerk (or Common Clerk) is mentioned in 1274 and the Common Serjeant in 1291.

Activities.—The work is assigned to a number of committees which present reports to the Court of Common Council. These Committees are:— City Lands and Bridge House Estates, Coal, Corn and Rates Finance, Planning and Communications, Central Markets, Billingsgate and Leadenhall Markets, Spitalfields Market, Police, Port and City of London Health, Library (Library, Records, Art Gallery and Museum), Schools, Music (Guildhall School of Music and Drama), General Purposes, Establishment, Housing, Gresham (City side), Epping Forest and Open Spaces, West Ham Park, Policy and Parliamentary, Privileges, Social Services, Guildhall Reconstruction, Barbican and Central Criminal Court (Extension).

The Honourable the *Irish Society*, which manages the Corporation's Estates in Ulster, consists of a Governor and 5 other Aldermen, the Recorder, and 19 Common Councilmen, of whom one is elected Deputy Governor.

The *City's Estate*, in the possession of which the Corporation of London differs from other municipalities, is managed by the City Lands and Bridge House Estates Committee, the Chairmanship of which carries with it the title of " Chief Commoner."

The Right Honourable the Lord Mayor 1975–1976★

Sir Lindsay Roberts Ring, G.B.E.; *born* 1914; Alderman of *Vintry*, 1968; *Sheriff of London*, 1967; *Lord Mayor*, 1975.
Secretary, Rear-Admiral E. W. Ellis, C.B., C.B.E.
Recorder, James William Miskin, Q.C., 1975; *Chamberlain*, John Percival Griggs, M.C., 1974; *Town Clerk*, Stanley James Clayton, 1974; *Common Serjeant*, John Mervyn Guthrie Griffith-Jones, M.C., 1964

The Aldermen

Aldermen.	Ward	Born.	C.C.	Ald.	Shff.	Lord Mayor
Sir Denis Henry Truscott, G.B.E., T.D.....	Bridge Without............	1908	1938	1947	1951	1957
Sir Bernard Nathaniel Waley-Cohen, Bt..	Portsoken................	1914	....	1949	1955	1960
Sir Robert (Ian) Bellinger, G.B.E........	Cheap	1910	1953	1958	1962	1966
Sir Gilbert (Samuel) Inglefield, G.B.E., T.D......................................	Aldersgate..............	1909	....	1959	1963	1967
Sir Edward de Coucey Howard, Bt., G.B.E.	Cornhill.................	1915	1951	1963	1966	1971
The Lord Mais, G.B.E., E.R.D., T.D........	Walbrook................	1911	....	1963	1969	1972
Sir Hugh Walter Kingwell Wontner, G.B.E., C.V.O..............................	Broad Street............	1908	....	1963	1970	1973
Sir Henry Murray Fox, G.B.E...........	Bread Street............	1912	1962	1966	1971	1974
Sir Lindsay Roberts Ring, G.B.E.......	Vintry..................	1914	1964	1968	1967	1975

All the above have passed the Civic Chair

Cdr. Robin Danvers Penrose Gillett, R.D., R.N.R...........................	Bassishaw...............	1925	1965	1969	1973	....
Air Cdre. Hon. Peter Beckford Rutgers Vanneck, C.B., O.B.E., A.F.C..........	Cordwainer.............	1922	....	1969	1974	....
Kenneth Russell Cork.................	Tower..................	1913	1951	1970	1975	....
Alan Seymour Lamboll................	Castle Baynard.........	1923	1949	1970	1976	....
Michael Herbert Hinton..............	Billingsgate............	1934	1970	1971	....	....
Peter Drury Haggerston Gadsden.......	Farringdon Wt..........	1929	1969	1971	....	....
Neville Bernard Burston..............	Farringdon Wn.........	....	1961	1971	....	....
Col. Ronald Laurence Gardner-Thorpe, T.D....................................	Bishopsgate............	1917	....	1972	....	....
Christopher Selwyn Priestley Rawson...	Lime Street.............	1928	1963	1972	1971	....
Christopher Leaver..................	Dowgate................	1937	1973	1974	....	....
George Peter Theobald...............	Queenhithe.............	1931	1968	1974	....	....
Anthony Stuart Jolliffe..............	Candlewick.............	1938	....	1975	....	....
Lady Donaldson.....................	Coleman St.............	1921	1966	1975	....	....
Alan T. Traill......................	Langbourn.............	....	....	1970	1975	....

★ The Lord Mayor for 1976–77 was elected on Michaelmas Day.

The Sheriffs 1976–1977

Alderman Alan Seymour Lamboll (*see above*) and Alexander Colin Cole, T.D., *elected* June 29; *assumed office* September 28, 1976.

THE COMMON COUNCIL OF LONDON

Allday, P. F. (1972)..............*Bishopsgate*
Amies, T. H. C. (1961)...........*Bridge*
Angell, O. D. (1964).............*Bishopsgate*
Ballard, K. A., M.C. (1969).......*Castle Baynard*
Balls, H. D. (1970)...............*Cripplegate*
Barratt, *Deputy* T. E. C., C.B.E.
(1944)........................*Candlewick*
Batty, J. G. (1968)..............*Portsoken*

Beck, R. T. (1963)..............*Farringdon Wn.*
Bell, A. M. (1971)..............*Bassishaw*
Bowen, I., C.M.G. (1971)........*Broad St.*
Brewer, *Deputy* H. G. (1970).....*Langbourn*
Brighton, A. G. (1966)..........*Portsoken*
Brooks, W. I. B. (1967).........*Cripplegate*
Brown, B. J. (1973).............*Aldersgate*
Brown, D. T. (1971)............*Walbrook*

Bull, P. A. (1968)..............*Cheap*
Burrow, G. W. (1965)..........*Lime Street*
Champness, *Deputy* P. H. (1966).. *Walbrook*
Charvet, R. C. L., R.D. (1970)....*Aldgate*
Clackson, *Deputy* D. L., M.B.E.
  (1951).....................*Farringdon Wt.*
Cleary, F. E., M.B.E. (1959).......*Coleman St.*
Clements, G. E. (1960)........*Farringdon Wt.*
Cohen, S. E., C.B.E. (1951)......*Farringdon Wt.*
Cole, A. C., T.D. (1964).........*Castle Baynard*
Collett, C. (1973)............*Broad Street*
Collett, *Deputy* Sir Kingsley, C.B.E.
  (1945)........................*Bridge*
Colover, D. (1975)..............*Bishopsgate*
Cook, J. E. Evan- (1972).........*Lime Street*
Cope, Dr. J. (1963).........*Farringdon Wt.*
Coulson, *Deputy* A. G. (1961)....*Broad St.*
Coven, *Deputy* Mrs. E. O. (1972).*Dowgate*
Coward, C. R. (1966)..........*Cripplegate*
Cresswell, P. H. (1958).........*Aldgate*
Daltrey, D. H. J. (1973).....*Billingsgate*
Davis, W. A. (1971)............*Queenhithe*
Dean, H. R. (1958)............*Cordwainer*
Deith, *Deputy* R. C. (1944).......*Farringdon Wn.*
Delderfield, D. W. (1971)........*Cripplegate*
Denny, A. M. (1971)............*Billingsgate*
Dewhirst, W. (1971)............*Cripplegate*
Donelly, T. A., M.B.E. (1973).....*Cheap*
Duckworth, *Deputy* H. (1960)...*Lime St.*
Durand, Mrs. B. J. (1975)......*Farrington Wt.*
Dyer, *Deputy* C. F. W., E.R.D. (1966)*Aldgate*
Ebbisham, The Lord, T.D., (1947) *Candlewick*
Ercolani, V. A. (1968)..........*Broad St.*
Eskenzi, A. N. (1971)..........*Farringdon Wn.*
Evans, D. I., T.D. (1952)........*Vintry*
Evans, Mrs. J. (1975)...........*Farringdon Wt.*
Ewin, *Deputy* Sir David Floyd-,
  M.V.O., O.B.E. (1963)...........*Castle Baynard*
Fairweather, C. H. F. (1958)......*Queenhithe*
Fellner, L. L. (1973)..........*Cripplegate*
Fisher, D. G. (1958)............*Cornhill*
Fordham, W. E. (1966)........*Aldgate*
Frankenberg, *Deputy* A. J. (1964)..*Portsoken*
Frappell, C. E. (1973)..........*Bread St.*
Game, *Deputy* D. S. (1950).......*Farringdon Wt.*
Gapp, *Deputy* J. G. (1956).......*Cheap*
Gardener, C. J. (1964)..........*Broad St.*
Gass, G. J. (1967)..............*Coleman St.*
Gold, R. (1965)................*Castle Baynard*
Goodinge, A. W. (1966).........*Aldersgate*
Gorman, R. W. (1975)..........*Aldersgate*
Green, A. E. C., M.B.E., T.D. (1971)*Bread Street*
Gugan, Dr. K. L. (1974).........*Dowgate*
Hall, N. L., C.B.E. (1952)........*Farringdon Wt.*
Harding, N. H. (1970)..........*Farringdon Wn.*
Harris, *Deputy* W. H. Wylie (1957) *Farringdon Wn.*
Hart, C. A. (1973)..............*Lime Street*
Hart, M. G. (1970).............*Bridge*
Hatfield, A. F. R. (1968).......*Bishopsgate*
Hedderwick, R. A. R. (1968)....*Walbrook*
Henfrey, Dr. A. W. (1974).......*Aldersgate*
Hill, *Deputy* E. W. F., T.D. (1962). *Tower*
Hoare, J. E. (1966)............*Bishopsgate*
Holland, J. (1972).............*Aldgate*
Horlock, H. W. S. (1969)........*Farringdon Wn.*
Howard, D. H. S. (1973).........*Cornhill*
Hunt, *Deputy* W. G. G. (1962)....*Cripplegate*
Ide, W. R. (1972)..............*Castle Baynard*
James, A. J. (1973).............*Cordwainer*
Jenks, M. A. B. (1972)..........*Coleman Street*

Keith, J. M., T.D. (1962)........*Candlewick*
Lascelles, J. C., D.F.C. (1970).....*Billingsgate*
Last, A. W. (1948).............*Bridge*
Laurie, P. D. Northall- (1975)....*Walbrook*
Lawson, G. C. H. (1972).........*Portsoken*
Lewis, *Deputy* C. F., C.B.E. (1936).. *Coleman Street*
Ley, A. H. (1964)..............*Bishopsgate*
Liss, H. (1965)................*Aldersgate*
Longman, M. H. (1967).........*Langbourn*
Luckin, I. F. (1964)............*Candlewick*
Luke, A. L. (1968)..............*Bishopsgate*
McAuley, C. (1957).............*Bread St.*
Mills, A. P. (1969).............*Bassishaw*
Mitchell, C. R. (1972)..........*Castle Baynard*
Morgan, *Deputy* B. L., C.B.E. (1963)*Bishopsgate*
Murkin, C. H. (1969)...........*Vintry*
Olson, A. H. F. (1972)..........*Dowgate*
Oram, *Deputy* M. H., T.D. (1963)..*Cordwainer*
Packard, Brig. J. J. (1973)......*Cripplegate*
Park, J. W. (1966).............*Tower*
Parkin, A. M. (1961)............*Cheap*
Peacock, *Deputy* R. W., C.B.E.
  (1956).......................*Vintry*
Peat, G. C. (1973)..............*Cheap*
Pettit, P. C. F. (1974)..........*Queenhithe*
Pike, *Deputy* H. T. (1946).......*Cornhill*
Prince, *Deputy* L. B., C.B.E. (1950).*Bishopsgate*
Quekett, D. A. F., E.R.D. (1965)..*Cornhill*
Rayleigh, R. (1973).............*Portsoken*
Rayner, N. (1960)..............*Farringdon Wt.*
Reed, J. L., M.B.E. (1967)........*Farringdon Wn.*
Rigby, P. P. (1972).............*Farringdon Wn.*
Rodgers, S. C. (1969)...........*Farringdon Wt.*
Roney, E. P. T. (1974)..........*Bishopsgate*
Rowlandson, Sir Graham, M.B.E.
  (1961)......................*Coleman Street*
Samuels, Mrs. I. (1972).........*Portsoken*
Saunders, D. (1975)............*Candlewick*
Shalit, D. M. (1973)............*Farringdon Wn.*
Sharp, Mrs. I. M. (1974).........*Queenhithe*
Sheppard, Mrs. J. (1975)........*Langbourn*
Sheppard, *Deputy* S., O.B.E. (1957)*Billingsgate*
Shindler, A. B. (1966)..........*Billingsgate*
Silk, D. (1974)................*Cripplegate*
Skilbeck, *Deputy* C. (1948)......*Queenhithe*
Smith, F. S., T.D. (1958)........*Cordwainer*
Smith, *Deputy* Sir John Newson-,
  Bt. (1954)...................*Bassishaw*
Smith, P. A. Revell- (1959)......*Vintry*
Spurrier, H. J. (1974)..........*Dowgate*
Steiner, F. N. (1962)...........*Bread St.*
Stevenson, J. M. (1970).........*Coleman Street*
Stitcher, G. M. (1966)..........*Farringdon Wt.*
Stunt, F. F. (1967).............*Farringdon Wn.*
Sudbury, Col. F. A., O.B.E., E.R.D.
  (1963)......................*Tower*
Sunderland, O., T.D. (1968)......*Billingsgate*
Titchener, H. B. (1966).........*Cripplegate*
Trentham, G. D. (1941).........*Bread St.*
Turner, R. L. (1973)...........*Tower*
Vine, G. M., C.B.E. (1955).......*Farringdon Wt.*
Walker, *Deputy* S. R., C.B.E. (1937)*Bread St.*
Ward, Maj. B. M., M.V.O. (1963)..*Bridge*
Welch, J. R. (1975)............*Walbrook*
Wilmot, R. T. D. (1973).........*Cordwainer*
Wilson, *Deputy* A. B. (1960).....*Aldersgate*
Wilson, E. S. (1971)...........*Aldersgate*
Wixley, G. R. A., O.B.E. (1964)...*Bassishaw*
Woodward, C. D. (1972)........*Cripplegate*
Yates, J. T., M.B.E. (1959).......*Cheap*

Deputies.—In the preceding list each Common Councilman so described serves as *Deputy* to the Alderman of his Ward.

THE CITY GUILDS (LIVERY COMPANIES)

The Livery Companies of the City of London derive their name from the assumption of a distinctive dress or livery by their members in the 14th century.

The order of precedence (according to 2nd Report of Municipal Corporations' Commissioners, 1837), omitting extinct companies, is given in parentheses after the name of each Company. There are 84 Guilds in existence.

About 10,000 Liverymen of the Guilds are entitled to vote at elections in *Common Hall*.

MERCERS (1). *Hall.* Ironmonger Lane, E.C.2. *Livery*, 214.—*Clerk*, G. M. M. Wakeford; *Master*, Sir James Scott, Bt.

GROCERS (2). *Hall*, Princes Street, E.C.2. *Livery* 265.—*Clerk*, A. S. Cox; *Master* Dr. J. G. D. Simpson.

DRAPERS (3). *Hall*, Throgmorton Street, E.C.2. *Livery*, 220.—*Clerk*, A. O'Neill; *Master* J. T. Eldrid.

FISHMONGERS (4) *Hall*, London Bridge, E.C.4. *Livery*, 286.—*Clerk*, E. S. Earl; *Prime Warden*, The Hon. H. W. Astor.

GOLDSMITHS (5). *Hall*, Foster Lane, E.C.2. *Livery*, 240.—*Clerk*, C. P. de B. Jenkins, M.B.E., M.C.; *Prime Warden*, R. Y. Goodden, C.B.E.

SKINNERS (6 and 7). *Hall*, 8 Dowgate Hill, E.C.4. *Livery*, 299.—*Clerk*, M. H. Glover; *Master*, The Hon. R. B. Holroyd Pearce.

MERCHANT TAYLORS (6 and 7). *Hall*, 30 Threadneedle Street, E.C.2. *Livery*, 330.—*Clerk*, J. M. Woolley, M.B.E., T.D.; *Master*, H. E. H. Jones, M.C., T.D.

HABERDASHERS (8). *Hall*, Staining Lane, E.C.2. *Livery*, 320.—*Clerk*, Cdr. W. R. Miller, R.N.; *Master*, Sir Guy Bracewell-Smith, Bt., M.B.E.

SALTERS (9). *Livery*, 150.—*Clerk*, J. M. Montgomery, 4, Fore St., Salters' Hall, E.C.2.; *Master*, H. I. Jory, T.D.

IRONMONGERS (10). *Hall*, Barbican, E.C.2., *Livery*, 36.—*Clerk*, R. B. Brayne, M.B.E.; *Master*, J. R. Crickmay.

VINTNERS (11). *Hall*, Upper Thames Street, E.C.4. *Livery*, 326.—*Clerk*, Cdr. R. D. Ross, R.N.; *Master*, A. J. Kentish.

CLOTHWORKERS (12). *Hall*, Dunster Court, Mincing Lane, E.C.3. *Livery*, 185.—*Clerk*, E. J. Reed; *Master*, W. R. B. Foster.

The above are the Twelve " Great " London Companies in order of Civic precedence.

AIR PILOTS AND AIR NAVIGATORS, GUILD OF (81). *Grand Master*, H.R.H. the Prince Philip Duke of Edinburgh, K.G.; *Clerk*, W. T. F. Rossiter, P.O. Box 13, Air Terminal, Buckingham Palace Road, S.W.1; *Master*, Air Cdre. and Ald. the Hon. P. Vanneck.

APOTHECARIES, SOCIETY OF (58), *Hall*, Black Friars Lane, E.C.4. *Livery*, 675.—*Clerk*, E. Busby, M.B.E.; *Master*, Prof. R. D. Teare.

ARMOURERS AND BRASIERS (22). *Hall*, 81 Coleman Street, E.C.2. *Livery*, 120.—*Clerk*, Col. G. F. H. Archer, M.B.E.; *Master*, A. F. R. Hatfield.

BAKERS (19). *Hall*, Harp Lane, Lower Thames Street, E.C.3. *Livery*, 300.—*Clerk*, H. M. Collinson; *Master*, P. L. Clarke.

BARBERS (17). *Hall*, Monkwell Square, E.C.2. *Livery*, 160.—*Clerk*, B. W. Hall, *Master*, G. S. Hamilton.

BASKETMAKERS (52). *Livery*, 395.—*Clerk*, B. Stroulger, Battlebridge House, 87–95 Tooley Street, S.E.1; *Prime Warden*, A. Breach, C.B.E.

BLACKSMITHS (40). *Livery*, 201.—*Clerk*, J. Green, 41 Tabernacle Street, E.C.2.; *Prime Warden*, D. H. F. Norris.

BOWYERS (38). *Livery*, 60.—*Clerk*, M. J. Smyth, 5 Giltspur Street, E.C.1.; *Master*, A. T. Reed.

BREWERS (14). *Hall*, Aldermanbury Square, E.C.2. *Livery*. 32.—*Clerk*, M. J. Adams; *Master*, Maj. L. J. Turner, T.D.

BRODERERS (48). *Livery*, 106.—*Clerk*, S. G. B. Underwood, 80 Bishopsgate, E.C.2.; *Master*, A. J. Hart, D.S.C.

BUTCHERS (24). *Hall*, Bartholomew Close, E.C.1. *Livery*, 387.—*Clerk*, W. M. Collins; *Master*, N. L. Hall, C.B.E.

CARMEN (77). *Livery*, 428.—*Clerk*, J. M. Donald, 2 Stratford Place, W.1; *Master*, Sir John Cohen.

CARPENTERS (26). *Hall*, Throgmorton Avenue, E.C.2. *Livery*, 150.—*Clerk*, Capt. G. B. Barstow, R.N.; *Master*, C. E. Keysell, M.B.E., T.D.

CITY OF LONDON SOLICITORS (79). *Livery*, 450.—*Clerk*, E. C. Robbins, C.B.E., Grindall House, 25 Newgate St., E.C.1.; *Master*, G. T. Clark.

CLOCKMAKERS (61). *Livery*, 248.—*Clerk*, R. C. Pennefather, M.B.E., 38 Bedford Place, Bloomsbury Square, W.C.1.; *Master*, R. G. Beloe.

COACHMAKERS (72). *Livery*, 356.—*Clerk*, A. T. Langdon-Down, 9 Lincoln's Inn Fields, W.C.2; *Master*, M. A. Smith, D.F.C.

COOKS (35). *Livery* 75.—*Clerk*, H. J. Lavington, T.D., 49 Queen Victoria Street, E.C.4.; *Master*, M. V. Kenyon, M.V.O.

COOPERS (36). *Livery*, 230.—*Clerk*, J. W. S. Clark, 13 Devonshire Square, E.C.2; *Master*, Ald. Sir Murray Fox, G.B.E.

CORDWAINERS (27). *Livery*, 137.—*Clerk*, E. J. Mander, Eldon Chambers, 30 Fleet Street, E.C.4.; *Master*, R. E. F. Peal.

CURRIERS (29). *Livery*, 65.—*Clerk*, I. R. McNeil, 43 Church Road, Hove; *Master*, A. O. R. Vick.

CUTLERS (18). *Hall*, 4 Warwick Lane, E.C.4. *Livery*, 100.—*Clerk*, K. S. G. Hinde; *Master*, N. W. Iorns.

DISTILLERS (69). *Livery*, 150.—*Clerk*, H. B. Dehn, Compter House, Wood Street, E.C.2; *Master*, Col. G. V. Churton, M.B.E., M.C., T.D.

DYERS (13). *Hall*, 10 Dowgate Hill, E.C.4. *Livery*, 110.—*Clerk*, A. J. Boyall; *Prime Warden*, C. A. Cooper.

FAN MAKERS (76). *Livery*, 163.—*Clerk*, E. J. H. Geffen, Africa House, 64–78 Kingsway, W.C.2; *Master*, J. A. Allen.

FARMERS (80). *Livery*, 284.—*Clerk*, Dr. B. A. C. Kirk-Duncan; 8 St. Mary at Hill, E.C.3. *Master*, Sir Nigel Strutt, T.D.; *Senior Warden*, M. C. Cheveley.

FARRIERS (55). *Livery*, 310.—*Clerk*, F. E. Birch, 3 Hamilton Road, Cockfosters, Barnet, Herts; *Master*, Prof. F. R. Bell.

FELTMAKERS (63). *Livery*, 350.—*Clerk*, E. J. P. Elliott, 53 Davies Street, Berkeley Square, W.1.; *Master*, G. F. D. Rice.

FLETCHERS (39). *Livery*, 69.—*Clerk*, F. N. Steiner, Compter House, 4–9 Wood Street, E.C.2.; *Master*, G. W. Burrow.

FOUNDERS (53). *Hall*, 13 St. Swithin's Lane, E.C.4. *Livery*, 136.—*Clerk*, H. W. Wiley; *Master*, R. C. Scott.

FRAMEWORK KNITTERS (64). *Livery*, 225.—*Clerk*, H. C. Weale, St. Saviour's School, New Kent Road, S.E.1.; *Master*, W. K. Lowe.

FRUITERERS (45). *Livery*, 220.—*Clerk*, D. L. Hohnen, 49 Berners St., W.1.; *Master*, J. J. Wells.

FURNITURE MAKERS (83). *Livery*, 182.—*Clerk*, G. Benbow, T.D., c/o J. Ward & Co., Robertsbridge, Sussex; *Master*, J. H. Nickson, T.D.

GARDENERS (66). *Livery*, 250.—*Clerk*, F. N. Steiner, Compter House, 4/9 Wood Street, E.C.2.; *Master*, C. R. Crosse.

GIRDLERS (23). *Hall*, Basinghall Avenue, E.C.2. *Livery*, 80.—*Clerk*, J. A. M. Rutherford; *Master*, R. H. Wilson.

GLASS-SELLERS (71). Livery, 160.—Hon. Clerk, H. K. S. Clark, 6 Eldon Street, E.C.2; Master, S. E. Matthews.

GLAZIERS (53). Livery, 250.—Clerk, W. L. T. Smith, 6 New Square, Lincoln's Inn, W.C.2.; Master, B. D. L. Thomas, O.B.E.

GLOVERS (62). Livery, 200.—Clerk, H. M. Collinson, Bakers Hall, Harp Lane, Lower Thames Street, E.C.3; Master, D. P. L. Amtill, T.D.

GOLD AND SILVER WYREDRAWERS (74). Livery, 325.—Clerk, D. Reid, 40a Ludgate Hill, E.C.4.; Master, R. A. R. Hedderwick.

GUNMAKERS (73). Livery, 84.—Clerk, F. B. Brandt, 12 Devonshire Square, E.C.3; Master, L. P. D. Salter.

HORNERS (54). Livery, 440.—Clerk, G. S. Wood, 28 Bush Lane, E.C.4.; Master, G. M. Pinker.

INNHOLDERS (32). Hall, College Street, Dowgate Hill, E.C.4. Livery, 107.—Clerk, J. H. Bentley, O.B.E.; Master, Dr. I. R. Haire.

JOINERS (41). Livery, 85.—Clerk, B. J. Turner, 14 Parkway, N.14; Master, D. A. Knight

LEATHERSELLERS (15). Hall, 15 St. Helens Place, E.C.3. Livery, 150.—Clerk, C. Davenport; Master, P. A. Preston, T.D.

LORINERS (57). Livery, 290.—Clerk, D. B. Morris, Africa House, 64–78 Kingsway, W.C.2.; Master, D. A. Walker-Arnott.

MASONS (30). Livery, 95.—Clerk, H. J. Maddocks, 9 New Square, W.C.2.; Master, J. G. Bentley.

MASTER MARINERS, HONOURABLE COMPANY OF (78). H.Q.S. Wellington, Temple Stairs, W.C.2. Livery, 300.—Clerk, D. H. W. Field; Admiral, H.R.H. the Prince Philip, Duke of Edinburgh, K.G.; Master, Capt. W. E. Warwick, C.B.E., R.D., R.N.R.

MUSICIANS (50). Livery, 220.—Clerk, W. R. I. Crewdson, 4 St. Paul's Churchyard, E.C.4.; Master, N. Abrahams.

NEEDLEMAKERS (65). Livery, 240.—Clerk, R. H. Lane, 8 Bolton St., W.1.; Master, Sir Martin Wilkinson.

PAINTER STAINERS (28). Hall, 9 Little Trinity Lane, E.C.4. Livery, 350.—Clerk, H. N. Wylie; Master, R. J. Green.

PATTERNMAKERS (70). Livery, 152.—Clerk, A. J. Hucker, 5/6 Raymond Bldgs., Gray's Inn, W.C.1.; Master, D. P. C. Weiner.

PAVIORS (56). Livery, 225.—Clerk, F. A. Barragan, 130 Mount Street, W.1.; Master, The Lord Mais, G.B.E., T.D., E.R.D.

PEWTERERS (16). Hall, Oat Lane, E.C.2. Livery, 110.—Clerk, C. G. Grant; Master, Rev. J. L. Mullens.

PLAISTERERS (46). Livery, 173.—Clerk, H. Mott, Plaisterers Hall, 1 London Wall, E.C.2; Master, P. J. Schryver.

PLAYING CARD MAKERS (75). Livery, 150.—Clerk, E. K. King, 21A Northampton Square, E.C.1; Master, D. T. Hill.

PLUMBERS (31). Livery, 250.—Clerk, M. E. C. Lewis, 218 Strand, W.C.2; Master, L. R. Holbrook.

POULTERS (34). Livery, 150.—Clerk, I. G. Williamson, 9 Staple Inn, Holborn, W.C.1.; Master, J. Gilpin.

SADDLERS (25). Hall, Gutter Lane, Cheapside, E.C.2. Livery, 90.—Clerk, Maj. A. D. Hathway-Jones, R.M. (ret.); Master, H. W. S. Horlock.

SCIENTIFIC INSTRUMENT MAKERS (84). Livery, 155.—Clerk, Maj. Gen. E. Younson, O.B.E., 20 Peel St., W.8.; Master, W. Logan.

SCRIVENERS (44). Livery, 136.—Hon. Clerk, D. V. O'Meara, Lower Court, Stationers Hall, Ludgate Hill, E.C.4.; Master, J. D. Heal.

SHIPWRIGHTS (59). Livery 500.—Hon. Clerk, D. J. Walker, 14–20 St. Mary Axe, E.C.3; Permanent Master, H.R.H. the Prince Philip Duke of Edinburgh, K.G.; Prime Warden, R. Hill.

SPECTACLEMAKERS (60). Livery, 220.—Clerk, C. J. Eldridge, Apothecaries' Hall, E.C.4; Master, F. M. Wiseman.

STATIONERS AND NEWSPAPER MAKERS (47). Hall, Stationers' Hall, E.C.4. Livery, 425.—Clerk, Col. R. A. Rubens; Master, J. Matson, C.B.E.

TALLOWCHANDLERS (21). Hall, 4 Dowgate Hill, E.C.4. Livery, 149.—Clerk, R. H. Monier-Williams; Master, R. T. D. Wilmot.

TIN PLATE WORKERS (67). Livery, 181.—Clerk, B. Dehn, Compter House, Wood Street, E.C.2; Master, F. Hayes.

TOBACCO PIPE MAKERS AND TOBACCO BLENDERS (82). Livery, 200.—Clerk, I. J. Kimmins, 9 Red Lion Court, E.C.4.; Master, R. S. Hargreaves, M.C.

TURNERS (51). Livery, 160.—Clerk, A. T. Reed, Giltspur House, 5–6 Giltspur Street, E.C.1; Master, D. L. Smithers.

TYLERS AND BRICKLAYERS (37). Livery, 90.—Clerk, J. C. Peck, 6 Bedford Row, W.C.1; Master, D. J. Parry-Crooke.

UPHOLDERS (49). Livery, 206.—Clerk, U. J. Burke, 26 St. Andrew's Hill, E.C.4.; Master, D. Horn.

WAXCHANDLERS (20). Hall, Gresham Street, E.C.2. Livery, 80.—Clerk, T. Wood; Master, A. J. Gregory.

WEAVERS (42). Livery, 125.—Clerk, J. G. Ouvry, 53 Romney Street, S.W.1; Upper Bailiff, R. E. Early.

WHEELWRIGHTS (68). Livery, 297.—Clerk, W. R. Rogers, 50 Chigwell Rd., E. 18.; Master, E. W. Bales.

WOOLMEN (43). Livery, 121.—Clerk, R. J. R. Cousins, 192–198 Vauxhall Bridge Rd., S.W.1; Master, R. O. Camac.

PARISH CLERKS (No livery) (Members, 90).—Clerk, R. H. Adams, T.D., F.S.A., 108 Dulwich Village, S.E.21; Master, R. T. Beck.

WATERMEN AND LIGHTERMEN (No livery).—Hall, 18 St. Mary-at-Hill, E.C.3.—Clerk, B. G. Wilson; Master, M. R. Francis.

LAUNDERERS (No livery).—Clerk, P. H. Jackson, V.R.D., 21 Whitefriars St., E.C.4.; Master, E. W. Swetman, O.B.E.

BUILDERS MERCHANTS OF THE CITY OF LONDON (No livery) (Members, 160).—Clerk, V. J. Fanstone, O.B.E., 34–35 Farringdon Street, E.C.4; Master, J. A. Hunter.

NOTE.—In certain companies the election of Master or Prime Warden for the year does not take place till the autumn. In such cases the Master or Prime Warden for 1975–76 is given.

LONDON BOROUGHS

City or Borough *Inner London Borough	Municipal Offices	Population (Reg. Gen.'s Est. June 1972)	Rateable Value April 1, 1976	Rate Levied 1976–77	Town Clerk (*Chief Executive)	Mayor or Lord Mayor
			£	p.		
CITY OF WESTMINSTER★	City Hall, Victoria St., S.W.1.	233,360	306,278,713	71	*Sir Alan Dawtry, C.B.E., T.D.	J. Gillett (*Lord Mayor*)
Barking.........	‡Dagenham, Essex.	158,710	26,404,856	79·5	S. W. Barker.	F. G. Tibble
Barnet..........	†The Burroughs, Hendon, N.W.4.	305,760	57,054,745	68·5	E. M. Bennett	A. Pares, M.B.E.
Bexley..........	†Erith, Kent.	216,980	28,883,379	78	*T. Musgrave.	Mrs. A. E. F. Orange
Brent...........	†Forty Lane, Wembley.	275,570	49,590,125	80	K. B. Betts.	L. Snow
Bromley........	†Bromley, Kent.	306,550	45,983,000	81·5	*P. J. Bunting.	Mrs. S. M. Stead
Camden★........	†Euston Road, N.W.1.	197,390	103,704,059	83·5	B. H. Wilson, C.B.E.	A. Soutter
Croydon........	†Taberner House, Park Lane, Croydon	334,000	66,343,415	69·03	*A. Blakemore, C.B.E.	Mrs. M. Parfitt
Ealing..........	†Ealing, W.5.	299,440	53,914,298	83·75	*P. J. Coomber.	J. I. Wood
Enfield..........	‡Silver St., Enfield.	265,910	46,580,722	74	*W. D. Day.	P. G. Elvidge
Greenwich★......	†Wellington St., Woolwich, S.E.18.	216,180	31,400,000	72·3	*R. L. Doble.	Mrs. H. Stroud
Hackney★.......	†Mare St., E.8.	215,270	36,348,584	62	*D. Wood	G. Silver
Hammersmith★..	†King St., W.6.	181,880	34,015,361	67	*A. Allen	L. Hilliard, C.B.E.
Haringey........	†High Road, N.22.	235,490	34,212,767	88	*R. C. Limb	V. Butler
Harrow.........	‡Station Rd., Harrow.	203,730	33,234,483	80	*R. Hill.	A. J. Lovell, B.E.M.,
Havering........	†Main Road, Romford, Essex.	247,130	36,484,455	78·5	*R. W. J. Tridgell.	H. J. S. Turner [I.S.M.
Hillingdon......	†Wood End Green Rd., Hayes, Middx.	236,390	54,151,085	81·4	*G. Hooper.	R. H. Collman
Hounslow.......	†I ampton Rd., Hounslow	206,460	48,041,602	79·9	*R. J. Jefferies	M. Digby
Islington★.......	†Upper St., N.1.	194,280	49,629,062	73	*H. M. Dewing.	Mrs. S. Gordon
Kensington and Chelsea (Royal Borough)★.....	†Kensington, W.8.	183,230	68,165,606	58·3	R. L. Stillwell D.F.C., D.F.M.	D. Collenette, M.C.
Kingston upon Thames.......	Guildhall, Kingston upon Thames	139,420	27,283,842	72·9	*J. S. Bishop.	F. J. Steptoe
Lambeth★.......	†Brixton Hill, S.W.2.	301,690	56,703,010	72·5	*F. D. Ward.	W. A. Hall
Lewisham★......	†Catford, S.E.6.	262,920	31,985,581	52·2	(vacant).	A. Patterson
Merton..........	†Broadway, Wimbledon, S.W.19.	176,820	29,559,185	79·5	*A. G. Robinson, D.F.C.	J. A. Watson
Newham........	†East Ham, E.6.	232,020	35,412,596	89·3	*J. J. Warren.	H. A. Taylor
Redbridge.......	†High Rd., Ilford, Essex.	238,300	35,680,000	76·5	*A. McC. Findlay.	F. Mountier
Richmond upon Thames.......	§Twickenham, Mddx.	172,560	30,004,307	77·5	A. W. B. Goode, MC	R. A. J. Alcock
Southwark★.....	†Peckham Rd., S.E.5.	253,260	50,242,035	79·5	S. T. Evans.	F. J. Francis
Sutton..........	‡3 Throwley Rd., Sutton, Surrey.	169,050	26,618,166	77·5	*T. M. H. Scott.	H. A. Bennett
Tower Hamlets★..	†Patriot Square, E.2.	159,200	40,353,041	80	*J. Wolkind.	D. Kelly
Waltham Forest..	†Walthamstow, E.17.	233,200	30,797,086	66·5	*L. G. Knox.	H. F. Fulton
Wandsworth★....	†Wandsworth, S.W.18.	287,080	41,352,389	67·5	*N. B. White.	S. P. Dougherty

† Town Hall. ‡ Civic Centre. § Municipal Offices.

Public and Private Buildings in London

ADELPHI, Strand, W.C.2.—Adelphi Terrace and district commemorate the four architect brothers, James, John, Robert and William ADAM, who laid out the district (formerly Durham House) at the close of the 18th century. Four of the streets in the Adelphi were formerly called James, John, Robert, and William Streets to commemorate these founders of the Adam style of architecture and internal decoration. They are now Adam Street, John Adam Street, Robert Street and Durham House Street. Extensive rebuilding took place between the two World Wars, and there are now few 18th-century houses left in the district. In the neighbourhood of the Adelphi was York House, built by the Duke of Buckingham in 1625 (the Water Gate of which still stands in Embankment Gardens), the commemorative streets being *Charles* Street, *Villiers* Street, *Duke* Street, *Of* Lane, *Buckingham* Street (Of Lane is now " York Buildings ").

AUSTRALIA HOUSE, Strand, W.C.2.—A handsome and imposing building, erected 1911-14 by the Commonwealth of Australia as the offices of the High Commissioner for the Commonwealth. NEW SOUTH WALES, QUEENSLAND, VICTORIA and WESTERN AUSTRALIA have separate offices in the Strand; TASMANIA at Golden Cross House, Charing Cross, and SOUTH AUSTRALIA at S.A. House, 50 Strand, W.C.2.

BALTIC EXCHANGE, St. Mary Axe, E.C.3.— The world market for the chartering of cargo ships. The present Exchange was built in 1903 and the new wing opened by Her Majesty the Queen on Nov. 21, 1956.

BANK OF ENGLAND, Threadneedle Street, E.C.2. (Not open to sightseers)—The Bank of England, founded in 1694, has always been closely connected with the Government. The present building, completed in 1940 to the designs of Sir Herbert Baker, incorporates features reminiscent of the earlier architects, Sampson (1734), Sir Robert Taylor (1765) and Sir John Soane (1788).

BRIDGES.—The bridges over the Thames (from East to West) are the *Tower Bridge* (built by the Corporation of London and opened in 1894), with its bascules, operated now by new electrically-run machinery; *London Bridge* (opened after rebuilding in 1831 by Rennie; the new London Bridge was completed in 1973 and opened by Her Majesty the Queen on March 16, 1973; *Southwark Bridge* (opened in 1819, also by Rennie; rebuilt by the Corporation of London, 1922); *Blackfriars Bridge* (opened in 1769, rebuilt, 1869, and widened by the Corporation of London in 1909); *Waterloo Bridge* (Rennie), opened in 1817, commanding a fine view of western London, rebuilt by L.C.C. and re-opened 1944; *Hungerford Bridge*, 1863 (railway bridge with a footbridge); *Westminster Bridge* (built in 1750 and then presenting a view that inspired Wordsworth's sonnet; rebuilt and re-opened in 1862; width, 84 ft.) with Thomas Thornycroft's *Boadicea* at the north-eastern end; this bridge leads from Westminster Abbey and the Houses of Parliament to the County Hall and St. Thomas's Hospital; *Lambeth Bridge* (built 1862, rebuilt 1932) leading from Lambeth Palace to Millbank; *Vauxhall Bridge* (built in 1811-16, rebuilt in 1906), leading to Kennington Oval; *Chelsea Bridge*, leading from Chelsea Hospital to Battersea Park (reconstructed and widened; 1937) and *Albert Bridge* (1873); *Battersea Bridge* (opened in 1890); *Wandsworth Bridge* (opened in 1873; rebuilt and re-opened in 1940); *Putney Bridge* (built 1729, rebuilt 1884, widened in 1933, where the Oxford and Cambridge Boat Race is started for Mortlake; *Hammersmith Bridge* (rebuilt 1887); *Barnes Bridge* (for pedestrians only, 1933); *Chiswick Bridge* (opened in 1933); *King Edward VII Bridge, Kew* (rebuilt in 1902, opened 1903, leading to the Royal Botanic Gardens, Kew; *Twickenham Lock Bridge; Twickenham Bridge* (opened 1933); *Richmond Bridge* (opened in 1777); *Kingston Bridge* (built 1828 and widened 1914) and *Hampton Court Bridge* (rebuilt, 1933).

BUCKINGHAM PALACE, St. James's Park, S.W.1. (Not open to the public.)—Was purchased by King George III in 1762 from the heir of the Duke of Buckingham, and was altered by Nash for King George IV. The London home of the Sovereign since Queen Victoria's accession in 1837. Re-fronted in stone (part of the Queen Victoria Memorial) by Sir Aston Webb in 1913.

The Queen's Gallery, containing a changing selection of the finest pictures and works of art from all parts of the royal collection, was opened to the public on July 25, 1962. Open: Tues.-Sat., and Bank Holidays 11-5 p.m.; Sundays, 2-5 p.m. Admission 30p; *Children, Students, OAPs* 10p, entering from Buckingham Palace Road.

The Royal Mews is open to visitors on Wednesdays and Thursdays throughout the year (except in Ascot Week), 2-4 p.m. The following charges, the net proceeds of which are devoted to charities, are payable on admission: *Adults*, 15p; *Children*, 5p.

CANADA HOUSE, Trafalgar Square, S.W.1.—A conspicuous building on the Western side of the Square, housing the Office of the High Commissioner for Canada in the United Kingdom. Designed by Sir Robert Smirke and built in 1824-7, it was renovated and embellished when acquired from the Union Club in 1924. Further major alterations have been completed to incorporate the former Royal College of Physicians building, also designed by Sir Robert Smirke, which was acquired in 1964. The renovated building was re-opened in March, 1967. The exteriors of the two buildings were originally designed to create the appearance of a single building by presenting a common façade facing Trafalgar Square. Certain interior features of the original building are preserved and the spacious, richly furnished room now occupied by the High Commissioner is much admired. Surrounded by Offices of Canadian Banks, Steamship, Railway and other Companies, the Canadian Building is one of London's landmarks. It was opened by King George V. in June, 1925.

CANONBURY TOWER, Canonbury, N.1.—The largest remaining part of a 16th-century house originally built by the Priors of St. Bartholomew, and since 1952 used as the headquarters of a non-professional theatre company. Contains the " Spencer " and " Compton " oak-panelled rooms. Other relics of Canonbury House can be seen nearby.

CARLYLE'S HOUSE, 24 Cheyne Row, Chelsea, S.W.3. The home of Thomas Carlyle for 47 years until his death in 1881, and containing much of his furniture, etc. Now the property of the National Trust. Open daily, except Mondays and Tuesdays, 11-1, 2-6, or dusk, if earlier. Sundays, 2-6. Closed New Year's Day, Good Friday and all December. Admission 25p; Children and Students 12p.

CATHOLIC CENTRAL LIBRARY, St. Francis Friary, 47 Francis Street, S.W.1.—Founded as a private library in 1914, it was taken over in 1959 by the Franciscan Friars of the Atonement. It is an up-to-date lending and research library of over 50,000 volumes, 120 periodicals, for the general reader, student and ecumenist. Books are sent by post

when required. Hours of opening: Mon.-Fri. 10.30-6.30; Sat. 10.30-4.30.

CEMETERIES.—In *Kensal Green Cemetery*, North Kensington, W.10 (70 acres), are tombs of W. M. Thackeray, Anthony Trollope, Sydney Smith, Shirley Brooks, Wilkie Collins, Tom Hood, W. Mulready, George Cruikshank, John Leech, Leigh Hunt, Brunel (" Great Eastern "), Ross (Arctic), Charles Kemble and Charles Mathews (Actors). In *Highgate Cemetery*, N.6, are the tombs of George Eliot, Herbert Spencer, Michael Faraday, Karl Marx and G. J. Holyoake. In *Abney Park Cemetery*, Stoke Newington, N.16, are the tomb of General Booth, founder of the Salvation Army, and memorials to many Nonconformist Divines. In the *South Metropolitan Cemetery*, Norwood, S.E.27, are the tombs of C. H. Spurgeon, Lord Alverstone, Douglas Jerrold, John Belcher, R.A., Theodore Watts-Dunton, Dr. Moffat (Missionary), Sir H. Bessemer, Sir H. Maxim, Sir J. Barnby, Sir A. Manns and J. Whitaker, F.S.A. (*Whitaker's Almanack*). In the churchyard of the former *Marylebone Chapel* are buried Allan Ramsay (poet), Hoyle (whist), Ferguson (astronomer), Charles Wesley (hymn writer) and his son Samuel Wesley (musician). The chapel itself was demolished in 1949. CREMATORIA.—*Ilford* (City of London); *Norwood; Hendon; Streatham Park; Finchley* (St. Marylebone) and *Golder's Green* (12 acres), near Hampstead Heath, with " Garden of Rest " and memorials to famous men and women.

CENOTAPH, Whitehall, S.W.1.—(Literally " empty tomb "). Monument erected " To the Glorious Dead ", as a memorial to all ranks of the Sea, Land and Air Forces who gave their lives in the service of the Empire during the First World War. Designed by Sir Edwin Lutyens. Erected as a temporary memorial in 1919 and replaced by a permanent structure in 1920. Unveiled by King George V on Armistice Day, 1920. An additional inscription was added after the 1939-45 War, to commemorate those who gave their lives in that conflict.

CHARTERHOUSE, The Hospital of King James, Sutton's Hospital, Charterhouse Square, E.C.1 (*Master*, O. Van Oss; *Registrar and Clerk to the Governors*, J. C. Moss), a Carthusian monastery until 1537, when it came into the possession first of Sir Edward (later the first Lord) North; and was eventually sold by the second Lord North to the former Duke of Norfolk, who renamed it " Howard House ". After his execution, following the Ridolfi Plot, hatched at Charterhouse, in due time the Crown restored the Lord Thomas Howard, later the Earl of Suffolk, and it was purchased from him in 1611 by Thomas Sutton as a hospital for aged " Brothers " and a School (removed to Godalming in 1872). The buildings are partly 14th (but mainly 16th) century. They suffered much damage during the 1939-45 War but are now restored and can accommodate nearly 40 " Brothers ". Visitors can be shown round at 2·45 p.m. on Wednesday during the months of April to July inclusive, except the Wednesdays immediately after Easter and Spring Holiday. (Charge for admission, 30p per person.) Roger Williams, the founder and governor of Rhode Island, U.S.A., was elected a scholar of the Foundation on June 25, 1621. Among many famous Carthusians are John Wesley; the poets Crashaw and Lovelace; Addison and Steele; Sir William Blackstone and Thackeray, who described " Greyfriars School " (Charterhouse) in " The Newcomes "; Baden-Powell and Vaughan Williams.

CHELSEA PHYSIC GARDEN, Royal Hospital Road, S.W.3.—A garden of general botanical research, established in latter part of 17th century by the Society of Apothecaries, occupies site presented in 1722 by Sir Hans Sloane. Transferred in 1899 to the Trustees of the London Parochial Charities. Applications for tickets of admission to the Clerk to the Trustees, 10 Fleet Street, E.C.4:—*Bona fide* students and teachers on any weekday. Unqualified persons limited to two special Open Days a year. 1977, May 5 and September 17.

CHELSEA ROYAL HOSPITAL (founded by Charles II, in 1682, and built by Wren; opened in 1692), Royal Hospital Road, Chelsea, S.W.3, for old and disabled soldiers. Great Hall and Chapel open daily 10 to 12 and 2 to 4 (Museum 10 to 12 and 2 to 5) and on Sunday afternoons. The extensive grounds include the former Ranelagh Gardens. *Governor*, General Sir Antony Read G.C.B., C.B.E., D.S.O., M.C.,; *Lieut-Governor and Secretary*, Major-Gen. P. R. C. Hobart C.B., D.S.O., O.B.E., M.C.

CITY BUSINESS LIBRARY (Corporation of London), 55 Basinghall Street, E.C.2. Open Mon.-Fri. 9.30-5.30.

COLLEGE OF ARMS OR HERALDS' COLLEGE, Queen Victoria Street, E.C.4.—Her Majesty's Officers of Arms (Kings, Heralds and Pursuivants of Arms) were first incorporated by Richard III, and granted Derby House on the site of the present College building by Philip and Mary. The building now in use dates from 1671-88. The powers vested by the Crown in the Earl Marshal (The Duke of Norfolk) with regard to State ceremonial are largely exercised through the College, which is the official repository of English coats of arms and pedigrees. Enquiry may be made to the Officer on duty in the Public Office, Mon.-Fri. between 10 a.m. and 4 p.m.

COMMONWEALTH INSTITUTE, Kensington High Street, W.8.— A permanent exhibition opened on Nov. 6, 1962, by Her Majesty the Queen, replacing the former Imperial Institute opened in 1893 in S. Kensington. An interesting feature of the building is its paraboloid copper-sheathed roof. The Institute contains, in 60,000 square feet arranged in 3 galleries, a visual representation of the history and geography of the Commonwealth countries and dependencies: on the ground floor, exhibits of Canada, Australia, New Zealand, India, Sri Lanka and Bangladesh and the smaller island territories in the southern hemisphere; on the middle gallery, the African territories; and on the upper gallery, the other countries of the Commonwealth. Art gallery; Cinema, showing documentary films daily.

Open, week-days, 10-5.30; Sundays, 2.30-6. Admission free, Closed Good Friday, Christmas Eve, Christmas Day, Boxing Day and New Year's Day.

COUNTY HALL, Westminster Bridge, S.E.1.— The Headquarters of the Greater London Council (*see* pp. 634-6) built on the Pedlar's Acre, Bishop's Acre, Four Acres and Float Mead, Lambeth, from the designs of Ralph Knott, with a river façade of 750 ft. The main building was completed in 1933. The building of the North and South blocks on a site to the East of the main building started in the early 1930s. They were occupied in 1939 but not finally completed until 1963. The Council, when in session, meets in public in the council chamber at three-weekly intervals on Tuesday afternoons at 2.30 p.m.

CUSTOM HOUSE, Lower Thames Street, E.C.3.— Built 1813-17, with a wide quay on Thames. The *Long Room* is about 190 ft. long.

DICKENS HOUSE, 48 Doughty Street, W.C.1.— In this house Charles Dickens lived from 1837 to 1839, and here he completed *Pickwick Papers*. It is the headquarters of the Dickens Fellowship and contains many relics of the novelist. It is open to the public daily, 10 to 5 (Sundays and Bank Holi-

days excepted); admission 40p; students, 30p; Children, 15p.

DR. JOHNSON'S HOUSE, Gough Square, Fleet Street, E.C.4.—A tall late 17th-century house in which Samuel Johnson (and his wife) lived between 1748 and 1759. His *Dictionary* was compiled here. The house is furnished with 18th century pieces and there is an excellent collection of Johnsoniana. Open daily (except Sundays and Bank Holidays) from 11 to 5.30 (Winter 5). Admission 20p; Students, 10p.

ELY PLACE, Holborn Circus, E.C.1.—The site of the London house of former Bishops of Ely, Ely Place is a private street (built in 1773) whose affairs are administered by Commissioners under a special Act of Parliament. The 14th-century chapel, now St. Etheldreda's (R.C.) Church, is open daily until dusk.

FULHAM PALACE, Bishop's Avenue, Fulham, S.W.6.—The courtyard is 16th century, remainder 18th and 19th century. Former residence of the Bishop of London. Grounds of about 9 acres.

GEFFRYE MUSEUM, Kingsland Road, E.2.—Open on Tuesdays to Saturdays 10 to 5, Sundays 2 to 5. Closed on Christmas Day and on Mondays except Bank Holidays. Admission free.

The Museum is housed in a building erected originally as almshouses in 1715. It was eventually purchased by the London County Council and opened as a museum in 1914. The exhibits are shown in a series of period rooms dating from 1600 to 1939, each containing furniture and domestic equipment of a middle-class English home. An 18th century woodworker's shop, an openhearth kitchen and the original chapel are also shown. Temporary exhibitions are held in the Exhibition Hall. There is a reference library of books on furniture, social history and art. Special arrangements for children visiting the Museum in school parties (which must be booked in advance) and in their leisure time. *Curator*, J. Daniels.

GEORGE INN, Southwark.—Near London Bridge Station. Given to National Trust in 1937. Last galleried inn in London, built in 1677. Open during licensed hours.

GUILDHALL, King Street, City, E.C.2.—Scene of civic government for the City for more than a thousand years. Built *c.* 1411–*c.* 1440; façade built 1788–9; damaged in the Great Fire, 1666, and by incendiary bombs, 1940. The main hall and crypt (the most extensive mediæval crypt in London) have been restored. Events in Guildhall include the annual election of Lord Mayor, election of Sheriffs, receptions in honour of Sovereigns and Heads of State, and the meetings of the Court of Common Council (*see* " Corporation of London "). Open free; weekdays, 10–5; Sundays (May to Sept.) 2–5. *Keeper of the Guildhall*, A.J. Marshall.

The Library and Museum of the Clockmakers' Company are housed in new premises, and are open to the public, Mon. to Sat., 10–5. Admission free (entrance in Aldermanbury). The Library contains Plans of London, 1570; Deed of Sale with Shakespeare's signature; first and second, fourth folios of Shakespeare's plays, etc. *see also* City Business Library).

HONOURABLE ARTILLERY COMPANY'S HEADQUARTERS, City Road, E.C.1.—The H.A.C. (*Sec.* Lt.-Col. P. Massey, M.C.) received its charter of incorporation from Henry VIII in 1537, and has occupied its present ground since 1641. The Armoury House dates from 1735. The present castellated barracks date from 1807. Four of its members who emigrated in the 17th century, founded in 1638 the Ancient and Honourable Artillery Company of Massachussetts. The H.A.C. is the senior regiment of the Territorial Army

Volunteer Reserves, and maintains a Headquarters with an Officer Training Wing, and four squadrons.

HORNIMAN MUSEUM AND LIBRARY, London Road, Forest Hill, S.E.23. Open daily except Christmas Eve and Christmas Day, 10.30 to 6, Sundays 2 to 6. Special arrangements on Boxing Day. Admission free. The Museum was presented in 1901 to the London County Council by the founder, Mr. F. J. Horniman, M.P. The Museum has three main departments, anthropology, musical instruments and natural history. In the anthropology department the large collections include exhibits illustrating man's progress in the arts and crafts from prehistoric times. The natural history department includes an aquarium. Reference library (except Mondays). Schools Service. Free concerts and lectures (autumn to spring). *Curator*, D. M. Boston.

HORSE GUARDS, Whitehall, S.W.1.—Archway and offices built about 1753. The mounting of the guard (Life Guards, or the Blues and Royals) at 11 a.m. (10 a.m. on Sundays) and the dismounting at 4 p.m. are picturesque ceremonies. Only those on the Lord Chamberlain's list may drive through the gates and archway into *Horse Guards' Parade* (230,000 sq. ft.), where the Colour is " trooped " on the Queen's Official Birthday.

HOUSES OF PARLIAMENT, Westminster, S.W.1.—After its destruction by fire in 1834, the Palace of Westminster was re-built in 1840–68 from the designs of Sir Charles Barry and Augustus Welby Pugin, at a cost of over £2,000,000.—Open (free) to visitors on Saturdays, on Easter Monday and Tuesday, Spring and late summer Bank Holiday Mondays and Tuesdays; Mon., Tues. and Thurs. in August and Thurs. in September, if neither House be sitting. Admission at the Norman Porch. House of Lords, on the above-mentioned days, from 10 a.m. to 4.30 p.m. Closed to visitors on Christmas Day, Boxing Day and Good Friday and the Saturday preceding the State Opening of Parliament. Admission to the Strangers' Gallery of the House of Lords as arranged by a Peer or by queue *via* the St. Stephen's Entrance. Admission to the Strangers' Gallery of the House of Commons, during session by Member's order, or order obtained on personal application at the Admission Order Office in St. Stephen's Hall after the House meets. The present House of Commons was used for the first time on October 26, 1950, the original Chamber having been destroyed by bombs in 1941. The Victoria Tower (House of Lords) is about 330 ft. high, and when Parliament is sitting the Union Jack flies by day from its flagstaff. The Clock Tower of the House of Commons is about 320 ft. high and contains " Big Ben," the Hour Bell, named after Sir Benjamin Hall, First Commissioner of Works when the original bell was cast in 1856. This bell which weighed 16 tons 11 cwt., was found cracked in 1857. The present bell 13½ tons) is a recasting of the original and was first brought into use in July, 1859. A light is displayed from this tower at night when Parliament is sitting.

INNS OF COURT.—The *Inner* and *Middle Temple*, S. of Fleet Street, E.C.4, and N. of Victoria Embankment, to which the gardens extend, have occupied (since early 14th century) the site of the buildings of the Order of Knights Templars. *Inner Temple Hall* (rebuilt in 1955 after bomb damage) is open to the public on Monday–Friday, 10–11.30 a.m. and 2.30–4 p.m., except during Vacations. *Temple Church*, restored in 1958 after severe damage by bombing, is open on weekdays 10–5 p.m. and the public are admitted to Sunday services. *Middle Temple Hall* (1562–70) is open to the public when not in use, Monday–Friday, 10–12 and 3–4.30 p.m.; Saturday, 10–4.30. Closed

1–2 p.m. and Sundays. In Middle Temple Gardens (not open to the public) Shakespeare (Henry VI, Part I) places the incident which led to the " Wars of the Roses " (1455–85). *Lincoln's Inn*, from Chancery Lane to Lincoln's Inn Fields, W.C.2, occupies the site of the palace of a former Bishop of Chichester and of a Black Friars monastery. The records show the Society as being in existence in 1422. The Hall and Library Buildings are of 1845, although the Library is first mentioned in 1474, and the old Hall early 16th century, the Chapel was rebuilt *c.* 1619–23. *Lincoln's Inn Fields* (7 acres); the Square contains many fine old houses with handsome interiors. *Gray's Inn*, Holborn/Gray's Inn Road, W.C.1. Early 14th century. Hall (1556–60); Chapel (largely rebuilt in 1698). (Services 11·15 a.m. during Law Dining Terms only). Holy Communion 1st Sunday in every month except Aug.–Sept. Public welcome. Library (33,000 vols., mss. and printed books) may be viewed by appointment. Gardens open to the public from 12 noon to 2 p.m. (May–July), 9.30 a.m.–5 p.m. (Aug.–Sept.). The Inn, although badly damaged during the last war has been completely restored to its former beauty with gracious old red brick buildings overlooking grass covered squares and gardens. Strong Elizabethan associations. No other " Inns " are active, but what remains of *Staple Inn* is worth visiting as a relic of Elizabethan London; though heavy damage was done by a flying-bomb, it retains a picturesque gabled front on Holborn (opposite Gray's Inn Road). *Clement's Inn* (near St. Clement Danes' Church), *Clifford's Inn*, Fleet Street, and *Thavies Inn*, Holborn Circus, are all rebuilt. *Serjeant's Inn*, Fleet Street (damaged by bombing) and another (demolished 1910) of the same name in Chancery Lane, were composed of Serjeants-at-Law, the last of whom died in 1922.

JEWISH MUSEUM, Woburn House, Upper Woburn Place, W.C.1.—Opened in 1932, the Museum contains a comprehensive collection of Jewish antiquities, liturgical items and " Anglo-Judaica ". Open free (Mon.–Thurs.), 2.30–5; (Fri. and Sun.), 10.30–12.45. Closed on Saturdays, Jewish Holy days and Bank Holidays. Conducted tours of parties by arrangement with the Secretary.

KEATS HOUSE, Keats Grove, Hampstead, N.W.3. —In two houses here, now made into one, John Keats lived at various times between 1818 and 1820. Restored 1974–75. Open weekdays, 10 a.m.–6 p.m.; Sundays and Bank Holidays, 2 p.m.–5 p.m. Closed—Christmas Day, Boxing Day, New Year's Day, Good Friday, Easter Eve. The Keats Memorial Library contains over 5,000 volumes.

KENSINGTON PALACE, W.8.—The original house was bought by William III in 1689 and rebuilt by Christopher Wren. The birthplace of Queen Victoria in 1819. The state apartments are open to the public and contain pictures and furniture from the royal collections. A suite of rooms devoted to the memory of Queen Victoria is also shown. *Hours of Opening:* (March 1–Sept. 30) 10 a.m.–6 p.m.; Sundays, 2–6 p.m.; (Feb. and Oct, 10–5; Sundays, 2–5; Jan, Nov. and Dec., 10–4; Sundays, 2–5) *Kensington Gardens* (*q.v.*) adjoin.

LAMBETH PALACE, S.E.1.—The official residence of the Archbishop of Canterbury, on south bank of Thames; the oldest part is 13th century, the house itself is early 19th century. For leave to visit the historical portions, applications should be made by letter to the Archbishop's Chaplain.

LIVERY COMPANIES' HALLS.—The Principal Companies (*see* pp. 640–1) have magnificent halls, but admission to view them has generally to be arranged beforehand. Among the finest or more interesting may be mentioned the following:

Goldsmiths' Hall, Foster Lane. The present hall was completed in 1835, and contains some magnificent rooms. Exhibitions of plate have been shown here periodically in recent years. Fishmongers' Hall, London Bridge (built 1831–3), now admirably restored after severe bomb damage, also contains fine rooms. Apothecaries' Hall, Black Friars Lane, was rebuilt in 1670, after the Great Fire, and has library, hall and kitchen which are good examples of this period, together with a pleasant courtyard. Vintners' Hall, Upper Thames Street, was also rebuilt after the Great Fire, and its hall has very fine late 17th century panelling. The Watermen and Lightermen's Company is not, strictly speaking, a Livery Company, but its hall, in St. Mary at Hill, is a good example of a smaller 18th century building, with pilastered façade. It was completed in 1780. Stationers' Hall, in Stationers' Hall Court, behind Ludgate Hill, another post-Fire Hall, standing in its own court, has a particularly finely carved screen; its façade dates from 1800. Barbers' Hall, Monkwell Street, with a Hall attributed to Inigo Jones, was completely destroyed by bombing, but has now been rebuilt. The new hall was built some 30 ft. from the old site to enable one of the bastions and part of the wall of the Roman fort to remain exposed to view.

LLOYD'S, Lime Street, E.C.3.—Housed in the Royal Exchange for 150 years and in Leadenhall Street from 1928–1957. The present building was opened by H.M. Queen Elizabeth the Queen Mother on Nov. 14, 1957. The underwriting space has an area of 44,250 sq. ft.

LORD'S CRICKET GROUND, St. John's Wood Road, N.W.8.—The headquarters (since 1814) of the Marylebone Cricket Club (founded 1787), the premier cricket club in England, the scene of some of the principal matches of the season and Middlesex County headquarters. Tennis court and squash courts in building behind members' pavilion.

The Cricket Memorial Gallery, a museum of cricket, open to the public on match days, until 5 p.m., and on other days by prior arrangement. Adults, 15p; children, 8p. In winter, admission is by prior arrangement.

MANSION HOUSE, City, E.C.4.—(Built 1739–53, reconstructed 1930–31.) The official residence of the Lord Mayor; the Egyptian Hall and Ballroom are the chief attractions. Admission by order from the Lord Mayor's Secretary.

MARKETS —The London markets (administered by the Corporation of the City of London) provide foodstuffs for 8,500,000 to 9,000,000 people. The dead meat market at Smithfields is the largest in the world, the supplies marketed amounting to nearly 500,000 tons annually. *Central Meat, Fish, Fruit, Vegetable, and Poultry Markets*, Smithfield (present buildings, 1866); *Leadenhall Market* (Meat and Poultry (built 1881, part recently demolished); *Billingsgate*, (Fish), Thames Street (built 1875, part recently demolished); *Spitalfields*, E.1. (Vegetables, Fruit, etc.), enlarged 1928, and opened by the late Queen Mary; *London Fruit Exchange*, Brushfield Street (built by Corporation of London 1928–29) faces Spitalfields Market. Other markets are— *Covent Garden* (now moved to Nine Elms) (established under a charter of Charles II, in 1661) and *Borough Market*, S.E.1, for vegetables, fruit, flowers, etc.

MARLBOROUGH HOUSE, Pall Mall, S.W.1.—The London home of Queen Mary until her death in 1953. Built by Wren for the great Duke of Marlborough and completed in 1711, the house finally reverted to the Crown in 1835. Prince Leopold lived there until 1831, and Queen Adelaide from 1837 until her death in 1849. In 1863 it became the London house of the Prince of Wales. The

Queen's Chapel, Marlborough Gate, begun in 1623 from the designs of Inigo Jones for the Infanta Maria of Spain, and completed for Queen Henrietta Maria, is open to the public for services during part of the year. In 1959 Marlborough House was given by the Queen as a Commonwealth centre for Government conferences and it was opened as such in March, 1962. It is open to the public at certain times when conferences are not taking place.

LONDON MONUMENT (commonly called " The Monument "), Monument Street, E.C.3.—Built from designs of Wren, 1671–77, to commemorate the *Great Fire of London*, which broke out in Pudding Lane, Sept. 2, 1666. The fluted Doric column is 120 ft. high (the moulded cylinder above the balcony supporting a flaming vase of gilt bronze is 42 ft. in addition), and is based on a square plinth 40 ft. high, with fine carvings on W. face (making a total height of 202 ft.). Splendid views of London from gallery at top of column (311 steps). Admission (until 20 minutes before closing time) 15p; children, 7p, Monday to Saturday, 9 a.m. to 6 p.m. (Oct.–March to 4 p.m.). Sundays—May to Sept. 2–6 p.m. Closed Christmas Day, Boxing Day and Good Friday.

MONUMENTS.—ALBERT MEMORIAL, South Kensington; AIR, Victoria Embankment; BEACONSFIELD, Parliament Square; BEATTY, JELLICOE and CUNNINGHAM, Trafalgar Square; BELGIAN (Reginald Blomfield), Victoria Embankment; BOADICEA (or " Boudicca "), Queen of the Iceni, E. Anglia (Thomas Thornycroft), Westminster Bridge; BURNS, Embankment Gardens; BRUNEL (Marochetti), Victoria Embankment; BURGHERS OF CALAIS (Rodin), Victoria Tower Gardens, Westminster; CARLYLE (Boehm), Cheyne Walk, Chelsea; CAVALRY, Hyde Park; CAVELL, St. Martin's Place (Frampton); CENOTAPH, Whitehall (Lutyens); CHARLES I, Trafalgar Square; CHARLES II. (Grinling Gibbons), inside the Royal Exchange; CHURCHILL, Parliament Square; CLEOPATRA'S NEEDLE (68½ ft. high c 1,500 B.C., erected on the Thames Embankment in 1877–8; the Sphinxes are Victorian; CLIVE, Whitehall; CAPTAIN COOK (Brock), The Mall; CRIMEAN, Broad Sanctuary; OLIVER CROMWELL (Thornycroft), outside Westminster Hall; DUKE OF CAMBRIDGE, Whitehall; DUKE OF YORK (124 ft.), Carlton House Terrace; EDWARD VII (Mackennal), Waterloo Place. ELIZABETH I (1586, oldest outdoor statue in London) (from Ludgate), Fleet Street; EROS (Shaftesbury Memorial) (Gilbert), Piccadilly Circus; MARECHAL FOCH, Grosvenor Gardens; CHARLES JAMES FOX, Bloomsbury Square; GEORGE III, Cockspur Street; GEORGE IV (Chantrey), riding without stirrups, Trafalgar Square; GEORGE V, Old Palace Yard; GEORGE VI, Carlton Gardens; GLADSTONE, facing Australia House, Strand; GUARDS' (Crimea), Waterloo Place; (Great War), Horse Guards' Parade; HAIG (Hardiman), Whitehall; IRVING (Brock), N. side of National Portrait Gallery; JAMES II. Trafalgar Square (Grinling Gibbons); KITCHENER, Horse Guards' Parade; ABRAHAM LINCOLN, Parliament Square; SAMUEL JOHNSON, opposite St. Clement Danes; MILTON, St. Giles, Cripplegate; MONUMENT, THE (*see above*); NELSON (170 ft. 1½ in.), Trafalgar Square, with Landseer's lions (cast from guns recovered from the wreck of the *Royal George*); FLORENCE NIGHTINGALE, Waterloo Place; PALMERSTON, Parliament Square; PEEL, Parliament Square; PITT, Hanover Square (Chantrey); PORTAL, Embankment Gardens; PRINCE CONSORT, Holborn Circus; RALEIGH, Whitehall; RICHARD COEUR DE LION (Marochetti), Old Palace Yard; ROBERTS, Horse Guards' Parade; FRANKLIN D. ROOSEVELT, Grosvenor Square (Reid Dick); ROYAL ARTILLERY (South Africa), The Mall; (Great War), Hyde Park Corner; CAPTAIN SCOTT,

Waterloo Place (Lady Scott); SHACKLETON, Kensington Gore; SHAKESPEARE, Leicester Square; SMUTS (Epstein), Parliament Square (Epstein); SULLIVAN, Victoria Embankment; TRENCHARD, Victoria Embankment; VICTORIA MEMORIAL, in front of Buckingham Palace; GEORGE WASHINGTON (Houdon copy) Trafalgar Square; WELLINGTON, Hyde Park Corner; WELLINGTON (Chantrey) riding without stirrups, Royal Exchange; JOHN WESLEY, City Road; WILLIAM III, St. James's Square; WOLSELEY, Horse Guards' Parade.

PERCIVAL DAVID FOUNDATION OF CHINESE ART, 53 Gordon Square, W.C.1.—Set up in 1951 to promote the study and teaching of the art and culture of China and the surrounding regions, and provide facilities necessary to that end. The Foundation contains the collection of Chinese ceramics formed by Sir Percival David and his important library of books on Chinese art. To these was added a gift from the Hon. Mountstuart Elphinstone of part of his collection of Chinese monochrome porcelains. The galleries were opened to the public in 1952. The Foundation is administered on behalf of the University of London by the School of Oriental and African Studies. *Hours of opening:* Galleries, Mon. 2 to 5 p.m.; Tues. to Fri. 10.30 a.m. to 5 p.m.; Sat. 10.30 a.m. to 1 p.m.; Closed Bank Holidays. Library available to ticket holders only; applications in writing to the Curator. Head of the Foundation, Prof. W. Watson.

PORT OF LONDON.—The Port of London comprises the tidal portion of the River Thames from Teddington to the seaward limit (Tongue light vessel), a distance of 95 miles and three dock systems and land for redevelopment covering an area of 4,512 acres, of which 512 acres are water. The governing body is the Port of London Authority, whose Head Office is in World Trade Centre, E.1. Particulars of the docks are as follows:— *India & Millwall Docks*, E.14.—Area 449 acres including 127 acres water. Principal commodities handled are hardwood, fruit, plywood, wood pulp and wine in bulk. *Royal Victoria & Albert & King George V Docks*, E.16.—Area 1,019 acres, including 230 acres water—have special facilities for grain and tobacco. Large quantities of fruit and general cargo are also dealt with. *Tilbury Docks, Essex.*—Area 1,059 acres, including 155 acres water. These docks are 26 miles below London Bridge and are used principally by vessels plying on the Australian, North American, Indian, other Eastern routes, West Africa and the Continent. Tilbury Passenger Landing Stage provides accommodation for liners at all states of the tide and adjoins Tilbury Riverside Station.

A development and extension scheme at Tilbury has added nearly 2 miles of deepwater quays, to provide 13 new berths, of which 6 are for container traffic and 3 for packaged timber. Also included are a freight-liner rail container terminal and a riverside grain terminal which can accommodate vessels up to 65,000 tons deadweight and provide a rated maximum discharge of 2,000 tons per hour. Cost of this development (including Grain Terminal) was estimated at about £35 million.

The St. Katharine Docks were sold to the G.L.C. in 1969 and the London Docks were closed on May 31, 1969 and sold to Tower Hamlets Council in 1976. Surrey Commercial Docks were closed in 1970 and a large proportion was sold to the G.L.C. and Southwark Council in 1976.

PRINCE HENRY'S ROOM, 17 Fleet Street, E.C.4.— Early 17th century timber-framed house containing fine room on first floor with panelling and moulded plaster ceiling. Open Mon. to Fri. 1.45 p.m. to 5 p.m.; Sat. to 4.30 p.m. Admission 10p. Closed Christmas Day and Good Friday. Available

occasionally for evening lettings on application to The Town Clerk, Guildhall, E.C.2.

ROMAN LONDON.—Though visible remains are very few, almost every excavation for the foundations of new buildings in the City reveals Roman remains. Sections of the City wall, often however merely a mediæval re-build on the Roman foundations, are the most striking remains still to be seen. Fragments may be seen near the White Tower in the Tower of London, Trinity Square, No. 1 Crutched Friars, All Hallows, London Wall—its semi-circular vestry being built on the remains of a round bastion—St. Alphage, London Wall, recently restored by the Corporation of London and showing a striking succession of building and repairs from Roman till later mediæval times, St. Giles, Cripplegate and, by permission only, the great bastion beneath the pavement of the yard of the G.P.O. in Giltspur Street. Recent excavations in the Cripplegate area have revealed that a fort was built in this area and later incorporated in the town wall in this north-west corner of the City. Evidence from these excavations proves that the fort was not built until about A.D. 100–120 and the date of the town wall must therefore be considerably later. Remains of a bath building are preserved beneath the Coal Exchange in Lower Thames Street and other foundations may be seen in the Crypt of All Hallows Barking by the Tower. The governmental headquarters of the town was a great basilica, more than 400 ft. long from east to west, the massive walls of which have been encountered, extending from Leadenhall Market across Gracechurch Street as far as St. Michael's, Cornhill. Excavations during the past few years have shown that buildings over the river front were erected on huge oaken piles and a framework of timber for a considerable distance both east and west of the present London Bridge. The " Roman Bath", in Strand Lane approached via Surrey Street, which is not now held by most authorities to be of Roman origin, is maintained by the G.L.C. on behalf of the National Trust, and is open to the public on weekdays from 10 a.m. to 12.30 p.m. (*Admission*, 10p). Excavations since 1948 on a bombed site in Walbrook, on the banks of the old Wall Brook, produced interesting discoveries, including a Temple of Mithras, from which the splendid marble statues have been placed in Guildhall Museum, now in the Royal Exchange, where many other relics from the Roman City may be seen.

ROYAL EXCHANGE, E.C.3 (founded by Sir Thomas Gresham, 1566, opened as " The Bourse " and proclaimed "The Royal Exchange " by Queen Elizabeth I, 1571, rebuilt 1667–69 and 1842–44).—Open to the public, free. Statues of Queen Elizabeth I, Charles II, Queen Victoria, Sir Thomas Gresham and others; mural paintings in the ambulatory by Leighton, Brangwyn, Wyllie, F. O. Salisbury and others. The carillon of the Royal Exchange (reinstated 1950) is temporarily out of use. With the exception of the courtyard and ambulatory (now used for exhibitions, art displays, etc.) and the shops the whole of the building is occupied by departments of the Guardian Royal Exchange Assurance Group and is administered by the Gresham Committee (*Clerk*, Mercers' Hall, Ironmonger Lane, E.C.2).

ROYAL GEOGRAPHICAL SOCIETY, Kensington Gore, S.W. 7.—Map Room open to public, *free*.

ST. JAMES'S PALACE, in Pall Mall, S.W.1.—(Not open to the public.) Built by Henry VIII; the Gatehouse and Presence Chamber remain, later alterations by Wren and Kent. The Chapel Royal and the Queen's Chapel (1623) opposite the Palace are open to the public for services. Representatives

of Foreign Powers are still accredited " to the Court of St. James's ". Clarence House (1825) in the palace precinct is the home of H.M. the Queen Mother.

ST. JOHN'S GATE, Clerkenwell, E.C.1.—Now the Chancery of the Order of St. John of Jerusalem, and formerly the entrance of the Priory of that Order, of which the gate house (early 16th century) and crypt of Church (12th century) alone survive, They may be inspected on application to the Curator.

SIR JOHN SOANE'S MUSEUM, 13 Lincoln's Inn Fields, W.C.2. The house and galleries, built 1812–24, are the work of the founder, Sir John Soane (1753–1837) and contain his collections, arranged as he left them, in pursuance of an Act procured by him in 1833. Exhibits include the Sarcophagus of Seti I (*c.* 1290 B.C.), classical vases and marbles, Hogarth's *Rake's Progress* and *Election* series, paintings by Canaletto, Reynolds, Turner, Lawrence, etc., and sculpture by Chantery, Flaxman, etc. Soane's library of 8,000 vols, and a collection of 20,000 architectural drawings are available for study. Open Tues.-Sat. inclusive, 10 a.m. to 5 p.m. Closed Bank Holidays. *Curator*, Sir John Summerson, C.B.E., F.B.A. *Inspectress*, Miss D. Stroud, M.B.E., F.S.A.

SOMERSET HOUSE, Strand, W.C.2, and Victoria Embankment, W.C.2.—The beautiful river façade (600 ft. long) was built in 1776–86 from the designs of Sir W. Chambers; the eastern extension, which houses part of King's College, was built by Smirke in 1829. Somerset House was the property of Lord Protector Somerset, at whose attainder in 1552 the palace passed to the Crown, and it was a royal residence until 1692.

STOCK EXCHANGE, E.C.2.—The market floor of the new Stock Exchange building in London opened for trading in June, 1973. A tower, 331 feet high, the new Market, and a separate Public Relations block replace the complex of buildings started in 1801 on the same site. The new building is the headquarters of The Stock Exchange, following the amalgamation of all the Stock Exchanges in Great Britain and Ireland on March 25, 1973.

The Stock Exchange provides a market for the purchase and sale of about 9,000 securities officially listed, and valued at over £250,000,000 and also securities listed on other Stock Exchanges throughout the World. At present the members of The Stock Exchange who consist of brokers (agents for clients) and Jobbers (dealers in specific securities) number about 4,150. The Visitors' Gallery is open between 10.00 a.m. and 3.15 p.m. Monday to Friday. Admission free and without ticket; film show, audio-visual exhibition. Advance bookings can be made; last complete programme begins at 2.50 p.m.

THAMES EMBANKMENTS.—The Victoria Embankment, on the N. side (from Westminster to Blackfriars), was constructed by Sir J. W. Bazalgette for the Metropolitan Board of Works, 1864–70 (the seats, of which the supports of some are a kneeling camel, laden with spicery, and of others a winged sphinx, were presented by the Grocers' Company, and by Rt. Hon. W. H. Smith, M.P., in 1874); the Albert Embankment on the S. side (from Westminster Bridge to Vauxhall), 1866–69; the Chelsea Embankment, 1871–74. The toal cost exceeded £2,000,000. Sir J. W. Bazalgette (1819–91) also inaugurated the London main drainage system, 1858–65. A medallion has been placed on a pier of the Victoria Embankment to commemorate the engineer of the Thames waterside improvements (" Flumini vincula posuit "). The headquarters of the G.L.C. include an embankment on the Surrey side.

THAMES TUNNELS.—The *Rotherhithe Tunnel*, constructed by the L.C.C. and opened in 1908, connects Commercial Road E.14, with Lower Road, Rotherhithe; the total length is 1 mile 332 yards, of which 474 yards are under the river. The cost of the tunnel and its approaches was £1,506,914. The first *Blackwall Tunnel* (foot passengers and vehicles) was constructed by the L.C.C. and opened in 1897, connecting East India Dock Road, Poplar, with Blackwall Lane, East Greenwich. The cost of the tunnel with its approaches was about £1,323,663. A second tunnel (for southbound vehicles only) was opened in August, 1967, at a cost of about £9,750,000 and the old tunnel was improved at a cost of about £1,350,000 and made one-way northbound. Both tunnels are for vehicles only. The relative lengths of the tunnels measured from East India Dock Road to the Gate House on the south side are 6,215 ft. (old tunnel) and 6,152 feet. *Greenwich Tunnel* (foot passengers only), constructed by the L.C.C. and opened in 1902, connects the Isle of Dogs, Poplar, with Greenwich. The length of the subway is 406 yards, and the cost was about £180,000. The *Woolwich Tunnel* (foot passengers only), constructed by the L.C.C. and opened in 1912, connects North and South Woolwich below the passenger and vehicular ferry from North Woolwich Station, E.16, to High Street, Woolwich, S.E.18. The length of the subway is 552 yards, and its cost was about £86,000. The *Thames Tunnel* (1,300 feet) was opened in 1843 to connect Wapping (N.) with Rotherhithe (S.). In 1866 it was closed to the public, and purchased by the East London Railway Company. The *Tower Subway* for foot passengers was opened in 1870, and has long been closed.

TOWER HILL, E.C.1 and E.C.3, was formerly the place of execution for condemned prisoners from the Tower, the site of the scaffold being marked in the gardens of Trinity Square.

TOWER OF LONDON, E.C.3.—Admission to a general view of the Tower, the White Tower (Armouries), the Beauchamp and Bloody Towers and the Chapels Royal—80p; children, 30p; to the Jewel House, 30p, children 10p. (Nov.-Feb. Adults 20p, children 10p; Jewel House 10p, children 5p). On Sundays throughout the year the public is admitted to Holy Communion, 9.15 a.m. and Morning Service, 11 a.m. Open on weekdays, March 1 to October 31, 9.30-5; Nov. 1-Feb. 28, 9.30-4; Sundays, 2 p.m. to 5 p.m., Mar. 1-Oct. 31 only; Tower closed Christmas Eve, Christmas Day, Boxing Day, Good Friday and New Year's Day. CONSTABLE, Field Marshal Sir Geoffrey Baker, G.C.B., C.M.G., C.B.E., M.C., *Lieutenant*, Lieut. Gen. Sir Napier Crookenden, K.C.B., D.S.O., O.B.E.; RESIDENT GOVERNOR AND KEEPER OF THE JEWEL HOUSE, Maj.-Gen. W. D. M. Raeburn, C.B., D.S.O., M.B.E.; MASTER OF THE ARMOURIES, A. R. Dufty, C.B.E., F.S.A.; CHAPLAIN AT THE CHAPEL ROYAL OF ST. PETER AD VINCULA, Rev. J. F. M. Llewellyn.

The White Tower is the oldest and central building in Her Majesty's Royal Palace and Fortress of the Tower of London. It was built at the order of William I and constructed by Gundulph, Bishop of Rochester, in the years 1078-98. The Inner Wall, with thirteen towers, was constructed by Henry III in the 12th century. The Moat was extended and completed by Richard I and the Wharf first mentioned in 1228. The Outer Wall was completed in the reign of Edward I and now incorporates 6 towers and 2 bastions. The last Monarch to reside in the Tower of London was James I. The Crown Jewels came to the Tower in the reign of Henry III. All coinage used in Great Britain was minted in the Outer Ward of the Tower of London until 1810 when the Royal Mint was formed. The Tower of London has had a military garrison since 1078. The Chapel Royal of St. John the Evangelist, within the White Tower (1080–1088) is the oldest Norman church in London. The chapel of St. Peter ad Vincula was built in the early 16th century.

WELLINGTON MUSEUM, Apsley House, 149 Piccadilly, at Hyde Park Corner, W.1.—Admission free on weekdays and Bank Holidays, 10 to 6; Sundays, 2.30 to 6. Closed Good Friday, Christmas Eve, Christmas Day, Boxing Day and New Year's Day. Apsley House was designed by Robert Adam for Lord Bathurst and built 1771–8. It was bought in 1817 by the Duke of Wellington, who in 1828–29 employed Benjamin Wyatt to enlarge it, face it with Bath stone and add the Corinthian portico. The museum contains many fine paintings, services of porcelain and silver plate and personal relics of the 1st Duke of Wellington (1769–1852) and was given to the Nation by the 7th Duke. It was first opened to the public in 1952, under the administration of the Victoria and Albert Museum.

WESTMINSTER HALL, S.W.1 (built by William Rufus, A.D. 1097–99 and altered by Richard II, 1394–1401), adjacent to and incorporated in the Houses of Parliament—Westminster Hall is part of the old Palace of Westminster and survived the fire, which destroyed most of the remainder of the Palace (Oct. 16, 1834) and the bombs of 1941. The Hall is about 240 ft. long, 69 ft. wide, and 90 ft. high. The hammer beam roof of carved oak, dating from 1396–98, is one of the principal attractions. King Charles I was tried in the Hall. Extensive repairs to the Hall have recently been carried out. Admission: During sessions—Mon. to Thurs., 10 a.m. until 1.30 p.m., provided neither House is sitting. Sat. 10 a.m.–5 p.m. During Recess—Mon. to Fri., except Good Friday, Christmas Day and Boxing Day, 10 a.m.–4 p.m.; Sat., 10 a.m.–5 p.m.

WHITECHAPEL ART GALLERY, High Street, E.1. Charitable institution founded in 1901 for the organization of temporary exhibitions of art. There is no permanent collection. Open: Tuesdays to Sundays, 11–6; closed Mondays. Admission Free.

PARKS, SPACES AND GARDENS

The principal Parks and Open Spaces in the Metropolitan area are maintained as under:—

By the Crown

BUSHY PARK (1,099 acres).

GREEN PARK (49 acres), W.1.—Between Piccadilly and St. James's Park with *Constitution Hill*, leading to Hyde Park Corner.

GREENWICH PARK (196½ acres), S.E. 10.

HAMPTON COURT GARDENS (54 acres).

HAMPTON COURT GREEN (17 acres).

HAMPTON COURT PARK (622 acres).

HYDE PARK (341 acres).—From Park Lane, W.1, to Kensington Gardens, W.2 containing the Serpentine. Fine gateway at Hyde Park Corner, with Apsley House, the Achilles Statue, Rotten Row and the Ladies' Mile. To the north-east is the *Marble Arch*, originally erected by George IV at the entrance to Buckingham Palace and re-erected in present position in 1851.

KENSINGTON GARDENS (275 acres), W.2.—From western boundary of Hyde Park to Kensington Palace, containing the Albert Memorial.

KEW, ROYAL BOTANIC GARDENS (300 acres).—Accessible by railway and omnibus. Open daily, except Christmas Day and New Year's Day from 10 a.m. The closing hour varies from 4 p.m. in mid-winter to 7 p.m. on week-days, and 8 p.m.

at week-ends and Bank Holidays, in mid-summer. Admission, 1p. Museums open 10 a.m.; Glasshouses, 11 a.m. to dusk or 4.50 p.m. (week-days); to dusk or 5.50 p.m. (Sundays). Dogs not admitted.

REGENT'S PARK and PRIMROSE HILL (464 acres), N.W.1.—From Marylebone Road to Primrose Hill surrounded by the Outer Circle and divided by the *Broad Walk* leading to the Zoological Gardens.

RICHMOND PARK (2,469 acres).

ST. JAMES'S PARK (93 acres), S.W.1.—From Whitehall to Buckingham Palace. Ornamental lake of 12 acres. The original suspension bridge built in 1857 was replaced in 1957. The *Mall* leads from the Admiralty Arch to the Queen Victoria Memorial and Buckingham Palace. *Birdcage Walk* from Storey's Gate, past Wellington Barracks, to Buckingham Palace.

By the Corporation of London

BURNHAM BEECHES and FLEET WOOD (504 acres), *see* col. 2.

COULSDON COMMON, Surrey (111 acres).

EPPING FOREST (6,000 acres).

FARTHINGDOWN, Surrey (121 acres).

HIGHGATE WOOD (70 acres).

KENLEY COMMON, Surrey (80 acres).

QUEEN'S PARK, Kilburn (30 acres).

RIDDLESDOWN, Surrey (87 acres).

SPRING PARK, West Wickham (51 acres).

WEST HAM PARK (77 acres).

WEST WICKHAM COMMON, Kent (25 acres).

With smaller open spaces within the City of London, including FINSBURY CIRCUS GARDENS.

By the Greater London Council

ABBEY WOOD PARK (18 acres), S.E.2.

ALEXANDRA PARK AND PALACE (188 acres).

ARCHBISHOP'S PARK (9 acres), S.E.1.

AVERY HILL (87 acres), S.E.9, with Winter Garden.

BATTERSEA PARK (200 acres), S.W.8 to S.W.11, with zoo and lake.

BLACKHEATH (271 acres), S.E.3.—*Morden College*, founded in 1695 as a home for " decayed Turkey merchants ", is near the S.E. corner. The building was designed by Wren and its Chapel doors have carvings attributed to Grinling Gibbons. Concerts and poetry recitals are held at Rangers House, an early 18th century mansion.

BOSTALL HEATH AND WOODS (159 acres), S.E.2.

CASTLEWOOD with Jackwood, Oxleas, Eltham Park, Eltham Common and Falcon Wood Field (249 acres), S.E.18 and S.E.9.

CRYSTAL PALACE (199 acres), S.E.19, with National Sports Centre. Zoo.

DULWICH PARK (72 acres), S.E.21.

FINSBURY PARK (115 acres), N.4.

GOLDER'S HILL (36 acres), adjoining West Heath, Hampstead.

HACKNEY MARSH (343 acres), E.5, E.9 and E.10. 112 football pitches.

HAINAULT FOREST (1,108 acres), Hainault, Essex.

HAMPSTEAD HEATH and Extension (294 acres), N.W.3.

HOLLAND PARK (55 acres), W.8. Open air theatre and concerts; floodlit gardens; King George VI Memorial Youth Hostel; Restaurant.

HORNIMAN GARDENS (21 acres), S.E.23. Adjoining Horniman Museum.

KENWOOD (200 acres), the northern part of Hampstead Heath. Part purchased in 1922 by public subscription. Open air symphony concerts each summer. The Iveagh Bequest, in an 18th-century Mansion (open to the public), includes valuable

art treasures. Recitals and poetry readings in the Orangery.

LESNES ABBEY WOODS (215 acres), Erith.—Ruins of an Augustinian abbey.

MARBLE HILL (66 acres).—Twickenham, Middlesex.—A beautiful park, running down to the riverside, on the left bank of the Thames; includes a mansion (open to the public, *see* under Environs of London). Open air theatre.

PARLIAMENT HILL (271 acres)—Part of Hampstead Heath. Lido and swimming bath. Important cross-country events are held here.

PARSLOES PARK (118 acres), Becontree, Essex.

SHAFTESBURY PARK (9 acres), Downham, Bromley, Kent.

THAMESMEAD (174 acres), S.E.2. Sailing.

TRENT PARK (560 acres), Cockfosters, Enfield. Country park with nature trail, riding school, golf course, picnic sites, fishing, etc.

VICTORIA PARK (217 acres), E.9.

WORMWOOD SCRUBS (200 acres), Hammersmith, W.12 and N.W.10. West London Stadium.

EXHIBITIONS, ETC., IN LONDON

MADAME TUSSAUD'S EXHIBITION, Marylebone Road, N.W.1. Oct.–Mar., 10–5.30; April–Sept., 10–6.30. Open every day, including Saturdays and Sundays.

LONDON PLANETARIUM, Marylebone Road, N.W.1. Presentations hourly from 11 a.m. daily.

ROYAL HORTICULTURAL SOCIETY, Vincent Square, S.W.1, holds regular exhibitions at its Halls in Greycoat Street and in Vincent Square, S.W.1, and the Chelsea Flower Show at the Royal Hospital Grounds, Chelsea (May).

ZOOLOGICAL GARDENS, Regents's Park, N.W.1. —Opened 1828. Admission: (Mar.–Oct.) Mondays to Saturdays, 9–5; Sundays and Bank Holidays, 9–7; (Nov.–Feb.), 10–5. Mondays throughout the year (except Bank Holidays), Adults £1.25 (Nov.–mid March £1.15), Children under 14, 60p. (Nov.–mid March 50p). Additional charge for admission to the Aquarium and the Children's Zoo. Special rates for parties.

WHIPSNADE ZOOLOGICAL PARK, Whipsnade Park, nr. Dunstable, Beds. (34 miles from London, 8½ miles from Luton and 3 miles from Dunstable). Open from 10 a.m. to 7. p.m., or sunset, whichever is the earlier. Charges as for London Zoo (*see* above). Cars admitted at extra charge. Special rates for parties.

MUSIC

ROYAL OPERA HOUSE, Covent Garden, W.C.2. —Opera and Ballet mid Sept.—early August. The (third) Covent Garden Theatre was opened May 15, 1858 (the first was opened Dec. 7, 1732). *General Administrator*, J. Tooley.

ROYAL ALBERT HALL, Kensington Gore, S.W.7— Regular seasons of Promenade Concerts. Also used for public meetings, concerts and other entertainments. The elliptical hall, one of the largest in the world, was completed in 1871.

ROYAL FESTIVAL HALL, South Bank, S.E.1.— Opened for the Festival of Britain, 1951, and administered by Greater London Council. Concerts and regular ballet seasons. Queen Elizabeth Hall and Purcell Room opened 1967. *Director, South Bank Concert Halls*, G. Mann, O.B.E.

KNELLER HALL, Twickenham.—Royal Military School of Music. A band of up to 250 instrumentalists gives concerts in the grounds on Wednesdays throughout the summer season, commencing at 8 p.m. Members of the public are welcome to attend; admission, 25p (including programme). Season tickets available.

ENVIRONS OF LONDON

BARNET AND HADLEY GREEN.—Scene of Battle, A.D. 1471. Hadley Woods.

BURNHAM BEECHES and FLEET WOOD, Bucks.— Magnificent wooded scenery, purchased by the Corporation of London for the benefit of the public in 1879, includes Fleet Wood (65 acres) presented in 1921. During summer omnibus runs daily. Sundays included, from Slough Station (Western Region), passing within 250 yards of " Gray's Elegy " Church. *See* " Stoke Poges".

BUSHY PARK (1,099 acres).—Adjoining Hampton Court, contains many fine trees and avenue of horse-chestnuts enclosed in a fourfold avenue of limes, planted by King William III. " Chestnut Sunday " (when the trees are in full bloom with their " candles ") is usually about May 1 to 15.

CHEQUERS, a country residence for Prime Ministers, was presented to the Nation (with an endowment to maintain the estate, etc.) by Lord and Lady Lee of Fareham, as the official country residence for the Prime Minister of the day, and the gift was approved by Parliament in the *Chequers Estate Act*, 1917. In 1921 the Chequers Estate of 700 acres was added to the gift by Lord Lee. Chequers is a mansion in Tudor style in the Chilterns about 3 miles from Princes Risborough, Bucks, and contains a collection of Cromwellian portraits and relics.

DARWIN AND DOWN HOUSE, Downe, Farnborough, Kent.—Where Charles Darwin thought and worked for 40 years and died in 1882. Maintained by the Royal College of Surgeons. Open 1 to 6. Closed Mondays (except Bank Holidays), Fridays, Christmas Eve, Christmas Day, Boxing Day and February. Admission, 50p. Children, 20p.

DORNEYWOOD, country house in 215 acres, near Burnham Beeches, Bucks., was presented to the nation by Lord Courtauld-Thomson (died 1954) as an official residence for any Minister of the Crown chosen by the Prime Minister during office. Administered by the National Trust. Garden and grounds open to the public on Saturdays only. (August and Sept, 2.15–6 p.m.) Admission 10p. Children, 5p.

DULWICH, S.E.21 (5 miles from London), contains *Dulwich College* (founded by Edward Alleyn in 1619), the *Horniman Museum and Dulwich Park* (72 acres). The *Dulwich Picture Gallery*, built by Sir John Soane to house the collection bequeathed by the artist, Sir Francis Bourgeois, was damaged by enemy action in the Second World War. The pictures, however, were saved, and the gallery has been rebuilt with the aid of a grant from the Pilgrim Trust. It was reopened by Queen Elizabeth the Queen Mother on April 27, 1953. In *Dulwich Village* the rural characteristics of the pre-suburban periods are preserved.

ELTHAM, Kent (10 miles from London by Southern Region). Remains of 13th-15th century Eltham Palace, the birthplace of John of Eltham (1316), son of Edward II. The hall, built by Edward IV, contains fine hammer-beam roof of chestnut. In the churchyard of St. John the Baptist is the tomb of Thomas Doggett, the comedian and founder of the Thames Watermen's championship (Doggett's Coat and Badge).

EPPING FOREST (6,000 acres, originally purchased by the Corporation of London for £250,000 and thrown open to the public in 1882; the present forest is 12 miles long by 1 to 2 miles wide, about one-tenth of its original area). LOUGHTON, BUCKHURST HILL, CHINGFORD, HIGH BEECH (London Transport and Eastern Region). Beautiful forest scenery.

ETON COLLEGE.—22 miles from London. The most famous of English schools, founded by Henry VI in 1440, the scholars numbering 1,195 in July, 1970. Buildings date from 1442.

GREENWICH, S.E.10.—*Greenwich Hospital* (since 1873, the Royal Naval College) was built by Charles II, largely from designs by John Webb, and by Queen Anne and William III, from designs by Wren, on the site of an ancient royal palace, and of the more recent *Placentia*, an enlarged edition of the palace, constructed by Humphrey, Duke of Gloucester (1391–1447), son of Henry IV. Henry VIII, Queen Mary I and Queen Elizabeth I were born in the Royal Palace (which reverted to the Crown in 1447) and King Edward VI died there. In the principal quadrangle is a marble statue of George II, by Rysbraeck. (For *National Maritime Museum*, see Index.) *Painted Hall* and *Chapel* open daily except Thursdays from 2.30 p.m. to 5 p.m. (closed on Sundays, Oct.–April inclusive). Visitors are also admitted to Morning Service in the Chapel at 11 a.m., summer and winter, except during College vacations. *Greenwich Park* (196½ acres) was enclosed by Humphrey, Duke of Gloucester, and laid out by Charles II, from the designs of Le Nôtre. The Queen's House, begun in 1616, was designed for Anne of Denmark by Inigo Jones. On a hill in Greenwich Park is the former Royal Observatory (founded 1675). Part of its buildings at Greenwich have been taken over by the Maritime Museum and named *Flamsteed House*, after John Flamsteed (1646–1719), first Astronomer Royal. The Parish church of Greenwich (*St. Alfege*) was rebuilt by Hawksmoor (Wren's pupil) in 1728, and restored after severe damage during the Second World War. General Wolfe (Heights of Abraham) and Tallis (" the father of Church Music ") are buried in the church. Henry VIII was christened in the former church. *Charlton House*: built in the early 17th century (1607–1612) for Adam Newton, tutor to Prince Henry, brother to Charles I. The house is largely in the Jacobean style of architecture. *Cutty Sark*, the last of the famous tea clippers, which has been preserved as a memorial to ships and men of a past era. The ship is fully restored and re-rigged, with a museum of sail on board, Open to visitors: weekdays, 11 to 5 (Summer, 6 p.m.); Sundays and Boxing Day, 2.30 to 5. The yacht *Gipsy Moth IV* in which Sir Francis Chichester sailed single-handed round the world, 1966–67, is preserved alongside *Cutty Sark*.

HAM HOUSE, Richmond.—A notable example of 17th-century domestic architecture, long the home of the Tollemache family (Earls of Dysart). The contents, described as " probably the finest and most varied collection of Charles II's reign to survive", were purchased for the Victoria and Albert Museum which now administers the house. Ham House may be seen on Tues.–Sun. inclusive and on Bank Holidays, 2–6 p.m., April–Sept., 12–4 p.m., Oct.–March. Closed Mon. (except Bank Holidays), Christmas Eve, Christmas Day, Boxing Day and Good Friday and New Year's Day. Admission, 20p; Children and Pensioners, 10p.

HAMPTON COURT.—Sixteenth-century Palace built by Cardinal Wolsey, with additions by Sir Christopher Wren for William and Mary, 15 miles from London. Fine view of river. Beautiful gardens with maze and prolific grape vine (planted in 1769). Old Royal Apartments and collection of pictures. Tennis Court, built by King Henry VIII in 1530. The Palace is *closed* on Christmas Eve, Christmas Day, Boxing Day, New Year's Day and Good Friday. April–September: State Apartments: 50p; (Oct.–March 20p). Mantegna Paintings 15p. (Oct.–March 15p, 5p). State Carriages 5p. Maze 2p. State Carriages, Tennis Court, *closed* Oct.–March. Maze *closed* Nov.–Feb. Open May–Sept. 9.30–6 (Sundays 11–6) (Maze 10–6; 11–6).

Nov.–Feb. 9.30–4 (Sundays 2–4). Oct., March and April 9.30–5 (Sundays 2–5) (Maze 11–5).

HARROW-ON-THE-HILL.—10 miles by Metropolitan and other railways. Large public school founded by John Lyon in 1571. The " Fourth Form Room " dates from 1608.

HUGHENDEN MANOR, High Wycombe, Bucks.—The home of Disraeli from 1847 till his death and contains much of his furniture, books, etc. Conveyed to the National Trust in 1947. Open daily including Sundays and Bank Holidays, 2–6 or till dusk. Saturdays and Sundays, 12.30 to 6. Closed Tuesdays and all December (1974), January, Good Friday and Christmas Day. Admission (non-members), 25p; Children, 12p.

JORDANS AND CHALFONT ST. GILES, near Beaconsfield, Bucks, contain the Old *Quaker Meeting House* (1688) at Jordans, in the burial ground of which lies William Penn (Pennsylvania); a barn built out of the timbers of the *Mayflower* by the 17th-century owner of Jordans (Gardener). At Chalfont St. Giles is the cottage where Milton lived during the Great Plague (1665–1666).

KEW, Surrey, was a favourite home of the early Hanoverian monarchs. Kew House, the residence of Frederick, Prince of Wales, and later of his son, George III, was pulled down in 1803, but the earlier Dutch House, now known as Kew Palace, survives. It was built in 1631 and acquired by George III as an annexe to Kew House in 1781. The famous Kew Gardens (*see* p. 649) were originally laid out as a private garden for Kew House for George III's mother in 1759 and were much enlarged in the nineteenth century, notably by the inclusion of the grounds of the former Richmond Lodge.

MARBLE HILL HOUSE, Twickenham, Middlesex.—Example of the English Palladian style, built 1724–9 for Henrietta Howard, Countess of Suffolk, mistress of George II. Reopened 1966, after restoration work on the elevations of the house, entrance hall, main staircase and first floor rooms. The Great Room and mahogany staircase are noteworthy. Open daily except Fri. Admission free.

NATIONAL ARMY MUSEUM, Royal Hospital Road, S.W.3. Established by Royal Charter (1960). Official Museum for British Army, Honourable East India Company, Indian Services and Colonial Forces. History of British, Indian and Colonial Forces, 1485 to 1914, in new building at Chelsea. Indian Army room remains open at R.M.A. Sandhurst, Camberley, Surrey.

OSTERLEY PARK, Isleworth.—House and park of 140 acres given to the National Trust by the Earl of Jersey in 1949. Part of the Elizabethan house, built in 1577 for Sir Thomas Gresham, remains, but it was largely remodelled by Robert Adam, and the staterooms are among the best examples of Adam decoration. Open daily, except Mondays, (April–Sept.) 2–6 p.m.; (Oct.–Mar.) 12 noon–4 p.m. Closed Monday (except Bank Holidays), Christmas Eve, Christmas Day, Boxing Day, New Year's Day and Good Friday. Admission 20p, children 10p.

RICHMOND, SURREY, contains the red brick gateway of *Richmond Palace* (Henry VIII, 1485–1509) and buildings of the Jacobean, Queen Anne, and early Georgian periods, including *White Lodge* in Richmond Park, the former home of Queen Mary's mother (the Duke of Windsor was born there, June 23, 1894). The *Star and Garter* Home for Disabled Soldiers, Sailors, and Airmen (the Women's Memorial of the Great War) was opened by Queen Mary in 1924. *Richmond Park* (2,469 acres) contains herds of fallow and red deer.

ROYAL AIR FORCE MUSEUM, Colindale, Hendon.—The museum was established in 1963 and officially opened by the Queen in November 1972. It covers all aspects of the history of the Royal Air Force and its predecessors and most of the history of aviation generally. The museum building is sited on ten acres of the historic former airfield at Hendon. Its aircraft hall, which occupies two hangars dating from the First World War, displays some 40 aircraft from the museum's total collection of over 100 machines. Open weekdays, 10 a.m.–6 p.m., Sundays, 2 p.m.–6 p.m. Admission free.

RUNNIMEDE.—A meadow of about 100 acres, on S. bank of Thames (part of the Crown Lands), between Windsor and Staines. From June 15–23, 1215, the hostile Barons encamped on this meadow during negotiations with King John, who rode over each day from Windsor. The 48 " Articles of the Barons " were accepted by the King on June 15, and were subsequently embodied in a charter, since known as *Magna Carta*, of which several copies were sealed on June 19. About half a mile N.E. of the meadow is *Magna Carta Island* (claimed as the actual site of the sealing), presented to the National Trust in 1930.

A memorial at *Cooper's Hill*, near Runnimede, to members of the Commonwealth air forces who lost their lives in the Second World War while serving from bases in the United Kingdom and north-western Europe and have no known grave, was unveiled by the Queen on October 17, 1953. Her Majesty on May 14, 1965, unveiled a memorial to the late President of the United States, John F. Kennedy, on ground nearby.

ST. ALBANS.—A city in Hertfordshire, on the River Ver, 22 miles N.W. of London. The abbey church, built partly of materials from the old Roman city of Verulamium by Paul of Caen, was consecrated in 1115. Parts still remain of the Norman structure. The city was the scene of the overthrow of Henry VI in 1455, and of the Earl of Warwick in 1461. The site of the pre-Roman city of King Tasciovanus and the remains of the ancient City of Verulamium, with well preserved theatre and many other features, excavated in recent years.

SYON HOUSE, Brentford.—The summer home of the Duke of Northumberland. The House is built on the remains of the Nunnery of Syon, founded by the order of Henry V in 1415. At the Dissolution of the Monasteries the estate reverted to the Crown. In 1594 it was granted to the 9th Earl of Northumberland, who altered and improved the property. In the eight years, 1762–1770, the interior was transformed and furnished by Robert Adam. Open Easter to Sept.

WALTHAM ABBEY (or WALTHAM HOLY CROSS), 13 miles from London (Eastern Region).—The Abbey ruins, Harold's Bridge (11th century), the Nave of the former cruciform Abbey Church (the oldest Norman building in England (consecrated May 3, 1060) and the traditional burial place of King Harold II (1066), and a Lady Chapel of Edward II, with crypt below. New evidence of the position and style of several buildings, which once stood on the site of the Augustinian monastery, were revealed by the prolonged drought in the summer of 1933. At Waltham Cross, 1 mile from the Abbey, is one of the crosses (partly restored) erected by Edward I to mark a resting place of the corpse of Queen Eleanor on its way to Westminster Abbey. (Ten crosses were erected, but only those at Geddington, Northampton and Waltham remain; " Charing " Cross originally stood near the spot now occupied by the statue of Charles I at Whitehall.)

WINDSOR CASTLE (begun by William the Conqueror, A.D. 1066-87).—22 miles from London, by Western and Southern Regions. The Castle Precincts are open daily, free of charge, from 10 a.m. to one hour before sunset or 4 p.m. (whichever is the later). When the Queen is not in official residence, the *State Apartments* of Windsor Castle are open to the public, during Her Majesty's pleasure, on every weekday and on certain Sunday afternoons during the summer months. When the State Apartments are open, the charges for admission are for Adults, 20p and for Children, 10p. By the Queen's command, the net proceeds go to charities. The hours of admission to the State Apartments are: Jan. to mid-March, 10.30-3; March to Dec., 10.30-3; March to mid-Oct., 10.30-5; Sundays, March to mid-Oct. 1.30-5; Closed, Nov.-Feb. *Queen Mary's Doll's House*, the *Exhibition of Dolls* and the Exhibition of Drawings by Holbein, Leonardo

da Vinci and other artists can be seen on the same days and hours as the State Apartments, admission 5p each person to each. When the State Apartments are closed, Queen Mary's Doll's House and the Exhibition of Drawings remain open to the public. The *Albert Memorial Chapel* is open free throughout the year from 10-1; 2-4; closed on Sundays; Admission free. A fee is charged to visit *St. George's Chapel*. The *Curfew Tower* may be seen under the guidance of the Keeper to whom application must be made at the entrance.

The *Royal Mausoleum*, Frogmore Gardens, Home Park, is open annually on two days in early May, usually the first Wednesday and Thursday in the month, in conjunction with the opening of Frogmore Gardens in aid of the National Garden Scheme, 10 a.m.-dusk. Also open on the Wednesday nearest to May 24 (Queen Victoria's birthday) from 11 a.m. to 4 p.m. Admission free.

HOUSES OPEN TO THE PUBLIC

Times of summer opening and admission fees shown are those which obtained in 1976, and are subject to modification. Space permits only a selection of some of the more noteworthy houses in England which are open to the public. A fuller description of some houses in or near London will be found in the preceding section.

ADLINGTON HALL, Cheshire.—Sun. and Bank Holidays (Sats., July and August), 2.30-6. Admission, 30p.

ALLINGTON CASTLE, Maidstone.—Daily, 2-4, Admission, 30p.

ALNWICK CASTLE, Northumberland. Seat of the Duke of Northumberland.—May-Sept., Daily (except Fri.) 1-5. Admission, 40p.

*ANGLESEY ABBEY, Cambs.—Easter to second week in Oct., Tues., Wed., Thurs., Sat., Sun., and Bank Holidays, 2-6. Admission 60p.

*ANTONY HOUSE, Cornwall.—Tues., Wed., Thurs. and Bank Holidays, 2-6. Admission 60p.

ARUNDEL CASTLE, Sussex. Seat of the Duke of Norfolk.—Easter to mid-June, Mon.-Thurs., 1-5; mid-June to end of Sept., Mon.-Fri. (and Suns. in August) also Easter Monday and Spring Bank Holiday, 12-5. Admission 60p.

ATHELHAMPTON, Dorset.—Sun., Wed., Thurs. and Bank Holidays, 2-6. Admission 50p.

AUDLEY END, Saffron Walden.—April-early Oct., daily, except Mon. (but including Bank Holidays), 10-5.30. Admission, 50p.

AVEBURY MANOR, Wiltshire. (Adjoining the famous Avebury stone circle, which is also on public view).—May-August, daily except Tues., 2-6; April and Sept., Sat. and Sun. 2-6, Bank Holidays, 10-6. Admission 40p.

*BATEMAN'S, Burwash, E. Sussex.—Former home of Rudyard Kipling. Daily except Fri., 2-6 Also 11-12.30, Mon.-Thurs., June-Sept. Admission, 50p.

BELVOIR CASTLE, nr. Grantham. Seat of the Duke of Rutland.—April-Sept., Wed., Thurs., Sat. and Tues. following Bank Holidays, 12-6; Bank Holidays, 11-7; Suns., 2-7. Admission 60p.

BERKELEY CASTLE, Glos.—April-Sept., daily, except Mon., (but including Bank Holidays), 11-5 (April 2-5); also Sun. from May, 2-5; Bank Holidays, 11-5. Admission, 50p.

BLENHEIM PALACE. Woodstock. Seat of the Duke of Marlborough and birthplace of Sir Winston Churchill.—April-Oct. daily, (except Spring Bank Holiday week-end) 11.30-5. Admission, 60p (1974).

BREAMORE HOUSE, Hants.—April-Sept., daily (except Mon. and Fri.), 2-5.30. Admission, 50p.

*BUCKLAND ABBEY, Tavistock.—Including Drake relics. Easter-Sept. 30, weekdays and Bank Holidays, 11-6. Sun. 2-6. Admission, 30p.

BURTON AGNES HALL, Bridlington.—Easter Sunday and Monday, May to mid-Oct. daily, (except Sat.) 1.45-5.00, Suns., 1.45-6.00. Admission, 35p.

CASTLE ASHBY, nr. Northampton. A home of the Marquess of Northampton.—Sundays and Bank Holidays; also Easter week-end. Also Thurs. and Sat., June-Aug., 2-5.30. Admission, 50p.

CASTLE HOWARD, Yorkshire.—Daily, 1.00-5.00; Bank Holidays, 11.30-5.30. Admission, 60p (1975).

*CHARLECOTE PARK, Warwicks. Associations with Shakespeare.—April, Sat., Sun., and daily in Easter Week. May-Sept., daily, except Mon., but incl. Bank Holidays, 11.15-5.45. Admission, 60p.

*CHARTWELL, Kent.—Home of the late Sir Winston Churchill. Sat., Sun. and Bank Holidays, 11-6; Tues. (except following Bank Holidays), Wed. and Thurs., 2-6. Admission, 80p.

CHASTLETON HOUSE, Oxfordshire.—Daily (except Wed.), 10.30-1, 2-5.30 Suns., 2-5. Admission, 50p.

CHICHELEY HALL, Newport Pagnell.—Wed., Thurs., Sat., Sun. and Bank Holidays (closed Sat. and Sun. in June). Admission, 40p.

*CLAYDON HOUSE, Bucks.—Daily except Mon., Fri. and Tues. following Bank Holiday, but including Bank Holiday, 2-6. Admission, 50p.

*CLEVEDON COURT, Avon.—April-Sept., Sun., Wed. and Thurs., and Bank Holidays, 2.30-5.30. Admission, 30p.

*CLIVEDEN, Bucks.—Wed., Sat. and Sun., 2.30-5.30. Admission, 10p.

*COMPTON CASTLE, nr. Paignton.—Fortified manor house. Mon., Wed. and Thurs., 10-12, 2-5. Admission, 30p.

COMPTON WYNYATES, Warwickshire. A home of the Marquess of Northampton.—Tues., Wed., Sat., Sun. and Bank Holidays. 2-5.30. Admission, 50p.

* Property of the National Trust.

CORSHAM COURT, Wilts.—April to mid-July, and mid-Sept. to Oct., Wed., Thurs., Sun. and Bank Holidays; mid-July to mid-Sept., daily except Mon. and Fri. (but incl. Bank Holiday), 11-12.30, 2-6. Admission, 50p.

★CROFT CASTLE, Herefordshire.—Sun., Wed., Thurs., Sat. and Bank Holiday Mondays, 2.30-5.30. Admission, 50p.

★DYRHAM PARK, Glos. (Avon).—Daily (except Mon. and Tues.), 2-6; Bank Holidays, 12-6 (Oct., Sat. and Sun., 2-6). Admission, 50p.

EYE MANOR, Herefordshire.—Sun., Wed., Thurs. and Sat. (also Bank Holidays and Tues. following) (July-Sept., daily), 2.30-5.30. Admission, 30p.

★FELBRIGG HALL, Norfolk. Easter-mid-Oct., Sun., Tues.-Thurs., Sat. and Bank Holidays, 2-6. Admission, 60p.

GAWSWORTH HALL, Cheshire.—Daily, 2-6. Admission, 35p.

GLYNDE PLACE, Lewes.—Easter week-end and Thurs., Sat., Sun. and Bank Holidays, May-first week in Oct. 2.15-5.30. Admission, 40p.

HADDON HALL, Derbyshire.—Tues.-Sat. and Bank Holidays, 11-6; Sun. preceeding Bank Holidays, 2-6. Admission, 60p.

HEVENINGHAM HALL, Suffolk.—Sun., Wed., Thurs., Sat. and Bank Holidays (also Tues., May-Sept.), 2-6. Admission, 50p.

★HUGHENDEN MANOR, High Wycombe. Former home of Disraeli. Daily, except Mon. and Tues., but including Bank Holidays, 2-6, Sat., Sun., and Bank Holidays, 12.30-6. Admission, 50p.

★ICKWORTH, Bury St. Edmunds.—Daily, except Mon. and Fri., but including Bank Holidays, 2-6. Admission, 60p.

KENTWELL HALL, Long Melford, Suffolk.—Wed., Thurs., Sun. and Bank Holidays, 2-6. Admission, 50p.

KNEBWORTH HOUSE, Herts.—Sat. and Sun., Easter-end of May. Daily, except Mon. (but including Bank Holidays) (Oct., Suns. only), 2-5.30. Admission, 30p.

★LACOCK ABBEY, Wilts.—Daily, except Mon. and Tues. in April, May and Oct., but including Bank Holidays, 2-6. Admission, 50p.

★LITTLE MORETON HALL, Cheshire. Famous example of " black and white " timbering.—Daily except Tuesday and Good Friday, 2-6. Admission, 50p.

LONGLEAT HOUSE, Wilts. Seat of the Marquess of Bath.—Daily, 10-6. Admission, 50p. (1975)

LUTON HOO, Beds.—Easter-Sept., Mon., Wed., Thurs. and Sat., 11-6; Sundays 2-6. Admission, 45p.

★LYME PARK, nr. Stockport.—Daily (except Mon.), 1-6. Admission 20p.

LYMPNE CASTLE, nr. Hythe.—April-June and Oct. Sun., Wed. and Bank Holidays, July-Sept. daily, 10.30-1, 2.30-6. Admission, 25p.

MELBOURNE HALL, Derbyshire.—April-mid-June, Suns. and Bank Holidays (and Tues. following. Mid-June-mid-Sept., daily, except Mon. and Fri. (but including Bank Holiday), 2-6, Bank Holidays, 11-6. Admission, 50p.

★MELFORD HALL, Suffolk.—April-Sept., Sun. Wed., Thurs. and Bank Holidays, 2.30-6. Admission, 50p.

MICHELHAM PRIORY, E. Sussex.—Daily, 11-1, 2-5.30. Admission 40p.

MILTON MANOR HOUSE, nr. Abingdon.—Easter-Sept., Sat., Sun. and Bank Holidays, 2-6. Admission, 40p.

NEWBY HALL, Yorks.—Sun., Wed., Thurs., Sat. and Bank Holidays, 2-6. Admission, 50p. (1975).

OSBORNE HOUSE, Isle of Wight. State and Private Apartments are shown, including the room in which Queen Victoria died.—Mon.-Fri., 11-5. (July and Aug., 10.30-5). Admission, 50p.

★OXBURGH HALL, Norfolk.—Sun., Tues., Wed., Thurs., Sat. and Bank Holidays, 2-6. Admission, 50p.

PARHAM, Pulborough, Sussex.—Sun., Wed., Thurs. and Bank Holidays, 2-5.30. Admission, 50p (last Sunday of each month, 70p).

★PAYCOCKE'S, Coggeshall, Essex. Tudor wool-merchant's town house.—April-Sept., Wed., Thurs., Sun. and Bank Holidays, 2-5.30. Admission, 25p.

★PECKOVER HOUSE, Wisbech, Cambs.—Sun., Wed., Thurs., Sat. and Bank Holidays, 2-6. Admission, 40p.

PENSHURST PLACE, Kent. Seat of Visct. De L'Isle, *V.C.*—Daily, except Mon. and Fri., but including Bank Holidays, 2-6 (July-Sept., 1-6, Bank Holidays, 11.30-6). Admission, 50p. (1975).

POWDERHAM CASTLE, Devonshire. Seat of the Earl of Devon.—Easter Sun. and Mon. and Suns. only to mid-May. Mid-May to mid-Sept., daily, except Fri. and Sat., 2-5.30. Admission, 60p.

RABY CASTLE, Co. Durham.—Easter week-end and May, Sun. and Spring Holiday week-end; June-Sept., Sun., Wed., Sat. and Bank Holidays (daily in Aug. except Fri.), 2-5. Admission, 35p (1975).

SHEFFIELD PARK, East Sussex.—Wed., Sat. and Sun., 2-5.30. Admission, 50p.

SKIPTON CASTLE, Yorkshire.—Weekdays, 10-6, Sundays 2-6. Admission, 25p.

★SMALLHYTHE PLACE, Tenterden.—Former home of Dame Ellen Tarry. Daily, except Tues. and Fri., 2-6. Admission, 40p.

★SNOWSHILL MANOR, Broadway.—April and Oct., Sat., Sun. and Bank Holidays. May-Sept. Daily, except Mon. and Tues., but including Bank Holidays, 11-1, 2-6 (Fri. 2-6 only). Admission, 60p.

STANFORD HALL, Lutterworth.—Thurs., Sat. and Sun., Bank Holidays and Tues. after Bank Holidays, 2.30-6. Admission, 45p.

★STOURHEAD, Wiltshire.—Daily, May-Aug., April and Sept., closed Mon. and Tues., but open Bank Holidays (Oct., Sat. and Sun. only), 2-6. Admission, 60p.

STRATFIELD SAYE, Hants. Seat of the Duke of Wellington. Daily (except Fri.), 11-5.30. Admission, 60p.

SULGRAVE MANOR, Northamptonshire. Former home of members of the Washington family.—Daily, except Weds., 10.30-1, 2-5.30 (closes at 4 p.m., Oct.). Admission, 30p.

★TATTON PARK, Cheshire.—Daily, except Mondays, but including Bank Holidays, 2-5.15 (2-5.45, first week in May to end of Aug.). Admission, 25p.

★TRERICE, Cornwall.—Daily, 11-1, 2-6. Admission, 50p.

★UPPARK, nr. Petersfield.—Sun., Wed., Thurs., and Bank Holidays, 2-6. Admission, 50p.

★THE VYNE, Basingstoke.—April-Sept., Wed. and Bank Holidays, 11-1, 2-6; Sun., Thurs. and Sat., 2-6. Admission, 60p.

★WADDESDON MANOR, Bucks.—Wed.-Sun., 2-6. Bank Holidays, 11-6. Admission, 55p (Fri. 75p).

WILTON HOUSE, Wilts. Seat of the Earl of Pembroke.—April-Sept., Tues.-Sat. and Bank Holidays, 11-6. Sun., 2-6. Admission, 40p.

★ *Property of the National Trust.*

HISTORIC MONUMENTS

A select list of monuments under the control of the Department of the Environment.

Reduced admission prices for retirement pensioners and children under 16. 10 per cent. discount for parties of 11 or more.

Standard hours of opening (marked *) are as follows:

	Weekdays	Sundays
Mar.–April	9.30 a.m.–5.30 p.m.	2–5.30 p.m.
May–Sept.	9.30 a.m.–7.00 p.m.	2–7.00 p.m.
October	9.30 a.m.–5.30 p.m.	2–5.30 p.m.
Nov.–Feb.	9.30 a.m.–4.00 p.m.	2–4.00 p.m.

Those marked † open on Sundays at 9.30 a.m. from April to September.

All monuments in England and Wales are closed on Christmas Eve, Christmas Day, Boxing Day and New Year's Day. Some smaller sites may close for the lunch-hour, which is normally 1–2 p.m.

BEESTON CASTLE, Cheshire. 20p†. Thirteenth-century inner ward with gatehouse and towers, and considerable remains of large outer ward.

BERKHAMSTED CASTLE, Hertfordshire. 10p.* Extensive remains of a large 11th-century motte-and-bailey castle with later stone wall.

BOLSOVER CASTLE, Derbyshire. 20p.† Established in Norman times, it is now notable for its exceptionally interesting 17th-century buildings.

BOSCOBEL HOUSE, Salop. 20p*. Timber-framed early 17-century hunting lodge with later alterations. Charles II's " Royal Oak " is nearby.

BRINKBURN PRIORY, Northumberland. 10p†. An Augustinian priory; the church (c. 1200, repaired in 1858) and parts of the claustral buildings survive.

BROUGHAM CASTLE, Cumbria. 10p†. Extensive remains of the keep (c. 1170), and of other buildings of periods up to the 17th century.

BUILDWAS ABBEY, Salop. 10p*. Beautiful 12th-century ruin of a Cistercian abbey with early 13th-century vaulted Chapter-house.

BYLAND ABBEY, North Yorkshire. 10p*. Considerable remains of church and conventional buildings date from the abbey's foundation in 1177 by the Cistercians.

CARISBROOKE CASTLE, Isle of Wight. Summer 50p, Winter 20p*. Extensive motte-and-bailey castle with shell keep.

CARLISLE CASTLE, Cumbria. Summer, 40p, Winter 20p†. The castle was begun by William Rufus. The keep houses the Regimental Museum of the Border Regiment.

CASTLE ACRE PRIORY, NORFOLK. 15p†. Extensive remains include the church with its elaborate west front, and the prior's lodgings.

CASTLE RISING, Norfolk. 15p†. A fine 12th-century keep stands in a massive earthwork with its gatehouse and bridge.

CHESTERS ROMAN FORT, Northumberland. Summer 30p, Winter 10p†.

CHYSAUSER ANCIENT VILLAGE Cornwall. 10p†. Iron-Age village of courtyard houses.

CLEEVE ABBEY, Somerset. 10p†. Much of the claustral buildings survive including timber-roofed frater, but only foundations of the church.

CORBRIDGE ROMAN STATION, Northumberland. Summer 30p, Winter 10p†. Excavations have revealed the central area of the Roman town and military base of Corstopitum.

DEAL CASTLE, Kent. 15p†. The largest and most complete of the castles erected by Henry VIII for coastal defence.

DOVER CASTLE, Kent. Keep—Summer 40p, Winter 20p†; Underground Works 20p*; Grounds —free. One of the largest and most important English castles.

DUNSTANBURGH CASTLE, Northumberland. 10p†. The castle, standing on a cliff above the sea, has a 14th-century gatehouse-keep.

FARLEIGH CASTLE, Somerset. 15p†. Late 14th-century castle of two courts. The chapel contains fine tomb of Sir Thomas Hungerford.

FARNHAM CASTLE, Surrey. 10p*. Keep, April–Sept. Built by the Bishops of Winchester, the motte of the castle is enclosed by a large 12th-century shell keep.

FINCHALE PRIORY, Durham. 10p†. Benedictine house on banks of River Wear with considerable remains of the 13th century.

FOUNTAINS ABBEY, North Yorkshire. Summer 40p, Winter 20p. Nov.–Feb. 9.30 a.m.–4 p.m. (Sundays 2–4 p.m.); March, April, Oct., 9.30 a.m.–5.30 p.m.; May, Sept. 9.30 a.m.–7 p.m.; June–Aug. 9.30 a.m.–9 p.m. Finest monastic ruin in W. Europe.

FRAMLINGHAM CASTLE, Suffolk. 15p†. Impressive castle with high curtain-walls of late 12th-century enclosing a poor-house of 1639.

FURNESS ABBEY, Cumbria. 10p*. Founded in 1127 by Stephen, afterwards King of England; extensive remains of church and conventual buildings.

GOODRICH CASTLE, Hereford and Worcester. 20p†. Extensive remains of beautiful 14th-century castle incorporating interesting 12th-century keep.

GRIMES GRAVES, Norfolk. 10p†. Extensive group of flint mines dating from the Stone Age. Several shafts can be inspected.

HAILES ABBEY, Gloucestershire. 10p*. Ruins of a Cistercian monastery founded in 1246. Museum contains some fine architectural fragments.

HELMSLEY CASTLE, North Yorkshire. 15p†. Twelfth-century keep and curtain wall with 16th-century domestic buildings against west wall.

HOUSESTEADS ROMAN FORT, Northumberland. Summer 30p, Winter 10p† Excavation has exposed this infantry fort on Hadrian's Wall with its extra-mural civilian settlement.

KENILWORTH CASTLE, Warwickshire. Summer 25p, Winter 10p†. One of the finest and most extensive castles in England, showing many styles of building from 1155 to 1649.

LANERCOST PRIORY, Cumbria. 10p*. The nave of the priory church is still used and there are remains of other claustral buildings.

LINDISFARNE PRIORY, Northumberland. 15p†. An Anglican monastery destroyed by the Danes, it was re-established by the Benedictine abbey of Durham.

LULLINGSTONE ROMAN VILLA, Kent. Summer 30p, Winter 10p†. A large villa occupied through much of the Roman period; fine mosaics and a unique Christian chapel.

MIDDLEHAM CASTLE, North Yorkshire. 10p*. The fine keep of 1170 stands in the centre of 13th-century inner ward.

MOUNT GRACE PRIORY, North Yorkshire. 15p†, but closed Mon. unless Bank Holiday. Carthusian monastery, with remains of monks' separate houses.

NETLEY ABBEY, Hampshire. 10p*. Extensive remains of 13th-century church, claustral buildings and abbot's house, incorporating much fine detail.

OLD SARUM, Wiltshire. 10p†. Large 11th-century earthworks enclosing the excavated remains of the castle and the cathedral.

ORFORD CASTLE, Suffolk. 15p†. Circular keep of c. 1170 and remains of coastal defence castle built by Henry II.

PENDENNIS CASTLE, Cornwall. 20p†. Well-preserved castle erected by Henry VIII for coast defence and enlarged by Elizabeth I.

PEVENSEY CASTLE, East Sussex. 15p†. Extensive remains of a Roman fort of the Saxon Shore enclosing an 11th-century castle.

PEVERIL CASTLE, Derbyshire. 15p†. In a picturesque and nearly impregnable position, this 12th-century castle is defended on two sides by precipitous rocks.

PORTCHESTER CASTLE, Hampshire. 20p†. A Roman fort of the Saxon Shore enclosing a fine Norman keep and priory church.

RECULVER CHURCH and ROMAN FORT, Kent. 10p. Church†. Fort at any reasonable time. Remains of Saxon church with 12th-century towers standing in a Roman fort.

RICHBOROUGH CASTLE, Kent. 10p†. The landing-site of the Claudian invasion, it became a supply-base and a Saxon Shore fort.

RICHMOND CASTLE, North Yorkshire. 15p†. This very fine 12th-century keep, with 11th-century curtain-wall and gatehouse, commands Swaledale.

RIEVAULX ABBEY, North Yorkshire. Summer 30p, Winter 10p†. Extensive remains include an early Cistercian nave (1140) and fine 13th-century choir and claustral buildings.

ROCHESTER CASTLE, Kent. 15p†. Eleventh-century wall, partly overlying the Roman city wall, encloses splendid square keep of c. 1130.

ST. AUGUSTINE'S ABBEY, Canterbury, Kent. 10p†. Sundays from 9.30 a.m. all the year. Founded by St. Augustine in 598; 7th- and 11th-century churches underlie the mediaeval abbey.

ST. MAWES CASTLE, Cornwall. 15p†. Coast defence castle built by Henry VIII consisting of central tower and three bastions.

SCARBOROUGH CASTLE, North Yorkshire. 20p†. Remains of 12th-century keep and curtain-walls dominating the town.

STONEHENGE, Wiltshire. Summer 40p, Winter 10p†. Sundays from 9.30 a.m. all year. World-famous prehistoric monument consisting of central stone circles surrounded by bank and ditch.

TILBURY FORT, Essex. 20p*. Built to guard the Thames against the Dutch, the fort is a fine example of 17th-century fortification.

TINTAGEL CASTLE, Cornwall. Summer 25p, Winter 10p†. Twelfth-century castle on cliff-top site and remains of a Celtic monastery.

TYNEMOUTH PRIORY and CASTLE, Tyne and Wear. 10p†. Anglian monastery destroyed by the Danes and re-established in 1090, with 14th-century defensive system.

WALMER CASTLE, Kent. Summer 30p, Winter 10p†. Closed Mon. (unless Bank Holiday) and when Lord Warden is in residence. One of Henry VIII's coast defence castles, it is the residence of the Lord Warden of the Cinque Ports.

WARKWORTH CASTLE, Northumberland. 15p†. Magnificent early 15th-century keep built by the Percys, with other remains from earlier periods.

WHITBY ABBEY, North Yorkshire. 15p†. A Saxon foundation destroyed by the Danes with considerable remains of fine 13th-century church.

WROXETER ROMAN CITY, Salop. 15p†. The public baths and part of the forum remain of the Roman town of Viroconium.

Wales

BEAUMARIS CASTLE, Anglesey, Gwynedd. Summer 25p, Winter 10p†. The finest example of the concentrically planned castle in Britain, it is still almost intact.

CAERLEON ROMAN AMPHITHEATRE, Gwent. 10p†. Late 1st-century oval arena surrounded by bank for spectators with entrance passages.

CAERNARFON CASTLE, Gwynedd. Summer 40p., Winter 10p†. The most important of the Edwardian castles, built together with the town wall in 1284.

CAERPHILLY CASTLE, Glamorgan. 15p†. Concentrically planned castle (c. 1300) notable for its great scale and use of water defences.

CHEPSTOW CASTLE, Gwent. 20p†. Fine rectangular keep in the middle of the fortifications.

CONWY CASTLE, Gwynedd. Summer 25p, Winter 10p†. Built by Edward I to guard the Conway ferry, it is a magnificent example of mediaeval military architecture.

CRICCIETH CASTLE, Gwynedd. 15p†. A native Welsh castle of the early 13th century, much altered by Edward I.

DENBIGH CASTLE, Clwyd, 15p†. The remains of the castle, which dates from 1282–1322, include unusual triangular gatehouse.

HARLECH CASTLE, Gwynedd. Summer 25p, Winter 10p†. Well preserved Edwardian castle with a concentric plan sited on rocky outcrop above the former shore-line.

NORTH WALES QUARRYING MUSEUM, LLANBERIS, Gwynedd, 20p†. Closed Oct.–March. The workshops of the Dinorwic Slate Quarry.

RAGLAN CASTLE, Gwent. 15p†. Extensive and imposing remains of 15th-century castle with moated hexagonal keep.

ST. DAVID'S, BISHOP'S PALACE, Dyfed. 15p†. Extensive remains of principal residence of Bishop of St. David's dating from 1280–1350.

TINTERN ABBEY, Gwent. 20p†. Very extensive remains of the fine 13th-century church and conventual buildings of this Cistercian monastery.

FREEMEN'S GUILDS

London.—Guild of Freemen of the City of London, 4 Dowgate Hill, E.C.4. *Clerk*, D. Reid.

Berwick upon Tweed.—Freemen's Guild of Berwick upon Tweed. *Sec.*, J. R. Reay, 9 Church Street.

Chester.—Freemen and Guilds of the City of Chester. *Hon. Sec.*, K. S. Astbury, The Guildhall, Chester.

Coventry.—City of Coventry Freemen's Guild. *Clerk.*—D. E. Sharpe, Milford House, Birdingbury, Rugby.

Grimsby.—Enrolled Freemen of Grimsby. *Clerk*, W. J. Savage, St. Mary's Chambers, Grimsby.

Lincoln.—Lincoln Freemen's Committee. *Clerk*, E. Mason, St. Swithin's Square, Lincoln.

Oxford.—Oxford Freemen's Committee. *Chairman*, E. H. Crapper, 15 Corbett Road, Carterton, Oxford.

Shrewsbury.—Association of Shrewsbury Freemen. *President*, M. Peele, 20 Dogpole, Shrewsbury.

York.—Gild of Freemen of the City of York. *Hon. Clerk.*, J. Buckle, 36 Oaken Grove, Haxby, York.

MUSEUMS AND ART GALLERIES OUTSIDE LONDON

BIRMINGHAM.—*City Museum and Art Gallery*. The art collection contains outstanding examples by British and European masters from 14th to 20th centuries, with particularly strong Pre-Raphaelite and Burne-Jones collections, sculpture, prints, drawings and water colours, British and European gold, silver and jewellery, pottery and porcelain, furniture, toys, textiles and costume, archaeology and natural history. Open, free, Weekdays, 10–6; Sundays 2–5.30. Closed Christmas Day, Boxing Day and Good Friday.

Museum of Science and Industry, Newhall Street. Founded 1950, the first provincial museum of its kind devoted to the history of science from the Industrial Revolution to the present. Locomotive Hall (1972) and many working machines under steam, gas, etc. Open, free, Weekdays, 10–5; Saturdays, 10–5.30; Sundays, 2–5.30. Open to 9 on first Wednesday evening of each month. Other Birmingham museums are: *Aston Hall, Blakesley Hall, Cannon Hill Nature Centre, Sarehole Mill, The Smithy* and *Weoley Castle*.

THE BOWES MUSEUM, Barnard Castle, Co. Durham. Important collections of British and European art, including paintings of Italian, Dutch, French and Spanish schools. Fine porcelain and pottery, tapestries and furniture. Music and costume galleries. English period rooms from Elizabeth I to Victoria; local antiquities from Stone Age to 20th century. Temporary Exhibitions. Open weekdays, May–Sept., 10–5.30; March, April and October, 10–5; Nov.–Feb., 10–4. Sundays, 2–5 (Summer); 2–4 (Winter). Admission 20p; children and OAPs, 5p. Curator, M. H. Kirkby.

BRADFORD.—*Cartwright Hall*, Lister Park, contains European and British paintings, drawings and watercolours from the 16th century onwards. *Bolling Hall* off Wakefield Road is a furnished house and local history museum dating from the 15th century. *Industrial Museum*, Moorside Mills, illustrates the local wool and worsted industries and transport. *Cliffe Castle*, Keighley. Natural history, local history. *Manor House*, Ilkley, is an Elizabethan Manor House with exposed wall of Roman Fort. All show changing temporary exhibitions. Open 10–5. Closed Good Friday and Christmas Day. Admission free.

BRIGHTON.—The *Royal Pavilion*, Palace of George IV. Chinoiserie interiors, much of the original furniture returned on loan from H.M. the Queen. Open daily 10–5 (10–8 during annual Regency Exhibition, July to September). Closed Christmas Day, Boxing Day and for three days before Regency Exhibition.

Art Gallery and Museum, Church Street (adjacent Royal Pavilion). Old master paintings; Willett pottery and porcelain collection, 20th-century decorative art and furniture, surrealist paintings; ethnography, archaeology. Open 10–6 winter, 10–7 summer (Sat. open 10–5; Sundays 2–5 winter, 2–6 summer). Closed Christmas, Boxing Day, Good Friday and Mondays.

Preston Manor, Preston Park. (Thomas-Stanford: Macquoid bequests of English period furniture, furnishings, china and silver.) Closed Christmas Day, Boxing Day, Good Friday and Mondays and Tuesdays. Open weekdays 10–5, Sundays, 2–5. Admission 15p; Children 5p. Gardens open, free.

The Grange, Rottingdean. Art Gallery, Sussex Room, Kipling Room and collections of National Toy Museum. Open, free, 10–7 (winter, 10–6); Saturdays, 10–5; Sundays, 2–6 (winter, 2–5). Closed Christmas Day, Boxing Day, Good Friday and Wednesdays.

BRISTOL.—*City Art Gallery*. Collection of Old Masters, 19th cent. and modern paintings, English watercolours, Chinese ceramics, glass, English silver, glass, porcelain and delftware, English and foreign embroideries. Open weekdays, 10–5.30. *Red Lodge*, Park Row. Furnished in style of 17th and very early 18th centuries. Open weekdays, 1–5. *Georgian House*, Great George Street. Furnished in Style of period. Open weekdays, 11–5.

CAMBRIDGE.—Fitzwilliam Museum. The Fine Art collections of the University, and one of the most important museums outside London. The chief collections, largely due to private benefaction, comprise Egyptian, Greek and Roman antiquities, coins and medals, mediæval manuscripts, paintings and drawings, prints, pottery and porcelain, textiles, arms and armour, mediæval and renaissance objects of art, and a library. Open free, Tuesday–Saturday 10–5; Sundays, 2.15–5. Closed Dec. 23–26, New Year's Day and Good Friday. Closed on Mondays, except Easter Monday and the Spring and Summer Bank Holidays.

CANTERBURY.—Royal Museum. Collections include archæology, geology and natural history, porcelain, prints and pictures. Open free weekdays, 9.30–5.30. Roman Pavement Museum. Roman material from post-war excavations of Canterbury. Westgate Tower Museum. Arms and armour and display of city walls and gates. (Roman and Westgate Museums open 10–1, 2–5, Oct.–March, 2–4 only.) Adm. 7p.

CARISBROOKE.—Castle Museum. Former home in Carisbrooke Castle of Governor of Isle of Wight. Collections cover archæology and history of Isle of Wight, and personal relics of Charles I, who was imprisoned in Castle from 1647 to 1648. Open, March–April and Oct. 9.30–5.30 (Sundays, 2–5.30); May–Sept. 9.30–7 (Sundays, 2–7); Nov.–Feb. 9.30–4. (Sundays, 2–4). Admission to Castle and Museum, 50p. (in winter, 20p).

COLCHESTER.—Colchester and Essex Museum, The Castle. The Norman Castle contains local archæological antiquities, expecially the extensive finds from Roman Colchester. The *Holly Trees Mansion* (1718) covers the antiquities of social life of the 18th and 19th centuries. *Natural History Museum*, All Saints Church. Natural history of Essex. *Museum of Social History*, Holy Trinity Church. Domestic life and crafts. Open, weekdays, 10–5 (branches closed 1–2 p.m.); Castle only, Sundays 2.30–5 (April–Sept.) Admission (April–Sept.) 15p; Children free. (Oct.–March) free.

DERBY.—Museum and Art Gallery, Strand. Archaeology, military, social history, natural history. Collection of paintings by Joseph Wright of Derby; Derby porcelain, costume. Open Tues.–Fri. 10–6 (Saturdays, 10–5).

Industrial Museum, Silk Mill, Full Street, Rolls Royce collection of aero engines etc. Tues.–Fri. 10–5.45 (Saturdays 10–4.45). Closed on all Bank Holidays.

DORCHESTER.—County Museum. Geology, archæology, local history, natural history and rural crafts of Dorset. Collection of Thomas Hardy's manuscripts, books, notebooks, drawings, etc.

GUILDFORD.—Guildford Museum, Castle Arch. Local museum for archæology and history of Surrey based on collections of the Surrey Archæological Society. Open every day except Sunday, 11–5.

HULL.—*Ferens Art Gallery.* Collection of foreign paintings includes works by Hals, Canaletto and Guardi; British 18th and 19th century works, especially sea-pieces and pictures by the Humberside marine painters, also a representative collection of British paintings to the present day and a constant programme of visiting exhibitions. *Wilberforce House.* Jacobean merchant's house, birthplace of William Wilberforce; collection of slavery relics, period furniture, costume and ceramics. *Transport and Archaeology Museum.* Veteran cars, trams, coaches and velocipedes; archæological finds from Humberside, including Roman mosaics. *Town Docks Museum.* Whales, whaling, fishing and trawling. Ferens Art Gallery and Town Docks Museum open weekdays, 10–5.30; Sundays, 2.30–4.30. Other museums open weekdays, 10–5.30; Sundays, 2.30–4.30.

HUNTINGDON.—*Cromwell Museum.* Housed in the only remaining portion of the 12th-century Hospital of St. John. Portraits of Cromwell, his family and Parliamentary notables (by Walker, Lely etc.); as well as reproductions and engravings covering the whole Puritan field. Unique collection of Cromwelliana—objects, documents, armour, coins and medals. Open free, Sundays 2–4; Tuesday to Friday, 11–1, 2–5, Saturday, 11–1, 2–4. Closed Mondays and Bank Holidays other than Good Friday.

IPSWICH.—*Ipswich Museum.* Refounded 1846. Present buildings 1880/1 with 1901 extension. Art Gallery attached. Collections of Suffolk geology, archaeology and natural history and general collections, including ethnology and industrial. Open weekdays 10–5, Sundays 2.30–4.30. Adm. free. Closed Good Friday, Dec. 24–25. *Christchurch* (Branch Museum) Tudor house, presented 1894. Furniture. Suffolk portraits and works by local artists (Gainsborough, Constable, Munnings, etc). Porcelain, pottery and glass. Modern prints. Sculpture. Open weekdays 10–5 (dusk in winter). Sundays 2.30–4.30. Closed Good Friday, Dec. 24–25.

LEEDS.—*City Art Gallery.* Important collection of early English watercolours. British and European painting, modern sculpture, etc. Print Room and Art library contains study collection of drawings and prints. Open weekdays, 10.30–6.30, Sundays, 2.30–5. (Print Room and Art Library 9–9, Saturdays, 9–4, closed Sundays.) *Temple Newsam House.* Tudor/Jacobean house altered in mid-18th cent. to make suite of state rooms. Collection of English furniture mostly of 17th and 18th cents., silver, European porcelain and pottery, pictures, etc. Open daily, 10.30–6.15 or dusk; Weds. (May–Sept.), 10.30–8.30. Admission 25p; Children (with adults), 5p. O.A.P.s free. *Lotherton Hall,* Gascoigne art collection, oriental gallery, costume collection, 19th century furniture, ceramics and silver, park and gardens. Open daily, 10.30–6.15 (or dusk in winter); Thursdays (May–Sept.), 10.30–8.30. Admission to Hall, 15p; children (with adult) 5p.

LEICESTER.—*Museum and Art Gallery,* New Walk (1849). *Newarke Houses,* The Newarke. Social history of Leicestershire from 1500 A.D.; musical instruments; local clocks. *Jewry Wall Museum,* St. Nicholas Circle. Archæology (prehistoric–1500). Roman Jewry Wall and Baths, mosaics *in situ.* *Belgrave Hall,* Church Road. A Queen Anne house with collection of furniture and garden of note. Coaches and agricultural collection. *Magazine Gateway,* Museum of Royal Leicestershire Regiment in a 14th century gatehouse. *Guildhall,* Guildhall Lane, 14th century timber-framed building. Used as town hall till 1876. *Museum of Tech-*

nology, Corporation Road. Horse-drawn vehicles, cycles, motor cycles and motor cars. Beam engines. *Wygston's House,* Museum of Costume, St. Nicholas Circle. Costume from 1789–1924.

All museums open weekdays 10–5.30; Sundays, 2–5.30 unless otherwise stated. Closed Christmas Day, Boxing Day and Good Friday.

LEWES.—*Barbican House Museum,* near Castle (Sussex Archæological Trust). Prehistoric Roman Saxon and mediæval collections relating to Sussex; local pictures and prints. Open weekdays, 10–5.30, Sundays (April–Oct.), 2–5.30. *Anne of Cleves, House,* Southover. Local history and folk museum. Open weekdays (Feb.–Nov.), 10.30–1; 2–5.30. Sundays (April–Oct.), 2–5.30. Admission, 20p; Children, 10p.

LINCOLN.—*Usher Gallery.* Collection of watches, miniatures, porcelain, silver, etc., Peter de Wint collection of oils and watercolours, Lincolnshire topographical drawings, *personalia* associated with Tennyson family. Open weekdays, 10–5.30; Sundays, 2.30–5. *City and County Museum.* In the Greyfriars, a 13th-cent. Franciscan building. Geology, natural history and archaeology of Lincolnshire. Special collection of armour. Open weekdays, 10–5.30; Sundays, 2.30–5. *Museum of Lincolnshire Life.* Collections illustrate life and work in Lincolnshire since 17th century. Open weekdays, 10–5.30; Sundays, 2.30–5. Closed Mondays.

LIVERPOOL.—*Walker Art Gallery.* One of the few Galleries outside London where a representative collection of European painting from the 14th century to the present day can be seen. Particularly strong in early Italian and Northern painting, Pre-Raphaelite and Academic 19th century paintings. Open, weekdays, 10–5; Sundays, 2–5. Closed on Good Friday, Christmas Eve, Christmas Day and Boxing Day. *Sudley Art Gallery* (Emma Holt Bequest), Mossley Hill Road. Collection of 18th and 19th-century paintings, mainly English, including Reynolds, Gainsborough and Romney, Wilkie, Mulready, Turner and Holman Hunt. Open as for Walker Art Gallery. *Merseyside County Museum,* William Brown Street. Founded 1851; buildings destroyed in 1941 and rebuilt 1966–69. The Museum was established on the important Mayer and Derby collections which have been supplemented to form an outstanding collection. These include the Mayer-Fejervary Gothic ivories, the Bryan Faussett group of Anglo-Saxon antiquities and the Lord Derby and Tristram ornithological collections. Gallery displays include material relating to Local History, Shipping, Egyptology, Ethnology, Decorative Art (including clocks and watches, pottery and musical instruments) and Transport. There is also an Aquarium and a Planetarium. Open weekdays, 10–5; Sunday, 2–5. Closed Good Friday, Christmas Day and Boxing Day. *Speke Hall.* A fine half-timbered Tudor house administered by the County Museums for the National Trust. Open weekdays and Bank Holidays 10–5, Sunday 2–7 (2–5 Sept.–April). Adults 25p, Children 10p.

NORWICH.—*Castle Museum.* Exhibits illustrating art, local archæology, social history and natural history. Open, weekdays 10–5; Sundays 2–5 (to 5.30, July–Aug.). *Strangers' Hall (Museum of Domestic Life,* Charing Cross). Late mediæval mansion furnished as a museum of urban domestic life, 16th–19th centuries, with displays of costume, transport, shop signs and toys. Open, weekdays, 10–5. *Bridewell Museum,* Bridewell Alley. Exhibits illustrating transport, crafts and industries of Norwich, Norfolk and North Suffolk. Open, weekdays, 10–5. *St. Peter Hungate Church Museum,*

Princes Street. Fifteenth century church used for display of church art and antiquities. Open, weekdays, 10–5.

NOTTINGHAM.—*Castle Museum*, housed in Nottingham Castle, built by Dukes of Newcastle in 17th century on site of mediæval royal castle. English and Netherlands paintings and drawings 17th–20th centuries; special collections of Bonington and Paul Sandby. Ceramics, silver, glass, mediæval Nottingham alabaster carvings, local historical and archaeological displays, classical, oriental and ethnographical antiquities; the regimental collection of the Sherwood Foresters. Open, Summer, 10–6.45; (Fri. 5.45; Sun., 4.45); Winter, 10–4.45. Closed Christmas Day. Admission free, 4p on Sun. and Bank Holidays.

Industrial Museum, Wollaton Park (in 18th century stables). Industries, lacemaking machinery, steam engines, transport. Open, Summer, Wed.–Sat., 10–7; Sunday, 2–5; Winter, Thurs. and Sat., 10–dusk; Sunday, 1.30–dusk. Admission free.

Natural History Museum, Wollaton Hall. Formal gardens, deer park and lake. Open, Summer 10–7 (Sun. 2–5); Winter 10 till dusk (Sun. 1.30–4.30). Admission free. Closed Christmas Day.

Newstead Abbey, 11½ miles N. of Nottingham. Originally a Priory founded *c.* 1170, later property of Byron family, 1540–1817. Collections associated with poet Byron. Abbey open Good Friday to end of September. Monday to Saturday conducted tours at 2, 3, 4 and 5 p.m. On Sundays and Bank Holidays except Good Friday the Abbey is open from 2 to 6.30 p.m. Admission, 11p; children, 5p. Gardens open all year, daily 10 till dusk. Closed Christmas Day and Dec. 31. Admission, 22p; children, 8p.

Museum of Costume and Textiles, Castle Gate. In row of Georgian terraced houses. Seventeenth century costume and embroideries and map tapestries; late 18th century period room. Open daily 10–5. Admission free.

OAKHAM, Rutland County Museum, Catmose Street.—Archæology, local history, craft tools and agricultural implements. Open Tues.–Sat., 10–1, 2–5; Sunday (April–Oct.) 2–5.

OXFORD, Ashmolean Museum.—Department of Western Art, Department of Antiquities, Heberden Coin Room, Department of Eastern Art, Cast Gallery. Open weekdays, 10–4, Sats. 10–5, Sundays 2–4 (Heberden Coin Room, weekdays, 10–12.30 and 2–4; Cast Gallery closed from 1 p.m. Saturdays and all day Sunday).

PORT SUNLIGHT, Merseyside. *Lady Lever Art Gallery*. Paintings and watercolour drawings, mainly of British School, antique, renaissance and British sculpture, English furniture, mainly 18th cent., Chinese pottery and porcelain, and important collection of old Wedgwood. Open weekdays 10–5, Sundays 2–5.

SHEFFIELD.—*City Museum, Weston Park*. Seven galleries are normally open to the public and the reference library and students' collections may be consulted on request. The exhibits cover a wide range of subjects, and include the Bateman Collection of antiquities from the Bronze Age barrows of the Peak District. Cutlery and Old Sheffield Plate collections. Open, weekdays, Sept.–May, 10–5; June–Aug. 10–8.; Sundays 11–5 (Closed Christmas Eve, Christmas Day and Boxing Day). *Abbeydale Industrial Hamlet*, Abbeydale Road South. A late 18th and early 19th century scythe and steel works with associated housing. Open, as for City Museum. *Shepherd Wheel*, Whiteley Wood. Water-powered cutlery grinding establishment. Open 10–12.30, 1.30–5 (opens at 11 on Sundays). Closed Mon. and Tues. *Bishops' House, Meersbrook Park*; museum of local history in late 15th century timber-framed domestic building with 16th and 17th century additions. Open, Wed.–Sat., 10–5; Sundays 11–5.

YORK.—*Castle Museum*. Folk museum of Yorkshire life of the past four centuries. Open weekdays, 9.30–6; Sats. and Bank Holidays 9.30–6.0.; Sundays, 10–6.0; Closes 4.30, Oct.–Mar. Admission, 40p; children, 20p (special party rates).

Yorkshire Museum and Gardens, Museum Street. Archæology, decorative arts, geology and natural history. Open weekdays, 10–5; Sundays, 1–5. Admission, 11p; Children, 5p. Gardens, Roman, Anglian and mediæval ruins. Open weekdays, 8 till dusk; Sundays 10 till dusk. Admission free.

Art Gallery, Exhibition Square. European paintings, 14th–20th century; watercolours and prints of Yorkshire; modern English stoneware pottery. Open weekdays, 10–5; Sundays, 2.30–5. Admission free.

St. Mary's Architectural Heritage Centre, Castlegate. Open Weekdays 10–5; Sundays 1–5. Admission: 20p; children 10p.

Treasurer's House (National Trust). Chapter House Street. Open, April–Oct., 10.30–6. Admission 40p; children 20p.

THE PRINCIPAL ENGLISH CITIES

BIRMINGHAM

BIRMINGHAM (West Midlands) is the second largest City in Britain and the chief centre of the hardware trade. In local government reorganization effective from April 1, 1974, Birmingham is merged with Sutton Coldfield as a Metropolitan District in the West Midlands Metropolitan County. It is estimated that over 1,500 distinct trades are carried on in the city, the chief industries being the manufacture of buttons, plastic goods, chocolate, chemicals, electroplate, guns, machine tools, glass, motor-cars and motor cycles, motor tyres, nuts and bolts, pens and nibs, tubes, paint and enamels, tools, toys, electrical apparatus, wire, jewellery and brass working, etc.

The first section of Birmingham's Queen Elizabeth Hospital, erected at Edgbaston at a cost of approximately £1,000,000, is claimed to be the finest of its type in Europe. A new maternity hospital adjoining was opened in 1969. The construction of an inner ring road round the centre was completed in 1971, hotel accommodation has been increased and there have been many improvements in the shopping centre including the redevelopment of the old market centre in the Bull Ring at a cost of £8,000,000. A new complex of buildings near the Town Hall includes a School of Music, Central Library, a shopping precinct and Corporation offices. A new television centre is in being and the City's new repertory theatre was opened in October, 1971. The National Exhibition Centre at Bickenhill opened in 1976.

The principal buildings are the Town Hall, built in 1832–1834; the Council House and Corporation Museum and Art Gallery (1878); Victoria Law Courts (1891); the University (1900); the Central Library; the 13th century Church of St. Martin (rebuilt 1873); the Cathedral (formerly St. Philip's Church); the Roman Catholic Cathedral of St. Chad (Pugin) and the Methodist Central Hall. Birmingham was incorporated as a borough in 1838, and was created a city in 1889. The generally accepted derivation of " Birmingham " is the *ham* or dwelling-place of the *ing* or the family of *Beorma* presumed to have been a Saxon. Between the 11th and 16th centuries the de Berminghams were Lords of the Manor.

The Lord Mayor (1976–77), H. Powell.
Stipendiary Magistrate, J. F. Milward (1951).
Chief Executive, F. J. C. Amos, C.B.E. (1974)

BRADFORD

BRADFORD (West Yorkshire), the principal town in the Metropolitan District of Bradford, is 192 miles N.N.W. of London and 8 miles W. of Leeds. The metropolitan area is 91,444 acres with a population (1974 estimate) 461, 000.

Although the area has always been associated with wool and textiles, industrial activity now covers a much wider range, Together with Keighley and Shipley in the Aire valley it is well known for its engineering and electrical industries, high quality machine tools, mail order firms, iron and printing works and quarries.

The chief public buildings of Bradford in addition to the 15th century Cathedral (formerly the Parish Church) and Bolling Hall (14th century), are the City Hall (1873), the tower of which contains a clock with dials, chimes and a carillon, Cartwright Hall (1904) commemorating the inventor of the power loom, Grammar School (Charter 1662), St. George's Hall (Concert Hall, 1853), Technical College (1882), Wool Exchange (1867), Britannia House (1933) and Bradford University. A new

Central Library, planned on the " subject department " principle was opened in 1967 and the new Magistrates' Courts were opened in 1972. The Civic Precinct was opened in 1974.

The Saxon township of Bradford was created a parliamentary borough in 1832, a borough in 1847, a county borough in 1889, and a city in 1897. The office of Lord Mayor was created in 1907. The Council consists of a Lord Mayor and 92 Councillors.

The Lord Mayor (1976–77), F. Hillam.
Chief Executive, G. C. Moore.

BRISTOL

BRISTOL, situated in the new county of Avon, is the largest non-metropolitan district in population in the country, and is 119 miles W. of London. The present municipal area is 27,068 acres, with a population (1975 estimate) of 421,000.

Among the various industries are aircraft and aero-engine construction, general and nuclear engineering, boot and shoe manufacture, chocolate and cocoa, tobacco, paper bags, cardboard and allied products, printing, chemical industry and shipbuilding and repairing. The principal imports are grain, flour and other cereal products, cocoa, tea, coffee, molasses, feeding stuffs, fruit, provisions, frozen meat, metals, ores, phosphates, paper, petroleum and chemicals, fertilizers, timber, tobacco, wood pulp and other goods, and the chief exports are metals and machinery, chemicals, unmanufactured clay, motor vehicles and parts, carbon black, electrical apparatus, tea, wines and spirits and manufactured goods.

The chief buildings, in addition to the 12th century Cathedral (with later additions), with Norman Chapter House and gateway, the 14th century Church of St. Mary, Redcliffe (described by Queen Elizabeth I as " the fairest, goodliest, and most famous parish church in England "), and Wesley's Chapel, Broadmead, are the Merchant Venturers' Almshouses, the Council House (opened by H.M. the Queen in April, 1956), Guildhall, Exchange (erected from the designs of John Wood in 1743), City Museum and Art Gallery, Central Library, Cabot Tower, the University and Clifton College, Red Lodge (Tudor), Georgian House, and Blaise Castle and Mansion with Folk Museum. The *Clifton Suspension Bridge*, with a span of 702 feet over the Avon, was projected by Brunel in 1836 but was not completed until 1864. The new Roman Catholic Cathedral at Clifton was opened in 1973.

Bristol was a Royal Borough before the Norman Conquest. In 1373 it received from Edward III a charter granting it county statutes and in 1899 its Mayor became a Lord Mayor. The Corporation includes 84 Councillors. The earliest forms of the name are *Brigstowe* and *Bristow*.

The Lord Mayor (1976–77), J. D. Fisk.
Chief Executive, P. M. McCarthy.

CAMBRIDGE

CAMBRIDGE, a settlement far older than its ancient University, lies on the Cam or Granta, 51 miles north of London and 65 miles south-west of Norwich. It has an area of 10,060 acres and a population (est., 1974) of 104,000.

The city is a parliamentary borough, county town and regional headquarters. Its industries, which include radio and electronics, flour milling, cement making and the manufacture of scientific instruments are extensive but nowhere obtrusive. Among its open spaces are Jesus Green, Sheep's Green, Coe Fen, Parker's Piece,

Christ's Pieces, the University Botanic Garden, and the Backs, or lawns and gardens through which the Cam winds behind the principal line of college buildings. East of the Cam, King's Parade, upon which stand Great St. Mary's Church, Gibbs' Senate House and King's College Chapel with Wilkins' screen, joins Trumpington Street to form one of the most beautiful throughfares in Europe.

University and College buildings provide the outstanding features of Cambridge architecture but several churches (especially St. Benet's, the oldest building in the City, and St. Sepulchre's the Round Church) also make notable contributions. The modern Guildhall (1939) stands on a site of which at least part has held municipal buildings since 1224.

The City Council has 42 members. The District was granted Borough status and reaccorded the style of City from April 1974.

Mayor (1976–77), R. E. Wright.
Chief Executive, G. G. Datson.

CANTERBURY

CANTERBURY, the Metropolitan City of the Anglican Communion, has an unbroken history going back to prehistoric times. It was the Roman Durovernum and the Saxon Cant-wara-byrig (stronghold of the men of Kent). Here in 597 St. Augustine began the re-conversion of the English to Christianity, when Ethelbert, King of Kent, was baptized. In 1170 the rivalry of Church and State culminated in the murder in Canterbury Cathedral, by Henry II.'s knights, of Archbishop Thomas Becket, whose shrine became a great centre of pilgrimage as described by Chaucer in his *Canterbury Tales*. After the Reformation pilgrimages ceased, but the prosperity of the City was strengthened by an influx of Huguenot refugees, who introduced weaving. In the first Elizabethan era Christopher Marlowe, the poetic genius and precursor of Shakespeare, was born and reared in Canterbury, and there are literary associations also with Defoe, Dickens and Barham, author of the *Ingoldsby Legends*, and Somerset Maugham.

The Cathedral, with its glorious architecture ranging from the eleventh to the fifteenth centuries, is world-famous. Modern pilgrims are attracted particularly to the Martyrdom, the Black Prince's Tomb and other historic monuments, the Warriors' Chapel and the many examples of mediæval stained glass.

Of the Benedictine St. Augustine's Abbey, burial place of the Jutish Kings of Kent (whose capital Canterbury was) only extensive ruins remain. St. Martin's Church, on the eastern outskirts of the City, is stated by Bede to have been the place of worship of Queen Bertha, the Christian wife of King Ethelbert, before the advent of St. Augustine.

The mediæval City Walls are built on Roman foundations and the fourteenth century West Gate is one of the finest buildings of its kind in the country.

The University of Kent at Canterbury admitted its first students in 1965.

The city has an area of 120 square miles, and a population of 115,000. Before the institution of the Mayoralty in 1448 it was governed by bailiffs and earlier still by prefects or provosts.

Mayor (1976–77), I. Fowler.
Sheriff (1976–77), J. H. Snell.
Chief Executive, C. C. Gay.

COVENTRY

COVENTRY (West Midlands) is a city 92 miles N.W. of London, and an important industrial centre. It has a population (estimated, 1973) of 336,000.

Coventry owes its beginning to Leofric, Earl of Mercia and his wife Godiva in 1043, when they founded a Benedictine Monastery. The beautiful guildhall of St. Mary dates from the 14th century, three of its churches date from the 14th and 15th centuries. Sixteenth century almshouses may still be seen. Coventry's first cathedral was destroyed at the Reformation, its second in the 1940 blitz (its walls remain) and the great new cathedral designed by Sir Basil Spence, consecrated in 1962, now draws innumerable visitors.

Post-war public buildings include the Art Gallery and Museum, Lanchester Polytechnic, the Civic Theatre and new swimming baths. The city centre has been redeveloped.

Coventry returns four M.P.'s. It is governed by a Lord Mayor and a Council of 54. Coventry produces cars, agricultural machinery, machine tools and telecommunications.

Lord Mayor (1976–77), R. F. Loosley.
Chief Executive, T. Gregory, O.B.E.

KINGSTON UPON HULL

HULL (officially " Kingston upon Hull ") is situated, from April, 1974 in the County of Humberside, at the junction of the River Hull with the Humber, 22 miles from the North Sea and 205 miles N. of London. The municipal area is 17,593 acres, with a population (1971 Census), of 285,970.

Hull is one of the great seaports of the United Kingdom. It has docks covering a water area of over 200 acres, well equipped for the rapid handling of cargoes of every kind, and its many industries include oil-extracting, saw-milling, flour-milling, engineering and chemical industries. New industries, such as electricals, and clothing and textiles are being developed. It also claims to be the premier distant-water fishing port and is an important centre for allied processing activities.

The City, restored after very heavy air raid damage during World War II, is well laid out with fine throughfares. It has good office and administrative buildings, its municipal centre being the Guildhall, its educational centre the University of Hull and its religious centre the Parish Church of the Holy Trinity.

Kingston upon Hull was so named by Edward I. City status was accorded in 1897 and the office of Mayor raised to the dignity of Lord Mayor in 1914. The Lord Mayor presides over a Council of 63 Councillors, representing the 21 wards of the City.

The Lord Mayor (1976–77), A. Parker.
Stipendiary Magistrate, I. R. Boyd (1973).
Chief Executive, A. B. Wood.

LEEDS

LEEDS (West Yorkshire), a Metropolitan District from April 1, 1974, is a junction for road, rail and canal services and an important commercial centre, situated in the lower Aire Valley, 195 miles by road N.N.W. of London.

Leeds has a wide variety of manufacturing industries, notably cloth and ready-made clothing, heavy and light engineering, leather and chemical products.

The municipal area is 138,441 acres, the population is 749,000.

The principal buildings are the Civic Hall (1933), the Town Hall (1858), the Municipal Buildings and Art Gallery (1884), the Corn Exchange (1863) and the University. The Parish Church (St. Peter's) was rebuilt in 1841; the 17th century St. John's Church has a fine interior with a famous 17th century renaissance screen; the last remaining 18th century church is Holy Trinity, Boar Lane (1727). Kirkstall Abbey (about 3

miles from the centre of the city), founded by Henry de Lacy in 1152, is one of the most complete examples of Cistercian houses now remaining. Temple Newsam, birthplace of Lord Darnley, was acquired by the Corporation in 1922. The present house, a stately building in red brick, was largely re-built by Sir Arthur Ingram in about 1620. Adel Church, about 5 miles from the centre of the city, is a fine Norman structure.

Leeds was first incorporated by Charles I in 1626, made a county borough in 1889, and created a city in 1893. The Lord Mayor presides over 96 Councillors. The earliest forms of the name are *Loidis* or *Ledes*, the origins of which are obscure.

The Lord Mayor (1976–77), E. H. Morris.
Stipendiary Magistrate, F. D. L. Loy (1972).
Chief Executive, K. H. Potts.

LEICESTER

LEICESTER is situated geographically in the centre of England, 100 miles north of London. The City dates back to pre-Roman times and was one of the five Danish *Burhs*. In 1589 Queen Elizabeth I granted a Charter to the City and the ancient title was confirmed by Letters Patent in 1919. The title of Lord Mayor was conferred upon the Chief Magistrate in 1928. Under local government reorganization Leicester's area remained unchanged at 18,141 acres, and with a population of 290,600 (1975 est.) it is the third largest non-metropolitan district in England and Wales in population. It retains its designation as a City Council.

The principal industries of the city are hosiery, boots and shoes, and light engineering. The growth of Leicester as a hosiery centre increased rapidly from the introduction there of the first stocking frame in 1670; in 1833 there were 14,000 knitting frames in the city, which to-day has some of the largest hosiery factories in the world. Hosiery and knitwear produced includes socks, stockings, dresses, underwear, pullovers, scarves and gloves, much of which is exported. Leicester is also a centre for the ancillary industries.

Engineering, developed partly for the supply of machinery to the hosiery and boot and shoe industries, has become one of the foremost industries in the city. Printing and the manufacture of electronic and plastic goods are also carried on.

The principal buildings in the city are the Town Hall; the University; Leicester Polytechnic; De Montfort Hall, one of the finest concert halls in the provinces, with accommodation for over 2,750 persons, and the Museum and Art Gallery. The ancient Churches of St. Martin (now Leicester Cathedral) St. Nicholas, St. Margaret, All Saints, St. Mary de Castro, and buildings such as the Guildhall, the 14th century Newarke Gate, the Castle and the Jewry Wall Roman site still exist. Leicester has a large number of parks and open spaces. The Sports Centre, which contains an athletics arena and cycle track, was the site of the 1970 World Cycling Championships. The Haymarket Theatre, an integral part of a large new shopping and car-parking complex, was opened in 1973.

The Lord Mayor (1976–77), B. Toft.
Chief Executive, J.S. Phipps.

LIVERPOOL

LIVERPOOL (Merseyside) a Metropolitan District, on the right bank of the river Mersey, 3 miles from the Irish Sea and 194 miles N.W. of London, is one of the greatest trading centres of the world and the principal port in the United Kingdom for the Atlantic trade. The municipal area is 27,819 acres (which includes 2,840 acres in the bed of the river

Mersey) (about 43 square miles, excluding the bed of the river), with a population of 574,560 (est. June 1973). Quays on both sides of the river are about 38 miles long, and the Gladstone Dock can accommodate the largest vessels afloat. Net tonnage of ships entering and leaving the port annually exceeds 45,000,000 tons. The main imports are petroleum, grain, ores, non-ferrous metals, sugar, wood, oil, fruit and cotton. The new Seaforth Container Terminal was opened in 1972, covering 500 acres and costing £50 m.

The Metropolitan District Council owns large industrial estates at Speke, Kirkby and Aintree, on which many modern factories have been built. These three estates have provided work for some 65,000 people. In 1943 a lease for 99 years was taken of the Elizabethan mansion at *Speke Hall* at a nominal rent.

The principal buildings are the Anglican Cathedral, erected from the designs of Sir Giles Gilbert Scott and consecrated in 1924; when completed this will be the largest ecclesiastical building in England; the Metropolitan Cathedral of Christ the King, designed by Sir Frederick Gibberd and consecrated in 1967; St. George's Hall, erected 1838–1854, and regarded as one of the finest modern examples of classical architecture; the Town Hall, erected 1754 from the designs of Wood; the Walker Art Gallery; Victoria Building of Liverpool University; The Royal Liver, Cunard and Mersey Docks building at Pier Head; the Municipal Offices; and the Philharmonic Hall.

Constructed between 1925 and 1934, the *Mersey Tunnel* connecting Liverpool and Birkenhead was opened to traffic on July 18, 1934, the total cost being estimated at £6,077,800. More than 17,000,000 vehicles pass through the Mersey Tunnel annually. A second tunnel between Liverpool and Wallasey was opened by the Queen on June 24, 1971, and a similar tunnel running adjacent to it was opened on Feb. 14, 1974.

Liverpool was incorporated as a borough early in the 13th century and was created a city in 1880. The Metropolitan District Council consists of a Lord Mayor and 98 Councillors.

The Lord Mayor (1976–77), R. F. Craine, M.B.E.
Stipendiary Magistrate, Leslie Mervyn Pugh (1965).
Chief Executive, A. J. Stocks.

MANCHESTER

MANCHESTER (Greater Manchester) (the *Mancunium* of the Romans, who occupied it in A.D. 78) is 189 miles N.W. of London. The municipal area is 28,720 acres (about 43 square miles) and the population (estimated 1973), 530,580.

Manchester is a commercial rather than an industrial centre, the industries being largely in the neighbouring towns. Within 25 miles radius, lives a population of 4,500,000 engaged in engineering, chemical, clothing, food processing and textile industries and providing the packing, transport, banking, insurance and other distributive facilities for those industries. The city is connected with the sea by the Manchester Ship Canal, opened in 1894, 35½ miles long, and accommodating ships up to 15,000 tons. Manchester Airport handles approximately 2,318,000 passengers yearly.

The principal buildings are the Town Hall, erected in 1877 from the designs of Alfred Waterhouse, R.A., together with a large extension of 1938; the Royal Exchange, built in 1869 and enlarged in 1921; the Central Library (1934); the Art Gallery; Heaton Hall; the Gallery of English Costume; the 17th century Chetham Library; the Rylands Library (1899), which includes the Althorp collection; the University (Owens College); the Univer-

sity Institute of Science and Technology; the 15th-century Cathedral (formerly the parish church) and the Free Trade Hall. Manchester is one of the principal centres of political, literary and scientific advancement, and the Hallé Concerts have placed the city in the forefront of musical development. as has the Royal Northern College of Music.

The town received its first charter of incorporation in 1838 and was created a city in 1853. The new charter and title of city, under local government reorganization, was presented in May, 1974. The City Council consists of 99 Councillors.

The Lord Mayor (1975–76) Dame Kathleen Ollerenshaw, D.B.E.

Stipendiary Magistrate, J. Bamber (1965).

NEWCASTLE UPON TYNE

NEWCASTLE UPON TYNE (Tyne and Wear) a Metropolitan District on the north bank of the River Tyne, 8 miles from the North Sea and 272 miles N. of London, has an area of 11,401 acres and a population of 295,700. A Cathedral and University City, it is the administrative commercial and cultural centre for north-east England and the principal port. It is an important manufacturing centre with a wide variety of industries.

The principal buildings include the Castle Keep (12th century), Black Gate (13th century), West Walls (13th century), St. Nicholas's Cathedral (15th century, fine lantern tower), St. Andrew's Church (12th–14th century), St. John's (14th–15th century), All Saints (1786 by Stephenson), St. Mary's Roman Catholic Cathedral (1844). Trinity House (17th century), Sandhill (16th century houses), Guildhall (Georgian), Grey Street (1834–39), Central Station (1846–50). Laing Art Gallery (1904), University of Newcastle Physics Building (1962), Civic Centre (1963), Central Library (1969) and Eldon Square Development (1976). Open spaces include the Town Moor (927 acres) and Jesmond Dene. Seven bridges span the Tyne at Newcastle.

The City derives its name from the " new castle " (1080) erected as a defence against the Scots. In 1400 it was made a County, and in 1882 a City. The City Corporation comprises a Lord Mayor (1906) and 78 Councillors.

Lord Mayor (1976–77), H. J. White.
Chief Executive, K. A. Galley.

NORWICH

NORWICH (Norfolk) is an ancient City 110 miles N.E. of London. It grew from an early Anglo-Saxon settlement near the confluence of the Rivers Yare and Wensum, and now serves as provincial capital for the predominantly agricultural region of East Anglia. The name is thought to relate to the most northerly of a group of Anglo-Saxon villages or " wics ". The present City comprises an area of 9,655 acres, with a population (1971 Census, preliminary) of 121,688.

Norwich serves its surrounding area as a market town and commercial centre, banking and insurance being prominent among the City's businesses. Continuously from the fourteenth century, however (when Flemish immigrants helped to establish Norwich as the centre of the woollen industry until the Industrial Revolution)· it has combined industry with commerce, and manufactures of a wide variety are now produced in the City. The biggest single industry is the manufacture of shoes and other principal trades are engineering, printing, and the production of chemicals, clothing, confectionery and other foodstuffs. Norwich is accessible to seagoing vessels by means of the River Yare, entered at Great Yarmouth, 20 miles to the east.

Among many historic buildings are the Cathedral (completed in the twelfth century and surmounted by a fifteenth century spire 315 feet in height), the Keep of the Norman Castle (now serving as a museum and also housing the Colman Collection of works by the Norwich School of painters), the fifteenth century flint-walled Guildhall, some thirty mediæval parish churches, St. Andrew's and Blackfriars' Halls, the Tudor houses preserved in Elm Hill and the Georgian Assembly House. The administrative centre of the City is the City Hall, built in 1938. A new central library, opened in 1963, is adjacent to the City Hall. The University of East Anglia has been established in Norwich and received its first students in 1963. The buildings of the University occupy a spacious site at Earlham on the City's western boundary.

The City's first known Charter was granted in 1158 by Henry II and its privileges and form of self government were prescribed successively by later Charters until the enactment of the Municipal Corporations Act, 1835. The City Council consists of 48 Councillors.

The Lord Mayor (1976–77), R. C. Frostick.
Chief Executive, G. G. Tilsley.

NOTTINGHAM

NOTTINGHAM (Nottinghamshire) stands on the River Trent, 124 miles N.N.W. of London in one of the most valuable coalfields of the country with excellent railway, water (being connected by canal with the Atlantic and the North Sea), and road facilities. The municipal area is 18,364 acres and population (estimated, 1975) of 287,790.

The principal industries are hosiery, lace, bleaching, dyeing and spinning, tanning, engineering and cycle works, brewing, the manufacture of tobacco, chemicals, furniture, typewriters and mechanical products.

The chief buildings are the 17th century Nottingham Castle (restored in 1878, and now the City Museum and Gallery of Art), Wollaton Hall (1580–88) owned by the City Council and now a Natural History Museum, St. Mary's, St. Peter's, and St. Nicholas's Churches, the Roman Catholic Cathedral (Pugin, 1842–4), the Council House (1929), the Guildhall and Court House (1888), Shire Hall, Albert Hall, the University, Trent Polytechnic and Newstead Abbey, home of Lord Byron.

Snotingaham or *Notingeham*, " the village or home of the sons of Snot " (the Wise), is the Anglo-Saxon name for the Celtic *Tuigogobauc*, " Cave Homes". The City possesses a Charter of Henry II, and was created a City in 1897. Under local government reorganization, the style of city was reaccorded from April, 1974. The City Council consists of 55 Councillors (including the Lord Mayor).

The Lord Mayor (1976–77), S. J. Rushton.
Chief Executive, M. H. F. Hammond.

OXFORD

OXFORD is a University City, an important industrial centre, and market town. A City from time immemorial, it has an area of 8,785 acres and a population of 115,100. Oxford is a parliamentary constituency returning one member and is governed by a Council of 45 members. Industry played a minor part in Oxford until the motor industry was established in 1912.

It is for its architecture that Oxford is of most interest to the visitor, its oldest specimens being the reputed Saxon tower of St. Michael's church, the remains of the Norman castle and city walls and the Norman church at Iffley. It is chiefly famous however, for its Gothic buildings, such as the Divinity Schools, the Old Library at Merton

College, William of Wykeham's New College, Magdalen College and Christ Church and many other college buildings. Later centuries are not represented by so many examples, but mention can be made of the exquisite Laudian quadrangle at St. John's College, the Renaissance Sheldonian Theatre by Wren, Trinity College Chapel, and All Saints Church; Hawksmoor's mock-Gothic at All Souls College, and the superb example of eighteenth century architecture afforded by Queen's College. In addition to individual buildings, High Street and Radcliffe Square, just off it, both form architectural compositions of great beauty. Most of the Colleges have gardens, those of Magdalen, New College, St. John's (designed by " Capability " Brown) and Worcester being the largest.

The visitor will always find some of the college chapels, halls and gardens open for public inspection between 10 a.m. and 5 p.m.

Lord Mayor (1976–77), Miss A. H. Spokes.
Chief Executive, E. J. Patrick.

PLYMOUTH

PLYMOUTH is situated on the borders of Devon and Cornwall at the confluence of the Rivers Tamar and Plym, 210 miles from London, with an area of 19,936 acres and a population (Reg. Gen. Estimate) of 257,900.

Following extensive war damage, the city centre comprising a large shopping centre, municipal offices, law courts and public buildings, has been re-built. The main employment is provided by H.M. Dockyard. Many new industrial firms have become established in the post-war period. In conjunction with the Cornwall County Council, the Tamar Bridge was constructed linking the City by road with Cornwall.

The Lord Mayor presides over a Council of 66 Councillors.

The Lord Mayor (1976–77), A. Floyd.
Chief Executive, A. F. Watson.

PORTSMOUTH

PORTSMOUTH, a city, and local government district, with an area of $14\frac{1}{2}$ sq. miles, occupies Portsea Island, Hampshire, with boundaries extending to the mainland. Portsmouth is 70 miles by road from London (90 minutes by electric train). It has a population (estimated, 1975) of 195,130.

Industries include H.M. Naval Base, the principal centre of employment with a labour force of 14,000, which occupies the south-western part of the Island. The holiday and tourist industry, centred on the coast at the resort area of Southsea, caters annually for 200,000 visitors and 1,000,000 day trippers. Other industries are shipbuilding and maintenance, electronics, aircraft engineering and the manufacture of corsets, cardboard boxes, confectionery, baby products, refrigerators and brushes. The commercial port (the Camber, Flathouse and Mile End is owned and run by the City Council. In 1976 a Continental Ferry Port was opened, with car ferries running to St. Malo and Cherbourg.

Among many tourist attractions are Lord Nelson's flagship, H.M.S. *Victory*; Charles Dickens' birthplace at 393 Old Commercial Road, now a Dickens museum; Southsea Castle, now a museum of military history, and the Round Tower and Point Battery, which for hundreds of years have guarded the entrance to Portsmouth Harbour. Southsea is particularly noted for its panoramic views of the busy shipping lanes of the Solent and Spithead.

Lord Mayor (1976–77), I. G. Gibson.
Chief Executive, J. R. Haslegrave, C.B.E., T.D.

SHEFFIELD

SHEFFIELD (South Yorkshire), the centre of the special steel and cutlery trades, is situated 159 miles N.N.W. of London, at the junction of the Sheaf, Porter, Rivelin and Loxley with the River Don. The City is set in a beautiful countryside, its residential suburbs penetrating the Peak District of Derbyshire.

Sheffield has an area of 91,000 acres (nearly 150 square miles), including 4,065 acres of publicly owned parks and woodland, and a population (est. 1975) of 559,800. Though its cutlery, silverware and plate have long been famous, Sheffield has other and now more important industries—special and alloy steels, engineering and tools in great variety. Refractory materials, silver refining, brush making, the manufacture of confectionery, canning, typefounding, pharmaceutical products, paper and the making of snuff are other contrasting industries in Sheffield. Research in glass, metallurgy, radiotherapy and other fields is carried on.

The parish church of St. Peter and St. Paul, founded in the twelfth century, became the Cathedral Church of the Diocese of Sheffield in 1914. Parts of the present building date from about 1435. The principal buildings are the Town Hall (1897 and 1923), the Cutlers' Hall (1832), the University (1905 and recent extensions, including 19-storey Arts Tower), City Hall (1932), Central Library and Graves Art Gallery (1934), City Museum (1937), Castle Market Building (1959), the new retail market (1973), the rebuilt Mappin Art Gallery and the Crucible Theatre.

Sheffield was created a borough on Aug. 24, 1843, a county borough in 1888 and a city in 1893, the Mayor becoming a Lord Mayor in 1897. On April 1, 1974 Sheffield became a Metropolitan District Council incorporating Stocksbridge and most of the Wortley Rural area, and retained city status.

The Lord Mayor (1976–77), R. E. Munn.
Master Cutler (1975–76) 352nd *Master of the Company of Cutlers in Hallamshire*, N. Hanlon.
Chief Executive, I. L. Podmore.

SOUTHAMPTON

SOUTHAMPTON, the principal city of Southern England, is Britain's premier passenger port. The first Charter was granted by Henry II and Southampton was created a county of itself in 1447. In February, 1964, Her Majesty the Queen granted city status by Royal Charter. The city has an area of 12,071 acres excluding tidal waters and a population of 213,000. The University of Southampton (1952) had 5,370 students in 1975–76.

The Civic Centre, completed in 1939, comprises four blocks, municipal offices and law courts, guildhall, library and art gallery. The tower, which is a notable land-mark for shipping using Southampton Water and which can be seen for many miles from vantage points in the surrounding countryside, incorporates a clock and bells. Public open spaces total over 1,000 acres in extent and comprise 9 per cent. of the city's area. The Sports Centre is 267 acres in extent. The Common covers an area of 328 acres in the central district of the city and is mostly natural parkland.

The City Council consists of 51 councillors.
Mayor (1976–77), Mrs. M. Key.
Chief Executive, D. Scouller.

STOKE-ON-TRENT

STOKE-ON-TRENT (Staffordshire), familiarly known as The Potteries, stands on the River Trent 157 miles N. of London. The present municipal area is 22,916 acres (36 square miles), with a

population (estimated, 1975) of 255,800. The City is the main centre of employment for the half-million population of North Staffordshire. It is the largest clayware producer in the world (chinaware, earthenware, sanitary goods, refractories, bricks and tiles) and has a large coal mining output drawn from one of the richest coalfields in Western Europe, with proved reserves exceeding one thousand million tons. The City has iron works, steelworks, foundries, chemical works, engineering plants, rubber works, paper mills, and a very wide range of manufactures including textiles, furniture, electrical goods, vehicle components, toys, machinery, plastic materials, metal stampings, glass and glazes.

Extensive reconstruction has been carried on since 1930. A unique feature of the city is that it has six " centres " and more shops and public halls than other areas of comparable size. The City was formed by the federation in 1910 of the separate municipal authorities of Tunstall, Burslem, Hanley, Stoke-upon-Trent, Fenton, and Longton, all of which are now combined in the present City of Stoke-on-Trent. Each of the six areas still has its own public buildings and amenities, but all civic administration is controlled by the City Council.

The City has 72 Councillors and elects 3 Members of Parliament.

The Lord Mayor (1976–77), W. Screen.
Town Clerk, S. W. Titchener.

STRATFORD UPON AVON

STRATFORD UPON AVON (in Warwickshire, on the banks of the River Avon) had a population of 19,452 at the Census of 1971. As the birthplace of Shakespeare the borough is visited annually by travellers from all parts.

Shakespeare's Birthplace. Half timbered house preserved by Shakespeare Birthplace Trust. Contains period furniture and a collection of rare books, mss. and objects of Shakespearian interest. Garden contains the new Shakespeare centre. *King Edward VI School.* Founded by the mediæval Guild of the Holy Cross of Stratford, and re-endowed by King Edward VI. Here Shakespeare acquired his " small Latin and less Greek." *Anne Hathaway's Cottage.* At Shottery, one mile from the centre of the town, is the thatched farmstead, the early home of Shakespeare's wife, Anne Hathaway. A fine specimen of domestic architecture. *Shakespeare Memorial.* Mainly due to munificence of C. E. Flower (1830–92) and his wife. Group comprises *Library*, with 10,000 volumes of Shakespeare editions and dramatic literature. *Gallery* of pictures. *Gardens*. *Royal Shakespeare Theatre* burnt down in 1926, rebuilt 1932, with 1,300 seats, chiefly by American generosity. The Shakespeare Festival takes place from spring to autumn each year at this theatre.

Chief Executive, T. J. W. Foy.

WINCHESTER

WINCHESTER, the ancient capital of England, is situated on the River Itchen 65 miles S.W. of London and 12 miles north of Southampton. The City has an area of 3,890 acres and a population (1971 Census, preliminary) of 31,041.

Occupation of the city area can be traced back to 1800 B.C. but organized settlements appeared later. Saxon history is somewhat obscure but Winchester became the capital of Wessex and in the 9th century capital of all England. Alfred the Great made Winchester a centre of education. William the Conqueror marched straight from his victory at Hastings to Winchester where he established a new Palace, his Treasury and his capital. Here he compiled Domesday Book as the returns came in from the shires. Winchester remained the capital for many years, but its decline as a capital began with the civil war between Stephen and Matilda; and by 1338 it had lost its favourable position.

Winchester is rich in architecture of all types but the Cathedral takes first place. The longest Gothic cathedral in the world, it was built in 1079–1093 and exhibits splendid examples of Norman, Early English and Perpendicular styles. Winchester College, founded in 1382, is one of the most famous public schools, the original building (of 1393) remaining almost unaltered. St. Cross Hospital, the third great mediæval foundation in Winchester, lies 1 mile south of the City. Founded in 1136 by Bishop Henry de Blois, the Almshouses were re-established in 1445 by Cardinal Henry Beaufort. The Chapel and dwellings are of great architectural interest, and visitors may still receive the " Wayfarer's Dole " of bread and ale.

It is not certain when Winchester was first designated a city but it is probable that the term was applied between 650 and 700. Winchester was one of the oldest corporations in the country; the first written record of a Mayor occurs in 1200.

Recent excavations in the Cathedral Close have revealed the sites of two earlier minsters, including the original burial place of St. Swithun, before his remains were translated to a site in the present Cathedral. Excavations in other parts of the city have thrown light on Norman Winchester, notably on the site of the Castle, where new Law Courts have been built.

Mayor (1976–77), Mrs. G. A. Shave.
Chief Executive, E. M. E. White.

YORK

The City of YORK is a District in the County of North Yorkshire, and is an archiepiscopal seat. The City has an area of 7,295 acres and a population of 102,700. It returns one member to Parliament and is governed by 39 Councillors.

The recorded history of York dates from A.D. 71, when the Roman Ninth Legion established a base under Petilius Cerealis which later became the fortress of Eboracum. By the 14th century the city had become prosperous and was used as the chief base against the Scots. It became a great mercantile centre, chiefly owing to its control of the wool trade, but under the Tudors its fortunes declined, though Henry VIII made it the headquarters of the Council of the North.

With its development as a railway centre in the 19th century the commercial life of York expanded and it is now a flourishing modern city. The principal industries are the manufacture of chocolate, railway coaches, scientific instruments, glass containers and sugar. The City is also an important tourist centre.

It is rich in examples of architecture of all periods. The earliest church (*built*, 627) was succeeded by several others until, in the 12th to the 15th centuries, the present Minster was built in a succession of styles. The finest features are the West front with its two towers, the spacious transepts and the stained glass. Other examples within the city are the mediaeval city walls and gateways, churches and guildhalls. Domestic architecture includes the Georgian mansions of The Mount, Micklegate and Bootham. Its museums are world-famous and include the Castle Museum which is one of the best-known folk museums in Great Britain and the new National Railway Museum.

Rt. Hon. Lord Mayor (1976–77), J. Archer.
Sheriff (1976–77), Mrs. D. C. Walker.
Chief Executive, R. Howell.

MUNICIPAL DIRECTORY OF ENGLAND

A list of METROPOLITAN BOROUGH AND CITY COUNCILS. Those accorded CITY status are in SMALL CAPITALS.

Metropolitan Boroughs	Population (Reg. G's Estimate)	Rateable Value 1976 £	Domestic Rate Levied p.	Chief Executive	Mayor †Lord Mayor 1976–77
GREATER MANCHESTER					
Bolton	263,300	25,957,065	77·1	B. Scholes	J. Rigby
Bury	180,500	18,500,000	75·5	J. A. McDonald	S. Pepperman
MANCHESTER	530,580	—	—	—	—
Oldham	224,700	21,184,635	87	T. M. C. Francis	C. McCall
Rochdale	211,500	19,580,754	92·1	J. Towey	J. L. Albiston
SALFORD	266,500	30,252,915	82·7	R. C. Rees	G. K. Edwards
Stockport	300,000	34,400,000	52	A. L. Wilson	H. Cook
Tameside	222,800	20,055,139	68·2	D. Spiers	E. C. Clark
Trafford	227,400	35,992,751	80·2	H. W. D. Sculthorpe	H. Pyper
Wigan	309,600	28,523,542	78·9–83·3	A. E. Hart	J. A. Eckersley
MERSEYSIDE					
Knowsley	191,400	21,400,000	100·2	D. Willgoose, O.B.E.	F. Lawler
LIVERPOOL	561,600	71,720,709	70·1	A. J. Stocks	†R. F. Craine, M.B.E.
St. Helens	194,700	21,192,056	87·1	B. S. Lace	T. Harvey
Sefton	305,300	34,801,661	49·5–68	J. P. McElroy	C. J. Currall
Wirral	348,200	39,623,672	77·2	I. G. Holt	J. E. Evans
SOUTH YORKSHIRE					
Barnsley	224,100	16,852,838	69–73·4	A. B. Bleasby	F. Kaye
Doncaster	285,000	26,088,866	104·42	W. J. Jackson	G. Gallimore
Rotherham	248,700	20,527,495	89·6–92·4	L. I. Frost	F. Cooper
SHEFFIELD	559,800	61,854,870	82·9	I. L. Podmore	†R. E. Munn
TYNE AND WEAR					
Gateshead	222,300	20,235,813	—	W. Miles	J. Handy
NEWCASTLE UPON TYNE	295,700	36,655,100	72–79	K. A. Galley	†H. J. White
North Tyneside	205,700	19,433,361	74	E. B. Lincoln	W. F. Fawcett
South Tyneside	171,800	14,978,697	86·9	A. Stansfield	Mrs. L. G. Jordison
Sunderland	298,000	24,579,250	—	L. A. Bloom	C. H. Slater
WEST MIDLANDS					
BIRMINGHAM	1,084,600	155,221,561	51·2—55·4	F. J. C. Amos, C.B.E.	†H. Powell
COVENTRY	337,000	42,175,545	67·36	T. Gregory, O.B.E.	†R. F. Loosley
Dudley	300,700	39,433,898	71·3	J. F. Mulvehill	D. Harty
Sandwell	315,500	48,443,863	85·7	K. Pearce	H. Roy
Solihull	199,700	25,600,000	77	D. W. Chapman, D.F.M.	P. F. Kellie
Walsall	271,000	36,376,019	58·1	J. A. Galloway	J. D. Winn
Wolverhampton	268,200	38,696,602	59·9	K. Williams	A. E. Steventon
WEST YORKSHIRE					
BRADFORD	461,000	39,238,530	84·6	G. C. Moore	†F. Hillam
Calderdale	190,736	15,297,088	83·5	A. W. Luke	Mrs. M. R. Mitchell,
Kirklees	375,100	29,924,879	48·6–51·9	E. S. Dixon	A. A. Mason [O.B.E.
LEEDS	748,300	78,719,000	68·2	K. H. Potts	†E. H. Morris
WAKEFIELD	305,300	27,746,992	95·3	A. I. Wylie	Mrs. D. Kenningham

DISTRICT COUNCILS

A list of non-Metropolitan District Councils in England. Those accorded CITY status are in SMALL CAPITALS, those with Borough status are distinguished by having § prefixed.

District	Population (Reg. G's Estimate)	Rateable Value 1976 £	Domestic Rate Levied p.	Chief Executive	Chairman 1976–7 (a) Mayor (b) Lord Mayor
Adur, West Sussex	55,050	7,663,376	65·4	Maj. Gen. R. J. D. E. Buckland	C. Robinson
Allerdale, Cumbria	94,800	7,977,034	57·5–71·5	A. C. Crane	L. Jefferson
Alnwick, Northumberland	28,900	2,331,803	73·5	A. G. A. Groome	(a) J. G. Young
Amber Valley, Derbyshire	106,300	10,035,685	52·5	J. Ragsdale	R. B. Ferro
Arun, West Sussex	108,100	14,406,421	58·9–62·9	E. H. Brown	A. A. Cookes
Ashfield, Nottinghamshire	102,800	8,729,153	63·02	S. Beedham	J. Barker
§Ashford, Kent	81,200	9,064,100	58·4	—	H. A. Watts

District	Population (Reg. G's Estimate)	Rateable Value 1976 £	Domestic Rate Levied p.	Chief Executive	Chairman 1976-7 (a) Mayor (b) Lord Mayor
Aylesbury Vale, Bucks..............	124,000	16,467,545	61·2	R. D. W. Maxwell	Mrs. E. D. Embleton
Babergh, Suffolk...................	67,700	7,811,478	82·4	H. A. Cooper	D. W. Wedgwood
§Barrow in Furness, Cumbria........	75,490	5,808,996	70	W. M. Robinson	(a) G. E. Smith
Basildon, Essex...................	138,100	20,500,000	64·5	R. C. Mitchinson	C. O'Brien
Basingstoke, Hants.................	117,900	15,476,762	58·5–61·9	D. W. Pilkington, R.D.	Mrs. B. Holmes
Bassetlaw, Notts....................	100,400	12,275,319	81·7–84·8	G. A. Yewdall	G. B. Ostick
BATH, Avon.......................	84,300	10,035,267	56·8–67·2	D. C. Beeton	(a) Miss M. Rawlings
Beaconsfield, Bucks...............	62,700	12,675,134	55·5–74	D. P. Harrison	A. G. Gasson
§Berwick upon Tweed, Northumberland.................	25,700	2,318,081	63·8	J. Healy	(a) R. C. Blackhall
§Beverley, Humberside............	106,800	10,922,050	53·8	W. J. H. Thomas	(a) Mrs. P. M. Byass
Blaby, Leics......................	76,600	7,891,580	64·8–67·1	T. Heap	R. Durrance
§Blackburn, Lancs.................	142,200	12,980,210	94–99·8	C. H. Singleton	(a) F. J. Beetham
§Blackpool, Lancs.................	150,100	17,780,840	—	I. B. Prosser	(a) A. Hudson
§Blyth Valley, Northumberland......	66,400	5,887,993	45–55	P. W. Ferry	(a) A. R. Hancock
§Bolsover, Derbys	70,980	4,938,110	65·5–71·9	E. Edwards	L. D. J. Fretwell
Boothferry, Humberside...........	56,000	4,397,876	64·76	Miss M. H. Sindell	F. Atkinson, O.B.E.
§Boston, Lincs....................	50,200	5,270,526	64·9	R. E. Coley	(a) F. Myatt
§Bournemouth, Dorset.............	153,000	22,587,192	71·5	K. Lomas	(a) A. W. Patton
Bracknell, Berks..................	68,970	11,268,021	65·6	C. S. McDonald	Mrs. M. D. B. Benwell
Braintree, Essex..................	101,300	12,571,782	60·1–61·8	P. W. Cotton	D. W. R. Claydon
Breckland, Norfolk................	87,500	8,854,423	82·8	J. B. Heath	E. H. J. Macro
Brentwood, Essex.................	74,000	11,942,297	72·9	G. Bowden	A. G. Gregg
Bridgnorth, Salop.................	48,500	5,174,259	52·1	G. C. Nutley	K. Worthington
§Brighton, East Sussex............	159,000	23,178,542	69·8	R. G. Morgan	(a) P. E. W. Best
BRISTOL, Avon...................	420,100	59,649,785	70·5	P. M. McCarthy	(b) J. D. Fisk
Broadland, Norfolk...............	92,000	8,443,755	59·7	P. M. Taylor	J. Mack
Bromsgrove, Hereford and Worcs....	77,900	10,024,376	58·9	G. F. Badham	J. L. Austin
§Broxbourne, Herts................	75,000	10,665,853	62·42	C. Campbell	G. F. Batchelor, M.B.E.
Broxtowe, Notts..................	102,500	10,739,159	69·01	A. E. Hodder	R. Hudson
§Burnley, Lancs...................	93,600	7,695,238	—	B. Whittle	(a) Mrs. R. I. Pilling
CAMBRIDGE....................	100,250	18,450,796	80·4	G. G. Datson	(a) R. E. Wright
Cannock Chase, Staffs.............	83,100	8,909,554	—	B. E. Rastall	J. Holston
CANTERBURY, Kent..............	116,780	13,048,089	69·58	C. C. Gay	(a) I. Fowler
Caradon, Cornwall................	60,500	5,378,907	79·85	H. Enever	W. V. S. Seccombe
CARLISLE, Cumbria...............	99,600	9,825,193	63	W. Hirst	(a) G. E. Dudson
Carrick, Cornwall.................	72,400	7,922,964	58·7	H. P. Dorey	B. R. Evea
§Castle Morpeth, Northumberland....	47,900	4,766,903	58·4–63·2	M. Cole	(a) J. D. Hutchinson
Castle Point, Essex...............	81,400	9,741,304	62·2	A. R. Neighbour	J. W. Pike
§Charnwood, Leics.................	131,000	16,732,341	48·78	D. L. Harris	(a) T. G. Deacon
Chelmsford, Essex................	127,800	19,303,233	56·5	R. M. C. Hartley	Mrs. H. How
§Cheltenham, Glos.................	86,500	13,676,000	58·57–60·91	B. N. Wynn	(a) V. G. Stanton
Cherwell, Oxon...................	103,800	13,066,068	65·42	A. M. Brace	H. R. H. Clifton
CHESTER, Cheshire...............	117,000	16,108,987	76·68	D. M. Kermode	(a) J. Arrowsmith
§Chesterfield, Derbys..............	95,600	10,334,146	87·1–90·1	R. A. Kennedy	(a) W. Everett, O.B.E.
Chester le-Street, Durham.........	47,000	3,915,944	84	J. Sanders	T. Scott
Chichester, West Sussex...........	95,000	12,069,339	57·95	P. G. Lomas	Mrs. M. E. L. Nicholson
Chiltern, Bucks...................	89,900	14,210,406	74	A. T. Rawlinson	W. C. Carvosso
§Chorley, Lancs...................	82,600	7,245,667	56·42–57·53	A. B. Webster	(a) J. Moorcroft
§Christchurch, Dorset.............	35,800	5,575,887	64·35	J. MacFadyen, D.F.C.	(a) E. N. S. Spreadbury
Cleethorpes, Humberside..........	70,400	8,073,048	47·16	R. Farmer	(a) A. Green
§Colchester, Essex................	129,200	15,647,190	77–78·8	J. Allen	(a) Mrs. J. M. Brooks
§Congleton, Cheshire..............	77,200	8,690,911	77	A. Molyneux	(a) L. Davis
§Copeland, Cumbria...............	70,960	6,233,686	74·8–80·8	P. N. Denson	(a) T. Broughton
Corby, Northants.................	55,300	8,002,664	76·5–80·5	C. E. Chapman	R. L. Webster
Cotswold, Glos...................	67,100	7,647,064	64	D. Waring	C. W. H. Staite
Craven, North Yorks..............	46,800	4,102,427	75·7	E. G. Sharp	G. Parker
§Crawley, West Sussex.............	73,500	12,756,444	58·3	K. J. L. Newell	(a) J. G. Smith
§Crewe and Nantwich, Cheshire.....	98,100	10,604,662	73·4	A. Brook	(a) Mrs. D. Kent
Dacorum, Herts...................	120,400	20,091,833	—	R. H. Davis	C. Fowler
§Darlington, Durham..............	97,800	11,621,502	85·9–86·3	H. Rogers, D.F.C., A.F.C.	(a) F. H. J. Robinson
Dartford, Kent...................	83,900	9,526,783	52·4–53·9	R. J. Duck	J. T. Clark
Daventry, Northants..............	53,000	6,856,496	—	R. C. Hutchison	F. W. Wright

District	Population (Reg. G's Estimate)	Rateable Value 1976 £	Domestic Rate Levied p.	Chief Executive	Chairman 1976–77 (a) Mayor (b) Lord Mayor
§Derby	215,200	27,086,497	68·2	—	(a) W. H. Baker
Derwentside, Durham	91,500	7,846,391	84–88	T. M. Hodgson	W. Bell
Dover, Kent	101,700	10,088,595	71·1–80·4	I. J. F. Paterson	P. W. Bean
DURHAM	86,500	7,845,782	86·1–90·1	Col. K. G. N. Miller, M.C., T.D.	(a) J. Mackintosh
Easington, Durham	105,700	6,521,071	75·5–78·5	D. C. Kelly	R. J. Todd
§Eastbourne, East Sussex	72,700	11,491,904	71·5	P. F. Humpherson	(a) Mrs. K. E. Raven
East Cambridgeshire	51,900	4,827,570	77·38	T. T. G. Hardy	Mrs. J. O'N. Smith
East Devon	100,800	10,924,297	58·6–64	R. Thompson	J. G. Alford
East Hampshire	84,200	9,818,560	57·6	R. H. Moores	J. S. G. Crosland
East Hertfordshire	105,100	14,169,303	62·1	J. J. B. Dutfield	W. H. Stripling
§Eastleigh, Hants	80,900	11,107,588	67·5–69·4	D. A. Tranah	(a) G. G. Olson
East Lindsey, Lincs.	100,100	10,169,650	47·41	B. C. V. Spence	R. H. Brackenbury
East Northamptonshire	59,800	5,786,244	60·6–65·3	D. B. Adnitt	W. H. Peasgood
East Staffordshire	96,500	11,468,045	78·7–84·2	F. N. Brammer	R. W. Robertson
Eden, Cumbria	41,800	3,524,374	—	J. D. Brown	J. J. Varty
§Ellesmere Port, Cheshire	85,100	15,841,216	—	R. J. Bernie	(a) E. E. Lalley
§Elmbridge, Surrey	112,800	20,820,776	66·5	E. G. Hubbard	(a) A. E. A. Charlton
Epping Forest, Essex	118,000	17,342,549	73·7	D. P. Brokenshire	G. C. Padfield
§Epsom and Ewell, Surrey	71,100	10,761,164	62·48	D. R. Grimes	(a) V. R. Barrett
§Erewash, Derbys.	100,800	10,201,000	—	J. M. Parker	(a) W. Evans
EXETER, Devon	93,900	12,937,249	71·76	J. D. McHardy	(a) J. F. Landers
§Fareham, Hants	85,700	9,618,955	62·5	L. E. Page	(a) D. B. Price
Fenland, Cambs.	65,700	6,653,487	60·1	W. G. E. Lewis	R. C. Heading
Forest Heath, Suffolk	46,600	4,890,801	65·3	J. F. Gale	Lady M. Petre
Forest of Dean, Glos.	69,800	5,818,592	49·5	L. W. Packer	E. Cooke
§Fylde, Lancs.	70,100	8,021,718	59·5–61·5	R. A. Cork	(a) H. L. Cartmell
§Gedling, Notts.	101,900	9,740,667	58·7	W. Brown	(a) G. Evans
§Gillingham, Kent	93,600	9,467,971	48·7	G. C. Jones	(a) H. Blease
§Glanford, Humberside	61,500	7,557,973	—	R. E. Crosby	(a) T. E. Atherton
GLOUCESTER	90,700	11,443,905	62·6	H. R. T. Shackleton	(a) T. B. Wathen
§Gosport, Hants	84,800	8,693,173	73·59	G. F. Burndred, T.D.	(a) R. H. Borras
§Gravesham, Kent	96,500	11,402,826	56·9	J. V. Lovell	(a) L. H. Hardy
§Great Yarmouth, Norfolk	76,100	9,636,329	63·4–68·5	K. G. Ward	(a) J. A. Laird
§Grimsby, Humberside	94,700	10,407,814	59·5	F. W. Ward, O.B.E.	(a) P. Ellis
§Guildford, Surrey	120,000	21,216,229	—	B. E. Twyford	(a) Mrs. P. E. Harding
§Halton, Cheshire	110,700	14,131,599	88·8–89·4	R. Turton	(a) W. N. Howell
Hambleton, North Yorks	72,300	6,609,415	77	D. Parkin	Mrs. A. W. Thompson
Harborough, Leics.	57,800	6,374,410	48·5–53·3	F. T. Berry	B. D. Beeson
Harlow, Essex	80,300	12,783,430	60·5	A. W. Medd	V. A. Phelps
§Harrogate, North Yorks	133,500	13,777,778	57·7	J. N. Knox	(a) W. R. Beaumont
Hart, Hants	69,900	8,128,531	54·2–56·1	E. Robinson	J. E. G. Todd
§Hartlepool, Cleveland	97,300	10,215,328	69·0–70·1	N. D. Abram	(a) J. C. Herbert
§Hastings, East Sussex	74,770	8,759,519	70·3	D. J. Taylor	(a) J. Hodgson
§Havant, Hants	115,900	13,569,724	80·97	J. L. Stubbs	(a) E. S. M. Chadwick
HEREFORD	47,300	6,056,138	70·98	H. G. Culliss	(a) W. A. Vowles
Hertsmere, Hertfordshire	87,400	14,896,510	87·7	J. Heath	Lt. Col. L. Jones
§High Peak, Derbys.	80,200	8,024,091	64·7–67·4	D. G. Jones	(a) R. Partridge
§Hinckley and Bosworth, Leics	80,600	9,042,574	73·8	B. D. Ainscough	(a) Mrs. A. A. Wainwright
Holderness, Humberside	42,800	4,032,738	50–60	D. B. Law	R. Richardson
Horsham, West Sussex	90,000	11,384,680	50·7	D. M. Balmford	W. S. Parsons
§Hove, East Sussex	88,700	14,068,012	58·25	R. Hinton	(a) R. D. F. Ireland
Huntingdon, Cambs	115,800	12,346,471	61·5	N. Godfrey	Mrs. W. M. Price
§Hyndburn, Lancs	80,000	6,371,581	82·2–84·2	N. D. Macgregor	(a) A. Critchlow
§Ipswich, Suffolk	122,600	17,670,460	69·2	R. L. Cross	(a) Mrs. H. R. Davis
Kennet, Wilts	68,600	5,811,698	61·3	S. L. A. Jaques	Dr. T. K. Maurice
Kerrier, Cornwall	80,400	7,238,213	42·7–60·7	F. J. Pearson	E. L. J. Spargo
§Kettering, Northants	70,200	7,145,302	70·7–72·6	K. C. Butler	(a) A. A. Morby
KINGSTON UPON HULL, Humberside	279,700	26,352,814	74·46	A. B. Wood	(b) A. Parker
Kingswood, Avon	78,900	7,004,393	59·6	A. Smith	C. W. Adams
LANCASTER, Lancs	125,500	12,368,865	60–72·6	J. D. Waddell, O.B.E.	(a) P. Sumner
§Langbaurgh, Cleveland	150,700	20,697,130	65·4–71·4	W. A. Middleham	(a) J. S. Dyball
LEICESTER	290,600	36,298,213	57·5	J. S. Phipps	(b) B. Toft
Leominster, Hereford and Worcs	34,900	3,004,895	82·3–84·3	G. A. Robson	D. P. Joyce
Lewes, East Sussex	76,400	10,243,243	59·86	D. N. Thompson	G. Kent
Lichfield, Staffs	87,700	10,290,129	59·9	N. Barton	A. G. Ward
LINCOLN	73,100	8,643,548	63·7	P. C. Watts	(a) C. P. Robinson
§Luton, Beds	166,100	27,187,327	81	A. Collins	(a) F. S. Lester
§Macclesfield, Cheshire	146,600	18,836,928	74·0	J. E. Sandford	(a) C. G. Taylor

District	Population (Reg. G's Estimate)	Rateable Value 1976 £	Domestic Rate Levied p.	Chief Executive	Chairman 1976–7 (a) Mayor (b) Lord Mayor
§Maidstone, Kent	125,357	14,443,514	59·88	A. F. Hargraves	(a) E. Marchesi
Maldon, Essex	43,300	6,049,169	66·3–69·4	E. Robinson	R. F. Daws
Malvern Hills, Hereford and Worcs.	80,000	8,555,353	81·1	L. J. Martin	P. G. A. Archer
Mansfield, Notts	96,900	8,437,010	86·75	G. R. Cottam	M. Warriner
§Medina, Isle of Wight	65,100	6,886,922	81·1	W. R. Wilks	(a) D. H. Gordon
§Medway, Kent	145,300	19,105,652	59·5–61·5	R. Hill	(a) F. P. Heppler
§Melton, Leics	41,000	4,724,108	54·6	J. P. Milburn	(a) G. W. Miller
Mendip, Somerset	82,300	8,427,781	44·9	C. Riley	B. R. S. Bush
Mid Bedfordshire	95,600	10,727,783	91·9–94·4	P. A. Freeman	K. G. Quince
§Middlesbrough, Cleveland	155,000	15,431,084	76	J. R. Foster	(a) N. Goldie
Mid Suffolk	64,500	6,447,768	82·1	H. McFarlane	H. A. Mitson
Mid Sussex	106,400	13,720,042	53·2	J. A. McGhee	A. L. Whitticks
§Milton Keynes, Bucks	82,100	12,075,875	63·7	E. C. Ray	(a) G. A. Neale
Mole Valley, Surrey	76,600	11,420,508	64	D. C. Hill	H. T. F. Layton
Newark, Notts	102,200	9,488,030	67·59	J. R. Spencer	Lt. Col. G. H. F. P Vere-Laurie
Newbury, Berks	111,400	15,354,097	68·35	B. J. Thetford	Mrs. P. M. Bodin
§Newcastle under Lyme, Staffs	121,200	11,657,233	58	A. G. Owen	(a) D. B. Westrup
New Forest, Hants	137,900	20,184,187	59·13	P. A. Bassett	Mrs. L. K. Errington
§Northampton	139,900	19,721,985	69·3	A. C. Parkhouse	(a) J. T. Barnes
Northavon, Avon	105,117	12,931,448	59·9	F. Maude	D. J. Winstone
§North Bedfordshire	130,500	17,394,302	75·6–79·9	T. R. B. Tiernay	(a) T. R. Donnelly
North Cornwall	60,400	5,885,742	61·74	I. Whiting	J. A. M. Kent
North Devon	72,280	—	—	—	—
North Dorset	47,200	4,153,777	62·2	J. L. Guest	Mrs. M. E. Cossins
North East Derbyshire	91,300	7,492,453	84–92	R. S. Billington	Mrs. B. Lees
North Hertfordshire	104,200	16,803,508	—	M. Kelly	C. J. Marshall
North Kesteven, Lincs	76,600	6,632,391	—	T. L. Hill	K. T. Godson
North Norfolk	79,700	8,861,272	62·7	T. V. Nolan	E. W. Harmer
North Shropshire	48,400	4,288,829	62·3	E. G. D. Healey	J. M. Boffey
§North Warwickshire	61,700	7,444,025	78·5	R. H. Kealy	(a) S. Chetwynd
North West Leicestershire	74,200	8,171,263	57·8–62·1	—	J. M. Dawkins
North Wiltshire	100,200	9,111,341	57·4–68·1	H. F. Hales	D. H. Reardon-Smith
§North Wolds, Humberside	69,500	5,745,727	—	E. Hutchinson	(a) K. Wilson
NORWICH, Norfolk	121,688	20,069,699	75·1	G. G. Tilsley	(b) R. C. Frostick
NOTTINGHAM	287,880	35,528,058	68·7	M. H. F. Hammond	(b) S. J. Rushton
§Nuneaton, Warwickshire	112,600	11,949,490	67	B. E. Walters	R. T. Walker
§Oadby and Wigston, Leics	52,350	6,118,494	68·2	J. B. Burton	(a) W. L. Boulter
§Owestry, Salop	31,000	2,714,850	64	D. T. David	(a) J. K. Stockbridge
OXFORD	116,600	19,308,597	68·5	E. J. Patrick	(b) Miss A. H. Spokes
Pendle, Lancs	86,100	5,851,712	59·5–65·5	C. A. Simmonds	J. Fletcher
Penwith, Cornwall	51,332	5,269,122	—	J. R. Eley	J. C. Laity
PETERBOROUGH, Cambs.	111,300	14,858,994	68·9	P. B. Sidebottom	(a) E. E. Titman
PLYMOUTH, Devon	257,900	26,679,544	45·5	A. F. Watson	(b) A. Floyd
§Poole, Dorset	112,800	16,657,267	84·8	I. K. D. Andrews	(a) R. G. W. Hewitt
PORTSMOUTH, Hants	200,900	25,119,744	72·7	J. R. Haslegrave, C.B.E., T.D.	(b) I. G. Gibson
§Preston, Lancs	132,000	14,295,295	63·8	H. T. Heap	(a) H. Parker
Purbeck, Dorset	38,800	4,734,780	49·5–64·8	D. R. Sansome	J. Spiller
§Reading, Berks	133,900	22,807,688	61·7	W. H. Tee	(a) Mrs. K. L. Sage
Redditch, Hereford and Worcs	48,000	7,240,640	69·5	J. D. Weth	H. Shakels
§Reigate and Banstead, Surrey	113,800	17,431,965	62·7–64·7	D. S. Walker	(a) G. H. Searle
§Restormel, Cornwall	74,800	8,713,576	78·1–82·5	D. W. Cross	W. J. Julyan
§Ribble Valley, Lancs	53,900	4,768,751	52–64·4	M. Jackson	(a) F. E. Green
Richmondshire, North Yorks	46,500	3,891,655	68·59	E. H. Hodge	F. W. Woodall
Rochford, Essex	69,100	8,800,000	61·7–64·6	E. J. Skevington	A. J. Harvey
§Rossendale, Lancs	62,300	4,590,087	74·1–75·5	W. B. Wolfe	(a) J. Holt
Rother, East Sussex	73,700	10,067,936	80·28	—	A. S. J. Stevens
§Rugby, Warwicks	86,400	10,593,627	82·3	J. A. Thwaites	(a) P. Clark
Runnymede, Surrey	75,300	10,810,063	60·3	L. W. Way	Mrs. P. M. Barry
§Rushcliffe, Notts	89,000	10,357,187	62·65	D. J. Ashford	(a) A. S. White
§Rushmoor, Hants	78,600	10,350,354	66	A. R. O'Dowd-Booth	G. J. Woolger
Rutland, Leics	30,800	3,144,120	56	R. L. Francis	D. G. Willmer
Ryedale, North Yorks	75,140	5,781,280	—	A. Pearson	M. J. Territt M.B.E.
ST. ALBANS, Herts	125,000	19,837,810	50·1–52·6	R. Braddon	(a) K. S. Hill
§St. Edmundsbury, Suffolk	80,556	9,848,000	—	E. G. Thomas	(a) A. F. S. Davies
Salisbury, Wilts	101,105	11,575,645	63	F. W. Colquhoun	G. H. A. Stocken
§Scarborough, North Yorks	97,900	9,812,255	67·1–77·1	R. Bradley	(a) A. T. F. Young
§Scunthorpe, Humberside	67,800	10,548,940	66	C. B. Jeynes	(a) Mrs. J. M. Abey

District	Population (Reg. G's Estimate)	Rateable Value 1976 £	Domestic Rate Levied p.	Chief Executive	Chairman 1976–7 (a) Mayor (b) Lord Mayor
Sedgefield, Durham...............	92,000	7,800,000	72·41	A. J. Roberts	J. Lee
Sedgemoor, Somerset..............	84,200	9,175,636	52·9	T. J. Shellard	E. J. Davies
Selby, North Yorks...............	70,700	8,881,399	80	J. A. Wakefield	E. A. Wright
Sevenoaks, Kent..................	102,100	11,389,700	—	D. A. Clarke	A. H. C. Branson
Shepway, Kent....................	86,500	10,678,453	56·5–61·3	K. H. G. Mills	L. C. Harrold
Shrewsbury and Atcham, Salop.....	83,900	10,489,582	52·8–56	L. C. W. Beesley	(a) Mrs. W. R. Jones
§Slough, Berks....................	101,800	22,044,071	62·8	M. F. Hulks	(a) J. McSweeney
SOUTHAMPTON, Hants...............	216,000	29,402,514	—	D. Scouller	(a) Mrs. M. Key
South Bedfordshire...............	97,300	15,878,882	77·5	R. C. Cranmer	E. S. Clarke
South Cambridgeshire.............	98,800	12,236,612	59·6	S. J. Flint	F. A. Rhead
South Derbyshire.................	63,100	7,631,158	63·32	R. V. Hawcroft	P. C. Hanbury
§Southend-on-Sea, Essex	159,400	25,435,735	60·9	F. G. Laws	(a) N. B. Moss
South Hams, Devon................	63,500	6,668,886	78·2–82	S. W. Bradley	Miss B. Breakwell, M.B.E.
South Herefordshire..............	44,800	3,775,801	64·7–69·6	E. N. Sheldon	W. W. Makin
South Holland, Lincs.............	58,200	5,459,453	80·77	J. T. Brindley	F. W. Hardwick
South Kesteven, Lincs............	91,700	9,260,199	65·4–66·9	K. R. Cann	G. Swallow
South Lakeland, Cumbria..........	93,100	9,069,666	49·7–58·9	N. C. Bizley	W. Dobson
South Norfolk...................	87,000	8,205,371	61·5	R. A. Gorham	B. A. Cook
South Northamptonshire...........	59,700	6,208,182	59·5–62·5	C. M. Major	Mrs. J. Green
South Oxfordshire................	140,600	17,291,131	58·1	J. B. Chirnside	A. H. Southorn, O.B.E.
§South Ribble, Lancs..............	90,500	8,091,464	—	C. E. Lea	(a) J. Crossley
South Shropshire.................	33,330	2,857,496	62·2	L. V. Atack	Maj. D. J. Brook
South Staffordshire..............	87,500	9,790,309	56	A. Roebuck	G. B. Roberts
South Wight, I.O.W...............	45,700	5,174,658	58–62	C. M. Simpson	(a) R. J. Callis
§Spelthorne, Surrey...............	97,300	19,580,958	57·5	G. F. Hilbert	(a) R. L. Schaffer
§Stafford........................	114,300	14,158,117	—	D. E. Almond	(a) R. E. Tonge
Staffordshire Moorlands..........	93,300	8,619,657	56·6	H. W. Henson	J. Dixon
§Stevenage, Herts.................	74,900	12,222,426	70·5	R. E. Hughes	(a) R. A. Clark
§Stockton-on-Tees, Cleveland......	164,000	23,566,436	71·1	G. F. Lyon	(a) J. A. Tatchell
STOKE-ON-TRENT, Staffs..........	255,800	28,835,941	85·9	W. S. Titchener	(b) W. Screen
Stratford-on-Avon, Warwicks.......	99,400	13,620,686	65·86	T. J. W. Foy	D. R. Fyfe
Stroud, Glos.....................	94,000	10,279,398	64·62	H. T. Arnold	M. W. Baker
Suffolk Coastal..................	94,300	11,068,598	67·7–82·1	D. L. Blay	Mrs. G. S. Agate
§Surrey Heath....................	70,500	11,073,692	63·06	D. J. L. Horn	(a) A. G. Mansfield
Swale, Kent.....................	106,500	10,968,276	60·8–66·5	D. Allen	R. W. Barnicott
§Tamworth, Staffs.................	55,500	5,635,740	81·3	H. B. Leake	(a) P. J. White
Tandridge, Surrey................	79,400	9,272,429	—	D. Brunton	C. J. Latilla
§Taunton Deane, Somerset..........	82,600	9,107,006	83·3	K. A. Horne	(a) R. H. May
Teesdale, Durham.................	24,100	1,931,041	59·5–68·5	J. A. Jones	J. L. Armstrong
Teignbridge, Devon...............	93,600	9,760,231	79·9–82·9	E. G. Loveys	L. Lamb
Tendring, Essex..................	107,000	13,538,506	—	C. H. Ramsden	A. Chappell
Test Valley, Hants...............	86,100	10,612,051	65·7–77	G. K. Waddell	A. E. Parke
§Tewkesbury, Glos.................	77,484	9,574,320	—	K. E. S. Smale	(a) F. J. Chamberlayne
§Thamesdown, Wilts...............	142,400	16,472,340	68·8–75·5	D. M. Kent	L. Gowing
Thanet, Kent....................	118,200	13,539,947	55·5–60	I. G. Gill	L. T. J. Corbitt
Three Rivers, Herts..............	80,610	12,250,905	85·69	J. D. Brown	D. P. Macdonald
§Thurrock, Essex.................	126,800	28,055,841	—	G. V. Semain	(a) P. P. Rice
Tiverton, Devon..................	55,800	4,766,076	73·68	R. C. Greensmith	E. H. Pennington
Tonbridge and Malling, Kent......	94,700	11,661,020	61·5	S. W. Stanford, T.D.	Mrs. J. Marwood
§Torbay, Devon...................	109,800	15,666,121	65	D. P. Hudson	(a) W. A. Beesley
Torridge, Devon..................	47,100	3,526,068	54·9–59·5	T. W. Frankland	R. E. J. Quance
§Tunbridge Wells, Kent.	95,200	10,619,340	61·8–70·6	W. E. Battersby	(a) Mrs. M. B. Streeten
Tynedale, Northumberland..........	54,700	5,010,684	72·5	A. Bates	M. D. Routledge
Uttlesford, Essex................	56,100	7,464,668	63·3–75·5	J. F. Vernon	F. G. Askew
Vale of White Horse, Oxon........	96,900	13,086,480	58·4	J. C. N. Wood	E. J. S. Parsons
Vale Royal, Cheshire.............	110,200	13,666,060	88·4–93·7	W. R. T. Woods	R. Carey, B.E.M.
Wansbeck, Northumberland..........	62,970	6,519,601	72	R. R. Nuttall	J. Haig
Wansdyke, Avon...................	73,500	7,529,719	81·85	B. L. Clifton	D. G. Miles
§Warrington, Cheshire.............	164,800	19,620,931	86·8–88·5	W. H. Lawton, T.D.	(a) T. Pye
Warwick.........................	111,700	16,050,824	61·1	M. J. Ward	M. E. Kerry
§Watford, Herts..................	78,100	15,384,868	81·12	R. B. McMillan	(a) D. J. Coleshill
Waveney, Suffolk	95,217	9,970,115	66·1	P. A. Taylor	Capt. R. E. S. Wykes-Sneyd

District	Popula-tion (Reg. G's Estimate)	Rateable Value 1976 £	Domestic Rate Levied p.	Chief Executive	Chairman 1976-7 (a) Mayor (b) Lord Mayor
Waverley, Surrey	106,290	15,410,601	84·07	C. J. Wagg	H. E. Buttery
Wealden, East Sussex	112,200	12,267,576	77·2	K. Wilson	Air Cdre. H. M. Russell,
Wear Valley, Durham	63,600	5,153,460	76	J. R. Passey	C. Wood [O.B.E.
§Wellingborough, Northants	62,200	6,992,739	73·3	J. Huxley	(a) J. L. H. Bailey
Welwyn Hatfield, Herts	93,900	17,563,725	75	L. Asquith	D. Lewis
West Derbyshire	66,200	6,221,663	84·89	R. Bubb	E. J. Smith
West Devon	40,200	3,396,886	54	G. E. G. Cotton	A. A. W. Brown
West Dorset	77,800	7,832,132	59·1-68·8	E. Andrews	H. W. Haward
West Lancashire	105,400	11,141,238	66·1	J. Cowdall	R. J. Kirby
West Lindsey, Lincs	73,600	6,032,000	83·78	W. McIntyre	A. Edlington
West Norfolk	115,100	12,645,179	63	J. E. Bolton	Sir John Bagge, Bt., E.D.
West Oxfordshire	81,933	8,609,437	—	M. G. Knapman	J. F. Swain
West Somerset	29,934	3,771,397	64·4	H. Close	Maj. M. P. Morris
West Wiltshire	93,500	9,569,882	67·85	R. Butterworth	M. M. Mortimer
§Weymouth and Portland, Dorset	56,300	5,652,889	63·6-65·6	E. J. Jones	(a) J. D. Blackburn
Wimborne, Dorset	57,600	7,395,752	73·1	W. G. Press	W. C. Tapper
WINCHESTER, Hants	88,700	11,276,917	67·6-73·3	E. M. E. White	(a) Mrs. G. A. Shave
§Windsor and Maidenhead, Berks	128,000	—	—	—	—
§Woking, Surrey	78,200	12,110,917	64·7	M. Shawcross	(a) I. S. McCallum
Wokingham, Berks	111,200	14,228,284	50-51·1	C. G. Cockayne	C. W. J. Rout
Woodspring, Avon	148,700	16,678,619	62	R. H. Moon	W. S. Dening
WORCESTER	74,300	11,529,832	71·5	B. Webster, O.B.E.	(a) A. E. Sage
§Worthing, West Sussex	92,800	12,862,000	50·8	H. Carroll [M.C.	(a) Mrs. W. M. Framp-
Wrekin, Salop	109,700	12,226,990	63·6	A. W. Flockhart	Mr. L. I. Butler [ton
Wychavon, Hereford and Worcs	85,800	11,354,441	88·2-91·8	P. G. Rust	R. J. Beckley
Wycombe, Bucks	150,500	24,800,075	58·1	D. I. Pendrill	(a) S. J. Mahoney
§Wyre, Lancs	98,800	9,966,059	57·5	W. F. Dolman	(a) W. G. Ball
Wyre Forest, Hereford and Worcs	92,100	12,141,426	69·8	N. A. James	A. H. Humphries
Yeovil, Somerset	122,800	12,478,337	62·3	K. C. Hermon	Rev. Preb. W. T. Tay-
YORK, North Yorks	102,700	10,307,261	69·4	R. Howell	(b) J. Archer [lor

PARTY REPRESENTATION

Abbreviations: *C.* = Conservative; *Comm.* = Communist; *D.Lab.* = Democratic Labour; *Ind.* = Independent, including Ratepayers' Association, etc.; *Lab.* = Labour; *L.* = Liberal; *P.C.* = Plaid Cymru.

Metropolitan Counties

Greater Manchester. *Lab.* 69, *C.* 23, *L.* 13, *Ind.* 1.
Merseyside. *Lab.* 53, *C.* 26, *L.* 19, *Ind.* 1.
West Midlands. *Lab.* 74, *C.* 26, *L.* 4.

Tyne and Wear. *Lab.* 74, *C.* 26, *Ind.* 3, *L.* 1.
South Yorkshire. *Lab.* 82, *C.* 13, *Ind.* 4, *L.* 1.
West Yorkshire. *Lab.* 51, *C.* 25, *L.* 11, *Ind.* 1.

Non-Metropolitan Counties

Avon. *C.* 36, *Lab.* 32, *Ind.* 3, *L.* 2.
Bedfordshire. *Lab.* 39, *C.* 32, *L.* 8, *Ind.* 3.
Berkshire. *C.* 42, *Lab.* 26, *L.* 13, *Ind.* 5.
Buckinghamshire. *C.* 36, *Lab.* 18, *Ind.* 12, *L.* 4.
Cambridgeshire. *C.* 28, *Lab.* 22, *Ind.* 13, *L.* 5.
Cheshire. *C.* 31, *Lab.* 29, *Ind.* 6, *L.* 1.
Cleveland. *Lab.* 52, *C.* 35, *Ind.* 2.
Cornwall. *Ind.* 75, *C.* 3, *Lab.* 1.
Cumbria. *Lab.* 38, *C.* 31, *Ind.* 11, *L.* 1.
Derbyshire. *Lab.* 60, *C.* 26, *Ind.* 7, *L.* 5.
Devon. *C.* 54, *Lab.* 20, *Ind.* 12, *L.* 11.
Dorset. *C.* 47, *Ind.* 20, *Lab.* 13, *L.* 11.
Durham. *Lab.* 56, *Ind.* 7, *L.* 6, *C.* 2.
East Sussex. *C.* 48, *Lab.* 19, *L.* 9, *Ind.* 8.
Essex. *C.* 50, *Lab.* 40, *L.* 5, *Ind.* 2.
Gloucestershire. *C.* 31, *Lab.* 18, *Ind.* 7, *L.* 5.
Hampshire. *C.* 44, *Lab.* 27, *Ind.* 20, *L.* 6.
Hereford and Worcester. *C.* 37, *Lab.* 30, *Ind.* 17, *L.* 8.
Hertfordshire. *C.* 33, *Lab.* 33, *L.* 3, *Ind.* 3.
Humberside. *Lab.* 51, *C.* 36, *Ind.* 7, *L.* 3.

Isle of Wight. *Ind.* 23, *L.* 7, *Lab.* 6, *C.* 6.
Kent. *C.* 63, *Lab.* 31, *L.* 7, *Ind.* 2.
Lancashire. *C.* 52, *Lab.* 33, *L.* 7, *Ind.* 4.
Leicestershire. *C.* 41, *Lab.* 37, *Ind.* 8, *L.* 7.
Lincolnshire. *C.* 34, *Ind.* 22, *Lab.* 10, *D.Lab.* 5, *L.* 3.
Norfolk. *C.* 52, *Lab.* 27, *Ind.* 4.
Northamptonshire. *Lab.* 47, *C.* 37, *Ind.* 4.
Northumberland. *Lab.* 28, *Ind.* 21, *C.* 10.
North Yorkshire. *C.* 39, *Ind.* 30, *Lab.* 12, *L.* 12.
Nottinghamshire. *Lab.* 54, *C.* 35.
Oxfordshire. *C.* 36, *Lab.* 21, *Ind.* 10.
Salop. *Ind.* 30, *Lab.* 16, *C.* 14, *L.* 3.
Somerset. *C.* 35, *Ind.* 12, *Lab.* 7, *L.* 2.
Staffordshire. *Lab.* 47, *C.* 28, *Ind.* 9, *L.* 1.
Suffolk. *C.* 47, *Lab.* 29, *L.* 3, *Ind.* 3.
Surrey. *C.* 46, *Lab.* 12, *L.* 9, *Ind.* 5.
Warwickshire. *C.* 27, *Lab.* 21, *L.* 5, *Ind.* 2.
West Sussex. *C.* 52, *Ind.* 14, *Lab.* 10, *L.* 7.
Wiltshire. *C.* 39, *Lab.* 22, *Ind.* 12, *L.* 6.

Metropolitan District Councils
(Elections of May 6, 1976)

GREATER MANCHESTER
Bolton..............C. 43, *Lab.* 20, *Ind.* 4, *L.* 2.
Bury..............C. 36, *Lab.* 11, *L.* 1.
Manchester........*Lab.* 54, *C.* 45.
Oldham...........C. 28, *Lab.* 20, *L.* 8, *Ind.* 1.
Rochdale..........C. 31, *Lab.* 19, *L.* 10.
Salford............*Lab.* 38, *C.* 24, *Ind.* 2, *L.* 2.
Stockport..........C. 39, *Lab.* 11, *L.* 7, *Ind.* 3.
Tameside..........C. 29, *Lab.* 22, *L.* 2, *Ind.* 1.
Trafford............C. 47, *Lab.* 12, *L.* 4.
Wigan............C. 56, *C.* 14, *Ind.* 1, *L.* 1.

MERSEYSIDE
Knowsley..........*Lab.* 42, *C.* 17, *Ind.* 2, *L.* 2.
Liverpool..........*Lab.* 42, *L.* 40, *C.* 17.
St. Helens.........*Lab.* 25, *C.* 19, *L.* 1.
Sefton..............C. 43, *Lab.* 21, *L.* 3, *Ind.* 2.
Wirral.............C. 42, *Lab.* 18, *L.* 6.

SOUTH YORKSHIRE
Barnsley...........*Lab.* 39, *Ind.* 15, *L.* 5, *C.* 1.
Doncaster.........*Lab.* 35, *C.* 17, *Ind.* 7, *Dem. Lab.* 1.
Rotherham........*Lab.* 45, *C.* 6, *Ind.* 3.
Sheffield..........*Lab.* 63, *C.* 22, *L.* 5.

TYNE AND WEAR
Gateshead.........*Lab.* 59, *C.* 13, *L.* 4, *Ind.* 2.
Newcastle upon
   Tyne............*Lab.* 44, *C.* 29, *L.* 3, *Ind.* 2.
North Tyneside....*Lab.* 44, *C.* 28, *Ind.* 2, *L.* 2.
South Tyneside....*Lab.* 34, *Ind.* 24, *C.* 4, *L.* 3.
Sunderland........*Lab.* 49, *C.* 26, *L.* 2, *Ind.* 1.

WEST MIDLANDS
Birmingham........C. 66, *Lab.* 52, *L.* 8.
Coventry..........*Lab.* 28, *C.* 26.
Dudley............C. 37, *Lab.* 26, *L.* 2, *Ind.* 1.
Sandwell..........*Lab.* 51, *C.* 39.
Solihull..........C. 34, *Lab.* 12, *Ind.* 4, *L.* 1.
Walsall............*Lab.* 28, *C.* 20, *Ind.* 11, *L.* 1.
Wolverhampton....*Lab.* 34, *C.* 24, *Ind.* 2.

WEST YORKSHIRE
Bradford..........C. 61, *Lab.* 27, *L.* 5.
Calderdale.........C. 34, *Lab.* 13, *L.* 4.
Kirklees..........C. 38, *Lab.* 25, *L.* 9.
Leeds.............C. 50, *Lab.* 38, *L.* 8.
Wakefield.........*Lab.* 42, *C.* 15, *Ind.* 9.

Non-Metropolitan District Councils

Adur..............L. 17, *C.* 16, *Ind.* 2, *Lab.* 2.
Allerdale..........*Ind.* 23, *Lab.* 23, *C.* 10.
Alnwick..........*Ind.* 21, *Lab.* 3, *C.* 2, *L.* 1.
Amber Valley......*Ind.* 26, *Lab.* 18, *L.* 14, *C.* 2.
Arun.............C. 51, *L.* 5, *Ind.* 3, *Lab.* 1.
Ashfield...........*Lab.* 22, *Ind.* 9, *C.* 2.
Ashford...........C. 30, *Lab.* 7, *Ind.* 5, *L.* 3.
Aylesbury Vale.....C. 28, *Ind.* 19, *Lab.* 9, *L.* 2.
Babergh...........*Ind.* 17, *C.* 16, *Lab.* 4, *L.* 1.
Barrow-in-Furness..C. 19, *Lab.* 12, *Ind.* 2.
Basildon..........*Lab.* 23, *C.* 17, *Ind.* 6.
Basingstoke........C. 35, *Lab.* 14, *Ind.* 9, *L.* 1.
Bassetlaw.........*Lab.* 24, *Lab.* 18, *Ind.* 7.
Bath.............C. 35, *Lab.* 13.
Beaconsfield.......C. 32, *Ind.* 10.
Berwick...........*Ind.* 21, *Lab.* 3, *L.* 3.
Beverley..........C. 44, *Ind.* 12, *L.* 3, *Lab.* 1.
Blaby............C. 21, *Ind.* 15, *L.* 1.
Blackburn.........C. 27, *Lab.* 17, *Ind.* 8, *L.* 6.
Blackpool.........C. 36, *Lab.* 6, *L.* 3.
Blyth Valley.......*Lab.* 23, *Ind. Lab.* 11, *C.* 6, *L.* 3.
Bolsover..........*Lab.* 25, *Ind.* 7, *C.* 4.
Boothferry........*Ind.* 20, *C.* 12, *Lab.* 3.
Boston............*Ind.* 15, *C.* 13, *Lab.* 3, *L.* 3.
Bournemouth......C. 46, *Ind.* 6, *Lab.* 3, *L.* 2.
Bracknell.........C. 27, *Lab.* 3, *L.* 1.
Braintree.........C. 39, *Ind.* 10, *Lab.* 8, *L.* 1.
Breckland........C. 21, *Ind.* 11, *Lab.* 9.
Brentwood........C. 34, *Lab.* 4, *Ind.* 1.
Bridgnorth........*Ind.* 24, *L.* 4, *C.* 2, *Lab.* 2.
Brighton..........C. 44, *Lab.* 15.
Bristol............*Lab.* 47, *C.* 34, *L.* 3.
Broadland.........C. 29, *Ind.* 17, *L.* 2, *Lab.* 1.
Bromsgrove........C. 32, *Lab.* 8, *Ind.* 2.
Broxbourne.......C. 36, *Lab.* 6.
Broxtowe.........C. 37, *Lab.* 11, *Ind.* 1.
Burnley...........*Lab.* 33, *C.* 19, *L.* 2.
Cambridge........C. 24, *Lab.* 16, *L.* 2.
Cannock Chase.....*Lab.* 24, *C.* 18.
Canterbury........C. 46, *Ind.* 4, *Lab.* 1.
Caradon...........*Ind.* 39, *L.* 1,
   Mabyon Kernow, 1.
Carlisle...........C. 22, *Lab.* 22, *Ind.* 3, *L.* 1.
Carrick...........*Ind.* 28, *C.* 9, *Lab.* 4, *L.* 4.
Castle Morpeth.....*Ind.* 15, *C.* 9, *Lab.* 5, *L.* 2.
Castle Point.......C. 36, *Lab.* 3.
Charnwood........C. 42, *Lab.* 13, *L.* 2, *Ind.* 1.
Chelmsford.......C. 46, *L.* 9, *Lab.* 3, *Ind.* 2.
Cheltenham.......C. 22, *Ind.* 7, *L.* 4, *Lab.* 2.

Cherwell..........C. 26, *Lab.* 10, *Ind.* 8.
Chester...........C. 44, *Lab.* 10, *Ind.* 6, *L.* 2.
Chesterfield.......*Lab.* 36, *C.* 14, *Ind.* 2, *L.* 2.
Chester-le-Street...*Lab.* 22, *L.* 6, *Ind.* 5.
Chichester........C. 37, *Ind.* 12, *L.* 1.
Chiltern..........C. 39, *Lab.* 6, *Ind.* 4, *L.* 1.
Chorley...........C. 33, *Lab.* 11, *Ind.* 3.
Christchurch.......C. 18, *Lab.* 4.
Cleethorpes.......*Ind.* 17, *C.* 13, *Lab.* 13, *L.* 5.
Colchester........C. 39, *Lab.* 18, *Ind.* 3.
Congleton.........C. 28, *Ind.* 7, *Lab.* 5, *L.* 2.
Copeland..........*Lab.* 22, *C.* 15, *Ind.* 11.
Corby............C. 16, *Lab.* 10, *Ind.* 1.
Cotswold..........*Ind.* 41, *C.* 4.
Craven...........C. 21, *Ind.* 6, *L.* 5, *Lab.* 2.
Crawley...........*Lab.* 14, *C.* 11.
Crewe............C. 28, *Lab.* 28, *Ind.* 8.
Dacorum..........C. 38, *Lab.* 21, *Ind.* 3.
Darlington........C. 30, *Lab.* 15, *Ind.* 4.
Dartford..........*Lab.* 25, *C.* 20.
Daventry..........C. 24, *Ind.* 9, *Lab.* 2.
Derby............C. 28, *Lab.* 26.
Derwentside.......*Lab.* 39, *Ind.* 9, *L.* 5, *C.* 2.
Dover............C. 36, *Lab.* 17, *Ind.* 2.
Durham..........*Lab.* 34, *Ind.* 17, *L.* 10.
Easington..........*Lab.* 45, *Ind.* 10, *L.* 4, *C.* 1.
Eastbourne........C. 25, *Lab.* 4, *L.* 1.
East Cambridgeshire *Ind.* 32, *C.* 3.
East Devon........C. 44, *Ind.* 12, *Lab.* 1.
East Hampshire....C. 31, *Ind.* 11.
East Hertfordshire...C. 28, *Ind.* 19, *Lab.* 1.
Eastleigh..........C. 36, *Lab.* 6, *Ind.* 1, *L.* 1.
East Lindsey.......*Ind.* 45, *C.* 10, *L.* 2, *Lab.* 1.
East Northampton-
   shire..............C. 28, *Lab.* 6, *Ind.* 3.
East Staffordshire..C. 37, *Lab.* 12, *Ind.* 10, *L.* 1.
Eden.............*Ind.* 36.
Ellesmere Port......*Lab.* 22, *C.* 17, *Ind.* 1, *L.* 1.
Elmbridge.........C. 36, *Ind.* 14, *Lab.* 7, *L.* 3.
Epping Forest......C. 53, *Ind.* 5, *Lab.* 1.
Epsom and Ewell...*Ind.* 36, *Lab.* 3.
Erewash..........C. 37, *Ind.* 8, *L.* 5, *Lab.* 4.
Exeter...........C. 24, *Lab.* 9, *L.* 1.
Fareham..........C. 24, *Ind.* 15, *Lab.* 2, *L.* 1.
Fenland..........C. 27, *Lab.* 8, *Ind.* 4, *L.* 1.
Forest Heath......C. 13, *Ind.* 11, *L.* 1.
Forest of Dean.....*Ind.* 26, *Lab.* 12, *C.* 7, *L.* 2.
Fylde............C. 26, *Ind.* 18, *L.* 4, *Lab.* 1.
Gedling...........C. 42, *Lab.* 10, *Ind.* 3.

Thamesdown.......C. 22, Lab. 21, Ind. 2, L. 1.
Thanet.............C. 39, Ind. 13, Lab. 11.
Three Rivers.......C. 32, Lab. 10, L. 5.
Thurrock..........Lab. 25, C. 11, Ind. 3.
Tiverton...........Ind. 35, L. 5.
Tonbridge and
   Malling.........C. 42, Lab. 4, Ind. 3.
Torbay............C. 34, Ind. 2.
Torridge...........Ind. 25, L. 7, C. 2, Lab. 2.
Tunbridge Wells...C. 36, Ind. 8, Lab. 4.
Tynedale...........Ind. 24, Lab. 11, C. 8, L. 4.
Uttlesford.........C. 29, Ind. 6, L. 4, Lab. 3.
Vale of White Horse C. 40, Lab. 4, Ind. 3, L. 1.
Vale Royal........C. 26, Ind. 16, Lab. 4, L. 4.
Wansbeck.........Lab. 46, Ind. 2, L. 1.
Wansdyke.........C. 26, Lab. 13, Ind. 8.
Warrington........C. 39, Lab. 19, Ind. 2.
Warwick...........C. 41, Lab. 14, L. 2.
Watford...........Lab. 19, C. 17.
Waveney..........C. 39, Lab. 13, L. 4, Ind. 1.
Waverley..........C. 45, L. 7, Ind. 6, Lab. 3.
Wealden..........C. 41, Ind. 15.
Wear Valley......Lab. 17, Ind. 11, L. 11, C. 2.
Wellingborough....C. 19, Lab. 9, Ind. 4, L. 1.
Welwyn Hatfield...C. 24, Lab. 19.
West Derbyshire....C. 29, Ind. 6, L. 3, Lab. 2.

West Devon.......Ind. 26, C. 4.
West Dorset.......Ind. 45, L. 7, C. 2, Lab. 1.
West Lancashire....C. 34, Lab. 15, Ind. 5, L. 1.
West Lindsey......Ind. 22, C. 7, Lab. 4, L. 4.
West Norfolk......C. 36, Ind. 12, Lab. 12.
West Oxfordshire..Ind. 22, C. 19, Lab. 4.
West Somerset....Ind. 25, C. 5, L. 1.
West Wiltshire....C. 19, Ind. 15, Lab. 7, L. 1.
Weymouth and
   Portland........C. 20, Lab. 13, Ind. 6.
Wimborne.........C. 19, Ind. 11, L. 3.
Winchester........C. 24, Ind. 23, Lab. 4, L. 3.
Windsor and
   Maidenhead....C. 55, Ind. 3, L. 1.
Woking...........C. 27, Lab. 8.
Wokingham.......C. 36, Ind. 8, L. 8.
Woodspring.......C. 50, Lab. 7, Ind. 4.
Worcester.........C. 24, Lab. 12.
Worthing.........C. 26, Ind. 3, L. 1.
Wrekin...........Lab. 30, C. 13, Ind. 12.
Wychavon........Ind. 31, C. 8, Lab. 4, L. 2.
Wycombe.........C. 51, Ind. 9.
Wyre............C. 49, Ind. 4, L. 2.
Wyre Forest.......C. 28, L. 9, Lab. 7, Ind. 1.
Yeovil...........C. 28, Ind. 24, Lab. 7, L. 1.
York............C. 26; Lab. 10, L. 3.

WALES
County Councils
(1973 elections)

Clwyd............Ind. 30, Lab. 20, C. 11, L. 4.
Dyfed............Ind. 41, Lab. 29, L. 8, P.C. 1.
Gwent...........Lab. 59, C. 12, Ind. 3, L. 3, P.C. 1.
Gwynedd.........Ind. 56, P.C. 6, Lab. 4.

Mid Glamorgan....Lab. 63, P.C. 9, Ind. 6, C. 3, Comm. 2, L. 2.
Powys...........Ind. 44, Lab. 7, L. 2.
South Glamorgan..Lab. 42, C. 35, Ind. 3.
West Glamorgan...Lab. 52, C. 9, Ind. 6, L. 2, P.C. 1.

District Councils

Aberconwy........Ind. 30, C. 6, L. 3, Lab. 2.
Afan.............Ind. 19, Lab. 11.
Arfon............Ind. 23, P.C. 13, Lab. 5.
Blaenau Gwent.....Lab. 26, Ind. 15, L. 5, P.C. 3, C. 1.
Brecknock........Ind. 29, Lab. 16, C. 5, L. 1.
Cardiff...........C. 44, Lab. 29, Ind. 2.
Carmarthen......Ind. 29, Lab. 6, L. 1.
Ceredigion.......Ind. 30, L. 7, Ind. 3, P.C. 2.
Colwyn..........C. 16, Ind. 11, L. 6.
Cynon Valley.....Lab. 23, P.C. 9, Ind. 5, Comm. 1.
Delyn............Ind. 20, Lab. 15, C. 2, P.C. 2, L. 1.
Dinefwr..........Ind. 17, Lab. 13, P.C. 2.
Dwyfor..........Ind. 22, P.C. 6, C. 1.
Islwyn...........Lab. 16, Ind. 13, P.C. 7.
Llanelli..........Lab. 24, Ind. 6, L. 2, P.C. 1.
Lliw Valley.......Lab. 19, Ind. 8, P.C. 5.
Meirionnyd......Ind. 28, P.C. 8, Lab. 3.
Merthyr Tydfil....P.C. 21, Lab. 8, Ind. 4.
Monmouth........C. 30, Lab. 7, Ind. 2.

Montgomery.......Ind. 42, L. 3, C. 1, Lab. 1, P.C. 1.
Neath............Lab. 17, Ind. 13, P.C. 2.
Newport.........C. 26, Lab. 22, Ind. 3.
Ogwr............Lab. 29, C. 13, Ind. 13, L. 1, P.C. 1.
Preseli...........Ind. 43.
Radnor...........Ind. 31.
Rhondda........Lab. 21, Ind. 8, P.C. 2, C. 1, Comm. 1.
Rhuddlan........Ind. 33, C. 1, L. 1, P.C. 1.
Rhymney Valley...P.C. 23, Lab. 19, Ind. 6.
Sth. Pembrokeshire..Ind. 31.
Swansea.........Ind. 32, C. 11, Lab. 7, P.C. 1.
Taff-Ely.........Lab. 24, Ind.'10, P.C. 8, L. 4.
Torfaen.........Lab. 24, Ind. 16, C. 1, Comm. 1, P.C. 1.
Vale of Glamorgan.C. 33, Lab. 10, Ind. 6.
Wrexham Maelor...Lab. 20, Ind. 14, C. 7, L. 2, P.C. 2.
Ynys Môn........Ind. 39, Lab. 5, P.C. 1.

GREATER LONDON BOROUGHS

The figures given in the press for Party Representation in the Greater London Boroughs after the elections of May, 1974, were as follows:

Barking..........Lab. 45, Ind. 4.
Barnet...........C. 46, Lab. 18, Ind. 1.
Bexley...........C. 37, Lab. 27.
Brent............Lab. 40, C. 25.
Bromley..........C. 47, Lab. 16, L. 2.
Camden..........Lab. 53, C. 12.
Croydon..........C. 43, Lab. 19, Ind. 5.
Ealing...........Lab. 41, C. 24.
Enfield...........C. 35, Lab. 29, L. 1.
Greenwich........Lab. 57, C. 8.
Hackney.........Lab. 65.
Hammersmith......Lab. 53, C. 10, L. 2.
Haringey.........Lab. 45, C. 19, Ind. 1.
Harrow..........C. 39, Lab. 14, Ind. 3.
Havering.........Lab. 31, C. 20, Ind. 9.
Hillingdon.........Lab. 32, C. 28.
Hounslow.........Lab. 42, C. 23.

Islington...........Lab. 65.
Kensington and
   Chelsea..........C. 48, Lab. 18.
Kingston..........C. 44, Lab. 15, L. 6.
Lambeth..........Lab. 51, C. 14.
Lewisham.........C. 29, Lab. 27, Ind. 3.
Merton...........C. 29, Lab. 27, Ind. 3.
Newham.........Lab. 56, Ind. 9.
Redbridge........C. 49, Lab. 16.
Richmond........C. 41, L. 10, Lab. 8.
Southwark.......Lab. 61, C. 4.
Sutton...........C. 30, Lab. 15, L. 6.
Tower Hamlets.....Lab. 65.
Waltham Forest....Lab. 40, C. 12.
Wandsworth.......Lab. 53, C. 12.
Westminster.......C. 39, Lab. 26.

AERODROMES AND AIRPORTS

There are 165 aerodromes in Great Britain, Northern Ireland, the Isle of Man and the Channel Islands which are either State owned, operated by the Civil Aviation Authority or licensed for use by civil aircraft. A number of unlicensed airfields not included in this list are also available for private use by permission of the owner or controlling authority.

> S = Aerodrome owned and operated by the State.
> CAA = Aerodrome operated by the Civil Aviation Authority.
> BAA = Aerodrome operated by the British Airports Authority.
> M = Aerodrome owned or operated by Municipal Authority.
> J = Military airfield available for civil use by prior permission.
> H = Licensed helicopter station.

Those aerodromes which are designated as Customs airports are printed in **bold** type. Customs facilities are available at certain other aerodromes by special arrangement.

ENGLAND AND WALES (118)

Abingdon, Oxon. J
Barrow (Walney Island), Cumbria.
Bembridge, I.O.W.
Biggin Hill, Kent.
Binbrook, Lincolnshire. J
Birmingham, W. Midlands. M
Bitteswell, Warwicks.
Blackbushe, Hants.
Blackpool, Lancs. M
Bournemouth (Hurn), Dorset. M
Bristol (Lulsgate). M
Cambridge.
Carlisle, Cumbria.
Chichester (Goodwood), Sussex.
Church Fenton, Yorks. J
Clacton, Essex.
Coltishall, Norfolk. J
Compton Abbas, Dorsetshire.
Coventry, W. Midlands. M
Cranfield, Beds.
Cranwell, Lincs. J
Culdrose, Cornwall. J
Denham, Bucks.
Dishforth, Yorks. J
Doncaster, Yorks.
Dunkeswell, Devon.
Duxford, Cambs.
East Midlands, Leics. M
Elstree, Herts.
Elvington, Yorks. J
Exeter, Devon.
Fair Oaks, Surrey.
Fenland, Lincs.
Finningley, Yorks. J
Glamorgan (Rhoose). M
Gloucester/Cheltenham (Staverton). M
Great Yarmouth (North Denes), Norfolk.
Grindale Field, Humberside.
Halfpenny Green, Staffs.
Hamble, Hants.
Hatfield, Herts.
Haverfordwest, Dyfed.
Hawarden, Clwyd.
Hucknall, Notts.
Humberside. M
Ipswich, Suffolk.
Kemble, Glos. J
Land's End (St. Just).
Lashenden, Headcorn, Kent.
Leavesden, Herts.
Leconfield, Humberside. J
Leeds and Bradford, Yorks. M
Leeming, Yorks. J
Lee-on-Solent, Hants. J
Leicester East, Leics.
Linton-on-Ouse, Yorks. J
Liverpool, Lancs. M
London (Gatwick). BAA

London (Heathrow). BAA
London (Westland Heliport). H
Luton, Beds. M
Lydd, Kent.
Lyneham, Wilts. J
Manchester. M
Manchester (Barton).
Manston, Kent. J
Nether Thorpe, S. Yorks.
Newcastle, Northumberland. M
Newton, Notts. J
Northampton (Sywell), Northants.
Northolt, Mddx. J
Norwich, Norfolk. M
Nottingham, Notts.
Odiham, Hants. J
Oxford (Kidlington), Oxfordshire.
Paull, Humberside
Penzance Heliport, Cornwall. H
Peterborough (Sibson), Cambs.
Plymouth (Roborough), Devon.
Portland Air Station, Dorset. JH
Redhill, Surrey
Rochester, Kent.
St. Mawgan, Cornwall. J
Scilly Isles (St. Mary's).
Seething, Norfolk.
Shawbury, Salop. J
Sherburn-in-Elmet, Yorks.
Shobdon, Herefordshire.
Shoreham, Sussex. M
Skegness (Ingoldmells), Lincs.
Sleap, Salop.
Southampton, Hants.
Southend, Essex. M
Southport (Birkdale Sands), Merseyside. M
Stansted, Essex. BAA
Stapleford Tawney, Essex.
Sturgate, Lincs.
Sunderland, Co. Durham. M
Swansea, Glam. M
Teesside, Co. Durham. M
Tern Hill, Salop. J
Thorney Island, West Sussex. J
Thruxton, Hants.
Topcliffe, Yorks. J
Valley, Anglesey. J
Waddington, Lincs. J
Warton, Lancs.
Wattisham, Suffolk. J
Weston-super-Mare, Avon.
White Waltham, Berks.
Wickenby, Lincs.
Wittering, Cambs. J
Woodford, Gtr. Manchester.
Woodvale, Merseyside. J
Wroughton, Wilts. J

Wycombe Air Park (Booker) Bucks.
Yeovil, Somerset.
Yeovilton, Somerset. J

SCOTLAND (38)

Aberdeen (Dyce). BAA
Barra, Hebrides.
Benbecula, Hebrides. CAA
Coll, Inner Hebrides. M
Dornoch.
Dounreay (Thurso).
Dundee, Angus. M
Eday. M
Edinburgh. BAA
Fair Isle.
Fetlar, Shetlands.
Glasgow. M
Glenforsa (Mull). M
Glenrothes. M
Hoy, Orkneys. M
Inverness (Dalcross). CAA
Islay (Port Ellen). CAA
Isle of Skye. M
Kinloss. J
Kirkwall. CAA
Leuchars. J
Lossiemouth. J
Machrihanish, Kintyre. J
Argyll. M
North Ronaldsay, Orkneys. M
Oban/North Connel, Argyll. M
Papa Westray, Orkneys. M
Perth (Scone).
Prestwick. BAA
Sanday, Orkneys. M
Stornoway, Hebrides. CAA
Stronsay, Orkneys. M
Sumburgh, Shetlands. CAA
Tiree. CAA
Unst. M
Westray, Orkneys. M
Whalsay, Shetlands. M
Wick. CAA

NORTHERN IRELAND (5)

Belfast (Aldergrove). S
Belfast (Harbour).
Enniskillen (St. Angelo). M
Londonderry (Eglinton).
Newtownards.

ISLE OF MAN (1)

Ronaldsway.

CHANNEL ISLANDS (3)

Alderney. S
Guernsey. S
Jersey. S

ENGLAND AND WALES

SCOTLAND

NORTHUMBERLAND

TYNE AND WEAR

Newcastle •

• Carlisle

NORTH SEA

Solway Firth

DURHAM   CLEVELAND

CUMBRIA

G.M. = Greater Manchester

W.M. = West Midlands

ISLE OF MAN

NORTH YORKSHIRE

York •

HUMBERSIDE

• Hull

IRISH SEA

Bradford • Leeds

LANCASHIRE

WEST YORKSHIRE

MERSEYSIDE

G.M.

SOUTH YORKSHIRE

Liverpool •

Manchester •

• Sheffield

CHESHIRE

DERBYSHIRE

NOTTS.

LINCOLNSHIRE

GWYNEDD

CLWYD

Stoke •

The Wash

POWYS

STAFFS.

Nottingham •

LEICS.

Norwich •

NORFOLK

SALOP

W.M.

Birmingham •

Leicester •

Coventry •

NORTHANT

CAMBRIDGE SHIRE

SUFFOLK

DYFED

HEREFORD AND WORCESTER

WARWICK.

Stratford •

BEDS.

BUCKINGHAM

HERTS.

ESSEX

WEST GLAMORGAN

GWENT

MID GLAMORGAN

GLOUCESTER

Oxford •

OXFORD.

GREATER LONDON

Swansea •

SOUTH GLAMORGAN

Cardiff •

Bristol •

AVON

WILTSHIRE

Reading •

BERKSHIRE

LONDON

SURREY

Canterbury •

KENT

Bristol Channel

SOMERSET

HAMPSHIRE

Winchester •

WEST SUSSEX

EAST SUSSEX

DEVON

DORSET

Southampton •

Portsmouth •

Exeter •

ISLE OF WIGHT

CHANNEL

CORNWALL

Plymouth •

ENGLISH

0   50   100 MILES

THE PRINCIPALITY OF WALES

Position and extent.—Wales occupies the extreme west of the central southern portion of the island of Great Britain, with a total area of 8,017 sq. miles (5,130,880 acres); it is bounded on the N. by the Irish Sea, on the S. by the Bristol Channel, on the E. by the English counties of Cheshire, Salop, Hereford and Worcester and Gloucester, and on the W. by St. George's Channel. Across the Menai Straits is the Welsh island of *Anglesey* or *Ynys Môn* (276 sq. miles), communication with which is facilitated by the Menai Suspension Bridge (1,000 ft. long), built by Telford in 1826 (freed from toll as from Jan. 1, 1941) and by the tubular railway bridge (1,100 ft. long) of the former L.M. & S. Railway, built by Stephenson in 1850. Holyheadharbour, on Holy Isle (N.W. of Anglesey), provides accommodation for a fast steam packet service to Dun Laoghaire and Dublin (70 miles).

Population.—The population at the Census of 1971 was 2,723,596 (preliminary figures), compared with 2,644,023 at the 1961 Census.

Relief.—Wales is mostly mountainous, the chief systems being those of North Wales (Snowdon 3,560 ft., Carnedd Llywelyn 3,484 ft., Carnedd Dafydd 3,426 ft.); Berwyn (Aran-mawddwy 2,970 ft.); Powys (Plinlimmon 2,468 ft., Drygan Fawr 2,115 ft., Radnor 2,163 ft.); and the Black Mountain, Brecknock Beacons and Black Forest ranges (Carmarthen Van 2,632 ft., Brecon Beacon 2,906 ft., Pen-y-gader fawr 2,660 ft.).

Hydrography.—The principal river of those rising in Wales is the *Severn* (*see* England), which flows from the slopes of Plinlimmon to the English border. The *Wye* (130 miles) also rises in the slopes of Plinlimmon. The *Usk* (56 miles) flows into the Bristol Channel, through Gwent. The *Dee* (70 miles) rises in Bala Lake and flows through the Vale of Llangollen, where an aqueduct (built by Telford in 1805) carries the Pontcysyllte branch of the Shropshire Union Canal across the valley. The estuary of the Dee is the navigable portion, 14 miles in length and about 5 miles in breadth, and the tide rushes in with dangerous speed over the " Sands of Dee". The *Towy* (68 miles), *Teifi* (50 miles), *Taff* (40 miles), *Dovey* (30 miles), *Taf* (25 miles), and *Conway* (24 miles), the last named broad and navigable, are wholly Welsh rivers.

The largest natural lake in Wales is *Bala* (Llyn Tegid) in Gwynedd, 4 miles long and about 1 mile wide; *Lake Vyrnwy* is an artificial reservoir, about the size of Bala, and forms the water supply of Liverpool, and Birmingham is supplied from a chain of reservoirs in the Elan and Clærwen valleys.

The Welsh Language.—Statistics published on Oct. 1, 1973, show that only 542,400 persons (of three years and over) in Wales were able to speak Welsh at the time of the 1971 Census, compared with 656,000 at the 1961 Census and 715,000 at the 1951 Census. One per cent. of the population could speak Welsh only, compared with 4 per cent. in 1931. The proportion of people speaking Welsh fell from 28·9 per cent. in 1951 to 20·8 per cent. in 1971. As in 1961, the Western Counties (75·9 per cent.), had the highest proportion of Welsh speakers.

Flag.—A red dragon on a green and white field (per fess argent and vert a dragon passant gules). The flag was augmented in 1953 by a royal badge on a shield encircled with a riband bearing the words *Ddraig Goch Ddyry Cychwyn* and imperially crowned. Only the unaugmented flag is flown on Government offices in Wales and, where appro-priate, in London. Both flags continue to be used elsewhere.

EARLY HISTORY

Celts and Romans.—The earliest inhabitants of whom there is any record appear to have been sub-dued or exterminated by the *Goidels* (a people of Celtic race) in the Bronze Age, and a further invasion of Celtic *Brythons* and *Belgae* followed in the ensuing Iron Age. The *Roman* conquest of South Britain and Wales was for some time successfully opposed by *Caratacus* (Caractacus or Caradog), Chieftain of the Catuvellauni and son of *Cunobelinus* (Cymbeline) King of the Trino-bantes. In A.D. 78 the conquest of Wales was completed under Julius Frontinus, and communi-cations were opened up by the construction of military roads from Chester to Caerleon-on-Usk and Caerwent, and from Chester to Conway (and thence to Carmarthen and Neath). *Christianity* was introduced (during the Roman occupation) in the 4th century.

The Anglo-Saxon Attacks.—The Anglo-Saxon invaders of South Britain drove the Celtic Goidels and Brythons into the mountain fastnesses of Wales, and into Strathclyde (Cumberland and S.W. Scotland) and Cornwall giving them the name of *Waelisc*, or Welsh (=Foreign). The West Saxons' victory of Deorham (577) isolated Wales from Cornwall and the battle of Chester (613) cut off communication with Strathclyde. In the 8th century the boundaries of the Welsh were further restricted by the annexations of Offa, King of Mercia, and counter-attacks were largely pre-vented by the construction of an artificial boundary from the Dee to the Wye (Offa's Dike). In the 9th century Rhodri Mawr united the country against further incursions of the Saxons by land and against the raids of Norse and Danish pirates by sea, but at his death his three provinces of *Gwynedd* (N.), *Powys* (Mid.) and *Dehenbarth* (S.) were divided among his three sons—Anarawd, Mervyn and Cadell—the son of the last named being Howel Dda, who codified the laws of the country, while Llewelyn ap Sitsyhlt (husband of the heiress of Gwynedd) again united the provinces and reigned as Prince from 1018 to 1023.

The Norman Conquest.—After the Norman con-quest of England, William I created Palatine counties along the Welsh frontier, and Robert FitzHamon, the Norman Earl of Gloucester, raided South Wales and erected fortresses from the Wye to Milford Haven. Henry I introduced Flemish settlers into South Wales, but after his death the Welsh rose under the leadership of Griffith ap Rhys and routed the Norman-Flemish forces at the fords of the Teifi (Cardigan) in 1136. From the early years of the 13th century the house of Gwynedd, in the north, gained an ascendancy over the whole of Wales, and Llywelyn ap Iorwerth was in constant strife with England for recognition as an inde-pendent sovereign. Llywelyn ap Gruffydd (grand-son of Llywelyn ap Iorwerth), the last native prince, was killed in 1282 during hostilities between the Welsh and English. On Feb. 7, 1301, Edward of Caernarvon, son of Edward I, was created *Prince of Wales*.

The Welsh are a distinct nationality, with a language and literature of their own, and the national bardic festival (Eisteddfod), instituted by Prince Rhys ap Griffith in 1176, is annually main-tained. These *Eisteddfodau* (sessions) form part of the *Gorsedd* (assembly), which is believed to date from the time of Prydian, a ruling prince in an age many centuries before the Christian era.

AREA AND POPULATION OF THE WELSH COUNTIES

County	Administrative Headquarters	Acreage	Population Reg. Gen.'s Est.	Rateable Value 1976	Rate Levied
				£	p.
Clwyd............	Shire Hall, Mold	599,481	374,000	36,504,760	64
Dyfed............	*Carmarthen	1,424,668	320,100	27,667,856	56·5
Gwent............	*Cwmbran	339,933	440,100	41,517,966	64
Gwynedd.........	Cty. Offices, Caernarvon	955,244	224,200	19,479,244	62
Mid Glamorgan....	*Cathays Park, Cardiff	251,732	545,206	34,312,011	63·5–70
Powys...........	*Llandrindod Wells	1,254,664	100,800	7,814,102	52·6
South Glamorgan...	Newport Rd., Cardiff	102,807	391,100	45,550,117	59
West Glamorgan...	Guildhall, Swansea	201,712	371,700	35,974,149	69·5

*County Hall

MUNICIPAL DIRECTORY OF WALES

District Councils

Those accorded CITY Status are shown in SMALL CAPITALS; those with Borough Status are distinguished by having § prefixed.

District	Popula-tion (Reg. G's Estimate)	Rateable Value 1976 £	Domestic Rate Levied p.	Chief Executive	Chairman 1976–77 (a) Mayor (b) Lord Mayor
§Aberconwy, Gwynedd............	50,200	4,933,129	87·4–97·9	J. P. Hughes	(a) H. L. Jones
§Afan, West Glamorgan...........	59,000	8,487,445	104·9	W. E. Griffiths	(a) S. R. Thomas
Alyn and Deeside, Clwyd..........	70,100	8,482,749	63·5	F. N. V. Meredith	T. M. Reidford
§Arfon, Gwynedd.................	53,300	3,706,308	63·1–71·7	D. L. Jones	(a) W. T. Hughes
Blaenau Gwent, Gwent............	84,000	5,429,881	—	R. Leadbeter	(a) W. D. R. Herbert
§Brecknock, Powys...............	37,200	2,874,277	70	D. H. Hughes, O.B.E.	(a) Rev. E. T. D. Lewis
CARDIFF, South Glamorgan........	287,000	34,322,706	78·3	H. Mansfield, O.B.E.	(b) I. Jones
Carmarthen, Dyfed...............	49,900	3,581,327	87·1	J. Thomas	W. D. Thomas
Ceredigion, Dyfed...............	57,400	4,246,041	55–61·8	J. K. Harris	W. T. K. Raw-Rees
§Colwyn, Clwyd.................	46,300	4,827,912	61·7–69·5	G. Edwards, M.B.E.	(a) D. Mars-Jones
Cynon Valley, Mid Glamorgan......	69,600	4,191,044	92·6–96·9	G. W. Hosgood	(a) T. C. McCue
§Delyn, Clwyd..................	61,600	5,163,793	106	G. A. McCartney	(a) M. I. Glazier
§Dinefwr, Dyfed................	36,429	1,978,374	—	E. W. Harries	(a) G. Davies
Dwyfor, Gwynedd...............	26,100	2,085,069	63·5	E. Davies	E. J. Williams
Glyndwr, Clwyd.................	39,000	2,987,739	61·7–67·9	W. T. Williams	E. Cunnah
§Islwyn, Gwent.................	66,052	3,858,949	104·63	J. E. Rogers	(a) P. G. Bullen, D.F.C.
§Llanelli, Dyfed................	76,800	6,014,007	60–69	A. B. Thomas	(a) A. Bowen
§Lliw Valley, West Glamorgan......	57,800	4,226,727	107·4	J. C. Howells	(a) J. G. I. Williams
Meirionydd, Gwynedd............	30,700	3,071,777	92·6–102·2	E. J. Lloyd-Jones	R. O. Lewis
Merthyr Tydfil, Mid Glamorgan.....	63,000	3,921,777	82·7	S. Jones	(a) J. V. Davies
Monmouth, Gwent...............	67,100	5,820,718	—	G. Cummings	D. I. C. Lewis
Montgomery, Powys..............	44,200	3,151,453	52·9	I. W. Williams	H. H. Bennett
§Neath, West Glamorgan..........	65,200	6,304,407	—	I. H. K. Thorne	(a) L. C. Adams
§Newport, Gwent................	133,500	18,088,051	64·3–67·7	J. R. Long	(a) S. J. Pritchard
§Ogwr, Mid Glamorgan...........	126,570	9,097,513	69·16	M. Matthews	(a) D. M. Thomas
Preseli, Dyfed..................	63,500	6,140,028	—	G. E. Jenkins, M.B.E.	W. G. Evans
Radnor, Powys..................	19,300	1,788,372	83·5–89·5	W. E. Price	J. D. A. Thompson
§Rhondda, Mid Glamorgan........	86,400	3,656,976	110·08	G. Evans	(a) Mrs. M. E. Collins
§Rhuddlan, Clwyd...............	49,900	5,434,376	107·71	F. J. K. Davies	(a) R. G. Spacey
Rhymney Valley, Mid Glamorgan....	105,700	6,439,815	78·69	D. W. C. Morgan	J. G. Davies
South Pembrokeshire, Dyfed.......	37,600	5,709,727	60·6–63·6	P. F. Klee	B. Williams
SWANSEA, West Glamorgan........	188,350	16,629,650	77	A. N. F. Rees	(a) W. W. Sivertsen
§Taff-Ely, Mid Glamorgan..........	89,600	7,359,625	76·8	G. Hockin	(a) D. J. Harrison
§Torfaen, Gwent.................	89,800	7,481,559	83·5–88·1	M. B. Mehta	(a) D. W. Puddle,
§Vale of Glamorgan, South Glamorgan	106,380	10,804,453	79·3	J. C. Colley	(a) P. C. Chapple [B.E.M.
§Wrexham Maelor, Clwyd..........	108,000	9,450,108	61·1–63·1	T. L. Williams, O.B.E.	(a) N. I. Wright
§Ynys Môn (Isle of Anglesey), Gwynedd......................	63,200	5,682,961	83–87	P. Lloyd	(a) Mrs. M. A. Edwards, M.B.E.

LORDS LIEUTENANT, HIGH SHERIFFS AND CHAIRMEN OF COUNTY COUNCILS

County	Lord Lieutenant	High Sheriff (1976–77)	Chairman of C.C.
(1) Clwyd...........	(vacant)	Capt. W. R. Williams	D. P. Schwarz
(2) Dyfed...........	Col. The Hon. R. H. Philipps, M.B.E.	T. A. Owen	C. M. George, O.B.E.
(3) Gwent...........	Col. E. R. Hill, D.S.O.	R. V. C. Jones	A. J. West
(4) Gwynedd........	Sir R. H. D. Williams-Bulkeley, Bt.	A. C. Maby, C.B.E.	R. G. Williams
(5) Mid Glamorgan...	Col. Sir Cennydd Traherne, K.G., T.D.	D. G. Badham, C.B.E.	C. Stanfield
(6) Powys...........	Col. J. L. Corbett-Winder, O.B.E., M.C.	Hon. H. J. L. Philipps	S. G. Pritchard
(7) South Glamorgan.	} *as Mid-Glamorgan*	J. G. Gaskell, T.D.	J. D. Leonard, O.B.E.
(8) West Glamorgan..		M. Thomas	W. Jones

WELSH COUNTY OFFICIALS

County	Chief Executive	County Treasurer	Chief Constable
(1) Clwyd...........	T. M. Haydn Rees, C.B.E.	E. Hughes	P. A. Myers, Q.P.M. (*a*)
(2) Dyfed...........	G. R. Peregrine	R. Silk	R. B. Thomas, Q.P.M. (*c*)
(3) Gwent.........	J. A. D. Bray	V. C. Vellacott	W. Farley, O.B.E., M.C., Q.P.M.
(4) Gwynedd......	D. E. A. Jones	W. E. Evans	(*see* Clwyd) (*a*)
(5) Mid Glamorgan...	T. V. Walters	R. K. Jacey	T. G. Morris, C.B.E., Q.P.M. (*b*)
(6) Powys...........	T. F. G. Young	S. V. Woodhouse	(*see* Dyfed) (*c*)
(7) South Glamorgan.	W. P. Davey	J. H. Dallard	} (*see* Mid Glamorgan) (*b*)
(8) West Glamorgan..	M. E. J. Rush	J. L. Couch	

(*a*) North Wales Police Authority; (*b*) South Wales Police Authority; (*c*) Dyfed & Powys Police Authority.

CARDIFF

CARDIFF (South Glamorgan) at the mouth of the rivers Taff, Rhymney and Ely, is the capital City of Wales and one of Britain's major administrative, commercial and office centres. It has many industries including steel works, car component manufacturing, cigars and a flourishing port with a substantial and varied trade, including citrus fruits and timber. There are many fine buildings in the civic centre started early this century which includes the City Hall, the National Museum of Wales, University Buildings, Law Courts, Welsh Office, County Hall, Police Headquarters and the Temple of Peace and Health. Also in the city are Llandaff Cathedral, the Welsh National Folk Museum at St. Fagans and Cardiff Castle.

New buildings include the Sherman Theatre and the Cardiff College of Music and Drama. The City returns four Members to Parliament. Population, 287,000.

Rt. Hon. Lord Mayor (1976–77), I. Jones.
Stipendiary Magistrate, Sir Lincoln Hallinan.
Chief Executive, H. Mansfield, O.B.E.

SWANSEA

SWANSEA (in Welsh, Abertawe), is a City and a seaport of West Glamorgan with its own municipal airport. The beautiful Gower Peninsula was brought within the City boundary under local Government reform on April 1, 1974. The trade of the port includes coal, patent fuel, ores, and the import and export of oil. The municipal area is 60,511 acres, with a population (1975 est.) of 188,350.

The principal buildings are the Norman Castle (rebuilt in 1330), the Royal Institution of South Wales, founded in 1835 (containing Museum and Library), the University College at Singleton and the Guildhall, containing the Brangwyn panels. Swansea was chartered by the Earl of Warwick, *circa* 1158–1184, and further charters were granted by King John, Henry III., Edward II., Edward III. and James II., 2 from Cromwell and 1 Lord Marcher.
Mayor (1976–77), W. W. Sivertsen.
Chief Executive, A. N. F. Rees.

THE KINGDOM OF SCOTLAND

Position and Extent.—The Kingdom of Scotland occupies the northern portion of the main island of Great Britain and includes the Inner and Outer Hebrides, and the Orkney, Shetland, and many other islands. The Kingdom lies between 60° 51′ 30″ and 54° 38′ N. latitude and between 1° 45′ 32″ and 6° 14′ W. longitude, its southern neighbour being the Kingdom of England, with the Atlantic Ocean on the N. and W., and the North Sea on the E. The greatest length of the mainland (Cape Wrath to the Mull of Galloway) is 274 miles, and the greatest breadth (Buchan Ness to Applecross) is 154 miles. The total area of the Kingdom is 29,798 square miles (or 19,068,724 acres) exclusive of inland water, tidal water and foreshore. The population (1971 Census, prelim.) was 5,227,706, an increase of 48,362 or 0.09 per cent. annually since the census of 1961. The average density of the population in 1971 was 175 persons per square mile, compared with 171 persons per square mile in 1951.

Land's End to John o' Groats.—The customary measurement of the Island of Great Britain is from the site of John o' Groat's house, near Duncansby Head, Caithness (at the N.E. extremity of the island) to Land's End, Cornwall (at the S.W. extremity), a total distance of 603 miles in a straight line and (approximately) 900 by road. But the site of the house of John de Groot (with its 8 doors and octagonal table, to solve the question of precedence between John and his 7 brothers) is about 4 miles S.W. of Duncansby Head, while Dunnet Head (also in Caithness) extends farther N. than Duncansby. John de Groot is believed to have obtained permission to settle in Caithness (from the Netherlands) in the reign of James IV (1488–1513).

Relief.—There are three natural orographic divisions of Scotland. The *Souther Uplands* have their highest points in Merrick (2,764 feet), Rinns of Kells (2,668 feet), and Cairnsmuir of Carsphairn (2,612 feet), in Kirkcudbright; Hartfell (2,651 feet) in Dumfries; and Broad Law (2,754 feet) in Peebles. The *Central Lowlands* include the valleys of the Tay, Forth and Clyde, and the cities of Edinburgh, the capital of the Kingdom, and Glasgow, its principal seaport. The heather-clad *Northern Highlands* extend almost from the extreme north of the mainland to the central lowlands, and are divided into a northern and southern system by the *Great Glen*; they contain, in the central Grampian Hills, Ben Nevis (4,406 feet), the highest point in the British Isles, and Ben Muich Dhui (4,296 feet). The *Cheviot Hills* form a natural boundary between Scotland and England, their highest point being The Cheviot (2,676 feet).

Hydrography.—The principal river of Scotland is the *Clyde* (106 miles), one of the most commercial rivers in the world, with the greatest commercial estuary in Scotland. The Clyde is formed by the junction of Daer and Portrail water, and flows through the city and port of Glasgow to the Firth of Clyde. During its course it passes over the picturesque *Falls of Clyde*, Bonnington Linn (30 feet), Corra Linn (84 feet), Dundaff Linn (10 feet) and Stonebyres Linn (80 feet), above and below Lanark. The *Tweed* (96 miles) has important woollen industries in its valley. The *Tay*, noted for its salmon, and the longest river in Scotland (117 miles, flows into the North Sea, with Dundee (the centre of the jute industry) on the estuary, which is spanned by the *Tay Bridge* (10,289 ft.), opened in 1887, and the *Tay Road Bridge* (7,365 ft.), opened by H.M. Queen Elizabeth the Queen Mother on Aug. 18, 1966. The *Dee* (90 miles), a noted salmon river, flows through scenery of unequalled beauty to the North Sea at Aberdeen. The *Spey* (110 miles),

the swiftest flowing river in the British Isles, and also noted for its salmon and its scenery, flows into the Moray Firth. The *Forth* (66 miles), navigable to Stirling, is spanned by the *Forth (Railway) Bridge* (1890), constructed at a cost of £3,000,000, with a length of 5,330 ft., and the *Forth (Road) Bridge*, with a total length of 6,156 ft. (over water) and a single span of 3,300 ft. The latter was completed in 1964 at a cost of £20,000,000.

The waterfall, *Eas-Coul-Aulin* in Sutherland with a total height of 658 ft. and the *Falls of Glomach* in Ross-shire, with a drop of 370 feet, are the highest in the British Isles; the *Grey Mare's Tail* (Dumfriesshire) is 200 feet.

The *lochs* are the principal hydrographic feature of the Kingdom, both on the mainland and in many of the Islands. The largest in the Kingdom and in Great Britain is *Loch Lomond* (24 miles long), with Lochs Awe, Tay, Rannoch and Ericht in the Grampian valleys; *Loch Ness* (24 miles long and 800 feet deep), with Lochs Oich and Lochy, in the Great Glen; and Lochs Shin (20 miles) and Maree in the northern Highlands.

Climate.—The general climatic values for Scotland are given below, together with the corresponding values for England and Wales within brackets—mean air temperature reduced to sea level 47.1° F. (49.7); *rainfall*, 50.3 inches (35.2); number of days with rain 217 (188); mean hours per day of bright sunshine, 3.36 (3.96).

Gaelic Language.—The preliminary report on the 1961 Census of Scotland showed that 76,587 persons were Gaelic speakers, compared with 95,447 in 1951. 1,079 persons spoke Gaelic only and not English (compared with 2,178 in 1951). The majority of Gaelic speakers lived in the counties of Ross and Cromarty (38.29 per cent.) and Inverness (24.44 per cent.). 75,508 persons spoke both Gaelic and English, compared with 93,269 in 1951.

Commerce.—The principal exports are machinery, ships and vehicles, iron and steel manufacturers, non-ferrous metals, woollen and worsted yarns and products, food and drink and textile materials. Whisky continues to be the leading export to dollar countries.

THE SCOTTISH ISLANDS

The preliminary report on the 1971 Census of Scotland showed a continued decline in the population of the islands. The populations at April 25, 1971, with 1961 populations in parenthesis, included: Islay, 3,825 (1961, *3,871*); Mull (including Iona, etc.), 1,560 (*1,635*); Coll and Tiree, 1,021 (*1,173*); Skye 7,372 (*7,772*); Barra, 1,087 (*1,564*); North Uist, 1,732 (*1,982*); South Uist, 3,781 (*4,000*).

Orkney.—About 6 miles N. of the Caithness coast, separated from the mainland by the *Pentland Firth*, is the island county of Orkney, a group of 90 islands and islets ("holms" and "skerries"), of which one-third are inhabited. The total area of the group is 375½ square miles, with a population (1971 Census, preliminary) of 17,075 (1961, *18,888*). 1971 populations of the islands (with 1961 figures in italic) are: Eday, 179 (*202*); Hoy and Walls, 531 (*699*); Mainland, 6,502 (*7,764*); N. Ronaldsay, 134 (*166*); Rousay, 256 (*350*); Sanday, 592 (*682*); Shapinsay, 346 (*432*); S. Ronaldsay, 990 (*1,275*); Stronsay, 440 (*497*); Westray 841 (*1,015*), Kirkwall (4,618), in *Mainland* (Pomona), the largest island of the group, is the capital of the county. Many of the Orkney (and Shetland) Islands contain *brochs* (Pictish towers) and other Pictish and Scandinavian remains. *Scapa Flow*, between *Mainland* and *Hoy*, was the war station of the Grand Fleet from 1914–19 and the scene of the scuttling of the surrendered German High Seas Fleet (June 21, 1919).

Zetland.—About 50 miles N. of Orkney (with the detached Fair Isle at 25 miles N.) is the island county of Zetland or Shetland, a group of about 100 islands and islets, of which one-fifth are in-habited. The total area of the group is 551 square miles, with a population (1971 Census, prelim.) of 17,298 (1961, 17,978). Lerwick (6,107), in *Main-land* (the largest and principal island), is the capital of the county. *Fair Isle*, the southernmost of the group is famous for handknitted hosiery, and *Unst* (with Fair Isle, 1,129) for the finest of the Shetland woollen work for which the county is famous. *Muckle Flugga*, about 1 mile N. of Unst, is the most northerly of the group and of the British Isles (60° 51′ 30″ N. lat.).

Western Islands.—Off the W. coast, at varying distances, and extending from Sutherland to Argyll, are over 500 islands and islets, of which 102 are inhabited. The total area of these Western Islands is 2,812 square miles, but owing to the mountainous surface of the land only about 300 square miles are under cultivation. *The Hebrides.*—Until the closing years of the 13th century " The Hebrides " included other Scottish islands in the Firth of Clyde, the peninsula of Kintyre (Argyllshire), the Isle of Man, and the (Irish) Isle of Rathlin. The ori-gin of the name is stated to be the Greek *Eboudai*, latinized as *Hebudes* by Pliny, and corrupted to its present form. The Norwegian name *Sudreyjar* (Southern Islands) was latinized as *Sodoreness*, a name that survives in the Anglican bishopric of " Sodor and Man." The *Inner Hebrides* include the island of *Skye* (643 square miles—capital, Por-tree, famous as a refuge of Prince Charlie after his defeat at Culloden, Inverness-shire, in 1746), which contains the *Cuillins* (Sgurr Alasdair 3,309 feet), *Red Hills* (Ben Caillich, 2,403 feet), and many other picturesque mountains; *Mull* (367 square miles), containing *Ben More* (3,169 feet), *Ben Buy* (2,354 feet), and *Ben Creach* (2,289 feet); *Jura* (160 square miles), with a chain of hills culmi-nating in the *Paps of Jura* (Beinn-an-Oir, 2,571 feet and Beinn Chaolais, 2,407 feet); *Islay* (235 square miles), and many smaller islands. The *Outer Hebrides*, separated from the mainland by the *Minch*, include *Lewis with Harris* (770 square miles), celebrated for its homespun " Tweeds," *North Uist, South Uist, Barra* and other islands. Thirteen miles W. of *Stornoway* (the largest town of Lewis and of the Hebrides) are the " Druidical " remains of *Callanish*, a well-preserved series of monolithic circles, cruciform in general arrange-ment, but usually regarded as a heathen monu-ment of the remote Stone Age.

EARLY HISTORY

Prehistoric Man.—The *Picts*, believed to be of non-Aryan origin, and stated to have been named *Picti* by the Romans on account of the tribal habit of painting the body, seem to have inhabited the whole of North Britain and to have spread over the north of Ireland. *Picts' Houses* are most fre-quent in the northern counties of Caithness and Sutherland and in the Orkney Islands. Celtic *Goidels, Brythons* and *Belgae* arrived from Belgic Gaul during the latter part of the Bronze Age and in the early Iron Age, and except in the extreme north of the mainland and in the islands the civilization and speech of the people were definitely Celtic at the time of the Roman Invasion of Britain.

The Roman Invasion.—In A.D. 80 Julius Agricola extended the Roman conquests in Britain by advancing into *Caledonia* as far as the " Grampian " Hills, but after a victory at *Mons Graupius* (since corrupted to " Grampius ") he was recalled, and no further advance was made for about 60 years, when the Roman frontier was carried to the isthmus between the Forth and Clyde and marked by the *Wall of Pius*, towards which ran military roads from the Cheviots. The Roman occupation of Southern Caledonia was not so effective as that of South Britain, and before the close of the second century the northern limit of Roman Britain had receded to *Hadrian's Wall* (Tyne to Solway Firth).

The Scots.—During the later years of the Roman occupation the garrison was continually harassed by Pictish tribes north of the Wall, aided by Scots (the Gaelic tribe then dominant in Ireland), and when the garrison was withdrawn these *Picts* and *Scots* were the principal enemies of the Celtic Brythons, who are believed to have called in the Saxons to protect them from the invasions of their neighbours. A relic of the struggle between Pict and Brython is still to be seen in the *Catrail*, or Picts' Work Dyke, of Roxburgh (from Torwood-lee, near Galashiels, to Peel Fell in the Cheviots). *Christianity* was introduced into Southern Caledonia about 380 by missionaries from Romanized Britain, who penetrated to the northern districts and islands. After the withdrawal (or absorption) of the Roman garrison of Britain there were many years of tribal warfare between the Picts and Scots, the Brythonic Waelisc (Welsh) of Strathclyde (South-west Scotland and Cumberland), and the Anglo-Saxons of the Lothians. The Waelisc were isolated from their kinsmen in Wales by the victory of the West Saxons at Chester (613), and towards the close of the 9th century the Scots under *Kenneth Macalpine* became the dominant power in Cale-donia. In the reign of Malcolm I (943–954) the Brythons of Waelisc (Welsh) of Strathclyde were brought into subjection, the lowland kingdom of the English (Lothian) being conquered by Mal-colm II (1005–1034). From the close of the 11th century until the middle of the 16th there were constant wars between Scotland and England, the outstanding figures in the struggle being *William Wallace*, who defeated the English at Stirling Bridge (1297) and *Robert Bruce*, who won the victory of Bannockburn (1314). James IV and many of his nobles fell at the disastrous battle of Flodden (1513), and in 1603 James VI, the Stuart King of Scotland and the heir to the Tudor line of England (his mother, Mary Queen of Scots, was the great-granddaughter of Henry VII), succeeded Queen Elizabeth I on the throne, his successors reigning as Sovereigns of Great Britain. After the abdication (by flight) of James VII and II, the crown devolved upon William III (grand-son of Charles I) and Mary (daughter of James VII and II) and, their issue failing, upon Anne (second daughter of James VII and II). Anne's children died young, and the throne developed upon George I (great-grandson of James VI and I). In 1689 Graham of Claverhouse " roused the High-lands " on behalf of James VII and II, but died after a military success at Killiecrankie. In 1715, armed risings led to the indecisive battle of Sheriff-muir, but the movement died down until 1745, when Prince Charles Edward defeated the Royalist troops under Sir John Cope at Prestonpans and advanced to Derby in England (1746). From Derby, the adherents of " James VIII and III " (the title claimed for his father by Prince Charles Edward) fell back on the defensive, and the *Jacobite* movement was finally crushed by the Royalist troops under the Duke of Cumberland at *Culloden* (April 16, 1746).

The Hebrides did not become part of the Kingdom of Scotland until 1266, when they were ceded to Alexander III by Magnus of Norway. Orkney and Shetland fell to the Scottish Crown as a pledge for the unpaid dowry of Margaret of Denmark, wife of James III, in 1468, the Danish suzerainty being formally relinquished in 1590.

SCOTLAND

SHETLAND
ISLAND
AREA

Lerwick

ORKNEY
ISLAND
AREA

Kirkwall

WESTERN
ISLES
ISLAND
AREA

Stornoway

H I G H L A N D

Inverness

GRAMPIAN

Aberdeen

REGION

R E G I O N

T A Y S I D E

Dundee

REGION

Cupar

FIFE

REGION

CENTRAL
Stirling
REGION

S T R A T H C L Y D E

Edinburgh

LOTHIANS REGION

BORDERS

Glasgow

Newtown,
St.Boswells
REGION

R E G I O N

50 miles

DUMFRIES AND
Dumfries
GALLOWAY REGION

NORTHERN
IRELAND

ENGLAND

AREA AND POPULATION OF SCOTTISH REGIONAL COUNCILS, ETC.

Region	Administrative Headquarters	Acres	Population	Rateable value	Rate Levied
				£	p
Borders	Newtown St. Boswells	1,154,288	99,409	4,620,699	117
Central	Stirling	650,022	269,281	19,878,899	110
Dumfries and Galloway	Dumfries	1,574,400	143,667	6,977,407	97—115
Fife	Glenrothes, Fife	322,560	337,690	19,357,801	92—95
Grampian	Aberdeen	2,151,000	450,000	23,000,000	108
Highland	Inverness	6,209,710	178,268	9,419,489	—
Lothian	Edinburgh	433,920	754,008	50,179,500	116
Orkney	Kirkwall	217,600	17,675	386,679	142
Shetland	Lerwick	352,640	19,135	463,641	113
Strathclyde	Glasgow	3,392,000	2,504,909	163,700,638	111
Tayside	Dundee	1,894,080	401,987	24,959,922	107
Western Isles	Stornoway, Lewis	716,800	29,615	702,240	141—168

CHIEF EXECUTIVES, CHAIRMEN AND CHIEF CONSTABLES

Region	Chief Executive	Chairman (a) Convener	Chief Constable
Borders	K. J. Clark	(a) J. M. Askew, C.B.E.	J. H. Orr, O.B.E.
Central	E. Geddes	(a) J. Anderson	E. Frizzell
Dumfries and Galloway	L. T. Carnegie	(a) J. F. Niven, C.B.E.	A. Campbell, Q.P.M.
Fife	J. M. Dunlop	(a) G. Sharp, O.B.E.	R. F. Murison, Q.P.M.
Grampian	J. L. Russell	(a) A. F. Mutch	A. Morrison
Highland	F. G. Armstrong	Rev. M. J. Nicolson	D. B. Henderson
Lothian	R. G. E. Peggie	(a) P. Wilson	J. H. Orr, O.B.E.
Orkney	H. A. G. Lapsley	G. R. Marwick	D. B. Henderson
Shetland	I. R. Clark	(a) A. I. Tulloch	D. B. Henderson
Strathclyde	L. Boyle, Ph.D.	Rev. G. M. Shaw	D. B. McNee, Q.P.M.
Tayside	A. H. Martin	(a) I. A. D. Millar, M.C.	J. R. Little
Western Isles	R. MacIver	Rev. D. Macaulay	D. B. Henderson

PRECEDENCE IN SCOTLAND

The Sovereign.

The Prince Philip, Duke of Edinburgh.

The Lord High Commissioner to the General Assembly (while that Assembly *is sitting*).

The Duke of Rothesay (eldest son of the Sovereign). H.R.H. Prince Andrew. H.R.H. Prince Edward.

Nephews of the Sovereign.

Lords Lieutenant of Counties, Lord Provosts of Counties of Cities, and Sheriffs Principal (successively — within their own localities and during holding of office).

Lord Chancellor of Great Britain.

Moderator of the General Assembly of the Church of Scotland.

The Prime Minister.

Keepers of the Great Seal and of the Privy Seal (successively —if Peers).

Hereditary Lord High Constable of Scotland. Hereditary Master of the Household.

Dukes (successively) of England, Scotland, Great Britain and United Kingdom (including Ireland since date of Union).

Eldest sons of Royal Dukes.

Marquesses, in same order as Dukes.

Dukes' eldest sons.

Earls, in order as Dukes.

Younger sons of Dukes of Blood Royal.

Marquesses' eldest sons.

Dukes' younger sons.

Keepers of the Great Seal and of the Privy Seal (successively —if not Peers).

Lord Justice General.

Lord Clerk Register.

Lord Advocate.

Lord Justice Clerk.

Viscounts, in order as Dukes.

Earls' eldest sons.

Marquesses' younger sons.

Lord-Barons, in order as Dukes.

Viscounts' eldest sons.

Earls' younger sons.

Lord-Barons' eldest sons.

Knights of the Garter.

Privy Councillors not included in above ranks.

Senators of Coll. of Justice (Lords of Session).

Viscounts' younger sons.

Lord-Barons' younger sons.

Sons of Life Peers.

Baronets.

Knights of the Thistle.

Knights of other Orders as in England.

Solicitor-General for Scotland.

Lord Lyon King of Arms.

Sheriffs Principal (except as shown in column 1).

Knights Bachelor.

Sheriffs Substitute.

Companions of Orders as in England.

Commanders of Royal Victorian and British Empire Orders.

Eldest sons of younger sons of Peers.

Companions of Distinguished Service Order.

Members (Class 4) Royal Victorian Order.

Officers of British Empire Order.

Baronets' eldest sons.

Knights' eldest sons successively (from Garter to Bachelor).

Members of Class 5 of Royal Victorian Order.

Members of British Empire Order.

Baronets' younger sons.

Knights' younger sons.

Queen's Counsel.

Barons-feudal.

Esquires.

Gentlemen.

LORD-LIEUTENANTS IN SCOTLAND

NAME	INFORMAL TITLE	PART OF REGION IN WHICH FUNCTIONS ARE DISCHARGED
	Lord-Lieutenant of:—	**Highland Region:—**
The Viscount Thurso	Caithness	The district of Caithness
Col. A. MacD. Gilmour, O.B.E., M.C.	Sutherland	The district of Sutherland
Capt. A. F. Matheson, R.N. (Ret.)	Ross and Cromarty	The districts of Ross and Cromarty and Skye and Lochalsh
Colonel Sir Donald Hamish Cameron of Lochiel, K.T., C.V.O., T.D.	Inverness	The districts of Lochaber, Inverness and Badenoch and Strathspey
The Earl of Leven and Melville	Nairn	The district of Nairn
		Grampian Region:—
Capt. I. M. Tennant	Morayshire	Such part of the county of Moray as existing before 16th May 1975 as lies within the region.
Colonel T. R. Gordon-Duff of Drummuir, M.C.	Banffshire	The county of Banff as existing before 16th May 1975
M. Mackie, C.B.E.	Aberdeenshire	The county of Aberdeen as existing before 16th May 1975 except the electoral divisions of Bucksburn, Newhills Landward, Old Machar and Stoneywood and the Parishes of Dyce and Peterculter
G. A. M. Saunders	Kincardineshire	The county of Kincardine as existing before 16th May 1975 except the electoral division of Nigg
		Tayside Region:—
The Earl of Dalhousie, K.T., C.B.E., M.C.	Angus	The district of Angus
Maj. D. H. Butter, M.C.	Perth and Kinross	The district of Perth and Kinross
		Fife Region:—
Major The Lord Kilmany, P.C., M.C.	Fife	The whole region
		Lothian Region:—
The Marquess of Linlithgow, M.C.	West Lothian	The district of West Lothian
Sir John Dutton Clerk of Penicuik, Bt., C.B.E., V.R.D.	Midlothian	The district of Midlothian
The Earl of Wemyss and March, K.T.	East Lothian	The district of East Lothian
		Central Region:—
The Earl of Mar and Kellie	Clackmannan	The district of Clackmannan
Colonel The Viscount Younger of Leckie, O.B.E.	Stirling and Falkirk	The districts of Stirling and Falkirk
		Borders Region:—
Sir Robert Heatlie Scott, G.C.M.G., C.B.E.	Tweeddale	The district of Tweeddale
The Duke of Buccleuch and Queensberry, V.R.D.	Roxburgh, Ettrick and Lauderdale	The districts of Roxburgh and of Ettrick and Lauderdale
Lt.-Col. W. B. Swan, C.B.E., T.D.	Berwickshire	The district of Berwickshire
		Strathclyde Region:—
The Lord Maclean, K.T., P.C., G.C.V.O., P.C., K.B.E.	Argyll and Bute	The district of Argyll and Bute
J. C. Robertson	Dunbartonshire	The districts of Dumbarton, Clydebank, Bearsden and Milngavie, Strathkelvin and Cumbernauld and Kilsyth
Col. The Lord Clydesmuir, K.T., C.B., M.B.E., T.D.	Lanarkshire	The districts of Monklands, Motherwell, Hamilton, East Kilbride and Lanark
The Viscount Muirshiel, K.T., P.C. C.H., C.M.G.	Renfrewshire	The districts of Eastwood, Renfrew and Inverclyde
Col. B. M. Knox, M.C., T.D.	Ayr and Arran	The districts of Cunninghame, Kilmarnock and Loudon, Kyle and Carrick and Cumnock and Doon Valley
		Dumfries and Galloway Region:—
The Earl of Stair, C.V.O., M.B.E.	Wigtown	The district of Wigtown
Col. G. G. M. Batchelor	The stewartry of Kirkcudbright	The district of Stewartry
Lt.-Gen. Sir William Turner, K.B.E., C.B., D.S.O.	Dumfries	The districts of Nithsdale and of Annandale and Eskdale
Col. R. A. A. S. Macrae, M.B.E.	Orkney	The islands area of Orkney
R. H. W. Bruce, C.B.E.	Shetland	The islands area of Shetland
Major S. Longbotham	Western Isles	The islands area of the Western Isles

NOTE.—The Lord Provosts of the four city districts of Aberdeen, Dundee, Edinburgh and Glasgow are Lord-Lieutenants for those districts *ex officio.*

PRINCIPAL SCOTTISH CITIES

EDINBURGH

EDINBURGH, the Capital of Scotland, has a municipal area of 34,781 acres, and a population of 475,042. The city is built on a group of hills and contains in Princes Street one of the most beautiful thoroughfares in the world. The principal buildings are the Castle, which includes St. Margaret's Chapel, the oldest building in Edinburgh, and near it, the Scottish National War Memorial; the Palace of Holyroodhouse; Parliament House, the present seat of the judicature; the University; St. Giles, Cathedral (restored 1879–83); St. Mary's (Scottish Episcopal) Cathedral (Sir Gilbert Scott); the General Register House (Robert Adam): the National and the Signet Libraries; the National Gallery; the Royal Scottish Academy; and the National Portrait Gallery. The city is governed by the City of Edinburgh District Council which includes the area of South Queensferry, Kirkliston, Currie, Ratho and Balerno and sends 9 Members to Parliament.

Rt. Hon. Lord Provost, J. Millar.
Chief Executive, E. G. Glendinning.

GLASGOW

GLASGOW, a Royal Burgh, City, largest District in the Strathclyde Region, and the principal commercial and industrial centre in Scotland, has a municipal area of 48,822 acres and a population of 880,617. The city occupies the north and south banks of the Clyde, one of the chief commercial estuaries in the world. The principal industries include ships, heavy engineering, motor cars, aero and marine engines, chemicals, printing, carpet, cotton thread, food processing, etc. The chief buildings are the Early Gothic former Cathedral, the University (Sir Gilbert Scott), the City Chambers, Pollok House, the Transport Museum, Kelvingrove Art Galleries and the Mitchell Library, Home of Scottish National Orchestra, Scottish Opera, etc. The city is governed by the City of Glasgow District Council with 72 Members and sends 15 Members to Parliament.

Rt. Hon. Lord Provost, P. T. McCann.
Chief Executive, C. Murdoch.

ABERDEEN

ABERDEEN, a City and a Royal, Municipal and Parliamentary Burgh, 126 miles N.E. of Edinburgh, received its charter as a Royal Burgh from William the Lion in 1179. The municipal area is 46,557 acres, with a resident population of 212,237. The chief industries are quarrying and granite working, white fish, salmon and herring fisheries, engineering, chemicals, plastics, ship-building, tourism, paper-making, clothing manufacture, wool and linen fabric. The city and surrounding area is now the principal centre of North Sea oil exploration. Aberdeen is famous for its many beautiful buildings, including Marischal College, reputed to be the most imposing white granite building in the world, King's College (1494), St. Machar Church (1378), the Auld Brig o'Balgownie (1320) and the Municipal Buildings. There is a sea beach promenade which stretches for fully two and a half miles along golden sands, and at Hazlehead an open public park of 800 acres, of which 200 are wooded, with one of the finest public golf courses in Scotland and a zoo. The climate is bracing and healthy. The city is governed by a District Council of 48 Members.

The Lord Provost (1975–77), R. S. Lennox.
Chief Executive, J. F. Watt.

CHIEFS OF CLANS AND NAMES IN SCOTLAND

THE ROYAL HOUSE: H.M. The Queen.

ARBUTHNOTT: Viscount of Arbuthnott, D.S.C., Arbuthnott House, Laurencekirk, Kincardineshire.

BARCLAY: Peter C. Barclay of that Ilk, Gatemans, Stratford St. Mary, Colchester, Essex.

BORTHWICK: Maj. J. H. S. Borthwick of Borthwick, T.D., Crookston, Midlothian.

BOYD: Lord Kilmarnock, Casa de Mondragon, Ronda (Malaga), Spain.

BRODIE: Ninian Brodie of Brodie, Brodie Castle, Forres.

BRUCE: Earl of Elgin and Kincardine, Broomhall, Dunfermline, Fife.

BUCHAN: David S. Buchan of Auchmacoy, Auchmacoy, Ellon, Aberdeenshire.

BURNETT: J. C. A. Burnett of Leys, Crathes Castle, Kincardineshire.

CAMERON: Col. Sir Donald Hamish Cameron of Lochiel, K.T., C.V.O., T.D., Achnacarry, Spean Bridge, Inverness.

CAMPBELL: Duke of Argyll, Inveraray, Argyll.

CARNEGIE: Earl of Southesk, K.C.V.O., Kinnaird Castle, Brechin.

CHISHOLM: Alastair Chisholm of Chisholm (*The Chisholm*), Silver Willows, Bury St. Edmunds.

CLAN CHATTAN: K. A. Mackintosh of Clan Chattan, Maxwell Park, Gwelo, Rhodesia.

COCHRANE: Earl of Dundonald, Lochnell Castle, Ledaig, Argyllshire.

COLQUHOUN: Sir Ivar Colquhoun of Luss, Bt., Rossdhu, Luss, Dunbartonshire.

DARROCH: Captain Duncan Darroch of Gourock. The Red House, Branksome Park Rd., Camberley.

DRUMMOND: Earl of Perth, P.C., Stobhall, Perth.

DUNBAR: Sir Adrian I. Dunbar of Mochrum, Bt., Mochrum Park, Wigtownshire.

DUNDAS: Ian H. Dundas of that Ilk and Inchgarvie, Moreson, Starke Road, Bergvliet, Cape Town, S. Africa.

ELIOTT: Sir Arthur Eliott of Stobs, Bt., Redheugh, Newcastleton, Roxburghshire.

ERSKINE: Earl of Mar and Kellie, Claremont House, Alloa.

FARQUHARSON: Capt. A. A. C. Farquharson of Invercauld, Invercauld, Braemar.

FERGUSSON: Sir Charles Fergusson of Kilkerran, Bt., Kilkerran, Maybole, Ayrshire.

FORBES: Lord Forbes, K.B.E., Balforbes, Alford, Aberdeenshire.

FRASER: Lord Saltoun, M.C., Cairnbulg Castle, Fraserburgh, Aberdeenshire.

FRASER (OF LOVAT)*: Lord Lovat, D.S.O., M.C., T.D., Beaufort Castle, Beauly, Inverness-shire.

GORDON: Marquess of Huntly, Aboyne Castle, Aberdeenshire.

GRAHAM: Duke of Montrose, Auchmar, Drymen, Stirlingshire.

GRANT: Lord Strathspey, 111 Elms Ride, West Wittering, Sussex.

HAIG: Earl Haig, O.B.E., Bemersyde, Melrose, Roxborough.

HAY: Countess of Erroll, Crimonmogate, Lonmay, Aberdeenshire.

KEITH: The Earl of Kintore, Keith Hall, Inverurie, Aberdeenshire.

KENNEDY: Marquess of Ailsa, O.B.E., Cassillis House, Maybole, Ayrshire.

KERR: Marquess of Lothian, Monteviot, Ancrum, Roxburgh.

KINCAID: A. C. Kincaid of Kincaid, Murarashi, Kenya.

LAMONT: Peter N. Lamont of that Ilk, 63 Patrick Street, Blacktown, Sydney, N.S.W.

LESLIE: Earl of Rothes, Strawberry House, Chiswick Mall, W.4.

LINDSAY: Earl of Crawford and Balcarres, K.T., G.B.E., Balcarres, Colinsburgh, Fife.

McBAIN: H. M. McBain of McBain, Kinchyle House, P.O. Box 2, Hubbard Woods, Illinois, 60093, U.S.A.

MALCOLM (MACCALLUM): Col. George Malcolm of Poltalloch, Duntrune Castle, Argyll.

MACDONALD: Lord Macdonald (*The Macdonald of Macdonald*), Ostaig House, Skye.

MACDONALD OF CLANRANALD*: Ranald A. Macdonald of Clanranald, 55 Compton Road, N.1.

MACDONALD OF SLEAT (CLAN HUSTEAIN)*: Sir Ian Bosville-Macdonald of Sleat, Bt., Thorpe Hall, Rudston, Driffield, Yorks.

MACDONELL OF GLENGARRY*: Air Cdre. Aeneas R. MacDonell of Glengarry, C.B., D.F.C., 5 Sydcote, Rosendale Rd., Dulwich, London S.E.21.

MACDOUGALL: Madame Coline MacDougall of MacDougall, Dunollie, Argyll.

MACGREGOR: Sir Gregor MacGregor of MacGregor, Bt., Edinchip, Lochearnhead, Perthshire.

MACKAY: Lord Reay, 11 Wilton Crescent, S.W.1.

MACKINNON: The Mackinnon of Mackinnon, Field End, Nailsbourne, nr. Taunton, Somerset.

MACKINTOSH: The Mackintosh of Mackintosh, O.B.E., Moy Hall, Inverness.

MACLACHLAN: Madam Marjorie MacLachlan of MacLachlan, Castle Lachlan, Argyll.

MACLAREN: Donald MacLaren of MacLaren and Achleskine, 53 Gordon Mansions, Torrington Place, W.C.1.

MACLEAN: Lord Maclean, P.C., K.T., G.C.V.O., K.B.E., Duart Castle, Mull.

MACLEOD: Dame Flora Macleod of Macleod, D.B.E., Dunvegan Castle, Skye.

MACMILLAN: Gen. Sir Gordon MacMillan of MacMillan, K.C.B., K.C.V.O., C.B.E., D.S.O., M.C., Finlaystone, Langbank, Renfrewshire.

MACNAB: J. C. Macnab of Macnab (*The Macnab*), Kinnell House, Killin, Perthshire.

MACNAGHTEN: Sir Patrick Macnaghten of Macnaghten and Dundarave, Bt., Dundarave, Bushmills, Co. Antrim.

MACNEIL OF BARRA: Ian R. Macneil of Barra (*The Macneil of Barra*), Kismull Castle, Barra.

MACPHERSON: William A. Macpherson of Cluny, Newtown of Blairgowrie, Perthshire.

MACTHOMAS: Andrew P. C. MacThomas of Finegand, The Bell House, Little Wilbraham, nr. Cambridge.

MAITLAND: Earl of Lauderdale, Moberty, Airlie, by Kirriemuir, Angus.

MAR: Countess of Mar, 10 Cranberry Drive, Stourport-on-Severn, Worcs.

MARJORIBANKS: William Marjoribanks of that Ilk, Kirklands of Forglen, Banffshire.

MATHESON: Sir Torquhil Matheson of Matheson, Bt., Sanderwick Court, Frome, Somerset.

MENZIES: David R. Menzies of Menzies, Mundena, Moora, Western Australia.

MONCREIFFE: Sir Iain Moncreiffe of that Ilk, Bt., Easter Moncreiffe, Bridge of Earn, Perthshire.

MONTGOMERIE: Earl of Eglinton and Winton, Skelmorlie Castle, Ayrshire.

MORRISON: Dr. Iain M. Morrison of Ruchdi, Ruchdi, by Lochmaddy, N. Uist.

MUNRO: Patrick G. Munro of Foulis, T.D., Foulis Castle, Ross.

MURRAY: Duke of Atholl, Blair Castle, Blair Atholl, Perthshire.

NICHOLSON OF SCORRYBRECK: Ian Nicholson of Scorrybreck, 18 Hamelin Crescent, Narrabundah. Canberra, A.C.T. 2604, Australia.

OGILVY: Earl of Airlie, Cortachy Castle, Kirriemuir, Angus.

RAMSAY: Earl of Dalhousie, K.T., G.B.E., M.C., Brechin Castle, Angus.

RATTRAY: James S. Rattray of Rattray, Craighall, Rattray, Perthshire.

ROBERTSON: Langton Robertson of Struan (*Struan-Robertson*), 7 Washington Drive, Devon Pen, P.O. Box 337, Halfway Tree P.O., Kingston 10, Jamaica.

ROSE: Miss Elizabeth Rose of Kilravock, Kilravock Castle, Nairn.

ROSS: David C. Ross of that Ilk, Strathdevon House, Dollar, Clackmannanshire.

RUTHVEN: Earl of Gowrie, Castlemartin, Kilcullen, Co. Kildare, Eire.

SINCLAIR: Earl of Caithness, Hampton Court Palace, East Molesey, Surrey.

SWINTON: W. F. H. Swinton of that Ilk, Box 596, Bozeman, Montana, U.S.A.

URQUHART: Kenneth T. Urquhart of that Ilk, 4713 Orleans Blvd., Jefferson, Louisiana, U.S.A.

WALLACE: Lt.-Col. M. R. Wallace of that Ilk, Kirklands of Damside, Auchterarder, Perthshire.

WEMYSS: Michael Wemyss of that Ilk, Wemyss Castle, Fife.

Only chiefs of *whole* Names or Clans are included (except certain special instances (marked *), who though not chiefs of a " whole name ", were, or are, for some reason, *e.g.* the Macdonald forfeiture, independent). Under decision (*Campbell-Gray*, 1950) that a bearer of a " double or triple-barrelled " surname cannot be held chief of a part of such, several others cannot be included in the list at present.

THE ARMS OF SCOTLAND

ARMS.—*Or*, a lion rampant *gules*, armed and langued *azure*, within a double-tressure flory counter-flory of the second. CREST.—An imperial crown *proper*, surmounted by a lion sejant-guardant *gules* crowned *or*, holding in his dexter paw a naked sword and in the sinister a sceptre both *proper*. SUPPORTERS.—Two unicorns *argent*, armed, tufted and unguled *or*, crowned with imperial and gorged with eastern crowns, chains reflexed over the backs *or*; the dexter supporting a banner charged with the arms of Scotland, the sinister supporting a similar banner *azure*, thereon a saltire *argent*. MOTTOES.—Over the arms, " In Defens "; under the arms " Nemo me impune lacessit."

SCOTTISH DISTRICT COUNCILS

District	Administrative Headquarters	Population	Rateable Value £	District Rate Levied p.	Chief Executive	Chairman (a) Convener (b) Provost (c) Lord Provost
Aberdeen City	Aberdeen	210,000	13,211,169	123	J. F. Watt	(c) R. S. Lennox
Angus	Forfar	86,849	4,200,000	—	W. S. McCulloch, M.C.	Col. L. Gray-Cheape
Annandale and Eskdale	Annan	35,148	1,581,820	107	G. F. Murray	R. G. Greenhow
Argyll and Bute	Lochgilphead	65,000	3,184,335	66	M. A. J. Gossip	E. T. F. Spence
Badenoch and Strathspey	Kingussie	9,380	620,000	30	H. G. McCulloch	Maj. A. C. Robertson
Banff and Buchan	Banff	75,150	3,558,700	122	N. S. McAlister	W. R. Cruickshank
Bearsden and Milngavie	Bearsden	37,500	2,650,000	111	A. R. Rae	(b) W. Hamilton
Berwickshire	Duns	17,513	823,000	29	D. Dunn	J. R. Ford
Caithness	Wick	29,604	876,679	35	A. Beattie	(a) J. M. Young
Clackmannan	Alloa	47,610	2,923,416	56	A. Stewart	(a) D. MacDonald
Clydebank	Clydebank	58,292	3,324,514	169	R. A. Nixon	R. A. Calder
Cumbernauld and Kilsyth	Cumbernauld	54,063	3,400,000	40	R. Kyle, M.B.E.	(b) G. S. Murray
Cumnock and Doon Valley	Cumnock	49,100	1,735,000	46	D. T. Hemmings	(a) T. P. McIntyre
Cunninghame	Irvine	131,362	6,936,727	145	J. M. Miller	D. White, Ph.D.
Dumbarton	Dumbarton	79,035	5,984,978	73–82	L. MacKinnon	(b) J. McKinley
Dundee City	Dundee	194,732	13,255,559	51	G. S. Watson	(c) C. D. P. Farquhar
Dunfermline	Dunfermline	121,000	6,916,324	93	G. Brown	L. G. Wood
East Kilbride	East Kilbride	81,299	5,794,000	40	W. G. McNay	(b) Mrs. S. Finlayson
East Lothian	East Lothian	78,000	4,200,000	40	D. B. Miller	T. White
Eastwood	Paisley	50,573	3,266,000	39	M. D. Henry	(b) I. S. Hutchison
Edinburgh City	Edinburgh	470,085	36,870,004	146	E. G. Glendinning	(c) J. Millar
Ettrick and Lauderdale	Galashiels	32,297	1,638,751	33	D. H. Cowan	G. R. Johnston
Falkirk	Falkirk	142,000	11,740,295	62	J. P. H. Paton	(b) W. Ure, M.B.E.
Glasgow City	Glasgow	880,617	67,608,000	67	C. Murdoch	(c) P. T. McCann
Gordon	Inverurie	47,900	1,937,600	44	A. C. Kennedy	J. B. Presly
Hamilton	Hamilton	106,780	5,985,000	47	W. Johnston	R. Sherry
Inverclyde	Greenock	105,801	5,790,689	159–188	I. C. Wilson	(b) J. Walsh
Inverness	Inverness	53,179	3,287,000	30	I. J. Miller	(b) I. C. Fraser
Kilmarnock and Loudoun	Kilmarnock	83,117	4,127,114	55	J. C. W. Nicol	W. Aitken
Kincardine and Deeside	Stonehaven	36,000	1,464,039	96	Miss E. M. G. Cockburn	I. M. Frain
Kirkcaldy	Kirkcaldy	148,028	8,466,107	37–40	C. D. Chapman, O.B.E.	(a) R. King
Kyle and Carrick	Ayr	111,316	6,413,942	33	J. R. Hill	(b) A. D. Paton
Lanark	Lanark	55,017	2,801,200	42	R. G. Dalkin, E.R.D.	(a) Col. R. C. M. Monteith, M.C., T.D.
Lochaber	Fort William	19,827	1,192,884	49	R. A. Christie	Lt.-Col. J. W. Forbes, M.B.E.
Midlothian	Dalkeith	83,841	4,250,360	33	D. W. Duguid	(a) D. R. Smith
Monklands	Coatbridge	108,689	5,713,265	191	J. S. Ness	(b) T. Clarke
Moray	Elgin	80,590	4,083,402	38	J. P. C. Bell	J. M. Anderson
Motherwell	Motherwell	159,640	10,433,000	64	F. C. Marks	H. B. Sneddon, O.B.E
Nairn	Nairn	9,305	410,889	20	J. R. McCluskey	(b) Lt.-Col. H. McLean, M.B.E.
Nithsdale	Dumfries	56,141	2,954,700	21	G. D. Grant	(b) F. H. Young
North-East Fife	Cupar	64,951	3,481,000	31	H. Farquhar	Capt. D. M. Russell, R.N.(Rtd.)
Perth and Kinross	Perth	119,169	6,476,625	29	R. T. Blair	(b) H. Young
Renfrew	Paisley	208,000	12,873,901	63	W. McIntosh	(b) E. G. Conway
Ross and Cromarty	Dingwall	39,200	2,188,300	40	T. M. Aitchison	(a) The Earl of Cromartie, M.C., T.D.
Roxburgh	Hawick	35,855	1,663,853	36	W. C. Hogg	D. Atkinson, M.B.E.
Skye and Lochalsh	Isle of Skye	9,672	341,074	26	D. H. Noble	R. S. Budge
Stewartry	Kirkcudbright	22,348	1,050,000	21	W. L. Dick-Smith	J. Nelson
Stirling	Stirling	78,892	5,190,603	49	D. M. Bowie	(a) Mrs. L. M. McCaig
Strathkelvin	Kirkintilloch	80,354	4,634,000	41	A. W. Harrower	I. MacBryde
Sutherland	Golspie	11,968	375,047	41	W. M. Martin	Col. A. M. Gilmour
Tweeddale	Peebles	13,877	865,364	26	G. Gardiner	T. Blyth
West Lothian	Bathgate	121,172	6,200,000	51	D. A. Morrison	(a) W. Connolly
Wigtown	Stranraer	30,024	1,312,200	25	D. R. Wilson	D. R. Robinson

NEW TOWNS IN GREAT BRITAIN

(Populations shown are amended 1971 Census preliminary figures; *see also* Municipal Directory.

Commission for the New Towns. Glen House, Stag Place, S.W.1.—The Commission was established on October 1, 1961, under the New Towns Act, 1959, to take over new towns in England and Wales from development corporations whose purposes have been achieved or substantially achieved.

Chairman, Sir Dennis Pilcher, C.B.E.

Deputy Chairman, C. Macpherson.

Members, S. R. Collingwood; J. Cousins; G. D. Hitchcock; W. F. Hodson; A. E. Pegler.

Secretary, M. G. McKenzie, M.B.E.

New Towns Association. Glen House, Stag Place, S.W.1.

Secretary, J. C. O'Neill.

Deputy Secretary, J. R. C. Pincombe, M.B.E.

CRAWLEY, Sussex.—*Chairman*, A. E. Pegler. *Manager*, R. M. Clarke, M.C. *Offices*, Broadfield House, Crawley, Sussex. Area 6,047 acres. Population, 74,000. Estimated eventual population, 100,000.

HATFIELD, Herts.—*Chairman*, Hatfield and Welwyn Garden City Local Committee, S. R. Collingwood. *Manager*, M. W. Biggs, C.B.E. *Offices:* Church Road, Welwyn Garden City, Herts. Area, 2,340 acres. Population, 26,000. Estimated eventual population, 29,000.

HEMEL HEMPSTEAD, Herts.—*Chairman*, G. D. Hitchcock. *Manager*, Brig. J. R. Blomfield, O.B.E., M.C. *Offices*, Swan Court, Waterhouse Street, Hemel Hempstead, Herts. Area, 5,910 acres. Population, 76,000. Estimated eventual population, 80,000.

WELWYN GARDEN CITY, Herts. *Chairman*, Hatfield and Welwyn Garden City Local Committee, S. R. Collingwood. *Manager*, M. W. Biggs, C.B.E. *Offices:* Church Road, Welwyn Garden City, Herts. Area, 4,317 acres. Population, 40,700. Estimated eventual population, 50,000.

Development Corporations

AYCLIFFE, Co. Durham.—Formed 1947. *Chairman*, H. D. Stevenson. *General Manager*, G. Philipson, D.F.C. *Offices*, Churchill House, Newton Aycliffe, nr. Darlington, Co. Durham. Area, 3,074 acres. Population, 25,700. Estimated eventual population, 45,000

BASILDON, Essex.—Formed 1949. *Chairman*, A. O. Kelting. *General Manager*, A. H. Mawer, D.F.C. *Offices*, Gifford House, Basildon, Essex. Area, 7,818 acres. Population, 89,100. Estimated eventual population, 134,000.

BRACKNELL, Berks.—Formed 1949. *Chairman*. J. W. Hughes. *General Manager*, G. J. Bryan, C.M.G., C.V.O., O.B.E., M.C. *Offices*, Farley Hall, Bracknell, Berks. Area, 3,303 acres. Population, 43,000. Estimated eventual population, 60,000.

CENTRAL LANCASHIRE NEW TOWN, Lancs.—Formed 1970. *Chairman*, Sir Frank Pearson. *General Manager*, R. W. Phelps. *Offices*, Cuerden Pavillion, Bamber Bridge, Preston, Lancs. Area, 35,225 acres. Population, 242,500. Estimated eventual population, 420,000.

CORBY, Northants.—Formed 1950. *Chairman*, Sir Henry Chisholm, C.B.E. *General Manager*, Brig. H. G. W. Hamilton, C.B.E. *Offices*, 9 Queen's Square, Corby, Northants. Area, 4,423 acres. Population, 53,500. Estimated eventual population, 70,000.

CWMBRAN, Gwent.—Formed 1949. *Chairman*, The Lord Raglan. *General Manager*, R. P. Menday, M.B.E., M.C. *Offices*, Gwent House, Town Centre, Cwmbran, Gwent. Area, 3,160 acres. Population, 45,000. Estimated eventual population, 55,000.

HARLOW, Essex.—Formed 1947. *Chairman*, B. J. Perkins. *General Manager*, A. T. Bardsley. *Offices*, Gate House, The High, Harlow, Essex. Area, 6,395 acres. Population, 83,500. Estimated eventual population, 90,000.

MILTON KEYNES, Bucks.—Formed 1967. *Chairman*, The Lord Campbell of Eskan. *General Manager*, F. L. Roche. *Offices*, Wavendon Tower, Wavendon, Milton Keynes, Bucks. Area, 22,000 acres. Population, 75,000. Estimated eventual population, 250,000.

NEWTOWN, Powys.—Formed 1967. *Chairman*, E. Roberts, M.B.E. *Chief Executive*, D. P. Garbett-Edwards. *Offices*, Ladywell House, Newtown, Powys. Area, 1,497 acres. Population, 7,280. Estimated eventual population, 13,000.

NORTHAMPTON.—Formed 1968. *Chairman*, A. R. Davis, C.B.E. *General Manager*, Dr. J. C. Weston. *Offices*, Cliftonville House, Bedford Road, Northampton. Area, 19,966 acres. Population, 148,000. Estimated eventual population, 240,000.

PETERBOROUGH.—Formed 1967. *Chairman*, C. T. Higgins. *General Manager*, W. Thomas. *Offices*, Touhill Close, City Road, Peterborough. Area, 15,952 acres. Population, 105,000. Estimated eventual population, 180,000.

PETERLEE, Co. Durham.—Formed 1948. *Chairman*, D. H. Stevenson. *General Manager*, G. Philipson, D.F.C. *Offices*, Shotton Hall, Peterlee, Co. Durham. Area, 2,799 acres. Population, 27,500. Estimated eventual population, 30,000.

REDDITCH, Worcs.—Formed 1964. *Chairman*, J. H. C. Chesshire, M.C. *General Manager*, W. C. Evans. *Offices*, Holmwood, Plymouth Road, Redditch, Worcs. Area, 7,180 acres. Population, 49,000. Estimated eventual population, 90,000.

RUNCORN, Cheshire.—Formed 1964. *Chairman*, W. H. Sefton. *General Manager*, D. F. Banwell. *Offices*, Chapel Street, Runcorn, Cheshire. Area, 7,234 acres. Population, 54,327. Estimated eventual population, 100,000.

SKELMERSDALE, Lancs.—Formed 1962. *Chairman*, A. J. E. Taylor, O.B.E. *Managing Director*, E. Bradbury. *Offices*, Pennylands, Skelmersdale, Lancs. Area, 4,124 acres. Population, 41,500. Estimated eventual population, 80,000.

STEVENAGE, Herts.—Formed 1946. *Chairman* Dame Evelyn Denington, D.B.E. *General Manager* J. N. Greenwood. *Offices*, Swingate House, Stevenage, Herts. Area, 6,256 acres. Population, 76,000. Estimated eventual population, 100,000.

TELFORD, Shropshire.—Formed 1963. *Chairman*, The Lord Northfield. *General Manager*, E. Thomas. *Offices*, Priorslee Hall, Telford, Salop. Area, 19,300 acres. Population, 96,700. Estimated eventual population, 250,000.

WARRINGTON, Cheshire.—Formed 1968. *Chairman*, The Lord Hamnett. *General Manager*, D. J. Binns. *Offices*, New Town House, Buttermarket St., Warrington, Cheshire. Area, 18,612 acres. Population, 132,750. Estimated eventual population, 188,000.

WASHINGTON, Tyne and Wear.—Formed 1964, *Chairman*, Sir James Steel, C.B.E. *General Manager*. W. S. Holley. *Offices*, Usworth Hall, Washington. Area, 5,583 acres. Population, 43,000. Estimated eventual population, 80,000.

Scotland

CUMBERNAULD, Dunbartonshire.—Formed 1956. *Chairman*, Sir Donald R. Liddle, LL.D. *Chief Executive*, Brig. C. H. Cowan. *Headquarters*, Cumbernauld House, Cumbernauld. Area, 7,750 acres. Population, 45,000. Estimated eventual population, 70,000.

EAST KILBRIDE, Lanarkshire.—Formed 1947. *Chairman*, The Lord Hughes of Hawkhill, P.C., C.B.E. *Managing Director*, G. B. Young. *Offices*, Atholl House, East Kilbride, Lanarkshire. Area, 10,250 acres. Population, 75,000. Estimated eventual population, 82,000.

GLENTROTHES, Fife.—Formed 1948. *Chairman*,

R. R. Taylor, C.B.E. *General Manager*, M. Cracknell. *Offices*, New Glenrothes House, Glenrothes, Fife. Area, 5,765 acres. Population, 35,000. Estimated eventual population, 70,000.

IRVINE, Ayrshire.—Designated, 1966. *Chairman*, J. H. F. MacPherson. *Managing Director*, J. D. Marquis, D.F.C. *Offices*, Perceton House, Irvine, Ayrshire. Area, 12,440 acres. Population, 52,600. Estimated eventual population, 120,000.

LIVINGSTON, West Lothian.—Designated, 1962. *Chairman*, B. D. Misselbrook. *Chief Executive*, S. E. M. Wright. *Offices*, Livingston, West Lothian. Area, 6,692 acres. Population, 25,000. Estimated eventual population, 100,000.

Northern Ireland

(For geographical and historical notes on Ireland, see Index)

The population of Northern Ireland in 1973 was 1,536,065 (males, 754,676; females, 781,389) compared with a total population of 1,484,775 at the Census of 1966. In 1971 the number of persons in the various religious denominations (expressed as percentages of the total population) were: Roman Catholic, 31·4; Presbyterian, 26·1; Church of Ireland, 22; Methodist, 4·7; others 5·8; not stated, 9·4. Northern Ireland has a total area of 5,452 sq. miles (land, 5,206 sq. miles; inland water and tideways, 246 sq. miles) with a density of population of 293 persons per sq. mile in 1971.

Constitution and Government. A separate parliament and executive Government was established for Northern Ireland in 1921 by the Government of Ireland Act. The Northern Ireland Constitution Act, 1973, abolished the post of Governor and Parliament of Northern Ireland and provided for the transfer of certain legislative functions to a Northern Ireland Assembly and Executive. Elections for a Northern Ireland Assembly took place on June 28, 1973. Devolved Government came into operation with effect from January 1, 1974 but when the Executive collapsed the Northern Ireland Assembly was prorogued on May 29 1974. The Northern Ireland Constitution Act, 1974, which became law in July 1974, made provision for temporary arrangements for the government of Northern Ireland by the Secretary of State for Northern Ireland and also provided for the holding of elections and a Constitutional Convention. The Convention which had the purpose of considering what provision for the government of Northern Ireland was likely to command the most widespread acceptance throughout the community there, reported on November 8, 1975. The Convention was reconvened on February 3, 1976 so that it might be determined whether agreement could be reached on the specific and crucial issue of a system of Government within Northern Ireland which provided for a form of partnership and participation. No further report was made and the Convention was dissolved on March 5, 1976. Direct Rule continues in being under the terms of the Northern Ireland Act 1974.

The Privy Council

Senator Sir John Andrews K.B.E. (1957); R. J. Bailie; D. W. Bleakley; R. H. Bradford; Capt. Viscount Brookeborough; W. Craig (1963); Sir Lancelot Curran (1957); J. Dobson (1969); A. B. D. Faulkner (1959); W. K. Fitzsimmons (1965); Sir Maurice Gibson (*Lord Justice*); Senator Col. the Lord Glentoran, H.M.L. (1953); Sir Edward Jones (*Lord Justice*) (1965); B. Kelly, Q.C. (1969); H. V. Kirk (1962); Capt. W. J. Long (1966); Sir Robert Lowry (*Lord Chief Justice*); R. W. B. McConnell (1964); W. B. McIvor (1971); The Lord MacDermott, M.C. (1940); Sir Ambrose McGonigal (*Lord Justice*) (1975); Sir Herbert McVeigh (1965); W. J. Morgan (1961); The Lord Moyola; Ivan Neill (1950); P. R. H. O'Neill; The Lord O'Neill of the Maine (1956); G. B. Newe, D.LITT. (1971); Sir Robert Porter, Q.C.; The Lord Rathcavan (1922); R. Simpson (1969); Capt. Sir Norman Stronge, Bt. M.C., H.M.L. (1946); J. D. Taylor; Judge W. W. B. Topping (1967); H. W. West (1960).

Government Offices

DEPARTMENT OF FINANCE

Permanent Secretary, W. E. Bell.
Deputy Secretaries, Dr. G. I. Dent; D. J. Clement.
First Legislative Draftsman, S. F. R. Martin.
Second Legislative Draftsman, T. R. Erskine.
Senior Asst. Secretaries, H. H. Wightman; Dr. A. T. Park; C. F. Darling.

Asst. Secretaries, F. G. Dougall; A. J. Green; R. M. MacDonald; J. Y. Malley, D.S.O., D.F.C.; E. J. A. Boston.

DEPARTMENT OF THE CIVIL SERVICE

Permanent Secretary, K. R. Shimeld.
Senior Asst. Secretaries, K. Darwin; S. H. Jamieson.
Asst. Secretaries, J. Armstrong; Miss Z. I. Davies; J. S. H. Gaw; J. Murray; L. J. McClelland.

DEPARTMENT OF EDUCATION

Permanent Secretary, A. C. Brooke, C.B.
Deputy Secretary, W. Slinger.
Senior Chief Inspector, J. Ferguson.
Asst. Secretaries, T. R. Meharg; E. J. Kirkpatrick; P. K. McHugh; J. B. McAllister; J. Saulters; E. G. Martin; P. Corvill.

ROYAL ULSTER CONSTABULARY
(Knock Road, Belfast 5)

Chief Constable, K. L. Newman.
Senior Deputy Chief Constable, H. Baillie, O.B.E.
Deputy Chief Constable, J. C. Hermon, O.B.E.

ULSTER OFFICE IN LONDON
11 Berkeley Street, W.1.

Director, H. S. Oliver.
Assistant Secretary, R. McClelland.

DEPARTMENT OF ENVIRONMENT

Permanent Secretary, K. P. Bloomfield.
Deputy Secretaries, J. H. Armstrong; L. V. D. Calvert; J. F. Irvine; J. P. McGrath.
Senior Assistant Secretaries, J. A. D. Higgins; T. J. McCormick; B. M. Rutherford.
Director, Town and Country Planning Service, G. Camblin, O.B.E.
Director, Water Service, H. T. Bergin.
Director, Roads Service, T. A. N. Prescott.
Assistant Secretaries, D. Barry; J. M. Beckett; G. F. Chambers; J. P. Hewlett; J. Marsh; W. P. McIlmoyle; J. G. McKinney; B. D. Palmer; J. L. Semple; R. B. Spence; T. A. Warnock; J. F. Younger; D. C. White; R. M. Wilson; J. B. Davidson; A. Hill.

DEPARTMENT OF HEALTH & SOCIAL
SERVICES

Permanent Secretary, N. Dugdale.
Deputy Secretary, J. H. Copeland.
Senior Assistant Secretaries, F. A. Elliott; C. G. Oakes; Dr. M. Hayes.
Assistant Secretaries, R. J. Christie; W. Bell; S. W. McDowell; G. Buchanan; Miss I. M. S. Jordan; S. H. O'Fee; N. I. Kells; R. F. Mills; W. S. Long; T. M. Lyness; W. J. Sloane.
Chief Medical Officer, Dr. T. T. Baird.
Deputy Chief Medical Officer, Dr. R. J. Weir.

DEPARTMENT OF COMMERCE

Permanent Secretary, Dr. W. G. H. Quigley.
Deputy Secretary, F. T. Mais.
Director of Industrial Development, H. S. Oliver.
Asst. Directors of Industrial Development, E. R. Jolley; W. McC. Taylor; J. T. B. Quan; J. Scott; A. I. Devitt.

Senior Asst. Secretary, Dr. A. J. Howard.
Assistant Secretaries, J. B. M. Thompson; J. A. G. Whitlaw; D. McVitty; T. McCrory.
Economic Adviser, Prof. W. Black.
Financial Controller, J. E. Hawkins.
Senior Industrial Development Officers, N. H. Sherrard; R. J. Browne; P. T. Bill.
Senior Principal Scientific Officers, Dr. W. McD. Morgan; J. T. McCullins.

DEPARTMENT OF MANPOWER SERVICES

Permanent Secretary, J. Finney.
Deputy Secretary, W. N. Drummond.
Senior Assistant Secretary, D. J. Perham.
Assistant Secretaries, J. S. Crozier; T. R. N. Balmer; D. G. Slattery; R. T. O'Connor; T. R. McKnight; J. B. C. Lyttle.

DEPARTMENT OF AGRICULTURE

Permanent Secretary, J. A. Young, C.B.
Deputy Secretary, R. Shaw.
Senior Assistant Secretaries, Dr. W. H. Jack; E. Mayne.
Chief Scientific Officer, Dr. W. O. Brown.
Chief Inspector, T. Moore.
Chief Veterinary Officer, E. Conn.
Assistant Secretaries, W. H. Parker; G. H. Hodgins; E. G. Sherrard; J. C. Chalmers; D. J. Alexander; A. J. Kissock.
Chief Forestry Officer, K. F. Parkin.

CENTRAL SECRETARIAT

Head of Northern Ireland Civil Service, R. H. Kidd, C.B.
Senior Assistant Secretary, J. M. C. Parke.
Assistant Secretary, R. Ramsay.
Director of Information, T. E. M. Roberts.

THE JUDICATURE

SUPREME COURT OF JUDICATURE, THE ROYAL
COURTS OF JUSTICE (ULSTER), BELFAST.

The Rt. Hon. Sir Robert Lowry, Lord Chief Justice of Northern Ireland
Rt. Hon. Lord Justice (Sir Edward Warburton) Jones; The Rt. Hon. Lord Justice (Sir Ambrose Joseph) McGonigal; The Rt. Hon. Lord Justice (Sir Maurice White) Gibson; The Hon. Mr. Justice (Turlough) O'Donnell; The Rt. Hon. Mr. Justice (John William Basil) Kelly; The Hon. Mr. Justice (John Clarke) MacDermott; The Hon. Mr. Justice (Donald Bruce) Murray.

Secretariat

Permanent Secretary to Supreme Court and Clerk of the Crown for Northern Ireland, J. A. L. McLean, Q.C.
Asst. Secretary to the Supreme Court and Legal Secretary to the Lord Chief Justice, J. W. Wilson.

Registrar's Department

Registrar, D. S. Stephens.
Asst. Registrar, V. A. Care.
Deputy Asst. Registrar, Miss M. Cullen, M.B.E.

Chief Clerk's Department

Chief Clerk (and Registrar in Lunacy), J. K. Davis, O.B.E.
Asst. Chief Clerk and Asst. Registrar in Lunacy, R. L. G. Davison.

Bankruptcy and Chancery Registrar's Department
Registrar, J. M. Hunter.
Asst. Registrar, V. G. Bridges.

Principal Probate Registry
Chief Registrar, T. S. Townley.
Asst. Registrar, Miss M. K. M. Aiken.

Official Assignee's Department
Official Assignee, R. B. Logan.
Deputy Official Assignee, J. B. Kell.

Accountant General's Department
Accountant General, R. A. Guiler.
Chief Clerk, R. J. King.

Taxing Office
Taxing Master, A. E. Anderson, C.B.E.

Recorders
Belfast, Rt. Hon. W. W. B. Topping, Q.C.
Londonderry, D. J. Little, Q.C.

County Court Judges
Judge Babington, D.S.C., Q.C.; Judge Brown, Q.C.; Judge Chambers, Q.C.; Judge Higgins, Q.C.; Judge Johnson, Q.C.; Judge McGrath, Q.C.; Judge Rowland, Q.C.; Judge Watt, Q.C.

Crown Solicitor, H. A. Nelson.
Director of Public Prosecutions, C. B. Shaw, C.B., Q.C.

FLAG.—The national flag is that of the United Kingdom.

BELFAST

BELFAST, a City, the seat of Government of Northern Ireland, situated at the mouth of the River Lagan at its entrance to Belfast Lough, has a municipal area of 16,017 acres, exclusive of tidal water (2,034) and a population (1973) of 353,700. The city received its first charter of incorporation in 1613 and has since grown, owing to its easy access by sea to Scottish coal and iron, to be a great industrial centre. The chief industries are ship-building and the manufacture of aircraft, machinery, textiles, ropes and tobacco. Belfast is an important seaport with extensive docks.

The principal buildings are of a relatively recent date and include the Parliament Buildings at Stormont, the City Hall, the Law Courts, the

Public Library and the Museum and Art Gallery. The Queen's University (previously Queen's College) was chartered in 1908.

The city returns 4 members to the House of Commons at Westminster. Belfast was created a city in 1888 and the title of Lord Mayor was conferred in 1892.

Lord Mayor, R. E. M. Humphreys.
Town Clerk, W. Johnston.

LONDONDERRY

LONDONDERRY, a City situated on the River Foyle, has a population (estimated, 1973) of 51,200 and was reputedly founded in 546 by St. Columba. Londonderry (formerly *Derry*) has important associations with the City of London. The Irish Society, under its royal charter of 1613, fortified the city and was for long closely associated with its administration. On April 2, 1969, the Corporation of Londonderry and Londonderry R.D.C. were dissolved and replaced by the Londonderry Development Commission. The Development Commission was dissolved in Sept. 1973, and its functions were taken over by the newly elected Local District Council and various Government departments and Area Boards.

Famous for the great siege of 1688–89, when for 105 days the town held out against the forces of James II until relieved by sea, Londonderry was an important naval base throughout the Second World War. Interesting buildings are the Protestant Cathedral of St. Columb's (1633) and the Guildhall reconstructed in 1912 and containing a number of beautiful stained glass windows, many of which were presented by the livery companies of London. The famous Walls are still intact and form a circuit of almost a mile around the old city. The manufacture of shirts and collars is the staple industry. Other industries include motor and mechanical engineering and fancy box making. New industries established in Londonderry in the post-war period include the manufacture of synthetic fibre and rubber, tyre cord and light engineering. A large part of Ulster's agricultural export trade passes through the port.

FINANCE

Taxation in Northern Ireland is largely imposed and collected by the United Kingdom Government. After deducting the cost of collections and of Northern Ireland's contributions to the European Economic Community the balance, known as the Attributed Share of Taxation, is paid over to the Northern Ireland Consolidated Fund. Northern Ireland's revenue is insufficient to meet its expenditure and is supplemented by a grant in aid.

	1975–76*	1976–77**
	£	£
Public Income....	1,083,716,594	1,144,503,000
Public expenditure	1,083,610,454	1,144,306,700

* Outturn ** Estimate

EXTERNAL TRADE*
Metric Tonnes

	1973	1974	1975
Total imports..	10,331	10,318	10,002
Total exports..	2,795	2,791	3,136

* Including cross-Channel trade with Great Britain.

PRODUCTION

Industries.—The total value of the industrial production of Northern Ireland in 1973 was approximately £1,693,000,000 and employment was given to about 195,000 persons. The products of the engineering, shipbuilding and aircraft industries which employed 47,000 persons, were valued at £208,000,000. The textile industries, employing 37,000 persons, produced yarns, fabrics, household textiles, handkerchiefs, carpets, hosiery, ropes and a wide variety of other products valued at approximately £294,000,000. The food and drink industry, giving employment to 20,000 persons, produced goods valued at £297,000,000 and clothing to the value of £69,000,000 was manufactured in 1973, of which £29,000,000 represented shirts and collars, which are manufactured principally in Londonderry. Other industries of importance to the economy of Northern Ireland are synthetic rubber and products, mineral oil refining, furniture and building materials and cardboard boxes and packing cases.

Minerals.—2,068 persons were employed in mining and quarrying operations in Northern Ireland in 1974 and the minerals raised were valued at £8,393,503.

Fisheries.—The total value of sea and freshwater fish caught in 1974 was £3,649,375.

COMMUNICATIONS

Seaports.—The net tonnage of shipping using the principal ports in 1975 was about 12,000,000 tons. *Belfast.*—Regular services operate to and from ports on the Western coast of Great Britain and the Continent of Europe. In addition there are frequent though less regular, calls by many other coastal and foreign-going ships. There are roll on/roll off services to Liverpool, Ardrossan and Heysham. Container services—with adequate cranage available—operate to Liverpool, Heysham, Holyhead, Garston, Ardrossan and Southampton and there are weekly sailings catering for palletised and container traffic to ports in France, Germany, Holland, Belgium, Sweden, Norway and Denmark. *Larne.*— Roll on/roll off ferry services carrying passengers, cars and commercial vehicles operate nine times daily to Stranraer and five times daily to Cairnryan, also a roll on/roll off service for commercial vehicles operates once daily to Fleetwood. There is a daily lift on/lift off service to Cairnryan. *Warrenpoint.*— Container services operate to Garston and Preston three times weekly, Rotterdam, bi-weekly and Gothenburg fortnightly. A roll on/roll off berth has now been provided.

Road and Rail Transport.—The reorganization of public transport in Northern Ireland was completed by the Transport Act (N.I.), 1967, which provided for the abolition of the Ulster Transport Authority and the establishment of the Northern Ireland Transport Holding Company. The Holding Company took over the assets of the Authority and is responsible for the supervision of the subsidiary companies, Northern Ireland Carriers, owned jointly with the National Freight Corporation, which operates road freight services, Ulsterbus Ltd. which operates the public road passenger services, Northern Ireland Railways Co. Ltd., which provides the railway services, and Northern Ireland Airports Ltd. which is responsible for running the main airport at Aldergrove, near Belfast. A few privately operated bus services are provided in rural areas under licence. Citybus Ltd. provides omnibus services in the Belfast area. Road freight services are also provided by a large number of hauliers operating competitively under licence.

Air Transport.—Passenger and freight services operate between Belfast Airport and airports throughout Great Britain. A limited number of services are also operated to North America. In 1975, 1,200,000 passengers, and 11,000 metric tons of freight, including mail, were carried making the Airport the sixth busiest in the United Kingdom. Plans for the improvement of terminal, airside and landside facilities have recently been agreed and a major development programme is due to begin early in 1977.

Counties of Northern Ireland

Counties and County Boroughs	Area★ sq. miles	Lord Lieutenant	High Sheriff, 1977
(1) Antrim.......................	1,099	Capt. R. A. F. Dobbs	Sir Ivan Ewart, Bt., D.S.C.
Belfast County Borough.......	25	Col. Lord Glentoran, P.C., K.B.E.	W. C. Corry
(2) Armagh....................	489	The Rt. Hon. Sir Charles Norman Lockhart Stronge, Bt., M.C.	A. H. C. Greer, T.D.
(3) Down......................	952	The Earl of Clanwilliam	C. F. C. Lindsay
(4) Fermanagh................	657	(vacant)	M. W. Scallon
(5) Londonderry†..............	810	Col. M. W. McCorkell, O.B.E., T.D.	J. R. Beresford-Ash
Londonderry City.............	3·4	T. F. Cooke	F. G. Gucklan
(6) Tyrone....................	1,218	The Duke of Abercorn	A. J. B. McFarland

★ Excluding tidal waters and large lakes.   † Excluding the City of Londonderry.

Municipal Directory of Northern Ireland

District and ★Borough Councils	Estimated Population	Annual Net Value	Council Clerk	Chairman 1976
		£		
Antrim......................	37,600	560,085	S. J. Magee	J. H. Allen, O.B.E.
★Ards.........................	52,100	678,466	W. C. Scott	H. S. Cosbey
Armagh.....................	47,500	437,942	N. C. H. Megaw	A. N. Creswell
★Ballymena..................	52,200	702,370	J. S. McIlroy	G. G. Sloane
Ballymoney.................	22,700	227,246	W. J. Regan	F. E. C. Holland
Banbridge..................	28,800	252,408	R. J. Wetherall	W. H. Davidson
Belfast City................	368,200	8,255,348	W. J. Johnston	R. E. M. Humphreys
★Carrickfergus..............	27,500	461,521	R. Boyd	H. McLean
Castlereagh................	63,600	936,120	A. D. Nicol	J. Scott
★Coleraine..................	44,900	689,257	W. E. Andrews	Col. A. N. Clarke, O.B.E.
Cookstown.................	27,500	262,285	W. A. Bownes	A. McConnell
★Craigavon..................	71,200	1,073,100	W. J. Mayes	T. H. Creith
Down.......................	48,800	513,103	J. Byrne	E. K. McGrady
Dungannon................	43,000	358,543	R. Paisley	Maj. J. H. Hamilton-Stubber
Fermanagh.................	50,900	363,644	G. Burns	R. Thornton
★Larne......................	29,000	470,397	R. Lyttle	T. Seymour
Limavady..................	25,000	248,998	M. S. Thompson	Miss F. Sloan
Lisburn....................	80,800	983,361	H. A. Duff	N. Bicker
Londonderry City..........	86,600	1,146,966	C. M. Geary	J. Hegarty
Magherafelt...............	32,200	254,674	W. J. McKinney, M.B.E.	P. J. Heron
Moyle......................	13,400	129,101	J. O'Kane	R. McKay
Newry and Mourne...........	75,300	660,567	P. J. O'Hagan	J. F. McEvoy
Newtownabbey...............	71,500	1,100,045	R. W. Blennerhassett	S. R. Cameron
★North Down................	59,600	955,437	J. McKimm	R. D. McConnell
Omagh.....................	41,800	331,614	D. R. D. Mitchell	G. E. McEnhill
Strabane..................	35,500	232,999	J. N. McMorran	Mrs. M. E. S. Britten
Northern Ireland............	1,537,200	22,285,597		

Note.—Since the reorganisation of Local Government, rates in Northern Ireland are now collected by the Department of Finance and consist of two rates. A regional rate of £2·99 was made by the Department of Finance. Each of the 26 District Councils made their own separate rate. The regional rate was subject to subsidy at varying levels to provide a gradual transition from the previous differing rates made by former rating authorities.

THE ISLE OF MAN (MONA)

An island in the Irish Sea, in lat. 54° 3′–54° 25′ N. and long. 4° 18′–4° 47′ W., nearly equidistant from England, Scotland, and Ireland. The total land area is 141,263 acres (221 sq. miles), of which 76,701 acres are under cultivation. An interim report on the 1971 Census showed a total population of 56,289 (males, 26,461; females 29,828). In 1973 the births numbered 807 and the deaths 921. 165 persons were returned at the Census of 1961 as able to speak the Manx language, compared with 4,657 in 1901 and 355 in 1951. The principal sectors of the Island's economy in terms of income generated and in order of importance (1971/72 figures) are Manufacturing Industry, Insurance, Banking and Finance, and Tourism.

Government.—The Isle of Man is governed by a Legislature, called the Tynwald, consisting of two branches—the Legislative Council and the House of Keys. The Council consists of the Lieutenant-Governor, the Bishop of Sodor and Man, the First Deemster, the Attorney-General and 7 members appointed by the House of Keys. The House

of Keys (possibly from the Scandinavian *keise=* chosen) is one of the most ancient legislative assemblies in the world. It consists of 24 members, elected by the adult male and female population, 13 from the six *sheadings*, 7 from Douglas, 2 from Ramsey, and 1 each from Castletown and Peel. Bills after having passed both Houses are signed by the members, and then sent for the Royal Assent. After receiving the Royal Assent, a Bill does not become law unless promulgated within the ensuing twelve months, and on the first "Tynwald Day" (July 5) following it is announced in the English and Manx languages on the Tynwald Hill. On the promulgation taking place a certificate thereof is signed by the Lieutenant-Governor and the Speaker of the House of Keys. The Isle of Man is associated for certain purposes with the Common Market under Protocol 3 of the Treaty of Accession. Community rules on agricultural trade, customs duties etc., apply to the Island.

Finance.—The Island's Budget for 1975/76 provided for revenue and capital expenditure of £31,765,620. The principal sources of Government revenue are a) Income Tax, charged at the rate of 21·25 per cent of all taxable income and b) Customs and Excise Duties, collected on behalf of the Island under the "Common Purse Agreement" by H. M. Customs and Excise. There are no surtax or death duties, although there is a Company Registration Tax, which is levied at the flat rate of £200 on every company incorporated in the Isle of Man which trades, and there is a Land Speculation Tax payable at the rate of 21·25 per cent.

An annual contribution of 5 per cent of the net "Common Purse" receipts is made towards the cost of defence and other common services provided by the United Kingdom Government.

There are also reciprocal Social Security arrangements with the U.K.

There are 36 primary, 6 secondary schools, a college of further education and a domestic science college, in addition to King William's College and the Buchan School for Girls.

CAPITAL, ΨDouglas. Population (1971), 20,389; ΨCastletown (2,820) is the ancient capital; the other towns are ΨPeel (3,081), and ΨRamsey (5,048).

FLAG.—Three legs in white and gold armed conjoined on a red ground.

Lieutenant-Governor, His Excellency Sir John Paul, G.C.M.G., O.B.E., M.C. (1973).

Government Secretary, T. Kelly.

Speaker, House of Keys, H. C. Kerruish, O.B.E.

THE CHANNEL ISLANDS

Situated off the north-west coast of France (at distances of from ten to thirty miles), are the only portions of the *Dukedom of Normandy* now belonging to the Crown, to which they have been attached ever since the Conquest. They consist of Jersey (28,717 acres) Guernsey (15,654 acres), Alderney (1,962 acres), Brechou (74), Great Sark (1,035), Little Sark (239), Herm (320), Jethou (44) and Lihou (38), a total of 48,083 acres, or 75 square miles. In 1971 the population of Jersey was 72,532; and of Guernsey, etc. (1975) (Guernsey, 51,620; Alderney, 1,785; Sark, 604).

The climate is mild, and the soil exceptionally productive. The land under cultivation is about 38,765 vergées (2¼ vergées=1 acre) in Jersey, and about 16,500 vergées (2½ vergées=1 acre) in Guernsey, the principal product of the soil of Jersey being potatoes, tomatoes and flowers, and of Guernsey, tomatoes, flowers and fern. The famous Jersey and Guernsey breed of cows have earned a well-deserved celebrity. The Lieutenant-Governors and Commanders-in-Chief of Jersey and Guernsey are the Personal Representatives of the Sovereign and the channel of communication between H.M. Government and the Insular Governments. The Bailiffs of Jersey and Guernsey, appointed by the Crown, are Presidents both of the Assembly of the States (the Insular Legislature) and of the Royal Courts respectively.

The official language is English and a Norman-French *patois* is also in use (except in Alderney). The principal imports are food, beverages, tobacco, manufactured goods, fuels and chemicals, and the chief exports potatoes, tomatoes, grapes, flowers and cattle. The chief town of Jersey is ΨSt. Helier on the south coast; the principal town of Guernsey is ΨSt. Peter Port, on the east coast, and of Alderney is St. Anne's.

JERSEY

Lieutenant-Governor and Commander-in-Chief of Jersey, His Excellency General Sir Desmond Fitzpatrick, G.C.B., D.S.O., M.B.E., M.C. £10,000

Secretary and A.D.C., Lt.-Comdr. O. M. B. de Las Casas, O.B.E., R.N.(*ret.*).

Bailiff of Jersey, Sir Frank Ereaut.

Dean of Jersey, Very Rev. T. A. Goss.

Attorney-General and Receiver-General, V. A. Tomes.

Solicitor-General, P. M. Bailhache.

States Treasurer, J. Clennett.

Year to Dec. 31:	1974	1975
Revenue........	£33,647,271	£46,984,000
Expenditure......	24,889,549	83,780,000
Public Debt......	5,538,940	4,138,690

The standard rate of Income Tax is 20p. in the £. No super tax or death duties are levied.

FLAG.—A white field charged with a red saltire.

GUERNSEY AND DEPENDENCIES

Lieutenant-Governor and Commander-in-Chief of Guernsey, His Excellency Vice-Adm. Sir John Martin, K.C.B., D.S.C. (1974). £7,000

Secretary and A.D.C., Capt. M. H. T. Mellish, O.B.E., E.R.D.

Bailiff of Guernsey, Sir John Loveridge, C.B.E.

Dean of Guernsey, Very Rev. F. W. Cogman.

Deputy Bailiff, E. P. Shanks, C.B.E., Q.C.

Attorney-General, C. K. Frossard.

Solicitor-General, G. M. Dorey.

States Supervisor, A. S. Forty.

Receiver-General, R. H. Collenette.

	1974	1975
Revenue.........	£14,793,118	£19,330,000
Expenditure......	11,308,363	16,013,713
Net Funded Debt.	2,538,371	2,127,926
Note and Coin issue.........	4,502,360	6,057,069

FLAG.—White, bearing a red cross of St. George.

ALDERNEY

President of the States, J. Kay-Mouat.

Clerk to the States, W. E. Jones.

Clerk to the Court, K. K. Lacey, V.R.D.

SARK

Le Seigneur of Sark, Michael Beaumont.

Deputy Seigneur, T. V. Gordon-Brown.

Seneschal, B. G. Jones.

The Commonwealth

The Commonwealth is a free association of the 36 sovereign independent states listed below together with their dependencies (mostly small islands which are dependencies of Britain, Australia or New Zealand) and the Associated States of the Eastern Caribbean.

UNITED KINGDOM	MALAWI
CANADA	MALAYSIA
AUSTRALIA	MALTA
NEW ZEALAND	MAURITIUS
BAHAMAS	NAURU (special member)
BANGLADESH	NIGERIA
BARBADOS	SEYCHELLES
BOTSWANA	SIERRA LEONE
CYPRUS	SINGAPORE
FIJI	SRI LANKA
GAMBIA	SWAZILAND
GHANA	TANZANIA
GRENADA	TRINIDAD AND TOBAGO
GUYANA	UGANDA
INDIA	ZAMBIA
JAMAICA	TONGA
KENYA	WESTERN SAMOA
LESOTHO	PAPUA NEW GUINEA

AREA AND POPULATION.—The total area of the independent British Commonwealth is 10,123,670 square miles (excluding the U.K.). Details of the areas and populations of the Member States and dependencies appear in the following pages and are also tabulated on pp. 199–203. The total population of the Commonwealth is estimated to be approaching 900,000,000.

GOVERNMENT.—Most members of the Commonwealth are parliamentary democracies, their laws being made with the consent of a freely elected parliament after discussion in that parliament, the executive government holding office by virtue of majority in parliament. However, Nigeria (1966) has suspended its constitution and is under military rule: the Constitution granted to Lesotho on independence in 1966 was suspended in January, 1970. In January, 1971, Uganda came under military rule.

Queen Elizabeth II is recognized as Queen and Head of State in the following member countries of the Commonwealth: United Kindom, Canada, Australia, New Zealand, Jamaica, Trinidad and Tobago, Fiji, Barbados, Mauritius, Bahamas, Grenada and Papua New Guinea. In each of these countries (except the United Kingdom) Her Majesty is personally represented by a Governor-General, who in many respects holds the same position in relation to the administration of public affairs as is held by the Sovereign in Britain (with the exception of certain constitutional functions which are performed by Her Majesty personally). The Governor-General is appointed by the Queen on the recommendation of the Government of the country concerned and is wholly independent of the British Government; in many cases he is a national of the country in which he holds office.

India, Ghana, Nigeria, Cyprus, Uganda, Tanzania, Kenya, Malawi, Zambia, Singapore, The Gambia, Guyana, Nauru, Sierra Leone, Botswana, Sri Lanka, Bangladesh, Malta and Seychelles are Republics with Presidents as Head of State, Malaysia has one of the State Rulers as elected Monarch (*Yang di-Pertuan Agong*) and Head of State; Lesotho, Tonga and Swaziland are monarchies which have their own Kings. Western Samoa has a Head of State whose functions are analogous to those of a constitutional monarch. All Members of the Commonwealth accept The Queen as the symbol of the free association of the member nations of the Commonwealth and as such, Head of the Commonwealth.

The status of member nations was defined by the Imperial Conference of 1926 and given legal substance by the *Statute of Westminster*, 1931, in which the Commonwealth nations were described as " autonomous communities within the British Empire, equal in status, in no way subordinate one to another, but united by a common allegiance to the Crown and freely associated as members of the British Commonwealth of Nations." Other parts of the Commonwealth, such as the Dependent Territories and Associated States, are regarded as forming part of the Commonwealth by virtue of their relationship with member states of the Commonwealth.

CONSULTATION.—The most important means of consultation between Governments are Heads of Government Meetings. These Meetings, which replaced the more formal pre-war Imperial Conferences, have been held at frequent intervals since 1944. They are a useful means whereby Commonwealth Heads of Government consult together on major issues of international affairs and other matters which affect them all. It is not their practice to pass Resolutions or to seek to formulate common and binding policies on international issues; but they have on occasion made general statements of principle to which they all subscribe—such as the Commonwealth Declaration agreed at Singapore in January 1971 and the statement on Nuclear Weapon Tests issued during the meeting held at Ottawa in August 1973—and the policies of individual Governments are clearly often influenced by the information and ideas exchanged at these Meetings. In addition to meetings of Heads of Government, there are annual meetings of Finance Ministers, as well as less frequent meetings between Ministers or officials responsible for subjects such as trade, education, medicine and law.

RHODESIA.—Southern Rhodesia was united with Northern Rhodesia and Nyasaland in a federation which lasted from 1953 until 1963, since when Nyasaland (as Malawi, 1964) and Northern Rhodesia (as Zambia, 1964) have become independent. Southern Rhodesia made a unilateral declaration of independence on Nov. 11, 1965. Its present constitutional status is as set out in the Southern Rhodesia Act, 1965.

CITIZENSHIP AND NATIONALITY.—Each member of the Commonwealth of Nations defines the citizenship and nationality of its own people and determines the status of other Commonwealth nationals within its own boundaries. In most cases, though not in all, they possess a common status as British subjects (or Commonwealth citizens). Even where there is no such provision for a common status, the Members of the Commonwealth differentiate, in greater or lesser degree, as regards the grant of privileges, between citizens of the Commonwealth and aliens. The Republic of Ireland, which in 1949 ceased to be a member of the Commonwealth, is not regarded by the other Commonwealth nations as a foreign country or her citizens as foreigners.

THE JUDICATURE.—The Supreme Judicial Authority for certain parts of the Commonwealth is the Judicial Committee of the Privy Council. Appeals may be brought to it from the Courts of the dependencies and also from the Courts of certain independent members of the Commonwealth which have not abrogated the right of appeal (i.e. Australian States, New Zealand, Jamaica, Trinidad

and Tobago, Malaysia, Singapore, The Gambia, Barbados, Mauritius, Fiji, The Bahamas and Grenada). The Committee consists of such members of the Privy Council as have held or are holding high judicial office in Great Britain or are or have been judges in certain Commonwealth countries. The Supreme Judicial Authority for Great Britain and Northern Ireland is the House of Lords.

DEFENCE.—Each of the independent members of the Commonwealth is completely responsible for its own defence and all are members of the United Nations. The United Kingdom and Canada belong to N.A.T.O.; the United Kingdom, Australia and New Zealand are members of S.E.A.T.O.; Australia and New Zealand are signatories of the Pacific Security Treaty. The United Kingdom has a defence agreement with Malta, and is a signatory to the Treaty of Guarantee of Cyprus. With Australia and New Zealand, the United Kingdom is also a partner in joint defence arrangements with Malaysia and Singapore.

THE ASSOCIATED STATES.—Early in 1967 the former colonies of Antigua, Dominica, Grenada, St. Kitts-Nevis-Anguilla and St. Lucia became " nondependent " States in association with Great Britain. Legal effect was given to this status by the West Indies Act, 1967. In October, 1969, St. Vincent also became an Associated State. The main features of the association are that each State is responsible for its own internal affairs, may amend its own Constitution and may sever the association by unilateral declaration, subject to the observance of procedures contained in the Constitution of each State. Her Majesty's Government retains responsibility for the external affairs and defence of each territory. On February 7, 1974, Grenada left the association on becoming an independent member of the Commonwealth.

OVERSEAS DEPENDENCIES.—The United Kingdom, Australia and New Zealand have dependencies for which they are independently responsible. (*See* following sections.)

Colony (or Settlement): a territory belonging by settlement, conquest or annexation to the British Crown.

Protectorate: a territory not formally annexed, but in respect of which, by treaty, grant, usage, sufferance, and other lawful means, Her Majesty has power and jurisdiction.

Protected State: a territory under a ruler which enjoys Her Majesty's protection, over whose foreign affairs she exercises control but in respect of whose internal affairs she does not exercise jurisdiction.

Condominium: a territory for which responsibility is shared by two administering powers.

Leased Territories: this term applies only to that part of the mainland of China which was in 1898 leased to Great Britain for 99 years and is administered by the Government of Hong Kong.

Other Commonwealth Dependencies.—Australia and New Zealand administer a number of island territories and extensive Antarctic areas.

DEVELOPMENT AND FINANCE.—Complete financial autonomy is enjoyed by all members of the Commonwealth. In some countries, customs tariffs are lower for merchandise of Commonwealth origin than for imports from foreign countries. The British Government provides guarantees for the capital issues made by dependent territories and also provides budgetary assistance in many cases as well as direct loans and grants to assist development.

Under the Colonial Development and Welfare Act, 1940, annual sums of £5,000,000 were made available for developments and £500,000 for research for a ten-year period. Succeeding Acts increased the total sum to be made available and extended the period to be covered. In 1965 the Act was extended for a final 5 years. It authorized Exchequer Loans towards the cost of approved development programmes amounting to £125,000,000 and a ceiling of £390,000,000 for development and welfare assistance in the period 1941–1970. Thereafter the development needs of the remaining dependencies have been dealt with under the provisions of the Overseas Aid Act, 1966.

COMMONWEALTH COUNTRIES NOW MEMBER STATES

1931 Canada; Australia; New Zealand

In 1931 the Statute of Westminster clarified the legal position of Canada, Australia and New Zealand which had long been self-governing and independent states.

1947 India (Republic, 1950)

1948 Sri Lanka (Republic, 1972; but originally a Republic as Ceylon, 1970)

1957 Ghana, *formerly* Gold Coast (Republic, 1960) Malaya (an elective monarchy, now MALAYSIA; *see* Sabah and Sarawak, 1963)

1960 Cyprus (Republic, 1960; Cwlth. Member, 1961)

1960 Nigeria (Republic, 1963)

1961 Sierra Leone (Republic, 1971) Tanganyika (Republic, 1962; united 1964 with Zanzibar as TANZANIA)

1962 Jamaica; Trinidad and Tobago; Uganda, (Republic, 1963); Western Samoa

1963 Zanzibar; Kenya (Republic, 1964) Sabah ⎫in Federation of Malaysia (an Sarawak⎭ elective monarchy) Singapore, as State in Federation of Malaysia, seceded as Republic, 1965

1964 Malawi (*formerly* Nyasaland Protectorate; Republic, 1966); Malta Zambia (Republic; *formerly* Northern Rhodesia)

1965 Gambia (The) (Republic, 1970)

1966 Guyana, *formerly* British Guiana (Republic, 1970) Botswana (Republic; *formerly* Bechuanaland Protectorate) Lesotho (*formerly* Basutoland); Barbados

1968 Mauritius; Nauru (Special Membership) Swaziland

1970 Fiji; Tonga

1972 Bangladesh (Republic, 1972; independent, originally as East Pakistan, 1948, although partitioned from India in 1947)

1973 Bahamas

1974 Grenada

1975 Papua New Guinea.

1976 Seychelles.

Associated States

From the dates shown, the following are fully self-governing states within the Commonwealth. The United Kingdom continues to be responsible for their defence and external relations:—

Antigua (Feb. 27, 1967); Dominica (March 1, 1967); St. Christopher Nevis and Anguilla (Feb. 27, 1967); St. Lucia (March 1, 1967); St. Vincent (Oct. 27, 1969).

Countries which have left the Commonwealth

1948 Burma; Palestine

1949 *Eire* or Republic of Ireland

1956 Sudan

1960 British Somaliland

1961 South Africa (on becoming a republic). Southern Cameroons

1963 Maldive Islands

1967 Yemen P.D.R. (*formerly* Aden).

1972 Pakistan.

Canada
AREA AND POPULATION

Provinces or Territories and Capitals (with official contractions)	Area (English Sq. Miles). Land and Water	Population	
		Census, 1971	Estimated (June 1, 1975)
Alberta, *Alta.* (Edmonton)	255,285	1,627,874	1,768,000
British Columbia, *B.C.* (Victoria)	366,255	2,184,621	2,457,000
Manitoba, *Man.* (Winnipeg)	251,000	988,247	1,019,000
New Brunswick, *N.B.* (Fredericton)	28,354	634,557	675,000
Newfoundland and Labrador, *Nfld.* (St. John's)	156,185	522,104	549,000
Nova Scotia, *N.S.* (Halifax)	21,425	788,960	822,000
Ontario, *Ont.* (Toronto)	412,582	7,703,106	8,226,000
Prince Edward Island, *P.E.I.* (Charlottetown)	2,184	111,641	119,000
Quebec, *Que.* (Quebec)	594,860	6,027,764	6,188,000
Saskatchewan, *Sask.* (Regina)	251,700	926,242	918,000
Yukon Territory, *Y.T.* (Whitehorse)	207,076	18,388	21,000
Northwest Territories, *N.W.T.* (Yellowknife)	1,304,903	34,807	38,000
Total	3,851,809	21,568,311	22,800,000

Land Area, 3,560,238 square miles; Water Area, 291,571 square miles. (For areas of individual provinces, excluding freshwater areas, *see* p. 200.)

Of the total immigration of 187,881 in 1974, 20,155 were from the United States, 34,978 from the United Kingdom, 11,132 from Hong Kong, 10,144 from India, and 11,472 from some 190 other countries including the Republic of Ireland (1,098).

Increase of the People

Census Year	Population			Decennial Increase	Immigrants during Census Year
	Males	Females	Total		
1901	2,751,708	2,619,607	5,371,315	538,076	55,747
1911	3,821,995	3,384,648	7,206,643	1,835,328	331,288
1921	4,529,643	4,258,306	8,787,949	1,581,306	91,728
1931	5,374,541	5,002,245	10,376,786	1,588,837	27,530
1941	5,900,536	5,666,119	11,506,655	1,129,869	9,329
1951	7,088,873	6,920,556	14,009,429	2,502,774	194,391
1956	8,151,879	7,928,912	16,080,791	..	164,857
1961	9,218,893	9,019,354	18,238,247	4,228,818	71,689
1966	10,054,344	9,960,536	20,014,880	..	194,743
1971	10,795,370	10,772,940	21,568,310	3,330,063	121,900

Origins	1961	1971	Religions	1961	1971
British Races	7,996,669	9,624,115	Roman Catholic	8,342,826	9,974,895
English	4,195,175	6,245,970	United Church of Canada	3,664,008	3,768,800
Scottish	1,902,302	1,720,390	Anglican Church of Canada	2,409,068	2,543,180
Irish	1,753,351	1,581,730	Presbyterian	818,558	872,335
Other	145,841	76,030	Baptist	593,553	667,245
European Races	9,657,195	11,139,800	Lutheran	662,744	715,740
French	5,540,346	6,180,120	Jewish	254,368	276,025
Austrian	106,535	42,120	Ukrainian (Greek) Catholic	189,653	227,730
Belgian	61,382	51,135	Greek Orthodox	239,766	316,605
Czech and Slovak	73,061	81,870	Mennonite	152,452	168,150
Finnish	59,436	59,215	Pentecostal	143,877	220,390
German	1,049,599	1,317,200	Salvation Army	92,054	119,665
Hungarian	126,220	131,890	Mormon	50,016	66,635
Italian	450,351	730,820	Church of Christ, Disciples.	19,512	16,405
Jewish	173,344	296,945	Christian Science	19,466	..
Netherlands	429,679	425,945	Adventist	25,999	28,590
Polish	323,517	316,430	Confucian and Buddhist	16,700	18,340
Rumanian	43,805	27,375	Others	543,627	1,567,580
Russian	119,168	64,475			
Scandinavian	386,534	384,795	Totals	18,238,247	21,568,310
Ukrainian	473,337	580,660			
Other	240,881	448,805			
Asiatic Races	121,753	285,540			
Chinese	58,197	118,815			
Japanese	29,157	37,260			
Other	34,399	129,460			
Indian and Eskimo	220,121	312,760	Indian population (1961), 208,286; (1971), 295,215;		
All other	242,509	206,095	Eskimo population (1961), 11,835; (1971), 17,550.		
Totals	18,238,247	21,568,310			

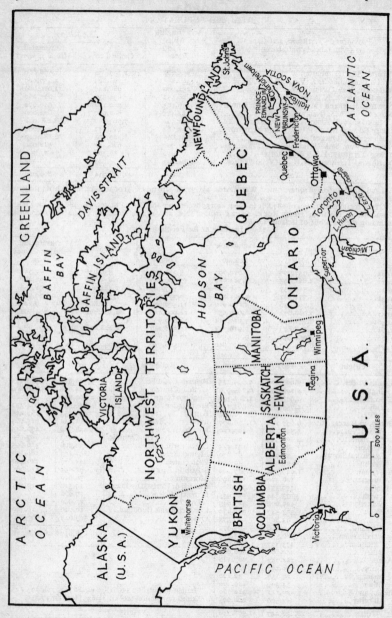

PHYSIOGRAPHY

Canada was originally discovered by Cabot in 1497, but its history dates only from 1534, when the French took possession of the country. The first permanent settlement at Port Royal (now Annapolis), Nova Scotia, was founded in 1605, and Quebec was founded in 1608. In 1759 Quebec was captured by the British forces under General Wolfe, and in 1763 the whole territory of Canada became a possession of Great Britain by the Treaty of Paris of that year. Nova Scotia was ceded in 1713 by the Treaty of Utrecht, the Provinces of New Brunswick and Prince Edward Island being subsequently formed out of it. British Columbia was formed into a Crown colony in 1858, having previously been a part of the Hudson Bay Territory, and was united to Vancouver Island in 1866.

Canada occupies the whole of the northern part of the North American Continent (with the exception of Alaska), from 49° North latitude to the North Pole, and from the Pacific to the Atlantic Ocean. In Eastern Canada, the southernmost point is Middle Island in Lake Erie, at 41° 41'.

Relief.—The relief of Canada is dominated by the mountain ranges running north and south on the west side of the Continent, by the pre-Cambrian shield on the east, with, in between, the northern extension of the North American Plain. From the physiographic point of view Canada has six main divisions. These are: (1) Appalachian-Acadian Region, (2) the Canadian Shield, (3) the St. Lawrence-Great Lakes Lowland, (4) the Interior Plains, (5) the Cordilleran Region and (6) the Arctic Archipelago. The first region occupies all that part of Canada lying southeast of the St. Lawrence. In general, the relief is an alternation of highlands and lowlands, and is hilly rather than mountainous. The lowlands area seldom rises over 600 feet above sea level. The great Canadian Shield comprises more than half the area. The interior as a whole is an undulating, low plateau (general level 1,000 to 1,500 feet), with the more rugged relief lying along the border between Northern Quebec and Labrador. Throughout the whole area water or muskeg-

filled depressions separate irregular hills and ridges, 150 to 200 feet in elevation. Newfoundland, an outlying portion of the shield, consists of glaciated, low rolling terrain broken here and there by mountains. The flat relief of the St. Lawrence-Great Lakes lowland varies from 500 feet in the east to 1,700 feet south of Georgian Bay. The whole area in the western part slopes gently to the Great Lakes. The most striking relief is provided by the eastward facing scarp of the Niagara escarpment (elevation 250 to 300 feet). The interior plains, comprising the Pacific Provinces, slope eastward and northward a few feet per mile. The descent from west to east is made from 5,000 feet to less than 1,000 feet in three distinct levels, with each new level being marked by an eastward facing *coteau* or scarp. Horizontal strata and peneplanation make for slight relief of the level to rolling type. Five fairly well-developed topographic divisions mark out the Cordilleran region of western Canada. These are: (1) coastal ranges, largely above 5,000 feet with deep fiords and glaciated valleys, (2) the interior plateau, around 3,500 feet and comparatively level, (3) the Selkirk ranges, largely above 5,000 feet, (4) the Rocky Mountains with their chain of 10,000 to 12,000-feet peaks, and (5) the Peace River or Tramontane region with its rolling diversified country. The Arctic Archipelago, with its plateau-like character has an elevation between 500 and 1,000 feet, though in Baffin Land and Ellesmere Island the mountain ranges rise to 8,500 and 9,500 feet. Two tremendous waterway systems, the St. Lawrence and the Mackenzie, providing thousands of miles of water highway, occupy a broad area of lowland with their dominant axis following the edge of the shield.

Climate.—The climate of the eastern and central portions presents greater extremes than in corresponding latitudes in Europe, but in the southwestern portion of the Prairie Region and the southern portions of the Pacific slope the climate is milder. Spring, summer, and autumn are of about seven to eight months' duration, and the winter four to five months.

GOVERNMENT

The Constitution of Canada has its source in the British North America Act of 1867 which formed a Dominion, under the name of Canada, of the four provinces: Ontario, Quebec, New Brunswick and Nova Scotia; to this Federation the other Provinces have subsequently been admitted. Under this Act Canada came into being on July 1, 1867 (Dominion Day), and under the Statute of Westminster, which received the royal assent on Dec. 11, 1931, Canada and the Provinces were exempted (in common with other self-governing Dominions of the Commonwealth of Nations) from the operation of the Colonial Laws Validity Act, the Statute of Westminster having removed all limitations with regard to the legislative autonomy of the Dominions. Provinces admitted since 1867 are: Manitoba (1870), British Columbia (1871), Prince Edward Island (1873), Alberta and Saskatchewan (1905) and Newfoundland (1949).

The Executive power is vested in a Governor-General appointed by the Sovereign on the advice of the Canadian Ministry, and aided by a Privy Council.

FLAG.—Red maple leaf with 11 points on white square, flanked by vertical red bars one half the width of the square.

GOVERNOR GENERAL'S HOUSEHOLD

Governor-General and Commander-in-Chief, His Excellency the Right Hon. Jules Léger, C.C., C.M.M., C.D. born April 4,1913, assumed office Jan. 14, 1974.
Secretary to the Governor-General, E. U. Butler, C.V.O.
Comptroller of the Household, D. C. McKinnon, C.V.O., C.D.
Administrative Secretary, E. A. C. Joly de Lotbinière.
Cultural Adviser, R. H. Hubbard.
Press Secretary, P. Cowan.
Attaché, C. Sirois.
Aides-de Camp, Capt. P. Collinge; Capt. A. Fenske; Capt. P. C. Leblanc.

THE CANADIAN MINISTRY
THE FEDERAL CABINET

Prime Minister, Rt. Hon. Pierre Elliott Trudeau.

President of the Queen's Privy Council for Canada, Hon. Allan Joseph MacEachen.

External Affairs, Hon. Donald Campbell Jamieson.
Science and Technology, Hon. James Hugh Faulkner.
Transport, Hon. Otto Emil Lang.
Finance, Hon. Donald Stovel Macdonald.
President of the Treasury Board, Hon. Robert Knight Andras.

Postmaster General, Hon. Jean Jacques Blais.

Energy, Mines and Resources, Hon. Alastair William Gillespie.

Labour, Hon. John Carr Munro.

Communications, Hon. Jeanne Sauvé.

National Revenue, Hon. Monique Begin.

Regional Economic Expansion, Hon. Marc Lessard.

Manpower and Immigration, Hon. Jack Sydney George Cullen.

Defence, Hon. James Armstrong Richardson.

Justice and Attorney General, Hon. Stanley Ronald Basford.

Supply and Services, Hon. Jean-Pierre Goyer.

Industry, Trade and Commerce, Hon. Jean Chrétien.

Agriculture, Hon. Eugene Francis Whelan.

Solicitor General, Hon. Francis Fox.

Secretary of Stat , Hon. John Roberts.

Veterans Affairs, Hon. Daniel Joseph MacDonald.

National Health and Welfare, Hon. Marc Lalonde.

Environment and Fisheries, Hon. Roméo leBlanc.

Leader of the Government in the Senate, Hon. Raymond Perrault.

Urban Affairs, Hon. Barnett Jerome Danson.

Indian and Northern Affairs, Hon. W. Warren Allmand.

Public Works, Hon. J. Judd Buchanan

Consumer and Corporate Affairs, Hon. Tony Abbott.

Minister of State (Fitness and Sport), Hon. Iona Campagnolo.

Small Business, Hon. Leonard Marchand.

The Prime Minister receives remuneration of $33,300; other ministers, each $20,000; without Portfolio, $7,500. In every case—including the Prime Minister's—a sessional allowance of $24,000 *per annum* is paid to members of the Senate and House of Commons. In addition, for each session of Parliament members of the House of Commons receive an expense allowance of $10,600, while members of the Senate receive an expense allowance of $5,300.

CANADIAN HIGH COMMISSION

Macdonald House, 1 Grosvenor Square, W.1.
[01-629-9492]

High Commissioner, His Excellency Hon. Paul Martin, P.C., Q.C.

Deputy High Commissioner, C. Hardy.

Minister, J. H. Stone (*Commercial*).

Minister-Counsellors, P. S. Cooper (*Administration*); W. Lavoie (*Economic*).

BRITISH HIGH COMMISSION

80 Elgin Street, Ottawa

High Commissioner, His Excellency Sir John Baines Johnston, K.C.M.G., K.C.V.O.

Deputy High Commissioner and Minister (Commercial), B. A. Flack.

Counsellors, T. Empson (*Head of Chancery*); F. A. Neal (*Commercial*); J. D. Campbell, M.B.E., M.C. (*Information*); J. F. C. Springford, O.B.E. (*Cultural Affairs*).

Defence Adviser, Air Commodore R. J. Carson, C.B.E., A.F.C.

Naval Adviser, Capt. A. A. Hensher, M.B.E., R.N.

Military Adviser, Col. T. W. Tilbrook.

Air Adviser, Group Capt. J. L. W. Towler.

1st Secretaries, G. W. Woodrow (*Admin.*); A. R. F. Burgess (*Commercial*); C. M. Carruthers; I. Woodroffe, O.B.E.; E. Jones-Parry; D. Thomson (*Defence Sales*); H. W. Benstead; L. J. Hobbs.

British Council Representative, J. F. C. Springford, O.B.E.

THE LEGISLATURE

Parliament consists of a Senate and a House of Commons. The *Senate* consists of 104 members, nominated by the Governor-General (age limit 75). They are distributed between the various provinces thus: 24 each for *Ontario* and *Quebec*, 10 each for *Nova Scotia* and *New Brunswick*, 6 each for *Newfoundland, British Columbia, Manitoba, Alberta*, and *Saskatchewan* and 4 for *Prince Edward Island*, 1 for *North West Territories* and 1 for *Yukon*; each Senator must be at least thirty years old, a resident in the province for which he is appointed, a natural-born or naturalized subject of the Queen, and the owner of a property qualification amounting to $4,000. The Speaker of the Senate is chosen by the Government of the day. The *House of Commons* is elected every five years at longest.

The House of Commons has 264 members. Representation by provinces is at present as follows: Newfoundland 7, Prince Edward Island 4, Nova Scotia 11, New Brunswick 10, Quebec 74, Ontario 88, Manitoba 13, Saskatchewan 13, Alberta 19, British Columbia 23, Yukon 1, Northwest Territories 1.

The Senate.

Speaker of the Senate, Hon. Renaude Lapointe (*with Members' annual indemnity $24,000, residence allowance $3,000, expense allowance $5,300, motor-car allowance $1,000 and Salary $12,000*)	$45,300
Clerk of the Senate & Clerk of the Parliaments, Robert Fortier	46,500

The House of Commons.

Speaker of the House of Commons, Hon. James Jerome (*with Member's annual indemnity $24,000, expense allowance $10,600, car allowance $1,000, residence allowance $3,000 and salary $20,000*) . . .	58,600
Deputy Speaker, Gérald Laniel (*with Member's annual indemnity $24,000, expense allowance $10,600, residence allowance, $1,500 and salary $8,000*)	44,100
Clerk of the House of Commons, Alistair Fraser	46,500

THE JUDICATURE

The Judicature is administered by judges following the Civil Law in Quebec Province and Common Law in other Provinces. All Superior and County Court Judges are appointed by the Governor-General, the others by the Lieutenant-Governors of the Provinces, until age 70, except present incumbents who may remain until age 75. Each Province has its Court of Appeal and the highest court is the Supreme Court of Canada, composed of a Chief Justice and eight puisne judges, which holds three sessions each year. There is only one other Dominion Court, the Federal Court of Canada which has both a trial and an appeal division and which replaces the Exchequer Court with expanded jurisdiction.

Supreme Court of Canada.

Chief Justice of Canada, Rt. Hon. Bora Laskin	$68,000
Puisne Judges, Hon. R. Martland; Hon. W. Judson; Hon. R. A. Ritchie; Hon. W. F. Spence; Hon. L-P. Pigeon; Hon. B. Dickson; Hon. J. Beetz; Hon. J. de Grandpré . . . . each	$63,000

Federal Court of Canada.

Chief Justice, Hon. W. R. Jackett, P.C.	$58,000
Associate Chief Justice, Hon. A. L. Thurlow	$58,000
Court of Appeal Judges, Hon. W. F. Ryan; Hon. L. Pratte; Hon. G. E. Le Dain; Hon. D. V. Heald; Hon. J. J. Urie . . each	$53,000
Trial Division Judges, Hon. A. A. Cattanach; Hon. H. F. Gibson; Hon. A. A. M. Walsh; Hon. J. E. Dubé; Hon. D. J. Heald; Hon. F. U. Collier; Hon. G. A. Addy; Hon. R. G. Decary; Hon. P. M. Mahoney . . . . each	$53,000

NATIONAL DEFENCE

On Aug. 1, 1964, the Headquarters of the Royal Canadian Navy, the Canadian Army and the Royal Canadian Air Force were integrated to form a single Canadian Forces Headquarters (C.F.H.Q.) under a single Chief of Defence Staff. The role of C.F.H.Q. is to provide military advice to the Minister of National Defence and to control and administer the Canadian Forces which are organized in seven major commands: *Mobile Command* (units for support of the United Nations or other peacekeeping operations; ground forces, with tactical air support, for the protection of Canadian territory; combat forces in Canada for support of overseas commitments); *Maritime Command* (all sea and air forces on the Atlantic and Pacific coasts for defence of Canada against attack by sea, provision of anti-submarine defence in support of N.A.T.O., conduct of search and rescue operations and sea transport in support of Mobile Command; No. 1 Air Division (the Canadian contribution to strike reconnaissance forces available to the Supreme Allied Commander Europe (SACEUR); *Air Defence Command* (participates with U.S.A. in air defence of North America through NORAD); *Air Transport Command* (air transport for all Canadian forces; search and rescue operations in Ontario and Quebec); *Training Command*; *Canadian Forces Communications System*. In addition there is a *Reserve and Survival Organization* (aid to the civil power, emergency forces for national survival). Armed Forces expenditure for the fiscal year ended March 31, 1976, was $2,797,855,782.

Chief of Defence Staff, Gen. J. A. Dextraze.

On March 31, 1976, the total strength of the Canadian Armed Forces was 78,412.

EDUCATION AND LANGUAGE

Education is under the control of the Provincial Governments, the cost of the publicly controlled schools being met by local taxation, aided by provincial grants. There were (1974–75) 15,191 publicly controlled elementary and secondary schools with 5,415,915 pupils. In addition there were 169,040 pupils in 1,094 private elementary and secondary schools. There are special schools for Indians with 33,825 pupils (1974–75). In 1974–75 there were 68 degree-granting universities with a full-time university enrolment of 350,960, as well as 211,260 students in other post-secondary, non-university institutions.

Canada has two official languages, English and French. At the 1971 census 67·1 per cent. of the total population gave English as their official language, 18·0 per cent. French, 13·4 per cent. both English and French, and the remaining 1·5 per cent. neither English nor French.

VITAL STATISTICS

Births, Deaths and Marriages, 1974

Province	Births	Deaths	Marriages
Alberta..........	29,813	11,252	16,691
British Columbia.	35,450	19,177	21,734
Manitoba........	17,311	8,430	9,231
New Brunswick..	11,444	5,205	6,108
Newfoundland...	10,236	3,286	4,276
Nova Scotia.....	12,941	6,899	7,112
Ontario.........	124,229	60,556	72,716
P.E.I...........	1,939	1,088	990
Quebec.........	85,627	42,767	51,532
Saskatchewan....	15,118	7,814	7,988
Yukon..........	495	114	190
N. W. Territories.	1,042	206	256
	345,645	166,794	198,824

Canada's Birth Rate per 1,000 population (1974) 15·0; Death Rate 7·4; Marriage Rate 8·9; Divorces 45,019.

REVENUE AND EXPENDITURE

Year ended March 31	Total Revenue ($)	Total Expenditure ($)
1972	14,226,557,770	14,840,865,151
1973	16,601,603,475	16,120,734,605
1974	19,383,016,716	20,055,659,307
1975	24,908,758,525	26,054,870,953

DEBT

Year ended March 31	Gross Public Debt ($)	Net Public Debt ($)
1972	47,723,635,726	17,936,681,625
1973	51,715,635,066	17,455,812,755
1974	55,557,065,787	18,128,455,346
1975	62,696,004,386	19,274,567,774

Banking.—There were 10 chartered banks on March 31, 1976, with assets of $111,828,051,000. Deposits were $101,515,330,000 of which $35,412,667,000 were personal savings.

TRADE

Total trade of Canada in 1975 was valued at $31,995,724,000 (exports) and $34,668,000,000 (imports). Value of trade with Canada's largest trading partners in 1975 was as follows:

Country	Imports ($)	Exports ($)
United States	23,516,282,000	20,862,455,000
Japan...........	1,232,812,000	2,115,266,000
United Kingdom .	1,226,635,000	1,798,614,000
West Germany...	796,137,000	583,526,000
Italy............	388,601,000	468,982,000
Netherlands......	160,342,000	460,356,000
U.S.S.R.........	28,556,000	407,097,000
People's Republic. of China.......	56,409,000	376,424,000
Belgium and Luxemburg....	144,256,000	374,598,000
France..........	493,008,000	331,629,000
Venezuela........	1,102,235,000	291,417,000
Australia........	344,957,000	224,890,000
Mexico..........	95,883,000	218,259,000
Cuba...........	85,548,000	217,992,000
Brazil...........	166,618,000	192,553,000
Norway.........	114,493,000	170,338,000
Iran............	758,100,000	145,384,000
South Africa.....	194,452,000	113,468,000
Sweden.........	206,950,000	93,609,000
Saudi Arabia.....	746,715,000	34,856,000

Canada's Trade with the United Kingdom

	1974	1975
Imports from U.K.	$1,126,489,000	$1,226,635,000
Exports to U.K...	$1,886,325,000	$1,798,614,000

CANADIAN PRODUCTION

Agriculture.—About 7 per cent. of the total land area of Canada is classified as farm land and approximately half of this is under cultivation, the remainder being woodland or suitable only for grazing purposes. More than three-quarters of the land now cultivated is found in the prairie region of Western Canada. Farm cash receipts from the sale of farm products in 1975 were $9,790,299,000. Livestock, poultry and eggs contributed $3,432,330,000; field crops $4,658,959,000 and dairy products $1,349,320,000.

Canadian grain crops (in thousands of bushels):

ALL CANADA	1973	1974	1975
Wheat........	604,738	488,513	627,515
Oats.........	326,880	254,745	289,619
Barley.......	469,570	404,286	437,251
Corn for grain	110,365	101,440	142,648
Rapeseed.....	53,200	51,300	72,100

Livestock.—In 1976, the livestock included 13,696,500 cattle, 504,500 sheep, 5,467,300 hogs & 36,772,000 poultry. The total milk production in 1975 was 17,674,949,000 lb.; butter, 291,865,000 lb.; factory cheese, 265,312,000 lb.; concentrated milk products 766,166,000 lb.; ice cream mix 31,555,000 gallons.

Fur Production.—Fur farms in Canada in 1974–5 produced 1,114,102 pelts valued at $16,587,286, mink contributing 99 per cent of the total. Wild life pelts totalled 3,241,148 with a value of $24,949,708.

Fisheries.—The total value of fishing products and by-products in 1974 was $709,033,000.

Forestry.—About 1,259,192 square miles, or 35 per cent. of the total land area is in forests, producing in 1973, about 673,160,000,000 cubic feet of merchantable timber. The value of forest products in 1973 was: newsprint $1,339,411,000; paper (other than newsprint) $912,869,000; lumber $2,227,156,000; wood pulp $1,301,486,000.

Minerals.—Canada was, in 1973, the world's leading producer of nickel, silver, zinc and asbestos, and ranked second in gypsum, molybdenum, potash and copper. The total value of mineral production in 1975 was $13,402,603,000. The value of principal minerals produced was: crude petroleum $3,781,067,000; copper $1,016,819,000; nickel $1,109,230,000; zinc $895,357,000; iron ore $719,036,000; natural gas $686,614,000; natural gas by-products $767,766,000; potash $346,806,000; asbestos $266,943,000; gold $276,125,000; silver $176,627,000; coal $575,800,000; cement $265,283,000; sand and gravel $260,340,000; lead $151,837,000.

COMMUNICATIONS

Railways.—The total first main track mileage of railways in operation on Dec. 31, 1974, was 44,266 miles, the capital of the railways being (1974) $6,141,787,049; operating revenues $2,568,993,823; and operating expenses $2,512,922,021. In 1974 the passengers carried on railways numbered 24,134,340, and revenue freight 138,655,302 ton-miles.

Shipping.—The registered shipping on Dec. 31, 1975 including inland vessels, was 31,288 vessels with gross tonnage 4,135,367. The volume of international shipping handled at Canadian ports in 1974 was 116,966,358 tons loaded and 66,930,216 tons unloaded.

Canals.—The bulk of canal shipping in Canada is handled through the Montreal-Lake Ontario and Welland Canal sections of the St. Lawrence Seaway. Total Seaway transits in 1975 (unduplicated between the two sections) numbered 7,099 carrying 66,895,989 cargo tons. Principal commodities carried were iron ore, wheat, corn, barley, soybeans, fuel oil, manufactured iron and steel, and coal.

Civil Aviation.—The number of passengers carried in 1974 (all carriers) was 24,621,126. 550,786,432 ton-miles of freight were carried.

Motor Vehicles.—Total motor vehicle registrations numbered 11,002,003 in 1974.

Post.—There were 8,665 postal facilities operating in Canada on March 31, 1975. 5,236,834 points of call were served by letter carriers on 11,968 full and 459 partial letter carrier routes. Mail was delivered to 887,338 customers through 4,956 rural routes and suburban services. Total postal revenue in the fiscal year 1974–75 was $617,743,000; total expenditure $938,682,000.

YUKON TERRITORY

The Yukon Act, 1970, as amended, provides for the administration of the Territory by a Commissioner acting under instructions from time to time given by the Governor in Council or the Minister of Indian Affairs and Northern Development. Legislative powers, analogous to those of a provincial government, are exercised by the Commissioner in Council. The Council comprises twelve members elected from electoral districts in the Territory. The area of the Territory is 207,076 square miles with a population (Jan. 1, 1976) of 21,000. Mining is the chief industry, though trapping remains important and there is considerable timber production. Mining production, including asbestos, copper, silver, lead, zinc, gold and nickel, was valued at $228,898,000 in 1975.

SEAT OF GOVERNMENT, Whitehorse. Pop. (1971) 11,217.

Commissioner, J. Smith.

NORTHWEST TERRITORIES

The Northwest Territories Act, 1970, as amended, provides for an executive, legislative and judicial structure. Legislative powers are exercised by the Commissioner in Council under the direction of the Minister of Indian Affairs and Northern Development. Council comprises 15 elected members.

The Northwest Territories are subdivided into the districts of Mackenzie, Keewatin and Franklin.

The area of the Northwest Territories is 1,304,903 square miles with a population of 38,000 (estimated Jan. 1, 1976). The chief industry is mining, with a total value of $189,477,000 in 1975. Zinc and lead contributed 74 per cent. of the total; gold and silver 21 per cent., and natural gas and petroleum 4 per cent.

SEAT OF GOVERNMENT, Yellowknife. Pop. (1971) 6,122.

Commissioner, S. M. Hodgson.

PROVINCES OF CANADA

ALBERTA

Area and Population.—The Province of Alberta has an area of 255,285 square miles, including about 6,485 square miles of water, with a population (estimated January, 1976) of 1,804,000.

Government.—The Government is vested in a Lieutenant-Governor and Legislative Assembly composed of 75 members, elected for five years, representing 75 electoral districts in the Province. At a provincial election held in March, 1975, the Progressive Conservative Party took 69 seats, Social Credit Party (in office for 36 years), 4, the

New Democratic Party, one seat and Independent one seat.

Lieut.-Governor, His Honour Ralph G. Steinhauer
special allowance

Executive

Premier, and President of Council, Hon. Peter Lougheed......................	$40,500
Speaker of the Legislative Assembly, Hon. G. Amerongen......................	21,500
Deputy Speaker, Dr. D. J. McCrimmon..	18,500
Leader of the Opposition, R. C. Clark.....	35,500
Clerk of the Executive Council, H. B. Hobbs.	

Clerk of the Legislative Assembly, (vacant)
The Judicature.
The Supreme Court of Alberta.
Appellate Division, Hon. William McGillivray (C.J.)......................... $55,000
Judges, Hons. J. M. Cairns; C. W. Clement; N. D. McDermid; G. H. Allen; W. R. Sinclair; D. C. Prowse; A. F. Moir; W. J. Haddad....... each 50,000
Trial Division, Hon. J. V. H. Milvain (C.J.) 55,000
Judges, Hons. N. Primrose; P. Greschuk; M. E. Manning; W. J. C. Kirby; A. M. Dechene; M. B. O'Byrne; H. J. MacDonald; S. S. Lieberman; J. C. Cavanagh; W. K. Moore; D. H. Bowen; M. E. Shannon; F. H. Quigley; G. A. C. Steer; D. C. McDonald; J. H. Laycraft........................... 50,000

London Office, 37 Hill Street, W.1.
Production.—The mining, manufacturing and construction industries have increased in economic impact so much more forcibly that agriculture is no longer of prime importance in Alberta.

The net value of production by industries (estimated 1975) is: mining $5,374,000,000; construction $1,570,000,000; manufacturing $1,407,000,000; electric power $221,000,000; agriculture $1,519,000,000; other $32,000,000. Total: $10,131,000,000.

Mining (1975 preliminary):—Crude oil $3,254,971,000; natural gas $1,639,898,000; natural gas by-products $748,063,000; coal $185,000,000; sulphur $87,749,000; cement $25,410,000.

Manufacturing.—The value of manufacturing shipments (1975 preliminary) was $3,812,000,000. Number of industrial establishments 1,860, total employees 60,168. The leading industries are slaughtering and meat processing, petroleum refining, chemicals and chemical products, primary metal and metal fabricating products.

Government Finance—Fiscal Year 1976–77 [Budgetary Estimates]—Revenue $2,930,000,000; Expenditure $2,961,400,000. NOTE: The Budgetary revenue figure does not include funds allocated to the Alberta Heritage Savings Trust Fund.

CAPITAL.—Edmonton. Population (June 30, 1975) 451,635. Other centres are Calgary (453,812), Lethbridge (44,522), Medicine Hat (30,174) and Red Deer (30,107).

BRITISH COLUMBIA

Area and Population.—British Columbia has a total area estimated at 366,255 square miles, with a population of 2,184,621 at the census of June 1, 1971.

Government.—The Government consists of a Lieutenant-Governor and an Executive Council together with a Legislative Assembly of 55 members.

Lieut.-Governor, Col. Hon. Walter Stewart Owen, Q.C., Ll.D.
Executive Council
Premier and President of the Council, Hon. William Richards Bennett........... $28,000
Provincial Secretary, Deputy Premier, and Minister of Recreation and Travel Industry, Hon. Grace Mary McCarthy......... 24,000
Attorney-General, Hon. Garde Basil Gardom, Q.C............................ 24,000
Finance, Hon. Evan Maurice Wolfe...... 24,000
Agriculture and Economic Development, Hon. Donald McGray Phillips............. 24,000
Education, Hon. Patrick Lucey McGeer.... 24,000
Municipal Affairs and Housing, Hon. Hugh Austin Curtis...................... 24,000

Mines and Petroleum Resources and Forests, Hon. Thomas Manville Waterland..... $24,000
Labour, Hon. Louis Allan Williams....... 24,000
Health, Hon. Robert Howard McClelland 24,000
Highways and Public Works, Hon. Alexander Vaughan Fraser.................. 24,000
Transport and Communications, Hon. Jack Davis.............................. 24,000
Human Resources, Hon. William Nick Vander Zalm....................... 24,000
Consumer Services, Hon. Kenneth Rafe Mair............................... 24,000
Environment, Hon. James Arthur Nielsen.. 24,000
Speaker, Legislative Assembly, Hon. D. E. Smith............................. $11,000
Note: These salaries have been reduced by 10 per cent. for the period April 1, 1976 to March 31, 1977.

The Judicature.
Court of Appeal—Chief Justice of British Columbia, Hon. J. L. Farris.......... $55,000
Justices of Appeal, Hons. E. B. Bull; H. A. Maclean; M. M. McFarlane; A. E. Branca; A. B. Robertson; J. D. Taggart; P. D. Seaton; W. R. McIntyre; A. B. C. Carrothers....................... 50,000
Supreme Court—Chief Justice, Hon. N. T. Nemetz............................ 55,000
Puisne Judges, Hons. J. G. Ruttan; D. R. Verchere; F. C. Munroe; J. S. Aikins; V. L. Dryer; J. G. Gould; J. A. Macdonald; W. K. Smith; G. G. S. Rae; A. B. Macfarlane; E. E. Hinkson; H. C. McKay; R. P. Anderson; T. R. Berger; D. E. Andrews; K. E. Meredith; A. A. Mackoff; W. A. Craig; E. D. Fulton; J. C. Bouck; S. M. Toy; H. E. Hutcheon; L. G. McKenzie; Hon. W. A. Schultz.......................each 50,000

Agent-General in London, R. M. Strachan, British Columbia House, 1 Regent Street, S.W.1.
Finances.—Estimated current Revenue for 1976–77, $3,615,250,000. Estimated current expenditure, $3,615,245,000. There was no direct debt at March 31, 1976.

Production and Industry.—The production levels of the four leading industries were estimated for 1975 as follows: wood manufactures, $1,500,000,000; paper and allied industries, $1,400,000,000; minerals, $1,223,300,000; agriculture, $373,000,000; fisheries, $146,000,000. Manufacturing activity is based largely on the processing of products of the main basic industries. The principal manufacturing centres are Vancouver, New Westminster, Victoria, North Vancouver and Port Moody. Forestry and forest-based industries form the most important economic activity, accounting for approximately 40 per cent. of total production. British Columbia is the leading province of Canada in the quantity and value of its timber and sawmill products. Mining, the second most important economic activity, is based on copper, zinc, lead, iron concentrates, molybdenum, coal, natural gas, crude petroleum, asbestos and nickel. Molybdenum production is approximately 90 per cent. of the Canadian total. The most important agricultural products are livestock, eggs and poultry, fruits and dairy products. Salmon accounts for approximately 75 per cent. of the value of fisheries Other species include halibut, herring, sole, cod, flounder, perch, tuna and shellfish. The climate is healthy, quite moderate on the coast and continental east of the coast mountains. The economy is dependent upon markets outside the province for

the disposal of most of the products of her industry. Canadian and world markets receive forestry, mineral, fishing and agricultural products.

Transport.—The province has deep water harbours which are well serviced by railways and modern paved highways. Vancouver is the base for regular scheduled air routes to other parts of Canada, the United States, Europe, Mexico, South America, Hawaii, Fiji, Australia, Japan, Hong Kong and the Middle East.

Principal Cities.—CAPITAL, Ψ VICTORIA, Metropolitan population (1972) 199,000. Ψ Vancouver (founded in 1886), the largest city in the Province, metropolitan population (1972) 1,098,000, is the western terminus of the Canadian Pacific Railway and the Canadian National Railways (the C.N.R. also has a terminus at Prince Rupert) and the southern terminus of the British Columbia Railway, and possesses one of the finest natural harbours in the world, servicing a variety of vessels, including large bulk cargo carriers. Other principal cities are Prince George (65,000), Kamloops (55,000), Kelowna (45,000) and Nanaimo (44,000).

MANITOBA

Area and Population.—Manitoba, originally the Red River settlement, is the central province of Canada. The Province has a considerable area of prairie land but is also a land of wide diversity combining 400 miles of sea-coast, large lakes and rivers covering an area of 30,225 square miles and Precambrian rock which covers about three-fifths of the Province. The total area is 251,000 square miles with a population estimated at 98,000 in 1973.

Government.—The Government is administered by a Lieutenant-Governor, assisted by an Executive Council of 15 Ministers, who are members of the Legislative Assembly of 57 members. Each member of the Legislative Assembly receives an annual sessional indemnity of $17,352.

The New Democratic Party has formed the government of Manitoba since June 25, 1969. The standing in the House at May 1, 1975 was: New Democrats 31, Progressive Conservative 21, Liberal 3.

Lieut.-Governor, His Honour Francis L. Jobin (1976).

Executive

Premier and President of the Council, Minister of Finances, Hon. Edward Schreyer . . $16,600
Minister of Labour and Deputy Premier, Hon. Russell Paulley.
Attorney-General and Minister of Municipal Affairs, Hon. Howard Pawley.
Health and Social Development, Hon. Laurent L. Desjardins.
Agriculture, Hon. Samuel Uskiw.
Northern Affairs, Hon. Ronald McBryde.
Tourism, Recreation and Cultural Affairs, Hon. René Toupin.
Education, Hon. Ben Hanushak.
Highways, Hon. Peter Burtniak.
Industry and Commerce, Hon. Leonard Evans.
Public Works, Hon. Russell Doern.
Mines, Resources and Environmental Management, Hon. Sidney Green.
Consumer, Corporate and Internal Services, Hon. Ian Turnbull.
Urban Affairs, Hon. Saul Miller.
Co-operative Development, Hon. Harvey L. Bostrom.
Minister Responsible for Public Insurance Corporation, Hon. William Uruski.
Minister Responsible for Corrections and Rehabilitative Services, Hon. J. R. Boyce.
            Ministers each $15,600

Speaker of the Legislative Assembly, Hon. P. Fox.

The Judicature

Court of Appeal:—
 Chief Justice of Manitoba, Hon. Samuel Freedman $39,000
 Puisne Judges, Hons. R. D. Guy; A. M. Mounin; R. J. Matos; G. C. Hall . each   35,000
Queen's Bench:—
 Chief Justice, Q.B.D. Hon. A. S. Dewar .   39,000
 Puisne Judges, Hons. I. Nitikman; L. Deniset; J. E. Wilson; J. M. Hunt; W. S. Wright; J. R. Solomon; A. C. Hamilton . . . . each   35,000

Finance.—The revenue of the provincial government, 1975–76, is estimated at $1,163,656,000 and the expenditure $1,176,490,000.

Agriculture and Livestock.—The total land area in Manitoba is 135,536,000 acres, of which 19,088,000 acres are in occupied farms. The gross value of agriculture production in 1975 was estimated at $1,106,000,000 and livestock $332,000,000. Farm animals in June 1974, numbered 1,300,000 cattle, 800,000 pigs, 29,000 sheep and 4,095,000 poultry.

Manufactures.—The gross annual value of manufactured products in 1975 was estimated at $2,493,000,000. Manufacturing enterprises employed about 50,300 persons in Sept. 1975. The chief manufacturing centres are Winnipeg, Brandon and Selkirk. The largest manufacturing industry is the food and beverage industry, followed by the clothing and metal fabricating industries.

CAPITAL.—Winnipeg, population (estimated, 1975), 553,000. Other centres are Brandon (35,237), Thompson (20,625) and Portage la Prairie (13,300).

The capital city of Winnipeg was amalgamated with its suburban municipalities on January 1, 1972 to form one city with a central government.

NEW BRUNSWICK

Area and Population.—New Brunswick is situated between 45°–48° N. lat. and 63° 47′–69° W. long. and comprises an area of 28,354 square miles with an estimated population (Jan. 1974) of 658,000. It was first colonized by British subjects in 1761, and in 1783 by inhabitants of New England, who had been dispossessed of their property in consequence of their loyalty to the British Crown.

Government.—The Government is administered by a Lieutenant-Governor, assisted by an Executive Council, and a Legislative Assembly of 58 members elected by the people. At the General Election of November 18, 1974, 33 Conservative and 25 Liberal members were returned.

Lieutenant-Governor, His Honour H. J. Robichaud (1969) $33,000

Executive

Premier, Hon. Richard B. Hatfield $38,000
Justice, Hon. P. S. Creaghan.
Transportation, Hon. W. G. Bishop.
Agriculture and Rural Development, Hon. Malcolm McLeod.
Economic Growth, Hon. Lawrence Garvie.
Health, Hon. G. W. N. Cockburn.
Education and Historical Resources Administration, Hon. G. S. Merrithew.
Natural Resources, Hon. Roland Boudreau.
Labour and Manpower, Hon. R. E. Logan.
Finance and Chairman, New Brunswick Electric Power Commission, Hon. Edison Stairs.
Municipal Affairs, Hon. Horace Smith.
Fisheries and Provincial Secretary, Hon. Omer Leger.
Tourism and Environment, Hon. Fernand Dube.
Chairman, Treasury Board, Hon. J. S. Brooks.
Social Services, Hon. Leslie Hull.
Youth, Hon. J. P. Ouellett.

Supply and Services, Hon. George Horton.
Ministers, each $26,500·00.
Speaker of the House, Hon. W. J. Woodroffe
$19,000

The Judicature
Court of Appeal
Chief Justice, C. J. A. Hughes.
Judges of Appeal, Hons. R. V. Limerick;
J. N. Bugold; Hon. H. C. Ryan.

Queen's Bench Division
Chief Justice, Q.B.D., Hon. A. J. Cormier. $39,000
Judges, Hons. D. Dickson; J. P. Barry;
C. I. L. Legere; R. C. Stevenson; S. G.
Stratton; G. A. Richard..........each $35,000
Finance.—The estimated revenue for the year
ending March 31, 1976, was $883,767,000 and
ordinary expenditure, $890,991,200.

Manufactures.—Forest products: pulp, paper and
timber form the major manufacture group, followed by foods, transportation equipment, metal
fabrication, chemicals and chemical products, non-
metallic mineral products, electrical products and
miscellaneous other products. Saint John is the
principal manufacturing centre. Total value of
manufactured products was $1,690,000,000 in 1975.

Agriculture and Livestock.—The total land area is
17,582,720 acres of which about 85 per cent. is
forested. The Province is the largest potato-pro-
ducing area of Canada, grown chiefly in the upper
Saint John River Valley. Dairy farming is next in
importance with, on Jan. 1, 1976, 106,000 cattle,
7,500 sheep, 41,000 hogs and 1,455,000 (approx.)
poultry. Farm cash receipts $99,052,000 in 1975.

Fishing.—The chief commercial fish are lobsters,
sardines, herring, tuna, crab, plaice, red fish and cod,
with an estimated market value of $105,000,000 in
1975.

Minerals.—Extensive zinc, lead and copper deposits are now being mined in the north-eastern
part of the Province with a lead smelter operating
in conjunction with one mine operation. The only
antimony mine in Canada is operating in the
Southern part of the Province and coal continues to
be mined at an increasing rate. High calcium
limestone, lightweight aggregates and horticultural
peat have also shown growth in recent years. Exploration by two major companies on two newly
discovered potash plants is under way. Total
mineral production was valued at $219,000,000 in
1974.

Principal Cities.—CAPITAL ΨFredericton: population (1973), 42,000. Ψ Saint John (pop. 106,745) is
one of the principal winter ports of Canada and is
connected by C.P.R. and Canadian National Railways with Montreal; Moncton (47,890); Bathurst
(16,675); Edmundston (12,365); Campbellton
(10,335).

NEWFOUNDLAND AND LABRADOR
Area and Population.—The Island of Newfoundland is situated between 46° 37′–51° 37′ N. latitude
and 52° 44′–59° 30′ W. longitude, on the north-
east side of the Gulf of St. Lawrence, and is
separated from the North American Continent by
the Straits of Belle Isle on the N.W. and by Cabot
Strait on the S.W. The island is about 317 miles
long and 316 miles broad and is triangular in shape,
with Cape Bauld (N.), Cape Race (S.E.) and Cape
Ray (S.W.) at the angles. It comprises an area of
43,359 sq. miles with a population (estimated Jan.
1975) (inclusive of Labrador) of 546,000.

Labrador forms the most easterly part of the
North American continent, and extends from Blanc
Sablon, at the northeast entrance to the Straits of
Belle Isle, on the south, to Cape Chidley, at the
eastern entrance to Hudson's Straits on the north.

It has an area estimated at 112,826 sq. miles.
Government.—On March 31, 1949 Newfound-
land became the 10th Province of the Dominion of
Canada. The Government is administered by a
Lieutenant-Governor, aided by an Executive Coun-
cil and a Legislative Assembly of 51 members.
Lieutenant-Governor, Hon. Gordon A.
Winter (July 2, 1974).

Executive
Premier, F. D. Moores.
President of the Council and Minister of Public Works
and Services, Dr. T. C. Farrell.
Minister of Justice, T. A. Hickman.
Education, H. W. House.
Finance, C. W. Doody.
Health, H. A. Collins.
Mines and Energy and Intergovernment Affairs, J. C.
Crosbie.
Social Services, R. C. Brett.
Municipal Affairs and Housing, B. Peckford.
Transportation and Communication, J. C. Morgan.
Industrial Development and Rural Development, J. H.
Lundrigan.
Manpower and Industrial Relations, E. Maynard.
Provincial Affairs and Environment, A. J. Murphy.
Fisheries, W. C. Carter.
Rehabilitation and Recreation, R. Wells (acting).
Tourism, T. V. Hickey.
Forestry and Agriculture, J. G. Rousseau, jr.

Speaker of the House of Assembly, G. Ottenheimer.
Clerk of the Executive Council, J. G. Channing.

The Legislature.
A General Election was held on Sept. 16, 1975,
when 30 Progressive Conservatives, 16 Liberals,
4 Liberal Reform and 1 Independent Liberal were
returned.
Finance.—The estimated net general revenue in
the fiscal year ending March 31, 1977, is
$651,661,000 and the net expenditure on current
and capital accounts $799,963,500.
Production and Industry.—The main primary
industries are fishing, forestry and mining. In 1974
shipments of fish products were valued at $86·1
million. In 1975 paper products from the 3 pulp
and paper mills were valued at $160·0 million and
the 12 mining operations plus the structural materials producers had combined shipments of
$568·2 million of which $486·6 million was from
the 3 iron ore mines located in Labrador. Manufacturing shipments with the exclusion of fish and
paper products totalled $435·8 million in 1974.
Transport.—The province is connected to mainland Canada by a ferry service from North Sydney,
Nova Scotia to Port aux Basques and Argentia.
The main line of the railway extends from St.
John's on the east coast to Port aux Basques on the
west coast. Transport between various points on
the island is by highway but the south coast and
Labrador still rely on the coastal boat service.
Principal Cities.—The Capital, St. John's (population 1971 Census, Greater St. John's 131,814) is
North America's oldest city, and thus of historical
interest and is the seat of the provincial legislature,
the site of most provincial and federal government
offices and the principal port for the island of Newfoundland. Newfoundland's second city of Corner
Brook (population 1971 Census, 26,309) is situated
on the west coast, its principal industry being its
pulp and paper mill.

LABRADOR
Labrador, the most northerly district in the
Province of Newfoundland, forms the most
easterly part of the North American continent, and
extends from Blanc Sablon, at the north-east

entrance to the Straits of Belle Isle, on the south, to Cape Chidley, at the eastern entrance to Hudson's Straits on the north. The territory under the jurisdiction of Newfoundland has an area estimated at 112,826 square miles, with a population (1971) of 28,165. Labrador is noted for its cod fisheries and also possesses valuable salmon, herring, trout and seal fisheries. Newfoundland (Labrador) supplies more iron ore than any other province in Canada and the huge hydro-electric plant on the Churchill River will be the largest in the world with a 5,250,000 kW. capacity when completed.

NOVA SCOTIA

Area and Population.—Nova Scotia is a peninsula between 43° 25'–47° N. lat. and 59° 40'–66° 25' W. long., and is connected with New Brunswick by a low fertile isthmus about thirteen miles wide. It comprises an area of 21,425 square miles including 1,023 square miles of lakes and rivers with a 6,479 miles of shoreline. No place is more than 35 miles from the Atlantic Ocean. Total population (1971 census) 788,960.

Government.—The Government consists of a Lieutenant-Governor and a 46-member elected Legislative Assembly, from which the Executive Council (Cabinet) is selected. The Lieutenant-Governor represents the Queen and is appointed by the Governor-in-Council.

Lieutenant-Governor, Hon. Clarence Gosse,
M.D. (*plus expense allowance* $12,000)... $35,000

Executive Council

Premier, Hon. Gerald A. Regan, Q.C.
(*plus members' sessional indemnity* $9,600
and expense allowance $4,800)......... $25,000
Finance, Hon. P. M. Nicholson, Q.C.
Recreation, Hon. A. Garnet Brown.
Attorney-General, Hon. L. L. Pace, Q.C.
Public Works, Hon. B. Comeau.
Social Services, Hon. W. M. MacEachern.
Education, Hon. M. C. MacAskill, M.D.
Development, Hon. G. M. Mitchell, Q.C.
Labour and Housing, Hon. W. R. Fitzgerald.
Consumer Affairs and Municipal Affairs, Hon. G. M. Bagnell.
Tourism, Hon. M. E. De Lory, M.D.
Environment and Agriculture and Marketing, Hon. J. Hawkins.
Highways, Hon. J. Fraser Mooney.
Lands and Forests and Fisheries, Hon. A. H. Cameron.
Public Health, Hon. A. E. Sullivan, Q.C.

Cabinet Ministers receive $21,000 a year, *plus* member's sessional indemnity $9,600 and expense allowance $4,800.

The Judicature
Supreme Court—Appeal Division

Chief Justice, Hon. I. M. MacKeigan..... $55,000
Judges, Hons. T. H. Coffin; A. G. Cooper;
A. L. Macdonald.................. 50,000

Trial Division

Chief Justice, Hon. G. S. Cowan........ 55,000
Judges, Hons. F. W. Bissett; G. L. S. Hart;
M. C. Jones; V. A. L. Morrison; A. J.
MacIntosh......................... 55,000
Finance.—The revenue for the fiscal year ending March 31, 1975, was $672,053,417 and expenditure was $794,529,807. The net direct debt was $319,065,487.

Manufacturing.—Manufacturing constitutes the single most important sector of the economy. Shipments were worth $1,711,500,000 in 1975 with a total value added of more than $466,800,000. Manufacturing plants provide employment for 43,000 or 15 per cent. of the labour force. Capital

expenditure has increased from $690,400,000 in 1975 to $758,100,000 (estimated) in 1976.

Utilities.—There is one major electrical utility; the Nova Scotia Power Corporation. With more than 2,300 employees, the Corporation delivered over 5·2 billion kilowatt hours of electrical energy during the year ending March 31, 1976. Power developed in the province is produced in fossil-fuelled thermal and hydro plants and is supported by auxiliary 85 MW gas turbines which provide rapid " peak demand " service. The Corporation, an agent of the provincial government, also operates seven retail electrical appliance outlets throughout the province.

Strait of Canso.—The Strait of Canso Superport in Nova Scotia is the largest deepwater harbour development on the Atlantic coast of North America. Government agencies and private corporations have been building this unique deepwater facility and related basic industries for more than 10 years. Existing industry includes an oil refinery, a thermal power generating station, a heavy water plant, bleached sulphate mill and newsprint mill. Major upgrading of the airport facilities at Port Hawkesbury was started in 1976 to enable commercial airlines to service the Strait area.

Tourism.—Between May 1 and October 31, 1975, 1,350,000 visitors spent $88,000,000 in the province. There was an increase of visitors of 4·3 per cent. over 1974.

Forest Products.—The estimated gross value of primary and secondary forestry is $213,000,000 annually. Forest lands total 10,982,000 acres or 80·1 per cent. of the land area. About 72 per cent. of forest land is privately owned. Forest based industries employ about 6,000.

Fishing.—The value of fish landed in 1975 was a record $88,793,000. Products have been diversified and enlarged into a variety of processed foods that are increasing in number. Primary fishing and fish processing employed 15,811 in 1974.

Mining.—The total value of mineral production in 1975 was estimated at $96,688,000, of which $47,600,000 was contributed by coal. Structural materials, gypsum ($12,410,000), salt ($12,355,000) and sand and gravel ($12,500,000) followed in dollar value.

Agriculture.—Farm cash receipts were estimated at about $115,784,000 in 1975. About 6 per cent. of the total area, or 1,781,000 acres, is classified as agricultural land, dairy products being the major sector.

Principal cities.—Capital ΨHALIFAX, including the neighbouring city of Dartmouth, has a population of over 225,000. In addition to a 56-acre container-handling terminal, a super autoport has been built at Port Halifax to handle both the export and import of motor vehicles. A second container port will be operational by 1977. A shipyard, with dry-dock, can build and repair the largest ocean-going liners. The harbour, ice-free the year round, is the main Atlantic winter port of Canada. Other cities and towns include Ψ Sydney (33,230), Ψ Glace Bay (22,400), Amherst (9,966) and New Glasgow (10,849).

CAPE BRETON ISLAND

This has been part of Nova Scotia since 1819. It is the centre of the steel manufacturing and coal mining industries, and is also noted for its large lakes and beautiful coastal scenery, making it a tourist attraction in Canada.

ONTARIO

Area and Population.—The Province of Ontario contains a total area of 412,582 sq. miles, with a population (estimated June 1976) of 8,300,000.

Government.—The Government is vested in a Lieutenant-Governor and a Legislative Assembly of 125 members elected for five years. The state of the parties in June 1976 was 51 Progressive Conservatives, 38 New Democrats, 36 Liberals.

Lieutenant-Governor, Hon. Pauline McGibbon, Q.C. (1974).

Executive Council

Premier and President of the Council, Hon. William G. Davis, Q.C.
Colleges and Universities, Hon. H. C. Parrott.
Education, Hon. T. L. Wells.
Health, Hon. F. S. Miller.
Community and Social Services, Hon. J. A. Taylor, Q.C.
Agriculture and Food, Hon. W. Newman.
Environment, Hon. G. A. Kerr, Q.C.
Labour, Hon. Bette M. Stephenson, M.D.
Natural Resources, Hon. L. Bernier.
Industry and Tourism, Hon. C. Bennett.
Transport and Communications, Hon. J. W. Snow.
Justice and Solicitor-General, Hon. J. P. MacBeth.
Consumer and Commercial Relations, Hon. S. B. Handleman.
Treasurer, Economics and Intergovernmental Affairs, Hon. W. D. McKeough.
Government Services, Hon. Margaret Scrivener.
Revenue, Hon. A. K. Meen, Q.C.
Management Board, Hon. J. A. C. Auld.
Resources Development, Hon. D. R. Irvine.
Energy, Hon. D. R. Timbrell.
Housing, Hon. J. R. Rhodes.
Social Development, Hon. Margaret Birch.
Culture and Recreation, Hon. R. Welch, Q.C.
Correctional Services, Hon. J. R. Smith.
Attorney-General, Hon. R. McMurtry, Q.C.
Without Portfolio, Hon. R. Brunelle (*Chairman of Cabinet*); Hon. L. C. Henderson.

Secretary of the Cabinet, Dr. E. E. Stewart.
Speaker, Legislative Assembly, Hon. R. D. Rowe.
Chief Justice of Ontario, Hon. G. A. Gale.
Chief Justice of the High Court, Hon. W. Z. Estey.

AGENT-GENERAL IN LONDON, W. A. Cornell, 13 Charles II Street, S.W.1.

Livestock.—In January 1976 the numbers of livestock included—cattle, 3,251,000; sheep and lambs, 133,000 and pigs, 2,000,000.

Forestry.—Productive forested lands cover 164,000 sq. miles or about 48 per cent. of the land area of the Province. Paper and allied industries are by far the most important sector of Ontario's forest industry.

Minerals.—Ontario leads other Canadian provinces in production of metallic minerals, producing more than 40 per cent. of the national total. Ontario produces all Canada's calcium, magnesium, platinum group metals and nepheline syenite, more than 80 per cent. of uranium, 70 per cent. of nickel, 60 per cent. of salt, 50 per cent. of elemental sulphur and 30 per cent. of zinc.

Electrical Power.—Ontario Hydro produced 84·2 billion kWh of primary electric energy in 1975.

Manufacture.—Ontario is the chief manufacturing province in Canada, producing over 51 per cent. of all manufactured goods. Seventy-five per cent. of Canada's fully manufactured exports are produced in Ontario.

CAPITAL.—Ψ Toronto (population, 2,741,000) has a wide range of manufacturing and service industries and is a centre of education, business and finance. Other major urban areas are: Ottawa, the national capital (626,000); Ψ Hamilton (498,523),

with iron and steel industry, metal fabrication, machinery, electrical and chemical industries; London (296,000), a business and manufacturing centre; Ψ Windsor (266,000); Kitchener (238,000) and Sudbury (154,000).

FEDERAL CAPITAL

OTTAWA, the Federal Capital, 111 miles west of Montreal and 247 miles north-east of Toronto, is a city on the south bank of the Ottawa river. The city was chosen as the Capital of the Province of Canada in 1857 and was later selected as the site of the Dominion capital. Ottawa contains the Parliamentary Buildings, the Public Archives, Royal Mint, National Museum, National Art Gallery and the Dominion Observatory.

A National Arts Centre opened on June 2, 1969, near the Parliament buildings. Facilities provided on 6½ acres of terraced land include an opera house with seating for 2,300, a theatre (800 seats), an experimental studio (300 seats) and a hall (100 seats).

Manufacturing is also carried on, food production, printing and publishing being of greatest importance. Ottawa is connected with Lake Ontario by the Rideau Canal. The City population was 302,341 at the Census of 1971; Metropolitan Ottawa (estimated, 1974), 626,000.

PRINCE EDWARD ISLAND

Area and Population.—Prince Edward Island lies in the southern part of the Gulf of St. Lawrence, between 46°-47° N. lat. and 62°-64° 30′ W. long. It is about 130 miles in length, and from 4 to 34 miles in breadth; its area is 2,184 square miles (rather larger than that of the English county of Norfolk), and its population (1975) 119,000.

Government.—The Government is vested in a Lieut.-Governor and an Executive Council, and Legislative Assembly of 32 members elected for a term of 5 years, 16 as Councillors and 16 as Assemblymen. Party representation at July 1, 1976 was: Liberal, 23; Conservative 6; *vacant*, 3.

Lieutenant-Governor, His Honour Gordon L. Bennett (1974) $35,000
(and expense allowance)

Executive

Premier, President of the Executive Council and Minister of Justice, Attorney and Advocate-General, Hon. A. B. Campbell $24,500
Development, Industry and Commerce, Hon. J. H. Maloney, M.D.
Provincial Secretary and Education, Hon. B. Campbell.
Health and Social Services, Hon. Catherine Callbeck.
Highways and Public Works, Hon. B. L. Stewart.
Finance, (vacant)
The Environment, Tourism, Parks and Conservation, and Municipal Affairs, Hon. G. R. Clements.
Fisheries and Labour, Hon. G. Henderson.
Agriculture, Hon. A. E. Ings.
Without Portfolio, Hon. G. Proude.
Ministers, each $14,500 (plus expenses)

Speaker of the Legislative Assembly, Hon. C. A. Miller $3,000
Members of the Legislative Assembly receive a salary of $7,000 *plus* $3,500 expense allowance; Ministers receive their salary and allowance as members in addition to their Ministerial salary.

Supreme Court

Chief Justice, Hon. C. St. C. Trainor $55,000
Associate Justices, Hon. J. P. Nicholson; Hon. F. Large; Hon. A. Peake; Hon. C. R. McQuaid . . . . each 50,000
Finance.—The ordinary revenue in 1975–76 was $175,000,000 and the expenditure was $183,000,000.
Education.—A university and a college of applied arts and technology were established in 1969,

estimated enrolment for 1975–76 being 2,350; college of applied arts and technology 900 students.

CAPITAL, ♆ Charlottetown (pop. 18,500), on the shore of Hillsborough Bay, which forms a good harbour.

QUEBEC

Area and Population.—The Province of Quebec contains an area estimated at 594,860 square miles with a population (June, 1975), of 6,188,000.

Government.—The Government of the Province invested in a Lieutenant-Governor, a Council of ministers and a National Assembly of 110 members elected for five years. There are at present 98 Liberals, one Social Credit Rally, 6 *Parti Quebecois* and one Union National and 4 Independents.

Lieut-Governor, The Hon. Hughes Lapointe, Q.C. (Feb. 22, 1966).

Executive
Prime Minister, Robert Bourassa.
Vice-Prime Minister and Minister for Justice, Gérard D. Lévesque.
Minister for Industry and Commerce, Guy Saint-Pierre.
Education, Jean Bienvenue.
Labour and Manpower, Gerald Harvey.
Social Affairs, Claude Forget.
Municipal Affairs and the Environment, Victor Goldbloom.
Public Works and Supply, William Tetley.
Tourism, Fish and Game, Claude Simard.
Transport, Raymond Mailloux.
Communications, Denis Hardy.
Lands and Forests, Normand Toupin.
Revenue, Robert Quenneville.
Cultural Affairs, Jean-Paul L'Allier.
Financial Institutions, Companies and Cooperatives and Immigration, Lise Bacon.
Agriculture, Kevin Drummond.
Natural Resources, Gilles Massé.
Finance, Raymond Garneau.
Civil Service, Oswald Parent.
Intergovernmental Affairs, François Cloutier.
Natural Resources, Jean Cournoyer.
Solicitor-General, Fernand Lalondé.
(and 8 Ministers of State).

AGENT-GENERAL IN LONDON.—Hon. Jean Fournier, 12 Upper Grosvenor Street, W.1.

The Judicature
Queen's Bench (Montreal):—
Chief Justice, Hon. L. Tremblay.
Puisne Judges (Montreal): Hons. P. C. Casey; G. E. Rinfret; G. R. W. Owen; G. H. Montgomery; R. Brossard; M. Crête; A. Mayrand; F. Kauffman; L. E. Bélanger.
Puisne Judges (Quebec).—Hons. A. Dube; J. Turgeon; F. Lajoie; J. Chouinard; Y. Bernier.
Superior Court:—
Chief Justice, Hon. Jules Deschênes.

Finance.—The revenue for the year 1974–5 was $6,474,366,987; expenditure amounted to $6,761,469,755. The net debt (March 31, 1975) was $3,154,696,671.

Production and Industry.—The principal manufacturing centres are Montreal, Montreal East, Quebec, Trois-Rivières, Sherbrooke, Shawinigan Drummondville and Lachine. Forest lands cover 685,480 sq. km., of which 490,693 sq. km. are productive. Forest products in 1974 included: wood pulp, 6,948,254 tons; paper and paperboard, 6,422,820 tons.

Total value of shipments in the manufacturing industries in 1975 was $23,822,200,000. Value of 1975 shipments in the chief industries: Food and beverages, $4,355,300,000; Paper and allied industries, $2,309,800,000; Primary metal industries,

$1,764,700,000; Textiles, $1,234,500,000; Clothing $1,477,300,000.

Agriculture and Fisheries.—In 1975 total farm receipts were: Crops, $137,053,000; Livestock and livestock products, $1,044,133,000; Other farm receipts, $155,282,000. 116,486,000 lb. of fish to the value of $14,452,377 were landed in 1975.

Mineral Production.—Minerals to the value of $1,142,457,000 were mined during 1975, compared with $1,192,440,000 in 1974. Distribution of the 1975 total was: copper, $163,440,000; zinc, $98,261,000; asbestos, $175,634,000.

Principal Cities.—CAPITAL, ♆ Quebec (population, estimated, 1975, 187,800) historic city visited annually by thousands of tourists, and one of the great seaport towns of Canada; and ♆ Montreal (municipal population, 1,210,200) with suburbs, 2,964,219 (Metropolitan Montreal), the commercial metropolis. Other important cities are Laval (246,200); Verdun (75,000) and Sherbrooke (86,000), Montreal-Nord (93,400) and La Salle (77,000).

SASKATCHEWAN

Area and Population.—The Province of Saskatchewan lies between Manitoba on the east and Alberta on the west and has an area of 251,700 square miles (of which the land area is 220,182 sq. miles), with a population (estimated, 1975) of 912,000. Saskatchewan extends along the Canada-U.S.A. boundary for 393 miles and northwards for 761 miles. Its northern width is 276 miles.

Government.—The Government is vested in the Lieutenant-Governor, with a Legislative Assembly of 61 members. There is an Executive Council of 18 members. The Legislative Assembly is elected for 5 years and the state of the parties in July 1975, was: N.P.D., 39; Liberals 15 and Progressive Conservative 7.

Lieut.-Governor, His Honour Stephen Worobetz, M.C., M.D. (1970) $18,000

Executive Council
Premier and President of the Council, Hon. A. E. Blakeney.......................... $32,500
Attorney-General and Deputy Premier, Hon. R. Romanow, Q.C.
Industry, Hon. J. R. Messer.
Finance, Hon. E. Cowley.
Health, Hon. W. E. Smishek.
Municipal Affairs, Hon. E. I. Wood.
Labour and Social Services, Hon. G. T. Snyder.
Northern Saskatchewan, Hon. G. R. Bowerman.
Highways and Transport, Hon. E. Kramer.
Education, Hon. G. MacMurchy.
Environment, Hon. N. E. Byers.
Government Services and Telephones, Hon. J. E. Brocklebank.
Agriculture, Hon. E. E. Kaeding.
Culture and Youth, Consumer Affairs and Provincial Secretary, Hon. E. Tchorzewski.
Tourism and Renewable Resources, Hon. J. Kowalchuk.
Minerals, Hon. E. C. Whelan.
Co-operation and Co-operative Development and Consumer Affairs, Hon. W. A. Robbins.
Ministers, each $27,500.

AGENT-GENERAL IN LONDON.—E. A. Boden, 14–16 Cockspur Street, S.W.1.

Finance.—Estimated revenue year ending March 31, 1976, is $1,143,708,620; expenditure, $1,140,643,250.

CAPITAL.—Regina. Population (estimated 1975), 147,000. Other cities: Saskatoon (126,449), Moose Jaw (32,000) and Prince Albert (28,500).

The Commonwealth of Australia

AREA AND POPULATION

States and Capitals	Area (English Sq. Miles)	Population		
		Census June 30, 1966	Census June 30, 1971	Estimated Dec. 31, 1975
States				
New South Wales (Sydney).........	309,433	4,237,901	4,601,180	4,811,100
Queensland (Brisbane)..............	667,000	1,674,324	1,827,065	2,015,100
South Australia (Adelaide)...........	380,070	1,094,984	1,173,707	1,241,700
Tasmania (Hobart).................	26,383	371,436	390,413	409,000
Victoria (Melbourne)...............	87,884	3,220,217	3,502,351	3,688,200
Western Australia (Perth)...........	975,920	848,100	1,030,469	1,138,300
Territories				
Australian Capital Territory (Canberra)	939	96,032	144,063	201,200
Northern Territory (Darwin)........	520,280	56,504	86,390	96,300
Total....................	2,967,909	11,599,498	12,755,638	13,601,000

Increase of the People

Year	Increase			Decrease			Net Increase†	Marriages
	Births	‡Overseas Arrivals	Total	Deaths	Overseas Departures	Total		
1969	250,176	898,858	1,149,034	106,496	769,812	876,308	261,600	112,470
1970	257,516	1,026,675	1,284,191	113,048	903,801	1,016,849	256,300	116,066
1971	276,362	1,078,798	1,355,160	110,650	994,193	1,104,843	244,800	117,637
1972	264,969	1,110,670	1,375,639	109,760	1,082,824	1,192,584	183,100	114,029
1973	247,670	1,290,360	1,538,030	110,822	1,249,942	1,360,764	177,300	112,700
1974	245,177	1,496,523	1,741,706	115,833	1,409,408	1,525,241	216,500	110,673

‡ Including the following arrivals under the Australian Government's various schemes for assisted immigration: 1969, 125,958; 1970, 134,428; 1971, 103,811; 1972, 63,710; 1973, 49,822; 1974, 52,194.
† = natural increase (excess of births over deaths), net overseas migration gain; adjusted to make the series of increases agree with total inter-censal increase shown by 1971 census.

Inter-Censal Increases, 1947–1971

Year of Census	Population at Census*			Inter-Censal Increase	Net Immigration during Period
	Males	Females	Total		
1947	3,797,370	3,781,988	7,579,358	949,519	1933–1947 .. 41,106
1954	4,546,118	4,440,412	8,986,530	1,407,172	1947–1954 .. 639,028
1961	5,333,185	5,215,082	10,548,267	1,561,737	1954–1961 .. 584,754
1966	5,841,588	5,757,910	11,599,498	1,051,231	1961–1966 .. 395,485
1971	6,412,711	6,342,927	12,755,638	1,156,140	1966–1971 .. 521,139

*Excludes full-blood Aborigines before 1961. Inter-censal increase figure for 1954–61 excludes full-blood Aborigines.

Races and Religions

Races	1966	1971	Religions	1966	1971
European...........	11,453,375	12,541,967	Church of England ...	3,885,018	3,953,204
Aboriginal†........	80,007	106,288	Roman Catholics*....	3,042,507	3,442,634
Torres Strait Islanders.	5,403	9,663	Methodists..........	1,126,960	1,099,019
Chinese.............	26,723	26,198	Presbyterians..........	1,045,564	1,028,581
			Other Christians......	1,130,363	1,466,941
Other..............	33,790	71,522	Hebrews	63,275	62,208
			Other‡..............	1,305,811	1,703,051

* Including Catholics, so described, 1,934,190 in 1966 and 1,913,402 in 1971.
† The 1966 figure relates to persons of half or more Aboriginal descent. The 1971 figure is for all persons who reported their race as Aboriginal.
‡ Including 1,159,474 and 781,247 who did not state their religion at the 1966 and 1971 Census respectively.

PHYSICAL FEATURES

Australia was separated from the other great land surfaces at a remote period, and exhibits therefore some very archaic types of fauna and flora. It may be regarded as the largest island or the smallest continent, being surrounded by the following waters:—*North*, the Timor and Arafura Seas and Torres Strait; *East*, Pacific Ocean; *South*, Bass Strait (which separates Tasmania from the Continent) and Southern Ocean; and *West*, Indian Ocean. The total area of the mainland is 7,614,500 sq kms, the island of Tasmania having an area of 67,800 sq kms and making a total area for the Commonwealth of 7,682,300 sq kms. The coastline of Australia is approximately 36,800 kms (including Tasmania, 3,200 kms), and its geographical positions is between 10° 41′–39° 8′ (43° 39′, including Tasmania) South latitude and 113° 9′–153° 30′ East longitude; the greatest length East to West is 4,000 kms, and from North to South 3,180 kms (3,680 kms, including Tasmania). Nearest distances from England *via* Cape of Good Hope are East Coast 22,957 and West Coast, 20,048 kms.

From a physical standpoint the continent of Australia is divisible into an eastern and a western area, the former containing a regular coast-line with a good harbourage, roadsteads, rivers, and inland waterways, and a greater development of fauna and flora; the latter a broken coast-line with estuaries rather than rivers, and but little inland water communication. The whole continent is, roughly speaking, a vast, irregular, and undulating plateau, part of which is below the level of the sea, surrounded by a mountainous coast-line, with frequent intervals of low and sandy shore on the north, west and south. The Great Barrier Reef extends parallel with the East coast of Queensland for 1,900 kms ranging in width from 19 kilometres in the north to 240 kilometres in the south. A large part of the interior, particularly in the west, consists of sandy and stony desert, covered with spinifex, and containing numerous salt-marshes, though reaches of grass-land occur here and there. The geological formation of Australia is remarkable for its simplicity and regularity; the *strike* of the rocks is, with a single exception, coincident with the direction of the mountain-chains, from N. to S.; and the tertiary formation to be found in the N., S., and W. develops in the S.E. into a gigantic tertiary plain, watered by the Darling and the Murray Rivers. Nearly all round the coast, however, and in eastern and south-eastern Australia, stretching far inland from the coastal range, is a fertile area devoted to agriculture, beef cattle and dairying, while the inland districts particularly are admirably adapted to the rearing of sheep. The most extensive mountain system takes its rise near the S.E. point, and includes a number of ranges known by different names in different places, none of them being of any great height. The highest peak, Mount Kosciusko, in New South Wales, reaches an elevation of 2,228 metres. The principal rivers are the Murray, which debouches on the south coast, after receiving the waters of its tributaries the Murrumbidgee, Lachlan, and Darling, in the S.E. part of the continent: on the east coast, the Hawkesbury, Hunter, Clarence, Richmond, Brisbane, Mary, Burnett, Fitzroy, and Burdekin; on the west, the

Swan, Murchison, Gascoyne, Ashburton, Fortescue. De Grey, and Fitzroy; on the north, the Drysdale, Ord, Victoria and Daly; and the Roper, Flinders, and Mitchell, which debouch into the Gulf of Carpentaria. The scarcity of the natural water supply in the interior has, however, been mitigated by successful borings and by the construction of large dams. The work of conserving the vast quantities of water which run to waste in the wet season is being vigorously prosecuted by a system of locks and weirs on some of the rivers. A major development is the use of the waters of the Snowy River in south-eastern New South Wales for hydro-electricity generation and irrigation.

Significant mineral resources comprise bauxite, coal, copper, crude petroleum, gems, gold, ilmenite, iron ore, lead, limestone, manganese, nickel, rutile, salt, silver, tin, tungsten, uranium, zinc and zircon. Recently, geological exploration has significantly increased the mineral resources of the nation.

Australia now has seven oilfields in production: Moonie, Alton and Bennett, Queensland; Barrow Island, Western Australia; and Barracouta, Kingfish and Halibut in the Gippsland Shelf area offshore from Victoria. In addition, a small amount of oil is being produced from several other wells in the Surat Basin in Queensland. The production of crude oil in 1975 from the Australian oil fields was 22,705,000 cubic metres, approximately 67 per cent. of the country's requirements. Work is at present in progress to develop the offshore Tuna and Mackerel oilfields on the Gippsland Shelf area.

Production from natural gas deposits to supply Brisbane, Melbourne and Adelaide began during 1969 and to supply Perth in 1971. Other natural gas reserves have since been discovered in South Australia and Queensland and off the shore of Western Australia and Victoria.

Climate.—The seasons are: summer, December to February; autumn, March to May; winter, June to August, spring, September to November. Australia is less subject to extremes of climate than are regions of similar size in low parts of the world, though the climate varies considerably from the tropical to the alpine.

GOVERNMENT

The Commonwealth of Australia was constituted by an Act of the Imperial Parliament dated July 9, 1900, and was inaugurated Jan. 1, 1901. The Government is that of a Federal Commonwealth within the British Commonwealth of Nations, the executive power being vested in the Sovereign (through the Governor-General), assisted by a Federal Ministry of twenty-four Ministers of State. Under the Constitution the Federal Government has acquired and may acquire certain defined powers as surrendered by the States, residuary legislative power remaining with the States. Trade and customs passed under Federal control immediately on the establishment of the Commonwealth; posts, telegraphs and telephones, naval and military defence, lighthouses and quarantine on proclaimed dates. The Federal Government also controls such matters as social services, patents and copyrights, naturalization, navigation, &c. The right of a State to legislate on these and other matters is not abrogated except in connection with matters exclusively under Federal control, but where a State law is inconsistent with a law of the Commonwealth the latter prevails to the extent of the inconsistency.

FLAG.—The British Blue Ensign, consisting of a blue flag, with the Union Jack occupying the upper quarter next the staff, differenced by a large white star (representing the six States of Australia and the Territories of the Commonwealth) in the centre of the lower quarter next the staff and pointing direct to the centre of the St. George's Cross in the Union Jack and five white stars, representing the Southern Cross, in the fly.

AUSTRALIA DAY.—January 26.

GOVERNOR-GENERAL AND STAFF

Governor-General, His Excellency the Hon. Sir John Robert Kerr, K.C.M.G., *born* Sept. 24, 1914 *assumed office* July 11, 1974.
Official Secretary, D. I. Smith.
Comptroller, W. H. J. Perring.

MINISTRY

Prime Minister, Rt. Hon. John Malcolm Fraser.
Deputy Prime Minister, Minister for National Resources and Minister for Overseas Trade, Rt. Hon. J. D. Anthony.
Treasurer, Hon. P. R. Lynch.
Minister for Primary Industry and Leader of the House, Hon. I. McC. Sinclair.
Minister for Administrative Services, Vice-President of the Executive Council and Leader of the Government in the Senate, Senator Hon. R. G. Withers.
Minister for Environment, Housing and Community Development, Senator Hon. I. J. Greenwood, Q.C.
Industry and Commerce, Senator Hon. R. C. Cotton.
Employment and Industrial Relations, Hon. A. A. Street.
Transport, Hon. P. J. Nixon.
Education and Federal Affairs, Senator Hon. J. L. Carrick.
Foreign Affairs, Hon. A. S. Peacock.
Defence, Hon. D. J. Killen.

Social Security, Senator Hon. Margaret Guilfoyle.
Attorney-General, Hon. R. J. Ellicott, Q.C.
Business and Consumer Affairs, Hon. J. W. Howard.
Health, Hon. R. J. D. Hunt.
Immigration and Ethnic Affairs, Hon. M. J. R. MacKellar.
Aboriginal Affairs, Hon. R. I. Viner.
Northern Territory, Hon. A. E. Adermann.
Post and Telecommunications, Hon. E. L. Robinson.
Construction, Hon. J. E. McLeay.
Repatriation, Hon. K. E. Newman.
Science, Senator Hon. J. J. Webster.
Capital Territory, Hon. A. A. Staley.

AUSTRALIAN HIGH COMMISSION
Australia House, Strand, London, W.C.2.
[01-438-8000]
High Commissioner, His Excellency Sir John Bunting, C.B.E.
Deputy High Commissioner, M. J. Cook.
Minister, A. F. Dingle.
Official Secretary, F. Murray.
Head, Australian Defence Staff, Maj.-General S. C. Graham.
Special Commercial Adviser, A. L. Paltridge.
Economic Adviser (Treasury), Dr. N. W. Davey.
Information Counsellor, H. E. Keen.
Migration Officer, B. L. Murray.
Defence, Scientific and Technical Representative, Air-Cmdre. F. A. Cousins, O.B.E.
Trade Commissioners, W. L. Scott; M. Letts (*Agriculture*).

BRITISH HIGH COMMISSION
Commonwealth Avenue, Canberra
High Commissioner, His Excellency the Rt. Hon. Sir Donald Tebbit (1976).
Consuls-General, R. F. Muston (*Adelaide*); H. A. Rogers, O.B.E. (*Brisbane*); I. F. S. Vincent, C.M.G., M.B.E. (*Melbourne*); A. F. R. Harvey, O.B.E. (*Perth*); A. H. Spire (*Sydney*).
Minister, H. A. Dudgeon, C.M.G.

Defence Adviser and Head of British Defence Liaison Staff, Maj.-Gen. J. M. W. Badcock, C.B., M.B.E.
Counsellors, B. L. Barder; R. J. Buller (*Technology*); M. H. 'Callender; P. G. P. D. Fullerton (*Commercial*) ; A. J. V. George O.B.E. (*Administration*); H. H. Tucker (*Information*).
First Secretaries, G. A. Duggan; B. F. Shorney (*Agriculture and Food*); G. W. Hewitt; J. F. Holding (*Economic*); M. Knight, M.B.E. (*Information*); J. K. Tolson.
Naval Adviser, Capt. P. A. Pinkster. R.N.
Military Adviser, Col. K. J. Carter.
Air Adviser, Group Capt. M. M. Dalston, A.F.C.
Cultural Attaché and British Council Representative, A. MacKenzie Smith, O.B.E., M.C., 203 New South Head Road, Edgecliff, Sydney.

THE LEGISLATURE

Parliament consists of the Queen, a Senate and a House of Representatives. The Constitution provides that the number of members of the House of Representatives shall be, as nearly as practicable, twice the number of Senators. An Act, assented to on May 18, 1948, provided for an increase in the number of members of the Senate from thirty-six to sixty, and as a result the number of members of the House of Representatives was increased from 74 to 123. There are now 127 members in the House of Representatives, including one member for the Northern Territory and two for the Australian Capital Territory. Members of the Senate are elected for six years by universal suffrage, half the members retiring every third year. Each of the six States returns an equal number of 10 Senators, the Australian Capital Territory, two Senators and the Northern Territory one Senator. The House of Representatives, similarly elected for a maximum of three years, contains members proportionate to the population, with a minimum of five members for each State. The state of parties in the House of Representatives after the general election held in November 1975 was Liberal Party 68, National Country Party, 23, Australian Labour Party 36. Members of both Houses received $A20,000 per annum, with allowances and free air and rail travel on parliamentary business.
President of the Senate, Senator Hon. C. L. Lancke.
Clerk of the Senate, J. R. Odgers, C.B.E.
Speaker, House of Representatives, Rt. Hon. B. M. Snedden, Q.C.
Clerk of the House, N. J. Parkes, O.B.E.

THE JUDICATURE

HIGH COURT OF AUSTRALIA
There is a Federal High Court with a Chief Justice and 6 Justices having original and appellate jurisdiction. The principal seat of the Court is at Sydney, New South Wales.
Chief Justice, Rt. Hon. Sir Garfield Edward John Barwick, G.C.M.G.
Justices, Rt. Hon. Sir Edward Aloysius McTiernan, K.B.E.; Rt. Hon. Sir Harry Talbot Gibbs, K.B.E.; Hon. Sir Ninian Martin Stephen, K.B.E.; Hon. Sir Anthony Frank Mason, K.B.E.; Hon. K. S. Jacobs; Hon. Lionel Keith Murphy.
Principal Registrar, L. B. Foley.

INDUSTRIAL COURT
Chief Judge, Hon. Sir John Spicer.
Judges, Hon. E. A. Dunphy; P. E. Joske, C.M.G.; R. A. Smithers; Sir John Nimmo, C.B.E.; A. E. Woodward, O.B.E.; R. J. A. Franki; J. B. Sweeney; P. Evatt; R. J. St. John.

CONCILIATION AND ARBITRATION COMMISSION
President, Hon. J. C. Moore.
Deputy Presidents, Hons. J. T. Ludeke; J. Robinson; P. A. Coldham, D.F.C.; E. A. Evatt; M. G. Gaudron; J. E. Isaac; M. D. Kirby; I. G. Sharp; J. F. Staples.

FEDERAL COURT OF BANKRUPTCY
Judges, Hon. C. A. Sweeny, C.B.E.; Hon. B. J. Riley.

SUPREME COURT OF THE AUSTRALIAN CAPITAL TERRITORY
Judges, Hons. R. W. Fox; E. A. Dunphy; P. E. Joske, C.M.G.; R. A. Smithers; R. A. Blackburn, O.B.E.; F. X. Connor; A. E. Woodward, O.B.E.; R. J. Franki; J. B. Sweeney; P. G. Evatt, D.S.C.; R. J. B. St. John; R. M. Northrop.

SUPREME COURT OF THE NORTHERN TERRITORY
Judges, Hon. W. E. S. Forster; Hon. J. H. Muirhead.
Additional Judges, Hons. E. A. Dunphy; P. E. Joske, C.M.G.; R. A. Smithers; R. E. Woodward, O.B.E.; A. J. A. Franki.

DEFENCE

A single Department of Defence was created on November 30, 1973, following the abolition of the Departments of the Navy, Army and Air. Legislation relating to the reorganization of the higher management of the Defence Force and Department of Defence was passed by the Commonwealth Parliament in September 1975 and the main provisions took effect on February 9, 1976.

The separate identities of the three services have been retained. The three Service Boards have been dissolved. Most of their previous powers are now exercised by the Minister for Defence or have been delegated by him to specific military or civilian appointments within the Department of Defence.

A new statutory appointment of Chief of Defence Force Staff has been created, under the Minister for Defence, responsible for command of the Defence Force through the three Service Chiefs of Staff (Navy, Army, Air Force) who are the professional heads of their respective arms of the Defence Force. The Chief of Defence Force Staff is also the principal military adviser to the Minister.

The Secretary to the Department of Defence has generally the powers and functions prescribed for such appointments in the Australian Public Service Act and the Audit Act. He is responsible to the Minister for Defence for advice on policy, resources and organization.

Royal Australian Navy

The Royal Australian Navy consists of an Anti-Submarine Warfare and strike aircraft carrier, 5 destroyers, 6 destroyer escorts, 4 submarines, 3 mines counter-measure vessels, 12 patrol boats, 2 survey ships, 2 fleet support ships, 6 landing craft heavy, 2 oceanographic ships and one training ship. The Fleet Air Arm is equipped with Skyhawk, Tracker, Macchi and HS748 fixed-wing aircraft, and with Sea King, Wessex, Iroquois and Bell 206 helicopters.

The strength of the Royal Australian Navy on 30 June 1976 was 2,100 officers and 14,015 sailors.

Army

In May 1976 the Australian Army comprised a volunteer Regular Army component of 31,415 and a volunteer Army Reserve component (formerly known as the Citizen Military Force) of 20,890.

The command structure of the Australian Army was reorganized in 1973, replacing the previous geographically based organization with a modernized functional organization.

The major development was the raising of three new functional commands which were invested with Australia-wide responsibilities for the command of units allocated to them and for the conduct of their specialist functions. Field Force Command, with its headquarters in Sydney, commands all field force units and is responsible for the operation of the Army's fighting formations. Logistic Command, with its headquarters in Melbourne, commands all logistic units and is responsible for the broad military functions of transport, supply and repair. Training Command, with its headquarters in Sydney, is responsible for the command of operation of all Army schools and training establishments.

Air

The total strength of the R.A.A.F. on June 1, 1976, was 21,268. There were 17 operational units, 5 maintenance squadrons, 3 control and reporting units, 3 aircraft depots, 3 stores depots, one ammunition depot, 22 training units, 7 Air Training Corps squadrons, 5 Citizen Air Force squadrons and supporting services. Three flying units, one maintenance squadron and supporting personnel were serving at Butterworth air base in Malaysia.

COMMONWEALTH FINANCE

Revenue and expenditure of the consolidated fund balanced at $A15,391,000,000 in 1974–75, compared with $A11,976,000,000 in 1973–74. Total loan fund expenditure was $A3,447,000,000 in 1974–75 (1973–74, $A1,828,000,000).

The unit of Australian currency is the $A. Rates of exchange in Mar. 1976, were $A1 = £0·645 (buying) and £0·639 (selling).

DEBT

The total of the Commonwealth Debt on June 30, 1975, was $A5,956,000,000. Adding the indebtedness of the States, viz. $A11,814,000,000, the "face" or "book" value of Australian government securities on issue amounted (June 30, 1975) to $A17,770,000,000.

The Debt per head of population at June 30, 1975, was $A1,319·34.

CONSOLIDATED REVENUE FUNDS (a)

State, etc.	1974–75		
	Revenue $Amillion	Expend're $Amillion	Surplus or Deficit $Amil.
N.S.W.	2,452	2,493	− 41
Victoria........	1,752	1,767	− 51
Queensland.....	1,113	1,121	− 8
S. Australia.....	789	781	+ 8
W. Australia....	734	743	− 9
Tasmania.......	269	282	− 14
Total Six States..	7,109	7,187	− 78
Australian Govt.	15,400	15,400	

(a) The particulars for the Australian Government and the States' consolidated revenue funds contain duplications of grants made by the Australian Government to the States as well as payments from the National Welfare Fund.

NATIONAL WELFARE FUND EXPENDITURE

Service	1973–74	1974–75
	$A,000	$A,000
Age and Invalid Pensions ...	1,372,409	1,918,900
Child Endowment	225,392	234,900
Commonwealth Rehabilitation Service.............	7,078	10,200
Funeral Benefits...........	1,578	1,600
Maternity Allowances......	7,782	7,500
Unemployment, Sickness Special Benefits..........	106,637	325,600
Widows' Pensions..........	180,957	241,400
Other Welfare	56,438	96,700
Hospital Benefits...........	226,523	302,900
Medical Benefits...........	198,866	243,600
Milk for Children..........	8,079	—
Pharmaceutical Benefits.....	218,292	262,300
Tuberculosis Campaign.....	12,083	14,300
Miscellaneous health services.	19,299	27,700
Rental Rebates.............	123	200
Home Savings Grants......	24,658	13,200
Total.................	2,666,196	3,691,000

BANKING

The average Australian liabilities and assets (excluding shareholders' funds, interbranch accounts and contingencies) of the 7 major trading banks operating in the Commonwealth in April, 1976, were: Liabilities in Australia, $A17,875,875,000 (1975, $A16,120,300,000); Assets in Australia, $A18,498,719,000 (1975, $A16,756,700,000). Total amount on deposit in savings banks in Australia in April 1976, was $A14,215,875,000 or $A1,053 per head of population (1975, $A12,258,619,000 or $A905 per head).

PRODUCTION AND INDUSTRY

The estimated gross values of production:—

	1973–74 ($A)	1974–75 ($A)
Crops.............	2,797,576,000	3,142,293,000
Livestock slaughterings....	1,695,956,000	1,026,092,000
Livestock products .	1,853,032,000	1,662,656,000

PRIMARY PRODUCTION

Year	Wool (million kg.)	Wheat ('000 tonnes)	Butter (million kg.)
1971–72	882	8,606	196
1972–73	735	6,590	185
1973–74	701	11,987	175
1974–75*	777	11,357	..

* Estimated.

Agriculture and Livestock.—The principal crops (1974–75) were:—

Crop	Tonnes
Wheat........................	11,357,000
Oats.........................	874,000
Barley.......................	2,513,000
Maize........................	133,000
Hay..........................	669,000
Sugar-cane*..................	20,418,000

* Cut for crushing.

Livestock (in thousands)

	1972	1973	1974	1975	p. 1976
Sheep.	162,910	140,029	145,174	151,652	148,770
Cattle.	27,373	29,101	30,839	33,279	33,655
Pigs...	3,199	3,259	2,505	2,197	2,183

p. = preliminary

In 1974–75 Australia produced 793,000,000 kg. of wool (as in the grease), estimated value, $A965,000,000; 175,498,000 kg. of butter; 95,793,000 kg. of cheese; and 17,638 tonnes of bone-in and 36,745 tonnes of bone-out bacon and hams. The total meat production (beef, veal, mutton, lamb and pig meat) in terms of carcass weight was 2,228,655 tonnes.

Mines and Minerals.—In 1974–75 the mine production of gold was 14,823 kg. and of black coal 70,338,694 tonnes. Smelter and refinery production of principal metals in 1974 was: pig iron, 10,006,000 tonnes; ingot steel 7,250,000 tonnes; copper (refined), 162,461 tonnes; blister copper, 196,129 tonnes; lead (incl. bullion), 336,960 tonnes; tin, 6,714 tonnes; zinc, 276,831 tonnes; silver, 256,475 kg. Value added by the mining industry in 1973–74 was estimated at $A1,985,340,000.

Manufactures.—In 1973–74 there were in Australia 37,144 industrial establishments, employing 1,338,444 persons; wages paid amounted to $A7,167·8 m; purchases, transfers in and selected expenses $A19,067·1 m; value added by manufacture $A13,149·2 m; and turnover $A31,246·9 m.

Trade Unions.—On December 31, 1975, there were 280 separate trade unions in Australia with a total membership of 2,814,000.

TOTAL EXTERNAL TRADE
(including Bullion and Specie.)

Years	Imports	Exports
1970–71	$A4,150,028,000	$A4,375,757,000
1971–72	4,008,365,000	4,893,368,000
1972–73	4,120,727,000	6,213,704,000
1973–74	6,085,004,000	6,913,395,000
1974–75	8,083,099,000	8,672,762,000

Country	Imports from	Exports to
		1974–75
United Kingdom	$A1,214,426,000	$A474,838,000
Canada	217,100,000	288,906,000
India	57,840,000	83,160,000
Pakistan	5,386,000	86,490,000
Malaysia	58,800,000	194,370,000
New Zealand	183,910,000	529,270,000
Hong Kong	172,240,000	105,179,000
Belgium and Luxemburg	73,026,000	73,543,000
China	81,150,000	253,967,000
France	139,838,000	175,069,000
Germany (Fed. Rep.)	580,039,000	308,503,000
Indonesia	18,693,000	175,251,000
Iran	76,796,000	116,411,000
Italy	208,818,000	150,042,000
Japan	1,420,862,000	2,396,265,000
Netherlands	123,399,000	145,898,000
Norway	45,578,000	14,223,000
Papua New Guinea	34,179,000	193,806,000
Poland	9,074,000	51,426,000
Saudi Arabia	171,136,000	27,863,000
South Africa	43,930,000	97,861,000
Sri Lanka	12,834,000	45,148,000
Sweden	183,229,000	34,581,000
Switzerland	104,790,000	9,391,000
U.S.A.	1,668,181,000	831,496,000
U.S.S.R.	6,376,000	243,086,000

IMPORTS FROM ALL COUNTRIES, 1974–75

	$A'000
Live animals	15,542
Meat and meat preparations	4,279
Dairy products and eggs	12,453
Fish	62,767
Cereals	8,037
Fruit and vegetables	76,862
Sugar	8,228
Coffee, tea, cocoa, spices, etc.	93,257
Feeding-stuff for animals	12,559
Miscellaneous preparations chiefly for food	8,512
Beverages	33,017
Tobacco	41,549
Hides and skins	2,418
Oil-seeds, etc.	7,260
Crude rubber	30,973
Wood, timber and cork	85,284
Pulp and waste paper	70,992
Textile fibres	43,562
Crude fertilizers and minerals	117,284
Metalliferous ores and metal scrap	9,802
Crude animal and vegetable materials	22,292
Coal and coke	1,851
Petroleum and products	722,362
Petroleum gases	99
Oils and fats	43,273
Chemical elements and compounds	302,695
Mineral tar, etc.	3,358
Dyeing, tanning and colouring materials	36,894
Medicinal and pharmaceutical products	105,837
Essential oils and perfume materials	30,694
Fertilizers, manufactured	13,105
Explosives	6,982
Plastic materials, etc.	188,076
Chemical materials and products	98,356
Leather	15,030
Rubber manufactures	124,187
Wood and cork manufactures	37,783
Paper, paperboard and manufactures	224,617
Textile yarn and fabrics	435,707
Non-metallic mineral manufactures	152,300
Iron and steel	251,683
Non-ferrous metals	51,666
Manufactures of metal	202,652
Machinery (except electric)	1,357,827
Electrical machinery, apparatus and appliances	719,160
Transport equipment	985,493
Sanitary, plumbing, heating and lighting fixtures and fittings	16,505
Furniture	24,413
Travel goods etc.	17,340
Clothing and clothing accessories	188,826
Footwear	50,361
Scientific instruments	245,779
Miscellaneous manufactured articles	417,417
Commodities and transactions of merchandise trade, not elsewhere classified	124,650
Commodities and transactions not included in merchandise trade	119,191

MAJOR EXPORTS 1974–75

Meat and meat preparations	$A443,767,000
Dairy products and eggs	165,611,000
Fish and fish preparations	69,186,000
Cereal grains and cereal preparations	1,466,399,000
Fruit and vegetables	99,208
Sugar, sugar preparations and honey	660,706
Hides, skins and fur skins, undressed	104,197
Textile fibres and their waste	762,651
Metalliferous ores and scrap	1,202,903,000
Coal, coke and briquettes	672,690,000
Petroleum and petroleum products	161,787,000
Animal oils and fats	50,070,000
Chemical elements and compounds	352,147,000
Chemical materials and products, n.e.s.	28,716,000
Non-metallic mineral manufactures, n.e.s.	48,065,000
Iron and steel	381,128,000
Non-ferrous metals	502,763,000
Manufactures of metal, n.e.s.	102,465,000
Machinery (except electric)	235,659,000

Electrical machinery, apparatus and
appliances..................... $A106,140,000
Transport equipment............. 223,175,000
Miscellaneous manufactured articles,
n.e.s......................... 58,140
Commodities and transactions of
merchandise trade, not elsewhere
classified..................... 141,709,000

FOOD EXPORTS TO U.K. 1974–75

Butter........................... $A ..
Cheese...........................   ..
Eggs.............................   ..
Meats:—
  Bovine animals................ 13,565,000
  Sheep, lambs and goats........ 5,883,000
  Preserved in airtight containers.. 1,264,000
Milk and Cream.................. 4,000
Dried fruit—grapes.............. 3,481,000
Fruit (preserved in airtight containers) 17,490,000
Flour (wheaten), plain white...... 73,000
Wheat........................... 2,000
Sugar-cane...................... 33,821,000

AUSTRALIA'S TRADE WITH U.K.

Year	Value of Merchandise	
	From U.K.	To U.K.
1972–73...........	$A764,577,000	$A575,267,000
1973–74...........	843,045,000	437,771,000
1974–75...........	1,206,630,000	426,242,000

COMMUNICATIONS

Railways.—Gross earnings during 1974–75:

	Gross Earnings
New South Wales...........	$A291,373,000 (a)
Victoria....................	129,942,000 (a)
Queensland..................	183,687,000
South Australia.............	47,950,000 (a)
Western Australia...........	106,844,000
Tasmania...................	8,266,000
Trans-Australian............	29,811,000
Central Australia...........	9,837,000
Northern Territory..........	1,446,000
Capital Territory...........	272,000
Total..................	$A809,429,000

(a) Excludes certain government subsidies
aggregating $A44,742,000.

The gross earnings of all Government lines in
1974–75 were $A809,429,000, working expenses
$A1,146,534,000, and net loss $A337,104,000. In
1974–75 passenger journeys numbered 339,954,000
and 103,465,000 tonnes of goods and livestock were
carried.

Shipping.—The entrances and clearances (one
entrance and one clearance per voyage, irrespective
of the number of ports visited) of vessels engaged
in overseas trade at the various Australian ports in
1974–75 were: entered 6,230 (80,313,404 tons);
cleared 6,254 (80,304,792 tons).

The total, including local shipping, entering the
ports of the capital cities during 1974–75 was:
Sydney, 2,725 vessels of 16,481,399 tons; Melbourne, 2,608 (13,059,935); Brisbane, 1,246
(8,572,573); Adelaide, 1,108 (4,087,016); Fremantle,
1,243 (9,555,935); Hobart 534 (1,594,330) tons. At
June 30, 1975, the Australian trading fleet vessels
200 tons gross and over comprised 120 vessels with a
total 1,572,124 tons gross. Of these, 106 vessels
totalling 1,363,950 tons gross were coastal trading
vessels.

Posts and Telegraphs.—In the year ended June 30,
1975, there were 6,068 post offices dealing with
2,273,531,000 letters, 373,657,000 packets and newspapers, 11,168,000 registered articles and 23,889,000

parcels. 16,092,000 internal telegrams and
2,427,000 international telegrams were despatched.
At June 30, 1975, there were 5,772 telephone
exchanges with 3,539,020 services and 5,266,845
instruments.

Broadcasting and Television.—On June 30, 1975, the
Australian Broadcasting Commission operated 100
stations, including 6 short-wave stations in Australia. Privately owned commercial broadcasting
stations totalled 118. Requirement for television
and radio licences was abolished on Sept. 17, 1974.
On June 30, 1975, 132 television stations were in
operation.

Motor Vehicles.—At June 30, 1975, there were
6,345,100 motor vehicles registered in Australia.
These comprised 4,899,700 cars and station wagons,
281,100 motor cycles, and 1,165,700 commercial
vehicles; revenue derived from motor registration
fees and motor tax, &c. in 1973–74 was
$A380,741,000.

Civil Aviation.—At June 30, 1975, there were 478
recognized landing grounds, including 378 licensed
public aerodromes, in the various States and Territories, and 5 flying boat bases and alighting areas.
Aircraft on the Australian Register at June 30,
1975, numbered 4,164.

CAPITAL

Canberra is the capital of Australia. It is
situated in the Australian Capital Territory which
has an area of 939 sq. miles and was acquired from
New South Wales in 1911. Canberra, which is the
seat of the federal government, had a population at
June 30, 1976, of 202,000. Apart from Parliament
House, the city also contains other National
institutions, such as the Australian War Memorial,
National Library, Royal Australian Mint and the
Australian National University. Most Government departments have their headquarters in
Canberra. An artificial lake is a central feature of
this planned city, based on Walter Burley Griffin's
design.

THE NORTHERN TERRITORY

The Northern Territory has a total area of
520,280 square miles, and lies between 129°–138°
east longitude and 11°–26° south latitude. The
administration was taken over by the Commonwealth on January 1, 1911, from the government of
the State of South Australia. The Department of
the Northern Territory, created in 1972. The
Northern Territory elects one member to the
Federal House of Representatives in Canberra and
is represented by two Senators in the Senate.

The Legislative Council for the Northern Territory, established in 1947 under the provisions of the
Northern Territory (Administration) Act, to make
Ordinances for the peace, order and good government of the Territory (subject to the assent of the
Administrator or Governor General), with 17 members, including 11 elected members, was superseded in October, 1974, by a fully elected Legislative Assembly of 19 members.

The estimated Aboriginal population in the
Northern Territory at the 1971 Census was 25,000.
Areas totalling 94,000 square miles, about one-fifth
of the Northern Territory, have been set aside as
reserves for the use and benefit of the Aboriginal
people. Legislation is to be introduced to enable
Aboriginal tenure of these lands and as a result of
recommendations of a Royal Commission the
Government set up land councils which are now
operating.

Approximately 16,000 Aboriginals live in communities which are now focal points for education,
health and social development.

About 4,000 Aboriginals live permanently on pastoral properties and the government aims to establish communal living areas for these communities. Other Aboriginals live in or around the main towns. In some of the more remote regions, the contact with European Australians has been relatively recent and traditional beliefs and customs are still strong.

The year 1974–75 saw an accelerating decline in the fortunes of the Territory's major rural industry, beef cattle raising, with total earnings down by 60 per cent. to $A10,400,000. The Katharine meat works was the only cattle export abattoir to open in 1975. Owing to a financial problem it was unable to open in the first half of 1976. Two buffalo abattoirs operated and sent buffalo meat, as game meat, overseas. Low beef prices and the limited abattoir season were factors in the continuing increase in cattle numbers which at June 30, 1975 stood at 1,335,000—a rise of 37,000 on the previous year. By-products earned $A920,000 of which $A595,000 came from the sale of buffalo meat.

The export of live buffalo breeders by air to New Guinea, Venezuela and Nigeria continued through 1975 and into 1976. The attraction of the Territory's buffaloes for overseas buyers is their freedom from serious stock diseases.

Research and extension activities towards the primary industries were maintained in the fields of animal production, animal health, economics, range management, agricultural crops, land surveys and soil conservation. There were considerable developments in the pig and poultry industries near Darwin to the stage of self sufficiency in these products.

Mineral industry projects are important to both regional and national economic development. The value of mine and quarry production for 1974–75 was just under $A140,000,000, derived mainly from bauxite ore and aluminal, manganese, copper, gold and bismuth ores. Recently, iron ore production ceased and copper production has been curtailed because of unfavourable world prices. The rich Alligator Rivers uranium deposits are not yet developed. In the McArthur River district a pilot plant has been established to develop an economic treatment method for the extensive, low-grade, but extremely finely disseminated, lead-zinc sulphides deposits, which pose a major dressing problem. The production of manganese from the extensive deposits at Groote Eylandt supplies all Australia's requirements of metallurgical grade manganese ore.

Tourism, an important industry, is estimated to be worth $A28,000,000 a year.

The chief rivers of the Territory are the Victoria, Adelaide, Daly, Roper, South Alligator and McArthur. These are navigable from 40–100 miles from their mouths for boats up to 4 ft. draft.

The north south axis route is the Stuart Highway. This is sealed from Darwin to Alice Springs (1,535 km) and from Alice Springs to the border with South Australia 207 km. is sealed and the remainder should be completed by December 1976.

The route to and from Queensland via Mt. Isa is via sealed Barkly Highway (648 km) which connects to the Stuart Highway near Tennant Creek.

The principal access route to Western Australia via Kununurra is the sealed Victoria Highway 467 km long that joins the Stuart Highway at Katherine.

The Government has a continuous programme of improvement and maintenance of the highways which are part of the National Highway System.

A rail line connects Alice Springs to Adelaide which is being replaced by a standard gauge line following a new route less susceptible to flood damage. The rail link extending from Darwin south to Larrimah (500 km) ceased operating in 1976.

Following the cyclone on Christmas Day 1974, which destroyed 90 per cent. of the city, the population of Darwin fell to 11,000. By June 1976, it was estimated at 41,000, 5,000 less than the pre-cyclone figure. Darwin, which is 97 ft. above sea level, overlooks Port Darwin. Alice Springs is situated in the MacDonnell Ranges. The climate of the Northern Territory ranges from dry in the south to wet-monsoonal in the north.

Judges of the Supreme Court, Hon. W. E. S. Forster; Hon. J. H. Muirhead; Hon. R. C. Ward.

Additional Judges, Hons. E. A. Dunphy; P. E. Joske, C.M.G.; J. A. Franki; P. G. Evatt; R. J. B. St. John; J. B. Sweeney; A. E. Woodward.

NORFOLK ISLAND

The island is situated in latitude 29° S. and longitude 168° E., being about 1,042 miles from Sydney and 400 miles north of New Zealand. It is about five miles in length by three in breadth, and was discovered by Capt. Cook in 1774. Its area is 8,528 acres and circumference 20 miles. The climate is mild, with a mean temperature of 68° and an annual rainfall of 53 inches. The descendants of the mutineers of the *Bounty* were brought here from Pitcairn Island in 1856. The island is a popular tourist resort, and a large proportion of the population depends on tourism and its ancillaries for employment. Estimated population (including tourists) (June 30, 1975), 1,870.

Seat of Government and Administration Offices, Kingston. The Norfolk Island Council advises the Administrator on policy and the control of public finance. The island is administered by the Australian Government through the Department of Administrative Services in Canberra.

Regular air services operate from Australia and New Zealand.

Administrator, Air Cdre. E. T. Pickerd, O.B.E., D.F.C. (*acting*).

COCOS (KEELING) ISLANDS

The Cocos (Keeling) Islands were declared a British possession in 1857. In 1878 they were placed under the control of the Governor of Ceylon and were later annexed to the Straits Settlements and incorporated with the colony of Singapore. On Nov. 23, 1955, their administration was transferred to Australia. They are two separate atolls comprising some 27 small coral islands with a total area of about 5½ square miles, situated in the Indian Ocean in latitude 12° 5′ South and longitude 96° 53′ East. The main islands are West Island (the largest, about 6 miles from north to south) on which are the aerodrome and the administrative centre, and most of the European community; Home Island, the headquarters of the Clunies Ross Estate; Direction Island, on which is situated the Department of Civil Aviation's marine base; and Horsburgh. North Keeling Island, which forms part of the Territory, lies about 15 miles to the north of the group and has no inhabitants. The climate is equable and pleasant, being usually under the influence of the south-east trade winds for about three-quarters of the year. A three weekly air charter service operates between Perth and the Cocos Islands and Christmas Island. Population (estimated June 30, 1975), 604.

Administrator, R. J. Linford.

CHRISTMAS ISLAND

Until the end of 1957 a part of the then Colony of Singapore. Christmas Island was administered

as a separate colony until October 1, 1958, when it became Australian territory. It is situated in the Indian Ocean about 224 miles S. of Java Head. Area 52 sq. miles. Population (estimated, June 30, 1975) 3,032. The island is densely wooded and contains extensive deposits of phosphate of lime. The Christmas Island Phosphate Commission is responsible for mining activities in the Territory on behalf of the Australian and New Zealand Governments. By agreement, the Commission's function of obtaining and distributing phosphates for the Australian and New Zealand markets is carried out by the British Phosphate Commissioners as managing agents.
Administrator, W. Worth.

THE ANTARCTIC CONTINENT

The area of the Antarctic Continent is estimated at approximately 14,000 square kilometres. The greater part of the coastline has been charted, but considerable portions of the interior have not been visited, or at best have been seen only from the air. The question of territorial rights is complicated and there is no general international agreement thereon.

The *Australian Antarctic Territory* was established by an Order in Council, dated February 7, 1933, which placed under the government of the Commonwealth of Australia all the islands and territories, other than Adélie Land, which are situated south of the latitude 60° S. and lying between 160° E. longitude and 45° E. longitude. The Order came into force on August 24, 1936, after the passage of the Australian Antarctic Territory Acceptance Act, 1933. The boundaries of Terre Adélie were definitely fixed by a French Decree of April 1, 1938, as the islands and territories south of 60° S. latitude lying between 136° E. longitude and 142° E. longitude. The Australian Antarctic Territory Act, 1954 declared that the laws in force in the Australian Capital Territory are, so far as they are applicable, in force in the Australian Antarctic Territory.

On February 13, 1954, the Australian National Antarctic Research Expeditions (ANARE) established a station on Mac. Robertson Land at latitude 67° 36′ S. and longitude 62° 53′ E. The station was named Mawson in honour of Sir Douglas Mawson and was the first permanent Australian station to be set up on the Antarctic continent. Scientific research conducted at Mawson includes upper atmosphere physics, meteorology, earth sciences, biology and medical science. Mawson is also the centre for coastal and inland exploration.

A second Australian scientific research station was established on the coast of Princess Elizabeth Land on January 13, 1957, at latitude 68° 35′ S. and longitude 77° 58′ E. The station was named in honour of Captain John King Davis, second in command of two of Mawson's expeditions and master of several famous Antarctic ships. The station was temporarily closed on Jan. 25, 1965 and reopened on Feb. 15, 1969. Scientific programmes carried out at Davis include meteorology, biology, upper atmosphere physics, with field investigations in geology. In February, 1959, the Australian Government accepted from the United States Government custody of Wilkes Station on the Budd Coast, Wilkes Land is about 66° 15′ S. and longitude 110° 33′ E. The station was closed in February 1969, and activities were transferred to Casey station. Casey station was named in honour of Lord Casey, former Governor-General of Australia, in recognition of his long association with Australia's Antarctic effort. The station, at 66° 17′ S., 110° 31′ E., is of advanced design and scientific programmes carried out there include upper atmosphere physics, cosmic ray physics, geophysics, meteorology with field programmes in glaciology, geology, etc.

Since 1948 ANARE has also operated a station on Macquarie Island, a dependency of Tasmania, situated at 54° 30′ S. and 158° 57′ E., about 900 miles north of the Antarctic Continent.

On December 1, 1959, Australia signed the Antarctic Treaty with Argentine, Belgium, Chile, France, Japan, New Zealand, Norway, South Africa, the United Kingdom, the United States and U.S.S.R., all countries which have been active in Antarctic operations and research. The Treaty reserves the Antarctic area south of 60° S. latitude for peaceful purposes, provides for international co-operation in scientific investigation and research, and preserves, for the duration of the Treaty, the *status quo* with regard to territorial sovereignty, rights and claims. The Treaty came into force on June 23, 1961, and has been acceded to by another four nations not actively engaged in the area.

For other Commonwealth dependencies in the Antarctic *see* New Zealand.

STATES OF THE COMMONWEALTH OF AUSTRALIA

NEW SOUTH WALES

The State of New South Wales is situated entirely between the 28th and 38th parallels of S. lat. and 141st and 154th meridians of E. long., and comprises an area of 309,433 square miles (exclusive of 939 sq. miles of Australian Capital Territory which lies within its borders).

POPULATION.—The estimated population at June 30, 1975 was: Males, 2,396,700; Females, 2,392,800. Total, 4,789,600.

Births, Deaths and Marriages

Year	Births	Deaths	Marriages
1972	95,278	41,652	43,038
1973	87,332	41,122	40,722
1974	86,162	43,999	39,327
1975	80,783	40,512	36,967

Vital Statistics.—Annual rate per 1,000 of mean population in 1974:—Births, 18·10; Deaths, 9·24; Marriages, 8·26. Deaths under 1 year per 1,000 live births, 16·58.

Religions

The members of the Church of England in New South Wales, according to the Census of 1971, number 1,639,316. Roman Catholic (including "Catholic") 1,319,250, Presbyterian 352,107, Methodist 302,856, Congregational 20,902, Baptist 59,541, Orthodox 129,178, Lutheran 33,776, Salvation Army 19,733, and Hebrew 25,971. The religion of 519,125 persons was either not stated in the census schedules or was stated as "none".

PHYSIOGRAPHY

Natural features divide the State into four strips of territory extending from north to south, viz., the Coastal Divisions; the Tablelands, which form the Great Dividing Range between the coastal districts and the plains; the Western Slopes of the Dividing Range; and the Western Plains. The highest points are Mounts Kosciusko, 7,328 feet, and Townsend, 7,266 feet. The coastal district is well watered by numerous rivers flowing from the ranges into fertile flats which form their lower basins. The western portion of the State is watered by the rivers of the Murray-Darling system and immense reservoirs have been constructed for

irrigation purposes, as well as many artesian bores. The Darling, 1,702 miles, and the Murrumbidgee, 981 miles, are both tributaries of the Murray, part of which forms the boundary between the States of New South Wales and Victoria. Other inland rivers are: Lachlan, Macquarie-Bogan, Castlereagh, Namoi and Gwydir.

Climate.—New South Wales is situated entirely in the Temperate Zone. The climate is equable and very healthy. At the capital (Sydney) the average mean shade temperature is 18°C. The mean (shade) temperature ranges for the various divisions of the State are as follows: coastal, 16°C in the south to 20°C in the north; northern and central tableland, 12°C to 16°C; southern tableland, 7°C to 14°C; and for the rest of the State (western slope, central plains, Riverina and western), 15°C in the south to 18°C in the north.

GOVERNMENT

New South Wales was first colonized as a British possession in 1788, and after progressive settlement a partly elective legislature was established in 1843. In 1855 Responsible Government was granted, the present Constitution being founded on the Constitution Act of 1902. New South Wales federated with the other States of Australia in 1901. The executive authority of the State is vested in a Governor (appointed by the Crown), assisted by a Council of Ministers.

GOVERNOR

Governor of New South Wales, His Excellency Sir (Arthur) Roden Cutler, $V.C.$, K.C.M.G., K.C.V.O., C.B.E., *assumed office* Jan. 20, 1966
$A40,000

Lieutenant-Governor, Hon. Laurence Whistler Street.

THE MINISTRY

Premier, Hon. N. K. Wran, Q.C., M.L.A.
Deputy Premier, Minister for Public Works, Ports and Housing, Hon. L. J. Ferguson, M.L.A.
Treasurer, Hon. J. B. Renshaw, M.L.A.
Transport and Highways, Hon. P. F. Cox, M.L.A.
Attorney-General, Hon. F. J. Walker, M.L.A.
Mines and Energy, Hon. P. D. Hills, M.L.A.
Industrial Relations and Vice-President of the Executive Council, Hon. D. P. Landa, M.L.C.
Decentralisation and Development, and Primary Industries, Hon. D. Day, M.L.A.
Education, Hon. E. L. Bedford, M.L.A.
Local Government and Planning, Hon. H. F. Jensen, M.L.A.
Lands and Environment, Hon. W. F. Crabtree, M.L.A.
Health, Hon. K. J. Stewart, M.L.A.
Consumer Affairs and Co-operative Societies, Hon. S. D. Einfield, M.L.A.
Justice and Services, Hon. R. J. Mulock, M.L.A.
Sport and Recreation, and Tourism, Hon. K. G. Booth, M.L.A.
Conservation and Water Resources, Hon. A. R. L. Gordon, M.L.A.
Youth and Community Services, Hon. R. F. Jackson, M.L.A.
Minister Assisting the Premier, Hon. W. H. Haigh, M.L.A.

The annual salaries of Ministers are: Premier, $A43,900; Deputy Premier, $A39,250; Leader of the Government in the Legislative Council, $A39,720; Deputy Leader of the Government on the Legislative Council, $A37,670; other Ministers $A36,860 each. Ministers also receive an expense allowance (Premier, $A9,830; Deputy Premier, $A4,920, and other Ministers $A4,420 each). In addition, Ministers who are members of the Legislative Assembly receive an Electoral Allowance, ranging from $A4,750 to $A7,100 according to the location of their electorate and those who represent outlying electorates receive a Special Expenses Allowance of $A3,410. Ministers who are members of the Legislative Council and who reside in outlying electorates also receive a special Expenses Allowance of $A3,410.

N.S.W. GOVERNMENT OFFICES IN LONDON, 66 Strand, W.C.2
Agent-General, Hon. Sir Davis Hughes (1972)

THE LEGISLATURE

The Legislature consists of the Sovereign and the two Houses of Parliament (the Legislative Council and the Legislative Assembly). The *Legislative Council* consists of 60 members, elected jointly by both Houses of Parliament. Membership is for 12 years, 15 members retiring in rotation triennially. The *Legislative Assembly* consists of 99 members. Natural-born or naturalized persons 18 years of age, who have resided 6 months in Australia, 3 months in the State and 1 month in the electoral district are entitled to the franchise. Voting is compulsory. At the State General Elections in November, 1973, there were 2,788,733 persons enrolled. In contested elections 2,560,653 persons voted, representing 93 per cent. of the persons enrolled.

President of the Legislative Council, Hon.
  Sir Harry Budd.........(incl. *allce.*) $A29,100
Chairman of Committees, Legislative Council, Hon. T. S. McKay....(incl. *allce.*). 19,030
Speaker, Legislative Assembly, Hon. L. B.
  Kelly.................(incl. *allce.*) 38,820
Chairman of Committees, Legislative Assembly, T. J. Cahill.....(incl. *allce.*) 27,160
Leader of Opposition, Legislative Assembly,
  Hon. Sir Eric Willis, K.B.E., C.M.G.
      (incl. *allce.*) 38,820
(Office-holders above who are members of the Legislative Assembly also receive electoral and accommodation allowances ranging from $A4,750 to $A10,510 according to the location of the electorate.)

THE JUDICATURE

The judicial system includes a Supreme Court with the Chief Justice, President, eight Judges of Appeal, and 29 Judges), Land and Valuation Court, Industrial Commission, District Courts, Workers' Compensation Commission, Courts of Quarter Sessions, Petty Sessions and Children's Courts.

Supreme Court

Chief Justice, Hon. L. W. Street
    (+ *allce* $A2,700)..$A50,660
Judges of Appeal, Hon. A. R. Moffitt
  (*President, Court of Appeal*) ($A47,710+
  allce. $A2,100); Hon. R. M. Hope;
  Hon. R. G. Reynolds; Hon. F. C.
  Hutley; Hon. N. H. Bowen (*Chief
  Judge in Equity*); Hon. H. H. Glass;
  Hon. G. J. Samuels; Hon. D. L. Ma-
  honey (+ *allce.* $A2,100)........... 46,380
Judges, Hon. R. L. Taylor (*Chief Judge
  of Common Law*); Hon. D. M. Selby,
  E.D. (*Chief Judge of the Family Law
  Division*); Hon. W. H. Collins; Hon.
  J. F. Nagle; Hon. C. E. Begg; Hon. P.
  P. H. Allen; Hon. J. O'Brien; Hon. J.
  A. Lee; Hon. M. M. Helsham; Hon.
  C. L. D. Meares; Hon. P. B. Toose,
  C.B.E.; Hon. G. Carmichael; Hon. J. P.
  Slattery; Hon. A. Larkins; Hon. P. M.
  Woodward; Hon. K. J. Holland;
  Hon. I. F. Sheppard; Hon. J. H.
  Wootten; Hon. A. F. Rath; Hon. A.
  V. Maxwell; Hon. T. W. Waddell;
  Hon. P. J. Jeffrey; Hon. D. A. Yeld-
  ham; Hon. G. D. Needham; Hon. W.
  P. Ash; Hon. H. L. Cantor (+ *allce.*
  $A2,100).......................... 46,350

Crown Employees Appeal Board
Chairman, Hon. W. B. Perrignon (+ *allce.*
$A2,100)........................ $A46,350

Industrial Commission

President, Hon. Sir Alexander Beattie
(+ *allce.* $A2,100)................. 47,710
Members, J. J. McKeon; J. A. Kelleher;
W. B. Perrignon; C. P. Sheehy;
J. J. Cahill; F. V. Watson; J. F. Dey;
J. J. Macken.....(+ *allce.* $A2,100)
.... each 46,350
Land and Valuation Court Judge, Hon.
The Chief Justice.
Workers' Compensation Commission, Chairman, His Honour C. C. Langsworth
(+ *allce.* $A2,100)................. 41,750
District Court, Chief Judge, His Honour
J. H. Staunton (+ *allce.* $A2,100)..... 41,750

EDUCATION

Education.—Education is compulsory between the ages of 6 and 15 years. It is non-sectarian and free at all state schools. The enrolment in August 1975 in 2,464 state schools was 788,943. In addition to the state schools there were, in 1975, 794 private colleges and schools, with an enrolment of 218,868 scholars. The six universities had an enrolment of 58,666 students in 1975; 17,667 at Sydney (incorporated 1850), 18,128 at New South Wales (1948), 7,395 at New England (1954), 8,917 at Macquarie (1964), 4,434 at Newcastle (1965) and 2,125 at Wollongong (1975). Colleges of Advanced Education which provide courses at tertiary level, but with a more vocational emphasis than universities, had 26,227 students enrolled in 1975. Students enrolled in technical colleges in 1975 numbered 226,292. The State expenditure on education was $A783,168,000 in the year 1974-75.

FINANCE

Year ended June 30th	Revenue	Expenditure
	$A	$A
1972............	1,429,341,000	1,434,825,000
1973............	1,641,920,000	1,645,117,000
1974............	1,878,509,000	1,895,052,000
1975............	2,452,089,000	2,492,634,000

The Public Debt of New South Wales at June 30, 1975, was $A3,834,052,000, of which an amount of $A58,241,000 was repayable in London (interest $A3,256,000), $A19,928,000 was repayable in New York (interest $A1,085,000), $A2,121,000 was repayable in Canada (interest $A122,000), $A4,775,000 was repayable in Switzerland (interest $A215,000), $A1,505,000 was repayable in the Netherlands (interest $A75,000) and $A3,747,843,000 was held in Australia, with an annual interest bill of $A238,427,000.

Banking, etc.—There were (Feb. 1976) 10 trading banks with deposits of $A7,237,300,000. Savings bank deposits amounted to $A4,154,100,000, representing $A864 per head of the population. The amount assured in New South Wales in *Life Insurance* in Feb. 1976 was $A8,820,166,000 ordinary, $A1,471,515,000 superannuation and $A570,498,000 industrial. The membership of *Friendly Societies* was 158,629, and the funds at June 30, 1975 were $A40,328,000. On Dec. 31, 1974, there were 191 separate *Trade Unions* in New

South Wales with a total membership of 1,059,700. Balances outstanding on *Instalment Credit* for retail sales on March 31, 1976, were $A846,600,000.

PRODUCTION AND INDUSTRY

Value of Production.—In 1974-5 the net value of production of the primary industries (excluding mining and quarrying), was $A1,520,422,000. Of that agriculture contributed $A682,448,000, livestock products (wool, milk, etc.) $A448,240, livestock slaughterings $A300,244,000 and other industries (forestry, fishing and trapping) $A76,098,000. Value added in mining and quarrying industries and manufacturing industries in 1973-4 was $A384,563,000 and $A5,184,450,000 respectively.

Agriculture.—The production of wheat in 1974-75 was 3,808,658 tonnes of grain and 42,713 tonnes of hay. Other important crops in 1974-75 were 407,553 tonnes of barley, 293,068 tonnes of oats, 376,232 tonnes of rice, besides other kinds of grain, 117,901 tonnes of potatoes, and 1,369,103 kilograms of dried leaf tobacco. Sugar-cane to the extent of 996,654 tonnes was crushed; while 77,954,994 kilograms of bananas were obtained; almost every kind of fruit and vegetable is grown.

Pastoral, etc.—A large area is suitable for sheepraising, the principal breed of sheep being the celebrated merino, which was introduced in 1797. On March 31, 1975, there were 8,935,074 cattle, 54,983,009 sheep and lambs, and 729,209 pigs. In 1974-75, 232,271,000 kg. (stated as in the grease) of wool were produced, 19,831,000 kg. of butter, 9,934,000 kg. of cheese, and 220,434,000 kg. of bacon and ham.

Mining Industry.—The principal minerals are coal, lead, zinc, rutile, zircon, copper and tin. The total value of minerals won in 1974-75 was $A784,097,000; the value of output of the coalmining industry was $A451,879,000 and of the silverlead-zinc industry, $A145,646,000. The mining industry gave employment to 23,575 miners during 1974-75. In 1974-75, 42,482,000 tonnes of coal were produced.

Manufacturing Industry.—At June 30, 1974, there were 13,807 manufacturing establishments. The average number of persons employed during 1973-74 was 516,221, and the value added to materials was $A5,184,450. Large iron and steel works with subsidiary factories are in operation at Newcastle and Port Kembla in proximity to the coalfields. Products of the regions include iron and steel of various grades, pipes, boilers, steel wire and wire netting, copper wire, copper and brass cables and tin-plate. The production (1974-75) of pig-iron was 5,942,000 tonnes, and of steel ingots 6,912,000 tonnes.

OVERSEAS TRADE

Year ended June 30	Overseas Imports $A(f.o.b.)	Overseas Exports $A(f.o.b.)
1972	1,764,769,000	1,204,938,000
1973	1,810,123,000	1,420,990,000
1974	2,590,179,000	1,513,202,000
1975	3,494,781,000	1,979,005,000

The chief exports in 1974-75 were wool, wheat, coal, meat, iron and steel, chemicals, raw sugar and machinery. Chief imports were machinery, tex-

tiles, motor vehicles, chemicals, petroleum, paper products, iron and steel, food stuffs, medical instruments, etc., pharmaceuticals, printed matter and plastic materials.

TRANSPORT AND COMMUNICATIONS.

Shipping.—Excluding coastal trade, 3,726 vessels entered ports of N.S.W. during the year ended June 30, 1975, the net tonnage being 30,693,539. The shipping entries at Sydney, including coastal, were 2,925 vessels of 16,481,399 net tonnage.

Roads and Bridges.—There are 207,971 kilometres of roads and streets in New South Wales, including 42,012 kilometres of natural surface and cleared only. The total expenditure by the Government and the local councils on roads, bridges, &c, in 1973–74 was $A317,033,000. Sydney Harbour Bridge which was completed and opened for traffic in March, 1932, carries eight lanes of roadway with a total width of 25·6 m, two footways each 3 m wide, and two lines of railway. At mean high water there is a headway of 52·6 m.

Motor Vehicles.—At June 30, 1975, there were 2,171,900 registered motor vehicles (cars, 1,420,600).

Railways.—The railways of New South Wales are controlled by the State, which also operates omnibus services. At June 30, 1975, the route kilometres of the State railways open for traffic was 9,756, revenue in the year 1974–75 being $A296,059,000.

Aviation.—Sydney is the principal overseas terminal in Australia. Traffic movements at Sydney airport in 1974–75 were: passengers 6,506,529 (4,953,051 domestic, 1,553,528 international); freight 100,620 tonnes (49,886 domestic, 50,734 international); aircraft, 112,427 (93,345 domestic, 190,82 international).

Posts, Telegraphs and Telephones.—The postal, telegraphic, telephonic and radio services are administered by the Australian Government. At June 30, 1975, there were 1,965 post offices in New South Wales. During the year 5,539,000 telegrams were despatched to places within Australia and 1,156,000 cablegrams to places outside Australia. Transit time between Sydney and London is approximately 2½ days for airborne mail and between 4 and 6 weeks for seaborne mail. The telephone services in operation numbered 1,362,817.

Radio and Television.—In June, 1975, there were 21 National Broadcasting Stations in New South Wales and 39 commercial stations operating under licence. At June 30, 1975, there were 28 television stations (14 national, 14 commercial) in operation.

TOWNS.

ΨSYDNEY, the chief city and capital and the largest city in Australia, stands on the shores of Port Jackson, with a water frontage of 245 kilometres; the depth of water at the entrance is not less than 24 m and at the wharves up to 12 m. There are extensive facilities for handling cargo, and for storing and loading grain in bulk or bags. For 21 kilometres Sydney Harbour extends inland, the finest harbour in the world, and is surrounded by scenery of surpassing beauty. The principal wharves are situated in close proximity to the business centre of the city. The total area of water in the harbour is about 55 square kilometres, of which approximately one-half has a depth of not less than 9 m; the average tidal range is 1 m.

The Sydney Statistical Division embraces an area of approximately 4,077 square kilometres, with a population of 2,922,760 (at June 30, 1975). The Newcastle and Wollongong Statistical Districts contain populations of 363,010 and 211,240 respectively.

The population of principal municipalities located outside the boundaries of these statistical areas are: Albury 32,250, Wagga Wagga 32,510, Broken Hill 28,160, Tamworth 25,360, Orange 24,830, Goulburn 22,160, Lismore 21,650, Blue Mountains 20,410 (part not included in Sydney Statistical Division), Armidale 20,300 and Dubbo 19,000.

DEPENDENCY OF NEW SOUTH WALES.

LORD HOWE ISLAND (702 kilometres north-east of Sydney). Lat. 31° 33′ 4″ S., Long. 159° 4′ 26″ E. Area 17 sq. km. Pop. June 30 1975, 240. The island is of volcanic origin with Mount Gower reaching an altitude of 366 m. The affairs of the Island and the supervision of the Kentia palm seed industry are controlled by an elected Island Committee and a Board at Sydney. *Office*, N.S.W. Department of Lands.

QUEENSLAND

This State, situated in lat. 10° 40′–29° S. and long. 138°–153° 30′ E., comprises the whole north-eastern portion of the Australian continent.

Queensland possesses an area of 1,728,000 square kms. (*i.e.*, equal to more than 5½ times the area of the British Isles).

POPULATION.—At Dec. 31, 1975, the population numbered 2,012,400 persons.

Births, Deaths and Marriages

Year	Births	Deaths	Marriages
1973	38,067	16,732	16,490
1974	37,852	18,128	16,086
1975	36,403	16,421	15,262

Vital Statistics:—Annual rate per 1,000 of mean population in 1975; Births, 18·2; Deaths, 8·2; Marriages 7·6. Deaths under 1 year, 15·0 per 1,000 live births.

Religions

At the Census of 1971 there were 544,432 Church of England, 467,203 Roman Catholics (including Catholics undefined), 192,079 Presbyterians, 182,887 Methodists, 45,228 Lutherans, 28,329 Baptists, 15,554 Orthodox, 10,608 Salvation Army, 10,196 Church of Christ, 9,627 Congregationalists, 75,668 other Christians, and 1,491 Hebrews.

PHYSIOGRAPHY

The Great Dividing Range on the eastern coast of the continent produces a similar formation to that of New South Wales, the eastern side having a narrow slope to the coast and the western a long and gradual slope to the central plains, where the Selwyn and Kirby Ranges divide the land into a northern and southern watershed. The Brisbane, Burnett, Fitzroy and Burdekin rise in the eastern ranges and flow into the Pacific, the Flinders, Mitchell, and Leichhardt into the Gulf of Carpentaria, and the Barcoo and Warrego rise in the central ranges and flow southwards.

GOVERNMENT

Queensland was constituted a separate colony with Responsible Government in 1859, having previously formed part of New South Wales. The executive authority is vested in a Governor (appointed by the Crown), aided by an Executive Council of 18 members.

GOVERNOR

Governor of Queensland, His Excellency Air Marshal
Sir Colin Thomas Hannah, K.C.M.G., K.B.E., C.B.
appointed March 21, 1972 $A50,000

EXECUTIVE COUNCIL.

(H.E. the Governor presides.)
Premier, Hon. J. Bjelke-Petersen....... $A39,640
Deputy Premier and Treasurer, Hon.
Sir Gordon Chalk, K.B.E............ $A33,990
Mines and Energy, Hon. R. E. Camm.
Minister for Justice and Attorney-General, Hon. W. E.
Knox.
Community and Welfare Services and Sport, Hon. J. D.
Herbert.
Industrial Development, Labour Relations and Consumer Affairs, Hon. F. A. Campbell.
Primary Industries, Hon. V. B. Sullivan.
Police, Hon. A. M. Hodges.
Water Resources, Hon. N. T. E. Hewitt.
Transport, Hon. K. W. Hooper.
Local Government and Main Roads, Hon. R. J. Hinze.
Tourism and Marine Services, Hon. T. G. Newbery.
Lands, Forestry, National Parks and Wildlife Services,
Hon. K. B. Tomkins.
Health, Hon. L. R. Edwards.
Education and Cultural Activities, Hon. V. J. Bird.
Works and Housing, Hon. N. E. Lee.
Aboriginal and Islanders Advancement and Fisheries,
Hon. C. A. Wharton.
Survey, Valuation, Urban and Regional Affairs, Hon.
W. D. Lickiss.
  Ministers, each $A31,190.

AGENT-GENERAL IN LONDON

Agent-General for Queensland, The Hon. Sir Wallace
Rae, 392–393 Strand, W.C.2.

THE LEGISLATURE.

Parliament consists of a *Legislative Assembly* of
82 members, elected by all persons aged 18 years
and over. Members of the Assembly receive
$A18,980 per annum and an electorate allowance
ranging from $A3,140 to $A7,670 p.a. The Assembly, as elected on December 7, 1974, was composed
of: National Party, 39; Liberal Party, 30; Australian
Labour Party, 11; Independent, 1; North Queensland Party, 1. The National and Liberal parties
formed a coalition government.
Speaker, Hon. J. E. H. Houghton....... $A26,060
Chairman of Committees, W. D. Hewitt. $A21,270

THE JUDICATURE

There is a Supreme Court, with a Chief Justice,
a Senior Puisne Judge and 12 Puisne Judges;
District Courts, with 17 Judges; and Industrial
Court, with a Supreme Court Judge as President;
a Land Appeal Court and a Medical Assessment
Tribunal, each presided over by a Judge of the
Supreme Court; a Local Government Court, presided over by a District Court Judge; and the
Industrial Conciliation and Arbitration Commission consisting of 5 members; and Inferior Courts
at all the principal towns, presided over by
Stipendiary Magistrates.

Chief Justice, Supreme Court, Hon.
Sir Mostyn Hanger, K.B.E........... $A47,890
Senior Puisne Judge, Hon. Sir Charles
Wanstall.......................... 40,820
Puisne Judges, Hons. N. S. Stable; G. A.
G. Lucas; J. A. Douglas; D. M. Campbell; M. B. Hoare, C.M.G.; W. B.
Campbell; R. H. Matthews; J. P. G.
Kneipp (*Northern Judge*); E. S. Williams; D. G. Andrews; J. L. Kelly
(*Central Judge*); J. D. Dunn.......*each* 40,820

EDUCATION.

Education is compulsory between the ages of
6 and 15, and is free in state primary and secondary
schools. On Aug. 1, 1975 there were 1,209 state
schools, including 225 providing secondary education, in operation, with 17,183 teachers and an
enrolment of 331,374 children, and 323 private and
8 grammar schools, with an enrolment of 91,148.
In 1974 tertiary level course enrolments at colleges
of advanced education (incl. government teachers'
colleges) and technical colleges, were 8,610 full-time
and 3,277 part-time. Sub-tertiary level course enrolments at these establishments and rural training
schools numbered 2,240 full-time and 32,401 part-time, including correspondence and apprenticeship
students. The three state-aided Universities had an
enrolment of 10,545 full-time students and 10,156
part-time students.

PRODUCTION AND INDUSTRY.

The gross value of primary industry commodities
produced (excluding mining) in 1974–75 was
$A1,261,880,000 (including crops $A866,348,000,
livestock disposals $A193,273,000, livestock products $A163,790,000, forestry $A25,163,000,
fisheries $A12,606,000 and hunting $A700,000.

Agriculture and Livestock.—The most important
crop in 1974–75 was sugar-cane, producing
2,727,533 tonnes of raw sugar. Wheat yielded
692,090 tonnes, maize 71,769 tonnes, sorghum
634,120 tonnes and barley 297,268 tonnes. The livestock on March 31, 1975 included 10,878,959
cattle, 515,298 being dairy cattle, 13,907,860 sheep
and 400,435 pigs.

Forestry.—Total Australian grown timber processed in 1974–75 amounted to 1,071,000 cubic
metres.

Minerals.—There are rich deposits of bauxite,
coal, copper, lead, phosphate, silver, uranium, and
zinc, and deposits of tin, limestone, ironstone,
wolfram and mineral sands. Coal is mined extensively in Central Queensland and on a lesser scale in
North Queensland and Ipswich districts. Commercial production of oil began at Moonie in South
Queensland in 1964 and at Alton nearby in 1966.
The output in 1975 included gold, $A1,190,168;
coal, $A448,291,946; copper $A155,520,261; tin
$A7,187,098; silver $A37,696,617; lead
$A62,296,640; zinc $A70,762,451; bauxite
$A54,829,000; mineral sands $A44,674,765.

Manufacturing.—At June 30, 1974, 4,290 establishments employed 121,012 persons. During the
year value added was $A1,220,170,000. Much
production was the processing of primary products,
e.g. meat, sugar, minerals, timber, fruit and vegetables, flour, and butter. Included in other factory
production were the products from engineering,
transport equipment, basic and fabricated, chemical
fertilizer works, cement, paper and woollen mills
and oil refineries.

Year	Revenue	Expenditure	Debt(Gross)[1]
	$A'000	$A'000	$A'000
1973	704,109	702,902	1,424,497
1974	853,676	855,184	1,485,255
1975	1,112,866	1,121,218	1,441,023

[1]At par rates of exchange.

Banking.—Advances made by Trading Banks
(including the Commonwealth Trading Bank of
Australia) at June 30, 1975, totalled
$A1,247,595,000. The deposits at the same date

amounted to $A2,148,915,000. Depositors' balances in Queensland savings banks at June 30, 1975, $A1,618,206,000, averaged $A808 for each inhabitant. There were 2,608,000 operative accounts.

COMMUNICATIONS

Road and Rail.—The State is served by 9,780 kilometres of railways, practically all of 1,067 millimetres gauge. During 1974–75, 36,632,000 passengers and 30,208,000 tonnes of goods and livestock were carried. At June 30, 1974, there were 131,412 kilometres of formed roads in the State, and 906,000 motor vehicles were on the register.

Aviation.—Regular services operate between Brisbane, the main Queensland coastal and inland towns and the southern capitals. Brisbane is also a port of call on several international services.

Radio and Television.—On June 30, 1975, 22 national and 26 commercial sound broadcasting and 32 national (including 5 microwave repeater stations) and 11 commercial television stations were operating in Queensland.

OVERSEAS TRADE

Year	Imports	Exports
1972–73	$A311,448,000	$A305,569,000
1973–74	542,646,000	1,380,764,000
1974–75	580,051,000	2,007,775,000

The chief overseas exports are minerals, meat, sugar, wool, alumina, and cereal grains.

TOWNS

CAPITAL, Ψ BRISBANE, is situated on the Brisbane River, which is navigable by large vessels to the city, over 23 kilometres from Moreton Bay. The population of the Brisbane Statistical Division at June 30, 1975 was 958,800. This area includes the cities of Brisbane (723,000), Ipswich (67,500) and Redcliffe (38,200).

Other cities and towns with population over 10,000 at June 30, 1975, are: Ψ Townsville, 82,500; Gold Coast, 80,250; Toowoomba, 62,900; Ψ Rockhampton, 51,500; Ψ Cairns, 35,200; Ψ Bundaberg, 29,100; Mount Isa,32,850; Ψ Maryborough, 19,000; Ψ Mackay, 20,550; Ψ Gladstone, 19,800; Gympie, 10,900.

Transmission of mails from London to Brisbane, by air, 3 days; by sea 5 to 6 weeks.

SOUTH AUSTRALIA

The State of South Australia is situated between 26° and 38° S. lat. and 129° and 141° E. long., the total area being 380,070 sq. miles.

POPULATION.—At 30 June, 1975, the population was estimated to be 1,234,100.

Births, Deaths and Marriages

Year	Births	Deaths	Marriages
1972	21,844	9,764	10,829
1973	20,407	9,835	10,806
1974	20,181	10,236	10,767
1975	19,980	9,947	9,843

Religions.

Religion is free and receives no State aid. At the Census, 1971, the persons belonging to the principal religious denominations were as follows: Church of England, 286,754; Methodists, 215,328;

Congregationalists, 15,238; Baptists, 22,010; Lutherans, 62,641; Roman Catholics, 242,166; Presbyterians, 39,920; Churches of Christ, 22,802; and Orthodox, 32,636.

PHYSIOGRAPHY

The most important physical features of South Australia are broad plains, divided longitudinally by four great secondary features, which form barriers to east-west movement, and which have thus largely determined the direction of roads and railways, the sites of towns and villages and the manner of distribution of the population. These four barriers are Spencer Gulf, Gulf St. Vincent, the Mt. Lofty-Flinders Ranges and the River Murray. The long, deeply-indented coast-line, which provides a few major, and a multitude of lesser harbours, trends generally south-eastward. Pleasant weather conditions and good rainfall are experienced in most coastal areas.

The north-western portion of the State is mostly desert, while north of latitude 32° S. the country is unpromising by comparison with the fertile land which surrounds the hill country of the east. The Murray, which flows for some 400 miles through the south-eastern corner, is the only river of importance.

The lack of rivers and fresh-water lakes in the settled areas has necessitated the building of a number of reservoirs, which have been supplemented since 1941 by the construction of pipelines from the River Murray.

Climate.—The mean annual temperature at Adelaide is 17·1°C, the winter temperature (June-August) averaging 11·8°C, and the summer (Nov-Mar.) 21·5°C. During the summer months the maximum temperature at times exceeds 40°C, but is associated with a relatively low humidity. The average annual rainfall at Adelaide, derived from over 130 years' record is 21 inches. This total is rather higher than the approximate average annual rainfall over the whole of the agricultural areas. In the Mount Lofty Ranges the mean yearly rainfall in places exceeds 40 inches, while in Adelaide precipitation has fallen as low as 10·11 inches.

GOVERNMENT

South Australia was proclaimed a British Province in 1836, and in 1851 a partially elective legislature was established. The present Constitution rests upon a Law of Oct. 24, 1856, the executive authority being vested in a Governor appointed by the Crown, aided by a Council of 12 Ministers.

GOVERNOR

Governor of South Australia, His Excellency Sir Mark Laurence Elwin Oliphant, K.B.E., F.R.S. (1971)
                                                        $A20,000
Lieut.-Governor, W. R. Crocker, C.B.E. (1973).

THE MINISTRY

($A284,297 was voted in 1974–75 as salaries and allowances to Ministers.)
Premier and Treasurer, Hon. D. A. Dunstan, Q.C., M.P.
Deputy Premier and Minister of Works and Marine, Hon. J. D. Corcoran, M.P.
Minister of Mines and Energy and Planning, Hon. H. R. Hudson, M.P.
Minister of Health and Chief Secretary, Hon. D. H. L. Banfield, M.L.C.
Minister of Transport and Minister of Local Government, Hon. G. T. Virgo, M.P.
Minister of Lands, Minister of Irrigation, Minister of Repatriation and Minister of Tourism, Recreation and Sport, Hon. T. M. Casey, M.L.C.

Minister of Education, Hon. D. J. Hopgood, M.P.

Minister of Agriculture, Minister of Forests and Minister of Fisheries, Hon. B. A. Chatterton, M.L.C.

Minister of Labour and Industry, Hon. J. D. Wright, M.P.

Minister of Community Welfare, Hon. R. G. Payne, M.P.

Attorney-General and Minister of Prices and Consumer Affairs, Hon. P. Duncan, M.P.

Minister for the Environment, Hon. D. W. Simmons, D.F.C., M.P.

AGENT-GENERAL IN LONDON

Agent-General and Trade Commissioner for South Australia, J. S. White, C.M.G., South Australia House, 50 Strand, W.C.2.

THE LEGISLATURE

Parliament consists of a *Legislative Council* of 22 members elected for 6 years, one-half retiring every 3 years; and a *House of Assembly* of 47 members, elected for a maximum duration of 3 years. Election is by ballot, with universal adult suffrage for both the Legislative Council and the House of Assembly for all British subjects, male and female. The number of electors in 1975 was 771,414.

The elections to the House of Assembly in July, 1975, returned 23 Labour members, 20 Liberals, 2 Liberal Movement, 1 Country Party and 1 Independent.

President of the Legislative Council, Hon.
F. J. Potter........................ $A22,550

Speaker of the House of Assembly, Hon.
E. Connelly........................ $A22,550

Leader of the Opposition, D. O. Tonkin.

THE JUDICATURE

Law and Justice.—The Supreme Court is presided over by the Chief Justice and nine Puisne Judges.

EDUCATION

Education at the primary and secondary level is available at Government schools controlled by the Education Department and at independent schools, most of which are denominational. In 1975 there were 619 Government schools with 234,712 students, and 151 independent private schools with 39,297 students. The Department of Further Education administers the South Australian College of External Studies, apprentice training and contributing education in 8 metropolitan and 4 country technical colleges and 5 metropolitan and 11 country further education centres.

There are two universities: the University of Adelaide, founded in 1874, and the Flinders University of South Australia, opened in 1966. In 1974 there was a total enrolment of 9,113 full-time students. There are also eight Colleges of Advanced Education.

FINANCE

Banking.—There are 8 trading banks in Adelaide, including the Commonwealth Trading Bank and the State Bank of South Australia, having total average deposits of $A973,499,000 in June 1975. The eight savings banks had deposits of $A1,394,585,000 at June 30, 1975.

Revenue and Expenditure
(For years ended June 30)

Year	Revenue	Expenditure	Debt
	$A	$A	$A
1972	455,245,000	456,312,000	1,333,720,000
1973	520,866,000	524,777,000	1,415,129,000
1974	641,967,000	645,368,000	1,481,337,000
1975	828,985,000	820,601,000	1,555,333,000

PRODUCTION AND INDUSTRY

The gross value of primary production in 1974–75 was: crops $A428,253,000, livestock slaughterings $A104,293,000, livestock products $A169,379,000, and other primary $A28,466,000.

Agriculture.—Wheat harvest 1974–75, 1,486,000 tonnes; barley, 1,134,000 tonnes. Oranges, lemons, apples, apricots, peaches, and all stone fruits and olives are successfully grown, and fruit drying is profitable. In 1974–75 214,349,000 litres of wine and 4,709 tonnes of currants and raisins were produced. Considerable quantities of fruits (fresh and dried), wine and brandy, are annually sent to overseas countries, and to other Australian States. Some areas of the State, particularly near Adelaide, are also very suitable for growing all kinds of root crops and vegetables.

Livestock (March 31, 1975).—There were 17,621,000 sheep, 1,869,000 cattle, 349,000 pigs. Wool production (1974–75), 107,452,000 kg.

Minerals.—Iron, pyrite, gypsum, salt, coal, limestone, clay, &c., are found. The total mineral output was valued at $A125,978,000 in 1974–75, including iron ore valued by the South Australian Director of Mines at $A48,195,000.

Manufactures.—In 1974–75 there were 2,968 factories, employing 128,142 hands, the value of production being $A1,104,400,000.

Transport and Communications.—There were (June, 1975) 6,030 kilometres of railway in South Australia, 765 kilometres of tram and bus routes and 100,255 kilometres of roads, including roads and tracks outside local government areas. There are a number of excellent harbours, of which Port Adelaide is the most important. The number of vessels (exceeding 200 net tons) entering South Australia from overseas and interstate during 1974–75 was 1,287 with net tonnage of 7,665,356. The total value of shipping at South Australian ports during 1974–75 was 10,984,701 net tons involving 2,459 recorded entries of vessels. The countries of registration of vessels entered were: Australia 1,413; United Kingdom 253; Greece 83; Norway 62; Sweden 43; New Zealand 61; Liberia 102; Japan 81; all other countries 361. There are 761 post offices in the State.

Civil Aviation.—There are 29 Government and licensed airports; the largest of these, Adelaide airport, recorded 1,425,860 passenger movements during 1974–75.

Motor Vehicles.—The registrations on 30 June, 1975, were 612,636, equal to 1 per 2·01 persons.

Wireless and Television (June 30, 1975)—Broadcasting stations 18; Television stations 11.

OVERSEAS TRADE

Year	Imports	Exports
	$A	$A
1971–72	189,748,047	394,063,996
1972–73	199,978,000	521,720,000
1973–74	313,915,000	622,881,000
1974–75	482,077,000	764,410,000

The principal exports are wool, wheat, barley, meat, lead and lead alloys, and ores and concentrates of iron, lead, zinc and motor vehicles.

TOWNS

ΨADELAIDE, the chief city and capital, according to population Census on June 30, 1971, 809,482, inclusive of suburbs. Other centres (with 1971 populations) are: Whyalla (32,109); Mt. Gambier

(17,934); Ψ Port Pirie (15,456); Ψ Port Augusta (12,224); and Ψ Port Lincoln (9,158).

Transit.—Transmission of mails from London to Adelaide, approximately 29 days by sea and 5 days by air.

TASMANIA

Tasmania is an island state of Australia situated in the Southern ocean off the south-eastern extremity of the mainland. It is separated from the Australian mainland by Bass Strait and incorporates King Island and the Furneaux group of islands which are in the Strait. It lies between 40° 38′–43° 39′ S. lat. and 144° 36′–148° 23′ E. long., and contains an area of 26,383 square miles.

POPULATION.—The estimated population at Dec. 31, 1975, was 409,000.

Year	Births	Deaths	Marriages
1972	7,824	3,277	3,426
1973	7,326	3,347	3,395
1974	7,398	3,484	3,567
1975	6,981	3,340	3,207

Vital Statistics.—The birth rate in 1974 was 18·4, death rate 8·7, marriage rate 8·9 per 1,000. Infant mortality (1974) 16·6 per 1,000 births.

Religions

In 1971 there were 169,089 members of the Church of England, 77,250 Roman Catholics, 42,173 Methodists, 17,281 Presbyterians, 4,134 Congregationalists and Independents, and 8,039 Baptists.

PHYSIOGRAPHY

The surface of the country is generally hilly and timbered, with mountains from 1,500 to 5,300 ft. in height, and expanses of level, open plains. There are numerous rivers, the Gordon, Derwent, Piemam and Esk being the largest. The climate is fine and salubrious, and well suited to European constitutions; the hot winds of Australia do not often reach the island. At Hobart the mean maximum temperature ranges from about 54°F in winter to 70°F in summer, the minimum from 40°F to 52°F. The western side of the island is very wet, the eastern side being much drier; the average rainfall varies from 20 inches to 140 inches in different parts.

GOVERNMENT

The island was first settled by a British party from New South Wales in 1803, becoming a separate colony in 1825. In 1851 a partly elective legislature was inaugurated, and in 1856 responsible government was established. In 1901 Tasmania became a State of the Australian Commonwealth. The State executive authority is vested in a Governor (appointed by the Crown), but is exercised by Cabinet Ministers responsible to the Legislature, of which they are members.

GOVERNOR

Governor of Tasmania, His Excellency Sir Charles Stanley Burbury, K.B.E.; *assumed office* Dec. 5, 1973.

THE MINISTRY

Premier, Treasurer and Minister for Immigration, Hon. W. A. Neilson, M.H.A.

Attorney-General and Minister for Police and Licensing, Hon. B. K. Miller, M.L.C.

Minister for Education, Recreation and the Arts, National Parks and Wildlife, Hon. N. L. C. Batt, M.H.A.

Minister of Transport, Hon. G. D. Chisholm, M.H.A.

Agriculture, Hon. E. W. Barnard, M.H.A.

Lands, Works and Tourism, Hon. M. T. C. Barnard, M.H.A.

Health, Hon. H. D. Farquhar, M.H.A.

Resources and Developments, Hon. S. C. H. Frost, M.H.A.

Industrial Relations, Planning and Environment, Hon. D. A. Lowe, M.H.A.

Housing and Social Welfare, Hon. D. J. Baldock, M.H.A.

AGENT-GENERAL IN LONDON

Agent-General for Tasmania, R. R. Neville, 458–9 Strand, Charing Cross, W.C.2.

THE LEGISLATURE

Parliament consists of two Houses, a *Legislative Council* of 19 members, elected for six years (3 retiring annually, in rotation, except in every sixth year, when four retire) and a *House of Assembly* of 35 members, elected by proportional representation for five years in five 7-member constituencies, the electors for both Houses being all Tasmanians of 18 years and over who have resided continuously in the State for 6 months. The current term of five years for the House of Assembly will be reduced to four years after the next General Election.

At the election held on April 22, 1972, the Labour Party was returned to power in the House of Assembly after the resignation of the Liberals who had held office for a little under three of the scheduled five year term. The Labour Party's previous term had lasted for 35 years. The composition of the House of Assembly after the election was: Labour 21; Liberal 14.

President of the Legislative Council, Hon. C. B. M. Fenton.

Clerk of the Council, G. B. Edwards.

Speaker of the House of Assembly, Hon. H. N. Holgate.

Clerk of the House, B. G. Murphy.

THE JUDICATURE

The *Supreme Court of Tasmania,* with civil, criminal ecclesiastical, admiralty and matrimonial jurisdiction, was established by Royal Charter on October 13, 1823.

Chief Justice, Hon. G. S. M. Green.

Puisne Judges, Hon. Sir George Crawford; Hon. F. M. Neasey; Hon. D. M. Chambers; Hon. R. R. Nettlefold; Hon. J. R. Rex.

Local Courts established under the Local Courts Acts, 1896, are held before Commissioners who are legal practitioners with a jurisdiction up to $A1,500 in the case of liquidated claims ($A1,000, unliquidated claims). Courts of General Sessions, constituted by a chairman who is a Justice of the Peace and at least one other Justice, are established in the municipalities for the recovery of debts and demands not exceeding $A100. Courts of Petty Sessions are established under the Justices Act, 1959, constituted by Police Magistrates sitting alone, or any two or more justices. A single justice may hear and determine certain matters.

EDUCATION

Government schools are of three main types: primary, secondary and matriculation schools. On Aug. 1, 1975, there were 80,917 scholars enrolled in 285 Government schools. There were also 68 independent schools with an enrolment of 14,597. The University of Tasmania at Hobart, established 1890, had 2,314 full-time students and 1,085 part-time (including external) students in 1975. A College of Advanced Education offering degree and

diploma courses was established in 1972. Enrolments in 1975 were 1,748 full-time students and 687 part-time students.

FINANCE

Revenue and expenditure of the Consolidated Revenue Fund and debt of Tasmania at current rates of exchange (June 30) was:—

Year	Revenue	Expenditure	Debt
	$A	$A	$A
1971–72	157,751,717	160,236,825	709,921,268
1972–73	181,866,413	185,998,130	751,990,198
1973–74	206,946,676	210,096,694	787,618,086
1974–75	268,521,721	282,065,237	833,861,830

Banking.—The weekly average of depositors' balances at trading banks in March 1976 was $A299,691,000; the savings bank balances at the end of March 1976, were $A424,449,000.

PRODUCTION AND INDUSTRY

Gross values of agricultural production in 1974–75 were: crops, $A53·9m.; livestock slaughtering and other disposals, $A31·7m., and livestock products, $A58·6m. Total value added in manufacturing in 1973–74 was $A340·3m.; value added in mining was $A72·9m. in 1974–75.

Agriculture and Livestock.—The principal crops are potatoes, apples and other fruit, hay, hops, oats, beans, oil poppies, green peas, turnips (for stock feed), barley and wheat. The livestock included (March 31, 1975) 921,000 cattle, 4,136,000 sheep and 64,000 pigs. The wool production (1974–75) was 18,888,000 kg.

Electrical Energy.—Tasmania, the smallest Australian state, ranks fourth as a producer of electrical energy—most of it derived from water power, with an assessed annual capacity of 7,610 million kWh. By reason of its low-cost electrical energy, Tasmania has large plants producing ferro-manganese and newsprint. A large aluminium plant is situated at Bell Bay and Tasmania is the source of the bulk of Australian requirements of electrolytic zinc and fine papers. The Hydro-electric Commission has completed a network of 22 stations including two oil fired stations at Bell Bay. Work is continuing on two hydro-electric developments in the remote western and south-western regions of the state, which will increase the installed generator capacity from 1·44 million kW to 2·20 million kW.

Forestry.—The quantity of timber (excluding firewood) of various species cut in 1974–75 was 3,937,610 cubic metres, including 2,866,340 cubic metres for woodchip and wood-pulp.

Minerals.—The chief ores mined are those containing copper, tin, iron, silver, zinc and lead. The gross value of output in all mines and quarries in 1974–75 was $A117·8m.

Manufactures.—The chief manufactures for export are: refined metals, pelletized iron ore, preserved fruit and vegetables, butter, cheese, woollen manufactures, alginates, paper, confectionery, wood chips and sawn timber. In 1973–74, 935 manufacturing establishments employed 31,527 persons, including working proprietors. Salaries and wages paid totalled $A161·4m.

COMMUNICATIONS

Road and Rail.—Tasmania is served by a 1,067 mm gauge Federal Government railway system of 985 route kms. An additional 134 route kms of the same gauge is privately operated. During 1974–75 the Government system carried 430,000 passengers and 1,731,000 tonnes of goods and livestock. At June 30, 1975 there were 20,993 kilometres of road

normally open to traffic. Of this total 6,937 kilometres were sealed. Motor vehicles on the register at Dec. 31, 1975 were: cars and station wagons, 159,200; commercial vehicles, 36,100 and motor cycles, 7,700.

Aviation.—Regular services operate between Tasmania and the other Australian States. During 1974–75 876,000 passengers were carried on these services. The main cities and towns in the State are served by regular internal services.

OVERSEAS TRADE

Year	Imports	Exports
	$A'000	$A'000
1972–73	45,045	218,712
1973–74	69,277	259,745
1974–75	100,610	226,154

The principal overseas exports are ores and concentrates, refined metals, fresh fruit, greasy wool, meat and butter.

TOWNS

CAPITAL, ΨHOBART, founded 1804. Population (June 30, 1975), 136,550.

Other towns (with estimated population at June 30, 1975) are ΨLaunceston (64,850), ΨDevonport (20,270), Burnie-Somerset (21,060), Ulverstone (8,680) and New Norfolk (6,870).

VICTORIA

The State of Victoria comprises the south-east corner of Australia, at the part where its mainland territory projects farthest into the southern latitudes; it lies between 34°–39° S. latitude and 141°–150° E. longitude. Its extreme length from east to west is about 493 miles, its greatest breadth is about 290 miles, and its extent of coast-line is about 980 geographical miles, including the length around Port Phillip Bay, Western Port and Corner Inlet, the entire area being 87,884 square miles.

Population.—The population at June 30, 1973, was 3,586,574 (1,792,201 males and 1,794,373 females).

Births, Deaths and Marriages

Year	Births	Deaths	Marriages
1971	75,498	30,598	31,729
1972	71,807	29,856	32,386
1973	67,123	30,696	30,203
1974	66,201	30,875	29,708

Vital Statistics.—Annual rate per 1,000 of population in 1974: Births, 18·25; Deaths,8·51; Marriages, 8·19. Deaths under 1 year per 1,000 births, 14.9.

Religions

Members of the Church of England at the date of the Census in 1971 numbered 892,568, Roman Catholics 1,003,826, Presbyterians 364,338, Methodists 256,058, Orthodox 140,600, Baptists 41,753, Churches of Christ 38,950, Lutheran 39,832 and Hebrew 30,117. The number of persons who did not state their religion was 215,212.

PHYSIOGRAPHY

The *Australian Alps* and the *Great Dividing Range* pass through the centre of the State, and divide it into a northern and southern watershed, the latter sloping down to the ocean and containing, especially in the south-east, well-wooded valleys. The length of the Murray River, which forms part of the northern boundary of Victoria, is about 1,200 miles along the Victorian bank. Melbourne,

the capital city, stands upon the Yarra-Yarra, which rises in the southern slopes of the Dividing Range.

Climate.—The climate of Victoria is characterized by warm summers, rather cold winters, and rain in all months with a maximum in winter or spring. Prevailing winds are southerly from November to February inclusive, with a moderate percentage of northerlies often associated with high temperatures. Northerly or westerly winds predominate from March to October inclusive. Rain on an average falls in Melbourne on 143 days per year, the annual average being 25·85 inches.

GOVERNMENT

Victoria was originally known as the Port Phillip District of New South Wales and was created a separate colony in 1851, with a partially elective legislature. In 1855 Responsible Government was conferred. The executive authority is vested in a Governor, appointed by the Crown, aided by an Executive Council of Ministers.

Governor of the State of Victoria, His Excellency Hon. Sir Henry Arthur Winneke, K.C.M.G., O.B.E., *born* Oct. 29, 1908; *assumed office* June 3, 1974).....................................$A20,500
Lieutenant-Governor, Hon. Sir John McIntosh Young, K.C.M.G., Q.C. (1974).

THE MINISTRY

Premier, Treasurer and Minister of the Arts, Hon. R. J. Hamer, E.D.
Deputy Premier and Minister of Education, Hon. L. H. S. Thompson, C.M.G.
State Development and Decentralization, Tourism and Immigration, Hon. Murray Byrne.
Housing, Hon. V. O. Dickie.
Transport, Hon. E. R. Meagher, M.B.E., E.D.
Fuel and Power and Mines, Hon. J. C. M. Balfour.
Chief Secretary, Hon. J. F. Rossiter.
Attorney-General, Hon. V. F. Wilcox, Q.C.
Conservation, Land, Soldier Settlement, Hon. W. A. Borthwick.
Labour and Industry, Consumer Affairs and Federal Affairs, Hon. J. A. Rafferty.
Agriculture, Hon. I. W. Smith.
Public Works, Hon. R. C. Dunstan, D.S.O.
Local Government and Planning, Hon. A. J. Hunt.
Health, Hon. A. H. Scanlan.
Social Welfare, Hon. W. V. Houghton.
Youth, Sport and Recreation, and Assistant Minister of Education, Hon. B. J. Dixon.
Water Supply and Forests, Hon. F. J. Granter.

AGENT-GENERAL IN LONDON

Agent-General for Victoria, Hon. J. F. Rossiter, Victoria House, Melbourne Place, Strand, W.C.2.

THE LEGISLATURE

Parliament consists of a *Legislative Council* of 36 members, elected for the 18 Provinces for 6 years, one-half retiring every 3 years; and a *Legislative Assembly* of 73 members, elected for a maximum duration of 3 years. By virtue of the Electoral Provinces and Districts Act 1974 the number of members of the Legislative Council will be increased to 44 elected for 22 provinces for 6 years, one half retiring every 3 years; the number of members of the Legislative Assembly will be increased to 81 elected for a maximum duration of 3 years. Voting is compulsory. The electors on the rolls at May 30, 1975 numbered 2,162,221.

President of the Legislative Council, Hon. Sir Raymond Garrett, A.F.C........ $A34,125
Speaker of the Legislative Assembly, Hon. K. H. Wheeler................... 34,125

THE JUDICATURE

There is a Supreme Court with a Chief Justice and 19 Puisne Judges, a County Court and Magistrates' Courts.

Supreme Court

Chief Justice, Hon. Sir John Young, K.C.M.G. $A42,400
Puisne Judges, Hon. Sir Gregory Gowans; Hon. Sir Oliver Gillard; Hon. J. E. Starke; Hon. E. H. E. Barber; Hon. M. V. McInerney; Hon. G. H. Lush; Hon. C. I. Menhennitt; Hon. H. R. Newton; Hon. F. Nelson; Hon. K. V. Anderson; Hon. W. C. Crockett; Hon W. Kaye; Hon. R. G. De B. Griffith; Hon. B. J. Dunn; Hon. P. Murphy; Hon. W. O. Harris; Hon. B. L. Murray; Hon. R. K. Fullagar; Hon. K. J. Jenkinson ....*each* 38,500

County Court

Chief Judge, Hon. D. Whelan.......... 38,000
Judges, Their Honours T. G. Rapke; H. T. Frederico; N. A. Vickery; A. Adams; D. W. Corson; J. X. O'Driscoll; J. H. Forrest; C. W. Harris; E. E. Hewitt; C. Just; R. J. Leckie; I. F. C. Franich; T. B. Shillito; J. P. Somerville; W. J. Martin; I. Gray; A. J. Southwell; J. R. O'Shea; J. G. Gorman; R. J. D. Wright; H. G. Ogden; G. M. Byrne; N. S. Stabey; B. F. McNab; K. F. Coleman; G. H. Spence; J. Mornane............*each* 31,750
Masters of the Supreme Court, C. P. Jacobs, M.B.E.; S. H. Collie; E. N. Bergere; G. S. Brett...................*each* 26,700

Law Department

Solicitor-General, D. Dawson, Q.C...... 38,500
Secretary to the Law Department, R. Glenister.......................... 27,400
Crown Solicitor, J. Downey............ 30,769

EDUCATION

Primary Education is compulsory, secular and free between the ages of 6 and 15. At Aug. 1, 1974, there were 1,724 Government Primary Schools attended by 366,303 pupils, 34 Primary-Secondary Schools with 8,588 pupils, and 262 Secondary Schools (excluding Junior Technical Schools) with an enrolment of 168,987. There were also 101 Government Junior Technical Schools with 61,599 pupils and 40 Special Schools with 3,166 pupils. In addition there are various Senior Colleges and Colleges of Advanced Education.

At Aug. 1, 1974, 196,420 pupils attended 571 non-Government schools, 466 of which were Roman Catholic.

There are three State-aided Universities—Melbourne, Monash and La Trobe. Enrolments for 1974 at Melbourne were 15,539, at Monash 12,837 and at La Trobe 6,481.

PRODUCTION AND INDUSTRY

The gross value of primary production (excluding mining and quarrying) in 1973–74 was $A1,467,007,979, agricultural $A461,231,870, pastoral $A597,851,098, dairying $A276,934,278, poultry and bee-keeping $A69,813,714, trapping $A5,633,632, forestry $A44,478,755 mining and quarries (including oil and natural gas) $A432,949,000, fisheries $A11,064,632. The net value of production of primary industries was $A1,081,611,136. Wool, wheat, flour, butter, live stock, fruits, milk and cream, meats, poultry and eggs are staple products.

Live Stock.—There were on rural holdings in March, 1974, 25,778,000 sheep, 5,840,000 cattle, and

424,000 pigs. The quantity of wool produced in 1973–74 was valued at A248,232,000 (preliminary figures).

Minerals.—Minerals raised include oil and natural gas, brown coal, limestone, clays and stone for construction material. Production of brown coal in 1973–74 amounted to 26,354,577 tonnes.

FINANCE

	Consolidated Fund		Debt at end of year
Year	Receipts	Payments	
	$A'000	$A'000	$A'000
1971–72	1,210,889	1,210,889	2,488,348
1972–73	1,381,153	1,381,153	2,632,910
1973–74	1,610,923	1,610,923	2,746,610

Banking, etc.—State Savings Bank deposits at June 30, 1974, amounted to $A1,861,972,000; in addition, deposits in the Commonwealth Savings Bank (in the State of Victoria) amounted to $A853,858,000, and in other savings banks $A1,214,312,000

Insurance (other than Life).—The total revenue of companies or other bodies transacting business in Victoria during the year 1973–74 amounted to $A522,897,000, made up of premium income $A486,197,000, and other income $A36,699,000. Expenditure totalled $A485,354,000 (excluding taxation), comprising claims $A361,053,000, commission and agents' charges $A39,555,000 and other expenditure $A84,746,000.

Crude Oil and National Gas.—In February, 1965 natural gas was first discovered in commercial quantities in the offshore waters of the Gippsland Basin in eastern Victoria. An even larger gas field was found early in 1966, and during 1967 two valuable oilfields were located in the same general area. These fields are still the largest yet found in Australia. Following the development of the four fields, commercial gas began to flow to consumers in Melbourne during April 1969, and crude oil came on stream in October, 1969. Production from the Gippsland fields during the calendar year 1974 was: stabilized crude oil, 20,136,889 cubic metres; treated natural gas, 2,128,154,045 cubic metres; commercial propane, 918,372 cubic metres and commercial butane, 1,055,219 cubic metres.

Secondary Industry.—In 1972–73 there were 11,734 manufacturing establishments in which 314,269 males and 141,004 females were employed. The principal industrial sub-divisions were: Transport equipment, 60,909 persons; basic and fabricated metal products 51,003 persons; other industrial machinery, 66,603 persons; clothing and footwear, 61,129 persons; and food, beverages and tobacco, 63,847 persons. Manufacturing activity is concentrated in the Melbourne Statistical Division. Important manufacturing centres are Geelong, Ballarat, Bendigo and in the shire of Morwell. Value added in the course of manufacture was $A3,738 million.

TRANSPORT
Victoria State Railways.—At June 30, 1974, there were 6,685 kms of railway open for traffic. The revenue and expenditure for the year ended June 30, 1974, were $A115,612,777 and $A156,119,624 respectively. Total distance travelled was 33,352,420 kms and passenger journeys numbered 114,589,353. The tonnage of goods and livestock carried was 11,231,160.

Shipping.—During the year ended June 30, 1974, 3,530 vessels with net tonnage 22,192,000 entered Victorian ports and 3,530 vessels with total net tonnage of 22,074,695 were cleared.

Motor Vehicle Registration.—The number of vehicles on the register at June 30, 1974, was: cars and stationwagons, 1,301,900; light commercial type vehicles, 150,100; trucks and omnibuses, 111,600, and motor cycles, 45,800.

OVERSEAS TRADE
The export trade (excluding inter-state trade) consists largely of agricultural and mining products. The principal overseas imports of the State are aircraft and parts, apparel and textiles, manufactured fibres, electrical and other machines and machinery, motor vehicles and tractors, metals and metal manufactures, iron and steel, rubber manufactures, crude petroleum, paper, drugs and chemicals, synthetic resins and professional, scientific and controlling instruments.

Year	Imports	Exports
	$A	$A
1969–70	1,347,053,000	912,596,000
1970–71	1,453,583,000	1,034,908,000
1971–72	1,431,076,000	1,139,731,000
1972–73	1,472,602,000	1,495,373,000
1973–74	2,155,908,000	1,594,870,000

CITIES, TOWNS AND BOROUGHS
ΨMELBOURNE, the capital city, which is an archiepiscopal see, was originally laid out in the year 1837 with wisdom and foresight; its wide streets, park lands, public gardens, university, public library, museum, art gallery and large churches are the principal features of the city. At the Census of June 30, 1971, the population of Urban Melbourne was 2,394,117. Other urban centres are ΨGeelong, 115,181; Ballarat, 58,620; Bendigo, 45,936; Moe-Yallourn, 20,863; Shepparton, 19,410; Ψ Warrnambool, 18,684; Morwell 16,858; Wangaratta, 15,586; Traralgon, 14,665.

WESTERN AUSTRALIA
Includes all that portion of the continent west of 129° E. long., the most westerly point being in 113° 9'E. long. and from 13° 44' to 35° 8' S. lat. Its extreme length is 1,480 miles, and 1,000 miles from east to west; total area 975,920 sq. miles.

POPULATION.—At June 30, 1975, the population was estimated at 1,122,559 (males, 572,703; females, 549,856). The figures include full-blood Aborigines.

Year	Births	Deaths	Marriages
1971	24,239	7,806	9,382
1972	22,177	7,441	9,120
1973	20,510	7,845	9,102
1974	20,207	7,778	9,295
1975(a)	20,349	8,014	9,026

(a) Preliminary figures.

Religions.—Census of 1971—Church of England 362,759, Roman Catholics 267,990, Methodists 85,283, and Presbyterians 48,367.

Physical Features.—Large areas of the State, for some hundreds of miles inland, are hilly and even mountainous, although the altitude, so far as ascertained, rises nowhere above that of Mount Meharry (4,082 ft) in the north-west division or that of Bluff Knoll (3,640 ft.) in the Stirling Range

in the south-west. The coastal regions are undulating, with an interior slope to the unsettled central portion of Australia. The Darling and Hamersley ranges of the west have a seaward slope to the Indian Ocean, into which flow many streams, notably the Preston, Collie, Murray, Swan, Murchison, Gascoyne, Ashburton, Fortescue and De Grey. In the north the Fitzroy flows from the King Leopold ranges into the Indian Ocean, and the Drysdale and Ord into the Timor Sea. The greater portion of the State may be described as an immense tableland, with an average elevation of 1,000 to 1,500 ft. above sea-level, the surface of which varies from stretches of clay soils to the sand dunes of the far interior. The climate is one of the most temperate in the world. The total rainfall at Perth during 1975 was 682 millimetres, the average for the previous 100 years 879. Of the total area two-thirds is suitable for pastoral purposes.

GOVERNMENT

Western Australia was first settled by the British in 1829, and in 1870 it was granted a partially elective legislature. In 1890 Responsible Government was granted, and the Administration vested in a Governor, a Legislative Council, and a Legislative Assembly. The present constitution rests upon the Constitution Act, 1889, the Constitution Acts Amendment Act, 1899, and amending Acts. The Executive is vested in a Governor appointed by the Crown and aided by a Council of responsible Ministers.

The Legislative Assembly (elected March, 1974) is composed of Liberal Party 23, Australian Labour Party 22, National Country Party 6.

Governor of Western Australia, Air Chief Marshal Sir Wallace Kyle, G.C.B., C.B.E., D.S.O., D.F,C, (1975).

Lieut.-Governor and Administrator, His Excellency Commodore J. M. Ramsay, C.B.E., D.S.C.

EXECUTIVE COUNCIL

Premier, Treasurer, and Minister Co-ordinating Economic and Regional Development, Hon. Sir Charles Court, O.B.E., M.I.A. $A42,683

Deputy Premier, Minister for Works, Water Supplies, and the North West, Hon. D. H. O'Neil, M.L.A. $A37,787

Minister for Justice, Chief Secretary and Leader of the Government in the Legislative Council, Hon. Neil McNeil, M.L.C. $A37,804

Minister for Agriculture, Hon. R. C. Old, M.L.A.

Minister for Transport, Police, and Traffic, Hon. R. J. O'Connor, M.L.A.

Minister for Education, Cultural Affairs, and Recreation, Hon. G. C. MacKinnon, M.L.C.

Minister for Labour and Industry, Consumer Affairs, and Immigration, Hon. W. L. Grayden, M.L.A.

Minister for Industrial Development, Mines and Fuel and Energy, Hon. A. Mensaros, M.L.A.

Minister for Local Government and Urban Development and Town Planning, Hon. E. C. Rushton, M.L.A.

Minister for Lands, Forests and Tourism, Hon. K. A. Ridge, M.L.A.

Minister for Health, and Community Welfare, Hon. N. E. Baxter, M.L.C.

Minister for Housing, Conservation and the Environment, and Fisheries and Wildlife, Hon. P. V. Jones, M.L.A.

Attorney-General and Minister for Federal Affairs, Hon. I. G. Medcalf, M.L.C.

(M.L.A.—Membership of the Legislative Assembly, M.L.C.—Member of the Legislative Council)

Ministers, each $A33,779 to $A38,579, according to location of electorate.

AGENT-GENERAL IN LONDON

Offices, Western Australia House
115 Strand, London, W.C.2.

Agent-General, J. A. Richards.

THE LEGISLATURE

Parliament consists of a *Legislative Council* and a *Legislative Assembly*, elected by adult suffrage subject to qualifications of residence and registration. The qualifying age for electors for both the Legislative Council and Legislative Assembly was lowered in 1970 from 21 to 18 years. There are 30 members in the Legislative Council, two from each Province, for a period of 6 years, one member from each Province retiring triennially. The Legislative Assembly is composed of 51 members, who are elected for a term of 3 years.

President of the Legislative Council, Hon.
  A. F. Griffith, M.L.C. $A27,612
Speaker of the Legislative Assembly, Hon.
  R. Hutchinson, D.F.C., M.I.A. 27,012

THE JUDICATURE

Chief Justice, Hon. Sir Lawrence Jackson, K.C.M.G. $A44,601
Senior Puisne Judge, Hon. F. T. P. Burt; 40,883
Puisne Judges, Hons. J. M. Lavan; A. R.
  A. Wallace; J. L. C. Wickham; R. E.
  Jones; P. F. Brinsden *each* 39,645

EDUCATION

Education.—In 1975 there were 629 government schools and 191 non-government schools (excluding kindergartens) with 195,024 and 43,373 pupils respectively. The total amount expended on education (from State Revenue) during the year ended June 30, 1975, was A179,890,614, including grants of $A4,643,727 to the University of Western Australia (6,279 full-time students in 1975), and $A145,577 to Murdoch University (417 full-time students in 1975).

PRODUCTION AND INDUSTRY

The gross value of primary production (excluding mining) in 1974–75 was: crops $A473,191,000; livestock slaughterings, etc., $A102,042,000; livestock products $A257,884,000; forestry $A14,314,000; fishing and whaling $A37,577,000; hunting $A1,663,000.

Crops and Livestock.—The production of wheat for grain in 1974–75 was 3,277,071 tonnes. On March 31, 1975, the livestock included 2,554,012 cattle, 34,476,337 sheep, and 264,157 pigs. The wool clip in 1974–75 was 172,221,000 kg. in the grease.

Manufacturing Industries.—There were 2,818 manufacturing establishments operating in the State at June 30, 1974. The total number of persons employed (including working proprietors) by these establishments at the end of June, 1974, was 69,711.

Forestry.—The forests contain some of the finest hardwoods in the world. The total quantity of sawn timber produced during 1974–75 was 392,481 cubic metres.

Minerals.—The State has large deposits of a wide range of minerals, many of which are being mined or are under development for production. The ex-mine value of all minerals produced during 1974–75 was $A860,451,000.

Communications.—On June 30, 1975, there were 6,075 kms. of State government railway open for general and passenger traffic; and 731 kms. of the Trans-Australian railway (Kalgoorlie-Port Pirie Junction). In the year ended June 30, 1975, 3,604 vessels (net tonnage 50,212,347) entered Western Australian ports and 3,623 (net tonnage 50,625,843) cleared. The total length of roads at June 30, 1975, was 161,654 kms. The number of registered motor vehicles at June 30, 1975, was 549,775 (414,402 motor cars and station wagons, 129,416 light and heavy commercials, and 25,957 motor cycles and motor scooters).

FINANCE

Total revenue of Western Australia in 1974–75 was $A734,239,941, compared with $A567,683,368 in 1973–74. Expenditure in 1974–75 totalled $A743,373,039 (1973–74 $A573,416,368). The net public debt of the State at June 30, 1975, was $A1,119,226,523 (1974, $A1,069,211,744).

TRADE

Year	Imports	Exports
	$A	$A
1972–73	1,013,446,826	1,313,686,247
1973–74	1,308,271,585	1,612,266,691
1974–75	1,711,929,244	2,098,694,885

Exports in 1974–75 included gold bullion ($A1,855,293), wool ($A169,333,487), wheat ($A409,758,410), salt ($A16,215,397), prawns ($A7,581,106), hides and skins ($A11,195,598), oats ($A9,997,543), timber ($A9,251,824), beef ($A24,789,145), mutton and lamb ($A22,106,931), live animals ($A15,160,673), rock lobster tails ($A25,257,769), apples ($A5,994,279), ilmenite ores and concentrates ($A9,893,221), iron ore ($A699,842,565), barley ($A38,129,002), petroleum and petroleum products ($A65,580,284), iron and steel ($A71,493,008), machines and machinery ($A42,193,578), transport equipment ($A25,235,530), furniture ($A11,506,536).

TOWNS

CAPITAL.—Ψ PERTH. Population (estimated, June 30, 1975) of Perth Statistical Division, including the port of Fremantle, 787,300.

Perth, the capital, stands on the right bank of the Swan River estuary, 12 miles from Fremantle. Other towns are Kalgoorlie-Boulder and environs (21,250), Ψ Bunbury (18,550); Ψ Geraldton (15,950); Ψ Albany (12,250).

DISTANCES FROM LONDON BY AIR

A list of the distances in statute miles from London to various places abroad. Distances given are Great Circle distances from London Heathrow Airport to destination airports. They have been supplied by International Aeradio Ltd., a Division of British Airways.

To	Miles	To	Miles	To	Miles
Ajaccio	790	Dublin	279	New York	3,440
Algiers	1,035	Düsseldorf	311	Nice	645
Alicante	911	Entebbe	4,033	Nicosia/Cyprus	2,008
Amsterdam	231	Faro	1,063	Oporto	806
Ankara	1,765	Frankfurt	406	Oslo	723
Athens	1,500	Geneva	468	Palermo	1,128
Auckland	11,404	Gibraltar	1,084	Palma/Majorca	836
Baghdad	2,550	Gothenburg	651	Paris	215; (Orly 227)
Bahrain	3,163	Hamburg	463	Perth/Australia	9,008
Bangkok	5,929	Hanover	437	Pisa	736
Barbados	4,192	Helsinki	1,147	Prague	649
Barcelona	712	Heraklion	1,685	Rangoon	5,581
Basle	447	Hong Kong	5,989	Reykjavik	1,167
Beirut	2,162	Honolulu	7,220	Rhodes	1,743
Bergen	648	Istanbul	1,560	Rome (Fiumicino)	896
Berlin	593	Johannesburg	5,634	Salzburg	652
Bermuda	3,428	Karachi	3,935	Shannon	369
Bombay	4,478	Khartoum	3,071	Singapore	6,754
Bordeaux	458	Kingston/Jamaica	4,668	Sofia	1,266
Bremen	406	Kuala Lumpur	6,557	Stockholm (Arlanda)	906
Brisbane	10,273	Kuwait	2,903	Stuttgart	469
Brussels	217	Leningrad	1,314	Sydney	10,568
Budapest	923	Lisbon	971	Tangier	1,120
Cagliari	959	Madrid	774	Teheran	2,741
Cairo	2,192	Malaga	1,041	Tel Aviv	2,229
Calcutta	4,958	Malta	1,305	Tokyo	5,955
Chicago	3,941	Marseilles	614	Toronto	3,545
Cologne	331	Mauritius	6,075	Trinidad	4,405
Colombo	5,413	Milan	609	Tripoli	1,468
Copenhagen	608	Montego Bay	4,687	Turin	570
Corfu	1,273	Montreal	3,239	Valencia	826
Dar-es-Salaam	4,661	Moscow	1,557	Venice	715
Darwin	8,613	Munich	588	Vienna	790
Delhi	4,180	Nairobi	4,247	Warsaw	912
Detroit	3,754	Naples	1,011	Zagreb	848
Doha	3,253	Nassau	4,332	Zürich	490

New Zealand
AREA AND POPULATION

Islands	Area (English) Sq. Miles)	Population	
		Census Mar. 23, 1971†	Estimated March 31, 1975
(a) *Exclusive of Island Territories:*			
North Island............................	44,281	2,051,363	2,251.420
South Island............................	58,093	811,268	853,983
Stewart Island..........................	670	414*	410*
Chatham Islands........................	372	716*	730*
Minor Islands:			
Inhabited—			
Kermadec Islands.....................	13	9*	9*
Campbell Island.......................	44	9*	9*
Uninhabited—			
Three Kings.........................	3	..	..
Snares..............................	1	..	..
Solander............................	½	..	..
Antipodes...........................	24	..	..
Bounty..............................	½	..	..
Auckland............................	234	..	..
Total exclusive of Island Territories......	103,736	2,862,631	3,105,430
(b) *Island Territories:*			
Tokelau Islands.........................	..	1,655	1,574‡
Niue Island............................	..	4,901	3,992§
Total, inclusive of Island Territories	103,939	2,869,187	3,110.966
(c) Cook Islands¶.........................	..	21,227	18 937§
Ross Dependency........................	175,000	..	..

Included in North Island and South Island totals.
† Excluding 1,482 members of the Armed Forces overseas.
‡ Sept. 25, 1974.   § Sept. 30, 1974.
¶ The Cook Islands have had complete internal self-government since Aug. 4, 1965, as has Niue since 19 Oct. 1974 but Cook Islanders and Niueans remain New Zealand citizens.
Maori Population included in the totals for New Zealand proper—1971 Census, 227,414 (males 114,948; females 112,466): estimated June 30, 1975, 252,800 (males 127,700; females 125,100).

Vital Statistics

Year	Births	Deaths	Natural Increase	Deaths of Infants under one year	Infant Mortality per 1,000 live births	Marriages
1972	63,215	24,801	38,414	988	15·63	26,868
1973	60,727	25,312	35,415	985	16·22	26,274
1974	59,336	25,261	34,075	922	15·54	25,412
1975	56,638	25,113	31,525	904	15·96	24,534

Birth rate (1975) 18·25; death rate 8·09; marriage rate 7·91.

Inter—Censal Increases

Year	Results of Census			Numerical Increase	Net Passenger Arrivals over inter-censal periods
	Males	Females	Total		
1956	1,093,211	1,080,851	2,174,062	234,590	+ 27,486
1961	1,213,376	1,201,608	2,414,984	240,922	+ 68,726
1966	1,343,743	1,333,176	2,676,919	261,935	+ 48,660
1971	1,430,856	1,431,775	2,862,631	185,712	..

Excluding 2,559 members of the Armed Forces overseas at the time of the 1961 census, 1,936 at the 1966 census and 1,482 at the 1971 census.

Races and Religions

Races	1966	1971	Religions	1966	1971
				Per cent.	Per cent.
Europeans.................	2,426,352	2,561,280	Church of England.......	33·7	31·3
Maoris....................	201,159	227,414	Presbyterians.............	21·8	20·4
Chinese..................	10,283	12,818	Roman Catholics.........	15·9	15·7
Polynesians (other than N.Z. Maoris).............	26,271	45,413	Methodists...............	7·0	6·4
Other races..............	12,854	15,706	Baptists.................	1·7	1·7

number of rainy days is generally in the neighbourhood of 160 to 180 in the North Island and between 110 and 140 in the South, except in the southern portion of the west coast. The amount of sunshine is generally over 2,000 hours per annum and ranges between 1,600 to 2,500 hours.

GOVERNMENT

The west coast of the South Island of New Zealand was discovered by Abel Janszoon Tasman, the navigator (voyaging under the direction of the Netherlands' East India Company), on December 13, 1642.

The islands were visited, and charted, in 1769 by Captain Cook, who returned to them in 1773, 1774 and 1777. From 1800 onwards sealers and whalers settled along the coasts, and trade in timber and flax followed. Christianity was introduced in 1814, and in 1832 a British Resident was appointed. In 1840 British sovereignty was proclaimed, and on May 3, 1841, New Zealand was, by letters patent, created a separate colony distinct from New South Wales. Organized colonization on a large scale commenced in 1840 with the New Zealand Company's settlement at Wellington. On Sept. 26, 1907, the designation was changed to *The Dominion of New Zealand*. The Constitution rests upon the Imperial Act of 1852, and on the New Zealand Constitution (Amendment) Act of Dec. 10, 1947. The Statute of Westminster was formally adopted by New Zealand in 1947. The executive authority is entrusted to a Governor-General appointed by the Crown and aided by an Executive Council, within a Legislature consisting of one chamber, the House of Representatives.

FLAG: Blue ground, with Union Jack in top left quarter, four five-pointed red stars with white borders on the fly. On June 20, 1968, a new naval ensign bearing the Southern Cross was adopted, replacing the British white ensign.

Governor General and Staff

Governor-General and Commander-in-Chief of New Zealand (1972–), His Excellency Sir (Edward) Denis Blundell, G.C.M.G., G.C.V.O., K.B.E.

$NZ 26,000

Official Secretary, D. C. Williams, C.V.O.

THE EXECUTIVE COUNCIL

His Excellency the GOVERNOR-GENERAL

Prime Minister and Minister of Finance, Rt. Hon. R. D. Muldoon.

Deputy Prime Minister and Minister of Foreign Affairs and Overseas Trade, Hon. B. E. Talboys.

Trade and Industry, Hon. L. R. Adams-Schneider.

Justice, Hon. D. S. Thornton.

Works and Development, Hon. W. L. Young.

Defence, Hon. A. McCready.

Social Welfare, Hon. H. J. Walker

Labour and State Services, Hon. J. B. Gordon.

Agriculture and Fisheries, and Maori Affairs, Hon. D. MacIntyre.

Local Government and Internal Affairs, Hon. D. A. Highet.

Transport, Hon. C. C. A. McLachlan

Education, Hon. L. W. Gandar.

Tourism and Environment, Hon. H. R. Lapwood.

Housing and Customs, Hon. G. F. Gair.

Health, Hon. T. F. Gill.

Minister of State, Rt. Hon. Sir Keith Holyoake.

Energy Resources, Hon. E. S. F. Holland.

Attorney-General, Hon. P. I. Wilkinson.

Lands, Hon. V. S. Young.

Broadcasting, Hon. H. C. Templeton.

PHYSIOGRAPHY

New Zealand consists of a number of islands of varying size in the South Pacific Ocean, and has also administrative responsibility for a large tract in the Antarctic Ocean. The two larger and most important islands, the North and South Islands of New Zealand, are separated by only a relatively narrow strait. The remaining islands are very much smaller and, in general, are widely dispersed over a considerable expanse of ocean. The boundaries, inclusive of the most outlying islands and dependencies, range from 8° South latitude to south of 60° South latitude, and from 160° East longitude to 150° West longitude.

Geographical Features.—The two principal islands have a total length of 1,040 miles, and a combined area of 102,374 square miles. A large proportion of the surface is mountainous in character. The principal range is that of the Southern Alps, extending over the entire length of the South Island and having its culminating point in Mount Cook (12,349 ft.). The North Island mountains include several volcanoes, two of which are active, others being dormant or extinct. Mt. Ruapehu (9,175 ft.) and Mt. Ngauruhoe (7,515 ft.) are the most important. Of the numerous glaciers in the South Island, the Tasman (18 miles long by 1¼ wide), the Franz Josef and the Fox are the best known. The North Island is noted for its hot springs and geysers. For the most part the rivers are too short and rapid for use in navigation. The more important include the Waikato (270 miles in length); Wanganui (180), and Clutha (210). Lakes (Taupo, 234 sq. miles in area; Wakatipu, 113; and Te Anau 133) are abundant, many of them of great beauty.

Climate.—New Zealand has a moist-temperate marine climate, but with abundant sunshine. A very important feature is the small annual range of temperature which permits of some growth of vegetation, including pasture, all the year round. Very little snow falls on the low levels even in the South Island. The mean temperature ranges from 15° C. in the North to about 9° C. in the South. Rainfall over the more settled areas in the North Island ranges from 35 to 70 inches and in the South Island from 25 to 45 inches. The total range is from approximately 13 to over 250 inches. The

The Prime Minister receives $27,500 per annum with a tax-free allowance of $5,000 for expenses of his office and the Ministerial residence. The salary of each Minister holding a portfolio is $18,000 with tax-free expense allowance of $2,000 and that of each Minister without portfolio $15,500, with $1,600 tax-free expense allowance.

NEW ZEALAND HIGH COMMISSION
New Zealand House, Haymarket, S.W.1
High Commissioner, Hon. D. J. Carter.
Deputy High Commissioner, D. B. G. McLean.
Minister (Commercial), E. A. Woodfield.
Defence and Naval Adviser, Cdre. F. H. Bland, O.B.E.
Counsellors, L. J. Watt *(Politcal)*; R. E. Alexander *(Finance)*; L. H. Jones *(Administration)*; Miss F. M. C. Lee *(Commercial).*
Army Adviser, Col. J. M. Morris, M.B.E.
Air Adviser, Group Capt. B. Stanley-Hunt, A.F.C.
1st Secretaries, Mrs. V. S. Blumhardt; G. D. Malcolm *(Economics)*; M. J. Taylor *(Press and Information).*
Agricultural Adviser, M. D. Gould.
Attaché (Scientific), C. M. Palmer.

BRITISH HIGH COMMISSION
Reserve Bank of New Zealand Building, 2 The Terrace (P.O. Box 1812), Wellington, 1
High Commissioner, His Excellency Harold Smedley, C.M.G. M.B.E. (1975)..................£15,000
Deputy High Commissioner and Counsellor (Commercial), T. D. O'Leary.
1st Secretary, G. R. Archer *(Head of Chancery).*
Defence Adviser, Capt. C. A. Johnson, R.N.
Asst. do., Squadron Leader P. R. Callaghan, R.A.F.
1st Secretaries, A. F. Baines *(Agriculture and Food)*; G. Rutherford *(Commercial)*; J. R. E. Carr-Gregg *(Information).*
2nd Secretaries, C. G. Patterson *(Administration)*; C. Thompson *(Commercial)*; R. D. Lavers.

———

British Council Representative, P. J. C. Dart.

THE LEGISLATURE
Parliament consists of a House of Representatives consisting of 87 members elected for 3 years. The General Election of November, 1975, returned 52 National members and 35 Labour. There are four Maori electorates. Women have been entitled to vote since 1893, and to be elected Members of the House of Representatives since the passing of the Women's Parliamentary Rights Act, 1919. There are at present 4 women members. Members of the House receive $NZ11,000 *per annum,* with an allowance of $NZ2,395 *per annum* for expenses, plus an electorate allowance. The Leader of the Opposition receives $NZ18,000 *per annum* and $NZ2,000 *per annum* for expenses, plus travelling allowance or $NZ2,000.
Speaker of the House of Representatives.
Hon. Sir Roy Jack *(plus expense allowance of $NZ1,500 per annum and residential quarters in Parliament House)* $NZ16,500

THE JUDICATURE
The judicial system comprises a Supreme Court and a Court of Appeal; also Magistrates' Courts having both civil and criminal jurisdiction.
Chief Justice, Rt. Hon. Sir Richard Wild. K.C.M.G., E.D................$NZ23,279
Court of Appeal, Rt. Hon. Sir Clifford Richmond *(President)*...........$NZ22,207
Judges, Rt. Hon. Sir Owen Woodhouse; R. B. Cooke...................... 21,130
Supreme Court Puisne Judges, Hons. A. C. Perry; J. N. Wilson; L. F. Moller; G. D. Speight; C. M. Roper; J. C. White; D. S. Beattie; J. P. Quilliam;

D. W. McMullin; P. T. Mahon; J. B. O'Regan; N. F. Chilwell; N. E. Casey; J. A. Ongley; J. F. Jeffries; E. J. Somers; D. H. M. Somers; J. S. Henry; R. I. Barker.............. 21,130
Supreme Court Administrative Divn., Rt. Hon. Sir Richard Wild *(Chief Justice)*; Hons. J. C. White; G. D. Speight.
Judge, Court of Arbitration, Judge A. P. Blair........................... 21,130

POLICE
On March 31, 1975 the strength of the Police Force was 4,119 of all ranks, equivalent to 1 for every 745 of the population. The total cost of police protection in 1975–76 was $NZ49,434,000.

DEFENCE
A unified Ministry of Defence was set up on Jan. 1, 1964. The Ministry is responsible, under the Minister of Defence, for the whole field of national defence. Defence expenditure in 1975–76 amounted to $NZ193,465,000.

Navy
The Royal New Zealand Navy was greatly expanded during the Second World War and a number of small vessels were built in New Zealand. The naval forces include the Women's Royal New Zealand Naval Service, and Volunteer Reserve forces in four divisions. The strength is 4 frigates, 1 survey ship. Active naval personnel number 303 officers and 2,850 ratings. A frigate is normally attached to the Far East Station.

Army
The New Zealand Army consists of the Regular Force, the Territorial Force and the Army Reserve. The strength of the Regular Force at March 31, 1975 was 5,523 and of the Territorial Force 5,618.
The Army is now organized on the basis of one integrated Regular/Territorial Brigade Group, with its own logistic support and reserves. In addition, a regular force battalion is stationed as part of the Commonwealth Far East strategic reserve in Malaysia.

Air
Operational elements of the R.N.Z.A.F. include one Strike Squadron, one ground attack squadron, one anti-submarine warfare squadron, one helicopter squadron and three transport squadrons, one of which is based in Singapore. Aircraft operated by the R.N.Z.A.F. include the Skyhawk, Strikemaster, Orion, Hercules and Bristol Freighter. The strength of the Regular Force at March 31, 1975, was 4,297.

FINANCE
Into the Consolidated Revenue Account (New Zealand's main public account) are paid the proceeds of income tax, sales tax, customs and excise duties and other taxes, also interest, profits from trading undertakings, and departmental receipts (departmental expenditure is included gross). Revenue from taxation is also paid into the National Roads Fund principally from a tax on motor spirits and registration and licence fees for motor vehicles.

Year ended March 31	Revenue	Expenditure
	$NZ	$NZ
1973	2,135,795,738	2,141,026,641
1974	2,512,164,904	2,509,778,874
1975	3,046,057,941	3,034,889,403
1976	3,682,505,390	3,684,091,613*

*Includes:

Education	$NZ631,751,000
Social Welfare	$NZ896,755,000
Health	$NZ602,546,000
Development of Industry	$NZ311,467,000
Defence	$NZ193,465,000
Debt sevices	$NZ322,761,000
Law and order	$NZ 88,508,000

Revenue from taxation in 1975–76 amounted to $NZ3,185,289,000 of which $NZ3,084,039,000 represented receipts into the Consolidated Revenue Account, and $NZ101,250,000 receipts into the National Roads Fund.

DEBT

The gross *Public Debt* amounted on March 31, 1975, to $NZ4,199,699,000, of which $NZ682,640,000 was domiciled in London and $NZ128,156,000 in the U.S.A.; $NZ54,955,000 represented World Bank loans.

CURRENCY

World recession has affected New Zealand through low export prices and high import prices, as shown in a rise in import prices in the two years ended March 31, 1974. To counter this trend, the Government devalued the New Zealand dollar by 15 per cent. on August 10, 1975.

BANKING

There are five trading banks (with numerous branches) doing business, two of which are predominantly New Zealand banks. Of these the Bank of New Zealand is owned by the State. At Mar. 31, 1976, assets of all trading banks in respect of New Zealand business amounted to $NZ2,584,000,000; liabilities, $NZ2,529,600,000; and the value of notes in circulation amounted to $NZ368,500,000. The Reserve Bank of New Zealand commenced business on August 1, 1934. The note-issuing powers of other banks have since been withdrawn and the Reserve Bank notes are legal tender. New Zealand's official overseas reserves at March 31, 1976, amounted to $NZ684,800,000, of which $NZ374,200,000 represented assets of the New Zealand banking system. Trading banks' advances, including discounts on Mar. 31, 1976, totalled $NZ1,787,600,000 compared with $NZ1,673,300,000 in the previous year. Deposits with trading banks on Mar. 31, 1976, amounted to $NZ2,459,500,000 (1974, $NZ2,102,900,000).

Post-office and trustee savings banks had, at the close of the year 1975–76, over 4 million accounts having $NZ2,136,547,000 to their credit. Private savings banks have been operated by the trading banks since Oct. 1964, and at March 31, 1976, deposits totalled $NZ556,848,000.

EDUCATION

Schools are free and attendance is compulsory between the ages of 6 and 15. There are opportunities for apt pupils to proceed to university. In 1974 there were 472,099 pupils attending public primary schools, and 50,574 pupils attending registered private primary schools. The secondary education of boys and girls in the cities and large towns is carried on in 233 state secondary schools, 48 state secondary departments of district high schools and 112 private secondary schools. The total number of pupils receiving full-time secondary education in July 1974 was 208,596 and in addition there were 107,507, students attending technical classes and 17,679 receiving part-time tuition from the Technical Correspondence School. The university system consists of the University of Auckland, the University of Waikato, Massey University of Manawatu, Victoria University of Wellington, the University of Canterbury and the University of Otago. The Lincoln university college of agriculture is associated with the University of Canterbury. The university system is co-ordinated by the University Grants Committee. The Universities had a total of 39,969 students in 1974.

The total expenditure on education out of public funds in 1975–76 was $NZ631,750,700.

PRODUCTION AND INDUSTRY

Gross Agricultural Production (Gross Output)

	Yrs. ended 30 June		
	1973	1974*	1975*
	$NZ(million)		
Sheep and lambs	349	305	197
Wool	364	315	216
Cattle	296	298	202
Pigs	27	35	37
Dairy Products	317	347	369
Crops and seeds	89	92	115
Fruit	39	40	39
Vegetables	42	48	46
Poultry and eggs	54	61	60
Agricultural services	73	74	69
Other—farm products	14	17	18
—non-farm products	4	3	4
Gross Agricultural Production (Gross Output)	1,668	1,676	1,329

* Provisional

Industrial Production

	1972–73 $NZ	1973–74 $NZ
Value of Production	4,611,300,000	5,250,900,000

Net Output (Net Value Added), consisting only of the rewards to the factors of production, *i.e.* salaries and wages, interest on borrowed capital, and proprietors' surplus, in 1973–74 amounted to $NZ1,502,400,000, compared with $NZ1,301,700,000 in the previous year.

Agricultural and Pastoral Production

	1973–74	1974–75
Wheat, bushels	12,800,000	12,800,000
Wool, metric tons	284,000	294,000
Butter, metric tons	215,900	240,100
Cheese, metric tons	89,000	88,600
Stock Slaughtered—	1973–74	1974–75
Lambs, No.	22,992,000	25,195,000
Sheep, No.	8,761,000	7,080,000
Cattle, No.	1,788,000	2,134,000
Calves, No.	1,244,000	1,438,000
Pigs, No.	747,000	719,000

Forestry.—The output of sawn timber for 1975 was 825,000,000 board ft., of which 676,000,000 board ft. represented exotic varieties, mainly pine.

Livestock.—Livestock on farms at Jan. 31, 1974, included 3,125,000 dairy cattle (of which 2,080,000 were dairy cows in milk during season), 6,528,000 beef cattle (of which 2,199,000 were beef breeding cows), and 500,000 pigs. At June 30, 1975, sheep numbered 55,320,000, including 41,108,000 breeding ewes.

Manufactures.—Statistics of factory production show (1973–74) 7,690 factories in operation, employing 244,522 persons. Salaries and wages amounted to $NZ1,042,214,000; cost of materials used, $NZ3,112,806,000. Total value of production, $NZ5,250,878,000.

Minerals.—Coal output in 1974 was 2,564,317 tons. Gold-mining was formerly an important industry, but production has declined greatly in recent years. Other minerals produced on a relatively small scale are copper, silver, iron ore, manganese ore, zinc, leads, cadmium, tungsten and asbestos. Valuable deposits of natural gas have been discovered in Taranaki, and this has been piped to some main North Island centres. New Zealand has large resources of potential iron ore in the black sands of many of its beaches of which 992,099 tons were exported in 1973 and steelworks have been built near Auckland to utilize such deposits.

TRADE

Provisional figures of New Zealand's trade during the year ended June, 1975, were; Imports (c.i.f.) $NZ2,737,460,000, compared with $NZ2,014,177,000 in 1973–74; Exports, (f.o.b.) $NZ1,612,607,000, compared with $NZ 1,787,563,000 in 1973–74.

Trade with U.K.

	1973	1974
Imports from U.K.	£167,287,000	£255,596,000
Exports to U.K.	276,171,000	247,603,000

New Zealand produce exported to the U.K. in the 12 months ending June, 1975, was valued at $NZ346,100,000 and included butter, valued at $NZ76,200,000, cheese ($NZ15,300,000; beef ($NZ6,800,000); wool ($NZ44,700,000); lamb ($NZ135,700,000).

Railways.—In March, 1975, there were 2,981 route miles of Government railway in operation. The number of passengers carried on Government lines in 1974–75, including season-ticket holders, was 18,896,000. Goods railed amounted to 12,883,000 tonnes. Railway total revenue and expenditure were $NZ153,911,000 and $NZ199,071,000 in 1974–75.

Motor Vehicles.—On December 31, 1975, there were 1,884,904 motor vehicles licensed, including 1,164,483 cars and 92,208 motor cycles and power cycles. The number of persons per passenger car was 2·8.

Shipping.—During 1975 the vessels entered from overseas ports numbered 3,692 (net tonnage 20,078,000) and those cleared for overseas 3,688 (net tonnage 19,976,000).

Post Office Statistics.—During 1974–75 internal postal services handled 699,026,000 items, including 351,148,000 letters and 329,605,000 items of printed matter. Overseas mails included 2,583,618 lb. of airmail received and 1,680,056 lb. despatched. Telephone subscribers totalled 980,307 at March 31, 1975.

Civil Aviation.—In 1975 domestic scheduled servies flew 25,171,000 kilometres and carried 2,312,000 passengers. Freight carried amounted to 62,900 tons. In 1975 international services to and from New Zealand carried 1,179,000 passengers, 30,877 tonnes of freight and 2,270 tonnes of mail.

CAPITAL, ΨWellington, in the North Island (pop. March 31, 1975, Wellington statistical division, 354,660).
Other large centres: ΨAuckland, 796,660; ΨChristchurch, 326,410; ΨDunedin, 120,890; Palmerston North, 87,000; Hamilton, 152,740; ΨWanganui, 38,480; ΨNew Plymouth, 43,050; Ψ Napier-Hastings, 109.360; Rotorua, 47,270; Ψ Tauranga, 48,360.

NATIONAL DAY (New Zealand Day).—Feb. 6.

THE ISLANDS OF NEW ZEALAND

In addition to North, South, Stewart and Chatham Islands:—

The Three Kings (discovered by Tasman on the Feast of the Epiphany), in 34° 9' S. lat. and 172° 8' 8" E. long. (uninhabited). *Auckland Islands*, about 290 miles south of Bluff Harbour, in 50° 32' S. lat. and 166° 13' E. long. The islands contain several good harbours, but are uninhabited. *Campbell Island* (used as a weather station). *Antipodes Group* (40° 41' 15 S. lat. and 178° 43' E. long.) uninhabited. *Bounty Islands* (47° 4' 43 S. lat., 170° 10 30 E. long.). *Snares Islands and Solander* (uninhabited).

The Kermadec Group (population normally 9 or 10) between 29° 10ı to 31° 30' S. lat., and 177° 45' to 179° W. long., includes Raoul or Sunday, Macaulay, Curtis Islands, L'Esperance, and some islets. All the inhabitants are government employees at a meteorological station.

Cook and other Islands, included in the boundaries of New Zealand since June, 1901, consist of the islands of Rarotonga, Aitutaki, Mangaia, Atiu, Mauke, Matiaro, Manuae, Takutea, Palmerston, Penrhyn or Tongareva, Manihiki, Rakahanga, Pukapuka or Danger, and Nassau. The total population of the group was 18,937 at Sept. 30, 1974. Niue, which is geographically part of Cook Islands, but which is administered separately, had an estimated population on Sept. 30, 1974 of 3,992. The chief exports of the Cook Islands are fruit juice, clothing, copra, bananas, citrus fruit and pulp, and pearl shell. The trade is chiefly with New Zealand, Australia, Japan, the U.K. and the U.S.A. Financial aid to the Cook Islands and Niue approved by the New Zealand Government totalled $NZ5·5 million for the 1973–74 financial year.

The High Commissioner of the Cook Islands is employed in a dual role, since he represents both the Queen and the New Zealand Government. Since Aug. 4, 1965, the Islands have enjoyed complete internal self-government, excecutive power being in the hands of a Cabinet consisting of the Premier and five other ministers. The new Constitution Act was passed by the New Zealand Parliament in November 1964, but did not come into force until it had been endorsed by the 22-member Legislative Assembly of the Cook Islands, elected in April 1965.

The New Zealand citizenship of the Cook Islanders is embodied in the Constitution, and assurances have been given that the changed status of the Islands will in no way affect the consideration of subsidies or the right of free entry into New Zealand for exports from the group.

A New Zealand Representative is stationed at Niue, which since October 1974 has been self-governing in free association with New Zealand, which is responsible for external affairs and defence. Executive power is in the hands of a Premier and a Cabinet of 3 drawn from the Assembly of 20 members.

Tokelau (or *Union Islands*.—A group of atolls (Fakaofo, Nukunono and Atafu) (population 1,574 in Sept. 1974), proclaimed part of New Zealand as from Jan. 1, 1948.

THE ROSS DEPENDENCY

The *Ross Dependency*, placed under the jurisdiction of New Zealand by Order in Council dated July 30, 1923, and defined as all the islands and territories between 160°E. and 150°W. longitude which are situated south of the 60°S. parallel. The Ross Dependency includes Edward VII Land and portions of Victoria Land. For some years there have been permanent bases in the area, staffed by survey and scientific personnel.

The Bahamas

The Bahama Islands are an archipelago lying in the Atlantic Ocean between 20° 55′–27° 22′ N. Lat; 72° 40′–79° 20′ W. Long. They extend from the coast of Florida on the north-west almost to Haiti on the south-east. The group consists of 700 islands, of which 30 are inhabited and 2,400 cays comprising an area of more than 5,380 square miles. The population, at the end of 1974, was estimated at 197,000. The principal islands include: Abaco, Acklins, Andros, Berry Islands, Bimini, Cat Cay, Cat Island, Crooked Island, Eleuthera, Exumas, Grand Bahama, Harbour Island, Inagua, Long Cay, Long Island, Mayaguana, New Providence (on which is located the capital, Nassau), Ragged Island, Rum Cay, San Salvador and Spanish Wells. San Salvador was the first landfall in the New World of Christopher Columbus on October 12, 1492.

The Bahamas were settled by British subjects when the islands were deserted. The ownership of the Bahamas was taken over in 1782 by the Spanish, but the Treaty of Versailles in 1783 restored them to the British.

Tourism is the economic mainstay of the Bahamas, whose salubrious climate and fine beaches attract over 1,000,000 visitors annually.

GOVERNMENT

The Bahamas gained independence on July 10, 1973. There are a Senate of 16 members and an elected House of Assembly of 38 members.

Governor-General, His Excellency Sir Milo Boughton Butler, G.C.M.G., G.C.V.O.
Prime Minister and Minister of Economic Affairs, Rt. Hon. L. O. Pindling.
Deputy Prime Minister and Minister of Finance, Hon. A. D. Hanna.
Transport, Hon. G. A. Smith.
Education, Hon. L. N. Coakley.
Health, Hon. A. L. Roker.
Agriculture and Fisheries, Hon. R. F. A. Roberts.
Development, Hon. A. Maycock.
Works, Hon. S. L. Bowe.
External Affairs and Attorney General, Hon. P. L. Adderley.
Labour and National Insurance, Hon. C. Darling.
Home Affairs, Hon. D. Rolle.
Tourism, Hon. C. T. Maynard.

Chief Justice, Sir Leonard Knowles.
Puisne Judges, Hon. S. Graham; Hon. K. Potter.

BAHAMAS HIGH COMMISSION
39 Pall Mall, S.W.1.
[01-930 6967]
High Commissioner, His Excellency Sir Alvin Braynen.

BRITISH HIGH COMMISSION
Bitco Building, East St.
P.O. Box N7516, Nassau.
High Commissioner, His Excellency Peter Mennell, C.M.G., M.B.E. (1975).
Deputy High Commissioner, J. G. Doubleday, O.B.E. (*Head of Chancery*).

Industries.—A plant for the manufacture of cement and an oil refinery have been established in Freeport, Grand Bahama, where there are also a number of light industries. A rum distillery is in operation in New Providence and a multi-million dollar aragonite operation is in progress off the island of Andros. Other industries are those associated with the treatment of local agriculture and marine produce, salt extraction and handwork, and timber-felling for plywood.

Education.—Education is compulsory between the ages of 5 and 14. More than 57,000 students are enrolled in Ministry of Education and Independent schools in New Providence and the Family Islands.

Civil Aviation.—Facilities for external traffic are provided by Bahamasair, Pan-American World Airways, British Airways, Air Canada, Air Jamaica, Eastern Air Lines, Delta Air Line, National Airlines, International Air Bahama, Flamingo Airways, Lufthansa, Sabena, and Mackey International Airline. Kivin Air provides inter schedule and charter flights to the Family Islands, and Bahamas Air Traders' Island Flying Service provides internal schedule and charter flights to the outlying islands. There are daily return flights between Nassau and Miami, several daily flights between Nassau–Palm Beach–Fort Lauderdale and Tampa, and a regular service between Nassau, Kingston and Montego Bay, Jamaica, besides regular trunk communication with London, New York, Chicago, Toronto, Montreal, Bermuda, Kingston and Haiti.

Communications.—There are a General Post Office in Nassau, 4 branch offices in New Providence and 109 sub-offices in the Family Islands. Wireless and telephone services are in operation to all parts of the world. There are 132 radio-telephone channels among the islands.

FINANCE AND TRADE

	1974	1975*
Public revenue	B$123,500,000	B$133,884,360
Expenditure	115,000,000	131,393,880

	1972	1973*
Total imports	484,894,662	764,260,752
Total exports	343,412,935	529,748,582
		*estimated

	1973	1974
Imports from U.K.	£8,164,000	£8,548,000
Exports to U.K.	19,253,000	10,552,000

The imports are chiefly foodstuffs, manufactured articles, building material, lumber and machinery. The chief exports in 1972 were pulpwood, cement, rum, crawfish, salt and aragonite.

CAPITAL.—ΨNassau. Estimated population (1974), 112,000. Nassau is distant from Liverpool 4,000 miles.

Bangladesh

Area, Population, Climate, etc.—The People's Republic of Bangladesh consists of the territory which was formerly East Pakistan (the old province of East Bengal and the Sylhet district of Assam), covering an area of 55,126 sq. miles in the region of the Gangetic delta, and has a population, according to the 1974 census, of 71,316,817, but official estimates place the current figure at 78,000,000.

The country is crossed by a network of navigable rivers, including the eastern arms of the Ganges, the Jumna (Brahmaputra) and the Meghna, flowing into the Bay of Bengal. The climate is tropical and

monsoon; hot and extremely humid during the summer, and mild and dry during the short winter. The rainfall is heavy, varying from 50 inches to 135 inches in different districts and the bulk of it falls during monsoon season (from June to September). The mean temperature during the winter (November to February) is about 20°C. (68°F.) and during the hot season 30°C (86°F.).

Prior to becoming East Pakistan, the territory had been part of British India. It acceded to Pakistan in October, 1947, and became a Republic on March 23, 1956.

By a proclamation of March 26, 1971, Bangladesh purported to secede from the central government, and a government-in-exile was set up in April in Calcutta. The short war between India and Pakistan, in both the East and the West, and India's overwhelming defeat of the Pakistani Army in the East, brought about a *de facto* secession of the East wing. The Indo-Pakistan war was concluded on December 16, 1971, and Mr. Zulfiqar Ali Bhutto became President on December 20. Sheikh Mujib was sworn in as Prime Minister on January 12. Recognition of the new state was accorded swiftly by many countries. Bangladesh was admitted to the Commonwealth on April 18, and to the United Nations in 1974. Pakistan and Bangladesh accorded one another mutual recognition in Feb. 1974 but they have yet to establish diplomatic relations.

Government.—A Constitution was promulgated on December 15, and provided for a multi-party system of democratic government. In Dec. 1974 the President declared a State of Emergency and suspended certain constitutional privileges. In January 1975 Sheikh Mujib introduced constitutional amendments which empowered him to assume the Presidency and to establish a one-party system of government. On August 15 Sheikh Mujib and his family were assassinated by dissident Army officers. The former Commerce Minister, Khandaker Moshtaque Ahmed, assumed the Presidency. On November 4 Brigadier Khaled Mosharraf, Chief of Army Staff, led a short-lived *coup* which displaced President Moshtaque, but Mosharraf was himself overthrown and killed a few days later. Since then a non-political administration under President Mr Justice A. M. Sayem (the former Chief Justice) has administered the country under martial law.

President and Chief Martial Law Administrators, Mr. Justice A. M. Sayem.
Members of Advisory Council, Maj.-Gen. Ziaur Rahman; Air Vice-Marshal M. K. Bashar; K. A. Haque; Dr. M. N. Huda; Mrs Benita Roy; Azizul Huq; Rear-Admiral M. H. Khan; Prof. Abul Fuzal; Mohommad Abdur Rashid; Dr. Mohammad Ibrahim; A. K. M. Hafizuddin; Col. M. M. Haque.

BANGLADESH HIGH COMMISSION
28 Queen's Gate, S.W.7
[01-584 0081]
High Commissioner, His Excellency A. F. M. Abul Fateh.
Deputy High Commissioner, Faruq Ahmed Choudhury.
Counsellors, M. R. Osmany; E. A. Chaudhury; M. H. Choudhury.
1st Secretaries, Q. A. M. A. Rahim; Syed Muhammad Hussain; Atiur Rahman.
2nd Secretaries, R. A. Khan; A. K. M. A. Rouf; A. Hai.

BRITISH HIGH COMMISSION
D.I.T. Buildings Annex, Dilkusha
(P.O. Box 90), Dacca 2
High Commissioner, His Excellency Barry Granger Smallman, C.M.G., C.V.O., (1974).
Deputy High Commissioner and Counsellor (*Economics*). D. M. Kerr, O.B.E.
1st Secretaries, D. P. Small, M.B.E. (*Head of Chancery*); G. T. Burgess, M.B.E. (*Commercial*) A. E. Montgomery; M. D. K. Halsey; M. C. McCulloch (*Aid*), H. Davidson O.B.E., (*Agricultural Advise*); W. A. Tincey (*Consular and Immigration*); J. R. Travis (*Aid*); N. H. B. Veriod (*Administration*).
2nd Secretaries, J. P. Bedingfield (*Commercial*); H. A. Condor (*Consular*); R. Brean (*Aid*).
British Council Representative, E. T. J. Phillips, 5 Fuller Road, Ramna, Dacca 2.
Education.—The present system of education is

under review. Primary education is free but not universal. There are six Universities: Dacca, Rajshahi, Chittagong, Bangladesh University of Engineering and Technology (at Dacca), Bangladesh Agricultural University (at Mymensingh), and Jahangirnagar (opened in 1970). In 1974 literacy was estimated at 22·21 per cent. of the whole of Bangladesh and 26 per cent. of the male population.

Transport and Communications.—Principal seaports with total import and export tonnages for 1975 in millions, were: ᴪ Chittagong 4·59, and ᴪ Chalna 1·54 The Bangladesh Shipping Corporation has been set up by the Government to operate the Bangladesh merchant fleet. The principal airports with runway lengths in feet are Dacca-Tejgaon (9,000) and Chittagong (7,500); a new international airport outside Dacca is scheduled for completion in 1977. A national airline, Bangladesh Biman, has been established with services to London and Calcutta, Bangkok, Karachi, Dubai and Katmandu, and an internal network.

There are about 3,900 miles of roads in Bangladesh; 2,400 miles are metalled. There are 2,600 miles of railway track.

Radio Bangladesh is the main national broadcasting service. A television service was introduced in 1965.

Production.—Bangladesh is the principal producer of raw jute in the world. Other agricultural products are rice, tea, oil seeds, pulses, and sugar cane. The chief industries are jute, cotton, tea, leather, paper, fertilizer and sugar.

Aid. Bangladesh is a major recipient of bilateral and multilateral development aid. Commitments in the financial year 1975–76 totalled U.S. $945,000,000, of which U.S. $905,000,000 derived from the Aid Group led by the I.B.R.D. Commitments were composed of U.S. $290,000,000 in food aid, U.S. $336,000,000 commodity aid and U.S. $319,000,000 project aid.

CAPITAL, Dacca. Population 2,539,991, according to the results of the 1974 census.

Barbados

Barbados, the most easterly of the West India islands, is situated in latitude 13° 14′ N. and longitude 59° 37′ W. The island has a total area of 166 square miles, the land rising in a series of tablelands marked by terraces to the highest point, Mt. Hillaby (1,104 ft.). It is nearly 21 miles long by 14 miles broad. Some 46 acres are covered by forest and 68,875 acres are cultivated. *Climate.*—Barbados has a pleasant climate with annual average temperature 26·5° C. (79·8° F.) and rainfall varying from a yearly average of 75 inches

in the high central district to 50 inches in some of the low-lying coastal areas. *Population.*—Since the Census held in April, 1970, the population has risen from 235,229 to an estimated total of 254,964 in 1975.

CAPITAL.—Ψ Bridgetown (population, estimated April, 1971, 18,789). Populations of other administrative areas (parishes) in 1970 were: St. Michael (88,097); Christ Church (36,033); St. Philip (17,230); St George (16,903); St. James (14,658); St. Peter (10,820) and St. Thomas (10,624). Bridgetown, the only port of entry, has a deep-water harbour with berths for 8 ships, opened in 1961. Oil is pumped ashore at one installation on the West Coast. FLAG.—Three vertical stripes, dark blue, gold and dark blue, with trident device on gold stripe. NATIONAL DAY—Nov. 30 (Independence Day).

Government.—Barbados was first settled by the British in 1627 and was a Crown Colony from 1652 until it became an independent state within the Commonwealth on November 30, 1966. The Legislature consists of the Governor-General, a Senate and a House of Assembly. The Senate comprises 21 members appointed by the Governor-General, of whom 12 are appointed on the advice of the Prime Minister, 2 on the advice of the Leader of the Opposition and 7 by the Governor-General at his discretion to represent religious, economic or social interests in the Island or such other interests as the Governor-General considers ought to be represented. The House of Assembly comprises 24 members elected every five years by adult suffrage. In 1963 the voting age was reduced to 18. In June, 1976, seats in the House of Representatives were distributed as follows: Democratic Labour Party 17, Barbados Labour Party 6, People's United Party 1.
Governor-General, Sir William Scott, G.C.M.G., G.C.V.O. (1967) (+ *duty allowance* $16,800) $36,000

CABINET★

Premier and Minister of Finance, Rt. Hon. E. W. Barrow.

Deputy Prime Minister and Minister of State for Parliamentary Affairs, Hon. C. E. Talma, C.B.E.

Health and Social Welfare, Senetor the Hon. L. E. Sandiford.

Labour, National Insurance, Housing and Lands, Hon. P. M. Greaves.

Trade, Industry and Commerce, Senator the Hon. B. M. Taitt.

Agriculture, Science and Technology, Hon. A. Morrison.

Education, Community Development, Youth Affairs and Sport, Hon. F. G. Smith, Q.C.

Communications and Works, Dr. the Hon. R. B. Caddle.

Minister without Portfolio, Capt. Hon. G. G. Fergusson.

External Affairs and Attorney-General, Senator the Hon. G. Moe, Q.C.

Tourism, Information and Public Relations, Hon. P. G. Morgan, C.B.E.

President of the Senate, Senator Sir Theodore Brancker, Q.C.

Speaker, House of Assembly, His Hon, P. A. E. Hoppin.

BARBADOS HIGH COMMISSION
[01-235 8686]
6 Upper Belgrave Street, S.W.1
High Commissioner, His Excellency Cecil Beaumont Williams, O.B.E., (1976).

BRITISH HIGH COMMISSION
147–9 Roebuck Street (P.O. Box 676C)
Bridgetown
High Commissioner, His Excellency Charles Stuart Roberts, C.M.G. (1973) £11,000
Deputy High Commissioner, R. P. de Burlet (*Head of Chancery*).

JUDICATURE
There is a Supreme Court of Judicature consisting of a High Court and a Court of Appeal. In certain cases a further appeal lies to the Judicial Committee of H.M. Privy Council. The Chief Justice and Puisne Judges are appointed by the Governor-

★A new Cabinet, with Mr. J. M. G. Adams as Prime Minister, was formed on Sept. 8, 1976.

General on the recommendation of the Prime Minister and after consultation with the Leader of the Opposition.
Chief Justice, Hon. Sir William Douglas . . . $31,200
Puisne Judges, A. J. H. Hanschell, C.M.G.; D. H. L. Ward; D. Williams.

Education.—Primary and secondary education is free in Government-aided schools.

Communications.—Barbados has some 840 miles of roads, of which about 780 miles are asphalted. There is an international airport at Seawell, 12 miles from Bridgetown, and frequent scheduled services connect Barbados with the major world air routes. There are a colour television service, and a radio broadcasting service operated by the Caribbean Broadcasting Corporation, and a wired broadcasting service operated by a local subsidiary of Rediffusion Ltd.

Production, etc.—The principal *exports* are sugar, molasses, rum, clothing, lard and margarine, and the *imports* food, manufactured goods, machinery, transport equipment and chemicals. Barbados' major trading partners are the U.K., U.S.A., CARICOM and Canada. The tourist industry is a major source of revenue.

TRADE

Goods to the value of BDS $217,120,000 were exported in 1975, including sugar ($95,137,000), molasses ($11,761,000), and rum ($4,347,000).

	1975
Total imports	$437,193,000
Total exports	$217,120,000

Trade with U.K.

	1974	1975
Imports from U.K.	£14,499,000	£17,184,000
Exports to U.K.	9,733,000	14,797,000

FINANCE

	1975–6	1976–7 (est.)
Revenue	$196,466,000	$182,480,000
Expenditure	146,173,000	208,865,000

Botswana

Botswana (formerly the British Protectorate of Bechuanaland) lies between latitudes 18° and 26° S. and longitudes 20° and 28° W. and is bounded by the Cape and Transvaal Provinces of South Africa on the south and east, by Rhodesia, the Zambesi amd Chobe (Linyanti) Rivers on the north and north-east and by South West Africa on the west. Botswana extends some 500 miles by 550 miles, with a total area of

220,000 square miles. The climate of the country is generally sub-tropical, but varies considerably with latitude and altitude. A plateau at a height of about 4,000 feet divides Botswana into two main topographical regions. To the east of the plateau streams flow into the Marico, Notwani and Limpopo Rivers; to the west lies a flat region comprising the Kgalagadi Desert, the Okavango Swamps and the Northern State Lands area. The Kgalagadi Desert is a level tract closely covered with thorn bush and grass, extending 300 miles to the west and bounded by the Makgadikgadi salt pans and the Boteti River in the north. Its rainfall varies from 20 inches in the east to 9 inches in the south-west. The Okavango Swamps, 6,500 square miles in area, lie in the remote north-western corner of Botswana, and, apart from the Limpopo and Chobe Rivers, are the only source of permanent surface water in the country. North of the Boteti River and the Makgadikgadi depression the Kgalagadi Desert gives way to forest and dense bush of the Northern State Lands. Large areas of the country support only herds of game. Elephant numbers have been estimated at 10,000.

Population.—At the census in August, 1971, it was recorded that Botswana had a population of 620,000. The eight principal Botswana tribes are Bakgatla, Bakwena, Bangwaketse, Bamalete, Bamangwato, Barolong, Batawana and Batlokwa. CAPITAL.—Gaborone, estimated population 18,000. Other business centres are Francistown (20,000) and Lobatse (13,000). FLAG.—Horizontal bands of blue, white, blue, with a black stripe on the white band.

Government.—On September 30, 1966, Bechuanaland became a Republic within the Commonwealth under the name Botswana. The President of Botswana is Head of State and appoints as Vice-President a member of the National Assembly who is his principal assistant and leader of Government business in the National Assembly. The Assembly consists of the President, 32 members elected on a basis of universal adult suffrage, 4 specially elected members, the Attorney-General (non-voting) and the Speaker. There is also a House of Chiefs.

President, Sir Seretse Khama, K.B.E.
Vice President, Dr. Hon. Q. K. J. Masire.

OFFICE OF THE PRESIDENT
Minister of State for External Affairs, Hon. A. M. Mogwe, M.B.E.
Minister of State for the Public Service and Broadcasting, Hon. D. K. Kwelagobe.
External Affairs Secretary, C. Tibone.

MINISTRY
Minister for Finance and Development Planning, Dr. Hon. Q. K. J. Masire.
Health, Hon. M. P. K. Nwako.
Home Affairs, Hon, B. K. Kgari.
Agriculture, Hon. E. S. Masisi.
Local Government and Lands, Hon. L. Makgekgenene.
Works and Communications, Hon. J. G. Haskins, O.B.E.
Commerce and Industry, Dr. Hon. G. K. T. Chiepe, M.B.E.
Education, Hon. K. P. Morake.
Mineral Resources and Water Affairs, Hon. M. K. Segokgo.

BOTSWANA HIGH COMMISSION
162 Buckingham Palace Road, S.W.1
High Commissioner, His Excellency B. M. Setshogo.

BRITISH HIGH COMMISSION
Private Bag 23, Gaborone
High Commissioner, Her Excellency Miss Eleanor Jean Emery, C.M.G. (1973).
British Council Representative, G. C. Stackhouse.

Chief Justice of Botswana, G. O. L. Dyke.
Attorney-General, M. D. Mokama.

The country is essentially pastoral, although sorghum, maize, beans, pumpkins and melons are sown. Cattle thrive, despite the drought of 1965–66, during which time the numbers of cattle decreased by 350,000. In 1972, after three years of good rain, the national herd numbered about 2,000,000. Plans for the development of agriculture and cattle production, for combating soil erosion, investigating the water resources of the country and improving water supplies are being carried out.

Mineral extraction and processing has recently become a major source of income for the country, following the opening of large mines for diamonds and copper-nickel. Very large deposits of coal have been discovered, and are being mined on a small scale; plans for comprehensive development remain to be formulated. Much of the country has yet to be fully prospected. Manufacturing industry is expected to grow rapidly in the future, as communications improve.

Education.—In 1972, there were 294 primary schools with enrolment of 81,662 and 15 secondary schools with enrolment of 5,564. There were also three teacher training establishments with enrolment of 332. The principal languages in use in the country are English and Setswana.

Communications.—The railway from Kimberley and Mafeking in South Africa to Bulawayo in Rhodesia passes through eastern Botswana. The main roads in the country are the north-south road, which closely follows the railway, and the road running east–west that links Francistown and Maun. A new road from Nata to Kazungula which will provide a direct link to Zambia from Botswana, is under construction. Air services are provided on a scheduled basis between the main towns, linking with services from South Africa and Zambia. There are telephone and telegraph links to South Africa and Rhodesia.

FINANCE

	1972–73	1973–74
Actual Revenue	R28,625,642	R42,400,000
Actual Expenditure	28,593,405	40,900,000

Currency: South African rand. R1·50= £1 approx.

TRADE

	1971–72	1973–74
Net Imports	R60,700,000	R99,000,000
Exports	33,000,000	64,500,000

Trade with U.K.

	1972	1974
Imports from U.K.	£906,000	£1,322,000
Exports to U.K.	3,820,000	2,532,000

Cyprus

Area, Climate and Population.—Cyprus with an area of 3,572 square miles, is the third largest island in the Mediterranean Sea, exceeded in size by Sicily and Sardinia. Its greatest length is 140 miles and greatest breadth 60 miles. It is situated at the extreme north-east corner of the Mediterranean in latitude 35° N. and longitude 33° 30′ E. It is about 40 miles distant from the nearest point of Asia Minor, 60 miles from Syria and 240 miles from Port Said. The main topographical features of Cyprus are: (*a*) A narrow limestone range of mountains extending in an unbroken chain for nearly 100 miles along the north coast, at an average height of 2,000 feet; (*b*) A broad central plain, running for some 60 miles from west to east; (*c*) An extensive igneous massif rising to over 6,000 feet in the west of the island; and (*d*) Narrow coastal plains between the mountains and the sea. The rivers are little more than mountain torrents. There is no permanent stream of any volume.

Cyprus has a somewhat intense Mediterranean climate (with a hot dry summer and a variable warm winter). There are two contrasted seasons, winter and summer, while the intermediate ones are short and transitional. The winter is generally sunny with frequent cold spells between the beginning of December and end of February. The mean temperatures of the coldest month range from 36° to 50° F.

The rainy season lasts from October to April with average total rainfall of about 20 inches.

The summers are hot, dry and almost cloudless. July and August are the warmest months, with mean temperatures ranging from 80°–85° F. in the lowlands, to 70° in the mountains. In April 1974 the estimated population was 632,000. There are two major communities, Greek Cypriots (78 per cent.) and Turkish Cypriots (18·2 per cent.); and minorities of Armenians, Maronites and others. The population increases on the average at 0·9 per cent. annually. The birth rate in 1973 was estimated to be 18·2 and the death rate 9·5 per thousand.

CAPITAL.—Nicosia, near the centre of the island, with a population of 235,000 (including suburbs); the other principal towns are ΨLimassol (population 125,300), ΨFamagusta (124,300), ΨLarnaca (60,900), Paphos (57,300) and Kyrenia (32,700). (Since the events of July and August 1974 (see below) there have been significant changes in population distribution). Nicosia is distant from London 2,028 miles by air.

FLAG.—Gold map of Cyprus on a white ground, surmounting crossed olive branches (green).

President, Archbishop Makarios, *elected* Dec. 14, 1959; *assumed office* Aug. 16, 1960; *re-elected* Feb. 25, 1968; *declared re-elected without opposition*, Feb. 8, 1973. [Following an uprising led by Greek Officers of the Cyprus National Guard, on July 15, 1974, Archbishop Makarios left Cyprus. On July 23, Mr. Olafkos Clerides, Speaker of the House of Representatives, was sworn in as Acting President.] Archbishop Makarios returned to Cyprus on Dec. 7, 1974 to resume his presidential functions.

COUNCIL OF MINISTERS

External Affairs, Ioannis Christophides.
Finance, Andreas Patsalides.
Interior and Defence, Christodoulos Veniamin.
Education, Andreas Mikellides.
Agriculture, Frixos Kolotas.
Commerce and Industry, Michael Colocassides.
Justice, George Ionnides.
Labour and Social Insurances, Marcos Spanos.
Communication and Works, George Touibazos.
Health, Christos Vakis.

CYPRUS HIGH COMMISSION
[01-499 8272]
93 Park Street, W.1
High Commissioner, His Excellency Costas Ashiotis, M.B.E.

BRITISH HIGH COMMISSION
Alexander Pallis Street (P.O. Box 1978)
Nicosia
High Commissioner, His Excellency Donald McDonald Gordon, C.M.G. (1975)..........£12,000
British Council Representative, S. C. Alexander, P.O. Box 1995, 3 Museum Street, Nicosia.

GOVERNMENT

Cyprus passed under British administration from 1878. Cyprus was formally annexed to Great Britain on Nov. 5, 1914, on the outbreak of war with Turkey. From 1925 to 1960 it was a Crown Colony administered by a Governor, assisted by an Executive Council and also for a time by a partly-elected Legislative Council. Following the launching in April 1955 of an armed campaign by EOKA in support of ENOSIS (union with Greece), a state of emergency was declared in November, 1955, and Archbishop Makarios was deported. Further proposals for a workable constitution made in 1956 and a seven-year-plan for the government of Cyprus in association with Greece and Turkey were rejected by the Greek Government and Greek Cypriots. Archbishop Makarios was released in March, 1957, but was not allowed to return immediately to Cyprus. Following a meeting at Zürich between the Prime Ministers of Greece and Turkey, a conference was held in London and an agreement was signed on February 19, 1959, between the United Kingdom, Greece, Turkey and the Greek and Turkish Cypriots which provided that Cyprus would be an independent Republic.

Constitution.—Under the Cyprus Act, 1960, the island became an independent sovereign republic on August 16, 1960. The constitution provides for a Greek Cypriot President and a Turkish Cypriot Vice-President elected for a five-year term by the Greek and Turkish communities respectively. The House of Representatives, elected for five years by universal suffrage of each community separately, consists of 35 Greek and 15 Turkish members. The 1960 Constitution proved unworkable in practice and led to the intercommunal troubles. Talks have been in progress between Greeks and Turks since 1968 on a new Constitution for the island assisted by the Special Representative in Cyprus of the U.N. Sec.-Gen. and more recently the Secretary General personally. The mandate of the U.N. Peace Keeping Force in Cyprus (UNFICYP) was last renewed for the twenty-seventh time on June 13, 1975, for a further period of six months.

A General Election was held for the 35 Greek Cypriot seats on July 5, 1970, resulting in the following state of parties: *Unified Party*, 15; *Akel* (Communist), 9; *Progressive Front*, 7; *Democratic Centre Union*, 2; and *Independents*, 2. On the same day elections were held in the Turkish sector to elect 15 members for Turkish Cypriot national seats and 15 Turkish communal seats which together form a temporary chamber in the Turkish Cypriot sector first set up in December, 1967, but which is not recognized by the Cyprus Government. On July 15, 1974, mainland Greek officers of the Greek Cypriot National Guard launched a *coup d'état*

against President Makarios and installed a former EOKA member Nikos Sampson in his place. Turkey, purportedly acting under the 1960 Treaty of Guarantee by which Britain, Greece and Turkey reserved to themselves the right to maintain constitutional order and the independence and territorial integrity of the island, invaded northern Cyprus on July 20, subsequently moving on August 13, to occupy approximately 40 per cent. of the island. Despite successive U.N. resolutions calling for the withdrawal of all foreign forces from the island and the return of refugees (who number about 210,000) to their homes, much of the northern part of Cyprus remains under Turkish military occupation with a " Turkish Federated State " declared in this area.

British Sovereign Areas.—The United Kingdom retained full sovereignty and jurisdiction over two areas of 99 square miles in all—Akrotiri–Episkopi–Paramali and Dhekelia–Pergamos–Ayios Nicolaos–Xylophagou—and use of roads and other facilities. The British Administrator of these areas is appointed by the Queen and is responsible to the Secretary of State for Defence.

Production and Industries.—About 36 per cent. of those gainfully employed take part in agriculture, the chief agricultural products being:—cereals, vine products, potatoes, carobs, carrots, citrus and other fresh and dried fruit, tobacco and legumes.

Various kinds of livestock are raised, principally sheep, goats, pigs and poultry. The value of agricultural and livestock exports in 1974 was about £28,250,000. Mining is an important industry in Cyprus; the value of minerals exported in 1974 was £9,742,000. The principal minerals are cupreous and copper concentrates, copper pyrites, and asbestos. There is no heavy industry, but a wide variety of light manufacturing industries. Tourism prior to July–August 1974, was an important source of revenue. Long-stay visitors to the island in 1973 numbered 257,000.

FINANCE

	1973	1974 (*prov.*)
Ordinary Revenue	C£59,603,000	C£55,208,000
Ord. Expenditure	£55,239,000	£60,840,000
Public Debt	20,235,000	....

TRADE

	1973	1974
Imports	C£157,442,000	C£148,028,000
Exports	63,132,000	55,287,000

	1973	1974
Imports from U.K.	C£35,251,000	C£30,652,000
Exports to U.K.	23,275,000	21,099,000

Fiji

This is a group of some 840 islands (of which about 100 are inhabited) in the South Pacific Ocean, about 1,100 miles north of New Zealand. The gross area of the group, which extends 300 miles from east to west, and 300 north to south, between 15° 45′—21° 10′ S. lat. and 176° E.—178° W. long. is 7,072 square miles. The International Date Line has been diverted to the east of the island group. Many of the islands are of volcanic origin, with lofty mountains, and well wooded. The principal are Viti Levu, Vanua Levu, Taveuni and Kandavu. The climate is oceanic. Shade temperatures seldom rise above 93° F. or fall below 60° F. except in the mountains. There is a great contrast in vegetation between the windward and leeward sides of the larger islands with rain forests and luxuriant vegetation giving way in the drier zones to grassland with scattered trees. The chief products are sugar cane, coconuts, (and coconut products, e.g., copra), gold, rice, bananas, pineapples, yams and dalo or taro (colocasia). Tourism is an increasingly important source of revenue.

The population (1974 estimate) was 569,800 (288,000 Indians, 251,000 Fijians, 10,000 part-Europeans, 4,000 Chinese, 2,000 Europeans, and 14,000 other Pacific races).

CAPITAL.—Ψ Suva, in the island of Viti Levu. Population 60,000.

Government.—Fiji was a British colony from 1874 until October 10, 1970, when it became an independent state and a member of the Commonwealth. Under the Constitution there is a Governor-General appointed by the Queen. An elected House of Representatives (52 members) consists of 12 Fijians, 12 Indians and 3 General members elected on Communal rolls; and 10 Fijians, 10 Indians and 5 General members elected on National rolls, in which members of all races vote on the same register. General members are in the main representatives of the European, part-European and Chinese communities.

There is a Senate of 22 members, 8 appointed by the Great Council of Chiefs, 7 by the Prime Minister, 6 by the Leader of the Opposition and one by the Council of Rotuma, an island dependency 400 miles from Suva, discovered in 1879 and annexed in 1881.

Governor-General, His Excellency Ratu Sir George Cakobau, G.C.M.G., O.B.E. (1973).

CABINET

Prime Minister, Rt. Hon. Ratu Sir Kamisese Mara, K.B.E.

Deputy Prime Minister and Minister for Home Affairs, Hon. Ratu Sir Penaia Ganilau, K.B.E., C.M.G., C.V.O., D.S.O.

Attorney-General, Hon. Senator Sir John Falvey, K.B.E., Q.C.

Minister for Counications, Works and Tourism, Hon. Jonati Maroa.

Finance, Hon. C. A. Stinson, O.B.E.

Agriculture, Fisheries and Forests, Hon. Ratu J. B. Toganivalu.

Labour, Hon. Ratu David Toganivalu.

Education, Youth and Sport, Hon. P. D. Nagasima.

Fijian Affairs and Rural Development, Hon. Ratu W. B. Toganivalu.

Lands and Mineral Resources, Hon. S. N. Waqanivavalagi.

Commerce, Industries and Co-operatives, Hon. E. J. Beddoes.

Health, Hon. J. S. Singh, M.B.E.

Urban Development, Housing and Social Welfare, Hon. M. Ramzan, M.B.E.

Information, Hon. J. B. Naisara.

Speaker, House of Representatives, Hon. Sir Vijay Singh, K.B.E.

Deputy Speaker, Hon. Mosese Qioniburavi.

President of the Senate, Hon. R. L. Munro, C.B.E.

FIJI HIGH COMMISSION
34 Hyde Park Gate, S.W.7
[01-493 6516]
High Commissioner, His Excellency J. D. Gibson.

BRITISH HIGH COMMISSION
Suva
High Commissioner, His Excellency James Stanley
Arthur (1974)..........................£11,000

JUDICIARY
Chief Justice of Fiji, Hon. C. H. Grant......$14,000
Puisne Judges, Hons. G. Mishra; T. Tuivaga; K.
Stuart; J. H. Williams................$12,500

FINANCE
	1974	1975*
Public Income........	$80,911,000	$102,107,000
Public Expenditure....	78,993,000	102,107,000
Public Debt (Dec. 31).	87,029,000	110,694,000
	* Estimated.	

TRADE
	1974	1975
Total Imports.......	$219,331,000	$221,753,000
Total Exports.......	123,740,000	141,763,000

	1973	1974
Imports from U.K...	£9,689,000	£9,744,000
Exports to U.K......	11,301,000	21,474,000

Currency.—Currency is the *Fiji dollar*, against
which the £ *sterling* floats. Current Exchange rate
approx. $1·58 = £1 *sterling*.
The principal exports are raw sugar, coconut oil,
gold, oil seed cake and meal, lumber, copra, ginger,
molasses, biscuits, fish, unmanufactured tobacco,
veneer sheets, paints and cement. The chief
imports are machinery, electrical goods, foodstuffs,
all types of fabrics, petroleum products, motor
vehicles and miscellaneous manufactured articles.
The tourist trade continues to expand.

Communications.—Fiji is approximately 11,000
miles from the United Kingdom; transit time from
London *via* Panama Canal about 28–30 days. Air
connections are provided between the United
Kingdom and Fiji *via* Canada, United States of
America, Hong Kong, Japan and U.S.S.R., and
the Middle East either through New Zealand and
Australia or through New Caledonia and Singapore.
The following trunk route operators provide
services through Nadi Airport; Qantas, Pan Ameri-
can, Air New Zealand, U.T.A., and CP Air.
Flights connecting with Fiji operate to Auckland,
Sydney–Perth and Darwin and points beyond;
Honolulu, San Francisco or Los Angeles or Van-
couver and points beyond; Tahiti and points
beyond; Pago Pago; Noumea and points beyond.
Fiji is one of the main aerial crossroads in the
Pacific.

Air Pacific Ltd. (previously Fiji Airways Ltd.)
is based at Nausori Airport near Suva and operates
scheduled domestic services within the Fiji islands
and from Suva provides connection to Nadi,
Labasa, Savusavu and Tavenni, and there are regional
services to Tonga, Western Samoa, Papua, New
Guinea (Port Moresby) *via* the New Hebrides
(Vila); the Solomon Islands (Honiara) and the
Republic of Nauru *via* the Gilbert Islands, and
Auckland, N.Z., *via* Tonga, Fiji Air Services Ltd.
operates Charter flights within the Fiji group of
islands and South Pacific and provides scheduled
services within the Fiji group.

The Gambia

The West African river Gambia was discovered by the Portuguese in 1447; and in 1588, the year of the
Spanish Armada, Queen Elizabeth I, being then at war with Spain and Portugal, gave a charter to a British
Company to trade with the Gambia, and as early as 1618 an effort to do so was made, but it was not successful. In 1686 a fort was built upon a rocky island, and, in honour of the new King, was named Fort James;
but the English merchants had formidable rivals in the Portuguese and French, and it was not until 1783 that
the river was recognized, by the *Treaty of Versailles*, as British. The Colony had no regular political
institutions until 1807, when it was put under the Government of Sierra Leone. The Colony of the Gambia
was created in 1843, and was constituted a separate government in 1888. It consists of a narrow strip of land,
estimated at 4,003 sq. miles, lying on both sides of the River Gambia to a distance of about 300 miles,
mainly between 13° 15′–13° 45′ N. and 13° 45′–13° 65′ W. The river is navigable to ocean-going vessels
for 150 miles and to river steamers up to 300 miles from its mouth. The capital and chief port, Banjul,
formerly Bathurst, is situated at the mouth of the river. The provisional figure for the total population of
the country at the 1973 Census was 493,499. The climate of Banjul is extremely pleasant except during
the rainy season from June to October, when it sometimes becomes uncomfortably humid. Rainfall,
30–60 inches a year.

CAPITAL.—Ψ Banjul. Population (1973 census), 39,476.
FLAG.—Horizontal stripes of red, blue and green, separated by narrow white stripes.

Government.—On February 18, 1965, the Gambia
became an independent monarchy within the Com-
monwealth, with the Queen as Head of State. On
April 24, 1970, following a referendum, the constitution was changed to that of a Republic (within the
Commonwealth) with an executive President. The
House of Representatives, which elects its own
Speaker, consists of 32 elected members, 4 elected
Head Chiefs, 3 nominated members and the
Attorney General (who is also a nominated member
with voting rights). The Vice-President, who is
the Government leader in the House, and other
Ministers are appointed by the President. The
latter's tenure of office is co-terminous with the life
of a Parliament.

PRESIDENT AND CABINET
President, Sir Dawda Jawara.
*Vice-President and Minister of Local Government and
Lands*, Hon. A. M. Camara.
Finance and Trade, Alhaji Hon. I. M. Garba Jahumpa.
Education, Youth and Sports, Alhaji Hon. M. C.
Cham.
Works and Communications, Alhaji Hon. Sir Alieu
Jack.
Agriculture and Natural Resources, Alhaji Hon.
Yaya Ceesay.

Health, Labour and Social Welfare, Alhaji Hon. K. Singhateh.
Attorney-General, Alhaji Hon. M. L. Saho.
External Affairs, Hon. A. B. N'jie.
Information and Tourism, Hon. B. L. K. Sanyang.
Economic Planning and Industrial Development, Hon. L. B. M'Boge.
Minister of State (President's office), Hon. K. N. Leigh.

Chief Justice, Hon. Sir Phillip Bridges, C.M.G.
Speaker, Dr. S. H. O. Jones. C.B.E.

GAMBIA HIGH COMMISSION
60 Ennismore Gardens, S.W.7.
[01-584 1242]

High Commissioner, His Excellency Bocar Ousman Semega-Janneh, M.B.E. (1971).

BRITISH HIGH COMMISSION
78 Wellington Street, Banjul
High Commissioner, His Excellency, M. H. G. Rogers (1975).

Communications.—Banjul is 2,600 miles from London. There are two direct air services weekly *via* Casablanca and Las Palmas and three weekly, changing at Dakar. There are no regular passenger or mails service by sea. Ocean-going vessels entering the ports in 1972 totalled 282 (net tonnage 668,000). There is an international aerodrome at Yundum, 17 miles from Banjul. Internal communication is by road and river. There are 794 miles of motor road, including 180 miles of bituminous surface roads, 330 miles of gravel roads and 284 miles of Commissioners' roads. There are eight Government wireless stations and a V.H.F. telephone service linking Banjul with the principal towns in the provinces. There is a broadcasting service.
Education.—There are 96 primary schools and 22 secondary schools, with a total enrolment of 26,338 pupils, including 8,071 girls. There are 99 students, including 31 females, at the Yundum Teacher Training College. Vocational and Training Centres operate at Banjul and Lamin, total enrolement, 196, including 11 girls.

Production.—Most of the population is engaged in agriculture. the chief product being ground-nuts which is the single important cash crop. Other crops are rice, millet and various kinds of fruit and vegetables. Fishing and livestock production are considerable. No minerals are at present being exploited and there are practically no manufactures other than ground-nut processing and a bottling plant.

FINANCE

| | 1972–73 (Actual) | | 1973–74 (Revised estimate) | |
	Re-current *D'ooo*	Develop-ment *D'ooo*	Re-current *D'ooo*	Develop-ment *D'ooo*
Revenue......	23,881	5,992	25,572	9,010
Expenditure...	20,970	4,519	23,692	10,068

The Government financial year begins on July 1.
Currency.—Decimal currency was introduced in the Gambia on July 1, 1971. The unit is the *dalasi* of 100 *butut.* The present rate of exchange is $D4 = £1$.

TRADE

	1974	1975
Total imports........	D79,410,000	D108,070,000
Total exports.........	72,110,000	85,030,000

	1974	1975
Imports from U.K...	£4,437,000	£7,554,000
Exports to U.K......	8,438,000	8,240,000

The chief exports are ground-nut products, which account for 95 per cent. of total exports, the main markets being Italy, the United Kingdom, W. Germany, Switzerland and the Netherlands. Other exports are palm kernels, dried fish and hides. Foodstuff imports include rice, sugar, flour and kola nuts. Tourism has been developed in recent years and is an increasing source of foreign exchange. Manufactured goods of all kinds are imported, the chief being textiles and apparel, vehicles, machinery, metal goods and petroleum products.

Ghana

Ghana (formerly the British Colony of the Gold Coast) is situated on the Gulf of Guinea, between 3° 07′ W. long. and 1° 14′ E. long. (about 334 miles), and extends 441 miles north from Cape Three Points (4° 45′ N.) to 11° 11′ N. It is bounded on the north by the Republic of Upper Volta, on the west by the Republic of Ivory Coast, on the east by the Republic of Togo, and on the south by the Atlantic Ocean. Although a tropical country, Ghana is cooler than many countries within similar latitudes.

Area and Population.—Ghana has a total area of 92,100 sq. miles with a total population (Census of 1970) of 8,545,561, some 27 per cent. more than the population at the Census of 1960. Almost all Ghanaians are Sudanese Negroes, although Hamitic strains are common in Northern Ghana.
CAPITAL.—ΨACCRA. Population of the Capital District (including Accra Tema City Council area, and Accra Rural area) (provisional, 1970) 851,614. Other towns are Kumasi, Tamale, Sekondi-Takoradi, Cape Coast, Sunyani, Ho, Koforidua, Tarkwa and Winneba. Accra is 3,920 miles by sea from Liverpool, transit 12 to 30 days.
FLAG.—Equal horizontal bands of red over yellow over green; five-point black star on gold stripe.
INDEPENDENCE DAY—March 6.

GOVERNMENT
The Gold Coast region of West Africa was first visited by European traders in the fifteenth century. The Gold Coast Colony, Ashanti, the Northern Territories and Trans-Volta-Togoland, the constituent parts of the new State, came under British administration at various times, the original Gold Coast Colony, the coastal and Southern areas, being first constituted in 1874; Ashanti in 1901; and the Northern Territories Protectorate in 1901. The territory of Trans-Volta-Togoland, part of Togo, a former German colony, was mandated to Britain by the League of Nations after the First World War, and remained under British administration as a United Nations Trusteeship after the Second World War. After a plebiscite in May,

1956, under the auspices of the United Nations, the territory was integrated with the Gold Coast Colony.

The former Gold Coast Colony and associated territories became the independent state of Ghana and a member of the British Commonwealth on March 6, 1957, under the *Ghana Independence Act, 1957*, and adopted a Republican constitution on July 1, 1960.

On Feb. 24, 1966, the Army seized power and Dr. Nkrumah and his ministers were dismissed.

Ghana was administered until October 1, 1969, by a National Liberation Council of four representatives each from the Army and the police, during which time a Constitution for the Second Republic of Ghana was evolved and brought into force by a 150 member Constituent Assembly on Aug. 22, 1969.

General elections were held on August 29, 1969, in which Dr. K. A. Busia's Progress Party won 105 seats and Mr. K. A. Gbedemah's National Alliance of Liberals 29, the remaining 6 seats being won by minority parties. Dr. Busia was appointed Prime Minister on Sept. 3, 1969, and the N.L.C. formally handed over to the civilian government on October 1, 1969. A three-man presidential commission was appointed under Brigadier Afrifa in September 1969. It was dissolved in July 1970, and a month later Mr. E. Akufo-Addo was elected President.

On January 13, 1972, the Busia administration was ousted in an army *coup d'état* led by Colonel I. K. Acheampong. The Constitution was withdrawn, political activity banned and the Presidency abolished. The National Redemption Council is the supreme governing body, assisted by an Executive Council. Rule is by decree.
Head of State and Chairman NRC, Col. I. K. Acheampong.

NATIONAL REDEMPTION COUNCIL
Head of State and Chairman of the NRC.; Commissioner for Defence, Finance and Sport; Commander in Chief of the Armed Forces, Col. I. K. Acheampong.
Labour, Social Welfare and Co-operatives, Lt. Col. K. B. Agbo.
Inspector General of Police and Commissioner for Internal Affairs, E. Ako.
Foreign Affairs, Lt. Col. R. M. Baah.
Economic Planning, Lt. Col. R. J. A. Felli.
Trade and Tourism, Lt. Col. D. A. Iddisah.
Works and Housing, Col. R. E. A. Kotei.
Attorney General and Commissioner for Justice, E. N. Moore.
Chief of Defence Staff and Commissioner for Special Duties, Maj. Gen. L. A. Okai.
Health, Lt. Col. A. H. Selormey.
N.R.C. Affairs, E. K. Buckman.

OTHER CENTRAL GOVERNMENT COMMISSIONERS
(Together with members of the N.R.C. forming the Executive Council.)
Local Government, Maj. Gen. N. A. Aferi.
Transport and Communications, Col. P. K. Agyekum.
Lands and Mineral Resources, Maj. Gen. D. C. K. Amenu.
Cocoa Affairs, Col. F. G. Bernasko.
Industries, Lt. Col. G. Minyila.
Agriculture, Lt. Col. P. K. Nkegbe.
Education and Culture, Col. E. O. Nyante.
Information, Col. C. R. Tachie-Menson.

GHANA HIGH COMMISSION
13 Belgrave Square, S.W.1
[01-235 4142]
High Commissioner, His Excellency Colonel Samuel McGal Asante (1975).

BRITISH HIGH COMMISSION
P.O. Box 296, High Street, Accra
High Commissioner, His Excellency Frank Mills, C.M.G. (1975) £6,250

British Council Representative, A. P. Weaver, Liberia Road, Accra, and an Office in *Kumasi.*

JUDICIARY
The Judiciary, headed by the Chief Justice, represents the judicial control of Ghana and has authority over all civil and criminal matters, except those heard by military tribunals. Fundamentally the Courts of Ghana consist of two divisions, the *Superior Court of Judicature* and the *Inferior Courts.* The former consists of the Court of Appeal and the High Court. The *Inferior Courts* consist of the Circuit Courts, approximately equivalent to the old British Assize Courts, now Crown Courts, and such courts as deal with judicial matters on a district and juvenile level.

The Court of Appeal, when constituted with five Justices, is the final Court of Appeal in Ghana. The Chief Justice has discretion to create divisions of the Court of Appeal.

The High Court of Justice.—This court has jurisdiction over criminal, industrial and labour matters. Consisting of the Chief Justice and a minimum of twelve Puisne Judges, it may also include any other judge appointed at the discretion of the Chief Justice. Individual courts may consist of up to three judges, with or without a jury.

PRODUCTION, ETC.
Agriculture.—Agriculture forms the basis of Ghana's economy, employing 70 per cent. of the working population. Crops of the *Forest Zone* include cocoa, which is the largest single source of revenue, rice and a variety of other foodstuff crops grown on mixed-crop farms. Fruits such as avocado pears, oranges and pineapples are grown. Cassava is the most important crop of the *Coastal Savannas Zone,* which consists of the Accra Plains (1,400 sq. miles) and Ho-Keta Plains (2,600 sq. miles) of the lower Volta area. Fishing is important in coastal areas and in the Volta itself. Production of pulses such as groundnuts, tiger nuts and cowpeas is widespread. Near the Togo border oil palms, yams, maize, cassava, fruit and vegetables are produced. Livestock is raised in the uncultivated areas. The *Northern Savanna Zone* is Ghana's principal cattle rearing area and other livestock production there is important for home consumption. Corn and millet crops are produced in the far north and maize, yams, rice and groundnut crops in more southerly parts of the Zone.

A State Farms Corporation, established in 1963 to further larger scale farming enterprise, has more than 100 farms in various parts of the country and operates from eight regional centres.

Fisheries.—Some 150,000 of the country's population are engaged in fisheries which now produce about 180,000 tons annually. Ghana's estimated annual requirement is at least 250,000 tons and there are considerable imports of fish products. About 80 per cent of home supply is obtained from sea fisheries, but production from the Volta Lake and other inland fisheries is increasing rapidly thanks to greatly increased fish population.

Mineral Production.—The area within a 60 mile radius of Dunkwa produces 90 per cent. of Ghana's mineral exports. Manganese production from Nsuta ranks among the world's highest and gold, industrial diamonds and bauxite are also produced. Some 30,000 persons are employed by the mining companies.

Manufactures.—Examples of the small-scale traditional industries are tailoring, goldsmithing and carpentry. Priority has been given in recent years to the establishment of a number of "Pioneer Industries " including sawmill furniture, prefabricated doors, plywood, vehicle assembly, cigarettes, boatbuilding, refrigerator assembly, food processing (biscuits, edible oils, confectionery, brewing, etc.), cotton textiles, clothing, footwear, printing and other light industries. A modern industrial complex is growing in the Accra–Tema area.

Volta River Project.—The Volta River is formed at the confluence of the Black and White Voltas, both of which rise in the neighbouring republic of Upper Volta. With its tributaries the Volta drains an area of 150,000 sq. miles of which 61,000 sq. miles lie in Ghana. The Volta Dam at Akosombo was inaugurated in January, 1966, to generate hydro-electric power for the processing of bauxite and feed a power transmission network for the Accra–Kumasi–Takoradi area. Electricity is now also sent to Togo and Dahomey, The lake raised by the Volta Dam has a maximum area of 3,275 sq. miles, a length of 250 miles and a shore line of 4,500 miles. A water transport service from Akosombo to various points on the lake has been instituted.

Power output from Akosombo is planned to reach 768 megawatts, 22 times the country's 1959 generating capacity. Smaller dams with 150 MW. and 93 MW. capacity are to be built at Kpong rapids and at Bui in the Northern Region. Planned aluminium output in Ghana by 1973 was 145,000 tons (1969, 103,000 tons).

COMMUNICATIONS

There are four aerodromes in Ghana, situated at Accra, Takoradi, Kumasi and Tamale. Accra Airport is an international airport and is the terminus for services from the United Kingdom, the Northern, Ashanti and Western Regions.

Railway communications consist of a main line running from Takoradi to Kumasi thence to Accra, a distance of 357 miles. From Huni Valley on the Kumasi line north of Takoradi a line runs to Kotoku on the railway about 17 miles north of Accra. Branch lines run to Sekondi, Prestea, Kade, Awaso and Tema. Total railway mileage open to traffic is 600. There are 20,245 miles of motorable roads, of which 2,335 are bitumen.

Takoradi Harbour consists of two breakwaters enclosing a water area of 220 acres. Seven quay berths are situated on the lee breakwater—five are used for the handling of general cargo, one is leased specially for manganese exports and one is used for shallow draft colliers. Tema Harbour—Africa's largest artificial harbour and a prospective major port of the South Atlantic—was opened in 1962. There are 10 berths for larger ocean going vessels and the harbour also has the largest dry dock on the West African coast. An oil berth has also been built to serve the Ghaip refinery which has been constructed at Tema.

TRADE

	1971	1974
Total imports...	N¢450,600,000	N¢046,800,000
Total exports....	387,900,000	873,400,000

Trade with U.K.

	1972	1974
Imports from U.K...	£16,474,000	£51,010,000
Exports to U.K......	33,136,000	70,700,000

FINANCE

The currency of Ghana is the *cedi* (¢) (of 100 *pesawas*) equivalent to 35 pence sterling.

Guyana

GUYANA, the former colony of British Guiana, which includes the Counties of Demerara, Essequibo and Berbice, is situated on the north-east coast of South America and has a total area of 83,000 square miles with a seaboard of about 270 miles. The population at December 31, 1970, was estimated at 714,233. There are about 31,460 Amerindians. The territory is bounded on the south by Brazil, on the east by Surinam, on the west by Venezuela, and on the north and N.E. by the Atlantic. The coastline is very like the Netherlands, below the level of the sea, and intersected with canals constructed by its former Dutch owners. At the junction of the Guyana-Venezuela-Brazil boundaries is Mt. Roraima, a flat topped mountain 9,000 feet above sea-level. There are many beautiful waterfalls in Guyana: on the Potaro River (a tributary of the Essequibo) is the *Kaieteur Fall*, with a clear drop of 741 feet and a total fall of 822 feet, and on the Essequibo, the *Horse Shoe Falls* (discovered in 1934); a fall, with a drop of some 500 feet, discovered in 1934 on the Ipobe River, a tributary of the Kuribrong, has been named the *Marina Fall*, and other falls were discovered in 1938 on the Kamarang River, 80 miles north-east of Mt. Roraima.

The seasons are divided into dry and wet, the two dry seasons lasting from the middle of February to the end of April, and from the middle of August to the end of November. The climate on the coast is pleasant and healthy for the greater part of the year. In the Aug.–Oct. period it is hot. The mean temperature is 80·3°, its extremes during 87 years ranging between 68° and 96°, but these are very rare, the usual extremes being 70° and 90°. In the interior the mean temperature is higher—82·6°, its extremes ranging from 66° to 103°. The yearly rainfall is subject to marked variation, its mean on the coast lands averaging about 90 inches with an average of 58 inches on the savannahs. The daily average sunshine is nearly 7 hours and, except when rain is falling, dull and cloudy weather is rarely experienced.

Government.—Guyana became independent on May 26, 1966, with a Governor-General appointed by the Queen. It became a Cooperative Republic on Feb. 23, 1970, and Mr. Arthur Chung was elected first President on March 17, 1970, for a term of six years. The electoral system is a Proportional Representation or " single list " system, each voter casting his vote for a party list of candidates. The Prime Minister and Cabinet are responsible collectively to a National Assembly of 53 members elected by secret ballot; the voting age is 21. Elections to the National Assembly are held every five years; the last election was on July 16, 1973.

An important feature of the Constitution is its provision for the appointment of an *Ombudsman*. The life of the Assembly, presided over by a Speaker, who may or may not be a Member of the Assembly, is five years.

CAPITAL.— ΨGeorgetown. Estimated population, including environs, 168,000. Other towns are: Linden (population 29,000); ΨNew Amsterdam (population 23,000); Corriverton (population 17,000).

FLAG.—Red triangle with black border, pointing from hoist to fly, on a yellow triangle with white border, all on a green field.

President.—His Excellency Arthur Chung, *re-elected for a further term of office*, March 12, 1976.

CABINET

Prime Minister, L. F. S. Burnham.
Deputy Prime Minister and Minister of National Development, Dr. P. A. Reid.
Finance, F. E. Hope.
Economic Development, H. D. Hoyte.
Education, Miss C. L. Baird.
Health, Dr. O. M. R. Harper.
Works and Housing, S. S. Naraine.
Labour, W. G. Carrington.
Information and Culture, Miss S. M. Field-Ridley.
Co-operatives and National Mobilization, H. Green.
Energy and Natural Resources, H. O. Jack.
Agriculture, G. B. Kennard.
Foreign Affairs, F. Wills.
Trade and Consumer Protection, G. A. King.
Home Affairs, C. V. Mingo.
Parliamentary Affairs and Leader of the House, B. C. Ramsaroop.
Ministers of State, O. E. Clarke; W. Haynes; A. Salim; P. P. Duncan; F. U. A. Carmichael; M. Kasim; C. A. Nascimento; J. Chowritmootoo; K. Bancroft.

GUYANA HIGH COMMISSION

3 Palace Court, Bayswater Road, W.2
[01–229 7684]

High Commissioner, His Excellency Lionel Samuels (*acting*).

BRITISH HIGH COMMISSION

44 Main Street (P.O. Box 625),
Georgetown

High Commissioner, His Excellency Peter Gautrey, C.M.G., C.V.O. (1975).

JUDICATURE

The Supreme Court of Judicature consists of a Court of Appeal and a High Court. There are also Courts of Summary Jurisdiction. The Court of Appeal consists of the Chancellor as President, the Chief Justice and such number of Justices of Appeal as may be prescribed by Parliament.

The High Court consists of the Chief Justice, as President, and nine Puisne Judges. It is a court with unlimited jurisdiction in civil matters and exercises exclusive jurisdiction in probate, divorce and admiralty, and certain other matters. It also sits as a Full Court of the High Court of the Supreme Court of Judicature comprising not less than 2 Puisne Judges and then its jurisdiction is almost entirely appellate.

Production, etc.—Much of the country is forest. The cultivated portion (about 600,000 acres, of which 107,182 are under sugar-cane and 316,950 in rice) is largely confined to the narrow coastal alluvial belt. There are extensive deposits of gold, diamonds, bauxite and mica.

Communications.—The Georgetown Automatic Exchange had 7,900 direct extension lines in 1972, involving 12,913 telephones. Twenty-six subsidiary exchanges provided a total of 1,465 direct exchange lines with 2,181 telephone stations. Thirty-nine land-line telegraph stations are maintained at coastal post offices and telegraph stations in the interior, providing communications with the coast. In Georgetown a central radio station, operated by the Guyana Telecommunication Corporation, provides radio-telephone communication with 5 branch offices, 20 stations operated by other Government departments, and 48 by private concerns. Overseas telephone, telex and telegraph services are provided by Cable and Wireless (W.I.) Ltd. in association with the Guyana Telecommunications Corporation. At the end of 1972 there were 50 district post offices (including two mobile post offices) at which all classes of postal business were transacted. There are two broadcasting stations operated on a commercial basis. The Guyana Airways Corporation provides internal and coastal air services.

Education.—At the end of the school year 1971–72 there were 390 primary schools with 130,671 pupils receiving first level education, or 81·27 per cent. of the 6–12 age group. Secondary education is offered in three types of school, 31 government-owned, 13 government-aided and approximately 50 privately-owned schools. In August 1972 there were 61,747 pupils receiving secondary education in government schools. This enrolment represented 45·4 per cent of the 12–17 age group. There were also about 10,000 pupils in private institutions.

The University of Guyana is the only institution which provides higher education. In 1971–72 1,232 students were enrolled in the Faculties of Arts, Natural Science, Social Science, Technical Studies and Education as well as in first-year studies in Law and in Diploma and Certificate courses. There are four established technical institutions: Georgetown and New Amsterdam Technical Institutes, the Carnegie School of Home Economics and the Guyana Industrial Training Centre. Besides these, there are 20 Home Economics and Industrial Arts Centres in various parts of the country. There are also Home Economics and Industrial Arts Department in many primary and secondary schools. Government trains teachers for both primary and secondary schools.

It was estimated that in 1973 the Government would spend G$35,200,000 on education, of which G$8,200.000 would be spent on building new schools and improving existing schools.

FINANCE

	1974	1975
Revenue	G$397,196,000	G$585,491,230
Expenditure	367,727,000	602,518,610
Public debt (Dec. 31	381,900,000	676,800,000

TRADE

	1973	1974
Total imports	G$320,245,000	G$567,054,570
Total exports	247,448,000	589,662,040

The leading exports are bauxite, sugar, alumina, rice, balata, rum, timber, molasses and diamonds.

India

AREA AND POPULATION.—The land area of the Republic of India is 1,261,816 sq. miles, and the population at the census of 1971, was 547,949,809. (In March 1976, it was officially announced that the population had reached 606,200,000).

FLAG.—The National Flag is a horizontal tricolour with bands of deep saffron, white and dark green in equal proportions. On the centre of the white band appears an Asoka wheel in navy blue.

CAPITAL.—Delhi (population in 1971 was 4,065,698).

NATIONAL DAY.—January 26 (Republic Day).

President of the Republic of India, Fakhruddin Aii Ahmed, *born* 1905, *elected* Aug. 20, 1974.
Vice-President, B. D. Jatti.

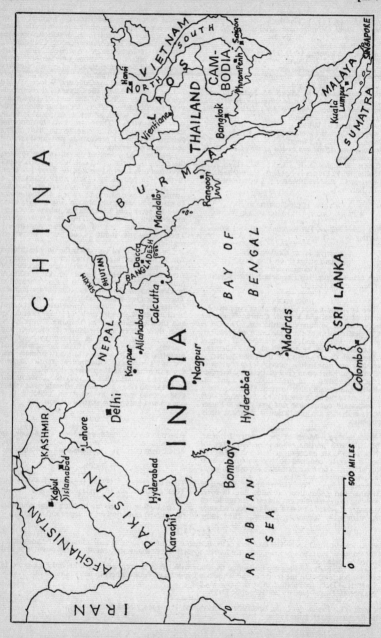

Members of the Cabinet (Jan. 1976)

Prime Minister and Minister of Atomic Energy, Mrs. Indira Gandhi.
External Affairs, Y. B. Chavan.
Finance, C. Subramaniam.
Railways, Kamlapati Tripathi.
Defence, Bansi Lal.
Works, Housing and Parliamentary Affairs, Raghu Ramaiah.
Tourism and Civil Aviation, Raj Bahadur.
Justice and Company Affairs, H. R. Gokhale.
Petroleum, K. D. Malaviya.
Home Affairs, K. Brahmananda Reddy.
Industry and Civil Supplies, T. A. Pai.
Agriculture and Irrigation, Jagjivan Ram.
Communications, S. D. Sharma.
Transport and Shipping, D. S. Dhillon.
Health and Family Planning, Dr. Karan Singh.
Chemicals and Fertilizers, P. C. Sethi.
Minister without Portfolio, Mir Qasim.

INDIAN HIGH COMMISSION

India House, Aldwych, W.C.2.
[01–836 8484]
High Commissioner, His Excellency B. K. Nehru (1973).
Deputy High Commissioner, K. Natwar-Singh.
Ministers, P. A. Nazareth (*Supply*); J. Abraham (*Consular*).

BRITISH HIGH COMMISSION

Chanakyapuri, New Delhi, 21.
High Commissioner, His Excellency Sir (Charles) Michael Walker, G.C.M.G. (1974).
British Council Representative in India, S. E. Hodgson, C.B.E., 21 Jor Bagh, New Delhi. Officers also at *Bombay*, *Madras* and *Calcutta*. There are British Council libraries at these four centres and at *Bangalore*, *Bhopal*, *Lucknow*, *Patna*, *Poona*, *Ranchi* and *Trivandrum*.

CONSTITUTION

The Constitution of India came into force on January 26, 1950. The Constitution provides for a single and uniform citizenship for the whole of India, with the right of vote for every adult citizen.

EXECUTIVE

The executive of the Indian Union consists of the President, the Vice-President and the Council of Ministers. The President is elected for five years by an electoral college consisting of all elected members of Parliament and of the various State Legislative Assemblies. The Vice-President is also elected for five years by members of the two Houses of Parliament. As head of the State the President exercises his functions with the aid and advice of the Council of Ministers headed by the Prime Minister. The Council is collectively responsible to the House of the People.

LEGISLATURE

The Legislature of the Union is called Parliament. It consists of two Houses known as the Council of States (*Rajya Sabha*) and the House of the People (*Lok Sabha*). The Council of States consists of not more than 250 members, of whom 12, having special knowledge or practical experience in literature, science, art or social service, are nominated by the President and the rest are indirectly elected representatives of the State and Union Territories. The Council is not subject to dissolution, one-third of its members retiring every two years. The House of the People at present consists of 524 members. Of these, 506 are directly elected from 21 States and 15 from eight Union Territories. One member is nominated by the President to represent the Union Territory of Arunachal Pradesh and two to represent the Anglo-Indian community. The House has a maximum duration of five years.

Subject to the provisions of the Constitution the Union Parliament can make laws for the whole of India and the State legislatures for their respective units. The distribution of legislative powers is governed by a system of three lists—the Union, the State and the Concurrent—under which all legislative activity has been mapped out. The Union Parliament has exclusive powers to legislate on 97 subjects of all-India importance, such as defence, foreign affairs, communications, railways, currency and banking, insurance, customs duties, etc. The State List contains 65 headings, *e.g.* public order and police, justice, education, public health, local government, agriculture, etc. The Concurrent List contains 48 subjects of common interest to the Union and the States.

OFFICIAL LANGUAGE

The Constitution (Art. 343) provides that the official language of the Union shall be Hindi in the Devanagari script and the form of numerals for official purposes shall be the international form of Indian numerals. English, which was originally to continue as the official language for a period of 55 years from the commencement of the Constitution (January 1950), will, under the Official Language Act, 1963, as amended, continue to be used for all the official purposes for which it was used before Jan. 26, 1965, and also for the transaction of business in Parliament.

THE JUDICATURE

The Supreme Court of India, consisting of a Chief Justice and not more than 13 other judges; is the highest court in respect of constitutional matters. It is also the final Court of Appeal in the country.

DEFENCE

The supreme command of the armed forces is vested in the President. Administrative and operational control resides in the Army, Navy and Air Headquarters under the supervision of the Ministry of Defence.

The *Army* has five Commands, Southern, Eastern, Northern, Western and Central. A Territorial Force was inaugurated in Oct. 1949. A National Cadet Corps, with senior, junior, and girls' divisions, has also been raised.

The *Indian Navy* consists of an aircraft-carrier, two cruisers, a number of frigate squadrons, including some of the latest type of anti-submarine and anti-aircraft frigates, a squadron of anti-submarine patrol vessels, a minesweeping squdron, conventional type submarines, a submarine depot ship and fast boats carrying surface-to-surface guided missiles. A Naval aviation wing and a hydrographic

office have also been set up. India has started building her own naval craft.

The *Indian Air Force* is organized in five major formations, the Western, Eastern and Central Air Commands, and the Training and Maintenance Commands and an independent Operational Group. Aircraft in use include SU-7, Hunter, Gnat, Mig 21 and HF24; Canberra bomber, helicopter and training planes.

PRODUCTION

About 70 per cent. of the inhabitants of India are dependent on agricultural pursuits. Most of the agricultural holdings are less than 5 acres. Food grains occupy three-fourths of the total cropped area. There are about 176,000,000 cattle, or about a quarter of the world's cattle population.

Production of Principal Crops, 1974–75

Crop	Production ('ooo tonnes)
Rice	40,250
Jowar	10,220
Bajra	3,230
Maize	5,720
Wheat	24,240
Barley, ragi and small millets	7,000
Pulses	10,400
Total food grains	101,660
Ground-nuts (in shell)	4,490
Rape and mustard	2,210
Cotton (lint)	7,080
Jute (dry fibre)	*4,490
Sugar-cane	143,100
Tea	493

* 'ooo bales.

Industrial

The output of coal in 1974–75 was 907 lakh tonnes: iron ore 355 lakh tonnes; finished steel 49·1 lakh tonnes; aluminium 126,600 tonnes; cement 147 lakh tonnes; machine tools Rs.92·50 crores; automobiles (commercial vehicles, passenger cars, etc.) 81,700; diesel engines (stationary) 114,300; sewing machines 335,000; sulphuric acid 1,434,000 tonnes; fertilizers 1,505,000 tonnes; petroleum products (refined), 195 lakh tonnes; cotton cloth 826·8 crore metres; cotton yarn, 102·5 crore kg.; rayon yarn 115,900 tonnes.

TRADE

Distribution of Trade, 1974

	Imports Rs. lakhs	Exports Rs. lakhs
United Kingdom	21,339	30,634
U.S.A.	72,909	34,527
U.S.S.R.	40,248	41,812
Germany (Federal Republic)	30,686	10,504
Italy	7,835	5,213
Netherlands	4,758	7,092
France	8,116	8,391
Japan	75,347	29,490
Australia	11,358	6,118
Canada	13,042	4,396
Kenya	983	1,464
Czechoslovakia	3,330	6,016
Egypt	2,283	5,244

Trade with U.K.

	1974	1975
Imports from U.K.	£127,133,000	£164,535,000
Exports to U.K.	203,330,000	237,136,000

Imports from All Countries, 1974–75

	Rs. lakhs
Petroleum oil and products	115,690
Machinery other than electric	39,680
Copper	7,298
Metal manufactures	466
Electric machinery and appliances	15,010
Medicinal and pharmaceutical products	3,420
Transport equipment	12,290
Chemical elements and compounds	17,880
Textile yarn and thread	999
Raw cotton	2,679
Rice	217
Wheat, unmilled	69,813

Exports to All Countries, 1974–75

	Rs. lakhs
Iron and steel	2,060
Cotton manufactures (excluding twist and yarn)	15,870
Iron ore and concentrates	16,040
Fresh fruits and nuts (excluding oil nuts)	4,716
Vegetable oils (non-essential)	4,290
Leather	14,490
Jute manufacture (excluding twist and yarn)	29,570
Coffee	5,140
Tea	22,400
Tobacco, unmanufactured	8,220

FINANCE

The budget estimates for 1976–77, as presented in the Lok Sabha on Feb. 16, 1976, placed expenditure (on revenue account) at Rs.76,89,62 lakhs including States' share of union excise duties as compared to Rs.71,16,68 lakhs (revised) in 1975–76 and revenue at Rs.81,78,70 lakhs as compared to Rs.80,22,83 lakhs (revised) in the previous year, resulting in a surplus of Rs.4,89,09 lakhs.

Revenue

Tax Revenue	1975/6	1976/7
	(in crores of rupees)	
Customs	1357	1470
Union Excise duties	3824	4085
Corporation tax	954	1025
Estate duty	9	9
Taxes on wealth	52	52
Gift tax	5	5
Other heads	1268	1191
	7469	7837
Non-Tax Revenue		
Interest receipts	995	1056
Others	1057	906

Expenditure

Taxes and duties	95	100
Debt services	1221	1352
Administrative services	371	363
Social and developmental services	83	87
Transport and communications	94	99
Currency and mint	72	74
Miscellaneous	3489	3329
Defence Services (net)	2192	2286

Banks and Banking.—The number of scheduled banks was 74 and the number of offices of banks was 18,730 in June 1976. The total credit at the end of June 1975 was *Rs.* 8.963 crores.

COMMUNICATIONS

Civil Aviation.—India occupies an important place in civil aviation among the nations of the world. All air lines were nationalized in 1953 and two corporations formed, Indian Airlines and Air India.

Four international aerodromes are managed by the International Airports Authority. The other 84 aerodromes are controlled and operated by the Civil Aviation Department of the Government.

Railways.—The railways are grouped into nine administrative zones, Southern, Central, Western, Northern, North-Eastern, North-East Frontier, Eastern, South-Eastern and South-Central.

Gross Traffic Receipts (1974–75), crores of rupees 1408·19. Working expenses, 1317·29. Net railway revenues, 73·64.

Ψ *Ports.*—The chief seaports are Bombay, Calcutta, Madras, Mormugao, Cochin, Visakhapatnam, Kandla, Paradip, Mangalore and Tuticorin. There are 167 intermediate and minor ports with varying capacity.

Shipping.—On Dec. 31, 1975, 471 ships totalling 38·69 lakh gross tons were on the Indian Register.

Postal.—On March 31, 1975, there were 117,222 post offices, and 1,744,088 telephones.

Jamaica

Jamaica is situated in the Caribbean Sea south of the eastern extremity of Cuba and lies between latitudes 17° 43′ and 18° 32′ North, and longitude 76° 11′ and 78° 21′ West. The island was discovered by Columbus on May 4, 1494, and occupied by the Spanish from 1509 until 1655 when a British expedition, sent out by Oliver Cromwell, under Admiral Penn and General Venables, attacked the island, which capitulated after a trifling resistance. In 1670 it was formally ceded to England by the Treaty of Madrid. Jamaica became an independent state within the British Commonwealth on August 6, 1962.

Area and Population.—Jamaica is 4,411 square miles in area and is divided into three counties (Surrey, Middlesex and Cornwall) and 14 parishes. The surface of the island is extremely mountainous, the highest peak being 7,402 ft. above sea level. The greatest length from east to west (Morant Point to Negril Point) is 146 miles and the extreme breadth 51 miles. At Dec. 31, 1975 Jamaica's population was estimated to be 2,060,300. Jamaica for climatic and other reasons is a popular tourist resort, attracting visitors mainly from the U.S.A. The total number of visitor arrivals in 1975 was 553,258. Tourist expenditure in 1975 was estimated at J$116·8 millions.

Physical Features.—The topography consists mainly of coastal plains, divided by the Blue Mountain Range in the east, and the hills and limestone plateaux which occupy the central and western areas of the interior. The central chain of high peaks of the Blue Mountains is over 6,000 feet above sea level, and the Blue Mountain Peak, the highest of these, reaches an elevation of 7,402 feet. The rivers flow down from the central mountainous area. Most of the rivers are narrow and fast flowing, and some have rapids. In general those flowing south are longer and are fed by more tributaries than those flowing north. None is navigable except the Black River, and that only for small craft.

Capital.—The seat of government is Kingston, the largest town and seaport (estimated population of the Corporate area of Kingston and St. Andrew in 1971, 572,653). Other towns are Montego Bay (42,800) and Spanish Town (41,600).

Flag.—Gold diagonal cross forming triangles of green at top and bottom, triangles of black at hoist and in fly. *National Day.*—First Monday in August (Independence Day).

GOVERNMENT

The Legislative consists of a Senate of 21 nominated members and a House of Representatives consisting of 53 members elected by universal adult suffrage. The number of members cannot be fewer than 45 nor more than 60. The Senate has no power to delay money bills for longer than one month or other bills for longer than seven months against the wishes of the House of Representatives. The Constitution provides for a Leader of the Opposition.

Governor-General, His Excellency Florizel Glasspole.

CABINET

Prime Minister, Hon. M. N. Manley.
Deputy Prime Minister and Minister of Finance, Hon. D. H. Coore, Q.C.
Industry, Tourism and Foreign Trade, Hon. P. J. Patterson.
Education, Hon. H. F. Cooke.
Pensions and Social Security, Hon. W. V. Jones.
Agriculture, Hon. A. U. Belinfanti.
Mining and National Resources, Hon. H. Clarke.
Health and Environmental Control, Hon. K. A. McNeil.
Labour and Employment, Hon. E. G. Peart.
Works and Communications, Hon. S. R. Pagon.
National Security, Hon. K. A. Munn.
Public Utilities and Transport, Hon. E. C. Bell.
Local Government, Hon. Mrs. R. A. Leon.
Housing, Hon. A. Spaulding.
Marketing and Commerce, Hon. V. Blake.
Youth and Community Development, Dr. Hon. D. Manley.
External Affairs, Hon. D. Thompson, Q.C.

Justice, Hon. C. Rattray, Q.C.
Minister of State, Senator S. Mullings.
Minister Without Portfolio, Hon. W. Isaacs.

Speaker, House of Representatives, Hon. R. McPherson.

JAMAICAN HIGH COMMISSION
48 Grosvenor Street, W.1
[01-499 8600]
High Commissioner, His Excellency Dr. Arthur S. Wint, C.D., M.B.E.

BRITISH HIGH COMMISSION
P.O. Box 575, Trafalgar Road, Kingston
High Commissioner, His Excellency John Kenneth Drinkall, C.M.G. (1976)

JUDICATURE
Chief Justice and Keeper of Records, Hon. K. G. Smith.

Judges of the Court of Appeal, Hon. L. B. Robinson (*President*); Hons. C. H. Graham-Perkin; W. H. Swaby; E. Zacca; E. H. Watkins (*acting*); K. C. Henry (*acting*).

Puisne Judges, Hons. U. N. Parnell (*Senior Puisne Judge*); V. C. Melville; V. O. Malcolm; L. Robotham; I. D. Rowe; W. B. Wilkie; H. V. T. Chambers; O. D. Marsh; C. A. B. Ross; R. O. C. White; V. K. G. McCarthy; W. D. Marsh; B. H. Carey; M. L. Wright; G. M. Vanderpump.

COMMUNICATIONS

There are several excellent harbours, Kingston being the principal port. The island is intersected by 2,700 miles of main road, of which 1,350 are asphalted. There are 229 miles of railway open. Telegraph stations and post offices are established in every town and in very many villages.

There are two international airports capable of handling the largest civil jet aircraft, the Norman Manley Airport on the south coast serving Kingston, and the Donald Sangster Airport on the north coast serving the major tourist areas. In addition there are licensed aerodromes at Port Antonio, Ocho Rios, Tinson Pen and Mandeville, which are used by Trans Jamaica Airlines on scheduled domestic flights. There are seven privately owned airstrips.

Air Jamaica, the national airline formed by the Government of Jamaica in association with Air Canada, operates scheduled services between the U.K., Canada, U.S.A., Nassau, Europe and Jamaica. Twelve other international carriers provide air communication with Europe, North, Central and South America and the Caribbean islands. They are: British Airways, British West Indian Airways, Air Canada, Pan American World Airways, A.L.M. Antillean, Cubana, Delta Lufthansa, Cayman Airways, Mexicana Airlines, Eastern Airlines and TACA International Airlines.

Scheduled internal routes are operated by Trans-Jamaica Airlines. There are also six non-scheduled air services catering for various services and activities.

PRODUCTION

Most of the staple products of tropical climates are grown. Sugar and rum are manufactured and exported (the latter is still counted the best in the world), and fine quality coffee is grown in certain areas of the Blue Mountains. Sugar production in 1975 amounted to 355,000 tons. There is trade in fruits, chiefly bananas, with U.K. Citrus, cocoa, coffee, pimento and ginger are important export crops. Jamaica has developed a breed of dairy cattle known as Jamaica Hope and a beef breed, the Jamaica Black. Jamaica is the second largest producer of bauxite in the world; output for 1975 was 11,388,000 tons. The bauxite deposits are worked by one of Canadian and five U.S. companies; the Canadian company and a consortium of the U.S. companies process bauxite into alumina. Further expansion of the industry is in progress. Gypsum is also mined, production in 1975 being 235,975 tons. Cement is manufactured locally, the output of the factory being 399,000 tons in 1975. The Esso Oil Refinery is designed to process 26,000 barrels of crude oil daily. The Jamaica Industrial Development Corporation is responsible for implementing the Government's industrial development programme. This Corporation administers incentive legislation which was enacted to stimulate the establishment of industries locally. In addition to undertaking promotional activities both locally and abroad, the Corporation maintains offices in the United States and the United Kingdom. In the last decade, manufacturing has grown from the processing of a few agricultural products into the production of a whole new range of commodities dependent on both local and foreign raw materials.

FINANCE

	1973–74	1974–75
Revenue	£177,500,000	J$445,134,000
Expenditure	235,550,000	841,000,000
Public Debt	241,000,000	539,000,000

TRADE

	1974	1975
Total imports	J$850,781,000	J$1,021,412,000
Total exports	664,446,000	712,667,000

	1973	1974
Imports from U.K.	£50,469,000	£50,122,000
Exports to U.K.	40,200,000	46,704,000

Chief Exports (1975).—Bauxite and alumina, J$453,800,000; sugar, rum and molasses, J$145,500,000; bananas, J$14,700,000; citrus, coffee, pimento, ginger, J$8,800,000; manufactured goods, J$70,900,000; clothing, J$4,200,000; mineral fuels, etc., J$10,300,000.

Kenya

Kenya is bisected by the equator and extends approximately from latitude 4° N. to latitude 4° S. and from longitude 34° E. to 41° E. From the coast of the Indian Ocean in the east, the borders of Kenya are with Somalia in the east and Ethiopia and Sudan in the north and north-west. To the west lie Uganda and Lake Victoria. On the south is Tanzania. The total area is 224,960 square miles (including 5,224 square miles of water). The population is estimated to be 12,934,000 and to be increasing by 3·5 per cent. annually. The country is divided into 7 Provinces (Nyanza, Rift Valley, Central, Coast, Western, Eastern and North-Eastern).

CAPITAL.—Nairobi, situated at latitude 2° S. and longitude 36° 49′ E. at 5,453 feet above sea level, covers an area of 266 sq. miles and has a population of about 509,000. It is 307 miles by road from Mombasa, the country's main port. Ψ Mombasa (246,000) possesses what is perhaps the finest harbour on the East Coast of Africa and is well served by shipping lines from Europe and Asia besides a frequent coastal service. Other centres are Nakuru (47,800), Kisumu (30,700), Eldoret (16,000), Thika (18,100) and Nanyuki (11,200).

Nairobi: transit from London about 25 days by sea; by air, 10 hrs.

FLAG.—Three equal horizontal bands of black over red over green; red and white spears and shield device in centre. NATIONAL DAY.—December 12.

GOVERNMENT

Kenya became an independent state and a member of the British Commonwealth on December 12, 1963, after six months of internal self-government. The national assembly consists of a single House of Representatives. Kenya became a Republic on Dec. 12, 1964. On July 4, 1974, the executive of the ruling Kenya African National Union decided that Swahili should become Kenya's official language, to be used in the National Assembly and in the country's administration, instead of English.

President, His Excellency Jomo Kenyatta, G.C.B., *elected* 1964; *re-elected* 1969.
Vice-President and Minister of Home Affairs, D. T. arap Moi.

CABINET

Minister of Finance and Economic Planning, M. Kibaki.
Defence, J. S. Gichuru.
Minister of State, Office of the President, M. Koinange.
Agriculture and Animal Husbandry, J. J. M. Nyagah.
Health, J. C. N. Osogo.
Local Government, R. S. Matano.
Works, N. W. Munoko.
Labour, J. Nyamweya.
Education, Dr. Z. Onyonka.
Tourism and Wildlife, M. J. Ogutu.
Lands and Settlement, J. H. Angaine.
Housing, T. A. Towett.
Power and Communications, I. Omolo Okero.
Attorney-General, C. Njonjo.
Information and Broadcasting, D. M. Mutinda.
Foreign Affairs, Dr. Munyua Waiyaki.
Co-operative Development, P. J. Ngei.
Water Development, Dr. J. G. Kiano.
Commerce and Industry, E. T. Mwamunga.
Natural Resources, S. S. Oloitiptip.

KENYA HIGH COMMISSION IN LONDON
45 Portland Place, W.1.
[01–636 2371]
High Commissioner, His Excellency Ng'ethe Njoroge (1970).

BRITISH HIGH COMMISSION
Bruce House, Standard Street, P.O. Box 30465 Nairobi
High Commissioner, His Excellency Stanley James Gunn Fingland, C.M.G. (1975).
British Council Representative, Dr. J. Barrott, P.O. Box 40751, Kenya Cultural Centre, Harry Thaku Road, Nairobi. There are offices at *Kisumu* and *Mombasa*.

JUDICATURE

Chief Justice, Sir James Wicks.
Puisne Judges, C. B. Madan, Q.C.; E. Trevelyan; Chana Singh; C. H. E. Miller; A. H. Simpson; L. G. E. Harris; K. G. Bennett; A. A. Kneller; J. M. Waiyaki; M. G. Muli; A. R. Hancox; J. G. Platt.
Registrar, Z. R. Chesoni.
Production.—Agriculture provides about 35 per cent. of the national income. The great variation in altitude and ecology provide conditions under which a wide range of crops can be grown. These include wheat, barley, pyrethrum, coffee, tea, sisal, coconuts, cashew nuts, cotton, maize and a wide variety of tropical and temperate fruits and vegetables. The total area of high potential land on which concentrated alternate husbandry can be practised amounts to only 16,761 sq. miles or 11·9 per cent. of the total land area. The remainder is arid or semi-arid country suitable for stock raising. In the areas of high potential, most of the old, large scale farms, formerly farmed by Europeans, have been bought by the Government for settlement of landless people and for transfer to African large-scale farmers.

In 1973 Kenya's forest area totalled 4,621,000 acres, of which 306,000 acres were under plantation.

Prospecting and mining are carried on in many parts of the country, the principal minerals produced being soda ash, salt and limestone. Major deposits of fluorite and galena are now being exploited. Small amounts of gold are also mined. Value of all minerals produced in 1973 was £K3,445,000.

Hydro-electric power has been developed, particularly on the Upper Tana River. Owen Falls Dam scheme in Uganda is connected to the Kenyan system, and supplies about 30 per cent. of consumption. Work is in progress on the second stage of the £37,000,000 Seven Forks Project which is expected to provide 300 MW on completion in the early 1980s.

There has been considerable industrial development over the last 15 years and Kenya has a wide variety of industries processing agricultural produce and manufacturing an increasing range of products from local and imported raw materials. New industries have recently come into being such as steel, textile mills, dehydrated vegetable processing and motor tyre manufacture as well as many smaller schemes which have added to the country's already considerable consumer goods. There is an oil refinery in Mombasa supplying both Kenya and Uganda, and a fuel pipeline to Nairobi is expected to open shortly. The market served comprises all the East African territories and the volume of exports to adjoining African and Indian Ocean countries is increasing year by year. Industrial areas have been developed in all the principal towns and light industrial estates are being developed for African *entrepreneurs*. The Kenya Government is actively encouraging investment in the industrial sector and has a Foreign Investments Protection Act to protect such investments.

The main imports are manufactured goods, classified chiefly as materials, machinery and transport equipment, mineral fuels, lubricants and related fuels and chemicals.

Communications.—The East African Railways and Harbours are self-contained and self-financing services of the East African Community; the railway, which is metre gauge, has a total route mileage of open line of 3,670 miles (1,270 miles in Kenya). In addition the East African Railways operate a marine service on Lakes Victoria and Tanganyika, with a route mileage of 3,469 miles. There are also 2,367 miles of road services providing regular transport to the Southern Highlands of Tanzania, and beyond the railhead at Pakwach in Uganda. East African Harbours control the four seaports of Mombasa, Tanga, Dar-es-Salaam amd Mtwara. Mombasa, Dar-es-Salaam and Mtwara have deep-water berths and Tanga is a lighterage port.

Scheduled trunk airline services are operated to and from Kenya, through Nairobi airport, by East African Airways, British Airways, Air India, Air France, Scandinavian Airlines System, Alitalia, Pan Am, K.L.M., Ethiopian Airlines, El Al Israel Airlines, Pakistan International Airlines, Lufthansa German Airlines, Sabena, Swissair, Olympic Airways, T.W.A. and Egyptair, while regional scheduled servies are also run by East African Airways, Ethiopian Airlines, Air Zaire, Air Malawi, Zambia Airways, Sudan Airways and Air Madagascar.

The country has approximately 26,000 miles of road including 3,850 miles of trunk roads and 6,200 miles of secondary roads. There is a total of 2,318 miles of bitumen-surfaced roads, apart from town streets, etc.

FINANCE

	1973–74	1974–75*
Revenue	K £235,500,000	K £261,130,000
Expenditure	234,960,000	276,690,000
	*Estimated	

Trade.—A large part of Kenya's trade is with the United Kingdom which in 1973 took 16 per cent. of her exports and supplied 25 per cent. of Kenya's imports (both figures excluding trade with Uganda

and Tanzania). The principal exports are coffee, tea, petroleum products, maize, meat products, pyrethrum flowers, powder and extract, and hides and skins.

	1973	1974
Imports from U.K....	£60,887,000	£78,681,000
Exports to U.K......	38,747,000	44,043,000

Lesotho

Lesotho is a landlocked state entirely surrounded by the Republic of South Africa. Of the total area of 11,716 sq. miles a belt between 20 and 40 miles in width lying across the western and southern boundaries and comprising about one-third of the total is classed as Lowlands, being between 5,000 and 6,000 ft. above sea level. The remaining two-thirds are classed as Foothills and Highlands, rising to 11,425 ft. The land is held in trust for the nation by the King. The population was estimated at 1,181,900 in April, 1975.

CAPITAL.—Maseru, population about 30,000.

FLAG.—Blue with conical white Basotho hat in centre, red and green vertical stripes (next staff).

Government.—Lesotho became a constitutional monarchy within the Commonwealth on October 4, 1966. The independence constitution was suspended in January, 1970, when the country was governed by a Council of Ministers, until the establishment of a National Assembly in April, 1974.

The country is divided into nine administrative districts. In each district there is a District Administrator who co-ordinates all Government activity in the area, working in co-operation with hereditary chiefs.

Judiciary.—The Lesotho Courts of Law consist of: the Court of Appeal, the High Court, Magistrates' Courts, Judicial Commissioners' Court, Central and local Courts. Magistrates' and higher courts administer the laws of Lesotho which are framed on the basis of the Roman–Dutch law. They also adjudicate appeals from the Judicial Commissioner's and Subordinate Courts.

Head of State, His Majesty King Moshoeshoe II.

CABINET

Prime Minister and Minister of Defence and Internal Security, Dr. Hon. Leabua Jonathan.
Deputy Prime Minister and Minister of Works and Communications, Hon. Chief Sekhonyana 'Maseribane.
Minister of Foreign Affairs, Hon. Joseph R. L. Kotsokoane.
Minister to the Prime Minister, Hon. Gabrial C. Manyali.
Finance, Hon. Evaristus R. Sekhonyana.
Health and Social Welfare, Hon. Patrick Mota.
Interior, Hon. Julius Monaleli.
Justice, Hon. Charles D. Molapo.
Agriculture, Hon. Khetla T. J. Rakhetla.
Commerce and Industry, Hon. Joel R. M. Moitse.
Education and Cultural Affairs, Hon. Anthony S. Ralebitso.

Chief Justice, Hon. Joseph T. Mapetla.

LESOTHO HIGH COMMISSION
16A St. James's Street (1st Floor), S.W.1
[01–839 1154]
High Commissioner, His Excellency T. E. Ntlhakana (1975).

BRITISH HIGH COMMISSION
P.O. Box 521, Maseru
High Commissioner, His Excellency Reginald H. Holden, D.F.C. (1976).
British Council Representative, G. A. Tindale, Hobson's Square, P.O. Box 429, Maseru.

Education.—There were 1,083 primary schools with 218,038 pupils enrolled in 1974, 58 secondary schools with 14,908 students and 7 teacher training colleges, with 383 trainees. There are also two main vocational training schools with 180 students and a training centre for civil servants. There is an Agricultural College with 120 students. The University of Botswana, Lesotho and Swaziland has its headquarters in Lesotho.

Health Services.—There are nine Government General hospitals, the largest being the Queen Elizabeth II Hospital in Maseru, one mental hospital, eight Mission hospitals and a leprosarium as well as 85 health centres and clinics run by Government, Missions and other voluntary organizations.

Communications.—The main north–south road of about 330 km (of which 176 km are bituminised) links Maseru and the lowlands. The mountainous areas are linked by a 1,200 km network of access tracks which are normally only suitable for four-wheel drive vehicles. Gravel roads link border towns in South Africa with the main towns in Lesotho. There is also an extensive network of about 900 km of gravel roads serving the lowlands and foothill areas, with about 1,000 km of bridle paths in the mountains. Maseru is connected by rail with the main Bloemfontein–Durban line of the South African Railways. Scheduled international services are operated three times a week between Maseru and Johannesburg. There are 32 airstrips. Internal scheduled services are operated by the Lesotho Airways Corporation. The telephone network is fully automated in all urban centres. Subscribers can dial direct to telephone exchanges in South Africa. Similar facilities exist for telex subscribers, who can also dial direct to a number of overseas countries. Radio telephone communication is used extensively in the remote rural areas.

Agricultural Production.—The economy of Lesotho is mainly agrarian. At the last enumeration livestock numbers were: cattle 465,500, sheep 1,556,900, goats 961,900, horses 114,000, poultry 578,800, 4,764,158 kg. of wool valued at R3,451,776 and 678,003 kg. of mohair valued at R1,589,162 were exported in 1974. Five large scale integrated agricultural development projects amounting to R25,330,000 are being implemented for increasing agricultural production, with emphasis on cash crops and livestock.

Finance, Trade and Industry.—The main sources of revenue are customs and excise duty. Estimates of expenditure and revenue for 1975–6 are: Recurrent Account, R25,000,000, Capital Account R16,500,000. Lesotho has few known and developed natural resources but it is intended to develop commercially the mineral resources of water and diamonds (the value of diamond exports for 1974–5 is R845,573). Drilling is being carried out for oil. Tourism is being developed and is rapidly playing a major role in the economic progress of the country. A National Park has been established at Sehlabathebe in the Maluti mountains. A number of light industries have recently been established. They include the manufacture of clothing, tapestries, carpets, sheepskin products, jewellery, pharmaceuticals, bricks and building materials; together with milling, diamond cutting and tractor assembly.

Malawi

MALAWI, formerly the Nyasaland Protectorate, comprises Lake Malawi (formerly Lake Nyasa) and its western shore, with the high table-land separating it from the basin of the Luangwa River, the watershed forming the western frontier with Zambia; south of the lake, Malawi reaches almost to the Zambesi and is surrounded by Mozambique; the frontier lying on the west on the watershed of the Zambesi and Shire Rivers, and to the east on the Ruo, a tributary of the Shire, and Lakes Chiuta and Chirwa. This boundary reaches the eastern shore of Lake Malawi and extends up to the mid-point of the lake for about half its length where it returns to the eastern and northern shores to form a frontier with Tanzania.

Malawi has a total area of 45,747 sq. miles (land area, 36,324). The population of Malawi at the Census of August, 1966, was 4,039,583 (52 per cent. female); estimated, mid-1976, 5,175,000.

CAPITAL.—Lilongwe (population, 1974, 87,000). The city of Blantyre, incorporating Blantyre and Limbe (population, 1974, 181,000), is the major commercial and industrial centre and headquarters of the Southern region. Other main centres are: Mzuzu, headquarters of the Northern Region; Thyolo, Mulanje, Mangochi, Mzimba, Nkhotakota and Zomba, the former capital.

FLAG.—Horizontal stripes of black, red and green, with rising sun in centre of the black stripe.

Government.—Malawi became a republic on July 6, 1966, having assumed internal self-government on February 1, 1963, and achieved independence on July 6, 1964, and is a member of the Commonwealth. There is a Cabinet consisting of the President and other Ministers. The National Assembly consists of 87 members, each elected by universal suffrage. Under the Constitution Act, 1966, the President exercises power to nominate in addition up to fifteen members to represent special interests. Being a one-party State (the Malawi Congress Party), all elected members are required to be members of the Party. The Assembly, which usually meets three times a year, is presided over by a Speaker, who need not himself be a member of it.

President, Minister of External Affairs, Works and Supplies, Agriculture and National Resources and Justice, Dr. H. Kamuzu Banda, *born* 1907, *elected* 1966, *sworn in as* President for Life July 6, 1971.

Minister of Youth and Culture, Hon. G. Chakuamba Phiri.

Central Region, Hon. A. E. Gadama.

Northern Region, Hon. M. M. Lungu.

Organization of African Unity Affairs, Hon. W. B. Deleza.

Finance, Hon. D. T. Matenje.

Transport and Communications and Labour, Hon. R. Chirwa.

Education and Health, Hon. R. T. C. Munyenyembe.

Southern Region, Hon. P. L. Makhumula Nkhoma.

Local Government, Community Development and Social Welfare, Hon. D. Kainja Nthara.

Minister without Portfolio, Hon. A. A. Muwalo-Ngumayo.

JUDICIARY

Chief Justice, J. J. Skinner.

Puisne Judges, L. Weston, L. A. Chatsikah.

Solicitor-General, D. R. Barwick, C.B.E.

MALAWI HIGH COMMISSION
47 Great Cumberland Place, W.1
[01-723 6021]

High Commissioner, His Excellency Robert B. Mbaya (1975).

BRITISH HIGH COMMISSION

Lingadzi Building (P.O. Box 30042), Lilongwe

High Commissioner, His Excellency Kenneth Gordon Ritchie, C.M.G.

Deputy High Commissioner, W. Jones.

British Council Representative, (vacant), P.O. Box 456, Glyn Jones Road, Blantyre. There is also an office at *Lilongwe.*

Education.—Primary education is the responsibility of local authorities in both urban and rural areas. About 35 per cent. of the population of school age can be taken into schools and only 10 per cent. of those successfully completing primary education can be placed in secondary schools. The Ministry is responsible for policy, school curricula, secondary education teachers' and technical training. Religious bodies, with Government assistance, still play an important part in primary and secondary education and teacher training. Further training is pursued at the University of Malawi, opened in September 1965. For the academic year 1974/75 there were 1,147 students studying for degrees and diplomas at the three constituent colleges.

Communications.—A single-track railway runs from the south-western area of Lake Malawi (itself served by two passenger and a number of cargo boats) through Blantyre to the southern frontier into Mozambique, crossing the Zambesi River by a bridge 12,050 feet long, and connecting with the Mozambique port of Beira, which handles the bulk of the country's imports and exports. In 1970 a 70-mile line was opened from Liwonde to Nayuci, linking the Malawi rail system with the Mozambique network to the port of Nacala. Construction of a new railway line from Salima to Lilongwe is in progress and was expected to be completed in 1976. Plans are underway and funds are available for another line from Lilongwe to Mchinji. A road system of 6,808 miles covers the whole country, of which 900 miles are bituminized from Mulanje through Blantyre and Zomba to Lilongwe, the new capital, and from there to the lakeshore at Salima, the northern terminus of the railway. Plans are underway for a bituminized road from Blantyre to the Mozambique border and onwards to Tete and Salisbury, Rhodesia.

FINANCE

	1973-4	1974-5
Revenue	K63,100,000	K66,788,000
Expenditure	61,700,000	67,605,000
(excluding Development Account)		

Decimal currency was introduced on Feb. 15, 1971. The unit is the *kwach* (=approx. 50p. sterling), divided into 100 *tambala.*

TRADE

	1974	1975
Imports	K157,700,000	K216,629,000
Exports	101,300,000	119,673,000
	1973	1974
Imports from U.K.	£7,866,000	£16,522,000
Exports to U.K.	17,436,000	16,088,000

Agriculture is the country's mainstay, the principal exports being tea, tobacco, cotton, sugar and groundnuts. The value of exports of these crops in 1975 was: tea, K20,827,000; tobacco, K50,390,000; groundnuts, K6,503,000; cotton, K1,933,000; sugar, K12,294,000. Other agricultural exports include tung oil, rice, sisal, casava, coffee and vegetables. A total of K94,654,000 of crops was exported in 1975. Imports are mainly clothing materials, vehicles, fuels and machinery.

Malaysia

Malaysia, comprising Malaya, Sabah and Sarawak, forms a crescent well over 1,000 miles long between latitudes 1° and 7° North latitude and longitudes 100° and 119° East. It occupies two distinct regions—the Malay Peninsula which extends from the Isthmus of Kra to the Singapore Strait and the North-West Coastal area of the Island of Borneo. Each is separated from the other by 400 miles of the South China Sea.

Area and Population.—The total area of the 13 states of Malaysia, including the Federal Territory of Kuala Lumpur (94 sq. miles) is estimated to be 130,000 sq. miles, containing a population of 10,434,034 at the Census of Housing and Population of Malaysia held in 1970. Details of individual states appear on p. 201.

Climate.—The whole region is open to maritime influences and is subject to the interplay of wind systems which originate in the Indian Ocean and the South China Sea. The year is commonly divided into the Southwest and Northeast monsoon seasons. Rainfall averages about 100 inches throughout the year, though the annual fall varies from place to place. The average daily temperature throughout Malaysia varies from 70° Fahrenheit to 90° Fahrenheit, though in higher areas temperatures are lower and vary widely.

CAPITAL.—Kuala Lumpur was proclaimed Federal Territory on February 1, 1974. Its population is about 770,000. The chief town of Sarawak is Ψ Kuching, and of Sabah is Ψ Kota Kinabalu.

Bahasa Malaysia (Malay) is the national language. In Sarawak English will continue as an official language as well as Bahasa Malaysia until 1979, when the Sarawak State Council will review the position.

RELIGION.—Islam is the official religion of Malaysia, each Ruler being the head of religion in his State, though the Heads of State of Sabah and Sarawak are not heads of the Muslim religion in their States. The Yang di-Pertuan Agung is the head of religion in Malacca and Penang. The Constitution guarantees religious freedom. NATIONAL DAY.—August 31 (*Hari Kebangsaan*).

FLAG.—Equal horizontal stripes of red (7) and white (7); 14 point yellow star and crescent in blue canton.

GOVERNMENT

The Federation of Malaya became an independent country within the Commonwealth on August 31, 1957, as a result of an agreement between H.M. the Queen and the Rulers of the Malay States, whereby Her Majesty relinquished all powers and jurisdiction over the Malay States and over the Settlements of Penang and Malacca which then became States of the Federation. On Sept. 16, 1963, the Federation was enlarged, by the accession of the further States of Singapore, Sabah (*formerly* British North Borneo) and Sarawak, and the name of MALAYSIA was adopted from that date. On Aug. 9, 1965, Singapore seceded from the Federation.

The Constitution was designed to ensure the existence of a strong Federal Government and also a measure of autonomy for the State Governments. It provides for a constitutional Supreme Head of the Federation (His Majesty the *Yang di-Pertuan Agung*) to be elected for a term of five years from among their number, and for a Deputy Supreme Head (His Royal Highness the *Timbalan Yang di-Pertuan Agung*) to be similarly elected. The Malay Rulers are either chosen or succeed to their position in accordance with the custom of the particular state. In other states of Malaysia choice of the Head of State is in the discretion of the *Yang di-Pertuan Agung* after consultation with the Chief Minister of the State. Save in certain instances provided in the Constitution, the Supreme Head acts in accordance with the advice of a Cabinet appointed by him from among the members of Parliament on the advice of the Prime Minister. The Supreme Head appoints as Prime Minister the person who in his judgement is likely to command the confidence of the majority of the members of the House of Representatives. He also has the powers to promulgate emergency ordinances. The National Operations Council was dissolved on February 19, 1971, and the Yang di-Pertuan Agung promulgated the reconvening of Parliamentary democracy the following day.

SUPREME HEAD OF MALAYSIA

Supreme Head of State, His Royal Highness Tuanku Yahya Putra Ibni-Marhum Sultan Ibrahim (*Sultan of Kelantan*). *assumed office for a term of 5 years*, Sept. 21, 1975.

Deputy Supreme Head of State, His Royal Highness Sultan Haji Ahmad Shah Al-Musta'in Billah Ibni Al-Marhum Sultan Abu Bahar Ri'ayatuddin Al-Mu'adzam Sha (*Sultan of Pohang*).

MINISTRY

Prime Minister and Minister of Defence, Dabuk Hussein bin Onn.

Deputy Prime Minister and Minister of Education, Dr. Mahathir bin Mohammed.

Works and Utilities, Datuk Haji Abdul Ghani Gilong.

Labour and Manpower, Datuk Lee San Choon.

Agriculture, Datuk Ali bin Haji Ahmadi.

Health, Tan Sri Lee Siok Yew.

Culture, Youth and Sports, Datuk Abdul Samad bin Idris.

Law and Attorney-General, Tan Sri Datuk Haji Abdul Kadir bin Yusoff.

Rural Economic Development, Encik Abdul Ghafar bin Baba.

Communications, Tan Sri V. Manickavasagam.

Welfare Services, Puan Hajjah Aishah binti Haji Abdul Ghani.

Primary Industries, Datuk Musa bin Hitam.

Land and Regional Development, Datuk Haji Mohamed Asri bin Haji Muda.

Home Affairs, Tan Sri Haji Muhammad Ghazali bin Shafie.

Local Government and Federal Territory, Tuan Haji Hassan Adli bin Haji Arshad.

Foreign Affairs, Tengku Datuk Ahmad Rithaudeen Al-Haj bin Tengku Ismail.

Finance, Tengku Tan Sri Razaleigh Hamzah.

Trade and Industry, Datuk Haji Hamzah bin Abu Samah.

Science, Technology and Environment, Tan Sri Ong Kee Hui.

Housing and Village Development, Encik Michael Chen Wing Sum.

Public Enterprises, Datuk Haji Mohamed bin Yacob.

Without Portfolio, Encik Mohamed Khir Johari.

NOTE.—The words " Tunku/Tengku ", " Tun ", " Tan Sri ", and " Datuk " are titles. The word " Tunka/Tengku " is equivalent to " Prince ".

" Tun " denotes membership of a high Order of Malaysian Chivalry and " Tan Sri " and " Datuk " (" Datu Sri " in Perak and " Datu " in Sabah) are each the equivalent of a knighthood. The wife of a " Tun " is styled " Toh Puan ", that of a " Tan Sri " is styled " Puan Sri " and of a " Datuk " " Datin ". The honorific " Tuan " or " Encik " is equivalent to " Mr." and the honorific " Puan " is equivalent to " Mrs." The words " Al-Haj " or " Haji " indicate that the person so named has made the pilgrimage to Mecca.

MALAYSIAN HIGH COMMISSION
45 Belgrave Square, S.W.1
[01-245 9221]
High Commissioner, His Excellency Datuk Abdallah Ali (1975).

BRITISH HIGH COMMISSION
Wisma Damansara, Jalan Semanton,
(P.O. Box 1030), Kuala Lumpur.
High Commissioner, His Excellency Sir Eric George Norris, K.C.M.G.
Deputy High Commissioner, J. D. B. Shaw, M.V.O.

———

British Council Representative, J. Lawrence, O.B.E., Jalan Bukit Aman, Kuala Lumpur, and offices at *Kota Kinabalu* (Sabah) and *Kuching* (Sarawak).

LEGISLATURE

The Federal Parliament consists of two houses, the Senate and the House of Representatives. The Senate (*Dewan Negara*) consists of 58 members, under a President (*Yang di-Pertua Dewan Negara*), 26 elected by the Legislative Assemblies of the States (2 from each) and 32 appointed by the *Yang di-Pertuan Agung* from persons who have achieved distinction in major fields of activity or are representative of racial minorities, including the Aborigines. The House of Representatives (*Dewan Rakyat*), consists of 154 members (Peninsular Malaysia, 114; Sarawak, 24; and Sabah, 16). Members are elected on the principle of universal adult suffrage with a common electoral roll. The House of Representatives is presided over by a Speaker who is either a member of the House or is qualified to be elected as a member. *Speaker,* Tan Sri Datuk Nik Ahmed bin Kamil.

The Constitution provides that each State shall have its own Constitution not inconsistent with the Federal Constitution, with the Ruler or Governor acting on the advice of an Executive Council appointed on the advice of the *Menteri Besar* or Chief Minister and a single chamber Legislative Assembly. Three *ex officio* members sit in the Executive Council besides these elected members. They are the State Secretary, the State Legal Adviser and the State Financial Officer. The State Constitutions provide for the Ruler or Governor to appoint as *Menteri Besar* or Chief Minister, to preside over the Executive Council, a member of the Legislative Assembly who in his judgement is likely to command the confidence of the majority of the members of the Assembly. The Legislative Assemblies are fully elected on the same basis as the Federal Parliament.

Legislative powers are divided into a Federal List, a State List and a Concurrent List, with residual powers vested in the State Legislatures. The Federal List comprises broadly, external affairs, defence, civil and criminal law and justice, the machinery of government, finance, commerce and industry, communications and transport, power, education, medicine and labour and social security. The State List includes land, agriculture and fores-

try, local government and services and the machinery of state government. In the Concurrent List are, *inter alia*, social welfare, wild-life, animal husbandry, town and country planning, public health and drainage and irrigation.

A State of Emergency was declared after disturbances on May 13, 1969. As Parliament was not then sitting, the *Yang di-Pertuan Agung* did not summon Parliament and instead established the National Operations Council and Y.A.B. Tun Abdul Razak bin Dato Hussein, the then Deputy Prime Minister, was appointed Director of Operations vested with the executive authority of the Federation including the powers to make essential regulations. The *Yang di-Pertuan Agung* remained as the Supreme Head of Federation with powers to promulgate emergency ordinances.

JUDICATURE

The Judicial System consists of a Federal Court and two High Courts, one in Peninsular Malaysia and one for Sabah and Sarawak (sitting alternately in Kota Kinabalu and Kuehing). The High Court in Peninsular Malaysia known as the High Court in Malaya has its principal registry in Kuala Lumpur while the High Court in Sabah/Sarawak known as the High Court in Borneo has its principal registry in Kuching.

The Federal Court comprises a President, the two Chief Justices of the High Courts and other judges. This court possesses appellate, original and advisory jurisdiction. In its capacity as an appellate court it has exclusive jurisdiction to determine appeals from the decisions of a High Court or of a judge thereof (except decisions of a High Court given by a registrar or other officer of the court and appealable under federal law to a judge of the Court). This appellate jurisdiction is subject to limitations imposed by or under federal law. It also has jurisdiction to determine disputes between the Federation and any of the States within the Federation, any challenge to the competence of the Federal or any State legislature to enact a particular law and any question as to the effect of any of the provisions of the Constitution which question has arisen in proceedings before another court. It also renders advisory opinions on questions referred to it by the *Yang di-Pertuan Agung* as regards the effect of any provisions of the Constitution which has arisen or is likely to arise.

Each of the High Courts consists of a Chief Justice and not less than 4 other judges. The Federal Constitution allows for a maximum of twelve such judges for Malaya and eight for Borneo. In Peninsular Malaysia the Subordinate Courts consist of the Sessions Courts and the Magistrates' Courts. In Sabah/Sarawak the Magistrates' Courts constitute the Subordinate Courts.

DEFENCE

The Malaysian Armed Forces consist of the Army, Navy and Air Force, together with volunteer forces for each arm. The defence of the country is largely borne by the army in its role of providing defence against external threat and counter-insurgency operations and also to assist the police in the performance of public order duties. The *Royal Malaysian Navy* (*RMN*) has the responsibility of defending the 3,000 miles of the country's coastline and maintaining constant patrol of 500 miles of the high seas that separate Sabah and Sarawak from the mainland. The *Royal Malaysian Air Force* (*RMAF*) is capable of providing close strategic and tactical support to the army and police in the defence and internal security of the country.

FINANCE

	1974	1975
Revenue......	4,400,000,000	4,815,000,009
Expenditure....	3,798,000,000	4,950,000,000

PRODUCTION AND TRADE

The agricultural sector continues to be the mainstay of the Malaysian economy. However diversification of crops and rapid growth in the manufacturing sector has made Malaysia less vulnerable to fluctuations in the price of its primary crop, natural rubber.

Malaysia is the largest exporter of natural rubber, tin, palm oil and tropical hardwoods. Other major export commodities are manufactured and processed products, petroleum, oil, and other minerals, palm kernel oil, tea and pepper.

Exports of the four major primary commodities: rubber, tin, palm oil and tropical hardwoods accounted for 62·7 per cent. of the total exports in 1975 (preliminary figures). With the rapid expansion in the manufacturing sector, Malaysia is also increasing her export of manufactured products.

Another commodity which is produced throughout Malaysia is rice, the staple food of Malaysians. Total output of *padi* in the 1974–75 season amounted to 1,099,000 tons. The level of self-sufficiency of rice has increased to 90 per cent. in Peninsular Malaysia. To achieve self-sufficiency, various measures aimed at increasing output and productivity are being introduced. They include wider use of improved seeds and fertilizers, expansion of double-cropping through the provisions of large-scale irrigation schemes and research programmes to improve rice yields.

Imports in 1973 consisted mainly of machinery and transport equipment, manufactured goods, food, mineral fuels, chemicals and inedible crude materials for her growing population and to accelerate the pace of her economic growth and development.

	1973 M'000,000	1974 M'000,000
Imports.........	5,899·1	8,591·0
Exports.........	7,372·2	9,252·4
Balance of trade..	+1,473·1	+661·4

Malaysia's Trade by Countries ($Mooo,000)

Countries	1972			1973			1974		
	Imports	Exports	Total Trade	Imports	Exports	Total Trade	Imports	Exports	Total Trade
Singapore........	356·5	1,126·8	1,473·3	463·4	1,714·7	2,178·1	820·2	2,208·0	3,028·2
Japan............	921·9	931·9	1,763·0	1,334·3	1,334·1	2,671·4	2,204·1	1,718·6	3,922·7
U.K............	581·8	342·4	924·2	604·1	582·9	1,187·0	928·5	673·6	1,602·1
Other Western Europe.......	—	—	—	—	—	—	1,400·5	1,702·8	3,103·3
U.S.S.R.........	—	—	—	—	—	—	10·0	421·1	431·1
China (Mainland)	194·6	76·4	271·0	364·7	199·5	564·2	492·9	210·6	703·5
Australia........	338·2	88·7	426·9	420·2	150·8	571·0	714·1	219·4	933·5
Indonesia........	153·1	37·1	191·0	149·3	37·4	186·7	232·2	51·7	283·9

Malta

Malta lies in the Mediterranean Sea, 58 miles from Sicily and about 180 from the African coast, about 17 miles in length and 9 in breadth, and having an area of 94·9 square miles. Malta includes also the adjoining island of *Gozo* (area 25·9 sq. miles); *Comino* and minor islets. The estimated population on Dec. 31, 1973, was 318,481 (including temporary visitors). Malta's climate, although not tropical, is hot in summer.

Malta was in turn held by the Phœnicians, Greeks, Carthaginians, Romans and Arabs. In 1090 it was conquered by Count Roger of Normandy. In 1530 it was handed over to the Knights of St. John, who made of it a stronghold of Christianity. In 1565 it sustained the famous siege, when the last great effort of the Turks was successfully withstood by Grandmaster La Vallette. The Knights expended large sums in fortifying the island and carrying out many magnificent works, until they were expelled by Napoleon in 1798. The Maltese rose against the French garrison soon afterwards, and the island was subsequently blockaded by the British fleet. The Maltese people freely requested the protection of the British Crown in 1802 on condition that their rights and privileges would be preserved and respected. The islands were finally annexed to the British Crown by the Treaty of Paris in 1814.

Malta was again closely besieged in the last war and again withstood the attacks of all its enemies. From June, 1940, to the end of the war, 432 members of the garrison and 1,540 civilians were killed by enemy aircraft, and about 35,000 houses were destroyed or damaged. In recognition of the part played by the Maltese people, King George VI awarded the George Cross to the island, but this honour is no longer used.

Government.—Following the report of a Constitutional Commission under the chairmanship of Sir Hilary Blood, a new Constitution for Malta was introduced by the Malta (Constitution) Order in Council, 1961, under which the Island became known as " the State of Malta ". On Sept. 21, 1964 under the Malta Independence Order, 1964, Malta became an independent state within the Commonwealth; on December 13, 1974, Malta became a republic within the Commonwealth. Elections under the 1964 Order were held in June, 1971, for the 55 seats in the House of Representatives and they resulted as follows: Nationalist Party, 27 seats; Malta Labour Party, 28 seats. The present state of the parties is Malta Labour Party 29 seats, Nationalist Party 26 seats. Maltese and English are the official languages of administration and Maltese is ordinarily the official language in all the courts of law and the language of general use in the islands.

CAPITAL.—Ψ Valletta. Population (estimated, Dec., 1973), 14,152. Valletta Grand Harbour is one of the finest in the world; it is very deep, and large vessels can anchor alongside the shore. It is an important port of call and ship repairing centre for vessels, being half-way between Gibraltar and Port Said.

FLAG.—Equal vertical stripes of white (next staff), and red; a silver George Cross outlined in red in top corner of white stripe.

President, His Excellency Sir Anthony Joseph Mamo, O.B.E., Q.C.

CABINET

Prime Minister and Minister of Commonwealth and Foreign Affairs, D. Mintoff.
Minister of Justice and Parliamentary Affairs, A. Buttigieg.
Labour, Employment and Welfare, Miss A. Barbara.
Finance and Customs, Dr. J. Abela.
Health, A. V. Hyzler, M.D.
Posts and Electricity, D. Piscopo, M.D.
Trade, Industry and Tourism, P. Xuereb.
Public Building and Works, L. Sant.
Education and Welfare, Dr. J. Cassar.
Development, W. Abela.
Agriculture and Fisheries, F. Micallef.
Housing and Land, Dr. P. Holland.

MALTESE HIGH COMMISSION
24 Haymarket, S.W.1
[01-930 9851]
High Commissioner, His Excellency Arthur J. Scerri (1971).

BRITISH HIGH COMMISSION
7 St. Anne Street, Floriana, Malta,
High Commissioner, (vacant).
British Council Representative, H. R. H. Salmon, Piazza Indipendenza, Valletta.

Education.—In October 1975 there were 104 Government Primary Schools with 22,681 pupils and 37 Secondary and Upper Secondary Schools with 22,769 pupils. Third level education is available at the Royal University of Malta (844 students in October 1975) and the Malta College of Arts, Science and Technology (1,284 students in October 1975). The Government also runs Trade Schools, a Nautical School, a Training Centre in Industrial Electronics, a School of Art, a School of Music, and a School of Nursing. A number of private schools offer more or less the same facilities that exist in Government Primary and Secondary (including sixth form) Schools. These are fee-paying and entry at Secondary level is selective.

In religion, the Maltese are Roman Catholics.

The Maltese language is of Semitic origin and held by some to be derived from the Carthaginian and Phoenician tongues.

Production.—The total labour force in 1975 was 112,708 of which 107,814 were gainfully employed.

Agriculture plays a significant role in the economy. There are 5,500 full time farmers and about 8,000 part time farmers. The yearly crop production is about 25,000 tons consisting mainly of potatoes, tomatoes, onions, cabbages and cauliflowers. Some 8,000 tons of fruit are produced. Grape is the largest fruit crop.

Industry.—The island's leading industry is the state-owned Malta Drydocks employing about 4,500 people. Local manufacturers include textiles, footwear, furniture, detergents, plastics, rubber products, electronic equipment and components, glass products and carpets. The private sector employs some 75,000.

Tourism.—In 1975, 334,519 tourists visited the island. Income from this industry stood at £M14·3 million.

FINANCE AND TRADE

	1973/4	1974/5
Revenue.........	£M55,850,000	£M74,500,000
Expenditure......	£M54,342,000	£M64,200,000

The Central Bank of Malta has the sole right of issuing legal tender currency notes and coins. The Maltese pound is divided into 100 cents and 1,000 milss. On 1 June 1976 the rate of exchange was £stg1 = £M1·3059.

Trade.—The principal imports for home consumption are foodstuffs—mainly wheat, meat and bullocks, milk and fruit—fodder, beverages and tobacco, fuels, chemicals, textiles and machinery (industrial, agricultural and transport). The chief domestic exports are potatoes, tomatoes, onions, smoking requisites, textile fabrics, rubber goods, gloves, hosiery, beer, mineral waters, edible oil, fresh flowers, fibres and yarns, rubber seals, flower cuttings, plastic goods, wine, mattresses, knitwear, stainless steel sinks, electronic equipment and components, carpets, etc.

Mauritius

Mauritius is an island group lying in the Indian Ocean, 550 miles east of Madagascar, between 57° 17′–57° 461 E. long. and lat. 10° 581–20° 33′ S., and comprising with its dependencies an area of 805 square miles. The resident population at the census of 1972 was: Mauritius, 826,199; Rodrigues, 24,769; Lesser Dependencies about 500, made up of Europeans (mainly of French extraction), Asiatic races and persons of mixed descent. The total population, including dependencies, was estimated in 1975 at 894,150.

Mauritius was discovered in 1511 by the Portuguese; the Dutch visited it in 1598, and named it Mauritius, in honour of the Stadtholder, Prince Maurice of Nassau. From 1638 to 1710 it was held as a small Dutch colony and in 1715 the French took possession but did not settle it until 1721. Mauritius was taken by a British Force in 1810. A British garrison remained on the island until its withdrawal in June 1960. The French language and French law have been preserved under British rule. English is the official language but French is in common use.

Climate.—Mauritius enjoys a sub-tropical maritime climate, with sufficient difference between summer and winter to avoid monotony; further variation is introduced by the wide range of rainfall and temperature resulting from the mountainous nature of the island. Humidity is rather high throughout the year and rainfall is sufficient to maintain a green cover of vegetation, except for a brief period in the driest districts.

CAPITAL.—Ψ Port Louis, population (1975), 140,800; other centres are Beau Bassin and Rose Hill (83,000); Curepipe (54,000); Vacoas and Phoenix (50,000) and Quatre Bornes (53,000) (all figures provisional). FLAG.—Red, blue, yellow and green horizontal stripes.

Government.—A Crown Colony for 158 years, Mauritius became an independent state within the Commonwealth on March 12, 1968. The Constitution defined by Order in Council in 1964 was slightly altered in 1966 on the recommendation of the Banwell Commission, the effect being to increase the membership of the Legislative Assembly to 70, 62 elected by block voting in multi-member constituencies (including 2 members for Rodrigues) and 8 specially-elected members. Of the latter, 4 seats go to the "best loser" of whichever communities in the island are under-represented in the Assembly after the General Election and the four remaining seats are allocated on the basis of both party and community. The Constitution provides for the appointment of a Governor-General who acts on the advice of the Council of Ministers,

collectively responsible to the Legislative Assembly. The present state of the parties in the Assembly is: Government; Labour, 40; *Comité d'Action Museilman* 5; Opposition; P.M.S.D. (*Parti Mauritien Social Democrate*) 15; Independent Forward Bloc 4, *Union Democratique Mauritienne* 5, *Mouvement Militant* 1, *Mauritien* (*Socialiste Progressiste*) 1.

Governor-General, His Excellency Sir Raman Osman, G.C.M.G., C.B.E. (1973).

COUNCIL OF MINISTERS

Premier and Minister of Defence, Information and Broadcasting and Internal Security, Dr. the Rt. Hon. Sir Seewoosagur Ramgoolam.

Minister of External Affairs, Tourism and Emigration, Sir Harold Walter.

Minister of Finance, Sir Veerasamy Ringadoo.

MAURITIUS HIGH COMMISSION
32–33 Elvaston Place, S.W.7
[01–581–0294]

High Commissioner, His Excellency Sir Leckraz Teelock, C.B.E. (1968).

Counsellor, Gian Nath.

BRITISH HIGH COMMISSION
Cerne House, Chaussée Street,
Port Louis

High Commissioner, His Excellency (Arthur) Henry Brind, C.M.G. (1974).

Deputy High Commissioner. R J. C. Pease (*Head of Chancery*).

1st Secretary, P. H. Charters (*Aid*).

British Council Representative, Miss M. E. Platon, O.B.E., Royal Road, Rose Hill.

Education.—At the primary level education is free and is provided for 136,564 children at 184 government primary schools and 50 aided primary schools. Although education is not compulsory it is estimated that about 90 per cent. of children of primary school age attend school. There are 6 government secondary schools—and also 119 private secondary schools, of which 25 are grant-aided. Total enrolment in secondary schools (1975) is 64,612. In addition there are 4 junior technical schools which provide education in practical subjects, 5 rural craft training centres (small scale industries) and 1 industrial trade training centre. There is a teacher training college for the training of primary school teachers. An institute of education has been set up for the purpose of training secondary school teachers and engaging in curriculum and examination reform. The University of Mauritius consists of a School of Administration, a School of Administration, a School of Agriculture and a School of Industrial Technology. There are 1,009 students (1975). Estimated expenditure on education in 1975–76 was: recurrent Rs. 107,514,000; capital Rs. 16,028,000.

Communications.—Port Louis, on the N.W. coast, has an excellent harbour which handles the bulk of the island's external trade. Goods unloaded in 1974 amounted to 861,000 metric tons and goods loaded to 820,000 metric tons. The international airport is located at Plaisance in the south-east of the island about 2 miles from Mahébourg. Freight unloaded there during 1974 totalled 952 metric tons and freight loaded totalled 1,360 metric tons. Scheduled services are operated by Air France, Air India, Air Malawi, Air Mauritius, British Airways, East African Airways, Lufthansa, Qantas, South African Airways, Zambia Airways, Air Malagasy and Alitalia. There are 27 telephone exchanges serving 24,300 individual telephone installations on the islands. There are 13 daily newspapers published, mostly in French with occasional articles in English, and 3 Chinese daily papers. The Mauritian Broadcasting Corporation has a monopoly of radio broadcasting in the country. Television was introduced in February 1965, educational television in 1969, and colour television in 1975.

Production.—In 1974, sugar cane was cultivated over an area of 214,000 acres compared with 13,500 acres under tea, 1,300 acres under tobacco and about 3,560 acres devoted to vegetables and other crops. The sugar crop in 1975 was 460,900 long tons.

Finance.—The main sources of Government revenue are private and company income tax, customs and excise duties, mainly on imports, but also on sugar exports.

	1975–76	1976–77*
Public revenue...	Rs.1,036,650,000	Rs.1,069,314,470
Public expenditure	1,035,088,210	1,057,463,600
	*Estimated.	

The National Debt in March 1976 was approx. Rs. 1,087,000,000.

Currency—*Rs.= Rupee*=8p.

Trade.—Most foodstuffs and raw materials have to be imported from abroad. Apart from local consumption (about 35,000 long tons per annum), the sugar produced is exported, mainly to Britain and Canada.

	1973	1974
Total imports...	Rs.915,800,000	Rs.1,756,000,000
Total exports....	748,400,000	1,786,400,000

Trade with U.K.

	1973	1974
Imports from U.K...	£10,528,000	£19,479,000
Exports to U.K.....	28,328,000	47,012,000

DEPENDENCIES OF MAURITIUS

Rodrigues, 350 miles east-north-east of Mauritius, area, 40 square miles. Population (1974) 25,700. Cattle, salt fish, sheep, goats, pigs and onions are the principal exports. The island is now administered by a Resident Commissioner, who was appointed in June 1974. *Resident Commissioner*, N. Heseltine.

Trade with Mauritius

	1973	1974
Total imports....	Rs.11,322,000	Rs.17,127,000
Total exports.....	3,401,000	6,885,000

In addition to Rodrigues, the islands of Agalea and St. Brandon are dependencies of Mauritius. Other small islands, formerly Mauritian dependencies, including Six Islands, Peros Banhos, Salomon, Diego Garcia and Trois Frères, have since 1965 constituted the British Indian Ocean Territory.

Nigeria

(For MAP, *see* Index).

Area and Population.—The Republic of Nigeria is situated on the the west coast of Africa. It is bounded on the south by the Gulf of Guinea, on the west by the Republic of Benin, on the north by Niger and on the east by Cameroun. It has an area of 356,669 sq. miles with a population (1963 Census) of 55,654,000. (The 1973 census provisional results give 79,760,000). The population is almost entirely African.

A belt of mangrove swamp forest 10–60 miles in width lies along the entire coastline. North of this there is a zone 50–100 miles wide of tropical rain forest and oil-palms. North of this the country rises

and the vegetation changes to open woodland and savannah. In the extreme north the country is semi-desert. There are few mountains, but in Northern Nigeria the central plateau rises to an average level of 4,000 feet. The Niger, Benue, and Cross are the main rivers.

The climate varies with the types of country described above, but Nigeria lies entirely within the tropics and temperatures are high. Temperatures of over 100° in the north are common while coast temperatures are seldom over 90°. The humidity at the coast, however, is much higher than in the north. The rainy season is from about April to October; rainfall varies from under 25 inches a year in the extreme north to 172 inches on the coast line. During the dry season the *harmattan* wind blows from the desert; it is cool and laden with fine particles of dust.

CAPITAL.—ΨLAGOS, estimated population, 1,000,000. Other important towns are Ibadan, Kano, Ogbomosho, Oyo, Oshogbo, Onitsha, Ife, Abeokuta, Enugu, Aba, Maiduguri, Katsina, ΨPort Harcourt, Sokoto, Zaria, Calabar, Benin, Jos and Ilorin. FLAG.—Three equal vertical bands, green, white and green. NATIONAL DAY.—October 1 (Republic Day).

GOVERNMENT

Following the military take-over of January 16, 1966, the Federal and Regional Constitutions were suspended, in relation to the offices of President, Prime Minister, Regional Governors and Regional Premiers, and Parliament and the Regional Legislatures were dissolved. The country was divided into 12 new States by decree in May, 1976, and this number was increased to 19 in January 1976. A Federal Military Government, made up of a Supreme Military Council, a Council of State composed of the State Military Governors, and a Federal Executive Council (the latter with some civilian members) perform the functions of the former Federal Government and Council of Ministers. A Military Governor administers each of the 19 States. *Head of State*, Lieut.-Gen. Olusegun Obasanjo.

NIGERIAN HIGH COMMISSION
Nigeria House, 9 Northumberland Avenue, W.C.2
[01-839 1244]
High Commissioner, His Excellency Sule Kolo.

BRITISH HIGH COMMISSION
Kajola House, 62-64 Campbell Street, Lagos.
High Commissioner, J. R. Williams, C.M.G. (*acting*).

British Council Representative in Nigeria, O. D. Elliott, Western House, 8-10 Broad Street, Lagos. Branch offices at Ibadan, Kano, Kaduna and Enugu.

Education.—There are six Universities, situated in Lagos, Ife, Zaria, Benin, Nsukka (with campuses at Nsukka, Calabar and Enugu) and Ibadan (with campuses at Ibadan and Jos). Four more universities are planned.

Railways.—The Nigerian railway system, which is controlled by the Nigerian Railway Corporation, is the most extensive in West Africa. There are 2,680 route miles of lines.

Civil Aviation.—Trunk route services operated by Nigerian and the principal international airlines bring Nigeria within less than 12 hours of the Western European capitals and South Africa. There are also services to other parts of Africa and to the United States. A network of internal air services connects the main centres. Comprehensive radio navigational aids are installed at Kano and Lagos airports, and basic radio naviga-

tional facilities are provided at the twelve other aerodromes in regular use. Several flying strips are also in use by light aircraft. There is a network of meteorological reporting stations.

Production and Industry.—Nigeria has a traditional but increasingly mixed economy: farming, forestry, and fishing activities contribute just under forty per cent. of the country's gross domestic product but manufacturing industry and, in particular, petroleum are gaining in importance. The export structure is diversified. Mineral oil is the principal source of export revenue, followed by cocoa and palm kernel products. Other crops include benniseed, capsicums, cassava, coffee, copra, cotton, ground nuts, guinea-corn, gum arabic, kola-nuts, maize, millet, piassava, rice, rubber, tobacco, and yams. There are important tin and coal-mining industries at Jós and Eriugu respectively. The coal is mainly used within the country. Nigeria is the principal source of supply of the world's requirements of columbite. Timber and hides and skins are other major exports. Some of the country's more important industrial installations include a steel-rolling mill, a tin smelter, a petroleum refinery, flour mills, a sugar factory, several cement plants and textile factories. Of growing importance is the local assembly of motor vehicles, bicycles, radio sets, fans and sewing machines. Other major manufactures include soap, cigarettes, beer, soft drinks, vegetable oils, canned food, confectionery, metal containers, plywood, footwear, tyres and tubes, paints, pharmaceuticals, plastic goods, glass containers, cement products, and roofing sheets.

Trade.—The principal imports are food, cotton yarn and thread, medicines and drugs, milk, motor vehicles and spares, general machinery and iron and steel bars, electrical goods, pipes and sheets. The principal export is crude oil.

	1973	1974
Total imports	MN1,224,800,000	1,715,400,000
Total exports	MN2,227,400,000	5,762,000,000
£1 = Naira 1·45.		

Trade with U.K.

	1973	1974
Imports from U.K.	£172,700,000	£222,400,000
Exports to U.K.	£206,800,000	£368,300,000

Papua New Guinea

Papua New Guinea extends from the equator to Cape Baganowa in the Louisiade Archipelago at 11 degrees 40 minutes south latitude and from the border with Irian Jaya to 160 degrees east longitude. The total area of Papua New Guinea is 178,260 square miles, of which approximately 152,420 are on the main island.

The main group of islands in Papua New Guinea is the Bismark Archipelago, portion of the Solomon Islands, the Trobriands, the D'Entrecasteaux Islands and the Louisiade Archipelago. The main islands of the Bismark Archipelago are New Britain, New Ireland and Manus. Bougainville is the largest of the Solomon Islands within Papua New Guinea.

Papua New Guinea lies wholly within the tropics between the continents of Asia and Australia and has a typically monsoonal climate. Atmospheric temperature and humidity are uniformly high throughout the year. The temperature may be slightly less in the dry areas around Port Moresby. The average rainfall is about 80 inches per year but there are wide variations—from 47 inches *per annum* at Port Moresby to 200 inches at Kikori in the Gulf of Papua.

Population.—At December 1974 the estimated total indigenous population of Papua New Guinea was 2,654,509. The indigenous inhabitants of the country comprise a great diversity of physical types and a large number of lingustic groups. The population increases by approximately 2·7 per cent. annually.

Capital.—Port Moresby. Estimated population 110,000. Other major towns are Lae, Rabaul, Madang, Wewak, Goroka and Mount Hagen.

Flag.—A rectangle divided diagonally from the top of the hoist to the bottom of the fly, the upper segment scarlet and containing a soaring yellow bird of paradise. The lower segment is black charged with five white five-pointed stars representing the Southern Cross.

Government.—New Guinea was sighted by Portuguese and Spanish navigators in the early sixteenth century. In 1884 Germany formally took possession of what came to be known as the Trust Territory of New Guinea. In 1914 the Territory was occupied by Australian troops and remained under military administration until 1921. In 1884, a British Protectorate was proclaimed over the southern coast of New Guinea and the islands adjacent thereto. British New Guinea, by which name the Protectorate was called, was annexed outright in 1888. In 1902 the Territory of British New Guinea was placed under the authority of the Commonwealth of Australia. In 1920 the League of Nations conferred on the Government of the Commonwealth of Australia a mandate for the government of the Territory of New Guinea.

New Guinea was administered under the Mandate until the Japanese invasion brought about the suspension of civil administration and the devastation of large areas of the country. Papua was administered under the Papua Act until the invasion by the Japanese in 1942 when the civil administration was suspended and an Australian Military Government established for the parts not occupied by the Japanese. With the surrender of the Japanese in 1945, civil administration of Papua New Guinea was progressively restored between October 1945 and June 1946, under the provisions of the Papua-New Guinea Provisional Administration Act 1945-1946.

The first House of Assembly opened in 1964 and had 64 members who included an elected indigenous majority and only ten nominated official members.

Elections held in April 1972 returned a Coalition Government to the House of Assembly. Elections are at present held every four years. The House of Assembly comprised 100 elected Members, 18 from Regional electorates, the remainder from Open electorates. After 1970 there was a gradual assumption of powers by the Papua New Guinea Government, culminating in formal self-government in December 1973. Final reserve powers held by Australia over defence and foreign relations were relinquished to Papua New Guinea in March 1975.

In June 1975, the Coalition Government obtained the approval of the House of Assembly for Papua New Guinea to achieve full independence on September 16, 1975.

Governor-General, Sir John Guise, G.C.M.G., K.B.E.

NATIONAL EXECUTIVE COUNCIL
(CABINET)

Prime Minister, and Acting Minister for National Resources, M. Somare.
Justice, assisting the Prime Minister, E. Olewale.
Provincial Affairs and Local Government, O. Tammur.
Primary Industry, B. Sali.
Culture, Recreation and Youth Development, M. Sasakila.
Foreign Affairs and Overseas Trade and Defence, Sir Maori Kiki, K.B.E. (*Deputy Prime Minister*).

Education, K. Kale.
Environment and Conservation, S. Tago.
Finance, J. Chan, C.B.E.
Health, Sir Paul Lapun, K.B.E.
Natural Resources, (vacant).
Labour, Commerce and Industry, G. Rea.
Police, J. Poe.
Transport and Works, B. Jephcott.
Posts and Telegraphs, K. Diria, O.B.E.
Housing and Supply, Y. Belo.
Public Utilities, D. Mola.
Corrective Institutions and Liquor Licensing, P. Lus, O.B.E.
Information and Broadcasting, Dr. R. Taureka.

BRITISH HIGH COMMISSION
P.O. Box 739, Port Moresby

High Commissioner, His Excellency George William Baker, O.B.E., V.R.D. (1971).

———

Communications.—The most important roads are those linking Lae with the populous and developing Highlands and with Wau, and those in the hinterlands of Port Moresby, Rabaul, Madang and Wewak.

Air Niugini (the National Airline) and Qantas operate regular air services from Australia to Port Moresby. Air Niugini also operates regular services to Manila (Philippines), Honiara (Solomon Islands) and Jayapura (Indonesia). Internal air services are operated by Air Niugini, Douglas Airways, Panga Airways and Talair.

Several shipping companies operate regular cargo and passenger services between Papua New Guinea and Australia, Europe, the Far East and U.S.A. Over 100 coastal vessels up to 1,000 tons provide cargo and limited passenger services between Papua New Guinea main ports, outports, plantations and missions.

Papua New Guinea is linked *via* the Seacom international cable to Australia, Guam, Hong Kong, Kota Kinabalu and Singapore. Further connections *via* the Compac cable are made to Canada, New Zealand and the United Kingdom. Direct dialling is available between the major towns and also with Australia. Telex services are also available.

Economy.—Papua New Guinea is essentially an agricultural nation and relies on primary industries for most of its overseas income. Before the mineral resources were tapped in any large quantities its wealth came from the primary crop products of coconuts, rubber, coffee, cocoa, tea and oil palm.

In the last few years the Bougainville copper project has become the country's major overseas money earner. Indications are that extensive mineral deposits exist in other parts of the country. Developers are investigating these and they could contribute significantly to the country's economic prosperity and development in the future.

Of the agricultural products, copra is the largest money earner but it has been losing ground in recent years. Coconuts grow in most coastal areas of Papua New Guinea and all exported nuts leave the country as copra or coconut oil.

Tea is a relative newcomer to Papua New Guinea. Experimental plantings were made in the early 1950s. The first commercial blocks were leased in 1965. Centrally placed processing factories on the large tea plantations provide facilities for smallholders in the vicinity.

A new crop for Papua New Guinea with considerable export potential is palm oil. Commercial plantings of the oil palm started in New Britain in 1967/68. As with tea, central processing factories on nucleus estates provide points of sale and processing facilities for smallholder blocks in their neighbourhood.

A beef cattle herd is being established in Papua

New Guinea and this is expected to reach 300,000 by 1980. The development of the livestock industry in Papua New Guinea is primarily directed towards the internal market. Small dairy herds exist in some main centres.

Secondary industry was originally orientated towards the processing of the local primary products. Emphasis has now swung to industries that service the expanding local market. Amongst those in successful operation are beer brewing, bottle and other packaging factories, paint manufacture, plywood, nails and other wire products, steel drums, clothing, match manufacture, louvred windows and doors, furniture, cement bricks and pipes and many others.

More and more Papua New Guinean entrepreneurs are starting their own businesses or are taking up equity in overseas operated companies. Papua New Guineans are increasingly entering the fields of retail trading, road transport and all aspects of the building industry.

OVERSEAS TRADE

	1973–74	1974–75
	Kina	Kina
Total Imports........	228,875,000	393,997,000*
Total Exports........	483,731,000	427,472,000*

Trade with U.K.

	1973	1974
Imports from U.K.....	£2,104,000	£3,124,000
Exports to U.K........	8,772,000	19,279,000

* provisional.

Currency.—Currency is the Kina, against which the £ Sterling floats. Exchange rate approximately K1·45 = £1 Sterling.

Sierra Leone

Area and Population, etc.—The peninsula of Sierra Leone, situated on the West Coast of Africa, was ceded to Great Britain in 1787 by the native chiefs to be used as an asylum for the many destitute negroes then in England. At a somewhat later date the Colony was used as a settlement for Africans from North America and the West Indies, and great numbers of Africans rescued from slave ships have from time to time been liberated and settled there. The total area of Sierra Leone is 27,925 sq. miles, and the total population (1974 Census) is 3,002,426. For administrative purposes, the interior portion of Sierra Leone is divided into 3 Provinces covering 12 Districts, each administered by a Resident Minister. The principal peoples are the Limbas and Korankos in the north, the Temnes in the centre, and the Mendis in the South.

CAPITAL.—Ψ Freetown (population 274,000). FLAG.—Three horizontal stripes of leaf green, white and cobalt blue. NATIONAL DAY.—April 19.

Government.—Sierra Leone became a fully independent state and a member of the British Commonwealth on April 27, 1961. There is a House of Representatives consisting of a Speaker and not fewer than 60 members, elected from constituencies established by an Electoral Commission.

After a period of martial law, and suspension of the Constitution, Parliament re-opened in June 1968.

A Bill instituting republican status for Sierra Leone and providing for the appointment of the *interim* Governor-General as its first President was approved on April 19, 1971, and the Prime Minister, Mr. (later Dr.) Siaka P. Stevius thereupon declared Sierra Leone a republic. He was elected President on April 20, 1971, and was sworn in for a four year term of office in April, 1976. A general election was held in May 1973. The Sierra Leone People's Party withdrew from the election and the All Peoples' Congress were unanimously returned. The number of seats actually held in Parliament at present (1975) is 85 elected members, 1 Paramount Chief from each of the 12 Districts, and 2 members elected by the President. There is provision for a third such elected member.

SIERRA LEONE HIGH COMMISSION
33 Portland Place, W.1.
[01–636 6483]
High Commissioner, His Excellency Ralph Emeric Kasope Taylor-Smith (1974)

BRITISH HIGH COMMISSION
Standard Bank Sierra Leone Building,
Wallace Johnson Street, Freetown.
High Commissioner, His Excellency David Arthur Roberts (1976).
British Council Representative, J. Mulholland, P.O. Box 124, Tower Hill, Freetown.

Communications.—The public railway has been phased out, but the Sierra Leone Development Company's railway runs for 52½ miles from the iron ore deposits at Marampa to the shipping port of Pepel. There are about 5,000 miles of road in the country, of which about 2,100 miles are surfaced.

The Freetown international airport is situated at Lungi, across the Sierra Leone River from Freetown. The main port is Freetown, which has one of the largest natural· harbours in the world, and where there is a deep water quay providing about six berths for medium sized ships. There are smaller ports at Pepel and Bonthe. The Sierra Leone Broadcasting Service operates a direct service. Broadcasts are made daily in several of the more important indigenous languages, in addition to English. There is also a television service.

Education.—There are 914 primary schools in Sierra Leone and 72 secondary schools. Technical education is provided in the two Government Technical Institutes, situated in Freetown and Kenema, in two Trade Centres and in the technical training establishments of the mining companies. Teacher training is carried out in two universities, one advanced college, five women's primary colleges and four Church training colleges in the Provinces, and in the Milton Margai Training College near Freetown. The University of Sierra Leone (1967), consists of Fourah Bay College (1960) and Njala University College (1964).

Production and Trade.—In the Western area, farming is largely confined to the production of cassava and garden crops, such as maize and vegetables, for local consumption. In the Provincial areas, the principal agricultural product is rice, which is the staple food of the country and export crops such as palm kernels, cocoa beans, coffee and ginger.

The economy depends largely on mineral exports (80 per cent), mainly diamonds and bauxite and, until 1975, iron ore. Exports of diamonds in 1975 totalled Le.67·3 million compared with Le.74·6 million in 1974.

Total exports in 1975 were valued at Le.116·8 million; imports Le.167·5 million.

	1974	1975
Imports from		
U.K.........	£18,700,000	£21,100,000(f.o.b.)
Exports to U.K.	£41,900,000	£32,600,000(c.i.f.)

Finance.—In August 1964, Sierra Leone adopted decimal currency. The basic unit is the Leone (worth 50p.). It is divided into 100 cents. Total revenue was estimated at Le.98·4 million in 1975/76; expenditure on ordinary budget Le.105·8 million. Development expenditure was estimated at Le.63·6 million.

Singapore

The Republic of Singapore consists of the island of Singapore and 54 smaller islands, covering a total area of 225·6 square miles. Singapore Island is 26 miles long and 14 miles in breadth and is situated just north of the Equator off the southern extremity of the Malay Peninsula, from which it is separated by the Straits of Johore. A causeway, carrying a road and railway, crosses the three-quarters of a mile to the mainland. The highest point of the island is 581 feet above sea level. *Climate.*—The climate is hot and humid and there are no clearly defined seasons. Rainfall averages 96 inches a year and temperature ranges from 24°–31° C (76°–87°F.). *Population.*—Estimated at 2,249,000 on June 30, 1975, the population is multi-racial with a preponderance of Chinese. The racial groups were estimated in 1975 to be divided as follows: Chinese—1,712,800; Malays—338,000; Indians, Pakistanis and Ceylonese—155,200; others (Europeans, Eurasians etc.)—43,100. At least 6 Chinese dialects are used and Malay, Mandarin, Tamil and English are the official languages. FLAG.—Horizontal bands of red over white; crescent with five five-point stars on red band near staff. NATIONAL DAY.—August 9.

Government.—Singapore, where Sir Stamford Raffles had first established a trading post under the East India Company in 1819, was incorporated with Penang and Malacca to form the Straits Settlements in 1826. The Straits Settlements became a Crown Colony in 1867. Singapore fell into Japanese hands in 1942 and civil government was not restored until 1946, when it became a separate colony. Internal self-government and the title " State of Singapore " were introduced in 1959. Singapore became a state of Malaysia when the Federation was enlarged in September, 1963, but left Malaysia and became an independent sovereign state within the Commonwealth on August 9, 1965. Singapore adopted a Republican constitution from that date, the Yang di-Pertuan Negara being re-styled President. There is a Cabinet collectively responsible to a fully-elected Parliament of 65 members.

HEAD OF STATE

President, Benjamin Henry Sheares, G.C.B., *assumed office as President,* Jan. 2, 1971 *(re-elected for second 4-year term from* Jan. 1, 1975).

CABINET

Prime Minister, Lee Kuan Yew, G.C.M.G., C.H.
Deputy Prime Minister and Minister of Defence, Dr. Goh Keng Swee.
Minister for Science and Technology, Dr. Lee Chiaw Meng.
Finance, Hon Sui Sen.
Foreign Affairs, S. Rajaratnam.
Home Affairs and Education, Chua Sian Chin.
National Development and Communications, Lim Kim San.
Culture, Jek Yeun Thong.
Social Affairs, Inche Othman bin Wok.
Law and Environment, E. W. Barker.
Health, Dr. Toh Chin Chye.
Labour, Ong Pang Boon.

Speaker of Parliament, Dr. Yeoh Ghim Seng.

SINGAPORE HIGH COMMISSION
2 Wilton Crescent, S.W.1
[01–235 8315]
High Commissioner, (vacant)

BRITISH HIGH COMMISSION
Tanglin Circus, Singapore 10
High Commissioner, His Excellency John Peter Tripp, C.M.G. (1974)
British Council Representative, J. P. Harmiman, 310 Cathay Building, Mount Sophia, Singapore 9.

Communications.—Singapore is one of the largest seaports in the world, with deep water wharves and ship repairing facilities. Ships also anchor in the roads, unloading into lighters. 52,100,000 tons of cargo were handled in 1975. The International Airport at Paya Lebar, 7½ miles from the centre of the city, has a runway 13,350 feet long. There are 28 miles of railway connected to the Malaysian rail system by the causeway across the Straits of Johore, and 1,337 miles of roads, 1,026 miles of which are metalled roads maintained by the Government. There are both wireless and wired broadcasting services carrying commercial advertising. Television was introduced in 1963 and a colour service on two channels in 1974.

Production, etc.—Historically Singapore's economy was largely based on the sale and distribution of raw materials from surrounding countries and on entre-pot trade in finished products. In the last decade, however, new manufacturing industries have been introduced, including ship building and repairing, iron and steel, textiles, footwear, wood products, micro-electronics, scientific instruments, detergents, confectionery, pharmaceuticals, petroleum products, sanitary-ware, building materials, domestic electrical appliances, plastic articles, transport equipment, etc. Singapore has also become a financial centre with over seventy banks established in the Republic.

Projects now being undertaken include the reclamation of 1,850 acres of land for a new International Airport at Changi for the 1980's; further reclamation of marshy land at Jurong Town where industrial sites and housing development already cover over 12,000 acres; extension of other industrial estates; the building of 148,000 low-cost housing units by the Housing & Development Board by 1979; a new drainage system throughout the island; and the development of additional water-supply catchments.

FINANCE

	1975–6	1976–7*
Revenue	S$2,647,461,000	S$3,107,570,000
Estimated	2,646,319,000	3,103,797,000

*Estimated.

Currency.—On June 12, 1967, the Singapore Currency Board began issuing its own currency, the $ *Singapore* (of 100 *cents*) approximately equivalent (June 1976) to 23p sterling. The S$ is freely interchangeable with the *$Brunei* (also issued on June 12, 1967). An interchangeability agreement with Malaysia was cancelled on May 8, 1973.

TRADE

	1974	1975
Total imports.	S$20,405,000,000	S$19,270,000,000
Total exports.	14,155,000,000	12,758,000,000

Trade with U.K.

	1974	1975
Imports from U.K.	£153,533,000	£157,096,000
Exports to U.K.	74,758,000	64,558,000

Sri Lanka

AREA AND POPULATION

Sri Lanka (formerly Ceylon) is an island in the Indian Ocean, off the southern tip of the peninsula of India and separated from it by a narrow strip of shallow water, the Palk Strait. Situated between 5° 55′–9° 50′ N. latitude and 79° 42′–81° 52′ E. longitude, it has an area of 25,332 square miles, including 33 square miles of inland water. Its greatest length is from north to south, 270 miles; and its greatest width 140 miles, no point in Sri Lanka being more than 80 miles from the sea.

At the Census of 1971, the population was 12,747,755.

Races and Religions

The races of Sri Lanka are low-country Sinhalese, Kandyan Sinhalese, Ceylon Tamils, Indian Tamils, Ceylon Moors, Indian Moors, Burghers and Eurasians, Malays and Veddahs. Generally Sinhalese who trace their descent to a low-country district are classified as low-country Sinhalese, others as Kandyan Sinhalese. The Western and Southern Provinces, the Southern (Chilaw) District and the Western parts of Puttalam District are low-country areas; the Central and North Central Provinces, Uva, Sabaragamuwa and Kurunegala are regarded as Kandyan districts. At the 1971 Census 42.8 per cent. of the population were low-country Sinhalese, 29.1 per cent. Kandyan Sinhalese. The religion of the great majority of inhabitants is Buddhism, introduced from India, according to ancient Sinhalese chronicles, in 247 B.C. Next to Buddhism, Hinduism has a large following.

PHYSIOGRAPHY

Sri Lanka is a compact area, except for the island of Mannar and an almost detached portion in the north, the Jaffna Peninsula and its satellite islands of Delft, Kayts, etc. The relief of the island includes a mountainous area in the south-central region of 3,000 to 7,000 feet above sea level, surrounded by an upland belt of about 1,000 to 3,000 feet and a narrow coastal plain broadening out to a vast tract in the north. The coastal plain continues for a distance out to sea as a continental shelf and a coral reef, for the most part submerged, lies close to the coast. On the Central Ridge of the hill country are some of the highest peaks in Sri Lanka, Pidurutalagala (8,281 ft.), Kirigalpotta (7,857 ft.) and Totapolakanda (7,741 ft.) and the high plains Nuwara Eliya (over 6,000 ft.), Elk Plains (6,000 ft.) and Horton Plains (over 7,000 ft.) The other principal peaks are Adam's Peak (7,360 ft.), Namunukula (6,679 ft.), Knuckles (6,112 ft.) and Haycock (2,167 ft.). The Peninsula of Jaffna and the island of Mannar are featureless level stretches.

The Mahaveli-ganga, 208 miles long, is the largest river of Sri Lanka. Rising on the western side of the central hilly ridge, it flows north and east to empty into the Koddiyar Bay on the east coast. Other rivers are the Kelaniganga (90 miles), Aruvi-aru (104), Kala-oya (92), Yam-oya (88) and Deduru-oya (88). Waterfalls girdle the central mountainous massif and offer some of the best scenic features in the island; Dunhinda (Badulla), Diyaluma (Koslanda), Elgin (Hatton Plateau) and Perawella are among the outstanding falls. Forests, jungle and scrub cover the greater part of the island, often being intermingled. The forests, of varying species, extend from fairly near the coast right into the hill country. In areas over 2,000 feet above sea level grasslands (*patanas* or *talawas*) are found. Their total area is some 250 square miles, principally in the Province of Uva.

Climate.—The climate of Sri Lanka is warm throughout the year, with a high relative humidity. Temperatures average 80° F. during the year in the lowlands, falling off in the hills to 60° F. at elevations over 6,000 ft. Day humidity is over 70 per cent. and night humidity over 85 per cent. Temperature ranges vary little between wet and dry seasons. In the hilly areas morning mists sometimes occur. Traces of ground frost appear occasionally at night, at the highest levels, and disappear at sunrise Thunderstorms occasionally give hail, but snow is completely absent. Rainfall is generally heavy, with marked regional variations; the heaviest falls (200–250 inches) are recorded on the south-west slopes of the central hills. Some depressional or cyclonic activity occurs generally during October to December.

GOVERNMENT

Early in the sixteenth century the Portuguese landed in Ceylon and founded settlements, eventually conquering much of the country. Portuguese rule in Ceylon lasted 150 years during which the Roman Catholic religion was established among the Sinhalese inhabitants and to some extent Portuguese modes of living adopted. In 1658, following a twenty-year period of decline, Portuguese rule gave place to that of the Dutch East India Company which was to exploit Ceylon with varying fortunes until 1796.

The Maritime Provinces of Ceylon were ceded by the Dutch to the British on February 16, 1798, becoming a British Crown Colony in 1802 under the terms of the Treaty of Amiens. With the annexation of the Kingdom of Kandy in 1815, all Ceylon came under British rule.

On February 4, 1948, Ceylon became a self-governing state and a member of the British Commonwealth of Nations under the *Ceylon Independence Act* 1947. Under this Act the Parliament of Ceylon consisted of (a) The Queen (represented by the Governor-General) and (b) two houses, namely, the Senate and the House of Representatives. The Executive consisted of the Prime Minister and a Cabinet chosen from the party which had the majority in the House of Representatives. The House of Representatives constituted itself as the constituent Assembly in July, 1970, to draft a republican Constitution for Ceylon. Accordingly, a new republican Constitution was adopted on May 22, 1972, and the country was renamed the Republic of Sri Lanka (meaning 'Resplendent Island'). The new republic continues to be in the Commonwealth.

CAPITAL.— Ψ Colombo, population (1971 Census), 563,705. Other principal towns are Ψ Jaffna (106,856), Kandy (91,942), Ψ Galle (71,060), Ψ Negombo (55,722) and Ψ Trincomalee (38,800).

REPUBLIC DAY.—May 22.

FLAG.—Yellow lion of Kandy on a maroon ground; Sinhalese pinnacle at the corners; yellow border; two vertical stripes of green and saffron at the staff side.

President, WILLIAM GOPALLAWA, *b.* 1897.

CABINET

Prime Minister and Minister of Defence and Foreign Affairs, Planning and Economic Affairs and Plan Implementation, Mrs. Sirimavo Bandaranaike.

Irrigation, Power and Highways, Maitripala Senana-yake.

Trade, Public Administration and Home Affairs, T. B. Illangaratne.

Education, Dr. Badiudin Mahmud.

Shipping, Aviation and Tourism, P. B. G. Kalugalle.

Labour, M. P. De Z. Siriwardene.

Finance and Justice, Felix Dias Bandaranaike.

Industries and Scientific Affairs, T. B. Subasinghe.

Plantation Industries, Ratnasiri Wickremanayake.

Agriculture and Lands, Hector Kobbekaduwa.

Housing and Construction, Pieter G. B. Keuneman.

Posts and Telecommunications, Chelliah Kumara-suriar.

Information and Broadcasting, R. S. Perera.

Cultural Affairs, T. B. Tennekoon.

Social Services, S. S. Kulatilake.

Parliamentary Affairs, Sport and Transport, K. B. Ratnayake.

Local Government, W. P. G. Ariyadasa.

Food, Co-operatives and Small Industries, S. K. K. Suriarachchi.

SRI LANKA HIGH COMMISSION
13 Hyde Park Gardens, W.2
[01–262 1841]

High Commissioner, His Excellency Vernon L. B. Mendis (1975).

BRITISH HIGH COMMISSION
Galle Road, Kollupitiya (P.O. Box 1433),
Colombo 3

High Commissioner, His Excellency David Pascoe Aiers, C.M.G.

British Council Representative, A. F. Keith, 190 Galle Road, Colombo 3.

THE LEGISLATURE

Under the Republican constitution which came into operation on May 22, 1972, the supreme legis-lative power is vested in the National State As-sembly, a unicameral legislative body.

THE JUDICATURE

The Judicial System includes a Supreme Court of Appeal, Supreme Court, District Courts, Magistrates' Courts, Courts of Requests and Rural Courts. Trial by jury obtains in the Supreme Court.

PRODUCTION

Agriculture.—The staple products of the island are agricultural, including paddy, tea, rubber and coconuts.

Industry.—Factories are established for the manu-facture or processing of ceramic ware, vegetable oils and by-products, paper, tanning and leather goods, plywood, cement, chemicals, sugar, salt, textiles, ilmenite, tiles, tyres, fertilizers and hard-ware and there is a petroleum refinery.

Trade with U.K.

	1974	1975
Imports from U.K....	£10,042,000	£15,882,000
Exports to U.K......	30,436,000	27,178,000

COMMUNICATIONS

There are 11,700 miles of motorable roads in Sri Lanka. A commercial wireless telegraph station has a range of 500 miles by day and about 1,000 to 2,000 miles by night and handles ship-to-shore traffic.

On May 6, 1976, Sri Lanka inaugurated a satellite earth station at Padukka, in south-west Sri Lanka. Constructed with assistance from the Asian De-velopment Bank, the earth satellite station provides instant telecommunication links via satellite with any part of the globe.

Air Ceylon currently operates a Trident 1 air-craft on twice-weekly flights to Kuala Lumpur, Singapore, Bangkok and Bombay; thrice weekly to Madras and once a week to Sharjah. A DC-8 is operated twice weekly on the Colombo, Karachi, Paris, London route; and an Avro HS 748 three times a week to Male and Trichinopoly.

Swaziland

Swaziland is the smallest of the former three High Commission Territories in Southern Africa. Geo-graphically and climatically, it is divisible into four physiographic provinces; the broken mountainous Highveld of the west, adjacent to the Drakensberg, with altitudes averaging over 4,000 ft., the Middleveld which is mostly mixed farming country, about 2,000 ft. lower and the Lowveld, a hot scrubland region, bounded on the east by the Lubombo mountains, with an average altitude of 1,500 ft. The Lubombo mountains form the fourth physiographic province. Four rivers, the Komati, Usutu, Mbuluzi and Ing-wavuma, flow from west to east, cutting their way through the Lubombo mountains to the Indian Ocean. The exploitation of these rivers is particularly important to the agricultural development of the middle and bush veld, where irrigation projects are giving the scenery a different aspect. The total area is 6,704 sq. miles and the population (estimated, 1976), 493,728.

CAPITAL.—Mbabane (population, estimated, 1975, 21,500), the headquarters of the Government, is situated on the hills at an altitude of 3,800 ft. Other main townships are: Manzini (population 18,000), Hlatikulu (2,000), Nhlangano (3,500), Pigg's Peak (3,000), Havelock (5,500), Big Bend (4,000) and Mhlume (3,000). FLAG.—Five horizontal bands, crimson, bearing shield and spears device, bordered by narrow yellow bands; blue bands at top and foot.

Government.—The Kingdom of Swaziland came into being on April 25, 1967, under a new internal self-government constitution and became an independent kingdom in membership of the Commonwealth on September 6, 1968. On April 12, 1973, the King, in response to a motion passed by both Houses of Parlia-ment, repealed the Parliamentary Constitution of 1968 and assumed supreme legislative, executive and judicial power, to be exercised in collaboration with a Council constituted by his Cabinet Ministers.

King of Swaziland, His Majesty Sobhuza II, K.B.E.

Prime Minister and Minister of Foreign Affairs, Colonel Mapheru Dlamini.

SWAZILAND HIGH COMMISSION
58 Pont Street, S.W.1.
[01–589 5447]

High Commissioner, His Excellency J. M. Fakudze (1973).

BRITISH HIGH COMMISSION
Mbabane

High Commissioner, His Excellency John Edwin Alfred Miles, O.B.E.

Education.—In 1974 the primary school enrolment was 86,110; secondary schools, 14,301.

Communications.—Swaziland's first railway was completed in 1964. It is about 140 miles long,

starting at Ngwenya, 13 miles north-west of Mbabane, and connecting at the Mozambique frontier with an extension to the existing line between Lourenco Marques and Goba. Principal export traffic on the railway is the iron ore mined at Bomvu Ridge, near Ngwenya, by the Swaziland Iron Ore Development Company. A large part of the country's passenger and goods traffic is carried by privately-owned motor transport services. Besides these, the South African Railways Road Motor Services maintain regular goods and passenger services between Mbabane and Manzini and the main railheads in South Africa which serve Swaziland—Breyten, Piet Retief, Komatipoort, Hectorspruit and Golela. There are post offices, telegraph and telephone offices at all the chief centres.

Production.—Exports in 1974 amounted to E.120,000,000 of which iron ore was worth E.12,289,000; sugar E.46,300,000; unbleached wood pulp E.31,328,400; wood and wood products E.5,433,500; asbestos E.5,682,200; citrus fruit E.4,516,700; live animals E.1,851,600; meat and meat products E.2,691,200; hides and skins E.426,400.

Finance.—Government revenue for 1974–75 was estimated at E.32,807,000 and expenditure at E.34,877,000. Of a capital budget of E.16,026,000, E.3,818,000 was estimated aid funds from the United Kingdom.

Currency.—The unit of currency is the Lilangeni (plural, Emalangeni). This currency was introduced on Sept. 6, 1974. Under the Currency Order of 1974 the value of one Lilangeni is equal to one South African Rand.

Trade with U.K.

	1973	1974
Imports from U.K...	£150,721	£511,000
Exports to U.K.....	£12,961,645	£16,119,100

Tanzania

Tanganyika, the mainland part of the United Republic of Tanzania (Tanganyika and Zanzibar) occupies the east-central portion of the African continent, between 1°–11° 45′ S. lat. and 29° 20′–40° 38′ E. long. It is bounded on the N. by Kenya and Uganda; on the S.W. by Lake Malawi, Malawi and Zambia; on the S. by Mozambique; on the W. it is bounded by Rwanda, Burundi and Zaire; on the E. the boundary is the Indian Ocean. Tanganyika has a coastline of about 500 miles and an area of 362,820 sq. miles (including 20,650 sq. miles of water). The greater part of the country is occupied by the Central African plateau from which rise, among others, Mt. Kilimanjaro, the highest point on the continent of Africa (19,340 ft.) and Mt. Meru (14,979 ft.). The Serengeti National Park, which covers an area of 6,000 sq. miles in the Arusha, Mwanza and Mara Regions, is famous for its variety and number of species of game.

The African population consists mostly of tribes of mixed Bantu race. The total population of Tanzania at the Census held in August, 1967, was 12,311,991 (estimated, July, 1973, 13,968,000); Africans form a very large majority, while the Europeans, the Asians, and other non-Africans form a small minority. Annual average population growth is 2·7 per cent. The total population of Zanzibar at the 1967 census was 354,815 (estimated, 1973, 403,000). Swahili is the national and official language. English is the second official language, both for educational and government purposes.

Zanzibar.—Formerly ruled by the Sultan of Zanzibar, and a British Protectorate until Dec. 10, 1963. Zanzibar consists of the islands of Zanzibar and Pemba. It has a total area of approximately 1,000 sq. miles The islands produce a large part of the world's supply of cloves and clove oil, and coconuts, coconut oil and copra are also produced.

Zanzibar became internally self-governing on June 24, 1963, and fully independent on Dec. 10, 1963. The revolutionary Afro-Shirazi party seized power on Jan. 12, 1964, and the Sultan was forced to leave the country. Later Zanzibar united with Tanganyika (*see* below).

CAPITAL.—ΨDar es Salaam (population about 300,000). Other towns are ΨTanga (61,061); Mwanza (34,861); Arusha (32,452); Moshi (26,853); Morogoro (25,262); Dodoma (23,559); Iringa (21,746); Tabora (20,994) and Mtwara (20,396). In Zanzibar, the chief town and seaport of that name (population, 68,490) provides facilities for shipping and trade. The principal international airport is Dar es Salaam. Other airports include Zanzibar, Arusha, Mwanza and Tanga. A new international airport has been opened at Kilimanjaro between Arusha and Moshi to take "Jumbo Jets".

FLAG.—Green (above) and blue; divided by diagonal black stripe bordered by gold, running from bottom (next staff) to top (in fly). NATIONAL DAY.—December 9 (anniversary of independence).

President of the United Republic, Julius Kambarage Nyerere, *b.* 1922; *elected* Nov. 1962; *took office* Dec. 9, 1962; *re-elected* Sept., 1965, Nov., 1970 and Oct., 1975.

Vice Presidents, Aboud Jumbe; R. M. Kawawa (also Prime Minister).

GOVERNMENT

Following a constitutional conference held in Dar es Salaam in March, 1961, Tanganyika became an independent state and a member of the British Commonwealth on December 9, 1961.

Tanganyika became a Republic, within the Commonwealth, on December 9, 1962, with an executive President, elected by universal suffrage, who is both the Head of State and Head of the Government. A presidential election will be held whenever Parliament is dissolved, and the presidency is closely linked with the official party, the Tanganyika African National Union (TANU), since Tanzania is a one-party state.

On April 25, 1964, following a Parliamentary ratification of an agreement signed by the President of the Republic of Tanganyika and the President of the People's Republic of Zanzibar and Pemba, Tanganyika united with Zanzibar to form a new sovereign state. By this agreement, the President of the United Republic is Julius K. Nyerere; the First Vice-President is Aboud Jumbe (also President of Zanzibar), and the Second Vice-President is Rashidi Mfaume Kawawa (of Tanganyika) who is also Prime Minister and the leader of the Government business in the National Assembly of the United Republic. The Vice-Presidents and Ministers form the Cabinet of the Union Government, which is presided over by the President. There are 4 Zanzibar Ministers and 2 Junior Ministers in the Union Government, and 35 others (15 backbenchers nominated from Zanzibar, 20 backbenchers nominated from Members of the Revolutionary Council) and 5 Zanzibar Regional Commissioners who are *ex officio* M.P.s in the National Assembly of the United Republic.

Zanzibar has its own legislature which legislates for matters which are not under the Union Govern-

ment, *e.g.* education, agriculture, health and community development.

CABINET

Minister for Foreign Affairs, Ibrahim M. Kaduma.
Agriculture, John Malecela.
Commerce, A. M. Rulegura.
Works, L. A. Sazia.
Finance and Planning, A. H. Jamal.
Health, Dr. Leader Stirling.
Home Affairs, Ali Hassan Mwinyi.
Natural Resources and Tourism, S. O. Saibul.
Information and Broadcasting, D. N. Mwakawago.
Water, Energy and Minerals, Dr. W. K. Chagulo.
Lands, Housing and Urban Development, Mrs. T. Siwale.
National Education, I. Elinewinga.
Defence and National Service, E. M. Sokoine.
Labour and Social Welfare, Crispin Tungaraza.
Communications and Transport, Alfred C. Tandau.
National Culture and Youth, Mrisho Sarakikya.
Justice, Miss Julie Manning.
Industries, C. D. Msuya.
Manpower Development, N. A. Kuhanga.
Ministers of State, P. Siyovelwa; H. N. Moyo; Hasnu Makame; H. R. Shekilangu.

Chief Justice, Hon. A. Saidi.

TANZANIA HIGH COMMISSION
43 Hertford Street, W.1
[01-499 8951]
High Commissioner, His Excellency Amon James Nsekela (1974)

BRITISH HIGH COMMISSION
Dar es Salaam.
High Commissioner, His Excellency Mervyn Brown,
C.M.G., O.B.E.........................£9,228

British Council Representative, G. W. Shaw.

EDUCATION

Education, almost entirely under state control, is characterised by official insistence that education must serve the aims of overall Government policy and planning. All Tanzanian Secondary Schools are expected to include practical subjects in the basic course. All who receive secondary (or equivalent) education are called up for a period of National Service. The school system is administered in Swahili and the intention is for the national language to become the medium at all levels. For higher education most Tanzanian students go to the University of Dar es Salaam, other East African universities, or to Universities and Colleges outside East Africa, mainly in Britain.

PRODUCTION AND TRADE

The economy is based mainly on the production and export of primary produce and the growing of foodstuffs for local consumption. The chief commercial crops are sisal, cotton, coffee, cashew nuts and oilseeds. The most important minerals are diamonds. Hides and skins are another valuable export. Industry is at present largely concerned with the processing of raw material for either export or local consumption. There is also a healthy growth of secondary manufacturing industries, including factories for the manufacture of leather and rubber footwear, knitwear, razor blades, cigarettes and textiles, and a wheat flour mill.

TRADE WITH U.K.

	1973	1974
Imports from U.K..	£29,129,000	£41,540,000
Exports to U.K....	49,105,000	31,865,000

Trinidad and Tobago

AREA AND POPULATION

Trinidad, the most southerly of the West Indian Islands, lies close to the north coast of the continent of S. America, the nearest point of Venezuela being 7 miles distant. The island is situated between 10° 3'–10° 50' N. lat. and 60° 55'–61° 56' W. long., and is about 50 miles in length by 37 in width, with an area of 1,864 sq. miles. *Population.*—Of the population (estimated at 1,027,900 in Dec. 1974), 43 per cent. are African, 36 per cent East Indian, 2 per cent. European, 1 per cent. Chinese, and the rest mixed.

The island was discovered by Colombus in 1498, was colonized in 1532 by the Spaniards, capitulated to the British under Abercromby in 1797, and was ceded to Britain under the Treaty of Amiens (March 25, 1802). Two mountain systems, the Northern and Southern Ranges, stretch across almost its entire width and a third, the Central Range lies somewhat diagonally across its middle portion; otherwise the island is mostly flat. The highest peaks are in the Northern Range (Aripo 3,085 ft., El Tucuche 3,072 ft.). The climate is tropical with temperatures ranging from 82° F. by day to 74° F. by night and a rainfall averaging 82·7 inches a year. There is a well-marked dry season from January to May and a wet season from June to December. The nights are invariably cool. The main tourist season is from December to April.

Tobago lies between 11° 9' and 11° 21' N. lat. and between 60° 30' and 60° 50' W. long., about 75 miles south-east of Grenada, 19 miles north-east of Trinidad, and 120 miles S.W. of Barbados. It was ceded to the British Crown in 1814 and amalgamated with Trinidad in 1888. The island is 26 miles long, and 7½ wide, and has an area of 116 sq miles. The population was 33,333 in the 1961 census and was estimated at 33,950 in Dec. 1974. It is one of the healthiest of the West Indies and a popular tourist resort. The main town is Ψ Scarborough.

Other Islands.—Corozal Point and Icacos Point, the N.W. and S.W. extremities of Trinidad, enclose the Gulf of Paria, and west of Corozal Point lie several islands, of which Chacachacare, Huevos, Monos and Gaspar Grande are the most important.

CAPITAL.—Ψ Port of Spain (population 100,000), one of the finest towns in the West Indies, with sewerage, electric lighting, omnibus and telephone services. Other towns of importance are Ψ San Fernando (population, 42,000★), and about 33 miles south of the capital, and Arima (population, 13,000★).

FLAG.—Black diagonal stripe bordered with white stripes, running from top by staff, all on a red field,
NATIONAL DAY.—August 31 (Independence Day).
★ Estimated

GOVERNMENT

The Territory of Trinidad and Tobago became an independent state and a member of the British Commonwealth on August 31, 1962, under the Trinidad and Tobago Independence Act, 1962. There is a Parliament consisting of a Senate and a

House of Representatives with an elected Speaker and 36 members. The Senate has 24 members of whom 13 are appointed on the advice of the Prime Minister, 4 on the advice of the Leader of the Opposition and 7 on the advice of the Prime Minister after consultation with religious, economic and

social organizations. Legislation was passed in April 1976 under which Trinidad and Tobago would become a Republic with a President as Head of State. General Elections under the new Constitution were due to take place before Sept. 14, 1976.

Governor-General, His Excellency Sir Ellis Emmanuel Innocent Clarke, G.C.M.G. (1973).

CABINET

Prime Minister and Minister of Finance, Rt. Hon. E. E. Williams, C.H., D.Phil.
Public Utilities, Hon. Shamshuddinq Mohammed.
Agriculture, Lands and Fisheries, Hon. O. R. Padmore.
National Security, Hon. V. L. Campbell.
Health and Local Government, Hon. Kamaluddin Mohammed.
Labour, Social Security and Co-operatives, Hon. B. M. Barrow.
Attorney-General and Legal Affairs, Hon. B. L. B. Pitt.
Education and Culture, Hon. G. M. Chambers.
Tobago Affairs, Hon. W. Winchester.
Industry and Commerce and Petroleum, Hon. E. E. Mahabir.
External Affairs, Dr. Hon. C. Joseph.
Ministers in the Ministry of Finance, Hon. L. M. Robinson (*Planning and Development*); Senator Hon. F. C. Prevatt (*Public Investment*); Hon. C. Gomes (*Pensions and Gratuities*).

President of the Senate, Dr. the Hon. W. Ali.
Speaker of the House of Representatives, Hon. C. A. Thomasos.

TRINIDAD AND TOBAGO HIGH COMMISSION
42 Belgrave Square, S.W.1
[01–245 9351]
High Commissioner, His Excellency Dr. Patrick Vincent Joseph Solomon (1971).
Deputy High Commissioner, L. E. Williams.
Counsellors, R. K. Ablack; B. Rambissoon.
BRITISH HIGH COMMISSION
Port of Spain
High Commissioner, His Excellency Christopher Ewart Diggines, C.M.G. (1973) £8,425

Education.—The system of education has been reformed to co-ordinate more closely the nursery, primary, junior secondary, senior secondary and university stages. The system provides for education of the pupils from 4–5 in nursery schools, 5–11 (or 15) in primary schools. Admission to secondary schools (11–18) is by common entrance examination at 11 years. A Primary School leaving Examination can be taken at 15. Junior secondary schools catering for the 11–14 group are being introduced to ease the shortage of places at secondary level. A General Certificate of Education giving admission to the University of the West Indies is taken in senior secondary schools. The Government Polytechnic Institute was established in 1959. There are two Technical Institutes, a government Vocational Centre and six Teacher Training Colleges. One of three branches of the University of the West Indies is ten miles from Port of Spain, at St. Augustine.

Communications.—There are some 4,000 miles of all-weather roads. The only general cargo port is Port of Spain but there are specialized port facilities elsewhere for landing crude oil, loading refinery products and sugar and for landing, storing and trans-shipping bauxite and cement. Regular shipping services call at Port of Spain, which is also a port for the many small inter-island craft. International scheduled airlines, including the national airline, B.W.I.A., use Piarco International Airport outside Port of Spain. A local airline flies between Piarco and Crown Point Airport in Tobago.

There are two commercial broadcasting stations, one rediffusion station and one commercial television station. There is an internal telephone system and good external telephone and telegraph connections.

Production.—Oil is extracted from land and sea wells for refining locally and large quantities of crude oil are also imported. The most important agricultural crop is sugar, but there is a growing diversification into other crops for local use and export. There is considerable industrialization, which already includes the manufacture of cement, chemicals, tyres, clothing, soap, furniture and foodstuffs.

Total exports in 1975 amounted to *T T*$3,847 million, of which *T T*$3,345 million was on account of exports of crude oil and petroleum products. Other main exports were sugar and sugar preparations, ammonium compounds, tar oils, coffee and cocoa beans and fertilizers. Total imports in 1975 were *T T*$3,232 million, of which *T T*$1,629 million was accounted for by imports of crude oil.

FINANCE

The following statistics show figures in *T T*$ millions.

	1975	1976
Revenue	1,212	2,104
Expenditure	1,294	2,104
Gross public debt	627	..

TRADE

	1974	1975
Imports	3,777	3,232
Exports	4,166	3,847
	1974	1975
Imports from U.K.	£37,169,000	£52,307,000
Exports to U.K.	15,312,000	34,844,000

Uganda

Situated in Eastern Africa, Uganda is flanked by Zaire, the Sudan, Kenya and on the south by Tanzania and Rwanda. Large parts of Lake Victoria, Idi Amin Dada and Mobutu Sese Seko are within its boundaries, as are Lakes Kyoga and Salisbury and the course of the River Nile from its outlet from Lake Victoria to the Sudan frontier post at Nimule. Despite its tropical location, Uganda's climate is tempered by its situation some 3,000 ft. above sea level, and well over that altitude in the highlands of the Western and Eastern Regions. Temperatures seldom rise above 85° F. (29° C.) or fall below 60°F. (15° C.). The rainfall averages about 50 inches a year which means that the country is covered in a lush green cloak for most of the year. Uganda has three National Parks with a wide variety of wildlife and flora.

Area and Population.—Uganda has an area of 91,000 sq. mile (water and swamp 16,400 sq. miles) and population (estimated, 1974) of 11,172,000. The official language of Uganda is Swahili, although English is commonly spoken and is used in commercial circles. The main local vernaculars are of Bantu, Luo and Hamitic origins. Ki-Swahili is generally understood in trading centres. CAPITAL.—Kampala (population of Greater Kampala, 331,900). FLAG.—Six horizontal stripes of black, yellow and red (repeated) with a crested emblem on a white orb in the centre. NATIONAL DAY.—October 9 (Independence Day).

Government.—Uganda became an independent state and a member of the Commonwealth on October 9, 1962, after some 70 years of British rule. A Republic was instituted on September 8, 1967, under an executive President, assisted by a Cabinet of Ministers.

Early on Jan. 25, 1971, while the President, A. Milton Obote, was in Singapore at the 1971 Commonwealth Prime Ministers' Meeting, the Uganda Army, with the co-operation of the police forces, assumed control of the country. All political activity in Uganda was suspended. On Jan. 26, 1971, Maj.-Gen. Idi Amin, the Army Commander, proclaimed himself Head of State, having previously announced that there would be an early return to civilian rule " after free and fair general elections ". There was some short-lived military opposition in northern parts of Uganda, by troops loyal to Dr. Obote. On Feb. 2, Gen. Amin announced the suspension of certain parts of the Constitution, dissolution of Parliament and the formation of a Defence Council under his own Chairmanship.

President and Commander in Chief of the Armed Forces and Minister of Defence, Field-Marshal Al-Hajji Idi Amin Dada, *born* 1926, *assumed office* Jan. 26,1971.

Diplomatic relations with Uganda were suspended by the United Kingdom in the summer of 1976.

Education.—Education is a joint undertaking by the Government, Local Authorities and, to some extent, Voluntary Agencies. The education system is divided into three distinct sectors—Primary, Secondary and Post-Secondary. The Primary course covers the first seven years of schooling. There were an estimated 786,899 pupils in grant-aided Primary Schools in 1972. Education at secondary level falls into four categories—Secondary schools, which are of the Grammar type of school with a course extending over six years to Higher School Certificate; Technical Schools;

Farm Schools; and Primary Teacher Training Colleges. Further education is provided at the Uganda Technical College, the National Teachers' College, the Uganda College of Commerce; and Agricultural Colleges. There are also in addition to these, several departmental training schools training staff for different departments. The Medical Department alone has eight such schools training nurses, midwives, medical assistants, health inspectors, and other medical staff.

University level education is available at Makerere University, Kampala: the University College, Nairobi, in Kenya, and the University College, Dar es Salaam, in Tanzania. Uganda students also go to universities and colleges outside East Africa for higher education.

Communications.—There is a first-class international airport at Entebbe, with direct flights to many places in Africa, Asia and Europe. There are 10 other state airports and airfields in Uganda. There are 1,700 kilometres of bituminized and 25,000 kilometres of gravel roads. Nearly 75 per cent. of all trunk roads are metalled, the remainder and all feeder roads are gravel roads of good standard. A railway network joins the capital to the western, eastern and northern centres. Lake, marine, road and rail services are operated by the E. African Railways and Harbours Administration.

Trade, etc.—The principal export commodities are coffee, cotton, copper, animal feeding-stuffs, hides and skins and unmanufactured tobacco. Other crops grown include sugar and groundnuts. Hydroelectric power is produced from the Owen Falls power station which has a capacity of 150,000 kWh. Plans are under way for increasing the output of electricity.

TRADE WITH U.K.

	1973	1974
Imports from U.K....	£ 4,913,000	£ 7,238,000
Exports to U.K......	20,788,000	24,412,000

Zambia

The Republic of Zambia lies on the plateau of Central Africa between the longitudes 22° E. and 33° 33' E. and between the latitudes 8° 15' S. and 18° S. It has an area of 290,587 square miles within boundaries 3,515 miles in length and a population (Census, 1969) of 4,054,000, including about 50,000 non-Africans.

With the exception of the valleys of the Zambesi, the Luapula, the Kafue and the Luangwa Rivers, and the Luano valley, the greater part of Zambia has a flat to rolling topography, with elevations varying from 3,000 to 5,000 feet above sea level, but in the north-eastern districts the plateau rises to occasional altitudes of over 6,000 feet. In many localities the evenness of the plateau is broken by hills, sometimes occurring as chains which develop into areas of broken country.

Although Zambia lies within the tropics, and fairly centrally in the great land mass of the African continent its elevation relieves it from the extremely high temperatures and humidity usually associated with tropical countries. The lower reaches of the Zambesi, Luangwa and Kafue rivers in deeper valleys do experience high humidity and trying extremes of heat, but these areas are remote and sparsely populated.

Government.—At the dissolution of the Federation of Rhodesia and Nyasaland, on December 31, 1963, Northern Rhodesia (as Zambia was then known) achieved internal self-government under a new constitution. Zambia became an independent republic with the Commonwealth on October 24, 1964—75 years after coming under British rule and nine months after achieving internal self-government. Until December 1972, when the 1964 Constitution was superseded, the country had a multi-party constitution. In July 1973, a new Constitution was introduced, providing that the United National Independence Party shall be the only party.

CAPITAL.—Lusaka, situated in the Central Province. Population (estimated, 1972), 347,900. Other centres are Livingstone, Kabwe, Chipata, Mazabuka, Mbala, Kasama, Solwezi, Mongu, Mansa, Ndola, Luanshya, Mufulira, Chingola, Chililabombwe, Kalulushi and Kitwe, the last six towns being the main centres on the Copperbelt. FLAG.—Green with three small vertical stripes, red, black and orange (next fly); eagle device on green above stripes.

President, Dr. Kenneth David Kaunda, *assumed office* October 24, 1964; *re-elected*, December 1973.

CABINET

The President (also *Minister of Defence*).
Prime Minister (also *Minister of National Guidance and Development*), E. H. K. Mudenda
Minister of Foreign Affairs, R. Banda.

Rural Development, P. Lusaka.
Home Affairs, A. M. Milner.
Local Government and Housing, P. W. Matoka.
Legal Affairs and Attorney-General, M. M. Chona.
Health, Dr. M. M. Bull.

Information and Broadcasting, C. M. Mwanansiku.
Lands, Natural Resources and Tourism, J. Mapoma.
Power, Transport and Works, Dr. N. S. Mulenga.
Education, F. M. Mulikita.
Labour and Social Services, H. D. Banda.
Mines and Industry, A. J. Soko.
Planning and Finance, A. B. Chikwanda.
Commerce, R. Kunda.

ZAMBIA HIGH COMMISSION
7–11 Cavendish Place, W.1
[01–580 0691]
High Commissioner, His Excellency L. H. Shamooya.
BRITISH HIGH COMMISSION
Lusaka
High Commissioner, His Excellency Frank Stephen
Miles, C.M.G. (1974)...................£12,000
British Council Representative, Dr. R. E. Wright,
Heroes Place, Cairo Road, Lusaka.

JUDICATURE
There is a Chief Justice appointed by the President, all other judges being appointed on the recommendation of the Judicial Service Commission consisting of the Chief Justice, the chairman of the Public Service Commission, a senior Justice of Appeal and one Presidential nominee.
Chief Justice of Zambia, Hon. A. M. Silungwe.
Deputy Chief Justice, L. S. Baron.
Justice of the Supreme Court, B. T. Gardener.

Puisne Judges, G. B. Muwo; W. S. Bruce-Lyle;
B. Cullinan; G. Care; M. Moodley; B. Bwewpe.

———

Education.—In 1973 there were 810,740 pupils in primary schools and 65,764 (1974) in secondary schools.
Full-time university enrolment in 1974 was 2,612.
Production and Employment.—Principal products are tobacco, maize, groundnuts, cotton, livestock and vegetables.
Mineral production was valued at K933,599,000 in 1974. The production of copper totalled 702,490 tonnes valued at K874,037,504. In 1973 an oil refinery at Ndola came into operation and the pipeline running through Zambia to Ndola was switched over to the transportation of crude oil.
In Dec. 1973, 383,830 persons were estimated to be in full employment. Included in this figure are: mining and quarrying, 62,590; agriculture, forestry and fishery, 36,500; construction, 75,560; manufacturing, 42,060.
Finance and Currency.—Zambia adopted decimal currency on Jan. 16, 1968, the unit being the *Kwacha.*

	1973	1974
Revenue...........	K329,300,000	K682,900,000
Expenditure........	356,600,000	490,000,000
Capital expenditure.	113,900,000	241,800,000

GRENADA

Grenada is situated between the parallels of 12° 13′–11° 58′ N. lat. and 61° 20′–61° 35′ W. long., and is about 21 miles in length and 12 miles in breadth; it is about 80 miles north of Trinidad, 68 miles S.S.W. of St. Vincent, and about 120 miles S.W. of Barbados. Area, including the Grenada Grenadines about 133 square miles; estimated population (including some of the Grenadines), 104,000 (1976). The country is mountainous and very picturesque, and the climate is healthy. Grenada was discovered by Columbus in 1498, and named Conception. It was originally colonized by the French, and was ceded to Great Britain by the Treaty of Versailles in 1783. It became an Associated State in 1967 and an independent nation on Feb. 1, 1974.
The soil is very fertile, and cocoa, bananas, nutmeg and other spices, coconuts, sugar cane and fruit are grown. The imports are chiefly dry goods, wheat, flour, dried fish and rice.
ΨSt. George's (population 8,600) on the southwest coast, is the chief town, and possesses a good harbour.

Trade
Total imports (1973)............... $42,537,790
Total exports (1974)............... $14,816,634
Includes Colonial Development and Welfare Grant.

Government
Grenada's legislature is bicameral consisting of Her Majesty (represented by a Governor-General), a Senate and a House of Representatives. The 13 Senators are appointed by the Governor-General, 7 on the advice of the Prime Minister, 3 on the advice of the Leader of the Opposition, and 3 on the advice of the Prime Minister after he has consulted interests which he considers Senators should be selected to represent. The Cabinet consists of the Prime Minister, the other Ministers, and at any time when his office is a public one, the Attorney-General.
Governor-General, Sir Leo de Gale (1974).
Premier, Hon. Eric M. Gairy.
The *Grenadines* are a chain of small islands lying between Grenada and St. Vincent, within which Governments they are included. The largest island is Carriacou, attached to the Government of Grenada, with area of 13 sq. miles and population of about 8,000.

GRENADA HIGH COMMISSION
King's House, 10 Haymarket, S.W.1
[01–930 7902]
High Commissioner, His Excellency Oswald M.
Gibbs, C.M.G. (1974).
British High Commission (see Trinidad and Tobago)

REPUBLIC OF NAURU

The Republic of Nauru is an island of 8·2 sq. miles in size, situated in 166° 55′ E. longitude and 32′ S. of the Equator. It has a population (estimated June, 1972) of 6,768, of whom two-thirds are Nauruans or other Pacific Islanders. There are Chinese and European minorities. About 43 per cent. of Nauruans are adherents of the Nauruan Protestant Church and there is a Roman Catholic Mission on the island.
Until 1968 Nauru was administered by Australia under an international trusteeship agreement which on Nov. 1, 1947, superseded a former League of Nations Mandate. It became an Independent State from February 1, 1968. It was announced in November, 1968, that a limited form of membership of the Commonwealth had been devised for Nauru at the request of its Government.

President, Premier and Minister for External Affairs, Internal Affairs, Island Development and Industry and Civil Aviation, His Excellency Hammer DeRoburt, O.B.E.
Minister for Finance, Hon. J. A. Bop.

Justice, Hon. J. D. Audoa.
Health and Education, Hon. A. Bernicke.
Works and Community Services, Hon. R. B. Detudamo.
Chief Justice, I. R. Thompson.

Judiciary.—The Nauruan judiciary consists of a District Court, a Central Court and a Court of Appeal.

Education and Welfare.—Nauru has a hospital service and other medical and dental services. There is also a maternity and child welfare service. Education is available in 9 primary and 2 secondary schools on the island with a total enrolment of 1,797 pupils.

Production, etc.—There are valuable deposits of phosphates on the island which were purchased from the Pacific Phosphate Company in 1919 by the Governments of Australia, New Zealand and the United Kingdom for £3,500,000 and vested in the British Phosphate Commissioners. Royalties on phosphate exports (about £5,000,000 annually) have been paid partly to the Nauruans and partly into a trust fund which used income from investments abroad to pay for Nauru's administrative and social services. Phosphate mining employs 1,369 persons out of a labour force of 2,208.

The assets on Nauru of the British Phosphate Commissioners have been purchased by the Nauruans, control of mining and marketing passing to the Nauru Phosphate Corporation on July 1, 1970.

FLAG.—Twelve-point star (representing the 12 original Nauruan tribes) below a gold bar (representing the Equator), all on a blue ground.

SEYCHELLES

The Republic of Seychelles, in the Indian Ocean, consists of two distinct collections of islands—the Mahé group, 45 islands in all, granitic with high hills and mountains (highest point about 2,990 ft.) and the outlying islands, the Coralline group, numbering 49 more and, for the most part, only a little above sea-level. Proclaimed as French territory in 1756, the Mahé group began to be settled as a dependency of Mauritius from 1770, was captured by a British ship in 1794 and was finally assigned to Great Britain in 1810. By Letters Patent of September, 1903, these islands, together with the Coralline group, were formed into a separate Colony. On June 28, 1976, the Islands became an independent republic within the Commonwealth.

The total area of the Granitic group is 190 square miles, of which Mahé, the largest island and the seat of Government, claims 57. The next largest island is Praslin, home of the unique double coconut, Coco de Mer. Islands of the Coralline group lie at distances from Mahé varying between 60 and 612 miles and have a total area of approximately 81 sq. miles. In 1965 the islands of Farquhar, Desroches and Aldabra were detached from Seychelles and with the Chagos Islands, formerly of Mauritius, formed the new British Indian Ocean Territory, but returned to Seychelles on independence. The coralline islands have no permanent population and, where worked, are supplied by contract labour from the Granitic group. The population at the 1971 Census was 52,650. Although only 4° S. of the Equator, the islands are healthy. There are 36 primary schools, 14 secondary schools, five vocational training centres and a teachers' training college.

A new Constitution was introduced in 1976. The National Assembly consists of 25 elected members and the Speaker.

TRADE

	1974	1975
Imports	Rs.160,500,000	Rs.191,400,000
Exports	18,700,000	12,900,000

The principal imports are rice, mineral oils, cotton piece goods, vehicles, manufactured items and building materials. The chief exports are tourism, cinnamon bark and copra; others include cinnamon leaf oil, guano, vanilla, patchouli oil and tortoise shell.

CAPITAL, Ψ Victoria (population, 1971, 13,736), on the N.E. side of Mahé.

President, Hon. J. R. Mancham.
Prime Minister, Hon. A. Rene.

Letters to and from London—5 to 10 days.

TONGA

The Tongan or *Friendly Islands*, a British-protected state for 70 years, became independent on June 7, 1970.

These islands are situated in the Southern Pacific some 450 miles to the E.S.E. of Fiji, with an area of 270 sq. miles, and population (estimated, 1974) of 97,157. The largest island, Tongatapu, was discovered by Tasman in 1643. Most of the islands are of coral formation, but some are volcanic (Tofua, Kao and Niuafoou or "Tin Can" Island). The limits of the group are between 15° and 23° 30′ S., and 173° and 177° W. Nuku'alofa, on the island of Tongatapu, is the seat of government. The present King Taufa'ahau Tupou IV, G.C.V.O., K.C.M.G., K.B.E., succeeded his mother, the late Queen Salote Tupou III, on December 16, 1965. The constitution provides for a Government consisting of the Sovereign, a privy council and cabinet, a legislative assembly and a judiciary. The legislative assembly has 22 members, with a Speaker, and includes the Ministers of the Crown, the two Governors of Island groups, and the representatives of the Nobles and of the people (seven of each), who are elected triennially.

Premier, Minister of Foreign Affairs and of Agriculture, H.R.H. Prince Fatafehi Tu'ipelehake, C.B.E.

Soil generally is fertile, the principal exports are copra and bananas. Revenue July 1974–June 1975 T$4,792,800; expenditure T$4,298,500. The national debt is T$1,363,305 (June 1975). Total imports (1974) T$11,819,247. Total exports (1974) T$4,561,494. The total shipping cleared in 1974 was 611,281 tons. Tongan currency is at parity with Australia.

CAPITAL.—Nuku'alofa (20,000).

FLAG.—Truncated red cross on rectangular white ground (next staff) on a red field.

TONGAN HIGH COMMISSION
New Zealand House, Haymarket, S.W.1
[01–839 3287]
High Commissioner, His Excellency 'Inoke Fotu Faletau.

BRITISH HIGH COMMISSION
Nuku'alofa
High Commissioner, His Excellency Humphrey Augustine Arthington-Davy, O.B.E.

WESTERN SAMOA

Head of State, H. H. Malietoa Tanumafili II, C.B.E. (April 15, 1963).

Prime Minister, Hon. Tupuola Efi.

Formerly administered by New Zealand (latterly with internal self-government), Western Samoa became, on January 1, 1962, the first fully-independent Polynesian State.

The State was treated as a member country of the Commonwealth until its formal admission on August 28, 1970.

Western Samoa consists of the islands of Savai'i (662 sq. miles) and of Upolu, which with nine other islands, has an area of 435 sq. miles. All islands are mountainous. Upolu, the most fertile, contains the harbours of ΨApia and ΨSaluafata and Savai'i the harbour of ΨAsau. The islanders are Christians of different denominations. In 1974 the population was estimated to be 152,000.

The chief exports are copra, cocoa, bananas and timber.

Total exports 1974 were $7,699,300.
Total imports 1974 were $17,459,900.

TRADE WITH U.K.

	1972	1974
Imports from U.K.	£1,116,000	£322,000
Exports to U.K.	124,000	387,000

CAPITAL.—ΨApia (population 28,800). Robert Louis Stevenson died and was buried at Apia in 1894.

FLAG.—Five white stars (depicting the Southern Cross) on a quarter royal blue at top next staff, and three quarters red.

Associated States, Colonies, Protectorates, etc.

Flags of the Dependencies.—Generally the dependencies use the Union Flag (" Union Jack ") or Blue Ensign bearing a badge of arms of the Dependency (with surrounding garland when used with the Union Flag). In a few cases, *e.g.* Bermuda, the Red Ensign is used with badge. (*See also* ANTIGUA (W. Indies); BRUNEI; ST. KITTS (W. Indies); ST. LUCIA (W. Indies).)

ASCENSION
See ST. HELENA

BELIZE

British Honduras, in Central America, was officially renamed Belize on June 1, 1973. It lies within 18° 29′ 50″ to 51° 53′ N. latitude and 89° 13′ 28″ to 87° 21′ 30″ W. longitude. Its extreme length and breadth are approximately 186 m. and 118 m. respectively; it is bounded on the north and north-west by Mexico, on the west and south by Guatemala; and on the east by the Caribbean Sea. The total area (including offshore islands) is about 8,867 sq. miles, with an estimated population (1947) of 140,000. The climate generally is damp and warm, but not unhealthy. The temperature ranges from 47° to 94° F. The average lies between 75° and 80°, but this is considerably tempered by the prevailing sea-breezes.

The greater part of the country is covered by forest, of which 50 per cent. is high rain forest, 15·5 pine forest and dry savannah, 5·5 wet savannah and mangrove forest, the remaining 20 per cent. being existing or recently abandoned cultivation. The wire grass and sedges of the dry savannahs make very poor pasturage for cattle. The north of the territory and the southern coastal plain (8 to 20 miles wide) are nearly flat. Near the sea the plain is low and swampy. The central mountain mass has a general altitude of 2,000 to 3,000 feet and 20 per cent. of the area of the territory is over 1,000 feet in elevation above mean sea-level.

The staple products are obtained from the forests, and include mahogany, cedar, and *chicle* (the basis of chewing-gum), Santa Maria, pine and rosewood. Agricultural crops which grow readily include sugar cane, coconuts, citrus fruit, plantains, pineapples, mangoes, maize, cucumbers, rice, varieties of beans and peas. Bananas also grow well in certain localities. All varieties of citrus fruits flourish, and in particular grape-fruit, of which a very high grade is exported. Lobster tails and shrimps are also exported.

In 1974 there were 181 Government and grant-aided primary schools and 8 unaided private elementary schools in the country, the total enrolment being 35,000. There are also 21 secondary schools with a total enrolment of 6,000.

There are 50 post offices in the country. A new transmitting and receiving station at Ladyville has been completed. External telegraph and radio telephone and telex services are operated by Cable and Wireless Ltd. Air services are scheduled 7 times weekly to and from the capitals of Panama, Honduras, Mexico, Salvador, Guatemala, Nicaragua, Costa Rica and twice weekly to and from Jamaica. There is a six times weekly service from and to New Orleans, a seven times weekly service from and to Miami and a weekly service to Mexico City. A local scheduled air service links the six districts into which the country is divided.

CAPITAL, Belmopan (estimated population, Dec. 31, 1974, 3,500). The largest city and the former capital is ΨBelize City (population, 1970, 38,000), which was badly damaged by a hurricane in October, 1961. It was announced in 1965 that a new capital would be built, 50 miles inland. Construction is proceeding on the new city, Belmopan, with U.K. aid of $24,000,000. The first phase was completed in 1970. Other towns are ΨCorozal (12,319), Cayo (16,484), ΨStann Creek (13,435) Orange Walk (13,266), Toledo (9,804).

FINANCE

	1974	1975
Revenue	$23,487,200	$31,606,444
Expenditure	23,487,200	27,647,259

Estimated revenue and expenditure on capital projects in 1974 balanced at $16,677,277.

Public Debt (Dec. 31, 1974), $17,469,814.

The Canadian Government has made a loan of $8,000,000 for modern water and sewerage systems in Belize City.

TRADE WITH U.K.

	1973	1974
Imports from U.K.	£3,770,000	£4,218,000
Exports to U.K.	2,730,000	4,975,000

GOVERNMENT

Under the Constitution introduced on Jan. 1, 1964, the Governor retains special responsibility for defence, external affairs, internal security and the safeguarding of the terms and conditions of service of public officers. For so long as the Government continues to receive grant-in-aid from the U.K. Government, the Governor also has special responsibility for maintaining or securing financial and economic stability and for ensuring that any condition attached to any financial grant or loan made by the U.K. Government is fulfilled. The Governor appoints as Premier the person who appears to him to be likely to command the support of a majority in the House of Representatives. Ministers are appointed by the Governor on the advice of the Premier.

The National Assembly comprises a House of Representatives and a Senate. The House of Representatives consists of 18 members elected by universal adult suffrage. The Speaker may be elected by the House from among its own members, or from outside; the Deputy Speaker is elected by the House from among its own members. The

Senate consists of 8 members appointed by the Governor (5 on the advice of the Premier, 2 on the advice of the leader of the Opposition and 1 after consulting such persons as he considers appropriate).

Governor and Commander-in-Chief, His Excellency Richard Neil Posnett, O.B.E. (1972).............................. $25,200
Chief Justice, D. Malone................ 14,000
Speaker of the House of Representatives, Hon. Sir Alexander Hunter, K.B.E..... 4,750
Premier and Minister of Finance and Economic Development, Hon. G. C. Price........ 9,700
Minister of Works and Communications, Hon. F. H. Hunter................... 9,000
Trade and Industry, Cooperative and Consumer Protection, Hon. S. A. Perdomo.. 9,000
Local Government and Social Welfare, and Labour, Hon. D. L. McKay............ 9,000
Education, Housing, Hon. G. Pech........ 9,000
Deputy Premier and Home Affairs and Health, Hon. C. L. B. Rogers......... 9,000
Agriculture and Lands, Hon. F. Marin..... 9,000
Attorney-General, Hon. A. Shoman...... 9,000

Belize is distant from London about 4,700 miles; transit, 17 days by sea, 18 hours by air *via* Miami.

BERMUDA

The Bermudas, or Somers Islands, are a cluster of about 100 small islands (about 20 only of which are inhabited) situated in the west of the Atlantic Ocean, in 32° 18′ N. lat. and 64° 46′ W. long., the nearest point of the mainland being Cape Hatteras in North Carolina, about 570 miles distant. The total area is now approximately 20·59 sq. miles which includes 2·3 sq. miles leased to, or reclaimed by, the U.S. authorities between 1941 and 1957 under the terms of the 99 year lease. The civil population was 53,000 at the Census taken in October, 1970. The colony derives its name from Juan Bermudez, a Spaniard, who sighted it before 1515, but no settlement was made until 1609, when Sir George Somers, who was shipwrecked here on his way to Virginia, colonized the islands.

Vegetation is prolific, the principal trees being the Bermuda cedar (juniper), formerly of great importance for shipbuilding, but since 1943 almost entirely destroyed by blight. At one time the islands enjoyed a flourishing export in onions, potatoes, and green vegetables, but the imposition of tariffs in U.S.A. and the growing shortage of arable land made further growing for export unprofitable. The lily bud trade with Canada and U.S.A. and locally manufactured concentrates and pharmaceuticals are now the Colony's leading exports. Little food is produced except vegetables and fish, other foodstuffs being imported.

The Colony's economic structure is based on its importance as a tourist resort and as a naval base and from these sources most of its revenue is derived. Bermuda is now within two hours' air travel from New York, and in 1972 a total of 488,271 visitors arrived in Bermuda. The airport is used by B.O.A.C., Pan-American Airways, Air-Canada, Eastern, North-East and Qantas air lines and most cruise ships dock at Hamilton.

Free elementary education was introduced in May, 1949. Free secondary education was introduced in 1965 for those children in the aided and maintained schools who were below the upper limit of the statutory school age (16 from 1969 onwards).

There are 4 radio and 2 television stations, one daily and 3 weekly newspapers and overseas telephone and telegraph services are maintained.

GOVERNMENT

Internal self-government was introduced on June 8, 1968. There are a Legislative Council of 11 Members and an elected House of Assembly of 40 Members. The Governor retains responsibility for external affairs, defence, internal security and the police.

Voters must be British subjects of twenty-one years of age or older at the time of registration, and if they do not possess Bermudian status, they must have been ordinarily resident in Bermuda for the whole of the period of three years immediately before registration. Registration is held every year during the month of February. Candidates for election must qualify as electors and must possess Bermudian status.

Governor and Commander-in-Chief, His Excellency Sir Edwin Hartley Cameron Leather, K.C.M.G., K.C.V.O. (1973) *(excluding allowances)* $28,512

Executive Council
CABINET

Premier, Hon. Sir Edward Richards, C.B.E.
Labour and Immigration, Hon. C. V. Woolridge.
Finance, Hon. J. H. Sharpe, C.B.E.
Education, Hon. Mrs. Gloria McPhee.
Tourism and Trade, Hon. de F. Trimingham.
Public Works and Agriculture, Hon. J. M. S. Patton, G.C.
Health and Water, Hon. Q. L. Edness.
Marine and Air Services, Hon. F. J. Barritt.
Planning, Hon. E. W. P. Vesey.
Transport, Hon. R. O. Marshall.
Organization, Hon. J. R. Plowman, C.B.E.
Youth and Sport, Hon. L. I. Swan.

President of the Legislative Council, Hon. Sir George Ratteray, C.B.E.
Speaker of the House of Assembly, Hon. Sir Arthur Spurling, C.B.E.

Chief Justice, Hon. Sir John Summerfield, C.B.E.
Puisne Judge, Hon. E. E. Seaton.
Deputy Governor, I. A. C. Kinnear, C.M.G.

FINANCE

	1973–74
Public revenue..................	52,245,598
Public expenditure..............	49,895,419
Public debt (March 31, 1971)......	6,093,600

Currency.—Bermuda Monetary Authority notes ($50, $20, $10, $5 and $1) and metal coinage (50c, 25c, 10c, 5c and 1c) became the currency of Bermuda on Feb. 6, 1970.

TRADE WITH U.K.

	1973	1974
Imports from U.K....	£12,717,000	£14,371,000
Exports to U.K......	5,947,000	4,154,000

CAPITAL, Hamilton, (Population (1970), 3,000).

THE BRITISH VIRGIN ISLANDS

The Virgin Islands are a group of islands at the eastern extremity of the Greater Antilles, divided between Great Britain and the U.S.A. Those of the group which are British number about 42, of which 11 are uninhabited, and have a total area of about 59 square miles. The principal are Tortola, the largest (situate in 18° 27′ N. lat. and 64° 40′ W. long., area, 21 sq. miles), Virgin Gorda (8½ sq. miles), Anegada (15 sq. miles) and Jost Van Dyke (3½ sq. miles). The 1970 Census of Population showed a total population of 10,030 (Tortola (8,676); Virgin Gorda (904); Anegada (269); Jost Van Dyke (123): and other islands 68). Apart from Anegada, which is a flat coral island, the British Virgin Islands are hilly, being an extension of the Puerto Rico and the U.S. Virgin Islands archipelago. The highest point is Sage Mountain on Tor-

tola which rises to a height of 1,780 feet. The islands are very picturesque and form one of the finest sailing areas in the world on account of their sheltered waters. The sea is rich in gamefish and there are said to be over 400 wrecks off Anegada. Tourism is the main industry, but there is some cattle raising and fishing. Other products are vegetables, fruit, charcoal and a small amount of rum.

The islands lie within the Trade Winds belt and possess a pleasant and healthy sub-tropical climate. The average temperature varies from 71° to 82° F. in winter and 78°–88° F. in summer. The summer heat is tempered by sea breezes and the temperature usually falls by about 10° at night. Average rainfall is 53 inches. Hurricanes are very rare—the last occurrence being in 1928.

The principal airport is on Beef Island, linked by bridge to Tortola, and an extended runway of 3,600 feet, opened in 1969, enables larger aircraft to call. There is a second airfield on Virgin Gorda and a third on Anegada. There are direct shipping services to the United Kingdom and the United States and fast passenger services connect the main islands by ferry.

FINANCE

	1975	1976
Revenue	\$U.S.5,374,250	\$U.S. 5,926,800
Expenditure	6,026,345	6,660,948

GOVERNMENT

The British Virgin Islands are partially internally self-governing, with a ministerial system. The Governor, appointed by the Crown, remains responsible for defence and internal security, external affairs, the civil service, administration of the courts and finance, and acts in accordance with the advice of the Executive Council. The Executive Council consists of the Governor as Chairman, two *ex officio* members (the Attorney-General and the Financial Secretary), the Chief Minister and two other ministers. The Legislative Council consists of a Speaker chosen from outside the Council, two *ex officio* members (the Attorney-General and Financial Secretary), one nominated member appointed by the Governor after consultation with the Chief Minister and seven elected members returned from seven one-member electoral districts. The islands are proud of their tradition of stable government.

Governor, His Excellency W. W. Wallace (1974) .... \$U.S. 14,200

Chief Minister, Hon. W. Wheatley, M.B.E. 10,300
Minister of Natural Resources and Public Health, Hon. H. L. Stoutt 8,400
Minister of Communications, Works and Industry, Hon. A. U. Anthony 8,400
Financial Secretary, Hon. J. A. Frost ... 12,480
Chief Secretary, A. E. Penn 12,480
Deputy Financial Secretary, D. Wheatley 11,136
Permanent Secretary, Chief Minister's Office, E. Georges 11,136
Permanent Secretary, National Resources and Public Health, Mrs. E. Todman-Smith 11,136
Permanent Secretary, Communications, Works and Industry, Miss Ethlyn Smith 11,136
Attorney-General, Hon. Paula Beaubrun 12,828
Chief Education Officer, Miss Enid Scatliffe 11,784
Chief of Police, R. Jones 10,236
Chief Medical Officer, Dr. H. P. Watson 12,384

Chief Medical Officer, H. P. Watson 12,384
Chief Engineer, Public Works, D. P. Grace 11,784
Chief Electrical Engineer, E. Garner 11,708
Chief Agricultural Officer, N. Vanterpool 7,584
CAPITAL.—Ψ Road Town (on the south-east of Tortola). Population, 2,129.

BRUNEI

Sultan, H. H. Hassanal Bolkiah Mu'izzadin Waddaulah, G.C.M.G., *acceded* 1967, *crowned* Aug. 1, 1968.

Brunei is situated on the north-west coast of the island of Borneo, total area about 2,226 sq. miles, population (estimated 1975), 162,200, of whom 71·7 per cent. are of Malay or other indigenous race and 23·4 per cent. Chinese. The chief town, Bandar Seri Begawan, with its nearby water village (groups of houses on stilts on the Brunei River) has a population of about 42,000. The country has a humid tropical climate.

In 1959, the Sultan of Brunei promulgated the first written Constitution, which provides for a Privy Council, a Council of Ministers and a Legislative Council. Under the 1959 Agreement, as amended in 1971, Britain is responsible for external affairs, and has an obligation to consult the Brunei Government on the defence of the State. The post of British Resident was abolished in 1959 and many of his functions were transferred to the Sultan in Council. A *Mentri Besar* (Chief Minister) is appointed by the Sultan, and is responsible to him for the exercise of executive authority. The Sultan presides over the Privy Council and the Council of Ministers.

FLAG.—Yellow, with diagonal bands of white over narrow black band (from top by staff), with red device on diagonal bands.

BRITISH HIGH COMMISSION
Jalan Residency, Brunei

High Commissioner, His Excellency James Alfred Davidson, O.B.E. (1974) £5,765

FINANCE

	1975	1976
Revenue	B\$1,290,992,350	B\$1,600,122,750
Expenditure*	445,000,000	495,811,271

Including development expenditure.

Currency.—Brunei issues its own currency, the *Brunei dollar* of 100 *cents*, which is fully interchangeable with the currency of Singapore.

Imports from the U.K. in 1974 totalled £5,113,000 (1973, £2,550,000).

FALKLAND ISLANDS

The Falkland Islands, the only considerable group in the South Atlantic, lie about 300 miles east of the Straits of Magellan, between 52° 15'–53° S. lat. and 57° 40'–62° W. long. They consist of East Falkland (area 2,610 sq. miles), West Falkland (2,090 sq. miles) and upwards of 100 small islands in the aggregate, the estimated population at the Census of Dec. 31, 1975 being 1,905. Mount Usborne, the loftiest peak, rises 2,312 feet above the level of the sea. The Falklands were discovered by Davis in 1592, and visited by Hawkins in 1594. A settlement was made by France in 1764; this was subsequently sold to Spain, but the latter country recognized Great Britain's title to a part at least of the group in 1771. The settlement was destroyed by the Americans in 1831. In 1833 occupation was resumed by the British for the protection of the seal-fisheries, and the islands were permanently colonized as the most southerly organized colony of the British Empire. The climate is cool. At Stanley the mean monthly temperature varies between 49° F. in January and 35·5° F. in July. The air temperature has never

been known to exceed 77° F. or to fall below 12° F.; it is notably windy. The islands are chiefly moorland. The population is almost totally British, and is principally engaged in sheep-farming to which practically all the land in the colony is devoted, 644,014 sheep being carried in 1974/5. Wool, hides and sheepskins are exported. The only town is Ψ Stanley on the coast of East Falkland.

GOVERNMENT

The Governor is assisted by a Legislative Council of 8 members, with the Governor as President, 2 *ex officio* (Chief Secretary and Financial Secretary), 2 non-official members (nominated by the Governor), and 4 representatives elected by the people.
Governor and Commander-in-Chief, His
  Excellency Neville Arthur Irwin French, C.M.G.,
  M.V.O........(1975) (+ *duty allce.* £936) £4,500
Chief Secretary, A. J. P. Monk £4,170
Financial Secretary, H. T. Rowlands (+ *allce.* £540)
                                    £3,120

FINANCE AND TRADE

	1974/75	1975/76†
Public Revenue	£862,176	£1,183,622
Expenditure	790,710	955,176
† Estimated.		

	1974	1975
Total imports	£805,237	£1,525,771
Total exports	4,921,746	1,172,732

Falkland Islands and Dependencies
Trade with U.K.

	1974	1975
Imports from U.K.	£506,878	£1,315,146
Exports to U.K.	4,921,746	1,172,732

CHIEF TOWN, ΨStanley, estimated population 1,079. Stanley is distant from England about 8,103 miles. Telegrams by wireless U.K. direct. The journey from U.K. to Falkland Islands can be accomplished in 4 to 5 days travelling to Comodoro Rivadavia, *via* Buenos Aires, thence by air to Stanley.

DEPENDENCIES.—*South Georgia,* an island 800 miles east-south-east of the Falkland group, with an area of 1,450 sq. miles. Some 22 persons reside at the British scientific base which has been established at King Edward Point. The South Sandwich Islands group, which is uninhabited and lies some 470 miles S.E. of South Georgia, is the only other dependency.

GIBRALTAR,

a rocky promontory, 3¾ miles in length, ¾ of a mile in breadth and 1,396 feet high at its greatest elevation, near the southern extremity of Spain, with which it is connected by a low isthmus. It is about 14 miles distant from the opposite coast of Africa. In a total area of 2¼ sq. miles, the population at the census of Oct. 1970 was 26,833. The estimated civilian population at the end of 1975 was 29,934.

Gibraltar is a naval base of strategic importance to Great Britain. It was captured in 1704, during the war of the Spanish Succession, by a combined Dutch and English force, under Sir George Rooke, and was ceded to Great Britain by the Treaty of Utrecht, 1713. Several attempts have been made to retake it, the most celebrated being the great siege in 1779–83, when General Eliott, afterwards Lord Heathfield, held it for 3 years and 7 months against a combined French and Spanish force. The town stands at the foot of the promontory on the W. side. Gibraltar enjoys the advantages of an extensive shipping trade. The chief sources of revenue are the port dues, the rent of the Crown estate in the town, and duties on consumer items. Import duties are low and Gibraltar is a popular

shopping centre. The gradual change from a fortress city to an attractive holiday centre has led to a flourishing tourist trade.

A total of 2,433 merchant ships (14,695,736 net tons) entered the port during 1975. Of these 1,787 were deep-sea ships (14,490,381 net tons). In addition 2,384 yachts (35,836 net tons) called at the port. There are 26·75 miles of roads.

Education is compulsory and free between the ages of 5 and 12 and scholarships are available for university or further education in Britain. There are 12 Government, 2 private and 2 Services primary schools, with 3,759 pupils in Dec. 1975. The two government secondary schools had 1,561 pupils in 1975. Government expenditure on education in 1975 was £928,698.

FINANCE AND TRADE

	1973/74	1974/75
Revenue	£6,710,196	£8,790,210
Expenditure	6,906,250	8,653,078

	1974	1975
Total imports	£25,088,714	£27,027,401
Total exports	10,484,352	10,753,448

	1974	1975
Imports from U.K.	£17,875,652	£18,003,000
Exports to U.K.	348,056	509,476

GOVERNMENT

The Constitution of Gibraltar, approved in 1969, made formal provision for certain domestic matters to devolve on Ministers appointed from among elected members of the House of Assembly then set up to replace the former Legislative Council. The House of Assembly consists of an independent Speaker, 15 elected members and the Attorney-General and Financial and Development Secretary.
Governor and Commander-in-Chief, His Excellency
  Marshal of the Royal Air Force Sir John Grandy,
  G.C.B., K.B.E., D.S.O. (1973) *(including* £1,500 *enter-*
  tainment allowance) £8,750
Flag Officer, Gibraltar, and Admiral Supr., H.M.
  Naval Base, Gibraltar, Rear Admiral M. L. Stacey.
Chief Minister, Sir Joshua Hassan, C.B.E., M.V.O.,
  Q.C.
Chief Justice, Sir Edgar Unsworth, C.M.G... £4,890
Speaker, A. J. Vasquez, C.B.E.
Deputy Governor, E. H. Davis, C.M.G., O.B.E. £4,890
Financial and Development Secretary, A.
  Collins................................ £4,490
Attorney-General, J. K. Havers, O.B.E., Q.C... £4,490
Distance from London 1,209 miles; transit, 3¼ days. British Airways operate regular direct air services to the U.K. (Some services are *via* Madrid.) Transit times average 3 hours.

GILBERT ISLANDS

Until October 1, 1975, the Gilbert Islands formed part of the Gilbert and Ellice Islands Colony.

On the recommendation of a Commissioner appointed by Her Majesty's Government to consider requests by the Ellice leaders to have their island group separated from the Gilberts, a referendum of Ellice Islanders was held in the autumn of 1974. This showed an overwhelming support for separation and this was effected on October 1 1975. The Ellice Islands became a separate Colony known as Tuvalu and the remainder of the original Gilbert and Ellice Islands changed its name to the Gilbert Islands. Separation of the Administration took place on January 1, 1976.

The Gilbert Islands which includes Ocean Island, the Phoenix Islands and the Line Islands is situated in the South West Pacific around the point at which the International Date Line cuts the Equator. The Colony consists of 33 coral atolls (of which 21 are permanently inhabited) with a total land area of

264 square miles spread over some 2 million square miles of ocean. Few of the atolls are more than 12 feet above sea level or more than half a mile in width. The vegetation consists mainly of coconut palms, breadfruit trees and pandanus. The total population based on a census in 1973 is approximately 48,000. The Phoenix and Line Islands now have no indigenous populations. Christianity is widespread, roughly half of the population being Protestant and the other half Roman Catholic. Most people still practice a subsistence economy, the main staples of their diet being coconuts and fish.

The Colony is administered by a Governor. In May 1974 a ministerial form of government was introduced providing for the establishment of a House of Assembly which comprised 28 elected members and three *ex officio* members, and a Council of Ministers which comprised the Governor, the three *ex officio* members of the House of Assembly, a Chief Minister (chosen by and from among the elected members) and between four and six Ministers appointed by the Governor on the advice of the Chief Minister. In May 1975 the constitution was slightly altered to take account of the separation of the Ellice Islands. Apart from reducing the number of seats in the House of Assembly (now 21) separation made little difference to the Gilbert Islands constitution.

Local Government services are provided by elected Island Councils. Under an agreement reached in 1939, Canton and Enderbury islands in the Phoenix Group are jointly administered by the United Kingdom and the United States.

The unit of currency is the Australian dollar. Estimated revenue for 1975 was $A24,944,500 and estimated expenditure $A24,942,500. The principal imports are foodstuffs, consumer goods and building materials. The only exports are phosphates from Ocean Island, and copra, most of which is produced by small landowners. There are three copra plantations in the Line Islands.

Communication between the islands is mainly by small ships operated by the Development Authority, a non-government organisation. There is a weekly service to Fiji. A few islands are served by an internal air service.

The Government maintains a teacher training college and a secondary school. Four junior secondary schools are maintained by missions. Throughout the Colony there are about a hundred primary schools. The total enrolment of children of school age is in the region of 13,000. The Marine Training School at Tarawa trains seamen for service with overseas shipping lines. There is a general hospital at Tarawa and the British Phosphate Commissioners maintain a general hospital on Ocean Island. The other inhabited islands have dispensaries, the larger ones being in the charge of qualified medical officers.

CAPITAL.—Tarawa.   Estimated   population, 17,000.

Governor, His Excellency John Hilary Smith, C.B.E. (1973).

HONG KONG

The Crown Colony of Hong Kong, consisting of a number of islands and of a portion of the mainland, on the south-eastern coast of China, is situated at the eastern side of the mouth of the Pearl River, between 22° 9′ and 22° 37′ N. lat. and 113° 52′–114° 30′ E. long.

The capital city, Victoria, situated on the island of Hong Kong, is about 81 miles S.E. of Canton and 40 miles E. of the Portuguese province of Macau at the other side of the Pearl River. It lies along the northern shore of the island and faces the mainland; the harbour (23 sq. miles water area) lies between the city and the mainland, on which is situated Kowloon with a population equalling that of Victoria. The total area of the territory is 403·8 sq. miles (including recent reclamation) with a population which has varied considerably during recent years owing to unsettled conditions in China: at the end of 1975 it was 4,379,900.

The island of *Hong Kong* is about 11 miles long and from 2 to 5 miles broad, with a total area of 29 square miles; at the eastern entrance to the harbour it is separated from the mainland by a narrow strait (Lei Yue Min), 500–900 yards in width. It was first occupied by Great Britain in January, 1841, and formally ceded by the Treaty of Nanking in 1842; *Kowloon* was subsequently acquired by the Peking Convention of 1860; and the *New Territories*, consisting of a peninsula in the southern part of the Kwangtung province, together with adjacent islands, by a 99-year lease signed June 9, 1898. Hong Kong Island is now linked to the Kowloon peninsula by a mile-long underwater road tunnel opened in 1972.

The island is broken in shape and mountainous, the highest point being Victoria Peak, which is 1,805 feet high. The New Territories contain several peaks higher than this, the highest being Tai Mo Shan, 3,140 ft.

Climate.—Although Hong Kong lies within the tropics it enjoys unusually varied weather for a tropical area. The mean monthly temperature ranges from 15° C. in February to 28° C. in July. Spring is cloudy and humid, often with spells of fog and drizzle. Summer days are hot with temperatures exceeding 33° C. several times in most years. The average annual rainfall is 2,168·8 mm., of which nearly 80 per cent. falls between May and September. Tropical cyclones passing at various distances from Hong Kong sometimes cause high winds and heavy rain, particularly in July, August and September. Autumn and early winter are the most pleasant seasons, with sunny, dry and mild weather. In late winter there is more cloud and strong northerly winds can cause temperatures to drop below 10° C. and frost is not uncommon.

Communications.—Hong Kong, one of the world's finest natural harbours, possesses excellent wharves at which vessels up to 800 ft. in length and 36 ft. draught can be berthed. An ocean terminal pier with an overall length of 1,250 ft. can accommodate large liners and cargo vessels. A recent addition is the Kwai Chung container terminal which opened in 1972. It has six berths, each 1,000 ft. in length, capable of berthing container ships drawing 40 ft. draught. Excellent dockyard facilities are available and include two floating drydocks, one of which can accommodate vessels up to 100,000 deadweight tons. The net tonnage of ocean-going shipping which entered the port in the year to December 31, 1975, amounted to 32,780,000.

Hong Kong International Airport, Kai Tak, situated on the North shore of Kowloon Bay, is an important link on the main air routes of the Far East. It is regularly used by 27 scheduled airlines and many charter airlines, providing frequent services throughout the Far East, to Europe, North America, Africa, Australia and New Zealand.

British Airways operate 20 passenger services per week to Britain, Australia, Africa and Japan. Cathay Pacific Airways, the Hong Kong based airline, operate 89 passenger and cargo services from Hong Kong weekly to points in the Far East. A total of 910 services is operated weekly to and from Hong Kong by scheduled airlines.

During the year ending Dec. 31, 1975, 51,904 aircraft on international flights arrived and departed, carrying 3,865,459 passengers, 141,619 metric tons of freight and 4,764 metric tons of mail.

Education.—In Sept. 1975 there were 2,805 schools with 1,305,918 pupils. About 62·4 per cent. of the pupils are financed wholly or in part by the Government. The University of Hong Kong has a full-time student strength of 3,802 in Faculties of Arts, Science, Medicine, Engineering and Architecture, and Social Sciences and Law. There is also a Centre of Asian Studies and a Department of Extra-Mural Studies. The Chinese University of Hong Kong, inaugurated in Oct. 1963, has a full time enrolment of 3,861 students in Faculties of Arts, Science, Social Science and Business Administration. There is also a Department of Extra-Mural Studies. The Hong Kong Polytechnic has an enrolment of 20,932 full-time and part-time students.

FINANCE

	1974–75	1975–76
Public revenue. . . .	$5,875,309,787	$6,519,539,700
Public expenditure.	6,255,150,535	6,032,190,492

TRADE

Hong Kong is now established as an industrial territory with an economy based on exports rather than the domestic market. Domestic industry, producing mainly light manufactures, has grown rapidly in recent years and now provides the bulk of goods for the export trade; but the secondary role as an *entrepôt*, has also been sustained. In 1974 the value of the re-export trade was 23·7 per cent. of total exports.

Hong Kong produces a wide range of articles, including cotton yarn, cotton piece-goods, garments of all types, woollen and man-made fibre knitwear, electronic products, watches and clocks, footwear, wigs, transistor radios, household enamel and aluminium ware, plastic articles (including household ware, toys and artificial flowers), iron and steel bars, photographic equipment, foodstuffs and beverages, cigarettes, jade, ivory, jewellery and goldsmiths' and silversmiths' ware, and an extensive range of metal products.

Diversification of manufacture continues to be a major feature of recent industrial development, as are industrial partnerships with foreign companies in a wide and varied field of manufactures. New products include quartz watches, shipping containers, air conditioners, automatic telephone dialling equipment, electric household appliances such as rice cookers and toasters, T.V. receiving sets and T.V. tuners and antennae, high grade semi-conductors, electronic modules, electronic flash bulbs, electronic desk calculators and other electronic components, steel pipes, rigid P.V.C. tubes and corrugated sheeting, P.V.C. covered fabrics, mixed cotton-synthetic fabrics, extruded aluminium sections, watches and clocks and fibreglass pleasure craft. Modern manufacturing processes have also been introduced to local industry; these include the permanent press for ready-made garments, soil release processing for garments and the manufacture of polyester fabrics. The marked improvement in both quality and output of items for which precision engineering is required, has continued.

The adverse balance on visible trade is offset by a favourable balance on invisible account-remittances from overseas Chinese, investments, exchange, shipping and insurance profits, and the spending of tourists, etc. In 1975 Hong Kong's principal customers for its domestic products, in order of value of trade, were U.S.A., the Federal Republic of Germany, the United Kingdom,

Australia, Japan, Canada, Singapore, the Netherlands, Sweden and Switzerland. Japan was its principal supplier, followed by China, U.S.A., Taiwan, Singapore, the United Kingdom, the Federal Republic of Germany, Switzerland, South Korea and Australia.

	1974	1975
	H.K. $	H.K. $
Total Exports. .	30,035,685,777	29,831,969,825
Total Imports. .	34,120,084,595	33,471,617,640

	1974	1975
Imports from U.K. . .	£167,400,505	£166,548,839
Exports to U.K.	238,624,317	269,660,845
$12·1 = £1.		

With effect from Nov. 26, 1974, the Hong Kong dollar was allowed to float—that is, market rates would not be maintained within 2¼ per cent. either side of the central rate of HK $5·0850 = US $1. The exchange rates used in the above conversions were the closing selling rates for the last working day of the respective years. Exchange Rates 1974, £1 = HK $11·60. 1975, £1 = HK $10·30.

GOVERNMENT

Hong Kong is administered as a Crown Colony with a Governor, aided by an Executive Council, consisting of 6 official and 8 unofficial members, and a Legislative Council, which consists of 14 official and 15 unofficial members. There is also an Urban Council, financially autonomous, in which is vested, *inter alia*, power of making byelaws in respect of certain matters of public health and sanitation, culture and recreation.

Governor, His Excellency Sir Crawford Murray MacLehose, G.B.E., K.C.M.G., K.C.V.O. (1971) (+ *allce.* £8,393)	£26,228
Commander, British Forces, Lt.-Gen. Sir John Archer, K.C.B., O.B.E.	20,825
Chief Justice, Hon. Sir Geoffrey Briggs . . .	20,825
Colonial Secretary, Hon. Sir Denys Roberts, K.B.E., Q.C.	20,825
Secretary for Administration, P. B. Williams	16,681
Attorney-General, Hon. J. W. D. Hobley, C.M.G., Q.C.	18,255
Secretary for Home Affairs, Hon. D. C. Bray, C.V.O.	18,255
Financial Secretary, Hon. C. P. Haddon-Cave, C.M.G.	19,514
Secretary for the Civil Service, A. J. Scott. .	16,681
Secretary for Economic Services, D. J. C. Jones.	16,681
Secretary for Environment, Hon. J. J. Robson, C.B.E.	16,681
Deputy Financial Secretary, D. G. Jeaffreson	16,681
Secretary for Housing, Hon. I. M. Lightbody, C.M.G.	£16,681
Secretary for Security, Hon. L. M. Davis, C.M.G., C.B.E.	16,681
Secretary for Social Services, Hon. Li Fook-kow	16,681
Secretary for the New Territories, Hon. D. Akers-Jones.	16,681
British Council Representative, K. Westcott, Star House, Kowloon.	

LONDON OFFICE

Hong Kong Government Office
6 Grafton Street, W.1.
Commissioner, S. T. Kidd.

THE NEW HEBRIDES

The New Hebrides Group, in the South Pacific Ocean, situated between the 13th and 21st degrees of South latitude and the 166th and 170th degrees

of East longitude. It includes 13 large and some 70 small islands, including the Banks and Torres Islands in the North, and has a total land area of about 6,050 square miles. The principal islands are Vanua Lava and Gaua (Banks), Espiritu Santo, Maewo, Pentecost, Aoba, Maleku, Ambrym, Epi, Efate, Erromango, Tanna and Aneityum.

The Territory is administered by an unique British-French Condominium Government. The British Resident Commissioner, exercising powers delegated to him by the High Commissioner for the Western Pacific, and the French Resident Commissioner, representing the High Commissioner for France in the Pacific Ocean, are the joint heads of the Administration. They each have staffs of national officers to assist them in general administrative work and the running of social services (health and education) financed from national funds. In addition they control the "joint" public services (posts and telegraphs, public works, mines, meteorology, etc.) which are financed from funds raised in the Territory. The Resident Commissioners are advised regarding policy and legislation by the Advisory Council, a composite body of New Hebrideans, French and British Nationals, some appointed and some elected, which meets twice a year.

The 1967 Census showed a population of 77,988 of whom 72,243 were New Hebrideans. There were 3,841 French Nationals and 1,629 British Nationals but only 1,773 of these were of European ethnic origin. Estimated population (Dec. 31, 1972), 89,031.

Principal products are frozen fish, copra, timber, frozen and canned meat, coffee, cocoa and manganese. Condominium Budget, 1973 (Recurrent and Development) \$A9,000,000; British National Service Budget \$A6,150,000; French National Service Budget NHF574,000,000. Two currencies are in use; the New Hebrides Franc and the Australian dollar.They may be converted at the official rate of exchanges as laid down by the Resident Commissioners.

Seat of New Hebrides Administration—Ψ Vila, Efate, population of Greater Vila, estimated, 1972, 12,715.

British Resident Commissioner, R. W. du Boulay, C.V.O.

French Resident Commissioner, R. Langlois.

PITCAIRN ISLANDS

Pitcairn, a small volcanic island of less than two square miles in area, is the chief of a group of Islands situated about midway between New Zealand and Panama in the South Pacific Ocean at longitude 130° 06′ W. and latitude 25° 04′ S.

The island rises in cliffs to a height of 1,100 feet and access from the sea is possible only at Bounty Bay, a small rocky cove, and then only by whaleboats. Mean monthly temperatures vary between 66° F. in August and 75° F. in February and the average annual rainfall is 80 inches. Moderate easterly and north-easterly winds predominate but short easterly and south-easterly gales occasionally occur from April to September. With an equable climate, the island is very fertile and produces both tropical and sub-tropical trees and crops.

The small community, descendants of the Bounty mutineers and their Tahitian companions who did not wish to remain on Norfolk Island (*see* p. 715) and returned here, numbers about 66 (1976). The Islanders live by subsistence farming and fishing, and their limited monetary needs are satisfied by the manufacture of wood carvings and other handicrafts which are sold to passing ships and to a few

overseas customers. Other than small fees charged for gun and driving licences there are no taxes and Government revenue is derived almost solely from the sale of postage stamps. Communication with the outside world is maintained by cargo vessels travelling between New Zealand and Panama which call at irregular intervals in each direction; and by means of a telegraphic link with Fiji.

The other three islands of the group (Henderson lying 105 miles E.N.E. of Pitcairn, Oeno lying 75 miles N.W. and Ducie lying 293 miles E.) are all uninhabited. Henderson Island is occasionally visited by the Pitcairn Islanders to obtain supplies of "miro" wood which is used for their carvings. Oeno is visited for excursions of about a week's duration every two years or so.

Under a scheme of co-operation, New Zealand supplies Pitcairn with a teacher for the one-teacher primary school on the Island. Education is compulsory between the ages of five and fifteen. Secondary education in Fiji and New Zealand is encouraged by the Administration which provides scholarships and bursaries for the purpose. Medical care is provided by a registered nurse and additional help is obtained when required from the surgeons of passing ships. Since 1887 the islanders have all been adherents of the Seventh Day Adventist Church.

Pitcairn became a British Settlement under the British Settlement Act, 1887, and was administered by the Governor of Fiji from 1952 until 1970, when the administration was transferred to the British High Commission in New Zealand and the British High Commissioner was appointed Governor. The local Government Ordinance of 1964 provides for a Council of ten members of whom four are elected.

Governor of Pitcairn, Ducie, Henderson and Oeno Islands, H. Smedley, C.M.G. (*British High Commissioner for New Zealand*).

––––––––––

Commissioner, R. J. Hicks (*British High Commission,* Auckland, New Zealand).

Island Magistrate and Chairman of Island Council, I. Christian.

Education Officer and Government Adviser, T. Whin.

RHODESIA

Rhodesia, comprising Matabeleland, Mashonaland, Manicaland, Midlands and Victoria, is that part of the territory named after Cecil Rhodes lying south of the Zambesi River, its political neighbours being Zambia and Portuguese East Africa on the N.; the Transvaal and Botswana on the S. and W.; and Portuguese East Africa on the E. Rhodesia has a total area of 150,820 square miles and a population (estimated, 1974) of 6,100,000 (Europeans, 273,000; Africans, 5,800,000; Asians and Coloured, 29,300).

The majority of Africans of Rhodesia (members of the so-called Bantu race), are known as Mashona. In the Western portion of the territory are the descendants of the Amandebele who conquered and settled down among the Mashona, and from whom the Province of Matabeleland derives its name.

Rhodesia was administered by the British South Africa Company from the date of occupation (1890) to 1923, when responsible government was granted. On this latter date the Company relinquished all rights and interests in the land of Rhodesia except in those estates which it was already developing on July 10, 1923. A Land and Agricultural Bank grants loans for farm development and acquisition

of residential property on easy terms of repayment. Under the Land Tenure Act, operative from March 2, 1970, Rhodesia is divided into three areas—European Area (44,950,000 acres), African Area (44,950,000 acres) and National Area (6,600,000 acres).

FINANCE AND TRADE

	1972–73	1973–74
Revenue	$290,100,000	$309,295,000
Expenditure	282,580,000	318,110,000

The expenditure from revenue funds for 1973–74 was estimated at $290,197,000.

TRADE WITH U.K.

	1973	1974
Imports from U.K.	£794,000	£831,000
Exports to U.K.	60,000	105,000

EDUCATION

African education comes under the Minister of Education in the Rhodesian Government. In 1974 there were 3,217 primary schools, 108 secondary schools, 20 teacher training schools, 6 special schools for the physically handicapped, 9 home-craft schools and 60 part-time classes. The total enrolment in African schools, exclusive of evening and part-time schools and study groups, was 835,760. The total enrolment of non-African pupils was 60,107.

GOVERNMENT

Rhodesia (then *Southern Rhodesia*) obtained self-government in 1923 and has a legislative Assembly of 66 members and a Cabinet of 14 members.

Municipal self-government has been established in the cities of Salisbury, Bulawayo, Umtali and Gwelo and the towns of Gatooma, Que Que and Fort Victoria. Smaller areas are administered by Town Management Boards. Over the past ten years local self-government among the Africans has been encouraged.

MINISTRY

On March 2, 1970, the Government of Mr. Ian Smith declared Rhodesia a republic and adopted a new constitution. The British Government has declared the assumption of republican status to be illegal.

The Parliament of Rhodesia, elected on April 10, 1970, consists of 50 Rhodesian Front, 7 Centre Party, 1 National People's Union and 8 Rhodesia Electoral Union Peoples' Party, 2 Democratic Party and 4 Independents.

Prime Minister, Hon. I. D. Smith.

CAPITAL.—SALISBURY, situated on the Mashonaland plateau, altitude 4,850 ft., population (Dec. 1973), 503,000 (European, 122,100; Asian and Coloured, 10,840; African, 370,000). BULAWAYO, the largest town in Matabeleland, altitude 4,450 ft., population (Dec. 1973), 308,000 (European, 58,200; Asian and Coloured, 9,730; African, 240,000). Other centres are Umtali, Gwelo, Gatooma, Que Que, Fort Victoria and Wankie.

Salisbury is 5,600 miles from London (air route) transit 12 hours; by sea, *via* Cape Town, 17 days (approx.).

FLAG.—Vertical stripes of green, white, green; Rhodesian coat of arms in centre of white stripe.

ST. HELENA

Probably the best known of all the solitary islands in the world, St. Helena is situated in the South Atlantic Ocean, 955 miles S. of the Equator, 760 S.E. of Ascension, 1,140 from the nearest point of the African Continent, 1,800 from the coast of S. America, 1,694 from Cape Town and 4,477 from Southampton (transit 3½ days and 9 days

respectively), in 15° 55′ S. lat. and 5° 42′ W. long It is 10½ miles long, 6½ broad, and encloses an area of 47 square miles, with a population in 1975 of 5,058.

St. Helena is of volcanic origin, and consists of numerous rugged mountains, the highest rising to 2,700 feet, interspersed with picturesque ravines. Although within the tropics, the south-east " trades " keep the temperature mild and equable. St. Helena was discovered by the Portuguese navigator, João de Nova, in 1502 (probably on St. Helena's Day) and remained unknown to other European nations until 1588. It was used as a port of call for vessels of all nations trading to the East until it was annexed by the Dutch in 1633. It was never occupied by them, however, and the English East India Company seized it in 1659. In 1834 it was ceded to the Crown. During the period 1815 to 1821 the island was lent to the British Government as a place of exile for the Emperor Napoleon Bonaparte who died in St. Helena on May 5, 1821. It was formerly an important station on the route to India, but its prosperity decreased after the construction of the Suez Canal. Since the collapse of the New Zealand flax (*phormuim tenax*) industry in 1965, there have been no significant exports, but a five year development plan, launched in 1974, seeks primarily to increase the island's productivity in its limited land and sea resources. Ψ St. James's Bay, on the north-west of the Island, possesses a good anchorage.

GOVERNMENT

The government of St. Helena is administered by a Governor, with the aid of a Legislative Council, consisting of the Governor, two *ex-officio* members (Government Secretary and Treasurer) and twelve elected members. Five committees of the Legislative Council are responsible for general oversight of the activities of Government Departments and have in addition a wide range of statutory and administrative functions. The Governor is also assisted by an Executive Council of the two *ex-officio* members and the Chairmen of the Council committees.

Governor, His Excellency Sir Thomas
  Oates, C.M.G., O.B.E., (1971) £3,750
Government Secretary, C. B. Kendall,
  (+ *allce.*)   3,450
Colonial Treasurer and Collector of Customs,
  P. E. Aldous. . . . . (+ *allce.*)   3,150
Chief Justice, Sir Peter Watkin Williams.
  £625 retainer (no fixed salary).
Senior Medical Officer, Dr. J. S. Noaks,
  O.B.E . . . . (+ *allce.*)   2,910
Agricultural and Forestry Officer, R. O.
  Williams . . . . (+ *allce.*)   2,670
Education Officer, C. S. Huxtable . . (+ *allce.*)   2,670

FINANCE AND TRADE

	1974–5	1975–6
Public revenue	£1,356,049	£1,481,539
Expenditure	1,520,101	1,544,027
Total imports	1,115,341	1,192,418

Imports from U.K. in 1975–76 were valued at £706,800.

CAPITAL, Ψ Jamestown. % Population (1974), 1,475.

ASCENSION

The small island of Ascension lies in the South Atlantic (7° 56′ S., 14° 22′ W.) some 700 miles north-west of the island of St. Helena. It is said to have been discovered by João de Nova, on Ascension Day, 1501, and two years later was visited by Alphonse d'Albuquerque, who gave the island its present name. It was uninhabited until the arrival of Napoleon in St. Helena in 1815 when

a small British naval garrison was stationed on the island. The population at December 31, 1975, was 1,131 of whom 698 were St. Helenian. The island remained under the supervision of the Board of Admiralty until 1922, when it was made a dependency of St. Helena by Royal Letters Patent and came under control of the Secretary of State for the Colonies.

Ascension is a rocky peak of purely volcanic origin, the highest point (Green Mountain) some 2,817 ft. is covered with lush vegetation, which with each rainy season is slowly creeping down to the lower areas. Cable & Wireless Ltd., maintains a farm of some 10 acres on the mountain, permitting the production of vegetables and livestock. The island is famous for Turtles, which land on the beaches from January to May to lay their eggs. It is also a breeding area for the sooty tern, or wide-awake, large numbers of which settle on the south-western coastal section every eighth month to hatch their eggs. Other wild life on the island includes feral donkeys and cats, rabbits and francolin partridge. All wild life except rabbits and cats is protected by law. The ocean surrounding the island abounds with shark, barracuda, tuna, bonito and many other fish.

Cable & Wireless Ltd. owns and operates a cable station which connects the Dependency with St. Helena, Sierra Leone, St. Vincent, Rio de Janeiro and Buenos Aires. A B.B.C. relay station was opened on the island in 1966.

Administrator, G. C. Guy, C.M.G., C.V.O., O.B.E.

TRISTAN DA CUNHA

Tristan da Cunha is the chief of a group of islands of volcanic origin lying in lat. 37° 6′ S. and long. 12° 2′ W., discovered in 1506 by a Portuguese admiral (Tristão da Cunha), after whom they are named. They have a total area of 45 square miles. The main island, with a peak rising to 6,760 ft., is about 1,500 miles W. of the Cape of Good Hope, 3,600 miles N.E. of Cape Horn, and about 1,320 miles S.S.W. of St. Helena. It was the resort of British and American sealers from the middle of the 18th century, and in 1760 a British naval officer visited the group and gave his name to Nightingale Island. On August 14, 1816, the group was annexed to the British Crown and a garrison was placed on Tristan da Cunha, but this force was withdrawn in 1817, William Glass, a corporal of artillery (*died* 1853), remaining at his own request, with his wife and two children. This party, with five others, formed a settlement. In 1827 five coloured women from St. Helena, and afterwards others from Cape Colony, joined the party.

The islands form a dependency of St. Helena, being administered by the Foreign and Commonwealth Office through a resident Administrator, with headquarters at the settlement of Edinburgh. Under a new constitution introduced in 1969, he is advised by an elected Island Council of 8 members of whom one must be a woman, and three appointed members, with universal suffrage at 18. The population numbered 292 persons in 1974, plus 7 expatriate Government officers and their families.

In October, 1961, a volcano, believed to have been extinct for thousands of years, erupted and lava was thrown up in some cases to a height of 75 feet. In view of the danger of further volcanic activity, the inhabitants were evacuated and reached the United Kingdom on Nov. 23, 1961, where they remained for nearly two years. An advance party returned to Tristan da Cunha in the spring of 1963, and the main body of the islanders has now returned to the island. Some went back to England in 1966, but most returned in August, 1967.

A boat harbour was completed in 1967. The first freezing factory was re-established in 1966. There are no taxes on Tristan, income being derived from royalties paid by the fishing company and from the sale of stamps. The new Camogli Hospital was opened early in 1971 and a new school was opened in 1975.

Administrator, S. G. Trees, M.V.O., O.B.E.
Chaplain, Rev. E. Buxton.

INACCESSIBLE ISLAND is a lofty mass of rock with sides 2 miles in length; the island is the resort of penguins and sea-fowl. Cultivation was started in 1937, but has been abandoned.

THE NIGHTINGALE ISLANDS are three in number, of which the largest is 1 mile long and ¾ mile wide, and rises in two peaks, 960 and 1,105 ft. above sea-level respectively. The smaller islands, Stoltenhoft and Middle Isle, are little more than huge rocks. Seals, innumerable penguins, and vast numbers of sea-fowl visit these islands.

GOUGH ISLAND (or Diego Alvarez), in 40° 20′ S. and 9° 44′ W., lies about 250 miles S.S.E. of Tristan da Cunha. The island is about 8 miles long and 4 miles broad, with a total area of 40 square miles, and has been a British possession since 1816. The island is the resort of penguins and sea-elephants and has valuable guano deposits. There is no permanent population, but there is a meteorological station maintained on the island by the South African Government and manned by South Africans.

SOLOMON ISLANDS

Governor, His Excellency Colin Hamilton Allan, C.M.G., O.B.E. (1976). (+ *allce.* §A5,000) $A12,850
Chief Justice, R. Davis, O.B.E. .... $A6,590★
Deputy Governor, A. J. Clark, C.B.E., M.V.O.
                      $A7,010★
Attorney General, P. J. Keenan ....★ $A6,505★
Financial Adviser, R. J. Wallace, O.B.E.

★Certain allowances are paid in addition under the Overseas Aid Scheme.

The Protectorate (officially called the Solomon Islands since June 1975), established in 1893, includes all the islands in the Solomons Archipelago S. and S.E. of the large island of Bougainville. The main islands in the Protectorate are Choiseul, Santa Isabel, the Shortlands Group, Vella Lavella, Kolombangara, Ranongga, Gizo, the New Georgia Group, the Florida Group, Guadalcanal, the Russell Islands, Malaita and San Cristobal, and the outlying islands of Bellona, Rennell, Santa Cruz, Vanikolo, Tikopia, Swallow (or Reef Islands) and Duff Groups, the Stewart Islands and the Ontong Java Atoll.

The Solomons are situated between 5–13° S. lat. and 155–170° 20′ E. long. They have a total land area of about 11,500 sq. miles. Distribution of population at the Census of 1970 was: Melanesian 149,667; Polynesian 6,399; Micronesian 2,362; European 1,280; Chinese 577; Others 713. Total 160,998.

CAPITAL, Honiara (population 14,993).

FINANCE AND TRADE

Estimated revenue (1976), $A18,420,000 (incl. British Development Aid $A5,750,000 and grant in aid of recurrent expenditure from the United Kingdom $A1,600,000).

The main imports are foodstuffs, consumer goods, machinery and building materials. Principal exports are copra, timber, fish. Other exports include cocoa, marine shells, tobacco and scrap metal.

GOVERNMENT

The British Solomon Islands Order 1974 came into effect in August 1974, thereby revoking the 1970 Order. The new constitution was drafted in accordance with the recommendations of a special select committee on constitutional development appointed by the former governing council, and established a new office of Governor of the Protectorate (replacing the High Commissioner so far as the Solomon Islands was concerned) and redesignating the Governing Council as the Legislative Assembly, with no increase in membership.

The first Chief Minister was elected from the Legislative Assembly and he in turn chose his Council of Ministers, the equivalent of the Cabinet, The British Solomon Islands (Amendment) Order 1975 increased the number of Ministers from six to eight, and replaced the Financial Secretary by an elected Minister of Finance. The Council of Ministers also includes two *ex officio* members (the Deputy Governor and the Attorney General).

Under the Solomon Islands (Amendment) Order 1975, the territory received a major measure of internal Self Government on January 2, 1976. The Chief Minister became the President of the Council of Ministers in place of the Governor, who is bound under the amended constitution to act in accordance with the advice of the Council. Responsibility for defence, external affairs, internal security and the public service remains however with the Governor.

A general election was held in June 1976 and returned 38 members of the Legislative Assembly, the Legislative having been increased from 24 seats under the Solomon Islands (Amendment) Order 1976. The new Government will negotiate the Independence constitution at a constitutional conference to be held with the British Government before Independence, scheduled for 1977.

JUDICIARY

The High Court of the Solomon Islands constituted by the Solomon Islands Court Order, consists of a Chief Justice and such number of Puisne Judges as may be prescribed by the Governor.

The Court is a Superior Court of Record and possesses all the jurisdiction which is vested in Her Majesty's High Court of Justice in England.

EDUCATION

In consequence of the withdrawal of some of the Churches from primary education, a new primary and secondary structure, with a national teaching service, is now being set up. Government participation in technical and teacher training and further education overseas continues.

COMMUNICATIONS

An internal air service, Solair, serves 19 airstrips, but the bulk of the inter-island traffic is by small ships. There are two air connections weekly each to Brisbane, Papua New Guinea, Fiji and Nauru. There are 283 miles of main roads in the country of which 14 miles are in Honiara. Guadalcanal has some 73 miles of main road along the north coast, with a further 100 miles of feeder roads; Malaita has 98 miles of main roads around the north of the Island; a coastal road is being built along the north coast of San Cristobal, of which some 34 miles has been completed. Except for timber roads, other islands only have short minor roads. All the main islands have transceivers (HF) to maintain communications with Honiara District Headquarters, and there is a VHF link between Honiara and Auki. There are telegraph and radio telephone links with the international networks *via* Fiji and Australia, and there are overseas airmail services on four days a week.

TUVALU

Tuvalu, formerly the Ellice Islands, formed part of the Gilbert and Ellice Islands Colony until October 1, 1975.

On the recommendation of a Commissioner appointed by Her Majesty's Government to consider requests by the Ellice leaders to have their island group separated from the Gilberts, a referendum was held in the autumn of 1974. This showed an overwhelming support for separation, which was formally implemented on October 1 1975. The Ellice Islands then became a separate Colony known as Tuvalu. The remainder of the former Gilbert and Ellice Island Colony became known as the Gilbert Islands. Separation of the Administration took place on January 1, 1976.

Tuvalu comprises nine coral atolls situated in the South West Pacific around the point at which the International Date Line cuts the Equator. The total land area is only about 10 square miles. Few of the atolls are more than 12 feet above sea level or more than half a mile in width. The vegetation consists mainly of coconut palms. The total population, based on a census in 1973, is approximately 10,000, of whom about 1,500 work in the phosphate industry in Nauru or serve in overseas ships. The entire population is Christian and is predominantly Protestant. Most people still practice a subsistence economy, the main staples of their diet being coconuts and fish.

Tuvalu came into being at the same level of constitutional development as that reached in the former joint Colony. The constitution provides for a Chief Minister and two other Ministers. The Queen's representative, who is responsible direct to the Secretary of State in London, is styled Her Majesty's Commissioner. He is chairman of the Cabinet which consists of the three Ministers and two *ex officio* members—the Attorney-General and Financial Secretary. The House of Assembly has eight elected members and the two *ex officio* members. Local Government services are provided by elected Island Councils.

The unit of currency is the Australian dollar. The main imports are foodstuffs, consumer goods and building materials.

The only export is a small amount of copra.

The capital, Funafuti, has a grass strip airfield from which a twice fortnightly service operates. There is no internal air service.

There are eight primary schools in Tuvalu and a church secondary school run jointly with the Government. The total of enrolled children of school age in 1975 was 1,728. There are no training institutes of any kind in the territory.

There is a new 31-bed hospital at Funafuti. All islands (except one which has no permanent population) are served by a dispensary.

CAPITAL.—Funafuti. Estimated population 1,000.

H. M. Commissioner, His Excellency Thomas H. Layng.

VIRGIN ISLANDS,
see BRITISH

THE WEST INDIES

The West Indies are a number of islands and islets, some of them mere rocks, situated between 10° to 27° North and 59° 30' to 85° West. The whole archipelago extends in a curve from the Florida Channel (North America) to within 7 miles of the coast of Venezuela (South America), and is divided into three main groups: I. GREATER ANTILLES, which contain the largest islands, *Cuba* (44,000 sq. miles) and *Hispaniola* (Haiti and the Dominican Republic) (30,000 sq. miles), Jamaica and Puerto Rico; II. BAHAMAS, which is now independent.

III. LESSER ANTILLES, which are variously divided; the British islands in the Lesser Antilles are the Leeward and Windward Islands. The total area of the archipelago is nearly 100,000 square miles, of which 72,000 square miles are *Independent*, 12,300 *British*, 3,890 *United States*, 1,350 *French*, 430 *Netherlands*, and 90 *Venezuelan*.

The West India Islands which lie nearest the East have been called the *Windward Islands*; the others the *Leeward Islands*, on account of the winds which in this area generally blow from the east.

COMMISSION FOR THE EASTERN CARIBBEAN
GOVERNMENTS
10 Haymarket, S.W.1
Commissioner, Dr. Claudius C. Thomas.

———

The British West Indies were governed under a series of federal arrangements, the last of which, a federation of the Leeward and Windward Islands with Barbados, was abandoned in 1966. The islands of Antigua, Dominica, Grenada, St. Kitts-Nevis-Anguilla and St. Lucia became States in association with Britain in February and March 1967. St. Vincent became an Associated State in October, 1969. Grenada became independent on Feb. 7, 1974. Britain's power and responsibilities are limited to defence and external affairs.

West Indies Associated States
The Associated States are described individually in the following sections. The Office of the British Government Representative is at George Gordon Building (P.O. Box 227), Castries, St. Lucia.
British Government Representative, E. G. Le Tocq, C.M.G.
Deputy do., C. G. Mortlock.
Development Adviser, Sir Bruce Greatbach, K.C.V.O., C.M.G., M.B.E. (*Resident at* Bridgetown, Barbados).

Supreme Court
Established by Order in Council (1967), which gives the Court additional jurisdiction in Montserrat and the British Virgin Islands. There are two constituents, a Court of Appeal and a High Court. The Chief Justice is appointed by Her Majesty and puisne judges by the Judicial and Legal Services Commission. Expenses of the Supreme Court, after allowing for contributions from Montserrat and the Virgin Islands, are met by the States in equal shares.
Chief Justice, Sir Maurice Davis, O.B.E., Q.C.
Justices of Appeal, E. L. St. Bernard; N. Peterkin (*acting*).
Puisne Judges, N. A. Berridge (*St. Vincent*); E. A. Bishop (*Antigua*); W. A. Bruno (*Dominica*); E. F. Glasgow (*St. Kitts-Nevis*); C. E. Hewlett (*Montserrat and British Virgin Islands*); R. A. Nedd (*Grenada*); J. D. B. Renwick (*St. Lucia*).

ANTIGUA
Antigua lies in 17° 6′ N. lat. and 61° 45′ W. long., and is nearly 108 square miles in area with a coast-line of about 70 miles. Antigua was first settled by the English in 1632, and was granted to Lord Willoughby by Charles II. Population in 1970 totalled 65,000. Antigua is much less hilly and wooded than the other Leeward Islands. Exports include petroleum products refined in the island. Cotton and rum are also exported. Tourism is the most important industry, with a good choice of resort hotels mostly built to take advantage of the many fine white sand beaches. There are frequent air services to Canada, U.S.A. and the United Kingdom.

FLAG.—Inverted triangle (centred on a red field) divided horizontally into three bands of black over blue over white; rising sun device in gold on black band.

Finance and Trade

	1973
Revenue	EC$27,644,000
Expenditure (recurrent)	23,718,000
Total imports	94,504,000

Governor, Sir Wilfred Ebenezer Jacobs, O.B.E., Q.C. (1967) (*plus* £1,000 allce. and house)..... $22,300

Trade with U.K.

	1973	1974*
Imports from U.K.	£4,215,000	£6,303,000
Exports to U.K.	135,000	2,532,000

* Including British Virgin Islands.

Barbuda, formerly a possession of the Codrington family, is situated 30 miles N. of Antigua, of which it is a dependency, in lat. 17° 35′ N., long. 61° 42′ W. Area, 62 square miles. Population, 1,000. The island is flat and mostly stony, producing cotton, corn and ground-nuts. Wild deer are found, and there is good tarpon and other fishing.
Redonda is uninhabited.
CAPITAL ♸ St. John's. Population 22,000.

THE CAYMAN ISLANDS
The Cayman Islands, between 79° 44′ and 81° 26′ W. and 19° 15′ and 19° 46′ N., consist of three islands, Grand Cayman, Cayman Brac, and Little Cayman, with a total area of 100 square miles. Population (Census, 1970), 10,652. The constitution provides for a Governor, Legislative Assembly and an Executive Council. The Legislative Assembly consists of the Governor, not fewer than two nor more than three official members and 12 elected members. The Executive Council consists of the Governor and three official members appointed by the Governor, and four elected members, chosen by the elected members of the Assembly from among their own number. The normal life of the Assembly is four years. Supervisory powers over the government of the Islands exercised by the Government of Jamaica came to an end in August, 1962.

The principal town is ♸ George Town, in Grand Cayman, population (1970 census) 3,000.

FINANCE

	1975
Revenue	CI$9,039,386
Expenditure	9,323,824
Public Debt	966,293

TRADE

	1975
Total imports	CI$22,519,253
Total exports	204,000

MONTSERRAT
Situated in 16° 45′ N. lat. and 61° 15′ W. long., 27 miles S.W. of Antigua, the island is about 11 miles long and 7 wide, with an area of 39 square miles; population (1972), 12,905. Discovered by Columbus in 1493, it was settled by Irishmen in 1632, conquered and held by the French for some time, and finally assigned to Great Britain in 1783. It is justly considered one of the most healthy and beautiful of the Antilles; it contains two active soufrières and several hot springs, while the scenery is charmingly diversified. About two-thirds of the island is mountainous, the rest capable of cultivation. The chief exports are sea island cotton, tomatoes and other fruits and vegetables. Real estate development and tourism have done much to aid the island's economy. Revenue (1974) EC$6,307,000; Expenditure EC$7,275,000.

Cabinet government was introduced in Montserrat in 1960. The Executive Council is composed of 4 elected members (the Chief and 3 other Ministers) and two official members (the Attorney-General and the Financial Secretary). The 4 Ministers are appointed from the members of the political party holding the majority in the Legislative Council. The present composition of the Legislative Council consists of the President (the Governor), two official members, one nominated unofficial member and 7 elected members.

Governor (vacant).

EXECUTIVE COUNCIL

Chairman, The Governor.
Chief Minister and Minister of Finance, Hon. P. A. Bramble.
Minister of Education, Health and Welfare, Hon. Mrs. M. R. Tuitt.
Agriculture, Trade, Lands and Housing, Hon. W. H. Ryan.
Communications and Works, Hon. E. A. Dyer.
Attorney-General, Hon. J. S. Weekes.
Financial Secretary, Hon. J. O. Whitaker.

Secretary to the Executive Council, K. A. Cassell.
CHIEF TOWN.— Ψ Plymouth (1,300).

ST. KITTS-NEVIS-ANGUILLA

Governor, His Excellency Sir Probyn Ellsworth Inniss, M.B.E. (1975).

The State of St. Kitts-Nevis-Anguilla is located at the northern end of the Eastern Caribbean. It comprises the islands of St. Kitts (65 sq. miles, population about 35,000), Nevis (36 sq. miles, 13,000), and Anguilla (35 sq. miles, 6,200).

St. Kitts, lat. 17° 18′ N. and long. 62° 48′ W. was the first island in the British West Indies to be colonised (1623). Its economy has been based on sugar for over three centuries. Tourism and light industry is being developed. The central area of the island is forest-clad and mountainous, rising to the 3,792 ft. Mount Misery. The capital, Basseterre, is a port of registry. Golden Rock airport can take large jet aircraft.

Nevis, lat. 17° 10′ N. and long. 62° 35′ W. is separated from the southern tip of St. Kitts by a strait two miles wide. The sea ferry route from Basseterre, St. Kitts to Charlestown, Nevis is 11 miles. Newcastle airstrip can take small aircraft, e.g. Islanders: no night landing facilities are available. The economy of Nevis centres on small peasant farmers. The island is dominated by the central Nevis Peak, 3,232 ft. The chief town, Ψ Charlestown, is a port of entry.

The Territory of St. Kitts-Nevis-Anguilla became a State in Association with Britain on Feb. 27, 1967. The State became responsible for internal affairs, while Britain became responsible for defence and external affairs. Her Majesty the Queen is represented by a Governor, appointed by her. There is a Cabinet Government with a Ministerial system.

CAPITAL: Basseterre (St. Kitts), population about 17,000. FLAG: Tricolor of green (next staff), yellow and blue vertical stripes; palm tree device on yellow stripe.

ANGUILLA

Anguilla is a flat coralline island about 70 miles N.W. of St. Kitts. The island is rather less than 16 miles in length, 3½ miles in breadth at its widest point and its area is about 35 sq. miles. The population is 6,500 (1974). Salt and lobster are the principal products.

The island is covered with low scrub and fringed with some of the finest white coral-sand beaches in the Caribbean. The climate is pleasant and healthy with temperatures in the range of 75-85°F. throughout the year.

Three months after the Associated State of Saint Christopher (St. Kitts)-Nevis-Anguilla came into being in 1967 the Anguillans repudiated government from St. Kitts. In 1971 the Anguilla Bill and Anguilla (Administration) Order were enacted, which provide for the administration of Anguilla by a Commissioner who is appointed by Her Majesty The Queen.

H.M. Commissioner for Anguilla, D. F. B. Le Breton (1974).

TURKS AND CAICOS ISLANDS

The Turks and Caicos Islands are situated between 21°-72°-30° West, about 100 miles north of Haiti and 50 miles West of the Bahamas of which they are geographically an extension.

There are over 30 islands of which eight are inhabited covering an estimated area of 192 square miles. The principal is Grand Turk. The 1970 Census of population showed a total population of 5,675 (Grand Turk 2,500). The most important industry is fishing but tourism is of increasing importance with over 8,000 visitors in 1975.

The Islands lie in the Trade Wind but with an excellent climate. The average temperature varies from 75°-80°F. in the Winter and 85°F.-90°F. in the summer and humidity is generally low. Average rainfall is 21 inches per annum. Hurricanes are rare, the last occurring in 1960.

The principal airports are on the islands of Grand Turk, South Caicos and Providenciales. There are direct shipping services to the U.S.A.(Miami). There is a twice weekly air service between Miami, Florida and Grand Turk and a weekly air service between Nassau, Bahamas and South Caicos. An internal air service provides a twice daily service between the principal islands. A comprehensive telephone and telex service is provided by Cable and Wireless (W.I.) Ltd.

FINANCE

	1974	1975
Revenue	$3,022,536	$3,378,000
Expenditure	$3,534,870	3,692,000

TRADE

	1973	1974
Imports	$3,625,404	$3,989,217
Exports	504,867	511,681

A new Constitution was agreed for introduction in 1976, providing for an Executive Council and Legislative Council, and for the appointment of a Chief Minister and three other Ministers from elected members of the Legislative.

Governor, His Excellency A. C. Watson.

The Windward Islands

The Windward Islands consist of Grenada, now independent, and the three Associated States of St. Vincent, St. Lucia and Dominica with their dependencies. Since March 1967, with the attainment of Associated Statehood, there has been a Governor in St. Lucia and Dominica and in St. Vincent since October, 1969. Each island has its own elected Parliament and a Premier. St. Vincent, St. Lucia and Dominica operate under single-chamber Parliaments, known in each case as the House of Assembly. The ministerial form of government was introduced in 1956. Grenada became independent in 1974.

ST. LUCIA

St. Lucia, the second largest and the most picturesque of the Windward group, situated in 13° 54′ N. lat. and 60° 50′ W. long., at a distance of about 90 miles W.N.W. of Barbados, 21 miles N. of St.

Vincent, and 24 miles S. of Martinique, is 27 miles in length, with an extreme breadth of 14 miles. It comprises an area of 238 square miles with an estimated population (1974) of 110,780. About 56,000 acres are devoted to agriculture. It possesses perhaps the most interesting history of all the smaller islands. Fights raged hotly around it, and it constantly changed hands between the English and the French. It is mountainous, its highest point being 3,145 feet above the sea, and for the most part it is covered with forest and tropical vegetation. The principal exports are bananas, copra, coconuts, cocoa, edible oil. Over 31,600 tons of bananas, valued at $17,539,000, were exported to the U.K. in 1975. The chief imports are flour, machinery, cotton piece goods, building materials and fertilisers.

CAPITAL.— Ψ Castries (estimated population, 47,000) is recognized as being one of the finest ports in the West Indies on account of its reputation as a safe anchorage in the hurricane season. FLAG.— Blue, bearing in centre a device of yellow over black over white triangles having a common base.

Government

There is a Cabinet of Ministers presided over by the premier and consisting of five other Ministers and the Attorney-General. There is a Legislature which consists of Her Majesty and a House of Assembly, of which the normal life is five years. The House of Assembly consists of a Speaker who may be elected from within or without the House, 17 elected and three nominated members and the Attorney General. The Constitution provides for a political Attorney-General if the Legislature or the Premier so decides.

Governor, Sir Allen Montgomery Lewis, Q.C.
Premier, J. G. M. Compton.

ST. VINCENT

St. Vincent achieved Associated Statehood with the United Kingdom on October 27, 1969. The territory of the State of St. Vincent includes certain of the Grenadines, a group of islands set across the Caribbean sea, stretching 40 miles south, some of the larger of which are Bequia, Canouan, Mayreau, Mustique, Union Island, Petit St. Vincent and Isle-a-Quatre. The territory extends 150 square miles (96,000 acres).

The main island, St. Vincent, is situated between 13° 6′ and 14° 35′ N. Latitude and 61° 6′ and 61° 20′ W. Longitude approximately 21 miles South West of St. Lucia and 100 miles West of Barbados. The island is 18 miles long and 100 miles wide at its extremities comprising an area of 133 square miles and an estimated population of 90,000 (1970). St. Vincent was discovered by Christopher Columbus in 1498. It was granted by Charles I to the Earl of Carlisle in 1627 and after subsequent grants and a series of occupations alternately by the French and English, it was finally restored to Britain in 1783. The capital and principal port is Ψ Kingstown, population approximately 23,000.

The economy is based mainly on agriculture but the tourist industry has been rapidly expanding, bringing approximately $5,500,000 to the State in 1972. The main products are bananas, arrowroot, coconuts, cocoa, spices, and various kinds of food crops. The main imports are foodstuffs (meat, rice, sugar, flour, butter and pickled and salted fish), textiles, lumber, cement and other building materials, fertilizers and motor vehicles.

The territory's education system provides a general primary and secondary education. Primary education is free but not compulsory. In 1972 there were 61 primary schools with a total enrolment of 27,609; and 16 secondary schools with a total enrolment of 4,015.

Government.—As an Associated State St. Vincent has a constitution under which there is a Governor who is Her Majesty's Representative. Except where otherwise provided, the Governor is required to act in accordance with the advice of the Cabinet. Statehood allows St. Vincent the full self-governing control of its internal affairs including the right to amend its own constitution and the power to end the Association and declare itself independent. The United Kingdom Government accepts the responsibility for the State's external affairs and defence.

Governor, His Excellency Sir Rupert Godfrey John.
Chief Minister, Hon. R. M. Cato.

The House of Assembly consists of 13 elected members, three nominated members and the Attorney-General. It is presided over by a Speaker elected by the House from within or without it.

DOMINICA

Dominica, the loftiest of the Lesser Antilles, was transferred from the Leeward to the Windward Group on Jan. 1, 1940. It is situated between 15° 20′ and 15° 45′ N. lat. and 61° 13′ and 61° 30′ W. long., 95 miles S. of Antigua, and is about 29 miles long and 15 broad comprising an area of 290 sq. miles, of which about 41,000 acres are under cultivation. The island is of volcanic origin and very mountainous and picturesque, abounding in streams fairly well stocked with fish, and the soil is very fertile. The temperature varies, according to the altitude, from 55° to 85°F. The climate is healthy, and during the winter months is very pleasant. The exports consist almost entirely of agricultural produce, principally bananas, lime oil, lime juice, oranges, bay oil, cocoa, copra, ground provisions, grapefruits, coconut oil and washing soap. Population (estimated, 1974, 74,000). The principal towns are Ψ Roseau, on the south-west coast population, 10,157 and Portsmouth, population, 2,379.

Education.—There are 57 elementary schools providing primary and post-primary education, with a total enrolment of 20,821 pupils and seven secondary (grammar) schools, including one for boys and two for girls, with a total enrolment of 2,269 pupils. The other secondary schools are co-educational. Primary education is free. There are 63 pre-schools in Dominica for the 3 to 5 year age group. There are also two post-secondary institutions and a Nursing School.

Finance and Trade

	1972	1973
Revenue (incl. Grants)	$19,140,895	$12,611,000
Expenditure (do.)....	19,670,419	19,267,000

Government

On March 1, 1967, Dominica became an Associated State of the United Kingdom. The Queen's Representative was redesignated the Governor.

The House of Assembly now comprises 21 elected and 3 nominated members, one nominated on the advice of the Leader of the Opposition. The Cabinet (Executive) presided over by the Premier, consists of 7 other Government Ministers and the Attorney-General (Official Member). The Premier is appointed by the Governor from the elected members of the House of Assembly. The other Ministers are appointed by the Governor on the advice of the Premier. The Speaker is elected from among the members of the House or from outside.

Governor, His Excellency Sir Louis Cools-Lartigue, O.B.E. (1967).
Premier, Hon. Patrick John.

UNIVERSITIES OF THE COMMONWEALTH
(outside the United Kingdom)

With date of foundation, number of full-time students and name of Executive Head

(*Vice-Chancellor, President or Principal*)

Australia

ADELAIDE (1874). (Full-time students, 6,533).—*Vice-Chancellor*, Prof. G. M. Badger, A.O., Ph.D., D.SC.

AUSTRALIAN NATIONAL (1946), Canberra. (3,810).—*Vice-Chancellor*, Prof. D. A. Low, D.Phil.

DEAKIN (1974), Geelong. (First students, 1978).—*Vice-Chancellor*, Prof. F. R. Jevons, Ph.D., D.SC.

FLINDERS, SOUTH AUSTRALIA (1966), Adelaide. (2,580).—*Vice-Chancellor*, Prof. R. W. Russell, Ph.D., D.SC.

GRIFFITH (1971), Brisbane. (398).—*Vice-Chancellor*, Prof. F. J. Willett, D.S.C., LL.D.

JAMES COOK, NORTH QUEENSLAND (1970), Townsville. (1,268).—*Vice-Chancellor*, K. J. C. Back, Ph.D.

LA TROBE (1964), Melbourne. (5,279).—*Vice-Chancellor*, Prof. J. F. Scott.

MACQUARIE (1964), Sydney. (4,542).—*Vice-Chancellor*, Prof. E. C. Webb, Ph.D.

MELBOURNE (1853). (11,079).—*Vice-Chancellor*, Prof. D. P. Derham, C.M.G., M.B.E., LL.D.

MONASH (1958), Melbourne. (9,746).—*Vice-Chancellor*, Prof. W. A. G. Scott.

MURDOCH (1973), Perth. (416).—*Vice-Chancellor*, Prof. S. Griew, Ph.D.

NEWCASTLE (1965). (2,597).—*Vice-Chancellor*, Prof. D. W. George, Ph.D.

NEW ENGLAND (1954), Armidale. (2,935).—*Vice-Chancellor*, Prof. A. Lazenby, Ph.D.

NEW SOUTH WALES (1949), Sydney. (13,129).—*Vice-Chancellor*, Prof. R. H. Myers, Ph.D.
W. S. & L. B. ROBINSON UNIV. COLL. (1967), Broken Hill.—*Director*, Prof. J. E. Andersen, Ph.D.

QUEENSLAND (1909), Brisbane. (9,508).—*Vice-Chancellor*, Prof. Sir Z. Cowen, C.M.G., Q.C., D.C.L., LL.D.

SYDNEY (1850). (13,668).—*Vice-Chancellor*, Prof. B. R. Williams, D.Litt.

TASMANIA (1890), Hobart. (2,314).—*Vice-Chancellor*, Sir George Cartland, C.M.G.

WESTERN AUSTRALIA (1911), Perth. (6,283).—*Vice-Chancellor*, Prof. R. F. Whelan, M.D., Ph.D., D.SC.

WOLLONGONG (1975). (1,116).—*Vice-Chancellor*, Prof. L. M. Birt, Ph.D., D.Phil.

Bangladesh

BANGLADESH AGRICULTURAL (1961), Mymensingh. (Full-time students, 2,730).—*Vice-Chancellor*, Prof. M. U. A. Choudhury.

BANGLADESH U. OF ENGINEERING AND TECHNOLOGY (1961), Dacca. (1,708).—*Vice-Chancellor*, Wahiduddin Ahmad, Ph.D.

CHITTAGONG (1966). (35,173).—*Vice-Chancellor*, Prof. A. Karim.

DACCA (1921). (66,223).—*Vice-Chancellor*, Prof. F. H. Choudhury.

JAHANGIRNAGAR (1970), Dacca. (904).—*Vice-Chancellor*, Prof. Z. R. Siddiqui.

RAJSHAHI (1953). (56,339).—*Vice-Chancellor*, Prof. S. Ali Ahsan.

Canada

ACADIA (1838), Wolfville. (Full-time students, 2,603).—*President*, J. M. R. Beveridge, M.D., Ph.D., D.SC., LL.D.

ALBERTA (1906), Edmonton. (19,155).—*President*, H. E. Gunning, Ph.D., D.SC.

BISHOP'S (1843), Lennoxville. (728).—*Vice-Chancellor*, C. I. H. Nicholl.

BRANDON (1967). (959).—*President*, A. L. Dulmage, Ph.D.

BRITISH COLUMBIA (1908), Vancouver. (19,866).—*President*, D. T. Kenny, Ph.D.

BROCK (1964), St. Catharines. (2,383).—*President*, A. J. Earp, LL.D.

CALGARY (1966). (9,578).—*President*, W. A. Cochrane, M.D.

CARLETON (1942), Ottawa. (8,448).—*President*, M. K. Oliver, Ph.D., LL.D.

CONCORDIA (1929), Montreal. (10,102).—*Principal*, J. W. O'Brien, Ph.D.

DALHOUSIE (1818), Halifax. (6,784).—*President*, The Hon. H. D. Hicks, C.C., Q.C., LL.D., D.Ed., D.C.L.
UNIV. OF KING'S COLL. (1789), Halifax. (253).—*President*, J. G. Morgan, D.Phil.

DOMINICAN COLL. OF PHILOSOPHY AND THEOLOGY (1967), Ottawa. (218).—*President*, Rev. Father G.-D. Mailhiot.

GUELPH (1964). (9,139).—*Vice-Chancellor*, D. F. Forster.

LAKEHEAD (1965), Thunder Bay. (2,387).—*Vice-Chancellor*, A. D. Booth, Ph.D., D.SC.

LAURENTIAN, SUDBURY (1960). (2,187).—*President*, (vacant).

LAVAL (1852), Quebec. (13,189).—*Rector Magnificus*, L. Kerwin, LL.D., D.SC.

LETHBRIDGE (1967). (1,156).—*President*, W. E. Beckel, Ph.D.

MCGILL (1821), Montreal. (16,379).—*Principal*, R. E. Bell, C.C., Ph.D., D.SC., LL.D.

MCMASTER (1887), Hamilton. (9,421).—*President*, A. N. Bourns, D.SC., Ph.D.

MANITOBA (1877), Winnipeg. (13,776).—*President*, Prof. R. Campbell, LL.D.
ST. JOHN'S COLL. (1866), Winnipeg.—*Warden*, Rev. Canon J. R. Brown, D.D.
ST. PAUL'S COLL. (1926), Winnipeg.—*Rector*, Very Rev. V. Jensen.

MEMORIAL, NEWFOUNDLAND (1949), St. John's. (5,944).—*Vice-Chancellor*, M. O. Morgan, C.C., LL.D., D.C.L.

MONCTON (1963). (3,080).—*Rector*, J. Cadieux, D.SC.ECON.

MONTREAL (1876). (32,870 full- and part-time).—*Rector*, P. Lacoste, D.U.

MOUNT ALLISON (1858), Sackville. (1,408).—*President*, W. S. H. Crawford, Ph.D.

MOUNT ST. VINCENT (1925), Halifax. (1,179).—*President*, Sister Mary Albertus, Ph.D.

NEW BRUNSWICK (1785), Fredericton. (5,424).—*President*, J. M. Anderson, Ph.D.

NOVA SCOTIA AGRICULTURAL COLL. (1905), Truro. (426).—*Principal*, H. F. MacRae, Ph.D.

NOVA SCOTIA COLL. OF ART AND DESIGN (1887), Halifax. (425).—*President*, G. N. Kennedy.

NOVA SCOTIA TECHNICAL COLL. (1909), Halifax. (465).—*Acting President*, A. E. Steeves.

OTTAWA (1848). (10,215).—*Rector*, Rev. R. Guindon, C.C., D.Th., LL.D.
ST. PAUL (1848), Ottawa (330).—*Rector*, Rev. Father M. Patry, D.Ph., Ph.D.

PRINCE EDWARD ISLAND (1969), Charlottetown (1,397).—*President*, R. J. Baker, LL.D.

QUEBEC (1968), Chicoutimi, Montreal, Rimouski, Trois-Rivières, and other centres (9,016).—*President*, R. Després.

QUEEN'S, KINGSTON (1841). (9,616).—*Principal*, R. L. Watts, D.Phil.

REGINA (1974). (3,599).—*President*, L. I. Barber, D.B.A.

ROYAL MILITARY COLL. OF CANADA (1876), Kingston. (679).—*Principal*, J. R. Dacey, M.B.E., Ph.D.

RYERSON POLYTECHNICAL INSTITUTE (1963), Toronto. (8,083).—*President*, W. G. Pitman.

COLL. STE.-ANNE, N. S.—*President*, L. Comeau.

ST. FRANCIS XAVIER (1853), Antigonish. (2,205).— *President*, Rev. M. MacDonell, LL.D.

COLL. OF CAPE BRETON, Sydney.—*President*, D. F. Campbell.

ST. MARY'S (1841), Halifax. (2,331).—*President*, D. O. Carrigan, Ph.D.

SASKATCHEWAN, (1907). Saskatoon (9,462).—*President*, R. W. Begg, M.D., D.Phil.

ST. THOMAS MORE COLL. (1936), Saskatoon.— *Principal*, Rev. P. J. M. Swan, Ph.D.

SHERBROOKE (1954). (5,031).—*Rector*, Y. Martin.

SIMON FRASER (1963), Burnaby. (5,305).—*President*, Pauline Jewett, Ph.D.

TORONTO (1827). (31,684).—*President*, J. R. Evans, D.Phil., M.D., LL.D., D.Sc.

UNIV. OF ST. MICHAEL'S COLL. (1852), Toronto. (2,248).—*President*, Rev. J. M. Kelly, Ph.D.

UNIV. OF TRINITY COLL. (1851), Toronto. (970).—*Vice-Chancellor*, G. Ignatieff, C.C., LL.D., D.C.L.

VICTORIA (1836), Toronto. (2,534).—*President*, G. S. French, Ph.D.

———

ONTARIO INSTITUTE FOR STUDIES IN EDUCATION (1965), Toronto. (534).—*Director*, C. C. Pitt, Ph.D.

TRENT (1963), Peterborough. (1,983).—*President*, Prof. T. E. W. Nind.

VICTORIA (1963), British Columbia. (5,216).— *President*, H. E. Petch, Ph.D.

WATERLOO (1959). (12,155).—*Vice-Chancellor*, B. C. Matthews, Ph.D.

ST. JEROME'S COLL., Waterloo.—*President*, C. L. Siegfried, LL.D.

WESTERN ONTARIO (1878), London. (17,202).— *President*, D. C. Williams, Ph.D., LL.D.

BRESCIA COLL. (1919), London.—*Principal*, Sister Frances Ryan, Ph.D.

HURON COLL. (1863), London.—*Principal*, Ven. J. G. Morden, D.D., D.Th.

KING'S COLL. (1912), London.—*Principal*, A. F. McKee, D.U.

WILFRED LAURIER (1973), Waterloo. (2,687).— *President*, F. C. Peters, Ph.D.

WINDSOR (1857). (6,001).—*Vice-Chancellor*, J. F. Leddy, O.C., D.Phil., D.Litt., D. ès L., LL.D., D.C.L.

WINNIPEG (1967). (2,661).—*President*, H. E. Duckworth, Ph.D., D.Sc.

YORK (1959), Toronto. (12,077).—*President*, H. I. Macdonald.

Ghana

CAPE COAST (1962). (Full-time students 1,131).— *Vice-Chancellor*, Prof. J. Y. Ewusie, Ph.D.

GHANA (1961), Legon. (2,834).—*Vice-Chancellor*, D. A. Bekoe, D.Phil.

UNIV. OF SCIENCE AND TECHNOLOGY (1961), Kumasi. (2,038).—*Vice-Chancellor*, E. B. Kwakye, Dr.Ing.

Guyana

GUYANA (1963), Georgetown. (Full-time students, 1,397).—*Vice-Chancellor*, D. H. Irvine, Ph.D.

Hong Kong

CHINESE UNIV. OF HONG KONG (1963). (Full-time students, 3,437).—*Vice-Chancellor*, C. M. Li, K.B.E.(hon.), Ph.D., LL.D., D.S.Sc.

HONG KONG (1911). (3,648).—*Vice-Chancellor*, R. L. Huang, D.Phil., D.Sc.

India

AGRA (1927). (Full-time students, 64,248).—*Vice-Chancellor*, B. P. Johari.

AGRICULTURAL SCIENCES (1964), Bangalore. (2,585). —*Vice-Chancellor*, H. R. Arakeri, Ph.D.

ALIGARH MUSLIM (1920). (10,478).—*Vice-Chancellor*, A. M. Khusro, Ph.D.

ALLAHABAD (1887). (11,583).—*Vice-Chancellor*, R. Sahay.

ANDHRA (1926), Waltair. (48,844).—*Vice-Chancellor*, M. R. Apparow.

ANNAMALAI (1928), Annamalainagar. (5,857).— *Vice-Chancellor*, S. Chandrasekhar, Ph.D.

ASSAM AGRICULTURAL (1969), Jorhat. (704).—*Vice-Chancellor*, Dr. L. S. Negi.

AWADHESH PRATAP SINGH VISHWAVIDYALAYA (1968), Rewa. (21,661).—*Vice-Chancellor*, N. Sinh.

BANARAS HINDU (1915). (13,483).—*Vice-Chancellor*, K. L. Shrimali, Ph.D.

BANGALORE (1964). (30,485).—*Vice-Chancellor*, H. Narasimhaiah, Ph.D.

BARODA (1949). (23,740).—*Vice-Chancellor*, Prof. P. J. Madan.

BERHAMPUR (1967). (10,075).—*Vice-Chancellor*, Justice B. K. Patra.

BHAGALPUR (1960). (23,425).—*Vice-Chancellor*, D. P. Singh.

BHOPAL VISHWAVIDYALAYA (1970). (16,602).—*Vice-Chancellor*, R. Prakash, Ph.D., D.Sc.

BIHAR (1952), Muzaffarpur. (52,554).—*Vice-Chancellor*, K. K. Mandal, Ph.D.

BIRENDRA NARAYAN CHAKRAVARTY (1956), Kurukshetra. (82,316).—*Vice-Chancellor*, S. K. Dutta, D.Litt.

BOMBAY (1857). (108,509).—*Vice-Chancellor*, T. K. Tope.

BURDWAN (1960). (68,254).—*Vice-Chancellor*, R. Mukherji, D.Phil., D.Litt.

CALCUTTA (1857). (210,634).—*Vice-Chancellor*, S. N. Sen, Ph.D.

CALICUT (1968). (50,440).—*Vice-Chancellor*, N. A. Noor Mahomed.

COCHIN (1971), Tripunithura. (504).—*Vice-Chancellor*, Dr. N. K. Panikkar.

DELHI (1922). (65,088).—*Vice-Chancellor*, R. C. Mehrotra, D.Phil.

DIBRUGARH (1965). (33,537).—*Vice-Chancellor*, J. N. Das.

GARHWAL (1973), Srinagar. (12,000).—*Vice-Chancellor*, B. D. Bhatt.

GAUHATI (1948). (46,256).—*Vice-Chancellor*, H. K. Baruah, Ph.D.

GORAKHPUR (1956). (63,379).—*Vice-Chancellor*, D. Sharma, Ph.D., D.Phil.

GOVIND BALLABH PANT U. OF AGRICULTURE AND TECHNOLOGY (1960), Pantnagar. (2,192).—*Vice-Chancellor*, S. P. Pande.

GUJARAT (1949), Ahmedabad. (98,857).—*Vice-Chancellor*, I. J. Patel.

GUJARAT AGRICULTURAL (1969), Ahmedabad. (1,843).—*Vice-Chancellor*, V. R. Mehta.

GURU NANAK DEV (1969), Amritsar. (47,737).— *Vice-Chancellor*, B. Singh Samundri.

HIMACHAL PRADESH (1970), Simla. (21,965).—*Vice-Chancellor*, B. S. Jogi.

INDIAN INSTITUTE OF SCIENCE (1909), Bangalore. (957).—*Director*, S. Dhawan, Ph.D.

INDIAN INST. OF TECHNOLOGY, BOMBAY (1958). (1,969).—*Director*, A. K. De, Ph.D.

INDIAN INST. OF TECHNOLOGY, DELHI (1961). (1,811).—*Director*, Prof. N. M. Swani, Ph.D.

INDIAN INST. OF TECHNOLOGY, KANPUR (1960). (1,899).—*Director*, J. Lal, Dr.Sc.Tech.

INDIAN INST. OF TECHNOLOGY, KHARAGPUR (1951). (2,387).—*Director*, Prof. C. S. Jha.

INDIAN INST. OF TECHNOLOGY, MADRAS (1959). (2,110).—*Director*, K. A. V. Pandalai.

INDIRA KALA SANGIT VISHWAVIDYALAYA (1956), Khairagarh. (3,150).—*Vice-Chancellor*, G. C. Jain.

INDORE (1964). (18,390).—*Vice-Chancellor*, Dr. P. G. Deo.

JABALPUR (1957). (21,312).—*Acting Vice-Chancellor*, R. S. Naidu.

JADAVPUR (1955), Calcutta. (3,365).—*Vice-Chancellor*, A. N. Bose, ph.d.

JAMMU (1969). (14,407).—*Vice-Chancellor*, J. D. Sharma.

JAWAHARLAL NEHRU KRISHI VISHWA VIDYALAYA (1964), Jabalpur. (2,240).—*Vice-Chancellor*, R. L. Kaushal.

JAWAHARLAL NEHRU TECHNOLOGICAL (1972), Hyderabad. (3,600).—*Vice-Chancellor*, M. V. Rajagopal.

JAWAHARLAL NEHRU U. (1969), New Delhi. (1,494). —*Vice-Chancellor*, B. D. Nag Chaudhuri.

JIWAJI (1964), Gwalior. (34,587).—*Vice-Chancellor*, G. N. Tandan.

JODHPUR (1962). (11,062).—*Vice-Chancellor*, Prof. S. C. Goyal.

KALYANI (1960). (1,909).—*Vice-Chancellor*, Prof. P. C. Mukherjee, D.Sc.

KANPUR (1965). (42,014).—*Vice-Chancellor*, B. Darshan.

KARNATAK (1949), Dharwar. (39,750).—*Vice-Chancellor*, R. C. Hiremath, ph.d.

KASHMIR (1969), Srinagar. (18,777).—*Vice-Chancellor*, R. H. Chishti.

KERALA (1937), Trivandrum. (112,327).—*Acting Vice-Chancellor*, R. S. Krishnan, D.Sc., ph.d.

LUCKNOW (1921). (30,410).—*Vice-Chancellor*, Dr. R. V. Singh.

MADRAS (1857). (136,059).—*Vice-Chancellor*, M. S. Adiseshiah, ph.d.

MADURAI (1966). (85,918).—*Vice-Chancellor*, S. V. Chittibabu.

MAGADH (1962), Gaya. (36,467).—*Vice-Chancellor*, L. P. Daya, ph.d.

MARATHWADA (1958), Aurangabad. (74,921).—*Vice-Chancellor*, S. R. Kharat.

MEERUT (1966). (52,179).—*Vice-Chancellor*, Prof. B. S. Mathur.

MYSORE (1916). (99,130).—*Vice-Chancellor*, D. V. Urs.

NAGPUR (1923). (99,620).—*Vice-Chancellor*, D. Y. Gohokar, D.Litt.

NORTH BENGAL (1962), Darjeeling. (21,229).—*Vice-Chancellor*, Prof. A. Datta.

NORTH-EASTERN HILL (1973), Shillong. (15,202).—*Vice-Chancellor*, C. D. S. Devanesen, ph.d.

OSMANIA (1918), Hyderabad. (64,823).—*Vice-Chancellor*, P. J. Reddy, LL.D.

PANJAB (1947), Chandigarh. (61,623).—*Vice-Chancellor*, Prof. R. C. Paul, ph.d., SC.D.

PATNA (1917). (14,007).—*Vice-Chancellor*, Prof. D. N. Sharma.

POONA (1948). (78,473).—*Vice-Chancellor*, D. A. Dabholkar.

PUNJAB AGRICULTURAL (1962), Ludhiana. (2,588).—*Vice-Chancellor*, M. S. Randhawa, D.Sc.

PUNJABI (1961), Patiala. (27,537).—*Vice-Chancellor*, Mrs. I. K. Sandhu.

PUNJABRAO KRISHI VIDYAPEETH (1969), Akola. (2,361).—*Vice-Chancellor*, N. Gopalkrishna.

RABINDRA BHARATI (1962), Calcutta. (4,215).—*Vice-Chancellor*, P. C. Gupta, ph.d.

RAJASTHAN (1947), Jaipur. (75,399).—*Vice-Chancellor*, Dr. G. C. Pande.

RANCHI (1960). (42,671).—*Vice-Chancellor*, Dr. A. K. Dhan.

RAVISHANKAR (1963), Raipur. (22,222).—*Vice-Chancellor*, J. C. Dikshit.

ROHILKHAND, Bareilly.—*Vice-Chancellor*, A. S. Raturi.

ROORKEE (1949). (2,083).—*Vice-Chancellor*, Prof. J. Krishna, ph.d.

SAMBALPUR (1967). (15,229).—*Vice-Chancellor*, Prof. B. Behera.

SAMPURNANAND SANSKRIT VISHWAVIDYALAYA (1958), Varanasi. (30,008).—*Vice-Chancellor*, K. P. Tripathi.

SARDAR PATEL (1955), Vallabh Vidyanagar. (14,600).—*Vice-Chancellor*, Prof. R. D. Patel, ph.d.

SAUGAR (1946), Sagar. (22,051).—*Vice-Chancellor*, Prof. T. S. Murty, ph.d.

SAURASHTRA (1966), Rajkot. (41,323).—*Vice-Chancellor*, H. S. Sanghvi.

SHIVAJI (1962), Kolhapur. (61,182).—*Vice-Chancellor*, P. G. Patil.

SHREEMATI N. D. THACKERSEY WOMEN'S (1951), Bombay. (20,534).—*Vice-Chancellor*, Mrs. Madhuri R. Shah, ph.d.

SOUTH GUJARAT (1966), Surat. (31,753).—*Vice-Chancellor*, A. R. Desai.

SRI VENKATESWARA (1954), Tirupati. (26,393).—*Vice-Chancellor*, K. S. Murthy.

TAMIL NADU AGRICULTURAL (1971), Coimbatore. (1,306).—*Vice-Chancellor*, G. Rangaswami, ph.d.

UDAIPUR (1962). (8,605).—*Vice-Chancellor*, P. S. Lamba, ph.d.

UTKAL (1943), Bhubaneswar. (49,206).—*Administrator*, G. Chand.

VIKRAM (1957), Ujjain. (15,813).—*Vice-Chancellor*, S. M. Singh Suman, ph.d., D.Litt.

VISVA-BHARATI (1951), Santiniketan. (2,641).—*Vice-Chancellor*, S. C. Sinha, ph.d.

Kenya

NAIROBI (1970). (Full-time students, 4,542).—*Vice-Chancellor*, J. N. Karanja, ph.d.

KENYATTA UNIV. COLL. (1972), Nairobi. (1,270).—*Principal*, D. Ireri, ph.d.

Lesotho

NATIONAL U. OF LESOTHO (1975), Roma.—*Actg. Vice-Chancellor*, M. T. Mashologu.

Malawi

MALAWI (1964), Zomba. (1,078).—*Vice-Chancellor*, Prof. G. Hunnings, ph.d.

Malaysia

UNIV. OF AGRICULTURE, MALAYSIA (1971), Serdang. (Full-time students, 2,109).—*Vice-Chancellor*, Prof. Tan Sri Mohd. Rashdan bin Haji Baba, ph.d.

MALAYA (1962), Kuala Lumpur. (8,430).—*Vice-Chancellor*, Prof. Ungku A. Aziz, D.Econ., D.Litt.H.

NATIONAL UNIV. OF MALAYSIA (1970), Kuala Lumpur. (1,977).—*Vice-Chancellor*, Anuwar bin Mahmud.

SCIENCE U., MALAYSIA (1969). (2,185).—*Vice-Chancellor*, Tan Sri Datuk Prof. Hamzah Sendut, D.Sc., LL.D.

U. OF TECHNOLOGY (1972), Kuala Lumpur. (1,745). —*Vice-Chancellor*, Ainuddin bin Abdul Wahid.

Malta

ROYAL UNIV. OF MALTA (1769), Valetta. (990).—*Vice-Chancellor*, Prof. E. J. Borg Costanzi.

Mauritius

MAURITIUS (1965), Réduit. (595).—*Vice-Chancellor*, R. Burrenchobay.

New Zealand

AUCKLAND (1882). (Full-time students, 6,605).—*Vice-Chancellor*, C. J. Maiden, D.Phil.

CANTERBURY (1873), Christchurch. (4,719).—
Vice-Chancellor, Emeritus Prof. N. C. Phillips,
C.M.G.
   LINCOLN COLL. (1878). (953).—*Principal*,
Emeritus Prof. J. D. Stewart, Ph.D.
MASSEY (1964), Palmerston North. (2,942).—*Vice-Chancellor*, A. Stewart, C.B.E., D.Phil.
OTAGO (1869), Dunedin. (5,045).—*Vice-Chancellor*, R. O. H. Irvine, M.D.
VICTORIA, WELLINGTON (1897). (4,123).—*Vice-Chancellor*, D. B. C. Taylor, Ph.D.
WAIKATO (1964), Hamilton. (1,936).—*Vice-Chancellor*, D. R. Llewellyn, D.Phil., D.Sc.

Nigeria

AHMADU BELLO (1962), Zaria. (Full-time students, 6,069).—*Vice-Chancellor*, Prof. I. Abubakar, Ph.D.
BENIN (1970). (1,054).—*Vice-Chancellor*, Prof. T. M. Yesufu, Ph.D.
CALABAR (1975).—*Vice-Chancellor*, Prof. E. A. Ayendele, Ph.D.
IBADAN (1948). (3,795).—*Vice-Chancellor*, Prof. T. N. Tamuno, Ph.D.
IFE (1961), Ile-Ife. (4,958).—*Vice-Chancellor*, Prof. O. Aboyade, Ph.D.
JOS (1975).—*Vice-Chancellor*, Prof. G. O. Onuagu-luchi, Ph.D.
LAGOS (1962). (3,626).—*Vice-Chancellor*, Prof. J. F. A. Ajayi, Ph.D., LL.D.
MAIDUGURI (1975).—*Vice-Chancellor*, Prof. E. U. Essien-Udom, Ph.D.
NIGERIA (1960), Nsukka and Enugu. (5,828).—*Vice-Chancellor*, Prof. J. O. C. Ezeilo, Ph.D.
SOKOTO (1975).—*Vice-Chancellor*, Prof. S. A. S. Galadanci, Ph.D.
AYERO UNIV. COLL. (1975), Kano.—*Principal*, Mallam M. Tukur.
UNIV. COLL., ILORIN (1975).—*Principal*, Prof. O. O. Akinkugbe.
UNIV. COLL., PORT HARCOURT (1975).—*Principal*, Prof. D. E. U. Ekong, Dr.rer.Nat.

Papua New Guinea

PAPUA NEW GUINEA (1965), Port Moresby. (Full-time students, 1,744).—*Vice-Chancellor*, G. B. Gris.
PAPUA NEW GUINEA UNIV. OF TECHNOLOGY (1973), Lae. (836).—*Vice-Chancellor*, J. A. Sandover, Ph.D.

Rhodesia

RHODESIA (1955), Salisbury. (Full-time students, 1,361).—*Principal*, Rev. Prof. R. Craig, Ph.D., D.D.

Sierra Leone

SIERRA LEONE (1966), with colleges at Freetown and Njala. (1,592).—*Vice-Chancellor*, A. T. Porter, Ph.D., L.H.D., LL.D.

Singapore

NANYANG (1953). (Full-time students, 2,426).—*Vice-Chancellor*, C. M. Lee, Ph.D.
SINGAPORE (1962). (5,762).—*Vice-Chancellor*, Kwan Sai Kheong.

South Pacific

SOUTH PACIFIC (1967), Suva. (Full-time students, 1,031).—*Vice-Chancellor*, J. A. Maraj, Ph.D.

Sri Lanka

SRI LANKA (1942), with campuses at Colombo (4,124), Gangodawila (1,863), Jaffna (104), Katubedde (1,283), Kelaniya (1,992), and Peradeniya (4,414).—*Vice-Chancellor*, Prof. P. P. G. L. Siriwardene, M.A.

Swaziland and Botswana

BOTSWANA, AND SWAZILAND (1964), with university colleges in Swaziland and Botswana.

Tanzania

DAR ES SALAAM (1970). (Full-time students, 2,444).—*Vice-Chancellor*, P. Msekwa.

Uganda

MAKERERE (1970), Kampala. (Full-time students, 3,721).—*Vice-Chancellor*, Prof. J. S. W. Lutwama.

West Indies

UNIV. OF THE WEST INDIES (1962), Jamaica, with campuses in Trinidad and Barbados. (Full-time students, 5,488).—*Vice-Chancellor*, A. Z. Preston.

Zambia

ZAMBIA (1965), Lusaka. (Full-time students, 2,605).—*Vice-Chancellor*, Dr. J. Mwanza.

H.M. COASTGUARD

The eleven Divisions of Her Majesty's Coastguard are administered by the Department of Trade, and co-ordinate search and rescue (SAR) operations around the 2,500-mile coastline of Great Britain and Northern Ireland. Approximately 600 regular and 8,000 Auxiliary Coastguard initiate and co-ordinate all SAR measures for vessels or persons in need of assistance; between January 1 and December 31,1975 they took part in 5,850 incidents and were responsible for the rescue of 7,363 persons.

Each Coastguard Division has three or four Districts within its boundaries, and each District comprises a number of Stations and Lookouts, of which there are four types. Constant Watch stations are manned at all times and keep a 24-hour watch. Day Watch Stations are manned by three or four Coastguards each keeping a four-hour watch in daylight, additional watch being kept in times of casualty risk (strong winds or poor visibilty). Auxiliary Lookouts and Auxiliary Rescue Stations are manned by Auxiliaries as and when the need arises. All are comprehensively equipped for rescue work.

From these stations, frequently located on bleak clifftops and headlands, the Coastguard are on the alert for oil slicks, shipping hazards, and vessels or people in distress. At the first sign of trouble, using their own modern telecommunications equipment and the extensive facilities provided by the Post Office Coast Radio Stations, they are in position to alert the most appropriate rescue facilities: the lifeboats of the Royal National Lifeboat Institution, Coastguard rescue companies, ships in the vicinity, Navy or RAF helicopters, fixed-wing aircraft, or Naval Vessels.

For those who regularly sail in local waters, or make longer passages, the Coastguard CG66 Boat Safety Scheme provides an invaluable service free. Its aim is to give the Coastguard a record of the movements of craft, information invaluable in an emergency. The scheme consists of cards CG66A and CG66B—" A " for the local sailor and " B " for longer voyages. Cards are available from all Coastguard Stations, Harbourmaster's Offices, and most yacht clubs and marinas.

From St. Margaret's Bay, Kent, Coastguards keep a constant watch on shipping traffic in the Dover

Strait, providing a Channel Navigation Information Service for all shipping in one of the busiest sea-lanes in the world.

Vital warning of impending bad weather is given to local shipping through the gale warning service. Most Coastguard stations hoist cones on their flag-masts, the direction of the gale being indicated by the positions of the cone; point upwards indicating a gale from the northern half of the compass, point downwards indicating a gale from the southern half.

Founded in 1822 to guard our coasts against smuggling, the Coastguard's role today is a very different one—that of complete dedication to the guarding and saving of all life at sea. Members of the public who see an accident or a potentially dangerous incident on or around the coast should without hesitation dial " 999 " and ask for the Coastguard. They will be connected to the nearest Coastguard Rescue Centre.

THE ZODIAC

The Zodiac is an imaginary belt in the heavens within which lie the apparent paths of the Sun, Moon and major planets. It is bounded by two parallels generally taken as lying 8° on either side of the ecliptic or path of the Sun in its annual course. The Zodiac is divided into twelve equal parts of 30° called Signs, which are not used by astronomers, but have some import in astrology, for which the division of the Zodiac was probably made origin-ally. The Signs of the Zodiac take their names from certain of the constellations with which they once coincided. They are assumed to begin at the vernal equinox or intersection of the plane of the ecliptic with that of the equator. This point is still called the First Point of Aries, although the Sign of Aries now lies in the constellation of Pisces,

some 30° to the west. This retrograding of the equinox by about 50″ a year is due to precession; the signs no longer coincide with the constellation; whose names they bear.

A catalogue has been made (Grimaldi, 1905) of all, so far as is known, sculptured or incised repre-sentations on ancient monuments or tablets of the traditional constellation figures, either Zodiacal or otherwise, together with many modern pictures of the Zodiac. The first in the list is a roughly shaped upright, black stone about 2½ feet high and 1½ feet broad in the Babylonian room of the British Museum on the front of which is lightly incised ten out of the twelve Signs and other constellation figures. This was found near Baghdad and its date is estimated to be about 1187–1175 B.C.

ARCHBISHOPS OF CANTERBURY SINCE 1414

1414 Henry Chichele	1633 William Laud	1828 William Howley
1443 John Stafford	1660 William Juxon	1848 John Bird Sumner
1452 John Kemp	1663 Gilbert Sheldon	1862 Charles Thomas Longley
1454 Thomas Bourchier	1678 William Sancroft	1868 Archibald Campbell Tait
1486 John Morton	1691 John Tillotson	1883 Edward White Benson
1501 Henry Dean	1695 Thomas Tenison	1896 Frederick Temple
1503 William Warham	1716 William Wake	1903 Randall Thomas Davidson
1533 Thomas Cranmer	1737 John Potter	1928 Cosmo Gordon Lang
1556 Reginald Pole	1747 Thomas Herring	1942 William Temple
1559 Matthew Parker	1757 Matthew Hutton	1945 Geoffrey Francis Fisher
1576 Edmund Grindal	1758 Thomas Secker	1961 Arthur Michael Ramsey
1583 John Whitgift	1768 Hon. Frederick Cornwallis	1974 Frederick Donald Coggan
1604 Richard Bancroft	1783 John Moore	
1611 George Abbot	1805 Charles Manners Sutton	

ARCHBISHOPS OF YORK SINCE 1606

1606 Tobias Matthew	1724 Launcelot Blackburn	1891 William Connor Magee
1628 George Montague	1743 Thomas Herring	1891 William Dalrymple Mac-lagan
1629 Samuel Harsnett	1747 Matthew Hutton	
1632 Richard Neile	1757 John Gilbert	1909 Cosmo Gordon Lang
1641 John Williams	1761 Robert Hay Drummond	1929 William Temple
1660 Accepted Frewen	1777 William Markham	1942 Cyril Forster Garbett
1664 Richard Sterne	1808 Edward Venables Vernon Harcourt	1956 Arthur Michael Ramsey
1683 John Dolben		1961 Frederick Donald Coggan
1688 Thomas Lamplugh	1848 Thomas Musgrave	1974 Stuart Yarworth Blanch
1691 John Sharp	1860 Charles Thomas Longley	
1714 William Dawes	1862 William Thomson	

Ireland

Position and Extent.—Ireland lies in the Atlantic Ocean, to the West of Great Britain, and is separated from Scotland by the North Channel and from Wales by the Irish Sea and St. George's Channel. The land area of the island is 32,408 sq. miles and its geographical position between 51° 26′ and 55° 21′ N. latitude and from 5° 25′ to 10° 30′ W. longitude. The greatest length of the island, from N.E. to S.W. (Torr Head to Mizen Head), is 302 miles, and the greatest breadth, from E. to W. (Dundrum Bay to Annagh Head), is 174 miles. On the N. coast of *Achill Island* (Co. Mayo) are the highest cliffs in the British Isles, 2,000 feet sheer above the sea. Ireland is occupied for the greater part of its area by the *Central Plain*, with an elevation 50 to 350 ft. above mean sea level, with isolated mountain ranges near the coastline. The principal mountains, with their highest points, are the *Sperrin Mountains* (Sawel 2,240 ft.) of County Tyrone; the *Mountains of Mourne* (Slieve Donard 2,796 ft.) of County Down, and the *Wicklow Mountains* (Lugnaquilla 3,039 ft.); the *Derryveagh Mountains* (Errigal 2,466 ft.) of County Donegal; the *Connemara Mountains* (Twelve Pins 2,695 ft.) of County Galway; *Macgillicuddy's Reeks* (Carrantuohill 3,414 ft., the highest point in Ireland); and the *Galtee Mountains* (3,018 ft.) of County Tipperary, and the *Knockmealdown* (2,609 ft.) and *Comeragh Mountains* (2,470 ft.) of County Waterford. The principal river of Ireland (and the longest in the British Isles) is the *Shannon* (240 miles), rising in County Cavan and draining the central plain. The Shannon flows through a chain of loughs to the city of Limerick, and thence to an estuary on the western Atlantic seaboard. The *Slaney* flows into Wexford Harbour, the *Liffey* to Dublin Bay, the *Boyne* to Drogheda, the *Lee* to Cork Harbour, the *Blackwater* to Youghal Harbour, and the *Suir, Barrow* and *Nore*, to Waterford Harbour. As in Scotland, the principal hydrographic feature is the *Loughs*, of which Lough *Neagh* (150 sq. miles) in the north-east is the largest in Ireland and the British Isles, others being the Shannon Chain of *Allen, Boderg, Forbes, Ree* and *Derg*, and the Erne Chain of *Gowna, Oughter, Lower Erne*, and *Erne; Melvin, Gill, Gara* and *Conn* in the north-west; and *Corrib* and *Mask* (joined by a hidden channel) in the west. In County Kerry, to the east of Macgillicuddy's Reeks, are the famous *Lakes of Killarney*. The climate of Ireland is more equable than that of Great Britain, the extreme range of temperature readings being from 2° F. to 90° F. (compared with − 17° F. to 100° F. over Great Britain). The average annual rainfall varies from 27 inches at Dublin to more than 100 inches in the mountains of Connemara. The rainfall is also more uniform from year to year than in Great Britain.

Primitive Man.—Although little is known concerning the earliest inhabitants of Ireland, there are many traces of neolithic man throughout the island; a grave containing a polished stone axehead assigned to 2,500 B.C. was found at Linkardstown, Co. Carlow, in 1944, and the use of bronze implements appears to have become known about the middle of the 17th century B.C. In the later Bronze Age a Celtic race of *Goidels* appears to have invaded the island, and in the early Iron Age *Brythons* from South Britain are believed to have effected settlements in the south-east, while *Picts* from North Britain established similar settlements in the north. Towards the close of the Roman occupation of Britain, the dominant tribe in the island was that of the *Scoti*, who afterwards established themselves in Scotland.

History.—According to Irish legends, the island of Ierne was settled by a Milesian race, who came from Scythia by way of Spain, and established the *Kingdom of Tara*, about 500 B.C. The supremacy of the *Ardri* (high king) of Tara was acknowledged by eight lesser kingdoms (Munster, Connaught, Ailech, Oriel, Ulidia, Meath, Leinster and Ossory) ruled by descendants of the eight sons of Miled. The basalt columns on the coast of Antrim, eight miles from Portrush, known as the *Giant's Causeway*, are connected with the legendary history of Ireland as the remnants of a bridge built in the time of Finn M'Coul (Fingal) to connect Antrim with Scotland (Staffa).

Hibernia was visited by Roman merchants but never by Roman legions, and little is known of the history of the country until the invasions of *Northmen* (Norwegians and Danes) towards the close of the 8th century A.D. The Norwegians were distinguished as Findgaill (White Strangers) and the Danes as Dubgaill (Black Strangers), names which survive in "Fingall," "MacDougall" and "MacDowell," while the name of the island itself is held to be derived from the Scandinavian *Ira-land* (land of the Irish), the names of the Provinces being survivals of Norse dialect forms (Ulaids-tir, Laigins-tir, Mumans-tir and Kunnak-tir). The outstanding events in the encounters with the Northmen are the *Battle of Tara* (980), at which the Hy Neill

king Maelsechlainn II defeated the Scandinavians of Dublin and the Hebrides under their king Amlaib Cuarán; and the *Battle of Clontarf* (1014) by which the Scandinavian power was completely broken. After Clontarf the supreme power was disputed by the O'Briens of Munster, the O'Neills of Ulster, and the O'Connors of Connaught, with varying fortunes. In 1152 Dermod MacMurrough (Diarmit MacMurchada), the deposed king of Leinster, sought assistance in his struggle with Ruaidhri O'Connor (the high king of Ireland), and visited Henry II, the Norman king of England. Henry authorized him to obtain armed support in England for the recovery of his kingdom, and Dermod enlisted the services of Richard de Clare, the Norman Earl of Pembroke, afterwards known as *Strongbow*, who landed at Waterford (Aug. 23, 1170) with 200 knights and 1,000 other troops for the reconquest of Leinster, where he eventually settled, after marriage with Dermod's daughter. In 1172 (Oct. 18) Henry II himself landed in Ireland. He received homage from the Irish kings and established his capital at Dublin. The invaders subsequently conquered most of the island and a feudal government was created. In the 14th and 15th centuries, the Irish recovered most of their lands, while many Anglo-Irish lords became virtually independent, royal authority being confined to the "Pale," a small district round Dublin. Though under Henry VII, Sir Edward Poynings, as Lord Deputy had passed at the *Parliament of Drogheda* (1494) the act later known as *Poynings' Law*, subordinating the Irish Legislature to the Crown, the Earls of Kildare retained effective power until, in 1534, Henry VIII began the reconquest of Ireland. Parliament in 1541 recognized him as King of Ireland and by 1603 English authority was supreme.

Christianity.—Christianity did not become general until the advent of St. Patrick. *St. Patrick* was born in Britain about 389, and was taken to Ireland as a slave about sixteen years later escaping to Gaul at the age of 22. In 432 he was consecrated Bishop at Auxerre and landed in Wicklow to establish and organize the Christian religion throughout the island.

Republic of Ireland

Area and Population.—The Republic has a land area of 26,600 sq. miles, divided into the four Provinces of LEINSTER (Carlow, Dublin, Kildare, Kilkenny, Laoighis, Longford, Louth, Meath, Offaly, Westmeath, Wexford and Wicklow); MUNSTER (Clare, Cork, Kerry, Limerick, Tipperary and Waterford); CONNACHT (Galway, Leitrim, Mayo, Roscommon and Sligo); and part of ULSTER (Cavan, Donegal and Monaghan). Total population of the Republic at the Census held on April 18, 1971, was 2,978,248 (males, 1,495,760; females 1,482,488), a density of 112 persons per sq. mile (Census, 1966, 2,884,002). Provisional figures showed 69,508 births, 21,103 marriages and 33,532 deaths in the year 1975.

THE PRESIDENT

*Uachtaran-na-hEireann (President),*Cearbhall O' Dálaigh (Carroll Daly), *born* 1911, *assumed office,* Dec. 19, 1974.

A new Irish Government took office on March 14, 1973. Following the victory of the National Coalition of the Fine Gael and Labour in the general election held on February 28, the leader of Fine Gael, Mr. Liam Cosgrave, was elected *Taoiseach* (Prime Minister) when the new *Dáil* (Lower House of Parliament) met for the first time on March 14. Later that evening, following his formal appointment by the President, Mr. de Valera, the new *Taoiseach,* Mr. Cosgrave, announced his Cabinet to the *Dáil.*

MEMBERS OF THE GOVERNMENT

Taoiseach, Liam MacCosgair (Liam Cosgrave).

Tanaiste and Minister for Health and Minister for Social Welfare, Brendán Mac Fheórais (Brendan Corish).

Minister for Defence, Padraig S. Ó Donnagáin (Patrick S. Donegan).

Minister for Local Government, Seamus Ó Táithligh (James Tully).

Finance and the Public Service, Risteárd O Riain (Richie Ryan).

Agriculture and Fisheries, Marcus Mac Giollafhionntáin (Mark Clinton).

Labour, Micheál Ó Laoire (Michael O'Leary).

Minister for the Gaeltacht, Tomás Ó Domhnaill (Tom O'Donnell).

Lands, Tomás Mac Giolla Phádraigh (Tom Fitzpatrick).

Foreign Affairs, Gearóid Mac Gearailt (Garret Fitz-Gerald).

Posts and Telegraphs, Conchubhar Crús O Brian (Conor Cruise-O'Brien).

Transport and Power, Peadur de Barra (Peter Barry).

Industry and Commerce, Saorbhreathach Céitinn (Justin Keating).

Education, Risteard de Búrca (Dick Burke).

Justice, Padraigh Ó Cuana (Patrick M. Cooney).

Parliamentary Secretaries

Parliamentary Secretary to the Taoiseach and to the Minister for Foreign Affairs, Seán Ó Ceallaigh (John Kelly).

Do. to the Minister for Agriculture and Fisheries, Micheál Pádraigh Ó Murchadha (Michael Pat Murphy).

Do. to the Minister for Health, Risteárd de Barra (Richard Barry).

Do. to the Minister for Finance, hAnnraoi Ó Cionaith (Henry Kenny).

Do. to the Minister for Social Welfare, Proinsias Mac Bhloscaidh (Frank Cluskey).

Do. to the Minister for Finance, and to the Minister for Defence, Micheál Ó Beaglaoi (Michael Begley).

Do. to the Minister for Education and to the Minister for Industry and Commerce, John Bruton.

Do. to the Minister for Local Government, Ochbheah Ó Flannagám (Oliver J. Flanagan).

Attorney-General, Declan Costello.

Secretary to the Government, Dónal Ó Súilleabháin (Daniel O'Sullivan).

Assistant Secretary to the Government, H. S. Ó. Dubha (H. J. Dowd).

Irish Embassy
17 Grosvenor Place, S.W.1

Ambassador Extraordinary and Plenipotentiary, His Excellency Dr. Donal O'Sullivan.

British Embassy
33 Merrion Road, Dublin 4

Ambassador Extraordinary and Plenipotentiary, His Excellency Walter Robert Haydon, C.M.G. (1976) £15,000

Counsellor, J. K. Hickman.
First Secretaries, P. J. Goulden (*Head of Chancery*); R. W. James (*Agriculture*).

GOVERNMENT

The Constitution.—The constitution approved by a plebiscite on July 1, 1937, came into operation on December 29, 1937.

The Constitution declares that Ireland is a sovereign independent democratic State and affirms the right of the Irish Nation to choose its own form of Government, to determine its relations with other nations, and to develop its life, political, economic and cultural, in accordance with its own genius and traditions. The national territory is declared to be the whole island of Ireland, its islands and the territorial seas. Pending the reintegration of the national territory, and without prejudice to the right of the Parliament and the Government established by the Constitution to exercise jurisdiction over the whole of the national territory, the laws enacted by that Parliament shall have the like area and extent of application as those of the Irish Free State, which did not include the six counties of Northern Ireland. The national flag is the tricolour of green, white and orange. The Irish language, being the national language, is the first official language. The English language is recognized as a second official language.

The President.—The President—*Uachtarán na hEireann*—is elected by direct vote of the people for a period of seven years. A former or retiring President is eligible for a second term. The President summons and dissolves Dáil Éireann on the advice of the *Taoiseach* (Head of the Government). He signs and promulgates laws. The supreme command of the Defence Forces is vested in him, its exercise being regulated by law. He has the power of pardon. The President, in the exercise and performance of certain of his constitutional powers and functions, is aided and advised by a Council of State.

The Legislature.—The National Parliament—*Oireachtas*—consists of the President and two Houses: a House of Representatives—*Dáil Eireann* —and a Senate—*Seanad Eireann.*

Dáil Eireann is composed of 144 members elected by adult suffrage on a basis of proportional representation.

Seanad Éireann is composed of 60 members, of whom 11 are nominated by the Taoiseach and 49 are elected; three by the National University of

Ireland three by the University of Dublin, and 43 from panels of candidates, established on a vocational basis.

Members of Dáil Éireann are paid an allowance of £5,403 per annum (and members of Seanad Éireann £3,087); are allowed free travelling facilities between Dublin and their constituencies and are, subject to certain restrictions granted free telephone and postal facilities from Leinster House and allowances for overnight stays in Dublin.

The Executive.—The executive authority is exercised by the Government subject to the Constitution. The Government is responsible to Dáil Éireann, meets and acts as a collective authority, and is collectively responsible for the Departments of State administered by the Ministers.

The Taoiseach is appointed by the President on the nomination of Dáil Éireann. The other members of the Government are appointed by the President on the nomination of the Taoiseach with the previous approval of Dáil Éireann. The Taoiseach appoints a member of the Government to be the *Tánaiste* who acts for all purposes in the place of the Taoiseach in the event of the death, permanent incapacitation, or temporary absence of the Taoiseach. The Taoiseach, the Tánaiste and the Minister for Finance must be members of Dáil Éireann. The other members of the Government must be members of Dáil Éireann or Seanad Éireann, but not more than two may be members of Seanad Éireann.

THE LEGISLATURE

The Legislature (*Oireachtas*) consists of the President and two Houses—a House of Representatives (*Dáil Eireann*) and a Senate (*Seanad Eireann*). Dáil Éireann has 144 Members, elected on the system of Proportional Representation by means of the single transferable vote. All citizens who have reached the age of 18 years and are not disqualified by law have the right to vote. Each Dáil may continue for a period not exceeding five years from the date of election.

The result of the general election on Feb. 28, 1973 was as follows: *Fine Gael and Labour Coalition*, 73; *Fianna Fáil*, 69; *Independent*, 2. Total membership including the *Ceann Comhairle* (Chairman),144.

THE JUDICIARY

The Judiciary consists of Courts of First Instance and a Court of Final Appeal called the Supreme Court—*Cúirt Uachtarach*. The Courts of First Instance include a High Court—*Ard-Chúirt*—invested with full original jurisdiction in and power to determine all matters and questions, whether of law or fact, civil or criminal, and also Courts of local and limited jurisdiction, with a right of appeal as determined by law. The High Court alone has original jurisdiction to entertain the question of the validity of any law having regard to the provisions of the Constitution. The Supreme Court has appellate jurisdiction from all decisions of the High Court, with such exceptions and subject to such regulations as may be prescribed by law. No law may, however, be enacted excepting from the appellate jurisdiction of the Supreme Court the question of the validity of any law, having regard to the provisions of the Constitution.

Chief Justice. Hon. Thomas F. O'Higgins £16,391
President of the High Court, Hon. Thomas
A. Finlay.......................... 14,211
Judges, Supreme Court, Hon. Brian Walsh;
Hon. Seamus Henchy; Hon. Francis
Griffin; Hon. Seán Kenny; Hon.
Weldon R. C. Parke............... 13,847

Judges, High Court, Hon. George Murnaghan; Hon. Seán Butler; Hon. John M. Gannon; Hon. Liam Hamilton; Hon. Thomas A. Doyle; Hon. James McMahon; Hon. Herbert R. McWilliam; Hon. John J. Durkan............*each* 12,029

DEFENCE

Under the direction of the President, and subject to the provisions of the Defence Act, 1954, the military command of the Defence Forces is exercisable by the Government through the Minister for Defence. To aid and counsel the Minister for Defence there is a Council of Defence consisting of the Parliamentary Secretary to the Minster, the Secretary of the Department of Defence, the Chief of Staff, the Adjutant-General and the Quartermaster-General. Establishments provide at present for a Permanent Defence Force of approximately 15,000 all ranks, including the Air Corps and the Naval Service. The Defence Estimates for the year ending Dec. 31, 1976, provide for approximately 22,800 all ranks of the Reserve Defence Force. Recruitment is on a voluntary basis. Minimum term of enlistment for the Army is three years in the Permanent Defence Force *or* three years in the Permanent Defence Force and nine years in the Reserve Defence Force. For the Naval Service, enlistment is for four years in the Permanent Defence Force *or* six years in the Permanent Defence Force and six years in the Reserve Defence Force. There are at present six Brigades in the Army. Each comprises three infantry Battalions and a squadron or company from each Corps (except Ordnance and Air). The Naval Service has three coastal minesweepers and a patrol vessel. The equipment of Air Corps includes Chipmunk, Provost, Dove and Cessna aircraft, Fouga Magister CM170 jet trainers and Alouette helicopters. The Defence Estimates for the year ending Dec. 31, 1976 provide for an expenditure of £72,960,000.

FINANCE

	1975 (Actual)	1976 (Estimated)
Revenue......	£1,071,230,000	£1,355,600,000
Expenditure...	1,349,994,000	1,682,600,000

In addition to the Expenditure figures shown above there were certain services of a capital nature regarded as proper to be met from borrowing. Issues for these services in 1975 amounted to £334,630,000, and for 1976 are estimated at £419,920,000.

The estimated *Revenue* for 1976 includes Customs Duties, £16,000,000; Excise Duties, £404,000,000; Estate etc. Duties, £70,000,000; Income Tax, £419,000,000; Corporation Profits Tax, £28,000,000; Motor Vehicle Duties, £37,500,000; Stamp Duties, £15,000,000; Post Office Services, £99,400,000; Value-added Tax, £212,500,000; Agricultural Levies, £3,000,000; Capital Taxes, £8,000,000. Total (including other items), £1,355,600,000.

The principal items of estimated current *Expenditure* for 1976 are Debt Service, £355,200,000; Agriculture, £118,200,000; Defence, £72,900,000; Police and Justice, £64,100,000; Education, £228,600,000; Social Welfare, £246,600,000; Health Services, £242,500,000; Transport, £60,500,000; Post Office, £78,400,000; Superannuation, £47,500,000; Industry, £51,600,000. Total (including other items), £1,682,600,000.

The Gross Debt on December 31, 1975 was £2,051,000,000 with capital assets of £1,076,000,000 at that date.

RELIGION
(Census of 1971)

Catholic	2,795,666
Church of Ireland	97,739
Presbyterians	16,052
Methodists	5,646
Others	63,145
Total	2,978,248

EDUCATION

Primary education is directed by the State, with the exception of approximately 120 private primary schools with an enrolment of about 23,000 in 1974-75.

There were 3,632 State-aided primary schools with an enrolment of 520,000 in 1974-75.

In 1974-75 there were 541 recognized secondary schools with 173,118 pupils under private management (mainly religious orders). Also, 63,772 full-time pupils (and approximately as many part-time pupils) received secondary education in 250 permanent secondary vocational schools (and a number of temporary centres), and 3 of the 8 Regional Technical Colleges—all these schools and colleges are controlled by some 38 statutory local Vocational Education Committees. There were 14 State comprehensive schools in 1974-75 with a total enrolment of 6,707 students, and 16 community schools with an enrolment of 6,818 students. There were also other miscellaneous second-level schools and the total full-time enrolment at second-level for 1974-75 was 256,652.

Third-level education is catered for by five University Colleges, a National Institute for Higher Education, and also by third-level courses offered by the Technical Colleges and Regional Technical Colleges and other miscellaneous third-level institutions. There were 30,989 full-time third-level students in 1974-75, of whom 20,711 were attending university courses.

The estimated State expenditure on education in the period Jan. 1, 1976 to Dec. 31, 1976, excluding administration and inspection, is Primary £104,631,000; Secondary £112,085,000. The vote for Universities and third-level Colleges amounted to £27,623,000, while, in addition, grants of £3,674,984 were provided in respect of the Facilities of General Agriculture, Veterinary Medicine and Dairy Science.

PRODUCTION AND INDUSTRY

Agriculture and Livestock.—In 1974 there were 860,400 acres under corn crops, 275,500 under root and green crops, 8,900 under fruit and 2,510,600 under hay, a total of 3,692,500 acres. The principal produce in 1974 was: oats, 154,000 tons; wheat, 241,000 tons; barley, 1,021,000 tons; turnips, 1,252,000 tons; potatoes, 1,096,000 tons; sugar beet, 1,911,000 tons; and hay, 3,726,000 tons. The *livestock* included, 7,216,500 cattle, 4,059,700 sheep, 922,600 pigs and 98,100 horses and ponies.

Minerals.—300 persons were employed in the coal mines in 1975 and 46,000 tons of coal won.

Sea Fisheries.—6,352 persons were employed in the fisheries in 1975. Total value of all fish (excluding salmon) landed in 1975 was £9,137,625.

COMMUNICATIONS

Railways.—In the nine months ended Dec. 31, 1974, there were 1,360 miles of railway all of standard (5 ft. 3 in.) gauge; 12,376,000 passengers and 2,652,000 tons of merchandise were conveyed; the receipts were £14,100,000 and expenditure £23,465,916. These figures are in respect of railway working by *Coras Iompair Eireann*, the national transport undertaking which is now the only concern operating a rail service in the State.

Road Motor Services.—In 1975 road motor (omnibus) vehicles carried 278,617,791 passengers, the gross receipts being £26,602,187.

Shipping.—In 1975 the number of ships with cargo and in ballast in the foreign trade which arrived at Irish ports was 12,464 (21,758,457 net registered tons); of these 1,650 (2,675,217 net registered tons) were of Irish nationality.

CIVIL AVIATION

Shannon Airport, 15 miles W. of Limerick, is on the main transatlantic air route. In 1975 the airport handled 1,031,325 passengers, 52,939 tonnes of cargo and 1,496 tonnes of mail.

Dublin Airport, 6 miles N. of Dublin, serves the cross-channel and European services operated by the Irish national airline *Aer Lingus* and other airlines. During 1975 the airport handled 2,195,690 passengers, 42,709 tonnes of cargo and 2,419 tonnes of mail.

Cork Airport, 5 miles S. of Cork, serves the cross-Channel and European services operated by *Aer Lingus* and other airlines. During 1975 the airport handled 255,627 passengers and 3,608 tonnes of cargo and 16 tonnes of mail.

There are 23 private aerodromes.

Trade with U.K.

	1974	1975
Imports from U.K.	£758,466,096	£828,158,039
Exports to U.K.	634,656,818	981,282,969

OVERSEAS TRADE

Year	Imports	Exports	Trade Balance
	£	£	£
1973	1,137,236,398	869,186,046	268,050,352
1974	1,626,311,286	1,136,279,721	492,031,565
1975	1,699,644,283	1,441,369,285	258,274,998

PRINCIPAL ARTICLES
Imports (1975)

The principal groups were: live animals, £14,071,282; food, drink and tobacco, £212,488,951; petroleum and petroleum products, £270,438,272; chemicals, £191,712,165; machinery (non-electric), £218,563,412; electrical machinery, £107,546,384; transport equipment, £93,096,165; metal and manufactures, £126,054,522; textiles and clothing, £158,931,863; paper, paperboard and manufactures, £49,793,122; professional, scientific, etc. goods, £26,029,672.

Exports (1975)

Principally live animals, £123,581,031; meat and meat preparations, £239,822,291; other food, drink, and tobacco, £310,587,525; machinery and transport equipment, £161,220,953; clothing, headgear and footwear, £57,506,331; textiles, £90,496,386; metal ores and scrap, £29,963,312; metals and manufactures, £42,403,271; non-metallic mineral manufactures, £27,912,300; chemicals, £108,125,299; professional, scientific, etc. goods, £35,370,703.

CAPITAL.—Dublin (*Baile Atha Cliath*) is a City and County Borough on the River Liffey at the head of Dublin Bay. In April, 1971, its population was 567,866.

Other cities and towns, with populations at the Census of 1971 are Ψ Cork (128,645); Ψ Limerick (57,161); Ψ Dun Laoghaire (53,171); Ψ Waterford (31,968); Ψ Galway (27,726); Ψ Dundalk (21,672).

FLAG.—Equal vertical stripes of green, white and orange.

NATIONAL DAY.—March 17 (St. Patrick's Day).

The United States of America

Area and Population

Population.—The total resident population of the United States on April 1, 1976 was estimated at 214,374,000, excluding Armed Forces stationed abroad. Civilian resident population at the same date was estimated at 212,705,000. Including Armed Forces stationed abroad (April 1, 1976), 214,850,000.

	Land Area, 1970 (sq. miles)	Population	
		Census 1960	Census 1970
The United States★...............	3,536,855	179,323,175	203,211,926
Commonwealth of Puerto Rico.....	3,435	2,349,544	2,712,033
Possessions.......................	463	123,151	..
Guam.........................	212	67,044	84,996
Virgin Islands of U.S............	133	32,099	62,468
American Samoa................	76	20,051	27,159
Midway Islands.................	2	2,356	2,220
Wake Island...................	3	1,097	1,647
Canton Island and Enderbury Island	27	320‡	..
Johnston Island and Sand Island....	—	156‡	1,007
Swan Islands....................	1	28‡	22
Other Outlying areas:			
Panama Canal Zone.............	553	42,122	44,198
Corn Islands..................	4	1,872	..
Pacific Islands Trust Territory.....	717	70,724‡	90,940
Population Abroad..............		1,374,421	1,737,836
Total.......................	3,542,481	183,285,009	207,682,378

★ The 50 States and the Federal *District of Columbia* (*see* p. 795).
‡ The islands of Enderbury, Sand, Little Swan and Little Corn were uninhabited at the time of enumeration.

REGISTERED BIRTHS AND DEATHS

Cal-endar Year	Live Births		Deaths	
	Number	Rate per 1,000	Number	Rate per 1,000
1966	3,606,274	18·4	1,863,149	9·5
1967	3,520,959	17·8	1,851,323	9·4
1968	3,501,564	17·5	1,930,082	9·7
1969	3,571,000	17·7	1,921,990	9·5
1970	3,731,386	18·4	1,921,031	9·5
1971	3,555,970	17·2	1,927,542	9·3
1972	3,258,411	15·6	1,963,944	9·4
1973	3,136,965	14·9	1,973,003	9·4
1974	3,159,958	14·9	1,934,388	9·2
1975★	3,149,000	14·8	1,910,000	9·0

Births based on 50 per cent. sample. ★Provisional.
Note.—Figures tabulated are for the United States. Deaths exclude fœtal deaths. Rates are based on the population as estimated on July 1 (1970, April 1).

IMMIGRATION AND NATURALIZATION

From 1820 to 1975, 47,008,919 immigrants were admitted to the United States. Of the 386,194 admitted during fiscal year 1975, 70 per cent. were born in the following countries: Mexico (62,205), the Philippines (31,751), Italy (11,552), Greece (9,984), Cuba (25,995), Jamaica (11,076), the United Kingdom (10,807), China and Taiwan (18,536), Canada (7,308), Portugal (11,845), the

Dominican Republic (14,066), India (15,773), Korea (28,362), Trinidad and Tobago (5,982) and Colombia (6,434). During 1975, 141,537 aliens residing permanently in the United States were naturalized, an increase of eight per cent. over 1974, and 27,731 persons acquired citizenship status at birth abroad, after birth by the naturalization of parents, through marriage, or by other reasons.

MARRIAGE AND DIVORCE

Laws of marriage and of divorce are within the exclusive jurisdiction of each State. Each State legislature enacts its own laws prescribing rules and qualifications pertaining to marriage and its dissolution.

Year	Marriages	Per 1,000 Pop.§	Estimated Divorces	Per 1,000 Pop.§
1966	1,857,000	9·5	499,000	2·5
1967	1,927,000	9·7	523,000	2·6
1968	2,069,000	10·4	584,000	2·9
1969	2,145,000	10·6	639,000	3·2
1970	2,159,000	10·6	708,000	3·5
1971	2,190,481	10·6	773,000	3·7
1972	2,282,154	11·0	845,000	4·1
1973	2,284,108	10·9	915,000	4·4
1974	2,229,677	10·5	977,000	4·6
1975★	2,126,000	10·0	1,026,000	4·8

★ Provisional.
§ Population as estimated on July 1.

Increase of the People

Year of Census	Total Population				Increase over preceding census	Inter-Censal Immigrants★
	White	Negro	Other Races	Total		
1930	110,395,753	11,891,842	915,065	123,202,660	17,181,092	4,107,209
1940	118,357,831	12,865,914	941,384	132,165,129	8,962,409	528,431
1950	135,149,629	15,044,937	1,131,232	151,325,798	19,161,229	1,035,039
1960	158,831,732	18,871,831	1,619,612	179,323,175	27,997,377	2,515,479
1970	177,748,975	22,580,289	2,882,662	203,211,926	23,888,751	3,321,677

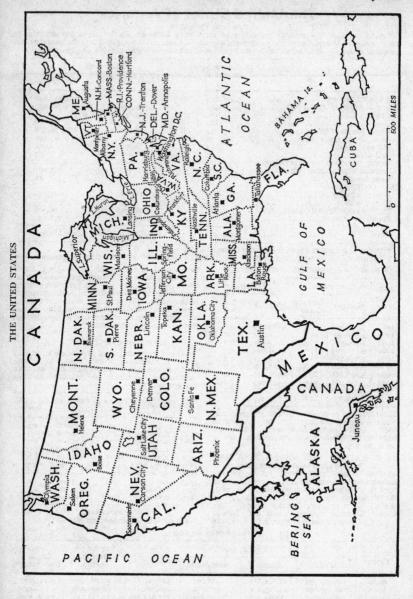

THE UNITED STATES

THE UNITED STATES

State (with date and *order* of admission)	Area Sq. M.★	Population, Census 1970	Capital	Governor (term of office in years, and starting year)	
Alabama (Ala.) (1819) (*22*)	51,609	3,444,165	Montgomery	George C. Wallace (D) (4—1975)	$29,000
Alaska (1959) (*49*)	586,400	302,173	Juneau	Jay S. Hammond (R) (4—1974)	50,000
Arizona (Ariz.) (1912) (*48*)	113,909	1,772,482	Phoenix	Raul H. Castro (D) (4—1975)	40,000
Arkansas (Ark.) (1836) (*25*)	53,104	1,923,295	Little Rock	David H. Pryor (D) (2—1975)	10,000
California (Cal.) (1850) (*31*)	158,693	19,953,134	Sacramento	Edmund G. Brown, Jr. (D) (4—1975)	49,100
Colorado (Colo.) (1876) (*38*)	104,247	2,207,259	Denver	Richard D. Lamm (D) (4—1975)	40,000
Connecticut (Conn.) § (1788) (*5*)	5,009	3,032,217	Hartford	Ella T. Grasso (D) (4—1975)	42,000
Delaware (Del.) § (1787) (*1*)	2,057	548,104	Dover	Sherman W. Tribbett (D) (4—1973)	35,000
Dist. of Columbia (D.C.) (1791)	69	756,510	‥	†	
Florida (Fla.) (1845) (*27*)	58,560	6,789,443	Tallahassee	Reubin O'D. Askew (D) (4—1975)	50,000
Georgia (Ga.) § (1788) (*4*)	58,876	4,589,575	Atlanta	George Busbee (D) (4—1975	50,000
Hawaii (1959) (*50*)	6,423	769,913	Honolulu	George R. Ariyoshi (D) (4—1974)	46,000
Idaho (1890) (*43*)	83,557	713,008	Boise	Cecil D. Andrus (D) (4—1975)	33,000
Illinois (Ill.) (1818) (*21*)	56,400	11,113,976	Springfield	Dan Walker (D) (4—1973)	50,000
Indiana (Ind.) (1816) (*19*)	36,291	5,193,669	Indianapolis	Otis R. Bowen (R) (4—1973)	37,000
Iowa (1846) (*29*)	56,290	2,825,041	Des Moines	Robert D. Ray (R) (4—1975)	40,000
Kansas (Kan.) (1861) (*34*)	82,276	2,249,071	Topeka	Robert F. Bennett (R) (4—1975)	35,000
Kentucky (Ky.) (1792) (*15*)	40,395	3,219,311	Frankfort	Julian M. Carroll (D) (4—1974)	35,000
Louisiana (La.) (1812) (*18*)	48,523	3,643,180	Baton Rouge	Edwin W. Edwards (D) (4—1972)	50,000
Maine (Me.) (1820) (*23*)	33,215	993,663	Augusta	James S. Longley (I) (4—1975)	35,000
Maryland (Md.) § (1788) (*7*)	10,577	3,922,399	Annapolis	Marvin Mandel (D) (4—1975)	25,000
Massachusetts (Mass.) § (1788) (*6*)	8,257	5,689,170	Boston	Michael S. Dukakis (D) (4—1975)	40,000
Michigan (Mich.) (1837) (*26*)	58,216	8,875,083	Lansing	William G. Milliken (R) (4—1975)	45,000
Minnesota (Minn.) (1858) (*32*)	84,068	3,805,069	St. Paul	Wendell R. Anderson (D) (4—1975)	41,000
Mississippi (Miss.) (1817) (*20*)	47,716	2,216,912	Jackson	Clift C. Finch (D) (4—1976)	43,000
Missouri (Mo.) (1821) (*24*)	69,674	4,677,399	Jefferson City	Christopher S. Bond (R) (4—1973)	37,500
Montana (Mont.) (1889) (*41*)	141,138	694,409	Helena	Thomas L. Judge (D) (4—1973)	30,000
Nebraska (Nebr.) (1867) (*37*)	77,227	1,483,791	Lincoln	J. James Exon (D) (4—1975)	25,000
Nevada (Nev.) (1864) (*36*)	110,540	488,738	Carson City	Mike O'Callaghan (D) (4—1975.)	40,000
New Hampshire (N.H.)§ (1788) (*9*)	9,304	737,681	Concord	Meldrim Thomson, Jr. (R) (2—1975)	34,070
New Jersey (N.J.)§ (1787) (*3*)	7,836	7,168,164	Trenton	Brendan T. Byrne (D) (4—1974)	60,000
New Mexico (N. Mex.) (1912) (*47*)	121,666	1,016,000	Santa Fé	Jerry Apodaca (D) (4—1975)	35,000
New York (N.Y.)§ (1788) (*11*)	49,576	18,190,740	Albany	Hugh L. Carey (D) (4—1975)	85,000
North Carolina (N.C.)§ (1789) (*12*)	52,712	5,082,059	Raleigh	James E. Holshouser, Jr. (R) (4—1973)	38,500
North Dakota (N. Dak.) (1889) (*39*)	70,665	617,761	Bismarck	Arthur A. Link (D) (4—1973)	18,000
Ohio (1803) (*17*)	41,222	10,652,017	Columbus	James A. Rhodes (R) (4—1975)	50,000
Oklahoma (Okla.) (1907) (*46*)	69,919	2,559,253	Oklahoma City	David L. Boren (D) (4—1975)	42,500
Oregon (Oreg.) (1859) (*33*)	96,981	2,091,385	Salem	Robert W. Straub (D) (4—1975)	38,500
Pennsylvania (Pa.)§ (1787) (*2*)	45,333	11,793,909	Harrisburg	Milton J. Shapp (D) (4—1975)	60,000
Rhode Island (R.I.)§ (1790) (*13*)	1,214	949,723	Providence	Philip W. Noel (D) (2—1975)	42,500
South Carolina (S.C.)§ (1788) (*8*)	31,055	2,590,516	Columbia	James B. Edwards (R) (4—1975)	39,000
South Dakota (S. Dak.) (1889) (*40*)	77,047	666,257	Pierre	Richard F. Kneip (D) (4—1975)	27,500
Tennessee (Tenn.) (1796) (*16*)	42,244	3,924,164	Nashville	Ray Blanton (D) (4—1975)	50,000
Texas (Tex.) (1845) (*28*)	267,339	11,196,730	Austin	Dolph Briscoe (D) (2—1975)	65,000
Utah (1896) (*45*)	84,916	1,059,273	Salt Lake City	Calvin L. Rampton (D) (4—1973)	35,000
Vermont (Vt.) (1791) (*14*)	9,609	444,732	Montpelier	Thomas P. Salmon (D) (2—1975)	36,100
Virginia (Va.)§ (1788) (*10*)	40,815	4,648,494	Richmond	Mills E. Godwin, Jr. (R) (4—1974)	50,000
Washington (Wash.) (1889) (*42*)	68,192	3,409,169	Olympia	Daniel J. Evans (R) (4—1973)	42,150
West Virginia (W. Va.) (1863) (*35*)	24,181	1,744,237	Charleston	Arch A. Moore, Jr. (R) (4—1973)	35,000
Wisconsin (Wis.) (1848) (*30*)	56,154	4,417,933	Madison	Patrick J. Lucey (D) (4—1971)	44,300
Wyoming (Wyo.) (1890) (*44*)	97,914	332,416	Cheyenne	Ed Herschler (D) (4—1975)	37,500
OUTLYING TERRITORIES AND POSSESSIONS					
Puerto Rico (1899)	3,435	2,712,033	San Juan	Rafael Hernández-Colón (4—1973)	35,000
Guam (1899)	206	86,926	Agaña	Ricardo J. Bordallo (D) (4—1975)	35,000
Samoa (1900)	76	27,769	Fagatogo	Earl B. Ruth (R) (2—1975)	45,000
Virgin Islands (1917)	133	63,200	Charlotte Amalie	Cyril E. King (I) (4—1975)	35,505

D.—Democratic Party. R.—Republican Party. § The 13 Original States.
★ Gross area, including water.
† The capital territory is governed by Congress through a Commissioner and City Council (*see* p. 796).

Largest Cities (Metropolitan Areas: Census 1970 (April)).

Ψ New York	9,973,716	Ψ Cleveland, Ohio	2,063,729	Denver–Boulder, Colo	1,239,477
Ψ Los Angeles–Long Beach, Calif.	7,041,980	Ψ Newark, N.J.	2,057,468	Riverside–San Bernardino–Ontario, Calif.	1,141,307
Ψ Chicago, Ill.	6,977,611	Ψ Houston, Texas	1,999,316	Indianapolis, Ind.	1,111,352
Ψ Philadelphia	4,824,110	Minneapolis–St. Paul, Minn.–Wis	1,965,391	Ψ Tampa–St. Petersburg, Fla.	1,088,549
Ψ Detroit, Mich.	4,435,051	Atlanta, Georgia	1,595,517	Ψ San José, Calif.	1,065,313
Ψ Boston, Mass.	3,376,328	Anaheim–Santa Ana–Garden Grove, Calif.	1,421,233	Ψ New Orleans, La.	1,046,470
Ψ San Francisco	3,108,782	Ψ Seattle–Evett, Wash.	1,424,605	Columbus, Ohio	1,017,847
Ψ San Francisco–Oakland, Calif.	3,108,782	Ψ Milwaukee, Wis.	1,403,884	Ψ Portland, Oreg.–Wash	1,007,130
Washington, D.C.	2,909,355	Cincinatti, Ohio–Ky–Ind.	1,385,103	Phoenix, Ariz.	969,425
Nassau–Suffolk, N.Y.	2,555,868	Ψ San Diego, Calif.	1,357,854	Ψ Rochester, N.Y.	961,516
St. Louis, Mo.–Ill.	2,410,492	Ψ Buffalo, N.Y.	1,349,211	San Antonio, Texas	888,179
Pittsburgh, Pa.	2,401,362	Kansas City, M.–Kans	1,273,296	Louisville, Ky.–Ind.	867,330
Dallas–Fort Worth, Texas	2,378,353	Ψ Miami, Florida	1,267,792	Dayton, Ohio	852,531
Ψ Baltimore, Md.	2,071,016				

Ψ Seaport

PHYSIOGRAPHY

The coterminous States of the Republic occupy nearly all that portion of the North American Continent between the Atlantic and Pacific Oceans, in latitude 25° 07′–49° 23′ North and longitude 66° 57′–124° 44′ West, its northern boundary being Canada and the southern boundary Mexico. The separate State of Alaska reaches a latitude of 71° 23′ N., at Point Barrow (2,502 miles from the U.S. geographic centre).

The general coastline of the 50 States has a length of about 2,069 miles on the Atlantic, 7,623 miles on the Pacific, 1,060 miles on the Arctic, and 1,631 miles on the Gulf of Mexico.

The principal river is the mighty Mississippi-Missouri-Red Rock, traversing the whole country from north to south, and having a course of 3,710 miles to its mouth in the Gulf of Mexico, with many large affluents, the chief of which are the Yellowstone, Platte, Arkansas, Ohio, and Red Rivers. The rivers flowing into the Atlantic and Pacific Oceans are comparatively small; among the former may be noticed the Hudson, Delaware, Susquehanna, Potomac, James, Roanoke and Savannah; of the latter, the Columbia-Snake, Sacramento, and Colorado. The Nueces, Brazos, Trinity, Pearl, Mobile-Tombigbee-Alabama, Apalachicola-Chattahoochee, Suwannee and Colorado of Texas fall into the Gulf of Mexico, also the Rio Grande, a long river partly forming the boundary with Mexico. The areas of the water-basins have been estimated as follows:—Rivers flowing to the Pacific, 647,300 square miles; to the Atlantic, 488,877; and to the Gulf of Mexico, 1,683,325 square miles, of which 1,234,600 are drained by the Mississippi-Missouri-Red Rock. The chain of the Rocky Mountains separates the western portion of the country from the remainder, all communication being carried on over certain elevated passes, several of which are now traversed by railroads; west of these, bordering the Pacific coast, the Cascade Mountains and Sierra Nevada form the outer edge of a high tableland, consisting in part of stony and sandy desert and partly of grazing land and forested mountains, and including the Great Salt Lake, which extends to the Rocky Mountains. Eastward the country is a vast, gently undulating plain, with a general slope southwards towards the partly marshy flats of the Gulf of Mexico, extending to the Atlantic, interrupted only by the Appalachian Highlands, of inferior elevation, in the Eastern States. Nearly the whole of this plain, from the Rocky Mountains to some distance beyond the Mississippi, consists of immense prairies. In the Eastern States (which form the more settled and most thickly inhabited portion of the country) large forests of valuable timber, as beech, birch, maple, oak, pine, spruce, elm, ash, walnut; and in the south, live oak, water-oak, magnolia, palmetto, tupil-tree, cypress, etc., still exist, the remnants of the forests which formerly extended over all the Atlantic slope, but into which great inroads have been made by the advance of civilization. The mineral kingdom produces much ore of iron, copper, lead, zinc, and aluminium, the non-metallic minerals include immense quantities of coal, anthracite, petroleum, stone, cement, phosphate rock, and salt. The highest point is Mount McKinley (Alaska), 20,320 ft. above sea level and the lowest point of dry land is in Death Valley (Inyo, California), 282 ft. below sea-level.

THE PRESIDENTS OF THE UNITED STATES OF AMERICA

Name (*with Native State*)	Party	Born	Inaug.	Died	Age
1. GEORGE WASHINGTON, *Va.*	Fed.	1732, Feb. 22	1789	1799, Dec. 14	67
2. John Adams, *Mass.*	,,	1735, Oct. 30	1797	1826, July 4	90
3. Thomas Jefferson, *Va.*	Rep.	1743, April 13	1801	1826, July 4	83
4. James Madison, *Va.*	,,	1751, Mar. 16	1809	1836, June 28	85
5. James Monroe, *Va.*	,,	1758, April 28	1817	1831, July 4	73
6. John Quincy Adams, *Mass.*	,,	1767, July 11	1825	1848, Feb. 23	80
7. Andrew Jackson, *S.C.*	Dem.	1767, Mar. 15	1829	1845, June 8	78
8. Martin Van Buren, *N.Y.*	,,	1782, Dec. 5	1837	1862, July 24	79
9. William Henry Harrison†, *Va.*	Whig.	1773, Feb. 9	1841	1841, April 4	68
10. John Tyler (*a*), *Va.*	,,	1790, Mar. 29	1841	1862, Jan. 17	71
11. James Knox Polk, *N.C.*	Dem.	1795, Nov. 2	1845	1849, June 15	53
12. Zachary Taylor† *Va.*	Whig.	1784, Nov. 24	1849	1850, July 9	65
13. Millard Fillmore (*a*), *N.Y.*	,,	1800, Jan. 7	1850	1874, Mar. 8	74
14. Franklin Pierce *N.H.*	Dem.	1804, Nov. 23	1853	1869, Oct. 8	64
15. James Buchanan, *Pa.*	,,	1791, April 23	1857	1868, June 1	77
16. Abraham Lincoln†§, *Ky.*	Rep.	1809, Feb. 12	1861	1865, April 15	56
17. Andrew Johnson (*a*), *N.C.*	,,	1808, Dec. 29	1865	1875, July 31	66
18. Ulysses Simpson Grant, *Ohio.*	,,	1822, April 27	1869	1885, July 23	63
19. Rutherford Birchard Hayes, *Ohio.*	,,	1822, Oct. 4	1877	1893, Jan. 17	70
20. James Abraham Garfield†§, *Ohio.*	,,	1831, Nov. 19	1881	1881, Sept. 19	49
21. Chester Alan Arthur (*a*), *Vt.*	,,	1830, Oct. 5	1881	1886, Nov. 18	56
22. Grover Cleveland, *N.J.*	Dem.	1837, Mar. 18	1893	1908, June 24	71
23. Benjamin Harrison, *Ohio.*	Rep.	1833, Aug. 20	1889	1901, Mar. 13	67
24. William McKinley†§, *Ohio.*	Rep.	1843, Jan. 29	1897	1901, Sept. 14	58
25. Theodore Roosevelt (*a*), *N.Y.*	,,	1858, Oct. 27	1901	1919, Jan. 6	60
26. William Howard Taft, *Ohio.*	,,	1857, Sept. 15	1909	1930, Mar. 8	72
27. Woodrow Wilson, *Va.*	Dem.	1856, Dec. 28	1913	1924, Feb. 3	67
28. Warren Gamaliel Harding†, *Ohio.*	Rep.	1865, Nov. 2	1921	1923, Aug. 2	57
29. Calvin Coolidge (*a*), *Vt.*	,,	1872, July 4	1923	1933, Jan. 5	60
30. Herbert Clark Hoover, *Iowa.*	,,	1874, Aug. 10	1929	1964, Oct. 20	90
31. Franklin Delano Roosevelt†‡, *N.Y.*	Dem.	1882, Jan. 30	1933	1945, April 12	63
32. Harry S. Truman (*a*), *Missouri.*	,,	1884, May 8	1945	1972, Dec. 26	88
33. Dwight D. Eisenhower, *Texas.*	Rep.	1890, Oct. 14	1953	1969, Mar. 28	78
34. John F. Kennedy, *Mass.*†§	Dem.	1917, May 29	1961	1963, Nov. 22	46
35. Lyndon B. Johnson (*a*), *Texas.*	,,	1908, Aug. 27	1963	1973, Jan. 22	64
36. Richard M. Nixon, *California.*	Rep.	1913, Jan. 9	1969	..	..
37. Gerald R. Ford *Michigan.*		1913, July 14	1974	..	..

† Died in office.   § Assassinated.   (*a*) Elected as Vice-President.

‡ Re-elected Nov. 5, 1940, the first case of a third term; re-elected for a fourth term Nov. 7, 1944.

GOVERNMENT

The United States of America is a Federal Republic consisting of 50 States and 1 Federal District (of which 13 are Original States, 7 were admitted without previous organization as Territories, and 30 were admitted after such organization), and of organized Territories. Hawaii formally entered the Union as the 50th State on Aug. 21, 1959, from which date the flag of the United States has 13 stripes and 50 stars in 9 horizontal rows of six and five alternatively. July 4 (Independence Day) is observed as the National Day.

THE CONSTITUTION.—By the Constitution of Sept. 17, 1787 (to which ten amendments were added on Dec. 15, 1791, and eleventh to twenty-sixth, Jan. 8, 1798, Sept. 25, 1804, Dec. 18, 1865, July 28, 1868, March 30, 1870, Feb. 25, 1913, May 31, 1913, Jan. 16, 1920, Aug. 26, 1920, Feb. 6, 1933, Dec. 5, 1933, Feb. 26, 1951, March 29, 1961, Jan. 23, 1964, Feb. 10, 1967 and June 30, 1971), the government of the United States is entrusted to three separate authorities—the Executive, the Legislative, and the Judicial.

THE EXECUTIVE

THE *Executive* power is vested in a President, who is elected every four years, and is eligible for re-election for one additional term. The mode of electing the President is as follows:—Each State appoints, in such manner as the Legislature thereof directs (they are now elected by popular vote on the *first Tuesday after the first Monday in November* of the year preceding the year in which the Presidential term expires), a number of electors, equal to the whole number of Senators and Representatives to which the State may be entitled in the Congress; but no Senator or Representative, or anyone holding office under Government, shall be appointed an elector. The electors for each State meet in their respective States on the *first Monday after the second Wednesday in December* following, and there vote for a President by ballot. The ballots are then sent to Washington, and opened on the *sixth day of January* by the President of Senate in presence of Congress, and the candidate who has received a majority of the whole number of electoral votes cast is declared President for the ensuing term. If no one has a majority, then from the highest on the list (not exceeding three) the House of Representatives elects a President, the votes being taken by States, the representation from each State having one vote. There is also a Vice-President, who, on the death of the President, becomes President for the remainder of the term. Under the XXth Amendment to the Constitution the terms of the President and Vice-President end at noon on the 20th day of January of the years in which such terms would have ended if the Amendment had not been ratified, and the terms of their successors then begin. In case of the removal or death of both President and Vice-President, a statute provides for the succession.

The President must be at least 35 years of age and a native citizen of the United States. He receives a taxable salary of $200,000 with a taxable expense allowance of $50,000 and a non-taxable travelling allowance not exceeding $100,000. Under the XXIInd Amendment to the Constitution, the tenure of the Presidency is limited to two terms. Executive duties:—(1) He is Commander-in-Chief of the Army and of the Navy (and of the Militias when they are in Federal service), and he commissions all officers therein. (2) With the consent of the Senate, he appoints the Cabinet officers and all the chief (and many minor) officials. (3) He exercises a general supervision over the whole Federal Administration and sees that the Federal Laws are duly carried out. Should disorder arise in any State which the authorities thereof are unable to suppress, the aid of the President is invoked. (4) He conducts the Foreign Policy of the Republic, and has power, " by and with the Advice and Consent of the Senate, to make Treaties, provided two thirds of the Senators present concur." The Declaration of War rests with Congress. (5) He makes recommendations of a general nature to Congress, and when laws are passed by Congress he may return them to Congress with a veto. But if a measure so vetoed is again passed by both Houses of Congress by a two-thirds majority in each House, it becomes law, notwithstanding the objection of the President.

President of the United States, GERALD RUDOLPH FORD, *born* July 14, 1913, *Sworn in* August 9, 1974. Republican.

Vice-President, Nelson A. Rockefeller, *born* July 8, 1908, *sworn in* Dec. 19,1974.

THE CABINET (*each* $60,000)

Secretary of State, Henry A. Kissinger, (*born* May 27, 1923), *appointed* Sept. 1973.
Secretary of the Treasury, William E. Simon (*born* 1927), *appointed* May 8, 1974.
Secretary of Defence, Donald H. Rumsfeld, *appointment confirmed* Nov. 18, 1975.
Attorney-General, Edward H. Levi (*born* 1911), *appointment confirmed* Feb. 5, 1975.
Secretary of the Interior, Thomas S. Klepper, *appointment confirmed* Oct. 9, 1975.
Secretary of Agriculture, Earl L. Butz (*born* 1909), *appointed* Nov. 11, 1971.
Secretary of Commerce, Elliot L. Richardson, *appointment confirmed* Dec. 11, 1975.
Secretary of Labour, William J. Usery, *appointment confirmed* Feb. 10, 1976.
Secretary of Health, Education and Welfare, F. David Mathews (*born* 1935), *nominated* June 27, 1975.
Secretary of Housing and Urban Development, Carla A. Hills (*born* 1934), *appointment confirmed* March 5, 1975.
Secretary of Transportation, William T. Coleman (*born* 1920), *appointment confirmed* March 3, 1975.

UNITED STATES EMBASSY
Grosvenor Square, W.1
[01-499 9000]

Ambassador Extraordinary and Plenipotentiary, Her Excellency the Hon. Anne L. Armstrong (1976).
Deputy Chief of Mission, Hon. Ronald I. Spiers.
Minister for Economic and Commercial Affairs, Hon. William K. Miller.
Counsellors, Michael T. F. Pistor (*Public Affairs*); Michael M. Conlin (*Administration*); Loren E. Lawrence (*Consular Affairs*); Borrie L. Hyman (*Commercial*); William M. Woessner (*Political Affairs*); John W. Holmes (*Economic Affairs*).

Defence Attaché, Naval Attaché and Naval Attaché for Air, Rear Admiral Frances T. Brown, U.S.N.
Army Attaché, Col. Robert B. Osborn, U.S.A.
Air Attaché, Col. Thomas G. McInerney, U.S.A.F.
1st Secretaries, Harry Pollack; H. Clay Black; (*Economic*); George H. Thigpen; William G. Hamilton, (*Public Affairs*); Lucien L. Kinsolving (*Politico-Military Affairs*); Lary C. Williamson (*Commercial*); Elwood J. McGuire (*Administration*); Raymond G. H. Seitz; Samuel Karp (*Consular*); Bruce R. Koch (*Cultural Affairs*); William Clappin; Frank M. Schroeder (*Administration*); Lenard R. Clarke (*Administration*);

Second Secretary, Denis A. Sandberg.
Attachés, William L. Rodman (*Agriculture*); William A. Kish (*Legal*); Michael G. MacDonald (*Politico-Military Affairs*); William M. McGhee; Ellen V. Watson (*Administration*); Charles M. Shaw (*Commercial*).

CAPITAL OF THE UNITED STATES

In 1790 Congress ratified the cession of 100 sq. miles by the States of Maryland and Virginia as a site for a Federal City to be the national capital of the United States. In 1791 it was decided to name the capital *Washington* and in 1793 the foundation-stone of the Capitol building was laid. In 1800 the seat of government was removed to Washington, which was chartered as a city in 1802. In 1846 the Virginia portion was retroceded and the present area of the *District of Columbia* (with which the City of Washington is considered co-extensive) is 61 square miles, with a population at the Census of 1970 of 756,510.

The District of Columbia has hitherto been governed by a Commissioner and assistant and a 9-member City Council, all appointed by the President. From Nov. 5, 1974, this body has been replaced by an elected mayor and City Council.

The *City of Washington* is situated on the west central edge of Maryland, opposite the State of Virginia, on the left bank of the Potomac at its confluence with the Anacostia, 107 miles from Chesapeake Bay and 186 from the Atlantic Ocean.

THE CONGRESS

The Legislative power is vested in two Houses, the Senate and the House of Representatives, the President having a *veto* power, which may be overcome by a two-thirds vote of each House. The Senate is composed of two Senators from each State, elected by the people thereof for the term of six years, and each Senator has one vote; and Representatives are chosen in each State, by popular vote, for two years. The average number of persons represented by each Congressman is 1 for 469,088. The *Senate* consists of 100 members. The salary of a Senator is $42,500 per annum, with mileage at 20 cents per mile each session. The *House of Representatives* consists of 435 Representatives, a resident commissioner from Puerto Rico and a delegate from the District of Columbia, Guam and the Virgin Isalnds. The salary of a Representative is $42,500 per annum, with mileage as for Senators. By the XIXth Amendment, sex is no disqualification for the franchise. On Nov. 1, 1972, there were 139,642,000 persons of voting age, excluding members of the armed forces overseas.

THE NINETY-FOURTH CONGRESS

President of the Senate, Nelson A. Rockfeller (*Vice-President of the United States*).
Speaker of the House of Representatives, Carl Albert, Oklahoma.
Secretary of the Senate, Francis R. Valeo, *District of Columbia*.
Clerk of the House of Representatives, W. Pat Jennings, *Va.*

Members of the 94th Congress were elected on Nov. 5, 1974.

The 94th Congress is constituted as follows:

Senate.—Democrats 62; Republicans, 38; Total, 100. *House of Representatives.*—Democrats, 291; Republicans, 144. Total, 435.

THE JUDICATURE

The *Federal Judiciary* consists of three sets of Federal Courts: (1) The *Supreme Court* at Washington, D.C., consisting of a Chief Justice and eight Associate Justices, with original jurisdiction in cases affecting Ambassadors, etc., or where a State is a party to the suit, and with appellate jurisdiction from inferior Federal Courts and from the judgments of the highest Courts of the States. (2) The *United States Courts of Appeals*, dealing with appeals from District Courts and from certain federal administrative agencies, and consisting of all the Circuit Judges within the circuit. (3) The 94 *District Courts* served by 399 District Court Judges.

THE SUPREME COURT

(U.S. Supreme Court Building, Washington, D.C.)
Chief Justice, Warren E. Burger, *Minn.*, *born* Sept. 17, 1907, *appointed* June 23, 1969.

Associate Justices

Name	Born	Apptd
William J. Brennan, Jr., *N.J.*	1906	1956
Potter Stewart, *Ohio*	1915	1958
Byron R. White, *Colo.*	1917	1962
Thurgood Marshall, *N.Y.*	1908	1967
Harry Blackmun, *Minn.*	1908	1970
Lewis F. Powell, Jr., *Va.*	1907	1971
William R. Rehnquist, *Ariz.*	1924	1971
John Paul Stevens, *Ill.*	1920	1975

Clerk of the Supreme Court, Michael Rodak, Jr.

CRIMINAL STATISTICS, U.S.

Crime	No. of offences	
	1972	1973
Murder	18,550	19,510
Rape	46,480	51,000
Robbery	374,790	382,680
Aggravated Assault	389,000	416,270
Burglary	2,352,800	2,540,900
Larceny—Theft	4,109,600	4,304,000
Thefts of Automobiles	882,200	923,600
Total	8,173,400	8,638,400

DEFENCE

Department of Defence

Secretary of Defence (in the Cabinet), Donald H. Rumsfeld.
Secretary of the Army, Martin R. Hoffman.
Secretary of the Navy, J. W. Middendorf II.
Secretary of the Air Force, Thomas C. Reed.
Chairman, Joint Chiefs of Staff, Gen. George S. Brown, U.S.A.F.

The Department of Defence includes the Secretary of Defence as its head, the Deputy Secretary of Defence, the Defence staff offices, the Joint Chiefs of Staff and the Joint Staff, the three military departments and the military services within those departments, the unified and specified commands, and other Department of Defence agencies as the Secretary of Defence establishes to meet specific requirements. The Defence staff offices and the joint Chiefs of Staff, although separately organized function in full coordination and cooperation. They include the offices of the Director of Defence Research and Engineering, the nine Assistant Secretaries of Defence, the General Counsel of the

Department of Defence and such other staff offices as the Secretary of Defence may establish. The Joint Chiefs of Staff, as a group, are directly responsible to the Secretary of Defence for the functions assigned to them. Each member of the Joint Chiefs of Staff, other than the Chairman, is responsible for keeping the Secretary of his military department fully informed on matters considered or acted upon by the Joint Chiefs of Staff.

Each military department is separately organized under its own Secretary and functions under the direction, authority and control of the Secretary of Defence.

The Department of Defence maintains and employs armed forces: (1) to support and defend the Constitution of the United States against all enemies, foreign and domestic; (2) to insure, by timely and effective military action, the security of the United States, its possessions, and areas vital to its interests; (3) to uphold and advance the national policies and interest of the United States; and (4) to safeguard the internal security of the United States. All functions in the Department of Defence and its component agencies are performed under the direction, authority and control of the Secretary of Defence.

Commanders of unified and specified commands are responsible to the President and the Secretary of Defence for the accomplishment of military missions assigned to them.

Unified Defence Commands

Commanders-in-Chief

U.S. European Command, Brussels.—Gen. Alexander M. Haig, Jr. (U.S.A.) (concurrently N.A.T.O. Supreme Allied Commander).

U.S. Southern Command, Quarry Heights, Panama Canal Zone.—Lt.-Gen. Dennis P. McAuliffe (U.S.A.).

Atlantic, Norfolk, Virginia.—Adm. Isaac C. Kidd (U.S. Navy) (concurrently N.A.T.O. Supreme Allied Commander, Atlantic).

Pacific, Hawaii.—Adm. Maurice Weisner (U.S. Navy).

†*U.S. Naval Forces, Europe, London.*—Adm. David Baglay (U.S. Navy).

North American Air Defence Command, Colorado Springs.—Gen. Daniel James (U.S.A.F.).

**Strategic Air Command, Omaha.*—Gen. Russell E. Dougherty (U.S.A.F.).

Alaskan Air Command, Anchorage, Alaska.—Lt.-Gen. James E. Hill (U.S.A.F.).

U.S. Readiness Command, MacDill, Florida.—Gen. John J. Hennessey (U.S. Army).

* A Specified Command.
† A subordinate component of *U.S. European Command.*

Army.—The Army of U.S. had a strength of 8,293,766 (including 2,310,436 Air Force) on V.E. Day, reduced by June 30, 1959, to 861,964 (excluding Air Force). The strength on March 31, 1976, was 771,301. Stationed in Germany were four divisions. There was one division in Korea.
Chief of Staff of the Army, Gen. Fred C. Weyand.

Navy.—The peak strength of the Navy (including Marine Corps in 1945, was 3,855,497. The strength of the U.S. Navy in 1975, was 535,900. Strength of the Marine Corps, 196,000.

The U.S. Navy had in service in 1976, 478 active fleet ships, including 14 attack carriers, 26 cruisers, 69 destroyers, 64 frigates, 116 submarines (65 nuclear, 41 SSBN and 10 diesel), 61 amphibious, 3 mine warfare, 117 auxiliaries and 18 patrol craft, *Chief of Naval Operations,* Adm. James Holloway.

Air.—The United States Air Force was established as a separate organization on September 18, 1947. At April 30, 1976, there were 595,988 officers and airmen on active duty, with 231,377 civilian employees. Air Force Reserve and Air National Guard numbered 137,103 on May 31, 1976.

To deter aggression the Air Force has about 140 strategic bombers maintaining constant alert as well as 1,054 inter-continental ballistic missiles in hardened silos. In addition, the Air Force maintains the capability to carry out limited war and special warfare operations. In March, 1961, the Air Force was assigned primary responsibility for the Department of Defence space development programmes and projects. By June 13, 1976, the United States had placed a total of 3,901 space-craft into earth orbit or deep space. These included Air Force, Army and N.A.S.A. shots.
Chief of Staff of the U.S. Air Force, Gen. David C. Jones.

NATIONAL ORIGINS OF THE POPULATION

About 102,200,000 of the approximately 205 million persons in the United States reported on a sample survey conducted in March, 1972, that they were of one of eight specific origin categories. Approximately 25·5 million persons reported German origin; 29·5 million, English, Scottish or Welsh; 16·4 million Irish; 9·2 million, Spanish; 8·8 million, Italian; 5·1 million, Polish; and 2·2 million, Russian. About 11 million persons living in the United States at the time of an earlier survey of 1969 were foreign born, Germany, Italy, Mexico and the United Kingdom were the major contributing countries. Two-thirds of them reported English as the language usually spoken in their homes. They were 23 years older on the average than the native population.

Countries of birth of the foreign-born population (1969) were: Austria (236,000), Cuba (504,000), Germany (1,004,000), Ireland (277,000), Italy (1,353,000), Mexico (938,000), Poland (550,000), Russia (412,000), Sweden (166,000), United Kingdom (1,006,000); other countries, 4,434,000.

SOCIAL WELFARE EXPENDITURE

The total value of government expenditure on social welfare (federal, state and local government) in 1975 was $286,547,000,0000 compared with $239,302,600,000 in 1974 and $52,293,000,000 in 1960. In 1975 expenditure per person (of the total population of U.S.A.) was $1,319—social insurance, $567; education, $361; public aid, $187; health and medical services, $77; veterans' welfare, $76; other services, $36 per person. Total expenditure by programmes was:

	$ million		
	1960	1973	1975
Social insurance.......	19,307	86,118	123,444
Education............	17,626	65,258	78,438
Public aid............	4,101	28,697	40,536
Health and medical...	4,464	12,640	16,636
Veterans.............	5,479	12,951	16,661
Other welfare services.	1,139	6,335	7,877
Housing.............	177	2,180	2,954
TOTAL.......	52,293	214,179	286,547

FINANCE

THE UNITED STATES BUDGET

[Fiscal years]

Description	Actual	
	1974	1975 Preliminary
Receipts by Source	$	$
Individual income taxes	118,951,031,000	122,321,565,000
Corporation income taxes	38,619,654,000	40,626,750,000
Social insurance taxes and contributions:		
Employment taxes and contributions	65,892,164,000	75,203,856,000
Unemployment insurance	6,836,545,000	6,764,177,000
Contributions for other insurance and retirement	4,051,342,000	4,460,650,000
Excise taxes	16,843,668,000	16,541,971,000
Estate and gift taxes	5,034,640,000	4,589,361,000
Customs	3,334,138,000	3,665,929,000
Miscellaneous	5,368,613,000	6,746,724,000
Total	264,932,400,000	280,920,983,000
Outlays by Function		
National defence	78,568,540,000	88,288,891,000
International affairs and finance	3,593,005,000	4,214,921,000
General science, space, and technology	4,154,043,000	4,156,821,000
Natural resources, environment, and energy	6,390,241,000	8,020,450,000
Agriculture	2,230,029,000	2,008,766,000
Commerce and transportation	13,100,014,000	15,545,907,000
Community and regional development	4,910,094,000	4,482,364,000
Education, manpower, and social services	11,600,144,000	15,060,808,000
Health	22,073,035,000	27,447,554,000
Income security	84,431,067,000	109,315,276,000
Veterans benefits and services	13,386,006,000	16,598,623,000
Law enforcement and justice	2,462,102,000	2,759,392,000
General government	3,327,174,000	3,582,264,000
Revenue sharing and general purpose fiscal assistance	6,746,029,000	6,695,095,000
Interest	28,072,121,000	31,035,387,000
Undistributed offsetting receipts	−16,651,661,000	−14,079,865,000
Total	$268,391,983,000	$325,132,657,000

PUBLIC DEBT

On June 30, 1976, the total gross *Federal Debt* of the United States stood at $631,285,027,000; the equivalent debt for 1975 was $544,131,193,000.

COST OF LIVING IN U.S.A.

The Consumer Price Index (for city wage-earner and clerical workers—single persons and families—in 50 cities representative of all cities in the United States) showed a monthly average during the calendar year 1975 of 161·2 (the basic figure of 100 being the 1967 average). The Consumer Price Index rose 6·2 per cent. in 1973, 11·0 per cent. in 1974 and 9·1 per cent. in 1975. From June 1974 to June 1975 the index rose 9·3 per cent. for all items, 8·8 per cent. for food, 9·3 per cent. for other commodities, 5·1 per cent. for rent and 10·5 per cent. for other services.

The Wholesale Price Index of all commodities averaged 160·1 in 1974 (compared to the base of 100·0 in 1967) and was 173·7 in June, 1975. From June, 1974 to June, 1975 the index rose 11·6 per cent. for all items, 10·4 per cent. for farm products, 14·2 per cent. for processed foods and feeds and 11·1 per cent. for industrial commodities.

PERSONAL INCOMES IN U.S.A.

Personal incomes in the United States rose from $944·9 billion in 1972 to $1,055·0 billion in 1973, $1,150·5 billion in 1974 and $1,220·8 billion in the second quarter of 1975. In the latter period, labour income was $885·5 billion, 4·4 per cent. above the level of the previous year. Business proprietors, professional and farm income totalled $86·0 billion in the second quarter of 1975 (4·2 per cent. decrease on previous year) and dividends, interest, and rent totalled $176·7 billion (up 10·6 per cent.). Transfer payments were $177·9 billion and personal contributions to social insurance, which are offsets to income, were $49·7 billion.

Disposition of personal incomes.—Personal taxes were $142 billion in the second quarter of 1975, leaving households with $1,078·8 billion of disposable income. Consumption expenditures were $938·1 billion; $130·0 billion for durable goods, $408·5 billion for non-durable goods and $399·6 billion for services. Personal saving was $114·6 billion. Disposable income per capita was $5,056 in the second quarter of 1975.

Private domestic investment.—The total gross private domestic investment rose from $179·3 billion in 1972 to $209·4 billion in 1973, and to $213·0 billion in the second quarter of 1974. It declined to $147·3 billion in the second quarter of 1975. Fixed investment in new residential construction declined to $46·0 billion in 1974 (1973 $57·2 billion) and other construction rose to $52·0 billion (1973 $47·0 billion). Investment in producers' durable equipment rose from $89·18 billion in 1973 to $97·1 billion in 1974.

EXTERNAL TRADE OF THE UNITED STATES

Year	General Imports	Total Exports and Re-exports excluding military aid	Balance of Exports and Imports
	$	$	$
1971	45,563,000,000	43,549,000,000	− 2,014,000,000
1972	55,583,000,000	49,199,000,000	− 6,384,000,000
1973	69,476,000,000	70,823,000,000	+ 1,347,000,000
1974	100,251,000,000	97,908,000,000	− 2,343,000,000
1975	96,140,000,000	107,191,000,000	+ 11,051,000,000

EXPORTS BY PRINCIPAL COMMODITIES OF DOMESTIC ORIGIN, 1975

Commodity	Value
	$
Food and Live Animals	15,487,000,000
Meat and Meat Preparations	528,000,000
Dairy Products and Eggs	134,000,000
Wheat and Wheat Flour	5,292,000,000
Rice	858,000,000
Corn and other grains	5,493,000,000
Fruit and Nuts	871,000,000
Vegetables	406,000,000
Soybean oil-cake and meal	639,000,000
Beverages and Tobacco	1,310,000,000
Cigarettes	368,000,000
Crude Materials (inedible), except fuels	9,784,000,000
Synthetic rubber	261,000,000
Raw cotton	991,000,000
Mineral fuels, etc.	4,465,000,000
Coal	3,259,000,000
Petroleum and products	907,000,000
Animal and Vegetable Oils and Fats	944,000,000
Chemicals	8,705,000,000
Machinery and Transport Equipment	45,710,000,000
Other Manufactured Goods	16,590,000,000

Commodity	Value
	$
Fruit, Nuts, Vegetables	992,000,000
Sugar	1,870,000,000
Coffee (green)	1,561,000,000
Beverages and Tobacco	1,419,000,000
Whisky	540,000,000
Crude materials (inedible), except fuels	5,564,000,000
Rubber (including latex)	353,000,000
Textile fibres and wastes	174,000,000
Ores and metal scrap	1,977,000,000
Mineral Fuels, etc.	26,476,000,000
Petroleum and Products	24,814,000,000
Animal and Vegetable Oils, Fats	554,000,000
Chemicals	3,696,000,000
Machinery and Transport Equipment	23,465,000,000
Electrical apparatus	4,911,000,000
Motor vehicles and parts	9,921,000,000
Other manufactured goods	23,929,000,000
Paper and manufactures	1,673,000,000
Metals and manufactures	8,944,000,000
Textiles other than clothing	1,219,000,000

UNITED STATES IMPORTS BY PRINCIPAL COMMODITIES, 1975

Commodity	Value
	$
Food and Live Animals	8,509,000,000
Meat and Meat Preparations	1,141,000,000
Fish	1,356,000,000

UNITED STATES FOREIGN TRADE BY ECONOMIC CLASS 1975

Class	Imports	Exports*
	$	$
Crude Materials	23,568,000,000	10,883,000,000
Crude Foodstuffs	3,642,000,000	11,804,000,000
Manufactured Foods	5,972,000,000	4,221,000,000
Semi-manufactures	17,323,000,000	12,815,000,000
Finished Manuf.	46,435,000,000	66,434,000,000
Total	96,940,000,000	106,157,000,000

* Excluding total military grant-aid of $105,696,000,000.

UNITED STATES FOREIGN TRADE BY PRINCIPAL COUNTRIES, 1975

Country	Exports and Re-exports to	General Imports from	Country	Exports and Re-exports to	General Imports from
	$	$		$	$
Australia	1,816,000,000	1,147,000,000	Japan	9,565,000,000	11,268,000,000
Belgium and Luxemburg	2,427,000,000	1,190,000,000	Korea	1,761,000,000	1,416,000,000
Brazil	3,056,000,000	1,464,000,000	Mexico	5,144,000,000	3,059,000,000
Canada	21,759,000,000	21,747,000,000	Netherlands	4,183,000,000	1,083,000,000
France	3,031,000,000	2,137,000,000	Spain	2,161,000,000	831,000,000
Germany, W.	5,194,000,000	5,382,000,000	Sweden	925,000,000	877,000,000
India	1,290,000,000	548,000,000	Switzerland	1,153,000,000	867,000,000
Israel	1,551,000,000	313,000,000	United Kingdom	4,525,000,000	3,784,000,000
Italy	2,867,000,000	2,397,000,000	Venezuela	2,243,000,000	3,624,000,000

UNITED STATES STOCK OF CURRENCY AND COIN
$ million

June 30	Gold★	Dollars†	Subsidiary Coin	Minor Coin	Silver Certificates§	United States Notes	Federal Reserve Notes	Total‡
1971	10,184·2	484·7	5,056·0	1,260·6	217·4	322·5	54,494·4	72,098·9
1972	10,401·1	711·9	5,394·8	1,344·0	215·2	322·5	58,285·5	76,761·5
1973	10,410·2	767·4	5,714·3	1,437·4	213·4	322·5	63,653·4	82,594·8
1974	11,566·8	792·5	5,969·3	1,553·0	211·9	322·5	69,489·3	89,980·4
1975	11,619·9	862·4	6,518·2	1,699·0	210·7	322·5	77,002·5	98,309·3

★ Held by U.S. Treasury only.

† Standard silver dollars only up to 1971. 1972, 1973, 1974 and 1975 figures consist of $481·8 m in standard silver and the balance in cupronickel clad dollars.

‡ Totals include value of early issue notes in process of withdrawal, not separately shown. Value, June 1975, $74·1 m.

§ In process of withdrawal. Not redeemable in silver.

AGRICULTURE AND LIVESTOCK

Agriculture.—The total land surface, including Hawaii and Alaska, is 2,263,591,000 acres of which about 50 per cent. is in farms. The total number of farms in 1975 was 2,818,580. The cash income from crops in 1974 was $52,677,000,000, and in 1973, $42,346,000,000. Cash income from live-stock and livestock products in 1974 was $46,244,000,000 and in 1973 $42,327,000,000.

Combined production of all crops in 1974 was about 8 per cent. less than in 1973. There were record outputs of wheat, rice, dry beans, peanuts, potatoes, and citrus fruits. Yields per acre were at new high levels for peanuts and potatoes. Farm output of livestock and livestock products was up 4 per cent. due largely to record high meat animal production.

Livestock on Farms, Jan. 1

	1973 'ooo head	1974 'ooo head	1975 'ooo head
Cattle	121,534	127,670	131,826
Cows	52,541	54,293	56,637
Hogs★	59,180	61,106	55,062
Stock sheep	14,852	13,744	12,480
Chickens★	406,241	412,503	382,793
Turkeys, hens	3,303	3,553	2,970

★ Dec. 1, preceding year.

MINERALS

The value of mineral production in the United States in 1975 totalled an estimated $63·1 billion compared with $54·9 billion in 1974 and $36·8 billion in 1973.

The value of processed minerals and mineral materials increased 22 per cent. to $270 billion. Imports and exports of minerals and mineral materials totalled $40 billion and $18 billion respectively.

Lead refinery production declined 7 per cent. from that of 1974 and aluminium primary production at 3·9 million tons decreased 22 per cent. from that of 1974. Mine production of zinc decreased 5·2 per cent. and iron ore dropped 3 per cent.; uranium concentrate mill production increased by 1 per cent.

About 72 per cent. of the mineral production of the United States (in value) consists of fuels. In 1975 U.S. production of crude petroleum amounted to 3·1 billion barrels. Total demand (domestic plus exports) averaged 12·5 million barrels daily, a 2·1 per cent. increase from 1974.

The 1975 average daily production in the three principal oil producing States declined: in Texas by 111,000 barrels (total average daily production 3,381,000 barrels); in Louisiana by 224,000 barrels

(total average daily production 1,846,000 barrels); and in California by 2,000 barrels (total average daily production 882,000 barrels).

Anthracite production declined for the second consecutive year in 1975. Production fell to 6·2 million tons, 6·3 per cent below 1974 output. The continued decline in production reflected competition from other fuels, particularly oil and gas, in domestic and foreign markets.

Bituminous coal and lignite output in 1975 rose to a record high of 640 million tons. Exports rose 9·1 per cent. to 66 million tons.

LABOUR

Organized Labour.—On December 5, 1955, the American Federation of Labour (AFL), founded in 1881, and the Congress of Industrial Organizations (CIO), formally established in 1928, merged into an organization called the American Federation of Labour and Congress of Industrial Organizations. The combined membership in 1974 was 16,938,000. There are also 4,705,000 members of unions not affiliated to the AFL-CIO. Of the 21,643,000 members of national and international unions with headquarters in U.S.A., 1,444,000 were employed in Canada.

Approximately 25·8 per cent. of the non-agricultural labour force of the United States is estimated to be organized.

Work Stoppages.—There were 5,031 stoppages recorded in 1975. There were 31,237,600 man-days of idleness, representing 0·16 per cent. of estimated working time of all non-agricultural workers.

Employment and Unemployment.—The civilian labour force (working population) was 94,557,000 in May, 1976. This includes self-employed, wage and salary-earners, and unpaid family workers,

Wages (Preliminary Figures) April 1976	Average Weekly Earnings $	Hours per Week	Average Hourly Earnings $
Manufacturing	198·74	39·2	5·07
Durable	214·24	39·6	5·41
Non-durable	176·33	38·5	4·58
Coal Mining	297·60	38·8	7·67
Bituminous Coal and Lignite Mining	297·99	38·7	7·70
Gen. Bldg. Contractors	271·58	36·9	7·36
Gas, Electricity and Sanitary Services	265·79	41·4	6·42
Wholesale trade	196·35	38·5	5·10
Retail trade (incl. eating and drinking places.	112·35	32·1	3·50
Laundries, Cleaners	112·70	35·0	3·22

employed and unemployed. Unemployment was estimated at 6,860,000 in May 1976 (7·3 per cent.)

Wages.—In April, 1976, gross average weekly earnings in industry ranged from $337·00 per week in malt liquors to $71·12 in eating and drinking places (28·0 hours and $2·54 average hourly earnings). The average for all manufacturing was $198·74 compared with $185·25 in May, 1975.

On Jan. 1, 1976, the minimum wage set by federal law became $2·30 an hour for most non-agricultural employees subject to the Fair Labour Standards Act. This law covers employees engaged in or producing goods for interstate commerce and employees of certain large enterprises. The law requires at least time and a half of an employee's regular rate of pay for all hours over 40 a week for most covered workers.

Other non-agricultural employees employed in enterprises or occupations made subject to the minimum wage provisions on or after February 1, 1967, became subject to a $2·20 minimum wage rate also on Jan. 1, 1976, and will become subject to the $2·30 minimum wage on Jan. 1, 1977. The minimum wage for hired farmworkers was increased to $2·00 on Jan. 1, 1976, will become $2·20 on Jan. 1, 1977, and $2·30 an hour on Jan. 1, 1978. The minimum wages for the three employment categories will be increased to $2·30 an hour over a 2 to 4 year period.

There are certain exemptions from these requirements in specific occupations and industries.

In addition to cash wages, most workers receive some type of " fringe " benefits—the most common forms being paid vacations, paid holidays, various types of insurance and health benefits financed by the employer or by employer and employees jointly.

COMMUNICATIONS
RAILWAYS

Data pertaining to Class I and II Carriers and their non-operating subsidiaries:—

	1972 $	1973 $
Capital Stock outstanding	5,904,814,000	5,894,304,000
Funded Debt outstanding	7,063,411,000	7,197,571,000
Total Rly. capital actually outsdg.	12,968,225,000	13,091,875,000
Dividends declared	531,908,000	482,362,000
Interest accrued	600,903,000	624,120,000
Total dividends and interest	1,132,811,000	1,106,482,000
Railway operating revenues	13,821,880,000	15,243,795,000
Railway operating expenses	11,016,037,000	12,067,957,000
Number of passengers carried earning revenue.	*Number* 262,010,000	*Number* 255,444,000
Number of passenger-train cars in service	7,762	7,362
Number of freight-train cars in service	1,415,004	1,391,448
Number of railway employees	537,038	533,766
Miles operated	218,024	216,405

ROADS

In 1974 there were 3,815,807 miles of roads and streets in the United States, of which 3,178,152 miles were in rural areas and 637,655 miles were in municipal areas. Surfaced roads and streets account for 3,067,438 miles of the total; 748,369 miles were unimproved and graded and drained. State primary roads, including extensions in municipal areas, total 476,982 miles (474,296 surfaced). Other roads and streets under State control total 313,404 miles (283,701 surfaced), 2,801,273 miles are under local control (2,238,753 surfaced); and 224,148 miles (70,688 surfaced) are under Federal control (in national forests and parks).

An estimated total of $24,506,000,000 was spent in 1974 for roads and streets in the United States. Of this total $15,832,000,000 was spent for State highways, $3,630,000,000 was spent for county and local rural roads, $4,509,000,000 was spent for city streets and $535,000,000 was spent on roads in Federal areas. Capital outlay accounts for 53·3 per cent. of the total expenditure; 26·5 per cent. was spent for maintenance, and 7·5 per cent. for administration; 8·3 per cent. for highway police and safety; and 4·4 per cent. for interest on highway bonds.

Motor Vehicles and Taxation.—The number of motor vehicles registered in 1974 in the United States was 129,893,311, an increase of 3·4 per cent. over the 1973 total of 125,669,992. The State governments received $13,121,049,000 in 1974 from motor fuel, motor vehicle and motor-carrier taxes. In 1974 the Federal Government received $5,846,038,000 from excise taxes on motor vehicles and parts, tyres and tubes, petrol, diesel and special fuels and lubricating oils.

Accidents.—In 1974 there were 46,200 deaths caused by motor vehicle accidents. The death rate per 100,000,000 vehicle-miles of travel was 3·6 in 1974, compared with 4·3 in 1973.

SHIPPING

The ocean-going Merchant Marine of the U.S. on April 1, 1975, consisted of 910 vessels of 1,000 gross tons and over, of which 553 were privately owned and 357 were government-owned ships. Of the 553 privately owned active vessels, 168 were freighters, 6 were combination passenger and cargo, 223 were tankers, 16 were bulk carriers and 140 were intermodal types. There were 310 ships in the National Defense Reserve Fleet of inactive government-owned vessels, of which 78 were to be sold for scrap.

AIR TRANSPORT

United States domestic and international scheduled airlines in 1974 were estimated to have carried 207,449,000 passengers over 162,917,241,000 revenue passenger miles. The freight flown by the scheduled airlines during 1974 totalled 4,890,074 ton miles and express 80,845,000 ton miles. In addition, the airlines flew 1,150,832,000 ton miles of mail, a decrease of 3·9 per cent. over 1973.

Total operating revenues of all U.S. scheduled airlines reached the record figure of $14,699,125,000 in 1974, an increase of 18·4 per cent. over 1973. Similarly, total operating expenses rose to a record high total of $13,973,385,000 last year, or a 11·9 per cent. increase over 1973. The net operating income (*i.e.* before deduction of taxes, interest, etc.). was $725,740,000, an increase of 24·0 per cent. from the previous year, resulting in a profit of $321,641,000 compared with a profit of $226,693,000 in 1973.

Ten principal classes of commercial air carriers can be distinguished in the United States, (a) The Domestic Trunk Lines (11); (b) Local Service Carriers, operating routes of lesser traffic density between the smaller traffic centres and between small and large centres (8); (c) The International and Territorial Carriers, including all U.S. flag air carriers authorized to operate between the

U.S.A. and foreign countries, other than Canada, and over international waters; also between foreign countries and into Mexico, the Caribbean (10); (d) Intra-Hawaiian Air Carriers, operating in Hawaii (2); (e) Intra-Alaskan Carriers, providing service within Alaska (4); (f) All Cargo Carriers (3); (g) Helicopter Carrriers (3); (h) Supplement Air Carriers (14); (i) Air Freight Forwarding Companies (181) and Air Taxi operators; and (j) Intra-State Carriers, with operations limited to State boundaries.

In 1974, 3,307,318 persons were employed by the domestic and international airlines, 1·3 per cent. more than in 1973.

U.S. SCHEDULED AIRLINE INDUSTRY STATISTICS, 1974 (Thousands)

	Domestic Trunk Airlines	Local Service Airlines	Intra-Hawaiian Carriers	Heli-copter Carriers	Interna-tional and Territorial Airlines	Intra-Alaskan Carriers	All Cargo Carriers
Revenue passengers carried	147,993	35,200	4,675	592	17,725	1,107	..
Revenue passenger miles..	117,616,261	10,808,141	644,685	10,298	33,186,199	635,222	..
Air mail ton miles........	620,348	33,432	1,182	4	337,060	11,647	147,159
Express ton miles........	70,961	6,929	..	2	857	206	1,885
Freight ton miles........	2,245,262	68,599	5,687	2	1,338,199	24,213	1,208,004
Revenue ton miles........	15,076,887	1,211,754	112,446	1,058	5,788,488	102,518	1,645,694
Revenue plane miles......	1,589,077	262,216	9,192	1,085	330,248	18,660	44,675

EDUCATION
State School Systems

Forty-nine of the fifty States in the Union have compulsory school attendance laws. In general, children are obliged to attend school from 7 to 16 years of age. In the States there are, connected with the local administrative units, officers charged with enforcing the compulsory attendance law, known in the majority of States as the truant or attendance officers.

In Oct. 1974 the total number of children in the United States of 5 to 17 years of age was 50,539,000, of whom 48,474,000 or 95·9 per cent. were enrolled in schools below the college level. Approximately 10 per cent. of these students attended non-public schools, and the remaining 90 per cent. were enrolled in public schools.

Preliminary data for the 1975–76 school year for public elementary and secondary schools were as follows: enrollment of 44,838,490; 2,203,089 classroom teachers with an average salary of $12,448; $59,149,733,000 for current expenditures; $5,982,539,000 for sites, buildings, furniture and equipment expenditures; and $1,970,297,000 expenditures for interest on school debt.

Revenue for public school purposes comes from the Federal, State, and local governments. Total receipts in 1973–74 were about $58,230,892,000; of this, approximately 8·5 per cent. ($4,930,351,000) came from the Federal Government, 41·4 per cent. ($24,113,409,000) from State governments, and 50.1 per cent. ($29,187,132,000) from local sources.

During the 1973–74 school year, the average daily attendance in public elementary and secondary schools was 41,438,000; the average length of the school term was 178·7 days; and the average number of days attended by each pupil enrolled was 159·5 days.

Institutions of Higher Education

In the autumn of 1975 enrolment in institutions of higher education numbered 9,731,431.

Institutions of higher education include universities, colleges, professional schools, and two-year colleges. The 1975 survey of enrolments covered 3,018 institutions classified as follows: 1,891 universities, colleges and professional schools enrolling 7,143,286 students; and 1,127 two-year colleges enrolling 2,818,507 students. Publicly controlled institutions of higher education enrolled 76·3 per cent. (7,425,772) of the students and privately controlled 23·7 per cent. (2,305,659).

During the school year 1973–74, an estimated 946,000 bachelor's degrees were conferred, 527,000 to men and 418,000 to women; 53,800 first-professional degrees, 48,500 to men and 5,200 to women; 277,000 master's degrees (157,800 to men and 119,100 to women), and 33,800 doctorates, 27,300 to men and 6,450 to women. There were 185,600 bachelor's degrees in Education, 150,800 in Social Sciences and 132,300 in Business and Management. The three leading fields of study for the master's degree were Education (112,250), Business and Management (32,750) and Social Sciences (17,300). The most popular fields of study on the doctorate level were Education (7,300), Social Sciences (4,100) and Physical Sciences (3,600).

Particulars of some of the Universities (with opening autumn enrolment figures, 1975) are: *Harvard* (20,498 students, including 7,883 women, founded at Cambridge, Mass. on Oct. 28, 1636, and named after John Harvard of Emmanuel College, Cambridge, England, who bequeathed to it his library and a sum of money in 1638; *Yale* (9,734 students, including 3,210 women), founded at New Haven, Connecticut, in 1701; *Bowdoin*, Brunswick, Me. (founded 1794; 1,348, including 437 women); *Brown*, Providence, R.I. (founded 1764); 6,766 students, including 2,717 women); *Columbia*, New York, N.Y. (founded 1754; 23,343 students, including 11,339 women); *Cornell* (founded at Ithaca, N.Y., 1865); 17,295 students, including 6,097 women); *Dartmouth*, Hanover, N.H. (founded 1769, 4,026 students, including 971 women); *Georgetown*, Washington, D.C. (founded 1789; 10,835 students, including 4,135 women); *North Carolina*, Chapel Hill, N.C. (founded in 1789; 20,536 students, including 9,151 women); *Pennsylvania*, Philadelphia, Pa. (founded 1740; 20,380 students, including 7,891 women); *Pittsburgh*, Pa. (founded 1787; 29,085 students, incl. 12,595 women); *Princeton*, N.J. (founded 1746; 5,975 men and 1,775 women); *Tennessee*, Knoxville, Tenn. (founded 1794; 29,999 students, including 12,820 women); *William and Mary*, Williamsburg, Va. (founded 1693; 6,200 students, including 2,934 women); *New York University*, founded in 1831 at New York, had 29,698 students, including 13,808 women.

WEIGHTS AND MEASURES

The weights and measures in common use in the United States are of British origin. They date

back to the American Revolution when practically all the standards were intended to be equivalent to those used in England at that period. The principal units were the yard, the avoirdupois pound, the gallon, and the bushel. More or less authentic copies of the English standards of the denominations mentioned had been brought over and adopted by the different colonies. Divergencies in these weights and measures were, however, quite common, due no doubt to the fact that the system of weights and measures in England was not itself well established, and hence the copies brought to this country were often adjusted to different standards.

Because of these discrepancies, the system of weights and measures in the United States (U.S. Customary System) is not identical with the British system. The U.S. bushel and the U.S. gallon, and their subdivisions differ from the corresponding British units. Also the British ton is 2,240 pounds, whereas the ton generally used in the United States is the short ton of 2,000 pounds. The American colonists adopted the English wine gallon of 231 cubic inches. The English of that period used this wine gallon and they also had another gallon, the ale gallon of 282 cubic inches. In 1824 these two gallons were abandoned by the British when they adopted the British Imperial gallon, equivalent to 277·42 cubic inches. At the same time, the bushel was redefined as 8 gallons. In the British system the units of dry measure are the same as those of liquid measure. In the United States these two are not the same, the gallon and its subdivisions being used in the measurement of liquids, while the bushel, with its subdivisions, is used in the measurement of certain dry commodities. The U.S. gallon is divided into 4 liquid quarts and the U.S. bushel into 32 dry quarts. All the units of capacity mentioned thus far are larger in the British system than in the U.S. system. But the British fluid ounce is smaller than the U.S. fluid ounce, because the British quart is divided into 40 fluid ounces, whereas the U.S. quart is divided into 32 fluid ounces.

The rapidly diminishing world-wide use of the U.S. Customary and British Systems of measurement and the corresponding rise in metric usage, promoted the passage of Public Law 90–472. Pursuant to this law, the National Bureau of Standards conducted a programme of investigation, research and survey to determine the impact on U.S.A. of such increasing world-wide and domestic use of the metric system (SI), reporting back to Congress in July, 1971. The study recommended a concerted, co-ordinated, but voluntary national effort to make the SI the predominant form of measurement in the United States. Legislation to effect this recommendation has been introduced in Congress.

The International System of Units—officially abbreviated SI—is a modernized version of the metric system. It was established by international agreement to provide a logical and interconnected framework for all measurements in science, industry and commerce.

TERRITORIES, ETC. OF THE UNITED STATES

The territories and the principal islands and island groups under the sovereignty of the United States of America comprise: Palmyra Island; Kingman Reef (about 1 sq. mile); Johnston (or Cornwallis) Island and Sand Island (about 1 sq. mile in all); Canton and Enderbury Islands (jointly administered with Great Britain); Midway Islands; Wake Island; Guam, Howland, Baker and Jarvis Islands (about 3 sq. miles in all); American Samoa (including the island of Tutuila, the Manua Islands, and all other islands of the Samoan group east of longitude 171° west of Greenwich together with Swains Island); the Commonwealth of Puerto Rico; the Virgin Islands of the United States, and Navassa Island (2 sq. miles).

The Canal Zone is under the jurisdiction of the United States.

The Trust Territory of the Pacific Islands is under the jurisdiction of the United States pursuant to a trusteeship agreement between the U.S. Government and the Security Council of the United Nations. It consists of the Mariana (except Guam), Caroline and Marshall Islands, with a land area of 687 square miles and a population of 101,592 in 1970. Nine individual languages are spoken in the Territory. Copra is the principal export of importance.

There are certain small guano islands, rocks, or keys which, in pursuance of action taken under the Act of Congress, August 18, 1856, subsequently embodied in Sections 5570–5578 of the Revised Statutes are considered as appertaining to the United States. Responsibility for territorial affairs generally is centred in the Director, Office of Territorial Affairs, Dept. of the Interior, Washington, D.C.

CANTON AND ENDERBURY

Under the Anglo-American Pact of Aug. 10, 1938, Canton and Enderbury (of the Phoenix Island Group in the Central Pacific) were declared to be for the common use of Great Britain and U.S.A. for aviation and communication. The islands, which are about midway between Hawaii and Australia, extend to a total of 27 sq. miles.

On April 6, 1939, the U.S. and Great Britain agreed to set up a joint regime for Canton and Enderbury Islands. Provision for the joint control of these islands was made by exchange of notes between the two Governments on April 6, 1939.

Canton Island was successively used for aviation support activities and as a missile tracking station by the U.S. National Aeronautics and Space Administration. These activities have been terminated. Enderbury has been uninhabited since World War II.

GUAM

Guam, the largest of the Ladrone or Mariana Islands in the North Pacific Ocean, lies in 13° 26′ N. lat. and 144° 39′ E. long., at a distance of about 1,506 miles east of Manila. The area of the island is estimated at 209 square miles, with an estimated civilian population (1974) of 105,000.

The Guamanians are of Chamorro stock mingled with Filipino and Spanish blood. The Chamorro language belongs to the Malayo-Polynesian family, but has had considerable admixture of Spanish. English is the language used throughout the island, although Chamorro is also used in Guamanian homes.

Guam was occupied by Japanese in Dec., 1941 but was recaptured and occupied throughout by U.S. forces before the end of August, 1944. Under the Organic Act of Guam of August 1, 1950 (Public Law 630 of the 81st Congress), Guam has statutory powers of self-government, and Guamanians are United States citizens. The Governor is popularly elected. In 1972 a non-voting delegate was elected to serve in the U.S. House of Representatives. A 21-member unicameral legislature is elected bien-

nially. There is also a District Court of Guam, with original jurisdiction in cases under federal law.
Governor, Ricardo J. Bordallo; *elected* Nov. 1974.
Lt. Governor, Rudolph G. Sablan; *elected* Nov. 1974.
CAPITAL, Agaña. Port of entry, Ψ Apra.

WAKE AND MIDWAY ISLANDS

Wake Island, annexed in 1898, has an area of about 3 sq. miles and lies in the N. Pacific about 2,300 miles from Hawaii on the direct route to Hong Kong. Wake Island was occupied by Japanese, Dec. 27, 1941; it was re-occupied by U.S. on Sept. 15, 1945. Population (1970), 1,647.

Midway Islands, with a total area of 28 sq. miles and a population (1970) of 2,220, lie in the N. Pacific about 1,300 miles from Hawaii. There is no indigenous population.

PUERTO RICO

Puerto Rico (Rich Port) is an island of the Greater Antilles group in the West Indies, and lies between 17° 50′–18° 30′ N. lat. and 65° 30′–67° 15′ W. long., with a total area of 3,435 square miles and a population (1973 Census preliminary) of 2,913,000. The majority of the inhabitants are of Spanish descent and Spanish and English are the official languages. The island is about 100 miles from west to east, and 35 miles from north to south at the western end, narrowing towards the eastern extremity. The capital is 1,600 miles distant from New York, and 1,000 miles from Miami. Puerto Rico was discovered in 1493 by Christopher Columbus. It was explored by Ponce de León in 1508. It continued a Spanish possession until Oct. 18, 1898, when the United States took formal possession as a result of the Spanish-American War. It was ceded by Spain to the United States by the Treaty ratified on April 11, 1899. Sugar is grown along the coastal plain and tobacco and coffee on the slopes of the hills; fruits, cotton, maize, sweet potatoes and yams are also grown. The trade is principally with the U.S. In 1973 there were 3,972 miles of highway under maintenance. There are good harbours at San Juan, Mayaguez and Ponce.

The Constitution approved by the Congress and the President of the United States, which came into force on July 25, 1952, establishes the Commonwealth of Puerto Rico with full powers of local government. Legislative functions are vested in the Legislative Assembly, which consists of 2 elected houses; the Senate of 29 members (2 from each of 8 senatorial districts and 13 at large) and the House of Representatives of 52 members (1 from each of 40 representative districts and 12 at large). Membership of each house may be increased slightly to accommodate minority representatives. The term of the Legislative Assembly is 4 years. The Governor is popularly elected for a term of 4 years. A Supreme Court of 9 members is appointed by the Governor, with the advice and consent of the Senate. There are 10 similarly appointed Secretaries at the head of permanent departments, but the selection of the Secretary of State must be approved also by the House of Representatives. The Governor appoints all judges. Puerto Rico is represented in Congress by a Resident Commissioner, elected for a term of 4 years, who has a seat in the House of Representatives, but not a vote, although he has a right to vote on certain committees within the House of Representatives, Great improvement has been made in the progress. industrialization and welfare of the island during the last two decades. A programme of tax exemption has raised income from industry to a level higher than that from agriculture. Public schools are

established throughout—enrolment in 1973 was 711,030.

CAPITAL.—Ψ San Juan, population 851,247; Other major towns are: Ψ Ponce (173,500); Bayamón (170,500); Ψ Mayagüez (92,900); and Ψ Arecíbo (73,283).

TRADE

	1973–74
Total Imports	$4,262,000,000
Total Exports	3,339,000,000

Trade with U.K.

	1973	1974
Imports from U.K.	£7,004,000	£8,548,000
Exports to U.K.	11,634,000	12,789,000

Governor, Rafael Hernández Colón, *elected* 1972.
Resident Commissioner, Jaime Benítez (1972).

AMERICAN SAMOA

American Samoa consists of the island of Tutuila, Aunu'u, Ofu, Olosega, Ta'u, Rose and Swains Islands, with a total area of 76·5 square miles and a population of 27,769 in 1970.

Tutuila, the largest of the group, has an area of 52 square miles and contains a magnificent harbour at Ψ Pago Pago (pop. 1960, 1,251). The constitution of American Samoa designates the village of Fagatogo as the seat of government. The remaining islands have an area of about 24 square miles. Tuna and copra are the chief exports.

Under an Executive Order of the President, which became effective on July 1, 1951, civilian administration under the Department of the Interior replaced the Naval administration which had existed since 1900. At present the Government consists of an executive, a bicameral legislature and a judiciary. Most of the Samoans are U.S. nationals, but some have acquired citizenship through service in the United States armed forces or other naturalization procedure.
Governor, Earl B. Ruth.

TRUST TERRITORY OF THE PACIFIC ISLANDS

The Trust Territory of the Pacific Islands consists of the Mariana (excluding Guam), Caroline and Marshall Islands which extend from latitude 1° to 20° north and from longitude 130° to 172° east. They cover an ocean area of 3,000,000 square miles but have a total land area of only 687 square miles. There are 96 separate islands and island groups in the Trust Territory. The population in 1970 was 101,592. The inhabitants of the Trust Territory are broadly classed as Micronesians. The native cultures vary considerably among island groups and even more among islands and atolls in the same geographic area. Nine different languages are spoken in the territory.

The Trust Territory is administered by the United States pursuant to a Trusteeship Agreement with the Security Council of the United Nations of July 18, 1947, administration being under the general jurisdiction of the Secretary of the Interior.

For administrative purposes, the territory is divided into six districts: The Marianas, Palau, Yap, Truk, Ponape and the Marshalls. Local governments exist within each district.

High Commissioner, Edward E. Johnston.
Deputy High Commissioner, Peter T. Coleman.
CAPITAL (Provisional).—Saipan, Mariana Islands.

Ψ Seaport.

VIRGIN ISLANDS

Purchased by the United States from Denmark for the sum of $25,000,000, and proclaimed, January 25, 1917. The total area of the islands is 133 sq. miles, with a population (estimated 1972), of 90,000. *St. Thomas* (28 sq. miles) had a population of 29,565; *St. Croix* (84 sq. miles) had a population of 31,892; *St. John* (20 sq. miles) had a population of 1,743.

CAPITAL, Ψ Charlotte Amalie contains one of the finest harbours in the West Indies. The government of the Virgin Islands is organized under the provisions of the Revised Organic Act of the Virgin Islands, enacted by the Congress of the United States on July 22, 1954. Legislative power is vested in the Legislature of the Virgin Islands, a unicameral body composed of 15 senators popularly elected for two-year terms. Virgin Islanders are citizens of the United States. From the elections of November, 1970, the Governor has been popularly elected. In 1972, a non-voting delegate was elected to serve in the U.S. House of Representatives. The Virgin Islands are now a favourite tourist area in the Caribbean. The climate of the islands is delightful at all times, and particularly so during the winter months.

Governor, Cyril E. King, *elected* Nov. 1974.
Lieut.-Governor, Juan F. Luis, *elected* Nov. 1974.

THE PANAMA CANAL

The Panama Canal, including the related commercial enterprises in the Canal Zone, are operated by the Panama Canal Company, which was formed on July 1, 1951, under the provisions of the Panama Canal Company Act. The Canal Zone is governed by the Canal Zone Government, which was established simultaneously with the new Canal Company. Both organizations are headed by Major-General H. R. Parfitt, U.S.A., who holds the joint title of Governor of the Canal Zone and President of the Panama Canal Company.

The Canal Zone has an area of 647 sq. miles (about 1 per cent. of the total area of Panama) (land area, 372 sq. miles) and a population in 1970 of 51,000.

Chief Towns.—Balboa Heights, Balboa, Ancon, Gamboa and Margarita.

Including only ocean-going commercial vessels, 300 Panama Canal net tons measurement or over, against which tolls were collected, the volume of commercial traffic passing through the Canal during each of the last 10 fiscal years (*see* table in col. 1). In 1974 the 14,033 vessels using the canal carried the highest tonnage so far recorded.

Fiscal Year	No. of Transits	Canal, Net Tons	Cargo Tons
1965	11,835	74,853,264	76,573,071
1966	11,926	78,918,013	81,712,940
1967	12,413	88,266,343	86,193,430
1968	13,199	96,487,843	96,550,165
1969	13,150	100,603,265	101,391,132
1970	13,658	108,141,640	114,257,260
1971	14,020	111,006,363	118,626,906
1972	13,766	112,971,058	109,233,725
1973	13,841	126,203,549	126,104,029
1974	14,033	135,715,628	147,906,914
1975	13,609	135,053,680	140,101,459

The canal is fifty statute miles long (44.08 nautical miles), and the channel is from 500 to 1,000 feet wide at the bottom. It contains 12 locks in twin flights; 3 steps at Gatun on the Atlantic side, 1 step at Pedro Miguel and 2 at Miraflores on the Pacific side. Each lock chamber is 1,000 feet long and 110 feet wide. Transit from sea to sea takes on average 8 to 10 hours. The least width is in Gaillard Cut, and the greatest in Gatun Lake, where the channel can be made much broader at any time by the cutting down of trees and a small amount of dredging.

The Panama Canal Company is engaged in a Canal improvement programme. The widening of Gaillard Cut from 300 to 500 feet was completed in August, 1970. The maximum draft allowable for ships using the Panama Canal is determined by the level of Lake Gatun, which is an average of 85 feet above sea level. During dry season, from December to April, the lake level drops, imposing draft restrictions. The all-time high maximum tropical fresh water draft was 40 feet for certain types of vessels in 1967.

BRITISH EMBASSY

3100 Massachusetts Avenue, N.W.
Washington, D.C. 200008

Ambassador Extraordinary and Plenipotentiary, His Excellency the Hon. Sir Peter Edward Ramsbotham, G.C.V.O., K.C.M.G. (1974) £14,000
Ministers, Sir John Moreton, K.C.V.O., C.M.G., M.C.; W. S. Pyrve (*Economic*); S. S. Shaylor (*Defence, Research and Development*); The Lord Bridges, C.M.G. (*Commercial*).
Head of British Defence Staff and Defence Attaché, Lt.-Gen. Sir Rollo Pain, K.C.B., M.C.
Naval Attaché, Rear Admiral R. W. Halliday, D.S.C.
Military Attaché, Brigadier A. L. Watson.
Air Attaché, Air Cdre. N. S. Howlett.
Counsellors, K. B. A. Scott; A. H. B. Herman (*Hong Kong Commercial Affairs*); D. G. Talintyre (*Labour*); K. P. Jeffs (*Defence Supply*); A. R. Gordon-Cumming, C.V.O. (*Civil Aviation and Shipping*); J. Gaunt; J. C. McKane; I. B. Bott (*Defence Research and Development*); C. T. Brant (*Energy*); R. A. Fyjis-Walker, C.V.O. (*Information*); J. C. Harrison; T. Sharp (*Commercial*); J. Parker; H. M. Griffiths (*Economic*); R. M. Russell; G. L. Scullard, O.B.E. (*Admin.* and *H.M. Consul-General*); R. F. R. Deare (*Overseas Development*); R. C. Samuel; P. Robinson (*Asst. Defence*

Research and Development); A. Smith (*Science and Technology*); Brig. J. P. Ferry (*Asst. Defence Research and Development*); D. A. Payne (*Civil Aviation Operations*); W. G. Codner (*Civil Aviation Telecommunications*); D. J. Walters (*Asst. Defence Research and Development*); G. R. Sanderson (*Education*); M. E. Pike.
1st Secretaries, A. Reeve; J. M. Knight; J. G. MacDonald (*Commercial*); S. H. Broadbent (*Economic*); C. J. A. Chivers (*Financial*); J. Thomas (*Commercial*); C. M. Cruickshank (*Civil Aviation and Shipping*); M. S. Baker-Bates (*Information*); B. L. Limbert (*Defence Supply*); J. E. Cornish; R. M. Muir; J. P. Millington; J. Davidson; D. C. Walker, M.V.O.; Dr. T. M. Moynehan (*Asst. Attaché (Science*); J. Q. Greenstock (*Private Secretary to the Ambassador*); P. W. Murphy (*Agriculture and Commercial*); J. McAuley (*Technology*); Miss O. Goodinson (*Consul*); W. H. Fletcher, M.B.E.; T. E. Colquhoun; A. A. Joy (*Energy*); A. Lovell; J. Smallwood (*Information*); Miss C. J. Tasch (*Administration*); R. Murphy; G. A. Gillespie (*Accountant*); J. H. R. Evans (*Commercial*).

The United Nations

CHARTER OF THE UNITED NATIONS

The foundations of the Charter of the United Nations were laid at the Conference of Foreign Ministers in Moscow in 1943, and upon those foundations a structure was built at the meetings at Dumbarton Oaks, Washington, D.C., Aug. 21–Oct. 7, 1944. The design was discussed and criticized at San Francisco from April 25 to June 26, 1945, on which date representatives of 50 Allied Nations appended their signatures to the Charter.

The United Nations formally came into existence on October 24, 1945. It was later decided that its seat should be in the United States. Permanent headquarters have been erected at Manhattan, New York. October 24 has been designated " United Nations Day ".

The following 144 states are members of the United Nations:—

Afghanistan, Albania, Algeria, Argentina,★ Australia,★ Austria, Bahamas, Bahrain, Bangladesh, Barbados, Belgium,★ Bhutan, Bolivia,★ Botswana, Brazil,★ Bulgaria, Burma, Burundi, Byelorussian Soviet Socialist Republic,★ Cambodia, Cameroon, Canada★, Cape Verde, Central African Republic, Chad, Chile★, China★ Colombia★, Comoros, Congo (Pop. Repub.), Costa Rica,★ Cuba,★ Cyprus, Czechoslovakia,★ Dahomey, Denmark,★ Dominican Republic,★ Ecuador,★ Egypt,★ El Salvador,★ Equatorial Guinea, Ethiopia,★ Fiji, Finland, France,★ Gabon, Gambia, Germany (East), Germany (West), Ghana, Greece,★ Guatemala,★ Guinea, Guyana, Haiti,★ Honduras,★ Hungary, Iceland, India,★ Indonesia, Iran,★ Iraq,★ Republic of Ireland, Israel, Italy, Ivory Coast, Jamaica, Japan, Jordan, Kenya, Kuwait, Laos, Lebanon,★ Lesotho, Liberia,★ Libya, Luxemburg,★ Madagascar, Malawi, Malaysia, Maldive Islands, Mali, Malta, Mauritania, Mauritius, Mexico,★ Mongolia, Morocco, Mozambique, Nepal, Netherlands,★ New Zealand,★ Nicaragua,★ Niger, Nigeria, Norway,★ Oman, Pakistan, Panama,★ Papua New Guinea, Paraguay,★ Peru,★ Philippines,★ Poland,★ Portugal, Qatar, Rumania, Rwanda, Sao Tome and Principe, Saudi Arabia,★ Senegal, Sierra Leone, Singapore, Somalia, South Africa,★ Spain, Sri Lanka, Sudan, Surinam, Swaziland, Sweden, Syria,★ Tanzania, Thailand, Togo, Trinidad and Tobago, Tunisia, Turkey,★ Uganda, Ukrainian Soviet Socialist Republic,★ Union of Soviet Socialist Republics,★ United Arab Emirates, United Kingdom,★ United States of America,★ Upper Volta, Uraguay,★ Venezuela,★ Yemen (Arab Repub.), Yemen (P.D.R.), Yugoslavia,★ Zaire, Zambia.

★ Original member (*i.e.* from 1945). (From October 25, 1971, " China " was taken to mean the People's Republic of China.)

The principal organs of the United Nations are:—
(1) The General Assembly; (2) The Security Council; (3) The Economic and Social Council; (4) The Trusteeship Council; (5) The International Court of Justice; (6) The Secretariat.

1. The General Assembly

The General Assembly consists of all the Members of the United Nations. Each Member is entitled to be represented at its meetings by five representatives, but has only one vote. The General Assembly meets once a year in regular session normally beginning on the third Tuesday in September. Special Sessions may also be held.

The work of the General Assembly is divided among seven Main Committees, on each of which every Member has the right to be represented:—
(1) Political and Security (including the regulation of armaments); (2) Economic and Financial; (3) Social, Humanitarian and Cultural; (4) Trusteeship (including Non-Self Governing Territories);

(5) Administrative and Budgetary; (6) Legal. There is also a Special Political Committee, to relieve the burden on the first Committee.

The Main Committees consider items referred to them by the General Assembly and recommend draft resolutions for submission to the Assembly's plenary meetings.

The Assembly has two procedural committees—a General Committee and a Credentials Committee; and three standing committees—an Advisory Committee on Administrative and Budgetary Questions, a Committee on Contributions and a Disarmament Commission.

The General Assembly appoints such *ad hoc* committees as may be required from time to time for special purposes. The Assembly is also assisted in its work by subsidiary bodies such as a Board of Auditors, an Investments Committee, a United Nations Staff Benefit Committee, and an International Law Commission. In 1964 the General Assembly set up the United Nations Conference on Trade and Development (UNCTAD) as a permanent body.

The United Nations Industrial Development Organization (UNIDO) was set up on Jan. 1, 1967, to promote industrialization and co-ordinate United Nations activities in this field.

President of the United Nations General Assembly, Gaston Thorn (*Luxemburg*) (1975).

2. The Security Council

The Security Council consists of fifteen Members, each of which has one representative and one vote. There are five *permanent Members* (China, France, U.K., U.S.A., U.S.S.R.) and ten non-permanent Members elected for a two-year term.

The Security Council bears the primary responsibility for the maintenance of peace and security. Decisions on procedural questions are made by an affirmative vote of seven Members. On all other matters the affirmative vote of nine Members must include the concurring votes of the *permanent Members,* and it is this clause which makes the *Veto* possible. The only exception to this rule is that with regard to measures for peaceful settlement a party to a dispute may refrain from voting.

The General Assembly, any member of the United Nations, or the Secretary-General, can bring to the Council's attention any matter considered to threaten international peace and security. A non-member State can bring a dispute before the Council provided it accepts in advance the U.N. Charter obligations for peaceful settlement.

A *Committee on the Admission of New Members* was set up by the Security Council on May 17, 1946, for the purpose of examining applications for admission to membership in the United Nations which may be referred to it by the Security Council. It is composed of a representative of each of the members of the Security Council.

The Security Council also establishes *ad hoc* committees and commissions which may be required from time to time for special purposes.

3. The Economic and Social Council

This body is responsible under the General Assembly for carrying out the functions of the

United Nations with regard to international economic, social, cultural, educational, health and related matters.

It has established the following Commissions: Statistical, Human Rights, Social, Status of Women, Narcotic Drugs, Population, Regional Economic Commissions for Europe, Asia and the Pacific, Western Asia, Latin America and Africa. The Council also supervises and co-ordinates the work of fourteen related agencies.

United Nations Children's Fund (UNICEF).—
UNICEF embraces all aspects of child welfare and assists the governments of the developing countries in developing maternal and child health services, the prevention and treatment of disease, nutrition and the preparation of children for adult life. It is financed by voluntary contributions from Governments and from the public and its work is carried out in co-operation with the relevant technical members of the United Nations.

4. Trusteeship Council

The Trusteeship Council is composed of countries administering Trust Territories, permanent members of the Security Council, and one other country elected by the General Assembly for a three-year term.

The Trusteeship Council considers reports from administering authorities; examines petitions in consultation with the administering authority; makes periodic inspection visits; and checks conditions with an annual questionnaire on the political, economic, social, and educational advancement of the inhabitants of trust territories.

5. International Court of Justice

The International Court of Justice is the principal judicial organ of the United Nations. The Statute of the court is an integral part of the Charter and all Members of the United Nations are *ipso facto* parties to it. The Court is composed of 15 judges, no two of whom may be nationals of the same State, and meets at The Hague.

If any party to a case fails to adhere to the judgment of the Court, the other party may have recourse to the Security Council.

THE SECRETARIAT

Secretary-General (1972–77), Kurt Waldheim (*Austria*).

Under-Secretaries–General

Inter-Agency Affairs and Co-ordination, C. V. Narasimhan (*India*).
Special Political Affairs, B. E. Urquhart (*U.K.*); Roberta Guyer (*Argentina*).
Conference Services, B. Lewandowski (*Poland*).
Economic and Social Affairs, Gabriel Van Laethem (*France*).
Political Affairs and Decolonization, Ming-Chao Tang (*China*).
Political and Security Council Affairs, A. Shevchenko (*U.S.S.R.*).
Director-General, U.N. Office, Geneva, V. Winspeare Guicciardi (*Italy*).
Office or Administration and Management, G. Davidson (*Canada*).
Legal Counsel, E. Suy (*Belgium*).

U.N. Information Centre, 14–15, Stratford Place, W.1.

BUDGET OF THE UNITED NATIONS

The budget is now approved for periods of two years, and the appropriation for the biennium 1975–76 is U.S.$745,813,800 (*gross*). The scale of assessments for 1974–76 includes: Australia, 1·44 per

cent.; Canada, 3·18 per cent.; India, 1·20 per cent.; New Zealand, 0·28 per cent.; United Kingdom, 5·31 per cent. The United States contribution is 25·00 per cent.; U.S.S.R. is 12·97 per cent.; France is 5·86 per cent.; Italy is 3.60 per cent and Japan is 7·15 per cent.

UNITED KINGDOM REPRESENTATIVES
845 Third Avenue, New York

Permanent Representative to the United Nations and Representative on the Security Council, Ivor Seward Richard, Q.C. (1974).
Minister and Deputy Permanent Representative, James Murray, C.M.G.
Minister (Economic and Social Affairs), P. H. R. Marshall, C.M.G.
Counsellors, J. C. Thomas (*Head of Chancery*); F. R. N. Fifoot (*Legal Adviser*); C. A. Lovitt, M.B.E. (*Administration*); M. F. H. Stuart (*Treasury Adviser*).
1st Secretaries, C. C. R. Battiscombe; A. D. Baighty; D. Broad; J. B. Donnelly; Miss S. E. Harden, M.B.E.; F. C. G. Hohler; D. B. C. Logan; M. A. Pattison; A. J. C. E. Rellie; T. L. Richardson; Miss E. C. Wallis, M.B.E.

INTERNATIONAL ATOMIC ENERGY AGENCY
Kärntnerring 11–13, P.O. Box 590, Vienna

Set up on July 29, 1957, to accelerate and enlarge the contribution of atomic energy to peace, health and prosperity throughout the world and to ensure that assistance provided by it or under its supervision is not used to further any military purpose. Agreements have been reached concerning the Agency's working relationship with the United Nations and some of the specialized agencies. In June, 1976, 109 states were members.

A General Conference of all members meets in regular annual session and in such special session as may be necessary. A Board of Governors (34 members) carries out the functions of the Agency and meets usually four times a year. The Budget in 1976 amounted to $37,002,000.

Director-General, Sigvard Eklund (*Sweden*).

INTERNATIONAL AGENCIES

Fourteen other international organizations, having wide responsibilities in economic, social, cultural, educational and other related fields, carry out their functions in co-operation with the United Nations under agreements made with a standing committee of the Economic and Social Council.

International Labour Organization (ILO)
Geneva (London Branch Office, 87–91 New Bond Street, W.1.). Established with the League of Nations in 1919 under the Treaty of Versailles, the ILO became in 1946 the first specialized agency associated with the United Nations. In June, 1976, the Organization had 132 member States. The aim of the ILO is to promote lasting peace through social justice, and to this end it works for better economic and social conditions everywhere. It was awarded the Nobel Peace Prize in 1969.

The ILO establishes international labour standards, which set guidelines for improving working conditions and protecting basic human rights; runs a world-wide programme of technical assistance to developing countries (with funds from all sources amounting in 1974–75 to about $80 million); conducts research and disseminates information on the human aspects of economic activity, with a view to improving social and economic well-being. Through its World Employment Programme, the ILO is attacking unemployment and its associated ills by aiding national and international efforts to

provide productive work for the world's fast-growing population.

The International Labour Conference, composed of national delegations of two government delegates, one worker delegate and one employer delegate, meets at least once a year. It formulates international labour standards and broad policies of the Organization, provides a forum for discussion of world labour and social problems, and approves the ILO's work programme and budget, which is financed by member States.

A 56-member Governing Body, composed of 28 government members, 14 worker members and 14 employer members, acts as the Organization's executive council. Ten governments hold seats on the Governing Body because of their industrial importance. These are Canada, China, France, the Federal Republic of Germany, India, Italy, Japan, U.S.S.R., the United Kingdom and the United States of America.

The International Labour Office, the secretariat of the Organization, collects and distributes information, assists governments on request in drafting legislation on the basis of international labour standards, directs technical co-operation activities, and issues publications.

Director-General, Francis Blanchard (*France*).

Food and Agriculture Organization of the United Nations (FAO), Viale delle Terme di Caracalla, Rome.—Established on October 16, 1945, to raise levels of nutrition and standards of living, to secure improvements in the efficiency of the production and distribution of all food and agricultural products and to better the condition of rural populations, and thus contributing to the expansion of world economy and ensuring man's freedom from hunger. Among its many activities the Organization promotes the global exchange of information in the fields of agriculture, forestry and fisheries, facilitates international agreement in these fields and provides technical assistance in such subjects as nutrition and food management, soil erosion control, re-afforestation, the establishment of paper industries, irrigation engineering, control of infestation of stored foods, production of fertilizers, control of crop pests and diseases, and improvement of fishing vessels, fish distribution and marketing. As well as its work as an intergovernmental agency the Organization also mobilizes the efforts of private individuals and associations through the world-wide *Freedom from Hunger Campaign*. Jointly with the United Nations it administers a $1,000,000,000 World Food Programme using food as capital backing for development programmes in developing countries. The 1975 session of the governing Conference approved a budget of $167,000,000 for the two years 1975–76. In addition FAO is carrying out field programmes involving expenditure of about $100,000,000 under the U.N. Development Programme and other aid programmes. Through its co-operative programme with the World Bank it is helping to increase international investment in agriculture and allied fields.

The policy of the Organization is directed by a two-yearly Conference of the 136 member countries. A council (42 members) acts for the Conference between its sessions.

Director-General, Edouard Saouma (*Lebanon*).

United Nations Educational, Scientific and Cultural Organization (UNESCO), 9 Place de Fontenoy, Paris 75700.—Under its constitution, the Organization makes its contribution to peace and security by promoting collaboration among its Member States in the fields of education, science, culture and communications. It aims at furthering a universal respect for justice, for the rule of law and for human rights, without distinction of race, sex, language or religion, in accordance with the Charter of the United Nations.

Unesco continues to work for the advancement of mutual knowledge and understanding of peoples ... to give fresh impulse to popular education and to the spread of culture ... to maintain, increase and diffuse knowledge.

The Organization is composed of three organs: (i) the *General Conference*, consisting of representatives of Member States, which meets biennially to decide the programme and budget; (ii) the *Executive Board*, composed of 40 members elected by the General Conference to supervise the execution of the approved programme and (iii) the *Secretariat*, which is responsible for Unesco's day-to-day functioning and the execution of the programme. In most Member States National Commissions serve as a link with Unesco and help carry out the programme. The broad objectives of Unesco: in education, its democratization and regeneration; in science, the development of science policy, the application of science and technology to development and the intensification of international programmes of scientific co-operation; in culture, the evolution of cultural policy; in communication, the improvement and development of the mass media in Member States as a means of increasing the flow of information. Member States in July, 1975, 136.

Director-General, Amadou-Mahtar M'Bow(*Senegal*).

U.K. National Commission for UNESCO, Ministry of Overseas Development, Stag Place, S.W.1.

Secretary, D. Bell.

World Health Organization (WHO), 1211 Geneva 27. Established on April 7, 1948, the aim of the World Health Organization is the attainment by all peoples of the highest possible level of health. Through its advisory services, it helps its member governments to develop health manpower, streamline health services, control communicable diseases, promote family health—including mother and child care, family planning, nutrition and health education—and strengthen environmental health. Its other services include the International Pharmacopoeia, drug evaluation and monitoring, biological standardization, epidemiological surveillance, medical research and scientific publications. Approved budget for 1977, $147,184,000. Membership (May 1976), 151.

Organs are a *World Health Assembly* meeting annually to frame policy, an *Executive Board* (30 members), meeting at least twice a year, and a *Secretariat*.

Director-General, H. T. Mahler (*Denmark*).

International Bank for Reconstruction and Development (*The World Bank*), 1818 H Street, Washington, D.C.; European office, 66 Ave. d'Iéna, 75116, Paris, France.—Established on Dec. 27,1945, to assist in the reconstruction and development of territories of member countries by facilitating the investment of capital for productive purposes; to promote private foreign investment and, when private capital is not readily available on reasonable terms, to supplement private investment by providing loans for productive purposes out of its own capital, funds raised by it, and its other resources. The 1,311 loans made by the Bank since its inception to June 30, 1976, totalled $32,552,000,000. Subscribed capital, June 30, 1976, $30,860,568,000.

The *Board of Governors* consists of one Governor and one alternative appointed by each of the 127 member countries.

Twenty *Executive Directors* exercise all powers of the Bank except those reserved to the Board of Governors. The *President*, selected by the Executive Directors, conducts the business of the Bank, with the assistance of an international staff.
President, Robert S. McNamara (*U.S.A.*).

International Development Association (IDA), 1818 H Street, Washington, D.C.; European office, 66 Ave. d'Iéna, 75116 Paris, France.—an affiliate of the World Bank established in September 1960. Its purposes are to promote economic development, increase productivity and thus raise standards of living in the less developed areas of the world included within the Association's membership, in particular by providing finance to meet their important developmental requirements on terms which are more flexible and bear less heavily on the balance of payments than those of conventional loans, thereby furthering the objectives of the World Bank and supplementing its activities. IDA's Board of Governors and Executive Directors are the same as those holding equivalent positions in the World Bank, serving *ex officio* in IDA. By June 30, 1976, IDA had extended 668 development credits totalling $9,993,000,000 in 68 countries for improved transportation, agriculture, electric power facilities, industry, education and municipal water supplies. The credits were for terms of 50 years, free of interest.

International Finance Corporation (IFC), 1818 H Street, Washington, D.C.; European office, 66 Ave. d'Iéna, 75116 Paris, France.—The IFC was established in 1956 as an affiliate of the World Bank to assist less developed member countries by promoting the growth of the private sector of their economies. IFC's share capital of $108,324,000 at June 30, 1976, had been subscribed by 100 countries. In addition, *IFC* is empowered to borrow up to approximately $685,000,000 from the World Bank for use in its lending programme. At the end of June, 1976, IFC had made commitments totalling more than $1,505,000,000 in 61 countries.
President, Robert S. McNamara (*U.S.A.*).

International Monetary Fund, 19th and H Streets, N.W. Washington, D.C.—Established on Dec. 27, 1945, the Fund exists to promote international monetary co-operation and the expansion of international trade; to promote exchange stability, maintain orderly exchange arrangements and avoid competitive exchange depreciations; and to assist in the establishment of a multilateral system of payments in respect of current transactions between members and in the elimination of foreign exchange restrictions which hamper world trade. 126 countries were in membership of the Fund in June, 1975.
The Fund's financial assistance takes the form of a foreign exchange transaction. The member pays to the Fund an amount of its own money equivalent to the amount of foreign currency it wishes to purchase. The member is expected to " repurchase " its own currency from the Fund within three, or at the outside five years, with a payment of gold or dollars or convertible currency acceptable to the Fund. These arrangements are subject to certain charges which rise in proportion to the amount of foreign exchange involved, and the length of time it is held.
Currencies drawn from the Fund may be used in a flexible way to relieve the member's payments difficulty, but its assets are not intended to be used for military purposes, or for programmes of economic development.
Each member of the Fund is assigned a quota

which approximately determines its voting power and the amount of foreign exchange that it may draw from the Fund. The subscription of each member is equal to its quota, and is payable partly in gold and partly in the member's own currency.
Managing Director, H. Johannes Witteveen (*Netherlands*).

International Civil Aviation Organization (ICAO), International Aviation Square, 1,000 Sherbrooke Street, W., Montreal, Quebec, Canada.—In existence since April 4, 1947, to study problems of international civil aviation and the establishment of international standards and regulations for civil aviation, ICAO encourages the use of safety measures, uniform regulations or operation, and simpler procedures at international airports. It promotes the use of new technical methods and equipment. With the co-operation of members, it has evolved a pattern for meteorological services, traffic control, communications, radio beacons and ranges, search and rescue organization, and other facilities required for safe international flight. It has secured much simplification of government customs, immigration, and public health regulations as they apply to international air transport. 134 states are now members of ICAO.
An *Assembly* of delegates from member states meets at least once every three years. A *Council* of 30 members is elected by the Assembly, taking into account the countries of chief importance in air transport and the need for representation of the main geographical areas of the world. The Council is the executive body, working through subsidiary committees.
President of Council, Assad Kotaite (*Lebanon*).
Secretary-General, Yves Lambert (*France*).

Universal Postal Union (UPU), Weltpoststrasse 4, 3000 Berne 15.—Established on October 9, 1874, by the postal Convention of Berne and in operation from July 1, 1875, UPU exists to form a single postal territory of all the countries, members of the Union, for the reciprocal exchange of correspondence in order to secure the organization and improvement of the various postal services and to promote in this sphere the development of international collaboration. Every member agrees to transmit the mail of all other members by the best means used for its own mail. The Union includes almost all the countries of the world. Budget, 1976, $U.S.6,353,000. A *Universal Postal Congress* meets at five-yearly intervals, the last Congress was held at Lausanne in 1974. The next is due to be held in Brazil in 1979.
Director-General, Mohammed I. Sobhi (*Egypt*).

International Telecommunication Union (ITU), Place des Nations, Geneva.—Founded at Paris in 1865 as the International Telegraph Union. ITU became a U.N. Specialized Agency in 1947 and as from Jan. 1, 1975, is governed by the Convention adopted by the Torremolinos Conference held in 1973. ITU exists to set up international regulations for telegraph, telephone and radio services to further their development and extend their utilization by the public, at the lowest possible rates; to promote international co-operation for the improvement and rational use of telecommunications of all kinds; the development of technical facilities and their most efficient operation. ITU allocates the radio frequency spectrum and registers radio frequency assignments. It studies, recommends, collects and publishes information on telecommunication matters, including space radio communications. The Budget for 1977 is 74,034,000 *Swiss francs*.
Secretary-General, M. Mili (*Tunisia*).

World Meteorological Organization (WMO), Geneva.—Came into existence in 1951. The present membership is 134 States and 11 Territories. WMO exists to facilitate world-wide co-operation in establishing networks of stations making observations related to meteorology, and to promote the establishment and maintenance of centres providing meteorological services; to promote the establishment of systems for the rapid exchange of weather information; to promote standardization of meteorological observations and to ensure their uniform publication; to further the application of meteorology to aviation, shipping, water problems, agriculture, and other human activities; to encourage research and training in meteorology and to co-ordinate their international aspects. Budget (1976–79), $U.S.40,542,000. A *World Meteorological Congress* meets at least once every four years. An *Executive Committee* (24 members), meeting at least annually carries out the resolutions of the Congress, initiates studies and makes recommendations on matters requiring international action. Other organs are six *Regional Meteorological Associations* (Africa, Asia, S. America, N. and Central America, Europe and South-West Pacific), eight technical commissions and a Secretariat. *Secretary-General*, D. A. Davies (*U.K.*).

Inter-Governmental Maritime Consultative Organization (IMCO), 101–104 Piccadilly, W.1. A United Nations Specialized Agency established on March 17, 1958, to provide means for co-operation and exchange of information among governments on technical matters related to international shipping, especially with regard to safety at sea and preventing marine pollution caused by ships.

IMCO is responsible for calling maritime conferences and drafting maritime agreements, *e.g.* Load Line Convention, 1966 and Convention on Tonnage Measurement of Ships. It has produced International Maritime Dangerous Goods Code; Code of Safe Practice for Bulk Cargoes; Code for the Construction and Equipment of Ships carrying Liquified Gases in bulk; revised International Code of Signals, and fire safety measures for ships. In June, 1976, 97 nations were in membership. Budget, 1976–77, $11,249,000.
Secretary-General, C. P. Srivastava (*India*).

International Trade. *General Agreement on Tariffs and Trade* (GATT), Villa le Bocage, Palais des Nations 1211, Geneva 10. A multilateral treaty, in operation since 1948, to which 83 countries are parties; a further 22 countries apply GATT *de facto*. Its rules thus govern over four-fifths of the world trade. Objectives of GATT are to expand international trade and promote economic development. GATT provides a permanent forum for discussion and solution of particular international trade problems, and for multilateral negotiations to reduce tariffs and other obstacles to the expansion of international trade. In September 1973, 102 countries agreed in Tokyo to launch comprehensive new negotiations in GATT, aimed at further reductions in both tariff and non-tariff barriers to industrial and agricultural trade. Special attention is given to trade problems of developing countries. An International Trade Centre, set up by GATT in 1964 to aid developing countries in export promotion, is now operated jointly by GATT and UNCTAD.
Director-General, O. Long (*Switzerland*).

VEHICLE LICENCES

From October 1, 1974, registration and first licensing of vehicles has been done through local offices (known as Local Vehicle Licensing Offices) of the Department of the Environment's Driver and Vehicle Licensing Centre in Swansea. The records of existing vehicles are now being transferred to Swansea in stages. Local facilities for relicensing will remain available as follows:—
  (i) Before transfer of the record to the centralised system through local authority Local Taxation Offices (on behalf of the Secretary of State for the Environment), and
  (ii) after transfer through DOE Local Vehicle Licensing Offices.
In certain circumstances licences are also issued by post offices. Details of the present duties chargeable on motor vehicles are set out in the Finance Act, 1975. The Vehicles (Excise) Act, 1971 provides *inter alia* that any vehicle kept on a public road but not used on roads is chargeable to excise duty as if it were in use.
Rates of duty for motor car and motor cycle licences are shown below. For Hackney Carriages the rates of duty are: Hackney Carriage with seating capacity not exceeding 20 persons, £20.00; additional for each person above 20 (excluding the driver) for which the vehicle has seating capacity, 50p.

Type of Vehicle	Exceeding	Not Exceeding	12 Months	4 Months
MOTOR CARS				
Electric and those first registered before January 1, 1947......	—	7 hp	28·80	10·55
Other than the above	—	—	40·00	14·65
MOTOR CYCLES				
With or without sidecar....................................	—	150 c.c.	4·00	—
With or without sidecar....................................	150 c.c.	250 c.c.	8·00	—
With or without sidecar....................................	250 c.c.	—	16·00	5·85
THREE WHEELERS				
Other than pedestrian-controlled........................	—	—	16·00	5·85
PEDESTRIAN-CONTROLLED VEHICLES..................	—	—	8·00	—

Rates

★ 'Till 70' Driving Licence............	£5·00
★Replacement of lost or defaced licence	0·25
★Amendment of licence (*e.g.* for additional Group of vehicles), for the unexpired period..................	0·25
Provisional Driving Licence: 12 months..	1·00
Public Service Vehicle Driving Licence: 3 years†.............................	0·15

★ But see opposite.
† Additional to ordinary driving licence.

Driving Licences

The Road Traffic Act 1974 contained provision for driving licences to run until the age of 70 with renewals on application at 3-yearly intervals thereafter. Full licences issued to commence on or after Jan. 1, 1976 to new drivers passing the driving test and to full licence holders upon renewal of their licences are now valid until their holder's 70th birthday on payment of the new once-and-for-all fee of £5 (£1 for people aged 65 and over). This fee will also cover subsequent issues. Drivers of any age with certain disabilities may be granted licences for one, two or three years.

Foreign Countries

THE following Articles have been revised under the direction of the various Governments or of the British Representatives at Foreign Capitals, to whom the Editor desires to express his warmest thanks. The Editor is also greatly indebted to the Embassies and Consulates-General in London for various corrections and additions.

Salaries and Allowances

The Salaries of Officers of H.M. Diplomatic Service are shown below. In addition foreign allowances are assigned to officers serving abroad:—

Grade 1—£18,675.
Grade 2—£14,000.
Grade 3—£12,465.
Grade 4—£9,115 to £11,465.
Grade 5S—£8,515 to £9,115.
Grade 5—£6,145 to £7,915.
Grade 6—£5,365 to £6,365.
Grade 7A—£4,869 to £5,898.
Grade 7E—£4,365 to £5,165.
Grade 8—£2,860 to £4,135.
Grade 9—£2,350 to £4,135.
Grade 10—£1,665 to £3,005.

NOTE.—Salaries of Ambassadors and of Ministers Plenipotentiary at British Embassies and Legations abroad shown in the following articles are in each case the maximum salary for the post and exclude *Frais de Représentation.*

ABYSSINIA. *See* Ethiopia

AFGHANISTAN
(Afghānistān)

Head of State (President), Mohammad Daoud, *born* 1909, assumed office, July 17, 1973. (Also *Prime Minister, Minister of National Defence and Foreign Affairs.*)

COUNCIL OF MINISTERS

Prime Minister, Mohammad Daoud.
First Deputy Prime Minister, Dr. Mohammad Hussan Sharq.
Second Deputy Prime Minister and Finance, Sayed Abdul Ellah.
Justice, Abdul Majid.
Interior, Abdul Qadir.
Education, Prof. Dr. Abdul Qayum.
Frontier Affairs, Faiz Mohammad.
Commerce, Mohammad Khan Jalalar.
Mines and Industries, Eng. Abdul Tawab Asafi.
Public Works, Ghausuddin Faeq.
Communications, Eng. Abdul Karim Attayee.
Health, Dr. Abdullah Omar.
Information and Culture, Prof. Dr. Abdul Rahim Navin.
Agriculture and Irrigation, Azizullah Wasefi.
Planning, Ali Ahmad Khoram.

EMBASSY IN LONDON
31 Princes Gate, S.W.7.
[01–589 8891/2]

Ambassador Extraordinary and Plenipotentiary, His Excellency Hamidollah Enayat-Seraj (1974).
1st Secretary, Mohammed Yussuf Samad.

Afghanistan lies to the N. and W. of Pakistan. Its ancient name was Aryana, by which title it is referred to by Strabo, the Greek geographer who lived in the 1st century B.C. The estimated area is 250,000 sq. miles, and the population (U.N. estimate, 1969) 16,516,000. The population is very mixed. The most numerous race is the Pathan which predominates in the South and West, the main divisions being the Durranis, from whom the Royal Family came, and the Ghilzais. Then come the Tadjiks, an Iranian people mainly cultivators and small traders. There are also Uzbeks and Turkomen in the North, Hazaras in the centre, Baluchis in the South-West and the Nuristanis who live near the Chitral border. All are Sunni Moslems, except the Hazaras and Kizilbashes, who belong to the Shia sect.

Afghanistan is bounded on the W. by Iran (boundary fixed 1857 and 1904), on the S. by Baluchistan (now Pakistan) (boundary fixed 1896–7), on the N. by Asiatic Russia (boundary fixed 1886–7 and 1893–5), and on the E. by the N.W. Frontier Province (now Pakistan) (boundary fixed 1895). The northern boundary runs from Zulfikar on the Iran frontier to Kushk, the Russian railway terminus, to the Oxus (or Amu Darya, "Mother of Rivers") which forms the boundary from Khamiab to Lake Victoria, whence the line to the Chinese frontier on the branch line from Mary and thence N.E. was fixed by the Pamir agreement of 1895. The Russo-Afghan frontier was demarcated by the Tashkent Boundary Commission in 1948. An Afghan-Chinese border treaty was signed in 1963 and the border demarcation in 1964. The Pakistan-Afghan frontier was settled by the Durand agreement of 1893.

Mountains, chief among which are the Hindu Kush, cover three-fourths of the country, the elevation being generally over 4,000 feet. There are three great river basins, the Oxus, Helmand, and Kabul. The climate is dry, with extreme temperatures.

Afghanistan is divided into 26 provinces each under a Governor.

Government.—The constitutional monarchy, introduced by the 1964 Constitution, was overthrown by a *coup d'état* on July 17, 1973. Pending a new constitution, which is in preparation, the country is under rule by Presidential Decree.

By treaty of Nov. 22, 1921 (renewed in 1930), Great Britain and Afghanistan agreed to respect one another's internal and external independence; to recognize boundaries then existent, subject to a slight re-adjustment near the Khyber; and to establish Legations and consular offices. As successor state to the British Government, Pakistan has agreed that her relations with Afghanistan shall be based on the 1921 treaty.

Judiciary.—Hitherto Afghanistan has been ruled on the basis of Shariat or Islamic law. However, the Constitution introduced in 1965 provided for the creation of a legal code, and for a new structure of courts, consisting of a lower court in each *wuluswal* (sub province), and a court of appeal in each province, with a Supreme Court in Kabul. The complete separation of executive and judiciary in this constitution was abolished by Presidential Decree in July, 1973.

Defence.—The Army has been reorganized and is recruited by yearly calls. Service is for one year for officers and 2 years for other ranks. The peace strength is about 100,000. A military academy and military colleges are located in Kabul; and provision is made for training of regular officers abroad. A small Air Force is maintained. All military and air force equipment is now of Russian pattern.

Production.—Agriculture and sheep raising are the principal industries. There are generally two crops a year, one of wheat (the staple food), barley, or lentils, the other of rice, maize, and *dal*. Sugar beet and cotton are grown. Afghanistan is rich in fruits. Sheep, including the Karakuli, and transport animals are bred. Silk, woollen and hair

cloths and carpets are manufactured. Salt, silver, copper, coal, iron, lead, rubies, lapis lazuli, gold, chrome and talc are found.

The following main roads are open to motor traffic. (a) Internal: Kabul–Kandahar (310 miles); Kandahar–Herat (350 miles); Herat–Maimana to Mazar-i-Sharif (500 miles); Mazar-i-Sharif–Kabul (380 miles). Also Kabul–Khanabad–Faizabad (450 miles); Kabul–Gardez (80 miles); Kabul–Bamian (140 miles). The road from Kabul to the North has now been shortened by the completion in 1964 of the Salang pass. (b) Roads to the frontiers: Kabul–Khyber (175 miles); Kandahar–Chaman (70 miles) and roads from Herat to the Russian and Iranian borders. Five of the major roads in Afghanistan have been surfaced by U.S. and Soviet Aid. The Kabul–Khyber, Kandahar–Spin Baldak and Kabul–Kunduz–Qizil Qala roads are also surfaced. A network of minor roads fit for motor traffic in fine weather links up all important towns and districts.

Motor transport has taken the place of pack transport as the chief means of conveyance. The chief trade routes to Pakistan and India are the Khyber Pass route, from Kabul to Peshawar (190 miles), and the road from Kandahar to Chaman (70 miles). Internal air services between the main towns are being developed.

Language and Literature.—The languages of the country are Persian and Pushtu, and Turki (spoken by Uzbeks and Turkoman tribes in the North). The Turki language is unwritten in Afghanistan. All schoolchildren learn both Persian and Pushtu. The Government is encouraging the spread of Pushtu, the language of the Pathans. Education is free and nominally compulsory, elementary schools having been established in most centres; there are secondary schools in large urban areas and a university (established in 1932) at the capital.

The annual revenue consists largely of payments in kind. There are taxes on land, sales of animals, a grazing tax, customs duties, stamps, fines, receipts from State lands, monopolies, and factories and mining royalties; in addition certain businesses and individuals have become eligible for income-tax.

Trade with U.K.

	1974	1975
Imports from U.K.	£3,345,000	£4,541,000
Exports to U.K.	12,887,000	8,645,000

Exports are mainly Persian lambskins (Karakul), fruits, cotton, raw wool, carpets, spice and natural gas, while the imports are chiefly oil, cotton yarn and piece goods, tea, sugar, machinery and transport equipment.

CAPITAL, Kabul (about 500,000). The chief commercial centres are Kabul and Kandahar (125,000). Other provincial capitals are Herat (86,000), Mazar-i-Sharif (42,000), Jalalabad (22,000).

FLAG.—Vertical stripes of black, red and green, with gold emblem.

NATIONAL DAY.—July 17.

BRITISH EMBASSY
(Kabul)
Ambassador Extraordinary and Plenipotentiary, His Excellency Kenneth Roy Crook (1976).
1st Secretary, J. A. Birch (*Consul*).
Oriental Secretary, Miss K. J. Himsworth.
2nd Secretary, B. W. V. Tomsett (*Commercial*).

British Council Representative.—P. A. Connell, P.O. Box 453, 855 Shehabuddin Wat, Kabul (British library).

Kabul is distant 5,000 miles from London, transit 21 days; by air 12 hours.

ALBANIA

Head of State, Haxhi Lleshi, *assumed office*, July 24, 1953.
Chairman, Council of Ministers, Mehmet Shehu.
Labour (= *Communist*) Party
Politbureau of the Central Committee, R. Alia; A. Carcani; K. Hazbiu; Enver Hoxha; H. Isai; H. Kapo; S. Koleka; R. Marko; P. Miska; M. Myftiu; M. Shehu; H. Toska (*full members*); L. Gegprifti; Q. Mihali; P. Peristeri; X. Spahiu (*candidate members*).
Secretariat of the Central Committee, Enver Hoxha (*First Secretary*); R. Alia; H. Isai; H. Kapo; H. Toska; P. Dode.

Situated on the Adriatic Sea, Albania is bounded on the north and east by Yugoslavia and on the south by Greece. The area of the Republic is estimated at 10,700 sq. miles, with a population (1974) of 2,377,600.

On Nov. 10, 1945, the British, U.S.A. and U.S.S.R. governments decided to recognize the Albanian administration under Colonel-General Enver Hoxha as the provisional government of Albania on the understanding that free elections would be held at an early date, in order that a truly representative government could be formed. Elections were held in December, 1945; on Jan. 11, 1946, the Constituent Assembly declared Albania an independent Republic. It was admitted to the United Nations in 1955. United Kingdom diplomatic relations with Albania ceased in 1946.

Although Albania was almost entirely an agricultural country (staple crops are wheat and maize), industrial expansion of her natural resources is now in process.

CAPITAL, Tirana (pop. 200,000).

FLAG.—Black-two-headed eagle surmounted by yellow outline star, all on a red field.

ALGERIA
(Republic of Algeria)

President of the Council of Revolution and Minister of National Defence, Houari Boumedienne, *assumed office* June 19, 1965.

CABINET

Minister of State, Cherif Belkacem.
Minister of State responsible for Transport, Rabah Bitat.
Minister of the Interior, Mohamed Ben Ahmed Abdelghani.
Foreign Affairs, Abdelaziz Bouteflika.
Information and Culture, Ahmed Taleb.
Health, Dr. Omar Boudjellab.
Justice, Boualem Benhamouda.
Industry and Energy, Belaid Abdesselam.
Public Works, Abdelkader Zaibek.
Agriculture and Agrarian Reform, Mohamed Larbi Tayebi.
Commerce, Layachi Yaker.
Labour and Social Affairs, Mohamed Said Mazouzi.
Higher Education and Scientific Research, Mohamed Benyahia.
Tourism, Abdelaziz Maoui.
Primary and Secondary Education, Abdelkrim Benmahmoud.
Religious Affairs, Mouloud Kassim.
Ex-Servicemen, Mahmoud Guennez.
Posts and Telecommunications, Said Ait Messaoudene.
Youth and Sports, Abdallah Fadel.
Finance, Abdelmalek Temam.

ALGERIAN EMBASSY IN LONDON
6 Hyde Park Gate, S.W.7
[01–584 9502]
Ambassador Extraordinary and Plenipotentiary, His Excellency Lakhdar Brahimi (1971).
Minister Plenipotentiary, Abdelkrim Chitour.

1st Secretary, Mohamed Larbi Tebbal.
Attachés, Lamri Khelif; Hamid Haraigue; Abdelkader Mesbahi; Abdelhamid Ghomari.

Algeria lies between 8° 45′ W. to 12° E. longitude,
37° 6′ N. to a southern limit about 19° N. Area,
855,900 sq. miles (estimated). The population
(U.N. estimate, 1970) is 13,547,000, of which 30 per
cent. are urban dwellers.

Government,—Algiers surrendered to a French
force on July 5, 1830, and Algeria was annexed to
France in Feb. 1842. From 1881 the three northern
departments of Algiers, Oran and Constantine
formed an integral part of France. Between 1955
and 1960 these were reorganized to form 13
departments: Algiers, Tizi-Ouzou, Orleansville,
(now El-Aznam) Médéa, Constantine, Bône (*now
Annaba*), Setif, Batna, Oran, Tlemcen, Mostaganem, Saida and Tiaret. The Southern Territories of the Sahara, formerly a separate colony,

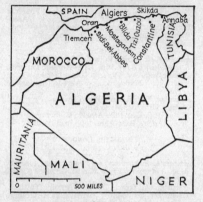

became an integral part of Algeria on the attainment of independence, forming the two additional
departments of the Saoura and the Oasis. An
armed rebellion led by the Moslem *Front de Libéra-
tion Nationale (F.L.N.)* against French rule broke
out on Nov. 1, 1954. French control of Algeria
came to an end when President de Gaulle declared
Algeria independent on July 3, 1962; by October,
1963, all agricultural land held by foreigners had
been expropriated and by 1965 more than 80 per
cent. of the French population had left Algeria.
More have left since.

Ben Bella was elected President of the Republic
in Sept., 1963, but was deposed and a Council of
the Revolution presided over by Col. Boumedienne
assumed power on June 19, 1965.

Development in Algeria is regulated by a series
of national development plans. The 1970–73 plan
provided for expenditure of approximately £3,200
million, with particular emphasis being placed on
industrial development. The 1974–77 Plan provides
for expenditure of the order of £13,000 million,
and places greater emphasis on infrastructure development, and the social services.

Trade with U.K.

	1973	1974
Imports from U.K.	£37,900,000	£54,700,000
Exports to U.K.	45,700,000	36,100,000

Algeria's main exports are crude oil and liquefied

natural gas. Principal imports from the United
Kingdom are capital plant and equipment for
industrial use.

Algeria's main industry is the hydrocarbons
industry. Oil and natural gas are pumped from the
Sahara to terminals on the coast before being
exported; the gas is first liquefied at liquefaction
plants at Skikda and Arzew.

Other major industries being developed include
a steel industry, motor vehicles, building materials,
paper making, chemical products and metal manufactures. All major industrial enterprises are now
under State control.

Algeria has a rapidly expanding network of roads
and railways. Considerable sums are also being
spent on the development of the State airline, the
national shipping company and telecommunications.

CAPITAL.— Ψ Algiers, population (census of 1966),
943,000. The large numbers of French inhabitants
who left the country have largely been replaced by
an influx of Algerians to the city. Other towns
include Ψ Oran (328,000); Constantine (254,000);
Ψ Annaba (*formerly* Bône) (168,000); Blida (99,000);
Setif (98,000); Sidi-Bel-Abbès (91,000); Tlemcen
87,000); Mostaganem (75,000); Ψ Skikda (*formerly*
Philippeville) (72,000); El Aznam (*formerly* Orleansville) (70,000) and Tizi Ouzou (53,000).

FLAG.—Red crescent and star on a vertically
divided green and white background.

NATIONAL DAY.—November 1.

BRITISH EMBASSY
Résidence Cassiopée, 7 Chemin de Glycines,
Algiers.
Ambassador Extraordinary and Plenipotentiary, His
Excellency John Armstrong Robinson, C.M.G.
(1974).
Cultural Attaché, British Council Representative,
K. R. Hunter, 6 Avenue Souidani Boudjemaa,
Algiers. There is a British Council library in
Algiers.

ANDORRA

A small, neutral principality situated on the
southern slopes of the Pyrenees, between Spain and
France, with an approximate area of 180 square
miles and population of about 28,500, one-third
of whom are native Andorrans. It is surrounded
by mountains of 6,500 to 10,000 feet. Historians
place the origin between the eight and ninth
centuries. Andorra is divided into six Parishes,
each of which has four Councillors elected by
vote to the Valleys of Andorra Council of Twenty-
four. Constitutionally, the sovereignty of Andorra is vested in two " Co-Princes ", the President
of the French Republic and the Spanish Bishop of
Urgel. These two " co-princes " can veto certain
decisions of the Council of the Valleys but cannot
impose their own decisions without the consent of
the Council. They are represented by Permanent
Delegates of whom one is the French Prefect of the
Pyrenees Oriental Department at Perpignan and
the other is the Spanish Vicar-General of the
Diocese of Urgel. They are in turn represented in
Andorra la Vella by two resident " Viguiers "
known as the Viguier Français and the Viguier
Episcopal, who have a joint responsibility for law
and order and overall administration policy, together with judicial powers as members of the
Supreme Court.

The official language of the country is Catalan,
but French and Spanish are also spoken. Spanish
pesetas and French *francs* are the accepted currency
and the Budget is expressed in *pesetas*. A good

road crossing the Valleys from Spain to France is open all year. Andorra has deposits of iron and quantities of alum and lead, stone quarries, granite, jasper and marble. Slate is abundant. Timber includes pine, fir, oak, birch and box-tree. Potatoes are produced in the highlands and tobacco in the plains. The climate is naturally cold for six months, but mild in spring and summer. The mountain slopes are suitable for skiing, and it is estimated that 2,250,000 tourists visit the Valleys during the year.

There are two radio stations in Andorra, one privately-owned and one operated by a French Government corporation. Both pay dues to the Council of the Valleys.

CAPITAL: Andorra la Vella (population 11,000).

FLAG.—Three vertical bands, blue, yellow, red; Andorran coat of arms frequently imposed on central (yellow) band but not essential.

H.M. Consul-General, L. J. Evans (*Resident at Barcelona*).

ANGOLA

President, Dr. Agostinho Neto.

Angola, which has an area of 488,000 square miles lies on the western coast of Africa; its population in 1970 was 5,673,046 although in the wake of fighting between the rival liberation movements, the white population, formally of several hundred thousand has been greatly reduced, by a mass exodus.

After a Portuguese presence of at least four centuries, and an anti-colonial war since 1961, Angola became independent on Nov. 11, 1975 in the midst of civil war. Soviet-Cuban military assistance to the Popular Movement for the Liberation of Angola (M.P.L.A.) enabled it to defeat its South African-assisted rivals early in 1976. Cuban troops remain in Angola which has entered a period of reconstruction.

Angola exports diamonds, iron ore, oil and coffee.

CAPITAL.—Ψ Luanda (346,763 in 1970).

FLAG.—Red and black with a yellow star, machete and cog-wheel.

ARABIA

Arabia is a peninsula in the south-west of the Asiatic continent, forming the connecting link between Asia and Africa, and lies between 30° 30′ —60° E, long. and 12° 45′—34° 50′ N. lat. The north-western limit is generally taken from 'Aqaba at the head of the Gulf of 'Aqaba, to a point in the Syrian Desert about 150 miles north-east, and thence northwards to a point about 50 miles due east of Damascus. The remaining land boundaries are in the form of a horse-shoe, encompassing the Syrian Desert, and descending in a south-easterly direction to the head of the Persian Gulf, and thus excluding the whole of Mesopotamia and the Euphrates Valley. The other boundaries of Arabia are the Red Sea and Gulf of Aden, the Arabian Sea, and the Persian Gulf and Gulf of Oman. Generally speaking, the peninsula consists of a plateau sloping from south-west to north-east towards the Euphrates Valley, except that the broad southeastern promontory, which encloses the Persian Gulf, contains a coastal range in Oman.

The total area is estimated at 1,200,000 sq. miles (of which nearly one-half is occupied by the Syrian, Nafud, Dahana, and Rub Al Khali deserts), and the total population is believed to be about 10,000,000.

Language and Literature.—Arabic is spoken not only in Arabia, but in many other countries, either as the principal or auxiliary tongue, notably in

Egypt and the Sudan, Libya, Morocco, Algeria, Iraq, Jordan, Syria, Lebanon; and to some extent also in Nigeria, Madagascar and Zanzibar. Owing to Moorish incursions it was formerly spoken in Spain, the Balearic Islands and Sicily. There are anthologies of pre- and post-Islamic poetry and a considerable prose literature, including popular romances and story cycles (such as " The Thousand Nights and One Night "), historical and biographical studies, and, resulting from the westernizing movement, there is a general revival of learning among Arabic speaking peoples. Many daily newspapers are published in Arabic and there is a native Arabic drama.

See also—BAHRAIN; KUWAIT; OMAN; QATAR; SAUDI ARABIA; THE YEMEN REPUBLICS: UNITED ARAB EMIRATES.

ARGENTINE REPUBLIC
(República Argentina)

Junta.—Lt.-Gen. Jorge Rafael Videla (also President of the Republic, *acceded* March 29, 1976); Adm. Emilio Eduardo Massera and Brig.-Gen. Orlando Ramón Agosti.

CABINET

Interior, Gen. Albano Eduardo Harguindeguy.
Foreign Affairs, Rear Adm. César Augusto Guzzetti.
Labour, Brig.-Gen. Horacio Tomás Liendo.
Treasury and Finance, Sr. José Alfredo Martínez de Hoz.
Education, Prof. Ricardo Pedro Bruera.
Defence, Gen. José María Klix.
Justice, Brig.-Gen. Julio Arnaldo Gómez.
Social Welfare, Rear Adm. Julio Juan Bardi.

EMBASSY IN LONDON.

9 Wilton Crescent, S.W.1.
[01–235 3717]

Ambassador Extraordinary and Plenipotentiary, (vacant).
Minister Plenipotentiary, Rafael M. Gowland (*Chargé d'Affaires*).
Naval Attaché, Rear Adm. Julio Antonio Torti.
Counsellors, Guillermo Figari; Rafael A. Ocampo Casco; Alejandro H. Piñeiro (*Consular*).
Military and Air Attaché, Cdre. Rodolfo A. Guerra.
Economic and Commercial Counsellor, Antonio E. Seward.
Senior Asst. Naval Attaché, Capt. Norberto M. Couto.
Asst. Naval Attachés, Cdr. Juan Arturo Dover; Cdr. Miguel José Guruceaga.
1st Secretaries, Horacio R. Basso; Federico Mirre.
2nd Secretaries, Pascual Adolfo Rossellini (*Consular*); Domingo Cullen; Luis D. Mendiola.
3rd Secretary, José Crescencio Quijano.
Consulate-General, 53 Hans Place, S.W.1 (01–584 1701).

There is also a Consulate in *Liverpool*.

Argentina is a wedge-shaped country, occupying the greater portion of the southern part of the South American Continent, and extending from Bolivia to Cape Horn, a total distance of nearly 2,300 miles; its greatest breadth is about 930 miles. It is bounded on the north by Bolivia, on the north-east by Paraguay, Brazil, and Uruguay, on the south-east and south by the Atlantic, and on the west by Chile, from which Republic it is separated by the Cordillera de los Andes. On the west the mountainous Cordilleras, with their plateaux, extend from the northern to the southern boundaries: on the east are the great plains. Those in the north are thickly wooded and are known as *El Gran Chaco*, and further south lie the treeless pampas extending from the Bolivian boundary in the north to the Río Negro; and south of the

Río Negro are the vast plains of Patagonia. Argentina thus contains a succession of level plains, broken only in Córdoba by the San Luís and Córdoba ranges, in the north-western states by the eastern spurs of the Andes, and in the southern portion of the Province of Buenos Aires by the Tandil Hills (about 1,000 ft.) and the Sierra Ventana, near Bahía Blanca (about 3,000 ft.). The Paraná River, formed by the junction of the Upper Paraná with the Paraguay River, flows through the north-eastern states into the Atlantic, and is navigable throughout its course in Argentina; the Pilcomayo, Bermejo, and Salado del Norte are also navigable for some distance from their confluence with the Paraná. In the Province of Buenos Aires the Salado del Sud flows south-east for some 300 miles into Samborombon Bay (Atlantic). In the south Colorado and Río Negro rise in the extreme west and flow across the pampas into the Atlantic, many similar streams in Patagonia (notably the Chubut and Santa Cruz) traversing the country from the Andes to the Atlantic. The climate ranges from sub-tropical to cold temperate.

The Republic consists of 22 provinces, one territory (Tierra del Fuego) and one federal district (Buenos Aires), comprising in all an area of 1,079,965 square miles, with a population (Census of 1970) of 23,360,000 (male 11,600,000; female 11,760,000).

Government.—The estuary of La Plata was discovered in 1515 by Juan Díaz de Solís, but it was not until 1534 that Pedro de Mendoza founded Buenos Aires. This city was abandoned and later founded once more by Don Juan de Garay in 1580. In 1810 (May 25) Spanish rule was defied, and in 1816 (July 9), after a long campaign of liberation conducted by General José de San Martín, the independence of Argentina was declared by the Congress of Tucumán.

Following months of crisis, marked by political and economic uncertainty, and continuous violence from guerilla forces, President María Estela Perón temporarily relinquished her powers on September 14, 1975, and handed over power to her constitutional successor, Sr. Italo Argentino Luder, speaker of the Senate.

President Perón resumed her powers on October 16, 1975, but continuing political and labour unrest, together with increased terrorist activity and the lack of any effective Government, led inevitably to a reluctant *coup d'état* by the Armed Forces Commanders, which took place bloodlessly on March 24, 1976; President Perón and many of her senior advisers and officials of her Government were arrested. A Junta, consisting of the three commanders of the Armed Forces, was established and one of their number, Lt.-General Videla, was also sworn in as President on March 29, 1976.

Agriculture.—Of a total land area of approximately 700,000,000 acres, farms occupy about 425,000,000. About 60 per cent. of the farmland is in pasture, 10 per cent. in annual crops, 5 per cent. in permanent crops and the remaining 25 per cent. in forest and wasteland. A large proportion of the land is still held in large estates devoted to cattle raising but the number of small farms is increasing. The principal crops are wheat, maize, oats, barley, rye, linseed, sunflower seed, alfalfa, sugar, fruit and cotton. Argentina is pre-eminent in the production of beef, mutton and wool, being self-sufficient in basic foodstuffs and conducting a large export trade in many others. Pastoral and agricultural products provide about 85 per cent. of Argentina's exports and they originate mainly from the pampas or rich central plain which embraces the provinces of Buenos Aires, Santa Fé, Entre Ríos, Córdoba and La Pampa.

The following table shows the yield of some of the more important crops:

	1973–74 metric tons
Maize	9,900,000
Wheat	6,560,000
Linseed	297,000
Oats	561,000
Barley	732,000
Rye	613,000
Rice	316,000
Sunflower seed	970,000
Cotton (gross bulk production)	418,400
Sugar cane	15,536,000
Millet	228,500
Tobacco	97,700
Soya	496,000

Livestock.—Livestock population in 1975 was: cattle, 57,000,000; sheep, 42,000,000; and pigs, 4,000,000. Meat exports to UK fell from 38,373 tons in 1974 to 19,558 tons in 1975. 11,975,602 cattle were slaughtered in 1975 (1974, 10,000,000).

Mineral Production.—Oil is found in various parts of the Republic and is obtained to a considerable extent at Comodoro Rivadavia (Chubut), Mendoza, Plaza Huincul (Neuquen), Tartagal (Salta) and in other districts. A natural gas pipeline between Comodoro Rivadavia and Buenos Aires has been in operation since 1949. An oil pipeline from Campo Duran (Salta) to a refinery in San Lorenzo (Santa Fé) was put in service in March, 1960, as was also a natural gas pipeline from the same source to the outskirts of Buenos Aires. Another project of importance was the construction of the natural gas pipeline between Neuquén and Bahía Blanca, completed in 1970. The production of oil is of first importance to Argentina's industries and, to

some extent, to her economic and financial development. Total petroleum output for 1975 was 22,953,000 cubic metres compared with 24,247,000 cubic metres in 1974.

Coal, lead, zinc, tungsten, iron ore, sulphur, mica and salt are the other chief minerals being exploited. There are small worked deposits of beryllium, manganese, bismuth, uranium, antimony, copper, kaolin, arsenate, gold, silver and tin. Coal production in 1975 was 502,300 tons, compared with 695,000 tons in 1974; this is produced at the Rio Turbio mine in the province of Santa Cruz. The output of other materials is not large but greater attention is now being paid to the development of these natural resources, especially copper for which the Government and private companies are carrying out exploration.

Industries.—Meat-packing is one of the principal industries; flour-milling, sugar-refining, and the wine industry are also important. In recent years great strides have been made by the textile, plastic and machine tool industries and engineering, especially in the production of motor vehicles and steel manufactures.

Communications.—There are 25,386 miles of railways of which 14,000 miles are broad gauge (5′ 6″), 2,000 miles standard (4′ 8½″), 8,720 miles of narrow 1 metre, 537 miles of 0·75 metre and 129 miles of 0·60 metre. They are all State property. Plans are in hand for complete re-organization of the railways in order to improve their operating efficiency and reduce a very large financial deficit. The combined national and provincial road network totals approximately 137,000 miles of which 23,180 miles are surfaced. There are air services between Argentina and all the neighbouring republics, Europe, Asia, Canada, the U.S.A. and South Africa. Total tonnage entering Argentine ports in 1974 was 12,179,235.

There are 16 short-wave broadcasting stations, 150 medium wave (of which 65 are official). In addition there are 65 television stations, of which 4 are in Buenos Aires. About 3·8 million television receivers are in use.

Defence.—The Army consists of four corps organized into ten brigades, including mountain, jungle, airborne and armoured troops. It numbers about 5,000 officers, 15,000 N.C.O.s and 65–70,000 conscripts who serve 1 year.

The Navy consists of 2 cruisers, 1 aircraft carrier, 9 destroyers, 4 frigates/corvettes, 4 submarines, 4 minesweepers, 1 minehunter and ancillary craft. Strength is about 3,000 officers and 30,000 ratings, including 11,000 conscripts.

The Air Force consists of 5 brigades and a training force, with a strength of 1,600 officers, 15,000 other ranks and 20,000 civilians. Aircraft total 321, including Meteor IV's, Skyhawk A.4 BS1, Lockheed C130, Fokker F27, Fokker F28, HS.748 and Mirage III.

Education—Primary and Secondary. The educational reform programme has been frozen since early 1971. The government is formulating a new education policy. At the moment, education is compulsory for the 7 grades of primary school (6 to 13). Secondary schools (14 to 17+) are available in and around Buenos Aires and in most of the important towns in the interior of the country. Most secondary schools are administered by the Central Ministry of Education in Buenos Aires, while primary schools are administered by the Central Ministry or by Provincial Ministries of Education. Private schools, of which there are many, are also loosely controlled by the Central Ministry. *Teacher-Training* now takes place at

post school level, courses lasting from 2 to 4 years. *Universities*—Many new universities have been created over the last two years. The total is now over 50 with 24 national (including the Federal Technological University), 25 private and a small number of provincial universities.

Language and Literature.—Spanish is the language of the Republic and the literature of Spain is accepted as an inheritance by the people. There is little indigenous literature before the break from Spain, but all branches have flourished since the latter half of the nineteenth century, particularly journalism. Under the first Perón régime many newspapers and reviews were closed down and others turned into Government mouthpieces. About 450 daily newspapers are published in Argentina, including 7 major ones in the city of Buenos Aires. The English language newspaper is the *Buenos Aires Herald* (daily). There are several other foreign language newspapers.

TRADE

	1973	1974
	Dollars U.S.	
Total Imports....	2,229,468,000	3,656,516,000
Total Exports....	3,266,003,000	3,930,882,000

Trade with U.K.

	1974	1975
Imports from U.K..	£49,204,000	£67,796,000
Exports to U.K.....	98,467,000	53,461,000

For Exchange Rate *see* p. 83.

CAPITAL.—Ψ Buenos Aires, Pop. (Dec. 1970), Metropolitan area 2,972,453; with suburbs, 8,774,529. Other large towns are: Ψ Rosario de Santa Fé (798,292), Córdoba (798,663), Ψ La Plata (408,300), Ψ Mar del Plata (317,444), San Miguel de Tucuman (326,000), Santa Fé (312,427) and Mendoza (118,568).

FLAG.—Horizontal bands of blue, white blue; gold sun in centre of white band.

NATIONAL DAY.—July 9.

BRITISH EMBASSY

Dr. Luis Agote 2412, Buenos Aires.

Ambassador Extraordinary and Plenipotentiary, His Excellency, Derick Rosslyn Ashe, C.M.G. (1975).

Minister, J. W. R. Shakespeare, M.V.O. (*Chargé d'Affaires a.i.*).

Counsellor (Commercial), E. J. Anglin (*Consul-General*).

1st Secretaries, J. Illman (*Head of Chancery*); S. M. J. Butler-Madden; I. I. Morgan, M.B.E. (*Administration*); R. A. M. Hendrie (*Commercial*).

Defence, Military and Air Attaché, Col. B. H. Bradbrook, O.B.E.

Naval Attaché, Capt. D. Leggatt, R.N.

Veterinary Attaché, R. L. Steele.

BRITISH CONSULAR OFFICES

There are British Consular Offices at *Buenos Aires, Cipolletti, Comodoro Rivadavia, La Plata, Rio Gallegos* and *Rio Grande (Tierra del Fuego).*

BRITISH COUNCIL

Representative in Argentina, F. M. Beatty, M.B.E., Marcelo T de Alvear, 590 Buenos Aires.

BRITISH CHAMBER OF COMMERCE
IN THE ARGENTINE REPUBLIC (INC.)

Calle 25 de Mayo 444, (5° Piso), Buenos Aires.

Manager, D. L. Briant.

Buenos Aires is 7,160 miles from Southampton; transit, 19 days by steamship; 18 hours by air.

AUSTRIA

President of the Austrian Republic, Dr. Rudolf Kirch-schläger, *born* 1915; *elected* June 23, 1974.

CABINET

Chancellor, Dr. Bruno Kreisky.
Vice-Chancellor and Minister of Social Affairs, Ing. Rudolf Häuser.
Minister for the Interior, Otto Rösch.
Justice, Dr. Christian Broda.
Transport, Erwin Lanc.
Foreign Affairs, Dr. Willibald Pahr.
Finance, Dkfm. Hannes Androsch.
Agriculture, Dip. Ing. Dr. Oskar Weihs.
Defence, Brig. Karl Lütgendorf.
Education, Dr. Fred Sinowatz.
Trade and Industry, Dr. Josef Staribacher.
Building, Josef Moser.
Science and Research, Frau Dr. Hertha Firnberg.
Health and Environment, Frau Dr. Ingrid Leodolter.

AUSTRIAN EMBASSY IN LONDON
18 Belgrave Square, S.W.1
[01-235 3731]

Ambassador Extraordinary and Plenipotentiary, His Excellency Dr. Kurt Enderl (1975).
Minister-Counsellor, Dr. Ingo Mussi, M.V.O.
Counsellor, Dr. Helga Winkler-Campagna.
1st Secretary, Dr. P. Lang.
Defence Attaché, Brig.-Gen. H. Wingelbauer.
Counsellor, Dr. B. Stillfried (*Cultural*).
Attachés, Dr. Ernst Menhofer (*Press*); Dr. P. Marginter (*Cultural*); Mrs. A. Schmidt, Mrs. D. Baldwin (*Administration*); Mrs. T. Stockert (*Social Welfare*); Mrs. M. Ballod (*Consular*).

Austria is a country of Central Europe bounded on the north by Czechoslovakia, on the south by Italy and Yugoslavia, on the east by Hungary, on the north-west by Germany and on the west by Switzerland. Its area is 32,376 square miles and its population (1975), 7,519,900.

Government.—The Austrian Federal Republic comprises nine provinces (Vienna, Lower Austria, Upper Austria, Salzburg, Tyrol, Vorarlberg, Carinthia, Styria and Burgenland) and was established in 1918 on the break-up of the Austro-Hungarian Empire. In March 13, 1938, as a result of the *Anschluss*, Austria (*Oesterreich*) was incorporated into the German *Reich* under the name *Ostmark*. After the liberation of Vienna in 1945, the Austrian Republic was reconstituted within the frontiers of 1937 and, after a period of provisional government, a freely-elected Government took office on December 20, 1945. The country was divided at this time into four zones occupied respectively by the U.K., U.S.A., U.S.S.R. and France, while Vienna was jointly occupied by the four Powers. On May 15, 1955, the Austrian State Treaty was signed in Vienna by the Foreign Ministers of the four Powers and of Austria. This Treaty recognized the re-establishment of Austria as a sovereign, independent and democratic state, having the same frontiers as on January 1, 1938. It entered into force on July 27, 1955.

There is a National Assembly of 183 Deputies. In the elections of October, 1975, the Socialists won an overall majority of the votes.

The state of the parties in June 1976, was:

Socialist Party	93
People's Party	80
Freedom Party (right wing)	10

Religion and Education.—The predominant religion is Roman Catholic. Elementary education is free and compulsory between the ages of 6 and 15 and there are good facilities for secondary, technical and professional education. There are Universities at Vienna, Graz, Innsbruck, Salzburg, Linz and Klagenfurt.

Language and Literature.—The language of Austria is German, but the rights of the Slovene- and Croat-speaking minorities in Carinthia, Styria and Burgenland are protected. The press is free. There are 6 daily papers in Vienna and 24 in the provinces, as well as numerous weeklies and monthlies.

Communications.—Internal communications in Austria are partly restricted because of the mountainous nature of the country, and road and rail routes must, of necessity, follow the river valleys. The railways in Austria are state-owned and have 5,901 km. of track of which 2,721 km. had

been electrified by June, 1976. While road surfaces in many cases are not up to British standards, the main roads linking the major towns are generally good and relatively fast. The *Westautobahn*, completed in 1967, links Munich, Salzburg, Linz and Vienna. A second major autobahn (*Inntal Autobahn*) is now complete between Kufstein, Innsbruck and the Brenner Pass, thus linking the West German and Italian autobahn networks through Austria. A third major autobahn (*Südautobahn*) linking Vienna with Graz, Klagenfurt and Villach is under construction and about half of it is already open for use.

Production and industry.—Agriculture is an important industry, the arable land producing wheat, rye, barley, oats, maize, potatoes, sugar beet, turnips, and miscellaneous crops. Many varieties of fruit trees flourish and the vineyards produce excellent wine. The pastures support horses, cattle and pigs. Timber forms a valuable source of Austria's indigenous wealth, about 39 per cent. of the total land area consisting of forest areas. Coniferous species predominate and account for more than 80 per cent. of the timber under cultivation. Hardwood trees are mainly confined to Lower Austria. Spruce is the most common among the conifers (about 60 per cent. of the total) and beech is the most prevalent of the broad leaf trees.

Austria has important heavy industries. Production figures for 1975 include (in thousands of metric tons): pig iron 3,055·8, steel 4,068, rolled products 2,857. Raw magnesite, nitrogenous fertilizers, paper, chemical pulp and synthetic fibres are produced in quantity. In addition, motor cycles, scooters, buses, tractors and motor lorries are produced.

Energy.—Of Austria's energy requirement in 1975, 42·8 per cent. was supplied from internal sources. Production of crude oil in Upper and Lower Austria amounted to 2 million metric tons in 1975, 25 per cent. of annual consumption. Imports of crude oil were 6 million tons, of which 2·8 million came from Iraq, 1·1 million from the U.S.S.R., 0·95 million from Libya and 0·57 million from Iran. Austria produced 1·8 billion cubic metres of natural gas in 1975 and imported 1·7 billion cubic metres from the U.S.S.R. Production of electric power in 1975 amounted to 35 million mwh and net exports of electric power were 4·5 million mwh. A 700 mw nuclear power station is under construction, due to commence operation in the summer of 1977 and tenders have been issued for a second.

Minerals.—There are iron ore and oil deposits. In addition there are useful deposits of brown coal, magnesite, salt and lead. There are also limited deposits of copper.

FINANCE.	1974	1975
	Schillings	'000,000
Ordinary Budget:		
Expenditure	160,303	188,173
Revenue	148,531	159,110
Extraordinary Budget:		
Expenditure	6,836	8,498
Revenue	104	403

Trade with U.K.

	1974	1975
Imports from U.K.	£153,139,000	£164,320,000
Exports to U.K.	203,659,000	204,115,000

Currency.—The unit of currency is the *Schilling* of 100 Groschen, reintroduced in December, 1945. The rate of exchange (June 1976) was 32·50 Austrian schillings= £1, at par.

CAPITAL, Vienna, on the Danube, population 1,614,841. Other towns are Graz (248,800),

Linz (208,000), Innsbruck (121,400), Salzburg (137,000), and Klagenfurt (84,700).

FLAG.—Horizontal stripes of red, white, red, with eagle crest on white stripe. NATIONAL DAY.—October 26.

BRITISH EMBASSY
Vienna.

Ambassador Extraordinary and Plenipotentiary, His Excellency Hugh Travers Morgan, C.M.G. (1976).
Counsellor, R. Brash.
Counsellor (IAEA/UNIDO), D. Slater.
1st Secretaries, M. F. Chapman (*Head of Chancery*); J. D. M. Blyth; R. Harrison; J. W. Cox; D. K. Urquhart (*Commercial*); P. J. Kirchner, M.B.E. (*H.M. Consul*); H. J. Bowe, M.V.O. (*Information*); Dr. W. Rhodes, M.B.E. (*Legal Adviser*); F. A. J. Archer (*Administration*).
Defence Attaché, Brig. J. N. Holden.
There are British Consular Offices at *Vienna* and *Innsbruck*.
British Council Representative, T. F. Hibbett, Schenkenstrasse 4, 1010 Vienna.

BAHRAIN

Amir, H. H. Shaikh Isa bin Sulman Al Khalifah, K.C.M.G., *born* 1932; *acceded* Dec. 16, 1961.

CABINET
Prime Minister, H.E. Shaikh Khalifa Isa bin Sulman Al-Khalifa.
Minister of Defence, H.E. Shaikh Hamed bin Isa Al-Khalifa (*Heir Apparent*).
Foreign Affairs, Shaikh Mohammed bin Mubarak Al-Khalifa.
Justice and Islamic Affairs, Shaikh Abdullah bin Khalid Al-Khalifa.
Development and Industry, Yusuf Ahmad Shirawi.
Health, Dr. Ali Fakroo.
Education, Shaikh Abdul Aziz bin Mohammed Al-Khalifa.
Legal Affairs, Dr. Hussain Al-Baharna.
Cabinet Affairs, Jawad Salim Al-Arayyed.
Transportation, Ibrahim Mohammed Humaidan.
Interior, Shaikh Mohammed bin Khalifa Al-Khalifa.
Information, Tariq Abdulrahman Almoayyed.
Labour and Social Affairs, Shaikh Isa bin Mohammed Al-Khalifah.
Works, Electricity and Water, Majid Jawad Al-Jishi.
Housing, Shaikh Khalid bin Abdullah Al-Khalifa.
Finance and National Economy, Ibrahim Abdulkarim Mohammed.
Commerce and Agriculture, Habib Ahmed Kassim.

BAHRAIN EMBASSY IN LONDON
98 Gloucester Road, S.W.7
[01-370 5132]

Ambassador Extraordinary and Plenipotentiary, His Excellency Ali Ebrahim Al-Mahroos.
Minister Plenipotentiary, Dr. Wasfi Nimer.
1st Secretary, Mustafa Kamal Mohamed (*Consul*).
2nd Secretary, Ebrahim Salahudin Ebrahim.

Area and population.—Bahrain consists of a group of low-lying islands situated about half-way down the Gulf, some 20 miles off the east coast of Arabia. The largest of these, Bahrain island itself, is about 30 miles long and 10 miles wide at its broadest. The capital, Manama, is situated on the north shore of this island. The next largest, Muharraq, with the town and airfield of the same name, is connected to Manama by a causeway 1½ miles long.

The Population (1971) is 216,000. There are about 5,000 British, 2,500 other Europeans and Americans, and 30,000 other resident foreigners, of whom about half are Iranians, Indians and Pakistanis. The Bahrainis are about equally divided between Sunnis and Shias; the ruling family and many of the most prominent merchants are Sunnis.

Climate.—The climate is humid all the year round, with rainfall of about 3 in., concentrated in the mild winter months, December to March; in summer, May to October, temperatures can exceed 110°F.

Economy.—The largest source of revenue is oil. The Bahrain field, discovered in 1932, is now owned 60 per cent. by the Government, represented by the Bahrain National Oil Co., and 40 per cent. by the Bahrain Petroleum Co. (BAPCO), a Caltex subsidiary, which operates the field. Production in 1975 was 22·3 million barrels. BAPCO owns the Sitra refinery, which derives about 70 per cent. of its crude by submarine pipeline from Saudi Arabia. Bahrain also has a half share, with Saudi Arabia, in the profits of the offshore Bu Sa'afa field. A reservoir of unassociated gas has recently been developed on Bahrain island.

The second source of revenue is the *entrepôt* trade to the mainland and to other Gulf states. This has fallen from some 70 per cent. of all imports a few years ago to about 35 per cent., in spite of the encouragement of a free transit area in the port.

Heavy industry is limited to the Aluminium Bahrain smelter, with an annual capacity of 120,000 tonnes of ingots, billets and slabs; it uses alumina from Australia and the local natural gas. The Bahrain Government owns 77·9 per cent. of the shares. A dry dock able to take tankers of 500,000 dwt is under construction for a consortium of the OAPEC countries.

The pearling industry, once the basis of the economy, has virtually ceased to exist. There is however a variety of light industries, and construction is thriving.

The state is being developed as a financial centre. Apart from commercial banks, led by the National Bank of Bahrain, the Chartered Bank, the British Bank of the Middle East and the Bank of Bahrain and Kuwait, many international banks are being licensed as " offshore banking units "; there are also money brokers and merchant banks.

The currency is the Bahraini Dinar (BD) divided into 1,000 fils. In June 1976 it was worth approximately US $2.53.

Trade with U.K.

	1974 million	1975 million
Imports from UK	BD25·7	BD42·8
Exports to UK	2·6	1·9

Communications.—The port of Mina Sulman has six alongside berths for ships up to 30' draft, and is being extended and deepened.

Muharraq airport is the main air traffic centre of the Gulf; it is the headquarters of Gulf Air, and a stopping point on routes between Europe and Australia and the Far East, including British Airways *Concorde*.

A world-wide telephone and telex service, by satellite, is operated by Cable and Wireless Ltd.

FLAG.—Red, with vertical serrated white bar next to staff.

CAPITAL.—Manama; population (1971) 89,608.

BRITISH EMBASSY
PO Box 114, Manama

Ambassador Extraordinary and Plenipotentiary, His Excellency Edward Ferguson Given, C.M.G. (1975).
1st Secretary and Consul, L. E. Walker, M.B.E.
2nd Secretary (Commercial), P. Nessling.
Vice-Consul, M. W. Tym.
British Council Representative, J. E. P. Ness, P.O. Box 452, Manama.

BELGIUM
(Royaume de Belgique.)

King of the Belgians, H.M. King Baudouin, K.G., born Sept. 7, 1930; succeeded July 17, 1951, on the abdication of his father, King Leopold III, after having acted as Head of the State since August 11, 1950; married Dec. 15, 1960, Doña Fabiola de Mora y Aragòn.

Heir Presumptive, H.R.H. Prince Albert, born June 6, 1934, brother of the King; married July 2, 1959, Donna Paola Ruffo di Calabria, and has issue Prince Philippe Léopold Louis Marie, b. April 15, 1960; Princess Astrid Josephine-Charlotte Fabrizia Elisabeth Paola Marie, b. June 5, 1962; Prince Laurent, b. Oct. 20, 1963.

CABINET
(October 4, 1974)

Prime Minister, M. Léo Tindemans (*CVP*).
Defence and Brussels Affairs, M. Paul Vanden Boeynants (*PSC*).
Finance, M. Willy de Clerq (*PVV*).
Foreign Affairs and Development Co-operation, M. Renaat van Elslande (*CVP*).
Health and Family Affairs, M. Joseph de Saeger (*CVP*).
Social Security, M. Placide de Paepe (*CVP*).
Justice, M. Herman Vanderpoorten (*PVV*).
Foreign Trade, M. Michel Toussaint (*PLP*).
Interior, M. Joseph Michel (*PSC*).
Agriculture, M. Albert Lavens (*CVP*).
Communications, M. Jozef Chabert (*CVP*).
Middle Classes, M. Louis Olivier (*PLP*).
Public Works, M. Jean Defraigne (*PLP*).
Economic Affairs, M. Fernand Herman.
Labour and Employment, Walloon Affairs, Housing and Land Use, M. Alfred Califice (*PSC*).
Dutch Culture and Flemish Affairs, Rita de Backer-Van Ocken (*CVP*).
French Culture, M. Henri-François van Aal (*PSC*).
Education (Dutch), M. Herman de Croo (*PVV*).
Education (French), M. Antoine Humblet (*PSC*).
Institutional Reform (French), M. François Perin (*RW*).
Institutional Reform (Flemish), M. Robert Vande-kerckhove (*CVP*).

STATE SECRETARIES

Wallon Regional Economy, M. Jean Gol (*RW*).
Flemish Regional Economy, Land Use and Housing, M. Luc Dhoore (*CVP*).
Regional Economy, assistant to the Minister for Brussels Affairs, M. August De Winter (*PVV*).
Civil Service, assistant to the Prime Minister, M. Louis d'Haeseleer (*PVV*).
Environment, assistant to the Prime Minister, M. Karel Poma (*PVV*).
Budget and Scientific Policy, assistant to the Prime Minister, M. Gaston Geens (*CVP*).
Economic Affairs assistant, M. Etienne Knoops (*RW*).
Social Affairs, assistant to the Minister for Walloon Affairs, M. Robert Moreau (*RW*).
[*CVP*=Christelijke Volkspartij
PSC=Parti social-chrétien
PVV=Partij voor Vrijheid en Vooruitgang
PLP=Parti pour la liberté et le progrès
RW=Rassemblement Wallon]

BELGIAN EMBASSY IN LONDON.
Chancery and Passport Office, 103 Eaton Square, S.W.1.
[01-235 5422]

Ambassador Extraordinary and Plenipotentiary, (vacant).
Minister Counsellors, M. Henri J. Perdieus; M. J. Kadijk (*Economic Affairs*).
Counsellors, M. C. Fellens (*Culture and Information*); M. Roger P. Martin; M. A. Adam; M. Maurice Cammaerts (*Agriculture*).

A Kingdom of Western Europe, with a total area of 11,775 square miles and a population, (Dec., 1970) of 9,650,944. The Kingdom of Belgium is bounded on the N. by the Kingdom of the Netherlands, on the S. by France, on the E. by Germany and Luxemburg, and on the W. by the North Sea.

Belgium has a frontier of 898 miles, and a sea-board of 41 miles. The Meuse and its tributary, the Sambre, divide it into two distinct regions, that in the west being generally level and fertile, while the table-land of the Ardennes, in the east, has for the most part a poor soil. The " polders " near the coast, which are protected by dykes against floods, cover an area of 193 sq. miles. The highest hill, Signal de Botranges, rises to a height of 2,276 feet, but the mean elevation of the whole country does not exceed 526 feet. The principal rivers are the Scheldt and the Meuse. Brussels has a mean temperature of 49° F. (summer 65°, winter 37°).

Belgium is divided linguistically between those who speak Dutch (the Flemings, who occupy the North) and those who speak French (the Walloons, who occupy the South) with a small German-speaking region east of Liège. Nearly all Belgians are Roman Catholics.

Government.—The kingdom formed part of the " Low Countries " (Netherlands) from 1815 until Oct. 14, 1830, when a National Congress proclaimed its independence, and on June 4, 1831, Prince Leopold of Coburg was chosen hereditary king. The separation from the Netherlands and the neutrality and inviolability of Belgium were guaranteed by a Conference of the European Powers, and by the *Treaty of London* (April 19, 1839), the famous " Scrap of Paper," signed by Austria, France, Great Britain, Prussia, The Netherlands, and Russia. On Aug. 4, 1914, the Germans invaded Belgium, in violation of the terms of the treaty.

The Kingdom was again invaded by Germany on May 10, 1940. The whole Kingdom eventually fell into enemy hands and was occupied by Nazi troops until the victorious advance of the Allies in September 1944. A monument at Hertain in the province of Hainault (where British forces crossed the frontier on Sept. 3, 1944), set up by the Anglo-Belgian Union, was unveiled on St. George's Day, 1949.

According to the Constitution of 1831 the form of government is a constitutional representative and hereditary monarchy with a bicameral legislature, consisting of the King, the Senate and the Chamber of Representatives. The Senate is partly directly and partly indirectly elected (or co-opted) for 4 years. 106 members out of 181 are directly elected. The Chamber of Representatives consists of not more than 1 per 40,000 inhabitants and is elected directly by all adult nationals.

The last election for the Chamber of Deputies was held on March 10, 1974, and M. Tindemans's Social Christians' Party won 32 per cent. of the votes. The results were as follows:

	Seats	
	1974	(1971)
Social Christians..........	72	(67)
Socialist..................	59	(61)
Liberals..................	30	(31)
French-speaking bloc......	25	(27)
Flemish Nationalist " People's Union ".................	21	(21)
Communists.............	4	(5)

Elections were also held for the Senate, 106 of whom were directly elected, 50 were appointed by the newly-elected provincial councils, and 25 co-opted by secret ballot. The overall distribution of seats in the Senate was as follows (*1971* results in parentheses): Social Christians, 66 (61); Socialists, 50 (49); Liberals, 27 (29); French-speaking bloc, 21 (19); Flemish Nationalists, 16 (19); Communists, 1 (1). H.R.H. Prince Albert is also a member of the Senate.

On April 24, 1974, M. Tindemans formed a minority coalition Government of Social Christians and Liberals, who were sworn in on April 25. M. Tindemans has since re-shuffled his Government on two occasions, and he has enlarged it to include the French-speaking Rassemblement Wallon.

Production.—Belgium is essentially a manufacturing country. With no natural resources except coal, annual production of which formerly averaged some 30,000,000 tons but which dropped to 8,841,000 metric tons in 1973 following the closing of uneconomic pits, industry is based largely on the processing for re-export of imported raw materials. In 1973 about 4·1 per cent. of the active population was engaged in agriculture and forestry, the former supplying four-fifths of the population's needs. Principal industries are coal, steel and metal products (Mons, Charleroi, Liège, Namur, Hainault, Brabant and Limburg), textiles (Ghent, Bruges, Courtrai, Verviers, etc.), glass nitrogen, heavy chemicals, sugar, breweries, etc. Crude steel output in 1973 was 15,527,000 metric tons.

Education.—The budget for education (over 100,000,000,000 Belgian francs) represents approximately a quarter of the national budget and does not include the amount spent by the Communes, provinces and the church in subsidized schools. The nursery schools provide free education for the 2½ to 6 age group. There are over 8,000 primary schools (6 to 12 years) of which approximately 5000 are administered by the State, province or commune and the remainder are free institutions (predominantly Roman Catholic). There are more than 1,100 secondary schools offering a general academic education slightly over half of which are free institutions (predominantly Roman Catholic but subsidized by the State) and the remainder official institutions. The official school leaving age is 14.

Language and Literature.—Dutch is spoken in the provinces of West Flanders, East Flanders, Antwerp, Limburg, and the northern half of

Brabant, and French in the provinces of Hainault, Namur, Luxemburg, Liège and the southern half of Brabant. Dutch is recognized as the official language in the northern areas and French in the southern (Walloon) area and there are guarantees for the respective linguistic minorities. Brussels is officially bi-lingual.

In July, 1971, the Belgian Parliament passed three Bills together implementing the constitutional amendments introduced in December 1970, to ease friction between the French-speaking and Dutch-speaking communities. The first Bill established a cultural council for each linguistic group, in operation from Dec. 1, 1971, all members of the Chamber of Representatives and the Senate being members of one council or the other. A Cultural Council for the German-speaking community also has since been established. The second Bill defined the powers of the cultural councils, providing that the councils would be responsible for certain aspects of cultural life; commissions for co-operation with the other council would be set up, with a statutory obligation to hold at least two meetings with the other council in each Parliamentary session. The third Bill provided for the establishment of five " agglomerations " of municipalities centred on Antwerp, Brussels, Charleroi, Ghent and Liège and the federation of small municipalities, with special provision in respect of the border boroughs of Brussels (which have a predominantly Flemish population) designed gradually to reduce the influence of the French speakers in that area. Regional councils for Flanders, Wallonia and Brussels were established in 1974.

The literature of France and the Netherlands is supplemented by an indigenous Belgian literary activity, in both French and Dutch. Maurice Maeterlinck (1862–1949) was awarded the Nobel Prize for Literature in 1911. Emile Verhaeren (1855–1916) was a poet of international standing. Of contemporary Belgian writers, perhaps the most celebrated is Georges Simenon (*born* at Liège in 1903). There are 45 daily newspapers (French, Dutch and some German) in Belgium.

FINANCE

Ordinary Budget	1973	1974
	B. Fr. (millions)	
Revenue	406,642	472,623
Expenditure	406,642	473,363

Extraordinary Budget		
Revenue	802	604
Expenditure	86,900	82,610

The unit of currency is the Belgian *franc*. Since June 1972 there has been no fixed rate. (*See also* p. 83)

TRADE

	1972	1973
	('000 *Francs*)	('000 *Francs*)
Total Imports	681,772,789	852,639,796
Total Exports	710,979,595	870,244,933

Trade with U.K.

	1972	1973
Imports from U.K.	£385,700,000	£612,200,000
Exports to U.K.	309,500,000	434,300,000

COMMUNICATIONS.—On Dec. 31, 1972, there were 4,080 kilometres of normal gauge railways operated by the Belgian National Railways, of which 1,232 kilometres were electrified; the length of regional railways operated in 1973 was 215·8 kilometres. Belgian National Railways also operate 4,425 kilometres of regular bus routes. Other operators run 14,179 km. of bus routes. On Dec. 31, 1973, there were 1,625,726 telephone subscribers in Belgium.

Ship canals include *Ghent-Terneuzen* (18 miles, of which half is in Belgium and half in the Netherlands; constructed 1825–27) which permits the passage to Ghent of ships up to 60,000 tons; the Canal of Willebroek Rupel-Brussels (20 miles, by which ships drawing 18 ft reach Brussels from the sea; opened in 1922); and *Bruges* (from Zeebrugge on the North Sea to Bruges, 6¼ miles; opened in 1922). The *Albert Canal* (79 miles), which figured prominently in the fighting (Sept. 1944) for the relief of Belgium and the Netherlands and for the invasion of Germany, links Liège with Antwerp; it was completed in 1939 and accommodates barges up to 1,350 tons. The modernization of the port of Antwerp begun in 1956 is well advanced. Inland waterway approaches to Antwerp are also to be improved. The river Meuse from the Dutch to the French frontiers, the river Sambre between Namur and Monceau, the river Scheldt from Antwerp-Ghent and the Brussels-Charleroi Canal are being widened or deepened to take barges up to 1,350 tons.

In 1973 there were 12,830 km. of trunk roads of which about 1,030 km. are motorways. Most of the maritime trade of Belgium is carried in foreign shipping, the mercantile marine consisting (1973) of 89 vessels (1,091,984 metric tons), in addition to which there were 268 fishing boats.

The Belgian National Airline *Sabena* operates regular services between Brussels and London, and many continental centres, as well as overseas services to the United States, Zaire, Canada, Mexico, Guatemala, Middle East, Far East, India, etc. Many foreign airlines call at Brussels.

CITIES AND TOWNS

The Capital, BRUSSELS, had an estimated population (Dec. 31, 1971) of 1,075,000 (with suburbs). Other towns are ΨAntwerp, the chief port (67,259); Ψ Ghent (229,687), which has large cotton and flax spinning mills, and is the second port of importance after Antwerp, while its flower shows are famous; Liège (446,990), the centre of the iron industry, and Charleroi (218,089), the important coal-mining and metallurgical centre; ΨBruges (118,000); Ψ Ostend (47,230); Malines (67,730). Brussels is 224 miles from London; transit, by rail and sea, 8 hrs.; by air, 1 hr.

NATIONAL FLAG.—Three vertical bands, black, yellow, red.

NATIONAL DAY.—July 21 (Accession of King Leopold I, 1831).

BRITISH EMBASSY.

28 Rue Joseph II, 1040 Brussels.

Ambassador Extraordinary and Plenipotentiary, His Excellency Sir David Muirhead, K.C.M.G., C.V.O. (1974).

Counsellors, I. S. Winchester (*Commercial*); The Viscount Dunrossil; C. P. H. T. Isolani, C.B.E., M.V.O. (*Information*).

Defence (Military and Naval) Attaché, Col. E. W. Nicoll.

Air Attaché, Wing Cdr. J. D. Evans.

BRITISH CONSULAR OFFICES

There are British Consular Offices at *Brussels*, *Antwerp*, *Ostend*, *Ghent* and *Liège*.

British Council Representative to Belgium and Luxembourg, C. H. Whistler, Galilée Building, Avenue Galilée 5, 1030, Brussels (Council Library at *Brussels*).

BRITISH CHAMBER OF COMMERCE FOR BELGIUM AND LUXEMBOURG (INC.), 30 Rue Joseph II, 1040 Brussels.

BENIN
(People's Republic of Benin)

President of the Military Revolutionary Government and Head of State, Lt.-Col. Mathieu Kerekou; *assumed office,* October 26, 1972.

A republic situated in West Africa, between 2° and 3° W. and 6° and 12° N., Benin (formerly known as Dahomey) has a short coast line of 78 miles on the Gulf of Guinea but extends northwards inland for 437 miles. It is flanked on the west by Togo, on the north by Upper Volta and Niger and on the east by Nigeria. It has an area of about 47,000 square miles and a population (estimate, 1973) of 2,948,000. Although poor in resources, Benin is one of the most thickly populated areas in West Africa, with a high level of education. It is divided into four main regions running horizontally: a narrow sandy coastal strip, a succession of inter-communicating lagoons, a clay belt and a sandy plateau in the north.

The first treaty with France was signed by one of the kings of Abomey in 1851 but the country was not placed under French administration until 1892. Benin became an independent republic within the French Community on Dec. 4, 1958; full independence outside the Community was proclaimed on August 1, 1960. In October, 1963, a popular revolution led to the fall of the government of the first President of Benin, Hubert Maga. The Army held power until Sourou-Migan Apithy was elected President and Justin Ahomadegbé Chief of Government in January, 1964, after a new constitution had been agreed. This government was overthrown in November, 1965, following a long-standing disagreement between Maga and Apithy. It was replaced by President Tahirou Congacou, who was in turn dismissed in December of the same year by the Army. Christophe Soglo then assumed control and dismissed the Assembly. Soglo was in his turn overthrown by an Army *coup d'état* on December 17, 1967. Seven months later Dr. Zinsou was installed, with the support of the Army, as President, an appointment which was confirmed by a national referendum on July 28, 1968.

Dr. Zinsou was overthrown by a military coup on December 10, 1969 and for five months the country was ruled by a military "Directoire". Following abortive elections in March, 1970, a Presidential Council was set up in May, 1970 consisting of MM Maga, Ahomadégbé and Apithy, with M. Maga as President of the Council and Head of State. He was succeeded in May, 1972 by M. Ahomadégbé, who in turn would have been succeeded in May 1974 by M. Apithy, but for the *coup d'état* of October 26, 1972 which brought the Military Revolutionary Government, headed by Lt.-Col. Kerekou, to power.

Benin is a member of the *Conseil de l'Entente*, the *Organisation Commune Africaine et Malgache* (OCAM) and the Organization of African Unity (O.A.U.). The official language is French.

Finance.—The currency of Benin is the *Franc CFA* (*Francs CFA* 50 = 1 French *Franc*) (*Francs CFA* 450 = £1·June, 1975).

Trade.—The principal exports are palm products (80 per cent.) followed by ground nuts, shea-nuts and coffee. Small deposits of gold, iron and chrome have been found.

Trade with U.K.

	1973	1974
Imports from U.K.	£2,032,006	£3,605,289
Exports to U.K.	53,595	457,891

CAPITAL.—Porto Novo (85,000). Principal commercial town and port, ΨCotonou (120,000).

FLAG.—Three stripes, one vertical, green, two horizontal yellow and red.
NATIONAL DAY.—August 1.
British Embassy (see Togo).

BHUTAN

King of Bhutan, Jigme Singye Wangchuck, *born* 1955; *succeeded his father,* July, 1972; *crowned,* June 2, 1974.

Bhutan, with an area of about 18,000 sq. miles and an estimated population (1972) of 1,010,000, mainly Buddhists, is an independent State bounded on the North and East by Tibet, on the South by India, and on the West by Sikkim, which is now a State of the Indian Union. In 1949, a treaty was concluded with the Government of India under which the Kingdom of Bhutan agreed to be guided by the Government of India in regard to its external relations, but it still retains complete independence, issues its own passports and has diplomatic representatives at the United Nations as well as in India. It also receives from the Government of India an annual payment of Rs.500,000 as compensation for portions of its territory annexed by the British Government in India in 1864. The principal cottage industries are weaving, metal works and crafts, and the main exports are timber, rice and wheat. A motor road runs 107 miles from Paro, the winter capital, to Phuntsholing in W. Bengal. Three other roads linking Bhutan with India are under construction or projected. The Government of India has a diplomatic representative in Bhutan.

CAPITAL. Thimphu. FLAG.—Orange and crimson divided diagonally, with dragon device in centre.

BOLIVIA
(República de Bolivia)

President, Col. Hugo Banzer, *assumed office* Aug. 22, 1971.

BOLIVIAN EMBASSY IN LONDON
106 Eaton Square, S.W.1.
[01-235 4248]
Ambassador Extraordinary and Plenipotentiary, His Excellency General Rogelio Miranda Baldivia (1974).
Consulate, 106 Eccleston Mews, S.W.1.
1st Secretary, Srta. Marta Bosacoma Bonel.
Mining Attaché, Sr. H. Zannier.

There are Bolivian Consular Offices in *Liverpool, Birmingham* and *Hull.*
The Republic of Bolivia extends between lat. 10° and 23° S. and long. 57° 30' and 69° 45' W. It has an area estimated at 415,000 square miles with an estimated population (1970) of 4,658,000. (*For* MAP, *see* Index.) The Republic derives its name from its liberator, Simón Bolívar born 1783, died 1830).

The chief topographical feature is the great central plateau (65,000 square miles) over 500 miles in length, at an average altitude of 12,500 feet above sea level, between the two great chains of the Andes, which traverse the country from south to north, and contain, in Illampu, Illimani, and Sajama, three of the highest peaks of the western hemisphere. The total length of the navigable streams is about 12,000 miles, the principal rivers being the Itenez, Beni, Mamore and Madre de Dios.

President Barrientos, who had held office since his election on July 3, 1966, was killed in a helicopter accident on April 27, 1969, and in accordance with the Constitution was succeeded by Vice-President Dr. Luis Adolfo Siles Salinas. On Sept. 26, 1969, the armed forces overthrew the constitutional Government and set up a civilian-military government under the Presidency of General Ovando. On October 7, 1970, Gen. Torres assumed the

Presidency after defeating the right-wing military group which had overthrown the Government of Gen. Ovando only the day before, and held office until August 22, 1971.

A *coup d'état* occurred in August 1971, when, after reported heavy fighting, the President was ousted by Army leaders headed by Col. Hugo Banzer, Gen. Florentino Mendieta and Col. Andres Selich. Col. Banzer was proclaimed President in La Paz on Aug. 22, and subsequently formed a national front embracing the Armed Forces and the two leading political parties. However, the political parties have now been excluded, and no elections will be held until 1980.

Mining, petroleum and agriculture are the principal industries. The ancient silver mines of Potosí are now worked chiefly for tin, but gold, partly dug and partly washed, is obtained on the Eastern Cordillera of the Andes; the tin output is, after that of Malaysia, the largest in the world. Copper, antimony, lead, zinc, asbestos, wolfram, bismuth salt and sulphur are found, and petroleum is also produced.

The Republic is now a net oil exporter. Production of crude oil in 1975 totalled 14,500,000 barrels (of 42 U.S. gallons). The Bolivian Gulf Oil Company was nationalised on October 17, 1969, and shortly afterwards exports diminished (4,662,004 barrels in 1970 compared with 8,807,834 barrels in 1969). Exports rose in 1975 to 40,000 barrels per day. Bolivia's agricultural produce consists chiefly of rice, barley, oats, wheat, sugarcane, maize, cotton, indigo, rubber, cacao, potatoes, cinchona bark, medicinal herbs, brazil nuts, etc. The development of manufacturing industry progresses slowly. However, Bolivia has joined the Latin American Free Trade Area, and on May 26, 1969, signed the Andean Pact which is designed to secure economic integration and co-operation within the Andean Group of countries. Total Exports (F.O.B.) in 1975 were U.S. $500 million.

Transport and Communications.—There are 2,200 miles of railways in operation including the lines from Corumbá to Santa Cruz (405 miles) and from Yacuiba to Santa Cruz (312 miles). There are about 10,950 miles of telegraphs, and wireless services between Riberalta, La Paz, Cobija, Capitandi (Chaco). There is direct railway communication to the sea at Antofagasta (32 hours), Arica (10 hours), and Mollendo (2 days), and also to Buenos Aires (3½ days); branch lines run from Oruro to Cochabamba, and from Río Mulato to Potosí, and from Potosí to Sucre, the legal capital. The Antofagasta (Chile) and Bolivia Railroad was formerly an all-British concern, but the Bolivian sector has now been nationalised. Communication with Peru is effected by rail to Guaqui and thence by steamer across Lake Titicaca to the railhead at Puno.

Commercial aviation in Bolivia is conducted by Braniff International Airways (American), Lufthansa, Iberia, Aerolineas Argentinas, and Lloyd Aereo Boliviano (Bolivian), providing international connections with U.S.A., West coast South American countries, Canal Zone, Europe and Argentina; Lloyd Aereo Boliviano, maintaining a service to Lima, São Paulo, Buenos Aires, Arica and Miami, and attending to local flights, links La Paz with Oruro, Cochabamba, Santa Cruz and Trinidad, etc. and connects with LAN of Chile, Argentine Airlines and Cruzeiro do Sul of Brazil.

Bolivia is without a sea-coast, having been deprived of the ports of Tocopilla, Cobija, Mejillones and Antofagasta by the " Pacific War " of 1879–1884.

Language and Literature.—The official language of the country is Spanish, but many of the Indian inhabitants (about two-thirds of the population) speak Quechua or Aymará, the two linguistic groups being more or less equal in numbers.

The Roman Catholic religion was disestablished in 1961 but relations between it and the State are good. Elementary education is compulsory and free and there are secondary schools in urban centres. Provision is also made for higher education; in addition to St. Francisco Xavier's University at Sucre, founded in 1624, there are six other universities, the largest being the University of San Andres at La Paz. Bolivian literature has not yet produced authors of world-wide renown. There are twelve principal daily newspapers in Bolivia, with an estimated daily circulation of 150,000.

FINANCE

The Budget for 1974, which included State industrial organisations (except the State Mining Corporation) and local authorities, envisaged an expenditure of $b26,742,172,500 showing a small deficit of just over $b349,000,000.

The Bolivian currency, after remaining stable for 15 years at 12 pesos to the U.S. dollar, was devalued in October 1972; the new rate is 20 pesos. A stand-by credit of U.S. $30,000,000 was granted by the I.M.F. and a stabilisation programme set up to effect a faster rate of growth and a balancing of the National Budget. Exchange cross-rate b48·2 = £1 (1974) (*see also* p. 83).

Bolivia has benefited considerably from the high prices of basic materials, notably oil, gas and tin, and her foreign exchange earnings for 1974 were U.S. $560,000,000.

Trade with U.K.

	1974	1975
Imports from U.K....	£4,300,000	£5,279,000
Exports to U.K.......	9,700,000	19,007,000

The principal exports are tin ore (most of which is exported to the U.K.), oil and gas, lead and antimony ores, silver, copper, wolfram, zinc, gold, nuts, hides and skins, cotton and coffee. The chief imports are wheat and flour, iron and steel products, machinery, vehicles and textiles.

Seat of Government.—La Paz. Population (estimated 1970) 553,000. Other large centres are Cochabamba (149,000), Oruro (119,700), Santa Cruz (124,900), Potosí (96,800), Sucre, the legal capital and seat of the judiciary (84,900) and Tarija (35,700).

FLAG: Three horizontal bands; Red, yellow, green.

NATIONAL DAY.—August 6 (Independence Day).

BRITISH EMBASSY.

Casilla 694, La Paz.

Ambassador Extraordinary and Plenipotentiary, His Excellency Ronald Christopher Hope-Jones, C.M.G. (1973).

1st Secretary, M. S. Green (*Commercial and Head of Chancery*).

Defence Attaché, Captain D. L. G. James, R.N. (*resident in Lima, Peru*).

2nd Secretaries, Miss J. D. Robertson (*Aid and Information*); B. A. Barrett (*Administration and Consul*).

Attaché, H. Kershaw (*Commercial*).

BRITISH CONSULAR OFFICES

There are British Consular Offices at *La Paz* and *Cochabamba*.

BRAZIL

(The Federative Republic of Brazil)

President, General Ernesto Geisel, *born*, August 3, 1908; *appointed*, Jan. 15, 1974; *acceded*, March 15, 1974.

Vice-President, General Adalberto Pereira dos Santos.

MINISTRY
(Feb. 21, 1974)

External Relations, Sr. Antônio F. A. da Silveira.
Interior, Sr. Maurício Rangel Reis.
Finance, Sr. Mário E. Simonsen.
Justice, Sr. Armando Falcão.
Planning, Sr. João P. dos R. Velloso.
Mines and Energy, Sr. Shigeaki Ueki.
Education, Sen. Ney Braga.
Agriculture, Sr. Alysson Paulinelli.
Labour, Sr. Arnaldo da C. Prieto.
Communications, Cdr. Euclides Q. de Oliveira.
Health, Dr. Paulo de A. Machado
Industry and Trade, Sr. Severo F. Gomes.
Transport, Gen. Dirceu de A. Nogueira.
Air Force, Gen. Joelmir de A. Macedo.
Army, Gen. Silvio Coelho da Frota.
Navy, Adm. Geraldo de A. Henning.
Welfare and Social Assistance, Sr. Luis G. do Nascimento Silva.

BRAZILIAN EMBASSY IN LONDON
32 Green Street, W.1.
[01-629 0155]

Ambassador Extraordinary and Plenipotentiary, His Excellency Roberto de Oliveira Campos (1975).
Minister-Counsellor, Ronaldo Costa.
Naval Advisers, Vice Adm. J. G. T. A. de Aratanha; Rear-Admiral T. B. Reifschneider; Captain F. M. B. da Costa.
Minister, Marcello Raffaelli (*Economic Affairs*).
Minister, O. de A. Melo (*Consular*).
Air Attaché, Colonel J. L. M. de Fonseca.
Naval and Military Attaché, Capt. M. H. B. de Carvalho.
Consular Section, 6 Deanery Street, W.1 (01-499 7441).
Commercial Section, 15 Berkeley Street, W.1 (01-499 6706).

There are also a Brazilian Consulate-General at *Liverpool* and honorary consular offices at *Cardiff*, *Newcastle upon Tyne*, and *Glasgow*.

POSITION AND EXTENT

Brazil, the most extensive State of South America, discovered in 1500 by Pedro Alvares Cabral, Portuguese navigator, is bounded on the north by the Atlantic Ocean, the Guianas, Colombia and Venezuela; on the west by Peru, Bolivia, Paraguay, and Argentina; on the south by Uruguay; and on the east by the Atlantic Ocean. Brazil extends between lat. 5° 16′ N. and 33° 45′ S. and long. 34° 45′ and 73° 59′ 22″ W., being 2,685 miles from north to south, and 2,690 from west to east, with a coast-line on the Atlantic of 4,604 miles. The Republic comprises an area of 3,289,440 square miles, with a population (1975) of 107,145,168.

The northern States of Amazonas and Pará are mainly wide, low-lying, forest-clad plains. The central state of Mato Grosso is principally plateau land and the eastern and southern States are traversed by successive mountain ranges interspersed with fertile valleys. The principal ranges are *Serra do Mar* in São Paulo; the *Serra Geral* (Caparao 9,393 feet) between Minas Gerais and Espírito Santo, the *Serra da Mantiqueira* (Itatiaia, 9,163 feet) and the *Serra do Espinhaco* (Itacolumi, 5,748 feet), in the south-east of Minas Gerais; the *Serra do Paraná*, between Goiás and Minas Gerais, the *Serra dos Aimorés*, which divide Espírito Santo from Minas Gerais; and the *Serra do Gurgueia*, *Branca* and *Araripe*, which envelop Piaui.

Brazil is unequalled for its rivers. The River *Amazon* has tributaries which are themselves great rivers, and flows from the Peruvian Andes to the Atlantic, with a total length of some 4,000 miles. Its principal northern tributaries are the *Rio Branco*, *Rio Negro*, and *Japurá*; its southern tributaries are the *Juruá*, *Purus*, *Madeira* and *Tapajós*, while the *Xingú* meets it within 200 miles of its outflow into the Atlantic. The *Tocantins* and *Araguaia* flow northwards from the Plateau of Mato Grosso and the mountains of Goiás to the Gulf of Pará. The *Parnaiba* flows from the encircling mountains of Piaui into the Atlantic. The *São Francisco* rises in the South of Minas Gerais and traverses Bahia on is way to the eastern coast, between Alagoas and Sergipe. The *Paraguai*, rising in the south-west of Mato Grosso, flows through Paraguay to its confluence with the *Paraná*, which rises in the mountains of that name and divides Brazil from Paraguay. On the *Iguaçu or Iguassú*, which unites with the Upper Paraná at the Brazil-Argentine-Paraguay boundary, are the majestic *Falls of the Iguaçu* (200 ft.), and on the *São Francisco* are the no less famous falls of *Paulo Afonso* (260 ft.).

Government.—Brazil was colonized by Portugal in the early part of the sixteenth century, and in 1822 became an independent empire under Dom Pedro, son of the refugee King Joao VI. of Portugal. On Nov. 15, 1889, Dom Pedro II., second of the line, was dethroned and a republic was proclaimed.

In October 1969, Congress confirmed the appointment of General Emilio Media as President for five years. A series of amendments to the Constitution came into effect on October 30, which codified the powers assumed by the régime, and which laid down that subsequent Presidents should be elected by an electoral college; previously the President had been chosen by the military, and approved by Congress. In January 1974, 66 Senators, 310 Deputies, and 127 delegates from the State Legislatures elected General Ernesto Geisel, the candidate of the Government party, to succeed President Medici, whose term of office was due to expire in March 1974.

Production.—There are large and valuable mineral deposits including among others, iron ore (hematite), manganese, bauxite, beryllium, chrome, nickel, tungsten, cassiterite, lead, gold, monazite (containing rare earths and thorium) and zirconium. Diamonds and precious and semi-precious stones are also found. The mineral wealth is being exploited to an increasing extent. The iron ore deposits of Minas Gerais and the untapped ones of the Amazon region are particularly rich and plans for mining them are advanced. Production is increasing all the time.

In 1974 10,114,294 cubic metres of oil was produced; 7,504,000 tons of steel ingots and almost 23,000,000 cubic metres of refined petroleum (including refining of imported oil); 59,000,000 tons of iron ore were exported at a value of U.S.$571,000,000.

Total foreign private investment in Dec. 1974 was estimated at almost U.S.$6,027,000,000.

In 1974 the Brazilian automobile industry produced 858,500 vehicles.

The main exports of agricultural produce in 1974 were:

	Metric tons	Value U.S.$
Coffee	731,000	1,002,000,000
Sugar	2,249,000	1,259,000,000
Soya	4,754,000	888,000,000

Coffee is grown mainly in the States of São Paulo and Paraná and to a lesser extent in Minas Gerais and Espírito Santo.

Defence.—The peace-time strength of the Army is 180,000 of which some 70 per cent are doing military service, with an immediate reserve of 250,000. The Navy consists of 1 Aircraft Carrier, 14 Destroyers and Escorts, 8 Submarines, 6 Minesweepers, 6 Survey Vessels, 10 Corvettes (tugs), 45 other vessels and 3 helicopter squadrons. The strength of the Navy is 57,000 including 13,000 marines. The Air Force, with a strength of 44,000, including approximately 1,600 pilots and aircrew, has 650 aircraft and is the largest in South America.

Education.—*Primary* education is compulsory and is the responsibility of State governments and municipalities. At this level approximately 10 per cent. attend private schools. *Secondary* education is largely the responsibility of the State and Municipal Governments, although a small number of very old foundations (the Pedro II Schools) remain under direct Federal control. Over 50 per cent. of all pupils at this level attend Private Schools. Higher education is available in Federal State, Municipal and private universities and faculties.

Language and Literature.—Portuguese is the language of the country, but Italian, Spanish, German, Japanese and Arabic are spoken by immigrant minorities, and newspapers of considerable circulation are produced in those languages. English and French are currently spoken by educated Brazilians.

Until the second quarter of the nineteenth century Brazilian literature was dominated by Portugal. French influence is traceable for the next half century, since when a national school has come into existence and there are many modern authors of high standing. Public libraries have been established in urban centres and there is a flourishing national press with widely circulated daily and weekly newspapers.

Communications.—In 1973 there were about 30,394 kilometres of railways in service, largely of 1 metre gauge, but including 3,880 kilometres of other gauges. During 1974, the ports of Brazil were used by 31,331 vessels, shipping a total of 110,348,000 tons. There are 7,800 kilometres of navigable inland waterways.

Varig of Brazil and 11 foreign airlines operate services between Brazil and Europe, 3 between Brazil and U.S.A., and there are connections with all Latin American countries. Four major domestic airlines, as well as the Brazilian Air Force, maintain services throughout the country.

FINANCE

	1972 Cruzeiros '000	1973 Cruzeiros '000
Revenue	39,419,929	52,726,000
Expenditure	38,198,339	50,767,000

In Dec. 1974, Brazil's foreign debt stood at U.S. $16,100,000,000. Reserves in Feb. 1975 were $4,750,000,000. The rate of exchange in May 1975 was Cr $7·9 = U.S.$1.

TRADE (1975)

Total imports..............U.S.$12,260,000,000
Total exports..............U.S.$ 9,420,000,000

Trade with U.K. (1975)

Imports from U.K................£160,890,000
Exports to U.K..................   174,883,000

The principal imports in 1971 and 1972 were machinery and aircraft, foodstuffs, raw materials, oil and chemicals, and manufactured goods. Principal exports were coffee, manufactured goods, iron ore and other minerals, foodstuffs and fruits.

CAPITAL.—Brasilia (inaugurated on April 21, 1960). Population (estimated 1970), 544,862. Other important centres are São Paulo (5,901,553); the former capital Ψ Rio de Janeiro (4,296,782); Ψ Belo Horizonte (1,232,708); Ψ Recife (1,078,819); Ψ Salvador (1,000,647); Ψ Porto Alegre (885,567); and Ψ Fortaleza (842,231).

FLAG.—Green, with yellow lozenge in centre; blue sphere with white band and stars in centre of lozenge.

NATIONAL DAY.—September 7 (Independence Day).

BRITISH EMBASSY

Avenida das Nacóes, Lote 8, Brasilia, D.F.
Ambassador Extraordinary and Plenipotentiary, His Excellency Sir Derek Sherborne Lindsell Dodson, K.C.M.G., M.C. (1973)
Counsellors, L. Bevan(*Economic*); S. F. St. C. Duncan (*Political, Head of Chancery and Consul-General*).
Defence and Military Attaché, Col. P. J. L. Wickes.
Naval Attaché, Capt. G. M. A. James, R.N.
Air Attaché, Wing Cdr. J. Cheesbrough.

BRITISH CONSULAR OFFICES

There are British Consulates-General at Rio de Janeiro and São Paulo.

BRITISH COUNCIL.—*Representative in Brazil,* P. B. Naylor, P.O. Box 142336, Brasilia D.F. Regional Directors in *Rio de Janeiro, Curitiba, Recife* and *Sao Paulo.* Book supply to libraries of *Sociedade Brasiliera de Cultura Inglesa* at *Rio de Janeiro* and *Sao Paulo.*
BRITISH AND COMMONWEALTH CHAMBER OF COMMERCE IN SÃO PAULO, Rua Barão de Itapetininga 275, Caixa Postal 1621, São Paulo. (Correspondents at *Santos* and *Porto Alegre.*)

Rio de Janeiro, 5,750 miles distant from London: transit, 15 days.

BULGARIA
(Bulgariya)

COUNCIL OF STATE

Chairman of the Council of State, Todor Zhivkov, elected July 7, 1971; re-elected, June 1976 (*Head of State*).
First Deputy Chairmen, Petur Tanchev; Krustyu Trichkov.
Deputy Chairmen, Peko Takov; Georgi Djagarov; Mitko Gregorov.
Secretary, Nikola Manolov.
Chairman of the Committee for State and Popular Control, Krustyu Trichkov.

COUNCIL OF MINISTERS

Chairman and Prime Minister, Stanko Todorov.
First Deputy Prime Minister, Tano Tsolov.
Deputy Prime Ministers, Krustyu Trichkov (*Chairman of the Committee for State and People's Control*); Kiril Zarev (*Chairman of the State Planning Committee*); Mako Dakov; Anrei Lukanov.
Finance, Brlcho Belchev.
Interior, Dimiter Stoyanov.
Defence, Dobri Djurov.
Foreign Affairs, Peter Mladenov.

Education, Nencho Stanev.
Mineral Resources, Stamen Stamenov.
Supply and State Reserve, Nikolai Zhishev.
Power, Hikola Todoroev.
Chemical Industry, Georgi Pankov.
Machine Building and Metallurgy, Nikola Kalchev.
Electronics and Electro Technics, Yordan Mladenov.
Light Industry, Stoyan Zhulev.
Agriculture and Food Industry, Gancho Krastev.
Construction and Architecture, Grigor Stoichkov.
Transport, Vassil Tsanov.
Internal Trade and Services, Georgi Karamanev.
Foreign Trade, Ivan Nedev.
Forests and Forest Industry, Yanko Markov.
Communications, Pando Vanchev.
Health, Angel Todorov.
Justice, Svetla Daskalova.
Ambassador to the U.S.S.R., Dimiter Zhulev.
Chairmen of the Committees, Ludmila Zhivkova (*Art and Culture*); Nacho Papazov (*Science, Technical Progress and Higher Education*).
Chairman of the Bulgarian National Bank, Vesselin Nikiforov.

THE COMMUNIST PARTY

The Politbureau of the Central Committee, A. Lilov; B. Velchev; G. Filipov; I. Mihailov; P. Kubadinski; S. Todorov; T. Tsolov; T. Zhivkov; T. Dragoicheva (*full members*); K. Trichkov; P. Takov; D. Zhurov; D. Vulcheva; P. Mladenov; T. Stoichev (*candidate members*).
The Secretariat of the Central Committee, Todor Zhivkov (1st); B. Velchev; A. Lilov; I. Primov; G. Filipov; O. Doinov.

BULGARIAN EMBASSY AND CONSULATE IN LONDON
12 Queen's Gate Gardens, S.W.7.
[01-584 9400]
Ambassador Extraordinary and Plenipotentiary, His Excellency Vladimir Velchev (1976).
Counsellors, Ivan Moutafchiev; Petko H. Kassarov (*Commercial*); Ilia I. Iliev (*Economic*).
Military, Naval and Air Attaché, Lt-Col. Dimitar Petkov Toskov.
Deputy Commercial Counsellor, Genadi M. Pankin.
1st Secretary, Mladen Galabov.

The Republic of Bulgaria is bounded on the north by Rumania, on the west by Yugoslavia, on the east by the Black Sea, and on the south by Greece and Turkey. The total area is approximately 43,000 square miles, with a population in December, 1972 of 8,594,493. The largest religion of the Bulgarians is the Bulgarian Orthodox Church. The Gregorian (Western) Calendar is in use.

A Principality of Bulgaria was created by the *Treaty of Berlin* (July 13, 1878) and in 1885 Eastern Roumelia was added to the newly-created principailty. In 1908 the country was declared to be an independent kingdom, the area at that date being 37,202 square miles, with a population of 4,337,500. In 1912–13 a successful war of the *Balkan League* against Turkey increased the size of the kingdom, but in August, 1913, a short campaign against the remaining members of the League reduced the acquired area, and led to the surrender of Southern Dobrudja to Rumania. On Oct. 12, 1915, Bulgaria entered the War on the side of the Central Powers by declaring war on Serbia. She thus became involved in the defeats of 1918, and on Sept. 29, 1918, made an unconditional surrender to the Allied Powers. On Nov. 29, 1919, she signed the *Treaty of Neuilly*, which ceded to the Allies her Thracian territories (later handed over to Greece) and some territory on the western frontier to Yugoslavia.

Nazi troops entered the country on March 3, 1941, and occupied Black Sea ports, but Bulgaria was not officially at war with the Soviet Union. On August 26, 1944, the government declared Bulgaria to be " neutral in the Russo-German war " and delegates to Cairo sought terms of peace from Great Britain and the United States. The Soviet Union refused to recognize the so-called " neutrality " and called upon Bulgaria to declare war against Germany, and no satisfactory reply being received on Sept. 5, 1944, the U.S.S.R. declared war on Bulgaria. Bulgaria then asked for an armistice and on Sept. 7 declared war on Germany, hostilities with U.S.S.R. ending on Sept. 10. The armistice with the Allies was signed in Moscow, Oct. 28. On Sept. 9 a *coup d'état* gave power to the Fatherland Front, a coalition of Communists, Agrarians, Social Democrats and Republican officers and intellectuals. In August, 1945, the main body of Agrarians and Social Democrats left the Government. The Peace Treaty with Bulgaria was signed on Feb. 22, 1947, and came into force on Sept. 15, 1947. It recognized the return of Southern Dobrudja to Bulgaria.

On Sept. 8, 1946, a referendum was held, at which, according to the published results, an overwhelming majority declared for the abolition of the Monarchy and the setting up of a Republic. On Oct. 27, a general election to a Grand National Assembly (with power to make a constitution) was held; the Opposition won 101 seats out of 465.

On May 16, 1971 a referendum was held, at which a new Constitution was adopted. According to the Constitution the legislature is a single chamber National Assembly of *Subranie* elected by adult suffrage for a maximum term of 5 years and consisting of 400 deputies representing constituencies of equal size. The 1971 Constitution also established the Council of State, being the supreme permanent body of the National Assembly with both legislative and executive functions. The opposition Agrarian Party was suppressed in 1947, but its remnant was later revived as the Agrarian Union which now constitutionally shares power with the Communist Party.

Production.—Until 1939 Bulgaria was a predominantly agricultural country, but has since pursued an elaborate programme of industrialization. About 90 per cent. of the country's agriculture has been turned over to co-operatives, and a smaller proportion mechanized. The principal crops are wheat, maize, beet, tomatoes, tobacco, oleaginous seeds, fruit, vegetables and cotton. The livestock includes cattle, sheep, goats, pigs, horses, asses, mules and water buffaloes.

There is now a substantial engineering industry producing *inter alia* machine tools, electric trucks of all kinds, agricultural machinery, cranes, electric motors and electronic components, which accounts for about two-thirds of Bulgaria's exports; and considerable production of ferrous and non-ferrous metals. In 1975 production of electricity was 25,232 million kilowatt-hours, of steel 2,265,000 tons and of coal 28,920,000 tons (of which about one-quarter was soft coal).

There are mineral deposits of varying importance. Bulgaria's heavy industry includes the Kremilkovski Steel Plant near Sofia and the Lenin steel mill at Pernik, the chemical complex at Devnia, the petro-chemical plant at Bourgas with an annual capacity of 6 million tons of processed oil and various other chemical and metallurgical works situated around the country. The Soviet-designed nuclear power station at Kozodui will have four reactors, each with a capability of producing 800 million kilowatt/hours; at present in 1976 two are in operation.

Defence.—Under the Peace Treaty signed between Bulgaria and the Allies, the Bulgarian Army is limited to 55,000 men, but it is believed at present to be at least 152,000 strong.

Education.—Free basic education is compulsory for children from 7 to 15 years inclusive. The Bulgarian educational system was reorganized on Soviet lines in September, 1950, and in 1975 there were 7,553 kindergartens, and a total of 4,485 educational establishments for primary and secondary education including vocational, technical and other specialized schools for secondary age pupils. The total number of pupils attending these establishments was 1,529,857. There are three Universities (at Sofia, Plovdiv and Veliko Turnovo) and 21 higher educational establishments whose pupils total 106,055.

Language and Literature.—Bulgarian is a Southern Slavonic tongue, closely allied to Serbo-Croat and Russian (*see* U.S.S.R.) with local admixtures of modern Greek, Albanian and Turkish words. There is a modern literature chiefly educational and popular. The alphabet is Cyrillic. In 1967 there were 8 daily newspaper in Sofia.

Finance.—Estimated budget revenue for 1976 is 8,778,000,000 *levs*, expenditure 8,757,000,000 *levs*. Currency in Bulgaria is the *lev*. Rate of exchange (June 1976) was 1·65 *levs*= £1.

TRADE

The principal imports are industrial and agricultural machinery, industrial raw materials, machine tools, chemicals, dyestuffs, pharmaceuticals, rubber, paper. The principal exports are non ferrous metals, electric trucks and motors, pumps, ships, accumulators and machine tools, cereals, tobacco, fruit, vegetables, oil seeds, oils, fats, textiles, eggs, chemicals and oils including attar of roses. In 1975 80 per cent. of Bulgaria's foreign trade was with the Soviet bloc, including about 50 per cent. with the Soviet Union.

Trade with U.K.

	1974	1975
Imports from U.K.	£18,042,000	£23,610,000
Exports to U.K.	13,549,000	7,410,000

CAPITAL.—Sofia, Pop. (1975), 965,728, at the foot of the Vitosha Range, the capital and commercial centre is on the main railway line to Istanbul, 338 miles from the Black Sea port of Ψ Varna (251,588) and 125 miles from Lom (28,500), on the Danube; Ψ Bourgas (144,000) is also a Black Sea Port, those on the Danube being Ψ Rousse (163,012), Ψ Svishtov (18,537), Ψ Vidin (43,000). Other important trading and industrial centres are Plovdiv (309,242), Pleven (108,180),

Stara Zagora (122,200), Pernik (87,432), Sliven (90,000), Yambol (75,861), Haskovo (75,031) and Tolbukhin (86,184).

FLAG.—3 horizontal bands, white, green, red; national emblem on white stripe near hoist.

NATIONAL DAY.—Sept. 9 (Day of Freedom).

BRITISH EMBASSY

Residence, 65 Boulevard Tolbuhin, Sofia.

Ambassador Extraordinary and Plenipotentiary, His Excellency John Cecil Cloake (1976).

1st Secretaries, J. W. D. Gray (*Consul and Head* of *Chancery*); N. Holland (*Commercial*).

2nd Secretary, K. Q. F. Manning (*Cultural Attaché*).

Defence, Naval, Military and Air Attaché, Lt.-Col. J. B. Grosvenor.

3rd Secretaries, G. M. Johnson; Miss V. Lemon; M. Corbett.

BURMA

(The Socialist Republic of the Union of Burma)

Government of the Union

President, U Ne Win.

BURMESE EMBASSY AND CONSULATE

19A Charles St., Berkeley Square, W.1.

[01-499 8841]

Ambassador Extraordinary and Plenipotentiary, His Excellency U Tha Kyaw (1975).

Counsellor, U Maung Maung Gyi.

Military Attaché, Lt.-Col. Soe Myint.

Cultural Attaché, U Mg Mg Soe Tint.

2nd Secretary, U Soe Thinn.

Area and Population.—Burma forms the western portion of the Indo-Chinese district of the continent of Asia, lying between 9° 58′ and 28° N. latitude and 92° 11′ and 101° 9′ E. longitude, with an extreme length of approximately 1,200 miles and an extreme width of 575 miles. It has a sea coast on the Bay of Bengal to the south and west and a frontier with Bangladesh along the Naaf River, defined in 1964 by a Memorandum of Agreements, and India to the north-west defined in 1967, in the north and east the frontier with China was determined by a treaty with the People's Republic in October, 1960, and has since been demarcated; there is a short frontier with Laos in the east, while the long finger of Tenasserim stretches southward along the west coast of the Malay Peninsula, forming a frontier with Thailand to the east. (*For* MAP, *see* Index). The total area of the Union is about 262,000 square miles, with an officially estimated population of 30,834,000 in 1975—about 118 persons to the square mile.

Political Divisions.—The Socialist Republic of the Union of Burma is comprised of fourteen States and Divisions. Amongst the former are the Kachin State (34,000 sq. miles), Kayah State (4,500 sq. miles); Karen (formerly Kawthoolei) State (12,000 sq. miles), Chin State (14,000 sq. miles), Mon State, Arakan State and the Shan State (60,000 sq. miles).

Physical Features.—Burma falls into four natural divisions, Arakan (with the Chin Hills region) the Irrawaddy basin, the old Province of Tenasserim, including the Salween basin and extending southwards to the Burma-Siam peninsula, and the elevated plateau on the east made up of the Shan States. Mountains enclose Burma on three sides, the highest point being Hka-kabo Razi (19,296 ft.) in the northern Kachin hills. Mt. Popa, 4,981 ft., in the Myingyan district is an extinct volcano and a well-known landmark in Central Burma. The principal river systems are the Kaladan-Lemro in Arakan, the Irrawaddy-Chindwin and the Sittang in Central Burma, and the Salween which flows through the Shan Plateau.

Races, Language and Religions.—The indigenous inhabitants who entered Burma from the north and east are of similar racial types and speak languages of the Tibeto-Burman, Mon-Khmer and Thai groups. The three important non-indigenous elements are Indians, Chinese and those from the former East Pakistan. Numbers of resident foreigners have shown a sharp decline in recent years. Burmese is the official language, but minority languages include Shan, Karen, Chin, and the various Kachin dialects. English is still spoken in educated circles in Rangoon and elsewhere. Buddhism is the religion of 85 per cent. of the people, with 5 per cent. Animists, 4 per cent. Moslems, 4 per cent. Hindus and rather less than 3 per cent. Christians.

Government.—Burma became an independent republic outside the British Commonwealth on January 4, 1948, and remained a parliamentary democracy for 14 years.

On March 2, 1962 the army took power, and suspended the parliamentary Constitution. A Revolutionary Council of senior officers under General Ne Win took measures to create a Socialist State in accordance with their policy statement "The Burmese Way to Socialism". The Burmese Socialist Programme or Lanzin Party was founded to provide political leadership for the country.

In January 1974 a new Constitution was adopted after a national referendum. In February elections to the People's Asssembly and local councils were held. On March 2 the Revolutionary Council transferred power to the bodies elected under the new Constitution. The highest authority is the People's Assembly (450 representatives) which is expected to meet twice a year. When the Assembly is not in session the Council of State (29 members) is vested with wide powers. The senior executive body is the Council of Ministers. The Chairman of the Council of State (U Ne Win) is also President of the Socialist Republic of the Union of Burma.

Education.—The literacy rate is high compared with other Asian countries, there is no caste system and women engage freely in social intercourse and play an important part in agriculture and retail trade.

Under the University Education Law of 1964, the Government reorganized the higher education system to encourage the expansion of medical and technical studies. The two existing Universities (Rangoon and Mandalay) retain their separate role but decentralisation has enhanced their faculties (at present there are two Medical Institutes in Rangoon and one in Mandalay, and an Institute of Dental Medicine in Rangoon), two independent institutes for medicine, technology, agriculture, economics, education and veterinary science. Under the two Universities are colleges at Bassein, Moulmein, Magwe, Akyab, Taunggyi and Myitkyina and the Workers' College (Rangoon).

There are teachers' training colleges in Rangoon, Moulmein and Mandalay which train junior assistant teachers and 13 State Teachers Training Institutes for primary assistant teachers. The Institute of Education in Rangoon trains senior assistant teachers and awards degrees. There are five Government technical institutes at Insein (near Rangoon), Mandalay, Kalaw, Chauk and Prome. There are 6 technical high schools, 2 in Rangoon, 1 in Mandalay, 1 in Maymo, 1 in Taunggyi and 1 in Moulmein. British aid to Burma under the Colombo Plan amounts to some £300,000 annually, over half of this being devoted of technical assistance awards.

Finance.—The chief sources of revenue are profits on state trading, income-tax, customs duties, commercial taxes and excise duties; the chief heads of expenditure are general administration, defence, education, police and development. The budget estimates for 1976–7 were: Revenue, *K*15,923,200,000; Expenditure, *K*16,726,300,000. The monetary unit is the *Kyat* of 100 *Pyas*. (For rate of exchange, *see* p. 83.)

Production, Industry and Commerce.—Three-quarters of the population depend on agriculture; the chief products are rice, oilseeds (sesamum and groundnut), maize, millet, cotton, beans, wheat, grain, tea, sugarcane, Virginia and Burmese tobacco, jute and rubber. Rice has traditionally been the mainstay of Burma's economy but the poor harvest of 1972–73 and increased home consumption have greatly reduced the quantity of exported rice. Exports in 1975 amounted to 283,500 tons, including by-products.

The net area sown to all crops in 1975–76 was 23,490,000 acres and reserved forests covered 37,655 square miles. The principal export after rice is teak, of which some 200,000 tons were exported annually before the war. The 1975 figure was 88,400 cubic tons.

Burma is rich in minerals, including petroleum, lead, silver, tungsten, zinc, tin, wolfram and gem-stones. Of these, petroleum products are the most important. Oil is now being produced from oil-fields in Myanaung, Prome and Shwepyitha and at Chauk, Yenangyaung, Mann, and Letpando. Production of crude oil in 1975 totalled 236,131,000 gallons. There is a refinery at the main oilfield, Chauk, and another at Syriam near Rangoon. Their combined output of petroleum products is almost sufficient for most of Burma's needs. The production and distribution of petroleum and the importation of oil products is a monopoly of Myanna Oil Corporation (formerly Burmah Oil Company (1954), Ltd.) which is owned by the Government of Burma.

Under the Government's development plan, a cement plant, a brick and tile factory, a steel rolling mill, a jute bag and twine mill, four cotton spinning and weaving mills, a pharmaceutical plant, a large hydro-electric scheme, five sugar factories, a paper factory and a plywood factory are in operation. West German soft loans have been made available to finance construction of a glass factory, a fertilizer plant, a textile mill, a natural gas liquefying plant, a soda ash factory and a formaldehyde plant, as well as a seismic survey for crude oil sources and technical assistance in the general field of mineral exploitation.

The Japanese Government has approved a third commodity loan of US $22,000,000. Loans amounting to US $102,500,000 have been extended by the World Bank as follows: forestry, US $24 million; telecommunications US $21 million; railways, US $16.7 million; inland water transport, US $16.3 million; irrigation, US $17 million; livestock development, US $7.5 million. The Asian Development Bank has loaned US $41,600,000 for the fishing (US $9.8 million), rice products (US $6.5 million) and jute mill (US $25.3 million) industries. The UNDP Governing Council has approved US $35,000,000 towards the Second Country Programme for Burma covering 1974 to 1978, and consisting of 52 large scale and 25 small scale projects. British grants in 1975 were £2 million for equipment, spare parts and commodities and £1·9 million for on-shore oil exploration.

Burma joined the Colombo Plan in 1952 and is now receiving important assistance from member countries and through the specialized agencies of the United Nations.

Trade with U.K.

	1974	1975
Imports from U.K...	£4,366,000	£6,221,000
Exports to U.K.....	4,099,000	2,510,000

Communications.—The Irrawaddy and its chief tributary, the Chindwin, form important waterways, the main stream being navigable beyond Bhamo (900 miles from its mouth) and carrying much traffic.

Ψ The chief seaports are Rangoon, Moulmein, Akyab and Bassein. Transit from London to Rangoon: by sea, 35 days; by air, 16 hours.

The Burma Railways network covers 2,780 route miles, extending to Myitkyina, on the Upper Irrawaddy. The first diesel locomotives were introduced in 1958 and there are now 164 diesel locomotives in service, as well as 229 steam. There were 2,452 miles of Union highways and 11,429 miles of other main roads in 1975–76. Since the war a considerable network of internal air services has come into being. The airport at Mingaladon, about 13 miles north of Rangoon, has been reconstructed and handles international traffic.

CAPITAL.—The chief city of Lower Burma, and the seat of the government of the Union is Rangoon, on the left bank of the Rangoon river, about 21 miles from the sea. The city contains the Shwe Dagon pagoda, much venerated by Burmese Buddhists. Population (1973), 3,186,886.

Mandalay, the chief city of Upper Burma, had a population of 781,819 in 1973, Moulmein of 679,484 and Bassein of 335,588. Pagan, on the Irrawaddy, S.W. of Mandalay, contains many sacred buildings of interest to antiquaries.

FLAG.—The Union flag is red, with a canton of dark blue, inside which are a cogwheel and two rice ears surrounded by 14 white stars.

NATIONAL DAY.—January 4.

BRITISH EMBASSY
(80 Strand Road, Rangoon.)

Ambassador Extraordinary and Plenipotentiary, His Excellency Terence John O'Brien, C.M.G., M.C. (1974).

1st Secretaries, B. E. Pauncefort (*Head of Chancery and Consul*); T. K. Blackman (*Commercial*).

Defence and Military Attaché, Lt.-Col. J. D. F. Alexander.

2nd Secretary, J. A. Stevens.

BURUNDI
(Republic of Burundi)

President, Michel Micombero, *assumed office*, Nov. 28, 1966.

CABINET

Foreign Affairs, Melchior Bwakira.
National Orientation, Bernard Bizindavyi.
Interior, Joseph Rwuri.
Justice, Philippe Minani.
Economy and Finance, Gabriel Mpozagara.
Agriculture, Pierre Bigayimpunzi.
Public Service, Grégoire Barakamfitiye.
National Education and Culture, Artemon Simbananiye.
Public Works, Transport and Equipment, Edouard Nzambimana.
Social Affairs and Labour, Damien Barakamfitiye.
Public Health, Joseph Nindorera.

Formerly a Belgian trusteeship under the United Nations, Burundi was proclaimed an independent State on July 1, 1962. Situated on the east side of Lake Tanganyika, the State has an area of 10,747 sq. miles and a population (estimated, 1969) of 3,475,000. There are some 2,500 Europeans and 1,500 Asians. The majority of the population are of the Bahutu tribe, but power rests in the hands of the minority Batutsi tribe.

Burundi became independent as a Constitutional monarchy but this was overthrown on November 28, 1966. The Constitution and Parliament were also abolished. The President rules through a Cabinet of Ministers and the UPRONA party apparatus. Burundi is a one-Party State.

The chief crop is coffee, representing about 80 per cent. of Burundi's export earnings, some 87 per cent. of which is exported to the United States. Cotton is the second most important crop. Minerals and hides and skins exports are also important. Joint economic arrangements of Burundi with Rwanda ended in 1964 and each country now has its own national bank, coffee organization, etc.

Trade with U.K.

	1974	1975
Imports from U.K...	£964,000	£1,003,000
Exports to U.K.....	590,000	476,000

The currency is the Burundi *Franc*. The rate of exchange was *Bu. Fr.* 16c=£1 (July 1976). Government expenditure for 1972 was *Bu. Fr.* 2,400,000,000 and revenue the same.

CAPITAL.—Bujumbura (*formerly* Usumbura), with about 70,000 inhabitants. Gitega (7,000 inhabitants) is the only other sizeable town. Official languages are Kirundi, a Bantu language, and French. Kiswahili is also used.

FLAG.—White diagonal cross on green and red quarters, with a circular white panel in the centre.

NATIONAL DAY.—July 1.

British Ambassador, His Excellency Richard James Stratton, C.M.G. (1974) (*resident at* Kinshasa, Zaire).

CAMBODIA
(Democratic Cambodia)

President of the State Presidium, Khieu Samphan, *acceded*, April 11, 1976.
First Vice-President, Sau Phim.
Second Vice-President, Nhim Ros.

Prime Minister, Pol Pot. (replaced by Nuon Chea, Oct. '76).
Deputy Premiers, Ieng Sary (*Foreign Affairs*); Vorn Veth (*Economic Affairs*); Son Sen (*Defence*).
Information and Propaganda, Hou Nim.
Health, Thiounn Thioeunn.
Social Affairs, Ieng Thirith.
Public Works, Toch Phoeun.
Education and Culture, Yun Yat.

Area and Population.—Situated between Thailand and the south of Vietnam and extending from the border with Laos on the north to the Gulf of Thailand, Cambodia covers an area of some 70,000 square miles. It has a population (March, 1976) of 7,735,279. (*For* MAP, *see* Index.)

History.—Once a powerful kingdom, which, as the Khmer Empire, flourished between the tenth and fourteenth centuries, Cambodia became a French protectorate in 1863 and was granted independence within the French Union as an Associate State in 1949. Two years earlier Prince (then King) Norodom Sihanouk had promulgated a constitution providing for parliamentary government. Full independence was proclaimed on November 9, 1953. The Geneva Conference of 1954 took Cambodia further along the road to independence by ensuring the withdrawal of French and Vietminh forces from the country, and the process was completed when, in January, 1955, the Kingdom of Cambodia became financially and economically independent not only of France but also of Laos and Vietnam. For the next fifteen years the political life of the country was dominated by Prince Norodom Sihanouk, first as King, then as Head of Government after he had abdicated in favour of his father and finally (following his father's death in 1960) as Head of State. Although

the *Sangkum Reastr Nyum* or Popular Socialist Community, which he set up to embody his political views still won all the seats in the National Assembly elections of September, 1966, his initial popularity was, towards the end of the sixties, increasingly dimmed by criticism both of his management of the economy and of the pro-communist slant of the neutralist policy he proclaimed, which condoned extensive use of Cambodian territory by the North Vietnamese in their military operations against South Vietnam.

On March 18, 1970, during his absence from the country, Prince Sihanouk was deposed as Head of State by a vote of the National Assembly. A Republic was declared on October 9, 1970, and the name of the country changed to the Khmer Republic. A constitution was adopted by referendum on April 30, 1972 and Marshal Lon Nol elected President. A bicameral parliament was elected in September 1972. Prince Sihanouk however maintained a rival government-in-exile in Peking (Royal Government of National Union of Cambodia—GRUNC).

In April 1970 widespread fighting developed between communist Viet-Namese and Khmer forces which gradually developed into a general civil war with republican forces controlling the major centres of population and large areas of the country falling under the control of the Khmer Rouge supported by North Viet-Namese. With large-scale assistance from the United States the armed forces of the Republic were increased from 35,000 in 1970 to 250,000 in 1973.

In March 1973 a State of National Emergency was declared, various clauses of the constitution were suspended and a coalition " government of exception " formed under the premiership of In Tam. Following In Tam's resignation in December 1973, Long Boret, formerly Foreign Minister, was appointed Prime Minister.

In April 1975 Phnom Penh fell to the Khmer Rouge. Khieu Samphan ran the government and Prince Sihanouk returned to Cambodia on September 9, to resume his role as Head of State. However, a new Constitution was promulgated in Jan. 1976 and elections to a People's Representative Assembly were held in March. Prince Sihanouk resigned as Head of State in April, and when the Assembly met on April 11 Khieu Samphan was elected President of the State Presidium. A Government led by Pol Pot was appointed.

Geography, Economy and Communications.—Cambodia has an economy based on agriculture, fishing and forestry, the bulk of its people being rice-growing farmers living in the basins of the Mekong and Tonlé Sap rivers. In addition to rice, which is the staple crop, the major products are rubber, livestock, maize, timber, pepper, palm sugar, fresh and dried fish, kapok, beans, soya and tobacco. Rice and rubber used to be the main exports though rubber production was brought to a standstill by the hostilities, and rice exports ceased in 1972, the country becoming for the first time a substantial importer. Following the Khmer Rouge victory, the populations of Phnom-Penh and other towns were forcibly evacuated to the country to work on the land. It was announced that the 1975 rice crop amounted to 2,200,000 tons, which was twice the amount needed to feed the population for a year. Subsequently, when the roads and railways had been repaired after war damage, many more of the population were redeployed to work on the land, and re-establish the plantations producing such crops as cotton, rubber and bananas. Factories, in particular textile mills, iron smelting works and cement works were put back in production.

Fifty per cent. of the total land area is forest or

jungle, abounding in wild life of all kinds, including big game. The climate is tropical monsoon with a rainy season from May to October.

The country has over 5,000 kilometres of roads, of which nearly half are hard-surfaced and passable in the rainy season. There are two railways. One runs from Phnom-Penh to the Thai border; the other from Phnom-Penh to Kampot and on to Kompong Som. Phnom-Penh is on a river capable of receiving ships of up to 2,500 tons all the year round. The deep water port at Kompong Som on the Gulf of Thailand can receive ships up to 10,000 tons. The port is linked to Phnom-Penh by a modern highway.

Religion and Education.—The state religion was Buddhism of the " Little Vehicle ". The new constitution guaranteed religious freedom, but " reactionary religion which is detrimental to Democratic Cambodia and the Cambodian People " was forbidden. There are also small Muslim and Christian communities. The national language is Khmer. In the years preceding the civil war considerable efforts were devoted to the development of education and new schools, colleges and technical institutes had been established. Until April 1975 there was a Buddhist University in Phnom-Penh, where there were also Faculties of Arts, Medicine and Law and a Technological Institute. Several residential teachers' training colleges were in operation.

CAPITAL, Phnom-Penh.

FLAG.—Red, with a yellow three-towered temple in the middle.

NATIONAL DAY.—October 9.

BRITISH EMBASSY
96 Moha Vithei 9 Tola,
Phnom-Penh.
(Diplomatic relations were resumed in August, 1976.)

CAMEROON REPUBLIC
(United Republic of Cameroon)

President, Ahmadou Ahidjo, *elected for* 5 *years*, May 5, 1960; *re-elected for* 5 *years*, May 7, 1965; Mar. 20, 1970 and April 5, 1975.

CAMEROON EMBASSY
84 Holland Park, W.11.
[01–727 0771]

Ambassador Extraordinary and Plenipotentiary, His Excellency Michel Koss Epangué (1975).

2nd Counsellor, Nkuo Thaddeus.

1st Secretary, Francis Isidore Wainchom Nkwain.

The United Republic of Cameroon lies on the Gulf of Guinea between Nigeria to the west, Chad and the Central African Republic to the east and Congo and Gabon and Equatorial Guinea to the south. It has an area of 183,381 sq. miles (432,000 sq. km.) and a population estimated (1976) at about 7,000,000. Principal products are cocoa, coffee, bananas, cotton, timber, ground-nuts,

aluminium, rubber and palm products. There is an aluminium smelting plant at Edéa with an annual capacity of 50,000 tons. Annual trade of the United Republic is approximately, Exports, *FCFA* 107,000,000; Imports, *FCFA* 132,000,000.

Rate of Exchange, July 1975, 426 Francs CFA= £1 (floating).

Trade with U.K.

	1974	1975
Imports from U.K.	£6,253,000	£7,730,000
Exports to U.K.	3,043,000	5,377,000

The whole territory was administered by Germany from 1884 to 1916. From 1916 to 1959, the former East Cameroon was administered by France as a League of Nations (later U.N.) trusteeship. On Jan. 1, 1960 it became independent as the Republic of Cameroon. The Republic was joined on October 1, 1961, by the former British administered trust territory of the Southern Cameroons, after a plebiscite held under United Nations auspices. Cameroon became a Federal Republic governed by a President, Vice-President and 19 Federal Ministers, with separate East and West Cameroon state governments. Subsequently in a plebiscite held in May, 1972, there was an overwhelming vote in favour of the proposal that Cameroon should become a United Republic and on July 3, 1972, the President appointed the first government of the United Republic.

Cameroon is the only country in Africa where French and English are both official languages enjoying equal status, and the government's declared long-term objective is to achieve complete " bilingualism " and " biculturalism ".

Unlike in neighbouring Nigeria and Gabon, oil has not yet been discovered in commercially significant quantities. The main economic emphasis is on agricultural development, both through encouraging small-scale peasant agriculture, and through the development of large-scale agro-industrial complexes, with the aim of making the country agriculturally self-sufficient and a major food exporter.

CAPITAL.—Yaoundé (180,000).   Ψ Douala (250,000), is an important commercial centre.

FLAG.—Vertical stripes of green, red and yellow with two five-pointed stars in upper half of green band.

NATIONAL DAY.—January 1 (Independence Day).

BRITISH EMBASSY
Yaoundé

Ambassador Extraordinary and Plenipotentiary, His Excellency Albert Edward Saunders, C.M.G., O.B.E. (1975).

1st Secretary, J. K. Gordon (*Head of Chancery and Consul*).

2nd Secretaries, C. A. Gregg; D. Wyatt.

British Council Representative, H. F. Grant.

CAPE VERDE ISLANDS

President, Aristides Pereira *born* 1924, *assumed office*, July 5, 1975.

The Cape Verde Islands, off the west coast of Africa, consist of two groups of islands, *Windward* (Santa Antão, São Vicente, Santa Luzia, São Nicolau Boa Vista and Sal) and *Leeward* (Maio, São Tiago, Fogo and Brava) with a total area of 1,516 sq. miles and a population (1970) of 272,071. *Capital*, Ψ Praia (1970, 6,000).

The Islands colonised in c. 1460 achieved independence from Portugal on July 5, 1975, after the decision of the Armed Forces Movement to give up the Portuguese colonies. Elections for a constituent assembly were held on June 30. President Pereira favours an eventual political union of the islands with neighbouring Guinea-Bissau and Article 1

of the latter's constitution expresses a similar wish. (Till 1879 Guinea-Bissau and the Islands were a single administrative unit.)

CENTRAL AFRICAN REPUBLIC

President, Marshal Jean Bedel Bokassa, *assumed office* Jan. 1, 1966.

Formerly the French colony of Ubanghi Shari, the Republic lies just north of the Equator between the Cameroon Republic and the southern part of Sudan. It has a common boundary with the Republic of Chad in the north and with Zaire in the south. The Republic has an area of about 234,000 sq. miles and a population of 3,200,000 (est. 1975). On December 1, 1958, Ubanghi Shari elected to remain within the French Community and adopted the title of the Central African Republic. It became fully independent on August 17,1960. The first President of the Central African Republic, M. David Dacko, held office from 1960 until Jan. 1, 1966, when he was replaced by the then Col. Bokassa after a *coup d'état*. Imports from U.K. 1974, £342,000; Exports to U.K., £287,000.

CAPITAL.—Bangui, near the border with the Zaire (301,793).

FLAG.—Four horizontal stripes blue, white, yellow, green, crossed by central vertical red stripe; a yellow star in centre of blue half-stripe next staff.

CHAD REPUBLIC

Head of State, Gen. Felix Malloum, *assumed office*, May, 1975.

Situated in north-central Africa, the Chad Republic extends from 23° N. latitude to 7° N. latitude and is flanked by the Republics of Niger and Cameroon on the west, by Libya in the north, by the Sudan on the east and by the Central African Republic on the south. (*For MAP, see* Index.) It has an area of 487,920 sq. miles and a population now estimated at 4,000,000. Chad became a member state of the French Community on Nov. 28, 1958, and was proclaimed fully independent on August 11, 1960. On April 14, 1962, a new Constitution was adopted involving a presidential-type régime. Mr. Tombalbaye accepted the formal title of President on April 23, 1962. He was killed in the military coup on April 13, 1975.

Trade with U.K.

	1974	1975
Imports from U.K.	£209,000	£823,000
Exports to U.K.	1,378,000	15,000

CAPITAL.—Ndjaména (formerly known as Fort Lamy) south of Lake Chad (126,000).

FLAG.—Vertical stripes, blue, yellow and red.

CHILE
(República de Chile)

Head of State, General Augusto Pinochet (Ugarte), *born*, November 25, 1915, Army Commander-in-Chief and President of the Military Junta that took power on September 11, 1973.

Other Junta Members, Admiral José Toribio Merino (Castro), C.-in-C. Navy; General Gustavo Leigh (Guzmán), C.-in-C. Air Force; General César Mendoza (Durán), Director-General of Carabineros.

CABINET
Foreign Affairs, Vice Adm. Patricio Carvajal.
Interior, Gen. César Benavides.
Defence, Gen. Herman Brady Roche.
Education, Rear Adm. Arturo Troncoso Daroch.
Mines, Sr. Luis E. Valenzeuela Blanquier.

Finance, Sr. Jorge Cauás.
Economy, Sr. Sergio de-Castro Spikula.
Justice, Sr. Miguel Schweitzer Speisky.
Public Works, Sr. Hugo Leon Puelma.
Transport, Gen. Raúl Vargas Miguel.
Agriculture, Gen. Mario Mackay.
Land and Settlement, Gen. Lautaro Recabarren.
Labour, Sr. Sergio Fernandez Fernández.
Health, Gen. Fernando Matthey Aubel.
Housing, Sr. Carlos Granifo Harms.
Minister without Portfolio, Gen. Hernán Bejares
    González (*Secretary General to the Government*).

CHILEAN EMBASSY AND CONSULATE IN LONDON
    12 Devonshire Street, W.1
        [01–580 6392]
Ambassador Extraordinary and Plenipotentiary, His
    Excellency Admiral Kaare Olsen.
Minister-Counsellor, Sr. Carlos Bustos.
Counsellor, Sr. Fernando Cousiño (*Commercial*).
Naval Attaché, Rear Adm. Maurice Poisson.
Air Attaché, Col. Guillermo Kaempffer.
1st Secretary, Sr. Jaime Pardo.
3rd Secretaries, Sr. Jorge Montero; Sr. Miguel
    Poklepovic.
Asst. Naval Attaché, Cdr. John Howard.
Cultural and Press Attaché, Sr. Igor Entralá.
Civil Attaché, Sr. Guillermo Santa Cruz.

A State of South America, of Spanish origin,
lying between the Andes and the shores of the
South Pacific, extending coastwise from just north
of Arica to Cape Horn south, between lat. 17° 15′
and 55° 59′ S. and long. 66° 30′ and 75° 48′ W.
Extreme length of the country is about 2,800 miles,
with an average breadth, north of 41°, of 100 miles.
The great chain of the Andes runs along its eastern
limit, with a general elevation of 5,000 to 15,000 feet
above the level of the sea; but numerous summits
attain a greater height. The chain, however,
lowers considerably towards its southern extremity.
The Andes form a boundary with Argentina, and at
the head of the pass where the international road
from Chile to Argentina crosses the frontier, has
been erected a statue of *Christ the Redeemer,* 26 feet
high, made of bronze from old cannon, to commemorate the peaceful settlement of a boundary
dispute in 1902. There are no rivers of great size,
and none of them is of much service as a navigable
highway. In the north the country is arid. (*For*
MAP, *see* p. 815.)
    Among the island possessions of Chile are the
Juan Fernandez group (3 islands) about 360 miles
distant from Valparaiso, where a wireless station has
been erected. One of these islands is the reputed
scene of Alexander Selkirk's (Robinson Crusoe)
shipwreck. *Easter Island* (27° 8′ S. and 109° 28′
W.), about 2,000 miles distant in the South Pacific
Ocean, contains stone platforms and hundreds of
stone figures, the origin of which has not yet been
determined. The area of the island is about 45
sq. miles.
    Chile is divided into 25 provinces and 13 admini-
strative and economic regions and the total area
of the Republic is estimated at 290,000 square
miles, with a population (estimated, 1971) of
10,000,000. Two of these provinces, Arica and
Antofagasta, were annexed from Peru and Bolivia
respectively after the War of the Pacific (1879–84).
The province of Tacna was also annexed but under
a treaty signed in 1929 was returned to Peru which
at the same time received payment of £1,200,000 for
Arica. The Chilean population has four main
sources: (*a*) Spanish settlers and their descendants;
(*b*) indigenous Araucanian Indians, Fuegians, and
Changos; (*c*) mixed Spanish Indians; and (*d*) European immigrants. Only the few remaining
indigenous Indians and some originally Bolivian

Indians in the north are racially separate. Following extensive inter-marriage there is no effective
distinction among the remainder.
    Government.—Chile was discovered by Spanish
adventurers in the 16th century, and remained
under Spanish rule until 1810, when a revolutionary
war, culminating in the *Battle of Maipu* (April 5,
1818), achieved the independence of the nation.
Chilean women obtained equal voting rights with
men on Dec. 21, 1948, before which they only
participated in municipal elections
    At a general election held on Sept. 4, 1970, the
Marxist candidate Dr. Allende was elected President by a narrow margin. A new Cabinet took
office on Oct. 30, 1970.
    Severe industrial unrest, notably a crippling
strike by the National Confederation of Lorry
Owners, which began in July 1973, led to sym-
pathy strikes in other occupations; there were
widespread violent incidents and a congressional
vote of censure against the Government, with
resultant resignations from the Cabinet. The
Government of Dr. Salvador Allende was overthrown on September 11, 1973, by a *coup* planned,
and carried out within a few hours, by leaders of
the Armed Forces and National Police. President
Allende was said to have committed suicide.
    Although the Constitution of 1925 is still notion-
ally in force, the National Congress has been dissolved, all political parties have been banned, as have
all political activities. As a temporary expedient
the Government has assumed wide-ranging civil
powers. Inflation is still the main problem; revaluation of the Peso (against the U.S. $) takes place con-
tinuously, approximately in line with the variation
in the internal value of the currency (i.e. cost of
living index).
    Production.—Wheat, maize, barley, oats, beans,
peas, rice, lentils, wines, tobacco, hemp, chili-
pepper, potatoes, sugar beet, onions and melons
are grown extensively and livestock accounts for
nearly 40 per cent. of agricultural production.
The vine and all European fruit trees flourish in
the central zone and fruit is a fairly important
export item. Good wines are produced and
exported and are becoming more widely known in
world markets. Sheep farming predominates in
the extreme south (Province of Magallanes).
There are large timber tracts in the central and
southern zones of Chile, some types of which are
exported, along with wood derivatives such as
cellulose, to Europe and the Argentine and other
markets. The mineral wealth is considerable,
the country being particularly rich in copper-ore,
iron-ore and nitrate. Uranium is also said to have
been discovered in small quantities. Copper production in 1975 totalled 836,015 metric tons.
Copper provides over 70 per cent. of Chile's
exports earnings, the remainder of which are
derived mainly from other minerals, wool, fruit,
fish and forestry derivatives. The rainless north is
the scene of the only commercial production of
nitrate of soda (Chile saltpetre) from natural resources in the world. Production in 1975 (including potassium nitrate) was 726,449 metric tons.
Chile also produces iodine, manganese ore, coal,
mercury, molybdenum, zinc, lead and a small
quantity of gold. 1,459,854 metric tons of coal
were produced in 1975. The country has also large
deposits of high grade sulphur, but mostly around
high extinct volcanoes in the Andes Cordillera,
difficult of access. Production of refined sulphur
has hitherto been in relatively small quantities, but
reached 96,323 metric tons in 1972. Oil was struck
in Magallanes (Tierra del Fuego) in December,
1945. Production in 1975 was 1,422,200 cu. metres
of crude oil and 7,096,900,000 cu. metres of natural

gas—all in the Magallanes area. This total production, and imported crude oil, amounting in 1975 to about 75 per cent. of the input, is refined at Concon and San Vicente in the central part of the country. A large steel plant was completed and started operation during 1950 at Huachipato, near Concepción. Current production capacity is about 600,000 metric tons of steel ingots per year, to be increased to one million metric tons per year.

Most consumer goods are manufactured locally—copper, steel and oil derivatives, pulp and paper, cement and other building materials, tobacco, cutlery, food products and beverages, sugar refining, textiles, clothing and footwear, plastic products, household equipment, tyres and other rubber products, radio and television sets, chemicals, pharmaceutical products, soaps, detergents and cosmetics. New classes of manufacture being developed are in the fields of motor-vehicle assembly, chemicals and petrochemicals, cellulose, metallurgy and some electrical, electronic and mechanical equipment.

Communications.—Chilean ships have a virtual monopoly in the coastwide trade, though, with the improvement of the roads, an increasing share of internal transportation is moving by road and rail. Foreign trade continues to be carried on mostly by foreign steamship lines operating either directly to the West Coasts of North and South America, or *viâ* the Straits of Magellan. Chilean vessels have also been participating for many years in foreign trade with North America and Europe. The Chilean mercantile marine numbers about 63 vessels (of over 100 tons gross) with a total deadweight tonnage of 678,556 (1976). Under a law promulgated in June, 1956, 50 per cent. of Chile's foreign trade must be carried by Chilean vessels with the intention of this figure eventually reaching 100 per cent. of bulk and refrigerated cargoes.

The first railway was opened in 1851 and there are now 6,575 miles of track. A metre-gauge line (the *Longitudinál*) runs from La Calera, just north of Santiago, to Iquique. The wide gauge railway (1·676 metres) runs from Valparaiso through La Calera, 60 miles inland, and after passing through Santiago ends at Puerto Montt.

With the completion of a section of 435 miles from Corumba, Brazil, to Santa Cruz, Boliva, the Trans-Continental Line will link the Chilean Pacific port of Arica with Rio de Janeiro on the Atlantic. Another line from Antofagasta to Salta (Argentine) was opened in 1948. Further south, the Trans-Andine Railway connects Valparaiso on the Pacific with Buenos Aires, crossing the Andes at 11,500 ft.

Chile is served by 15 international airlines. The domestic traffic is carried almost exclusively by the State-owned Linea Aerea Nacional, which also operates internationally. Chile has an extensive system of airports which are being modernized with international financial assistance.

Chile's road system is about 65,000 kilometres in length, but only an estimated 7,000 kilometres are first-class paved highways. At the end of 1974 there were registered 216,122 cars, 15,682 buses and taxis and 166,308 goods vehicles, excluding about 15,000 tractors.

Defence.—Military service is compulsory, but not all those who are liable are required. Recruitment for the Navy is voluntary. The Army's total strength is 50,000, which includes 3,000 officers and 25,000 conscripts (2 years). In addition there is a police force of " Carabineros " of 30,000 officers and men. The Air Force has 800 officers and 8,700 other ranks with a strength of 200 aircraft. The Navy consists of 3 cruisers, 12 destroyers, frigates and escorts, some patrol vessels and FPBs and 3 sub-

marines. There is a support force of transports, tankers, 1 submarine depôt ship and ancillary small craft. The strength of the Navy is 1,000 officers and 14,000 men, plus a Marine Force of 60 officers and 2,000 men.

Education.—Elementary education is free, and has been compulsory since 1920. There are 8 Universities (3 in Santiago, 2 in Valparaiso, 1 in Antofagasta, 1 in Concepción and 1 in Valdivia). The religion is Roman Catholic.

Language and Literature.—Spanish is the language of the country, with admixtures of local words of Indian origin. Recent efforts have reduced illiteracy and have thus afforded access to the literature of Spain, to supplement the vigorous national output. The Nobel Prize for Literature was awarded in 1945 to Señorita Gabriela Mistral, for Chilean verse and prose, and in 1971 to the poet Pablo Neruda. There are over 100 newspapers and a large number of periodicals, including some devoted to professional, scientific and social subjects.

Finance.—Total revenue for 1975 was estimated at Pesos 18,725,666,000 and expenditure at Pesos 17,540,966,000. Foreign debt in December 1975 was estimated at some U.S. $4,802,000,000.

The official rate of exchange, (July 1976), was about Pesos ($) 23 = £1.

EXTERNAL TRADE
(Final figures)

	1974	1975
Total imports.	$U.S.2,178,400,000	1,811,000,000
Total exports .	2,043,400,000	1,548,000,000

Trade with U.K.

	1974	1975
Imports from U.K...	£36,878,000	£36,195,000
Exports to U.K....	86,516,000	62,091,000

The principal exports are metallic and non-metallic minerals (refined copper, ingots and bars, iron ore, etc.), wood derivatives, some metal products, fish products, vegetables, fruit and wool. The principal imports are wheat and other food products, industrial raw materials, machinery, equipment and spares, oil fuels, lubricants, transportation equipment and raw cotton.

CAPITAL, Santiago, 4,000,000 (Greater Santiago), Other large towns are:—Ψ Valparaiso (500,000), Concepción (170,000), Temuco (110,000), Ψ Antofagasta (110,000), Chillán (79,461), Ψ Talcahuano (75,643), Talca (75,354); Ψ Valdivia (70,000), Ψ Iquique (50,000), Ψ Punta Arenas (50,000). Punta Arenas, on the Straits of Magellan, is the southernmost city in the world.

FLAG.—2 horizontal bands, white, red; in top sixth a white star on blue square, next staff.

NATIONAL DAY.—September 18 (National Anniversary).

BRITISH EMBASSY.
Avenida La Concepción 177, Piso 4° Santiago (Casilla 72D)

Ambassador Extraordinary and Plenipotentiary (vacant).

1st *Secretaries*, D. K. Haskell (*Head of Chancery*); R. Bedford (*Commercial*).

Defence Attaché, Capt. S. K. Sutherland, R.N.

2nd *Secretaries*, A. W. Shave (*Commercial*); P. Langmead (*Information*); M. I. P. Webb (*Chancery*); A. J. Abbott (*Consul/AO*).

BRITISH CONSULAR OFFICES
There are British Consular Offices at *Santiago, Antofagasta, Arica, Valparaiso, Concepción, Coquimbo* and *Punta Arenas.*

BRITISH COUNCIL
Representative in Chile, Dr. V. A. Atkinson, Calle Eliodoro Yañez 832, Santiago (Casilla 154-D).

The Council supplies books to the libraries of the *Instituto Chileno-Britanico* in *Santiago* and in *Viña del Mar/Valparaiso.*

Valparaiso is distant from London 9,000 miles *viâ* Panama, and 11,000 *viâ* the Strait; transit 28 to 45 days; by air, 22 hrs.

CHINA

(Zhonghua Renmin Gongheguo— The People's Republic of China.)

Chairman of the Standing Committee of the Fourth National People's Congress (vacant).
Secretary-General of the Fourth NPC Standing Committee, Chi Peng-fei.
Premier, Hua Kuo-feng.
Vice-Premiers, Chang Chun-chiao; Li Hsien-nien; Chen Hsi-lien; Chi Teng-kuei; Hua Kuo-feng; Chen Yung-kuei; Wu Kuei-hsien; Wang Chen; Yu Chiu-li; Ku Mu; Sun Chien.

MINISTERS

Foreign Affairs, Chiao Kuan-hua.
National Defence, Yeh Chien-ying.
State Planning Commission, Yu Chiu-li.
State Capital Construction Commission, Ku Mu.
Foreign Trade, Li Chiang.
Economic Relations With Foreign Countries, Fang Yi.
Agriculture and Forestry, Sha Feng.
Metallurgical Industry, Chen Shao-kun.
Machine Building, Li Shui-ching, (*1st Ministry*); Liu Hsi-yao (*2nd*); Li Chi-tai (*3rd*); Wang Cheng (*4th*); Li Cheng-fang (*5th*); Pien Chiang (*6th*); Wang Yang (*7th*).
Coal Industry (vacant).
Petroleum and Chemical Industries, Kang Shih-en.
Water Conservancy and Power, Chien Cheng-ying.
Light Industry, Chien Chih-kuang.
Railways, (vacant).
Communications, Yeh Fei.
Posts and Telecommunications, Chung Fu-hsiang.
Finance, Chang Ching-fu.
Commerce, Fan Tzu-yu.
Culture, Yu Hui-yung.
Public Health, Liu Hsiang-ping.
Physical Culture and Sport, Chuang Tse-tung.

THE CHINESE COMMUNIST PARTY

Chairman of the Central Committee, (vacant).
First Vice Chairman of the Central Committee, Hua Kuo-feng.
Vice-Chairmen of the Central Committee, Wang Hung-wen; Yeh Chien-ying.
The Standing Committee of the Politbureau of the Central Committee, Wang Hung-wen; Yeh Chien-ying; Chang Chun-chiao.
The Politbureau, Wang Hung-wen; Wei Kuo-ching; Yeh Chien-ying; Liu Po-cheng; Chiang Ching; Hsu Shih-yu; Hua Kuo-feng; Chi Teng-kuei; Wu Teh; Wang Tung-hsing; Chen Yung-kuei; Chen Hsi-lien Li Hsien-nien; Li Te-sheng; Chang Chun-chiao; Yao Wen-yuan (*full members*); Wu Kuei-hsien; Su Chen-hua; Ni Chih-fu; Saifudin (*alternate members*).

EMBASSY IN LONDON
31 Portland Place, W.1
[01–636 5726]

Ambassador Extraordinary and Plenipotentiary, His Excellency Sung Chih-kuang.
Counsellors, Chu Chi-yuan; Peng Jun-min (*Commercial*); Hu Ting-yi; Ting Wen-pin.
Military, Naval and Air Attaché, Shih Hsin-Jen.
1st Secretaries, Hung Lung (*Consular*); Hou Ping-Lin; Lin Hsiang-ming; Chiang Ta; Shen Chao-chi (*Maritime*).
2nd Secretaries, Madame Hsieh Heng; Hu Nan-sheng; Sung Kuei-pao; Lei Wei-tsung; Wu Sheng-yuan; Chiang En-chu.

AREA AND POPULATION.—The area of China is about 3,700,000 square miles. Estimates of the present population vary considerably, but the U.N. estimate for 1974 gave a figure of 827,850,000. The Chinese also now make public reference to a population of 800,000,000. According to figures published in 1957 by the National Bureau of Statistics, the total population of China was 656,630,000, not including Chinese living in Hong Kong, Macau or abroad. A birth-rate of 32 per 1,000 and death rate of 17 per 1,000 were estimated for 1970. In 1953 the percentage distribution of the population was as follows:

Han, 94·13; Mongolian, 0·26; Tibetan, 0·48; Manchu, 0·41; Tribal, 3·57; Others, 1·15. There is no reason to suppose that the proportions have significantly changed.

THE PROVINCES OF CHINA.

Population figures made public in 1967–76 were as follows:

Anhwei	40,000,000
Chekiang	34,000,000
Chinghai	2,000,000
Fukien	18,000,000
Heilungkiang	25,000,000
Honan	60,000,000
Hopei	50,000,000
Hunan	38,000,000
Hupeh	38,000,000
Kansu	14,000,000
Kiangsi	28,000,000
Kiangsu	47,000,000
Kirin	20,000,000
Kwangsi Chuang Autonomous Region	24,000,000
Kwangtung	43,000,000
Kweichow	20,000,000
Liaoning	28,000,000
Inner Mongolian Autonomous Region	8,000,000
Ningsia Autonomous Region	2,000,000
Shansi	20,000,000
Shantung	57,000,000
Shensi	21,000,000
Sinkiang Uighur Autonomous Region	10,000,000
Szechuan	70,000,000
Tibet	1,000,000
(Taiwan)	16,050,000)
Yunnan	23,000,000

Sinkiang is the largest region or province in area (about 1/6th of the whole area of the country) and Szechuan the most populous.

Government.—On October 10, 1911, the party of reform forced the Imperial dynasty to a "voluntary" abdication, and a Republic was proclaimed at Wuchang.

On September 30, 1949, the Chinese People's Political Consultative Conference (C.P.P.C.C.) met in Peking and appointed the National People's Government Council under the Chairmanship of Mao Tse-tung. On October 1, Mao proclaimed the inauguration of the Chinese People's Republic. The Soviet Union broke off relations with the Nationalists and established relations with the new *régime* on October 2. The *régime* was recognized by all the Communist *bloc* countries in quick succession, and soon after by the Asian countries of the Commonwealth, the United Kingdom and by a number of other countries. France recognized the Chinese People's Republic on January 27, 1964. Canada agreed to recognize the People's Republic in October 1970. From 1970 to 1975 the Chinese People's Republic has established or renewed diplomatic relations with over 50 countries. The United States and certain other countries continue to recognize the Nationalist *régime* in Formosa.

The C.P.P.C.C. continued to be the supreme legislative body of the new state until September 20, 1954, when a new constitution was adopted. It was then replaced as the highest organ of state power by the National People's Congress which exercised legislative power.

With the adoption of the 1954 Constitution, the National People's Government Council was replaced by the State Council, composed of the Premier, 16 Vice-Premiers and the heads of ministries and commissions. This body was the supreme administrative body, responsible for the day-to-day running of the country.

In January 1975 a new Constitution was adopted by the Fourth National People's Congress, which established the leading role of the Chinese Communist Party in all spheres of national life. Institutions such as the National People's Congress and the State Council and the system of People's Congresses remain, but their powers are less clearly defined under the new Constitution, or are curtailed. The post of State Chairman has been abolished, and the Standing Committee of the National People's Congress now appears to act as a kind of collective Head of State. Among its powers is that of acting for the country in its dealings with foreign states, i.e. in the despatch and recall of Chinese representatives abroad and the reception of foreign diplomatic envoys. The National People's Congress, which is supposed to hold one session a year, is empowered to amend the Constitution, make laws, appoint and remove the Premier and members of the State Council on the recommendation of the Party Central Committee, and to approve the national economic plan, the state budget and the final state accounts. Command over the armed forces is now vested in the Chairman of the Chinese Communist Party.

The system of elections to local People's Congresses and to the National People's Congress is maintained under the new Constitution; but there is no reference to deputies to congresses at the primary level being " directly elected by the voters ". Deputies to congresses at all levels are now to be elected " through democratic consultation ". Deputies to the National People's Congress are, as before, elected by provinces, autonomous regions, municipalities directly under the Central Government and by the armed forces, but no longer by Chinese resident abroad.

Local government is now entrusted to local Revolutionary Committees. These bodies, which emerged during the Cultural Revolution to replace the former People's Councils, were firmly established under the new Constitution as the permanent organs of the local people's congresses by which they are elected and to which they are accountable, in each instance at the corresponding level. They are also accountable to the " organ of state at the next higher level " (this would appear to mean the people's congress at the next higher level).

Autonomous regions, prefectures and counties continue to exist for national minorities and are described as self-governing. The system prevailing is that found elsewhere, i.e. people's congresses and revolutionary committees. Peking, Shanghai and Tientsin continue to come directly under the central government.

It is only in the 1975 Constitution that the leading role of the Chinese Communist Party is spelt out; but its complete dominance over the Government, which includes " united-front " figures from lesser parties, has always been achieved by ensuring that all the really important positions at whatever level have been filled by Party members.

During the Cultural Revolution both Party and State organs were disrupted. The system of

" Revolutionary Committees " was devised to replace the People's Councils at provincial level and below. Party Committees have been reconstituted at all levels. The leadership in both Party and Revolutionary Committees is for the most part identical, thus providing for an interlocking relationship between the two bodies. Until April, 1959, Mao Tse-tung was Chairman both of the Republic and the Communist Party. When he stood down from his position as Head of State his place was taken by Liu Shao-ch'i who was then First Vice-Chairman of the Party. In October 1968, the Party's Central Committee resolved to strip Liu of all his posts both in the Party and in the State. The 10th Congress of the Chinese Communist Party was held in Peking from August 24 to 28, 1973. The Congress was unusual in several respects; the Party Constitution provides that congresses should normally be held every five years, and only four years had passed since the previous one; the Congress was unusually short, lasting only five days compared to 24 days for the ninth congress, and its also took place in unusual secrecy, no official announcement being made until after it had finished. It was stated that 1,249 delegates, representing 28,000,000 party members, attended. The agenda consisted of three items, adoption of the Central Committee's political report, which was presented by Chou En-lai, a report on the revision of the new party constitution adopted in 1969, presented by Wang Hung-wen and election of a new Central Committee of 195 full and 124 alternate members.

Armed Forces.—All three military arms in China are parts of the People's Liberation Army (P.L.A.) The size of this body has not been formally given, but it is estimated that China has between $2\frac{1}{2}$ and 3 million men under arms, with a further 12 million (or perhaps many more) reserves who take part in militia activities. Until 1955 the P.L.A. did not have a rank structure, but one was introduced in that year similar to that of the Russian Army. In the same year compulsory military service was introduced for all men between the ages of 18 and 40. This service was on a selective basis. In January, 1965, the length of service for those conscripted was increased by one year, to four years for the Army, five years for the Air Force and six years for the Navy; and with effect from June 1, 1965, the rank structure was abolished, together with all marks of distinction of branch of service (although members of the services may still be distinguished from one another by the colour of their uniforms). This means a reversion to the previous system by which members of the armed forces are known only by their appointment.

China exploded her first experimental nuclear device on October 16, 1964 and made further tests in 1965 and in May, October and December, 1966. Her first hydrogen bomb was tested in June, 1967, and further tests of nuclear devices were detected up to January, 1976. China launched her first earth-satellite in April, 1970, a second one in March, 1971 and others in July, November and December, 1975.

Religion.—The indigenous religions of China are Confucianism (which includes ancestor worship), Taoism (originally a philosophy rather than a religion) and, since its introduction in the first century of the Christian era, Buddhism. There are also Chinese Moslems and Christians. Since 1949, the practice of all religions has been severely curtailed, although not actually prohibited.

Education.—Although primary education was compulsory under the Nationalists, mass education did not become a fact until after the Communists had

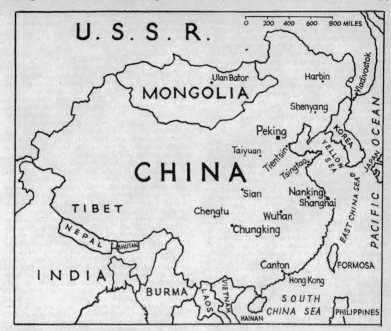

taken over. All major educational establishments closed down at the start of the Great Proletarian Cultural Revolution in 1966. Primary and middle school education was interrupted and it was announced that the entire education system was to be reformed. School classes are being resumed, and, among the reforms observable are a reduction in the number of years in primary and middle schools, and the application of the principle of part-work part-study. In the summer of 1970 some of the major institutes of higher education started to enrol new students, and courses started in the autumn. Students are being selected from among workers, peasants, soldiers and also middle-school graduates who have had two-three years experience of manual labour in factories or in the rural areas. The new courses are from 2-3 years duration.

Language and Literature.—The Chinese language has many dialects, Cantonese, Hakka, Swatow. Foochow, Wenchos, Ning-po and Wu (Shanghai). The Common Speech or *Putonghua* (often referred to as " Mandarin ") which is being taught throughout the country is based on the Peking dialect. The Communists, when they came into power, continued the Kuomintang policy of promoting it as the national language and made much more intensive efforts to propagate it throughout the country. Since the most important aspect of this policy is the use of the spoken language in writing, the old literary style of writing has fallen into disuse.

Chinese writing is ideographic and not phonetic. The number of sounds in *Putonghua* is strictly limited; each sound may have a large number of different characters and meanings. Whereas originally the language was monosyllabic and confusion was avoided by the use of different characters, thus producing texts which were visually clear but ambiguous to the ear, with the increasing use of the spoken language for writing people are increasingly making use of polysyllabic compounds both in speech and writing in order to avoid confusion. In 1956, after some 4 years of study, the Government decided to introduce 230 simplified characters with a view to making reading and writing easier. The list was enlarged; there are now about 1,000 simplified characters in use. In January, 1956, all Chinese newspapers and most books began to appear with the characters printed horizontally from left to right, instead of vertically reading from right to left, as previously.

In November 1957, after some experimentation, the Government introduced a system of Romanization, using 25 of the letters of the Latin alphabet (not v). This has been used within the country largely for assisting school children and others to learn the pronunciation of characters in *Putonghua*. It has been announced that there is no intention of using the alphabet to replace characters.

Although the pinyin system of romanisation of names was due to be brought into use from Sept. 1, 1975, it was announced in Peking on Aug. 27 that it would not then be introduced.

Chinese literature is one of the richest in the world. Paper has been employed for writing and printing for nearly 2,000 years. The Confucian classics which formed the basis of the traditional Chinese culture date from the Warring States period (4th–3rd centuries B.C.) as do the earliest texts of the rival tradition, Taoism. Histories, philosophical and scientific works, poetry, literary and art criticism, novels and romances survive from most periods. Many have been translated into

English. In the past all this considerable literature was available only to a very small class of *literati*, but with the spread of literacy in the 20th century, a process which has received enormous impetus since the Communists took over in 1950, the old traditional literature has been largely superseded by modern works of a popular kind and by the classics of Marxism and modern developments from them.

Three daily (and one monthly) newspapers are published in Peking of which the most important is the People's Daily, the organ of the Chinese Communist Party.

Currency.—The *yuan* was revalued with effect from March 1, 1955, on the basis 10,000 old *yuan* for one new *yuan*. (*See also* p. 83.)

Production and Industry.—China is essentially an agricultural and pastoral country: peasants constitute about 80 per cent. of the population. After the establishment of the Chinese People's Government at which time land for the most part was privately owned, there occurred several stages of land reform culminating in the formation of the people's communes in 1958. With the exception of a few State farms, the communes embrace the whole rural population. In all there are 74,000 communes and each is sub-divided into production brigades and teams. Work is assigned on a collective basis and the production team (of about 45 families) is the normal unit of accounting and labour. Wheat, barley, maize, millet and other cereals, with peas and beans, are grown in the northern provinces, and rice and sugar in the south. Rice is the staple food of the inhabitants. Cotton (mostly in valleys of the Yangtze and Yellow Rivers), tea (in the west and south), with hemp, jute and flax, are the most important crops.

Livestock is raised in large numbers. Silkworm culture is one of the oldest industries. Cottons, woollens and silks are manufactured in large quantities. The mineral wealth of the country is very great. Coal of excellent quality is produced. Iron ore, tin, antimony, wolfram, bismuth and molybdenum are also abundant. Oil is produced in Kansu, Sinkiang, Sining and three new major oilfields located in the northeast and east of the country. No reliable figures for industrial production have been published since 1959. The figures given below are those estimated for 1974.

Steel, 23,800,000 tons; Pig Iron, 31,500,000 tons; Coal, 389,000,000 tons; Electric Power, 108,000,000,000 kWh.; Crude oil, 65,300,000 tons; Cement, 31,600,000 tons; Timber 53,000,000 cubic metres; Chemical Fertilizers, 24,880,000 tons; Cotton Cloth, 7,600,000,000 metres; Motor Vehicles, 110,000 (1973); Machine Tools, 80,000 (1973).

Following the Great Leap Forward in 1958 and during three subsequent years of difficult conditions for agriculture, there was a cut back in both agricultural and industrial production which then recovered to its pre-1958 level. During the Cultural Revolution there was some economic dislocation. Industrial policy is governed by the need to build up agriculture, and some branches of industry, especially those such as machine tools and chemical fertilizers which have a direct relevance to agriculture have gone ahead more quickly. China is now self-sufficient in petrol and oil.

A new (third) Five Year Plan began in 1966. The Fourth Five Year Plan ran from 1971 to 1975; as with the Third Plan, no details of it were published, but it has been announced that it has been successfully completed. The Fifth Five Year Plan began in 1976.

The principal articles of export are animals and animal products; oils; textiles; ores, metals and tea. The principal imports are raw cotton, cotton yarn and thread; motor vehicles; machinery; chemical fertilizer plants; wheat; aircraft; books, paper and paper-making materials; chemicals; metals and ores; and dyes.

Trade with U.K.

	1974	1975
Imports from U.K.	£71,738,000	£80,368,000
Exports to U.K.	66,681,000	59,423,000

Communications.—Of the total area of China about half consists of tableland and mountainous areas where communications and travel are generally difficult. By 1949, the communications system, as a result of years of neglect and civil war, was more or less completely paralysed. In any case such roads and railways as did exist were largely confined to the eastern plains. After the Communists achieved complete control they devoted much attention to restoring and improving the communication system. By the end of 1958 the total length of railways was 19,000 miles (42 p.c. more than 1949), the total length of roads was 250,000 miles (about 5 times as much as in 1949) and of inland waterways about 100,000 miles (twice as much as 1949). In addition, internal civil aviation has been developed; routes total more than 20,000 miles. As a result the communications network now covers most of the country. In the past where roads did not exist the principal means of communications east to west was provided by the rivers, the most important of which are the Yangtze (3,400 miles long), the Yellow River (2,600 miles long) and the West River (1,650 miles long). These, together with the network of canals connecting them are still much used, but their overall importance is less than it was. In the past 10 years great progress has been made in developing postal services and telecommunications. It is now claimed that 95 p.c. of all rural communes are on the telephone and that postal routes reach practically every production brigade headquarters.

SPECIAL TERRITORY

Tibet, a plateau seldom lower than 10,000 feet, forms the northern frontier of India (boundary imperfectly demarcated), from Kashmir to Burma, but is separated therefrom by the Himalayas. The area is estimated at 463,000 square miles with a population (estimated, 1957) of 1,270,000.

From 1911 to 1950, Tibet was virtually an independent country but its status was never officially so defined. In October, 1950, Chinese Communist forces invaded Eastern Tibet. The Dalai Lama later left Lhasa and set up his Government at Yatung, near the Sikkim frontier. On May 23, 1951, an agreement was reached whereby the Chinese army was allowed entry into Tibet. A Communist military and administrative headquarters was set up. In 1954 the Government of India recognized that Tibet was an integral part of China, in return for the right to maintain trade and consular representation there.

A series of revolts against Chinese rule over several years culminated on March 17, 1959, in a rising in Lhasa. Heavy fighting continued for several days before the rebellion was suppressed by Chinese troops and military rule imposed. The Dalai Lama fled to India where he and his followers were granted political asylum. On May 4, the Indian Government announced that an estimated 9,000 Tibetans had entered India or the Himalayan hill states. On March 28, 1959, the Chinese Prime Minister issued an order dissolving the Tibetan Government. In its place the 16-member Preparatory Committee for the Tibetan Autonomous Region, originally set up in 1955 with the Dalai

Lama as Chairman, was to administer Tibet under the State Council. The Preparatory Committee was to have the Panchen Lama as Acting Chairman and also to include 4 Chinese Officials. Elections were held to choose local People's Congresses in Tibet, thus indicating that the government organization there no longer differed significantly from that of any ordinary province in China. The Dalai Lama, now exiled in India, announced a " new constitution " in March, 1963.

In December, 1964, the Dalai Lama, although absent, was declared to be a traitor, and both he and the Panchen Lama were dismissed. The position of Acting Chairman of the Preparatory Committee was assumed by Jigme, who had long been the most prominent secular figure in Tibet. This move marked the end of the period of co-operation by the Chinese Government with the traditional religious authorities, and the eclipse of the latter. The Preparatory Committee completed its work with the setting up of Tibet as an Autonomous Region of China on Sept. 9, 1965.

CAPITAL.—Peking, population (U.N. estimate, 1972), 7,570,000. The population of ΨShanghai was estimated at 10,820,000 (U.N. 1972); Nanking, 2,000,000 (Chinese est.); figures for the other principal towns are those for 1957; Tientsin, 3,220,000; Shenyang (Mukden), 2,411,000; Wuhan (*formerly* Hankow, Hanyang and Wuchang), 2,146,000; Chungking, 2,121,000; ΨCanton, 1,840,000; Harbin, 1,552,000; ΨPort Arthur (Lushun)/Dairen, 1,508,000; Sian, 1,310,000; ΨTsingtao, 1,121,000; Chengtu, 1,107,000; Tai-yuan, 1,020,000.

FLAG.—Red, with large gold five-point star and four small gold stars in crescent, all in upper quarter next staff.

NATIONAL DAY.—October 1 (Founding of People's Republic).

BRITISH EMBASSY
11 Kuang Hua Lu,
Chien Kuo Men Wai, Peking.
Ambassador, His Excellency Edward Youde, C.M.G., M.B.E. (1974).
Counsellors, N. M. Fenn (*Head of Chancery*); E. T. Davies (*Commercial*).
Defence Attaché, Col. P. J. L. Tustin.
1st Secretaries, R. R. Garside; R. E. Allen (*Commercial*); J. H. C. Gerson.
2nd Secretaries, W. H. H. Sanders; R. P. Margolis; R. J. Shaw; W. G. Ehrman.
Attachés, Miss P. Stones; A. J. Slater; G. W. Hawkes; D. H. Hugill; J. B. Cave; F. A. Doherty; D. A. McKellar; A. P. Nash.

FORMOSA
(Taiwan)

President, Dr. C. K. Yen (Yen Chia-kan), *sworn in*, April 6, 1975.
Premier, Gen. Chiang Ching-kuo (June 1, 1972).

An island of some 13,800 sq. miles in the China Sea, Formosa lies 90 miles east of the Chinese mainland in latitude 21° 45′ N.—25° 38′ N. The population (15,353,291 in March, 1973), is almost entirely Chinese in origin and includes about 2,000,000 mainlanders who came to the island with Chiang Kai-Shek in 1947–49. The territory of Formosa includes the Pescadores Islands (50 sq. miles), some 35 miles west of Formosa, as well as Quemoy (68 sq. miles) and Matsu (11 sq. miles) which are only a few miles from the mainland. Settled for centuries by the Chinese, the island has been known as Ryukyu and Taiwan. It was administered by Japan as a province from 1895 to 1945. General Chiang Kai-shek withdrew to Formosa in 1949, towards the end of the war against the Communist *régime* accompanied by 500,000 Nationalist troops,

since when the territory continued under his presidency. Gen. Chiang Kai-Shek died on April 5, 1975 and was succeeded by the Vice-President, Dr. C. K. Yen. A mutual defence treaty between the United States and Formosan Governments was signed in 1954.

The eastern part of the main island is mountainous and forest covered. Mt. Morrison (Yu Shan) (13,035 ft.) and Mt. Sylvia (Tzu'ukaoshan) (12,972 ft.) are the highest peaks. The western plains are watered by many rivers and the soil is very fertile, producing sugar, rice, tea, bananas, pineapples and tobacco. Coal, sulphur, iron, petroleum, copper and gold are mined. There are important fisheries. The principal seaports ΨKeelung (305,545) and ΨKaohsiung (724,222) are situated in the northern and southern sections of the island.

Trade with U.K.

	1974	1975
Imports from U.K...	£39,152,000	£33,829,000
Exports to U.K.....	66,663,000	73,045,000

CAPITAL.—Taipei (population March, 1973, 1,921,736). Other towns are ΨKaohsiung (915,035); Tainan (495,454); Taichung (490,992); and ΨKeelung (333,998).

FLAG.—Red, with blue quarter at top next staff, bearing a twelve-point white sun.

BRITISH CONSULATES
The British Consulate was withdrawn from Taiwan on March 31, 1972.

COLOMBIA
(República de Colombia)

President (1974–78), Alfonso López Michelsen, *elected* April 21, 1974; *assumed office*, August 7, 1974.

COLOMBIAN EMBASSY IN LONDON
3 Hans Crescent, S.W.1
[01–589 9177]
Ambassador Extraordinary and Plenipotentiary, His Excellency Alfredo Vázquez-Carrizosa (1975).
Counsellors, Srta. N. Millán; Dr. F. Corredor (*Economic*).
1st Secretary, Dr. A. Arango.
2nd Secretaries, Sra. B. de Perdomo; Dr. J. M. Santos (*Coffee Affairs*).
There are *Consulates-General* in *London* and *Liverpool*.

The Republic of Colombia lies in the extreme north-west of South America, having a coast-line on both the Atlantic and Pacific Oceans. It is situated between 4° 13′ S. to 12° 30′ N. lat. and 68° to 79° W. long., with an approximate area of 440,000 square miles, and a population (estimated 1973) of 23,500,000.

The Colombian coast was visited in 1502 by *Christopher Colombus*, and in 1536 a Spanish expedition under Jiménez de Quesada penetrated to the interior and established on the site of the present capital a government which continued under Spanish rule until the revolt of the Spanish-American colonies of 1811–1824. In 1819 *Simón Bolívar* (born 1783, died 1830) established the Republic of Colombia, consisting of the territories now known as Colombia, Panama, Venezuela and Ecuador. In 1829–1830 Venezuela and Ecuador withdrew from the association of provinces, and in 1831 the remaining territories were formed into the Republic of New Granada. In 1858 the name was changed to the Granadine Confederation and in 1861 to the United States of Colombia. In 1886 the present title was adopted. In 1903 Panama seceded from Colombia, and became a separate Republic.

There are three great ranges of the Andes, known as the Western, Central, and Eastern Cordilleras; the second contains the highest peaks, but the latter is the most important, as it consists of a series of vast tablelands, cool and healthy. This temperate region is the most densely peopled portion of the Republic. The highest mountain in Colombia is Cristobal Colon (18,946 feet) in the Sierra Nevada de Santa Marta on the Caribbean coast.

The principal rivers are the Magdalena, Guaviare, Cauca, Atrato, Caqueta, Putumayo and Patia. The Patia flows through the famous *Minima Gorge* of the Western Cordilleras, and one of its tributaries (the Carchi, or Upper Guiatara) is spanned by the Rumichaca Arch, or *Inca's Bridge*, of natural stone. On the Rio Bogotá is the great *Fall of Tequendama*, 482 ft. in height.

Government.—During the early nineteenth-fifties Colombia suffered a period of virtual civil war between the supporters of the traditional political parties, the Conservatives and the Liberals. The dictatorship of Gen. Rojas Pinilla (1953–57) put an end to the worst of the violence and on May 10, 1957, following Pinilla's summary dismissal, a military junta took over, preparing the way for a return to democratic government. Congressional elections were held on March 16, 1958, which yielded a Liberal majority. This led, the same year, to the institution of the National Front system, to run for a period of 16 years. The Presidency alternated every four years between the Liberals and Conservatives while parity of appointment was maintained between the two parties in Congress, the Government and all Government Departments.

During the presidency of Dr. Carlos Lleras (May, 1966 to April, 1970) the country made considerable economic advances, but the National Front system was nearly overthrown at the 1970 presidential election, when Gen. Rojas, with his political movement, the National Popular Alliance, almost defeated the Government candidate, Dr. Misael Pastrana.

In 1974 the first election not subject to the National Front system for the Presidency and Congress was won by the Liberal candidate, Alfonso Lopez Michelsen; parity in administrative appointments between the traditional parties will continue, however, until 1978.

Production.—The Colombian forests are extensive; among the trees are mahogany, cedar, fustic, and other dye-woods and medicinal plants. The mineral productions are emeralds, gold, silver, platinum, copper, iron, lead and coal. In 1975 the country was producing 156,000 barrels of oil per day after a peak production figure of 218,000 in 1970. Measures have recently been taken to encourage exploration for new reserves, but since early 1975 Colombia has exchanged its rôle of net-exporter for that of net-importer of crude oil. The principal agricultural products are coffee (which accounts for nearly 50 per cent. of total exports by value) cotton, bananas, rice, cocoa, sugar, tobacco, maize, cut flowers, wheat and other cereals. Manufactures (mainly for home consumption, but with an increasing export trade) consist of woollen, cotton and artificial silk textiles, leather goods, chemicals, asbestos-cement goods, many pharmaceutical products, rubber goods, including motor tyres, furniture, boots and shoes, confectionery cigarettes, beer, cement, glass containers and steel. The Government, backed by massive international finance and technical aid, has continued to encourage the development of new industries, including the local assembly and partial manufacture of motor vehicles, radio sets and office machinery. The importation of many consumer goods is restricted, although there has recently been a slight relaxation of controls.

Defence.—The Army peace effective strength is 41,000; war effective 300,000. The Navy consists of 4 destroyers, 4 frigates, 2 submarines, some gunboats and other small craft, with personnel about 5,000 including one battalion of marines; a battalion of the Colombian army and elements of the Navy served with the United Nations forces in Korea. The Air Force, with 4,000 personnel, has jet trainers and a front-line squadron equipped with Mirage fighters.

Communications.—The first railway was opened in 1855, about 1,914 miles being open in 1949. The "Atlantic Railway" running through the Magdalena Valley, which links the departmental lines running down to the river, and completes the connection between Bogota and Santa Marta, was opened in July, 1961. There are about 2,200 miles of rail in use at present. The total road network (1973) consists of 39,900 km. of roads of all types, of which 7,000 km. are classified as main trunk and transversal roads. A programme of road improvement and construction is under way, financed by a tax on petrol. The national telephone and telegraph system consists primarily of wireless links between the more important centres. Large appropriations have been made for modernization of the country's telecommunication system. There are daily passenger and cargo air services between Bogota and all the principal towns. There are daily services to other countries in South America, and services to London daily *via* Miami, *via* Paris and once a week by British Caledonian to London. Air mail is delivered to the United Kingdom 3 to 5 days after leaving Bogotá. There are wireless stations in the main cities, and a television station in Bogotá with relays to most parts of the country.

Roman Catholicism is the established religion.

Language and Literature.—Spanish is the language of the country and education has been free since 1870. Great efforts have been made in reducing illiteracy and it is estimated that about 60 per cent. of those over 10 years of age can read and write. In addition to the National University with headquarters at Bogotá there are 26 other universities. There is a flourishing press in urban areas and a national literature supplements the rich inheritance from the time of Spanish rule.

Finance.—For rate of exchange, *see* p. 83.

	1974	
	$U.S.	
Total imports (c.i.f.)	1,337,000,000	
Total exports (f.o.b.)	1,345,000,000	

Trade with U.K.

	1974	1975
Imports from U.K.	£24,213,000	£28,696,000
Exports to U.K.	12,458,000	24,096,000

CAPITAL, Bogotá, population (estimated, 1975) 3,200,000. Bogotá is an inland city in the Eastern Cordilleras, at an elevation of 8,600 to 9,000 ft. above sea level. Other centres are Medellin (1,100,000); Cali (950,000); Barranquilla (700,000); Bucaramanga (320,000); Manizales (300,000); Cucuta (230,000); Ψ Cartagena (340,000).

FLAG.—Broad yellow band in upper half, surmounting equal bands of blue and red.

NATIONAL DAY.—July 20 (National Independence Day).

BRITISH EMBASSY

Calle 38, No. 13–35, Bogotá.

Ambassador Extraordinary and Plenipotentiary, His Excellency Geoffrey Allan Crossley, C.M.G.

1st Secretaries R. B. Hervey (*Head of Chancery and Consul*); R. G. Osborn, M.B.E. (*Commercial*); Mrs. M. F. Das (*Technical Assistance*).

Defence Attaché, Lt.-Col. M. Liley.
2nd Secretaries, M. Leach (Commercial and Information); A. T. R. Oaten.
There are British Consular Offices at Bogotá, Barranquilla and Cali.
British Council Representative, R. S. Newberry, Calle 11, No. 5–16, Bogotá.

CONGO
(People's Republic of the Congo)
President of the PCT, Commandant Marien Ngouabi.
Prime Minister, Head of Government, President of the Committee for the Plan, Louis Sylvain Goma.

The Republic lies on the Equator between Gabon on the west and Zaire on the east, the River Congo and its tributary the Ubanghi forming most of the eastern boundary of the state. The Congo has a short Atlantic coastline. Area of the Republic of Congo is 129,960 sq. miles, with a population of approximately 2,100,000. Formerly the French colony of Middle Congo, it became a member state of the French Community on November 28, 1958, and was proclaimed fully independent on August 17, 1960.

M. Fulbert Youlou held office as President of the Republic from Aug. 7, 1960. Growing discontent with the régime culminated in riots in Brazzaville and led to the President's resignation on Aug. 15, 1963, and the dissolution by the Army of the National Assembly. A provisional Government led by M. Alphonse Massemba-Débat took office on Aug. 16, and a new constitution, giving the provisional Government full powers, came into operation in December, 1963.

On Jan. 12, 1968, the President dismissed the Prime Minister, M. Noumazalay, with three other members of his Cabinet and himself assumed office as Prime Minister with a reformed Ministry. He was himself arrested after heavy fighting during the last few days of August and resigned on Sept. 4 1968. Conduct of affairs was assumed by a National Council of Army officers.

Commandant Marien Ngouabi became President of the Republic on December 31, 1968. The Parti Congolais du Travail (PCT) was created by the Congress of December 29–31, 1969. The People's Republic of the Congo was established, and a new Constitution was promulgated. Following the Second Extraordinary Congress of the Party in December 1972, a new Constitution and a reorganization of the structures of the Party and the State were submitted to a people's referendum, in July 1973.

Trade with U.K.

	1974	1975
Imports from U.K...	£1,324,0000	£1,460,000
Exports to U.K....	5,266,000	6,765,000

Currency.—The Congolese currency is the CFA Franc, currently pegged to the French Franc at 1 CFA Franc=0·02 French Franc.
CAPITAL.—Brazzaville (156,000); ΨPointe Noire (76,000). FLAG.—Red, with hammer and sickle in centre.

BRITISH EMBASSY
Ambassador Extraordinary and Plenipotentiary, His Excellency Richard James Stratton, C.M.G. (1974). (Resident at Kinshasa, Zaire.)

COSTA RICA
(República de Costa Rica)
President (1974–78), Lic. Daniel Oduber Quirós, born 1923, elected February 8, 1974; assumed office, May 8, 1974.

COSTA RICAN EMBASSY
1 Culross St., W.1.
[01–286 7898]
Ambassador Extraordinary and Plenipotentiary, His Excellency Sr. Don Eduardo Echeverría-Villafranca (1974).
Minister-Counsellor, Sr. Julio Revollo Acosta (Economic and Consular).
2nd Secretary, Srta. Ana María Aranaz.

The Republic of Costa Rica, in Central America extends across the isthmus between 8° 17′ and 11° 10′ N. lat. and from 82° 30′ to 85° 45′ W. long., contains an area of 19,653 English sq. miles, and a population (estimated January, 1974) of 1,875,000. The population is basically of European stock, in which Costa Rica differs from most Latin American countries. The Republic lies between Nicaragua and Panama and between the Caribbean Sea and the Pacific Ocean.

For nearly three centuries (1530–1821) Costa Rica formed part of the Spanish-American dominions, the seat of government being at Cartago. In 1821 the country obtained its independence, although from 1824 to 1839 it was one of the United States of Central America.

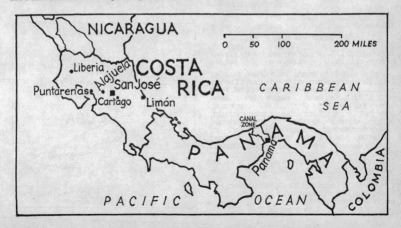

On Dec. 1, 1948, the Army was abolished, the President declaring it unnecessary, as the country loved peace.

The coastal lowlands by the Caribbean Sea and Pacific have a tropical climate but the interior plateau, with a mean elevation of 4,000 feet, enjoys a temperate climate. The capital is 103 miles from the Atlantic and 72 miles from the Pacific by rail.

The principal agricultural products are coffee (of a high quality), bananas, rice, maize, sugar-cane, potatoes, cocoa beans and hemp, the soil being extremely fertile. Increasing attention is being paid to cattle raising.

The chief ports are Ψ Limón, on the Atlantic coast, through which passes most of the coffee exported, and Ψ Puntarenas on the Pacific coast. A new Pacific port, Caldera, currently under construction with Japanese aid, is likely to divert traffic from Puntarenas in a few years.

Bananas are exported from Golfito, on the Pacific Coast, by the United Fruit Co., and from Limón by the Standard Fruit Co. In 1973, 1,605 ships entered at Costa Rican ports bringing in approximately 1,539,000 tons of goods. About 500 miles of railroad are open. The country is well provided with airways, and Pan-American Airways, Iberia, Viasa, TACA, SAHSA and COPA call at San José, while feeder services link the main centres of population with the capital. LACSA is the national airline with BAC-111 flights to Miami, Mexico, Central American capitals and Caracas, Barranquilla and Maracaibo in South America, besides internal flights to local airports.

Spanish is the language of the country. Education is compulsory and free. The literacy rate is the highest in Latin America. In post-war years there has been a big advance in the provision of social services.

GNP.—1975 $U.S. 1,000,000,000.

FINANCE

	1974	1975
	Colones, millions	
Revenue	2,020·5	2,501·4
Expenditure	2,416·0	3,073·0
Public Debt	3,351·0	—

Currency is the _colon_ of 100 _centimes_. Exchange rate in 1973 was C8·54= U.S. $1.

TRADE

	1974	1975
	$U.S., millions	
Total imports	·719·7	698·6
Total exports	440·3	487·7

Trade with U.K.

	1974	1975
Imports from U.K.	£7,025,000	£9,144,000
Exports to U.K.	1,085,000	8,946,000

The chief exports (1973) were coffee, bananas, meat, chemical products, sugar and cacao. The imports, 32 per cent. from U.S.A., 20 per cent. from other Central American Common Market countries, 7 per cent. from Germany and 10 per cent. from Japan, consisted of machinery, motor vehicles, bicycles, chemicals, textiles, fuel and lubricants, rubber manufactures, non-ferrous metals, etc.

CAPITAL, San José pop. (May 1973); 215,441; Alajuela (96,325); Ψ Puntarenas (65,562); Cartago (65,310); Ψ Limón (40,830); Heredia (36,487); Liberia (21,781). (Populations shown are of the Central Cantons of provincial capitals at May, 1973.)

FLAG.—Five horizontal bands, blue, white, red, white, blue (the red band twice the width of the others with emblem near staff).

NATIONAL DAY.—September 15.

BRITISH EMBASSY

3202 Paseo Colon, Apartado 10056, San José

Ambassador Extraordinary and Plenipotentiary and Consul-General, His Excellency Keith Hamylton Jones (1974).

1st Secretary and Consul, S. E. Warder (_Head of Chancery_).

Commercial Attaché, J. Coneso.

San José is 5,687 miles from London; sea transit direct 18 days; _via_ New York, 20 days; Air Mails (_via_ New York) 3 to 5 days from London. Ocean Mail, 8 to 16 weeks.

CUBA
(Republica de Cuba)

President, Dr. Osvaldo Dorticós Torrado, _appointed_ July 17, 1959.

COUNCIL OF MINISTERS

Prime Minister, Dr. Fidel Castro Ruz.

First Deputy Prime Minister and Minister for Armed Forces, Cdte de Div. Raúl Castro Ruz.

Deputy Prime Ministers, Cdte. de la Revolucion Ramiro Valdes Menendez; Cdte. de la Revolucion Guillermo Garcia Fria; Sr. Flavio Bravo Pardo; Sr. Belarmino Castilla Más; Sr. Diocleo Torralba González; Dr. Carlos Rafael Rodriguez; Sr. Joel Domenech Benitez.

Minister of Foreign Affairs, Dr. Raúl Roa Garcia.

Justice, Dr. Armando Torres Santrayill.

Interior, Sr. Sergio del Valle.

Communications, Sr. Pedro Guelmes González.

Foreign Trade, Sr. Marcelo Fernandez Font.

Internal Trade, Sr. Serafín Fernández Rodriguez.

Chemical Industry, Sr. Antonio Esquivel Yedra.

Mining and Geology, Sr. Manuel Cespedes Herrandez.

Sidero-Mechanic Industry, Sr. Lester Rodriguez Pérez.

Electricity Industry, Sr. José Luis Beltran Fernandez.

Light Industry, Sra. Nora Frometa Silva.

Public Health, Dr. José A. Gutiérrez Muñiz.

Education, Sr. José Fernandez Alvarez.

Labour, Sr. Oscar Fernandez Padilla.

Merchant Marine and Ports, Sr. Angel Joel Chaveco Morales.

Transport, Sr. Enrique Lussón Battle.

Sugar Industry, Ing. Marcos Lage Cuello.

Food Industry, Sr. José A. Naranjo Morales.

President, National Bank, Sr. Raúl León Torras.

Industrial Development, Ing. Angel Gomez Trueba.

Industrial Construction, Sr. Raciel Alvarez.

Social and Agriculture Buildings Development, Sr. Levi Farah Balmaseda.

Agricultural Development, Sr. Mario Oliva Perez.
Building Materials Industry, Sr. José Valle Roque.

CUBAN EMBASSY IN LONDON
57 Kensington Court, W.8
[01–937 8226]

Ambassador Extraordinary and Plenipotentiary, His Excellency Dr. Lionel Soto Prieto (1973).

Cuba (the largest of the " West India " Islands) lies between 74° and 85° W. long., and 19° and 23° N. lat., with a total area of 44,178 sq. miles and a population at the Census of 1970 of 8,553,395.

The island of Cuba was visited by Christopher Columbus during his first voyage, on October 27, 1492, and was then believed to be part of the Western mainland of India. Early in the 16th century the island was conquered by the Spaniards, to be used later as a base of operations for the conquest of Mexico and Central America, and for almost four centuries Cuba remained under a Spanish Captain-General. [The island was under British rule for one year, 1762–1763, when it was returned to Spain in exchange for Florida.] Separatist agitation culminated in the closing years of the 19th century in a fierce and blood-thirsty war. In 1898 the government of the United States intervened and despatched the battleship *Maine* to Havana harbour, where in February of that year the vessel was sunk by an explosion, the cause of which remains an unsolved mystery. On April 20, 1898, the U.S. Government demanded the evacuation of Cuba by the Spanish forces, and a short Spanish-American war led to the abandonment of the island, which was occupied by U.S. troops. From Jan. 1, 1899, to May 20, 1902, Cuba was under U.S. military rule, and reforms of the widest and most far-reaching character were instituted. On May 20, 1902, an autonomous government was inaugurated with an elected President, and a legislature of two houses. The island was, however, again the prey of revolution from Aug. to Sept., 1906, when the U.S. Government resumed control. On Jan. 28, 1909, a republican government was again inaugurated. In 1933 a revolution was followed by provisional government until May, 1936, when a constitutional government was elected. A new Constitution was promulgated in 1940, but its operation was suspended for various periods until February 24, 1955, when the Government elected on November 1, 1954, took office.

A revolution led by Dr. Fidel Castro overthrew the Government of General Batista on January 1, 1959. A provisional government was set up and elections were promised within four years. Dr. Castro has since proclaimed the revolution to be Socialist and himself to be a Marxist-Leninist.

In October, 1965, the Communist Party of Cuba was formed to succeed the United Party of the Socialist Revolution. It is the only authorized political party. Elections are no longer to be held. The First Congress of the Communist Party of Cuba was held in December 1975. The new Socialist Constitution came into force on February 24, 1976.

The Revolutionary Government has carried out programmes of land and urban reform and of nationalization of the means of production and distribution. By June, 1963, 90 per cent. of industrial production, all foreign trade and about 50 per cent. of small commercial companies were in state hands. In March, 1968, virtually all remaining private commercial enterprises were nationalised, About 70 per cent. of the cultivated land is in state farms or co-operatives. Private smallholders, who own the remainder, also come under a measure of Government control.

Although efforts are being made to diversify the economy, sugar is still its mainstay and Cuba's principal source of foreign exchange. It still accounts for some 80 per cent. in value of total Cuban exports. The largest sugar harvest ever was produced in 1969/70, when total production reached about 8,500,000 tons. This was achieved at considerable expense to the rest of the economy, however, and the declared target of 10 million tons, which was to have been reached in 1970, has been delayed. Cuba's other main exports are nickel, tobacco and rum, while increases are expected shortly in the availability of fish, meat and citrus fruit.

Despite increased trade with Western Europe and Japan, the Communist countries, particularly the Soviet Union, form Cuba's main trading partners, covering about 60 per cent. of imports and exports. In addition, the U.S.S.R. offers substantial aid from an imbalance in the annual trade profits in Cuba's favour which has recently been in the region of 250 to 350 million roubles.

11,915 miles of railway are open (public service 4,880; sugar plantations and mining areas 7,035) and about 12,000 miles of telegraph line. There are about 8,291 miles of road. At present scheduled international air services run to Mexico City, Moscow, Prague, Madrid, Rabat, Algiers, Georgetown, Kingston, Montreal, Panama, Lima, Berlin and Brussels.

Language and Literature.—Spanish is the language of the island, but English is widely understood. Education is compulsory and free. The University of Havana was founded in 1728, but until its enlargement under American auspices in the first quarter of the twentieth century no great progress was made in secondary or higher education. There are universities at Santiago de Cuba and Santa Clara. Public libraries have been established. The daily press and broadcasting and television are under the control of the Government.

Finance.—The public revenue rose from an estimated $365,247,946 in 1958 to $2,399,006,000 for 1964, including profits from State trading concerns, etc. No up-to-date figures are available for the public debt—at the end of 1958 this stood at $760,300,000.

Currency.—Average, Pesos 1·45 = £1, U.S. currency ceased to be legal tender in Cuba on June 30, 1951 (*see also* p. 83).

Trade.—Exports in 1973 were valued at Pesos 1,150·8m, compared with Pesos 770·9m, in 1972; imports, 1973, Pesos 1,390·6m (1972, Pesos 1,189·8m).

Trade with U.K.

	1974	1975
Imports from U.K.	£23,926,000	£36,977,000
Exports to U.K.	19,952,000	6,318,000

The exports are principally sugar and tobacco; the imports are mainly machinery.

CAPITAL, ψHavana (pop., Census 1970), 1,755,360; other towns are ψSantiago (292,251), Santa Clara (213,296), Camagüey (196,854), Holguín (183,115), and ψCienfuegos (164,061).

FLAG.—Five horizontal bands, blue and white (blue at top and bottom) with red triangle, close to staff, charged with 5-point white star.

NATIONAL DAY.—January 1 (Day of Liberation).

BRITISH EMBASSY
Edificio Bolivar, Capdevila No. 101,
e Morro y Prado, Apartado 1069, Havana.

Ambassador Extraordinary and Plenipotentiary, His Excellency John Edward Jackson (1975).

Counsellor, A. S. Papadopoulos, M.V.O., M.B.E. (*Head of Chancery*).

1st Secretary, M. W. Marshal (*Commercial and H.M. Consul*).

2nd Secretary, W. V. Fell (*Commercial*).

3rd Secretary, Miss P. J. Taylor.

Defence Attaché, Lt.-Col. B. D. O. Smith (*Resident at Mexico City*).
Attachés, G. W. Soden; A. Hay (*Administration and Vice-Consul*).
Vice-Consul, Miss M. L. Reid, M.B.E.

CZECHOSLOVAKIA
(Československá Socialistická Republika)
President, Gustáv Husák, *born* Jan. 10, 1913; *elected*, May 29, 1975.

Federal Government
Prime Minister, Lubomír Štrougal.
Deputy Prime Ministers, Petr Colotka; Václay Hůla; Josef Korčák; Karol Laco; Matej Lučan; Rudolf Rohlíček; Josef Šimon; Jindřich Zahradník.

Ministers
Agriculture and Food, (vacant).
Finance, Leopold Ler.
Foreign Affairs, Bohuslav Chňoupek.
Foreign Trade, Andrej Barčák.
Fuel and Power, Vlastimil Ehrenberger.
Interior, Jaromir Obzina.
Labour and Social Affairs, Michal Štancel.
Metallurgy and Heavy Engineering, Zdeněk Půček.
National Defence, Martin Dzúr.
Telecommunications, Vlastimil Chalupa.
Technical and Investment Development, Ladislav Šupka.
Transport, Vladimir Blažek.
People's Control, František Ondřich.
Prices, Michal Sabolčík.
General Engineering, Pavol Bahyl.
Deputy Chairman of State Planning Commission, Vladimir Janza.

_____

Prime Minister of the Czech Socialist Republic, Josef Korčák.
Prime Minister of the Slovak Socialist Republic, Dr. Petr Colotka.

CZECHOSLOVAK COMMUNIST PARTY
Presidium of the Central Committee, V. Bilak; P. Colotka; K. Hoffman; V. Hůla; G. Husák; A. Indra; A. Kapek; J. Kempny; J. Korčák; J. Lenárt; L. Štrougal (*full members*); M. Hruškovic; J. Baryl (*alternate members*).
Secretariat of the Central Committee, Gustáv Husák (*General Secretary*); J. Baryl; V. Bilak; J. Fojtík; J. Havlín; J. Kempny (*secretaries*); M. Kabrhelová; C. Lovětínský; J. Poledník; O. Švestka (*members*).

CZECHOSLOVAK EMBASSY
25 Kensington Palace Gardens, W.8.
[01–229 1255]

Ambassador Extraordinary and Plenipotentiary, Mečislav Jablonský (1974).
Minister-Counsellor, Dr. František Telička.
Commercial Counsellor, Martin Sakál.
Military and Air Attaché, Col. Miroslav Dvořák.
2nd Secretaries, František Pavlis; Jiří Novotný.
Commercial Attachés, Václav Levora; Josef Maruniak.
Assistant Military and Air Attachés, Col. Miroslav Merhaut; Maj. Gustav Opremčák.
3rd Secretaries, Jan Příkopa; Dr. Miloslav Ježil.
Attaché, Milan Pokorný.

Area and Population.—Czechoslovakia, formerly part of the Austro-Hungarian Monarchy, declared its independence on Oct. 28, 1918 (Czechoslovak Independence Day), the territory affected having an area of 53,700 square miles, reduced, by the cession of Ruthenia to U.S.S.R. in 1945, to 49,400 square miles. The population of Czechoslovakia was 14,686,255 in 1974.

Government.—The Communist Party, with the aid of Action Committees, seized power in Czechoslovakia in February, 1948, and Communist control of the country is now unqualified. On July 11, 1960, a new constitution was proclaimed, replacing that of 1948. Its purpose was to express the fact that Czechoslovakia is now deemed to have completed the construction of Socialism and to be on the road to true Communism. The official title of the State was accordingly changed to " The Czechoslovak Socialist Republic ".

In January, 1968, pressures for reform of the system were realized with the removal of the First Secretary of the Communist Party, Novotný, and his replacement by Alexander Dubček. They were translated into a Party Action Programme adopted in April. Shortly afterwards the country's supreme legislative body, the National Assembly, began work on new legislation, which envisaged the democratisation of the country's political life, greater guarantees of fundamental liberties and the establishment of a federal system.

The speed of events and their implications for the internal development of the other communist regimes in Eastern Europe and the Soviet Union, as well as for the system of alliances among these countries, alarmed the Soviet Union. On the night of August 20, Czechoslovakia was invaded by Soviet, Polish, East German, Hungarian and

Bulgarian troops, the capital and all major towns being occupied.

The Russians were unable to depose the Czechoslovak leadership, but forced them to sign on August 26 an Agreement modifying their policies and, on October 18, a treaty legalising the presence of Soviet troops on Czechoslovak territory.

On April 17, 1969, Gustáv Husák took over the leadership of the Communist Party, and the reforms of 1968 were abandoned with exception of the Federal system of government, which had been set up in October 1968. Czechoslovakia now consists of the Czech Socialist Republic and the Slovak Socialist Republic, each of which has its own government responsible to its legislative body—the National Council. Areas such as the Constitution, Defence, Foreign Affairs, State Material Reserves and Currency are the responsibility of the Federal Administration. The Federal Government is responsible to the Federal Assembly, which is composed of two Chambers, the Chamber of the People, whose duties are elected throughout the Federation, and the Chamber of the Nations, consisting of an equal number of Czech and Slovak Deputies. The federal system was not extended to the organization of the Communist Party.

The Economic System.—Czechoslovakia has long been one of the most highly-industrialised countries of Central Europe. Under the present political system industry is state-owned, while nearly all agricultural land is cultivated by state or co-operative farms. Economic planning is centralised, and state economic plans have the force of law. In 1965 the system was reformed to allow for a greater devolution of responsibility to enterprises and factories, and greater emphasis was placed on profitability and competition within a centrally planned economy. After the events of 1968-69 there was a sharp swing back to the present highly centralised system. There are at present no signs of substantial economic reform.

Language and Literature.—Czech and Slovak are the official languages, each having its own literature. The Reformation gave a wide-spread impulse to Czech literature, the writings of Jan Hus (who was martyred in 1415 as a religious and social reformer) familiarizing the people with Wyclif's teaching. This impulse endured to the close of the 17th century when Jan Amos Komensky or Comenius (1592-1670) was expelled from the country. He is still recognized as an outstanding educationist and a thinker of first magnitude. Under Austrian repression and with the persistent pursuit of Germanization, there was a period of stagnation until the national revival in the first half of the 19th century. Modern prose, drama and fiction, penned between the Wars, are represented by several authors, of international reputation, notably K. M. Capek-Chod (1860-1927), Viktor Dyk (1877-1931), Jaroslav Hašek (1883-1923) Karel, Čapek (1890-1938), Vladimír Vančura (1891-1942), and Ivan Olbracht (1882-1952). Liberty of the press ceased with the loss of independence and the Nazi occupation in 1939. It was temporarily restored on the liberation of the country. After the Communist take-over of February, 1948, however, freedom of the press was curtailed. All papers and periodicals were forced to follow the Party line and a number of publications were banned. Following the thaw of 1956 and after the relapse into dogmatism after the Hungarian Revolution, the new wave of freedom started in 1962-1963 and led to increased recognition of Czech and Slovak literature in the world. Greater international recognition is hampered by translation difficulties. In 1966 nearly 250 Czech and Slovak books were published abroad, including roughly one-third in non-Socialist

countries. The prominent writers include František Hrubín (b. 1910), Bohumil Hrabal (b. 1914), Václav Havel (b. 1936), Ladislav Mňačko (b. 1919), Ladislav Novomeský (b. 1904), Arnošt Lustig (b. 1926), Jiří Mucha (b. 1915), and others. Poetic writing ranges from traditional lyric (Jaroslav Seifert) to " concrete " and typographic modernism (Jiří Kolář, Josef Hiršal). In the present political conditions few of these writers are published in Czechoslovakia.

Education.—Education is compulsory and free for all children from the ages of 6 to 15. The number of pupils in basic nine-year schools is 1,890,081 (1973-74). There are 127,451 students in the secondary grammar schools and the number given for technical schools of all kinds is 277,945. There are five universities in Czechoslovakia of which the most famous is Charles University in Prague (founded 1348), the others being situated at Bratislava, Brno, Olomouc and Košice. In addition there are a considerable number of other institutions of university standing, technical colleges, agricultural colleges, etc. In 1973-74, there were 135,874 students in centres of higher education of which 23,811 were part-time.

Finance.—The Czechoslovak currency is the Czechoslovak *Koruna* (*Kčs*= Czechoslovak crown) of 100 *heller*. The present Czechoslovak rate of exchange is Kčs. 10·45= £1 (June 1976) with a bonus of 75 per cent. for non-commercial travellers (*see also* p. 83).

Trade with U.K.

	1974	1975
Imports from U.K...	£44,770,000	£51,210,000
Exports to U.K.....	55,400,000	59,090,000

CAPITAL, Prague (Praha), on the Vltava (Moldau), the former capital of Bohemia with a population (1973) of 1,091,449. Other towns are Brno (Brünn), capital of Moravia (353,866), Bratislava (Pressburg), capital of Slovakia (325,035), Ostrava (290,828), Košice (163,359) and Plzen (Pilsen) (153,119).

FLAG.—Two equal horizontal stripes, white (above) and red; a blue triangle next to staff.

NATIONAL DAY.—May 9.

BRITISH EMBASSY

Thunovská Ulice 14, Prague 1.

Ambassador Extraordinary and Plenipotentiary, His Excellency Edward Gervase Willan, C.M.G. (1974)
Counsellor, K. G. MacInnes (*Head of Chancery*).
Defence and Military Attaché, Col. P. F. Rodwell.
Air Attaché, Wing-Cdr. B. M. Burley.
1st Secretaries, B. Sparrow (*Commercial*); D. S. Broucher; G. M. Chittenden; R. E. Escritt (*Commercial*).
2nd Secretary (*Consul/AO*), P. H. Johnson.
3rd Secretaries, N. Carter (*Commercial*); B. M. Bennett (*Press*); L. Etheridge; G. Cleave.
Cultural Attaché, K. L. Pearson.

DENMARK
(Kongeriget Danmark)

Queen, Margrethe II, eldest daughter of King Frederik IX, *born* April 16, 1940, *succeeded* Jan. 14, 1972, *married* June 10, 1967, Count Henri de Monpezat (Prince Henrik of Denmark) and has issue Crown Prince Frederik *born* May 26, 1968; and Prince Joachim, *born* June 7, 1969.

CABINET

Prime Minister, Anker Jørgensen.
Foreign Affairs, K. B. Andersen.
Finance, Knud Heinesen.
Economic Affairs, Per Hækkerup.
Labour, Erling Dinesen.
Foreign Economic Affairs, Ivar Nørgaard.
Housing and Environment, Helge Nielsen.
Interior, Egon Jensen.

Public Works and Cultural Affairs, Niels Matthiasen.

Social Affairs, Eva Gredal.

Commerce, Erling Jensen.

Justice and Defence, Orla Møller.

Education, Ritt Bjerregaard.

Inland Revenue, Svend Jakobsen.

Ecclesiastical Affairs and Greenland, Jørgen Peder Hansen.

Agriculture and Fisheries, Poul Dalsager.

ROYAL DANISH EMBASSY IN LONDON
29 Pont Street, S.W.1
[01–584 0102]

Ambassador Extraordinary and Plenipotentiary, His Excellency Erling Kristiansen, G.C.V.O. (1964).

Minister Plenipotentiary, K. E. Willumsen, K.C.V.O.

1st Secretaries, E. H. Schmiegelow, M.V.O.; E. Hedegard.

Minister Plenipotentiary, Press and Culture, H. Agerbak, C.V.O.

Economic Counsellor, B. V. Blønd.

Agricultural Counsellor, M. Hermansen.

Defence Attaché, Col. H. H. Prince Georg of Denmark K.C.V.O.

Commercial Counsellor, J. Marcussen.

Area and Population.—A Kingdom of Northern Europe, consisting of the islands of Zeeland, Funen, Lolland, etc., the peninsula of Jutland, and the outlying island of Bornholm in the Baltic, the Faroes and Greenland. Denmark is situated between 54° 34'–57° 45' N. lat., and 8° 5'–15° E. 12' long., with an area of 17,000 square miles, and a population estimated (April 1975) of 5,054,909. In 1972 there were 75,505 live births, 50,445 deaths and 31,073 marriages.

Government.—Under the Constitution of the Kingdom of Denmark Act of June 5, 1953, the legislature consists of one chamber, the *Folketing*, of not more than 179 members, including 2 for the Faröes and 2 for Greenland. Voting age has been 18 since 1971.

A Social Democrat minority Government was formed in February 1975. The representation in the *Folketing* following the 1974 election was as follows; Social Democrats 53; Venstre 42; Progress Party 24; Radicals 13; Conservatives 10; Christian People's Party 9; Socialist People's Party 9; Communists 7; Centre Democrats 4; Left Socialists 4; Greenland 2; Faroes 2.

In 1973 Denmark joined the European Economic Community. Denmark is also a member of NATO, and the Nordic Council.

Education is free and compulsory, the schools being maintained by taxation. Special schools are numerous, technical and agricultural predominating. There are Universities at Copenhagen (founded in 1478), Aarhus (1933), Odense (1966), Roskilde (1972) and Aalborg (1974). A further University at Esbjerg is planned.

Language and Literature.—The Danish language is akin to Swedish and Norwegian. Danish literature, ancient and modern, embraces all forms of expression, familiar names being Hans Christian Andersen (1857–1875), Sören Kierkegaard (1813–1855) and Georg Brandes (1842–1927), with Henrik Pontoppidan (1857–1943) and Karl Gjellerup (1857–1919), who shared the Nobel Prize for Literature in 1917, and Johannes V. Jensen (1873–1950), who received the same award in 1944. Among recent authors of note are Klaus Rifbjerg (b. 1931) and Leif Panduro (b. 1923). Some 52 newspapers are published in Denmark. 10 daily papers are published in Copenhagen.

Production and Industry.—Nine per cent. of the labour force is engaged in agriculture, fishing, forestry, etc.; 35 per cent. in manufacturing, building and construction; 17 per cent. in commerce and 28 per cent. in administration, the liberal professions, etc. The chief agricultural products are pigs, cattle, dairy products, poultry and eggs, seeds, cereals and sugar beet; manufactures are mostly based on imported raw material but there are also considerable imports of finished goods.

COMMUNICATIONS.—Mercantile marine (ships above 100 gross tonnage) at end of 1972, 1,567 ships, with a gross tonnage of 4,069,017. On March 31, 1973, there were 2,522 km. of railway. In 1973 the capacity of the telecommunications network in circuit km. was 12,366,000.

FINANCE 1976–77
Revenue (*Budget estimate*)..... Kr. 67,000,000,000
Expenditure (*Budget estimate*).. 79,300,000,000

Denmark's balance of payments on current account showed a deficit for 1975 of Kr. 3,050,000,000 (1974, Kr. 5,755,000,000).

Rate of Exchange.—Kr. 10·80–11·00 = £1 (floating) (June 1976) (*see also* p. 83).

TRADE

	1974	1975
	Kr. million	
Total Imports..............	60,138	59,491
Total Exports..............	46,915	50,053

Trade with U.K.

	1974	1975
Imports from U.K..	£427,074,000	£443,122,000
Exports to U.K.....	577,115,000	621,704,000

The principal imports are petroleum and its products, machinery, vehicles and textile products. The chief exports are agricultural produce, fish products, butter, bacon, eggs, meat and livestock and machinery.

CAPITAL, Ψ Copenhagen, pop. (1970), 802,226; Greater Copenhagen, 1,380,118. Other centres are: ΨAarhus, 198,980; Ψ Odense 137,288; ΨAalborg, 100,255; ΨEsbjerg, 68,085; ΨRanders, 58,411; Roskilde, 44,245; ΨKolding, 41,612; ΨHorsens, 44,121; ΨFredericia, 36,154; ΨVejle, 43,876.

FLAG.—Red, with white cross

NATIONAL DAY.—June 5 (Constitution Day).

Copenhagen, distant from London 728 miles; transit 26 hours by rail and sea.

BRITISH EMBASSY
Offices, Kastelsvej 36–40, Copenhagen.

Residence, Bredgade 26, Copenhagen.

Ambassador Extraordinary and Plenipotentiary, Her Excellency Anne Marion Warburton, C.V.O. (1976).

Counsellor, R. J. T. McLaren.

Counsellor (Commercial), G. L. Simmons, M.V.O.

Defence, Naval, Military and Air Attaché, Cdr. D. Monsell, R.N.

1st Secretaries, J. P. Davies; W. E. W. Mattey (*Administration and H.M. Consul*); F. S. Napier (*Information*); J. R. Cowling (*Commercial*); P. S. Astley; G. L. Jones (*Agric. and Fisheries*); C. Marshall (*Labour*) (*resident in Stockholm*).

Asst. Military Attaché, Major R. N. L. Denyer.

Asst. Air Attaché, Sqn. Ldr. C. P. Russell-Smith.

2nd Secretaries, D. G. Parker (*Commercial*); D. A. Rogers.

Attachés, Miss P. A. Terry (*Consular*); Miss B. Brett-Rooks (*Commercial*).

Chaplain, Rev. D. H. T. Picton.

There are Consulates at *Aabenraa*, *Aalborg*, *Esbjerg*, *Aarhus* and *Odense*; and at *Thorshavn* and *Klaksvig* (Faröes).

———

British Council Representative and Cultural Attaché, D. B. Pickersgill, Montergade 1, Copenhagen.

Outlying Parts of the Kingdom

The outlying parts of Denmark have about 81,000 inhabitants. The FARÖES, or Sheep Islands (540 sq. m.; pop. (1969) 38,000), capital, Thorshavn, are governed by a *Lagting* of 26 members, a *Landstyr* of 4 members which deals with special Faröes affairs, and send 2 representatives to the *Folketing* at Copenhagen. On Sept. 14, 1946, the *Lagting*, with the consent of the Danish Government, for its own guidance held a plebiscite on the Faröes. About one-third of the electors did not, however, take part in the voting: of the rest a little more than half the votes cast were in favour of separation from Denmark and the establishment of a republic. At subsequent general election for the *Lagtime* a great majority voted in favour of remaining part of the Kingdom of Denmark with a certain measure of home rule and in 1948 the Faröes received this. GREENLAND (ice-free portion about 132,000 sq. m., total area about 840,000 sq. m., population, 1965, 48,792) is divided into 3 provinces (West, North and East). Greenland (capital, Godthaab) has a *Landsraad* of 17 members and sends 2 representatives to the *Folketing* at Copenhagen. The trade of Greenland is mainly under the management of the Royal Greenland Trade Department. Mineral and oil prospecting revealed deposits of lead, zinc, iron ore, oil and gas. Commercial exploitation of these resources has not yet begun. The United States of America has acquired certain rights to maintain air bases in Greenland.

DOMINICAN REPUBLIC
(República Dominicana)

President, Joaquin Balaguer, *born* Sept. 1, 1907; *elected* June 1, 1966; *re-elected* May 16, 1970; *re-elected*, May 16, 1974.

EMBASSY AND CONSULATE

4 Braemar Mansions, Cornwall Gardens, S.W.7
[01–937 1921]

Ambassador Extraordinary and Plenipotentiary, His Excellency Alfredo A. Ricart (1975).

Cultural Attaché, Mrs. N. Barletta.

There are also Consular Offices at *Liverpool*, *Birmingham*, *Manchester*, *Nottingham*, *Grimsby*, *Southampton*, *Plymouth*, *Cardiff*, *Edinburgh*, *Glasgow* and *Belfast*.

The Dominican Republic, formerly the Spanish portion of the island of Hispaniola, is the oldest settlement of European origin in America. The western part of the island forms the Republic of Haiti. (*For Map, see* p. 870.)

The island lies between Cuba on the west and Puerto Rico on the east and the Republic covers an area of about 19,322 square miles, with a population (U.N. estimate, 1970) of 4,012,000. The climate is tropical in the low lands and semi-tropical to temperate in the higher altitudes.

Government.—Santo Domingo was discovered by Christopher Columbus in December, 1492, and remained a Spanish Colony until 1821. In 1822 it was subjugated by the neighbouring Haitians who remained in control until 1844 when the Dominican Republic was proclaimed. The country was occupied by American marines from 1916 until the adoption of a new Constitution in 1924. In July, 1924, a properly elected Constitutional Government was installed. From 1930 until May 30, 1961 (when he was assassinated) Generalissimo Rafael Trujillo ruled the country.

A Council of State headed by Rafael F. Bonnelly was set up in 1962, and Professor Juan Bosch, elected President in December 1962, held office until September, 1963, when he was deposed by a military junta. A revolt in favour of ex-President Bosch in April, 1965, developed into civil war lasting until September the same year when a provisional President was elected. At a further election on June 1, 1966, Dr. Joaquin Balaguer was elected President; re-elected May 16, 1970 and again on May 16, 1974.

Communications.—According to local classification there are 2,932 miles of first class and 1,392 miles of second class and inter-communal roads in the Republic. There is a direct road from Santo Domingo to Port-au-Prince, the capital of Haiti, but that part of it in the border area has fallen into disuse and although road travel is possible, it is preferable to travel direct between the two capitals by air. The frontier has been closed since Sept., 1967, except for that section crossed by the main road linking the two capitals. A telephone system connects practically all the principal towns of the republic and there is a telegraph service with all parts of the world. There are more than 90 commercial broadcasting stations and there is a television station operated by Radiotelevision Dominicana, which with the help of relay stations provides receptions of its programmes in the major cities. Three other television stations in Santo Domingo—Rahintel, Tele-Inde and Color-Vision —transmit to the local area.

Spanish is the language of the Republic.

The Republic is served by two national and six foreign airlines, and an international airport 18 miles to the east of the capital is in operation. Another is being constructed near Puerto Plata on the north coast.

Sugar, coffee, cocoa, and tobacco are the most important crops. Other products are peanuts, maize, rice, bananas, molasses, salt, cement, ferronickel, bauxite, gold, silver, cattle, sisal products, honey and chocolate. There is a growing number of light industries producing beer, tinned foodstuffs, glass products, nylon and cotton textiles, soap, cigarettes, construction materials, plastic articles, shoes, papers, paint, rum, matches, peanut oil and other products.

FINANCE

Budget	1975 (est.)	1976 (est.)
Revenue.....	*RD*$486,308,238	*RD*$530,000,000

One *Dominican Peso*= $1·00 U.S.

TRADE

	1974	1975
Imports......	*RD*$673,000,000	*RD*$773,000,000
Exports......	650,000,000	920,000,000

Trade with U.K.

	1974	1975
Imports from U.K....	£6,396,000	£6,123,000
Exports to U.K......	10,553,000	7,522,000

The chief imports are machinery, food stuffs, iron and steel, cotton textiles and yarns, mineral oils (including petrol), cars and other motor vehicles, chemical and pharmaceutical products, electrical equipment and accessories, construction material, paper and paper products, and rubber and rubber products; the chief exports are sugar, coffee, cocoa, tobacco, chocolate, molasses, bauxite, ferro-nickel and gold.

The principal export to U.K. over a number of years has been sugar by-products; ferro-nickel and bauxite are also exported in considerable quantities to the U.S.A. and Europe.

CAPITAL, Ψ Santo Domingo, population of the Capital District (1970 census), 817,000. Other centres, with populations (1970 census); Santiago de los Caballeros (245,000); La Vega (156,000); San Francisco de Macoris (126,000); San Juan (114,000); San Cristóbal (106,000).

FLAG.—Red and blue, with white cross bearing an emblem at centre.

NATIONAL DAY.—February 27 (Independence Day, 1844).

BRITISH EMBASSY

Avenida Independencia 506, Santo Domingo
Ambassador Extraordinary and Plenipotentiary, His Excellency Clement Spearman (1976).
First Secretary and Consul, E. F. Barrett.

BRITISH CONSULAR OFFICES

There are British Consular Offices at *Santo Domingo, Puerto Plata* and *San Pedro de Macoris.*

ECUADOR
(Republica del Ecuador)

Junta, Vice Admiral Alfredo Poveda Burbano; Colonel Luis Guillermo Durán Arcentales; General Luis Leoro Franco, *assumed power,* January 11, 1976.

CABINET

Interior, Col. Richelieu Levoyer.
Foreign Affairs, Dr. Armando Pesantes.
Defence, Gen. Andrés Arrata Macias.
Natural Resources and Energy, Col. René Vargas Pazos.
Finance, Sr. César Robalino.
Education, Capt. Anibal Carrillo.
Public Works, Gen. Angel Polivio Vega.
Agriculture and Livestock, Col. Oliveiro Vásconez.
Industry, Commerce and Integration, Sr. Galo Montaño.
Labour and Social Welfare, Col. Francisco Aguirre Armendariz.
Public Health, Col. Raúl Maldonado Mejía.
Secretary to Cabinet, Capt. Victor Garces.

EMBASSY AND CONSULATE

Flat 3B, 3 Hans Crescent, S.W.1
[01-584 1367]
Ambassador Extraordinary and Plenipotentiary, His Excellency Gustavo Ycaza.
1st Secretary, Lic. J. Marchan.
Counsellor (Commercial), Sra. E. de Sancho.
3rd Secretary, Srta. G. Moreno.
There are consulates at *Liverpool, Birmingham* and *Glasgow.*

Area and Population.—Ecuador is an equatorial State of South America, the mainland extending from lat. 1° 38′ N. to 4° 50′ S., and between 75° 20′ and 81° W. long., comprising an area reduced by boundary settlements with Peru (Jan. 29, 1942) to about 226,000 sq. miles. (*For* MAP, *see* Index.)

The Republic of Ecuador is divided into 20 provinces. It has a population estimated (1973) at 7,000,000, mostly descendants of the Spaniards, aboriginal Indians, and Mestizoes. The territory of the Republic extends across the Western Andes, the highest peak of which is Aconcagua, in the Chilean sector (22,976 ft.), the highest peaks in Ecuador being Chimborazo (20,408 ft.), Ilinza (17,405 ft.), Carihuairazo (16,515 ft.), Cotocachi (16,301 ft.), and Pichincha (16,000 ft.) in the Western Cordillera; and Cotopaxi (19,612 ft.), Antisana (18,864 ft.), Cayambe (19,160 ft.), Altar (17,730 ft.), Sangay (17,464 ft.), Tungurahua (16,690 ft.), and Sincholagua (16,365 ft.) in the Eastern Cordillera. Ecuador is watered by the Upper Amazon, and by the rivers Guayas, Mira, Santiago, Chone, and Esmeraldas on the Pacific coast. There are extensive forests, and the cinchona bark tree is common.

The *Galápagos* (Giant Tortoise) *Islands* forming the province of the Archipelago de Colón, were annexed by Ecuador in 1832. The archipelago lies in the Pacific, about 500 miles from Saint Elena peninsula, the most westerly point of the mainland. There are 12 large and several hundred smaller islands with a total area of about 3,000 sq. miles and an estimated population (1973) of 4,000. The capital is San Cristobal, on Chatham Island. Although the archipelago lies on the equator, the temperature of the surrounding water is well below equatorial average owing to the *Antarctic Humboldt Current.* The province consists for the most part of National Park Territory, where unique marine birds, iguanas, and the giant tortoises are conserved. There is some local subsistence farming; the main industry, apart from tourism, is tuna and lobster fishing.

Government.—The former *Kingdom of Quito* was conquered by the Incas of Peru in the latter part of the 15th century. Early in the 16th century Pizarro's conquests led to the inclusion of the present territory of Ecuador in the Spanish Viceroyalty of Peru. The independence of the country was achieved in a revolutionary war which culminated in the battle of Mount Pichincha (May 24, 1822). On Jan. 11, 1976, a military junta assumed power from President Guillermo Rodríguez Lara.

Production and Industry.—The chief products are petroleum, bananas, cocoa, coffee, sugar, rice, straw hats, pyrethrum, xanthophyll, scopolamine, vegetable ivory and balsa wood. The oil deposits in the Oriente are estimated at between 10-15,000,000,000 barrels. The oil is evacuated by a trans-Andean pipeline to the port of Balao (near Esmeraldas). In the highlands the principal crops are maize, wheat, potatoes and other temperate products. Small amounts of gold, silver and lead are mined, and emeralds and rubies are occasionally found. A Five-Year industrialisation programme was introduced in 1973, and industry is being rapidly diversified; textiles have traditionally been predominant.

Communications.—There are 23,256 km. of permanent roads and 5,044 km. of roads which are only open during the dry season. There are about 750 miles of railway, including the railway from Quito to Guayaquil. Nine commercial airlines operate international flights, linking Ecuador with New York, Miami, Panama, Lima, Santiago, Rio de Janeiro, Paris, Frankfurt, Madrid, etc. There are internal services between all important towns.

Defence.—The standing Army has a strength of about 15,000. There is an Air Force of some 90 aircraft of various kinds and a small Navy.

Language and Literature.—Spanish is the language of the country. The electorate is confined to adult

male and female citizens who can read and write, and in recent years considerable headway has been made in reducing the high figure of illiteracy. 3 daily newspapers are published at Quito and 4 at Guayaquil. Elementary education is free and compulsory. In 1973 there were 8,062 primary schools with 1,091,102 pupils and 894 high schools with 278,400 pupils. The 9 Universities, at Quito (2), Guayaquil (3), Cuenca, Machala, Loja and Portoviejo, the Polytechnic Schools at Quito and Guayaquil and the 8 technical colleges in other provincial capitals had 70,138 students in the same year.

FINANCE
		1973
Revenue(*Budget Estimates*)..	Sucres	8,700,000,000
Expenditure(*Budget Estimates*).....		8,700,000,000
		1974
Revenue(*Budget Estimates*)....	Sucres	9,427,000,000
Expenditure (*Budget Estimates*).....		9,427,000,000
Internal Debt (Sept. 30, 1967).....		4,516,570,000
External Debt (Dec. 31, 1972)..	U.S.	$343,295,000

The official rate of Exchange: Sucres 57 = £1, is used for most legal imports and exports. There is also a free rate of exchange. *See also* p. 83.

TRADE
Import licences are required for all merchandise and these are issued by the Central Bank of Ecuador.

	1971	1972
Imports....	$U.S.289,793,000	$U.S.279,128,000
Exports....	221,544,000	279,783,000

Trade with U.K.
	1974	1975
Imports from U.K.....	£13,600,000	£17,307,000
Exports to U.K........	2,170,000	2,065,000

The chief exports are petroleum, bananas, cocoa, coffee and sugar. Other exports are rice, balsa wood, castor-oil seeds, hats, pharmaceuticals, fish, ivory, nuts and pyrethrum. Manufactured goods and machinery are the main imports.

CAPITAL.—Quito. Population (estimated 1972), 700,000; Ψ Guayaquil (1,000,000) is the chief port; other centres are Cuenca (100,000); (est. 1968) Ambato (69,766); Riobamba (50,710); ΨEsmeraldas (51,573); and Ψ Manta (42,750). The foregoing figures of urban populations have been revised by the Census and Statistics Office to exclude from 1968 figures for rural areas of the cities (*i.e.* areas not supplied by city fuel or water services).

FLAG.—Three horizontal bands, yellow, blue and red (the yellow band twice the width of the others); emblem in centre.

NATIONAL DAY.—August 10 (*Dia de la Independencia*).

BRITISH EMBASSY
Calle G. Suarez, 111 (P.O. Box No. 314), Quito.
Ambassador Extraordinary and Plenipotentiary, His Excellency Norman Ernest Cox, C.M.G. (1974)
1st Secretary, D. V. Thornley (*Commercial, Head of Chancery*).
There is a British Consular Office at *Guayaquil.*

EGYPT
(Arab Republic of Egypt)
President, Mohammad Anwar El Sadat, *elected President,* Oct. 15, 1970.

CABINET
Prime Minister, Mamduh Salem.
Deputy Prime Ministers
Social Development and Services, Dr. Mohamed Hafez Ghanem.
Foreign Affairs, Ismail Fahmy.
War, General Mohamed Abdul Ghany al Gamassy.
Production, Power and Energy, Ahman Sultan.

Manpower and Training, Abdul Latif Boltia.
Tourism and Aviation, Ibrahim Naguib.
Social Affairs, Dr. Aisha Rateb.
Information and Culture, Dr. Gamal el Oteify.
Health, Dr. Ahmad Fuad Muhieddin.
Petroleum, Ahmad Ezzedin Hilal.
Justice, Samih Talat.
Maritime Transport, Mahmoud Fahmy.
Planning, Dr. Mohamed Mahmoud el Imam.
Interior, El-Sayed Hussein Fahmy.
Trade and Supply, Zakaria Tawfiq Abdul Fattah.
Agriculture and Irrigation, Abdul Azim Abdul Ata.
Industry and Mineral Wealth, Issa Shaheen.
Finance, Dr. Ahmad Abu Ismail.
Economy and Economic Cooperation, Dr. Mohamed Zaky Shafei.
Housing and Reconstruction, Osman Ahmad Osman.
Education, Dr. Mustafa Kamel Helmy.
Transport and Communications, Abdul Fattah Abdullah.
WAQFS and Azhar Affairs, Dr. Mohamed Hussein el Dahaby.
Ministers of State, Dr. Fuad Sherif (*Cabinet Affairs and Administrative Development*); Albert Barsoum Salama (*People's Assembly Affairs*); Mohamed Hassan Bahgat Hassanein (*Housing and Reconstruction*); Mohamed Hamed Mahmoud (*Local Government and People's Organisations*); Gamaleedin Sidky (*War Production*); Dr. Abdul Aziz Hussein (*Agriculture and Sudan Affairs*); Dr. Ahmad Abdul Maaboud el Gebeilly (*Scientific Research and Atomic Energy*); Mohamed Riad (*Foreign Relations*).

EMBASSY IN LONDON
26 South Street, W.1
[01-499 2401]

Ambassador Extraordinary and Plenipotentiary, His Excellency Mohammed Samih Anwar (1974).
Minister-Counsellor, Abdel Halim Abdel Hamid Badawi.
Minister-Counsellor, Magdy Sabry (*Consular*).
Counsellors, Gamal Mohamed Said; Mahmoud Abdel Rahim Pasha; Hassan Shakir Abdel-Aal; Emad El Din Aly El-Kadi; Mohamed Salah El-Din Mohamed Abboud; Ahmed Amin Waly; Farouk Mohammed Youssef El-Kady.

1st *Secretaries*, Mohammed Abdel Rahim Mohamed (*Consular*); Nabil Rihan (*Consular*); Ali Mutwalli Hegazi; Farouk Helmy Ali Helmy; Hamdi Mohamed Nada.

AREA AND POPULATION.—The total area of Egypt is estimated at 1,000,000 square kilometres (385,110 square miles), the inhabited area being only 35,168 square kilometres (13,578 square miles), with a population (estimated May, 1971) of 34,000,000.

There are three distinct elements in the native population. The largest, or " Egyptian " element, is a Hamito-Semite race, known in the rural districts as *Fellahin* (*fellâh*—ploughman, or tiller of the soil). The *Fellahin* have been mainly of the Moslem faith since the conquest of the country in the 7th century. A second element is the *Bedouin*, or nomadic Arabs of the Libyan and Arabian deserts, of whom about one-seventh are real nomads, and the remainder semi-sedentary tent-dwellers on the outskirts of the cultivated end of the Nile Valley and the Fayûm. The third element is the *Nubian* of the Nile Valley between Aswân and Wadi-Halfa of mixed Arab and Negro blood. The Bedouin and Nubians are Moslems.

The territory of Egypt comprises (1) *Egypt Proper*, forming the N.E. corner of the African continent, divisible into (*a*) the valley and delta of the Nile, (*b*) the Libyan or Western Desert, and (*c*) the Arabian or Eastern Desert; (2) *The Peninsula of Sinai*, forming part of the continent of Asia; and (3) a number of *Islands* in the Gulf of Suez and Red Sea, of which the principal are Jubal, Shadwan, Gafatin and Zeberged (or St. John's Island). This territory lies between 22° and 32° N. lat. and 24° and 37° E. long. The northern boundary is the Mediterranean, and in the south Egypt is conterminous with the Sudan. The western boundary runs from a point on the coast 10 kilometres N.W. of Sollüm to the latitude of Siwa and thence due S. along the 25th meridian to the parallel of 22° N. (the N. boundary of the Sudan) at 'Uweinat Mountain. The E. boundary follows a line drawn from Rafa on the Mediterranean (34° 15′ E. long.) to the head of the Gulf of 'Aqaba, from which point the remainder of the E. boundary is washed by the waters of the Gulf of 'Aqaba and the Red Sea. The " settled land area " is stated officially at 7,667,000 *feddâns* (12,431 square miles) and the area of lakes at 641,000 *feddâns* (1,039 square miles), a total of 8,308,000 *feddâns* (13,470 square miles).

Physical Features.—The Nile valley varies in width from less than half a mile in the southern granitic region to over 10 miles in the northern limestone region, and the cliffs in some places rise to heights of over a thousand feet above the river. The fertile lands, on which the prosperity of the country depends, occupy the floor of the valley between the river and the bounding cliffs, while to the north of Cairo they spread out into the irregular fan-shaped formation of the Delta which comprises the six provinces of Lower Egypt, with the richest soil in the country.

The *Nile* has a total length of 4,160 miles. In the 960 miles of its course through Egypt it receives not a single tributary stream. The river formerly had a regular yearly rise and fall of about 13 feet at Cairo, but since the commencement of storage in the reservoir of the Aswan High Dam in 1965, there has been no flood downstream of the Dam and the water level remains almost constant throughout the year. Westward from the Nile Valley into Tripolitania stretches the *Libyan Desert*, an arid region, containing some depressions, whose springs irrigate small areas known as *Oases*, of which the principal, from S.E. to N.W., are known as Kharga, Dakhla, Farafra, Baharia and Siwa.

On the eastern edge of the Libyan Desert, a few miles south-west of Cairo stand the Pyramids of Gizeh, of which the highest, the *Great Pyramid*, is 451 feet high. Close to the pyramids is the *Great Sphinx*, 189 feet long. In the Eastern Desert a great backbone of high and rugged mountains extends north-westwards from Ethiopia to near Suez, and reappears as a detached mass in the Peninsula of Sinai. Flanking this mountain chain on the west, between the axis of the range and the Nile, are plateaux of sandstones and limestones, dissected by *wadis* (dry water-courses), often of great length and depth, with some wild vegetation and occasional wells and springs. The roads follow the course of the main *wadis* from well to well, and here and there are to be found small encampments of wandering Arabs.

Religions.—The predominant religion is Islam but there are about 2,000,000 Christians (mainly Copts). By 1968 nearly all the Jews had left the country. The chief Moslem religious authorities in Egypt are the *Sheik el Gami el Azhar* and the *Mufti Gumhuriya Misr al Arabiya.*

Government.—From 30 B.C. to A.D. 639 Egypt was a province of the Roman Empire, but in A.D. 640 the Christian inhabitants were subjugated by Moslem invaders and Egypt became a province of the Eastern Caliphate. In 1517 the country was incorporated in the Ottoman Empire under which it remained until early in the 19th century.

A British Protectorate over Egypt declared on Dec. 18, 1914, lasted until Feb. 28, 1922, when Sultan Ahmed Fuad was proclaimed King of Egypt. Following closely on the accession of King Farouk, the *Anglo-Egyptian Treaty* was signed in London (Aug. 26, 1936) and the military occupation by British troops was terminated.

In July, 1952, following a military *coup d'état*, King Farouk abdicated in favour of his infant son, who became King Ahmed Fuad II. In June, 1953, however, Gen. Neguib's military council deposed the young king, and declared Egypt a Republic, Gen. Neguib himself assuming the Presidency. In November, 1954, General Neguib was deposed by Lt.-Col. Gamal Abdel Nasser and the military council. On June 23, 1956, Col. Nasser assumed office as President, after an election at which voting was compulsory, and he was the only candidate.

A union with Syria was affected in 1958 and lasted until September, 1961, when Syria seceded after a *coup d'état*. The title and flag of the United Arab Republic were, however, retained for Egypt until Sept. 2, 1971.

President Nasser died suddenly on Sept. 28, 1970, and the duties of Head of State were assumed by Mr. Anwer Sadat who was elected President in a referendum on Oct. 15.

Agriculture.—Despite increased industrialization and the discovery of new oil fields, agriculture continues to provide the most substantial contribution to the national economy. Cotton (10 million *kanbars* in 1974) is the most important export, but sugar cane, onions, potatoes and citrus fruits are also sold extensively to overseas markets. Nearly all cultivation is carried out by peasant farmers whose operations are funded and generally controlled by co-operative organizations. Productivity is usually good. Irrigation and land reclamation schemes have contributed to a small increase in the cultivable area, and a $147 million drainage project, financed partly by the International Bank for Reconstruction and Development, is intended ultimately to irrigate nearly one million acres.

Railways.—The principal lines radiate from Cairo to Alexandria (and on to Rosetta), Damietta and Ismailia (continuing northwards to Port Said and

southward to Suez). From Cairo the line runs southwards for a distance of 554 miles to a new port being constructed upstream of the High Dam. At this point a steamer connection runs to New Halfa, connecting Egypt with the Sudan Government Railways. Westwards from Alexandria (and close to the coast) runs a line to the frontier at Sollûm, thus joining Libya to Egypt. The gauge is standard (4 ft. 8½ in.).

Roads and Caravan Routes.—A sea coast motor road exists from Alexandria to Mersa Matruh, with an extension along the coast to Sollûm and thence to connect with the coast road in Libya. A bitumen road leads to Kharga and Dakhla, from the former of which there is a route, known as the Darb el 'Arbain, leading to Dar Fûr and the south of the Sudan. There are many well-known routes across the Arabian Desert to the Red Sea, that from Qena to Qoseir, a metalled road, being probably the most frequently used.

Shipping.— Ψ Apart from the three great seaports of Alexandria, Port Said and Suez, the last two of which are now undergoing reconstruction following several years of disuse after the 1967 war, Egypt has but few harbours and anchorages adapted for large craft; the principal are those of Sollûm and Matruh on the Mediterranean, Tor, Abu Zenima, Zeitia, Jemsa and Hurghada in the Gulf of Suez, and Safaga and Qoseir on the Red Sea.

Currency.—£E (Egyptian *pound* of 100 piastres) =97p sterling. Floating Official Rate of Exchange, plus a Preferential Rate of Exchange for visitors, about 50 per cent. above the Official Rate.

Trade with U.K.

	1974	1975
Imports from U.K.	£52,000,000	£108,000,000
Exports to U.K.	27,000,000	41,000,000

The principal imports are metals, and manufactures thereof, chemicals and pharmaceuticals, machinery and transport equipment, foodstuffs, beverages and textile fibres. The exports are principally raw cotton, textile yarns, rice, fruit and vegetables, petroleum products and a growing list of secondary exports, many of them manufactured goods.

CAPITAL.—Cairo (population, estimated in 1975 at 8,143,000), stands on the E. bank of the Nile, about 14 miles from the head of the Delta. Its oldest part is the fortress of Babylon in old Cairo, with its Roman bastions and Coptic churches. The earliest Arab building is the Mosque of 'Amr, dating from A.D. 643, and the most conspicuous is the Citadel, built by Saladin towards the end of the 12th century and containing in its walls the Mosque of Mohamed Ali built in the 19th century.

Ψ ALEXANDRIA (estimated population, 1,900,000), founded 332 B.C. by Alexander the Great, was for over 1,000 years the capital of Egypt and a centre of Hellenic culture which vied with Athens herself. Its great *pharos* (lighthouse), 480 feet high, with a lantern burning resinous wood, was one of the "Seven Wonders of the World". Other towns are: Ismailia; Ψ Port Said; Mansura (102,709); Asyût (284,000); Faiyûm (162,000); Tanta (139,965); Mahalla el Kubra (115,509); Ψ Suez; Ψ Damietta (97,000).

CAIRO is 2,520 miles from London: transit *via* Trieste, 5 days; *via* Marseilles, 6 days.

FLAG.—Horizontal bands of red, white and black, with two 5-point green stars in white band. NATIONAL DAY.—July 23 (Anniversary of Revolution in 1952).

BRITISH EMBASSY
Kasr el Doubara, Garden City, Cairo
Ambassador Extraordinary and Plenipotentiary, His

Excellency Willie Morris, C.M.G. (1975).
Counsellor, P. J. S. Moon.
Defence and Military Attaché, Col. W. C. Deller, O.B.E.
H.M. Consul, D. H. G. Rose.
1st *Secretaries*, A. J. Coles (*Head of Chancery*); K. J. Gullick (*Information*); A. P. a'C. Bergne; D. H. Parker (*Aid*); M. Dougall (*Commercial*); P. W. Ford.
2nd *Secretaries*, K. J. Passmore; T. Airey (*Administration*); N. R. Brice (*Commercial*).
British Consulate-General, Alexandria
Consul-General, F. W. Hall.
Vice-Consul, G. B. B. Chavasse.
British Council Representative, Dr. N. A. Daniel, C.B.E., 192 Sharia el Nil Agouza, Cairo.

EQUATORIAL GUINEA

President, Francisco Macias (Nguema), *elected* October 12, 1968.

Formerly the territory of " Spanish Guinea ", Equatorial Guinea consists of the Island of Macias Nguema (formerly known as Fernando Póo), an island in the Bight of Biafra about 20 miles from the west coast of Africa, Pagalu Island (formerly Annobon) in the Gulf of Guinea, the Corisco Islands (Corisco, Elobey Grande and Elobey Chico) and Rio Muni, a mainland area between Cameroon and Gabon. It has a total area of about 11,000 sq. miles and a population (U.N. estimate, 1969) of 286,000.

Macias Nguema is a mountainous island with forests of oil palm, ebony, mahogany and oak, and sugar-cane, cotton and indigo. Cocoa, coffee, sugar, tobacco, vanilla nut and kola nut are cultivated and cocoa and other products are exported.

Government.—Former colonies of Spain, the territories now forming the Republic of Equatorial Guinea were from April 1, 1960, constituted as two provinces of Metropolitan Spain, the inhabitants having the same rights as Spanish citizens. As a result of a plebiscite held on Dec. 15, 1963, an autonomous *régime* was instituted on June 2, 1964, with the approval of the Spanish Government. Equatorial Guinea became fully independent on October 12, 1968, after a referendum on the new constitution held in August, 1968, and presidential elections on Sept. 22, 1968. The latter were supervised by a U.N. Mission. The first President, Señor Francisco Macias, assumed office on Independence Day.

Severe disorders occurred during February and March, 1969, following incidents at the town of Bata (in Rio Muni). Spanish residents left Equatorial Guinea in large numbers, having had to seek the protection of residual Spanish forces while awaiting evacuation to Spain. Some 600 Spanish civilians elected to remain in Macias Nguema and about 80 in Rio Muni, but most of these have subsequently left. Following Nigerian allegations of continuing mistreatment, most of the Nigerian labour force, on whom cocoa production largely depended, were repatriated in late 1975 and early 1976. The economy is now mainly dependent on outside aid, mostly from Communist countries.

CAPITAL, Ψ Malabo (formerly known as Santa Isabel) on the island of Macias Nguema (population 9,000). Ψ Bata is the principal town and port of Rio Muni. FLAG.—Three horizontal bands, green over white over red; blue triangle next staff; coat of arms in centre of white band.

British Ambassador, His Excellency, Albert Edward Saunders, C.M.G., O.B.E. (1975) (Resident at *Yaoundé, Cameroon*).

ETHIOPIA

Provisional Military Administrative Council
Chairman, Brig.-Gen. Teferi Benti.
First Vice-Chairman, Major Mengistu Haile Mariam.
2nd Vice-Chairman, Lt.-Col. Atenafu Abate.

EMBASSY IN LONDON
17 Prince's Gate, S.W.7
[01-589 7212]
Ambassador Extraordinary and Plenipotentiary, His Excellency Ato Zaudie Makuria (1976).
1st Secretaries, Ato Mismaku Asrat; Ato Tesfaye Demeke; Ato Aklilu Gebre Kidan.
3rd Secretary, Ato Getahun Dessalegn.
Attaché, Ato Demelesh Teshome.

Position and Extent.—Ethiopia, with which Eritrea was federated from 1952 to 1962 when it was incorporated as a province, is in North-Eastern Africa, bounded on the north west by the Sudan; on the south by Kenya; on the east by Afars and Issas Territory and the Republic of Somalia; and on the north-east by the Red Sea. The area is estimated at 400,000 square miles, with a population of 26,000,000 of whom about one-third are of the ruling race of Semitic origin (Amharas and Tigres) and the remainder mainly Gallas, Guraghi, Sidama, Agao, negro tribes on the west and south frontiers, and Danakil and Somalis on the east.

Ethiopia is mainly a mountainous country, volcanic in origin, with several peaks of about 14,000 ft., notably in the centre and in the Simien range in the north; many other mountains exceed 10,000 ft. Eritrea consists of a mountainous hogs-back range up to 10,000 ft., interposed between the Red Sea and the Sudan, flanked on east and west by flatter territory. The lower country and valley gorges are very hot; the higher plateaux are well watered, with a genial climate. On the high plateaux there are two main seasons in the year, a dry winter, October to May, and a rainy summer from June to September, with a season of " small rains " occurring generally in March. The chief river is the Blue Nile, issuing from Lake Tana; the Atbara and many other tributaries of the Nile also rise in the Ethiopian highlands.

Those of Semitic origin (Amharas and Tigres), who inhabit the southern highlands of Eritrea, provinces of Tigre, Begemdir, Gojjam, parts of Shoa, and many of the Gallas, are Christians of the Ethiopian Orthodox Church, which was formerly led by the head of the Coptic Church, the Patriarch at Alexandria. Since 1959, however, the Ethiopian Church has been autocephalous and the new Patriarch, Abuna Theophilos, was enthroned by the Ethiopian archbishops in May, 1971. Moslems predominate in some areas, notably northern Eritrea, Harar and Jimma and Arussi, the Moslem centre being at Harar. The province of Gamu Gofa and parts of Sidamo and Arussi have considerable pagan elements.

Following considerable military and civil unrest in early 1974 the Emperor Hailé Selassié I announced on March 5 the convening of a commission to revise the Constitution, and the setting up within six months of a conference to consider the commission's proposals. It appeared likely that more power would devolve on to Parliament. Internal unrest continued through the summer, however, and at the end of June, the armed forces assumed effective control of the country by establishing an " Armed Forces Committee " now entitled the Provisional Military Administrative Council. Their demands for far-reaching reforms were acceded to by the Government, with the agreement of the Emperor, who was finally deposed on Sept. 12, 1974.

Eritrea.—Eritrea was administered by Great Britain from the end of the Second World War until September 15, 1972, when in accordance with a resolution of the United Nations Assembly of December 2, 1950, it was federated with Ethiopia under the Ethiopian Crown, becoming a province of Ethiopia in 1962. An armed campaign for independence has accompanied the collapse of the imperial régime.

Production and Industry.—The principal pursuits are agriculture and cattle breeding. In the hotter regions, sugar-cane, cotton, &c., flourish; in the middle zone maize, wheat, barley, coffee, oranges and other fruit trees, tobacco, potatoes and oil seeds are cultivated; and above 6,000 feet are excellent pastures with some corn cultivation. Coffee provided approximately 64 per cent. of the country's total exports by value in 1974. The forests are a potential source of wealth. Horses, mules, donkeys, cattle, oxen, goats, and sheep, and camels in the lowlands, form a large portion of the wealth of the people. Industry is small, the main products being textiles, foodstuffs, tyres, beer and cement. Hydro-electric power production and telecommunications are expanding rapidly, however, mainly with loans from the World Bank, which in 1971 had approved a number of loans for agricultural development.

Communications.—A railway links Addis Ababa, the capital, *via* Dire Dawa, with Djibouti, 486 miles away. In Eritrea a narrow gauge line runs from Massawa to Asmara and on to Agordet. Several roads were constructed before and during the Italian occupation; the principal road runs from Addis Ababa to Dessie and on to Asmara, with a branch from Dessie to Assab on the Red Sea Coast. Addis Ababa and Asmara are linked by a road running through Gondar and along Lake Tana. Others run from Addis Ababa west to Lekempti, south-west to Jimma, Gore and Gambela, south to the Kenya frontier, and in the East to Dire Dawa, Harar and the northern region of the Somali Republic. Partly financed by large loans from the International Bank for Reconstruction and Development, much further improvement and extension of roads is being undertaken. The Ethiopian Air Lines maintain regular services from Addis Ababa to many provincial towns. External services are operated to Athens, Frankfurt, Rome, Paris, Aden, Djibouti, Sana'a, Taiz, Jedda, Cairo, Khartoum, Nairobi, Dar-es-Salaam, Entebbe, Lagos,

Accra, Douala, Kigali, Kinshasa, Bombay, New Delhi, Peking and London.

Defence.—Under the Ministry of Defence the armed forces comprise the Army the Air Force and the Navy. The Army consists of four infantry divisions, including one mechanized brigade with armour, with normal artillery, engineer units and supporting arms including a parachute battalion. An American Military Advisory and Assistance Group (MAAG) assists the forces, mainly the Army, with training and advice,under an agreement signed with the Ethiopian Government. There is a military academy at Harar and a military training centre at Holleta with a specialist training wing. The Air Force comprises a transport squadron, a bomber squadron, three fighter squadrons, a training squadron, a jet conversion squadron, and an elementary training unit. The Air Force Headquarters is situated at Debre Zeit. The aircraft are mostly of American manufacture but also include Canberras.

The Navy has a headquarters in Addis Ababa with a main base at Massawa and a smaller one at Assab. The principal units are an ex-U.S. seaplane tender (*Ethiopia*), a patrol craft squadron of 5, an MTB squadron of 4, and an ex-Dutch minesweeper.

Education.—Elementary education is provided without religious discrimination by Government schools in the main centres of population; there are also Mission schools, and cadet-schools for the Army, Air Force, and Police. Government secondary schools are found mainly in Addis Ababa, but also in most of the provincial capitals. In 1961 the Hailé Selassié I University was founded to co-ordinate the existing institutions of higher education (University College, Engineering, Building and Theological Colleges in Addis Ababa, Agricultural College at Alemaya, near Harar, and Public Health Centre in Gondar, etc.) and to provide a framework for future development. There is also a Catholic-run university in Asmara. Amharic is the official language of instruction, with English as the first foreign language. Arabic is taught in Koran Schools; and Ge'ez (the ancient Ethiopic) in Christian Church Schools, which abound. Adult education is met to some extent by institutes which provide evening classes in Addis Ababa. In 1971 the International Development Agency granted a loan of U.S. $95 million for the development of secondary education.

Finance.—Total revenue for 1974–75 was estimated at £180 m., while expenditure was expected to reach £188 m. The Ethiopian dollar has a value of 5.52 grains of fine gold and is divided into 100 cents. At Jan. 31, 1975, the combined note and coin issue amounted to £128,000,000. Foreign exchange and gold reserves of the National Bank amounted to £115,000,000 at the same date. Eth. $4·90= £1 (May 1975). (*See also* p. 83.)

Trade.—The chief imports by value are machinery and transport equipment, manufactured goods, chemicals, beverages and tobacco (from U.K.); the principal exports by value being coffee, oilseeds, hides and skins, and pulses.

TRADE

	1973	1974
Total Imports	£85,000,000	£116,000,000
Total Exports	122,000,000	143,000,000
	1974	1975
Imports from U.K.	£9,815,000	£8,709,000
Exports to U.K.	4,804,000	3,762,000

CAPITAL, Addis Ababa (population, estimated 912,000), also capital of the province of Shoa; Asmara (population 250,000) is the capital of the Province of Eritrea. Dire Dawa is the most important commercial centre after Addis Ababa and Asmara, Ψ Massawa and Ψ Assab (recently enlarged) are the two main ports. There are ancient architectural remains at Aksum, Gondar, Lalibela and elsewhere.

ETHIOPIAN FLAG.—Three horizontal bands; green, yellow, red; bearing crowned lion at centre.

NATIONAL DAY.—July 23.

BRITISH EMBASSY
(Addis Ababa)

Ambassador Extraordinary and Plenipotentiary, His Excellency Derek Malcolm Day, C.M.G. (1975).

There are British Consular Offices at *Addis Ababa* and *Asmara*.

British Council Representative, E. C. Pugh, Artistic Building, Adua Avenue, Addis Ababa.

FINLAND
(Suomi)

President, Dr. Urho Kaleva Kekkonen, G.C.B., *born* 1900, *elected* Feb. 15, 1956; re-elected 1962 and 1968; term extended until 1978 by Act of Parliament (1973).

CABINET

Prime Minister, Martti Miettunen (*CP*).
Foreign Minister, Kalevi Sorsa (*SDP*).
Minister in the Cabinet Office, Reino Karpola (*CP*).
Justice, Kristan Gestrin (*SPP*).
Interior, Paavo Tiilikainen (*SDP*); Olavi Hänninen (*Deputy*) (*FPDL*).
Defence, Ingvar Melin (*SPP*).
Finance, Paul Paavela (*SDP*); Esko Rekola (*Deputy*).
Education, Paavo Väyrynen (*CP*); Kalevi Kivistö (*Deputy*) (*FPDL*).
Agriculture, Heimo Linna (*CP*).
Communications, Kauko Hjerppe (*FPDL*).
Labour, Paavo Aitio (*FPDL*).
Trade and Industry, Eero Rantala (*SDP*).
Foreign Trade, Sakari T. Lehto.
Social Affairs, Irma Toivanen (*LPP*); Pirkko Työläjärvi (*Deputy*) (*SDP*).
(*CP*=Centre Party, *SDP*=Social Democratic Party, *FPDL*=Finnish People's Democratic League, *SPP*=Swedish People's Party, *LPP*= Liberal People's Party.)

FINNISH EMBASSY AND CONSULATE
38 Chesham Place, S.W.1
[01-235 9531]

Ambassador Extraordinary and Plenipotentiary, His Excellency Richard Björnson Tötterman, K.C.V.O., O.B.E. (1975).
Counsellor, Erkki Mäentakanen.
1st Secretary, Juhani Muhonen.
2nd Secretaries, Erkki Palmqvist; Esko Hamilo.
Press Counsellor, Kristofer Gräsbeck.
Cultural Counsellor, Henrik Antell.
Defence Attaché, Lt.-Col. Pertti Nykänen.

Area and Population.—A country situated on the Gulfs of Finland and Bothnia, with a total area of 130,165 square miles, of which 70 per cent. is forest, 10 per cent. cultivated, 9 per cent. lakes and 11 per cent. waste and other land, population (1975), 4,720,259. In 1975 the birth rate was 14·1, death rate 9·4 per 1,000. The infant mortality rate was 10·2 per 1,000 live births. 92·6 per cent of the people are Lutherans, 1·2 per cent. Greek Orthodox and 6·2 per cent. others.

The Åland Archipelago (Ahvenanmaa), a group of small islands at the entrance to the Gulf of Bothnia, covers about 572 square miles, with a population (1973) of 21,800 (96·3 per cent. Swedish-speaking). The islands have a semi-autonomous status.

Government.—Under the Constitution there is a single Chamber (*Eduskunta*) for which women are

eligible, composed of 200 members, elected by universal suffrage of both sexes. The legislative power is vested in the Chamber and the President. The highest executive power is held by the President who is elected for a period of 6 years.

The present government came into office on Dec. 1, 1975. The five parties in the coalition are the Social Democratic Party, the Centre Party, the Finnish People's Democratic League (which includes the Finnish Communist Party), the Swedish People's Party and the Liberal People's Party.

Defence.—By the terms of the Peace Treaty (Feb. 10, 1947) with U.K. and U.S.S.R., the Army is limited to a force not exceeding 34,400. The Navy is limited to a total of 10,000 tons displacement with personnel not exceeding 4,500. The Air Force, including naval air arm, is limited to 60 machines with a personnel not exceeding 3,000. Bombers or aircraft with bomb-carrying facilities are expressly forbidden. The Defence Forces contain a cadre of regular officers and N.C.O.'s, but their bulk is provided by conscripts who serve for 8–11 months. None of the Defence Forces has the full complement permitted.

Education.—Primary education is compulsory for children from 7 to 16 years, and free in certain State and municipal schools. In the autumn of 1975, there were 128,172 in primary schools, 449,942 in comprehensive schools, 16,391 in experimental comprehensive schools and 196,807 in secondary schools. There are 11 Higher Schools and 6 Universities (1975); Helsinki University (1975), 20,894 students. Combined enrolment at Higher Schools and Universities was 72,502.

Language and Literature.—Most Finns are bilingual. 93·2 per cent. speak Finnish as their first language, 6·6 Swedish and the remaining 0·2 per cent. other languages (mainly Lapps living a nomadic life in the North). Since 1883 Finnish has been on an equal footing with Swedish as the official language of Finland, but since independence in 1917 Finnish has slowly been displacing Swedish. In literature also, until the close of the eighteenth century, Swedish was dominant, but awakening Finnish nationalism in the early years of the nineteenth century and the establishment of an association for the promotion of Finnish literature in 1831 gave Finnish the status of a literary language. There is a vigorous modern literature. Eemil Sillanpää was awarded the Nobel Prize for Literature in 1939. There are 62 daily newspapers in Finland which appear on 4 or more days per week (55 Finnish language, and 7 Swedish).

Production and Industry.—Finland is a highly industrialised country producing a wide range of capital and consumer goods. Timber and the products of the forest-based industries remain the backbone of the economy, accounting for about half of her export earnings, but the importance of the metal-working, shipbuilding and engineering industries is growing. This sector in 1975 accounted for over a quarter of Finland's exports. The textile industry is well developed and Finland's glass, ceramics and furniture industries enjoy international reputations. Other important industries are rubber, plastics, chemicals and pharmaceuticals, footwear, foodstuffs and electronic equipment.

Communications.—There are 5,900 kilometres of railroad and a well-developed telegraph and telephone system. There is railway connection with Sweden and U.S.S.R., passenger boat connection with Britain, Sweden, Denmark and West Germany. Vessels on the London to Leningrad route call at Helsinki. There are also passenger/cargo services between Britain and Helsinki, Korka and other Finnish ports. External civil air services are maintained by British Airways, Finnair, Kar Air, Scandinavian Airlines, Maley, Lufthansa, Interflug, Pan American, LOT (Polish Airlines), Aeroflot, Czechoslovak Airlines and Swiss Air. The merchant fleet at the end of 1975 totalled 450 vessels (2,048,100 tons gross); 24 steamers (13,300 tons gross); 365 motor vessels (896,200) and 61 tankers (1,138,600).

FINANCE

	1975	1976*
	Finnmarks	*Finnmarks*
Revenue (*Budget*)	24,779,000,000	29,010,000,000
Expenditure (*Budget*)	27,050,000,000	29,009,000,000

* Proposed budget figures for 1976.

TRADE

	1974	1975
	Finnmarks	*Finnmarks*
Total Imports	25,676,000,000	27,974,000,000
Total Exports	20,687,000,000	20,248,000,000
	1974	1975
Imports from U.K.	£228,000,000	£264,466,000
Exports to U.K.	493,000,000	400,402,000

The principal imports are raw materials, foodstuffs, machinery and manufactured goods. The exports are principally the output of the timber and forest based industries and metal industry (*e.g.* paper-working machinery and ships).

CAPITAL.— Ψ Helsinki (Helsingfors). Population 505,719; other towns are Tampere (Tammerfors), 164,423; Ψ Turku (Abo), 162,210; Lahti, 93,396; Ψ Oulu (Uleaborg) 89,039; Ψ Pori (Björneborg) 79,295; Jyväskylä, 59,930; Kuopio, 69,569; Lappeenranta, 52,052; and Ψ Vaasa (Vasa) 54,115.

NATIONAL DAY.—December 6 (Day of Independence).

FLAG.—White with blue cross.

BRITISH EMBASSY
Helsinki

British Ambassador's Residence, It. Puistotie 15. *Chancery Offices*, Uudenmaankatu 16–20.

Ambassador Extraordinary and Plenipotentiary, His Excellency Sir James Eric Cable, K.C.V.O., C.M.G. (1975).

Counsellor (*Commercial*), M. S. Berthoud (*and Consul-General*).

1st Secretaries, Miss M. I. Rothwell; H. B. Herring (*Commercial*); H. O. Spankie; P. J. Monk (*Consul*).

Defence, Military Attaché and Air, Lt.-Col. J. O. Lawes, M.C., M.V.O.

Naval Attaché, Capt. R. J. F. Turner, R.N.

2nd Secretaries, J. B. Midgley (*Commercial*); G. Berg, M.V.O.; R. O. L. Fraser-Darling.

3rd Secretaries, M. Edwards (*Vice-Consul*); Miss E. A. Sketchley.

There are British Consular offices at *Helsinki, Tampere, Turku, Pori, Kotka, Oulu*, and *Vaasa*.

British Council Representative, R. B. Lodge, Eteläsplanadi 22A, Helsinki 13.

FRANCE
(La République Française)

President of the French Republic, Valéry Giscard d'Estaing, born Feb. 2, 1926, elected May 19, 1974, assumed office, May 27, 1974.

CABINET

Prime Minister, Economy and Finance, M. Raymond Barre.

Foreign Affairs, M. Louis de Guiringaud.

Interior, M. Michel Poniatowski.

Justice, M. Olivier Guichard.

Planning and Development, M. Jean Lecanuet.

Minister-Delegate to Economy and Finance Minister, M. Michel Durafour.

Defence, M. Yvon Bourges.

Education, M. René Haby.

Co-operation, M. Robert Galley.

Supply, M. Jean-Pierre Fourcade.

Parliamentary Relations, M. Robert Boulin.

Agriculture, M. Christian Bonnet.

Foreign Trade, M. André Rossi.

Labour, M. Christian Beullac.

Health, Mme. Simone Veil.

Industry and Research, M. Michel d'Ornano.

Quality of Life, M. Vincent Ansquer.

Trade and Crafts, M. Pierre Brousse.

Posts and Telecommunications, M. Norbert Segard.

Secretaries of State, M. André Bord (*Ex-Servicemen*); Mme. Françoise Giroud (*Culture*).

FRENCH EMBASSY IN LONDON

Residence: 11 Kensington Palace Gardens, W.8 [01–229 9411]

Chancery: 58 Knightsbridge, S.W.1. [01–235 8080].

Ambassador Extraordinary and Plenipotentiary, His Excellency Monsieur Jacques de Beaumarchais (1972).

Minister-Counsellor, M. Jean-Max Bouchaud.

2nd Counsellors, M. Charles Crettien; M. Robert Delos Santos.

Press Counsellor, M. Daniel Contenay.

1st Secretaries, M. Denis Nardin; M. Jean-Paul Réau; M. Henri Vignal.

2nd Secretary, M. Philippe Selz.

3rd Secretary, M. Dominique Raoux (*Press*).

Area and Population.—The largest state in Central Europe, extending from 42° 20′ to 51° 5′ N. lat., and from 7° 85′ E. to 4° 45′ W. long., bounded on the north by the English Channel and the Straits of Dover (*Pas de Calais*), which separate it from England. Its circumference is estimated at about 3,000 miles and its area at 213,000 sq. miles divided into 95 departments, including the island of Corsica, in the Mediterranean, off the west coast of Italy. The population of France (estimated) in 1975 was 52,590,000.

DEPARTMENTS AND REGIONS

Paris.....2,317,217			Calvados.... 572,421	
Seine-et-			Manche.... 466,319	
Marne..... 755,762			Orne........ 300,375	
Yvelines.....1,081,255				
Essonne..... 923,061			*Basse-Nor-*	
Hauts-de-			*mandie*...1,339,115	
Seine.....1,438,930				
Seine-Saint-			Côte-d'Or... 467,557	
Denis.....1,322,127			Nièvre..... 249,996	
Val-de-			Saône-et-	
Marne.....1,215,674			Loire...... 580,060	
Val-d'Oise... 840,885			Yonne...... 307,347	
Paris			*Bourgogne*..1,604,960	
Region....9,895,911				
			Nord.......2,534,906	
			Pas-de-	
Ardennes.... 309,306			Calais....1,403,035	
Aube 284,823				
Marne...... 549,485			*Nord*.....3,937,941	
Marne				
(Haute).... 221,437			Meurthe-et-	
			Moselle.... 741,437	
Champagne 1,365,061			Meuse..... 214,398	
			Moselle....1,020,957	
			Vosges..... 409,599	
Aisne....... 549,372				
Oise........ 620,450			*Lorraine*....2,396,391	
Somme...... 549,564				
			Rhin (Bas).. 896,185	
Picardie...1,719,386			Rhin (Haut).. 647,209	
Eure........ 433,529			*Alsace*.....1,543,394	
Seine-				
Maritime..1,187,919			Doubs...... 484,483	
			Jura........ 247,370	
Haute-Nor-			Saône (Haute) 229,357	
mandie...1,621,448			Belfort (Terr.	
			de)........ 131,359	
Cher....... 322,924				
Eure-et-Loir . 342,281			*Franche-*	
Indre....... 256,147			*Comté*...1,092,569	
Indre-et-				
Loire..... 486,884			Corrèze..... 250,559	
Loir-et-Cher.. 289,474			Creuse..... 151,341	
Loiret...... 502,213			Vienne	
			(Haute).... 359,365	
Centre.....2,199,923				
			Limousin... 761,265	
Loire-Atlan-				
tique 948,307			Ain......... 386,943	
Maine-et-			Ardèche.... 263,790	
Loire...... 644,458			Drôme..... 370,571	
Mayenne.... 268,108			Isère........ 875,525	
Sarthe...... 502,306			Loire....... 751,598	
Vendée..... 461,928			Rhône.....1,449,527	
			Savoie..... 315,098	
Pays de la			Savoie	
Loire....2,825,107			(Haute).... 458,885	
			Rhône-	
Côtes-du-			*Alpes*....4,872,117	
Nord...... 547,871			Charente.... 345,445	
Finistère..... 832,158			Charente-	
Ille-et-			Maritime... 513,478	
Vilaine.... 719,320			Sèvres (Deux) 342,383	
			Vienne...... 366,530	
Morbihan.... 581,348				
			Poitou-Char-	
Bretagne...2,680,697			*entes*....1,567,836	

Dordogne...	381,797
Gironde.....	1,082,074
Landes......	298,585
Lot-et-Garonne...	299,157
Pyrénées (*Atlantiques*)	552,615
Aquitaine..2,614,228	
Ariège......	141,436
Aveyron.....	289,352
Garonne (Haute)....	793,569
Gers........	180,501
Lot.........	157,079
Pyrénées (Hautes)..	234,112
Tarn........	346,775
Tarn-et-Garonne...	189,547
Midi-Pyrenees....2,332,371	
Allier.......	386,489
Cantal......	173,758
Loire (Haute)	214,269
Puy-de-Dôme	596,699
Auvergne...1,371,215	

Aude........	279,003
Gard........	506,607
Hérault......	658,858
Lozère......	80,234
Pyrénées-Orientales.	305,730
Languedoc-Roussillon	1,830,432
Alpes-de-Haute-Provence..	115,697
Alpes (Hautes)	102,694
Alpes-Maritimes......	823,731
Bouches-du-Rhône....1,646,679	
Var........	643,740
Vaucluse....	398,540
Provence-Côte d'Azur...3,731,081	
Corsica....	220,000

Government.—Following the death of President Pompidou in 1974, M. Giscard d'Estaing was elected President. He assumed office on May 27. After the most recent parliamentary elections held on March 4 and 11, 1973, the strengths of the party groups in the National Assembly were established as follows:—

Union of Democrats for the Republic (Gaullist)	183
Socialists and left-wing Radicals	102
Communists	73
Independent Republicans (Government Supporters)	55
Reformers	34
Central Union (Government Supporters)	30
Others	13

Parliament consists of the National Assembly and the Senate. Bills may be presented in either House, except money bills, which must originate in the National Assembly. The normal session of Parliament is confined to 5½ months each year and it may also meet in extraordinary session for 12 days at the request of the Prime Minister or a majority of the Assembly. Voting rights are personal and can only be delegated in special circumstances.

The *Prime Minister* is appointed by the President, as is the Cabinet on the Prime Minister's recommendation. They are responsible to Parliament. But the executive is constitutionally separate from the legislature and Ministers may not sit in Parliament. The Prime Minister is assumed to have the Assembly's confidence unless the Opposition moves a censure motion signed by not less than one-tenth of the deputies; such motion must be approved by an absolute majority; if defeated, its sponsors must not introduce another no-confidence motion in the same session.

A *Constitutional Council* is responsible for supervising all elections and referenda and must be consulted on all constitutional matters and before the President of the Republic assumes emergency powers. At the request of the Government, the *Economic and Social Council* gives advice on bills, ordinances or decrees referred to it. Any economic or social plan or bill must be submitted to it.

Production.—The chief agriculture products are wheat, barley, rye, maize, oats, potatoes, beetroot (for the manufacture of sugar), hops, &c. Rice is being grown in parts of the Camargue (Rhône delta). Fruit trees abound, and are very productive, the principal being the olive, chestnut, walnut, almond, apple, pear, citron, fig, plum, &c. The harvest in 1974–75 was:—

	(Quintals)
Wheat	159,685,000 (1974–75)
Oats	36,868,000 (1975)
Barley	61,803,000 (1974–75)
Rye	3,892,000 (1975)
Maize	52,206,900 (1975)

Forestry is an important industry, the principal forests being those of the Ardennes, Compiègne, Fontainebleau, and Orléans, consisting chiefly of oak, birch, pine, beech, elm, chestnut and the corktree in the south. The vine is cultivated to a very great extent, as the names Bordeaux, Burgundy, Champagne, &c., universally testify. Production of wine in 1974 was 62,100,000 hectolitres. Cidermaking is also an important industry. The mineral resources include coal, natural gas, pig iron, bauxite, lead, silver, antimony and salt. The most important manufactures are of metals, cars, aircraft, watches, jewellery, cabinet-work, carving, pottery, glass, chemicals, dyeing, paper making, cottons, woollens, carpets, linen, silk and lace.

Language and Literature.—French is the universal language of France and of a large proportion of the people of Belgium, Luxembourg, Switzerland, Tunisia, Algeria, Mauritius, Haiti and the Province of Quebec, Canada, to whom the almost inexhaustible literature of France is a treasured heritage. The work of the *French Academy*, founded by Richelieu in 1635, has established *le bon usage*, equivalent to " The King's English " in Great Britain. French authors have been awarded the Nobel Prize for Literature on 11 occasions:— R.F.A. Sully-Prudhomme (1901), F. Mistral (1904), Romain Rolland (1915), Anatole France (1921), Henri Bergson (1927), Roger M. du Gard (1937), André Gide (1947), François Mauriac (1952), Albert Camus (1957), St. John Perse (Alexis Léger) (1960) and Jean Paul Sartre (1964).

Defence.—The personnel of the Defence Forces in September 1975 totalled: ARMY 331,500; AIR FORCE 102,000; NAVY 69,000; GENDARMERIE 70,000. National nuclear forces include medium-range ballistic missiles, submarine-launched ballistic missiles and *Mirage IV* medium bombers. The Army has a variety of new French-made equipment in service, including medium tanks, field and anti-aircraft SP guns, trucks and radio equipment.

Defence Budget for 1974, 38,221,000,000,000 francs.

Education.—The educational system is highly developed and centralized. It is administered by the Ministry of National Education, comprising (a) the *Direction des Enseignements Supérieurs; Direction de la Pédagogie, des Enseignements Scholaires et de l'Orientation; Direction des Personnels d'Enseignement Général Technique et Professionnel; Direction des Services Administratifs et Sociaux; Direction de l'Equipement Scolaire, Universitaire et Sportif; Direction des Bibliothèques et de la Lecture Publique; Direction de la Coopération;* (b) the Superior Council of National Education (consultative); and (c) the Inspectorate. *Local Administration* comprises 25 Territorial Academies, with inspecting staff for all grades, and Departmental Councils presided over by the *Préfet*, and charged especially with *primary* education.

Primary and secondary education are compulsory, free and secular, the school age being from 6 to 16. Schools are for boys, for girls, or mixed. (i) *Primary* education is given in *écoles maternelles* (nursery schools), *écoles primaires élémentaires* (primary schools) and *collèges d'enseignement général* (4-year secondary modern course); (ii) *Secondary* education in *collèges d'enseignement technique, collèges d'enseignement secondaire* and *lycées* (7-year course leading to one of the five *baccalauréats*). *Baccalauréat A* consists largely of philosophy and languages with a little mathematics, and provides entry into the faculties of Letters and Law. *Baccalauréat B* groups languages, mathematics and economics with philosophy classes oriented towards psychology and sociology. It provides entry to the faculties of Letters for the social sciences and to the faculty of Law for economics. *Baccalauréat C*, consisting of mathematics and physics with some languages, provides entry to the faculty of Sciences for those studying for a degree in mathematics and physics. *Baccalauréat D* has the same language component as *Baccalauréat C*, but its main feature is the natural sciences. It provides entry to the faculty of Sciences for natural science degrees, and also to the Medicine and Pharmacy Faculties. *Baccalauréat E* is largely scientific and technical with a language element, and provides entry to engineering schools and the Faculty of Science. (iii) *Special schools* are numerous. (iv) There are numerous *Grandes Ecoles* in France which award diplomas in many subjects not taught at university, especially applied science and engineering. Most of them are State institutions but have a competitive system of entry, unlike the universities. (v) The reform of the French university structure continues, and there are now universities in twenty-four towns in France. In the major provincial towns the existing university has been reorganized to form two, or three universities, and in Paris and the immediate surrounding district there are, since autumn 1970, thirteen universities.

Archæology, etc.—There are dolmens and menhirs in Brittany, prehistoric remains and cave drawings in Dordogne and Ariège, and throughout France various megalithic monuments erected by primitive tribes, predecessors of Iberian invaders from Spain (now represented by the Basques), Ligurians from northern Italy and Celts or Gauls from the valley of the Danube. Julius Cæsar found Gaul " divided into three parts " and described three political groups—Aquitanians south of the Garonne, Celts between the Garonne and the Seine and Marne, and Belgae from the Seine to the Rhine. Roman remains are plentiful throughout France in the form of aqueducts, arenas, triumphal arches, &c., and the celebrated Norman and Gothic Cathedrals, including Notre Dame in Paris, and

those of Chartres, Reims, Amiens (where Peter the Hermit preached the First Crusade for the recovery of the Holy Sepulchre), Bourges, Beauvais, Rouen, etc., have survived invasions and bombardments, with only partial damage, and many of the renaissance and the XVIIth and XVIIIth century châteaux survived the French Revolution.

Roads.—The length of the *Routes Nationales* at the end of 1974 was 73,306 km. and of motorways 2,628 km. The principal rivers of France are the Seine, Loire, Garonne, and Rhône, the navigable waterways in general use in 1975 were 8,623 km.

Railways.—The system of railroads in France is very extensive. The length of lines of general interest, exclusive of local lines, open for traffic at the end of 1974 was 34,810 km., of which 9,325 km. were electrified. Traffic at the end of 1974 totalled 47,100,000,000 passenger-km. and 77,054,000,000 ton-km.

Shipping.—The French mercantile marine consisted in Jan. 1973, of 531 ships of 7,440,004 tons gross, of which 26 were passenger vessels (229,696 tons gross), 129 tankers (4,658,995 tons gross) and 376 cargo vessels (2,551,313 tons gross).

FINANCE

	1973	1974
	F. millions	
Total revenue (*Budget*)	225,278	272,898
Total expenditure (*do.*)	220,018	254,148

The *Public Debt* on Dec. 31, 1972, was F.87,810,000,000 of which the external debt amounted to F.38,400,000,000.

Currency.—The unit of currency is the *franc* of 100 *centimes*, which was devalued on Aug. 10, 1969. Bank notes in 10, 50, 100 and 500 *franc* denominations and coins in 1, 5, 10 and 20 *francs* are issued.

EXCHANGE RATE (at May 14, 1976).—F.8·53/8·63 = £1 (*see also* p. 83).

COMMERCE

The principal imports are machinery, mineral fuels, chemical products, automobiles, iron, electrical equipment, minerals and non-ferrous metals, textile and leather goods, meat, fish, poultry and other agricultural products and precision instruments. The principal exports are automobiles, chemical products, iron and steel, textile and leather goods, machinery, electrical equipment, cereals and flour, wine and other agricultural products.

FRENCH FOREIGN TRADE

	1974	1975
	Francs	Francs
Imports	245,847,000,000	223,691,000,000
Exports	210,464,000,000	212,348,000,000

Trade with U.K.

	1974	1975
Imports from U.K.	£914,639,000	£1,164,441,000
Exports to U.K.	1,349,153,000	1,627,770,000

OVERSEAS DEPARTMENTS

With effect from Jan 1, 1947, the colonies of Guyane (French Guiana), Martinique, Guadeloupe and La Réunion with its dependencies have been theoretically administered in exactly the same way as the Metropolitan Departments, but in practice somewhat greater discretion is allowed to the Prefects and the locally elected bodies.

La Réunion.—Formerly Ile de Bourbon, about 420 miles E. of Madagascar, Réunion has been a French possession since 1643. Area, about 1,000 sq. miles. Population (1974), 476,675. Capital,

St. Denis (104,603). Assigned to the administration of Réunion are the distant islands of St. Paul (3 sq. miles), New Amsterdam (27 sq. miles) and Kerguelen containing whaling and fishing stations 1,100 sq. miles). The Crozet Islands (200 sq. miles) and Adélie Land in the Antarctic Continent are also dependencies of Réunion. Imports from U.K., 1975, £1,138,000.

Martinique.—An island situated in the Windward Islands group of the West Indies, between Dominica in the north and St. Lucia in the south. Population 324,832. Capital ΨFort de France (100,576). Other towns are ΨTrinité (11,214) and ΨMarin (6,104).

Guadeloupe.—In the Leeward Islands of the West Indies, the island of Guadeloupe, together with Marie Galante, the Ile des Saintes, Petite Terre, St. Barthélemy and St. Martin, form the other West Indian Department of France. Population 324,530. Capital ΨPointe à Pitre 23,889). Other towns are ΨBasse Terre (15,778) in Guadeloupe and ΨGrand Bourg (6,611) in Marie Galante.

French Guiana.—Area, 35,000 sq. miles. Population (U.N. estimate, 1969), 48,000. Capital, ΨCayenne (20,000). Situated on the north-eastern coast of South America, French Guiana is flanked by Surinam on the west and by Brazil on the south and east. Under the administration of French Guiana is a group of islands (St. Joseph, Ile Royal and Ile du Diable), known as Iles du Salut. On Devil's Isle, Captain Dreyfus was imprisoned from 1894 to 1899. Imports from U.K. in 1975 were valued at £422,,000.

CAPITAL OF FRANCE. Paris, on the Seine.
Population (estimated, 1975), 2,317,227) (town); 6,293,958 (incl. suburbs).

District of Paris.—Created by legislation promulgated on August 10, 1966, the District consists of 8 Departments one of which is the City of Paris (*see* list of Departments, p. 855).

Paris is administered by the Council of Paris which is composed of 90 members elected for six years by popular vote within the city/Department. The President and four Vice-Presidents of the Council are elected for one year by the members. The President presides over the meetings of the Council and is the representative of Paris on all official occasions. The administrative functions exercised in all other towns by the Mayor are exercised in Paris by two Government nominees: the Prefect of Paris, and the Prefect of Police. But Mayors are elected in each of the 20 arrondissements of Paris to carry out local civil duties.

The following towns have a population of over 150,000 inhabitants:—Paris (2,317,227); Ψ Marseilles (914,356); Lyons (452,841); Toulouse (383,176); Ψ Nice (346,620); ΨNantes (263,689); Strasbourg (257,303); ΨBordeaux (226,281); Saint-Etienne (221,775); Ψ Le Havre (219,583); Rennes (205,733); Montpellier (195,603); Ψ Toulon (185,050); Reims (183,610); Lille (177,218); ΨBrest (172,176); Grenoble (169,740); Clermont-Ferrand (161,203); Dijon (156,787); Le Mans (155,245).

The chief towns of Corsica are Ψ Ajaccio (44,659) and ΨBastia (51,022).

Paris is distant from London 267 miles; transit by air, 1 hr.

FLAG.—The "tricolour", three vertical bands, blue, white, red (blue next to flagstaff).

NATIONAL DAY.—July 14.

BRITISH EMBASSY

(35 rue du Faubourg St. Honoré, Paris 8e)
Ambassador Extraordinary and Plenipotentiary, His Excellency Sir Nicholas Henderson, K.C.M.G., (1975).

Minister, C. M. James.
Minister (Economic), R. Arculus, C.M.G.
Defence Attaché, Air Cdre. W. J. Herrington.
Counsellor and Consul-General, J. McAdam Clark, C.V.O., M.C.

BRITISH CONSULAR OFFICES

There are British Consulates-General in Metropolitan France at *Paris, Bordeaux, Lille, Lyons, Marseilles* and *Strasbourg*.

BRITISH CHAMBER OF COMMERCE
6 Rue Halévy, Paris 9e

President, O. G. Longley, M.C.
Vice-Presidents, D. H. Goodchild; K. G. W. Bartell.

BRITISH COUNCIL

Representative in Paris, R. M. Auty, O.B.E., 9 rue de Constantine, 75007 Paris.

There is a British Council office at *Toulouse*; British Council libraries at *Paris, Bordeaux, Lille, Lyons* and *Strasbourg*.

THE FRENCH COMMUNITY

The Constitution of the Fifth French Republic promulgated on Oct. 6, 1958, envisaged the establishment of a French Community of States closely linked with common institutions. A number of the former French States in Africa have seceded from the Community but for all practical purposes continue to enjoy the same close links with France as those that remain formally members of the French Community. The Community Institutions in fact never operated as envisaged. Nevertheless, with the exception of Guinea, which opted out of the Community in the 1958 referendum, all the former French African colonies are closely linked to France by a series of financial, technical and economic agreements.

Francophone Countries.

In the following countries French is either the official or national language or the language of instruction; where there is another national language the name of it is shown after the name of the country:—Algeria (*Arabic*); Belgium (*Flemish*); Benin; Burundi (*Kirundi*); Cambodia (*Khmer*); Cameroon (*English*); parts of Canada (in Quebec, parts of Ontario and New Brunswick) (*English*); Central African Republic (*Sangho*); Chad; Congo (P.D.R.); France; Gabon; Guinea; Haiti (*Creole*); Ivory Coast; Laos (*Laotian*); Lebanon (*Arabic*); Luxembourg (*German and Letzeburgesch*); Madagascar (*Malagasy*); Mali; Morocco (*Arabic*); Mauritania (*Arabic*); Niger; Rwanda (*Kinyarwanda*); Senegal; Switzerland (1,000,000 French speaking); Togo; Tunisia (*Arabic*); Upper Volta; Vietnam (*Vietnamese*); Zaire. French is also spoken in the Overseas Departments (*see* above).

OTHER TERRITORIES

French Territory of the Afars and Issas.— Situated on the north-east coast of Africa, the Territory has an area of 9,000 sq. miles with a population (estimate, 1970) of about 81,200.

Formerly French Somaliland, the Territory was renamed on July 6, 1967, to emphasize the existence of the two main ethnic groups in the population. A renamed Chamber of Deputies succeeded the former territorial assembly to which a governing council is responsible for the administration of the territory. The French High Commissioner retains responsibility for foreign policy, defence, currency, credit, citizenship and law, other than traditional civil law. Capital, Ψ Djibouti (62,000).

New Caledonia.—Area, 7,200 sq. miles. Population (estimate, 1971), 100,600. Capital Ψ Noumea (12,000). A large island in the Western Pacific, 700 miles E. of Queensland. Dependencies are

the Isle of Pines, the Loyalty Islands (Mahé, Lifou, Urea, etc., the Huon islands and Alofis). New Caledonia was discovered in 1774 and annexed by France in 1854; from 1871 to 1896 it was a convict settlement. It is the world's third largest producer of nickel, after Canada and U.S.S.R.

Wallis and Futuna Islands.—Following a request from local kings and chiefs, it was decided by referendum (Dec. 27, 1959) that the islands would become the sixth Overseas Territory of France. Population of the islands, formerly dependencies of New Caledonia, is about 8,550, mostly Polynesians.

French Polynesia.—Area, 2,500 sq. miles. Population (estimate, 1971), 119,200. Capital, Ψ Papeete (15,220), in Tahiti. Includes the Society Islands (Tahiti, Moorea, Makatea, etc.), the Marquesas (Nukahiva, Hiva-oa, etc., 500 sq. miles, population, 3,000); the Leeward Isles (Huahine, Raiatea, Tahaa, Bora Bora, Maupiti, etc.); the Gambier Islands (Mangareva, etc.); the Tubuai Islands (Tubuai, Rurutu, Raivavae, Rimatara and Rapa Island; and Maiao Island).

Comoro Archipelago.—Area, 800 sq. miles. Population (estimated 1970), 275,227. Capital, Moroni Includes the islands of Great Comoro, Anjouan, Mayotte and Mohilla and certain islets in the Indian Ocean. Except for Mayotte, the islands voted in favour of independence in a referendum in December, 1974.

St. Pierre and Miquelon—Area, 93 sq. miles. Population (1968), 5,200. Two small groups of Islands off the coast of Newfoundland.

GABON
(Gabonese Republic)
(*For MAP, see* Index).

President, Omar Bongo, *assumed office*, December, 1967.

EMBASSY IN LONDON
48 Kensington Court, W.8.
[01-937 5285]

Ambassador Extraordinary and Plenipotentiary, His Excellency Joseph N'Goua.

Gabon lies on the Atlantic coast of Africa at the Equator and is flanked on the north by Equatorial Guinea and Cameroon and on the east and south by the People's Republic of Congo. It has an area of 101,400 sq. miles and a population (estimated 1972) of 500,000. Gabon elected on Nov. 28, 1958, to remain an autonomous republic within the French Community and was proclaimed fully independent on August 17, 1960.

Over the past decade Gabon has known one of the fastest economic growth rates in Africa, based almost entirely on oil, production of which attained 11·5 million tonnes in 1975, making Gabon the fourth largest oil producer in Africa. Other wealth includes okoumé wood, manganese, uranium and iron.

The budget increased by 575 per cent. between 1970 and 1975, and for 1975 stands at £424,000,000. Gabon became an associate member of OPEC in 1973 and a full member in 1975.

Trade with U.K.

	1974	1975
Imports from U.K.	£3,565,000	£2,828,000
Exports to U.K.	28,397,000	3,759,000

CAPITAL.— Ψ Libreville (31,000).
FLAG.—Horizontal bands, green, yellow and blue.
NATIONAL DAY.—August 17.
British Ambassador (vacant).
Chargé d'Affaires, 1st Secretary and Consul, J. K. Gordon (resident at *Yaoundé*).
Consul, S. Prince (resident at *Douala*).

GERMANY
★ Deutsches Reich (German Realm)

THE HISTORY OF GERMANY from 1863–1945 is marked by wars of aggression. In 1864, Prussia, in company with Austria, attacked Denmark, and after a short campaign annexed the peninsula of Schleswig-Holstein. In 1866, as a result of war with Austria (the Seven Weeks' War), Prussia acquired the hegemony of the North Germanic Confederation from Austria. After the Franco-Prussian War of 1870, when Prussia wrested Alsace-Lorraine from France, the North Germanic Confederation and three South German States became the Germanic Confederation, the King of Prussia being proclaimed German Emperor at Versailles on Jan. 18, 1871.

At the outbreak of the War of 1914–1918, Germany was a Confederate League bearing the name German Empire under the hereditary presidency of the King of Prussia holding the title of German Emperor. At the close of the war, Germany lost most of the gains she had acquired since 1863, including all her colonies.

THE WAR OF 1939–1945.—After concluding a Treaty of Non-Aggression with Soviet Russia (Aug. 24, 1939), Germany invaded Poland (Sept. 1, 1939), thus precipitating war with France and Great Britain, which had (March 31) given a pledge to support Poland against aggression.

On May 8, 1945, the unconditional surrender of all German forces was accepted by representatives of the Western Allied and Soviet Supreme Commanders.

Hitler committed suicide on April 30, 1945.

THE POST WAR PERIOD.—After the surrender the Allied Powers assumed supreme authority in Germany. Power was to be exercised by the Commanders-in-Chief, each in his own zone of occupation and jointly in matters affecting Germany as a whole through a Control Council. Berlin was to be governed jointly by the four occupying powers. The guiding lines of policy were laid down in the agreement reached between the U.K., U.S. and U.S.S.R. Governments at Potsdam in August, 1945, which was to remain in force until a Peace Treaty should confirm or revise its directives. It was decided that " for the time being no Central German Government shall be established," but that central German administrative departments acting under the direction of the Control Council should be established in the fields of finance, transport, communications, foreign trade and industry. The Eastern frontier of Germany was provisionally redrawn (pending final settlement in the Peace Treaty) to transfer the northern area of East Prussia, including Königsberg (now Kaliningrad), to the U.S.S.R. and the rest of East Prussia and all the area lying east of the Oder and Western Neisse rivers to Polish control. On Oct. 15, 1947, the Saar, enlarged at the expense of German territory, voted for economic union with France, but following a plebiscite was incorporated in the Federal Republic of Germany on Jan. 1, 1957. The Potsdam agreement also laid down that Germany should be disarmed and prohibited from producing armaments, that production of certain other goods should be limited to the amount needed to support a peacetime economy and that

existing capital equipment surplus to these requirements should be removed as reparations and distributed by the Inter Allied Reparations Agency among the nations who had suffered war damage, in proportion to their losses. (The proportions were fixed by the Paris Conference of November, 1945.) The agreement further dealt with denazification, democratization, refugees, restitution, decartelization, etc.

Though certain details of the Potsdam agreement (not yet superseded by a Peace Treaty) have been carried out, differences in interpretation among the Allies have made it impossible to apply the provisions in full. Quadripartite control became a dead letter when the Russians withdrew from the Control Council in March, 1948.

FEDERAL REPUBLIC OF GERMANY

President, Walter Scheel, *born* July 8, 1919, *elected* July 1, 1974, *for five years*.

CABINET

Federal Chancellor, Helmut Schmidt (*SPD*).
Foreign Minister and Vice-Chancellor, Hans Dietrich Genscher (*FDP*).
Interior, Dr. Werner Maihofer (*FDP*).
Justice, Jochen Vogel (*SPD*).
Finance, Hans Apel (*SPD*).
Economics, Dr. Hans Friderichs (*FDP*).
Food, Agriculture and Forestry, Josef Ertl (*FDP*).
Labour and Social Affairs, Walter Arendt (*SPD*).
Defence, Georg Leber (*SPD*).
Transport, Posts and Telecommunications, Kurt Gscheidle (*SPD*).
Regional Planning, Building and Urban Development, Karl Ravens (*SPD*).
Intra-German Relations, Egon Franke (*SPD*).
Health, Family and Youth Questions, Dr. Katharina Focke (*SPD*).
Education and Science, Hans Rohde (*SPD*).
Research and Technology, Hans Matthöfer (*SPD*).
Economic Co-operation, Egon Bahr (*SPD*).
FDP=Free Democrats; *SPD*=Social Democrats.

EMBASSY IN LONDON
23 Belgrave Square, S.W.1
[01–235 5033]

(*Consular, Passports, etc.*:
6 Rutland Gate, S.W.7.)

Ambassador Extraordinary and Plenipotentiary, His Excellency Karl-Günther von Hase, K.C.M.G. (1970).
Minister Plenipotentiary, H. H. Noebel.
Minister-Counsellor, Dr. K. Stöckl.
Minister, Herr Hans Freiherr von Stein (*Head of Economic Dept.*).
1st Counsellors, Dr. Rolf Breitenstein (*Press*); Frau Dr. Brigitte Lohmeyer (*Cultural*); Dr. Hans-Peter Lorenzen (*Scientific Affairs*); Dr. Christian Hofman (*Agriculture*); Herr Lothar Schiebschick (*Defence Research*).
Counsellors, Herr Hans-Wolfgang Neugebauer; Herr Dietrich Lincke; Dr. Rudolf Vollmer (*Labour*); Dr. Mario Graf von Matuschka; Dr. Hans-Cajetan Schmidt-Dahlenburg (*Commodities*); Dr. Christopher Niemöller (*Legal and Consular*).
1st Secretaries, Fräulein Margarete Stark; Dr. Wilhelm Dünwald; Herr B. Oetter; Herr Günter Habelt; Frau Dr. Jutta Grützner; Frau Dr. Elke Schmitz; Herr Jörg-Rainer Wendicke, Herr Bertold Brandenstein (*Finance*); Herr Klaus Metscher.

★ Nazi historians referred to the National Socialist régime as *Drittes Reich*. The *First* was the Holy Roman Empire, established in A.D. 962 by Otto I of Saxony, enduring until 1806. The *Second* was established by Prince Otto von Bismarck, after the Franco-Prussian war in 1871, and endured until 1918. The *Third* was established by Adolf Hitler in 1933.

Note.—Except where otherwise indicated statistical data on the Federal Republic of German include Berlin (West).

Area and Population.—The area of the Federal Republic is approximately 95,993 sq. miles. Total population of the Federal Republic on December 31, 1975, was 61,644,600. Distribution of the population among the *Länder* in 1975 was:

Schleswig-Holstein	2,582,400
Hamburg	1,717,400
Lower Saxony	7,238,500
Bremen	716,800
North Rhine Westphalia	17,129,600
Hessen	5,549,800
Rhineland Palatinate	3,665,800
Baden-Wurttemberg	9,152,700
Bavaria	10,810,400
Saarland	1,096,300
Berlin (West)	1,984,800

The population of the principal cities and towns in the Federal Republic on Dec. 31, 1975, was:

Berlin (West)	1,984,837	Mainz	183,880
ΨHamburg	1,717,383	Freiburg	175,371
Munich	1,314,865	Hamm	172,210
Cologne	1,013,771	Solingen	171,810
Essen	677,568	Ludwigshaven	170,374
Düsseldorf	664,336	Leverkusen	165,947
Frankfurt/Main	636,157	Osnabrück	161,671
Dortmund	630,609	Neuss	148,198
Stuttgart	600,421	ΨBremerhaven	143,836
Duisburg	591,635	Darmstadt	137,018
ΨBremen	572,969	Oldenburg	134,706
Hanover	552,955	Remscheid	133,145
Nuremberg	499,060	Regensburg	131,886
Bochum	414,842	Heidelberg	129,368
Wuppertal	405,369	Wolfsburg	126,298
Gelsenkirchen	322,584	Göttingen	123,797
Bielefeld	316,058	Recklinghausen	122,437
Mannheim	314,086	Koblenz	118,394
Bonn	283,711	Salzgitter	117,341
Karlsruhe	280,448	Siegen	116,552
Brunswick	268,519	Offenbach/	
Münster	264,546	Main	115,251
ΨKiel	262,164	Heilbronn	113,177
Mönchen-		Würzburg	112,584
Gladbach	261,367	Witten	108,771
Wiesbaden	250,592	Pforzheim	108,635
Augsburg	249,943	Hildesheim	105,290
Aachen	242,453	Paderborn	103,705
Oberhausen	237,147	ΨWihelms-	
ΨLübeck	232,270	haven	103,417
Hagen	229,224	Fürth	101,639
Krefeld	228,463	Moers	101,511
Kassel	205,534	Bottrop	101,495
Saarbrücken	205,336	Kaiserslautern	100,886
Herne	190,561	Erlangen	100,671
Mülheim/Ruhr	189,259	Trier	100,338

Vital Statistics.—There were 10·1 live births per 1,000 inhabitants in the Federal Republic in 1974, compared with 19·5 per 1,000 for the same area in 1938.

Government.—The Federal Republic grew out of the fusion of the three western zones. The economic union of the U.K. and U.S. zones followed the Fusion Agreement of December, 1946. The Bizone was later joined by the French zone and in 1948–49 Parliamentary Council, elected by the Diets of the three zones, drafted a provisional democratic federal constitution for Germany. This Basic Law came into force in the three western zones on May 23, 1949. It provides for a President, elected for a five-year term, a Lower House, with a four-year term of office, elected by direct universal suffrage, and an Upper House

composed of delegates of the *Länder*, without a fixed term of office.

The preliminary results of the elections held for the lower House (*Bundestag*) on October 3, 1976, were as follows:

Party	Numbers
Social Democrats	213
Christian Democratic Union	191
Christian-Social Union	53
Free Democrats	39
Total	496

with an additional 22 representatives of Berlin elected by the Berlin Chamber of Deputies (Social Democrats, 12; Christian Democrats, 9; Free Democrats, 1). The Social Democrats form a coalition with the Free Democrats. The Christian Democratic and the Christian Social Unions are the Parliamentary Opposition.

When the Federal Government took office the Allied Military Governors were replaced by High Commissioners. In 1952 a contractual agreement was signed between the Federal Republic and the western Allies, whereby the Republic, in return for certain promises regarding a defence contribution, a foreign debt settlement, and the continuation of allied policies concerning decartelization, democratization, restitution, etc., regained virtual sovereignty in May, 1955, after ratification by all the parties concerned. The High Commissioners then became Ambassadors.

The Prime Ministers of the *Länder* governments in June, 1976, were:—

Ministers-President
Baden-Württemberg.—Dr. Hans Filbinger.
Bavaria.—Dr. Alfons Goppel.
Berlin.—Klaus Schütz (*Governing Mayor*).
Bremen.—Hans Koschnick (*Mayor*).
Hamburg.—Peter Schulz (*Mayor*).
Hessen.—Albert Osswald.
Lower Saxony.—Dr. Ernst Albrecht.
North Rhine-Westphalia.—Heinz Kühn.
Rhineland-Palatinate.—Dr. Helmut Kohl.
Saarland.—Dr. Franz-Josef Röder.
Schleswig-Holstein.—Dr. Gerhard Stoltenberg.

Economic position.—Despite the difficulties arising from the division of Germany, which cut off from the Federal Republic the main food producing areas of Eastern Germany and some of the principal centres of light industry, German economic recovery has made rapid strides since the currency reform of 1948. As a result of United States and British economic aid and of successful economic policies pursued by the Federal Government, Germany has regained her position as the main industrial power on the Continent, and is the most economically powerful member of the European Common Market. The Gross National Product at current prices in 1975 was estimated at $DM.1,040·4$ milliard, an increase of $DM.44·7$ milliard or 4·5 per cent. over 1974.

Agriculture.—In 1975 total area of farmland was 13,303,100 hectares, of which 7,538,000 hectares were arable land. Forest areas cover 7,161,600 hectares. The 1975 harvest yielded 9,241,900 metric tons of bread grains, 10,853,200 metric tons of potatoes. The livestock population at the end of 1975 included 14,511,462 cattle, 341,562 horses, 1,093,844 sheep, 19,853,250 pigs and 91,248,575 fowl.

Industrial Production.—The index of industrial net production adjusted for irregularities of the calendar (1970= 100) has developed in the Federal Republic, including Berlin, as follows:

	1973	1974	1975
Mining......................	92·3	91·4	84·8
Manufacturing industry......	112·6	110·6	103·2
(i) Basic materials........	116·3	116·0	101·6
(ii) Capital goods........	110·3	107·2	102·1
(iii) Consumer goods......	112·2	107·7	101·9
(iv) Foodstuffs...........	111·9	113·7	114·0
Power (electricity and gas)....	139·8	159·8	155·7
Building Industry...........	110·3	104·8	93·8
Total industry.......	113·1	111·5	104·5

Productivity of labour in industry (excluding electricity, gas and building industries) per man-hour: 1968, 90·5; 1969, 96·5; 1970, 100; 1971, 106·1; 1972, 114·6; 1973, 122·7; 1974, 128·3; 1975, 134 per cent.

Some production figures are shown below (monthly averages):

	1974	1975
	Number	
Passenger cars...............	214,607	224,212
Commercial vehicles..........	18,786	20,386
	Tons	
	1974	1975
Sulphuric acid (SO3).........	348,983	282,819
Chlorine....................	227,094	191,329
	Tons	
	1974	1975
Artificial plastic material.......	522,601	420,503

	1974	1975
Man-made fibres..............	78,302	62,394
Cotton yarn.................	17,831	16,027
Woollen yarn................	4,565	4,285

436,800 new dwellings were completed in 1975 in the Federal Republic (1974, *604,400*).

Labour.—Of 25,350,000 employed in 1975 (annual average), 15,978,000 were men. The average number of unemployed was 1,074,217 of whom 622,627 were men (1974=*582,481* and *324,685*). On September 30, 1975, 2,038,800 foreign workers were employed in the Federal Republic. An average of 7,615,882 (1974=*8,143,537* were employed in industry (establishments employing 10 or more persons).

	1974	1975
Coal mining...............	224,422	225,867
Iron and steel production...	316,046	310,242
Mechanical engineering.....	1,700,155	1,606,866
Chemicals.................	600,498	582,577
Textiles and clothing.......	703,997	645,192

Finance.—As from January 1, 1975, the distribution of taxes in the Fed. Rep. of Germany between Federation, Länder, communities and local authorities has been regulated by an amendment of the Basic Law (Constitution) as follows:—

(1) Of the yields of wage tax and assessed income tax, Federation and Länder receive 43 per cent. each, and the communities 14 per cent. The

yields of capital yield tax and corporation tax are distributed to Federation and Länder with 50 per cent. each.

(2) The turnover taxes have been made joint taxes of which the Federation obtains 68·25 per cent. and the Länder 31·75 per cent, after deduction of the E.C. share.

(3) Of the trade tax which so far had been fully allocated to the communities, the Federation and the Länder receive equal shares (about 20 per cent. of the trade tax receipts).

(4) The yields of capital transactions taxes, insurance and bill taxes accrue to the Federation.

Excise duties, other than the beer tax, accrue to the Federal Government, all other taxes (with the exception of local taxes, *i.e.* particularly taxes on land and buildings) to the *Länder*.

Preliminary figures of budgetary expenditure in 1976 are: total expenditure *DM*.164,047,000,000 (*1975,156,262,000,000*); Defence *DM*.33,384,000,000 (*1975, 32,101,000,000*); Social expenditure, *DM*.61,478,000,000 (*1975, 57,051,000,000*) (about 37 per cent.); Agriculture and food, *DM*.2,465,000,000 (*1975, 2,255,000,000*) (about 1·5 per cent.); Transport, *DM*.11,750,000,000 (*1975, 11,468,000,000*).

Currency.—The currency of the Federal Republic is the *Deutsche Mark* of 100 *Pfennig*, the rate of exchange with sterling being at April 30, 1976, *DM*.4·679 = £1. The rate of exchange of the pound sterling has been floating since 23 June 1972. (*See also* p. 83.)

Foreign Trade.—In 1975, imports were valued at *DM*.184,312,510,000 (*1974, 179,732,599,000*); and exports at *DM*.221,588,594,000; 16·9 per cent. of imports consisted of foodstuffs and 16·4 per cent. of industrial raw materials; 49·5 per cent. came from the Common Market* countries; 8·7 per cent. from the E.F.T.A.† and 8·7 per cent. from the United States and Canada. The Common Market countries took 43·6 per cent. of all exports, the E.F.T.A. 14·5 per cent. and the United States and Canada 6·8 per cent.

Trade with U.K.

	1974	1975
Imports from U.K.	£1,011,271,000	£1,272,446,000
Exports to U.K....	1,892,651,000	1,996,903,000

Communications.—In December, 1975, the state-owned railways of the Federal Republic measured 17,910 miles of which 6,215 miles were electrified, and the privately owned railways 1,919 miles, a total of 19,829 miles. In 1975 the railways handled 329,203,032 tons of goods and the inland waterways 227,329,886 tons. Railway rolling stock (*Deutsche Bundesbahn*) included, in 1975, 256 steam locomotives, 2,629 electric locomotives, 3,097 diesel locomotives, 17,548 passenger coaches, 627 rail buses and 287,755 goods waggons. Classified roads measure 104,940 miles. On Jan. 1, 1976, there were registered 18,161,179 cars, 1,293,158 commercial vehicles (incl. buses) and 1,441,778 tractors. Ocean-going shipping under the German flag in Dec., 1975, amounted to 8,700,371 tons gross (1,742 ships). Civil aircraft in service at the same date totalled 162 aircraft.

Social Welfare.—There is compulsory insurance against sickness, accident, old age and unemployment. Children's allowances are payable in respect of the second and subsequent children. Pension schemes for widows and orphans of public servants are in operation. Public assistance is given to persons unable to earn their living, or with insufficient income to maintain a decent standard of living.

Law and Justice.—Judicial authority is exercised by the Federal Constitutional Court, the Supreme Federal Court, and the courts of the *Länder*. Judges are independent and subject only to the law. The death sentence has been abolished.

Language and Literature.—Modern (or New High) German has developed from the time of the Reformation to the present day, with differences of dialect in Austria and Alsace and in the German-speaking cantons of Switzerland. The literary language is usually regarded as having become fixed by Luther and Zwingli at the Reformation, since which time many great names occur in all branches, notably philosophy, from Leibnitz (1646–1716) to Kant (1724–1804), Fichte (1762–1814), Schelling (1775–1854) and Hegel (1770–1831); the drama from Goethe (1749–1832) and Schiller (1759–1805) to Gerhart Hauptmann (1862–1946); and in poetry, Heine (1797–1856). German authors have received the Nobel Prize for Literature on seven occasions—Theodore Mommsen (1902), R. Eucken (1908), P. Heyse (1909), Gerhart Hauptmann (1912), Thomas Mann (1929), N. Sachs (1966) and Heinrich Böll (1972). In 1973 there were 404 daily papers.

Education.—School attendance is compulsory for all children and juveniles between the ages of 6 and 18. Compulsory education comprises 9 years of schooling at primary schools (*Volksschulen*)—full-time compulsory education—and 3 years of compulsory vocational education on a part-time basis. Preliminary figures showed that in autumn, 1974, there were in the Federal Republic 18,094 primary schools (*Volksschulen*) with 6,451,775 pupils. Intermediate schools (*Realschulen*) numbered 2,320 with 1,099,887 pupils. There were 2,543 secondary schools (*Gymnasien* including *Gesamtschulen*) with 1,914,001 pupils.

There were also 2,631 special schools (*Sonderschulen*) for retarded, physically and mentally handicapped and socially maladjusted children in the Federal Republic with 384,952 pupils.

The secondary school leaving examination (*Abitur*) entitles the holder to a place of study at a university or another institution of higher education. The number of examinations passed in 1974 was 109,967.

Juveniles below the age of 18 who are not attending an intermediate school, a secondary or a full-time vocational school (*Berufsfachschule*) are obliged to take a three-year course (part-time) at a vocational school. In November, 1974, there were 1,776 part-time vocational schools (*Berufsschulen*) and 500 vocational extension schools (*Berufsaufbauschulen*) with 1,680,518 pupils, 2,840 full-time vocational schools with 274,989 pupils, 1,409 advanced vocational schools (*Fachschulen*) with 130,835 pupils; 819 schools for secondary technical studies (*Fachoberschulen/Fachgymnasien*) with 117,517 students and 1,789 Public Health Schools with 80,674 pupils. [State expenditure for primary schools per annum amounted to *DM*.2,100 per pupil, for intermediate schools *DM*.2,300 and for grammar schools *DM*.3,300. State expenditure per pupil for part-time vocational, full-time vocational and advanced vocational schools per annum amounted to *DM*.1,500.] According to preliminary results, in the winter term 1975/76 there were 60 universities—including a college for physical education (*Sporthochschule*)—(599,226 students), 11

---

*Common Market: Belgium and Luxembourg, Denmark, France, Italy, Netherlands, Rep. of Ireland, U.K. W. Germany.

† E.F.T.A. (European Free Trade Association): Austria, Iceland, Norway, Portugal, Sweden, Switzerland.

colleges of theological philosophy (*Theologische Hochschulen*) (1,768 students), 33 teachers' training colleges (*Pädagogische Hochschulen*) (79,163 students), 26 colleges of arts (*Kunsthochschulen* (15,395 students) and 124 vocational colleges (*Fachhochschulen*) (145,205 students); a total of 254 institutions of higher education with 840,757 students. The largest universities were in Munich, Berlin, Hamburg, Münster (Westf.), Cologne, Bonn and Frankfurt-am-Main.

Religion.—In 1970 there were 29,696,571 Protestants in the Republic, 27,060,826 Roman Catholics, 31,684 Jews and 3,861,518 others.

CAPITAL, Bonn, in North Rhine Westphalia, 15 miles distant from Cologne. Population 283,711 (Dec. 31, 1975).

FLAG.—Horizontal bars of black, red and gold.

BRITISH EMBASSY

Friedrich-Ebert Allee 77, 5300 Bonn

Ambassador Extraordinary and Plenipotentiary, His Excellency Sir (John) Oliver Wright, K.C.M.G., D.S.C (1975).

Ministers, J. L. Bullard, C.M.G.; H. T. A. Overton, C.M.G.

Counsellors, J. S. Whitehead, C.M.G. (*Head of Chancery*); J. R. Rich (*Commercial*); J. S. P. MacKenzie, O.B.E. (*Labour*); C. A. Alldis, C.B.E., D.F.C., A.F.C. (*Defence Supply*); R. I. T. Cromartie (*Scientific*); P. W. Unwin (*Economic*); B. Hitch; W. C. Lyall, M.B.E. (*Administration*); P. H. Towers-Picton, O.B.E.; T. J. Clark (*Press and Information*).

1st Secretaries, P. Yarnold; K. J. Chamberlain; G. M. Stephens; C. A. K. Cullimore; C. D. Powell; A. O'B. ffrench Blake; H. L. Davies; A. S. Payne; R. F. Cornish; A. Carter; R. G. Bowen; J. F. MacCulloch; E. T. Hanley; H. Davies; G. Brook, M.B.E.; A. F. Blake-Pauley; G. Hay, M.B.E.; W. B. McCleary.

2nd Secretaries, Miss P. E. Lambe; A. E. Gay; A. J. Frost; S. Macpherson; N. J. Guthrie; T. G. Longdon-Griffiths; R. Tempest; R. C. Cutler.

Defence and Military Attaché, Brig. C. M. A. Mayes.

Asst. Military Attaché, Lt.-Col. J. C. McQ. Johnston.

Naval Attaché, Captain B. J. Williams, R.N.

Asst. Naval Attaché, Lt.-Cdr. L. S. J. Barry, R.N.

Air Attaché, Air Cdre. L. G. P. Martin.

Head of Visa Section (*Düsseldorf*), Miss D. M. Symes.

Chaplain, Rev. F. H. Mountney.

There are British Consulates-General at *Berlin, Hamburg, Hanover, Düsseldorf, Frankfurt, Munich* and *Stuttgart* and a British Consulate at *Bremen*.

BRITISH COUNCIL

Representative, Dr. J. M. Mitchell, C.B.E., Hahnenstrasse 6, Cologne. Offices at *Berlin, Hamburg* and *Munich* and British Council libraries at *Berlin, Cologne* and *Munich*.

BERLIN

G.O.C. British Sector, Maj.-General R. M. F. Redgrave, M.C.

Minister and Deputy Commandant, J. H. Lambert, C.M.G.

Counsellor, D. A. S. Gladstone (*Political Adviser and Head of Chancery*).

GERMAN DEMOCRATIC REPUBLIC

Area and Population.—The German Democratic Republic comprises the five former German *Länder* of Brandenburg, Mecklenburg, Saxony, Saxony-Anhalt and Thuringia (an area of 41,768 sq. miles). The seat of Government is East Berlin (156 sq. miles). The population of the Republic, including

East Berlin, (end of 1974) is 16,890,800. In 1952 the former *Länder* were replaced by fourteen *Bezirke* (regions): Potsdam, Cottbus and Frankfurt (*formerly* Brandenburg); Rostock, Schwerin and Neubrandenburg (*formerly* Mecklenburg); Karl-Marx-Stadt, Dresden and Leipzig (*formerly* Saxony); Halle and Magdeburg (*formerly* Saxony-Anhalt); Erfurt, Gera and Suhl (*formerly* Thuringia.)

The present Constitution, which defines the GDR as a Socialist state, came into force on April 9, 1968 after endorsement by a referendum. It replaced the first Constitution of October 7, 1949. Among items of the 1949 Constitution omitted from that of 1968 were the rights of trade unions to strike, of citizens to emigrate and of newspapers to publish without censorship. Further amendments came into force on October 7, 1974 after adoption by the *Volkskammer* on September 27, 1974. They mainly involved (*a*) the deletion of all references to the German nation and to the possibility of reunification, and (*b*) the recording of the transfer of certain governmental functions from the State Council to the Council of Ministers which had their origin in the Law on the Council of Ministers of October 16, 1972. The supreme organ of State power is the *Volkskammer*, which has power to elect and dismiss the State Council, the Council of Ministers, the Chairman of the National Defence Council, the Supreme Court and the Procurator-General. The State Council retains the presidential powers which it has exercised since the abolition of the office of President on September 12, 1960, together with responsibility for the organization of defence with the help of the National Defence Council. The Council of Ministers is responsible to the *Volkskammer* for the conduct of State policy. The present *Volkskammer* is that elected on November 14, 1971.

As with other communist countries, effective power lies with the ruling Marxist-Leninist Party, in this case the Socialist Unity Party of German (SED). The other parties and mass organizations are members of the SED-controlled National Front.

Council of State

Chairman, Herr Willi Stoph.

Deputy Chairmen, Herr Friedrich Ebert; Herr Gerald Götting; Dr. Heinrich Homann; Dr. Manfred Gerlach; Herr Hans Rietz.

Members, Herr K. Anclam; Herr F. Clermont; Prof. E. Correns; Herr W. Grandetzka; Herr E. Grützner; Frau B. Hanke; Prof. Lieselott Herfurth; Herr E. Honecker; Herr F. Kind; Frau M. Müller; Herr B. Quandt; Prof. H. Rodenberg; Herr K. Sorgenicht; Herr P. Strauss; Frau I. Thiele; Herr P. Verner; Frau R. Walther; Herr H. Tisch.

Council of Ministers

Prime Minister, Herr Horst Sindermann.

1st Deputy Prime Ministers, Dr. Günter Mittag; Herr Alfred Neumann.

Total membership of the Council is 41, including 9 other Deputy Prime Ministers, 13 holding principal portfolios and 15 holding portfolios of a mainly technical nature.

SOCIALIST UNITY PARTY OF GERMANY.

Politbureau of the Central Committee, H. Axen; F. Ebert; W. Felfe; G. Grüneberg; K. Hager; Gen. H. Hoffman; E. Honecker; W. Krolikowski; W. Lamberz; E. Mielke; G. Mittag; E. Mückenberger; K. Naumann; A. Neumann; A. Norden; H. Sindermann; W. Stoph; H. Tisch; P. Verner (*full members*); H. Dohlus; J. Herrmann; W. Jarowinsky; G. Kleiber; E. Krenz; Frau I. Lange; Frau M. Mueller; G. Schürer; W. Walde (*candidate members*).

Secretariat of the Central Committee, E. Honecker (*General Secretary*); H. Axen; G. Grüneberg; K. Hager; J. Herrmann; W. Jarowinsky; W. Lamberz; A. Norden; P. Verner; W. Krolikowski; I. Lange; H. Dohlus (*secretaries*).

EMBASSY IN LONDON
34 Belgrave Square, S.W.1
[01–235 9941]

Ambassador Extraordinary and Plenipotentiary, His Excellency Karl-Heinz Kern.

Economic Position.—Before the 1939–45 war, the economy of the area at present occupied by the GDR was largely devoted to agriculture and light industry, most heavy industry being concentrated in other parts of the Reich. In spite of this imbalance, compounded by severe war damage, a declining population, a shortage of labour and a lack of basic raw materials, East Germany has made considerable economic progress and is now in the world's top ten industrial nations in terms of G.N.P., and is second to the U.S.S.R. in Eastern Europe as a major producer of industrial goods. East Germany has a number of highly developed industries including basic chemicals and petro-chemicals, machine tools and industrial plant, ship-building and transport equipment, electronic and engineering equipment, precision tools and optical instruments.

The East German economy, including the control of industry and foreign trade, is centrally planned and administered. The State Planning Commission, which is subordinate to the Council of Ministers, is responsible for drawing up the 5- and 1-Year Plans. The 5-Year Plans determine the future development and structure of the economy; the 1-Year Plans have to achieve these aims. The implementation of these plans is the responsibility of the State Production Enterprises under the supervision of the economic and industrial Ministries.

The economy is very closely integrated with those of other member countries of C.M.E.A. and particularly with the U.S.S.R.

Trade with U.K.

	1974	1975
Imports from U.K...	£39,230,000	£32,580,000
Exports to U.K.....	£44,880,000	£39,230,000

Principal cities and towns (population, 1974): East Berlin (1,094,147); Leipzig (570,972); Dresden (507,692); Karl-Marx-Stadt (Chemnitz) (303,811); Magdeburg (276,089); Halle/Saale (241,425); Rostock (210,167); Erfurt (202,979); Zwickau (123,069).

FLAG.—Horizontal bands of black, red, gold; hammer, compasses and corn device at centre.

BRITISH EMBASSY
(108 Berlin, Unter den Linden 32/34)

Ambassador Extraordinary and Plenipotentiary, His Excellency Percy Cradock, C.M.G. (1975).

Counsellors, J. Mellon (*Commercial*); Miss C. E. Pestell.

1st Secretaries, P. J. Fowler (*Head of Chancery*); G. H. Grubb (*Administration and Consul*); R.McL. Greenshields; G. P. Lockton, M.B.E. (*Commercial*).

2nd Secretaries, P. J. Talbot, M.B.E.; R. T. Jenkins; G. G. Wetherell.

GREECE
(Hellas)

President of the Hellenic Republic, Constantine Tsatsos, *born* 1899 (*assumed office* June 20, 1975).

CABINET

Prime Minister, Constantine Karamanlis.
Coordination and Planning, Panayotis Papaligouras.
Alternate Minister of Coordination and Planning, John Boutos.

Minister to the Prime Minister, Education and Religion, George Rallis.
Foreign Affairs, Dimitiros Bitsios.
National Defence, Evangelos Averoff-Tositsas.
Interior, Constantine Stephanopoulos.
Justice, Constantine Stephanakis.
Public Order, George Stamatis.
Culture and Science, Constantine Trypanis.
Finance, Evangelos Devletoglou.
Agriculture, Hippocrates Iordanoglou.
Industry, Constantine Konofagos.
Commerce, John Varvitsiotis.
Employment, Constantine Laskaris.
Social Services, Constantine Chrysanthopoulos.
Public Works, Christophoros Stratos.
Transport and Communications, George Voyatzis.
Merchant Marine, Alexandros Papadongonas.
Northern Greece, Nikolaos Martis.

GREEK EMBASSY IN LONDON
1a Holland Park, W.11
[01–727 8040]

Ambassador Extraordinary and Plenipotentiary, His Excellency Stavros Georgiou Roussos (1974).

Minister, N. E. Athanassiou.

Counsellors, L. Mavromichalis (*Consular Affairs*); A. Philon; A. Zaphiropoulos (*Commercial*); C. Kondoyiannis (*Agricultural*); M. Dragoumis (*Press*).

Armed Forces Attaché, Capt. N. Pappas.
Tourist Adviser, C. Analytis.

There are Honorary Consulates at *Birmingham*, *Bradford*, *Bristol*, *Falmouth*, *Hull*, *Immingham*, *Leeds*, *Liverpool*, *Manchester*, *Newcastle*, *Plymouth*, *Portsmouth*, *Southampton*, *Cardiff*, *Edinburgh* and *Glasgow*, and at *Belfast*.

A maritime State in the south-east of Europe, bounded on the N. by Albania, Yugoslavia and Bulgaria, on the S. and W. by the Ionian and Mediterranean seas, and on the E. by Turkey, with an estimated area of 51,182 sq. miles. A census held throughout the country on March 14, 1971, recorded a population of 8,768,641.

The area of the mainland is 41,328 sq. miles, and of the islands 9,854 sq. miles. The main divisions are: *Macedonia* (which includes Mt. Athos and the island of *Thasos*), *Thrace* (including the island of *Samothrace*), *Epirus*, *Thessaly*, *Continental Greece* (which includes the island of *Euboea* and the *Sporades*, or "scattered islands," of which the largest is *Skyros*), the *Peloponnese* (or *Morea*), the *Dodecanese* or *Southern Sporades* (12 islands occupied by Italy in 1911 during the Italo-Turkish War and ceded to Greece by Italy in 1947) consisting of Rhodes, Astypalaia, Karpathos, Kassos, Nisyros, Kalymnos, Leros, Patmos, Kos, Symi, Khalki and Tilos, the *Cyclades* (a circular group numbering about 200, with a total area of 923 sq. miles; the chief islands are Syros, Andros, Tinos, Naxos, Paros, Santorini, Milos and Serifos), the *Ionian Islands* (Corfu, Paxos, Levkas, Ithaca, Cephalonia, Zante and Cerigo), the *Aegean Islands* (Chios, Lesbos, Limnos and Samos). In *Crete* there was for over 1,500 years (300 to 1400 B.C.) a flourishing civilization which spread its influence far and wide throughout the Aegean, and the ruins of the palace of Minos at Cnossos afforded evidence of astonishing comfort and luxury. Greek civilization emerges about 1300 B.C. and the poems of Homer, the blind poet of Chios, which were probably current about 800 B.C., record the 10-year struggle between the Achaeans of Greece and the Phrygians of Troy (1194–1184 B.C.).

Government.—A military *coup* on April 21, 1967, suspended parliamentary government and, following an unsuccessful royal counter *coup* on December 13, 1967, King Constantine went into voluntary

exile in Rome. A new constitution was approved in 1968 in a national referendum. On June 1, 1973, following allegations of a plot within the Navy to overthrow the government, the monarchy was abolished and a republic established under the Presidency of Mr. George Papadopoulos.

A referendum held on July 29, 1973, confirmed the new presidential Constitution with Mr. Papadopoulos as President until 1981. In early October a civilian government, headed by Mr. Markezinis, was appointed. Following student demonstrations in early November the Army, on November 17, was called in to restore order and martial law was declared. On November 25, following an Army coup, the Markezinis Government was overthrown and General Gizikis was sworn in as President of the Republic.

The overthrow of Archbishop Makarios, President of Cyprus, on July 15, by a military coup led by Greek Officers of the Cypriot National Guard caused an international crisis, in the wake of which the heads of the Greek armed forces decided, on July 23, to relinquish power. President Gizikis called upon Mr. Konstantinos Karamanlis, Prime Minister between 1955 and 1963, to return from his self-imposed exile in Paris and form a provisional Government. On August 1, Mr. Karamanlis announced that the Constitution of 1952 would be reintroduced, pending a new Constitution.

The first elections for ten years were held on November 17, 1974. Mr. Karamanlis' New Democracy Party polled 54·3 per cent. of the vote and gained 220 out of the 300 seats in Parliament (this was later reduced in by-elections to 216 seats). Mr Karamanlis formed a new Government on November 21.

The constitutional position of the King, however, remained unsettled until December 8, when by a referendum the Greek people rejected " crowned democracy " by 69·2 per cent. to 30·8 per cent. and Greece became a republic.

On December 18, 1974 Mr. Michael Stassinopoulos was elected by Parliament President of the Hellenic Republic until a new constitution should be passed. The draft of the new constitution was presented by the Government to Parliament in January 1975 and was formally passed on June 7, coming into force on June 11, 1975.

On June 19 the Greek Parliament elected Mr. Constantine Tsatsos President of the Hellenic Republic under the new constitution. He assumed office on June 20, 1975.

Defence.—The Navy consists of 17,500 men and is equipped with a balanced fleet of destroyers, submarines, fast patrol boats and amphibious warfare vessels, mostly of U.S., French and German origin. The strength of the Army is 122,000. The Air Force consists of 23,000 men and is equipped with a modern inventory of aircraft disposed in 12 combat squadrons supported by the necessary transport, training, helicopter and reconnaissance squadrons.

Communications.—The 2,650 kilometres of Greek railways are State-owned with the exception of the Athens-Piraeus Electric Railway. The railway from Athens to the Peloponnese, serving Patras and southern Greece, is metre gauge, but the other lines, except one or two minor ones, are standard gauge. Greek roads total somewhat over 35,500 kilometres, of which about 25 per cent. are classified as national highways and just under 30,000 km. are classified as provincial roads.

On Dec. 31, 1975, the Greek Mercantile fleet numbered 2,971 ships with a total tonnage of 25,108,441 tons gross. On the same day Greek-owned ships registered under foreign flags numbered 1,359 with a total tonnage of 23,189,995 tons gross. (N.B. These figures exclude Greek-owned vessels under 100 tons gross). Athens has direct airline links with Australasia, North America, most countries in Europe, Africa and the Middle East.

Religion.—Over 97 per cent. of the people are adherents of the Greek Orthodox Church, which is the State religion, all others being tolerated and free from interference. The Church of Greece recognizes the spiritual primacy of the Œcumenical Patriarch of Constantinople, but is otherwise a self-governing body administered by the Holy Synod under the Presidency of the Archbishop of Athens and All Greece. It has no jurisdiction over the Church of Crete, which has a degree of autonomy under the Œcumenical Patriarch, nor over the Monastic Community of Mount Athos and the Church in the Dodecanese, both of which come directly under the Œcumenical Patriarch.

Education is free and compulsory from the age of 6 to 12 and is maintained by State grants. There are four Universities, Athens, Salonika, Patras and Joannina. There are several other institutes of higher learning, mostly in Athens.

Language and Literature.—The *spoken* language of modern Greece is descended by a process of natural development from the " Common Greek " of Alexander's empire. Official and technical matter is mostly composed in *Katharevousa*, a conservative literary dialect evolved by Adamantios Corais (Diamant Coray), who lived and died in Paris (1748-1833) but novels and poetry are mostly composed in *dimotiki*, a progressive literary dialect which owes much to John Psycharis (1854-1929). The poets Solomos, Palamas, Cavafis, Sikelianos and Seferis have won a European reputation.

Production.—Though there has in recent years been a substantial measure of industrialization, Greece is still largely an agricultural country. Agriculture employs about 40 per cent. of the working population, the most important product and export being tobacco, which accounts for about one-tenth of the value of total visible exports from Greece. Since the war the production of wheat, cotton, sugar and rice has been greatly increased, partly in an attempt to make the country's economy less dependent upon tobacco. The most important of the fruit trees are the olive, vine, orange, lemon, fig, peach, almond, pomegranate and currant-vine, and

considerable efforts have lately been made to develop exports of Greek fresh fruit and vegetables as well as currants and other dried fruits. Currants, grown mainly around Patras, remain one of Greece's main exports, the United Kingdom being the principal purchaser.

The principal minerals mined in Greece are nickel, bauxite, iron ore, iron pyrites, manganese, magnesite, chrome, lead, zinc and emery, and prospecting for petroleum is being carried on. Oil refineries are in operation near Athens and at Salonika, where there is also a petro-chemical plant. The chief industries are textiles (cotton, woollen, silk and rayon), chemicals, cement, glass, metallurgy, shipbuilding, domestic electrical equipment and footwear. In recent years new factories have been opened for the production of aluminium, nickel, iron and steel products, tyres, chemicals fertilizers and sugar (from locally-grown beet). Food processing and ancillary industries have also grown up throughout the country. The development of the country's electric power resources, irrigation and land reclamation schemes and the exploitation of Greece's lignite resources for fuel and industrial purposes are also being carried out, and the television network is being expanded. Tourism is developing rapidly. Greece has announced her intention of becoming a full member of the E.E.C., but has yet to negotiate transitional arrangements.

Currency.—The Greek *drachma* has a floating exchange rate of about 65 = £1 (July 1976) and 36 = $1 U.S.

(See also p. 83)

TRADE

	1974	1975
Total imports	$4,635,200,000	$4,875,700,000
Total exports	1,774,100,000	1,959,600,000

Trade with U.K.

	1974	1975
Imports from U.K.	£105,079,000	£117,207,000
Exports to U.K.	68,180,000	65,297,000

CAPITAL, Athens. Population (including ΨPiraeus and suburbs), 2,540,241 (1971 Census). Other large towns are ΨSalonika (557,360); ΨPatras (111,607), ΨVolos (71,245); Larissa (72,336); and ΨKavalla (46,234); in Crete—ΨHeraklion or Candia (77,506), ΨCanea (40,564), and ΨRethymnon (14,969); in the Ionian Islands—ΨCorfu (28,630); in the Dodecanese—ΨRhodes (32,092); in the Cyclades—ΨSyros Hermoupolis (13,502); in Lesbos—Ψ Mytilene (23,426); in Chios—Ψ Chios (24,084).

FLAG.—9 horizontal bands, alternately blue and white, with white cross, on blue ground, at top next hoist.

NATIONAL DAY.—March 25 (Independence Day).

BRITISH EMBASSY
(Ploutarchou 1, Athens)

Ambassador Extraordinary and Plenipotentiary, His Excellency Sir (Francis) Brooks Richards, K.C.M.G., D.S.C. (1974).

Counsellors, J. B. Denson, C.M.G., O.B.E. (*Political and Consul-General*); T. J. Everard (*Commercial*).

1st Secretaries, P. W. M. Vereker; C. C. Smellie, C.B.E., M.V.O.; M. S. R. Heathcote (*Information*); S. T. Corcoran (*Labour*); D. T. Wallis (*Commercial*); J. K. B. Davenport (*Administration*).

2nd Secretaries, J. W. Forbes-Meyler (*Consul*); M. J. H. Wood.

3rd Secretary, M. D. Hanman (*Commercial*).

Defence and Military Attaché, Brigadier Sir Gregor MacGregor of MacGregor, Bt.

Naval and Air Attaché, Capt. D. G. Mather, R.N.

Attachés, E. C. Duckworth, M.B.E. (*Commercial*); E. Tragoutsi, O.B.E.; H. Byatt, M.B.E. (*Press*).

Embassy Chaplain, Ven. S. R. Skemp.

Hon. Attaché, H. W. Catling, D.Phil. (*Director, British School of Archæology*).

BRITISH CONSULAR OFFICES
There are British Consular Offices at *Athens, Piraeus, Corfu, Samos, Rhodes, Salonika, Heraklion, Kavalla* and *Patras*.

BRITISH COUNCIL
17 Philikis Etairias Street, Kolonaki Square, Athens 138

Representative, P. G. Lloyd, C.B.E.
There is also an office at *Salonika* and British Council libraries at both centres.

GUATEMALA
(República de Guatemala)

President, Gen. Kjell Eugenio Laugerud García, *elected*, March, 1974; *assumed office*, July 1, 1974.

Guatemala, the most northerly of the Republican States of Central America, is situated in N. lat. from 13° 45′ to 17° 49′, and in W. long. from 88° 12′ 49″ to 92° 13′ 43″, and has an area of 42,042 square miles, and a population of 5,400,000 (*for* MAP, *see* p. 871). The constitutionally elected president, Gen. Miguel Ydigoras Fuentes, who had taken office on March 3, 1958, was overthrown on March 31, 1963, by the Army, which handed executive and legislative powers to the Minister of Defence, Col. Enrique Peralta Azurdia. Important changes were included in a new constitution promulgated on Sept. 15, 1965, including the reduction of the presidential term from 6 to 4 years and the establishment of a Council of State under the chairmanship of a Vice-President. Elections for a new Congress and for President and Vice-President took place on March 6, 1966. Dr. Mendez was chosen as President at the first meeting of the new Congress and was succeeded by Col. Arana in 1970.

The Republic is divided into 22 departments, and is traversed from W. to E. by an elevated mountain chain, containing several volcanic summits rising to 13,000 feet above the sea; earthquakes are frequent, and the capital (which is at an altitude of 4,800 ft.) was destroyed by an upheaval in Dec. 1917. An earthquake in Feb. 1976 killed about 25,000 people, and caused considerable damage to property and the infrastructure. The country is well watered by numerous rivers; the climate is hot and malarial near the coast, temperate in the higher regions. The rainfall in the capital is 57 in. per annum. The chief seaports are San José de Guatemala and Champerico on the Pacific and Livingston, Santo Tomás de Castilla and Puerto Barrios on the Atlantic side.

Language and Literature.—Spanish is the language of the country, and since the establishment of the University in the capital education has received a marked impulse and the high figure of illiteracy is being reduced. The National library contains about 80,000 volumes in the Spanish tongue.

Finance.—Actual revenue and expenditure in 1974 were *Quetzales* 282,245,200 and *Quetzales* 322,912,800 respectively, compared with *Quetzales* 214,706,800 and *Quetzales* 253,484,000 in 1973.
At par 1 *Quetzal* = $1 U.S. (*See also* p. 84).

TRADE

	1973	1974
	Quetzales	*Quetzales*
Imports (c.i.f.)	431,002,200	700,473,700
Exports (f.o.b.)	436,151,300	572,133,300

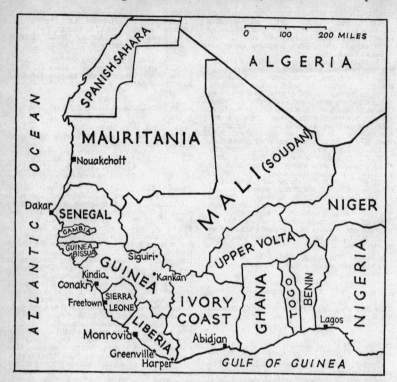

Trade with U.K.

	1974	1975
Imports from U.K.	£6,948,000	£9,838,000
Exports to U.K.	7,410,000	31,918,000

The principal export is coffee, other articles being manufactured goods, sugar, bananas, cotton, beef and essential oils. The chief imports are petroleum, vehicles, machinery and foodstuffs.

CAPITAL, Guatemala. Population: 790,311. Quezaltenango (second city of the Republic), has a pop. of 54,487. Other towns are Ψ Puerto Barrios (29,435), Mazatenango (23,932), and Antigua (17,270).

FLAG.—Three vertical bands, blue, white, blue; coat of arms on white stripe.

BRITISH EMBASSY
(Diplomatic relations suspended, July 31, 1963).

GUINEA
(Republic of Guinea)

President, Ahmed Sékou Touré, *elected* for seven year terms, January 1961, 1968 and on Dec. 27, 1974.

President of National Assembly, Léon Maka.

SUPER MINISTERS

Prime Minister, Dr. Lansara Beavogui.
Interior and Security, Moussa Diakite.
Culture and Education, Mamady Keita.
Social Domain, Alpha Bocar Barry.
Exchanges Domain, N. Famara Keita.
Economy and Finance, Ismael Touré

As from the Government changes of May 22, 1975, there were 31 Ministers in the domains of the Super Ministers, including the President.

Formerly part of French West Africa, Guinea has a coastline on the Atlantic Ocean between Guinea-Bissau and Sierra Leone and in the interior is adjacent to Senegal, Mali, Ivory Coast, Liberia and Sierra Leone (*see* below). Area, 96,865 sq. miles. The population (U.N. estimate, 1969), is 3,890,000, mostly the Fullah, Malinké and Soussou tribes. It is estimated that there are about 2,000 Europeans in the country.

Government.—Guinea was separated from Senegal in 1891 and administered by France as a separate colony until 1958. In the referendum held in Metropolitan France and the overseas territories on Sept. 2, 1958, Guinea rejected the new French Constitution. Accordingly, on Sept. 28, it was declared that Guinea had separated itself from the other territories of French West Africa which had adopted the Constitution. French administrative and financial assistance was terminated; and Guinea left the French Community. On October 2, 1958, Guinea became an independent republic governed by a Constituent Assembly. M. Sékou Touré, Prime Minister in the Territorial Assembly, assumed office as head of the new Government.

A provisional constitution, adopted on Nov. 12, 1958, declared Guinea " a democratic, secular and social republic ", powers of government being exercised by a president assisted by the Cabinet. The President, eligible for a term of 7 years and for re-election, is head of state and of the armed forces. M. Sékou Touré was elected President of the Republic by an overwhelming vote in an election (in which he was the sole candidate) in January, 1961 and re-elected in 1968. General recognition of Guinea as an independent state was followed by her admission to membership of the United Nations in December, 1958.

Guinea withdrew from the Franc Zone on March 1, 1960, and established her own currency, the *Guinea franc* (at par with the *franc C.F.A.*). This led to the rupture of commercial relations with France, hitherto her most important supplier and purchaser. Guinea is in receipt of economic aid and technical assistance from a number of countries, including the United States, Federal Republic of Germany, Yugoslavia, the Soviet Union and China. The Government's foreign policy is one of " positive neutralism " and non-alignment. In May, 1963, Guinea signed agreements with France covering *inter alia* the settlement of Governmental claims and technical co-operation. Diplomatic relations with U.K., suspended in December, 1965, were resumed on Feb. 20, 1968.

Production, etc.—The principal products of Guinea are alumina, iron-ore, palm kernels, millet, rice, coffee, bananas, pineapples and rubber. Principal imports are cotton goods, manufactured goods, tobacco, petroleum products, sugar, rice, flour and salt; exports, alumina, iron-ore, diamonds, coffee, hides, bananas, palm kernels and pineapples. In the mountains in the hinterland of Guinea (Fouta Djalon, 4,970 feet), where the rivers Senegal, Gambia and Niger have their sources, large deposits of bauxite (the raw material of aluminium) are worked and alumina is produced for export. Bauxite has been worked and exported from the Conakry area where there are also rich deposits of iron-ore and large-scale mining is carried on. There are a British-built cotton mill and a Chinese-built cigarette and match factory. Guinea imported goods to the value of £3,644,000 from U.K. and exported to U.K. goods to be the value of £22,000 in 1975.

CAPITAL.—Ψ Conakry (120,000). Other towns are Kankan (29,000), which is connected with Conakry by a railway, Kindia (25,000), N'Zérékoré, Mamou, Siguiri and Labé.

FLAG.—Three vertical stripes of red, yellow and green.

NATIONAL DAY.—October 2 (Anniversary of Proclamation of Independence.

BRITISH EMBASSY
Ambassador Extraordinary and Plenipotentiary, His Excellency John Ernest Powell-Jones, C.M.G. (1976) *(resident at Dakar).*

GUINEA–BISSAU
President of the Council of State, Sr. Luis Cabral.

Guinea-Bissau, formerly Portuguese Guinea, lies in western Africa, between Senegal and Guinea; it has an area of 14,000 sq. miles and had a population in 1972 of 544,000 (est. 1975—600,000).

Guinea-Bissau achieved independence on Sept. 10, 1974.

Currency, it is planned to replace the *escudo* in 1978 by Guinea-Bissau's own unit of currency, the *peso*.

Economy, The country produces rice, coconuts and ground-nuts. Cattle are raised, and there are bauxite deposits in the south.

Provisional Capital, Medina de Boe. The former capital and chief port is Ψ Bissau.

BRITISH EMBASSY
Ambassador Extraordinary and Plenipotentiary, His Excellency John Ernest Powell-Jones, C.M.G. (1976) *(resident at Dakar).*

HAITI
(République d'Haïti)

President, Jean Claude Duvalier, *born* 1951, *installed as President for life*, April 21, 1971.

CABINET
Interior and Defence, Pierre Biamby.
Agriculture and Rural Development, Remillot Leveille.
Labour and Social Affairs, Dr. Achille Savant.
Public Health and Population, Dr. Willy Verrier.
Public Works, Transport and Communications, Fernand Laurin.
National Education, Dr. Raoul Pierre-Louis.
Finance and Economic Affairs, Emmanuel Bros.
Justice, Aurélien C. Jeanty.
Co-ordination and Information, Pierre Gousse.
Foreign Affairs, Edner Brutus.
Commerce and Industry, Antonio André.

EMBASSY AND CONSULATE
17 Queen's Gate, S.W.7
[01–581 0577]

Ambassador Extraordinary and Plenipotentiary, His Excellency Dr. Hervé Boyer.

The Republic of Haiti occupies the western third of the island of Hispaniola, which, next to Cuba, is the largest island in the West Indies.

The area of the Republic, including off-shore islands, is about 10,700 sq. miles with a population (estimated, 1969) of 4,768,000. The people are mainly negroes but there are numbers of mulattoes and others with some admixture of European blood. About 250 British subjects, many of West Indian origin, reside in Haiti.

A French colony under the name of Saint-Domingue from 1697, the slave population, estimated at 500,000, revolted in 1791 under the leadership of Toussaint L'Ouverture, who was born a slave and made himself Governor-General of the colony. He capitulated to the French in 1802 and died in captivity in 1803. Resistance was continued by Jean Jacques Dessalines, also a former negro slave, who, on January 1, 1804, declared the former French colony to be an independent state. It was at this time that the name Haiti, an aboriginal word meaning mountainous, was adopted. Dessalines became Emperor of Haiti, but was assassinated in 1806. In 1915, following a period of political upheaval, the country was occupied by a force of U.S. marines. The occupation came to an end in 1934, and U.S. control of the revenue of Haiti officially ended on October 1, 1947.

Dr. Duvalier was installed as President in 1957 and was re-elected as President for life on June 15, 1964. He died on April 21, 1971. He was succeeded as President for life on the same day by his son, Jean Claude Duvalier, whom he had nominated as his successor under Article 102 of the Constitution of 1964 as amended on January 14, 1971.

Production, Industry, etc.—In French colonial times, Haiti was one of the most productive countries in the world and the richest French possession. Improvident methods of peasant agriculture succeeded the plantation system and resulted in the gradual impoverishment of natural resources through exhaustion of the soil, deforestation and erosion.

In recent years measures for agricultural rehabilitation have been taken with the aim of a gradual restoration of productivity. The main project is a scheme for the irrigation of more than 70,000 acres of the Artibonite valley.

The principal products are coffee, sugar, essential oils, sisal, cocoa and cotton. Coffee accounts for about one third of total exports and is still a mainstay of the country's economy though exports now rarely exceed 300,000 bags (of 60 kg.). Exports of bauxite began in 1957. Production of copper in the Terre Neuve area started in 1960, but was suspended as uneconomic at the end of 1971. Industry is still on a small scale but the last few years have seen a steady and considerable expansion of light industry (the so-called transformation industries) taking advantage of cheap local labour (minimum wage $U.S.1.30 per day) to assemble or manufacture labour-intensive goods for the U.S. market (baseballs, brassieres, electronic equipment, etc.). Exports of manufactures now rank second after coffee at about 40 per cent. of total exports. The tourist industry is again expanding and many French Canadians are now attracted to Haiti for winter holidays. The country is one of the most beautiful in the Caribbean.

Communications.—There are very few asphalted roads and internal communications are bad although the situation is improving. Air services are maintained between the capital and the principal provincial towns. The principal towns and villages are connected by telephone and/or telegraph. The telephone company is now state owned (51 per cent.) and the service both in Port-au-Prince and Inter-urban has been greatly improved. External telegraph, telephone and postal services are normal. There are several commercial radio stations and a television station at Port-au-Prince.

Haiti is very well served by air from New York, Miami and Kingston to the North and from Martinique, Puerto Rico and other points to the South, with daily services by one line or another in both directions. The airlines touching Port-au-Prince International Airport include Pan American, Air France, American Air Lines, Eastern Airlines, and A.L.M. Regular passenger liner services to New York have ceased, but cruise ships call regularly, one Norwegian line operating a weekly cruise service to Kingston and Miami. Freight sailings are frequent for the U.S.A., Canada, Europe, Latin America (except Cuba) and the main Caribbean ports. (Airmail: U.K./Port-au-Prince, 4–14 days—extremely variable.)

Climate.—The climate is tropical with comparatively little difference in the temperatures between the summer (March-Oct.) and the winter (Nov.-Feb.). The temperature at Port-au-Prince rarely exceeds 95° F., but the humidity is high, especially in the autumn.

Language and Literature.—French is the language of the government and the press, but it is only spoken by the educated minority. The usual language of the people is Creole. Education is free but estimates of illiteracy are as high as 75 per cent. There are 3 French daily newspapers and one monthly in English. The total circulation is very small.

Finance.—The International Monetary Fund has granted Haiti a stand-by credit of $U.S.4,000,000

	1974-75*	1975-76*
	$U.S.	$U.S.
Revenue..............	38,916,000	43,300,000
Expenditure..........	38,916,000	43,300,000

* Haitian budget figures: there is also non-fiscal revenue—e.g. from the Tobacco Monopoly.
Exchange Rate: 5 *Gourdes*= $1 (U.S.). (*See also* p. 84.)

Trade.—Value of imports 1974 $U.S. 119,900,000 (est.); exports 1974 $U.S. 100,800,000 (est.)

Trade with U.K.

	1974	1975
Imports from U.K......	£2,000,000	£2,143,000
Exports to U.K........	199,000	139,000

The principal exports are listed above; the principal imports are foodstuffs, machinery, vehicles, chemicals and miscellaneous manufactured goods.

CAPITAL, Ψ Port-au-Prince. Population (estimated, 1974), 400,000. Other centres are: ΨCap Haitien (24,957); Ψ Gonaives (13,534); Ψ Les Cayes (11,835); Jérémie (11,138); Ψ St. Marc (10,485); Ψ Jacmel (8,545); Ψ Port de Paix (6,309) (1960 Census figures).

FLAG.—Two vertical bands, black (next staff) and red; arms in centre on a white background.

NATIONAL DAY.—January 1.

BRITISH EMBASSY
(Port-au-Prince)
Ambassador Extraordinary and Plenipotentiary, His Excellency John Kenneth Drinkall, C.M.G. (1976) (*resident at Kingston, Jamaica*).

HEJAZ, *see* Saudi Arabia

HONDURAS

(Republica de Honduras)
Head of State, Brigadier-General Juan Alberto Melgar Castro, *assumed office* April 22, 1975.

CABINET
[April 23, 1975]

Interior and Justice, Col. Alonso Flores Guerra.
Defence, Brig.-Gen. Mario Carcamo Chinchilla.
Economy and Commerce, Vicente Díaz.
Finance, Sr. Porfirio Zabala.
Foreign Affairs, Roberto Perdomo Paredes.
Education, Sra. Lídia Arias de Williams.
Health and Social Security, Dr. Enrique Aguilar Paz.
Natural Resources, Sr. Fernando Montes Matamoros.
Labour and Social Affairs, Sr. Enrique Flores Valeriano.
Economic Planning, Sr. Arturo Corletto.
Telecommunications, Col. Mario Flores Theresin.

Director of National Agrarian Institute, Sr. Rigoberto Sandoval Correa.

HONDURAS EMBASSY IN LONDON
48 George Street, W.1.
[01–486 3380]
Ambassador Extraordinary and Plenipotentiary (vacant).

Honduras, one of the five Republican States of Central America, lies between lat. 13° and 16° 30′ N. and long. 83° and 89° 41′ W. with a seaboard of about 400 miles on the Carribbean Sea and an outlet, consisting of a small strip of coast 77 miles in length on the Pacific. Its frontiers are contiguous with those of Guatemala, Nicaragua and El Salvador.

The Republic contains a total area of approximately 43,278 sq. miles and a population (preliminary, March 1974, census) of 2,646,828, of mixed Spanish and Indian blood. There is a strong foreign negro (British West Indian) element in Northern Honduras. The country is very mountainous, being traversed by the Cordilleras. Most of the soil is poor and acid, except for a few acres along the North coast and in the interior. Rainfall is seasonal, May to October being wet and November to April dry. The climate varies with the altitude, being tropical throughout the year in the coastal belts and temperate and mainly healthy in the uplands.

Originally discovered and settled by the Spaniards at the beginning of the sixteenth century Honduras formed part of the Spanish American Dominions for nearly three centuries until 1821 when independence was proclaimed.

On December 4, 1972, General López Arellano took over the Government from the previous National/Liberal Coalition headed by Dr. Ramón Ernesto Cruz, in a bloodless *coup*, and set up a military régime. President López Arellano was removed on April 22, 1975, and replaced by Colonel Juan Alberto Melgar Castro. The coup followed allegations of corruption, involving bribes alleged to have been paid by the American banana concern, United Brands, to obtain a reduction in a banana export tax.

Following the cancellation of special privileges and concessions to foreign banana companies, the establishment of the Honduran Banana Corporation was decreed, the Corporation taking control of all operations concerned with bananas as well as ports and railways owned by the banana companies.

The Republic is divided into 18 departments, the newest of which, Gracias a Dios, formed in Feb. 1957, covers all the territory previously known as La Mosquitia, together with portions of the Departments of Olancho and Colón. It is inhabited by Indian tribes and largely unexplored.

The chief industry is the production of bananas. Other products are coffee, tobacco, beans, maize, rice, cotton, sugar cane, cement and tropical fruits. Cattle raising is becoming an increasingly important industry, a number of cattle being exported to the neighbouring countries every year. Honduras is also a timber producing country, the most important woods being pine, mahogany and cedar. There are large tracts of uncultivated land.

There are about 730 miles of railway in operation, chiefly to serve the banana plantations and the Caribbean ports. There are 5,943 km. of

roads, of which 1,228 are paved. Improvements are being made and new roads built. There are 33 unpretentious airports and three international airports in use in Honduras. A new international airport suitable for jet aircraft has been built near San Pedro Sula. There are numerous small landing and emergency fields. There are four international air services (AVIATECA, SAHSA, PAA and TAN) and 3 domestic air services (SAHSA, Aero Servicios and LANSA).

The language of the country is Spanish. Primary and secondary education is free, primary education being compulsory, and, although there is still a great deal of illiteracy, it is gradually diminishing.

ΨThe chief ports are Puerto Cortes, Tela and La Ceiba on the North Coast, through which passes the bulk of the trade with the United States and Europe, and Amapala, situated on Tiger Island in the Gulf of Fonseca, on the Pacific side.

FINANCE	1975 Lempiras	1976 Lempiras
Revenue		
(Budget estimate)	281,000,000	343,000,000
Expenditure	240,000,000	282,000,000
Public Debt—		
External............	330,200,000	420,000,000
Internal............	219,200,000	—

The unit of currency is the *Lempira* (named after a native chief), value of 50 cents, U.S. and Lps 5·20 to the £. (*See also* p. 84.)

TRADE	1975
Imports..................*Lempiras*	410,000,000
Exports.................. ,,	296,700,000

Trade with U.K.

	1975
Imports from U.K.................	£4,187,000
Exports to U.K....................	714,000

CAPITAL.—Tegucigalpa. Pop. 267,754 (March 1974 census); other towns are San Pedro Sula (146,842), ΨLa Ceiba (38,582), ΨPuerto Cortes (25,661), Choluteca (25,120) and ΨTela (19,268).

FLAG.—Three horizontal bands, blue, white, blue (with five blue stars on white band).

NATIONAL DAY.—September 15.

BRITISH EMBASSY

Ambassador Extraordinary and Plenipotentiary and Consul-General, His Excellency Keith Hamylton Jones (1975) (resident at San José).

Tegucigalpa is 5,930 miles from London; transit, *via* New York, 14 days; *via* Panama 20 days. By air *via* New York or Miami 2 days.

HUNGARY
(Magyarország)

President of the Presidential Council of the Republic, Pál Losonczi, elected April, 1967.

COUNCIL OF MINISTERS

Prime Minister, György Lázár.
Deputy Prime Ministers, György Aczél; János Borbándi; Ferenc Havasi; István Huszár; Gyula Szekér.
Foreign Affairs, Frigyes Puja.
Interior, András Benkei.
Defence, Lajos Czinege.
Finance, Dr. Lajos Faluvégi.
Justice, Dr. Mihály Korom.
Metallurgy and Machine Industry, Tivadar Nemeslaki.
Heavy Industry, Dr. Pál Simon.
Light Industry, Mrs. János Keserü.
Foreign Trade, Dr. József Biró.
Internal Trade, István Szurdi.
Agriculture and Food, Dr. Pál Romány.

Health, Dr. Emil Schultheisz.
Education, Dr. Károly Polinszky.
Culture, Dr. László Orbán.
Building and Town Planning, Jozsef Bondor.
Labour, László Karakas.
Transport and Postal Affairs, Károly Rödönyi.
President National Planning Office, István Huszár.
President, Technical Development Committee, Miklós Ajtai.

THE COMMUNIST PARTY

Politbureau of the Central Committee, G. Aczél; A. Apró; V. Benke; B. Biszku; J. Fock; S. Gáspar; J. Kádár; I Huszár; G. Lázár; P. Losonczi; L. Maróthy; D. Nemes; K. Németh; M. Ovári; I. Sárlos.

Secretariat of the Central Committee, János Kádár (1st Secretary); B. Biszku; I. Györi; A. Gyenes; K. Németh; M. Ovári; A. Pullai.

HUNGARIAN EMBASSY AND CONSULATE
35 Eaton Place, S.W.1

[01–235 4048, 7191; Consulate: 01–235 4462]

Ambassador Extraordinary and Plenipotentiary, His Excellency Dr. Vencel Házi (1970).
Counsellors, M. T. Antalpéter (Commercial); Dr. E. Simonyi; Mrs. E. Ábri (Cultural Affairs).
Military and Air Attaché, Col. Károly Mészáros.
1st Secretaries, M. Dezsö Takács; Miss Piroska Szögyéni (Administration); M. Géza Kollár (Commercial).
2nd Secretary, M. Károly Kovács (Press).
3rd Secretary, M. Laszlo Merklin (Consul).
Attaché, Dr. Istvan Földesi.

Area and Population.—The area of Hungary may be stated as approximately 36,000 sq. miles with a population (1976) of 10,572,000.

Government.—Hungary was reconstituted a kingdom in 1920 after having been declared a republic on Nov. 17, 1918. She joined the Anti-Comintern Pact on Feb. 24, 1939, and entered the 1939–45

War on the side of Germany in 1941. On Jan. 20, 1945, a Hungarian provisional government of liberation, which had been set up during the preceding December, signed an armistice under the terms of which the frontiers of Hungary were withdrawn to the limits existing in 1937.

After the liberation, a coalition of the Smallholder, National Peasant, Social Democrat and Communist parties carried out major land reform and mines, heavy industry, banks and schools were nationalized. By 1949 the Communists had suc-

ceeded in gaining a monopoly of power. A campaign was opened to collectivize agriculture and by 1952 practically the entire economy had been " socialized ".

In mid-1953 Mr. Imre Nagy became Prime Minister, replacing Mr. Rákosi, who remained as First Secretary of the Party. Mr. Nagy introduced a more moderate policy based largely on the development of agriculture rather than heavy industry. However, in April 1955 he was removed from his position as Prime Minister and subsequently expelled from the Party. But opposition to Mr. Rákosi within the Hungarian Communist Party mounted and on July 18, 1956, he was removed from his post as First Secretary and succeeded by Mr. Gerö, who had been one of his closest associates.

The period from July to the outbreak of the national revolution on Oct. 23, 1956, was marked by growing ferment in intellectual circles and increased discord within the Party. The immediate signal for the revolt was a series of students' demonstrations, first in Szeged on Oct. 22 and in Budapest a day later. The chief demands put forward by students and other demonstrators were for the return of Mr. Nagy as Prime Minister, for the withdrawal of Soviet troops from the country and for free elections. Fighting broke out on the night of Oct. 23 between demonstrators, who had been joined by large numbers of factory workers, and the State Security Police (A.V.H.). Soviet forces intervened in strength early the next morning. By Oct. 30 Soviet troops had withdrawn from Budapest and on Nov. 3 Mr. Nagy formed an all-party coalition government. This government was overthrown and the revolution suppressed as the result of a renewed attack by Soviet forces on Budapest in the early hours of Nov. 4. Simultaneously the formation of a new Hungarian Revolutionary Worker Peasant Government under the leadership of Mr. Kádár, Mr. Gerö's successor as First Secretary of the Party, was announced. The trial and execution of Imre Nagy and three of his associates was announced on June 17, 1958.

Industrialization has made considerable progress in the last decade and now produces 68 per cent. of national income. Industry is mainly based on imported raw materials, but Hungary has her own coal (mostly brown), bauxite, considerable deposits of natural gas (some not yet under full exploitation), some iron ore and oil. Output figures in 1975 (1,000 tons), coal, 24,900; bauxite, 2,890; steel 3,671; crude oil, 2,006; cement, 3,759. Natural gas production totalled 20,457 million cubic metres.

Agriculture still occupies an important place in the Hungarian economy. 10·6 per cent. of the entire land area is owned by State farms and a further 63·8 per cent. is within co-operative farms. Production of the most important crops in 1975 was as follows (1,000 tons): wheat, 4,005; rye 147; barley 699; maize 7,088; rice 69; oats 87; sugar beet 4,089; green maize and silage maize 5,105; lucerne 2,328.

In 1975 most plan targets were fulfilled apart from that for agriculture. National income grew by 5 per cent., and industrial output by 6 per cent. Agricultural production was only 1 per cent. higher than in 1973. The index of retail prices rose 3·6 per cent. The new Fifth Five Year Plan will run from 1976–1980. Targets in this Plan are slightly lower than the performance in 1971–75.

Since 1968 the Hungarian economy has been run according to a system which allows more decentralized decision-making than in some other Eastern European countries. More difficult economic circumstances have led to some slight moves to more central control in vital areas such as the allocation of fuels and raw materials.

Religion and Education.—About two-thirds of the population are Roman Catholics, and the remainder mostly Calvinist. There are five types of schools under the Ministry of Education—kindergartens 3–6, general schools 6–14 (compulsory). vocational schools (15–18), secondary schools (15–18), universities and adult training schools (over 18). In the academic year 1974–75 there were 103,390 students at higher education institutions, 374,569 (incl. 209,646 attending day courses) at secondary schools, and 1,039,600 at general schools.

Language and Literature.—Magyar, or Hungarian, is one of the Finno-Ugrian languages. Hungarian literature began to flourish in the second half of the sixteenth century. Among the greatest writers of the nineteenth and twentieth centuries are Mihály Vörösmarty (1800–1855), Sándor Petöfi (1823–1849), János Arany (1817–1882), Imre Madach (1823–1864), Kálmán Mikszáth (1847–1910), Endre Ady (1877–1918), Attila József (1905–1937), Mihály Babits (1883–1941) and Dezsö Kosztolányi (1885–1936).

Finance.—The budget estimates for the year 1975 were: Revenue, Forints 318,500,000,000; Expenditure, Forints 323,400,000,000. The tourist rate of exchange for the Forint (of 100 Filler) was 38·53 Forints= £1 (July, 1 1976).

TRADE

	1974	1975
	Forints	*Forints*
Imports	51,010,000,000	61,537,400,000
Exports	46,927,000,000	52,169,800,000

Trade with U.K.

	1974	1975
Imports from U.K.	£44,050,000	£44,449,000
Exports to U.K.	25,007,000	26,137,000

CAPITAL: Budapest, on the Danube; population (1975), 2,055,646. Other large towns are: Miskolc (196,049); Debrecen (182,326); Szeged (167,220) and Pecs (161,612).

FLAG.—Red, white, green (horizontally).

NATIONAL DAY.—April 4 (Anniversary of Liberation, 1945).

BRITISH EMBASSY
6 Harmincad Utca, Budapest V
Ambassador Extraordinary and Plenipotentiary, His Excellency Richard Edmund Parsons (1976).
1st Secretaries, C. W. Long (*Head of Chancery*); S. N. P. Hemans (*Commercial*), M. J. Reynolds.
Defence and Military Attaché, Lt.-Col. K. H. J. Reynolds.
Air Attaché, Wg.-Cdr. R. G. Reekie.
Consul and Administration Officer, J. W. O. Smith, M.V.O., M.B.E.
2nd Secretaries, S. C. Johns (*Commercial*); D. B. Merry (*Information*).
Cultural Attaché, J. M. E. Took, M.B.E.
Attaché and Vice Consul, C. J. W. Forrester.
Assistant Cultural Attaché, Miss M. J. Cole.
Budapest is distant 1,126 miles from London, transit by rail 30 hours; by air 2 hrs. 20 mins.

ICELAND
(Island)
President, Dr. Kristjan Eldjarn, *born* 1917, *elected* July 1, 1968; *assumed office* Aug. 1, 1968, *re-elected* 1972 and 1976.
Prime Minister, Geir Hallgrimsson (*Ind.*).
Foreign Affairs, Einar Augustsson (*Pr.*).

ICELAND

Industries and Social Affairs, Gunnar Thoroddsen (*Ind.*).
Finance, Matthias A. Mathiesen (*Ind.*).
Fisheries, Health and Social Security, Matthias Bjarnason (*Ind.*).
Justice and Commerce, Ólafur Jóhanneson (*Pr.*).
Agriculture and Communications, Halldór Sigurdsson (*Pr.*).
Education, Vilhjalmur Hjalmarsson (*Pr.*).
(*Ind.*—Independence Party; *Pr.*—Progressive Party).

EMBASSY IN LONDON
1 Eaton Terrace, S.W.1
[01-730 5131]

Ambassador Extraordinary and Plenipotentiary, His Excellency Sigurdur Bjarnason (1976).
Minister-Counsellor, M. Eiríkur Benedikz.
1st Secretary, M. Helgi Ágústsson.

Iceland is a large volcanic island in the North Atlantic Ocean, extending from 63° 23' to 66° 33' N. lat., and from 13° 22' to 24° 35' W. long., with an estimated area of 40,500 square miles, or about one-sixth greater than that of Ireland. The population was 218,682 on Dec. 1, 1975.

Iceland was uninhabited before the ninth century, when settlers came from Norway. For several centuries a form of republican government prevailed, with an annual assembly of leading men called the *Althing,* but in 1241 Iceland became subject to Norway, and later to Denmark. During the colonial period, Iceland maintained its cultural integrity but a deterioration in the climate, together with frequent volcanic eruptions and outbreaks of disease led to a serious fall in the standard of living and to a decline in the population to little more than 40,000. In the nineteenth century a struggle for independence began which led first to home-rule for Iceland under the Danish Crown (1918), and later to complete independence under a republican form of rule in 1944.

The Icelandic Cabinet normally consists of seven Ministers, responsible to the *Althing,* a Parliamentary assembly of 60 members. A coalition of Progressives, Left Wing Liberals and members of the People's Alliance (Communists) held office from 1971 until the general election of June 30, 1974, in which government and opposition parties obtained an equal number of seats. After prolonged discussions between the party leaders, a new coalition of members of the Independence Party (25 seats) and Progressives (17 seats) took office on Aug. 28, 1974.

The principal exports are frozen fish fillets, salt fish, stock fish, fresh fish on ice, frozen scampi, fishmeal and oil, skins and aluminium; the imports consist of almost all the necessities of life, the chief items being petroleum products, transport equipment, textiles, foodstuffs, animal feeds, timber, and alumina.

At January 1, 1976, the mercantile marine consisted of 635 vessels of under 100 gross tons and 360 ships of 100 gross tons and over; a total of 995 vessels (175,207 gross tons), of which 898 were fishing boats and trawlers and 48 were coasters. There is a regular shipping service between Reykjavik and Felixstowe and between Reykjavik and Weston Point on the Mersey and the Continent.

In the period since Iceland attained independence in 1944, relations between Britain and that country have come under strain on several occasions as a result of unilateral action by Iceland to extend the area of her exclusive fishery jurisdiction. In 1952, Iceland extended her fishing limits from 3 miles to 4 miles from new base lines across bays and estuaries, and the consequent dispute with Britain lasted until 1956. In 1958, Iceland extended her fishing limits from 4 to 12 miles. The ensuing dispute with Britain (and West Germany) was settled in March 1961 by an Exchange of Notes in which it was agreed, *inter alia,* that Iceland would give Britain 6 months' notice of any further extension of her fisheries jurisdiction and that in the event of a dispute about such extension the matter could be referred to the International Court of Justice at the request of either party.

The Icelandic Government which came to power in July 1971, declared their intention of extending the fishing limits to 50 miles from September 1, 1972, and on February 15, 1972, passed legislation purporting to have this effect. Britain then referred the matter to the International Court. As an interim measure, the Court granted Britain an injunction restraining Iceland from enforcing the 50 mile limit against British vessels and at the same time ordered Britain to limit her catch in the area to 170,000 tons a year (the average for 1967–1971). The Court subsequently decided that it had jurisdiction, but the Icelandic Government refused to recognize the Court's competence in the matter and sought to apply the new fishing limit by force. After September 1, 1972, British trawlers were subjected to warp cutting and harassment by Icelandic Coastguard vessels. On May 19, 1973, the British Government ordered naval vessels into the disputed zone to provide protection for British trawlers. An interim settlement recorded in an Exchange of Notes dated Nov. 13, 1973, established maximum numbers for British trawlers fishing off Iceland and a system of rotating areas around the coast in which it was agreed that they should fish, with certain other areas reserved for conservation purposes. This agreement was valid for 2 years.

Negotiations failed to produce a further agreement before its expiry, and the sequence of warp-cutting and naval protection once again ensued, this time leading to a breach of diplomatic relations on Feb. 19, 1976. Informal contacts within NATO subsequently prepared the way for an agreement signed in Oslo on June 1, 1976, which provided for a daily average of 24 trawlers to fish in designated areas for a period of 6 months, at the end of which British vessels would fish only to the extent provided for in arrangements agreed with the Government of Iceland.

A regular air service is maintained between

Glasgow and London and Reykjavik. There are also air services from the island to Scandinavia, U.S.A., Germany and Luxemburg.

Road communications are adequate in summer but greatly restricted by snow in winter. Only roads in town centres and a few key highways are metalled the rest being of gravel, sand and lava dust. The climate and terrain make first-class surfaces for highways out of the question. Total number of vehicles licensed is about 75,000 (private cars, 60,000).

Language and Literature.—The ancient Norraena (or Northern tongue) presents close affinities to Anglo-Saxon and as spoken and written in Iceland to-day differs little from that introduced into the island in the ninth century. There is a rich literature with two distinct periods of development, from the middle of the eleventh to the end of the thirteenth century and from the beginning of the nineteenth century to the present time.

FINANCE

	1974	1975
	Krónur ('000)	*Krónur* ('000)
Revenue.............	29,178,000	47,625,000
Expenditure.........	29,402,000	47,225,000
External Debt.......	13,358,000	—
Internal Debt........	4,473,000	—

TRADE

	1974	1975
	Krónur ('000)	*Krónur* ('000)
Exports.............	32,877,000	47,436,000
Imports.............	52,568,000	75,062,000

TRADE WITH U.K.

	1974	1975
Imports from U.K....	£24,575,000	£23,205,000
Exports to U.K.......	12,059,000	13,675,000

The Icelandic *Krónur* was devalued by 10·7 per cent. on Dec. 19, 1972, by 10 per cent. on Feb. 15, 1973, by 3·6 per cent. on Sept. 14, 1973, by 4 per cent. on May 17, 1974, and by 20 per cent. on Feb. 14, 1975, the present par value being expressed as *Krónur* 184= \$U.S. 1. (*see also* p. 83).

CAPITAL: ΨReykjavik. Population (Dec. 1, 1975), 84,423.

Other centres in approximate order of importance are Akureyri, Kopavogur, Hafnarfjördur, Keflavik, Westmann Islands, Akranes, Isafjördhur and Siglufjördur.

FLAG.—Blue, with white-bordered red cross.
NATIONAL DAY.—June 17.

BRITISH EMBASSY
Laufasvegur 49, Reykjavik

Ambassador Extraordinary and Plenipotentiary and Consul-General, His Excellency Kenneth Arthur East, C.M.G. (1975).

1st Secretary and Consul, E. Young, O.B.E.

BRITISH CONSULAR OFFICES

There are Consular Offices at *Reykjavik, Akureyri* and *Isafjördhur*.

INDONESIA
(Republic of Indonesia)

President, General Soeharto, *born* June 9, 1921. *Acting President*, March 12, 1967; *confirmed as President*, Mar. 28, 1968, *re-elected for a term of 5 years*, March, 1973.
Vice-President, Sultan Hamengku Buwono IX.

SECOND DEVELOPMENT CABINET
Ministers of State
Economic, Financial and Industrial Affairs, Prof. Dr. Widjojo Nitisastro.

Administrative Reform, Dr. Johanes Baptista Sumarlin.
Research, Prof. Dr. Sumitro Djojohadikusumo.
Public Welfare, Prof. Dr. Sunawar Sukowati, S.H.
State Secretary, Maj.-Gen. Sudharmono, S.H.
Ministers
Home Affairs, Lt.-Gen. Amir Machmud.
Foreign Affairs, Hadji Adam Malik.
Defence/Security, Gen. Maraden Panggabean.
Justice, Prof. Dr. Muchtar Kusumaatmadja.
Information, Mashuri S.H.
Finance, Prof. Dr. Ali Wardhana.
Trade, Drs. Radius Prawiro.
Agriculture, Prof. Dr. Ir. Thojib Adiwadjaja.
Industry, Lieut.-Gen. M. Jusuf.
Mining, Prof. Dr. Ir. M. Sadli.
Public Works and Electricity, Ir. Sutami.
Communications, Prof. Dr. Emil Salim.
Education and Culture, Dr. Syarif Thayeb.
Health, Prof. Dr. G. A. Siwabessy.
Religion, Prof. Dr. H. A. Mukti Ali.
Manpower, Transmigration, Co-operatives, Prof. Dr. Subroto.
Social Affairs, H. M. S. Mintaredja S.H.

INDONESIAN EMBASSY AND CONSULATE
38 Grosvenor Square, W.1.
[01-499 7661]

Ambassador Extraordinary and Plenipotentiary, His Excellency Admiral Ricardus Subono (1974).
Minister, K. Noermattias (*Political*).
Minister-Counsellor, U. Notodirdjo (*Economic*).
Defence, Air and Military Attaché, Col. J. H. Sumarjono.
Naval Attaché, Lt.-Col. Aboe.
Attachés, K. Sunoto (*Information*); S. Boedjang (*Commercial*); Capt. T. Surahardja (*Communications*).
Counsellor, J. Sutantio (*Political*).
1st Secretaries, K. Kartadisastra (*Administration*); A. Surjadi (*Economic*).
2nd Secretaries, Abdul Rahman Siata (*Economic*); Ibnu Ash Djamil, S.H. (*Protocol*).
3rd Secretaries, E. S. Suryodiningrat, S.H. (*Consular*); Miss Soerochmah (*Administration*).

Situated between latitudes 6° North and 11° South and between longitudes 95° and 141° East, Indonesia comprises the islands of *Java* and *Madura*, the island of *Sumatra*, the *Riouw-Lingga Archipelago* which with Karimon, Anambas, Natuna Islands, Tambelan, and part of Sumatra, forms the province of Riau), the islands of *Bangka* and *Billiton*, part of the island of *Borneo* (Kalimantan), *Sulawesi* (formerly *Celebes*) *Island*, the *Molucca Islands* (Ternate, Halmahera, Buru, Seram, Banda, Timor-Laut, Larat, Bachiam, Obi, Kei, Aru, Babar, Leti and Wetar), part of *Timor Island*, the islands of *Bali* and *Lombok* and the western half of the island of New Guinea (*Irian Jaya*), with a total area of 735,000 sq. miles, and a population of about 129,000,000.

From the early part of the 17th century much of the Indonesian Archipelago was under Netherlands rule. Following the World War 1939–45, during which the Archipelago was occupied by the Japanese, a strong nationalist movement manifested itself and after sporadic fighting the formal transfer of sovereignty by the Netherlands of all the former Dutch East Indies except W. New Guinea took place on December 27, 1949.

Dr. Sukarno was elected President of Indonesia and held office until his deposition in 1967. He died on June 21, 1970.

Following the establishment of Malaysia (including Sabah and Sarawak) in 1963, President Sukarno pursued a policy of " confrontation " against it, involving border incursions in both West and East Malaysia. Commonwealth forces

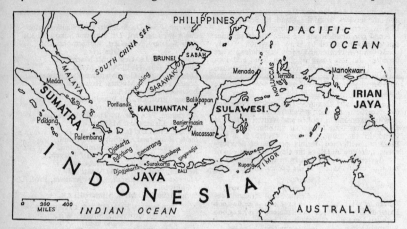

assisted Malaysian resistance. Western New Guinea became part of Indonesia in 1963 under the name West Irian (now Irian Jaya), this interpretation being confirmed in an " Act of Free Choice " in July, 1969, of which the United Nations took note in November 1969.

On Sept. 30, 1965, an attempted *coup d'état* assisted by the Palace Guard resulted in the murder of six generals. The Indonesian Communist Party was charged with plotting to destroy the power of the Army and to set up a Peking-oriented régime, nominally under President Sukarno. The coup was swiftly crushed and a widespread massacre of Communists and their supporters followed. Sukarno remained in office but his Foreign Minister, Dr. Subandrio, among others, was arrested and later sentenced to death. The sentence had not been carried out by the summer of 1976.

Following a three-week period of unrest and violent student demonstrations the Minister of the Army, General Soeharto, took over effective political power in March, 1966, and announced the banning in Indonesia of the Communist Party. The new régime concluded an agreement ending the " confrontation " with Malaysia on Aug. 11, 1966, and Indonesia resumed membership of the United Nations Organization which it had left in 1965. General Soeharto was made Acting President with full powers, on March 11, 1967.

Using his powers as Acting President, General Soeharto revised the membership of the two Houses of Parliament, and on March 28, 1968, the MPRS (Provisional People's Consultative Congress), the highest constitutional body, appointed him full President for a period of five years. The 1971 elections resulted in the Government faction Golkar (functional groups) achieving a large majority.

In accordance with another instruction General Soeharto on June 6 replaced the Ampera Cabinet with the Development Cabinet, *i.e.* one which was intended to reflect the emphasis to be placed henceforward on the development of the country, economic affairs, efficiency and expertise in general, and to reduce the direct influence of the military in the Government.

From March 12–24, 1973, the M.P.R. (Peoples' Consultative Assembly) met at Jakarta, the first time that it had assembled in its proper form during Indonesian independence. The primary outcome was the re-election of President Soeharto for a further term of 5 years, the election of Hamengku Buwono IX, Sultan of Yogyakarta, as Vice-President, and the determination of the broad lines of State policy. In March a new Cabinet, called the Second Development Cabinet, was sworn in. The Government have announced that the next elections will take place in May 1977, and that the M.P.R. will meet in 1978.

Finance.—Following new measures introduced by the Government in October, 1966, inflation declined from the rate of 600 per cent. in 1966 to about 2 per cent. in 1971. At the end of 1972, a rice shortage, followed by a rise in other prices, increased inflationary pressure on the economy and inflation rose to 27 per cent. in 1973 and 40 per cent. in early 1974 but special measures reduced this to about 2 per cent. for the year. Following the agreement on the re-scheduling of Indonesia's debts in 1966, Western creditor nations agreed to make available aid amounting to $200,000,000 as balance of payments support. Commitments undertaken by these countries in May 1974 amounted to over $900,000,000.

The new measures adopted by the Government in October, 1966, included the abolition of State controls and the introduction of a free market policy with more realistic exchange rates geared to a floating rate for the purchase of foreign exchange in the form of bonus export certificates for essential imports. The rate had risen to a peak of Rps.480= $1 by mid-1968, but fell to Rps.378 = $1 by mid-1969. It has remained stable since then even though on April 17, 1970, the Government abolished the bonus exports certificate system and introduced a free market for foreign exchange. Rps.415= U.S. $1 (July 1974).

Production.—Nearly 70 per cent. of the population of Indonesia is engaged in agriculture and related production. Copra, kapok, nutmeg, pepper and cloves are produced, mainly by smallholders; palm oil, sugar, fibres and cinchona are produced by large estates. Rubber, tea, coffee and tobacco are also produced by both in large quantities. Timber is now the second largest foreign exchange earner after oil. Rice is a traditional staple food for the people of Indonesia and the islands of Java and Madura are important producers, but production

is only gradually rising and up to 1976 has been insufficient to meet home demands.

Oil is the most important asset with production in 1974 earning some U.S. $7,500,000,000 in foreign exchange.

Indonesia is rich in minerals; petroleum, tin, coal and bauxite are the principal products; gold, silver, manganese phosphates, nickel and sulphur were produced in quantity before the Second World War and there are considerable deposits. Aid to Indonesia is channelled through the Inter-Governmental Group on Indonesia (IGGI), which pledged U.S. $940,000,000 in May 1975.

The first five-year development programme announced on Dec. 30, 1968, concentrating particularly on agriculture and communications, was inaugurated on April 1, 1969. The second five-year plan began in April 1974 and envisages a five-fold increase in the Government's development expenditure and a 7½ per cent. annual rate of growth in Gross National Product.

Trade with U.K.

There was a progressive decline in British exports to Indonesia after 1960. This became more marked during Indonesia's policy of " confrontation " against Malaysia which resulted in a disruption of normal commercial relations and stringent import controls due to lack of foreign currency, but exports have improved markedly since the restoration of normal commercial relations in 1967.

	1974	1975
Direct Imports from U.K.	£46,693,000	59,500,000
Exports to U.K.	14,419,000	15,100,000

Principal exports to the United Kingdom are rubber, tea, coffee, spices and sugar. Imports from the United Kingdom are mainly of machinery, chemicals, electrical equipment, motor vehicles, cycles, lubricating and heavy oils, and metal goods

Language.—The National Language is Bahasa Indonesia; common spelling for Malay and Bahasa Indonesia was introduced in August 1972.

Transport.—In Java a main line connects Jakarta with Surabaya in the East of Java and there are several branches, including a line from Semarang on the North coast to Yogyakarta in the South. In Sumatra the important towns of Medan, Padang and Palembang are the centres of short railway systems.

Sea communications in the archipelago are maintained by the State-run shipping companies Djakarta-Lloyd (ocean-going) and Pelni (coastal and inter-island) and other smaller concerns. Transport by small craft on the rivers of the larger islands plays an important part in trade. Air services in Indonesia are operated by Garuda Indonesian Airway and other local airlines, and Jakarta is served by various international services. There are approximately 50,000 miles of roads.

CAPITAL.— Ψ Jakarta, formerly Batavia (population 5,000,000). Other important centres are: (Java), Ψ Surabaya, Ψ Semarang, Bandung, Ψ Cirebon, Ψ Surakarta and Yogyakarta; (1971 *populations*) (Madura) Pamekesan (180,000); (Sumatra) Palembang (582,961); Medan (800,000); and Ψ Padang; (Sulawesi) Ψ Ujung Pandang (*formerly* Makassas) (600,000); and Ψ Menado; (Kalimantan, Borneo) Banjarmasin, Ψ Balikpapan and Ψ Pontianak; (Moluccas) Ternate (70,000); (Bali) Denpasar and Singaraya (120,000); (W. Timor) Kupang (10,000); (W. Irian) Jayapura.

NATIONAL DAY.—August 17 (Anniversary of Proclamation of Independence).

FLAG.—Equal bands of red over white.

BRITISH EMBASSY
Jakarta

Ambassador Extraordinary and Plenipotentiary, His Excellency John Archibald Ford, C.M.G., M.C. (1975).

Counsellors, A. C. Stuart; R. B. Crowson (*Commercial*).

Defence and Military Attaché, Col. D. T. Grantham, O.B.E.

Naval Attaché, Capt. C. G. Le Mesurier, R.N.

1st *Secretaries,* S. Muir; J. C. A. Rundall; Miss S. E. Hunt (*Information*); R. K. Buist (*Commercial*); Miss M. Clay (*Aid*); T. E. F. Williams (*Consul*).

2nd *Secretaries,* R. J. C. Allen; P. J. Torry (*Commercial*).

3rd *Secretaries,* R. H. Gozney; Miss H. M. Thomas (*Commercial*); Miss V. B. M. Steele (*Vice-Consul*); R. C. Huxley (*Aid*); R. D. Leighton; G. T. Squires (*Commercial*); Miss L. Fleming (*Aid*).

Attaché, J. F. Pitman (*Agricultural*).

BRITISH CONSULAR OFFICES

There are British Consular Offices at *Jakarta, Medan* and *Surabaya.*

BRITISH CONSULAR OFFICES

There are British Consular Offices at *Jakarta* and *Medan.*

BRITISH COUNCIL

Representative, Dr. J. H. F. Villiers, Jalan Imam Bonjol 57–59 Jakarta. There is also an office at *Bandung.*

IRAN
(Persia)

Shanshah of Iran, H.I.M. Mohammed Reza Pahlavi, *born* Oct. 26, 1919; *acceded* Sept. 16, 1941 (on abdication of his father Reza Shah Pahlevi); *married* (March 15, 1939), Princess Fawzieh, sister of ex-King Farouk of Egypt (marriage dissolved Nov. 17, 1948). and has issue a daughter *born* 1940. The Shah *married* (Feb. 12, 1951) Suraya Esfandiari Bakhtiari (marriage dissolved, April 6, 1958); *married* Dec. 21, 1959, Farah Dibah (Empress Farah Pahlevi) and has issue Crown Prince Reza, *born* Oct. 31, 1960; Princess Farahnaz, *b.* March 12, 1963; Prince Ali Reza, *b.* April 28, 1966; Princess Leila, *b.* Mar. 27, 1970.

Prime Minister, Amir Abbas Hoveida

IRANIAN EMBASSY IN LONDON
16 Princes Gate, S.W.7
[01–584 8101]

Ambassador Extraordinary and Plenipotentiary, His Excellency Dr. Parviz Radji (1976).

Area and Population.—Iran has an area of 628,000 sq. miles, with a population of 25,781,090 (Census of 1966); U.N. estimate, March, 1970, 28,448,000. It is mostly an arid table-land, encircled, except in the east, by mountains, the highest in the north rising to 18,934 ft. The central and eastern portion is a vast salt desert.

The Iranians are mostly Shi'ah Moslems but among them are a few hundred thousand Zoroastrians, Bahais, Sunni Moslems and Armenian and Assyrian Christians. There is also a substantial Jewish community. Civil and Penal codes based on those of France and Switzerland are in force.

Government.—Iran was ruled from the end of the 18th century by Shahs of the Qajar Dynasty, with despotic power, subject only to the influence of interpreters of the sacred law. A nationalist movement became active in Dec., 1905, and in Aug., 1906, the Shah, Muzaffer-ud-Din, admitting the need for reforms, granted a Constitution. After the war of 1914–18, the subsequent troubles and the signature of the Soviet-Iranian

Treaty of 1921, a vigorous Prime Minister, Reza Khan, formerly an officer of the Persian Cossack Regiment, re-established general order. On Oct. 31, 1925, the last representative of the Qajar Dynasty, Sultan Ahmed Shah, who had been absent from the country for some time, was deposed by the National Assembly, which handed over the government to the Prime Minister, Reza Khan, who was elected Shah on Dec. 13, 1925, by the Constituent Assembly, and took the title Reza Shah Pahlavi.

Owing to Nazi German penetration before and during the early part of the war of 1939-45, the Shah and his Government tended so far to favour the Axis powers that, after the German invasion of the U.S.S.R. in 1941, counter-measures became necessary; British and Soviet Forces entered the country from south and north on August 25, 1941, and expelled the agents of the Axis. On September 16, 1941, Reza Shah abdicated and left the country, nominating the Crown Prince as his successor. The Prince ascended the throne under the title of Mohammed Reza Shah Pahlavi.

In March 1949, the Shah issued an Imperial Farman convoking a Constituent Assembly to make certain revisions to the Constitution and the Assembly was duly elected and convened on April 21. After this Assembly the Senate was formed for the first time.

On February 26, 1963, the Shah announced his six point "White Revolution". The six points are: 1. A land reform designed to redistribute land and place it in the hands of the peasants. 2. Nationalization of all forest land. 3. The sale of government shares in factories and industrial enterprises to raise money for the implementation of the land reform. 4. The distribution of factory profits among the factory employees. 5. The granting of the vote to women. 6. The creation of a Literacy Corps to bring basic education to the rural areas. Six additional points have since been added.

On March 2, 1975, the Shah dissolved the two-party system, and announced the formation of the *Rastakhiz* (National Resurrection) Party, which would be the only political party. On June 20, general elections were held for the *Majhs* (Chamber of Deputies) and the Senate.

For the purposes of local government the country is divided into 14 Provinces (Ustans) and 8 Countries (*Farmandariye Kol*), comprising 147 Sub-

Provinces (*Shahristans*), under Governors-General and Governors, respectively.

Defence.—The Army has a strength of about 175,000 men, in 3 armoured divisions, 2 infantry divisions and 4 independent brigades. Two years' military service is compulsory. The Air Force has a strength of about 50,000, with over 200 aircraft. The Navy, with personnel of about 13,000, consists of 3 destroyers, 4 frigates, 4 corvettes, 6 mine-sweepers, and patrol boats, landing craft and hover-craft. The Gendarmerie is an all regular, para-military force of about 70,000 men which provides frontier guards and mans small posts throughout the country.

Education.—Since 1943 primary education has been compulsory and free, but there is large scale absenteeism, particularly outside the towns. The establishment in 1963 of the Literacy Corps (a body of National Servicemen who are seconded to the Ministry of Education to work as Primary School teachers in rural districts) has brought schooling to hitherto deprived villages and is making a valuable contribution in increasing educational opportunities for country people. There are in Iran eight universities (Tehran 3, Tabriz, Meshed, Isfahan, Shiraz, Rezayeh and Ahwaz).

Language and Literature.—Persian, or Farsi, the language of Iran, and of some other areas formerly under Persian rule, is an Indo-European tongue with many Arabic elements added; the alphabet is mainly Arabic, with writing from right to left. Among the great names in Persian literature are those of Abu'l Kásim Mansúr, or Firdausi (A.D. 939-1020), Omar Khayyám, the astronomer-poet (died A.D. 1122), Muslihu'd-Din, known as Sa'di (born A.D. 1184) and Shems-ed-Din Muhammad, or Hafiz (died A.D. 1389).

Finance.—The budget for the Iranian year beginning March 21, 1971, including development expenditure, balanced at Rls. 481,000,000,000 an increase of 18 per cent. over 1970-71. The unit of currency is the *Rial* of 100 *Dinars* (for rate of exchange, *see* p. 84).

Production and Industry.—While petroleum is the principal product and by far the greatest export Iran, except for its desert areas, is primarily an agricultural country and more than half of the inhabitants depend of their living on the land. Wheat is the principal crop, using about half the area under cultivation. Other important crops are barley, rice, cotton, sugar beet, fruits and vegetables. Wool is also produced—sheep, as well as goats, being numerous. There are extensive forests in the north and west, the conservation of which is an urgent problem. Rapid progress has been made in the development of industry. Apart from oil, the principal industrial products are carpets, textiles (mainly cotton), sugar, cement and other construction materials, ginned cotton, vegetable oil and other food products, leather and shoes, metal manufactures, pharmaceuticals, automobiles, fertilizers, plastics, matches and cigarettes. A steel mill at Isfahan began the production of pig iron at the end of 1971. There are now three petro-chemical plants in operation, producing fertilizers plastics, detergents, sulphur and liquid petroleum gas. Large-scale copper deposits have been found in the south-eastern part of the country.

The oilfields had produced over 200,000,000 metric tons of oil from their first output to Dec. 31, 1946. Production had risen to a total of 35,000,000 metric tons in 1950, the last full year before nationalization. Oil shipments ceased in 1951 and were not resumed until Oct. 30, 1954.

The former functions of A.I.O.C. (now renamed "British Petroleum Company") in Iran were

taken over for an initial period of 25 years by a consortium of 8 oil companies (including A.I.O.C., one French, one Dutch and five U.S.), A.I.O.C. receiving from Iran £25,000,000 cash in the 10 years from Jan. 1. 1957, in compensation for its old assets in Northern Iran and in settlement of losses since 1951; and from the other members of the consortium for their shares, about £214,000,000 payable over 20-25 years. The consortium is responsible for the production, refining and sale of Iranian oil through two operating companies, while " non-basic " operations are undertaken by the National Iranian Oil Company.

Oilfields outside the Consortium area are being developed by several oil companies formed jointly by N.I.O.C. with western oil companies, notably S.I.R.P., I.P.A.C., L.A.P.C.O. and I.M.I.N.C.O. Production from offshore oil wells in the Persian Gulf developed by these companies is increasing rapidly.

Recent oil production figures are (in long tons): 1966, 105,100,000; 1967, 129,300,000; 1968, 142,200,000; 1969, 168,100,000; 1970, 194,000,000.

Communications.—The principal roads are from the frontier of Iraq at Khosravi to Tehran; from Tehran *via* Saveh and Hamadan to Ahwaz and Khorramshahr; from Tehran *via* Qum, Isfahan and Shiraz to Bushire; from Tehran into Azerbaijan, through Tabriz to Julfa (on the Soviet frontier) with a branch road into Turkey; from Tehran to Meshed; three roads through the Elbruz mountains to the Caspian coast and the Soviet borders east and west of the Caspian Sea; and from Isfahan, *via* Yezd and Kerman to Zahidan and thence to Meshed. Zahidan is connected by road with Quetta (Pakistan). Meshed is connected by road with Herat (Afghanistan). Some of these roads traverse extremely difficult mountainous country; others are desert tracks. The *Trans-Iranian Railway,* from Bandar Shah, on the Caspian Sea, to Bandar Shahpur, on the Persian Gulf, was inaugurated in 1938; this line has a total length of 872 miles, the total cost, after eleven years' work, being approximately £30,000,000. The branch lines from Tehran to Meshed and to Tabriz have now been completed. There are also railroads from Tabriz to Julfa and from Zahidan to Mirjawa and thence to Quetta and branch lines from Ahwaz to Khorramshahr and Khorramshahr to Tanuma in Iraq (on the Shatt al Arab, opposite Basrah) were opened during the war. An extension from Qum to Yezd *viâ* Kashan is now in operation as is one from Bandar Shah to Gorgan. Extensions from Yezd to Kerman and from Tabriz to Van (Turkey) are being built. It is hoped to connect the Iranian rail system with the Turkish and with the Pakistan systems, thereby offering a through route from Europe to Pakistan.

Civil Aviation.—In May, 1946, a Department of Civil Aviation was created, subordinate to the Ministry of Roads. Progress has been made towards establishing first-class International Airports at Tehran and Abadan, with secondary airfields in accordance with ICAO standards. The *Iranian National Airlines Corporation* was formed from the former *Iranian Airways* and *Persian Air Services* in February, 1962. The Company is 51 per cent. Government-owned and operates internal and international routes. Air France, K.L.M., S.A.S., Iraqi, M.E.A., P.A.A., Lufthansa, British Airways, Qantas, P.I.A., Aeroflot, Alitalia, Aryana Airways and El Al operate services to Tehran.

TRADE

	1968-69	1969-70
Imports.	Rials106,723,875,715	Rials115,567,000,000
Exports.	16,268,001,537	18,533,000,000

These figures are calculated at the commercial rate of exchange and exclude oil exports. Total exports, including oil exports for 1969-70, *Rials* 612,357,000,000.

Trade with U.K.

	1974	1975
Imports from U.K	£278,580,000	£494,621,000
Exports to U.K.	513,270,000	700,933,000

Imports into Iran consist mainly of industrial and agricultural machinery, iron and steel (including manufactures), electrical machinery and goods, sugar, chemicals and pharmaceuticals, motor vehicles and certain textile fabrics and yarns. The principal exports, apart from oil, are cotton, carpets, dried fruits and nuts, hides and skins, mineral ores, wool, gums, caviare, cummin seed and animal casings. West Germany, the U.S.A. and the U.K. are Iran's three leading suppliers. West Germany, the U.S.S.R., the U.K. and the U.S.A. are the main customers for non-oil exports.

CAPITAL: Tehran, population (1970), 3,150,000. Other large towns are Tabriz (388,000), Isfahan (340,000), Meshed (312,000), Shiraz (206,000), Resht (119,000), Kerman (73,000), Hamadan (115,000), Yezd (74,000), Kermanshah (152,000), ΨAbadan (273,000), Ahwaz (145,000).

FLAG.—Equal horizontal bands of green, white and red; with arms (lion and sun) in centre.

NATIONAL DAY.—October 26 (Anniversary of Birthday of the Shahanshah).

BRITISH EMBASSY
Avenue Ferdowsi, Tehran

Ambassador Extraordinary and Plenipotentiary, His Excellency Sir Anthony Derrick Parsons, K.C.M.G., M.V.O., M.C. (1974).

Counsellors, G. B. Chalmers; M. K. O. Simpson-Orlebar (*Commercial*); A. B. Milne, O.B.E.
Defence and Military Attaché, Col. M. H. Jones.
Naval Attaché, Capt. C. R. V. Doe, R.N.
Air Attaché, Group Capt. J. Fennell, M.B.E., A.F.C.

BRITISH COUNCIL
Representative, J. G. Hanson, Kh. Ferdaussi 53 and 38 Tehran. Centres and libraries at *Isfahan, Meshed, Shiraz, Tabriz* and *Tehran.*

IRAQ

REVOLUTIONARY COMMAND COUNCIL
Chairman, President of the Republic, and *Supreme Commander of the Armed Forces,* Field Marshal Ahmad Hasan al Bakr, *assumed office* July 17, 1968.
Members, Saddam Hussain (*Vice-Chairman*); General Sa'dun Ghaidan (*Minister of Communications*); Dr. Izzat Mustafa (*Minister of Labour and Social Affairs*); Sd Izzat Ibrahim al Duri (*Minister of the Interior*); Sd Taha al Jazrawi (*Minister of Works and Housing*).
In addition to those members of the R.C.C. holding departmental portfolios listed above, there are 23 other ministers, including 5 ministers of State.

EMBASSY OF THE REPUBLIC OF IRAQ
21-22 Queen's Gate, S.W.7
[01-584 7141]

Ambassador Extraordinary and Plenipotentiary, H. E. Abdul Malik Ahmed Ali-Yasin.

Area, etc.—Traversed by the Rivers Euphrates and Tigris, Iraq extends from Turkey on N. and N.E. to the Persian Gulf on the S. and S.E. and from Iran on E. to Syria and Arabian Desert on W. the approximate position being between 37½° to 48½° E. long., and from 37½° to 30° N. lat. (*see*

MAP, p. 878). The area of Iraq is officially estimated at 172,000 sq. miles of which 37 per cent. is desert land. About 35 to 40 per cent. of the remainder is potentially cultivable either by rainfall or by irrigation.

Population.—At the Census of 1965 Iraq had a total population of 8,097,230; estimated 1970, 9,498,362.

The *Euphrates* (which has a total length of 1,700 miles from its source to its outflow in the Persian Gulf) is formed by two arms, of which the Murad Su (415 miles) rises in the slopes of the Ala Dagh, a mountain of Eastern Erzurum, and flows westwards to a junction with the Kara Su, or Frat Su (275 miles); the other arm rises in the north-west of Erzurum in the Dumlu Dagh. The *Tigris* has a total length of 1,150 miles from its source to its junction with the Euphrates at Qurna, 70 miles from the Persian Gulf, and rises in two arms south of the Taurus mountains, in Kurdistan, uniting at Til, where the boundaries of the districts of Diarbekir, Van and Bitlis conjoin.

Antiquities.—In 1944 excavations at Tell Hassuna, near Shura (on the Tigris in North Iraq) unearthed abundant traces of culture dating back to 5000 B.C. Excavations in 1948 at Tel Abu Shahrain, 14 miles south of " Ur of the Chaldees," confirm Eridu's claim to be the most ancient city of the Sumerian world. Hillah, the ancient city on the left bank of the Shatt el Hillah, a branch of the Euphrates, about 70 miles south of Baghdad, is near the site of Babylon and of the " house of the lofty-head " or " gate of the god " (Tower of Babel). Mosul *Liwa* covers a great part of the ancient kingdom of *Assyria*, the ruins of Ninevah, the Assyrian capital, being visible on the banks of the Tigris, opposite Mosul. Qurna, at the junction of the Tigris and Euphrates, is the traditional site of the *Garden of Eden*. The " *Tree of Knowledge*," which had stood there " from time immemorial," withered and died in December, 1946. It has been replaced by a shoot said to be from the original tree.

Government.—Under the Treaty of Lausanne (1923), Turkey renounced the sovereignty over Mesopotamia. A provisional Arab Government was set up in Nov., 1920, and in Aug., 1921, the Emir Faisal was elected King of Iraq. The country was a monarchy until July, 1958, when King Faisal II was assassinated. From 1958 Iraq has been under Presidential rule.

Diplomatic relations with the United Kingdom were broken in June 1967 and resumed in May 1968 They were again broken in Dec. 1971 and resumed once more in April 1974.

Language.—The language is mainly Arabic (*see* Arabia) and English is widely used in commerce, science and the arts.

Education.—In 1974 Iraq had 149 infant schools, with 867 teachers and 16,831 pupils; 6,731 primary schools, with 58,455 teachers and 1,408,929 pupils; and 1,193 intermediate and preparatory secondary schools, with 14,871 teachers and 388,624 full-time students. There were 5 universities and 4 other public institutes of higher education, with 2,669 teachers and lecturers and 58,351 students. In 1974 there were 64 vocational schools (agriculture, commerce and industry, home economics).

Communications and Trade.—New roads are being rapidly built, and communications between Baghdad and the provincial capitals are being improved and secured. The port of Basrah is not at present able to handle expeditiously all seaborne traffic. Continuous dredging of the Shatt-al-Arab has provided a navigable channel of 22½ feet at low water (as compared with 9 feet before dredging was begun). The port of Um Qasr near the Kuwaibi

border has been developed for freight and sulphur handling. Road routes from Turkey and the Mediterranean are well used, and carry through traffic to Kuwait and the south.

There are international airports at Baghdad and Basrah. Iraqi Airways provide a London/Baghdad service six days a week. British Airways and other European airlines operate frequently. Iraqi Airways and Middle East Airlines operate within the area, including (Iraqi) services to Basrah and Mosul. Iraqi Republican Railways provide regular passenger and goods services on a standard gauge line between Basra, Baghdad and Mosul, which links up through Syria and Turkey with the Mediterranean and the Bosphorus. There is also a metre gauge line connecting Baghdad with Khanaqin, Kirkuk and Arbil.

Agriculture and Industry.—Iraq is capable of supporting a considerably greater population if irrigation is developed and extended. The Government's concern with agricultural development is shown in the large financial allocations made to the sector. Apart from the valuable revenues to be derived from oil the wealth of the country depends upon agricultural development and two harvests can usually be gathered in the year. Production fluctuates from year to year according to rainfall. During the five years 1964–69 crops of barley, millet, rice, wheat, dates, cotton and tobacco were produced in sufficient quantities to allow a margin for export. However, due to a poor harvest in 1969–70 dates were the only important agricultural export. All crops improved in 1971–72 but fell to 1970 levels in 1973.

Few industries with the exception of the oil industry are yet established on any scale, but increasing industrialization is taking place, mainly in the public sector. Priority is being given to petrochemicals, food industries, construction industries and engineering. Existing industries include cement, building materials, flour milling, cigarettes, soap, beer, steel fabrications, furniture, tanning, textiles, footwear and vegetable oils. In 1972 there were 1,319 industrial establishments employing an average number of 121,409 persons annually. Turnover of these establishments was ID.235,986,000. Iraq's major industry is oil production, and this accounts for approximately 98 per cent. of the country's foreign exchange receipts, 90 per cent. of total government revenue and 45 per cent. of the Gross National Product. Production figures in long tons are:

1970.....75,241,000	1972.....71,207,000
1971.....82,450,046	1973.....97,802,000

Total revenues from exports of crude oil have not been published since 1972, but they are believed to have been worth some ID.2,120,000,000 in 1974. The Iraq Petroleum Company was nationalized on June 1, 1972, and its associate, Basrah Petroleum Company, was nationalized on Dec. 8, 1975. Following nationalization, Iraq's oil production fell to an estimated 65,000,000 long tons in 1972. However, as a result of an agreement reached between the Iraq Petroleum Company and the Government in March 1973 Iraq's oil production has since risen to meet market requirements and reached some 97,800,000 long tons in 1973.

FINANCE

	1973–74	1974–75*
Total revenue...	ID1,270,300,000	ID2,747,851,776
Total expenditure	1,375,200,000	2,993,458,195
	* Budget estimates.	

The Iraqi *Dinar* of 1,000 *Fils*= £1·40 sterling. Exchange rate (July, 1976), 524 *Fils*= £1 (*see also* p. 84).

TRADE
(Excluding oil)

	1973	1974
Total imports	ID270,316,788	ID700,100,000
Total exports	32,522,820	28,100,000

Trade with U.K.

	1974	1975
Imports from U.K.	£59,838,000	£136,500,000
Exports to U.K.	106,577,000	102,500,000

In 1974, petroleum accounted for some £103,000,000 of exports to the U.K.

The principal imports are iron and steel, mechanical and electrical machinery, motor cars, cotton and rayon piecegoods, sugar and tea; and the chief exports are crude petroleum, dates, cement, raw wool, raw hides and skins and raw cotton.

CAPITAL.—Baghdad. Population of the governorate (estimated 1970), 2,696,000. Other towns of importance are Ψ Basrah and Mosul.

FLAG.—Horizontal stripes of red, white and black, with three green stars on the white stripe.

BRITISH EMBASSY
Sharia Salah Ud-Din,
Karkh, Baghdad

Ambassador Extraordinary and Plenipotentiary, His Excellency John Alexander Noble Graham, C.M.G. (1974).
Counsellor, R. G. Giddens.
Commercial Secretary, N. W. Lomas.
Defence Attaché, Col. A. J. Adcock.
Air Attaché, Wg. Cdr. A. A. Hutchinson.
Consul, W. J. Dixon.
Second Secretaries, N. Witney; R. Austen.
Attachés, D. White (*Commercial*); S. H. Palmer (*Consular*).
There are no British Consular Offices outside Baghdad.

British Council Representative, R. A. K. Baker, 7/2/9 Waziriya, Baghdad.

ISRAEL
(Yisrael)

President of Israel, Professor Ephraim Katzir, *born* May 16, 1916, *elected President* May 24, 1973.

CABINET

Prime Minister, Yitzhak Rabin.
Deputy Prime Minister and Minister for Foreign Affairs, Yigal Allon.
Interior, Dr. Joseph Burg.
Education and Culture, Aharon Yadlin.
Agriculture and Communications, Aharon Uzan.
Labour, Moshe Bara'm.
Defence, Shimon Peres.
Police, Shlomo Hillel.
Health, Victor Shemtov (*Mapam*).
Finance, Yehoshua Rabinowitz.
Commerce and Industry, Haim Bar-Lev.
Transport, Gad Yaacobi.
Justice, Haim Yosef Zadok.
Housing, Avraham Ofer.
Immigration Absorption, Shlomo Rosen (*Mapam*).
Religious Affairs, Itzhak Raphael.
Tourism, Moshe Kol (*I.L.P.*).
Social Welfare, Zevulun Hammer.
Without Portfolio, Israel Galili; Gideon Hausner (*I.L.P.*).

Apart from Ministers marked otherwise, members of the Cabinet belong to the Israel Labour Party, a merger (Jan. 21, 1968) of the former *Mapai, Ahdut Avodah* and *Rafi* parties. *Mapam*= United Workers' Party; *I.L.P.*= Independent Liberal Party.

EMBASSY IN LONDON
2 Palace Green, Kensington, W.8
[01-937 8050]

Ambassador Extraordinary and Plenipotentiary, His Excellency Efrain Evron (1976).

Area and Population.—Israel lies on the western edge of the continent of Asia at the eastern extremity of the Mediterranean Sea, between lat. 29° 30′-33° 15′ N. and longitude 34° 15′-35° 40′ E. Its political neighbours are Lebanon on the North, Syria on the North and East, Jordan on the East and the Egyptian province of Sinai on the South-West.

The area is estimated at 7,992 square miles out of the 10,429 square miles which comprised the pre-1948 mandated territory of Palestine (the remainder being occupied by Israel since the Six Day War in June, 1967, together with the Sinai Peninsula and the Golan Heights in Syria). The population was estimated in 1973 at 3,230,000. Jewish immigration has made rapid progress since the establishment of the State in 1948. In 1912 there were only 83,790 Jews in Palestine out of a total population of 752,048. During the upheavals of 1948-49 a large number of Arabs left the country as refugees and settled in neighbouring countries. Since 1948 the population of Israel has more than quadrupled.

Hebrew and Arabic are the official languages of Israel. Arabs are entitled to transact all official business with Government Departments in Arabic, and provision is made in the *Knesset* for the simultaneous translation of all speeches into Arabic.

Physical Features.—Israel comprises four main regions: (*a*) the hill country of Galilee and Judæa and Samaria, rising in places to heights of nearly 4,000 feet; (*b*) the coastal plain from the Gaza strip to North of Acre, including the plain of Esdraelon running from Haifa Bay to the south-east, and cutting in two the hill region; (*c*) the Negev, a semi-desert triangular-shaped region, extending from a base south of Beersheba, to an apex at the head of the Gulf of 'Aqaba; and (*d*) parts of the Jordan valley, including the Hula Region, Tiberias and the south-western extremity of the Dead Sea. The principal river is the Jordan, which rises from three main sources in Israel, the Lebanon and Syria, and flows through the Hula valley and the canals which have replaced Lake Hula, drained in 1958. Between Hulata and Tiberias (Sea of Galilee) the river falls 926 ft. in 11 miles and becomes a turbulent stream. Lake Tiberias is 696 ft. below sea-level and liable to sudden storms. Between it and the Dead Sea the Jordan falls 591 ft. The other principal rivers are the Yarkon and Kishon. The largest lake is the *Dead Sea* (shared between Israel and Jordan); area 393 sq. miles, 1,286 feet below sea-level, 51·5 miles long, with a maximum width of 11 miles and a maximum depth of 1,309 ft.; it receives the waters of the Jordan and of six other streams, and has no outlet, the surplus being carried off by evaporation. The water contains an extraordinarily high concentration of mineral substances. The highest mountain peak is Mount Meron, 3,962 feet above sea-level, near Safad, Upper Galilee.

Climate.—The climate is variable, similar to that of Lower Egypt, but modified by altitude and distance from the sea. The summer is hot but tempered in most parts by daily winds from the Mediterranean. The winter is the rainy season lasting from November to April, the period of maximum rainfall being January and February.

Antiquities.—The following are among the principal historic sites in Israel: Jerusalem: the Church of the Holy Sepulchre; the Al Aqsa Mosque and Dome

of the Rock, standing on the remains of the Temple Mount of Herod the Great, of which the Western (wailing) Wall is a fragment; the Church of the Dormition and the Cœnaculum on Mount Zion; Ein Karem: Church of the Visitation, Church of St. John the Baptist. Galilee: The Sea; Church and Mount of the Beatitudes, ruins of Capernaum and other sites connected with the life of Christ. Mount Tabor: Church of the Transfiguration. Nazareth: Church of the Annunciation and other Christian shrines associated with the childhood of Christ. There are also numerous sites dating from biblical and mediæval days, such as Ascalon, Cæsarea, Atlit, Massada, Megiddo and Hazor. Other antiquities in the West Bank of Jordan, Sinai or the Golan Heights at present occupied by Israel can now be visited from Israel.

Government.—There are a Cabinet and a single-chamber Parliament (*Knesset*) of 120 members. A general election is held at least once every four years. The last took place on Dec. 31, 1973.

A "Government of National Unity" was formed on December 11, 1969, headed by Mrs. Golda Meir. It was a broad coalition and, with one exception, embraced the same parties as were in the two previous governments formed in June, 1967, and March, 1969, by the late Mr. Levi Eshkol and Mrs. Meir respectively. In August, 1970, the *Gahal* bloc left the Government because they were opposed to a resumption of the Jarring negotiations. Following the General Election held on December 31, 1973 (postponed from October 30 owing to the outbreak of war), there was a prolonged ministerial crisis, finally resolved when Mrs. Meir succeeded in forming a new Coalition Government, and the Cabinet was chosen on March 6. The Government received a vote of confidence in the Knesset on March 10. However, on April 10, Mrs. Meir announced her resignation; on April 22 the Labour Party chose General Itzhak Rabin as Prime Minister-designate, and on April 26 President Katzir asked him to form a new Government, which was chosen on May 28, and received a vote of confidence in the Knesset on June 3. The present coalition government commands 57 seats in the Knesset, as follows: *Alignment*, 50; *Arab & Druse Lists* (affiliated to Labour Party), 3; *Independent Liberals* 4. The Opposition commands 59 seats in the Knesset as follows: *Likud*, 39; *National Religious*, 10; *Agudat Blo*, 5; *Ya'ad* (the former C.R.M. with *Lyiova Fliar* from the Labour Party) 4; *New Communists*, 4; *Israel Communists*, 1.

Immigration.—The Declaration of Independence of May 14, 1948, laid down that "the State of Israel will be open to the immigration of Jews from all countries of their dispersion." The Law of Return, passed by the *Knesset* on July 5, 1950, provides that an immigrant visa shall be granted to every Jew who expresses his desire to settle in Israel. From the establishment of the State until April 1975, more than 1½ million immigrants had entered Israel from over 100 different countries.

Education.—Elementary education for all children from 5 to 15 years is compulsory. The Law also provides for working youth, age 15-18, who for some reason have not completed their primary education, to be exempted from work in order to do so.

In 1974-75 enrolment in all educational establishments was 1,012,300: kindergartens 192,600 (including 37,000 in private schools; elementary education, 503,500; teacher's training colleges, 11,100; secondary education, 175,300; academic institutions, 51,000.

Finance.—Government expenditure for the fiscal year 1974-75 totalled I£40,650,000,000.

The unit of account is the Israel pound of 100 *agorot*. Exchange rate, *see* p. 84.

COMMUNICATIONS

Railways and Roads.—Israel State Railways started operating in August 1949. Towns now served are Haifa, Tel Aviv, Jerusalem, Lod, Nahariya, Beersheba, Domona, Oron, Ashdod and intermediate stations. In March 1973 the total railway network amounted to 795 km. There were over 10,000 km. of paved road and 375,340 licensed vehicles in 1974.

Shipping.—Israel's merchant marine had reached a total of 3,435,076 tons deadweight by December, 1973.

The chief ports are Haifa, a modern harbour, with a depth of 30 ft. alongside the main quay; the harbour on the Red Sea at Eilat, inaugurated in September 1965, has a capacity of 10,000 tons a day; Acre has an anchorage for small vessels; the deep-water port at Ashdod, 20 miles south of Tel Aviv, which started operations at the end of 1965, handled 3,363,000 million tons of cargo in 1973. In 1974 Israel's three main ports handled 9,989,000 tons of cargo (excluding petroleum).

Civil Aviation.—In 1974, El Al carried 862,000 passengers. El Al operates Boeing jets exclusively and has bought three Boeing 747's. Arkia, the internal airline, has had a steep increase in traffic since the Six-Day War and in 1974 carried 363,000 passengers. Arkia uses five Heralds and five Viscounts.

PRODUCTION AND INDUSTRY

Agriculture.—The country is generally fertile and climatic conditions vary so widely that a large variety of crops can be grown, ranging from temperate crops, such as wheat and cherries, to subtropical crops such as sorghum, millet and mangoes. The famous " Jaffa " orange is produced in large quantities mostly in the coastal plain for export; other kinds of citrus fruits are also grown and exported. The citrus yield during the 1972-73 season was 1,495,038 tons. Of this total, 846,770 tons were exported, of which 182,000 tons went to the U.K. Olives are cultivated, mainly for the production of oil used for edible purposes and for the manufacture of soap. The main winter crops are wheat and barley and various kinds of pulses, while in summer sorghum, millet, maize, sesame and summer pulses are grown. Large areas of seasonal vegetables are planted; potatoes can be grown in autumn and in the winter. Since the establishment of the State of Israel, beef, cattle and poultry farming have been developed and the production of mixed vegetables and dairy produce has greatly increased. Tobacco and medium staple cotton are now grown. Fishing has also been extended, and production (mostly from fish ponds) reached 23,737 tons in 1973. All kinds of summer fruits such as figs, grapes, plums and apples are produced in increasing quantities for local consumption. Water supply for irrigation is the principal limiting factor to greater production. The area under cultivation during 1972-73 was

4,225,000 dunams, of which 1,815,000 were under irrigation. The largest of these is the Kinneret-Negev Project. Much of the dairy industry is dependent on the production of fodder crops under irrigation; areas under fodder crops have doubled. The Israel land measure is the *dunam*, equivalent to 1,000 square metres (approximately a quarter of an acre).

Industry.—In value polished diamonds now account for more than one-third of Israel's total exports. Amongst the most important of her exporting industries are textiles, foodstuffs, chemicals (mainly fertilisers and pharmaceuticals). Her metal-working and science-based industries have been developed to a highly sophisticated and technologically advanced level. These include the aircraft and military industries. Other important manufacturing industries include plastics, rubber, cement, glass, paper and oil refining.

TRADE

	1973	1974
Imports..	$U.S.3,080,174,000	$U.S.4,339,910,000
Exports..	1,647,490,000	2,129,214,000

Trade with U.K.

	1974	1975
Imports from U.K...	£219,206,000	£237,243,000
Exports to U.K......	78,701,000	91,253,000

The principal imports are foodstuffs, crude oil, machinery and vehicles, iron, steel and manufactures thereof, and chemicals. The principal exports are citrus fruits and by-products, polished diamonds, plywood, cement, tyres, minerals, finished and semi-finished textiles.

CAPITAL.—Most of the Government departments are in Jerusalem (population, 1974, 380,000). A resolution proclaiming Jerusalem as the capital of Israel was adopted by the Israel parliament on Jan. 23, 1950. It is not, however, recognized as the capital by the United Nations. Other principal towns are ΨTel Aviv and district (947,000); ΨHaifa and district (514,000) and Beersheba and district (228,000).

FLAG.—White, with two horizontal blue stripes, the Shield of David in the centre. NATIONAL DAY (1976)—May 5.

JERUSALEM

Until 1967 Jerusalem was divided between Israel and Jordan, two of the 36 recognized Christian Holy Places (in the New City) being under Jewish administration, the remainder under Arab administration in the Old City. At the conclusion of hostilities between Israel and the surrounding Arab countries in 1967 the entire city was under Israeli control.

BRITISH EMBASSY

192 Hayarkon Street, Tel Aviv.
Ambassador Extraordinary and Plenipotentiary (vacant).
Counsellor, M. J. Newington (*Head of Chancery and Consul-General*).
Defence and Air Attaché, Group Capt. A. Musker.
Counsellor, E. V. Vines, O.B.E. (*Commercial*).

British Council Representative, Miss M. A. J. Swinley, 140 Hayarkon Street, Tel Aviv. There is an office and library in *Tel Aviv* and a library in *Jerusalem*.

ITALY
(Repubblica Italiana)
President of the Italian Republic, Giovanni Leone, *born* at Naples in 1908. *Elected* December 24, 1971.

COUNCIL OF MINISTERS

(July 30, 1976)

Prime Minister, Giulio Andreotti (*CD*).
Foreign Affairs, Arnaldo Forlani (*CD*).
Interior, Francesco Cossiga (*CD*).
Grace and Justice, Paolo Bonifacio.
Budget and Economic Planning, Tummaso Morlino (*CD*).
Finance, Filippo Pandolfi (*CD*).
Treasury, Gaetano Stammati.
Defence, Vito Lattanzio (*CD*).
Education, Franco Malfatti (*CD*).
Public Works, Antonio Gullotti (*CD*).
Agriculture, Giovanni Marcora (*CD*).
Transport and Civil Aviation, Attilio Ruffini (*CD*).
Posts and Telecommunications, Vittorino Colombo (*CD*).
Industry, Commerce and Arts and Crafts, Carlo Donat Cattin (*CD*).
Labour and Social Security, Sra. Tina Anselmi (*CD*).
Foreign Trade, Rinaldo Ossola (*CD*).
Merchant Marine, Francesco Fabri (*CD*).
State Participation, Antonio Bisaglia (*CD*).
Health, Luciano Dafalco (*CD*).
Tourism and Entertainment, Dario Antoniozzi (*CD*).
Culture, Mario Pedini (*CD*).
Minister without Portfolio:
   South, Ciriaco de Mita (*CD*).
CD= Christian Democrat.

ITALIAN EMBASSY IN LONDON

14 Three Kings Yard, Davies Street, W.1
[01-629 8200]

Ambassador Extraordinary and Plenipotentiary, His Excellency Signor Roberto Ducci (1975).
Minister, Signor R. Paolini.
Minister-Counsellor, Sig. M. Egidi (*Commercial*).
First Counsellor, Sig. G. Borga.
Counsellors, Sig. L. M. Falconi (*Labour*); Sig. C. Civiletti (*Press*); Sig. G. Lenzi.
1st Secretary, Sig. B. Uguccioni (*Commercial*).
2nd Secretaries, Sig. F. Mistretta; Sig. F. Trupiano.
Defence and Naval Attaché, Rear-Admiral F. Mottolese.
Asst. Defence and Naval Attaché, Lt.-Cdr. C. Bruno.
Military Attaché, Lt.-Col. L. Caligaris.
Asst. Military Attaché, Lt.-Col. N. Russo.
Air Attaché, Col. G. Batazzi.
Asst. Air Attaché, Capt. T. Lusi.
Financial Attaché, Sig. F. Anzilotti.
Cultural Attaché, Prof. M. Montuori.
Italian Consulate General, 38 Eaton Place, S.W.1.
(01-235 4831).
Consul General, Sig. M. Manea.

Italy is a Republic in the South of Europe, consisting of a peninsula, the large islands of Sicily and Sardinia, the island of Elba and about 70 islands. Italy is bounded on the N. by Switzerland and Austria, on the S. by the Mediterranean, on the E. by the Adriatic and Yugoslavia, and on the W. by France and the Ligurian and Tyrrhenian Seas. The total area is about 324,000 sq. kilometres (131,000 sq. miles).

The peninsula is for the most part mountainous, but between the Apennines, which form its spine, and the East coastline are two large fertile plains; of Emilia/Romagna in the north and of Apulia in the south. The Alps form the northern limit of Italy, dividing it from France, Switzerland, Austria and Yugoslavia. Mont Blanc (15,782 feet), the highest peak, is in the French Pennine Alps, but partly within the Italian borders are Monte Rosa (15,217 feet), Matterhorn (14,780 feet) and several peaks from 12,000 to 14,000 feet.

The chief rivers are the Po (405 miles), which flows through Piedmont, Lombardy and the Veneto, and the Adige (Trentino and Veneto) in the north, the Arno (Florentine Plain) and the Tiber (flowing through Rome to Ostia). The *Rubicon*, a small stream flowing into the Adriatic near Rimini formed the boundary between Italy and Cisalpine Gaul: " crossing the Rubicon " (as Cæsar did in 49 B.C., thus " invading " Italy in arms) is used to indicate definite committal to some course of action.

Population.—Italy has a resident population estimated at 56,024,000 at the end of 1975 about 428 persons per sq. mile. Live births in 1970 totalled 917,496, deaths, 528,622 and marriages 395,321 (estimated).

Government.—Italian unity was accomplished under the House of Savoy, after an heroic struggle from 1848 to 1870, in which the great patriots Mazzini (1805-72), Garibaldi (1807-82) and Cavour (1810-61) were the principal figures. It was completed when Lombardy was ceded by Austria in 1859 and Venice in 1866, and through the evacuation of Rome by the French in 1870. In 1871 the King of Italy entered Rome, and that city was declared to be the capital.

Benito Mussolini, known as *Il Duce* (The Leader) was born July 29, 1883, and was continuously in office as Prime Minister from Oct. 30, 1922, until July 25, 1943, when the Fascist *régime* was abolished. He was captured by Italian partisans while attempting to escape across the Swiss frontier and was put to death on April 28, 1945.

In fulfilment of a promise given in April, 1944, that he would retire when the Allies entered Rome a decree was signed on June 5, 1944, by the late King Victor Emmanuel III under which Prince Umberto, the King's son, became " Lieutenant-General of the Realm." The King remained head of the House of Savoy and retained the title of King of Italy until his abdication on May 9, 1946, when he was succeeded by the Crown Prince.

A general election was held on June 2, 1946, together with a referendum on the question of Republic or Monarchy. The Referendum resulted in 12,717,923 votes for a Republic and 10,719,284 for a Monarchy. The Royal Family left the country on June 13, and on June 28, 1946, a Provisional President was elected.

Constitution.—The constitution of the Republic of Italy, approved by the Constituent Assembly on December 22, 1947, provides for the election of the President by an electoral college which consists of the two Houses of Parliament (the Chamber of Deputies and the Senate) sitting in joint session together with three delegates from each region (one in the case of the Valle d'Aosta). The President, who must be over 50 years of age, holds office for 7 years. He has numerous carefully defined powers, the main one of which is the right to dissolve one or both Houses of Parliament, after consultation with their Speakers.

Senator Leone was elected President at the twenty-third ballot on December 24 with 518 votes (the required majority was 505). The new President was sworn in before Parliament in joint session on December 29, 1971.

Since the General Election of 1948, governments have been formed by Signor de Gasperi (1948-53, coalition); Signor Pella (1953-54, *Christian Democrat*); Signor Scelba (1954-55, coalition); Signor Segni (July, 1955-May, 1957, coalition); Signor Zoli (June, 1957-May, 1958, *Christian Democrat*); Signor Fanfani (May, 1958-Feb., 1959, coalition); S. Segni (Feb., 1959-Feb., 1960, *Christian Democrat*, with *Liberal* support). Signor Tambroni (March 25-July 1960, *Christian Democrat*, with Neo-Fascist support); Signor Fanfani (July 27, 1960-Feb., 1962,

Christian Democrat); Signor Fanfani (Feb. 1962–June, 1963, coalition); Signor Leone (June–Nov., 1963, *Christian Democrat*); Signor Moro (coalitions formed, Nov., 1963; July, 1964; Feb., 1966); Sen. Leone (May, 1968–December, 1968, *Christian Democrat*); Sig. Rumor (December, 1968–June, 1969, Centre Left coalition); Sig. Rumor (second Government) (August, 1969–April, 1970, *Christian Democrat*); Sig. Rumor (third Government, April–Aug., 1970, Centre Left coalition); Sig. Colombo (Aug., 1970–Feb., 1972, Centre Left coalition); Sig. Andreotti (Feb., 1972, *Christian Democrat*); Sig. Andreotti (June, 1972–June, 1973, *Christian Democrat, Social Democrat and Liberals*); Sig. Rumor (July, 1973–March, 1974, *Centre Left Coalition*); Sig. Rumor (March 1974–Oct. 1974, *Centre Left Coalition*); Sig. Moro (Nov., 1974–Jan. 1976, *Christian Democrat and Republican*); Sig. Moro (Feb.–June, 1976, *Christian Democrat*); Sig. Andreotti (July, 1976, *Christian Democrat*).

Sig. Rumor's fifth government (Centre-Left Coalition) was forced to resign on Oct. 3, 1974, owing to differences among the coalition parties. After an unsuccessful attempt by Sig. Fanfani to form a Government, Sig. Moro (*CD*) formed a two-party coalition of Christian Democrats and Republicans, supported in Parliament by the Socialists and Social Democrats, which received its final vote of confidence in the National Assembly in December, 1974.

This government survived throughout 1975, but resigned on Jan. 7, 1976 after the Socialists had withdrawn their parliamentary support, mainly because of disagreements over economic policy. Following the usual consultations, Sig. Moro formed his fifth government on Feb. 11, consisting only of Christian Democrats, with non-parliamentarians as ministers of Justice and Finance. Dependent on the abstention of the Socialists in Parliament, this government was weakened by a serious financial crisis. The refusal of the Socialists (and of the Communists, who were consulted) to agree to an emergency economic programme proposed by the government, led Sig. Moro to tender his resignation on April 30. After consultations, President Leone dissolved Parliament on May 1, and general elections were held on June 20, 1976.

In the Chamber of Deputies, the Christian Democrats won 263 seats, the Communists 228, Socialists 57, Republicans 14, Social Democrats 15, Italian Social Movement 35, Liberals 5, Radicals 4, Democratic Proletarians 6 and South Tirol Party 3. In the Senate the Christian Democrats won 135 seats, the Communists 116, Socialists 29, Republicans 6, Social Democrats 6, Liberals 2 and Italian Social Movement 15.

Consequently, Sig. Andreotti formed a minority Christian Democrat government, which received a vote of confidence on Aug. 11, through Communist abstentions.

Defence.—The period of conscription is 18 months for the Army and Air Force and 12 months for the Navy. The *Army* consists of 300,000 men including 22,000 officers. It has two armoured divisions, five infantry divisions, four independent infantry brigades, five Alpine brigades, one independent armoured brigade, one missile brigade, one parachute brigade and one amphibious regiment. There is also a para-military force, the *Carabinieri*, about 84,000 strong. The *Navy* consists of 3 cruisers, 37 escorts including four G.W. destroyers, 10 submarines, 60 minesweepers and also coastal craft and fleet auxiliaries. Approximate strength: 43,000 uniformed personnel. The *Air Force* consists of 500 aircraft; approximate strength: 75,000 men.

REGIONS OF ITALY

Rome and Central Italy.—Rome was founded, according to legend, by Romulus in the year now known as 753 B.C. It was the focal point of Latin civilization and dominion under the Republic and afterwards under the Roman Empire and became the capital of Italy when the Kingdom was established in 1871. With a metropolitan population of 2,842,616, Rome has been recreating herself as a major capital in the 100 years since Italy's reunification. The capital is concerned mainly with tourism and government, but owing partly to the fact that the power of the Central Government is increasingly felt by industry, and that the headquarters of the giant State and parastatal companies are located there, Rome's importance as a business centre, although far from rivalling that of Milan, is steadily increasing.

Lombardy and Milan.—In the small area around Milan, which has a metropolitan population of 1,724,819, are to be found some 22 per cent. of Italy's commercial and banking services and some 30 per cent. of her industry. Here too, a market for consumer goods greatly exceeds that of any other comparable area in Italy. Lombardy's population of some 8·3 million is growing fast, both naturally and by immigration, and enjoys a *per capita* income some 40 per cent. above the national average. The whole range of Italian industry is there. Most important are the steel, machine tool and motor car factories.

Turin and Piedmont.—Turin between 1861 and 1865 was Italy's first capital as the home of the Piedmontese Royal Family. Now with a metropolitan population of 1,187,832 it is famous as the headquarters of Europe's largest manufacturer of motor cars, produces 75 per cent. of Italy's motor vehicles and over 80 per cent. of its roller bearings. Turin is also Italy's second largest steel producing city. Piedmont is the centre of the Italian textile industry based mainly on Biella.

Genoa and the Ligurian Riviera.—Genoa, with a metropolitan population of 842,114, is Europe's fourth largest port and handles one-third of Italy's foreign trade. About 80 per cent. of the goods handled are imports. Anglo-Genoese trade goes back to the 13th century and 20 per cent. of Genoa's imports still come from Britain. Genoa is Italy's third most important industrial city.

Venice and the North-East.—Venice, with a metropolitan population of 367,528 is primarily a tourist attraction of unique beauty. It was founded in the middle of the 5th century by refugees fleeing from the mainland fleeing from Barbarian attacks. At the beginning of the 16th century it was one of the strongest and richest states of Europe, dominating Eastern Mediterranean trade. It lost its independence in 1797 when Napoleon handed it over to Austria. Industry is now developing in the Venice area, particularly on the autostrada linking Venice with her historical and now developing rivals, Verona, Vicenza, Padua and in the areas around Pordenone. Padua is known for mechanical equipment, Verona for paper and stationery, Treviso for consumer goods, and Valdagno for its woollen industry. An important electrical appliance industry is based near Treviso and at Pordenone. Near Trieste, which has a population of 277,135, is the modern Monfalcone shipyard. Present-day Trieste itself consists of Zone A, the area which was administered by the Allied Military Government from June 12, 1945, to October 26, 1954, when it was handed over to the Italian authorities. The remainder of the area of Trieste was administered by Yugoslavia after the War and handed over to that country in 1954 after the free territory of Trieste, an arrangement agreed in the Italian Peace Treaty of 1947, had proved to be unworkable. An agreement was reached in 1975 between Italy and Yugoslavia for each country to abandon its residual claims to the other's zone.

Tuscany, Emilia and Romagna.—Before the last war this area was the agricultural centre of Italy and there was little industry. Now there are large industrial centres at Bologna (metropolitan population, 493,700), Florence (metropolitan population, 460,944), Modena, Pistoia and Ravenna. Most of the new firms are small or medium-sized. In Prato there are about 1,000 textile firms. The footwear industry is based on Florence, reproduction furniture at Cascina and Poggibonsi, ceramics at Sassuolo, and glass and pottery at Empoli and Montelupo. Bologna is an important centre for the food industry. Florence, the capital of Tuscany was one of the greatest and most creative cities in Europe from the 11th to the 16th centuries. Under the Medici family in the 15th century flourished many of the greatest names in Italian art, including Filippo Lippi, Botticelli, Donatello and Brunelleschi. In the 16th century the tide turned to Rome where great Florentine artists like Michelangelo and Leonardo da Vinci flourished.

Naples and the Toe of Italy.—Naples (metropolitan population 1,258,721), formerly the capital and administrative centre of the Kingdom of Naples and Sicily, remains the dominant city in the area, but it is beset with great problems of unemployment and the need for modernization. Around it, however, helped by Government incentives, industry is slowly developing, northwards to Caserta, southwards to Salerno and eastwards to Benevento.

Puglia.—Bari (metropolitan population, 356,250) has always been a commercial centre. Fairly rapid industrial development is now taking place in the areas of Taranto, Bari, Brindisi and Foggia. At Taranto there are a highly-mechanized steel-works and a modern oil refinery. The Bari industrial zone has factories producing electronic and pneumatic valves, specialized vehicle bodies and tyres, etc. The main industry of Brindisi is a petro-chemical plant. At Foggia there is a textile factory.

Sicily.—The main source of income is agriculture, particularly citrus fruits, almonds and tomatoes, but this faces severe competition. Oil and oil products have recently supplanted citrus fruits as Sicily's main exports. The island is the scene of intense activity in the fields of oil, natural gas and petrochemicals. Small and medium sized industries, benefiting from the Government's incentives, are developing. Of the island's 279 factories, some 90 are in the Catania area and 60 around Palermo (metropolitan population, 657,326), the capital of the island. Tourism is bringing an increasing amount of revenue to Sicily.

Sardinia.—Sardinia is another autonomous region, with its capital at Cagliari (metropolitan

population, 225,812). Six main industrial development areas have been officially designated; they are at Cagliari, Porto Vesme, Oristano, Sassari, Olbia and Arbatax. Lead and zinc mining are important. At Porto Vesme, a large smelting plant has been constructed. In the same area, a company is investing some £60 million in an aluminium plant. There is a flourishing tourist industry.

THE ECONOMY

Italian gross domestic product in 1975 was *lire* 135,120 milliards, as compared with *lire* 119,840 milliards in 1974. The economy developed fast in the fifties and early sixties with an average real annual increase in the gross national output of about 7 per cent. But its recovery after a setback caused by labour unrest in the last quarter of 1969, has been slower than was expected. After a partial recovery came the energy crisis of 1973/74. In 1975 the balance of payments deficit was reversed and inflation halved but this was accompanied by stagnation and increasing unemployment.

Currency.—The market rate of exchange on June 16, 1976, stood at *lire* 1,517=£1.

Industry.—The general index of industrial production (1970=100) stood at 108·1 in 1975. The State-owned sector of Italian industry is important, dominated by the holding companies IRI (mechanical, steel, airlines), ENI (petro-chemicals) and ENEL (electricity).

Mineral Production.—Italy is generally poor in mineral resources but since the war deposits of natural methane gas and smaller deposits of oil have been discovered and rapidly exploited. Production of lignite has also increased. Other minerals produced in significant quantities include iron ores and pyrites, mercury (over one-quarter of the world production), lead, zinc and aluminium. Marble is a traditional product of the Massa Carrara district. Tobacco is still a Government monopoly.

Agriculture.—Agriculture accounted for 9·2 per cent. of gross domestic product in 1972, and at the end of 1974 employed about 16·5 per cent. of the working population. Some three-quarters of the 3,785,000 farms and small holdings are privately owned and operated. In the period 1964–71 Italy was a net exporter of rice, vegetables, fresh and dried fruit and wine, but the rising standard of living has increased imports of foodstuffs, particularly meat and animal food.

Tourist Traffic.—About 32,910,000 visitors entered Italy in 1974, a decline of 9 per cent. from 1973.

Communications.—The main railway system is State-run by the *Ferrovia dello Stato.* A network of motorways (*autostrade*) covers the country, built and operated mainly by the IRI State-holding company and ANAS the State highway authority. The autostrada network covered 5,176 kms. in 1974. *Alitalia,* the principal international and domestic airline, is also State-controlled by the IRI group. Other smaller companies, including ATI (an *Alitalia* subsidiary) and *Itavia* operate on domestic routes. The Italian mercantile marine total of 8,378,000 tons in December, 1972, compared with 3,500,000 tons before the War.

FOREIGN TRADE

Total Italian imports in 1975 were *lire* 25,092 milliards (a decrease of 5·7 per cent. over 1974). Exports were *lire* 22,752 milliards (an increase of 15·6 per cent. over 1974).

The main markets for Italian exports in 1974 were West Germany (22·9 per cent.), France (14·2 per cent.) and U.S.A. (9·8 per cent.). The U.K. accounted for 4·3 per cent. of Italian exports. The main commodities exported were: machinery, motor vehicles, iron and steel, footwear, textiles and clothing, plastic and artificial resins and materials. The main commodities imported were petroleum products, iron and steel, meat, copper and motor vehicles. The E.E.C. provides the largest share in Italy's imports (55·7 per cent. in 1974). The U.K.'s share has decreased from 6·3 per cent. in 1963 to 3 per cent. in 1974.

Trade with U.K.

	1974	1975
Imports from U.K.	£510,100,000	£563,258,000
Exports to U.K.	723,800,000	809,641,000

Language and Literature.—Italian is a Romance language derived from Latin. It is spoken in its purest form at Siena (Tuscany), but there are numerous dialects, showing variously French, German, Spanish and Arabic influences. Sard, the dialect of Sardinia, is accorded by some authorities the status of a distinct Romance language. Italian literature (in addition to Latin literature, which is the common inheritance of the civilized world) is one of the richest in Europe, particularly in its golden age (Dante, 1265–1321; Petrarch, 1304–1374; and Boccaccio, 1313–1375) and in the renaissance during the fifteenth and sixteenth centuries (Ariosto, 1474–1533; Machiavelli, 1469–1527; Tasso, 1544–1595). Modern Italian literature has many noted names in prose and verse, notably Manzoni (1785–1873), Carducci (1835–1907) and Gabriele d'Annunzio (1864–1938). The Nobel Prize for Literature has been awarded to Italian authors on four occasions—G. Carducci (1906), Signora G. Deledda (1926), Luigi Pirandello (1934) and Salvatore Quasimodo (1959). In 1971, there were 85 daily newspapers published in Italy, of which 22 were published in Rome and 10 in Milan.

Education.—Education is free and compulsory between the ages of 6 and 14; this comprises five years at primary school and three in the " middle school ", of which there are about 8,000. Pupils who obtain the middle school certificate may seek admission to any " senior secondary school ", which is roughly equivalent to a U.K. grammar school but may be a lyceum with a classical or scientific or artistic bias, or may be an institute or school for teacher training, or may be an institute directed at technology (of which there are eight different types) or trade or industry (including vocational schools). Courses at the lyceums and technical institutes usually last for five years and success in the final examination qualifies for admission to university. There are 35 State and 14 private universities, some of ancient foundation; those at Bologna, Modena, Parma and Padua were started in the 12th century. University education is not free, but entrants with higher qualifications are charged reduced fees according to a sliding scale. In general, schools, lyceums and universities are financed by local taxation and central government grants.

CAPITAL, Rome. Metropolitan population (estimated Oct. 1971), 2,842,616.

Oct. 1971 estimates of the metropolitan population of the principal cities and towns are Milan, 1,724,819; Ψ Naples 1,258,721; Turin, 1,187,832; Ψ Genoa, 842,114; Bologna, 493,007; Florence, 460,944; Ψ Venice, 367,528; Ψ Bari, 356,250; Ψ Trieste, 277,135; Verona, 262,014; Padua, 228,854; Ψ Taranto, 223,392; Brescia, 209,659; Modena, 170,450; Ψ Reggio Calabria, 167,087; Ψ Salerno, 152,780; and Bergamo, 126,504; in *Sicily;* Ψ Palermo, 657,326; Ψ Catania, 414,619; Ψ Messina, 274,740; in *Sardinia;* Ψ Cagliari, 225,812.

ISLANDS.—*Pantelleria Island* (part of Trapani Province) in the Sicilian Narrows, has an area of

31 sq. miles and a population of 9,601. The *Pelagian Islands* (Lampedusa, Linosa and Lampione) are part of the Province of Agrigento and have an area of 8 sq. miles, pop. 4,811. The Tuscan Archipelago (including Elba), area 293 sq. km., pop. 31,861; Pontine Archipelago (including Ponza, area 10 sq. km., pop. 2,515); Flegrean Islands (including Ischia, area 60 sq. km., pop. 51,883); Capri; Eolian Islands (including Lipari, area 116 sq. km., pop. 18,636); Tremiti Islands (area 3 sq. km., pop. 426).

FLAG.—Vertical stripes of green, white and red.
NATIONAL DAY.—June 2.

BRITISH EMBASSY
Via XX Settembre 80a, Rome.
Ambassador Extraordinary and Plenipotentiary, His Excellency Sir Alan Hugh Campbell, K.C.M.G. (1976).
Ministers, A. J. Williams, C.M.G., A. A. W. Landymore, C.B.E. (*FAO*).
Defence and Military Attaché, Col. P. E. B. Madsen.
Naval Attaché, Capt. M. A. George, R.N.
Air Attaché, Group-Capt. R. G. Churcher, D.S.O., M.V.O., D.F.C.
Counsellors, M. R. Morland (*Head of Chancery*); A. F. R. Harvey, O.B.E. (*Commercial*); K. Kenney, O.B.E. (*Labour*); C. de L. Herdon, O.B.E.
1st Secretaries, A. M. Layden; M. Pellen (*Information*); N. H. Young (*Administration*); E. F. Macleod; J. H. Bailey (*Consul*); A. A. C. Nash, M.B.E. (*Commercial*); P. M. Scola (*Agriculture*); R. A. Fulton.
2nd Secretaries, J. Smith; C. P. P. Baldwin.
Asst. Defence Attaché, Maj. N. Boggis-Rolfe.
3rd Secretaries, H. R. Mortimer; J. M. G. Freeman.
Chaplain, Rev. D. Murfet.

BRITISH CONSULAR OFFICES
There are British Consular Offices at *Milan, Rome, Naples, Genoa, Florence, Palermo, Turin, Venice, Trieste, Messina* and *Cagliari* and a trade representative at *Bari.*

British Council Representative, R. E. Cavaliero, Palazzo del Drago, Via delle Quattro Fontane 20, 00184, Rome.
There are *British Council Institutes* at Milan and Naples, each with a library.

IVORY COAST
(République de Côte d'Ivoire)

President, Félix Houphouët-Boigny, *elected* for five years in 1960; *re-elected* 1965, 1970 and 1975.
President of National Assembly, Philippe Yacé.
President of Economic and Social Council, Mamadou Coulibaly.
President of Supreme Court, Alphonse Boni.
Ministers of State, Auguste Denise; Mathieu Ekra; Jean-Baptiste Mockey; Loua Diomandé; Nanlo Bamba.
Minister for Foreign Affairs, Arsène Assouan Usher.

IVORY COAST EMBASSY IN LONDON
2 Upper Belgrave Street, S.W.1
[01-235 6991]
Ambassador Extraordinary and Plenipotentiary, His Excellency Louis-Antoine Aduko (1973).
1st Counsellor, M. Patrice K. Anoh.
Counsellors, M. J. M. Kacou Gervais (*Head of Commercial Section*); M. Benjamin Amuah.
2nd Secretary, M. Raymond T. Diecket.
3rd Secretary, M. Kouakou G. Loukou.
Financial Attaché, M. Gérard Biatchon.

The Ivory Coast is situated on the Gulf of Guinea between 5° and 10° N. and 3° and 8° W. and is flanked on the West by Guinea and Liberia, on the North by Mali and Upper Volta and on the East by Ghana. It has an area of about 127,000 square miles—tropical rain forest in the southern half and savannah in the northern—and a population of 5,400,000 (1972 estimate) divided into a large number of ethnic and tribal groups.

Although official French contact was made in the first half of the 19th century, the Ivory Coast became a Colony only in 1893 and was finally pacified in 1912. It decided on December 5, 1958 to remain an autonomous republic within the French Community; full independence outside the Community was proclaimed on August 7, 1960. Special agreements with France, covering financial and cultural matters, technical assistance, defence, etc., were signed in Paris on April 24, 1961. The Ivory Coast was a founder member of the *Conseil de l'Entente,* established on May 29, 1959, as a loose union embracing also, without abrogation of sovereignty, Dahomey, Niger and Upper Volta. Togo also adhered in June, 1966. The Ivory Coast is also an Associated State of E.E.C. and a member of the *Organisation Commune Africaine et Malgache* (O.C.A.M.), the Organization of African Unity (O.A.U.) and the 'Communauté Economique de l'Afrique de l'Ouest (C.E.A.O.). The official language is French.

The Ivory Coast has a presidential system of government modelled on that of the United States and the French Fifth Republic. The single Chamber National Assembly of 120 members was elected in 1975 for five years. The defence of the Constitution which was promulgated on Nov. 3, 1960, is vested in a Supreme Court.

Finance.—The unit of currency of the Ivory Coast is the Franc CFA (Francs CFA 50= 1 French franc). In 1975, the Ivory Coast Budget totalled Francs CFA 180,841,000,000.

Trade.—The principal exports are coffee, cocoa, timber and bananas all of which are exported to the U.K. Diamonds are exported. There are a few deposits of minerals including manganese and iron. Trade in 1975 was valued at: Imports, Francs CFA 241,393,158,663; Exports, Francs CFA 254,571,664,570.

Trade with U.K.
	1974	1975
Imports from U.K.	£6,528,000	£12,288,000
Exports to U.K.	19,928,000	18,836,000

CAPITAL, Ψ Abidjan (population, 900,000) which is also the main port.
FLAG.—3 vertical stripes, orange, white and green.
NATIONAL DAY.—December 7.

BRITISH EMBASSY
Immeuble Shell, Abidjan, B.P. 2581.
Ambassador Extraordinary and Plenipotentiary, His Excellency Joe Booth Wright (1975).
(also Ambassador to *Niger* and *Upper Volta*).
1st Secretary, F. M. A. Cargill (*Commercial*).
2nd Secretary, P. J. Wilson.
3rd Secretary, G. B. Anderson (*Admin. and Vice-Consul*).

JAPAN
(Nihon Koku—Land of the Rising Sun)

Emperor of Japan, His Majesty Hirohito, *born* April 29, 1901; *succeeded* Dec. 25, 1926; *married* (1924) Princess Nagako (*born* March 6, 1903), daughter of the late Prince Kuniyoshi Kuni, and has issue two sons and four daughters.
Heir-Apparent, His Imperial Highness Prince Akihito, *Crown Prince, born* Dec. 23, 1933; *married* April 10, 1959, Miss Michiko Shoda and has issue Prince Naruhito Hironomiya, *born* Feb. 23, 1960, Prince Fumihito, *born* Nov. 30, 1965 and Princess Sayako, *born* April 18, 1969.

CABINET

Prime Minister, Takeo Miki.
Deputy Prime Minister (and Director-General, Economic Planning Agency), Takeo Fukuda.
Justice, Osamu Inaba.
Foreign Affairs, Zentaro Kosaka.
Finance, Masayoshi Ohira.
Education, Michio Nagai.
Health and Welfare, Masami Tanaka.
Agriculture, Shintaro Abe.
International Trade and Industry, Toshio Komoto.
Transport, Mutsuo Kimura.
Posts and Telecommunications, Isamu Murakami.
Labour, Takashi Hasegawa.
Construction, Nobaru Takeshita.
Home Affairs, Hakime Fukuda.
Ministers of State, Ichitaro Ide (*Chief Cabinet Secretary*); Mitsunori Ueki (*Prime Minister's Office, and Director-General, Okinawa Development Agency*); Yuzo Matsuzawa (*Director General, Administrative Management Agency*); Michita Sakata (*Director-General, Defence Agency*); Yoshitake Sasaki (*Director-General, Science and Technology Agency*; *Chairman, Atomic Energy Commission*); Tatsuo Ozawa (*Director-General, Environment Agency*); Shin Kanemaru (*Director-General, Land Development Agency*).

JAPANESE EMBASSY AND CONSULATE
43–46 Grosvenor Street, W.1
Information Centre: 9 Grosvenor Square, W.1
[01–493 6030]

Ambassador Extraordinary and Plenipotentiary, His Excellency, Tadao Kato (1975).
Minister Plenipotentiary, Keiichi Tachibana.
Minister, Yasuhiko Sano (*Commercial*).
Minister, Yoshihito Amano (*Financial*).
Counsellor, Hiroshi Hashimoto (*Consul General*).
Counsellors, Masanori Ho (*Consular*); Takashi Onda; Jutaru Sakamoto (*Press and Information*); Makoto Hata (*Agriculture*); Mitsumasa Iwata (*Transport*); Yutaka Kubota (*Agriculture*).
1st Secretaries, Capt. Hideo Sato (*Defence Attaché*); Yasuo Yashima (*Labour*); Issei Nomura; Kenji Ogawa (*Transport*); Koichi Kikuchi; Miss Moto Uwano (*Press and Information*); Kazuo Ichinose; Ryusuke Sakai; Yasuhide Hayashi; Masaharu Wakasa (*Scientific*); Katsuhisa Uchida; Yasuyuki Shimizu; Akihiko Hayashi (*Commercial*); Hiroyuki Ieda; Michio Hamano.

Area and Population.—Japan consists of 4 large and many small islands situated in the North Pacific Ocean between longitude 128° 6′ East and 145° 49′ East and between latitude 26° 59′ and 45° 31′ N., with a total area of 142,812 square miles and a population (1974) of 110,050,000.

Japan Proper consists of *Honshū* (or Mainland), 230,448 sq. k. (88,839 sq. m.), *Shikoku*, 18,757 sq. k. (7,231 sq. m.), *Kyūshū*, 42,079 sq. k. (16,170 sq. m.), *Hokkaido*, 78,508 sq. k. (30,265 sq. m.). Formosa and the Kwangtung Province, which had been throughout the years of Japanese expansion and aggression leased or annexed, reverted to Chinese sovereignty after the War of 1939–45.

After the unconditional surrender to the Allied Nations (Aug. 14, 1945), Japan was occupied by Allied forces under General MacArthur (Sept. 15, 1945). A Japanese peace treaty conference opened at San Francisco on Sept. 4, 1951, and on Sept. 8, 48 nations signed the treaty, which became effective on April 28, 1952. Japan then resumed her status as an independent power.

British participation in the occupation of Japan was virtually over by May, 1950. However, the outbreak of hostilities in Korea in June, 1950, resulted in the despatch to Korea of British Forces, from the United Kingdom, Australia, New

Zealand and Canada to participate in the United Nations action. The main base of this force was established in Japan at Kure. On July 1, 1956, the base was moved to Inchon, Korea, and all Commonwealth troops had left Japan by the middle of 1957.

Under the terms of the Japan–U.S.A. Security Treaty of Sept. 8, 1951, United States forces remained to assist in the defence of Japan. However, as Japan's own Self Defence Forces have been built up, U.S. ground troops have been withdrawn. A revised version of the security treaty, which went into effect on June 23, 1960, was the subject of considerable controversy in the summer of that year.

Vital Statistics.—The birth rate in 1973 was 19.4 per 1,000 (1947, 34 per 1,000; 1967, 19.7 per 1,000). It has been stated that a considerable part in reducing the birth rate to its present level was played by drastic methods, induced abortion and sterilization, the legal grounds for which had been extended by the Eugenics Law, 1948, to include economic and social hardships. The improving standard of living has also played an important part in keeping the birthrate down.

The death rate in 1973 was 6.6 per 1,000, compared with 17 per 1,000 in pre-war years, natural increase of the population being 1,382,500 in 1973.

Physiography.—The coastline exceeds 17,000 miles and is deeply indented, so that few places are far from the sea. The interior is very mountainous, and crossing the mainland from the Sea of Japan to the Pacific is a group of volcanoes, mainly extinct or dormant. Mount Fuji, the loftiest and most sacred mountain of Japan, about 60 miles from Tokyo, is 12,370 ft. high and has been dormant since 1707, but there are other volcanoes which are active, including Mount Aso in Kyūshū. There are frequent earthquakes, mainly along the Pacific coast near the Bay of Tokyo. Japan proper extends from sub-tropical in the south to cool temperate in the north. Heavy snowfalls are frequent on the western slopes of Hokkaidō and Honshū, but the Pacific coasts are warmed by the Japan current. There is a plentiful rainfall and the rivers are short and swift-flowing

offering abundant opportunities for the supply of hydro-electric power.

Government.—According to Japanese tradition, Jimmu, the First Emperor of Japan, ascended the throne on Feb. 11, 660 B.C. Under the constitution of Feb. 11, 1889, the monarchy was hereditary in the male heirs of the Imperial house. A new constitution approved by the Supreme Allied Commander was published on March 6, 1946, superseding the " *Meiji Constitution* " of 1889, and containing many radical changes based on the constitutional practices of the United Kingdom, U.S.A. and France.

The new constitution came into force on May 3, 1947. Legislative authority rests with *The Diet*, which is bicameral, consisting of a *House of Representatives* and a *House of Councillors*, both Houses being composed of elected members. Executive authority is vested in the Cabinet which is responsible to the Legislature.

A General Election was held in December 1972, in which the Liberal Democratic Party was once more returned to power. The strength of the parties in the House of Representatives on May 23, 1976, was: Liberal Democratic Party, 274; Japan Socialist Party, 114; Japan Communist Party, 39; Komeito, 30; Democratic Socialist Party, 19; Independent, 1; vacant, 14.

A regular election for the House of Councillors was held in 1974. The Liberal Democratic Party maintained their overall majority in the Upper House. The state of the parties there is now: Liberal Democratic Party, 129; Japan Socialist Party, 62; Komeito, 24; Japan Communist Party, 20; Democratic Socialist Party, 10; Niin Club, 5; Independent, 3.

Agriculture and Livestock.—Owing to the mountainous nature of the country not more than one-sixth of its area is available for cultivation. The forest land includes Cryptomeria japonica, Pinus massoniana, Zeikowaskeaki, and Pawlonia imperialis, in addition to camphor trees, mulberry, vegetable wax tree and a lacquer tree which furnishes the celebrated lacquer of Japan. The soil is only moderately fertile, but intensive cultivation secures good crops. The tobacco plant, tea shrub, potato, rice, wheat and other cereals are all cultivated: rice is the staple food of the people, about 13,165,000 metric tons being produced in 1975. The floral kingdom is rich, beautiful and varied. Fruit is abundant, including the mandarin, persimmon, loquat and peach; European fruits such as apples, strawberries, pears, grapes and figs are also produced.

Minerals.—The country has mineral resources, including gold and silver, and copper, lead, zinc, iron chromite, white arsenic, coal, sulphur, petroleum, salt and uranium, but iron ore, coal and crude oil are among the principal post-war imports to supply deficiencies at home.

Industry.—Japan is the most highly industrialized nation in the Far East, with the whole range of modern light and heavy industries, including mining, metals, machinery, chemicals, textiles (cotton, silk, wool and synthetics), cement, pottery, glass, rubber, lumber, paper, oil refining and shipbuilding. The labour force of Japan in 1975 (average) was 52,770,000, of which 990,000 were unemployed. Of the total labour force, some 45,630,000 were engaged in non-agricultural industries, 6,150,000 in agriculture, forestry and fisheries.

Communications.—There were 26,852 kilometres of Government and private railroad (steam and electric) in March, 1976. The merchant fleet (ocean-going ships over 3,000 tons gross) consisted of 1,167 vessels totalling 33,006,116 tons gross in July, 1975.

Armed Forces.—After the unconditional surrender of August, 1945, the Imperial Army and Navy were disarmed and disbanded and all aircraft confiscated by the occupying forces.

Although the Constitution of Japan prohibits the maintenance of armed forces, an internal security force, known as the National Police Reserve, came into being in August, 1950, and a Maritime Safety Force was established in April, 1952. In August, 1952, these Forces were renamed the National Safety Force and the Coastal Safety Force and were placed under a National Safety Agency. In July, 1954, the Agency was renamed the Defence Agency, the Forces under it the Ground Self Defence Force and the Maritime Self Defence Force respectively, and a new arm, the Air Self Defence Force, was created. At the same time the mission of the forces was extended to include the defence of Japan against direct and indirect aggression.

A Treaty of Mutual Co-operation and Security between Japan and the U.S.A. was signed in January, 1960, replacing an earlier Security Treaty signed in 1951 at the same time as the Peace Treaty. By this Treaty each country recognised that an armed attack against either in the territories under the administration of Japan would be dangerous to its own safety and declared that it would act to counter the danger.

The defence budget allocated for the fiscal year 1976/77 amounted to *Yen* 1,512 billion, equivalent to 0·90 per cent. of Japan's Gross National Product, or 6·22 per cent. of the total budget. The authorised uniformed strength was: Ground Self-Defence Force (GSDF) 180,000 (Reserve 36,000); Maritime Self-Defence Force (MSDF) 41,388 (Reserve 300); Air Self-Defence Force (ASDF) 44,575 (Reserve 490).

In 1976 the GSDF was organised into five Armies of thirteen Divisions. In addition, in the Northern Army there were one Artillery Brigade, one Anti-Aircraft Artillary Brigade and one Tank Brigade; the Eastern Army had one Airborne Brigade and all five Armies had one Engineer Brigade. Under the Ground Staff Office there were one Helicopter Brigade and one Signal Brigade. Seven divisions had an authorised strength of almost 9,000 (four combat groups) and the remainder of about 7,000 (three combat groups). Major equipment included 700 tanks, 700 APCs, 1,427 artillery pieces, 50 missiles, 140 Hawks, and 410 aircraft. Equipment is now largely manufactured in Japan.

The MSDF has 161 warships totalling 159,775 tons and including two DDH, two TARTAR-equipped GMDs, 41 escort ships, 16 submarines and 96 others. The MSDF has a total of 286 aircraft (75 helicopters, 30 S2F-1, 30 P2V-7, 46 P2J-1, 14 PS1 A/S flying boats and 91 others).

The ASDF has about 940 aircraft (160 F104J, 185 F86F (with 70 in reserve), 63 F4EJ, 14 RF4E; 284 trainers T34, Fuji T-1, MHIT-2, T-33, F104DH; 24 transports and about 100 search and rescue and communications). The principal fighter is the F104J augmented by the F4EJ. Domestically designed and built supersonic T2 trainers and C1 cargo planes have entered service. There are about 5 Nike surface to air missile units.

Religion.—All religions are tolerated. The principal religions of Japan are Mahayana Buddhism and Shinto. The Roman Catholic Church has 1 Cardinal, 1 archbishop and 14 bishops. The Nippon Seikokai (Holy Catholic Church of Japan) has 11 Japanese bishops (1968) and is an autonomous branch of the Anglican communion. There is also a United Protestant Church.

Education.—Under the Education Law of 1948 education at elementary (6 year course) and lower secondary (3 year course) is free, compulsory and co-educational. They have courses in general, agricultural, commercial, technical, mercantile marine, radio-communication and home-economics education, etc. 32·2 per cent. of upper secondary school leavers went on to higher education in 1973. There are 2 or 3 year junior colleges and 4 year universities. Some of the 4 year universities have graduate schools. In May 1973 there were 905 universities and junior colleges, 101 state maintained, 78 local authority maintained and 726 privately maintained. The most prominent universities are the seven State Universities of Tokyo, Kyoto, Tohoku (Sendai), Hokkaido (Sapporo), Kyushu (Fukuoka), Osaka and Nagoya, and the two private universities, Keio and Waseda.

Language and Literature.—Japanese is said to be one of the Uro-Altaic group of languages and remained a spoken tongue until the fifth–seventh centuries A.D., when Chinese characters came into use. Japanese who have received school education (99·8 per cent. of the population) can read and write the Chinese characters in current use (about 1,800 characters) and also the syllabary characters called Kana. English is the best known foreign language. It is taught in all middle and high schools. By 1973, the number of public libraries was 915, with 33,587,084 volumes. In addition there are 1,059 university libraries with 66,485,099 volumes. There are 123 daily newspapers in Japan. Japan's total newspaper circulation was estimated at 39,847,332 copies and 1·25 per household at the end of 1973. The National Diet Library contained in 1973 2,866,956 books; 135,602 atlases; 140,098 public records; 47,382 items of microfilm; and 26,695 periodicals.

FINANCE

The Budget for the financial year 1976–77, ending on March 31, was initially estimated at Yen 24,296,011,447,000 for revenue and expenditure on the general account, an increase of 14·1 per cent. over the preceding financial year, before the Supplementary Budget and 16·6 per cent. after the Supplementary Budget.

The market rate of exchange with Sterling in June 1976, was Yen 532= £1. (*see also* p. 83).

PRODUCTION AND TRADE

Being deficient in natural resources, Japan has had to develop a complex foreign trade. Principal imports in 1975 consisted of mineral oils (33·9 per cent.), raw materials (20·1 per cent.) e.g. metal ores, 7·6 per cent., timber, 4·5 per cent.; raw cotton, 1·5 per cent.; and soya beans, (1·6 per cent.), foodstuffs (15·3 per cent.) (e.g. wheat and sugar) machinery (7·4 per cent.), chemicals (3·6 per cent.) and textiles (2·3 per cent.). Principal exports consist of steel (18·2 per cent.), ships (10·8 per cent.), automobiles (11·1 per cent.), electric machinery and appliances (11·0 per cent.), non-electric machinery (12·1 per cent.), chemicals (7·0 per cent.) and textile goods (6·7 per cent.).

FOREIGN TRADE

	1974 ($1,000)	1975 ($1,000)
Total imports........	62,110,456	57,863,088
Total exports........	55,535,755	55,752,805

TRADE WITH U.K.

	1974	1975
Imports from U.K...	£319,047,000	£308,470,000
Exports to U.K......	570,009,000	671,745,000

CAPITAL.—TOKYO. Population (estimated Oct. 1, 1975), 11,671,138. The other chief cities had the following populations at the beginning of 1971: Ψ Osaka (2,778,973); Ψ Nagoya (2,079,676); Ψ Yokohama (2,621,704); Kyoto, the ancient capital (1,461,053); Ψ Kobé (1,360,601); Kita-Kyushu (1,058,067); Ψ Sapporo (1,240,617); Ψ Kawasaki (1,014,909); Ψ Fukuoka (1,002,221).

FLAG.—White, charged with sun (red).

NATIONAL DAY.—April 29 (Birthday of the Emperor).

Yokohama, by sea *via* Cape Town, 14,653 miles (50 days); *via* Panama, 12,544 miles (35 days); Tokyo, by air (B.O.A.C., polar route), 8,382 miles distant from London: transit, 17 hrs.; (B.O.A.C. trans-Siberia route (13 hrs.).

BRITISH EMBASSY

(No. 1 Ichiban-cho, Chiyoda-ku, Tokyo)

Ambassador Extraordinary and Plenipotentiary, His Excellency Sir Michael Wilford, K.C.M.G. (1975).

Minister (Commercial and Economic), C. S. R. Giffard, C.M.G.

Counsellors, R. A. H. Duke, C.V.O., C.B.E. (*Cultural*); H. A. J. Prentice (*Scientific*); N. C. R. Williams (*Economic*); B. Thorne, M.B.E. (*Commercial*); J. N. T. Spreckley (*Head of Chancery*); W. K. Slatcher, C.V.O. (*Information*.

1st Secretaries, R. A. Kidd; A. J.-J. Dunn (*Cultural*); M. S. Baker-Bates (*Commercial*); C. A. Axworthy (*Administration*); J. G. Dearlove; P. M. Newton (*Economic*); Dr. P. E. Roe (*Scientific*); A. C. Thorpe (*Economic*); P. B. Preece; J. W. Mac-Donald (*Commercial*); R. S. Howe, M.B.E. (*Commercial*); R. Irving, M.B.E. (and *Consul General*).

2nd Secretaries, T. Havey (Administration); D. F. Bleakley (*Vice-Consul*); G. Julian (*Commercial*); J. A. Towner; G. H. Fry (*Commercial*); S. J. Gomersall; D. F. Parsons (*Commercial*); S. D. M. Jack; J. McLaren.

Defence and Military Attaché, Col. D. F. Ryan, O.B.E.

Naval Attaché, Captain C. McK. Little, A.F.C., R.N.

Air Attaché, Group Captain R. H. B. Dixon.

Financial Attaché, J. E. W. Kirby.

Assistant Defence Attaché, Lt.-Col. D. O. Caton.

There is a British Consulate-General at *Osaka* and an Honorary Consulate at *Kita Kyushu*.

JORDAN

(The Hashemite Kingdom of The Jordan)

King of the Jordan, Hussein, G.C.V.O., *born* November 14, 1935, *succeeded* on the deposition of his father, King Talal, Aug. 11, 1952, *assumed constitutional powers*, May 2, 1953, on coming of age.

Crown Prince, Prince Hassan, third son of King Talal of Jordan, *born* 1948, *appointed Crown Prince*, April 1, 1965.

CABINET

(Feb. 8, 1976)

Prime Minister, Foreign Affairs and Defence, Zaid al Rifai.

Construction and Development, Dr. Subhi Amin Amer.

Culture and Information, Salah Abu Zaid.

Education, Thouqan al Hindawi.

Finance, Salim Massadeh.

Tourism and Antiquities, Ghalib Barakat.

Public Works, Ahmed al Shawbaki.

Agriculture, Marwan al Humoud.

Islamic Affairs, Sheikh Abed al Aziz Khayat.

Transport, Mahmoud Hawamdeh.

Interior, Tharwat al Telhouni.

Justice, Naji al Tarawneh.

Health, Dr. Trad Saud al Qadi.

Communications, Dr. Mohammed Addoub al Zabin.

Trade and Industry, Dr. Rajai al Muashir.
Supplies, Salah Juma'ah.
Labour, Isam Ajlouni.
Municipal Affairs, Isma'el Armouti.
Ministers of State, Rakan Inad al Jazi (*Cabinet Affairs*); Hassen Ibraheem (*Foreign Affairs*).

JORDANIAN EMBASSY AND CONSULATE
6 Upper Phillimore Gardens, W.8
[01–937 3685]
Ambassador Extraordinary and Plenipotentiary, His Excellency, Ma'an Abu Nowar.
Minister Plenipotentiary, Hani B. Tabbara.
Counsellor, Hassan Abu Nimah.
Counsellor, Miss Zein Samir Rifai (*Press*).
Military, Naval and Air Attaché, Brig. Riad Kat Khuda.

Service Office: 16 Upper Phillimore Gardens, W.8. (01-937-9611).

Area and Population.—The Kingdom, which covers 37,700 sq. miles, is bounded on the north by Syria, on the west by Israel, on the south by Saudi Arabia and on the east by Iraq. Since the hostilities of June, 1967, that part of the country lying to the west of the Jordan River has been under Israeli occupation. The majority of the population are Sunni Moslems and Islam is the religion of the State. Total population (1974) is 2,660,000, of whom 1,890,000 live in East Jordan and the remainder on the West Bank and in East Jerusalem. (*For Map, see* p. 882.)

History and Government.—After the defeat of Turkey in the First World War the Amirate of Transjordan was established in the area east of the River Jordan as a state under British mandate. The mandate was terminated after the Second World War and the Amirate, still ruled by its founder, the Amir Abdullah, became the Hashemite Kingdom of Jordan. Following the 1948 war between Israel and the Arab States, that part of Palestine remaining in Arab hands (but excluding Gaza) was incorporated into the Hashemite Kingdom. King Abdullah was assassinated in 1951; his son Talal ruled briefly but abdicated in favour of the present King, Hussein, in 1952. All of Jordan west of the River has been under Israeli occupation since 1967. As a result of the wars of 1948 and 1967 there are about 750,000 refugees and displaced persons living in East Jordan, about 200,000 of whom live in refugee and displaced persons camps established by the U.N. Relief and Works Agency (UNRWA). In addition there are some 300,000 entirely self-supporting Palestinian members of the East Jordanian community. It was largely among the refugee population that the Palestinian *fedayeen* (commando) movement which had come into existence some years earlier grew considerably in strength during 1969 and 1970. The *fedayeen* organizations conducted a number of operations against Israel but during 1970 came more and more into conflict with the Jordanian Government. After the civil war between the Jordan Army and the *fedayeen* the Jordan Government re-established its authority. The *fedayeen* were finally expelled from Jordan in the summer of 1971. In March 1972 King Hussein put forward a plan for the "United Arab Kingdom" which was to be implemented after liberation of the West Bank. The plan provides for the creation of a federal State, composed of two autonomous regions, Palestine and East Jordan. During the war of October 1973 between the Arab countries and Israel, Jordan sent two armoured brigades into Syria to support the Syrian campaign on the Golan Heights.
The present constitution of the Kingdom came into force in 1952. It provides for a senate of 30 members (all appointed by the King) and an elected

House of Representatives of 60 persons. The King himself appoints the members of the Council of Ministers. Crown Prince Hassan normally acts as Regent when King Hussein is away from Jordan.

Production and Industry.—West Jordan is fertile, though many areas have suffered from soil erosion. In East Jordan the main agricultural areas are the east part of the Jordan Valley, the hills overlooking the Valley and the flatter country to the south of Amman and around Madaba and Irbid. The rest of the country is desert and semi-desert. The principal crops are wheat, barley, vegetables, olives and fruit (mainly grapes and citrus fruits). Agricultural production in the Jordan Valley has suffered from the continued hostilities in the area, though the East Ghor Canal, vital to the irrigation of the area, has now been restored and is being extended. The only important industrial product is raw phosphates (production 1974: 1,674,800 tons), most of which is exported. There are schemes under consideration for the production of copper, potash and phosphate fertilizers. Tourism was a major industry and foreign currency earner before the 1967 war but dwindled considerably as most of the tourist sites are now in Israeli occupied territory. In recent years it has begun to increase once more, with numbers of tourists visiting the archæological sites of East Jordan and the resort of Aqaba. The Trans-Arabian oil pipeline (Tapline) runs through North Jordan on its way from the eastern province of Saudi Arabia to the Lebanese coast of Sidon. A branch pipeline feeds a refinery at Zerqa (production 1974: 748,400 tons) which meets most of Jordan's requirements for refined petroleum products.

Communications.—The trunk road system is good. Amman is linked to Damascus, Baghdad and Jedda by tarred roads which are of considerable importance in the overland trade of the Middle East. The former Hejaz Railway enters Jordan east of Ramtha and runs through Zerqa and Amman to Ma'an with a spur to the top of the Raz al-Naqb escarpment. The formerly abandoned section from Ma'an to Medina in Saudi Arabia has been partially reconstructed. A total of 299 vessels called at Aqaba in 1974 and 1,483,300 tons of cargo were handled. Much of Jordan's trade moves overland to and from the ports in Syria and Lebanon. The Royal Jordanian Airline (ALIA) operates from Amman Airport to other cities in the Middle East and to Rome, London, Paris, Frankfurt, Athens, Istanbul and Madrid. There is a service to the newly constructed airport at 'Aqaba.

FINANCE

	1974 JD (Million)	1975 JD (Million)
Expenditure	165·7	218·2
Domestic Revenue	56·7	95·8
Budgetary Supports	51·4	60·4
Compensatory Finance	3·2	Nil
Development Loans	45·0	50·2
Deficit	12·6	11·9

Trade with U.K.

Britain has been a leading source of supply of imported goods to Jordan for some time. Jordan's exports to U.K. are negligible.

	1974	1975
Imports from U.K.	£20,648,000	£36,847,000
Exports to U.K.	1,631,000	733,000

CAPITAL.—Amman. Population, 615,000 (1974).

FLAG.—Black, white and green horizontal stripes, surcharged with white seven-point star on red triangle.

NATIONAL DAY.—May 25 (Independence Day).

BRITISH EMBASSY, AMMAN
Ambassador Extraordinary and Plenipotentiary, His

Excellency John Campbell Moberly, C.M.G. (1975).

Counsellor, J. K. E. Broadley.

Defence, Naval and Air Attaché, Col. R. B. Robertson.

Air Attaché, Wing-Cdr. D. E. Brett.

1st Secretaries, M. St. E. Burton (*Head of Chancery and Consul*), J. A. N. Brehony.

2nd Secretaries, B. J. McDowell (*Commercial*); A. J. R. Pitt (*Administration*); B. E. Stewart (*Information*).

3rd Secretary, P. Willis (*Development*).

BRITISH COUNCIL

Representative, J. G. Mills, Box 634, Jebel Amman, Amman.

KOREA

Korea is situated between 124° 11″ and 130° 57′ E. long., and between 33° 7′ and 43° 1″ N. lat. It has an area of 85,256 sq. miles with an estimated population of about 48,000,000, of whom about 33,500,000 live south of the present dividing line. The southern and western coasts are fringed with innumerable islands, of which the largest, forming a province of its own, is Chejudo (Quelpart).

Agriculture.—The soil is fertile, but the arable land is limited by the mountainous nature of the country. The staple agricultural products are rice, barley, and other cereals, beans, cotton, tobacco and hemp. Fruit-growing and seri-culture are also practised. Gingseng, a medicinal root much affected by the Chinese, forms a rich source of revenue.

Minerals.—Gold, copper, coal, iron, graphite, tungsten and other minerals are distributed throughout the country, but are more abundant in the north.

In pre-war days the south was mainly agricultural and most of the limited industries were in the north. Since 1966, however, rapid industrialization has taken place in the south.

History.—The last native dynasty (Yi) ruled from 1392 until 1910, in which year Japan formally annexed Korea. The country remained an integral part of the Japanese Empire until the defeat of Japan in 1945, when it was occupied by troops of the U.S.A. and the U.S.S.R.; the 38th parallel being fixed as the boundary between the two zones of occupation. The U.S. Government endeavoured to reach agreement with the Soviet Government for the creation of a Korean Government for the whole country and the withdrawal of all Russian and American troops. These efforts met with no success, and in September, 1947, the U.S. Government laid the whole question of the future of Korea before the General Assembly of the United Nations. The Assembly in November, 1947, resolved that elections should be held in Korea for a National Assembly under the supervision of a temporary Commission formed for that purpose by the United Nations and that the National Assembly when elected should set up a Government. The Soviet Government refused to allow the Commission to visit the Russian Occupied Zone and in consequence it was only able to discharge its function in that part of Korea which lies to the south of the 38th parallel.

The Korean War.—The country remained effectively divided into two along the line of the 38th parallel until the aggression of June 25, 1950, when the North Korean forces invaded South Korea. On the same day, at an emergency meeting of the United Nations Security Council, a resolution was adopted calling for immediate cessation of hostilities, and the withdrawal of the North Korean armed forces to the 38th parallel. The Communist forces ignored this demand and continued their advance. In response to a Security Council recommendation that United Nations members should furnish assistance to repel the attack, 16 nations, including the United States of America and the United Kingdom, came to the aid of the Republic of Korea. A unified command under the leadership of the United States was established on July 8. Shortly afterwards U.S. troops were landed in Korea but were at first unable to stem the Communists' onslaught. Finally the United Nations and South Korean forces were able to stabilize a front around the Pusan perimeter. On September 15, U.S. Marines made a successful surprise landing at Inchon which was quickly followed by a break-out from the Pusan perimeter and a general advance to the north. The Communist forces had been pushed back almost to the Manchurian frontier when, at the beginning of November, hordes of Chinese " Volunteers " began to pour over the Yalu River and by sheer weight of numbers forced the U.N. troops to withdraw once again south of Seoul. However, the latter quickly regrouped and threw the Communist forces back to approximately the old dividing line.

The fighting was ended by an armistice agreement signed by the U.N. Commander-in-Chief and the commanders of the North Korean army and the Chinese People's " Volunteers " on July 27, 1953. By this agreement (which was not signed by the government of the Republic of Korea) the line of division between North and South Korea remained in the neighbourhood of the 38th parallel. The Geneva Conference discussed Korea from April 26 to June 15, 1954, but failed to agree on measures for reunifying the country.

Republic of Korea

President, Park, Chung Hee, *assumed office,* March 22 1962; *re-elected for four years* 1963, 1967 and 1971; *and for six years* in 1972.

Prime Minister, Choi Kyu Hah (1975).

KOREAN EMBASSY
4 Palace Gate, W.8.
[01-581 0247]

Ambassador Extraordinary and Plenipotentiary, His Excellency Yong Shik Kim (1974).

Ministers, Jong Ick Choi; Dong Kun Kim.

Counsellors, In Hwan Choi; Jai Sung Kim; Chu Won Yoon.

Defence Attaché, Col. Dong Yull Seo.

The Republic of Korea has been officially recognized by the Governments of the United States, France, Great Britain, and most other countries except the U.S.S.R. and its satellites. It has an area of 38,452 sq. miles and a population of 33,459,000.

A general election was held on May 10, 1948, and the first National Assembly met in Seoul on May 31. The Assembly passed a Constitution on July 12, and on July 20 elected the late Dr. Syngman Rhee as the first President of the Republic of Korea, an office which he held until 1960. On August 15, 1948, the Republic was formally inaugurated and American Military Government came to an end.

President Syngman Rhee was overthrown by a widespread popular rising in 1960. After a year of unstable and ineffectual governments a new régime was set up by an army officers' coup on May 16, 1961 led by Major-Gen. Park Chung Hee. On March 22, 1962, he took over as acting President, retaining his post as Chairman of the Supreme Council. Elections were originally promised for May and August, 1963, respectively, but when political

activities were allowed to start again at the beginning of that year there was considerable confusion, so that the military government decided to retain power until December, 1963. Elections were then held in which General Park was elected and the Democratic Republican Party secured a majority. At further elections held in 1967, Pres. Park was returned by a comfortable majority for a new four-year term. In 1969 a constitutional amendment was passed to enable Pres. Park to stand for a third term and he was re-elected on April 27, 1971.

In 1972 a new constitution was inaugurated under which there was no limit to the number of terms which the President could serve. President Park was then elected in December 1972 to a six-year term.

The Republic of Korea has an army of about 550,000 men, a small navy mainly for coast protection duties, a small air force and a Marine Corps which includes one division trained in amphibious operations.

Finance.—The Budget for 1976 totalled *Won* 2,036 billion, of which 35 per cent. was for defence.

The unit of Korean currency is the *Won*. In 1976 the rate of exchange was about 854 *Won* to £1.

Trade.—The Republic of Korea's main exports are textiles, plywood and wood products, fish and fish preparations, electrical and electronic equipment, chemicals, footwear, rubber, petroleum products, cement, ships, musical instruments, toys, sports goods, iron and steel products and metalliferous ores and scrap. Her main customers are Japan and the U.S.A. Imports greatly exceed exports. In 1975 exports totalled $U.S. 5,081,016,000; imports amounted to $U.S. 7,274,434,000.

Trade with U.K.

	1974	1975
Imports from U.K....	£36,045,000	£52,577,000
Exports to U.K.......	50,985,000	74,543,000

CAPITAL.—Seoul, population (1973), 6,289,556. Other main centres are Ψ Pusan (pop. 2,015,162), Taegu (pop. 1,082,750) and Ψ Inchon (pop. 646,013), Pusan on the south-east coast, and Inchon on the

west coast, only 28 miles from Seoul, are the main ports but the development of Inchon is hampered by a tide variation of 28–30 feet.

FLAG.—White, with red over blue device in centre, three black parallel bars, some broken, in each quarter.

NATIONAL DAY.—August 15 (Independence Day).

BRITISH EMBASSY
Seoul

Ambassador Extraordinary and Plenipotentiary, His Excellency William Stanley Bates, C.M.G. (1975).
Counsellor, R. G. Tallboys, O.B.E. (*Commercial*).
1st Secretaries, I. C. Sloane (*Head of Chancery and Consul*); P. J. D. Whitehead (*Political*).
Defence Attaché, Brig. K. Neely, M.B.E.
2nd Secretary, R. J. Griffiths (*Commercial*).
Vice-Consul, R. D. Stainton.
Attachés, P. Fluck (*Commercial*); F. A. Wilson (*Administration*).
Cultural Attaché, G. E. B. Coe (British Council Representative). There is an Honorary British Consul at Pusan.

Democratic People's Republic of Korea—Meanwhile in the Russian-occupied zone north of the 38th parallel the Democratic People's Republic had been set up with its capital at Pyongyang; a Supreme People's Soviet was elected in September 1948, and a Soviet-style Constitution adopted. Recognition had been given by the U.S.S.R. and its satellites. The population is around 14,500,000.

Korean Workers (= *Communist*) Party
Political Committee of the Central Committee, Kim Il Sung; Choe Yong Kun; Kim Il; Pak Song Chol; Kim Yong Chu; O Chin U; Kim Tong Kyu; So Chol; Kim Chung Im; Han Ik Su, Yi Kun Mo; Yang Hyang Sop; Yi Yong Mu (*full members*); Hyon Mu Kwang; Kim Man Kim; Kang Song San; Ch'oe Chae U; Kim Yong Nam; Yu Chang Sik; Chan Mun Sop (*alternate members*).
Secretariat of the Central Committee, Kim Il Song (*Secretary-General*); Choe Yong Ko; Kim Il; Kim Yong Chu; O Chin U; Kim Tong Kyu; Kim Chung Im; Han Ik Su; Hyon Mu Kwang; Yang Hyong Sop; Yon Hyong Muk; Kim Yong Nam; Yu Chang Sik.
FLAG.—Broad red horizontal band bordered by white lines bearing a five-point red star on a white disc in centre; blue horizontal bands at top and bottom.

KUWAIT
(The State of Kuwait)

Amir, H.H. Shaikh Sabah as-Salem as-Sabah, *born* 1915; acceded Nov. 24, 1965.
Crown Prince and Prime Minister (Dec. 1965), H.H. Shaikh Jabir al-Ahmed-as-Sabah; *appointed Crown Prince*, May 31, 1966.

KUWAIT EMBASSY IN LONDON
40 Devonshire Street, W.1
[01–580 8471]

Ambassador Extraordinary and Plenipotentiary, His Excellency Sheikh Saud Nasir Al-Sabah (1975).

Area and Population.—Kuwait extends along the shore of the Persian Gulf from Iraq to Saudi Arabia, with an area of about 7,500 square miles and a population (Census, 1975) of 990,000. It is officially estimated that about 47 per cent. of this total are Kuwaitis, the remainder being large numbers of other Arab peoples, Persians, Indians and Pakistanis. The total European and American population is about 7,000. Kuwait has a hot, dry climate with a summer season extending from April to September. During the coldest month

(January) the temperatures can fall below freezing, but normally range between 50° to 60°F. Shade temperatures are about 85°F; and can reach 130°F.; 180°F. has been recorded in the sun. Humidity rarely exceeds 60 per cent. except in July and August.

Government.—Although Kuwait had been independent for some years, the " exclusive agreement " of 1899 between the Shaikh of Kuwait and the British Government was formally abrogated by an exchange of letters dated June 19, 1961. This exchange was immediately followed by Iraqi claims to sovereignty over Kuwait and, in accordance with the terms of the exchange, the Amir requested British military assistance to help him maintain his sovereignty and independence, which was immediately supplied. British troops were withdrawn in October, 1961, and replaced by the Arab League Security Force composed of contingents from various Arab States. The withdrawal of this Force was completed in January, 1963. On May 7, 1963, Kuwait was admitted to the United Nations and on Oct. 4, 1963, Iraq recognized Kuwait's independence. On May 13, 1968, an exchange of Notes was signed giving notice that the 1961 defence agreement with the United Kingdom would end on May 13, 1971.

Elections were held in December, 1961, for a Constituent Assembly, which held its first meeting in January, 1962. A council of Ministers including non-members of the ruling family was formed in January, 1962, to replace the former Supreme and Joint Councils. Under the Constitution drafted by the Constituent Assembly, the first 50-member National Assembly was elected in January, 1963. The present National Assembly was elected for four years in January, 1975. The Constitution provides that the Assembly must pass all laws and approve the Heir Apparent nominated by the Amir. The Prime Minister is appointed by the Amir and can appoint his Ministers from the members of the Assembly or from outside. The Assembly has the right to pass a vote of no confidence in any Minister except the Prime Minister.

Education, etc.—As a result of the very considerable oil revenues, the Kuwait Government embarked on a large scale development scheme and plans for social services. Education and medical treatment are free. New hospitals and schools continue to be built. Kuwait University was opened in 1966. In 1974, 488 students graduated out of a total 2,600. In 1975 there were over 182,778 pupils at 285 government schools.

Public Utilities.—Kuwait has a domestic water supply from water distillation plants which operate on waste natural gas from the oil fields. These plants can produce over 40,000,000 gallons of fresh water daily. For storage there are two 15,000,000 gallon reservoirs and one of 3,000,000 gallons. There are also two 7,500,000 gallon reservoirs at Shuaiba and two of similar capacity at Abraq Kheitan.

In 1961 a natural source of fresh water was discovered at Raudhatain in the north of the State. This has been developed to produce 5,000,000 gallons per day for at least 20 years and a pipeline has been built to carry the water to Kuwait town. Kuwait signed an agreement with Iraq on Feb. 11, 1964, allowing her to draw up to 120,000,000 gallons of sweet water a day from the Shatt-al-Arab, but this has yet to be implemented. Electricity is produced by three power stations in Kuwait (160 MWh) and two at Shuaiba (400 MWh). Twal town is served by a network of dual carriageway roads and more are under construction.

Communications.—Ships of British, Dutch, Kuwaiti and other lines make regular calls at Kuwait.

British Airways, Kuwait Airways, K.L.M., Lufthansa and several international and Middle Eastern airlines operate regular air services, and other companies make non-scheduled flights to Kuwait under charter. Wireless communications, telephone and postal services are conducted by the Kuwait Government, which has built an earth satellite station.

Finance.—Banking is carried out by the National Bank of Kuwait, the Commercial Bank, the Gulf Bank, the Ahli Bank, and by the Bank of Kuwait and the Middle East. The banking system is controlled by the Central Bank of Kuwait.

Revenue for the financial year 1975–76 was budgeted at $KD1,736,166,000$. Estimated total expenditure for 1975–76 was $KD826,000,000$ including $KD45,111,000$ on health, $KD65,750,000$ on defence, $KD86,740,000$ on education, and $KD 50,756,000$ on public works.

Production and Trade.—Until 1974, the Kuwait Oil Company was wholly owned by the British Petroleum Company and the American Gulf Oil Corporation. The Government of Kuwait then began to participate by stages in the ownership of the Company and an agreement was signed in November 1975 which brought 100 per cent. government ownership.

The centre of the Kuwait Oil Company's production is at Burgan, south of Kuwait City. Oil is exported through a specially constructed port at Mina al Ahmadi, which is about five miles from the Company's administrative and residential centre at Ahmadi. Production of crude oil in 1975 was approximately 103 million metric tons. The Company employs about 3,000 people, including Kuwaitis, British, Americans, Indians, Pakistanis and citizens of other Arab Countries.

Oil is also lifted in the Kuwait/Saudi Arabia Partitioned Zone, south of the State. Concessions for this area are held by the American Independent Oil Company (AMINOIL) from Kuwait and the Getty Oil Company from Saudi Arabia. AMINOIL's production in 1975 (i.e. Kuwait's share) was approximately 4 million metric tons.

The Arabian Oil Company of Japan, having been awarded in 1958 the oil concession for the Partitoned Zone offshore sea-bed by Kuwait and Saudi Arabia for their respective half shares, commenced exploratory drilling in the summer of 1959 and struck oil in commercial quantity early in 1960. The first shipment of crude oil was made in March 1961; production in 1972 was approximately 8·5 million metric tons. A concession covering the offshore area of Kuwait proper was awarded to the Shell Company in November 1960, and the concession agreement in the name of the Kuwait Shell Petroleum Development Company was signed in Kuwait on January 15, 1961. Exploratory drilling began in 1962 but was suspended in the autumn of 1963. The establishment of the Kuwait National Petroleum Company was authorised by an Amiri Decree on October 5, 1960. This company took over the distribution of petroleum products in Kuwait from the Kuwait Oil Company on June 1, 1961, and was, in partnership with the Spanish Company Hispanoil, awarded the concession to exploit an area relinquished by the KOC Ltd in 1962.

In addition to petroleum products, wooden prefabricated office accommodation, skins and wool are also exported. Trade in 1974 amounted to: Imports, $KD331,300,000$; Exports (including re-exports), $KD79,100,000$, excluding oil.

Trade with U.K.

	1974	1975
Imports from U.K.	£59,800,000	£99,200,000
Exports to U.K.	600,000,000	419,300,000

CAPITAL.—ΨKuwait (population, excluding suburbs, 400,000).

FLAG.—Three horizontal stripes of green, white and red, with black trapezoid next to staff.

NATIONAL DAY.—February 25.

BRITISH EMBASSY
Arabian Gulf Street, Kuwait

Ambassador Extraordinary and Plenipotentiary, His Excellency Albert Thomas Lamb, C.M.G., M.B.E., D.F.C. (1974).

Counsellor, G. E. Fitzherbert.

1st Secretaries, P. R. M. Hinchcliffe (*Head of Chancery*); J. Long, M.B.E. (*Consul*); J. Gallacher; J. S. Khoury (*Commercial*); A. S. M. Marshall.

2nd Secretaries, A. H. Ellis (*Admin.*); H. G. Hogger.

British Council Office, P.O. Box Safat 345 Kuwait.
Representative, R. L. S. Tong.
There is a library in *Kuwait*.

LAOS
(People's Democratic Republic of Laos)

President, Souphanouvong, *assumed office*, Dec. 2, 1975.

Prime Minister, Kaysone Phomvihane.

EMBASSY IN LONDON
5 Palace Green, W.8

Ambassador Extraordinary and Plenipotentiary, His Excellency Platthana Chounlamany (1976).

Position and Extent.—The People's Democratic Republic of Laos is in the northerly part of Indo-China, lying between China and Viet-nam, on the north and east, and Burma and Thailand on the west. Laos has a common boundary with Cambodia to the south. The area of the country is approximately 90,000 sq. miles, with a population (estimated, 1976) of about 3,000,000.

History.—The Kingdom of Lane Xang, the Land of a Million Elephants, was founded in the 14th century, but broke up at the beginning of the 15th century into the separate kingdoms of Luang Prabang and Vientiane and the Principality of Champassac, which together came under French protection in 1893. In 1945 the Japanese executed a *coup de force* and suppressed the French administration. Under a Constitution of 1947 Laos became a constitutional monarchy under King Sisvang Vong of the House of Luang Prabang, and an independent sovereign state in 1949.

The next twenty-five years in Laos were marked by power struggles and civil war. International conferences were held in Geneva in 1954 and 1961–2 to produce a settlement based on neutrality and independence. But the resulting Coalition Governments were short-lived. Personalities involved include the present adviser to the Government, Prince Souvanna Phouma, who in 1957 formed a Government of National Union, including *Pathet Lao* (Communist) ministers, and held office as Prime Minister with intervals from 1962 to 1975; Prince Boun Oum of Champassac who formed a rightist Government in December 1960, fled Laos in 1975 and was consequently condemned to death, and Prince Souphanouvang, who took part in a later coalition with Souvanna Phouma and Boun Oum in 1962–63. Attempts to seize power by Capt. Kong Le (1960), Gen. Phoumi Nosavan (1965) and Gen. Thoa Ma (1966 and 1973) were unsuccessful.

Recent Events.—After 1967 North Vietnamese forces steadily increased their military activities in Laos. Although there were regular seasonal fluctuations in the fighting, which resulted in many areas of the country changing hands several times, Government forces gradually lost ground. By

February 21, 1973, when a ceasefire agreement was signed in Vientiane between the *Pathet Lao* and the Government in Vientiane, Communist forces had occupied or dominated most of the strategic areas of Laos, including the Plain of Jars in the north, and the Bolovens Plateau in the south. The 1973 Vientiane Agreement and its Protocol of September 1973, provided for a cease-fire; a timetable for the withdrawal of foreign forces; a halt to U.S. bombing and the " neutralization " of Vientiane and of the Royal capital, Luang Prabang. The agreement also made provisions for a Provisional Government of National Union and for a Political Consultative Council (eventually formed on April 5, 1974) with equal representation from the *Pathet Lao* (now known as the Lao Patriotic forces) and the Vientiane Government, which would hold office until new elections could be held. After the fall of Saigon in April 1975, internal resistance to the Pathet Lao crumbled; Communist troops occupied the whole country and, though still paying lip-service to the 1973 Agreement and maintaining a façade of coalition, the *Pathet Lao* took over the government and began to implement an authoritarian régime with policies of austerity and economic self-sufficiency. On December 2, 1975, following the abdication of the King, Laos was declared a People's Democratic Republic and the *Pathet Lao* assumed full charge of the country.

Finance.—Budget estimates for the fiscal year 1976/77 are not available. The unit of currency is the *Kip* (*K*). In July 1976 the official exchange rate was 60 *Kip* to US $.

CAPITAL.—Vientiane population (estimated 1973) 174,000.

FLAG.—Blue background with a central white circle, framed by 2 horizontal red stripes.

NATIONAL DAY.—December 2.

BRITISH EMBASSY
Vientiane

Ambassador Extraordinary and Plenipotentiary, His Excellency Donald Paul Montagu Stewart Cape (1976) £12,410

1st Secretary, P. S. Fairweather (*Head of Chancery and Consul*).

2nd Secretary, D. G. Taylor (*Admin. and Vice-Consul*).

3rd Secretary, Miss R. M. Lowry (*Chancery, Information, Commercial, Aid.*)

LEBANON

President of the Republic of Lebanon, Elias Sarkis, elected May 8, 1976; *assumed office*, Sept. 23, 1976.

CABINET
[Sept. 15, 1976]

Prime Minister, Agriculture, Tourism and Information, Rachid Karamé.

Interior, Defence and Foreign, Camille Chamoun.

Justice, Public Works and Transport, and Economy and Commerce, Adel Osseiran.

Health, Agriculture, Housing and Co-operatives, Emir Magid Arslan.

Foreign Affairs, Education and Fine Arts, and Planning, Philippe Takla.

Labour and Social Affairs, Tourism, Industry and Oil, Ghassan Toueini.

Finance, Economy and Trade, George Skaff.

LEBANESE EMBASSY IN LONDON
21 Kensington Palace Gardens, W.8
[01–229 7265]

Ambassador Extraordinary and Plenipotentiary, His Excellency Nadim Dimechkie (1966).

Counsellor, Chawki Nicholas Choueri.

1st Secretary, Nizar Farhat.

2nd Secretary, Gilbert Aoun.
Attaché (Tourism), Mounir El-Sheikh.
Military Attaché, Col. Fouad El-Houssami.
Consular Section, 15 Palace Gardens Mews, W.8 (01-229 8485).

Area and Population.—Lebanon forms a strip about 120 miles in length and varying in width from 30 to 35 miles, along the Mediterranean littoral, and extending from the Israel frontier on the south to the Nahr al Kebir (15 miles north of Tripoli) on the north; its eastern boundary runs down the Anti-Lebanon range and then down the Great Central depression, the *Beqaa,* in which flow the rivers Orontes and Litani. It is divided into 5 districts, North Lebanon, Mount Lebanon, Beirut, South Lebanon and Beqaa. The seaward slopes of the mountains have a Mediterranean climate and vegetation. The inland range of Anti-Lebanon has the characteristics of steppe country. There is a mixed Arabic-speaking population of Christians, Moslems and Druses. The total area of Lebanon is about 4,300 sq. miles, population (U.N. estimate, 1969), 2,645,000. (*For* MAP, *see* p. 882.)

Government.—Lebanon became an independent State on Sept. 1, 1920, administered under French Mandate until Nov. 26, 1941. Powers were transferred to the Lebanese Government from Jan. 1, 1944, and French troops were withdrawn in 1946.

Suleiman Franjieh was elected President in 1970, for a term of six years. In April 1975, serious fighting broke out in Beirut between members of the predominantly Christian Phalangist Party and Palestinian guerrillas based in Lebanon. On May 15, the Government of M. Rashid Solh resigned, and the President appointed a military government led by Brig. Noureddin Rifai on May 23, which lasted only three days. After a renewed outbreak of violence on June 24, the country was on the verge of civil war. On June 30, a new cabinet was formed with the sole intention of restoring peace. It was led by Rachid Karamé, and contained a representative of each of the main religious communities.

However, the government was powerless to stop the fighting, which continued and increased throughout 1975 and 1976. In April 1976 a constitutional amendment facilitated the resignation of President Frangié. On May 8, the Lebanese Parliament elected Mr. Elias Sarkis President.

Production.—Fruits are the most important products and include citrus fruit, apples, grapes, bananas and olives. There is a small but growing industry, geared mainly to the production of consumer goods. The most important industries are foods and drinks (confectionery, jams, sugar, wines and beer, etc.), textiles, chemicals, furniture, plastics, leather, clothing and footwear, refrigerators, cast and forged metal products, and building materials. There is little remaining of the famous cedars of Lebanon.

Railways.—A narrow-gauge railway runs from Beirut to Damascus, connecting at Rayak with a branch of the standard-gauge line which runs from Tripoli through Homs, Hama and Aleppo to the Turkish frontier, from Nusaybin to the Iraq frontier at Tel Kotchek. A standard gauge railway also runs up the coast from Beirut to Tripoli.

Archæology, etc.—Lebanon has some important historical remains, notably Baalbek (Heliopolis) which contains the ruins of first to third century Roman temples and Jubail (Biblos), one of the oldest continuously inhabited towns in the world, and ancient Tyre which is in course of excavation.

Language and Literature.—Arabic is the principal language (*see* Arabia), and French is also widely used. The use of English is increasing. About 40 daily papers are published, including 2 in French, 1 in English and 4 in Armenian; and a further 30 periodicals.

Education.—There are four universities in Beirut, the American and the French (R.C.) Universities established in the last century, and the Lebanese National University and the Arab University which are recent foundations in the early stages of development. There are several institutions for vocational training and there is a good provision throughout the country of primary and secondary schools, among which are a great number of private schools.

Finance.—Revenue and Expenditure, 1974 (Estimated) £L1,385,300,000. The monetary unit is the Lebanese £(L). (*See also* p. 84.)

Principal Imports.—Gold and precious metals, machinery and electrical equipment, textiles and yarns, vegetable products, iron and steel goods, motor vehicles, mineral products, chemicals and chemical products, pharmaceuticals, prepared foods, beverages, tobacco products, live animals and animal products.

Principal Exports.—Gold and precious metals, fruits and vegetables, textiles, building materials, furniture, plastic goods, foodstuffs, tobacco and wine.

Trade with U.K.

	1974	1975
Imports from U.K.	£60,800,000	£69,528,000
Exports to U.K.	28,640,000	8,025,000

There is also a considerable transit trade through Beirut, including gold, crude oil and a wide range of machinery and consumer goods. Lebanon is the terminal for two oil pipe lines, one belonging to the Iraq Petroleum Company, debouching at Tripoli, the other belonging to the Trans-Arabian Pipeline Company, at Sidon. There are refineries at the end of each pipeline which can supply Lebanon's needs.

CAPITAL.— Ψ Beirut (population, excluding suburbs, about 600,000). Other towns are Ψ Tripoli (210,000), Zahlé (45,000), Ψ Sidon (42,000), Aley (14,500), Ψ Tyre (12,000).

FLAG.—Horizontal bands of red, white and red with a green cedar of Lebanon in the centre of the white band.

NATIONAL DAY.—November 22.

BRITISH EMBASSY
Beirut
Ambassador Extraordinary and Plenipotentiary, His Excellency Peter George Arthur Wakefield, C.M.G. (1975)

LIBERIA
(Republic of Liberia)

President, Dr. William R. Tolbert.
Vice President, J. E. Greene.
Presidential Affairs, F. R. Townsend.
Finance, J. T. Phillips.
Foreign Affairs, C. Cecil Dennis.
National Defence, H. A. Greaves.
Health and Welfare, O. Bright.
Commerce, Industry and Transportation, W. E. Dennis.
Planning and Economic Affairs, D. F. Neal.
Public Works, G. J. Tucker.
Agriculture, L. A. Russ.
Education, Dr. A. A. Hoff.
Local Government, Rural Development and Urban Reconstruction, E. J. Goodridge.

Mines and Lands, A. Holmes.
Information, Cultural Affairs and Tourism, Dr. E. B. Kesselly.
Labour and Youth, J. J. Peal.
Posts and Telecommunications, Mrs. A. Jones.
Justice, E. Bernard (acting).
Without Portfolio, Dr. C. A. Clarke.
Director of Cabinet, S. Kla-Williams.
Action for Development and Progress, J. K. L. Moulton.

LIBERIAN EMBASSY IN LONDON
21 Prince's Gate, S.W.7
[01-589 9405]

Ambassador Extraordinary and Plenipotentiary, His Excellency Herbert Richard Wright Brewer (1975).
1st Secretary and Consul, W. E. Greaves.
2nd Secretary and Vice-Consul, J. D. Moulton.

An independent republic of Western Africa, occupying that part of the coast between Sierra Leone and the Ivory Coast, which is between the rivers Mano in the N.W. and Cavalla in the S.E., a distance of about 350 miles, with an area of about 43,000 square miles, and extending to the interior to latitude 8° 50′, a distance of 150 miles from the seaboard. It was founded by the American Colonization Society in 1822, and has been recognized since 1847 as an independent State. The population at the Census of 1974 was 1,481,524.

The executive power is vested in a President elected for 4 years (8 years in the first instance) assisted by a Cabinet; there are two houses of Legislature, the Senate and the House of Representatives. The Senate is composed of 19 members elected from each of the nine Counties. They hold office for a period of six years. The House of Representatives is composed of 70 members, each member holding office for four years. William V. S. Tubman, President of Liberia since 1944, died on July 23, 1971, and was succeeded by Dr. Tolbert (see above). The Army of Liberia consists of one division of 2 brigades of militia, three regular infantry battalions, one engineer battalion and a small coastguard. The artificial harbour and free port of Monrovia was opened on July 26, 1948. There are 9 ports of entry, including 3 river ports.

Liberia is receiving assistance from the U.S. A.I.D. (successor to I.C.A.), and technicians have been sent from U.S.A. to advise on various projects. Technical assistance is also being provided by several other countries, including the United Kingdom. UNESCO, WHO and FAO have missions in the country providing technical assistance. The U.S.A. and more recently I.B.R.D., has also made loans for the improvement of power and water supplies, roads and hospitals.

FINANCE

	1974	1975
Revenue	$96,000,000	$117,000,090
Expenditure	96,000,000	117,200,000

$=U.S. Dollar.

TRADE

	1973	1974
Imports	$193,468,586	$288,400,000
Exports	324,039,251	400,200,000

Trade with U.K.

	1974	1975
Imports from U.K.	£13,990,000	£23,752,000
Exports to U.K.	6,494,000	6,085,000

The principal exports are iron ore, crude rubber, uncut diamonds, palm kernels, cocoa and coffee. The chief imports are manufactured goods of all kinds, transport and iron-ore mining equipment and foodstuffs.

The language of the Republic is English. American weights and measures are used.

CAPITAL, Ψ Monrovia. Est. Pop. 201,600. Other ports are Ψ Buchanan, Ψ Greenville (Sinoe) and Ψ Harper (Cape Palmas).
FLAG.—Alternate horizontal stripes (5 white, 6 red), with 5-pointed white star on blue field in upper corner next to flagstaff.
NATIONAL DAY.—July 26.

BRITISH EMBASSY
Monrovia

Ambassador Extraordinary and Plenipotentiary and Consul-General, His Excellency John Henry Reiss, O.B.E. (1973).
1st Secretary and Consul, L. Underwood.
3rd Secretary and Vice-Consul, G. Tippett.

Monrovia, 3,650 miles distant; transit by English steamers from Liverpool, 11 to 20 days; also by French, Netherlands, German and U.S. vessels from Continent and U.S.A., British Caledonian, U.T.A., Pan American Airways, Iberia, Nigerian Airways, K.L.M., Sabena, S.A.S., Swissair, Middle East Airlines and Air Afrique aircraft call at Robertsfield, 35 miles from Monrovia. Ghana and Nigerian Airways call at Spriggs Payne airfield, on the outskirts of Monrovia.

LIBYA

Chairman of the Revolutionary Command Council, Commander in Chief of the Armed Forces, Minister of Defence and President of the General People's Congress, Col. Mu'ammar al-Qadhafi (or " Gaddafi ").
Prime Minister and Secretary General of the General People's Congress, Maj. Abdul Salam Jalud.
Minister of the Interior, Maj. Khweldi al Humaidi.
Foreign Minister, Maj. Abdul Munim al Huni.

LIBYAN EMBASSY IN LONDON
58 Prince's Gate, S.W.7
[01-589 5235]

Ambassador Extraordinary and Plenipotentiary, His Excellency Mahmood Suleiman Maghribi (1973).
Minister Plenipotentiary, Suleiman M. Grada.
Counsellors, Ahmed I. Al Fakih; Khalifa A. Bazelya; Sayed M. Gadafeddam.
2nd Secretaries, Fawzi T. Hamza; Salah Eddin M. Msallem.

Libya, on the Mediterranean coast of Africa, is bounded on the East by Egypt and the Sudan, on the South by the Republics of Chad and Niger, and on the West by Algeria and Tunisia. It consists of the three former provinces of Tripolitania, Cyrenaica and the Fezzan, with a combined area of approximately 810,000 square miles and a population (1973 Census preliminary results) of 2,257,037. The people of Libya are principally Arab with some Berbers in the West and aboriginal tribes in the Fezzan. Islam is the official religion of Libya, but all religions are tolerated. The official language is Arabic.

Vast sand and rock deserts, almost completely barren, occupy the greater part of Libya. The Southern part of the country lies within the Sahara Desert. There are no rivers, and, as rainfall is precarious, a good harvest is infrequent. Agriculture is confined mainly to the coastal areas of Tripolitania and Cyrenaica, where barley, wheat, olives, almonds, citrus fruits and dates are produced, and to the areas of the oases, many of which are well supplied with springs supporting small fertile areas. Among the important oases are Jaghbub, Gadames, Jofra, Sebha, Murzuch, Brach, Gat, Jalo and the Kufra group in the South-East. Exports from Libya are dominated by crude oil, but some wool, cattle, sheep and horses, esparto grass, olive oil, sponges and hides and skins

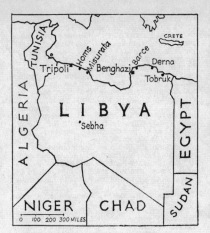

are also exported. Principal imports are food-stuffs, including sugar, tea and coffee and most constructional materials and consumer goods. The major producing companies are Esso, Oasis, Mobil, Um Al Jawabi (*formerly* Amoseas), A.G.I.P., Occidental, Aquitane and Libyan National Oil Co. In September 1973, the Libyan Government announced that it would be taking a 51 per cent. share in all foreign-owned companies. A few companies have been completely nationalized. In addition to the Esso main pipeline from Zelten to the terminal at Mersa Bregha and the Oasis Company's pipeline from Dahra to Ras-es-Sider, Mobil operates a 176-mile pipeline from Amal to Ras Lanuf and the Occidental line from Intisar field to Zuetina. A new gas liquefaction plant run by Esso was opened at Mersa Bregha in June 1970. Production of crude oil in 1973 was approximately 105 million tons (2·1 million barrels per day) which was a decrease of 4·6 per cent. over 1972.

The ancient ruins in Cyrenaica, at Cyrene, Ptolemais (Tolmeta) and Apollonia, are outstanding, as are those at Leptis Magna near Homs, 70 miles from Tripoli and at Sabratha, 40 miles west of Tripoli. An Italian expedition has found in the S.W. of the Fezzan a series of rock-paintings more than 5,000 years old. The Museum in the Castello at Tripoli has been completely re-organized and is of great interest to visitors.

Communications in Libya are good in the coastal area where a motor road (of international standards) runs from the Tunisian frontier through Tripoli to Benghazi, Tobruk and the Egyptian border, serving the needs of the main population centres. A road from the coast to Sebha, in the Fezzan, was completed in Oct. 1962. A Czech-built road between Nalut and Ghadames was completed in 1972. Elsewhere roads are poor and the transport inland is confined to caravan and occasional motor bus routes. There are airports at Tripoli and Benghazi (Benina), Tobruk, Mersa Bregha, Sebha, Ghadames and Kufra regularly used by commercial airlines and military airfields at Jamal Abdul Nasser (formerly El Adem near Tobruk) Okba ben Nafi' (formerly Wheelus Field near Tripoli) and at Al Watiyah south of Zuara.

Government.—Libya was occupied by Italy in 1911–12 in the course of the Italo-Turkish War,

and under the Treaty of Ouchy (Oct. 1912) the sovereignty of the province was transferred by Turkey to Italy. In 1939 the four Provinces of Libya (Tripoli, Misurata, Benghazi and Derna) were incorporated in the national territory of Italy as *Libia Italiana*. After the Second World War Tripolitania and Cyrenaica were placed provisionally under British and the Fezzan under French administration, and in conformity with a resolution of the General Assembly on Nov. 21, 1949, Libya became on Dec. 24, 1951, the first independent state to be created by the United Nations. The monarchy was overthrown by a revolution on Sept. 1, 1969, and the country was declared a republic. In 1971 a Libyan Arab Socialist Union was created as the country's sole political organisation. In January 1976 the General People's Congress was designated the supreme constitutional authority.

Local Government.—Until the amendment of the Constitution in 1963, Libya was a Federal State, each of the three Provinces, Tripolitania, Cyrenaica and Fezzan, being administered by a Governor assisted by Executive and Legislative Councils. In April 1963, however, comprehensive unity was proclaimed and the Federal system (together with the Governors and the Executive and Legislative Councils) abolished. The country is now divided into ten divisions, each administered by an Inspectorate (*Muraaqiba*).

Currency.—The Libyan *pound* was abolished in August, 1971, and a new currency the Libyan *dinar* of 1,000 *dirham* was introduced. *Dinar*= £1·90 sterling (*see also* p. 83).

Technical assistance is being provided by the United Nations to foster Libya's economic and educational development.

A treaty of alliance and friendship between the United Kingdom and Libya, together with military and financial agreements, was signed at Benghazi on July 29, 1953, but terminated at the Libyans' request in January, 1972.

Trade with U.K.

	1974	1975
Imports from U.K...	£62,500,000	£107,041,000
Exports to U.K.....	390,132,000	127,000,000

CAPITAL.—Tripoli.

The principal towns with the latest available estimates of population are: ΨTripoli (551,477); ΨMisurata (103,302); ΨBenghazi (282,192); Homs-Cussabat (88,695); Zawia (72,207); Gharian (65,439); ΨTobruk (58,869).

FLAG.—Libya uses the flag of the Confederation of Arab Republics (Libya, Egypt, Syria) which is a red, white and black tricolor with an eagle in gold in the centre. NATIONAL DAY.—Sept. 1.

BRITISH EMBASSY

30 Trigal Fatah, Tripoli.

Ambassador Extraordinary and Plenipotentiary, His Excellency Donald Frederick Murray, C.M.G. (1974).

Counsellor, R. L. Balfour, M.V.O.

1st Secretaries, D. J. Easton; G. H. Boyce; I. S. Lockhart, M.B.E. (*Commercial*); C. O. Wood (*Consul*).

2nd Secretaries, K. Farnworth (*Administration*); T. Millson (*Commercial*).

There is a British Consular Office at *Tripoli*.

LIECHTENSTEIN
(Fürstentum Liechtenstein)

Prince, Franz Josef II., *b.* Aug. 16, 1906; *suc.* July 26, 1938; *married* March 7, 1943, Countess Gina von Wilczek. *Heir*, Crown Prince Hans Adam,

b. Feb. 14, 1945; *married* July 30, 1967, Countess Marie Kinsky.

Prime Minister, Dr. Walter Kieber.

Liechtenstein is represented in diplomatic and consular matters in the United Kingdom by the Swiss Embassy, *q.v.*

At the General Election on Feb. 1 and 3, 1974, the Progressive Citizens' Party won 8 seats and Patriotic Union Party 7. Dr. Walker Kieber was asked to form a new Government.

A Principality on the Upper Rhine, between Vorarlberg (Austria) and Switzerland, with an area of 65 square miles and a population in 1974 of 23,745. The main industries are metal goods, cotton spinning and weaving, measuring instruments, coating of lenses, manufacture of vacuum apparatus, electronic microscopes, ceramics, artificial teeth and sausage casings, textiles, various apparatus, foodstuffs, leatherware and woodwork. The chief products are cotton yarn, cotton material, screws, bolts and bolt-shooting apparatus, needles, knitting machinery, ceramics, artificial teeth, precision measuring instruments, vacuum pumps, coated lenses, shoes, leather gloves, bed down, conveyor belts, boilers, preserves, damask cloth, socks and stockings, and furniture. Revenue 1974, *Swiss francs* 114,763,727. Expenditure 1974, *Swiss francs* 114,734,931.

The language of the Principality is German.

CAPITAL, Vaduz. Pop. (1974), 4,382.

FLAG.—Equal horizontal bands of blue over red; gold crown on blue band near staff.

British Consul General, James Ernest Reeve (*office at* Dufourstrasse 56, 8008 Zürich). *Consul*, O. E. Goddard (*office at* Bellerivestrasse 5, 8008 Zürich).

LUXEMBURG
(Grand-Duché de Luxembourg)

Grand Duke, H.R.H. Jean, *born* Jan 5, 1921, *married*, April 9, 1953, Princess Joséphine-Charlotte of Belgium, and has issue, 3 sons and 2 daughters; *succeeded* (on the abdication of his mother) Nov., 1964. *Heir Apparent*, Prince Henri, *born* April 16, 1955.

Prime Minister and Minister for Foreign Affairs and Sport, M. Gaston Thorn.

Deputy Prime Minister and Minister of Finance, of the Budget and of Planning, M. Raymond Vouel.

Minister of Economic Affairs, of the Middle Classes, of Transport, of Energy and of Tourism, M. Marcel Mart.

Minister of Employment and Social Affairs, M. Benny Berg.

Minister of Public Health, of the Environment, of the Civil Service and of the Armed Force, M. Emile Krieps.

Minister of Agriculture, of Viticulture and of Public Works, M. Jean Hamilius.

Minister of the Interior, M. Jos. Wohlfart.

Minister of Justice and of National Education, M. Robert Krieps.

State Secretaries, M. Maurice Thoss; M. Guy Linster; M. Albert Berchem.

EMBASSY AND CONSULATE
27 Wilton Crescent, S.W.1
[01–235 6961]

Ambassador Extraordinary and Plenipotentiary, His Excellency André Philippe, G.C.V.O. (1972).

A Grand Duchy in Western Europe, bounded by Germany, Belgium, and France. Established as an independent State under the sovereignty of the King of the Netherlands as Grand Duke by the Congress of Vienna in 1815, it formed part of the Germanic Confederation, 1815–66, and was included in the German " Zollverein ". In 1867 the Treaty of London declared it a neutral territory. On the death of the King of the Netherlands in 1890 it passed to the Duke of Nassau. The territory was invaded and overrun by the Germans at the beginning of the war in 1914, but was liberated in 1918. By the *Treaty of Versailles*, 1919, Germany renounced her former agreements with Luxemburg in respect of the customs union, etc., and in 1921 an economic union was made with Belgium (B.L.E.U.). The Grand Duchy was again invaded and occupied by Germany on May 10, 1940. The constitution of the Grand Duchy was modified on April 28, 1948, and the stipulation of permanent neutrality was then abandoned. Luxemburg is now a fully effective member of the Western association of powers and a signatory of the Brussels and North Atlantic Treaties. She is also a member of the European Communities.

Besides B.L.E.U., Luxemburg is also a member of the Belgium–Netherlands–Luxemburg Customs Union (Benelux, 1960). The Court of the European Communities has its seat in Luxemburg, as does the Secretariat of the European Parliament, the European Investment Bank and the European Monetary Co-operation fund.

The area is 1,000 square miles; the population (Jan. 1975) 357,300, nearly all Roman Catholics. There is a Chamber of 59 Deputies, elected by universal adult suffrage for 5 years. Legislation is submitted to the Council of State. The Grand Duchy is rich in iron-ore and possesses an important iron and steel industry with an annual productive capacity over 6,000,000 tons. Government revenue for 1975 was estimated at L.F. 30,510,318,000, expenditure L.F.30,781,613,000. The Luxemburg *franc* has at present the same value as the Belgian *franc* and the latter is legal tender in the Grand Duchy, Approximate Exchange Rate, 70 *Francs*= £1 (June 1, 1976). There are 170 miles of railway.

Trade with U.K.

	1972	1973
Imports from U.K.	£8,030,000	£8,580,000
Exports to U.K.	6,363,000	7,847,000

The capital, Luxemburg, pop. (1972), 78,300, is a dismantled fortress. The country is well wooded, with many deer and wild boar. The language is Letzeburgesch but French is the official language; all speak German and many English.

FLAG.—Three horizontal bands, red, white and blue. NATIONAL DAY.—June 23.

BRITISH EMBASSY
Luxemburg

Ambassador Extraordinary and Plenipotentiary, His Excellency Antony Arthur Acland, C.M.G. (1975).

1st Secretary and Consul, J. M. Crosby.

2nd Secretary, R. Kincher.

3rd Secretary and Vice Consul, W. F. Harris.

MADAGASCAR
(The Democratic Republic of Madagascar)

President, Capt. de Frégate Didier Ratsiraka.

CABINET
[Jan. 13, 1976]

Prime Minister, Defence, (vacant).

Interior, Lt.-Col. Mampila Joana.

Public Service and Labour, Dr. Marius Randranto.

Posts and Telecommunications, Rakotovao Andriantina.

Counsellor to the Presidency, Lucian M. X. Andrianarahirjaka.

Economy and Commerce, Justin Rarivoson.

Finance and Planning, Rakotovao Razakaboana.

Public Works, Radio Célestin.

National Education, Justin Rakotoniaina.
Rural Development, Pierre Rajyaonah.
Scientific Research, Dr. Rémi Tiandrazana.
Health, Dr. Jean-Jacques Séraphin.
Transport, Supply and Tourism, Evariste Vazaha.
Population and Social Conditions, George T. Indrian-jafy.
Justice, Ampy Porthos.
Youth, Christian R. Richard.
Foreign Affairs, Jean Bemananjara.
Art and Revolutionary Culture, Gaston Lahy.

Madagascar lies 240 miles off the east coast of Africa and is the fifth largest island in the world. It has an area of 228,000 sq. miles and a population of about 8,000,000. It became a French protectorate in 1895, and a French colony in 1896 when the former queen was exiled. Republican status was adopted on October 14, 1958. Independence was proclaimed on June 26, 1960, when agreements confirming Madagascar's membership of the French community and co-operation with France on defence, monetary, judicial, educational and other matters were signed.

Following demonstrations in Tananarive on May 13, 1972, the Parti Social Democrate (PSD) Government which had been in power since independence under Monsieur Tsiranana (President 1959–1972) was replaced by a military government under General Ramanantsoa who resigned in January 1975. His successor, Col. Ratsimandrava, was assassinated on February 11 after only 6 days in office. A mutiny in a police camp in the capital was put down with about 20 casualties. A Directoire Militaire under General Andriamahazo then took over and martial law was declared. The Directoire was replaced by a Supreme Council of the Revolution of 8 members of the armed forces under Capitaine de Frégate Didier Ratsiraka on June 15, 1975. Twelve civilian ministers whose activities are coordinated and directed by the Supreme Council were also appointed. The first act of the new Government was to nationalise insurance and banking.

Both houses of the Malagasy Parliament, and the activities of political parties were suspended.

In December 1975 a new constitution was approved in a referendum, and Lt. Cdr. Ratsiraka was appointed President.

Revised agreements with France were signed on June 4, 1973, providing for the withdrawal of the French forces stationed in the country since independence. The French naval base at Diégo Suarez has been turned into a civilian ship repair yard and French influence has been greatly reduced. Madagascar has also withdrawn from the Franc Zone and has announced a claim to the Islands of Juan de Nova, Glorieuses, Isle de l'Europe, Bassa da India and Tromelin which had remained integral parts of the French Republic after independence.

The people are of mixed Polynesian, Arab and Negro origin. The languages spoken are Malagasy and French. There are sizeable French, Chinese and Indian communities.

The island's economy is still almost wholly based on agriculture, which accounts for three-quarters of its exports. Development plans have placed emphasis on increasing agricultural and livestock production, the improvement of communications and the creation of small industries.

Total exports in 1973 amounted to FMG 44·7 million. The principal exports in order of value were coffee (25 per cent. of total), cloves (10 per cent.), vanilla, rice, meat and meat products, sugar and butter beans. Minerals exported include chrome ore, graphite and mica.

Total imports in 1973 amounted to FMG 45·1 million compared with FMG 51 million in 1972.

The main imports are manufactures, petroleum, fertilizers, cement and rice.

TRADE WITH U.K.

	1972	1973
Imports from U.K.	£817,000	£763,000
Exports to U.K.	1,213,000	1,902,000

The rate of exchange is about Malagasy francs (FMG) 460 = £1 (June 1975).

CAPITAL.—Tananarive (population about 400,000). Other main towns are the chief port Tamatave (55,000); Majunga (50,000); Fianarantsoa (47,000); Diégo Suarez (41,000).

FLAG.—Equal horizontal bands of red (above) and green, with vertical white band by staff.

NATIONAL DAY.—June 26 (Independence Day).

BRITISH EMBASSY
Ambassador Extraordinary and Plenipotentiary and Consul-General, His Excellency Mervyn Brown, C.M.G., O.B.E. (1975) (resides at Dar-es-Salaam).
1st Secretary and Consul, R. B. Hammond.
Commercial Officer and Vice-Consul, A. J. Marcelin.

THE MALDIVES

President, His Excellency Amir Ibrahim Nasir.

Area, etc.—The Maldives are a chain of cora atolls, some 400 miles to the south-west of Sri Lanka, stretching from just south of the equator for about 600 miles to the north. There are 12 clearly defined atolls, separated from each other by deep channels through which the currents run strongly. No point in the entire chain of islands is more than 8 feet above sea-level. The total number of islands is over 2,000, some being very small; about 220 of them are inhabited. The population of the islands (estimated, 1975) is 123,000. The people are Moslems and the Maldivian language is akin to Elu or old Sinhalese. They are highly civilized and are great navigators and traders.

Government.—The Maldives form a Republic which is elective. There is a Parliament (the Citizens' Majlis) with representatives elected from all the atolls. The life of the Majlis is 5 years. The Government consists of a Cabinet, which is responsible to the Majlis. By the agreement signed with the British Government in 1965, the Maldives form a composite sovereign and fully independent state, free to conduct their own external relations with other countries.

On March 6, 1975, the Prime Minister, Ahmed Zaki, was arrested and exiled, and presidential rule was imposed.

With the agreement of the Maldivian Government, the R.A.F. maintain a staging post on Gan Island, in Addu Atoll, the most southerly atoll, lying just south of the equator.

Production, etc.—The islands are thickly covered with coconut palms, and coir and ropes are exported. The principal industry is fishing and considerable quantities of fish are exported to Japan. Dried fish is exported to Sri Lanka, where it is a delicacy. The tourist industry is expanding very rapidly.

CAPITAL.—Malé (population, estimated 1970, 13,610). There is an air strip on Hulule Island about 1 mile from Malé.

FLAG.—Green field bearing a white crescent, with wide red border.

BRITISH REPRESENTATION
Ambassador Extraordinary and Plenipotentiary, His Excellency Harold Smedley, C.M.G., M.B.E. (1973) (concurrently British High Commissioner to Sri Lanka).

MALI
(Republic of Mali)

Chairman, National Liberation Committee, Col. Moussa Traore, *born* 1937, *assumed office* Nov. 20, 1968.

The Republic of Mali, an inland state in north-west Africa has an area of 465,000 square miles and a population (U.N. estimate, 1969) of 4,929,000.

Formerly the French colony of Soudan, the territory elected on Nov. 24, 1958, to remain as an autonomous republic within the French Community. It associated with Senegal in the Federation of Mali which was granted full independence on June 20, 1960. The Federation was effectively dissolved on August 22 by the secession of Senegal. The title of the Republic of Mali was adopted on Sept. 22, 1960. The Republic is no longer a member of the French Community. On July 1, 1962, a Mali *franc* equal in value to the *Franc CFA* was introduced and a new State bank set up. The *Franc Malien* now has a fixed rate of exchange of 2*FM* = 1 *CFA Franc*.

The *régime* of Modibo Keita was overthrown on Nov. 19, 1968, and the President arrested by a group of Army officers, who formed a National Liberation Committee and appointed a Prime Minister. Lieut. Traore assumed the functions of Head of State. A new civil constitution to come into being in 1979 was approved in a national referendum on June 21, 1974.

Mali's principal exports are groundnuts (raw and processed), cotton fibres, meat and dried fish. The principal rivers are the Niger and the Senegal. Goods to the value of £1,697,000 were imported from the United Kingdom in 1975 (1974 £1,436,000). Exports to U.K. 1975 £576,000 (1974 £2,505,000).

CAPITAL.—Bamako (170,000). Other towns are Gao, Kayes, Mopti, Sikasso and Segou (all regional capitals), and Timbuktu.

FLAG.—Vertical stripes of green (by staff), yellow and red. NATIONAL DAY.—September 22.

BRITISH EMBASSY

Ambassador Extraordinary and Plenipotentiary, His Excellency John Ernest Powell-Jones, C.M.G. (resident at *Dakar*).

MAURITANIA
(Islamic Republic of Mauritania)

President and Prime Minister, Moktar Ould Daddah, *assumed office* Nov. 28, 1958; *re-elected for 5 years*, 1966, 1971 and 1976.

Mauritania lies on the north-west coast of Africa immediately to the north of Senegal. It is bounded on the south and on the east by the Republic of Mali. To the north it is bounded by the territory formerly known as Spanish Sahara. (Mauritania and Morocco took possession of that territory in February 1976 when Spain formally relinquished all right to it and in April 1976 agreed on a new frontier dividing the territory between them). Area 419,000 sq. miles. The population was estimated at 1,200,000 in 1972. (For MAP, *see* p. 868.) The Republic of Mauritania elected on November 28, 1958, to remain within the French Community as an autonomous republic. It became fully independent on Nov. 28, 1960. In 1972 Mauritania broke with the franc zone and established its own unit of currency, the *Ougiya*, equal in value to 5 *francs CFA*. Mauritania's main source of potential wealth lies in rich deposits of iron ore around Fort Gouraud, in the north of the country. Exports began in 1963, via a railway laid for the purpose from the mine to the port of Nouadhibou. The deposits are being exploited under the aegis of the *Société Nationale Industrielle Miniere* following the nationalisation on November 28, 1974 of the internationally based company MIFERMA. There are copper deposits at Akjoujt which are being exploited by SOMIMA, a company which had an international base but was nationalised on Feb. 25, 1975.

	1974	1975
Imports from U.K.	£4,554,000	£3,950,000
Exports to U.K.	13,303,000	15,238,000

FLAG.—Yellow star and crescent on green ground
NATIONAL DAY.—November 28.
CAPITAL.—Nouakchott (30,000).

British Ambassador, His Excellency John Ernest Powell-Jones, C.M.G. (Resident at *Dakar*).

MEXICO
(Estados Unidos Mexicanos)

President (1976–82), Lic. José López Portillo, *born* 1916, *elected* July 4, 1976; *to assume office*, Dec. 1, 1976.

CABINET

Minister of the Interior, Lic. Mario Moya Palencia.
Foreign Affairs, Lic. Alfonso García Robles.
National Defence, Gen. Hermenegildo Cuenca Díaz.
Navy and Marine, Almirante C. G. Luís M. Bravo Carrera.
Finance, Lic. Mario Ramon Beteta Monsalve.
National Patrimony, Lic. Francisco Javier Alejo.
Industry and Commerce, Lic. José Campillo Sainz.
Agriculture and Livestock, Dr. Oscar Brauer Herrera.
Communcations and Transport, Ing. Eugenio Méndez Docurro.
Public Works, Ing. Luís Enriquez Bracamontes.
Hydraulic Resources, Ing. Leandro Rovirosa Wade.
Education, Ing. Victor Bravo Ahuja.
Labour and Social Affairs, Lic. Carlos Galvez Betancourt.
Secretariat of the Presidency, Lic. Ignacio Ovalle Fernández.
Agrarian Reform, Lic. Felix Barra García.
Federal District, Lic. Octavio Senties Gomez.
Health and Public Welfare, Dr. Ginés Navarro Díaz de León.
Attorney-General, Lic. Pedro Ojedo Paullada.
Tourism, Lic. Julio Hirschfield Almada.

MEXICAN EMBASSY IN LONDON
8 Halkin St. S.W.1
[01–235 6393]

Ambassador Extraordinary and Plenipotentiary, His Excellency Hugo B. Margain, G.C.V.O.
Minister-Counsellors, Sr. Donaciano Gonzalez Gomèz; Sr. Horacio Flores-Sánchez.

Consul-General, Sr. Mario Tapia Ponce.
Naval Attaché, Rear Adm. Carlos López Sotelo.
Counsellors, Sra. Francisca Celis-Campos, M.V.O.
(*Information*); Sr. Lic. Oliver Farrés (*Commercial*);
Sr. Lic. Andrés Rozental; Sr. Lic. José Gurría
Treviño; Sr. Lic. Guillermo Guevara Botello;
Sr. Manuel de Araoz, C.V.O.

Area and Population.—Mexico occupies the
southern part of the continent of North America,
with an extensive seaboard to both the Atlantic
and Pacific Oceans, extending from 14° 33′ to 32°
43′ N. lat. and 86° 46′ to 117° 08′ W. long., and
comprising one of the most varied zones in the
world. It contains 31 states and the federal district
of Mexico, making in all 32 political divisions,
covering an area of 761,604 square miles. At the
Mexican General Census taken on Jan. 28, 1970,
the total population was 48,313,000, but a present
day estimate is 61,000,000.

The two great ranges of North America, the
Sierra Nevada and Rocky Mountains, are prolonged from the north to a convergence towards
the narrowing Isthmus of Tehuantepec, their
course being parallel with the west and east coasts.
The surface of the interior consists of an elevated
plateau between the two ranges, with steep slopes
both to the Pacific and Atlantic (Gulf of Mexico).
In the west is the Peninsula of Lower California,
with a mountainous surface, separated from
the mainland by the Gulf of California. The
Sierra Nevada, known in Mexico as the *Sierra
Madre*, terminates in a transverse series of volcanic
peaks, from Colima on the west to Citlaltepetl
(" El Pico de Orizaba ") on the east. The low-
lying lands of the coasts form the *Tierra Caliente*,
or tropical regions (below 3,000 ft.), the higher
levels form the *Tierra Templada*, or temperate
region (from 3,000 to 6,000 ft.), and the summit
of the plateau with its peaks is known as *Tierra
Fria*, or cold region (above 6,000 ft.). The only
considerable rivers are the *Rio Grande del Norte*
which forms part of the northern boundary, and
is navigable for about 70 miles from its mouth
in the Gulf of Mexico, and the *Rio Grande de
Santiago*, the *Rio Balsas* and *Rio Papaloapan*. The
remaining streams are governed by the formation
of the land, and run in mountain torrents between
deep-cut cañons or " barrancas ". The largest
fresh-water lakes are *Chapala* (70 miles long and
20 miles wide), and *Pátzcuaro*. In the north-west
are saline lakes amid bare and dry regions. The
climate varies according to the altitude, the rainy
season lasting from June to October.

History and Archæology.—The present Mexico
and Guatemala were once the centre of a remarkable
indigenous civilization, which had unknown
beginnings in the centuries before Christ, flowered
in the periods from A.D. 500 to 1100 and A.D. 1300
to 1500 and collapsed before the little army of
Spanish adventurers under Hernán Cortés in the
years following 1519. Pre-Columbian Mexico
was divided between different but connected
Indian cultures, each of which has left distinctive
archæological remains: the best-known of these
are Chichén Itzá, Uxmal, Bonampak and Palenque,
in Yucatán and Chiapas (Maya); Teotihuacan,
renowned for the Pyramid of the Sun (216 feet
high) in the Valley of Mexico (Teotihuacáno);
Monte Albán and Mitla, near Oaxaca (Zapotec);
El Tajín in the State of Veracruz (Totonac); and
Tula in the State of Hidalgo (Toltec). The last and
most famous Indian culture of all, the Aztec, based
on Tenochitlán, suffered more than the others
from the Spaniards and only very few Aztec
monuments remain.

A few years after the Conquest, the Spaniards
built Mexico City on the ruins of Tenochitlán,
and appointed a Viceroy to rule their new dominions, which they called New Spain. The country
was largely converted to Christianity, and a
distinctive colonial civilization, representing a
marriage of Indian and Spanish traditions, developed
and flourished, notably in architecture and sculpture. In 1810 a revolt began against Spanish rule.
This was finally successful in 1821, when a precarious independence was proclaimed. Friction
with the United States in Texas led to the war of
1845–48, at the end of which Mexico was forced to
cede the northern provinces of Texas, California
and New Mexico. In 1862 Mexican insolvency led to
invasion by French forces which installed Archduke
Maximilian of Austria as Emperor. The empire
collapsed with the execution of the Emperor in 1867
and the austere reformer, Juárez, restored the
republic. Juárez's death was followed by the
dictatorship of Porfirio Diaz, which saw an
enormous increase of foreign, particularly British
and United States, investment in the country. In
1910 began the Mexican Revolution which reformed the social structure and the land system,
curbed the power of foreign companies and ushered
in the independent industrial Mexico of today.

Government.—Under the Constitution of Feb. 5,
1917 (as subsequently amended), Congress consists
of a Senate of 64 members, elected for six years,
and of a Chamber of Deputies, at present numbering
213, elected for three years. Presidents, who wield
full executive powers, are elected for six years;
they cannot be re-elected.

There are four political parties registered in
Mexico, of which by far the largest and most
influential is the *Part do Revolucionario Institucional*
(P.R.I.) which has for many years constituted the
governing party.

Communications.—Veracruz, Tampico and Coat-
zacoalcos are the chief ports on the Atlantic, and
Guaymas, Mazatlán, Puerto Lázaro Cárdenas,
Acapulco, Salina Cruz and Puerto Madero on the
Pacific. The total tonnage of registered merchant
marine in May, 1976, was 1,053,679 tons. There
were 25,864 kilometres of railway track open in
Mexico in 1974. Work is proceeding on the
reorganization, rehabilitation and re-equipment of
the whole system; help in this has been forthcoming
from the World Bank, the Export-Import Bank
and private sources in the United States. The railways were completely nationalised in 1970.

The total length of road at the end of 1974 was
175,540 kilometres, of which 53,140 were paved,

68,900 dressed and 53,500 gravelled. Mexico City may be reached by at least three excellent highways (with 14 entry points) from the United States, and work is complete on roads southward from Mexico City to Yucatán as well as on two principal highways to the Guatemalan border (with three entry points).

At the end of February 1976, the national telegraph system had a network of 58,215 kilometres. The total length of lines within the network was 220,422 kilometres. International telegraph services to the United States frontier are provided by the government-owned Mexican Telegraph Company and then through the United States to Canada and Europe.

Teléfonos de México, a state-controlled company, controls about 98 per cent. of all telephone services; there were slightly more than 3·5 million telephones in service in mid-1975 and installations are expanding at an annual rate of 15 per cent. In 1976 there were 9,708,000 kilometres of long distance lines. Satélite Latinoamericano, S.A. (SATELAT) is a joint government/private sector venture disseminating television programmes to Latin America through Intelstat IV satellite facilities leased by the Mexican Government.

There is a good national and international network of air services. There are 1,113 airports and landing fields in Mexico, of which eighteen are equipped to handle long-distance flights. There are 166 airline companies, including two of the major national airlines—*Mexicana de Aviación* and *Aeroméxico.* Passenger traffic is growing by about 18 per cent. yearly, while cargo increases by some 14 per cent. a year.

Production.—The principal agricultural crops are maize, beans, rice, wheat, sugar cane, coffee, cotton, tomatoes, chili, tobacco, chick-peas, groundnuts, sesame, alfalfa, vanilla, cocoa and many kinds of fruit, both tropical and temperate. The maguey, or Mexican cactus, yields several fermented drinks, mezcal and tequila (distilled) and pulque (undistilled). Another species of the same plant supplies sisal-hemp (henequen). The forests abound in mahogany, rosewood, ebony and chicle trees.

The volume of the fishing industry has grown from 187,922 tons in 1965 to 451,330 tons in 1975 for human consumption and 26,446 tons in 1965 to 157,795 tons in 1975 for industrial use.

The principal industries (apart from agriculture) are mining and petroleum, but during recent years there has been very considerable expansion of both light and heavy industries. The mining industry has shown a growth of 20 per cent. in two years. The steel industry has expanded rapidly and produced 5,077,000 tons of steel in 1975. The mineral wealth is great, and principal minerals are gold, silver, copper, lead, zinc, quicksilver, iron and sulphur. Substantial reserves of uranium have been found. Production in 1974 amounted to: gold, 4,182 kilograms; silver, 1,200 tons; lead, 218,021 metric tons. In the non-metals sector, Mexico continues to produce 25 per cent. of the world's supply of fluorspar with a yearly output of 1·1 million metric tons. Sulphur production rose 70·3 per cent. in 1973 and jumped an additional 44·3 per cent. in 1974 to a total of 2·32 million metric tons.

The total proven petroleum reserves were 7,000 million barrels in 1975. Crude oil production in 1975 was 39,403,000 cubic metres and current daily production is 895,000 barrels. Daily production of natural gas is 223,577 cubic metres. Oil reserves were increased substantially due to very important new discoveries in Tabasco and Chiapas

states. A new refinery at Tula, State of Hidalgo, is the nation's largest; and new refineries in Monterrey, State of Nuevo Leon, and Salina Cruz, State of Oaxaca, will be in operation by the end of 1977.

Paper production is growing about 9 per cent. per year and reached 1·2 million metric tons in 1974, but imports are still necessary to meet domestic demand.

Textile production is led by the artificial fibres sector, which is growing by about 9 per cent. each year, and produced 160,000 tons in 1974. The natural fibre textile industry has not registered dynamic growth in the past two years and continues to lose its share of the market to the synthetics, but is being re-structured to make it more efficient and competitive.

An indication of the rapid industrial expansion of Mexico is that output of electricity increased from 3,048 thousand kilowatts in 1960 to 9,629 thousand kilowatts in 1974. It is estimated that electric energy production increases by about 11 per cent. yearly and generating capacity will be at least 13·3 million killowatts by the end of 1976 and 15·7 million kilowatts in 1978.

Defence.—The regular army has a strength of 58 infantry battalions, one infantry brigade and a Presidential Guard of three battalions, 20 cavalry regiments, 3 parachute battalions and a small number of artillery and engineer units. There is also a conscript army of about 250,000 men organized into National Service divisions, each 6,000–7,000 strong. The Navy has some 60 ships of all kinds and the Air Force some 200 aircraft.

Language and Literature.—Spanish is the official language of Mexico and is spoken by about 95 per cent. of the population. In addition to Spanish, there are five basic groups of Indian languages spoken in Mexico. The 1970 Census showed that of the 3,111,415 inhabitants speaking an Indian language, 25·7 per cent. spoke Náhuatl; 14·6 per cent. Maya; 9·1 per cent Zapotec; 7·1 per cent. Otomí; 7·5 per cent. Mixtec and 36 per cent. one or other of the 59 dialects derived from these basic languages. The National Library in the capital contained 1,034,000 volumes in 1976 and has a yearly increment of 30,000 volumes. The Press of Mexico is in a flourishing condition with many daily newspapers in the capital and in other urban centres. The first printing press and the first regularly issued newspaper in the New World were established by the Spaniards in Mexico City.

Education.—Education is divided into primary, secondary, preparatory and university. Primary education is free, secular and nominally compulsory. Total school population at all levels rose to 16,000,000 in 1975–76, from 11,500,000 in 1970–71. There were 53,489 kindergarten and primary schools in 1974–75 and 12,700,000 pupils at these levels at the end of 1975; 5,900 secondary schools with an estimated 2,024,042 pupils in 1976. Preparatory, vocational and technical schools in 1974–75 numbered 1,326 with 590,089 students, while there were 299 teacher training colleges with 89,865 students and 507 professional schools, including universities, with 452,000 students.

The National Autonomous University of Mexico (1533) had 238,300 students in 1975. In 1975, illiteracy had fallen to 10·5 per cent. of the population above 6 years of age from 21 per cent. in 1965. Between 1971 and 1976, the number of schools increased by 137 per cent. and the number of pupils by 38 per cent.

The prevailing religion is Roman Catholic.

Finance. (Pesos).

The proposed budget expenditure for 1976 amounts to 392,389,000,000 pesos, 209,510,000,000 from the Federal Government and 182,879,000,000

from the decentralised agencies. 29·7 per cent. is allotted to the industrial sector, 22·9 per cent. to social welfare programmes, 20 per cent. to agricultural development, 16·8 per cent. to general administrative expenses, 10·2 per cent. to transportation and communication projects. It was record budget and represented a 10 per cent. increase over the 1975 budget.

As from April 19, 1954, by agreement with the International Monetary Fund, the Rate of Exchange has been fixed at 12·50 pesos = 1 $U.S. (See also p. 84).

	1975
Total Imports	Pesos 82,251,950,000
Total Exports	Pesos 35,732,810,000

Trade with U.K.

	1974	1975
Imports from U.K.	£60,012,000	£111,734,000
Exports to U.K.	17,868,000	10,889,000

Imports consist largely of machinery and implements for industry, mining and agriculture, and raw materials for industry. Principal exports are cotton, coffee, sisal (henequen), sugar, tomatoes and shrimps, lead, silver, zinc and other metals, tobacco, sulphur and heavy fuel oil.

CAPITAL.—Mexico City, est. pop. 1976–77 8,941,912; metropolitan area 12,578,420. Other cities (est. pop. 1976–77) are: Guadalajara (1,725,107); Monterrey (1,350,000); Ciudad Juárez (570,401); León (557,030); Puebla (516,197); Mexicali (360,556); Chihuahua (386,645); San Luis Potosi (303,571); and Mérida (250,206).

FLAG.—Three vertical bands in green, white, red, with the Mexican emblem (an eagle on a cactus devouring a snake) in the centre.

NATIONAL DAY.— September 16 (Proclamation of Independence).

BRITISH EMBASSY

(Calle Río Lerma 71, Colonia Cuauhtémoc, Mexico 5, D.F.)

Ambassador Extraordinary and Plenipotentiary, His Excellency Sir John Edgar Galsworthy, K.C.V.O., C.M.G. (1972).

Counsellors, A. J. Payne; I. P. Allnutt, O.B.E. (*Cultural*).

Defence, Naval, Military and Air Attaché, Lt.-Col. B. D. O. Smith, M.V.O.

1st Secretaries, P. J. Streams (*Head of Chancery*); E. V. Nelson, M.V.O. (*Information*); P. G. Harborne (*Commercial*); Dr. I. Baker (*Scientific*).

2nd Secretaries, A. C. W. Culbert (*Consul*); M. J. Peart; A. S. Green, M.V.O. (*Administration*); P. J. Smith (*Commercial*); G. Thomas (*Cultural*).

Assistant Information Officer, Mrs. M. Jolly.

Vice-Consul, A. D. Morales.

There are British Consular Offices at *Mexico City*, *Guadalajara*, *Acapulco*, *Mérida*, *Monterrey*, *Tampico* and *Veracruz*.

British Council Representative.—I. P. Allnutt, O.B.E., Calle M. Antonio Caso 127, Mexico 4, D.F.

BRITISH CHAMBER OF COMMERCE, Calle Tiber 103, 6th Floor, Mexico 5, D.F.—*Manager*, T. D. Thornton.

Transit from London to Mexico City:—By air, 13 hours; By sea, U.K.–New York, 5 to 10 days; New York–Mexico City, by rail, 3 days; by air, 4 hours. There is a direct freight service from Liverpool to ports on both the Mexican Gulf and the Pacific Coast.

MONACO
(Principauté de Monaco)

Sovereign Prince, H.S.H. Rainier III–Louis–Henri–Maxence Bertrand, *born* May 31, 1923, *succeeded*

his grandfather (H.S.H. Prince Louis II), May 9, 1949; *married* April 19, 1956, Miss Grace Patricia Kelly and has issue Prince Albert Alexandre Louis Pierre, *born* March 14, 1958, Princess Caroline Louise Marguerite, *born* January 23, 1957; and Princess Stephanie Marie Elisabeth, *born* Feb. 1, 1965.

President of the Crown Council, M. Pierre Blanchy.

President of the National Council, M. Auguste Medecin.

Minister of State, André Saint-Mleux, *appointed* 1972.

CONSULATE-GENERAL IN LONDON
4 Audley Square, W.1
[01-629 0734]

Consul-General, I. S. Ivanović.

Consul, A. J. Hucker, 3 Gray's Inn Square, W.C.1 [01-242 5323].

A small Principality on the Mediterranean, with land frontiers joining France at every point, and consisting of the old town of Monaco, La Condamine, and Monte Carlo, where is the famous casino. The Principality comprises a narrow strip of country about 2 miles long (area approx. 467 acres), with 24,500 inhabitants (est. 1975) and a yearly average of over 600,000 visitors. The whole available ground is built over, so that there is no cultivation, though there are some notable public and private gardens. Monaco has a small harbour (30 ft. alongside quay) and the import duties are the same as in France. The National Council consists of 18 members and the Council of Government of the Minister of State, as President, and three State Counsellors. There is a local police force of 160 men.

A new constitution was promulgated by Prince Rainier on Dec. 17, 1962, which is subject to modification only with the approval of the elected National Council. It maintains the traditional hereditary monarchy and gives guarantees for the right of association, trade union freedom and the right to strike.

CAPITAL.—Monaco-viller (2,422).

FLAG.—Two equal horizontal stripes, red over white.

H.M. Consul-General, D. J. Swan, M.V.O. (*Resident at Marseilles*).

(OUTER) MONGOLIA
(Mongolian People's Republic—
Bugd Nairamdakh Mongol Ard Uls)

President: Yu Tsedenbal.

Prime Minister: J. Batmounkh.

Mongolian People's Revolutionary
(= Communist) Party

Politbureau of the Central Committee, Yu Tsedenbal; J. Batmounkh; N. Jagvaral; S. Jalan-Aajav; N. Luvsanravdan; D. Maydar; D. Molomjamts; T. Ragchaa (*full members*); B. Altangerel; D. Gombojav (*deputy members*).

Secretariat of the Central Committee, Yu Tsedenbal (*1st*); D. Molomjamts; N. Jagvaral; S. Jalan-Aajav; D. Chimidorj.

MONGOLIAN EMBASSY
7 Kensington Court, W.8
[01-937 0150]

Ambassador Extraordinary and Plenipotentiary, His Excellency Denzengiin Tserendondov (1973).

Area and Population.—The Mongolian People's Republic (Outer Mongolia) is a large and sparsely populated country to the north of China. Its area is over 600,000 square miles. Its population, 1976 is about 1,450,000. However, this total

constitutes only part of the Mongolians of Asia, a number of whom are to be found in China and in the neighbouring regions of the Soviet Union (especially the Mongolian Buryat Autonomous Region). This country, which is almost nowhere below 1,000 feet above sea level, forms part of the Central Asiatic Plateau and rises towards the west in the high mountains of the Mongolian Altai and Khanggai Ranges. The Khentai Mountain Range, situated to the north-east of the capital Ulan Bator, is less high. The Gobi region covers the southern half of the country. It contains some sand deserts, but between these less hospitable areas there is steppe land which provides pasture for great numbers of cattle, sheep, goats, camels and horses (the latter is still the characteristic means of transport for the population). There are several long rivers and many lakes, but good water is scarce since much of the water is salty. The climate is hard, with a short mild summer giving way to a long winter when temperatures can drop as low as minus 50° Centigrade.

History.—Mongolia, under Genghis Khan the conqueror of China and much of Asia, was for many years a buffer state between Tsarist Russia and China, although it was under general Chinese suzerainty. The outbreak of the Chinese Revolution in 1911 was the signal for a declaration of independence which was confirmed by the Sino-Russian Treaty of Kiakhta (1915), but cancelled by a unilateral Chinese declaration in 1919. Later the country became a battleground of the Russian Civil War, and Soviet and Mongolian troops occupied Ulan Bator in 1921: this was followed by another declaration of independence. However, in 1924 the Soviet Union in a Treaty with China again recognized the latter's sovereignty over Mongolia; but this was never properly exercised because of China's pre-occupation with internal affairs, and later by the anti-Japanese war. The Mongolian People's Republic was formally established in 1924. Under the Yalta Agreement, Chiang Kai-shek agreed to a plebiscite, held in 1945, in which the Mongolians declared their desire for independence; this was granted. The country entered the United Nations in 1961. The heroes of Mongolian history during the earlier part of the century were Sukhebator, who died in 1923, and the Communist Choibalsang (died 1952), who did much to turn the country into the Communist state it is today, and carried out a systematic destruction of the power of the Lamas and the old princely houses which had previously been the dominant force in both the economy and the government.

Production, etc.—The total of Mongolia's livestock was planned to reach 25 million in 1975. Traditionally the Mongolian is a herdsman, tending his flock of sheep, goats and horses, cows and camels and leading a totally nomadic life. With the coming of the Communist régime (under the Mongolian People's Revolutionary Party) and especially since 1952, great efforts have been made to settle the population, but a large proportion still live nomadically or semi-nomadically in the traditional *ger* (circular tent). The pastoral population was collectivized at the end of the 1950s into huge *negdels* (co-operatives) and State farms which have hastened the process of settlement, but within these the herdsmen and their families still move with their *gers* from pasture to pasture as the seasons change. The country, except for the capital, is today divided into 18 *aimaks* (provinces) and beneath these into 259 *somons* (counties), and these form the basis of the State organization of the country, parallel with which runs the apparatus of the Revolutionary Party.

Membership of the Communist bloc has brought Mongolia considerable quantities of aid from other Socialist countries, especially the Soviet Union and China, both of which supplied many thousands of workers to help with various construction projects. Mongolia's support of the Soviet Union in the Sino-Soviet dispute resulted in the cessation of Chinese aid and a halt in the supply of Chinese workers. Mongolia is now relying on eastern European, especially Czech, Polish and East German aid to supplement the massive assistance from the Soviet Union. Soviet and Bloc aid is hastening the process of industrialization; for although the economy remains based on the herds of animals, and the principal exports of the country are still animal by-products (especially wool, hides and furs) and cattle, factories serving the needs of the country have been started up and the coal and electricity industries are being developed to provide an industrial base. A joint Mongolian/Soviet enterprise for copper and molybdenum mining has been started in northern Mongolia. In 1976 a major geological survey is being carried out by the CMEA countries, in order to prepare for the extraction of the considerable mineral deposits known to exist in Mongolia. Coal production is expected to rise to 4·5–4·9 million tons by 1980.

Ulan Bator, which contains a quarter of the country's population, is the main seat of industry. Under the third 5-year plan, a new industrial centre was founded at Darkhan, north of the capital near the Soviet frontier. This was being continued in the fourth 5-year plan (1966–70), and a start has been made with the development of Choibalsan in the east as a third industrial town (mostly for the processing of animal and agricultural products). Agriculture, formerly little practised, is now being extended. By the end of the sixth 5-year plan (1976–80), total cereal production is expected to be 500,000 to 530,000 tons. Communication is still difficult in the country as there are virtually no roads. The trans-Mongolian railway, following the line of the old north-south trade route, was opened in 1955 and links Mongolia with both China and Russia. Mongolia's fundamental difficulty is its very small population and labour force.

Foreign trade is dominated by the Soviet Union, with the eastern European countries taking most of what is left. Trade with western countries is developing slowly.

CAPITAL.—Ulan Bator. (Pop. 334,000.)
FLAG.—Vertical tri-colour red, blue, red and in the hoist the traditional Soyombo symbol in gold.
NATIONAL DAY.—July 11 (Anniversary of the Mongolian People's Republic).

BRITISH EMBASSY
Ulan Bator
Ambassador Extraordinary and Plenipotentiary, His Excellency Myles Walker Ponsonby, C.B.E. (1974)
3rd Secretary, J. D. Clark, M.B.E.
Attachés, K. McWilliam; J. N. C. Church.

MOROCCO
(Kingdom of Morocco)
King, H.M. King Hassan II, *born* July 9, 1929; *acceded* February 26, 1961, *on the death of his father*, King Mohammad V. Heir, Crown Prince Sidi Muhammad, *b.* August 21, 1963.

CABINET
(April 1974)
Prime Minister, Ahmed Osman.
Cultural Affairs, Hadj M'Hamed Bahnini.
Co-operation and Training of Cadres, Dr. Mohamed Benhima.

Foreign Affairs, Dr. Ahmed Laraki.
Information, Ahmed Taibi Benhima.
Justice, Abbas El Kissi.
Interior, Mohamed Haddou Echiguer.
Religious Endowments and Islamic Affairs, Dey Ould Sidi Baba.
Posts, Telegraphs and Telephones, Gen. Driss Ben Omar el Alami.
Finance, Abdelkader Benslimane.
Agriculture and Agrarian Reform, Salah M'Zily.
Urbanism, Housing, Tourism and the Environment, Hassan Zemmouri.
Administrative Affairs and Secretary General of the Government, M'Hamed Benyakhlef.
Public Health, Dr. Abolerrahman Touhami.
Commerce, Industry, Mines and Merchant Marine, Abdellatif Ghissassi.
Public Works and Communications, Ahmed Tazi.
Higher Education, Abdellatif Ben Abdeljalil.
Primary and Secondary Education, Mohamed Bouamoud.
Labour and Social Affairs, Mohamed Larbi el Khattabi.
Secretaries of State, Abdallah Gharnit (*National Co-operation and Traditional Industry*: Kamal Raghaye (*Finance*); Abdeslam Znined (*General and Saharan Affairs*); Mohamed Belkhayat (*Economic Affairs*); Tayeb Bencheikh (*Planning and Regional Development*); Dr. Mohamed Tahiri Jotti (*Youth and Sports*); Driss Basri (*Interior*); Jalal Said (*Urbanism, Housing, Tourism and Environment*); Hassan Loukach (*Religious Endowments and Islamic Affairs*); Moussa Saadi (*Commerce, Industry, Mines and Merchant Marine*); Moulay Ahmed Cherkaoui (*Foreign Affairs*).

ROYAL MOROCCAN EMBASSY AND CONSULATE
49 Queen's Gate Gardens, S.W.7
[01–584 8827]

Ambassador Extraordinary and Plenipotentiary, His Excellency M. Abdellah Chorfi.
Military, Naval and Air Attaché, Col. Ahmed Benomar Sbay.

Area and Population.—Morocco is situated in the north-western corner of the African continent between latitude 27° 40'–36° N. and longitude 1°–13° W. with an area estimated at approximately 180,000 sq. miles, and a population (1971) of 15,379,259. It is traversed in the north by the Riff Mountains and in a general S.W. to N.E. direction, by the Middle Atlas, the High Atlas, the Anti-Atlas and the Sarrho ranges. The northern flanks of the Middle and High Atlas Mountains are well wooded but their southern slopes, exposed to the dry desert winds, are generally arid and desolate, as are the whole of the Anti-Atlas and Sarrho ranges. The north-westerly point of Morocco is the peninsula of Tangier which is separated from the continent of Europe by the narrow strait of Gibraltar. The Jebel Mousa dominates the promontory and, with the rocky eminence of Gibraltar, was known to the ancients as the *Pillars of Hercules*, the western gateway of the Mediterranean.

Climate.—The climate of Morocco is generally good and healthy, especially on the Atlantic coast, (where a high degree of humidity is, however, prevalent) the country being partially sheltered by the Atlas mountains from the hot winds of the Sahara. The rainy season may last from November to April. The plains of the interior are intensely hot in summer. Average summer and winter temperatures for Rabat are 81° F. and 45° F.; for Marrakesh 101° F. and 40° F. respectively.

Government.—Morocco became an independent sovereign state in 1956, following joint declarations made with France on March 2, 1956, and with

Spain on April 7, 1956. The Sultan of Morocco, Sidi Mohammad ben Youssef, adopted the title of King Mohammad V.

A constitution, adopted by referendum on December 7, 1962, was in force from December 14, 1962, until June 7, 1965.

Following serious disturbances in Casablanca in March, 1965, attempts were made by King Hassan, in consultation with all political parties, to form a government of national union. These efforts were unsuccessful and on June 7, 1965, the King proclaimed a " state of exception " and suspended Parliament. Assuming himself the office of Prime Minister, he announced the formation of a new government and indicated that constitutional changes were to follow. A revised Constitution was approved by a national referendum on July 24, 1970 and brought into effect soon after. It was superseded by another constitution, also approved by a national referendum, on March 1, 1972. This provides that not only political parties, but trade unions, chambers of commerce and professional bodies will participate in the organization of the State and representation of the people; specifies that the King is the supreme representative of the people; makes changes in the composition of the Regency Council and the Sovereign's rights; establishes a unicameral legislature in which members' tenure of office is six years. The new Chamber is to have 240 members, 180 elected by direct universal suffrage and 60 members elected by electoral colleges representing local government, industry, agriculture and working class groups. However the election expected in April 1973 did not take place. Parliamentary elections have now been promised for early 1977, so that Parliament will be able to meet in April 1977.

Defence.—The Moroccan army, formed in 1956, is about 50,000 strong. A Moroccan air force was formed in 1959 and a navy in 1960. The armed forces possess quantities of French, Soviet and American equipment, including aircraft.

Production and Trade.—Morocco's main sources of wealth are agricultural and mineral. The current Five Year Plan (1973–77) for economic development places particular emphasis on social improvement. Other priority sectors are industrial development, agriculture and tourism.

Agriculture employs more than 70 per cent. of the working population and accounts for about 40 per cent. of Morocco's exports. The main agricultural products are cereals, citrus fruits, olives, grapes, tomatoes and vegetables. Dates and figs are

also grown and exported. Cork and wood-pulp are the most important commercial forest products. Esparto grass is also produced. There is a fishing industry and substantial quantities of canned fish, mainly sardines, are exported. Livestock in 1972 included about 11,900,000 sheep, 4,600,000 goats, 2,785,000 horned cattle and smaller numbers of donkeys, camels, horses and pigs.

Morocco's mineral exports are phosphates, anthracite, manganese, iron ore, lead and zinc, while the following are also produced: petroleum, cobalt, graphite, copper, molybdenum, tin, antimony, ochre and gypsum. Production of phosphates totalled 17,800,000 tons in 1975. There are oil refineries at Mohammedia and Sidi Kacem, and oil sold in Morocco in 1975 amounted to 2,270,117 cu. metres. Production of crude oil in 1974 amounted to 25,159 tons.

Morocco's main import requirements are petroleum products, motor vehicles and tyres, building materials, fabrics, agricultural and other machinery, chemical products, clothing, household-ware, sugar, green tea and other foodstuffs.

The trade of Morocco, which is chiefly with France, the U.S.A., W. Germany, Italy, the United Kingdom and Spain, was valued in 1974 at Imports, DH 4,683,587,000; Exports, DH 3,745,948,000 (both involving very small variations on 1973).

Trade with U.K.

	1974	1975
Imports from U.K....	£28,127,000	£35,500,000
Exports to U.K.......	52,506,000	51,900,000

There is a British Chamber of Commerce at Casablanca (c/o B.B.M.E., 80 Avenue Lalla Yacout).

Finance and Currency.—The unit of currency is the *dirham*. Exchange rate (*see* p. 84).

The 1976 Ordinary Budget amounted to DH 8,213,000,000 (1975: DH 8,849,000,000).

Communications.—The railway runs south from Tangier to Sidi Kacem. From this junction, one line runs eastwards through Fez and Oujda to Algeria, and another continues southwards, through Rabat and Casablanca, to Marrakesh. A line running due south from Oujda skirts the Morocco-Algeria frontier and reaches Colomb-Bechar in Algeria, the beginning of the Mediterranean–Niger project. Moroccan railroads cover 1,250 miles and traction is electric or diesel. An extensive network of well-surfaced roads covers all the main towns in the kingdom.

Tangier is distant from London about 1,200 miles or a matter of hours by air, 4 days by sea. Royal-Air-Maroc and British Caledonian Airways operate services between Casablanca and London. There are air services between Tangier, Agadir, Marrakesh (seasonal) and London, and also between Tangier and Gibraltar connecting with London. Royal Air Inter operates internal services. There are also regular services by many airlines with many parts of the world.

Language.—Arabic is the official language. Berber is the vernacular mainly in the mountain regions. French and Spanish are also spoken, mainly in the towns. The foreign population is estimated at 112,000 (1971). The national daily press consists of 3 Arabic and 4 French newspapers.

Education.—There are government primary, secondary and technical schools. At Fez there is a theological university of great repute in the Moslem world. There is a secular university at Rabat. Schools for special denominations, Jewish and Catholic, are permitted and may receive government grants.

CAPITAL.— Ψ Rabat (population 565,000). The other chief towns are: Ψ Casablanca (1,638,000);

Marrakesh (407,000); Fez (399,000); Meknes (376,000); Oujda (323,000); Tetuan (285,000). Ψ Tangier (187,894), Ψ Kenitra (139,105). The towns of Fez, Marrakesh and Meknes were capitals at various times in Morocco's history.

FLAG.—Red, with green pentagram (the Seal of Solomon). NATIONAL DAY.—March 3 (Anniversary of the Throne).

BRITISH EMBASSY
Rabat

Ambassador Extraordinary and Plenipotentiary, His Excellency John Spenser Ritchie Duncan, C.M.G., M.B.E. (1975).

1st Secretary, P. K. Williams (*Head of Chancery and Consul*).

Defence Attaché, Lt.-Col. J. R. Nias.

2nd Secretaries, Mrs. A. Massouh, M.B.E.; C. P. M. Griffith.

Vice-Consul, J. S. Taylor.

BRITISH CONSULAR OFFICES

There are British Consular Offices at *Tangier* and *Casablanca*.

British Council Representative, W. E. N. Kensdale, P.O. Box 427, 6 Avenue Moulay Youssef, Rabat.

MOZAMBIQUE
(Moçambique)

President, Samora Moises Machel.

Area and Population.—The People's Republic of Mozambique lies on the east coast of Africa, and is bounded by South Africa in the south and west, Rhodesia in the west, Zambia and Malawi in the north-west and Tanzania in the north. It has an area of 297,657 square miles, with a population (census 1970) of 8,233,834.

Government.—Mozambique, discovered by Vasco da Gama in 1498, and colonized by Portugal in 1505, achieved complete independence from Portugal on June 25, 1975. The date had been agreed in September 1974 by Portugal and *Frelimo*, (*Frente da Libertação de Moçambique*) the Marxist liberation movement. A transitional government, containing Portuguese and *Frelimo* elements, had been sworn in on Sept. 20, 1974.

A constitution was published on June 25, 1975, which stated, *inter alia*, that the President of *Frelimo* would be President of the People's Republic of Mozambique, and head of state. The legislative body would be the People's Assembly, consisting of 210 members.

It was announced that the basis of the economy would be collectivised agriculture. Main exports are sugar, cashew nuts, copra, cotton, tea and sisal.

CAPITAL.— Ψ Maputo (pop. 441,363). Other main ports are Beira and Nacala.

FLAG.—Red, green, black and yellow diagonals, divided by white stripes; motif in top left-hand corner of a rifle crossed with a hoe, on a book inside a cog-wheel.

BRITISH EMBASSY

Av. Augusto Castilho, 310, Maputo.

Ambassador Extraordinary and Plenipotentiary, His Excellency John Henry Lewen (1975).

2nd Secretaries, C. R. L. de Chassiron; A. Vittery.

3rd Secretary, J. E. Kingsbury, M.B.E., B.E.M.

(NEJD. *See* Saudi Arabia)

NEPAL

Sovereign, King Birendra Bir Bikram Shah Deva, born 1945; *succeeded* January 31, 1972; *crowned* Feb. 24, 1975.

COUNCIL OF MINISTERS

Prime Minister and Minister for Private Affairs and Defence, Dr. Tulsi Giri.
Food, Agriculture and Irrigation, and Land Reforms, Khadga Bahadur Singh.
Foreign Affairs, Krishna Raj Aryal.
Home Affairs and Panchayat, Bhoj Raj Ghimire.
Law and Justice and Communications, Jog Meher Shrestha.
Finance and General Administration, Dr. Bhekh Bahadur Thapa.
Ministers of State.—Harischandra Mahat (*Water and Electricity*); Mrs. Sushila Thapa (*Health*); Balaram Gharti Magar (*Works and Transport*); Bola Nath Jha (*Forests*); Dr. Harka Bahadur Gurung (*Industry and Commerce and Education*).
There are also four Assistant Ministers.

ROYAL NEPALESE EMBASSY IN LONDON
12A, Kensington Palace Gardens, W.8.
[01-229 6231]
Ambassador Extraordinary and Plenipotentiary, His Excellency The Rt. Hon. General Kiran Shumshere J. B. Rana, K.C.V.O., K.B.E. (1974).
1st Secretary, Bhanu Prasad Thapliya.
Military Attaché, Lt.-Col. Madan Krishna Kharel.
Attaché, Khadga Bahadur Khadka.

Nepal lies between India and Tibet on the slopes of the Himalayas, and includes Mt. Everest (29,028 ft.). It has a total area of 54,362 sq. miles and a population (1971 census) of 11,289,000. Amid the mountains lie many fertile valleys. The lower hills and Terai Plains are covered with jungle, in which wild animals abound. Rice, wheat, maize, etc., are grown. (*For* MAP, *see* p. 744.) Kathmandu, the capital, is connected with India by a road, the mountain section of which was built by India under the Colombo Plan, and to Tibet by a road from Kathmandu to Kodari on the border, which was built by the Chinese and opened on May 26, 1967. The Indian-aided Sunauli Pokhara road (128 miles) was inaugurated in April, 1972, and construction by the Chinese of a road between Kathmandu and Pokhara was opened in 1973. The East–West Highway (*Mahendra Raj Marg*) to run the length of the country, is now under construction. The road is complete from the Eastern border to Butwal except for two major bridges (which will restrict traffic during the monsoon). Work is in progress from Butwal westwards. Sections of the highway have been, or are being built, with aid from India, Great Britain, U.S.S.R., America and the Asian Development Bank.

Nepal exports rice and other grains, hides, oilseeds, *ghi*, cattle, jute, large quantities of timber, etc., and imports cotton goods and yarn, sugar, salt, spices, petrol, metals, etc. Nepalese imports from U.K. were valued at £1,485,000 in 1974 (1973, £1,532,000); exports to U.K., £452,400 (1973, £221,000).

Finance.—Revenue for the fiscal year 1975–76, mainly from land rent and taxes, is estimated at *N.Rs.*2,146,900,000. A State Bank was inaugurated on April 26, 1956, to issue bank notes, regulate the Nepalese currency, fix foreign exchange rates and help in the preparation of a national budget. Since the sterling pound was floated, the exchange rate has fluctuated. On June 23, 1976, it was *NRs.*22·10 Buying Rate and *NRs.*22·60 Selling Rate= £1. There are three commercial banks with branches throughout Nepal.

The inhabitants are of mixed stock with Mongolian characteristics prevailing in the north and Indian in the south, and their religions are Hinduism and Buddhism. They were originally divided into numerous hill clans and petty principalities, one of which, Gorkha, whose ruler founded the present Nepalese dynasty, became predominant in 1768.

During the 1914–18 and the 1939–45 wars, the Nepalese Government rendered unstinted and unconditional assistance to the British Government.

From the middle of the nineteenth century, Nepal was ruled by the Rana family which provided the hereditary prime ministers of the country. After the Second World War, a revolutionary movement in 1950 and 1951 achieved the aim of breaking the hereditary power of the Ranas and of restoring to the monarchy the powers which it had lost 104 years before. After ten years, during which various parties and individuals tried their hand at government, the late King Mahendra resumed direct powers on December 16, 1960, with the object of leading a united country to basic democracy.

The state of emergency ended on April 13, 1963, the King appointing a Cabinet consisting of a Prime Minister and seven other ministers, all of whom have seats in the indirectly elected *Rastriya Panchayat* (Parliament). A State Council (*Raj Sabha*) of 69 members, to advise the King on state affairs, constitutional matters and on the choice of the heir to the throne was also appointed on April 2, 1963. An Act was passed at the same time maintaining the existing ban on political parties.

CAPITAL.—Kathmandu, population (1971) 353,756. Other towns of importance are Morang (301,557), Lalitpur (154,998) and Bhaktapur (110,157). These population figures include some adjacent rural areas.

FLAG.—Double pennant of crimson with blue border on peaks; white moon with rays in centre of top peak; white quarter sun, recumbent in centre of bottom peak. NATIONAL DAY.—February 18.

BRITISH EMBASSY
Ambassador Extraordinary and Plenipotentiary, His Excellency Michael Scott, M.V.O. (1974).
1st Secretaries, R. E. Holloway (*Head of Chancery and Consul*); D. A. Spain, O.B.E. (*Aid*).
Defence Attaché, Lt.-Col. P. T. Bowring.
2nd Secretary, M. H. Connor.
Vice-Consul, P. H. Chase.

British Council Representative, D. M. Waterhouse, P.O.Box 640, Kanti Path, Kathmandu.

NETHERLANDS (or HOLLAND)
(Koninkrijk der Nederlanden)
Queen of the Netherlands, Her Majesty JULIANA, K.G., *born* April 30, 1909; *married* January 7, 1937, Prince Bernhard of Lippe-Biesterfeld, G.C.B., G.C.V.O., G.B.E. (THE PRINCE OF THE NETHERLANDS), *born* June 29, 1911; *succeeded*, September 4, 1948, upon the abdication of her mother Queen Wilhelmina who died Nov. 28, 1962. Issue:
(1) H.R.H. Princess Beatrix Wilhelmina Armgard, G.C.V.O., *born* Jan. 31, 1938; *married* March 10, 1966, H.R.H. Prince Claus George Willem Otto Frederik Geert of the Netherlands, Jonkheer van Amsberg; and has issue, Prince Willem Alexander, *b.* April 27, 1967; Prince Johan Friso, *b.* Sept. 25, 1968; Prince Constantijn Christof, *b.* Oct. 11, 1969.
(2) H.R.H. Princess Irene Emma Elisabeth, *born* Aug. 5, 1939; *married* April 29, 1964, Prince Carlos Hugo of Bourbon-Parma and has issue, Prince Carlos, *b.* Jan. 27, 1970; Princess Margarita and Prince Jaime, *b.* Oct. 13, 1972; and Princess Maria Carolina Christina, *b.* June 23, 1974.
(3) H.R.H. Princess Margriet Francisca, *born* (at Ottawa, Canada), Jan. 19, 1943; *married* Jan. 10, 1967, Mr. Pieter van Vollenhoven;

and has issue, Prince Maurits, *b.* April 17, 1968; and Prince Bernhard, *b.* Dec. 25, 1969; and Prince Pieter-Christiaan, *b.* March 22, 1972; and Prince Floris, *b.* April 10, 1975.

(4) H.R.H. Princess Maria Christina, *born* Feb. 18, 1947. married June, 28, 1975, Jorge Guillermo.

CABINET

Prime Minister and Minister of General Affairs, J. M. den Uyl (*Labour*).

Deputy Prime Minister and Minister of Justice, A. A. M. van Agt (*Catholic*).

Foreign Affairs, M. van der Stoel (*Labour*).

Home Affairs, W. F. de Gaay Fortman (*Anti-Revolutionary*).

Education and Sciences, J. A. van Kemenade (*Labour*).

Finance, W. F. Duisenberg (*Labour*).

Defence, H. Vredeling (*Labour*).

Housing and Planning, J. P. A. Gruijters (*Democrats '66*).

Transport and Waterways, T. E. Westerterp (*Catholic*).

Economic Affairs, R. F. M. Lubbers (*Catholic*).

Agriculture and Fisheries, A. P. J. J. M. van der Stee (*Catholic*).

Social Affairs, J. Boersma (*Anti-Revolutionary*).

Culture, Recreation and Social Welfare, H. W. van Doorn (*Radical*).

Public Health and Environment, Mrs I. Vorrink (*Labour*).

Development Co-operation, J. P. Pronk (*Labour*).

Without Portfolio in charge of Science Policy, F. H. P. Trip (*Radical*).

NETHERLANDS EMBASSY IN LONDON
38 Hyde Park Gate, S.W.7
[01-584 5040]

Ambassador Extraordinary and Plenipotentiary, His Excellency Robbert Fack (1976).

Ministers Plenipotentiary, H. T. Schaapveld; C. H. A. Plug.

Counsellors, A. U. W. van Werven; A. P. van Walsum; D. J. van Wijnen, C.V.O.

1st Secretaries, R. de Beaufort, C.V.O.; J. Schoen; J. A. Krijgsman; J. A. van Alphen; J. Huisman.

Naval Attaché and Air Attaché, Capt. J. R. Roele.

Assistant Naval Attaché and Assistant Air Attaché, Cdr. H. Prinselaar.

Military Attaché, Col. W. Epke.

Area and Population.—The Kingdom of the Netherlands is a maritime country of Western Europe, situated on the North Sea, in lat. 50° 46′–53° 34′ N. and long. 3° 22′–7° 14′ E., consisting of 11 provinces plus Eastern and Southern Flevoland (reclaimed parts of the Ysselmer) and containing a total area of 13,500 sq. miles (34,830 sq. km). The population in Jan. 1976 was estimated at 13,700,000. The live birth rate in Jan., 1975 was 13 per 1,000 of the population, and the death-rate was 8·3.

The land is generally flat and low, intersected by numerous canals and connecting rivers—in fact, a network of water courses. The principal rivers are the Rhine, Maas, Yssel and Scheldt.

The chief agricultural products are potatoes, wheat, rye, barley, corn, sugar beet, cattle, pigs, milk and milk products, cheese, butter, poultry, eggs, beans, peas, flax seed, vegetables, fruit, flower bulbs, and cut flowers and there is an important fishing industry. Among the principal industries are engineering, both mechanical and electrical, electronics, nuclear energy, petro-chemicals and plastics, shipbuilding, steel, textiles of all types, leather goods, electrical appliances, metal ware, furniture, paper, cigars, sugar, liqueurs, beer, clothing, rubber products, etc.

Production of crude oil (1975) 14,190,000,000,000 K.cal and refined oil 439,920,000,000,000 K.cal; steel 4,823,000,000 Kgs. and gas 90,853,000,000 cubic metres. Diamond cutting, though still an important industry, has declined considerably in importance.

Government.—In 1815 the Netherlands became a constitutional Kingdom under King William I, a Prince of Orange-Nassau, a descendant of the house which has taken a leading part in the destiny of the nation since the 16th century. The States-General comprise the *Eerste Kamer* (First Chamber) of 75 members, elected for 6 years by the Provincial Council; and the *Tweede Kamer* (Second Chamber) of 150 members, elected for 4 years by men and women voters of 18 years and upwards. Members of the *Tweede Kamer* are paid.

General elections were held on Nov. 29, 1972 for the Second Chamber of the States-General. Party Representation is: Labour Party, 43; Catholic People's Party, 27; Liberal, 22; Anti-Revolutionary, 14; Democrats '66, 6; Christian Historical Union, 7; Democratic Socialists '70, 6; Communists, 7; Radicals, 7; Political Reformed, 3; Reformed Political Union, 2; Pacifist Socialists, 2; Farmers' Party, 3; Roman Catholic National Party, 1.

The First (Upper) Chamber of the States-General was elected by the Provincial Councils in June, 1974 Party Representation is: Labour, 21; Catholic People's Party, 16; Liberal, 12; Christian Historical Union, 7; Anti-Revolutionary, 6; Radicals, 4; Communists, 4; Democrats '66, 3; Political Reformed, 1; Farmers' Party, 1.

Defence.—The armed forces are almost entirely committed to NATO. As a result of a far-reaching defence review, completed in 1974 and revised in 1976 the three services are expected to be reduced in size but to be re-equipped over the next decade with new ships, aircraft and Army vehicles. Under this plan, the Royal Netherlands Navy is to be modernized to provide three escort groups, each consisting of a Command ship and six frigates, for use under NATO Command in the Atlantic and North Sea. The Royal Netherlands Army is to be reorganized into two active and one reserve Divisions each containing three Brigades. These units are fully integrated into the NATO Central Army Command. The Royal Netherlands Air Force comprises nine squadrons of jet aircraft, the principal roles of which are offensive support, air defence,

and reconnaissance. All these squadrons are assigned to the NATO Central Region. In addition there are various missile units stationed in Germany, also assigned to NATO.

Language and Literature.—Dutch is a West-Germanic language of Saxon origin, closely akin to Old English and Low German. It is spoken in the Netherlands and the northern part of Belgium. It is also used in the Netherlands Antilles. Afrikaans, one of the two South African languages, has Dutch as its origin, but differs from it in grammar and pronunciation. There are eight national papers, four of which are morning papers, and there are many regional daily papers.

Education.—Illiteracy is practically non-existent. Primary and secondary education is given in both denominational and State schools, the denominational schools being eligible for State assistance on equal terms with the State schools. Attendance at primary school is compulsory. Secondary schools are numerous, well equipped and well attended. The principal Universities are at Leiden, Utrecht, Groningen, Amsterdam (2), Nijmegen (R.C.) and Rotterdam, and there are technical Universities at Delft (polytechnic); Eindhoven (polytechnic), Enschede (polytechnic) Wageningen (agriculture).

Communications.—The total extent of navigable rivers including canals, is 4,359·9 km. and of metalled roads 86,354 km. In 1975 the total length of the railway system amounted to 3,832 km., of which 1,719 km. were electrified. The mercantile marine in 1975 consisted of 915 ships of total 3,223,000 gross registered tons. The total length of air routes covered by K.L.M. (Royal Dutch Airlines) in the course of April, 1974, to April, 1975, was 369,232 km.

FINANCE
Estimates, 1976
Aggregate Budget Revenue. . . . Fls.71,940,000,000
Aggregate Budget Expenditure. 87,011,000,000

TRADE

The Dutch are traditionally a trading nation. *Entrepôt* trade, banking and shipping are of particular importance in their economy. The geographical position of the Netherlands, at the mouths of the Rhine, Meuse and Scheldt, brings a large volume of transit trade to and from the interior of Europe to Dutch ports.

Principal trading partners are the Federal Republic of Germany and Belgium/Luxemburg. Britain supplied 6·4 per cent. of Netherlands imports in 1975 (Fls. 5,096,679,000) and took 10·4 per cent. of Netherlands exports (Fls. 8,120,932,000).

In common with other members of the European Economic Community, the Netherlands on July 1, 1968, removed remaining duties on imports from EEC countries and brought down duties on imports from other countries into line with the Common External Tariff of the EEC.

Excluding the building industry, the index of industrial production in the Netherlands (1970= 100) fell from 121 in 1974 to 115 in 1975 and the index of industrial production per worker (1970= 100) fell from 132 in 1974 to 129 in 1974. In 1975 Dutch imports amounted to Fls.76,500,000,000 and exports to Fls.76,375,000,000 (excluding Belgium and Luxembourg).

Trade with U.K.
	1974	1975
Imports from U.K.	£982,300,000	£1,113,460,000
Exports to U.K.	1,637,000,000	1,872,819,000

SEAT OF GOVERNMENT, The Hague (Den Haag or, in full, 's-Gravenhage). Pop. (1975) 479,369.

PRINCIPAL TOWNS.— Ψ Amsterdam, 770,805; Ψ Rotterdam, 625,361; Utrecht, 269,574; Eindhoven, 191,842; Haarlem, 168,243; Groningen,

167,571; Tilburg, 152,500; Nijmegen, 148,219; Enschede, 142,851; Arnhem, 126,585; Leiden, 97,154; Breda, 119,186; Maastricht, 111,314; Dordrecht, 101,279; Apeldoorn 131,979; Hilversum, 96,841.

FLAG.—Three horizontal bands of red, white and blue. NATIONAL DAY.—April 30 (The Queen's Birthday).

BRITISH EMBASSY
(Lange Voorhout, 10, The Hague)
Ambassador Extraordinary and Plenipotentiary, His Excellency Sir John Barnes, K.C.M.G., M.B.E. (1972).
Counsellors, J. A. Sankey; D. F. Ballentyne (*Commercial*).
Defence and Naval Attaché, Capt. J. R. Hill, R.N.
Air Attaché, Wing-Comdr. D. B. Hives.
Military Attaché, Lt.Col. P. G. Duffield.
1st Secretaries, D. J. Moss (*Head of Chancery*); J. D. B. McKibbin (*Chancery*); A. D. F. Findlay (*Agriculture*); W. K. Prendergast (*Economic*); K. H. Jones (*Commercial*); Miss P. M. Kelly (*Information*).

BRITISH CONSULAR OFFICES
Amsterdam, Johannes Vermeerstraat 7.—*Consul-General*, T. J. Trout, M.B.E.
Rotterdam, Parklaan 18.—*Consul-General*, W. F. B. Price.
There is an Honorary British Consul at *Aruba*, Netherlands Antilles.
British Council Representative, C. N. P. Powell, D.S.O., O.B.E., Keizersgracht 343, Amsterdam (Library).

OVERSEAS TERRITORIES
The Netherlands West Indies formerly comprised Surinam in South America and certain islands in the West Indies known as the *Netherlands Antilles* (Curaçao, Bonaire, Aruba, part of St. Martin, St. Eustatius, and Saba). The area of the Netherlands Antilles is 394·1 sq. miles with a population of 234,400. Under the Realm Statute which took effect on December 29, 1954, Surinam and the Netherlands Antilles received autonomy in domestic affairs as parts of the Netherlands Realm under the Crown. The statue was amended in 1975 to provide for the full independence of *Surinam* on November 25, 1975. Henceforth the Realm comprises the Netherlands and the Netherland Antilles only.

Governor
Netherlands Antilles, Dr. B. M. Leito (1970).

Trade with U.K.
Netherlands Antilles	1974	1975
Imports from U.K.	£8,684,000	£12,044,000
Exports to U.K.	38,760,000	31,219,000

The capital of Curaçao is Ψ Willemstad (pop. 154,928), of Aruba, Ψ Oranjestad; of Bonaire, Ψ Kralendijk; of St. Martin, Philipsburg; of Statius (St. Eustatius), Oranjestad; and of Saba, Bottom.

NICARAGUA
(República de Nicaragua)
President of the National Emergency Committee and Supreme Chief of the Armed Forces, Gen. Anastasio Somoza Debayle, *assumed office*, Dec. 1, 1974.
Foreign Affairs, Dr. Alejandre Montiel Arguello.

NICARAGUAN EMBASSY AND CONSULATE GENERAL
8 Gloucester Road, S.W.7
[01-584 3231]
Ambassador Extraordinary and Plenipotentiary (vacant).
Minister-Counsellor, Dr. José Rizo Castellon.

Area and Population.—Nicaragua is the largest State of Central America, with a long seaboard on both the Atlantic and Pacific Oceans, situated between 10° 45′–15° N. lat. and 83° 40′–87° 38′ W.

long., containing an area of 57,145 English square miles (*see* MAP, p. 872). It has a population of 2,400,000 of whom about threequarters are of mixed blood. Another 15 per cent. are white, mostly of pure Spanish descent and the remaining 10 per cent. are Indians or negroes. The latter group includes the Mosquitos, who live on the Atlantic coast and were formerly under British protection.

Government.—The eastern coast of Nicaragua was touched by Columbus in 1502, and in 1519 was overrun by Spanish forces under Davila, and formed part of the Spanish Captaincy-General of Guatemala until 1821, when its independence was secured. From 1972 the country was headed by a three-man National Governing Council A new Constitution, adopted in April 1974, provided for presidential elections to be held on Sept. 1, 1974. General de Division Anastasio Somoza, Debayle was re-elected President (formerly in office, 1967–72) of the Republic, and took office on December 1, 1974 for a term expiring on April 31, 1981. Nicaragua is now a democratic representative republic divided into sixteen Departments and the National District, which includes Managua and its surroundings. The Government is divided into four branches: Legislative, Executive, Judicial and Electoral. Legislative power is vested in a Senate of 30 members and the ex-President, and a chamber of Deputies with not less than 70 members.

Agriculture and Industry.—The country is mainly agricultural. The major crops are cotton, coffee, sugar, sesame and bananas. Beans, rice, maize and ipecacuanha are also important. Livestock and timber production, already considerable, are expanding. Nicaragua possesses deposits of gold and silver, both of which are mined and exported by United States and Canadian concessionaires.

Communications.—There are 252 miles of railway, all on the Pacific side and approximately 5,500 miles of telegraph. There are 27 radio stations and two television stations in Managua. An automatic telephone system has been installed in the capital and extended to the provincial towns of León, Granada, Matagalpa, Chinandega, Diriamba and Jinotepe. The system in the capital, however, suffered heavy damage as a result of the earthquake in December 1972. A ground station for satellite communication was inaugurated in 1973. Transport except on the Pacific slope, is still attended with difficulty but many new roads have either been opened or are under construction. The Inter-American Highway runs from the Honduras frontier in the north to the Costa Rican border in the south; the interoceanic highway runs from the Corinto on the Pacific coast viâ Managua to Rama, where there is a natural waterway to Bluefields on the Atlantic. The country's main airport is at Managua. It is used by several airlines, including Panam and Lanica, the Nicaraguan national airline.

Language and Literature.—The official language of the country is Spanish. There are 2 daily newspapers published at Managua, apart from the official Gazette (*La Gaceta*) and 4 in the provinces. About 40 per cent. of the population are illiterate. There are universities at León and Managua.

Trade with U.K.

	1974	1975
Imports from U.K.	£7,706,000	£5,247,000
Exports to U.K.	1,385,000	9,980,000

Considerable quantities of foodstuffs are imported as well as cotton goods, jute, iron and steel, machinery and petroleum products. The chief exports are cotton, coffee, beef, gold, sugar, cottonseed, bananas, copper and soluble coffee.

CAPITAL, Managua, population post-earthquake,

400,000. The centre was almost totally destroyed in the earthquake of December 1972, and reconstruction will take several years. León, 119,347; Granada, 100,334; Masaya, 96,830; Chinandega, 95,437; ΨBluefields, 17,706; Matagalpa, 65,928; Jinotepe, 15,957. ΨCorinto (9,650), on the Pacific is the chief port, handling about 70 per cent. of the total trade; Bluefields and Puerto Somoza on the E. coast are mainly concerned in the fish, banana and timber trade to the United States.

FLAG.—Three horizontal bands, blue, white, blue (the arms of the Republic on the white band, displaying five volcanoes surmounted by a cap of liberty under a rainbow).

BRITISH REPRESENTATION

Ambassador Extraordinary and Plenipotentiary and Consul-General, His Excellency Keith Hamylton Jones (resides at *San José*).

NIGER
(République du Niger)

President, Lt.-Col. Seyni Kountché, *assumed power* April 15, 1974.
Minister of Foreign Affairs, Capt. Moumouni Djermakoye Amadou.

Situated in West Central Africa, between 12° and 24° N. and 0° and 16° E., Niger has common boundaries with Algeria and Libya in the north, Chad, Nigeria, Benin, Mali and Upper Volta.

It has an area of about 459,000 square miles with a population (U.N. estimate, 1972) at 4,030,000. Apart from a small region along the Niger Valley in the south-west near the capital the country is entirely savannah or desert. The main races in Niger are the Haussas in the east, the Djermas in the south-west and the nomadic Touaregs in the north.

The first French expedition arrived in 1891 and the country was fully occupied by 1914. It decided on December 18, 1958, to remain an autonomous republic within the French Community; full independence outside the Community was proclaimed on August 3, 1960. Special agreements with France, covering financial and cultural matters, technical assistance, defence, etc., were signed in Paris on April 24, 1961.

The constitution of Niger, adopted on November 8, 1960, provided for a presidential system of government, modelled on that of the United States and the French Fifth Republic, and a single Chamber National Assembly. In April 1974 Lt.-Col. Seyni Kountché seized power, suspended the Constitution, dissolved the National Assembly, and suppressed all political organizations. He then set up a Supreme Military Council with himself as President and eleven other officers together with a temporary Government in which all the major portfolios are held by military officers. Niger is a member of the United Nations, the *Conseil de l'Entente*, O.C.A.M., O.A.U. and C.E.A.O. (*see* Ivory Coast). The official language is French.

Finance.—The currency of Niger is the *franc CFA* (*Francs CFA* 50 = 1 *French Franc*). In 1975 the total budget amounted to *Francs CFA* 16,670,000,000.

Trade.—The cultivation of ground-nuts and the production of livestock are the main industries and provide the two main exports. A company formed by the Government, the French Atomic Energy Authority and private interests is exploiting uranium deposits at Arlit. Total value of trade in 1974 was: Imports, *Francs CFA* 23,144,000,000; Exports, *Francs CFA* 12,621,000,000. Imports from U.K. (1975) — £2,667,000; exports to U.K. (1975) — £1,485,000.

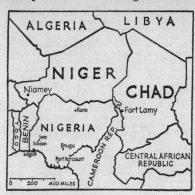

CAPITAL.—Niamey (100,000).

FLAG.—Three horizontal stripes, orange, white and green with an orange disc in the middle of the white stripe. NATIONAL DAY.—December 18.

British Ambassador, His Excellency Joe Booth Wright (*resident at Abidjan*).

NORWAY
(Norge)

King, Olav V, K.G., K.T., G.C.B., G.C.V.O., *b.* July 2, 1903; *succeeded*, Sept. 21, 1957, on death of his father King Haakon VII; *married* March 21, 1929, Princess Marthe of Sweden (*born* March 29, 1901; *died* April 5, 1954); having issue, Harald (*see below*) and two daughters.

Heir-Apparent, H.R.H. Prince Harald, G.C.V.O., *b.* Feb. 21, 1937; *m.* Aug. 29, 1968, Sonja Haraldsen, and has issue Princess Märtha Louise, *b.* Sept. 22, 1971; and Prince Haakon Magnus, *b.* July 20, 1973.

CABINET

Prime Minister, Odvar Nordli.
Foreign Affairs, Knut Frydenlund.
Agriculture, Oskar Øksnes.
Justice, Fru Inger Louise Valle.
Education and Ecclesiastical Affairs, Kjølv Egeland.
Defence, Rolf Hansen.
Commerce, Hallvard Bakke.
Industry, Bjartmar Gjerde.
Consumer Affairs and Administration, Fru Annemarie Lorentzen.
Communications, Ragnar Christiansen.
Fisheries, Eivind Bolle.
Labour and Municipal Affairs, Leif J. Aune.
Social Affairs, Ruth Ryste.
Environment, Fru Gro Harlem Brundtland.
Finance and Customs, Per Kleppe.
Without Portfolio, Jens Evensen.

ROYAL NORWEGIAN EMBASSY IN LONDON
Offices: 25 Belgrave Square, S.W.1
[01–235 7151]

Ambassador Extraordinary and Plenipotentiary, His Excellency Frithjo Halfdan Jacobsen (1975).
Minister-Counsellor, Olav Sole.
Counsellors, Herman Pedersen (*Press and Information*), Semund Remøy (*Fisheries*); Øivind Johnsen (*Consular*); Hans Hoegh Henrichsen (*Commercial*); Nils Oskar Dietz (*Economic*).
1st Secretaries, Jan Wessel Hegg; Sven Smaaland; Oscar Torgersen (*Consular*); D. R. Nielson (*Commercial*).

Defence Attaché, Lt.-Col. Jørgen Mørtvedt.
Asst. Defence Attaché, Maj. B. Schaathun.
2nd Secretaries, Ole F. Knudsen (*Commercial*); Arne Walther (*Political*).
Attachés, Sigfred Hungnes (*Consular*); Kari Foldøy (*Welfare*).

Area and Population.—Norway (" The Northern Way "), a kingdom in the northern and western portion of the Scandinavian peninsula, was founded in 872. It is 1,752 km. in length, its greatest width about 430 km. The length of the coastline is 2,650 km., and the frontier between Norway and the neighbouring countries is 2,531 km. (Sweden 1,619 km., Finland 716 km. and U.S.S.R. 196 km.). It is divided into 19 counties (*fylker*) and comprises an area of 323,877 sq. km. (125,016 sq. miles) with a population (estimated, Dec., 1973) of 3,972,990. In 1972 there were for every 1,000 inhabitants: 16·1 live births; 10·0 deaths; 11·8 deaths during first year of age (per 1,000 live births); 7·2 marriages. The Norwegian coastline is extensive, deeply indented with numerous fiords, and fringed with an immense number of rocky islands. The surface is mountainous, consisting of elevated and barren tablelands, separated by deep and narrow valleys. At the North Cape the sun does not appear to set from the second week in May to the last week in July, causing the phenomenon known as the *Midnight Sun*; conversely, there is no apparent sunrise from about Nov. 18 to Jan. 23. During the long winter nights are seen the multiple coloured *Northern Lights* or *Aurora Borealis*, which have a maximum intensity in a line crossing North America from Alaska to Labrador and Northern Europe to the Arctic coast and Siberia.

Production.—The cultivated area is about 10,000 sq. km. (3·4 per cent. of total surface area); forests cover nearly 25 per cent.; the rest consists of highland pastures or uninhabitable mountains.

The *Gulf Stream* pours from 140 to 170 million cubic feet of warm water per second into the sea around Norway and causes the temperature to be higher than the average for the latitude. It brings shoals of herring and cod into the fishing grounds and causes a warm current of air over the west coast, making it possible to cultivate potatoes and barley in latitudes which in other countries are perpetually frozen.

The chief industries are manufactures, agriculture and forestry, fisheries, mining and shipping. In the fourth quarter of 1973, 1,660,000 persons were employed in Norwegian industry. Manufactures are aided by great resources of water power, estimated at 14,120 MW. Actual production in 1972 amounted to 67·8 GW*. Oil was discovered on the Norwegian continental shelf in 1968. In normal years the quantity of fish caught by Norwegian fishing vessels is greater than that of any other European country except U.S.S.R. In 1973 the total catch amounted to 2,692,392 metric tons. In 1972 herring oil production amounted to 189,549 metric tons.

Government.—From 1397 to 1814 Norway was united with Denmark, and from Nov. 4, 1814, with Sweden, under a personal union which was dissolved on June 7, 1905, when Norway regained complete independence. Under the constitution of May 17, 1814, the *Storting* (Parliament) itself elects one-quarter of its members to constitute the *Lagting* (Upper Chamber), the other three-quarters forming the *Odelsting* (Lower Chamber). Legislative questions alone are dealt with by both parts in separate sittings.

On April 8–9, 1940, Germany invaded Norway, and it was not until June 7, 1945, that the late

* Gigawatt = 1,000 million watts.

King Haakon was able to return from Great Britain to Oslo.

On October 14, 1973, Mr. Trygve Bratteli, leader of the Labour Party, formed his second minority Government since March 1971, in succession to the three-party coalition of Mr. Lars Korvald, which resigned on October 12.

Defence.—Norway is a member of the North Atlantic Treaty Organization, and the Headquarters of Allied Forces, Northern Europe, is situated near Oslo. The period of compulsory national service is 15 months (without refresher training) in the Navy and Air Force, and 12 months (with refresher training) in the Army.

Education from 7 to 16 is free and compulsory in the " basic schools " maintained by the municipalities with State grants-in-aid. From 1976 all schools catering for the 16–19 age groups will be organised along comprehensive lines, the aim being to offer facilities for some 85–90 per cent. of the age groups. In 1971 47·4 per cent. of all 18 year olds received full time schooling. In addition to the many specialized schools and industrial and technical institutes, there are 29 colleges of education and 7 new regional colleges. There are 4 universities and 7 state colleges of university level, with a total in autumn 1973 of 36,694 students, 32·4 per cent. of them women. Oslo University (founded 1811) had 19,367; Bergen University (1948) 7,351, and Trondheim University (created in 1968 by merging the State Institute of Technology, the State College for Teachers, and the Royal Norwegian Society of Science Museum) 6,230; the newest, Tromsø University, started teaching in 1972 with 871 students in science, the humanities and medicine.

Language and Literature.—Norwegian is one of the Scandinavian languages and is the language of the mainland and of Svalbard. Old Norse literature is among the most ancient (and the richest) in Europe. Modern Norwegian became formed in the time of the Reformation and Ludvig Holberg (1684–1754) is regarded as the founder of Norwegian literature, although modern Norwegian literature dates from the establishment of a national university at Christiania (Oslo) in 1811 and with the writings of Henrik A. Wergeland (1805–1845). Some of the famous names are Henrik Ibsen (1828–1906) the dramatist, Björnstjerne Björnson (1832–1910) journalist, dramatist and novelist and Nobel Prizewinner in 1903, Jonas Lie (1833–1908) novelist, Knut Hamsun (1859–1952) novelist and Nobel Prizewinner in 1920, and Sigrid Undset (1882–1949), champion of Norwegian womanhood and herself a Nobel Prizewinner in 1928. In 1973 there were 67 daily newspapers in the country with a total circulation of 1,555,000, and 77 newspapers published 1 to 5 times a week with a total circulation of 331,000.

Communications.—The total length of railways open at the end of 1971 was 4,242 km., excluding private lines. The extension of the main line from Fauske to Bodö, 60 miles north of the Arctic Circle, was completed in 1962 and opened on June 7 by King Olav. The number of telephones at the end of 1972 was 1,262,254 which is 32 telephones per 100 inhabitants. There are 74,796 km. of public roads in Norway (including urban streets). At the end of 1973, 1,468,517 road motor vehicles were registered.

Civil Aviation.—Scheduled airlines are operated by Scandinavian Airlines System (SAS) on behalf of Det Norske Luftfartselskap (DNL), by Braathens South American and Far East Airtransport (SAFE), and by Wideröes Flyveselskap A.S.

Mercantile Marine.—The Mercantile Marine, December 31, 1972, consisted of 2,117 vessels of 23,328,000 gross tons (vessels above 100 gross tons, excluding fishing boats, floating whaling factories, tugs, salvage vessels, icebreakers and similar types of vessel). The fleet ranks fourth among the merchant navies of the world.

FINANCE

	1974	1975
	million *Kroner*	
Revenue	25,737	29,693
Expenditure	30,505	37,034
National Debt	33,943	—

Rate of Exchange (1976) Kr.10·20= £1. See also p. 83.

TRADE

	1973	1974
	million *Kroner*	
Total imports	36,041	54,630
Total exports	21,625	34,862

Trade with U.K.

	1975
Imports from U.K.	Kr.284,792,000
Exports to U.K.	356,361,000

The chief imports are raw materials, motor vehicles, chemicals, motor spirit, fuel and other oils; coal, ships and machinery; together with manufactures of silk, cotton and wool. The exports consist chiefly of fish and products of fish (as canned fish, whale oils), pulp, paper, iron ore and pyrites, nitrate of lime, stone, calcium carbide, aluminium, ferro-alloys, zinc, nickel, cyanamide, etc.

CAPITAL.—Ψ Oslo (incl. Aker). Pop. (Jan. 1, 1975), 464,900. Other towns are Ψ Trondheim, 133,213; Ψ Bergen, 214,580; Ψ Stavanger, 84,359; Ψ Kristiansand, 58,975; Ψ Drammen, 50,573; Ψ Tromsö, 42,253; Ψ Aalesund, 40,662; Ψ Haugesund, 27,283; Moss, 25,523.

FLAG.—Red, with white-bordered blue cross.

NATIONAL DAY.—May 17 (Constitution Day).

AIR TRANSIT FROM U.K.—London–Bergen or Oslo, 1 hr. 50 mins.

BRITISH EMBASSY
Thomas Heftyesgate, 8 Oslo 2.

Ambassador Extraordinary and Plenipotentiary, His Excellency Charles Peter Scott, C.M.G., O.B.E. (1975).

BRITISH CONSULAR OFFICES
There are British Consular Offices at *Bergen* and *Olso* and Honorary Consulates at *Tromso, Aalesund, Kristiansand N., Narvik, Stavanger, Trondheim, Tønsberg, Kristiansand S.* and *Haugesund.*

BRITISH COUNCIL
Representative, J. D. Edmondston, O.B.E., Fridtjof Nansen Plass 5, Oslo 1.

SVALBARD
(Spitsbergen and Bear Island)

By Treaty (Feb. 9, 1920) the sovereignty of Norway over the Spitsbergen (" Pointed Mountain ") Archipelago was recognized by the Great Powers and other interested nations, and on Aug. 14, 1925, Norway assumed sovereignty. In September, 1941, Allied forces (British, Canadian and Norwegian) landed on the main island. After destruction of the accumulated stocks of coal and dismantling of mining machinery and the wireless installation, the Norwegian inhabitants (about 600) were evacuated to a British port and the Russians (about 1,500) to the U.S.S.R. After the war the Norwegian mining plants were rebuilt. 873,406 metric tons of coal were shipped from Norwegian and Russian mines in Svalbard in 1973 (Norwegian mines, 411,503 metric tons).

The Svalbard Archipelago lies between 74°–81° N. lat. and between 10°–35° E. long., with an estimated area of 24,295 square miles. The archipelago consists of a main island, known as Spitsbergen (15,200 sq. miles); North East Land, closely adjoining and separated by Hinlopen Strait; the Wiche Islands, separated from the mainland by Olga Strait; Barents and Edge Islands, separated from the mainland by Stor Fjord (or Wybe Jansz Water); Prince Charles Foreland, to the W.; Hope Island, to the S.E.; Bear Island (68 square miles) 127 miles to the S.; with many similar islands in the neighbourhood of the main group. In addition to those engaged in coal-mining, the archipelago is also visited by hunters for seal, foxes and polar bears.

South Cape is 355 miles from the Norwegian Coast. Ice Fjord is 520 miles from Tromsö, 650 miles from Murmansk, and 1,300 miles from Aberdeen. Transit from Tromsö to Green Harbour 2 to 3 days; from Aberdeen 5 to 6 days.

JAN MAYEN, an island in the Arctic Ocean (70° 49′–71° 9′ N. lat. and 7° 53′–9° 5′ W. long.) was joined to Norway by law of Feb. 27, 1930.

Norwegian Antarctic
BOUVET ISLAND (54° 26′ S. lat. and 3° 24′ E. long.) was declared a dependency of Norway by law of Feb. 27, 1930.

PETER THE FIRST ISLAND (68° 48′ S. lat. and 90° 35′ W. long.), was declared a dependency of Norway by resolution of Government, May 1, 1931.

PRINCESS RAGNHILD LAND (from 70° 30′ to 68° 40′ S. lat. and 24° 15′ to 33° 30′ E. long.' has been claimed as Norwegian since Feb. 17, 1931.

QUEEN MAUD LAND.—On Jan. 14, 1939, the Norwegian Government declared the area between 20° W. and 45° E., adjacent to Australian Antarctica, to be Norwegian territory.

OMAN
(The Sultanate of Oman)

Sultan, Qaboos bin Said, *succeeded* on deposition of Sultan Said bin Taimur, July 23, 1970.

COUNCIL OF MINISTERS
Personal Adviser and Governor of the Capital, Sayyid Thuwaini bin Shihab.

Communications, Abdul Hafidh Salim Rajab.

Public Works, Karim Ahmad al Haremi.

Diwan Affairs, Sayyid Hamad bin Hamud.

Education, Ahmed Al-Ghazali.

Health, Dr. Mubarak al-Khadduri.

Information and Culture, Sayyid Fahd bin Mahmoud al-Said.

Justice, Sayyid Hilal bin Hamad al-Sammar.

Interior, Sayyid Muhammad bin Ahmed.

Land Affairs, Dr. Asim Al-Jamali.

Social Affairs and Labour, Khaitan bin Nasr al-Wahaibi.

Awkaf and Islamic Affairs, Shaikh Walid bin Zahir al Hinai.

Commerce and Industry, Mohamed Zubair.

Agriculture, Fisheries, Petroleum, and Minerals, Said Ahmed al-Shanfari.

Youth Affairs, Sayyid Fahar bin Taimur.

National Heritage, Sayyid Faisal bin Ali.

Minister of State (Foreign Affairs), Qais Abdul Munim Al-Zawawi.

Minister without Portfolio, Shaikh Braik bin Hamud al-Ghafari.

(The Sultan acts as his own Minister of Foreign Affairs and Defence.)

OMAN EMBASSY IN LONDON
64 Ennismore Gardens, S.W.7.
[01–584 6782]

Ambassador, His Excellency Nassir Seif El Bualy.

The independent Sultanate of Oman lies at the eastern corner of the Arabian Peninsula. Its seaboard is nearly 1,000 miles long and extends from near Tibat on the west coast of the Musandam Peninsula round to Ras Darbat Ali, with the exception of the stretch between Dibba and Kalba on the east coast which belongs to Sharjah and Fujairah of the United Arab Emirates. Ras Darbat Ail marks the boundary between the Sultanate and the People's Democratic Republic of Yemen. The Sultanate extends inland to the borders of the Rub al Khali, or "Empty Quarter" as the South Eastern Arabian Desert is called.

Physically and historically modern Oman can be split into two main parts, the North and the South, divided by a large tract of desert. *Northern Oman* has three main sections. The *Batinah*, the coastal plain, varies in width from 30 miles in the neighbourhood of Suwaiq to almost nothing at Muscat where the mountains descend abruptly to the sea. The plain is fertile, with date gardens extending over its full length of 150 miles. The dates, which ripen in early July, well before the Basra product, are famous for their flavour. The *Hajjar*, a mountain spine running from North East to South West, reaching nearly 10,000 feet in height on Jabal Akhdar. For the most part the mountains are barren, but numerous valleys penetrate the central massif of Jabal Akhdar and in these there is considerable cultivation irrigated by wells or a system of underground canals called *falages* which top the water table. The two plateaus leading from the western slopes of the mountains, the *Dhahirah* or back, in the north and the *Sharqia* in the south east also have centres of settlements and cultivation. They fall from an average height of 1,000 feet into sands of the Empty Quarter. Camels

raised in this area are prized throughout Arabia. The *Wahiba Sands* separate the North from the South with nearly 400 miles of inhospitable country crossed by one motorable track, the only land link. *Dhofar*, the Southern Province, is the only part of the Arabian Peninsula to be touched by the South West Monsoon. Temperatures are more moderate than in the North and sugar cane and coconuts are grown on the coastal plain, while cattle are bred on the mountains.

Muscat is the original capital of Oman, but Matrah, 3 miles away, where a new port has been built and where there is more room for expansion, is the commercial centre, and government offices and private houses are moving out to Ruwi and Qurum along the road to Seeb Airport. The other main towns on the northern coast are Sur, Khaburah and Sohar, all of which are ports but without sheltered anchorage. In the interior Nizwa and Rostaq, both former capitals, are the centres of population. The main town of Dhofar is Salalah, and Raysut and Murbat are the ports.

The area of Oman has been estimated at 120,000 sq. miles and the population at 750,000 (1973). The inhabitants of the North are for the most part Arab but along the coast there is a strong infusion of negro blood, while in the Capital Area which stretches from Muscat to Seeb there are large communities of Hindus, Khojas and Baluch, in addition to Zanzibaris of Omani origin. In Dhofar there is also an infusion of negro blood around Salalah, but in the mountains the inhabitants are either of pure Arab descent or belong to tribes of pre-Arab origin, the Qarra and Mahra, who speak their own dialects of semitic origin.

Since 1972 ships have been using Port Qaboos at Matrah, where 8 deep water berths have been constructed as part of the new harbour facilities (£20m.). In 1974, 361 vessels entered the port. 169 tankers called at the oil company port at Mina al Fahal and carried away over 106 million barrels of crude oil.

The telegraph office, an automatic telephone service in Muscat and Matrah and an international telephone service have been operated since January 1975 by OMANTEL. The Sultanate of Oman and Cable & Wireless share in the company in the ratio of 60/40. There are cleared or graded motorable tracks linking most main population centres of the country with the coast and with the towns of the United Arab Emirates. Over 300 miles of tarmac road are now open linking the capital area with the new international airport at Seeb and the town of Sohar and others are being built, for example to link Muscat and Nizwa.

Finance.—On May 7, 1970, a new currency was brought into circulation. The main unit is the *Rial Oman* RO 0·770= £1 (July 1975). Each *Rial* is divided into 1,000 new *Baiza*. There are notes of *Rials* 10, 5, 1, ½, ¼ and 100 *Baiza* and coins of *Baiza* 100, 50, 25, 10, 5 and 2. The Indian External Rupee ceased to be legal tender from May 21, 1970. The metric system was introduced in 1975 but there is also a local system in which one *kiyas*=the weight of six dollars or 5·9375 oz.; 24 *liyas*=one Muscat *maund*; 10 *maunds*=one *Farasala*; 200 *maunds*=1 *Bahar*. Rice is sold by the bag, other cereals by the following measurement: 40 *Palis*=one *Farrah*; 20 *Farrahs*=one *Khandi*.

Trade with U.K.

	1974	1975
Imports from U.K.	£42,900,000	£97,994,000
Exports to U.K.	32,800,000	113 997,000

Commerce and Trade.—Trade is mainly with the United Kingdom, Japan, the Netherlands, U.S., West Germany and India. Imports for the year 1975 exceeded RO 231m. Chief imports were

machinery, cars, building materials, refined petroleum and food and telecommunications equipment.

Petroleum Development (Oman) Ltd. (owned 60 per cent. by Oman Government and 34 per cent. by Shell) began exporting oil on Aug. 1, 1967. Exports are currently at a rate of 368,000 barrels a day. Wintershall A.-G., Sun Oil and ELF-ERAP have off-shore concessions and Eif-Aquitane Sumitomo has a new inland oil concession.

Development.—For many years the Sultanate was a poor country with a total annual income of less than £1,000,000. The advent of oil revenues since 1967 and the change of régime in 1970 have improved prospects and have enabled the initiation of a wide-ranging development programme, especially concerned with health, education and communications. New hospitals have been completed in the main provincial centres. 180 primary schools were in operation in Sept. 1974. At Salalah, the main coastal town of the southern province of Dhofar, a new civil airport is planned. A metalled road joins Salalah to Taqa and the port of Rayzut and several housing schemes have been completed. A thermal power station and desalination plant is under construction near Muscat and work has recently begun on a flour mill. There are also plans to build a cement factory near Muscat.

CAPITAL.—Ψ Muscat, population (estimated), 7,000.

FLAG.—Red, green and white with crossed daggers in red sector.

BRITISH EMBASSY
Muscat

Ambassador Extraordinary and Plenipotentiary, His Excellency Charles James Treadwell, C.M.G. (1975).
First Secretary, D. E. Tatham (*Head of Chancery*).
Defence Attaché, Col P. G. Rosser, M.B.E.
Air Attaché, Wing Cdr. P. J. Hirst.
1st Secretaries, D. R. Gallwey; E. T. A. Parsons.
British Council Representative, M. R. W. Dexter, Mutrah, Oman.

PAKISTAN

President, Fazal Elahi Chaudhry, *born* 1905, *elected* Aug. 10, 1973.
Prime Minister, Defence, Foreign Affairs and Atomic Energy, Zulfiqar Ali Bhutto.
Interior and States and Frontier Regions, Abdul Qayyum Khan.
Labour, Health, Manpower and Population Planning, Mir Taj Mohammad Khan Jamali.
Education and Provincial Coordination, Abdul Hafiz Pirzada.
Communications, Mumtaz Ali Bhutto.
Production, Rafi Raza.
Religious Affairs, Maulana Kausar Niazi.
Finance, Planning and Development, Rana Mohammad Hanif Khan.
Fuel, Power and Natural Resources, Mohammad Yusuf Khattak.
Commerce and Tourism, Afzal Khan.
Food and Agriculture, Co-operatives, Underdeveloped Areas and Land Reforms, Sheikh Mohammad Rashid.
Social Welfare, Local Government and Rural Development, Malik Meraj Khalid.
Railways, Hafeezullah Cheema.
Industries, Kashmir Affairs and Northern Areas, Syed Qaim Ali Shah Jilani.
Law and Parliamentary Affairs, Malik Mohammad Akhtar.
Information and Broadcasting, Mohammad Hanif Khan.
Housing, Works and Urban Development, Syed Nasir Ali Shah Rizvi.

Attorney-General, Yahya Bakhtiar.

Ministers of State.—Aziz Ahmad (*Defence, Foreign Affairs*); Maj.-Gen. Jamal Dar (*Establishment*); Abdul Sattar Gabol (*Labour*); Chaudhry Jehangir Ali (*Health and Population Planning*); Malik Mohammad Jaffer (*Science and Technology, Cultural Affairs and Provincial Coordination*); Shehzada Saeed-ur-Rashid Abbasi (*Tourism*); Abdul Aleem (*Kashmir and Northern Affairs*); Mian Mohammad Ataullah (*Education*); Makhdoomzada Mohammad Amin (*Cabinet*); Ch. Mumtaz Ahmad (*Food*).

PAKISTAN EMBASSY
35 Lowndes Square, S.W.1
[01-235 2044]

Ambassador Extraordinary and Plenipotentiary, His Excellency Mian Mumtaz Mohammad Khan Daultana.

Ministers, Bakhtiar Ali (*Head of Chancery*); Elahi Bakhsh Soomro.

Counsellors, Zafar Hussain Qureshi (*Chancery*); Khalid Hasan (*Press*); Zafar Iqbal (*Economic and Commercial*); Nasim Ahmad (*Investment*); Javaid Qayum Khan; Nazir Ahmad (*Education*).

1st Secretary, Muhammad Abdul Wasay Farouqi.

Area and Population.—The Islamic Republic of Pakistan consists of country situated to the north-west of the Indian sub-continent, bordered by Iran, Afghanistan, the disputed territory of Kashmir and India. It covers a total area of 310,403 sq. miles. The Government of Pakistan census in 1972 showed a population figure of 64,892,000. (A mid-1976 estimate was 72,400,000.) Of these, about 88 per cent. are Moslems, about 6 per cent. Scheduled Caste Hindus, 5 per cent. Caste Hindus, under 1 per cent. Christians, and ½ per cent. Buddhists.

Running through Pakistan are five great rivers, the Indus, Jhelum, Chenab, Ravi and Sutlej. The upper reaches of these rivers are in Kashmir, and their sources in the Himalayas.

Government.—Until April 17, 1972, when the Republic of Bangladesh seceded and was formally created to replace East Pakistan, Pakistan consisted of two geographical units, West and East Pakistan, which were separated by about 1,100 miles of Indian territory. Pakistan was constituted as a Dominion under the Indian Independence Act, 1947, which received Royal Assent on July 18, 1947.

In terms of the Act the Dominion of Pakistan consisted of former territories of British India. The States of Bahawalpur and Khairpur (in Punjab and Sind), with a Muslim population of almost 80 per cent. and with Muslim rulers, acceded to Pakistan in October, 1947. Boundaries of the Provinces of East Bengal and of Punjab (West Punjab) were defined by a Boundary Commission presided over by Sir Cyril Radcliffe, K.B.E., Q.C. (now Viscount Radcliffe). The following States also acceded to Pakistan: the Baluchistan States of Kalat, Mekran, Las Bela and Kharan, and the North-West Frontier States of Amb, Chitral, Dir and Swat. (All these States have since been merged in the relevant Provinces of what is now Pakistan). The States of Junagadh and Manavadar which had acceded to Pakistan were occupied by India on November 8, 1947.

Pakistan became a Republic on March 23, 1956, when a Parliamentary Constitution came into force. On October 7, 1958, however, this Constitution was abrogated and Pakistan came under martial law. General (later Field Marshal) Mohammed Ayub Khan, Commander-in-Chief of the Pakistan Army, was appointed the Chief Martial Law Administrator. On October 28, 1958, General Ayub Khan also became President of Pakistan. Following a period of unrest in both East and West Pakistan, marked by rioting and massed strikes, President Ayub Khan on March 24, 1969, announced his resignation and handed over control of the country to the armed forces. The Commander-in-Chief, General Yahya Khan, proclaimed martial law on March 25 and appointed military governors for East and West Pakistan. The Constitution was abrogated, National and Provincial Assemblies dissolved and Provincial Governors dismissed. Law and order were rapidly restored. On March 31, 1969, Gen. Yahya Khan assumed the Presidency and formed a Council of Administration.

A Legal Framework Order, published by the President in March. 1070. laid down the principles on which a new Constitution for Pakistan would be based, including the division of West Pakistan into four provinces—The Punjab, Sind, Baluchistan and the North-West Frontier Province.

The first general elections ever held in Pakistan on a basis of " one man, one vote ", were held on Dec. 7, 1970, with a postponement until January 17, 1971, in 9 East Pakistan constituencies which had been severely affected by the cyclone disaster in the Ganges delta. The Awami League in East Pakistan, led by Sheikh Mujibur Rahman, and the Pakistan People's Party in West Pakistan, led by Zulfikar Ali Bhutto, won large majorities, the latter party in Punjab and Sind. Following the elections there was total disagreement between the two main parties on the question of a new Constitution for Pakistan, Sheikh Mujib insisting on complete autonomy for East Pakistan. The proposed opening of the National Assembly at Dacca on March 25, 1971, was postponed by the President. Civil war broke out.

The unofficially styled " Bangladesh " seceded from the Government of Pakistan by unilateral declaration on March 26, 1971, and Sheikh Mujibur Rahman was flown to West Pakistan where he was in due course tried for treason. Meanwhile, in East Pakistan, fierce and brutal fighting continued between West Pakistan forces and Bengali guerrillas. Several million Bengali refugees fled to India. Fighting in East Pakistan intensified towards the end of the year and on December 3 it spread to West Pakistan where Pakistan and Indian forces were engaged. On December 16 the Pakistan forces on the eastern front surrendered, and the following day Pakistan accepted a cease-fire in the West. Following the resignation of Gen. Yahya Khan as President and the succession of Mr. Bhutto on December 20 Sheikh Mujibur Rahman was released from detention and flown to London on January 8, 1972. From there he proceeded to Dacca where he reasserted that Bangladesh was an independent country and that all ties with West Pakistan were severed. " The Democratic Government of Bangladesh " was formally proclaimed on April 17, 1972.

The United Kingdom had recognized Bangladesh on February 4; but already, on January 30, 1972, President Bhutto announced that Pakistan had left the Commonwealth as a protest against the decision by Britain, Australia and New Zealand to recognize Bangladesh. His decision, taken with regret, was, he said, " final and irrevocable " and " essential to Pakistan's self-respect ".

A new Constitution was adopted by the National Assembly on April 10, 1973. It was enforced on Aug. 14, 1973 and provides for a federal parliamentary system with the President as constitutional head and the Prime Minister as chief executive.

Education.—Formal education in Pakistan is organized into five stages. These are five years of primary education (5–9 years), 3 years of middle or

lower secondary (general or vocational), 2 years of upper secondary, 2 years of higher secondary (intermediate) and 2 to 5 years of higher education in colleges and universities. Education is free to upper secondary level.

Examinations for the first two stages are conducted by the Provincial Education Departments for the award of certificates. Public examinations are conducted at secondary and higher secondary/intermediate levels by the concerned Boards of Intermediate and Secondary education. Public examinations are also held for scholarships and conducted by the Directorates of Education. Examinations at higher levels of education are conducted by the universities.

Provincial Governments are responsible for the total financial support of the government institutions and for grants to non-government institutions. But policy making is authorized by the national Government, which makes annual grants. The Government of Pakistan announced in March, 1972, the Education Policy, 1972–80, the main objects of which are to promote ideological solidarity and eradicate illiteracy. According to the Policy, education in classes I–VIII has been made free since Oct. 1, 1972. It is anticipated that primary education will become universal for boys and girls by 1984.

Education in classes IX and X has been made free in all schools from 1973. The present rate of increase in enrolment at secondary and intermediate levels is about 10 per cent. per annum. By 1980, it is estimated that the enrolment will be more than double, rising from 400,000 to 850,000 in classes IX and X and from 160,000 to 360,000 in classes XI and XII.

The number of existing school teachers is about 160,000. It is estimated that an additional 235,000 elementary and secondary school teachers and an additional 300,000 adult and further education teachers, men and women, will be needed by 1980. The number of primary schools in 1970 was 39,000. There were 3,435 secondary schools and 300 general colleges.

Production.—Pakistan's economy is chiefly based on agriculture which, following the secession of East Pakistan, is the occupation of about 54·8 per cent. of the labour force. The principal crops are cotton, rice, wheat, sugar cane, maize and tobacco. There are large deposits of rock salt. Pakistan has one of the longest irrigation systems in the world. The total area irrigated is 33 million acres.

Other Products: Pakistan also produces hides and skins, leather, wool, fertilizers, paints and varnishes, soda ash, paper, cement, fish, carpets, sports goods, surgical appliances and engineering goods, including switchgear, transformers, cables and wires.

Trade.—Pakistan imported manufactured goods and raw materials to the value of $2,113·7 million in 1974–75 and exported mainly agricultural products valued at $1,039 million. Principal imports are listed as: machinery, food grains, iron and steel manufactures, transport equipment, electrical goods, mineral oils, chemicals, fertilizers, drugs and medicines, and vegetable oils. Principal exports are raw cotton yarn and cloth, carpets, sports goods, rice, raw skins and fish.

Trade with U.K.

	1974	1975
Imports from U.K....	£45,808,000	£77,203,000
Exports to U.K.......	39,779,000	38,012,000

Finance.—The unit of currency is the *Rupee* of 100 *Paisa* (1 *crore*=10 million *Rupees*). For rate of exchange, see p. 83.

The State Bank has a capital of about Rs.30,000,000 and is wholly owned by the Government. Total bank deposits in Pakistan in Dec. 1975, were Rs.2,793 *crores*.

The 1976–77 Budget anticipated Revenue receipts of Rs. 1819·87 *crores* and expenditure (excluding development expenditure) of Rs.1614·71 *crores*.

Communications—The main seaport is Karachi (annual handling capacity 6,000,000 tons of cargo). The main airport at Karachi occupies an important position on international trunk routes and is equipped with modern facilities and equipment. Pakistan International Airlines (P.I.A.) operates air services between the principal cities within the country as well as abroad.

Post and telegraph facilities are available to every country in the world.

CAPITAL.—Islamabad, pop. 235,000. ΨKarachi (pop. 1972, 3,469,000) is the largest city and seaport; Lahore had a population of 2,148,000 at the 1972 Census.

FLAG.—The National Flag of Pakistan is dark green, with white vertical stripes at the mast, the green portion bearing a white crescent in the centre and a five-pointed heraldic star.

NATIONAL DAYS.—March 23 (Pakistan Day), August 14 (Independence Day).

BRITISH EMBASSY

Diplomatic Enclave, Ramna 5,
P.O. Box 1122, Islamabad.

Ambassador Extraordinary and Plenipotentiary, His Excellency John Christopher Wyndowe Bushell, C.M.G. (1976).

Counsellors, A. W. B. Strachan, O.B.E. (*Economics*); C. H. Imray (*Head of Chancery*).

Defence and Military Attaché, Brig. G. N. Powell.
Naval Attaché, Cdr. N. J. Cocks, R.N.
Air Attaché, Wing Cdr. J. K. Craven.
1st Secretaries, G. A. Shepherd; H. Thompson, M.B.E. (*Administration*); D. M. Harrison; D. H. Doble; A. R. Murray; C. P. Burdess; P. A. Timothy (*Works*); J. H. Turner (*Commercial*).

There is a British Consulate-General at *Karachi*.
British Council Representative, A. J. Herbert, P.O. Box 1135, Islamabad.

PROVINCES OF THE ISLAMIC REPUBLIC OF PAKISTAN

The Establishment of West Pakistan Act, 1955, came into force on October 3, 1955, and incorporated: (1) the former Governors' Provinces of the Punjab, North-West Frontier and Sind; (2) the former Chief Commissioners' Provinces of Baluchistan and Karachi; (3) the States of Bahawalpur and Khairpur and the Baluchistan States Union; (4) the Tribal Areas of Baluchistan, the Punjab and the North-West Frontier and the States of Amb, Chitral, Dir and Swat, into the Province of *West Pakistan* with effect from October 14, 1955. The Province was reorganized with effect from July 1, 1970, into the four separate Provinces of Punjab (including Bahawalpur), Sind (including Karachi), North West Frontier Province and Baluchistan together with Islamabad Capital Territory and the Tribal Areas.

PANAMA
(República de Panama)

President of the Republic, Ing. Demetrio Lakas, appointed, Dec. 18, 1969, re-appointed, Oct. 11, 1972, *for a term of six years*.
Vice-President, Lic. Gerardo González Vernaza.

CABINET

Interior and Justice, Lic. Jorge E. Castro.
Foreign Affairs, Lic. Aquilino Boyd.
Finance, Sr. Miguel Sanchiz.

Commerce and Industry, Lic. Julio Sosa.
Public Works, Sr. Néstor T. Guerra.
Agricultural Development, Lt. Col. Rubén Dario Paredes.
Health, Sr. Abraham Saied.
Education, Sr. Aristides Royo.
Labour and Social Affairs, Lic. Adolfo Ahumada.
Planning, Sr. Nicolas Ardito Barletta.
Housing, Lic. Tomás Altamirano Duque.
Controller General, D. Castillo.
Minister to the Presidency, Lic. Fernando Manfredo.

PANAMANIAN EMBASSY IN LONDON
39 Montpelier Square, Knightsbridge, S.W.7
[01-589 8751]
Ambassador Extraordinary and Plenipotentiary, His Excellency Roger Decerega (1976).
Minister-Counsellor, Sr. Miguel Chavez-Boyd.
1st Secretary, Sra. Carlina Roquebert (Consular).
Attachés, Sr. Fernando Perez Bedolla; Srta. Nitzia Eugenia Martin; Sr. Hugo Torrijes Richa; Sra. Brunhilda de Garcia-Navarro; Sra. Cecillia G. Revilla de Prudhoe; Sr. Marcos A. Villareal; Sr. Carlos Domingo de Puy.

CONSULATE—Wheatsheaf House, 4 Carmelite Street, E.C.4 [01-353 4792/3].
There are also Consular Offices of the Republic at Glasgow and Liverpool.
Panama lies on the isthmus of that name which connects N. and S. America (see MAP, p. 842). After a revolt (Nov. 3, 1903) it declared its independence from Colombia and established a separate Government.
Since 1968 control of Panama has been increasingly taken over by Gen. Omar Torrijos, Commander of the National Guard, following a military coup. On October 11, 1972, at an assembly of representatives from the 505 electoral districts, the President and Vice-President were installed for a six-year term, and General Torrijos was designated as " Leader of the Revolution " with wide overriding powers.
The area of the Republic is 31,890 sq. m., the population (1975 est.) 1,678,000. The soil is moderately fertile, but nearly one-half of the land is uncultivated. The chief crops are bananas, sugar, coconuts, cacao, coffee and cereals. The shrimping industry plays an important rôle in in the Panamanian economy. A railway 47 miles in length joins the Atlantic and Pacific oceans.
Education is compulsory and free from 7 to 15 years. In 1972 there were 1,906 official primary schools and 65 private primary schools; 69 official secondary and 138 private secondary schools. Primary students numbered 273,324 in official and 14,241 in private schools in 1971; secondary students, 60,352 official and 26,443 private. The average number of students at Panama University in 1973 was 21,216 and at the Catholic University (Universidad Santa Maria Le Antigua) about 718.
Language and Literature.—The official language is Spanish. There are 4 Spanish language and 2 English language newspapers published daily in the capital.
Finance.—Budget estimates for 1976 showed revenue and expenditure in balance at B.463,000,000.
The monetary unit is the Balboa (= $1 U.S.); no Panamanian paper currency is issued, and U.S. dollar bills of all values are in circulation in the Republic and in the Canal Zone.

TRADE

	1973 Balboas	1974 Balboas
Imports	448,881,000	767,800,000
Exports	135,655,000	203,100,000

Trade with U.K.†

	1973	1974
Imports from U.K.	£13,654,000	£12,196,000
Exports to U.K.	773,000	2,092,000

† Including Colon Free Zone.

The imports are mostly manufactured goods, machinery, lubricants, chemicals and foodstuffs; exports are bananas, petroleum products, shrimps, sugar, meat and fishmeal.

CAPITAL, ΨPanama City. Population (1970 Census, preliminary), 418,000.
FLAG.—Four quarters; white with red star (top, next staff), red (in fly), blue (below, next staff) and white with red star. NATIONAL DAY.—November 3.
Dependencies of Panama.—Taboga Island (area 4 sq. miles) is a popular tourist resort some 12 miles from the Pacific entrance to the Panama Canal. Tourist facilities are also being developed in the Las Perlas Archipelago in the Gulf of Panama. There is a penal settlement at Guardia on the island of Coiba (area 19 sq. miles) in the Gulf of Chiriqui.

BRITISH EMBASSY
(120 Via España, Panama)
Ambassador Extraordinary and Plenipotentiary, His Excellency Robert Michael John (1974).
1st Secretary and Consul, A. C. Hunt.
There is a British consular office at Panama City, and an honorary consul at Colon.
Panama, 4,650 miles; transit from Liverpool, 15 to 19 days; from Southampton 15 days; via N.Y., 14 days.

PARAGUAY
(República del Paraguay)

President, General Alfredo Stroessner, inaugurated Aug. 15, 1954, re-elected 1958, 1963, 1968 and 1973.
Foreign Affairs, Dr. Alberto Nogués.
Finance, General César Barrientos (ret.).
Interior, Dr. Sabino A. Montanaro.
Defence, General Marcial Samaniego (ret.).
Justice and Labour, Dr. Saúl González.
Education and Worship, Dr. Raúl Peña.
Public Works and Communications, General de División Juan A. Cáceres.
Agriculture and Livestock, Ing. Hernando Bertoni.
Industry and Commerce, Dr. Delfin Ugarte Centurión.
Without Portfolio, Arq. Tomás Romero Pereira.
President of Central Bank, Dr. César Romeo Acosta.

PARAGUAYAN EMBASSY IN LONDON
Braemar Lodge, Cornwall Gardens, S.W.7
[01-937 1253]
Ambassador Extraordinary and Plenipotentiary, His Excellency Numa Alcides Mallorquín (1969).
Minister-Counsellor and Consul General, Bernardo Galeano.
1st Secretaries, Jorge A. Colmán; Mrs. G. S. de Jauregui.
There is a Paraguayan Consulate in Liverpool.
Area and Population.—Paraguay is an inland subtropical State of South America, situated between Argentina, Bolivia and Brazil.
The area is computed at 157,000 square miles, with a population (est. 1975) of 2,500,000.
Eastern Paraguay consists of a series of plains, intersected by abrupt ranges of hills, none of which exceeds 2,300 feet above sea level. The Paraguay and Alto Paraná rivers are normally navigable for vessels of 6 to 7 feet draught. Some of the tributary streams are also navigable. The Pilcomayo river is navigable for small craft for 180 miles from Asunción. Paraguay is a country of grassy plains and dense forest, the soil being marshy in many parts and liable to floods; while the hills are covered for the most part with immense forests.

The streams flowing into the Alto Paraná descend precipitously into that river. In the angle formed by the Paraná-Paraguay confluence are extensive marshes, one of which, known as " Neembucú," or " endless," is drained by *Lake Ypoa*, a large lagoon, south-east of the capital. The *Chaco*, lying between the rivers Paraguay and Pilcomayo and bounded on the north by Bolivia, formed the subject of a long-standing dispute with that country and led to war between Paraguay and Bolivia from 1932 to 1935. The Chaco is a flat plain, rising uniformly towards its western boundary to a height of 1,140 feet; it suffers much from floods and still more from drought, but the building of dams and reservoirs has converted part of it into good pasture for cattle raising.

Government.—In 1535 Paraguay was settled as a Spanish possession. In 1811 it declared its independence of Spain.

The 1967 constitution provides for a two-chamber parliament consisting of a 30-member Senate and a 60-member Chamber of Deputies. Two-thirds of the seats in each chamber are allocated to the majority party and the remaining one-third shared among the minority parties in proportion to the votes cast. Voting is compulsory for all citizens over 18.

The President is elected for 5 years and may be re-elected for a further term. He appoints the Cabinet, which exercises all the functions of government. During parliamentary recess it can govern by decree through the Council of State, the members of which are representative of the Government, the armed forces and various other bodies.

The first elections under the new constitution were held on Feb. 11, 1968.

Production.—About three-quarters of the population are engaged in agriculture and cattle raising. Canned and frozen beef, timber, tobacco, cotton, soya, edible oils and essential oils are the main exports. The forests contain many varieties of timber which find a good market abroad. Paraguay's hydroelectric power station at Acaray produces 90,000 kW. of which a surplus is exported to Argentina and Brazil.

Brazil and Paraguay are carrying out a project to develop the potential of the River Paraná—annual output is planned at 10·7 million kWh. Similarly, Paraguay and Argentina are to develop the hydroelectric complex at the Yacyreta rapids. This has a potential annual output of 3·5 million kWh. Work on the Itaipú hydroelectric scheme began early in 1976 and work on the Jacyretá scheme is scheduled to begin in 1977.

Communications.—A railway, 985 miles in length, connects Asunción with Buenos Aires. The journey takes 55 hours. Train ferries enable the run to be accomplished without break of bulk. River steamers also connect Buenos Aires and Asunción (3 to 5 days). This service is liable to cancellation without warning when the river is low or in flood. There are direct shipping services between Hamburg, Antwerp, Amsterdam and Asunción; New York, Philadelphia, Baltimore and Asunción; and Liverpool, London and Asunción. Eight airlines operate services from Asunción.

There are 810 km. of asphalted roads in Paraguay, connecting Asunción with São Paulo (26 hrs.) *via* the Bridge of Friendship and Foz de Yguazú and with Buenos Aires (24 hrs.) *via* Puerto Pilcomayo, and about 4,050 miles of earth roads in fairly good condition, but liable to be closed or to become impassable in wet weather. A 1000 km. unpaved road links Asunción with the Bolivian border. There are services to Buenos Aires, São Paulo and Paranagua, a port on the Brazilian coast.

Defence.—There is a permanent military force of about 14,000 all ranks, most of whom are conscripts doing their military service; and about 6,500 armed police (again mostly conscripts). Three gunboats and a number of small armed launches patrol inland waters.

Language and Literature.—Spanish is the official language of the country but outside the larger towns *Guaraní*, the language of the largest single unit of original Indian inhabitants, is widely spoken. Three morning, one afternoon and three weekly newspapers are published in Asunción.

Education.—In 1976 there were 2,850 primary schools. They had 15,100 teachers and 458,000 students. The National University in Asunción had in 1976 a teaching staff of 1,125 and 9,280 students. The Catholic University had 4,560 students and about 438 teachers.

FINANCE

| | 1975 | 1976 |
	Guaranies	*Guaranies*
Revenue	50,481,591,141	61,655,000,000
Expenditure	49,259,984,666	59,175,000,000

Currency.—A free exchange system was introduced in August, 1957. The rate of exchange in June 1976 was Gs.225=£1. (*See also* p. 86.)

Trade.—The imports are chiefly articles of food and drink, consumer goods, textiles, vehicles and machinery. Main exports: Meat and by-products, tobacco, seeds, yerba maté, maize, fruit (lemons, grapefruit, oranges), coffee, cotton fibre, essential oils, vegetable oil, castor seed oil, and timber.

Trade with U.K.

	1974	1975
Imports from U.K.	£4,452,000	£6,484,000
Exports to U.K.	2,466,000	6,837,000

CAPITAL, Ψ Asunción, about 1,000 miles up the River Paraguay from Buenos Aires. Pop. (census, 1970), 437,000; other centres being ΨEncarnación, 47,333; Concepción, 52,826; and Villarica 38,052.

FLAG.—Three horizontal bands, red, white, blue with the National seal on the obverse white band and the Treasury seal on the reverse white band.

NATIONAL DAY.—May 14.

BRITISH EMBASSY
Casilla de Correo 404, Asunción
Ambassador Extraordinary and Plenipotentiary and Consul-General, His Excellency Charles William Wallace, C.V.O. (1976)
1st Secretary and Consul, J. D. Edgerton.
Defence Attaché, Col. R. W. Millo (resident in *Buenos Aires*).
3rd Secretary and Vice-Consul, G. L. Minter.

Asunción is approximately 4,000 miles distant from London by air. Transit by sea 25 days. By air approximately 21 hours flying time *via* Rio de Janeiro.

PERSIA. See IRAN

PERU
(República del Peru)

President, General de División EP Francisco Morales Bermudez, *assumed office*, Aug. 29, 1975.
Prime Minister and Minister of War, General de División EP Jorge Fernandez Maldonado Solari.
Foreign Affairs, Gen. de División EP Miguel de la Flor Valle.
Interior, Gen. Luis Cisneros Vizquerra.
Energy and Mines, Gen. Arturo la Torre di Tolla.
Economy and Finance, Dr. Luis Barúa Castañeda.

PERUVIAN EMBASSY AND CONSULATE
52, Sloane Street, S.W.1
[01–235 1977]
Ambassador Extraordinary and Plenipotentiary, His
Excellency Señor Don Adhemar Montagne
(1969).
Minister, Sr. Dr. Don Alejandro San Martin Caro.
Naval Attaché, Rear-Adm. Daniel Masías Abadía.

Air and Military Attaché, Maj. Gen. José Aste.

Area and Population.—Peru is a maritime Republic
of South America, situated between 0° 00′ 48″ and
18° 21′ 00″ S. latitude and between 68° 39′ 27″ and
81° 20′ 13″ W. longitude. The area of the Republic including 4,440 square kilometres of the Peruvian section of Lake Titicaca and 32 square kilometres of the coastal islands, is about 531,000
square miles with a total population (census,
1972) of 14,121,564.

Physical Features.—The country is traversed
throughout its length by the Andes, running parallel
to the Pacific coast, the highest points in the Peruvian
sector being *Huascaran* (22,211 feet), *Huandoy*
(20,855 feet), *Ausangate* (20,235 feet), *Misti* volcano
(18,364 feet), *Hualcan* (20,000 feet), *Chachani*
(19,037 feet), *Antajasha* (18,020 feet), *Pichupichu*
(17,724 feet), and *Mount Meiggs* (17,583 feet).

There are three main regions, the *Costa*, west of
the Andes, the *Sierra* or mountain ranges of the
Andes, which include the *Punas* or mountainous
wastes below the region of perpetual snow and the
Montana, or *Selva*, which is the vast area of jungle
stretching from the eastern foothills of the Andes to
the eastern frontiers of Peru. The coastal area,
lying upon and near the Pacific, is not tropical,
though close to the Equator, being cooled by the
Humboldt Current; its chief products are cotton,
sugar, and petroleum. It contains the capital,
Lima, and most of the white population.

In the mountains, where most of the Indians live,
are to be found minerals in great richness and
variety, and cattle, sheep, llamas and alpacas are
bred there. In the mountain valleys maize,
potatoes and wheat are grown. Upon the eastern
slopes of the Andes are to be found very large tracts
suitable for cultivation and stock raising. The
main products of the jungle are timber, barbasco
and leche caspi.

Government.—Peru was conquered in the early
16th century by Francisco Pizarro (born 1478,
died 1541). He subjugated the Incas (the ruling
caste of the Quechua Indians), who had started
their rise to power some 500 years earlier, and for
nearly three centuries Peru remained under Spanish
rule. A revolutionary war of 1821–1824 established its independence, declared on July 28, 1821.
The constitution rests upon the fundamental law
of Oct. 18, 1856 (amended in 1860, 1919, 1933,
1936 and in 1939), and is that of a democratic
Republic. The Constitution provides for the
election for six years of a President by direct vote
of the people and of a Congress composed of a
Senate and Chamber of Deputies.

Presidential and Congressional elections on a basis
of proportional representation were held on June 9,
1963, and a new President, Sr. Belaúnde Terry,
held office from July 28 until deposed by a revolutionary junta on Oct. 3, 1968, and sent out of the
country. The junta appointed a Cabinet composed
of officers from the three armed services and named
General Velasco as President. In a bloodless coup
on August 29, 1975, Gen. Valasco was replaced by
Gen. Francisco Morales Bermudez.

Production.—Agriculture employing 46 per cent.
of the labour force accounted for only about
14·5 per cent. of the Gross Domestic Product in 1973.
The chief crops are cotton, potatoes and other
vegetables, sugar, fruit, maize, rice, wheat, barley,
grapes and coffee. Mineral exports in 1974 were
valued at U.S. $562,103,000 and included lead, zinc,
copper, iron ore and silver,

Peru is normally the world's largest exporter of
fishmeal. The value of fishmeal exports dropped
from U.S. $267,000,000 in 1971 to U.S. $233,254,000
in 1972 and U.S. $135,894,000 in 1973 because of
adverse climatic conditions, but is now recovering.

Communications.—In recent years the coastal
and sierra zones have been opened up by means of
roads and air routes and there is air communication,
as well as communication by protracted land routes,
with the tropical eastern zones, which lie east of
the Andes towards the borders of Brazil, and consist mainly of unexplored or little known country
inhabited by Indians in a savage state. The completion in 1944 of the trunk road of the *Andean
Highway* from the Pacific port of Callao, *via* Lima,
Oroya, Cerro de Pasco (14,700 ft.), Huanuco, Tingo
Maria, to Pucallpa, the river port on the Ucayali,
forms a link between the Pacific, the Amazon and
the Atlantic. The trunk road runs through the
Boqueron del Padre Abad, a pass rediscovered on July
22, 1937, in the backbone of the Blue Cordillera.
The Peruvian section of the Pan American highway
is complete and is asphalted throughout.

The first railway was opened in 1850 and the
2,400 miles of track are now administered by the
Government. There is also steam navigation on
the Ucayali (*see* Andean Highway above) and
Huallaga, and in the south on Lake Titicaca. Air
services are maintained throughout Peru, and a
number of international services call at Lima.

Defence.—The Army is recruited by voluntary
enlistment, supplemented by conscription (2 years),
and numbers about 45,000 of all ranks. Armoured
units are equipped with American, Russian and
French vehicles. Engineer units are employed on
the construction of roadways in Peru using American equipment. *Navy.*—The Navy consists of 3
cruisers; 4 destroyers; 2 frigates; 2 corvettes; 6
U.S. submarines and 2 German submarines, the
latter added to the fleet in 1974 and 1975; 4 LST's;
5 river gun-boats; 4 fleet oilers; 4 fleet auxiliaries;
2 river transports; 14 patrol boats; 2 patrol launches;
1 floating dock and 2 tugs. The main Naval base is

in Callao and supports all ships of the Fleet. There are training establishments in Callao and La Punta. The Naval Air Arm consists of U.S. and French helicopters; U.S. anti-submarine aircraft and DC3's. *Air Force.*—The Air Force is equipped with British Hunter and Canberra aircraft; American training, fighter and transport aircraft plus helicopters; French Mirage aircraft and Alouette helicopters. There are military airfields at Talara, Piura, Chiclayo, Lima, Pisco, Joya, Iquitos and Arequipa plus a seaplane base at Iquitos. There are also a Civil Guard and a Republican Guard whose members number respectively 30,000 and 5,000.

Education.—Education is compulsory and free for both sexes between the ages of 6 and 15. In 1972 a new Law of Education radically changed the structure of the system. There are to be three levels: Initial (up to 6 years), Basic (6-15 years) and Higher (over 15 years). Basic education corresponds approximately to the former Primary and Secondary level pupils. In 1975 there were 3,729,028 pupils attending in the normal basic level of education. State basic education schools numbered 19,167 with 106,496 teachers. Technical education numbered 250,788 pupils, 377 schools and 10,320 teachers. Private basic schools numbered 3,517, teachers 11,535 and pupils 376,169. A new system of Higher Schools of Professional Education is being developed to cater for pupils from 15 years to 18 or 19 years. In 1975 there were 9 such schools, with 234 teachers and 5,523 pupils. These schools will replace the top three classes of the former secondary school (16-18 years) and from them pupils may enter University. In 1975 there were 22 state (134,979 students) and 11 private (51,532 students) Universities in Peru: 14 of the universities are located in Lima: the oldest, San Marcos, was founded in 1551.

Language and Literature.—Spanish, the language of the original Spanish stock from which the governing and professional classes are mainly recruited, was formerly the only official language of the country. However, in May 1975, the Quechua language was declared by Decree Law as the second official tongue. Quechua and Aymara are widely spoken by more than half the population of the country. Before the arrival of Pizarro, the Incas had attained a high state of culture, some traces of which survived three centuries of Spanish rule. Modern Peruvian literature includes a national drama in the Spanish tongue and many Peruvian writers have attained international fame. The national library founded at Lima in 1821 was pillaged by Chileans in the Pacific War of 1879-1882, but many of the scattered manuscripts and books have since been recovered. The greater part of the historical section of the library was destroyed by fire in 1943. The first printed news-sheet in South America was issued at Lima in 1594 and in 1976 there were 7 main morning papers, including the official gazette *El Peruano*, one afternoon paper daily and about 50 provincial papers.

Finance.—The unit of currency is the *Sol* of 100 *centavos*. For rate of exchange, *see* p. 84.

	1973-74 (two years)
Public revenue	*Soles* 143,219,000,000
Public expenditure	146,219,000,000

In 1975, Peru's balance of payments deficit was U.S.$565,077,000.

Trade.—Import trade of Peru in 1975 totalled U.S.$2,491,000,000 and exports U.S.$1,378,460,000.

Trade with U.K.

	1974	1975
Imports from U.K.	£21,884,000	£51,034,000
Exports to U.K.	35,788,000	28,794,000

The principal imports are machinery, foodstuffs, metal and manufactured metal goods, chemicals and pharmaceutical products. The chief exports are minerals and metals, fishmeal, sugar, cotton and coffee.

CAPITAL.—Metropolitan Lima (including ΨCallao), population 3,595,000. Arequipa (561,338) ΨIquitos (540,560), ΨChiclayo (533,266).

FLAG.—Three vertical bands, red, white, red; coat of arms on white band. NATIONAL DAY.—July 28 (Anniversary of Independence).

BRITISH EMBASSY

Edificio El, Pacifico-Washington (Piso 12), Plaza Washington, Avenida Arequipa, Lima.

Ambassador Extraordinary and Plenipotentiary, His Excellency Kenneth Douglas Jamieson, C.M.G. (1974).

1st Secretaries, D. W. R. Lewis (*Head of Chancery*); M. Elliott (*Commercial*).

Defence, Naval, Military and Air Attaché, Capt. D. L. G. James, R.N.

2nd Secretaries, S. S. Calder (*Commercial*); R. G. Lewington (*Information*); G. S. Cowling (*Technical Assistance*).

BRITISH CONSULAR OFFICES

There are British Consular Offices at *Lima* and *Callao*.

British Council Representative, O. R. Siddle, Apartado 11114, Edif. Pacifico-Washington, Ave Arequipa, Lima

Lima, 7,020 miles; transit, *via* New York and Colon, 21-27 days: *via* Liverpool and Colon, 17-30 days. Direct British Airways service Lima-London.

THE PHILIPPINES
(República ng Pilipinas)

President, Ferdinand Marcos, *b.* 1917, *elected* Nov. 10, 1965, *assumed office* Dec. 30, 1965, re-elected for 4 years, Nov. 11, 1969.

CABINET

Foreign Affairs, Carlos P. Romulo.
Justice, Vicente Abad Santos.
Finance, Cesar Virata.
Defence, Juan Ponce Enrile.
Education, Juan L. Manuel.
Labour, Blas F. Ople.
Trade, Troadio Quiazon.
Public Works, Alfredo L. Juinio.
Health, Clemente S. Gatmaitan.
Agriculture, Arturo Tanco.
[The above are the principal appointments.]

PHILIPPINE EMBASSY
9a Palace Green, W.8
[01-937 3646]

Ambassador Extraordinary and Plenipotentiary (vacant).
Minister-Counsellor, Pablo A. Araque.
Armed Forces Attaché, Capt. Artemio Tadiar.
3rd Secretary, Hector K. Villarroel.

Area and Population.—The Philippines are situated between 21° 20'-4° 30' N. lat. and 116° 55'-126° 36' E. long., and are distant about 500 miles from the south-east coast of the continent of Asia.

The total land area of the country is 114,834 square miles, of which total 106,914 square miles are contained in the eleven largest islands, the 7,079 other islands having a combined area of 7,929 square miles.

The principal islands are:—

Name	sq. miles	Name	sq. miles
Luzon	40,422	Mindoro	3,759
Mindanao	36,538	Leyte	2,786
Samar	5,050	Cebu	1,703
Negros	4,906	Bohol	1,492
Palawan	4,550	Masbate	1,262
Panay	4,446		

Other groups in the Republic are the Sulu islands (Capital, Jolo), Babuyanes and Batanes; the Catanduanes; and Culion Islands.

The population of the Philippines was estimated in 1975 at 42,517,300.

The inhabitants, known as Filipinos, are basically all of Malay stock, with a considerable admixture of Spanish and Chinese blood in many localities, and over 90 per cent. of them are Christians, predominantly Roman Catholics. Most of the remainder are Moslems, in the south, and Pagans, mainly in the north. There is a Chinese minority estimated at 350,000, and other much smaller foreign communities, notably Spanish, American and Indian.

The Portuguese navigator Magellan came to the Philippines in 1521 and was slain by the natives of Mactan, a small island near Cebu. In 1565 Spain undertook the conquest of the country which was named "Filipinas", after the son of the King of Spain, and in 1571 the city of Manila was founded by the conquistador Legaspi, who subdued the inhabitants of almost all the islands, their conversion from barbarism and paganism being undertaken by the Augustinian friars in Legaspi's reign. In 1762 Manila was occupied by a British force, but in 1764 it was restored to Spain. In the nineteenth century there were frequent disturbances in the islands, and at the outbreak of the Spanish–American War of 1898 a rebellion under Aguinaldo, a native leader, had just died down. After the Spanish fleet had been destroyed in Manila Bay (May 1, 1898), Manila was captured by American troops with the help of Filipinos, on Aug. 13, 1898, and the Islands were ceded to the United States by the *Treaty of Paris* of Dec. 10, 1898. However, the Filipinos, under Aguinaldo, rose up in arms on Feb. 4, 1899, against the U.S. Government, maintaining a desultory rebellion until it was quelled in 1902. Following this, the Philippine Commission was established, consisting of a Governor-General and Commissioner appointed by the President of the United States, who exercised a large measure of executive and legislative authority.

A measure of local independence was granted under the Jones Act of August 29, 1916. On March 24, 1934, the Tydings-McDuffie Law, gave the Philippines a "Commonwealth" Status. The Republic of the Philippines came into existence on July 4, 1946 with a presidential form of government based on the American system. On January 17, 1973, a revised constitution, providing for a parliamentary form of government with a unicameral legislative, was proclaimed after its ratification in a national referendum. Since September 21, 1972, however, the country has been under martial law: the President, who has also assumed the position of Prime Minister under the new constitution, has postponed indefinitely elections for the new National Assembly, while he attempts to carry out a programme of social reforms. In the meantime government functions by presidential decrees.

Language and Literature.—The official languages are Pilipino and English. Pilipino, the national language, is based on Tagalog, one of the Malay-Polynesian languages which according to the 1960 census is spoken by 44 per cent. of the population. English, which is the language of government and

of instruction in secondary and university education, is spoken by at least 40 per cent. of the population. Spanish, which ceased to be an official language in 1973, is now spoken by only 2 per cent. 73 per cent. of the population are literate. There is a National Library in the capital with branches in other urban centres and a flourishing press. Education accounts for about 30 per cent. of local expenditure in the national budget. Secondary and higher education is extensive and there are 37 private universities recognized by the Government, including the Dominican University of Santo Thomas (founded in 1611), the first in the Far East and 25 years older than Harvard; there are also 6 State-supported universities, including the University of the Philippines, founded 1908. It is estimated that students at private and state colleges and universities in 1975–76 will number 1,234,170.

Roads and Railways.—Communications suffered

serious damage during the War of 1941–45 owing to the lack of proper maintenance during the Japanese occupation and destruction by bombardment. The highway system is undergoing rehabilitation and extension and, including all types of services, covered 74,768 kilometres in 1972. In 1974 there were 792,253 road vehicles registered. Before the war the railways, which were largely Government owned, operated approximately 845 miles of track of which some 740 miles are still operated. The Philippine National Railway, on Luzon Island, has been converted to diesel traction.

Shipping.—There are 92 ports of entry in the Philippines and 3,377 vessels of various types, totalling 591,443 tons, are engaged in inter-island traffic. There are 154 ocean-going vessels registered in the Philippines, totalling 740,233 gross tons.

Civil Aviation.—Air transport plays a key part in inter-island travel and an important one in communications overseas. Philippine Air Lines have regular flights to Hong Kong, Taipei, Sydney, Singapore, Saigon, and Tokyo and operate four trans-Pacific flights a week to San Francisco, in addition to inter-island services. Air Manila (Inc.) also operate charter international and local air services.

FINANCE

	1974	1975
Receipts	P.9,498,000	P.16,833,000
Expenditure	8,574,000	18,511,000

P.=Philippine Peso. Official rate of exchange:

P1·00=U.S.26c. Rate of exchange (1974) for imports is P.6·772=U.S.$1; exports P.6·791= U.S.$1.
(*See also* p. 84.)

TRADE

	1974	1975
Total imports....	$3,143,260,000	$3,459,000,000
Total exports....	2,724,900,000	2,294,000,000

Trade with U.K.

	1974	1976
Imports from U.K...	£49,276,000	£54,606,000
Exports to U.K.....	16,791,000	40,574,000

The Philippines is a predominantly agricultural country, the chief products being rice, coconuts, maize, sugar-cane, abaca (manila hemp), fruits, tobacco and lumber. There is, however, an increasing number of manufacturing industries and it is the policy of the Government to diversify its economy.

The principal Philippine exports in both natural and manufactured states are coconuts, sugar, abaca, base metals, lumber, pineapples, bananas, embroideries and tobacco.

CAPITAL.— Ψ Manila, in the island of Luzon: population (1975): City area, 1,438,252; Manila with suburbs (incl. Quezon City, Pasay City, Caloocan City, Makati, Parañaque, San Juan Mandaluyong and Navota), 3,356,404. The next largest cities are Ψ Cebu (418,517), Ψ Davao (515,520), Ψ Iloilo (247,956), Ψ Zamboanga (240,066), and Bacolod (196,492).

FLAG.—Equal horizontal bands of blue (above) and red; gold sun with three stars on a white triangle next to staff. NATIONAL DAY.—June 12 (Independence Day).

BRITISH EMBASSY
Manila

Ambassador Extraordinary and Plenipotentiary, His Excellency James Alexander Turpin, C.M.G. (1972)
Counsellor, P. J. George, O.B.E.
Defence Attaché, Cdr. A. L. Thorpe, R.N.
1st Secretary, W. E. Quantrill (*Head of Chancery*).
2nd Secretaries, C. J. Gunnell (*Commercial*); A. J. F. Caie; I. J. Towner (*Administration and Consul*).

POLAND
(Polska Rzeczpospolita Ludowa)
COUNCIL OF STATE

Chairman, Henryk Jabloński.
Deputy Chairmen, Edward Babiuch; Wladyslaw Kruczek; Tadeusz Witold Mlynczak; Zdzislaw Tomal.
Secretary, Ludomir Stasiak.

CABINET

Prime Minister, Piotr Jaroszewicz.
Deputy Premiers, Mieczyslaw Jagielski; Franciszek Kaim; Jozef Tejchma; Kazimierz Olszewski; Tadeusz Pyka; Longin Cegielski; Tadeusz Wrzaszczyk; Alojzy Karkoszka.
Foreign Affairs, Stefan Olszowski.
Defence, Gen. Wojciech Jaruzelski.
Internal Affairs, Stanislaw Kowalczyk.
Finance, Henryk Kisiel.
Mining, Jan Kulpinski.
Heavy and Agricultural Machinery Industry, Franciszek Adamkiewicz.
Internal Trade, Jerzy Gawrysiak.
Transport, Tadeusz Bejom.
Culture and Art, Jozef Tejchma.
Forestry and Timber Industry, Tadeusz Skwirzynski.
Communications, Edward Kowalczyk.
Chemical Industry, Maciej Wirowski.
Machine Industry, Aleksander Kopec.
Light Industry, Tadeusz Kunicki.
Food Industry, Emil Kolodziej.

Agriculture, Kazimierz Barcikowski.
Justice, Jerzy Bafia.
Foreign Trade and Marine Economy, Jerzy Olszewski.
Health and Social Welfare, Marian Sliwinski.
Building and Building Materials, Adam Glazur.
Chairmen of Committees, Tadeusz Wrzaszczyk (*Planning Commission*); Jaroslaw Nowicki (*Main Customs Office*).
Science, Technology and Higher Schooling, Sylwester Kaliski.
Education and Schooling, Jerzy Kuberski.
Labour, Wages and Social Affairs, Tadeusz Rudolf.
Regional Economy and Protection of the Environment, Emil Wojtaszek.
Power Industry and Nuclear Power, Andrzej Szozda.
Raw Materials, Eugeniusz Szyr.
War Veterans' Affairs, Gen. Mieczyslaw Grudzien.
Religious Affairs, Kazimierz Kakol.
Metallurgy, Franciszek Kaim.

UNITED WORKERS' (=Communist) PARTY

Politbureau of the Central Committee, E. Gierek; E. Babiuch; H. Jablonski; M. Jagielski; P. Jaroszewicz; W. Jaruzelski; W. Kruczek; S. Olszowski; J. Szydlak; J. Tejchma; Z. Grudzien; S. Kania; J. Kepa; Stanistaw Kowalczyk (*full members*); K. Barcikowski; T. Wrzaszczyk; J. Lukaszewicz.
Secretariat of the Central Committee, E. Gierek (*First*); E. Babiuch; W. Krasko; J. Pinkowski; S. Kania; J. Lukaszewicz; J. Szydlak; A. Werblan; R. Frelek; Z. Zandarowski (*Secretaries*); Z. Kurowski (*member*).

POLISH EMBASSY IN LONDON
47 Portland Place, W.1
[01-580 4324]

Ambassador Extraordinary and Plenipotentiary, His Excellency Artur Starewicz (1971).
Minister Plenipotentiary and Counsellor, Janusz Mickiewicz.
Counsellors, Leonard Lachowski (*Commercial*); Marian Spaliński (*Press*); Janusz Czamarski (*Scientific*); Jan Rabś; Ernest Bryll (*Cultural*).
1st Secretaries, Mieczyslaw Schwarz; Jerzy Cendrowski.
2nd Secretaries, Jerzy Poziomek; Lech Zembrzuski.
Military, Air and Naval Attaché, Col. Antoni Wasilewski.

Area and Population.—In 1939 the area of the Polish Republic was 150,572 square miles with a population of about 35,000,000, of whom 30 per cent. were national minorities (including over 3,000,000 Jews). Frontier changes took place at the end of the war as foreshadowed at the Tehran Conference in 1943. About 69,000 square miles of territory in the east were ceded to the Soviet Union. In exchange Poland received in the west 39,000 square miles of Eastern Germany. The southern boundary was not affected except for minor adjustments to that part formerly dividing Poland from Ruthenia (Czechoslovakia). The western boundary is formed by the Rivers Oder and Neisse. Poland now has a maritime frontier stretching from west of Kaliningrad (formerly Königsberg) to west of Szczecin (formerly Stettin). As a result of the change of frontier and of very great war-time losses, at the census of December 3, 1950, the population had fallen to 24,977,000 in an area of 121,000 square miles. In 1975, it was estimated to be 34,186,000. Roman Catholicism is the religion of 95 per cent. of the inhabitants.

Government.—The Republic of Poland (reconstituted within the limits of the old Polish Commonwealth) was proclaimed at Warsaw in November, 1918, and its independence guaranteed by the signatories of the Treaty of Versailles. The Polish Commonwealth had ceased to exist in 1795 after three successive partitions in 1772, 1793 and 1795,

in which Prussia, Russia and Austria shared. During the Napoleonic wars, the small Grand Duchy of Warsaw was created but was dissolved by the final act of the Congress of Vienna. The so-called " Congress Kingdom " was then established on the Polish territory which had fallen to Russia's share and the Tsar assumed the title of King of Poland. Prussia acquired Poznania and Polish Pomerania, Austria acquired Galicia and the small Republic of Cracow came into existence under the joint control of Prussia, Russia and Austria. In 1831, after an insurrection, the Congress Kingdom was dissolved and annexed by Russia and in 1848 the Austrians absorbed the Cracow Republic, Poland as an independent state ceasing to exist until the end of the War of 1914–18, when she became independent once again, after 150 years of foreign rule.

In March, 1939, Great Britain entered into a treaty with Poland (France had done so in 1921) guaranteeing Polish territory against aggression, and on Hitler's invasion France and Britain implemented their guarantee. On September 17,

1939, Russian forces invaded eastern Poland and on September 21, 1939, Poland was declared by Germany and Russia to have ceased to exist. A line of demarcation was established between the areas occupied by German and Russian forces. At the end of the war a Coalition Government was formed in which the Polish Workers' Party played a large part. In December, 1948, the Polish Workers' Party and the Polish Socialist Party fused in the new Polish United Workers' Party. This is a Communist Party which closely controls every branch of State activity. A new Constitution modelled on the Soviet Constitution of 1936 was adopted on July 22, 1952, and was modified in February 1976. It changed the title of the country to the Polish People's Republic (*Polska Rzeczpospolita Ludowa*). It made no provision for a President of the Republic, whose functions were to be jointly exercised by a Council of State. Private ownership of land and freedom of religion were recognized. Church and State were to be separate.

Despite the guarantee of religious freedom in the Constitution, a campaign of encroachment in 1953 culminated in the arrest of the Primate of the Roman Catholic Church, Cardinal Wyszyński. Dissatisfaction with the *régime* and conditions of life led to riots in Poznań in June, 1956, and subsequently M. Wladyslaw Gomülka, who had been expelled from the Party in 1949, was reinstated and elected First Secretary of the Party. At the same time Cardinal Wyszyński was allowed to resume his functions. In Jan., 1957, elections to the *Sejm* were held and in Feb., 1957, a reconstructed Government, still led by M. Cyrankiewicz, took office. Elections to the *Sejm* have been held in 1961, 1965, 1972 and 1976. The expression of severe popular discontent in December 1970, in the form of rioting in the northern parts of Gdansk, Gdynia and Szczecin led to the ousting of Gomulka, and substantial Government and Party changes followed. Edward Gierek succeeded as First Secretary.

Education.—Elementary education (ages 7–15) is compulsory and free. Secondary education is optional and free. There are universities at Kraków Warsaw, Poznan, Lódź, Wroclaw, Lublin and Toruń and a considerable number of other towns.

Language and Literature.—Polish is a western Slavonic tongue (*see* U.S.S.R.), the Latin alphabet being used. Polish literature developed rapidly after the foundation of the University of Cracow (a printing press was established there in 1474 and there Copernicus died in 1543). A national school of poetry and drama survived the dismemberment and the former era of romanticism, whose chief Polish exponent was Adam Mickiewicz, was followed by realistic and historical fiction, including the works of Henryk Sienkiewicz (1846–1916), Nobel Prize-winner for Literature in 1905, Boleslaw Prus (1847–1912), and Stanislaw Reymont (1868–1925), Nobel Prize-winner in 1924. There are now 42 daily papers published in Poland, 11 of them in Warsaw.

Production and Industry.—On January 3, 1946, a decree was issued to provide for the nationalization of mines, petroleum resources, water, gas and electricity services, banks, textile factories and large retail stores. At present over 99 per cent. of Polish industry is stated to be " socialized ", but 74·1 per cent. of agricultural land is privately farmed.

FINANCE

	1974	1975
	Zloty	*million*
Revenue†	604,100	720,000
Expenditure†	602,300	713,800
† Budget.		

The basic exchange rate is 7·54 *zloty*= £1 but this is not used in practice. A special rate of 35·70 *zloty*= £1 (June 1976) is in force for non-commercial transactions with western countries. All foreign trade is conducted in foreign currencies. (*See also* p. 84.)

Trade with U.K.

	1973	1974
Imports from U.K...	£111,192,000	£138,700,000
Exports to U.K.....	95,124,000	11C,300,000

CAPITAL.—Warsaw, on the Vistula, pop. (1975) 1,436,100. Other large towns are Lódz (798,300); Kraków (684,000); Wroclaw (575,900); Poznan (516,000); Gdansk (421,000); Szczecin (369,700); Katowice (343,700); Bydgoszcz (322,700); Lublin (271,900); Bytom (234,400); Zabrze (203,700); Czestochowa (200,300).

FLAG.—Equal horizontal stripes of white (above) and red. NATIONAL DAY.—July 22.

BRITISH EMBASSY
(No. 1 Aleja Róz, Warsaw)

Ambassador Extraordinary and Plenipotentiary, His Excellency George Frank Norman Reddaway, C.B.E. (1974).

Counsellors, J. H. Fawcett (*Head of Chancery*); K. E. H. Morris (*Commercial*).

Defence and Air Attaché, Gp.-Capt. M. C. N. Smart, A.F.C.
Naval and Military Attaché, Lt.-Col. J. P. Mac-Donald.
1st Secretaries, Dr. R. R. B. Baxendine; J. H. Potter, M.B.E.; G. G. Collins; K. C. James.
2nd Secretaries, N. C. MacKenzie (*Consul*); A. H. Banks (*Administration*); N. H. J. Ferguson (*Commercial*); P. A. Burrowes; D. G. Manning.
British Council Representative, Dr. B. M. Lott, O.B.E., Al. Jerozolimskie 59, 00–697 Warsaw.

PORTUGAL
(República Portuguesa)
President of the Republic, General António Ramalho Eanes, *assumed office*, July, 1976.

CABINET
(July 23, 1976)
Prime Minister, Dr. Mário Soares.
Ministers of State, Prof. Henrique de Barros; Prof. Jorge Campinos.
Defence, Lt. Col. Firmino Miguel.
Foreign Affairs, Dr. Medeiros Ferreira.
Interior, Lt. Col. Costa Brás.
Agriculture and Fisheries, Eng. Lopes Cardoso.
Social Affairs, Dr. Armando Bacelar.
Public Works, Eng. Almeida Pina.
Transport and Communications, Dr. Rui Vilar.
Labour, Dr. Marcelo Curto.
Finance, Dr. Medina Carreira.
Justice, Dr. António Almeida Santos.
Trade and Tourism, Dr. António Barreto.
Industry and Technology, Eng. Walter Rosa.
Education and Scientific Research, Dr. Mário Sotto-mayor Cardia.
Planning and Economic Coordination, Eng. António Sousa Gomes.
Housing, Town Planning and Construction, Eng. Eduardo Pereira.

EMBASSY IN LONDON
11 Belgrave Square, S.W.1
[01–235 5331]
Ambassador Extraordinary and Plenipotentiary, His Excellency Dr. Albano Pines Fernandes Nogueira.
Counsellor, Sr. J. D. N. Barata, O.B.E.
1st Secretary, Sr. F. A. Guimarães.

Area and Population.—Continental Portugal occupies the western part of the Iberian Peninsula, covering an area of 34,000 square miles. It lies between 36° 58′–42° 12″ N. lat. and 6° 11′ 48″–9° 29′ 45″ W. long., being 302 miles in length from N. to S., and averaging about 117 in breadth from E. to W. The population (including the Azores and Madeira) of 8,611, 125 (1970 census) has been swollen by the arrival since 1974 of approximately 600,000–700,000 refugees from the former colonies.

New statutes granted greater autonomy to the North Atlantic islands of the Azores and Madeira in 1976.

Government.—From the eleventh century until 1910 the government of Portugal was a monarchy. and for many centuries included the Vice-Royalty of Brazil, which declared its independence in 1822. In 1910 an armed rising in Lisbon drove King Manoel II and the Royal family into exile, and the National Assembly of Aug. 21, 1911, sanctioned a Republican form of government.

After the fall of the monarchy in 1910, a period of great political instability ensued until eventually the military stepped in. In 1928 Dr. Salazar was appointed Finance Minister, with very wide powers, and in 1932 he became Prime Minister. The Constitution of 1933 gave formal expression to the corporative "Estado Novo" (New State) which he came to personify. Dr. Caetano succeeded Salazar as Prime Minister in 1968 but his failure to liberalize the régime or to provide any alternative to continuing the wars in the African colonies resulted in his government's overthrow by a military coup on April 25, 1974. The next two years were characterized by great political turmoil. No fewer than 6 provisional governments held office between April 1974 and July 1976. The first post-coup President, General Spínola, resigned in September 1974, and was succeeded by General Costa Gomes, who remained in office until a presidential election was held in 1976.

During 1975 Communist and other extreme left elements, both civilian and military, made determined and repeated attempts to control the Government. The political situation was confused and unstable for most of the year, but with the failure of an attempted coup by the extreme left in November 1975 the situation began to become more stable. Elections for a Constituent Assembly were held on April 25, 1975, and for the Assembly of the Republic on April 25, 1976. Both showed that the Communists and the extreme left generally lacked wide support among the population. The results of the 1976 elections were:

Socialist Party	106 seats	(34·87%)
Popular Democratic Party	73 ,,	(24·38%)
Centre Social Democrats	42 ,,	(16%)
Communist Party	40 ,,	(14·35%)
Popular Democratic Union	1 ,,	(1·67%)

General Ramalho Eanes was elected President on June 27, 1976, with 61·54% of the vote.

Defence.—All physically fit males are liable for military service, but conscription is becoming increasingly selective as the armed forces are being greatly reduced following the end of the colonial wars, and reorganized and re-equipped for a conventional national defence rôle. The present strength of the Army is about 33,000. One brigade is earmarked for N.A.T.O. service. The Navy consists of about 12,000 officers and men, including 2,000 marines, manning about 70 craft of various types, many of which are obsolete. The present serving strength of the Air Force is about 9,000, (including paratroops) and about 200–300 aircraft of various types.

Education is free and compulsory for six years from the age of 7. Secondary education is mainly conducted in State lyceums, commercial and industrial schools, but there are also private schools. There are also military, naval, technical and other special schools. There are old established Universities at Coimbra (founded in 1290), Oporto and Lisbon. Three new Universities have been established at Lisbon, Braga and Aveiro.

Language and Literature.—Portuguese is a Romance language with admixtures of Arabic and other idioms. It is the language of Portugal and Brazil, and is the *lingua franca* of Angola, Mozambique and Guinea-Bissau.

Portuguese language and literature reached the culminating point of their development in the *Lusiadas* (dealing with the voyage of Vasco da Gama) and other works of Camoens (Camões), born in 1524, died in 1580. Until the second quarter of the nineteenth century Portuguese literature dominated that of Brazil. Modern literature, both prose and verse, is flourishing.

Newspapers and Broadcasting.—Many new newspapers have sprung up since 1974 and there are now 10 main daily newspapers in Lisbon and 3 in Oporto, and 3 main weekly newspapers. Most have been losing money and the Government has announced plans for a radical reorganization of the newspaper industry. There are 2 TV channels (both black and white) and 5 radio stations (3 state controlled) broadcasting nationwide.

Civil aviation is controlled by the Ministry of Communications. There is an international airport at Portela, about 5 miles from Lisbon, and the airport of Pedras Rubras near Oporto is also used for some international services. There are direct flights between London and Faro in the Algarve.

Agriculture.—The chief agricultural products are cork, maize, wheat, rye, rice, oats, barley, potatoes, beans, onions, olives, oranges, lemons, figs, almonds, tomatoes, timber, port wine and table wines. There are extensive forests of pine, cork, eucalyptus and chestnut covering about 20 per cent. of the total area of the country.

Industry.—The country is so far only moderately industrialized, but is fairly rapidly extending its industries. The principal manufactures, some of which are still protected by high tariffs, are textiles, clothing and footwear, machinery (including electric machinery and transport equipment), foodstuffs (tomato concentrates and canned fish), chemicals, fertilizers, wood, cork, furniture, cement, glassware and pottery. There is a modern steelworks, and two modern and very large shipbuilding and repair yards at Lisbon and Setúbal working mainly for foreign ship-owners. There are several hydro-electric power stations and a new thermal power station. *Minerals.*—The principal mineral products are pyrites, wolfram, tin, iron ores, copper and sodium and calcium minerals.

Finance.—Portugal is a member of the European Monetary Agreement, the World Bank, the International Monetary Fund and the International Finance Corporation. The country has substantial, but declining, gold and foreign exchange reserves. The 1976 Budget showed a deficit of *Escudos* 34,778 million. Total revenue, *Escudos* 105,521 million; expenditure *Escudos* 70,743 million.

Currency.—*Escudo* (of 100 *Centavos*). *Conto* consists of 1,000 escudos. The rate of exchange (July 1976) was *Escudos* 55·50 = £1 (*see also* p. 83).

Trade.—Total trade of Portugal in 1975 amounted to imports valued at *Escudos* 97,692 million and exports valued at *Escudos* 49,310 million. The British share of the Portuguese import market amounted to 8·7 per cent. and the United Kingdom imported 21·1 per cent. of all Portuguese exports.

Portugal is a member of EFTA, GATT and OECD. Portugal has signed a Trade Agreement with EEC and the Government has announced its intention of achieving full membership of the E.E.C. The principal imports are cereals, meat, raw and semi-manufactured iron and steel, industrial machinery, chemicals, crude oil, motor vehicles, dried cod fish and raw materials for textiles.

The principal exports for 1975 were textiles, foodstuffs, timber, cork, diamonds, electrical and other machinery, and chemicals.

Trade with U.K.

	1974	1975
Imports from U.K....	£185,637,000	£157,600,000
Exports to U.K......	236,176,000	201,081,000

CAPITAL, Ψ Lisbon. Population (estimated, 1970), 783,000. Ψ Oporto 310,000; Ψ Setubal 100,000.

Lisbon distance 1,110 miles; transit 50 hours; by air, 2½ hours.

FLAG.—Vertical band of green (next staff) and square of red, bearing arms of the Republic, framed. NATIONAL DAY.—April 25.

BRITISH EMBASSY
Lisbon

Ambassador Extraordinary and Plenipotentiary, His Excellency The Hon. (Richard) John (McMoran) Wilson, C.M.G. (1976).

Counsellors, J. B. Ure, M.V.O.; L. E. Hanham (*Consul-General*).

Defence and Military Attaché, Lt. Col. C. A. S. Hinton.

Naval and Air Attaché, Cdr. P. B. Reynolds, O.B.E., R.N.

1st Secretaries, G. E. Clark (*Head of Chancery*); G. C. Gullan (*Commercial*); Lt. Col. F. G. E. Walford, O.B.E. (*Economic*); D. Dawson (*Labour*); R. P. Ralph (*Information*).

2nd Secretaries, R. Mowforth (*Commercial*); D. W. Fitzwilliam (*Administration*); C. H. Woodland (*Consul*); S. A. Brooks.

British Council Representative, M. G. Elterton.

MADEIRA AND THE AZORES
Madeira and The Azores are two administratively autonomous provinces of Portugal, having locally elected Assemblies and Governments.

Madeira is a group of islands in the Atlantic Ocean about 520 miles south-west of Lisbon, and consist of Madeira Porto Santo and 3 uninhabited islands (Desertas). The total area is 314 square miles with a population of 253,220 (1970). Ψ Funchal in Madeira, the largest island (270 square miles), is the capital, with a population of 54,068; Machico (10,905). Trade with U.K., 1972: Imports from U.K., £1,745,000; Exports, £866,000.

The Azores are a group of 9 islands (Flores, Corvo, Terceira, São Jorge, Pico, Faial, Graciosa, São Miguel and Santa Maria) in the Atlantic Ocean, with a total area of 922 square miles and a population of 291,028 (1970). Ψ Ponta Delgada, the capital of the group, has a population of 21,347. Other ports are Ψ Angra, in Terceira, (16,476) and Ψ Horta (2,509). Trade with U.K., 1972: Imports from U.K., £609,000; Exports, £63,000.

PORTUGUESE OVERSEAS PROVINCES
The former Portuguese overseas territories of Guinea-Bissau, Mozambique and Angola achieved independence in 1974, 1975 and 1976 respectively.

Ψ MACAU, in China, on an island in the Canton River, has an area of 5 square miles and a population (1970) of 248,316.

After some months of confused fighting between rival indigenous factions, PORTUGUESE TIMOR (the eastern part of the island) was incorporated into Indonesia in July 1976. Situated in the Malay Archipelago, it has an area of 7,329 square miles, with a population (1970), 610,541. Capital, Ψ Dili, pop. 7,000.

QATAR

Amir of Qatar, H.H. Sheikh Khalifa Bin Hamad Al-Thani; *assumed power* February 22, 1972 (*also Prime Minister and Minister of Defence*).

COUNCIL OF MINISTERS

Minister of Education, Shaikh Jassem Bin Hamad Al-Thani.

Foreign Affairs, Shaikh Suhaim Bin Hamad Al-Thani.

Finance and Petroleum Affairs, Shaikh Abdul Aziz bin Khalifa Al Thani.

Municipal Affairs, Shaikh Mohamed Bin Jablr Al-Thani.

Economy and Commerce, Shaikh Naser Bin Khaled Al-Thani.

Justice (vacant).

Electricity and Water, Shaikh Jasem Bin Moh'd Al-Thani.

Industry and Agriculture, Shaikh Faisal Bin Thani Al-Thani.
Health, Sayed Khalid Bin Mohammed Al-Mana.
Public Works, Sayed Khaled Bin Abdullah Al-Attiyah.
Labour and Social Welfare Affairs, Sayed Ali Bin Ahmed Al-Ansari.
Communications and Transport, Sayed Abdullah Bin Naser Al-Suwaidi.
Information, Sayed Issa Ghanim Al-Kawari.

EMBASSY IN LONDON
10 Reeves Mews, W.1.
[01-499 8831]
Ambassador Extraordinary and Plenipotentiary, His Excellency Shaikh Ahmed Bin Saif Al-Thani.
Counsellor, Ahmed Abdullah Al-Khal.

Until 1971, Qatar was one of the nine independent Emirates in the Arabian Gulf in special treaty relations with the Government of the United Kingdom. In that year, with the withdrawal of H.M. Forces from the area, these special treaty relations were terminated. On April 2, 1970 a Provisional Constitution for Qatar was proclaimed, providing for the establishment of a Council of Ministers and for the formation of a 20-member Consultative Council to assist the Council of Ministers in running the affairs of the State. The first Cabinet was formed of 10 members on May 29, 1970. A permanent constitution will be formulated in the light of experience gained during the current transitional stage to supersede the Provisional Constitution. Qatar is a member of the Arab league as well as of the United Nations.

The state of Qatar covers the peninsula of Qatar from approximately the Northern shore of Khor al Odaid to the Eastern shore of Khor al Salwa. The area is about 4,000 sq. miles, with a population estimated in 1975 at about 180,000.

The great majority of the population is concentrated in the urban district of the capital Doha. Only a small minority still pursue the traditional life of the semi-nomadic tribesmen and fisherfolk. There are townships on the coast at Khor, Dukhan, Wakra and Umm-Said. There are many gardens and farms near Doha and to the North and encouragement is being given to the development of agriculture.

Doha is an expanding town with good shopping facilities and services and an airport built to international standards. Regular air services connect Qatar with Bahrain and the United Arab Emirates, Kuwait, Muscat, Iran, Saudi Arabia, Jordan, Lebanon, Egypt, the Indian sub-continent and Europe.

In April, 1973, the new Qatar *Riyal* was introduced.

Current industrial development projects include a fertilizer plant, a cement factory, and a natural gas liquids plant. In addition the government is developing an iron and steel and ore reduction plant, and a petrochemical complex. The township of Umm-Said is being developed as an industrial area. Qatar is also rapidly expanding its infrastructure including electrical generation and water distillation, roads, ports, hotels, houses, and Government buildings.

The Qatar Broadcasting Authority transmits on medium, shortwave, and V.H.F. Regular television transmissions in colour began in 1974 and a second channel is planned.

Oil deposits on land are being exploited by the Qatar Petroleum Company who first shipped oil on December 31, 1949. An offshore concession is held by the Shell Company of Qatar which is exporting oil from its terminal on Halul Island at a rate of about 7,000,000 long tons per annum.

Further offshore concessions are held by a consortium headed by Wintershall, who also hold an onshore concession. On January 1, 1975, the Amir signed an act establishing the Qatar General Petroleum Corporation, empowering it to establish subsidiaries, offices or agencies inside or outside Qatar. It will be responsible for all oil production in the country once current negotiations for a 100 per cent. takeover of Q.P.C. and Shell Company of Qatar are completed.

Trade with U.K.
	1974	1975
Imports from U.K.	£22,100,000	£55,700,000
Exports to U.K.	166,000,000	156,700,000

CAPITAL.—Doha. Population (estimated) 180,000.

FLAG.—White and maroon, white portion nearer the mast; vertical indented line comprising 17 angles divides the colours.

BRITISH EMBASSY
(Doha)
Ambassador Extraordinary and Plenipotentiary, His Excellency David Gordon Crawford (1974).
1st Secretary, D. L. Hardinge (*Commercial*).
2nd Secretary, D. Moorhouse (*Vice Consul and Administration*).
Attaché, D. Meadowcroft (*Commercial*).
3rd Secretary, E. A. Mohan.
British Council Representative, W. H. Jefferson.

RUMANIA
(Republica Socialistă România)
President of the Republic, Nicolae Ceauşescu, *elected*, March 28, 1974.
State Council, N. Ceausescu (*President*); Emil Bobu; Stefan Voitec (*Vice-Presidents*); Silviu Curticeanu (*Presidential Secretary of the State Council*).

COUNCIL OF MINISTERS
Prime Minister, Manea Manescu.
Deputy Prime Ministers, Emil Drăgănescu; Janos Fazekas; Mikhai Marinescu; Angelo Miculescu; Paul Niculescu; Georghe Oprea; Ion Pătan; George Rădulescu; Gen. Ion Ioniţă.
Minister of National Defence, Colonel-General Ion Coman.
Interior, Teodor Coman.
Foreign Affairs, George Macovescu.
President of the State Planning Committee, Mihai Marinescu.
Agriculture, Food Industry and Water, Angelo Miculescu.
Finance, Florea Dumitrescu.
Technical Material Supply, Maxim Berghiann.
Metallurgical Industry, Neculai Agachi.
Machine Building, Ioan Avram.
Chemical Industry, Mihai Florescu.
Electric Power, Nicolae Manescu.
Petroleum Industry, Bujor Almăşan.
Transport and Telecommunications, Traian Dudaş.
Light Industry, Lina Ciobanu.
Industrial Construction, Vasile Bambacea.
Timber Industry, Vasile Patilineţ.
Health, Nicolae Nicolaescu.
Labour, Petre Lupe.
Tourism, Ion Cosma.
Internal Trade, Janos Fazekas.
Foreign Trade, Ion Pătan.
Education, Suzana Gadea.
Justice, Emil Nicolcioiu.
Presidents of:
　Committee for People's Council Affairs, Iosif Uglar.
　State Committee for Prices, Gheorghe Gaston Marin.
　Central Council of the General Union of Trade Unions, Gheorghe Pană.

Council of Socialist Culture and Education, Dumitru Popescu.

National Union of Agricultural Co-operatives, Aldea Militaru.

National Council for Science and Technology, Ioan Ursu.

National Council of Water Resources, Florin Iorgulescu.

State Department for Food Industry, Constantin Iftodi.
Department for Agriculture, Marin Capisizu.
Minister Secretaries of State, Emilian Dobrescu; Nicolae Ionescu; Nicolae M. Nicolae.

THE COMMUNIST PARTY

Executive Political Committee, N. Ceauşescu;; M. Mănescu; E. Ceauşescu; G. Cioara; L. Ciobanu; E. Bobu; C. Burtică; G. Oprea; I. Pāţan; I. Uglar; E. Drăgănescu; J. Fazekas; P. Lupu; P. Niculescu; G. Pană; D. Popescu; G. Rădulescu; L. Răutu; V. Trofin; I. Verdet; V. Vîlcu; S. Voitec (full members); I. Banc; M. Dalea; M. Dobrescu; I. Iliescu; S. Andrei; N. Giosan; I. Ioniţă; V. Patilinet; R. Winter; I. Ursu; M. Telescu (alternate members).

Secretariat of the Central Committee, N. Ceausescu (Secretary General); G. Pană; D. Popescu; I. Verdet; C. Burtică; I. Uglar; E. Bobu; I. Banc; S. Andrei.

RUMANIAN EMBASSY IN LONDON
4 Palace Green, W.8
[01-937 9666]

Ambassador Extraordinary and Plenipotentiary, His Excellency Pretor Popa (1973).

Counsellors, Ioan Amariei (Political); Adrian Gheorghiu; Nicu Bujor (Political).
Military Attaché, Col. Cornel Popa.

Area and Population.—Rumania is a republic of South-Eastern Europe, formerly the classical Dacia and Scythia Pontica, having its origin in the union of the Danubian principalities of Wallachia and Moldavia under the Treaty of Paris (April, 1856). The area of Rumania is 237,500 sq. km. and the population in July, 1973 was 20,827,525.

Government.—The principalities remained separate entities under Turkish suzerainty until 1859, when Prince Alexandru Ion Cuza was elected Prince of both, still under the suzerainty of Turkey. Prince Cuza abdicated in 1866 and was succeeded by Prince Charles of Hohenzollern-Sigmaringen, in whose successors the crown was vested. By the Treaty of Berlin (July 13, 1878) the Principality

was recognized as an independent State, and part of the Dobrudja (which had been occupied by the Rumanians) was incorporated. On March 27, 1881, it was recognized as a Kingdom.

The outcome of the War of 1914–18 added Bessarabia, the Bukovina, Transylvania, The Banat and Crisana–Maramures, these additions of territory being confirmed in the Treaty of St. Germain, 1919, and the Treaty of Petit Trianon, 1920.

On June 27, 1940, in compliance with an ultimatum from U.S.S.R., Bessarabia and Northern Bukovina were ceded to the Soviet Government, the area affected being about 20,000 sq. miles, with a population of about 4,000,000.

In August, 1940, Rumania ceded to Bulgaria the portion of Southern Dobrudja (about 3,000 sq. miles) taken from Bulgaria in 1913. Rumania became "The Rumanian People's Republic" in December, 1947, on the abdication of King Michael.

A new Constitution, modelled on the Soviet Constitution of 1936, was adopted unanimously on September 24, 1952, by the Grand National Assembly. The Assembly was later dissolved and elections were held for a new Grand National Assembly on November 30, 1952; in each constituency there was only one candidate for election, representing the People's Democratic Front. Further elections on similar lines were held in February, 1957; in March, 1961, and in March, 1965. A new Constitution was approved by the Grand National Assembly in 1965 when the name of the state was changed to The Socialist Republic of Rumania. The Constitution states (Art. 3) that the leading political force of the whole society is the Rumanian Communist Party. The Constitution was modified in March, 1974.

Agriculture.—The soil of Wallachia and Moldavia is among the richest in Europe producing wheat, maize, millet, oats, barley, rye, beans, peas and other vegetables. Grape vines and fruits are abundant. The fertile plain of Transylvania yields large crops of maize, wheat, rye, oats, flax and hemp. Agriculture and sheep and cattle raising are the principal industries of Rumania, but the climate of this part of South-Eastern Europe is of the Continental character, and the intense winter cold and summer heat, and fierce summer drought sometimes defeat these principal industries. The forests of the mountainous regions are extensive, and the timber industry is important.

Socialization of agriculture was completed when plans for collectivization were fulfilled in the spring of 1962, some three years ahead of the planned date.

Natural Resources and Industry.—Before the war petroleum and agriculture were the backbone of the Rumanian economy. Though the production of both industries has increased, they no longer hold the same dominant position. Rumania's oil resources enabled her to produce 14,287,000 tons of crude oil in 1973 and there are plentiful supplies of natural gas, together with various mineral deposits including coal, iron ore, bauxite, lead, zinc, copper and uranium in quantities which allow a substantial part of the requirements of industry to be met from local resources. Since 1948 industrialization has proceeded rapidly and the State is well on the way to establishing a mixed industrial economy. Heavy investments have been made in electrical power, the chemical industry, the metallurgical industry and the engineering industry and growing attention is being paid to light industry. The economy is certainly organized on the basis of Five-Year Plans which cover all branches of national activity including investment and production.

1973 production figures were: crude oil, 14,287,000 tons; coal, 26,664,000 tons; electric power, 46,779 million kWh; methane gas, 23,639 million cu. metres; steel, 8,161,000 tons; pig iron, 5,713,000 tons; wheat, 5,528,500 tons; maize, 7,397,200 tons; sugar-beet, 4,380,200 tons.

Language and Literature.—Rumanian is a Romance language with many archaic forms and with admixtures of Slavonic, Turkish, Magyar and French words. The folk-songs and folk-lore, composed by the people themselves, and transmitted orally through many centuries (and collected in the 19th century), form one of the most interesting of such collections. The publication of all books and reviews is controlled and authorized by the Council for Socialist Culture and Education, which has the status of a Ministry. In 1972, 75 daily newspapers were published. The leading religion is that of the Rumanian Orthodox Church; the Roman Catholics and some Protestant denominations are of importance numerically. The Jewish community has declined through emigration.

Education is free and nominally compulsory, with 3,308,381 in attendance in 1973–74, including 143,656 in higher education. There are Universities at Bucharest, Iasi, Cluj, Timisoara, Craiova and Brasov. A "Marxist-Leninist" University was opened in Bucharest in 1951. There are polytechnics at Bucharest, Timisoara, Cluj, Brasov, Galati and Iasi, two commercial academies at Bucharest and Brasov, and agricultural colleges at Bucharest, Iasi, Cluj, Craiova and Timisoara.

Communications.—In 1972 there were 11,023 km. of railway open for traffic. The mercantile marine, as a result of war losses, seizure and reparations, was reduced to a few moderate-sized sea-going steamers and a number of coastal and river craft. The principal ports are Constanta (on the Black Sea), Sulina (on the Danube Estuary), Galati, the most important, Braila, Giurgiu and Turnu Severin. Rumania is a member of the Danube Commission whose seat is at Budapest.

FINANCE

	1971	1973
	Lei	*Lei*
Revenue	153,382,200,000	175,972,100,000
Expenditure	145,432,300,000	168,090,700,000

Up-to-date figures of the Public Debt are not available. No foreign loans (other than short-term commercial loans) are known to have been contracted since March, 1947. The internal debt was virtually wiped out by stabilization in August, 1947; there has been no internal loan issue since that date.

The Rumanian *Lei* (of 100 *Bani*) had been re-valued three times since the war by Feb. 1, 1954. With a 189·33 per cent. premium on all "capitalist" currencies for non-commercial transactions, the effective exchange rate on May 1975 was *Lei* 28·08 = £1. (*See also* p. 84.)

TRADE

	1972	1973
	Lei	*Lei*
Imports	14,465,200,000	17,417,700,000
Exports	14,373,000,000	18,575,000,000

No complete figures for foreign trade have been published since the start of the Communist *régime*. Imports are chiefly semi-manufactured goods, raw materials, machinery and metals; exports consist principally of maize, wheat, barley, oats, petroleum, timber, cattle, machines and industrial equipment. Trade with U.K., although relatively small, has increased notably since the signature of an Anglo-Rumanian trade arrangement in 1960. External trade with Communist countries dropped from 80 per cent. in 1960 to 50 per cent. in 1970.

Trade with U.K.

	1973	1974
Imports from U.K.	£34,160,000	£33,485,000
Exports to U.K.	31,710,000	34,252,000

CAPITAL, Bucharest, on the Dimbovita, population (1975), 1,528,562. Other large towns are: Cluj (212,690); Timisoara (204,687); Iasi (202,052); Brasov (193,089); Ψ Galati (191,111); Craiova (188,333); Ploiesti (171,668); Ψ Braila (161,057); Oradea (148,587); Arad (142,960); Sibiu (127,146); Tîrgu-Mures (109,873); Baia Mare (86,602).

FLAG.—Three vertical bands, blue, yellow, red, with the emblem of the Republic in the centre band. NATIONAL DAY.—August 23 (Liberation Day, 1944).

BRITISH EMBASSY
24 Strada Jules Michelet, Bucharest 22
Ambassador Extraordinary and Plenipotentiary, His Excellency Jeffrey Charles Petersen, C.M.G. (1975).
Counsellor, R. B. Dorman (*Commercial*).
Defence, Naval and Military Attaché, Lt.-Col. B. A. Allum.

RWANDA
(Republic of Rwanda)

President, Major General Juvénal Habyarimana, *assumed office*, July 5, 1973.

Rwanda became an independent republic on July 1, 1962. Formerly part of the Belgian-administered trusteeship of Ruanda-Urundi, it has an area of 10,169 sq. miles and a population of 4,000,000, mainly of the Bahutu tribe, with Batutsi and Batwa minorities. Coffee, cotton and tea are grown and there is some mineral production. Hides, extract of quinine and pyrethrum flowers are also exported.

A University was opened at Butare in 1963.

The currency is the *Rwanda franc.* In 1975 total imports were valued at *Rw.Fr.*8,3662,00,000; total exports, *Rw.Fr.*5,640,000,000; imports from U.K. 1974, *Rw.Fr.*226,700,000; exports to U.K., *Rw.Fr.* 91,100,000. Revenue in 1975 totalled: *Rw.Fr.*. 13,213,000,000; Expenditure *Rw.Fr.* 14,447,000,000

At a referendum held in September, 1961, under supervision of the United Nations, a large majority voted against the retention of the monarchy which was accordingly abolished on Oct. 2, 1961. Elections for a new Legislative Assembly were also held in September, 1961, and the Assembly elected M. Kayibanda as President of the National Council, to hold office as Head of State and Head of the Government. He was deposed in 1973, and replaced by a military government under Maj.-Gen. Juvénal Habyarimana. Admission of Rwanda to membership of the United Nations was approved on July 26, 1962.

CAPITAL.—Kigali (7,000).

FLAG.—Three vertical bands, red, yellow and green with letter R on yellow band.

NATIONAL DAY.—July 1.

British Ambassador, His Excellency James Patrick Ivan Hennessy, C.M.G., O.B.E. (resident at Kampala).

EL SALVADOR
(República de El Salvador)

President, Col. Arturo Armando Molina; *elected* February 20, 1972; *assumed office* July 1, 1972, *for* a five-year term.

Vice-President, Dr. Enrique Mayorga Rivas.

Minister of Foreign Affairs, Ing. Mauricio Borgonovo.

SALVADOREAN EMBASSY AND CONSULATE
9B Portland Place, W.1.
[01-636 9563]
Ambassador Extraordinary and Plenipotentiary, His Excellency Alvaro Ernesto Martínez (1974).

1st Secretary and Consul, Señor Lic. Oscar Manuel Gutiérrez-Rosales.
Attachés, Dr. David Castro-Escobar; Dr. Rafael Lemus-Corleto.

Area and Population.—The Republic of El Salvador extends along the Pacific coast of Central America for 160 miles with a general breadth of about 50 miles, and contains an area of 7,722 square miles with a population (July 1973) of 3,863,793. El Salvador is therefore a densely populated country with some 500 persons per square mile. It is divided into 14 Departments. (*For* MAP, *see* p. 84.)

The surface of the country is very mountainous, many of the peaks being extinct volcanoes. The highest peaks are the Santa Ana volcano (7,700 ft.) and the San Vicente volcano (7,200 ft.). Much of the interior has an average altitude of 2,000 feet. The lowlands along the coast are generally hot, but towards the interior the altitude tempers the severity of the heat. Much has been done in recent years to improve sanitary conditions and services. There is a wet season from May to October, and a dry season from November to April. Earthquakes have been frequent in the history of El Salvador, the most recent being that of May 3, 1965, when considerable damage was done to San Salvador.

The principal river is the Rio Lempa. There is a large volcanic lake (Ilopango) a few miles to the east of the capital, while farther away and to the west lies the smaller but very picturesque lake of Coatepeque, which appears to have been formed in a vast crater flanked by the Santa Ana volcano.

Government.—El Salvador was conquered in 1526 by Pedro de Alvarado, and formed part of the Spanish vice-royalty of Guatemala until 1821. Under a new Constitution adopted in 1950, the President is elected for six years and the Legislature for two. In the legislative elections under proportional representation held in March, 1974, the result was, 36 deputies of the Official party, and 16 opposition deputies. In the presidential elections held on February 20, 1972, the candidate of the Official Party, Col. Arturo Armando Molina, secured a narrow margin over his closest opponent, Ingeniero José Napoléon Duarte, therefore his election had to be confirmed by the National Assembly.

Agriculture.—The principal cash crops are coffee, which is grown under shade-trees principally on the slopes of the volcanoes, cotton, which is cultivated on the coastal plains, and cane sugar. Also cultivated are maize, sesame, indigo, rice, balsam, etc. In the lower altitudes towards the east, sisal is produced and used in the manufacture of coffee and sugar bags. Diversification and modernization of agriculture are in progress, including the exportation of meat, principally to the U.S.A.

Industry.—There is growing industrialization and existing factories make textiles, constructional steel, furniture, cement and household items. El Salvador is a leading exporter to the Central American Common Market, of which she is a member. The first trade zone was inaugurated in November 1974 and the National Assembly approved a new Export Development Law. The free-trade scheme has already attracted several industries.

Education.—The illiteracy rate is about 50 per cent. Primary education is nominally compulsory, but the number of schools and teachers available is too small to enable education to be given to all children of school age. In recent Budgets, however, a high percentage of the national revenue has been devoted to education and great efforts are being made to eliminate the existing shortage of schools and teachers.

Language and Literature.—The language of the country is Spanish. Indigenous literature has not yet produced work of international repute. There are 4 daily newspapers published at the capital, and 4 in the provinces.

Communications.—The former El Salvador Railways and the Salvadorean Section of International Railways of Central America have been merged under the Executive Autonomous Port Commission (CEPA) which will also administer the previously foreign-owned port of Cutoco. The new railroad organization is styled FENADESAL. There is continuous railway communication between San Salvador and Guatemala City and Puerto Barrios on the Caribbean coast. The roads are paved and in good condition. There are good motor roads between Acajutla, the principal port, and the capital (23 miles), and between the capital and Guatemala City. The Pan-American Highway from the Guatemalan frontier follows this route and continues to the Honduran frontier. Pan American Airways, TACA, LANICA, COPA, AVIATECA, SAM, Iberia and LACSA connect El Salvador with the rest of the world. British Airways, SABENA, Iberia and other important airway companies are represented in San Salvador. The Ilopango international airport can receive jet aircraft. The new Cascatlán Airport is expected to be finished in 1977.

There are post and telegraph offices throughout the country. There are many broadcasting stations and six television stations.

FINANCE

	1976
	Colones
Revenue (*Budget*)	762,032,445
Expenditure (*do.*)	709,608,962
Surplus	52,423,483
Public Debt (Dec. 31)	727,135,200
Direct Governmental Debt	397,269,100
Internal	117,107,600
External	280,161,500
Guaranteed by the Government	266,494,800
Internal	77,136,700
External	189,358,100
Non-Guaranteed Debt	63,371,300

TRADE

	1974	1975
	Colones	*Colones*
Imports	1,409,200,000	1,511,691,000
Exports	1,156,200,000	1,289,987,000

Trade with U.K

	1974	1975
Imports from U.K	£3,857,000	£8,333,000
Exports to U.K	897,000	6,143,000

Par of Exchange 2·50 *Colones*= $1 (U.S.) (*see also* p. 84).

Coffee to the value of ₡568,500,000 was exported in 1975. Exports of cotton were valued at ₡167,000,000. Other exports are sugar (₡191,000,000), shrimps, sisal (in the form of bags used for exporting coffee, sugar, etc.), balsam, towels, hides and skins. The chief imports are iron and steel goods, motor cars, fertilizers, manufactured goods, chemical products and petroleum.

CAPITAL.—San Salvador. Population, 620,000. Other towns are Santa Ana (204,000), San Miguel (120,700), ΨLa Union (Cutoco), ΨLa Libertad and ΨAcajutla.

FLAG.—Three horizontal bands light blue, white, light blue; coat of arms on white band. NATIONAL DAY.—September 15.

BRITISH EMBASSY
11A Avenida Norte (BIS), No. 611, Colnia Dueñas, (Apartado 23-50), San Salvador

Ambassador Extraordinary and Plenipotentiary and Consul-General, His Excellency Albert Henry Hughes, O.B.E. (1975).
1st Secretary, J. F. Taylor (*Head of Chancery and Consul*).
San Salvador is 5,700 miles from London.

SAN MARINO
(Repubblica di San Marino)
Regents, Two " Capitani Reggenti ".
CONSULATE GENERAL IN LONDON
Saxone House, 74A Regent St., W.1.
Consul General, Sir Charles Forte.
Vice-Consul, R. E. Rudge.
A small Republic in the hills near Rimini, on the Adriatic, founded, it is stated, by a pious stonecutter of Dalmatia in the 4th century. The Republic always resisted the Papal claims, and those of neighbouring dukedoms, during the 15th–18th centuries, and its integrity and sovereignty is recognized and respected by Italy. The Republic is governed by a State Congress of 10 members, under the Presidency of two Heads of State. The Great and General Council, a legislative body of 60 members, is elected by a universal suffrage for a term of 5 years. A Council of Twelve forms in certain cases a Supreme Court of Justice. The area is approximately 23 square miles, the population (June, 1973) is 21,000. The city of San Marino, on the slope of Monte Titano, has three towers, a fine church and Government palace, a theatre and museums. The principal products are wine cereals, and cattle, and the main industries are ceramics, lime, concrete, cotton yarns, colour and paints. A Treaty of Extradition between the Governments of Great Britain and the Rebublic of San Marino has been in force since 1899.
FLAG.—Two horizontal bands, white, blue (with coat of arms of the Republic in centre).

SÃO TOMÉ AND PRÍNCIPE

President and Minister of Agriculture, Land Reform and Defence, Dr. Manuel Pinto da Costa.
Prime Minister, Economic Co-ordination and Tourism, Sr. Miguel Trouvoada.
Foreign Affairs, Sr. Leonel Mario d'Alva.
Interior, Sr. José Fret Lau Chong.
Health and Social Affairs, Dr. Carlos Alberto Dias da Graça.
Labour and Justice, Sr. Manuel Quaresma dos Santos Costa.
Education and Culture, Sr. Alda Graça do Espirito Santo.
Domestic Administration, Maj. Daniel Daio.
Social Equipment and Environment, Sr. Xavier Daniel Dias.
The islands of São Tomé and Príncipe are situated in the Gulf of Guinea, off the west coast of Africa. They have an area of 372 square miles, and a population (1970) of 74,500.
Following Portugal's decision to grant independence, a transitional government was installed on Dec. 21, 1974, and the islands became an independent democratic republic on July 12, 1975.
Cacao is the main product.
CAPITAL.— Ψ São Tomé (3,187).

SAUDI ARABIA
(Al Mamlaka al Arabiya as-Sa'udiyya.)
King of Saudi Arabia, H.M. King Khalid bin Abdul Aziz Al Saud, *born* 1912, *ascended the throne* March 25, 1975.
Crown Prince, H.R.H. Amir Fahd bin Abdul Aziz, *born* 1921.

COUNCIL OF MINISTERS
Prime Minister, H.M. King Khalid bin Abdul Aziz.
First Deputy Prime Minister, H.R.H. Amir Fahd bin Abdul Aziz.
Second Deputy Prime Minister and Commander of the National Guard, H.R.H. Amir Abdullah bin Abdul Aziz.
Defence and Aviation, H.R.H. Amir Sultan bin Abdul Aziz.
Public Works and Housing, H.R.H. Amir Mut'eb bin Abdul Aziz.
Interior, H.R.H. Amir Nayef bin Abdul Aziz.
Municipal and Rural Affairs, H.R.H. Amir Majid bin Abdul Aziz.
Foreign Affairs, H.R.H. Amir Saud al-Faisal bin Abdul Aziz.
Finance and National Economy, Shaikh Muhammad Al Ali Aba al-Khail.
Agriculture and Water, Dr. Abdul Rahman bin Abdul Aziz bin Hassan Al al-Shaikh.
Higher Education, Shaikh Hassan bin Abdullah Al al-Shaikh.

Commerce, Dr. Sulaiman Al-Abdul Aziz al-Sulaim.
Communications, Shaikh Muhammad Omar Tawfiq.
Petroleum and Mineral Resources, Shaikh Ahmad Zaki Yamani.
Justice, Shaikh Ibrahim bin Muhammad bin Ibrahim Al al Shaikh.
Labour and Social Affairs, Shaikh Ibrahim bin Abdullah al-Angari.
Information, Dr. Muhammad Abdo Yamani.
Health, Dr. Hussein Abdul Razzak al Jazeyeri.
Pilgrimage and Trusts, Shaikh Abdul Wahhab Ahmed Abdul Wasi'.
Education, Dr. Abdul Aziz Al-Abdullah al-Khuwaiter.
Planning, Shaikh Hisham Mohiyiddin Nazer.
Telegraphs, Posts and Telephones, Dr. Alawi Darwish Kayyal.
Electricity and Industry, Dr. Ghazi Abdul Rahman al-Qusaibi.
Ministers of State, Shaikh Muhammad Ibrahim Mas'oud; Dr. Muhammad al-Amran; Dr. Muhammad Abdul Latif al-Melhem.

SAUDI ARABIAN EMBASSY
30 Belgrave Square, S.W.1.
[01–235 0831]
Ambassador Extraordinary and Plenipotentiary, His Excellency Sheikh Abdul Rahman Al Helaissi, G.C.V.O. (1966).

Counsellor, Salem Azzam, C.V.O.
1st Secretaries, Saleh al-Fouzan; Yasien Khalil Allaf; Hassan M. Attar; Amin Malki; Abdullah O. Barry.
Defence Attaché, Maj.-Gen. Mohammad Sabri.
Cultural Counsellor, Abdul Aziz Mansour Al-Turki.

The Kingdom of Saudi Arabia, so named since Sept. 20, 1932, is a personal union of two countries, the Sultan of Nejd becoming also King of the Hijaz.

By the *Treaty of Jedda* (May 20, 1927) Great Britain recognized Ibn Saud as an independent ruler, King of the Hijaz and of Nejd and its Dependencies.

The total area of the Kingdom is about 927,000 sq. miles, with a population (U.N. estimate, 1969) of 7,200,000.

In the 18th century Nejd was an independent State and the stronghold of the Wahhabi sect. It subsequently fell under the Turkish yoke, but in 1913 Ibn Saud threw off Turkish rule and captured from the Turks the Province of Hasa. In 1921 he added to his dominions the territories of the Rashid family of Jebel Shammar, which he captured by force of arms; in 1925 he completed the conquest of the Hijaz, and in 1926 accepted the surrender of the greater part of Asir, the whole of which is now part of the Kingdom.

Nejd (" Plateau ") has no definite frontiers, but may be said to extend over about 800,000 square miles of Central Arabia, including the Nafud and Dahana Deserts, and reaches eastward to the Persian Gulf (Hasa). The population is largely nomadic and is estimated at about 3,500,000, the majority being Muslims of the Wahhabi persuasion. There is little agriculture, but wheat and barley are grown, and there is an experimental farm, irrigated from natural deep pools and covering 3,000 acres, at al-Kharj, about 50 miles south of Riyadh. The principal occupation of the bulk of the population is camel and sheep raising, but oil makes by far the largest contribution to the economy of the country. Oil was found in commercial quantities at Dammam, near Dhahran in the Hasa, in 1938, and in 1973 total production of crude oil for the whole country, including off-shore concessions, averaged some 8,000,000 barrels per day. Exports other than oil are negligible. The capital is Riyadh (666,840), and the principal trading centres are Hofuf (the chief town of the Hasa province) (101,271). Ψ Al Khobar (44,817) and Ψ Dammam (127,844) on the Persian Gulf littoral, Anaiza, Buraida, Hail and Jauf. The old ports (Persian Gulf) were Ψ Qatif, Ψ Uqair and Ψ Al Khobar, which were suitable only for sailing craft, but the Arabian-American Oil Company, which is exploiting the Hasa oil under a 60 years' lease, has built a deep-water port for its own purposes at Ψ Ras Tannura, and a civil deep-water port, with a pier seven miles long, was brought into use at Ψ Dammam in 1950. A railway is in operation from Dammam through Hofuf to Riyadh.

The *Hijaz* (" The Boundary "—between Nejd and Tihama) extends from Asir in S. to Jordan in N., and from the Red Sea and the Gulf of 'Aqaba in the W. to the ill-defined boundaries of Central Arabia. The coastline on the Red Sea is about 800 miles, and the total area is about 112,500 sq. miles, with a population of from 1,000,000 to 1,500,000, including many nomad tribes. On the coast are the small ports of Al-Wajh, Yanba'u, Raabigh and Jizzan. Jedda contains the ruins of the reputed " tomb of Eve, the mother of mankind "; and in-land are many settlements through which runs the course of the disused Saudi-Arabian section of the Hijaz Railway. The *Oasis of Khaibar,* east of the railway, contains a considerable population, descendants of former negro slaves, with a centre at

Kast al Yahudi. The importance of the Hijaz depends upon the pilgrimages to the holy cities of Medina and Mecca. *Medina (al Madinah al Munawwarah,* " The City of Light "), once the terminus of the Hijaz Railway, 820 miles from Damascus, has a permanent population of about 137,000 and is celebrated as the burial place of Muhammad, who died in the city on June 7, 632 (12 Rabia, A.H. 11). The Mosque of the Prophet (500 feet in length and over 300 in breadth) contains the sacred tomb of Muhammad. *Mecca,* the birth-place of the Prophet, is 45 miles east of the sea-port of Jedda, and about 200 miles south of Medina, and has a population estimated at 301,000. The city contains the great mosque surrounding the *Kaaba,* or sacred shrine of the Muslim religion, in which is the black stone " given by Gabriel to Abraham ", placed in the south-east wall of the Kaaba at such a height that it may be kissed by the devout pilgrim. 1,557,867 Muslim pilgrims visited Mecca during the ten day " Haj " period in 1975. Ψ *Jedda* (561,104) is the principal port and commercial centre of Saudi Arabia. A new deep-water port was completed in 1971.

Asir (" The Inaccessible ") extends, geographic-ally, from a line drawn inland from Birk on the southern limit of Hijaz to the northern boundary of the Yemen, some 12 miles N. of the port of Meidi. Its breadth extends about 180 miles east-wards to Bisha in the north and to the boundary of the Beni Yam in the south. The territory includes the Farsan Islands, where prospectors have searched for oil, but without success. The maritime low-land is interspersed with fertile areas near the wadis, which afford pasturage and bear grain. Capital, Abha (30,150).

Finance and Trade.—Oil is the main source of the country's wealth, though customs revenues and other taxes, as well as the foreign exchange accruing from the annual Pilgrimage to Mecca, also bring in a significant income. In the fiscal year 1974-75 the budget was balanced at *SR* 98,247,000,000, of which 96 per cent. was derived from oil. 57·7 per cent. of total Government expenditure was allocated to development projects. The rate of exchange was *SR* 7·60 = £1 (June 1976). (*See also* p. 84.) The currency is strong, and backed by gold and foreign exchange reserves, second only to West Germany, of more than £14,000,000,000. With few exceptions, such as the ban on alcohol, there are no restrictions on trade or payments including foreign exchange transactions. There is no public debt. Imports in 1974 were valued at *SR* 15,286,000,000, the United States of America being the leading supplier followed by Japan, West Germany and the United Kingdom.

Trade with U.K.

	1974	1975
Imports from U.K.	£119,698,000	£199,700,000
Exports to U.K.	1,178,149,000	856,600,000

Communications.—The railway from the port of Dammam to the oilfields at Abqaiq and through Hofuf to Riyadh was opened late in 1951. Metal-led roads connect all the main cities in the northern half of the country, and a road linking Abha, in the south, to this network will shortly be opened. The Government-owned Saudi Arabian Airlines, in association with Transworld Airlines operate Lockheed Tristars, Douglas DC3, Convair 340, and Boeing 707, 720 and 737 aircraft. Scheduled services are flown to all the main towns of the country. There are first class airports at Dhahran, where a new airport was opened in 1962, and at Jedda. A new airport is under construction at Jedda and a new airport is planned for Riyadh; other airports, for internal flights, are also in the planning stage. Saudi

Arabian Airlines have an extensive overseas operation including 15 flights to London per week. A large number of international airlines operate into Jedda and Dhahran.

Education.—With four exceptions, all schools are Government-run. In 1974 there were (including schools for both boys and girls) a total of 2,675 primary, 589 intermediate, 160 general secondary and 11 vocational secondary schools. There are Islamic Universities in Medina and Riyadh and Universities in Jedda (with a branch at Mecca), Riyadh and Dammam. There is a University of Petroleum and Minerals at Dhahran. Education at all levels is free.

CAPITAL.—Riyadh, population about 666,840.

SAUDI ARABIAN FLAG.—Green oblong, white Arabic device in centre: " There is no God but God, Muhammad is the Prophet of God," and a white scimitar beneath the lettering.

BRITISH EMBASSY
Kilo 5, Medina Road, Jedda

Ambassador Extraordinary and Plenipotentiary, His Excellency Arthur John Wilton, C.M.G., M.C. (1976).

Counsellors, J. C. Kay (*Economic*); R. O. Miles.

1st Secretaries, D. I. Lewty (*Head of Chancery*); H. V. B. Brown (*Commercial*); W. K. F. Boswell.

2nd Secretaries, M. J. Copson (*Commercial*); D. J. Plumbly; W. I. Rae (*Consul*); P. W. James, M.B.E.; R. O. Barnes (*Commercial*).

3rd Secretaries, A. R. A. Dearing (*Vice-Consul*); A. R. Michael (*Commercial*); T. Rooney (*Archivist*).

Defence and Military Attaché, Col. B. M. Lees.

Attaché, D. J. Sones.

British Council Representative, B. Vale, P.O. Box 2701, Riyadh.

SENEGAL
(République du Sénégal)

President and Head of Government, Léopold Senghor, elected President, Sept. 5, 1960; re-elected for five years, 1973.

Prime Minister, Abdou Diouf.

MINISTERS OF STATE
Armed Forces, Amadou Cledor Sall.
Interior, Jean Collin.
Finance and Economic Affairs, Babacar Bâ.
National Education, Doudo Ngom.
Foreign Affairs, Assane Seck.
Justice, Alioune Badara M'Bengue.
Relations with Assemblies, Information, Posts and Tele-communications, Daouda Sow.

MINISTERS
Rural Development, Adrian Senghor.
Higher Education, Ousmare Camara.
Industrial Development, Louis Alexandrenne.
Planning and Co-operation, Ousmane Seck.
Public Works, Town Planning and Transport, Mamadou Diop.
Culture, Alioune Sène.
Public Health and Social Affairs, Dr. Matar N'Diaye.
Civil Service, Labour and Employment, Arnadou Ly.
There are also 2 Secretaries of State, following Cabinet reorganization on Nov. 21, 1975.

SENEGAL EMBASSY IN LONDON
11 Phillimore Gardens, W.8.

[01-937 0925]

Ambassador Extraordinary and Plenipotentiary (vacant).

Senegal lies on the west coast of Africa between Mauritania in the north and the Republic of Guinea in the south. (*For MAP, see* p. 871.) It has an area of 77,814 sq. miles and a population (estimated, 1970) of 3,800,000.

Formerly a French colony, Senegal elected on Nov. 25, 1958, to remain within the French Community as an autonomous republic. Foundation of a Federation of Mali, to consist of the State of Senegal, (French) Soudan, Benin and Upper Volta, was announced in January, 1959, and the Federation came into existence on April 4, consisting of Senegal and the Sudanese Republic only, the others having meanwhile withdrawn. Mali was proclaimed fully independent by the President of the Federal Assembly, M. Léopold Senghor, on June 20, 1960. However, these arrangements proved short-lived as on August 22, 1960, the Senegal Legislative Assembly formally approved measures to secede from the Federation and continue as an independent state. In March, 1963 (after an attempted *coup d'état* by the then Prime Minister in the previous December) a new constitution was approved giving executive powers to the President, on the lines of the present French constitution. Senegal's principal exports are ground-nuts (raw and processed) and phosphates.

Trade with U.K

	1974	1975
Imports from U.K.	£3,260,000	£5,659,000
Exports to U.K.	9,637,000	14,637,000

CAPITAL.—ΨDakar (581,000).

FLAG.—Three vertical bands, green, yellow and red; a green star on the yellow band. NATIONAL DAY.—April 4.

BRITISH EMBASSY
B.P. 6025, Dakar.

Ambassador Extraordinary and Plenipotentiary, His Excellency John Ernest Powell-Jones, C.M.G. (1976).

1st Secretary, T. Grady, M.B.E. (*Head of Chancery and Consul*).

2nd Secretaries, C. Dyer; J. C. J. Ramsden.

3rd Secretary, R. Daly.

Cultural Attaché (*British Council Representative*), H. B. Bending.

SIAM. *see* Thailand

SOMALIA
(Somali Democratic Republic)

President of the Supreme Revolutionary Council, Maj.-Gen. Mohamed Siyad Barreh, *assumed office* Oct. 21, 1969.

EMBASSY
60 Portland Place, W.1

[01-580 7148]

Ambassador Extraordinary and Plenipotentiary, His Excellency Ahmed Mohamed Adan (1975).

1st Secretary, Abdi Haji Ahmed Liban.

The Somali Democratic Republic occupies part of the north-east horn of Africa, with a coast-line on the Indian Ocean extending from the boundary with Kenya (2° South latitude) to Cape Guardafui (12° N.); and on the Gulf of Aden to the boundary with the Territory of the Afars and Issas. Somalia is bounded on the west by the Territory of the Afars and Issas, Ethiopia and Kenya and covers an area of approximately 246,000 sq. miles. The population, of which a large proportion is nomadic, is estimated (June, 1969) at 2,730,000. Livestock raising is the main occupation in Somalia and there is a modest export trade in livestock on the hoof, skins and hides. Italy imports the bulk of the banana crop, the second biggest export under agreement with the Somali Government. Imports from U.K. in 1973 totalled £2,050,000.

Government.—The Somali Republic, consisting of the former British Somaliland Protectorate and the former Italian trust territory of Somalia, was set up on July 1, 1960. British rule in Somaliland lasted

from 1887 until June 26, 1960, with the exception of a short period in 1940–41 when the Protectorate was occupied by Italian forces. Somalia, formerly an Italian colony, was occupied by the United Kingdom from 1941 until the end of 1950, when it was placed under Italian administration by resolution of the United Nations. This trusteeship came to an end on July 1, 1960, when Somalia became independent and united with the former British Somaliland Protectorate under the title of the Somali Republic. Aden Abdulle Osman was returned to office as the first substantive President of the Republic in 1961, after a year as provisional President. Following national elections on June 10, 1967, Dr. Shermarke suceeded to the Presidency and on July 6 appointed Mr. Egal as Prime Minister. On October 15, 1969, the President was assassinated and Army commanders assisted by the police took over the Government without resistance. A Revolutionary Council under Major. Gen. Siad assumed full control of the state. The Somali Socialist Revolutionary Party became the only legal political organization following its inaugural congress in June 1976. The Government thenceforth comprised a Political Bureau, of five members including the President, 17 Departmental Ministers and a Minister of State.

CAPITAL.—Ψ Mogadishu (Mogadiscio), population (estimated 1971), 220,000. Other towns are Hargeisa (50,000), Kisimayu (18,000), Ψ Berbera (19,000) and Burao (10,000).

FLAG.—Five-pointed white star on blue ground. NATIONAL DAY.—October 21.

SOUTH AFRICA
(Republiek van Suid-Afrika)
State President, Dr. Nicolaas Diederichs, *elected President*, Feb. 21, 1975; *inaugurated April 10, 1975.*

Area and Population.—The Republic occupies the southernmost part of the African continent from the courses of the Limpopo, Molopo and Orange Rivers (34° 50′ 22″ South latitude) to the Cape of Good Hope, with the exception of the Transkei, Lesotho, Botswana and Swaziland, and part of Mozambique. It has a total area of 1,180,042 square kilometres (455,616 square miles) and the Transkei has an area of 41,000 sq. km. (15,830 sq. miles) and a total population (census of May, 1970) of 22,469,000 (White 3,835,000; African, 15,918,000; Coloured, 2,074,000 and Asian, 642,000). Mid-year estimates for 1974 show a total population of 24,920,000 (White, 4,160,000; African, 17,745,000; Coloured, 2,306,000 and Asian, 642,000). Populations of the Provinces at the 1970 census were: Cape Province (278,380 sq. miles), 4,293,000; Natal (33,578 sq. miles), 2,164,000; Transvaal (109,621 sq. miles), 6,478,000; Orange Free State (49,866 sq. miles), 1,682,120; African Homelands, 7,138,197.

Zululand, annexed in 1897, comprises about two-thirds of the country formerly under Zulu kings, and is bounded on the south and south-west by the Tugela River; on the south-east by the Indian Ocean; on the north by the ex-Portuguese possessions; and on the west by the districts of Babanango, Vryheid and Ngotshe and by Swaziland. In 1951, the appointment was confirmed of Cyprian Bekuzulu, grandson of Dinizulu and great-grandson of Cetewayo, as Paramount Chief of the Zulus in Natal.

The southernmost province contains many parallel ranges, which rise in steps towards the interior. The south-western peninsula contains the famous *Table Mountain* (3,582 feet), while the *Great Swartberg* and *Langeberg* run in parallel lines from west to east of the Cape Province. Between these two ranges and the *Roggeveld* and *Nieuwveld* ranges to the north is the Great Karroo Plateau, which is bounded on the east by the *Sneeuberg*, containing the highest summit in the province (Kompasberg, 7,800 feet). In the east are ranges which join the *Drakensberg* (11,000 feet) between Natal and the Orange Free State.

The Orange Free State presents a succession of undulating grassy plains with good pasture-land, at a general elevation of some 3,800 feet, with occa-

sional hills or kopjes. The Transvaal is also mainly an elevated plateau with parallel ridges in the *Magaliesberg* and *Waterberg* ranges of no great height. The veld or plains of this northernmost province is divisible into the High Veld of the south, the Bankenveld of the centre, and the Low Veld of the north and east, the first and second forming the grazing and agricultural region of the Transvaal and the last a fertile sub-tropical area. The eastern province of Natal has pastoral lowlands and rich agricultural land between the slopes of the Drakensberg and the coast, the interior rising in terraces as in the southern provinces. The *Orange*, with its tributary the *Vaal*, is the principal river of the south, rising in the Drakensberg and flowing into the Atlantic between the Territory of South West Africa and the Cape Province. The *Limpopo*, or Crocodile River, in the north, rises in the Transvaal and flows into the Indian Ocean through Mozambique (Portuguese East Africa.) Most of the remaining rivers are furious torrents after rain, with partially dry beds at other seasons.

Government.—The self-governing colonies of the Cape of Good Hope, Natal, the Transvaal and the Orange River Colony became united on May 31, 1910, under the South Africa Act, 1909, in a legislative union under the name of the Union of South Africa, the four colonies becoming Provinces of the Union. The Union of South Africa continued as a member of the British Commonwealth until 1961. A referendum held among white voters on October 5, 1960, decided by a narrow majority in favour of Republican status. 1,633,772 votes were cast—a poll of 90·73 per cent.—with 52·05 per cent. in favour. The Union of South Africa became a republic on May 31, 1961, and withdrew from the Commonwealth. On October 26, 1976, the Transkei became the first of the Bantu homelands to be given independence.

The *Senate* as reconstituted by the Senate Act, 1960, consists of 54 members, appointed or elected for a term of five years. Eleven are appointed by the Government (8 for the Republic, 2 for South West Africa and a Coloured representative). Forty-three are elected (Transvaal, 14; Cape Province, 11; Natal and Orange Free State, each 8; and South West Africa, 2). The Act of 1960 reintroduced proportional representation at elections to the Senate and excluded Native representation.

The *House of Assembly* consists of 171 elected members, 55 of whom represent the Cape of Good Hope, 20 Natal, 76 Transvaal, 14 the Orange Free State, and 6 South West Africa. Members of both Houses must be South African citizens of white descent. White female franchise was introduced under the provision of Act No. 18 of 1930. Cape Bantu voters ceased to be entitled to elect 3 members in Nov. 1959.

In July 1976 the party representation in the House of Assembly was as follows: Nationalist Party, 123; United Party, 36; Progressive Reform Party, 12.

Defence.—The South Africa Defence Act, 1957, became law on Nov. 1, 1958. This Act, as amended in 1961, provides that every citizen between the ages of 17 and 65 is liable to render personal service in time of war, and those between 17 and 65 are liable to undergo a prescribed course of peace training with the Citizen Force or Commandos spread over a period of four consecutive years. Thereafter citizens are required to serve with the Reserve for a prescribed period of time.

Education.—The Provinces have been relieved of all vocational education (technical and industrial), and the Departments of Cultural Affairs and Higher Education under the Minister are concerned with universities, technical colleges, schools of industries, reformatories and State technical, housecraft and commercial high schools. State-aided vocational schools and State and State-aided special schools for the physically handicapped.

Communications.—The total open mileage of Government-owned railway lines at the end of March 1975 was 22,149 km., of which 4,650 km. were electrified. Working expenditure (excluding depreciation) amounted to R.1,540,924,918 (railways, harbours, airways, pipelines and road transport). Internal air services are operated between all the major centres in South and South West Africa.

Production and Trade.—Final figures for the principal crops produced in 1974–75 were: Wheat, 1,596,000 metric tons; Maize, 9,100,000 mt.; Barley, 50,000 mt.; Oats, 103,000 mt.; ground nuts, 179,050. mt.

Mineral production is of the greatest importance in the South African economy. Value of mineral production in 1975: gold, R.2,560,395,000; diamonds, 7,295,133 metric carats; silver, R.10,012,472. Production in 1975: coal, 67,848,885 metric tons; copper, 178,927 metric tons; tin, concentrates and metallic, 6,432 metric tons; asbestos, 354,710 metric tons.

Value of trade in 1975, Imports, R.5,568,471,716; Exports, R.3,906,945,372.

Trade with U.K.

	1974	1975
Imports from U.K.	£526,291,000	£684,769,000
Exports to U.K.	465,194,000	540,289,000

Currency.—The South African £ reached parity with the £ sterling in 1946. A new decimal currency the *Rand* (R.) was introduced in South Africa on Feb. 14, 1961, with a par value of 10s(50p). Sterling. Rate of exchange (July 1975) R.1·55= £1.

Finance.—Estimated revenue for the year ended March 31, 1977, was RM6,455 (1976 RM5,909); total estimated expenditure RM7,792 (1976 RM6,679). The total government debit as at December 31, 1975 was RM10,094.

Capital.—The administrative seat of the Government is PRETORIA, Transvaal; population (census 1970), 563,384; the seat of the Legislature is ΨCAPE TOWN, population (1970), 1,107,764. Cape Town is 5,979 miles from Southampton; transit by mail steamship 11 days, and by air mail two days. There is a modern and well-equipped aerodrome seventeen miles by road from the centre of the city. Cape Town's harbour and docking facilities, existing and projected, are in keeping with its status as a world port of commercial and strategic importance. Other large towns are Johannesburg, Transvaal (1,441,335); ΨDurban, Natal, the largest seaport (350,935); ΨPort Elizabeth, Cape (475,869); Germiston, Transvaal (221,972); BLOEMFONTEIN, capital of Orange Free State (182,329); Springs, Transvaal (142,812); Benoni Transvaal (151,294); ΨEast London, Cape (124,763); Welkom, O.F.S. (210,629); and PIETERMARITZBURG, capital of Natal (160,847).

Flag.—Three horizontal stripes of equal width; from top to bottom, orange, white, blue; in the centre of the white stripe, the old Orange Free State flag hanging vertical, towards the pole the Union Jack horizontal, away from the pole the old Transvaal Vierkleur, all spread full.

NATIONAL DAY.—May 31.

BRITISH EMBASSY
6 Hill Street, Pretoria
91 Parliament Street, Cape Town (Jan.–June)
Ambassador Extraordinary and Plenipotentiary, His Excellency Sir David Scott, K.C.M.G. (1976).

Minister, D. M. Summerhayes. C.M.G.
Counsellors, J. M. O. Snodgrass (*Head of Chancery*); R. Carter.
Naval Attaché, Capt. W. E. C. Perkins. R.N.
Military Attaché, Col. D. A. Polley, O.B.E.
1st Secretaries, W. J. Vose (*Labour*); M. Hime (*Economic*); P. J. W. Le Breton (*Political and Press*); E. F. Lewis, M.B.E. (*Administration*); J. B. Noss (*Economic*).
2nd Secretaries, P. K. C. Thomas; W. F. L. Coleshill (*Vice-Consul*).
Cultural Attaché and British Council Representative, D. J. Sharp, 170 Pine Street, Pretoria.
There are British Consular Offices at *Cape Town, Johannesburg, Durban, East London* and *Port Elizabeth*.

South West Africa
Administrator, B. J. van der Walt.
South West Africa stretches from the southern border from Angola (lat. 17° 23′ S.) to part of the northern (Orange River) and north-western borders of the Cape Province of the Republic of South Africa; and from the Atlantic Ocean in the west to Botswana in the east.

The territory has an area of 318,261 sq. miles, including the area of Walvis Bay (434 sq. miles) which, although part of the Republic of South Africa, is for convenience administered as part of South West Africa. The population was 746,328 in 1970 (Census) and the main population groups are: Ovambo (342,455), Whites (90,658), Damara (64,973), Kavango (49,577), Herero (49,203), Nama (32,853), Coloured (28,275), East Caprivians (25,009), Bushmen (21,909), Rehoboth Baster (16,474), Kaokovelders (6,457), Tswana (3,719) and others (14,766).

Government.—A German protectorate from 1880 to 1915, South West Africa was administered until the end of 1920 by the Union of South Africa. In terms of the Treaty of Versailles the Territory was declared a "C" Mandate and entrusted to South Africa with full powers of administration and legislation over the Territory. After the dissolution of the League of Nations and in the absence of a trusteeship agreement, South Africa informed the United Nations that she would continue to administer South West Africa in the spirit of the Mandate. Since the establishment of the United Nations, South West Africa has been the subject of dispute.

The South African Government announced on Oct. 2, 1968, the formation of a Legislative Council of 42 members for Ovamboland, six members nominated by each of the seven tribal authorities in the territory and a nominated Executive Council of seven members, with a Chief Councillor elected by the Legislative Council. Certain administrative powers held in South West Africa were in February, 1969, transfered to the South African Government.

On June 21, 1971, the International Court of Justice at The Hague delivered an advisory opinion as requested by the U.N. Security Council on the legal consequences for States of the continued presence of South Africa in "Namibia" (South West Africa). The Court decided by 13 votes to 2, that (*inter alia*) "the continued presence of South Africa being illegal, South Africa is under obligation to withdraw its administration from Namibia immediately and thus put an end to its occupation of the Territory". Dissenting opinions were submitted by the British and French judges; several other judges issued separate opinions in respect of parts of the Court's advisory opinion. A member of the South African legal team had contended at the hearings that South Africa had no obligation to submit to general international supervision of its administration of South West Africa, as the Mandate by the League of Nations had come to an end at the dissolution of that organization. The South African Prime Minister rejected the Court's majority opinion in a statement also made on June 21, 1971. In September 1975 constitutional talks were begun in Windhoek between delegates from the 11 ethnic groups of the territory in order to determine the future of South West Africa.

Production and Education.—Mining, agriculture and fisheries are important. Animal husbandry accounts for 99 per cent. of the total gross output of commercial agriculture. The average rainfall over 70 per cent. of the Territory is below 400 mm. per annum. In 1970 there were 480 native schools, with 2,649 teachers and 107,572 Native pupils. For the Whites there were 83 schools with 1,155 teachers and 22,253 pupils.

Trade with U.K.

	1974	1975
Imports from U.K.	£1,735,000	£684,000
Exports to U.K.	21,857,000	24,257,000

CAPITAL.—Windhoek (population, 1970 census, 61,260). The ports are Ψ Walvis Bay and Ψ Lüderitz.

SPAIN
(España)
Head of the Spanish State, King Juan Carlos I de Borbón y Borbón, *born* Jan. 5, 1938, *acceded to the throne*, Nov. 22, 1975.
President of the Government, Sr. Adolfo Suárez Gonzalez, *appointed* July 3, 1976.

CABINET
(July 8, 1976)
1st Vice-President, Defence, Lt. Gen. Manuel Gutiérrez Mellado Hernández.
2nd Vice-President, Presidency, Sr. Alfonso Osorio García.
Foreign Affairs, Sr. Marcelino Oreja Aguirre.
Justice, Sr. Landelino Lavilla Alsina.
Army, Lt.-Gen. Félix Alvarez-Arenas y Pacheco.
Air, Lt.-Gen. Carlos Franco Iribarnegaray.
Navy, Adm. Gabriel Pita de Velga y Sanz.
Finance, Sr. Eduardo Carriles Galarraga.
Education and Science, Sr. Aurelio Menéndez Menéndez.

Relations with Trade Unions, Sr. Enrique de la Mata Gorostizaga.
Information and Tourism, Sr. Andrés Reguera Guajardo.
Secretary-General of the Movement, Sr. Ignacio Garcia López.
Public Works, Sr. Leopoldo Calvo-Sotelo y Bustelo.
Agriculture, Sr. Fernando Abril Martorell.
Housing, Sr. Francisco-Javier Lozano Vicente.
Industry, Sr. Carlos Pérez de Bricio Olarriaga.
Commerce, Sr. Josè Lladó y Fernández-Urrutia.
Interior, Sr. Rodolfo Martín Villa.
Labour, Sr. Alvaro Rengifo Calderón.

SPANISH EMBASSY IN LONDON
24 Belgrave Square, S.W.1
[01-235 5555]

Ambassador Extraordinary and Plenipotentiary, His Excellency The Marqués de Perinat (1976).
Minister-Counsellor, Sr. Don Manuel Gómez Acebo.

Area and Population.—A National State in the south-west of Europe, between 36°–43° 45′ N. lat. and 4° 25′ E. – 9° 20′ W. long., bounded on the south and east by the Mediterranean, on the west by the Atlantic and Portugal, and on the north by the Bay of Biscay and France, from which it is separated by the Pyrenees. Continental Spain occupies about eleven-thirteenths of the Iberian peninsula, the remaining portion forming the Republic of Portugal. Its coast-line extends 1,317 miles—712 formed by the Mediterranean and 605 by the Atlantic—and it comprises a total area of 196,700 square miles, with a population (1970) of 34,032,801. Returns for 1970 gave 656,102 births, 281,777 deaths and 247,492 marriages.

Physical Features.—The interior of the Iberian Peninsula consists of an elevated tableland surrounded and traversed by mountain ranges—the Pyrenees, the Cantabrian Mountains, the Sierra Guadarrama, Sierra Morena, Sierra Nevada, Montes de Toledo, &c. The principal rivers are the Douro, the Tagus, the Guadiana, the Guadalquivir, the Ebro and the Minho.

Government.—In April, 1931, the last monarch of Spain, Alfonso XIII, left the country; a Republic was immediately proclaimed and a Provisional Government, drawn from the various Republican and Socialist parties, was formed. The Republican Assembly (*Cortes*) was a single Chamber Congress of Deputies. On July 18, 1936, a counter-revolution broke out in many military garrisons in Spanish Morocco and spread rapidly throughout Spain. The principal leader was General Francisco Franco Bahamonde, formerly Governor of the Canary Islands. The struggle, in its later phases, threatened to embroil some of the European Powers, those of Nazi-Fascist tendency lending aid to General Franco (leader of the Military-Fascist fusion, or *Falange*) while those of Communist views supported the Azaña (*Popular Front*) government. In October, 1938, many of the supporting troops were withdrawn, and on March 29, 1939, the Civil War was declared to have ended, the popular Front Governments in Madrid and Barcelona surrendering to the *Nationalists* (as General Franco's followers were then named). On June 5, 1939, the Grand Council of the *Falange Española Tradicionalista y de las Juntas Ofensivas Nacional-Sindicalistas*, which replaced the former *Cortes*, met at Burgos to legislate for the reorganization of the country under the Presidency of General Franco, who had assumed the title of *Caudillo* (*Leader*) *of the Empire and Chief of the State*. In the Civil War of 1936–39 over 1,000,000 lives were lost.
On July 1, 1942, General Franco announced the reinstitution of the *Cortes de España*. This was re-organized by an Organic Law of 1966 and is composed of approximately 564 members—ministers, 19; members of the National Council of the Movement, 109; Presidents of various State bodies, 5; representatives of the national syndicates, 150; 100 members elected by heads of families and married women; university rectors, 12; representatives of professional, academic and scientific bodies, 28; 1epresentatives of local administration, 116; and 25 members directly appointed by the Head of State.
A referendum held in 1967 approved an Organic Law of the State introducing a number of changes in state institutions. The offices of Head of State and Head of Government were separated, but General Franco continued to hold both offices until June 1973.
On July 22, 1969, General Franco nominated Prince Juan Carlos (Alfonso) of Bourbon (*born* Jan. 5, 1938; grandson of the late King Alfonso XIII) to succeed him as head of state at his death or retirement. The nomination was approved in the *Cortes* by a large majority. Following the death of General Franco, on November 20, 1975, Juan Carlos acceded to the throne on Nov. 22, 1975.

Defence.—*Army:* There are in Spain one armoured, one mechanized, one motorized, and two mountain divisions; one cavalry brigade, two artillery brigades, one air-transportable brigade, 1 parachute brigade, 11 infantry brigades, 2 artillery brigades, 1 mountain brigade (Independent) and 1 battalion surface to air missiles. The *Guardia Civil* also forms part of the Army though it operates as a gendarmerie in the rural areas under the control of the Ministry of the Interior.
The active Spanish *Navy* consists of 1 cruiser, 1 helicopter carrier, 20 destroyers, 11 frigates and corvettes, 3 anti-submarine launches, 23 minesweepers, 6 submarines, 14 landing craft, 4 squadrons of helicopters, and a large number of auxiliary and small craft.
The *Air Force* is divided geographically into 3 Regions covering Spain plus an Air Zone for the Canaries. There are also separate functional Air Defence, Tactical and Transport Commands. The Air Force consists of 11 fighter-bomber squadrons, one anti-submarine squadron, and one search and rescue squadron. There are also a variety of training and miscellaneous aircraft and some helicopters.

Education.—A new law of education (1970) providing free education for all children aged 6 to 13 is now in the process of implementation. 30 per cent. of primary schools and 80 per cent. of secondary schools are still run privately, although state spending on education multiplied fourfold between 1960 and 1970. There are eighteen state universities, the oldest of which, Salamanca, was founded in 1230. Other ancient foundations are Valencia (1245), Oviedo (1317), Valladolid (1346), Barcelona (1450), Zaragoza (1474), Santiago (1501), Seville (1502), Granada (1526), and Madrid (1590). Private universities are Deusto in Bilbao, and Navarra in Pamplona. Student numbers in the universities have risen to over 200,000.

Language and Literature.—Castilian is the language of more than three-quarters of the population of Spain and is the form of Spanish spoken in Mexico, Central and (except in Brazil) Southern America. Basque, reported to have been the original language of Iberia, is spoken in the rural districts of Vizcaya, Guipuzcoa and Alava. Catalan is spoken in Provençal Spain, and Galician, spoken in the north-western provinces, is allied to Portuguese. The literature of Spain is one of the oldest and richest in the world, the *Poem of the Cid*, the earliest and best of the heroic songs of Spain, having been written about A.D. 1140. The outstanding writings of its golden

age are those of Miguel de Cervantes Saavedra (1547–1616), Lope Felix de Vega Carpio (1562–1635) and Pedro Calderón de la Barca (1600–1681). The Nobel Prize for Literature has three times been awarded to Spanish authors—J. Echegaray (1904), J. Benavente (1922) and Juan Ramón Jimenez (1956).

FINANCE

	1974 million Pesetas	1975 million Pesetas
Estimated Revenue	653,400	782,400
Estimated Expenditure	642,700	766,300

Public Debt (Dec. 31, 1964) excluding parastatal organizations and State-guaranteed issues: *Pesetas* 186,928,600,000.

The rate of exchange for the *peseta* in July, 1976 was 121 *pesetas* = £1 sterling (*see also* p. 83).

Production and Industry.—The country is generally fertile, and well adapted to agriculture and the cultivation of heat-loving fruits—olives, oranges, lemons, almonds, pomegranates, bananas, apricots and grapes. The agricultural products include wheat, barley, oats, rice, hemp and flax. The orange crop is exported mainly to Germany, France and the United Kingdom. The vine is cultivated widely; in the south-west, Jerez, the well-known sherry and tent wines are produced.

Spain's mineral resources of coal, iron, wolfram, copper, zinc, lead and iron ores are variously exploited. Many of the richer and more easily worked deposits have been exhausted, but the authorities are actively engaged in stimulating the exploitation of hitherto unworked or lower grade deposits. In 1970 the coal output amounted to 13,150,000 metric tons. 4,150,000 metric tons of iron ore and 7,366,000 metric tons of steel were produced in 1970. Other production figures included ('000 metric tons): cement, 16,500; sulphuric acid, 2,015; cotton yarn, 117 and wool yarn, 37. Production of electric power was 56,484 million kWh. The fishing industry is important.

The principal goods produced are manufactured goods, textiles, chemical products, footwear and other leather goods, ceramics, sewing machines and bicycles. 24,105,000 tourists visited Spain in 1970 and spent £700,000,000. The Gross National Product is approximately £13,400 million.

Communications.—In 1970 there were over 13,402 km. of railways in service and 138,670 km. of paved roads. The sea-going mercantile marine in 1970 (excluding fishing boats) registered a total on 3,338,190 gross tons. Civil aviation is under the control of the Air Ministry; there are several inland and international services in operation.

TRADE

	1974 $ million	1975 $ million
Imports	14,287	15,067
Exports	7,241	7,789

The balance of payments on current account showed a deficit of $3,477 million in 1975 and reserves stood at $5,799 m. at the end of the year.

Trade with U.K.

	1974	1975
Imports from U.K.	£296,000.000	£332,000,000
Exports to U.K.	301,000,000	308,000,000

Inclusion of the Canary Islands trade with U.K. raises the 1974 figures to: Imports from U.K., £294,519,000; Exports, £301,143,000.

The principal imports are cotton, tobacco, cellulose, timber, coffee and cocoa, fertilizers, dyes, machinery, motor vehicles and agricultural tractors, wool and petroleum products. The principal exports include iron ore, cork, salt, vegetables, citrus fruits, wines, olive oil, potash,

mercury, pyrites, tinned fruit and fish, bananas and tomatoes.

CAPITAL, Madrid. Population 3,146,071. Other large cities are ΨBarcelona (1,750,000), Valencia (648,000), ΨSeville (546,000), Zaragoza (470,000), ΨMálaga (361,000), Bilbao (410,000); Murcia (244,000).

FLAG.—Three horizontal bands, red, yellow and red, with coat of arms on yellow band. NATIONAL DAY.—July 18 (*Fiesta Nacional Espanola*).

AIR TRANSIT FROM U.K.—London–Barcelona (713 miles), 2 hrs. 25 mins.; Madrid (775 miles), 2 hrs. 5 mins.; Valencia, 2 hrs. 10 mins.

BRITISH EMBASSY

(Calle de Fernando el Santo, 16, Madrid 4)

Ambassador Extraordinary and Plenipotentiary, His Excellency Charles Douglas Wiggin, C.M.G., D.F.C., A.F.C. (1974).

Minister, R. L. Wade-Gery.

Counsellor, A. White, O.B.E. (*Commercial*).

Defence and Military Attaché, Brig. J. I. Dawson.

Air Attaché, Wing. Cdr. J. W. Everitt, M.B.E.

Naval Attaché, Cdr. J. M. Lee, O.B.E., R.N.

1st Secretary, A. R. Thomas (*Head of Chancery*).

British Council Representative, G. R. Sanderson, Almagro 5, Madrid 4.

The BALEARIC ISLES form an archipelago off the east coast of Spain. There are four large islands (Majorca, Minorca, Ibiza and Formentera), and seven smaller (Aire, Aucanada, Botafoch, Cabrera, Dragonera, Pinto and El Rey). The islands were occupied by the Romans after the destruction of Carthage and provided contingents of the celebrated Balearic slingers. The total area is 1,935 square miles, with a population of 558,287. The archipelago forms a province of Spain, the capital being ΨPalma in Majorca, pop. 234,098; ΨMahon (Minorca), pop. 16,547.

The CANARY ISLANDS are an archipelago in the Atlantic, off the African coast, consisting of 7 islands and 6 uninhabited islets. The total area is 2,807 square miles, with a population of 1,170,224. The Canary Islands form two Provinces of Spain.—*Las Palmas* (Gran Canaria, Lanzarote (38,500), Fuerteventura (19,500) and the islets of Alegranza, Roque del Este, Roque del Oests, Graciosa, Montaña Clara and Lobos), with seat of administration at ΨLas Palmas (pop. 287,038) in Gran Canaria, where major oil companies have installations for re-fuelling shipping; and *Santa Cruz de Tenerife* (Tenerife, La Palma (76,000), Gomera (31,829), and Hierro (10,000)), with seat of administration at ΨSanta Cruz in Tenerife, pop. 151,361.

Trade with U.K.

	1973	1974
Imports from U.K.	£27,812,000	£34,227,000
Exports to U.K.	29,667,000	39,317,000

ISLA DE FAISANES is an uninhabited Franco-Spanish condominium, at the mouth of the Bidassoa in La Higuera bay.

ΨCEUTA is a fortified post on the Moroccan coast, opposite Gibraltar. The total area is 5 square miles, with a population (1970) of 67,187.

ΨMELILLA is a town on a rocky promontory of the Rif coast, connected with the mainland by a narrow isthmus. Melilla has been in Spanish possession since 1492. Population (1970) 64,942. Ceuta and Melilla are parts of Metropolitan Spain.

OVERSEAS TERRITORIES

The former provinces of Spanish Guinea, Fernando Póo and Rio Muni achieved independence on October 12, 1968, under the title of Equatorial Guinea.

Ifni, the former enclave in Morocco, was incorporated in the latter state by treaty, on June 30, 1969, and the Spanish Sahara came under joint Moroccan and Mauritanian control in November 1975.

SPANISH MOROCCO.—In addition to Ceuta and Melilla, Spain exercised until 1956 a protectorate over a part of Northern Morocco. Moroccan independence was proclaimed after negotiations with France and Spain in 1956 (*see* "Morocco"). Remaining Spanish settlements on the Moroccan seaboard are:—

Alhucemas, the bay of that name includes six islands: population 366.

Peñon de la Gomera (or *Peñon de Velez*) is a fortified rocky islet about 40 miles west of Alhucemas Bay; population 450.

The Chaffarinas (or *Zaffarines*) are a group of three islands near the Algerian frontier, about 2 miles north of Cape del Agua; population 610.

SUDAN
(Democratic Republic of the Sudan)
President, Major-General Gaafar Mohamed El Nimeri, *assumed office* May 25, 1969.
Prime Minister, Sayed Al Rashid Tahir.
Defence, Field Marshal Bashir Mohammed Ali.
Minister of Foreign Affairs, Mahgoub Makawy.

SUDANESE EMBASSY IN LONDON
3 Cleveland Row, S.W.1.
[01-839 8080]
Ambassador Extraordinary and Plenipotentiary, His Excellency Amir El Sawi (1976).

Area and Population.—The Sudan extends from the southern boundary of Egypt, 22° N. lat., to the northern boundary of Uganda, 3° 36′ N. lat., and reaches from the Republic of Chad about 21° 49′ E. (at 12° 45′ N.) to the north-west boundary of Ethiopia in 38° 35′ E. (at 18° N.). The greatest length from north to south is approximately 1,300 miles, and east to west 950 miles.

The northern boundary is the 22nd parallel of North latitude; on the east lie the Red Sea and Ethiopia; on the South lie Kenya, Uganda and Zaire; and on the west the Central African Republic, Chad, and Libya.

The *White Nile* enters from Uganda at the Sudan frontier post of Nimule in Equatoria Province, as the *Bahr el Jebel*, and leaves the Sudan at Wadi Halfa. The *Blue Nile* flows from Lake Tana on the Ethiopian Plateau. Its course in the Sudan is nearly 500 miles long, before it joins the White Nile at Khartoum. The next confluence of importance is at Atbara where the main Nile is joined by the River Atbara. The total length of the Nile, now accepted as the longest river in the world, is estimated to be 4,160 miles from its source to the Mediterranean Sea. Between Khartoum and Wadi Halfa lie five of the six *Cataracts*.

The estimated area is about 967,500 sq. miles with a population (estimated, 1974) of 16,900,000, partly Arabs, partly Negroes, and partly of mixed Arab-Negro blood, with a small foreign element, including some 8,000 Europeans. The Arabs are Moslems. The Nilotics of the Bahr el Ghazal and Upper Nile Valleys are generally animists, but some have been converted to Christianity and others are Moslems.

Government.—The Anglo-Egyptian Condominium over the Sudan which had been established in 1899 ended when the Sudan House of Representatives on Dec. 19, 1955, voted unanimously a declaration that the Sudan was a fully independent sovereign state. A Republic was proclaimed on Jan. 1, 1956, and was recognized by Great Britain and Egypt, a Supreme Commission being sworn in to take over sovereignty. The Sudan was under military rule from Nov., 1958, until 1964 when a new civilian Cabinet was appointed. Following a crisis in the coalition Cabinet of Mr. Mahgoub, the Prime Minister resigned on April 23, 1969, and was unable to form a new coalition. Government of the country was taken over on May 25, 1969, by a ten-man revolutionary council headed by Col. Gaafar Mohamed El Nimeri. A *coup d'état* by a Communist group on July 19, 1971, was short-lived. The leader of the group, Lt.-Col. Babikr al Noor, had been in London for medical treatment when power was seized by Maj. Hashem Atta. The B.O.A.C. plane in which the former was returning to Khartoum on July 22 was forced down at Benghazi by Libyan fighter aircraft and Lt.-Col. Noor and an aide were arrested. They were later returned to the Sudan and executed. Maj.-Gen. Nimeri was overwhelmingly elected President in an uncontested election in October 1971. In February 1972 an agreement was signed at Addis Ababa which brought to an end nearly 17 years of insurrection and civil war in the three southern provinces, and which recognized southern regional autonomy within a unified Sudanese State.

Education.—School education is free for most children, but not compulsory, beginning with Primary School (of which there are 4,000) which continues for 6 years. The final examination at Primary School is highly competitive and selects children for General Secondary Schools (of which there are 700) which continues for 3 years. The Higher Secondary Stage comprises 80 academic Higher Secondary schools (3 years); 15 vocational schools—Technical (4 years); Agricultural and Commercial (3 years) and 15 Primary Teacher Training Colleges (4 years). The medium of instruction is Arabic. English is taught as the principal foreign language in all schools.

Teacher Training is carried out in 15 Primary Teacher Training Colleges, 2 General Secondary Teacher Training Institutes and 1 Higher Teacher Training Institute.

Khartoum University is the largest educational institution and had 9 faculties and 5,478 students in 1971–72. There is an Islamic University at Omdurman.

Selection for higher education is normally based on the Sudan School Certificate.

In addition to the three universities there are various technical post-secondary institutes as well as professional and vocational training establishments.

Production.—The principal grain crops are wheat and *dura* (great millet), the staple food of the people in the Sudan. Sesame and ground-nuts are other important food crops, which also yield an exportable surplus and a promising start has been made with castor seed. The principal export crop is cotton. Main production is of long-staple (mainly Egyptian type) cotton of which the Sudan is a major producer, but increasing quantities of short and medium staple (American) type cotton are being grown. Production in 1974–75 totalled 1,200,000 bales. Much of the high quality, long-staple cotton is provided by the Sudan Geriza Scheme (a Government-controlled project irrigated from the Sennar Dam on the Blue Nile) and its extension, the Managil Scheme. The Sudan also produces the bulk of the world's supply of gum arabic. Sugar is an increasingly important crop. The Sudan aims to be self-sufficient in sugar by 1976 and then to produce an exportable surplus; Livestock is the mainstay of the nomadic Arab tribes of the desert and the negro tribes of the swamp and wooded grassland country in the South. A new dam at Khashm el Girba began to store water in May, 1964, and will eventually provide irrigation to about 500,000 acres, most of which is being used to resettle the population of the Wadi Halfa area which has been flooded by the reservoir of the Egyptian High Dam. Another dam at Roseires on the Blue Nile will enable new or increased irrigation on a further 3,000,000 acres as well as providing hydro-electric power.

Communications.—The railway system (3 ft. 6 in. gauge) has a route length of about 3,200 miles, linking Khartoum with Wadi Halfa, Port Sudan, Wad Medani, Sennar, Kosti, El Obeid and Nyala. A line branches out southwards to Wau from the Sennar/Nyala western line. Regular rail and Nile steamer services connect Khartoum with Juba in Equatoria Province which in turn is connected by a bus service with Nimule on the Uganda border. Ψ Port Sudan is a well-equipped modern seaport. Sudan Airways fly regular services from Khartoum to many parts of the Sudan and to Egypt, Greece, Italy, the Lebanon, the United Kingdom, Ethiopia, Uganda and W. Germany, Iraq and Bahrain and are equipped with 2 Boeing 707's and 4 Fokker F27 aircraft as well as some smaller machines; they have contracted to buy 2 Boeing 737.

FINANCE

	1972–73	1974
Revenue	£S 191,286,658	£S 268,291,000
Expenditure	190,136,658	264,791,000

£S = Sudanese *Pound* of 100 Piastres.
Exchange Rate £S. 0·847 = £1 sterling, £S. 0·349 = U.S.$1. (May 1974) (*see also* p. 84).

TRADE

	1972	1974
Total Imports	£S 123,100.000	£S 223,580,000
Exports	125,500,000	122,010,000

Trade with U.K.

	1973	1974
Imports from U.K.	£26,900,000	£36,000,000
Exports to U.K.	8,400,000	8,000,000

The principal exports are cotton and cotton seed, ground-nuts and gum arabic. The chief imports are cotton piece goods, base metals, vehicles and transport equipment, machinery, petroleum products, sugar, tea, coffee, chemicals and pharmaceuticals.

CAPITAL, Khartoum (est. pop. 194,000). The town contains many mosques, a Catholic cathedral and an Anglican cathedral, which is no longer open for worship, and the University with extensive government buildings. Khartoum North and Omdurman have estimated populations of 58,000 and 167,000 respectively.

FLAG.—Three horizontal stripes of red, white and black with a green triangle next to the hoist.
NATIONAL DAY.—January 1 (Independence Day).

BRITISH EMBASSY
Khartoum

Ambassador Extraordinary and Plenipotentiary, His Excellency John Fleetwood Stewart Phillips, C.M.G. (1973).
Counsellor, R. W. Newman.
Defence and Military Attaché, Col. P. L. F. Baillon.
1st Secretary, R. E. Palmer (*Head of Chancery*).
British Council Representative, D. D. Reid, Gama'a Avenue, P.O. Box 1253, Khartoum. There are British Council libraries at *Khartoum, El Fasher, El Obeid, Omdurman* and *Wad Medani.*

SURINAM

President, Dr. J. H. E. Ferrier.
Prime Minister, Henck Arron.

Surinam is situated on the north coast of South America and is bounded by French Guiana in the east, Brazil in the south and Guyana in the west. It has an area of 63,250 square miles, with a population of 480,000 (December, 1971).

Formerly known as Dutch Guiana, Surinam remained part of the Netherlands West Indies until November 25, 1975, when it achieved complete independence. Surinam had received autonomy in domestic affairs under the Realm Statute which took effect on December 29, 1954.

Surinam has large timber resources. Rice and sugar cane are the main crops. Bauxite is mined, and is the principal export.

TRADE

	1971	1972
	Surinam Guilders	
Imports	237,800,000	258,200,000
Exports	294,500,000	305,700,000

Trade with U.K.

	1973	1974
Imports from U.K.	£2,904,000	£4,099,000
Exports to U.K.	4,071,000	4,873,000

CAPITAL.— Ψ Paramaribo (population, 1971, 110,000).
British Ambassador, His Excellency Peter Gautrey C.M.G., C.V.O. (resides at *Georgetown*).
There is a *British Consulate* at Paramaribo.
Honorary Consul, J. T. Healy.

SWEDEN
(Sverige)

King of Sweden, Carl XVI Gustaf, *grandson* of the late King Gustaf VI Adolf, *born* April 30, 1946.

Prime Minister, Thorbjoern Faelldin.

SWEDISH EMBASSY IN LONDON
Residence, 27 Portland Place, W.1; *Chancery*, 23 North Row, W.1.
[01–499 9500]
Ambassador Extraordinary and Plenipotentiary, His Excellency Olof Rydreck (1976).
Minister Plenipotentiary, L. Bergquist.
Counsellors, Baron C. G. von Platen, C.V.O. (*Economic and Financial*); D. Winter (*Press*); G. Westin, M.V.O. (*Consular*).

1st Secretaries, N. G. Revelius, M.V.O.; L. G. Carlsson (Consular); Miss K. Rosenstrom (Administration); Mrs. W. Tornberg (Consular); T. Westlund (Commodities).

Naval Attaché, Capt. L. Jedeur-Palmgren.

Air and Military Attaché, Col. J. Winqvist, M.V.O.

Trade Commissioner, S. Widenfelt, M.V.O. (73 Welbeck St., W.I.)

Area and Population.—Sweden occupies the eastern area of the Scandinavian peninsula in N.W. Europe and comprises 24 local government districts, "*Län*", with an area of 173,436 sq. miles, and population Jan. 1, 1975 of 8,177,000. In 1975 there were 103,421 births (12·62 per 1,000 inhabitants); death rate was 10·75 per 1,000 inhabitants and infant mortality rate (under one year of age) 0·9 per cent. of all live births.

Government. Under the Act of Succession of June 6, 1809 (with amendments) the throne is hereditary in the House of Bernadotte. Jean-Baptiste Jules Bernadotte, Prince of Ponte Corvo, a Marshal of France, was invited to accept the title of Crown Prince, with succession to the throne. He landed at Hälsingborg on Oct. 20, 1810, and succeeded Charles XIII in 1818. There is a unicameral Diet (*Riksdag*) of 349 members elected for 3 years. The Council of Ministers (*Statsrad*) is responsible to the *Riksdag*.

Production and Industry.—Since the end of the First World War Sweden has become one of the leading industrial nations of Europe. Agriculture is still one of the main activities, but its relative importance is declining and in 1975 less than 6 per cent. of the working population was engaged in farming and forestry. The country's industrial prosperity is based on an abundance of natural resources in the form of forests, mineral deposits and water power. The forests are very extensive, covering about half the total land surface, and sustain flourishing timber, pulp and paper milling industries. The mineral resources include iron ore of excellent quality, lead, zinc, sulphur, granite and marble. There are also extensive deposits of low grade uranium ore. Important industries based on mining include iron and steel, aluminium, and copper. The engineering industry has expanded largely on the basis of products invented or developed by Swedish engineers. Sweden has now one of the most important shipbuilding industries in the world. Motor car manufacturing is a major industry. The establishment of a petro-chemicals industry has led to a rapid expansion in the output of chemicals and plastics.

Communications.—The total length of Swedish railroads is about 7,500 miles. At the end of 1974 there were 633 telephones for every 1,000 of the population, and in January, 1976, the number of broadcast receiving licences issued had reached 2,909,000. The number of private cars in use on December 31, 1975 was 2,761,000.

The Mercantile Marine amounted on December 31, 1975 to 7,731,000 gross tonnage, of which 3,494,000 comprised the tanker fleet. The Board of Civil Aviation under the control of the Ministry of Communications handles civil aviation matters. Regular domestic air traffic is maintained by the Scandinavian Airlines System and by A. B. Linjeflyg. . Regular European and inter-continental air traffic is maintained by the Scandinavian Airlines System.

Defence.—Based on the policy of non-alignment in peace leading to neutrality in war Sweden maintains a Total Defence intended to make any attack on her costly. Total Defence includes peacetime organizations for civil, economic and psychological defence as well as compulsory national service for all acceptable males. Some 50,000 National Servicemen are called up for up to 11 months training each and all are recalled every fourth year for refresher training. On mobilization the Army strength totals 600,000 men including 50 tank, artillery and infantry battalions, 6 tank brigades and 20 infantry brigades. The Navy has 8 destroyers, 4 frigates, 20 submarines, 35 torpedo boats, a large number of minor craft and auxiliaries and 65 coast artillery units. The Air Force has modern supersonic aircraft of Swedish manufacture forming a standing force of 300 air defence, 150 attack and 100 reconnaissance aircraft supported by a modern air defence radar system. Facilities exist for rapid dispersal from main bases in war.

Religion.—The State religion is Lutheran Protestant, to which over 95 per cent. of the people officially adhere.

Language and Literature.—Swedish belongs, with Danish and Norwegian, to the North Germanic language group. Swedish literature dates back to King Magnus Eriksson, who codified the old Swedish provincial laws in 1350. With his translation of the Bible, Olaus Petri (1493–1552) formed the basis for the modern Swedish language. Literature flourished during the reign of Gustavus III, who founded the Swedish Academy in 1786. Swedish literature is studded with names such as Kellgren (1751–1795), Atterbom (1790–1855), Almquist (1795–1866), Rydberg (1828–1895), Levertin (1862–1906), Strindberg (1849–1912) and Lagerlöf (1858–1940), Nobel Prize Winner in 1909. Contemporary authors include Lagerquist (1891–1973), Nobel Laureate in 1951, Martinson (b 1904) and Johnson (b. 1900), Nobel Laureates jointly in 1974. The Swedish scientist Alfred Nobel (1833–1896) founded the Nobel Prizes for Literature, Science and Peace. In 1975 there were 146 daily newspapers with a total circulation of 4,677,800 copies, 4 major papers being published at Stockholm, 2 at Göteborg and 4 at Malmö.

Education.—Well developed and recently reorganized to provide (i) 9 years' compulsory schooling from the age of 7 to 16 in the *Grundskolan*; (ii) further education from 16 to 18/19 in the *Gymnasia*, which offer a number of courses preparing for entry to the universities, other centres of higher education, the professions, etc.; (iii) the universities. There are six universities—Uppsala (founded 1477); Lund (founded 1668); Stockholm (founded 1878); Gothenburg (founded 1887); Umea (founded 1963) and Linköping (founded 1967); three affiliated university branches, empowered to grant first degrees only in the humanities, social sciences and natural sciences, at Örebro, Växjö and Karlstad; and three universities of technology, at Stockholm, Gothenburg and Luleå. Another institution of university status is the Karolinska Institute, which specializes in medicine and dentistry. Tuition within the State system, which is maintained by the State and by local taxation, is free.

FINANCE

	1975–76 'ooo Kronor	1976–77 'ooo Kronor
Revenue (Estimated)	89,810	99,197
Expenditure (Estimated)	99,895	111,099

The Swedish *Krona* (of 100 *Ore*) exchanges at about 7.85 *Kronor*= £1 sterling (June, 1976). (*See also* p. 83.)

TRADE

	1973 'ooo Kronor	1974 'ooo Kronor
Imports	69,993	79,180
Exports	70,390	72,228

Trade with U.K.

	1974	1975
Imports from U.K.	£723,340,000	£825,000,000
Exports to U.K.	929,112,000	886,000,000

The chief imports from Britain are machinery and engineering goods, transport equipment, petroleum products, chemicals, plastics, raw materials, iron and steel and other metals, textile fabrics, clothing, instruments and some foodstuffs. Sweden's chief exports to Britain are timber, pulp and paper, machinery, motor vehicles, iron ore, and iron and steel.

CAPITAL.—Ψ Stockholm. Population (1975): City 665,202; Greater Stockholm, 1,357,558; Ψ Gothenburg (Göteborg) (444,651); Ψ Malmö (243.591); Västerås (117,911); Uppsala (138,116); Ψ Norrköping (119,169); Örebro (117,837); Ψ Helsingborg (101,685); Linköping (109,236); Ψ Gävle (86,911); Borås (105,177); Eskilstuna (92,663).

FLAG.—Yellow cross on a blue ground. NATIONAL DAY.—June 6 (Day of the Swedish Flag).

BRITISH EMBASSY
(*Residence*, Laboratoriegatan 8; *Chancery*, Skarpögatan 8, Stockholm.)
Ambassador Extraordinary and Plenipotentiary, His Excellency Sir Samuel Falle, K.C.V.O., C.M.G., D.S.C. (1974).
Counsellors, R. M. Evans (*Commercial*); D. J. Wyatt (*Head of Chancery*).
1st Secretaries, J. G. B. Weait (*Commercial*); C. Marshall, O.B.E. (*Labour*); D. G. H. Brookfield, M.B.E.; A. L. Free-Gore (*Economic*); A. Lindsay (*Consul*); P. R. Holmes (*Information*).
Defence and Air Attaché, Gp. Capt. K. J. Barratt.
Naval Attaché, Cdr. C. McK. Marr, R.N.
Military Attaché, Lt.-Col. P. J. Watson.
British Council Representative, W. D. Sharrocks.

BRITISH CONSULAR OFFICES
There are British Consular Offices at *Gävle*, *Göteborg*, *Hälsingborg*, *Luleå*, *Malmö*, *Norrköping*, *Stockholm* and *Sundsvall*.

British-Swedish Chamber of Commerce in Sweden: Birger Jarlsgatan 6B, Stockholm.

SWITZERLAND
(Schweizerische Eidgenossenschaft—Confédération Suisse—Confederazione Svizzera.)

CABINET
President of the Swiss Confederation (1976) *and Head of the Military Department*, M. Rudolf Gnaegi.
Vice-President (1976) *and Justice and Police*, M. Kurt Furgler.
Public Economy, M. Ernst Brugger.
Political Department, M. Pierre Graber.
Transport and Power, M. Willi Ritschard.
Interior, M. Hans Huerlimann.
Finance and Customs, M. Georges-André Chevallaz.
Federal Chancellor, M. Karl Huber.

SWISS EMBASSY IN LONDON
16–18 Montagu Place, W.1.
[01-723 0701]
Ambassador Extraordinary and Plenipotentiary, His Excellency, Dr. Ernesto Thalmann (1976).
Minister Plenipotentiary, Dr. K. Fritschi.
Counsellors, J. P. Zehnder (*Economic and Labour*); J.-J. Indermuehle (*Cultural Affairs*); M. R. Serex.
Defence Attaché, Col. Hans W. Fischer.
1st Secretary, Paul A. Ramseyer.
Counsellor, H. H. Buchmann (*Commodities and Agriculture*).
Consul and Head of Administration, C. Glauser.
There is a Swiss Consulate-General in *Manchester*.

Area and Population.—The Helvetia of the Romans, a Federal Republic of Central Europe, situated between 45° 50′–47° 48′ N. lat. and 5° 58′–10° 3′ E. long. It is composed of 22 Cantons, 3 subdivided, making 25 in all, and comprises a total area of 15,950 square miles with a population (estimated Jan. 1, 1973) of 6,385,000. In 1972 there were 91,342 (1973, 84,187) live births, 56,489 deaths and 43,081 marriages. The infant mortality rate was 13 per 1,000 live births. In 1970, out of a total of 6,169,800, 47·8 per cent. of the population was Protestant, 49·4 per cent. Roman Catholic and 0·3 per cent. Jewish.

Physical Features.—Switzerland is the most mountainous country in all Europe. The Alps, covered with perennial snow and from 5,000 to 15,217 feet in height, occupy its southern and eastern frontiers, and the chief part of its interior;

and the Jura mountains rise in the north-west. The Alps occupy 61 per cent., and the Jura mounains 12 per cent., of the country. The *Alps* are at crescent-shaped mountain system situated in France, Italy, Switzerland, Bavaria and Austria, covering an area of 80,000 square miles from the Mediterranean to the Danube (600 miles). The highest peak, Mont Blanc, Pennine Alps (15,732 feet) is partly in France and Italy; Monte Rosa (15,217 feet) and Matterhorn (14,780 feet) are partly in Switzerland and partly in Italy. The highest wholly Swiss peaks are Dufourspitze (15,203 ft.), Finsteraahorn (14,026), Aletschhorn (13,711), Jungfrau (13,671), Mönch (13,456), Eiger (13,040), Schreckhorn (13,385), and Wetterhorn (12,150) in the Bernese Alps, and Dom (14,918), Weisshorn (14,803) and Breithorn (13,685).

The Swiss lakes are famous for their beauty and include Lakes Maggiore, Zürich, Lucerne, Neuchâtel, Geneva, Constance, Thun Zug, Lugano, Brienz and the Walensee. There are also many artificial lakes.

Production and Industry.—Agriculture is followed chiefly in the valleys, where wheat, oats, maize, barley, flax, hemp, and tobacco are produced, and nearly all English fruits and vegetables as well as grapes are grown. Dairying and stock-raising are the principal industries, about 3,000,000 acres being under grass for hay and 2,000,000 acres pasturage. The forests cover about one-quarter of the whole surface. The chief manufacturing industries comprise engineering and electrical engineering, metal-working, chemicals and pharmaceuticals, textiles, watchmaking, woodworking, foodstuffs and footwear. Banking, insurance and tourism are major industries.

Government.—The legislative power is vested in a Parliament, consisting of two Chambers, a National Council (*Nationalrat*) of 200 members, and a Council of States (*Ständerat*) of 44 members; both Chambers united are called the Federal Assembly, and the members of the National Council are elected for four years, an election taking place in October. The executive power is in the hands of a Federal Council (*Bundesrat*) of 7 members, elected for four years by the Federal Assembly and presided over by the President of the Confederation. Each year the Federal Assembly elects from the Federal Council the President and the Vice-President. Not more than one of the same canton may be elected member of the Federal Council; on the other hand, there is a tradition that Italian and French-speaking areas should between them be represented on the Federal Council by at least two members.

Defence.—All Swiss males must undertake military service in the Army. *Elite* (ages 20 to 32) initial training, 118 days. Subsequently 8 training periods of 21 days; then *Landwehr* (33–42) and *Landsturm* (43 to 50). Flying personnel of the Air Force, which is part of the Army (ages 20–36): Initial training 1 year, totalling 200 hours of flying. 6 weeks with squadron each year and completion of 80 to 100 hours of flying. After 36 revert to ground duties with Air Force or Army. Swiss Army equipment includes many British items, notably Centurion tanks, Bloodhound missiles, and Venom, Vampire and Hunter aircraft.

Communications.—By the end of 1974 there were 4,992 km of railway tracks (Swiss Federal Railways, 2,926 km; Swiss privately owned railways 2,066 km); the whole system is electrified. At the end of 1973, there were 89,940 km of telegraph and telephone lines. By December 1974 the number of telephone subscribers amounted to 2,390,852 and

the network was fully automatic throughout the country. In 1974 there were 2,036,431 licensed radio receivers and 1,714,336 television receivers.

At the end of 1975 the total length of motorways was 916 km. The number of motor vehicles licensed at the end of 1974 was 2,011,378.

A merchant marine established in 1940, consisted in 1975 of 27 vessels with a total displacement of 211,201 tons (gross). In addition 496 vessels with a total tonnage of 588,121 were engaged in Rhine shipping. In 1974 goods handled at the Basle Rhine ports amounted to 9,340,192 tons. 121 lake vessels transported 9,733,000 passengers and 236,362 tons of freight in 1973. The national airline, Swissair, has a network covering 230,769 km and in 1973 carried a total of 5,152,106 passengers. Its fleet of 45 aircraft includes 2 Jumbojets, with 5 aircraft on order (5 DC9's). It flies to and from the Swiss airports at Zürich, Geneva and Basle.

Education.—Control by cantonal and communal authorities. No central organization. Illiteracy practically unknown. (i) *Primary:* Free and compulsory. School age varies, generally 7 to 14. (ii) *Secondary:* Age 12–15 for boys and girls. Schools numerous and well-attended, and there are many private institutions. (iii) *Special schools* make a feature of commercial and technical instruction. (iv) *Universities:* Basle (founded 1460), Berne (1834), Fribourg (1889), Geneva (1873), Lausanne (1890), Zürich (1832), and Neuchâtel (1909), and the technical University of Zürich and commercial University of St. Gall.

Language and Literature.—There are three official languages: French, German and Italian. In addition Romansch is recognized as a national, but not an official language. German is the dominating language in 19 of the 25 cantons; French in Fribourg, Geneva, Neuchâtel, Valais and Vaud; Italian in Ticino, and Romansch in parts of the Grisons.

Many modern authors, alike in the German school and in the Suisse Romande, have achieved international fame. Karl Spitteler (1845–1924) and Hermann Hesse (1877–1962) were awarded the Nobel Prize for Literature, the former in 1919, the latter in 1946.

FINANCE

	Budget 1975	Budget 1976
	Swiss Francs	*Swiss Francs*
Revenue	12,908,000,000	14,485,000,000
Expenditure	13,366,000,000	15,658,000,000
Federal Public Debt (Dec., 1975):		
Internal consolidated		2,609,000,000

The approx. rate of exchange is *Sw. Frs.* 4·40 = £1 (*see also* p. 83).

TRADE

	1974	1975
	Sw. Frs.	*Sw. Frs.*
Total Imports	42,909,358,510	34,268,000,000
Total Exports	35,353,101,852	33,429,700,000

Trade with U.K.
(including Liechtenstein)

	1974	1975
Imports from U.K.	£600,450,000	£711,338,000
Exports to U.K.	717,143,000	710,046,000

The principal imports are machinery, electrical and electronic equipment, textiles, motor vehicles, non-ferrous metals, chemical elements, clothing, food, medicinal and pharmaceutical products. The principal exports are machinery, chemical elements, non-ferrous metals, watches, electrical and electronic equipment, textiles, dyeing, tanning and colouring products. Switzerland is a member of E.F.T.A.

CAPITAL, Berne. Population (1975) 162,405. Other large towns are Zürich (422,640), Basle (212,857), Geneva (173,618), Lausanne (173,383), Winterthur (91,400), St. Gallen (80,300), Lucerne (67,400), Bienne (61,600) and La Chaux-de-Fonds (41,800).

FLAG.—Red, with white cross. NATIONAL DAY. —August 1.

AIR TRANSIT FROM U.K.—London-Basle (446 miles), 1 hr. 20 mins.; Geneva (468 miles), 1 hr. 20 mins.; Zürich (491 miles), 1 hr. 20 mins; Berne, 2 hrs. 20 mins.

RAIL TRANSIT FROM U.K.—London-Berne, 16 hrs.

BRITISH EMBASSY
(Thunstrasse 50, 3005 Berne)

Ambassador Extraordinary and Plenipotentiary, His Excellency Alan Keir Rothnie, C.M.G. (1976).

Counsellor, P. A. Grier, O.B.E.

1st Secretary, H. L. O'Bryan-Tear, O.B.E.

2nd Secretaries, A. V. Hill; G. D. Darby (*Consul*).

Defence, Naval and Military Attaché, Lt.-Col. A. A. Taylor.

Air Attaché, Wing. Cdr. D. T. McCann.

Attaché, D. L. Wetton, M.B.E. (*Commercial*).

Press and Information Attaché, P. A. Arengo-Jones.

BRITISH CONSULAR OFFICES
There is a Consular Section at H.M. Embassy, Berne; *Consulates-General* at *Zürich* and *Geneva*, a Consulate in *Basle* and Consular offices at *Lugano* and *Montreux*. The Directorate of British Export Promotion in Switzerland is in the Consulate-General Office in *Zürich*.

British Council Representative (vacant).

BRITISH-SWISS CHAMBER OF COMMERCE FOR SWITZERLAND, Dufourstrasse, 51, 8008 *Zürich* (Branch at 1 Galeries Benjamin Constant, 1,000 *Lausanne*).

SWISS-BRITISH SOCIETY, Berne.—*President*, Dr. Th. von Mandach.

SWISS-BRITISH SOCIETY, Zürich.—*President*, Dr. R. Schneebeli.

SWISS-BRITISH SOCIETY, Basle.—*President*, Mr. Simons.

SYRIA
(Syrian Arab Republic)

President, Lt.-Gen. Hafez el Assad, *b.* 1930, *assumed office* March 14, 1971, *for a term of 7 years.*

Prime Minister, Maj.-Gen. Abdul Rahman Khleifawi.

SYRIAN EMBASSY IN LONDON
5 Eaton Terrace, S.W.1.

[01-730 0384]

Ambassador Extraordinary and Plenipotentiary, His Excellency Adnan Omran (1974).

Area and Population.—Syria is in the Levant, covering a portion of the former Ottoman Empire, with an estimated area of 70,800 sq. miles and a population (Census of 1970) of 6,294,000, Arabic speaking and mainly Moslems. (*For Map, see* p. 883.) The Orontes flows northwards from the Lebanon range across the northern boundary into Antakya (Antioch, Turkey). The Euphrates crosses the northern boundary near Jerablus and flows through north-eastern Syria to the boundary of Iraq.

Archæology, etc.—The region is rich in historical remains. Damascus (*Dimishq ash-Sham*) is the oldest continuously inhabited city in the world, having an existence as a city for over 4,000 years. It is situated on the river Abana (now known as Barada), in an oasis at the eastern foot of the Anti-Lebanon, and at the edge of the wide sandy desert which stretches to the Euphrates. The city contains the Omayed Mosque, the Tomb of Saladin, and the " Street Called Straight " (Acts ix. 11), while to the North-East is the Roman outpost of Dmeir and further east is Palmyra.

On the Mediterranean coast at Amrit are ruins of the Phœnician town of Marath, where the *well* has been found and is being excavated and also ruins of Crusaders' fortresses at Markab, Sahyoun, and Krak des Chevaliers. At Tartous (also on the coast) the cathedral of Our Lady of Syria, built by the Knights Templars in the 12th and 13th centuries has been restored as a museum.

Hittite cities dating from 2,000 to 1,500 B.C., have recently been explored on the west bank of the Euphrates at Jerablus and Kadesh.

Government.—Syria, which had been under French mandate since the 1914-18 war, became an independent Republic during the 1939-45 war. The first independently elected Parliament met on August 17, 1943, but foreign troops were in part occupation until April, 1946. Syria remained an independent Republic until February, 1958, when it became part of the United Arab Republic. It seceded from the United Arab Republic on Sept. 28, 1961.

A new Constitution was promulgated in March 1973; this declared that Syria is a " democratic, popular, socialist State ", and that the Ba'ath Party, which has been the ruling party since 1963, is " the leading party in the State and society ". Elections to the 186-seat Peoples' Council in May 1973 resulted in a large majority for the Ba'ath Party.

Production and Industry.—Agriculture is the principal source of production; wheat and barley are the main cereal crops, but the cotton crop is the highest in value. Tobacco is grown in the maritime plain in Sahel, the Sahyoun and the Djebleh district of Lattakia; skins and hides, leather goods, wool and silk, textiles, cement, vegetable oil, glass, soap, sugar, plastics and copper and brass utensils are locally produced. Large new areas are coming under irrigation and cultivation in the north-east of the country as a result of the Tabqa dam. There are also some light assembly plants. Mineral wealth is modest but oil has been found at Karachuk and other parts in the north-eastern corner of the country and drilling is continuing. A pipeline has been built to the Mediterranean port of Tartous, *via* Homs. An oil refinery is in production at Homs. and revenue is derived from the Kirkuk-Banias oil pipeline and the pipeline from the oilfields of Saudi Arabia to Sidon in Lebanon (Tapline). Oil production in 1975 was estimated at about 8 million tons per annum. Syria also has deposits of phosphate and rock salt.

Language and Literature.—Arabic is the principal language (*see* Arabia), but a few villages still speak Aramaic, the language spoken by Christ and the Apostles. There are 2 daily newspapers and several periodicals in Arabic published in Damascus and one daily newspaper in Aleppo.

Education.—Education in Syria is under State control and, although a few of the schools are privately owned, they all follow a common system and syllabus. Elementary education is free at State Schools, and is compulsory from the age of seven. Secondary education is not compulsory and is free only at the State Schools. Because of the shortage of places, entry to these State Schools is competitive. Damascus University, founded in 1924, has faculties of law, medicine, engineering, science, arts, commerce, agriculture, divinity, fine arts, and a Higher Teachers' Training College. The number of students has risen from a few hundred in 1943 to about 20,000. There are

also over 4,500 students at Aleppo University (founded 1961). Approximately 10 per cent. of all students receive scholarships, and at the present time Palestinian refugees are admitted free. The rest pay fees.

Communications.—A narrow-gauge railway runs from Beirut in the Lebanon to Damascus, connecting at Rayak (Lebanon) with the standard-gauge line which runs from Beirut and Tripoli (in the Lebanon) through Homs, Hama and Aleppo to the Turkish frontier, from Nusaybin to the Iraq frontier at Tel Kotchek. From Damascus the Hejaz railway runs southwards to Jordan. Railway lines are under construction to link the ports of Lattakia and Tartous with Aleppo and Qamishli. All the principal towns in the country are connected by roads of varying quality. An internal air service operates between Damascus and Aleppo, and between Aleppo and Qamishli. There are also flights from Damascus to Palmyra and Deir-ez-Zor. Damascus is also on international air routes.

Currency.—The monetary unit is the Syrian paper pound (£Syr.). Exchange rate, *see* p. 84.

Trade.—The principal imports are foodstuffs (fruit, vegetables, cereals, meat and dairy products, tea, coffee and sugar), mineral and petroleum products, yarn and textiles, iron and steel manufactures, machinery, chemicals, pharmaceuticals, fertilizers and timber.

Principal Exports.—Raw cotton, cereals, fruit, livestock and dairy products, other foodstuffs, textiles and raw wool.

Trade with U.K.

	1973	1974
Imports from U.K.	£11,630,000	£20,854,000
Exports to U.K.	1,154,000	20,572,000

CHIEF TOWNS.—Damascus (population (estimate, 1971), 557,252) is the capital of Syria. Other important towns being Aleppo (population 425,467), Homs (137,217) and Hama (97,390), and the principal port is Ψ Lattakia (67,604).

FLAG.—Red over white over black horizontal bands, with three green stars on central white band.
NATIONAL DAY.—April 17.

BRITISH EMBASSY
(Quartier Malki, 11 rue Mohammad Kurd Ali, Imm. Kotob, Damascus.)
Ambassador Extraordinary and Plenipotentiary, His Excellency Albert James MacQueen Craig, C.M.G. (1976).

THAILAND (Siam)

King, His Majesty Bhumibol Adulyadej, *born* 1927; *succeeded his brother*, June 9, 1946; *married* Princess Sirikit Kityakara, April 28, 1950; *crowned* May 5, 1950; daughter *born*, April 6, 1951; son and heir *born*, July 28, 1952; second daughter *born* April 2, 1955; third daughter *born* July 4, 1957.

CABINET
(April 1976)
Prime Minister, Seni Pramoj.
Deputy Prime Minister and Agriculture and Co-operatives, Maj. Gen. Pramarn Adireksarn.
Deputy Prime Minister and Finance, Sawet Piamphongsant.
Deputy Prime Minister and Public Health, Air Chief Marshal Dawee Chullasapya.
Ministers to Prime Minister's Office, Surin Masdit; Chuan Leekpai.
Defence, Gen. Tawit Seniwong Na Aynthaya.
Foreign Affairs, Bhichai Rattakul.
Communications, Tavich Klinpratoom.
Commerce, Damrong Lathapipat.
Justice, Prasit Kanchananat.

Education, Maj. Gen. Siri Siriyodhin.
Industry, Maj.-Gen. Chatichai Choonhavan.
State Universities, Nibonh Sasidhorn.
There are also 17 Deputy Ministers.

ROYAL THAI EMBASSY IN LONDON
30 Queen's Gate, S.W.7
[01–589 0173]
Ambassador Extraordinary and Plenipotentiary, His Excellency Konthi Suphamongkhon, G.C.V.O. (1970).

Area and Population.—The Kingdom of Thailand, formerly known as Siam, has an area of 198,247 sq. miles with a population (estimated 1975) of 42,000,000. For position, *see* MAP, p. 744. It has a common boundary with Malaysia in the south, is bounded on the west by Burma and on the north-east and east by the People's Democratic Republic of Laos and Cambodia, which were formerly part of the French Colony of Indo-China. Although there is no common boundary between Thailand and China, the Chinese province of Yunnan is separated from the Thai northern border only by a narrow stretch of Burmese and Laotian territory.

The capital, Bangkok, with a population of about 4,500,000, is situated in the south of the central plain area. To the north-east there is a plateau area and to the north-west mountains. The south of Thailand consists of a narrow mountainous peninsula. The principal rivers are the Chao Phraya with its tributary the Meping and the Mekong and its tributaries, which water the eastern plateau.

Government.—Thailand is a Constitutional Monarchy. The Constitution promulgated in October 1974 provides for a bicameral National Assembly, consisting of an elected House of Representatives, currently with 279 members and an appointed senate of 100 members.

Following the dissolution of parliament in January 1976, a general election was held on April 4, 1976, resulting in the coalition government of Mom Rachawongse (M.R.) Kukrit Pramoj being replaced by the present coalition government led by M. R. Seni Pramoj.

Language, Religion and Education.—Thai is basically a monosyllabic, tonal language, a branch of the Indo-Chinese linguistic family, but its vocabulary especially has been strongly influenced by Sanskrit and Pali. It is written in an alphabetic script derived from ancient Indian scripts. The principal religion is Buddhism. In 1973 93·6 per cent. of the population were Buddhists, 3·9 per cent. Moslems, 0·6 per cent. Christians and 1·9 per cent. other religions. Primary education is compulsory and free and secondary education in Government Schools is free. In 1974 there were 33,448 schools of all kinds with 7,321,797 pupils and 250,300 teachers. There are 10 Universities attended by 136,349 students, 34 training colleges and 196 vocational schools (all types). New universities were opened at Chiengmai and Khon Kaen in 1966 and a further university has subsequently been opened at Songkhla in the south. In 1972 an open university (Ramkhamhaeng) was established in Bangkok with some 45,000 students.

Production and Industry.—The agricultural sector provides just under half the national income and employs about 70 per cent. of the working population. Rice remains the most important crop, accounting for 63 per cent. of the area planted. After rice (14,700,000 tons est. in 1975) the main crops are cassava (7,430,000 tons of roots), maize (2,540,000 tons), and rubber (435,000 tons). Other crops of some importance are sugar cane, kenaf,

groundnuts, tobacco, and coconuts. There is also a substantial forest extraction industry, the most valuable product of which is teak.

Mineral resources are mainly tin, antimony, tungsten, gypsum and fluorite. The most important of these, tin, is seeing something of a decline, mainly because of the exhaustion of reserves. The importance of lignite as a source of energy increased with higher oil prices.

Before the war, industry was mainly confined to the basic processing industries—sawmilling, rice-milling, etc. After the war, the Government set up a number of factories run by the Civil Service or the Armed Forces. The Government still has a sizeable stake in industry—notably the tobacco monopoly and factories for the manufacture of cement, glass, paper, jute, textiles, sugar and beer and spirits.

The then Government in 1962 instituted a policy of encouraging the private sector to invest in industry, by means of tax reliefs and other incentives. The private sector industries are almost entirely of a secondary nature; soap products, gunny bags, textiles, car assembly, pharmaceutical preparations and packaging, dry batteries, etc. Over the last decade the size of the manufacturing sector has grown rapidly and now provides 18 per cent. of national income.

Communications.—Rivers and canals provide the traditional mode of transport for much of the country. Navigable waterways have a length of about 1,100 km. in the dry season and 1,600 km. in the wet season. About 3,830 km. of State-owned railways were open to traffic in 1974. The track is metre gauge. Main lines run from Bangkok to Aranya Prathet, on the Cambodian border (160 miles E.); *via* Korat to Ubol (about 352 miles E.) and to Nongkhai (415 miles N.E.) the ferry terminal on the River Mekong opposite Vientiane, capital of Laos; to Chiengmai (411 miles N.); and to Haadyai (600 miles S.), whence lines go down the eastern and western sides of the Malay Peninsula, *via* Sungei Golok and Penang respectively, to Singapore.

Thailand has some 18,000 km. of highways and provincial roads, of which 63 per cent. are paved.

Bangkok has an international airport of importance, and services connect it direct with cities in Europe, America, and Australia, as well as countries in Asia. Thai Airways International (THAI), was formed in 1960 in association with SAS to operate international routes. Domestic routes are operated by Thai Airways Corporation. A private airline, Air Siam, operates a limited number of services to Hong Kong, Japan, Singapore and the West Coast of the United States. There are some 22,000 km. of telegraph lines and improvements are being made to an already extensive micro-wave communications system. The harbour at Bangkok, which can take vessels up to 10,000 tons dead weight is congested, but six new berths are presently being constructed. A new deep-water port has been constructed on the east side of the Gulf of Thailand, but is not yet in full use.

FINANCE

	1974	1975
	millions of *Baht*	
Total revenue	43,800	42,000
Total expenditure	41,800	52,100

The exchange rate for the *Baht* was officially fixed at Baht 20·0 = $1 U.S. (*See also* p. 84.)

TRADE

	1974	1975†
	millions of *Baht*	
Total imports	64,044	50,399
Total exports	50,245	36,195

† Jan.–Sept.

Trade with U.K.

	1974	1975
Imports from U.K.	£57,000,000	£55,800,000
Exports to U.K.	18,300,000	13,600,000

Thailand's main exports in 1975 (in millions of *Baht*) were: rice, 5,773, maize 5,614, tapioca products 4,589, rubber 3,451 and tin 2,240. Other exports include ready-made garments, textiles, shrimps, tobacco, cement, beans, sorghun and teak. Main imports for the same period were machinery 23,075, petroleum products 11,160, manufactured goods 10,461, chemicals 9,143 and raw materials 3,948.

CAPITAL, ΨBangkok (population 4,300,000); in the delta of Chao Phraya. Other centres are Chiengmai, Nakorn Sawan, Korat and Haadyai, but no other town approaches Bangkok in size or importance.

FLAG.—Five horizontal bands, red, white, dark blue, white, red (the blue band twice the width of the others). NATIONAL DAY.—December 5 (King's Birthday).

BRITISH EMBASSY
(Bangkok)

Ambassador Extraordinary and Plenipotentiary, His Excellency Sir David Lee Cole, K.C.M.G., M.C. (1973).
Counsellors, H. A. J. Staples; J. P. Law, Q.P.M.
Defence and Military Attaché, Col. I. T. C. Wilson, M.B.E., M.C.
Naval and Air Attaché, Cdr. G. C. Roberts, O.B.E., R.N.
1st Secretaries, R. Goring-Morris, O.B.E. (*Head of Chancery*); O. H. Robinson; J. N. Howard (*Consul*); P. B. Cormack; J. L. Brooke; G. D. Quinn; Miss C. Swan.
British Council Representative, I. Ll. Watts.

TOGO
(Republic of Togo)

President and Minister of Defence, Gen. Gnassingbé Eyadéma, *born* 1937, *assumed office as Head of State*, April 14, 1967.
Minister for Foreign Affairs, M. Houenou Hunlédé.

The Republic is situated in West Africa between 0°–2° W. and 6°–11° N., with a coastline only 35 miles long on the Gulf of Guinea, and extends northward inland for 350 miles. It is flanked on the west by Ghana, on the north by Upper Volta and in the east by Benin (*see* MAP, p. 953). It has an area of 21,000 sq. miles and a population (estimate, Dec. 1972) of 2,089,900, including people of several African races.

The first President of Togo, Sylvanus Olympio, assassinated on January 13, 1963, was succeeded by Nicolas Grunitzky, who was himself overthrown by an army *coup d'état* on January 13, 1967. On April 14, 1967, the Commander-in-Chief of the Togolese army, Lt. Colonel (later promoted General) Eyadéma named himself President. Togo is a member of the *Conseil de l'Entente*, the *Organisation Commune Africaine et Malgache* (O.C.A.M.), and the Organization of African Unity (O.A.U.). The official language is French.

Finance.—The currency of Togo is the *Franc C.F.A.* (*Francs* C.F.A. 50 = 1 *French Franc*) (*Francs* C.F.A. 450 = £1, at June, 1975).

Production and Trade.—Although the economy of Togo remains largely agricultural exports of phosphates have superseded agricultural products as the main source of export earnings, being 75 per cent. of the total in the first 10 months of 1974 compared with 11 per cent. for cocoa and 6 per cent. for coffee. Other exports include palm

kernels, copra and manioc. The production of phosphates entirely for export was begun by a Franco-American consortium in 1958 but the Togolese Government has increased its participation in recent years and took over completely in February 1974.

Trade with U.K.

	1973	1974
Imports from U.K.	£3,008,958	£3,333,933
Exports to U.K.	173,896	542,210

CAPITAL.— ΨLomé, population (1974), 214,200.

FLAG.—Five alternating green and yellow horizontal stripes; a quarter in red at top next staff bearing a white star. NATIONAL DAY.—April 27 (Independence Day).

BRITISH EMBASSY

Ambassador Extraordinary and Plenipotentiary and Consul-General, His Excellency Frank Mills, C.M.G. (resides at *Accra*).

TUNISIA
(Tunisian Republic)

President, Habib Bourguiba, *elected* July 25, 1957; *re-elected* 1959, 1964, 1969 and 1974.

CABINET

Prime Minister, Hédi Nouira.
Minister delegué in the Prime Minister's Office, Mohamed Sayah.
Justice, Slaheddine Baly.
Foreign Affairs, Habib Chatti.
Interior, Tahar Belkhodja.
National Defence, Abdallah Farhat.
Finance, Mohamed Fitouri.
National Economy, Abdelaziz Lasram.
Agriculture, Hassan Belkhodja.
National Education, Mohamed M'Zali.
Public Health, Mongi Kooli.
Cultural Affairs, Mahmoud Messadi.
Transport and Communications, Abdelhamid Sassi.
Social Affairs, Mohamed Ennaceur.
Youth and Sport, Fouad M'Bazaa.
Equipment, Lassaad Ben Osman.
Relations with National Assembly, Moncef Belhaj Amor.

In addition there are 5 Secretaries of State.

TUNISIAN EMBASSY IN LONDON
29 Princes Gate, S.W.7
[01-584 8117]

Ambassador, His Excellency Brahim Turki (1974).
Counsellor, Mohamed Maherzi.
Assistant Military Attaché, Lt. Habib El Helmi.
Attachés, Azouz Rafrari; Mahmoud Slim; Belgacem Gabchoug.

Area and Population.—Tunisia lies between Algeria and Libya and extends southwards to the Sahara Desert, with a total area of 63,380 sq. miles and the estimated population in 1975 was 5,600,000.

Government.— A French Protectorate from 1881 to 1956, Tunisia became an independent sovereign State with the signing on March 20, 1956, of an agreement whereby France recognized Tunisia's independence and right to conduct her own foreign policy and to form a Tunisian Army. The United Kingdom formally recognized Tunisia as an independent and sovereign state on May 10, 1956.

Following a first general election held on March 25, 1956, a Constituent Assembly met for the first time on April 8. On July 25, 1957, the Constituent Assembly deposed the Bey, abolished the monarchy and elected M. Bourguiba first President of the Republic. On June 1, 1959, the Constitution was promulgated and on December 7, 1959, the National Assembly held its first session.

In March 1975 the National Assembly proclaimed M. Bourguiba as President for life.

Important changes in the system of local government were decreed on June 16, 1956. The country was divided into 13 regions (*gouvernorats*) each administered by a Governor. In 1972, the number of regions was increased to 14 by the division of the Tunis region into two regions. By 1974, the number increased to eighteen.

Production, Trade, etc.—The valleys of the northern region support large flocks and herds, and contain rich agricultural areas, in which wheat, barley, and oats are grown. The vine and olive are extensively cultivated.

The chief exports are crude oil, olive oil, phosphates and wine. The chief imports are machinery, food-stuffs, iron and steel, textiles and crude petroleum, etc. Some oil has been discovered in Tunisia and production was 4,500,000 tons in 1975. In 1975 Tunisia's total imports were equal in value to *Dinars* 572,815,000 and total exports *Dinars* 345,580,000. France remains Tunisia's main trading partner, supplying 34 per cent. of the country's imports and purchasing 19 per cent. of Tunisia's exports.

Trade with U.K.

	1974	1975
Imports from U.K.	£11,465,000	£26,729,000
Exports to U.K.	6,192,000	2,968,000

Currency.—The Tunisian *dinar* was adopted on Nov. 3, 1958. At the same time a new Central Bank of Tunisia became responsible for the issue of notes. Although Tunisia remains in the Franc Zone the *dinar* is not tied to the French *franc*. The current rate of exchange is *dinars* 0·75= £1 (June, 1976).

So far as trade is concerned Tunisia was effectively part of metropolitan France until September, 1959, when she abrogated the Customs Union with the latter and a new trade and payments agreement was negotiated. This reduced or eliminated the tariff advantages enjoyed by certain French goods. Under commercial agreements concluded in November, 1962, and February, 1964, import quotas were established for certain French goods. In June, 1964, however, following Tunisian measures regarding the take-over of foreign-owned lands in Tunisia, France gave notice that she would not renew the 1959 Trade Agreement, due to expire on Sept. 30, 1964. In May 1966, France opened import quotas for a wide range of Tunisian goods (but excluding wine). Within these quota limits these goods can be admitted into France customs-free. In 1966 a policy of severe import restriction was adopted in order to reduce the country's chronic imbalance of trade. An ambitious programme of co-operative schemes for most areas of the economy was reversed in September, 1969, and gave way to a more orthodox economic policy. Tunisia became an associate member of EEC early in 1969, and signed a new agreement with the E.E.C. in 1976.

CAPITAL, ΨTunis, connected by canal with La Goulette on the coast, has a population of 1,127,000. The ruins of ancient Carthage lie a few miles from the city. Other towns of importance are: ΨSfax (482,000); ΨBizerta (316,000); ΨSousse (586,000); Kairouan (302,000).

FLAG.—Red crescent and star in a white orb, all on a red ground. NATIONAL DAY.—June 1.

BRITISH EMBASSY
Place de la Victoire, Tunis
Ambassador Extraordinary and Plenipotentiary and Consul-General, His Excellency Hugh Glencairn Balfour-Paul, C.M.G. (1975)

1st Secretary, G. S. Burton (*Head of Chancery*).
2nd Secretary, G. F. Noble (*H.M. Consul*).
Commercial Attaché, I. Whitting.

British Council Representative, J. E. Lankester. There is a British Council Library in *Tunis*.

TURKEY

President of the Republic, Fahri Korutürk, *born* 1903; elected President April 6, 1973.

Prime Minister, Süleyman Demirel (*JP*).
Deputy Prime Ministers, Prof. Necmettin Erbakan (*NSP*); Prof. Turhan Feyzioglu (*RRP*); Col. Alpaslan Türkes (*NAP*).
Justice, Ismail Müftüoglü (*NSP*).
Defence, Sen. Ferit Melen (*RRP*).
Interior, Oguzhan Asiltürk (*NSP*).
Foreign Affairs, Sen. Ihsan Sabri Caglayangil (*JP*).
Finance, Yilmaz Ergenekon (*JP*).
Education, Ali Naili Erdem (*JP*).
Public Works, Fehim Adak (*NSP*).
Trade, Halil Başol (*JP*).
Health, Dr. Kemal Demir (*RRP*).
Customs and Monopolies, Orhan Öztrak (*RRP*).
Food, Agriculture and Animal Breeding, Prof. Korkut Özal (*NSP*).
Communications, Nahit Mentese (*JP*).
Labour, Ahmet Tevfik Paksu (*NSP*).
Energy, Selähattin Kiliç (*JP*).
Tourism, Sen. Lütfü Tokoglu (*JP*).
Housing, Nurettin Ok (*JP*).
Villages, Sen. Vefa Poyraz (*JP*).
Forestry, Sen. Turan Kapanli (*JP*).
Youth and Sports, Ali Sevki Erek (*JP*).
Culture, Rifki Danisman (*JP*).
Social Security, Ahmet Mahir Ablum (*JP*).
Industry and Technology, Abdulkerim Doğru (*NSP*).
Ministers of State, Soyfi Özturk (*JP*); Hasan Aksay (*NSP*); Mustafa Kemal Erkovan (*NAP*); Giyasettin Karaca (*JP*).

(*JP*=Justice Party; *NSP*=National Salvation Party; *RRP*=Republican Reliance Party; *NAP*= Nationalist Action Party.)

TURKISH EMBASSY IN LONDON
Chancery: 43 Belgrave Square, S.W.1
[01-235 5252]
Ambassador Extraordinary and Plenipotentiary, His Excellency Turgut Menemencioğlu (1972).

Area and Population.—Turks are to be found scattered throughout a wide belt extending from China through the Soviet Union, Afghanistan and Iran to the present day Turkish State.

Turkey itself extends from Edirne (Adrianople) to Transcaucasia and Iran, and from the Black Sea to the Mediterranean, Syria and Iraq. Total population at the Census of October, 1975 was estimated at 40,197,669.

Turkey in Europe consists of Eastern Thrace, including the cities of Istanbul and Edirne, and is separated from Asia by the Bosphorus at Istanbul and by the *Dardanelles*—about 40 miles in length with a width varying from 1 to 4 miles—the political neighbours being Greece and Bulgaria on the west. Population (Census, 1975), 3,773,705.

Turkey in Asia comprises the whole of Asia Minor or *Anatolia* (" Land of the Rising Sun " or Orient), and extends from the Aegean Sea to the western boundaries of Georgia, Soviet Armenia and Iran, and from the Black Sea to the Mediterranean and the northern boundaries of Syria and Iraq. Population (Census, 1975), 36,423,964.

Government.—On October 29, 1923, the National Assembly declared Turkey a Republic and elected Gazi Mustafa Kemal (later known as Kemal Ataturk) President. Following the introduction of a multi-party régime in 1945, the Democrat Party was returned to power in 1950 and re-elected in 1954 and 1957. On May 27, 1960, the D.P. Government was overthrown by the Turkish Armed Forces which ruled through the Committee of National Union, a body of military officers. The committee ruled from January to November, 1961, in conjunction with a civilian House of Representatives, the two bodies together forming the Constituent Assembly.

At elections held in October, 1969, the Justice Party obtained 256 seats, the People's Republican Party 143 and the Reliance Party 15. Mr. Demirel's Justice Party Government (in office since Oct., 1965) resigned on March 12, 1971, following a memorandum to the President by the Chiefs of Staff of the Armed Forces. Three all-party governments, two under Prof. Erim and the third under Senator Ferit Melen were in office between March 26, 1971 and April 1973. After the resignation of the latter Senator Naim Talu formed a further government drawn mostly from the Justice and

Republican Reliance Parties. Elections were held in October 1973 and PRP obtained 185 seats, JP 149 seats, DP 45 seats and NSP 48 seats. After several unsuccessful attempts to form a government, a coalition under PRP party leader Mr. Bülent Ecevit with NSP as minority partner was formed on January 25, 1974.

However, this coalition collapsed in September, but continued to rule Turkey on a caretaker basis until a new administration was formed by Senator Prof. Sadi Irmak in November. This largely technocratic government was denied a vote of confidence by Parliament, but continued in office until March 31, 1975, when a right-wing coalition of the Justice, National Salvation, Republican Reliance and Nationalist Action Parties was formed, under the Premiership of Süleyman Demirel, Chairman of the Justice Party.

Turkey is divided for administrative purposes into 67 *vilayet* with subdivisions into *kaza* and *nahiye*. Each *vilayet* has a governor (*vali*) and elective council.

Religion and Education.—98·99 per cent. of the population are Moslems. The main religious minorities, which are concentrated in Istanbul and on the Syrian frontier, are: Orthodox, 107,000; Armenian Apostolic, 71,000; Catholic, 25,000; Protestant, 17,000; others, 10,000 (Total Christians, 230,000); Jewish, 44,000. On April 10, 1928, the Grand National Assembly passed a law in virtue of which Islam ceased to be the State religion of the Republic. Education is compulsory, free, and secular. There are elementary, secondary and vocational schools.

In 1975 there were 41,060 primary schools, with 5,354,593 pupils. There are two universities at Istanbul (one being a Technical University), three in Ankara, one each at Izmir, Erzurum and Trabzon. There is also a Faculty of Agriculture at Adana, a Faculty of Veterinary Science in Elazig, and Faculties of Economics in Bursa and Eskişehir. The expenditure allocated to education in the 3rd Five Year Plan (1973–77) is TL14,000,000,000, compared with TL7,002,000,000 actually spent from 1968–72, but past experience has shown that targets in this field are not always met.

Language and Literature.—Until 1926, Turkish was written in Arabic script, but in that year the Roman alphabet was substituted for use in official correspondence and in 1928 for universal use, with Arabic numerals as used throughout Europe. Mainly as a consequence of this change the number of Turks who can read and write is rising steadily, from about 10 per cent. in 1927 to nearly 80 per cent. by 1970. Ancient Turkish literature aped the Arabic manner, but the revolution of 1908 was followed by a popular reaction against the writings of the past (which appealed only to a small class) and led to the introduction of a native literature free from foreign influences and adapted to the understanding of the people. The vehicle first employed was the newspaper, printed in the neo-Latin alphabet, with supplements for prose and dramatic fiction, poetry and literary criticism. The leading Turkish newspapers are centred in Ankara and Istanbul, although most provincial towns have their own daily papers. There are foreign language papers in French, Greek, Armenian and English and numerous magazines and weeklies on various subjects, but few trade commercial publications.

Agricultural Production.—1975 was a year of significant growth in several sectors. Agricultural production rose to 28·8 per cent. of the gross domestic product at constant factor prices, while exports of agricultural commodities represented 56·6 per cent. of the total exports. Over 9,000,000, about 70 per cent. of the working population, are in the rural sector, but agriculture is still primitive in many areas and agricultural productivity is low. Estimated production figures for the principal crops in 1975 were ('000 tons): Wheat, 14,750 (a record); barley, 4,500; rice, 165; pulses, 684·3; cotton, 480; tobacco, 200; olives 588·2; sugar beet, 7,000; peaches, 170; apples, 800; citrus fruits, 750; sultanas, 110; hazelnuts, 350. With the important exception of wheat, which is mostly grown on the arid Central Anatolian Plateau, most of the crops are grown on the fertile littoral. Tobacco, sultana and fig cultivation is centred around Izmir, where substantial quantities of cotton are also grown. The main cotton area is in the Cukurova Plain around Adana. In 1974 it was estimated that there were 76,427,000 head of livestock, including sheep, 40,539,000; goats, 18,746,000; and cattle, 13,387,000. The forests which lie between the littoral plain and the Anatolian Plateau, contain beech, pine, oak, elm, chestnut, lime, plane, alder, box, poplar and maple. During recent years the Government has attempted, so far not altogether successfully, to combat the depredations of peasant and goat which threaten to destroy the existing forests within the next 25 years.

Industry.—After agriculture, Turkey's second most important industry is based on her considerable mineral wealth which is, however, as yet comparatively unexploited. Coal production in 1975 amounted to 8,361,000 tons, and 11,759,000 tons of lignite. The main export mineral is chromite. Production of iron ore in 1975 was 2,238,108 tons; chrome ore, 933,240 tons; manganese, 35,928 tons; sulphur, 83,832 tons; blister copper, 26,952 tons and boracite, 970,920 tons. The research and exploitation of the principal mineral deposits are mainly in the hands of the Mineral Research and Exploration Institute of Turkey and the State-owned Etibank respectively. The latter controls directly, on behalf of the Government, all the copper, sulphur and pyrite output of Turkey, as well as much of the colemenite and chrome production. Since State-sponsored industrialization began in 1935, industry has played an increasing part in the Turkish economy. Here, also, as in the case of minerals, much of the industry of the country is controlled by the Government.

The progress made in the manufacture of sugar, cotton, woollen and silk textiles, and cement, has been such that the bulk of the country's requirements can now be produced locally, while other industries contributing substantially to local needs include vehicle assembly, paper, glass and glassware, iron and steel, leather and leather goods, sulphur refining, canning and rubber goods, soaps and cosmetics, pharmaceutical products, prepared foodstuffs and a host of minor industries. Legislation was passed in 1954 to encourage the investment of foreign capital in Turkey and to promote the exploitation of Turkey's petroleum resources by foreign countries. Local production of crude petroleum in 1975 totalled 3,095,486 tons, a decrease of 6.9 per cent. from 1974.

In common with other developing countries, Turkey's economy was adversely affected by the steep rises in oil prices from 1973 onwards. Remittances from workers overseas, which had risen to $1·2 billion in 1973, flattened out and declined owing to the recession in Western Europe. Exports at $1,401m. fell in 1975 by 8·6 per cent. compared with 1974. At the same time, industrial growth continued at a high level (8·6 per cent.).

Since the Second World War the United States Government has given Turkey financial aid totalling over 5 billion dollars, half of which has been for military and half for economic purposes. The other main official sources of foreign aid have been

the O.E.C.D., and more recently the I.B.R.D., while the I.M.F. has made medium term loans for balance of payment support. The United Kingdom has pledged nearly £66,000,000 of aid to Turkey since 1963.

The third of Turkey's three Five Year Development Plans, for the years 1973–77, began in January 1973. The basic economic objective of the third plan is to achieve an average growth rate of 7·9 per cent. per annum in the gross national product.

COMMUNICATIONS

Railways.—The complete network became the property of the State Railways Administration in 1948. The total length of lines in operation at the end of 1974 was 8,141 kilometres. In 1974, the railways carried 128,424,000 passengers and 13,770,000 metric tons of freight.

Roads.—At the end of 1974 there were 34,918 km. of national roads (32,696 of which were surfaced). Total all-weather roads, both national and provincial, amounted to 51,176 km. The estimated number of motor vehicles in use at the end of 1974 was 735,033 of which there were 303,845 motor cars, 34,421 minibuses, 21,287 buses, 175,014 trucks and 200,466 tractors.

Posts.—In 1974 the number of telephone subscribers in Turkey was over 599,000. There is a considerable shortage of telephone lines in some of Turkey's major cities.

Shipping.—At the end of 1973, the Turkish Merchant Navy consisted of 2,516 cargo ships of 18 tons gross and over totalling 1,023,261 gross tons, 117 passenger ships of a gross tonnage of 114,850 tons and 99 tankers with a gross tonnage of 253,036 tons.

Civil Aviation.—The State airlines (T.H.Y.) operate all internal services and have services to London, Paris, Athens, Beirut, Brussels, Amsterdam, Zürich, Frankfurt, Munich, Rome, Milan, Geneva, Copenhagen, Nicosia, Tel Aviv and Vienna. Most of the leading foreign airlines, including British Airways, operate services to Istanbul and some also to Ankara. The T.H.Y. fleet is composed of D.C.10's, D.C.9's, Fokker Friendships, Fokker Fellowships and Boeing 707's.

FINANCE
(Financial year, March 1 to February 28)

	1975–76	1976–77
	TL'000,000	
Estimated Expenditure	106,888	151,520
Estimated Revenue	99,442	142,264

Currency.—The Turkish *Lira (TL)* is divided into 100 *Kurus*. The official rate of exchange is *TL* 29·90=£1 (June 1976) and *TL*16=U.S.$1. (*See also* p. 84.)

TRADE

	1974	1975
Total imports	$3,778,000,000	$4,739,000,000
Total exports	1,532,000,000	1,401,000,000

All imports are subject to licence and the issue of licences is limited to goods considered necessary for the country's economy. Lists of permitted imports are published annually at the beginning of January. The main imports are machinery, crude oil and petroleum products, iron and steel, vehicles, medicines and dyes, fabrics and yarns. The principal exports are cotton, tobacco, fruits, nuts, minerals, livestock and textiles.

Trade with U.K.

	1975
Imports from U.K.	£344,600,000
Exports to U.K.	70,000,000

CAPITAL OF TURKEY, ANKARA (Angora), an inland town of Asia Minor, about 275 miles E.S.E. of Istanbul, with a population (1975) of 1,698,542. Ankara (or Ancyra) was the capital of the Roman Province of *Galatia Prima*, and a marble temple (now in ruins), dedicated to Augustus, contains the *Monumentum* (*Marmor*) *Ancyranum*, inscribed with a record of the reign of Augustus Cæsar. A new city was laid out on modern lines, with parks, statues and avenues. ΨISTANBUL (2,534,839), the former capital, was the Roman city of Byzantium. It was selected by Constantine the Great as the capital of the Roman Empire about A.D. 328 and renamed Constantinople. Istanbul contains the celebrated church of St. Sophia, which, after becoming a mosque, was made a museum in 1934; it also contains Topkapi, former Palace of the Ottoman Sultans, which is also a museum. Other cities are ΨIzmir (636,078); Adana (467,122); Bursa (346,084); Gaziantep (300,801); and Eskişehir (258,266).

FLAG.—Red, with white crescent and star. NATIONAL DAY.—October 29 (Republic Day).

BRITISH EMBASSY
(Ankara)

Ambassador Extraordinary and Plenipotentiary, His Excellency Sir Horace Phillips, K.C.M.G. .. £11,000

Counsellors, D. N. Lane; A. B. Ball, O.B.E. (*Economic and Commercial*).
1st Secretaries, W. H. Fullerton (*Head of Chancery*); L. C. R. Seeley; M. A. Goodfellow; J. R. Leeland; A. H. G. Amy; H. C. Waller.
2nd Secretary, H. Warren-Gash.
Consul, J. Hanratty.
Defence and Military Attaché, Brig. J. P. Sellers, D.F.C.
Naval Attaché, Cdr. M. T. H. Styles, R.N.
Air Attaché, Wing-Cdr. K. J. Ryall, D.F.C.

BRITISH CONSULAR OFFICES
There is a British Consulate-General at *Istanbul* and a British Consulate at *Izmir*.

BRITISH COUNCIL.—27 Adakale Sokak, Yenisehir, Ankara, *Representative*, J. Goatly, O.B.E.—There are also a centre and library at *Istanbul* and a library at *Ankara*.
BRITISH CHAMBER OF COMMERCE OF TURKEY INC., Mesrutiyet Caddessi No. 34, Tepebasi Beyoğlu, Istanbul (Postal Address, P.O. Box 190 Karaköy, Istanbul). *Chairman*, S. E. P. Nowill.

UNITED ARAB EMIRATES

President, Sheikh Zayed bin Sultan Al Nahayyan (Abu Dhabi).
Vice-President, Sheikh Rashid bin Sa'id Al Maktum (Dubai).
Prime Minister, Sheikh Maktum bin Rashid Al Maktum (Dubai).
Minister of Finance, Economy and Industry, Sheikh Hamdan bin Rashid Al Maktum (Dubai).
Minister of Interior, Sheikh Mubarak bin Mohammed Al Nahayyan (Abu Dhabi).
Minister of Defence, Sheikh Mohammed bin Rashid Al Maktum (Dubai).
Minister of Foreign Affairs, Sayed Ahmed Khalifa Al Suwaidi (Abu Dhabi).

EMBASSY IN LONDON
30 Prince's Gate, S.W.7
[01–581 1281]

Ambassador Extraordinary and Plenipotentiary, His Excellency Sayed Mohammed Mahdi Al-Tajir.

The United Arab Emirates (formerly the Trucial States) is composed of seven Emirates (Abu Dhabi,

Ajman, Dubai, Fujeirah, Ras al Khaimah, Sharjah and Umm al Qaiwain) which came together as an independent state on December 2, 1971, when they ended their individual special treaty relationships with the British Government (Ras al Khaimah joined the other six on February 10, 1972).

The British Government, by virtue of a treaty made in 1892, had been responsible for the external affairs of the states through the British Political Resident in the Arabian Gulf and the British Political Agents in each state but on independence the Union Government assumed full responsibility for all internal and external affairs apart from some internal matters that remained the prerogative of the individual Emirates. Six of the Emirates lie on the shore of the Gulf between the Musandam peninsula in the East and the Qatar peninsula in the West while the seventh, Fujeirah, lies on the Gulf of Oman.

Area and Population

The approximate area of the U.A.E. is 32,000 square miles and the population (according to a census in December 1975) is 655,937, more than double the 1972 estimate. Security in the area is maintained under one central command by the Union Defence Forces (formerly the Trucial Scouts). Until May 1976 Abu Dhabi, Dubai, Sharjah and Ras al Khaimah had their own separate defence forces, of which the Abu Dhabi Defence Force was the largest, but they were then merged with the Union Defence Forces. Some of the separate police forces have also been merged.

Revenue is chiefly derived from oil and from customs dues on imports. Other formerly important sources of revenue, such as the export of dried fish and pearling, are now almost negligible. A substantial amount is spent on overseas aid, where commitments in 1975 reached a quarter of the gross national product, and on agriculture where more than half of the cultivable area of more than 50,000 acres has already been brought into use.

Trade with U.K.

	1974	1975
Imports from U.K.	£103,800,000	£198,650,000
Exports to U.K.	220,300,000	159,161,000

Abu Dhabi is the largest Emirate of the U.A.E. in area, stretching from Khor al Odaid in the west to the borders with Dubai in the Jebel Ali area. It includes six villages in the Buraimi oasis, the other three being part of the Sultanate of Oman, and a number of settlements in the Liwa Oasis system. Following negotiations with Saudi Arabia, some adjustment of the border has now been made in the Khor al Odaid region, but the agreement has not yet been ratified.

The Abu Dhabi Government owns a sixty per cent. interest in oil operations in the Emirate, through the Abu Dhabi National Oil Company. Several companies are operating; the two most important are the Abu Dhabi Petroleum Co. Ltd., on land and Abu Dhabi Marine Areas Ltd. in the offshore concession area. The most important offshore field is near Das Island where Abu Dhabi Marine Areas has its headquarters and which began production in 1962. Production from the on-shore Murban field began in December 1963. Abu Dhabi's oil revenues for 1975 are estimated at £1,650 million.

With its oil wealth the Emirates are expanding rapidly, not only in Abu Dhabi, now a fast growing modern town, but also elsewhere such as at Al Ain in the Buraimi Oasis. There are airfields at Abu Dhabi and Das Island, and an airstrip at Al Ain, and a new harbour, Port Zaid, at Abu Dhabi. The population of the Emirates is 235,662 (1975 census).

Dubai is the second largest Emirate both in size and in population, which was 206,861 at the last census. The town of Dubai is the main port for the import of goods into the U.A.E. and the interior of the Sultanate of Oman, and there is also a lively entrepôt trade. Oil was discovered offshore in 1966 and production began in September 1973. A second offshore field was discovered in September 1973. The main operator is the Dubai Petroleum Company.

Development is proceeding fast. A new deep water harbour was completed in 1972 and is now being expanded, while a major dry dock has also been built. An international airport opened in May 1971, served on a schedule basis by ten international airlines and by two regular freight services. More than thirty banks are now operating in Dubai and telegraphic and telex communications, managed by Cable and Wireless, are good.

Sharjah, with a present population of 88,188, has declined from its position 50 years ago as principal town in the area. It became the third oil producing Emirate in the summer of 1974, following the discovery of oil offshore by the Crescent Petroleum Company, a consortium of six companies from the United States headed by Buttes Oil and Gas. The offshore concessions on Sharjah's west coast, in the Arabian Gulf, are held by Shell Hydrocarbons, while Shell Minerals hold both the offshore and on-shore concessions for Sharjah's eastern dependencies on the Gulf of Oman coast. Linked by metalled roads to Dubai and Ras al Khaimah on the Arabian Gulf coast, Sharjah is centrally placed within the U.A.E., and is now experiencing a construction and business boom. More than a dozen banks are already in operation. Sharjah harbour has been deepened and expanded, while construction of a new port at Khor Fakkan, on the Gulf of Oman coast, is under way. A small airport is in use while a new one, which will be the biggest in the Middle East, is approaching completion.

Ras al Khaimah has a population of 57,282 of whom more than half live in the town. An ancient sea-port, near which archaeological remains have been found, Ras al Khaimah is the most agricultural of the Emirates, producing vegetables, dates, fruit and tobacco. The offshore oil concession is held by Vitol Exploration and the on-shore concession by Shell Hydrocarbons. Some oil has been found off the coast, but not in commercial quantities.

Fujeirah, with a population of 26,498, is the poorest and most remote of the seven Emirates, lying on the Gulf of Oman coast, and only connected by a metal road to the rest of the country since the end of 1975. Largely agricultural, its population is spread between the slopes of the inland Hajar mountain range and the town of Fujeirah itself, together with a number of smaller settlements on the comparatively fertile plain on the coast. Shell Minerals hold the on-shore concession and offshore drilling by Reserve Oil and Minerals was due to begin by the end of 1976.

Ajman and *Umm al Qaiwain* are the smallest Emirates having populations of 21,566 and 16,879 respectively. Both lie on the Arabian Gulf coast although Ajman has two inland enclaves at Manama and Masfut. Both are beginning to benefit from the rapid development taking place in their neighbours, Sharjah and Ras al Khaimah. Occidental of Ajman Incorporated hold both the major on-shore and offshore oil concessions, while in Umm al Qaiwain the on-shore concession is held by Shell Hydrocarbons and the offshore by Occidental of Umm al Qaiwain Incorporated and by a consortium headed by Zapata Exploration who made a non-commercial oil find early in 1975.

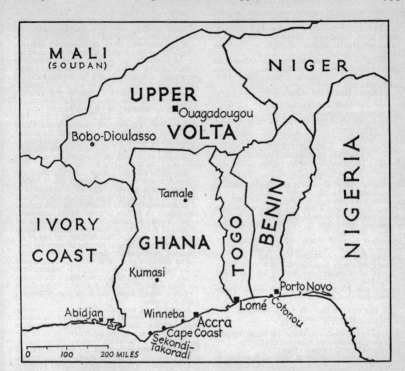

BRITISH EMBASSY
(Abu Dhabi)
Ambassador Extraordinary and Plenipotentiary, His
Excellency Daniel John McCarthy, C.M.G. (1973).
British Council Representative, M. A. Evans, P.O.
Box 1636, Dubai.

UPPER VOLTA
(République de Haute Volta)

President, Gen. Sangoulé Lamizana, *assumed power*
in 1966.
Foreign Affairs, Alfred Kabore.
Justice, François-Xavier Zongo.
Finance, Capt. Léonard Kalmogo.
Information and Posts and Telecommunications, Capt.
Koulidiati.
Interior and Security, Maj. Gabriel Some Yorgman.
Public Service and Labour, Zoumana Traore.
Planning, Boubac ar Soumana.
Tourism, Emile Bassano.

Upper Volta is an inland savannah state in
West Africa, situated between 9° and 15°N and
2°E and 5°W with an area of about 100,000
square miles and a population estimated in 1972 at
5,514,000. It has common boundaries with Mali on
the west, Niger and Benin on the east and Togo,
Ghana and the Ivory Coast on the south. The
largest tribe is the Mossi whose king, the Moro
Naba, still wields a certain moral influence.

Upper Volta was annexed by France in 1896 and
between 1932 and 1947 was administered as part
of the Colony of the Ivory Coast. It decided on
December 11, 1958, to remain an autonomous
republic within the French Community; full
independence outside the Community was proclaimed on August 5, 1960. Special agreements
with France, covering financial and cultural
matters, technical assistance, etc., were signed in
Paris on April 24, 1961. Upper Volta is a
member of the *Conseil de l'Entente*, *OCAM*, *OAU*
and *C.E.A.O.* (*see* Ivory Coast). The official language is French. The 1960 constitution provided
for a presidential form of government with a single
chamber National Assembly, but in January, 1966,
the Army assumed power after popular demonstrations in Ouagadougou against the *régime* of the
former President Yaméogo. A new constitution
allowing for a partial return to civilian rule but with
the Army still in effective control was adopted by
a referendum held on June 14, 1970. Following
internal political manoeuvering the President
suspended the constitution on Feb. 8, 1974 and
dissolved the National Assembly. A Government
of National Renewal was formed, with a majority
of military members.

Finance and Trade.—The currency of the Republic is the *Franc CFA* (*Francs CFA* 50= 1 *French
Franc*). The 1974 Budget totalled *Francs CFA*
12,490,000,000.

The principal industry is the rearing of cattle
and sheep and the chief exports are livestock,
groundnuts, shea-nuts and cotton. Small deposits

of gold, manganese, copper, bauxite and graphite have been found. Value of trade in 1973 amounted to: Imports, *francs CFA* 21,897,000; Exports, *francs CFA* 5,598,000. Imports from U.K.— £299,000 (1975); Exports to U.K. — £718,000 (1975).

CAPITAL.—Ouagadougou (125,000). Other principal town: Bobo-Dioulasso (80,000).

FLAG.—Three horizontal stripes, black over white over red.

NATIONAL DAY.—December 11.

BRITISH REPRESENTATION

Ambassador Extraordinary and Plenipotentiary, His Excellency Joe Booth Wright (*resident in Abidjan*).

URUGUAY
(República Oriental del Uruguay)
President, Dr. Aparicio Méndez (1976).

CABINET

Minister of Interior, General Hugo Linares Brum.
Foreign Affairs, Dr. Juan Carlos Blanco.
Economy and Finance, Col. Valentín Arismendi
Transport and Public Works, Ing. Eduardo Sampson
Public Health, Dr. Antonio Cañellas.
Labour and Social Security, Dr. José Enrique Etcheverry Stirling.
Agriculture and Fishing, Ing. Agr. Julio Aznarez.
Education and Culture, Dr. Daniel Darracq.
National Defence, Dr. Walter Ravenna.
Industry and Energy, Ing. Quím Luis Meyer.
Director of Planning and Budget, Sr. Juan José Anichini.
Secretariat of Planning, Coordination and Diffusion, Brig. José D. Cardozo.

URUGUAYAN EMBASSY AND CONSULATE
48 Lennox Gardens, S.W.1
[01-589 8835]
Ambassador Extraordinary and Plenipotentiary (vacant).
Minister-Counsellor, Sr. Ramiro Píriz Ballón.
1st Secretary, Señor Alfredo Cazes.

Area and Population.—The smallest Republic in South America, on the east coast of the Rio de la Plata situated in lat. 30°-35°S. and long. 53° 25′-57° 42′ W., with an area of 72,172 square miles, and a population of 2,763,964, almost entirely white and predominantly of Spanish and Italian descent. Many Uruguayans are Roman Catholics. There is complete freedom of religion and no church is established by the State.

Physical Features.—The country consists mainly (and particularly in the south and west) of undulating grassy plains. The principal chains of hills are the Cuchilla del Haedo, which cross the Brazilian boundary and extend southwards to the Cuchilla Grande of the south and east. In no case do the peaks exceed 2,000 feet.

The principal river is the *Rio Negro* (with its tributary the Yi), flowing from north-east to south-west into the *Rio Uruguay*. The boundary river *Uruguay* is navigable from its estuary to Salto, about 200 miles north, and the Negro is also navigable for a considerable distance. Smaller rivers are the Cuareim, Yaguaron, Santa Lucia, Queguay and the Cebollati. On the south-east coast are several lagoons, and the north-east boundary crosses the (Brazilian) Lake Merin.

The climate is reasonably healthy. The summer is warm, but the heat is often tempered by the breezes of the Atlantic. The winter is, on the whole, mild, but cold spells, characterized by winds from the South Polar regions, are experienced in June, July and August. Rainfall is regular throughout the year, but there are occasional droughts.

Government.—Uruguay—or the *Banda Oriental*, as this territory lying on the eastern bank of the Uruguay River was then called—resisted all attempted invasions of the Portuguese and Spaniards until the beginning of the 17th century, and 100 years later the Portuguese settlements were captured by the Spaniards. From 1726 to 1814 the country formed part of Spanish South America and underwent many vicissitudes during the Wars of Independence. In 1814 the armies of the Argentine Confederation captured the capital and annexed the province, and it was afterwards annexed by Portugal and became a province of Brazil. In 1825, the country threw off the Brazilian yoke. This action led to war between Argentina and Brazil which was settled by the mediation of the United Kingdom, Uruguay being declared an independent state in 1828. In 1830 a Republic was inaugurated.

Elections were held on Nov. 28, 1971, which gave the Colorado Party a narrow majority.

According to the Constitution the President appoints a council of 11 ministers and the Vice-President presides over Congress. The legislature consists of a Chamber of 99 deputies and a Senate of 30 members (plus the Vice-President), elected for five years by a system of proportional representation. Voting is obligatory and extends to all citizens of good repute and certain long standing residents who are not citizens, from the age of 18. However, since February, 1973 the country has been governed by presidential rule with military support.

The Republic is divided into 19 Departments each with a chief of police and a Departmental Council. The most important cities of the interior are Salto and Paysandu, both situated on the River Uruguay, which forms the main line of division from Argentina.

Production and Industry.—Wheat, barley, maize, linseed, sunflower seed and rice are cultivated. The wealth of the country is obtained from its pasturage, which supports large herds of cattle and sheep, the wool of which is of excellent quality. The 1970 livestock census showed figures of 8,563,747 cattle, 19,892,758 sheep, 420,972 horses, 418,709 hogs. It was estimated that in 1973 the number of cattle rose to 11,000,000. In addition to the meat packing industry, other foodstuffs, wine, beer and textiles are of importance.

The development of local industry continues and during and since the Second World War, in addition to the greatly augmented textile industry, marked expansion in local production is notable in respect of tyres, sheet-glass, three-ply wood, cement, leather-curing, beet-sugar, plastics, household consumer goods, edible oils and the refining of petroleum and petroleum products.

Mineral Deposits.—Iron is now being quarried; estimated yearly production is 1,000,000 tons of first quality pellets.

Communications.—There are about 7,820 km. of national highways, and about 12,083 km. of telegraph, with 48,375 miles of telephones.

There are about 2,398 km. of standard gauge railway in use in Uruguay. A State Autonomous Entity was formed to administer the railway systems purchased by the Government from four British companies in 1948.

An airline, PLUNA, which is owned by the State, runs a limited daily service to southern Brazil, Paraguay and Argentina. The principal capitals of the interior and a limited freight service are connected to Montevideo by TAMO, another State owned airline, using principally military aircraft and personnel. International passenger and freight services are maintained by American, South American and European airlines. The airport of Carrasco lies 12 miles outside Montevideo.

Education and Social Services.—Uruguay is one of the most advanced of the South American states, with old-age pensions, maternity and child welfare centres, accident insurance, etc. Primary education is compulsory and free, and technical and trade schools and evening courses for adult education are state controlled. There are about 322,053 pupils in the 2,362 state schools. In 1969 there were 140,700 pupils in secondary schools. The University at Montevideo (founded in 1849) had, in 1969, 18,000 students enrolled in its ten faculties.

Language and Literature.—Spanish is the language of the Republic. Modern literature has provided some authors with international reputations and the literature of Spain is accessible in all public libraries. Four daily newspapers are published in Montevideo with an estimated total circulation of 200,000. Most of them are distributed throughout the country.

Finance.—No recent figures of revenue and expenditure are available. The national debt at Dec. 31, 1972 amounted to $Ur. 61,597,140,427.

Currency.—The monetary unit is the *peso*. In May, 1963, the gold content of the *peso* was fixed at 0·059245 grammes of pure gold. After several devaluations the commercial exchange rate stood at June 8, 1976, at UrN $3·63=$U.S.1. Sterling exchange stood at June 8, 1976, at $UrN 6·40=£1. The quotations of the U.S. dollar and pound sterling in the financial (fluctuating) market as at the same date were 1·360 and 3·280 Uruguayan *pesos* respectively. Sterling exchange, *see p.* 84.

TRADE

	1974	1975
Total exports	$U.S.381,182,000	$U.S.381,197,781
Total imports	481,259,000	516,197,876

Trade with U.K.

	1974
Imports from U.K.	£6,604,000
Exports to U.K.	9,211,000

The major exports are meat and by-products, wool and by-products, hides and bristle and agricultural products. The principal imports are raw materials, construction materials, oils and lubricants, automotive vehicles, kits and machinery.

The principal export item to the U.K. is wool and the main imports are automotive vehicles, kits, machinery, raw materials and metals.

CAPITAL, ΨMontevideo. Population (1975 census 1,229,748). Other centres (with 1967 estimates) are ΨSalto (60,000), ΨPaysandu (60,000), ΨMercedes (34,000), Minas (34,000), Melo (30,000), and Rivera (40,000).

FLAG.—Four blue and five white horizontal stripes surcharged with sun on a white ground in the top corner, next flagstaff. NATIONAL DAY.—August 25 (Declaration of Independence, 1825).

Time of transit from London to Montevideo, by air, 20–22 hours.

BRITISH EMBASSY
Montevideo

Ambassador Extraordinary and Plenipotentiary, His Excellency Peter Richard Oliver, C.M.G. (1972).

1st Secretary, E. J. Sharland.

2nd Secretary, R. Backhouse.

Naval Attaché, Capt. J. Thomas, R.N. (resident at Buenos Aires).

Defence and Air Attaché, Gp. Capt. R. W. Millo (resident at Buenos Aires).

BRITISH CONSULAR OFFICES

There is a British Consular Office at *Montevideo*.

ANGLO-URUGUAYAN CULTURAL INSTITUTE, San José 1426, Montevideo.

There are branch Institutes at Salto, Paysandú, Fray Bentos, Rivera, Las Piedras, Melo, Mercedes, Trinidad and Treinta y Tres.

BRITISH-URUGUAYAN CHAMBER OF COMMERCE, Avenida Agraciada 1641, Piso 2°, *Montevideo*.

U.S.S.R.

Soyuz Sovetskikh Sotsialisticheskikh Respublik = Union of Soviet Socialist Republics

THE COMMUNIST PARTY OF THE SOVIET UNION

(K.P.S.S.=Kommunisticheskaya Partiya Sovetskogo Soyuza)

Constitutionally, the highest executive organ of the C.P.S.U. is its *Central Committee*, as elected by the *Party Congress*. The present Central Committee (elected at the XXVth Party Congress in March, 1976) consists of 287 full members; there are also 139 candidate members with a consultative voice and 85 members of the *Central Revision Commission*. The real power in the Party is vested, however, in the *Politbureau*, the *Secretariat* and the permanent Departments of the Central Committee.

Politbureau, Yu. V. Andropov; L. I. Brezhnev; V. V. Grishin; A. A. Gromyko; A. P. Kirilenko; A. N. Kosygin; F. D. Kulakov; D. A. Kunayev; K. T. Mazurov; A. Ya Pel'she; N. V. Podgorny; G. V. Romanov; V. V. Shcherbitsky; M. A. Suslov; D. F. Ustinov: (full members); G. A. Aliev; P. N. Demichev; P. M. Masherov; B. N. Ponomarev; Sh. R. Rashidov; M. S. Solomentsev (candidates for membership).

Secretariat, Leonid Ilyich Brezhnev (General Secretary) (since October 14, 1964); K. U. Chernenko; V. I. Dolgikh; I. V. Kapitonov; K. F. Katushev; A. P. Kirilenko; F. D. Kulakov; B. N. Ponomarev; M. A. Suslov; D. F. Ustinov; M. V. Zimyanin.

Committee of Party Control, A. Ya Pel'she (Chairman).

Komsomol (Young Communist League). Ye. M. Tyazhelnikov (1st Secretary).

GOVERNMENT OF THE U.S.S.R

The Presidium of the Supreme Soviet of the U.S.S.R.

Chairman (=President of the U.S.S.R.), Nikolay Viktorovich Podgorny (since December 9, 1965).

Secretary, M. P. Georgadze.

The Supreme Soviet (=Parliament) consists of two chambers.

Chairman (=Speaker) of the Council of the Union, A. P. Shitikov.

Chairman (=Speaker) of the Council of Nationalities, V. P. Ruben.

The Council of Ministers of the U.S.S.R.

Chairman (=Prime Minister), Alexei Nikolayevich Kosygin (since October 14, 1964).

1st Vice-Chairmen, K. T. Mazurov; N. A. Tikhonov.

Vice-Chairmen, I. V. Arkhipov; N. K. Baybakov; V. E. Dymshits; V. A. Kirillin; M. A. Leschenko; I. T. Novikov; V. N. Novikov; Z. N. Nuriyev; L. V. Smirnov.

Ministries.—There are three groups of departmental ministries, with a total of 76 ministers—31 All Union Ministries, *i.e.* federal ministries, 31 Union Republican Ministries (co-ordinating ministries of individual republics) and 14 Chairmen of State committees, etc., ranking as Ministers. The more important posts are occupied by:

Foreign Affairs, A. A. Gromyko.

Defence, D. F. Ustinov.

Foreign Trade, N. S. Patolichev.

Internal Affairs, N. A. Shchelokov.

Planning, N. K. Baybakov.

Science and Technology, V. A. Kirillin.
Buildings, I. T. Novikov.
State Security, Yu V. Andropov.
The Prime Ministers of the 15 constituent
republics belong to the Council *ex officio*.

EMBASSY OF THE U.S.S.R. IN LONDON
13 Kensington Palace Gardens, W. 8.
[01–229 2666]
Ambassador Extraordinary and Plenipotentiary, His
Excellency Nikolai M. Lunkov (1973).

AREA AND POPULATION
The U.S.S.R. is composed of 15 Union Re-
publics (*see* below). Before the outbreak of the
Second World War (1941–45 in U.S.S.R.), the
U.S.S.R. consisted of 11 Republics—the Russian
Socialist Federal Soviet Republic (R.S.F.S.R.) and
the Ukrainian, Belorussian, Armenian, Azerbaidjan,
Georgian, Turkmen, Uzbek, Tadjik, Kazakh and
Kirghiz Soviet Socialist Republics. After the
collapse of Poland in September, 1939, the Soviet
Government by agreement with Germany seized
five-eighths of Poland's territory, the so-called
Western Ukraine and *Western Belorussia*, subsequently
incorporated into the Ukrainian and Belorussian
Republics respectively.
In March, 1940, some territories ceded by
Finland under the 1940 Treaty were joined to
the Karelian Autonomous Soviety Socialist Re-
public to form a Karelo-Finnish S.S.R. which
became the 12th constituent Republic of the
U.S.S.R., while others, including the town of
Viipuri (Vyborg), were added to the R.S.F.S.R.
Similarly, in August of the same year, the major
part of *Bessarabia* ceded by Rumania in June was
joined to the Moldavian A.S.S.R. to form a
Moldavian S.S.R. as the 13th Soviet Republic,
while a smaller part of Bessarabia, including the
Danube estuary port of Izmail, and *Northern
Bukovina*, also ceded by Rumania, became part
of the Ukraine. The new Soviet-Rumanian
frontier was confirmed by the 1947 Peace Treaty
with Rumania.
In August, 1940, the three independent Baltic
States, *Estonia*, *Latvia* and *Lithuania*, were forcibly
incorporated into the Soviet-Union to form the 14th,
15th and 16th Republics respectively. In June, 1945,
Ruthenia was ceded by Czechoslovakia and became
part of the Ukranian S.S.R. under the name of
Transcarpathia. After the defeat of Germany, a part
of *East Prussia* with its capital Königsberg (renamed
Kaliningrad in July, 1946) became part of the
R.S.F.S.R., while the port and district of *Memel*
(Klaipeda) was incorporated into the Lithuanian
S.S.S. By the 1947 Peace Treaty with Finland,
the district of *Petsamo* (Pechenga) was added
to the territory of the R.S.F.S.R. In the Far East,
the southern half of *Sakhalin* and the whole of the
Kurile Islands were incorporated into the last-
named Republic in 1945, after the defeat of Japan. In
October, 1944, *Tannu-Tuva*, until the Second World
War a nominally independent state lying to the
N.W. of Outer Mongolia, became the autonomous
province of *Tuva* and, in 1961, the Autonomous
Republic of Tuva, within the R.S.F.S.R.
In July, 1956, the Karelo-Finnish Republic
reverted to the status of an Autonomous (*Karelian*)
Republic within the R.S.F.S.R.
Area and population (January 1, 1975 estimate)
of the constituent Republics of the U.S.S.R.
with their capitals:—

	Republic (Capital)	Sq. miles	Population
I.	R.S.F.S.R.		
	(Moscow)	6,593,391	133,741,000
II.	Ukraine (Kiev)	252,046	48,817,000
III.	Belorussia (Minsk)	80,300	9,331,000
IV.	Uzbekistan		
	(Tashkent)	157,181*	13,689,000*
V.	Kazakhstan		
	(Alma-Ata)	1,064,980*	14,168,000*
VI.	Georgia (Tbilisi)	26,911	4,923,000
VII.	Azerbaidjan (Baku).	33,436	5,607,000
VIII.	Lithuania (Vilnius)..	26,173	3,290,000
IX.	Moldavia (Kishinev)	13,012	3,812,000
X.	Latvia (Riga)	24,695	2,478,000
XI.	Kirghizia (Frunze)..	76,642	3,298,000
XII.	Tadjikistan		
	(Dushanbe)	54,019	3,387,000
XIII.	Armenia (Erevan)..	11,306	2,785,000
XIV.	Turkmenistan		
	(Ashkhabad)	188,417	2,506,000
XV.	Estonia (Tallinn)	17,413	1,429,000

* (Adjusted to include transfer of 3 border regions
—888 sq. miles and 162,000 inhabitants—by Uzbek
S.S.R., Kazakh S.S.R. and U.S.S.R. decrees of
May–June 1971.)
The total area of the U.S.S.R. is 8,620,822 sq.
miles; the total population: 253,261,000.
A striking demographic feature is the rapid
urbanization. While in 1939 the proportion of
urban population was 32 per cent. of the total, in
1975 it reached 60 per cent., owing to migration to
the towns, growth of new towns, incorporation of
villages into conurbations and a higher birth-rate in
urban areas. There are now 36 towns with over
500,000 (11 in 1939).
The proportion of women to men is 53·6 to 46·4.
(In 1973 the birth-rate was 17·6; the mortality rate,
8·6; the natural increase, 9·0 per 1,000.
More than four-fifths of the people were born
after the 1917 Revolution.

Main Nationalities
(1970 Census)
The most numerous national groups of U.S.S.R.
are: Russian, 129 m and Ukrainian, 41 m. There
are between 5 and 9 million Belorussians, Uzbeks,
Kazakhs, and Tatars respectively. Azerbaidjani,
Armenians and Georgians number between 3 and
5 million each group. There are some 2·5 million
Lithuanians, Jews, Moldavians and Tadjiks respectively. In each of the following nationality
groups the population numbers between 1·05 and
1·8 million: Germans, Chuvashes, Latvians, Poles,
Mordovians, Turkmens, Kirghizians, Bashkirs and
Estonians.
The 1970 census revealed a remarkable difference
between the growth rates of individual nationalities:
while the Slav nations showed an annual increase of
roughly one per cent., certain Central-Asian and
Caucasian (mostly Moslem) nations recorded an
annual net growth of three to four per cent.

CONSTITUTION
Under the 1936 (" Stalin ") Constitution, the
Union of Soviet Socialist Republics is " a socialist
state of workers and peasants " (§ 1) in which " all
power belongs to the working people as represented by the Soviets [Councils] of Working
People's Deputies " (§ 3), while its economy is
based on " the socialist ownership of the instruments and means of production " (§ 4). " The
land, its mineral wealth, waters, forests, mills,
factories, mines, rail, water and air transport, banks,
communications, large state-organized agricultural
enterprises, as well as municipal enterprises and the
bulk of dwelling-houses in the cities and industrial
localities, are state property " (§ 6), while " the
joint enterprises of collective farms and co-operative organizations . . . constitute the common,
socialist property of the collective farms and co-
operative organizations " (§ 7). " The law [also]
permits the small private economy of individual

ALASKA

NORTH PACIFIC OCEAN

WRANGEL I.

ARCTIC CIRCLE

KAMCHATKA

NEW SIBERIAN IS.

ARCTIC OCEAN

SAKHALIN

Okhotsk

JAPAN

Nikolayevsk

Vladivostok

UNION OF SOVIET SOCIALIST REPUBLICS

MONGOLIA

CHINA

Krasnoyarsk

Irkutsk

Novosibirsk

Omsk

BARENTS SEA

NOVAYA ZEMLYA

Perm
Sverdlovsk
Chelyabinsk

INDIA

PAKISTAN

AFGHANISTAN

Gorky
Kazan
Ufa
Kuibyshev
Saratov
Volgograd

CASPIAN SEA

IRAN

Leningrad

FINLAND

Moscow

Voronezh
Rostov

BLACK SEA

TURKEY

POLAND
CZECH.
RUMANIA
BULG.
YUGO.

0 200 400 600 800 1000 MILES

peasants and handicraftsmen based on their own labour and precluding the exploitation of the labour of others " (§ 9). " The personal property right of citizens in their incomes and savings from work, in their dwelling-houses and subsidiary home enterprises, in household articles . . . as well as the right of citizens to inherit personal property, is protected by law " (§ 10). The whole economic life, however, is subordinated to the state economic plan (§ 11).

The U.S.S.R. is a federal state, " formed on the basis of a voluntary union of equal Soviet Socialist Republics " (§ 13); every Republic has " the right to secede from the U.S.S.R." (§ 17).

" The highest organ of state power in the U.S.S.R. is the Supreme Soviet of the U.S.S.R." (§ 30) which exercises exclusively the legislative power (§ 32). It consists of two Chambers, the *Soviet of the Union* (elected on the basis of one deputy for every 300,000 of the population) and the *Soviet of Nationalities* (elected at the ratio of 25 deputies from each Union Republic, 11 from each Autonomous Republic, 5 from each Autonomous Province and 1 from each National Territory) (§§ 33–35). At elections held on June 16, 1974, for the two Chambers, approximately 161 million persons voted *for* candidates (99·82 per cent. of voters) and under 400,000 against. The *Supreme Soviet* which, as a rule, meets twice a year for about a week, delegates most of its power to its *Presidium* which acts as a kind of collective President of the U.S.S.R. between the sessions.

" The highest executive and administrative organ of state power is the Council of Ministers of the U.S.S.R." (§ 64). It is appointed by the Supreme Soviet (§ 70) and is accountable to it, or, in the intervals between the sessions, to its Presidium (§ 65).

The Supreme Court of the U.S.S.R. and the Special Courts of the U.S.S.R. are elected by the Supreme Soviet for a term of five years (§ 104). Similarly, the Procurator-General, who exercises " supreme supervisory power to ensure the strict observance of law " (§ 113), is appointed by the Supreme Soviet for a term of seven years.

Citizens of the U.S.S.R. have the right to work, to rest and leisure, to maintenance in old age and sickness and disability relief and to education (§§ 118–121). " Women are accorded equal rights with men " (§ 122). Citizens are accorded equal rights irrespective of their nationality or race (§ 123). The citizens are also guaranteed freedom of speech, of the press, of assembly and of street processions and demonstrations, " in conformity with the interests of the working people and in order to strengthen the socialist system " (§ 125).

Section 126 of the Constitution is remarkable for containing the only reference to the real master of the country, the Communist Party. It says that " the most active and politically conscious citizens in the ranks of the working class and other sections of the working people unite in the Communist Party of the Soviet-Union, which is the vanguard of the working people in their struggle to strengthen and develop the socialist system and is the leading core of all organizations of the working people, both public and state." The new Party programme, adopted in November, 1961, envisages a great increase of the economic capacity of the country and promises the transition to " full Communism " some time after 1980.

A special committee was set up in November, 1961, to draft a new constitution.

Local Government.—The State power in regions, provinces, autonomous provinces, territories, districts, towns and rural localities is vested in the *Soviets of Working People's Deputies* (§ 94), elected by the working people of the respective administrative units for a term of two years (§ 95). The executive and administrative organ of a Soviet is its Executive Committee elected by it (§ 99). The Union Republics and the Autonomous Republics have Supreme Soviets and Councils of Ministers of their own (§§ 57–63 and 79–88), although their jurisdiction is severely circumscribed in favour of the central Government. Since February, 1944, the Union Republics have had the right to enter into direct relations with foreign states and to conclude agreements and exchange diplomatic and consular representatives with them (§ 18A). So far, however, the only important activity of this kind has been the individual membership of the Ukraine and of Belorussia in the United Nations Organization. Similarly, the 1944 law allowing each Union Republic to possess its own Republican military formations (§ 18B) seems to have remained a paper provision.

The Union Republics possess Ministries of their own for internal affairs, certain branches of heavy and light industry, agriculture, public health, trade, finance and the like. The work of these Ministries is co-ordinated by respective federal Ministries and/or the *Gosplan*. Nominally, the Union Republics possess exclusive jurisdiction over such matters as motor transport, housing, social security, municipal affairs, local industry, education and, since 1956, inland water transport and justice.

Religion.—Section 124 of the Constitution lays down that " in order to ensure to citizens freedom of conscience, the church in the U.S.S.R. is separated from the state, and the school from the church," and that " freedom of religious worship and freedom of anti-religious propaganda is recognized for all citizens." Churches have remained open in virtue of contracts concluded between the congregations and the local authorities. The clergy live on voluntary donations from their parishioners. A new *modus vivendi* between the Government and the religious communities was created during the War of 1939–1945. In September, 1943, Stalin agreed to the election of the Patriarch of Moscow and All Russia, a post which had been vacant since the death of Patriarch Tikhon in 1925. Patriarch Sergius, elected by the Council of the Russian Church in 1943, died in May, 1944, and was succeeded in February, 1945, by Patriarch Alexius (*d.* 1970). A new Patriarch, Pimen, was elected in 1971.

The proselytizing successes of the religious communities have become of great concern to the authorities; there has been a great increase of anti-religious articles in the press since 1959, and a number of religious institutions were once again closed or banned. Harassment of individuals active in all religions and denominations continues.

Education.—Under the Constitution, citizens of the U.S.S.R. have the right to education. Since 1956 the entire educational course, including higher education at universities, technical colleges, etc., has been free.

The state controls all educational institutions, theatres, cinemas, museums, libraries and picture galleries, as well as the press and the radio. The main centre of research and learning is the Academy of Sciences of the U.S.S.R., which is in effect a vast government-controlled pool of scientists.
President, A. Paleksandrov.

Chronological System.—On February 14, 1918, the Soviet Government adopted the Gregorian (Western) Calendar, and by a decree of June 16, 1930, the Soviet Government advanced all the

clocks in the Union by one hour, thus adopting permanent Summer Time. The country is divided into several time zones (Moscow time is 3 hours ahead of G.M.T.).

LANGUAGE, LITERATURE AND ARTS

Language and Literature.—Russian is a branch of the Slavonic family of languages which is divided into the following groups: *Eastern*, including Russian, Ukrainian and White Russian; *Western*, including Polish, Czech, Slovak and Sorbish (or Lusatian Wendish); and *Southern*, including Serbo-Croat, Slovene, Macedonian and Bulgarian. The Western group and part of the Southern group are written in the Latin alphabet, the others in the Cyrillic, said to have been instituted by SS. Cyril and Methodius in the ninth century, and largely based on the Greek alphabet. Before the Westernization of Russia under Peter the Great (1682–1725), Russian literature consisted mainly of folk ballads (*byliny*), epic songs, chronicles and works of moral theology. The eighteenth and particularly the nineteenth centuries saw a brilliant development of Russian poetry and fiction. Romantic poetry reached its zenith with Alexander Pushkin (1799–1837) and Mikhail Lermontov (1814–1841). The 20th century produced great poets like Alexander Blok (1880–1921), the Nobel Prize laureate of 1958 Boris Pasternak (1890–1960), Vladimir Mayakovsky (1893–1930) and Anna Akhmatova (1888–1966). Realistic fiction is associated with the names of Nikolai Gogol (1809–1852), Ivan Turgenev (1818–1883), Fedor Dostoyevsky (1821–1881) and Leo Tolstoy (1828–1910), and later with Anton Tchekhov (1860–1904), Maxim Gorky (1868–1936), Ivan Bunin (1870–1953) and Alexander Solzhenitsyn (b. 1918).

Great names in music include Glinka (1804–1857), Borodin (1833–87), Mussorgsky (1839–1881), Rimsky-Korsakov (1844–1908), Rubinstein (1829–1894), Tchaikovsky (1840–1893), Rakhmaninov (1873–1943), Skriabin (1872–1915), Prokofiev (1891–1953), Stravinsky (1882–1971) and Shostakovich (1906–1975). Performers include Igor Oistrakh, M. Rostropovich, and S. Richter and the famous conductor Rozhdestvensky.

FINANCE

A new "heavy" Rouble was introduced on January 1, 1961. Prices and wages have been changed accordingly at the rate of 10 old Roubles = 1 new Rouble. The official exchange rate is now approx. £1 = R.1·33. It bears little relation to the actual purchasing power of the two currencies. Banknotes in circulation are those valuing R. 1, 3, 5, 10, 25, 50 and 100. There are also coins valuing Kopecks 1, 2, 3, 5, 10, 15, 20 and R. 1.

DEFENCE

Defence expenditure in the U.S.S.R. for 1975–76 is put officially at 17·4 billion roubles (or 7·8 per cent. of total budget). It is believed, however, that this does not represent the total spent on defence in the U.S.S.R. Much of this is concealed in estimates for other ministries. The general trend is a continuing emphasis on nuclear weapons while improving the levels and capabilities of conventional arms.

The basic military service is two years in the Army and Air Force and two to three years in the Navy and Border Guards.

The total size of the Soviet regular forces is now estimated to be about 3,525,000.

Operational ICBMs, i.e. Inter-Continental Ballistic Missiles, now total about 1,575. SLBMs number 720. The number of MRBMs and IRBMs appears to be fixed at about 600. The operational personnel of the Strategic Rocket Forces totals about 350,000.

The Air Forces comprise about 11,790 operational aircraft (including about 8,250 combat aircraft). The total strength of the Air Forces, excluding the Naval Air Force, is about 550,000 men. The total personnel of the separate Air Defence Command is estimated at 500,000 men.

The total size of the Soviet Army is estimated at 1,800,000 men. It is thought to be organized in 167 divisions, distributed as follows: 63 divisions in European U.S.S.R., 28 in Central and Southern U.S.S.R., 45 in the Sino-Soviet border area, 31 in Eastern Europe.

The total strength of the Soviet Navy and Naval Air Force is 475,000 men. In total tonnage, it is the second largest navy in the world, and its main strength lies in the submarine fleet. There are now 130 nuclear-powered and 250 diesel-powered submarines.

The Soviet Navy will soon have its first two aircraft-carriers; the first one was expected to enter service in mid-1976. The land-based Naval Air Force comprises about 650 bombers and 420 other aircraft. The surface ships comprise 35 cruisers and 100 destroyers.

The para-military forces number some 130,000 security and 180,000 border troops. There are also about 2½ million DOSAAF members who participate in such activities as athletics, shooting and parachuting.

Minister of Defence, D. F. Ustinov (with rank of Army General).

Chief of General Staff, Army General V. G. Kulikov.

Chief, Political Administration, Soviet Armed Forces, Army Gen. A. A. Yepishev.

On May 14, 1955, a Treaty of Friendship, Mutual Assistance and Co-operation was signed in Warsaw between the Soviet Union and its European associates (Bulgaria, East Germany, Hungary, Poland, Rumania, and Czechoslovakia) (and Albania which left the Pact in Sept. 1968) to serve as a counterpoise to NATO. A united military command was set up in Moscow (*Secretary-General,* N. P. Firyubin; *C.-in-C.,* Marshal I. I. Yakubovsky; *Chief of Staff* (vacant)).

INDUSTRY AND AGRICULTURE

One of the most remarkable aspects of the Soviet economy has been the transformation of an essentially agricultural country into the second-strongest industrial power in the world. The 1975 output amounted to 103,900,000* tons of pig-iron, 141,000,000* tons of steel, 115,000,000* tons of rolled metal, 701,000,000* tons of coal, 482,000,000* tons of crude oil, 122,000,000* tons of cement, 1,038,000 million kW/h of electricity and 1,964,000 motor vehicles.

Agricultural development has been far slower, mainly owing to lack of incentives among peasants organized in *kolkhozy* (collective farms). Repeated droughts, such as in 1975, were a contributing factor to a permanent shortage of grain. Stock breeding has also suffered from the general mismanagement of farming. The livestock at Jan. 1, 1976 included 110,000,000 cattle, including 41,900,000 cows, and 146,900,000 sheep and goats. The level of productivity remains very low. It remains to be seen whether new incentives for peasants introduced in 1966 and 1970 and a variety of administrative reforms recently introduced in Moldavia and elsewhere will bring about a radical change in the situation. *Forests* cover nearly 40 per cent. of the whole area of the Union and form a considerable source of wealth.

---

* Metric.

Trade with U.K.

	1974	1975
Imports from U.K..	£110,016,000	£210,297,000
Exports to U.K.....	395,457,000	408,421,000

COMMUNICATIONS

European Russia is relatively well served by railways, Leningrad and Moscow being the two main focal points of rail routes. The centre and south have a good system of north-south and east-west lines, but the eastern part (the Volga lands), traversed as it is by trunk lines between Europe and Asia which enter Siberia *via* Sverdlovsk, Chelyabinsk, Magnitogorsk and Ufa, lacks north-south routes. In Asia, there are still large areas of the U.S.S.R., notably in the Far North and Siberia, with few or no railways. Railways built since 1928 include the Turkestan-Siberian line (*Turksib*) which has made possible a large-scale industrial exploitation of Kazakhstan, a number of lines within the system of the *Trans-Siberian Railway* (Magnitogorsk-Kartaly-Troitsk, Sverdlovsk-Kurgan, Novosibirsk-Proyektnaya, etc.), which are of great importance for the industrial development in the east, the Petropavlovsk-Karaganda-Balkhash line which has made possible the development of the Karaganda coal basin and of the Balkhash copper mines, and the Moscow-Donbass trunk line. In the northern part of European Russia, the North Pechora Railway has been completed, while in the Far East a second Trans-Siberian line (the Baikal-Amur Railway) is under construction; it will follow a more northerly alignment than the existing Trans-Siberian and will terminate in the Pacific port of Sovetskaya Gavan.

Sea Ports and Inland Waterways.—The most important ports (Odessa, Nikolayev, Batumi, Taganrog, Rostov, Kerch, Sevastopol and Novorossiisk) lie around the Black Sea and the Sea of Azov. The northern ports (Leningrad, Murmansk and Archangel) are, with the exception of Murmansk, icebound during winter. Several new ports have been built along the Arctic Sea route (between Murmansk and Vladivostok) and are now in regular use every summer. The great Far Eastern port of Vladivostok, the Pacific naval base of the U.S.S.R., is kept open by icebreakers all the year round. Inland waterways, both natural and artificial, are of great importance in the country, although all of them are icebound in winter (from 2½ months in the south to 6 months in the north). The great rivers of European Russia flow outwards from the centre, linking all parts of the plain with the chief ports, an immense system of navigable waterways which carried about 419,000,000 tons of freight in 1973. They are supplemented by a system of canals which provide a through traffic between the White, Baltic, Black and Caspian Seas. The most notable of them, built largely by forced labour, are the *White Sea-Baltic Canal*, and the *Moscow-Volga Canal*. The 63-miles long *Volga-Don Canal* linking the Baltic and the White Seas in the North to the Caspian, the Black Sea and the Sea of Azov in the South, was completed in May 1952.

FLAG OF THE U.S.S.R.—Red, with five-pointed star above hammer and sickle.

NATIONAL DAY OF THE U.S.S.R.—November 7 (Commemorating the October Bolshevist Revolution of 1917).

BRITISH EMBASSY

(Naberezhnaya Morisa Toreza 14, Moscow)

Ambassador Extraordinary and Plenipotentiary, His Excellency Sir Howard Frank Trayton Smith, K.C.M.G. (1975).

Minister, I. J. M. Sutherland, C.M.G.

Counsellors, K. J. Uffen (*Commercial*); Dr. J. C. J.

Thynne (*Scientific*); C. L. G. Mallaby (*Head of Chancery*); B. Spencer (*Admin.*).

Defence and Air Attaché, Air Cdre. P. D. Thorne, O.B.E., D.F.C.

Military Attaché, Brig. D. H. Bush.

Naval Attaché, Capt. R. J. F. Turner, R.N.

British Council Representative, A. A. Edmondson (*Asst. Cultural Attaché*).

There are no British Consulates in the U.S.S.R. apart from the Consular Section attached to the Embassy.

I.—R.S.F.S.R.

(The Russian Soviet Federal Socialist Republic)

Chairman of the Presidium of the Supreme Soviet, M.A. Yasnov.

Chairman of the Council of Ministers, M. S. Solomentsev.

The R.S.F.S.R. has no Communist Party Central Committee of its own.

The R.S.F.S.R., the largest and the most important of the Republics, occupies the major half of the European part of the U.S.S.R. and the major northern half of its Asiatic part and makes up 77 per cent. of the total territory of the U.S.S.R. with 53 per cent. of the total population. It consists of 16 Autonomous Republics (the Bashkir, Buryat, Checheno-Ingush, Chuvash, Daghestan, Kabardin-Balkar, Kalmyk, Karelian, Komi, Mari, Mordovian, North-Osetian, Tatar, Tuva, Udmurt and Yakut A.S.S.R.s); 6 regions (Altai, Khabarovsk, Krasnodar, Krasnoyarsk, Maritime and Stavropol) containing in their turn 5 autonomous provinces; 49 provinces (Amur, Archangel, Astrakhan, Belgorod, Bryansk, Chelyabinsk, Chita, Gorky, Irkutsk, Ivanovo, Kalinin, Kaliningrad, Kaluga, Kamchatka, Kemerovo, Kirov, Kostroma, Kuibyshev, Kurgan, Kursk, Leningrad, Lipetsk, Magadan, Moscow, Murmansk, Novgorod, Novosibirsk, Omsk, Orel, Orenburg, Penza, Perm, Pskov, Rostov, Ryazan, Sakhalin, Saratov, Smolensk, Sverdlovsk, Tambov, Tomsk, Tula, Tyumen, Ulyanovsk, Vladimir, Volgograd, Vologda, Vorenezh and Yaroslavl).

Physical Features.—The R.S.F.S.R. may be conveniently divided into three areas, a low-lying flat Western part stretching eastwards up to the Yenisei and divided in two by the Ural ridge; an eastern part, between the Yenisei and the Pacific, consisting of a number of tablelands and ridges, and a southern mountainous part. Climatically, the R.S.F.S.R. extends over all zones, except the tropics, and may be divided into the following belts (from north to south): Arctic, Tundra, Forest, Mixed Forest-Steppe, Steppe, Sub-Tropics.

The Republic has a very long coast-line, including the longest Arctic coast-line in the world (about 17,000 miles). The most important rivers in the European Part of the R.S.F.S.R. are the Volga with its tributaries Kama and Oka, the Northern Dvina and the Pechora, the short but wide Neva, the Don and the Kuban, and in the Asiatic part, the Obi with the Irtysh, the Yenisei, the Lena and the Amur, and, further north, the Khatanga, Olenek, Yana, Indigirka, Kolyma and Anadyr. Lakes are abundant, particularly in the north-west. The huge Baikal Lake in Eastern Siberia is the deepest lake in the world. There are also two large artificial water reservoirs within the Greater Volga canal system, the Moscow and Rybinsk " Seas."

Minerals.—The Republic occupies one of the first places in the world for mineral wealth. Coal is mined in the Kuznetsk area, in the Urals, south of Moscow, in the Donets basin (its Eastern part lies in the R.S.F.S.R.) and in the Pechora area in the North. Oil is produced in the Northern

Caucasus, in the area between the Volga and the Ural (the so-called "Second Baku") and in Western Siberia. The Ural mountains contain a unique assortment of minerals—high-quality iron ore, manganese, copper, aluminium, gold, platinum, precious stones, salt, asbestos, pyrites, coal, oil, etc. Iron ore is mined, in addition to the Urals, near Kursk, Tula, Lipetsk, Khopper, in several areas in Siberia and in the Kola Peninsula. Non-ferrous metals are found in the Altai, in Eastern Siberia, in the Northern Caucasus, in the Kuznetsk-Basin, in the Far East and in the Far North. Nine-tenths of all U.S.S.R. forests are located in the R.S.F.S.R.

Production and Industry.—The vastness of the territory of the Republic and the great variety in climatic conditions cause great differences in the structure of agriculture from north to south and from west to east. In the Far North stag breeding, hunting and fishing are predominant. Further south, timber industry is combined with grain growing. In the southern half of the forest zone and in the adjacent forest-steppe zone, the acreage under grain crops is far larger and the structure of agriculture more complex. An extensive programme of land improvement mainly involving this zone, announced early in 1974, aims to double its total agricultural output by 1990. In the eastern part of this zone, between the Volga and the Urals, cericulture is predominant (particularly summer wheat), with cattle breeding next. Beyond the Urals, we find another important grain-growing and stock-breeding area in the southern part of the Western-Siberian plain. The southern steppe zone is the main wheat granary of the U.S.S.R., containing also large acreages under barley, maize and sunflower. In the extreme South (Krasnodar region, Stavropol region) cotton is now cultivated. Vine, tobacco and other Southern crops are grown on the Black Sea shore of the Caucasus.

Industrially, the R.S.F.S.R. occupies the first place among the Soviet Republics. Major changes in the location of industry have occurred since the revolution and again since the war with two new industrial areas being developed in the Urals and in the Kuznetsk basin, although Moscow and Leningrad are still the two largest industrial centres in the country. Most of the oil produced in the U.S.S.R. now comes from two areas in the R.S.F.S.R.—the Bashkir and Tatar Autonomous Republics. All industries are represented in the R.S.F.S.R., including iron and steel and engineering. Industrial centres include Magnitogorsk, Chelyabinsk, Novokuznetsk, Tula, Komsomolsk, Perm, Ufa, Irkutsk, Kuibyshev, Krasnoyarsk, Nizhny-Tagil, Novosibirsk, Omsk, Volgograd, Gorky, Saratov, Grozny, Rostov and Taganrog.

CAPITAL, MOSCOW. Population 7,466,000 (Jan. 1, 1975). Moscow, founded about A.D. 1147 by Yuri Dolgoruki, became first the centre of the rising Moscow principality and, later, in the 15th century, the capital of the whole of Russia (Muscovy). In 1325, it became the seat of the Metropolitan of Russia. In 1703 Peter the Great transferred the capital to the newly built St. Petersburg, but on March 14, 1918, Moscow was again designated as the capital. Ψ Leningrad (before the First World War "St. Petersburg" and from 1914–1924 "Petrograd") has a population of 3,853,000 (Jan. 1, 1975).

Other towns with populations exceeding 500,000 are:—

Gorky (Nizhny-Novgorod)	1,283,000
Novosibirsk (Novonikolayevsk)	1,265,000
Kuibyshev (Samara)	1,164,000
Sverdlovsk (Yekaterinburg)	1,147,000
Chelyabinsk	969,000
Omsk	968,000
Kazan	946,000
Perm (Molotov)	939,000
Volgograd (Stalingrad; Tsaritsyn)	900,000
Ufa	895,000
Ψ Rostov-on-Don	888,000
Saratov	834,000
Voronezh	746,000
Krasnoyarsk	748,000
Yaroslavi	568,000
Novokuznetsk	524,000
Krasnodar	532,000

Ψ Seaport.

About 83 per cent. of the population are Russians.

II.—UKRAINE

First Secretary of the Party Central Committee, V. V. Shcherbitsky.

Chairman of the Presidium of the Supreme Soviet, A. F. Vatchenko.

Chairman of the Council of Ministers, A. P. Lyashko.

This Republic, second largest in population, lying in the south-western part of the European half of the U.S.S.R., was formed in December, 1917. It consists of 25 provinces—Cherkassy, Chernigov, Chernovtsy, Crimea, Dnepropetrovsk, Donetsk, Ivano-Frankovsk, Kharkov, Kherson, Khmelnitsky, Kiev, Kirovograd, Lvov, Nikolayev, Odessa, Poltava, Rovno, Sumy, Ternopol, Transcarpathia, Vinnitsa, Volhynia, Voroshilovgrad, Zaporozhye and Zhitomir.

Physical Features.—The larger part of the Ukraine forms a plain with small elevations. The Carpathian mountains lie in the south-western part of the Republic. The climate is moderate, with relatively mild winters (particularly in the southwest) and hot summers. The main rivers are the Dnieper with its tributaries, the Southern Bug and the Northern Donets (a tributary of the Don).

Production and Industry.—The main centre of Soviet coal mining and iron and steel industry is situated in the southern part of the Ukraine. Engineering and chemical industry have been greatly developed under the Soviet régime. In 1970, the Ukraine provided 40 per cent of the total Soviet steel, 40 per cent. of metal goods and 33 per cent. of coal. The central forest-steppe region (mainly on the right bank of the Dnieper) is the greatest sugar-producing area in the U.S.S.R. The Ukraine also leads in grain-growing and stock-raising.

There are large deposits of coal and salt in the Donets Basin, of iron ore in Krivoy Rog and near Kerch in the Crimea, of manganese in Nikopol, and of quicksilver in Nikitovka.

CAPITAL (since 1934), Kiev, the oldest city in the U.S.S.R. founded in the 9th century A.D., was the capital of the Russian State from 865 to 1240. Population (Jan. 1, 1975), 1,947,000. Other towns with population over 500,000 are:—

Kharkov	1,357,000
Ψ Odessa	1,002,000
Dnepropetrovsk (Yekaterinoslav)	958,000
Donetsk (Stalino; Yuzovka, *i.e.* Hughes-ovka)	950,000
Zaporozhye (Aleksandrovskaya)	744,000
Krivoy-Rog	628,000
Lvov (Lviv; Lwow; Lemberg)	617,000

III.—BELORUSSIA
(White Russia)

First Secretary of the Party Central Committee, P. M. Masherov.

Chairman of the Presidium of the Supreme Soviet, F. A. Surganov.

Chairman of the Council of Ministers, T. Ya. Kiselev.

The Belorussian S.S.R., lying in the western part of the European area of the U.S.S.R., was formed early in 1919. It now consists of six provinces (Brest, Gomel, Grodno, Minsk, Mogilev and Vitebsk). It is largely a plain with many lakes, swamps and marshy land. Before the revolution of 1917 the area was one of the most backward parts of European Russia. Since then, agriculture has been greatly developed, thanks to draining of swamps. Most of the Republic's industry is also of recent growth. Woodworking is of great importance, but engineering has also been greatly extended with several major plants built in Gomel and Minsk.

The main rivers are the upper reaches of the Dnieper, of the Niemen and of the Western Dvina.

CAPITAL, Minsk. Population 1,133,000 (Jan. 1, 1975).

Belorussians make up four-fifths of the population, with Russians and Poles coming next.

IV.—UZBEKISTAN

First Secretary of the Party Central Committee, Sh. R. Rashidov.

Chairman of the Presidium of the Supreme Soviet, N. M. Matchanov.

Chairman of the Council of Ministers, N. D. Khudayberdyev.

The Uzbek S.S.R. was formed in 1924 and consists of the Kara-Kalpak A.S.S.R. and of 11 provinces (Andizhan, Bokhara, Dzhizak, Ferghana, Kashka-Darya, Khorezm, Namangan, Samarkand, Surkhan-Darya, Syr-Darya and Tashkent). It lies between the high Tienshan Mountains and the Pamir highlands in the east and south-east and sandy lowlands in the west and north-west. The major part of the territory is a plain with huge waterless deserts and several large oases, which form the main centres of population and economic life. The largest is the Ferghana valley, watered by the Syr-Darya. Other oases include Tashkent, Samarkand, Bokhara and Khorezm. The climate is continental and dry. Minerals include gold, natural gas, oil, copper, lead, zinc and coal.

The Uzbeks, a Turkic people, make up 65·5 per cent. of the population, the Russians (12·5 per cent.), Tatars (5 per cent.) and Kazakhs (4 per cent.) come next.

There are major agricultural and textile machinery plants and several chemical combines. Uzbekistan is the main cotton-growing area of the U.S.S.R. producing more than 60 per cent. of all Soviet cotton. Irrigation has always been of decisive importance in this area, and the Soviet Government has done much in this field, including the contruction of the Great Ferghana Canal (230 miles).

CAPITAL, Tashkent. Population 1,595,000 (Jan. 1, 1975). Samarkand contains the Gur-Emir (Tamerlane's Mausoleum), completed A.D. 1400 by Ulugbek, Tamerlane's astronomer-grandson, and a 15th-century observatory. Heavy damage was done to Tashkent by the series of earthquakes in April and May, 1966.

V.—KAZAKHSTAN.

First Secretary of the Party Central Committee, D. A. Kunayev.

Chairman of the Presidium of Supreme Soviet, S. B. Niyazbekov.

Chairman of the Council of Ministers, B. A. Ashimov.

The Kazakh S.S.R., the second-largest Union-Republic, stretching from the lower reaches of the Volga and the Caspian in the west to the Altai and Tienshan in the east and bordering on China, was formed in 1920 as an autonomous republic (under the name of the Kirghiz A.S.S.R.) within the R.S.F.S.R., and was constituted a Union Republic in 1936. It consists of the 19 Provinces: Aktyubinsk, Alma-Ata, Chimkent, Dzhambul, Dzhezkazgan, East-Kazakhstan, Guryev, Karaganda, Kokchetav, Kustanay, Kzyl-Orda, Mangyshlak, Semipalatinsk, Taldy-Kurgan, Tselinograd, North-Kazakhstan, Pavlodar, Turgay and Uralsk.

Kazakhstan is a country of arid steppes and misedeserts, flat in the west, hilly in the east and mountainous in the south-east (Southern Altai and Tienshan). The climate is continental and very dry. The main rivers are the (Upper) Irtysh, the Ural, the Syr-Darya and the Ili. Kazakhstan is very rich in minerals: copper in Kounrad and Dzhezkazgan, lead and zinc in the Altai and Karatau mountains, iron ore in Radryg and Lisakovsk, coal in Ekibastuz and Karaganda and oil and natural gas in the Maangyshlak peninsula. Major centres of metal industry exist now in the Altai Mountains, in Chimkent, north of the Balkhash Lake and in Central Kazakhstan. Stock-raising is highly developed, particularly in the central and south-western parts of the Republic. Grain is grown in the north and north-east and cotton in the south and south-east. In 1954 an ambitious programme of development of " virgin " lands in the steppes was launched by the Government to increase grain production.

The Kazakhs (a Turkic people) are now in a minority in the Republic named after them; they constitute only 33 per cent. of its population. Russian settlers make up 42 per cent. and Ukrainians 7 per cent.

CAPITAL, Alma-Ata (formerly Verny). Population, 837,000 (Jan. 1, 1975). Karaganda, a major mining centre, has a population of 565,000 (Jan. 1, 1975).

VI.—GEORGIA

First Secretary of the Party Central Committee, E. A. Shevardnadze.

Chairman of the Presidium of the Supreme Soviet, P. G. Gilashuili.

Chairman of the Council of Ministers, Z. A. Pataridze.

The Georgian S.S.R., occupying the north-western part of Transcaucasia, lies on the shore of the Black Sea and borders in the south-east on Turkey. It was formed in 1921; in 1922 it joined the Transcaucasian Federation which, in its turn, adhered to the U.S.S.R. in the same year. After the liquidation of the Transcaucasian S.F.S.R. in 1936 Georgia became a Union Republic. It contains two Autonomous Republics (Abkhazia and Adjaria) and the South-Osetian Autonomous Province. Georgia is a country of mountains, with the Greater Caucasus in the north and the Smaller Caucasus in the south. A relatively low-lying land between these two ridges is divided into two parts by the Surz Ridge: Western Georgia with a mild and damp climate and Eastern Georgia with a more continental and dry climate. The Black Sea shore and the Rion lowlands are subtropical in their climatic character. The most important mineral deposits are manganese (Chiatura), coal (Tkibuli and Tkvarcheli) and oil (Kakhetia). Georgia is leading as regards production of manganese in the U.S.S.R. There are also many oil refineries. Viniculture and tobacco-growing are the two main agricultural industries. The Black Sea coast harbours many famous holiday resorts. Georgians make up 67 per cent. of the population, the remainder being composed of Armenians, Russians, Azerbaidjani and Osetians.

CAPITAL, Tbilisi (Tiflis), population 1,006,000 (Jan. 1, 1975).

VII.—AZERBAIDJAN

First Secretary of the Party Central Committee, G. A. Aliyev.

Chairman of the Presidium of the Supreme Soviet, K. A. Khalilov.

Chairman of the Council of Ministers, A. I. Ibragimov.

The Azerbaidjan S.S.R. occupies the eastern part of Transcaucasia, on the shore of the Caspian Sea, and borders on Iran. It was formed in 1920. Between 1922 and 1936 it formed part of the Transcaucasian Federation. In 1936 it became a Union Republic. It contains the Nakhichevan Autonomous Republic and the Nagorno-Karabakh Autonomous Province.

The north-eastern part of the Republic is taken up by the south-eastern end of the main Caucasus ridge, its south-western part by the smaller Caucasus hills, and its south-eastern corner by the spurs of the Talysh Ridge. Its central part is a depression irrigated by the Kura and by the lower reaches of its tributary Araks. Sheltered by the mountains from the humid west winds blowing from the Black Sea, Azerbaidjan has a continental climate. The land requires artificial irrigation. Industry is dominated by oil and natural gas extraction and related chemical and engineering industries centred on Baku and Sumgait. A large power station on the Kura (Mingechaur) was completed in 1954. Azerbaidjan is also important as a cotton growing area. The Azerbaidjani (Turks) make up three-quarters of the population of the Republic, Armenians, about 9 per cent., and Russians, 10 per cent.

CAPITAL, Ψ Baku. Population 929,000 (Jan. 1, 1975).

VIII.—LITHUANIA

First Secretary of the Party Central Committee, P. P. Grishkyavichus.

Chairman of the Presidium of the Supreme Soviet, A. K. Barkauskas.

Chairman of the Council of Ministers, I. A. Manyushis.

Lithuania, formerly a Province of the Russian Empire, was declared an independent Republic at Vilna in 1918 and was incorporated into the U.S.S.R. in August, 1940. It was occupied by German forces from June, 1941, until the autumn of 1944. The Republic forms a plain with a large number of lakes and swamps. The forests occupy 19 per cent. of the whole area. The main river is the Niemen with its tributaries.

The chief industries are agriculture and forestry, the chief products being rye, oats, wheat, barley, flax, sugar-beet and potatoes. Before its incorporation into the Soviet Union, Lithuania exported a large quantity of meat and dairy produce.

The Lithuanians make up four-fifths of the population, Russians and Poles, 8–9 per cent. each.

CAPITAL, Vilnius (Vilna, restored to Lithuania by U.S.S.R. after the collapse and partition of Poland in 1939, and recaptured by Soviet forces in 1944). Population 433,000 (Jan. 1, 1975).

IX.—MOLDAVIA

First Secretary of the Party Central Committee, I. I. Bodyul.

Chairman of the Presidium of the Supreme Soviet, K. F. Ilyashenko.

Chairman of the Council of Ministers, P. A. Paskar.

Moldavia, occupying the south-western corner of the U.S.S.R., borders in the west on Rumania with the Pruth forming the frontier. In 1918, Rumania seized the Russian Province of Bessarabia. In 1924 a Moldavian Autonomous Republic was formed within the Ukraine, and in 1940 the U.S.S.R. forced Rumania to give back Bessarabia, the major part of which was merged with the Moldavian A.S.S.R. to form a Moldavian Union Republic. Moldavia was occupied by the Germans and Rumanians from 1941 to 1944.

The northern part of the Republic consists of flat steppe lands, now all under plough. Some forests skirt the Dniester. Further south, around Kishinev, there are woody hills and further south again, low-lying steppe lands. The climate is moderate. The main river is the Dniester, navigable along the whole course.

The main industry is agriculture (viniculture, fruit-growing and market-gardening). Industry is insignificant in both parts of Moldavia, but the Republic has the densest population in the U.S.S.R. Moldavians make up 64 per cent. of the population, with Ukranians, and Russians next.

CAPITAL, Kishinev (Chisinau). Population, 452,000 (Jan. 1, 1975).

X.—LATVIA

First Secretary of the Party Central Committee, A. E. Voss.

Chairman of the Presidium of the Supreme Soviet, P. Ya. Strautmanis.

Chairman of the Council of Ministers, Yu. Ya. Ruben.

The Latvian S.S.R., lying on the shores of the Baltic and of the Gulf of Riga, was formerly a Baltic Province of the Russian Empire. It was proclaimed an independent state in 1918 and was forcibly incorporated into the U.S.S.R. in August 1940. Between 1941 and 1944 the Republic was occupied by the German forces.

The surface of the country is generally flat, interspersed by occasional chains of hills. The climate is moderately-continental. The main rivers are the lower reaches of the Western Dvina and its tributaries. Forests occupy 20 per cent. of the total territory.

The Latvians make up 57 per cent. of the Republic's population, Russians 30 per cent.

Latvian industry was always highly developed, with shipbuilding, engineering, chemical industry, textile industry, wood-working and dairying being the chief occupations. Both Riga and Liepaja (Libava, Liebau) are important sea-ports.

As in other newly-acquired Republics an agrarian reform was carried out in Latvia in 1940–41 and again after 1944.

CAPITAL, Ψ Riga. Population, 796,000 (Jan. 1, 1975).

XI.—KIRGHIZIA

First Secretary of the Party Central Committee, T. U. Usubaliyev.

Chairman of the Presidium of the Supreme Soviet, T. Kulatov.

Chairman of the Council of Ministers, A. S. Suyumbayev.

The Kirghiz S.S.R. occupies the north-eastern part of Soviet Central Asia and borders in the south-east on China. In 1924, a Kara-Kirghiz Autonomous Province was formed within the R.S.F.S.R. In 1926 it became a Kirghiz Autonomous Republic, and in 1936 a Union Republic. It contains three provinces, Issyk-Kul, Naryn and Osh. The Kirghiz Republic is a mountainous country, the major part being covered by the ridge of the Central Tienshan, while mountains of the Pamir-Altai system occupy its southern part. There are a number of spacious mountain valleys, the Alai, Susamyr, the Issyk-kul lake and others. The majority of the population is concentrated in plains, lying at the foot of mountains—Chu, Talass, part of the Ferghana Valley where agriculture prospers. Crops include sugar beet and cotton, and sheep are important in the mountains. Industry is being developed and some mining is done. The Kirghiz constitute 44 per cent. of the population, the Russians 29 per cent. The Uzbeks (in Eastern Ferghana) amount to 11 per cent.

CAPITAL, Frunze (formerly Pishpek). Population, 486,000 (Jan. 1, 1975).

XII.—TADJIKSTAN

First Secretary of the Party Central Committee, D. Rasulov.

Chairman of the Presidium of the Supreme Soviet, M. Kholov.

Chairman of the Council of Ministers, R. N. Nabiev.

The Tadjik S.S.R. lies in the extreme south-east of Soviet Central Asia and borders in the south on Afghanistan and in the east on China. It was originally formed in 1924 as an Autonomous Republic within the Uzbek S.S.R. and became a Union Republic in 1929. It includes the Gorno-Badakhshan Autonomous Province and the Kulyab and Leninabad Provinces.

The country is mountainous: in the east lie the Pamir highlands with the highest point in the U.S.S.R., Pik Kommunizma (24,500 feet), in the centre the high ridges of the Pamir-Altai system. Plains are formed by wide stretches of the Syr-Darya valley in the north and of the Amu-Darya in the south.

Like the other Central-Asiatic Republics, Tadjikistan is a cotton-growing country. Its climatic conditions favour the cultivation of Egyptian cotton. Irrigation is of great importance. Fifty-six per cent. of the population are Tadjiks (linguistically and culturally akin to the Persians), 23 per cent. Uzbeks, the rest Russians and others.

CAPITAL, Dushanbe (formerly Stalinabad; Dyushambe). Population, 436,000 (Jan. 1, 1975).

XIII.—ARMENIA

First Secretary of the Party Central Committee, K. S. Demirchyan.

Chairman of the Presidium of the Supreme Soviet, B. E. Sarkisov.

Chairman of the Council of Ministers, G. A. Arzumanyan.

The Armenian S.S.R. occupies the south-western part of Transcaucasia: it was formed in 1920. In 1922 it joined the Transcaucasian Federation, and on its liquidation in 1936 became a Union Republic. In the south it borders on Turkey. It is a mountainous country consisting of several vast table lands surrounded by ridges. The population and the economic life are concentrated in the low-lying part of Armenia, the Aras valley and the Erevan hollow; the climate is continental, dry and cold, but the Aras valley has a long, hot and dry summer. Irrigation is essential for agriculture. At the junction of the former Turkish, Persian and Russian boundaries is *Mount Ararat* (17,160 ft.), the traditional resting place of "Noah's Ark." Industrial and fruit crops are grown in the low-lying districts, grain in the hills. Armenia is traditionally noted for her wine. There are large copper ore and molybdenum deposits and other minerals. The Armenian Church centred in Etchmiadzin is the oldest established Christian Church, Christianity having been recognized as the State religion in A.D. 300.

Nearly 90 per cent. of the population is Armenian.

CAPITAL, Erevan. Population, 899,000 (Jan. 1, 1975).

XIV.—TURKMENISTAN

First Secretary of the Party Committee, M. Gapurov.

Chairman of the Presidium of the Supreme Soviet, A.-M. Klychev.

Chairman of the Council of Ministers, B. Yazkuliev.

Turkmenia occupies the extreme south of Soviet Central Asia, between the Caspian and the Amu-Darya and borders in the south on Iran and

Afghanistan. It was formed in 1924 and contains five Provinces: Ashkhabad, Chardjou, Knasnovodsk, Mary and Tashauz. The country is a low-lying plain, fringed by hills in the south. Ninety per cent. of the plain is taken up by the arid Kara-Kum desert. Of all Central-Asiatic Republics, Turkmenia is the lowest and driest. The cultivation of cotton, stock-raising and mineral extraction are the principal industries. The republic produces 16 per cent. of the Soviet Union's natural gas, as well as astrakhan furs and carpets. Most of the land under plough is artificially irrigated. The oil and silk industries are of old standing. There are also some fisheries in the Caspian.

Turkmens, nomadic in the past, make up two-thirds of the population, Russians 15 per cent., and Uzbeks eight per cent.

CAPITAL, Ashkhabad (formerly Askhabad, Poltoratski). Population, 289,000 (Jan. 1, 1975).

XV.—ESTONIA

First Secretary of the Party Central Committee, I. G. Kebin.

Chairman of the Presidium of the Supreme Soviet, A. P. Vader.

Chairman of the Council of Ministers, V. I. Klauson.

Estonia, formerly a Baltic province of the Russian Empire, was proclaimed an independent Republic in 1918. In 1940, it was forcibly incorporated into the U.S.S.R. It lies on the shores of the Baltic and of the Finnish Gulf in the north and of the Gulf of Riga in the south-west. Some 800 islands, among them Dagö and Ösel, form part of Estonian territory. Between 1941 and 1944, Estonia was occupied by the German forces.

The country forms a low-lying plain with many lakes, among them the Chud (or Pskov) Lake, on the border with the R.S.F.S.R. Forests take up about one-fifth of the territory. Agriculture and dairy-farming are the chief industries, rye, oats, barley, flax and potatoes being the chief crops, and butter, bacon and eggs the chief products of dairy farming. There are important manufactures, including textiles, engineering, shipbuilding, wood-working, etc.

The population consists of Estonians (68 per cent.) and Russians (25 per cent.).

CAPITAL, ΨTallinn (formerly Reval). Population, 399,000 (Jan. 1, 1975).

THE VATICAN CITY STATE
(Stato della Città del Vaticano)

Sovereign Pontiff, His Holiness Pope Paul VI (Giovanni Battista Montini), *born* at Concesio (Brescia), Sept. 26, 1897, *elected* Pope (in succession to John XXIII), June 21, 1963.

Secretary of State, Cardinal Jean Marie Villot, *appointed* April 30, 1969.

The office of the ecclesiastical head of the Roman Catholic Church (Holy See) is vested in the Pope, the Sovereign Pontiff. For many centuries the Sovereign Pontiff exercised temporal power, and in 1859 the Papal States had an area of 17,218 square miles, with a population of 3,124,688. During the reign of Pius IX (1846–1878), the Papal States of Romagna, Umbria and the Marches were incorporated in the Kingdom of Sardinia and with the remaining States (Rome, Comacchio, Viterbo, Civita Vecchia, Velletri and Frosinone) became part of unified Italy in 1870. The territory of the Papacy was confined to the palaces of the Vatican and the Lateran and the Villa of Castel Gandolfo and the temporal power of the Pope was in suspense until the treaty of Feb. 11, 1929, which recognized the full and independent sovereignty of the Holy See in the City of the Vatican. Accompanying

the treaty were conventions regulating the condition of religion and the Catholic Church in Italy and agreeing to pay 750,000,000 lire in cash and the income at 5 per cent. on 1,000,000,000 lire State bonds as a final settlement of the claims of the Holy See against Italy for the loss of temporal power. The population of the Vatican City in 1975 was 1,000.

FLAG.—Square flag; equal vertical bands of yellow (next staff), and white; crossed keys and triple crown device on white band.

BRITISH LEGATION
(91 Via Condotti, Rome)

Envoy Extraordinary and Minister Plenipotentiary to the Holy See, His Excellency Dugald Malcolm, C.M.G., C.V.O., T.D. (1975).

1st Secretary, R. M. Purcell.

VENEZUELA
(La Republica de Venezuela)

President, Sr. Carlos Andrés Pérez, _elected_ Dec. 9, 1973, _assumed office_ March 12, 1974.

CABINET
Home Affairs, Dr. Octavio Lepage.
Foreign Affairs, Dr. Ramón Escovar Salom.
Finance, Dr. Héctor Hurtado Navarro.
Defence, General Francisco Eloy Alvarez Torres.
Public Works, Dr. Arnoldo José Gabaldón Berti.
Development, Dr. José Ignacio Casal.
Education, Dr. Luis Manuel Peñalver.
Health and Social Assistance, Dr. Antonio Parra León.
Agriculture, Dr. Carmelo Contreras Barbuesa.
Labour, Dr. José Manzo González.
Communications, Ing. Leopoldo Sucre Figarella.
Justice, Dr. Armando Sánchez Bueno.
Mines and Hydrocarbons, Dr. Valentín Hernández Acosta.
Goods and Services, Dr. Carmelo Lauría Lesseur.
Social Development, Dr. Roberto Padilla Fernández.
Minister of State for Planning, Dr. Gumersindo Rodríguez.
Minister of State for Information, Dr. Guido Groscors.
Governor of Federal District, Dr. Diego Arria Salicetti.
Governor of Miranda State, Dr Manuel Mantilla.

VENEZUELAN EMBASSY IN LONDON
3 Hans Crescent, S.W.1
[01-584 4206]

Ambassador Extraordinary and Plenipotentiary, His Excellency Dr. Carlos Pérez de la Cova (1970).
Minister-Counsellor, Lic. José Miguel Quintana.
Minister-Counsellor, Dr. Luis Eloy Añez (_Economic_).
1st Secretaries, Hedy Hernández-Ortega Lic.; José Parada.
2nd Secretary, Lic. Rafael Hernández-Sanchez.
Counsellor, Dr. Miriam Blanco-Fombona de Hood (_Cultural_).
Attaché, O. Senior (_Education_).

Consulate-General: 71A Park Mansions, S.W.1.
General Consul, Roberto Erwin Lascano.
There is also a Consulate-General at _Liverpool_.

Area and Population.—A South American Republic, situated approximately between 0° 45′ S. lat. and 12° 12′ N. lat. and 59° 45′–73° 09′ W. long. It consists of one Federal District, 20 states and 2 territories. Venezuela has a total area of 353,894 sq. miles and a population (estimate, 1975) of 11,992,700 increasing annually at a rate of 3·4 per cent.

Venezuela lies on the north of the South American continent, and is bounded on the north by the Caribbean Sea, west by the Republic of Colombia,

east by Guyana, and south by Brazil. Included in the area of the Republic are 72 islands off the coast, with a total area of about 14,650 square miles, the largest being _Margarita_, which is politically associated with Tortuga, Cubagua and Coche to form the State of _Nueva Esparta_. Margarita has an area of about 400 square miles. In 1942 Great Britain ceded to Venezuela the small island of _Patos_ (170 acres) about 3 miles from the mainland.

Physical Features.—The Eastern Andes from the south-west cross the border and reach to the Caribbean Coast, where they are prolonged by the Maritime Andes of Venezuela to the Gulf of Paria on the north-east. The main range is known as the Sierra Nevada de Merida, and contains the highest peaks in the country in Pico Bolivar (16,411 feet) and Picacho de la Sierra (15,420 feet), the maritime ranges containing the Silla de Caracas (8,531 feet). Near the Brazilian border the Sierras Parima and Pacaraima, and on the eastern border the Sierras de Rincote and de Usupamo, enclose the republic with parallel northward spurs, between which are valleys of the Orinoco tributaries. The Sierra Parima contains Yaparana (7,175 feet) and Duida (8,120 feet), and Pacaraima contains Maraguaca (8,228 feet) and Roraima (9,000 feet), the latter being on the Venezuela-Guyana boundary. The slopes of the mountains and foothills are covered with dense forests, but the basin of the Orinoco is mainly _llanos_, or level stretches of open prairie, with occasional woods.

The principal river of Venezuela is the _Orinoco_, with innumerable affluents, the main river exceeding 1,600 miles in length from its rise in the southern highlands of the republic to its outflow in the deltaic region of the north-east.

A Franco-Venezuelan Expedition, led by Major Frank Risquez, claimed to have discovered the source of the Orinoco, on Nov. 27, 1951, at 63° 15′ W. long., 2° 18′ N. lat., and about 1,100 metres above sea-level.

The Orinoco is navigable for large steamers from its mouth for 700 miles, and by smaller vessels as far as the Maipures Cataract, some 200 miles farther up-stream. Dredging operations completed at the beginning of 1954 opened the Orinoco to ocean-going ships, of up to 40 ft. draft, as far as

Puerto Ordaz (about 150 miles up-stream), which with the adjacent town of San Felix is now officially known as Ciudad Guayana. Among the many tributaries of the main stream are the Ventuari, Caura and Caroni from the south, and the Apure (with its tributary the Portuguesa), Arauca, Meta, and Guaviare from the west, the Meta and Guaviare being principally Colombian rivers. The upper waters of the Orinoco are united with those of the Rio Negro (a Brazilian tributary of the Amazon) by a natural river or canal, known as the *Casiquiare.* A British scientific expedition travelled in April-May, 1968, by Hovercraft from Manaos in Brazil *viâ* the Rio Negro, Casiquiare canal and Orinoco River to Trinidad. The coastal regions of Venezuela are much indented and contain many lagoons and lakes, of which *Maracaibo,* with an area of 8,296 square miles, is the largest lake in South America. Other lakes are Zulia (290 square miles), south-west of Maracaibo, and Valencia (216 square miles) about 1,400 ft. above sea-level in the Maritime Andes. The *llanos* also contain lakes and swamps caused by the river floods, but they are dry in the summer seasons.

The climate is tropical and, except where modified by altitude or tempered by sea breezes, is unhealthy, particularly in the coastal regions and in the neighbourhood of lowland streams and lagoons. The hot, wet season lasts from April to October, the dry, cooler season from November to March.

Government.—On January 23, 1958, the military dictatorship of Maj-Gen. Marcos Pérez Jiménez, which had lasted since 1953 and covered a period of remarkable economic expansion due to the Venezuelan oil boom, was overthrown by a popular and military uprising. Since 1958 Venezuela has had a freely-elected democratic government. In elections in December, 1958, *Accion Democratica* (A.D.) gained a clear majority and Sr. Rómulo Betancourt of A.D. was elected President. For most of his five-year term of office Sr. Betancourt governed in coalition with the Christian Socialist Party, *Copei.* Further national elections were held on December 1, 1963, in which A.D. retained a reduced majority. Dr. Raúl Leoni of A.D. was elected President. The inauguration of the new Government took place on March 11, 1964. Formation of a broad-based coalition government composed of A.D., U.R.D. (*Union Republicana Democratica*) and F.N.D. (*Frente Nacional Democratico*) was announced on Nov. 5, 1964. The F.N.D. left the Government in 1965 and U.R.D. in April, 1968. A general election held in Dec., 1968, was narrowly won by *Copei* and Dr. Rafael Caldera assumed the Presidency in March, 1969. *Copei,* however did not have a majority in Congress, and to some extent governed with the consensus of A.D., who were returned to power with a Congressional majority in the General Election of Dec. 1973. President Carlos Andrés Pérez's term of office lasts until March 1979.

Language and Literature.—Spanish is the language of the country. Some Venezuelan literature is of international repute. There are 44 daily newspapers in Venezuela, of which ten are published in Caracas, and about 60 to 70 weekly news magazines. There are also a large number of fortnightly, monthly and quarterly publications.

Education is free and primary education compulsory from the age of 7 years. There are ten universities in Venezuela, five in Caracas and the others in Maracaibo, Mérida, Valencia, Cumaná and Barquisimeto.

Production and Industry.—The produce of Venezuelan forest and fields includes the following: (*a*) Tropical forest region: orchids, wild rubber, timber, mangrove bark, balata gum and tonka beans. (*b*) Agricultural areas: cocoa beans, coffee, cotton, rice, maize, sugar, sesame, groundnuts, potatoes, tomatoes, other vegetables, sisal and tobacco. There is an extensive beef and dairy farming industry. The country does not produce all the grain it requires but is practically self-sufficient for its other food requirements.

The principal industry is that of *Petroleum,* which last year contributed 97 per cent. of Venezuela's foreign exchange income. Daily production of the oilfields was reduced by direct government policy in 1974, and this policy of reduction in offtake is to continue until 1976 as a conservation measure. Before the war of 1939-45 over 80 per cent. of the crude oil was exported to Netherlands Antilles refineries. In 1942 small refineries were established in Venezuela, capable of handling about 200,000 barrels daily. The large Shell plant at Punta Cardon went into production in February, 1949, and the Creole refinery at Amuay a year later. Both companies have invested heavily in desulphurization plant to satisfy anti-pollution measures in Eastern U.S.A., whither most of their product goes in the form of fuel oil. Other refineries are being operated at Caripitó, San Lorenzo, Puerto La Cruz, Tucupeido, El Chaure and El Palito. New contracts have been signed for exploitation of petroleum resources in parts of the Maracaibo region. The Venezuelan Government has unified income tax on firms involved in mining and petroleum at 60 per cent., and reformed the basis on which tax is calculated.

Rich iron ore deposits in Eastern Venezuela have been developed and production was 17,000,000 metric tons in 1972. Secondary processes for pelletizing and briqueting ore for export have been installed. The government-owned steel mill at Matanzas in the Guayana uses local iron ore and obtains its electric power from hydro-electric installations on the Caroni River. It produces seamless steel tubes, billets, wire and profiles. The production of more steel products is planned over the next few years. A new mill at Ciudad Guayana for the production of centrifugally-cast iron pipe came into operation at the end of 1970, with an annual capacity of 30,000 tons. It is planned to increase steel production to 15,000,000 tons a year by 1985.

Other industries include petrochemicals, gold, diamonds and asbestos; textiles and clothing; plastics; manufacture of paper, cement, glass and plate glass; beer and other alcoholic beverages; tyres, cigarettes, soap, animal feeding concentrates, non-alcoholic drinks, simple steel products, shoes, tins, jewellery, rope, metal and wooden furniture, sacks, paint and motor-vehicle assembly; preparation of pharmaceutical goods, lard, powdered milk, vegetable oil, flour, biscuits and other foods; fishing and fish-canning; pearl fishing, sanitary ware, electric home appliances, pumps, aluminium and aluminium products, toys, agricultural machinery, bicycles, electronic components, cosmetics and many others.

Communications.—There are about 39,563 km. of all-weather roads. The State has now acquired all but a very few of the railway lines, whose total length is only some 372 kilometres. Road and river communications have made railways of negligible importance in Venezuela except for carrying iron-ore in the south-east. However, the government now plans a new railway from Guayana to the industrial zones round Valencia for carrying steel. British, U.S. and European airlines provide Venezuela with a wide range of services. There are three Venezuelan airlines (two of them state-owned) which between them have a comprehensive

network of internal lines and also connect Caracas with the United States, Central America, South America, the Caribbean and Europe. In 1972 the Venezuelan state-owned merchant fleet had 16 ships with a total deadweight tonnage of 115,950. Foreign vessels are not permitted to engage in the coast trade. The telegraph, radio-telegraph and radio-telephone services are state-owned. There are one government-controlled, 96 commercial and one cultural, FM, broadcasting stations. There are three television stations in Venezuela, all in Caracas. One is government controlled.

FINANCE

	1972	1973
	(in millions of *Bs.*)	
Revenue	12,450	16,440
Expenditure	12,618	14,036

National income per head in Venezuela in 1973 was $U.S.1260, the highest in Latin America.

Currency.—The unit of currency is the gold *Bolivar* of 100 *centimos*. The selling rate for foreign exchange for all purposes is *Bs.* 4·30= U.S. $1. The rates for other currencies fluctuate according to their quotations against the U.S. dollar. The Government still subsidises the imports of certain basic commodities.

TRADE

	1972	1973†
Imports	*Bs.*9,301,000,000	*Bs.*10,895,000,000
Exports	13,060,000,000	23,418,000,000
	† Estimate.	

The principal imports are machinery, foodstuffs, durable and non-durable consumer goods, iron, steel and chemicals. The principal exports are petroleum and petroleum products, iron ore, coffee and cocoa, and diamonds.

Trade with U.K.

	1974	1975
Imports from U.K.	£50,311,000	£91,630,000
Exports to U.K.	135,226,000	165,425,000

CAPITAL.—Caracas (3,000 ft.). Population, 1971, 2,183,935. Other principal towns are ΨMaracaibo (650,000), Barquisimeto (330,000), Valencia (360,000), Maracay (250,000), San Cristobal (150,000), Cumaná (120,000) and Ciudad Guayana (150,000).

FLAG.—Three horizontal bands, yellow, blue, red (with seven white stars on blue band and coat of arms next staff on yellow band). NATIONAL DAY.—July 5.

BRITISH EMBASSY
Edificio La Estancia, Apartado 1246, Ciudad Comercial Tamanaco, Caracas.
Ambassador Extraordinary and Plenipotentiary, His Excellency John Lang Taylor, C.M.G. (1975).
Counsellors, P. W. Heap; D. A. Hamley (*Commercial*).
Defence Attaché, Cdr R. D. G. Williams, R.N.
British Council Representative, D. Aspinall.

BRITISH CONSULAR OFFICES
There are British Consular Offices at *Caracas, Maracaibo, Puerto La Cruz* and *Valencia.*

VIETNAM
(Socialist Republic of Vietnam)
President, Ton Duc Thang.
Vice-Presidents, Nguyen Luong Bang; Nguyen Huu Tho.
Prime Minister, Pham Van Dong.

Deputy Premiers, Pham Hung; Huynh Tan Phat; Gen. Vo Nguyen Giap (*National Defence*); Nguyen Dug Trinh (*Foreign Affairs*); Le Thanh Nghi (*Chairman of State Planning Commission*); Vo Chi Cong (*Marine Products*); Do Muoi (*Construction*).

EMBASSY IN LONDON
89 Belsize Park Gardens, N.W.3.
[01-586 2577]
Ambassador, (vacant).
Chargé d'Affaires, Lai Van Ngoc.
Attaché, Le Van Chan.

Vietnam, with an area of 129,000 square miles, and an estimated population of 43,700,000, is bordered on the north by China and the west by Laos and Cambodia.

Government.—Following the end of the war in Vietnam in 1975, and the establishment of a Provisional Revolutionary Government to administer South Vietnam, a National Assembly representing the whole of Vietnam was elected on April 25, 1976. The Assembly met in Hanoi on June 24, and on July 2 approved the reunification of North and South Vietnam under the name of the Socialist Republic of Vietnam. The national flag, anthem and capital of North Vietnam were unanimously adopted for the Socialist Republic, and Saigon was renamed Ho Chi Minh City.

A committee was elected to draft a constitution, pending the introduction of which the 1959 Constitution of North Vietnam applied to the whole country.

The President of North Vietnam since 1969, Ton Duc Thang, was elected President and Pham Van Dong was elected Prime Minister.

CAPITAL.—Hanoi (1,378,335).
FLAG.—Red, with yellow five-point star in centre.
NATIONAL DAY.—September 2.

BRITISH EMBASSY
16 Pho Ly Thuong Kiet, Hanoi
Ambassador Extraordinary and Plenipotentiary, His Excellency Robert Mathieson Tesh, C.M.G.
1st Secretary, I. F. M. Lancaster (*Consul*).

YEMEN
(Yemen Arab Republic)
Chairman of Command Council, Lieutenant-Colonel Ibrahim Mohammed al Hamdi, *assumed office,* June 13, 1974.
Prime Minister, Abdul Aziz Abdul Ghani.

YEMENI EMBASSY
41 South Street, W.1
[01-499 5246]
Ambassador Extraordinary and Plenipotentiary, His Excellency Mohammed Abdullah al-Eryani (1974).
Minister-Plenipotentiary, Abdul Wahab Mohammed Al-Shami.

Yemen, the *Arabia Felix* of the ancients, occupies the S.W. corner of Arabia between the kingdom of Saudi Arabia and the People's Democratic Republic of Yemen, with an estimated area of 75,000 square miles and a population of about 6,500,000 including about 1,250,000 emigrant workers in the Arabian peninsula and elsewhere, including the U.K. The highlands and central plateau of Yemen, and the highest portions of the maritime range, form the most fertile part of Arabia, with an abundant but irregular rainfall.

Trade.—The main exports are cotton, hides and skins, and cotton seeds. Imports from U.K. in 1975 were valued at £9,000,000.

The ruins of Marib, the ancient Sabæan capital and its dam are in the Yemen.

Government.—Following a bloodless military coup in Sana'a on June 13, 1974, a Military Command Council seized power. The Presidential Council resigned; the Constitution and the Consultative Council were suspended. On Oct. 23, 1974 the Constitution was revived, but the Consultative Assembly, whilst in theory reconvened, remained in suspense. The Command Council, no longer exclusively formed of military members, replaced the Republican Council as the supreme Constitutional body. In October 1975, by Constitutional Decree, the Chairman of the Command Council became Head of State and Commander in Chief.

CAPITAL, Sana'a (pop. 135,000). Other main cities are Taiz (80,000) and Hodeida (80,000).

FLAG.—Horizontal bands of red, white and black, with 5-point green star in centre of white band. (Adopted Dec., 1962).

BRITISH EMBASSY
Sana'a

Ambassador Extraordinary and Plenipotentiary, His Excellency Derrick Charles Carden, C.M.G. (1973).
1st Secretaries, D. Pragnell (*Commercial, Head of Chancery and Consul*); H. R. Leach, M.B.E.
Military Attaché, Lt.-Col. B. M. Lees (resides at Jedda).
Attaché, C. S. M. Shelton (*Technical Assistance*).
Vice-Consul, S. N. Lee.
British Council Representative, C. K. Smith.

YEMEN
(People's Democratic Republic of Yemen)
Presidential Council, Salim Rubi'a Ali (*Chairman*); Ali Nasser Muhammed; Abdul Fattah Isma'il.

Prime Minister and Minister of Defence and Education, Ali Nasser Muhammed.
Foreign Affairs, Mohammed Saleh Yafai Muti.
There are 13 other departmental Ministers.

EMBASSY
57 Cromwell Road, S.W.7
[01-584 6607]

Ambassador Extraordinary and Plenipotentiary, His Excellency Muhammed Hadi Awad.
Minister-Plenipotentiary, Abdullah Ahmed Muheirez.
Area and Population.—The Democratic Republic of Yemen lies at the southern end of the Arabian peninsula, having a frontier with the Yemen Arab Republic, and a coastline extending 700 miles from the Red Sea eastwards along the Gulf of Aden. The area is largely composed of mountains and desert. Rainfall is generally scarce and unpredictable. The population outside Aden is concentrated in the fertile districts. In the more extensive desert and near-desert areas nomadic communities depend on their livestock for a livelihood.

Included in the State are the offshore islands of Perim (in the Bab al-Mandeb Straits) and Socotra, formerly part of the sultanate of Qishn and Socotra, now merged in the People's Republic. Sovereignty over the island of Kamaran (area 70 sq. miles) in the Red Sea is under dispute following its occupation by forces of the Yemen Arab Republic during border conflicts in October, 1972. The area of the People's Democratic Republic is 180,000 sq. miles, with a population of 1,598,275 (Census, May 1973). The population of Aden alone (75 sq. miles) is about 250,000. The principal districts of Aden township are: Crater, Khormaksar, Tawahi, and Ma'alla. Neighbouring communities are at Sheikh Othman, Medinat al-Shaab, and Little Aden, which is linked to the main town by a

sandy strip of coastline, and is the site of a British Petroleum oil refinery. The other major coastal town is Mukalla.

Government.—The People's Republic of South Yemen was set up on Nov. 30, 1967 when the British government ceded power to the National Liberation front, thus bringing to an end 129 years of British rule in Aden and some years of protectorate status in the hinterland. Its name was changed to People's Democratic Republic of Yemen on Nov. 30, 1970. Territory of the Republic is that of the former Federation of South Arabia and the Aden Protectorates, consisting of the State of Aden and some 17 sultanates and emirates. It is now divided into six Governorates. Negotiations held between the British Government and representatives of the N.L.F. at Geneva from Nov. 21–29, 1967, ended in agreement on financial aid to South Yemen for civil and military purposes for a period of six months from the date of independence. Evacuation of British military forces which had begun in April, 1967, was completed on Nov. 29.

The Secretary-General of the National Liberation Front, Mr. Qahtan as-Shaabi, who had been appointed President from Nov. 30, 1967, held office until June 22, 1969, when he was deposed in a bloodless *coup d'état* and replaced by a Presidential Council led by Salim Rubi' a Ali. Under a constitution promulgated on Nov. 30, 1970, a Supreme People's Council of 101 members was appointed in May, 1971.

The Government receives substantial development and other aid from China, U.S.S.R. and other Socialist Bloc countries.

Kuria Muria Islands.—The Kuria Muria Islands, which had been administered by Gt. Britain from Aden although 200 miles distant from Yemen territory, were retroceded to the Sultanate of Oman on Nov. 30, 1967.

Production.—Agriculture is the main occupation of the inhabitants of the 60,000 square miles of the Republic, outside Aden town. This is largely of a subsistence nature, sorghum, sesame and millets being the chief crops, with wheat and barley widely grown at the higher elevations. Of increasing importance, however, are the cash crops which have been developed since the Second World War, by far the most important of which is long-staple cotton, which is now a major export, and revenue from which averages about £1,500,000 annually.

Under the Five Year Development Plan 1974–79 much importance is attached to the development of agricultural and fisheries projects. It is expected, that together, there will be a production increase of 54·1 per cent. by 1978–80 over the base year 1972–73. Light industries are being established which will replace imports and use locally produced raw materials.

Trade with U.K.

	1974	1975
Imports from U.K.	£5,968,000	£8,394,000
Exports to U.K.	8,118,000	3,630,000

Following the closure of the Suez Canal in 1967 the once prosperous trading economy of Aden fell into a steady decline, which has not been reversed by the re-opening of the Canal. The British Petroleum refinery exports almost 2,500,000 tons of petroleum products annually. In the main harbour, cargo handling for larger vessels is by lighter, but wharves at Maalla can accommodate alongside vessels up to 300 feet in length and 18 feet in draught.

Finance and Currency.—In the financial year 1974–75 revenue was estimated at about £18,000,000 and expenditure £38,000,000. Currency is the South

Yemen *dinar* (SYD), the total circulation of which is about £48,000,000.

Communications.—There are no railways in the Republic. Aden has 400 miles of good roads and construction of a further 300 miles will proceed under the Five Year Plan. A system of undeveloped but motorable roads links the towns and villages outside Aden. There is an international airport at Aden (Khormaksar) into which a limited number of international airlines operate.

CAPITAL.—Aden (population, 250,000).

FLAG.—A tricolour, red, white and black horizontal bands, with a triangle of light blue at the hoist pointing towards the fly and charged with a five pointed red star.

NATIONAL DAYS.—Independence Day, Nov. 30; Revolution Day, Oct. 14.

BRITISH EMBASSY
Khormaksar, Aden.
Chargé d'Affaires, John Single Martyn Roberts.
1st Secretary, W. J. A. Buckley (*Consul*).
3rd Secretary, N. Coleman (*Vice Consul*).

YUGOSLAVIA
(Socijalistička Federativna Republika Jugoslavije)

President of the Republic, President of the Presidency, President of the League of Communists of Yugoslavia, Chairman of the National Defence Council and Supreme Commander o f the Armed Forces, Josip Broz Tito, *assumed office,* Jan. 14, 1953, *re-elected for 4 years,* 1954, 1958, 1963, 1967 *and July 29,* 1971 (5 yrs.). In May, 1974 he was elected

President of the Federal Republic for an un-
limited term.
Vice President of the Republic, Vidoje Žarković (*elected
May, 1976 for one year*).
President of the SFRJ Assembly, Kiro Gligorov.
President of the Federal Executive Council, Džemal
Bijedić.
*President of the Socialist Alliance of the Working People
of Yugoslavia*, Dušan Petrović.
Vice-Presidents of the SFRJ Assembly, Marijan
Cvetković; Peko Dapčević; Sinan Hasani;
Branko Pešić; Rudi Kolak.
Vice-Presidents of the Federal Executive Council, Anton
Vratusa; Dobrosav Čulafić; Borislav Šefer;
Miloš Minić.
Secretary of the Federal Executive Council, Ivica
Čačić.
Foreign Affairs, Miloš Minić.
Defence, Nikola Ljubičić.
Internal Affairs, Franjo Herljević.
Finance, Momčilo Cemović.
Foreign Trade, Dr. Emil Ludviger.
Justice and General Adminnstrative Matters, Ivan
Franko.
Market and Prices, Imer Pulja.
President of the Constitutional Court, Nikola Sekulić.
Federal Committee Presidents:—
    Social Planning, Milorod Birovljev.
    Power and Energy, Dušan Ilijević.
    Agriculture, Ivo Kuštrak.
    Tourism, Milan Vukasović.
    Transport and Communications, Boško Dimitrijević.
    Economic Cooperation with Developing Countries,
    Stojan Andov.
    Labour and Employment, Svetozar Pepovski.
    War Veterans, Mara Radić.
    Health and Social Policy, Zora Tomić.
    Science and Culture, Trpe Jakovlevski.
    Information, Muharem Berberović.

LEAGUE OF YUGOSLAV COMMUNISTS
President, Josip Broz Tito.
Praesidium, R. Albreht; D. Alimpić; M. Bakali;
V. Bakarić; I. Balint; M. Baltić; D. Bijedić;
J. Billić; A. Čemerski; R. Dugonjič; S. Dolanc;
S. Doronjski; V. Djuranović; K. Gligorov; A.
Grličkov; F. Hodža; E. Kardelj; L. Koliševski;
T. Kurtović; N. Ljubičić; K. Markovski; B.
Mikulić; C. Mijatović; M. Minić; D. Petrović;
M. Popović; F. Popit; M. Planinc; D. Ristić;
D. Šarac; P. Stambolić; M. Spiljak; J. Smole;
J. Vrhovec; T. Vlaškalić; J. Vujadinović; V.
Zarković.
Executive Committee, J. Bilić; S. Dolanc; T. Kurto-
vić; D. Popović; V. Srzentić; A. Grličkov;
I. Kukoč; M. Mesihović; D. Popović; D.
Stavrev; A. Šukrija; D. Vidić.

YUGOSLAV EMBASSY IN LONDON
5–7 Lexham Gardens W.8.
[01–370 6105]
Ambassador Extraordinary and Plenipotentiary, His Ex-
cellency Gen. Bogdan Orescanin (1973).
Minister-Counsellor, Vladislav Jovanović.
Minister Plenipotentiary, Branko Komatina (*Eco-
nomic*).
Counsellors, Dušan Bogdanović (*Press and Culture*);
Momcilo Bajcetic (*Consular*); Petar Boskovic
(*Scientific*).
Defence Attaché, Col. Milos Surlan.
Ast. Defence Attaché, Lt.-Col. Miroslav Ribner.
First Secretary, Jovan Cvejić (*Consular*).
2nd Secretaries, Radoslav Maksimović (*Press and
Culture*); Jovica Prodanović.
3rd Secretary, Miss Sonja Biserko.
Consulate, 7 Lexham Gardens, W.8.

Area and Population.—Yugoslavia is a Federation
comprising the Socialist Republics of Serbia,
Croatia, Slovenia, Montenegro, Bosnia and Herzegovina, and Macedonia, Serbia includes the Socialist
Autonomous Provinces of the Vojvodina and
Kosovo. In July, 1946, Pelagosa and adjacent
islands with all territory east of the line known as
the *French Line* in Istria (including Pola and Fiume)
were ceded by Italy to Yugoslavia. By an agreement concluded in London on Oct. 5, 1954,
between Yugoslavia, Italy, the United Kingdom
and the United States, Zone B of the Trieste
Territory was transferred to the civil administration
of Yugoslavia, under whose military administration it had been since 1945. The area of Yugoslavia
is estimated at 255,804 square kilometres (98,725
square miles) and the population in June, 1975,
at 21,352,000. As a result of the war there was a
decrease of nearly 2,000,000 in the population of
Yugoslavia, and this loss has only recently been
made up.

Government.—On Nov. 29, 1945, the Constituent
Assembly of Yugoslavia at a joint session of the
Skupšatina and the House of Nationalities, proclaimed Yugoslavia a Republic. In January, 1953,
a new Constitution became effective, under which
two houses (the Federal Council and Council of
Producers) were established. Elections to these
houses were held in November, 1953 and March,
1958.

On April 7, 1963, a new Constitution was proclaimed under which the official name of the country
was changed to " The Socialist Federal Republic of
Yugoslavia". The existing two Councils of the
Federal Assembly were replaced by five Chambers
of 120 members each (Federal Chamber, Economic
Chamber, Educational-Cultural Chamber, Social
Welfare and Health Chamber, and Organizational/
Political Chamber), plus a Chamber of Nationalities
of 70 members. A Constitutional Court was
created. Elections to the new Federal Assembly
were held in 1963 and in April, 1967.

In 1969 the Federal Assembly was reconstructed
by the abolition of the Federal and Organizational/
Political Chambers and the addition of one new
chamber, the Social/Political. All Chambers continued to have 120 members each except the Chamber of Nationalities which doubled its size to 140.
Elections to this Assembly were held in April, 1969.
Several amendments to the Constitution were
made in 1971. The most important formed a new
ruling body called the Presidency. The intention
is that its members will take it in turns to become
President of the Republic for a period of 12 months
each. President Tito will however have the title
of Life President. A new Constitution was proclaimed in 1974 followed by the reconstitution of
the Federal Assembly, after elections based on the
new delegatory system, into two chambers consisting of the Federal Chamber (220 delegates) and
the Republican/Provincial Chamber (88 delegates).
A new Federal Executive Council (i.e. government)
was also formed.

Defence.—The Army, Navy and Air Force on a
peace footing consist of 222,000 officers and men.

Religion and Education.—The Orthodox, Roman
Catholic, Protestant, Islamic and Judaic faiths are
recognized by the State. The 1953 Census revealed
that 2,127,875 of the population were without
religion, 6,984,686 were Orthodox, 5,370,760
Catholic, 157,702 Protestant, 61,274 other Christians, 2,090,380 Moslem, 2,565 Jews, 495 other non-
Christians, 10,096 undecided and 130,740 unknown.
The Church is separated from the State. All religious instruction in schools has been forbidden
since January 1952. Priests are allowed to teach in

churches. Eight years' elementary education is compulsory and all education is free. In 1969–70 there were 14,043 elementary schools with 116,895 teachers and 2,854,579 pupils and 2,974 secondary schools (including adult and special schools) with 33,702 teachers and 801,169 pupils. In addition, in the 1970–71 academic year there were 13 art academies with 483 teachers and 2,225 pupils, 10 high schools with 557 teachers and 7,456 pupils, and 119 higher schools with 3,986 teachers and 79,325 pupils. There are nine universities: Belgrade, Zagreb, Ljubljana, Sarajevo, Skopje, Novi Sad, Nis, Pristina and Titograd.

Language and Literature.—The languages of the country are Serbo-Croat, Slovenian and Macedonian, all South-Slav tongues. Serbo-Croat predominates and is the language of the Federal Government. In Serbia, Macedonia and Montenegro the Cyrillic script is used and in the rest of the country the Latin; Hungarian, Turkish, Rumanian, Albanian, Italian, Slovak and Ruthenian are also used in certain districts. The desire for the political union of the South Slavs led to a cultural unity and a revival of Slav literature. There are 4

Serbian daily newspapers in Belgrade, 2 Slovene dailies in Ljubljana (Laibach), 2 Croat dailies in Zagreb, 2 dailies in Novi Sad, one in Hungarian, 2 dailies in Rijeka, one in Italian and daily papers at Skopje, Sarajevo, Priština, Split, Maribor and Osijek.

Production and Industry.—About 47 per cent. of the population is engaged in agriculture, although in recent years industry has expanded rapidly and industrial production has grown sevenfold since 1939. Recent emphasis has been on the integration of small industrial enterprises into more efficient complexes. In agriculture the main emphasis is on increased investment in mechanization and fertilizers in the large socially-owned agricultural combines but now the private sector is being encouraged to mechanize and become more efficient and small size tractors, farm machinery and implements are being supplied.

The main crops are wheat and maize, of which the yields in 1974 were 6,282,000 and 7,989,000 tons

respectively. The forest areas produced 17,430,000 cubic metres of cut timber in 1973. According to Yugoslav official estimates, the livestock population in 1974 was approximately as follows: cattle, 5,681,000; sheep, 7,852,000; pigs 7,401,000; poultry, 54,685,000. Minerals are an important source of wealth particularly in the central and south-eastern regions. Estimated production in 1974 included the following ('ooo tons): coal 33,583; coke 1,315; electrolytic copper 150; pig iron 2,126; steel (total) 2,833; aluminium 147; zinc 56; mercury 546 and crude petroleum 3,458.

Communications.—In 1973 there were approximately 10,400 kms of standard and narrow gauge railway and approximately 98,400 kms of classified roads. The 476 km. Belgrade–Bar railway was opened in June 1976. In 1974 there were 1,143,000 telephones in use in the country. The principal Ψports on the long Adriatic seaboard of Yugoslavia are Rijeka, Šibenik, Split, Zadar, Ploče, Dubrovnik, Bar, Kotor (Carraro) and Koper. A new port is still under construction at Bakar. The Danube forms a great commercial highway and the tributary rivers Sava and Tisa provide other shipping routes.

FINANCE

	1973	1974
	million *Dinars*	
Revenue	59,314	82,302
Expenditure	58,742	81,492

The rate of exchange is variable and in mid-1976 was 32/33 *dinars*= £1 (*see also* p. 84).

Trade with U.K.

	1974	1975
Imports from U.K.	£83,100,000	£94,200,000
Exports to U.K.	30,600,000	24,300,000

The chief exports to the United Kingdom are meat and meat products, textiles, furniture and timber. The main imports from the United Kingdom are machinery of all kinds, chemicals, wool tops and metal manufactures.

CAPITAL.—Belgrade, population (Greater Belgrade, 1971), 1,204,000. Other towns are Zagreb (602,000); Skopje (388,000); Ljubljana (258,000); Sarajevo (292,000); Novi Sad (214,000); Priština (153,000); Ψ Split (152,000); Ψ Rijeka (133,000); Titograd (99,000).

FLAG.—Five-point red star outlined by narrow yellow stripe, on a ground of three horizontal bars, blue, white and red. NATIONAL DAY.—November 29.

BRITISH EMBASSY

Generala Ždanova 46, Belgrade.
Ambassador Extraordinary and Plenipotentiary, His Excellency Sir Dugald Leslie Lord Stewart, K.C.V.O., C.M.G. (1971).
Counsellors, C. L. Booth; L. J. Middleton (*Economic and Commercial*).
Defence Attaché, Col. T. Holloway.
Naval and Air Attaché, Wing-Cdr. I. Scott.
1st Secretaries, A. M. Wood; G. D. G. Murrell (*Information*); S. T. Corcoran (*Labour*) (*resident at* Athens); D. J. Young (*Admin. and Consular*).
2nd Secretary, P. L. Thomas.
3rd Secretaries, A. Marshall; N. A. S. Jones.

BRITISH CONSULAR OFFICES

There are British Consular Offices at *Belgrade, Zagreb* and *Split.*

British Council Representative, Dr. D. S. Coombs, Generala Ždanova 34, Belgrade. British Council Reading Room Knez Mihajlova 45, Belgrade. There are also a centre and library at *Zagreb.*

ZAIRE
(The Republic of Zaire)

President of the Republic and Minister of Defence, Gen. Mobutu Sésé Seko, *born* Oct. 30, 1930; *assumed office* November 25, 1965; *elected for 7-year term*, Nov. 5, 1970.

CABINET
(As at Feb. 1976)

Political Affairs, Engulu Baangampongo Bakokele Lokanga.

Foreign Affairs and International Cooperation, Nguza Karl-I-Bond.

National Orientation, Mandungu Bulu Nyati.

Justice, Mulenda Shamwenge Mutebi.

Sports, Elonga Mali Mazungu.

Finance, Bofosa W'Amb'Ea Nkoso.

National Economy and Industry, Mwarairi Mitima Taneno.

Mines, Brig.-Gen. Molongya Mayi Kusa Moi Bongenye.

Agriculture, Kayinga Onsi Ndal.

Trade, Duga Kugbeto Lo.

National Education, Mbula Nzenge Mokwambe.

Public Works and Land Management, Takizala Luyanu Musimbimbi.

Transport and Communications, Dzbo Kaloji.

Land Affairs, Mbala Mbaba.

Energy, Muntu Kakubi Tshiono Kabaza Wa Mintege.

Public Health, Ngweti Kinkela.

Labour and Social Security, Bokonga Ekanga Botombele.

Posts and Telecommunications, Col. Wabali Bakitambisa.

Culture and Arts, Citoyenne Mbemba Yowa Mabinda Kapinga.

Environment, Conservation of Nature and Tourism, Citoyenne Lessedjina Kiaba Lema.

State Portfolio, Mambu Ma Nkenzu Makwala.

ZAIRE EMBASSY
26 Chesham Place, S.W.1.
[01-235 6137]

Ambassador Extraordinary and Plenipotentiary, His Excellency Kaninda Mpumbua Tshingomba, G.C.V.O.

The State of the Congo, founded in 1885, became a Belgian Colony on Nov. 15, 1908, and was administered by Belgium until June 30, 1960, when it became the Democratic Republic of the Congo. In October 1971 the name changed to the Republic of Zaire. Situated between long. 12°–31° E. and lat. 5° N.–13° S., the Zairian Republic comprises an area of 905,582 sq. miles, with a population (Census, 1970) of 21,637,000, including 932,000 foreigners. The State is divided into 8 provinces (*see* below).

Government.—On June 30, 1960, the Belgian Congo became an independent unitary state under the Presidency of M. Kasavubu with a provisional constitution, the *Loi Fondamentale*, drawn up by the metropolitan Belgian Parliament. On July 11, M. Moise Tshombe announced the independence of the State of Katanga although he failed to obtain international recognition. Katanga did not come under the Government at Leopoldville until January 14, 1963.

The constitutional and political situation remained unsettled, the United Nations having mixed forces in the country until 1964. By the middle of 1965, the Congolese Government formed by M. Tshombe in July, 1964, had succeeded in gaining control of all the towns from the rebels and depriving them of military aid from outside the Congo. At elections held in the spring of 1965 the Government party won an overall majority of 86, but the

elections in three provinces were annulled on the grounds that they had been irregularly conducted. Following fresh elections held in these provinces in August, 1965, M. Tshombe's Government was dismissed by the President. A new Cabinet was formed by M. Evariste Kimba on October 19 and held office until the deposition on Nov. 25 of the President.

General Joseph-Desiré Mobutu, Commander-in-Chief of the Congolese National Army, announced on November 25, 1965, that he had assumed the Presidency. After re-organizations in Dec. 1966, and Oct. 5, 1967, a new Cabinet, with the President again as Prime Minister, took office on Mar. 5, 1969.

The office of Prime Minister was later dropped and a Presidential régime instituted. The *Mouvement Populaire de la Révolution*, formed in 1967, was made the sole political party. With its deliberative assembly, the Party Congress, it is the supreme political institution of the country. Its executive body, the 15-man Political Bureau, is headed by the President and takes precedence over the single-chamber 420-person National Assembly as well as over the Government. The President changed his name to Mobutu Sésé Séko Kuku Ngbendu Wa Zabanga in 1972, but is usually known by the first three of these names only.

Climate.—Apart from the coastal district in the West which is fairly dry, the rainfall averages between 60 and 80 inches. The average temperature is about 80° F., but in the South the winter temperature can fall nearly to freezing point. There has been some increase in sleeping-sickness since independence. Malaria, formerly under control in Leopoldville (*now* Kinshasa) and Matadi, has also begun to increase.

Extensive forest covers the central districts.

Provinces.—On December 24, 1966, the number of provinces was reduced from 21 to 8, each under a Governor and provincial administration. They have recently been redesignated as "regions" and are now as follows with names of capitals in brackets: Bas-Zaire (*Matadi*); Bandundu (*Bandundu*); Equateur (*Mbandaka*); Haut-Zaire (*Kisangani*); Kivu (*Bukavu*); Shaba, *formerly* Katanga (*Lubumbashi*); East Kasai (*Mbuji-Mayi*); West Kasai (*Kananga*).

Production.—The cultivation of oil palms is widespread, palm oil being the most important agricultural cash product. Rubber, coffee, cocoa and timber are the next most important agricultural exports. The production of cotton, pyrethrum and copal fell sharply on independence but is now

increasing. The country is rich in minerals, particularly Shaba (*ex*-Katanga) province. Copper is widely exploited and is the country's major source of foreign exchange earnings. Extensive radium deposits exist near Lubumbashi and reef-gold exists in the north-east of the country.

There is a wide variety of small but flourishing secondary industries, the main products being: cotton fabrics, blankets, sacks, footwear, beer, cigarettes, cement, paint, sugar, furniture, metal goods and tyres, and local assembly of motor vehicles is now beginning. There are very large reserves of hydro-electric power and the huge Inga dam on the river Zaire is now supplying electricity to Matadi and Kinshasa.

The chief exports are copper, palm oil and palm-kernels, coffee, diamonds, rubber, cobalt, cassiterite, zinc and other metals.

Currency.—The present unit of currency, the *Zaire*, was introduced in 1967, replacing 1,000 Old Congolese francs. In March 1976 it was divorced from the U.S. dollar and devalued to a parity of 1 *Zaire*=1 S.D.R. Rate against Sterling, £1= 1·60 Zaire.

Trade with U.K.

	1974	1975
Imports from U.K....	£20,428,000	£23,609,000
Exports to U.K......	36,496,000	29,933,000

Language, Religion and Education.—The people are mainly of Bantu-Negro stock, divided into semi-autonomous tribes, each speaking a Bantu tongue.

Swahili, a Bantu dialect with an admixture of Arabic, is the nearest approach to a common language in the East and South, while Lingala is the language of Kinshasa, and of a large area along the river and in the north. It is estimated there are 5,000,000 African Christians in the Republic (Roman Catholic 4,200,000, Protestant 800,000). The local Kimbanguist religion has over a million adherents. The National University of Zaire has campuses in Kinshasa, Kisangani and Lubumbashi, with approximately 12,000 students.

CAPITAL, Kinshasa (*formerly* Leopoldville), population (estimated, 1971) 1,300,000. Principal towns, Lubumbashi (*formerly* Elisabethville) (182,638); Kisangani (*formerly* Stanleyville) (79,941); Likasi (74,478); Kananga (59,935); ΨMatadi (59,184); Kolwezi (47,712); Mbandaka (37,587); and ΨBoma (31,598).

FLAG.—Dark brown hand and torch with red flame in yellow roundel on green background.

NATIONAL DAY.—June 30.

BRITISH EMBASSY
Kinshasa.

Ambassador Extraordinary and Plenipotentiary, His Excellency Richard James Stratton, C.M.G. (1974).

Counsellor, D. J. Reid (*Consul General*).

Defence, Naval, Military and Air Attaché, Col. R. C Wigglesworth.

1st Secretaries, J. D. Massingham (*Head of Chancery*); T. E. Martin (Commercial); E. K. Green (*Vice Consul*).

EUROPEAN FREE TRADE ASSOCIATION (EFTA)

Member States: Austria, Iceland, Norway, Portugal, Sweden, Switzerland. Associate Member: Finland.

Following the unsuccessful attempt to create a European Free Trade Area linking the E.E.C. with other members of the O.E.E.C., seven European States above came together in 1959 to form the European Free Trade Association. The seven were Austria, Denmark, Norway, Portugal, Sweden, Switzerland and the United Kingdom. The EFTA Convention became effective on May 3, 1960, and just over a year later, on June 26, 1961, Finland became an associate member. Iceland applied for full membership in November, 1968, and acceded to the Association and to the Finland–EFTA Agreement on March 1, 1970.

In 1973 all the EFTA Member States entered into a new relationship with the EEC. Two—Denmark and the United Kingdom—withdrew from EFTA at the end of December 1972 to become members of the EEC on January 1, 1973. Agreements establishing industrial free trade between five of the other EFTA Member States (Austria, Iceland, Portugal, Sweden and Switzerland) and the EEC came into force on that same date. Similar agreements with Norway and Finland came into force on July 1, 1973, and January 1, 1974, respectively.

The Convention defines the objects of the Association as (1) to promote economic expansion in the area of the Association and in each member state; (2) to ensure that trade between member states takes place in conditions of fair competition; (3) to avoid significant disparity between member states in the condition of supply of raw materials produced within the area; and (4) to contribute to

the harmonious development and expansion of world trade and to the progressive removal of barriers to it.

Members agreed to reduce progressively their tariffs on imports of industrial goods originating in the area with a view to their complete elimination by January 1, 1970. They also undertook to abolish quantitative restrictions on imports of goods from the free trade area. Provision was made for alterations in these timetables and in May, 1963, when tariffs had been reduced to 50 per cent. of the original rates, members agreed to bring forward the date when tariffs and quotas would be finally eliminated to December 31, 1966. Since that date therefore the member countries of the Association have constituted a virtually complete industrial free trade area. There is no common external tariff for the Association, each member country being free to fix the level of its tariffs against countries outside the area. The Convention includes rules governing the origin of goods manufactured in the area. It also contains provisions relating to the "rules of competition"—government subsidies, restrictive business practices, etc. There are special provisions relating to trade in agricultural and fish products.

The Council of EFTA consists of one ministerial or official representative from each member country. Each state has a single vote and recommendations must normally be unanimous. Decisions of the Council are binding on member countries.

Secretary-General, Charles Müller, 9–11 rue de Varembé, 1211 Geneva 20.

EUROPEAN COMMUNITY

The nine member states: Belgium, Denmark, France, Germany, Ireland, Italy, Luxemburg,
The Netherlands, the United Kingdom.

The beginnings of the European Community date from May 9, 1950, when Robert Schuman, France's Foreign Minister, proposed that France and Germany should pool their coal and steel in-

dustries under an independent ("supranational") High Authority, in a Community open to the membership of any other European country wishing to join. Not only Germany, but also Italy,

Belgium, the Netherlands, and Luxemburg accepted this invitation.

The Coal and Steel Community (ECSC), Common Market and Euratom share a single institutional framework: a Commission, Council of Ministers, Parliament and Court of Justice. The core of the Community policymaking process is the "dialogue" between the Commission, which initiates and implements policy, and the Council of Ministers, which takes major policy decisions. The beginnings of democratic control are exercised by the European Parliament, while the Court of Justice ensures the rule of law and is the final arbiter in all matters arising from the Community Treaties.

Since the start of the Common Market and Euratom in 1958, the Parliament and Court of Justice have been common to all three Communities. Up to July, 1967, each Community had its own executive body (the EEC and Euratom Commissions, and the ECSC High Authority) and its own Council of Ministers.

In April, 1965, the Six signed a treaty providing for the merger of the three executive bodies in a single Commission and the three Councils in a single Council, with a view to the eventual merger of the three Communities themselves. The merger treaty came into force on July 1, 1967; the single Commission and single Council then took office. They enjoy the same powers under the three Community Treaties as did their predecessors.

On December 1 and 2, 1969, the Heads of State or Government of the Six met at the Hague and decided on the completion, strengthening, and, provided that other European countries wished to accept the Treaties of Rome, enlargement of the Community. They instructed the Commission to draw up a plan for economic and monetary union, and the Foreign Ministers to report by the end of July on possible moves towards political unification. They also resolved to intensify the co-ordination of research and development programmes.

In accordance with the Hague decisions the Council of Ministers agreed in April, 1970, that as from 1975 the Community would have its own revenue, independent of national contributions. The Foreign Ministers agreed (May, 1970) to hold formal political consultations twice a year.

In June, 1970, the Six invited Britain, the Irish Republic, Denmark and Norway to open negotiations on June 30 at Luxemburg on their applications to join the Community. Negotiations continued in 1971 and were concluded with the United Kingdom Government for all major questions by the end of June; on July 8, H.M. Government issued a White Paper on the results. On Jan. 22, 1972, the four applicant countries signed the Treaty of Accession in Brussels. Norway conducted a referendum on its Common Market entry and as a result withdrew its application. The enlarged Community of the Nine came into existence on Jan. 1, 1973.

With the advent of a Labour Government in the U.K. in 1974, there followed a period of renegotiation of the terms of Britain's entry into the Community, culminating in a referendum on June 5, 1975, as to whether or not the country should remain a member of the E.E.C. The result of the referendum showed two to one in favour of staying in. British Labour Party representatives who had hitherto boycotted the European Parliament now took up their 18 allotted seats.

In January 1976 the European Parliament approved a Report urging direct elections to the Parliament in 1978. On July 12–13, 1976, the Heads of Government or State, meeting in European Council, decided to approve a 410 member Parliament with Britain, France, West Germany and Italy allocated 81 seats each; the Netherlands 25, Belgium 24, Denmark 16, Ireland 15 and Luxemburg 6. Mr. Roy Jenkins was expected to be appointed President of the European Commission in 1977.

The "European Council", an addition to the institutionalized meetings provided under the Treaties, evolved from the "summit" conference of December 1974, when the Heads of Government decided to meet at least three times a year in order to deal with Community problems and with matters requiring political co-operation.

At the end of 1975 Mr. Leo Tindemans, the Belgian Prime Minister, who had been invited to prepare a report on *European Union* submitted his conclusions. The Report was discussed by the European Council during 1976, but no immediate action was taken on it.

OFFICE OF THE UNITED KINGDOM PERMANENT REPRESENTATIVE TO THE EUROPEAN COMMUNITIES
Rond-point Robert Schuman 6, 1040 Brussels
Ambassador and U.K. Permanent Representative, Sir Donald Maitland, C.M.G., O.B.E. (1975).

The Commission

On July 1, 1970, the Commission was reduced from 14 members to nine, two each from Germany, France, and Italy, and one each from Belgium, the Netherlands and Luxemburg. After the three new countries joined, the number rose to 13, with two seats each from Britain, France, Germany, and Italy and one each for the other members.

The members of the Commission are appointed by agreement among the nine member governments for a four-year renewable term; the president and vice-presidents are appointed from among the members for a two-year term, also renewable.

The members of the Commission are pledged to independence of the governments and of national or other particular interests. They accept joint responsibility for their decisions, which are taken by majority vote.

In addition to being the initiator of Community action and having specific powers, the Commission acts as a mediator between the member governments in Community affairs and is the guardian of the Community Treaties.

Commission of the European Communities
200 Rue de la Loi, Brussels 1049
President, François-Xavier Ortoli (French).
Vice-Presidents, Wilhelm Haferkamp (German); Carlo Scarascia Mugnozza (Italian); Sir Christopher Soames (British); Patrick Hillery (Irish); Henri Simonet (Belgian).

The Commission maintains information offices in London (20 Kensington Palace, Gardens, W.8), Washington (Suite 707, 2100 M Street, N.W., Washington, D.C. 20037), New York (277 Park Avenue, New York, N.Y. 10017) and other cities.

The new 13-member Commission was appointed by the Government of the Nine and was sworn in on Jan. 9, 1973.

The Council of Ministers
170 Rue de la Loi, 1040 Brussels

This consists of ministers from each member government, the ministers concerned depending on the subject under discussion. It is the Community's main decision-taking body but its authority is not as great in ECSC matters as in those relating to the European Economic Community and Euratom. The powers of the Commission are proportionately greater under the ECSC Treaty. For coal and steel, decisions are usually by majority vote; on E.E.C. and Euratom matters decisions usually had to be unanimous in the early stages but many decisions can now be taken by a qualified majority vote. For certain important questions,

however, unanimity is still required. (Admission of new members is not decided by the Council, but by a unanimous decision of the member governments.) Although the Council is the Community's ultimate decision-taking body, in almost all cases it can act only on the basis of proposals submitted by the Commission. The Council acts by issuing (a) " regulations " which are generally and directly binding throughout the Community; (b) " directives " which set out the aims of policy but leave national governments to implement; (c) " decisions " which bind only those addressed (normally member states); (d) " recommendations " and (e) " opinions ", which have no binding force. The meetings of the Council are prepared by a Committee of Permanent Representatives of the member states.

The Presidency of the Council is held in rotation for periods of six months.

European Parliament

Secretariat: Centre Européen, Kirchberg, Luxemburg.

The first direct elections to the European Parliament are due to be held in mid-1978. Of 410 seats, the United Kingdom, France, Germany and Italy will have 81 each, the Netherlands 25, Belgium 24, Denmark 16, Ireland 15 and Luxemburg 6. At present the Parliament which meets in Luxemburg and Strasbourg has 198 members nominated by the national parliaments of the nine European Community member countries—the United Kingdom, France, Germany and Italy have 36 each, Belgium and the Netherlands 14 each, Denmark and Ireland 10 each and Luxemburg 6. Set up under the European Coal and Steel Community Treaty of 1952, the Parliament's authority was extended by the 1952 Treaty of Rome to cover the European Economic Community and Euratom. It must be consulted on all major issues and has the right to dismiss the Commission by a vote of censure. Apart from general powers of supervision and consultation, it questions the Commission and the Council of Ministers and has a large measure of control over the Community's annual budget including its final adoption. It can reject the budget as a whole and can amend items of non-obligatory expenditure (i.e. expenditure not specified in the original treaties—amounting to some 20 per cent. of the total budget). The Members of the Parliament serve on a dozen specialised committees and currently sit in six political groups—Socialists, Christian Democrats, Liberals, European Conservatives, European Progressive Democrats and Communists. There are also six independents. *President,* Georges Spénale (*Socialist, France*).

European Court of Justice
Boîte postale 1406, Luxemburg

The European Court superseded the Court of Justice of ECSC and is common to the three European Communities. It exists to safeguard the law in the interpretation and application of the Community treaties, to decide on the legality of decisions of the Council of Ministers or the Commission and to determine violations of the Treaties. Cases may be brought to it by the member States, the Community institutions, firms or individuals. Its decisions are directly binding in the member countries. The nine judges of the court are appointed by the member Governments in concert and are partially replaced every three years, being eligible for re-appointment.

Judges, R. Lecourt (*President*); H. Kutscher; A. O'Keefe; A. M. Donner; J. Mertens de Wilmars; P. Pescatore; M. Sørensen; Lord Mackenzie Stuart; F. Capotorti.

Advocates-General, H. Mayras; A. Trabucchi; J.-P. Warner; G. Reischl.
Registrar, A. Van Houtte.

The European Investment Bank
2 Place de Metz, Luxemburg

The European Investment Bank (EIB) was set up in 1958 under the terms of the Treaty of Rome with the essential function that of contributing to the balanced development of the Common Market.

It grants long-term loans to enterprises, public authorities and financial institutions to finance projects which assist the development of less advanced regions and areas where the conversion or modernisation of older, exhausted industries is required. Another important role of the EIB is that of helping to finance projects which serve the interests of the Community as a whole or more than one member country (such as motorways, railways and telecommunications, development and diversification of the EEC's energy sources).

The members of the European Investment Bank are the nine member countries of the Community, who have all subscribed to the Bank's capital, which currently stands at 3543·75 million units of account.★ The funds required to carry out its tasks are borrowed on the capital markets of the Community and non-member countries, and on the international markets.

As it operates on a non-profit-making basis, the interest rates charged by the E.I.B. are therefore close to the average rates charged on the markets where it obtains its funds.

The Board of Governors of the European Investment Bank consists of Ministers nominated by the member countries, usually the Finance Minister, who lay down general directives on the policy of the Bank and appoint members to the Board of Directors, which takes decisions on the granting and raising of loans and the fixing of interest rates.

A Management Committee, also appointed by the Board of Governors, is responsible for the day-to-day operations of the Bank.
President, Yves Le Portz.
Vice-Presidents, Sjoerd Boomstra; Horst-Otto Steffe; Sir Raymond Bell; Giorgio Bombassei Fraseani de Vettor.
(The President and Vice-Presidents also sit as Chairman and Vice-Chairmen at meetings of the Board of Directors.)
Secretary General, Henri Lenaert.

★ The financial statements of the European Investment Bank are drawn up in terms of the European Unit of Account which in June 1976 was equivalent to £0·58.

EUROPEAN COAL AND STEEL COMMUNITY

This, the first of the European Communities, was established in 1952. Since then, for coal, iron ore and scrap, it has abolished customs duties, quantitative restrictions, the dual pricing system whereby prices charged on exported coal or steel differed from those charged to home consumers, currency restrictions and discrimination in transport rates based on the nationality of customers and the special frontier charges which made international transport of these goods within the Community dearer than transport within national frontiers. It has applied rules for fair competition and a harmonized external tariff for the whole Community.

In the period 1952 to 1968 Community steel production rose rapidly from 41·9 to 99 million tons. The coal industry, however, after expanding initially in conditions of acute energy shortage, found that a growing share of the energy market

was being won by oil. The task of the ECSC thus came to be to ensure the orderly retreat of coal at a price which would avoid social or economic dislocation. So far, since the start of the crisis, in 1957, the Community's coal industry has lost a third of its labour force. The ECSC has been especially active in meeting the social problems raised by such changes.

Between 1954 and 1973 joint expenditure in retraining and resettling or assisting the retirement of workers came to over £228 millions. ECSC loans in the same period helped to provide over 120,000 new jobs. New priorities, for avoiding further rundown in the coal industry and enhancing its status, have been put forward since 1973. The ECSC also conducts its own housing programme for coal and steel workers.

Decisions of the European Commission in ECSC matters are directly binding on the industries concerned. The Commission now supervises the smooth working of the common market in ECSC products, ensures that the Treaty rules of fair competition are observed, stimulates investment and research, and aids workers threatened with unemployment. The Paris Summit of 1972 recognized the need for the EEC to prepare an energy policy covering all sources. Attempts to formulate such a policy have become a dominant issue in EEC affairs since the energy crisis. Of the various forms of energy, coal falls within the competence of the ECSC, nuclear energy within that of Euratom and all others within the EEC.

The United Kingdom, Ireland and Denmark joined the ECSC on Jan. 1, 1973.

EUROPEAN ECONOMIC COMMUNITY (THE COMMON MARKET)

Discussions were held at Messina, Sicily, in 1955 between the foreign ministers of the six member states of ECSC (Belgium, France, Germany, Italy, Luxemburg and The Netherlands) on proposals for further advances towards economic integration in Europe, and after intensive study of these proposals, a treaty was signed at Rome on March 25, 1957, setting up the European Economic Community.

The Treaty aimed to lay the foundations of an enduring and closer union between the European peoples by gradually removing the economic effects of their political frontiers. The Common Market was established during a transition period of twelve years which ended on Dec. 31, 1969. The Treaty provides for the elimination of customs duties and quotas in trade between member states; the establishment of a common customs tariff and a common trade policy towards third countries; the abolition of the obstacles to free movement of persons, services and capital between member states; the inauguration of common policies for agriculture and transport; the establishment of a system ensuring that competition shall not be distorted in the Common Market; the co-ordination of economic policies; the harmonization of social and economic legislation to the extent necessary in order to enable the Common Market to work; the creation of a European Social Fund in order to improve the possibilities of employment for workers and to contribute to the raising of their standard of living; the establishment of an Economic and Social Committee which must be consulted on major proposals, consisting of representatives of employers, workers, consumers and other groups; the establishment of a European Investment Bank intended to aid investment in underdeveloped areas and help to finance modernization; and the association of overseas countries and territories with the Community with a view to increasing trade and to

pursuing jointly their effort towards economic and social development.

To date, this programme has been put into effect as follows:

Reduction of trade barriers.—A first 10 per cent. reduction in customs duties between member countries took place on January 1, 1959. Decisions taken by the Council of Ministers in May, 1960, and July, 1963, resulted in a speeding up of the rate of tariff cutting. On May 11, 1966, the Council of Ministers agreed that the abolition of internal duties should be completed on July 1, 1968, and this advanced target date was met. Quota restrictions on trade within the Common Market were completely removed on January 1, 1962. Customs tariffs between the three new member states and the original Six will be phased out by three stages ending in July 1977. A determined effort is being made to speed up the removal of non-tariff barriers to trade, *e.g.* different safety regulations and technical specifications.

Common external tariff.—The Common Market has a common external tariff (CET) which came into effect in July 1968 along with the abolition of customs duties among the Six, thus forming a customs union. The CET is based on the arithmetical average of those national tariffs it replaced, and after two international tariff-cutting rounds now stands at an average of 6 per cent. The three new members are gradually aligning their industrial tariffs up or down towards the CET and should join in full customs union by 1977.

In international tariff and trade negotiations in the GATT framework, the Community is represented by the Commission, which negotiates under a mandate from the Council of Ministers.

Trade between the six member countries of the E.E.C. increased from 6,864 million u.a. equivalent (unit of account=pre-1971 U.S. $) to 112,251 million u.a. in 1972. Community exports to the rest of the world increased from 15,911 u.a. equivalent in 1958 to 56,681 million u.a. in 1972; imports rose to 52,526 million u.a. in 1972.

Although the Community was enlarged in 1973, the oil crisis of that year affected the trading pattern with the onset of economic recession in some of the member States. Levelling off of demand during 1975 reduced overall imports by 3 per cent., while exports rose by only 2 per cent. over 1974 to 225 bn. u.a. The Community's trade with the rest of the world, however, was marked by a 6 per cent. decline in imports (mainly oil) to 117·8 bn. u.a., while exports rose by 5 per cent. to 113·98 bn. u.a.

The deficit in the overall trade balance of the Community contracted to about 2·89 bn. u.a. in 1975 from 14·5 bn. u.a. in 1974. Excluding internal E.E.C. trade, the Community's 1975 external trade deficit shrank to 3·82 bn. u.a. from 15·8 bn. u.a. in 1974.

Free movement of labour.—Freedom of movement for workers was achieved within the Common Market in July 1968, and those who work in member countries other than their own are ensured of rights equal to those of local workers, and of full transferability of social security benefits. They enjoy equal treatment in applying for jobs and receive priority over workers from non-member countries.

Services.—The right of Community firms to establish business in member countries other than their own is being progressively freed, as is the right of Community citizens to engage in professional activities in member countries other than their own. In parallel with this programme, the mutual recognition of professional qualifications is being achieved. Freedom of establishment for a number

of liberal professions was delayed for years, but with provision by the end of 1976 for doctors to practise throughout the Community, progress elsewhere may improve.

Capital.—So far unconditional and complete freedom of movement has been achieved for direct investments, transfers of personal funds and emigrants' remittances, short and medium term commercial loans and the buying and selling of stocks and shares. For other transactions, such as capital issues, there is conditional liberalization. Progress is being made towards equalizing access to domestic capital markets within the Nine.

Rules for Fair Competition.—The Common Market Treaty bans agreements which prevent, restrain or distort competition and, in particular, price-fixing, market-sharing, restriction of production or of technical development and discriminatory supply conditions if they are likely to affect trade between member states. The abuse of a dominant position in the market by a firm or firms is also banned. Implementing regulations adopted by the Council have caused some 36,000 restrictive agreements to be registered with the Commission. Decisions banning or authorizing particular agreements have begun to be taken, and a body of case-law is being established.

Agriculture.—The basic machinery for a common organization of agricultural markets throughout the Community was established by decision of the Council of Ministers in January 1962. It involved the setting of target prices, support buying, levies on imports, and export rebates. Community funds can be allotted for the modernization of farming and the improvement of agricultural productivity in the Community.

Under a decision reached in December, 1964, common price levels throughout the Community came into effect in July, 1967, for grains, pigmeat, and eggs and poultry. Further decisions taken on July 24, 1966, established common marketing regulations and common price levels for fruit and vegetables, sugar, dairy produce and fats and oils; to come into force between July 1, 1967, and July 1, 1968. On July 24, also, common price levels were fixed for beef and veal, milk and other dairy produce.

On July 1, 1967, grains, pigmeat, eggs and poultry reached the full single-market stage, thus bringing half the Community's farm production under the common agricultural policy's marketing and financial provisions. On May 29, 1968, the Six agreed on the pricing system for dairy produce and beef and veal in the single-market stage from July 1, 1968, having failed to agree by the original planned date of May 1. The policy has developed and changed along the lines of the 1975 "stocktaking" of the common agricultural policy, which aimed to reduce the cost of the policy and tailor it to changing priorities.

Firm proposals accepted in principle in March, 1971 and formally adopted in March, 1972 provided for Community part-financing of pensions for farmers retiring between the ages of 55 and 65 and other measures to reduce the number of small, scattered farms and to improve agricultural efficiency by offering modernization aid. The Community has now adopted a hill farming policy which applies to difficult farming areas throughout the Nine.

Economic Policy.—Member States are required by the Treaty to consider their economic policies as a matter of common concern and to consult their partners and the Commission in the concertation of these policies. From 1959 regular discussions took place in the Monetary Committee (senior officials from the national treasuries and Central Banks), the Central Bank Committee and others devoted to economic policy (later, in 1974, replaced by a single committee, the Economic Policy Committee). Regular finance ministers' meetings were held.

Following the currency crisis of 1969 and the Hague Summit, a short-term reserve fund of $2,000 millions was set up. Then, in 1971, the Six embarked on the first steps towards Economic and Monetary Union. The Werner Plan (named after the Luxemburg Prime Minister who chaired the Committee) laid down the path to be followed in the first phase up to 1973; establishment of a $2,000 million medium-term reserve pool; intensification of short-term monetary policy co-ordination; concertation in international affairs; the progressive harmonisation of taxes and budgetary affairs; and the centrepiece, the narrowing of the permitted margin of fluctuation of members' currencies from the central rate from 4·5 per cent. (world margin) to 2·25 per cent.

The goal of economic and monetary union was affirmed by the 1972 Summit of the Nine, and the target date of 1980 affixed. But by this time (long before the Nine were due to move towards the second phase in December 1973) the international monetary crisis, devaluation of the dollar and floating of the EEC currencies in 1971 had curtailed further progress towards EMU. The floating, first of the Pound Sterling and then of the Lira in 1972, outside the joint float of EEC currencies, left only six countries effectively coordinating their monetary policies. Between January 1974 when France allowed the franc to float separately and July when the franc rejoined the "snake" or fluctuation margin, there were only five.

During 1973 the Nine set up the embryonic Monetary Cooperation Fund but at the end of the year failed to consolidate this action by a significant pooling of reserves. By this time they were faced with the impact of quadrupling oil prices on their economies and prospects of world-wide recession. During 1974 and 1975 inflation, balance of payments deficits and their financing through "recycling", the coordination of policies internationally and structural economic problems occupied the centre of discussions. On October 21, 1974, the Finance Ministers agreed to launch an initial $3,000 million EEC loan to assist member states in balance of payments difficulties and help recycle "petrodollars" accumulating to the oil-exporting countries. The Nine heads of Government reaffirmed the goal of Economic and Monetary Union at the September 1974 Summit, but the weakness of sterling and the *Lira* and consequent wide fluctuations in the value of Community currencies hindered any practical move in that direction.

Industrial Policy.—The Council of Ministers has adopted a number of directives aimed at removing technical barriers to trade in foodstuffs and industrial products.

The Commission has put forward proposals for harmonizing company law and taxation and the creation of a European Company Statute, as well as proposals for the improvement, greater independence and cohesion of the Community aircraft, shipbuilding, paper and data-processing industries.

Transport.—The Treaty aims to establish a common policy on transport, with common rules for international transport within the Common Market, covering road, rail and inland water transport. Rates for freight which discriminate as to the national origin or destination of goods trans-

ported are to be eliminated within the transitional period. In June, 1965, the Council adopted a Commission proposal setting out the principles of a common policy to be put into force by the end of the transition period. The member governments did not agree on the implementation of these principles, but late in 1967 and early in 1968 a number of steps were agreed, on controlling social and economic conditions in intra-Community transport, especially road-haulage. Other measures covering railways were agreed by the Commission later in 1968 and early in 1969. In December, 1974, the Council agreed to lay down a uniform basis for calculating costs and financing railways. In the middle of 1974 substantial new road haulage quotas were agreed for the three new Member States.

Social Policy.—Under the Treaty, member states agree upon the necessity to promote improvement of the living and working conditions of labour so as to permit the equalization of such conditions in an upward direction. They also cooperate closely on matters relating to employment, labour legislation and working conditions, occupational training, social security, industrial accidents and diseases, industrial hygiene and trade union law. The main instrument for social policy is the Social Fund, established under the Treaty and reformed in 1972. Since then, the Nine's agreement in 1974 on the principles of a social action programme has enlarged the scope for the Fund's operation, which now includes special provisions for migrants, the handicapped, young and redundant workers. In the two years since the Programme was initiated in 1974 the Council has adopted a directive, due to come into effect by February 1977, seeking to ensure that no firm or public authority can dismiss or make redundant 10 or more employees without proper consultation with the trade unions; two directives require member States to introduce pay and equaity of treatment for men and women; pilot schemes have been introduced to test and develop new methods of helping the poor; and special help has been allocated from the Social Fund to offset unemployment among young people, as well as extra aid to the handicapped and migrant workers. The total budget for the Social Fund for 1976 is 440 million u.a. (approx. £183m). Under the rules of the Fund the Commission can assist in training and retraining schemes by reimbursing 50 per cent. of the cost financed by a public authority.

In 1975 a European Centre for the Development of Vocational training was established in West Berlin; in May 1976 the new European Foundation for the Improvement of Living and Working Conditions held its first meeting in Dublin, the first Community institution to be set up in Ireland.

Regional development policy.—On December 10, 1974, the Summit of the Nine meeting in Paris approved a Regional Development Fund of 1,300 million units of account (£540 million) to be spent over the three years (1975–77). The money will be used to help to provide or maintain jobs in the poorer areas of the Community; during the three years the Community will seek to coordinate the regional development policies of the Nine. By April 1976 the R.D.F. had committed 460 m.u.a. (£192m.) since it made its first grants in October 1975.

The Community's external relations.—Under its common external trade policy the EEC has trade agreements of varying kinds with the following countries: Argentine, Brazil, Uruguay, Mexico, India, Pakistan, Bangladesh, Thailand, Sri Lanka, Philippines, Spain, Yugoslavia, Egypt, Lebanon, Israel, Malta, Cyprus, Morocco and Tunisia. Some of these arrangements are being remade and new trade agreements being considered or negotiated with other countries including Syria, Jordan and Algeria in the context of the EEC's Mediterranean policy which will lead to links with 14 countries bordering on the Mediterranean. The first of these was concluded with the Maghreb countries of Algeria, Morocco and Tunisia at the end of April 1976.

In January 1975 the EEC completed negotiations for a trade, aid and cooperation agreement (Lomé Convention) with 46 developing countries of Africa, the Caribbean and the Pacific, among them 22 ex-Commonwealth countries. (Protocol 22 of Britain's accession Treaty had held out the offer of a relationship with the enlarged Community for these countries equivalent to that associating the 18 African French-speaking countries with the EEC under the Yaoundé Convention.) The convention came into force on April 1, 1976. A different kind of association—holding out the possibility of eventual membership—with Greece and Turkey dates back to 1961 and 1963.

Separate agreements, leading to an industrial free trade area by 1977, were concluded in 1972 with those members of the European Free Trade Association which did not seek candidature for EEC membership when Britain, Denmark and Norway filed their applications: Sweden, Finland, Iceland, Austria, Switzerland, Portugal. These were joined by Norway when the referendum went against entry in the autumn of 1972.

Member states' bilateral agreements with the East European state-trading countries (which was officially due to expire at the end of 1974) are still due to be reshaped into a common commercial policy. The first steps have been made towards this with agreement among the Nine on the draft outlines, or models, for agreements with each of these countries.

Political cooperation.—Cooperation on general foreign policy questions began through the machinery set up in 1970 (Davignon Committee), and takes the form of frequent meetings of the foreign affairs ministers of the Nine. They worked closely together at ministerial level and committee level during the years of preparation and the final summit at Helsinki of the Conference on Security and Cooperation in Europe. Actual military matters are not within the scope of political cooperation: all the members of the EEC except for Ireland are members of the Atlantic Alliance, although France is no longer a member of NATO's integrated military organization. Consultation on foreign affairs is exemplified by the EEC's joint positions on the Middle East, Cyprus and United Nations matters. The Community is also to participate as an entity in the Conference on International Economic Co-operation (North-South Dialogue) that is due to take place in Paris on December 16–18, 1976.

Scientific and technical collaboration.—In March, 1970, Britain and eight other European countries accepted an invitation by the Six to start discussing concrete projects for Europe-wide scientific and technical collaboration. Seven working parties have so far been set up covering data-processing, telecommunications, new forms of transport, metallurgy, pollution, meteorology and oceanography. The Paris Summit of October 1972 affirmed the aim of increasing collaboration in the fields of scientfic research and advanced technology. In May 1976 the Commission proposed a four-year rolling programme of research for the Joint Research Centre (JRC) centring on nuclear safety and the environment.

Enlargement.—The question of possible enlargement of the Community played an important part in its development from the autumn of 1961

when Britain, the Irish Republic, Denmark and Norway first sought membership, and Austria, Sweden, Switzerland, Spain and Cyprus sought association with the Community. The negotiations were vetoed by France in January, 1963. In May, 1967, Britain, the Irish Republic and Denmark formally submitted applications for Community membership. In July Norway followed suit and Sweden announced that it would seek to participate in the enlargement of the Community on terms compatible with its neutrality. These applications made very slow progress and appeared to come to a standstill when in December, 1967, France declared that Britain's economy would have to be strengthened before negotiations could begin. But shortly after taking office as President of France, Georges Pompidou stated in July, 1969, that there was no objection in principle to the admission of Britain to the Community. At the Hague " summit " meeting in December, 1969 (*see above*) the Six decided that provided that the completion of the Community was not prejudiced, and provided that the Community was strengthened to provide for enlargement, then the entry of other European countries would be desirable. After deciding on a common negotiating position, the Six invited Britain and the other applicants to begin negotiations for membership, and these were opened in Luxemburg on June 30, 1970, and settled in outline, as far as Britain is concerned, on June 23, 1971.

The Entry Terms.—A single overall transitional period of five years, during which the Three were to adopt Community rules and regulations, started on January 1, 1973, giving time for the gradual integration of the economies of the Three with the Six. The five-year period covers both agriculture and industry. The industrial tariff reductions take the form of five moves of 20 per cent., the first on April 1, 1973, a further three on January 1 of 1974,

1975 and 1976, and the final reduction on July 1, 1977.

The first 40 per cent. alignment on the Community's Common External Tariff (CET)—i.e. 40 per cent. of the difference between the new members' tariffs and the CET—was made at the beginning of 1974, and three further alignments of 20 per cent. each will follow the same rhythm as internal tariff-cutting, so that from July 1, 1977, the Three will apply the same tariffs as the Six on goods from non-member states.

EUROPEAN ATOMIC ENERGY COMMUNITY (EURATOM)

A second treaty, arising from the Messina discussions between the ECSC powers on additional means of co-operation, was signed in Rome on March 25, 1957, setting up the European Atomic Energy Community. The task of *Euratom*, defined in detail in the Treaty, is to create within a short period the technical and industrial conditions necessary to utilize nuclear discoveries and especially to produce nuclear energy on a large scale. Other sections of the Treaty cover the establishment and growth of nuclear industries, the procurement, ownership and control of nuclear materials, matters affecting health and safety, including training, and external relations, the stimulation of scientific research and the training of specialists, to assure through a Supply Agency adequate supplies of nuclear fuels, the supervision of the nuclear common market, inspection and control of the use of fissile material, and the safeguarding of both workers and the population at large by laying down basic standards for the protection of health. The United Kingdom, Denmark and Ireland joined Euratom on Jan. 1, 1973.

CURRENCIES OF THE WORLD

Country	Monetary Unit	Denominations in Circulation	
		Notes	Coins
Afghanistan.......	Afghani of 100 Puls	Afghanis 1,000, 500, 100, 50, 20, 10	Afghanis 5, 2, 1; Puls 50, 25
Albania..........	Lek of 100 Qindarka	Leks 100, 50, 25, 10, 5, 3, 1	Lek 1: Quindarka 50, 20, 10, 5
Algeria...........	Dinar of 100 Centimes	Dinars 500, 100, 10, 5	Dinars 5, 1; Centimes 50, 20, 10, 5, 2, 1
Angola...........	Escudo of 100 Centavos	Escudos 1,000, 500, 100, 50, 20	Escudos 20, 10, 5, 2½, 1; Centagos 50, 20, 10
Argentina........	Peso of 100 Centavos or 100 Old Pesos	Pesos 1,000, 500, 100, 50, 10, 5, 1; Old Pesos 10,000, 5,000, 1,000, 500, 100, 50, 20	Old Pesos 25, 10, 5, 1; Pesos 5, 1; Centavos 50, 20, 10, 5, 1
Australia........	Dollar of 100 Cents	$A 50, 20, 10, 5, 2, 1	Cents 50, 20, 10, 5, 2, 1
Austria...........	Schilling of 100 Groschen	Schillings 1,000, 500, 100, 50, 20	Schillings 100, 50, 25, 10, 5, 1; Groschen 50, 10, 5, 2, 1
Bahamas.........	Bahamian Dollar of 100 Cents	B.$ 100, 50, 20, 10, 5, 3, 1; Cents 50	B.$ 5, 2, 1; Cents 50, 25, 15, 10, 5, 1
Bahrain..........	Dinar of 1,000 Fils	Dinars 10, 5, 1, ½, ¼; Fils 100	Fils 500, 250, 100, 50, 25, 10, 5, 1
Bangladesh.......	Bangladesh: Taka = 100 Paise	Taka 100, 50, 10, 5, 1	Paise 50, 25, 10, 5, 2, 1
Barbados.........	Dollar of 100 Cents	$100, 20, 10, 5, 1	$1; Cents 25, 10, 5, 1
Belgium..........	Belgian Franc of 100 Centimes	Frs. 5,000, 1,000, 500, 100, 50, 20	Frs. 100, 50, 10, 5 1; Centimes 50, 25
Belize............	Dollar of 100 Cents	$20, 10, 5, 2, 1	Cents 50, 25, 10, 5, 1
Bermuda..........	Dollar of 100 Cents	$50, 20, 10, 5, 1	Cents 50, 25, 10, 5, 1
Bolivia...........	Peso of 100 Centavos	Pesos 100, 50, 20, 10, 5, 1	Peso 1; Centavos 50, 25, 20, 10, 5
Botswana	Pula	Pula 10, 5, 2, 1	
Brazil............	Cruzeiro of 100 Centavos	Cruzeiros 500, 100, 50, 10, 5, 1	Cruzeiros 300, 20, 1; Centavos 50, 20, 10, 5, 2, 1
Brunei...........	Brunei Dollar of 100 Sen	$100, 50, 10, 5, 1	Sen 50, 20, 10, 5, 1
Bulgaria..........	Lev of 100 Stotinki	Léva 20, 10, 5, 2, 1	Léva 2, 1; Stotinki 50, 20, 10, 5, 2, 1
Burma...........	Kyat of 100 Pyas	Kyats 25, 20, 10, 5, 1	Pyas 50, 25, 10, 5, 1; Kyat 1.
Burundi..........	Burundi Franc	Frs. 5,000, 1,000, 500, 100, 50, 20, 10	Frs. 10, 5, 1
Cameroon (Federal Republic of)	Franc C.F.A.	Frs. 10,000, 5,000, 1,000, 500, 100	Frs. 100, 50, 25, 10, 5, 2, 1
Canada...........	Dollar of 100 Cents	Dollars 1,000, 100, 50, 20, 10, 5, 2, 1	Dollars 1; Cents 50, 25, 10, 5, 1
Cape Verde Islands	Escudo of 100 Centavos	Esc 500 $00, 100 $00, 50 $00, 20 $00	Esc 10 $00, 5 $00, 2 $50, 1 $00, Centavos $50, $20, $10, $05,
Cayman Islands...	Dollar of 100 Cents	$25, 10, 5, 1	Cents 25, 10, 5, 1
Chile............	New Peso of 1000 old Escudos	Pesos 50, 10, 5; Escudos 10,000, 5,000, 1,000, and smaller	Escudos 100, 50, 10, 5, 1
China............	Renminbi or Yuan of 10 Jiao or 100 Fen	Yuan 10, 5, 2, 1; Jiao 5, 2, 1	Fen 5, 2, 1
Colombia........	Peso of 100 Centavos	Pesos 100, 50, 20, 10, 5, 2, 1	Pesos 5, 1; Centavos 50, 20, 10, 5, 1
Congo	Franc C.F.A.	Frs. 10,000, 5,000, 1,000 500, 100	Frs. 100, 50, 25, 10, 5, 2, 1
Costa Rica	Colon of 100 Céntimos	Colones 1,000, 500, 100, 50, 20, 10, 5	Colones 20, 10, 5, 2, 1; Centimos 50, 25, 10, 5
Cuba............	Peso of 100 Centavos	Pesos 100. 50. 20, 10, 5, 1	Centavos 40, 20, 5, 2, 1
Cyprus...........	Cyprus Pound of 1,000 Mils	£C5, 1; Mils 500, 250	Mils 500, 100, 50, 25, 5, 3, 1
Czechoslovakia....	Koruna (Crown) of 100 Halëru (Heller)	Korunas 500, 100, 50, 20, 10	Korunas 5, 2, 1; Heller 50, 20, 10, 5, 3, 1
Dahomey (Republic of)	Franc C.F.A.	Frs. 5,000, 1,000, 500, 100, 50	Frs. 100, 50, 25, 10, 5, 2, 1
Denmark.........	Krone of 100 Ore	Krone 1,000, 500, 100, 50, 10	Kroner 5, 1; Ore 25, 10, 5
Dominican Republic	Peso of 100 Centavos	Pesos 1,000, 500, 100, 50, 20, 10, 5, 1	Peso 1; Centavos 50, 25, 10, 5, 1
East Caribbean Territory	East Caribbean Dollar of 100 Cents	$100, 20, 5, 1	Cents 50, 25, 10, 5, 2, 1
Ecuador..........	Sucre of 100 Centavos	Sucres 1,000, 100, 50, 20, 10, 5	Sucre 1; Centavos 50, 20, 10
Egypt............	Egyptian Pound of 100 Piastres or 1,000 Millièmes	£E 10, 5, 1, ½, ¼; Piastres 10, 5	Piastres 10, 5; Millièmes 20, 10, 5, 2, 1
El Salvador.......	Colón of 100 Centavos	Colones 100, 25, 10, 5, 2, 1	Centavos 50, 25, 10, 5, 3, 2, 1

Country	Monetary Unit	Denominations in Circulation	
		Notes	Coins
Equatorial Guinea	*Ekuele*	E. 1000, 500, 100, 50, 25	
Ethiopia..........	*Ethiopian Dollar of 100 Cents*	Dollars 500, 100, 50, 20, 10, 5, 1	Cents 50, 25, 10, 5, 1
Falkland Islands...	*Pound of 100 Pence*	£10, 5, 1; 50p	As in U.K., except no 50p
Faröe Islands......	*Krone*	Kr. 100, 50, 10, 5★	As in Denmark
Fiji..............	*Fiji Dollar of 100 Cents*	$20, 10, 5, 2, 1	Cents 50, 20, 10, 5, 2, 1
Finland...........	*Markka of 100 Penniä*	Markkas 500, 100, 50, 10, 5, 1	Markkas 5, 1; Penniä 50, 20, 10, 5, 1
Formosa..........	*New Taiwan Dollar of 100 Cents*	NT$ 100, 50, 10, 5, 1	$5, $1; Cents 50, 20, 10
France...........	*Franc of 100 Centimes (1 Franc = 100 old Francs)*	Francs 500, 100, 50, 10	Francs 50, 10, 5, 1, ½; Old Francs 2, 1; Centimes 20, 10, 5, 1
French Community (Republics of Gabon, Congo Central Africa and Chad)	*Franc C.F.A.*	Frs. 10,000, 5,000, 1,000, 500, 100	Frs. 100, 50, 25, 10, 5, 2, 1
Gambia (The).....	*Dalasi of 100 Bututs*	Dalasis 25, 10, 5, 1	Dalasi 1; Bututs 50, 25, 10, 5, 1
Germany (East)....	*Mark der Deutschen Demokratischen Republik (M.) of 100 Pfennig*	M. 100, 50, 20, 10, 5	M. 20, 10, 5, 2, 1; Pfennig 50, 20, 10, 5, 1
Germany (Federal Republic of)	*Deutsche Mark of 100 Pfennig*	D.M. 1,000, 500, 100, 50, 20, 10, 5	D.M. 10, 5, 2, 1; Pfennig 50, 10, 5, 2, 1
Ghana...........	*Cedi of 100 Pesewa*	Cedis 10, 5, 2, 1	Pesewas 20, 10, 5, 2½, 1, ½
Gibraltar.........	*Pound of 100 pence*	£5, £1	As in U.K.
Greece...........	*Drachma of 100 Lepta*	Drachmae 1,000, 500, 100, 50	Drachmae 20, 10, 5, 2, 1; Lepta 50, 20, 10, 5
Guatemala........	*Quetzal of 100 Centavos*	Quetzales 100, 50, 20, 10, 5, 1; Centavos 50	Centavos 25, 10, 5, 1
Guinea (Republic of)	*Syli*	Sy 100, 50, 25, 10	Sy 5, 2, 1, ½
Guinea-Bissau (Republic of)	*Escudo of 100 Centavos*	Escs. 1,000, 500, 100, 50	Escs. 20, 10, 5, 2·50, 1; Centavos 50, 20, 10, 5
Guyana..........	*Guyana Dollar of 100 Cents*	Dollars 20, 10, 5, 1	Cents 100, 50, 25, 10, 5, 1
Haiti..............	*Gourde of 100 Centimes★*	Gourdes 500, 250, 100, 50, 10, 5, 2, 1	Centimes 50, 20, 10, 5
Honduras.........	*Lempira of 100 Centavos*	Lempiras 100, 50, 20, 10, 5, 1	Lempira 1; Centavos 50, 20, 10, 5, 2, 1
Hong Kong......	*Hong Kong Dollar of 100 Cents*	Dollars 500, 100, 50, 10, 5; Cents 1	Dollar 5, 1; Cents 50, 20, 10, 5
Hungary.........	*Forint of 100 Fillér*	Forints 500, 100, 50, 20, 10	Forints 10, 5, 2, 1; Fillér 50, 20, 10, 5, 2
Iceland...........	*Króna of 100 Aurar*	Króna 5,000, 1,000, 500, 100	Króna 10, 5, 1
India..............	*Rupee of 100 Paise*	Rupees 10,000, 5,000, 1,000, 100, 50, 20, 10, 5, 2, 1	Rupees 50, 10; Paise 50, 25, 20, 10, 5, 3, 2, 1
Indonesia.........	*Rupiah of 100 Sen*	Rupiahs 10,000, 5,000, 1,000, 500, 100; Sen 50, 25, 10, 5, 1	Rupiahs 100, 50, 25, 10, 5, 2, 1
Iran..............	*Rial of 100 Dinars*	Rials 10,000, 5,000, 1,000, 500, 100, 100, 50, 20, 10	Rials 20, 10, 5, 2, 1; Dinars 50
Iraq..............	*Iraqi Dinar of 1000 Fils*	Dinars 10, 5, 1, ½, ¼	Dinars 5, 1; Fils 500, 250, 100, 50, 25, 10, 5, 1
Ireland (Republic of)	*Pound of 100 Pence*	£100, 50, 20, 10, 5, 1; 10s.	New Pence 50, 10, 5, 2, 1, ½
Israel.............	*Israel Pound of 100 Agorot (formerly 1,000 Prutot)*	Pounds 100, 50, 10, 5, 1, ½; Prutot 500, 250, 100, 50	Pounds 1, ½; Agorot 25, 10, 5, 1; Prutot 250, 100, 50, 25, 10, 5, 1
Italy..............	*Lira*	Lire 100,000, 50,000, 20,000, 10,000, 5,000, 2,000, 1,000, 500	Lire 1,000, 500, 100, 50, 20 10, 5, 2, 1
Ivory Coast (Republic of)	*Franc C.F.A.*	Frs. C.F.A. 5,000, 1,000, 500, 100	Frs. C.F.A. 100, 50, 25, 10, 5, 2, 1
Jamaica..........	*Jamaican Dollar of 100 Cents*	$20, 10, 5, 2, 1; Cents 50	$1, Cents 50, 25, 20, 10, 5, 1
Japan.............	*Yen*	Yen 10,000, 5,000, 1,000, 500	Yen 1,000, 100, 50, 10, 5, 1

★ U.S.A. Currency also used.

Country	Monetary Unit	Denominations in Circulation	
		Notes	Coins
Jordan (Hashemite Kingdom of)	Jordanian Dinar of 1,000 Fils	J. Dinars 10, 5, 1, ½	Fils 250, 100, 50, 25, 20, 10, 5, 1
Kenya..........	Kenya Shilling of 100 Cents	Shillings 100, 20, 10, 5	Shillings 1; Cents 50, 10, 5
Korea, Republic of (South Korea)	Won of 100 Jeon	Won 10,000, 5,000, 1,000, 500, 100, 10, 5, 1; Jeon 50, 10	Won 100, 50, 10, 5, 1
Korea (North)....	Won of 100 Jeon	Won 100, 50, 10, 5, 1; Jeon 50	Jeon 10, 5, 1
Kuwait..........	Kuwait Dinar of 1,000 Fils	Dinars 10, 5, 1, ½, ¼	Fils 100, 50, 20, 10, 5, 1
Laos.............	Kip of 100 Ats	Kips 1,000, 500, 200, 50, 20, 10, 5, 1	—
Lebanon..........	Lebanese Pound of 100 Piastres	Pounds 100, 50, 25, 10, 5, 1	Piastres 50, 25, 10, 5, 2½, 1
Liberia..........	Liberian $ of 100 Cents	Dollars 20, 10, 5, 1 (U.S. notes)	Dollar 1; Cents 50, 25, 10, 5 1*
Libya.............	Libyan Dinar of 1,000 Dirhams	Libyan Dinars 10, 5, 1, ½, ¼	Dirham 100, 50, 20, 10, 5, 1
Luxembourg......	Franc of 100 Centimes†	Francs 100, 50, 20	Francs 250, 100, 10, 5, 1; Centimes 25
Macau..........	Pataca of 100 Avos	Patacas 500, 100, 50, 10, 5	Patacas 5, 1; Avos 50, 10, 5
Malagasy Republic	Franc Malgache (F.M.G.)	Frs. 5,000, 1,000, 500, 100, 50	Frs. 20, 10, 5, 2, 1
Malawi..........	Malawi Kwacha of 100 Tambala	KM. 10, 5, 1; Tambala 50	Tambala 20, 10, 5, 2, 1
Malaysia..........	Malaysian Dollar (Ringgit) of 100 Cents	Dollars 1,000, 100, 50, 10, 5, 1	Dollar 1; Cents 50, 20, 10, 5, 1
Mali (Republic of)	Franc Malien	Frs. 10,000, 5,000, 1,000, 500, 100	Frs. 25, 10, 5
Malta.............	Maltese Pound of 100 cents or 1,000 Mils	£M10, £M5, £M1	Cents 50, 10, 5, 2, 1; Mils 5, 3, 2
Mauritania........	Ouguiya of 5 khoums	UM 1,000, 200, 100	UM 20, 10, 5, 1, ⅕
Mauritius.........	Rupee of 100 Cents	Rs. 50, 25, 10, 5	R. 1; Cents 50, 25, 10, 5, 2, 1
Mexico..........	Peso of 100 Centavos	Pesos 10,000, 1,000, 500, 100, 50, 20, 10, 5, 1	Peso 25, 10, 5, 1; Centavos 50, 20, 10, 5, 1
Mongolian People's Republic	Tugrik of 100 Mongo	Tugriks 100, 50, 25, 10, 5, 3, 1	Tugrik 1; Mongo 50, 20, 15, 10, 5, 2, 1
Morocco..........	Dirham of 100 Centimes	Dirham 100, 50, 10, 5	Dirham 5, 1; Centimes 50, 20, 10, 5, 2, 1
Mozambique......	Escudo of 100 Centavos	Escudos 1,000, 500, 100, 50	Escudos 20, 10, 5, 2½, 1; Centavos 50, 20, 10
Nepal.............	Rupee of 100 Paisa	Rupees 1,000, 500, 100, 10, 5, 1	Rupee 1; Paisa 50, 25, 10, 5, 2, 1
Netherlands (The).	Florin (Guilder) of 100 Cents	Florins 1,000, 100, 25, 10, 5, 2½, 1	Florins 10, 2½, 1; Cents 25, 10, 5, 1
Netherlands Antilles (The)	N.A. Guilder of 100 Cents	Guilders 500, 250, 100, 50, 25, 10, 5, 2½, 1	Guilders 2½, 1, ¼, 1/10; Cents 5, 2½, 1
New Zealand.....	New Zealand Dollar of 100 Cents	N.Z.$ 100, 20, 10, 5, 2, 1	Cents 50, 20, 10, 5, 2, 1
Nicaragua........	Córdoba of 100 Centavos	Córdobas 1,000, 500, 100, 50, 20, 10, 5, 2, 1	Cordobas 1; Centavos 50, 25, 10, 5
Niger (Republic of)	Franc C.F.A.	Frs. C.F.A. 5,000, 1,000, 500, 100	Frs. C.F.A. 100, 50, 25, 10, 5, 2, 1
Nigeria (Federal Republic of)	Naira = 100 Kobo	N.10, 5, 1 and Kobo 50	k.25, 10, 5, 1, ½
Norway..........	Krone of 100 Ore	Kroner 1,000, 500, 100, 50, 10, 5	Kroner 5, 1; Ore 50, 25, 10, 5, 2, 1
Oman...........	Rial Omani of 1,000 Baiza	Rial Omani 10, 5, 1, ½, ¼; Baiza 100	Baiza 100, 50, 25, 10, 5, 2
Pakistan..........	Rupee of 100 Paisa	Rupees 100, 50, 10, 5, 1	Rupee 1, ½, ¼; Paisa 50, 25, 10, 5, 2, 1
Panama..........	Balboa of 100 Cents (= U.S.$)	As in U.S.A.	Balboa 1, ½, ¼, 1/10, 1/20, 1/40; Cent 1.*
Papua New Guinea	Kina = 100 Toea	Kina 10, 5, 2	Kina 1; Toea 20, 10, 5, 2, 1
Paraguay.........	Guarani of 100 Céntimos	Guaranies 10,000, 5,000, 1,000, 500, 100, 50, 10, 5, 1	
Peru.............	Gold Sol of 100 Centavos	Soles 1,000, 500, 200, 100, 50, 10, 5	Soles 10, 5, 1; Centavos 50, 25, 20, 10, 5, 1

* U.S. coins also circulate.   † Belgian currency is also legal tender.

Country	Monetary Unit	Denominations in Circulation	
		Notes	Coins
Philippines........	Philippine Peso of 100 Centavos	Pesos 100, 50, 20, 10, 5	Peso 1; Centavos 50, 25, 10, 5, 1
Poland...........	Zloty of 100 Groszy	Zlotys 1,000, 500, 100, 50, 20	Zlotys 200, 100, 50,20, 10, 5,2, 1; Groszy 50, 20, 10, 5, 2, 1
Portugal..........	Escudo of 100 Centavos	Escudos 1,000, 500, 100, 50, 20	Escudos 50, 20, 10, 5, 2½, 1; Centavos 50, 20, 10
Portuguese Timor.	Escudo of 100 Centavos	Escs. 1,000, 500, 100, 50, 20	Escs. 10, 5, 2½, 1; Centavos 50, 20, 10
Qatar............	Qatar Riyal of 100 Dirhams	Q.R. 500, 100, 50, 10, 5, 1	Dirhams 50, 25, 10, 5, 1
Reunion Island....	Franc (C.F.A.)	Frs. 5,000, 1,000, 500	Frs. 100, 50, 20, 10, 5, 2, 1
Rhodesia.........	Dollar of 100 cents	RH$ 10, 5, 2, 1	Cents 2½, 1, ½
Rumania.........	Leu of 100 Bani	Lei 100, 50, 25, 10, 5, 3, 1	Lei 3, 1; Bani 25, 15, 10, 5, 3, 1
Rwanda..........	Rwanda Franc	Frs. 1,000, 500, 100, 50, 20	Frs. 10, 5, 2, 1, ½
St. Helena	St. Helena Pound of 100 Pence	£5, 1	As in U.K.
Samoa (Western)..	Tala of 100 Sene	Tala 10, 2, 1	Sene 50, 20, 10, 5, 2, 1
St. Tomé and Princípé	Escudo of 100 Centavos	Escs. 1,000, 500, 100, 50, 20	Escs. 50, 20, 10, 5, 2½, 1; Centavos 50, 20, 10
Saudi Arabia......	Riyal of 20 Qursh or 100 Halalas	Riyals 100, 50, 10, 5, 1	Qursh 4, 2, 1; Halala 50, 25, 10, 5, 1
Seychelles........	Rupee of 100 Cents	Rs. 100, 50, 20, 10, 5	Rupees 10, 5, 1; Cents 50, 25, 5, 1
Sierra Leone......	Leone of 100 Cents	Leone 5, 2, 1; Cents 50	Cents 50, 20, 10, 5, 1, ½
Singapore........	S. Dollar of 100 Cents	$10,000, 1,000, 500, 100, 50, 25, 10, 5, 1	$10, 1; Cents 50, 20, 10, 5, 1
Solomon Islands...	Solomon Islands Dollar of 100 cents	Dollars 10, 5, 2	Dollars 1; Cents 20, 10, 5, 2, 1
Somali Democratic Republic	Somali Shilling of 100 Cents	S. Shillings 100, 20, 10, 5	Shillings 1, ½; Cents 10, 5, 1
South Africa (Republic of)	Rand of 100 Cents	Rands 20, 10, 5, 2, 1; £SA 100, 20, 10, 5, 1; 10s.	Rand 1; Cents 50, 20, 10, 5, 2, 1, ½
Spain............	Peseta of 100 Céntimos	Pesetas 1,000, 500, 100	Pesetas 100, 50, 25, 5, 2½, 1; Céntimos 50, 10
Sri Lanka (Ceylon)	Rupee of 100 Cents	Rupees 100, 50, 10, 5, 2	Rupees 5, 2, 1; Cents 50, 25, 10, 5, 2, 1
Sudan............	Sudanese Pound of 100 Piastres or 1,000 Milliemes	£S 10, 5, 1; Piastres 50, 25	Piastres 10, 5, 2; Milliemes 10, 5, 2, 1
Surinam..........	Guilder of 100 Cents	Guilders 1,000, 100, 25, 10, 5, 2½, 1	Guilder 1; Cents 25, 10, 5, 1
Swaziland........	Lilangeni (plural Emalangeni) of 100 cents	E. 10, 5, 2; L. 1	L. 1; Cents 50, 20, 10, 5, 2, 1
Sweden..........	Krona of 100 Ore	Kronor 10,000, 1,000, 100, 50, 10, 5	Kronor 10, 5, 2, 1; Ore 50, 25, 10, 5, 2, 1
Switzerland.......	Franc of 100 Centimes	Francs 1,000, 500, 100, 50, 20, 10, 5	Francs 5, 2, 1; Centimes 50, 20, 10, 5, 2, 1
Syria............	Syrian Pound of 100 Piastres	Pounds 500, 100, 50, 25, 10, 5, 1	Pound 1, ½; Piastres 50, 25, 10, 5, 2½
Tanzania.........	T. Shilling of 100 Cents	Shillings 100, 20, 10, 5	Shilling 5, 1; Cents 50, 20, 5
Thailand.........	Baht of 100 Stangs	Bahts 500, 100, 20, 10, 5, 1; Stangs 50	Baht 1; Stangs 50, 25, 20, 10, 5, 1, ½
Togo (Republic of)	Franc C.F.A.	Frs. C.F.A. 5,000, 1,000, 500, 100	Frs. C.F.A. 100, 50, 25, 10, 5, 2, 1
Tonga...........	Pa'anga (T$) of 100 Seniti	Pa'anga 10, 5, 2, 1, ½	Pa'anga 2, 1; Seniti 50, 20, 10, 5, 2, 1
Trinidad and Tobago	Trinidad and Tobago Dollar of 100 Cents	Dollars 20, 10, 5, 1	Dollar 1; Cents 50, 25, 10, 5, 1
Tunisia..........	Tunisian Dinar of 1,000 Millimes	Dinars 10, 5, 1, ½	Dinar ½; Millimes 100, 50, 20, 10, 5, 2, 1
Turkey..........	Turkish Lira of 100 Kuru	TL 1,000, 500, 100, 50, 20, 10, 5	TL 10, 5, 2, 1; Kuru 50, 25, 10, 5, 1
Uganda..........	U. Shilling of 100 Cents	Shillings 100, 50, 20, 10	Shillings 5, 2, 1; Cents 50, 20, 10, 5
United Arab Emirates	Dirham of 100 Fils	Dirhams 1,000, 100, 50, 10, 5, 1	Dirham 1; Fils 50, 25, 10, 5, 1
United Kingdom.. (See pp. 1209–10)	Pound of 100 new pence	£20, £10, £5, £1	Pence 50, 10, 5, 2, 1, ½; 5s. (25p); 6d. (2½).
United States of America	Dollar of 100 Cents	$100, 50, 20, 10, 5, 2, 1	$1; Cents 50, 25, 10, 5, 1

Country	Monetary Unit	Denominations in Circulation	
		Notes	Coins
Upper Volta (Republic of)	Franc C.F.A.	Frs. C.F.A. 5,000, 1,000, 500, 100	Frs. C.F.A. 100, 50, 25, 10, 5, 2, 1
Uruguay........	Peso of 100 Centésimos	Pesos 10, 5, 1, 0·50	Pesos 1,000, 50, 20, 10, 5, 1
U.S.S.R.........	Rouble of 100 Copceks	Roubles 100, 50, 25, 10, 5, 3, 1	Rouble 1; Copecks 50, 20, 15, 10, 5, 3, 2, 1
Venezuela.......	Bolivar	Bolivares 500, 100, 50, 20, 10, 5	Bolivares 100, 20, 10, 5, 2, 1, ½, ¼, ⅛, ¹⁄₂₀
Vietnam (North)..	Dong of 10 Hào or 100 Xu	Dong 10, 5, 2, 1; Hào 5, 2, 1; Xu 5	Xu 5, 2, 1
Vietnam (South)...	Dong of 100 Xu	Dong 50, 10, 5, 2, 1; Xu 50, 20, 10	Xu 5, 2, 1
Yemen (Arab Republic).........	Riyal of 100 Fils	Riyals 100, 50, 20, 10, 5, 1;	Fils 50, 25, 10, 5, 1
Yemen (People's Democratic Republic)	Southern Yemen Dinar (YD) of 1,000 Fils	YD 10, 5, 1; Fils 500, 250	Fils 50, 25, 5, 2½, 1
Yugoslavia.......	Dinar of 100 Paras.....	Dinars 1,000, 500, 100, 50, 20, 10, 5	Dinar 5, 2, 1; Paras 50, 20, 10, 5
Zaire (Congolese Republic)	Zaire of 100 Makuta or 10,000 Sengi	Zaires 10, 5, 1; Makuta 50, 20, 10	Makuta 5, 1; Sengi 10
Zambia..........	Kwacha of 100 Ngwee	Kwacha 20, 10, 5, 2, 1; Ngwee 50	Ngwee 50, 20, 10, 5, 2, 1

THE COUNCIL OF EUROPE

Headquarters: 67006 Strasbourg, France.   *Secretary-General*, G. Kahn-Ackermann.

A European organization founded in 1949 whose aim is to achieve greater unity between its Members to safeguard their European heritage and to facilitate their economic and social progress. The aim of the Council is pursued through discussion and common action in economic, social, cultural, educational, scientific, legal and administrative matters and in the maintenance and furtherance of human rights and fundamental freedoms.

The following 18 countries belong to the Council: Austria, Belgium, Cyprus, Denmark, France, the Federal Republic of Germany, Greece, Iceland, the Republic of Ireland, Italy, Luxemburg, Malta, Netherlands, Norway, Sweden, Switzerland, Turkey and the United Kingdom.

The organs are the Committee of Ministers, consisting of the Foreign Ministers of member countries: and the Parliamentary Assembly of 147 members, elected or chosen by the national parliaments of member countries in proportion to the relative strength of political parties. There is also a Joint Committee of Ministers and Representatives of the Parliamentary Assembly.

The Committee of Ministers is the executive organ of the Council. Certain of its conclusions take the form of international agreements or recommendations to governments. On certain major matters the Committee votes by unanimity but abstentions are permitted. Decisions of the Ministers may also be embodied in partial agreements to which a limited number of member governments are party. The Committee of Ministers meets twice yearly. All Ministers have appointed Deputies to act on their behalf. The Committee of Deputies meets monthly to transact business and to take decisions on behalf of Ministers. Member governments accredit Permanent Representatives to the Council in Strasbourg, who are also the Ministers' Deputies.

The Committee is a forum for discussion between member governments on political and other matters, supervises the work of the technical expert committees and considers recommendations received from the Parliamentary Assembly. The Assembly's conclusions may take the form of recommendations to the Committee of Ministers

or resolutions. Ministers, including Ministers other than those for Foreign Affairs, may address the Assembly and take part in its debates.

The Parliamentary Assembly holds three week-long sessions a year. It debates reports on, *inter alia*, political, economic, agricultural, social, educational, legal and regional planning affairs. The Chairman in office of the Committee of Ministers presents a report at each session. The Assembly also debates reports received annually from the O.E.C.D., other European organizations and certain specialized agencies of the United Nations. It holds an annual joint meeting with the members of the European Parliament of the " Nine ". Matters of mutual interest to the Committee of Ministers and the Assembly are discussed in the joint Committee. The Council's budget is voted annually in December and is met by agreed contributions of member countries.

One of the principal achievements of the Council of Europe is the European Convention on Human Rights (1950) under which was established the European Commission and the European Court of Human Rights. These organs have built up a valuable system of European jurisprudence in the field of Human Rights. Other major achievements of the Council of Europe are the European Cultural Convention (1953) and the European Social Charter (1960). Eighty-seven conventions and agreements have been concluded by the Council covering matters in all the fields of its competence, such as social insurance, equivalence of European diplomas for university entrances, equivalence of university degrees, public health patents, extradition, etc.

The Council's cultural and educational programme is administered by the Council for Cultural Co-operation to which in addition to members of the Council of Europe belong Finland, Portugal, Spain and the Holy See. A European Committee for Legal Co-operation administers the Council's legal programme. A few non-member states take part as observers in several of the Council's inter-governmental activities.

Permanent U.K. Representative, His Excellency Peter John Foster, C.M.G. (1974) £6,475

RETROSPECT OF SPORT 1975–76

OLYMPIC GAMES

The XXIst Olympic Games took place in Canada from July 17 to August 1, 1976. The Main Events were held in Montreal, and the Yachting in Kingston, Ontario. The following 21 Sports were included: Archery, Athletics, Basketball, Boxing, Canoeing, Cycling, Equestrian, Football, Gymnastics, Handball, Hockey, Judo, Modern Pentathlon, Rowing, Shooting, Swimming, Volley Ball, Water Polo, Weight-lifting, Wrestling, and Yachting.

Previous Games have been held as follows: I, 1896, Athens; II, 1900, Paris; III, St. Louis, 1904; IV, London, 1908; V, Stockholm, 1912; VII, Antwerp, 1920; VIII, Paris, 1924; IX, Amsterdam, 1928; X, Los Angeles, 1932; XI, Berlin, 1936; XIV, London, 1948; XV, Helsinki, 1952; XVI, Melbourne, 1956; XVII, Rome, 1960; XVIII, Tokyo, 1964; XIX, Mexico, 1968; XX, Munich, 1972; XXI, Montreal, 1976.

The VIth Games scheduled for Berlin in 1916, the XIIth for Tokyo and then Helsinki in 1940, and the XIIIth did not take place owing to World Wars. The XXIInd Games will be held in Moscow in 1980.

OLYMPIC GOLD MEDALLISTS 1976

ARCHERY

			points
Men's Double F.I.T.A. Round			
	D. Pace	U.S.A.	2,571*
Women's Double F.I.T.A. Round			
	L. Ryon	U.S.A.	2,499*

ATHLETICS

Metres	*Men's Events*		min. sec.
100	H. Crawford	Trinidad	10·06
200	D. Quarrie	Jamaica	20·23
400	A. Juantorena	Cuba	44·28
800	A. Juantorena	Cuba	1 43·5†
1,500	J. Walker	N.Z.	3 39·2
5,000	L. Viren	Finland	13 24·8[1]
10,000	L. Viren	Finland	27 40·5
20 km. *Walk*	D. Bautista	Mexico	1 hr 24 40·6*
Marathon	W. Cierpinski	G.D.R.	2 hr 09 55·0*
110 *Hurdles*	G. Drut	France	13·30
400 *Hurdles*	E. Moses	U.S.A.	47·64†
Steeplechase	A. Garderud	Sweden	8 08·0†
4 × 100 *Relay*	U.S.A.		38·33
4 × 400 *Relay*	U.S.A.		2 59·52
			metres/ft. in
High Jump	J. Wazola	Poland	2·25/7 4¾*
Pole Vault	T. Slusarski	Poland	5·50/18 0½*[3]
Long Jump	A. Robinson	US.A.	8·35/27 4
Triple Jump	V. Saneyev	U.S.S.R.	17·29/56 8¾
Shot	U. Beyer	G.D.R.	21·05/69 6½[2]
Discus	M. Wilkins	U.S.A	67·50/221 5*[4]
Hammer	Y. Sedyn	U.S.S.R.	77·52/254 4*
Javelin	M. Nemeth	Hungary	95·48/310 4†
Decathlon	B. Jenner	U.S.A.	8,618 points†

Metres	*Women's Events*		min. sec.
100	A. Richter	Germany	11·10 [5]
200	B. Eckert	G.D.R.	22·37*
400	I. Szewinska	Poland	49·29†
800	T. Kazankina	U.S.S.R.	1 54·9†
1,500	T. Kazankina	U.S.S.R.	4 05·5
4 × 100 *Relay*	G.D.R.		42·55*
4 × 400 *Relay*	G.D.R.		3 19·23†
Hurdles	J. Schaller	G.D.R.	12·77
			metres/ft. in.
High Jump	R. Ackermann	G.D.R.	1·93/6 4*
Long Jump	A. Voigt	G.D.R.	6·72/22 2½
Shot	I. Christova	Bulgaria	21·16/68 5¼*
Discus	E. Schlaak	G.D.R.	69·00/226 4*
Javelin	R. Fuchs	G.D.R.	65·94/214 4*
Pentathlon	S. Siegl	G.D.R.	4,745 points

Notes

[1] 5,000 *metres*, Olympic Record 13 min. 20·4 sec by Brendan Foster, G.B., in heat.

[2] *Shot* Olympic Record 21·32/69′ 11½″ by A. Barisnikov, U.S.S.R., in qualifying round.

[3] *Pole Vault* Olympic Record tied also by A. Kalliomaki, Finland, and D. Roberts, U.S.A.

[4] *Discus* Olympic record in qualifying round, 68·28/224′0″ by Mac Wilkins in qualifying round.

[5] *Women's 100 metres* 11·01 World and Olympic Record by A. Richter, Germany, in semi-final.

* Olympic Record † World & Olympic Record

BASKETBALL

Men: U.S.A. *Women*: U.S.S.R.

BOXING

Light-Flyweight	J. Hernandez	Cuba
Flyweight	L. Randolph	U.S.A.
Bantamweight	Y. J. Gu	N. Korea
Featherweight	A. Herera	Cuba
Lightweight	H. Davis	U.S.A.
Light-Welterweight	R. Leonard	U.S.A.
Welterweight	J. Bechfeld	G.D.R.
Light-Middleweight	J. Rybicki	Poland
Middleweight	M. Spinks	U.S.A.
Light-Heavyweight	L. Spinks	U.S.A.
Heavyweight	T. Stevenson	Cuba

CANOEING

(Men) Kayak

500 *Metres, Singles*—V. Diba, Roumania 1m 46·41 sec.

1,000 *Metres, Singles*—R. Helm, G.D.R., 3 48·20

500 *Metres, Pairs*—G.D.R., 1 35·87

1,000 *Metres, Pairs*—U.S.S.R., 3 29·01

1,000 *Metres, Fours*—U.S.S.R., 3 08·69

Canadian

500 *Metres, Singles*—A. Rogov, U.S.S.R., 1 59·23

1,000 *Metres, Singles*—M. Ljubek, Yugoslavia, 4 08·51

500 *Metres, Pairs*—U.S.S.R., 1 45·81

2,000 *Metres, Pairs*—U.S.S.R., 3 52·76

(Women) Kayak

500 *Metres, Singles*—C. Zirzov, G.D.R., 2 01·05

500 *Metres, Pairs*—U.S.S.R., 1 51·15

CYCLING

	hr. min. sec.
1000 *metres Sprint*, A. Tkac Czechoslovakia	
1,000 *metres Time*, K-J. Grunke, G.D.R.	1 05·927
4,000 *metres Pursuit*, G. Braun, Germany	4 47·61
4,000 *metres Team Pursuit*, Germany	4 21·06
Road Race, Individual, B. Johansson	4 46 52·0
Team Road Race, U.S.S.R.	2 8 53

EQUESTRIAN

Grand Prix Jumping—Individual, A. Schockemoehle, Germany

Grand Prix Jumping—Team, France

Dressage—Individual, C. Stückelberger, Switzerland

Dressage—Team, Germany

Three Day Event—Individual, E. Coffin, U.S.A.

Three Day Event—Team, U.S.A.

FENCING

Men

Foil, Individual	B. Talvard	France
Foil, Team	Germany	
Epee, Individual	G. Kulscar	Hungary
Epee, Team	Germany	

Sabre, Individual	V. KROVOPOUSKOV	U.S.S.R.	
Sabre, Team	U.S.S.R.		
Women			
Foil, Individual	I. SCHWARCZENBERGER	Hungary	
Foil, Team	U.S.S.R.		

FOOTBALL
GERMAN DEMOCRATIC REPUBLIC

GYMNASTICS
Men

Team Classification	JAPAN	576·85 points	
Combined Exercises	N. ADRIANOV	U.S.S.R.	
116·650 points			
Floor	N. ADRIANOV	U.S.S.R.	
19·450 points			
Side Horse	Z. MAGYAR	Hungary	
19·700 points			
Rings	N. ADRIANOV	U.S.S.R.	
19·650 points			
Horse Vault	N. ADRIANOV	U.S.S.R.	
19·450 points			
Parallel Bars	S. KATO	Japan	
19·675 points			
Horizontal Bars	M. TSUKAHARA	Japan	
19·675 points			

Women

Combined Exercises (Team)	U.S.S.R. 390·35 points	
Combined Exercises (Individual)	N. COMANECI	Roumania
79·275 points		
Asymmetrical Bars	N. COMANECI	Roumania
20·000 points		
Horse Vault	N. KIM	U.S.S.R.
19·800 points		
Balance Beam	N. COMANECI	Roumania
19·950 points		
Floor Exercises	N. KIM	U.S.S.R
19·850 points		

HANDBALL

Men	U.S.S.R.
Women	U.S.S.R.

HOCKEY NEW ZEALAND

JUDO

Lightweight (63 Kg)	H. RODRIGUEZ	Cuba
Light-Middlewt. (70 Kg)	V. NEVZOROV	U.S.S.R.
Middleweight (80 Kg)	I. SONODA	Japan
Light-Heavywt. (93 Kg)	K. NIMONIYA	Japan
Heavyweight (93+)	S. NOVIKOV	U.S.S.R.
Open Category	H. UEMURA	Japan

MODERN PENTATHLON

Individual	J. PYCIAK-PECIAK Poland	5,520 points
Team	GREAT BRITAIN	15,559 points

ROWING
Men

		min. sec.
Single Sculls	P. KARPINNEN Finland	7 29·03
Double Sculls	NORWAY	7 13·20
Coxless Quadruple Sculls	G.D.R.	6 28·65
Coxless Pairs	G.D.R.	7 23·31
Coxed Pairs	G.D.R.	7 58·99
Coxed Fours	U.S.S.R.	6 40·22
Coxless Fours	G.D.R.	6 37·42
Eights	G.D.R.	5 58·29

Women

		min. sec.
Single Sculls	C. SCHEIBLICH G.D.R.	4 05·56
Double Sculls	BULGARIA	3 44·36
Coxless Pairs	BULGARIA	4 01·22
Coxed Quadruple Sculls	G.D.R.	3 29·99
Coxed Fours	G.D.R.	3 45·08
Eights	G.D.R.	3 33·32

SHOOTING

		points
Free Pistol	U. POTTECK G.D.R.	573‡
Small Bore Rifle (Prone)	K. SMIESZEK Germany	599†

★ Olympic Record. ‡ World & Olympic Record.

Small Bore (3 positions)	L. BASSHAM	U.S.A.	1162
Rapid Fire Pistol	N. KLAAR	G.D.R.	587★
Olympic Trap			
Shooting	D. HALDEMAN	U.S.A.	190
Skeet	J. PANACEK	Czech.	198†
Running Game Target	A. GAZOV	U.S.S.R.	579‡

SWIMMING
Men

Metres			min. sec.
100 *Freestyle*	J. MONTGOMERY	U.S.A.	49·99‡
200 *Freestyle*	B. FURNISS	U.S.A.	1 50·29‡
400 *Freestyle*	B. GOODELL	U.S.A.	3 51·93‡
1,500 *Freestyle*	B. GOODELL	U.S.A.	15 02·40‡
100 *Backstroke*	J. NABER	U.S.A.	55·49‡
200 *Backstroke*	J. NABER	U.S.A.	1 59·19‡
100 *Breaststroke*	J. HENCKEN	U.S.A.	1 03·11‡
200 *Breaststroke*	D. WILKIE	G.B.	2 15·11‡
100 *Butterfly*	M. VOGEL	U.S.A.	54·35
200 *Butterfly*	M. BRUNER	U.S.A.	1 59·23‡
400 *Individual Medley Relay*	R. STRACHAN	U.S.A.	4 23·68‡
4 × 200 *Freestyle Relay*	U.S.A.		7 23·22‡
4 × 100 *Medley Relay*	U.S.A.		3 42·22‡
Springboard Diving	P. BOGGS	U.S.A.	619·05 points
Platform Diving	K. DIBIASI	Italy	600·51 points

Women

Metres			min. sec.
100 *Freestyle*	K. ENDER	G.D.R.	55·65‡
200 *Freestyle*	K. ENDER	G.D.R.	1 59·26‡
400 *Freestyle*	P. THUMER	G.D.R.	4 09·89‡
800 *Freestyle*	P. THUMER	G.D.R.	8 37·14‡
100 *Backstroke*	U. RICHTER	G.D.R.	1 01·83‡
200 *Backstroke*	U. RICHTER	G.D.R.	2 13·43‡
100 *Breaststroke*	H. ANKE	G.D.R.	1 11·16[1]
200 *Breaststroke*	M. KOSHEVAIA	U.S.S.R.	2 33·35‡
100 *Butterfly*	K. ENDER	G.D.R.	1 00·13‡
200 *Butterfly*	A. POLLACK	G.D.R.	2 11·41‡
400 *Freestyle Relay*	U.S.A.		3 44·22‡
400 *Medley Relay*	G.D.R.		4 07·95‡
400 *Individual Medley Relay*	U. TAUBER	G.D.R.	4 42·77‡
Springboard Diving	J. CHANDLER U.S.A.		506·19 points
Platform Diving	E. VAYTSEKHOVSKAIA		
	U.S.S.R. 406·59 points		

NOTE
[1] 100 *Breaststroke* 1·10·86 World Record in pre-limary.

WATER POLO—HUNGARY
VOLLEY BALL

Men	POLAND
Women	JAPAN

WEIGHT-LIFTING

			Kg	lbs
Flyweight	A. VORONIN	U.S.S.R.	242·5	534★
Bantam	N. NURIKYAN	Bulgaria	262·5	579‡
Feather	N. KOLESNIKOV			
		U.S.S.R.	285	628★
Light	Z. KACZMAREK			
		Poland	307·5	678★
Middleweight	Y. MITKOV	U.S.S.R.	335	738★
Light-Heavy	V. SHARY	U.S.S.R.	365	804★
Middle-Heavy				
	D. RIGERT	U.S.S.R.	382·5	843★
Heavy	V. KHRISTOV	Bulgaria	400	882★
Super Heavy	V. ALEXEEV	U.S.S.R.	440	970★

† Equal Olympic Record.

WRESTLING—Freestyle		
Light-Flyweight	K. ISSAEV	Bulgaria
Flyweight	Y. TAKADA	Japan
Bantamweight	V. UMIN	U.S.S.R.
Featherweight	J-N. YANG	Korea
Lightweight	P. PINIGIN	U.S.S.R.
Welterweight	J. DATE	Japan
Middleweight	J. PETERSON	U.S.A.
Light-Heavywt.	L. TEDIASHVILI	U.S.S.R.
Heavyweight	I. YARYGIN	U.S.S.R.
Super-Heavywt.	S. ANDIEV	U.S.S.R.
Graeco-Roman		
Light-Flyweight	A. SHUMAKOV	U.S.S.R.
Flyweight	V. KONSTANTINOV	U.S.S.R.
Bantamweight	P. UKKOLA	Finland

Featherweight	K. LIPIEN	Poland
Lightweight	S. NALBANDYAN	U.S.S.R.
Welterweight	A. BYKOV	U.S.S.R.
Middleweight	M. PETKOVIC	Yugoslavia
Light-Heavywt.	V. REZANTSEV	U.S.S.R.
Heavyweight	N. BOLBOSHIN	U.S.S.R.
Super-Heavywt.	A. KOLCHINSKI	U.S.S.R.
YACHTING		
Soling		DENMARK
Tempest		SWEDEN
Flying Dutchman		GERMANY
Finn		J. SCHUMAN, G.D.R.
470		GERMANY
Tornado		GREAT BRITAIN

WORLD'S ATHLETIC RECORDS

(All the world records given below have been accepted by the International Amateur Athletic Federation up to August 1976.)

At the Congress of the International Amateur Athletic Federation held in Montreal in July 1976 it was decided that in future (a) with the exception of the one mile both the men and women world records should be accepted only at metric distances (b) up to 400 metres only records timed by fully automatic timekeeping apparatus should be accepted, (c) records up to 400 metres should be accepted to 1/100 sec. and (d) all other records should be accepted to 1/10 second.

Running

Distances	Time			Name	Nation	Year
	hr.	min.	sec.			
100 metres			9·90	J. Hines	U.S.A.	1968
200 metres (turn)			19·78	T. Smith	U.S.A.	1968
400 metres			43·81	L. Evans	U.S.A.	1968
800 metres		1	43·5	A. Juantorena	Cuba	1976
1,000 metres		2	13·9	R. Wohihuter	U.S.A.	1974
1,500 metres		3	32·2	F. Bayi	Tanzania	1974
1 mile		3	49·4	J. Walker	New Zealand	1975
2,000 metres		4	51·4	J. Walker	N.Z.	1976
3,000 metres		7	35·2	B. Foster	G.B.	1974
5,000 metres		13	13·0	E. Puttemans	Belgium	1972
10,000 metres		27	30·8	D. Bedford	G.B.	1973
20,000 metres		57	44·4	G. Roelants	Belgium	1972
20,944 metres (13 miles)	1	00	00·0	J. Hermens	Netherlands	1976
25,000 metres	1	14	16·8	P. Paivarinta	Finland	1975
30,000 metres	1	31	30·4	J. Alder	G.B.	1970
3,000 metres steeplechase		8	08·0	A. Garderud	Sweden	1976

Hurdling

Hurdles	sec.	Name	Nation	Year
110 metres	13·24	R. Milburn	U.S.A.	1973
400 metres	47·64	E. Moses	U.S.A.	1976

Relay Racing

Distance	Time	Nation	Year
	min. sec.		
4 × 100 metres	38·19	U.S.A.	1968 and 1972
4 × 200 metres	1 21·5	Italy	1972
4 × 400 metres	2 56·1	U.S.A.	1968
4 × 800 metres	7 08·6	Germany	1966
4 × 1,500 metres	14 49·0	France	1965

Jumping and Throwing

	ft.	in.	metres	Name	Nation	Year
High Jump	7	7¼	2·31	D. Stones	U.S.A.	1976
Pole Vault	18	8½	5·80	D. Roberts	U.S.A.	1976
Long Jump	29	2½	8·90	R. Beamon	U.S.A.	1968
Triple Jump	58	8½	17·89	J. de Oliveira	Brazil	1975
Shot	72	2¼	22·00	A. Baryshnikov	U.S.S.R.	1976
Discus	232	6	70·86	M. Wilkins	U.S.A.	1976
Hammer	260	2	79·30	W. Schmidt	Germany	1975
Javelin	310	4	94·58	M. Nemeth	Hungary	1976
Decathlon	8,618 points			B. Jenner	U.S.A.	1976

Walking

Distance	Time			Name	Nation	Year
	hr.	min.	sec.			
20,000 metres	1	24	45·0	B. Kannenberg	Germany	1974
27,153 metres (16 miles 1,535 yards)	2	00	00·0	B. Kannenberg	Germany	1974
30,000 metres	2	12	58·0	B. Kannenberg	Germany	1974
50,000 metres	4	00	27·0	G. Weidner	Germany	1973

WOMEN'S EVENTS

Running

Distance	Time min. sec.	Name	Nation	Year
100 metres	11·01	A. Richter	Germany	1976
200 metres	22·21	I. Szewinska	Poland	1974
400 metres	49·29	I. Szewinska	Poland	1976
800 metres	1 54·9	T. Kazankina	U.S.S.R.	1976
1500 metres	3 56·0	T. Kazankina	U.S.S.R.	1976
1 mile	4 29·5	P. Cacchi	Italy	1973
3,000 metres	8 27·1	L. Bragina	U.S.S.R.	1976
100 metres hurdles (2 ft. 0 in.)	12·3	A. Ehrhardt	G.D.R.★	1973
400 metres hurdles	56·5	K. Kasperczik	Poland	1974

★ German Democratic Republic (East Germany).

Relays

Distance	Time min. sec.	Nation	Year
4 × 100 metres	42·50	G.D.R.	1976
4 × 200 metres	1 33·8	G.B.	1968
4 × 400 metres	3 19·23	G.D.R.	1976
4 × 800 metres	8 05·2	Bulgaria	1975

Women's Jumping and Throwing

	ft.	in.	metres	Name	Nation	Year
High Jump	6	5¼	1·96	R. Ackermann	G.D.R.	1976
Long Jump	22	11¼	6·99	S. Siegl	G.D.R.	1976
Shot Putt	71	10	21·89	I. Khristova	Bulgaria	1976
Discus	231	9	70·50	F. Melnik	U.S.S.R.	1976
Javelin	226	9	69·12	R. Fuchs	G.D.R.	1976
Pentathlon	4,932 pts.			B. Pollak	G.D.R.	1973
Hurdles	12·59			A. C. Ehrhardt	G.D.R.	1973

UNITED KINGDOM (ALL COMERS') RECORDS
(Records made in the United Kingdom of Great Britain and Northern Ireland by any athlete.)

MEN

Distance	Time hr. min. sec.	Name	Nation	Year
100 metres	10·26	S. Schenke	G.D.R.	1973
100 metres	10·26	D. Quarrie	Jamaica	1975
200 metres	20·31	S. Williams	U.S.A.	1975
400 metres	45·01	C. Asati	Kenya	1970
800 metres	1 45·1	A. Carter	G.B.	1973
1000 metres	2 17·5	I. Van Damme	Belgium	1976
1,500 metres	3 36·6	K. Keino	Kenya	1969
1 mile	3 53·4	K. Keino	Kenya	1966
2,000 metres	5 00·6	J. Walker	N.Z.	1976
3,000 metres	7 35·2	B. Foster	G.B.	1974
5,000 metres	13 17·2	D. Bedford	G.B.	1972
10,000 metres	27 30·8	D. Bedford	G.B.	1973
20,000 metres	58 39·0	R. Hill	G.B.	1976
12 miles 1268 yards	1 00 00·0	R. Hill	G.B.	1968
25,000 metres	1 15 22·6	R. Hill	G.B.	1968
30,000 metres	1 31 30·4	J. Alder	G.B.	1970
3,000 metres steeplechase	8 18·2	B. Malinowski	Poland	1975
110 metres hurdles	13·70	G. Drut	France	1973
400 metres hurdles	48·85	A. Pascoe	G.B.	1975
4 × 100 metres	39·36	——	U.S.S.R.	1975
4 × 400 metres	3 03·6	——	Kenya	1970
4 × 1500 metres	15 12·6	——	England Team	1975

	ft.	in.	Name	Nation	Year
High Jump	7	5	D. Stones	U.S.A.	1976
Pole Vault	17	9¾	T. Slusarskki	Poland	1976
Long Jump	26	10	R. Boston	U.S.A.	1965
Triple Jump	55	7½	V. Saneyev	U.S.S.R.	1975
Shot	70	8½	G. Capes	G.B.	1976
Discus	218	3	M. Wilkins	U.S.A.	1976
Hammer	252	3	V. Dmitrenko	U.S.S.R.	1975
Javelin	297	6	K. Wolfermann	Germany	1973
Decathlon	7,985 pts.		W. Toomey	U.S.A.	1968

Walking	hr. min. sec.	Name	Nation	Year
20,000 metres	1 28 45·8	K. Matthews	G.B.	1964
16 miles 315 yards	2 00 00·0	R. Wallwork	G.B.	1971
30,000 metres	2 28 44·0	P. Nihill	G.B.	1972
50,000 metres	4 17 29·8	D. Thompson	G.B.	1960

U.K. (All Comers') Records—*continued*

WOMEN

Distance	Time min. sec.	Name	Nation	Year
100 metres	11·16	A. Lynch	G.B.	1975
200 metres	22·81	R. Stecher	G.D.R.	1973
400 metres	50·32	I. Szewinska	Poland	1974
800 metres	1 58·9	G. Hoffmeister	G.D.R.	1973
1,500 metres	4 08·5	T. Kazankina	U.S.S.R.	1975
1 mile	4 35·1	G. Reiser	Canada	1973
3,000 metres	8 54·0	I. Knutsson	Sweden	1975
4 × 100 metres	42·95	——	G.D.R.	1973
4 × 200 metres	1 33·8	——	G.B.	1968
4 × 400 metres	3 28·5	——	U.S.S.R.	1975
4 × 800 metres	8 25·0	——	G.B.	1970
100 metres hurdles	12·95	A. Ehrhardt	G.D.R.	1973
400 metres hurdles	57·84	C.Warden	G.B.	1976
	ft. in.			
High Jump	6 2¼	R. Witschas	G.D.R.	1974
Long Jump	22 0¾	S. Sherwood	G.B.	1972
Shot	68 1¾	N. Chizhova	U.S.S.R.	1973
Discus	227 11	F. Melnik	U.S.S.R.	1973
Javelin	216 10	R. Fuchs	G.D.R.	1973
Pentathlon	4,630 pts.	M. Peters	G.B.	1972

UNITED KINGDOM (NATIONAL) RECORDS

(Records made anywhere by athletes eligible to represent Great Britain and Northern Ireland)

Men

100 *metres*—10.29 sec. (P. Radford, 1958).
200 *metres*—20·66 sec. (R. Steane, 1968, D. Jenkins, 1972).
400 *metres*—44·93 (D. Jenkins, 1975).
800 *metres*—1 min. 45·1 sec. (A. Carter, 1973).
1,000 *metres*—2 min. 18·2 sec. (J. P. Boulter, 1969).
1,500 *metres*—3 min. 37·4 sec. (F. Clement, 1974).
1 *mile*—3 min. 55·0 sec. (F. Clement, 1975).
2,000 *metres*—5 min. 03·0 sec. (B. Foster, I. Stewart, 1975).
3,000 *metres*—7 min. 35·2 sec. (B. Foster, 1974).
5,000 *metres*—13 min. 14·6 sec. (B. Foster, 1974).
10,000 *metres*—27 min. 30·8 sec. (D. Bedford, 1973).
20,000 *metres*—58 min. 39·0 sec. (R. Hill, 1968).
12 *miles* 1,268 *yards* 1hr. (R. Hill, 1968).
25,000 *metres*—1 hr. 15 min. 22·6 sec. (R. Hill, 1965).
30,000 *metres*—1 hr. 31 min. 30·4 sec. (J. Alder, 1970).
3,000 *metres Steeplechase*—8 min. 19·0 sec. (D. Coates, 1976).
110 *metres Hurdles*—13·69 sec. (B. Price, 1973).
400 *metres Hurdles*—48·12 sec. (D. P. Hemery, 1968).
4 × 100 *metres Relay*—39·33 sec. (British Team, 1968).
4 × 200 *metres*—1 min. 24·1 sec. (British Team, 1961).
4 × 400 *metres*—3 min. 00·5 sec. (British Team, 1972).
4 × 800 *metres*—7 min. 17·4 sec. (British Team, 1970).
4 × 1,500 *metres*—15 min. 04·4 sec. (G.B. Team, 1976).
High Jump—7 ft. 0½ in. (B. Burgess, 1976).
Pole Vault—17 ft. 5½ in. (B. Hooper, 1976).
Long Jump—27 ft. 0 in. (L. Davies, 1968).
Triple Jump—54 ft. 2½ in. (A. Moore, 1976).
Shot—76 ft. 8½ in. (G. Capes, 1974).
Discus—209 ft. 11 in. (W. Tancred, 1973).
Hammer—246 ft. 0 in. (C. Black, 1976).
Javelin—278 ft. 7 in. (C. Clover, 1974).
Decathlon—7,905 pts. (D. Thompson, 1976).
Walking
20,000 *metres*—1 hr. 28 min. 45·8 sec. (K. Matthews, 1964).

2 *Hours*—16 miles 315 yds. (R. Wallwork, 1971).
30,000 *metres*—2 hr. 24 min. 18·2 sec. (R. Thorpe, 1974).
50,000 *metres*—4 hr. 11 min. 22·0 sec. (R. Dobson, 1974).

Women

100 *metres*—11·16 sec. (A. Lynch, 1974).
200 *metres*—22.81 sec. (S. Lannaman, 1976).
400 *metres*—51·28 sec. (D. Murray, 1975).
800 *metres*—2 min. 00·2 sec. (R. Stirling, 1972).
1,500 *metres*—4 min. 04·8 sec. (S. Carey, 1972).
1 *mile*—4 min. 36·2 sec. (J. Allison, 1973).
3,000 *metres*—8 min. 55·6 sec. (J. Smith, 1974).
100 *metres Hurdles*—13·11 sec. (S. Colyear, 1976).
400 *metres Hurdles*—57·84 sec. (C. Warden, 1976).
4 × 100 *metres Relay*—43·44 sec. (G.B. Team, 1976).
4 × 200 *metres Relay*—1 min. 33·8 sec. (G.B. Team, 1968).
4 × 400 *metres*—3 min. 26·6 sec. (G.B. Team, 1975).
4 × 800 *metres Relay*—8 min. 23·8 sec. (G.B. Team, 1971).
High Jump—6 ft. 1¼ in. (B. Lawton, 1973).
Long Jump—22 ft. 2¼ in. (M. Rand, 1964).
Shot—53 ft. 6¼ in. (M. Peters, 1966).
Discus—190 ft. 4 in. (R. Payne, 1972).
Javelin—187 ft. 7 in. (T. Sanderson, 1976),
Pentathlon—4,801 pts. (M. Peters, 1972).

A.A.A. AND W.A.A.A. INDOOR CHAMPIONSHIPS

Held at Cosford, January 24/25, 1976

Men's Events

Metres		min.	sec.
60—C. Monk (Leicester)			6·9
200—A. McMaster (Edinburgh A.C.)			22·0
400—S. Scutt (Loughborough)			49·0
800—P. Lewis (Wolverhampton)		1	50·0
1,500—D. Moorcroft (Coventry)		3	45·6
3,000—R. Smedley (Birchfield)		7	59·2
Steeplechase—A. Asgeirsson (Iceland)		5	36·8
60 Hurdles—B. Price (Cardiff)			8·1
		ft.	in.
High Jump—M. Butterfield		7	1
Pole Vault—B. Hooper (Woking)		16	6¼

Long Jump—R. Mitchell (Enfield)	25	2¼
Triple Jump—A. Moore (Birchfield)	51	10
Shot—W. Tancred (Wolverhampton)	59	1¼

Women's Events

Metres	min.	sec.
60—A. Lynch		7·3
400—V. Elder (Wolverhampton)		54·1
800—M. Stewart (Birchfield)	2	08·2
1,500—L. Harvey (LOAC)	4	29·8
60 *Hurdles*—E. Sutherland (Edinburgh S.H.)		8·3
Relay—Wolverhampton & Bilston		48·7
	ft.	in.
High Jump—D. Cooper (Bristol)	5	8½
Long Jump—S. Reeve (Birchfield)	20	7¼
Shot—J. Kerr (Mitcham)	51	10

GREAT BRITAIN v. GERMAN DEMOCRATIC REPUBLIC

Held at Cosford, January 31, 1976

Men's Events

Metres	min.	sec.
60—E. Ray (G.D.R.)		6·6
400—A. Bennett (G.B.)		48·5
800—G. Stolle (G.D.R.)	1	49·6
1,500—K-P Justus (G.D.R.)	3	46·1
3,000—F. Baumgartl (G.D.R.)	7	57·8
60 Hurdles—T. Munkelt (G.D.R.)		7·7
4×200 Relay—G.D.R.	1	27·3
High Jump—E. Kirst (G.D.R.)	7	4¼
Pole Vault—W. Reinhardt (G.D.R.)	17	4½
Long Jump—P. Rieger (G.D.R.)	24	10
Triple Jump—A. Moore (G.B.)	52	5½
Shot—H.-J. Rothenburg (G.D.R.)	66	9¾

German Democratic Republic beat Great Britain by 78½ points to 48½.

Women's Events

Metres	min.	sec.
60—A. Lynch (G.B.)		7·3
400—D. Maletzki (G.D.R.)		53·6
800—C. Neumann (G.D.R.)	2	05·8
1,500—W. Strotzer (G.D.R.)	4	12·4
4×200 *Relay*—G.B.	1	37·7
60 *Hurdles*—A. Ehrhardt (D.G.R.)		8·1
	ft.	in.
High Jump—R. Ackermann (G.D.R.)	6	2
Long Jump—A. Voigt (G.D.R.)	21	2
Shot—J. Schoknecht (G.D.R.)	62	11¼

German Democratic Republic beat Great Britain by 55 points to 27.

WOMEN'S NATIONAL CROSS COUNTRY

Held at Blackburn on January 31, 1976

Senior Race:
A. Ford (Feltham), 17 min. 23 sec. Team: London Olympiads A.C.

INTERNATIONAL CROSS COUNTRY

Held at Chepstow on February 28, 1976

Senior Men (12 Km)	min.	sec.
1 C. Lopes (Portugal)	34	48
2 A. Simmons (England)	35	04
3 B. Ford (England)	35	07
4 K. Lismont (Belgium)	35	08
5 D. Uhlemann (Germany)	35	17
6 E. Sellik (U.S.S.R.)	35	17

Team Result:

	points
1 England (2, 3, 15, 16, 26, 28)	90
2 Belgium (4, 13, 17, 19, 27, 38)	118
3 France (9, 18, 25, 32, 46, 57)	187

4. U.S.S.R. (219 points); 5, Italy (224); 6. U.S.A. (243); 7. Germany (292); 8, Wales (304); 9. Finland (348); 10. Scotland (348); 11. Spain (390); 12. Portugal (394); 13. Eire (397); 14. Morocco (482); 15. Algeria (498); 16. Tunisia (574); 17. Sweden (600); 18. N. Ireland (742).

Junior Men (7·8 km)	min.	sec.
1 E. Hulst (U.S.A.)	23	54
2 T. Hunt (U.S.A.)	24	07
3 N. Muir (Scotland)	24	17

Team Result: U.S.A. (16 pts.); 2. Spain (60); 3. England (91); 4. Italy (97); 5. Morocco (106); 6. Germany (115); 7. Canada (120); 8. Belgium (125); 9. Scotland (143); 10. Finland (144); 11. France (160); 12. Algeria (168); 13. Wales (187); 14. Eire (235); 15. N. Ireland (315).

Women (4·8 Km)	min.	sec.
1 C. Valero (Spain)	16	19
2 T. Kazankina (U.S.S.R.)	16	39
3 G. Dorio (Italy)	16	56

Team Result—1. U.S.S.R. (33 points); 2. Italy (59); 3. U.S.A. (64); 4. England (78); 5. Poland (87); 6. France (107); 7. Belgium (120); 8. Eire (122); 9. Scotland (127); 10. Spain (129); 11. Finland (137); 12. Wales (247).

EUROPEAN INDOOR CHAMPIONSHIPS

Held in Munich, February 21/22, 1976

Men's Events

Metres	min.	sec.
60—V. Borzov (U.S.S.R.)		6·6
400—J. Bratanov (Bulgaria)		48·2
800—I. Van Damme (Belgium)	1	49·2
1,500—P-H. Wellmann (Germany)	3	45·1
3,000—I. Sensburg (Germany)	8	01·6
60 *Hurdles*—V. Myasnikov (U.S.S.R)		7·8
	ft.	in.
High Jump—S. Senyukov (U.S.S.R.)	7	3½
Pole Vault—T. Prokhorenko (U.S.S.R.)	17	10½
Long Jump—J. Rousseau (France)	25	11
Triple Jump—V. Sanyeyev (U.S.S.R.)	56	1¼
Shot—G. Capes (G.B.)	67	8¾

Women's Events

Metres	min.	sec.
60—L. Haglund (Sweden)		7·2
400—R. Wilden (Germany)		52·3
800—N. Shtereva (Bulgaria)	2	02·2
1,500—B. Kraus (Germany)	4	15·2
Hurdles—G. Rabsztyn (Poland)		8·0
	ft.	in.
High Jump—R. Ackermann (G.D.R.)	6	3½
Long Jump—L. Alfeyeva (U.S.S.R.)	21	9½
Shot—I. Khristova (Bulgaria)	67	1¼

NATIONAL CROSS COUNTRY

Held at Leicester, March 13, 1976

Senior Race, 9 miles		
1 B. Ford (Aldershot)	43	26
2 D. Moorcroft (Coventry)	43	39
3 S. Kenyon (Bolton)	44	02
4 G. Tuck (Cambridge)	44	16
5 A. McKean (Edinburgh)	44	25
6 D. Slater (Leeds)	44	32

Team Result:

	points
1 Gateshead H. & A.C. (7, 33, 38, 56, 61, 62)	257
2 Cambridge & Coleridge A.C. (4, 26, 27, 34, 70, 138)	299
3 Cardiff A.A.C. (25, 31, 32, 66, 82, 98)	334

Junior, 6 miles
Won by N. Muir (Shettleston) in 30 min. 40 sec. Team: Sale H., 128 pts.

Youth, 4 miles
Won by N. Martin (Bracknell) in 20 min. 12 sec. Team: Brighton & Hove A.C., 134 points.

R.W.A. 10 MILES WALK

Held at York on March 20, 1976

	min.	sec.
1 O. Flynn (Basildon)	69	59
2 B. Adams (Leicester)	71	00
3 R. Mills (Ilford)	71	09

Team Event: Borough of Enfield, 40 points.

GREAT BRITAIN *v.* GERMAN DEMOCRATIC REPUBLIC *v.* JUGOSLAVIA

Held in Split, May 1/2, 1976

Men's Events

Metres	min.	sec.
100—K-D. Kurrat (G.D.R.)		10·5
200—S. Schenke (G.D.R.)		20·9
400—A. Scheibe (G.D.R.)		46·3
800—L. Susanj (J.)	1	47·1
1,500—B. Bozinovic (J.)	3	39·6
5,000—D. Black (G.B.)	13	31·8
10,000—K-H. Leiteritz (G.D.R.)	28	35·0
110 *Hurdles*—T. Munkelt (G.D.R.)		13·8
400 *Hurdles*—S. McCallum (G.B.)		51·4
Steeplechase—D. Coates (G.B.)	8	32·8
4×100 *Relay*—G.D.R.		39·4
4×400 *Relay*—G.D.R.	3	06·2
	ft.	in.
High Jump—R. Beilschmidt (G.D.R.)	7	2½
Pole Vault—B. Hooper (G.B.)	17	0¼
Long Jump—N. Stekic (J.)	25	9½
Triple Jump—A. Moore (G.B.)	53	11
Shot Putt—U. Beyer (G.D.R.)	68	8½
Discus—W. Schmidt (G.D.R.)	213	2
Hammer—J. Sachse (G.D.R.)	250	8
Javelin—D. Michel (G.D.R.)	277	11

Match Result: German Democratic Republic, 188 points; Great Britain, 128 points, Jugoslavia, 106 points.

Women's Events

Metres	min.	sec.
100—S. Lannaman (G.B.)		11·2
200—R. Stecher (G.D.R.)		22·7
400—C. Brehmer (G.D.R.)		50·4
800—E. Zinn (G.D.R.)	2	01·4
1,500—W. Strotzer (G.D.R.)	4	11·0
100 *Hurdles*—A. Ehrhardt (G.D.R.)		13·2
4×100 *Relay*—G.D.R.		43·0
4×400 *Relay*—G.D.R.	3	25·0
	ft.	in.
High Jump—R. Kirst (G.D.R.)	6	1½
Long Jump—A. Voigt (G.D.R.)	21	8¼
Shot—M. Adam (G.D.R.)	68	4¼
Discus—G. Hinzmann (G.D.R.)	215	3
Javelin—R. Fuchs (G.D.R.)	206	11

Match Result: German Democratic Republic, 137 points; Great Britain, 82 points, Jugoslavia 47 points.

GREAT BRITAIN *v.* NETHERLANDS (Women)

Held at Grangemouth, May 8, 1976

Metres	min.	sec.
100—S. Lannaman (G.B.)		11·2
200—V. Elder (G.B.)		24·2
400—E. Barnes (G.B.)		54·0
800—A. Creamer (G.B.)	2	08·4
1,500—H. Hollick (G.B.)	4	22·1
3,000—A. Ford (G.B.)	9	29·6
Hurdles—E. Sutherland (G.B.)		13·2
	ft.	in.
High Jump—R. Ahlers (N.)	6	0½
Long Jump—M. Nimmo (G.B.)	21	2
Shot—B. Bedford (G.B.)	50	10
Discus—I. Stalman (N.)	180	3
Javelin—T. Sanderson (G.B.)	180	4

Great Britain beat The Netherlands by 182 points to 95.

THE "KRAFT" GAMES

Held at Crystal Palace, June 4/5, 11/12, 1976

Men's Events

Metres	min.	sec.
100—S. Green (T.V.H.)		10·7
200—A. McMaster (Edinburgh A.C.)		21·6
400—D. Jenkins (Gateshead)		45·5
800—S. Ovett (Brighton)	1	46·7
1,500—S. Ovett (Brighton)	3	39·6
5,000—B. Foster (Gateshead)	13	33·8
10,000—B. Foster (Gateshead)	27	53·8
110 *Hurdles*—B. Price (Cardiff)		14·0
400 *Hurdles*—P. Kelly (Wolverhampton)		51·0
Steeplechase—D. Coates (Gateshead)	8	27·0
	ft.	in.
High Jump—M. Butterfield (R.A.F.)	6	10¾
Pole Vault—J. Gutteridge (Windsor)	16	4¾
Long Jump—R. Mitchell (Enfield)	25	9¼
Triple Jump—A. Moore (Birchfield)	54	2½
Shot—G. Capes (Enfield)	69	0½
Discus—P. Tancred (Wolverhampton)	202	2
Hammer—P. Dickenson (Hillingdon)	235	11
Javelin—D. Ottley (Thurrock)	261	5

Women's Events

Metres	min.	sec.
100—S. Lannaman (Solihull)		11·5
200—S. Lannaman (Solihull)		22·9
400—V. Elder (Wolverhampton)		52·0
800—A. Creamer (Rotherham)	2	03·5
1,500—M. Stewart (Birchfield)	4	10·3
Hurdles—S. Colyear (Stretford)		13·4
	ft.	in.
High Jump—M. Walls (Edinburgh S.H.)	5	11½
Long Jump—R. Howell (Birchfield)	20	9¼
Shot—J. Oakes (Croydon)	52	3¾
Discus—M. Ritchie (Edinburgh S.H.)	176	0
Javelin—T. Sanderson (Wolverhampton)	184	2

GREAT BRITAIN *v.* U.S.S.R.

Held in Kiev on May 22/23, 1976

Men's Events

Metres	min.	sec.
100—N. Kolesnikov (U.S.S.R.)		10·2
200—A. Aksinin (U.S.S.R.)		21·0
400—G. Cohen (G.B.)		46·5
800—V. Anokhin (U.S.S.R.)	1	46·6
1,500—A. Mamontov (U.S.S.R.)	3	38·9
5,000—A. Simmons (G.B.)	13	21·2
10,000—B. Ford (G.B.)	28	07·2
4×100 *Relay*—U.S.S.R.		39·4
4×400 *Relay*—G.B.	3	07·6
110 *Hurdles*—V. Myasnikov (U.S.S.R.)		13·5
400 *Hurdles*—Y. Gavrilenko (U.S.S.R.)		50·2
Steeplechase—A. Staynings (G.B.)	8	30·4
	ft.	in.
High Jump—S. Budalov (U.S.S.R.)	7	3
Pole Vault—Y. Prokhorenko (U.S.S.R.)	18	0½
Long Jump—A. Pereverzev (U.S.S.R.)	26	11¼
Triple Jump—V. Shevchenko (U.S.S.R.)	54	6½
Shot—A. Baryshnikov (U.S.S.R.)	69	11
Discus—V. Penzikov (U.S.S.R.)	208	7
Hammer—A. Spridonov (U.S.S.R.)	257	11
Javelin—A. Chupulko (U.S.S.R.)	277	0

U.S.S.R. 254 points; G.B. 153 points.

Women's Events

Metres	min.	sec.
100—S. Lannaman (G.B.)		10·8
200—S. Lannaman (G.B.)		22·6
400—V. Elder (G.B.)		51·4
800—V. Gerasimova (U.S.S.R.)	1	59·7
1,500—L. Bragina (U.S.S.R.)	4	05·9
3,000—S. Ulmasova (U.S.S.R.)	8	53·8
4×100 *Relay*—U.S.S.R.		43·1
4×400 *Relay*—U.S.S.R.	3	26·8
Hurdles—V. Anisimova (U.S.S.R.)		12·8
	ft.	in.
High Jump—G. Filatova (U.S.S.R.)	6	2¾
Long Jump—L. Alfeyeva (U.S.S.R.)	21	5¼
Shot—N. Chizhova (U.S.S.R.)	68	2½
Discus—F. Melnik (U.S.S.R.)	215	3
Javelin—S. Babich (U.S.S.R.)	207	0

U.S.S.R. 174 points; Great Britain, 100 points.

R.W.A. 20 MILES WALK

Held at Stevenage on June 19, 1976

		hr.	min.	sec.
1	R. Mills (Ilford)	2	32	13·0
2	R. Dobson (Southend)	2	33	30·0
3	R. Thorpe (Sheffield)	2	36	53·0

Team Result: Sheffield, 44 points; Southend, 49; Brighton, 62.

GREAT BRITAIN *v.* WEST GERMANY WALKING

Held in Salzgitter on June 6, 1976

20 *Km.*

		hr.	min.	sec.
1	B. Kannenberg (W.G.)	1	27	31·0
2	G. Weidner (W.G.)	1	29	17·8
3	R. Mills (G.B.)	1	29	55·4

Team Result: West Germany, 13 points; G.B. 9 points.

35 *Km.*

		hr.	min.	sec.
1	R. Thorpe (G.B.)	2	51	02·8
2	H. Schubert (W.G.)	2	51	20·4
3	H. Binder (W.G.)	2	51	31·8

Team Result: W.G. 12 points; G.B. 10 points.

Match Result: West Germany, 25 points; G.B. 19 points.

R.W.A. 2 KM. WALK

Held at Southend on May 15, 1976

		hr.	min.	sec.
1	O. Flynn (Basildon)	1	30	00
2	G. de Jonckheere (Belgium)	1	31	33
3	P. Nihill (Croydon)	1	31	38

Team Result: Sheffield, 34 points; Southend 52; Leicester, 86.

INTERNATIONAL DECATHLON AND PENTATHLON

Held in Copenhagen June 26/27, 1976

Decathlon

1. M. Cordon (G.B., 7,750 points; 2. N. Phipps (G.B.), 7,532; 3. R. Lobo (Spain), 7,228.

Team: G.B., 21,921 points; 2, Denmark, 20,991; 3, Spain, 20,451; 4, Netherlands, 20,270.

Pentathlon

1, S. Longden (G.B.), 4,422 points, 2. H. Oakes (G.B.), 4,229; 3. N. v.d. Laar (Netherlands), 4,160.

Teams: G.B., 12,622; Netherlands, 12,003; Denmark, 11,833.

GREAT BRITAIN *v.* POLAND
GREAT BRITAIN *v.* CANADA

Held at Crystal Palace, July 3/4, 1976

GREAT BRITAIN *v.* POLAND

Men's Events

Metres	min.	sec.
100—A. Swierczynski (P.)		10·44
200—M. Woronin (P.)		20·73
400—D. Jenkins (G.B.)		45·65
800—S. Ovett (G.B.)	1	46·7
1,500—B. Foster (G.B.)	3	42·9
5,000—N. Rose (G.B.)	14	03·8
10,000—R. Kopijasz (P.)	29	27·6
110 *Hurdles*—B. Price (G.B.)		13·73
400 *Hurdles*—A. Pascoe (G.B.)		50·62
Steeplechase—B. Malinowski (P.)	8	22·6
4× 100 *Relay*—Poland		39·02
4× 400 *Relay*—Poland	3	04·7
	ft.	in.
High Jump—J. Wszola (P.)	7	3
Pole Vault—T. Slusarski (P.)	17	0¾
Long Jump—R. Mitchell (G.B.)	25	10¾
Triple Jump—A. Moore (G.B.)	53	10¼
Shot—G. Capes (G.B.)	68	4¼
Discus—S. Wolodko (P.)	200	7
Hammer—C. Black (G.B.)	237	6
Javelin—J. Damszel (P.)	264	1

Great Britain beat Poland by 106 points to 103.

Women's Events

Metres	min.	sec.
100—S. Lannaman (G.B.)		11·28
200—S. Lannaman (G.B.)		22·86
400—D. Murray (G.B.)		51·89
800—E. Katolik (P.)	2	02·2
1,500—P. Yule (G.B.)	4	13·9
Hurdles—S. Colyear (G.B.)		13·39
4× 100 *Relay*—Great Britain		43·68
4× 400 *Relay*—Great Britain	3	28·5
	ft.	in.
High Jump—A. Gilson (G.B.)	5	10¾
Long Jump—S. Reeve (G.B.)	20	10½
Shot—L. Chewinska (P.)	62	8
Discus—D. Rosani (P.)	199	2
Javelin—D. Jaworska (P.)	187	2

Great Britain beat Poland by 74½ points to 71½.

GREAT BRITAIN *v.* CANADA

Men's Events

Metres	min.	sec.
100—S. Green (G.B.)		10·49
200—D. McMaster (G.B.)		20·94
400—D. Jenkins (G.B.)		45·65
800—S. Ovett (G.B.)	1	46·7
1,500—D. Hill (C.)	3	41·9
5,000 N. Rose (G.B.)	14	03·8
10,000—G. Tuck (G.B.)	29	52·8
110 *Hurdles*—B. Price (G.B.)		13·73
400 *Hurdles*—A. Pascoe (G.B.)		50·62
Steeplechase—T. Staynings (G.B.)	8	28·6
4× 100 *Relay*—Canada		39·24
4× 400 *Relay*—Canada	3	05·3
	ft.	in.
High Jump—G. Joy (C.)	7	0½
Pole Vault—K. Wenman (C.)	16	8¾
Long Jump—R. Mitchell (G.B.)	25	10¾
Triple Jump—A. Moore (G.B.)	53	10¼
Shot—G. Capes (G.B.)	68	4¼
Discus—P. Tancred (G.B.)	193	7
Hammer—C. Black (G.B.)	237	6
Javelin—D. Ottley (G.B.)	262	9

Great Britain beat Canada by 127 points to 81.

Women's Events

	min.	sec.
100—S. Lannaman (G.B.)		11·44
200—S. Lannaman (G.B.)		22·86
400—D. Murray (G.B.)		51·89
800—Y. Saunders (C.)	2	01·6
1,500—P. Werthner (C.)	4	10·6
3,000—A. Ford (G.B.)	9	06·8
4× 100 *Relay*—Great Britain		43·68
4× 400 *Relay*—Great Britain	3	28·5
Hurdles—S. Colyear (G.B.)		13·39
	ft.	in.
High Jump—A. Gilson (G.B.)	5	10¾
Long Jump—D. Jones (C.)	20	11¾
Shot—L. Moreau (C.)	52	9½
Discus—J. Haist (C.)	182	6
Javelin—T. Sanderson (G.B.)	182	10

Great Britain beat Canada by 71 points to 64.

ENGLISH SCHOOLS CHAMPIONSHIPS

Held at Cannock, July 9/10, 1976

Boys' Events

Metres	min.	sec.
100—A. Pitts		11·1
200—D. Baptiste		22·1
400—M. Francis		49·1
800—N. Brooks	1	50·8
1,500—S. Cahill	3	56·4
5,000—K. Tesh	14	39·8
Steeplechase—J. Wilson	5	52·4
110 *Hurdles*—I. Ratcliffe		14·5

400 *Hurdles*—C. Preston		54·9
	ft.	in.
High Jump—T. Foulger	6	4¾
Pole Vault—R. Goodall	15	1
Long Jump—J. Bramble	22	7¼
Triple Jump—N. Stoppard	48	7½
Shot—M. Eyres	51	11
Discus—C. Wilkinson	150	5
Hammer—S. Watson	162	2
Javelin—R. Good	187	5

Girl's Events

Metres	min.	sec.
100—H. Hunte		11·9
200—C. Thomas		25·2
400—H. Oakes		55·1
800—J. Prictoe	2	09·2
1,500—A. Mason	4	24·9
Hurdles—T. O'Nions		14·6
	ft.	in.
High Jump—D. Cooper	5	8½
Long Jump—K. Murray	18	11¾
Shot—J. Oakes	48	10
Discus—V. Watson	140	9
Javelin—H. McDonald	143	3

A.A.A. CHAMPIONSHIPS

Held at Crystal Palace, August 13/14, 1976

Metres	min.	sec.
100—D. Quarrie (Jamaica)		10·42
200—D. Quarrie (Jamaica)		20·35
400—D. Jenkins (Gateshead)		45·86
800—S. Ovett (Wolverhampton)	1	47·3
1,500—R. Dixon (New Zealand)	3	41·2
5,000—B. Foster (Gateshead)	13	33·0
10,000—G. Tebroke (Netherlands)	28	04·0
Marathon*—B. Watson (Cambridge) 2hr	15	08·0
3,000 *Walk*—R. Mills (Ilford)	12	22·6
10,000 *Walk*†—B. Adams (Leicester)	42	58·0
110 *Hurdles*—B. Price (Cardiff)		13·80
400 *Hurdles*—A. Pascoe (Polytechnic)		49·57
	ft.	in.
High Jump—M. Palmer) (Wolverhampton)	6	9
Pole Vault—M. Tully (U.S.A.)	17	5¾
Long Jump—R. Mitchell (Navy)	26	0¼
Triple Jump—A. Moore (Birchfield)	53	5¾
Shot—G. Capes (Enfield)	68	7¾
Discus—J. Powell (U.S.A.)	214	11
Hammer—C. Black (Edinburgh)	238	4
Javelin P. Maync (Switzerland)	246	7
Decathlon§—D. Thompson (Essex)	7,684 pts.	

* Held at Rotherham on May 8.
† Held at West London Stadium on March 27.
§ Held at Cwmbran on May 22 and 23.

WOMEN'S A.A.A. CHAMPIONSHIPS

Held at Crystal Palace on August 20/21, 1976

Metres	min.	sec.
100—A. Lynch (Mitcham)		11·22
200—D. Hyman (Ramsden)		23·48
400—V. Elder (Wolverhampton)		52·08
800—A. Creamer (Rotherham)	2	04·6
1,500—P. Yule (Portsmouth)	4	15·1
3,000—M. Purcell (Ireland)	9	08·0
5,000 *Walk*—M. Fawkes (North Shields)	24	10·0
100 *Hurdles*—S. Colyear (Stretford)		13·47
400 *Hurdles*—C. Warden (Hull)		57·84
	ft.	in.
High Jump—D. Brown (Wolverhampton)	5	10½
Long Jump—S. Reeve (Birchfield)	20	7¼
Shot—J. Kerr (Mitcham)	52	1¼
Discus—J. Thompson (Bracknell)	168	7
Javelin—T. Sanderson (Wolverhampton)	186	11

*Pentathlon**—S. Wright (Essex)	4,196 pts.	

* Held at Crystal Palace on May 26.

A.A.A. JUNIOR (UNDER 20) CHAMPIONSHIPS

Held at Wolverhampton on August 7/8, 1976

Metres	min.	sec.
100—R. Denham (Edinburgh)		10·7
200—A. McMaster (Edinburgh)		21·0
400—J. Griffiths (Swansea)		47·2
800—S. Caldwell (Bolton)	1	50·4
1,500—R. Flynn (Ireland)	3	44·1
5,000—N. Lees (Derby)	14	13·2
Steeplechase—J. Wilson (Epsom)	5	47·4
10,000 *Walk*—M. Dunion (Essex)	47	24·4
110 *Hurdles*—J. Holtam (Stoke)		14·5
400 *Hurdles*—G. Oakes (Haringey)		53·1
	ft.	in.
High Jump—M. Palmer (Wolverhampton)	6	11
Pole Vault—R. Goodall (Stoke)	14	5¼
Long Jump—L. Tyson (T.V.H.)	23	6¼
Triple Jump—K. Connor (Windsor)	50	9½
Shot—G. McEvoy (Ballymena)	49	5¾
Discus—L. Strutt (Q.P.H.)	143	5
Hammer—R. Gibson (Crusaders)	167	4
Javelin—J. Brooks (Southport)	212	8

BRITISH INTERNATIONAL GAMES

Held at Crystal Palace on August 30, 1976

Men's Events

Metres	min.	sec.
100—A. Wells (Edinburgh)		10·74
200—A. Wells (Edinburgh)		21·59
800—M. Edwards (Wolverhampton)	1	49·3
"*Emsley Carr*" *Trophy*		
Mile—D. Moorcroft (Loughborough)	3	57·1
5,000—G. Tebroke (Netherlands)	13	37·6
Steeplechase—P. Griffiths (Tipton)	8	40·0
110 *Hurdles*—B. Danville (Wolverhampton)		14·67
400 *Hurdles*—A. Pascoe (Poly.)		50·09
4×400 *Relay*—Great Britain	3	08·9
	ft.	in.
Pole Vault—B. Hooper (Woking)	17	1
Long Jump—G. Cybulski (Poland)	25	10¼
Triple Jump—A. Moore (Birchfield)	52	7¼
Javelin—M. Nemeth (Hungary)	280	8

Women's Events

Metres	min.	sec.
100—S. Colyear (Stretfield)		11·72
200—B. Goddard (Reading)		23·69
800—C. McMeekin (Glasgow)	2	05·9
1,500—M. Stewart (Birchfield)	4	13·3
Hurdles—S. Colyear (Stretfield)		14·02
	ft.	in.
Javelin—T. Sanderson (Wolverhampton)	187	8

BRITISH ATHLETICS LEAGUE

Div. I—Wolverhampton & Bilston, 22 points; Edinburgh South H., 16½.
Div. II—Enfield, 18 points, Stretford, 17.
Div. III—Essex Beagles, 21 points; Polytechnic, 18.
Div. IV—Liverpool, 19 points; Southampton, 19.
"*Pye*" *Gold Cup*—Wolverhampton & Bilston, 128 points.
British Women's Cup—Stretford, 94 points.

OXFORD *v.* CAMBRIDGE

Cambridge beat Oxford in the Annual Oxford *v.* Cambridge Sports held at the Crystal Palace on May 19, 1976 by 115 points to 94. Of the 102 contests held since 1864, Oxford have won on 51 occasions, Cambridge on 45. There have been 7 draws. In the Women's contest held since 1975,

Cambridge won for the second time by 67 points to 64.

Oxford won the Cross Country Race (1975) by 29 points to 53.

WORLD 50KM. WALKING CHAMPIONSHIP
held in Malmo, September 18, 1976

		hr.	min.	sec.
1.	V. Soldatenko (U.S.S.R.)	3	54	40
2.	E. Vera (Mexico)	3	58	14
3.	R. Alaonen (Finland)	3	58	33

GREAT BRITAIN JUNIORS v. GERMANY v. POLAND
Held in Bremen, September 11 and 12

MATCH v. GERMANY
Men's Events

Metres		min.	sec.
100—D. Thompson (G.B.)			10·90
200—B. Sattler (G.)			21·57
400—L. Zander (G.)			46·92
800—M. Edwards (G.B.)		1	49·4
1,500—P. Ilg (G.)		3	47·3
3,000—H. Hudak (G.)		8	25·0
5,000—W. Grommisch (G.)		14	16·4
10,000 Walk—W. Werner (G.)		46	45·0
4 × 100 Relay—Great Britain			40·74
4 × 400 Relay—Germany		3	08·4
110 Hurdles—W. Kessel (G.)			14·60
400 Hurdles—H. Schmid (G.)			49·92
2,000 Steeple—A. Howden (G.B.)		5	48·0

		ft.	in.
High Jump—A. Ketterer (G.)		6	10¼
Pole Vault—D. Wesp (G.)		15	9
Long Jump—W. Klepsch (G.)		24	9¼
Triple Jump—K. Connor (G.B.)		52	1¼
Shot—U. Gelhausen (G.)		55	5
Discus—T. Berlep (G.)		170	3
Hammer—K. Ploghaus (G.)		215	2
Javelin—K. Tafelmeier (G.)		257	7

Germany beat Great Britain by 249 points to 182

GERMANY (JUNIORS) v. GREAT BRITAIN
Women's Events

Metres		min.	sec.
100—H. Barnett (G.B.)			11·98
200—M. Probert (G.B.)			23·60
400—E. Rauhut (G.)			54·77
800—E. Schact (G.)		2	05·2
1,500—J. Williamson (G.B.)		4	24·8
4 × 100 Relay—Germany			44·38
4 × 400 Relay—Great Britain		3	41·1
100 Hurdles—D. Schenten (G.)			13·89

		ft.	in.
High Jump—B. Holzapfel (G.)		6	0¾
Long Jump—K. Hanel (G.)		20	7¼
Shot—B. Phillip (G.)		57	11¼
Discus—D. Galler (G.)		147	1
Javelin—H. Repser (G.)		182	8

Germany beat Great Britain by 151 points to 110

MATCH v. POLAND
Men's Events

Metres		min.	sec.
100—M. Woronin (P.)			10·88
200—L. Dunecki (P.)			21·66
400—J. Jank (P.)			47·18
800—M. Edwards (G.B.)		1	49·4
1,500—J. Robson (G.B.)		3	47·6
3,000—S. Broslawksi (P.)		8	24·8
5,000—E. Stacha (P.)		14	17·0
10,000 Walk—W. Cieslak (P.)		46	34·0
4 × 100 Relay—Great Britain			40·74
4 × 400 Relay—Poland		3	10·0
110 Hurdles—R. Giegel (P.)			14·42
400 Hurdles—G. Adamczyk (P.)			52·35
Steeplechase—E. Rolbiecki (P.)		5	42·4

		ft.	in.
High Jump—J. Wszola (P.)		7	2¾
Pole Vault—M. Klimeyk (P.)		17	0¾
Long Jump—L. Dunecki (P.)		24	9
Triple Jump—K. Connor (G.B.)		52	1¼
Shot—P. Durczynski (P.)		53	0
Discus—J. Dariusz (P.)		171	1
Hammer—R. Weinar (P.)		200	9
Javelin—R. Zwierzchowski (P.)		245	4

Poland beat Great Britain by 139 points to 81

Women's Events

Metres		min.	sec.
100—Z. Filip (P.)			11·97
200—M. Probert (G.B.)			23·60
400—A. Baldock (G.B.)			54·90
800—E. Glodz (P.)		2	07·2
1,500—J. Williamson (G.B.)		4	24·8
4 × 100 Relay—Poland			45·12
4 × 400 Relay—Great Britain		3	41·1
100 Hurdles—E. Szulc (P.)			13·52

		ft.	in.
High Jump—E. Cludzinska (P.)		5	9¼
Long Jump—S. Hearnshaw (G.B.)		19	11
Shot—J. Oakes (G.B.)		50	4½
Discus—U. Plusa (P.)		164	11
Javelin—E. Namierowska (P.)		157	11

Poland beat Great Britain by 72 points to 63

GREAT BRITAIN v. FRANCE DECATHLON AND PENTATHLON
Held at Lille, September 11 and 12

Senior Decathlon	Points
1. N. Phipps (G.B.)	7,231

Team Event   Great Britain beat France by 27,788 points to 27,439

Junior Decathlon	
1. G. Watson (G.B.)	6,703

Team Event   France beat Great Britain by 25,674 points to 24,230

Senior Pentathlon	
1. S. Longden (G.B.)	4,350

Team Event   Great Britain beat France by 12,254 points to 11,504

Junior Pentathlon	
1. Y. Wray (G.B.)	3,739

Team Events   Great Britain beat France by 10,991 points to 10,630

THE TURF

The Turf in Great Britain is under the control of the Jockey Club.

The *Jockey Club* (incorporating the National Hunt Committee, 42 Portman Square, London, W.1.). Stewards are: The Lord Howard de Walden (*Senior Steward*); Capt. H. M. Gosling; R. N. Richmond-Watson (*Deputy Senior Stewards*); Lt. Col. P. H. G. Bengough, O.B.E.; J. Hambro; Major E. M. Cameron; Sir John Thompson, K.B.E., T.D.; The Lord Manton; J. B. Sumner.

Leading Owners and Trainers, 1976
(Flat Season up to Oct. 8)

Winning Owners		Winning Trainers	
D. Wilden-		H. Cecil...	£260,077
stein......	£244,500	A. Penna (Fr.)	240,819
C. D'Alessio	169,018	H. R. Price..	177,422
N. B. Hunt..	122,108	P. Walwyn...	164,016
J. H. Whitney	88,913	W. R. Hern..	150,977
C. F. Spence.	53,342	B. Hobbs....	141,289
G. Cambanis.	52,437	B. W. Hills..	112,026
C. A. B. St		M. Zilber (Fr.)	111,825
George....	48,750	M. W. Easter-	
R. E. Sangster	46,913	by.........	107,978
R. D. Hol-		C. E. Brittain	101,434
lingsworth.	45,463	J. Dunlop....	81,883
G.A.Pope,jun.	43,889	M. Stoute....	81,132
H. J. Joel....	41,773		
Capt. M. D.			
Lemos.....	35,727		

Leading Breeders, 1976
(Up to Oct. 8)

	Races Horses won		Value
Dayton Ltd..............	5	10	£232,599
Tally Ho Stud............	1	5	166,389
N. B. Hunt.............	4	5	128,202
J. H. Whitney...........	7	17	75,080
E. A. Dandy............	1	4	53,342
R. D. Hollingsworth.....	5	11	45,463
G. A. Pope, jun.........	3	8	43,889
H. J. Joel..............	12	26	41,095
Société Aland............	1	3	40,318
G. Cambanis.............	1	2	35,461
Trowell Hall Stud........	4	10	33,321
Late Duke of Norfolk.....	11	13	30,301

Winning Jockeys, 1975
(Up to Oct. 3)

	1st	2nd	3rd	Unpl.	Total Mts.	Per. cent.
P. Eddery......	146	125	88	353	712	20·51
W. Carson....	130	129	94	425	778	16·71
B. Taylor......	93	68	61	257	479	19·42
J. Mercer......	92	82	73	263	510	18·04
E. Hide........	88	87	90	333	598	14·72
M. L. Thomas..	84	63	68	360	575	14·61
L. Piggott.....	82	64	44	181	371	22·10
P. Cook.......	66	70	61	318	515	12·82
G. Starkey.....	63	47	51	239	400	15·75
G. Lewis.......	61	60	53	255	429	14·22
E. Johnson.....	56	56	46	260	417	13·45
D. Dineley.....	52	31	27	167	277	18·77
B. Raymond...	52	58	53	259	422	12·32

Winning Sires, 1975
(Up to Oct. 8)

	Races Horses won		Value
Wolver Hollow (1964), by			
Sovereign Path.......	17	31	£188,513
Carvin (1962), by Marino..	1	2	131,625
Vaguely Noble (1965), by			
Vienna...............	5	5	117,518
Lucky Debonair (1962), by			
Vertax...............	1	2	86,746
Habitat (1966), by Sir Gay-			
lord.................	14	18	85,581
Exbury (1959), by Le Haar.	4	7	75,612
Yellow God (1967), by Red			
God.................	18	26	70,663
Le Levanstell (1957), by Le			
Lavandou............	14	21	70,121
Hotfoot (1966), by Fire-			
streak...............	10	19	66,909
Nijinsky (1967), by North-			
ern Dancer..........-	6	14	61,605
Busted (1963), by Crepello.	27	40	60,112
Sea Hawk II (1963), by			
Herbager.............	14	23	57,419

THE DERBY, 1966–1976
For particulars of the Derby from 1780–1965 see 1921–66 editions.

The *Distance* of the Derby course at Epsom is 1½ miles. Lord Egremont won Derby in 1782, 1804, 5, 7, 26 (also, 5 Oaks); Duke of Grafton, 1802, 9, 10, 15 (also, 9 Oaks); Mr. Bowes, 1835, 43, 52, 3; Sir J. Hawley, Teddington (1851), Beadsman (1858), Musjid (1859), and Blue Gown (1868), the 1st Duke of Westminster, Bend Or (1880), Shotover (1882), Ormonde (1886), and Flying Fox (1899). Lady James Douglas is the first lady to win the Derby—War Substitute at Newmarket (1918); at Epsom, Mrs. G. B. Miller (1937). First winner was Sir Charles Bunbury's Diomed in 1780. From 1940 to 1945 a substitute Derby was run at Newmarket. By winning his 5th Derby, the late Aga Khan equalled Lord Egremont's record. He also won 2 Oaks.

Year	Owner and Name of Winner	Betting	Jockey	Trainer	No. of Run'rs
1966	Lady Zia Wernher's Charlottown......	5 to 1	A. Breasley...	G. Smyth....	22
1967	Mr. H. J. Joel's Royal Palace*..........	7–4 F.	G. Moore....	N. Murless...	25
1968	Mr. R. R. Guest's Sir Ivor* (Ir.)	4–5 F.	L. Piggott....	M. V. O'Brien	22
1969	Mr. A. M. Budgett's Blakeney.........	15–2	E. Johnson....	A. M. Budgett	13
1970	Mr. C. W. Engelhard's Nijinsky*°(Ir.)..	11–8 F.	L. Piggott....	M. V. O'Brien	26
1971	Mr. P. Mellon's Mill Reef...........	100–30 F.	G. Lewis.....	I. Balding....	11
1972	Mr. J. Galbreath's Roberto (Ir.).......	3–1 F.	L. Piggott....	M. V. O'Brien	21
1973	Mr. A. M. Budgett's Morston..........	25–1	E. Hide......	A. M. Budgett	22
1974	Mrs. N. Phillips' Snow Knight.........	50–1	B. Taylor....	P. M. Nelson.	25
1975	Dr. C. Vittadini's Grundy.............	5–1	P. Eddery....	P. Walwyn....	18
1976	Mr. N. B. Hunt's Empery (Fr.)	10–1	L. Piggott....	M. Zilber....	23

Marked* also won the Two Thousand Guineas; °the St. Leger.

Record times, 2 min. 34 secs. by Hyperion in 1933; Windsor Lad in 1934; 2 min. 33·8 sec. Mahmoud in 1936.

TWO THOUSAND GUINEAS. First Run, 1809. Rowley Mile. Newmarket. 9 st.

Year	Owner and Name of Winner	Betting	Jockey	Trainer	No. of Run'rs
1972	Sir Jules Thorn's High Top	85 to 40F.	W. Carson	B. van Cutsem	12
1973	Mrs. B. Davis's Mon Fils	50 to 1	F. Durr	R. Hannon	18
1974	Mme. M. Berner's Nonoalco (Fr.)	19 to 2	Y. Saint-Martin	F. Boutin	12
1975	Mr. C. d'Alessio's Bolkonski	33 to 1	F. Dettori	H. Cecil	24
1976	Mr. C. d'Allessio's Wollow	Evens F.	G. Dettori	H. Cecil	17

ONE THOUSAND GUINEAS. 1814. Rowley Mile. Newmarket. Fillies. 9 st.

Year	Owner and Name of Winner	Betting	Jockey	Trainer	No. of Run'rs
1972	Mrs. R. Stanley's Waterloo	8 to 1	E. Hide	B. Watts	18
1973	Mr. G. H. Pope's Mysterious	11 to 1	G. Lewis	N. Murless	14
1974	H.M. The Queen's Highclere	12 to 1	J. Mercer	W. R. Hern	15
1975	Mrs. D. O'Kelly's Nocturnal Spree	14 to 1	J. Roe	N. Murless	16
1976	Mr. D. Wildenstein's Flying Water (Fr.)	2 to 1 F.	Y. Saint-Martin	A. Penna	25

OAKS. 1779. Epsom. 1½ Mile. Fillies. 9 st.

Year	Owner and Name of Winner	Betting	Jockey	Trainer	No. of Run'rs
1972	Mr. C. St. George's Ginevra	8 to 1	A. Murray	H. R. Price	17
1973	Mr. G. H. Pope's Mysterious	13 to 8 F.	G. Lewis	N. Murless	10
1974	Mr. L. Freedman's Polygamy	3 to 1 F.	P. Eddery	P. Walwyn	15
1975	Mr. J. Morrison's Juliette Marny	12 to 1	L. Piggott	J. Tree	12
1976	Mr. D. Wildenstein's Pawneese (Fr.)	6 to 5 F.	Y. Saint-Martin	A. Penna	14

ST. LEGER. 1776(8). Doncaster. 1¾ mile, 127 yards.

Year	Owner and Name of Winner	Betting	Jockey	Trainer	No. of Run'rs
1972	Mr. O. Phipps's Boucher (Ir.)	3 to 1	L. Piggott	M. V. O'Brien	7
1973	Col. W. Behrens's Peleid	28 to 1	F. Durr	W. Elsey	13
1974	Lady Beaverbrook's Bustino	11 to 10 F.	J. Mercer	W. R. Hern	10
1975	Mr. C. St. George's Bruni	9 to 1	A. Murray	R. Price	12
1976	Mr. D. Wildenstein's Crow (Fr.)	6 to 1 JF.	Y. Saint-Martin	A. Penna	15

	Lincolnshire Handicap Doncaster—1 mile.	Free Handicap Newmarket—3yrs.—7f.	Jockey Club Stakes Newmarket—1½ miles.	Coronation Cup Epsom—1½ miles.
1973	Bronze Hill 4y 7st 9lb	Pitskelly 8st 5lb	Our Mirage 4y 9st 3lb	Roberto (Ir.) 4y 9st 3lb
1974	Quizair 5y 7st 13lb	Charlie Bubbles 8st 3lb	Relay Race 4y 8st 9lb	Buoy 4st 9lb
1975	Southwark Star 4y 7st 3lb.	Green Belt 8st 9lb	Shebeen 4y 8st 10lb	Bustino 4y 9st
1976	The Hertford 5y 8st 6lb	Man of Harlech 8st 4lb	Orange Bay 4y 9st 8lb	Quiet Fling 4y 9st

	Ascot Stakes 2½ miles.	Gold Cup Ascot—2½ miles.	Coventry Stakes Ascot—2 yrs—6 furlongs.	Grand Prix de Paris 1 mile 7½ furlongs.
1973	Full of Beans 5y 7st 11lb	Lassalle (Fr.) 4y 9st	Doleswood 8st 11lb	Tennyson
1974	Kambalda 4y 8st 9lb	Ragstone 4y 9st	Whip it Quick 8st 11lb	Sagaro
1975	Crash Course 4y 9st 4lb	Sagaro 4y 9st	Galway Bay 8st 11lb	Matahawk
1976	Tudor Crown 5y 7st 7lb	Sagaro 5y 9st	Cawston's Clown 8st 11lb	Exceller

	Chester Cup Chester—2¼m. 97yd.	Jubilee Handicap Kempton Park—1¼m.	Eclipse Stakes Sandown Park—1¼m.	King George VI and Queen Elizabeth Stakes Ascot—1½ miles.
1973	Crisalgo 5y 7st 7lb	Brigade Major 4y 8st 5 lb	Scottish Rifle 4y 9st 5lb	Dahlia 3y 8st 4lb
1974	Attivo 4y 7st 5lb	Jumpabout 4y 7st 12lb	Coup de Feu 5y 9st 5lb	Dahlia 4y 9st 4lb
1975	Super Nova 5y 7st 7lb	Jumpabout 5y 8st 5lb	Star Appeal 5y 9st 7lb	Grundy 3y 8st 7lb
1976	John Cherry 5y 9st 4lb		Trepan 4y 9st 7lb	Pawneese 3y 8st 5lb

	Prix de L'Arc de Triomphe Longchamp—1½ m.	Cheltenham Gold Cup abt. 3¼ m.	Cambridgeshire Newmarket—9f.	Middle Park Stakes Newmarket—2yrs.—6f.
1973	Rheingold 4y 9st 6lb	The Dikler 10y 12st	Siliciana 4y 8st 5lb	Habat 9st
1974	Allez France 4y 9st 3lb	Captain Christy 7y 12st	Flying Nelly 4y 7st 7lb	Steel Heart 9st
1975	Star Appeal 5y 9st 6lb	Ten Up 8y 12st	Lottogift 4y 8st 7lb	Hittite Glory 9st
1976	Ivanjica 4y 9st 1lb	Royal Frolic 7y 12st	Intermission 3y 8st 6lb	Tachypous 9st

	Cesarewitch Newmarket—2¼m.	Washington Int'national Laurel Park—1½ m.	Champion Stakes Newmarket—1¼ m.	Grand National Liverpool—4m. 856 yds.
1973	Flash Imp 4y 7st 13lb	Dahlia (France)	Hurry Harriet (Ir.)3y8st7lb	Red Rum 8y 10st 5lb
1974	Ocean King 8y 7st 7lb	Admetus (France)	Giacometti 3y 8st 10lb	Red Rum 9y 12st
1975	Shantallah 3y 8st 10lb	Nobiliary (France)	Rose Bowl 3y 8st 7lb	L'Escargot 12y 11st 3lb
1976	John Cherry 5y 9st 13lb	....	Vitiges 3y 8st 11lb	Rag Trade 10y 10st 12lb

CRICKET

Marylebone Cricket Club (1787), Lord's, N.W.8. *Pres.*, W. H. Webster; *Sec.*, J. A. Bailey; *Asst. Sec. Admin.*, Gp. Capt. W. R. Ford, C.B.E., R.A.F.(*ret.*); *Asst. Sec. Cricket*, J. G. Lofting; *Curator*, S. E. A. Green.

TEST MATCHES

Australia v. West Indies, 1975–76

First Test.—(Brisbane, Nov. 28–Dec. 2). Australia won by eight wickets. West Indies 214 and 370. Australia 366 and 219 for 2.

Second Test.—(Perth, Dec. 12–16). West Indies won by an innings and 87 runs. West Indies 585; Australia 329 and 169.

Third Test.—(Melbourne, Dec. 26–30). Australia won by eight wickets. West Indies 224 and 312; Australia 485 and 55 for 2.

Fourth Test.—(Sydney, Jan. 3–7). Australia won by seven wickets. West Indies 355 and 128; Australia 405 and 82 for 3.

Fifth Test.—(Adelaide, Jan. 23–28). Australia won by 190 runs. Australia 418 and 345; West Indies 274 and 299.

Sixth Test.—(Melbourne, Jan. 31–Feb. 5). Australia won by 165 runs. Australia 351 and 300 for 3 (dec.); West Indies 160 and 326.

AUSTRALIA BATTING

Batsmen	Innings	Times not out	Runs	Highest Score	Average
G. S. Chappell	11	5	702	182★	117·00
G. J. Cosier	3	0	174	109	58·00
I. R. Redpath	11	0	575	103	52·27
I. M. Chappell	12	2	449	156	44·90
G. N. Yallop	5	1	179	57	44·75
A. Turner	11	0	439	136	36·58
R. W. Marsh	8	0	236	66	29·50
R. B. McCosker	8	2	172	109★	28·66
G. J. Gilmour	7	0	185	95	26·42
D. K. Lillee	6	3	77	25	25·66
A. A. Mallett	8	2	66	18★	11·00
J. R. Thomson	7	0	63	44	9·00
M. H. N. Walker	4	0	13	8	3·25

Also batted: T. J. Jenner 6★.

BOWLING

Bowlers	Overs	Maidens	Runs	Wickets	Average
G. J. Gilmour	97·6	17	406	20	20·30
D. K. Lillee	129·3	7	712	27	26·37
J. R. Thomson	150·5	15	831	29	28·65
M. H. N. Walker	79·3	14	320	11	29·09
A. A. Mallett	119·1	19	506	11	46·00

Also bowled: G. S. Chappell 21·2—1—69—3; I. M. Chappell 12·6—4—54—2; T. J. Jenner 24—3—90—2; G. J. Cosier 12—1—51—0.

WEST INDIES BATTING

Batsmen	Innings	Times not out	Runs	Highest Score	Average
K. D. Boyce	7	2	240	95★	48·00
C. H. Lloyd	11	1	469	149	46·90
I. V. A. Richards	11	0	426	101	38·72
A. I. Kallicharran	11	0	421	101	38·27
R. C. Fredericks	11	0	417	169	37·90
D. L. Murray	11	0	342	66	31·09
B. D. Julien	5	1	124	46★	31·00
L. G. Rowe	11	0	270	107	24·54
V. A. Holder	6	1	82	24	16·40
M. A. Holding	9	0	95	34	10·55
L. R. Gibbs	11	6	43	13	8·60
A. M. E. Roberts	11	0	40	17	4·44
C. G. Greenidge	4	0	11	8	2·75

Also batted: Inshan Ali 12 and 24; L. Baichan 3 and 20.

BOWLING

Bowlers	Overs	Maidens	Runs	Wickets	Average
A. M. E. Roberts	141·6	14	580	22	26·36
B. D. Julien	68·4	6	303	11	27·54
V. A. Holder	109·0	7	513	13	39·46
K. D. Boyce	82·2	6	361	9	40·11
L. R. Gibbs	232·4	48	652	16	40·75
M. A. Holding	138·5	15	614	10	61·40

Also bowled: A. I. Kallicharran 3·1—1—21—1; R. C. Fredericks 13—1—62—1; Inshan Ali 27—1—124—1; C. H. Lloyd 17—4—56—0; I. V. A. Richards 8·1—0—44—0; C. G. Greenidge 1—1—0—0; L. G. Rowe 1—0—6—0.

★ Not out.

New Zealand v. India, 1976

First Test.—(Auckland, Jan. 24–28). India won by eight wickets. New Zealand 266 and 215; India 414 and 71 for 2.

Second Test.—(Christchurch, Feb. 5–10). Drawn. India 270 and 255 for 6; New Zealand 403.

Third Test.—(Wellington, Feb. 13–17). New Zealand won by an innings and 33 runs. India 220 and 81; New Zealand 334.

West Indies v. India, 1976

First Test.—(Bridgetown, March 10–13). West Indies won by an innings and 97 runs. India 177 and 214; West Indies 488 for 9 (dec.).

Second Test.—(Port-of-Spain, March 24–29). Drawn. West Indies 241 and 215 for 8; India 402 for 5 (dec.).

Third Test.—(Port-of-Spain, April 7–12). India won by six wickets. West Indies 359 and 271 for 6 (dec.); India 228 and 406 for 4.

Fourth Test.—(Kingston, April 21–25). West Indies won by ten wickets. India 306 for 6 (dec.) and 97; West Indies 391 and 13 for no wicket.

England v. West Indies, 1976

First Test.—(Trent Bridge, June 3–8). Drawn. West Indies 494 and 176 for 5 (dec.); England 332 and 156 for 2.

Second Test.—(Lord's, June 17–22). Drawn. England 250 and 254; West Indies 182 and 241 for 6.

Third Test.—(Old Trafford, July 8–13). West Indies won by 425 runs. West Indies 211 and 411 for 5 (dec.); England 71 and 126.

Fourth Test.—(Headingley, July 22–27). West Indies won by 55 runs. West Indies 450 and 196; England 387 and 204.

Fifth Test.—(The Oval, Aug. 12–17). West Indies won by 231 runs. West Indies 687 for 8 (dec.) and 182 for no wkt. (dec.); England 435 and 203.

ENGLAND BATTING

Batsmen	Innings	Times not out	Runs	Highest Score	Average
J. H. Edrich	4	1	145	76*	48.33
D. B. Close	6	1	166	60	33.20
D. S. Steele	10	0	308	106	30.80
A. W. Greig	9	1	243	116	30.37
A. P. E. Knott	9	0	270	116	30.00
P. Willey	4	0	115	45	28.75
R. A. Woolmer	9	0	245	82	27.22
C. M. Old	3	0	65	33	21.66
J. A. Snow	5	2	54	20*	18.00
J. M. Brearley	4	0	70	40	17.50
J. C. Balderstone	4	0	39	35	9.75
F. C. Hayes	4	0	25	18	6.25
M. W. W. Selvey	4	2	10	4*	5.00
D. L. Underwood	9	0	40	31	4.44
P. I. Pocock	3	1	13	7	4.33
M. Hendrick	3	1	5	5	2.50
R. G. D. Willis	4	2	5	5*	2.50

Also batted: D. L. Amiss 203, 16; G. Miller 36, 24; A. Ward 0, 0; B. Wood 6, 30.

BOWLING

Bowlers	Overs	Maidens	Runs	Wickets	Average
R. G. D. Willis	57.3	11	234	9	26.00
J. A. Snow	106.4	16	423	15	28.20
A. Ward	24	2	128	4	32.00
D. L. Underwood	224	59	631	17	37.11
C. M. Old	68.3	11	248	6	41.33
P. I. Pocock	61	15	173	4	43.25
M. W. W. Selvey	67	8	263	6	43.83
M. Hendrick	69	14	192	4	48.00
A. W. Greig	98	15	336	5	67.20

Also bowled: J. C. Balderstone 16—0—80—1; G. Miller 27—4—106—1; D. S. Steele 3—0—18—0; P. Willey 4—0—15—0; R. A. Woolmer 40—2—194—1.

WEST INDIES BATTING

Batsmen	Innings	Times not out	Runs	Highest Score	Average
I. V. A. Richards	7	0	829	291	118.42
C. G. Greenidge	10	1	592	134	65.77
R. C. Fredericks	10	1	517	138	57.44
L. G. Rowe	3	0	126	70	42.00
C. L. King	5	1	167	63	41.75
A. I. Kallicharran	6	1	180	97	36.00
C. H. Lloyd	9	0	296	84	32.88
D. L. Murray	8	2	123	36	20.50
V. A. Holder	6	3	50	19*	16.66
B. D. Julien	4	0	38	21	9.50
A. M. E. Roberts	5	0	45	19	9.00
W. W. Daniel	4	2	18	10	9.00
M. A. Holding	5	0	41	32	8.20
H. A. Gomes	3	0	11	3	3.66

Also batted: R. R. Jumadeen 0*; A. L. Padmore 8*.

BOWLING

Bowlers	Overs	Maidens	Runs	Wickets	Average
M. A. Holding	159.1	54	356	28	12.71
A. M. E. Roberts	221.4	69	537	28	19.17
W. W. Daniel	108	28	317	13	24.38
V. A. Holder	158	48	367	15	24.46

Also bowled: R. C. Fredericks 43.4—11—119—1; H. A. Gomes 13—2—26—0; R. R. Jumadeen 28—8—64—1; B. D. Julien 86—28—168—2; A. I. Kallicharran 10—3—18—0; C. L. King 39—11—95—2; C. H. Lloyd 7—3—9—0; A. L. Padmore 3—2—1—0; I. V. A. Richards 31—12—56—1.

* Not out.

County Championship Table, 1976

County Order for 1976 1975 in brackets	Played	Won	Lost	Drawn	Bonus Btg.	Bonus Blng.	Points
Middlesex (11)	20	11	5	4	57	67	234
Northamptonshire (8)	20	9	5	6	54	74	218
Gloucestershire (16)	20	9	5	6	54	66	210
Leicestershire (1)	20	9	3	8	51	68	209
Warwickshire (14)	20	6	7	7	65	70	195
Essex (7)	20	7	4	9	57	62	189
Somerset (12)	20	7	8	5	47	63	180
Yorkshire (2)	20	6	8	6	49	67	176
Surrey (6)	20	6	4	10	54	61	175
Sussex (17)	20	5	8	7	49	71	170
Worcestershire (10)	20	6	3	11	50	59	169
Hampshire (3)	20	4	10	6	52	67	159
Nottinghamshire (13)	20	4	7	9	58	60	158
Kent (5)	20	5	7	8	48	57	155
Derbyshire (15)	20	4	7	9	39	70	149
Lancashire (4)	20	3	7	10	43	75	148
Glamorgan (9)	20	3	10	7	37	60	127

Gillette Cup Final.—Northamptonshire beat Lancashire by four wickets. Lancashire 195 for 7; Northamptonshire 199 for 6.

Benson and Hedges Cup Final.—Kent beat Worcestershire by 43 runs. Kent 236 for 7; Worcestershire 193.

John Player Sunday League Competition.—Kent won title on faster scoring rate for season.

Universities.—Oxford University beat Cambridge University by ten wickets. Oxford 297 for 5 (dec.) and 86 for no wkt.; Cambridge 116 and 263.

Eton v. Harrow.—Match drawn. Eton 220 and 112 for 9; Harrow 328 for 9 (dec.).

MISCELLANEOUS CRICKET RECORDS

Highest Individual Scores.—In first-class cricket in England: A. C. MacLaren, 424, for Lancashire v. Somerset at Taunton, July, 1895. In Australia: D. G. Bradman (Australia), 452 (not out) for N.S.W. v. Queensland, Sydney, 1929-30. In India: B. B. Nimbalkar (Maharashtra v. W. Indian States), Poona, 1948-49, 443 (not out). In Pakistan: Hanif Mohammad, 499, Karachi v. Bahawalpur, 1959. In a minor inter-county match: F. E. Lacey (Hampshire v. Norfolk), Southampton, 1887, 323 (not out). In other minor matches: A. E. J. Collins, aged 13, scored 628 (not out) in a Junior House match playing for Clarke's House v. North Town at Clifton College in 1899.

Highest Team Innings.—Australia: Victoria 1,107 v. N.S.W., Melbourne, 1926; England: England 903 (for 7 dec.) v. Australia, 1938.

Smallest Totals.—Oxford University (one man absent), 12 v. M.C.C. at Oxford, May 1877; Northamptonshire v. Gloucestershire, June 11, 1907.

Highest Aggregate.—Bombay, 651 and 714 for 8 dec. v. Maharashtra, 407, 604, Poona, 1948-49. Total: 2,376 (38 wkts.).

Highest Partnership.—Gul Mahomed (319) and V. S. Hazare (288) made 577 for 4th wkt. for Baroda v. Holkar, March 7, 1947.

BATTING AND BOWLING AVERAGES

English Batting Averages, 1976
(Qualification, 8 Innings)

English Bowling Averages, 1976
(Qualification, 10 Wickets)

Batsmen	Number of Innings	Times not out	Total Runs	Highest Innings	Average
Zaheer Abbas	39	5	2,554	230★	75·11
G. Boycott	24	5	1,288	207★	67·78
D. L. Amiss	38	6	2,110	203	65·93
Javed Miandad	10	1	523	162	58·11
B. F. Davison	41	9	1,818	132	56·81
K. W. R. Fletcher	36	7	1,588	128★	54·75
H. Pilling	35	5	1,569	149★	52·30
Mushtaq Mohammad	36	4	1,620	204★	50·62
G. M. Turner	37	2	1,752	169	50·05
G. D. Barlow	37	7	1,478	160★	49·26
K. S. McEwan	38	1	1,821	156	49·21
B. A. Richards	34	2	1,572	179	49·12
Sadiq Mohammad	39	2	1,759	163★	47·54
R. A. Woolmer	39	2	1,749	143	47·27
E. J. O. Hemsley	14	5	421	157	46·77
J. H. Edrich	37	4	1,526	179	46·24
A. Jones	40	3	1,692	156★	45·72
B. C. Rose	39	4	1,624	177	45·40
J. H. Hampshire	31	2	1,303	153	44·93
B. Wood	27	7	890	198	44·50
G. W. Humpage	37	7	1,329	125★	44·30
J. A. Jameson	40	0	1,727	144	43·17
D. W. Randall	37	1	1,546	204★	42·94
G. A. Gooch	34	4	1,273	136	42·43
C. E. B. Rice	37	3	1,438	246	42·29
B. L. d'Oliveira	26	6	840	113	42·00
J. A. Ormrod	38	2	1,507	166	41·86
P. Willey	29	2	1,115	227	41·29
C. J. Tavaré	36	6	1,229	105★	40·96
G. R. J. Roope	43	12	1,266	156★	40·83
Imran Khan	31	4	1,092	166	40·44
J. M. Brearley	45	3	1,695	153	40·35
M. J. Harris	31	6	1,006	140★	40·24
Younis Ahmed	41	5	1,439	161	39·97
D. B. Close	34	5	1,137	88	39·20
J. D. Hopkins	13	2	429	105	39·00
J. N. Shepherd	29	6	895	87	38·91
M. J. Smedley	36	8	1,077	130	38·46
G. P. Howarth	41	0	1,554	124	37·90
K. D. Smith	30	3	1,023	124	37·88
R. D. V. Knight	38	4	1,240	165★	37·57
A. P. E. Knott	29	4	938	144	37·52
S. B. Hassan	29	3	970	162	37·30
B. Leadbeater	15	4	408	140★	37·09
G. Richards	25	4	774	102★	36·85
J. Birkenshaw	30	9	770	74★	36·66
F. M. Engineer	33	7	952	96	36·61
D. R. Turner	40	5	1,269	130★	36·25
C. T. Radley	33	1	1,154	171	36·06
R. B. Kanhai	28	4	864	111★	36·00
D. I. Gower	13	4	323	102★	35·88
J. Whitehouse	42	4	1,363	169★	35·86
T. E. Jesty	39	3	1,288	159★	35·77
M. J. Procter	38	3	1,209	131	34·54
P. J. Sharpe	37	0	1,277	228	34·51
R. T. Virgin	40	5	1,207	145	34·48
R. W. Tolchard	32	6	895	88★	34·42
A. Hill	40	2	1,303	160★	34·28
M. J. Smith	41	1	1,368	148	34·20
I. T. Botham	35	5	1,022	167★	34·06
J. C. Balderstone	44	2	1,409	125	33·54
A. G. E. Ealham	40	7	1,105	134★	33·48
D. S. Steele	34	4	992	139	33·06
C. M. Old	18	2	526	112	32·87
P. J. Graves	40	4	1,178	133★	32·72
F. C. Hayes	33	4	948	137	32·68
M. H. Denness	33	5	913	83	32·60
B. E. A. Edmeades	24	3	674	155	32·09
N. G. Featherstone	35	4	995	78	32·09
D. Lloyd	34	2	1,017	146	31·78
B. Dudleston	20	4	502	103★	31·37
D. A. Francis	27	5	658	88	31·22
A. W. Stovold	39	1	1,185	83	31·18
A. J. Hignell	39	2	1,140	119	30·81
J. D. Love	20	0	615	163	30·75
R. E. East	30	7	702	113	30·52
F. W. Swarbrook	36	15	638	80	30·38
P. A. Neale	33	1	949	143	29·65
D. P. Patel	25	3	648	107	29·45
R. Illingworth	37	7	879	135	29·30

Bowlers	Overs	Maidens	Runs	Wickets	Average
N. G. Featherstone	232	64	569	26	15·80
R. M. H. Cottam	213·5	54	584	36	16·22
Asif Iqbal	69·4	12	214	13	16·46
P. J. Sainsbury	572·3	228	1,236	66	18·72
E. J. Barlow	308·5	60	897	46	19·50
P. B. Clift	572·5	128	1,493	74	20·17
W. Larkins	67·2	9	245	12	20·41
R. D. Jackman	563·4	120	1,760	85	20·70
M. W. W. Selvey	644·3	130	1,913	90	21·25
K. Higgs	473·4	114	1,175	55	21·36
R. Illingworth	389·2	143	772	36	21·44
G. Miller	565·2	147	1,660	77	21·55
F. J. Titmus	640·4	188	1,553	72	21·56
S. P. Perryman	392	115	892	41	21·75
J. R. T. Barclay	240·1	63	660	30	22·00
R. Arrowsmith	182·5	74	399	18	22·16
Sarfraz Nawaz	639·2	143	1,867	82	22·76
T. M. Lamb	167	44	503	22	22·86
A. A. Jones	552	113	1,626	71	22·90
A. W. Allin	334·3	96	1,011	44	22·97
P. H. Edmonds	887	286	2,029	88	23·05
S. Turner	749·4	189	1,869	81	23·07
P. Willey	218·4	52	601	26	23·11
J. Spencer	725·1	183	1,833	79	23·20
A. L. Robinson	379	89	1,006	43	23·39
Imran Khan	523·4	117	1,522	65	23·41
G. G. Arnold	376	100	962	41	23·46
J. D. Inchmore	480·2	95	1,485	63	23·57
R. G. D. Willis	238·5	41	757	32	23·65
A. S. Brown	350·2	80	983	41	23·97
F. W. Swarbrook	651	194	1,562	65	24·03
G. A. Cope	916·4	289	2,245	93	24·13
J. Simmons	503	157	1,194	49	24·36
D. P. Hughes	452·5	129	1,114	45	24·75
B. L. d'Oliveira	208·5	54	520	21	24·76
A. Ward	388·5	83	1,164	47	24·76
J. C. Balderstone	282·2	77	744	30	24·80
H. R. Moseley	582·1	156	1,440	58	24·82
R. M. Ratcliffe	434·5	122	1,167	47	24·82
D. A. Graveney	751·1	253	1,817	73	24·89
P. G. Lee	633	165	1,651	66	25·01
R. Le Q. Savage	400·5	84	1,151	46	25·02
J. A. Snow	488·2	100	1,488	59	25·22
A. J. Good	117·3	26	381	15	25·40
N. M. McVicker	317	60	1047	41	25·53
D. L. Acfield	718	131	1,850	72	25·69
J. F. Steele	300·3	93	747	29	25·75
D. J. Brown	615·3	122	1,703	66	25·80
C. E. Waller	674·1	180	1,845	71	25·98
C. E. B. Rice	451·1	109	1,254	48	26·12
J. N. Graham	294·1	88	656	25	26·24
B. S. Bedi	564·5	172	1,339	51	26·25
S. Oldham	258·3	45	765	29	26·37
K. Cooper	340·4	69	1,139	43	26·48
B. M. Brain	303·2	39	1,097	41	26·75
J. C. J. Dye	437·4	77	1,388	51	27·21
J. K. Lever	682·1	147	1,909	70	27·27
D. L. Underwood	859·2	317	2,139	78	27·42
D. R. Gurr	515·1	113	1,682	61	27·57
P. J. Lewington	230·4	78	524	19	27·57
M. Hendrick	524·3	119	1,298	47	27·61
J. H. Childs	345·1	100	1,024	37	27·67
C. M. Old	277·4	66	803	29	27·68
S. J. Rouse	393·2	79	1,221	44	27·75
A. Hodgson	355·4	70	1,142	41	27·85
T. E. Jesty	492	132	1,173	42	27·92
M. J. Procter	635	146	1,908	68	28·05
J. N. Shepherd	496·2	106	1,347	48	28·06
F. Booth	384·2	66	1,275	45	28·33
I. T. Botham	565·5	100	1,880	66	28·48
W. A. Bourne	536·2	101	1,630	57	28·59
K. D. Boyce	301·4	64	834	29	28·75
Mushtaq Mohammad	384·3	101	1,072	37	28·97
N. Gifford	686·2	200	1,715	59	29·06
R. P. Baker	212·5	39	727	25	29·08
T. J. Mottram	193·2	50	496	17	29·17
D. Lloyd	124	42	321	11	29·18
M. N. S. Taylor	301	67	908	31	29·29
P. I. Pocock	685·5	172	1,937	66	29·34
P. Lever	417·1	91	1,147	39	29·41

★ Denotes not out.

LIST OF COUNTY CRICKET CHAMPIONS.

1934	Lancashire	1950	{ Lancashire	1960	Yorkshire	1971	Surrey
1935	Yorkshire		{ Surrey	1961	Hampshire	1972	Warwickshire
1936	Derbyshire	1951	Warwickshire	1962	Yorkshire	1973	Hampshire
1937	Yorkshire	1952	Surrey	1963	Yorkshire	1974	Worcestershire
1938	Yorkshire	1953	Surrey	1964	Worcestershire	1975	Leicestershire
1939	Yorkshire	1954	Surrey	1965	Worcestershire	1976	Middlesex
1946	Yorkshire	1955	Surrey	1966	Yorkshire		
1947	Middlesex	1956	Surrey	1967	Yorkshire		
1948	Glamorgan	1957	Surrey	1968	Yorkshire		
1949	{ Middlesex	1958	Surrey	1969	Glamorgan		
	{ Yorkshire	1959	Yorkshire	1970	Kent		

RUGBY FOOTBALL

International Union Table, 1975-76

Country	Played	Won	Lost	Drawn	Points Scored		Points
					For	Against	
Wales..................	4	4	0	0	102	37	8
France.................	4	3	1	0	82	37	6
Scotland...............	4	2	2	0	49	59	4
Ireland................	4	1	3	0	31	87	2
England................	4	0	4	0	42	86	0

CALCUTTA CUP
England v. Scotland

1967	England 27–14
1968	England 8–6
1969	England 8–3
1970	Scotland 14–5
1971	Scotland 16–15
1972	Scotland 23–9
1973	England 20–13
1974	Scotland 16–14
1975	England 7–6
1976	Scotland 22–12

COUNTY CHAMPIONSHIP

Surrey and Durham.
Middlesex.
Lancashire.
Staffordshire.
Surrey.
Gloucestershire.
Lancashire.
Gloucestershire.
Gloucestershire.
Gloucestershire.

INTERNATIONAL MATCHES, 1975-76

1975			
Sept. 21	Osaka:	Japan 12	Wales 56
Sept. 24	Tokyo:	Japan 6	Wales 82
Dec. 6	Edinburgh:	Scotland 10	Australia 3
Dec. 20	Cardiff:	Wales 28	Australia 3
1976			
Jan. 3	Twickenham:	England 23	Australia 6
Jan. 10	Edinburgh:	Scotland 6	France 13
Jan. 17	Twickenham:	England 9	Wales 21
	Dublin:	Ireland 10	Australia 20
Feb. 7	Cardiff:	Wales 28	Scotland 6
	Paris:	France 26	Ireland 3
Feb. 21	Edinburgh:	Scotland 22	England 12
	Dublin:	Ireland 9	Wales 34
Mar. 6	Cardiff:	Wales 19	France 13
	Twickenham:	England 12	Ireland 13
Mar. 20	Paris:	France 30	England 9
	Dublin:	Ireland 6	Scotland 15
June 5	Wellington:	N.Z. 11	Ireland 3

COUNTY CHAMPIONSHIP FINAL
Gloucestershire beat Middlesex 24–9

OTHER CHIEF MATCHES, 1975-76

Universities. 1975. Cambridge University beat Oxford University 34–12 at Twickenham on Dec. 9.

Hospitals Cup Final.—St. Bartholomew's beat The London 12–0.

Services.—Army beat R.A.F. 6–3; Army beat Royal Navy 15–6; Royal Navy beat R.A.F. 21–13.

John Player Cup.—Gosforth beat Rosslyn Park 23–14 at Twickenham on April 24, 1976.

Middlesex Seven-a-Side Final.—Loughborough Colleges beat Harlequins 21–20.

RUGBY FOOTBALL LEAGUE (Est. 1895)
INTERNATIONAL MATCHES

World Championship

1975					
Sept. 20	Warrington:	Wales	16	England	22
	27	Auckland:	N.Z.	8	Australia 24
Oct. 11	Bordeaux:	France	2	England	48
	17	Marseilles:	France	12	N.Z.	12
	19	Swansea:	Wales	6	Australia 18
	25	Bradford:	England	27	N.Z.	12
	26	Perpignan:	France	2	Australia 41
Nov. 1	Wigan:	England	16	Australia 13
	2	Swansea:	Wales	25	N.Z.	24
	6	Salford:	Wales	18	France	2

Winners: Australia
Runners-up: England

Rugby League Challenge Cup.—Final. St. Helens beat Widnes 20–5 pts. at Wembley Stadium on May 8, 1976.

County Champions.—Yorkshire.

Premiership.—St. Helens beat Salford 15–2 pts. at Swinton.

First Division Champions.—Salford.

Second Division Champions.—Barrow.

Yorkshire Cup.—Leeds beat Hull Kingston Rovers 15–11 pts.

Lancashire Cup.—Widnes beat Salford 16–7 pts.

HOCKEY, 1975–76
MEN'S HOCKEY
INTERNATIONAL CHAMPIONSHIP

					Goals	
	P.	W.	D.	L.	F.	A.
Wales...............	2	1	1	0	3	0
Ireland.............	2	1	1	0	3	1
Scotland............	2	0	0	2	1	6
England.............	–	–	–	–	–	–

Universities.—Oxford University beat Cambridge University 7–0.

County Championship Final.—Hertfordshire beat Lancashire 3–0.

Services Championship.—R.A.F.

National Club Championship.—Final. Nottingham beat Hounslow 2–1.

WOMEN'S HOCKEY
LEADING MATCHES

England drew with Wales 1–1; England beat Scotland 3–0; England lost to Ireland 1–2; England beat Rest of Great Britain 2–0; England lost to Holland 0–2.

I.F.W.H.A. World Cup.—Final. England beat Wales 2–0 in Edinburgh.

ASSOCIATION FOOTBALL
International Table, 1975-76

Country	Played	Won	Drawn	Lost	Goals		Points
					For	Against	
Scotland...........	3	3	0	0	8	2	6
England...........	3	2	0	1	6	2	4
Wales.............	3	1	0	2	2	4	2
Ireland...........	3	0	0	3	0	8	0

ENGLAND v. SCOTLAND

g. g.
1967 Scotland...3—2
1968 Draw.......1—1
1969 England...4—1
1970 Draw.......0—0
1971 England...3—1
1972 England...1—0
1973 England...1—0
1974 Scotland...2—0
1975 England...5—1
1976 Scotland...2—1

LEAGUE COMPETITION, 1975-76

Div. I.—Liverpool, 60 pts. Runners-up: Q.P.R., 59 pts. Relegated: Wolves, 30 pts.; Burnley, 28 pts.; Sheffield Utd., 22 pts.
Div. II.—Promoted: Sunderland, 56 pts.; Bristol C., 53 pts.; W.B.A., 53 pts. Relegated: Oxford Utd., 33 pts.; York C., 28 pts.; Portsmouth, 25 pts.
Div. III.—Promoted: Hereford Utd., 63 pts.; Cardiff C., 57 pts.; Millwall, 56 pts. Relegated: Aldershot, 39 pts.; Colchester Utd., 38 pts.; Southend Utd., 37 pts.; Halifax T., 35 pts.
Div. IV.—Promoted: Lincoln C., 74 pts.; Northampton T., 68 pts.; Reading, 60 pts.; Tranmere R., 58 pts.
SCOTTISH LEAGUE.—*Premier Div.*—Rangers, 54 pts. *Div. I.*—Partick T., 41 pts. *Div. II.*—Clydebank, 40 pts.

REPRESENTATIVE MATCHES, 1975-76
HOME INTERNATIONAL CHAMPIONSHIP

1976
May   6 Hampden
         Park: Scotland 3 Wales   1
May   8 Cardiff: Wales   0 England 1
May   8 Hampden
         Park: Ireland 0 Scotland 3
May 11 Wembley: England 4 Ireland 0
May 14 Swansea: Wales   1 Ireland 0
May 15 Hampden
         Park: Scotland 2 England 1

OTHER INTERNATIONALS

1975
Sept. 3 Basle: Switzerland 1 England 2
1976
Mar. 24 Wrexham: Wales   1 England 2
May   23 Los
         Angeles: England   0 Brazil 1
May   28 New York:England   3 Italy   2

EUROPEAN CHAMPIONSHIPS

1975
Oct. 30 Bratislava: Czechoslovakia 2 England 1
Nov. 19 Lisbon: Portugal   1 England 1

WORLD CUP

1976
June 13 Helsinki: Finland   1 England 4

INTER-LEAGUE MATCH

Mar. 17 Hampden Scottish   Football
         Park: League   0 Lge   1

FOOTBALL ASSOCIATION CUP

g. g.
Tottenham H. b. Chelsea...2—1
W.B.A. b. Everton.........1—0
Manchester C. b. Leicester..1—0
Chelsea b. Leeds U.........2—1
Arsenal b. Liverpool.......2—1
Leeds U. b. Arsenal.......1—0
Sunderland b. Leeds U.....1—0
Liverpool b. Newcastle....3—0
West Ham U. b. Fulham...2—0
Southampton b. Man.U.....1—0

EUROPEAN UNDER-23 CHAMPIONSHIP

1975
Oct. 28 Trnava: Czechoslovakia 1 England 1
Nov. 18 Selhurst
         Park: England   2 Portugal 0
1976
Mar. 10 Budapest: Hungary   3 England 0
Mar. 23 Old
         Trafford:England   3 Hungary 1

CUP FINALS, 1975-76

F.A. CUP.—*S.F.:* April 3 (Hillsborough), Manchester United beat Derby 2—0; (Stamford Bridge), Southampton beat Crystal Palace 2—0.
Final: May 1 (Wembley Stadium), Southampton beat Manchester United 1—0. Attendance 100,000. Receipts £420,000.
FOOTBALL LEAGUE CUP. *Final:* February 28 (Wembley Stadium), Manchester City beat Newcastle 2—1. Attendance 100,000.
F.A. VASE. *Final:* Billericay beat Stamford 1—0 at Wembley Stadium.
F.A. CHALLENGE TROPHY.—*F.:* Scarborough beat Stafford Rangers 3—2 at Wembley Stadium.
F.A. YOUTH.—*F.:* W.B.A. beat Wolves (on aggregate) 5—0.
SCOTTISH F.A. CUP.—*S.F.:* Rangers beat Motherwell 3—2; Hearts beat Dumbarton 3—0. (after 0—0 draw).
Final: May 1 (Hampden Park), Rangers beat Hearts 3—1. Attendance 85,000.
SCOTTISH LEAGUE CUP.—*F.:* Rangers beat Celtic 1—0.
EUROPEAN CUP.—*S.F.:* St. Etienne beat PSV Eindhoven (on aggregate) 1—0; Bayern Munich beat Real Madrid (on aggregate) 3—1.
F.: Bayern Munich beat St. Etienne 1—0 at Hampden Park.
EUROPEAN CUP-WINNERS' CUP.—*S.F.:* West Ham beat Eintracht Frankfurt (on aggregate) 4—3; Anderlecht beat Sachsenring Zwickan (on aggregate) 5—0.
F.: Anderlecht beat West Ham 4—2 in Brussels.
U.E.F.A. CUP.—*F.:* Liverpool beat Bruges (on aggregate) 4—3.

Universities.—Oxford University beat Cambridge University 2—0.
Arthur Dunn Cup.—Malvernians beat Brentwoods, 5—3.
Services Championship.—Royal Navy.

WORLD CUP WINNERS, 1930-1974

1930 *(Played in Uruguay)*...............Uruguay
1934 *(Italy)*................................Italy
1938 *(France)*...............................Italy
1950 *(Brazil)*............................Uruguay
1954 *(Switzerland)*...............West Germany
1958 *(Sweden)*...........................Brazil
1962 *(Chile)*..............................Brazil
1966 *(England)*.........................England
1970 *(Mexico)*............................Brazil
1974 *(West Germany)*...........West Germany

GOLF, 1974–75

CHAMPIONSHIPS

OPEN
(Instituted 1860)

1966 J. Nicklaus (U.S.A.), 282.
1967 R. de Vicenzo (Argentina), 278.
1968 G. Player (S. Africa), 289.
1969 A. Jacklin (G.B.), 280.
1970 J. Nicklaus (U.S.A.) beat D. Sanders (U.S.A.) after tie, 283.
1971 L. Trevino (U.S.A.), 278.
1972 L. Trevino (U.S.A.), 278.
1973 T. Weiskopf (U.S.A.), 276.
1974 G. Player (S. Africa), 282.
1975 T. Watson (U.S.A.) beat J. Newton (Australia) after tie, 279.
1976 J. Miller (U.S.A.), 279.

PROFESSIONAL MATCH PLAY TOURNAMENT
1966 P. W. Thomson (Aust.).
1967 P. W. Thomson (Aust.).
1968 B. Huggett.
1969 M. Bembridge.
1970 T. Horton.
1972 J. Garner.

1973 N. C. Coles.
1974 J. Newton (Aust.).
1975 E. Polland.
1976 B. Barnes.

AMATEUR
(1885)
1966 R. Cole (S. Africa).
1967 B. Dickson (U.S.A.).
1968 M. F. Bonallack.
1969 M. F. Bonallack.
1970 M. F. Bonallack.
1971 S. N. Melnyk (U.S.A.).
1972 T. Homer.
1973 R. Siderowf (U.S.A.).
1974 T. Homer.
1975 M. Giles (U.S.A.).
1976 R. Siderowf (U.S.A.).

LADIES
(1893)
1966 Miss D. E. Chadwick.
1967 Miss D. E. Chadwick.
1968 Mlle. B. Varangot (France).
1969 Mlle. C. Lacoste (France).
1970 Miss D. L. Oxley.
1971 Miss M. Walker.
1972 Miss M. Walker.
1973 Miss A. Irvin.
1974 Miss C. Semple (U.S.A.).
1975 Mrs. N. Syms (U.S.A.).
1976 Miss C. Panton.

CURTIS CUP
(Royal Lytham and St. Annes, June 1976)

U.S.A. won by 11½ to 6½.

Winners—

Singles—U.S.A.—Miss B. Daniel (2); Mrs. N. Syms; Miss D. Massey (2); Miss N. Lopez; Miss D. Horton.
Great Britain and Ireland—Mrs. D. Henson; Miss J. Greenhalgh; Miss T. Perkins; Miss M. McKenna.
Foursomes—U.S.A.—Miss D. Massey and Miss D. Horton; Miss B. Daniel and Miss C. Hill (2); Miss N. Lopez and Miss B. Barrow.
Great Britain and Ireland—Miss A. Irvin and Miss T. Perkins; Mrs. D. Henson and Miss T. Perkins.

OTHER GOLF EVENTS, 1975–76

Australian Open.—J. Nicklaus (U.S.A.).
President's Putter.—M. J. Reece beat C. Edginton 4 and 3.
Halford Hewitt Cup (Final).—Merchiston beat Whitgift, 3–2.
English Amateur.—P. Deeble.
Piccadilly Medal.—S. Torrance.
Brabazon Trophy.—P. J. Hedges.
Penfold P.G.A. Championship.—N. Coles.
Madrid Open.—F. Abreu (Spain).
Club Professionals' Champioship.—W. Ferguson.
Berkshire Trophy.—P. J. Hedges.
Grafton Morrish Old Boys' Tournament.—Charterhouse.
World Cup (Bangkok, Dec. 1975).—1, U.S.A., 554; 2, Taiwan, 564; 3, Japan, 565.

Golf Illustrated Gold Vase.—A. Brodie.
Martini International Tournament.—S. Torrance.
Scottish Amateur.—G. Murray.
Welsh Amateur.—D. Adams.
British Seniors' Championship.—C. O'Connor.
Uniroyal International.—T. Horton.
Boys' International Match.—Scotland beat England 8–7.
Avia International Women's Foursomes.—Mrs. A. Bonallack and Mrs. S. Barber.
Newmark Ladies Open Stroke Play Tournament.—Miss J. Lee-Smith.
U.S.A. Masters.—R. Floyd.
U.S.A. Open.—J. Pate.
U.S.A., P.G.A. Championship.—D. Stockton.
Universities.—Cambridge beat Oxford by 9 matches to 4, with 2 halved.
English Women's County Championship.—Staffordshire.
British Youth Championship.—M. Lewis.
British Boys' Championship.—M. Mouland.
British Girls' Championship.—Miss G. Stewart.
Girls' Home International Series.—Scotland.
Home International Championship.—Scotland.
English Women's Championship.—Miss L. Harrold.
Women's Home International Championship.—England.
South African Open.—D. Hayes.
French Open.—V. Tshabalala (S. Africa).
Spanish Open.—E. Polland.
Lytham Trophy.—M. Kelley.
Benson and Hedges International.—G. Marsh (Australia).
Carris Trophy.—H. Stott.
World Under-25 Championship.—E. Darcy.
Italian Open.—W. Casper (U.S.A.).
Sunningdale Foursomes.—C. Clark and M. Hughesdon.
Double Diamond World Classic.—England.
Double Diamond Individual Championship.—S. Owen (New Zealand).
Kerrygold International Classic.—A. Jacklin.
Greater Manchester Open.—J. O'Leary.
British Women's Open Championship.—Miss J. Lee-Smith.
World Senior Professional Championship.—C. O'Connor.
Colgate European Women's Tournament.—Mrs. C. Higuchi (Japan).
English Girls' Championship.—H. Latham.
German Open.—S. Hobday (Rhodesia).
Swiss Open.—M. Pinero (Spain).
Dutch Open.—S. Ballesteros (Spain).
Sumrie Better-Ball Tournament.—C. O'Connor, Jnr. and E. Darcy.
Carrolls Irish Open.—B. Crenshaw (U.S.A.).
Scandinavian Open.—H. Baiocchi (S. Africa).
Portuguese Open.—S. Balbuena (Spain).
British P.G.A. Under-25.—H. Clark.
Canadian Open.—J. Pate.
Dunlop Masters.—B. Dassu (Italy).
World Open.—R. Floyd (U.S.A.).
Piccadilly Match-Play.—D. Graham (Australia).
St. Andrews Trophy.—Great Britain and Ireland beat Continent of Europe by 18½ matches to 11½.
County Championship (Final).—Warwickshire beat Yorkshire 7–2.

LAWN TENNIS

THE DAVIS CUP CHALLENGE ROUNDS

(Founder—Dwight Filley Davis (1879–1945), First Played, 1900.)

1931 France beat Great Britain....3–2	1950 Australia beat U.S.A.........4–1
1932 France beat U.S.A...........3–2	1951 Australia beat U.S.A.........3–1
1933 Great Britain beat France....3–2	1952 Australia beat U.S.A.........4–1
1934 Great Britain beat U.S.A.....4–1	1953 Australia beat U.S.A.........3–2
1935 Great Britain beat U.S.A.....5–0	1954 U.S.A. beat Australia........3–0
1936 Great Britain beat Australia..3–2	1955 Australia beat U.S.A.........5–0
1937 U.S.A. beat Great Britain....4–1	1956 Australia beat U.S.A.........5–0
1938 U.S.A. beat Australia........3–2	1957 Australia beat U.S.A.........3–2
1939 Australia beat U.S.A.........3–2	1958 U.S.A. beat Australia........3–2
1946 U.S.A. beat Australia........5–0	1959 Australia beat U.S.A.........3–2
1947 U.S.A. beat Australia........3–1	1960 Australia beat Italy.........4–1
1948 U.S.A. beat Australia........5–0	1961 Australia beat Italy.........5–0
1949 U.S.A. beat Australia........4–1	1962 Australia beat Mexico........5–0

1963 U.S.A. beat Australia........3–2
1964 Australia beat U.S.A.........3–2
1965 Australia beat Spain.........4–1
1966 Australia beat India.........4–1
1967 Australia beat Spain.........4–1
1968 U.S.A. beat Australia.........4–1
1969 U.S.A. beat Rumania.........5–0
1970 U.S.A. beat W. Germany.....5–0
1971 U.S.A. beat Rumania.........3–2
1972 U.S.A. beat Rumania.........3–2
1973 Australia beat U.S.A.........5–0
1974 S. Africa won by default.
1975 Sweden beat Czechoslovakia..3–2

THE CHAMPIONSHIPS (WIMBLEDON)
1976

Men's Singles.—B. Borg (Sweden) beat I. Nastase (Rumania), 6–4, 6–2, 9–7.

Women's Singles.—Miss C. M. Evert (U.S.A.) beat Mrs. R. Cawley (Australia), 6–3, 4–6, 8–6.

Men's Doubles.—B. Gottfried (U.S.A.) and R. Ramirez (Mexico) beat R. L. Case and G. Masters (Australia), 3–6, 6–3, 8–6, 2–6, 7–5.

Women's Doubles.—Miss C. M. Evert (U.S.A.) and Miss M. Navratilova (Czechoslovakia) beat Mrs. L. W. King (U.S.A.) and Miss B. F. Stove (Holland), 6–1, 3–6, 7–5.

Mixed Doubles.—A. D. Roche (Australia) and Miss F. Durr (France) beat R. L. Stockton and Miss R. Casals (U.S.A.), 6–3, 2–6, 7–5.

All England Plate:
  Men's Singles.—B. E. Fairlie (N. Zealand) beat R. Taylor (G.B.), 4–6, 6–3, 6–4.
  Women's Singles.—Miss M. Wikstedt (Sweden) beat Miss B. Bruning (U.S.A., 4–6, 6–3, 6–3.

Junior International Invitation Tournament:
  Boy's Singles.—H. Guenthardt (Switzerland) beat P. Elter (W. Germany), 6–4, 7–5.
  Girl's Singles.—Miss N. Chmyreva (U.S.S.R.) beat Miss M. Kruger (S. Africa), 6–3, 2–6, 6–1.

Veteran's Doubles.—L. Bergelin (Sweden) and B. Patty (U.S.A.) beat H. K. Richards and R. C. Sorlien (U.S.A.), 6–1, 4–6, 6–1.

BRITISH HARD COURT CHAMPIONSHIPS
(Bournemouth)

Men's Singles.—W. Fibak (Poland).

Women's Singles.—Mrs. H. Mastoff (W. Germany).

Doubles.—Men's: F. McNair (U.S.A.) and W. Fibak (Poland).

Women's: Miss L. Boshoff and Miss I. Kloss (S. Africa).

U.S.A. Championships:
  Men's Singles.—J. Connors (U.S.A.).
  Women's Singles.—Miss C. M. Evert (U.S.A.).
  Men's Doubles.—T. Okker (Holland) and M. Riessen (U.S.A.).
  Women's Doubles.—Miss L. Boshoff and Miss I. Kloss (S. Africa).
  Mixed Doubles.—Mrs. L. W. King (U.S.A.) and P. Dent (Australia).

French Championships:
  Men's Singles.—A. Panatta (Italy).
  Women's Singles.—S. Barker (G.B.).
  Men's Doubles.—F. McNair and S. Stewart (U.S.A.).

  Women's Doubles.—Miss F. Bonicelli (Uruguay) and Miss G. Lovera (France).
  Mixed Doubles.—K. Warwick (Australia) and Miss I. Kloss (S. Africa).

Federation Cup.—U.S.A.

Public Schools.—Youll Cup: St. Paul's beat Magdalen College School, 3–1; *Clark Cup.*—Millfield beat Manchester G.S., 2–1.

County Championship.—Men: Essex; *Women:* Surrey.

GREEN SHIELD JUNIOR CHAMPIONSHIPS
(Eastbourne)

Boys' Singles.—C. Bradman beat N. Rayner, 2–6, 6–3, 6–4.

Girls' Singles.—Miss J. Durie beat Miss K. Glancy, 7–6, 6–7, 6–4.

Boys' Doubles.—M. Grave and N. Rayner beat P. Goodman and A. Payton, 6–3, 6–4.

Girls' Doubles.—Miss J. Durie and Miss C. Harrison beat Miss A. Hobbs and Miss C. Drury, 6–4, 7–6.

TENNIS, 1976

Amateur Singles Championship.—H. R. Angus beat J. Ward, 3–0.

Amateur Doubles Championship.—H. R. Angus and D. Warburg beat J. Reiss and J. Walsh, 3–0.

Open British Doubles Championships.—F. Willis and D. Cull beat C. Ennis and M. Dean, 3–1.

British Open Singles Championship.—H. R. Angus beat F. Willis.

Henry Leaf Cup.—Winchester beat Rugby, 3–0.

Universities.—Oxford University beat Cambridge University, 6–0.

BADMINTON, 1976
ALL-ENGLAND CHAMPIONSHIPS, 1976

Men's Singles.—R. Hartono (Indonesia) beat Liem Swie King (Indonesia), 2–0.

Ladies' Singles.—Mrs. M. A. Gilks (G.B.) beat Mrs. M. Lockwood (G.B.), 2–0.

Men's Doubles.—B. Froman and T. Kihlstrom (Sweden) beat S. Pri and S. Skovgaard (Denmark), 2–0.

Ladies' Doubles.—Mrs. M. A. Gilks and Mrs. P. E. Whetnall (G.B.) beat Mrs. M. Lockwood and Miss N. C. Gardner (G.B.), 2–0.

Mixed Doubles.—D. Talbot and Mrs. M. A. Gilks (G.B.) beat M. G. Tredgett and Miss N. C. Gardner (G.B.), 2–0.

SQUASH RACKETS, 1975–76

World and British Open Championship.—G. Hunt (Australia) beat Mohibullah Khan (Pakistan), 3–2.

British Amateur Championship.—K. Shawcross (Australia) beat A. Aziz (Egypt), 3–0.

Women's Championship.—Mrs. H. McKay (Australia) beat Miss S. Newman (Australia), 3–0.

University Match.—Oxford University beat Cambridge University, 4–1.

Londonderry Cup.—Barnard Castle beat Lancing, 4–1.

Inter-County Championship.—Yorkshire beat Sussex, 3–2.

Drysdale Cup.—G. P. Briars (Gresham's).

Inter-Services.—Army.

British Amateur Closed Championship.—P. N. Ayton beat S. H. Courtney, 3–2.

Home International Amateur Team Championships.— Men: England; Women: England.

FENCING, 1975–76

British Championships:
   Foil.—B. Paul (Salle Paul).
   Sabre.—J. Philbin (Polytechnic).
   Epée.—E. O. Bourne (Salle Boston).
   Ladies Foil.—Miss L. Martin (Polytechnic).
Sporting Record Cup.—Salle Paul.
Granville Cup.—Salle Boston.
Magrini Cup.—Salle Boston.
Public Schools Championship:
   Foil.—R. Hill (Whitgift).
   Epée.—J. C. Steventon (Brentwood).
   Sabre.—C. Webb (Brentwood).
Inter-Schools (Graham Bartlett Cup).—Brentwood.
Savage Shield.—Salle Boston.
Martin Edmunds Cup.—London.
Universities.—Cambridge University beat Oxford University, 15–12.
Schools' Home International Championship.—England.

RACKETS, 1975–76

British Open Championship.—H. R. Angus beat J. A. N. Prenn, 4–1.

Amateur Singles Championship.—W. R. Boone beat J. A. N. Prenn, 3–2.

Amateur Doubles Championship.—C. T. M. Pugh and W. R. Boone beat J. A. N. Prenn and C. J. Hue Williams, 4–3.

Public Schools Championship.—Singles (H. K. Foster Cup).—A. Pigott (Harrow) beat P. C. Nicholls (Malvern), 3–2. Doubles: Marlborough (D. K. Watson and M. N. P. Mockridge) beat Malvern (P. C. Nicholls and M. A. Tang), 4–3.

Noel Bruce Cup.—Harrow (C. J. Hue Williams and J. A. N. Prenn) beat Tonbridge (R. M. K. Gracey and M. G. M. Smith), 4–1.

Universities.—Oxford University beat Cambridge University, 3–0.

RUGBY FIVES, 1976

Schools Competition.—Singles.—A. M. Lloyd-Williams (Bedford) beat R. N. Barr (Sedbergh), 2–0.

   Doubles: St. Dunstan's (D. R. Trew and G. A. Handy) beat St. Paul's (T. P. J. MacAskie and D. R. Lee), 2–1.

Amateur Doubles Championship.—J. H. M. East and G. W. Enstone beat D. Gardner and S. Reid, 2–1.

POLO, 1976

Queen's Cup.—San Flamingo beat Jersey Lilies 5–4½.

Cowdray Park Gold Cup.—Stowell Park beat Greenhill Farm 8–6.

Cowdray Park Challenge Cup.—Jersey Lilies beat Stowell Park 4½–3.

Royal Windsor Cup.—Jersey Lilies beat Golden Eagles 5–4.

Harrison Cup.—Sladmore beat Cowdray Park 3–2.

Brecknock Cup.—Cowdray Park beat Jersey Lilies 4–2.

Benson Cup.—Apaches beat Pirates 4–3.

Barrett Cup.—Jersey Lilies beat Ambersham 5–4.

Bass Charrington Cup.—Cowdray Park beat Jersey Lilies 8–7.

Jersey Lilies Challenge Cup.—Cowdray Park beat Jersey Lilies 5½–5.

Maidensgrove Cup.—Rangatiki beat Los Locos 6–5.

Midhurst Town Cup Final.—Jersey Lilies beat Blue Devils 11–4.

Holden White Cup.—Edgeworth beat Maidensgrove 3–2.

Cicero Cup.—Jersey Lilies beat Cowdray Park 6–4.

Ruins Cup.—Woolmers beat Apaches 6–3.

Coronation Cup.—South America beat England 6–2.

Smith's Lawn Cup.—Rangitiki beat Roundwood Park 6–4½.

Combermere Cup.—Eaglesfield beat Westcroft Park 5–4½.

TABLE TENNIS, 1976

INTERNATIONAL CHAMPIONSHIPS
(Brighton)

Singles.—Men: S. Bengtsson (Sweden) beat A. Stipancic (Yugoslavia).
   Women: Mrs. J. Hammersley (G.B.) beat Miss A. C. Hellman (Sweden).

Doubles.—Men: D. Douglas and D. Neale (G.B.) beat Z. Kosanovic and A. Stipancic (Yugoslavia).
   Women: I. Uhlikova and B. Silhanova (Czechoslovakia) beat C. Knight and K. Rogers (G.B.).

Mixed: S. Bengtsson and Miss A. C. Hellman (Sweden) beat M. Schenk and I. Uhlikova (Czechoslovakia).

Team Event.—Men: England; *Women:* Sweden.

WRESTLING, 1976

British Amateur Championships

52 *kg.*—B. Singh (Midlands); 57 *kg.*—A. Singh-Gill (Northern); 62 *kg.*—K. Dawes (South); 68 *kg.*—J. Gilligan (North); 74 *kg.*—K. Haward (South); 82 *kg.*—M. Nylin (U.S.A.); 90 *kg.*—G. M. Allan (Scotland); 100 *kg.*—A. Singh (Midlands); and +100 *kg.*—R. Bradley (South).

CANOEING, 1976

Devizes–Westminster Race (124 miles) *Senior Class.*—1, G. Mitchell and C. Norton (Royal Engineers C.C.), 19 hr. 50 m. 20 s.; 2, B. Kidston and A. Wheeler (562 Para RCT and J. L. Regt.), 20 hr. 12 m. 45 s.; 3, J. Hayden and D. Thom (Royal Engineers C.C.), 20 hr. 59 m. 10 s.

ANGLING
National Championship

Year	Venue	No. of teams	Individual Winner	Weight	Team winners	Points	Division
				lb. oz.			
1972	Bristol Avon, Wilts.	80	P. Coles (Leicester)	33 8	Birmingham A.A.	248 pts.	(*1st Div.*)
	R. Welland, Spalding	80	J. Hart (Whittlesey)	54 14½	Coleshill A.C.	216 pts.	(*2nd Div.*)
1973	R. Witham, Lincs.	—	A. Wright (Derby)	41 10¼	Grimsby	717 pts.	(*1st Div.*)
	Gt. Ouse Relief Channel, Norfolk	92	J. Wilkinson (Elthorn)	43 1½	Leigh	826 pts.	(*2nd Div.*)
1974	R. Welland and Coronation Channel, Lincs.	80	P. Anderson (Cambridge F.P. & A.S.)	40 2½	Leicester A.S.	—	(*1st Div.*)
	R. Avon, between Bidford and Tewkesbury	115	C. Hibbs (Leigh Miners)	47 3½	Stockport Federation	—	(*2nd Div.*)
1975	R. Nene, Peterborough	78	M. Hoad-Reddick (Rotherham)	63 7	—	—	(*1st Div.*)
	R. Trent, Nottingham	71	A. Webber (Wigan)	16 2½	—	—	(*2nd Div.*)

SWIMMING

Amateur Swimming Association Championships, 1976

Men:

400 *metres Free Style.*—A. McClatchey, 4 m. 5·46 s.
100 *metres Butterfly.*—J. Mills, 56·68 s.
200 *metres Individual Medley.*—J. Carter, 2 m. 12·60 s.
200 *metres Free Style.*—A. McClatchey, 1 m. 55·94 s.
200 *metres Back Stroke.*—J. Carter, 2 m. 9·80 s.
1,500 *metres Free Style.*—D. Parker, 16 m. 10·7 s.
200 *metres Butterfly.*—P. Hubble, 2 m. 7·04 s.
200 *metres Breast Stroke.*—D. Goodhew, 2 m. 25·98 s.
100 *metres Back Stroke.*—E. Abrahams, 1 m. 1·00 s.
400 *metres Individual Medley.*—A. McClatchey, 4 m. 35·25 s.
100 *metres Free Style.*—K. Burns, 54·84 s.
Medley Team Relay.—1, Southampton, 4 m. 3·28 s. (English record); 2, Cardiff, 4 m. 4·09 s.; 3, Coventry, 4 m. 5·34 s.

Women:

800 *metres Free Style.*—A. Nelson (Canada), 9 m. 14·19 s.
100 *metres Back Stroke.*—A. James, 1 m. 8·50 s.
200 *metres Free Style.*—M. Houston, 2 m. 8·00 s.
200 *metres Butterfly.*—A. Nelson (Canada), 2 m. 23·5 s.
400 *metres Individual Medley.*—S. Davies, 5 m. 3·53 s. (British record).
100 *metres Free Style.*—C. Brazendale, 59·58 s. (British record).
200 *metres Individual Medley.*—S. Davies, 2 m. 26·46 s.
100 *metres Breast Stroke.*—M. Kelly, 1 m. 14·23 s.
400 *metres Free Style.*—M. Houston, 4 m. 28·20 s. (British record).
100 *metres Butterfly.*—L. Taylor, 1 m. 4·97 s.
200 *metres Back Stroke.*—S. Davies, 2 m. 23·63 s.
Free Style Team Relay.—1, Cardiff, 4 m. 7·09 s.; St. James's Ladies, 4 m. 11·40 s.; 3, Coventry, 4 m. 14·35 s.
Medley Team Relay.—1, Coventry, 4 m. 31·06 s. (English record); 2, St. James,'s Ladies, 4 m. 40·78 s.; 3, Beckenham Ladies 4 m. 43·06 s.

HENLEY REGATTA, 1976

Grand Challenge Cup.—Thames Tradesmen beat Leander by ⅝ length, 6 m. 25s.
Ladies Challenge Plate.—Trinity College, Hartford (U.S.A.) beat Queen's Univ., Belfast by 1⅓ lengths, 6 m. 49 s.
Princess Elizabeth Cup.—Holy Spirit H.S. (U.S.A.) beat Emanuel School by ⅝ length, 6 m. 37 s.
Thames Cup.—Harvard Univ. (U.S.A.) beat Henley R. C. by a canvas, 6 m. 39 s.
Stewards' Cup.—Univ. of British Columbia, Vancouver (Canada) beat Thames Tradesmen by ⅓ length, 7 m. 10 s.
Prince Philip Cup.—Thames Tradesmen rowed over, Leander scratched.
Visitors' Cup.—Univ. of London beat Salisbury School (U.S.A.), not rowed out, 7 m. 21 s.
Wyfold Cup.—London R.C. beat Potomac B.C. (U.S.A.) by ½ length, 6 m. 56 s.
Britannia Challenge Cup.—Tideway Scullers School beat Wallingford Schools by 2½ lengths, 7 m. 22 s.
Silver Goblets.—I. A. Luxford and C. D. Shinners (Sydney, Australia) beat J. M. Lecky and W. R. Crooker (Club d'Avirion de Boucherville, Canada), early, 7 m. 30 s.
Double Sculls.—R. Prentice and M. S. Spencer (London R. C.) beat J. H. van Drooge and R. Nolet (A.S.R. Nereus, Holland) by 2 lengths, 7 m. 22 s.
Diamond Sculls.—E. O. Hale (Sydney R. C., Australia) beat P. Zeun (Peterborough City R. C.), easily, 7 m. 42 s.

THE UNIVERSITY BOAT RACE
(Putney-Mortlake, 4m. 1f. 180 yds)

Year	Winner	m. s.	Won by
1962	Cambridge....	19 46	5 lengths
1963	Oxford.......	20 47	5 lengths
1964	Cambridge....	19 18	6½ lengths
1965	Oxford.......	18 45	4 lengths
1966	Oxford.......	19 12	3¾ lengths
1967	Oxford.......	18 52	3¼ lengths
1968	Cambridge....	18 22	3½ lengths
1969	Cambridge....	18 4	4 lengths
1970	Cambridge....	20 22	3½ lengths
1971	Cambridge....	17 58	10 lengths
1972	Cambridge....	18 36	9½ lengths
1973	Cambridge....	19 21	13 lengths
1974	Oxford.......	17 35	5½ lengths
1975	Cambridge....	19 27	3¾ lengths
1976	Oxford......	16 58*	6 lengths

Cambridge have won 68 times, Oxford 53 and there has been 1 dead-heat.
* Record.

OTHER AQUATIC EVENTS

Head of the River (Thames, Mortlake-Putney).— 1, National Squad; 2, Tideway Scullers I; 3, Leander.

*Oxford Torpids,—*Oriel

*Oxford Summer Eights.—*Oriel.

*Cambridge Lents.—*Lady Margaret.

*Cambridge Mays.—*Pembroke College.

*Doggett's Coat and Badge (Estab. 1715, 26 2nd Race, London Bridge-Chelsea, 4½ miles).—*P. Prentice (Wapping).

SKATING, 1975–76
WORLD CHAMPIONSHIPS
(Gothenburg)

*Men's Figure.—*J. Curry (G.B.).

*Ladies' Figure.—*Miss D. Hamill (U.S.A.).

*Pairs.—*A. Zaitsev and Miss I. Rodnina (U.S.S.R.)

*Ice Dancing.—*A. Gorshkov and Miss L. Pakhomova (U.S.S.R.)

EUROPEAN CHAMPIONSHIPS
(Geneva)

*Men's Figure.—*J. Curry (G.B.).

Ladies' Figure. Miss D. de Leeuw (Holland).

*Pairs.—*A. Zaitsev and Miss I. Rodnina (U.S.S.R.)

*Ice Dancing.—*A. Gorschkov and Miss L. Pakhomova (U.S.S.R.).

BRITISH CHAMPIONSHIPS (Ice)

*Men's Figure.—*J. Curry.

*Ladies' Figure.—*Miss K. Richardson.

*Pairs.—*C. Taylforth and Mrs. E. Taylforth.

*Dancing.—*G. Watts and Miss H. Green.

SHOOTING–BISLEY, 107th N.R.A., 1976

*Queen's Prize.—*1, Maj. W. H. Magnay, 287 pts; 2, N. E. C. Molyneux, 287; 3, Mrs. L. Felton, 287.

*St. George's Challenge Vase.—*M. G. Gordon, 144.

*Grand Aggregate.—*1, J. S. Spaight, 585; 2, J. R. Killian, 581; 3, A. E. Clarke, 581.

*Elcho Challenge Shield.—*1, Scotland, 1,450; 2, England, 1,428; 3, Ireland, 1,413.

*The Kolapore.—*1, Australia, 1,164; 2, Mother Country, 1,159; 3, New Zealand, 1,144; 4, Guernsey, 1,136; 5, Canada, 1,130; 6, Jersey, 1,122.

*Universities—Chancellor's Challenge Plate.—*1, Cambridge University, 1,128; 2, Oxford University, 1,087.

*Inter-Services Long Range.—*1, Regular Army, 549; 2, R.A.F., 549; 3, R.N., 548.

*United Service.—*1, Canadian Forces, 1,212; 2, R.A.F., 1,203; 3, R.M., 1,194.

*Ashburton Shield.—*1, Uppingham, 517; 2, Lancing, 509; 3, Victoria College, Jersey, 506.

*National Match.—*1, England, 2,016; 2, Scotland, 1,974; 3, Ireland, 1,936; 4, Wales, 1,920.

CLAY PIGEON SHOOTING, 1976

*International Cup (Down-the-Line).—*1, England, 7,289/7,500; 2, Scotland, 7,244; 3, Wales, 7,134; 4, Ireland, 7,100.

*Mackintosh Trophy.—*1, Australia, 7,358/7,500; 2, England, 7,289; 3, Scotland, 7,244.

*British Open Down-the-Line Championship.—*M. Campbell (Thurso), 295/300.

*British Open Skeet Championship.—*D. Ellis (USA), 100/100 (after shoot-off).

*British Open Sporting Championship.—*P. R. Howe (Norfolk), 90/100.

*Coronation Cup.—*T. Poskitt (S. Yorks), 373/400.

*Grand Prix of Great Britain (Olympic Trap).—*J. Tennison (Humberside), 193/200.

Grand Prix of Great Britain (International Skeet).— B. J. Wells (Worcs), 197/200.

BOXING, 1976
A.B.A. CHAMPIONSHIPS
(Winners)

*Light-Flyweight.—*P. Fletcher (St. Theresa's); *Flyweight.—*C. Magri (Arbour Youth); *Bantam.—* J. Bambrick (Edinburgh City Transport); *Feather.—* P. Cowdell (Warley); *Light.—*S. Mittee (Repton); *Light-Welter.—*C. McKenzie (Sir Philip Game). *Welter.—*C. Jones (Penyrheol); *Light-Middle.—* W. Lauder (MacTaggart Scott); *Middle.—*E. Burke (Woodside); *Light-Heavy.—*G. Evans (Liverpool); *Heavy.—*J. Rafferty (Monkland).

THE UNIVERSITIES

Cambridge University beat Oxford University by 6 bouts to 3.

PROFESSIONAL BOXING
WORLD CHAMPIONS
Title Holders in Sept. 1976

*Semi-Flyweight.—*L. Estaba (Venezuela); *Flyweight.* —M. Canto (Mexico); *Bantamweight.—*C. Zarate (Mexico); *Super-Bantamweight.—*D. Yum (Korea); *Featherweight.—*D. Koety (Ghana); *Semi-Lightweight.—*A. Escalera (Puerto Rico); *Light-Welterweight.—*M. Velasquex (Spain); *Lightweight.—* E. Dejesus (Puerto Rico); *Welterweight.—*C. Palomino (Mexico); *Light-Middleweight.—*E. Dagge (Germany); *Middleweight.—*C. Monzon (Argentina); *Light-Heavyweight.—*J. Conteh (England); *Heavyweight.—*Muhammad Ali (U.S.A.).

BRITISH CHAMPIONS
Title Holders in Sept. 1976

*Flyweight.—*J. McClusky; *Bantam-weight.—*P. Maguire; *Featherweight.—*V. Sollas; *Lightweight.—*J. Watt; *Light Welterweight.—*D. Green; *Welterweight.—*P. Thomas; *Light Middleweight.—*M. Hope; *Middleweight.—*A. Minter; *Light-Heavyweight.—*T. Wood; *Heavyweight.—*R. Dunn.

COMMONWEALTH CHAMPIONS
Title Holders in Sept. 1976

*Flyweight.—*P. Mambire (Zambia); *Bantamweight.—*P. Ferrari (Australia); *Featherweight.—* vacant; *Semi-Lightweight.—*B. Moeller (Australia); *Lightweight.—*J. Dele (Nigeria); *Light Welterweight.—* H. Thompson (Australia); *Welterweight.—*C. Gray (Canada); *Light Middleweight.—*M. Hope (England); *Middleweight.—*M. Betham (N.Z.); *Light-Heavyweight.—*T. Mundine (Australia); *Heavyweight.—*R. Dunn (England).

EUROPEAN CHAMPIONS
Title Holders in Sept. 1976

*Flyweight.—*F. Udella (Italy); *Bantamweight.—* S. Fabrizio (Italy), *Featherweight.—*E. Contena (Italy); *Semi-lightweight.—*R. Cazeaux (France); *Lightweight.—*F. Roelands (Belgium); *Light Welterweight.—*C. Cemaci (Austria); *Welterweight.—* M. Scano (Italy); *Light Middleweight.—*vacant; *Middleweight.—*A. Jacopucci (Italy); *Light Heavyweight.—*M. Parlov (Yugoslavia); *Heavyweight.—* R. Dunn (England).

BILLIARDS AND SNOOKER

World Professional Billiards Championship.—A. L. Driffield (England) beat A. Johnson (Australia) by 9,204 to 4,696.

World Open Billiards Championship.—A. L. Driffield (England) beat P. Morgan (Ireland) by 3,055 to 2,404.

World Professional Snooker Championship.—R. Reardon beat A. Higgins by 27–16 frames.

World Amateur Snooker Championship.—R. Edmonds (England) beat G. Thomas (Wales) by 11–9 frames.

World Amateur Billiards Championship.—N. Dagley (England) beat M. Ferreira (India) by 3,386 to 2,268.

English Amateur Billiards Championship.—R. Close beat C. Everton by 2,413 to 2,194.

English Amateur Snooker Championship.—C. Ross beat R. Andrewartha by 11–7.

Women (Amateur).—*Billiards:* Mrs. V. Selby; *Snooker:* Miss A. Johnson.

BOWLS, 1976

English Bowling Association Championships (Worthing).

Fours.—S.F.: Baldock Town (Herts.) beat Banbury Boro' (Oxford) 21–18; Clevedon (Somerset) beat Gosforth (Northumberland) 28–19; F.: Baldock Town beat Clevedon 25–8.

Triples.—S.F.: Wymondham Dell (Norfolk) beat Andre (Surrey) 19–14; Wigton (Cumberland) beat Beech Hill (Beds.) 22–12; F.: Wigton beat Wymondham Dell 18–11.

Pairs.—S.F.: Plessey (Nottingham) beat Roker Marine (Durham) 23–19; Thames Poly. (Kent) beat Summertown (Oxford) 25–16; F.: Plessey beat Thames Poly. 16–12.

Singles.—S.F.: A. O'Connell (Wimbledon Durnsford, Surrey) beat D. J. Bryant, (Clevedon, Somerset) 21–20; W. Hobart (Sleaford Road, Boston, Lincs.) beat S. Bunting (Courtfield, Cumberland) 21–15; F.: O'Connell beat Hobart 21–17.

Inter-County Championship (Middleton Cup)—S.F.: Surrey beat Durham 117–107; Lincolnshire beat Worcestershire 115–114; F.: Lincolnshire beat Surrey 132–114.

International Championship.—Not played.

BRITISH SHOW JUMPING, 1976

ROYAL INTERNATIONAL HORSE SHOW, WEMBLEY

King George V Gold Cup.—M. Saywell on Chain Bridge; 2, E. Macken on Boomerang; 3, H. Steenken on Goya.

Horse and Hound Cup.—H. Smith on Olympic Star; 2, J. Whitaker on Ryan's Son; 3, G. Meier on Casimir.

Queen Elizabeth II Cup.—Mrs. M. Mould on Elizabeth Ann; 2, Miss C. Bradley on Marius; Miss A. Ferguson on Freelance IV and Miss L. Chapman on Grays China, equal third.

Moss Bros. Puissance.—1, J. Whitaker on Bericote Golden Vale; J.-R. Dechamps on Don Juan de Mirande and H. Schulz-Siehoff on Ferro, equal second.

John Player Trophy.—1, G. Meier on Casimir; 2, H. Smith on Graffiti; four tied for third place.

Daily Mail Cup.—1, D. Broome on Sportsman; 2, J. Whitaker on Ryan's Son; 3, G. Billington on Talk of the North.

OXFORD AND CAMBRIDGE

Principal Events and Winners, 1975–76

Event (with date of first meeting)	Summary of Results			Results 1975–76
	Ox.	Camb.	Drawn	
Cricket (1827)............	45	51	36	Oxford
Boat Race (1829).........	53	68	1	Oxford
Athletics (1864).........	49	46	7	Camb.
Football—				
Association (1873–4)...	33	41	19	Oxford
Rugby (1871–2)........	42	39	13	Camb.
Golf (1878).............	34	46	5	Camb.
Hockey (1890)..........	27	32	14	Oxford

OTHER UNIVERSITY EVENTS AND WINNERS 1975–76

Squash Rackets.......................Oxford
Boxing ....Cambridge
Shooting............................Cambridge
Real Tennis............................Oxford
Rackets..............................Oxford

CYCLING, 1976

Tour de France.—L. Van Impe (Belgium).

Tour of Britain.—W. Nickson (G.B.).

MOTOR CYCLING, 1976

Senior T.T., Isle of Man.—1, T. Herron (Yamaha), 2 hr. 9 m. 10 s. (105·15 m.p.h.); 2, I. Richards (Yamaha), 2 hr. 9 m. 13·4 s.; 3, W. Guthrie (Yamaha), 2 hr. 9 m. 35 s.

Junior 350 c.c. TT., Isle of Man.—1, C. Mortimer (Yamaha), 1 hr. 46 m. 2 s. (106·78 m.p.h.); 2, T. Rutter (Yamaha), 1 hr. 46 m. 7 s.; 3, W. Guthrie (Yamaha), 1 hr. 49 m. 1·8 s.

250 c.c. Lighweight T.T., Isle of Man.—1, T. Herron (Yamaha), 1 hr. 27 m. 26·8 s. (103·55 m.p.h.); 2, T. Katayama (Yamaha), 1 hr. 27 m. 52·2 s.; 3, C. Mortimer (Yamaha), 1 hr. 28 m. 43·2 s.

Motor Cycle News Superbikes (1,000 c.c.) (Oulton Park.)—1, M. Grant (Kawasaki), 16 m. 47·2 s. (98·69 m.p.h.); 2, R. Ditchburn (Kawasaki); 3, B. Sheene (Suzuki).

MOTOR RACING 1975–76

24-hours (Le Mans.)—1, J. Ickx and G. van Lennep (Porsche); 2, J. L. Lafosse and F. Migault (Mirage) 3, A. de Cadenet and C. Craft (de Cadenet-Lola).

Spanish Grand Prix.—1, J. Hunt (McLaren), 1 hr. 42 m. 20·43 s.; 2, N. Lauda (Ferrari), 1 hr. 42 m. 51·40 s.; 3, G. Nilsson (Lotus-Ford), 1 hr. 43 m. 8·45 s.

Monaco Grand Prix.—1, N. Lauda (Ferrari), 1 hr. 59 m. 51·47 s. (80·82 m.p.h.); 2, J. Scheckter (Tyrrell), 2 hr. 0 m. 2·6 s.; 3, P. Depailler (Tyrrell), 2 hr. 0 m. 56·31 s.

French Grand Prix.—1, J. Hunt (McLaren), 1 hr. 40 m. 58·6 s. (116·51 m.p.h.); 2, P. Depailler (Tyrrell), 1 hr. 41 m. 11·3 s.; 3, J. Watson (Penske), 1 hr. 41 m. 22·15 s.

British Grand Prix (Brands Hatch).—1, J. Hunt (McLaren); 2, N. Lauda (Ferrari); 3, J. Scheckter (Tyrrell). (*Hunt was later disqualified and the race awarded to Lauda*).

German Grand Prix.—1, J. Hunt (McLaren), 1 hr. 41 m. 42·7 s. (117·17 m.p.h.); 2, J. Scheckter (Tyrrell), 1 hr. 42 m. 10·4 s.; 3, J. Mass (McLaren), 1 hr. 42 m. 35·1 s.

South African Grand Prix.—1, N. Lauda (Ferrari), 1 hr. 42 m. 18·4 s.; 2, J. Hunt (McLaren), 1 hr. 42 m. 19·7 s.; 3, J. Mass (McLaren), 1 hr. 43 m. 40·3 s.

Brazilian Grand Prix.—1, N. Lauda (Ferrari), 1 hr. 45 m. 16·78 s. (113·42 m.ph.); 2, P. Depailler (Tyrrell), 1 hr. 45 m. 38 s.; 3, T. Pryce (Shadow), 1 hr. 45 m. 40·62 s.

Swedish Grand Prix.—1, J. Scheckter (Tyrrell), 1 hr. 46 m. 53·72 s. (100·86 m.p.h.); 2, P. Depailler (Tyrrell), 1 hr. 47 m. 13·49 s.; 3, N. Lauda (Ferrari), 1 hr. 47 m. 27·59 s.

Italian Grand Prix.—1, R. Peterson (March), 1 hr. 30 m. 35·6 s. (124·11 m.p.h.); 2, C. Regazzoni (Ferrari), 1 hr. 30 m. 37·9 s.; 3, J. Laffitte (Ligier Matra), 1 hr. 30 m. 38·6 s.

Austrian Grand Prix.—1, J. Watson (Penske), 1 hr. 30 m. 7·8 s. (131·99 m.p.h.); 2, J. Laffitte (Ligier Matra), 1 hr. 30 m. 18·65 s.; 3, G. Nilsson (JPS), 1 hr. 30 m. 19·84 s.

Belgian Grand Prix.—1, N. Lauda (Ferrari), 1 hr. 42 m. 53·13 s. (108·10 m.p.h.); 2, C. Regazzoni (Ferrari), 1 hr 42 m. 56·9 s.; 3, J. Laffitte (Ligier Matra), 1 hr 43 m. 28·61 s.

U.S. Grand Prix West.—1, C. Regazzoni (Ferrari), 1 hr. 53 m. 18·47 s. (85·51 m.p.h.); 2, N. Lauda (Ferrari); 3, P. Depailler (Tyrrell).

Canadian Grand Prix.—1, J. Hunt (McLaren); 116·70 m.p.h.; 2, P. Depailler (Tyrrell); 3, M. Andretti (Lotus).

THE WINTER OLYMPIC GAMES, 1976

The Games took place in Innsbruck from February 4 to 15.   The following is a list of the gold medallists:

Alpine Skiing
Men's Downhill.—F. Klammer (Austria).
Men's Slalom.—P. Gros (Italy).
Men's Giant Slalom.—H. Hemmi (Switzerland).
Women's Downhill.—R. Mittermaier (West Germany).
Women's Slalom.—R. Mittermaier (West Germany).
Women's Giant Slalom.—K. Kreiner (Canada).

Ski Jumping
90 Metres.—K. Schnabl (Austria).
70 Metres.—H.-G. Aschenbach (East Germany).

Biathlon
Individual.—N. Kruglov (U.S.S.R.).
Relay.—U.S.S.R.

Nordic Skiing
Men's 15 km.—N. Bajukov (U.S.S.R.).
Men's 30 km.—S. Saveliev (U.S.S.R.).
Men's 50 km.—I. Formo (Norway).
Men's Relay.—Finland.
Combined.—U. Wehling (East Germany).
Women's 5 km.—H. Takalo (Finland).
Women's 10 km.—R. Smetanina (U.S.S.R.).
Women's Relay.—U.S.S.R.

Ice Hockey
Winners.—U.S.S.R.

Speed Skating
Men's 500 m.—E. Kulikov (U.S.S.R.).
Men's 1,000 m.—P. Mueller (U.S.A.).
Men's 1,500 m.—J. E. Storholt (Norway).
Men's 5,000 m.—S. Stenson (Norway).
Men's 10,000 m.—P. Kleine (Netherlands).
Women's 500 m.—S. Young (U.S.A.).
Women's 1,000 m.—T. Averina (U.S.S.R.).
Women's 1,500 m.—G. Stephanskaya (U.S.S.R.).
Women's 3,000 m.—T. Averina (U.S.S.R.).

Ice Skating
Men's Figure.—J. Curry (G.B.).
Women's Figure.—D. Hamill (U.S.A.).
Pairs.—I. Rodnina and A. Zaitsev (U.S.S.R.).
Ice Dancing.—L. Pakhomova and A. Gorshkov (U.S.S.R.).

Bobsleigh
Two-man.—East Germany.
Four-man.—East Germany.

Tobogganing
Men.—D. Guenther (East Germany).
Two-man.—H. Rinn and N. Hahn (East Germany).
Women.—M. Schumann (East Germany).

SPORTS REPRESENTATIVE BODIES

ASSOCIATION FOOTBALL.—The Football Association. *Sec.*, E. A. Croker, 16 Lancaster Gate, W.2.

ATHLETICS.—Amateur Athletic Association. *Hon. Sec.*, B. E. Willis, 70 Brompton Road, S.W.3.
—British Amateur Athletic Board. *Hon. Sec.*, A. Gold, C.B.E., 70 Brompton Road, S.W.3.
— Women's Amateur Athletic Association. *Hon. Sec.*, Miss M. Hartman, M.B.E., 70 Brompton Road, S.W.3.

BADMINTON.—Badminton Association of England. *Sec.*, J. B. H. Bisseker, 44/45 Palace Road, Bromley, Kent.

BASKET BALL.—English Basket Ball Association. *Sec.*, K. K. Mitchell, Dept. of Physical Education, The University, Leeds.

BILLIARDS.—Billiards and Snooker Control Council. *Chairman*, W. H. Cottier, Alexandra Chambers, 32 John William Street, Huddersfield.

BOBSLEIGH.—British Bobsleigh Association. *Hon. Sec.*, G. Renwick, 515 Watford Way, N.W.7.

BOWLS.—English Bowling Association. *Sec.*, J. F. Elms, 4 Lansdowne Crescent, Bournemouth, Hants.

BOXING.—Amateur Boxing Association, 70 Brompton Road, S.W.3.—*Hon. Sec.*, W. S. Cox.
— British Boxing Board of Control, Ramillies Buildings, Hills Place, W.1.—*Gen. Sec.*, R. L. Clarke.

CANOEING.—British Canoe Union, 70 Brompton Road, S.W.3.—*Dir.*, G. Richards, M.B.E.

CLAY PIGEON SHOOTING.—Clay Pigeon Shooting Association. *Dir.*, A. P. Page, 107 Epping New Road, Buckhurst Hill, Essex.

CRICKET.—Marylebone Cricket Club, Lord's Ground, N.W.8. *Sec.*, J. A. Bailey.

CYCLING.—British Cycling Federation, 70 Brompton Road, S.W.3.—*Sec.* L. Unwin.

FENCING.—Amateur Fencing Association. *Sec.*, Cmdr. F. A. Booth, R.N., 83 Perham Road, W. Kensington, W.14.

GOLF.—Royal and Ancient Golf Club, St. Andrews. *Sec.*, K. R. T. Mackenzie, M.C.
— English Golf Union. *Sec.*, I. R. H. M. A. Erskine, 12A Denmark Street, Wokingham, Berks.
— Ladies' Golf Union, 2 Fairways, Sandwich Bay, Kent.—*Sec.*, Mrs. G. Anderson.

GYMNASTICS.—British Amateur Gymnastics Association. *Gen. Sec.*, Lt. Cdr. B. W. C. Middleton, R.N. (*ret.*), 23A High Street, Slough, Bucks.

HOCKEY.—Hockey Association.—*Sec.* Col. D. M. R. Eagan, 70 Brompton Road, S.W.3.

— All England Women's Hockey Association, 160 Great Portland Street, W.1. *Sec.*, Miss P. A. Brooker.

JUDO.—British Judo Association, 70 Brompton Road, S.W. 3. *Gen. Sec.*, A. C. G. Johnson.

LACROSSE.—English Lacrosse Union. *Hon. Sec.* R. Balls, 64 Broad Walk, Hockley, Essex.

LAWN TENNIS.—Lawn Tennis Association. *Sec.*, P. M. Johns, Barons Court, West Kensington, W.14.

— International Lawn Tennis Federation, *Gen. Sec.* D. Gray, International Lawn Tennis Federation, Barons Court, West Kensington, W.14.

MOTOR CYCLING.—Auto-Cycle Union, 31 Belgrave Square, S.W.1. *Sec. Gen.*, K. E. Shierson.

MOUNTAINEERING.—British Mountaineering Council, Crawford House, Precinct Centre, Booth Street East, Manchester. *Gen. Sec.*, D. D. Gray.

NETBALL.—All England Netball Association. *Organising Sec.*, Mrs. B. Thomson, 70 Brompton Road, S.W.3.

ORIENTEERING.—British Orienteering Federation, Lea Green, near Matlock, Derbyshire. *Professional Officer*, A. Walker.

RACING.—The Jockey Club (incorporating National Hunt Committee), 42 Portman Square, W.1. *Sec.*, S. M. Weatherby.

RIFLE SHOOTING.—National Rifle Association, *Sec.*, Air Commodore A. B. Riall, C.B.E., R.A.F. (*ret.*), Bisley Camp, Brookwood, Woking, Surrey.

— National Small-bore Rifle Association. *Sec.*, R. C. Russell, Codrington House, 113 Southwark Street, S.E.1.

ROWING.—Amateur Rowing Association. *Dir.-Sec.*, M. C. Stamford, 6 Lower Mall, W.6.

RUGBY FIVES.—Rugby Fives Association. *Sec.*, T. Wood, Fairbourne Lodge, Epping Green, Essex.

RUGBY FOOTBALL.—The Rugby Football Union, Whitton Road, Twickenham, Middx. *Sec.*, Air Commodore R. H. G. Weighill, C.B.E., D.F.C.

— The Rugby Football League, *Sec.-Gen.*, D. S. Oxley, 180 Chapeltown Road, Leeds.

SKATING.—National Skating Association of Great Britain. *Gen. Sec.*, A. R. Drake, Charterhouse, E.C.1.

SKI-ING.—National Ski Federation of Great Britain. *Sec.*, Maj. Gen. I. R. Graeme, C.B., O.B.E., 118 Eaton Square, S.W.1.

SQUASH RACKETS.—Squash Rackets Association. *Sec.*, E. P. Woods, 70 Brompton Road, S.W.3.

— Women's Squash Rackets Association. *Sec.*, Miss C. Myers, 345 Upper Richmond Road West, East Sheen, Surrey.

SWIMMING.—Amateur Swimming Association, Harold Fern House, Derby Square, Loughborough, Leics.

TABLE TENNIS.—English Table Tennis Association, *Gen. Sec.*, A. W. Shipley, 21 Claremont, Hastings, East Sussex.

TOBOGANNING.—British Racing Toboganning Association.—*Pres.*, Dr. R. Liversedge, 82 Firtree Road, Banstead, Surrey.

UNDERWATER SWIMMING.—British Sub-Aqua Club, *Dir.-Gen.*, R. L. Vallintine, 70 Brompton Road. S.W.3.

WATER SKI-ING.—British Water Ski Federation, 70 Brompton Road, S.W.3.—*Sec.*, G. Hill.

WEIGHT-LIFTING.—British Amateur Weight Lifters Association. *Hon. Sec.*, W. W. R. Holland, 3 Iffley Turn, Iffley, Oxford.

WRESTLING.—English Olympic Wrestling Association.—*Chairman*, H. Jacob, O.B.E., 2 Huxley Drive, Bramhill, Stockport, Cheshire.

YACHTING.—Royal Yachting Association, Victoria Way, Woking, Surrey. *Sec.- Gen.*, J. Durie.

DUKE OF EDINBURGH'S AWARD SCHEME

The Duke of Edinburgh's Award Scheme is meant to provide an incentive and a challenge to young people to reach certain standards in leisure-time activities with the voluntary help of adults. Entrants in the United Kingdom and in other Commonwealth countries, must be between their 14th and 23rd birthdays and can enter through their school, the firm where they work, a youth organization, or on their own. Bronze, Silver and Gold Awards can be gained by those who qualify in four of the five sections of the Scheme: Service, Expedition, Interest, Design for Living, and Physical Activity. The qualifying standards are expressed in terms of proficiency, perseverance or sustained effort, participants being assessed on the use they make of their personal abilities and aptitudes and not in competition with others.

In 1975, there were 73,767 new entrants from the United Kingdom and 25,522 from overseas; a total of 30,195 Awards were gained in the U.K. and 10,832 overseas. There have now been more than a million entrants since the Scheme began.

Head Office: 5 Prince of Wales Terrace, W.8. Director: A. Blake, C.V.O., M.C.

THE AMERICAN BICENTENNIAL

In 1976 The United States of America celebrated its 200th year of independence from Britain. Events were held all over the world to mark the occasion and Britain, especially, although the defeated party in 1776, took the opportunity to remember the constructive aspects of Anglo-American friendship and also simply to enjoy herself. The following give some idea of the range of activities which resulted from the Bicentennial: A jazz festival was held in New Orleans; John Wayne, the film star, made a record singing the praises of his homeland; the South Korean, Mr. Sun Myung Moon and his Unification Church put on a £½m " God Bless America " extravaganza in New York's Yankee Stadium; trees were ceremonially planted in literally hundreds of parks and in Kent (Britain's not America's) three were laid down by descendants, respectively, of Cornwallis, Lord North and Lafayette in a symbolic act of reconciliation; a plaque to the anglophile American author, Henry James, was unveiled at Poets Corner in Westminster Abbey; an attempt, as it turned out unsuccessful, was made to recover the bones of Pocahontas, the famous Indian girl, from her tomb at Gravesend in order to transport them to Jamestown, Virginia; Michael Foot gave a major address on Tom Paine; the Mormons sang their hearts out in a festival of music in Utah; the London Hilton organised a Festival of American Culinary Heritage.

B.P. donated a statue of Captain Cook, greatly admired in America, to the new Resolution Park, (in Anchorage, Alaska), named after the explorer's ship; Leonard Bernstein's musical on the theme of America's Presidents " 1600 Pennsylvania Avenue ", opened in Broadway (and flopped); American money (£200,000) was contributed towards the £690,000 spent by the British Government on buying the site of the Battle of Hastings, the assistance being rendered as " a tangible token of the enduring link between the U.K. and U.S. in this bicentennial year "; American money was also forthcoming to help in the restoration of Washington Old Hall near Gateshead, the ancestral home of America's first president.

In Ulster an Irish-American folk park was opened which included the restored cottage of the Mellon family; in January, there took place the first performance in Europe for 35 years of Benjamin Britten's operetta, *Paul Bunyan* (with libretto by W. H. Auden) about the founding of America; Richard Rodney Bennett's *Zodiac* and Malcolm Arnold's concerto, both composed for the bicentennial, were also given their first performances; in late May, Britain presented a golden replica of the Magna Carta in Westminster Hall to 25 members of Congress which would reside permanently in the Capitol, to symbolise the shared political origins of the two democracies. It is to be set in a two-ton piece of stone taken from a remote shore of the Outer Hebrides, which is the nearest point in Britain to the New World. This permanent gift is in lieu of the original copies of the Great Charter which were temporarily lent to America; a huge Indian Pow-Wow was held with 10,000 representatives from 40 Indian tribes, including the few surviving Aztecs, where the Red Indians were able to mark not only the 200th year of America but the 100th since Custer's last stand (in 1876); in a special series of football matches " Team America " represented the host; the bicentennial wing of the Metropolitan Museum of Modern Art in New York was opened specifically to hold American art, including a complete room designed by Frank Lloyd Wright.

In England discussions were held on restoring 36 Craven Street off the Strand, which was occupied by Benjamin Franklin, perhaps as a museum to the great man; in Boston, Massachusetts, where the firm has a new 40 storey office block, Commercial Union helped in the restoration of the Old State House, the scene of the 1770 Massacre; throughout the country the American Freedom Train made a slow trek by rail—24 carriages pulled by an old steam engine and containing such mementoes as Washington's personal copy of the Constitution, the first Bible printed in America, Will Rogers' rope, Judy Garland's dress from The Wizard of Oz and a collection of moon rocks. It was due to travel 16,000 miles and reach 10 million people. Similarly a Bicentennial Wagon Train rolled its way along the legendary Oregon Trail entertaining thousands as it went; a folklife festival with displays from 34 nations also toured 90 American cities; Britain produced a special 11p stamp depicting Franklin, who among his many accomplishments was a postmaster in Philadelphia; coins and medals were cast —the Washington Crown, for example, the first British legal tender to portray the Queen and an American president on the same coin. A series of plates, designed by Annigoni, also portraying Queen Elizabeth and President Ford, was put on the market. Similarly the wealthy consumer was offered " American Royal Family " spoons showing the 10 colonial monarchs who were the American Heads of State before the Revolution. Wedgwoods sent ½m pieces to America including basalt busts of Washington, one copy of which was given to the U.S. National Portrait Gallery, very appropriately, for the first Wedgwood had bravely backed American independence in 1776; 1976 also saw many books, TV programmes and exhibitions, in Britain and America. The biggest exhibition here, visited by many Americans, and opened by the Queen, was held at Greenwich and was impressive in its use of full-scale mock-ups, of a Georgian coffee house, and American colonial inn and life-size statues, for example, of George III receiving John Adams as the first ambassador of the new nation.

Several very ambitious plans failed to materialise: among them was the intention of holding the Winter Olympics for 1976 in Denver which was also celebrating its own single centenary. However the taxpayers revolted.

The highlight of the year was the Queen's six-day visit to America (her second in fact), designed to express the complete reconciliation between the former belligerents, as well as our common ideology. As the Queen told her hosts: " Both our peoples believe in the world of the individual and the family, in freedom of religion and expression, and the right to change a government by the ballot box, rather than the gun, perhaps the best definition of democracy." The Queen and the Duke of Edinburgh's first port of call (literally for they came in the Royal yacht, *Britannia*, rather than the supersonic airliner, Concorde, as originally planned) was Philadelphia, " cradle of the Revolution ". There she presented to America a new " Liberty Bell " cast by the same Whitechapel foundry that made the original in 1752, which was cracked in 1855. In Washington, the royal party was met by the president on the White House lawn and while in the city, attended a Scottish military tattoo and the consecration of the nave of the cathedral, among many engagements. In Boston, scene of the Tea Party, the Queen received as warm a welcome as she received all over the country, despite the city's Irish Republican presence. In Virginia, the oldest English settlement on the

continent, the Queen deliberately made her trip a tribute to the state's greatest son, Jefferson. From America Her Majesty went to Canada to open the Olympics.

Throughout the year, other Heads of State also came to participate in America's celebrations, including the King of Spain. More aptly, in view of the vital military help France had given the youthful nation in its fight for independence, in May President Giscard d'Estaing spent six days in America and among his official visits was one to Yorktown, where Britain surrendered.

All in all, this sizeable foreign role in the Bicentenary (and some 40 nations held events) was itself very appropriate given that America is the world's quintessential " nation of immigrants ". The immigration rate is still running at 350,000 a year—in 1975 some 125,000 South Vietnamese arrived. Part of the great July 4th celebrations this year was a moving mass pledging of allegiance by immigrants to their new land, and like Britain, America's most noble role in history has been as a haven for the oppressed or restless.

Of course the climax of the Bicentennial was July 4th (when the Queen was in the country); the day annually celebrated by Americans but never so grandly as this year. Plans to land *Viking II*, the unmanned spaceshot, on Mars, 400m miles away, on July 4th did not come off (for the landing was delayed till the 20th) but other events took place as planned. The Parade of Tall Ships in New York harbour was a glorious display involving scores of ships from several dozen nations, including some from behind the Iron Curtain. Britain sent her largest sailing ship, *Sir Winston Churchill* (named after a man with an American mother), and this vessel was one of the 225 ships which took part in the Transatlantic Tallships Race beforehand. The parade was the largest assemblage of sailing ships for 150 years and took its theme from sail's role in bringing settlers to America and that of the clippers in developing U.S. trade. On the same day " the biggest birthday cake in the world " was unveiled in Baltimore and liberty bells rang out across the continent from Independence Hall, Philadelphia to the Alamo in Texas.

America celebrated its first centenary, in 1876, fairly modestly. Only one major city, rather than the whole country, was chosen as the forum for the festivities. This was Philadelphia, where the Declaration of Independence was signed. Here a large exhibition was mounted which attracted millions and one of the exhibits was a 50 foot statue of William Penn. Much larger of course was the most famous product of the celebrations, the Statue of Liberty, designed by Eiffel and Bartholdi and finally dedicated in 1886. It was the gift of France and given in expression of the Franco-American " Love of Liberty ". (It is being restored in 1976.) Germany's main contribution was an overture composed by Wagner, and Britain also marked the event—an important Congregational church just south of the river in London, for example, put up a " Lincoln Tower and Spire ".

If the celebrations of 1876 were large and those of 1976 much larger, what can we expect in 2076? The Americans of that time will not be short of inspiration for all over the great country children have been burying time capsules containing instructions for their great grandchildren to be read 100 years from now on the tercentenary. Perhaps the greatest wish is that the reverence for " Life, Liberty and The Pursuit of Happiness ", so eloquently enunciated in 1776, will still be deep in the hearts of America (and Britain).

THE DROUGHT OF 1975–76 OVER ENGLAND AND WALES

" Drought " and " partial drought " were formally defined in *British Rainfall* in 1887; " drought " as a given number of consecutive days on none of which more than a stated, tiny amount of rain fell (at a selected location) and " partial drought " as a larger number of consecutive days over which the total rainfall, shared over the whole period, did not exceed a slightly larger amount per day. These definitions were later recognized as being artificial and misleading and a new system, based on the shortfall of rain in relation to the local average, was introduced in the 1961 issue of *British Rainfall*.

This new system of looking at drought is very meaningful since it rates dry weather in a normally dry area as a commonplace but highlights the occurrence of prolonged dry weather in an area where the rainfall is usually both frequent and abundant.

To the water supply industry a dry winter half-year (October to March) gives cause for concern. Two or more dry " winters " in succession or in close proximity present very serious problems. To the farmer, the horticulturalist and the gardener unusual dryness in the growing season (which corresponds more or less to the other half-year, April to September) may be merely a nuisance or an expensive disaster. Some crops are too expensive to irrigate and must rely on rainfall; for others irrigation is cost-beneficial and the grower relies upon some form of water storage. After a dry winter and a dry spring these reserves are likely to be slender or to fail altogether. Thus after a dry winter the water suppliers fear a dry summer and high demands on their dwindling water stocks, and in a dry summer the grower is poorly placed if the previous winter was also dry.

Those who are neither water suppliers nor growers of fruit, flowers and vegetables may welcome prolonged fine weather until called upon to pay the price in terms of heath and forest fires, closed canals, dried-up lakes and rivers more than usually polluted and offering poor angling, factories reduced to short-time, poor crops and high food prices and, finally, the severe inconvenience or even misery of water restrictions and trips to standpipes in the streets.

In winter the soil normally becomes fully moistened without being waterlogged; this state is technically described as " field capacity ". The energy received in Great Britain from the winter sun is low and hence there is not much winter evaporation. Only a small amount of all winter rainfall evaporates and the rest goes to stock up the water-holding layers below ground (aquifers) and to feed lakes, reservoirs and rivers. Summer rainfall is normally all used up by plant life; some being evaporated as the plants transpire and some contributing to plant bulk. Only a very wet spell in the summer half-year can make any worthwhile contribution to water storage, since this requires the soil to be moistened to " field capacity " status first. A knowledge of the frequency with which high and low rainfalls and high and low river flows occur is essential for water management and for long-term planning. Frequency is often expressed as " return period "; the return period of any event is the number of years which elapse, *on average*, between successive occurrences of the event. In the present context an " event " would be unusually low rainfall or river flow.

In the 1931 issue of *British Rainfall*, F. J. Nicholas and J. Glasspoole published general monthly and annual rainfall values for England and Wales for the period 1727 to 1931. This series of general values

has been extended up to the present by the Meteorological Office. In 1971, B. G. Wales-Smith published monthly and annual totals of rainfall representative of Kew, Surrey, from 1697 to 1970. Observations have been made at Kew since the 1850s and rainfall is still measured there. Thus some 250 years of general values for England and Wales and some 280 years of values and estimated values (from measurements made elsewhere) for Kew are available for analysis. The once in 25 year event occurs, on average, only 10 times in 250 years and rarer events proportionately less frequently. Accepted statistical methods can be used to obtain estimates of the sizes of events corresponding to large return periods. It is important, however, to interpret such estimates sensibly. So far as rainfall deficiency is concerned, it is prudent to accept a return period of 200 years as meaning somewhere between 100 and 400 years (i.e. as lying between half and twice the estimated value).

Droughts can be studied in many ways. A fairly comprehensive picture can be built up using totals of measured rainfall, estimates of the evaporative demand (potential evapotranspiration) and estimates of the proportion of rainfall which has contributed to the recharge of water storage in the aquifers and to increasing the levels of rivers, lakes and reservoirs. Some meteorologists have called this " hydrologically effective rainfall "; hydrologists and water engineers often call it " residual rainfall ".

Estimates of potential evapotranspiration can be calculated from measurements of sunshine duration, temperature, humidity and wind speed, using a formula published by H. L. Penman in 1948. Estimates of effective rainfall can be calculated from rainfall and potential evapotranspiration values, provided that the rooting characteristics of the vegetation which is transpiring the moisture from the soil to the air are known. Broadly speaking, the deeper the root systems the more soil moisture can be reached and extracted from the soil.

Considering, first, rainfall alone we can add up measured totals over various periods and compare them with what happened in the past. In the 16-month period May 1975 to August 1976, for instance, the general value for England and Wales, 759 mm (just under 30 inches) was only 64·2 per cent of the 1916–50 average. It was the driest 16-month spell in the whole series right back to 1727, the earliest date from which records are available. One technique for estimating the probability of occurrence of such rare deficiencies of rainfall suggests that such a low 16-month total, starting in May, has a return period of 1,000 years or more; perhaps somewhere between 500 and 2,000 years.

In Table 1 winter and summer half-year and annual rainfall totals from the England and Wales series and at Kew Observatory, Surrey, for the period 1971–6 are expressed as per cent. of average and are given tentative return periods. The averages are as follows:

	Year	Apr–Sep	Oct–Mar
	mm	mm	mm
England and Wales	904	414	490
Kew Observatory..	608	305	303

1916–50 averages are used here because averages for the new standard period 1941–70 are not quite ready. In the table " % " stands for per cent. of the averages given above. The estimated return periods are given in years. Negative signs indicate values below average and positive signs show that values were above average. Return periods of 5 years and less are preceded by the " less than " symbol <. Values given in brackets are provisional and may be amended, slightly, after careful scrutiny of the data. The significance of the winter and summer half-years in hydrometeorological studies has been clearly established. Examination of the annual totals, percentages and return periods shows that analyses based on annual data alone can be misleading. It is essential to consider accumulated deficiencies of rainfall over *any* period.

In Table 2 the lowest winter half-year rainfalls for England and Wales and for Kew and the lowest summer half-year rainfalls at Kew are set out. Percentages are given to the nearest whole figure.

Each table has been extended far enough to contain either the 1975 winter half-year or the 1976 summer half-year. It is of interest to examine the summer half year recently ended in more detail.

Rainfall at Kew accumulated through the summer half-year:

April 9·5 mm

April and May 36·7 mm
   a once in 20 year low total

April to June 44·6 mm
   a once in 200 year low total; 3rd lowest since 1697

April to July 68·6 mm
   over once in 500 year low total; 2nd lowest since 1697

Table 1

	England and Wales			Kew Observatory		
	mm	%	Return period	mm	%	Return period
APR 1971–SEP 1971..........	387	93	− <5	359	118	+ <5
OCT 1971–MAR 1972.........	458	93	− <5	288	95	− <5
APR 1972–SEP 1972.........	358	87	− <5	143	47	−300
OCT 1972–MAR 1973.......	343	70	−20	172	57	−35
APR 1973–SEP 1973........	454	110	+ <5	343	113	+ <5
OCT 1973–MAR 1974........	439	90	− <5	248	82	− <5
APR 1974–SEP 1974..........	436	105	+ <5	316	104	+ <5
OCT 1974–MAR 1975........	525	107	+ <5	425	140	+25
APR 1975–SEP 1975.........	364	88	− <5	279	91	− <5
OCT 1975–MAR 1976........	302	62	−65	158	52	−60
APR 1976–SEP 1976.........	(320)	77	−10	(189)	62	−30
1971........................	798	88	− <5	620	102	+ <5
1972........................	848	94	− <5	423	70	−25
1973........................	739	82	−11	476	78	−10
1974........................	994	110	+ <5	714	117	+6
1975........................	752	83	−10	575	95	− <5

April to August   82·1 mm
over once in 500 year low total; lowest since 1697

April to September   188·7 mm
close to a once in 20 year low total; joint 7th lowest since 1697

Considering, next, potential evapotranspiration (the evaporative demand, which can only be satisfied if water is sufficiently available) the 1916–50 averages for green vegetation completely covering the ground (e.g. a lawn) at Kew were:

Year mm	Apr–Sep mm	Oct–Mar mm
543	460	83

Approximate values for evaporation from lakes, reservoirs, etc. may be obtained by multiplying these figures by 1·2 giving some 652 mm for the year, 552 mm for the "summer" and 100 mm for the "winter".

The six winter half-years having the highest evaporative demand since 1871 and perhaps even since 1698 (although this is not certain) were 1966, 1964, 1959, 1965, 1884 and 1911 with between 109 and 102 mm. These figures would have to be multiplied by 1·2 to give estimates for open water. The 1975 value for a vegetated surface was a mere 93 mm. The seven summer half-years with the highest evaporative demand were 1959, 1911, 1975, 1957, 1846, 1893 and 1899 with between 565 and 516 mm for a vegetated surface. It has not been possible to complete the 1976 summer computations yet but the evaporative demand this summer can be studied on a progressive basis.

The April value was 63 mm; a once in 20 year high value

the May value was 100 mm; the total 163 mm is the 4th highest calculated so far and is assessed as a 1 in 80 year high

the June value was 119 mm; the 282 mm total is the 2nd highest calculated so far and is assessed above 200 years

the July value was 138 mm; the 420 mm total is the highest calculated so far and is assessed well above 200 years

It can be seen that a reservoir in the west London area might have lost 76 mm in April, 120 mm in May, 143 mm in June and 166 mm in July, a total of 540 mm (or nearly 20 inches). These losses would have been compensated a little by rain falling directly into the reservoir; if totals were the same as measured at Kew this would have amounted to only some 69 mm (or only 2·7 inches).

Finally we can consider the estimated effective rainfall for a grassed surface at Kew since 1871. The 1916–50 averages are 156 mm for October to March and only 10 mm for April to September; estimated value below 50 mm are as follows for 6-month periods beginning in October in the years listed:

1890, 1933, 1964 and 1972 Nil
1897 7, 1943 34, 1901 37, 1921 43, 1908 45, 1873 46, 1900 47, 1948 48 and 1947 49 mm i.e. between 0 and 31 per cent of average.

Of summer half-years since 1871 60 years (out of 105) had no effective rainfall under grass at Kew and only 3 summers had more than 50 mm.

Although no forecasting value should be ascribed to the fact, it is interesting to note that of the 13 winter half-years estimated to have had less than 50 mm of effective rainfall (for a grassed surface at Kew) two were followed by even drier winter half-years but the remaining 11 were followed by winter half-years yielding amounts of effective rainfall 65 to 70 mm greater, although only three of these exceeded the average value of 156 mm.

A study was carried out to see whether extremely dry 16-month periods beginning in May are followed by wet or dry winter half-years over England and Wales as a whole; the results showed no statistically significant bias.

Table 2

Rainfall in Winter half-year (October–March)

England and Wales			Kew Observatory		
Year	Rain mm	% of average	Year	Rain mm	% of average
1739	244	50	1724	141	47
1784	270	55	1879	148	49
1879	270	55	1890	156	51
1829	279	57	1975	158	52
1730	287	59	1933	159	53
1788	292	60	1931	163	54
1975	303	62			

Rainfall in Summer half-year (April–September)

Kew Observatory		
Year	Rain mm	% of average
1921	131	43
1972	143	47
1959	152	50
1870	173	57
1893	175	57
1705	176	58
1976	189	62
1714	189	62

DRAMATIC SUMMARY, 1975–76

Among London productions between October 1, 1975 and September 30, 1976, were the following:

ADELPHI: (1976) *June* 15. *Irene.*

ALBERY: (1975) *Oct.* 2. Wendy Hiller and Michael Aldridge in *Lies* by Trevor Baxter. *Nov.* 20. *A Month in the Country* (Dorothy Tutin, Timothy West, Derek Jacobi, John Turner). *Nov.* 27. *A Room With a View* (Jane Lapotaire, Timothy West, Pauline Jameson, Lynn Farleigh). (1976) *Apr.* 20. *Equus* by Peter Shaffer, directed by John Dexter (Colin Blakely).

ALDWYCH: (1975) *Oct.* 23. George Bernard Shaw's *Too True To Be Good* (Ian McKellen, Anna Calder-Marshall, Judi Dench, directed by Clifford Williams). *Dec.* 4. Denholm Elliot and Paul Rogers in *The Return of A. J. Raffles* by Graham Greene. (1976) *Jan.* 20. Alan Howard as Shakespeare's Henry V. *Jan.* 29. *Henry IV Part 1* and *Henry IV Part 2* (Alan Howard, Emrys James, Brewster Mason). *Mar.* 26. *The Merry Wives of Windsor. Apr.* 28. Mia Farrow in *The Zykovs* by Maxim Gorky. *May* 25. *The Iceman Cometh* by Eugene O'Neill (Ian Holm, Patrick Stewart, Norman Rodway). *July* 5. *The Devil's Disciple* by Bernard Shaw (Royal Shakespeare Company.) *Sept.* 7. Royal Shakespeare Company in Chekhov's *Ivanov* (in repertoire with *The Devil's Disciple*).

APOLLO: (1976) *Mar.* 16. Barry Humphries in *Housewife-Superstar! May* 19. *Confusions* by Alan Ayckbourn (Pauline Collins, John Alderton).

CAMBRIDGE: (1976) *June* 23. *The Black Mikado.* Jonathan Miller's production of *The Three Sisters* with Janet Suzman, Nigel Davenport, June Ritchie, Angela Down, Peter Eyre, Susan Engel, John Shrapnel, Peter Bayliss and Sebastian Shaw.

COMEDY: (1976) *Mar.* 4. Adam Faith in *City Sugar* by Stephen Poliakoff. *May* 24. *Dimetos* by Athol Fugard (Paul Scofield). *June* 23. Kenneth Williams, Peggy Mount, Brian Pringle in *Signed and Sealed. July* 21. *Getting Away with Murder* by J. Lee Thompson (Barry Foster, Anthony Bate, Hildegard Neil, Ernest Clark).

CRITERION: (1976) *Mar.* 24. *Gaslight* (Nicola Pagett, Anton Rogers, Peter Vaughn). *June* 5. Alec McCowan, Michael Bryant, Judy Parfitt and Annette Crosbie in *The Family Dance* by Felicity Browne.

DRURY LANE: (1976) *July* 22. *A Chorus Line.*

DUKE OF YORK'S: (1975) *Nov.* 3. *Roger's Last Stand* (Leslie Phillips and Roy Kinnear). (1976) *Apr.* 14. Elizabeth Seal and Sheila Steafel in *Salad Days. Aug.* 11. Alan Bates in *The Seagull.*

FORTUNE: (1975) *Nov.* 6. The Charles Pierce Show. (1976) *Feb.* 3. *The Lady or the Tiger. May* 5. *Gigi* by Colette and Anita Loos (Lila Kedrova, Simon Williams, Veronica Quilligan).

GLOBE: (1976) *Mar.* 10. Tony Britton in *The Chairman* by Philip Mackie. *July* 15. Peter Barkworth, Penelope Keith, Peter Jeffrey in *Donkeys' Years* by Michael Frayn.

HAYMARKET: (1975) *Oct.* 22. Herbert Lom and Nigel Stock in William Douglas Home's *Betzi. Dec.* 16. *On Approval* by Frederick Lonsdale (Edward Woodward, Geraldine McEwan, Jennie Linden, Edward Hardwicke, Stephanie Beacham and Geoffrey Palmer).

HER MAJESTY'S: (1975) *Oct.* 16. Richard Johnson, James Smilie, Dilys Hawlett & Caroline Villiers in *Thomas and The King. Nov.* 19. Ipi Tombi.

JEANETTA COCHRANE: (1976) *Aug.* 16. National Youth Theatre. *Here Comes The Sun* by Barry Keeffe. *Aug.* 31. National Youth Theatre in *Stag Night* by Willis Hall.

LYRIC: (1975) *Oct.* 28. Anton Chekhov's *The Seagull,* directed by Lindsay Anderson (Joan Plowright, Helen Mirren, Peter McEnery, John Moffatt, Frank Grimes). *Dec.* 9. Anderson's production of the Ben Travers farce *The Bed Before Yesterday* (Joan Plowright, Frank Grimes, John Moffatt).

LYTTELTON: (1976) *Mar.* 15. *Plunder* by Ben Travers, transferred from the Old Vic. Also transferred were *Hamlet, John Gabriel Borkman, Happy Days, No Man's Land, Watch It Come Down* and *Playboy of the Western World. June* 19. *Blithe Spirit* by Noel Coward. *July* 1. *Weapons of Happiness* by Howard Brenton.

MAYFAIR: (1976) *May* 22. *What's A Nice Country Like U.S. Doing In A State Like This? Aug.* 16. Libby Morris in a new musical revue, *Just Libby.*

MERMAID: (1976) *Jan.* 22. Richard Beckinsale in *Funny Peculiar* by Mike Stott. *May* 4. *Side by Side,* by Sondheim (Millicent Martin, Julia McKenzie, David Kernan, Ned Sherrin). *July* 9. Patrick Cargill, Moira Redmond, Hugh Paddick, in *Some of My Best Friends are Husbands* by Hugh Leonard. *Aug.* 4. Michael Rothwell in *Crocodiles in Cream. Sept.* 2. *The Worst of Kenneth Robinson.*

NEW LONDON: (1976) *June* 2. Brian Protheroe in *Leave Him to Heaven.*

OLD VIC: (1975) *Oct.* 29. *Playboy of the Western World* by J. M. Synge (Stephen Rea). *Dec.* 10. Albert Finney, Angela Lansbury, Denis Quilley in *Hamlet,* directed by Peter Hall. (1976) *Jan.* 14. *Plunder* by Ben Travers; directed by Michael Blakemore. *Feb.* 24. *Watch It Come Down* by John Osborne. *July* 12. Glenda Jackson, Patrick Magee, Jack Shephard in *The White Devil* by John Webster, directed by Michael Lindsay-Hogg.

OPEN AIR, REGENT'S PARK: (1976) *June* 9. Shakespeare's *Othello* (Robert Stephens and Edward Fox). *July* 21. *Love's Labours Lost.*

PALLADIUM: (1976) *Feb.* 2 for 2 weeks, and *May* 17–*June* 5, Shirley Maclaine. *June* 9. Julie Andrews. *July* 8–28. Australian Ballet in *The Merry Widow. Aug.* 2. Johnnie Ray, Billy Daniels, Francis Faye, *The Ink Spots.*

PHOENIX: (1975) *Oct.* 15. *Tarantara! Tarantara!* (1976) *Jan.* 21. *I Do! I Do!* (Rock Hudson and Juliet Prowse). *Mar.* 17. Glynis Johns and Louis Jourdan in 13 *Rue de L'Amour. May* 12. Lee Remick, Keir Dullea, Alfred Marks and Miriam Karlin in *Bus Stop. July* 7. Douglas Fairbanks Jr, Dinah Sheridan, David Langton and Wilfred Hyde White in *The Pleasure of His Company. Sept.* 30. *Carte Blanche.*

PRINCE OF WALES: (1975) *Oct.* 8. Harry Secombe in *The Plumber's Progress.* (1976) *Mar.* 18. *Mardi Gras.*

ST. GEORGE'S: (1976) *Apr.* 21. *Twelfth Night* (Eric Porter, Lynn Farleigh). *June* 2. *Romeo and Juliet* (Peter McEnery and Sarah Badel). *July* 8. *Richard III* (Alan Badel).

SAVOY: (1976) *July* 19. Robert Morley and George Cole in Ben Travers' *Banana Ridge.*

SHAFTESBURY: (1975) *Oct.* 2. Arthur Lowe, John Le Mesurier and Clive Dunn in *Dad's Army. June* 8. Somerset Maugham's *Liza of Lambeth,* musical.

SHAW: (1976) *Jan.* 26. *The Ginger Man* by J. P. Donleavy. *Apr.* 6. Fulton Mackay in Pinter's *The Caretaker. June* 28. Timothy Dalton, Maggie Fitzgibbon in *Black Comedy and White Liars* by Peter Shaffes. *Aug.* 18. National Youth Theatre. *The Bread and Butter Trade* by Peter Terson.

VAUDEVILLE: (1975) *Nov.* 5. *Double Edge* (Margaret Lockwood, Paul Daneman and Barrie

Ingham). (1976) *June 17*. *Baggage* (Gerald Harper, Hannah Gordon, Una Stubbs, Prunella Gee).

VICTORIA PALACE: (1976) *Apr. 8*. Terry Scott and June Whitfield in *A Bedful of Foreigners*.

WHITEHALL: *Aug. 26*. Brian Rix, Terence Alexander and Jane Bonns in *Fringe Benefits*.

WYNDHAMS: (1976) *May 26*. *Teeth 'N' Smiles* written and directed by David Hare (Helen Mirren, Dave King, Martin Shaw).

On March 15, 1976 a Charity Preview of the Ben Travers farce *Plunder* introduced the first repertory season at Britain's new £15 million National Theatre. It was performed in the Lyttelton Theatre, the first of the three stages to become available. The Theatre, designed by Denys Lasdun, is built on a South Bank site of almost five acres and can accommodate up to 2,500 people. The list of playwrights whose plays opened the first season is very impressive—Shakespeare, Ibsen, Beckett, Travers, Pinter, Osborne and Synge—but it must remain so to be able to attract an audience that can cover the vast commercial requirements the cost of building put on the Theatre.

It seems a fairly remarkable achievement to have the National actually open at last. As long ago as the 1840s a national theatre based on London was suggested, albeit tentatively. Then in 1946 a council was appointed and three years later an Act of Parliament was passed allowing the spending of up to one million pounds on a theatre. In 1951 a foundation stone was laid by the Queen Mother but work on the site was not started until 1969. Now in 1976 we have 3 stages housed in one massive complex. The Olivier Theatre, named after Lord Laurence Olivier who created the National Company at the Old Vic in 1963 and was its artistic director for ten years. This theatre has a capacity of 1,160 and its stage is built on a drum-revolve 40 feet in diameter and 45 feet high and split into halves which are on lifts that can bring up complete stage sets in 30 seconds if necessary. The Lyttelton Theatre is named after Oliver Lyttelton, Lord Chandos, chairman of the National Theatre Board from 1963–1971 and holds 890 people. This is to be used exclusively for new plays once the Theatre is in full swing. Finally there is the smaller Cottesloe Theatre named after the chairman of the South Bank Theatre Board, in which it is possible to adapt the seating arrangements to suit almost any style of acting space a director may require.

So the nation's theatre is now open to everybody to watch a choice of three plays a night or to enjoy the facilities—bars, buffets or restaurant—or simply to look round and have a sit down. Peter Hall hopes to introduce other spectacles including some plays at lunch-time, late-night events, music, poetry-readings and street-theatre shows on the terraces. He hopes to concentrate on attracting a wider range of people who have been put off attending West End theatre in recent years by high ticket prices, and a limited and non-committal fare of entertainment that has more to do with the profit motive than art.

The Theatres Trust Bill received the Royal Assent on July 22 in the House of Lords. This Act, as it now is, sets up a Theatres Trust aimed at protecting Britain's theatres from planners and demolition men. The Trust, members of which will be appointed by the Education Secretary, will have to be consulted before planning authorities allow any changes to be made to theatre buildings.

The Act was designed to make it more difficult to add to the demise of live theatres by demolishing them or radically altering their nature. Lord Harmar-Nicholls said that there was much more to this Bill than just rescuing a theatre or two from bankruptcy; the one thing in which this country truly led the world was British theatre and British acting. Viscount Norwich's view was that in the present, rather grim period through which they were passing, it was marvellous to think that the theatre had in the past few years gone from strength to strength. The Arts Minister (Lord Donaldson of Kingsbridge) said that the Government agreed with the aims of the Bill and hoped it would turn out to be one more weapon in the armoury they had to defend the theatre.

LITERATURE OF THE YEAR

Alexander Solzhenitsyn, the exiled Russian author, has further enhanced his already formidable reputation, and his position as the dominant figure in modern world literature. At the end of 1975, the second volume of his work on the Soviet prison camps was published. *The Gulag Archipelago, Vol. II* contains the third and fourth parts of the seven that comprise the whole. Solzhenitsyn attributes the whole concept of forced labour to Lenin, and not, as is popularly supposed, to Stalin, who merely inherited the system and perfected and expanded it. *Lenin in Zurich*, published this year, forms part of Solzhenitsyn's major project, which is to rescue Russian history for the people from the distortions of Soviet propaganda. The first volume of this work was *August 1914*, published when the author was still resident in Russia, and Chapter 22 was omitted from it at his request. The reason for this is now apparent, as it concerned Lenin. It now forms part of this volume; further chapters from the as yet unpublished *October 1916* and *March 1917* have been added, and expanded since Solzhenitsyn's researches in the West to make a compelling psychological portrait of the architect of the revolution during the crucial period of his frustrating exile in Switzerland. The work is a skilful blend of history, biography and novel.

MALORY.—The only extant manuscript of Sir Thomas Malory's *Morte d'Arthur* was sold by Winchester College to the British Library in March for a reported fee of £150,000. Little is known of Malory, but it is believed that he was a member of parliament, fought on both sides in the Wars of the Roses, and spent some time in prison for various offences, where he may well have written his great Arthurian romance. Malory gave coherence to the many Arthurian legends, and constructed a continuous narrative around the two main themes of the reign of Arthur and the Knights of the Round Table, and the quest for the Holy Grail. He worked from a combination of sources, including French, and finished it in about 1469. Caxton printed an edition of it in 1485, and may well have worked from the Winchester manuscript, but it contains much material omitted from Caxton's edition. The manuscript was identified in Winchester College Library in 1934 by Dr. W. F. Oakeshott, and published under the title *The Works of Sir Thomas Malory*, edited by Professor Eugene Vinaver, in three volumes in 1947. A facsimile of the manuscript is to be published.

BYRON.—In the words of Lady Caroline Lamb, he was " Mad, bad and dangerous to know ", yet his life and works continue to attract authors and readers. Two more volumes of Byron's letters and journals have now been published, admirably edited as before by Leslie A. Marchand. In " *So Late Into the Night* ": *Byron's Letters and Journals, Vol. V, 1816–17* the principal event is Byron's separation from his wife, Anne Isabella Milbanke, an attractive heiress whom he had married in 1815. Following the birth of their daughter, she had, on a visit to her parents, resolved not to return to Byron. The real reason for her departure has never been established, and is not revealed in these letters, but it is known that Byron had given her ample cause, by his abominable behaviour towards her. Between February and April of 1816 he wrote frequently, seeking a reconciliation, but she would not be swayed, and he eventually agreed to a separation to keep his half-sister Augusta out of the proceedings " although they had no business with anything previous to my marriage with that infernal fiend ". So to escape the social stigma, Byron went abroad, where he eventually recaptured his old gaiety, and, with Canto IV of *Childe Harold's Pilgrimage, Beppo* and eventually *Don Juan*, produced his finest poetry. In *The Flesh is Frail: Byron's Letters and Journals, Vol. VI, 1818–19*, Byron is ensconced in Venice for much of the time, leading a life of extravagant debauchery, in love with the Countess Teresa Guiccioli and writing the first cantos of *Don Juan*.

Lady Longford has written in *Byron* a sympathetic and informative biography, which provides a useful accompaniment to the Letters and Journals by providing the essential background details, for those not familiar with Professor Marchand's own three volume work. Lady Longford establishes the fine balance between his greatness in writing, and weakness in character, and shows that his poetry has to be considered in relation to his life for full appreciation. Byron also features in a fascinating account of the Greek War of Independence by David Howarth entitled *The Greek Adventure: Lord Byron and Other Eccentrics in the War of Independence*.

Also published were *Selected Letters of James Joyce*, edited by Richard Ellman, which provide valuable background material for an understanding of the man and his work, and *Dante Gabriel Rossetti and Jane Morris, Their Correspondence* edited by John Bryson in association with Janet Camp Troxell.

PEPYS.—The final volume of the complete edition of *The Diary of Samuel Pepys* has now appeared in the much-praised edition edited by Robert Latham and William Matthews. Volume IX covers the years 1668 and 1669 until, at the age of 35, Pepys closed it on May 31 with the famous words, " And so I betake myself to that course, which is almost as much as to see myself go into my grave, for which, and all the discomforts that will accompany my being blind, the good God prepare me "; this was perhaps premature, as he retained his sight until his death at the age of 70. This volume sees Pepys becoming increasingly important and wealthy, and includes a great personal triumph for him, when on March 5, 1668, he defended the Navy Board in a speech to the House of Commons against charges of irregular payments to seamen, and spoke " most acceptably and smoothly " for three hours, fortified with claret and brandy. His private life was as complex as ever, and Pepys found the attractions of his wife's maid, Deborah Willett, too much for him. However, Pepys was caught by his wife in a compromising situation, and " was at a wonderful loss upon it and the girl also ", and his wife made him dismiss her, and promise not to see her again, an injunction he immediately ignored. It is this combination of domestic trivia, and the politics of the day as seen by an original and inquiring mind, that make the diary such an enduring masterpiece, and when the two concluding volumes, of commentary and index, are published, the whole will stand as the definitive edition of the classic example of the art of keeping a diary.

The Diaries of Evelyn Waugh were published during the year. Extracts first appeared in *The Observer* newspaper three years ago, when no complete edition was anticipated, but they have now been edited by Michael Davie and appear all but complete. Since they amount to some 340,000 words, the editor removed some of Waugh's Lancing Diary, for being too tedious, and other passages, have been excised for being libellous, or " intolerably offensive or distressing ". Waugh kept a diary throughout most of his life, except for some periods of emotional crisis; the diary of his Oxford days he later destroyed as the events described were too depraved, and he did not keep a diary during the breakdown of his first marriage, or during the period of "lunacy", described in *The Ordeal of Gilbert Pinfold*, in 1954. The Diaries will add nothing to Waugh's literary reputation, and

should not be considered in relation to the novels, but they do add to the portrait of a remarkable figure, albeit not favourably.

Albert Speer, Hitler's architect and armaments minister, served twenty years in Spandau Prison for his part in the Second World War. During that time, he secretly kept a diary, written on any available scraps of paper, which he managed to smuggle out of the prison. His first book, *Inside the Third Reich*, has now been followed by the publication of these fragments as *Spandau: The Secret Diaries*. Of them, Speer says that " Diaries are usually the accompaniment of a lived life. This one stands in place of a life ". They provide a fascinating insight into the Nazi régime, through Speer's vivid recollections of the period, and into life in Spandau.

The other six inmates included Admiral Dönitz, Nazi Chancellor after Hitler's suicide, and Hitler's deputy Rudolf Hess, sentenced to life imprisonment, and sole occupant of Spandau for the last ten years. Speer's relationship with the others was often strained, as Speer was the only defendant at Nuremberg to plead guilty, and the description of how he kept his sanity, with his imagined walk around the world in the prison garden and his remarkable resilience, make these thoughts of a repentant Nazi leader a unique and valuable postscript to the Second World War.

Memoirs of William Hickey first appeared in Peter Quennell's abridged edition in 1960, and they have now been republished. They were written by Hickey from memory after his retirement in 1808, and are an entertaining and enthralling account of the full life of this remarkable lawyer with his numerous travels abroad, to India, China and the West Indies, and his weakness for wine and women. They first appeared in four volumes between 1913 and 1925.

LITERARY LIVES.—T. E. Lawrence, archaeologist, soldier, leader of the Arab revolt, and author of *Seven Pillars of Wisdom* was a complex and intriguing figure, who has been frequently, if not always well, served by biographers. However, in *A Prince of Our Disorder: The Life of T. E. Lawrence*, Dr. John E. Mack, a distinguished American psychiatrist, has well utilised his professional skills in writing a convincing analysis of Lawrence's genius in an absorbing, thoroughly researched account of the legendary " Lawrence of Arabia ".

Oscar Wilde said to André Gide before his trial that the drama of his life was that " I've put my genius into my life; I've only put my talent into my works." H. Montgomery Hyde has already written of *The Trials of Oscar Wilde* and *Oscar Wilde: The Aftermath*, and now, in *Oscar Wilde: a Biography* he presents the complete picture of that tragic genius. A brilliant talker and wit, playwright novelist, essayist and poet, Wilde had attracted attention with his founding of the aesthetic movement, caricatured in the Gilbert and Sullivan opera *Patience*, and thenceforth until his exile was seldom out of the public eye. Yet he brought about his own downfall, and seemed to court disaster. If any good came of the affair, it was surely in the *Ballad of Reading Gaol* and *De Profundis*, both produced during his imprisonment. Also published was *Oscar Wilde* by Sheridan Morley, which contains many excellent illustrations, and *The Cleveland Street Scandal*, also by H. Montgomery Hyde, about another Victorian *cause célèbre*, involving misdoings in high places.

The tragedy of Mervyn Peake was that he was struck by a crippling illness, which dominated his later years until it gradually destroyed him. Peake was a great book illustrator and a novelist with a rare and original talent, which was not universally appreciated during his lifetime. It is only in comparatively recent years that his marvellous, gothic *Gormenghast* trilogy has reached the audience it deserves. John Watney's *Mervyn Peake* is a sound and very moving account of his life, and his drawnout death.

It is perhaps appropriate that Mrs. Winifred Gérin, who has herself written a distinguished biography of Charlotte Brontë, should now turn her talents to a life of Charlotte's first biographer, Mrs. Gaskell. Besides her novels, it is for her classic *Life of Charlotte Brontë* that she is best known, and in *Elizabeth Gaskell: A Biography*, her full and varied life, as minister's wife and crusading novelist, is well evoked.

Catherine Dupré has written a fine biography in *John Galsworthy* of the Nobel Laureate for Literature in 1932, whose works, in particular *The Forsyte Saga*, have recently enjoyed a resurgence of popularity. Mrs. Dupré sees Galsworthy's relationship with his wife Ada as the dominant influence on his life and work, and she examines it in depth. Ada had married Galsworthy's cousin Major Arthur Galsworthy in 1891. She had met John in 1893, and they lived together openly following the death of his father, thus forcing her husband to divorce her. They married in 1905. The relationship of Soames and Irene is based on that of Arthur and Ada, and Ada provided the model for many of Galsworthy's heroines. His first novel, *Jocelyn*, has now been reprinted with an introduction by Mrs. Dupré. First published pseudonymously in 1898, it is an immature work, and largely autobiographical, but it contains many of the themes which were to recur throughout Galsworthy's writings.

THE ZOO.—The Zoological Society of London was founded in 1825, and its 150th anniversary has been marked by the publication of several books. In its early days, the public were not admitted, but the increasing animal population in Regent's Park, and the cost of maintaining them, caused the Society to open its gates to the public in 1847, thus hastening its development to the Institution we know today, a place not so much of entertainment, but of serious research. Among the books published were *The Ark in the Park: the Zoo in the Nineteenth Century*, an entertaining account of the Zoo in the first half of its existence by Wilfrid Blunt; *London's Zoo* by Gwynne Vevers, Curator of the Aquarium in the Zoo and son of a former Superintendent of the Society, an excellent anthology covering the whole history; *Golden Days: Historic Photographs of the London Zoo*, a marvellous collection of pictures, with a foreword by Lord Zuckerman, present Secretary of the Society; and *The London Zoo* by Sally Holloway.

Among the remarkable occurrences noted in WHITAKER, 1883 for the previous year was the following item for March 24th; " Jumbo, the Zoological Society's large African Elephant, shipped to New York ". This was undoubtedly a black day in the annals of the Zoo, and caused immense resentment at the time. In *Jumbo*, W. P. Jolly relates the whole sad business. Jumbo had been the zoo's star attraction for 17 years, but his behaviour had become erratic, and when the impresario Phineas T. Barnum agreed to pay £2,000 for him, the zoo must have felt relief at disposing of their irascible old inmate. The public however were loath to see him go, and when Jumbo several times refused to be packed up in a crate for the voyage, the uproar increased. Jumbo eventually died in Canada, knocked down by a train.

OXFORD.—The sixth edition of *The Concise Oxford Dictionary of Current English*, edited by

J. B. Sykes, is, the publishers state, " the most radical revision yet undertaken of a dictionary that for over sixty years has held its place as the most widely accepted authority on current English ". Drawing on the material assembled for the *Supplement to the Oxford English Dictionary*, which is now in preparation, it contains entries for nearly 40,000 headwords, with a total of 74,000 vocabulary items. There has as usual been some controversy over the inclusion of the modern usage or abusage of words and phrases, but a language is inevitably the sum of its words at any given time, and *The Concise Oxford Dictionary* is an invaluable list of those ingredients, at the reasonable price of £4·75. Also published was *The Oxford Companion to Film*. Edited by Liz-Anne Bawden, it contains some 3,000 entries on all aspects of the cinema, with entries on some 700 individual films, and is illustrated with frame enlargements taken from the films themselves.

THEATRE.—Edmund Kean was one of the great tragic actors on the English stage, and one of the great dissolutes off it. He made his reputation at Drury Lane in 1814 with his Shylock, and enhanced it with his passionate and powerful performances as Hamlet, Richard III and Othello. The London Stage was an undignified place in those days. Actors and theatres were supported much as football teams are now; rivalries were intense, notably between Covent Garden and Drury Lane, and audiences would applaud an actor his points in a play as if a goal had been scored. It is thus appropriate that Kean should have collapsed on stage after speaking the words " Othello's occupation's gone ", a phrase he had made his own, and died soon afterwards. Raymond Fitzsimons relates the story of this flawed genius of the stage in his *Edmund Kean: Fire from Heaven*, which is complemented by Christopher Murray's *Robert William Elliston: A Theatrical Biography*, for Elliston was manager of the Drury Lane Theatre. He was also one of the great impresarios and innovators of the age, and apparently as drunk and debauched as Kean, with whom he was in frequent conflict. Also published was *Theatre in the Age of Kean*, an admirable survey of the period by Joseph Donohue.

MONTY.—Soon after his death this year, the biography of *Montgomery of Alamein* by Alun Chalfont was published. Montgomery had told Lord Chalfont that he would have to find out what made him tick, as this was " the hub of the whole thing ", and the author has delved deep into his past, from his unhappy childhood, to his school and Sandhurst days, in order to do just that. Although Montgomery was prepared to give his biographer frequent interviews, and to answer his questions, he refused him any access to his diaries or papers, and so this is by no means an official biography. The portrait that emerges is of a flamboyant, eccentric personality, an undoubtedly brave soldier, but not perhaps the military genius that he himself would have us believe.

AMERICA.—No significant literary works have so far appeared on this side of the Atlantic in response to the American Bicentennial. However, a work by the American author Gore Vidal entitled *1876* can inevitably be taken as a comment on the present through his treatment of the people and events surrounding the Philadelphia Centennial Exposition of that year. *1876* complete's Vidal's trilogy of historical novels on America, the other volumes being *Washington, D.C.* and *Burr*. Written as the journal of Charles Schuyler, who in *Burr* discovered that he was the illegitimate son of the third Vice-President, Colonel Aaron Burr, the book is a marvellous account of the period, notably the disputed

election, won by Rutherford Hays with a quarter of a million votes less than his opponent. The present contest for that office pales in comparison.

That enduring symbol of America, the Statue of Liberty Enlightening the World on New York Harbour, was finally unveiled on October 28, 1886. The hand of the statue holding the torch had already been exhibited in Philadelphia ten years earlier to mark the Centennial. The intriguing story of this monument is related by Marvin Trachtenberg in *The Statue of Liberty*. Conceived in the 1870s to commemorate Franco-American friendship, it was the work of Frederic Auguste Bartholdi. It was made from sheets of copper hammered into shape on wooden battens, on a framework of steel supports designed by Gustave Eiffel. The statue was completed in France in 1884, dismantled and shipped to New York in over 200 packing cases. Eiffel's engineering masterpiece, the huge tower that bears his name in Paris, which was designed to mark the Paris Exposition of 1889, is similarly commemorated in a well-illustrated volume by Joseph Harriss, *The Eiffel Tower*.

FIRST OF THE YEAR.—One of the most readable books of the year was *The First Cuckoo: Letters to The Times 1900–1975*, a selection of some 250 letters from *The Times* edited by Kenneth Gregory. Among the many delights in this volume is a letter from P. G. Wodehouse discoursing on the Wooster chin, and a letter on the inevitable " First Cuckoo ", which was later explained away as an uncommonly fine imitation by a labourer. Correspondents include Thomas Hardy, A. P. Herbert, John Galsworthy, G. B. Shaw, Winston Churchill and many more in an informative, provocative and often amusing compilation, well introduced and annotated by its editor.

POLITICS.—Among the many books published during the year by or about politicians, were the following: *The Way the Wind Blows*, the autobiography of Lord Home; *Another World, 1897–1917*, by Anthony Eden, who having written three volumes of memoirs now turns to his early life; *Stanley Baldwin*, by Kenneth Young, about the man whom Churchill called " the most formidable politician I have ever known in public life "; *The Making of Lloyd George* by his nephew W. R. P. George, which relates his life up to his election to Parliament in 1890, based on family papers; *The Elder Pitt* by Stanley Ayling; *Castlereagh* by John W. Derry; *Canning: Politician and Statesman* by Peter Dixon; *Lord North* by Peter D. G. Thomas; *Sir Robert Walpole* by Betty Kemp; *Asquith* by Stephen Koss; *Peel* by Norman Gash, and *Melbourne* by Philip Ziegler.

NOVELS.—Among novels published were *The Alteration* by Kingsley Amis; *Sleeping Murder* by Agatha Christie; *In the Frame* by Dick Francis; *The Death of the King's Canary* by Dylan Thomas and John Davenport; *The Malacia Tapestry* by Brian Aldiss; *A Fringe of Leaves* by Patrick White.

BIOGRAPHIES.—Other biographies published included *Bismarck* by Alan Palmer; *The Black Prince* by Barbara Emerson; *Julian Grenfell: His Life and the Times of His Death, 1885–1915* by Nicholas Mosley; *Albert Schweitzer* by James Brabazon; *A. P. Herbert* by Reginald Pound; *Edward VII* by Christopher Hibbert.

OTHER BOOKS.—Other books published included *Lyndon Johnson and the American Dream* by Doris Kearns; *The Tolkien Companion* by J. E. A. Tyler. edited by S. A. Tyler; *The Thirteenth Tribe* by Arthur Koestler; *Hitler's Decision to Invade Russia, 1941* by Robert Cecil; *Peking Man* by Harry L. Shapiro; *Infants of the Spring* by Anthony Powell.

SCIENCE, DISCOVERY AND THE ENVIRONMENT 1975-76

BREAKUP OF A COMET.—One of the most predictable things one can say about comets is that their behaviour cannot be predicted. The splitting of a comet into two or three fragments has been recorded on about a dozen occasions but splitting into four or more components is relatively rare. This has been observed only on three occasions—the famous sun-grazing comet of 1882, Comet Brooks 2 in 1889 and lastly Comet West, visible in the spring of 1976.

Comet West was discovered in November 1975 on photographic plates taken at the European Southern Observatory at La Silla, Chile. Initially it could only be seen from the southern hemisphere and it behaved in a fairly normal manner, steadily brightening as it approached the Sun. Towards the end of February 1976, it could be seen with the naked eye from latitudes such as those of the southern United States. It reached perihelion (point nearest to the Sun) on February 28 and reappeared as a morning object next day. It was observed from the British Isles in early March but was relatively low in the morning sky at dawn. It was during this period that the comet behaved in an extraordinary manner.

At the beginning of March, it was a brilliant object with a very long tail. The structure of the tail was complex, photographs showing a delicate fibrous structure. The comet had in fact two distinct tails, one slender and straight about 5 to 10 degrees long, gaseous in composition with a distinct bluish colour. The other, a broad white fan curving northwards consisted of dust particles expelled from the head and measured about 30° in length. The head of the comet consisted of an apparently bright starlike nucleus surrounded by a fairly bright coma, although detailed studies showed a complex cluster of tightly packed nuclei. This split into two separate parts on about March 8 and then four days later into four parts. One component faded rapidly and by the end of the month there were only three parts visible, separating from each other at a slow rate. The motion, brightness and structure of each component have been studied in detail, thus providing for the first time interesting information on the structure and bonding forces existing in comets.

In addition to the wealth of information gained from the study of the breakup of the head, the tail provided interesting information. The fibrous structure mentioned earlier originated not from the head but from the edge of the dust tail nearest to the Sun. Zdenek Sekanina, of the Harvard-Smithsonian Center for Astrophysics, said that these bands were caused by particles released during the perihelion passage breaking down into a very fine dust, this dust then being dissipated by solar radiation pressure. (Source: *Sky and Telescope*.)

CONTINENTAL DRIFT.—The majority of geologists in recent years have been unanimous in assigning the distribution of the continents to a process known as " continental drift ". Research into this process, however, which involves determining when and how continents have separated and joined, is by no means over and developments are frequently publicised. The most obvious evidence pointing to a different arrangement of the continents in the past is the similar shape of the Atlantic coast lines of South America and Africa, two continents or " plates " which figure largely in research into the process. Recent enlightenment has come from studies into orogenic belts and past glacial conditions; palaeomagnetism, which acknowledges that iron bearing rocks betray their position in relation to the pole at the time they were laid down (or solidified, in the case of igneous magma), is also an accurate source of information.

As well as providing evidence for continental drift, palaeomagnetic directions have also provided " proof " of seafloor spreading, and have shown that ridges in ocean floors are seismically active. So far from being inactive and old, ocean floors are regions where new material from the earth's mantle rises and becomes new crust, spreading slowly away from the ridges.

Recently a British geophysicist, Dr. Girdler of Newcastle University, has suggested that the East African Rift Valley represents an early stage of continental drift. The feature is marked by low gravity values, known as a negative Bouguer anomaly, which run from Southern Ethiopia southwards to Lake Malawi and then turns westwards to the Angolan coast. Until now the western extent of this feature had remained undetected.

The low gravity values in such areas arise when two surface lithographic plates stretch apart, for then underlying lighter material wells up underneath. The light material gives lower gravity values than ideal theoretical values. Dr. Girdler has found evidence in existing seismic data and with the coincidence of the extension with surface volcanic rock to support his view. It is therefore reasonably certain that the rifting of Eastern Africa continues in a western branch and it should be interesting to see the results of further experiments.

EXCAVATION OF WRECK.—Sir William Hamilton British Minister to the Court of the Two Sicilies, from 1764 to 1800, formed two large and important collections of classical antiquities during his life at Naples. In 1772, his first collection was acquired by the British Museum and included vases which formed the nucleus of what is today one of the best collections of Greek vases to be found anywhere in the world.

By 1796, Hamilton had amassed a second collection: it included one thousand vases and was in his own judgement " finer than the first ". In 1798 when, during the Napoleonic war, Italy faced the threat of invasion, Sir William and his second wife, Emma, fled Naples when the court evacuated the city. Hamilton's collection was hastily packed and part of it put on board *HMS Colossus* which set sail for England in November. On December 10, 1798, the *Colossus* sank in a fierce storm off the Scillies and Hamilton, who believed that eight cases of his best vases were on board—" all the cream of my collection "—was heartbroken at their loss. He was to some extent mollified in 1801 by the arrival of the rest of his vases on the *Foudroyant*. The number of vases on board has never been known, but the quality of the pieces had fortunately been captured in elegant outline drawings of selected specimens by Wilhelm Tischbein.

In July, 1976, an experienced team of divers at Penzance were granted a licence under the Protection of Wrecks Act 1973 to excavate the site of the wrecked ship. Excavation was supervised by Dr. Ann Birchall of the British Museum. The results of the first season far exceeded expectation: 7,400 fragments of Greek pottery from painted vases dating from the seventh to the fourth centuries B.C. have already been raised from the sea bed. The majority of the finds come from Athens in the fifth century B.C. or in the Greek colonies of southern Italy in the fourth. There are handles, rims, bases and body fragments, from cups, bowls, jars, pitchers, jugs and oil flasks. A high proportion is decorated. An outstanding set of fragments is a group of nineteen which depict the drunken Hephaestus with Dionysus, god of wine, and

revelling satyrs. The pieces were readily put together with the aid of one of Tischbein's drawings. The excavation is to continue this year and the British Museum hopes to acquire the fragments eventually.

EXPLODING BLACK HOLES.—The 1976 British Association Meeting was held at Lancaster University and it was not surprising that the inevitable lecture on black holes was included, especially in the light of the very interesting facts that had been published earlier in the year. The lecture was given by one of Britain's leading theoretical physicists, Dr. Dennis Sciama.

Black holes are postulated as the end product of a collapsing star, in which the gravitational forces are so great that nothing, not even light, can escape from them. With such properties, it is virtually impossible to identify them directly and much effort has been made in recent years in trying to find evidence for their existence. Indirect observational evidence has indicated that they might exist as components in some binary stellar systems.

Dr. Sciama said that recent work by Dr. Stephen Hawking had shown theoretically that black holes are not necessarily completely black. Although not capable of radiating energy from its interior, it could radiate heat from its surface. This implies that black holes are losing mass in the process. The rate at which heat could be radiated depends, according to Hawking, on the inverse square of the mass of the black hole. This means that with time the rate of emission would increase and eventually reach an explosive condition. The black hole would flash into extra-ordinary brilliance and in its last one tenth of a second of its life, when the diameter was one ten-thousandth of that of an electron, it would emit high energy X-rays with an energy of a billion billion megawatts.

The predicted time to reach this catastrophic condition turns out to be longer than the age of the universe except in cases where the black hole is smaller than 10^{-13}cm. It is therefore possible that such an event from very small objects could be observed, in which case much information would be gained on the behaviour of matter at exceedingly high temperatures and conditions existing in the universe at early times.

FIRST ARTIFICIAL GENE SYNTHESISED.—It was announced at the annual meeting of the American Chemical Society in August 1976 that scientists at the Massachusetts Institute of Technology had synthesised the first man-made gene which was fully functional in a living cell. In 1973, Dr. Khorana reported that the structural part of the gene had been synthesised but now he and his research team have succeeded in synthesising the " start and stop signals " for the gene.

The gene is the basic unit of all heredity and consists primarily of a long double stranded molecule of deoxyribonucleic acid (DNA) the two strands twisting to form a double helix. The units of DNA are called nucleotides, of which there are various types, adenine, thymine, guanine and cytosine, in the double stranded DNA molecule, each adenine on one strand pairs with thymine on the other, and guanine and cytosine acting similarly. They bond naturally because of their mutually attractive chemical properties.

When information from the gene is to be transmitted into protein molecules in a cell, enzymes begin transcribing information by building a complementary strand of ribonucleic acid (RNA) along one strand of the DNA. When the synthesis is complete, the RNA strand breaks away and is used to synthesise protein molecules. There are basically three types of RNA synthesised on the DNA. The first, messenger RNA, represents the cell's method of transmitting information from the gene to the protein. The second, ribosomal RNA, folds up after leaving the gene to form ribosomes which are used to provide a holder which the messenger RNA uses to translate its information into the protein. The third type, transfer RNA, locates and grabs the amino acids (the building blocks of the protein) and carries them to the ribosomes.

Dr. Khorana and his team have synthesised the gene that codes for a particular kind of transfer RNA, the type that grabs the amino acid tyrosine. The name given to this gene is tyrosine transfer RNA gene.

The start and stop signals, consisting of additional sequences of nucleotides, direct the enzymes to form the RNA strand. In the tyrosine transfer RNA gene, the start signal consists of 59 and the stop signal 23 nucleotides. The new synthesised gene and its controls have functioned correctly in test-tube experiments as well as in a bacterium. The method developed allows completely controlled manipulation of the gene structure. Dr. Khorana stated that with chemical analysis it is possible to alter specific parts of the gene, carry out deliberate mutations in order to study their influence on the gene function.

FISH IN THE THAMES.—In 1957 a survey by Dr. Alwyne Wheeler of the British Museum showed that, with the possible exception of eels, there were no fish whatsoever in the thirty miles of London Thames. This was attributed to the high toxic content of the water which, even had dissolved oxygen been in the water, which is doubtful, was effectively inhibiting all forms of fish life. Since then pollution has been severely countered and the toxic content of the water, and dissolved oxygen level, have taken corresponding changes for the better. The Thames Water Authority, in rebuilding sewage works and thereby improving the quality of effluent discharged into the river, is to a large extent responsible for the re-establishment of fish fauna in the lower Thames.

Since 1964 ninety-four species of fish and one hybrid have been found in a forty mile stretch of the Thames between Brentford, where fresh water is to be found, and Northfleet, where the water is brackish. Six of these species are new to the river since September, 1975. Worthy of particular mention is a salmon weighing 8lbs. $4\frac{1}{2}$ ozs. which was caught at West Thurrock Power Station in 1975. The last catches of salmon in the Thames are said to have been in 1833, though at one time Thames salmon was a common enough dish in London.

FOSSIL METEORITIC CRATER.—Photographs of the Moon, Mercury, Mars and its satellites all show abundant evidence of craters, the majority of which are currently thought to have been caused by meteoritic bombardment. Although we cannot see the surface of Venus, radar studies also indicate a heavily cratered surface. It is thought that intensive cratering occurred during the early days of the formation of the solar system and that the present rate of formation is relatively low. The reason why the Earth, the other major body in the inner region of the solar system has not a heavily cratered surface is that such formations would be eroded away in a relatively short time by the wind and rain. Therefore any feature currently visible is thought to be of a relatively young age, geologically speaking.

Recent work has shown that there are in fact many features on the Earth's surface which in the past were large circular meteoritic craters. Even

the British Isles, a very small land mass, has two such features, both in the Shetland Isles. The most famous crater is of course the one in the Arizona Desert. Its diameter of approximaely 1,200 metres is dwarfed by the huge crater known as the Popingay depression in the Soviet Union, which is 75 km. in diameter and thought to have been formed about 300 million years ago.

Until recently, there has been no evidence of craters existing in rocks lying beneath the present surface of the Earth, i.e. fossil craters. Information given in a recent Novosti Press release gives details of such a discovery made by geologists drilling in the Minsk region of the Soviet Union. A large conical depression was located at a depth of 80 to 140 metres in which the overlying sedimentary rocks and the lower granitic material were damaged. The bottom of the cone was bounded by partially re-melted rocks. Studies of the rock fragments within the disturbed region indicate that the rocks have been subjected to intense shock. The conclusion reached by the geologists is that a large meteorite exploded there about 70 million years ago. With the amount of drilling going on at the present time, it is quite likely that more of these fossil craters wil be identified.

GRIBBLES DEVOUR BOATS.—Bridlington Harbour, North Humberside, has been attacked by vast numbers of gribbles. These small mites, a quarter of an inch long, have derived a lively pleasure from eating the wooden craft on the harbour since the summer of 1975, and no treatment of the timber has yet succeeded in spoiling their appetite. *Linnoria Lignorum* thrives in salt water and it seems that their recent abundance may originally have been caused by the hot summer of 1975 when the salinity of the harbour water would have been increased by a reduction in the inflow of fresh water. At the time of the report scientists from ICI were working at possible ways in which to end the danger. It is to be hoped that a cure will have been found soon since a succession of dry summers could prove very expensive to boat owners.

HADRIAN'S WALL WESTERN EXTENSION.—Professor G. D. B. Jones of Manchester University has never been satisfied with the conventional view of the western termination of Hadrian's wall, whatever may have been the precise nature of the Morecambe estuary before extensive flooding in the thirteenth century. He states that the termination of the elaborate wall and vallum system at Bowness and its replacement there by an apparently far weaker system dependent on isolated milefortlets and towers has always been against the dictates of both common sense and topography, as there is no natural change in the Solway coastline until the Wampool estuary further west, whatever form it took. Professor Jones found that parallels from linear defensive systems in Germany show that it is unlikely that this system depended entirely on isolated towers. He therefore predicted that under suitable crop conditions evidence of a more integrated system would appear.

In the drought of June to July, 1975, close study of Milefortlet 1 at Biglands revealed, under parching, the evidence of two parallel ditches forty-six metres apart approaching the front and rear of the site from the north-east, some thirty metres from the present edge of the coastal moss. Further evidence was forthcoming at Campfield where the site of Tower 2B was clearly recognised from the air, with indications of an unbroken ditch seven metres in front of the tower. Further west, near Cardurnock, parallel ditches (thirty metres apart)

were traced for over a kilometre which, like the other ditches, have been tested by excavation.

The northern ditch of the two parallel ditches near Biglands proved to have been cut into the gravel sub-soil to a depth of eighty centimetres. As the exposed face dried it became evident that the ditch had been recut on at least two, and probably three, occasions. The southern ditch comprised a simple cut into similar sub-soil with the "ankle breaker" sump well defined. The middle part of the ditch had filled with fine silt in which a fragment of pottery was found. This single sherd derived from a wide-mouthed jar of a type unusual in North Britain, which was identified as Severn Valley fabric. This ware occurs only in installations of Hadrian's Wall in Period 1, and thus the newly discovered Solway system probably belongs to the initial establishment of the wall.

The site of Tower 2B had been noted earlier in the century but photographs in July 1975 showed the tower plan complete with doorway, and even with traces of what may have been a service track to either side. Photographs taken earlier in the same month revealed that at the foot of the raised beach on which the tower sat there was probably a ditch. On excavation a ditch system appeared that had undergone three modifications.

A final section was cut near Cardurnock. A forward ditch was located running on the brow of the first raised beach south of the present coastline, and it was flanked to the north by evidence of a continuous slot for stakes pointing upwards at about seventy to eighty degrees. This ditch had been recut at least once with major changes to its shape. Thirty metres to the south the rearward trench was located in great detail. The primary ditch sump was clearly preserved below the top-soil level and had twice been recut.

In addition to these discoveries it is thought that the success of this barrier lay in creating a hinterland of farmsteads, of which 154 examples were located in 1975 where only some twenty were previously known.

"HIDDEN" LEONARDO DRAWINGS.—Sir Robert Mackworth-Young, librarian at Windsor Castle, has used a lamp purchased for £28 to show up details in drawings by Leonardo da Vinci that have faded away over the centuries. On thirty drawings the ultraviolet light has caused shapes to appear, whole figures in some cases, which for many years have been invisible. The process operates because Leonardo, who worked before pencils existed, prepared his papers with a special ground on which he scratched his drawings with a metal point; the metal deposit left in the paper absorbs ultraviolet light and shows up in black lines. The first public exhibition of the drawings was expected to be held at the Royal Academy in the autumn of 1976.

"HOMO ERECTUS" DISCOVERY.—In August, 1975, Mr. Richard Leakey found a human skull almost identical to that of Peking Man. It was discovered near Lake Torkana (formerly Rudolph) in North Kenya, and is said to be the oldest and most complete fossil skull of *Homo Erectus* yet brought to light. It was given a dating of one and a half million years which, if correct, would mean that Peking Man is considerably more ancient than has been suspected. Mr. Leakey, who is director of the National Museum of Kenya, is unsatisfied with Chinese methods for dating archaeological sites.

In June, 1976, a fossilised skeleton was discovered imbedded in a stalagmite in a cave in Greece. It was reported to be 400,000 years old. The discovery was made by the Greek Anthropological Society in the Halkidiki peninsula, south-east of

Salonika. In dating the skeleton to the lower Mindel-Riss interglacial period tools and other evidence in the locality were considered.

HOURS OF THE VIRGIN.—A formerly unknown early sixteenth century illuminated manuscript on vellum, Hours of the Virgin, was sold at Sotheby's in July, 1976, for £407,000, the highest ever price for a manuscript. The manuscript came from a German collection and contains eighty-four perfectly preserved miniatures from Europe's leading workshop of the time, which operated in Ghent and Bruges. The Flemish manuscript throws a new light on the Grimani Breviary from the same workshop, for it is apparent that a number of miniatures were copied from the former to the latter. Two English dealers and a Brussels dealer were outbid by H. P. Kraus of New York, the world's foremost dealer in this field.

INCREASE IN EARTHQUAKE ACTIVITY.—During the last twelve months there has been a significant increase in the number of major earthquakes. Scientists at the International Earthquake Center at Golden, Colorado, have reported that the number of events of magnitude 8 or more on the Richter scale average at one per year, but already in the first seven months of 1976 four such events have been recorded, Kermadec Islands (Jan. 14), Guatemala (Feb. 4) China (July 27) and Philippine Islands (Aug. 17). In addition to these there have been many quite severe events, nine occurring in the last three months of 1975 and 28 in the first eight months of 1976, in addition to those mentioned above. This increase in activity is a continuation of a trend reported over the last few years. Earthquakes have occurred along all the major zones of activity but there is no evidence to connect events in one zone with those in another. Even within a single belt, the events are random and not connected.

To the general public the severity of an earthquake is not measured by the intensity of the shock waves produced but by the damage caused and the number of people killed. The largest earthquake ever recorded took place in Alaska in 1964 but because it occurred in a not too densely populated area, only 300 people lost their lives. It should be pointed out that on an average about 10,000 people are killed every year by earthquakes. If the centre of the earthquake lies out at sea, the production of tsunamis often cause considerable loss of life as was the case in the Philippines on August 17, when over 8,000 people were killed. On this occasion a 5 metre high tsunami was reported. The severe earthquake which occurred in the Tangshan area of China must have killed many thousands of people because the area is densely populated. No casualty figures have yet been published. In addition to that event, several other shocks have been reported in the area. Another region hit by a series of shocks has been northern Italy. A strong foreshock was recorded one minute before the main quake and during the two hours following, 14 strong after shocks were reported. The casualties included nearly 1,000 killed and over 2,000 injured. Approximately 100,000 people were made homeless. The main tremor was the strongest recorded in that part of the world this century. The Guatemala Earthquake of February 4 was the worst event in central America this century. Over 22,000 people were reported killed, 74,000 people injured and over 1 million made homeless. The strongest quake to hit Hawaii since 1868 occurred on November 29, 1975. Although by no means as severe as those in Italy and China, it caused extensive damage. It is thought that it was responsible for the eruption of the volcano Kilauea. Lava flowed in the floor of the caldera less than one hour after the main shock.

Earthquakes generally occur at the edges of lithospheric plates and are caused by the readjustment of the crustal rocks to relieve the stresses caused by the movement of the plates.

INDUSTRIAL ARCHAEOLOGY AWARDS.—Nine industrial archaeology groups received cash awards under the B.P. Industrial Heritage scheme announced in July, 1975, by B.P. industrial division. The scheme was devised in conjunction with the Association for Industrial Archaeology and it gives support to industrial archaeological work, particularly in those fields not eligible for grant aid from official sources.

The award winning projects were selected from 130 applications by a joint committee from the Association for Industrial Archaeology and B.P. Of the awards announced on November 24, 1975, the most valuable were: £500 to the Arkwright Society in Cromford, Derbyshire, to assist in the development of local history trails at Cromford, Belper and Shardlow; £500 to the Tyne and Wear Industrial Monuments Trust, to help make a cine film record of the surviving glass industry in the North East; and £400 to the Veteran Steamship Society Ltd., Essex, to help restore the *Resolute*, a steam-driven river steamer. Other awards ranged from £325 to £50, and similar assistance from industry to the A.I.A. will be forthcoming in the future.

JUPITER'S MAGNETIC TAIL.—In December 1973, *Pioneer* 10 passed close to the planet Jupiter and whilst doing so sent back to Earth many interesting facts about its magnetic field and also pictures of its surface in greater detail than was possible from Earth-based observatories. The probe then carried on its journey towards the outer regions of the solar system, passing the orbit of Saturn early in 1976. It will eventually become the first manmade object to leave the solar system completely.

During March 1976, the probe's solar wind instrument suddenly fell to zero for a period of about 24 hours. Because of the unlikelihood of this being due to solar conditions, another explanation had to be found. Analysis of the orbital parameters showed that at that particular time, the probe was in a position which suggested it was passing through Jupiter's magnetic tail and was hence shielded from the solar wind. If this explanation is found to be correct, it implies that the magnetic tail of Jupiter extends well beyond the orbit of Saturn and is at least 700 million kilometres in length.

Experiments on the Earth's magnetic tail have indicated a length of about 6·5 million kilometres, so the Jovian tail makes that of the Earth very insignificant. One interesting feature is that at the time of encounter with the tail, the probe was 6° above the plane of Jupiter's orbit. The width of the magnetic envelope in the region of Jupiter is about 18 million kilometres and this will increase with increasing distance from the planet. The solar wind blows radially outwards from the Sun and hence the tail should remain in the orbital plane. Even at distances of the outer planets, it is known to be very turbulent and so a position well above the orbital plane does not present too big an objection.

If the above explanation for the solar wind cutoff is correct, it means that Saturn itself will pass through the tail about every 20 years. This will next occur in 1981 and the appearance of the planet will be watched with very great interest.

LARGEST STONY METEORITE.—The number of meteorites falling on the Earth every year is far higher than is generally imagined but the number that are actually located and studied is very low. As far as the British Isles is concerned there have been three such cases since the last war, the largest fall known to have taken place in the British Isles occurring at Barwell, Leicestershire in December, 1965. On that occasion about 50 kg. of meteorite were collected. It was classed as one of the commonest types of stony meteorite. Stony meteorites make up about 96% of all falls, the rest being mostly "iron" meteorites consisting of virtually 100% mixture of iron and nickel. The stony types have in the region of about 7% iron and nickel.

On March 8, 1976, a very large number of such stones fell in northern China near Kirin City, rivalling and possibly surpassing the previoulsy accepted largest fall which took place in Mexico in 1969. At 1502 hrs. local time, a brilliant fireball crossed the Kirin Province travelling in a southwesterly direction and exploded above the outskirts of Kirin City. Most of the fragments were scattered over a fairly wide area but three large pieces continued along the flight path and fell much further away. By April 21, more than 100 meteorites had been recovered from an area larger than 500 sq km. Three of the stones weighed more than 100 kg., the largest weighing 1,770 kg. The largest individual stone prior to this fall was found in Kansas, U.S.A. and weighed 1,078 kg.

The local population have been intimately associated with the collection of the stones and information relating to the event. Although only provisional information is currently available, studies of the stones show that they contain mainly augite and olivine, with smaller amounts of kamacite, taenite, magnetite and other metals. The stones have a typical chondritic structure and have been classed as an olivine bronzite chondrite. The whole event lasted for 37 seconds and the last fragment to reach the ground penetrated through 1·7 metres of frozen soil to a depth of 6·5 metres, forming a crater 3 metres deep and 2 metres across. Clumps of earth were thrown 100 metres from the crater.

Depending on the size and number of fragments ultimately collected, the Kirin fall may prove to be bigger than the Hidalgo de Parral fall in Mexico, but regardless of this, it is certainly assured of a place in the list of major falls.

MAPPING THE OCEAN FLOOR.—We are all familiar with the very detailed maps of the continents and land masses in general. We are also quite conversant with the extremely detailed maps of the Moon and more recently, of Mars. It comes as a shock when it is realised that apart from a few very selected areas, detailed maps of the ocean floor are virtually non-existent. Even on the continental shelves, detail is scanty. Unfortunately, one cannot use normal photographic or television cameras because of the lack of light. Consequently it is necessary to use techniques involving sound waves, but even so sea floor mapping is in its very early stages. Echo sounders are relatively inefficient since they do not give a high resolution and even then it is a very slow process.

A technique involving scanning the sea bed with a narrow sound beam and which had previously been used on the continental shelves, has been successfully used on the deep ocean bed, according to Dr. A. S. Laughton, when he addressed the British Association this year. Dr. Laughton is head of the Marine, Geology and Geophysical Group at the Institute of Oceanographic Sciences. The extension of this technique to the deep ocean bed has been achieved using long range sonar, called *Gloria*, housed in a streamlined shell and towed behind a ship. Speeds of up to 7 knots have been used with success. Strips of the ocean bed are scanned and a picture of the contour obtained. By combining the strips, a mosaic of large areas can be built up. So far, 30,000 square kilometres of parts of the Mid-Atlantic Ridge and ocean basin in the north east Atlantic have been scanned, revealing complex fault patterns. This information should provide the data on which can be built a better understanding of the origins of the sea floor.

METALLIC HYDROGEN.—Theoretical work over the last half century has forecast that under certain critical conditions, hydrogen, the simplest of all the elements and normally non-metallic in properties would exist in metallic form. Much effort and research has taken place in trying to produce this metallic phase. In the United States, the main line of attack has been to use shock waves to produce very high pressures of the order of 100 megabars (100 million atmospheres) but it has been reported that success has been achieved in the Soviet Union using static pressures.

Theory has predicted that all substances will be transformed into a metallic state if the pressure is high enough. Soviet workers have converted diamond and silica into the metallic phase using pressures in the region of 1 megabar. Further studies showed that the critical pressure for hydrogen lay in the range of 1 to 10 megabars. The apparatus used in their experiments consisted of two diamond anvils, one flat and the other very slightly conical, which were capable of being brought very close together, thus producing very high pressures on any substance trapped between them.

The diamond anvils were cooled to a temperature of 4·2° K. and the hydrogen trapped between the anvils became frozen. The shape of the anvils was such that although a very high pressure could be produced in the central region, it fell off rapidly towards the edges, thus reducing the problems of the surrounding equipment having to support and contain these pressures. The anvils were connected electrically and when the hydrogen turned into the metallic state, a current flowed. This took place when the pressure was in the region of 1 to 3 megabars. When the current flowed the electrical resistance of the circuit dropped from 100 million to just 100 ohms. It was therefore concluded that metallic hydrogen had at last been produced.

The production of metallic hydrogen is, of course, not the end of the road. It is necessary to learn something of the crystalline structure of this new metal. Evidence suggests that it should have a body centred cubic structure, the system with the lowest energy. This is in line with the structure of the metals lying below hydrogen in the periodic table. The determination of the structure of metallic hydrogen however presents many problems which so far have nowhere near been solved. (Source: *New Scientist*.)

METEOROID IMPACTS ON THE MOON.—We on Earth are protected from the continual bombardment from space of small meteoroids by our atmosphere. However, such bodies as our Moon, having no atmosphere, are at the mercy of these interplanetary fragments. Impacts of masses greater than about 50 g can be recorded by the seismometers left on the lunar surface by the various *Apollo* missions. This provides a source of information as to the spatial distribution and masses of these particles. The seismic network set up by the *Apollo* astronauts consists of 3 stations located at the corners of an equilateral triangle of sides about

1,100 km, with a fourth about 180 km from one of them.

Analysis of the records have shown that the number of impacts varied considerably with time and it has been concluded that for the more massive objects there exist clouds of meteoroids superimposed on the random impacts. These clouds are very diffuse and are detectable only because of the large catchment area. Typical size of a cloud is 0·1 astronomical units with impact rates of the order of one every three days over an area of 100 square kilometres.

They cannot be linked with the well-known meteor showers seen on Earth at specific times in the year because these latter particles are much smaller and the clouds detected so far show no periodicity. They appear to be sporadic. Most lie close to the plane of the ecliptic and their orbits have aphelia between 2 and 5 astronomical units.

Over two and a half years, from January 1973 to July 1975, 815 impacts were recorded and peaks of activity were noted in November and December 1974 and January 1975. For the last event, calculations have been made as to the possible mass of the cloud, about 10^{13} grams confined to a sphere 17 million kilometres in diameter. If concentrated into a single body it would be equivalent to a mass of a body about 300 metres in diameter. However, to put this into real perspective, it is estimated that spacecraft would have to travel through a cloud for 9,000 years before being hit by a fragment.

The discovery of these clouds is of fundamental importance to solar system astronomers, but it is felt that one will have to wait some time before it is found how they fit into the overall picture and the links if any with the meteor showers, comets, minor planets and random meteoroids. (Source: *Science*.)

METHANE ICE ON PLUTO.—The planet Pluto is so far away that the amount of energy it receives from the Sun is so small that temperatures on its surface must be exceedingly low and could be only a little above absolute zero. It is difficult to determine any reliable facts about the planet because of its distance, faintness and size, currently thought to be about 6,000 km in diameter. In the spring of 1976, astronomers from the University of Hawaii, using the 4 metre reflector at Kitt Peak National Observatory in Arizona, showed that the surface was covered, at least partially, with methane ice.

They observed Pluto in infra-red light by passing the light through two very narrow band filters, one selected to admit a bright reflection from water ice and the other from methane ice and these were then compared with the results from earth bound sources. The response was exactly as expected from methane ice. To check the technique, the experiments were repeated using Saturn's satellites as targets with results indicating water ice, a result in accordance with previous knowledge. So far, only Pluto has given methane ice. The existence of this means that the surface must be colder than 50° K, the temperature at which pure methane condenses at low pressures.

Although methane has been detected in the atmosphere of the major planets and also in the atmosphere of Titan, Saturn's largest moon, this is the first time in which solid methane has been identified. It is too early to say that the whole of the surface is covered with it but the information collected has provided evidence that suggests that Pluto is even smaller than was previously thought, it having a diameter possibly as low as 3,500 km, roughly the size of our own Moon.

Based on the discovery of methane ice, several theories have been proposed for the structure of the planet but much will depend on the obtaining of reasonably accurate values for the diameter and mass. (Source: *Science*).

NESSITERAS RHOMBOPTERYX.—Just as G. K. Chesterton says that " The rolling English drunkard made the rolling English road ", so a great many men claiming to be sober say that it is pure Scotch that has created the Loch Ness Monster. Apparently the monster rolls in an equally fetching manner. The problem until recently has been that the rolling roads have been rather more in evidence than the monster, but during the last forty years, and especially in the summer of 1975, the monster has made a number of seemingly genuine appearances (and the roads are being straightened).

The first recorded appearance of the Loch Ness monster was in A.D. 565 by St. Columba, whose biographer recorded that the monster " rushed up with a great roar and open mouth ". St. Columba, evidently not in the mood for such frivolity, commanded the "beastie" to retreat, and it obeyed, " going faster than it had approached ". One of the latest books on the subject, *The Loch Ness Story* by Nicholas Witchell, thoroughly recounts the many subsequent appearances, and gives a critical appraisal of the vast quantity of material in a remarkably lucid fashion. Mr. Witchell is only one person out of thousands who seriously believe in the existence of a species generally thought to be extinct. He finds it puzzling, as does Gerald Durrell, who wrote the foreword to his book, that the witness of so many intelligent people of spotless repute should be flippantly set aside by both scientists and the media.

Since 1934 many sightings of unidentified animate objects have been reported; statements have been made under oath and photographs have been developed under strict security procedures. The Russians may compare the Loch Ness monster with flying saucers and the abominable snowman, but scientists have been urged many times to examine the evidence without prejudice. In 1972 an underwater photograph was taken and developed showing a recognisable flipper, about eight foot long, attached to a roughly textured body. The British Museum of Natural History states the photograph was genuine and that a large moving object was visible in it, but they were not prepared to try to identify the object.

The climax of the monster hunt came in 1975 when, after years of unsuccessful underwater photography, it was claimed that close-up photographs showed the neck, head and body of one of the animals, which bore a resemblance to plesiosaurs. The authorities are obviously not convinced by the evidence as yet.

Meanwhile, scientific explanations of the monster are in spate. One of the latest says that an atmospheric phenomenon known as a water-devil could explain many sightings. This occurs when warm air on a loch surface is covered by a layer of cooler air, causing the water to rise from the surface.

To solemnise the new interest in the monster, it has been given a new name: *Nessiteras Rhombopteryx*. That this is an anagram of " Monster hoax by Sir Peter S." should not be allowed to discourage believers!

NEW SUB-ATOMIC PARTICLES.—If the results recently announced from California's Lawrence Berkeley Laboratory and the Stanford Linear Accelerator Center are confirmed, this is the first discovery of a fundamental sub-atomic particle for about 25 years. The new particle, as yet unnamed, has a large mass, nearly twice that of the proton and survives for a

relatively long time before decaying into lighter more common particles. These properties and the way in which it decays, are in line with theoretical ideas associated with a whole family of sub-atomic particles referred to as " charmed " particles. Charmed particles have been predicted and are described as a new property of matter analogous to an electric charge. Although none have so far been isolated, there have been many claims that such particles have been identified. Until all the properties of these new particles have been determined, a direct link with the predicted charmed particles cannot be confirmed.

The existence of charmed particles has been based on the results from experiments carried out at the world's leading laboratories. Generally the particles detected showed many of the features expected of charms but vital information on their manner and mode of decay has not been established. In the LBL/SLAC experiments, beams of electrons collide head-on with their anti-particles, positrons. Both particles are annihilated producing a state of energy from which sub-atomic particles are formed. Many of these particles are involved in nuclear binding forces and are termed hadrons. When the energy of the electron-positron colliding beam is raised above 4,000 million volts, the rate of hadron formation was found to increase markedly. Using improved sensitivity techniques, the scientists found that in about 0·5% of the cases, there was evidence of the existence of a new particle which decayed into two hadrons. Subsequent work showed particles decaying into four hadrons.

It is fairly certain that it will not be long before the main problems associated with charmed particles will be sorted out and only time will tell how much significance will be attached to this new discovery.

PARTHENON EXHIBITION AT BRITISH MUSEUM.— A new gallery at the British Museum completes the Museum's permanent exhibition on the Parthenon, displaying for the first time since the war some splendid fragments of the sculptures as well as architectural elements of the building itself. An important feature of the exhibition is the detailed explanation of the objects, accompanied by a wide range of illustrations, including casts, photographs and copies of drawings and engravings from the 17th and 18th centuries. This approach was dictated by the fragmentary state of many of the objects shown. The Parthenon was severely damaged by an explosion in 1687, when a Venetian shell touched off the gunpowder that the beleagured Turks had stored there. The side walls and colonnades of the temple were blown down and many of its sculptures were destroyed or badly broken. The sculptures suffered further deterioration as the result of neglect and deliberate damage.

Among the slabs of the frieze that were still substantially intact when the architect James Stuart visited Athens in 1752 was one showing a group of horsemen. When Lord Elgin's party arrived half a century later, all that survived of this slab was a small fragment some two feet square. Fortunately Stuart had drawn the slab and published an engraving of it, which makes it possible to appreciate the surviving detail.

This fragment was among those brought to England by Lord Elgin and acquired for the British Museum in 1816. Other fragments were purchased from H. Inwood in 1843, some came from France and Germany in the nineteenth century, and a head that had found its way to Chatsworth was presented by the Duke of Devonshire in 1854. This head joins a torso from the Elgin collection and the whole figure may be seen in a drawing made before the explosion by an artist who is usually identified

as Jacques Carrey. His drawings are now preserved in Paris and, made in 1674, they remain our only source of knowledge for pieces that did not survive the explosion. Carrey's drawing of the whole metope is here exhibited beside the surviving fragments, enabling the visitor to reconstruct the whole action in his mind's eye. One imposing item in the exhibition is a complete Doric capital resting on the topmost drum of one of the columns of the colonnade; the capital was carved from a single block of marble weighing about five tons. Regrettably it was sawn in two to facilitate its voyage to England.

QUASAR DISTANCES CONFIRMED.—One of the big problems that have puzzled astronomers since the discovery of quasars in the early 1960s has been the difficulty in deciding how far away they are. The core of the trouble has been that they have a star-like appearance. If they are very distant objects, the energies emitted are comparable with that of galaxies and therefore their small size immediately suggests physical processes not capable of explanation in the light of current knowledge. On the other hand, if they are relatively near, the energy outputs are much lower but their large red shifts of the spectral lines cannot be explained by the Doppler shift, and must therefore be due to some other physical process. Until recently the solution to this problem has eluded astronomers.

Astronomers at the National Radio Astronomy Observatory in West Virginia and at the Arecibo Observatory in Puerto Rico have investigated a quasar called 3C 286 (3C stands for the third Cambridge catalogue and 286 is the number in that list) and have shown that this quasar at least is a very distant object. They have deduced this by searching for a quasar which lies exactly in the same line of sight as part of an independent galaxy. Quasar 3C 286 is partially obscured by a hydrogen cloud that is thought to be associated with a nearby galaxy. The red-shift measurement of the galaxy gives a distance of 17,000 million light years. The red-shift distance relationship for galaxies is generally accepted by astronomers. The quasar is therefore thought to be at a greater distance. This is in line with the red-shift given by the quasar, a value indicating that it is about 5,000 million light years farther away than the galaxy.

It is therefore concluded that the red-shifts given by the spectral lines from quasars are a measure of their distances from the Earth. The acceptance of such distances creates many problems relating to the methods of generating such vast amounts of energy and so these objects will be the centre of study for many years to come.

RADAR STUDIES OF VENUS.—Until recently photography of the surface of the planet Venus has not been possible, but radar studies have provided much detailed information about the general surface features. This has been predominantly the work of scientists at the Goldstone tracking station of the Jet Propulsion Laboratory, Pasadena, California and the Arecibo Observatory in Puerto Rico. Earlier radar maps had shown a few bright spots but by using the 64-metre steerable dish at Goldstone and the fixed 330-metre dish at Arecibo, sufficient data has been obtained to start a study of the geology of the planet.

Features identified include a 1,500 km. long linear trough near to the equator, comparable with the East African Rift on the Earth and Coprates Canyon on Mars. These features are interpreted as evidence of crustal movement. There is also a long arc of mountains crossed by another linear feature. At another place, a region covering an area 300 by

400 km. and rising to a height of 1 km., has been identified as a huge volcano having a crater 80 km. in diameter at its centre. Although this by no means rivals the Olympic Mons on Mars, it is comparable in size with other Martian volcanoes and is indeed larger than the Earth's Hawaiian volcanic complex.

Other circular features ranging in size from 30 to several thousand kilometres in diameter have also been recorded, the larger ones being comparable in size with the lunar Mare Imbrium and the martian Hellas basin, both of which are currently thought to have been formed by impact. The Arecibo pictures also show a circular feature about 1,000 km. in diameter and having a bright sharp rim, but the shape of the basin does not suggest an impact origin.

The Arecibo dish is being refitted to permit improved radar studies and it is hoped that the resolution will be reduced from 20 to 5 km. Being a fixed dish, observations can only be made for two hours each day, whereas the Goldstone dish, designed specifically for deep space tracking, can follow the planet for about 8 hours with a current resolution in the region of 10 km.

So far the radar maps cover only a small portion of the surface of the planet, that near to the equator, but they have provided a picture which shows that, in spite of its thick cloud cover, underneath it is basically similar to the other inner planets. (Source: *Science.*)

RAINFALL FORECASTS.—The preliminary results of a long-term research study called the Dee Weather Radar Project, indicate that rainfall forecasts could be improved. Over the last fifteen years there have been many investigations into the technique of using radar to measure surface rainfall, and during the last three years comparisons have been made between estimates of areal rainfall using radar and estimates derived from a network of rain gauges over the River Dee catchment area in North Wales. These comparisons show that many conditions prevail in summer and winter which are at present incorrectly forecast, and the research aims at showing how to improve the system.

Meanwhile, the drought of 1975 and 1976 has been so severe that even with average rainfall it will probably take two years before natural underground reservoirs are filled again. When they are filled it will probably be to no more than the low level of the last decade, to which they have been reduced by the high water consumption of industry. Shortage of water is a problem that will outlive a few months of low rainfall.

SATURN'S FOURTH RING.—When Galileo first turned his telescope on Saturn, he thought it was three stars in line. Later observations, made at a time when the Earth lay in the plane of the rings, showed a single object. With the advent of better optical systems, it was realised that the planet had a ring system consisting of two rings separated by what is known as the Cassini Division. Later on, a third ring, now known as the Crepe Ring because of its relative faintness, was discovered lying inside the bright rings.

During the last ten years there have been several claims to have observed a fourth ring, by some, outside the three main ones, and yet by others, inside the Crepe ring. The existence of an inner ring was claimed by Pierre Guérin of the Institut d'Astrophysique in Paris in 1970 and since then Guérin has confirmed his original observation by scanning the rings with a point microphotometer. The results show quite distinctly a faint but definite ring separated from the Crepe ring by a distinct gap. The signal to noise ratio obtained using this photometer is about 5 times better than that obtained in earlier photometric measurements. Even the very clear results obtained by Guérin are not universally accepted. Many planetary astronomers are still reluctant to believe that the presence of this ring is a fact, their suspicions being centred on the difficulties of observing a faint object so near to the brilliant planet.

John Murray, of the University of London, has however observed the ring visually on four occasions using the 107 cm telescope at the Pic du Midi Observatory in the Pyrenees. The measurements made were in complete agreement with those of Guérin. Murray is also of the opinion that the equatorial band on the planet could be the shadow of the Guérin ring on the disc and he contends that observational evidence supports this theory.

A very interesting and exciting situation will arise in 1979 when *Pioneer* 11, now on its journey across the solar system after providing a fund of data on Jupiter, is due to fly by Saturn, passing in between the planet and the Crepe Ring. If the probe is still fully functional, the question of the existence of this rather elusive ring could be solved.

SILICA GLASS IN LIBYA.—Following up an earlier discovery, P. A. Clayton and L. J. Spencer embarked on an expedition into the Libyan Desert in 1934, and identified a well defined oval area measuring 130 by 53 km, in which was found many specimens of silica glass. The largest weighed 7·25 kg. The presence of silica glass makes the region of even greater interest because of the presence nearby of two circular structures, now thought to have been caused by impact. A recent investigation carried out by geologists from universities in Texas, V. E. Barnes (University of Texas, Austin, Texas) and J. R. Underwood (West Texas State University, Canyon, Texas) concentrated on the collecting of further specimens and on the problems associated with the origin of the glass.

The glasses collected were found in the sandy desert floor scattered amongst pebbles and cobbles of quartz, chert and petrified wood. No glass was found in direct contact with the local bedrock consisting of sandstone. Many fragments were found but most were retained by the University of Libya. Based on the ten specimens kept by the American geologists, it has been concluded that they originated from the Nubian sandstone, the country rock found in the region where the glass was found. In the glass, included minerals were found to be partially altered through shock and temperature effects. Both the glass and the sandstone were found to contain zircon and elbaite, a variety of tourmaline. The specimens ranged from transparent and colourless to milky translucent and they had a wide range in colour. The degree to which the specimens contained bubbles varied between samples and, in a particular sample, from layer to layer.

One of the circular features, known as the Oasis Circular Structure, was visited by the team but no decision was reached as to whether this and the other feature, 80 km to the NNW, are related to the silica glass. The nearest glass to the Oasis Structure was found at a distance of 140 km. The age of the glass, determined by fission track methods, has been given as 28·5 million years.

Silica glass is normally found only in locations close to and associated with meteoritic craters, e.g. Arizona, Wabar, Henbury. Volcanic processes are generally thought to be incapable of producing temperatures high enough to form the glass. (Source: *Planetary and Space Science.*)

SOFT TISSUE X-RAYS.—The Albert and Mary Lasker Foundation has awarded a prize to Mr. Godfrey Hounsfield for developing a machine capable of photographing soft tissues, including the brain. Mr. Hounsfield, who is head of E.M.I.'s medical systems section at Hayes, Middlesex, has said that various organs of the body which were previously transparent to X-ray, such as the liver and the kidney, can now be clearly seen. The development of this machine is said to be one of the most important contributions in this field since the discovery of X-ray in 1895, and means that a number of conditions can be recognised more quickly in early stages.

SOLAR ENERGY.—An analysis published by the International Solar Energy Society, *Solar Energy: A U.K. Assessment*, states that a fifth of energy supplies could derive from solar energy. The report was compiled by seven teams of specialists, including scientists, engineers, economists and industrialists, who express concern at the dwindling reserves of fossil fuels. Although the United Kingdom has only half the solar radiation of, for example, the United States, it is pointed out that such a source of energy has the value of being inexhaustible, and that fossil fuel reserves of the earth are not renewable and are equivalent to only about a week's supply of solar energy.

In America, where £35 million was spent in 1976 on research into solar energy, machines have already been developed for heating and cooling buildings while the next phases envisage the design of electrical generators and water pumps. In Japan, £18 million was spent in 1976, in West Germany £3 million, and in France £3 million. In the Japanese and German research programmes industrial machinery figures more prominently than in America. The sun's irradiation of the British Isles has already been systematically analysed, but the annual British expenditure in this field is estimated at not more than £500,000. Already solar water heaters are economically attractive compared with " on peak " electricity at the standard domestic rate, and it is hoped that before long solar energy will be harnessed on a much larger scale.

SOVIET UNION CONTINUES LUNAR STUDIES.—After the close of the Apollo project, lunar exploration seemed to fall into the background with planetary missions taking the lead. The Soviet Union has however continued its systematic study of the Moon, the latest probe, *Luna* 24, successfully achieving its objectives in August 1976.

The station was placed in selenographic orbit on August 14. On August 16 and 17, adjustments were made in its orbit so that its height above the lunar surface ranged between 12 and 120 km. The following day, braking rockets were fired and six minutes later, the probe soft landed in the south-eastern corner of Mare Crisium (12° 45' N, 62° 12' E). On command from the Earth, the lunar surface was drilled to a depth of 2 metres, samples collected and placed in containers which were then sealed. On August 16th, a capsule was launched from the landing stage, making its way back to the Earth, where it landed successfully, 200 km south-east of Surgut in Western Siberia. The lunar rock was then handed over to the Academy of Sciences for study.

The *Luna* 24 experiment is one of a series of lunar probes which started in 1970 when *Luna* 16 brought back a core of material from Mare Foecunditatis. In 1972, *Luna* 20 obtained samples from the mountainous region lying between Mare Crisium and Mare Foecunditatis, but an attempt by *Luna* 23 in 1974 to sample the rocks from Mare

Crisium failed due to a damaged drill. This was designed to penetrate to a depth of 7·5 metres and consequently it is felt that the mere two metre penetration by *Luna* 24 did not achieve its full design potential.

" SPOT THE HOMER."—Professor David West of Newcastle University, talking at the Classical Association's conference in Aberystwyth in April, 1976, said that a German scholar examining Virgil's debt to Homer had turned the *Aeneid* into a literary game called " Spot the Homer ". During the last decade lists of Homeric material found in Virgil's *Aeneid* have been systematically drawn up, showing better than ever the extremely close linguistic connections between the two. Professor West, while discussing borrowings from the *Odyssey* in *Aeneid* 1, made it clear that he thought that Knauer, an authoritative German classicist, had taken the comparisons too far.

Professor Milman Parry had in fact found in the late 1920s that recurrent expressions in the Homeric epic were not accidental, nor amateurish, but the result of a long-established tradition, and from this point of view Virgil is seen as a respectable vehicle of that same tradition, In Hebrew poetry the same characteristics are to be found as in Greek poetry— " Spot the Deuteronomist ". Typical of this is parallelism, in which pairs of words and phrases recur in different contexts and by different authors. Again this is neither accidental nor indicative of a lack of imagination. The phenomenon of dependence on a fixed poetic diction is particularly a feature of oral poets, but modes of composition do not change rapidly, and Virgil's borrowings show the intentional perpetuation of old techniques.

STABILITY BEYOND URANIUM.—Until recently one has always been led to believe that uranium was the heaviest of the naturally occurring elements. Over the last few decades there has been a gradual extension of the list of elements using synthetic processes but all have been unstable and subject to fairly rapid radio-active decay. So far, fourteen elements have been made reaching an atomic number of 106. Recently, however, physicists have suspected that there may be a group of elements, well beyond number 92 (uranium) which would be relatively stable, i.e. having lifetimes comparable with that of the Earth. Proof of the existence of such elements came to light during the study of the mineral monazite, found in Madagascar.

These new nuclei were located as trace elements in small inclusions in monazite, a form of calcium phosphate. The intrusions themselves were trapped between layers of the Madagascar mica. Alpha particles (helium nuclei) ejected during the decay of the heavy nuclei penetrated the mica to distances depending on their emission energies. Within this range the mica is discoloured giving rise to spherical haloes which can be readily identified. The mica is easily cleaved into flat plates and on them can be seen the haloes as rings surrounding the radio-active source. Such haloes have been the target of much research during recent years and during these studies haloes were found having radii far too large to correspond to any known source. A team of U.S. scientists, headed by Dr. Robert Gentry, studied the X-ray taken from these extra large haloes and found evidence for new super heavy but stable elements. They have atomic numbers 116 and 126 and the preliminary results suggest the existence of other elements in the atomic number range 114-127. The results of these investigations were announced in Canada and at a seminar in Oxford in June, 1976.

The possibility of the existence of these stable super heavy elements has been of considerable in-

terest to the nuclear physicist for some time. It has been shown that the nucleus of an atom arranges its constituent neutrons and protons into shells, somewhat analogous to the periodic classification of the elements by their electron configuration. Theory had shown that nuclei with atomic numbers such as those just discovered should be stable. In fact it has been suggested that further stable elements of even higher mass could exist. Some of the team think they have found evidence of these but there are many problems to be sorted out before a categoric identification can be made.

SURFACE OF VENUS REVEALED.—The fact that Venus has a surface pressure in the region of 100 bars (100 times that of the Earth's sea level pressure) and a temperature in the region of 450° C suggested that it would be virtually impossible for automated probes to reach the surface of the planet, carry out experiments and transmit the information back to Earth. One major problem would be the difficulty of sophisticated electronic systems to survive such hostile conditions. However, the Soviet Union have successfully softlanded two spacecraft on the planet, taken photographs of the surrounding landscape and transmitted the information back.

On 22 October, 1975, *Venus* 9 entered the atmosphere and by aerodynamic braking slowed down from 10·7 km sec⁻¹to 250 m sec⁻¹, when a parachute system was brought into action. At a height of 50 km, the parachute was discarded and the probe continued to descend by free fall. It impacted the surface at a speed of about 7 metres per second, the impact being cushioned by a ring of crushable metal supported by shock-absorbing trusses. During the descent and for 53 minutes after landing, information was sent back on the atmosphere and conditions existing on the surface. At the landing site, estimated to be 2,500 m above the Venusian " sea level ", the temperature was 485°C and pressure 90 bars.

Venus 10 behaved in a similar way on arrival at the planet and reached the surface on 25 October 1975 at a point 2,300 km from the earlier landing site. At this new site the temperature was 465°C and pressure 92 bars. A wind speed of 3½ metres per second was recorded. It transmitted information on the surface for 65 minutes.

At the *Venus* 9 site, the surface was fairly level and strewn with sharp edged, unweathered rocks. It was considered that these rocks were debris from tectonic activity or meteoritic impact. The *Venus* 10 site, on the other hand, showed rocks resembling huge pancakes with sections of cooled lava or debris of weathered rocks in between. A surprising fact which emerged was that the surface of the planet is relatively dust free. No dust cloud was sent up when the probes landed and the atmosphere appears to be free of dust absorption, since the horizon could be seen as a very sharp line.

After releasing the capsules which descended through the atmosphere, the spacecraft went into orbit round the planet and sent back photographs of the upper cloud surface in ultraviolet light. This information, together with that collected by the capsules, has provided some clues to the structure and composition of the atmosphere. The clouds extend over a height range of 30 to 40 km not as a single thick belt but as a series of layers. The lower layers are about 35 km from the surface. The uppermost layers have been found to be composed of droplets of concentrated sulphuric acid with hydrochloric and hydrofluoric acids also present.

The information given is provisional. Subsequent analysis of the data will no doubt give a more accurate picture.

SYNTHETIC TOBACCOS.—Cigarette smoking during pregnancy has for some years been considered dangerous for the foetus, resulting in a smaller baby and reducing the grown child's intelligence by as much as ten per cent., according to some estimates. The ingredient in tobacco which is responsible for these effects has not been identified with certainty, but the Nuffield Institute for Medical Research in Oxford has now produced strong evidence that nicotine is the cause. The breathing pattern of a foetus is known to be a reasonably good indication of health, and it has been shown that smoking two consecutive cigarettes of the normal kind reduces the time occupied by foetal breathing activities from seventy per cent. to fifty per cent. Chewing gum containing nicotine had the same results, whereas smoking herbal tobacco had no effect on breathing. The conclusion drawn from the experiments is that regular smoking during pregnancy deprives the foetus of some oxygen, thereby constricting growth.

A different substitute for tobacco, New Smoking Material (NSM), appears to reduce the health hazard in smoking without affecting satisfaction. The substitute is manufactured from cellulose and for the experiments, conducted at the Royal Postgraduate School, cigarettes were made up with thirty per cent. NSM. As with the herbal tobacco, the effect of NSM was to reduce the nicotine content.

THESE TREELESS DAYS.—In Warwickshire alone some 400,000 trees have been ravaged by Dutch elm disease, nearly half of the elms in the country. This presents a challenge which must be met with careful deliberation. Some reports have been made of suckers appearing from the root systems of felled trees and it has been suggested that these should be given a chance to grow. However, an authority on trees, Mr. G. D. Roper of Forde Abbey in Dorset, has said that many diseased trees will not regenerate and that any that do will be in extreme danger of a similar fate. He considers it would be unwise to plant elms in the neighbourhood of diseased trees for the next ten years. The best thing to do is to plant either beech or oak on the site of felled trees; a beech particularly recommended is a fast-growing Chilean tree, *nothofagus obliqua*.

Man, however, is the most hostile and widespread enemy of trees. Reports during 1976 show that tropical rain forest is being so heavily cut that rainfall is considerably lessened, while in North Africa desert is moving over previously fertile land at the rate of twenty miles a year. In England it is common for trees to be felled without thought of restocking; alternatively, quick-growing softwoods replace oaks that have stood for nearly two centuries. Certainly the *Andredsweald*, the impenetrable Sussex Forest of Saxon days, is something which today is very difficult to imagine; and Sherwood forest hardly provides cover for outlaws nowadays. Mr. Roper, who has plantations in which two rows of oak alternate with three rows of Norway spruce, points out that if eighty per cent. conifers are cultivated the planting should pay and every fifth tree could be a hardwood such as oak: " You must plant ahead; someone has done it for you."

The best trees are not the product of haphazard planting and forgetfulness. Seeds must come from trees of good provenance, known as " plus trees ", and must be planted in suitable soil conditions. In plantations trees should not be more than six feet apart (five feet for some conifers) to avoid excessive bottom growth. The growth on a tree should always be under careful control: up to

twenty feet high only the top half of a tree should be in growth; after twenty feet only a third. If care is taken trees need not be a profitless use of land, but whatever the financial aspect of plantations may be, the sight of dwindling woodlands should encourage any landowner with a spare corner to plant trees rather than let it waste.

UNUSUAL METEORITE.—Apart from the material brought back from the Moon, the only extra-terrestrial rocks available for study are meteorites. Since the time of their formation they will have remained almost unaltered and this gives scientists the opportunity to study the various conditions which have existed in the past. Of special interest is a relatively rare type of stony meteorite, the ureilites, Their composition is very similar to that of the ultra basic terrestrial rocks called dunites, the material forming the Earth's mantle. The ureilites are also of particular interest because they are the only type in which are found diamonds.

Only seven ureilites are known, the last, the Havero meteorite, falling in Finland on 2 August 1971. It was a relatively small stone weighing only 1·5 kg and fell on a farm, penetrating through a tiled roof and three wooden floors. Recently a detailed account of the research on the meteorite has been published in *Space Science Review* and this certainly confirms the special place filled by these objects. The total carbon content is high (2%) in line with the others of this class of meteorite. This carbon is found in the form of large diamond-graphite inclusions up to 4 mm in diameter and fairly evenly distributed. The meteorite is strongly recrystallised, the chief mineral olivine having been transformed into a mosaic of small grains amongst which kamacite with a low nickel content is distributed. The meteorite is penetrated by a system of cavities, all elongated in a common direction. In some of these cavities are found kamacite plates containing a much higher percentage of nickel. These facts all indicate an origin similar to that of the other ureilites in that they were formed at a time when conditions were very turbulent and that shock waves generating pressures in the region of 300–600 kilobars existed. One possible explanation is that these shock waves originated from solar flares in the early days of the solar system.

Detailed analysis has shown that 60 per cent of the material ablated during the passage through the atmosphere. Isotope studies have shown that before Earth encounter, the orbit had an eccentricity of at least 0·25 and an aphelion of about 4·3 astronomical units (the distance between the Earth and the Sun).

VIKING'S VIEW OF MARS.—After each visit by a spacecraft to Mars, there has been a drastic modification of our ideas of the conditions existing there. Incorrect ideas however started centuries before the space age. In 1659, Huygens made a sketch of the most prominent feature and called it Syrtis Major (giant quicksand). In the 17th and 18th centuries it was widely accepted that Mars was inhabited. These ideas were strengthened by the identification of the polar caps and their fluctuation in size with the seasons. The peak of the belief was reached by the work of Schaparelli and Lowell, who made detailed maps of the " canali ", but it was Lowell who was convinced that these canals were constructed by Martians.

The first fly-by in 1964 by *Mariner* 4 showed a cratered surface similar to that of the Moon. This was strengthened by the results sent back by *Mariners* 6 and 7 in 1969. Only 10 per cent of the surface had been photographed in detail but they showed a relatively uniform cratered surface. *Mariner*

9, in 1971, gave a completely different picture. In addition to the cratered highlands of the southern hemisphere, it revealed gigantic volcanoes, a rift valley many thousands of kilometres long and evidence of dried up river beds. The probe thus revealed a dynamic, evolving Mars, not at all like the Moon. It also showed the non-existence of the canals or even extensive linear markings. All the probes so far had carried out experiments to study conditions on the planet to see if life was possible. No experiment was included to try to detect life.

The purpose of the *Viking* missions was to extend and pursue the study of the planet, with a special emphasis on the search for evidence of life there. The prime targets for examination were therefore the atmosphere, the surface and its physical evolution and the question of any possible biological evolution. Of paramount importance was the question of the presence, either now or in the past, of water.

It was known that water existed in small quantities in the atmosphere but with a surface atmospheric pressure of only about 1 per cent of that of the Earth, the Martian atmosphere could not sustain large quantities of liquid water. The principal question was whether there were large amounts locked in the permafrost. The presence of braided channels had suggested that water had existed in large quantities in the geologic past.

The contrasting surface features of Mars are of special interest. Geologists would like to learn more about the high concentration of huge volcanoes near Tharsis, the great rift valley, Valles Marineris, and the stratified terrain of the polar regions. This last feature suggests a marked precession of the polar axis over a long period. Another mystery that it is hoped can be clarified is the fate of the gas nitrogen, not identified by the previous probes. Was it lost by outgassing or is it locked up in the surface in the form of nitrates? The answer to this question is vital if one is to investigate the possibility of life on the planet.

It was with this background knowledge that two *Viking* spacecraft were launched from the United States with the aim of softlanding on the planet and carrying out a complex series of experiments. *Viking 1* went into orbit round Mars on June 14 and immediately went into action, photographing the various possible landing sites. All earlier photographs had a resolution of about 100 metres and before a landing could take place, far greater detail of the landing sites was required. Analysis of the pictures showed that the sites were far rougher than had been hoped but it was finally decided to choose a position about 900 km southwest of the primary site in the Chryse Basin. The orbit of the spacecraft was modified accordingly and on July 20, the landing capsule was detached from the orbiter and landed successfully at the desired place.

During its descent, *Viking 1* showed that the atmosphere consisted of about 2 per cent argon, 3 per cent nitrogen and some oxygen, the main constituent being carbon dioxide. Mars skies were found to be a faint pink due to the scattering of sunlight by dust. The surface of the planet is decidedly red, the result of oxidation of iron. It is not possible at this stage to determine whether the oxidation has been due to a rapid process early on in the planet's history or a continual process of photooxidation by ultraviolet light in an atmosphere deficient in oxygen, as it is today.

The first pictures transmitted back to Earth were in the low resolution mode and showed just a rock strewn landscape, but later transmissions in higher resolution revealed a wealth of detail. Early on, three distinct types of rock were identified, rough

textured igneous rocks which appeared to have cooled slowly, finely textured rocks (indicating rapid cooling) and very smooth light coloured material. Most of the loose rocks seemed to be associated with the rocky outcrops, with dark rocks near to the dark outcrops and the lighter coloured material near to the light outcrops. The coloured pictures released were in fact transmitted back to Earth as black and white scans of an area seen through three separate filters and these were then combined together at the Jet Propulsion Laboratory at Pasadena, California.

The first weather report from Mars was quite interesting. The meteorological team leader, Seymour Hess, commented that at the landing site there were light winds from the east in the late afternoon, changing to light winds from the south-west after midnight. Maximum wind speed was 15 miles per hour. Temperatures ranged from $-122°F$ just after dawn to $-22°F$. The pressure was steady at 7·70 millibars.

On July 28, the lander scooped up a sample of the martian soil and began the search for microscopic life. The soil was cooked in an incubator for 5 days. One biological experiment was designed to detect any microorganism that lived by photosynthesis. The second, labelled the release experiment, was designed to look for signs of metabolism, evidence that organisms in the soil are maintaining and reproducing themselves. A third biological experiment was designed to detect any exchange of gases between microorganisms in the soil and the atmosphere in the test chamber. Like all experimental work, the results were not as clear cut as expected. In the gas exchange test, large amounts of oxygen were given off when the soil was exposed to the laboratory conditions. In the labelled release experiment, large amounts of radio-active carbon 14 were released from the soil. Unfortunately in the early stages it was not possible to decide whether this was a biological reaction or a chemical one between active ingredients. With the information gleaned during the first few days, American scientists are endeavouring to duplicate martian soil back in the laboratory but many difficulties are being encountered.

Whilst the lander had been busy with studying conditions at the surface, the orbiter was studying large scale weather conditions. It revealed turbulent swirls around the giant volcanoes, with clouds forming over areas up to 600 km across and others streaming away from the mountain tops at speeds up to 200 km per hour. In the huge canyon near to the equator, clouds formed below the rims obscuring the canyon floor. The onset of winter in the southern hemisphere is being monitored in detail.

Viking 2, following in the footsteps of its predecessor, successfully arrived in the vicinity of the planet and on September 3, its orbiter made a perfect soft landing in an area called Utopia, about 1,400 km farther north than the Chryse region and on the other side of the planet. The preliminary results from this probe showed that the rocks in this region were very similar to those at the other site.

VOLCANIC ACTIVITY (1975–76).—Although volcanoes have been active in all the well-known regions, including the famous names of Etna and Cotopaxi, the most severe and dangerous eruptions have taken place in Alaska and the Central-America West Indies regions.

La Soufrière, a strato volcano at the southern end of Basse Terre, Guadeloupe, has erupted frequently over the last 300 years but this time local volcanologists came to the conclusion that this latest round of activity could be catastrophic. Activity increased suddenly on July 8, 1976, when a surface fracture opened on the southeast flank and solfataric gases and old ash began to be ejected from the fracture. The authorities evacuated residents living in the area. Activity intensified again on August 12 with a sudden increase in seismic phenomena. This build-up continued as can be shown by the number of seismic events reported on consecutive days: August 20, 26; 21, 88; 22, 156; 23, 116; 24, 1162; 25, 471 and the next few days about 200 per day. For the whole of August 5,989 tremors were recorded. On the 30, continuous tremors accompanied volcanic emission for the first time. On the same day, a roaring sound, like a jet engine, gradually increased in intensity and the volcano started to eject blocks up to a metre across as well as considerable quantities of ash. Activity has since died down considerably. Scientists had however predicted a very high probability of an eruption on the same scale as that, in 1902, of Mt. Pelée on the neighbouring island of Martinique, when 28,000 people were killed.

WATER MILL CONSERVATION.—Two Cornish water mills have recently gone into operation and it has been reported that " astronomical savings have been made " since they have been used. At one time there were twenty tide mills, filled at flood tides, on Cornish creeks and inlets; in addition to these there was a great number of tidal and wind-and-tide mills on rivers and streams in the Duchy. The two mills in question are near Liskeard and Lanivet; with technical innovations it would apparently be possible to re-establish many other mills that would prove highly efficient. Mr. John Pardoe, M.P. for North Cornwall, who has demanded a " tough and brutal programme of energy conservation ", is also involved in a tidal barrage scheme for the Severn Estuary. This scheme has already been investigated by Bristol University and pronounced feasible.

WHO FOUND AMERICA?—For some years now people have searched for evidence in a variety of places to support the theory that Bristol men discovered America before Columbus. Oscar Wilde, who always enjoyed a harmless jibe at the Americans, said that " Of course America had often been discovered before, but it had always been hushed up ", and it is almost certain that he was right.

In the harbour of Louisbourg in the " Baie des Anglais ", Nova Scotia, a primitive cannon was dredged up of a type in use about A.D. 1500. It is not altogether certain that this was discarded ballast from an Elizabethan or later ship, which is how it has normally been explained.

Mr. Forbes Taylor of Bristol has recently found peculiarities in the customs accounts of Bristol imports and exports from 1479 onwards. Certain ships, reported to have been trading with Ireland, took up to three times as long for their voyages as the distance merited, and it has been suggested that in reality a secret of rich trans-Atlantic fishing grounds was being jealously guarded. This suggestion has been meticulously backed up with analyses of patterns of cargoes and sailings.

Though there is little information which serves as definite proof of these ideas, the chances are fairly high that at some time British or Portuguese fishermen, and Bretons and Basques as well, were in a position to be taken to Newfoundland by unexpected winds. The Basques, who were in the majority, would probably have been among the first to have landed there. Whatever the relationship of probability and fact, the discussion is so vigorous that if further evidence is available it will not remain hidden for long.

ARCHÆOLOGY IN 1975-76

Sir Mortimer Wheeler

In July, 1976, Sir Mortimer Wheeler, who has been described as " the outstanding British archaeologist of his generation ", died at the age of 85. From 1913, apart from distinguished service in both the World Wars, Sir Mortimer (as he became in 1952) held a succession of posts beginning in the Royal Commission on Historical Monuments, moving to the National Museum of Wales and the London Museum, culminating in 1944 with his appointment as Director-General of Archaeology to the Indian Government. He held many offices, including that of President of the Society of Antiquaries from 1954 until 1959 and also the Secretaryship of the British Academy from 1949 to 1968; he was a Trustee of the British Museum from 1963 and was Chairman of the Ancient Monuments Board for England from 1964 to 1966; in 1968 he was elected a Fellow of the Royal Society.

His archaeological excavations were not only carried out with great technical expertise but were also publicised in such a way as to catch the public imagination; especially notable were those at Caerleon, Verulamium and, perhaps above all, at Maiden Castle in Dorset; his investigations into the pre-history of the Great Indus Valley civilisation added very greatly to the knowledge of the archaeology of the Indian sub-continent.

Apart from his skills as an archaeologist, there is no doubt that Sir Mortimer will be remembered as the person above all others who has made archaeology popular in the 20th century; not only did his great interest in furthering the education of the public cause him to argue for the establishment of the Institute of Archaeology at London University, which opened in 1937, but he also understood the potentiality of television; his appearances especially on " Animal, Vegetable, or Mineral ?" contributed to him being declared in 1954 " Television Personality of the Year ". Sir Mortimer Wheeler will long be remembered as one of the most influential figures in British archaeology.

Ancient Monuments Board

The 22nd Annual Report of the Ancient Monuments Board for England, covering the year 1975, was ordered to be printed in June, 1976. The Report includes a description of a tour by the Ancient Monuments Board based on Chester; in that city a number of buildings restored under the Chester Conservation Scheme were inspected, and of the Agricola Tower, the only part of the Castle held by the Department of the Environment, the Board notes " we consider that the monument could be made more intelligible to the public if certain later buildings were removed from the site and we therefore urged the Department to try to enlarge the area under their control." Norton Priory was then visited; this was an Augustinian foundation of 1134 which is now within the confines of Runcorn New Town; the Development Corporation in consultation with the Department of the Environment has been undertaking excavation and consolidation over the last six years and the Board " congratulate all concerned in this work, which has received a Civic Trust Heritage Year Award in the conservation category." It had also noted that some thirteen thousand people were present at the public opening on May 1, 1975.

Visits were also made to the Roman fortress at Abbey Green, Chester, (" in our view, the remains are eminently suitable for display "), Wroxeter, the fourth largest city of Roman Britain, of which the Department of the Environment has acquired over two hundred acres, Beeston and Whittington Castles, at the latter of which members of the Board were told about the new single-span concrete bridge to the inner ward; it is remarked that " it was the hope of your Board that in future the Department would bring to their attention any such major departure from current practice before it was put into effect ". At Baguley Hall, described as " one of the series of great timber-framed hall-houses of Cheshire and South Lancashire ", the Board was " concerned by the quality of some of the repairs so far undertaken," and recommended " that the most careful consideration be given both to the method of repair and to the detailed recording of the building in its present state and during the course of the Department's work ". Two very different types of monuments also engaged the Board's attention, namely the two Anglo-Saxon Sandbach Crosses, which are deteriorating through the action of the weather at their present, but not original, position on a large stepped base in the Market Place; by contrast, the Board inspected Marple Aqueduct, which is noted as being " one of the few surviving structures built by Samuel Oldknow and was one of the earliest industrial monuments to be scheduled "; now considerably restored, the Aqueduct was reopened for boats in 1967.

In the section on individual cases, it is reported that three monuments have been removed from the list, namely a Fairbairn crane at Hartlepool Docks which was demolished before an alternative site for it could be found, part of the site of the Royal Palace at King's Langley, which was excavated prior to redevelopment, and part of the wall of Hyde Abbey, Winchester, which had collapsed.

Twelve cases of the use of compulsory powers by the Secretary of State are recorded; sites range in date from Neolithic to medieval times and include the three Thornborough Circles which are described as being " among the finest henge monuments in the North of England and are an important focus for the extensive late Neolithic settlement of North Yorkshire ". For the Roman period, sites included the Brancaster Roman fort in Norfolk, which was one of the Saxon shore forts which formed part of a defensive system stretching from Brancaster to Portchester; streets and sites of buildings have been found by aerial photography and field work in the vicinity of the fort indicates an extensive civil settlement. An Interim Preservation Notice was served to encourage the protection of the Roman site at Chesterton, Huntingdon and Peterborough, which " is of exceptional importance, since it is known to contain extensive Roman buildings "; the Board recommended that the whole of the scheduled area north of the A1 road should be preserved under grass for all time because finds of gold and silver indicate that the Roman levels are very near the surface. " As well as affording legal protection, this course of action would make looting to 'treasure-hunters' using metal-detectors more difficult. This is a most destructive practice because it disturbs valuable archaeological evidence within the superimposed soil strata." Planning permission for housing given by Stratford-upon-Avon District Council covering six acres of the Roman town of Alcester in Warwickshire, where the fourteen acre scheduled site contains stone buildings, some of them having frescoed walls, led to the Secretary of State serving an Interim Preservation Notice " in order to save the site from destruction and to allow time for its future to be further considered." Compulsory

powers were also used by the Secretary of State in connection with some eight medieval sites, including the twenty foot high motte at Yockleton Hall at Westbury in Shropshire which was threatened with levelling for the cultivation of sugar beet, the motte of Eardisley Castle in Herefordshire threatened with infilling by a flood alleviation scheme and the motte at Bampton in Devon, which the Town Council wished to level to improve the area for recreation; two threats of particular importance were that arising from the intention of the Dean and Chapter of St. Albans Cathedral and Abbey to seek planning permission to build a three storey pilgrim centre on the site of the chapter house; an Interim Preservation Notice was served and the full excavation of the chapter house site is recommended should planning permission for the pilgrim centre be granted; the second particularly noteworthy threat arose from the recommendation of the Diocesan Parsonages Board to demolish the tower and adjoining lengths of wall, the only standing remains of the former summer palace of the Bishops of Exeter, at Bishop's Palace, Torquay in Devon, on the grounds of the expense of repairs and maintenance; an Interim Preservation Order was served and a recommendation made that the permanent preservation of the monument should be ensured.

The Ancient Monuments Board advised on some twelve cases during the year, including the threat of total destruction by quarrying of the Palaeolithic site at Westbury-sub-Mendip in Somerset, described as " possibly the earliest Palaeolithic site in Britain "; in 1949 part of a cave system was found and the roofs of caves had been blasted by the quarry owners in 1974, thereby destroying four of the most important levels from an archaeological point of view; the Board recommended the immediate excavation of the remaining top layers, which because of their condition were very difficult to preserve. The very important Neolithic site of Grimes Graves flint mines in Norfolk also claimed the attention of the Board, which was consulted as to whether or not an excavated pit should be left open for specialist inspection or whether it ought to be filled in again to preserve the contents; the Board recommended that the pit should be kept open if this could be done without damage.

Threats to four Roman sites were considered by the Board, the first being the Beaufront Red House military site at Corbridge in Northumberland, which was discovered in the course of excavations in advance of road construction; the east and western military ditches were located together with the remains of some fifteen timber-framed buildings between them, and the indications are that the whole fort covered perhaps some thirty acres; it was decided to schedule the remainder of the site immediately. So far as the Vindolanda Roman fort and civil settlement at Chesterholm in Northumberland is concerned, the Board considered the Report of a monitoring team which it had set up to review the development of the excavation and post-excavation work. The Board supported the Department of the Environment's proposed excavation of the Romano-British settlement at Hibaldstow, Humberside, in advance of the construction of a dual carriageway link with the M.180, which would affect a five mile stretch of Ermine Street; excavations during 1975 showed the settlement to be quite extensive and the Board asked the Department to consider urgently the possibility of re-routing the new road. At Verulamium at St. Albans in Hertfordshire ploughing is adversely affecting large areas of the Roman town and the Board " recommended that the Department should take steps to have these areas taken out

of arable cultivation in order to protect the Roman remains from further damage ".

For the medieval, period the Board's advice was sought over the bulldozing by Swale District Council of the site of the fourteenth century Queenborough Castle at Queenborough in Sheppey in Kent; the Board recommended that the site should remain scheduled despite the damage and " were pleased to hear that at a meeting with senior officers of the Department the Chief Executive had given an assurance that his Council would co-operate with the Department in preserving archaeological sites in his district and displaying them more effectively to the public ". Unauthorised bulldozing also took place at a motted site north of Park Barn Farm at Boughton Aluph in Kent; another threatened castle was Wallingford in Oxfordshire, where it is proposed to build a retirement home on a site below which are the remains of medieval buildings buried by the levelling up of the area in the early thirteenth century to form an extension to the Norman castle; the cob walls of these buildings had been preserved to a height of about six feet and it was believed that the remains of the Saxon town would lie beneath them; the planning application concerning this site has been called in by the Secretary of State.

Two later buildings were brought to the Board's attention, namely Witley Court in Worcestershire and The Grange at Northington in Hampshire; the former is now a ruin, having suffered for thirty five years from fire, neglect and vandalism; this ruined mansion was taken into the guardianship of the Department of the Environment in 1973 and the Board recommended that " all worthwhile parts of the ruins including interior features should be preserved in such a way as to permit the eventual opening of at least some of the interior to the public ". The necessary arrangement for the Department of the Environment to take over the remains of the late seventeenth century Grange at Northington were made this year; it was designed by William Samwell and later encased within a neo-classical skin by Wilkins; it is intended to consolidate the remains of the building and possibly to add a new roof; the Board " accepted that as the house is internally totally ruinous it would be impracticable to allow the public inside ".

In July 1974 the Ancient Monuments Board set up a Committee for Rescue Archaeology " to advise the Department on policies and priorities for surveys and excavations, on allocation of grants and on bank-up facilities to aid early completion and publication of reports "; the Committee met three times in 1974 and five times in 1975. In its Report on its work the Committee reviews the present position and recent developments, and draws attention to where improvements are needed. " There are two major problems in providing for satisfactory processing and storage of excavated material. These are the need to improve laboratory and museum storage facilities in the provinces and the need to train more conservators." The Committee, realising that these were matters largely beyond the responsibility of the Secretary of State for the Environment, has had discussions with the Standing Commission on Museums and Galleries on these subjects. At its October meeting the Committee set up a working party to consider in detail how conservation and scientific back-up facilities could be improved. Similar concern was expressed with regard to the field of scientific investigations, while " funds for improving conservation facilities throughout the country are a major problem. At the meeting with the Standing Commission on Museums and Galleries. . . . it was agreed to approach the Department of Education and

Science, which is responsible for museums, to ask them to consider contributing towards the cost of improving conservation facilities ... there is an acute shortage of trained personnel at present. At the end of 1974 it was estimated that less than 100 (probably nearer 80) conservators were engaged, as part of their duties, on the conservation of material from past and present excavations in England. Furthermore only approximately one-third of this number were believed to hold a conservation qualification ". The Committee was also concerned over the years in question with the " serious backlog " of unpublished reports on archaeological excavations; a working party was set up and a report entitled " Principles of Publication in Rescue Archaeology " was produced and the Ancient Monuments Board recommended that it should be published for the guidance of excavators throughout the country and this was done in November, 1975.

Rescue Archaeology

Rescue Archaeology was also the theme of a paper presented by the Chief Inspector of Ancient Monuments and Historic Buildings, who considers it " opportune to consider the relationship between the traditional role of the Department as an agency for the preservation for posterity of surviving sites and monuments of national importance and its developing role as the principal agency for preserving, by means of survey, excavation and record, the archaeological evidence contained within selected sites also of national importance whose destruction cannot be prevented. Essentially there is a single factor linking these two facets of the Department's work in terms of the Ancient Monuments Acts: Preservation." Although preservation is the ideal, economic circumstances dictate that selection is the order of the day, " cost effectiveness is now a fashionable term in archaeological circles ", and the conclusion is reached that " what is needed is a strategy for rescue archaeology in terms of its potential contribution to current and long-term research needs ". The Chief Inspector summarises the position thus: " Excavation should be regarded more and more as a selective though essential weapon in the battle to save the archaeological heritage ... in order to dispose of the Department's resources in the most economical way and to further the long-term objective of saving the nation's past for the future, greater attention needs to be focused on the policy and practice of preservation. The future lies with a clearer definition of long-term aims, the better management of available resources including the co-ordination of excavation, conservation and publication and the achievement of a satisfactory balance between conservation and development, particularly agricultural, which will respect the interest of everyone concerned with the exploitation of the land."

It is recorded in the Report that thirteen monuments have been taken into the care of the Department of the Environment during the year under review, and these include Nympsfield Long Barrow, Frocester, Gloucestershire, Piercebridge Roman Bridge, Manfield in North Yorkshire; Bramber Castle, Sussex; The Iron Bridge, Shropshire and Landguard Fort, Felixstowe, Suffolk. Some 321 monuments were recommended for scheduling by the Ancient Monuments Board during 1975, of which 51 are in Cornwall, 22 in both Devon and Cornwall and 20 in Cumbria. These 321 monuments are divided up into the following categories: caves, 3; burial mounds or groups of mounds, megalithic monuments and ritual and ceremonial sites, 50; camps and settlements, 53; Roman remains, 32; Saxon remains, 3; linear

earthworks, 5; ecclesiastical buildings, 15; crosses, 5; castles and fortifications, 25; deserted villages, settlements and motted sites, 45; industrial monuments, 37; other secular sites, 38; bridges, 10.

Archaeological Excavations 1975

The Department of the Environment published a summary of pre-historic Roman and medieval sites excavated in advance of destruction under the title of *Archaeological Excavations in* 1975. In the introduction it is stated that in the financial year 1975/76 money made available for rescue archaeology in England, Scotland and Wales was increased by £566,000 to a total of £1,629,000; in the calendar year 1975 £906,191 was made available towards the cost of surveys and excavations in England, £281,782 for post-excavation work and £34,055 towards publication costs; for Scotland £23,289 was provided in grants and £81,587 in Wales; further, fees for supervisors and assistants working on direct and sponsored excavations totalled £50,123, £14,653 going to those engaged on post-excavation work; £16,416 was spent on central excavation in England, £37,443 in Scotland and £4,622 in Wales. To help to spread more fairly the available resources, some fourteen major projects of national importance have been removed from area funding and now have their grants allocated centrally; these major projects include very important urban excavations in London, York, Hull and Lincoln, as well as rural sites such as the Somerset levels, the route of the M.3 Motorway through the Wessex Chalk and the important group of sites in the area of Peterborough New Town. It did not prove possible to constitute or expand archaeological rescue units as had been intended, because most extra funds during 1975 were allocated to post-excavation work. " This period of retrenchment and financial restriction, which will continue through 1976/77 and beyond, gives an opportunity to concentrate on survey work. It is intended to have at least one Field Officer, on a three year contract, in each of the English counties, where there is no one already employed by other agencies, with the aim of basic coverage for survey and general intelligence on the rescue situation. By the end of 1975 there were only a few counties where this had not been achieved."

Central Excavation Unit

A significant innovation was that the Inspectorate of Ancient Monuments set up its own Central Excavation Unit, a mobile organisation designed to complement archaeological rescue work being done by a number of bodies with grant-aid from the Department of the Environment. " The purpose of the unit is to operate a flexible programme of excavations in England: (1) in areas where no suitable organisation exists (2) in areas where units have insufficient resources (3) on special sites of national importance and (4) on sites which the DOE becomes committed to excavate with three months' notice." The report considers the executive organisation region by region, giving details of the current administrative arrangements. The attention to survey work is stressed and is summarised thus: " the emphasis has therefore been on establishing what antiquities exist, relating these to specific areas and assessing their relative importance. The Field Officers are also playing an increasingly important part in the conservation of sites." It is noted that despite the economic situation, requests for excavation grants for threatened sites were for double the amount of money which it was possible to allocate; the principal threat to archaeological sites have come from urban

rebuilding, mineral extraction, road construction and intensive agriculture. "Broadly speaking, the year has been one in which many archaeological organisations have 'marked-time', concentrating on post-excavation work and on general survey work. This, while undoubtedly desirable, has resulted in a drop in the number of excavations carried out."

Among the more important pre-historic sites noted in the Report were a Mesolithic occupation at Monk Moors at Eskmeals in Cumbria, where four hearths and some probable stake-holes have been excavated, and a Neolithic causewayed camp excavated at Orsett in Essex; the investigation of the causewayed camp on Hambledon Hill in Dorset continued as did the Somerset Levels Project, which has led to the discovery of quantities of pre-historic timber. The investigation of Neolithic barrows continues and a particularly interesting one at Callis Wold, Humberside, known as Mortimer's barrow 275, was finished, having revealed a Neolithic mortuary enclosure, structure and façade, associated with a large amount of Neolithic Towthorpe ware. Moving on in time, three beaker burials were excavated at Smeeton Westerby in Leicestershire and a Late Bronze Age cemetery being excavated at Long Benington in Lincolnshire has led to the discovery of at least thirty bucket urns; at Burton Fleming, Humberside, the excavation of the major La Tène cemetery has revealed more square barrows and four additional sword-burials; at Barnack in Cambridgeshire a barrow of three periods was excavated, the primary phase of which produced a beaker, dagger and gold-studded wrist guard. For the period of the hill-forts, the most important excavation was at Danebury in Hampshire, where excavations within the rampart revealed remains of stratified timber buildings, while the investigation of the Iron Age landscape at Mucking in Essex, revealed a further nine roundhouses. An interesting multi-period site was on downland at Bishopstone in Sussex, which on completion was found to consist of Iron Age and Romano-British settlements as well as twenty timber structures of Anglo-Saxon date.

Under the heading Roman military sites, the Report notes that a new section of the Turf Wall, ditch and vallum was recorded at Appletrees in Cumbria where a gas-pipe trench cut through the Roman frontier; the first milefortlet at Biglands in Cumbria beyond the west end of Hadrian's wall was found to have three periods of second century occupation, while an investigation of the east end of the fort of Wallsend in Northumberland showed a succession of structures beginning with a timp building but no evidence of violent destruction by fire in any period; at Hyton, Humberside, the Flavian fort found by aerial photography was investigated and the excavation was undertaken of the north-west and south-east gates, as well as two corner towers and barrack blocks; traces of early Saxon occupation were also found in the central area of the fort. Work also continued on the two legionary fortresses of York and Chester, at the latter place an internal tower, rampart building and parts of the centurion's quarters of barrack blocks being examined. Among excavations in Roman towns those at Leicester are noted as having revealed a large cemetery on the west side of the town overlying earlier industrial development, which includes, possibly, a pottery kiln site; at Colchester in Essex, the excavation of the extra-mural settlement to the west led to the discovery of a complex system of wooden water pipes which is taken to imply the existence of some form of water tower, while at St. Albans in Hertfordshire a bath house dating to the second century A.D. was investigated. At Southwark, the bridge-head suburb of Londinium is starting to appear, while in the City of London, major excavations are revealing more of the Roman waterfront and its history; a defensive wall along the river bank was found and it had in it many sculptured stones from earlier monuments. At Poundbury in Dorset another 155 graves were recorded in the late Roman Christian cemetery and another 3 in the nearby pagan cemetery, bringing the total for the two cemeteries to 960.

From sites of the earlier medieval period described in the Report may be noticed the excavation of Anglo-Saxon cemeteries at, for example, Elsham, Humberside, where a large cremation cemetery was investigated and at Wigber Low, Derbyshire, where five secondary inhumation burials were found in a much earlier Bronze Age barrow. The excavations at Mucking in Essex continue to be of the greatest importance, and particular mention must be made of a Norse farmstead excavated at Ribblehead in North Yorkshire which produced four ninth-century coins, including some of Aethelred II and Wylfhere. The remains of industrial activity in Lincoln in the ninth and tenth centuries have been found on the Flaxengate site and important discoveries have been made in the urban sites of Northampton and Norwich. For the later medieval period, an interesting discovery was made in York where a fifteenth-century pit was found containing debris from a glazier's workshop; in Hull, excavations in advance of major roadworks led to the discovery of traces of medieval and post-medieval properties, the earliest of which can be identified in the Hull Rental of 1347. The most significant excavation of a castle was undertaken at Stanford, Lincolnshire, where the complex series of halls discovered in 1974 was investigated and an early kitchen complex was found below the first stone wall. Compared to the extensive number of medieval ecclesiastical, urban, castle and village excavations that were undertaken during the year, the Report draws attention to the only specifically post-medieval investigation that took place, which was of a water-powered industrial site at Ardingly in Sussex.

Council for British Archaeology

The Council for British Archaeology's 25th Annual Report for the year ended 30th June, 1975, was published during the winter of that year, and in it is noted that the year under review had been dominated by two major issues—the publication of *Archaeology and Government* and the proposal to set up a professional institute for archaeologists. *Archaeology and Government: A Plan for Archaeology in Britain*, a publication produced jointly by the Council for British Archaeology and the organisation known as Rescue, was widely circulated and promoted much discussion, culminating in a delegation being received by Baroness Birk, Minister of State in the Department of the Environment, whose responsibilities include archaeology, on January 15, 1975; one of the results of this meeting was the publication of a memorandum by the Department of the Environment for distribution to local authorities; the memorandum treated archaeology under a number of heads—what it is, why it has developed, how it is financed, existing organisations, the resources of the Department of the Environment, departmental staff, local organisations and the role of local authorities, and training.

EDUCATION IN THE UNITED KINGDOM

There are nearly 12 million pupils and students in full-time attendance at schools and institutions of further and higher education in Britain. In 1974–75 estimated total public expenditure on education was over £4,500 million, about 13 per cent of all public expenditure (includes school meals, milk, local libraries and museums).

ENGLAND AND WALES

Department of Education and Science

Those responsibilities of the Secretary of State for Education and Science that relate to civil science and the arts and (exercised through the University Grants Committee) the universities cover the whole of Great Britain, but her functions in connection with schools, further education and teachers relate to England and Wales only, except that responsibility for nursery, primary and secondary education in Wales is in the hands of the Secretary of State for Wales. Most of the work of the 520 H.M. Inspectors (who inspect schools and other educational establishments apart from universities, and provide the Secretary of State with information and advice) is in the local education authority areas. The Department of Education and Science does not run any schools or colleges, or engage any teachers, or prescribe textbooks or curricula, but it does set minimum standards of educational provision; control the rate, distribution, nature and cost of educational building; and control the training, supply and distribution of teachers. The Secretary of State's requirements under the Act are issued, and guidance is given, mainly in the form of regulations, orders and circulars addressed to local education authorities and other bodies, and in booklets. A report and six volumes of statistics are published annually.

Local Education Authorities

The educational service is a national service locally administered. Among its main features are:—

(a) Its administration is decentralized, the responsibility for providing state primary, secondary and further education (but not university education) to meet the needs of their areas being that of the 162 local education authorities (L.E.A.'s).

These elected councils appoint education committees consisting of some of their own members (a majority of the committee) and other people with experience in education and knowledge of the local education situation. The L.E.A.'s maintain schools and colleges and build new ones, employ teachers and provide equipment. Most of the public money spent on education is disbursed by the local authorities. Education is the largest item of their expenditure. L.E.A.'s are financed by rate support grants from the Department of the Environment and from the rates; and employ more than one million people, half of them teachers, whose salaries account for almost half of the national expenditure on education.

Voluntary Agencies

(b) Voluntary agencies play an important part in educational provision often in co-operation with the State. Some indication of its nature and extent is given below.

SCHOOLS AND PUPILS

Schooling is compulsory for all children between 5 and 16 years. No fees are charged in any publicly maintained school.

There are four main categories of school: (a) those *maintained* by local education authorities, the authorities meeting their expenditure partly from local rates and partly from grants made by the Department of the Environment; (b) *direct grant grammar* schools which have been assisted by grants from the Department of Education and Science (in 1975 the Secretary of State announced the government's intention to withdraw financial support from these schools by stages from 1976 unless, by the end of 1975 they indicated an intention to seek entry to the maintained sector); (c) *recognized independent* schools, *i.e.* independent schools which have sought and obtained recognition as efficient after inspection by H.M. Inspectors of Schools; (d) *other independent* schools.

County and Voluntary Schools

Maintained schools are of two types: (i) *county schools* (19,000) which are built, maintained and staffed by local education authorities. Their managers (primary schools) and governors (secondary schools) are appointed by the L.E.A.'s. (ii) *Voluntary schools* (8,600) which although built by voluntary bodies (mainly religious denominations) are maintained by an L.E.A. About two-thirds of the voluntary schools are Church of England schools and about 2,600 are Roman Catholic. Voluntary schools are of three kinds: controlled, aided, and special agreement. In *controlled* schools the L.E.A. nominates two-thirds of the managers or governors (the rest are nominated by the voluntary body), bears all costs and appoints the teachers.

In *aided* schools the managers or governors (two-thirds appointed by the voluntary interest and one-third by the L.E.A.) are responsible for repairs to the outside of the school building and for improvements and alterations to it though the Department of Education and Science may reimburse up to four-fifths of approved capital expenditure. The L.E.A. meets all running costs. The managers or governors control the appointment of teachers. *Special agreement* schools are those where the L.E.A. may, by special agreement, pay between one-half and three-quarters of the cost of building a new, or extending an existing, voluntary school, almost always a secondary school. Two-thirds of the governors are appointed by the voluntary body and the remainder by the L.E.A. Expenditure is normally apportioned between the authority and the voluntary body as for an aided school.

Direct Grant Schools

Direct grant grammar schools are being phased out starting from 1976. By the end of 1975, 51 of these schools had said they intended to seek entry to the maintained sector as comprehensive schools; others announced their intention of becoming independent.

Public Schools

By the term *public schools* is usually meant the independent schools in the membership of the Headmasters' Conference, the Governing Bodies Association or the Governing Bodies of Girls' Schools Association.

Independent schools charge fees and do not receive grants from the State. *Preparatory schools* are mainly for boys from about 8 to 13 years who wish to enter public schools. All independent schools are open to inspection and must register with the Department of Education and Science which lays down certain minimum standards and can make

schools remedy any unacceptable features of their building or instruction and exclude any unsuitable teacher or proprietor. To be designated "recognized as efficient", an independent school must satisfy the D.E.S. that its standards are broadly comparable with those of grant-aided schools.

The State System

Nursery Education is for children under 5 years who may attend a nursery school or a nursery class attached to a primary school. In the public sector there are some 580 nursery schools accommodating about 46,000 children two-thirds of whom attend part-time. In addition there are 270,000 boys and girls under compulsory school age who attend maintained primary schools full-time.

Primary Stage.—This begins at 5 years and the transfer to secondary school is generally made at 11 years. Over half the primary schools take 5 to 11-year olds; about a quarter are schools for infants (up to 7 years only); and most of the rest take juniors only (7 to 11 year olds). Most primary schools take both boys and girls. More than half have between 100 and 300 children each; most of the rest are smaller.

First Schools.—In some areas, first schools cater for ages from 5 to 8, 9 or 10; they are the first stage of a three-tier system.

Middle Schools.—Middle schools (which take children from first schools) cover the age-ranges 8 to 12, 9 to 12, 9 to 13, 10 to 13 or 10 to 14.

Secondary Stage.—Secondary Schools are for children aged 11 to 16 and over. The largest have over 2,000 pupils but more than half the schools take between 300 and 600 pupils. In January, 1974, when there were 3,550,598 full-time pupils in maintained secondary schools the main types were: (a) *comprehensive* schools (2,136,958 pupils), whose admission arrangements are without reference to ability or aptitude and cater for the secondary education of all pupils in an area; (b) *secondary modern* schools (856,749 pupils) providing mainly a general education with a practical bias, with an increasing number of pupils staying on after the school-leaving age; (c) *grammar* schools (411,195 pupils) providing an academic course from 11 to 16-18 years; and (d) *technical* schools (21,144 pupils) providing an integrated academic and technical course.

By 1976, 70% of the maintained secondary school population were in comprehensive schools. The policy of the Government is to develop a fully comprehensive system of secondary education and to end selection at eleven plus or at any other stage. The *Further Stage* is treated separately below.

Primary and Secondary Schools

There was a slight drop in the number of full-time primary school-children in 1974. This was the first time that there has been a reduction in numbers since 1962 and reflects the continuous decline in the birthrate since 1964. But the number of full-time pupils in all schools—primary and secondary—rose by 370,000, 250,000 of this increase being due to the raising of the school-leaving age.

In January 1974, there were 33,100 schools, of which 30,365 were maintained by local education authorities, 302 were direct grant schools, 1,379 were independent schools recognized as efficient, and 1,054 were other independent schools. There were at school in 1974, 9,560,015 children (4,907,014 boys and 4,653,001 girls) of whom 9,009,988 were in maintained schools, 130,880 in direct grant schools, 324,326 in recognized independent schools and 94,821 in other independent schools. Of those in maintained schools, 4,971,994 were in primary,

347,697 in middle, and 3,550,598 in secondary schools and the rest in nursery (15,431) or special (122,990) schools including hospital or immigrant centres (2,278). Almost all maintained primary schools, and about 70 per cent. of the maintained secondary schools, are for both boys and girls. At secondary level most recognized independent schools are for boys only or girls only.

Class sizes.—Between January 1973 and January 1974 the pupil/teacher ratio in primary schools dropped from 25·5:1 to 24·9:1, but in secondary schools, it rose from 17·0:1 to 17·3:1. In primary schools the average size of class as registered dropped from 30·8 to 30·3 while in secondary schools the average size of class as taught rose from 22·3 to 22·7.

School Meals.—L.E.A.'s must provide school dinners to all maintained school pupils who require them. In October 1975, 5,552,000 or 70·3 per cent. of pupils at maintained schools took the school dinner; 13·1 per cent. of the dinners were free of charge. Free school milk is available to pupils in special schools, children in other maintained schools up to the end of the summer term after they become seven, and other junior children for whom it is recommended on health grounds by a school medical officer.

Work Experience.—Many schools provide opportunities for pupils in their later secondary years to see something of the work and other activities of their neighbouring communities, as part of their curriculum. In recent years there has been a marked growth in the provision of "work experience" schemes which involve the participation of pupils in the work of industrial, commercial and other firms.

Educational Disadvantage.—As part of a policy of special educational help to children suffering from particular social difficulties, including immigrants, the Government in 1974 established an Educational Disadvantage Unit and a related non-government advisory committee. Both work in co-operation with an Assessment of Performance Unit with the wider brief of finding out why some children of all ranges of ability fall below their potential. In addition a government grant of about £1 million has been allocated to promote measures to reduce adult illiteracy.

Examinations.—Secondary school pupils (and others) can take the General Certificate of Education (G.C.E.) or the Certificate of Secondary Education (C.S.E.). The examinations for the G.C.E., which are conducted by eight examining bodies (most connected with universities) are set at two levels: Ordinary level (" O ") and Advanced level (" A "). " A " level is usually taken after two years in the sixth form following " O " level, which is normally taken at 16 years (earlier only if the head teacher agrees). The G.C.E. is not a " grouped subject " examination and candidates at either level may take one or more subjects as they wish. At " A " level passes are awarded in five grades. " A " level candidates may take Special papers which are usually set on the same syllabus as the basic " A " level papers but contain more searching questions.

Under a new grading system for " O " level, attainment in an " O " level subject is indicated by a grade A, B, C, D or E of which grade A is the highest and grade E the lowest. Candidates awarded grade A, B or C have reached the standard of the former subject pass at " O " level. Grades D and E indicate lower levels of attainment.

Like the G.C.E. the Certificate of Secondary Education (C.S.E.) can be taken in one or more subjects. It is open to boys and girls in any school completing five years of secondary education, and is meant for pupils of about 16 years who are

around the average in terms of ability for their age groups. Five grades are awarded. The C.S.E. can be examined in a number of ways, internal and external, and is controlled largely by serving teachers sitting on the 14 regional examining boards. More than a quarter of a million candidates take the C.S.E. examinations each summer.

Co-ordinating the work of the G.C.E. and C.S.E. examining boards, and advising them, is the *Schools Council for the Curriculum and Examinations* which was established in 1964 by the Secretary of State for Education and Science as an independent advisory body financially supported by the D.E.S. and the L.E.A.'s and representing all educational interests with teachers forming a majority of its members. The Council is particularly concerned with promoting and encouraging curriculum study and development. It carries out research and development work on curricula, teaching methods and examinations in primary and secondary schools. It is also concerned *inter alia* with maintaining comparability of standards between boards and also between the two examinations (grade 1 in the C.S.E. is intended to indicate a standard such that a candidate achieving it might reasonably have been expected to obtain a pass at " O " level in the G.C.E. had he followed a course leading to that examination).

School-leavers. There were (provisional figure) 692,000 school-leavers in 1975, 10,000 more than in 1974. In 1974–75, for the first time, just over 80 per cent of school-leavers achieved some graded examination results. The increase came mainly at junior levels of attainment with nearly 400,000 leavers gaining one to four " O " levels or C.S.E. grades. Leavers gaining one or more " A " level passes in the G.C.E. numbered 106,000, 1,000 more than the previous year. Over a period of five years, about one in five leavers has continued direct to full-time further or higher education.

TEACHERS

Although it is the duty of each Local Education Authority to ensure that there is efficient education to meet the needs of the local population, what is taught in the schools is normally decided on their behalf by the head teachers of schools.

Teachers are appointed by local education authorities, school governing bodies or managers. Those in maintained schools must (except student teachers and instructors) be approved as "qualified " by the Department of Education and Science. Most teachers become qualified by successfully completing a course at a college of education or at a university department of education.

In Transition. Colleges of education are in a transitional period. The profession is moving towards an all-graduate entry and some of the colleges are extending their work beyond teacher training into other forms of higher education. Some are amalgamating with other institutions and still others will close. Under present plans, 18 colleges are expected to close by 1981 and four to amalgamate with universities. There would then be some 25 education departments in polytechnics, 40 institutions combining teacher and further education, and 30 colleges engaged almost wholly in teacher training, a reduction from 163 establishments to about 100. The 1977 intake to initial teacher training will be limited to 12,000 non-graduate students and 10,000 postgraduate students.

In the next ten years or so the number of newly trained teachers required to meet the needs of the schools will decline substantially because of the expected drop in pupil numbers. This expected fall in school population could, in the long term,

allow continued improvement in the pupil-teacher ratio (about 20 to one) without further expansion of the teacher force.

There are, however, still shortages of graduate teachers in certain subjects—in particular, in mathematics, the physical sciences, handicrafts, French, German, and business studies.

An *Advisory Committee on the Supply and Training of Teachers* was set up in 1973 to advise the Secretary of State on the supply and training of teachers for maintained schools and establishments of further education. It met seven times in 1975.

Training to be Teachers. In autumn 1975, the estimated number of students in courses of initial teacher training (excluding universities) was 100,198 compared with 106,295 a year earlier. Estimated *admissions* to full-time courses of initial teacher training in 1975 (1974 figures in brackets) were: non-graduate entrants to colleges and departments of education: 28,138 (31,660); colleges of education (technical): 1,620 (1,526); art teacher training centres: 788 (667); graduates taking one-year course of professional training in university departments of education: 4,989 (4,670); graduates taking one-year course of professional training in colleges or departments of education: 5,638 (4,800). The non-graduate intake in 1976 to initial training is being reduced to 20,000 compared with 30,000 in 1975.

Training Institutions. Teachers are trained in institutions of various types. In October 1973, there were 121 colleges maintained by local education authorities and 52 by voluntary bodies, and 33 departments of universities. These included 30 university departments of education providing mainly one-year courses for graduates; 152 colleges of education providing mainly three-and four-year courses; 7 departments of education in polytechnics, which also offered mainly three- and four-year courses; 13 art teacher training centres offering one-year specialist courses; and 4 colleges of education (technical) providing one-year and four-term specialist courses and initial training courses for serving teachers.

Serving Teachers. There were 508,516 full-time teachers in maintained schools and colleges in January 1975 compared with 488,993 a year earlier and 463,948 in January 1973.

The 508,516 full-time teachers were employed thus:—in secondary schools 212,869; primary schools 202,130; miscellaneous primary and secondary schools 4,427; further education 64,541; special schools 14,967; colleges of education 7,173; nursery schools 1,519; others 890.

Salaries. There are national salary scales for teachers in schools and other educational institutions maintained from public funds. There is a superannuation scheme administered by the Department of Education and Science.

HIGHER EDUCATION

" Higher Education " consists of the education provided by universities, polytechnics, colleges of education and in the advanced courses offered by colleges of further education. For details, *see under* " Universities ", " Teachers " and " Further Education ".

FURTHER EDUCATION

The term " Further Education " usually means all post-school education except that provided by universities.

Local Education Authorities are responsible for providing full-time and part-time courses of post-secondary education (other than university education) in their areas. There are ten Regional Advisory Councils which co-ordinate further education in

their regions and nominate a majority of the members of the National Advisory Council on Education for Industry and Commerce which advises the Secretary of State for Education and Science on national educational policy relating to industry and commerce.

The 7,523 further education establishments (November 1973 enrolment: 3,534,370 students, more than half of them women) other than the colleges of education, may be grouped in the following main categories of which all, except the last, are grant-aided:—

1. *Polytechnics.*—Thirty major centres in which a wide range of full-time, sandwich and part-time courses are provided for students at all levels of higher education, and entirely or almost entirely for those of 18 years or more. They have governing bodies with a large measure of autonomy and are mainly teaching institutions though provision is made for certain research where it is essential to the proper fulfilment of teaching functions and the maintenance of close links with industry. They complement the universities and colleges of education. By November 1973 there were 156,704 students (23% of them women) enrolled in polytechnics, 116,496 of them taking advanced courses.

2. *Other Maintained and Assisted Major Establishments* (566).—Including all major establishments, other than polytechnics, maintained or assisted by local education authorities and providing courses in art, agricultural, commercial, technical and other subjects. 1,626,528 students.

3. *Direct-Grant Establishments* (16) which receive financial aid direct from the D.E.S. 4,407 students.

4. *Evening Institutes* (6,812) offering a wide range of courses, many of them recreational, for evening students, and often housed in premises used by day for other educational purposes.—1,730,059 students.

5. *Independent Establishments* which may apply to the Department of Education and Science for recognition as efficient; in 1973 there were 99 such recognized establishments with 16,672 students.

For Colleges of Education, *see* under " Teachers " above.

The number of students taking advanced courses in 1973 (full-time, part-time, sandwich, or evening only) leading to recognized qualifications at grant-aided establishments was 208,320 of whom 20 per cent were women. Of the 208,320, 66,490 were on full-time courses, 33,570 were sandwich course students, 72,600 were taking part-time day courses and 35,660 were attending evening only classes. 8,580 of the total were working for a university first degree, 37,220 for a C.N.A.A. first degree (*see below*), 2,440 for a university or a C.N.A.A. higher degree, and 52,790 for an H.N.D. or H.N.C. qualification.

In 1973 there was set up a *Technician Education Council* to develop a unified national system of courses for technicians in England,Wales and Northern Ireland; and in 1974 the *Business Education Council* which is concerned with the development of policies for a uniform national system of courses, in further and higher education, for people in business and commerce.

An important body with few, if any, parallels in other countries is the *Council for National Academic Awards* (C.N.A.A.) which awards degrees to students taking courses approved by it in non-university institutions. Following a recommendation of the Robbins Committee it was established by Royal Charter in 1964 as an autonomous body. More than 100 colleges in Britain conduct courses leading to its degrees: B.A., B.Ed., B.Sc., and the higher degrees of M.A. and M.Sc. (for post-graduate course work) and M.Phil. and Ph.D. (for re-

search which may be undertaken jointly in industry and college). In 1975–76, 77,548 students were working for C.N.A.A. qualifications. Of these, 72,627 (44,687 full-time, 23,291 sandwich and 4,649 part-time) were studying for first degrees in: science and technology 30,422; arts and social studies 25,712; art and design 10,699; education 4,725; and modular courses 1,069. Of the 77,548, 1,451 were working for an M.A. or M.Sc. and 2,122 for a research degree (M. Phil. or Ph.D.).

The new *Diploma of Higher Education* (Dip.H.E.) is a two-year diploma intended to serve as either a terminal qualification or as a stepping stone to a degree or other further study; it has a normal entry requirement of two " A " levels. The Dip. H.E. is awarded by either the Council for National Academic Awards (*see above*) or by a university. Courses leading to it are offered by nearly 40 polytechnics and colleges. At present the emphasis in most Dip. H.E. courses is on the humanities and social sciences but many colleges offer scientific options.

Adult Education.—"Adult Education " is generally taken to mean courses of post-school education outside the main areas of higher, professional and technical education. A wide variety of such courses for the education and recreation of adults is provided by local education authorities, the Workers' Educational Association and other voluntary bodies, the extra-mural departments of universities and certain residential colleges. In 1974 nearly 3 million people registered for these courses.

The Youth Service.—Provides for the spare-time activities of young people. The Local Education Authorities co-operate with voluntary bodies in their areas and may maintain their own youth clubs. There are various national voluntary youth organizations which receive grants from the Department of Education and Science. There are about 3,000 full-time youth leaders on the Department's register. In addition there are many thousands of part-time paid and unpaid workers.

A *Further Education Information Service* is provided each summer by the local education authorities in cooperation with the polytechnics and other colleges offering full-time degree and higher national diploma courses, and the Department of Education and Science. Its purpose is to provide up-to-date information and advice about full-time degree, H.N.D. and Dip.H.E. courses in the colleges for those who find themselves, late in the summer, without a place on a course. A list of local advisory officers is available from the D.E.S.

SCOTLAND

The educational system of Scotland has developed independently of that of England and has a number of distinctive features. The general supervision of the national system of education, except for the universities, is the responsibility of the Secretary of State for Scotland acting through the Scottish Education Department. The duty of providing education locally rests with the nine regional councils and three island councils. Educational facilities of various kinds are also provided by the governing bodies of grant-aided schools, independent schools, " central institutions ", and national voluntary organizations in the field of informal further education.

Schools in Scotland fall into three main categories, viz. *education authority schools* which are managed by education authorities and financed partly from local rates and partly from rate support grant: *grant-aided schools*, conducted by voluntary managers who receive grants direct from the department; and *independent schools* which receive no direct grant, but which are subject to inspection and registration.

As at January 1974 there were 3,541 education authority and grant-aided schools and departments of which 301 were nursery, 2,524 primary, 478 secondary and 174 special, together with 64 occupational centres catering for the most severely mentally handicapped. There were also 105 registered independent schools. The total number of pupils in education authority and grant-aided schools and departments (including special) was 1,060,439 (541,807 boys, 518,632 girls) of which 19,832 (10,152 boys, 9,680 girls) received nursery education.

Schooling normally starts at the age of 5, and the primary school course lasts for 7 years. Primary schools usually take both boys and girls. Pupils transfer from the primary course to secondary courses about the age of 12.

Over 98 per cent of secondary pupils in education authority schools attend schools with a comprehensive intake to the first year. The majority of these schools provide a full range of courses appropriate to all levels of ability from first to sixth year, although a decreasing number offer only 2- and 4-year courses, on completion of which children may continue their secondary education at the nearest 6-year comprehensive. There are also a few schools which are selective in that they admit only the less able pupils and which offer only non-certificate courses or courses leading to the Ordinary grade in the Scottish Certificate of Education examinations. Pupils from these schools wishing to continue their education to the Higher grade of the S.C.E. may also transfer to the fifth and sixth year local comprehensive.

The Scottish Certificate of Education examination is conducted by the S.C.E. Examination Board. Pupils may attempt as many of a wide range of subjects as they are capable of, on either the Ordinary grade which corresponds to the Ordinary level of the General Certificate of Education, or on the Higher grade which is normally taken a year earlier than the G.C.E. Advanced level and is therefore not of so high a standard. The Board grants a Certificate of Sixth Year Studies designed to give direction and purpose to sixth-year work by encouraging pupils who have completed their main subjects at Higher grade to study a particular subject in depth.

Further Education.—Facilities for further education are provided by 14 Central Institutions (grant-aided colleges administered by independent Boards of Governors) and by 69 further education day centres managed by education authorities. The Central Institutions provide mainly advanced courses in science and technology, commerce, art, music, domestic science, and other subjects, leading to their own diplomas, to professional qualifications or, in certain cases, to C.N.A.A. degrees.

The further education centres normally provide less advanced courses which are mainly part-time covering vocational and non-vocational subjects, but a few offer courses of degree level. Courses are offered in a wide variety of subjects but to make the most economic use of resources, provision of certain courses is made on a regional or even a national basis.

Teachers.—All teachers in permanent posts in public or grant-aided schools in Scotland are required to be registered with the General Teaching Council for Scotland (which is independent of the Scottish Education Department) and normally to hold a teaching qualification awarded by a Scottish college of education. There are ten of these colleges, seven of which provide both one- and three-year courses leading to a Teaching Qualification (Primary Education) or a Teaching Qualification (Secondary Education). Of the remaining three colleges, one is a residential college of physical education for women and the other two provide only courses leading to a Teaching Qualification (Primary Education). Nine of the colleges, in conjunction with local universities or the Council for National Academic Awards, also provide four-year combined courses leading to the degree of B.Ed.

The basic scales of teachers' salaries are for primary and secondary levels, with additional payments for qualifications and for posts of special responsibility.

NORTHERN IRELAND

The statutory system of education in Northern Ireland is broadly comparable to that in Great Britain. Under the 1947 Act (and later amendments) primary education is provided for children up to about 11½ years of age when they are transferred to secondary school. The main types of secondary school are: grammar and secondary (intermediate). Selection for secondary education is based on verbal reasoning tests at eleven-plus combined with teachers' assessments of performance in school subjects. Fees are charged at grammar schools but qualified pupils there receive scholarships from their local education authority.

In January 1975 there were 26 nursery schools with 1,192 pupils and 39 full-time teachers; 1,123 primary schools with 212,510 pupils and 7,908 full-time teachers; 261 secondary schools with 154,322 pupils and 8,683 full-time teachers; 27 special schools with 2,349 pupils and 239 full-time teachers. In 1974–75, 36,902 students were enrolled in institutions of further education; of these 4,390 were taking advanced courses, 12,190 were full-time, 11,765 were on day-release, 739 were on block release, and 12,208 were other part-time. The training of teachers is carried out in 5 colleges, and in the department of education of the Queen's University of Belfast and the education centre of the New University of Ulster.

Expenditure from public funds on education in Northern Ireland during 1973–74 was £121,231,000.

UNIVERSITIES

There are 44 universities in the United Kingdom (*see* pp. 501–10). Of these, 33 are in England, eight in Scotland, two in Northern Ireland and one (a federal institution) in Wales. In addition, there is the " *Open University* " which provides courses leading to degrees by a combination of television, radio, correspondence, tutorials, short residential courses and local audio-visual centres. The Open University offers undergraduate (no qualifications needed for entry), post-experience and post-graduate courses. It is grant-aided directly by the Department of Education and Science and does not come within the University Grants Committee system. More than 5,000 students graduate each year from the Open University.

A University College at Buckingham, the nucleus of an Independent University, admitted its first students in February 1976; it provides a two-year course leading to a Licence and its tuition fees were £1,500 for its first year (which consisted of 4 terms of 10 weeks each).

In December 1973 there were 251,226 full-time students enrolled at universities in the United Kingdom; of these, 80,396 were women and 24,880 from overseas. For postgraduate students. The number of new undergraduate entrants (full-time) in 1972–73 was 68,998; the corresponding figures for 1958–59 and 1965–66 were 29,054 and 52,446. The full-time total of 251,226 in 1973–74 compares with just over 50,000 in 1938–39. In 1971–72, 52,477 first degrees (including

honours degrees) and 13,085 higher degrees were awarded by universities. In 1973–74 there were 37,069 full-time teaching and research staff in U.K. universities; 3,944 of them were professors, 7,408 readers or senior lecturers, 23,549 lecturers or assistant lecturers.

By October 1975 the full-time student population had risen to about 263,200.

In 1975 the new Universities' Superannuation Scheme (U.S.S.) was introduced. It provides for retirement benefits based on terminal salary.

Students applying for admission to a first degree course at a university do so through the Universities Central Council on Admissions (U.C.C.A.) which was set up by the universities in 1961 on the initiative of the Committee of Vice-Chancellors and Principals. All universities participate fully in the U.C.C.A. Scheme except certain Scottish universities. The U.C.C.A. office is in Cheltenham.

The requirements for entry to first degree courses may vary somewhat from one university to another but the universities publish co-operatively an annual Compendium which describes these requirements in detail.

Students who are normally resident in Britain, have certain minimum qualifications and have been admitted to a university in the United Kingdom are entitled to an award from public funds; the amount varies according to the financial circumstances of the students and their parents. Tuition fees for first degree courses in 1977–78 will be £650.

In 1973–74 the total income of universities in the U.K. was £598,606,000 of which £468,337,000 was recurrent income. The largest items of recurrent income were £349,734,000 of recurrent exchequer grant, £52,626,000 of research grants and £23,437,000 of fees income. Payments for buildings and other non-recurrent grant were £51,536,000 and the furniture and equipment grant was £38,926,000.

The University Grants Committee advises the Secretary of State for Education and Science on university matters. Most of its members are academics or businessmen.

Although the universities have freedom in academic matters, the Government, through the U.G.C., determines the total size of the university student population, strongly influences its distribution between arts, science, medicine, etc., and determines the part which the university sector plays in the whole higher education system.

The Comptroller and Auditor General has access to the books and records of the U.G.C. and of the universities.

SCHOOLS COUNCIL FOR CURRICULUM AND EXAMINATIONS
160 Great Portland Street, W.1

Established in 1964, the Schools Council is an independent body representing all sections of the education service in England and Wales—with a majority of teacher members on its main committees. It undertakes research and development in the curriculum and keeps under review teaching methods and examinations in schools, including aspects of school organization in so far as they affect the curriculum.

The Schools Council is jointly financed by the Department of Education and Science and local education authorities.

Chairman, Sir Alex Smith.

Joint Secretaries, V. H. Stevens; J. G. Raitt; P. M. Dines.

THE STOCK EXCHANGE IN THE UNITED KINGDOM AND IRELAND

THE STOCK EXCHANGE

Broker Members of the Stock Exchange buy and sell shares for members of the public. This is done for individual investors, for their advisers such as bank managers, solicitors and accountants, and for investing institutions like insurance companies, pension funds, unit trusts and merchant banks. For this the stockbroker is paid a fixed scale of commission based on the value of the securities. In addition to this service, brokers advise their clients, according to their particular circumstances and needs, on how to invest their money to greatest advantage. In addition, they will undertake to review periodically the portfolios of their clients.

The Stock Exchange provides facilities for raising capital for industry. Any Broker will give advice on how a company can finance its growth by getting a listing. For companies already listed, other methods are possible—such as rights issues and debenture or loan stocks—for obtaining additional funds. Brokers' advice is also available to industrialists on matters such as mergers and acquisitions.

All listed British companies are incorporated under the Companies' Acts, which contain stringent regulations for their management and control. They are limited liability companies, which means that if you are a shareholder in such a company you cannot be called upon to pay any part of its debt or liabilities if it gets into difficulties, unless, in quite exceptional cases, you are a holder of partly-paid shares, in which event your liability is limited to the amount required to make the shares fully paid. The Stock Exchange serves investors, whether inexperienced or expert, big or small, and the authorities of the Stock Exchange insist on compliance with stringent regulations to ensure that the public are fully informed of the constitution and record of every company whose securities are admitted to the market.

In London the foundation stone of the building was laid in 1801, but the building was almost entirely reconstructed in 1854 from the designs of Thomas Allason. The Stock Exchange has now been rebuilt as a large tower block, 321 feet high with a new Trading Floor to the west of the block.

There are other Trading Floors in Liverpool, Manchester, Birmingham, Glasgow, Belfast and Dublin.

The Stock Exchange provides a market for the purchase and sale of about 9,000 securities valued at over £250,000,000,000, and also securities listed on overseas Exchanges. At present, the Members of the Stock Exchange, consisting of Brokers (agents for clients) and jobbers (dealers as principals in specific securities), number about 4,100. Visitor's Gallery in London is open between 10 a.m. and 3.15 p.m. from Monday to Friday. Admission free and without ticket. Film show.

The Stock Exchange
Chairman, N. P. Goodison; *Deputy Chairmen*, J. W. Robertson; F. T. Powell, M.B.E.; G. R. Simpson, D.S.O., T.D.; *Chief Exec.*, R. Fell, C.B.E.

Administrative Units

The Stock Exchange, London, E.C.2; the Stock Exchange, Margaret Street, Birmingham; the Stock Exchange, Norfolk Street, Manchester; the Stock Exchange, 69 St. George's Place, Glasgow; the Stock Exchange, 28 Anglesea Street, Dublin 2; the Stock Exchange, Northern Bank House, 10 High Street, Belfast; the Stock Exchange, Melrose House, 3 St. Sampson's Square, York.

THE NOBEL PRIZES

The Nobel Prizes are awarded each year from the income of a trust fund established by the Swedish scientist Alfred Nobel, the inventor of dynamite, who died on December 10, 1896, leaving a fortune of £1,750,000. They are awarded to those who have contributed most to the common good in the domain of (*a*) Physics; (*b*) Chemistry; (*c*) Physiology or Medicine; (*d*) Literature; (*e*) Peace. The first awards were made in 1901 on the fifth anniversary of Nobel's death. The awarding authorities are the Swedish Academy of Sciences: (*a*) Physics—(*b*) Chemistry; the Royal Caroline Institute, Stockholm—(*c*) Physiology or Medicine; the Swedish Academy—(*d*) Literature; a committee of five persons elected by the Norwegian Storting—(*e*) Peace. The Trust is administered by the Board of Directors of the Nobel Foundation, Stockholm. The Board consists of five members and three deputy members. The Swedish Government appoints a chairman and a deputy chairman, the remaining members being appointed by the awarding authorities.

The nationality of prizewinners is indicated as follows: (a) Great Britain; (b) U.S.A.; (c) France; (d) Sweden; (e) Belgium; (f) U.S.S.R.; (g) Germany; (h) Netherlands; (i) Switzerland; (k) Denmark; (l) Norway; (m) Spain; (n) Poland; (o) Austria; (p) Italy; (q) India; (r) Hungary; (s) Finland; (t) Canada; (u) Chile; (v) Argentina; (w) Japan; (x) Portugal; (y) Irish Free State; (z) Republic of Ireland; (aa) South Africa; (bb) Iceland; (cc) China; (dd) Czechoslovakia; (ee) Australia; (ff) Yugoslavia; (gg) Greece; (hh) Israel; (ii) Guatemala. The distribution by nationalities is shown at foot of table.

For prize winners for the years 1901-1964, *see* earlier editions of WHITAKER'S ALMANACK.

Year	(a) PHYSICS	(b) CHEMISTRY	(c) PHYSIOLOGY OR MEDICINE	(d) LITERATURE	(e) PEACE
1965	S. I. Tomonaga (w) J. Schwinger (b) R. P. Feynman (b)	R. B. Woodward (b)	A. Lwoff (c) F. Jacob (c) J. Monod (c)	M. Sjolochov (f)	U.N. Children's Fund
1966	A. Kastler (c)	R. S. Mulliken (b)	P. Rous (b) C. B. Huggins (b)	S. Y. Agnon (hh) N. Sachs (g)	*No award*
1967	Prof. H. A. Bethe (b)	Prof. M. Eigen (g) Prof. G. Porter (a) Prof. R. Norrish (a)	Prof. R. Granit (d) Prof. H. K. Hartline (b) Prof. G. Wald (b)	M. A. Asturias (ii)	*No award*
1968	Prof. L. W. Alvarez (b)	Prof. L. Onsager (b)	R. W. Holley (b) H. G. Khorana (b) M. W. Nirenberg (b)	Y. Kawabata (w)	R. Cassin (c)
1969	M. Gell-Mann (b)	D. H. Barton (a) O. Hassel (l)	M. Delbrück (b) A. D. Hershey (b) S. E. Luria (b)	S. Beckett (z)	International Labour Organization
1970	H. Alfven (d) L. Néel (c)	L. F. Leloir (v)	Sir Bernard Katz (a) U. von Euler (d) J. Axelrod (b)	A. Solzhenitsyn (f)	N. E. Boriaug (b)
1971	Prof. D. Gabor (a)	G. Herzberg (t)	E. W. Sutherland (b)	P. Neruda (u)	W. Brandt (g)
1972	J. Bardeen (b) L. N. Cooper (b) J. R. Schrieffer (b)	C. H. Anfinsen (b) S. Moore (b) W. H. Stein (b)	G. R. Porter (a) G. M. Edelman (b)	H. Böll (g)	*No award*
1973	B. D. Josephson (a) L. Esaki (w) I. Giaever (b)	G. Wilkinson (a) E. O. Fischer (g)	K. Lorenz (o) N. Tinbergen (h) K. von Frisch (o)	P. V. M. White (ee)	H. A. Kissinger (b)
1974	Sir Martin Ryle (a) A. Hewish (a)	P. J. Flory (b)	A. Claude (b) C. de Duve (e) G. E. Palade (e)	E. Johnson (d) H. Martinson (d)	S. McBride (z) E. Sato (w)
1975	Prof. J. Rainwater (b) Prof. A. Bohr (k) Prof. B. Mottelson (k)	Prof. J. W. Cornfort (ee) Prof. V. Prelog (i)	Prof. D. Baltimore (b) Prof. R. Dulbecco (b) Prof. H. M. Temin (b)	E. Montale (p)	Dr. A. S. Sakharov (f)

The awards have been distributed as follows: PHYSICS (104).—*U.S.A.* 33; *Gt. Britain*, 19; *Germany*, 14; *France*, 9; *U.S.S.R.* 6; *Netherlands*, 5; *Austria*, 3; *Denmark*, 3; *Japan*, 3; *Sweden*, 3; *China*, 2; *Italy*, 2; *India*, 1; *Ireland*, 1.

CHEMISTRY (88).—*Germany*, 23; *U.S.A.*, 20; *Gt. Britain* 19; *France*, 6; *Sweden*, 4; *Switzerland*, 4; *Netherlands*, 2; *Australia* 1; *Austria*, 1; *Czechoslovakia*, 1; *Finland*, 1; *Hungary*, 1; *Italy* ,1; *Norway*, 1; *U.S.S.R.*, 1; *Argentina*, 1; *Canada*, 1.

PHYSIOLOGY OR MEDICINE (116).—*U.S.A.*, 45; *Gt. Britain*, 17; *Germany*, 10; *France*, 6; *Austria*, 5; *Belgium*, 4; *Denmark*, 4; *Sweden*, 4; *Switzerland*, 4; *Netherlands*, 3; *Australia*, 2; *Canada*, 2; *Hungary*, 2; *Italy*, 2; *U.S.S.R.*, 2; *Argentina*, 1; *Portugal*, 1; *South Africa*, 1; *Spain*, 1.

LITERATURE (72).—*France*, 11; *Germany*, 7; *Gt. Britain*, 6; *Sweden*, 6; *U.S.A.*, 6; *Italy*, 5; *U.S.S.R.*, 4; *Denmark*, 3; *Norway*, 3; *Spain*, 3; *Chile*, 2; *Ireland*, 2; *Poland*, 2; *Switzerland*, 2; *Australia*, 1; *Belgium*, 1; *Finland*, 1; *Greece*, 1; *Guatemala*, 1; *Iceland*, 1; *India*,1; *Israel*, 1; *Japan*, 1; *Yugoslavia*, 1.

PEACE (69).—*U.S.A.*, 16; *Institutions*, 10; *France*, 9; *Gt. Britain*, 7; *Germany*, 4; *Sweden*, 4; *Belgium*, 3; *Switzerland*, 3; *Austria*, 2; *Norway*, 2; *Argentina*, 1; *Canada*, 1; *Denmark*, 1; *Ireland*, 1; *Italy*, 1; *Japan*, 1; *Netherlands*, 1; *South Africa*, 1; *U.S.S.R.*, 1.

In 1969 a Nobel Prize for Economic Sciences was instituted. Prize-winners have been: 1969, J. Tintergen (h) and R. Frisch (1); 1970, P. A. Samuelson (b); 1971, S. Kuznets (b); 1972, Sir John Hicks (a) and K. J. Arrow (b); 1973, W. Leontief (b); 1974, F. von Hayek (1) and G. Myrdal (d); 1975, Prof. L. V. Kantorovich (f) and Prof. T. C. Koopmans (b).

BRITISH ARCHITECTURE OF 1975–76

EDDINGTON STREET CHILDREN'S DAY CENTRE, LONDON, N.4

The site for the children's day centre lies behind a group of shops on the south side of Tollington Park. Originally it was intended that the single storey building, within an open space, should be built as part of a new housing scheme, but the council subsequently decided to rehabilitate the existing properties.

The architects' brief required a 60 place nursery to Department of Health and Social Security standards with six group rooms for eight or nine children and two babies rooms for five children each; with adjacent lavatories and lockers, laundry room and kitchen.

The day centre is located near the northern corner of the site to provide a maximum open area to be seen from the group rooms. These group rooms are ranged along the southern and eastern side of the plan with staff rooms and a kitchen to the north. The babies rooms are separated from the other group rooms by the main entrance, to reduce the chance of disturbance by the older children. The walled garden area for the babies is separated for the same reason. Parents arriving with their prams reach the shelter of the roof canopy and can either take their pram to the store and then directly in to the babies room, or in through the main entrance to see the matron. The flooring in the central lavatory/nursing area is of washable vinyl tiles, whereas the play area is carpeted.

The group rooms are arranged in pairs with integral coat hanging and lavatory area, bed and toy stores. A sliding door links the paired rooms to ease supervision and to provide one large room when required. These doors have been introduced to reduce the risk of accidents and to make maximum use of the space available. Children therefore have direct access to a sheltered outside play area while being supervised by their own nursery nurse. The door to the coat hanging area has been glazed to allow the children a sight of their coats, providing security by suggesting to them that they will be collected at the end of the day. The children have an after lunch sleep in their group rooms on camp beds which are kept in the adjoining store.

The outdoor play area has been subdivided by shrubs and trees to allow different activities to take place simultaneously, without fear of disturbance to one another. Instead of the various parts of the building being linked on a corridor system, a central play area has been created. This is the focal point where parents, children and staff meet.

To overcome the disadvantage of the northern location of the staff accommodation, high level windows pierce the partition to the central play area and allow sunlight into the matron's and staff rooms, cloakroom, laundry and kitchen. In addition, the matron's and staff rooms have windows opening on to the courtyard garden. The kitchen in the northern corner of the layout has direct access from the service area and parking space. It is equipped for the preparation of all meals, including a special milk preparation area for the babies. The children eat their meals in the group rooms.

It is rarely easy to achieve satisfactory massing for a single storey building but in this instance the pitched roof, deeply overhanging eaves and large areas of glazing have given the centre a clear form and a strong identity. Window sills are low to be at a suitable height for the children to see out. The underside of the roof is stained bright red and the rafters and ties dark brown; with the clerestory lights above the external walls the roof takes on the character of an all-enveloping tent.

There can be little doubt that the building is most successful. It is clearly enjoyed by the children, who find it a resource which they can explore and use with pleasure, and is equally appreciated by the staff, who can develop their relationships with the children in congenial surroundings. The building is highly practical, and the strong visual stimulus that it provides seems valuable for the children and staff. The detailing is robust, straightforward and entirely in keeping with the character of a building which will clearly be required to take on much of the imprint of personality of those who use it.

The jury who awarded the 1976 Royal Institute of British Architects Award for the London Area to the architects of the day centre, Darbourne and Darke, was most impressed with this small scheme, on the design of which, much thought, care and skill had been exercised. They state in their report that, " It had clearly been designed for its principal users, the children, and the architects had succeeded in producing a building which not only satisfied the needs of the adult supervisors but was giving much pleasure to the young children.... With an economy of means they had produced a building which should improve with age rather than deteriorate."

HOUSING, POTTERNEWTON GARDENS, LEEDS

This housing development stands on a site in North Leeds formerly occupied by a disused laundry and some old back to back houses. The site is surrounded on four sides by existing roads and is situated in the centre of a densely populated urban area consisting of two and three storey domestic property of all types and ages.

The site was planned with the objectives of providing a high density development with low rise house types, using low occupancy dwellings to redress the balance in the area, and using new designs of patio type dwellings produced by Yorkshire Development Group as additions to their existing range of houses. The scheme retains the surrounding existing streets for vehicular access, but pedestrian areas have been created in the centre of the development with seats in sheltered positions where people can meet and talk. The character of these areas is clean and severe with hard surfaces of smooth buff brick and concrete paving slabs relieved at carefully selected points with restrained planting using low shrubs, creepers and the occasional specimen tree.

Integral with the plan of each dwelling is an outdoor space which is sited and screened to give a small private garden where young children can play in safety and the occupants can sit in complete seclusion. Some rooms in each dwelling have been designed to overlook this outdoor space, thus ensuring privacy for these rooms and effectively preventing a feeling of overcrowding and being overlooked on this densely developed site.

All dwellings are of traditional construction with smooth buff brick walls, timber window frames and a pitched roof covered with concrete slates. The heating is by low pressure hot water radiators supplied by gas boilers. The twenty-eight dwellings include five bungalows, four ground floor flats, four first floor flats and fifteen houses.

The scheme was designed by the Director of Architecture and Landscape, Leeds City Council. The development was given the 1976 Architecture Award for the Yorkshire Region. " The careful solution to the problem of infill housing, with three dimensional effect of hanging gardens, walled

patios, hard landscaping with accent planting " the judges stated, added up " to a considerable achievement." It was felt that the scheme demonstrated a " socially and environmentally acceptable development which answers the adverse criticism of the high-rise residential buildings."

CIGARETTE FACTORY, BRISTOL

This industrial complex consists of two main buildings, an office building and a low spreading factory. The buildings stand on a prominent undulating 56 acre site south of the city centre, adjacent to a bypass, which provides the principal access. There are hills in the distance and the surroundings are built up with suburban housing. As the impact of the project on the adjoining residential community would be considerable, landscaping assumed exceptional significance. The architects' response has been to exploit the character of the site by damming a small stream to form a lake, providing the main entrance *via* an underpass and planting over one thousand semi-mature trees.

The plan of the factory clearly indicates the manufacturing process being carried out. Tobacco is delivered into a bonded store from where it is taken into the " Primary " area for preparation and blending. From here the tobacco is transferred to stores which are provided with exact environmental conditions controlled by computer. The next stage in the production is the " Secondary " process, which involves the making and packing of up to 2,500 cigarettes per minute, giving a total output of 380-400 million cigarettes per week. The final stage is the transfer of cigarettes into the warehouse ready for dispatch.

The concept of the factory to house this process is a single level manufacturing floor. The central area is occupied by the " Secondary " operation in a " great " production room uninterrupted by columns. It is marked externally by nine large " Warren " trusses of bridge-building scale. The " Primary " area is on one side of this vast room and the warehouse is on the other, both separated from it by two storey high spines containing offices, lavatories, tea bays and other ancillary accommodation. The tobacco stores are in the basement between the two main production areas. The basement also contains services which supply the machines above. A power house containing four gas-fired boilers is located to the north west of the factory building.

The clients' head offices are sited to the south west and linked to the factory by a subway. The office building sitting astride the artificial lake is made up of an " L " shaped podium of two storeys containing a restaurant, with a five storey tower block rising above it.

The factory building is basically a single storey steel structure sitting on a concrete podium which contains the basement service zone, tobacco stores and car parking. Externally all the steelwork is in " Cor-ten " steel which undergoes limited oxidizing process during its first two or three years, i.e., rusting, giving it a deep red-brown colour. Infill panels between stanchions are in " earth " colour ribbed metal sheeting. The office tower is finished in a similar manner with exposed steelwork and infilled with bronze tinted glazing, the podium being clad in precast concrete panels.

The interiors of the office block are simply treated, with brown-beige carpet and near white walls. Colour is provided by the furnishings and art work. The theme is followed through in the factory area with beige painted walls and light beige floor tiles.

The building is considered by many to be the most ambitious " Cor-ten " building in England.

The Chicago architects Skidmore, Owings and Merrill, in conjunction with the London architects Yorke, Rosenberg, Mardell, have developed a cool, underplayed architecture based on a clear structure and on careful detailing which won them the 1976 RIBA Award for the South West Region.

CEFNDY HOSTEL, RHYL, WALES

This scheme which won the 1976 Royal Institute of British Architects Award for Wales provides residential accommodation for 24 mentally handicapped adults. The buildings house three home units accommodating eight people in each on both a permanent and semi-permanent basis. The lounge and recreation rooms are shared with a central kitchen serving the living/dining rooms with accommodation included for resident staff.

The design philosophy was to create a domestic and non-institutional character with small scale units using familiar domestic materials. The design of the workshop closely follows that of the Home. Honey coloured facing brickwork and brown concrete tile roofs, with low eaves lines and exposed stained timber, have been used, with traditional constructional methods. Earth moulding and generous shrub and tree planting have been employed about the building to develop the domestic idiom, and to serve as foils to the man-made form.

The Hostel, which was designed by the Bowen, Dann, Davies Partnership in association with the Clwyd County Architect was praised by the RIBA jury: " using a traditional vocabulary of brown brickwork and single pitch tiled roofs together with stained timber creates an environment of great unity.... On a site otherwise featureless the imaginative landscaping, both soft and hard, combines to make this an outstanding scheme."

HOUSING, PERSHORE, WORCESTERSHIRE

Architectural romanticism is not at all what it was thought to be at the beginning of the Modern Movement. It is not a casual, inappropriate taste lightly worn, but is to be thought of as a serious return to an older wisdom which the march of modern life has inadvertently trampled underfoot. Behind its charming and whimsical form is an iron will powered by a strong and perceptive intellect.

The rustic idyll at Pershore, which won for the architects, Darbourne and Darke, a 1976 RIBA Award, is a fine example of modern romanticism.

The redevelopment area of about 6·22 acres is near the historic centre of the town, and is to provide housing (70 per cent. family dwellings) with provision for both local Authority and private sale. 150 per cent. car spaces per dwelling were required along with a high degree of safety for pedestrians.

It was decided that the existing character of the town should be retained, deriving architectural scale and materials for the new buildings from the old. Dwellings were designed to allow the maximum possible flexibility of use, from a basic plan providing a good sized second living room in addition to a kitchen which can act as a dining room. There are also two person dwellings suitable for older people, which retain as far as possible a " house " quality with a small garden. There is an unusual variety of house and flat types and the architects have eschewed the more usual (and easy) practice of lumping like with like—the elderly together, the flats together—and have jumbled them up. This has the advantage of giving the semblance of a " real " piece of town: a locality which has grown over a period as a result of diverse pressures, not one which has been dumped down all at one time.

The jury of the RIBA found " the development delightful, full of character and appropriate."

" The layout is sensitive, the retention of mature trees and the varying roof line, the type of railings, footpath and road surfaces all contribute to achieving a specific atmosphere of homeliness. The architects have shown great skill in relating the character of the new development to that of Pershore. There is consistency of character, materials and detailing and the whole should mature gracefully."

WINE AND SPIRIT STORE, BURY ST. EDMUNDS

The architects' brief was to design a building of approximately 4,000 square metres to house a centralized storage and distribution unit for wines and spirits, close to the clients' main offices and brewery in Bury St. Edmunds. The warehouse was to replace a number of existing cellars dispersed about East Anglia.

The site selected was a southward facing slope of disused allotments adjoining the clients' main offices. The clients' need for possible future expansion and the local river authority's requirement that no part of the building should be within the 1968 flood plane restricted the building to the north east corner of the site. This siting necessitated considerable earth moving and the construction of retaining walls. To minimize the effect which such a large building would have on adjacent housing and the backcloth of traditional buildings, the lowest possible ground floor level was chosen, an extensive perimeter planting scheme was incorporated and a muted colour scheme of dark brown cladding and framing adopted.

The structure for the building comprises an exposed steel frame of columns and beams with exposed diagonal tubular steel braces supporting a felt covered metal deck roof. The building is clad between the columns with a double skin of profiled sheet steel, P.V.C. coated externally and galvanized internally, with a central layer of fibreglass insulation. A matching P.V.C. coated curtain walling system is used for the associated offices. Heating and ventilation are by means of high level oil-fired heaters and fresh air intakes with localized roof extractors. With the exception of the office area it is artificially lit throughout by means of fluorescent light fittings. Fire protection is provided by smoke vents and fire compartment doors activated by gas and heat detectors.

The building, which was designed by Lyster, Grillet and Harding, was given a Structural Steel Design Award. The judge commented: " large warehouses on backland sites are often crude eyesores. This building is outstanding with sophisticated and simple steelwork. Its excellent proportions and subtle colouring reduce its apparent bulk and enhance its setting."

AGNEW HOUSE, CAMBRIDGE

Agnew House is the first stage in the up-grading and extension of the Evelyn Nursing Home, Cambridge. The new building is a hostel for nurses which replaces a converted Victorian house.

The Home is situated off the Trumpington Road within a mile of the city centre of Cambridge and stands in delightful gardens, which most of the patients' rooms overlook. The building consists of twelve bedsitting rooms and two single bedroom, two persons flats providing accommodation for sixteen nurses. In addition there are four kitchenettes, four bathrooms and a utility room. A communal lounge is provided within the main home. The building was required to be separate from the Home and to have if possible its own

garden. This latter requirement has been only partially solved in order to gain good orientation.

The new hostel is faced externally with brick colour washed white and roofed with "Eternit" asbestos slates. Recessed dormer windows and screens are set in the roof with slatted duckboard balconies in front. Purpose made timber, horizontal sliding and top hung windows perforate the building. Internally the building is finished with painted blockwork, plastered ceilings and carpeted floors. The entrance hall is floored with quarry tiles. The building is heated by a gas fired low pressure hot water boiler serving various radiators and convector heaters.

Agnew House won the Royal Institute of British Architects' 1976 annual award for the best new building in the Eastern Region. The RIBA jury reported that " this is an excellent and very human building, displaying a fresh and relevant approach to the use of traditional materials. Money has been spent in the right places and the building has a refreshing quality and clarity which make it not only a cheerful place in which to live, but one that will survive a lot of knocks and changes. Particularly successful are the sitting-out spaces at first floor level, the bright clerestory-lit corridors and the use of colour and natural lighting." The Hostel was designed by the local architectural practice, Cambridge Design Group.

ICI PETROCHEMICALS DIVISION HEADQUARTERS, WILTON

The building is designed to accommodate the headquarters and research department of the Petrochemicals Division of I.C.I. Located directly opposite the main production site at Wilton, it provides offices, laboratories and drawing offices with catering and other facilities for 1,200 people.

The buildings, which use red rustic bricks externally with stained cedar windows, are generally three storeys, with an additional storey where the ground falls. Designed to be flexible, the complex can be extended by adding further wings creating more courtyards.

The entire building complex, from the main approach on the west, forms a broad background to the natural shape of the newly-formed lake and contoured landscaping. In contrast, within the main building, the formal courtyards contain soft landscaping. Enclosed on all sides and visible from the interior of the building, the courtyards provide a constant source of interest as well as linking the various parts of the building through a series of pathways passing under the wings at the lower ground floor level.

The architects, Building Design Partnership, received one of the Royal Institute of British Architects coveted awards for this scheme. The jury considered it to be " a building excellent of its type, making full use of a fine site."

THE OLD GAOL, ABINGDON

The conversion of a gaol into a community centre for public use is in itself an unusual task to undertake but to commission the Project Office of the Royal College of Art in London added a further ingredient to make this project an interesting and novel one.

In 1804 the Town Clerk of Abingdon put his name to plans for a new "House of Correction" to be built on the site of White Hart Inn where the London Road crosses the Thames". During the following eight years 3,000 tons of stone were made into what is still one of the largest buildings in Abingdon. The gaol was one of the first to be built under the Prison Reform Act of 1771, which decreed that all

prison cells should be built above ground level and close to a running stream or river for sanitation.

Abingdon Gaol was to be an object of civic pride putting the town one step ahead of its old rival Reading. The new building was not only a gaol but also a court and lodgings for the travelling judges. The architect who prepared the earliest drawings (possibly Wyatville, who later rebuilt Windsor Castle for George IV) followed the most up to date examples. Three wings containing single stone vaulted cells radiated from a central octagonal block. The gaol served for roughly 50 years until 1861 when Reading became the centre of local government and the new Reading Gaol took over. The building passed into private hands. A range of meagre tenements was crammed into one wing and the rest became a cornmill.

In recent years a growing number of local residents came to recognize the qualities of the Old Gaol and in particular its position facing south over the Thames close to the heart of Abingdon. In 1971 Abingdon Council approached the Royal College of Art and subsequently schemes to develop the Old Gaol for the community were prepared by ten students.

The schemes which they suggested were put to the local community by means of a questionnaire for discussion. Once a scheme had been selected the same group of students worked on the drawings and supervised the site with the help of the staff of the College.

The building provides a sports hall with four badminton courts, swimming pool, combat room for fencing and judo, cinema/lecture/recital hall, viewing galleries to the sports room including a bar, special exhibition room, four teaching rooms, two rehearsal rooms and supporting changing rooms, cloakrooms, offices, kitchen and an administrative wing. Most of the accommodation has been housed in the existing building, two new extensions being added to contain the swimming pool and sports hall.

The existing Old Gaol is a listed building. New extensions were planned so that they did not obscure the river views of and from the old building nor dominate its rich and forbidding character. Stone which was saved from the demolition work on the original boundary wall was used in the external walls and flooring of the new buildings.

The scheme overcomes a number of structural difficulties. The entire interior of the existing building was demolished and the foundations and external walls were strengthened before the construction of new floors.

The original builders of the gaol built with an eye to economy and durability. They used common materials very simply but with generosity and good sense. This example has been followed, using a wider vocabulary of materials, such as steel, glass, concrete, timber and stone.

The Old Gaol, Abingdon, was the only rehabilitation project to win an RIBA Award in 1976. The jury commenting that " the Architects had successfully used a significant old building which was strongly linked to the social and historical centre of the town."

THE ARCTIC OCEAN

The Arctic Ocean consists of a deep sea over 2,000 fathoms, on the southern margin of which there is a broad continental shelf with numerous islands. Into this deeper sea there is only one broad channel, about 700 miles, between Greenland and Scandinavia. Behring Strait is only 49 miles wide and 27 fathoms deep. The southern boundary of the Arctic Ocean is the Wyville-Thomson and Faeroe-Icelandic submarine ridge, which separates the North Atlantic from the Norwegian and Greenland Seas. The Norwegian Deep lies between Norway and Jan Mayan and Iceland; it exceeds 1,500 fathoms. The Greenland Deep, of similar depth, lies between Spitsbergen and Greenland. These two depressions are separated by a somewhat deeply submerged ridge from the east of Jan Mayen to Bear Island, south of Spitsbergen. A shallow ridge from the north-west of Spitsbergen to Greenland separates the Greenland Sea from the deep North Polar, Basin. This extends from the north of Spitsbergen and Franz Josef Land to the north of the New Siberia Islands and of the North American Arctic Archipelago. Another more shallow depression is Baffin Bay, less than 1,000 fathoms. This is separated from the North Atlantic by a submarine ridge. Barent's Sea, between Spitsbergen, Norway and Novaya Zemlya, and the Kara Sea, between Novaya Zemlya and the Siberian coast, are respectively below 200 and 100 fathoms. The total area of the Arctic Sea is about 5·5 million square miles, of which 2·3 million square miles are probably covered with floating ice.

THE COST OF LIVING

The first cost-of-living index to be calculated in Great Britain was the one which took July, 1914, as 100 and was based on the pattern of expenditure of working class families in 1904. Since 1947 the Index of Retail Prices has superseded the cost-of-living index, although the older term is still often popularly applied to it. This index is designed to reflect the month-by-month changes in the average level of retail prices of goods and services purchased by the "majority" of households in the United Kingdom, including practically all wage-earners and most small and medium salary-earners. For spending coming within the scope of the index, a representative list of items is selected and the prices actually charged for these items are collected at regular intervals. In working out the index figure, the price changes are "weighted"—that is, given different degrees of importance—in accordance with the pattern of consumption of the average family.

A more widely used guide when considering changes in the average level of prices of all consumer goods and services, particularly over a number of years, is the consumer price index, now renamed the consumers' expenditure deflator. This index, which has been calculated back to 1938, covers the expenditure of all consumers as defined for national income purposes, and compares the price of goods and services actually purchased in a given year with the prices of the same goods and services in a base year.

During 1973 the Central Statistical Office constructed an annual index of prices of consumer goods and services over the period 1914 to 1972. This index has been constructed by linking together the pre-war cost of living index for the period 1914–1938, the consumers' expenditure deflator for the period 1938 and 1946–62* and the General Index of Retail Prices for the period 1962–1972.

In 1974 the index was rebased taking January 1974 = 100. Using this index the following table has been constructed:

	Price Index Jan. 1974 = 100	Comparable Purchasing power of £1 in 1975
1914........	11·1	12·14
1915........	13·7	9·84
1920........	27·7	4·87
1930........	17·6	7·66
1938........	17·4	7·75
1946........	29·4	4·59
1950........	35·6	3·79
1955........	44·1	3·06
1960........	49·6	2·72
1961........	51·0	2·64
1962........	53·0	2·54
1963........	54·0	2·50
1964........	55·8	2·42
1965........	58·1	2·31
1966........	60·7	2·22
1967........	62·3	2·16
1968........	65·2	2·07
1969........	68·7	1·96
1970........	73·1	1·84
1971........	80·0	1·69
1972........	85·7	1·57
1973........	93·5	1·44
1974........	108·5	1·24
1975........	134·8	1·00

By employing this table an annual purchasing power of the pound index may be derived by taking the inverse of the price index. So, for example, if the purchasing power of the pound is taken to be 100p in 1955, then its comparable purchasing power in 1975 would be:

$$100 \times \frac{44 \cdot 1}{134 \cdot 8} = 33\text{p}$$

It should be noted that these figures can only be approximate.

*There are no official figures for 1939–45.

TEMPERATURE AND RAINFALL RECORDS

WORLD: The maximum air temperature recorded is 57·8° C. (136° F.) at San Louis, Mexico on Aug. 11, 1933; the minimum air temperature recorded is −88·3° C. (−127° F.) at Vostok Antarctica on Aug. 24, 1960. The greatest rainfall recorded in one day is 1870 mm. (73·62 ins.) at Cilaos, Ile de Réunion on Mar. 16, 1952; the greatest rainfall in one calendar month is 9,300 mm. (366·14 ins.) at Cherrapunji, Assam in July 1861; the greatest annual total being 22,990 mm. (905·12 ins.) also at Cherrapunji in 1861.

UNITED KINGDOM: The maximum air temperature recorded is 38·1° C. (100·5° F.) at Tonbridge, Kent on July 22, 1868; the minimum air temperature recorded is −27·2° C. (−17° F.) at Braemar, Aberdeen on Feb. 11, 1895. The greatest rainfall recorded in one day is 280 mm. (11 ins.) at Martinstown, near Dorchester on Jul. 18, 1955; the greatest annual total is 6,528 mm. (257 ins.) at Sprinkling Tarn in 1954.

THE QUEEN'S AWARDS FOR EXPORT AND TECHNOLOGY

The Queen's Award for Export Achievement and The Queen's Award for Technological Achievement were instituted by Royal Warrant in 1976, the two separate Awards taking the place of The Queen's Award to Industry which had been instituted in 1965. This was the major change made as a result of a number of recommendations by a committee chaired by the Duke of Edinburgh that reviewed all aspects of the Award scheme in 1975 after its second 5-year period of operation; all the recommendations were accepted by the Government. The reports of the 3 committees that have considered the scheme, in 1965, 1970, and 1975—under the chairmanship of the Duke of Edinburgh, Lord McFadzean and the Duke of Edinburgh respectively—are available from Her Majesty's Stationery Office.

The Awards are designed to recognize and encourage outstanding achievements in exporting goods or services from the United Kingdom and in advancing process or product technology. They differ from a personal Royal honour in that they are given to a unit as a whole—management and employees working as a team.

They may be applied for by any organization within the United Kingdom, the Channel Islands or the Isle of Man producing goods or services which meet the criteria for the Awards. Eligibility is not influenced in any way by the particular activities of the unit applying, its location, or size. Units or agencies of central and local government with industrial functions, as well as research associations, educational institutions and bodies of a similar character, are also eligible, provided that they can show they have contributed to industrial efficiency.

The criteria on which recommendations for the Awards are based are:

1. Export Achievement

A substantial and sustained increase in export earnings to a level which is outstanding for the products or services concerned and for the size of the applicant unit's operations. Account will be taken of any special market factors described in the application. Applicants for the Award will be expected to explain the basis of the achievement (e.g. improved marketing organization or new initiative to cater for export markets) and this will be taken into consideration. Export earnings considered will include receipts by the applicant unit in this country from the export of goods produced in this country, and the provision of services to non-residents. Account will be taken of the overseas expenses incurred other than marketing expenses. Income from profits (after overseas tax) remitted to this country from the applicant unit's direct investments in its overseas branches, subsidiaries or associates in the same general line of business will be taken into account, but not receipts from profits on other overseas investments or by interest on overseas loans or credits.

2. Technological Achievement

A significant advance, leading to increased efficiency, in the application of technology to a production or development process in British industry or the production for sale of goods which incorporate new and advanced technological qualities.

Each award is formally conferred by a Grant of Appointment and is symbolized by a representation of its emblem cast in stainless steel and encapsulated in a transparent acrylic block. Presentations are usually made on behalf of The Queen by Her Majesty's Lord Lieutenants at the principal place of business or production of the unit. A reception is given annually by The Queen at Buckingham Palace for representatives of the winners of the Awards.

Awards are held for five years and holders are entitled to fly the appropriate Award flag and to display the emblem on the packaging of goods produced in this country, on the goods themselves, on the unit's stationery, in advertising and on certain articles used by employees: units may also display the emblem of any previous current Awards during the 5 years.

Awards are announced on April 21 each year—the actual birthday of Her Majesty the Queen—and published formally in a special supplement to the London Gazette.

All enquires about the scheme and requests for application forms should be made to:

The Secretary,
The Queen's Awards Office,
Williams National House,
11–13 Holborn Viaduct,
Telephone: 01-222 2277

Exports Achievement Awards

In 1976, the Queen's Award was conferred on the following concerns for export achievement: Acrow Ltd., London, W.2; The Angus Fire Armour Division of George Angus & Co. Ltd., Thame, Oxfordshire; Aquascutum and Associated Companies Ltd., London, W.1; Associated British Maltsters Ltd., Newark-on-Trent, Nottinghamshire; The Associated Octel Co. Ltd., London, W.1; Avery Export Ltd., Warley, West Midlands; BOC Ltd., London, W.6; Barbour Threads Ltd., Lisburn, Co. Antrim; Barr & Murphy Ltd., London, N.W.1; The Bemrose Transfer Prints Division of Bemrose Spondon Ltd., Derby; Bibby Line Ltd., Liverpool; British Aircraft Corporation Ltd., Weybridge, Surrey; British Engine, Boiler & Electrical Insurance Co. Ltd., Manchester; E. Brown (Leathers) Ltd., London, N.3; Brush Switchgear Ltd., Loughborough, Leicestershire; James Burn Bindings Ltd., Esher, Surrey; James Burrough Ltd., London, S.E.11; Cambridge Analysing Instruments Ltd., Royston, Hertfordshire; Caterpillar Tractor Co. Ltd., Glasgow; Chivas Brothers Ltd., Paisley; Contractors Plant (London & Midland) Ltd., London, N.3; Cook Bolinders Ltd., Leighton Buzzard, Bedfordshire; Costain International Ltd., London, S.E.1; Courtaulds Ltd., London, W.1; Crosfield Electronics Ltd., London, N.19; The Darlington Division of Cummins Engine Co. Ltd., Darlington, Co. Durham; Davy Ashmore International Ltd., Stockton-on-Tees, Cleveland; Decca Ltd., London, S.E.1; C. H. Dexter Ltd., Duns, Berwickshire; Druce & Co. Ltd., London, W.1; The Oil and Marine Division of Dunlop Ltd., Grimsby, South Humberside; EMI Medical Ltd., Hayes, Middlesex; Engineering Laboratory Equipment Ltd., Hemel Hempstead, Hertfordshire; The Military Products Division of Fairey Engineering Ltd., Stockport, Greater Manchester; S. W. Farmer & Son Ltd., London, S.E.13; The Fertilizer Division of Fisons Ltd., Felixstowe, Suffolk; Ford Motor Co. Ltd., Brentwood, Essex; Gestetner Holdings Ltd., London, N.17; A. Grantham Ltd., Brighton, East Sussex; Guest, Keen & Nettlefolds Ltd., Warley, West Midlands; Guinness Peat Group Ltd., London, E.C.3; Sir William Halcrow & Partners, London, W.11; Harris-Intertype Ltd., Slough; T. S. Harrison & Sons Ltd., Heckmondwike, West Yorkshire; Henley Forklift Group Ltd.,

Blackwood, Gwent; Hield Brothers Ltd., Bradford, West Yorkshire; R. G. Holland & Co. Ltd., Sheffield.; Howard Rotavator Co. Ltd., Bury St. Edmunds, Suffolk; The Plant Protection Division of Imperial Chemical Industries Ltd., Haslemere, Surrey; Inductotherm Europe Ltd., Droitwich, Hereford and Worcester; International Computers Ltd., London, S.W.15; Dick James Music Ltd., London, W.C.1; Johnston Brothers (Engineering) Ltd., Dorking, Surrey; Lancer Boss Group Ltd., Leighton Buzzard, Bedfordshire; P. Leiner & Sons (Encapsulations) Ltd., Treforest, Mid-Glamorgan; Lindsay & Williams Industries Ltd., Manchester; R. A. Lister & Co. Ltd., Dursley, Gloucestershire; Sir M. MacDonald & Partners, Cambridge; Manchester Liners Ltd., Manchester; Martin-Black Ltd., Coatbridge, Lanarkshire; The Mercantile & General Reinsurance Co. Ltd., London, E.C.2; The Royal Ordance Factories of the Ministry of Defence, London, W.C.2; The Monotype Corporation Ltd., Redhill, Surrey; Munton & Fison Ltd, Stowmarket, Suffolk; The Manufacturing Division of NCR Ltd., Dundee; Newell Dunford Engineering Ltd., Surbiton, Surrey; P.M.C. (Sheffield) Ltd., Sheffield; Pauling & Co. Ltd., London, S.W.1; Penlon Ltd., Abingdon, Oxfordshire; Petbow Ltd., Sandwich, Kent; Edgar Pickering (Blackburn) Ltd., Blackburn, Lancashire; Victor Pyrate Ltd., South Ockendon, Essex; Racal Communications Ltd., Bracknell, Berkshire; Racal-Mobilcal Ltd., Reading, Berkshire; John Ratcliff & Sons Ltd., Leeds; Charles Richards Fasteners Ltd., Wednesbury, West Midlands; The Ryvital Co. Ltd., Poole, Dorset; Saunders Valve Co. Ltd., Cwmbran, Gwent; The Serck Tubes Division of Serck Industries Ltd., Birmingham; Silverline Caravan Co. Ltd., Full Sutton, Nr. York; 600 Services Ltd., Colchester, Essex; David Skellon Yachts Ltd., Hamble, Hampshire; The Aviation Division of Smiths Industries Ltd., Cheltenham, Gloucestershire; Standard Chartered Bank Ltd., London, E.C.4; The Large Cylinder Division of TI Chesterfield Ltd., Chesterfield, Derbyshire; TI Desford Tubes Ltd., Leicester; The International Division of Thorn Lighting Ltd., London, W.C.2; The International Trade Finance Division of Tozer, Kemsley & Millbourn (Holdings) Ltd., London, E.C.3; Transprints (UK) Ltd., Manchester; Viking Engineering Co. Ltd., Stockport, Greater Manchester; Viking Marine Co. Ltd., Gosport, Hampshire; Vogt & Maguire Ltd., London, E.C.3; John Walker & Sons Ltd., London, S.W.1; Josiah Wedgwood & Sons Ltd., Stoke-on-Trent, Staffordshire; The Wellcome Foundation Ltd., London, N.W.1.

Awards for Technological Achievement

In 1976, the following concerns received the Queen's Award for technological achievement: The A.P.V. Co. Ltd., Crawley, West Sussex (*Computer control of beverage and liquid food processing*); Chas. A. Blatchford & Sons Ltd., Basingstoke, Hampshire (*A modular system for the production of artificial limbs*); The Guided Weapons Division of British Aircraft Corporation Ltd., Stevenage, Hertfordshire (*The " Rapier " guided weapon system*); The Forties Project Team of British Petroleum Co. Ltd., London, E.C.2 (*Development of the North Sea Forties oilfield*); Central Research Laboratories of EMI Ltd., Hayes, Middlesex (*The " EMI Whole Body Scanner " X-ray machine*); Ecko Instruments Ltd., Southend-on-Sea, Essex (*Automatic safe load indication systems for cranes*); Ford Motor Co. Ltd., Brentwood, Essex (*A " sonic idle " carburettor for motor vehicles*); Froude Engineering Ltd., Worcester (*Hydraulic dynamometers for programmed engine testing*); The Hatfield Unit of Hawker Siddeley Aviation Ltd., Hatfield, Hertfordshire (*Aerodynamic design of a wing for the European Airbus aircraft*); Instron Ltd., High Wycombe, Buckinghamshire (*The Model 1122 material testing instrument*); Marconi Communication Systems Ltd., Chelmsford, Essex (*The B3404 integrated telecine unit*); The Tobacco Machinery Division of Molins Ltd., London, S.E.8. (*Tobacco machinery*); The Optoelectronics and Microwave Unit of the Microsystems Division of The Plessey Co. Ltd., Towcester, Northamptonshire (*Gallium arsenide microwave devices*); Rothamsted Experimental Station, Harpenden, Hertfordshire (*Highly active safe insecticides*); The Pump Division of William R. Selwood Ltd., Eastleigh, Hampshire (*High speed reciprocating diaphragm pumps*); The Missile Systems Division of Short Brothers & Harland Ltd., Belfast (*The " Short Blowpipe " guided weapon system*); John Thurley Ltd., Harrogate, North Yorkshire (*Vaporisers for liquid natural gas and other cryogenic liquids*); Victor Products (Wallsend) Ltd., Wallsend, Tyne & Wear (*Intrinsically safe coal face lighting*); Welsh Plant Breeding Station, Plas Gogerddan, Nr. Aberystwyth (*Breeding of hybrid ryegrasses*); Wilson & Longbottom Ltd., Barnsley, South Yorkshire (*Rapier looms for the weaving of industrial fabrics*).

A TABLE OF THE NUMBER OF DAYS FROM ANY DAY IN ONE MONTH TO THE SAME IN ANY OTHER MONTH IN ORDINARY YEARS

	Jan.	Feb.	Mar.	April	May	June	July	Aug.	Sept.	Oct.	Nov.	Dec.
January	365	31	59	90	120	151	181	212	243	273	304	334
February	334	365	28	59	89	120	150	181	212	242	273	303
March	306	337	365	31	61	92	122	153	184	214	245	275
April	275	306	334	365	30	61	91	122	153	183	214	244
May	245	276	304	335	365	31	61	92	123	153	184	214
June	214	245	273	304	334	365	30	61	92	122	153	183
July	184	215	243	274	304	335	365	31	62	92	123	153
August	153	184	212	243	273	304	334	365	31	61	92	122
September	122	153	181	212	242	273	303	334	365	30	61	91
October	92	123	151	182	212	243	273	304	335	365	31	61
November	61	92	120	151	181	212	242	273	304	334	365	30
December	31	62	90	121	151	182	212	243	274	304	335	365

WEATHER IN THE UNITED KINGDOM, 1975-1976

(1975) *July*.—Monthly rainfall totals were generally near or above average in the central highlands, parts of northern and central England, southwest England and in Wales but below average elsewhere. A few places in Northern Ireland and southeast England had less than a quarter of the average amount. Until the 20th and again towards the end of the month fog was reported from time to time along southwestern and western coasts and more frequently on Scottish coasts. Fog became widespread for a short time in the Midlands and eastern England on the 9th. The first week of the month was mainly dry apart from some thundery outbreaks on the 3rd and 4th. Most districts had periods of rain between the 7th and 24th, thunderstorms being reported in many areas. Gales were reported in the English Channel on the 15th and on the 18th a violent whirlwind lifted a heavy grain-storage bin to a height of about 12 metres (39·4 feet) near St. Boswells (Borders Region). The storms were particularly violent in northern and eastern England and the Midlands where they were accompanied by squalls and large hail. Hailstones 3 to 4 cms. (1 to 1½ ins.) in diameter were reported from several places in the north Midlands. During these storms two men lost their lives and several people were injured. Property and crops were severely damaged by lightning, hail and torrential rain. Public services were disrupted. On the 14th 104·9 mm. (4·14 ins.) of rain fell at Inverbeg (Strathclyde Region) and 31·5 mm. (1·24 ins.) fell in 15 minutes at Wiserton (Nottinghamshire). On the 22nd gales were reported in northern England when a gust of 72 knots (83 m.p.h.) was recorded at Snaefell (Isle of Man) and 156 mm. (6·15 ins.) of rain fell at Honister Pass (Cumbria). Gales were reported on western coasts on the 23rd. From the 25th most of England and Wales became sunny and very warm. Several places in eastern, southeastern and central England recorded maxima of at least 30° C. (86° F.) on the 30th whilst 32° C. (89·6° F.) was recorded at Bromley (Greater London). Scattered thunderstorms occurred in southern England on the 31st. Monthly mean temperatures were mostly above average in all areas except Shetland and it was the warmest July in Northern Ireland for 20 years. Monthly sunshine totals were generally near or above average but parts of eastern and northern Scotland were less sunny than normal. Lerwick (Shetlands) had its dullest July since 1962.

August.—Rainfall was generally below average except for a few scattered places. It was less than half the average in parts of Northern Ireland, central and southern Scotland, west Wales, south Devon and central England. Eastern England had less than a quarter of the normal amount in places. Thunderstorms were fairly frequent between the 4th and 15th. On the 5th a tornado with very heavy rain and hail occurred near Coventry (Warwickshire) and 5 major roads into the City were blocked by fallen trees. On the 8th a whirlwind in Derbyshire caused the main road to be blocked by trees between Bakewell and Rowsley. Thunderstorms were widespread on the 8th and 9th. On the 10th three people were killed in a collision in fog near Alnwick (Northumberland) and on the 13th two coasters collided in thick fog off the Norfolk coast. On the 14th thunderstorms occurred over eastern districts of England and an unusually severe storm struck northwest London. A total of 170·8 mm (6·72 ins.) of rain, most of which fell in 2½ hours on the evening of the 14th was measured at Hampstead on the morning of the 15th. This is the largest daily total ever recorded in London and severe flooding resulted. One man was drowned and two people were struck by lightning. There

was considerable damage and public services were disrupted. Occasional rain or showers occurred in many places in the second half of the month but southern and central parts of England and Wales were mostly dry between the 24th and 29th. Scattered thunderstorms were reported on the last few days. Monthly mean temperatures were above average everywhere. Maximum temperatures occurred mainly between the 3rd and the 8th and exceeded 33° C. (91·4° F.) in the Midlands, East Anglia and southern England. On the 4th a temperature of 31·2° C. (88·16° F.) at Glasgow was the highest recorded in any month since 1868 whilst at London/Heathrow Airport a temperature of 34·2° C. (93·56° F.) was the highest temperature since records began in 1946. In central England it was probably the warmest August for 300 years and in England and Wales as a whole and in Scotland it was the warmest since 1947. Nights were often warm and on the night of the 4th/5th the temperature at the London Weather Centre did not fall below 22·2° C. (71·96° F.). Monthly sunshine totals were slightly below average in Cornwall, the western part of Northern Ireland, the Western Isles and parts of west Scotland. Most other districts had above average sunshine. In the north Midlands, parts of east and northeast England and eastern Scotland sunshine exceeded 150 per cent of average. Braemar (Grampian Region) had its sunniest August since 1947.

September.—Rainfall was below average in parts of northeast England, the west of Northern Ireland, parts of west Wales and in a wide belt extending from Cheshire and Salop to the east coast from the Tees to the Wash. Elsewhere monthly totals were above normal. The coast of east Kent received over three times the average amount. Except in western Scotland and Northern Ireland the month started dry but became increasingly unsettled. Gales were reported on exposed coasts from the 9th onwards. Showers and thunderstorms between the 10th and 12th brought the first significant rain for several weeks to parts of southern England. On the 10th funnel clouds were reported over the sea west of Alderney(Channel Isles). Waterspouts were observed over the Irish Sea on the 11th when whirlwinds were reported in Blackpool (Lancashire) and Swansea (West Glamorgan). On the 13th and 14th rain and gales swept across southern counties causing loss of life when a small boat foundered in the Severn Estuary. Southampton (Hampshire) had its wettest day of the century on the 13th when 54·4 mm. (2·15 ins.) of rain were recorded. On the 14th a whirlwind caused extensive damage to glasshouses and crops in a nursery garden at Barnham (West Sussex). From the 20th gales became more frequent in the west and north. Many places in Scotland recorded gusts exceeding 50 knots (57 m.p.h.) between the 20th and 24th. 101 mm. (3·98 ins.) of rain fell at Honister Pass (Cumbria) on the 24th. Heavy rain and gales reached most areas on the 27th and snow fell in the scottish mountains, heavy falls being reported in the Cairngorms. Gales were severe in places and gusts reached at least 70 knots (81 m.p.h.) on exposed coasts in the southwest. Monthly mean temperatures were below average almost everywhere but at a few places along the coast of East Anglia and around the Thames Estuary they were a little above average. On the 8th temperatures exceeded 24° C. (75·2° F.) at several places in central, southern and eastern districts of England. Temperatures were exceptionally low in southern England on the 14th. 10° C. (50° F.) at London Weather Centre was the lowest September day temperature there since 1940. Monthly sunshine totals were

near average over most of Scotland but were above average in the Isle of Lewis and the extreme south-west. Sunshine was generally above average in Northern Ireland, Wales and England but a little below average along the south coast of England. The sunniest places were in the North Midlands and Merseyside.

October.—Rainfall was below average in all districts except for a few places in Northern Ireland and Kent. North and east Scotland, most of England and much of Wales had less than half the average amount whilst a number of places from central southern England through the south Midlands to East Anglia had only about a quarter of the average. Although dry there were some outbreaks of heavy rain and at Pickering (North Yorkshire) 35 mm. (1·38 ins.) were recorded in 100 minutes on the 2nd. A marked feature of the month was the absence of snowfall particularly in northern areas. In northern and western districts winds and gales occurred until the 6th. On the 2nd a gust of 84 knots (97 m.p.h.) was recorded at Snaefell (Isle of Man) and on the 5th gusts of 68 and 74 knots (78 and 85 m.p.h.) were recorded at Lerwick (Shetland) and Cairngorm (Highland Region) respectively. On the 15th a funnel of cloud was observed over the sea near Alderney (Channel Islands). From the 16th onwards fog affected many parts of the country persisting all day in places, as in the Forth and Clyde valleys on the 17th and 18th. After the 18th eastern districts were mainly dry but there was rain at times in the west and north. Gales again affected the western coasts of Scotland from the 19th. On the 24th fog was widespread in southern England and extended north-eastwards across the Midlands to eastern areas. Yorkshire and Humberside had a foggy day on the 27th. On this day 19 lorries and 11 cars were involved in three collisions near Huddersfield (West Yorkshire) and 25 people were taken to hospital. Fog was also slow to clear in eastern areas on the 29th, persisting all day in parts of Lincolnshire and Yorkshire. Monthly mean temperatures were below average almost everywhere in England and Wales, southern and central Scotland. In Northern Ireland and northern Scotland they were near or above normal. On the 1st the temperature rose to 19·9° C. (67·82° F.) at Newton Rigg (Cumbria). From the 10th to the 13th many areas had a cold spell and at Bastreet (Cornwall) the temperature fell to − 3·7° C. (25·34° F.) on the 13th. The cold weather lasted longer in northern districts and on the 18th the temperature fell to − 6·5° C. (20·3° F.) at Lagganlia (Highland Region). Many places had their highest temperatures during the last week and on the 27th 22·0° C. (71·6° F.) was recorded at Loggerheads (Clwyd). At Balmacara (Highland Region) 19·4° C. (66·92° F.) was recorded on the 28th. Monthly sunshine totals were below average along the coasts of Sussex, Kent and eastern England, parts of northern England, Northern Ireland, the east coast of Scotland and parts of western Scotland. Elsewhere sunshine was above average.

November.—Rainfall was near or above average in the Channel Islands, extreme southwest and southeast England, parts of East Anglia, west Wales, the west of Northern Ireland and much of western Scotland. Elsewhere the month was drier than usual, less than half the average amount falling in the west and north Midlands, southeast Scotland and a few places in northern England. Apart from the beginning of the month, when most places had some rain, the first two weeks were mostly dry. On the night of the 10th/11th extensive fog, dense and freezing in places, developed in central and eastern England. The fog became persistent and wide-spread on the 14th before clearing on the 16th. From the 15th onwards the weather became less settled, rain spreading to all areas at times, but most persistently in the west and north where there were gales. Most stations recorded their highest gusts on the 16th, 17th or 27th, 60 knots (69 m.p.h.) being recorded at a few places. Whitland in southwest Wales had 57·4 mm. (2·26 ins.) of rain in 16 hours on the 23rd. On the 22nd fog lingered in the Severn Valley for much of the day. Hail showers were more frequent in the second half of the month and thunderstorms, which were occasionally reported earlier, occurred during the last few days. Snow or sleet showers fell in northern areas and in the Welsh mountains during the third week and again towards the end of the month. Depths of about 10 cms. (3·94 ins.) were measured in the Grampians. Reports of snow or sleet were few in other areas although there were slight falls in Devon between the 25th and 30th. On the 29th and 30th dense, freezing fog occurred in central, east and southeast England affecting coastal shipping and disrupting road and air traffic. On the evening of the 29th 10 people were killed when two light aircraft crashed on landing in fog, one at Elstree and the other at Birmingham. Monthly mean temperatures were near average everywhere. The highest temperatures recorded during the month being 16·7° C. (62·06° F.) at Aldenham (Hertfordshire) on the 1st, 15·5° C. (59·9° F.) at Nettlecombe (Somerset) on the 15th and 15·7° C. (60·26° F.) at Perth (Tayside Region) on the 19th. Minimum temperatures were − 7·3° C. (18·86° F.) at Lagganlia (Highland Region) on the 21st and − 7·1° C. (19·22° F.) at Aylesbury (Buckinghamshire) on the 22nd. Monthly sunshine totals were below average in northwest Scotland, the west of Northern Ireland, Cornwall and parts of the east coast of Kent and Suffolk but totals were above average everywhere else. Manchester Airport and Liverpool Airport with 89 and 95 hours respectively had almost twice their normal sunshine for November.

December.—Rainfall was below average except in some places in northern Scotland, a part of Lincolnshire and around the Humber. Most of southern England, south Wales and the extreme north of England had less than half the average amount and many places in Devon, Cornwall, Northern Ireland and eastern Scotland had only about a quarter of the average amount. Perth (Tayside Region) with a monthly total of 7 mm. (0·28 ins.) and the Edinburgh area with a similar amount had their driest December since 1908. The month began with rain in all districts, a number of places in Wales recording amounts well in excess of 50 mm. (2 ins.) on the 1st, 99·5 mm. (3·92 ins.) were recorded at Moel Cynnedd (Powys) in 18 hours. There were showers of hail, snow and sleet in the north. Gales swept across many areas on the 1st and gusts exceeding 50 knots (57 m.p.h.) were recorded widely in southern districts. Six cross-channel ferries rode out the storm on the night of the 1st/2nd before entering port. Also on the 1st there was freezing fog in central and southern England. After the 2nd the month was generally dry although there was rain on every day in parts of north and west Scotland. Many districts had rain on the 12th. Fog was reported fairly often between the 4th and 21st and in southern England persistent freezing fog on the 15th and 16th disrupted road, rail and air traffic. Thirty people were taken to hospital following a series of 70 road accidents near Bexley (Greater London). Gales blew around northern coasts from the 21st. Many districts had rain on the 23rd and 24th and again during the last few days of the month when wintry showers and thunder occurred in the north. Monthly mean temperatures ranged from 1 deg. C. below average at a few places along the southern coasts of England to 2·5 deg. C. above average in parts of eastern

Scotland. On the 5th the temperature rose to 14·4°
C. (57·9° F.) at Banchory (Grampian Region) and
fell on the night of the 12th/13th to −8·5° C. (16·7°
F.) at Dalwhinnie and Dall (Grampian Region) and
to −9·1° C. (15·6° F.) at Moor House (Cumbria).
Ground frost was reported at a number of places
during the month. Monthly sunshine totals were
near or above average in southeast England, in much
of northern and central England and in southeast
Scotland. Totals were more than 150 per cent of
average in northeast England and in the Forth/Clyde
area. All other districts had less sunshine than normal.

Year (1975)—Annual rainfall was near or a little
above average in most of southeast England, parts of
Essex and some places in northwest Scotland. It
was less than normal in all other areas. The most
notable feature of the rainfall was the exceptional
dryness of the months October to December inclusive. There has been no drier corresponding
period in England and Wales since 1879, in Northern
Ireland since 1922 and in Scotland since 1937. January was mainly, wet and very mild. Gales were
severe at times. Shipping ran aground and lives
were lost on several occasions. Heavy rain caused
flooding in Wales and southern England towards
the end of the month. The weather changed suddenly at the beginning of February and became dry
and much less windy. Fog often formed, freezing at
times, but the month was generally mild. After the
first week March became much colder. It was dry
and sunny in the north but wet elsewhere with some
widespread flooding in eastern England and the Midlands. There were gales in southern districts. Cross-
Channel services were affected and a stretch of sea-
wall collapsed at Lowestoft. A man was killed in
Essex. The cold weather continued into April and
there were blizzards in Scotland. A skier lost his
life at Aviemore. After mid-month it was generally milder with rain at times and fog on the coasts.
May brought cool conditions to all areas. There
were gales at times and a tree blown into a bus in
Wiltshire killed the driver. Western and northern
districts were very dry and sunny but eastern England
was rather wet. Northern Ireland had its driest May
this century. June started cold with snow and heavy
rain in places and gales in the north. Scattered
showers of snow or sleet spread even as far south as
London. Within a few days most districts became
dry, sunny and very warm and continued like this
through the first week of July. During the next
two weeks heavy rain and thunderstorms occurred
in which two men lost their lives and property and
crops were severely damaged. Sunny and very
warm weather then returned and during the first
fortnight of August it was often very hot. Glasgow
recorded its highest temperature since 1868 and it
was the warmest August in central England for over
300 years. Thunderstorms were frequent and the
highest daily rainfall ever recorded in London occurred in an exceptionally severe storm. Flooding
followed and one man was drowned. Two people
were struck by lightning. Damage to property was
considerable. Lives were lost in fog in Northumberland and whirlwinds caused roads to be blocked
by trees in Warwickshire and Derbyshire. The rest
of August was cooler and September was cool and
wet with gales at times. Southampton had its wettest day of the century. The remaining months
were rather changeable but rainfall amounts were
small. As in the early months snow or sleet occurred
less frequently than normal but fog was sometimes
persistent. Three multiple accidents occurred in
fog in October injuring 25 people. Two light aircraft crashed in fog in November killing 10 people
and in December 30 people were injured in no less
than 70 accidents in fog near Bexley. Annual mean
temperatures were above average in all districts.

Annual sunshine totals were generally above normal.
Only the summer of 1911 sunnier was this century
in England and Wales. Manchester had its sunniest
summer since 1877 and in Paisley the combined
May and June total was the highest since 1885.

(1976) January.—Rainfall was above average in
Northern Ireland and most of Scotland. It was up
to 2½ times the average in northern Scotland. Parts
of north Wales and much of northern England
were also wetter than usual. In general, however,
rainfall decreased southwards and was less than half
the average in southern counties. The month started
wet everywhere and at Yspytty-Ifan (Gwynedd)
124 mm. (4·88 ins.) were recorded on the 2nd. One
of the most severe gales this century swept across
the British Isles on the 2nd causing at least 23 deaths.
Public services were widely disrupted and the total
national damage was estimated at up to £100
million. At Lawther Hill (Strathclyde Region) a
gust of 116 knots (133 m.p.h.) was recorded and at
Wittering (Cambridgeshire) a gust of 91 knots (105
m.p.h.) was reported. The gale was followed by a
tidal surge along the east coast which breached the
sea defences at a few places, mainly in Humberside
and Norfolk. Precipitation occurred on almost
every day of the month in north and northwest
Scotland but southern districts of England and Wales
were often dry between the 7th and 17th. Gales
returned to many areas between the 19th and 22nd
and were severe in places. Most areas had rain or
showers from the 18th to 26th but the rest of the
month, except in the southwest was mainly dry. It
became very cold from the 24th to the 26th. Heavy
falls of snow in Scotland and northeast England on
the 24th soon spread southwards, affecting eastern
counties until the 26th. Heavy snowfall occurred
on Dartmoor on the 30th. Monthly mean temperatures were above average almost everywhere in
spite of the cold spell. Only in Shetland and the
extreme northwest of Scotland were mean temperatures below average. At Braemar (Grampian
Region) a temperature of −13° C. (8·6° F.) was
recorded on the night of the 1st/2nd but on the 11th
the temperature rose to 15·1° C. (59·2° F.) at Stone-
haven (Grampian Region). On the night of the
27th/28th the temperature fell to −10·6° C. (12·92°
F.) at Honington (Suffolk). Monthly sunshine totals
were near or above average in southeast England,
in much of central and eastern England and in south-
west Scotland and the central lowlands. The London
area with 180 per cent of average had the most sunshine. Elsewhere, sunshine was below average and
the Northern Isles, one or two places on western
coasts and the Channel Islands had only about half
the average amount.

February.—Rainfall was near or above average in
parts of northern, western and southern Scotland
and in a few scattered places in Wales, the western
half of England and the Channel Islands. Rainfall
was below normal elsewhere and in England and
Wales this was the fifth successive month with less
than average rainfall. Some eastern districts of
England were particularly dry with several places
having monthly totals of less than 10 mm.
(0·39 ins.). Snow or sleet fell in many areas until
the 6th and fog was extensive and slow to clear in
eastern, central and southern districts of England on
the 7th. Some rain fell between the 9th and 12th
and at Winstitchen (Somerset) 75·3 mm. (2·96 ins.)
fell in 16 hours 6 minutes on the 12th. Snow or
sleet showers from the 10th to the 12th mainly
affected northern districts. Gales were reported on
eastern coasts on the 13th. Fog was reported from
the 19th to the end of the month and was extensive
and slow to clear in eastern, central and southern
districts on the 20th and 21st. There was further

rain from the 21st to the 24th. On the 24th a gust of 90 knots (103 m.p.h.) was recorded at Cairngorm (Highland Region) and a gust of 74 knots (85 m.p.h.) was recorded at Lerwick (Shetland) on the 29th. On the night of the 24th/25th the Hastings lifeboat rescued the crew of a coaster which had collided with another vessel in fog off Beachy Head. Monthly mean temperatures were above average almost everywhere but near normal in coastal districts of southern England, in south Wales and in the Channel Islands. This is the sixth successive year in which monthly mean temperatures for February have been above normal in Scotland and in England and Wales together. On the night of the 1st/2nd the temperature at Lagganlia (Highland Region) fell to − 14·9° C. (5·18° F.) and in parts of southern England and south Wales temperatures occasionally remained below freezing all day until the 6th. The last week was very mild in many districts and the temperature rose to 16·6° C. (61·88° F.) at Aberdeen Airport on the 25th, a temperature which has only been exceeded in Scotland on two previous Februarys this century. Monthly sunshine totals were above average in parts of northern Scotland and west Wales and in an arc from north Wales to Cheshire to the northwest Midlands. They were below normal everywhere else,

March.—Rainfall was above average almost everywhere in Scotland and Northern Ireland, in extreme northern England, northwest and southwest England and in parts of the west Midlands and southern Wales. Parts of west Cornwall and eastern Scotland had almost twice the average amount. Remaining districts had less rain than normal and most of the eastern half of England had less than half the average amount. The month was dry at first with night frosts. From the 6th it became much colder and snow and sleet fell in the north and east. The snow continued intermittently in the north until the 17th. Many areas had rain at times from the 9th to the end of the month. Gales affected much of England, Wales and eastern Scotland on the 12th and there were many distress calls from shipping in the western approaches to the English Channel. Some lives were lost. Avalanches were reported in the Cairngorms on the 12th and seven climbers were taken to hospital. On the 21st, 125·0 mm.(4·92 ins.) of rain were recorded at Spegla Dam (Co. Down) and on the 22nd 81·7 mm. (3·22 ins.) were measured at Bugle (Cornwall). Snowfall was much more general on the 21st and 22nd blocking roads and mountain passes in Scotland, Cumbria and northern Wales and affecting roads in southwest England. It remained generally cold until the 24th with rain or drizzle and hill fog. Milder weather then reached most districts and although rain fell at times and there were wintry showers and gales in the north sunny periods also occurred and the southeast became warm. On the 28th a gust of 94 knots (108 m.p.h.) was recorded at Cairngorm (Highland Region). Heavy snow was reported in Shetland on the 31st. Monthly mean temperatures were below normal in all areas. On the night of the 8th/9th the temperature fell to − 10·5° C. (13·1° F.) at Alwen (Clwyd) and on the 28th it rose to 17·1° C. (62·78° F.) at Gillingham (Kent). Monthly sunshine totals were near or above average in parts of northern Scotland, northern England, the north Midlands, East Anglia and in most of southeastern and central England. Elsewhere monthly totals were a little below average. Eskdalemuir (Dumfries and Galloway Region) had its dullest March since 1936.

April.—Rainfall was near or above average in a few places in northwest and southern Scotland and in an area round the Firth of Forth but below normal in all other areas. Parts of northeast Scotland, Northern Ireland and most of England and

Wales had considerably less than half the average amount. A number of places in southernmost counties had less than 10 per cent of average and Callington (Cornwall) had no rain at all. Although it was a mostly dry month there were outbreaks of rain or showers in many areas on the 1st and 2nd and a man was killed by lightning on the Isle of Lewis. The heavy snow at the end of March in Shetland continued to the 1st of April and snowdrifts were up to 1 metre (3·3 ft.) deep. Snow or sleet showers fell in other northern and some western districts at the beginning of the month. There were gales at times during the first half of the month and on the 6th a gust of 85 knots (98 m.p.h.) was recorded at Snaefell (Isle of Man). Rain or showers, wintry in the north, continued to occur at times during the first two weeks and affected many districts on the 13th and 14th, 55·7 mm. (2·2 ins.) of rain was measured at Braithwaite (Cumbria). A little snow or sleet fell on Dartmoor on the 14th and 15th. The second half of the month was dry over England and Wales but Scotland had occasional outbreaks of rain. Fog occurred frequently around Scottish coasts and islands and was persistent on southern coasts of England on the 17th and 18th and on eastern coasts of England and Scotland on the 20th. Widespread frost occurred towards the end of the month. Monthly mean temperatures were below average in Shetland, a few places in northern and southeastern Scotland and almost everywhere in England and Wales. They were above normal in Northern Ireland, the Isle of Man and most of Scotland. At Achnashellach and Lock Oich (Highland Region) the temperature rose to 21·6° C. (70·88° F.) on the 20th and central London had its warmest Easter (16th to 19th) since 1952. Monthly sunshine totals were near or above average in East Anglia, southern England, west Wales, Northern Ireland and parts of northern England and western Scotland. Values were below average elsewhere and Fortrose (Highland Region) had its dullest April since 1910.

May.—Rainfall was generally below average in extreme north and northeast Scotland, southern Wales and in England south of a line from the west Midlands to the Wash. Totals were above average elsewhere. Less than half the average fell in southern England with some places along the south coast recording less than a quarter of the average amount. By contrast some places in Humberside and North Yorkshire recorded more than 2½ times the average. Outbreaks of rain or showers reached most areas on the 1st and on the 2nd Honister Pass (Cumbria) had 76·2 mm. (3·0 ins.) of rain. Fog, which was reported from time to time throughout the month in coastal areas, particularly affected northeast coasts of England on the 6th. Thunderstorms occurred fairly frequently but were particularly widespread from the 7th to the 10th. Gales occurred occasionally around mid month and on the 16th a gust of 78 knots (90 m.p.h.) was recorded at Edinburgh. Fog affected the northeast coast of England on the 24th and extended along the English Channel from the southwest on the 31st. Monthly mean temperatures were slightly below average in the Hebrides, the Glasgow area, Northern Ireland, the Isle of Man, southwest Wales and most of Cornwall. In other areas mean temperatures were near or above average. On the 1st at Bastreet (Cornwall) a temperature of − 5·0° C. (23·0° F.) was recorded and on the night of the 4th/5th − 3·0° C. (26·6° F.) was recorded at Fyvie Castle (Grampian region). At Ulcombe (Kent) and at Waddon (Greater London) the temperature rose to 29·0° C. (84·2° F.) on the 7th. The difference between the night minimum and the day maximum at several places in the southeast on the 7th was 22° C. (39·6° F.). Monthly sunshine totals were near or above average in southeast and central south-

ern England, parts of southwest England, parts of East Anglia and in Caithness and the Northern Isles. Sunshine was below normal elsewhere and Onich (Highland Region) had its dullest May since 1929.

June.—Rainfall was above average in west and northwest Scotland but everywhere else rainfall was below average. Parts of the east and much of the south coasts of England had less than a quarter of average. Exmouth (Devon) and Guernsey (Channel Islands) had only 4 per cent of normal. It was the driest June in England and Wales since 1925 and following the previous dry months 17 counties had a serious shortage of water. The month started unsettled but by the 3rd it had become dry over much of the country and many central and eastern districts stayed dry until the middle of the month. On the 19th rain spread over the whole of England and Wales as far north as Lancashire and Yorkshire. At Fullaford (Devon) 68 mm. (2·68 ins.) were recorded and 62·4 mm. (2·46 in s.) fell at Blackpits Gate (Somerset). There were gales in the English Channel on the 19th. From the 21st most of England and Wales stayed dry although there were a few thunderstorms on the southeast coast on the 23rd and in parts of the southwest on the 27th and 28th. Monthly mean temperatures were above average in all areas except the

Western Isles. The night of the 24th/25th was the warmest June night in London since 1947, the minimum temperature never falling below 21·3° C. (70·3° F.). On the 25th, 26th, 27th and 28th temperatures exceeded 32° C. (90° F.) over much of London, the first occasion in at least 135 years that 32° C. (90° F.) has been reached on 4 consecutive days. On the 26th and 28th temperatures over much of southern England were up to 14° C. (25° F.) above normal and at Plumpton (East Sussex) the temperature reached 36° C. (96·8° F.) on the 28th, the highest June temperature ever recorded in Britain. On the 30th, 30·8° C. (87·4° F.) at Knockaraven (Co. Fermanagh) was the highest temperature ever recorded in Northern Ireland. The hot spell from the 23rd onwards caused traffic congestion, industrial troubles, heat exhaustion, etc., and fires. Towards the end of the month large fires were reported in Norfolk, Suffolk, Surrey, Essex, Hampshire and North Yorthshire. The army were called in to control the moor fires near Whitby (North Yorkshire). Sunshine was above normal in most areas but in much of central and western Scotland and west coast regions of England and Wales it was less than normal. It was the dullest June on record at Benbecula (Western Isles).

Average and General Values, 1974–1976 (June)

Month	Rainfall (mm.)				Temperature (°C.)				Bright Sunshine (hrs. per day)			
	Aver. 1916–1950	1974	1975	1976	Aver. 1941–1970	1974	1975	1976	Aver. 1941–1970	1974	1975	1976
					England and Wales							
January........	92	117	117	60	4·0	6·5	7·2	6·2	1·6	1·7	1·7	1·7
February	66	99	31	40	4·2	6·1	5·2	5·0	2·4	2·3	2·3	1·7
March..........	57	47	81	43	6·2	6·2	5·3	5·4	3·7	3·4	3·0	3·6
April..........	60	14	71	21	8·8	8·3	8·6	8·3	5·3	5·1	4·5	5·4
May...........	63	40	47	64	11·6	11·3	10·1	12·2	6·3	6·7	6·3	5·6
June...........	55	65	21	17	14·7	14·0	14·1	17·1	6·8	6·7	9·2	8·5
July...........	79	77	66	—	16·3	15·5	7·5	—	5·9	5·4	6·8	—
August.........	81	95	52	—	16·1	15·7	18·7	—	5·5	6·1	7·4	—
September......	76	144	106	—	14·3	12·6	13·9	—	4·4	4·7	5·0	—
October........	92	99	36	—	11·2	8·2	10·5	—	3·3	2·9	3·5	—
November.....	95	125	73	—	7·2	7·2	6·7	—	1·9	1·8	2·5	—
December......	88	72	52	—	5·1	8·3	5·6	—	1·5	1·5	1·5	—
YEAR......	904	994	753	—	10·0	10·0	10·4	—	4·0	4·0	4·4	—
					Scotland							
January........	154	228	245	185	3·5	5·9	5·3	5·0	1·4	1·1	1·2	1·1
February	106	118	48	87	3·7	5·4	4·8	5·2	2·5	1·8	3·0	1·7
March..........	89	73	58	130	5·4	5·4	4·5	4·9	3·4	3·3	3·8	3·0
April..........	88	18	100	60	7·5	7·6	7·3	7·8	5·0	6·0	3·9	4·2
May...........	87	78	48	118	9·9	10·3	8·6	10·2	5·7	5·5	7·2	4·5
June...........	87	71	67	65	12·7	12·3	12·6	13·9	5·8	6·4	7·5	4·9
July...........	114	102	112	—	14·1	13·4	14·9	—	4·8	4·7	4·9	—
August.........	122	97	86	—	14·0	13·9	16·2	—	4·5	4·5	5·4	—
September......	128	141	184	—	12·5	11·0	11·6	—	3·7	4·0	3·7	—
October........	158	106	78	—	9·9	7·7	10·2	—	2·7	2·5	2·7	—
November.....	143	190	128	—	6·3	6·1	6·4	—	1·7	1·7	1·9	—
December......	143	226	88	—	4·6	6·5	6·1	—	1·1	1·1	1·1	—
YEAR......	1419	1448	1242	—	8·7	8·8	9·0	—	3·5	3·5	3·9	—

TEMPERATURE, RAINFALL AND SUNSHINE
IN THE UNITED KINGDOM

The following table gives mean air temperature (°C.) total monthly rainfall (mm.) and mean daily bright sunshine (hrs.) at a representative selection of climatological reporting stations in the United Kingdom during the year July 1975 to June 1976 and the calendar year 1975. The heights (metres) of the reporting stations above mean sea level are also given. Fuller details of the weather are given in the *Monthly Weather Report* published by the Meteorological Office.

Station	Ht. in m.	July			August			September			October		
		Temp. °C	Rain mm.	Sun hrs.	Temp. °C	Rain mm.	Sun hrs.	Temp. °C	Rain mm.	Sun hrs.	Temp. °C	Rain mm.	Sun hrs.
Aberporth........	133	15·9	48	6·3	16·4	47	5·7	12·8	67	5·1	10·7	59	4·5
Aberystwyth......	4	—	61	—	—	33	—	—	103	—	—	43	—
Aldergrove.......	68	16·1	78	5·4	16·5	44	5·7	12·1	147	3·5	10·5	59	2·3
Bath.............	118	—	—	—	—	—	—	—	—	—	—	—	—
Birmingham......	163	17·7	58	6·5	19·1	35	6·6	13·3	70	4·9	10·2	23	3·6
Bournemouth.....	40	17·3	21	8·6	18·1	49	8·2	13·9	177	5·5	10·9	15	4·4
Braemar.........	339	14·1	73	4·9	15·3	68	6·8	9·7	88	3·2	7·9	31	2·6
Buxton...........	314	15·3	105	—	16·9	53	—	11·2	91	—	7·9	47	—
Cambridge........	26	18·0	27	7·3	19·4	26	7·6	14·4	70	5·4	10·2	6	4·1
Cardiff...........	62	18·1	63	6·5	—	—	—	—	—	—	—	—	—
Cheltenham.......	65	18·7	53	7·4	19·9	38	7·6	14·2	67	4·8	11·0	22	4·1
Clacton-on-Sea....	16	17·4	14	6·5	19·0	26	8·2	14·9	110	5·4	10·8	18	3·6
Douglas..........	87	15·5	56	6·2	16·2	67	6·6	12·3	124	4·7	10·8	93	3·3
Dumfries.........	49	15·7	129	5·7	17·2	70	6·4	11·6	167	3·8	9·5	83	2·6
Dundee...........	45	16·0	78	4·6	16·9	51	4·8	11·8	92	3·4	9·9	35	2·7
Durham..........	102	15·9	61	4·7	17·5	85	7·2	11·9	79	4·1	8·8	21	2·9
Eastbourne.......	7	17·2	37	7·6	18·9	52	8·9	15·4	160	5·4	11·6	35	3·6
East Malling.......	37	17·4	17	7·3	19·0	25	7·3	14·4	139	5·1	9·9	30	3·7
Edinburgh........	134	15·7	42	5·3	17·1	82	5·5	11·7	156	3·6	9·7	29	2·9
Falmouth.........	51	16·9	87	7·6	17·3	119	5·5	13·8	94	5·1	11·6	49	3·7
Glasgow..........	107	15·4	75	5·3	16·9	47	5·6	11·1	154	3·3	9·2	78	1·7
Hartland Point....	91	16·3	70	6·9	17·1	60	5·4	13·8	67	5·7	11·7	57	4·9
Hastings..........	45	17·0	35	6·8	19·1	41	8·1	15·1	132	5·1	11·2	34	3·8
Huddersfield......	99	16·9	57	5·9	18·9	40	7·0	13·3	67	5·7	9·5	34	3·4
Hull.............	2	17·7	40	6·8	18·7	26	7·9	14·3	27	4·8	10·3	25	2·9
Inverness.........	4	14·7	71	4·8	—	59	5·0	—	54	3·4	—	39	3·3
Lincoln..........	7	16·7	20	6·3	18·7	44	7·7	13·1	27	4·7	9·8	16	3·2
London (Kew).....	6	17·9	26	7·7	18·9	13	7·6	14·3	120	5·0	9·9	21	3·9
Lowestoft.........	25	16·7	47	7·2	18·3	31	8·6	14·7	93	5·5	10·9	41	3·4
Manchester Airport	75	17·1	55	6·1	18·5	37	7·3	13·1	99	5·0	10·3	31	3·7
Margate..........	16	17·5	15	7·5	19·2	25	8·1	15·7	167	5·8	11·3	45	3·3
Morecambe.......	7	17·1	105	5·2	18·6	62	7·1	13·5	153	4·8	10·2	38	3·3
Newton Rigg.....	171	15·5	75	4·9	16·9	79	5·9	11·5	115	4·3	9·1	48	2·9
Nottingham.......	59	17·8	44	5·9	19·9	33	7·1	13·9	55	4·2	10·7	35	2·8
Oxford...........	63	18·6	34	7·8	19·6	30	7·1	14·3	95	4·9	10·3	11	3·9
Penzance.........	19	17·1	71	7·2	17·5	119	5·6	14·1	143	5·8	12·0	66	4·6
Plymouth.........	36	—	70	7·6	18·1	51	6·0	13·9	91	5·0	11·7	42	—
Prestwick.........	16	15·5	68	6·0	16·6	41	5·4	12·0	121	3·9	10·1	57	2·4
Ross-on-Wye......	68	18·0	53	—	—	—	—	—	—	—	—	—	—
St. Mawgan.......	103	16·7	66	7·7	17·2	133	5·7	13·5	131	5·7	11·5	39	4·5
Sandown..........	4	17·5	20	8·6	18·1	60	8·5	14·5	136	5·5	11·3	18	4·5
Scarborough......	53	16·3	81	6·2	17·3	23	7·9	13·2	48	5·1	9·7	29	2·9
Scilly............	48	17·1	51	7·0	17·3	84	—	14·8	106	6·1	12·5	51	4·3
Sheffield.........	131	17·5	82	5·5	19·3	47	7·6	13·4	35	4·5	9·9	27	2·9
Shoeburyness.....	2	17·7	17	7·3	18·7	24	7·9	15·5	119	5·3	10·9	20	3·5
Shrewsbury.......	56	17·5	57	5·9	18·3	45	6·3	13·1	36	4·9	9·8	17	3·4
Skegness.........	5	17·3	26	7·6	18·2	20	—	14·1	37	5·2	10·7	11	2·2
Southampton.....	3	18·7	25	8·0	19·5	36	8·0	14·8	164	4·8	11·7	31	4·2
Stornoway........	3	13·1	75	4·4	14·2	43	3·7	10·7	132	4·3	10·3	69	2·9
Tiree............	9	13·9	100	5·7	14·7	56	4·6	11·9	164	3·7	10·9	100	1·6
Torbay...........	8	17·9	37	8·6	18·4	31	7·0	14·3	91	5·6	11·8	35	3·8
Tregaron	178	15·7	82	5·3	16·3	74	5·1	11·5	130	4·4	9·1	67	3·7
West Kirby.......	8	17·8	35	5·4	18·7	47	7·4	13·6	60	—	10·7	83	—
Weymouth........	23	17·3	29	8·6	18·2	46	7·7	14·9	99	5·7	11·7	35	4·0
Worthing.........	2	17·0	23	7·4	18·5	44	8·4	14·5	133	5·4	11·1	34	3·6
York.............	20	16·9	146	5·8	18·9	12	7·9	13·0	51	4·8	9·4	32	2·7

TEMPERATURE, RAINFALL AND SUNSHINE IN THE UNITED KINGDOM

Mean Temperature of the air (°C.), Rainfall (mm.) and Bright Sunshine (as mean hours per day) at a representative selection of reporting stations during the year July, 1975 to June, 1976. Fuller details of the weather are given in the *Monthly Weather Report* published by the Meteorological Office.

Station	1975									1976					
	November			December			Year			January			February		
	Temp.	Rain	Sun	Temp.	Rain	Sun	Temp.	Rain	Sun	Temp.	Rain	Sun	Temp.	Rain	Sun
	°C.	mm.	hrs.	°C.	mm.	hrs.	°C.	mm.	hrs.	°C.	mm.	hrs.	°C.	mm.	hrs.
Aberporth	7·5	69	2·0	6·6	60	0·8	9·9	655	4·7	6·7	48	1·0	5·0	41	2·9
Aberystwyth	—	84	—	—	54	—	—	722	—	—	61	—	—	43	—
Aldergrove	6·5	58	2·1	5·6	23	0·8	9·5	693	4·3	5·3	86	1·3	5·1	46	1·8
Bath	6·9	66	—	4·8	40	—	—	—	—	—	23	—	4·4	15	—
Birmingham	6·2	57	3·0	5·3	52	1·3	10·0	582	4·1	5·9	34	1·7	4·3	38	2·0
Bournemouth	7·5	76	3·5	5·1	31	1·9	10·5	678	5·4	6·5	10	2·2	4·8	41	1·3
Braemar	3·7	72	1·2	4·3	31	0·6	7·3	757	—	2·3	106	0·5	2·2	31	1·7
Buxton	4·8	88	—	4·3	120	—	8·9	994	—	4·1	176	—	2·8	76	—
Cambridge	5·7	38	2·3	4·5	—	1·0	10·2	—	4·4	5·7	25	1·7	4·3	14	1·8
Cardiff	—	—	—	—	—	—	—	—	—	6·7	17	1·0	4·5	36	1·4
Cheltenham	7·1	48	3·1	5·5	37	1·1	10·9	527	4·5	6·3	21	1·7	5·3	31	1·7
Clacton-on-Sea	6·9	66	2·3	4·5	24	2·1	10·2	535	4·4	5·4	19	2·3	4·1	20	1·6
Douglas	7·5	122	2·5	6·7	54	1·3	9·7	995	4·9	6·1	142	1·5	5·0	70	1·6
Dumfries	5·6	84	2·4	5·5	32	1·3	9·1	986	4·4	5·5	96	1·6	4·5	75	1·4
Dundee	5·9	41	2·3	5·3	17	2·0	9·3	547	3·6	4·3	48	1·6	4·7	35	1·5
Durham	5·3	34	2·5	5·3	23	2·1	8·9	548	3·8	4·7	46	1·7	4·1	17	1·4
Eastbourne	8·0	112	2·4	5·4	29	2·0	10·9	817	5·0	6·5	25	2·2	4·9	43	1·5
East Malling	5·8	61	2·3	4·3	30	1·7	10·1	639	4·4	5·9	18	1·9	4·5	25	1·4
Edinburgh	5·8	25	2·3	5·5	18	1·8	9·0	603	3·9	4·5	37	1·6	4·5	26	1·2
Falmouth	8·6	131	1·8	6·7	36	1·3	10·9	885	4·8	7·3	44	1·5	6·4	77	2·4
Glasgow	5·3	86	1·6	5·2	42	1·5	8·9	866	3·8	4·7	122	1·4	4·3	49	1·1
Hartland Point	8·9	116	2·0	7·5	29	0·7	10·7	711	4·9	7·4	34	1·0	5·4	46	2·3
Hastings	7·6	114	2·7	4·9	27	2·1	10·7	763	4·8	5·7	20	2·2	4·5	33	1·4
Huddersfield	5·7	33	2·4	5·7	47	1·6	9·8	539	—	5·4	118	1·2	4·4	32	1·1
Hull	6·2	56	2·0	5·5	63	2·0	10·2	513	—	5·7	67	—	5·1	20	—
Inverness	—	53	1·7	6·8	38	0·7	—	597	3·5	4·7	85	1·1	4·5	25	3·1
Lincoln	5·1	37	2·2	4·3	58	1·6	9·5	461	—	5·3	38	1·8	4·5	15	1·9
London (Kew)	6·2	64	2·7	4·7	28	1·5	10·3	575	4·6	6·1	15	2·1	4·9	21	1·5
Lowestoft	6·6	72	1·9	4·3	30	1·0	9·8	585	4·5	5·3	45	1·8	4·1	13	2·1
Manchester Airport	6·2	58	3·0	5·6	62	1·1	10·0	646	4·5	6·1	91	1·3	5·1	40	2·1
Margate	7·5	78	1·7	5·3	20	1·4	10·5	651	4·3	6·1	21	2·3	4·8	21	1·4
Morecambe	6·3	97	2·5	5·7	31	1·1	10·3	844	4·7	5·8	104	1·4	5·1	36	1·9
Newton Rigg	4·7	65	2·1	4·5	35	1·3	8·7	755	4·2	—	—	—	4·0	43	1·3
Nottingham	6·7	55	2·1	5·5	43	1·5	—	539	—	6·1	61	1·1	4·9	16	1·4
Oxford	6·1	38	2·8	4·6	22	1·1	10·5	538	4·4	5·9	19	2·3	4·8	19	1·5
Penzance	9·6	169	2·0	7·1	59	1·3	11·4	1078	5·0	7·8	59	1·4	6·8	70	2·4
Plymouth	8·5	91	2·3	6·5	20	1·4	—	701	—	7·1	38	1·3	5·7	48	2·0
Prestwick	6·3	85	1·8	6·4	47	1·0	9·3	740	4·5	5·7	100	1·8	5·1	44	1·2
Ross-on-Wye	—	—	—	—	—	—	—	—	—	—	—	—	—	—	—
St. Mawgan	8·7	119	1·8	6·5	39	1·2	10·8	919	5·1	7·3	70	1·1	5·7	57	2·4
Sandown	8·1	60	3·4	5·5	34	2·3	10·9	706	5·3	6·7	16	2·0	5·3	37	1·3
Scarborough	6·5	57	2·5	5·5	50	1·6	9·4	595	4·3	5·5	79	1·8	4·7	14	1·7
Scilly	10·3	108	2·4	8·5	39	0·9	11·8	765	—	8·7	53	1·3	7·7	53	2·4
Sheffield	6·1	29	2·3	5·8	43	1·6	9·9	560	4·0	5·4	94	1·3	4·4	34	1·5
Shoeburyness	6·9	61	2·4	4·9	20	1·7	10·5	575	4·5	6·2	15	2·1	4·4	20	1·3
Shrewsbury	6·0	39	2·7	5·5	37	0·9	9·9	459	3·9	6·1	38	1·7	4·5	37	2·6
Skegness	6·6	50	2·3	5·1	46	1·6	9·9	475	—	5·5	40	1·9	4·6	11	1·9
Southampton	7·7	59	3·4	5·3	33	1·9	11·3	690	5·0	6·4	12	1·8	5·4	31	1·4
Stornoway	6·3	129	1·6	5·9	116	0·6	8·3	1021	3·8	4·4	165	1·0	5·1	77	2·5
Tiree	7·7	152	1·5	7·4	66	0·8	9·3	1107	4·1	6·3	136	0·7	5·8	72	1·4
Torbay	8·9	59	3·3	6·5	27	1·5	11·3	560	5·3	7·5	29	1·8	6·1	54	1·6
Tregaron	5·7	115	1·5	4·7	93	0·5	9·1	1040	3·9	5·4	115	1·1	4·3	85	2·1
West Kirby	7·1	67	2·6	6·5	83	—	10·5	610	—	6·9	65	—	5·3	43	—
Weymouth	8·5	97	3·3	5·9	25	1·6	11·1	611	5·2	7·1	10	2·1	5·2	41	1·3
Worthing	7·5	50	3·2	5·0	26	2·2	10·5	679	5·1	5·9	11	2·1	4·7	16	1·4
York	5·2	40	2·4	4·9	57	2·1	9·4	529	4·2	5·3	46	1·9	4·1	20	1·6

TEMPERATURE, RAINFALL AND SUNSHINE IN THE UNITED KINGDOM

Mean Temperature of the air (°C.), Rainfall (mm.) and Bright Sunshine (as mean hours per day) at a representative selection of reporting stations during the year July, 1975 to June, 1976. Fuller details of the weather are given in the *Monthly Weather Report* published by the Meteorological Office.

Station	March			April			May			June		
	Temp. °C.	Rain mm.	Sun hrs.	Temp. °C.	Rain mm.	Sun hrs.	Temp. °C.	Rain mm.	Sun hrs.	Temp. °C.	Rain mm.	Sun hrs.
Aberporth	5·3	62	3·8	7·5	19	6·0	10·5	57	5·1	14·9	11	7·5
Aberystwyth	—	43	—	—	18	—	—	76	—	—	9	—
Aldergrove	5·5	61	2·5	8·1	23	5·9	10·5	79	4·0	15·4	55	6·2
Bath	5·1	56	—	8·4	8	—	12·3	34	—	17·6	35	—
Birmingham	4·7	42	3·3	8·0	11	4·0	11·9	51	4·7	17·5	21	8·7
Bournemouth	5·5	34	4·6	8·3	6	7·2	12·3	23	8·3	17·1	5	9·5
Braemar	2·4	58	2·9	6·1	19	4·0	8·5	105	3·7	13·4	11	5·5
Buxton	2·7	75	—	6·1	37	—	9·9	131	—	14·9	24	—
Cambridge	4·9	16	3·7	8·4	21	5·8	12·7	31	6·4	17·9	8	9·3
Cardiff	5·5	58	3·7	8·9	3	5·4	12·3	59	5·3	—	—	—
Cheltenham	5·4	29	3·4	8·4	15	5·3	12·8	46	5·4	18·4	19	8·1
Clacton-on-Sea	5·1	9	3·8	7·7	10	6·9	12·9	19	6·5	17·1	11	9·6
Douglas	5·2	104	2·9	7·9	35	5·8	10·1	93	5·4	13·7	47	7·2
Dumfries	4·3	92	3·1	7·9	32	4·1	10·4	112	3·9	14·5	41	6·1
Dundee	4·4	87	2·7	8·0	23	4·0	10·5	85	3·6	15·3	25	5·4
Durham	4·1	26	3·3	7·1	31	3·5	10·5	79	3·8	15·3	25	7·1
Eastbourne	5·5	20	4·5	8·5	15	8·1	13·1	9	8·7	17·2	5	10·8
East Malling	5·2	11	4·4	8·3	10	7·0	12·9	24	7·3	17·7	8	10·2
Edinburgh	4·1	61	2·8	7·2	52	3·8	10·7	60	4·2	14·9	20	5·0
Falmouth	6·9	104	2·7	8·5	14	7·0	11·3	39	6·3	16·2	6	—
Glasgow	3·9	100	2·6	7·7	50	3·9	10·3	133	4·0	14·5	46	4·9
Hartland Point	5·9	65	3·9	8·3	11	7·1	11·1	45	6·5	14·8	37	6·7
Hastings	5·3	15	4·3	8·3	12	7·8	12·9	17	8·2	17·2	5	10·6
Huddersfield	4·4	42	3·2	7·7	21	4·1	11·7	108	4·8	16·9	14	7·9
Hull	5·2	29	3·6	8·3	17	5·1	12·1	144	4·8	17·5	3	9·1
Inverness	5·5	59	3·8	7·9	20	3·1	10·9	39	4·7	14·9	15	4·4
Lincoln	4·9	23	3·8	7·3	16	4·6	11·9	55	4·6	16·7	6	8·7
London (Kew)	5·5	9	4·2	8·4	9	6·5	13·3	22	7·4	18·3	8	8·9
Lowestoft	4·7	11	4·0	7·4	9	5·8	11·8	20	6·9	16·5	9	10·5
Manchester Airport	5·0	54	3·8	8·2	23	5·1	11·8	97	4·4	16·7	22	7·8
Margate	5·4	10	4·1	8·0	11	7·4	13·1	13	8·3	17·9	9	10·9
Morecambe	4·9	69	3·7	8·4	41	5·1	11·7	91	4·3	16·0	26	6·9
Newton Rigg	3·8	44	2·9	—	—	—	—	—	—	15·1	27	7·0
Nottingham	5·2	22	2·4	8·6	10	2·7	12·4	37	—	—	13	—
Oxford	5·3	16	3·5	8·5	8	5·0	13·1	44	5·5	18·5	17	8·7
Penzance	7·3	142	3·4	8·6	16	7·9	11·6	56	6·8	16·3	13	7·8
Plymouth	6·4	98	3·1	8·9	3	6·9	12·1	31	6·8	16·1	9	8·3
Prestwick	4·9	71	2·8	7·9	46	4·9	10·5	79	4·8	14·2	26	6·3
Ross-on-Wye	—	—	—	—	—	—	—	—	—	—	—	—
St. Mawgan	6·3	132	3·7	8·5	12	8·0	11·3	41	6·5	15·9	17	7·5
Sandown	5·6	12	4·8	8·2	5	7·7	12·5	8	8·9	16·5	7	9·5
Scarborough	4·6	23	3·5	7·3	17	4·5	10·8	77	5·0	16·0	7	9·9
Scilly	8·3	65	3·2	9·5	22	7·8	11·9	39	6·6	15·9	7	7·3
Sheffield	4·6	40	3·5	8·1	16	3·9	11·9	80	4·8	17·1	17	8·3
Shoeburyness	5·3	5	3·9	8·1	9	7·1	13·5	11	7·2	17·8	11	10·1
Shrewsbury	4·6	42	3·0	7·9	9	3·9	12·1	54	4·4	16·7	14	7·3
Skegness	5·1	16	3·3	—	11	4·8	11·9	66	5·6	16·9	6	10·1
Southampton	5·9	17	4·3	9·2	10	6·6	13·3	32	7·9	18·5	11	8·9
Stornoway	5·5	102	3·9	7·1	78	5·1	9·0	73	4·9	12·0	101	3·9
Tiree	5·9	98	2·6	8·2	51	5·8	9·8	84	5·3	12·6	103	4·4
Torbay	6·5	76	3·5	8·9	4	7·1	12·3	25	7·6	17·3	7	9·9
Tregaron	4·3	60	3·5	7·1	30	4·7	10·7	103	4·2	14·7	14	6·5
West Kirby	5·3	58	—	8·6	13	—	12·4	91	—	16·7	15	—
Weymouth	5·9	48	4·4	8·6	4	7·0	12·3	22	7·9	16·7	3	8·5
Worthing	5·4	21	4·6	8·3	8	7·8	12·7	13	8·4	17·0	7	9·7
York	4·7	13	3·3	7·7	11	4·8	11·3	113	4·2	16·5	5	8·1

Weather Record, July, 1975

Day	Max. °C.	Min. °C.	Wind Speed knots	Rainfall mm.	Sunshine hrs.
1	23.0	11.9	4.6	0.0	13.8
2	23.1	10.3	4.7	0.0	14.6
3	22.2	10.6	6.3	0.0	6.9
4	20.2	14.8	10.0	0.0	0.9
5	18.6	12.2	6.5	0.0	0.0
6	22.3	12.2	8.3	0.0	12.0
7	23.9	12.3	10.8	7.3	13.0
8	25.8	13.3	6.0	0.0	6.7
9	23.1	14.1	6.5	0.0	7.5
10	22.9	14.6	8.8	0.1	7.1
11	23.8	15.6	7.9	0.0	10.1
12	21.2	14.1	7.1	1.1	3.7
13	24.7	15.3	8.1	0.0	4.9
14	24.5	17.4	11.9	0.1	10.4
15	22.5	16.0	13.7	8.6	5.0
16	23.6	14.0	8.9	0.7	13.3
17	23.8	16.4	5.4	0.6	4.7
18	24.6	15.1	5.5	2.1	7.6
19	22.4	13.5	6.8	0.1	3.5
20	21.9	16.9	6.3	1.7	1.9
21	22.8	12.8	5.0	0.0	10.4
22	22.8	14.7	11.8	0.2	2.8
23	21.2	15.2	11.6	0.8	6.9
24	18.7	11.3	9.7	0.0	8.1
25	21.0	11.4	5.4	0.0	11.4
26	25.9	13.5	4.2	0.0	11.1
27	27.2	14.7	1.4	0.0	3.7
28	28.0	15.1	2.3	0.0	9.2
29	30.3	14.0	2.2	0.0	12.2
30	30.5	13.8	1.9	0.0	12.6
31	26.4	18.3	6.5	2.4	1.2
Total ..	—	—	—	25.8	237.2
Mean ..	23.6	14.0	7.0	—	—
Temp. °F.	74.5	57.2	—	—	—
Average ..	21.6	13.4	6.8	62	197

Weather Record, August, 1975

Max. °C.	Min. °C.	Wind Speed knots	Rainfall mm.	Sunshine hrs.	Day
25.4	16.2	6.6	0.0	7.8	1
27.6	10.5	4.8	0.0	13.1	2
29.3	9.2	3.7	0.0	13.8	3
31.6	14.7	7.8	0.1	12.3	4
28.3	18.6	3.7	1.0	5.5	5
29.4	11.5	3.7	0.0	12.8	6
32.2	13.9	2.5	0.0	10.4	7
33.2	14.5	5.5	0.3	11.7	8
25.0	14.7	5.5	0.0	7.3	9
21.8	14.4	2.8	0.9	3.9	10
25.1	15.3	3.4	0.0	5.4	11
27.0	15.8	1.8	0.0	8.0	12
29.1	13.1	2.2	0.0	11.1	13
28.4	11.5	2.3	1.8	9.6	14
23.9	16.5	9.0	3.4	5.1	15
22.0	16.2	10.0	0.6	7.0	16
23.3	14.4	2.5	0.0	5.1	17
22.8	11.7	2.7	0.8	2.7	18
23.9	15.9	8.7	0.2	0.3	19
19.9	18.0	10.7	0.2	0.0	20
21.1	13.6	3.0	0.0	3.5	21
19.3	7.5	4.8	0.3	8.0	22
19.5	7.3	5.9	2.9	7.8	23
20.2	13.2	4.0	0.0	5.1	24
23.6	8.0	3.7	0.0	12.3	25
25.2	7.1	1.3	0.0	11.2	26
24.9	9.2	4.0	0.0	11.9	27
26.7	8.0	4.5	0.0	10.8	28
27.3	7.7	2.2	0.0	10.9	29
18.6	13.2	3.5	0.0	0.2	30
18.4	13.1	7.0	0.0	0.0	31
—	—	—	12.5	234.6	.. Total
25.0	12.7	4.6	—	—	.. Mean
77.0	54.9	—	—	—	Temp. °F.
21.0	13.1	6.2	57	183	.. Average

Weather Record, September, 1975

Day	Max. °C.	Min. °C.	Wind Speed knots	Rainfall mm.	Sunshine hrs.
1	22.6	11.4	5.5	0.0	9.4
2	20.0	9.2	1.4	0.0	0.5
3	22.4	14.3	4.3	0.0	6.4
4	20.4	8.9	2.7	0.0	6.3
5	20.6	5.7	3.1	0.0	5.6
6	21.2	8.8	2.0	0.0	5.2
7	22.6	12.5	2.3	0.0	1.5
8	23.5	8.4	7.1	0.0	6.8
9	20.1	15.1	11.7	0.5	0.9
10	21.6	13.0	8.2	0.0	8.4
11	18.3	9.1	9.5	1.9	8.3
12	15.3	6.7	9.6	0.8	6.5
13	17.0	6.6	8.1	43.2	6.5
14	10.8	7.5	12.5	8.4	0.0
15	14.9	7.7	8.2	0.0	4.4
16	15.2	4.3	5.8	4.7	0.1
17	19.3	7.9	5.5	1.1	7.2
18	19.7	10.6	7.7	0.8	8.3
19	20.7	9.6	5.9	0.9	4.9
20	20.0	14.3	5.7	0.8	6.5
21	18.6	5.6	3.5	0.0	8.1
22	18.5	5.1	5.7	0.0	6.5
23	17.5	10.8	7.4	0.1	2.5
24	18.3	6.3	10.4	0.1	6.5
25	16.1	13.8	13.1	23.1	0.0
26	15.4	7.9	8.8	19.9	9.8
27	17.5	9.2	13.9	8.7	0.9
28	17.7	4.2	6.9	0.2	6.0
29	21.8	12.5	6.7	3.6	6.5
30	16.0	12.7	6.0	1.1	0.1
31					
Total ..	—	—	—	119.9	150.7
Mean ..	18.8	9.3	7.0	—	—
Temp. °F.	65.8	48.7	—	—	—
Average ..	18.5	11.4	6.6	50	143

Weather Record, October, 1975

Max. °C.	Min. °C.	Wind speed knots	Rainfall mm.	Sunshine hrs.	Day
15.7	9.3	7.7	3.6	3.7	1
17.2	3.3	9.2	0.9	2.3	2
15.8	11.6	11.5	0.0	9.0	3
15.8	5.5	9.3	0.0	5.1	4
15.4	11.2	8.2	0.0	1.5	5
17.1	7.9	5.8	0.0	1.5	6
15.4	4.5	4.8	0.0	9.1	7
13.4	1.2	1.4	0.0	5.9	8
15.4	1.6	1.9	3.1	6.6	9
13.5	8.1	8.9	0.1	8.0	10
12.3	6.5	11.3	0.0	5.8	11
12.4	7.0	10.3	0.0	5.9	12
11.6	4.5	6.6	0.0	3.8	13
12.3	0.4	3.3	2.9	0.6	14
14.9	5.4	6.0	0.0	0.0	15
12.1	2.6	1.4	3.3	0.2	16
11.8	2.6	5.8	4.4	0.5	17
14.7	10.3	5.3	0.0	5.0	18
13.0	1.6	3.1	0.0	2.0	19
12.7	5.1	6.0	0.0	0.1	20
11.5	8.6	5.6	0.0	0.0	21
13.1	1.8	6.8	0.0	5.1	22
17.0	5.6	4.2	0.0	8.7	23
14.3	4.2	1.4	0.0	1.5	24
11.7	5.0	2.2	0.0	0.0	25
11.6	8.6	3.3	0.0	0.1	26
16.1	9.1	2.6	0.0	6.3	27
10.4	2.6	2.7	0.0	2.6	28
15.6	4.9	2.5	0.0	3.9	29
17.6	4.6	5.0	0.0	5.6	30
16.5	6.9	7.3	3.2	2.6	31
—	—	—	21.5	121.1	.. Total
14.1	5.6	5.5	—	—	.. Mean
57.4	42.1	—	—	—	Temp. °F.
14.7	8.5	6.6	57	102	.. Average

Entries of Maximum Temperature cover the day period 9–21 h.; Minimum Temperature the night period 21–9 h. entered to the day of reading: Rainfall is for the 24 hours commencing at 9 h. on the day of entry: Sunshine is for the 24 hours 0–24 h.: Mean Wind Speed 10 metres above the ground.

100 knots = 115·1 m.p.h.; 100 mm = 3·94 ins.; °F = 9/5°C + 32

Weather Record, November, 1975

Day	Max. °C.	Min. °C.	Wind Speed knots	Rain-fall mm.	Sun-shine hrs.
1	14.1	1.9	6.1	2.3	3.4
2	12.3	8.5	4.5	4.5	5.5
3	12.9	8.6	6.6	0.6	3.8
4	12.4	−1.7	1.9	0.0	6.7
5	13.2	3.8	5.3	0.1	0.0
6	12.3	9.1	6.7	0.0	5.2
7	10.7	4.4	9.5	0.2	5.7
8	11.4	7.0	13.5	0.0	1.8
9	9.8	8.6	13.3	0.0	0.1
10	8.2	4.5	3.9	0.0	4.1
11	9.5	0.7	4.3	0.0	5.9
12	9.3	2.1	10.1	0.0	3.7
13	7.1	−1.6	4.7	0.0	2.0
14	3.7	−4.5	0.6	0.4	0.0
15	14.3	2.0	6.1	19.2	0.0
16	9.5	9.4	10.5	4.5	0.0
17	6.7	3.6	18.0	0.9	0.0
18	7.7	3.1	10.6	1.2	7.3
19	12.3	1.5	7.8	4.7	0.0
20	12.2	11.5	8.8	0.0	1.2
21	7.1	−2.8	0.9	0.0	6.0
22	7.2	−1.2	1.6	0.0	6.7
23	10.8	−2.9	6.7	0.0	3.8
24	9.0	−0.3	2.9	0.4	6.8
25	12.3	1.1	7.6	2.1	0.0
26	6.9	0.3	4.2	1.5	0.1
27	12.8	−2.6	10.5	0.7	1.2
28	8.3	6.3	7.5	21.1	0.4
29	4.8	0.9	1.1	0.0	0.0
30	1.6	0.3	1.6	0.0	0.0
31					
Total ..	—	—	—	64.4	81.5
Mean ..	9.7	2.7	6.6	—	—
Temp. °F.	49.5	36.9	—	—	—
Average ..	9.8	5.3	6.8	63	58

Weather Record, December, 1975

Max. °C.	Min. °C.	Wind Speed knots	Rain-fall mm.	Sun-shine hrs.	Day
12.0	−1.9	12.5	14.5	0.0	1
8.4	6.7	12.6	0.0	3.9	2
5.8	2.9	6.8	0.0	3.8	3
8.2	−1.6	4.9	0.0	0.1	4
10.4	7.4	4.9	0.0	0.0	5
11.1	8.4	2.5	0.0	0.0	6
9.4	7.1	4.3	0.0	0.0	7
6.9	−1.3	1.7	0.0	2.2	8
7.1	−4.1	1.2	0.0	5.3	9
7.1	4.0	1.0	0.1	0.0	10
7.0	4.9	1.0	0.2	2.0	11
5.7	−3.6	4.3	1.2	0.0	12
2.4	0.7	12.7	0.0	6.7	13
3.3	−5.1	1.1	0.0	6.0	14
−0.3	−5.5	0.5	0.0	0.0	15
0.5	−4.0	0.7	0.4	0.1	16
5.1	0.4	10.5	0.0	2.4	17
4.3	−1.1	3.9	0.8	3.7	18
7.5	2.0	3.8	0.0	1.1	19
5.5	−2.5	1.0	0.0	0.0	20
8.3	0.8	4.8	0.0	0.0	21
8.2	6.2	4.8	0.0	0.0	22
8.8	5.9	8.7	2.7	0.1	23
7.2	4.1	8.7	5.2	6.6	24
11.1	1.5	8.0	0.4	0.0	25
10.6	5.3	6.1	0.0	0.0	26
7.6	2.3	8.0	0.0	0.0	27
8.7	6.7	8.5	0.0	0.0	28
8.4	1.0	4.0	0.0	0.0	29
10.4	7.2	11.9	0.0	0.9	30
11.6	8.7	15.3	2.3	0.0	31
—	—	—	27.8	44.9	.. Total
7.4	2.0	5.8	—	—	.. Mean
45.3	35.6	—	—	—	Temp. °F.
7.2	3.4	7.6	52	43	.. Average

Weather Record, January, 1976

Day	Max. °C.	Min. °C.	Wind Speed knots	Rain-fall mm.	Sun-shine hrs.
1	12.1	4.2	8.8	0.2	0.0
2	12.8	7.2	15.3	1.0	0.0
3	7.5	5.7	13.4	0.0	6.1
4	8.8	−2.9	6.2	6.4	0.0
5	11.4	8.6	9.4	0.0	0.1
6	11.8	7.6	8.0	0.0	3.1
7	9.8	6.3	10.9	0.0	0.0
8	11.3	8.2	11.5	0.0	0.0
9	12.0	6.5	10.7	3.1	5.3
10	11.4	8.3	10.5	0.1	0.0
11	12.4	11.1	10.3	0.0	0.6
12	12.4	8.1	9.5	0.0	3.7
13	11.5	6.1	5.5	0.0	0.4
14	11.2	6.2	10.6	0.0	4.5
15	8.3	0.7	3.9	0.0	4.5
16	8.1	0.7	3.6	0.0	0.0
17	9.2	2.3	2.2	0.0	0.0
18	8.8	1.2	6.2	0.1	0.1
19	9.3	2.2	11.7	0.0	2.7
20	12.3	9.2	17.3	0.2	2.1
21	8.8	5.1	13.6	0.0	2.2
22	11.8	8.4	13.7	0.0	0.6
23	7.8	7.0	10.8	0.1	4.4
24	3.3	−0.4	8.3	1.6	3.1
25	1.6	0.2	13.3	0.6	3.3
26	2.3	−0.9	8.7	1.4	0.5
27	5.5	0.8	5.8	0.0	2.4
28	2.6	−6.9	8.0	0.0	5.1
29	3.4	0.8	14.9	0.0	5.5
30	0.3	−3.3	20.5	0.0	6.3
31	−0.2	−1.7	15.7	0.0	0.0
Total ..	—	—	—	14.8	66.6
Mean ..	8.4	3.8	10.3	—	—
Temp. °F.	47.1	38.8	—	—	—
Average	6.1	2.3	8.1	55	48

Weather Record, February, 1976

Max. °C.	Min. °C.	Wind Speed knots	Rain-fall mm.	Sun-shine hrs.	Day
0.4	−0.9	10.2	0.0	0.0	1
1.6	−0.3	7.3	0.3	0.0	2
0.4	−0.1	6.8	0.1	0.0	3
2.5	−0.9	10.1	0.4	0.0	4
3.0	1.5	15.0	0.0	0.0	5
9.1	2.5	7.8	0.0	2.1	6
8.1	0.7	2.4	0.0	0.0	7
10.1	0.1	6.3	1.1	0.4	8
10.9	−4.5	8.4	1.4	4.3	9
8.5	6.2	9.2	2.0	7.9	10
7.1	2.7	12.0	0.0	6.8	11
10.0	2.7	10.9	13.1	0.0	12
6.2	5.7	15.9	0.0	0.0	13
5.9	2.3	8.2	0.0	2.9	14
5.1	−3.9	2.7	0.0	0.5	15
2.0	1.0	13.0	0.0	0.0	16
3.9	1.9	5.6	0.2	0.0	17
5.1	2.1	2.5	0.0	0.0	18
6.1	−0.2	4.7	0.0	0.0	19
9.3	−0.6	2.8	0.0	0.0	20
12.4	−0.7	5.5	0.9	3.3	21
12.3	8.3	6.8	0.0	1.0	22
11.6	6.1	7.1	1.0	0.0	23
13.7	10.1	6.9	0.0	2.6	24
13.2	6.8	7.7	0.0	6.7	25
12.3	6.5	4.0	0.0	0.1	26
9.9	2.5	3.3	0.0	0.0	27
9.4	1.2	3.7	0.1	0.2	28
14.8	0.8	8.5	0.3	4.2	29
					30
					31
—	—	—	20.9	43.0	.. Total
7.8	2.1	7.4	—	—	.. Mean
46.0	35.8	—	—	—	Temp. °F.
6.8	2.3	8.3	39	65	.. Average

Weather Record, March, 1976

Day	Max. °C.	Min. °C.	Wind Speed knots	Rain-fall mm.	Sun-shine hrs.
1	10.6	− 3.9	3.0	0.0	9.2
2	11.1	− 5.1	6.0	0.0	7.6
3	9.5	3.4	10.5	0.0	8.2
4	12.7	0.0	5.1	0.0	7.9
5	9.9	− 4.3	8.6	0.0	8.5
6	4.8	− 1.1	12.6	0.0	9.4
7	2.7	0.5	12.9	0.5	2.4
8	4.1	− 0.2	6.7	0.0	6.8
9	7.1	− 0.3	2.6	0.0	5.6
10	9.1	− 4.4	6.9	0.0	1.6
11	8.5	4.2	10.5	0.9	0.5
12	8.6	5.3	9.5	2.9	1.3
13	7.8	4.4	10.0	0.0	1.7
14	6.8	3.0	4.7	0.4	0.0
15	6.7	3.0	8.0	1.3	0.0
16	7.7	5.0	2.0	0.4	0.0
17	8.4	4.8	4.1	0.1	0.0
18	9.7	6.0	6.7	0.0	1.1
19	6.9	0.7	9.8	0.0	1.9
20	9.6	1.1	8.8	0.0	10.1
21	8.9	− 2.2	8.7	0.0	3.3
22	5.7	2.1	14.5	0.0	4.9
23	5.8	− 0.7	10.0	0.0	6.9
24	8.8	− 1.5	8.5	1.7	8.0
25	13.5	7.0	11.9	0.2	1.1
26	11.9	8.6	11.3	0.4	4.0
27	12.9	4.2	11.4	0.0	0.9
28	14.4	6.7	11.1	0.0	9.7
29	11.8	4.0	11.4	0.0	3.0
30	12.5	5.7	9.8	0.0	4.1
31	13.9	6.0	12.5	0.0	1.2
Total ..	—	—	—	8.8	130.9
Mean ..	9.1	2.0	8.7	—	—
Temp. °F.	48.4	35.6	—	—	—
Average ..	9.8	3.4	8.0	37	112

Weather Record, April, 1976

Max. °C.	Min. °C.	Wind Speed knots	Rain-fall mm.	Sun-shine hrs.	Day
13.2	8.0	7.7	0.0	1.4	1
11.6	7.3	7.5	0.8	2.2	2
11.8	1.1	7.7	0.0	9.8	3
11.7	− 0.3	6.5	0.1	4.7	4
13.0	1.3	8.2	0.0	7.0	5
14.8	6.5	9.2	0.0	4.8	6
11.6	5.7	9.3	0.6	2.3	7
12.1	− 3.9	3.7	0.0	8.3	8
12.7	2.4	1.9	0.0	0.4	9
15.6	2.0	3.4	0.0	2.2	10
15.3	0.3	5.5	0.0	5.8	11
13.9	1.4	7.7	0.0	2.3	12
13.6	2.1	7.3	2.6	3.2	13
10.0	7.3	11.0	5.4	0.4	14
14.5	6.7	12.5	0.0	6.9	15
10.8	5.5	5.3	0.0	3.9	16
16.5	2.0	2.0	0.0	8.7	17
18.4	1.8	4.5	0.0	5.8	18
18.4	5.0	9.7	0.0	11.9	19
18.4	6.3	12.7	0.0	13.1	20
15.9	6.9	12.2	0.0	12.1	21
12.9	5.9	12.7	0.0	8.3	22
10.1	2.4	14.0	0.0	11.4	23
11.6	2.3	13.2	0.0	12.6	24
13.2	5.2	13.0	0.0	10.1	25
12.7	4.3	12.9	0.0	10.8	26
9.0	6.5	11.8	0.0	1.3	27
10.7	1.2	8.7	0.0	12.6	28
13.1	− 3.5	2.7	0.0	12.9	29
13.4	6.0	2.6	0.0	5.4	30
					31
—	—	—	9.5	202.6	.. Total
—	—	—	—	—	.. Mean
13.3	3.5	8.2	—	—	Temp. °F.
55.9	38.3	—	—	—	Temp. °F.
13.3	5.7	8.1	46	162	.. Average

Weather Record, May, 1976

Day	Max. °C.	Min. °C.	Wind Speed knots	Rain-fall mm.	Sun-shine hrs.
1	16.6	2.5	8.5	0.2	7.9
2	14.6	7.8	10.9	0.0	1.9
3	15.1	8.3	11.5	0.4	7.2
4	16.1	7.6	9.2	0.2	8.6
5	18.3	9.3	4.3	0.1	1.6
6	22.9	11.7	7.8	0.0	9.9
7	28.4	5.7	2.5	0.0	13.0
8	26.3	7.9	3.5	0.0	11.8
9	25.6	10.3	4.7	0.0	11.5
10	18.4	14.4	6.9	0.0	5.5
11	16.6	5.1	8.7	0.1	6.6
12	15.4	10.0	12.5	0.5	5.6
13	14.9	7.3	6.2	0.0	9.5
14	18.1	3.0	5.6	0.0	10.7
15	17.9	1.7	10.6	0.0	12.0
16	17.0	6.7	9.7	0.0	10.3
17	20.9	5.1	7.7	0.6	12.1
18	19.5	6.5	6.3	1.5	8.3
19	14.8	7.3	11.3	3.9	3.9
20	15.1	7.3	8.3	5.6	7.2
21	17.5	6.3	7.0	0.0	9.2
22	18.7	10.9	4.8	0.0	2.8
23	21.9	6.1	5.9	0.0	12.6
24	22.0	11.0	9.9	3.0	10.7
25	16.9	10.5	6.0	0.0	6.2
26	16.4	8.8	8.5	0.0	3.2
27	17.5	7.3	3.4	0.0	6.9
28	19.7	7.3	5.1	0.0	3.4
29	20.5	11.8	7.5	0.8	5.8
30	17.4	8.1	8.5	0.0	1.7
31	17.8	11.7	6.7	4.9	1.3
Total ..	—	—	—	21.8	228.9
Mean ..	18.7	7.9	7.4	—	—
Temp. °F.	65.7	46.2	—	—	—
Average ..	16.8	8.4	7.4	46	203

Weather Record, June, 1976

Max. °C.	Min. °C.	Wind Speed knots	Rain-fall mm.	Sun-shine hrs.	Day
18.4	12.5	10.5	0.0	8.5	1
15.9	11.6	4.3	0.0	0.4	2
16.9	6.3	6.4	0.0	8.4	3
21.5	7.8	2.5	0.0	4.1	4
22.6	5.1	4.3	0.0	7.1	5
24.6	10.0	5.2	0.0	6.3	6
26.1	10.2	4.4	0.0	14.0	7
28.9	11.7	4.7	0.0	14.6	8
31.0	10.1	7.1	0.0	11.7	9
20.5	12.0	5.6	0.0	10.0	10
21.4	9.2	6.5	0.0	7.9	11
23.5	11.1	7.9	0.0	4.0	12
25.7	10.9	4.4	0.0	13.9	13
26.3	13.5	6.1	0.0	12.6	14
26.1	13.1	4.9	0.2	7.6	15
16.9	14.1	4.8	0.3	0.0	16
18.1	12.3	2.6	0.0	0.0	17
24.8	10.8	7.0	0.0	9.6	18
15.3	13.7	10.9	7.3	0.0	19
19.5	12.3	7.2	0.1	5.9	20
22.5	8.8	4.2	0.0	2.5	21
26.6	10.2	2.0	0.0	13.4	22
31.0	14.3	5.6	0.0	13.5	23
30.3	13.0	3.2	0.0	14.8	24
32.4	12.3	1.6	0.0	13.6	25
34.2	16.4	1.4	0.0	12.6	26
33.7	18.0	2.5	0.0	10.9	27
33.7	16.4	3.3	0.0	10.1	28
29.1	14.4	6.7	0.0	15.0	29
29.9	15.3	10.7	0.0	15.2	30
					31
—	—	—	7.9	268.2	.. Total
—	—	—	—	—	.. Mean
24.8	11.9	5.3	—	—	Temp. °F.
76.6	53.4	—	—	—	Temp. °F.
20.2	11.5	7.2	44	214	.. Average

MERCHANT SHIPPING

PRINCIPAL MERCHANT FLEETS OF THE WORLD

Source: Lloyd's Register of Shipping

Flag	1960 No.	1960 Tons Gross	1965 No.	1965 Tons Gross	1970 No.	1970 Tons Gross	1975 No.	1975 Tons Gross
Liberia	977	11,282,240	1,287	17,539,462	1,869	33,296,644	2,520	65,820,414
Japan	3,124	6,931,436	5,836	11,971,157	8,402	27,003,704	9,932	39,739,598
United Kingdom	5,246	21,130,874	4,437	21,530,264	3,822	25,824,820	3,622	33,157,422
Norway	2,725	11,203,246	2,742	15,641,498	2,808	19,346,911	2,706	26,153,682
Greece	747	4,529,234	1,377	7,137,244	1,850	10,951,993	2,743	22,527,156
U.S.S.R.*	1,138	3,429,472	1,845	8,237,847	5,924	14,831,775	7,652	19,235,973
U.S.A.†	4,059	24,837,169	3,416	21,527,349	2,938	18,463,207	4,346	14,586,616
Panama	607	4,235,983	692	4,465,407	886	5,645,877	2,418	13,667,123
France	1,456	4,708,728	1,558	5,198,435	1,420	6,457,900	1,393	10,745,999
Italy	1,312	5,122,240	1,413	5,279,493	1,639	7,447,610	1,732	10,136,989
Germany, Fed. Rep. of.	2,449	4,536,591	2,525	4,290,103	2,868	7,881,000	1,964	8,516,567
Sweden	1,211	3,746,866	1,123	4,891,041	995	4,920,704	775	7,486,196
Netherlands	1,891	4,884,049	1,847	2,132,002	1,598	5,206,663	1,348	5,679,413
Spain	1,453	1,800,721	1,814	2,561,599	2,234	3,440,952	2,667	5,433,354
Denmark	808	2,269,847	923	93,882	1,210	3,314,330	1,371	4,476,112
Singapore	115	116,144	124	1,522,663	153	424,417	610	3,891,902
India	257	858,916	354	46,454	399	2,401,056	471	3,886,187
Cyprus	2	991	9	551,143	207	1,138,229	735	3,221,070
China, People's Rep. of.	201	402,417	213	1,039,966	248	867,994	466	2,828,290
Poland	262	619,144	390	1,252,968	516	1,580,298	696	2,817,129
Brazil	423	1,054,733	397	1,829,741	422	1,721,608	482	2,601,408
Canada	1,085	1,578,077	1,154	1,009,486	1,266	2,399,949	1,257	2,565,501
Finland	334	714,483	420	999,846	388	1,397,232	361	2,001,618
Yugoslavia	237	661,061	353	8,864	348	1,515,563	414	1,873,482
Somali Republic**	Not recorded		4	129,999	79	369,118	273	1,813,313
Korea (South)	35	100,936	74	200,063	329	849,457	828	1,623,532
Bermuda	10	60,093	29	638,274	48	683,529	59	1,450,387
Taiwan	68	281,662	128	1,288,056	274	1,166,230	428	1,449,957
Argentina	355	1,041,507	323	591,106	327	1,265,510	374	1,447,165
German Democratic Rep.	49	149,988	274	831,976	423	988,640	437	1,380,000
Belgium	206	728,981	220	697,627	230	1,062,152	252	1,358,425
Portugal	331	602,867	333	726,999	376	870,008	440	1,209,701
Australia	330	619,996	306		344	1,074,112	419	1,205,248
WORLD TOTAL	36,311	129,769,500	41,865	160,391,504	52,444	227,489,864	63,724	342,162,363

* Information incomplete   ** Independence established in 1960.   † Including ships of the United States Reserve Fleet.

TONNAGE CLASSED WITH LLOYD'S REGISTER.

At July 1975, 29 per cent (99,331,765 tons) of the tonnage owned in the world was classed by Lloyd's Register.

MERCHANT SHIPPING

STEAMSHIPS AND MOTORSHIPS COMPLETED IN THE WORLD* DURING 1975

Source: *Lloyd's Register of Shipping*

Country of Build	Steamships No.	Steamships Tons Gross	Motorships No.	Motorships Tons Gross	Total No.	Total Tons Gross	For Registration in	Total Steamships and Motorships No.	Total Steamships and Motorships Tons Gross
Japan	61	7,985,555	869	9,005,675	930	16,991,230	Liberia	227	9,705,125
Germany, Fed. Rep. of	17	1,801,774	147	666,795	164	2,468,569	Norway	184	3,478,728
Sweden	4	649,627	43	1,537,898	47	2,187,525	Japan	402	3,066,083
Spain	3	458,855	207	1,133,667	210	1,592,522	United Kingdom	156	2,961,881
United Kingdom	3	431,211	111	738,305	114	1,169,516	Panama	166	1,328,140
France	12	989,745	47	159,984	59	1,149,729	U.S.S.R.	260	1,189,558
Norway	4	503,299	134	548,909	138	1,052,208	Singapore	57	1,117,145
Netherlands	5	705,110	138	323,366	143	1,028,476	Greece	57	1,044,590
Denmark	4	648,465	54	320,703	58	969,168	Sweden	36	1,037,191
Italy	2	97,500	39	694,042	41	791,542	France	71	930,081
Poland			99	735,021	99	735,021	Germany, Fed. Rep. of	70	912,552
Yugoslavia			25	638,001	25	638,001	Italy	36	847,462
U.S.A.	7	287,323	120	188,198	127	475,521	India	32	766,641
Korea (South)	3	315,369	28	94,286	31	409,655	Spain	175	693,587
†U.S.S.R.			148	395,686	148	395,686	Poland	47	586,554
German Democratic Rep.			63	350,636	63	350,636	Denmark	95	571,092
Brazil			25	295,279	25	295,279	Netherlands	58	483,661
Finland			31	267,083	31	267,083	U.S.A.	104	461,437
Belgium			16	200,565	16	200,565	Kuwait	7	323,982
Canada	1	12,862	35	158,790	36	171,652	Iran	22	321,463
Portugal			10	162,931	10	162,931	Finland	16	318,239
†Rumania			21	131,916	21	131,916	Brazil	27	310,017
Greece			29	120,299	29	120,299	Belgium	10	143,648
Taiwan			4	88,410	4	88,410	Australia	26	122,324
Australia			24	73,431	24	73,431	China, People's Rep. of	50	120,532
Bulgaria			5	65,112	5	65,112	Rumania	10	111,317
Singapore			55	49,126	55	49,126	Iraq	20	83,784
India			7	46,805	7	46,805	Libya	6	77,009
Irish Republic			2	30,500	2	30,500	Cuba	13	76,138
Peru			4	16,787	4	16,787	Hong Kong	1	69,602
Other Commonwealth Countries			13	8,652	13	8,652	Other Commonwealth C.	63	194,611
Other Countries			51	38,961	51	38,961	Other Countries	226	658,339
WORLD TOTAL	126	14,886,695	2,604	19,315,819	2,730	34,202,514	WORLD TOTAL	2,730	34,202,514

Tonnage completed to Lloyd's Register Class.—Of the world tonnage completed during 1975, 30 per cent. (10,254,958 tons) was to Lloyd's Register Class.

* Excluding People's Republic of China.   † Information incomplete.

THE LARGEST SHIPS IN THE WORLD FLEET
As recorded at Lloyd's Register at December 1975

NAME	Propulsion	Flag	Tons Gross	Length	Breadth	Draught	Year Built	Owners
Oil Tankers								
Nissei Maru	Tb	Japan	238,517	1243·0	203·0	91·0	1975	Tokyo Tanker K. K. & Chisu Kaiun K.K.
Globtik Tokyo	Tb	U.K.	238,252	1243·0	203·0	92·0	1973	Globtik Tankers Ltd.
Globtik London	Tb	U.K.	238,207	1243·0	203·0	92·0	1973	Globtik Tankers London Ltd.
Berge Emperor	Tb	Norway	211,360	1285·0	223·0	74·0	1975	Sig. Bergesen d.y. & Co.
Aiko Maru	Tb	Japan	207,000	1200·0	229·0	74·0	1976	Sanko Kisen
Hilda Knudson	Tb	Norway	202,406	1240·0	226·0	73·0	1975	D/S A/S Jeanette Skinner
Coraggio	Tb	Italy	201,000	1181·0	226·0	73·0	1976	Pluto Soc. Di. Nav.
Andros Petros	Tb	Liberia	198,000	1241·0	223·0	82·0	1976	Northern Sealanes Corp.
Al Andalus	Tb	Kuwait	191,006	1188·0	175·0	85·0	1975	Kuwait Oil Tanker Co. S.A.K.
Malmros Mariner	Tb	Sweden	190,401	1193·0	208·0	74·0	1975	Malmros R/A
Hemland	Tb	Sweden	190,367	1193·0	208·0	74·0	1974	Angfartygs A/B Tirfing
†Oppama	Tb	Liberia	189,000	1174·0	209·0	73·0	1976	Atlantian Shipping Co.
Titus	Tb	Norway	189,000	1225·0	209·0	75·0	1975	A/S Kosmos
Esso Japan	Tb	Liberia	189,000	1225·0	209·0	75·0	1976	W. Wilhelmsen
Nisseki Maru	Tb	Japan	184,855	1138·0	179·0	88·0	1971	Tokyo Tanker K.K.
Sea Scape	Tb	Sweden	178,515	1190·0	197·0	73·0	1975	Salenrederierna A/B
Sea Saint	Tb	Sweden	178,515	1190·0	197·0	73·0	1974	Salenrederierna A/B
Sea Symphony	Tb	Sweden	178,515	1190·0	197·0	73·0	1975	Salenrederierna A/B
Sea Stratus	Tb	Sweden	178,515	1190·0	197·0	73·0	1975	Salenrederierna A/B
Vassiliki Colocotronis	Tb	Greece	176,100	1213·0	210·0	73·0	1975	Panseguro Armadora S.A.
Ioannis Colocotronis	Tb	Greece	176,070	1213·0	210·0	73·0	1975	Viavela Armadora S.A.
Brazilian Hope	Tb	Germany, Fed. Rep.	176,053	1213·0	210·0	73·0	1975	Unknown
Shat-Alarab	Tb	Iraq	176,000	1213·0	209·0	73·0	1976	Arab Maritime Petroleum Transport Co.
Santa Maria	Tb	Spain	175,560	1189·0	175·0	85·0	1975	CIA. Maritima Gulf S.A.
Ocean Park	Tb	Korea (South)	172,336	1141·0	175·0	81·0	1974	Pan Ocean Bulk Carriers Ltd.
Karoline Maersk	Tb	Denmark	167,207	1215·0	185·0	73·0	1976	A/S D/S Svendborg & D/S at 1912 A/S
Kirsten Maersk	Tb	Denmark	167,207	1215·0	185·0	73·0	1975	A/S D/S Svendborg & D/S at 1912 A/S
Kristine Maersk	Tb	Denmark	167,204	1215·0	185·0	74·0	1974	A/S D/S Svendborg & D/S at 1912 A/S
Katrine Maersk	Tb	Denmark	167,204	1215·0	185·0	73·0	1974	A/S D/S Svendborg & D/S at 1912 A/S
Stavros G. L.	Tb	Greece	163,810	1187·0	196·0	72·0	1976	South Caribbean Shipping Co.
Tina	Oe	Greece	163,801	1187·0	196·0	73·0	1976	North Caribbean Shipping Co.

THE LARGEST SHIPS IN THE WORLD FLEET (*cont.*)

NAME	Propulsion	Flag	Tons Gross	Length	Breadth	Draught	Year Built	Owners
Arteaga..............	Tb	Spain	163,795	1141·0	175·0	81·0	1972	Refinería de Petroleos del Norte S.A.
Butron..............	Tb	Spain..	163,795	1141·0	175·0	81·0	1973	Refinería de Petroleos del Norte S.A.
Maasbracht.........	Tb	Netherlands	162,911	1155·0	181·0	73·0	1975	Schepv. Maats, Maasbracht B.V.
Protam Waal........	Tb	Netherlands	162,287	1148·0	181·0	73·0	1975	Produkten Tanker Maats.
Liofina.............	Tb	Germany, Fed. Rep.	162,226	1153·0	181·0	73·0	1974	Deutsche Shell A.G.
Amica..............	Tb	Norway	162,030	1152·0	181·0	73·0	1975	C. H. Sorensen & Sonner
Belfri.............	Tb	Norway	162,028	1153·0	181·0	73·0	1975	Belships Co. Ltd. S/A
Passenger Liners								
Queen Elizabeth 2..	Tb	U.K.	66,852	963·0	105·0	32·0	1969	Cunard Line Ltd.
France.............	Tb	France	66,348	1035·0	110·0	34·0	1961	Cie. Générale Transatlantique
Raffaello..........	Tb	Italy	45,933	904·0	101·0	30·0	1965	"Italia" Soc per Azioni di Nav.
Michelangelo.......	Tb	Italy	45,911	904·0	101·0	30·0	1965	"Italia" Soc per Azioni di Nav.
Canberra...........	Te	U.K.	44,807	818·0	102·0	32·0	1961	P. & O. Steam Nav. Co.
Oriana.............	Tb	U.K.	41,910	804·0	97·0	32·0	1960	P. & O. Steam Nav. Co.
United States......	Tb	U.S.A.	38,216	990·0	101·0	32·0	1952	United States Lines Co.
Rotterdam..........	Tb	Netherlands	37,783	748·0	94·0	29·0	1959	N. V. Nederl.-Amerika Stoomv. Maats.
Windsor Castle......	Tb	U.K.	36,277	783·0	92·0	32·0	1960	Union Castle Mail S.S. Co. Ltd.

† Name not officially confirmed.   Oe= Oil engine   Tb= Turbine engines.   Te= Turbo-electric.

Principal Book Publishers and Their Addresses

More than 8,000 firms, individuals and societies have published one or more books in recent years. The list which follows is a selective one comprising, in the main, those firms whose names are most familiar to the general public. An interleaved list containing some 2,500 names and addresses is available, price 80p post free, from the publishers of "Whitaker".

Abelard-Schumann, Intertext House, 450 Edgware Rd., W.2.
Allan (Ian), Terminal House, Shepperton, Mddx.
Allen (J. A.), 1 Lower Grosvenor Pl., S.W.1.
Allen, (W. H.), 44 Hill St., W.1.
Allen & Unwin, 40 Museum St., W.C.1.
Angus & Robertson, 2 Fisher St., W.C.1.
Architectural Press, 9 Queen Anne's Gate, S.W.1.
Arlington Books, 3 Clifford St., W.1.
Armada Books, 14 St. James's Place, S.W.1.
Arms & Armour Press, 2 Hampstead High St., N.W.3.
Arnold (E.), & Co., 25 Hill St., W.1.
Arnold (E. J.) & Son, Butterley St., Leeds.
Arrow Books, 3 Fitzroy Square, W.1.
Athlone Press, 4 Gower St., W.C.1.
Autobooks, Golden Lane, Brighton.
Baillière, Tindall, 35 Red Lion Sq., W.C.1.
Baker (John) 35 Bedford Row, W.C.1.
Barker (Arthur), 11 St. John's Hill, S.W.11.
Barrie & Jenkins, 24 Highbury Cresc., N.5.
Bartholomew & Son, Duncan St., Edinburgh.
Batsford, 4 Fitzhardinge St., Portman Square, W.1.
Bell (Geo.) & Sons, 6 Portugal St., W.C.2.
Benn (Ernest), Sovereign Way, Tonbridge, Kent.
Bingley (Clive), 16 Pembridge Rd., W.11.
Black (A. & C.), 35 Bedford Row, W.C.2.
Blackie, Glasgow, and 450 Edgware Road, W.2.
Blackwell (Basil), 108 Cowley Rd., Oxford.
Blackwood (W.), 32 Thistle St., Edinburgh.
Blandford Press, West St., Poole, Dorset.
Blond & Briggs, 12 Caroline Pl., W.2.
Bodley Head, 9 Bow St., W.C.2.
Bowes & Bowes, 9 Bow St., W.C.2.
Brown, Son & Ferguson, 52 Darnley St., Glasgow.
Burke Pub. Co., 14 John St., W.C.1.
Butterworth & Co., Borough Green, Sevenoaks, Kent.
Calder & Boyars, 18 Brewer St., W.1.
Cambridge Univ. Press, 200 Euston Rd., N.W.1, and Cambridge.
Cape (Jonathan), 30 Bedford Square, W.C.1.
Cassell & Co., 35 Red Lion Sq., W.C.1.
Centaur Press, Fontwell, Arundel, Sx.
Chambers (W. & R.), 11 Thistle St., Edinburgh.
Chapman & Hall, 11 New Fetter Lane, E.C.4.
Chapman (Geoffrey), 35 Red Lion Sq., W.C.1.
Chatto & Windus, 40-42 William IV St., W.C.2.
Churchill Livingstone, 23 Ravelston Terr., Edinburgh.
Collier-Macmillan, 35 Red Lion Sq., W.C.1.
Collins, Sons & Co., 14 St. James's Place, S.W.1.
Constable & Co., 10 Orange St., W.C.2.
Cooper (Leo), 196 Shaftesbury Ave., W.C.2.
Corgi Books, 61 Uxbridge Road, W.5.
Darton, Longman & Todd, 85 Gloucester Rd., S.W.7.
David & Charles, Brunel House, Newton Abbot, Devon.
Davies (Christopher), 4 Thomas Row, Swansea.
Davies (Peter), 15 Queen St., W.1.
Davis (R. Hart-), MacGibbon, Frogmore, St. Albans, Herts.
Dean & Son, 43 Ludgate Hill, E.C.4.
Dent (J. M.) & Sons, 26 Albemarle St., W.1.
Deutsch (A.), 105 Gt. Russell St., W.C.1.
Dobson Books, 80 Kensington Church St., W.8.
Dolphin Pub. Co., Milton Rd., Aylesbury, Bucks.
Duckworth & Co., 43 Gloucester Crescent, N.W.1

E.P. Group, 10 Snow Hill, E.C.1.
Elek, 54 Caledonian Rd., N.1.
Elliot Right Way Books, Kingswood Bldg., Kingswood, Surrey.
Encyclopædia Britannica, 156 Oxford St., W.1.
English Universities Press, Mill Rd., Dunton Green, Kent.
Evans Bros., Montague House, Russell Sq., W.C.1.
Eyre & Spottiswoode, 11 New Fetter Lane, E.C.4.
Faber & Faber, 3 Queen Square, W.C.1.
Focal Press, 31 Fitzroy Square, W.1.
Fontana, 14 St. James's Place, S.W.1.
Foulis (G. T.), Sparkford, Yeovil, Som.
Foulsham & Co., Yeovil Rd., Slough, Berks.
Fountain Press, 14 St. James Rd., Watford, Herts.
French (Samuel), 26 Southampton St., W.C.2.
Frewin (Leslie), 5 Goodwin's Court, W.C.2.
Gall & Inglis, 12 Newington Road, Edinburgh, 9.
Garnstone, 59 Brompton Rd., S.W.3.
Gee & Co., 151 Strand, W.C.2.
Geographia, St. Albans, Herts.
Gibbons (Stanley), 391 Strand, W.C.2.
Gibson (Robert), 17 Fitzroy Place, Glasgow.
Ginn & Co., Elsinore Ho., Buckingham St., Aylesbury, Bucks.
Gold Lion Books, 138 Park Lane, W.1.
Gollancz (Victor), 14 Henrietta St., W.C.2.
Gower Press, Epping, Essex.
Graham (Frank), 6 Queen's Terrace, Newcastle.
Green (W.), St. Giles St., Edinburgh.
Griffin (Charles), 5A Crendon St., High Wycombe, Bucks.
Guinness Superlatives, 2 Cecil Court, London Road, Enfield.
H.M. Stationery Office, Atlantic House, Holborn Viaduct, E.C.1.
Hale (Robert), Clerkenwell Green, E.C.1.
Hamilton (Hamish), 90 Gt. Russell St., W.C.1.
Hamlyn, Astronaut Ho., Hounslow Road, Feltham, Mddx.
Harrap (G. G.) & Co., 182 High Holborn, W.C.1.
Harvill Press, 30A Pavilion Rd., S.W.1.
Haynes (J. H.), Sparkford, Yeovil, Som.
Heinemann (Wm.), 15 Queen St., W.1.
Hodder & Stoughton, 47 Bedford Sq., W.C.1.
Hodge & Co., 34 N. Frederick St., Glasgow.
Hogarth Press, 40-42 William IV St., W.C.2.
Hollis & Carter, 9 Bow St., W.C.2.
Holmes-Macdougall, 137 Leith Walk, Edinburgh.
Holt-Saunders, 1 St. Annes Rd., Eastbourne, Sx.
Hughes & Son, 4 Thomas Row, Swansea.
Hurst & Blackett, 3 Fitzroy Square, W.1.
Hutchinson & Co., 3 Fitzroy Square, W.1.
Independent Press, 86 Tavistock Pl., W.C.1.
Jackdaw Publications, 30 Bedford Sq., W.C.1.
Jarrold & Sons, Barrack Street, Norwich.
Jarrolds, 3 Fitzroy Square, W.1.
Johnson Pubns., 55 Langley Pk. Rd., Sutton, Sy.
Johnston & Bacon, 35 Red Lion Sq., W.C.1.
Jordan & Sons, 15 Pembroke Rd., Bristol.
Joseph (Michael), 52 Bedford Sq., W.C.1.
Kaye & Ward, 21 New St., E.C.2.
Kelly's Directories, Neville House, Eden St., Kingston, Surrey.
Kimber (Wm.), 22A Queen Anne's Gate, S.W.1.
Kimpton (Henry), 7 Leighton Place, N.W.5.
Ladybird, Beeches Rd., Loughborough.
Lane (Allen), 17 Grosvenor Gdns., S.W.1.
Lawrence & Wishart, 46 Bedford Row, W.C.1.

Lewis (H. K.), 136 Gower St., W.C.1.
Lockwood (Crosby) Frogmore, St. Albans, Herts.
Long (John), 3 Fitzroy Square, W.1.
Longman Group, Burnt Mill, Harlow, Essex.
Low (S.), Marston & Co., Queen St., Maidenhead, Berks.
Lund Humphries, 26 Litchfield St., W.C.2.
Lutterworth Press, Farnham Rd., Guildford, Sy.
Macdonald & Evans, Estover Rd., Plymouth.
Macdonald & Jane's, 8 Shepherdess Walk, N.1.
McGraw-Hill, Shoppenhangers Rd., Maidenhead, Berks.
Machinery Pub. Co., New England St., Brighton.
Macmillan Publishers, Little Essex St., W.C.2.
Marshall Cavendish, 58 Old Compton St., W.1.
Marshall, Morgan & Scott, 116 Baker St., W.1.
Mayflower, Frogmore., St. Albans, Herts.
Methodist Publishing, Wellington Rd., S.W.19.
Methuen & Co., 11 New Fetter Lane, E.C.4.
Mills & Boon, 17 Foley St., W.1.
Mitchell Beazley, 14 Manette St., W.1.
Mowbray, The Alden Press, Osney Mead, Oxford.
Muller (F.), Victoria Works, Edgware Rd., N.W.2.
Murray (John), 50 Albemarle St., W.1.
Museum Press, 39 Parker St., W.C.2.
National C.E.C., Robt. Denholm House, Nutfield, Surrey.
Nelson (T.), Lincoln Way, Sunbury, Mddx.
New Authors, 3 Fitzroy Square, W.1.
New English Library, Barnard's Inn, E.C.1.
Nisbet & Co., Digswell Pl., Welwyn, Herts.
Nonesuch Library, 9 Bow St.,W.C.2.
Novello & Co., Borough Green, Sevenoaks, Kent.
Oak Tree Press, 116 Baker St., W.1.
Octopus Books, 59 Grosvenor St., W.1.
Odhams Books, Astronaut Ho., Hounslow Rd., Feltham, Mddx.
Oliphants, 116 Baker St., W.1.
Oliver & Boyd, 23 Ravelston Terr., Edinburgh.
Owen (Peter), 73 Kenway Rd., S.W.5.
Oxford Univ. Press, 37 Dover St., W.1.
Pall Mall Press, St. Ebbes St., Oxford.
Pan Books, 18 Cavaye Place, S.W.10.
Panther, Frogmore, St. Albans, Herts.
Paul (Kegan), 39 Store St., W.C.1.
Paul (Stanley), 3 Fitzroy Square, W.1.
Pelham Books, 52 Bedford Sq., W.C.1.
Penguin Books, Harmondsworth, Mddx.
Pergamon Press, Headington Hill Hall, Oxford.
Phaidon Press, St. Ebbes St., Oxford.
Pharmaceutical Press, 17 Bloomsbury Sq., W.C.1.
Philip (George), 12 Long Acre, W.C.2.
Photo Precision, Caxton Rd., St. Ives, Hunts.
Pickering & Inglis, 26 Bothwell St., Glasgow, C.2.
Pitkins, 11 Wyfold Rd., S.W.6.
Pitman Publishing, Parker St., W.C.2.
Purnell Books, Queen St., Maidenhead, Berks.

Putnam & Co., 9 Bow St., W.C.2.
Quartet Books, 27 Goodge St., W.1.
Queen Anne Press, 8 Shepherdess Walk, N.1.
Rapp & Whiting, 105 Great Russell Street, W.C.1.
Reinhardt (Max), 9 Bow St., W.C.2.
Religious Education Press, Hennock Rd., Exeter.
Rider & Co., 3 Fitzroy Square, W.1.
Rivingtons, Montague House, Russell Sq., W.C.1.
Routledge & Kegan Paul, 39 Store St., W.C.1.
Scripture Union & C.S.S.M., 47 Marylebone Lane, W.1.
Secker & Warburg, 14 Carlisle St., W.1.
Seeley Service, 196 Shaftesbury Av., W.C.2.
Sheed & Ward, 6 Blenheim St., W.1.
Sheldon Press, Holy Trinity Church, Marylebone Rd., N.W.1.
Sidgwick & Jackson, 1 Tavistock Chambers, W.C.1.
Smith (M. Temple), 37 Gt. Russell St., W.C.1.
Smythe (Colin), Gerrards Cross, Bucks.
S.P.C.K., Holy Trinity Church, Marylebone Rd., N.W.1.
Souvenir Press, 43 Gt. Russell St., W.C.1.
Spearman (N.), 112 Whitfield St., W.1.
Sphere Books, 30 Gray's Inn Rd., W.C.1.
Spon (E. & F. N.), 11 New Fetter Lane, E.C.4.
Sporting Handbooks, 13 Bedford Square, W.C.1.
Stanford Maritime, 12–14 Long Acre, W.C.2.
Stephens (Patrick), Bar Hill, Cambridge.
Stevens & Sons, 11 New Fetter Lane, E.C.4.
Student C. M. P., 58 Bloomsbury St., W.C.1.
Studio Vista, 35 Red Lion Sq., W.C.1.
Sweet & Maxwell, 11 New Fetter Lane, E.C.4.
Tabard Press, 10 Snow Hill, E.C.1.
Talbot Press, Ballymount Rd., Dublin.
Tavistock Publications, 11 New Fetter Lane, E.C.4.
Technical Press, Freeland, Oxford.
Thames & Hudson, 30 Bloomsbury St., W.C.1.
Turnstone Press, 37 Upper Addison Gdns., W.14.
University of London Press, Mill Rd., Dunton Green, Kent.
University of Wales Press, Gwennyth St., Cardiff.
University Tutorial Press, 9 Gt. Sutton St., E.C.1.
Vallentine Mitchell, 10 Woburn Walk, W.C.1.
Ward, Lock, 116 Baker St., W.1.
Warne, 40 Bedford Square, W.C.1.
Watts & Co., 39 Parker St., W.C.2.
Weidenfeld & Nicolson, 11 St. John's Hill, S.W.11.
Wheaton (A.), Hennock Rd., Exeter.
"Whitaker," 13 Bedford Square, W.C.1.
Wildwood House, 29 King St., W.C.2.
Witherby (H. F. & G.), 5 Plantain Place, S.E.1.
Wolfe Publishing, 10 Earlham St., W.C.2.
World Distributors, 12 Lever St., Manchester.
World's Work, Kingswood, Tadworth, Surrey.
Wright (John), 42 Triangle West, Bristol.

Most of the principal book publishers are members of The Publishers Association, whose address is 19 Bedford Square, London, W.C.1.—*President*, Peter Allsop (Associated Book Publishers, Ltd.); *Chief Executive*, Clive Bradley.

BOOK PRODUCTION AND BOOK EXPORTS

These figures for book production and exports are issued by the Department of Industry. The totals for the years 1964 to 1975 are shown below:

Year	Total value of Books produced in U.K.	Total value of Books exported from U.K.	Year	Total value of Books produced in U.K.	Total value of Books exported from U.K.
1964	£98,489,220	£43,225,649	1970	£153,676,000	£67,842,000
1965	104,876,998	46,123,190	1971	179,099,000	77,856,000
1966	119,578,145	51,417,786	1972	205,266,000	81,207,000
1967	125,782,262	53,838,418	1973	230,106,000	95,855,000
1968	137,748,324	61,741,160	1974	281,508,000	119,359,000
1969	145,893,000	68,523,000	1975(Provisional)	350,648,000	143,460,000

BOOKS PUBLISHED IN GREAT BRITAIN IN 1975

This table, from *The Bookseller* of December 27, 1975, shows the books published in 1975 with the number of new editions, translations and limited editions.

Books and pamphlets priced at less than 12½p have been omitted, as are also all Government publications except the more important issued by H.M. Stationery Office.

	Total	Reprints and New Editions	Translations	Limited Editions
Aeronautics	90	30	1	—
Agriculture and Forestry	327	82	7	—
Architecture	392	97	7	1
Art	1,322	306	52	11
Astronomy	89	25	3	—
Bibliography and Library Economy	554	89	2	1
Biography	1,211	281	60	1
Chemistry and Physics	972	95	27	—
Children's Books	2,688	589	99	2
Commerce	771	190	2	—
Customs, Costume, Folklore	126	38	9	—
Domestic Science	478	115	12	—
Education	1,036	181	5	1
Engineering	1,047	261	11	—
Entertainment	513	135	19	2
Fiction	4,198	1,809	137	14
General	216	46	12	—
Geography and Archæology	255	64	4	3
Geology and Meteorology	275	50	11	—
History	1,324	413	55	1
Humour	91	11	1	—
Industry	462	112	11	—
Language	312	66	7	—
Law and Public Administration	1,062	208	8	1
Literature	907	152	48	12
Mathematics	539	87	26	—
Medical Science	1,844	406	29	—
Military Science	134	14	2	1
Music	297	91	6	—
Natural Sciences	1,130	165	45	1
Occultism	240	69	19	—
Philosophy	289	69	35	—
Photography	144	33	3	—
Plays	203	58	20	2
Poetry	707	86	59	81
Political Science and Economy	2,629	390	106	—
Psychology	602	109	11	—
Religion and Theology	1,098	293	119	1
School Textbooks	2,099	399	75	—
Science, General	62	10	—	—
Sociology	957	126	14	—
Sports and Outdoor Games	586	143	10	2
Stockbreeding	208	68	7	2
Trade	389	90	—	1
Travel and Guidebooks	560	183	11	1
Wireless and Television	174	27	2	—
Totals	**35,608**	**8,361**	**1,209**	**142**

COPYRIGHT

The Government Department dealing with Copyright is the *Industrial Property and Copyright Dept., Department of Trade*, 25 Southampton Bldgs., W.C.2.

Subject to the provisions of the Copyright Act, 1956, copyright subsists automatically in every original literary, dramatic, musical and artistic work and continues to subsist until the end of the period of fifty years from the end of the calendar year in which the author died and shall then expire. *No registration nor other formalities are required in order to obtain the protection of the Act.* Protection is conferred not only against reproduction but also against the public performance of a work without permission. Copyright may also subsist in sound recordings, cinematograph films and television and sound broadcasts. Libraries entitled, under a provision still in force of the Copyright Act, 1911, to receive free copies of books published in the United Kingdom are the British Library, the Bodleian Library, Oxford, University Library, Cambridge, the National Library of Wales, the National Library of Scotland and Trinity College, Dublin.

Voluntary Registration at Stationers' Hall.—Compulsory registration at Stationers' Hall was terminated by the Copyright Act of 1911, but in 1924 the Stationers' Company esablished a *new* Register in which Books and Fine Arts can be registered. A copy has to be filed at Stationers' Hall and certified copies of the entries are issued, the fees being £5 for a Book, or a Fine Art; certified copies £3 in either case. The fee for a search is £2·50.

ANNUAL REFERENCE BOOKS

Advertiser's Annual—Neville Ho., Eden St., Kingston-upon-Thames, Sy. £10·50.

Aeromodeller Annual.—14 St. James Rd., Watford. £2·25.

Aircraft.—Terminal House, Shepperton, Middx. £2·75.

Annual Art Sales Index.—Pond Ho., Weybridge, Sy. (Nov.). £19·50.

Annual Register of World Events.—Longman Ho., Burnt Mill, Harlow, Essex. £15·00.

Antiques in Britain.—Amadines, Coln St. Dennis, Cheltenham, Glos. £2·75.

Architects & Planners Directory of Official.—2 Catherine Street, W.C.2. £6·50.

Astronomical Ephemeris.—H.M. Stationery Office, Atlantic House, Holborn Viaduct, E.C.1. (Jan.) £7·10.

Automobile Year.—Bar Hill, Cambridge. (Feb.) £11·95.

B.B.C. Handbook.—144 Bermondsey St., S.E.1. £1·50.

Baily's Hunting Directory.—1 Lower Grosvenor Place, S.W.1 (Oct.) £5·25.

Banker's Almanac & Year Book.—R.A.C. House, Lansdowne Rd., Croydon. (Feb.) £20·00.

Benedictine Year Book.—St. Albans Priory, Bewsey St., Warrington, Lancs. (Dec.) 25p.

Bloodstock Breeders Annual Review.—26 Charing Cross Rd., W.C.2. £18·50.

Boat World.—39 East St., Epsom, Surrey. (Jan.) £2·25.

Boxing News Annual.—135 Wardour St., W.1. £1·00.

Brassey's Defence Year Book.—81A Endell St., W.C.2. £8·50.

British Antiques Year Book.—Chestergate Ho., Vauxhall Bridge Rd., S.W.1. £7·50.

British Books in Print.—13 Bedford Square, W.C.1. £27·00.

British Film & Television Year Book.—142 Wardour St., W.1. (Jan./Feb.) £6·00.

British Industry & Services in the Common Market.—Neville Ho., Eden St., Kingston-upon-Thames, Sy. £10·00.

British Music Year Book.—Erasmus Ho., Epping, Essex. £10·50.

British Textile Register.—R.A.C. House, Lansdowne, Rd., Croydon. (Mar.) £10·50.

Brown's Nautical Almanack.—52 Darnley St., Glasgow, S.1. (Sept.) £6·00.

Building Societies Yearbook.—2–3 Burgon St., E.C.4. (July.) £9·60.

Buses Annual.—Terminal Ho., Shepperton, Mddx. £2·75.

Caravan & Chalet Sites Guide.—54 Regent St., W.1. 50p.

Carpet Annual.—54 Regent St., W.1. (Jan.). £7·95.

Catholic Directory.—21 Fleet St., E.C.4. £6·00.

Charities Digest.—88 Kingsway, W.C.2. (Jan.) £2·80.

Chemical Industry Directory & Who's Who.—Sovereign Way, Tonbridge, Kent. (Nov.) £15·00.

Chemist & Druggist Directory.—Sovereign Way, Tonbridge, Kent. £12·00.

Christies' Review of the Season.—3 Fitzroy Sq., W.1. (Dec.) £10·00.

Church of England Year Book.—Church House, Dean's Yard, Westminister, S.W.1. (Jan.) £4·50.

Church of Scotland Year Book.—121 George St., Edinburgh 2. (Apr.) £2·50.

City Connections, Directory of.—4 New Burlington St., W.1. £20·00.

Clean Air Year Book.—134 North St., Brighton. (May.) £1·25.

Clothing Export Council Directory.—1–5 Bath St., E.C.1. £8·00.

Commercial Television Yearbook & Directory.—103–119 Waterloo Road, S.E.1. £5·00.

Commonwealth Universities Year Book.—36 Gordon Square, W.C.1. (Sept.) £21·00.

Computer Users' Year Book.—18 Queen's Rd., Brighton, Sx. £14·80.

Concrete Year Book.—Wexham Springs, Slough, Bucks. £4·00.

Consulting Engineers Who's Who.—10–16 Elm St., W.C.1. £3·75.

Containerization International Year Book.—Chestergate Ho., Vauxhall Bridge Rd., S.W.1. (Mar.). £9·50.

Contractors and Public Works, Annual Directory of.—68 High St., Northwood, Middx. (Apr.) £7·00.

Coventry Evening Telegraph Year Book and Who's Who.—Coventry Newspapers Ltd., Corporation St., Coventry. (Nov.) £2·50.

Current Law Year Book.—11 New Fetter La., E.C.4. £12·50.

"Daily Mail" Year Book.—Carmelite House, Fleet St., E.C.4. (Dec.) £1·20; 90p.

Decorating Contractor Annual Directory.—2 Queensway, Redhill, Surrey. £3·70.

Decorative Art in Modern Interiors.—35 Red Lion Sq., W.C.1. £10·50.

Diplomatic Service List.—H.M.S.O., Atlantic House, Holborn Viaduct, E.C.1. (April.) £5·00.

Directory of Directors.—R.A.C. House, Lansdowne Rd., Croydon. (Apr.) £9·00.

Directory of Opportunities for Graduates.—54 Regent St., W.1. £6·00.

Do-it-Yourself Annual.—Link House, Dingwall Ave., Croydon. (Jan.) 25p.

Dod's Parliamentary Companion.—39 East St., Epsom, Surrey. (Sept.) £8·00.

Education Authorities' Directory and Annual.—Derby House, Bletchingley Rd., Merstham, Surrey. (Jan.) £8·00.

Electrical & Electronic Trader Year Book.—40 Bowling Green Lane, E.C.1. £6.00.

Electrical & Electronics Trades Directory.—P.O. Box 8, Southgate House, Stevenage. (Feb.) £16·50.

Electrical Contractor's Yearbook.—55 Catherine Place, S.W.1. £2·00.

Electricity Supply Handbook.—40 Bowling Green Lane, E.C.1. (Apr.) £1·50.

"Engineer" Buyers' Guide, 30 Calderwood St., S.E.18. £2·30.

Europa Year Book.—18 Bedford Square, W.C.1. 2 vols. (Apr.) £29·00.

European Glass Directory & Buyer's Guide, European.—2 Queensway, Redhill, Surrey. £6·50.

European Offshore Oil & Gas Year Book.—116A Pentonville Rd., N.1. £20·00.

European Plastics Buyers' Guide.—40 Bowling Green Lane, E.C.1. £15·00.

Export Data: Exporter's Year Book.—Sovereign Way, Tonbridge, Kent. (Dec./Jan.) £14·00.

Extel Issuing House Year Book.—37–45 Paul St., E.C.2. £20·00.

Farm and Garden Equipment Guide.—40 Bowling Green Lane, E.C.1. £3·50.

Finishing Handbook and Directory.—4 Ludgate Circus, E.C.4. £5·65.

Fire Protection Directory.—Sovereign Way, Tonbridge, Kent. (Nov.) £8·50.

Fishing Industry Index International.—54 Regent St., W.1. £5·50.

"Flight" Directory of British Aviation.—40 Bowling Green Lane, E.C.1. £6·50.

Food Processing and Packaging Directory.—40 Bowling Green Lane, E.C.1. £12·00.

Frozen Foods Yearbook.—2 Queensway, Redhill, Surrey. £3·00.

Fruit Trades World Directory.—54 Regent St., W.1. (Jan.) £5·57.

Furnishing Trade, Directory to the.—Sovereign Way, Tonbridge, Kent. (Jan.) £15·00.

Gas Directory.—Sovereign Way, Tonbridge, Kent. (Jan.) £8·50.

Gibbon's Stamps of the World Catalogue.—392 Strand, W.C.2. (Oct.) £7·00.

Girls' School Year Book.—35 Bedford Row, W.C.1. (May.) £2·75.

Good Food Guide.—14 Buckingham St., W.C.2. £3·50.

Government & Municipal Contractors Register.—39 East St., Epsom, Surrey. (Jan.) £7·00.

Guild of Agricultural Journalists Year Book.—151 Gt. Portland St., W.1. £1·50.

Guinness Book of Records.—2 Cecil Court, London Rd., Enfield. (Oct.) £2·95.

Hardware Directory.—Sovereign Way, Tonbridge, Kent. £10·00.

Harper's Directory & Manual of Wine & Spirit Trades.—Southbank House, Black Prince Rd., S.E.1. (June.) £4·00.

Harper's Guide to the Sports Trade.—Southbank House, Black Prince Rd., S.E.1. (Jan.) £2·50.

Health Services Buyers' Guide.—39 East St., Epsom, Surrey. £8·00.

Hi-fi Year Book.—40 Bowling Green Lane, E.C.1. £3·00.

Hollis Press and P.R. Annual.—Contact House, Lower Hampton Rd., Sunbury-on-Thames. (Oct.) £10·00; £6·00.

Horse & Hound Yearbook.—P.O. Box 21, Tower House, Southampton St., W.C.2. (Winter.) £2·50.

Horseman's Year.—52 Bedford Sq., W.C.1. (Apr.) £4·25.

Hospitals & Health Services Yearbook.—75 Portland Place, W.1. (Nov.) £15·60.

Hotel Catering and Institutional Managers' Yearbook.—116A Pentonville Rd., N.1. £4·24.

Hotel, Restaurant & Canteen Supplies.—39 East St., Epsom, Sy. £4·00.

Hutchins' Priced Schedules.—33 Station Rd., Bexhill-on-Sea. £7·50.

Hydraulic Handbook.—Crown House, Morden, Surrey. £14·00.

Insurance Directory & Yearbook.—The Butts, Half Acre, Brentford, Middx. £7·00.

International Antiques Yearbook.—29 Maddox St., W.1. (Jan.). £7·50.

International Finishing Industries Manual.—157 Hagden La., Watford. (Jan.) £5·50.

International Shipping & Shipbuilding Directory.—Sovereign Way, Tonbridge, Kent. £20·00.

International Yearbook & Statesman's Who's Who.—Neville Ho., Eden St., Kingston-upon-Thames, Surrey (Apr.) £20·00.

Iron & Steel Year Book.—Atlantic House, Holborn Viaduct, E.C.1. £2·20.

Jane's All The World's Aircraft.—8 Shepherdess Walk, N.1. (Oct.). £25·00.

Jane's Fighting Ships.—8 Shepherdess Walk, N.1. (Aug.) £25·00.

Jane's Freight Containers.—8 Shepherdess Walk, N.1. (Nov.). £25·00.

Jane's Infantry Weapons.—8 Shepherdess Walk, N.1. (May.) £25·00.

Jane's Major Companies of Europe.—8 Shepherdess Walk, N.1. (May.) £30·00.

Jane's Surface Skimmer Systems.—8 Shepherdess Walk, N.1. (Dec.). £16·50.

Jane's Weapon Systems.—8 Shepherdess Walk, N.1. (Dec.). £25·00.

Jane's World Railways.—8 Shepherdess Walk, N.1. £25·00.

Jewish Year Book.—25 Furnival St., E.C.4. (Jan.) £3·50.

Journal of Commerce Annual Review.—213 Tower Bldg., 22 Water St., Liverpool. 75p.

Kelly's Handbook to the Titled, Landed and Official Classes.—Neville House, Eden St., Kingston-upon-Thames, Surrey. £12·00.

Kelly's Post Office London Directory.—Neville House, Eden St., Kingston-upon-Thames, Surrey. (Jan.) £10·50.

Kempe's Engineers Year Book.—30 Calderwood St., S.E.18. £11·00.

Kemp's Directory.—1–5 Bath St., E.C.1. (Sept.) £12·00.

Kemp's International Film & T.V. Directory.—1–5 Bath St., E.C.1. (May.) £6·50.

Kime's International Law Directory.—170 Sloane St., S.W.1. (June.) £4·00.

Law List.—11 New Fetter Lane, E.C.4. (May.) £10·00.

Law List, International.—Pitman Ho., Parker St., W.C.2. £12·50.

Laxton's Building Price Book.—Neville House, Eden St., Kingston-upon-Thames, Surrey. £5·00.

Library Assocation Yearbook.—7 Ridgmount St., Store St., W.C.1. (May.) £6·25.

Lloyd's Calendar.—Lime St., E.C.3. (Oct.). £2·50.

London Chamber of Commerce and Industry Directory.—2 Queensway, Redhill, Surrey. (Nov.) £5·00.

Manufacturers & Merchants Directory.—Neville House, Eden St., Kingston-upon-Thames, Surrey. £10·85.

Markets (Retail) Yearbook.—Union St., Oldham. 90p.

"Mechanical World" Electrical Year Book.—14 St. James Rd., Watford. £2·50.

"Mechanical World" Year Book.—14 St. James Rd., Watford. £3·00.

Medical Annual.—42–44 Triangle West, Bristol. (Sept.) £8·00.

Medical Directory.—23 Ravelston Terr., Edinburgh. (Apr.) £20·00.

Medical Register.—44 Hallam St., W.1. (Mar.) £13·00.

Metal Bulletin Handbook.—46 Wigmore St., W.1. £7·00.

Middle East & North Africa.—18 Bedford Sq., W.C.1. (Oct.) £15·50.

Mining International Yearbook.—10 Cannon St., E.C.4. (June.) £8·00.

Modern Publicity.—35 Red Lion Sq., W.C.1. (Sept.) £10·50.

Motor Industry of Great Britain.—Forbes House, Halkin St., S.W.1. (Oct.) £11·50.

Municipal Yearbook & Public Services Directory, 178 Gt. Portland St., W.1. (Dec.) £13·50.

Music Trades Directory.—157 Hagden Lane, Watford. £4·50.

National Trust Year Book.—18 Bedford Sq., W.C.1. £4·00.

Nautical Almanac.—H.M.S.O., Atlantic House, Holborn Viaduct, E.C.1. (Oct.) £2·20.

Newspaper Press Directory.—Sovereign Way, Tonbridge, Kent. (Feb.) £20·00.

Oil & Gas International Yearbook.—10 Cannon St., E.C.4. (Dec.) £10·00.

Old Moore's Almanac.—Yeovil Rd., Slough, Bucks. (July.) 7p.

Owen's Commerce and Travel and International Register.—886 High Rd., N.12. (Mar.) £8·00.

Packaging Directory.—9 Chiswick High Rd., W.4. 2v. ea. £4·00.

Paper Trade Directory of the World, Phillips'.—Sovereign Way, Tonbridge, Kent. (Jan.) £16·00.

Paperbacks in Print.—13 Bedford Sq., W.C.1. £8·00.

Pears Cyclopedia.—52 Bedford Square, W.C.1. £3·75.

Penrose Annual.—10–16 Elm St., W.C.1. (Apr.) £8·50.

Personnel & Training Management Year Book.—116A Pentonville Rd., N.1. £7·95.

Photography Year Book.—14 St. James Rd., Watford. £6·50.

Polymers, Paint, Colour Year Book.—2 Queensway, Redhill, Surrey. £6·00.

Ports of the World.—Sovereign Way, Tonbridge, Kent. £20·00.

Printing Industries Annual.—11 Bedford Row, W.C.1. £8·00.

Printing Trades Directory.—Sovereign Way, Tonbridge, Kent. £12·50.

Public and Preparatory Schools Year Book.—35 Bedford Row, W.C.1. (May.) £3·75.

Publishers in the United Kingdom and their Addresses.—13 Bedford Square, W.C.1. (Feb.) 80p.

Publishing, Directory of.—35 Red Lion Square, W.C.1. (Oct.) £3·50.

R.A.C. Guide & Handbook.—85 Pall Mall, S.W.1. (Apr.) £3·00.

Raceform Up-to-date Form Book: Flat Racing.—Thomson Ho., Withy Grove, Manchester. (Dec.) £3·50.

Raceform Up-to-date Form Book: National Hunt.—Thomson Ho., Withy Grove, Manchester. (Aug.) £2·00.

Railway Directory & Year Book.—40 Bowling Green Lane, E.C.1. (Dec.) £8·00.

Reed's Nautical Almanac.—36–37 Cock Lane, E.C.1. (Oct.) £4·95.

Register of Defunct & Other Companies.—R.A.C. House, Lansdowne Rd., Croydon. £5·00.

RIBA Directory of Practices.—Royal Institute of British Architects, 66 Portland Place, W.1. (Oct.) £5·00.

Royal Society Year Book.—6 Carlton Ho. Terr., S.W.1. (Feb.) £3·20.

Ruff's Guide to the Turf.—9 New Fetter Lane, E.C.4. (Dec.) £6·00.

Salvation Army Year Book.—117–121 Judd St., W.C.1. (Nov.) £1·50.

Scottish Current Law Year Book.—St. Giles St., Edinburgh. £16·00.

Scottish Law Directory.—34–36 North Frederick St., Glasgow. £6·50.

Screen World.—Victoria Works, Edgware Rd., N.W.2. £5·75.

Sell's British Aviation.—39 East St., Epsom, Surrey. £6·00.

Sell's British Exporters Register & National Directory.—39 East St., Epsom, Surrey. £7·00.

Sell's Building Index.—39 East St., Epsom, Surrey. £10·00.

Sell's Directory of Products and Services.—39 East St., Epsom, Surrey. (July.) £9·00.

Sheet Metal Industries Year Book.—2 Queensway, Redhill, Surrey. £6·00.

Shipowners, Shipbuilders & Marine Engineers. Directory of.—40 Bowling Green Lane, E.C.1. £10·00.

Sociological Yearbook of Religion in Britain.—56–58 Bloomsbury St., W.C.1. (May.) £2·80.

Specification.—9–13 Queen Anne's Gate, S.W.1. (May.) £8·50.

Spoon's Architects' & Builders' Price Book.—11 New Fetter La., E.C.4. (Oct.) £5·50.

Spon's Mechanical & Electrical Services Prices Book.—11 New Fetter La., E.C.4. £7·75.

Statesman's Yearbook.—Little Essex St., W.C.2. (Aug.) £7·95.

Stock Exchange Official Year Book.—R.A.C. Ho., Lansdowne Rd., Croydon. £27·00.

Stone's Justices' Manual.—88 Kingsway, W.C.2. 2v. (May.) £30·00.

Stores, Shops, Supermarkets Retail Directory.—48 Poland St., W.1. £18·00.

T.V. & Radio: Guide to Independent Television.—70 Brompton Rd., S.W.3. £1·30; £1·60.

Tanker Register.—52 Bishopgate, E.C.2. (May.) £18·00.

Theatre.—3 Fitzroy Sq., W.1. (Oct.) £4·50.

Timber Trades Directory.—Sovereign Way, Tonbridge, Kent. £15·00.

Trades Register of London.—1–5 Bath St., E.C.1. (Jan.) £4·50.

Travel Trade Directory.—30 Calderwood St., S.E.18. (July.) £4·50.

U.K. Kompass Register of British Industry & Commerce.—R.A.C. House, Lansdowne Rd., Croydon. £20·75.

Unit Trust Year Book.—30 Finsbury Sq., E.C.2. (Mar.) £2·75.

United Reformed Church Year Book.—86 Tavistock Pl., W.C.1. (Sept.) £3·50.

Veterinary Annual.—42–44 Triangle West, Bristol. (Dec.) £10·50.

Watchmaker, Jeweller & Silversmith Directory.—40 Bowling Green Lane, E.C.1. £3·00.

Water Services Handbook.—2 Queensway, Redhill, Surrey. (Oct.) £3·75.

Which Company?—116A Pentonville Rd., N.1. (Mar.). £1·25; £3·75.

Which University?—54 Regent St., W.1. £12·00.

Whitaker's Almanack.—13 Bedford Sq., W.C.1. (Dec.) £1·60, £3·50, £4·75.

Who Owns Whom?—24 Tufton St., S.W.1. £32·00.

Who's Who.—35 Bedford Row, W.C.1. (Apr.). £18·00.

Who's Who, International.—18 Bedford Sq., W.C.1. (Sept.) £20·00.

Willing's Press Guide.—R.A.C. House, Lansdowne Rd., Croydon. (Apr.) £6·00.

Wine & Spirit International Year Book.—54 Regent St., W.1. £7·95.

Wisden Cricketers' Almanack.—13 Bedford Square, W.C.1. (Apr.) £3·00; £3·50.

World of Learning.—18 Bedford Square, W.C.1. (Jan.) £21·00.

World Radio & Television Year Book.—14 St. James Rd., Watford. £3·75.

Writers' & Artists' Year Book.—35 Bedford Row, W.C.1. (Jan.) £1·50.

Year Book of World Affairs.—11 New Fetter Lane, E.C.4. £8·00.

Principal Daily Newspapers

LONDON

Daily Express (*Ind.*) Fleet St., E.C.4.
Daily Mail (*Ind.*) Northcliffe House, E.C.4.
Daily Mirror (*Ind.*) Holborn, E.C.1.
Daily Telegraph and Morning Post (*Cons.*) 135 Fleet St., E.C.4.
Financial Times (*Ind.*) 10 Cannon St., E.C.4.
The Guardian (*Ind.*) 192 Gray's Inn Rd., W.C.1.
Lloyd's List, Lloyd's, E.C.3.
Morning Advertiser (*Ind.*) 57 Effra Rd., S.W.2.
Morning Star (*Communist*) 75 Farringdon Rd., E.C.1.
Sporting Life, 9 New Fetter Lane, E.C.4.
The Sun, 30 Bouverie St., E.C.4.
The Times (*Ind.*) Gray's Inn Road, W.C.1.
Evening News (*Ind.*) Carmelite House, E.C.4.
Evening Standard (*Ind.*) 47 Shoe Lane, E.C.4.

ABERDEEN........Press and Journal (*Ind.*)
　　　　　　　　Evening Express (*Ind.*)
BARROW.........North-Western Evening Mail (*Ind.*)
BATH...........Bath and West Evening Chronicle (*Cons.*)
BELFAST........Belfast Telegraph (*Ind.*)
　　　　　　　　Irish News (*Nat.*)
BIRMINGHAM.....Birmingham Post (*Ind.*)
　　　　　　　　Evening Mail (*Ind.*)
BLACKBURN......Lancs. Evening Telegraph (*Ind.*)
BLACKPOOL......W. Lancs. Ev. Gazette (*Ind.*)
BOLTON.........Evening News (*Ind.*)
BOURNEMOUTH....Evening Echo (*Ind.*)
BRADFORD.......Telegraph and Argus (*Ind.*)
BRIGHTON.......Evening Argus (*Ind.*)
BRISTOL........Evening Post
　　　　　　　　Western Daily Press (*Ind.*)
BURNLEY........Evening Star (*Ind.*)
BURTON.........Burton Daily Mail (*Un.*)
CAMBRIDGE......Cambridge Evening News (*Ind.*)
CARDIFF........South Wales Echo (*Ind.*)
　　　　　　　　Western Mail (*Ind.*)
CARLISLE.......Cumberland Evening News (*Ind.*)
CHELTENHAM.....Gloucestershire Echo (*Ind.*)
CLEVELAND......Evening Gazette (*Ind.*)
COLCHESTER.....Evening Gazette (*Ind.*)
COVENTRY.......Coventry Evening Telegraph (*Ind.*)
DARLINGTON.....Northern Echo (*Ind.*)
　　　　　　　　Evening Despatch (*Ind.*)
DERBY..........Derby Evening Telegraph (*Ind.*)
DONCASTER......Doncaster Evening Post (*Ind.*)
DUNDEE.........Courier and Advertiser (*Ind.*)
　　　　　　　　Evening Telegraph and Post (*Ind.*)
EDINBURGH......Scotsman (*Ind.*)
　　　　　　　　Evening News (*Ind.*)
EXETER.........Express and Echo (*Ind.*)
GLASGOW........Glasgow Herald (*Ind.*)
　　　　　　　　Daily Record (*Ind.*)
　　　　　　　　Evening Times (*Ind.*)
GLOUCESTER.....Citizen (*Ind.*)
GREENOCK.......Greenock Telegraph (*Lib.*)
GRIMSBY........Evening Telegraph (*Ind.*)
GUERNSEY.......Guernsey Evening Press and Star (*Ind.*)
HALIFAX........Halifax Evening Courier (*Ind.*)
HUDDERSFIELD....Huddersfield Daily Examiner (*Lib.*)

HULL...........Daily Mail (*Ind.*)
IPSWICH........East Anglian Daily Times (*Ind.*)
　　　　　　　　Evening Star (*Ind.*)
JERSEY.........Evening Post (*Ind.*)
KETTERING......Northants Evening Telegraph (*Ind.*)
LEAMINGTON SPA..Leamington Spa Morning News (*Ind.*)
LEEDS..........Yorkshire Post (*Cons.*)
　　　　　　　　Evening Post (*Cons.*)
LEICESTER......Leicester Mercury (*Ind.*)
LINCOLN........Lincolnshire Echo (*Ind.*)
LIVERPOOL......Liverpool Daily Post (*Ind.*)
　　　　　　　　Liverpool Echo (*Ind.*)
　　　　　　　　Journal of Commerce (*Ind.*)
LUTON..........Evening Post (*Ind.*)
MANCHESTER.....Manchester Evening News (*Ind.*)
　　　　　　　　Sporting Chronicle
NEWCASTLE......Evening Chronicle (*Ind.*)
　　　　　　　　Journal
NEWPORT........South Wales Argus (*Ind.*)
NORTHAMPTON...Chronicle and Echo (Northampton) (*Ind.*)
NORWICH........Eastern Daily Press (*Ind.*)
　　　　　　　　Eastern Evening News (*Ind.*)
NUNEATON......Nuneaton Evening Tribune (*Ind.*)
OLDHAM........Oldham Evening Chronicle (*Lib.*)
OXFORD.........Oxford Mail (*Ind.*)
PAISLEY........Paisley Daily Express (*Ind.*)
PETERBOROUGH...Peterborough Evening Telegraph (*Ind.*)
PLYMOUTH.......Western Morning News (*Ind.*)
　　　　　　　　Western Evening Herald (*Ind.*)
PORTSMOUTH.....The News (*Ind.*)
PRESTON........Lancashire Evening Post (*Ind.*)
READING........Evening Post (*Ind.*)
SCARBOROUGH....Scarborough Evening News (*Ind.*)
SHEFFIELD......Morning Telegraph (*Ind.*)
　　　　　　　　Star (*Ind.*)
SOUTH SHIELDS..Shields Gazette and Shipping Telegraph (*Ind.*)
SOUTHAMPTON....Southern Evening Echo (*Ind.*)
STOKE..........Evening Sentinel (*Ind.*)
SUNDERLAND.....Echo (*Ind.*)
SWANSEA........South Wales Evening Post (*Ind.*)
SWINDON........Evening Advertiser (*Ind.*)
TORQUAY........Herald Express (*Ind.*)
WATFORD........Evening Echo (*Ind.*)
WEYMOUTH.......Dorset Evening Echo (*Ind.*)
WOLVERHAMPTON..Express and Star (*Ind.*)
WORCESTER......Evening News (*Ind.*)
YORK ....Yorkshire Evening Press (*Ind.*)

SUNDAY NEWSPAPERS

News of the World (*Ind.*)—30 Bouverie St., E.C.4.
Observer (*Ind.*)—160 Queen Victoria St., E.C.4.
Sunday Express (*Ind.*)—Fleet St., E.C.4.
Sunday Mail (*Ind.*)—Anderston Quay, Glasgow.
Sunday Mercury (*Ind.*)—Colmore Circus, Birmingham.
Sunday Mirror (*Ind.*)—Holborn, E.C.1.
Sunday News (*Ind.*)—51-59 Donegall St., Belfast.
Sunday People (*Ind.*)—9 New Fetter Lane, E.C.4.
Sunday Post (*Ind.*)—144 Port Dundas Road, Glasgow.

Sunday Sun (*Ind.*)—Groat Market, Newcastle-on-Tyne.
Sunday Telegraph (*Cons.*)—135 Fleet St., E.C.4.
Sunday Times (*Ind.*)—200 Gray's Inn Rd., W.C.1.

RELIGIOUS PAPERS

[*W.*=Weekly; *M.*=Monthly; *Q.*=Quarterly]
Baptist Times—4 Southampton Row, W.C.1. *W.*
British Weekly and Christian World—69 Fleet St., E.C.4. *W.*
Catholic Herald—63 Charterhouse Street, E.C.1. *W.*
Challenge—Revenue Buildings, Chapel Rd., Worthing, Sussex. *W.*
Christian Herald—South Wharf, Aldrington Basin, Portslade, Brighton, Sussex. *W.*
Church of England Newspaper—69 Fleet St., E.C.4. *W.*
Church of Ireland Gazette—468 Lisburn Rd., Belfast. *W.*
Church Times—7 Portugal St., W.C.2. *W.*
Crusade—19 Draycott Pce, S.W.3. *M.*
English Churchman—P.O. Box 217, S.E.5. *Alt. W.*
Friend—Drayton House, Gordon St., W.C.1. *W.*
Inquirer—1–6 Essex St., W.C.2. *Alt. W.*
Jewish Chronicle—25 Furnival St., E.C.4. *W.*
Jewish Gazette—18 Cheetham Parade, Manchester, 8. *W.*
Jewish Telegraph—Levi House, Bury Old Road, Manchester, 8. *W.*
Life and Work—121 George St., Edinburgh 2. *M.*
Methodist Recorder—176 Fleet St., E.C.4. *W.*
Sunday—Udimore Vicarage, Rye, Sussex. *M.*
Tablet—48 Great Peter St., S.W.1. *W.*
Universe—Universe House, 21 Fleet St., E.C.4. *W.*
War Cry—101 Queen Victoria St., E.C.4. *W.*

PERIODICALS, MAGAZINES AND REVIEWS

[*W.*=Weekly; *M.*=Monthly; *Q.*=Quarterly]
Amateur Gardening—189 High Holborn, W.C.1. *W.*
Amateur Photographer—1 Throwley Way, Sutton, Surrey. *W.*
Angler's Mail—Hatfield House, 54 Stamford St., S.E.1. *W.*
Angling—30 Langham St., W.1. *M.*
Angling Times—Oundle Rd., Woodston, Peterborough. *W.*
Antiquaries' Journal—Oxford U. Press, Press Rd., N.W.10. *Twice a year.*
Antique Collector—Chestergate House, Vauxhall Bridge Rd., S.W.1. *M.*
Apollo—10 Cannon St., London, E.C.4. *M.*
Art and Antiques Weekly—181 Queen Victoria St., E.C.4.
Art and Artists—75 Victoria St., S.W.1. *M.*
Asia and Africa Review—38 Kennington Lane, S.E.11. *M.*
Autocar—Dorset House, Stamford St., S.E.1. *W.*
Birds and Country Magazine—79 Surbiton Hill Park, Surbiton, Surrey. *Q.*
Blackwood's Mag.—32 Thistle St., Edinburgh. *M.*
Books & Bookmen—75 Victoria St., S.W.1. *M.*
Boxing News—30 Langham St., W.1. *W.*
Brain—The Clarendon Press, Oxford. *Q.*
Brides and Setting-up Home—Vogue House, Hanover Sq., W.1. *Alt. M.*
British Birds—4 Little Essex St., W.C.2. *M.*
British Books News—The British Council, 65 Davies St., W.1. *M.*
Bunty—185 Fleet St., E.C.4. *W.*

Burlington Mag.—10–16 Elm St., W.C.1. *M.*
Buses—Terminal House, Shepperton. *M.*
Cage and Aviary Birds—1 Throwley Way, Sutton, Surrey. *W.*
Caravan—Link House, Dingwall Ave., Croydon, Surrey. *M.*
Classical Quarterly—The Clarendon Press, Oxford. *Twice a Year.*
Classical Review—The Clarendon Press, Oxford. *Twice a Year.*
Coal News—Hobart House, Grosvenor Place, S.W.1. *M.*
Coin Monthly—Sovereign House, High St., Brentwood, Essex.
Coins—Link House, Dingwall Ave., Croydon, Surrey. *M.*
Connoisseur—Chestergate House, Vauxhall Bridge Road, S.W.1. *M.*
Contemporary Review—37 Union St., S.E.1. *M.*
Country Life—King's Reach Tower, Stamford St., S.E.1. *W.*
Countryman—23/27 Tudor St., E.C.4. *Q.*
Cricketer—Beech Hanger, Ashurst, Kent. *M.*
Criminologist—9 Old Bailey, E.C.4. *Q.*
Cycling—1 Throwley Way, Sutton, Surrey. *W.*
Dalton's Weekly—Windsor Ave., Merton, S.W.19. *W.*
Dance and Dancers—75 Victoria St., S.W.1. *M.*
Dancing Times—18 Hand Court, W.C.1. *M.*
Disc—Calderwood St., S.E.18. *W.*
Dog World—32 New St., Ashford, Kent. *W.*
Do It Yourself—Link House, Dingwall Ave, Croydon. *M.*
Drama—9 Fitzroy Sq., W.1. *Q.*
Drive—Fanum House, Basingstoke, Hants. *Alt.M.*
Economic Journal—Bentley House, 200 Euston Rd., N.W.1. *Q.*
Economica—Lond. Sch. of Economics, Houghton St., Aldwych, W.C.2. *Q.*
Economist, The (*Ind.*)—25 St. James's St., S.W.1. *W.*
Edinburgh Gazette (*Official*)—Exchequer Offices, 102 George St., Edinburgh 2. *Twice a week.*
Encounter—59 St. Martin's Lane, W.C.2. *M.*
English Historical Review—5 Bentinck St., W.1. *Q.*
Exchange and Mart—Link House, 25 West St., Poole, Dorset. *W.*
Family Circle—Elm House, Elm St., W.C.1. *M.*
Field, The—8 Stratton St., W.1. *W.*
Films and Filming—75 Victoria St., S.W.1. *M.*
Freethinker, The—698 Holloway Rd., N.19. *M.*
Fur and Feather—Idle, Bradford. *Alt. W.*
Gardeners' Chronicle—Regent House, 54 Regent St., W.1. *W.*
Garden News—Park House, 117 Park Rd., Peterborough. *W.*
Geographical Journal—Kensington Gore, S.W.7. *Three times a year.*
Geographical Magazine—128 Long Acre, W.C.2. *M.*
Golf Illustrated—8 Stratton St., W.1. *W.*
Golf Monthly—113 St. Vincent St., Glasgow. *M.*
Good Housekeeping—Chestergate House, Vauxhall Bridge Road, S.W.1. *M.*
Good Motoring—2 Elis St., S.W.1. *M.*
Gramophone—179 Kenton Road, Kenton, Mx. *M.*
Greece and Rome—The Clarendon Press, Oxford. *Twice a year.*
Guider—17–19 Buckingham Palace Rd., S.W.1. *M.*
Harper's Queen—Chestergate House, Vauxhall Bridge Rd., S.W.1. *M.*
Health & Strength—20–30 Holborn, E.C.1. *M.*

Health Education Journal—78 New Oxford St., W.C.1. Q.

Hers—30–32 Southampton St., W.C.2. M.

History—59A Kennington Park Road, S.E.11. *Three times a year.*

History Today—388–389 Strand, W.C.2. M.

Homefinder—10 East Road, N.1. M.

Homemaker—189 High Holborn, W.C.1. M.

Homes and Gardens—Tower House, Southampton St., W.C.2. M.

Homoeopathy—27A Devonshire St., W.1. M.

Honey—Tower House, Southampton St., W.C.2. M.

Horse and Hound—189 High Holborn, W.C.1. W.

House and Garden—Vogue House, Hanover Sq., W.1. *Ten times a year.*

Ideal Home—189 High Holborn, W.C.1. M.

Illustrated London News—Elm House, Elm Street, W.C.1. M.

In Britain—B.T.A., 4 Bromells Rd., S.W.4. M.

International Affairs—Chatham House, St. James's Square, S.W.1. Q.

Jazz Journal—1 Upper James St., W.1. M.

Kennel Gazette—1–4 Clarges St., Piccadilly, W.1. M.

Labour Monthly—134 Ballards Lane, N.3.

Labour Research—78 Blackfriars Rd., S.E.1. M.

Lady—39–40 Bedford St., W.C.2. W.

Land and Liberty—177 Vauxhall Bridge Rd., S.W.1. *Alt.* M.

Lawn Tennis—Lowlands, Wenhaston, Suffolk. M.

Liberal News—7 Exchange Ct., Strand, W.C.1. W.

Light (*Psychic*)—16 Queensbury Place, S.W.7. Q.

Light Horse—19 Charing Cross Rd., W.C.2. M.

Listener, The—35 Marylebone High St., W.1. W.

Living—Elm House, Elm St., W.C.1. M.

Local Government Chronicle (*Ind.*)—11–12 Bury St., St. Mary Axe., E.C.3. W.

London Gazette (*Official*)—Atlantic House, Holborn Viaduct, E.C.1. *Four times a week.*

London Magazine—30 Thurloe Place, S.W.7. *Six times a year.*

London Weekly Advertiser—Regent House, 54 Regent St., W.1.

London Weekly Diary of Social Events—39 Hertford St., W.1.

Look and Learn—Fleetway House, Farringdon St., E.C.4. W.

Look and Listen—75 Victoria St., S.W.1. M.

Man—36 Craven St., W.C.2. Q.

Mayfair—95a Chancery Lane, W.C.2. M.

Meccano Magazine—Binns Rd., Liverpool 13. Q.

Melody Maker—1 Throwley Way, Sutton, Surrey. W.

Meteorological Magazine—P.O. Box 569, Cornwall House, S.E.1. M.

Mind—108 Cowley Rd., Oxford. Q.

Mirabelle—Tower House, Southampton St., W.C.2. W.

Model Boats—13–15 Bridge St., Hemel Hempstead, Herts. M.

Model Railway Constructor—Terminal House, Shepperton. M.

Model Railways—13–15 Bridge St., Hemel Hempstead, Herts. M.

Modern Caravan—Link House, Dingwall Avenue, Croydon. M.

Modern Languages—35 Lewisham Way, S.E.14.

Month—114 Mount St., W.1. M.

Monthly Digest of Statistics (*Official*)—P.O. Box 569, Cornwall House, S.E.1.

Mother—189 High Holborn, W.C.1. M.

Motor Cycle News—Dryland St., Kettering. W.

Movie Maker—13–15 Bridge Street, Hemel Hempstead, Herts. M.

Municipal & Public Services Journal—178–202 Gt. Portland St., W.1. W.

Municipal Engineering and Environmental Technology—178–202 Gt. Portland St., W.1. W.

Municipal Review—36–38 Old Queen St., Westminster, S.W.1. M.

Museums Journal—87 Charlotte St., W.1. Q.

Music and Letters—32 Holywell, Oxford. Q.

Music and Musicians—75 Victoria St., S.W.1. M.

My Weekly—185 Fleet St., E.C.4.

Nature—4 Little Essex St., W.C.2. W.

Nautical Magazines—52 Darnley Street, Glasgow, M.

Navy International—River Hall Farm, Biddenden, Kent. M.

Needlewoman—Bromley Cross, Bolton, Lancs. Q.

New Musical Express—128 Long Acre, W.C.2. W.

New Scientist—128 Long Acre, W.C.2. W.

New Society—128 Long Acre, W.C.2. W.

New Statesman (*Ind.*)—10 Great Turnstile, High Holborn, W.C.1. W.

19—Tower House, Southampton St., W.C.2. M.

Notes and Queries—Oxford U. Press, Press Rd., N.W.10. M.

Nursery World—Clifford's Inn, Fetter Lane, E.C.4.

Opera—6 Woodland Rise, N.10. M.

Our Dogs—Oxford Road, Station Approach, Manchester. W.

Oxford—8 Wellington Square, Oxford. *Twice a year.*

Parade—135 Wardour Street, W.1. M.

Parliamentary Debates (Lords) (Hansard)—P.O. Box 569, Cornwall House, S.E.1. *Daily during Session.*

Parliamentary Debates (Commons) (Hansard)—P.O. Box 569, Cornwall House, S.E.1. *Daily during Session.*

Penthouse—2 Bramber Rd., W.14. M.

People's Friend—7 Bank Street, Dundee. W.

Philosophy—Bentley House, 200 Euston Rd., N.W.1. Q.

Photography—13–15 Bridge St., Hemel Hempstead, Herts. M.

Photoplay Film Monthly—12–18 Paul St., E.C.2. M.

Pins and Needles—Elm House, Elm Street, W.C.1. M.

Playhour and Bonnie—Fleetway House, Farringdon St., E.C.4. W.

Plays and Players—75 Victoria St., S.W.1. M.

Poetry Review—21 Earls Court Square, S.W.5. Q.

Political Quarterly, The—Elm House, Elm Street, W.C.1.

Pony—19 Charing Cross Rd., W.C.2. M.

Popular Gardening—189 High Holborn, W.C.1. W.

Poultry World—1 Throwley Way, Sutton, Surrey. W.

Practical Boat Owner—54 Stamford Street, S.E.1.

Practical Camper—Regent House, 54 Regent St. M. W.1.

Practical Caravan—Regent House, 54 Regent St. M. W.1.

Practical Gardening—Park House, Peterborough. M.

Practical Householder—Fleetway House, Farringdon St., E.C.4. M.

Progress (*Braille Type*)—224–8 Great Portland St., W.1. M.

Punch—23–27 Tudor St., E.C.4. *W.*

Racing Calendar—42 Portman Sq., W.1. *W.*

Radio Control Models and Electronics—13 Bridge St., Hemel Hempstead, Herts. *M.*

Radio Times—35 Marylebone High St., W.1. *W.*

Railway Magazine—Dorset House, Stamford St., S.E.1. *M.*

Railway World—Terminal House, Shepperton. *M.*

Readers Digest—25 Berkeley Sq., W.1. *M.*

Record and Recording—75 Victoria St., S.W.1. *M.*

Red Star Weekly—185 Fleet St., E.C.4.

Riding—Tower House, Southampton St., W.C.2. *M.*

Round Table—18 Northumberland Ave., W.C.2. *Q.*

Scotland's Magazine—114–116 George St., Edinburgh. *M.*

Scots Independent—9 Upper Bridge St., Stirling. *M.*

Scottish Field—57–59 Buchanan St., Glasgow. *M.*

Scouting—Baden Powell House, Queen's Gate, S.W.7. *M.*

Seafarer—207 Balham High Rd., S.W.17. *Q.*

She—Chestergate House, Vauxhall Bridge Road, S.W.1. *M.*

Shoot!—Fleetway House, Farringdon St., E.C.4. *W.*

Shooting Times and Country Magazine—Clivemont Rd., Maidenhead. *W.*

Sociological Review—University of Keele, Staffs. *Q.*

Spectator—56 Doughty Street, W.C.1. *W.*

Sporting Chronicle Handicap Book—Thomson House, Withy Grove, Manchester. *W.*

Stitchcraft—Belmont Rd., W.4. *M.*

Strad—1 Upper James St., W.1. *M.*

Studio International—14 West Central St., W.C.1. *Alt.M.*

Tatler and Bystander—15 Berkeley St., W.1. *M.*

Tennis World—171b High St., Beckenham, Kent. *Ten times a year.*

Theatre Quarterly—39 Goodge St., W.C.1.

Time (British Isles)—Time and Life Bldg., New Bond St., W.1. *W.*

Time & Tide—13 New Bridge St., E.C.4. *M.*

Times Educational Suppl't.—Gray's Inn Rd., W.C.1. *W.*

Times Higher Education Suppl't.—Gray's Inn Rd., W.C.1. *W.*

Times Literary Suppl't.—Gray's Inn Rd., W.C.1. *W.*

Tribune—24 St. John St., E.C.1. *W.*

Trout and Salmon—21 Church Walk, Peterborough. *M.*

True Magazine—Tower House, Southampton St., W.C.2. *M.*

True Romances and True Story Magazine—12–18 Paul St., E.C.2. *M.*

TV Times—247 Tottenham Court Rd., W.1. *W.*

Universities Quarterly—10 Gt. Turnstile, W.C.1.

Vacher's Parliamentary Companion—15 Cochrane Mews, N.W.8. *Q.*

Vogue—Vogue House, Hanover Square, W.1. *Sixteen times a year.*

Weather—Cromwell House, Bracknell, Berks. *M.*

Weekend—Carmelite House, E.C.4. *W.*

Welsh Nation—8 Heol Frenhines, Caerdydd, Cardiff. *W.*

West Africa—Bath House, 53 Holborn Viaduct, E.C.1. *W.*

Woman—189 High Holborn, W.C.1. *W.*

Woman and Home—40 Long Acre, W.C.2. *M.*

Woman's Journal—Tower House, Southampton St., W.C.2. *M.*

Woman's Own—Tower House, Southampton St., W.C.2. *W.*

Woman's Realm—189 High Holborn, W.C.1. *W.*

Woman's Weekly—40 Long Acre, W.C.2.

World Today—Chatham House, St. James's Sq., S.W.1. *M.*

Yachting Monthly—Hatfield House, Stamford St., S.E.1.

Yachting World—Dorset House, Stamford St., S.E.1. *M.*

Yachts and Yachting—196 Eastern Esplanade, Southend-on-Sea. *Alt. W.*

TRADE, PROFESSIONAL AND BUSINESS JOURNALS

[*W.*= Weekly; *M.*= Monthly; *Q.*= Quarterly]

Accountancy—56 Goswell Rd., E.C.1. *M.*

Accountant—151 Strand, W.C.2. *W.*

Accountants' Magazine—27 Queen St., Edinburgh. *M.*

Achievement—50 London Rd., Riverhead, Kent. *M.*

Advertising Quarterly—Abford House, Wilton Rd., S.W.1.

Agricultural Machinery Journal—1 Throwley Way, Sutton, Surrey. *M.*

Anti-Corrosion—127 Stanstead Rd., S.E.23. *M.*

Antique Dealer and Collector's Guide—1 Wine Office Court, Fleet St., E.C.4. *M.*

Architects' Journal—9–13 Queen Anne's Gate, S.W.1. *W.*

Architectural Review—9–13 Queen Anne's Gate, S.W.1. *M.*

Artist—41 Parker St., W.C.2. *M.*

Bakers' Review—886 High Rd., Finchley, N.12. *M.*

Banker—10 Cannon St., E.C.4. *M.*

Bankers' Magazine—Holywell House, Worship St., E.C.2. *M.*

Bookseller—13 Bedford Square, W.C.1. *W.*

Brewer's Guardian—93–99 Goswell Rd., E.C.1. *M.*

Brewing Review—42 Portman Square, W.1. *M.*

British Baker—69–77 High St., Croydon. *W.*

British Clothing Manufacturer—20 Soho Sq., W.1. *M.*

British Dental Journal—64 Wimpole St., W.1. *Twice a month.*

British Food Journal—Peterson House, Northbank, Droitwich. *Alt. M.*

British Jeweller and Watch Buyer—27 Frederick St., Birmingham. *M.*

British Journal for Philosophy of Science—Farmers Hall, Aberdeen. *Q.*

British Journal of Photography—24 Wellington Street, W.C.2. *W.*

British Medical Journal—B.M.A. House, Tavistock Square, W.C.1. *W.*

British Printer—30 Old Burlington St., W.1. *M.*

British Steelmaker—5 Pond St., Hampstead, N.W.3. *Alt. M.*

British Sugar Beet Review—P.O. Box 26, Oundle Rd., Peterborough. *Q.*

British Tax Review—11 New Fetter Lane, E.C.4. *Alt.*

British Veterinary Journal—7–8 Henrietta St., W.C.2. *Alt. M.*

Brushes International—157 Hagden Lane, Watford. *M.*

Builders' Merchants Journal—Sovereign Way, Tonbridge, Kent. *M.*

Building—4 Catherine St., W.C.2. *W.*

Cabinet Maker and Retail Furnisher—25 New Street Square, E.C.4. *W.*

Cage and Aviary Birds—1 Throwley Way, Sutton, Surrey. *W.*

Campaign—Regent House, 54 Regent St., W.1. *W.*

Canoe-Camper—Bulls Green, Knebworth, Herts. Q.

Carpet and Floor Covering World—25 New Street Square, E.C.4. *M.*

Carpet Review—Regent House, 54 Regent St., W.1. *M.*

Caterer and Hotel Keeper—40 Bowling Green Lane, E.C.1. *W.*

Catering and Hotel Management—Pembroke House, Wellesley Rd., Croydon. *M.*

Catering Times—Northwood House, 93–99 Goswell Rd., E.C.1. *W.*

Chemical Age—Morgan Grampian House, Calderwood St., S.E. 18. *W.*

Chemist and Druggist—25 New Street Square, E.C.4. *W.*

Chemistry and Industry—14 Belgrave Sq., S.W.1. *Twice a month.*

Chemistry in Britain—Burlington House, W.1. *M.*

Child Education—Montague House, Russell Sq., W.C.1. *M.*

Chiropodist—8 Wimpole St., W.1. *M.*

Civil Engineering and Public Works Review—Morgan Grampian House, Calderwood St., S.E.18. *M.*

Club Mirror—18 Queen's Rd., Brighton. *M.*

Colliery Guardian—Queensway House, Redhill, Surrey. *M.*

Commerce International—69 Cannon St., E.C.4. *M.*

Commercial Grower—Sovereign Way, Trowbridge, Kent. *W.*

Commercial Motor—Dorset House, Stamford St., S.E.1. *W.*

Computer Survey—42–43 Gerrard St., W.1. *Alt. M.*

Concrete—52 Grosvenor Gdns., S.W.1. *M.*

Contract Journal—1 Throwley Way, Sutton, Surrey. *W.*

Control and Instrumentation—Morgan Grampian House, Calderwood St., S.E.18. *M.*

Cordage, Canvas and Jute World—157 Hagden Lane, Watford. *M.*

C.S.E. News (Camping and Sports Equipment)—4 Spring St., W.2. *M.*

Dairy Farmer—Fenton House, Ipswich. *M.*

Dairy Industries International—42–43 Gerrard St., W.1. *M.*

Design—28 Haymarket, S.W.1. *M.*

Display International—Pembroke House, Wellesley Rd., Croydon. *M.*

Dock and Harbour Authority—19 Harcourt St., W.1. *M.*

Drapers' Record—20 Soho Sq., W.1. *W.*

Education—10 Queen Anne St., W.1. *W.*

Education Equipment—125 High St., Colliers Wood, S.W.19. *M.*

Electrical & Electronic Trader—Dorset House Stamford St., S.E.1. *W.*

Electrical and Radio Trading—Dorset House, Stamford St., S.E.1. *W.*

Electrical Review—Dorset House, Stamford St., S.E.1. *W.*

Electrical Times—Dorset House, Stamford St., S.E.1. *W.*

Electronic Engineering—Morgan Grampian House, Calderwood St., S.E.18. *M.*

Electronics Weekly—Dorset House, Stamford St., S.E.1. *W.*

Embroidery—73 Wimpole St., W.1. Q.

Engineer—Morgan Grampian House, Calderwood St., S.E.18. *W.*

Engineering—28 Haymarket, S.W.1. *M.*

Engineers' Digest—120 Wigmore St., W.1. *M.*

Estates Gazette—151 Wardour St., W.1. *W.*

Export News, Benn's—Lyon Tower, Colliers Wood, S.W.19. *W.*

Fairplay International Shipping Weekly—1 Pudding Lane, E.C.3. *W.*

Far East Trade & Development—3 Belsize Crescent., N.W.3. *M.*

Farmers' Weekly—1 Throwley Way, Sutton, Surrey. *W.*

Fire (British Fire Service)—34 Dudley Rd., Tunbridge Wells, Kent. *M.*

Fire Protection Review—125 High St., Colliers Wood, S.W.19. *M.*

Fish Friers' Review—289 Dewsbury Road, Leeds. *M.*

Fish Trade Gazette—2 Queensway, Redhill, Surrey. *W.*

Flight International—Dorset House, Stamford St., S.E.1. *W.*

Food Trade Review—7 Garrick St., W.C.2. *M.*

Forestry and Home Grown Timber—25 New Street Square, E.C.4. *Alt. M.*

Foundry Trade Journal—Queensway House, Redhill, Surrey. *W.*

Frozen Foods—2 Queensway, Redhill, Surrey. *M.*

Fruit Trades Journal—6–7 Gough Square, E.C.4. *W.*

Fuel—32 High St., Guildford. Q.

Funeral Service Journal—King & Hutchings, Cricketfield Rd., Uxbridge, Middx. *M.*

Fur & Leather Review—27 Garlick Hill, E.C.4. *M.*

Fur Weekly News—87 Lamb's Conduit St., W.C.1.

Games and Toys—30–31 Knightrider St., E.C.4. *M.*

Gas Marketing—25 New Street Square, E.C.4. *M.*

Gas World and Gas Journal—25 New Street Square, E.C.4. *W.*

Gifts—Lyon Tower, Colliers Wood, S.W.19. *M.*

Glass—Queensway House, Redhill, Surrey. *M.*

Grocer—5–7 Southwark St., S.E.1. *W.*

Grower—49 Doughty St., W.C.1. *W.*

Hair and Beauty—62 Oxford St., W.1. *M.*

Hairdressers' Journal—40 Bowling Green Lane, E.C.1. *W.*

Handy Shipping Guide—12–16 Laystall St., E.C.1. *W.*

Hardware Trade Journal—Sovereign Way, Tonbridge, Kent. *W.*

Harper's Sports and Camping—Southbank House, Black Prince Rd., S.E.1. *Alt. W.*

Harper's Wine and Spirit Gazette—Southbank House, Black Prince Rd., S.E.1. *W.*

Heating and Ventilating Engineer—886 High Rd., Finchley, N.12. *M.*

Hospital and Health Services Review—75 Portland Place, W.1. *M.*

Ice Cream & Frozen Confectionery—90 Grays Inn Rd., W.C.1. *M.*

Industrial Daily News—49 Hatton Garden, E.C.1.

Industrial Society—48 Bryanston Square, W.1. *Alt. M.*

Insurance Mail—44 Fleet St., E.C.4. *M.*

Insurance Record—9 Chiswick High Rd., W.4. *M.*

Investor's Chronicle and Stock Exchange Gazette—30 Finsbury Sq., E.C.2. *W.*

Investors' Review—100 Fleet St., E.C.4. *Alt. W.*

Jeweller—39 High St., Wheathampstead, Herts. *M.*

Journalist—314 Gray's Inn Rd., W.C.1. *M.*

Journal of the Chemical Society—Burlington House, W.1. *In six parts.*

Journal of the Institute of Bankers—10 Lombard St., E.C.3. *Alt. M.*

Junior Age—Pembroke House, Wellesley Rd., Croydon. *M.*

Justice of the Peace—Little London, Chichester. *W.*

Knitting and Haberdashery Review—6 Ludgate Square, E.C.4. *Alt. M.*

Lancet—7 Adam Street, W.C.2. *W.*

Law Quarterly Review—11 New Fetter Lane, E.C.4.

Law Reports—3 Stone Buildings, Lincoln's Inn, W.C.2. *M.*

Law Society's Gazette—113 Chancery Lane, W.C.2. *W.*

Leather—125 High St., Colliers Wood, S.W.19. *M.*

Leathergoods—125 High St. Colliers Wood, S.W.19. *M.*

Library Review—98-100 Holm St., Glasgow. *Q.*

Light and Lighting—York House, Westminster Bridge Road, S.E.1. *Alt. M.*

Lithoprinter—Regent House, 54 Regent St., W.1. *M.*

Lloyd's Loading List—Sheepen Rd., Colchester, Essex. *W.*

Locomotive Journal—9 Arkwright Rd., N.W.3. *M.*

London Corn Circular—63 Crutched Friars, E.C.3. *W.*

Machinery and Production Engineering—New England House, New England St., Brighton. *W.*

Machinery Market—146A Queen Victoria St., E.C.4. *W.*

Management Accounting—63 Portland Place, W.1. *M.*

Management Decision—200 Keighley Rd., Bradford. *Six times a year.*

Management Today—Regent House, 54 Regent St., W.1. *M.*

Manufacturing Chemist and Aerosol News—Morgan Grampian House, Calderwood St., S.E.18. *M.*

Manufacturing Clothier—42 Gerrard St., W.1. *M.*

Marine and Air Catering—125 High St., Colliers Wood, S.W.19. *M.*

Marketing—Regent House, 54 Regent St., W.1. *M.*

Materials Reclamation Weekly—69-77 High St. Croydon. *W.*

Meat Trades Journal—49 Hatton Garden, E.C.1. *W.*

Mechanical Handling International—33-40 Bowling Green Lane, E.C.1. *M.*

Medico-Legal Journal—129 Long Lane, S.E.1. *Q.*

Men's Wear—20 Soho Sq., W.1. *W.*

Metal Bulletin—46 Wigmore St., W.1. *Twice a week.*

Metallurgia and Metal Forming—Queensway House, Redhill, Surrey. *M.*

Milk Industry—20 Eastbourne Terrace, W.2. *M.*

Mining Journal—15 Wilson St., Moorgate, E.C.2. *W.*

Mining Magazine—15 Wilson St., Moorgate, E.C.2. *M.*

Model Engineer—13-15 Bridge St., Hemel Hempstead, Herts. *Twice a month.*

Modern Law Review—11 New Fetter Lane, E.C.4. *Alt. M.*

Modern Railways—Terminal House, Shepperton. *M.*

Motor—1 Throwley Way, Sutton, Surrey. *W.*

Motor Boat and Yachting—Dorset House, Stamford St., S.E.1. *M.*

Motor Cycle—1 Throwley Way, Sutton, Surrey. *W.*

Motor Cycle and Cycle Trader—157 Hagden Lane, Watford. *Alt. W.*

Motor Trader—Dorset House, Stamford Street, S.E.1. *W.*

Motor Transport—Dorset House, Stamford St., S.E.1. *W.*

Musical Times—1-3 Upper James St. W.1. *M.*

National Builder—82 New Cavendish St., W.1. *M.*

Natural Gas—25 New Street Square, E.C.4. *M.*

New Law Journal—Butterworths, Borough Green, Sevenoaks, Kent. *W.*

Nuclear Engineering International—Dorset House, Stamford St., S.E.1. *M.*

Nurseryman & Garden Centre—Sovereign Way, Tonbridge, Kent. *W.*

Nursing Mirror—1 Throwley Way, Sutton, Surrey. *W.*

Nursing Times—4 Little Essex St., W.C.2. *W.*

Off Licence News—5-7 Southwark St., S.E.1. *W.*

Official Journal (Patents)—Patent Office, St. Mary Cray, Orpington. *W.*

Ophthalmic Optician—65 Brook St., W.1. *Alt. W.*

Optician—40 Bowling Green Lane, E.C.1. *W.*

Packaging—9 Chiswick High Road, W.4. *M.*

Packaging Review—Dorset House, Stamford St., S.E.1. *M.*

Paint Manufacture—157 Hagden Lane, Watford. *Ten times a year.*

Painting and Decorating Journal—30 Princes St., Southport, Merseyside. *M.*

Paper—Lyon Tower, Colliers Wood, S.W.19. *Alt. W.*

Personnel Management—Mercury House, Waterloo Rd., S.E.1. *M.*

Petroleum Times—Dorset House, Stamford St., S.E.1. *Alt. W.*

Pharmaceutical Journal—17 Bloomsbury Square, W.C.1. *W.*

Philatelic Magazine—42 Maiden Lane, W.C.2. *M.*

Philatelic Trader—42 Maiden Lane, W.C.2. *Alt. W.*

Photographer, The—Amwell End, Ware, Herts. *Six to Ten issues a Year.*

Physics Bulletin—Netherton House, Marsh St., Bristol. *M.*

Physics Education—Netherton House, Marsh St. Bristol. *Seven issues a Year.*

Physics in Technology—Netherton House, Marsh St., Bristol. *Alt. M.*

Plumbing Equipment News and Heating Engineer—Peterson House, Northbank, Droitwich. *M.*

Police Review—14 St. Cross St., E.C.1. *W.*

Policy Holder—Waterloo Rd., Stockport. *W.*

Post Magazine and Insurance Monitor—12-13 Henrietta St., W.C.2. *W.*

Power Farming—1 Throwley Way, Sutton, Surrey. *M.*

Power Laundry and Cleaning News—40 Bowling Green Lane, E.C.1. *Alt. W.*

Practical Wireless—Fleetway House, Farringdon St., E.C.4. *M.*

Practical Woodworking—Fleetway House, Farringdon St., E.C.4. *M.*

Practitioner—5 Bentinck St., W.1. *M.*

Printing Trades Journal—Sovereign Way, Tonbridge, Kent. *M.*

Printing World—Lyon Tower, Colliers Wood, S.W.19. *W.*

Product Finishing—127 Stanstead Rd., S.E.23. *M.*

Professional Administration—388/389 Strand, W.C.2. *M.*

Public Law—11 New Fetter Lane, E.C.4. Q.
Public Ledger—11 Tokenhouse Yard, E.C.2. *Daily.*
Public Service—1 Mabledon Place, W.C.1. M.
Quarry Management and Products—7 Regent St., Nottingham. M.
Quarterly Journal of Experimental Psychology—24–28 Oval Rd., N.W.1.
Quarterly Journal of Medicine—The Clarendon Press, Oxford.
Railway Gazette International—Dorset House, Stamford Street, S.E.1. M.
Railway Review—205 Euston Rd., N.W.1. W.
Rating and Valuation Reporter—2 Paper Bldgs., Temple, E.C.4. W.
Resale Weekly—Unit 4, Sewell St., Plaistow, E.13. W.
Retail Jeweller—93/99 Goswell Rd., E.C.1. *Alt. W.*
Retail Newsagent—21–25 Earl Street, E.C.2. W.
Review (Insurance)—42–43 Gerrard St., W.1. *Alt. W.*
Review of Economic Studies—Faculty of Economics, Sidgwick Ave., Cambridge. Q.
Review of English Studies—The Clarendon Press. Oxford. Q.
Safety at Sea International—Queensway House, Redhill, Surrey. M.
Scottish Farmer—39 York St., Glasgow. W.
Scottish Grocer—34–6 North Frederick St. Glasgow. W.
Scottish Schoolmaster—41 York Place, Edinburgh, *Alt. M.*
Service Station—178–202 Gt. Portland St., W.1. M.
Sheet Metal Industries—Queensway House, Redhill, Surrey. M.
Shipping World and Shipbuilder—125 High St., Colliers Wood, S.W.19. M.
Shoe and Leather News—84–88 Great Eastern St., E.C.2. W.
Soap, Perfumery and Cosmetics—42–43 Gerrard St., W.1. M.
Solicitors' Journal—237 Long Lane, S.E.1. W.
Sports Trader—125 High St., Colliers Wood, S.W.19. M.
Stage and Television Today—19 Tavistock St., W.C.2. W.
Structural Engineer—11 Upper Belgrave St., S.W.1. M.
Surveyor and Public Authority Technology—1 Throwley Way, Sutton, Surrey. W.
Tableware International—2 Queensway, Redhill, Surrey. M.
Taxation—98 Park St., W.1. W.
Teacher—Derbyshire House, Kettering, Northants. W.

Teacher's World—Montague House, Russell Sq., W.C.1. W.
Teaching History—59A Kennington Park Rd., S.E.11. *Twice a year.*
Television—Fleetway House, Farringdon St., E.C.4. M.
Textile Institute and Industry—10 Blackfriars St., Manchester. M.
Textile Manufacturer—33 King St., Manchester. *Ten times a year.*
Textile Month—Statham House, Talbot Rd., Stretford, Manchester. M.
Timber and Plywood—21 New St., E.C.2. W.
Timber Trades Journal and Woodworking Machinery—25 New Street Square, E.C.4. W.
Tobacco—2 Queensway, Redhill, Surrey. M.
Tooling—127 Stanstead Rd., S.E.23. M.
Town and Country Planning—17 Carlton House Terrace, S.W.1. M.
Town Planning Review—Dept. of Civic Design, Liverpool University. Q.
Toy Trader—157 Hagden Lane, Watford. M.
Trade and Industry (*Official*)—1 Victoria St., S.W.1. W.
Trade Marks Journal—25 Southampton Bldgs., W.C.2. W.
Traffic Engineering and Control—29 Newman St., W.1. M.
U.K. Press Gazette—Cliffords Inn, Fetter Lane, E.C.4. W.
Ultrasonics—32 High St., Guildford. *Alt. M.*
Universities Quarterly—10 Great Turnstile, W.C.1.
Watchmaker, Jeweller and Silversmith—40 Bowling Green Lane, E.C.1. M.
Weekly Law Reports—3 Stone Buildings, Lincoln's Inn, W.C.2.
Welding and Metal Fabrication—32 High St., Guildford. *Ten times a year.*
Which?—14 Buckingham St., W.C.2. M.
Whitaker's Books of the Month and Books to Come—13 Bedford Sq., W.C.1. M.
Whitaker's Cumulative Book List—13 Bedford Sq., W.C.1. Q.
Wire Industry—157 Station Road East, Oxted, Surrey. M.
Wireless World—Dorset House, Stamford St., S.E.1. M.
Woodworker—13–35 Bridge St., Hemel Hempstead. M.
Woodworking Industry—25 New Street Square, E.C.4. M.
Wool Record and Textile World—91 Kirkgate, Bradford. *Alt. W.*
World Crops—9 Botolph Alley, E.C.3. *Alt. M.*
World's Fair—Union St., Oldham. W.

NORTHERN IRISH NEWSPAPERS

LONDON OFFICES:

Ballymena Observer—30 Fleet St., E.C.4.
Banbridge Chronicle—30 Fleet St., E.C.4.
Belfast Telegraph—Greater London House, Hampstead Road, N.W.1.
Coleraine Chronicle—30 Fleet St., E.C.4.
Derry Journal—30 Fleet St., E.C.4.
Down Recorder—30 Fleet St., E.C.4.
Impartial Reporter (Enniskillen)—30 Fleet St., E.C.4.
Irish News—70 Hatton Garden, E.C.1.

Irish Weekly—70 Hatton Garden, E.C.1.
Lurgan Mail—30 Fleet St., E.C.4.
Mid Ulster Mail—30 Fleet St., E.C.4.
Northern Constitution (Coleraine)—30 Fleet St., E.C.4.
Portadown News—30 Fleet St., E.C.4.
Strabane Weekly News—30 Fleet St., E.C.4.
Tyrone Constitution—30 Fleet St., E.C.4.
Ulster Gazette (Armagh)—30 Fleet St., E.C.4.
Ulster Herald (Omagh)—80 Fleet Street, E.C.4.

REPORTING AND NEWS AGENCIES IN LONDON

ASSOCIATED PRESS LTD.,
83–86 Farringdon Street, E.C.4. 01–353 1515.

BRENARD PRESS LTD.,
Heathrow Airport, Hounslow, Middx. 01–759 1235.

CAPEL COURT PRESS AGENCY LTD.,
20 Copthall Avenue, E.C.2. 01–628 3580.

CENTRAL PRESS FEATURES,
80 Fleet Street, E.C.4. 01–353 7792.

EXCHANGE TELEGRAPH CO., LTD.,
Extel House, East Harding Street, E.C.4. 01–353–1080.

HAYTERS SPORTS.
41–42 Shoe Lane, E.C.4. 01–353–0971.

NATIONAL PRESS AGENCY LTD.,
Newspaper House, 8–16 Great New Street, E.C.4. 01–353 1030.

PARLIAMENTARY NEWS SERVICES.
92 Fleet Street, E.C.4. 01–583 7848.

PRESS ASSOCIATION LTD.,
85 Fleet Street, E.C.4. 01–353 7440.

REUTERS LTD.,
85 Fleet Street, E.C.4. 01–353 6060.

UNITED PRESS INTERNATIONAL, LTD.,
8 Bouverie St., E.C.4. 01–353 2282.

UNIVERSAL NEWS SERVICES, LTD.,
Gough Square, Fleet St., E.C.4. 01–353 5200.

LETTER POST SINCE 1972

The following list shows the cost of sending within the United Kingdom an ordinary letter not exceeding the weight shown:

Feb., 1972		First-Class		Second-Class
2 oz.	for ..	3p	..	2½p
4 oz.	for ..	4p	..	3½p
6 oz.	for ..	6p	..	5½p
8 oz.	for ..	8p	..	6½p
10 oz.	for ..	10p	..	7½p
12 oz.	for ..	13p	..	8½p
14 oz.	for ..	15p	..	9½p
1 lb.	for ..	17p	..	11½p
1 lb. 8 oz.	for ..	24p	..	13½p
2 lb.	for ..	34p		Limit of weight
Each extra lb.	..	17p		1 lb. 8 oz.

Sept., 1973		First-Class		Second-Class
2 oz.	for ..	3½p	..	3p
4 oz.	for ..	5p	..	4p
6 oz.	for ..	8p	..	5½p
8 oz.	for ..	10p	..	7p
10 oz.	for ..	12p	..	8½p
12 oz.	for ..	14p	..	10p
14 oz.	for ..	16p	..	11½p
1 lb.	for ..	18p	..	13p
1 lb. 8 oz.	for ..	27p	..	18½p max.
2 lb.	for ..	36p	..	—
each additional				
½ lb.	for ..	9p	..	—

June, 1974		First-Class		Second-Class
2 oz.	for ..	4½p	..	3½p
4 oz.	for ..	6½p	..	5p
6 oz.	for ..	10p	..	7p
8 oz.	for ..	12½p	..	9p
10 oz.	for ..	15p	..	11p
12 oz.	for ..	17½p	..	13p
14 oz.	for ..	20p	..	15p
1 lb.	for ..	22½p	..	17p

1 lb. 8 oz. for	..	32½p	..	22½p max.
2 lb. for	..	42½p	..	—
each additional				
½ lb.		10p		

March, 1975		First-Class		Second-Class
2 oz.	for ..	7p	..	5½p
4 oz.	for ..	10p	..	8p
6 oz.	for ..	12½p	..	9½p
8 oz.	for ..	15p	..	11p
10 oz.	for ..	17½p	..	13p
12 oz.	for ..	19½p	..	14½p
14 oz.	for ..	22p	..	16½p
1 lb.	for ..	24p	..	18p
1 lb. 8 oz.	for ..	34p	..	24p max.
2 lb.	for ..	44p	..	
each additional				
½ lb or part ½ lb: 10p			..	—

Sept., 1975		First-Class		Second-Class
60 g (2.1 oz.)	for ..	8½p	..	6½p
100 g (3.5 oz.)	for ..	11½p	..	9p
150 g (5.3 oz.)	for ..	15p	..	11p
200 g (7.1 oz.)	for ..	18p	..	13½p
250 g (8.8 oz.)	for ..	21p	..	16p
300 g (10.6 oz.)	for ..	24p	..	18½p
350 g (12.3 oz.)	for ..	27p	..	21p
400 g (14.1 oz.)	for ..	30p	..	23½p
450 g (15.9 oz.)	for ..	33p	..	26p
500 g (1.1lb.)	for ..	36p	..	28½p
750 g (1.7 lb.)	for ..	51p	..	42p max.
1000 g (2.2 lb.)	for ..	66p	..	
each additional				
250 g (8.8 oz.)		15p		

THE PRESS COUNCIL

1 Salisbury Square, E.C.4.
[01-353 1248]

In April, 1947, a Royal Commission was appointed to enquire into the control, management and ownership, etc., of the Press and news agencies and to make recommendations thereon. The Commission, in its report of June, 1949, recommended *inter alia* that a voluntary Press Council be formed.

A constitution ultimately set up provided for the establishment of such a council on July 1, 1953. This constitution was materially amended in 1963 by the introduction of an independent chairman and up to 20 per cent. lay membership. In 1973, the Council was increased to 30 (excluding the Chairman) of whom one-third are lay members. The objects of the Council are (1) to preserve the established freedom of the British press; (2) to maintain the character of the British Press in accordance with the highest professional and commercial standards; (3) to consider complaints about the conduct of the Press or the conduct of persons and organizations towards the Press; to deal with these complaints in whatever manner might seem practical and appropriate and record resultant action; (4) to keep under review developments likely to restrict the supply of information of public interest and importance; (5) to report publicly on developments that may tend towards greater concentration or monopoly in the Press (including changes in ownership, control and growth of Press undertakings) and to publish statistical information relating thereto; (6) to make representations on appropriate occasions to the Government, organs of the United Nations and Press organizations abroad; and (7) to publish periodical reports recording the Council's work and to review, from time to time, developments in the Press and the factors affecting them.

The membership of the Council consists of editorial and managerial nominees of The Newspaper Publishers Association Ltd. (5), The Newspaper Society (3), The Periodical Publishers Association Ltd. (2), The Scottish Daily Newspaper Society (1), Scottish Newspaper Proprietors' Association (1), The Guild of British Newspaper Editors (2), The National Union of Journalists (4), The Institute of Journalists (2) plus (10) lay members appointed by the Press Council Appointments Commission. In addition each constituent body nominates one official as a non-voting member.

Chairman, The Lord Shawcross, P.C., G.B.E., Q.C.

Vice-Chairman, D. R. W. Greenslade.

Professional Members, W. J. Bailey; M. Bower; W. R. A. Breare; C. N. D. Cole; T. H. Cooke; H. R. Douglas; H. French; Sir Denis Hamilton, D.S.O.; The Hon. A. V. Hare, M.C.; W. Heald; F. P. M. Johnston; I. McColl; A. J. Miles; F. Owens, O.B.E.; K. J. Peters; E. Pickering; M. Randolph; R. J. P. Swingler; G. Withy.

Lay Members, Capt. G. C. Baldwin, C.B.E., D.S.C.; Dr. A. C. Copisarow; Dame Mary Green, D.B.E.; R. M. Harrold; T. Jackson; Prof. C. H. Lawrence; Mrs. J. Martin; Sir Ian Morrow; Dame Jean Rivett-Drake, D.B.E.; Rt. Rev. W. J. Westwood.

Secretary, N. S. Paul.

WEATHER INFORMATION AND FORECASTS

Recorded weather forecasts for the areas listed below are available by telephoning the numbers shown:

Bedford area	Bedford 8091	Kent Coast	Medway 8091	North Wales Coast	Chester 8091
Bishops Stortford 8091		Lancs, Merseyside,	051-246 8091		Colwyn Bay 8091
	01-246 8099	Gtr. Manchester	061-246 8091	Notts., Leics. and	
Peterborough 8091		and Cheshire	Blackburn 8091	Derby	Nottingham 8091
Northampton 8091			Blackpool 8091		Leicester 8091
	Luton 8091	Leeds/Bradford and			Derby 8091
Belfast area	Belfast 8091	Huddersfield area	Bradford 8091	Sheffield area	Sheffield 8091
Birmingham area	021-246 8091		Huddersfield 8091		Doncaster 8091
	Coventry 8091		Leeds 8091	Southern Hants. and I.O.W.	
Bristol area	Bristol 8091	London area	01-246 8091	(including coastal area	
	Swindon 8091		Tunbridge Wells 8091	between Poole Harbour and	
Cardiff area	Cardiff 8091		Guildford 8091	Chichester)	Bournemouth 8091
	Newport 8091	Norfolk and Suffolk			Portsmouth 8091
Devon and Cornwall	Exeter 8091		Norwich 8091		Southampton 8091
	Plymouth 8091		Ipswich 8091	South-West Midlands	
	Torquay 8091	North East England			Cheltenham 8091
Edinburgh area	031-246 8091		Middlesbrough 8091		Gloucester 8091
Essex Coast	Chelmsford 8091		Newcastle-upon-Tyne 8091		Hereford 8091
	01-246 8096	North Lincs. and		Sussex Coast	01-246 8097
	Colchester 8091	Retford area	Grimsby 8091		Brighton 8091
	Southend 8091		Lincoln 8091	Thames Valley	01-246 8090
Glasgow area	041-246 8091	North Wales Coast			High Wycombe 8091
Kent Coast	01-246 8098	from Conwy	051-246 8093		Oxford 8091
	Canterbury 8091	to Chester	061-246 8093		Reading 8091

Principal London Clubs

Club and Address	Secretary	Subscription		Remarks
		Entr.	Ann.	
		£	£	
Alpine (1857), 74 S. Audley St., W.1.	M. F. Baker (*Hon.*)...	4·00	2·00 to 6·00	Mountaineering.
American (1919), 95 Piccadilly, W.1.	I. B. Macfarlane.....	100·00	75·00	Americans in London.
American Women's (1899), 1 Cadogan Gardens, S.W.3.	Mrs. K. E. Hayward..	15·00	5·00 to 25·00	American Women in London.
Anglo-Belgian (1955), 6 Belgrave Square, S.W.1.	Baron de Gerlache de Gomery, M.V.O.	30·00 & 20·00	30·00 & 20·00	Social.
Army and Navy (1837), 36 Pall Mall, S.W.1.	J. Gordon............	Nil	45·00 & 23·00	Commissioned officers of H.M. Forces.
Arts (1863), 40 Dover Street, W.1.	A. E. Eldon-Edington.	50·00	70·00	Art, Literature, Science.
The Athenæum (1824), 107 Pall Mall, S.W.1.	G. L. E. Lindow.....	52·50	95·00	Literature and Science, Public Services, The Arts.
Authors' (1891) 40 Dover Street, W.1.	E. Walsh............	10·00	70·00	Literary and Social
The Bath (1896), 43 Brook St., W.1.	H. A. Style..........	110·00	110·00	Social: non-political.
Beefsteak (1876), 9 Irving Street, W.C.2.	W. E. Usher.........	30·00	30·00	Dining and Social.
Boodle's (1762), 28 St. James's St., S.W.1.	R. J. Edmonds.......	150·00	142·00	Social: non-political.
Brooks's (1764), St. James's Street, S.W.1.	J. O. Robson........	55·00	88·40	Social: non-political.
Buck's (1919), 18 Clifford Street, W.1.	Miss H. Pocock......	100·00	90·00	Social: non-political.
Caledonian (1897), 9 Halkin St., S.W.1.	Capt. G. G. Wilson, C.B.E., R.N.	Nil	75·00 to 8·00	Strictly Scottish.
Canning (1910), 42 Half Moon Street, W.1.	R. B. Baker.........	50·00	45·00	Social: S. American.
Carlton (1832), 69 St. James's St., S.W.1.	R. P. McDouall......	50·00	100·00	Conservative and Unionist.
Cavalry and Guards (1891), 127 Piccadilly, W.1.	Sqn.-Ldr. A. F. O'Connor (*Hon.*)	34·65	60·00	Officers of Mounted and Guards Regiments.
Challoner (1949), 61 Pont Street, S.W.1.	Brig. P. B. Cuddon, C.B.E., M.C. (*Hon.*)	..	Various	Roman Catholic residential.
Chelsea Arts (1891), 143 Old Church Street, S.W.3.	A. G. Hartmann......	..	33·00	Arts and Literature.
Chemical (1918), 1 Whitehall Place, S.W.1.	P. F. Corbett........	Nil	25·00 & 20·00	Chemical and Social.
City Livery (1914), Sion College, E.C.4.	B. L. Morgan, C.B.E.	25·00	25·00	Liverymen of City only.
City of London (1832), 19 Old Broad Street, E.C.2.	P. Merritt...........	200·00	90·00	Merchants, Bankers, &c.
City University (1885), 50 Cornhill, E.C.3.	G. O. Puckle........	55·00	55·00	Primarily Oxford and Cambridge Graduates.
Constitutional (1883), 86 St. James's Street, S.W.1.	S. F. Head...........	Nil	75·00	Social and Political.
East India, Devonshire, Sports and Public Schools (1849), 16 St. James's Square S.W.1.	P. H. Wallace........	50·00 & 25·00	85·00 & 20·00	Social and Residential.
Eccentric (1890), 9 Ryder Street, S.W.1.	J. McKeown	50·00	50·00	Social.
Farmers' (1842), 3 Whitehall Ct., S.W.1.	Vacant..............	30·00 to 15·00	30·00 to 5·00	Agricultural Interests.
Flyfishers' (1884), 86 St. James's Street, S.W.1.	H. A. Rickett.......	50·00 & 25·00	35·00 to 10·00	Flyfishing and Social.
Garrick (1831), Garrick Street, W.C.2.	M. Harvey..........	125·00	100·00	Dramatic and Literary.
Golfers' (1893), 10 Old Burlington Street, W.1.	Mrs. M. A. Pearse....	..	11·55 to 6·93	Members of Golf Clubs.
Green Room (1887), 9 Adam Street, W.C.2.	C. Clopet...........	10·00	35·00	Dramatic Profession.
Gresham (1843), 15 Abchurch Lane, E.C.4.	P. N. Owen..........	100·00	100·00	Bankers, Merchants, Social.
Hurlingham (1869), Ranelagh Gardens, S.W.6.	D. F. A. Trewby.....	100·00	65·00	Tennis, Swimming, Croquet, Squash, Bowls, Social, Golf, Cricket.

Club and Address	Secretary	Subscription		Remarks
		Entr.	Ann.	
		£	£	
Junior Carlton (1864), 30 Pall Mall, S.W.1.	W. A. Jolly..........	Nil	75·00	Conservative.
Kempton Park (1878), Sunbury-on-Thames.	Mrs. V. J. Blackford..	..	40·00	Racing.
Kennel (1873), 1 Clarges St., W.1.	Lt.-Cdr. J. S. Williams.	25·00	15·00	For improving breed of dogs.
Lansdowne (1935), 9 Fitzmaurice Place, Berkeley Square, W.1.	E. A. Jeffreys.........	Nil	32·00 to 5·00	Social, Sports and Residential.
London Fencing (1848), 83 Perham Road, W.14.	E. J. Morten (Hon.)...	Nil	25·00	Fencing.
London Rowing (1856), Embankment, Putney, S.W.15.	K. C. W. King.......	2·00	Various	Amateur Rowing.
M.C.C. (Marylebone Cricket Club) (1787), Lord's Cricket Ground, N.W.8.	J. A. Bailey..........	10·00	20·00	Headquarters of Cricket.
Mining (1910), 3 London Wall Bldgs, E.C.2.	G. Sumner..........	10·00	25·00 to 5·00	Mining and metallurgical interests.
National (1845), c/o Constitutional Club (q.v.).	E. Scott (Hon.).......	Nil	22·00	Clerical and social.
National Liberal (1882), 1 Whitehall Place, S.W.1.	G. M. de Chabris (Hon.)	10·00	45·00 to 30·00	Social and Liberal.
Naval (1943), 38 Hill Street, W.1.	P. M. Wass..........	Nil	Various	Serving and retired Naval Officers, R.M. and yacht club members.
Naval and Military (1862), 94 Piccadilly, W.1.	Maj. W. E. Anderson, M.B.E., M.C.	63·00	63·00	Officers of R.N., Army, Marines, R.A.F.
Oriental (1824), Stratford House, Stratford Place, W.1.	R. N. Rapson, M.V.O..	55·00	75·00 to 10·00	Social.
Portland (1816), 42 Half Moon Street, W.1.	Cdr. D. A. Becker, R.N. (ret.)	100·00	70·00	Social: Non-political.
Pratt's (1841), 14 Park Place, S.W.1.	Maj. G. C. Hackett, M.B.E.	Nil	20·00	Social.
Press (1882), International Press Centre, 76 Shoe Lane, E.C.4.	J. H. Horrocks.......	10·00	25·00	Strictly Journalistic.
Queen's (1886), Palliser Road, W. Kensington, W.14.	N. K. Haugh........	64·80	81·15	Lawn Tennis, Tennis, Rackets and Squash Rackets.
Railway (1899), 112 High Holborn, W.C.1.	C. F. Wells (Hon).....	1·00	8·00	Railway interests.
Reform (1832), 104–5 Pall Mall, S.W.1.	R. G. Tennant.......	55·00	136·00	Social.
Roehampton (1901), Roehampton Lane, S.W.15.	J. Maples............	100·00 to 30·00	95·00 to 30·00	Golf, Lawn Tennis, Squash, Croquet, Swimming.
Royal Air Force (1918), 128 Piccadilly, W.1.	J. Swaffield..........	25·00*	12·50*	Officers of R.A.F., R.A.F.V.R., W.R.A.F., etc.
Royal Automobile (1897), 89–91 Pall Mall, S.W.1.	G. E. Samson........	34·00 to 10·00	60·00 to 10·00	And at Woodcote Park, Epsom.
Royal Cruising (1880), 42 Half Moon Street, W.1.	A. P. Gray (Hon.).....	10·00	7·00	Cruising and Social.
R.A.F. Reserves (1948), c/o Naval Club, 38 Hill Street, W.1.	Sqn. Ldr. H. C. Room, M.B.E. (Hon.)	Nil	5·25 to 1·00	Officers of R.A.F., R.A.F.V.R., R.A.F. Reserve and ex-officers.
Royal Ocean Racing (1925), 20 St. James's Place, S.W.1.	Mrs. M. Pera........	6·75	27·00	Off-shore Yacht Racing.
Royal Thames Yacht (1775), 60 Knightsbridge, S.W.1.	Capt. K. Stobbs......	35·00 & 75·00	Various to 105·00	Yachting and Social.
St. Stephen's (1870), 34 Queen Anne's Gate, S.W.1.	Maj. P. J. Browning..	20·00 & 10·00	60·00 to 5·00	Conservative and Social.
Sandown Park (1875), Esher, Surrey.	F. J. Bates..........	Nil	27·50	Racing.
Savage (1857), 9 Fitzmaurice Place, Berkeley Square, W.1.	A. Wykes (Hon.).....	25·00	50·00 & 25·00	Drama, Literature, Art, Music, Science, Law.
Savile (1868), 69 Brook Street, W.1.	P. Aldersley.........	65·00	78·00	Social: Non-political.

* Non-Serving Officers.

Club and Address	Secretary	Subscription		Remarks
		Entr.	Ann.	
		£	£	
Sesame Pioneer and Lyceum (1895), 49 Grosvenor Street, W.1.	Miss C. Sutton.......	15·00	22·00 to 9·00	Social and Residential: Men and Women.
Ski Club of G.B. (1903), 118 Eaton Square, S.W.1.	Brig. L. E. Madrell...	Nil	12·00 & 8·00	Ski-ing and Social.
Thames Rowing (1860), Embankment, Putney, S.W.15.	K. A. Williams (Hon.)	2·00	18·00	Men and Women.
Travellers' (1819), 108 Pall Mall, S.W.1.	R. A. Williams......	55·00	100·00	Social: Non-political.
Turf (1868), 5 Carlton House Terrace, S.W.1.	J. D. Thomson.......	110·00 to 70·00	110·00 to 70·00	Social: Non-political.
United Nursing Services (1921), 40 South Street, W.1.	W. Oakes..........	3·50	9·25	Social.
United Oxford & Cambridge University (1972), 71–7 Pall Mall, S.W.1.	D. J. McDougall.....	Nil	70·00	Oxford & Cambridge.
United Wards (1877)	D. Munro..........	1·15	5·00	Freemen, Liverymen, Ward Club members, Civic.
University Women's (1886), 2 Audley Square, W.1.	Miss M. F. Lindsay...	10·80	15·12 to 14·04	University Graduates.
V.A.D. Ladies (1920), 44 Great Cumberland Place, W.1.	Miss M. A. Sample...	2·20	13·20 & 8·80	Social and residential.
Victoria (1863), 150–162 Edgware Road, W.2.	L. A. Holland........	Nil	36·75	Sporting and Social.
Victory Services (1907), 63–79 Seymour Street, W.2.	D. G. Stovey........	Nil	3·00	Social and residential; Serving and Ex-Service Men and Women.
White's (1693), 37–8 St. James's St., S.W.1.	W. H. West.........	100·00	100·00	Social: Non-political.
Wig and Pen (1908), 229–230 Strand, W.C.2.	R. A. Brennan.......	7·00	7·50	Law and Journalism.

CLUB AND LIBRARY EDITION OF WHITAKER, 1977

The Club and Library Edition of Whitaker's Almanack, 1977, contains 1,220 pages, illustrations and additional coloured maps (The World, The British Isles, Baltic States, Russia and her neighbours, Germany and her neighbours, France and Spain, The Far East, India, Pakistan and Burma, Africa, Canada, and Newfoundland, The United States, South America, Australia, New Zealand) in strong leather binding, with gilt top and silk headband. Price £5·75 net.

| Club and Address (with date of foundation) | Secretary or *Hon Sec. | Subscription | |
		Entr.	Ann.
		£	£
Aldershot (Officers) (1846), Farnborough Road.	B. A. Harvey........	15·00	29·00
Bath (Bath and County) (1858), 21–22 Queen Square.	R. A. L. Belben......	Nil	..
Birmingham—			
(Birmingham Club) (1888), Winston Churchill House, 8 Ethel Street.	N. J. Masterton......	Nil	46·00
(Chamber of Commerce) (1922), 75 Harborne Road.	J. R. Dixon..........	Nil	21·00
(St. Paul's) (1859), 34 St. Paul's Square.	A. E. Shipton........	Nil	59·40 to 10·80
(Union) (1850), 87 Colman Row	*J. McFea	Nil	Various
Bishop Auckland (The Club) (1870), Victoria Street.	T. W. Walton........	5·00	9·00
Bradford (The Club) (1870), 41 Bank Street.	★W. E. B. Holroyd; D. R. Hobbs	5·00	61·56
Bridport and West Dorset (1921), 12 South Street.	R. M. Mayles........	Nil	10·00
Bristol (Clifton) (1882), 22 The Mall.	Lt.-Col. A. W. Thompson, O.B.E., M.C., T.D.	Nil	40·00
(Constitutional) (1885), Marsh Street.	Brig. H. A. Hardy, M.B.E., M.C.	11·05	35·00 to 15·00
Cambridge (Amateur Dramatic) (1855), Park Street.	N. Hytner...........	Nil	3·50
(Hawks) (1874), Jesus Lane.	*D. B. Williams, Ph.D.	3·00 to 6·50	†25·00
(Union) (1815), Bridge Street.	B. Thoday (Chief Clerk)	Nil	10·50
Canterbury (Kent and Canterbury) (1868), 17 Old Dover Road.	A. G. A. Cooper......	10·00	20·00
Cardiff (Cardiff and County) (1866), 2 Westgate Street.	★G. V. Wynne-Jones, O.B.E.	40·00	70·00
Cheltenham (The New Club) (1890), Mountpellier Parade.	*Dr. H. G. Dowler...	Nil	33·00
Chester (Grosvenor) (1866), 3 Vicars Lane.	M. J. D. Roberts.....	Nil	18·90
(City) (1807), St. Peter's Church Yard.	R. Edwards..........	20·00	20·00
Chichester (W. Sussex County) (1873), 38 East St.	C. W. Hayden........	..	11·00 & 5·50
Colchester (The Club) (1874), 3–5 Culver Street, E.	P. A. Witard........	Nil	18·00
Devizes (Devizes & District) (1932), 17 St. John Street.	*C. S. D. Hall.......	5·50	7·50
Douglas, Isle of Man (Ellan Vannin Club) (1893), 20 Finch Road.	*T. E. Osborne......	1·05	20·00
Durham (County) (1894), 52 Old Elvet.	*E. P. Timm........	Nil	10·00
Eastbourne (Devonshire) (1872), Westdown House, Hartington Place.	*J. B. Neal..........	9·00	9·00
Exeter (Exeter and County) (1871), 5 Cathedral Close.	M. P. Saunders......	5·00	24·00 to 12·00
Folkestone Radnor Club) (1874), 136 Sandgate Rd.	Vacant..............	5·50	13·20
Harrogate (The Club) (1857), 36 Victoria Avenue.	*C. L. Leslie........	..	25·00 & 5·25
Haverfordwest (Pembrokeshire County) (1877), 48 High Street.	*B. J. Radley........	4·00	6·00
Henley-on-Thames (Leander) (1818), Henley.	*H. R. P. Steward, T.D.	10·00	11·00
(Phyllis Court) (1906), Marlow Road.	D. C. Ferguson......	Nil	35·00
Hove (The Hove Club) (1882), 28 Fourth Avenue.	Sqn. Ldr. G. A. Inverarity, D.F.C.	10·00	25·00
Jersey (United) (1846), Royal Sq.; St. Helier.	*R. J. Michel........	20·00	20·00
(Victoria) (1853), Beresford St., St. Helier.	C. G. Mitchell.......	30·00 to 15·00	25·00 to 12·50
Leamington (Tennis Court) (1847), 50 Bedford Street.	*O. D. R. Dixon.....	10·00	25·00
Leeds (The Leeds Club) (1850), 3 Albion Place.	*J. W. Bosomworth..	Nil	40·00
Leicester (Leicestershire Club) (1873), 9 Welford Place.	A. B. Proctor........	10·00	52·00
Liverpool (Artists) (1886), 5 Eberle Street.	*M. S. Dawson......	11·00	48·60
(Athenæum) (1797), Church Alley.	*F. J. Smith.........	Nil	35·00
(Racquet) (1877), 102 Upper Parliament Street.	*R. L. Packer........	Nil	50·00
Manchester (The Manchester Club) (1871), 50 Spring Gardens.	F. C. T. Baker.......	27·50	55·00 to 7·70
Newcastle upon Tyne (Northern Constitutional) (1908), 37 Pilgrim Street.	Mrs. G. Whitham....	Nil	64·80
Northampton (Northampton and County) (1873), George Row.	Sqdn. Ldr. J. V. Hadland, D.F.C.	5·00 to 20·00	12·00 to 31·50
Norwich (Norfolk) (1864), 17 Upper King Street.	Mrs. S. M. Gostling...	15·00	45·00 to 15·00

† Life Membership.

Club and Address (with date of foundation)	Secretary or *Hon. Sec.	Subscription Entr. £	Subscription Ann. £
Oxford (Frewen) (1869), 98 St. Aldate's.	*W. H. Miller, B.E.M..	11·00	14·00
(Vincent's) (1863), King Edward Street.	G. J. Brazier (*Steward*).	..	..
Peterborough (City and Counties) (1867), 21 Priestgate.	D. A. S. Parker......	2·00	20·00
Portsmouth (Royal Naval and Royal Albert Yacht) (1867), 17 Pembroke Road.	Capt.D.J.Bateman,R.N.	10·00	*Various*
Reading (Berkshire Athenæum) (1776), 53 Blagrave Street.	*B. H. Powell.......	*Nil*	20·00
Rochester (Castle) (1865), 3 Esplanade.	*L. F. Fagg..........	15·00	24·00
Rugby (The Rugby) (1865), 35 North Street.	*V. M. Roberts, O.B.E.	15·00	5·00
Rye (Dormy House) (1896), East Cliff, Rye.	*H. A. Fowler.......	5·00	20·00 & 10·00
St. Leonards on Sea (East Sussex) (1893), 1 Warrior Square.	*S. G. Bradbury......	1·05	10·50
Sheffield (The Club) (1843), George Street.	Lt.-Col. J. R. Pattison.	30·00	50·00 to 22·00
Shrewsbury (Salop) (1972), 6 The Square.	S. Davies, T.D.........	*Nil*	21·00 to 7·00
Teddington (Royal Canoe) (1866), Trowlock Island, Middx.	Mrs. G. Barnard......	3·00 to 2·00	15·60 to 11·90
Torbay (The Paignton Club) (1882), The Esplanade.	P. Grafton...........	20·00	10·00
Worcester (Union and County) (1861), 49 Foregate Street.	*P. J. Seward........	*Nil*	20·00
York (Yorkshire) (1839), River House, Museum St.	S. A. Free, O.B.E......	22·00	40·00
(City) (1876), 4 Museum Street.	*I. R. Washington....	3·00	30·00

Scotland

Club and Address	Secretary or *Hon. Sec.	Entr.	Ann.
Ayr (County) (1872), Savoy Park Hotel.	*W. W. McHarg.....	*Nil*	8·00 to 5·00
Dundee (Eastern) (1865), 2 Euclid Street.	....	*Nil*	54·00
Edinburgh (Caledonian) (1877), 32 Abercromby Place.	Mrs. M. W. Hutton...	*Nil*	30·00 to 15·00
(Ladies' Caledonian) (1908), 13–14 Charlotte Square.	Miss P. D. Bremner...	*Nil*	40·00 to 5·50
(New) (1787), 86 Princes Street.	R. Pettie, T.D........	35·00	60·00 to 33·00
Glasgow (Art) (1867), 185 Bath Street.	G. Cowan............	21·60 to 5·00	28·03
(Royal Scottish Automobile) (1899), 11 Blythswood Square.	Maj. R. T. Reid, M.C..	34·00 or 17·00	40·00 or 15·00
(The Western Club) (1825), 32 Royal Exchange Square.	Lt.-Col. A. Gordon, M.C.	25·00	50·00
Inverness (Highland) (1870), 39 High Street.	C. J. Sedgwick.......	25·00	30·00

Northern Ireland

Club and Address	Secretary or *Hon. Sec.	Entr.	Ann.
Belfast (Ulster) (1837), River House, High Street.	*S. M. P. Cross.......	10·50	61·56
(Ulster Reform) (1885), 4 Royal Avenue.	S. F. Hodge, M.B.E....	*Nil*	40·00

YACHT CLUBS

Club and Address (with date of foundation)	Secretary or *Hon. Sec.	Subscription Entr. £	Subscription Ann. £
Beaumaris (Royal Anglesey) (1802), 6–7 Green Edge.	*R. R. M. Jones.....	30·00 to 20·00	10·00 to 1·05
Bembridge, I. of W. (Sailing) (1886), Isle of Wight.	K. J. Hawker........	15·00	25·00
Birkenhead (Royal Mersey) (1844), 8–10 Bedford Road, Rock Ferry.	*C. J. Kay...........	20·00	25·00
Bridlington (Royal Yorks) (1847), 1 Windsor Crescent.	*Lt.-Col. G. R. Saltoustall, O.B.E.	10·00	30·00 to 5·00
Burnham-on-Crouch. (Royal Corinthian) (1872), Burnham-on-Crouch	Cdr. I. McL. Methven, R.N. (*ret.*)	6·00	*Various*
Caernarvon (Royal Welsh) (1847), Porth-Sr-Aur.	*N. Cottam..........	5·00	8·00
Cowes (Royal Yacht Squadron) (1815), The Castle, Cowes	Maj. J. D. Dillon, D.S.C., R.M.	260·00	130·00
(Royal London) (1838), The Parade.	Sqn.-Ldr. C. A. A. Davis	50·00	35·00
Dover (Royal Cinque Ports) (1872), 4–5 Waterloo Crescent.	Mrs. E. A. Parker.....	5·00	20·00 to 6·00
Essex (1890), Leigh-on-Sea.	Lt.-Cdr. C. Stokes, M.B.E.	7·45	14·90
Fishbourne, I. of W. (Royal Victoria) (1844), Fishbourne.	D. E. Hurles.........	3·15	12·00 to 3·00

Club and Address (with date of foundation)	Secretary or *Hon. Sec.	Subscription Entr. £	Subscription Ann. £
Fowey (Royal Fowey) (1894), Fowey.	*T. K. Jones.........	Various	Various
Harwich (Royal Harwich) (1843), Woolverstone, nr. Ipswich.	Col. C. H. Bavin.....	15·00	15·00
Jersey (Royal Channel Islands) (1862), Le Boulevard, St. Aubin, Jersey.	A. K. Jackson........	..	..
Kingswear (Royal Dart.) (1866), Kingswear, S. Devon.	*Miss A. M. Hine-Haycock, M.B.E.	10·00	10·00 to 2·00
London (Cruising Association) (1908), Ivory House, St. Katharine Dock, E.1.	Miss E. Rider........	5·00	12·00 to 2·00
(Royal Cruising) (1880), 42 Half Moon Street, W.1.	*A. P. Gray.........	10·00	7·00
Lowestoft (Royal Norfolk and Suffolk) (1859), Royal Plain.	Capt. I. A. B. Quarrie, C.B.E., V.R.D.	10·00	Various
Penarth (Penarth) (1880), The Esplanade.	D. E. Morse.........	5·00	18·00
Plymouth (Royal Western) (1827), 9 Grand Parade, West Hoe.	Sqn.-Ldr. J. E. R. Vosper	Various	Various
(Royal Plymouth Corinthian) (1877), Madeira Road.	*E. J. Stanley........	Various	Various
Poole (East Dorset Sailing) (1875), Sandbanks Rd.	Mrs. B. V. Okey.....	10·50	9·00
(Parkstone) (1895), Pearce Avenue, Parkstone.	Col. T. A. Hunt......	30·00	28·00
(Poole Harbour) (1949), Salterns Way, Lilliput.	Mrs. E. M. Perry.....	Various	Various
(Royal Motor Yacht) (1905), Sandbanks.	Mrs. M. C. Hardie....	26·25	21·00
(Yacht) (1865), New Quay Road, Hamworthy.	Capt. G. E. Thornton	20·00	22·00
Ramsgate (Royal Temple) (1857), West Cliff Mansions.	C. R. De Silva.......	37·80	Various
Southampton:			
Royal (Air Force) (1932), Riverside Ho., Hamble.	Sqn.-Ldr. A. R. Middleton, D.S.O., D.F.C.	25·00	22·00
(Royal Southern) (1837), Hamble, Hants.	Mrs. W. J. F. Clampett	33·00	Various
(Royal Thames) (1775), Shore House, Warsash, Hants.	Capt. K. R. Stobbs...	52·50 & 26·25	105·00 to 35·00
Southend (Alexandra) (1873), The Cliffs, Clifton Terrace.	*E. Green............	10·00	20·00 to 10·00
Southsea (Royal Naval and Royal Albert) (1864), 17 Pembroke Road, Portsmouth.	Capt. D. J. Bateman, R.N. (ret.)	10·00	Various
Swansea (Bristol Channel) (1875), 744 Mumbles Road, Mumbles.	*P. G. Cawker.......	30·00	30·00 to 20·50
Westcliff-on-Sea (Thames Estuary) (1947), 3 The Leas.	*A. H. Basgallop.....	7·50	10·00
Weymouth (Royal Dorset) (1875), 51 The Esplanade.	*J. C. T. Plummer....	15·00	25·00
Windermere (Royal Windermere) (1860), Fallbarrow Road, Bowness.	*A. Murdoch.........	25·00	17·00 & 14·00
Yarmouth (Royal Solent) (1878), Yarmouth, I.O.W.	Col. R. W. Stephenson, O.B.E.	14·00 to 20·00	24·00 to 1·00

Scotland

Dundee (Royal Tay) (1891), 34 Dundee Road, Broughty Ferry.	*W. Anderson.......	10·00	8·00
Edinburgh (Royal Forth) (1868), 1 Boswall Road, Edinburgh, 5.	*G. Laing...........	35·00	35·00
Glasgow (Royal Clyde) (1856), Rhu, Dunbartonshire.	D. M. Paul, 111 Union Street, Glasgow	5·00	15·00
(Royal Western) (1875), (None).	*Lt.-Col. R. King-Clark, M.B.E., M.C., Amberwood, Shandon, Dunbartonshire.	1·00	1·00 and 0·50
Oban (Royal Highland) (1881).	W. Melville.......	Nil	2·10
Rhu (Royal Northern) (1824), Rhu, Dunbartonshire.	*R. G. K. Hardey....	30·00	44·00

Northern Ireland

Bangor (Royal Ulster) (1866), Clifton Road, Bangor, Co. Down.	*G. D. Ralston.......	20·00	55·00

Principal British and Irish Societies and Institutions

THE ROYAL ACADEMY OF ARTS (1768), Burlington House, W.1.—*President*, Sir Hugh Casson (1976); *Keeper*, Peter Greenham, R.A.; *Treas.*, Roger de Grey, R.A.; *Sec.*, Sidney C. Hutchison, M.V.O., F.S.A.; *Reg.*, K. J. Tanner.

Royal Academicians

1972 Adams, Norman, C.B.E.	1970 Hayes, Colin
1963 Aldridge, John	1961 Hepple, Norman
1970 Ardizzone, Edward, C.B.E.	1971 Hermes, Miss Gertrude
1955 Bawden, Edward, C.B.E.	1967 Hillier, Tristram
1976 Blackadder, Miss Elizabeth	1968 Holford, Lord, O.B.E.
1975 Blamey, Norman	1965*Jones, Allan Gwynne, D.S.O.
1975 Bowey, Miss Olwyn	1973 Jones Ivor Roberts
1971 Bratby, John R.	1974 Kneale, Bryan
1937‡Brockhurst, G. L.	1962*Lowry, L. S.
1972 Brown, Ralph	1963 McFall, David
1955 Buhler, Robert	1955 Machin, Arnold, O.B.E.
1962*Burn, Rodney J.	1933*McMillan, W., C.V.O.
1972 Butler, James	1973 MacTaggart, Sir William
1975 Brown, H. T. Cadbury-, O.B.E.	1973 Middleditch, Edward
1970 Casson, Sir Hugh	1938 Monnington, Sir Thomas
1975 Clarke, Geoffrey	1951*Nash, John, C.B.E.
1973 Clatworthy, Robert	1967*Nimptsch, Uli
1972 Coker, Peter	1953*Pitchforth, R. V.
1972 Cooke, Miss Jean	1966*Roberts, William
1938 Cowern, Raymond T.	1969 Rosoman, Leonard
1974 Cuming, Frederick	1961 Sanders, Christopher C.
1969 de Grey, Roger	1972 Sheppard, Richard, C.B.E.
1976 Dickson, Miss Jennifer	1963*Sisson, Marshall A., C.V.O., C.B.E.
1955 Dring, William	1959 Skeaping, John R.
1968 Dunstan, Bernard	1969 Soukop, Willi
1953 Eurich, Richard	1954 Spear, Ruskin
1974 Fell, Miss Sheila	1960 Spence, Sir Basil, O.M., O.B.E., T.D.
1954*Fitton, James	1945*Thomson, A. R.
1942‡Frampton, Meredith	1954 Tunnicliffe, C. F.
1965 Freeth, H. Andrew	1965 Ward, John
1972*Fry, E. Maxwell, C.B.E.	1965 Weight, Carel, C.B.E.
1969 Gibberd, Sir Frederick, C.B.E.	1974 Williams, Kyffin
1975 Goldfinger, Ernö	1945*Woodford, James, O.B.E.
1972 Gore, Frederick	1972*Wolfe, Edward
1960 Greenham, Peter	

Associates

1974 Blake, Peter	1974 Harpley, Sydney
1971 Blow, Miss S.	1974 Hogarth, Paul
1974 Bowyer, William	1975 Levene, Ben
1974 Camp, Jeffrey	1976 Manasseh, Leonard
1975 Chamberlin, Peter	1972 Paolozzi, Eduardo
1976 Dalwood, Hubert	1973 Phillipson, Robin
1976 Eyton, Anthony	1972 Powell, Sir Philip, O.B.E.
1975 Fraser, Donald Hamilton	1975 Stephenson, Ian
1971 Frink, Miss Elisabeth, C.B.E.	1972 Swanwick, Miss Betty
1971 Green, Anthony	1973 Tindle, David

*Senior Academician.
‡ Honorary Retired Academician.

Former Presidents of the Royal Academy

Sir J. Reynolds, 1768	Sir F. Dicksee, 1924
Benjamin West, 1792	Sir W. Llewellyn, 1928
James Wyatt, 1805	Sir E. Lutyens, 1938
Benjamin West, 1806	Sir A. J. Munnings, 1944
Sir T. Lawrence, 1820	
Sir M. A. Shee, 1830	Sir G. F. Kelly, 1949
Sir C. Eastlake, 1850	Sir A. E. Richardson, 1954
Sir F. Grant, 1866	
Lord Leighton, 1878	Sir C. Wheeler, 1956
Sir J. Millais, 1896	Sir T. Monnington, 1966
Sir E. Poynter, 1896	
Sir A. Webb, 1919	

ROYAL CAMBRIAN ACADEMY OF ART (1881), Plas Mawr, Conway.—*Pres.*, K. Williams, R.A.; *Hon. Sec.*, J. R. Webster; *Curator and Sec.*, L. H. S. Mercer.

THE ROYAL SCOTTISH ACADEMY (1826), Princes Street, Edinburgh—*Pres.*, Sir Robin Philipson, R.S.A.; *Sec.*, E. Gordon, R.S.A.; *Treas.*, J. Cumming, R.S.A.; *Librarian*, J. Houston, R.S.A.; *Asst. Sec.*, J. Marshall.

Hon. Retired Academicians:
1939 McGlashan, Arch. A.
1946 Thomson, Adam B., O.B.E.
1964 Miller, James

Royal Scottish Academicians

1958 Armour, Mrs. M.	1973 Littlejohn, William
1966 Armour, William	1957 Lorimer, Hew
1972 Blackadder, Elizabeth	1971 McClure, David
1971 Cameron, Gordon S.	1948 MacTaggart, Sir William
1962 Coia, J. A., C.B.E.	1976 Malcolm, Ellen
1974 Collins, Peter	1972 Michie, David
1956 Crawford, H. Adam	1963 Morrocco, Alberto
1974 Crosbie, William	1957 Patrick, J. McIntosh
1970 Cumming, James	
1962 Donaldson, David A.	1966 Peploe, Denis
1956 Fleming, Ian	1962 Philipson, Sir Robin
1967 Gordon, Esmé	1976 Reeves, Philip
1972 Houston, John	1937 Schotz, Benno
1966 Johnston, Ninian	1970 Sutherland, Scott
1956 Kininmonth, Sir William	1975 Wheeler, H. Anthony, O.B.E.

Associates

Baillie, W. J. L.	Morris, James
Balmer, Barbara	Morrison, James
Bone, W. Drummond	Morrocco, Leon
Brown, Neil Dallas	Pelly, Frances
Bryce, Gordon	Reiach, Alan, O.B.E.
Buchan, Dennis	Richards John
Butler, Vincent	Robertson, James
Campbell, A. Buchanan	Robertson, R. Ross
Campbell, Alex.	Scott, William
Dick, Miss Alix	Shanks, Duncan F.
Donald, George	Smart, Alastair
Evans, David	Smith, Ian McKenzie
Fairgrieve, James	Snowden, Michael
Fraser, Alexander	Steedman, Robert R.
Glover, John Hardie, O.B.E.	Stewart, S. Birnie
Johnstone, Miss Dorothy	Thomson, Sinclair
Johnstone, John	Walker, Frances
Knox, Jann	Whiston, Peter
	Womersley, Peter

Hon. Retired Associates, Miss Elizabeth Dempster; J. H. Clark. Non-Resident Associates, Charles Pulsford; Sir Basil Spence, O.M., O.B.E., T.D., R.A.

ROYAL IRISH ACADEMY (1786), 19 Dawson Street, Dublin.—*Pres.*, G. F. Mitchell; *Treas.*, P. Lynch; *Sec.*, T. Walsh.

ABBEYFIELD SOCIETY, 35A High Street, Potters Bar, Herts.—Provides small households for lonely elderly people.—*Gen. Sec.*, D. A. L. Charles.

ACCOUNTANTS, INSTITUTE OF CHARTERED, in England and Wales (1880), Chartered Accountants' Hall, Moorgate Place, E.C.2.—*Pres.* (1976–77), S. Kitchen; *Secretary*, J. P. Hough.

ACCOUNTANTS AND AUDITORS, BRITISH ASSOCIATION OF (1923), Stamford House, W.4.—*Sec.*, G. F. Garrad.

ACCOUNTANTS, ASSOCIATION OF CERTIFIED (1904), 22 Bedford Square, W.C.1.—*Pres.*, H. Hill; *Sec.*, R. A. Dudman.

ACCOUNTANTS OF SCOTLAND, THE INSTITUTE OF CHARTERED (1854), 27 Queen Street, Edinburgh —*Pres.*, G. R. G. Stewart; *Sec.*, A. B. Richards.

ACCOUNTANTS IN IRELAND, INSTITUTE OF CHARTERED (1888), 7 Fitzwilliam Place, Dublin 2, and 11 Donegall Square, South, Belfast.—*Dir.*, R. F. Hussey.

ACCOUNTANTS, SOCIETY OF COMPANY AND COMMERCIAL (1974), 11 Portland Road, Edgbaston, Birmingham.—*Exec. Dir.*, J. H. Tresman.

ACTORS' BENEVOLENT FUND (1882), 6 Adam Street, W.C.2.—*Sec.*, Miss A. G. Marks.

ACTORS' CHARITABLE TRUST (incorporating DENVILLE HALL), Gloucester House, 19 Charing Cross Road, W.C.2.—Assists children of theatrical parentage who are in need; home for elderly and infirm actors and actresses.—*Pres.*, The Lord Olivier; *Admin. Sec.*, Miss M. M. Brisley.

ACTORS' CHURCH UNION (1899), St. Paul's Church, Bedford Street, W.C.2.—*Senior Chaplain*, Rev. M. Hurst-Bannister.

ACTUARIES IN SCOTLAND, THE FACULTY OF (1856), Hall and Library, 23 St. Andrew Square, Edinburgh.—*Sec.*, W. W. Mair.

ACTUARIES, INSTITUTE OF (1848), Staple Inn Hall, W.C.1.—*Pres.*, C. M. O'Brien; *Sec.*, N. J. Page, M.C.

ADDICTION (TO ALCOHOL AND OTHER DRUGS), SOCIETY FOR THE STUDY OF (1884).—*Sec.*, N. H. Rathod, c/o 1 Wimpole St., W.1.

ADDITIONAL CURATES SOCIETY; HOME MISSIONS OF CHURCH OF ENGLAND AND THE CHURCH IN WALES (1837), St Mark's Church House, 264a Washwood Heath Road, Birmingham.—*Sec.*, Rev. A. J. Prescott.

ADMINISTRATIVE MANAGEMENT, INSTITUTE OF (1915), 205 High Street, Beckenham, Kent.—*Sec.*, J. L. Cousins.

ADMINISTRATIVE ACCOUNTING, INSTITUTE OF (1916), Walter House, 418-422 Strand, W.C.2.—*Sec.-Gen.*, D. W. Bradley.

ADVERTISING ASSOCIATION, Abford House, 15 Wilton Road, S.W.1.—*Director-General*, R. Underhill.

ADVERTISING BENEVOLENT SOCIETY, NATIONAL (1913), 3 Crawford Place, W.1.—*Gen. Sec.*, Miss R. Bell.

ADVERTISING, INSTITUTE OF PRACTITIONERS IN, 44 Belgrave Square, S.W.1.—*Dir.*, J. P. O'Connor.

ADVERTISEMENT MANAGEMENT ASSOCIATION, Incorporated (founded 1932, inc. 1958), Mansfield House, Bulstrode Lane, Felden, Hemel Hempstead, Herts.—*Hon. Sec.*, M. A. Geddes.

AERONAUTICAL SOCIETY, ROYAL (1866) (incorporating the Institution of Aeronautical Engineers and the Helicopter Association of Great Britain), 4 Hamilton Place, W.1.—*Pres.*, (1976–77) C. Abell; *Sec.* E. M. J. Schaffter.

AFRICAN INSTITUTE, INTERNATIONAL (1926), 210 High Holborn, W.C.1—*Dir.*, Dr. D. Dalby.

AFRICAN MEDICAL AND RESEARCH FOUNDATION, 27 Dover Street, W.1.—*Administration*, Mrs E. Young.

AGED PILGRIMS' FRIEND SOCIETY (1807), 175 Tower Bridge Road, S.E.1.—*Sec.*, G. Reid.

AGED POOR SOCIETY (1708) AND ST. JOSEPH'S HOUSE, 39 Eccleston Square, S.W.1.—*Sec.*, Major A. R. W. Shipley.

AGRICULTURAL BENEVOLENT INSTITUTION, ROYAL, Vincent House, Vincent Square, S.W.1.—*Hon. Treas.*, J. D. S. Ainscow; *Sec.*, Cdr. O. C. Wright.

AGRICULTURAL BENEVOLENT INSTITUTION, ROYAL SCOTTISH (1897), 8 Dublin Street, Edinburgh.—*Sec.*, K. M. Campbell, W.S.

AGRICULTURAL BOTANY, NATIONAL INSTITUTE OF (1919), Huntingdon Road, Cambridge.—*Director*, P. S. Wellington, D.S.C., Ph.D.

AGRICULTURAL ENGINEERS ASSOCIATION, LIMITED (1877), 6 Buckingham Gate, S.W.1.—*Dir.-Gen.*, F. D. Swift, O.B.E.

AGRICULTURAL SOCIETY, EAST OF ENGLAND, East of England Showground, Peterborough.—*Sec.*, R. W. Bird.

AGRICULTURAL SOCIETY, GLASGOW (1860).—*Sec.*, S. Gilmour, 24 Beresford Terrace, Ayr.

AGRICULTURAL SOCIETY, ROYAL ULSTER (1826), The King's Hall, Balmoral, Belfast.—*Sec.*, J. T. Kernohan, O.B.E.

AGRICULTURE, ASSOCIATION OF (1947), 78 Buckingham Gate, S.W.1.—*Gen. Sec.*, Miss J. Bostock.

AIRBROKERS ASSOCIATION (1949), 25 Bury Street, E.C.3.—*Sec.*, G. E. K. Ireland.

AIRCRAFT NOISE, BRITISH ASSOCIATION FOR THE CONTROL OF, 30 Fleet Street, E.C.4.

AIR LEAGUE, THE (1909), 99 New Cavendish Street, W.1.—*Chairman*, K. G. Bergin, M.D.; *Dir.* J. Motum.

ALEXANDRA ROSE DAY FUND, 1 Castelnau, Barnes, S.W.13.—*Organizer*, Mrs. E. Day.

ALMSHOUSES, NATIONAL ASSOCIATION OF, Billingbear Lodge, Wokingham, Berks.—*Gen. Sec.*, D. M. Scott.

AMATEUR CINEMATOGRAPHERS, INSTITUTE OF (1932), 63 Woodfield Lane, Ashtead, Surrey.—*Admin. Sec.*, Mrs B. Wood.

ANAESTHETISTS OF GREAT BRITAIN AND IRELAND, ASSOCIATION OF (1932). Room 475, Tavistock House South, Tavistock Square, W.C.1.

ANCIENT BUILDINGS, SOCIETY FOR THE PROTECTION OF (1877), 55 Great Ormond Street, W.C.1.—*Sec.*, Mrs. M. Dance, M.B.E.

ANCIENT MONUMENTS SOCIETY (1924).—*Hon. Sec.*, I. Bulmer-Thomas, F.S.A., 33 Ladbroke Square, W.11.

ANGLO-ARAB ASSOCIATION (1961), West End House, 11 Hills Place, W.1.

ANGLO-BELGIAN UNION (1918), 6 Belgrave Square, S.W.1.—*Hon, Sec.*, Dr. Sheelagh O'Hara.

ANGLO-BRAZILIAN SOCIETY (1943), 2 Belgrave Square, S.W.1.—*Sec.*, Mrs. M. J. Fyfe.

ANGLO-DANISH SOCIETY (1924), 7 St. Helen's Place, Bishopsgate, E.C.3.—*Chairman*, Sir Robert Bellinger, G.B.E.

ANGLO-NORSE SOCIETY, 25 Belgrave Square, S.W.1.

ANGLO-SWEDISH SOCIETY, 52 Ennismore Gardens, S.W.7.

ANGLO-THAI SOCIETY (1962).—*Hon. Sec.*, Miss B. I. Crewe, 95 Kennington Park Road, S.E.11.

ANTHROPOLOGICAL INSTITUTE, ROYAL (1843), 36 Craven Street, W.C.2.—*Hon. Sec.*, Prof. Lucy Mair.

ANTHROPOSOPHICAL SOCIETY IN GREAT BRITAIN, Rudolf Steiner House, 35 Park Road, N.W.1.

ANTIQUARIES, SOCIETY OF (1717), Burlington House, W.1.—*Pres.*, A. J. Taylor; *Treas.*, R. M. Robbins; *Director*, Prof. J. D. Evans; *Sec.*, I. H. Longworth.

ANTIQUARIES OF SCOTLAND, SOCIETY OF (1780), National Museum of Antiquities of Scotland, Queen Street, Edinburgh.—*Sec.*, B. C. Skinner; *Treas.*, J. A. Donaldson.

ANTI-SLAVERY SOCIETY FOR THE PROTECTION OF HUMAN RIGHTS (1839), 60 Weymouth Street, W.1.—*Sec.*, Col. J. R. P. Montgomery, M.C.

ANTI-VIVISECTION: BRITISH UNION FOR THE ABOLITION OF VIVISECTION (INC.) (1898), 47 Whitehall, S.W.1.—*Gen. Sec.*, S. Hicks.

ANTI-VIVISECTION SOCIETY, THE NATIONAL (1875), 51 Harley Street, W.1.

ANTI-VIVISECTION SOCIETY, SCOTTISH, 121 West Regent Street, Glasgow.

APOSTLESHIP OF THE SEA (1920). For active seafarers. *National Headquarters.*—Anchor House, 81 Barking Road, E.16.—*Dir.*, Rt. Rev. D. McGuinness.

APOTHECARIES, SOCIETY OF (1617).—Black Friars Lane, Queen Victoria Street, E.C.4.—*Clerk and Registrar*, E. Busby, M.B.E.

ARCHÆOLOGICAL ASSOCIATION, BRITISH (1843), 61 Old Park Ridings, Winchmore Hill, N.21.—*Hon. Asst. Treas.*, Miss I. B. McClure.

ARCHÆOLOGICAL ASSOCIATION, CAMBRIAN (1846).—*President* (1976–77) D. J. Cathcart King, M.C., F.S.A.; *Gen. Sec.*, H. D. Rees, Llyswen, Bow Street, Dyfed.

ARCHÆOLOGICAL INSTITUTE, ROYAL (1843).—*Hon. Sec.*, S. D. T. Spittle, M.A., F.S.A., A.R.I.B.A.; *Asst. Sec.*, Miss W. E. Phillips, 304 Addison House, Grove End Road, N.W.8.

ARCHÆOLOGY, COUNCIL FOR BRITISH (1944), 7 Marylebone Road, N.W.1.—*President*, N. Thomas; *Hon. Sec.*, R. T. Rowley, F.S.A.; *Dir.*, H. F. Cleere, F.S.A.

ARCHITECTS, THE ROYAL INSTITUTE OF BRITISH (1834), 66 Portland Place, W.1.—*President*, E. Lyons; *Chief Executive*, W. D. Edmonds.

ARCHITECTS REGISTRATION COUNCIL OF THE UNITED KINGDOM, 73 Hallam Street, W.1.—*Chairman*, D. Waterhouse; *Registrar*, Mrs. N. Dawson, M.B.E.

ARCHITECTS AND SURVEYORS, INCORPORATED ASSOCIATION OF (1925), 29 Belgrave Square, S.W.1.—*Pres.* D. M. Walker; *Sec.*, M. G. Tatch.

ARCHITECTS AND SURVEYORS, THE FACULTY OF, LTD: (incorporating The Institute of Registered Architects Ltd), 68 Gloucester Place, W.1.—*Sec.*, A. D. G. Webb.

ARCHITECTS BENEVOLENT SOCIETY (1850), 66 Portland Place, W.1.—*Hon. Sec.*, Howard Lobb, C.B.E.

ARCHITECTS IN SCOTLAND, ROYAL INCORPORATION OF (1922), 15 Rutland Square, Edinburgh.—*Sec. and Treas.*, P. G. D. Clark.

ARCHITECTURAL ASSOCIATION (INC.) (1847), 34–36 Bedford Square, W.C.1.—*Pres.*, R. Andrews, M.B.E.; *Sec.* E. Le Maistre.

ARCHIVISTS, SOCIETY OF (1946), *Hon. Sec.*, P. Walne, County Hall, Hertford.

AREA MEDICAL OFFICERS, ASSOCIATION OF (1974).—*Hon. Sec.*, Dr P. C. Moore, The Limes, Belle Vue Road, Shrewsbury, Salop.

ARLIS (Art Libraries Society) (1969).—*Sec.*, Mrs. F. Robinson, Cambridgeshire College of Arts and Technology Library, Cambridge.

ARMY BENEVOLENT FUND (1944), "G" Block, Duke of York's H.Q., Chelsea, S.W.3.—*Controller*, Maj.-Gen. D. N. H. Tyacke, C.B., O.B.E.

ARMY CADET FORCE ASSOCIATION (1930), 58 Buckingham Gate, S.W.1.—*Sec.*, W. F. L. Newcombe, O.B.E., T.D.

ARMY HISTORICAL RESEARCH, SOCIETY FOR (1921).

Hon. Sec., Maj. B. Mollo, T.D., c/o National Army Museum, Royal Hospital Road, S.W.3.

ART-COLLECTIONS FUND, NATIONAL (1903), 24–28 Bloomsbury Way, W.C.1.—*Sec.*, J. Christian, F.S.A.

ART EDUCATION, NATIONAL SOCIETY FOR (1888), 3rd Floor, Champness Hall, Drake Street, Rochdale, Lancs.—*Gen. Sec.*, G. F. Williams.

ART WORKERS GUILD (1884), 6 Queen Square, Bloomsbury, W.C.1.—*Master*, A. Bultitude; *Sec.* R. Murry.

ARTHRITIS AND RHEUMATISM COUNCIL FOR RESEARCH, Faraday House, 8–10 Charing Cross Road, W.C.2.—*Gen. Sec.*, M. C. G. Andrews.

ARTISTS' GENERAL BENEVOLENT INSTITUTION (1814) AND ARTISTS' ORPHAN FUND (1871), Burlington House, Piccadilly, W.1.—*Sec.*, Miss D. P. Laidman.

ARTISTS UNITED SOCIETY OF (1921), 17 Carlton House Terrace, S.W.1.—*Pres.* G. Gunn; *Sec.*, C. de Winter.

ARTS COUNCIL OF GREAT BRITAIN, 105 Piccadilly W.1.—*Chairman*, The Lord Gibson; *Secretary-General*, R. Shaw.

ASLIB (1924). (Formerly Association of Special Libraries and Information Bureaux), 3 Belgrave Square, S.W.1.—*Director*, L. Wilson.

ASSISTANT MASTERS ASSOCIATION, 29 Gordon Square, W.C.1.—*Sec.*, A. W. S. Hutchings, C.B.E.

ASSISTANT MISTRESSES, ASSOCIATION OF, 29 Gordon Square, W.C.1.—*Sec.*, Miss S. D. Wood, C.B.E.

ASTHMA RESEARCH COUNCIL, 12 Pembridge Square, W.2.—*Chairman*, D. M. Walters, M.B.E., M.P.

ASTRONOMICAL ASSOCIATION, BRITISH.—*Office*, Burlington House, Piccadilly, W.1. Meetings at 23 Savile Row, W.1.—*President*, H. B. Ridley; *Sec.*, N. J. Goodman; *Asst, Sec.*, J. L. White.

ASTRONOMICAL SOCIETY, ROYAL (Incorporated (1820), Burlington House, W.1.—*Pres.*, Prof. F. G. Smith, F.R.S.; *Secs.*, Dr. J. A. Hudson; Prof. R. J. Tayler; Dr. J. R. Shakeshaft.

A.T.S. and W.R.A.C. BENEVOLENT FUNDS (1964), Queen Elizabeth Park, Guildford, Surrey.—*Sec.*, Mrs E. Laurence-Smith.

AUDIT BUREAU OF CIRCULATIONS LTD., 19 Dunraven Street, W.1.—*Dir.*, K. Derbyshire.

AUTHORS, PLAYWRIGHTS AND COMPOSERS, INCORPORATED SOCIETY OF, 84 Drayton Gardens, S.W.10.—*Secs.*, G. D. Astley; V. Bonham-Carter; Phillippa Macliesh.

AUTOMOBILE ASSOCIATION (1905), Fanum House, Basingstoke, Hants.—*Chairman*, The Lord Erroll of Hale, P.C.; *Dir.-Gen.*, A. C. Durie, C.B.E.; *Sec.*, W. Lynch.

AVICULTURAL SOCIETY (1894).—*Hon. Sec.*, H. J. Horswell, 20 Bourdon Street, W.1.

AYRSHIRE CATTLE SOCIETY OF GREAT BRITAIN AND IRELAND (1877), 1 Racecourse Road, Ayr.—*Gen. Sec.*, J. Lawson.

BALTIC EXCHANGE (1903), St. Mary Axe, E.C.3.—*Chairman*, B. H. F. Fehr; *Sec.*, D. J. Walker.

BANKERS, THE INSTITUTE OF (1879), 10 Lombard Street, E.C.3.—*Pres.*, C. J. Montgomery; *Sec.-Gen.*, G. H. Dix.

BANKERS IN SCOTLAND, THE INSTITUTE OF (1875), 20 Rutland Square, Edinburgh.—*Sec.*, B. McKenna.

BAPTIST MISSIONARY SOCIETY (1792), 93–97 Gloucester Place, W.1.—*Secs.*, Rev. A. S. Clement (*Home*); Rev. H. F. Drake, O.B.E. (*Overseas*).

(DR.) BARNARDO'S (1866), *Head Offices:* Tanner's Lane, Barkingside, Essex. More than 220,000 children have been helped. 7,000 boys and girls are helped each year in residential and non-residential settings.

BARONETAGE, STANDING COUNCIL OF THE (1898), 6–10 Eldon Street, E.C.2.—*Sec. and Regr.*, P. L. Forwood.

BARRISTERS' BENEVOLENT ASSOCIATION (1873), 3 Raymond Buildings, Grays Inn, W.C.1.—*Hon. Treasurers*, M. Nolan, Q.C.; P. Medd, Q.C.; *Sec.*, Miss K. M. Hopper.

BEIT MEMORIAL FELLOWSHIPS (for Medical Research) (1909).—*Sec.*, Prof. W. G. Spector, Pathology Dept., St. Bartholomew's Hospital, E.C.1.

BIBLE AND MEDICAL MISSIONARY FELLOWSHIP (formerly Zenana Bible and Medical Mission) (1852), 352 Kennington Road, S.E.11.—*Gen. Sec.*, A. M. S. Pont.

BIBLE CHURCHMEN'S MISSIONARY SOCIETY (1922), 251 Lewisham Way, S.E.4.—*Gen. Sec.*, Rev. Canon A. S. Neech.

BIBLE SOCIETY, BRITISH AND FOREIGN (1804), 146 Queen Victoria Street, E.C.4.

BIBLIOGRAPHICAL SOCIETY (1892), c/o British Academy, Burlington House, W.1.—*Hon. Secs.*, Mrs. M. M. Foot; R. J. Roberts.

BIBLIOGRAPHICAL SOCIETY, EDINBURGH (1890), c/o National Library of Scotland, Edinburgh, 1.—*Hon. Sec.*, J. R. Seaton.

BIOCHEMICAL SOCIETY, THE (1911), 7 Warwick Court, W.C.1.—*Sec.*, A. I. P. Henton.

BIOLOGICAL ENGINEERING SOCIETY.—*Hon. Sec.*, K. Copeland, Biophysics Dept., Faculty of Medical Sciences, University College London, Gower Street, W.C.1.

BIOLOGISTS, ASSOCIATION OF APPLIED. — *Hon. Gen. Sec.*, Dr. D. G. Jones, Dept. of Agricultural Botany, University College of Wales, Penglais, Aberystwyth.

BIOLOGY, INSTITUTE OF, 41 Queen's Gate, S.W.7.—*Pres.*, Prof. G. E. Fogg, F.R.S.; *Gen. Sec.*, D. J. B. Copp.

BIRD PRESERVATION, INTERNATIONAL COUNCIL FOR (BRITISH SECTION), c/o Natural History Museum, Cromwell Road, S.W.7.—*Hon. Sec.*, Miss Phyllis Barclay-Smith, C.B.E.

BLIND, GREATER LONDON FUND FOR THE, 2 Wyndham Place, W.1.—*Pres.*, The Lord Mayor of London; *Gen. Sec.*, A. C. Jay, D.S.C.

BLIND, GUIDE DOGS FOR THE, ASSOCIATION, Alexandra House, 113 Uxbridge Road, Ealing, W.5. *Director-Gen.*, A. R. Clark.

BLIND, INCORPORATED ASSOCIATION FOR PROMOTING THE GENERAL WELFARE OF THE (1854), 8–22 Curtain Road, E.C.2.

BLIND, LONDON ASSOCIATION FOR THE (1857), 14–16 Verney Road, S.E.16. A national voluntary organization helping the blind and partially-sighted throughout the country. Training and employment; homes, holiday hotels and hostels; self-contained flats; pensions and special grants fund.—*Gen. Sec.*, G. W. Guy.

BLIND, ROYAL COMMONWEALTH SOCIETY FOR THE (1950), Commonwealth House, Haywards Heath, Sussex.—*Dir.*, Sir John Wilson, C.B.E.

BLIND, ROYAL NATIONAL INSTITUTE FOR THE (1868), 224 Great Portland Street, W.1.—*Director-General*, E. T. Boulter. Branches of the Institute: *Queen Elizabeth Homes of Recovery, Homes for Blind and Deaf Blind, School of Physiotherapy, Schools for Blind Girls and Boys, School for Shorthand-Typing and Telephony, Sunshine Home Nursery Schools, Braille and Moon Periodicals and Books, Braille Music, Talking Books, Students' Library, Professional, Commercial and Industrial Placement, Vocational Assessment Centre for Blind Adolescents, Apparatus and Appliances, Personal Services, Prevention of Blindness, etc.*

BLIND, NATIONAL LIBRARY FOR THE (1882), 35 Great Smith Street, S.W.1.—Books in embossed and large type are sent free on loan and post free to blind and partially-sighted readers. Stock of volumes, 400,000.—*Director-General*, W. A. Munford, M.B.E., PhD.

BLIND, ROYAL LONDON SOCIETY FOR THE (1838), *Head Office and Workshops*, 105–9 Salusbury Road, Brondesbury, N.W.6; *School*, Dorton House, Seal, nr. Sevenoaks, Kent; *Home Workers' Scheme* and *Residential Clubs.—Gen. Manager and Sec.*, W. H. Pascoe, O.B.E.

BLIND, ROYAL NORMAL COLLEGE (1872). Further education for visually-handicapped. Rowton Castle and Albrighton Hall, nr. Shrewsbury.—*Principal*, A. W. Laurie.

BLIND, ROYAL SCHOOL FOR THE INDIGENT (1799), Leatherhead.—*Resident Principal and Chaplain*, Rev. B. A. E. Coote.

BLIND (LONDON) SPORTS CLUB FOR THE (1932), *Chairman*, R. D. Birrell, Grants, Grants Lane, Limpsfield, Oxted, Surrey.

BLOOD TRANSFUSION. See GREATER LONDON RED CROSS BLOOD TRANSFUSION SERVICE.

BLUE CROSS, THE (Incorporating Our Dumb Friends' League) (1897), Animals' Hospital, Hugh Street, Victoria, S.W.1.—*Sec.*, P. Carpmael, M.B.E.

BODLEIAN, FRIENDS OF THE, Bodleian Library, Oxford.—*Sec.*, J. P. Feather.

BOOK-KEEPERS, INSTITUTE OF (1916), (see under Administrative Accounting, Institute of).

BOOKSELLERS ASSOCIATION OF GREAT BRITAIN AND IRELAND (1895), 154 Buckingham Palace Road, S.W.1.—*Dir.*, G. R. Davies.

BOOK TRADE BENEVOLENT SOCIETY (1967), 19 Bedford Square, W.C.1, formerly the National Book Trade Provident Institution (1962).—*Pres.*, T. Joy, F.R.S.A.; *Hon. Sec.*, (vacant).

BOTANICAL SOCIETY OF THE BRITISH ISLES (1836), c/o Dept. of Botany, British Museum (Natural History), S.W.7.

BOTANICAL SOCIETY OF EDINBURGH, Royal Botanic Garden, Edinburgh.—*Hon. Gen. Sec.*, R. Watling, Ph.D.

BOY SCOUTS ASSOCIATION, *see* SCOUT ASSOCIATION, THE.

BOYS' BRIGADE, THE (INCORPORATED) (1883), Brigade House, Parsons Green, S.W.6. Membership: British Isles, 160,185; Overseas, 145,695 in 60 countries; World strength, 305,880.—*Sec.*, A. A. J. Hudson.

BOYS' CLUBS, NATIONAL ASSOCIATION OF, INCORPORATED (1925), 17 Bedford Square, W.C.1. Responsible for the development and co-ordination of boys' club work throughout the country, and has affiliated to it, either directly or through local organizations, 1,970 clubs—*Gen. Sec.*, Brig. E. G. B. Davies-Scourfield, C.B.E., M.C.

BOYS' CLUBS, NORTHERN IRELAND ASSOCIATION OF (1940), 28 Bedford Street, Belfast.—*Gen. Sec.*, C. E. Larmour.

BREWING, INSTITUTE OF (1886), 33 Clarges Street, W.1.—*Sec.*, Capt. S. Le H. Lombard-Hobson, C.V.O., O.B.E., R.N.

BRIDEWELL ROYAL HOSPITAL, King Edward's School, Witley, Surrey (1553).—*Treas.*, The Earl of Selborne; *Clerk to the Governors*, Lt.-Col. S. A. Faith.

BRITISH ACADEMY, THE (1901), Burlington House, Piccadilly, W.1.—*President*, Sir Isaiah Berlin, O.M., C.B.E.; *Treas.* Prof. W. G. Beasley; *Sec.* Dr. N. J. Williams; *Foreign Sec.*, Prof. A. G. Dickens, C.M.G.

BRITISH AND FOREIGN SCHOOL SOCIETY (1808). South Road, Saffron Walden, Essex.—*Sec.*, W. O. Bell.

BRITISH ARTISTS FEDERATION OF (1959), 17 Carlton House Terrace, S.W.1.—*Chairman*, R. Lister; *Sec. Gen.*, M. B. Bradshaw.

BRITISH ASSOCIATION FOR THE ADVANCEMENT OF SCIENCE (1831), Fortress House, 23 Savile Row, W.1.—*President*, Sir Andrew Huxley, F.R.S.; *Gen. Secs.*, Sir Lincoln Ralphs; Dr. T. Emmerson; Prof. J. Heslop-Harrison, F.R.S.; *Gen. Treas.*, Dr. J. A. Pope; *Sec.* Dr. Magnus Pyke, F.R.S.E.

BRITISH ASSOCIATION FOR EARLY CHILDHOOD EDUCATION (formerly Nursery School Association of Gt. Britain and N. Ireland), Montgomery Hall, Kennington Oval, S.E.11.—*Sec.*, Miss D. E. Warren, O.B.E.

BRITISH ASSOCIATION OF THE HARD OF HEARING.—*Sec.-Gen.*, C. H. Mardell, M.B.E., 16 Park Street, Windsor, Berks.

BRITISH BEE-KEEPERS' ASSOCIATION (1874), 55 Chipstead Lane, Riverhead, Sevenoaks, Kent.—*Gen. Sec.*, O. Meyer.

BRITISH BOARD OF FILM CENSORS, 3 Soho Square, W.1.—*Sec.*, J. Ferman.

BRITISH COMMONWEALTH EX-SERVICES LEAGUE, 49 Pall Mall, S.W.1.—*Sec.-Gen.*, Air Commodore B. J. R. Roberts.

BRITISH COMPUTER SOCIETY (1957), 29 Portland Place, W.1., *Sec.-Gen.*, M. C. Ashill.

BRITISH COTTON GROWING ASSOCIATION LTD. (1904), Stanley Hall, Edmund Street, Liverpool.—*Managing Director*, R. Derbyshire.

BRITISH CYCLING FEDERATION (1878), 70 Brompton Road, S.W.3.—*Sec.*, L. Unwin.

BRITISH DENTAL ASSOCIATION (1880), 64 Wimpole Street, W.1.—*Pres.*, J. Booth; *Sec.*, R. B. Allen.

BRITISH DIABETIC ASSOCIATION (1934), 3–6 Alfred Place, W.C.1.—*Sec.-Gen.*, R. Allard.

BRITISH DRIVING SOCIETY, 10 Marley Avenue, New Milton, Hants.—*Sec.*, Mrs. P. Candler.

BRITISH EDUCATIONAL ADMINISTRATION SOCIETY (1971).—*Sec.*, Dr. E. A. Ewan, Moray House College of Education, Edinburgh.

BRITISH EQUESTRIAN FEDERATION, National Equestrian Centre, Kenilworth, Warwicks.—*Dir. Gen.*, Maj.-Gen. J. R. Reynolds, C.B., O.B.E.

BRITISH FIELD SPORTS SOCIETY (1930), 26 Caxton Street, S.W.1.—*Sec.*, Maj. Gen. J. M. Brockbank, C.B.E., M.C.

BRITISH FILM INSTITUTE (1933), 81 Dean Street, W.1.—*Director*, K. Lucas; *Deputy Dir.*, G. Rawlinson; *Controller, National Film Theatre*, L. Hardcastle.

BRITISH GLIDING ASSOCIATION (1930), affiliated to Royal Aero Club. Kimberley House, Vaughan Way, Leicester.—*Gen. Sec.*, B. Rolfe.

BRITISH GOAT SOCIETY (1879). *Sec.*, Mrs. T. T. F. May, Lion House, Rougham, Bury St. Edmunds, Suffolk.

BRITISH HEART FOUNDATION (1963), 57 Gloucester Place, W.1.—*Sec.*, D. A. Blake, M.B.E.

BRITISH HORSE SOCIETY, National Equestrian Centre, Kenilworth, Warwicks.—*Dir.*, Col. N. F. Grove-White.

BRITISH INSTITUTE IN EASTERN AFRICA, 1 Kensington Gore, S.W.7. *Sec.*, Mrs. J. Filson.

BRITISH INSTITUTE OF ARCHÆOLOGY AT ANKARA, c/o British Academy, Burlington House, W.1.—*Hon. Sec.*, A. S. Hall, F.S.A.

BRITISH INSTITUTE OF INTERNATIONAL AND COMPARATIVE LAW, Charles Clore House, 17 Russell Square, W.C.1.—*Sec.*, H. H. Marshall, C.M.G.

BRITISH INSTITUTE OF INTERIOR DESIGN (1899), 162 Derby Road, Stapleford, Nottingham.—*Sec.*, N. Parker.

BRITISH INSTITUTE OF PERSIAN STUDIES (1961), *Asst. Sec.*, Mrs. M. E. Gueritz, 85 Queen's Road, Richmond, Surrey.

BRITISH INSTITUTE OF RADIOLOGY, 32 Welbeck Street, W.1.—*Gen. Sec.*, Miss B. J. Bashford.

BRITISH INSTITUTE OF RECORDED SOUND (1948), 29 Exhibition Road, S.W.7.—*Dir.*, P. Saul.

BRITISH INTERPLANETARY SOCIETY (1933), 12 Bessborough Gardens, S.W.1.—*Exec. Sec.*, L. J. Carter.

BRITISH ISRAEL WORLD FEDERATION (1919), 6 Buckingham Gate, S.W.1.—*Sec.*, H. E. Stough.

BRITISH LEGION, ROYAL. *Headquarters*, Pall Mall, S.W.1.—*Gen. Sec.*, D. E. Coffer, C.B.E.

BRITISH LEGION SCOTLAND, ROYAL, Haig House, 23 Drumsheugh Gardens, Edinburgh.—*Gen. Sec.*, Brig. F. H. Coutts, C.B.E.

BRITISH MEDICAL ASSOCIATION (1832), B.M.A. House, Tavistock Square, W.C.1.—*President*, B. O'Donnell, F.R.C.S.; *Sec.*, E. Grey-Turner, M.C., T.D.

BRITISH MIGRAINE ASSOCIATION, Evergreen, Offermead Lane, Offenshaw, Surrey.

BRITISH MUSIC INFORMATION CENTRE, 10 Stratford Place, W.1.—*Sec.*, Miss E. Yeoman.

BRITISH NATURALISTS' ASSOCIATION (1905).—*Hon. Sec.*, Mrs. L. K. Butcher, Willowfield, Boyneswood Road, Four Marks, Alton, Hants.

BRITISH NUTRITION FOUNDATION (1967), 93 Albert Embankment, S.E.1.—*Dir. Gen.* Miss D. Hollingsworth, O.B.E.

BRITISH OPTICAL ASSOCIATION, THE, 65 Brook Street, W.1.—*Sec.*, P. A. Smith.

BRITISH POULTRY BREEDERS AND HATCHERIES ASSOCIATION LTD., 52–54 High Holborn, W.C.1.—*Gen. Sec.*, T. J. Aley.

BRITISH PROPERTY FEDERATION (formerly National Association of Property Owners), 35 Catherine Place, S.W.1; *Sec.*, C. E. F. Gough.

BRITISH RECORDS ASSOCIATION (1932), The Charterhouse, Charterhouse Square, E.C.1.—*Pres.*, The Master of the Rolls; *Hon. Sec.*, A. J. Farrington.

BRITISH RECORD SOCIETY (1887).—*Hon. Sec.*, P. Spufford, Dept. of History, The University, Keele, Staffs.

BRITISH RED CROSS SOCIETY (1870).—*National Headquarters*, 9 Grosvenor Crescent, S.W.1.—*Dir.-Gen.*, R. J. H. Edwards.

BRITISH RHEUMATISM AND ARTHRITIS ASSOCIATION (1947), 1 Devonshire Place, W.1.

BRITISH SCHOOL AT ATHENS—*Chairman of the Managing Committee*, R. A. Higgins, F.B.A., F.S.A.; *Director*, H. W. Catling, D. Phil.; *Sec.*, Mrs. S. Bicknell, 31–34 Gordon Square, W.C.1.

BRITISH SCHOOL AT ROME (1901).—*Chairman of Executive Committee*, A. G. Shepherd Fidler, C.B.E.; *Director*, D. B. Whitehouse, F.B.A.; *Hon. Sec.*, C. A. H. James, 1 Lowther Gardens, Exhibition Road, S.W.7.

BRITISH SCHOOL OF ARCHÆOLOGY IN JERUSALEM (1919), 2 Hinde Mews, Marylebone Lane, W.1.—*Pres.*, Sir Mortimer Wheeler, C.H., C.I.E., M.C.; *Dir.*, Mrs. C-M. Bennett, F.S.A.

BRITISH SEAMEN'S BOYS' HOME, Rock House, Brixham.—*Supt.*, Capt. W. G. Parry, R.N.

BRITISH SHIP ADOPTION SOCIETY, *see* SEAFARERS EDUCATION SERVICE.

BRITISH SHIPPING, GENERAL COUNCIL OF (1975), 30–32 St. Mary Axe, E.C.3.—*Pres.* (1976–77) The Earl of Inchcape; *Dir.-Gen.*, J. N. Wood.

BRITISH SOCIAL BIOLOGY COUNCIL, 69 Eccleston Square, S.W.1.—*Sec.*, H. M. Thomas.

BRITISH STANDARDS INSTITUTION, 2 Park Street, W.1.—*Dir.-Gen.*, G. B. R. Feilden, C.B.E., F.R.S.

BRITISH THEATRE ASSOCIATION (*formerly* British Drama League) (1919), 9–10 Fitzroy Square, W.1.—*Dir.*, W. Lucas.

BRITISH THORACIC AND TUBERCULOSIS ASSOCIATION 30 Britten Street, S.W.3. *Admin. Sec.*, A. N. Hutchins.

BRITISH UNITED PROVIDENT ASSOCIATION LIMITED Provident House, 24 Essex Street, W.C.2.—*Chief Exec.*, D. V. Damerell.

BRITISH VETERINARY ASSOCIATION (1881), 7 Mansfield Street, W.1.—*Sec.*, P. B. Turner, M.A.

BUILDING, INSTITUTE OF (1834), Englemere, King's Ride, Ascot, Berks.—*Exec. Dir.*, D. A. Neale, O.B.E., M.C.

BUILDING SERVICES, CHARTERED INSTITUTION OF (1897), 49 Cadogan Square, S.W.1.—*Sec.*, B. A. Hodges, O.B.E.

BUILDING SOCIETIES ASSOCIATION, 14 Park Street, W.1.—*Sec.-Gen.*, N. E. Griggs, C.B.E.

BUILDING SOCIETIES INSTITUTE, THE, Fanhams Hall, Ware, Hertfordshire.

BUSINESS and PROFESSIONAL WOMEN, UNITED KINGDOM FEDERATION OF (1938), 54 Bloomsbury Street, W.C.1.—*Gen. Sec.*, Miss E. M. Young.

BUSINESS ARCHIVES COUNCIL, 37-45 Tooley Street, S.E.1.—*Hon. Sec.*, Dr. D. Avery.

BUTCHERS' CHARITABLE INSTITUTION (1828).—*Sec.*, J. A. Fordyce, 61 West Smithfield, E.C.1.

BUYERS, THE INSTITUTION OF (1974) (see Sales Engineers).

CALOUSTE GULBENKIAN FOUNDATION, LISBON, United Kingdom and British Commonwealth Branch (1956), 98 Portland Place, W.1.—*Dir.*, P. Brinson.

CAMBRIDGE PRESERVATION SOCIETY (1929).—*Chairman*, S. C. Bowles; *Sec.*, C. P. R. Clarke, Gatehouse Lodge, Gog Magog Hills, Babraham, Cambridge.

CAMERA CLUB (1885), 8 Great Newport Street, W.C.2.—*Hon. Sec.*, W. A. J. Paul.

CANADA UNITED KINGDOM CHAMBER OF COMMERCE (1921), British Columbia House, 1–3 Lower Regent Street, S.W.1.—*Pres.*, J. M. Breen; *Sec. Gen.*, J. W. Webber.

CANCER RESEARCH CAMPAIGN (Brit. Empire Cancer Campaign for Research), 2 Carlton House Terrace, S.W.1.—For research into the disease of cancer in all its forms.—*Sec. Gen.*, Brig. K. D. Gribbin, M.B.E.

CANCER COUNCIL, BRITISH (1968).—*Sec.*, Dr. Graham Bennette, 19 St. Michael's Road, S.W.9.

CANCER RELIEF, NATIONAL SOCIETY FOR (1911), Michael Sobell House, 30 Dorset Square, N.W.1. *Admin. Sec.*, Miss T. Scrope.

CANCER RESEARCH FUND, IMPERIAL (1902), Lincoln's Inn Fields, W.C.2. Research into causes, prevention, treatment and cure of all forms of cancer; in own laboratories and extra-mural units.—*Sec.*, A. B. L. Clarke, O.B.E.

CANCER RESEARCH, INSTITUTE OF: ROYAL CANCER HOSPITAL (1911), Fulham Road, S.W.3.—*Sec.*, F. Kelly.

CARAVAN MISSION TO VILLAGE CHILDREN (1893), 47 Marylebone Lane, W.1.—*Sec.*, H. P. M. Warde.

CARNEGIE DUNFERMLINE TRUST (1903) (social and cultural purposes in Dunfermline).—*Sec.*, F. Mann, Abbey Park House, Dunfermline, Fife.

CARNEGIE HERO FUND TRUST (1908). Income £50,000. Makes grants and allowances to people injured or the dependants of people killed in saving human life within the British Isles and territorial waters.—*Sec.*, F. Mann, Abbey Park House, Dunfermline, Fife.

CARNEGIE UNITED KINGDOM TRUST (1913). Comely Park House, Dunfermline, Fife.—*Object*, The improvement of the well-being of the masses of the people of Great Britain and Ireland by means which are " charitable " in law and are to be selected by the Trustees themselves. The Trust is particularly concerned with social welfare schemes of a pioneer or experimental kind; grants are not made to individuals or in response to general appeals for subscriptions. Management—By trustees. *Sec.*, (vacant).

CAREER TEACHERS, ASSOCIATION OF, Hillsboro. Castledine Street, Loughborough, Leics.—*Gen. Sec.*, Miss R. Yaffé.

CATHEDRALS ADVISORY COMMITTEE, 83 London Wall, E.C.2.—*Sec.*, D. C. Mandeville, O.B.E.

CATHOLIC MARRIAGE ADVISORY COUNCIL (National Office), 15 Lansdowne Road, W.11; (London Centre), 33 Willow Place, Francis Street, S.W.1. *Chairman*, G. Steer (*acting*).

CATHOLIC RECORD SOCIETY (1904).—*Hon. Sec.*, Miss R. Rendel, c/o 114 Mount Street, W.1.

CATHOLIC TRUTH SOCIETY (1868), P.O. Box 422, 38–40 Eccleston Square, S.W.1.—*Gen. Sec.*, D. Murphy.

CATHOLIC UNION OF GREAT BRITAIN.—*Pres.*, The Duke of Norfolk, C.B., C.B.E., M.C.; *Sec.*, Mrs. J. Stuyt, 18 The Boltons, S.W.10.

CATTLE BREEDER'S CLUB, BRITISH (1949), Lavenders, Isfield, nr. Uckfield, Sussex.—*Sec.*, C. R. Stains.

CATTLE VETERINARY ASSOCIATION, BRITISH.—*Sec.*, A. H. Andrews, P.O. Box 44, Queensway House, Bletchley, Milton Keynes, Bucks.

CECIL HOUSES (Inc.), 190–192 Kensal Road, W.10. —*Sec.*, Mrs. J. M. Bolton.

CEREALS AND BALTIC SOCIETY (1908), 14/20 St. Mary Axe, E.C.3.—*Sec.*, R. T. Wheelans.

CERAMIC SOCIETY, BRITISH (1900), Shelton House, Stoke Road, Shelton, Stoke-on-Trent, Staffs.— *Pres.*, P. Popper.

CERAMICS INSTITUTION OF (1955), Federation House, Station Road, Stoke-on-Trent, Staffs.—*Sec.*, W. A. Evans.

CEYLON ASSOCIATION IN LONDON, 2/3 Crosby Square, Bishopsgate, E.C.3.—*Sec.*, R. J. Barber.

CHADWICK TRUST (1895) (for the promotion of health and prevention of disease), 13 Grosvenor Place, S.W.1.—*Clerk*, D. S. Wilson.

CHAMBERS OF COMMERCE.—See COMMERCE.

CHANTREY BEQUEST (1875).—*Sec. to the Trustees*, The Secretary, Royal Academy of Arts, Burlington House, Piccadilly, W.1.

CHARTERED SECRETARIES AND ADMINISTRATORS, INSTITUTE OF (1891), 16 Park Crescent, W.1.— *Sec.*, B. Barker, M.B.E.

CHEMICAL ENGINEERS, INSTITUTION OF (1922), 15 Belgrave Square, S.W.1.—*Pres.*, H. D. Anderson; *Gen. Sec.*, Maj.-Gen. A. M. McKay.

CHEMICAL INDUSTRY, SOCIETY OF, 14 Belgrave Square, S.W.1.—*Pres.*, D. M. Bell, C.B.E.; *Sec.* D. H. Sharp.

CHEMICAL SOCIETY, Burlington House, Piccadilly, W.1.—*Pres.*, Prof. C. C. Addison, F.R.S.; *Gen. Sec.*, J. R. Ruck Keene, M.B.E., T.D.

CHEMISTRY, THE ROYAL INSTITUTE OF, 30 Russell Square, W.C.1.—*Pres.*, Prof. C. Kemball, F.R.S.; *Sec. and Registrar*, R. E. Parker, PH.D.

CHESS FEDERATION, BRITISH, 4 The Close, Norwich.—*Gen. Sec.*, P. Buswell.

CHEST, HEART AND STROKE ASSOCIATION (1899), Tavistock House North, Tavistock Square, W.C.1.—*Gen.*, Air Marshal Sir Ernest Sidey, K.B.E., C.B., M.D.

CHILDREN'S COUNTRY HOLIDAYS FUND, 1 York Street, W.1.—*Gen. Sec.*, Mrs. J. M. Meekins, M.B.E.

CHILDREN'S RELIEF INTERNATIONAL (1959), Overstream House, Cambridge.—*Dir.*, T. Hardy.

CHINA ASSOCIATION (1889), 18 Diamond House, Hatton Garden, E.C.1.—*Sec.*, E. S. Bush.

CHIROPODISTS, THE SOCIETY OF, 8 Wimpole Street, W.1.—*Sec.*, G. C. Jenkins.

CHOIR SCHOOLS ASSOCIATION (1921).—*Hon. Sec.*, Rev. D. Thomson, Cathedral Choir School, Ripon, Yorks.

CHRISTIAN ACTION (1949), 2 Amen Court, E.C.4. —*Sec.*, Mrs. F. Champion.

CHRISTIAN EDUCATION MOVEMENT (1965), 2 Chester House, Pages Lane N.10. *Gen. Sec.*, Rev. J. M. Sutcliffe.

CHRISTIAN EVIDENCE SOCIETY (1870), St. Margaret-Pattens, Eastcheap, E.C.3.—*Hon. Sec.*, Rev., S. E. Alford.

CHRISTIAN KNOWLEDGE, SOCIETY FOR PROMOTING (1698), Holy Trinity Church, Marylebone Road, N.W.1.—*Gen. Sec.*, P. N. G. Gilbert.

CHRISTIANS AND JEWS COUNCIL OF (1942), 48 Onslow Gardens, S.W.7.—*Org. Sec.*, L. Goss.

CHURCH ARMY, C. S. C. House, North Circular Rd., N.W.10. *Chief Sec.*, Rev. A. M. A. Turnbull.

CHURCH BUILDING SOCIETY, INCORPORATED (1818), 24 Great Peter Street, S.W.1.—*Sec.*, W. A. Carter.

CHURCH EDUCATION CORPORATION, The Oyster Building, Horsebridge, Whitstable, Kent.—*Sec.*, W. F. Holmes.

CHURCH HOUSE, THE CORPORATION OF (1888), Dean's Yard, S.W.1.—*Sec.*, Maj. G. C. Hackett, M.B.E.

CHURCH LADS' BRIGADE (1891), *National Headquarters*, 15 Etchingham Park Road, N.3.—*Gen. Sec.*, Rev. C. Grice.

CHURCH MISSIONARY SOCIETY (1799), 157 Waterloo Road, S.E.1. Income, 1974 £1,423,424.—*Secs.*, Rev. Canon S. Barrington-Ward (*General*); A. Forrester-Paton (*Depy. Gen. Sec.*); J. J. Hillman (*Overseas*); Rev. H. W. Moore (*Home*); Miss M. H. Beaver (*Candidates*); G. A. Hill (*Financial*).

CHURCH OF ENGLAND CHILDREN'S SOCIETY (1881) (formerly Waifs and Strays), Old Town Hall, Kennington Road, S.E.11.—*Dir.*, D. F. T. Bowie.

CHURCH OF ENGLAND MEN'S SOCIETY (1899). 24 Tufton Street, S.W.1.—*Gen. Sec.*, Rev. B. Dawson.

CHURCH OF ENGLAND PENSIONS BOARD (1926), 53 Tufton Street, S.W.1.—*Sec.*, D. Thackray.

CHURCH OF ENGLAND SOLDIERS', SAILORS' AND AIRMEN'S CLUBS (1891), and CHURCH OF ENGLAND SOLDIERS', SAILORS' AND AIRMEN'S HOUSING ASSOCIATION LTD. (1974), 1 Shakespeare Terrace, 126 High Street, Portsmouth. *Chairman*, Rear-Adm. J. L. Blackham, C.B.; *Gen. Sec.*, Group Capt. J. A. S. Brown.

CHURCH OF SCOTLAND COMMITTEE ON SOCIAL RESPONSIBILITY, 121 George Street, Edinburgh 2.—*Dir.*, Rev. L. Beattie Garden.

CHURCH PASTORAL AID SOCIETY (1836), Falcon Court, 32 Fleet Street, E.C.4.

CHURCH UNION (1859), 7 Tufton Street, S.W.1.—*Sec.*, G. Evans.

CHURCHES, BRITISH COUNCIL OF (1942), 10 Eaton Gates, S.W.1.—*Gen. Sec.*, Rev. H. O. Morton, M.A.

CHURCHES, COUNCIL FOR CARE OF, (see Places of Worship, Council for).

CHURCHES, FRIENDLESS, FRIENDS OF (1957), 12 Edwardes Square, W.8.—*Hon. Dir.*, I. Bulmer-Thomas; *Hon. Sec.*, L. E. Jones.

CHURCHES MAIN COMMITTEE (1941), Fielden House, Little College Street, S.W.1.—*Sec.*, A. E. L. Parnis, C.B.E., M.A.

CIRCUS PROPRIETORS OF GREAT BRITAIN, ASSOCIATION OF, The Pheasantry, Longleat, Warminster, Wilts.—*See* R. Cawley.

CITY PAROCHIAL FOUNDATION (Trustees of the London Parochial Charities), 10 Fleet Street, E.C.4.

CIVIL DEFENCE, INSTITUTE OF (1942). P.O. Box 229, 3 Little Montague Court, E.C.1.—*Hon. Gen. Sec.*, V. G. B. Atwater.

CIVIL DEFENCE AND EMERGENCY PLANNING OFFICERS, ASSOCIATION OF, 8 Meadow Road, Harborne, Birmingham 17.—*Hon. Gen. Sec.*, G. E. Willcock.

CIVIL ENGINEERS, INSTITUTION OF (1818), Great George Street, S.W.1.—*Pres.*, J. W. Baxter, C.B.E.; *Sec.*, J. G. Watson, C.B.

CIVIL LIBERTIES, NATIONAL COUNCIL FOR (1934), 186 King's Cross Road, W.C.1.—*Sec.*, Miss P. Hewitt.

CIVIL SERVICE COUNCIL FOR FURTHER EDUCATION.—*Sec.*, R. W. Farrington, Riverwalk House, 157-161 Millbank, S.W.1.

CLASSICAL ASSOCIATION (1903).—*Hon. Treas.*, G. R. Watson, Dept. of Classical and Archæological Studies, The University, Nottingham.

CLASSICAL TEACHERS, JOINT ASSOCIATION OF (1962) 31-34 Gordon Square, W.C.1.—*Exec. Sec.*, D. W. Taylor.

CLAY TECHNOLOGY INSTITUTE OF (1927), c/o Butterley Building Materials Ltd., Wellington Street, Ripley, Derbyshire.—*Acting Sec.*, B. A. Robinson.

CLERGY ORPHAN CORPORATION (1749), 5 Verulam Buildings, Gray's Inn, W.C.1.—*Sec.*, Miss V. B. Warters, O.B.E.

CLERKS OF THE PEACE OF SCOTLAND, ASSOCIATION OF (1908).—*Hon. Sec.*, J. B. McGowan, 135 Irish Street, Dumfries.

CLERKS OF WORKS OF GREAT BRITAIN INCORPORATED, INSTITUTE OF (1882), 6 Highbury Corner, N.5.—*Sec.*, A. P. Macnamara.

CLYDESDALE HORSE SOCIETY OF GREAT BRITAIN AND IRELAND (1877), 24 Beresford Terrace, Ayr.

COACHING CLUB (1871), 65 Medfield Street, S.W.15.—*Sec.*, R. A. Brown, O.B.E.

COAL TRADE BENEVOLENT ASSOCIATION (1889), 63 Narrow Street, Limehouse, E.14.—*Sec.*, A. R. Bruce.

COKE OVEN MANAGERS' ASSOCIATION, Waveney House, Adwick Road, Mexborough, South Yorks.

COLLEGE OF THE SEA, *see* SEAFARERS EDUCATION SERVICE.

COMBINED CADET FORCE ASSOCIATION (1952), 58 Buckingham Gate, S.W.1.—*Sec.*, W. F. L. Newcombe, O.B.E., T.D.

COMMERCE, ASSOCIATION OF BRITISH CHAMBERS OF (1860).—*Pres.*, The Earl of Limerick; *Dir-Gen.*, W. A. Newsome, 6-14 Dean Farrar Street, S.W.1.

COMMERCE AND INDUSTRY, LONDON CHAMBER OF (1881), 69 Cannon Street, E.C.4.—*Pres.*, The Lord Mais, G.B.E. E.R.D., T.D.; *Dir.*, W. F. Nicholas, O.B.E.

COMMERCE, ASSOCIATION OF SCOTTISH CHAMBERS OF, 30 GEORGE SQUARE, Glasgow.—*Sec.*, M. Neil, C.B.E.

COMMERCE AND MANUFACTURES, EDINBURGH CHAMBER OF (1786), 20 Hanover Street, Edinburgh 2.—*Chief Executive*, D. M. Mowat.

COMMERCE AND MANUFACTURES, GLASGOW CHAMBER OF (1783), 30 George Square, Glasgow.—*Sec.*, M. Neil, C.B.E.

COMMERCIAL AND INDUSTRIAL EDUCATION, BRITISH ASSOCIATION FOR (BACIE), 16 Park Crescent, W.1.—*Dir.*, P. J. C. Perry, O.B.E.

COMMERCIAL TRAVELLERS' BENEVOLENT INSTITUTION (1849), No. 1 London Bridge, S.E.1.—*Sec.*, E. B. Auger.

COMMISSIONAIRES, THE CORPS OF (1859), founded by the late Captain Sir Edward Walter; for the employment of ex-Soldiers, Sailors and Airmen and ex-police, fire service and merchant navy servicemen. *Headquarters*, Exchange Court, 419A Strand, W.C.2 (3 Crane Court, E.C.4. from early 1977). *Outquarters*, War Memorial Building, Waring St., Belfast 1.; Room 53,

Guildhall Buildings, Navigation Street, Birmingham; 87 Park Street, 1st Floor, Bristol; 99 Shandwick Place, Edinburgh; 180 W. Regent Street, Glasgow; Room 23, 10–12 East Parade, Leeds; 21 Dale Street, Liverpool; 2 St. John Street, Deansgate, Manchester; 10 Bigg Market, Newcastle-upon-Tyne 1. Total strength, 3,900—*Commandant*, Col. G. L. V. Pring; *Adjutant*, Col. A. M. Thorburn.

COMMONS, OPEN SPACES AND FOOTPATHS PRESERVATION SOCIETY (1865), Suite 4, 166 Shaftesbury Avenue, W.C.2.—*Sec.* P. Clayden.

COMMONWEALTH AND CONTINENTAL CHURCH SOCIETY (1823), 175 Tower Bridge Road, S.E.1. —*Secs.*, Rev. T. P. Watson; Rev. D. R. Steele.

COMMONWEALTH ASSOCIATION OF PLANNERS (1971), 18 Northumberland Avenue, W.C.2.—*Sec.*, R. J. Harvey.

COMMONWEALTH GAMES FEDERATION, THE—*Hon. Sec.*, K. S. Duncan, O.B.E., 12 Buckingham Street, W.C.2.

COMMONWEALTH INDUSTRIES ASSOCIATION, LTD., 55 Park Lane, W.1.—*Dir.*, E. Holloway.

COMMONWEALTH PARLIAMENTARY ASSOCIATION.— *Sec.*, *U.K. Branch*, P. G. Molloy, M.C., Westminster Hall, S.W.1.

COMMONWEALTH PRESS UNION (1909), Studio House, 184 Fleet Street, E.C.4.—*Sec.*, Lt.-Col. T. Pierce-Goulding, M.B.E., C.D.

COMMONWEALTH SETTLEMENT, CHURCH OF ENGLAND COUNCIL FOR (1925), (see OVERSEAS SETTLEMENT, C. of E. COMMITTEE FOR).

COMMONWEALTH SOCIETY FOR THE DEAF (1959), 83 Kinnerton Street, S.W.1.—*Exec. Chairman*, Lady Templer.

COMMONWEALTH UNIVERSITIES, ASSOCIATION OF, 36 Gordon Square, W.C.1.—*Sec. Gen.*, Sir Hugh Springer, K.C.M.G., C.B.E.

COMMUNIST PARTY OF GREAT BRITAIN EXECUTIVE COMMITTEE (1920), 16 King Street, W.C.2.— *Gen. Sec.*, G. McLennan.

COMMUNITY MEDICINE, CENTRE FOR EXTENSION TRAINING IN (London School of Hygiene and Tropical Medicine) (1972), 31 Bedford Square, W.C.1.—*Admin.*, P. F. V. Waters.

COMMUNITY MEDICINE, SOCIETY OF (1856), (formerly Society of Medical Officers of Health), Tavistock House South, W.C.1.—*Pres.*, Dr. A. M. Nelson; *Sec.*, N. G. T. Taylor.

COMPOSERS' GUILD OF GREAT BRITAIN, THE (1945), 10 Stratford Place, W.1.—*Sec.*, Miss E. Yeoman.

CONFEDERATION OF BRITISH ROAD PASSENGER TRANSPORT (1974), Sardinia House, 52 Lincoln's Inn Fields, W.C.2.—*Dir.-Gen.*, D. R. Quin.

CONGREGATIONAL AND REFORMED, COUNCIL FOR WORLD MISSION (1973), Livingstone House, Carteret Street, S.W.1.—Formerly the Congregational Council for World Mission, the London Missionary Society, the Commonwealth Missionary Society and the Presbyterian Church of England Overseas Mission.—*Gen. Sec.*, The Rev. B. G. Thorogood.

CONSERVATION OF HISTORIC AND ARTISTIC WORKS, INTERNATIONAL INSTITUTE FOR, 608 Grand Buildings, Trafalgar Square, W.C.2.—*Pres.*, S. Keck; *Sec. Gen.*, N. Brommelle.

CONSERVATION SOCIETY, LTD. (1966), 12 London Street, Chertsey, Surrey.—*Dir.*, Dr. J. Davoll.

CONSERVATIVE AND UNIONIST ASSOCIATIONS, NATIONAL UNION OF (1867), 32 Smith Square, S.W.1.—*Sec.*, J. A. Smith: *Women's National Advisory Committee.*—*Sec.*, Mrs. S. Hewitt; *Young Conservative and Unionist National Advisory Committee.*—*Sec.*, P. Houlden.

CONSERVATIVE AND UNIONIST CENTRAL OFFICE, 32 Smith Square, S.W.1.—*Chairman*, The Lord Thorneycroft, P.C.; *Deputy Chairmen*, W. G.

Clark, M.P.; A. E. U. Maude, M.P.; *Vice-Chairmen*, R. E. Eyre, M.P.; G. Finsberg, M.B.E., M.P.; J. M. Fox, M.P.; J. E. M. Moore, M.P.; The Baroness Young; *Treasurers*, The Lord Chelmer, M.C., T.D.; The Lord Ashdown; A. McAlpine; *Dir. of Organization*, A. S. Garner.

CONSERVATIVE CLUBS, LTD., ASSOCIATION OF (1894), 32 Smith Square, S.W.1.—*Sec.*, L. G. Waterman.

CONSTRUCTION SURVEYORS' INSTITUTE (1952), 203 Lordship Lane, S.E.22.—*Exec. Dir.*, S. L. J. Cook.

CONSULTING ENGINEERS, ASSOCIATION OF (1913), Hancock House, 87 Vincent Square, S.W.1.— *Sec.*, Maj.-Gen. M. W. Prynne, C.B., C.B.E.

CONSULTING SCIENTISTS, ASSOCIATION OF, 47 Belgrave Square, S.W.1.—*Asst. Sec.*, F. B. Lucas.

CO-OPERATIVE SOCIETIES AND ASSOCIATIONS:—
Central Council for Agricultural and Horticultural Co-operation, 301–344 Market Towers, New Covent Garden Market, 1 Nine Elms Lane, S.W.8.—*Chief Exec.*, P. R. Dodds.
Co-operative Party, 158 Buckingham Palace Road, S.W.1.—*Sec.*, D. Wise.
Co-operative Productive Federation (1882), 42 Western Road, Leicester.—*Sec.*, J. Leonard.
Co-operative Union (1869), Holyoake House, Hanover Street, Manchester.—*Gen. Sec.*, D. L. Wilkinson.
Co-operative Wholesale Society (C.W.S.) (1863), New Century House, Manchester 4.—*Chief Exec. Officer*, A. Sugden; *Sec.*, G. J. Melmoth
Co-operative Women's Guild, 342 Hoe Street, Walthamstow, E.17.—*Gen. Sec.*, Mrs. K. Kempton.
Fisheries Organization Society, Ltd. (1914), 558 London Road, Sutton, Surrey.—*Gen. Sec.*, E. B. Hamley.
International Co-operative Alliance (1895), 11 Upper Grosvenor Street, W.1.—*Dir.*, S. K. Saxena.
Plunkett Foundation for Co-operative Studies (1919), 31 St. Giles, Oxford.—*Chief Executive Officer*, F. H. Webster.

COPYRIGHT COUNCIL, BRITISH (1953), 29–33 Berners Street, W.1.

CORONERS' SOCIETY OF ENGLAND AND WALES (1846).—*Hon. Sec.*, J. Burton, Coroner's Court, 77 Fulham Palace Road, W.6.

CORPORATE TRUSTEES, ASSOCIATION OF, Juxon House, St. Paul's Churchyard E.C.4.—*Sec.*, J. S. Rawlings.

CORRESPONDENCE COLLEGES, ASSOCIATION OF BRITISH (1955), 4 Chiswell Street, E.C.1.—*Sec.*, F. L. Cowham.

COUNTRY LANDOWNERS' ASSOCIATION (1907), 16 Belgrave Square, S.W.1.—*Sec. Gen.*, J. M. Douglas.

COUNTY CHIEF EXECUTIVES, ASSOCIATION OF.— *Hon. Sec.*, W. U. Jackson, County Hall, Maidstone, Kent.

COUNTY COUNCILS, ASSOCIATION OF (1973), Eaton House, 66A Eaton Square, S.W.1.—*Sec.*, A. C. Hetherington, C.B.E.

COUNTY SECRETARIES, SOCIETY OF.—*Hon. Sec.*, M. J. Le Fleming, County Hall, Hertford.

COUNTY SURVEYORS' SOCIETY (1884).—*President*, C. R. Chadwick, County Hall, Trowbridge; *Hon. Sec.*, D. B. Charnock, Phoenix Causeway, Lewes, E. Sussex.

COUNTY TREASURERS, SOCIETY OF (1903), Shire Hall, Reading, Berks.—*Hon. Sec.*, M. C. Beasley.

CRAFT EDUCATION, INSTITUTE OF.—*Gen. Sec.*, H. N. Deslow, 59 Dovedale Avenue, Clayhall, Ilford, Essex.

CRAFTS CENTRE, BRITISH (1948), 43 Earlham Street, W.C.2.—*Dir.*, M. Sellers.

EDUCATION OFFICERS' SOCIETY, COUNTY.—*Hon. Sec.*, J. A. Springett, Threadneedle House, Market Road, Chelmsford, Essex.

EDUCATION, SCOTTISH COUNCIL FOR RESEARCH IN, 16 Moray Place, Edinburgh.

EDUCATION THROUGH ART, SOCIETY FOR, Bath Academy of Art, Corsham, Wilts.—*Chairman*, D. Pope.

EDUCATIONAL CENTRES ASSOCIATION, Walthamstow Adult Education Centre, Greenleaf Road, E.17.—*Sec.*, Ray Lamb, M.B.E.

EDUCATIONAL FOUNDATION FOR VISUAL AIDS, 33 Queen Anne Street, W.1.—*Dir.*, G. C. Marchant.

EDUCATIONAL INSTITUTE OF SCOTLAND (1847), 46 Moray Place, Edinburgh.—*Gen. Sec.*, J. D. Pollock.

EDUCATIONAL RESEARCH IN ENGLAND AND WALES, NATIONAL FOUNDATION FOR, The Mere, Upton Park, Slough, Berks.—*Dir.*, A. Yates.

EDUCATIONAL VISITS AND EXCHANGES, CENTRAL BUREAU FOR, 43 Dorset Street, W.1.—*Dir.*, J. Platt.

EDWARDIAN STUDIES ASSOCIATION, 125 Markyate Road, Dagenham, Essex.—*Sec.*, E. Ford.

EGYPT EXPLORATION SOCIETY (1882), 3 Doughty Mews, W.C.1.—*Chairman*, Prof., E. G. Turner; *Sec.*, Miss M. Crawford.

ELDERLY INVALIDS FUND AND OLD PEOPLES ADVISORY SERVICE, 10 Fleet Street, E.C.4.

ELECTORAL REFORM SOCIETY OF GREAT BRITAIN AND IRELAND (founded 1884 as Proportional Representation Soc.), 6 Chancel Street, S.E.1.—*Dir.*, Miss E. Lakeman.

ELECTRICAL ENGINEERS, INSTITUTION OF (1871), Savoy Place, W.C.2.—*Sec.*, Dr. G. F. Gainsborough.

ELECTRONIC AND RADIO ENGINEERS, INSTITUTION OF (1925), 8–9 Bedford Square, W.C.1.—*Sec.*, G. D. Clifford, C.M.G.

ENGINEERING DESIGNERS, INSTITUTION OF (1945), Courtleigh, Westbury Leigh, Westbury, Wilts.—*Gen. Sec.*, P. J. Booker.

ENGINEERING INDUSTRIES ASSOCIATION, Equitable House, Lyon Road, Harrow, Middx.—*Dir.*, T. R. Wade.

ENGINEERING INSTITUTIONS, COUNCIL OF (1965), 2 Little Smith Street, S.W.1.—*Sec.*, M. W. Leonard.

ENGINEERS AND SHIPBUILDERS IN SCOTLAND, INSTITUTION OF (1857), 183 Bath Street, Glasgow, C.2.—*Pres.*, Prof. A. W. Scott; *Sec.*, W. McLaughlin.

ENGINEERS AND SHIPBUILDERS, N.E. COAST INSTITUTION OF (1884), Bolbec Hall, Newcastle upon Tyne—*Sec.*, Capt. H. G. S. Brownbill, D.S.C., R.N.

ENGINEERS, INSTITUTION OF BRITISH (1928), Regency House, 3 Marlborough Place, Brighton.—*Sec.*, Mrs. D. Henry.

ENGINEERS, SOCIETY OF (Incorporated) (1854), 21–23 Mossop Street, S.W.3.—*Sec.*, L. T. Griffith.

ENGLISH ASSOCIATION (1906), 1 Priory Gardens, W.4.—*Sec.*, Lt. Col. R. T. Brain, M.C.

ENGLISH FOLK DANCE AND SONG SOCIETY (1932), Cecil Sharp House, 2 Regent's Park Road, N.W.1.—*Dir.*, S. A. Matthews.

ENGLISH PLACE-NAME SOCIETY (1923).—*Hon. Director*, Prof. K. Cameron, Ph.D., The University, Nottingham.

ENGLISH-SPEAKING UNION OF THE COMMONWEALTH (1918), 37 Charles Street, Berkeley Square, W.1.—*Chairman*, Sir Patrick Dean, G.C.M.G.; *Dir.-Gen.*, W. N. Hugh Jones, M.V.O.

ENGLISH WOODLANDS LTD., 109 Upper Woodcote Road, Caversham Heights, Reading.

ENHAM VILLAGE CENTRE (1918), The White House, Enham Alamein, Andover, Hants. For rehabilitation, employment and housing of the physically handicapped.—*Sec.*, R. H. Hebbourn, M.B.E.

ENTOMOLOGICAL SOCIETY OF LONDON, ROYAL (1833), 41 Queen's Gate, S.W.7.—*Hon. Sec.*, P. E. S. Whalley.

ENTOMOLOGY, COMMONWEALTH INSTITUTE OF (1913), 56 Queen's Gate, S.W.7.—*Director*, A. H. Parker, Ph.D. (*acting*).

ENVIRONMENTAL CONSERVATION, COMMITTEE FOR (1909), 29–31 Greville Street, E.C.1.—*Sec.*, F. D. Webber, C.M.G., M.S., T.D.

ENVIRONMENTAL (*formerly Public*) HEALTH OFFICERS ASSOCIATION, 19 Grosvenor Place, S.W.1.—*Sec.*, R. Johnson.

EPILEPSY ASSOCIATION, BRITISH, 3–6 Alfred Place, W.C.1.—*Dir.*, L. Fitzgibbon.

EPILEPTICS, THE NATIONAL SOCIETY FOR (1892), Chalfont Centre for Epilepsy, Chalfont St. Peter, Bucks.—*Sec.*, Col. H. V. Trewhella.

ESPERANTO ASSOCIATION (LTD.), BRITISH (1907), 140 Holland Park Avenue, W.11.—*Sec.*, H. E. Platt.

EUGENICS SOCIETY (1907), 69 Eccleston Square, S.W.1.—*Gen. Sec.*, Miss S. E. Walters.

EVANGELICAL ALLIANCE (1846), 19 Draycott Place, S.W.3.—*Sec.*, G. J. T. Landreth.

EVANGELICAL LIBRARY, THE, 78A Chiltern Street, W.1.—*Librarian*, G. R. Sayer.

EXAMINERS UNDER SOLICITORS (SCOTLAND) ACTS (1933–1965), Law Society's Hall, 26–27 Drumsheugh Gardens, Edinburgh.—*Clerk*, K. W. Pritchard.

EXECUTIVES ASSOCIATION OF GREAT BRITAIN (1929), 16 West Central Street, W.C.1.—*Sec.*, M. C. Waddilove.

EXPORT, INSTITUTE OF, World Trade Centre, E.1. *Dir.-Gen.*, A. J. Day, O.B.E.

EX-SERVICES MENTAL WELFARE SOCIETY (for ex-Service men and women suffering from psychoses and neuroses arising from active or long regular service), 37 Thurloe Street, S.W.7.

FABIAN SOCIETY (1884), 11 Dartmouth Street, S.W.1.—*Gen. Sec.*, D. Hayter.

FAIRBRIDGE SOCIETY (1909) (formerly Fairbridge Farm Schools), 119–125 Bush House (N.E.), Aldwych, W.C.2.—*Dir.*, Maj.-Gen. W. T. Campbell, C.B.E.

FAIR ISLE BIRD OBSERVATORY TRUST, 21 Regent Terrace, Edinburgh.—*Hon. Sec.*, Dr. George Waterson, O.B.E., F.R.S.E.

FAMILY PLANNING ASSOCIATION, 27–35 Mortimer Street, W.1.—*Chief Exec. Officer*, T. E. Parker.

FAMILY SERVICE UNITS, 207 Old Marylebone Road, N.W.1.—*Dir.*, J. R. Halliwell.

FAMILY WELFARE ASSOCIATION Ltd. (Founded 1869 as CHARITY ORGANIZATION SOCIETY), 501–5 Kingsland Road, E.8.—*Dir.*, Mrs. P. A. Thomas.

FAUNA PRESERVATION SOCIETY (1903).—*Office*, c/o Zoological Society of London, Regent's Park, N.W.1.—*Hon. Sec.*, R. S. R. Fitter.

FAWCETT SOCIETY (1866), 27 Wilfred Street, S.W.1.—*Sec.*, O. Braman.

FELLOWSHIP HOUSES TRUST (Flatlets for the elderly) (1937), Clock House, Byfleet, Surrey.—*Sec.*, L. P. Leech.

FIELD STUDIES COUNCIL (1943), 9 Devereux Court, W.C.2.—*Sec.*, R. S. Chapman.

FIRE ENGINEERS, INSTITUTION OF, 148 New Walk, Leicester.—*Gen. Sec.*, D. S. Ramsey.

FIRE PROTECTION ASSOCIATION, Aldermary House, Queen Street, E.C.4.—*Dir.*, N. C. Strother Smith, O.B.E., T.D.

FIRE SERVICES ASSOCIATION, BRITISH, 86 London Road, Leicester.—*Gen. Sec.*, D. G. Varnfield.

FIRE SERVICES NATIONAL BENEVOLENT FUND (1943), Marine Court, Fitzalan Road, Littlehampton, Sussex.—*Hon. Organizing Sec.*, R. W. Greene, M.B.E.

FOLKLORE SOCIETY, c/o University College London, Gower Street, W.C.1.—*Hon. Sec.*, Mrs. V. J. Newall.

FORCES HELP SOCIETY AND LORD ROBERTS WORK-SHOPS (1899), 122 Brompton Road, S.W.3. *Comptroller*, Maj. L. F. E. James, M.B.E.

FOREIGN BONDHOLDERS, COUNCIL OF (1873), 9–12 Cheapside, E.C.2.—*Director-General*, C. E. N. Wyatt, M.C.

FOREIGN PRESS ASSOCIATION IN LONDON, 11 Carlton House Terrace, S.W.1.—*Pres.*, P. Deured.

FORENSIC SCIENCES, BRITISH ACADEMY OF (1959).—*Sec.-Gen.*, Prof. J. M. Cameron, Dept. of Forensic Medicine, The London Hospital, Turner Street, E.1.

FORESTERS OF GREAT BRITAIN, INSTITUTE OF (1973), 6 Rutland Square, Edinburgh.—*Hon. Sec.*, Dr. C. J. Taylor.

FORESTRY ASSOCIATION, COMMONWEALTH (1921). 11 Keble Road, Oxford.—*Editor-Sec.*, C. J. W. Pitt.

FORESTRY SOCIETY OF ENGLAND, WALES AND NORTHERN IRELAND, ROYAL (1882), 102 High Street, Tring, Herts.—*Dir.*, E. H. M. Harris.

FORESTRY SOCIETY, ROYAL SCOTTISH (1854), 18 Abercromby Place, Edinburgh.—*Sec. and Treas.*, W. B. C. Walker.

FRANCO-BRITISH SOCIETY, 1 Old Burlington Street, W.1.—*Sec.*, Miss M. Coate, M.B.E.

FREE CHURCH FEDERAL COUNCIL, 27 Tavistock Square, W.C.1.—*Moderator*, Rev. J. Huxtable, D.D.; *Gen. Sec.*, Rev. G. A. D. Mann.

FREEMASONS, GRAND LODGE OF SCOTLAND (1736), (Freemasons' Hall, Edinburgh.—*Grand Master Mason of Scotland*, Capt. R. Wolrige Gordon of Esslemont; *Grand Sec.*, E. S. Falconer.

FREEMASONS, UNITED GRAND LODGE OF ENGLAND, Freemasons' Hall, Great Queen Street, W.C.2.—*Grand Master*, H.R.H. the Duke of Kent, G.C.M.G., G.C.V.O.; *Pro Grand Master*, The Earl Cadogan, M.C.; *Deputy Grand Master*, Hon. Fiennes Cornwallis, O.B.E.; *Asst. Grand Master*, Hon. E. L. Baillieu; *Grand Wardens*, The Earl of Elgin and Kincardine; The Lord Mais, G.B.E., E.R.D., T.D.; *Grand Chaplain*, The Bishop of Dunwich, *Grand Sec.*, J. W. Stubbs, T.D.

FREEMEN OF CITY OF LONDON, GUILD OF (1908), 4 Dowgate Hill, E.C.4.—*Master*, D. F. Dunstan; *Clerk*, D. Reid.

FREEMEN OF ENGLAND (1966), 4 Lindsay Close, Epsom, Surrey.—*Pres.*, H. Ward.

FREIGHT FORWARDERS LTD., THE INSTITUTE OF, Suffield House, 9 Paradise Road, Richmond, Surrey.

FRESHWATER BIOLOGICAL ASSOCIATION (1929), The Ferry House, Far Sawrey, Ambleside, Cumbria. —*Sec. and Director of Laboratories*, E. D. Le Cren, M.A.

FRIENDS OF THE CLERGY CORP. (incorporating the Friend of the Clergy Corp. and the Poor Clergy Relief Corp.), 27 Medway Street, S.W.1.—*Sec.*, C. L. Talbot.

FRIENDLY SOCIETIES, NATIONAL CONFERENCE OF—*Sec.*, P. M. Madders, Room 341, Hamilton House, Mableton Place, W.C.1.

FRIENDS OF CATHEDRAL MUSIC (1956), Holy Trinity Church, Marylebone Road, N.W.1.—*Hon. Gen. Sec.*, N. T. Barnes.

FRIENDS OF THE NATIONAL LIBRARIES, c/o The British Library, W.C.1.—*Chairman*, The Lord Kenyon, C.B.E.; *Hon. Sec.*, T. S. Blakeney.

FRIENDS OF THE ELDERLY & GENTLEFOLK'S HELP

(1905), 42 Ebury Street, S.W.1.—*Gen. Sec.*, Miss P. M. Lethbridge.

FUEL, INSTITUTE OF (1927), 18 Devonshire Street, Portland Place, W.1.—*Sec.*, H. M. Lodge.

FURNITURE HISTORY SOCIETY (1964).—*Hon. Sec.*, Dr. L. Boynton, c/o Dept. of Furniture, Victoria and Albert Museum, S.W.7.

GAME CONSERVANCY, Fordingbridge, Hants.—*Dir.*, C. L. Coles.

GARDEN HISTORY SOCIETY (1965).—*Hon. Sec.*, Mrs. M. Batey, 12 Charlbury Road, Oxford.

GARDENERS' ROYAL BENEVOLENT SOCIETY (1839), Palace Gate, Hampton Court, East Molesey, Surrey.—*Dir.*, W. J. Hayward.

GAS ENGINEERS, INSTITUTION OF (1863), 17 Grosvenor Crescent, S.W.1.—*Sec.*, D. C. Elgin.

GEMMOLOGICAL ASSOCIATION OF GREAT BRITAIN (1931), St. Dunstan's House, Carey Lane, E.C.2. —*Sec.*, H. J. Wheeler.

GENEALOGICAL RESEARCH SOCIETY, IRISH.—*Sec.*, Mrs. L. Rosbottom, 82 Eaton Square, S.W.1.

GENEALOGISTS AND RECORD AGENTS, ASSOCIATION OF (1968).—*Hon. Sec.*, Miss I. Mordy, 123 West End Road, Ruislip, Middx.

GENEALOGISTS, SOCIETY OF (1911), 37 Harrington Gardens, S.W.7.—*Sec.*, Miss. M. Surry.

GENERAL PRACTITIONERS, ROYAL COLLEGE OF (1952), 14 Princes Gate, S.W.7.—*Sec.*, J. Wood, D.S.C.

GENTLEPEOPLE, GUILD OF AID FOR (1904), 10 St. Christopher's Place, W.1.—*Sec.*, Miss P. Roden.

GEOGRAPHICAL ASSOCIATION, 343 Fulwood Road, Sheffield.—*Joint Hon. Secs.*, R. A. Dougherty; G. M. Lewis.

GEOGRAPHICAL SOCIETY, ROYAL (1830), Kensington Gore, S.W.7.—*Pres.*, Sir Duncan Cumming, K.B.E., C.B.; *Hon. Secs.*, Prof. W. R. Mead; Dr. G. C. L. Bertram; *Hon. Foreign Sec.*, Lt.-Col. D. N. Hall; *Hon. Treas.*, H. Gould; *Director and Sec.*, J. Hemming; *Keeper of the Map Room*, Brig. R. A. Gardiner, M.B.E.; *Librarian*, G. S. Dugdale.

GEOGRAPHICAL SOCIETY, MANCHESTER (1884), 274, The Corn Exchange Buildings, Manchester. —*Sec.*, Mrs. A. Wood.

GEOGRAPHICAL SOCIETY, ROYAL SCOTTISH (1884), 10 Randolph Crescent, Edinburgh 3.—*Sec.*, D. G. Moir.

GEOLOGICAL SOCIETY (1807), Burlington House, Piccadilly, W.1.—*Pres.*, Prof. W. S. Pitcher, D.SC.; *Secs.*, A. H. B. Stride, PH.D.; M. G. Audley-Charles, PH.D.; *Foreign Sec.*, J. V. Hepworth, PH.D.; *Exec. Sec.*, D. G. Clayton.

GEOLOGISTS' ASSOCIATION.—*Hon. Gen. Sec.*, Joanna P. Edwards, 23 Green Dragon Lane, Flackwell Heath, Bucks.

GEORGIAN GROUP (1937), 2 Chester Street, S.W.1.

GIFTED CHILDREN, NATIONAL ASSOCIATION FOR (1966), 27 John Adam Street, W.C.2.—*Dir.*, H. J. G. Collis, T.D.

GILBERT AND SULLIVAN SOCIETY.—*Hon. Sec.*, C. Lambert, 273 Northfield Avenue, W.5.

GIRL GUIDES ASSOCIATION.—An organization founded by the first Lord Baden-Powell as a sister movement to the Scouts and incorporated by Royal Charter in 1922. In 1975 the total membership in Great Britain and Northern Ireland was 806,030. *Commonwealth Headquarters*, 17–19 Buckingham Palace Road, S.W.1.

GIRLS' BRIGADE, THE, Brigade House, 8 Parsons Green, S.W.6.—*Brigade Sec. for Eng. & Wales*, Miss M. I. Taylor.

GIRLS' FRIENDLY SOCIETY AND TOWNSEND FELLOWSHIP (1875), 126 Queens Gate, S.W.7.

GIRLS OF THE REALM GUILD (1900).—Educational grants towards schooling or initial training of single girls. Applications before February for ensuing academic year to: Mrs. L. Jennens, Wistaria, Church Street, Chiswick, W.4.

GIRLS' VENTURE CORPS, 33 St. George Drive, S.W.1. A uniformed youth movement for girls between 13 and 20.

GLASS TECHNOLOGY, SOCIETY OF (1916), 20 Hallam Gate Road, Sheffield.—*Hon. Sec.*, T. S. Busby.

GORDON BOYS' SCHOOL (1885), West End, Woking. —*Head Master*, G. Leadbeater.

GRAPHIC ARTISTS, SOCIETY OF (1919), 17 Carlton House Terrace, S.W.1.—*Pres.*, F. J. Winter.

GREATER LONDON PLAYING FIELDS ASSOCIATION (1926), 25 Ovington Square, S.W.3.—*Sec.*, Capt. D. N. Forbes, D.S.C., R.N. (*ret.*).

GREATER LONDON RED CROSS BLOOD TRANSFUSION SERVICE (1921), 4 Collingham Gardens, S.W.5 [01-373 1056/7]. Hours, 9 a.m. to 10 p.m. every day.

GREEK INSTITUTE (1969) (for the promotion of modern Greek studies), 34 Bush Hill Road, N.21. —*Dir.*, Dr. Kypros Tofallis.

GRENFELL ASSOCIATION OF GREAT BRITAIN AND IRELAND, Hope House, 45 Great Peter Street, S.W.1. For medical and social work among the fishermen, Eskimos and Indians of Labrador and N. Newfoundland.—*Sec.*, Miss S. A. Yates.

GULBENKIAN FOUNDATION, *see* CALOUSTE.

HAKLUYT SOCIETY (1846), c/o Map Library, The British Library, Ref. Div., Great Russell Street, W.C.1—*Joint Hon. Secs.*, Dr. T. E. Armstrong; Prof. E. M. J. Campbell.

HANSARD SOCIETY FOR PARLIAMENTARY GOVERN- MENT (1944), 12 Gower Street, W.C.1.—*Sec.*, Mrs. M. Vlieland.

HARLEIAN SOCIETY (1869), Ardon House, Mill Lane, Godalming, Surrey.—*Hon. Sec.*, J. P. Heming.

HARVEIAN SOCIETY OF LONDON.—*Hon. Sec.*, Dr. I. Murray-Lyon, 11 Chandos Street, Cavendish Square, W.1.

HEADMASTERS, INCORPORATED ASSOCIATION OF, 29 Gordon Square, W.C.1.—*Pres.* (1977), A. H. Jennings; *Joint Hon. Secs.*, B. H. Holbeche; D. A. Frith; *Hon. Treas.*, A. R. Barnes; *Sec.*, E. J. Dorrell; *Deputy Sec.*, B. C. Harvey.

HEAD MISTRESSES, ASSOCIATION OF, 29 Gordon Square, W.C.1.—*President*, Miss M. N. Blake; *Sec.*, Miss S. M. Chapman.

HEADMISTRESSES OF PREPARATORY SCHOOLS, ASSO- CIATION OF.—*Vice Pres.*, Miss M. McVicar, Rookesbury Park, Wickham, Hants.

HEAD TEACHERS, NATIONAL ASSOCIATION OF.—*Gen. Sec.*, R. J. Cook, Maxwelton House, 41-43 Boltro Road, Haywards Heath, West Sussex.

HEALTH EDUCATION COUNCIL, THE (1968), 78 New Oxford Street, W.C.1.—*Dir.-Gen.*, A. C. L. Mackie, C.B.E.

HEALTH EDUCATION, INSTITUTE OF.—*Sec.*, Dr. L. Bariç, 14 High Elms, Hale Barnes, Cheshire.

HEALTH, GUILD OF (1904), Edward Wilson House, 26 Queen Anne Street, W.1.—*Chairman*, Rev. B. Coote.

HEALTH SERVICE ADMINISTRATORS, INSTITUTE OF (1902), 75 Portland Place, W.1.—*Sec.*, J. F. Milne.

HELLENIC STUDIES, SOCIETY FOR THE PROMOTION OF (1879), 31-34 Gordon Square, W.C.1.—*Pres.*, Prof. R. Browning; *Hon. Sec.*, Prof. R. P. Winnington-Ingram, F.B.A.

HENRY GEORGE FOUNDATION, 177 Vauxhall Bridge Road, S.W.1.—*Sec.*, V. H. Blundell.

HERALDIC AND GENEALOGICAL STUDIES, INSTITUTE OF (1961), 80-82 Northgate, Canterbury, Kent.— *Dir.*, C. R. Humphery-Smith.

HERALDRY SOCIETY, THE (1947), 28 Museum Street, W.C.1.—*Sec.*, Mrs. J. C. G. George.

HIGHWAY ENGINEERS, INSTITUTION OF (1930). 3 Lygon Place, S.W.1.—*Sec.*, Miss P. A. Steel.

HISTORICAL ASSOCIATION (1906), 59A Kennington Park Road, S.E.11.—*Sec.*, Miss C. M. Povall.

HISTORICAL SOCIETY, ROYAL (1868), University College, London, Gower Street, W.C.1.—*Pres.*, Prof. G. R. Elton, M.A., Ph.D., D.Litt, F.B.A.; *Exec. Sec.*, Mrs. J. Chapman.

HOMELESS CHILDREN'S AID AND ADOPTION SOCIETY, and F. B. Meyer Children's Home (1920), 54 Grove Avenue, Muswell Hill, N.10.—*Gen. Sec.*, Rev. R. H. Johnson.

HONG KONG ASSOCIATION (1961), 18 Diamond House, Hatton Garden, E.C.1.—*Sec.*, E. S. Bush.

HORATIAN SOCIETY (1933).—*Hon. Sec.*, Lady Templeman, Manor Heath, Knowl Hill, The Hockering, Woking, Surrey.

HOROLOGICAL INSTITUTE, BRITISH (1858), Upton Hall, Upton, Newark, Notts.—*Exec. Dir.*, F. West, M.B.E.

HOROLOGICAL SOCIETY, ANTIQUARIAN (1953), New House, High Street, Ticehurst, Wadhurst, Sussex.—*Hon. Sec.*, Cdr. G. Clarke.

HORTICULTURAL ADVISORY BUREAU, INTERNATIONAL, Arkley Manor, Arkley, nr. Barnet, Herts.—*Dir.*, W. E. Shewell-Cooper, M.B.E., D.Litt.

HOSPITAL FEDERATION, INTERNATIONAL (1947), 126 Albert Street, N.W.1.—*Dir. Gen.*, M. C. Hardie;

HOSPITALS CONTRIBUTORY SCHEMES ASSOCIATION, BRITISH (1948), 30 Lancaster Gate, W.2.—*Hon. Sec.*, Air Vice-Marshal A. A. Case, C.B., C.B.E.

HOSPITAL SATURDAY FUND, THE (1873).—*Head Office*, 192-198 Vauxhall Bridge Road, S.W.1.— *Sec.*, Miss I. Gleeson.

HOSPITAL SAVING ASSOCIATION, THE, 30 Lancaster Gate, W.2.—*Gen. Sec.*, Air Vice-Marshal A. A. Case, C.B., C.B.E.

HOTEL CATERING AND INSTITUTIONAL MANAGEMENT ASSOCIATION, 191 Trinity Road, S.W.17.—*Sec.*, Miss E. Gadsby.

HOTELS, RESTAURANTS AND CATERERS ASSOCIATION, BRITISH (1907), 13 Cork Street, W.1.—*Chief Exec.*, C. Derby.

HOUSE OF HOSPITALITY LTD., Holy Cross Priory, Cross-in-Hand, Heathfield, Sussex. Twenty homes for old people.—*Sec.*, Sister Mary Garson.

HOUSE OF ST. BARNABAS IN SOHO (House of Charity for Distressed Women in London) (1846), 1 Greek Street, Soho Square, W.1.

HOUSING AID SOCIETY, CATHOLIC (1956), 189a Old Brompton Road, S.W.5.—*Dir.*, D. Pollard.

HOUSING AND TOWN PLANNING COUNCIL, NATIONAL (1900), 34 Junction Road, N.19.— *Sec. Gen.*, A. H. Small.

HOUSING ASSOCIATION FOR OFFICERS' FAMILIES (1916), Alban Dobson House, Green Lane, Mor- den, Surrey.—*Gen. Sec.*, R. Davis.

HOVERCRAFT SOCIETY, UNITED KINGDOM (1971), Rochester House, Little Ealing Lane, W.5.—*Sec.*, P. A. Bartlett.

HOWARD LEAGUE FOR PENAL REFORM (1866), 125 Kennington Park Road, S.E.11. For the advancement of knowledge of constructive penal and social policies.—*Dir.*, M. Wright.

HUGUENOT SOCIETY OF LONDON (1885), c/o Barclays Bank, Ltd., 1 Pall Mall East, S.W.1.— *Hon. Sec.*, Miss I Scouloudi, M.SC., F.S.A., F.R.Hist.S.

HUNTERIAN SOCIETY, The Hunterian Room, The Wellcome Building, Euston Road, N.W.1. *Secs.*, Dr. N. Thorne; Dr. Anne Jepson.

HUNTERS' IMPROVEMENT AND NATIONAL LIGHT HORSE BREEDING SOCIETY (1885), 8 Market Square, Westerham, Kent.—*Sec.*, G. W. Evans.

HYDROFOIL SOCIETY, INTERNATIONAL, 17 Melcombe Court, Dorset Square, N.W.1.—*Chairman*, M. Thornton.

HYDROGRAPHIC SOCIETY (1972), North East London Polytechnic Dept. of Land Surveying, E.17.— *Hon. Sec.*, A. E. Ingham.

ILLUMINATING ENGINEERING SOCIETY (1909), York House, Westminster Bridge Road, S.E.1.—*Sec.*, G. F. Cole.

INCOME TAX PAYERS' SOCIETY, P.O. Box 443, 5 Plough Place, Fetter Lane, E.C.4.—*Dir.*, E. C. L. Hulbert-Powell.

INDEPENDENT SCHOOLS CAREERS ORGANIZATION (*formerly* Public Schools Appointments Bureau), 12A–18A Princess Way, Camberley, Surrey.—*Dir.*, R. F. B. Campbell, M.A.

INDEPENDENT SCHOOLS INFORMATION SERVICE (I.S.I.S.) (1972), 47 Victoria Street, S.W.1.—*Dir.*, D. D. Lindsay, C.B.E.

INDEXERS, SOCIETY OF, 28 Johns Avenue, N.W.4.—*Hon. Sec.*, J. A. Gordon.

INDUSTRIAL ARTISTS AND DESIGNERS, SOCIETY OF (1930), 12 Carlton House Terrace, S.W.1.—*Sec.*, G. V. Adams.

INDUSTRIAL CHRISTIAN FELLOWSHIP (1877), St. Katharine Cree Church, Leadenhall Street, E.C.3.

INDUSTRIAL MARKETING RESEARCH ASSOCIATION.—*Admin. Sec.*, 11 Bird Street, Lichfield, Staffs.

INDUSTRIAL PARTICIPATION ASSOCIATION (1884), 25–28 Buckingham Gate, S.W.1.—*Sec.*, D. Wallace Bell.

INDUSTRIAL SAFETY OFFICES, INSTITUTION OF, 222 Uppingham Road, Leicester.—*Sec.*, Maj. A. Poole (*ret.*).

INDUSTRIAL SOCIETY, THE (1918), Robert Hyde House, 48 Bryanston Square, W.1.—*Dir.*, W. J. P. M. Garnett, C.B.E.; *Sec.*, D. Fazakerley.

INLAND WATERWAYS ASSOCIATION, 114 Regent's Park Road, N.W.1.—*Gen. Sec.*, R. J. Taunton.

INNER WHEEL CLUBS IN GREAT BRITAIN AND IRELAND, ASSOCIATION OF (1934), 51 Warwick Square, S.W.1.—*Sec.*, Miss J. Dobson.

INSURANCE ASSOCIATION, BRITISH (1917), Aldermary House, Queen Street, E.C.4.—*Sec. Gen.*, R. C. W. Bardell.

INSURANCE BROKERS, CORPORATION OF (1906), 15 St. Helen's Place, E.C.3.—*Sec.*, J. E. Fryer.

INSURANCE INSTITUTE, CHARTERED (1897), 20 Aldermanbury, E.C.2.—*Sec.*, D. C. McMurdie.

INTERNATIONAL LAW ASSOCIATION (1873), 3 Paper Buildings, Temple, E.C.4.—*Chairman*, The Lord Wilberforce, P.C., C.M.G., O.B.E.; *Sec.-Gen.*, J. B. S. Edwards.

INTERNATIONAL POLICE ASSOCIATION (British Section).—*National Headquarters*, 1 Fox Road. West Bridgford, Nottingham.—*Chief Exec, Officer*, K. H. Robinson.

INTERNATIONAL SHIPPING FEDERATION (1909), 146–150 Minories, E.C.3.—*President*, F. B. Bolton, M.C.; *Sec.*, M. R. Brownrigg.

INTERNATIONAL SOCIETY FOR THE PROTECTION OF ANIMALS (1959), *Headquarters*, 106 Jermyn Street, S.W.1.—*Exec. Dir.*, T. H. Scott.

INTERNATIONAL STUDENTS TRUST (1962), 229 Gt. Portland Street, W.1.—*President*, The Duke of Grafton, K.G.; *Dir.*, H. A. Shaw, O.B.E.

INTERNATIONAL UNION FOR LAND VALUE TAXATION AND FREE TRADE, 177 Vauxhall Bridge Road, S.W.1.—*Sec.*, V. H. Blundell.

INTERNATIONAL VOLUNTARY SERVICE (1920), Ceresole House, 53 Regent Road, Leicester.—*Sec.-Gen.*, G. L. Hewitt.

INVALID CHILDREN'S AID ASSOCIATION (LONDON), INCORPORATED (1888), 126 Buckingham Palace Road, S.W.1.—Advisory service on care of handicapped children; family social work in London and Home Counties; special schools. *Dir.*, Miss M. Coubrough.

INVALIDS-AT-HOME (1966).—*Hon. Sec.*, Mrs. J. Pierce, 23 Farm Avenue, N.W.2. Helps seriously disabled people living at home.

IRAN SOCIETY (1936), 42 Devonshire Street, W.1.—*Pres.*, The Lord Carrington, P.C., K.C.M.G., M.C.

IRISH LINEN MERCHANTS' ASSOCIATION (1872), Lambeg, Lisburn, N. Ireland.—*Sec.*, E. O. L. Seccombe.

IRISH SOCIETY, THE HONOURABLE THE (1613), Irish Chamber, Guildhall Yard, E.C.2.—*Sec.*, E. H. Shackcloth; *Representative* (*N. Ireland*), Cmdr. P. C. D. Campbell-Grove, M.V.O., R.N.

IRON AND STEEL INSTITUTE, *see* METALS SOCIETY.

JAPAN ASSOCIATION (1950), 18 Diamond House, Hatton Garden, E.C.1.—*Sec.*, E. S. Bush.

JAPAN SOCIETY OF LONDON (1891), 630 Grand Buildings, Trafalgar Square, W.C.2.—*Hon. Sec.*, Mrs. E. F. Dobson, O.B.E.

JERUSALEM AND THE MIDDLE EAST CHURCH ASSOCIATION (1887), 24 The Borough, Farnham, Surrey.—*Gen. Sec.*, J. B. Wilson.

JEWISH ASSOCIATION FOR THE PROTECTION OF GIRLS, WOMEN AND CHILDREN (administered by the Jewish Welfare Board) (1885).

JEWISH WELFARE BOARD (1859), Lionel Cohen House, 315 Ballards Lane, N.12.

JEWISH HISTORICAL SOCIETY OF ENGLAND, Mocatta Library, University College, W.C.1.—*Hon. Sec.*, Dr. J. Israel, 33 Seymour Place, W.1.

JEWISH YOUTH, ASSOCIATION FOR (1899), A.J.Y. House, 50 Lindley Street, E.1.—*Gen. Sec.*, Michael Goldstein, M.B.E.

JEWS, CHURCH'S MINISTRY AMONG THE, Vincent House, Vincent Square, S.W.1.—*Secs.*, Rev. W. F. Barker; Rev. B. F. Adeney.

JEWS AND CHRISTIANS, LONDON SOCIETY OF (1927), 28 St. John's Wood Road, N.W.8.—*President*, The Very Rev. E. S. Abbott, K.C.V.O., M.A., D.D.; *Joint Chairman*, Rabbi Leslie I. Edgar, M.A., D.D.; The Dean of Westminister; *Sec.*, Mrs. E. Hathan.

JOHN INNES INSTITUTE (1910), Colney Lane, Norwich.—*Director*, Prof. R. Markham, PH.D., F.R.S.

JOURNALISTS, THE INSTITUTE OF, 1 Whitehall Place, S.W.1.—*Gen. Sec.*, R. F. Farmer.

JUSTICES' CLERKS' SOCIETY (1839).—*Hon. Sec.*, P. J. Halnan, County Hall, Hobson Street, Cambridge.

KEEP BRITAIN TIDY GROUP (1954), Bostel House, 37 West Street, Brighton, Sussex.—*Dir. Gen.*, D. J. Lewis.

KING EDWARD'S HOSPITAL FUND FOR LONDON (1897), 14 Palace Court, W.2.—A charity which uses its annual income to help hospitals improve the effectiveness and efficiency of their service to patients. The Fund divides its income between several major activities: making grants to hospitals both within and outside the National Heath Service but confined to those in or serving the Greater London area; providing education for hospital staffs through the King's Fund College; sponsoring experiment and enquiry and providing information through its various experts and through the King's Fund Centre; providing the special service of the Emergency Bed Service.—*Chairman of Management Committee*, The Lord Hayter; *Treasurer*, R. J. Dent; *Secretary*, G. A. Phalp.

KING GEORGE'S FUND FOR SAILORS (1917), 1 Chesham Street, S.W.1. The central fund for all charities which support seafarers in need and their families. Distributes over £400,000 in grants annually.—*Gen. Sec.*, Capt. E. G. Brown, R.N.

KING GEORGE'S JUBILEE TRUST, 8 Buckingham Street, W.C.2.—Inaugurated in 1935 in commemoration of the Silver Jubilee of King George V. Its objects are the advancement of the physical, mental and spiritual welfare of the younger generation.—*Sec.*, Sir Michael Hawkins, K.C.V.O., M.B.E.

KING'S FUND, THE (1940), Norcross, Blackpool, Lancs.—To give temporary assistance in directions which are beyond the province of State liability to war-disabled members of the Navy, Army, Air Force, Auxiliary Services, Home Guard, Merchant Navy and Civil Defence

organizations and to widows, children and other dependants of those who lost their lives through war service. *Sec.*—T. Mann.

LABOUR PARTY, Transport House, Smith Square, S.W.1.—*Gen. Sec.*, R. G. Hayward, C.B.E.

LADIES IN REDUCED CIRCUMSTANCES, SOCIETY FOR THE ASSISTANCE OF (1886), Lancaster House, Malvern, Worcs.—*Sec.*, Mrs. A. R. White.

LANCASTRIANS IN LONDON, ASSOCIATION OF (1892), Burnley House, 129 Kingsway, W.C.2.—*Hon. Sec.*, H. Butler.

LANDSCAPE INSTITUTE (incorporating the Institute of Landscape Architects), 12 Carlton House Terrace, S.W.1.—*Registrar*, P. C. Bird.

LAND-VALUE TAXATION LEAGUE, 177 Vauxhall Bridge Road, S.W.1.—*Pres.*, V. G. Saldji.

LAW REPORTING FOR ENGLAND AND WALES, INCORPORATED COUNCIL OF (1865), 3 Stone Buildings, Lincoln's Inn, W.C.2.

LEAGUE OF THE HELPING HAND, Edgeleys, Manor Farm, East Worldham, Alton, Hants.—*Sec.*, Mrs. L. E. M. Stacey.

LEAGUE OF REMEMBRANCE, 48 Great Ormond Street, W.C.1.—*Hon. Administrator*, Mrs. D. A. Jeffreys.

LEAGUE OF WELLDOERS (incorporated) (1893), 129 & 133 Limekiln Lane, Liverpool, 5.—*Warden and Sec.*, W. J. Horn.

LEATHER AND HIDE TRADES' BENEVOLENT INSTITUTION (1860), 82 Borough High Street, S.E.1.—*Sec.*, H. G. Forward.

LEGAL EXECUTIVES, INSTITUTE OF, Ilex House, Barrhill Road, S.W.2.—*Sec.*, L. W. Chapman, M.B.E.

LEISURE GARDENERS, NATIONAL SOCIETY OF (*formerly* National Allotments and Gardens Society), 22 High Street, Flitwick, Beds.

LEPROSY GUILD (St. Francis) (1895), 20 The Boltons, S.W.10.

LEPROSY MISSION, THE (*formerly* The Mission to Lepers) (1874), 50 Portland Place, W.1.—*Chairman*, Sir E. Richardson, C.B.E., PH.D.; *Int. Gen. Sec.*, A. D. Askew.

LEUKAEMIA RESEARCH FUND (1962), 43 Great Ormond Street, W.C.1.—*Dir.*, G. J. Piller.

LIBERAL PARTY ORGANIZATION, 7 Exchange Court, Strand, W.C.2.—*Head of Organization*, E. Wheeler, O.B.E.

LIBERAL PUBLICATION DEPARTMENT (1887), 9 Poland Street, W.1.—*Sec.*, Mrs. E. Hill.

LIBRARY ASSOCIATION (1877), Ridgmount Street, W.C.1.—*Sec.*, R. P. Hilliard.

LIFEBOATS. See "ROYAL NATIONAL."

LIFE OFFICES' ASSOCIATION, THE (1889), Aldermary House, Queen Street, E.C.4.—*Sec. Gen.*, T. H. M. Oppé.

LINGUISTS, INSTITUTE OF (1910), 91 Newington Causeway, S.E.1.—*Sec.*, M. D. Payne.

LINNEAN SOCIETY OF LONDON (1788), Burlington House, W.1.—*Pres.*, Dr. P. H. Greenwood; *Treas.*, J. C. Gardiner; *Secs.*, Dr. F. H. Perring (*Botany*); Dr. B. Gardiner (*Zoology*); D. C. McClintock, T.D. (*Editorial*); *Exec. Sec.*, T. O'Grady.

LIVERPOOL COTTON ASSOCIATION, 620 Cotton Exchange Buildings, Edmund Street, Liverpool, 3.—*Sec.*, J. R. A. Daglish.

LLOYD'S Lime Street, E.C.3.—*Chairman* (1976), H. H. T. Hudson; *Deputy Chairmen*, A. W. Higgins; P. L. Foden-Pattinson; *Sec. Gen.*, C. A. Thomas; International Insurance Market.

LLOYD'S PATRIOTIC FUND (1803), Lloyd's, Lime Street, E.C.3.—*Sec.*, A. J. Carter.

LLOYD'S REGISTER OF SHIPPING (1760), 71 Fenchurch Street, E.C.3.—*Chairman*, R. A. Huskisson; *Deputy Chairman and Chairman of the Sub-Committees of Classification*, P. B. Arthur; *Deputy Chairman and Treas.*, J. N. S. Ridgers; *Exec.*

Director, C. M. Glover; *Technical Director*, B. Hildrew; *Chief Ship Surveyor*, J. McCallum; *Chief Engineer Surveyor*, S. N. Clayton; *Secretary*, W. T. Leadbetter; Office of *Lloyd's Register Book*, *Lloyd's Register of Yachts*, etc.

LOCAL AUTHORITIES, INTERNATIONAL UNION OF (1913), British Section, 36 Old Queen Street, S.W.1.—*Joint Secs.*, A. C. Hetherington, C.B.E.; T. H. Caulcott; S. Rhodes, O.B.E.; G. H. Speirs.

LOCAL GOVERNMENT ADMINISTRATORS, INSTITUTE OF.—*Hon. Sec.*, B. J. N. Gleave, 127 Lexden Road, Colchester, Essex.

LOCAL GOVERNMENT BARRISTERS, SOCIETY OF.—*Hon. Sec.*, N. A. L. Rudd, Council Offices, Pontypool, Gwent.

LONDON APPRECIATION SOCIETY (1932), 17 Manson Mews, S.W.7. Visits to places of historic and modern interest in and around London.—*Hon. Sec.*, H. L. Bryant Peers.

LONDON BOROUGHS ASSOCIATION (1964), Westminster City Hall, Victoria Street, S. W.1.—*Hon. Sec.*, Sir Alan Dawtry, C.B.E., T.D. (*Chief Exec. of Westminster*).

LONDON CITY MISSION (1835), 175 Tower Bridge Road, S.E.1.—*Gen. Sec.*, Rev. D. M. Whyte.

LONDON CORNISH ASSOCIATION (1898), *Hon. Gen. Sec.*, N. S. Bunney, 119 Warwick Road, N.11.

LONDON COURT OF ARBITRATION (1892), 75 Cannon Street, E.C.4.—*Chairman*, L. B. Prince, C.B.E.; *Registrar*, B. W. Vigrass, O.B.E., V.R.D.

LONDON DIOCESAN FUND AND LONDON DIOCESAN HOME MISSION, 33 Bedford Square, W.C.1.—*Sec.*, Ven. J. D. R. Hayward.

LONDON LIBERAL PARTY, St. Margaret's Mansions, 53 Victoria Street, S.W.1.—*Hon. Sec.*, George B. Patterson.

LONDON LIBRARY, THE (1841), 14 St. James's Square, S.W.1.—*Librarian*, S. G. Gillam.

LONDON MAGISTRATES' CLERKS' ASSOCIATION (1889), *Hon. Sec.*, C. D. H. Wolstenholme, Deputy Chief Clerk. Inner London Juvenile Courts, 185A Marylebone Road, N.W.1.

LONDON MISSIONARY SOCIETY, *see* CONGREGATIONAL COUNCIL.

"LONDON OVER THE BORDER" CHURCH FUND (1878), Guy Harlings, New Street, Chelmsford. —*Sec.*, H. R. Lovell.

LONDON PLAYING FIELDS SOCIETY (1890), Headquarters, Boston Manor Playing Field, Boston Gardens, Brentford, Middlesex. *Sec.*, Lt.-Col. C. E. B. Sutton, T.D.

LONDON SOCIETY, THE (1912), Wheatsheaf House, 4 Carmelite Street, E.C.4.

LONDON TOPOGRAPHICAL SOCIETY, 50 Grove Lane, S.E.5.—*Hon. Sec.*, S. N. P. Marks.

(LORD MAYOR) TRELOAR TRUST (incorporating Lord Mayor Treloar College and Florence Treloar School for physically handicapped boys and girls), Froyle, nr. Alton, Hants.—*Sec.*, *and Bursar*, B. E. T. Roberts.

LORD'S DAY OBSERVANCE SOCIETY (1831), 47 Parish Lane, Penge, S.E.20.—*Gen. Sec.*, H. J. W. Legerton.

LORD'S TAVERNERS, THE, 1 St. James's Street, S.W.1.—*Sec.*, Capt. J. A. R. Swainson, O.B.E., R.N.

MAGISTRATES' ASSOCIATION (1920), 28 Fitzroy Square, W.1.—*Pres.*, The Lord Chancellor; *Sec.*, A. J. Brayshaw, C.B.E.

MALAYSIA-SINGAPORE COMMERCIAL ASSOCIATION INC. (1955), Cereal House, 58 Mark Lane, E.C.3. —*Secs.*, The Rubber Growers' Association, Ltd.

MALAYSIAN RUBBER PRODUCERS' RESEARCH ASSOCIATION (1938), 19 Buckingham Street, W.C.2. —*Sec.*, P. O. Wickens.

MALCOLM SARGENT CANCER FUND FOR CHILDREN.— *Gen. Administrator*, Miss S. Darley, 56 Redcliffe Square, S.W.10.

MALONE SOCIETY (for the study of Early English Drama).—*Hon. Sec.*, Miss K. M. Lea, 2 Church Street, Beckley, Oxford.

MANAGEMENT, BRITISH INSTITUTE OF, Management House, Parker Street, W.C.2.—*Dir.-Gen.*, R. Close.

MARIE CURIE MEMORIAL FOUNDATION (1948) (for the welfare of cancer sufferers), 124 Sloane Street, S.W.1.—*Sec.*, Sqdn. Ldr. T. B. Robinson, O.B.E.

MARINE ARTISTS, ROYAL SOCIETY OF (1939), 17 Carlton House Terrace, S.W.1.—*Pres.*, K. Shackleton; *Sec.*, C. de Winter.

MARINE BIOLOGICAL ASSOCIATION OF THE U.K. (1884), The Laboratory, Citadel Hill, Plymouth. —*Sec. to Council and Director of Plymouth Laboratory*, E. J. Denton, C.B.E., SC.D., F.R.S.

MARINE ENGINEERS, INSTITUTE OF (1889), 76 Mark Lane, E.C.3.—*Dir. and Sec.*, J. Stuart Robinson.

MARINE SOCIETY, THE (1756), Hanway House, Clark's Place, E.C.2.—*Sec.*, Capt. C. W. Malins, D.S.O., D.S.C., R.N. (*ret.*).

MARKET AUTHORITIES, NATIONAL ASSOCIATION OF BRITISH, 3 St. Jude's Avenue, Mapperley, Nottingham.

MARKETING, INSTITUTE OF (1911), Moor Hall, Cookham, Maidenhead, Berks.—*Sec.*, W. E. Hinder.

MARK MASTER MASONS, GRAND LODGE OF (1856), Mark Masons' Hall, 40 Upper Brook Street, W.1.—*Grand Master*, The Earl of Stradbroke; *Deputy Grand Master*, Col. E. Perry Morgan, M.B.E., T.D.; *Grand Sec.*, W. J. Leake.

MASONIC BENEVOLENT INSTITUTION, ROYAL (1842), 20 Great Queen Street, W.C.2.—*Sec.*, Sqn.-Ldr. D. A. Lloyd, D.F.C., D.F.M.

MASONIC BENEVOLENT INSTITUTIONS IN IRELAND; *Masonic Girls' School* (1792); *Masonic Boys' School* (1867); *Victoria Jubilee Masonic Annuity Fund* (1887).—*Sec.*, R. J. Clinton, 19 Molesworth Street, Dublin 2.

MASONIC DEGREES—ORDER OF THE TEMPLE, Mark Masons' Hall, 40 Upper Brook Street, W.1.— *Grand Master*, H. D. Still; *Great Vice-Chancellor*, W. J. Leake.

MASONIC INSTITUTION FOR BOYS, ROYAL (Incorporated) (1798), 26 Great Queen Street, W.C.2.— *Sec.*, A. R. Jole.

MASONIC INSTITUTION FOR GIRLS, ROYAL (1788). *School*, Rickmansworth; *Offices*, 31 Great Queen Street, W.C.2.—*Sec.*, A. A. Huckle.

MASTER BUILDERS, FEDERATION OF, 33 John Street, W.C.1.—*Nat. Dir.*, W. S. Hilton.

MASTERS OF FOXHOUNDS ASSOCIATION (1856), Parsloes Cottage, Bagendon, Cirencester, Glos.— *Hon. Sec.*, A. H. B. Hart.

MATERNAL AND CHILD WELFARE, NATIONAL ASSOCIATION FOR (1911), Tavistock House (North), Tavistock Square, W.C.1.—*Gen. Sec.*, W. Rice.

MATHEMATICAL ASSOCIATION (1871), 259 London Road, Leicester.—*Pres.*, Dr. E. Kerr; *Hon Secs.*, Miss N. L. Squire; Dr. A. Howson.

MATHEMATICS AND ITS APPLICATIONS, INSTITUTE OF (1964), Maitland House, Warrior Square, Southend, Essex.—*Sec.*, N. Clarke.

MEASUREMENT AND CONTROL, INSTITUTE OF (1944), 20 Peel Street, W.8.—*Sec.*, E. Eden.

MECHANICAL ENGINEERS, INSTITUTION OF, 1 Birdcage Walk, S.W.1.—*Pres.*, E. McEwen, C.B.E., D.SC.; *Sec.*, A. McKay, C.B.

MEDIC-ALERT FOUNDATION, 9 Hanover Street, W.1.—*Chairman*, A. J. Hart. For the protection, in emergencies, of those with a medical disability; to prevent mistakes.

MEDICAL COUNCIL, GENERAL, 44 Hallam Street, W.1.—*Registrars*, M. R. Draper (*General Council*

of England and Wales); W. Russell (*Branch Council for Scotland*), 8 Queen Street, Edinburgh; Miss M. Hoolan (*Branch Council for Ireland*), 6 Kildare Street, Dublin 2.

MEDICAL SOCIETY OF LONDON (1773), 11 Chandos Street, Cavendish Square, W.1.—*Pres.*, A. W. Woodruff, M.D.; *Hon. Sec.*, D. Garfield Davies, F.R.C.S.; *Registrar*, Maj. H. R. Mitchell, T.D.

MEDICAL WOMEN'S FEDERATION (1917), Tavistock House (North), Tavistock Square, W.C.1.—*Pres.*, Mrs. J. Williamson; *Hon. Sec.*, Dr. Jean Lawrie.

MEN OF THE TREES (1922), Crawley Down, Crawley, Sussex.

MENTAL AFTER CARE ASSOCIATION (1879), for the care and rehabilitation of those recovering from mental illness.—*Sec.*, Mrs. J. Moore, 110 Jermyn Street, S.W.1.

MENTAL HEALTH FOUNDATION (1940), 8 Wimpole Street, W.1.—*Dirs.*, Maj.-Gen. C. M. F. Deakin, C.B., C.B.E.; Air Vice-Marshal A. A. Adams, C.B., D.F.C.

MERCANTILE MARINE SERVICE ASSOCIATION (1857) (Shipmasters in command). Affiliated to the Officers (Merchant Navy) Federation. Nautilus House, Mariners' Park, Wallasey, Merseyside.— *Gen. Sec.*, Capt. W. W. P. Lucas; *London Office*, 750/760 High Road, Leytonstone, E.11.

MERCHANT NAVY WELFARE BOARD, 19–21 Lancaster Gate, W.2.—*Sec.*, R. E. Haerle.

MERSEY MISSION TO SEAMEN (1857). *Headquarters, Hotel and Registered Office*, Kingston House, James Street, Liverpool 2.

METALLURGISTS, THE INSTITUTION OF, Northway House, High Road, Whetstone, N.20.—*Registrar-Sec.*, T. B. Marsden.

METALS SOCIETY, THE (1974) (*Amalgamation of* Institute of Metals and Iron and Steel Institute), 1 Carlton House Terrace, S.W.1.—*Sec.-Gen.*, M. J. Hall.

METEOROLOGICAL SOCIETY, ROYAL (1850), James Glaisher House, Grenville Place, Bracknell, Berks.—*Pres.*, Dr. J. T. Houghton, F.R.S.; *Hon. Secs.*, D. E. Pedgley; A. J. Gadd, PH.D.; J. R. Milford, D.Phil.

METHODIST MISSIONARY SOCIETY (1786), 25 Marylebone Road, N.W.1. Income, 1974 £1,717,596.

METROPOLITAN AND CITY POLICE ORPHANS FUND (1870), 30 Hazlewell Road, Putney, S.W.15.— *Sec.*, E. R. Hall, M.B.E.

METROPOLITAN AUTHORITIES, ASSOCIATION OF (1974), 36 Old Queen Street, S.W.1.—*Sec.*, T. H. Caulcott.

METROPOLITAN HOSPITAL-SUNDAY FUND (1872), P.O. Box 15, 206b Station Road, Edgware, Middx. In 1975, £47,650 was distributed as maintenance grants and grants for specific purposes to Hospitals and Homes not controlled by the State; £21,400 to State Hospitals for the use of their medical and psychiatric social workers; £3,900 to other medical charities.—*Sec.*, Miss B. F. Ambler.

METROPOLITAN PUBLIC GARDENS ASSOCIATION (1882), 4 Carlos Place, W.1.

MIDDLE EAST ASSOCIATION (1961), Bury House, 33 Bury Street, S.W.1.—*Dir.-Gen.*, Sir Richard Beaumont, K.C.M.G., O.B.E.

MIDWIVES, ROYAL COLLEGE OF (1881), 15 Mansfield Street, W.1.—*Gen. Sec.*, Miss B. D. Mee.

MIGRAINE TRUST (1965), 23 Queen Square, W.C.1. —*Dir.*, D. R. Mullis.

MILITARY HISTORICAL SOCIETY.—*Hon. Sec.*, J. Gaylor, Duke of York's Headquarters, Chelsea, S.W.3.

MIND (National Association for Mental Health), 22 Harley Street, W.1.—*Dir.*, A. Smythe.

MINERALOGICAL SOCIETY (1876).—*Pres.* (1976), Sir Kingsley Dunham, F.R.S.; *Hon. Gen. Sec.*, J. E. T. Horne, 41 Queen's Gate, S.W.7.

MINIATURE PAINTERS, SCULPTORS AND GRAVERS, ROYAL SOCIETY OF (1895), 17 Carlton House Terrace, S.W.1.—*Pres.*, R. Lister; *Sec.*, C. de Winter.

MINIATURISTS, SOCIETY OF (1895), R. W. S. Galleries, 26 Conduit Street, W.1.—*Sec.*, M. Fry.

MINING AND METALLURGY, INSTITUTION OF (1892), 44 Portland Place, W.1.—*Pres.*, S. H. U. Bowie; *Sec.*, M. J. Jones.

MINING ENGINEERS, THE INSTITUTION OF (1889), Hobart House, Grosvenor Place, S.W.1.—*Pres.* (1976–77) G. D. Nussey; *Sec.*, G. R. Strong.

MINING INSTITUTE OF SCOTLAND, c/o National Coal Board, Green Park, Greenend, Edinburgh.—*Sec.*, E. R. Rodger.

MISSIONS TO SEAMEN, THE, AND ST. ANDREW'S WATERSIDE CHURCH MISSION FOR SAILORS, St. Michael Paternoster Royal, College Hill, E.C.4. —*Gen. Sec.*, Rev. W. J. D. Down.

MODERN CHURCHMEN'S UNION (1898), for the Advancement of Liberal Religious Thought— *Pres.*, The Dean of Westminster; *Hon. Sec.*, Rev. F. E. Compton, Caynham Vicarage, Ludlow, Salop.

MODERN LANGUAGE ASSOCIATION (incorporating the Association of Teachers of German), 35 Lewisham Way, S.E.14.—*Hon. Sec.*, S. R. Ingram.

MONUMENTAL BRASS SOCIETY (1887), *Hon. Sec.*, W. Mendelsson, 57 Leeside Crescent, N.W.11.

MORAVIAN MISSIONS, LONDON ASSOCIATION IN AID OF (1817), Moravian Church House, 5/7 Muswell Hill, N.10.—*Sec.*, Rev. R. S. Burd.

MORDEN COLLEGE (1695), Blackheath, S.E.3. *Treasurer*, A. A. Snashall.

(WILLIAM) MORRIS SOCIETY AND KELMSCOTT FELLOWSHIP (1918).—*Hon. Sec.*, R. C. H. Briggs, Kelmscott House, 26 Upper Mall, W.6.

MOTOR INDUSTRY, THE INSTITUTE OF THE (1920), Fanshaws, Brickendon, Hertford.—*Dir.*, E. V. Tipper.

MOUNTBATTEN (EDWINA) TRUST, 1 Grosvenor Crescent, S.W.1.—*Sec.*, Miss V. W. Henderson, M.B.E.

MULTIPLE SCLEROSIS SOCIETY, 4 Tachbrook Street, S.W.1.—*Gen. Sec.*, A. C. Waine, M.B.E., T.D.

MUNICIPAL ENGINEERS, INSTITUTION OF (1873), 25 Eccleston Square, S.W.1.—*Sec.*, A. Banister, O.B.E., B.SC.

MUSEUMS ASSOCIATION (1889), 87 Charlotte Street, W.1.—*Sec.*, Miss B. Capstick, O.B.E.

MUSICIANS' BENEVOLENT FUND, St. Cecilia's House, 16 Ogle Street, W.1. *Convalescent Home*, Westgate-on-Sea. *Permanent Homes*, Westgate, Hereford and Bromley.

MUSICIANS, INCORPORATED SOCIETY OF (1882) 10 Stratford Place, W.1.—*Gen. Sec.*, S. M. Alcock.

MUSICIANS OF GREAT BRITAIN, ROYAL SOCIETY OF (1738), 10 Stratford Place, W.1.—*Sec.*, Mrs. M. E. Gleed.

MUSIC SOCIETIES, NATIONAL FEDERATION OF (1935), 1 Montague Street, W.C.1.—*Sec.*, J. Crisp.

MYCOLOGICAL SOCIETY, BRITISH.—*Sec.*, B. E. J. Wheeler, Ph.D., Imperial College Field Station, Silwood Park, Sunninghill, Berks.

NATIONAL ADULT SCHOOL UNION (1899), Drayton House, Gordon Street, W.C.1.—*Gen. Sec.*, L. A. Sanders.

NATIONAL ALLIANCE OF PRIVATE TRADERS (1943), 388 Corn Exchange, Hanging Ditch, Manchester 4.

NATIONAL AND UNIVERSITY LIBRARIES, STANDING CONFERENCE OF (1950).—*Sec.*, A. J. Loveday,

c/o The Library, School of Oriental and African Studies, Malet Street, W.C.1.

NATIONAL ASSOCIATION OF ESTATE AGENTS (1962), Walton House, 11–15 The Parade, Royal Leamington Spa.—*Sec.*, J. S. Perry.

NATIONAL ASSOCIATION OF FIRE OFFICERS, 6 Westow Hill, S.E.19.—*Gen. Sec.*, W. R. J. Hitchin.

NATIONAL ASSOCIATION OF LOCAL COUNCILS (1947), 100 Great Russell Street, W.C.1.—*Sec.*, C. Arnold-Baker, O.B.E.

NATIONAL BENEVOLENT INSTITUTION (1812), 61 Bayswater Road, W.2.—*Sec.*, Lt.-Col. G. G. Robson.

NATIONAL BIRTHDAY TRUST FUND (1928), 57 Lower Belgrave Street, S.W.1. For Extension of Maternity Services.—*Consultant Adviser*, Miss D. V. Riddick, M.B.E.

NATIONAL BOOK LEAGUE (1925), 7 Albemarle Street, W.1.—*Dir.*, M. Goff.

NATIONAL CATTLE BREEDERS' ASSOCIATION, Jenkins Lane, St. Leonards, nr. Tring, Herts.—*Sec.*, J. Thorley.

NATIONAL CHILDREN'S HOME (1869). *Chief Office*, 85 Highbury Park, N.5. Cares for 5,000 socially mentally, or physically handicapped children annually in residental homes, special schools, family centres and community projects in the U.K. and Jamaica.—*Principal*, Rev. G.E. Barritt.

NATIONAL CHRISTIAN EDUCATION COUNCIL (*incorporating* International Bible Reading Association and Denholm House Press), Robert Denholm House, Nutfield, Redhill, Surrey.

NATIONAL CORPORATION FOR THE CARE OF OLD PEOPLE, Nuffield Lodge, Regent's Park, N.W.1. —*Sec.*, H. W. Mellor.

NATIONAL COUNCIL OF LABOUR COLLEGES, 5 Mount Boone, Dartmouth, Devon.—*Gen. Sec.*, J. P. M. Millar.

NATIONAL COUNCIL OF SOCIAL SERVICE, 26 Bedford Square, W.C.1.—*Dir.*, J. K. Owens.

NATIONAL COUNCIL OF WOMEN OF GREAT BRITAIN, 36 Lower Sloane Street, S.W.1.—*Gen. Sec.*, Mrs. J. Simpson.

NATIONAL FEDERATION OF OLD AGE PENSIONS ASSOCIATIONS, 91 Preston New Road, Blackburn, Lancs.—*Sec.*, G. Dunn.

NATIONAL FEDERATION OF OWNER-OCCUPIERS' AND OWNER-RESIDENTS' ASSOCIATIONS.—*Hon. Sec.*, J. W. Clark, 29 Norview Drive, East Didsbury, Manchester.

NATIONAL FEDERATION OF YOUNG FARMERS' CLUBS, Y.F.C. Centre, National Agricultural Centre, Kenilworth, Warwicks.

NATIONAL FUND FOR RESEARCH INTO CRIPPLING DISEASES (1952), Vincent House, Springfield Road, Horsham, Sussex.—*Dir.*, D. Guthrie.

NATIONAL MARKET TRADERS' FEDERATION (1899).— *Pres.*, Mrs. F. Gaunt; *Gen. Sec.*, J. Coates, 87 Spital Hill, Sheffield 4.

NATIONAL MARRIAGE GUIDANCE COUNCIL, Herbert Gray College, Little Church Street, Rugby, Warwicks.—*Chief Officer*, N. J. Tyndall.

NATIONAL MONUMENTS RECORD (*incorporating* the National Buildings Record) (1941), Fortress House, 23 Savile Row, W.1.—*Curator*, E. Mercer, F.S.A.

NATIONAL OPERATIC AND DRAMATIC ASSOCIATION (1899), 1 Crestfield Street, W.C.1.—*Sec.*, W. A. J. Rogers.

NATIONAL PEACE COUNCIL (1908), 29 Great James Street, W.C.1.—*Gen. Sec.*, Miss S. Oakes.

NATIONAL PURE WATER ASSOCIATION (1960).— *Sec.*, Mrs. A. R. Cooper, 225 Newtown Road, Worcester.

NATIONAL SECULAR SOCIETY (1866), 702 Holloway Road, N.19.—*Gen. Sec.*, W. McIlroy.

NATIONAL SOCIETY FOR CLEAN AIR (1899), 136 North Street, Brighton, Sussex.—*Sec.-Gen.*, Rear-Adm. P. G. Sharp, C.B., D.S.C.

NATIONAL SOCIETY (CHURCH OF ENGLAND) FOR PROMOTING RELIGIOUS EDUCATION (1811), Church House, Dean's Yard, S.W.1.—*Gen. Sec.*, Rev. Canon R. T. Holtby.

NATIONAL SOCIETY FOR THE PREVENTION OF CRUELTY TO CHILDREN (1884), *Headquarters*, 1 Riding House Street, W.1.—*Chairman*, Lady Holland-Martin, O.B.E.; *Hon. Treas.*, G. Edmiston; *Director*, Rev. Arthur Morton, O.B.E.

NATIONAL TRUST for places of Historic Interest or Natural Beauty (1895), 42 Queen Anne's Gate, S.W.1.—*Dir. Gen.*, J. D. Boles.

NATIONAL TRUST FOR SCOTLAND for places of historic interest or natural beauty (1931), 5 Charlotte Square, Edinburgh 2.—*Dir.*, J. C. Stormonth Darling, C.B.E., M.C., T.D., W.S.

NATIONAL UNION OF STUDENTS, 3 Endsleigh Street, W.C.1.—*Admin. Sec.*, D. G. Metheringham.

NATIONAL VIEWERS' AND LISTENERS' ASSOCIATION. —*Hon. Gen. Sec.*, Mrs. M. Whitehouse, Blacharnae, Ardleigh, Colchester, Essex.

NATION'S FUND FOR NURSES, 1a Henrietta Place, W.1.—*Sec.*, Mrs. M. Wynne Williams.

NATURE CONSERVATION, SOCIETY FOR PROMOTION OF (1912).—*Gen. Sec.*, A. E. Smith, O.B.E., The Green, Nettleham, Lincs.

NAUTICAL RESEARCH, SOCIETY FOR (1911), c/o National Maritime Museum, Greenwich, S.E.10. —*Hon. Sec.* G. P. B. Naish.

NAVAL, MILITARY AND AIR FORCE BIBLE SOCIETY (1780), Radstock House, Eccleston Street, S.W.1. Copies and portions of the Scriptures circulated to the Forces (1975), 174,286.—*Sec.*, N. Brown.

NAVAL ARCHITECTS, ROYAL INSTITUTION OF (1860), 10 Upper Belgrave Street, S.W.1.—*Sec.*, P. W. Ayling.

NAVIGATION, ROYAL INSTITUTE OF, at the Royal Geographical Society, 1 Kensington Gore, S.W.7. *Dir.*, M. W. Richey, M.B.E.

NAVY LEAGUE (INC.) (1895), Broadway House, Broadway, S.W.19.—*Pres.*, The Earl Cairns, G.C.V.O., C.B.; *Dir.-Gen.*, Rear Adm. I. G. W. Robertson, C.B., D.S.C.

NAVY RECORDS SOCIETY, Royal Naval College, Greenwich, S.E.10.—*Hon. Secs.*, M. A. M. Rodger; A. N. Ryan.

NEWCOMEN SOCIETY (1920), for the Study of the History of Engineering and Technology, Science Museum, S.W.7.—*Exec. Sec.*, J. W. Butler.

NEW ENGLISH ART CLUB (1886), 17 Carlton House Terrace, S.W.1.—*Sec.*, C. de Winter.

NEWMAN ASSOCIATION (1942), Newman House, 15 Carlisle Street, W.1.

NEWSPAPER EDITORS, GUILD OF BRITISH (1946), Whitefriars House, Carmelite Street, E.C.4.— *Pres.*, T. H. Cooke (*St Regis Newspapers, Bolton*); *Sec.-Treas.*, C. Gordon Page.

NEWSPAPER PRESS FUND (1864), Dickens House, 35 Wathen Road, Dorking, Surrey.—*Sec.*, P. W. Evans.

NEWSPAPER PUBLISHERS ASSOCIATION, LTD. (1906), 6 Bouverie Street, E.C.4.—*Dir.*, J. Dixey, O.B.E.

NEWSPAPER SOCIETY (1836), Whitefriars House, Carmelite Street, E.C.4.—*Pres.*, J. L. Brown (*Birmingham Post and Mail*); *Dir.*, D. Lowndes.

NEWSVENDORS' BENEVOLENT INSTITUTION (1839), Dutch House, 307 High Holborn, W.C.1.—*Sec.*, J. E. Llewellyn-Jones.

NOISE ABATEMENT SOCIETY, 6 Old Bond Street, W.1.—*Chairman*, John Connell.

NON-SMOKERS, NATIONAL SOCIETY OF (1926)—*Sec.*, Rev. H. V. Little, 125 West Dumpton Lane, Ramsgate, Kent.

NORE R. N. and R. M. CHILDREN'S TRUST, H.M.S. *Pembroke*, Chatham.—*Sec.*, Lt.-Cdr. H. Blease, R.N. (*ret.*).

NORTHERN IRELAND TOURIST BOARD, River House, 48 High Street, Belfast 1.—*Chief Executive*, R. C. C. Hall.

NORTHUMBERLAND AND DURHAM ASSOCIATION IN LONDON (1920).—*Hon. Sec.*, H. J. Luxton, 7 Havannah Street, E.14.

NORWOOD HOMES FOR JEWISH CHILDREN (Jewish Orphanage) (1795), 315/317 Ballards Lane, N.12. —*Exec. Dir.*, H. Altman.

NUCLEAR ENERGY SOCIETY, BRITISH (1962), 1–7, Great George Street, S.W.1.—*Sec.*, J. G. Watson, C.B.

NUFFIELD FOUNDATION (1943), Nuffield Lodge, Regent's Park, N.W.1.—*Dir.*, J. Maddox.

NUFFIELD PROVINCIAL HOSPITALS TRUST (1939), 3 Prince Albert Road, N.W.1.—*Gen. Sec.*, G. McLachlan, C.B.E.

NUMISMATIC SOCIETY, BRITISH.—*Hon. Sec.*, W. Slayter, 63 West Way, Edgware, Middx.

NUMISMATIC SOCIETY, ROYAL, c/o Dept. of Coins and Medals, The British Museum, W.C.1.—*Pres.*, R. A. G. Carson; *Hon. Sec.*, Miss M. M. Archibald.

NURSES', RETIRED, NATIONAL HOME, Riverside Avenue, Bournemouth.

NURSES, ROYAL NATIONAL PENSION FUND FOR, 15 Buckingham Street, W.C.2.—*Manager and Actuary*, C. M. O'Brien.

NURSING COUNCIL FOR ENGLAND AND WALES, GENERAL, 23 Portland Place, W.1.—*Registrar*, Miss E. Bendall.

NURSING COUNCIL, GENERAL, for Scotland, 5 Darnaway Street, Edinburgh 3.—*Registrar*, Miss J. G. M. Main, O.B.E.

NURSING, ROYAL COLLEGE OF, Henrietta Place, W.1.—*Gen. Sec.*, Miss C. M. Hall, C.B.E.

NUTRITION SOCIETY (1941).—*Hon. Sec.*, G. L. S. Pawan, D.SC., Middlesex Hospital Medical School, W.1.

OBSTETRICIANS AND GYNAECOLOGISTS, ROYAL COLLEGE OF (1929), 27 Sussex Place, Regent's Park, N.W.1.—*Pres.*, Prof. C. J. Dewhurst; *Sec.*, D. B. Lloyd.

OFFICERS' ASSOCIATION, THE (1920), 28 Belgrave Square, S.W.1. Affords relief to ex-officers of The Royal Navy, Army and R.A.F. and their widows and dependants in distress; assists such persons with disability pension and other claims, and to find accommodation in homes for the elderly; helps unemployed ex-officers to find employment.—*Gen. Sec.*, Maj.-Gen. M. Janes, C.B., M.B.E.

OFFICERS' FAMILIES FUND (1899), 28 Belgrave Square, S.W.1.—*Sec.*, Mrs. E. R. Sword.

OFFICERS' PENSIONS SOCIETY, LTD., 15 Buckingham Gate, S.W.1.—*Gen. Sec.*, Rear Adm. F. B. P. Brayne-Nicholls, C.B., D.S.C.

OIL PAINTERS, ROYAL INSTITUTE OF (1883), 17 Carlton House Terrace, S.W.1.—*Pres.*, M. Noakes; *Sec.*, C. de Winter.

OILSEED, OIL AND FEEDINGSTUFFS TRADES BENEVOLENT ASSOCIATION, THE, 14–20 St. Mary Axe, E.C.3.

OLYMPIC ASSOCIATION, BRITISH (1905), 12 Buckingham Street, W.C.2.—*Gen. Sec.*, G. M. Sparkes.

ONE PARENT FAMILIES, NATIONAL COUNCIL FOR (*formerly* National Council for the Unmarried Mother and Her Child), 255 Kentish Town Road, N.W.5.—*Dir.*, Mrs. M. E. Bramall, O.B.E.

OPEN-AIR MISSION (1853), 19 John Street, W.C.1. —*Sec.*, A. J. Greenbank.

OPTICAL COUNCIL, GENERAL, 41 Harley Street, W.1.—*Registrar*, J. D. Devlin.

ORDERS AND MEDALS RESEARCH SOCIETY.—*Gen. Sec.*, N. G. Gooding, 11 Maresfield, Chepstow Road, Croydon.

ORIENTAL CERAMIC SOCIETY (1921), 31B Torrington Square, W.C.1.—*Sec.*, Vice-Admiral Sir John Gray, K.B.E., C.B.

ORNITHOLOGISTS' CLUB, THE SCOTTISH, 21 Regent Terrace, Edinburgh.—*Sec.*, Maj. A. D. Peirse-Duncombe.

ORNITHOLOGISTS' UNION, BRITISH, c/o Zoological Society of London, Regent's Park, N.W.1.—*Sec.*, P. J. S. Olney.

ORNITHOLOGY, BRITISH TRUST FOR (1932), Beech Grove, Tring, Herts.—*Administrator*, C. W. N. Plant.

ORNITHOLOGY, FIELD, THE EDWARD GREY INSTITUTE OF (1938), Dept. of Zoology, South Parks Road, Oxford.

ORTHOPÆDIC ASSOCIATION, BRITISH (1918), c/o Royal College of Surgeons, Lincoln's Inn Fields, W.C.2.—*Hon. Sec.*, R. Q. Crellin, F.R.C.S.

OUTWARD BOUND TRUST, Iddesleigh House, Caxton Street, S.W.1.—*Exec. Dir.*, Lt. Col. C. Wylie.

OVERSEAS DEVELOPMENT INSTITUTE LTD. (1960), 10–11 Percy Street, W.1.—*Dir.*, R. N. Wood.

OVERSEAS GRADUATES, LONDON HOUSE FOR, Mecklenburgh Square, W.C.1.

OVERSEAS SERVICE PENSIONERS' ASSOCIATION (1960), 408–412 Coastal Chambers, 172 Buckingham Palace Road, S.W.1.—*Sec.*, K. M. Cowley, C.M.G., O.B.E.

OVERSEAS SETTLEMENT, CHURCH OF ENGLAND COMMITTEE FOR (1925), Church House, Dean's Yard, S.W.1.—*Admin.-Sec.*, Miss P. J. Hallett.

OWNERS OF CITY PROPERTIES, ASSOCIATED.—*Sec.*, C. E. F. Gough, 35 Catherine Place, S.W.1.

OXFORD AND CAMBRIDGE SCHOOLS EXAMINATION BOARD (1873). *Offices*, 10 Trumpington Street, Cambridge and Elsfield Way, Oxford.—*Secs.*, A. R. Davis, Oxford; H. F. King, Cambridge.

OXFORD PRESERVATION TRUST (1927), 10 Turn Again Lane, St. Ebbes, Oxford.—*Sec.*, R. S. W. Malcolm.

OXFORD SOCIETY (1932), 8 Wellington Square, Oxford.—*Sec.*, Mrs. D. M. Lennie.

PAINTER-ETCHERS AND ENGRAVERS, ROYAL SOCIETY OF (1880), 26 Conduit Street, W.1.—*Pres.*, H. N. Eccleston; *Sec.*, M. Fry.

PAINTERS IN WATER COLOURS, ROYAL INSTITUTE OF (1831), 17 Carlton House Terrace, S.W.1. —*Pres.*, A. Sykes; *Treas.*, E. Wesson; *Sec.-Gen.*, M. B. Bradshaw.

PAINTERS IN WATER COLOURS, ROYAL SOCIETY OF (1804), 26 Conduit Street, W.1.—*Pres.*, E. Greenwood; *Sec. and Curator*, M. Fry.

PAINTERS, SCULPTORS AND PRINTMAKERS, NATIONAL SOCIETY OF (1930), 17 Carlton House Terrace, S.W.1.—*Pres.*, K. Barratt; *Sec.*, C. de Winter.

PALÆONTOGRAPHICAL SOCIETY (1847). *Sec.*, F. G. Dimes, c/o Institute of Geological Sciences, Exhibition Road, S.W.7.

PALÆONTOLOGICAL ASSOCIATION (1957).—*Sec.*, Dr. C. T. Scrutton, Dept. of Geology, The University, Newcastle upon Tyne.

PALESTINE EXPLORATION FUND (1865), 2 Hinde Mews, Marylebone Lane, W.1.—*Chairman*, Brig. A. Walmesley White, C.B.E., M.A., F.R.G.S.

PARENTS' NATIONAL EDUCATIONAL UNION, P.N.E.U. (1888), Murray House, Vandon Street, S.W.1.—*Dir.*, C. S. Smyth.

PARKINSON'S DISEASE SOCIETY (1969), 81 Queens Road, S.W.19.—*Exec. Dir.*, C. A. A. Kilmister.

PARLIAMENTARY AND SCIENTIFIC COMMITTEE.—*Sec.*, Lt.-Cdr. C. Powell, 30 Farringdon Street, E.C.4.

PARLIAMENTARY LABOUR PARTY.—*Leader*, Rt. Hon. L. J. Callaghan, M.P.; *Deputy Leader*, Rt. Hon.

E. W. Short, M.P.; *Chief Whip*, Rt. Hon. M. F. L. Cocks, M.P.; *Chairman*, Rt. Hon. Cledwyn Hughes, M.P.; *Leader of Labour Peers*, The Lord Shepherd, P.C.; *Sec.*, F. H. Barlow, C.B.

PASTEL SOCIETY (1899), 17 Carlton House Terrace, S.W.1.—*Pres.*, A. Sykes; *Sec.*, M. B. Bradshaw.

PASTORAL PSYCHOLOGY, GUILD OF (1936).—*Hon. Sec.*, Mrs. R. Cole, 9 Phoenix House, 5 Waverley Road, N.8.

PATENT AGENTS, CHARTERED INSTITUTE OF (1882), Staple Inn Buildings, W.C.1.—*Sec.*, P. E. Lincroft, M.B.E.

PATENTEES AND INVENTORS, INSTITUTE OF (1919), Whiteley Building, 165 Queensway, W.2.—*Sec.*, A. L. T. Cotterell, M.B.E.

PATHOLOGISTS, ROYAL COLLEGE OF, 2 Carlton House Terrace, S.W.1.

PATIENTS ASSOCIATION (1963), Suffolk House, Banbury Road, Oxford—*Pres.*, Dame Elizabeth Ackroyd, D.B.E.

PEACE SOCIETY, INTERNATIONAL (1816), Fellowship House, Browning Street, S.E.17. (*Continental Offices*, 5 rue Charles Bonnet, Geneva).—*Dir.*, Rev. H. Rathbone Dunnico.

PEARSON'S FRESH AIR FUND, 112 Regency Street, S.W.1.—*Gen. Sec.*, G. Franklin, O.B.E.

PEDESTRIANS' ASSOCIATION FOR ROAD SAFETY, 166 Shaftesbury Avenue, W.C.2.—*Sec.*, P. Claydon.

P.E.N., INTERNATIONAL (1921), 62 Glebe Place, S.W.3. World association of writers.—*Gen. Sec.*, P. Elstob.

PENSION FUNDS, NATIONAL ASSOCIATION OF (1923), —*Sec.*, J. D. Cran, Prudential House, Wellesley Road, Croydon, Surrey.

PEOPLE'S DISPENSARY FOR SICK ANIMALS (1917), P.D.S.A. House, South Street, Dorking, Surrey. —*Gen. Sec.*, E. Rowling.

PERFORMING RIGHT SOCIETY LTD. (1914), 29–33 Berners Street, W.1.—*Gen. Manager*, M. J. Freegard; *Sec.*, G. M. Neighbour.

PERIODICAL PUBLISHERS ASSOCIATION LTD., Imperial House, Kingsway, W.C.2.—*Dir.-Gen.*, D. Burnett.

PESTALOZZI CHILDREN'S VILLAGE TRUST, Sedlescombe, Battle, Sussex.—*Sec.*, S. G. Dibley.

PETROLEUM, INSTITUTE OF (1913), 61 New Cavendish Street, W.1.—*Gen. Sec.*, D. C. Payne.

PHARMACEUTICAL SOCIETY OF GREAT BRITAIN, 1 Lambeth High Street, S.E.1.—*Pres.*, J. P. Bannerman; *Sec.*, D. F. Lewis.

PHARMACOLOGICAL SOCIETY, BRITISH.—*Gen. Sec.*, Prof. J. F. Mitchell, Dept. of Pharmacology, The Medical School, University Walk, Bristol.

PHILOLOGICAL SOCIETY (1842), University College, Gower Street, W.C.1.—*Hon. Secs.*, Prof. H. L. Shorto; Prof. R. H. Robins.

PHILOSOPHY, ROYAL INSTITUTE OF, 14 Gordon Square, W.C.1.—*Director*, Prof. G. N. A. Vesey.

PHOTOGRAPHERS, INSTITUTE OF INCORPORATED (1901), Amwell End, Ware, Herts.—*Gen. Sec.*, E. I. N. Waughray.

PHYSICAL EDUCATION ASSOCIATION OF GREAT BRITAIN AND N. IRELAND, THE, Ling House, 10 Nottingham Place, W.1.—*Gen. Sec.*, P. Sebastian.

PHYSICAL RECREATION, CENTRAL COUNCIL OF (1935), 70 Brompton Road, S.W.3.

PHYSICIANS, ROYAL COLLEGE OF (1518), 11 St. Andrew's Place, N.W.1.—*Pres.*, Sir Cyril Clarke, K.B.E., M.D., P.R.C.P., F.R.S.; *Treas.*, N. D. Compston, M.D.; *Registrar*, D. A. Pyke, M.D.; *Sec.*, G. M. G. Tibbs.

PHYSICIANS AND SURGEONS, ROYAL COLLEGE OF (GLASGOW) (1599), 242 St. Vincent Street, Glasgow.—*Pres.*, Sir Ferguson Anderson; *Hon. Sec.*, Dr. N. Mackay.

PHYSICIANS OF EDINBURGH, ROYAL COLLEGE OF (1681), *Hall and Library*, 9 Queen Street, Edinburgh —*Sec.*, D. H. A. Boyd.

PHYSICS, INSTITUTE OF (1874), 47 Belgrave Square, S.W.1.—*Pres.*, Dr. B. J. Mason, F.R.S.; *Sec.*, L. Cohen, Ph.D.

PHYSIOLOGICAL SOCIETY (1876), Physiological Laboratory, Downing Street, Cambridge.—*Hon. Sec.*, S. M. Hilton, Ph.D.

PIG BREEDERS ASSOCIATION, NATIONAL (1884), 51a Clarendon Road, Watford, Herts.—*Sec.*, A. J. Manchester.

PILGRIM TRUST, THE (1930), Fielden House, Little College Street, S.W.1.—*Sec.*, Sir Patrick Hancock, G.C.M.G.

PILGRIMS OF GREAT BRITAIN, THE (1902), Savoy Hotel, W.C.2.—*Chairman*, The Lord Astor of Hever; *Hon. Sec.*, Lt.-Col. S. W. Chant-Sempill, O.B.E., M.C.

PILGRIMS OF THE U.S., THE (1903).—*Pres.*, Hugh Bullock, K.B.E., 74 Trinity Place, New York, N.Y. 10006, U.S.A.

PLACES OF WORSHIP, COUNCIL FOR, 83 London Wall, E.C.2. (*formerly* Council for the Care of Churches) —*Sec.*, D. C. Mandeville, O.B.E.

PLAID CYMRU (Welsh National Party), 8 Heol y Frenhines, Cardiff.

PLANT ENGINEERS, INSTITUTION OF, 138 Buckingham Palace Road, S.W.1.—*Sec.*, J. K. Bennett.

PLASTICS AND RUBBER INSTITUTE, THE (1931), 11 Hobart Place, S.W.1.—*Sec.*, J. N. Ratcliffe.

PLAYING FIELDS ASSOCIATION, NATIONAL (1925), 25 Ovington Square, S.W.3.—*Chairman*, A. C. Gilmour; *Gen. Sec.*, Lt. Col. R. G. Satterthwaite, O.B.E.

POETRY SOCIETY (1909), 21 Earl's Court Square, S.W.5.—*Gen. Sec.*, R. Vas Dias.

POLIO FELLOWSHIP, BRITISH (1939), Bell Close, West End Road, Ruislip, Middlesex.— *Gen. Sec.*, D. S. Powell.

POLITICAL AND ECONOMIC PLANNING (PEP) (1931), 12 Upper Belgrave Street, S.W.1.—*Jt. Dirs.*, J. Pinder, O.B.E.; R. Davies.

POLYTECHNICS, COMMITTEE OF DIRECTORS OF, 309 Regent Street, W.1.—*Chairman*, Dr. A. Suddaby; *Sec.*, P. L. Flowerday.

POLYTECHNIC TEACHERS, ASSOCIATION OF (1973), 11 Queen's Keep, Clarence Parade, Southsea, Hants.—*Chief Executive*, Miss V. S. Gay.

PORTRAIT SCULPTORS, SOCIETY OF (1962), 17 Carlton House Terrace, S.W.1.—*Pres.*, R. Thomas; *Sec.*, M. B. Bradshaw.

POULTRY CLUB, THE (1877) (incorporating the British Bantam Association).—*Gen. Sec.*, Mrs. S. Jones, 72 Springfields, Gt. Dunmow, Essex.

PRECEPTORS, COLLEGE OF, Bloomsbury House, 130 High Holborn, W.C.1. All persons engaged in education who have obtained a Diploma of the College are admissible as members.—*Secretary*, J. V. Chapman.

PREHISTORIC SOCIETY (1908).—*Hon. Sec.*, I. A. Kinnes, Ph.D., F.S.A., Dept. of Prehistoric and Romano-British Antiquities, British Museum, W.C.1.

PRESBYTERIAN HISTORICAL SOCIETY OF ENGLAND (1913), c/o United Reformed Church History Society, 86 Tavistock Place, W.C.1.

PRESBYTERIAN HOUSING LIMITED (1929), 86 Tavistock Place, W.C.1.—*Sec.*, D. J. Rawson.

PRESS ASSOCIATION (1868), 85 Fleet Street, E.C.4.—*Chairman* (1976–77), C. N. D. Cole (*Thomson Regional Newspapers*); *General Manager*, I. H. N. Yates; *Sec.*, J. Purdham.

PRINCESS LOUISE SCOTTISH HOSPITAL EOR LIMBLESS SAILORS AND SOLDIERS (1916), Erskine, Bishopton, Renfrewshire.—*Treasurer*, J. A. Young, Erskine Hospital, Bishopton, Renfrewshire.

PRINTERS' CHARITABLE CORPORATION (1827), 61 Doughty Street, W.C.1. Homes for elderly printers and widows at Basildon and Bletchley, holiday hotel and convalescence at Eastbourne.— *Gen. Sec.*, A. Reynolds.

PRINTING HISTORICAL SOCIETY (1964), St. Bride Institute, Bride Lane, E.C.4.—*Hon. Sec.*, D. Chambers.

PRINTING, INSTITUTE OF (1961), 10–11 Bedford Row, W.C.1.—*Sec.*, M. A. Smith.

PRISON VISITORS, NATIONAL ASSOCIATION OF (1922), 47 Hartington Street, Bedford.—*Gen. Sec.*, Mrs. A. G. McKenna.

PRIVATE LIBRARIES ASSOCIATION (1957), Ravelston, South View Road, Pinner, Middlesex.—*Hon. Sec.*, F. Broomhead.

PRIVATE PATIENTS PLAN (The Provident Association for Medical Care Ltd.), Eynsham House, Tunbridge Wells, Kent.—*Man. Dir.*, G. D. Lock.

PROCURATORS IN GLASGOW, ROYAL FACULTY OF (1600).—*Treas.*, *Clerk and Fiscal*, J. G. L. Robinson, 55 West Regent Street, Glasgow.

PRODUCTION CONTROL, INSTITUTE OF, Beaufort House, Rother Street, Stratford-upon-Avon, Warwickshire.—*Gen. Sec.*, K. Roberts.

PRODUCTION ENGINEERS, INSTITUTION OF, Rochester House, 66 Little Ealing Lane, W.5.

PROFESSIONAL CLASSES AID COUNCIL, 10 St. Christopher's Place, W.1.—*Sec.*, Miss P. Roden.

PROFESSIONAL SALESMEN—*See* Sales Engineers.

PROFESSIONAL WORKERS, NATIONAL FEDERATION OF (1920), 30a Station Road, Harpenden, Herts.

PROFESSIONS SUPPLEMENTARY TO MEDICINE, COUNCIL FOR, York House, Westminster Bridge Road, S.E.1.—*Registrar*, B. L. Donald, Ph.D.

PROPAGATION OF THE GOSPEL, UNITED SOCIETY FOR THE (U.S.P.G.), 15 Tufton Street, S.W.1.—*Sec.*, Rev. Canon J. S. Robertson.

PROTECTION OF LIFE FROM FIRE, SOCIETY FOR THE (1836), Aldermary House, Queen Street, E.C.4.—*Sec.*, E. H. Gledhill.

PROTESTANT ALLIANCE, THE (1845), 112 Colin Gardens, N.W.9.—*Sec.*, Rev. A. G. Ashdown.

PROVINCIAL NOTARIES SOCIETY (1907), 132 High Street, Portsmouth, Hants.—*Sec.*, G. E. Delafield.

PSYCHIATRISTS, ROYAL COLLEGE OF (1971, *formerly* Royal Medico-Psychological Association founded in 1841), 17 Belgrave Square, S.W.1.— *Registrar*, M. Markowe, M.D.

PSYCHICAL RESEARCH, SOCIETY FOR (1882), 1 Adam and Eve Mews, W.8.—*Pres.*, Prof. A. J. Ellison.

PSYCHOLOGICAL SOCIETY, THE BRITISH (1901), 18–19 Albemarle Street, W.1.—*Pres.*, Miss M. A. Davidson; *Sec. Gen.*, Dr. R. R. Hetherington.

PUBLIC ADMINISTRATION, ROYAL INSTITUTE OF (1922), Hamilton House, Mabledon Place, W.C.1 —*Dir.-Gen.*, R. Nottage, C.M.G.

PUBLIC FINANCE AND ACCOUNTANCY, CHARTERED INSTITUTE OF (1885) (*formerly* Institute of Municipal Treasurers and Accountants).—*Sec.*, R. A. Emmott, 1 Buckingham Place, S.W.1.

PUBLIC HEALTH AND HYGIENE, THE ROYAL INSTITUTE OF (1937), Postgraduate Medical School, 28 Portland Place, W.1.; Harben Laboratories, 23 Queen Square, W.C.1.—*Sec.*, A. R. Horsham.

PUBLIC HEALTH ENGINEERS, INSTITUTION OF (1895), 32 Eccleston Square, S.W.1.—*Sec.*, I. B. Muirhead.

PUBLIC RELATIONS, INSTITUTE OF (1948), 1 Great James Street, W.C.1.—*Dir.*, J. Wild.

PUBLIC SCHOOLS, ASSOCIATION OF GOVERNING BODIES OF (BOYS) (1941).—*Sec.*, F. J. Walesby, 27 Church Road, Steep, Petersfield, Hants.

PUBLIC SCHOOLS, ASSOCIATION OF GOVERNING BODIES OF GIRLS' (1942).—*Sec.*, F. J. Walesby (*see above*).

PUBLIC SCHOOLS BURSARS' ASSOCIATION (1932).—
Sec., Capt. I. G. Mason, R.N., 69 Crescent Road,
Alverstoke, Gosport, Hants.

PUBLIC TEACHERS OF LAW, SOCIETY OF (1908).—
Pres., Prof. L. C. B. Gower; *Hon. Sec.*, Prof. P. B.
Fairest, Faculty of Law, The University, Hull.

PUBLISHERS ASSOCIATION (1896), 19 Bedford
Square, W.C.1.—*Pres.*, P. Allsop; *Chief Exec. and
Sec.*, C. Bradley.

PURCHASING AND SUPPLY, INSTITUTE OF (1967),
York House, Westminster Bridge Road, S.E.1.—
Dir.-Gen., I. G. S. Groundwater.

QUALITY ASSURANCE, INSTITUTE OF (*formerly the
Institution of Engineering Inspection*), 54 Princes
Gate, Exhibition Road, S.W.7.—*Sec.*, R.
Knowles, C.B.E.

QUANTITY SURVEYORS, INSTITUTE OF, 98 Gloucester
Place, W.1.—*Dir.*, Brig. F. H. Lowman.

QUARRIER'S HOMES (1871), Bridge of Weir, Renfrewshire, Scotland.

QUARRYING, INSTITUTE OF (1917), 7 Regent Street,
Nottingham.—*Sec.*, R. Oates.

QUEEN ELIZABETH'S FOUNDATION FOR THE DISABLED
(1967), Leatherhead, Surrey.—*Dir.*, R. N. Smith,
O.B.E., M.C., T.D. Incorporating Queen Eliza-
beth's Training College (1934), Banstead Place
Assessment and Further Education Centre for
Handicapped School Leavers (1973), Dorincourt
Residential Sheltered Workshop (1958) and
Lulworth Court Holiday and Convalescent
Home (1959).

QUEEN VICTORIA CLERGY FUND (1897), *Central
Fund*, Church House, Dean's Yard, S.W.1.—
Sec., Maj. G. C. Hackett, M.B.E.

QUEEN VICTORIA SCHOOL, Dunblane, Perthshire.—
Commandant, Brig. H. H. M. Marston, M.C. (*ret.*);
Headmaster, J. R. F. Melluish, M.A.

QUEEN'S NURSING INSTITUTE (1887), 57 Lower
Belgrave Street, S.W.1.—*Gen. Sec.*, Miss M.
Faulkner.

RADIO SOCIETY OF GREAT BRITAIN (Incorporated),
35 Doughty Street, W.C.1.—*Gen. Manager*,
G. R. Jessop.

RADIOLOGISTS, ROYAL COLLEGE OF (1934), 28
Portland Place, W.1.—*Sec.*, Miss P. D. Thomson.

RAILWAY AND CANAL HISTORICAL SOCIETY.—*Hon.
Sec.*, M. R. Prew, 435 Upper Richmond Road,
Putney, S.W.15.

RAILWAY BENEVOLENT INSTITUTION (1858), 29
John Street, W.C.1.; Railway Children's Home
at Derby and Old People's Home near Dorking.
—*Gen. Sec.*, E. A. Palmer.

RAILWAY INVIGORATION SOCIETY (1954), BM-RIS,
W.C.1.—*Gen. Sec.*, J. M. Stanley.

RAINER FOUNDATION, 89a Blackheath Hill, S.E.10.
A voluntary society providing residential and
remedial help for children and young people.—
Gen. Sec., R. Howell.

RAMBLERS' ASSOCIATION (1935), 1–4 Crawford
Mews, York Street, W.1.—*Sec.*, A. Mattingly.

RATEPAYERS' ASSOCIATIONS, NATIONAL UNION OF,
47 Victoria Street, S.W.1.

RATING AND VALUATION ASSOCIATION (1882), 115
Ebury Street, S.W.1.—*Sec.*, B. L. Hill.

RED CROSS SOCIETY, BRITISH. *See* BRITISH.

RED POLL CATTLE SOCIETY AND BRITISH DANE
CATTLE SOCIETY OF GREAT BRITAIN AND IRELAND,
28 Riseholme Lane, Riseholme, Lincoln.—*Sec.*,
W. Dunnaway.

REEDHAM SCHOOL (Incorporated) (1844), Purley,
Surrey.—*Sec.*, Mrs. M. J. Pupius.

REED'S SCHOOL (1813), *Offices*, 8 Little Trinity
Lane, E.C.4.—*Sec.*, D. Cooper.

REFRIGERATION, INSTITUTE OF (1899), 272 London
Road, Wallington, Surrey.—*Sec.*, D. T. Lee.

REGULAR FORCES EMPLOYMENT ASSOCIATION (1885),
25 Bloomsbury Square, W.C.1. Finds employment for non-commissioned ex-Regulars.—
General Manager, Maj.-Gen. P. F. Claxton, C.B.,
O.B.E.

REINDEER COUNCIL OF THE UNITED KINGDOM
(1949), Newton Hill, Harston, Cambridge.—
Hon. Sec., Dr. E. J. Lindgren, M.A.

RELIGION AND MEDICINE, INSTITUTE OF (1964).—
Organizing Sec., Mrs. E. A. Wye, St. Mary
Abchurch, Abchurch Lane, E.C.4.

RENT OFFICERS, INSTITUTE OF.—*Hon. Sec.*, D. A. G.
Sargent, D.F.C., Moulsham House, 48 Moulsham
Street, Chelmsford, Essex.

RESEARCH DEFENCE SOCIETY, 11 Chandos Street,
Cavendish Square, W.1.—*Hon. Sec.*, Prof. H.
Barcroft, M.D., F.R.C.P., F.R.S.; *Sec.*, Mrs. C. Ewen.

RETAIL ALLIANCE, 3 Berners Street, W.1.—*Sec.*,
J. Hussey.

RICHARD III SOCIETY.—*Gen. Sec.*, Mrs. P. Hester,
65 Howard Road, Upminster, Essex.

RIVERS PROTECTION, CENTRAL COUNCIL FOR,
Fishmongers' Hall, E.C.4.—*Joint Hon. Secs.*, E. S.
Earl; Leonard Millis, C.B.E.

ROAD SAFETY OFFICERS, INSTITUTE OF (1971), 53
Knightlow Road, Harborne, Birmingham.—
Sec., D. E. Clarke.

ROADS IMPROVEMENT ASSOCIATION, Comet Way,
Southend-on-Sea, Essex.

ROAD TRANSPORT ENGINEERS, INSTITUTE OF (1945),
1 Cromwell Place, S.W.7.—*Sec.*, J. A. Fletcher,
M.B.E.

ROMAN AND MEDIAEVAL LONDON EXCAVATION
COUNCIL.—*Hon. Sec.*, R. A. Woods, F.S.A., 31
Goodyers Avenue, Radlett, Herts.

ROMAN STUDIES, SOCIETY FOR PROMOTION OF,
31–34 Gordon Square, W.C.1.—*Pres.*, A. N.
Sherwin-White, F.B.A.; *Sec.*, Mrs. P. Gilbert.

ROTARY INTERNATIONAL IN GREAT BRITAIN AND
IRELAND (1914), Sheen Lane House, Sheen Lane,
S.W.14.—*Sec.*, J. H. Jackson.

ROYAL AFRICAN SOCIETY (1901), 18 Northumberland Avenue, W.C.2.—*Sec.*, Miss M. Edgedale.

ROYAL AGRICULTURAL SOCIETY OF ENGLAND (1838),
National Agricultural Centre, Stoneleigh,
Kenilworth, Warwicks.—*Chief Exec.*, J. D. M.
Hearth.

ROYAL AGRICULTURAL SOCIETY OF THE COMMON-
WEALTH (1957).—*Hon. Sec.*, F. R. Francis, M.B.E.,
Robarts House, Rossmore Road, N.W.1.

ROYAL AIR FORCE BENEVOLENT FUND (1919), 67
Portland Place, W.1.—*Controller*, Air Marshal
Sir Denis Crowley-Milling, K.C.B., C.B.E., D.S.O.,
D.F.C.

ROYAL AIR FORCES ASSOCIATION, 43 Grove Park
Road, W.4.—*Sec. Gen.*, G. R. Boak, C.B.E.

ROYAL ALEXANDRA AND ALBERT SCHOOL (1758),
Offices, Gatton Park, Reigate, Surrey.—*Comptroller*, E. A. Corner.

ROYAL ALFRED MERCHANT SEAMEN'S SOCIETY
(1865), Weston Acres, Woodmansterne Lane,
Banstead, Surrey.—*Gen. Sec.*, D. J. Lafferty,
M.B.E.

ROYAL ARMOURED CORPS BENEVOLENT FUND,
Headquarters, R.A.C. Centre, Bovington Camp,
Wareham, Dorset; *Sec.*, Lt.-Col. C. H. Rayment,
M.B.E.

ROYAL ARTILLERY ASSOCIATION, Artillery House,
Connaught Barracks, Grand Depot Road, S.E.18.
—*Gen. Sec.*, Col. R. H. Haynes, M.B.E.

ROYAL ASIATIC SOCIETY (1823), 56 Queen Anne
Street, W.1.—*Sec.*, Miss D. Crawford.

ROYAL ASSOCIATION OF BRITISH DAIRY FARMERS
(1876), Robarts House, Rossmore Road,
N.W.1.—*Sec.*, F. R. Francis, M.B.E.

ROYAL BRITISH NURSES ASSOCIATION, 94 Upper
Tollington Park, N.4.—*Hon. Sec.*, Mrs. H. M.
Vorstermans, M.B.E.

ROYAL CALEDONIAN SCHOOLS (1815), Bushey, Herts.—*Chief Exec.*, Capt. R. E. Wilson, C.B.E., D.F.C., R.N. (*ret.*)

ROYAL CAMBRIDGE HOME FOR SOLDIERS' WIDOWS, 82–84 Hurst Road, East Molesey, Surrey.—*Sec.*, Miss G. M. East.

ROYAL CELTIC SOCIETY (1820), 49 Queen Street, Edinburgh.—*Sec.*, J. G. S. Cameron, W.S.

ROYAL CHORAL SOCIETY (1871), Royal Albert Hall, S.W.7.—*Gen. Man.*, M. de Grey.

ROYAL COLLEGE OF VETERINARY SURGEONS, 32 Belgrave Square, S.W.1.—*Pres.*, Dr. O. Uvarov; *Registrar*, A. R. W. Porter.

ROYAL COMMONWEALTH SOCIETY (1868), Northumberland Avenue, W.C.2.—(26,000 members). —*Sec.-Gen.*, A. S. H. Kemp, O.B.E.

ROYAL DESIGNERS FOR INDUSTRY, FACULTY OF (1936) (Royal Society of Arts), John Adam Street, W.C.2.—*Master*, J. Howe, R.D.I., F.R.I.B.A.; *Sec.*, K. Grant.

ROYAL DRAWING SOCIETY (1902), 17 Carlton House Terrace, S.W.1.—*Pres.*, J. Mills, F.R.S.A.; *Sec.*, D. Flanders.

ROYAL ECONOMIC SOCIETY (1890), P O. Box 86, Cambridge.—*Sec.-Gen.*, R. C. Tress.

ROYAL ENGINEERS ASSOCIATION, *Headquarters*, R.S.M.E., Chatham, Kent.—*Controller*, Col. R. R. L. Harradine, T.D.

ROYAL ENGINEERS, THE INSTITUTION OF (1875), Chatham.—*Sec.*, Col. E. E. Peel.

ROYAL HIGHLAND AND AGRICULTURAL SOCIETY OF SCOTLAND (1784), Ingliston, Newbridge, Midlothian.—*Sec.*, T. W. M. Alder.

ROYAL HORTICULTURAL SOCIETY (1804).—*Offices*, Vincent Square, S.W.1. *Garden*, Wisley, Ripley, Woking, Surrey.—*Sec.*, J. R. Cowell.

ROYAL HOSPITAL AND HOME FOR INCURABLES, PUTNEY (1854), West Hill, S.W.15.—*Sec.*, Col. N. F. Gordon-Wilson, M.B.E.

ROYAL HOSPITAL SCHOOL, Holbrook, nr. Ipswich, Suffolk.—*Headmaster*, N. B. Worswick.

ROYAL HUMANE SOCIETY (1774).—In 1975, 721 persons were rewarded by the R.H.S. for saving 451 lives, and attempting to save the lives of 69 others.—*Offices*, Watergate House, York Buildings, Adelphi, W.C.2.—*Sec.*, J. M. Leadbitter, O.B.E.

ROYAL INSTITUTE OF INTERNATIONAL AFFAIRS (1920), Chatham House, St. James's Square, S.W.1.—*Director*, A. Shonfield.

ROYAL INSTITUTION OF GREAT BRITAIN (1799), 21 Albemarle Street, W.1.—*Pres.*, H.R.H. The Duke of Kent, G.C.M.G., G.C.V.O.; *Dir.*, Prof. Sir George Porter, F.R.S.; *Sec.*, J. S. Porterfield, M.D.

ROYAL INSTITUTION OF SOUTH WALES, Swansea (1835).—*Hon. Sec.*, F. M. Gibbs.

ROYAL LIFE SAVING SOCIETY, THE (1891), Desborough House, 14 Devonshire Street, W.1.—*Dir. and Sec.*, O. S. M. Bayley.

ROYAL LITERARY FUND (1790), 11 Ludgate Hill, E.C.4. Grants to necessitous authors of some published work of approved literary merit or to their immediate dependants.—*Pres.*, Janet Adam Smith, C.B.E.; *Sec.*, V. Bonham-Carter.

ROYAL MEDICAL BENEVOLENT FUND (1836), 24 King's Road, Wimbledon, S.W.19.—*Dir.*, Col. A. J. S. Crockett, O.B.E.

ROYAL MEDICAL SOCIETY (1737), Students Centre, Bristo Street, Edinburgh.—*Sec.*, R. Elliott.

ROYAL METAL TRADES BENEVOLENT SOCIETY (1843), 223 Cranbrook Road, Ilford, Essex.—*Sec.*, L. H. Lindsay, M.B.E.

ROYAL MICROSCOPICAL SOCIETY, 37–38 St. Clements, Oxford.—*Administrator*, Lt.-Col. P. G. Fleming.

ROYAL MILITARY POLICE ASSOCIATION (1946), Regimental Headquarters, Corps of Royal Military Police, Roussillon Barracks, Chichester, Sussex.—*Sec.*, Major R. J. R. Whistler.

ROYAL MUSICAL ASSOCIATION (1874) c/o British Museum, W.C.1.—*Sec.*, M. Turner.

ROYAL NATIONAL LIFE-BOAT INSTITUTION, THE (1824).—*Income* (1975) £5,271,312, expenditure £5,539,126; rescued in 1975, 1,038. 135 lifeboats and 122 fast inshore lifeboats are maintained on the coasts of Great Britain and Ireland. *Offices*, West Quay, Poole, Dorset.—*Dir.*, Capt. N. Dixon, R.N.

ROYAL NATIONAL MISSION TO DEEP SEA FISHERMEN (1881), 43 Nottingham Place, W.1.—*Sec.*, J. C. Lewis, O.B.E.

ROYAL NATIONAL ROSE SOCIETY, Chiswell Green Lane, St. Albans, Herts.—*Sec.*, L. G. Turner.

ROYAL NAVAL AND ROYAL MARINE CHILDREN'S HOME (1834), Waterlooville.—*Sec.*, Mrs. J. P. Thorpe, H.M.S. *Nelson*, Portsmouth.

ROYAL NAVAL BENEVOLENT SOCIETY (1739), 1 Fleet Street, E.C.4.—*Sec.*, Lt. Cdr. S. W. Birse, O.B.E., D.S.C., R.N., (*ret.*)

ROYAL NAVAL BENEVOLENT TRUST (1922) (Grand Fleet and Kindred Funds), High Street, Brompton, Gillingham, Kent (Local Committees at Chatham, Devonport and Portsmouth).—*Gen. Sec.*, Lt.-Cdr. D. C. Lawrence, R.N. (*ret.*).

ROYAL NAVAL FUND (1891). Administered by the Royal Naval Benevolent Trust. *See above.*

ROYAL NAVY OFFICERS, ASSOCIATION OF (Trafalgar Day, 1925), 70 Porchester Terrace, W.2.—*Sec.-Treas.*, Lt. Cdr. J. V. Watson, R.N. (*ret.*).

ROYAL PATRIOTIC FUND CORPORATION (1854), 1 Cambridge Gate, N.W.1. Administers funds for the benefit of widows, children and other dependants of deceased officers and servicemen of the Armed Forces.—*Sec.*, Brig. H. E. Boulter, C.B.E., D.S.O.

ROYAL PHILANTHROPIC SOCIETY'S SCHOOL, Redhill, Surrey.—*Princ.*, L. H. Crew.

ROYAL PHILATELIC SOCIETY, LONDON (1869), 41 Devonshire Place, W.1.—*Hon. Sec.*, J. O. Griffiths.

ROYAL PHILHARMONIC SOCIETY (1813), 124 Wigmore Street, W.1.—*Hon. Sec.*, W. Cole, M.V.O., D.MUS., F.R.A.M., F.R.C.O.

ROYAL PHOTOGRAPHIC SOCIETY (1853), 14 South Audley Street, W.1.—*Sec.*, K. R. Warr.

ROYAL PINNER SCHOOL FOUNDATION, 110 Old Brompton Road, S. Kensington, S.W.7. Assists by grants and bursaries in the education of commercial travellers' children where families are struck by misfortune.—*Sec.*, W. H. Drayton.

" ROYAL SAILORS' RESTS " (Miss Agnes Weston's) (1876). *Head Office*, South Street, Gosport, Hants. Centres for naval personnel at Devonport, St. Budeaux, Ilchester, Gosport, Portsmouth and Faslane.

ROYAL SCHOOL OF NEEDLEWORK (1872), 25 Princes Gate, S.W.7.—*Dir.*, D. Lloyd.

ROYAL SCOTTISH COUNTRY DANCE SOCIETY (1923), 12 Coates Crescent, Edinburgh.—*Sec.*, Miss M. M. Gibson.

ROYAL SCOTTISH SOCIETY FOR PREVENTION OF CRUELTY TO CHILDREN (1884), 16 Melville Street, Edinburgh.—*Gen. Sec.*, A. M. M. Wood.

ROYAL SCOTTISH SOCIETY OF ARTS (1821) (Science and Technology).—*Sec.*, G. Brash, 70 Cumberland Street, Edinburgh.

ROYAL SEAMEN'S PENSION FUND (Incorporated) (1919), 58 High Street, Sutton, Surrey.—*Sec.*, R. F. Van Houten

ROYAL SIGNALS INSTITUTION (1950), Cheltenham Terrace, S.W.3.—*Sec.*, Lt.-Col. E. J. Beale.

ROYAL SOCIETY, THE (1660), 6 Carlton House Terrace, S.W.1.—*Pres.*, The Lord Todd; *Treas. and Vice-Pres.*, Sir James Menter; *Secretaries and Vice-Presidents*, Sir Bernard Katz; Sir Harrie Massey; *Foreign Secretary and Vice-Pres.*, Sir Kingsley Dunham; *Executive Sec.*, Sir David Martin, C.B.E.

ROYAL SOCIETY FOR ASIAN AFFAIRS (1901), 42 Devonshire Street, W.1.—*Pres.*, The Lord Greenhill of Harrow, G.C.M.G., O.B.E.; *Sec.*, Miss M. FitzSimons.

ROYAL SOCIETY FOR THE PREVENTION OF ACCIDENTS, Cannon House, Priory Queensway, Birmingham.—*Dir.-Gen.*, J. P. Weston.

ROYAL SOCIETY FOR THE PREVENTION OF CRUELTY TO ANIMALS (1824), Causeway, Horsham, Sussex. *Exec. Dir.*, Maj. R. F. Seager.

ROYAL SOCIETY FOR THE PROTECTION OF BIRDS (1889), The Lodge, Sandy, Beds.—*Dir.*, I. Prestt.

ROYAL SOCIETY OF ARTS (1754), 6–8 John Adam Street, Adelphi, W.C.2.—*Chairman*, The Lord Nathan; *Sec.*, K. Grant.

ROYAL SOCIETY OF BRITISH ARTISTS (1823), 17 Carlton House Terrace, S.W.1.—*Pres.*, P. Greenham, R.A.; *Vice-President*, D. J. Winfield; *Keeper*, C. de Winter.

ROYAL SOCIETY OF BRITISH SCULPTORS (1904), 108 Old Brompton Road, S.W.7.—*Pres.*, M. Rizzello; *Sec.*, Mrs. F. McGregor-Eadie.

ROYAL SOCIETY OF EDINBURGH (1783), 22 George Street, Edinburgh 2.—*Pres.*, Prof. R. A. Smith, C.B.E., F.R.S.; *Gen. Sec.*, Prof. R. M. S. Smellie, Ph.D., D.Sc.; *Treas.*, The Lord Balerno, C.B.E., T.D., D.Sc.; *Curator*, H. E. Butler, Ph.D.

ROYAL SOCIETY OF HEALTH (1876), to promote the health of the people, 13 Grosvenor Place, S.W.1.—*Sec.*, D. S. Wilson.

ROYAL SOCIETY OF LITERATURE (1823), 1 Hyde Park Gardens, W.2.—*Sec.*, Mrs. J. M. Patterson.

ROYAL SOCIETY OF MEDICINE (1805), 1 Wimpole Street, W.1.—*Pres.*, Sir Gordon Wolstenholme, O.B.E., F.R.C.P.; *Exec. Dir.*, R. T. Hewitt, O.B.E.

ROYAL SOCIETY OF PORTRAIT PAINTERS (1891), 17 Carlton House Terrace, S.W.1.—*Pres.*, E. I. Halliday, C.B.E.; *Sec.*, M. B. Bradshaw.

ROYAL SOCIETY OF ST. GEORGE (1894), 4 Upper Belgrave Street, S.W.1.—*Gen. Sec.*, Miss J. Wynn.

ROYAL STATISTICAL SOCIETY (1834), 25 Enford Street, W.1.—*Pres.*, Miss S. V. Cunliffe; *Sec.*, I. H. Blenkinsop.

ROYAL TANK REGIMENT ASSOCIATION and BENEVOLENT FUND, H.Q. R.A.C. Centre, Bovington Camp, Wareham, Dorset.—*Sec.*, Lt.-Col. C. H. Rayment, M.B.E.

ROYAL UNITED KINGDOM BENEFICENT ASSOCIATION (1863), 6 Avonmore Road, W.14.—*Gen. Sec.*, Maj.-Gen. R. D. Houghton, C.B., O.B.E., M.C.

ROYAL UNITED SERVICES INSTITUTE FOR DEFENCE STUDIES, Whitehall, S.W.1.—*Dir.-Gen.*, Maj. Gen. A. E. Younger, D.S.O., O.B.E.

RURAL ENGLAND, COUNCIL FOR THE PROTECTION OF (1926), 4 Hobart Place, S.W.1.—*Dir.*, C. Hall.

RURAL SCOTLAND, ASSOCIATION FOR PROTECTION OF (1927), 20 Falkland Avenue, Newton Mearns, Renfrewshire.—*Sec.*, R. Livingstone.

SAILORS' CHILDREN'S SOCIETY, THE (1821), Newland, Hull. Cares for British seamen's children who have lost a parent and for short periods during a mother's illness if father is at sea. Provides welfare facilities for seamen in Humber area, including Homes for aged seafarers at Hull and S. Shields.

ST. DEINIOL'S LIBRARY (1895), Hawarden, Clwyd.—*Warden*, Rev. Canon R. S. Foster.

ST. DUNSTAN'S, for men and women blinded on War Service, P.O. Box 58, 191 Old Marylebone Road, N.W.1. In March 1976, the number of blinded men and women in the care of the organization was 1,753.—*Pres.*, Sir Neville Pearson, Bt.; *Chairman*, I. Garnett-Orme; *Sec.*, C. D. Wills.

ST. JOHN AMBULANCE ASSOCIATION AND BRIGADE, 1 Grosvenor Crescent, S.W.1.—*Chief Commander*, Sir Maurice Dorman, G.C.M.G., G.C.V.O.; *Commissioner-in-Chief*, Maj.-Gen. D. S. Gordon, C.B., C.B.E. *Brigade Strengths* (U.K. 1975), Men, 19,115; Women, 15,508; Boy Cadets, 17,920; Girl Cadets, 34,375.—*Registrar*, L. E. Hawes.

SALES ENGINEERS, INSTITUTION OF (1966), Concorde House, 24 Warwick New Road, Royal Leamington Spa. *Dir.-Gen.*, J. E. Fenton.

SALMON AND TROUT ASSOCIATION (1903), Fishmongers' Hall, E.C.4.—*Sec.*, J. Rose, C.M.G., M.B.E., D.F.C.

SALTIRE SOCIETY (1936), Gladstone's Land, 483 Lawnmarket, Edinburgh 1. *Org. Sec.*, A. C. Davis.

SALVAGE CORPS (FIRE)—
 London (1866), 140 Aldersgate Street, E.C.1.
  Chief Officer, K. G. Smith.
 Liverpool (1842), 46 Derby Road, Liverpool.
  Chief Officer, A. H. Jones.
 Glasgow (1873), 90 Maitland Street, Glasgow.
  Chief Officer, W. C. Borland.

SAMARITANS, THE (to help the suicidal and despairing).—*Gen. Secs.*, Miss J. Burt; Rev. D. Evans, 17 Uxbridge Road, Slough, Berks.

SAMUEL PEPYS CLUB.—*Sec.*, R. H. Adams, T.D., F.S.A., 108 Dulwich Villages, S.E.21.

SANITARY ENGINEERS, INSTITUTION OF. *See* PUBLIC HEALTH ENGINEERS.

SAVE THE CHILDREN FUND, THE (1919), 157 Clapham Road, S.W.9.—*Dir. Gen.*, J. A. Cumber, C.M.G., M.B.E., T.D.

SAVINGS BANKS INSTITUTE, Knighton House, 52–66 Mortimer Street, W.1.—*Sec.*, A. J. F. Miller.

SCHOOL LIBRARY ASSOCIATION, Victoria House, 29–31 George Street, Oxford.—*Hon. Sec.*, C. A. Waite.

SCHOOL NATURAL SCIENCE SOCIETY, 2 Bramley Mansions, Berrylands Road, Surbiton, Surrey.—*Hon. Gen. Sec.*, M. Jenny Sellers.

SCHOOLMASTERS, SOCIETY OF (1798) (for the relief of Necessitous Schoolmasters and of their Widows and Orphans), 308 Galpins Road, Thornton Heath, Surrey.—*Sec.*, Mrs. H. E. Closs.

SCHOOLMISTRESSES AND GOVERNESSES BENEVOLENT INSTITUTION, 39 Buckingham Gate, S.W.1. Helps schoolmistresses, matrons and secretaries in independent schools, and self-employed women teachers; annuities, grants, a home.—*Sec.*, C. J. Page.

SCHOOLS MUSIC ASSOCIATION, THE (1938), 4 Newman Road, Bromley, Kent.—*Sec.*, S. S. Moore.

SCHOOLTEACHERS' ASSOCIATION, SCOTTISH, 41 York Place, Edinburgh.—*Gen. Sec.*, R. McClement.

SCIENCE AND LEARNING, SOCIETY FOR THE PROTECTION OF, 3 Buckland Crescent, N.W.3.—*President*, Prof. A. V. Hill, C.H., O.B.E., F.R.S.; *Sec.*, Miss E. Simpson, O.B.E.

SCIENCE EDUCATION, ASSOCIATION FOR (1963), College Lane, Hatfield, Herts.

SCOTTISH ASSESSORS' ASSOCIATION. *Sec.*, J. S. Gardner, 30/31 Queen Street, Edinburgh.

SCOTTISH CONSERVATIVE AND UNIONIST ASSOCIATION, 11 Atholl Crescent, Edinburgh 3.—*Sec.*, A. Strang, M.B.E.

SCOTTISH CONSERVATIVE AND UNIONIST CENTRAL OFFICE, 11 Atholl Crescent, Edinburgh 3.—*Dir.*, A. M. G. Macmillan.

SCOTTISH GENEALOGY SOCIETY (1953).—*Hon. Sec.*, Miss J. P. S. Ferguson, 21 Howard Place, Edinburgh.

SCOTTISH HISTORY SOCIETY (1886).—*Hon. Sec.*, D. Stevenson, PH.D., Dept. of History, Taylor Building, King's College, Aberdeen.

SCOTTISH LANDOWNERS' FEDERATION (1906).—*Dir.*, A. F. Roney Dougal, 18 Abercromby Place, Edinburgh.

SCOTTISH LAW AGENTS SOCIETY, 61 High Street, Dunblane, Perthshire.

SCOTTISH LIBERAL PARTY (1946), 2 Atholl Place, Edinburgh.—*Admin. Sec.*, Mrs. M. Aitken.

SCOTTISH MARINE BIOLOGICAL ASSOCIATION (1914), Dunstaffnage Marine Research Laboratory, P.O. Box 3, Oban, Argyll.—*Dir., and Sec.*, R. I. Currie, F.R.S.E.

SCOTTISH NATIONAL BLOOD TRANSFUSION ASSOCIATION (1940), 5 St. Colme Street, Edinburgh.—*Sec.*, Neil A. Milne, W.S.

SCOTTISH NATIONAL PARTY, 6 North Charlotte Street, Edinburgh.—*Sec.*, Miss M. M. Gibson.

SCOTTISH RECORD SOCIETY, Scottish History Dept., Univ. of Glasgow.—*Hon. Sec.*, Dr. J. Kirk.

SCOTTISH SECONDARY TEACHERS' ASSOCIATION, 15 Dundas Street, Edinburgh.—*Gen. Sec.*, J. Docherty.

SCOTTISH SOCIETY FOR PREVENTION OF CRUELTY TO ANIMALS (1839), 19 Melville Street, Edinburgh, —*Sec.*, G. F. S. Brian.

SCOTTISH SOCIETY FOR THE PROTECTION OF WILD BIRDS (1927), 125 Douglas Street, Glasgow.—*Treas.*, James M. MacKellar.

SCOTTISH TOURIST BOARD (1969), 23 Ravelston Terrace, Edinburgh.—*Chief Exec.*, P. Taylor.

SCOTTISH WOMEN'S RURAL INSTITUTES (1917), 42 Heriot Row, Edinburgh.—*Gen. Sec.*, Mrs. J. A. Noble.

SCOUT ASSOCIATION, THE, *Headquarters*, Baden-Powell House, Queen's Gate, S.W.7.—*Chief Scout*, Sir William Gladstone, Bt.; *Sec.*, E. W. Hayden. Membership in U.K. (1975), 596,934; World Membership over 14,000,000 in over 100 countries.

SCRIBES AND ILLUMINATORS, THE SOCIETY OF.—*Hon. Sec.*, G. K. Jacklin, 6 Queen Square, W.C.1.

SCRIPTURE GIFT MISSION (1888), Radstock House, Eccleston Street, S.W.1. Copies and selections of the Scriptures circulated (1975), 14,629,173.—*Sec.*, N. Brown.

SCRIPTURE UNION (1867), 47 Marylebone Lane, W.1.—*Gen. Dir.*, N. W. H. Sylvester.

SEAFARERS EDUCATION SERVICE (1919), Mansbridge House, 207 Balham High Road, S.W.17 (incorp. College of the Sea and British Ship Adoption Society).—*Director*, R. Hope, O.B.E., D.Phil.

SEAMEN'S CHRISTIAN FRIEND SOCIETY (1846), 87 Brigstock Road, Thornton Heath, Surrey.

SELDEN SOCIETY (1887), Faculty of Laws, Queen Mary College, Mile End Road, E.1. To encourage the study and advance the knowledge of the History of English Law.—*Pres.*, Sir Richard Southern, F.B.A.; *Sec.*, V. Tunkel.

SHAFTESBURY HOMES AND *Arethusa* (founded 1843); *Headquarters*, 3 Rectory Grove, S.W.4.; *Gen. Sec.*, Maj. R. P. A. de Berniere-Smart.

SHAFTESBURY SOCIETY (1844), Shaftesbury House, 112 Regency Street, S.W.1.—Engaged in social service among the physically handicapped and the poor. Maintains Residential Schools for physically handicapped children, Hostels for Muscular Dystrophy sufferers over 16 years, Holiday centres for the disabled and Missions in Greater London.—*Sec.*, G. A. Franklin, O.B.E.

SHAW SOCIETY (1941), 125 Markyate Road, Dagenham, Essex.—*Sec.*, E. F. J. Ford.

SHEEP ASSOCIATION, NATIONAL, Jenkins Lane, St. Leonards, nr. Tring, Herts.—*Sec.*, J. Thorley.

SHELLFISH ASSOCIATION OF GREAT BRITAIN, Fishmongers' Hall, London Bridge, E.C.4.—*Hon. Sec.*, E. S. Earl.

SHELTER (National Campaign for the Homeless), 157 Waterloo Road, S.E.1.

SHERLOCK HOLMES SOCIETY (1951), 5 Manor Close, Warlingham, Surrey.—*Hon. Sec.*, Capt. W. R. Michell, R.N. (*ret.*).

SHIPBROKERS, INSTITUTE OF CHARTERED (1911), 25 Bury Street, E.C.3.—*Sec.*, J. H. Parker.

SHIPWRECKED FISHERMEN AND MARINERS' ROYAL BENEVOLENT SOCIETY (1839), 1 North Pallant, Chichester, West Sussex.—*Sec.*, J. F. Byford.

SHIRE HORSE SOCIETY (1878), East of England Showground, Peterborough.—*Sec.*, R. W. Bird.

SIMPLIFIED SPELLING SOCIETY (1908).—*Hon. Sec.*, G. O'Halloran, 83 Hampden Road, N.8.

SIR OSWALD STOLL FOUNDATION, 446 Fulham Road, S.W.6.—*Sec.*, Maj. L. F. H. Kershaw, D.S.O.

SMALL INDUSTRIES IN RURAL AREAS, COUNCIL FOR, 11 Cowley Street, S.W.1.—*Sec.*, S. A. Jackson.

SOCIAL CREDIT CENTRE.—*Hon. Sec.*, V. R. Hadkins, Montagu Chambers, Mexborough, Yorkshire.

SOCIAL WORKERS, BRITISH ASSOCIATION OF (1970), 16 Kent Street, Birmingham.—*Gen. Sec.*, C. Andrews.

SOCIALIST PARTY OF GREAT BRITAIN (1904), 52 Clapham High Street, S.W.4.—*Gen. Sec.*, W. Valinas.

SOIL ASSOCIATION, Walnut Tree Manor, Haughley, Stowmarket, Suffolk.—*Pres.*, Dr. E. F. Schumacher, C.B.E.; *Gen. Sec.*, Brig. A. W. Vickers, D.S.O., O.B.E.

SOLDIERS' AND AIRMEN'S SCRIPTURE READERS ASSOCIATION, THE (1838), 75–79 High Street, Aldershot, Hants.—*Gen. Sec.*, G. H. Stokes.

SOLDIERS' DAUGHTERS' SCHOOL, ROYAL (1855) 65 Rosslyn Hill, Hampstead, N.W.3.—*Sec.*, Col. J. G. Palmer.

SOLDIERS', SAILORS' AND AIRMEN'S FAMILIES ASSOCIATION (1885). 27 Queen Anne's Gate, S.W.1.—*Chairman*, Lt.-Gen. Sir Napier Crookenden, K.C.B., D.S.O., O.B.E.; *Controller*, D. Smithers; *Sec.*, Lt.-Cdr. R. G. Brown, V.R.D., R.N.R.

SOLDIERS, SAILORS AND AIRMEN'S HELP SOCIETY (Incorporated) (1899), *see* FORCES HELP SOCIETY.

SOLICITORS' BENEVOLENT ASSOCIATION (1858), 58 Clifford's Inn, Fetter Lane, E.C.4.—*Sec.*, Lt.-Col. P. B. Wakelin, M.C.

SOLICITORS IN THE SUPREME COURTS OF SCOTLAND, SOCIETY OF.—*Sec.*, A. R. Brownlie, 2 Abercromby Place, Edinburgh 3; *Treas.*, A. Stewart.

S.O.S. SOCIETY, THE (1929), 14 Culford Gardens, S.W.3. Old people's homes (5), Mental Rehabilitation homes (2), Ex-offenders and Homeless Men's hostel (1), Young's Men's Hostel (1).—*Dir.*, Lt.-Col. P. Rew.

SOUTH AMERICAN MISSIONARY SOCIETY, Allen Gardiner House, Pembury Road, Tunbridge Wells, Kent.—*Gen. Sec.*, Rev. P. D. King.

SOUTH WALES INSTITUTE OF ENGINEERS (1857), Institute Buildings, Park Place, Cardiff.—*Hon. Sec.*, T. G. Dash.

SPASTICS SOCIETY, THE (1952), 12 Park Crescent, W.1.—*Sec.*, A. V. M. Diamond, M.B.E.

SPINA BIFIDA AND HYDROCEPHALUS ASSOCIATION, Devonshire Street House, 30 Devonshire Street, W.1.—*Gen. Sec.*, Miss M. E. Oughtred.

SPORTS MEDICINE, INSTITUTE OF (1963), 10 Nottingham Place, W.1.—*Hon. Sec.*, P. Sebastian.

SPURGEON'S HOMES (1867), Park Road, Birchington, Kent.—*Sec.*, P. E. Johnson.

STAIR SOCIETY (to encourage the study and advance the knowledge of the history of Scots Law).—*Sec.*, G. R. Thomson, T.D., PH.D., 2 St. Giles' Street, Edinburgh.

STAR AND GARTER HOME FOR DISABLED SAILORS, SOLDIERS, AND AIRMEN (1916), Richmond-upon-Thames.—*Commandant*, Maj.-Gen. J. Sheffield, C.B., C.B.E.

STATISTICIANS, INSTITUTE OF (1948), 36 Churchgate Street, Bury St, Edmunds, Suffolk.—*Hon. Sec.*, E. Hunter.

STEWART SOCIETY (1899), 48 Castle Street, Edinburgh.—*Hon. Sec.*, D. F. Stewart, W.S.

STRUCTURAL ENGINEERS, INSTITUTION OF (1908), 11 Upper Belgrave Street, S.W.1.—*Sec.*, C. D. Morgan, O.B.E.

STUDENT CHRISTIAN MOVEMENT OF GREAT BRITAIN AND IRELAND (1889), Wick Court, Wick, Bristol.

SURGEONS OF ENGLAND, ROYAL COLLEGE OF (1800), Lincoln's Inn Fields, W.C.2.—*Pres.*, Sir Rodney Smith; *Sec.*, R. S. Johnson-Gilbert, O.B.E.

SURGEONS OF EDINBURGH, ROYAL COLLEGE OF (1505), 18 Nicolson Street, Edinburgh.—*Sec.*, I. F. MacLaren, F.R.C.S.Ed.

SURGICAL AID SOCIETY, ROYAL (1862), 1 Dorset Buildings, Salisbury Square, E.C.4.—*Sec.*, Maj. R. F. Crichton, M.C.

SURGICAL TECHNOLOGISTS, BRITISH INSTITUTE OF, 21 Tothill Street, S.W.1.—*Sec.*, R. Nunn.

SURVEYORS, ROYAL INSTITUTION OF CHARTERED (1868), 29 Lincolns Inn Fields, W.C.2.—*Pres.*, (1976–77), C. P. Franklin, M.B.E.; *Sec.*, R. Steel.

SUSSEX CATTLE SOCIETY (1887), Station Road, Robertsbridge, E. Sussex.—*Sec.*, H. J. Hancorn.

SUTTON HOUSING TRUST (1901), Sutton Court, Tring, Herts.—*Gen. Manager*, R. G. Poulter.

SWEDENBORG SOCIETY (1810), 20–21 Bloomsbury Way, W.C.1.—*Sec.*, Madeline G. Waters.

TAIL WAGGERS' CLUB TRUST, 4–6 Cannon Street, E.C.4. *Sec.*, J. Minister.

TAVISTOCK INSTITUTE OF HUMAN RELATIONS, Tavistock Centre, Belsize Lane, N.W.3.—*Sec.*, S. G. Gray.

TAXATION, INSTITUTE OF (1930), 3 Grosvenor Crescent, S.W.1. *Sec.*, A. A. Arnold.

TEACHERS IN COMMERCE LTD., FACULTY OF, 141 Bedford Road, Sutton Coldfield, West Midlands. —*Sec.*, J. Snowdon.

TEACHERS OF DOMESTIC SCIENCE, ASSOCIATION OF, Hamilton House, Mabledon Place, W.C.1.—*Gen. Sec.*, Miss P. Hedley.

TEACHERS OF MATHEMATICS, ASSOCIATION OF.— c/o *Sec.*, Market Street Chambers, Nelson, Lancs.

TEACHERS OF SPEECH AND DRAMA, SOCIETY OF, St. Bride Institute, Fleet Street, E.C.4.—*Hon. Sec.*, Marguerite Turnbull, Abbot's Lodging, Marshside, Canterbury.

TEACHERS OF THE DEAF, BRITISH ASSOCIATION OF.— *Hon. Sec.*, A. Bates, Thomasson Memorial School, Devonshire Road, Bolton, Lancs.

TEACHERS' UNION, ULSTER (1919), 94 Malone Road, Belfast.—*Sec.*, B. K. Toms.

TELEPHONE USERS' ASSOCIATION (1965), 34 Grand Avenue, N.10.—*Sec.*, M. Elwes.

TELEVISION SOCIETY, ROYAL, Tavistock House East, Tavistock Square, W.C.1.—*Dir.* D. Gurton.

TEMPERANCE SOCIETIES:—
British National Temperance League (1834), Livesey-Clegg House, 44 Union Street, Sheffield, 1.—*Sec.*, Miss M. Daniel.
British Women's Temperance Association, S.C.U. (1876), 8 North Bank Street, Edinburgh 1.— *Hon. Sec.*, Mrs. G. M. McKinlay.
Church of England Council for Social Aid, Church House, Dean's Yard, S.W.1.—*Gen. Sec.*, Rev. E. W. F. Agar.
Division of Social Responsibility of the Methodist Church No. 1 Central Buildings, Matthew Parker St., S.W.1.—*Gen. Sec.*, Rev. J. H. Atkinson.

Independent Order of Rechabites, Salford Unity Friendly Society, London District (1870), No. 30, 18 Doughty Street, W.C.1.

Order of the Sons of Temperance, 21 Victoria Avenue, Harrogate.—*Sec.*, K. Unsworth.

Royal Naval Temperance Society (auxiliary of Royal Sailors' Rests), The Bus Station, South Street, Gosport, Hants.

Social Responsibility Dept., General Assembly of Unitarian and Free Christian Churches, Essex Hall, Essex Street, W.C.2.

Social Service Board of the Episcopal Church in Scotland (1919).—*Sec.*, I. D. Stuart, 21 Grosvenor Crescent, Edinburgh.

Temperance Council of the Christian Churches (1915) (incorporating the Overseas Temperance Council), Drayton House, Gordon Street, W.C.1.—*Gen. Sec.*, Rev. A. C. Davies.

Temperance Education Board (Ireland) (1918), c/o 98 Lisburn Road, Belfast.—*Sec.*, (vacant).

United Kingdom Band of Hope Union, Hope House, 45 Great Peter Street, S.W.1.—*Gen. Sec.*, A. Candler Page.

TERRITORIAL, AUXILIARY AND VOLUNTEER RESERVE ASSOCIATIONS, COUNCIL OF (1908), Centre Block, Duke of York's Headquarters, Chelsea, S.W.3.— *Sec.*, Maj. Gen. W. Bate, C.B., O.B.E.

TEXTILE INSTITUTE (1910), 10 Blackfriars Street, Manchester.—*Gen. Sec.*, R. G. Denyer.

THEATRE RESEARCH, SOCIETY FOR (1948).—*Hon. Secs.*, Miss K. M. Barker, J. Reading, 14 Woronzow Road, N.W.8.

THEATRICAL FUND ASSOCIATION, ROYAL GENERAL (1839), 11 Garrick Street, W.C.2.—*Sec.*, G. S. Hall.

THEATRICAL LADIES' GUILD OF CHARITY (1892), Gloucester House, 19 Charing Cross Road, W.C.2.—*Sec.*, Mrs. G. Hammill.

THEOSOPHICAL SOCIETY IN ENGLAND (1875), 50 Gloucester Place, W.1.—*Gen. Sec.*, Miss I. H. Hoskins, M.A.

THISTLE FOUNDATION, THE (1945), 22 Charlotte Square, Edinburgh 2.—*Secs.*, Graham, Smart and Annan, Chartered Accountants.

THORACIC SOCIETY, THE.—*Hon. Sec.*, J. E. Cotes, D.M., M.R.C., Pneumoconiosis Unit, Llandough Hospital, Penarth, South Glamorgan.

TIBET SOCIETY OF THE UNITED KINGDOM AND TIBET RELIEF FUND (1959), 46 Belgrave Square, S.W.1.

TIN RESEARCH INSTITUTE (1932), Fraser Road, Perivale, Greenford, Middlesex.—*Dir.*, D. A. Robins, Ph.D.

TOC H (TALBOT HOUSE) (1915), *Headquarters*, 1 Forest Close, Wendover, Bucks.—*Gen. Sec.*, G. A. Francis.

TOWN AND COUNTRY PLANNING ASSOCIATION, 17 Carlton House Terrace, S.W.1.—*Dir.*, D. Hall.

TOWN PLANNING INSTITUTE, ROYAL (1914), 26 Portland Place, W.1.

TOWNSWOMEN'S GUILDS, NATIONAL UNION OF (1929), 2 Cromwell Place, S.W.7.—*Nat. Sec.*, Mrs. M. Erskine-Wyse.

TRADE MARK AGENTS, INSTITUTE OF (1934), 69 Cannon Street, E.C.4.—*Sec.*, R. A. Marshall.

TRADE, NATIONAL CHAMBER OF (1897), Enterprise House, Henley-on-Thames, Oxon.—*Dir. Gen.*, L. E. S. Seeney.

TRADES UNION CONGRESS (T.U.C.).—*See* p. 1117.

TRADING STANDARDS ADMINISTRATION, INSTITUTE OF—*Admin. Officer*, J. T. Fisher, Estate House, 319D London Road, Hadleigh, Benfleet, Essex.

TRAFFIC ADMINISTRATION, INSTITUTE OF (1944), 8 Cumberland Place, Southampton.—*National Sec.*, G. C. McCarthy.

TRANSPORT, CHARTERED INSTITUTE OF (1919), 80 Portland Place, W.1.—*Dir.-Gen.* Brig. D. N. Locke, O.B.E.

TRAVEL AGENTS, ASSOCIATION OF BRITISH (1950), 53–54 Newman Street, W.1.—*Chief Exec.*, M. A. Elton.

TROPICAL MEDICINE AND HYGIENE, ROYAL SOCIETY OF (1907), Manson House, 26 Portland Place, W.1.—*Pres.*, C. E. Gordon Smith, C.B., M.D., F.R.C.P., *Sec.*, Mrs. B. Harrison.

TRUSTEE SAVINGS BANKS CENTRAL BOARD (1976), 3 Gracechurch Street, E.C.3.—*Chief Gen. Man.*, T. Bryans, M.B.E.

UFAW (Universities Federation for Animal Welfare) (1926), 6 Hamilton Close, Potters Bar, Herts.—*Sec.*, Mrs. C. Brockhurst.

ULSTER SOCIETY IN LONDON, THE, 11 Berkeley Street, W.1.—*Pres.*, The Lord Rathcavan, P.C.; *Hon. Sec.*, Miss P. Bell.

UNIT TRUST ASSOCIATION (1959), Park House, 16 Finsbury Circus, E.C.2.—*Sec.*, W. J. Burnett.

UNITED COMMERICAL TRAVELLERS' ASSOCIATION OF GREAT BRITAIN AND IRELAND (U.K.C.T.A.), (1883), Bexton Lane, Knutsford, Cheshire.—*Gen. Sec.*, R. Tomlinson.

UNITED NATIONS ASSOCIATION OF GREAT BRITAIN AND NORTHERN IRELAND (1945), 93 Albert Embankment, S.E.1.—*Dir.*, Rev. D. Harding.

UNITED SOCIETY FOR CHRISTIAN LITERATURE, THE, Luke House, Farnham Road, Guildford, Surrey. —*Gen. Sec.*, Rev. A. Gilmore; *Gen. Manager*, M. E. Foxell.

UNITED SYNAGOGUE (1870).—*Pres.*, A. Woolf.— *Sec.*, N. Rubin, Woburn House, Upper Woburn Place, W.C.1.

UNIVERSITIES CENTRAL COUNCIL ON ADMISSIONS (1961), P.O. Box 28, Cheltenham, Glos.—*Sec.*, L. R. Kay.

UNIVERSITY TEACHERS, ASSOCIATION OF (1919), United House, 1 Pembridge Road, W.11.—*Sec.* L. J. Sapper.

UNIVERSITY WOMEN, BRITISH FEDERATION OF (1907), Crosby Hall, Cheyne Walk, S.W.3.— *Sec.*, Mrs. E. Bianco, LL.B.

VALUERS AND AUCTIONEERS, INCORPORATED SOCIETY OF, 3 Cadogan Gate, S.W.1.—*Sec.*, (vacant).

VEGETARIAN SOCIETY (U.K.) LTD., Parkdale, Dunham Road, Altrincham, Cheshire.

VENEREAL DISEASES, MEDICAL SOCIETY FOR THE STUDY OF, 11 Chandos Street, W.1.—*Hon. Sec.*, C. B. S. Schofield, M.D., F.R.C.P., The Clinic, 67 Black Street, Glasgow.

VICE-CHANCELLORS AND PRINCIPALS OF THE UNIVERSITIES OF THE UNITED KINGDOM, COMMITTEE OF, 29 Tavistock Square, W.C.1.—*Chairman*, Sir John Habakkuk.

VICTORIA INSTITUTE (Philosophical Society of Great Britain).—*Pres.*, Sir Norman Anderson, O.B.E., Q.C., F.B.A.; *Asst. Sec.*, B. H. T. Weller, 130 Wood Street, E.C.2.

VICTORIA LEAGUE FOR COMMONWEALTH FRIENDSHIP (1901), 18 Northumberland Avenue, W.C.2. —*Sec.*, Mrs. C. Barnett, O.B.E.

VICTORIAN SOCIETY (1958), 1 Priory Gardens, Bedford Park, W.4.—*Sec.*, Mrs. E. Fawcett, M.B.E.

VICTORY (SERVICES) ASSOCIATION LTD. AND CLUB, THE, 63–79 Seymour Street, W.2.—*Sec.*, D. G. Stovey.

VIKING SOCIETY FOR NORTHERN RESEARCH, University College, Gower Street, W.C.1.—*Hon. Secs.*, Prof. G. Turville-Petre, M.A., B.Litt.; Prof. P. G. Foote, M.A.

VITREOUS ENAMELLERS, INSTITUTE OF, Ripley, Derby.—*Sec.*, J. D. Gardom.

VOLUNTARY SERVICE OVERSEAS (1958), 14 Bishop's Bridge Road, W.2.—*Dir.*, D. W. A. Collett.

WAR BLINDED, SCOTTISH NATIONAL INSTITUTION FOR THE. Workshops at Edinburgh, Glasgow and Linburn. *Appeals Director*, Maj. D. F.

Callander, M.C., P.O. Box 304, 38 Albany Street, Edinburgh.

WATER ENGINEERS AND SCIENTISTS, INSTITUTION OF, 6–8 Sackville Street, W.1.—*Pres.* (1976–77), L. R. Bays; *Sec.*, J. P. Banbury, M.B.E.

WELDING INSTITUTE, THE, Abington Hall, Cambridge and 54 Princes Gate, S.W.7.—*Dir.-Gen.*, Dr. R. Weck, C.B.E., F.R.S.

WELFARE OFFICERS, INSTITUTE OF (1945), Red Cross House, 73 Penrhyn Road, Kingston upon Thames, Surrey.—*Gen. Sec.*, Miss B. M. Langridge.

WELLCOME TRUST (1936), 1 Park Square West, N.W.1.—*Dir.*, P. O. Williams, M.B., F.R.C.P.

WELLS (H. G.) SOCIETY, 24 Wellin Lane, Edwalton, Nottingham.—*Sec.*, J. R. Hammond.

WELSH JOINT EDUCATION COMMITTEE (1948), 245 Western Avenue, Cardiff.—*Sec.*, D. A. Davies.

WESLEY HISTORICAL SOCIETY (1893).—*Gen. Sec.*, Rev. T. Shaw, 39 Fair Street, St. Columb Major, Cornwall.

WEST AFRICA COMMITTEE (1956), Chronicle House, 72–78 Fleet Street, E.C.4.—*Secs.*, W. G. Syer, C.V.O., C.B.E.; Group Capt. P. R. Magrath.

WEST INDIA COMMITTEE (1750), 18 Grosvenor Street, W.1.—*Sec.*, Lt.-Col. M. R. Robinson, D.S.O., O.B.E.

WEST LONDON MISSION (1887), Kingsway Hall, W.C.2.—*Supt.*, Rev. The Lord Soper, M.A., Ph.D.

WIDOWS, SOCIETY FOR THE RELIEF OF DISTRESSED (1823) (residing within five miles of Charing Cross and applying within two months of widowhood), 175 Tower Bridge Road, S.E.1.— *Sec.*, W. N. Barr.

WILDLIFE ARTISTS, SOCIETY OF (1962), 17 Carlton House Terrace, S.W.1.—*Pres.*, Sir Peter Scott, C.B.E., D.F.C.; *Sec.*, M. B. Bradshaw.

WINE AND SPIRIT ASSOCIATION OF GREAT BRITAIN (INC), Five King's House, Kennet Wharf Lane, Upper Thames Street, E.C.4.—*Dir.*, R. H. Insoll, E.R.D.

WOMEN ARTISTS, SOCIETY OF (1855), 17 Carlton House Terrace, S.W.1.—*Sec.*, M. B. Bradshaw.

WOMEN, NATIONAL ADVISORY CENTRE ON CAREERS FOR (formerly Women's Employment Federation) (1933), 251 Brompton Road, S.W.3.—*Dir.*, Miss K. M. Menon.

WOMEN PILOTS' ASSOCIATION, BRITISH (1955), c/o P.O. Box 13, British Airways Victoria Terminal, S.W.1.

WOMEN, SOCIETY FOR PROMOTING THE TRAINING OF (1859) (Women's Loan Training Fund) The Dean Cottages, Hedgerley, Bucks.—*Sec.*, Mrs. W. M. Golding.

WOMEN'S ENGINEERING SOCIETY (1920), 25 Foubert's Place, W.1.—*Sec.*, Miss T. Davison.

WOMEN'S HOLIDAY FUND (1895), 125 Wilton Road, S.W.1.—*Sec.*, Mrs. U. Muirhead.

WOMEN'S INSTITUTES, NATIONAL FEDERATION OF (1915), 39 Eccleston Street, S.W.1.—*Gen. Sec.*, Mrs. A. Ballard, M.A.

WOMEN'S INTERNATIONAL LEAGUE FOR PEACE AND FREEDOM (1915), British Section, 29 Great James Street, W.C.1.—*Sec.*, Miss R. Adams.

WOMEN'S LIBERAL FEDERATION, 42 King Street, Covent Garden, W.C.2.—*Pres.*, Mrs. M. Budd; *Sec.*, Mrs. S. Bruce.

WOMEN'S NATIONAL CANCER CONTROL CAMPAIGN, 1 South Audley Street, W.1.—*Senior Administrator*, Mrs. M. K. Cooper.

WOMEN'S PROTESTANT UNION (INC.), WORLD PROTESTANT UNION, and THE SENTINELS' UNION, Sentinels Court, 130 South Coast Road, Peacehaven, Newhaven, Sussex.

WOMEN'S ROYAL NAVAL SERVICE BENEVOLENT TRUST, 2 Lower Sloane Street, S.W.1.

WOMEN'S ROYAL VOLUNTARY SERVICE (WRVS) (1938), 17 Old Park Lane, W.1.

WOMEN'S TRANSPORT SERVICE (FANY) (1907), Duke of York's H.Q., Chelsea, S.W.3.—*Corps Commander*, Mrs. S. Y. Parkinson.

WOOD PRESERVING ASSOCIATION, BRITISH, 62 Oxford Street, W.1.—*Dir.*, J. Bick.

WORCESTERSHIRE ASSOCIATION (1926).—*Hon. Sec.*, S. Driver White, 5 Deansway, Worcester.

WORK STUDY, ORGANIZATION AND METHODS, INSTITUTE OF PRACTITIONERS IN (1975), 9–10 River Front, Enfield, Middx.—*Dir.*, *and Gen. Sec.*, E. A. King.

WORKERS' EDUCATIONAL ASSOCIATION, Temple House, 9 Upper Berkeley Street, W.1.—*Gen. Sec.*, R. J. Jefferies.

WORKS AND HIGHWAYS TECHNICIAN ENGINEERS, INSTITUTION OF, 26 Bloomsbury Way, W.C.1.—*Gen. Sec. and Registrar*, S. H. Crowle.

WORKS MANAGERS, INSTITUTION OF, 45 Cardiff Road, Luton, Beds.

WORLD CONGRESS OF FAITHS (1936), Younghusband House, 23 Norfolk Square, W.2.

WORLD EDUCATION FELLOWSHIP (1921), *International Headquarters*, 33 Kinnaird Avenue, W.4.

WORLD ENERGY CONFERENCE (1924). *Central Office*, 34 St. James's Street, S.W.1.—*Sec.-Gen.*, *International Executive Council*, E. Ruttley.

WORLD SHIP SOCIETY (1946).—*Sec.*, S. J. F. Miller, 35 Wickham Way, Haywards Heath, Sussex.

WRITERS TO H.M. SIGNET, SOCIETY OF, PARLIAMENT Square, Edinburgh.—*Deputy Keeper of the Signet*, R. K. Will; *Sub-Keeper and Clerk*, P. C. Millar.

YEOMANRY BENEFIT FUND, 206 Brompton Road, S.W.3.—*Sec.*, Mrs. M. L. Bernard, O.B.E.

YORKSHIRE AGRICULTURAL SOCIETY (1837), Great Yorks Showground, Hookstone Oval, Harrogate.—*Sec.-Gen.*, R. G. G. English.

YORKSHIRE FIELD STUDIES LTD.—*Gen. Sec.*, D. H. Smith, Westland, Westfields, Kirbymoorside, York.

YORKSHIREMEN IN LONDON, SOCIETY OF (1899), AND THE YORKSHIRE SOCIETY (1812), 200 High Street, Brentford, Middx.—*Sec.*, G. G. Prince.

YOUNG MEN'S CHRISTIAN ASSOCIATION, *National Council*, 640 Forest Road, E.17.—*Gen. Sec.*, S. Charlesworth.

YOUNG WOMEN'S CHRISTIAN ASSOCIATION (1855), *National Headquarters*, 2 Weymouth Street, W.1.—*Nat. Gen. Sec.*, Miss B. Cowderoy.

YOUTH CLUBS, NATIONAL ASSOCIATION OF, P.O. Box 1 Blackburn House, Bond Gate, Nuneaton, Warwicks. (London Centre—30 Devonshire St., W.1.)—*Chief Exec. Officer*, J. M. Butterfield.

YOUTH CLUBS, NORTHERN IRELAND ASSOCIATION OF, Hampton, Glenmachan Road, Belfast.—*Dir.*, G. Johnston.

YOUTH HOSTELS ASSOCIATION (ENGLAND AND WALES) (1930), *National Office*, Trevelyan House, St. Albans, Herts.—*Sec.*, H. B. Livingstone.

YOUTH HOSTELS ASSOCIATION (SCOTTISH) (1931), *National Office*, 7 Glebe Crescent, Stirling.

YOUTH HOSTELS ASSOCIATION OF NORTHERN IRELAND LTD. (1931), 93 Dublin Road, Belfast.—*Hon. Sec.*, E. R. Henderson.

ZOOLOGICAL SOCIETY OF LONDON, Regent's Park, N.W.1.—*Sec.*, Prof. Lord Zuckerman, O.M., K.C.B., D.SC., F.R.S. Attendances (1975), Regent's Park, 1,795,000, and Whipsnade Park, 453,000.

ZOOLOGICAL SOCIETY OF SCOTLAND, ROYAL, Scottish National Zoological Park, Murrayfield, Edinburgh 12.—*Dir.*, R. J. Wheater.

THE CIVIC TRUST

17 Carlton House Terrace, S.W.1
[01-930 0914]

Founded in 1957 with the object of improving the appearance of town and country. The Trust is a recognized charity, supported by voluntary contributions. Four Associate Trusts are linked with it in Scotland, Wales, the North West and the North East.

The Trust gives support and advice to over 1,200 local civic and amenity societies throughout Britain. It has initiated hundreds of schemes to brighten and tidy up drab streets. It has promoted new techniques for moving semi-mature trees as part of a wider campaign to plant more trees. It stimulates voluntary action to remove eyesores which mar town and countryside. It makes awards annually for good development of all kinds. Its proposals led to the creation of the Lee Valley Regional Park Authority. It was closely associated with the drafting of the Civic Amenities Act 1967 and of the Town and Country Amenities Act 1974. It makes available on hire films, photographs, slides and exhibitions. By conferences, projects and reports, it focuses attention on major issues in town planning and architecture. The Trust also provided the central Secretariat for the United Kingdom campaign for European Architectural Heritage Year, 1975.

LOCAL ARCHAEOLOGICAL SOCIETIES

England and Wales

Anglesey.—ANGLESEY ANTIQUARIAN SOCIETY. *Hon. Sec.*, D. O. Jones, 22 Lôn Ganol, Menai Bridge, Anglesey.

Bedfordshire.—SOUTH BEDFORDSHIRE ARCHÆOLOGICAL SOCIETY. *Hon. Sec.*, D. H. Kennett, 55 Mount Grace Road, Stopsley, Luton.

Berkshire.—BERKSHIRE ARCHÆOLOGICAL SOCIETY. *Hon. Sec.*, L. J. Over, 42 Laburnam Road, Maidenhead, Berks.

Berkshire.—NEWBURY DISTRICT FIELD CLUB, Donnington Dene, Newbury. *Hon. Sec.*, Mrs. M. E. Kaines-Thomas, D.LIT., F.S.A.

Buckinghamshire.—BUCKS ARCHÆOLOGICAL SOCIETY. *Hon. Sec.*, E. Viney, County Museum, Church Street, Aylesbury, Bucks.

Cambridgeshire. — CAMBRIDGE ANTIQUARIAN SOCIETY. *Sec.*, Miss J. Liversidge, 20 Manor Court, Grange Road, Cambridge.

Cheshire.—CHESTER ARCHÆOLOGICAL SOCIETY, Grosvenor Museum, Chester.—*Hon. Sec.*, J. T. Driver, 25 Abbot's Grange, Chester. *See also under Lancashire.*

Cornwall.—ROYAL INSTITUTION OF CORNWALL, County Museum and Art Gallery, Truro. *Hon. Sec.*, A. J. Lyne.

Cumberland and Westmorland.—CUMBERLAND AND WESTMORLAND ANTIQUARIAN AND ARCHÆOLOGICAL SOCIETY. *Hon. Sec.*, Mrs. J. Cherry, 68 Santon Way, Seascale, Cumbria.

Derbyshire.—DERBYSHIRE ARCHÆOLOGICAL SOCIETY, 35 St. Mary's Gate, Derby. *Hon. Sec.*, M. A. B. Mallender.

Devonshire.—DEVON ARCHÆOLOGICAL SOCIETY. Hon. Sec., Miss S. M. Pearce, City Museum, Queen Street, Exeter.

Dorset.—DORSET NATURAL HISTORY AND ARCHÆOLOGICAL SOCIETY, Dorset County Museum, Dorchester. *Curator and Sec.*, R. N. R. Peers.

Durham. — DURHAM AND NORTHUMBERLAND ARCHITECTURAL AND ARCHÆOLOGICAL SOCIETY, *Hon Secs.*, P. Clack, Dept. of Archaeology, Saddler Street, Durham; J. T. Lang, 4 Heathways, High Shincliffe, Durham.

SUNDERLAND ANTIQUARIAN SOCIETY.—*Hon. Sec.*, J. R. Salkeld, 72 The Broadway, Grindon Sunderland.

Dyfed.—CEREDIGION ANTIQUARIAN SOCIETY.—*Hon. Sec.*, D. M. Jones, 26 Alban Square, Aberaeron.

Essex.—ESSEX ARCHÆOLOGICAL SOCIETY, Hollytrees Museum, High Street, Colchester. *Hon. Sec.*, J. E. Sellers.

Gloucestershire.—BRISTOL AND GLOUCESTERSHIRE ARCHÆOLOGICAL SOCIETY, 9 Pembroke Road, Bristol 8. *Hon. Sec.*, Miss E. Ralph.

Hampshire.—HAMPSHIRE FIELD CLUB AND ARCHÆOLOGICAL SOCIETY, *Hon. Sec.*, Miss E. R. Lewis, City Museum, The Square, Winchester, Hants.

Herefordshire.—WOOLHOPE NATURALISTS' FIELD CLUB. *Hon. Sec.*, c/o The Hereford Library, Broad Street, Hereford.

Hertfordshire. — EAST HERTFORDSHIRE ARCHÆOLOGICAL SOCIETY. *Hon. Sec.*, C. L. Lee, 107 Queen's Road, Hertford.

ST. ALBANS AND HERTFORDSHIRE ARCHITECTURAL AND ARCHÆOLOGICAL SOCIETY.—*Hon. Sec.*, G. L. Wilde, 5 Townsend Drive, St. Albans.

Kent.—KENT ARCHÆOLOGICAL SOCIETY. *Gen. Sec.*, c/o The Museum, Maidstone.

Lancashire.—HISTORIC SOCIETY OF LANCASHIRE AND CHESHIRE.—*Hon. Sec.*, P. J. Andrews, 15 Woodley Field, Penketh, Warrington.

Leicestershire.—LEICESTERSHIRE ARCHÆOLOGICAL AND HISTORICAL SOCIETY, The Guildhall, Guildhall Lane, Leicester. *Hon. Sec.*, D. Tomkins.

London and Middlesex.—CITY OF LONDON ARCHAEOLOGICAL SOCIETY.—*Hon. Sec.*, Miss A. Gallagher, 41 Honley Road, S.E.6.

LONDON AND MIDDLESEX ARCHAEOLOGICAL SOCIETY, Bishopsgate Institute, 230 Bishopsgate, E.C.2.—*Hon. Sec.*, J. Clark.

Norfolk.—NORFOLK AND NORWICH ARCHÆOLOGICAL SOCIETY. *Hon. Gen. Sec.*, I. Cresswell, F.S.A., The Old Rectory, Shelton, Norwich.

Northumberland.—SOCIETY OF ANTIQUARIES OF NEWCASTLE UPON TYNE. *Admin. Sec.*, Dr. C. M. Fraser, c/o Department of Adult Education, University of Newcastle upon Tyne.

Nottinghamshire.—THOROTON SOCIETY OF NOTTINGHAMSHIRE, Bromley House, Angel Row, Nottingham. *Hon. Sec.*, M. G. Dobbin.

Oxfordshire.—OXFORDSHIRE ARCHITECTURAL AND HISTORICAL SOCIETY.—*Hon. Sec.*, Mrs. J. Young, c/o Ashmolean Museum, Oxford.

Powys: Montgomery District; POWYSLAND CLUB. *Hon. Sec.*, W. G. J. Hughes, County Branch Library, Red Bank, Welshpool, Powys.

Radnor District; RADNORSHIRE SOCIETY. *Hon. Secs.*, E. V. Howells, The White House, Cefnllys Lane, Llandrindod Wells; C. W. Newman, Wynberg, Dyffryn Road, Llandrindod Wells.

Somerset.—SOMERSET ARCHÆOLOGICAL AND NATURAL HISTORY SOCIETY, Taunton Castle, Taunton. *Hon. Sec.*, Dr. P. C. Davey.

Staffordshire.—NORTH STAFFORDSHIRE FIELD CLUB, *Hon. Sec.*, R. A. Tribbeck, Dept. of Chemistry, North Staffordshire Polytechnic, Stoke-on-Trent.

CITY OF STOKE-ON-TRENT MUSEUM ARCHÆOLOGICAL SOCIETY, City Museum, Stoke-on-Trent. *Chairman*, A. R. Mountford.

SOUTH STAFFORDSHIRE ARCHÆOLOGICAL AND HISTORICAL SOCIETY. *Hon. Sec.*, Dr. J. G. L. Cole, 11 Bracebridge Road, Sutton Coldfield, West Midlands.

Suffolk.—SUFFOLK INSTITUTE OF ARCHÆOLOGY.—*Hon. Sec.*, D. G. Penrose, Suffolk Record Office, County Hall, Ipswich.

Surrey.—SURREY ARCHÆOLOGICAL SOCIETY, Castle Arch, Guildford.—*Hon. Sec.*, Dr. G. P. Moss.

Sussex.—SUSSEX ARCHÆOLOGICAL SOCIETY, Barbican House, High Street, Lewes.

Warwickshire.—BIRMINGHAM AND WARWICKSHIRE ARCHÆOLOGICAL SOCIETY, Birmingham and Midland Institute, Margaret Street, Birmingham 3.—*Hon. Sec.*, Mrs. R. Taylor.

Wight.—ISLE OF WIGHT NATURAL HISTORY AND ARCHAEOLOGICAL SOCIETY, 66 Carisbrooke Road, Newport.—*Sec.*, Miss H. Blount.

Wiltshire. — WILTSHIRE ARCHÆOLOGICAL AND NATURAL HISTORY SOCIETY, The Museum, 41 Long Street, Devizes. *Sec.*, C. P. Barber.

Worcestershire.—WORCESTERSHIRE ARCHÆOLOGICAL SOCIETY.—*Hon. Sec.*, R. F. Panton, Birchdale, 4 Orchard Road, Gt. Malvern.

Yorkshire.—HUNTER ARCHÆOLOGICAL SOCIETY. *Hon. Sec.*, F. L. Preston, Grove Cottage, Moorgate Grove, Rotherham.

YORKSHIRE ARCHÆOLOGICAL SOCIETY.—*Hon. Sec.*, P. B. Davidson, Claremont, 23 Clarendon Road, Leeds.

HALIFAX ANTIQUARIAN SOCIETY. *Hon. Sec.*, R. L. Sunderland, 37 Lombard Street, King Cross, Halifax.

THORESBY SOCIETY, Claremont, 23 Clarendon Road, Leeds 2.—*Hon. Sec.*, D. Keighley.

Isle of Man and Channel Islands

ISLE OF MAN NATURAL HISTORY AND ANTIQUARIAN SOCIETY, c/o The Manx Museum, Douglas.

SOCIETE JERSIAISE, The Jersey Museum, Pier Road, St. Helier.—*Hon. Sec.*, Mrs. W. E. Macready.

Scotland

AYRSHIRE ARCHÆOLOGICAL AND NATURAL HISTORY SOCIETY. Carnegie Library, Ayr.—*Hon. Sec.*, R. Waite, Ph.D., 74 Doonfoot Road, Ayr.

DUMFRIESSHIRE AND GALLOWAY NATURAL HISTORY AND ANTIQUARIAN SOCIETY. *Hon. Sec.*, Mrs. E. Adamson, 39 Westerlea, Roberts Crescent, Dumfries.

GLASGOW ARCHÆOLOGICAL SOCIETY. *Hon. Secs.*, Miss H. C. Adamson, Art Gallery and Museum, Glasgow; E. J. Talbot, Dept. of Archæology, University of Glasgow.

HAWICK ARCHÆOLOGICAL SOCIETY. *Hon. Sec.*, T. I. Storie, 6 Park Terrace, Hawick.

SHETLAND ARCHÆOLOGICAL AND HISTORICAL SOCIETY, County Museum, Lerwick.—*Pres.*, T. Henderson.

EMPLOYERS' AND TRADE ASSOCIATIONS

AEROSPACE COMPANIES, SOCIETY OF BRITISH (1916), 29 King Street, S.W.1.—*Dir.*, Vice-Adm. Sir Richard Smeeton, K.C.B., M.B.E.

BAKERS, CONFECTIONERS AND CATERERS, NATIONAL ASSOCIATION OF MASTER, Queen's House, Holly Road, Twickenham, Middx.—*Dir.*, M. F. Zimmerman.

BAKERS, THE FEDERATION OF, 20 Bedford Square, W.C.1.

BOOT TRADES ASSOCIATION, LTD., ST. CRISPINS, St. Crispin's House, Desborough, nr. Kettering, Northants.—*Gen. Sec.*, Mrs. P. J. Copley.

BRUSH MANUFACTURERS' ASSOCIATION, BRITISH, 4 Southampton Row, W.C.1.—*Sec.*, R. F. Knox, M.B.E.

BUILDING AND ALLIED HARDWARE MANUFACTURERS FEDERATION, NATIONAL, 5 Greenfield Crescent, Edgbaston, Birmingham 15.—*Dir. and Sec.*, E. C. Skelding.

BUILDING TRADES EMPLOYERS, NATIONAL FEDERATION OF (1878), 82 New Cavendish Street, W.1. —*Sec.*, H. L. Foster.

CEMENT MAKERS' FEDERATION, Terminal House, 52 Grosvenor Gardens, S.W.1.—*Dir.*, Rear Adm. C. K. T. Wheen, C.B.

CERAMIC MANUFACTURERS' FEDERATION, BRITISH, Federation House, Station Road, Stoke-on-Trent.—*Sec.*, D. Turner, M.B.E.

CHEMICAL INDUSTRIES ASSOCIATION LTD. (1966), Alembic House, 93 Albert Embankment, S.E.1.— *Dir.-Gen.*, M. E. Trowbridge.

CINEMATOGRAPH EXHIBITORS' ASSOCIATION OF GREAT BRITAIN AND IRELAND, 22–25 Dean Street, W.1.—*Gen. Sec.*, R. S. Camplin.

CIVIL ENGINEERING CONTRACTORS, FEDERATION OF, Romney House, Tufton Street, S.W.1.—*Dir.*, D. V. Gaulter.

CLOTHING MANUFACTURERS' FEDERATION OF GREAT BRITAIN LTD., 14–16 Cockspur Street, S.W.1.— *Dir.*, M. K. Reid, O.B.E.

COAL MERCHANTS' FEDERATION OF GREAT BRITAIN, Victoria House, Southampton Row, W.C.1.— *Dir.*, J. H. Thomas.

COCOA, CHOCOLATE AND CONFECTIONERY MANUFACTURERS' INDUSTRIAL GROUP, 11 Green Street, W.1.—*Sec.*, E. T. Beauchamp.

COLD STORAGE FEDERATION, NATIONAL, 272 London Road, Wallington, Surrey.—*Sec.*, D. T. Lee.

COOPERAGE FEDERATION, NATIONAL, 27 Queen Charlotte Street, Leith, Edinburgh 6.—*Sec.*, J. Steven.

CUTLERY AND SILVERWARE ASSOCIATION, Light Trades House, Melbourne Avenue, Sheffield, 10.—*Sec.*, Miss M. Arnold, M.B.E.

CYCLE AND MOTOR CYCLE TRADERS, NATIONAL ASSOCIATION OF, 31A High Street, Tunbridge Wells, Kent.—*Gen. Sec.*, J. E. F. Davies.

DAIRY TRADE FEDERATION, 20 Eastbourne Terrace, W.2.—*Dir.-Gen.*, J. R. Owens.

DECORATORS ASSOCIATION, BRITISH, 6 Haywra Street, Harrogate, N. Yorks.—*Dir.*, K. A. C. Blease.

DRAPERS' CHAMBER OF TRADE, North Bar, Banbury, Oxfordshire.—*Chief Exec.*, S. D. Russell.

ELECTRICAL AND ALLIED MANUFACTURERS ASSOCIATION, BRITISH (1905), 8 Leicester Street, W.C.2. —*Chief Executive*, A. K. Edwards.

ELECTRICAL CONTRACTORS' ASSOCIATION, 32–34 Palace Court, W.2.—*Dir.* B. E. Gray.

ENGINEERING EMPLOYERS' FEDERATION, Broadway House, Tothill Street, S.W.1.—*Sec.*, H. K. Mitchell.

FARMERS' UNION, NATIONAL (1908), Agriculture House, Knightsbridge, S.W.1.—*Dir. Gen.*, G. H. B. Cattell.

FISH FRIERS, NATIONAL FEDERATION OF, 289 Dewsbury Road, Leeds 11.—*Gen. Sec.*, P. Worthington.

FISHMONGERS, NATIONAL FEDERATION OF, 21 John Adam Street, W.C.2.—*Sec.*, R. W. Stote.

FLAT GLASS ASSOCIATION, THE, 6 Mount Row, W.1.—*Sec.*, M. G. Stretton-Hill.

FOOD MANUFACTURERS FEDERATION, 1–2 Castle Lane, Buckingham Gate, S.W.1.—*Gen. Sec.*, H. R. Evans.

FOOD AND DRINK, NATIONAL FEDERATION OF (incorp. National Grocers' Federation and the National Off-Licence Federation), 17 Farnborough Street, Farnborough, Hants.—*Chief Exec.*, L. E. Reeves-Smith.

FOOTWEAR MANUFACTURERS FEDERATION, BRITISH, Royalty House, 72 Dean Street, W.1.—*Dir. Gen.*, M. O. Feilden.

FRESH MEAT WHOLESALERS, FEDERATION OF, Columbia House, 69 Aldwych, W.C.2.

FURNISHERS, NATIONAL ASSOCIATION OF RETAIL, 3 Berners Street, W.1.—*Dir.*, H. L. Calder-Jones, O.B.E.

GLASS MANUFACTURERS FEDERATION, 19 Portland Place, W.1.—*Dir.*, O. C. T. R. Normandale.

GRAIN, SEED, FEED AND AGRICULTURAL MERCHANTS, BRITISH ASSOCIATION OF, 3 Whitehall Court, S.W.1.—*Sec.*, H. S. Leech.

GROCERS AND PROVISION MERCHANTS, NATIONAL FEDERATION OF WHOLESALE, 18 Fleet Street, E.C.4.—*Sec.*, D. Ellam.

HYDRAULIC EQUIPMENT MANUFACTURERS LTD., ASSOCIATION OF (1959), 54 Warwick Square, S.W.1.—*Dir.*, J. F. Nosworthy.

JEWELLERY AND GIFTWARE FEDERATION LIMITED, BRITISH, St. Dunstan's House, Carey Lane, E.C.2. —*Dir.-Gen.*, S. R. Simmons.

JUTE SPINNERS AND MANUFACTURERS ASSOCIATION, Kandahar House, 71 Meadowside, Dundee.— *Dir.*, D. A. Borrie.

LAUNDERERS AND CLEANERS, ASSOCIATION OF BRITISH, LTD., Lancaster Gate House, 319 Pinner Road, Harrow, Middlesex.—*Dir.*, E. W. Swetman, O.B.E.

LONDON CLEARING BANK EMPLOYERS, FEDERATION OF, 10 Lombard Street, E.C.3.—*Dir. and Sec.*, E. S. Richards.

MALTSTERS' ASSOCIATION OF GREAT BRITAIN, Prince Rupert House, 64 Queen Street, E.C.4.—*Sec.*, Group Capt. V. Fairfield, O.B.E.

MEAT TRADERS, NATIONAL FEDERATION OF, 29 Linkfield Lane, Redhill, Surrey.

MENSWEAR ASSOCIATION OF BRITAIN LTD., Palladium House, 1–4 Argyll Street, W.1.—*Dir.*, K. E. Smith.

MILLERS, NATIONAL ASSOCIATION OF BRITISH AND IRISH, LTD. (1878), 21 Arlington Street, S.W.1.— *Sec.*, E. T. J. Hurle.

MINES OF GREAT BRITAIN, FEDERATION OF SMALL, 9 Winchester Road, Billinge, Wigan, Lancs.— *Chairman and Sec.*, J. Wainwright.

MOTOR AGENTS' ASSOCIATION, LTD., 201 Great Portland Street, W.1.—*Dir.-Gen.*, A. M. Dix.

MOTOR MANUFACTURERS AND TRADERS, SOCIETY OF, LTD. (1902), Forbes House, Halkin Street, S.W.1.—*Sec.*, M. G. Feather.

PAINTMAKERS ASSOCIATION OF GREAT BRITAIN LIMITED, Prudential House, Wellesley Road, Croydon, Surrey.—*Dir.*, M. J. Levete.

PAPER AND BOARD INDUSTRY FEDERATION, BRITISH, (Industrial Relations Division), 1 Clements Inn, W.C.2.—*Dir.*, W. J. Bartlett.

PAPER MERCHANTS, NATIONAL ASSOCIATION OF, 35 New Bridge Street, E.C.4.—*Dir.*, S. R. W. Bailey.

PLUMBING, HEATING AND MECHANICAL SERVICES CONTRACTORS NATIONAL ASSOCIATION OF, 6 Gate Street, W.C.2.—*Sec.*, C. D. Webster.

PORT EMPLOYERS, NATIONAL ASSOCIATION OF, 3/5 Queen Square, W.C.1.—*Gen. Manager*, E. Bainbridge.

PRECAST CONCRETE FEDERATION, BRITISH, 60 Charles Street, Leicester.—*Dir.-Gen.*, J. P. Metcalfe.

PRINTING INDUSTRIES FEDERATION, BRITISH, 11 Bedford Row, W.C.1.—*Dir.*, H. W. Kendall.

RADIO, ELECTRICAL AND TELEVISION RETAILERS ASSOCIATION, 100 St. Martin's Lane, W.C.2.—*Dir.*, R. T. Edom.

READY MIXED CONCRETE ASSOCIATION, BRITISH, Shepperton House, Green Lane, Shepperton, Middlesex.—*Dir.-Gen.*, K. Newman.

ROAD HAULAGE ASSOCIATION LTD., 22 Upper Woburn Place, W.C.1.—*Dir.-Gen.*, G. K. Newman.

ROOFING CONTRACTORS, NATIONAL FEDERATION OF, 15 Soho Square, W.1.—*Gen. Sec.*, H. S. Kitching.

SAND AND GRAVEL ASSOCIATION LIMITED, 48 Park Street, W.1.—*Sec. Gen.*, A. C. F. Hey.

SAWMILLING ASSOCIATION, NATIONAL, Clareville House, Whitcomb Street, W.C.2.—*Sec.*, P. A. T. Smith.

SCIENTIFIC INSTRUMENT MANUFACTURERS' ASSOCIATION OF GREAT BRITAIN, 20 Peel Street, W.8.

SCOTCH WHISKY ASSOCIATION, 20 Atholl Crescent, Edinburgh.—*Dir. Gen. and Sec.*, Col. H. F. O. Bewsher. *Information and Development Office*, 17 Half Moon Street, W.1.

TAILORS, FEDERATION OF MERCHANT, Alderman House, 37 Soho Square, W.1.—*Exec. Sec.*, C. W. Allen.

TEXTILE EMPLOYERS' ASSOCIATION, BRITISH, 5th Flr., Royal Exchange, Manchester.—*Sec.*, J. Platt, M.B.E.

TIMBER TRADE FEDERATION, Clareville House, Whitcomb Street, W.C.2.—*Sec.*, H. J. Bocking.

TOBACCONISTS, FEDERATION OF RETAIL, 546-548 Commercial Road, E.1.—*Sec.*, G. J. Alden.

TRAWLERS FEDERATION LTD., BRITISH, Trinity House Chambers, 12 Trinity House Lane, Hull. *Sec.*, I. C. Thorburn.

VEHICLE BUILDERS AND REPAIRERS ASSOCIATION, Belmont House, 102 Finkle Lane, Gildersome, Leeds.—*Sec.*, J. G. Mellor.

WALLCOVERING MANUFACTURERS ASSOCIATION, Prudential House, Wellesley Road, Croydon, Surrey.—*Dir.*, M. J. Levete.

WATER COMPANIES' ASSOCIATION, 14 Great College Street, S.W.1.—*Dir.*, R. P. Owen.

CLUB AND LIBRARY EDITION OF WHITAKER, 1977

The Club and Library Edition of Whitaker's Almanack, 1977, contains 1,220 pages, including illustrations and coloured maps (The World, The British Isles, Baltic States, Russia and her neighbours, Germany and her neighbours, France and Spain, The Far East, India, Pakistan and Burma, Africa, Canada and Newfoundland, The United States, South America, Australia, New Zealand) in strong leather binding, with gilt top and silk headband. Price £5.75 net.

TRADES UNION CONGRESS (T.U.C.)

Congress House, 23–28 Great Russell Street, W.C.1.

[01–636–4030]

The Trades Union Congress, founded in 1868, is a voluntary association of Trade Unions, the representatives of which meet annually to consider matters of common concern to their members. The Congress has met annually since 1871 (with the exception of 1914) and in recent years has met normally on the first Monday in September, its sessions extending through the succeeding four days. Congress is constituted by delegates of the affiliated unions on the basis of one delegate for every 5,000 members, or fraction thereof, on whose behalf affiliated fees are paid. Affiliated unions (in 1975/6) totalled 113 with an aggregate membership of 11,036,326.

The main business of the annual Congress is to consider the report of its General Council dealing with the activities of the Congress year, along with motions from affiliated societies on questions of policy and organization. Some of these unions, especially in cotton, are themselves federal bodies including over 100 more unions.

One of the important responsibilities of the annual Congress is to elect a General Council to keep watch on all industrial movements, legislation affecting labour and all matters touching the interest of the trade union movement, with authority to promote common action on general questions, and to assist trade unions in the work of organization. The General Council is elected by Congress and is composed of 38 members (36 representing 18 trade groups and two representing women workers). Following is a list of these trade groups with the aggregate membership of unions in each group and with the number of representatives each group is entitled to have on the General Council. *Women Members.*—In 1976, a total of 3,033,591 women were members of unions in the T.U.C. The largest groups were members of the National Union of General and Municipal Workers (289,283), National Union of Public Employees (382,638), Transport and General Workers' Union (289,582), National Union of Teachers (211,894), National and Local Government Officers' Association (267,221), and Union of Shop, Distributive and Allied Workers (223,649).

Among the powers vested in it by consent of the Unions in Congress is the responsibility of adjusting disputes and differences between affiliated organizations; such cases being dealt with by a Disputes Committee of the General Council which investigates matters referred to it and issues its findings thereon, which are invariably accepted by the parties to the dispute. The General Council has power also, if there appears to be justification, to institute an investigation into the conduct of any affiliated organization on the ground that its activities are detrimental to the interests of the trade union movement or contrary to the declared principles and policy of the Congress; but membership of the Congress is voluntary and Unions retain full control of their own affairs, and a penalty of suspension from membership of the Congress or exclusion from membership is the only measure that can be taken to enforce Congress decisions. Through the General Council, the trade union movement maintains systematic relations with the Government and Government Departments, with the Confederation of British Industry and with a large number of other bodies. The General Council is represented on the National Economic Development Council, established to examine problems associated with faster economic growth. The Council includes Ministers dealing with economic and industrial affairs, representatives of public and private industry and independent members. The General Council nominates members to serve on numerous other bodies, e.g., Manpower Services Commission, Health and Safety Commission and the Council of the Advisory, Conciliation and Arbitration Service.

Chairman (1976–77), D. McGarvey, C.B.E.

General Secretary, Rt. Hon. L. Murray, O.B.E.

Trade Group (with numbers of unions)	Membership
Mining and Quarrying (2)	282,460
Railways (3)	283,721
Transport (other) (6)	1,961,058
Shipbuilding (1)	136,193
Engineering, Founding and Vehicle Building (10)	1,434,735
Technical Engineering and Scientific (4)	557,438
Electricity (1)	420,000
Iron and Steel and Minor Metal Trades (10)	141,984
Building, Woodworking and Furnishing (5)	364,149
Printing and Paper (6)	406,582
Textiles (16)	124,600
Clothing, Leather and Boot and Shoe (6)	249,178
Glass, Ceramics, Chemicals, Food, Drink, Tobacco, Brushmaking, and Distribution (10)	527,844
Agriculture (1)	85,000
Public Employees (10)	1,888,223
Civil Servants and Post Office (11)	918,739
Professional, Clerical and Entertainment (10)	373,066
General Workers (1)	881,356
TOTAL (113)	11,036,326

SCOTTISH TRADES UNION CONGRESS

16 Woodlands Terrace, Glasgow

The Congress was formed in 1897 and acts as a national centre for the trade union movement in Scotland. In 1976 it consisted of 75 unions with a membership of 962,499 and 45 directly affiliated Trades Councils. The majority of the unions organize throughout Britain and affiliate on their membership in Scotland.

The Annual Congress in April elects a 20-member General Council on the basis of 11 industrial sections. Congress has been prominent in pressing for economic expansion and full employment in Scotland and the development of the social services, most of which are separately organized in Scotland.

Chairman (1976–77), H. D'Arcy.

General Secretary, J. Milne.

TRADE UNIONS AFFILIATED TO T.U.C.

A list of the Trade Unions affiliated to the Trades Union Congress in September, 1976. The number of members of each Union is shown in parenthesis.

ACTORS' EQUITY ASSOCIATION, BRITISH (22,373).—*Gen. Sec.*, P. Plouviez, 8 Harley St, W.1.

AGRICULTURAL AND ALLIED WORKERS, NATIONAL UNION OF (85,000).—*Sec.*, R. N. Bottini, C.B.E., 308 Gray's Inn Road, W.C.1.

ASPHALT WORKERS, THE AMALGAMATED UNION OF (3,018).—*Sec.*, H. M. Wareham, Jenkin House, 173A Queen's Road, Peckham, S.E.15.

BAKERS UNION (52,676), Stanborough House, Great North Road, Stanborough, Welwyn Garden City, Herts.—*Gen. Sec.*, S. Maddox.

BAKERS AND ALLIED WORKERS, SCOTTISH UNION OF (8,780).—*Sec.*, A. H. Mackie, Baxterlee, 127 Fergus Drive, Glasgow 20.

BANK EMPLOYEES, NATIONAL UNION OF (101,922).—*Sec.*, L. A. Miles, Sheffield House, Portsmouth Road, Esher, Surrey.

BEAMERS, TWISTERS AND DRAWERS (HAND AND MACHINE), AMALGAMATED ASSOCIATION OF (955).—*Gen. Sec.*, F. Sumner, 27 Every Street, Nelson, Lancs.

BLASTFURNACEMEN, ORE MINERS, COKE WORKERS AND KINDRED TRADES, THE NATIONAL UNION OF (16,328).—*Sec.*, H. C. Smith, 93 Borough Road West, Middlesbrough. Cleveland.

BLIND AND DISABLED, NATIONAL LEAGUE OF THE (4,250).—*Sec.*, T. J. Parker, O.B.E., Tottenham Trades Hall, 7 Bruce Grove, N.17.

BOILERMAKERS, SHIPWRIGHTS, BLACKSMITHS AND STRUCTURAL WORKERS, AMALGAMATED SOCIETY OF (136,193).—Lifton House, Eslington Road, Newcastle-upon-Tyne 2.—*Pres.*, D. McGarvey, C.B.E.

BOOT, SHOE AND SLIPPER OPERATIVES, ROSSENDALE UNION OF (5,635).—*Sec.*, T. Whittaker, 7 Tenterfield Street, Waterfoot, Rossendale, Lancs.

BRITISH AIR LINE PILOTS ASSOCIATION (4,495).—*Gen. Sec.*, M. Young, 81 New Road, Harlington, Hayes, Middlesex.

BROADCASTING STAFF, ASSOCIATION OF (13,889), King's Court, 2 Goodge Street, W.1.—*Gen. Sec.*, D. A. Hearn.

BRUSHMAKERS AND GENERAL WORKERS, NATIONAL SOCIETY OF (1,620).—*Sec.*, A. W. Godfrey, 20 The Parade, Watford.

CARD SETTING MACHINE TENTERS' SOCIETY (142).—*Sec.*, G. Priestley, 36 Greenton Avenue, Scholes, Cleckheaton, Yorks.

CARPET TRADE UNION, NORTHERN (2,189).—*Gen. Sec.*, L. R. Smith, 22 Clare Road, Halifax, Yorks.

CERAMIC AND ALLIED TRADES UNION (44,096).—*Gen. Sec.*, L. R. Sillitoe, 5 Hillcrest Street, Hanley, Stoke-on-Trent.

CINEMATOGRAPH, TELEVISION AND ALLIED TECHNICIANS, ASSOCIATION OF (18,690).—*Sec.*, A. Sapper, 2 Soho Square, W.1.

CIVIL AND PUBLIC SERVANTS, SOCIETY OF (99,925). *including Customs and Excise Group*).—*Gen. Sec.*, B. A. Gillman, 124-6 Southwark Stteet, S.E.1.

CIVIL AND PUBLIC SERVICES ASSOCIATION (224,242). —*Sec.*, R. R. Thomas, 215 Balham High Road, S.W.17.

CIVIL SERVANTS, INSTITUTION OF PROFESSIONAL (103,502).—*Gen. Sec.*, W. McCall, 3-7 Northumberland Street, W.C.2.

CIVIL SERVICE UNION (46,784).—*Sec.*, J. O. N. Vickers, 17-21 Hatton Wall, E.C.1.

CLOTH PRESSERS' SOCIETY (180).—*Sec.*, G. Kaye, 34 Southgate, Honley, Huddersfield, Yorks.

COLLIERY OVERMEN, DEPUTIES AND SHOTFIRERS, NATIONAL ASSOCIATION OF (20,589).—*Sec.*, A. E. Simpson, Argyle House, 29-31 Euston Road, N.W.1.

CONSTRUCTION, ALLIED TRADES AND TECHNICIANS, UNION OF (274,786).—*Sec.*, G. F. Smith, C.B.E., Ucatt House, 177 Abbeville Road, S.W.4. STAMP (Supervisory, Technical, Administrative, Managerial and Professional Section).—*Sec.*, J. L. Jones, Ucatt House, 177 Abbeville Road, S.W.4.

CO-OPERATIVE OFFICALS, NATIONAL ASSOCIATION OF (5,499).—*Sec.* A. W. Potts, Saxone House, 56 Market Street, Manchester 1.

COOPERS' AND ALLIED WORKERS FEDERATION OF GREAT BRITAIN (1,066).—*Gen. Sec.*, W. Marshall, 13 Gayfield Square, Edinburgh 1.

DOMESTIC APPLIANCE & GENERAL METAL WORKERS, NATIONAL UNION OF (5,342).—*Sec.*, J. Higham, M.B.E., Imperial Bldgs., Corporation Street, Rotherham.

DYERS, BLEACHERS AND TEXTILE WORKERS, NATIONAL UNION OF (54,737), National House, Sunbridge Road, Bradford 1.—*Sec.*, F. Dyson.

ELECTRICAL, ELECTRONIC, TELECOMMUNICATION, AND PLUMBING UNION (420,000).—*Sec.*, F. J. Chapple, Hayes Court, West Common Road, Bromley, Kent.

ELECTRICAL POWER ENGINEERS' ASSOCIATION (34,207).—*Gen. Sec.*, J. Lyons, Station House, Fox Lane North, Chertsey, Surrey.

ENGINEERING WORKERS, AMALGAMATED UNION OF (1,204,720), 110 Peckham Road, S.E.15.—*Gen. Sec.*, J. M. Boyd, C.B.E.
CONSTRUCTION SECTION (25,000).—*Sec.*, J. Baldwin. Construction House, 190 Cedars Road, Clapham, S.W.4.
FOUNDRY SECTION (57,815).—*Sec.*, R. Garland, 164 Chorlton Road, Manchester 16.
TECHNICAL, ADMINISTRATIVE AND SUPERVISORY SECTION (140,784).—*Sec.*, K. Gill, Onslow Hall, Little Green, Richmond, Surrey.

FELT HATTERS AND ALLIED WORKERS, AMALGAMATED SOCIETY OF JOURNEYMEN (703).—*Sec.*, H. Walker, 14 Walker Street, Denton, nr. Manchester.

FELT HAT TRIMMERS AND WOOL FORMERS, AMALGAMATED (664).—*Sec.*, H. Walker, 14 Walker Street, Denton, nr. Manchester.

FILM ARTISTES' ASSOCIATION, THE (1,559).—*Sec.*, S. Brannigan, 61 Marloes Road, W.8.

FIRE BRIGADES UNION, THE (30,000).—*Sec.*, T. Parry, O.B.E., 59 Fulham High Street, S.W.6.

FOOTWEAR, LEATHER AND ALLIED TRADES, NATIONAL UNION OF (62,455). The Grange, Earls Barton, Northampton.—*Sec.*, S. F. Clapham.

FUNERAL SERVICE OPERATIVES, NATIONAL UNION OF (1,179).—*Sec.*, D. R. Coates, 16 Woolwich New Road, S.E.18.

FURNITURE, TIMBER AND ALLIED TRADES UNION (84,100).—Fairfields, Roe Green, Kingsbury, N.W.9.

GENERAL AND MUNICIPAL WORKERS UNION (881,356), Thorne House, Ruxley Ridge, Claygate, Esher, Surrey.—*Gen. Sec.*, D. Basnett.

GOLD, SILVER AND ALLIED TRADES, NATIONAL UNION OF (2,756).—*Gen. Sec.*, B. H. Bridge, Kean Chambers, 11 Mappin Street, Sheffield 1.

GOVERNMENT SUPERVISORS AND RADIO OFFICERS, ASSOCIATION OF (11,838).—*Sec.*, P. L. Avery, 90 Borough High Street, S.E.1.

GRAPHICAL AND ALLIED TRADES, SOCIETY OF (195,522).—*Sec.*, W. H. Keys, Sogat House, 274-288 London Road, Hadleigh, Benfleet, Essex.

SCOTTISH GRAPHICAL DIVISION.—*Sec.*, E. Smith, 136 West Regent Street, Glasgow.

GRAPHICAL ASSOCIATION, NATIONAL (107,441).—*Sec.*, J. F. Wade, Graphic House, 63–67 Bromham Road, Bedford.

GREATER LONDON COUNCIL STAFF ASSOCIATION (19,767).—*Sec.*, F. T. Hollocks, 164–8 Westminster Bridge Road, S.E.1.

HEALDERS AND TWISTERS TRADE AND FRIENDLY SOCIETY, HUDDERSFIELD (211).—*Sec.*, G. Booth, 20 Uppergate, Hepworth, Huddersfield.

HEALTH SERVICE EMPLOYEES, CONFEDERATION OF (167,200).—*Gen. Sec.*, E. A. G. Spanswick, Glen House, High Street, Banstead, Surrey.

HEALTH VISITORS' ASSOCIATION (8,603).—*Sec.*, Mrs. J. Wyndham-Kaye, 36 Eccleston Square, S.W.1.

HOSIERY AND KNITWEAR WORKERS, NATIONAL UNION OF (70,292).—*Sec.*, D. A. C. Lambert, 55 New Walk, Leicester.

INLAND REVENUE STAFF FEDERATION (60,584).—*Sec.*, A. M. G. Christopher, 7 St. George's Square, S.W.1.

INSURANCE WORKERS, NATIONAL UNION OF (25,582).—*Sec.*, F. H. Jarvis, 185 Woodhouse Road, N.12.

IRON AND STEEL TRADES CONFEDERATION (104,485).—*Sec.*, W. Sirs, Swinton House, 324 Gray's Inn Road, W.C.1.

JOURNALISTS, NATIONAL UNION OF (28,274).—*Sec.*, K. Morgan, Acorn House, 314–320 Gray's Inn Road, W.C.1.

JUTE, FLAX AND KINDRED TEXTILE OPERATIVES, UNION OF (1,740).—*Gen. Sec.*, Mrs. M. Fenwick, M.B.E., 93 Nethergate, Dundee.

LAMINATED AND COIL SPRING WORKERS' UNION (254).—*Sec.*, B. Nuttall, 120 Burngreave Road, Sheffield.

LICENSED HOUSE MANAGERS, NATIONAL ASSOCIATION OF (12,187).—*Sec.*, H. Shindler, 9 Coombe Lane, S.W.20.

LITHOGRAPHIC ARTISTS, DESIGNERS, ENGRAVERS AND PROCESS WORKERS, SOCIETY OF (16,819).—*Sec.*, J. A. Jackson, 55 Clapham Common (South Side), S.W.4.

LOCK AND METAL WORKERS, NATIONAL UNION OF (6,648).—*Sec.*, J. Martin, Bellamy House, Wilkes Street, Willenhall, Staffs.

LOCOMOTIVE ENGINEERS AND FIREMEN, ASSOCIATED SOCIETY OF (29,000).—*Sec.*, R. W. Buckton, 9 Arkwright Road, N.W.3.

LOOM OVERLOOKERS, THE GENERAL UNION OF ASSOCIATIONS OF (3,183).—*Gen. Sec.*, H. Brown, 6 St. Mary's Place, Bury.

MANAGERS AND OVERLOOKERS' SOCIETY (1,303).—*Sec.*, L. Smith, Textile Hall, Westgate Bradford.

MERCHANT NAVY AND AIRLINE OFFICERS' ASSOCIATION (30,050).—*Sec.*, E. Nevin, 750–760 High Road, Leytonstone, E.11.

METALWORKERS' UNION, ASSOCIATED (5,003).—*Sec.*, E. Tullock, 92 Deansgate, Manchester 3.

METAL MECHANICS, NATIONAL SOCIETY OF (47,100).—*Sec.*, J. H. Wood, 70 Lionel Street, Birmingham 3.

MILITARY AND ORCHESTRAL MUSICAL INSTRUMENT MAKERS TRADE SOCIETY (145).—*Gen. Sec.*, G. W. Lock, 56 Avondale Crescent, Enfield, Middx.

MINEWORKERS, NATIONAL UNION OF (261,871).—*Sec.*, L. Daly, 222 Euston Road, N.W.1.

MUSICIANS' UNION (35,982).—*Gen. Sec.*, J. Morton, 29 Catherine Place, Buckingham Gate, S.W.1.

NATIONAL AND LOCAL GOVERNMENT OFFICERS ASSOCIATION (625,163).—*Sec.*, G. A. Drain, Nalgo House, 1 Mabledon Place, W.C.1.

PATTERNMAKERS AND ALLIED CRAFTSMEN, ASSOCIATION OF (9,979).—*Sec.*, G. Eastwood, 15 Cleve Road, W. Hampstead, N.W.6.

PATTERN WEAVERS' SOCIETY (150).—*Gen. Sec.*, D. G. Hawley, 21 Kaye Lane, Almondbury, Huddersfield.

POST OFFICE ENGINEERING UNION (124,682).—*Sec.*, B. C. Stanley, Greystoke House, Hanger Lane, Ealing, W.5.

POST OFFICE EXECUTIVES, SOCIETY OF (22,601).—*Gen. Sec.*, J. K. Glynn, 116 Richmond Road, Kingston-on-Thames, Surrey.

POST OFFICE MANAGEMENT STAFFS ASSOCIATION (19,343).—*Gen. Sec.*, L. F. Pratt, 52 Broadway, Bracknell, Berks.

POST OFFICE WORKERS, UNION OF (185,000).—*Sec.*, T. Jackson, U.P.W. House, Crescent Lane, Clapham Common, S.W.4.

POWER LOOM CARPET WEAVERS AND TEXTILE WORKERS' ASSOCIATION (5,740).—*Sec.*, A. Hatton, Callows Lane, Kidderminster.

POWER LOOM OVERLOOKERS, YORKSHIRE ASSOCIATION OF (1,377).—*Sec.*, E. D. Sleeman, Textile Hall, Westgate, Bradford.

POWER LOOM OVER-LOOKERS, SCOTTISH UNION OF (350).—*Sec.*, A. Stobie, 1 Osnaburg Street, Forfar.

PRINTERS, GRAPHICAL AND MEDIA PERSONNEL, NATIONAL SOCIETY OF OPERATIVE (53,826).—*Sec.*, O. O'Brien, Caxton House, 13–16 Borough Road, S.E.1.

PRISON OFFICERS' ASSOCIATION (19,728).—*Sec.*, K. A. Daniel, Cronin House, 245 Church Street, N.9.

PROFESSIONAL, EXECUTIVE, CLERICAL AND COMPUTER STAFF, ASSOCIATION OF (136,097).—*Gen. Sec.*, R. Grantham, 22 Worple Road, S.W.19.

PUBLIC EMPLOYEES, NATIONAL UNION OF (584,485).—*Sec.*, A. W. Fisher, Civic House, Aberdeen Terrace, Blackheath, S.E.3.

RADIO AND ELECTRONIC OFFICERS UNION (3,548).—*Sec.*, K. A. Murphy. 4–6 Branfill Road, Upminster, Essex.

RAILWAYMEN, NATIONAL UNION OF (180,429).—*Sec.*, S. Weighell, Unity House, Euston Road, N.W.1.

ROLL TURNERS' TRADE SOCIETY, BRITISH (752).—*Sec.*, B. W. Johnson, 44 Collingwood Avenue, Corby, Northants.

SAWMAKERS' PROTECTION SOCIETY, SHEFFIELD (245).—*Sec.*, A. Marples, 27 Main Avenue, Totley, Sheffield.

SCALEMAKERS, NATIONAL UNION OF (1,892).—*Gen. Sec.*, S. W. Parfitt, Herbert Morrison House, 195 Walworth Road, S.E.17.

SCHOOLMASTERS, NATIONAL ASSOCIATION OF, AND UNION OF WOMEN TEACHERS (82,763).—*Sec.*, T. A. Casey, P.O. Box 65, Swan Court, Waterhouse Street, Hemel Hempstead, Herts.

SCIENTIFIC, TECHNICAL AND MANAGERIAL STAFFS, ASSOCIATION OF (374,000).—*Gen. Sec.*, C. Jenkins, 10–26A Jamestown Road, N.W.1.

   MEDICAL PRACTITIONERS' SECTION (5,106).

SCREW, NUT, BOLT AND RIVET TRADE UNION (2,524).—*Sec.*, H. Cater, 368 Dudley Road, Birmingham 18.

SEAMEN, NATIONAL UNION OF (44,300).—*Gen. Sec.*, J. Slater, Maritime House, Old Town, Clapham, S.W.4.

SHEET METAL WORKERS, COPPERSMITHS AND HEATING AND DOMESTIC ENGINEERS, NATIONAL UNION OF (75,086).—*Gen. Sec.*, L. W. Buck, 75–77 West Heath Road, N.W.3.

SHOP, DISTRIBUTIVE AND ALLIED WORKERS, UNION OF (377,302).—*Sec.*, The Lord Allen of Fallowfield, C.B.E., "Oakley," 188 Wilmslow Road, Fallowfield, Manchester 14.

SHUTTLEMAKERS, SOCIETY OF (129).—*Gen. Sec.*, E. V. Littlewood, 21 Buchan Towers, Manchester Road, Bradford.

SPRING TRAPMAKERS' SOCIETY (90).—*Sec.*, J. Martin, Bellamy House, Wilkes Street, Willenhall, Staffs.

TAILORS AND GARMENT WORKERS, NATIONAL UNION OF (109,429), Radlett House, West Hill, Aspley Guise, Milton Keynes.—*Gen. Sec.*, J. Macgougan.

TEACHERS, NATIONAL UNION OF (281,855).—*Sec.*, F. Jarvis, Hamilton House, Mabledon Place, W.C.1.

TEACHERS IN FURTHER AND HIGHER EDUCATION, NATIONAL ASSOCIATION OF (59,750).—*Gen. Sec.* T. Driver, Hamilton House, Mabledon Place, W.C.1.

TEXTILE WAREHOUSE OPERATIVES, AMALGAMATED (3,201).—*Gen. Sec.*, N. Wareing, 80 St. George's Road, Bolton, Lancs.

TEXTILE WORKERS AND KINDRED TRADES, AMALGAMATED SOCIETY OF (5,372).—*Gen. Sec.*, H. Lisle, O.B.E., Foxlowe, Market Place, Leek, Staffs.

TEXTILE WORKERS' UNION, AMALGAMATED (46,292). —*Gen. Sec.*, F. G. Hague, Textile Union Centre, 5 Caton Street, Rochdale, Lancs.

THEATRICAL, TELEVISION AND KINE EMPLOYEES, THE NATIONAL ASSOCIATION OF (15,739).—*Gen. Sec.*, J. L. Wilson, 155 Kennington Park Road, S.E.11.

TOBACCO MECHANICS' ASSOCIATION (360).—*Gen. Sec.*, W. D. Brunt, 9 Wootton Crescent, St. Anne's Park, Bristol.

TOBACCO WORKERS' UNION, THE (21,074).—*Sec.*, C. D. Grieve, 9 Station Parade, High Street, E.11.

TRANSPORT AND GENERAL WORKERS' UNION (1,856,165).—*Sec.*, J. L. Jones, M.B.E., Transport House, Smith Square, S.W.1.

TRANSPORT SALARIED STAFFS' ASSOCIATION (74,292). —*Gen. Sec.*, D. A. Mackenzie, Walkden House, 10 Melton Street, N.W.1.

TRANSPORT UNION, UNITED ROAD (22,500).—*Sec.*, J. Moore, 76 High Lane, Chorlton-cum-Hardy, Manchester.

UNIVERSITY TEACHERS, ASSOCIATION OF (28,687).— *Sec.*, L. J. Sapper, United House, 1 Pembridge Road, W.11.

WALLCOVERINGS, DECORATIVE AND ALLIED TRADES, NATIONAL UNION OF (4,700).—*Gen. Sec.*, R. W. Tomlins, 223 Bury New Road, Whitefield, Manchester.

WIRE DRAWERS AND KINDRED WORKERS, THE AMALGAMATED SOCIETY OF (10,399).—*Sec.*, L. Carr, Prospect House, Alma Street, Sheffield 3.

WOOL SHEAR WORKERS' TRADE UNION, SHEFFIELD (27).—*Sec.*, J. Billard, 19 Rivelin Park Drive, Sheffield 6.

WOOL SORTERS' SOCIETY, NATIONAL (779).—*Sec.*, N. Newton, M.B.E., 40 Little Horton Lane, Bradford 5.

WRITERS GUILD OF GREAT BRITAIN (1,233).—*Sec.*, Mrs. E. Steel, 430 Edgware Road, W.2.

OTHER TRADE UNIONS

The following Trade Unions were not affiliated to the Trades Union Congress at the time of going to press.

CHAIN MAKERS AND STRIKERS' ASSOCIATION (228). —*Sec.*, A. E. Head, M.B.E., Unity Villa, Sidney Road, Cradley Heath, Warley, West Midlands.

ENGINEERS' AND FIREMEN'S UNION, GRIMSBY STEAM AND DIESEL FISHING VESSELS (200).—10 Orwell Street, Grimsby.

PROFESSIONAL FOOTBALLERS' ASSOCIATION (2,160).— *Sec.*, C. Lloyd, O.B.E., 124 Corn Exchange Buildings, Manchester 4.

RETAIL BOOK, STATIONERY AND ALLIED TRADES EMPLOYEES' ASSOCIATION, THE (6,226).—*Gen. Sec.*, A. J. Johnson, 7 Grape Street, Shaftesbury Avenue, W.C.2.

TEXTILE CRAFTSMEN, YORKSHIRE SOCIETY OF (1,014) —*Sec.*, C. Hall, Textile Hall, Westgate, Bradford 1.

INDUSTRIAL RESEARCH ASSOCIATIONS

A notable development in modern industry is the growth in numbers and importance of Industrial Research Associations and their increasing influence on the scientific and economic life of the country.

The Government Scheme for Co-operative Industrial Research was launched by the Department of Scientific and Industrial Research in 1917. Its aim was to stimulate the industries of the United Kingdom to undertake co-operative research as a means of increasing their efficiency.

Research Associations formed under this scheme are registered companies, limited by guarantee of a nominal sum and working without the division of profits in the form of dividends. To assist the formation of such Associations the Department of Trade and Industry kept a model Memorandum and Articles of Association, to which Research Associations under the scheme conform in all essential points.

The Research Associations are autonomous bodies free to determine their own policy for the development of their research programmes and the use to be made of the results of their research. Membership is open to any British firm in the particular industry, subject to the approval of the Councils of the Research Associations. The Department of Industry's Research Requirement Boards, now offer work to the Research Associations in a contractual capacity, this system having replaced general purpose grants.

Brushes.
BRITISH BRUSH MANUFACTURERS' RESEARCH ASSOCIATION, 90 Cowcross Street, E.C.1.—*Dir.*, D. I. Fothergill.

Cast Iron.
BRITISH CAST IRON RESEARCH ASSOCIATION, Bordesley Hall, Alvechurch, Birmingham.—*Dir.*, H. Morrogh, C.B.E., F.R.S.

Ceramics.
BRITISH CERAMIC RESEARCH ASSOCIATION, Queen's Road, Penkhull, Stoke-on-Trent.—*Dir.*, A. Dinsdale, O.B.E.

Civil Engineering.
CONSTRUCTION INDUSTRY RESEARCH AND INFORMATION ASSOCIATION, Old Queen Street House, 6 Storey's Gate, S.W.1.—*Dir.*, A. R. Collins, M.B.E., D.SC., Ph.D.

Coke and Tar.
BRITISH CARBONIZATION RESEARCH ASSOCIATION, Research Centre, Wingerworth, Chesterfield, Derbyshire.—*Dir.*, J. P. Graham.

Cotton, Silk, etc.
COTTON, SILK AND MAN-MADE FIBRES RESEARCH ASSOCIATION, Shirley Institute, Didsbury, Manchester, 20.—*Dir.*, L. A. Wiseman, O.B.E.

Cutlery.
CUTLERY AND ALLIED TRADES RESEARCH ASSOCIATION, Henry Street, Sheffield, 3.—*Dir.*, E. A. Oldfield.

Drop Forging.
DROP FORGING RESEARCH ASSOCIATION, Shepherd Street, Sheffield, 3.—*Director*, S. E. Rogers, Ph.D.

Electrical.
ELECTRICAL RESEARCH ASSOCIATION, Cleeve Road, Leatherhead, Surrey.—*Man. Dir.*, B. C. Lindley, Ph.D.

Flour Milling and Baking.
FLOUR MILLING AND BAKING RESEARCH ASSOCIATION, Research Station, Chorleywood, Rickmansworth, Herts.—*Dir.*, C. T. Greenwood, D.SC., Ph.D.

Food Manufacture.
BRITISH FOOD MANUFACTURING INDUSTRIES RESEARCH ASSOCIATION, Randalls Road, Leatherhead, Surrey.—*Dir.*, A. W. Holmes, Ph.D.

Fruit and Vegetable Canning.
CAMPDEN FOOD PRESERVATION RESEARCH ASSOCIATION, Chipping Campden, Glos.—*Dir.*, H. R. Hinton.

Furniture.
FURNITURE INDUSTRY RESEARCH ASSOCIATION, Maxwell Road, Stevenage, Herts.—*Dir.*, D. M. Heughan.

Glass.
BRITISH GLASS INDUSTRY RESEARCH ASSOCIATION, Northumberland Road, Sheffield 10.—*Dir.*, C. Thorpe.

Heating and Ventilating.
BUILDING SERVICES RESEARCH & INFORMATION ASSOCIATION, Old Bracknell Lane, Bracknell, N. S. Billington, O.B.E.

Hosiery.
HOSIERY AND ALLIED TRADES RESEARCH ASSOCIATION (Hatra), Thorneywood, 7 Gregory Boulevard, Nottingham.—*Dir.*, W. A. Dutton.

Hydromechanics.
BRITISH HYDROMECHANICS RESEARCH ASSOCIATION, Cranfield, Bedford.—*Dir.*, G. F. W. Adler.

Industrial Powders, Chalk & Lime.
WELWYN HALL RESEARCH ASSOCIATION, Edgeworth House, Arlesey, Beds.—*Dir.*, R. R. Davidson.

Instrumentation.
SIRA INSTITUTE LTD., South Hill, Chislehurst, Kent.—*Man. Dir.*, S. S. Carlisle.

Leather.
BRITISH LEATHER MANUFACTURERS' RESEARCH ASSOCIATION, Milton Park, Egham, Surrey.—*Dir.*, R. L. Sykes, Ph.D.

Linen.
LAMBEG INDUSTRIAL RESEARCH ASSOCIATION, Research Institute, Lambeg, Lisburn, Co. Antrim, N. Ireland.—*Dir.*, H. A. C. Todd, O.B.E.

Machine Tools.
MACHINE TOOL INDUSTRY RESEARCH ASSOCIATION, Hulley Road, Hurdsfield, Macclesfield, Cheshire. —*Dir.*, A. E. De Barr, O.B.E.

Motor Vehicles.
MOTOR INDUSTRY RESEARCH ASSOCIATION, Watling Street, Nuneaton, Warwickshire.—*Dir.*, R. H. Macmillan.

Mycology.
COMMONWEALTH MYCOLOGICAL INSTITUTE, Ferry Lane, Kew, Surrey.—*Dir.*, A. Johnston.

Non-Ferrous Metals.
BRITISH NON-FERROUS METALS TECHNOLOGY CENTRE, The Grove Laboratories, Denchworth Road, Wantage, Berks.—*Dir.*, A. J. Kennedy, D.SC., Ph.D.

Paint.
PAINT RESEARCH ASSOCIATION, Paint Research Station, Waldegrave Road, Teddington, Middlesex.—*Dir.*, G. de W. Anderson, Ph.D.

Paper, Board, Printing and Packing.

RESEARCH ASSOCIATION FOR THE PAPER AND BOARD, PRINTING AND PACKAGING INDUSTRIES (Pira), Randalls Road, Leatherhead, Surrey.—*Dir.*, N. K. Bridge, ph.D.

Production Engineering.

PRODUCTION ENGINEERING RESEARCH ASSOCIATION OF GREAT BRITAIN, Melton Mowbray, Leics.— *Dir.*, D. F. Galloway, C.B.E., ph.D.

Rubber and Plastics.

RUBBER AND PLASTICS RESEARCH ASSOCIATION OF GREAT BRITAIN, Shawbury, Shrewsbury, Shropshire.—*Dir.*, W. F. Watson, D.SC., ph.D.

Ships.

BRITISH SHIP RESEARCH ASSOCIATION, Research Station, Wallsend, Northumberland.—*Dir.*, R. Hurst, G.M., C.B.E., ph.D.

Shoes.

SHOE AND ALLIED TRADES RESEARCH ASSOCIATION, Satra House, Rockingham Road, Kettering, Northants.—*Dir.* (vacant).

Springs.

SPRING RESEARCH ASSOCIATION, Henry Street, Sheffield 3.—*Dir.*, J. A. Bennett.

Steel Castings.

STEEL CASTINGS RESEARCH AND TRADE ASSOCIATION. East Bank Road, Sheffield 2.—*Director* J. C. Wright, ph.D.

Timber.

TIMBER RESEARCH AND DEVELOPMENT ASSOCIATION, Hughenden Valley, High Wycombe, Bucks.— *Dir.*, J. S. McBride.

Toxicology.

BRITISH INDUSTRIAL BIOLOGICAL RESEARCH ASSOCIATION, Woodmansterne Road, Carshalton, Surrey.—*Dir.*, R. F. Crampton, ph.D.

Water.

WATER RESEARCH CENTRE, Ferry Lane, Medmenham, Marlow, Bucks.—*Dir.*, R. G. Allen, O.B.E., ph.D.

Welding.

WELDING INSTITUTE, Abington Hall, nr. Cambridge.—*Dir.-Gen.*, R. Weck, C.B.E., ph.D.

Wool.

WOOL INDUSTRIES RESEARCH ASSOCIATION (Wira), Headingley Lane, Leeds 6.—*Dir.*, B. E. King, ph.D.

AGRICULTURAL RESEARCH INSTITUTES AND UNITS

The following research institutes are under the direct control of the Agricultural Research Council (*see* p. 372):—

Unit Of Animal Genetics, Institute of Animal Genetics, West Mains Road, Edinburgh 9.— *Director*, Prof. D. S. Falconer, SC.D., F.R.S.

Unit of Developmental Botany, 181A Huntingdon Road, Cambridge.—*Director.*, Prof. P. W. Brian, SC.D., F.R.S.

Unit of Invertebrate Chemistry and Physiology, University of Sussex, Falmer, Brighton.—*Hon. Director*, Prof. A. W. Johnson, F.R.S.

Unit of Invertebrate Chemistry and Physiology (Subgroup), University of Cambridge, Zoology Dept., Downing Street, Cambridge.—*Associate Director*, J. E. Treherne, ph.D., SC.D.

Unit of Muscle Mechanism and Insect Physiology, Dept. of Zoology, University of Oxford, South Parks Road, Oxford.—*Hon. Dir.*, Prof. J. W. S. Pringle, M.B.E., SC.D., F.R.S.

Unit of Nitrogen Fixation, University of Sussex, Brighton.—*Director*, Prof. J. Chatt, ph.D., SC.D., F.R.S.

Unit of Reproductive Physiology and Biochemistry, 307 Huntingdon Road, Cambridge.—*Director*, Prof. T. R. R. Mann, C.B.E., M.D., SC.D., ph.D., F.R.S.

Unit of Soil Physics, 219C Huntingdon Road, Cambridge.—*Dir.*, E. G. Youngs, ph.D. (*acting*).

Unit of Statistics, University of Edinburgh, 21 Buccleuch Place, Edinburgh 8.—*Hon. Director*, Prof. D. J. Finney, SC.D., F.R.S., F.R.S.E.

Statistics Group, Dept. of Applied Biology, Downing Street, Cambridge.

Systemic Fungicide Unit, Wye College, Ashford, Kent.—*Hon. Director*, Prof. R. L. Wain, C.B.E., D.SC., ph.D., F.R.S.

Institute for Research on Animal Diseases, Compton, Newbury, Berks.—*Director*, J. M. Payne, ph.D.

Institute of Animal Physiology, Babraham, Cambs.—*Director*, B. A. Cross, ph.D., SC.D., F.R.S.

Animal Breeding Research Organisation, West Mains Road, Edinburgh 9.—*Director*, J. W. B. King, ph.D., F.R.S.

Poultry Research Centre, King's Buildings, West Mains Road, Edinburgh, 9.—*Director*, T. C. Carter, O.B.E., ph.D., D.SC., F.R.S.E.

Letcombe Laboratory, Letcombe Regis, Wantage, Oxon.—*Director*, R. Scott Russell, C.B.E., D.SC., ph.D.

Weed Research Organisation, Begbroke Hill, Sandy Lane, Yarnton, Oxford.—*Director*, J. D. Fryer.

Food Research Institute, Colney Lane, Norwich.— *Director*, Prof. S. R. Elsden, ph.D.

Meat Research Institute, Langford, nr. Bristol.— *Director*, J. R. Norris, ph.D. (also Weston Laboratory, Bridge Road, Weston-super-Mare).

GRANT-AIDED RESEARCH INSTITUTES

In addition to the above there are other institutes which, while retaining their own individuality, are financed wholly or in the main by grants made from Government funds. Most of these Institutes have governing bodies of their own to which they are directly responsible. The maintenance grants for Institutes in England and Wales are met from funds voted by Parliament and administered by the Agricultural Research Council; the Scottish Institutes are borne on the vote of the Department of Agriculture and Fisheries for Scotland.

Long Ashton Research Station, Bristol.—*Director*, Prof. J. M. Hirst, D.SC., ph.D., F.R.S.

Animal Diseases Research Association (Scotland), Moredun Institute, 408 Gilmerton Road, Edinburgh.—*Dir.*, J. T. Stamp, D.SC., F.R.S.E.

Animal Virus Research Institute, Pirbright, Surrey. —*Director*, J. B. Brooksby, C.B.E., D.SC., F.R.S.E.

East Malling Research Station, Maidstone, Kent.— *Director*, A. F. Posnette, C.B.E., ph.D., SC.D., F.R.S.

Glasshouse Crops Research Institute, Worthing Road, Rustington, Littlehampton, Sussex.—*Director*, D. Rudd-Jones, ph.D.

Grassland Research Institute, Hurley, nr. Maidenhead, Berks.—*Director*, Prof. E. K. Woodford, o.b.e., ph.D.

Hannah Research Institute, Ayr.—*Director*, Prof. J. A. F. Rook, ph.D., d.sc.

Hill Farming Research Organisation, Bush Estate, Penicuik, Midlothian.—*Director*, J. M. M. Cunningham, ph.D.

Hop Research Centre, Wye College, Ashford, Kent. *Head of Dept.*, R. A. Neve, ph.D.

Houghton Poultry Research Station,* Houghton, Huntingdon.—*Director*, P. M. Biggs, ph.D., f.r.s.

John Innes Institute, Colney Lane, Norwich.—*Director*, Prof. R. Markham, ph.D., f.r.s.

Macaulay Institute for Soil Research, Craigiebuckler, Aberdeen.—*Director*, R. L. Mitchell, ph.D., f.r.s.e.

National Institute of Agricultural Engineering, Wrest Park, Silsoe, Bedford.—*Director*, C. J. Moss.

Scottish Institute of Agricultural Engineering, Scottish Station, Bush Estate, Penicuik, Midlothian.—*Director*, W. J. West, f.r.s.e.

National Institute for Research in Dairying, Shinfield, nr. Reading.—*Director*, Prof. B. G. F. Weitz, o.b.e., d.sc.

National Vegetable Research Stn. Wellesbourne, Warwick.—*Director*, Prof. D. W. Wright.

Plant Breeding Institute, Maris Lane, Trumpington, Cambridge.—*Director*, Prof. R. Riley, d.sc., f.r.s.

Welsh Plant Breeding Station, Plas Gogerddan, nr. Aberystwyth.—*Director*, Prof. J. P. Cooper, ph.D., d.sc.

Scottish Plant Breeding Station, Pentlandfield, Roslin, Midlothian.—*Director*, J. H. W. Holden, ph.D. (*acting*)

Rowett Research Institute, Bucksburn, Aberdeen. —*Director*, K. L. Blaxter, d.sc., f.r.s.

Rothamsted Experimental Station, Harpenden, Herts.—*Director*, L. Fowden, ph.D., f.r.s.

Scottish Horticultural Research Institute, Invergowrie, Dundee.—*Director*, C. E. Taylor, ph.D.

*Financed jointly by the Agricultural Research Council and the Animal Health Trust.

PROGRESS OF THE NEW TOWNS (To Dec. 31, 1975)

Town	New Industries		New Shops and Offices	New Houses and Flats	Net Capital advances at March 31, 1975 £
	Number of firms	Number Employed			
Aycliffe	—	238	113	7,176	25,252,106
Basildon	237	22,440	—	26,092	102,264,497
Bracknell	79	9,828	274	13,944	45,423,551
Central Lancs	21	100	1	5,611	27,209,184
Corby	45	5,022	301	12,368	29,330,756
Crawley	93	16,790	357	21,138	
Harlow	303	19,330	474	24,894	60,971,649
Hatfield	20	1,568	136	6,895	
Hemel Hempstead	78	14,000	375	—	
Milton Keynes	119	24,000	83	10,925	99,115,626
Northampton	215	8,845	232	11,130	41,682,630
Peterborough	—	6,900	—	8,104	59,031,828
Peterlee	52	4.143	157	7,930	33,340,435
Redditch	242	—	130	7,837	58,319,338
Runcorn	64	3,748	143	9,024	64,946,285
Skelmersdale	104	10,050	217	9,312	70,046,488
Stevenage	47	15,300	437	22,288	66,398,477
Telford	175	5,300	116	10,902	89,638,649
Warrington	18	940	—	8,211	39,972,061
Washington	236	8.770	136	8,929	48,863,676
Welwyn Garden City	25	5,000	182	8,536	—
Cwmbran	117	5,530	254	11,921	36,883,859
Newtown	32	756	7	917	7,619,352
Cumbernauld	184	8,000	160	12,310	67,847,085
East Kilbride	313	18,540	323	21,859	72,905,713
Glenrothes	140	7,544	159	9,658	38,571,837
Irvine	96	8,600	140	4,773	29,561,442
Livingston	74	4,702	76	7,172	55,610,984
Stonehouse	—	—	—	207	—
TOTAL	3,129	235,978	5,372	310,063	1,362,981,674

PRINCIPAL CHARITABLE BEQUESTS OF THE YEAR

The following alphabetical list comprising 29 women and 22 men shows the principal charitable bequests since our last issue. Legacies and certain other charges are deductible from gross estates before the amounts for charity can be arrived at.

Barbara Hepworth, the sculptor, who was found dead after a fire at her Cornwall studio, left £10,000 to Westminster Hospital, London, for cancer research, to be known as " The Dame Barbara Laboratory of Tumor Biology ", and three cancer charities share the whole of Mrs. Jeanne O. J. Western's estate—she died in hospital after jumping from a first-floor window to escape a fire in Peter Street, Soho.

The Friends Service Council receive half the estate of Peter R. Selwood, of Southampton, who left £978,077, and St. Mary's Parish Church Council, Petworth, Sussex, are left a £10,000 legacy under the will of Donal W. Morphy.

A retired engineer from Bournemouth—Ernest W. Davies—and Reginald F. Gard, of Bristol, both left the whole of their estates to the Salvation Army, and Oxfam inherit £44,000, the whole of Miss Violet E. Olney's property.

The National Trust benefit under certain wills—Leslie Forder left them all his property to purchase coastal land in the West Country and Edward D. Jackson, of Bellister Castle, Haltwhistle, left the Bellister Castle Estate, other than endowment land, to the Trust, provided they pass a resolution declaring that the estate " is proper to be held for the benefit of the nation and shall be inalienable ", and the said endowment land held as a source of income for the estate.

Oswald Claus and the Rt. Rev. Ronald O. Hall both left varying amounts for such general charitable purposes as their respective trustees select, whereas Jabes J. Hancock, left all his £179,649 estate for such charities for the welfare of old aged and lonely people as his executor selects.

Wilson P. Grant, a caretaker, left all his property to Chertsey and Walton Constituency Labour Party, and the RAF Benevolent Fund receive most of Mrs. Miriam E. M. Lousada's £248,852 estate, in memory of her son Ormond, an Air Gunner in the RAF, killed on active service on air operations on November 13, 1944.

The principal figure in the list below is that of the *gross* estate.

Miss Mildred Dorothy Bellamy, of Shirley, Solihull...............................£75,463
(Residue equally between RSPCA, PDSA, and St. Dunstan's.)

Mr. Leslie Birkett, of Chigwell, Essex... £429,607
(Residue to Imperial Cancer Research Fund.)

Mrs. Bertha Bradbury, of Wembley.... £104,271
(Residue equally between the Greater London Fund for the Blind, Dr. Barnardo's and the RSPCA.)

Mrs. Edith Bragg, of Sittingbourne, Kent. £30,684
(Residue equally between the PDSA, Dr. Barnardo's, The Poplar Mission, and Royal National Mission to Deep Sea Fishermen.)

Mr. Oswald Claus, of Blackburn........£33,294
(Residue to such charities as his executors select.)

Mr. John Solomon Cohen, of London... £194,821
(£50,000 each to the John S. Cohen Foundation and the Friends of the Hebrew University of Jerusalem.)

Mr. Herbert Samuel Jared Cook, of Weston super Mare..........................£32,265
(Residue equally between the Imperial Cancer Research Fund and Arthritis and Rheumatism Council.)

Mr. Edward Owen Crosse, of Reading.. £73,359
(All property equally between RNIB, British Sailors Society and RNLI.)

Grace Marion Davidson, of Bristol......£24,777
(All property to Bristol Dogs Home.)

Mr. Ernest William Davies, of Bournemouth
£41,814
(All property to the Salvation Army.)

Miss Gertrude Jane Dickinson, of Washington, Tyne and Wear......................£25,998
(All property to the RSPCA.)

Mr. John Emmott, of Keighley, Yorks.,... £35,443
(All property to the Yorkshire Naturalists Trust.)

Miss Edith Winifred Evans, of Epsom, Surrey
£102,201
(Residue equally between the PDSA and Cats Protection League.)

Mr. Leslie Forder, of London...........£47,325
(All property to the National Trust.)

Mr. Reginald Frederick Gard, of Bristol.. £20,461
(All property to the Salvation Army.)

Mr. Wilson Phelps Grant, of Ottershaw, Surrey
£28,164
(All property to Chertsey and Walton Constituency Labour Party.)

Rt. Rev. Ronald Owen Hall, of Lewknor, Oxon............................£214,818
(£50,000 for such charitable purposes in the UK or the Diocese of Hong Kong as his trustees select.)

Mr. Jabes James Hancock, of Brighton... £179,649
(All property to such charities for the welfare of old aged and lonely people as his executor selects.)

Miss Annie Dewar Henderson, of London. £65,835
(Residue equally between the RNLI, Dr. Barnardo's and Bank Clerks Orphans Fund.)

Mr. William Henry Horden, of Bournemouth
£104,712
(£25,000 to RNLI, £500 to RSPCA, and residue equally between the Imperial Cancer Research Fund and Cheshire Homes.)

Mr. George Newman Horne, of Bidborough, Kent.............................£301,893
(£50,000 to the Copthall Trust Fund.)

Mr. Percy Henry Horsford, of Rushden, Northants...............................£21,535
(Half property to the National Society for Mentally Handicapped Children, and half property equally between RNIB and Wellingborough and District Chest Care Association.)

2nd Baron Inverforth of London.......£532,362
(£10,000 each to Salvation Army, Wildfowl Trust, Imperial Cancer Research Fund, and Distressed Gentlefolks Aid Association, and £5,000 to the Baltic Exchange Benevolent Fund.)

Mr. Edward Donaldson Jackson, of Haltwhistle, Northumberland...................£395,299
(Bellister Castle Estate, other than endowment lands, to National Trust.)

Deana Kurlander, of London...........£22,619
(All property to Jewish Blind Society.)

Mrs. Miriam Evelyn Mary Lousada, of Todenham, Gloucs.......................£248,852
(Residue to RAF Benevolent Fund.)

Miss Mollie Marsden, of Skellow, near Doncaster
£35,859
(Residue equally between Marie Curie Memorial Foundation, Imperial Cancer Research Fund and Royal Commonwealth Society for the Blind.)

Mr. Herbert Miller, of Chelmsford...... £633,878
(£600 and two thirds of residue to USPG and a third of residue to British and Foreign Bible Society.)

Mr. Donal William Morphy, of Byworth, Petworth, Sussex...................... £280,669
(£10,000 to St. Mary's Parish Church Council, Petworth.)

Dame Barbara Hepworth-Nicholson, of St. Ives, Cornwall........................ £2,970,049
(£10,000 to Westminster Hospital, London, for cancer research.)

Miss Violet Elizabeth Olney, of Rhos on Sea, N. Wales............................. £44,322
(All property to Oxfam.)

Mrs. Diana Margaret Pannett, of Basingstoke, Hants............................... £74,557
(All property to the National Trust.)

Mrs. Olga Parbury, of Bexhill, Sussex.... £52,146
(All property to the Imperial Cancer Research Fund.)

Mrs. Ethel Elizabeth Pepper, of Ashtead, Surrey £213,746
(Residue equally between NSPCC, Dr. Barnardo's, Children's Society, National Childrens Home, Shaftesbury Society, Save the Children Fund, and Cheshire Homes.)

Miss Annie Perry, of Clayton le Moors, Lancs. £28,767
(All property equally between Marie Curie Memorial Foundation and Accrington and District Institution for the Blind.)

Doris Beatrice Pink, of Wallington, Surrey £41,157
(All property to the PDSA.)

Miss Emily Matilda Potter, of Burgess Hill, Sussex............................. £24,113
(All property to St. Dunstan's.)

Mr. John Reach, of Westcliff on Sea...... £82,794
(£2,000 to National Art Collection Fund, £1,000 each to Imperial Cancer Research Fund and British Heart Foundation, and residue to Jewish National Fund.)

Mr. Christopher Herbert Renny Reeves, of Podington, Beds.................. £3,620,914
(£20,000 to his executors " to be given by them on my behalf as they may in their absolute discretion decide ".)

Miss Vera Muriel Robertson, of Godalming, Surrey.............................. £30,167
(Residue to PDSA.)

Miss Esme Dorothy Theresa Roe, of Southsea, Hants............................... £59,204
(£10,000 each to CMS, London City Mission and London Embankment Mission, £3,000 to the Commonwealth and Continental Church Society, £1,000 to two churches in Southsea, £500 to the Bible Flower Mission, and residue to British and Foreign Bible Society.)

Mrs. Agnes Eveline Rowland, of Seaton Delaval, Tyne and Wear.................... £31,681
(All property to Imperial Cancer Research Fund.)

Mrs. Mary Jocelyn St. Barbe, of Falmouth, Cornwall............................... £393,643
(£42,000 and some effects to National Trust, and £4,000 each to Guide Dogs for the Blind Association, Distressed Gentlefolks Aid Association, Help the Aged and the Samaritans.)

Mr. Peter Richard Selwood, of Bassett, Southampton........................... £978,077
(Half property to Friends Service Council.)

Mrs. Martha Ellen Spedding, of Barnsley.. £86,453
(£100 to Kendray Hospital, Barnsley, and residue equally between RNIB and Royal Association in Aid of the Deaf and Dumb.)

Miss Marjorie Helen Victoria Strong, of Trowbridge........................... £57,187
(Residue to Musicians Benevolent Fund.)

Mrs. Bertha Thompson, of Manchester... £46,436
(Residue to PDSA.)

Miss Sarah Witham Thompson, of Ingleton, Yorks............................... £447,428
(£50,000 to RNLI, £5,000 to Thornton in Lonsdale Parish Church, and £2,000 each to RUKBA and Salvation Army.)

Mrs. Elsie Turner, of Sheffield........... £28,105
(All property equally between RNLI, RSPB and RSPCA.)

Miss Alice Annie Webb, of London...... £59,426
(All property equally between Salvation Army, Cancer Research Campaign, Save the Children Fund, National Association for Mental Health, RNIB and NSPCC.)

Mrs. Jeanne Odette Juliette Western, of London £32,258
(All property equally between Cancer Research Campaign, Imperial Cancer Research Fund and Institute of Cancer Research.)

BRITISH INSURANCE COMPANIES IN 1975

In 1975, the worldwide general business premium income of the insurance companies increased by £712 million to £4,641 million, an increase of 18% over 1974.

The general insurance funds and the shareholders' capital and free reserves held as security for policyholders at the end of 1975 amounted to £6,507 million and represented 140% of premium income, compared with £5,272 million (134% of premiums) at the end of 1974.

Investment income earned on these funds was £465 million. Against this, companies sustained an underwriting loss on general worldwide business of £180 million (4·0% of premiums) compared with a loss of 2·9% of premiums (£107·0 million) in 1974.

RESULTS IN MAJOR TERRITORIES

United Kingdom

There was a small motor underwriting loss of £4·6 million (0·7% of premiums). Claims costs were increased by factors which included increases in the cost of spare parts (18%), garage charge out rates (21%), car prices (over 20%) and payments for bodily injuries (30%).

The outturn of fire and accident (non motor) business was a modest profit of £20·3 million (2·1% of premiums).

United States

The loss on underwriting in the U.S.A. was £117·5 million (£46·1 million in 1974). Motor results deteriorated with a loss of £74·7 million (£11·3 million in 1974). Fire and accident (non motor) underwriting losses were £42·8 million (£34·8 million in 1974).

British companies operating in the U.S.A. are intensifying their policy of very selective underwriting to counteract the poor experience in that territory, especially in motor business.

Rest of the World

The deterioration in the motor account was seen also in other overseas territories, where there was a loss in this class of business of £70·5 million or 12% of premiums (£41·6 million, 8·6% of premiums in 1974).

There was a marked improvement in fire and

accident classes which produced a marginal loss of £2·7 million, compared with a £52·3 million loss in 1974.

Factors particularly influencing this improvement included much reduced losses in Australia and Canada. Experience in South Africa became generally unfavourable.

MARINE, AVIATION AND TRANSPORT

Worldwide premium income for marine and aviation rose by 8·6% to £408 million and transfers from profit and loss accounts totalled £5·0 million.

Towards the end of the year, two of the largest tankers, "Kriti Sun" and "Burge Istra", blew up in the Far East. Each was insured for over £10 million, more than 70% covered by British insurers. Since then, these losses have been overshadowed by the "Olympic Bravery" which went aground on its maiden voyage. Two wide-bodied jet aircraft were destroyed in 1975 and two others severely damaged although fewer people were killed in aviation accidents.

OVERSEAS EARNINGS

60% of general premium income relates to overseas operations and a major contribution is made to foreign currency earnings. The most recent figures put the annual invisible earnings, from all insurance activities (comprising companies, Lloyd's and brokers), at £372 million.

INVESTMENTS

Invested funds arising from long term insurance totalled £21,877 million at book values at 31st December 1975. Income from these funds was £1,727 million.

As already stated, invested funds arising from general business totalled £6,507 million at book values at 31st December 1975. Income from these funds was £465 million.

Market values for both long term and general funds were some 8% above the corresponding book values.

NOTE: Insurance company figures refer to British Insurance Association members who transact some 95% of the world-wide business of the British insurance company market.

WORLDWIDE GENERAL PREMIUMS 1974 AND 1975

	1974	1975	Increase
	£m	£m	%
Fire and Accident (non-motor)......................	2,271	2,687	18·3
Motor...	1,282	1,546	20·6
Marine, Aviation and Transport.....................	376	408	8·6
TOTAL...................................	3,929	4,641	18·1

NOTE: 1. These tables are compiled from worldwide figures provided by those members of the BIA which have head offices in the U.K. and U.K. premiums for those members with head offices outside the U.K.
2. The above figures include business transacted by specialist reinsurers, and business written on a 3 year account basis which is not included in later tables.

WORLDWIDE UNDERWRITING RESULTS 1974 AND 1975

	1974			1975		
	Premiums	Profit/ Loss	% of Premiums	Premiums	Profit/ Loss	% of Premiums
	£m	£m	%	£m	£m	%
Fire and Accident (non-motor)...	2,154	−65·7	−3·1	2,597	−25·2	−1·0
Motor..........................	1,252	−51·1	−4·1	1,533	−149·8	−9·8
TOTAL..................	3,406	−116·8	−3·4	4,130	−175·0	−4·2

NOTE: In 1975, there was a transfer *from* profit and loss account for marine, aviation and transport business of £5 million and in 1974 a transfer *to* profit and loss account of £9·8 million.

WORLDWIDE LONG-TERM PREMIUMS 1974 AND 1975

	1974	1975	Increase
	£m	£m	%
Ordinary Long-Term U.K........................	1,927	2,120	10·0
Ordinary Long-Term (Overseas)....................	489	573	17·2
Industrial Long-Term (U.K.).......................	382	418	9·4
TOTAL...................................	2,798	3,111	11·2

U.K. UNDERWRITING 1974 AND 1975

	1974			1975		
	Premiums	Profit/Loss	% of Premiums	Premiums	Profit/Loss	% of Premiums
	£m	£m	%	£m	£m	%
Fire and Accident (non-motor)...	789	+21·4	+2·7	970	+20·3	+2·1
Motor.........................	507	+1·8	+0·4	623	−4·6	−0·7
TOTAL.................	1,296	+23·2	+1·8	1,593	+15·7	+1·0

NOTE: In 1975 U.K. premiums were increased by the inclusion of business transacted by new members, amounting to £22 million for fire and accident and £20 million for motor.

USA UNDERWRITING 1974 AND 1975

	1974			1975		
	Premiums	Profit/Loss	% of Premiums	Premiums	Profit/Loss	% of Premiums
	£m	£m	%	£m	£m	%
Fire and Accident (non-motor)...	486	−34·8	−7·2	584	−42·8	−7·3
Motor	262	−11·3	−4·3	320	−74·7	−23·3
TOTAL.................	748	−46·1	−6·2	904	−117·5	−13·0

REST OF THE WORLD UNDERWRITING 1974 AND 1975

	1974			1975		
	Premiums	Profit/Loss	% of Premiums	Premiums	Profit/Loss	% of Premiums
	£m	£m	%	£m	£m	%
Fire and Accident (non-motor)...	879	−52·3	−5·9	1,043	−2·7	−0·3
Motor.........................	483	−41·6	−8·6	589	−70·5	−12·0
TOTAL.................	1,362	−93·9	−6·9	1,632	−73·2	−4·5

LLOYD'S OF LONDON

Lloyd's of London is an international market for almost any type of insurance. Ships, aircraft, oil rigs, cargo of all descriptions, motor cars, civil engineering projects, fire, personal accident and third party liability are a few random examples of the everyday risks placed at Lloyd's which bring some £750 million of premiums to underwriters each year. Two thirds of this business comes from outside Great Britain and makes a valuable contribution to the country's balance of payments.

Today, as it was three centuries ago, a policy is subscribed at Lloyd's by private individuals with unlimited liability. Now that Lloyd's members are numbered in their thousands, however, the method of underwriting is the same only in principle. The merchant of the past, signing policies in a coffee house as a sideline to his main business, has long since given way to the specialist underwriter who accepts risks at Lloyd's on behalf of members grouped in a syndicate. There are currently about 270 syndicates of varying sizes, some with up to several hundred names and each managed by a full-time underwriting agent.

Lloyd's membership today is drawn from many sources. Industry, commerce and the professions are strongly represented while many members are, of course, actively engaged at Lloyd's either on the broking or the underwriting side.

Underwriting membership of Lloyd's is open to men and women of any nationality provided that they meet the stringent financial requirements of the Committee of Lloyd's. Assets of at least £75,000 have to be shown and a minimum deposit of £10,000 must be lodged with the Corporation of Lloyd's as security for underwriting liabilities.

Lloyd's also provides the most comprehensive shipping intelligence service available in the world. The enormous volume of shipping information received from Lloyd's agents, radio stations, shipowners and other sources is collated and distributed to newspapers, radio and television services, and throughout the marine and commercial communities in general.

This information is edited, printed and published at Lloyd's and sent all over the world. " Lloyd's List " is London's oldest daily newspaper and contains news of general commercial interest as well as shipping information. " Lloyd's Shipping Index " also published daily, lists some 18,000 ocean-going vessels in alphabetical order and gives the latest known report of each.

LLOYD'S UNDERWRITERS
SUMMARY OF ACCOUNTS AS AT DECEMBER 31, 1973

In the summaries: (1) Premiums include the reinsurance premium (if any) received from a previous closed account; and (2) Claims include the reinsurance premium paid or amount placed to reserve at close of third year.

	Net Premium Income	Interest and other credits	Claims	Expenses and other debits	Balance
	£	%	%	%	%
1971 A/C (end Year 3)		5·98			
Life	966,483	5·98	78·02	9·90	18·06
Motor	52,078,934	3·40	89·57	9·96	3·87
Marine, Aviation and Transit		3·85	87·72	3·43	12·70
Other than Aviation	336,410,895		89·15		
Aviation	83,646,809		81·98		
All other	398,162,435	3·58	95·24	2·83	5·51
	871,265,556	3·70	91·26	3·55	8·89
1972 A/C (end Year 2)					
Life	929,313	2·87	60·81	12·43	29·63
Motor	66,333,656	1·73	40·46	9·38	51·89
Marine, Aviation and Transit		1·32	23·47	2·77	75·08
Other than Aviation	362,637,499		23·53		
Aviation	85,561,588		23·22		
All other	442,019,411	1·09	21·72	2·36	77·01
	957,481,467	1·24	23·88	3·05	74·31
1973 A/C (end Year 1)					
Life	874,604	0·91	14·90	9·07	76·94
Motor	55,885,358	0·84	15·84	11·67	73·33
Marine, Aviation and Transit		0·84	23·05	5·46	72·33
Other than Aviation	180,968,302		22·71		
Aviation	34,480,695		24·83		
All other	169,200,510	0·84	13·65	5·89	81·30
	441,409,469	0·84	18·52	6·42	75·90

LIFE ASSURANCE IN 1975

These figures take into account all forms of ordinary and industrial life assurance, including business written under occupational pension schemes, and business written overseas by U.K. offices and their subsidiaries.

In 1975 the total of yearly premiums for life assurance and annuities rose to £2,760 million from £2,420 million in 1974, an increase of 14%. Single premiums decreased from £890 million to £640 million, this reduction being mainly due to a fall in the issue of guaranteed income bonds.

Benefits paid to policyholders, including amounts paid on death and maturity and payments to annuitants, totalled £2,190 million.

Investment income earned on life assurance and annuity funds totalled £1,830 million in 1975, against £1,570 million the previous year.

Amounts put aside to meet future claims totalled £2,560 million, representing new money made available for investment in 1975 through life assurance savings.

The total value of life funds increased from £19,600 million to £23,000 million, reflecting both new money put aside and also the recovery in market values of assets from the low levels existing at the end of 1974.

LIFE ASSURANCE NEW BUSINESS 1975

	1975 £m	1974 £m
New yearly premiums	943	746
Single premiums and considerations for immediate and deferred annuities	248	546
Benefits secured by these premiums		
New sums assured	34,100	26,000
New annuities, deferred and immediate	1,100 p.a.	941 p.a.

INDUSTRIAL LIFE ASSURANCE 1975

The following figures are based on returns from 18 "home service" insurance offices, which together transact over 99% of all industrial assurance business. While they, unlike all other insurers, transact industrial life assurance, they also carry on a very considerable volume of ordinary life and general insurance business, much of it in policyholders' homes.

	1975	1974
Industrial Life Business	£m	£m
1. Premium Income	418·0	382·1
2. Investment Income (Gross)	239·9	214·1
3. Industrial Assurance Fund as at the end of the year (after transfers to and from investment reserves, etc.)	2,904.0	2,644·6
4. New Business:		
(a) New Sums Assured	1,402·8	1,206·6
(b) New Premiums per annum	85·9	73·2
5. Payments to policyholders:		
(a) On death	90·7	88·6
(b) On maturity	141·0	135·7
(c) On surrender	76·8	74·6
TOTAL	308·5	298·9
6. Expenses including pension fund contributions, staff bonuses	184·7	149·9

NEW BUSINESS IN LINKED LIFE ASSURANCE POLICIES

	Year ended Dec. 31, 1974	Year ended Dec. 31, 1975
	£m	£m
1. *New Annual Premiums*		
(a) Ordinary business	35·748★	38·241
(b) Pension (including retirement annuity)	17·583	27·596
Total New Annual Premiums	£53·331★	£65·837
2. *New Single Premiums*		
(a) Ordinary business	101·186★	80·889
(b) Pension (including retirement annuity)	11·521★	13·125
Total New Single Premiums	£112·707★	£94·014
3. Number of policies in force at end of period	2,247,167★	2,308·047
(a) Number of policies involving investment directly or indirectly, and wholly or partly, in authorised unit trusts	1,155·486★	1,274·916
Investment in authorised unit trusts in respect of policies falling under 3 (a)		
4. Net amount invested during period	50·842★	69·583
5. Aggregate market value at end of period	240·076★	507·846

★ Revised figure, February 1976.

INSURANCE COMPANY INVESTMENTS
Long Term Funds

	1974		1975	
	£m	%	£m	%
British Government authority securities	2,496	13·6	3,689	16·9
Foreign and Commonwealth Government, provincial and municipal stocks	693	3·8	913	4·2
Debentures, loan stocks, preference and guaranteed stocks and shares	2,771	15·2	3,100	14·2
Ordinary stocks and shares	4,203	23·0	5,410	24·7
Mortgages	3,079	16·8	3,266	14·9
Real property and ground rents	3,649	19·9	4,313	19·7
Other investments	1,402	7·7	1,186	5·4
TOTAL	18,293	100·0	21,877	100·0
INCOME	1,459		1,727	

INSURANCE COMPANY INVESTMENTS

Other Funds

	1974		1975	
	£m	%	£m	%
British Government authority securities	345	6·5	757	11·6
Foreign and Commonwealth Government, provincial and municipal stocks............................	818	15·5	1,163	17·9
Debentures, loan stocks, preference and guaranteed stocks and shares....................................	884	16·8	981	15·1
Ordinary stocks and shares...........................	1,407	26·7	1,583	24·3
Mortgages..	366	6·9	408	6·3
Real property and ground rents......................	547	10·4	655	10·1
Other investments.................................	905	17·2	960	14·7
TOTAL...................................	5,272	100·0	6,507	100·0
INCOME.................................	377		465	

THE LIFE ASSURANCE COMPANIES

The list on the following pages contains the names of all the more important British life offices, and of Commonwealth offices (marked C) which transact life business in this country.

Class of business. The second column shows whether the company is conducted on the mutual system whereby the whole of the divisible profit is allotted to participating policyholders (M), or whether the company has proprietors by whom part (usually a very small proportion) of such profits received (P). Life offices transacting other business are marked (O) in this column. In such cases the life funds are kept separately, and are not liable for the claims of other departments. The share capital is usually liable for the claims of all branches. Those having an industrial branch are indicated by letter (I).

Figures. These are taken from the latest annual accounts available at date of going to press and in the majority of cases refer to annual reports for the financial year ended December 31, 1975.

Life funds. The amounts of these funds, though of interest, are not in themselves a sufficient indication of the financial stability of a company, which cannot be judged unless liabilities are actually compared with assets.

Premium income. The annual premium income is in all cases stated after deduction of the amount paid to other companies for reassuring parts of the risk.

Consideration for annuities.—These are the amounts received to provide various types of annuities.

Interest.—The rate of interest earned is important for comparison with the rate assumed in valuing liabilities, since the greater the margin between these rates the greater is the surplus available from this source bonus declaration. The rate of interest given is before deduction of Income Tax except where marked (N)—net.

Valuation.—The valuation returns which are required to be made by the companies to the Department of Trade and Industry indicate liability under existing policies, after making allowance for the amounts to be paid and received. It is assumed that deaths will occur in accordance with a mortality table (various tables are used) and that interest will be earned at a certain rate. If a company assumes that it will earn a high rate of interest in the future the net liability will appear less than if it assumes a low rate, while the liability on account of mortality appears greater when some tables than by others. The position of an office is most satisfactory when a stringent basis of valuation is adopted, because the margin between the calculated and experienced

liability is larger and the surplus available for bonuses is greater. The lower the rate of interest assumed the more stringent is the valuation. The foregoing remarks, however, do not apply in the case of an office which has adopted a Bonus Reserve Valuation.

Types of policy.—Although there are scores of life offices in Britain each offering their own particular products under a wide variety of labels, there are really only four basic types of contract. These are:

1. " Term " assurance (sometimes called " temporary " assurance). With this type of policy the assurer, in return for a regular premium agrees to pay the sum assured if the person assured should die within the term of years stated by the policy.

Such policies take care of the temporary need for protection of the family while the children are growing up, and the family is therefore most vulnerable. The commonest and most popular forms are to cover the mortgage on the family home or to assume a regular tax-free income for the family over so many years should the breadwinner die. This is much the cheapest form of life assurance because the majority of policies invariably do not result in claims.

2. " Whole-life " assurance is one under which the assurer undertakes to keep the assurance in force provided the premiums are paid for the whole life of the assured. They will then pay the agreed sum whenever death takes place.

This costs a good deal more than term, naturally. All policies end in claims.

3. " Endowment " assurance. This contract really is one which uses a fund for saving to a particular target sum by a particular future date and at the same time secures payment of the sum assured should the saver die before that date arrives. In return for the continued payment of a regular premium over a fixed number of years, the assurer agrees to pay the sum assured at the end of that time, or earlier if the assured person should die. The bulk of an endowment assurance premium is savings; consequently the premium of such a contract is a lot higher than that for a whole life assurance.

4. " Annuities ". Life assurance can be divided broadly speaking into death or survival benefits. Death benefits are paid to a policyholder's dependants if and when he dies. Survival benefits are paid to the policyholder himself either in the form of a cash sum when he reaches a certain age or in the form of a guaranteed annual income for life, which is known as an annuity. Pensions are annuities of a kind and a very large proportion of the pension due to people are being and will be paid by funds run by life offices.

PRINCIPAL LIFE ASSURANCE COMPANIES

Established	Class	Name of Office	Annual Accounts				Interest % assumed at Valuation
			Life and Annuity Funds	Life Premium Income	Consideration for Annuities	Rate of Interest % Earned	
			£m	£,000	£,000	£	£
1961	P	Abbey Life..................	287·9	45,987	13,186		3·5
1849	M	Australian Mutual (C)..........	60·5	5,159	285	8·06	Various
1925	PO	Avon......................	9·6	1,616	112	10·44	Various
1961	P	Bedford Life†...............	6·9	1,089	55	8·5	4·25
1866	PIO	Britannic (Ord.)..............	107·2	10,330	456	7·075	3·00
1920	PO	British National..............	5·8	967	254	6·1	2·5–4·00
1963	P	Cannon.....................	113	30,588	1,936	8·41	Various
1862	MI	City of Glasgow (Ord.)........	4	480	1	8·00	3·00
1824	M	Clerical Medical..............	235·5	14,748	34,446	9·00	7·00
1873	M	Colonial Mutual (C)...........	764		107,060	8·03	Various
1861	PO	Commercial Union.............	1,537·3	114,959	87,581	8·56	3·00
1871	M	Confederation (C)†...........	45·5	7,996	469	9·25	Various
1867	MIO	Co-operative.................	609	92,600	1,800	7·82	3·50
1900	M	Crown Life..................	600		114,000	7·07	Various
1899	PO	Crusader....................	94·3	14,217	2,232	8·60	Various
1904	PO	Eagle Star...................	683·1	52,500	23,200	8·37	Various
1887	MO	Ecclesiastical................	8·4	1,668	79	10·61	4·5
1844	P	Equity & Law................	354	34,656	25,531	—	Various
1832	M	Friends Provident.............	448·4	51,290	5,883	8·86	2·75
1848	P	Gresham.....................	57	7,179	172	9·65	3·0 and 5·5
1821	PO	Guardian Royal Exchange.......	1048·7	115,000	33,900	7·26	Various
1965	P	Hambro.....................	288	32,400	31,900	—	—
1960	P	Hill Samuel..................	230·8	13,061	21,235	—	Various
1897	P	Imperial Life (C).............	305	47,053	—	7·34	Various
1939	PI	Irish Life...................	165·2	30,273	3,589	7·69	3·5
1836	PO	Legal and General............	1,792	268,515	11,540	83	Various
1838	P	Life Assoc. of Scotland†.......	48·5	3,293	3,640	8·85	Various
1843	MI	Liverpool Victoria (Ord.).......	62·3	6,591	—	7·48	3·00
1869	PIO	London and Manchester........	102·5	10,556	37	10·37	3·00
1806	M	London Life.................	209	27,547	937	8·31	Various
1852	M	MGM Assurance..............	44	6,364	86	8·69	Various
1884	M	Medical Sickness.............	16·9	1,501	40	8·76	Various
1890	M	Nalgo Assurance..............	6·2	626	—	7·9	2·5
1935	P	National Employers...........	56·5	19,179	8	10·08	4·5–4·75
1910	MO	National Farmers Union........	99·9	7,796	3,144	9·84	Various
1830	M	Natl. Mutual Life†............	68·3	5,730	4,740	8·04	Various
1835	M	National Provident............	165·2	22,078	4,673	—	4·0
1808	M	Norwich Union...............	894·8	130,179	4,805	10·74	5·0
1864	PIO	Pearl (Ord.).................	398·9	40,594	3,312	8·95	3·0
1782	PO	Phoenix.....................	273·3	41,515	1,310	7·70	3·5–4·0
1891	MI	Pioneer Mutual (Ord.)..........	19·2	1,714	40	9·34	4·5
1877	P	Prov. Life Assoc..............	75·3	9,321	280	6·49	2·5–9·5
1840	M	Prov. Mutual................	211·7	12,605	23,776	8·18	Various
1848	PIO	Prudential (Ord.).............	2,223·8	290,043	8,482	7·83	3·0–3·5
1864	PIO	Refuge (Ord.)................	146·4	13,294	966	9·93	3·25
1911	MI	Reliance (Ord.)...............	7·5	995	24	8·1	4·25
1845	PO	Royal.......................	536	41,970	35,574	8·99	3·0–3·75
1850	MI	Royal Liver (Ord.)............	127·1	20,721	—	8·84	3·75
1861	MIO	Royal London (Ord.)†.........	73·6	11,577	29	9·72	5·00
1826	M	Scottish Amicable.............	311·9		45,041	11·46	Various
1831	M	Scottish Equitable............	162·2	25,558	5,795	10·68	Various
1881	M	Scottish Life.................	115·8	19,016	1,521	10·81	4·75–5·5
1883	MO	Scottish Mutual..............	128·7	15,986	1,790	8·45	2·75–3·5
1837	M	Scottish Provident............	184·3	31,543	1,327	11·46	Various
1825	M	Standard Life................	1,274·6	140,858	30,196	8·67	Various
1710	PO	Sun Alliance.................	303·5	41,114	1,239	—	Various
1810	P	Sun Life Society.............	595·7		34,800	8·13	Various
1865	M	Sun of Canada (C)............	1,810·4	172,111	43,606	7·15	Various
1908	P	United Friendly..............	32·6	5,926	—	8·12	3·00
1804	M	United Kingdom Provident......	214·1	15,579	4,595	7·5	Various
1825	P	University...................	36·1	1,528	2,556	9·1	9·25
1974	P	Vanbrugh...................	31·5	11,700	—	10·13	—
1841	MIO	Wesleyan & General (Ord.).....	45	4,637	81	9·60	2·75–4·0
1837	P	Yorkshire General.............	315·5	29,117	11,420	8·82	4·5

† 1974 figures

(C) denotes Commonwealth Office

INDUSTRIAL COMPANIES

Estab-lished	Class	Name of Office	Life Funds	Life Premium Income	Rate of interest % Earned	Interest % assumed at Valuation
			£m	£,000		
1866	PO	Britannic....................	186·9	30,994	8·779	3·00
1862	M	City of Glasgow..............	8·6	1,150	8	4·00
1939	P	Irish Life....................	40·7	6,048	8·55	4·00
1843	M	Liverpool Victoria............	309·9	32,630	7·44	3·00
1869	PO	London and Manchester.......	80·6	10,934	10·38	3·00
1864	PO	Pearl........................	380·5	60,115	8·97	2·50
1891	M	Pioneer Mutual..............	20·7	3,392	7·80	4·00
1848	PO	Prudential...................	904·8	122,250	8·87	3·00
1864	PO	Refuge......................	150·5	23,292	9·43	4·00
1911	MI	Reliance.....................	6·5	1,328	8·58	4·25
1850	M	Royal Liver..................	38·2	5,140	8·84	3·5
1861	MO	Royal London†...............	186·7	18,194	9·82	4·00
1841	MO	Wesleyan and General........	58·9	7,979	9·85	3·00

† 1974 figures

LIFE ASSURANCE NEW BUSINESS 1975

Name of Office	No. of policies issued	Net sums assured	Net annual premiums	Net single premiums
		£	£	£
Abbey Life.............................	66,159	406,883,000	11,269,000	19,206,000
Australian Mutual.....................	9,130	51,369,891	976,643	321,110
Avon.................................	2,994	19,359,688	287,774	6,185
Britannic (Ord.).......................	26,565	73,604,764	1,673,834	106,888
British National.......................	2,441	15,579,000	265,211	—
Cannon...............................	40,247	261,130,775	2,699,149	2,878,292
City of Glasgow (Ord.).................	900	2,630,000	78,700	49,500
Clerical Medical.......................	18,305	103,460,662	2,099,058	67,270
Colonial Mutual.......................	—	1,025,729,798	20,546 752	—
Commercial Union.....................	139,607	1,814,898,500	18,288,253	2,314,572
Confederation†........................	8,139	36,424,957	951,963	6,263
Co-operative..........................	668,490	663,000,000	15,800,000	16,000
Crown Life............................	54,000	840,000,000	—	—
Crusader..............................	20,349	535,000,000	4,834,000	174,000
Eagle Star............................	24,219	656,000,000	10,700,000	26,100,000
Ecclesiastical..........................	1,111	8,371,899	119,560	382
Equity & Law.........................	98,525	999,572,189	16,436,436	7,944,730
Friends Provident......................	44,094	645,100,000	12,200,000	4,000,000
Gresham..............................	10,394	62,301,344	1,117,840	7,404
Guardian Royal Exchange..............	147,789	2,014,400,000	29,300,000	13,000,000
Hambro...............................	58,000	376,900,000	19,900,000	24,400,000
Hill Samuel...........................	33,730	145,951,000	1,828,000	6,158,000
Imperial Life..........................	31,280	403,518,000	5,727,000	2,666,239
Irish Life.............................	31,543	272,842,000	7,394,000	6,366,000
Legal and General.....................	131,988	2,562,629,000	59,362,000	146,618,000
Life Assoc. of Scotland†...............	4,710	52,727,674	1,502,294	707,788
Liverpool Victoria (Ord.)..............	18,978	30,503,015	1,099,882	—
London and Manchester...............	13,906	50,368,230	1,693,730	242,624
London Life...........................	17,694	100,282,703	1,903,754	202,100
MGM Assurance......................	5,311	35,873,621	668,792	998
Medical Sickness......................	2,234	25,815,457	185,421	47,565
Nalgo Assurance......................	1,966	11,819,490	92,950	—
National Employers'...................	14,114	202,000,000	6,370,000	550,000
National Farmers Union...............	6,742	44,862,344	904,009	2,393
National Mutual Life†.................	5,422	42,400,313	1,030,193	9,603
National Provident....................	15,531	155,819,000	5,931,000	4,714,000
Norwich Union........................	165,304	1,204,207,106	28,609,572	11,937,891
Pearl (Ord.)..........................	86,034	347,307,000	7,348,000	4,083,000
Phoenix...............................	43,900	961,000,000	10,023,000	1,790,000
Pioneer Mutual (Ord.).................	5,626	15,629,802	197,820	46,815
Prov. Life Assoc......................	14,428	156,275,293	2,478,790	690,356
Prov. Mutual.........................	36,486	355,521,589	9,723,469	3,307,752
Prudential (Ord.)......................	362,978	4,172,393,816	53,470,221	26,953,006
Refuge (Ord.).........................	23,136	61,810,328	1,781,042	383,938
Reliance (Ord.)........................	2,694	11,308,486	169,887	93,863
Royal.................................	79,000	752,976,000	14,350,000	14,800,000
Royal Liver (Ord.)....................	20,951	32,525,305	1,192,068	23,882
Royal London (Ord.)†.................	26,533	78,147,000	2,160,000	178,000
Scottish Amicable.....................	42,795	407,108,866	11,909,478	2,032,413
Scottish Equitable.....................	21,582	166,289,309	8,385,443	5,812,761

† 1974 figures
LIFE ASSURANCE NEW BUSINESS 1975—*continued*

Name of Office	No. of policies issued	Net sums assured	Net annual premiums	Net single premiums
		£	£	£
Scottish Life..............................	12,443	222,798,669	4,910,525	1,524,042
Scottish Mutual...........................	13,952	121,382,828	3,382,618	49,702
Scottish Provident.........................	42,398	352,689,000	3,594,000	29,000
Standard Life..............................	86,263	1,081,514,750	31,118,568	19,037,811
Sun Alliance..............................	61,952	508,618,000	8,405,000	2,560,000
Sun Life Society...........................	79,000	806,400,000	51,600,000	
Sun of Canada............................	134,932	1,684,215,000	23,470,000	25,996,000
United Friendly...........................	23,631	82,626,302	1,379,193	176
United Kingdom Provident..................	24,306	128,278,211	3,355,686	20,264
University................................	5,872	11,456,928	580,551	932,681
Vanbrugh.................................	6,225	16,300,000	1,400,000	10,400,000
Wesleyan & General (Ord.).................	6,757	23,043,000	604,000	24,000
Yorkshire General.........................	50,589	651,685,354	4,468,576	339,148

INDUSTRIAL LIFE NEW BUSINESS 1975

Name of Office	Policies issued	Net sums assured	Net annual premiums
		£	£
Britannic....................................	336,653	100,210,317	7,746,543
City of Glasgow..............................	18,000	4,420,000	251,397
Irish Life....................................	61,800	18,244,000	1,037,000
Liverpool Victoria............................	378,100	103,800,000	5,587,000
London and Manchester.......................	92,739	36,936,881	2,599,451
Pearl..	487,394	201,614,000	13,011,000
Pioneer Mutual..............................	21,393	4,339,694	347,100
Prudential...................................	856,414	444,742,820	25,532,725
Refuge......................................	237,876	81,054,605	—
Reliance....................................	15,114	3,834,997	217,584
Royal Liver.................................	266,141	53,777,159	—
Royal London†..............................	158,792	48,667,000	—
Wesleyan and General........................	66,451	22,799,000	1,464,000

† 1974 figures

POLICYHOLDERS PROTECTION BOARD

Aldermary House, Queen Street, London E.C.4

The Policyholders Protection Act 1975 put into effect the scheme whereby private policyholders of companies in liquidation will normally be granted 90 per cent. (100 per cent. in the case of compulsory insurance) of the benefits promised under their policies. The scheme will be financed mainly by a compulsory levy on insurance companies limited to a maximum of 1 per cent. of their annual net premium income. The Board consists of five members, of whom three are drawn from the management of insurance companies and at least one must be qualified to represent the interests of policyholders.

DIRECTORY OF INSURANCE COMPANIES

The class of Insurance undertaken is shown in the second column as follows: A—Accident (which includes Motor, Employers' Liability, etc.); F—Fire (including Burglary); L—Life; and M—Marine. A number of offices are now included in a Group—the initials of which appear after the name. The main Groups are as follows—E.S.—Eagle Star; C.U.—Commercial Union; G.R.E.—Guardian Royal Exchange; G.A.—General Accident; N.U.—Norwich Union; R—Royal; S.A.—Sun Alliance & London.

Est'd	Nature of Business	Name of Company	Address
1961	L	Abbey Life	1-3 St. Paul's Churchyard, E.C.4.
1960	AFLM	Ansvar	St. Leonards Rd., Eastbourne.
1951	AFM	Albion	14 Fenchurch Ave., E.C.3.
1824	AFM	Alliance............S.A.	1 Bartholomew Lane, E.C.2.
1921	L	American Life	12-14 Sydenham Rd., Croydon.
1904	AFM	Army, Navy & General..E.S.	1 Threadneedle St., E.C.2.
1808	ALFM	Atlas...........G.R.E.	Royal Exchange, E.C.3.
1849	L	Australian Mutual Provident..	A.M.P. Ho., Dingwall Rd., Croydon.
1925	AFL	Avon	1 Church St., Stratford-upon-Avon.
1905	AFM	Baptist	4 Southampton Row, W.C.1.
1883	AFM	Beacon............S.A.	1 Bartholomew Lane, E.C.2.
1960	L	Bedford Life	Fairfax Ho., Fulwood Pl., High Holborn, W.C.1.
1894	AFM	Bedford General	Fairfax Ho., Fulwood Pl., High Holborn, W.C.1.
1925	AFM	Black Sea and Baltic	106 Fenchurch St., E.C.3.
1959	AFLM	Bradford	North Park, Halifax.
1863	M	British & Foreign Marine..R.	Liverpool & London Chambers, Exchange, Liverpool 2.
1878	Machinery	British Engine, &c........R.	Longbridge House, Manchester 4.
1854	AFL	British Equitable......G.R.E.	Royal Exchange, E.C.3.
1904	AFM	British General........C.U.	St. Helen's, 1 Undershaft, E.C.3.
1888	AFM	British Law............S.A.	1 Bartholomew Lane, E.C.2.
1896	L	British Life	Reliance House, Tunbridge Wells, Kent.
1920	AFL	British Nat. Life	Framlington Hse., Ireland Yd., E.C.4.
1908	AFM	British Oak.........G.R.E.	Royal Exchange, E.C.3.
1881	A	Builders' Accident	31 & 32 Bedford St., Strand, W.C.2.
1805	AFLM	Caledonian..........G.R.E.	Royal Exchange, E.C.3.
1934	AFM	Cambrian..........G.R.E.	Royal Exchange, E.C.3.
1847	AL	Canada Life	6 Charles II St., S.W.1.
1932	Dog Ins.	Canine Ins. Assoc.	610 Chiswick High Rd., W.4.
1903	AFM	Car & General.......G.R.E.	Royal Exchange, E.C.3.
1885	AFM	Century	4-5 King William St., E.C.4.
1922	AFMex-motor	Chemists' Mutual	321 Chase Rd., Southgate, N.14.
1862	L	City of Glasgow Friendly	200 Bath Street, Glasgow C.2.
1824	L	Clerical, Medical & Gen.	15 St. James's Square, S.W.1.
1873	L & Pers. Acc.	Colonial Mutual	24 Ludgate Hill, E.C.4.
1919	AFM	Comrcl. Ins. Co. of Ireland...	5 Donegall Square, S., Belfast.
1861	AFLM	Commercial Union	St. Helen's, 1 Undershaft, E.C.3.
1871	L	Confederation	120 Regent St., W.1.
1891	AF	Congregational	21-22 Apsley Crescent, Bradford 8.
1867	AFLM	Co-operative	Miller St., Manchester.
1905	AFM	Cornhill	32 Cornhill, E.C.3.
1900	L	Crown Life	NLA Tower, Addiscombe Rd., Croydon.
1899	AFLM	Crusader	Woodhatch, Reigate, Surrey.
1908	AFM	Dominion	92/94 Gracechurch St., E.C.3.
1904	AFLM	Eagle Star	1 Threadneedle St., E.C.2.
1887	AFL	Ecclesiastical	Beaufort House, Brunswick Rd., Gloucester.
1901	AFLM	Economic	Lloyd's Building, 19 Leadenhall St., E.C.3.
1823	AFM	Edinburgh...........C.U.	St. Helen's, 1 Undershaft, E.C.3.
1880	AFM	Employers' Liability.....C.U.	St. Helen's, 1 Undershaft, E.C.3.
1762	L	Equitable Life	4 Coleman St., E.C.2.
1844	L	Equity & Law	20 Lincoln's Inn Fields, W.C.2.
1802	AF	Essex & Suffolk.......G.R.E.	Royal Exchange, E.C.3.
1894	AFM	Excess	The Warren, Warren Rd., Worthing.
1925	AFL	Federation Mutual	29 Linkfield Lane, Redhill, Surrey.
1890	AF	Fine Art & General.....C.U.	St. Helen's, 1 Undershaft, E.C.3.
1832	L	Friends' Prov.	Dorking, Surrey.
1899	L	FS Assurance	190 West George St., Glasgow.
1885	AFM	General Accident	General Buildings, Perth, Scotland.
1848	L	Gresham Life	2-6 Prince of Wales Rd., Bournemouth.
1910	AFM	Gresham Fire & Accident	11 Queen Victoria St., E.C.4.
1840	AFM	Guarantee Society.......G.A.	Ibex House, Minories, E.C.3.
1821	ALFM	Guardian...........G.R.E.	Royal Exchange, E.C.3.
1965	L	Hambro	7 Old Park Lane, W.1.

Est'd.	Nature of Business	Name of Company	Address
1908	AFM	Hibernian..................	Hawkins St., Dublin, 2.
1960	L	Hill Samuel.................	NLA Tower, Addiscombe Rd., Croydon.
1966	AF	Household & General....S.A.	1 Bartholomew Lane, E.C.2.
1932	FL	Ideal.......................	Pitmaston, Birmingham, 13.
1896	L	Imperial Life of Canada.....	London Road, Guildford, Surrey.
1935	AFM	Insurance Corpn. of Ireland...	33–36 Dame St., Dublin 2
1939	L	Irish Life..................	Mespil Road, Dublin 4.
1880	A	Iron Trades Employers'......	Iron Trades Ho., 21–24 Grosvenor Pl., S.W.1.
1845	AF	Law Fire...............S.A.	1 Bartholomew Lane, E.C.2.
1806	AFM	Law Union & Rock......R.	1 North John St., Liverpool.
1907	AFM	Legal....................R.	1 North John St., Liverpool, 2.
1836	AFLM	Legal and General...........	Temple Court, 11 Queen Victoria St., E.C.4.
1890	AFLM	Licenses & General....G.R.E.	Royal Exchange, E.C.3.
1838	L	Life Assoc. of Scotland......	10 George St., Edinburgh.
1836	AFM	L'pool & London & Globe.R.	1 North John St., Liverpool.
1918	AFM	Liverpool Marine & General..	4–5 King William St., E.C.4.
1843	L	Liverpool Victoria Friendly...	Victoria House, Southampton Row, W.C.1.
1890	AFM	Local Government Guarantee G.R.E.	Royal Exchange, E.C.3.
1836	AFM	Lombard Insurance..........	3 & 4 Lime St., E.C.3.
1720	AFLM	London Assurance.......S.A.	1 Bartholomew Lane, E.C.2.
1869	AFM	London Guar. & Accident....	4 King William St., E.C.4.
1919	AFM	London & Lancashire........	Bread St., E.C.4.
1806	L	London Life................	81 King William St., E.C.4.
1919	AFLM	London & Edinburgh........	Warren Rd., Worthing.
1869	AFL	London & Manchester.......	50 Finsbury Square, E.C.2.
1860	AFM	London & Provincial Marine . G.A.	Lloyd's Building, Lime St., E.C.3.
1862	AFM	London & Scottish......C.U.	St. Helen's, 1 Undershaft, E.C.3.
1887	L	Manufacturers Life..........	St. George's Way, Stevenage.
1836	M	Marine...................R.	15–18 Lime St., E.C.3.
1852	L	Marine & General..........	MGM House, Heene Rd., Worthing.
1864	M	Maritime...............N.U.	Surrey St., Norwich.
1884	L Sickness A	Med., Sickness, Ann. and Life.	7–10 Chandos St., Cavendish Sq., W.1.
1907	Reinsurance	Mercantile & General.......	Moorfields House, Moorfields, E.C.2.
1871	M	Merchants' Marine......C.U.	4 Fenchurch Ave., E.C.3.
1872	AF	Methodist..................	51 Spring Gardens, Manchester.
1940	AFM	Minster....................	Minster House, Arthur St., E.C.4.
1906	AFM	Motor Union.........G.R.E.	Royal Exchange, E.C.3.
1903	AF	Municipal Mutual...........	22 Old Queen St., Westminster, S.W.1.
1886	L	Mutual Life & Citizens'......	1 Lancaster Place, Strand, W.C.2.
1890	AFL	Nalgo Insurance Association ..	8 Harewood Row, N.W.1.
1935	L	National Employers' Life.....	Milton Court, Dorking, Surrey.
1914	AFM	National Employers' Mutual..	National Employers House, Bury Street, E.C.3.
1910	AFL	National Farmers' Union.....	Church St., Stratford-upon-Avon.
1863	Fidelity Guar.	Natl. Guaran. & Suretyship C.U.	St. Helens, 1 Undershaft, E.C.3.
1894	AF	National Ins. & Guarantee Cor.	11–13 Holborn Viaduct, E.C.1.
1830	L	National Mutual Life........	5 Bow Churchyard (off Cheapside), E.C.4.
1869	L	National Mutual of Australasia	Australia House, Basinghall Ave., E.C.2.
1835	L	National Provident..........	48 Gracechurch St., E.C.3.
1854	Plate Glass	National Provincial....G.R.E.	Royal Exchange, E.C.3.
1921	{Naval Officers} risks, etc.	Navigators & General....E.S.	1 Threadneedle St., E.C.2.
1924	L	New Ireland................	11/12 Dawson St., Dublin, C.2.
1809	AFLM	North British & Mercantile C.U.	St. Helen's, 1 Undershaft, E.C.3.
1862	FM	North Pacific.........G.R.E.	Royal Exchange, E.C.3.
1836	AFLM	Northern..............C.U.	St. Helen's, 1 Undershaft, E.C.3.
1797	AFM	Norwich Union Fire.........	Surrey St., Norwich.
1808	L	Norwich Union Life........	Surrey Street, Norwich.
1871	AFM	Ocean Accident.........C.U.	St. Helen's, 1 Undershaft, E.C.3.
1859	M	Ocean Marine..........C.U.	4 Fenchurch Ave., E.C.3.
1931	AFM	Orion......................	70–72 King William St., E.C.4.
1886	AF	Palatine................C.U.	St. Helen's, 1 Undershaft, E.C.3.
1864	AFLM	Pearl......................	High Holborn, W.C.1.
1958	Sickness A	Permanent.................	7–10 Chandos Street, Cavendish Sq., W.1.
1782	AFLM	Phœnix....................	Phœnix House, King William St., E.C.4.
1891	L	Pioneer Mutual............	16 Crosby Rd. N., Liverpool.
1920	AFM	Planet Assurance........S.A.	1 Bartholomew Lane, E.C.2.
1877	L	Prov. Life Assocn. of London .	246 Bishopsgate, E.C.2.

Est'd.	Nature of Business	Name of Company	Address
1840	L	Provident Mutual Life.......	25–31 Moorgate, E.C.2.
1903	AFM	Provincial.................	Kendal, Stramongate.
1848	AFLM	Prudential.................	Holborn Bars, E.C.1.
1849	AF	Railway Passengers......C.U.	St. Helen's, 1 Undershaft, E.C.3.
1864	AFL	Refuge.....................	Oxford St., Manchester 1.
1911	L	Reliance Mutual............	Reliance House, Tunbridge Wells, Kent.
1906	AF	Reliance Fire & Accident....	Reliance House, Tunbridge Wells, Kent.
1881	AFM	Reliance Marine......G.R.E.	Royal Exchange, E.C.3.
1823	Reversions	Reversionary Interest Society .	4 Coleman St., E.C.4.
1918	AF	Road Transport & General G.A.	77 Upper Richmond Rd., S.W.15.
1845	AFLM	Royal.....................	New Hall Place, Liverpool.
1720	AFL	Royal Exchange............	Royal Exchange, E.C.3.
1850	L	Royal Liver Friendly........	Royal Liver Buildings, Liverpool 3.
1861	AFL	Royal London..............	Royal London House, Finsbury Square, E.C.2.
1887	L	Royal Nat. Pensions (Nurses).	15 Buckingham St., W.C.2.
1909	AFM	Salvation Army.............	101 Queen Victoria St., E.C.4.
1963	L	Save and Prosper...........	4 Great Helens, E.C.3.
1826	L	Scottish Amicable...........	35 St. Vincent Place, Glasgow, C.1.
1881	FM	Scottish Boiler..........G.A.	22 Queen St., Glasgow, C.1.
1831	L	Scottish Equitable..........	28 St. Andrew Square, Edinburgh.
1919	AFM	Scottish General.........G.A.	100 West Nile St., Glasgow, C.2.
1852	L	Scottish Legal.............	95 Bothwell St., Glasgow, C.2.
1881	L	Scottish Life..............	19 St. Andrew Square, Edinburgh, 2.
1876	AF	Scottish Metropolitan.....C.U.	St Helen's, 1 Undershaft, E.C.3.
1883	AL	Scottish Mutual.............	109 St. Vincent Street, Glasgow, C.2.
1837	L	Scottish Provident.........	6 St. Andrew Square, Edinburgh.
1824	AFLM	Scottish Union & National N.U.	Surrey St., Norwich.
1815	L	Scottish Widows'...........	9 St. Andrew Square, Edinburgh 2.
1875	AFM	Sea.....................S.A.	1 Bartholomew Lane, E.C.2.
1904	AFL	Sentinel...................	11–13 Holborn Viaduct, E.C.1.
1968	L	Slater Walker Insurance......	30 Uxbridge Road, W.12.
1872	AFM	South British..............	26/28 Fenchurch Street, E.C.3.
1825	L	Standard Life..............	3 George Street, Edinburgh.
1891	AFM	State..................G.R.E.	Royal Exchange, E.C.3.
1710	AFM	Sun.....................S.A.	1 Bartholomew Lane, E.C.2.
★	AFLM	Sun Alliance & London......	1 Bartholomew Lane, E.C.2.
1810	AFL	Sun Life..................	107 Cheapside, E.C.2.
1865	L	Sun Life of Canada..........	2, 3 & 4 Cockspur St., S.W.1.
1936	FL	Teacher's Assurance........	12 Christchurch Rd., Bournemouth.
1916	AF	Timber & General..........	158 Fenchurch St., E.C.3.
1969	L	Trident....................	19 Hanover Sq., W.1.
1869	L	Tunstall & District.........	Station Chambers, Tunstall, Stoke on Trent.
1867	M	Ulster Marine...........G.A.	5 Donegall Sq., S., Belfast.
1714	AFM	Union Assurance........C.U.	St. Helen's, 1 Undershaft, E.C.3.
1835	AFM	Union Ins. Soc. of Canton G.R.E.	Royal Exchange, E.C.3.
1863	M	Union Marine..............	4–5, King William St. E.C.4.
1915	AFM	United British........G.R.E.	Royal Exchange, E.C.3.
1908	AFL	United Friendly............	42 Southwark Bridge Road, S.E.1.
1840	L	United Kingdom Prov.......	33–36 Gracechurch St., E.C.3.
1825	L	University.................	4 Coleman St., E.C.2.
1919	Reinsurance	Victory Insurance...........	155–157 Minories, E.C.3.
1859	Machinery	Vulcan Boiler and General S.A.	1 Bartholomew Lane, E.C.2.
1875	AFM	Warden.................R.	1 North John St., Liverpool.
1911	AF	Welsh Insurance Corpn..C.U.	St. Helen's, 1 Undershaft, E.C.3.
1841	AFL	Wesleyan & General........	Colmore Circus, Ringway, Birmingham, 4.
1886	AF	West of Scotland.......C.U.	26 George St., Edinburgh 2.
1851	AFM	Western Assurance........R.	Liverpool and London Chambers, Exchange, Liverpool.
1912	AFLM	Western Australian..........	107–111 Fleet St., E.C.4.
1717	AF	Westminster Fire........S.A.	1 Bartholomew Lane, E.C.2.
1865	AF	White Cross............C.U.	St. Helen's, 1 Undershaft, E.C.3.
1894	AFM	World Marine & General C.U.	4 & 7 Fenchurch Avenue, E.C.3.
1837	L	Yorkshire General Life...G.A.	Rougier St., York.
1872	AF	Zurich.....................	Fairfax Ho., Fulwood Place, W.C.1.

★ Sun Alliance & London—Incorporating Funds established 1720, 1824 and 1883.

NORTH ATLANTIC TREATY ORGANIZATION

Headquarters: Brussels 1110, Belgium.

The North Atlantic Treaty was signed on April 4, 1949, by the Foreign Ministers of twelve nations. The twelve are Belgium, Canada, Denmark, France, Iceland, Italy, Luxembourg, the Netherlands, Norway, Portugal, the United Kingdom and United States. Greece and Turkey acceded to the Treaty in 1952 and the Federal Republic of Germany in 1955. The North Atlantic Council is the highest authority of the Alliance and is composed of permanent representatives of the fifteen member countries. It meets at ministerial level at least twice per year. The permanent representatives head national delegations of advisers and experts.

Permanent U.K. Representative, His Excellency Sir John Killick, K.C.M.G. (1975)

The senior military authority in NATO is the Military Committee composed of a Chief-of-Staff of each member country except France. The Military Committee, which is assisted by an international military staff, functions in permanent session with permanent military representatives and is responsible for higher strategic direction throughout the North Atlantic Treaty area.

Secretary-General, J. M. A. H. Luns (*Netherlands*).
Deputy Secretary-General, P. Pansa Cedronio (*Italy*).
Assistant Secretaries-General, Dr. E. F. Jung (*Fed. Republic of Germany*) (*Political Affairs*); D. C. Humphreys (*U.K.*) (*Defence Planning and Policy*); Dr. W. B. LaBerge (*U.S.*) (*Defence Support*); Prof. Nimet Özdas (*Turkey*) (*Scientific Affairs*).
Supreme Allied Commander, Europe, Gen. Alexander M. Haig (U.S.).
Supreme Allied Commander, Atlantic, Admiral Isaac C. Kidd (U.S.).
Allied Commander-in-Chief, Channel, Admiral Sir John Treacher, K.C.B. (U.K.).
Chairman, Military Committee, Admiral of the Fleet Sir Peter Hill-Norton, G.C.B. (U.K.).

SOUTH-EAST ASIA TREATY ORGANIZATION

Headquarters: Bangkok, Thailand.

The South-East Asia Collective Defence Treaty (The Manila Pact) was signed on September 8, 1954, by representatives of Australia, France, New Zealand, Pakistan, the Philippines, Thailand, the United Kingdom and the United States. Pakistan withdrew from the Treaty and ended its participation in SEATO on November 7, 1973. France, which had ceased to participate in the military activities of SEATO in 1967, terminated financial contributions on June 30, 1974, and ended its limited participation in the Organization's civil activities. France nevertheless remains a party to the Manila Pact.

At their Twentieth Annual Meeting in New York City on September 26, 1975, the SEATO Council of Ministers announced that while the Organization had over the years made a useful contribution to stability and development in the region, they had decided that in view of the changing circumstances it should now be phased out in an orderly and systematic manner. The phasing-out process is now under way.

The Manila Pact consists of eleven Articles, with the Parties undertaking mutual defence responsibilities in the Treaty Area. Other articles deal with mutual economic assistance, including technical assistance, designed to promote economic progress and social well-being; the rights and obligations of the parties under the Charter of the United Nations; and the area to which the Treaty applies. The United States executed the Treaty with the understanding that its recognition of the effect of aggression and armed attack apply only to Communist aggression, but agreed to consult with the other signatories in the event of any other armed attack.

In an accompanying declaration of principles, The Pacific Charter, the Treaty powers uphold the principle of equal rights and self-determination of peoples. They state that they will earnestly strive by every peaceful means to promote self-government and to secure the independence of all countries whose people desire it and are able to undertake its responsibilities. They state that they will continue to co-operate in the economic, social and cultural fields in order to promote higher living standards, economic progress and social well-being in the region. They express their determination to prevent or counter by appropriate means any attempt in the Treaty Area to subvert their freedom or destroy their sovereignty or territorial integrity.

Member countries are represented on a Council of Ministers which normally meets annually to review and determine policy. The Council Representatives, composed of the Ambassadors to Thailand of the member countries and a Thai Foreign Ministry official of ambassadorial rank, meet periodically in Bangkok to supervise the work of the Organization.

Secretary-General, Sunthorn Hongladarom (Thailand).
Deputy Secretary-General, Commodore Rachel R. Cruz (Philippines).

CENTRAL TREATY ORGANIZATION

Headquarters: Ankara, Turkey.

A mutual security and defence treaty was concluded between Turkey and Iraq at Baghdad on Feb. 24, 1955. Three further states, the United Kingdom, Iran, and Pakistan signed the *Baghdad Pact* later in the same year. The United States, although not a full member of the Council, participates in an observer capacity, is a member of all major committees, and contributes an equal share to the international staff and budget, as well as a large share of economic and military assistance. Iraq formally withdrew from the Pact on March 24, 1959, and the title Central Treaty Organization (C.E.N.T.O.) was adopted on Aug. 21, 1959.

Secretary-General, U. Haluk Bayülken (1975).

BRITAIN'S OVERSEAS TRADE

IMPORTS: Section and Division	1973	1974	1975	1976 1st quarter	1976 2nd quarter
	£ million	£ million	£ million	£ million	£ million
Food and live animals	2,710·3	3,355·6	3,931·4	972·9	1,143·7
Live animals	80·2	76·9	108·0	17·3	18·2
Meat and meat preparations	715·8	681·3	701·9	186·2	208·9
Dairy products and eggs	225·1	332·8	522·6	136·8	98·3
Fish and fish preparations	132·1	122·0	136·7	39·3	34·6
Cereals and cereal preparations	369·8	560·9	612·3	136·5	226·2
Fruit and vegetables	561·3	655·0	700·3	221·6	293·7
Sugar, sugar preparations and honey	174·6	367·0	632·5	99·9	106·7
Coffee, cocoa and preparations, tea and spices	248·6	322·1	321·8	86·8	101·0
Feeding stuffs for animals	153·6	127·0	110·6	30·3	35·5
Miscellaneous food preparations	49·1	80·6	84·7	18·1	20·8
1. *Beverages and tobacco—*	383·5	406·8	414·2	84·1	118·5
Beverages	229·8	221·3	222·2	39·9	55·8
Tobacco	153·7	185·4	192·0	44·1	62·8
2. *Crude materials, inedible—*	1,833·6	2,344·2	2,049·1	621·3	731·2
Hides, skins and furskins, undressed	112·5	106·3	106·8	36·5	38·9
Oil seeds, oil nuts and oil kernels	104·0	141·9	127·8	49·6	43·9
Crude rubber (including synthetic and re-claimed)	74·8	100·3	92·9	32·3	32·6
Wood, lumber and cork	458·1	587·2	363·1	98·8	123·4
Pulp and waste paper	201·1	329·8	358·0	102·0	121·7
Textile fibres, not manufactured and their waste	322·2	310·3	263·4	101·2	113·7
Crude fertilizers and minerals	80·9	140·1	156·5	43·8	49·7
Metalliferous ores and metal scrap	389·1	518·4	475·9	123·2	180·2
Crude animal and vegetable materials	91·0	109·9	104·7	33·8	27·1
3. *Mineral fuels, lubricants, etc.—*	1,723·7	4,626·2	4,309·9	1,369·3	1,386·9
Petroleum and petroleum products	1,678·3	4,532·6	4,168·5	1,336·9	1,350·0
4. *Animal and vegetable oils and fats—*	129·4	216·2	164·6	44·7	51·0
5. *Chemicals—*	896·6	1,578·7	1,409·0	438·5	484·9
Chemical elements and compounds	360·4	711·7	672·3	188·1	211·7
Essential oils and perfume materials	51·5	76·2	68·6	19·9	22·7
Plastic materials and artificial resins	204·7	360·9	262·3	97·7	114·0
All other	280·0	430·0	405·8	132·8	136·6
6. *Manufactured goods classified chiefly by materials*	3,379·8	4,785·3	4,741·1	1,328·6	1,519·0
Leather, leather manufactures and dressed furs	67·4	60·6	68·9	20·9	26·3
Rubber manufactures	57·1	87·7	97·2	26·7	30·6
Wood and cork manufactures	244·4	232·2	217·7	59·1	72·6
Paper, paperboard and manufactures thereof	401·9	725·1	623·3	178·3	194·4
Textile yarn, fabrics and articles	514·6	687·6	682·7	212·7	225·3
Non-metallic mineral manufactures	855·2	974·2	1,077·8	301·6	360·4
Iron and steel	373·3	716·3	821·0	220·7	233·5
Non-ferrous metals	660·6	1,015·6	820·2	209·1	264·7
Other metal manufactures	205·2	286·0	332·3	94·5	111·3
7. *Machinery and transport equipment—*	3,292·8	3,902·9	4,522·7	1,301·9	1,630·3
Machinery other than electric	1,526·2	1,958·8	2,297·9	630·3	868·8
Electrical machinery, apparatus and appliances	847·4	1,009·4	1,045·3	298·6	320·7
Transport equipment	919·2	934·7	1,179·4	373·0	440·8
8. *Miscellaneous manufactured articles—*	1,338·8	1,646·5	1,872·4	554·7	600·7
Furniture	62·9	70·0	92·3	28·0	31·0
Clothing	333·2	402·4	505·1	158·3	166·4
Footwear	84·3	109·1	123·3	46·3	40·6
Professional, scientific and controlling instruments; photographic and optical goods	281·7	376·8	446·7	121·6	135·9
Other	576·7	688·3	705·0	200·6	226·7
5–8. *Manufactured goods—*	8,908·0	11,913·5	12,545·1	3,618·7	4,235·0
9. *Commodities and transactions not classified according to kind*	151·2	371·9	749·0	109·5	109·6
Total United Kingdom imports	15,839·8	23,234·4	24,163·2	6,820·4	7,775·9

BRITAIN'S OVERSEAS TRADE—*continued*

EXPORTS: Section and Division	1973	1974	1975	1976	
				1st quarter	2nd quarter
	£ million	£ million	£ million	£ million	£ million
Food and live animals—	512·1	610·4	884·8	235·6	235·5
Live animals	58·8	45·4	53·4	13·6	11·9
Meat and meat preparations	79·9	80·0	140·1	47·4	49·6
Dairy products and eggs	44·4	41·1	51·5	20·3	27·3
Fish and fish preparations	43·1	51·7	57·8	16·7	16·6
Cereals and cereal preparations	54·5	76·7	169·4	35·4	28·7
Fruit and vegetables	43·3	52·7	67·7	19·2	15·5
Sugar, sugar preparations and honey	61·5	94·8	162·0	30·8	30·2
Coffee, cocoa preparations, tea and spices	61·3	91·6	101·0	29·2	30·3
Other food and food preparations	65·1	76·4	81·8	23·0	25·4
1. *Beverages and tobacco—*	363·5	452·9	543·5	146·8	144·7
Beverages	305·4	384·0	437·1	116·2	111·5
Tobacco	58·1	68·9	106·3	30·6	33·2
2. *Crude materials, inedible*	416·3	544·2	533·3	169·7	184·1
Hides, skins and furskins, undressed	80·7	91·6	102·4	41·3	35·5
Crude rubber (including synthetic and reclaimed)	37·9	53·6	41·8	13·5	16·4
Textile fibres, not manufactured and their waste	172·1	201·7	183·5	57·6	64·8
Crude fertilizers and minerals	60·2	79·5	80·1	23·1	28·5
Metalliferous ores and metal scrap	36·1	72·0	86·5	21·9	26·6
Other crude materials	29·4	45·9	39·1	12·3	12·4
3. *Mineral fuels, lubricants, etc.—*	370·1	767·1	813·7	241·2	265·1
Petroleum and petroleum products	340·6	696·1	720·9	219·8	242·9
Coal, coke, gas and electric energy	29·5	71·1	92·8	21·4	22·2
4. *Animal and vegetable oils and fats*	17·1	31·5	27·3	6·6	7·4
5. *Chemicals—*	1,272·3	2,143·8	2,179·3	675·7	765·9
Chemical elements and compounds	364·4	730·4	653·7	217·0	273·6
Dyeing, tanning and colouring materials	140·5	213·8	201·5	56·4	70·0
Medicinal and pharmaceutical products	221·2	301·2	373·0	104·3	106·9
Essential oils and perfume materials	96·8	145·5	169·4	48·9	56·9
Plastic materials and artificial resins	225·2	366·0	354·9	117·7	133·9
All other	224·2	387·0	426·8	131·4	124·6
6. *Manufactured goods classified chiefly by materials—*	3,258·8	4,002·7	4,269·3	1,231·5	1,456·8
Leather manufactures and dressed furs	83·8	94·4	98·8	32·3	36·9
Rubber manufactures, not elsewhere specified	121·2	166·5	221·2	70·3	74·5
Wood and cork manufactures	15·5	25·4	28·5	7·8	9·9
Paper, paperboard and manufactures thereof	128·8	199·2	205·8	60·1	66·3
Textile yarn, fabrics and articles	589·5	745·1	698·2	203·4	230·9
Non-metallic mineral manufactures	1,010·1	1,060·0	1,177·9	371·0	448·2
Iron and steel	433·2	552·5	683·0	167·8	206·8
Non-ferrous metals	537·8	689·4	538·9	135·4	180·3
Other metal manufactures	338·9	470·2	617·1	183·3	202·9
7. *Machinery and transport equipment*	4,774·2	6,058·8	8,236·0	2,418·7	2,594·6
Machinery other than electric	2,413·2	3,082·9	4,254·5	1,243·4	1,282·7
Electric machinery, apparatus and appliances	807·3	1,131·6	1,529·4	466·7	514·7
Transport equipment	1,553·6	1,844·2	2,452·0	708·6	797·2
8. *Miscellaneous manufactured articles*	1,149·8	1,479·3	1,779·7	504·7	575·6
Sanitary, plumbing, heating and lighting fittings	28·5	43·6	56·0	14·2	13·9
Furniture	44·2	69·4	98·5	29·7	33·2
Clothing	179·6	229·7	265·4	74·1	87·7
Footwear	35·6	47·2	52·9	15·6	13·9
Professional, scientific and controlling instruments, photographic and optical goods, watches and clocks	343·8	424·3	518·0	145·6	159·5
Other	518·2	655·1	789·0	225·6	267·5
5–8. *Manufactured goods*	10,455·0	13,684·6	16,464·3	4,830·5	5,392·9
9. *Commodities and transactions not classified according to kind*	320·2	509·3	662·4	187·6	163·5
Total United Kingdom exports	12,454·3	16,600·1	19,929·2	5,818·1	6,393·1

UNITED KINGDOM REVENUE AND EXPENDITURE

Consolidated Fund: revenue
(Years ended March 31)

£ million

	1970–71	1971–72	1972–73	1973–74	1974–75
TAXATION					
INLAND REVENUE: Total	8,174·6	9,133·7	9,245·4	10,633·3	14,191·2
Income Tax	5,728·3	6,449·0	6,475·3	7,135·8	10,238·7
Surtax	240·3	349·1	340·9	307·3	185·8
Profits Tax	2·3	2·0	0·8	1·0	1·0
Corporation Tax.............	1,589·0	1,557·6	1,532·7	2,262·2	2,849·7
Capital Gains Tax............	138·8	155·5	208·4	323·6	380·4
Death Duties................	356·3	452·4	458·5	412·2	337·8
Stamp Duties................	116·2	166·3	227·6	190·3	197·4
Special Charge..............	3·4	1·8	1·2	0·9	0·4
CUSTOMS AND EXCISE: Total.....	4,709·1	5,325·3	5,743·5	6,219·6	7,406·5
Beer........................	466·9	480·0	491·7	365·1	450·1
Wines and spirits............	464·2	524·0	581·8	588·3	682·9
Tobacco....................	1,139·8	1,124·0	1,182·6	1,084·9	1,337·4
Hydrocarbon Oils............	1,395·2	1,439·0	1,553·2	1,585·1	1,547·6
Protective Duties............	262·8	269·3	348·5	437·1	500·5
Purchase Tax................	1,270·7	1,429·0	1,387·4	379·5	1·2
Agricultural Levies...........	—	—	4·1	25·4	25·2
Betting.....................	130·4	155·0	171·3	185·4	238·4
Temporary Charge on Imports.	—	—	—	—	—
Import Levies...............	—	6·0	16·0	—	—
V.A.T......................	—	—	—	1,447·4	2,496·5
Car Tax....................	—	—	—	117·7	122·1
Other......................	2·6	11·0	11·2	9·3	9·5
Import Deposits.............	423·5	112·0	—	—	—
less Export rebates..........	—	—	4·3	5·6	4·9
MOTOR VEHICLE DUTIES........	421·2	473·3	485·0	533·5	532·1
SELECTIVE EMPLOYMENT TAX.....	1,989·6	1,323·7	993·5	45·0	2·0
Total taxation............	15,294·5	16,256·0	16,467·4	17,431·4	22,131·8
MISCELLANEOUS RECEIPTS:					
Interest and Dividends........	99·6	100·5	99·4	106·5	170·5
Broadcast receiving licences....	100·7	122·0	136·4	152·9	164·3
Other.......................	348·0	453·3	474·9	535·6	1,103·5
Total revenue............	15,842·8	16,931·8	17,178·1	18,226·4	23,570·1

Consolidated Fund: expenditure
(Years ended March 31)

£ million

	1970–71	1971–72	1972–73	1973–74	1974–75
SUPPLY SERVICES................	13,447·8	14,817·8	16,617·5	18,624·2	25,605·3
CONSOLIDATED FUND STANDING SERVICES:					
National Loans Fund in respect of service of the National Debt	324·7	333·5	543·6	676·7	576·3
Northern Ireland—share of Taxes, etc.................	277·2	341·6	357·7	349·5	420·7
Payments to European Communities, etc..............	—	—	37·9	219·3	242·9
Contingencies Fund...........	7·0	26·0	14·0	63·0	68·0
OTHER SERVICES:					
War Damage Payments.....	0·5	0·2	—	—	—
Repayment of post-war Credits.................	14·1	18·0	132·6	14·8	3·7
Miscellaneous..............	15·0	11·7	13·8	17·8	21·6
Total expenditure........	14,086·3	15,548·8	17,689·1	19,965·3	26,802·5

AGRICULTURE

Agriculture in the national economy

July/June years	1970/1	1971/2	1972/73	1973/74	1974-5 (provisional)	
Home production as percentage of UK food supplies†	53·2	53·6	54·6	54·5	54·3	
Home production as percentage of indigenous-type supplies.	66·9	66·8	66·8	68·2	67·9	
(calendar years)	1970	1971	1972	1973	1974	1975 (provisional)
Agriculture's contribution to gross domestic product						
£ million...	1,126	1,234	1,437	1,688	1,940	2,248
percentage...	2·6	2·6	2·6	2·7	2·7	—
Agriculture's share of gross fixed capital formation						
£ million...	250	286	351	441	552	654
percentage...	2·7	2·8	3·1	3·1	3·4	—
Manpower engaged in agriculture ('000)	750	716	790	704	678	654
Percentage of total manpower in all occupations	3·1	3·0	3·0	2·9	2·7	2·7
Agricultural price index (1968/9-1971/2=100)						
All products—sales	99·4	106·3	112·9	144·7	165·5	204·0
Inputs—selected indicators						
Feedingstuffs	100·0	110·7	108·9	156·6	209·2	206·9
Fertilisers (excl. lime)	90·4	109·8	128·0	143·3	211·4	261·5
Fuel	96·5	106·8	111·1	117·8	171·8	202·0
Labour	97·9	111·3	124·7	145·8	190·1	241·8
Machinery	99·1	108·4	118·1	129·9	157·7	194·0
Imports of food, feed & alcoholic beverages						
£ million...	2,079	2,214	2,214	3,174	4,007	4,508
Import volume index (1970=100)	100·0	100·0	101·8	102·9	97·4	98·8
Import price index (1970=100)	100·0	107·1	113·5	151·2	200·9	219·6
Exports of food, feed & alcoholic beverages						
£ million...	484	567	625	838	1,049	1,368
Export volume index (1970=100)	100·0	109·5	114·6	137·3	143·8	153·8
Export price index	100·0	105·5	113·0	126·2	150·8	177·9
Consumers' expenditure on food and alcoholic beverages				(Jan.-Sept. only)		
£ million...	9,684	10,665	11,549	13,336	15,342	13,588
Percentage of total consumers' expenditure	30·9	30·6	29·2	29·7	29·7	29·9
Retail price index January 1962=100)						(Jan.-Nov. only)
Food	140·1	155·6	169·4	194·9	230·0	288.8
Alcoholic beverages	143·9	152·7	159·0	164·2	182·1	274·4
All items	140·2	153·4	164·3	179·4	208·2	258·6

† The value of food moving into manufacture or distribution derived from home agricultural output.

Crop areas and livestock numbers

At June of each year

	1970	1971	1972	1973	1974	1975 (provisional)
A. Crop areas ('ooo acres)						
Total area..................	47,255	47,234	47,045	46,920	46,974	46,911
of which:						
Wheat.....................	2,495	2,710	2,786	2,831	3,046	2,555
Barley....................	5,542	5,654	5,653	5,603	5,471	5,790
Oats......................	929	896	777	695	624	574
Mixed corn...............	196	137	150	126	104	87
Rye.......................	11	16	16	13	11	15
Maize....................	—	3	5	3	3	2
Total cereals†.............	9,174	9,416	9,386	9,271	9,260	9,023
Potatoes..................	669	634	584	555	532	503
Sugar beet................	463	471	468	480	482	488
Oilseed rape..............	10	13	17	34	61	98
Hops.....................	17	18	17	17	16	16
Vegetables gorwn in the open...................	505	452	441	462	480	487
Orchard fruit.............	160	154	146	141	136	131
Soft fruit.................	45	45	45	45	44	43
Ornamentals..............	37	36	38	40	38	37
Total horticulture........	751	690	674	694	704	698
Total tillage.............	12,888	12,139	12,021	11,905	11,955	11,890
Temporary grass..........	5,700	5,718	5,825	5,798	5,722	5,282
Total arable.............	17,788	17,857	17,846	17,703	17,677	17,177
Permanent grass..........	12,217	12,172	12,132	12,143	12,157	12,537
Rough grazing...........	16,537	16,501	16,342	16,320	16,220	16,220
Other land..............	712	704	725	753	920	928
B. Livestock numbers ('ooo head)						
Total cattle and calves........	12,581	12,804	13,483	14,445	15,227	14,641
of which:						
Dairy cows..............	3,244	3,234	3,325	3,436	3,402	3,221
Beef cows...............	1,300	1,378	1,476	1,678	1,889	1,891
Heifers in calf...........	863	831	954	898	1,049	898
Total sheep and lambs........	26,080	25,981	26,877	27,943	28,639	28,125
of which:						
Ewes....................	10,544	10,422	10,668	10,921	11,213	11,224
Shearlings...............	2,263	2,263	2,438	2,733	2,673	2,454
Total pigs.................	8,088	8,724	8,619	8,979	8,621	7,471
of which:						
Sows for breeding........	794	862	832	859	791	706
Gilts in pigs..............	159	121	128	156	107	103
Total poultry..............	143,430	139,016	140,045	144,079	139,957	136,249
of which:						
Table fowls (incl. broilers)..............	49,783	49,730	50,933	58,366	56,781	56,609
Laying fowls.............	55,237	53,703	53,831	51,766	50,130	49,227
Growing pullets..........	24,599	22,465	21,678	18,808	18,958	18,156

† For threshing.

Number of persons engaged in agriculture

At June of each year
'ooo persons

	1970	1971	1972	1973	1974	1975 (provisional)
Workers						
Whole-time:						
Hired: male	186	181	175	170	164	156
female	16	16	15	16	16	15
Family: male:	53	50	48	45	39	37
female	14	15	14	15	14	13
All male	239	231	223	215	203	193
All female	30	31	29	31	30	28
Total	(269)	(262)	(252)	(246)	(233)	(220)
Part-time: All male	80	78	78	81	78	77
All female	76	78	76	82	80	76
Total	(156)	(156)	(154)	(163)	(158)	(153)
Salaried managers	—	—	6	7	8	7
Total employed	425	418	412	416	398	380
Farmers, partners and directors						
Whole-time	216	230	229	222	214	211
Part-time	56	68	68	66	66	63
Total	697	716	709	704	678	654

Estimated average yields of crops and livestock products

June/May years

	Unit	1970/71	1971/72	1972/73	1973/74	1974/75	1975/76 (forecast)
Crops							
Wheat	tons/acre	1·67	1·75	1·69	1·74	1·95	1·71
Barley	,, ,,	1·34	1·49	1·61	1·58	1·63	1·43
Oats	,, ,,	1·30	1·50	1·58	1·53	1·54	1·37
Potatoes	,, ,,	11·0	11·5	11·0	12·1	12·6	9·3
Sugar	,, ,,	2·3	2·7	2·2	2·4	1·5	1·7
Oilseed rape	cwts./acre	15	15	17	18	15	0·6 (tons/acre)
Apples:							
Desert	tons/acre	5·2	5·4	3·5	5·0	3·7	4·4
Culinary	,, ,,	6·1	4·8	4·2	5·1	4·4	3·9
Pears	,, ,,	5·1	5·0	3·6	3·2	3·8	1·9
Tomatoes	,, ,,	41·8	42·1	43·7	46·9	48·3	51·5
Cauliflowers	,, ,,	7·6	7·8	8·2	8·4	8·3	7·4
Hops	centals/acre	15·4	14·6	11·6	13·7	13·6	31·6
Livestock products							
Milk	galls/cow	847	867	888	864	864	917
Eggs	no./bird	219·5	225·5	232·5	225·5	232	233·5

BRITISH MONETARY UNITS

COIN

GOLD COINS	CUPRO-NICKEL (SILVER)
†Five Pound £5	Crown 5s. (25p)
†Two Pound £2	Florin 2s. (10p)
†Sovereign £1	Shilling 1s. (5p)
†Half-Sovereign 10s.	Sixpence 6d. (2½p)
† Discontinued	*50 New Pence 50p
	*10 New Pence 10p
BRONZE COINS	*5 New Pence 5p

*2 New Pence 2p
*1 New Penny 1p
*½ New Penny ½p
*For further details of decimal coins, *see* p. 1142.

SILVER
Maundy Money‡

Fourpence 4p	Twopence 2p
Threepence 3p	Penny 1p

‡ Gifts of special money distributed by the Sovereign annually on Maundy Thursday to the number of aged poor persons corresponding to the Sovereign's own age.

Gold Coin.—Gold ceased to circulate during the First World War. An Order of April 27, 1966, made it illegal for U.K. residents to continue holding more than 4 gold coins minted after 1837, or to acquire such coins unless they had been licensed as genuine collectors by the Bank of England. This Order was revoked on April 1, 1971, by the Exchange Control (Gold Coins Exemption) Order, 1971, whereby residents of the United Kingdom, Channel Islands and the Isle of Man may freely buy and sell and hold gold coins.

The 1971 order was revoked on April 15, 1975, by the Exchange Control (Gold Coin Exemption) Order, 1975. Under this Order Section 1 of the Exchange Control Act 1947 (which prohibits dealings in gold or foreign currency except with Treasury permission) is exempted for gold coins minted in or before 1837. But in relation to gold coins minted after 1837, the Order exempts from Section 1 the following transactions only:

(a) Buying and selling such coins if held in the U.K. and if the seller is resident in the U.K. and is not selling on behalf of a non-resident.

(b) Borrowing and lending such coins if held in the U.K. and if the borrower and lender are resident in the U.K.

Accordingly any other transactions in gold coins minted after 1837 (if prohibited by Section 1) now require Treasury permission.

The English sovereign, however, is still used as currency in certain Middle East countries and to meet foreign demand during the years 1958–1968 the Royal Mint struck some 44·5 million sovereigns.

Silver.—Prior to 1920 our silver coins were struck from standard silver—an alloy of which 925 parts in 1,000 were silver. In 1920 the proportion of silver was reduced to 500 parts. From January 1, 1947 all 'silver' coins, except Maundy money, have been struck from cupro-nickel- an alloy of copper 75 parts and nickel 25 parts. Maundy coins since 1947 have been struck from standard silver.

Bronze, introduced in 1860 to replace copper, is an alloy of copper 97 parts, zinc 2½ parts and tin ½ part. These proportions are subject to slight variation.

The ' Remedy ' is the amount of variation from standard permitted in weight and fineness of coins when first issued from the Mint.

Legal tender of coin.—Gold, dated 1838 onwards, if not below least current weight, is legal tender to any amount. Since Decimal Day (Feb. 15, 1971) cupro-nickel (silver) coins with values up to and including the 10p have been legal tender up to £5. The 50p coin has been legal tender up to £10 from

the date of its introduction. Bronze coins are legal tender for amounts up to 20p. Farthings ceased to be legal tender on December 31, 1960, the halfpenny on August 1, 1969, the halfcrown on January 1, 1970, and the threepence and penny on August 31, 1971.

THE WORK OF THE ROYAL MINT DURING 1975

During the year under review, the Royal Mint produced some 1671 million coins, almost all of which were struck at Llantrisant. Tower Hill concentrated on the manufacture of sovereigns, coinage blanks, official and commercial medals and the production of embossing seals and revenue dies until these operations too were transferred to Llantrisant at the end of October 1975.

The domestic coinage production in 1975 was made up as follows:

Sovereigns	4,000,000
UK 50p	41,500,000
10p	166,075,000
5p	83,850,000
2p	111,199,000
1p	241,800,000
½p	209,200,000
UK Decimal Proof Coin	22,158
Maundy Money	4,594
Overseas Coin	813,252,839
Overseas Proof Coin	638,053

Coinage for overseas governments accounted for nearly 49% of the year's total production. In addition, some 458 million coins for export were struck by sub-contractors working under Royal Mint supervision. Countries and territories to which coins have been supplied include:—

Afghanistan, Bahamas, Bahrain, Belize, Bermuda, Brunei, Cayman Islands, Costa Rica, Dominica, Eire, Eastern Caribbean, Ecuador, El Salvador, Equatorial Guinea, Ethiopia, The Gambia, Ghana, Gibraltar, Guyana, Guernsey, Hong Kong, Iceland, Iraq, Jamaica, Jersey, Jordan, Kenya, Kuwait Liberia, Libya, Malawi, Malta, Mauritius, Morocco, Nepal, New Zealand, Nicaragua, Oman, Papua New Guinea, Seychelles, Sierra Leone, Swaziland, Tanzania, Thailand, Uganda, United Arab Emirates, Venezuela, Yemen Arab Republic, Zaire and Zambia.

The output of medals during the year totalled 107,891. Among medals of new design were:—Dictionary of International biography 10th Anniversary: FAO " Ceres " (Dame Margot Fonteyn de Arias, Kathleen Kenyon, Iris Murdoch, Mother Teresa, Matsuyo Yamamoto): International Who's Who in Music: International Who's Who in Poetry: New Zealand Queen's Service Medal, New Zealand Queen's Service Order: Numismatic Society: Royal Observatory Tercentenary and Tower Hill Closure Medal.

Among the seals manufactured were a number for various British Embassy posts and for Government Departments in this country.

BANK NOTES

Bank of England notes are currently issued in denominations of £1, £5, £10 and £20 for the amount of the Fiduciary Note Issue, and are legal tender in England and Wales. Only £1 notes are legal tender in Scotland and Northern Ireland.

The last of the old white £5 notes dated up to September 20, 1956, and the £5 notes issued between 1957 and 1963, bearing a portrait of Britannia, ceased to be legal tender on March 14, 1961, and June 27, 1967, respectively. The next series of £5 notes—the first to bear a portrait of the

Queen—were first issued in 1963 and ceased to be legal tender on September 1, 1973. The old series of £1 notes issued during the years 1928 to 1960 and the 10s. notes of the same type issued from 1928 to 1961—those without the royal portrait—ceased to be legal tender on May 29 and October 30, 1962, respectively. The 10s. note was replaced by the 50p coin in October 1969, and ceased to be legal tender on November 21, 1970. Bank notes which are no longer legal tender are payable when presented at the Head Office of the Bank of England in London.

The old white notes for £10, £20, £50, £100, £500 and £1,000, which were issued until April 22, 1943, ceased to be legal tender in May 1945. However, on February 29, 1976 the value of these notes still outstanding amounted to some £881,000.

The £10 note—after an interval of 21 years was restored on February 21, 1964. This completed the original series bearing portraits of the Queen, plans for which were announced in November 1959.

In 1968 the Bank announced that a new series of Bank notes generally smaller in size than the notes they replace, would be issued in the 1970's. First of the series was a £20 note, which the Bank of England introduced on July 9, 1970. This was followed by the new £5 note introduced on November 11, 1971, and the new £10 note introduced on February 20, 1975. A new £1 note will be introduced in due course to complete the series.

Note circulation is highest at the two peak spending periods of the year—around Christmas and the Summer holiday period. On December 24, 1975 it reached a peak of £6,514 million which was £555 million more than the previous peak of £5,959 million reached on July 30, 1975.

£5 notes continue to enjoy popularity and now represent over 54 per cent of the total value of notes in circulation as against 14 per cent in 1956. On the other hand, the proportion of £1 notes has dropped from 76 per cent to a fraction over 13 per cent. The percentage of £10 notes in circulation has increased steadily since 1965 and now represents over 19 per cent of the total. The proportion of £20 notes in circulation now amounts to 8 per cent of the total compared with just over 2 per cent in 1971. On February 29, 1976 the values of notes in circulation were:—£20: £499,977,000; £10: £1,157,022,000; £5: £3,261,425,000; £1: £831,173,000; 10s: £12,923,000.

Partly because of the rapidly growing preference by the public for new notes rather than used ones, the demand for new bank notes has increased greatly in recent years. Between 1957 and 1975 the average life of a £1 note fell from 19 months to 9, and consequently it has been necessary for the Bank of England to print more notes per head of the population than in comparable countries abroad. To alleviate the high cost of the note replacement, the 50p coin was introduced in October, 1969, in place of the 10s. note. The Bank of England has been conducting a campaign, in conjunction with the commercial banks, to encourage the public to accept more used but clean notes and this has been successful in reducing the public's requirements of new notes.

Other Bank Notes.—Bank Notes are issued by three Scottish banks—Bank of Scotland, Clydesdale Bank Ltd., Royal Bank of Scotland Ltd. Notes of the latter's constituent banks—Royal Bank of Scotland and National Commercial Bank of Scotland Ltd.—are being withdrawn from circulation, as are those of the former British Linen Bank. These banks issue notes for £1, £5, £10, £20 and £100. Scottish notes are not legal tender, but in Scotland they enjoy a status equal to that of the Bank of England note.

Channel Isles and the Isle of Man.—The States of Jersey and Guernsey issue notes for £10, £5 and £1. The Government of the Isle of Man issues notes for £10, £5, £1 and 50 new pence. These are legal tender only in their respective islands.

Although none of the series of notes specified above is legal tender in the United Kingdom they are generally accepted by the banks irrespective of their place of issue. At one time English banks made a small commission charge for handling Scottish and Irish notes but this was abolished some years ago.

Currency Notes.—Under the provision of the Currency and Bank Notes Act 1928, Currency Notes (popularly known as Treasury Notes) of the value of 10s and £1 were replaced by the issue of Bank of England Notes of the same denominations as from November 22, 1928. Although no longer legal tender, Currency Notes are payable on presentation at the Head Office of the Bank of England.

Denomination	Metal	Standard Weight (grams)	Standard Diameter (centimetres)
New halfpenny	bronze	1·78200	1·7145
New penny	bronze	3·56400	2·0320
2 New pence	bronze	7·12800	2·5910
5 New pence	cupro-nickel	5·65518	2·3595
10 New pence	cupro-nickel	11·31036	2·8500
50 New pence	cupro-nickel	13·5	3·0

ROADS

On April 1, 1975, the provisional total mileage of public roads in Great Britain, including green lanes, was 213,687 of which 162,372 were in England, 30,031 in Scotland and 21,284 in Wales.

Highway Authorities.—The powers and responsibilities of highway authorities in England and Wales are set out in the Highways Act 1959–1971. They are concerned mainly with the construction, improvement and maintenance of highways. The Secretaries of State for the Environment and for Wales are the highway authorities for the trunk roads in England and in Wales respectively. (Trunk roads constitute the national system of routes for through traffic and include most motorways.) Under the Local Government Act 1972, from April 1, 1974, the new county councils are the highway authorities for all highways in England (outside Greater London) and Wales, other than trunk roads. However, the new district councils have a right to maintain unclassified urban roads, footpaths and bridleways and may under agency arrangements carry out other highway functions on behalf of the county councils. In Greater London the most important non-trunk roads are metropolitan roads, for which the Greater London Council is highway authority. The Common Council of the City of London and the London borough councils are highway authorities for all other non-trunk roads in their areas.

For Scotland there is separate legislation under which the Secretary of State for Scotland is the highway authority for trunk roads. The highway authorities for non-trunk public roads are the town councils of large burghs for all such roads and the town councils of small burghs for unclassified roads in their respective areas (under the Roads and Bridges (Scotland) Act 1878), and county councils for all other non-trunk public roads (under the Local Government (Scotland) Act 1889). Under the Local Government (Scotland) Bill the highway authorities for all non-trunk public roads would, after May 15, 1975, be the councils of the proposed new regions and island areas who will have general powers of delegation which will enable them, if they wish, to delegate road functions to district councils.

The system of grant-aiding local authority expenditure on highways has recently been revised. From April 1, 1975, the GLC and all county councils in England and Wales became eligible for an annual grant towards their total transport needs. The grant, known as the transport supplementary grant, represents about one-third of Central Government's aid towards all local transport services; the remaining two-thirds is assisted through the rate support grant along with other rate-borne expenditure. For the financial year beginning April 1, 1976, local authorities received a total of £295,000,000 in transport supplementary grants.

Motorways

The network in England and Wales is based on six main routes—London–Yorkshire (M1), London–South Wales (M4). Birmingham–Bristol–Exeter (M5), Birmingham–Carlisle (M6), London–Folkestone (M20) and Lancashire–Yorkshire (M62). Other motorways in use or under construction include M2 Medway Towns, M3 London–Basingstoke, M18 Rotherham–Goole, M40 London–Oxford, M53 Mid-Wirral, M56 North Cheshire, M73 Maryville, (M74)–Mollisburn (A80), M74 Draffen–Stonehouse (A74)–Glasgow, M9 Edinburgh–Stirling and M90 Inverkeithing–Perth.

At the end of March 1975, 1212·1 miles of motorway were open to traffic in England and Wales and 113·9 miles were under construction, with a further 313·9 miles in the firm programme.

Motor Vehicles.—The number of vehicles in Great Britain with current licences in 1975 totalled 17,489,000; cars 13,746,000; motor cycles, scooters and mopeds 1,160,000; public transport vehicles 112,000; goods vehicles 1,774,000; agricultural tractors 414,000. There were 167,000 vehicles exempt from licensing.

Driving Tests.—The number of driving tests conducted in Great Britain in the year 1975 was 1,825,032, of which 54·6 per cent. resulted in failure.

Expenditure on roads in Great Britain rose from £1,042,500,000 in 1973–74 to about £1,149,500,000 in 1974–75. The expenditure during 1974–75 may be broken down as follows: New Construction and Improvement, £687,000,000 (Trunk roads, £336,000,000; Principal roads, £270,000,000; Other roads, £81,000,000); Maintenance £292,000,000 (Trunk roads, £44,000,000; Principal roads, £66,000,000; Other roads, £182,000,000); Cleansing, Gritting and Snow-Clearing, £52,000,000 Other roads, £43,000,000); Administration £118,000,000 (Non-trunk roads) £110,000,000. In addition to the 1974–75 total of expenditure on roads, the cost of road lighting was £60,000,000, and of vehicle parks £51,000,000 (gross).

Expenditure on new construction and improvement of trunk roads in England during 1974–75 was £285,000,000. In Scotland and Wales, the figures were £31,000,000 and £20,000,000 respectively. Grants made to local highway authorities for the improvement of principal roads in the same financial year were: England, £101,000,000; Scotland, £24,000,000; Wales £9,000,000.

Road Casualties

In 1975 there were 82 vehicles for every mile of road or one vehicle for every 21 yards. Seventeen road users were killed and 873 injured on an average day.

Year	Killed	Injured	Year	Killed	Injured
1958	5,970	293,797	1967	7,319	362,659
1959	6,520	326,933	1968	6,810	342,398
1960	6,970	340,581	1969	7,365	345,529
1961	6,908	342,859	1970	7,499	355,869
1962	6,709	334,987	1971	7,699	344,328
1963	6,922	349,257	1972	7,779	352,013
1964	7,820	377,679	1973	7,406	346,874
1965	7,952	389,985	1974	6,876	317,726
1966	7,985	384,472	1975	6,366	318,546

BRITISH AIRWAYS

Financial	1974–75 £m	1975–76 £m
Turnover...	748·1	930·7
Group Profit before interest and taxation............................	5·4	10·1
Profit (loss) attributable to British Airways........................	(9·4)	(16·3)

Airline Activity (European, Overseas & Regional Divisions)	1974–75	1975–76
All services		
Available tonne kilometres offered (mills).........................	5,832	6,247
Scheduled services		
Available tonne kilometres offered (mills).........................	5,388	5,856
Revenue tonne kilometres sold (mills).............................	2,997	3,249
Passengers carried (thousands).....................................	13,349	13,792
Revenue. Passenger kilometres (mills).............................	24,171	27,280
Freight tonne kilometres (mills)....................................	721	659

Staff & Productivity	1974–75	1975–76
British Airways total strength.....................................	59,407	58,207
Airline Activities		
Strength at year end...	53,066	52,351
Average number of employees..................................	53,591	52,476
Available tonne kilometres per employee........................	109,000	119,000
Revenue per employee...	£12,450	£15,330
Average number of staff employed per week by British Airways in the U.K..	48,650	48,585
Aggregate remuneration payable to the above employees for the year.	£161·5m	£196·6m

Aircraft Fleet

The following types of aircraft were in service with British Airways: *Tristar*, 7; *Boeing 747*, 17; *Boeing 707-336*, 11; *Boeing 707-436*, 14; *Super VC10*, 15; *Standard VC10*, 4; *Trident Three*, 26; *Trident Two*, 15; *Trident One*, 10; *Trident 1E*, 3; *Super 1-11*, 18; *1-11/400*, 7; *Merchantman*, 4; *Viscount*, 29; *Concorde*, 2; *HS 748*, 2. On order: *Concorde*, 3; *Tristar*, 8; *Boeing 747*, 4.

BUCHAN'S WEATHER PERIODS OR RECURRENCES OF WEATHER

Dr. Alexander Buchan, F.R.S., Secretary of the Scottish Meteorological Society, published in 1867 a paper in the Journal of that Society entitled " Interruptions in the regular rise and fall of temperature in the course of the year ". Buchan gave six cold periods and three warm periods, based on his examination of the mean daily temperature as recorded at stations in Scotland covering long periods. The cold periods were February 7–14, April 11–14, May 9–14, June 29–July 4, August 6–11, November 6–13, and the warm periods July 12–15, August 12–15, and December 3–14. This early work aroused considerable interest later. It should be noted, however, that Buchan claimed no more than the existence of tendencies for short spells of relatively cold or warm weather to occur at certain times of the year.

In recent years these smaller fluctuations of weather super-imposed on the normal seasonal changes have been examined from the aspect of tendencies to stormy or anticyclonic spells over the British Isles and have been referred to as " singularities ". Stormy periods are relatively warm in winter and cool in summer. The following tendencies have been given:—Jan. 5–17 stormy; Jan. 18–24 anticyclonic; Jan. 24–Feb. 1 stormy; Feb. 8–16 anticyclonic; Feb. 21–25 cold; Feb. 26–Mar. 9 stormy; Mar. 12–19 anticyclonic; Mar. 24–31 stormy; April 10–15 stormy; April 23–26 unsettled; June 1–21 summer monsoon; July 10–24 warm; Aug. 20–30 stormy; September 1–17 anticyclonic; Sept. 17–24 stormy; Sept. 24–Oct. 4 anticyclonic; Oct. 5–12 stormy; Oct. 16–20 anticyclonic; Oct. 24–Nov. 13 stormy; Nov. 15–21 anticyclonic; Nov. 24–Dec. 14 stormy; Dec. 18–24 anticyclonic; Dec. 25–Jan. 1 stormy.

BRITISH RAILWAYS IN 1975

The British Railways Board was set up, along with our other separate nationalized transport undertakings, by the terms of the Transport Act, 1962. This Act dissolved the British Transport Commission and shared its assets between the new bodies which assumed their responsibilities on January 1, 1963. Under the Act the finances of the railways were reconstructed and previous restrictions were modified to give them greater commercial freedom than they had enjoyed in the past.

The Transport Act of 1968 reduced the railways' commencing debt from £1,562,000,000 to £300,000,000. The Act also enabled the Secretary of State for the Environment to make grants for the maintenance of unremunerative passenger services.

The Railways Act of 1974 introduced a new system of financial support in accordance with EEC regulations and from January 1 1975 the Board's capital debt was reduced to £250,000,000 and their borrowing limit, including commencing debt, was increased to £600,000,000 extendable to £900,000,000.

The power to make grants for unremunerative passenger services is withdrawn. The Secretary of State is authorised to impose general obligations on the Board in respect of passenger services and is empowered to compensate the Board for providing adequate transport services. Aggregate compensation is limited to £900,000,000 extendable to £1,500,000,000, subject to Parliamentary approval.

For the purposes of management and operation the railways are divided into Regions. They cover the following areas:

1. London Midland Region—bounded by a line joining Carlisle, Oldham, Nottingham, Bedford, London, Banbury, Kidderminster, Aberystwyth.

2. Western Region—west of a line joining Yeovil, Westbury, Reading, London and the southern border of the L.M. Region.

3. Southern Region—south of a line joining Dorchester, Salisbury, London and the Thames.

4. Eastern Region—east of a line joining London, Peterborough, Sheffield, Bradford and Carlisle.

5. Scottish Region—north of a line joining Carlisle and Berwick.

Staff.—On Dec. 31, 1975, British Rail employed a total staff of 189,931, compared with 194,891 on Dec. 31, 1974.

Financial Results, 1975.—The balance sheet for 1975 showed a deficit of £60,800,000, compared with a deficit of £157,800,000 for 1974 while the railway working loss (before taking interest charges or revenue from other activities into account) was £42,339,000, compared with £96,914,000 for the previous year.

Railways	£ million 1975
Gross receipts:	
Passenger (including Grants)....	752.9
Freight (including parcels and mails)......................	332.5
Miscellaneous.................	12.8
TOTAL....................	1,098.2
Working expenses:	
Train services.................	517.9
Terminal.....................	161.6
Miscellaneous traffic expenses...	10.6
Track and signalling...........	272.9
General expenses..............	187.9
TOTAL................	1150.9
Railway net loss.....................	52.7
Net income from Operational Property (Letting), Advertising and Catering....	10.3
OPERATING LOSS..................	42.4

OPERATING STATISTICS

At the end of 1975, British Rail had 28,872 miles of standard gauge lines and sidings in use, representing 11,258 miles of route of which 2,271 miles were electrified. Standard rail on main line has a weight of 110 lbs. per yard. British Rail had 3,860 locomotives (diesel and diesel electric, 3,508 and electric, 352); 3,412 diesel multiple-unit vehicles, 7,225 electric multiple-unit vehicles and 6,826 locomotive-hauled passenger carriages with a capacity of 1,099,391 seats or berths in 1975. Loaded train miles run in passenger service totalled 198,193,000. 714,695,000 passenger journeys were made during the year, including 282,136,000 made by holders of season tickets. The average distance of each passenger journey on ordinary fare was 28.6 miles; and on season ticket, 18.4 miles. Passenger stations in use in 1975 numbered 2,358 and freight stations 515.

Freight.—There were 216,367 freight-vehicles and 5,439 other vehicles in the non-passenger-carrying stock. 97,231,000 tonnes of coal and coke were carried in 1975, 25,727,000 tonnes of iron and steel and 53,490,000 tonnes of other traffic. Loaded train miles run in freight service totalled 47,248,000.

Casualties in Train Accidents
(includes British Railways, London Transport and other railways).

	Average 1970-74	1974
Fatal Accidents........	16	6
Passengers killed......	6	1
Passengers seriously injured..............	17	14
Railwaymen killed....	5	4
Railwaymen seriously injured............	7	9
Other persons killed...	5	1
Other persons seriously injured............	5	3
Passengers carried per passenger killed.....	420,883,000	1,280,000,000
Passenger miles run per passenger killed....	7,158,376,000	22,410,000,000

RAILWAY ACCIDENTS IN WHICH 20 PERSONS AND OVER WERE KILLED IN THE UNITED KINGDOM SINCE 1948

Year	Date	Name of Accident	Railway	Number Killed	Cause
1948	Apl. 17	Winsford	L.M. Region	24	Collision.
1952	Oct. 8	Harrow	L.M. Region	112	Collision.
1957	Dec. 4	Lewisham	S. Region	90	Collision in fog.
1967	Nov. 5	Hither Green	S. Region	49	Track failure
1975	Feb. 28	Moorgate	L.T.E.	43	Terminal overrun

FUEL AND POWER

ELECTRICITY SUPPLY
England and Wales

In the year ended March 31, 1976, the electricity industry sold 189,438 million units to all consumers, a decrease of 3·3 per cent. over 1974–75. Average price per unit to consumers was 1·718p compared with 1·243p in 1974–75. At the end of the year there were 19,526,000 consumers, 1·2 per cent. more than at March 31, 1975.

75,307 million units were supplied to industry (a decrease of 3·5 per cent.), 75,063 million to domestic users (5·5 per cent. less) and 31,132 million to commercial users (2·9 per cent. more), 19,495 million units were sold on off-peak tariffs, a decrease of 10·1 per cent. over 1974–75.

On March 31, 1976, the Central Electricity Generating Board had 161 power stations (1975, 168) with a maximum output capacity of 58,677 MW, an increase in capacity of 0·3 per cent. over 1975. In 1975/76 1,165 MW of new plant was commissioned. C.E.G.B. power stations supplied 204,623 million kWh in 1975–76, 3·0 per cent. less than in 1974–75. Maximum simultaneous demand met during the year was 41,353 MW (1974–75, 40,973).

Transmission lines in service at the end of the year totalled 13,820 circuit km. and distribution lines 581,059 circuit km.

The industry employed 166,826 persons at March 31, 1976, 5,657 less than in 1974–75.

The following results are those of the Electricity Council and Boards in England and Wales, the figures being rounded off.

Electricity Industry Finance 1974–76

	£ million	
	1974–75	1975–76
Revenue		
Sales of Electricity	2,434·9	3,255·0
Other	20·3	21·8
Total	2,455·2	3,276·8
Expenditure		
Generation and Purchases	1,549·7	1,910·7
Main Transmission and Distribution	133·7	171·0
Consumer Service	40·2	51·8
Administration, Collection of Accounts, etc.	137·2	176·7
Rates	95·8	115·2
Depreciation	344·3	376·3
Other	34·1	42·1
TOTAL	2,335·0	2,843·8
Operating Profit	120·2	433·0
Deduct Interest Payable	385·5	424·5
Profit or Loss	(–) 265·3	(–) 8·5

COAL PRODUCTION
million tons

Year (*March*)	NCB Mines	Open Cast	Other	Total
1970	139·8	6·2	1·4	147·4
1971	133·3	7·9	1·2	142·4
1972	109·2	9·9	1·2	120·4
1973	127·0	9·9	1·3	138·3
1974	97·1	8·9	1·1	107·1
1975	115·0	9·1	1·1	125·2
1976	112·6	10·2	1·0	123·8

power stations 71,465,000 tons, gas works 55,000 tons, coke ovens 20,183,000 tons colliery consumption 1,288,000 tons and others 6,608,000.

	£ million	
Income	1974–75†	1975–76†
From Sales (Net)	1,552·2	1,924·4
Principal Items:—		
Coal	1,284·3	1,671·2
Coke	128·9	111·6
Gas, Benzole, Tar, etc.	32·6	17·1
Processed Fuel	34·0	42·6
Other Receipts	114·9	269·4
NET INCOME	1,667·1	2,193·8
Expenditure		
Wages, Salaries, Pensions, etc.	939·6	1,239·0
Contract work	76·4	114·8
Materials, Repairs, Power	419·5	558·2
Depreciation and other expenses	191·2	229·6
TOTAL EXPENDITURE	1,626·7	2,141·6
PROFIT/*Loss*	40·4	52·2
Less Interest Payable, etc.	40·4	46·9
SURPLUS or *DEFICIENCY*	—	5·3

† April to March.

GAS SUPPLY

	1974–75	1975–76
	(Million Therms)	
Natural gas for supply direct to customers	12,426	13,867
Natural gas for town gas manufacture	808	364
Coal and oil based gas made and bought	458	115
Total gas available	13,692	14,346

Consumption of coal for gas making fell from 17·5 million tons in 1965–66 to 8 thousand tons in 1975–76. Total oil used was 2·7 million tons in 1965–66 compared with 5·9 million tons in 1968–69 and 0·2 million tons in 1975–76.

In 1965–66 8·2 per cent. of total gas available was based on natural gas but by 1975–76 the proportion based on natural has had risen to 99·2 per cent.

Gas Industry Finance

	£ million	
	1974–75	1975–76
Gross Revenue		
Sales—Gas	1,023·8	1,339·2
Products	0·8	1·2
Appliances	83·8	105·7
Other Revenue	110·9	133·6
TOTAL REVENUE	1,219·3	1,580·4
Gross Expenditure		
Process Materials—Natural Gas.	198·6	242·2
Oil	27·0	11·0
Other	5·5	2·0
Payments to employees	279·4	374·2
Cost of Appliances	57·8	72·0
Depreciation	247·3	283·0
Interest	162·8	176·7
Rates	22·9	30·8
Other materials and services	262·2	363·4
TOTAL EXPENDITURE	1,263·5	1,555·3
SURPLUS or *DEFICIENCY*	44·2*	25·1

* £42·3m Government compensation receivable.

ADMINISTRATION OF THE NATIONAL HEALTH SERVICE

Since its inception in 1948 the N.H.S. has been administered according to its three main branches—the hospital and specialist services, the general practitioner services and the local health authority services. These have now been unified under the provisions of the National Health Service Reorganization Act 1973 which came into force on April 1, 1974. The services which were brought together are:

(a) the hospital and specialist services previously administered by Regional Hospital Boards, Hospital Management Committees and Boards of Governors of undergraduate Teaching Hospitals;

(b) the family practitioner services previously administered by Executive Councils;

(c) the personal health services (*e.g.* ambulance services, epidemiological work, family planning, home nursing and midwifery, maternity and child health care, etc.) previously administered by local authorities through their health committees;

(d) the school health service previously administered by local education authorities.

Under the new structure all these services are administered by Regional and Area Health Authorities.

Regional Health Authorities

There are 14 Regional Health Authorities in England based on the former Hospital Regions. The R.H.A. develops strategic plans and priorities based on a review of the needs identified by the Area Health Authorities and on its judgement of the right balance between individual areas' claims on resources. It is also responsible for identifying in consultation with the A.H.A.s, services which need a regional approach rather than an area approach and arranging for their provision. The R.H.A. allocates resources between the A.H.A.s, after having agreed area plans with them, and monitors their performance. One of the R.H.A.s executive functions is the design and construction of new buildings and works. The R.H.A. will itself undertake the more important projects on behalf of the A.H.A.

Area Health Authorities

There are 90 Area Health Authorities in England whose boundaries generally match those of the non-metropolitan counties and metropolitan districts of local government, or of one or more London boroughs. The A.H.A. is the operational health authority, responsible for assessing needs in its area and for planning, organizing and administering area health services to meet them. The day-to-day running of the services for which the A.H.A. is responsible is based on health districts. These normally contain a district general hospital or a number of hospitals providing the services of a district general hospital and usually have a population of between 150,000 and 300,000. There are 205 Health districts in England, including 34 single district areas.

Under the new N.H.S. the status of general medical and dental practitioners, ophthalmic medical practitioners, opticians and pharmacists as independent contractors remains unchanged. Each A.H.A. is required to set up a Family Practitioners Committee to administer family practitioner services.

Community Health Councils have been established for each health district. The Council's basic job is to represent to the Area Health Authority the interests of the public in the health services in its district. Councils have power to secure information, to visit hospitals and other institutions, and have access to the A.H.A. and in particular to its senior officers administering the district services. The A.H.A. is required to consult the Community Health Council(s) on its plans for health service developments and the full A.H.A. will meet representatives of all its Community Health Councils at least once a year. The Council will publish an annual report and the A.H.A. is required to publish replies recording action taken on the issues raised.

Complaints

One of the most important innovations in the reorganized N.H.S. is the establishment of a Health Service Commissioner to investigate complaints against N.H.S. authorities. The Commissioner began work on October 1, 1973, and since April 1, 1974 his jurisdiction has covered the whole of the unified N.H.S. Further details of the Commissioner's work and the procedure for making complaints can be obtained from the Office of the Health Service Commissioner, Church House, Great Smith Street, London S.W.1.

NAUTICAL MEASURES

Distance is measured in nautical (or sea) miles. The nautical mile is traditionally defined as the length of a minute of arc of a great circle of the earth; but as this length varies in different latitudes (owing to the fact that the earth is not a perfect sphere), 6,080 feet, a "rounded off value" of the mean length, has been adopted in British practice as the standard length of the nautical mile. On this basis 38 nautical miles exactly equal 38 statute miles; the statute (land) mile contains 5,280 feet. A *cable*, as a measure used by seamen, is 600 feet (100 fathoms) approximately one-tenth of a nautical mile. *Soundings at sea* are recorded in fathoms (6 feet).

6 feet= 1 fathom.
100 fathoms= 1 cable length.
10 cables= 1 nautical mile.

Note.—Some other countries, including the United States in 1954, have adopted the nautical mile of 1,852 metres as recommended by the International Hydrographic Bureau in 1929.

Speed is measured in *nautical miles per hour*, called *knots*. A knot is a measure of speed and is not used to express distance. A ship moving at the rate of 30 nautical miles per hour is said to be "doing 30 knots" and as the nautical mile is longer than the land or statute mile this represents a land speed of over 34½ miles per hour.

Knots	m.p.h.	Knots	m.p.h.	Knots	m.p.h.
1	1.1515	15	17.2727	29	33.3939
2	2.3030	16	18.4242	30	34.5454
3	3.4545	17	19.5757	31	35.6969
4	4.6060	18	20.7272	32	36.8484
5	5.7575	19	21.8787	33	38.0000
6	6.9090	20	23.0303	34	39.1515
7	8.0606	21	24.1818	35	40.3030
8	9.2121	22	25.3333	36	41.4545
9	10.3636	23	26.4848	37	42.6060
10	11.5151	24	27.6363	38	43.7575
11	12.6666	25	28.7878	39	44.9090
12	13.8180	26	29.9393	40	46.0606
13	14.9696	27	31.0908	41	47.2121
14	16.1212	28	32.2424	42	48.3636

Net tonnage.—The gross tonnage less certain deductions for crew space, engine room, water ballast and other spaces not used for passengers or cargo.

Gross tonnage.—The total volume of all the enclosed spaces of a vessel, the unit of measurement being a ton of 100 cubic feet.

Friendly Societies—Great Britain

Act 1974

Friendly societies are mutual insurance societies in which the members subscribe for provident benefits, in particular sickness, death, endowment and old age benefits. Those friendly societies that are known as "collecting societies" because they collect members' premiums for life assurance by house-to-house visits of collectors or agents are subject to the provisions of the Industrial Assurance Acts as well as the Friendly Societies Act. The totals in ordinary type in the table below relate to registered friendly societies proper (including both centralized societies and the Orders with their branches); those in italics relate to collecting societies.

End of Year	No. of Societies on Register		Member-ship	Assurances or Policies	Total Funds	
			Thousands		£000	
1974............	5,490	*64*	4,354	*24,423*	399,741	*582,225*
1938............	19,600	*149*	8,491	*25,738*	151,613	*84,837*
1913............	25,475	*71*	6,783	*7,481*	51,489	*11,165*

The first column headed "No. of Societies on Register" in the above table includes (for 1974) 559 societies without branches and 28 societies with branches ("Orders"), the remainder being the separately registered branches of the Orders.

Although recent years have seen the growth of societies registered for such specific purposes as the provision of Institutional treatment or assuring annuities and pensions, most friendly societies continue to provide the customary benefits in sickness and at death. During 1974 Friendly Societies proper paid out £4·5 millions in sickness benefit and £2·3 millions in death benefit.

As compared with the previous year the number of societies without branches decreased in 1974 by 25 and the number of branches by 330. Total membership fell to under 4·4 millions.

Many societies still operate mainly on the old system of accumulating funds on a mutual basis. Others, usually termed deposit societies, allocate all or the greater part of their funds annually to the individual credit of the members to be withdrawn by them as the rules provide. Apart from the National Deposit Society's method of a uniform contribution throughout membership there are several systems operated on individual account lines, one of which (known as the "Holloway" principle) is worked by a contribution increasing with each year of attained age after the member reaches age 30 up to age 65.

The latest available figures of membership and funds set out below indicate the relative strength of several leading old established societies, including the three largest Orders which operate through registered districts and branches subject to a central body:—

FRIENDLY Socs.—Name with (in brackets) Year Established	Membership	Total Funds
		£000
National Deposit Friendly Society (1868)...............................	313,000	25,220
Hearts of Oak Benefit Society (1842)....................................	315,000	26,752
Independent Order of Odd Fellows, Manchester Unity (1810).............	261,000	34,611
Ancient Order of Foresters (1834).......................................	232,000	28,983
Independent Order of Rechabites, Salford Unity (1835)..................	97,000	7,662

COLLECTING Socs.—Name and Year Established	No. of Industrial Assurances		Total Funds
	Premium Paying	Free Paid-up	
			£000
Liverpool Victoria Friendly Society (1843).................	8,306,000	4,171,000	295,604
Royal Liver Friendly Society (1850).......................	5,328,000	2,248,000	126,475
Scottish Legal Life Assurance Society (1852)................	1,533,000	1,074,000	30,583

Long before the term "Friendly Society" came into use, the seeds of voluntary mutual insurance had been sown in the ancient religious and trade "Guilds." As is evident from the many extant parchment returns detailing their rules and possessions under a decree of Richard II, Guilds had become widespread in Britain by the 14th century. By then, the purely charitable character of the original Guilds had largely changed with the emergence of numerous small institutions adopting primitive mutual insurance methods of a regular flat rate contribution to insure relief when sick or in old age and a payment to the widow in the event of death.

The present register of Friendly Societies includes several societies which have been in existence for upwards of 200 years, the oldest, operating in Scotland, being the "Incorporation of Carters in Leith" established as long ago as 1555.

The first Act for the encouragement and protection of "Friendly Societies" in this country was not passed until 1793, but various amending Acts were put on the Statute Book during the next century as the result of the recommendations of successive Select Committees (including a Royal Commission in 1871). For example, it was not until the 1829 Act that all registered Friendly Societies were required to keep proper records of individual sickness and mortality amongst their members, which data enabled the construction of standard actuarial tables showing the expected (average) duration or sickness at successive ages, and also (with data from the Census) the corresponding mortality rates.

The rules and other documents of societies deposited with local justices passed into the custody of the Registrar following the Act of 1846 and are of considerable interest to social historians.

Those relating to some societies no longer on the register have been transferred to the Public Record Office for permanent preservation.

The Friendly Societies Act 1974, which came into force in April, 1975, consolidated the nine Acts which comprised the Friendly Societies Acts 1896 to 1971 and a few other minor enactments relating to societies to which those Acts applied. The Act allows various specific classes other than " Friendly Societies " to be registered thereunder, but tax exemption (irrespective of the extent of interest income) is enjoyed only by registered " Friendly Societies."

Industrial and Provident Societies—Great Britain

Acts 1965–1968

The familiar " Co-op " societies are amongst the wide variety which are registered under the Industrial and Provident Societies Act 1965. This consolidating Act, which like the Friendly and the Building Societies Act is administered by the Chief Registrar of Friendly Societies, provides for the registration of societies and lays down the broad framework within which they must operate. Internal relations of societies are governed by their registered rules.

Registration under the Act confers upon a society corporate status by its registered name with perpetual succession and a common seal, and limited liability. A society qualifies for registration if it is carrying on an industry, business or trade, and it satisfies the Registrar that either (a) it is a bona fide co-operative society or (b) in view of the fact that its business is being, or is intended to be, conducted for the benefit of the community there are special reasons why it should be registered under the Act rather than as a company under the Companies Act.

During 1975 the number of registered societies decreased by 93 to 9,583, the first decrease since 1957. The largest single group was the 4,104 housing societies which accounted for most of the new registrations in 1975. The largest group in terms of turnover was that consisting of the retail, wholesale and productive societies which includes the " co-ops " with sales in 1975 of £1·929 million and the Co-operative Wholesale Society Limited with 1975 sales of £1,070 million. The principal statistics at the end of 1975 are given in the table below.

	Retail	Wholesale and Productive	Social and Recreational Clubs	General Service	Housing	Agricultural	Fishing	Total
Number of Societies	313	73	3,576	228	4,104	1,204	85	9,583
Number of Members	000's 10,402	000's 40	000's 2,531	000's 428	000's 140	000's 442	000's 10	000's 13,993
Funds of Members	£000's 264,723	£000's 163,635	£000's 82,996	£000's 663,130	£000's 62,380	£000's 70,048	£000's 867	£000's 1,307,778
Total Assets	£000's 650,624	£000's 308,800	£000's 133,653	£000's 794,987	£000's 905,713	£000's 145,184	£000's 2,179	£000's 2,941,141

Building Societies—Great Britain

Act 1962

Building Societies are associations incorporated with limited liability under the Building Societies Act. All Building Societies are required to register their rules and file their accounts with Registry of Friendly Societies. The following particulars showing the growth of Building Societies (as also that of Friendly and Industrial and Provident Societies) are based on the Chief Registrar's Annual Reports.

The year 1975 was one of unparalleled achievement for building societies, with record progress being made in practically every department of their affairs. Assets increased by 20·5 per cent. and totalled £24,204 million at the end of the year.

Share and deposit receipts of £9,154 million were 44 per cent more than in 1974, but withdrawals increased by only 14 per cent to £5,920 million. The ratio of withdrawals to receipts fell to 65 per cent. from the high level of 82 per cent. in 1974.

The amount advanced on mortgage reached a new peak in 1975 and totalled £4,908 million compared with £2,945 million in 1974. 798,000 advances were made compared with 546,000 in 1974.

Despite the substantial increase in their lending, societies added £1,281 million to their cash and investment holdings in 1975. At the end of the year, cash and investments represented 20·9 per cent. of total assets and amounted to £5,064 million.

In view of the growth of assets in the year, and the small margins on which societies were operating it was inevitable that the ratio of reserves to assets should fall. The amount added to reserves was more in 1975 than in 1974, £100 million compared with £73 million, but the average reserve ratio fell from 3·43 per cent. to 3·26 per cent. Working margins, which had been eroded by successive rises in the composite rate at which societies pay income tax on investors' interest, were improved to some extent in June 1975 when the recommended rate on shares was reduced to 7·0 per cent. However, 1975 also saw a notably sharp increase in management expenses reflecting both the growth of business and the effect on costs of inflation over the year. Margins were also affected in some cases by the issue of term shares at rates above the ordinary share rates.

Societies co-operated with the Department of the Environment during the year to establish a scheme whereby societies set aside £100 million to be advanced by them to assist in making good the shortfall in local authority lending for owner occupation which had been curtailed in 1975. The year also saw the introduction on a fairly wide scale of differential mortgage rates. A majority of the 30 largest societies now operate schemes which in varying ways are based on the practice of charging a higher rate for advances above a certain size—usually in the region of £13,000 to £15,000. The average advance in 1975 amounted to just under £7,500.

The number of societies merging in 1975 was very much in line with the 1974 experience, but the indications are that the numbers in 1976 will be smaller. 31 societies transferred engagements to other societies and two united to form a new society in 1975. In 1974 30 societies transferred their engagements. At the end of 1975 there were 382 building societies on the register.

Under sections 48 and 51 of the Building Societies Act 1962 the Chief Registrar, with Treasury consent, exercises power of control over the activities of building societies. Under section 55 there is further power to control in relation to small societies. His report for 1975 discloses that orders prohibiting or restricting investment were in force against 13 societies at the end of 1975, whilst directions controlling advertising were in force in respect of four societies.

A society meeting certain basic requirements as to assets and liabilities, liquid funds, reserves and other matters may be designated by the Chief Registrar under section 1 of the House Purchase and Housing Act 1959 for the purposes of trustee status. The requirements are set out in The Building Societies (Designation for Trustee Investment) Regulations 1972. The shares and deposits of a society so designated become authorised investments for trustee subject to the provisions of the Trustee Investments Act 1971. Designated societies are identified in the list below by a letter " D " in the first column.

Nearly 70 per cent. of all building societies have an accounting year which ends on 31st December, the remainder at various dates. Statistics in the tables below are taken from accounts made up to dates between 1st February and the following 31st January. References in the tables below to years or to the financial year should be understood accordingly. In a very few cases the latest information available at the time of compilation has been included in the list of societies.

BUILDING SOCIETIES, GREAT BRITAIN, 1975—with 1974 in Italics.

Class	Number	Share Investors	Advances during Year *	Amount due to Share-holders †	Deposi-tors ‡	General Reserve and Balances C/fd.	Mortgage Assets	Total Assets
		000's	£000	£000	£000	£000	£000	£000
Assets over								
£2 m.......	213	17,852	4,893,400	22,061,100	759,700	785,200	18,734,300	24,121,400
Other Societies..	*169*	*65*	*14,600*	*73,000*	*2,200*	*4,700*	*67,500*	*82,400*
1975 TOTALS.	382	17,916	4,908,000	22,134,000	761,900	790,000	18,801,900	24,203,700
1974 TOTALS.	*416*	*15,856*	*2,945,100*	*18,021,400*	*632,800*	*689,800*	*16,029,600*	*20,093,500*

* Total Borrowers, 4,397,000   † Total Share Investors, 17,916,000   ‡ Total Depositors, 677,000

SOCIETIES WITH TOTAL ASSETS EXCEEDING £500,000 AT END OF FINANCIAL YEAR 1975

Year Estab-lished	* Name of Society (abbreviated) Head Office	Share Investors	Assets Total £'000
1849D	Abbey National, Abbey House, Baker St., London NW1 6XL.......	3,377,626	3,701,776
1869D	Accrington Savings and Bldg. Soc., 60 Blackburn Road, Accrington, Lancs. BB5 1LD..	4,265	5,151
1873	Advance, Advance Bldgs, Surtees St., Hartlepool..................	416	857
1885	Aid to Thrift, 38 Finsbury Sq.,`London EC2A 1PT.................	454	889
1866D	Alfreton, 103 High St., Alfreton, Derby DE5 7DP.................	2,339	2,936
1863D	Alliance. Alliance House, Hove Park, Hove, Sussex BN3 7AZ........	425,921	862,942
1886	Anchor, 8 Coronation St., South Shields...........................	773	1,079
1848D	Anglia, Abington St., Northampton NN1 2BJ.....................	465,323	503,213
1870D	Argyle, Argyle Ho., 105 Seven Sisters Rd., Holloway, London N7 7QH	4,368	8,386
1945	Ashton-Stamford, Booth St. Chambers, Ashton-u-Lyne, Lancs OL6 7LQ	735	1,258
1871	Banffshire, 186 Mid Street, Keith.................................	525	760
1965	Banner, Banner Cross Hall, Sheffield S11 9PD.....................	5	4,434
1853D	Barnsley P., Regent St., Barnsley, South Yorks. S70 2EH..........	15,096	23,231
1922D	Barry Mutual, Lombard Bldgs., 1 Lombard St., Barry, S. Glam. CF6 6SG...	1,535	2,480
1953D	Bath Investment and Bldg. Soc., 20 Charles St., Bath, BA1 1HY.....	8,260	7,177
1863	Bede P., 5 Grange Road West, Jarrow, NE32 3JA...................	926	1,204
1881D	Bedford, 65 Midland Rd., Bedford................................	7,875	8,923
1879D	Bedford Crown, 117 Midland Rd., Bedford, MK40 1DE............	2,740	2,746

* P.=Permanent; B.=Benefit. The words " Building Society " are the last words in every society's name.

Year Established	Name of Society (abbreviated) Head Office	Share Investors	Assets Total £'000
1866D	Beverley, 16 Lairgate, Beverley, Yorks. HU17 8EE...............	3,656	3,010
1914D	Bexhill-on-Sea, 2 Devonshire Sq., Bexhill-on-Sea, Sussex TN40 1AE..	2,121	3,341
1853D	Bideford and North Devon, 5 The Quay, Bideford, Devon..........	3,823	6,346
1889D	Birmingham Citizens, 20 Bennetts Hill, Birmingham B2 5QL.......	17,050	27,435
1847D	Birmingham Incorporated, 42–44 Waterloo St., Birmingham B2 5QB	35,457	51,741
1903D	Blackheath, Cranford Ho., 14 Long Lane, Rowley Regis, Warley, Worcs.	7,694	10,426
1957	Blackheath, Kidbrooke and Charlton, National Westminster Bank Chambers, Blackheath Village, London, SE3...................	493	557
1873	Blyth and Morpeth Dt. P. B., 3 Stanley St., Blyth, Nbld...........	816	966
1864D	Bolton, 213 Baker St., London NW1 6HY...................	2,209	6,740
1851D	Bradford and Bingley, P.O. Box 2, Bingley, Yorks................	458,834	600,648
1921D	Bridgwater, 1 King Sq., Bridgwater, Som...................	63,086	84,726
1849D	Brierley Hill and Stourbridge Incorporated, 12 Hagley Rd., Stourbridge, Worcs DY8 1PS...................	8,896	10,830
1867D	Brighton and Shoreham, 115 Western Rd., Brighton, Sussex BN1 2AB	568	1,201
1853D	Bristol Econ. Broad St., Bristol BS1 2HE...................	2,600	4,303
1850D	Bristol and West, Broad Quay, Bristol BS99 7AX..........	264,269	373,870
1856D	Britannia, P.O. Box 20, Newton House, Leek, Staffs. ST13 5RG......	524,221	688,443
1883D	Bromley, 182 High St., Bromley, Kent BR1 1HE................	2,382	3,400
1907D	Buckinghamshire, High St., Chalfont St., Giles, Bucks..........	5,529	6,444
1850D	Burnley, 12 Grimshaw St., Burnley, Lancs..................	301,267	432,780
1866D	Bury St. Edmunds P. B., 87 Guildhall St., Bury St. Edmunds IP33 1PU	2,169	4,141
1886	Calne and District P.B., 1 Patford St., Calne, Wilts................	652	804
1850D	Cambridge, 32 St. Andrew's St., Cambridge CB2 3AR..........	18,530	29,629
1865D	Cardiff, 92 St. Mary St., Cardiff CF1 1LT...................	2,651	5,417
1960D	Catholic, 7 Strutton Ground, London SW1P 2HY...........	1,714	2,207
1899	Century, 21–23 Albany St., Edinburgh EH1 3QW................	1,096	2,473
1862	Chatham, 27 Lord St., Liverpool L2 9SG...................	522	615
1898D	Chatham Reliance, Reliance House, Manor Rd., Chatham, Kent.....	22,140	22,954
1875D	Chelsea, 110/112 King's Rd., London SW3 4TY.................	77,121	141,232
1850D	Cheltenham and Gloucester, 37–43 Clarence St., Cheltenham, Glos. GL50 3JR...................	240,331	350,082
1845D	Chesham, 12 Market Sq., Chesham, Bucks...................	5,398	7,275
1888D	Chesham and Dt. Mut. & P., Norfolk House, Station Rd., Chesham, Bucks...................	1,898	2,448
1870D	Cheshire and Northwich, Castle St., Macclesfield SK11 6AH........	48,431	55,262
1861D	Cheshunt, 100 Crossbrook St., Waltham Cross, Herts. EN8 8JJ.......	25,146	28,497
1859D	Chorley and Dt., 51 St. Thomas's Rd., Chorley, Lancs...........	3,439	5,708
1866	Chorley P.B., 41 Chapel St., Chorley, Lancs................	690	868
1905D	Citizens Regency, Citizens Hse., Marlborough Pl., Brighton, Sussex BN1 1WW...................	16,323	2,005
1946D	City and Metropolitan, 37 Ludgate Hill, London EC4M 7NA........	8,794	16,129
1862D	City of London, 34 London Wall, London EC2Y 5JD...............	17,095	43,059
1931D	Civil Service, 26 Caxton St., London SW1H 0RE...............	8,064	14,151
1894D	Clacton, 72 Station Rd., Clacton-on-Sea, Essex...............	889	1,362
1859D	Clay Cross Benefit, 42 Thanet St., Clay Cross, Chesterfield........	2,424	2,279
1912D	Coalville P., 42 High St., Coalville, Leicester LE6 2AG...........	1,854	2,451
1869D	Colchester Eq., 1–3 Pelhams Lane, Colchester CO1 1JT...........	3,869	6,329
1856D	Colchester P., 11 Sir Isaac's Walk, Colchester CO1 1JL...........	2,116	4,275
1866D	Colne, Albert Rd., Colne, Lancs. BB8 0AJ................	5,566	10,507
1878D	Cotswold, 11 Long St., Wotton-under-Edge, GL12 7ES...........	3,110	3,401
1884D	Coventry Economic, P.O. Box 9, Little Park St., Coventry CV1 2JZ..	144,728	153,243
1848D	Coventry and Warwickshire B., 23 Bayley Lane, Coventry, Warws...	712	964
1872D	Coventry Provident, Provident Hse., 25 Warwick Rd., Coventry CV1 2ER...................	21,030	28,937
1906D	Cradley Heath, 194 High St., Cradley Heath, Warley, Worcs........	5,165	6,749
1850D	Cumberland, 38 Fisher St., Carlisle...................	40,256	46,674
1946D	Darlington, Tubwell Row, Market Pl., Darlington, Co. Durham.....	27,350	33,028
1847D	Deal and Walmer, 7 Victoria Rd., Deal, Kent................	761	1,437
1865	Denton, 37 Ashton Rd., Denton, Manchester................	1,093	1,373
1859D	Derbyshire, 7 Iron Gate, Derby DE1 3FW...................	110,180	134,946
1923	Dillwyn P., 11 Cradock St., Swansea, Glam. SA1 3EW...........	1,473	3,631
1879	Dorking, Haybarn Hse., 118 South St., Dorking, Surrey...........	957	2,042
1861	Dover Dt., 3 Market Sq., Dover, Kent...................	712	1,231
1883	Dover and Folkestone, 27–29 Castle St., Dover, Kent...........	688	1,077
1865	Driffield, 51 Market Place, Driffield, Yorks................	967	914
1886	Duchess of Kent, Marcol Hse., 289–293 Regent St., London, W.1...	346	668
1858D	Dudley, Dudley Hse., Stone St., Dudley, Worcs...............	7,194	9,798
1869D	Dunfermline 48–56, East Port, Dunfermline, Fife................	25,625	42,340
1927D	Ealing and Acton, 55 The Mall, Ealing, London, W5 3TG..........	2,428	5,995
1857D	Earl Shilton, 22 The Hollow, Earl Shilton, Leicester LE9 7NB........	6,215	7,356
1903D	East Surrey, 54 Station Rd., Redhill, Surrey................	6,104	8,466

Year Established	Name of Society (abbreviated) Head Office	Share Investors	Assets Total £'000
1877D	Eastbourne Mut., 147 Terminus Rd., Eastbourne, Sussex............	24,042	41,641
1870D	Edinburgh, 32 Castle St., Edinburgh EH2 3JB......................	5,440	10,339
1847D	Essex Eq., 5 Brooke Road, Grays, Essex..........................	3,566	4,709
1862D	Falkirk, Manse Place, Falkirk, Stirlingshire......................	3,131	3,278
1860D	Frome Selwood P., 3 Market Pl., Frome, Som......................	6,200	8,008
1865D	Furness, 51–55 Duke Street, Barrow-in-Furness, LA14 1RT........	30,095	31,908
1911D	Gainsborough, 26 Lord St., Gainsborough, Lincs. DN21 2DB........	1,688	2,665
1924D	Gateway, P.O. Box 18, Worthing, W. Sussex BN13 2QD..........	230,386	387,918
1886	General Thrift P., 3/4 Turnpike Parade, Green Lanes, London N15 3LA	861	1,459
1906D	Glantawe P., 47 Mansel St., Swansea, Glam......................	1,051	2,864
1957D	Grainger, Hood St., Newcastle upon Tyne NE1 6JP................	27,788	40,752
1875	Grantham, 15 Market Place, Grantham, Lincs......................	563	927
1880D	Grays, 22 New Rd., Grays, Essex RM17 6PH......................	7,876	10,250
1852D	Greenwich, 281 Greenwich High Rd., London, SE10 8NL..........	15,043	21,153
1848D	Grimsby, Osborne Chambers, Osborne St., Grimsby, Lincs..........	925	2,045
1871D	Guardian, Guardian Hse., 120 High Holborn, London WC1V 6RH...	53,416	159,384
1928D	Hadrian, 30 Fowler St., South Shields, Co. Durham..............	3,757	4,630
1853D	Halifax, P.O. Box 60, Trinity Rd., Halifax, Yorks..............	3,214,961	4,576,736
1866D	Hampshire, 29–31 Guildhall Walk, Portsmouth, Hants. PO1 2RW...	5,676	10,629
1854D	Hanley Econ., 42 Cheapside, Hanley, Stoke-on-Trent, Staffs. ST1 1EX	21,291	21,376
1953D	Harpenden and Dt., 14 Station Rd., Harpenden, Herts............	1,873	2,984
1882D	Harrow, Cunningham Hse., Bessborough Rd., Harrow, Middx. HA1 3DA...	4,772	8,644
1866	Hartlepool and Dt., 17 Scarborough St., Hartlepool, Co. Durham....	608	1,178
1851D	Hasbury and Cradley, 5 Summer Hill, Halesowen, Worcs............	3,910	4,251
1931	Haslemere, 18 High Street, Haslemere, Surrey....................	754	1,158
1849D	Hastings and Thanet, 12–14 Wigmore St., London W1H 0DA........	289,790	394,560
1890D	Haywards Heath and Dt., 33 The Broadway, Haywards Heath, Sussex	12,327	16,153
1863D	Heart of England, 22–26 Jury St., Warwick......................	78,955	82,398
1875D	Hearts of Oak and Enfield, 47–49 Oxford St., London, W1R 2BN...	40,666	64,000
1884D	Hemel Hempstead, 43 Marlowes, Hemel Hempstead, Herts..........	8,822	13,253
1926D	Hendon, Central Circus, Hendon, London, N.W.4................	4,995	6,957
1888D	Herne Bay, 39 William St., Herne Bay CT6 5NS..................	2,758	5,417
1888D	Herts and Essex P., 4 Market Sq., Bishop's Stortford, Herts........	3,204	5,580
1874D	Hibernian P., 22 High St., Cardiff, Glam......................	2,061	2,987
1865D	Hinckley P., Upper Bond St., Hinckley, Leics....................	19,445	24,654
1855D	Holmesdale B., 43 Church St., Reigate, Surrey RH2 0AE..........	7,015	10,360
1856D	Horsham, 30 Carfax, Horsham, Sussex RH12 1EE..................	3,959	5,326
1864D	Huddersfield and Bradford, Permanent Hse., Westgate, Bradford BD1 2AU...	244,491	372,354
1868D	Hyde, 5 Corporation St., Hyde, Cheshire SK14 1AF..............	2,228	3,186
1853D	Ilkeston P., Queen St., Ilkeston, Derby DE7 5HQ................	2,316	3,198
1849D	Ipswich, 44 Upper Brook St., Ipswich IP4 1DP..................	17,228	19,653
1847	Kent and Canterbury P.B., 3 The Parade, Canterbury, Kent........	485	1,026
1869D	Kettering P.B., 26–28 Headlands, Kettering......................	950	1,455
1961	Kidderminster Eq., 30 Church St., Kidderminster................	638	1,161
1851	Kidderminster P.B., 29 Church St., Kidderminster, Worcs..........	1,405	2,662
1864D	Kilmarnock, 57 The Foregate, Kilmarnock......................	866	1,417
1917	King Edward, 19 Castle St., Liverpool..........................	113	607
1865D	Kingston, 6 Eden St., Kingston-on-Thames, Surrey..............	7,094	12,746
1852D	Lambeth, 118–120 Westminster Bridge Rd., London SE1 7XE........	29,432	59,636
1867D	Lancashire, 127 Union St., Oldham, Lancs......................	2,990	5,082
1853D	Leamington Spa, 118–120 Warwick St., Leamington Spa, Warws.......	16,618	22,944
1875D	Leeds and Holbeck, 105 Albion St., Leeds LS1 5AS..............	83,915	126,117
1848D	Leeds P., Permanent Hse., The Headrow, Leeds LS1 1NS..........	1,124,090	1,354,598
1863D	Leek United and Midlands, 50 St. Edward St., Leek, Staffs. ST13 5DH	33,966	40,303
1875D	Leicester, Oadby, Leicester LE2 4PF..........................	485,935	793,966
1875	Leigh P., 12a Leigh Road, Leigh, Lancs........................	897	1,704
1854	Liverpool Charter, 3 Brunswick St., Liverpool L2 0PQ..........	550	510
1877D	Liverpool, 375 Stanley Road, Bootle L20 2HS..................	39,747	64,213
1859	London B., 85 Blackfriars Rd., London SE1 8HA................	1,250	2,177
1863D	London Commercial, Guildford Hse., Gray's Inn Rd., London, W.C.1.	1,978	3,918
1883D	London and Essex, Security Hse., 2 Romford Rd., London, E.15....	4,374	7,353
1879D	London Goldhawk, 15/17 Chiswick High Road, London W4 2NG...	45,312	76,867
1878D	London Grosvenor and Middlesex, 5 Old Brompton Rd., SW7 3H7..	882	1,161
1848	London P., 14 Tufton St., London SW1P 3QZ....................	1,751	3,674
1867D	Loughborough P., 6 High St., Loughborough, Leics. LE11 2QB......	4,795	9,232
1877	Louth, Mablethorpe and Sutton P.B., 3 Eastgate, Louth, Lincs. LN11 9NA	908	1,218
1848D	Magnet & Planet, Planet House, 215 Strand, London WC2R 1AY....	83,897	139,498
1922D	Manchester, 18–20 Bridge St., Manchester M3 3BU..............	3,559	6,663
1956	Mancunian, 22 Dickinson St., Manchester M1 4LF................	771	1,427
1870D	Mansfield, Regent Hse., Regent St., Mansfield, Notts..............	10,877	17,547

Year Established	Name of Society (abbreviated) Head Office	Share Investors	Assets Total £'000
1867	Margam, 18 Station Rd., Port Talbot SA13 1BU.................	457	1,074
1870D	Market Harborough, Welland Hse., The Sq., Market Harborough, Leics.	16,419	16,772
1860D	Marsden, 6–20 Russell St., Nelson, Lancs. BB9 7NJ.................	26,742	34,512
1874D	Melton Mowbray, 43 Nottingham St., Melton Mowbray, Leics.......	12,753	20,125
1966D	Mercantile, 75 Howard St., North Shields......................	7,629	11,602
1851D	Mercia, 52 Lower High Street, Wednesbury, Staffs.................	22,520	23,181
1882	Merseyside, 41 North John St., Liverpool L2 6RR.................	429	824
1886D	Metrogas, Katherine Hse., Katherine St., Croydon CR9 1JU........	1,868	1,971
1872D	Middleton, 99 Long St., Middleton, Manchester M24 3UR..........	20,421	25,629
1886D	Mid-Glamorgan, 4 Gelliwastad Rd., Pontypridd, Glam.............	3,044	6,175
1933	Midland P., 3 Lower High St., Cradley Heath, Warley, Worcs.......	646	898
1859D	Midshires, 5/9 St. Nicholas St., Worcester......................	42,804	55,371
1880D	Mid-Sussex, Mid-Sussex Hse., 66 Church Rd., Burgess Hill, Sussex...	3,237	4,153
1883D	Mitcham, 173 London Rd., Mitcham, Surrey CR4 2JB.............	1,976	1,441
1869D	Monmouthshire, 119/120 Commercial St., Newport, Gwent NPT 1PX	7,455	12,900
1866D	Mornington P., 158 Kentish Town Rd., London NW5 2BT..........	12,819	18,762
1866	Musselburgh, 8 Bridge St., Musselburgh.......................	1,592	1,143
1896D	National Counties, Waterloo Hse., High St., Epsom, Surrey.........	26,817	67,592
1884D	Nationwide, New Oxford Hse., High Holborn, London, WC1 6PW..	1,499,818	1,905,059
1877D	Nelson and Premier, 3 Westoe Village, South Shields, Co. Durham...	2,203	3,417
1866D	New Cross, 58 Deptford High St., London, SE8 4RT................	4,093	7,626
1882D	New Swindon, 36 Regent Circus, Swindon, Wilts.................	1,836	3,316
1856D	Newbury, 17–20 Bartholomew St., Newbury, Berks................	15,752	23,768
1863D	Newcastle and Gateshead, St. Nicholas Sq., Newcastle upon Tyne NE1 1DX..	3,845	5,172
1861D	Newcastle upon Tyne P., 37–41 Grainger St., Newcastle upon Tyne..	22,905	44,575
1876D	North East Globe, 18 Ridley Place, Newcastle upon Tyne NE1 8JW..	2,603	4,003
1866D	North Kent, North Kent Hse., Windmill St., Gravesend, Kent DA12 1AZ..	14,510	15,647
1886	North London, 105 Seven Sisters Rd., London N7 7QR...........	813	2,115
1877D	North of England, 57 Fawcett St., Sunderland, Co. Durham SR1 1SQ	17,481	29,725
1899D	North Wilts Eq., 18 and 19 Commercial Rd., Swindon, Wilts........	4,046	6,446
1850D	Northern Rock, Northern Rock Hse., Gosforth, Newcastle upon Tyne NE3 4PL..	234,980	304,101
1852D	Norwich, St. Andrew's Hse., St. Andrew St., Norwich, Norfolk.....	27,969	52,067
1850D	Nottingham, 5–13 Upper Parliament St., Nottingham NG1 2BX.....	45,223	60,975
1935D	Nottingham Oddfellows, Imperial Bldg., Victoria St., Nottingham...	4,004	3,328
1849	Nuneaton and Warwickshire, 9 Queen's Rd., Nuneaton, Warws......	889	1,131
1848D	Otley, 34 Boroughgate, Otley, Yorks.........................	6,918	10,828
1869D	Over Darwen, 24 Railway Rd., Darwen BB3 2AG.................	3,636	4,026
1879D	Paddington, 125 Westbourne Grove, London W2 4UP.............	2,266	6,330
1877D	Padiham, 34 Burnley Rd., Padiham, Lancs.....................	4,510	6,815
1853D	Paisley, 7 Glasgow Rd., Paisley, Renfrew.....................	6,447	11,108
1879D	Peckham Mut., Hanover Park Hse., 14/16 Hanover Park, London, S.E.15	6,514	9,013
1855D	Peckham P., 6–8 Queens Rd., London SE15 2PP.................	1,956	3,229
1856D	Peebles, 90 High St., Peebles.............................	1,117	1,739
1877D	Penrith, 7 King St., Penrith, Cumb.........................	3,550	5,655
1860D	Peterborough, 5 Cathedral Sq., Peterborough.................	26,444	38,162
1884	Pioneer P., 51 Lincoln's Inn Fields, London WC2A 3LZ..........	544	1,234
1875	Poole, 50 Parkstone Road, Poole, Dorset BH15 2QB............	450	903
1881D	Portman, 40 Portman Sq., London W1H 9FH.................	64,444	116,114
1896D	Portsmouth, 176 London Rd., North End, Portsmouth PO2 9DL.......	12,483	25,228
1860D	Principality, Principality Bldgs., Queen St., Cardiff CF1 4NA........	62,389	89,725
1941D	Property Owners, 4 Cavendish Place, London W1M 0AQ...........	19,869	53,346
1849D	Provincial, Provincial Hse., Market St., Bradford BD1 1NL........	428,557	755,181
1886D	Queen Victoria Street, Pearl Assurance Hse., 1A Katherine St., Croydon CR0 1NX..	975	2,004
1846D	Ramsbury, The Square, Ramsbury, Marlborough, Wilts. SN8 2PF...	34,880	40,220
1883	Rowland Hill P., Victoria Hse., Southampton Row, London WC1B 4DW..	835	1,733
1888D	Rowley Regis, 223 Halesowen Rd., Crawley Heath, Warley, Worcs..	11,134	12,689
1861D	Rugby Prov., 34 North St., Rugby, Warwicks...................	3,557	4,153
1850	Rye P., 18 High St., Rye, Sussex...........................	872	987
1849D	Saffron Walden and Dt., Market Place, Saffron Walden, Essex.......	7,682	12,493
1867D	St. Andrew's, 26 Ridley Place, Newcastle upon Tyne NE1 8DY......	1,841	2,163
1937D	St. Pancras, 200 Finchley Rd., London NW3 6DA..............	3,739	8,936
1850	St. Philip's B., 121–123 Edmund Street, Birmingham B3 2HZ........	766	1,793
1852D	Sandbach, 5 Middlewich Rd., Sandbach, Chesh.................	2,301	4,188
1875D	Sandy, 6 Bedford Rd., Sandy, Beds.........................	3,672	4,610
1846D	Scarborough, York Hse., York Place, Scarborough, Yorks...........	13,692	20,448
1848D	Scottish, 2 York Place, Edinburgh EH1 3ER...................	4,645	6,812
1935D	Sheffield, 66 Campo Lane, Sheffield, Yorks S1 2EG.................	2,404	4,346

Year Estab- lished	Name of Society (abbreviated) Head Office	Share Investors	Assets Total £'000
1879D	Shepshed, Bull Ring, Shepshed, Loughborough, Leics. LE12 9QD....	4,777	4,663
1864	Shields and Washington, 15 Beach Rd., South Shields...............	602	848
1875D	Shields Commercial, Barrington St., South Shields, Co. Durham.....	2,413	3,555
1853D	Skipton, 59 High St., Skipton, Yorks.............................	72,846	115,605
1859D	South of England, 58 King St., Maidenhead, Berks..................	96,385	153,813
1874	South Metropolitan, 44 Woodcote Road, Wellington, Surrey........	317	708
1876	South Shields, Sun P., Suc Bldgs., Beach Rd., Sth. Shields, Co. Durham	601	1,175
1875D	South West Wales, 17 The Kingsway, Swansea, Glam...............	3,187	6,186
1877D	Stafford Railway, 4 Market Sq., Stafford.........................	4,977	7,351
1902D	Staffordshire, 5 Princes St., Wolverhampton, Staffs. WV1 1HJ......	79,105	77,475
1873	Stamford, The Grey House, 3 Broad St., Stamford, PE9 1PR........	433	647
1875D	Standard, 64 Church Way, North Shields, Nbld....................	2,483	3,108
1970	Stanley, Cromarty Hse., Front St., Stanley, Co. Durham...........	1,974	2,441
1876	Stockport, 20 Market Place, Stockport...........................	447	989
1877	Stockport and County P., Carlyle Hse., 109 Wellington Rd. Sth., Stockport, Chesh...	524	1,037
1898D	Stockport Mersey, 72–74 Wellington Rd. South, Stockport, Chesh. SR1 3SU...	1,114	2,131
1852D	Stoke-on-Trent P., 66–68 Liverpool Rd., Stoke-on-Trent, Staffs. ST4 1BQ..	1,301	2,431
1889D	Stourbridge, Lye and Dt. P., Victoria Chambers, 97 High St., Stour- bridge, Worcs..	4,782	6,111
1882	Strand and County P., 10 New Fetter Lane, London, EC4 1AD......	517	697
1850D	Stroud, 7 Russell St., Stroud, Glos..............................	19,960	20,922
1901D	Summers, Shotton Steel Works, Shotton, Deeside, Flint CH5 2NH...	7,435	5,156
1853D	Sunderland and Shields, 51 Fawcett St., Sunderland, Co. Durham SR1 1SA..	44,728	58,099
1870D	Sussex County, Bank House, 62 High St., Steyning, W. Sussex BN4 3RT..	31,408	47,726
1872D	Sussex Mutual, Sussex Hse., 130 Western Rd., Hove, Sussex BN3 1DR	16,070	46,985
1887	Swansea Albion and Gower, 60 Mansel St., Swansea, Glam..........	581	1,039
1868D	Swindon P., 1 Commercial Rd., Swindon, Wilts....................	3,657	6,352
1904	Sydenham, 72 Sydenham Rd., Sydenham.........................	467	676
1899	Strathclyde, 98 Bata St., Glasgow G2 2EN.......................	1,248	1,728
1970	Target, Target Hse., 7–9 Breams Bldgs, London, EC4A 1EU.........	1,795	3,138
1854D	Tamworth P.B., 6 Victoria Rd., Tamworth, Staffs.................	3,351	4,286
1966	Teachers, 12 Christchurch Rd., Bournemouth.....................	9,189	17,642
1901D	Tipton and Coseley, 57–60 High St., Tipton, Staffs. DY4 8HG......	10,078	9,467
1853D	Town and Country, 1 Castle Street, Hinckley, Leicester LE10 1DF....	26,582	40,635
1866D	Tyldesley, 213–215 Elliott St., Tyldesley, Manchester M29 8EB.......	5,460	7,878
1877D	Tyne, 10 Grange Rd., West, Jarrow, Co. Durham.................	4,211	5,185
1855D	Tynemouth, 53–55 Howard St., North Shields, Nbld...............	4,615	5,202
1887D	Tynemouth Victoria, 23 West Percy St., North Shields, Nbld........	2,532	5,108
1861	United Provinces, Hamilton Hse., 56 Hamilton St., Birkenhead, Cheshire L41 5HZ..	432	529
1863D	Universal, 36 Grey St., Newcastle upon Tyne NE1 6BT.............	16,859	22,009
1924D	Vernon, 26 St. Petersgate, Stockport, Chesh......................	4,696	8,668
1846D	Wakefield, 57 Westgate, Wakefield, Yorks........................	19,554	20,974
1847D	Waltham Abbey, 5 Church St., Waltham Abbey, Essex..............	8,428	11,928
1877D	Walthamstow, 869 Forest Rd., Walthamstow, London E17 4BB.....	22,288	38,382
1867	Warrington, 3 Springfield St., Warrington........................	579	749
1857	Wellington (Somerset) and Dist., 15 High St., Wellington, Somerset..	651	810
1878D	Welsh Economic, Old Bank Chambers, Pontypridd, Glam...........	964	1,939
1949D	Wessex, 115 Old Christchurch Rd., Bournemouth, Hants BH1 1HB ..	8,784	20,427
1849D	West Bromwich, 321 High St., West Bromwich, Staffs.............	108,917	127,018
1882D	West Cumbria, Cumbria House, Murray Rd., Workington, CA14 2AD	2,317	-3,899
1907	Westbury and Dt. P., 88 The Butts, Westbury, Wilts..............	706	1,232
1862D	Western Counties, 20 The Quay, Bideford, Devon.................	28,104	37,891
1866D	West Yorkshire, Church St., Dewsbury, Yorks....................	30,180	42,865
1873D	Wigan, 14 Library St., Wigan, Lancs............................	3,312	4,178
1849D	Wolverhampton, 37–41 Lichfield St., Wolverhampton, Staffs. WV1 1EL	46,329	66,355
1847D	Woolwich Eq., Equitable Hse., London SE18 6AB.................	964,126	1,259,162

WATER AUTHORITIES

The Water Act 1973, which provided for the re-organisation of the water services in England and Wales, resulted in the disappearance of 29 river authorities, 157 water undertakings and 1,393 sewerage and sewage disposal authorities and the creation of ten autonomous multi-purpose water authorities (nine regional authorities in England and the Welsh National Water Development Authority). The Act also created the National Water Council and the Water Space Amenity Commission.

The water authorities are responsible for water supply, water conservation, sewerage and sewage disposal, prevention of river pollution, fisheries, land drainage and the recreational use of their waters. Between them the new authorities employ about 65,000 people, have an annual revenue of some £850 million and an investment budget of about £500 million a year.

The National Water Council is the national consultative and advisory body for the water services and consists of a chairman appointed by the Secretary of State for the Environment, the chairmen of the regional water authorities and ten other members appointed by the Secretary of State and the Minister of Agriculture, Fisheries and Food.

The Council advises water authorities and the Government on national water policy and promotes and assists the efficient performance by water authorities of their functions in research and planning.

To undertake this work the Council has manpower and training divisions, and sections dealing with technical services, testing of appliances, public relations, information, legal and financial matters and a secretariat.

THE NATIONAL WATER COUNCIL, 1 Queen Anne's Gate, London, S.W.1.—*Dir.-Gen.*, P. F. Stott.

Regional Water Authorities

THAMES WATER AUTHORITY, New River Head, Rosebery Avenue, London, E.C.1.—*Chief Executive*, A. Morrison.

SOUTHERN WATER AUTHORITY, Guildborne House, Worthing, Sussex.—*Chief Executive*, B. R. Thorpe.

SEVERN TRENT WATER AUTHORITY, Abelson House, 2297 Coventry Road, Sheldon, Birmingham.—*Chief Executive*, J. E. Beddoe.

WESSEX WATER AUTHORITY, Techno House, Redcliffe Way, Bristol.—*Chief Executive*, K. F. Roberts.

ANGLIAN WATER AUTHORITY, Diploma House, Grammar School Walk, Huntingdon.—*Chief Executive*, P. H. Bray.

SOUTH WEST WATER AUTHORITY, P.O. Box 22, 3-5 Barnfield Road, Exeter.—*Managing Director*, H. R. Slocombe.

NORTHUMBRIAN WATER AUTHORITY, Northumbria House, Regent Centre, Gosforth, Newcastle-upon-Tyne.—*Chief Executive*, A. S. Robertson.

NORTH WEST WATER AUTHORITY, Dawson House, Great Sankey, Warrington.—*Chief Executive*, J. G. Lloyd.

YORKSHIRE WATER AUTHORITY, West Riding House, 67 Albion Street, Leeds.—*Chief Executive*, A. B. Baldwin.

WELSH NATIONAL WATER DEVELOPMENT AUTHORITY, Cambrian Way, Brecon, Powys.—*Chief Executive*, Dr. H. H. Crann.

THE ENGLISH MILE COMPARED WITH OTHER EUROPEAN MEASURES

	English Mile	English Geog. M.	French Kilom.	German Geog. M.	Russian Verst	Austrian Mile	Dutch Ure	Norweg. Mile	Swedish Mile	Danish Mile	Swiss Stunde
English Statute Mile.	1·000	0·868	1·609	0·217	1·508	0·212	0·289	0·142	0·151	0·213	0·335
English Geog. Mile..	1·153	1·000	1·855	0·250	1·738	0·245	0·333	0·164	0·169	0·246	0·386
Kilometre.........	0·621	0·540	1·000	0·135	0·937	0·132	0·180	0·088	0·094	0·133	0·208
German Geog. Mile.	4·610	4·000	7·420	1·000	6·953	0·978	1·333	0·657	0·694	0·985	1·543
Russian Verst.....	0·663	0·575	1·067	0·144	1·000	0·141	0·192	0·094	0·100	0·142	0·222
Austrian Mile......	4·714	4·089	7·586	1·022	7·112	1·000	1·363	0·672	0·710	1·006	1·578
Dutch Ure.........	3·458	3·000	5·565	0·750	5·215	0·734	1·000	0·493	0·520	0·738	1·157
Norwegian Mile....	7·021	6·091	11·299	1·523	10·589	1·489	2·035	1·000	1·057	1·499	2·350
Swedish Mile......	6·644	5·764	10·692	1·441	10·019	1·409	1·921	0·948	1·000	1·419	2·224
Danish Mile........	4·682	4·062	7·536	1·016	7·078	0·994	1·354	0·667	0·705	1·000	1·567
Swiss Stunde.......	2·987	2·592	4·808	0·648	4·505	0·634	0·864	0·425	0·449	0·638	1·000

UNIT TRUSTS

A Unit Trust is a method of investment by which money subscribed in varying amounts by individual investors is pooled in a fund, the investment and management of which is subject to the strict legal provisions of a Trust Deed. The fund is invested in carefully-selected stocks and shares by a management company and the investments so acquired are held by a Trustee (usually a bank or insurance company). The management company and the Trustee, who must be effectively independent of each other, are parties to the Trust Deed which must be authorized by the Department of Trade (or the Ministry of Commerce in Northern Ireland) before any public offer of units for sale may be made.

Units are readily marketable, being bought or sold at the price (based on the value of the underlying securities) ruling at the time the order for sale or repurchase is received by the Management Company. The Department of Trade regulates the charges which Unit Trust managers may make. These charges are taken by way of an initial service charge (which is included in the sale price unit), and a semi-annual management fee levied on the value of the fund and taken out of either income or capital. Over a 20-year life of a Trust, the initial service charge, together with management fees, may not total more than 13¼ per cent. In order to avoid the need for quoting unit prices with awkward fractions of a penny the managers are also entitled to round off the price of a unit by 1·25p or 1 per cent., whichever is the lower.

Through his subscription to the Trust Fund each subscriber acquires a fractional interest in the block of securities in which the fund is invested, while the dividends received from the investments form the income of the trust. The net income is paid to all investors in the Trust Fund in proportion to the size of their holdings. The dividend income is either paid directly to the investor every six months, or can be used by arrangement to purchase further units for his account. In either case any unit-holder who is not liable to tax at the basic rate of tax deducted can claim appropriate relief from the Inland Revenue.

The past performance of unit trusts has generally been better than direct investment in stocks and shares but being an investment in equities they cannot escape stock market trends. A unit trust investment neither guarantees an increasing income nor ensures continual capital appreciation. They are essentially a long-term form of investment.

Savings Schemes

Most management companies operate savings schemes whereby an investor is able to make contributions at intervals which are utilized to purchase units at the current price, the cash balance remaining from any such purchase being carried forward and added to the next contribution. Savings schemes can be for a direct purchase of units or linked with life assurance. The latter have provided one of the most rapid growth sectors of the Unit Trust movement in recent years. The unit linked schemes enable a person to accumulate a sum of money for retirement, etc., with the protection of life assurance cover for the duration of the planned period of saving. At the end of this period, the investor receives all the units acquired or their cash value. If death occurs beforehand, the dependents receive all the units bought up to date, plus a cash sum equivalent to the total remaining contributions necessary to have completed the savings programme. Tax relief is available on these contributions as with other life assurance premiums.

Arrangements for Children

In general, units cannot be registered in the name of a child but they can be registered in the name of a parent or any other adult, and the registered holding can be designated with the initials of the child. Alternatively, money can be settled on a child under one of the various children's gift plans operated and the units held in trust. Income distributions, less income tax, are invested in further units, and additional units may be purchased at any time. When the child reaches 18 or some chosen later age, the units become his property.

Unit Trust Association

The unit trust industry has been in operation for some forty-five years.

The Unit Trust Association of Park House, 16, Finsbury Circus, EC2M 7JP, was formed on October 13, 1959, and membership is open to any management company of an authorized unit trust scheme. The associations' main object is to act as a consulting body amongst its members in order to agree strict standards of unit trust practices for the protection of the interest of unit holders and to maintain the good name of the Unit Trust industry.

At December 31, 1975, the Association represented 328 of the 395 trusts in existence (83%); 97 per cent of all unit holdings being in these trusts.

The total value of all funds under management was £2.51 billion, and out of a total of 95 management groups five had funds in excess of £100 million; 23 between £10 million and £100 million and 46 between £1 million and £10 million.

The following details relating to the management groups operating in Great Britain and Northern Ireland have been extracted from the *Unit Trust Year Book 1976*, published by Fundex Ltd. (Addresses correct to March 1, 1976.)

Unit Trusts 1975–1976

(With value of funds managed and number of unit holdings as at December 31, 1975.)

★ABBEY UNIT TRUST MANAGERS LTD., 72–80 Gatehouse Road, Aylesbury, Bucks. HP19 3EB. *Funds Managed* £36·1 million; *Holdings* 4,645.

ALBEN TRUST MANAGERS LTD., 14 Finsbury Circus, London EC2M 7DS. *Funds Managed* £0·7 million; *Holdings* 100.

★ALLIED HAMBRO GROUP, Hambro House, Rayleigh Road, Hutton, Brentwood, Essex CM13 1AA. *Funds Managed* £183·7 million; *Holdings* 106,428.

ANDERSON UNIT TRUST MANAGERS LTD., 158 Fenchurch Street, London EC3M 6AA. *Funds Managed* £0·2 million; *Holdings* 140.

★ANSBACHER UNIT MANAGEMENT COMPANY LTD., 1 Noble Street. Gresham Street, London EC2V 7JH. *Funds Managed* £0·2 million; *Holdings* 22.

★ANTONY GIBBS UNIT TRUST MANAGERS, 23 Blomfeld Street, London EC2M 7NL. *Funds Managed* £0·4 million; *Holdings* 199.

★ARBUTHNOT SECURITIES LTD., 21 Leven Street, Edinburgh EH3 9LH. *Funds Managed* £15·8 million; *Holdings* 29,110.

★ARCHWAY UNIT TRUST MANAGERS LTD., 24 St. Mary Axe, London EC3 8EN. *Funds Managed* £1·1 million; *Holdings* 411.

★BARCLAYS UNICORN LTD., Head Office, Unicorn House, 252 Romford Road, London E7 9JB. *Funds Managed* £284·2 million; *Holdings* 285,827.

★Bishopsgate Progressive Unit Trust Management Company Ltd., 9 Bishopsgate, London EC2N 3AD. *Funds Managed £4·6 million; Holdings* 1,628.

Bridge Talisman Fund Managers Ltd., Plantation House, 5–8 Mincing Lane, London EC3M 3DX. *Funds Managed £5·3 million; Holdings* 2,770.

★British Life Office Ltd. (The), Reliance House, Tunbridge Wells, Kent. *Funds Managed £7·2* million; *Holdings* 587.

★Cabot Unit Trust Management Company Ltd., The Bristol & West Building, Broad Quay, Bristol BS1 4DD. *Funds Managed £1·9 million; Holdings* 499.

Canada Life Unit Trust Managers Ltd., 6 Charles II Street, London SW1Y4 AD. *Funds Managed £5·3 million; Holdings* 624.

★James Capel and Company Unit Trust Management Ltd., Winchester House, 100 Old Broad Street, London EC2N 1BQ. *Funds managed £o·6 million; Holdings* 100.

Carliol Unit Fund Managers Ltd., A Floor, Milburn House, Newcastle upon Tyne NE1 1LU. *Funds Managed £o·9 million; Holdings* 380.

★Charterhouse Japhet Unit Management Ltd., 1 Paternoster Row, St. Pauls, London EC4M 7DH. *Funds Managed £4·0 million; Holdings* 2,451.

College Hill Unit Trust Managers Ltd., 6 Wardrobe Place, London EC4V 5HR. *Funds managed £o·1 million; Holdings* 45.

★Confederation Funds Management Ltd., 120 Regent Street, London W1R 6AY. *Funds Managed £o·7 million; Holdings* 155.

★Cosmopolitan Fund Managers Ltd., 56 Copthall Avenue, London EC2 7JX. *Funds Managed £o·2 million; Holdings* 954.

Coyne Investment Management Ltd., Fairhill Courthouse, Hildenborough, Kent. *Funds Managed £o·2 million; Holdings* 247.

★Crescent Unit Trust Managers Ltd., 4 Melville Crescent, Edinburgh EH3 7JB. *Funds Managed £16·9 million; Holdings* 19,053.

Discretionary Unit Fund Managers Ltd., Finsbury House, 22 Blomfield Street, London EC2M 7AL. *Funds Managed £2·2 million; Holdings* 834.

★Emblem Fund Management Company Ltd. (The) 20 Copthall Avenue, London EC2. *Funds managed £o·2 million; Holdings* 152.

★Equitas Securities Ltd., 5 Rayleigh Road, Hutton, Brentwood, Essex CM13 1AA. *Funds Managed £2·5 million; Holdings* 227.

Equity & Law Unit Trust Managers Ltd., Amersham Road, High Wycombe, Bucks. HP13 5AL. *Funds Managed £7·5 million; Holdings* 426.

Founders Court Management Services Ltd., Founders Court, Lothbury, London EC2R 7HE. *Funds Managed £o·8 million; Holdings* 254.

Framlington Unit Management Ltd., Framlington House, 5–7 Ireland Yard, London EC4V 5DH. *Funds Managed £3·1 million; Holdings* 1,176.

★Friends' Provident Unit Trust Managers Ltd., Pixham End, Dorking, Surrey RH4 1QA. *Funds Managed £1·0 million; Holdings* 659.

★G and A Unit Trust Managers Ltd., 5 Rayleigh Road, Hutton, Brentwood, Essex CM13 1AA. *Funds Managed £2·2 million; Holdings* 7,596.

★Gartmore Fund Managers Ltd., 2 St. Mary Axe, London EC3A 8BP. *Funds Managed £12·0* million; *Holdings* 5,474.

Glenfriars Unit Trust Management Ltd., 25 Austin Friars, London EC2N 2JB. *Funds Managed* not disclosed; *Holdings* not disclosed.

Grieveson Management Company Ltd., 59 Gresham Street, London EC2P 2DS. *Funds Managed £19·6 million; Holdings* 6,164.

★John Govett Unit Management Ltd., Winchester House, 77 London Wall, London EC2N 1DH. *Funds Managed £6·7 million; Holdings* 4,594.

GT Unit Managers Ltd., (6th floor) 16 St. Martins-le-Grand, London EC1A 4EP. *Funds Managed £5·0 million; Holdings* 1,892.

★Guardian Royal Exchange Unit Managers Ltd., The Royal Exchange, London EC3P 3DN. *Funds Managed £34·7 million; Holdings* 1,888.

★Henderson Unit Trust Management Ltd., 11 Austin Friars, London EC2N 2ED. *Funds managed £33·4 million; Holdings* 61,077.

★Hill Samuel Unit Trust Managers Ltd., 45 Beech Street, London EC2P 2LX. *Funds managed £94·3 million; Holdings* 46,229.

★Intel Funds (Management) Ltd., 15 Christopher Street, London EC2A 2HA. *Funds managed £3·6 million; Holdings* 1,360.

Ionian Unit Trust Management Ltd., 64 Coleman Street, London EC2R 5BD. *Funds Managed £1·7 million; Holdings* 393.

★Key Fund Managers Ltd., 25 Milk Street, London EC2V 8JE. *Funds Managed £3·0 million; Holdings* 710.

★Kleinwort Benson Unit Managers Ltd., PO Box 560, 20 Fenchurch Street, London EC3P 3DB. *Funds Managed £1·7 million; Holdings* 101.

★L & C Unit Trust Management Ltd., The Stock Exchange, London EC2N 1HA. *Funds managed £o·6 million; Holdings* 212.

Lawson Securities Ltd., 63 George Street, Edinburgh EH2 2JG. *Funds Managed £8·6 million; Holdings* 9,072.

Lazard Brothers & Company Ltd., 21 Moorfields, London EC2P 2HT. *Funds managed £40·0* million (estimated); *Holdings* not disclosed.

Legal & General—Tyndall Fund Managers Ltd., 18 Canynge Road, Bristol BS99 7UA. *Funds Managed £3·4 million; Holdings* 671.

Leonine Administration Ltd., 28 Throgmorton Street, London EC2 2AN. *Funds Managed £o·2* million; *Holdings* 50.

★Lloyds Bank Unit Trust Managers Ltd., 71 Lombard Street, London EC3P 3BS. *Funds managed £57·6 million; Holdings* 83,028.

Lloyd's Life Unit Trust Managers Ltd., 72–80 Gatehouse Road, Aylesbury, Buckinghamshire HP19 3EB. *Funds Managed £o·5 million; Holdings* 17.

★London Wall Group of Unit Trusts Ltd., 1 Finsbury Square, London EC2A 1PD. *Funds Managed £17·1 million; Holdings* 29,339.

★M & G Group Ltd., Three Quays, Tower Hill, London EC3R 6BQ. *Funds Managed £288.8* million; *Holdings* 139,310.

Manulife Management Ltd., PO Box 21, Manulife House, St. George's Way, Stevenage, Hertfordshire SG1 1HP. *Funds Managed £o·4* million; *Holdings* 44.

Mayflower Management Company Ltd., Clements House, Gresham Street, London EC2. *Funds Managed £1·1 million* (estimated); *Holdings* not disclosed.

★Mercury Fund Managers Ltd., St. Albans House, Goldsmith Street, London EC2P 2DL. *Funds Managed £3·6 million; Holdings* 445.

Metropolitan Exempt Fund Managers Ltd., 28 Haymarket, London SW1Y 4SR. *Funds managed £2·4 million; Holdings* 34.

★Midland Bank Group Unit Trust Managers Ltd., Courtwood House, Silver Street Head, Sheffield S1 3RD. *Funds managed £11·5 million; Holdings* 13,545.

*MINSTER FUND MANAGERS LTD., Minster House, Arthur Street, London EC4R 9BH. *Funds Managed* £1·2 million; *Holdings* 126.

*MUTUAL UNIT TRUST MANAGERS LTD., Throgmorton House, 15 Copthall Avenue, London EC2R 7BU. *Funds Managed* £9·3 million; *Holdings* 17,270.

*NATIONAL PROVIDENT INVESTMENT MANAGERS LTD., PO Box 227, 48 Gracechurch Street, London EC3P 3HH. *Funds Managed* £2·2 million; *Holdings* 715.

*NATIONAL WESTMINSTER UNIT TRUST MANAGERS LTD., 41 Lothbury, London EC2P 2BP. *Funds Managed* £52 million; *Holdings* 68,250.

NEL TRUST MANAGERS LTD., Milton Court, Dorking, Surrey. *Funds Managed* £7·0 million; *Holdings* 1,180.

NEW COURT FUND MANAGERS LTD., New Court, St. Swithin's Lane, London EC4. *Funds managed* £22·4 million; *Holdings* 3,462.

*NORWICH GENERAL TRUST LTD., Surrey Street, Norwich NR1 3NJ. *Funds Managed* £4·0 million; *Holdings* 48.

*OCEANIC UNIT TRUST MANAGERS LTD., 15 Great St. Thomas Apostle, London EC4V 2BB. *Funds Managed* £11·9 million; *Holdings* 56,343.

*PEARL TRUST MANAGERS LTD., 252 High Holborn, London WC1V 7EB. *Funds Managed* £1·9 million; *Holdings* 3,120.

*PELICAN UNITS ADMINISTRATION LTD., Fountain House, 81 Fountain Street, Manchester M2 2EE. *Funds Managed* £2·0 million; *Holdings* 284.

*PERPETUAL UNIT TRUST MANAGEMENT LTD., 48–50 Hart Street, Henley-on-Thames, Oxon. RG9 2AZ. *Funds Managed* £0·2 million; *Holdings* 113.

PICCADILLY UNIT TRUST MANAGERS LTD., 65 London Wall, London EC2M 5UA. *Funds Managed* £4·5 million; *Holdings* 3,200.

PRACTICAL INVESTMENT COMPANY LTD., Europe House, World Trade Centre, London E1 9AA. *Funds Managed* £30·9 million; *Holdings* 4,253.

PROVINCIAL LIFE INVESTMENT COMPANY LTD., 222 Bishopsgate, London EC2M 4JS. *Funds Managed* £6·7 million; *Holdings* 1,020.

PRUDENTIAL UNIT TRUST MANAGERS LTD., Holborn Bars, London EC1N 2NH. *Funds Managed* £15·0 million; *Holdings* 1,980.

*QUILTER MANAGEMENT COMPANY LTD., Gerrald House, 31–35 Gresham Street, London EC2V 7LH. *Funds Managed* £1·0 million; *Holdings* 525.

RAPHAEL UNIT TRUST MANAGERS LTD., 10 Throgmorton Avenue, London EC2N 2DP. *Funds Managed* £0·2 million; *Holdings* 64.

*RELIANCE UNIT MANAGERS LTD., Reliance House, Tunbridge Wells, Kent. *Funds Managed* £0·1 million; *Holdings* 20.

*REMINGIUM MANAGEMENT LTD., 1st Floor, City-Gate House, 39–45 Finsbury Square, London EC2A 1JA. *Funds Managed* £1·7 million; *Holdings* not disclosed.

ROTHSCHILD & LOWNDES MANAGEMENT LTD., New Court, St. Swithin's Lane. London EC4. *Funds Managed* £9·0 million. *Holdings* 127.

*ROWE & PITMAN MANAGEMENT LTD., 1st Floor, City-Gate House, 39–45 Finsbury Square, London EC2A 1JA. *Funds Managed* £1·9 million *Holdings* 46.

*ROYAL TRUST COMPANY OF CANADA FUND MANAGEMENT LTD. (THE), Royal Trust House, 54 Jermyn Street, London SW1Y 6NQ. *Funds Managed* £1·5 million; *Holdings* 240.

*SAVE & PROSPER GROUP LTD., 4 Great St. Helens, London EC3P 3EP. *Funds Managed* £632·5 million; *Holdings* 649,933.

*SCHLESINGER TRUST MANAGERS LTD., 19 Hanover Square, London W1R 9DA. *Funds Managed* £20·0 million; *Holdings* 8,981.

*J. HENRY SCHRODER WAGG & COMPANY LTD., 120 Cheapside, London EC2V 6DS. *Funds Managed* £47·3 million; *Holdings* 10,847.

*SCOTTISH EQUITABLE FUND MANAGERS LTD., 28 St. Andrew Square, Edinburgh EH2 1YF. *Funds managed* £1·8 million; *Holdings* 160.

SEBAG UNIT TRUST MANAGERS LTD., PO Box 511, Bucklersbury House, 3 Queen Victoria Street, London EC4N 8DX. *Funds Managed* £1·1 million; *Holdings* 271.

SECURITY SELECTION LTD., 8 The Crescent Minories, London EC3N 2LY. *Funds Managed* £0·2 million; *Holdings* 40.

*STEWART UNIT TRUST MANAGERS LTD., 45 Charlotte Square, Edinburgh EH2 4HW. *Funds Managed* £3·1 million; *Holdings* 1,809.

*STRATTON TRUST MANAGERS LTD., Temporary address, 88 Leadenhall Street, London EC3A 3DT. *Funds Managed* £3·9 million; *Holdings* 803.

*SLATER, WALKER TRUST MANAGEMENT LTD., Leith House, 47–57 Gresham Street, London EC2V 7EP. *Funds Managed* £186·0 million; *Holdings* 319,297.

SUN ALLIANCE FUND MANAGEMENT LTD., 1 Bartholomew Lane, London EC2. *Funds Managed* £3·8 million; *Holdings* 453.

*TARGET TRUST MANAGERS LTD., Target House, 7–9 Breams Buildings, London EC4A 1EU. *Funds Managed* £67·8 million; *Holdings* 86,300.

*TARGET TRUST MANAGERS (SCOTLAND) LTD., 19 Atholl Crescent, Edinburgh EH3 8HQ. *Funds Managed* £2·8 million; *Holdings* 3,700.

*TRADES UNION UNIT TRUST MANAGERS LTD., 100 Wood Street, London EC2P 2AJ. *Funds Managed* £9·0 million; *Holdings* 478.

*TRANSATLANTIC AND GENERAL SECURITIES COMPANY LTD., 91–99 New London Road, Chelmsford CM2 0PY. *Funds Managed* £21·0 million; *Holdings* 5,470.

*TRUSTEE SAVINGS BANKS UNIT TRUST MANAGERS LTD., White Bear House, 21 Chantry Way, Andover, Hants. SP10 1PG. *Funds Managed* £42·5 million; *Holdings* 55,592.

TYNDALL MANAGERS LTD., 18 Canynge Road, Bristol BS99 7UA. *Funds Managed* £71·1 million; *Holdings* 23,823.

*ULSTER BANK UNIT TRUST MANAGERS LTD., PO Box 233, Waring Street, Belfast BT1 2ER. *Funds managed* £1·4 million; *Holdings* 2,270.

UNIT TRUST ACCOUNTING & MANAGEMENT LTD., Plantation House, 5–8 Mincing Lane, London EC3M 3DX. *Funds Managed* £1·2 million; *Holdings* 650.

* *Members of the Unit Trust Association.*

Legal Notes

IMPORTANT

The Purpose of these notes is to outline some of the more common parts of the law as they may affect the average person, and they are, of course, believed to be correct at the time of going to press. The law is constantly developing and changing, however, and it is dangerous for the layman to seek to be his own lawyer— he may not have access to completely up to date books and his case may, because of its special facts, come within an exception to the general rules set out herein.

It is always best to take expert advice, and if you have a Solicitor who has acted for you in the past you should take any legal problems you have to him. If you do not have a Solicitor a friend may be able to recommend one. Failing this your local Citizens' Advice Bureau (whose address can be obtained from the Telephone Directory or from any Post Office or Town Hall) has a list of Solicitors in your area who deal with that particular type of problem which you have. If you are not able to find a Solicitor in any of these ways you should ask for help in doing so from The Law Society, 113 Chancery Lane, London, W.C.2 or 27 Drumsheugh Gardens, Edinburgh.

The Legal Aid and Legal Advice and Assistance schemes (see pages 1178–9) exist to make the help of the trained lawyer available to everyone whatever their means as of right. The best policy is if in doubt go to a Solicitor without delay—timely advice will set your mind at rest but sitting on your rights can mean that you lose them.

Remember also that it is not necessary for a dispute to have arisen before you go to a Solicitor—the Legal Advice and Assistance Scheme enables him to advise you on your rights say under a tenancy agreement, the estate of a deceased person or in connection with matrimonial and consumer matters, and to write letters or take other steps on your behalf. He can also act for you where there is no question of a dispute at all, e.g. in the making of a will.

Your entitlement to take advantage of the Scheme depends on your means (see below) but a Solicitor will be able to tell you whether you are covered by it.

BRITISH NATIONALITY AND CITIZENSHIP OF THE UNITED KINGDOM AND COLONIES

General.—The law as to British Nationality is now to be found mainly in the British Nationality Act 1948, which came into force on Jan. 1, 1949.

The Act introduces a new term, " citizenship." Every person who under the Act is a citizen of the United Kingdom and Colonies, or any citizen (by virtue of legislation in that country) of Canada, Australia, New Zealand, India, Southern Rhodesia, Sri Lanka, Ghana, Malaysia, Cyprus, Nigeria, Sierra Leone, Tanzania, Jamaica, Trinidad and Tobago, Uganda, Kenya, Malawi, Zambia, Malta, Gambia, Guyana, Botswana, Lesotho, Singapore, Barbados, Mauritius, Swaziland, Tonga, Fiji, The Bahamas, Bangladesh and Grenada (hereafter referred to as " the Dominions ") has by virtue of that citizenship the status of a British subject and may be known either as a British subject or as a Commonwealth citizen. Under s. 2 of the Newfoundland (Consequential Provisions) Act 1950, potential citizens of Newfoundland under the British Nationality Act 1948, are deemed to have been potential citizens of Canada.

Nationality *before* Jan. 1, 1949, was determined mainly by the British Nationality and Status of Aliens Acts 1914–1943, though these Acts did not affect the status of any person born *before* Jan. 1, 1915.

Retention of nationality by persons born in or who are citizens of Eire (now by virtue of the Ireland Act 1949, styled the Republic of Ireland).

By the Ireland Act 1949, a person who was born before Dec. 6, 1922, in what is now the Republic of Ireland (Eire) and was a British subject immediately before Jan. 1, 1949, is not deemed to have ceased to be a British subject unless either (i) he was domiciled in the Irish Free State on Dec. 6, 1922, or (ii) was on or after April 10, 1935, and before Jan. 1, 1949, permanently resident there, or (iii) had before Jan. 1, 1949, been registered as a citizen of Eire under the laws of that country.

In addition, by the British Nationality Act 1948, any citizen of Eire who immediately before Jan. 1, 1949, was also a British subject can retain that status by submitting at any time a claim to the Home Secretary on any of the following grounds: (a) he has been in the service of the United Kingdom government; (b) he holds a British passport issued in the United Kingdom or in any colony, protectorate, United Kingdom mandated or trust territory; (c) he has associations by way of descent, residence or otherwise with any such place; or on complying with similar legislation in any of the " Dominions."

Citizenship of the United Kingdom and Colonies

In the majority of cases, a person who is a British subject becomes also a " citizen," either of one of the " Dominions " by virtue of legislation in that country, or of the United Kingdom and Colonies under the 1948 Act. In the latter case, citizenship is acquired by:—

1. *Birth* on or after Jan. 1, 1949, in the United Kingdom and Colonies (which term does not include the " Dominions "), except

   (a) children born to non-citizen fathers enjoying diplomatic immunity from suit or legal process;

   (b) children born to fathers who are enemy aliens in enemy occupied territory.

2. *Descent*, if the father was a citizen by *birth*. If the father was a citizen by *descent* only, the child acquires citizenship by descent if either:—

   (a) the child is or his father was born in a protectorate, protected state, mandated territory or trust territory, or in a foreign country where Her Majesty then had jurisdiction over British subjects; or

   (b) the birth (occurring elsewhere than (a)) is registered at a United Kingdom consulate within one year; or

   (c) the father is at the time of birth in the service of the Crown under Her Majesty's United Kingdom government; or

   (d) the child is born in one of the " Dominions " in which a citizenship law has then taken effect and does not become a citizen thereof by birth.

3. *Registration* by the Home Secretary upon application by:—

   (a) a citizen of one of the " Dominions " or of the Republic of Ireland who can show that he has been (a) ordinarily resident in the United Kingdom; or (b) in Crown service under Her Majesty's Government in the United Kingdom; or (c) partly the one and partly the other throughout the period of five years ending with the date of his application, or such shorter period so ending as the Home Secretary may in the special circumstances of any particular case accept; or, in certain circumstances, if he is

serving under an international organization of which the United Kingdom government is a member, or is in the employment of a body established in the United Kingdom;

By the provisions of the Immigration Act 1971, registration as of right in these circumstances is restricted to Commonwealth citizens who are " patrial ", i.e. born to or legally adopted by a parent who at the time of the birth or adoption had citizenship of the United Kingdom and Colonies by his birth in the United Kingdom. In the case of non-patrials, there are additional conditions and the Home Secretary has a discretion whether or not to register.

(b) a woman married to a United Kingdom, etc. citizen. (A woman who marries on or after Jan. 1, 1949, does not by virtue of that marriage acquire citizenship.)

A minor child of a citizen can be registered upon application being made by his parent or guardian.

A person in respect of whom a recommendation for deportation or a deportation order is in force is not entitled to be registered, although the Home Secretary may register such a person.

4. *Naturalization.*—In order to be eligible for a certificate of naturalization an alien must:—

(a) during the eight years preceding his application have resided for not less than five years (of which not less than one year immediately preceding the application *must* have been spent in the United Kingdom) in the United Kingdom or in any colony, protectorate, United Kingdom mandated or trust territory, or have been for five years in the service of the Crown; and

(b) be of good character and have a sufficient knowledge of the English language; and

(c) intend to reside in the United Kingdom or any colony, etc., or to enter or continue in the service of the Crown or in the service of certain organizations.

A British protected person who satisfies (b) and (c) above can apply for naturalization if he can show that he has been (a) ordinarily resident in the United Kingdom; or (b) in Crown service under Her Majesty's Government in the United Kingdom; or (c) partly the one and partly the other throughout the period of five years ending with the date of his application, or such shorter period as the Home Secretary may in any particular case accept.

Instructions for the guidance of persons desiring to apply for a Certificate of Naturalization are supplied with the form of application which may be obtained from H.M. Stationery Office.

5. *Incorporation of Territory* when citizenship is granted to such persons as are specified by Order in Council.

6. *Transitional provisions,* which confer citizenship on a person who was a British subject immediately before Jan. 1, 1949, if either:—

(i) (a) he would, if born after that date, have qualified for citizenship by birth; or

(b) he is a person naturalized in the United Kingdom and Colonies; or

(c) he became a British subject by reason of annexation of territory which on Jan. 1, 1949, was included in the United Kingdom and Colonies; or

(ii) at the time of his birth his father was a British subject and possessed any of the above qualifications; or

(iii) he was born within territory comprised on Jan. 1, 1949, in a protectorate, protected state or United Kingdom trust territory; or

(iv) he was not on that date a citizen or potential citizen of one of the " Dominions "; or

(v) being a woman, had before Jan. 1, 1949, been married to a man who becomes, or would but for his death have become, a citizen.

A British subject who is merely a potential citizen of one of the " Dominions " continues as a British subject without citizenship until he becomes a citizen of such " Dominion " or of the Republic of Ireland, or an alien. If none of these has happened at the date when a citizenship law is passed in the country of which he is potentially a citizen, he becomes a citizen by descent of the United Kingdom and Colonies.

A woman who lost British nationality by reason of marriage to an alien regained it on Jan. 1, 1949.

By the Adoption Act 1958 an adopted child becomes a citizen of the United Kingdom and Colonies as from the date of the adoption order if the adopter or, in the case of a joint adoption, the male adopter, is a citizen of the United Kingdom and Colonies.

Citizenship of the United Kingdom and Colonies can be lost—

(i) by declaration in the prescribed manner by a person who is also a citizen of a " Dominion " or of the Republic of Ireland or a national of a foreign country. The Home Secretary can withhold registration of the declaration in time of war. Under the British Nationality Act 1964 a person who has ceased to be a citizen of the United Kingdom and Colonies as a result of a declaration of renunciation is entitled to registration as a citizen of the United Kingdom and Colonies if he can satisfy the Home Secretary on a number of matters;

(ii) where the Home Secretary is satisfied that citizenship by registration or naturalization was obtained by fraud, false representation, etc.;

(iii) by the Home Secretary depriving a *naturalized* person of citizenship if such person has:—

(a) shown himself by act or speech to be disloyal or disaffected towards Her Majesty; or

(b) in time of war, traded with the enemy; or

(c) within five years after becoming naturalized, been sentenced in any country to a term of twelve months' imprisonment; or

(d) continuously resided in foreign countries for seven years, and during that period has neither at any time been in the service of the Crown or of certain international organizations, nor registered annually at a United Kingdom consulate his intention to retain citizenship;

and the Home Secretary is satisfied that it is not conducive to the public good that such person should retain his citizenship;

(iv) where a naturalized person is deprived of citizenship of a " Dominion " or of the Republic of Ireland, the Home Secretary can also deprive him of citizenship of the United Kingdom and Colonies.

(v) Under a series of Acts, 1958–1973, which contain special provisions relating to Ghana, Cyprus, Nigeria, Sierra Leone, Tanzania, Jamaica, Trinidad and Tobago, Uganda, Malaysia, Kenya, Malawi, Zambia, Malta, Gambia, Guyana, Botswana, Lesotho, Barbados, Aden, Perim and Kuria Muria Islands, Mauritius, Swaziland, Fiji, The Bahamas and Bangladesh.

STATUS OF ALIENS.—Property may be held by an alien in the same manner as by a natural-born British subject, but he may not hold public office, exercise the franchise or own a British ship or aircraft. The Republic of Ireland Act 1949 declares that the Republic, though not part of H.M. Dominions, is not a foreign country, and any reference to an Act of Parliament to foreigners, aliens, foreign countries, etc., shall be construed accordingly.

CONSUMER LAW

1. THE SUPPLY OF GOODS

(a) The Sale of Goods Act 1893 as amended by the Supply of Goods (Implied Terms) Act 1973 provides protection to the purchaser of goods, by implying certain terms into every contract for the Sale of Goods. These implied terms are:—

(i) A condition that the seller will pass good title to the buyer (unless the seller agrees to transfer only such title as he or his principal has) and warranties that the goods will be free from undisclosed encumbrances, and that the buyer will enjoy quiet possession of the goods.

(ii) Where there is a sale of goods by description, a condition that the goods will correspond with that description, and where the sale is by sample and description, a condition that the bulk of the goods shall correspond with both sample and description.

(iii) Where the seller sells goods in the course of a business, a condition that the goods will be of merchantable quality, unless before the contract is made, the buyer has examined the goods and ought to have noticed the defect, or the seller has specifically drawn the attention of the buyer to the defect. Merchantable quality means fit for the purpose for which goods of the kind are commonly bought, taking into account any description applied to them, the price and other relevant circumstances.

(iv) A condition that where the seller sells goods in the course of a business, the goods are reasonably fit for any purpose made known to the seller by the buyer, unless the buyer does not rely on the sellers skill and judgment, or it would be unreasonable for him to do so.

(v) Where there is a sale of goods by sample, conditions that the bulk of the goods shall correspond with the sample in quality, that the buyer will have a reasonable opportunity of comparing the bulk with the sample, and that the goods are free from any defect rendering them unmerchantable, which would not be apparent from the sample.

For these purposes, the broad difference between a condition and a warranty is that the remedy for a breach of an implied condition may enable the buyer to reject the goods and recover damages if he has suffered loss whereas the remedy for a breach of warranty will only enable the buyer to recover damages.

It is possible for a seller to exclude some of the above terms from a contract, subject to restrictions imposed by the 1973 Act given below. These restrictions give more protection to a consumer sale than a non-consumer sale. A consumer sale is a sale by a seller in the course of a business where the goods are of a type ordinarily bought for private use or consumption, and are sold to a person who does not buy or hold himself out as buying them in the course of a business. A sale by auction or competitive tender is never a consumer sale.

The 1973 Act prohibits the exclusion of the implied terms given in (ii) to (v) above, in consumer sales. In non-consumer sales, terms purporting to exclude these implied terms, may be relied upon only to the extent that it would be reasonable to allow reliance. The Act provides guidelines for determining whether it would be reasonable to allow reliance. The implied terms in (i) above cannot be excluded in consumer or non-consumer sale.

(b) *Trading Stamps.*—The 1973 Act provides protection for a person taking goods in exchange for trading stamps, and implies warranties as to title, freedom from encumbrances, quiet possession and merchantable quality, similar to those implied by the Sale of Goods Act.

(c) The Trade Descriptions Act 1968 provides that it is a criminal offence for a trader or businessman to apply a false trade description to any goods, or to supply or offer to supply any goods to which a false trade description has been applied. A trade description includes a description as to quantity, size, method, place and date of manufacture, other history, composition, other physical characteristics, fitness for purpose, behaviour or accuracy, testing or approval. Prosecutions are brought by Inspectors of Weights and Measures.

(d) The Fair Trading Act 1973 is also designed to protect the consumer. It provides for the appointment of a Director General of Fair Trading, whose duties include keeping under review commercial activities in the U.K. relating to the supply of goods or services to consumers, and to collect information to discover practices that may adversely affect the economic interests of the consumer. He may refer certain consumer trade practices to the Consumer Protection Advisory Committee, or, of his own initiative take proceedings against firms that are trading unfairly. He may also publish information and advice to consumers. Examples of practices with which he may be concerned include the use of void exclusion clauses, double pricing, false bottoms in bottles, and the size or complexity of print and wording.

Scotland

The Sale of Goods Act, 1893, as amended by the Supply of Goods (Implied Terms) Act 1973, the Trading Stamp Act, 1964, the Trade Description Act, 1968, and the Fair Trading Act, 1973, all apply with some modification to Scotland. For example, it is not necessary in Scotland to distinguish between the words condition and warranty. The remedies of the buyer in both cases are the same, that is, he can either within a reasonable time reject the goods and treat the contract as repudiated, or retain the goods and treat the failure to perform such material

part as a breach which may give rise to a claim for compensation or damages.

2. HIRE PURCHASE
England and Wales

At present, protection of the hirer against unscrupulous dealings and against delivery of shoddy goods is given by the Hire-Purchase Act, 1965, which applies to hire-purchase agreements under which the hire-purchase price, *i.e.*, the total sum payable by the hirer to complete the purchase of the goods, does not exceed £2,000. The Act also provides that where the hirer is a body corporate, the Act is not to apply at all.

Before any agreement is made, the owner of the goods must state in writing to the hirer the cash price at which the goods can be purchased, and the agreement must be in writing signed by the hirer himself and by or on behalf of the owner and any guarantor. The agreement must contain (i) the cash price, (ii) the hire-purchase price, (iii) the amount of each instalment, (iv) when each instalment falls due, (v) a list of the goods, and (vi) a notice informing the hirer of his rights to terminate the agreement (*below*), and of the restrictions on the owner's right to recover the goods (*below*). If the agreement is complete as soon as the hirer signs it he must be given a copy there and then; in all other cases he must be given one copy when he signs and another within seven days of the completion of the agreement. There are also Department of Trade and Industry regulations dealing with such matters as the size of the print. In breach of any of these conditions the owner can neither recover the goods from the hirer nor enforce the agreement or any security given, although the Court can dispense with any of the conditions save that as to the signed agreement. The same results ensures (while default continues) if the owner fails without reasonable cause within four days after written request (with a tender of 12½p for expenses) to supply to the hirer a copy of the agreement and a statement of amounts paid, in arrear, and not yet payable. Before the last instalment becomes due, the hirer may by writing determine the agreement, and, although he remains liable for any instalments already due, he will be under no further obligation *under the agreement*. Under the Act, however, he must allow the owner to retake the goods and, if one-half of the hire-purchase price exceeds the total of the sums paid and due he must pay the difference to the owner unless the court considers that a lesser sum is sufficient to compensate the owner. These rights of the hirer cannot be taken away from him, but he can enforce more favourable rights (if any) under the agreement.

An important new provision in the Act gives the hirer the right to cancel the agreement and recover all sums paid if he signed it at a place other than trade premises. This right (which was designed to cover the activities of door-step salesmen) must be exercised within 4 days of receiving the second copy.

Any provision in the agreement giving the owner a right to enter any premises for the purpose of seizing the goods is invalidated by the Act. Further, even though the agreement may have been terminated because the hirer has broken it, or because the owner has exercised a right to terminate it, if one-third of the hire-purchase price has been paid or tendered, the owner cannot recover the goods otherwise than by action in a County Court, in which the Court can ensure that the hirer is fairly treated. If the owner disregards this provision, the hirer cannot recover the goods, but can recover all sums paid under the agreement.

The Trade Descriptions Act, 1968, further protects the consumer by making it a criminal offence for traders falsely to describe or advertise the quantity or price of goods or services; prosecutions are brought by Inspectors of Weights and Measures. The Act provides no civil remedies.

An important new provision is the Supply of Goods (Implied Terms) Act 1973 which applies to agreements made on or after 18th May 1973. Sections 8–12 which apply to all hire-purchase agreements whether governed by the 1965 Act or not provide that clauses purporting to exclude the owner from liability for defects in the goods shall be void in the case of consumer agreements, and in non-consumer agreements are valid only if they are fair and reasonable in the circumstances.

Consumer Credit Act. This Act has received the Royal Assent, but most of its provisions are not yet in force. It provides a new system for the protection of the consumer, of licensing and control of all matters relating to the provision of credit, or the supply of goods on hire or hire-purchase, administered by the Director-General of Fair Trading. The Act takes the place of previous Acts of Parliament relating to moneylenders, pawnbrokers and hire-purchase traders, and the protection provided by the Trade Description Act 1968 and Supply of Goods (Implied Terms) Act 1973 will be retained. The Act extends to the United Kingdom.

Scotland

The Hire Purchase (Scotland) Act 1965 provides a Scots code corresponding to, but not identical with English law. The Supply of Goods (Implied Terms) Act 1973 also applies to Scotland.

The Sale of Goods Act, 1893, as amended by the Supply of Goods (Implied Terms) Act, 1973, the Trading Stamp Act, 1964, the Trade Description Act, 1968, and the Fair Trading Act, 1973, all apply with little modification to Scotland. The Consumer Credit Act (see above) also extends to Scotland, and goes far in assimilating the Scots law on this topic with English law.

3. RECEIPTS

The law on receipts in Scotland is governed by the Prescription and Limitation (Scotland) Act 1973, which for this purpose came into force on July 25 1976. Now, receipts need only be kept for a period of five years and if a creditor does not make a relevant claim within that period no action can be raised.

CROWN—PROCEEDINGS AGAINST

Before 1947 proceedings against the Crown were generally possible only by a procedure known as a petition of right, which placed the litigant at a considerable disadvantage and which was not normally available at all in cases of tort (i.e., civil wrongs other than breach of contract). Thus, no proceedings would normally lie against the Government if a subject were injured by the negligent driving of a Government vehicle (although the driver could be sued) or if a Government employee were injured by the defective condition of the Crown premises on which he worked. Now however, by the Crown Proceedings Act 1947, which came into operation on Jan. 1, 1948, the Crown, in its public capacity, is largely placed in the same position as a subject, although some procedural disadvantages remain. Exceptions to the Act include the immunity of the Crown and any member of the armed forces from liability in tort in respect of death of, or personal injury to, another

member of the armed forces on duty, provided that the death or injury is certified as attributable to service for purposes of pension.

Scotland.—The Act extends to Scotland and has the effect of bringing the practice of the two countries as closely together as the different legal systems will permit. While formerly actions against the Crown, when permissible, were confined to the Court of Session, proceedings may now be brought in the Sheriff Court.

The Act lays down that arrestment of money in the hands of the Crown or of a Government Department is competent in any case where arrestment in the hands of a subject would have been competent, but an exception is made in respect of National Savings Bank deposits. Section 2 (1) of the Law Reform (Miscellaneous Provisions) (Scotland) Act 1966 removes the privilege whereby the wages of Crown servants, other than serving members of the armed forces, are exempt from arrestment in execution.

DEATHS

REGISTRATION, BURIAL AND CREMATION

REGISTRATION

(For Certificates, *see* under FAMILY LAW–CERTIFI-CATES)

In England and Wales.—When a death takes place, personal information of it must be given to the local Registrar of Births and Deaths, and the register signed in his presence, by one of the following persons: (1) A relative of the deceased present at the death, or in attendance during the last illness. If they fail (2) some other relative of the deceased. In default of any relatives (3) a person present at the death; or, the occupier of the house in which the death happened. If all the above-named fail (4) an inmate of the house. A person (other than a relative) registering the death must be causing the disposal of the body. Relatives present or in attendance are first required to attend to the registration. The registration must be made within five days of the death, or within the same time written notice of the death sent to the Registrar. If the deceased was attended during his last illness by a registered medical practitioner, a certificate of cause of death must be sent by the doctor to the Registrar. The doctor must give to the informant of the death a written notice of the signing of the certificate, which must be delivered to the Registrar. It is essential that a certificate for disposal should be obtained from the Registrar before the funeral and delivered to the clergyman or other person in charge of the churchyard or cemetery. No fee is chargeable for this certificate. If the death is not registered within five days (or fourteen days if written notice of the occurrence of the death is sent to him) the Registrar may require any one of the above-mentioned persons to attend to register at a stated time and place. Failure to comply involves a penalty of ten pounds. The registration of a death is free of charge. After twelve months no death can be registered without the Registrar General's consent.

A body must not be disposed of until (1) either the Registrar has given a certificate to the effect that he has registered or received notice of the death, or (2) until the Coroner has made a disposal order (*Births and Deaths Registration Act* 1926, S. 1).

A person disposing of a body must within ninety-six hours deliver to the Registrar a notification as to the date, place, and means of the disposal of the body (*ib.*, S. 3).

" Still-born " child (*see* under Births (Registration), p. 1169).

Death at Sea.—The master of a British ship must record any death on board and send particulars to the Registrar General of Shipping.

Death Abroad.—Consular Officers are authorized to register deaths of British subjects occurring abroad. Certificates are procurable at the Registrar General's Office, London. If the deceased was of *Scottish* domicile, particulars are sent to the Registrar General for Scotland.

With regard to the registration of deaths of members of the armed forces, and deaths occurring on H.M. ships and aircraft, *see* the Registration of Births, etc. Act 1957.

Deaths (Registration) in Scotland.—New provisions are included in the Registration of Births, Deaths and Marriages (Scotland) Act 1965 which amends and re-enacts provisions in former Acts.

Personal notification within 8 days must be given to the registrar of (*a*) the registration district in which the death took place or (*b*) any registration district in which the deceased was ordinarily resident immediately befor his death, and (*c*) when a body is found and the place of death is not known, either the registration district in which the body was found or any other registration district appropriate by virtue of the preceding paragraph. When a person dies (in or out of Scotland) in a ship, aircraft or land vehicle during a journey and the body is conveyed therein to any place in Scotland the death shall, unless the Registrar General otherwise directs, be deemed to have occurred at that place.

The register must be signed in the presence of the registrar by one of the following: (*a*) any relative of the deceased; (*b*) any person present at the death; (*c*) the deceased's executor or other legal representative; (*d*) the occupier, at the time of the death, of the premises where the death took place; (*e*) if these fail, any other person having knowledge of the particulars to be registered. Failure to comply involves a penalty not exceeding £20.

The medical practitioner who attended the deceased during the last illness must sign a certificate of the cause of death. If there is no such medical practitioner, any medical practitioner who is able to do so, may sign the certificate. At the time of registering the death the registrar shall, without charge, give the informant a certificate of registration, and the person to whom the certificate is given must hand it to the undertaker previous to cremation. A body may, however, be interred before the death is registered, in which case the undertaker must deliver a certificate of burial to the Registrar within three days.

BURIAL

The duty of burial is incumbent on the deceased person's Executors (if any appointed); it is also a recognized obligation of the husband of a woman, and the parent of a child, also of a householder where the body lies. Funeral expenses of a reasonable amount will be repayable out of deceased's estate in priority to any other claims. Directions as to place and mode of burial are frequently contained in the deceased's will or in some memorandum placed with private papers, or may have been communicated verbally to a relative. Consequently steps should immediately be taken to ascertain the deceased's wishes from the above sources. If the wishes are considered objectionable, they are not necessarily enforceable; legal advice should be taken. A person may legally leave directions for the anatomical examination of his body. As to the place of burial—unless closed by Order in Council—the parish churchyard is the normal burying place for parishioners, or any person dying in the Parish, but nowadays this will apply only in villages and the smaller towns. In

populous districts cemeteries and crematoria have been established either by the local council, or a private company, and burials will take place there in accordance with the regulations. For an exclusive right to a burial space in the churchyard a faculty is required from the Ecclesiastical Court. Poor persons may be buried at the public expense by the local authority. As to the necessity for obtaining a registrar's certificate or authority from the Coroner for disposal, *see* above.

CREMATION

Under the Cremation Acts, 1902 and 1952, regulations are made by the Home Secretary dealing fully with the cremation of a body, disposal of ashes, etc., and containing numerous essential safeguards.

If Cremation is desired it is advisable for instructions to be left in writing to that effect.

To arrange for Cremation the Executor or near relative should instruct the undertaker to that effect and obtain from him the Statutory Forms required as given in the Cremation Regulations issued in 1930 (Statutory Rules and Orders, 1930, No. 1016), as amended by the Cremation Regulations 1965 (No. 1146).

INTESTACY
ENGLAND AND WALES

As regards deaths on or after July 1, 1972, the position is governed by the Administration of Estates Act, 1925, as amended by the Intestates' Estates Act, 1952, the Family Provision Act, 1966 and Orders made thereunder. The 1952 and 1966 Acts and S.I. 1972/916 increased the benefits of a surviving spouse of an intestate. These notes deal with the present position, so that if the death occurred before July 1, 1972 reference must be made elsewhere. If the intestate leaves a spouse and issue, the spouse takes (i) the "personal chattels"; (ii) £15,000 with interest at 4 per cent. from death until payment; and (iii) a life interest in half of the rest of the estate. This life interest can be capitalized at the option of the spouse. "Personal chattels" are articles of household use or ornament (including motor-cars), not used for business purposes. The rest of the estate goes to the issue. If the intestate leaves a spouse and no issue, but leaves a parent or brother or sister of the whole blood or issue of such brothers and sisters the spouse takes (i) the "personal chattels"; (ii) £40,000 with interest at 4 per cent. from death until payment, and (iii) half of the rest of the estate absolutely. The other half of the rest of the estate goes to the parents, equally if more than one, or, if none, to the brothers and sisters of the whole blood. If the intestate leaves a spouse, but no issue, no parents and no brothers or sisters of the whole blood or their issue, the spouse takes the whole estate absolutely. If resident therein at the intestate's death, the surviving spouse may generally require the personal representatives to appropriate the interest of the intestate in the matrimonial home in or towards satisfaction of any absolute interest of the spouse, including the capitalized value of a life interest. In certain cases, leave of Court is required. On a partial intestacy any benefit (other than personal chattels specifically bequeathed) received by the surviving spouse under the will must be brought into account against the statutory legacy of £15,000 or £40,000, as the case may be. If there is no surviving spouse, the estate is distributed among those who survive the intestate in the following order (those entitled under earlier numbers taking to the exclusion of those entitled under later numbers):—(1) children (2) father or mother (equally, if both alive); (3) brothers and sisters of the whole blood; (4) brothers and sisters of the half blood; (5) grandparents

(equally, if more than one alive); (6) uncles and aunts of the whole blood; (7) uncles and aunts of the half blood; (8) the Crown.

In cases (1), (3), (4), (6) and (7) the persons entitled lose their interests unless they or their issue not only survive the intestate, but also attain eighteen or marry under that age, their shares going to the persons (if any) within the same group who do attain eighteen or marry. Moreover, in the same cases, succession is not *per capita*, but *per stirpes*, *i.e.*, by stocks or families. Thus, if the intestate leaves one child and two grandchildren, being the children of a child of the intestate, who pre-deceased the intestate, the two grandchildren represent their deceased parent and take between them one-half of the issue's share, the remaining half going to the surviving child. Similarly, nephews and nieces represent a deceased brother, and so on.

When the deceased died partially intestate (*i.e.*, leaving a will which disposed of only part of his property), the above rules apply to the intestate part.

Children must bring into account (hotchpot) any substantial advances received from the intestate during his lifetime before claiming any further share under the intestacy. Special hotchpot provisions apply to partial intestacy.

By the Family Law Reform Act, 1969, the position of an illegitimate child is equated with that of a legitimate child in respect of all deaths occurring on or after January 1, 1970. In respect of deaths after March 1976 the provisions of the Inheritance (Provision for Family and Dependents) Act 1975 may allow other persons to claim provision out of the estate. See *post* under "Wills".

For personal application for Letters of Administration—see p. 1168.

SCOTLAND

The Succession (Scotland) Act, 1964, provides that the whole estate of any person dying intestate shall devolve without distinction between heritable and moveable property. By that Act the surviving spouse of an intestate may, as a prior right (in addition to legal rights, *see* below), claim the matrimonial home to a maximum of £30,000, or a choice of one matrimonial home if more than one (or in certain circumstances the value thereof), with its furniture and plenishings not exceeding £8,000 in value, plus the sum of £4,000 if the deceased left issue or, if no issue, the sum of £8,000. These figures may be increased from time to time by order of the Secretary of State.

The Act has been modified by the Law Reform (Miscellaneous Provisions) (Scotland) Act, 1968, which provided that an illegitimate child had exactly the same rights of succession in the estate of his parents as a legitimate child. However, the position still remains that an illegitimate child has no succession rights in the estate of a grandparent even though such would have fallen to his predeceasing parent.

Legal rights, referred to above, are:—

Jus relicti (æ): the right of a surviving spouse to one half of the deceased's net moveable estate after satisfaction of prior rights if there are no surviving children, or to one third if there are any surviving children.

Legitim: right of surviving children to one-half or one-third of the net moveable estate of deceased parents after satisfaction of prior rights. There are no legal rights in heritage.

In general, the lines of succession are: (1) descendants; (2) collaterals; (3) ascendants and their collaterals, and so on in the ascending scale. The Crown is ultimus haeres. The right of representation, *i.e.*, the right of the issue of a person, who

would have succeeded if he had survived the intestate, is open to any line of succession where previously it was limited to apply only when there were next of kin or the issue of predeceasing next of kin. The surviving mother of an intestate now has equal rights of succession with the surviving father, where formerly these were restricted. The intestate's maternal relations, who prior to the Act had no rights of succession, are now on an equal footing with his paternal relations. Where the intestate is survived only by parents, and by brothers and sisters (collaterals) half of the estate is taken by the parents and the other half by the brothers and sisters, those of the whole blood being preferred to those of the half blood; where, however, succession opens to collaterals—(which expression can include the brothers and sisters of an ancestor of the intestate)—of the half blood, they shall rank equally amongst themselves, whether related to the intestate (or his ancestor) through their father or their mother.

WILLS

IMPORTANT NOTE.—The following notes and those on Intestacy must be read subject to the provisions of the Inheritance (Provision for Family and Dependents) Act 1975 which can affect the estate of anyone dying domiciled in England and Wales after March 1976. Very broadly a spouse, former spouse who has not remarried, a child of the deceased himself or one treated by him as a child of his family, or any person maintained by him at his death may apply to the Court under the Act. If the Court thinks that the will or the law of intestacy or both do not make reasonable provision for the applicant it may order payment out of the net estate of maintenance or a lump sum. It may also order the transfer of property, vary certain trusts and the powers can affect property disposed of by the deceased in his lifetime intending to defeat the Act. It is up to the applicant to take the initiative, and the application must generally be made within six months of the grant of Probate or Letters of Administration.

In respect of earlier deaths, earlier Acts apply with a narrower class of applicants and less ample powers for the Court.

REASONS FOR MAKING A WILL.—Every person over the age of 18 should make a will. However small the estate the rules of Intestacy (see above) may not reflect a person's wishes as to his property; in any case a will can do more than just deal with property—it can in particular appoint executors, give directions as to the disposal of the body and appoint guardians to take care of children in the event of the parents' death. For the wealthier person an appropriately drawn will can operate to reduce the burden of Capital Transfer Tax.

It is considered desirable for a will to be properly drawn up by a Solicitor, and the making of a will is one of the services which he can provide under the Legal Advice and Assistance Scheme (see above).

In no circumstances should one person prepare a Will for another person where the former is to take any benefit under it—this can easily lead to a suggestion of undue influence which may cause the will to be held bad.

Assuming a lawyer is not employed, a person having resolved to make a will must remember that it is only after a person is dead, and cannot explain his meaning, that his will can be open to dispute. It is the more necessary, therefore, to express what is meant in language of the utmost clearness, avoiding the use of any word or expression that admits of another meaning than the one intended. Avoid the use of " legal terms," such as " heirs " and " issue," when the same thing may be expressed in plain language. If

in writing the will a mistake be made, it is better to rewrite the whole. Before a will is executed (*see below*) an alteration *may* be made by striking through the words with a pen, but opposite to such alteration the testator and witnesses should write their names or place their initials. Never scratch out a word with a knife or other instrument, and no alteration *of any kind whatever* must be made after the will is executed. If the testator afterwards wishes to change the disposition of his estate, it is best to make a new will, revoking the old one. The use of *codicils* should be left to the lawyer. *A will should be written in ink and very legibly, on a single sheet of paper.* Although, of course, forms of wills must vary to suit different cases, the following forms may be found useful to those who, in cases of emergency, are called upon to draw up wills, either for themselves or others.

Nothing more complicated should be attempted. The forms should be studied in conjunction with the notes following.

This is the last will and testament of me [*Thomas Smith*] of [*Vine Cottage, Silver Street, Reading, Berks*] which I make this [*thirteenth*] day of [*February, 1973*] and whereby I revoke all previous wills and testamentary dispositions.

1. I hereby appoint [*John Green of —— and Richard Brown of ——*] to be the executor(s) of this my will.

2. I give all my property real and personal to [*my wife Mary* or *my sons Raymond and David equally* or as the case may be].

Signed by the testator in the presence of us both present at the same time who,
at his request, in his presence ⎫ Thomas Smith
and in the presence of each ⎬ *Signature of*
other have hereunto set our ⎭ *Testator;*
names as witnesses.

William Jones (*signed*) of Green Gables, South Street, Reading, tailor.

Henry Morgan (*signed*) of 16, North Street, Reading, butcher.

Should it be desired to give legacies and/or gifts of specific property, instead of giving the whole estate to one or more persons, the form above should be used with the substitution for clause 2 of the following clauses:—

2. I give to —— of —— the sum of £—— and to —— of —— the sum of £—— and to —— of —— all my books (*or as the case may require*).

3. All the residue of my property real and personal I give to —— of ——.

TERMS.—Real property includes freehold land and houses; while personal property includes debts due, arrears of rents, money, leasehold property, house furniture, goods, assurance policies, stocks and shares in companies, and the like. The words " my money," apart from the context, will normally only include actual real money. The expression " goods and chattels " should not be used. In giving *particular* property, ordinary language is sufficient, *e.g.*, " my house, Vine Cottage, Silver Street, Reading, Berks." Such specific gifts fail if not owned by the testator at his death.

RESIDUARY LEGATEES.—It is well in all cases where legacies or specific gifts are made, to leave to some person or persons " the residue of my property," although it may be thought that the whole of the property has been disposed of in legacies, etc., already mentioned in the will. *It should be remembered that a will operates on property acquired after it has been made.*

EXECUTION OF A WILL, AND WITNESSES.—The testator should sign his name at the foot or end of the will, in presence of two witnesses, who will immediately afterwards sign their names in

his and in each other's presence. A person who has been left any gift or share of residue in the will, or whose wife or husband has been left such a gift, should not be an attesting witness. Their attestation would be good, but they would forfeit the gift. It is better that a person named as executor should not be a witness. Husband and wife may both be witnesses, provided neither is a legatee. If a solicitor be appointed executor, it is lawful to direct that his ordinary fees and charges shall be paid; but in this case he (as an interested party) must not be a witness to the will.

It is desirable that the witnesses should be fully described, as they may possibly be wanted at some future time. If the testator should be too ill to sign, even by a mark, another person may sign the testator's name to the will for him, in his presence and by his direction, and in this case it should be shown that the testator knew the contents of the document. The attestation clause should therefore be worded: " Signed by Thomas Brown, by the direction and in the presence of the testator, Thomas Smith, in the joint presence of us, who thereupon signed our names in his presence and in the presence of each other, the will having been first read over to the testator, who appeared fully to understand the same."

Where there is any suspicion that the Testator is not, by reason of age or infirmity, fully in command of his faculties it is desirable to ask his Doctor to act as a witness (see Testamentary capacity below).

A *blind person* may make a will in Braille. If the testator be blind the will should be read aloud to him in the presence of the witnesses, and the fact mentioned in the attestation clause. A blind person cannot witness a will.

If by inadvertence the testator should have signed his will without the witnesses being present, then the attestation should be:—" The testator acknowledged his signature already made as his signature to his last will and testament, in the joint presence," etc. Any omission in the observance of these details may invalidate the will. *The stringency of the law as to signature and witnessing of a will is only relaxed in favour of soldiers, sailors and airmen in certain circumstances.*

EXECUTORS.—It is usual to appoint two executors, although one is sufficient; any number up to and including four may be appointed. The name and address of each executor should be given in full. An executor may be a legatee. Thus a child of full age or wife to whom the whole or a portion of the estate is left may be appointed sole executor, or one or two executors. The addresses of the executors are not essential; but it is desirable here as elsewhere, to avoid ambiguity or vagueness.

LAPSED LEGACIES.—If a legatee dies in the lifetime of the testator, the legacy generally lapses and falls into the residue. Where a residuary legatee predeceases the testator, his share of the residuary estate will not generally pass to the other residuary legatees, but will pass to the persons entitled on the deceased's intestacy. In all such cases it is desirable to make a new will.

TESTAMENTARY CAPACITY.—A person under the age of 18 cannot make a will (except for soldiers, sailors and airmen and then only in exceptional circumstances).

So far as mental capacity is concerned the Testator must be able to understand and appreciate the nature and effect of making a will, the property of which he can dispose and the claims to which he ought to give effect. If a person is not mentally able to make a will provision exists under the

Mental Health Act, 1959 as amended) for the Court to do this for him.

REVOCATION.—A will is revoked by a subsequent will (but if it does not expressly revoke former wills, only so far such subsequent will operates as an implied revocation as by making other provisions inconsistent with the previous will, for this reason a will should always have a clause revoking previous testamentary dispositions), or by burning, tearing or otherwise *destroying* the will with the intention of revoking it. Such destruction must either be by the testator or by some other person in his presence and at his direction. *It is not sufficient to obliterate the will with a pen.* Marriage in every case acts as the revocation of a will, unless, in the case of a will made on or after Jan. 1, 1926, it is expressed to have been made in contemplation of a particular marriage (Law of Property Act, 1925, s. 177); so that after marriage a new will should be made, except in this last case.

PERSONAL APPLICATION FOR PROBATE OR LETTERS OF ADMINISTRATION

Application for probate or for letters of administration may be made *in person* at the Personal Application Dept. of the Principal Registry of the Family Division, a district probate registry or sub-registry, or a probate office by the executors or persons entitled to a grant of administration. Applications should bring (1) the will, if any; (2) a certificate of death; (3) particulars of all property and assets left by the deceased; and (4) a list of debts and funeral expenses.

Intending applicants, before attending at a registry or probate office, should write or telephone to the nearest probate registry or sub-registry for the necessary forms. Postal or telephone applications cannot be dealt with at the local probate offices, which are part-time only.

Certain property can be disposed of on death without a grant of probate or administration, or in pursuance of a nomination made by the deceased, provided the amount involved does not exceed £1,500. *See* the Administration of Estates (Small Payments) Act, 1965.

WHERE TO FIND A PROVED WILL

A will proved since 1858 must have been proved either at the Principal Registry at Somerset House, or a District Registry. In the former case the original will itself is carefully preserved at Somerset House, the copy of which probate has been granted is in the hands of the executors who proved the will, and another copy for Parliament is bound up in a folio volume of wills made by testators of that initial and date; the indices to these volumes fill a room of considerable size at Somerset House, where the indices may be examined and a copy of any will read. In the latter case, the original will proved in the District Registry, is kept there, and may be seen or a *copy* obtained, but a copy is sent to and filed at Somerset House, where also it may be seen. A general index of grants, both probates and administrations, is prepared and printed annually in lexicographical form, and may be seen at either the Principal or a District Registry. This index is usually ready by about October of the following year.

RECENT DEATHS.—A newly introduced system enables a person to discover when a grant of Probate or Letters of Administration is made which may be invaluable to a creditor of the deceased or applicant under the Inheritance (Provision for Family and Dependents) Act 1975—see above. A "standing search" may be made by sending a request in the form set out below to the Record Keeper at the Principal Registry of the Family Division with £1 fee. The

searcher will receive particulars of any grant made in the previous 12 months or the following 6 months, including names and addresses of the executors or administrators and the Registry in which the grant was made.

FORM OF SEARCH

In the High Court of Justice
Family Division
The Principal Registry (Probate)

I/We apply for the entry of a standing search so that there shall be sent to me/us an office copy of every grant of representation in England & Wales in the estate of:—
Full name of deceased:
Alternative or alias name
Full address
Exact date of death
Which either has issued not more than 12 months before the entry of this application or issues within 6 months hereafter
Sgd.—(full address).

SCOTS LAW OF WILLS

A domiciled Scotsman, unlike a domiciled Englishman, cannot in certain circumstances dispose effectively of the entirety of his estate. If he leave a widow and children, the widow is entitled to a one-third share in the whole of the moveable estate (her *jus relictae*), and the children are entitled to another one-third share equally between them (their *legitim*). If he leave a widow but no children —or children but no widow—the *jus relictae* or *legitim* is increased to a one-half share of the estate. The remaining portion is known as the *dead's part*. A surviving husband and children have comparable rights (*jus relicti* and *legitim*) in the wife's estate. It should be noted that the amount of any claim of *jus relecti*, *jus relictae* or *legitim* out of an estate on intestacy, shall be calculated by reference to so much of the net moveable estate as remains after the satisfaction of any prior claims under the Succession (Scotland) Act, 1964—*see* Illegitimacy, Scotland and Intestacy, Scotland, *supra*. The *dead's part* is the only portion of which the testator can freely dispose. All debts are payable out of the whole estate before any division. Burdens in the nature of legacies are payable out of the *dead's part*. Pupils cannot make wills. Formerly a minor could dispose only of movables but since the passing of the Succession (Scotland) Act, 1964 he has a like capacity to test on heritable property. A will must be in writing and may be typewritten or even in pencil. A will may be either (1) *holograph*, i.e. written and subscribed by the testator himself, in which case no witnesses are necessary; a printed form filled up by the testator is not necessarily *holograph* but may be made effectual when it has clearly been adopted as *holograph*. Words written on erasure or marginal additions or interlineations in *holograph* writings, if proved to be in the handwriting of the maker of the deed, are valid; (2) *tested*, i.e. signed in presence of two witnesses. It is not necessary that these witnesses should sign in presence of one another, or even that they should see the testator signing so long as the testator acknowledges his signature to the witnesses. The Conveyancing and Feudal Reform (Scotland) Act, 1970 whilst altering generally the rules for the description of deeds, specifically (s. 44 (2)) makes no change in the rules applying to wills which must still be signed by the testator on every page. If the testator cannot write, or is blind, his will may be authenticated by a notary and two witnesses. It is better that the will be not witnessed by a beneficiary thereunder, although this circumstance will not invalidate the attestation of the will or (as it would in England) the gift. A parish minister may act as a notary for the purpose of subscribing a will in his own parish.

Wills are registered in the Books of the Sheriffdom in which the deceased died domiciled, and in the Books of Council and Session, H.M. General Register House, Edinburgh. The original deed may be inspected on payment of a small fee and a certified official copy may be obtained. A Scottish will is not revoked by the subsequent marriage of the testator. The subsequent birth of a child, no testamentary provision having been made for him, may revoke a will in whole or in part. A will may be revoked by a subsequent will, either expressly or by implication; but in so far as the two can be read together both wills have effect. If a subsequent will is revoked, the earlier will is revived.

"Confirmation," the Scottish equivalent of Probate, is obtained in the Sheriff Court of the Region in which the deceased was domiciled at the date of his death or, where he had no fixed domicile or died abroad in the commissariat of Edinburgh. Executors are either "nominate" or "dative." An Executor nominate is one nominated by the deceased in his will or, where such person has predeceased the testator, by the residuary beneficiary. An Executor dative is one appointed by the Court (1) in the case of intestacy or (2) where the deceased had failed to name an executor in his will. In the former case the deceased's next-of-kin are all entitled to be declared executors dative. An inventory of the deceased's estate and a schedule of debts, together with an affidavit, must first be given up. In estates under £1,000 nett and under £3,000 gross confirmation is obtained under a simplified procedure at reduced fees.

Presumption of Survivorship.—The Succession (Scotland) Act, 1964, referred to above provides that where two persons die in circumstances indicating that they died simultaneously or if it is uncertain which was the survivor, the younger will be deemed to have survived the elder unless the elder person left testamentary provision in favour of the younger, whom failing in favour of a third person, the younger person having died intestate (partially or wholly); but if the persons so dying were husband and wife, neither shall be presumed to have survived the other.

EMPLOYMENT

WAGES AND HOLIDAYS

Under the Truck Acts, it is in general forbidden for an employer to pay wages other than in current coin of the realm, and it is illegal for an employer to deduct from the employee's wages sums alleged to be due to the employer. However, the application of these Acts is confined to manual workers, and domestic servants are specifically excluded from their operation. Even in the case of payments to workmen, certain deductions, including rent and the price of food to be consumed on the employers' premises, are not forbidden where the employee's written consent is obtained. Further, under the Payment of Wages Act, 1960, it is permissible for wages to be paid otherwise than in cash at the request of the employee, *e.g.*, by cheque, money order, postal order or into a banking account.

The Equal Pay Act 1970, which extends to Scotland, and which came into force on December 29, 1975, prevents discrimination, as regards terms and conditions of employment between men and women.

PARTICULARS OF TERMS OF EMPLOYMENT

Under the Contracts of Employment Act 1972, an employer must give each employee within 13 weeks of the beginning of the employment a

written statement containing the following particulars of the contract between them:

(1) the date when the employment began with an indication whether previous work counts as continuous with this job;
(2) the rate of remuneration (or how it is calculated);
(3) the intervals at which wages are paid;
(4) the hours of work;
(5) the employee's entitlement to holidays (including public holidays) and holiday pay;
(6) the title of the employee's job;
(7) terms relating to sickness, injury and sick pay;
(8) the length of notice which the employee should give and receive in order to terminate the contract.

In addition, the written particulars must identify the person to whom the employee can apply to seek redress of any grievance and what further steps may ensue.

TERMINATION OF EMPLOYMENT

An employee may be dismissed without notice if he is guilty of gross breach of contract, such as disobedience to a lawful order or dishonesty. He is then only entitled to wages accrued due at the date of dismissal.

In other cases, the employee is entitled to reasonable notice which, under the contracts of Employment Act 1972, as amended by the Employment Protection Act 1975, must not be less than one week when he has been continuously employed for up to 2 years; then it is one week for each full year worked with a maximum of 12.

An employer who wrongfully dismisses an employee (i.e. with less than the length of notice to which he is entitled) is generally liable to pay wages for the period of proper notice.

An employee who has a fixed term contract has no claim against his employer for wrongful dismissal if his contract is not renewed when it expires. He may, however, have a claim for a redundancy payment or compensation for unfair dismissal. If he is wrongfully dismissed before his contract expires, he is generally entitled to remuneration payable over the full period of the contract.

Unless the employee has been guilty of misconduct, he may be entitled to a redundancy payment or to compensation for unfair dismissal if he has been continuously employed for at least certain periods and the employment has been terminated by the employer (with or without proper notice) or he has a fixed term contract which expires without being renewed.

Under the Redundancy Payments Act 1965, an employee who satisfies the foregoing conditions and is dismissed by reason of redundancy may be entitled to a redundancy payment calculated by reference to his age, pay and length of service.

The Trade Union and Labour Relations Act 1974 enables an employee who is unfairly dismissed to complain to an Industrial Tribunal (generally within 3 months of dismissal). The onus will then be on the employer to prove that the dismissal was due to capability, conduct, redundancy, illegality or some other substantial reason justifying dismissal, and that he acted reasonably in dismissing the employee. If the tribunal finds that the employer did not act reasonably the dismissal will be unfair, in which case the tribunal can

(a) recommend re-engagement or
(b) award compensation consisting of a basic or compensatory award.

For an employee to bring himself within the unfair dismissal provisions, he must have been continuously employed for a period not less than 26 weeks.

All complaints of unfair dismissal are referred to a conciliation officer or the Department of Employment and a very high proportion of complaints are disposed of in this way.

OFFICES, SHOPS AND RAILWAY PREMISES

The Offices, Shops and Railway Premises Act, 1963, which extends to Scotland with minor modifications, applies to office premises, shop premises and railway premises being, in each case, premises where persons are employed to work. Shop premises include a building which is not a shop but of which the main use is the carrying on there of a retail trade or business; a building occupied by a wholesaler where goods are kept for sale wholesale (except a warehouse belonging to the owner of a dock, wharf or quay); and a building to which the public can resort for the purpose of having goods repaired. However, the Act does not apply to premises if the only employees are the spouse, parent, grandparent, child, grandchild or brother or sister of the employer, and it does not apply to premises if the period of time worked there during each week does not normally exceed 21 hours.

The following is a very brief summary of the main provisions affecting premises to which the Act applies—

1. The premises and all furniture etc., must be kept clean, and no dirt or refuse must be allowed to accumulate.
2. No overcrowding so as to cause risk of injury to health is permitted.
3. Provisions must be made for maintaining a reasonable temperature in rooms, and a thermometer must be provided on each floor of a building.
4. Provision must be made for securing adequate ventilation.
5. Provision must be made for securing sufficient and suitable lighting.
6. Suitable and sufficient sanitary conveniences and washing facilities (including a supply of clean, running hot and cold or warm water and, in addition, soap and clean towels or other suitable means of cleaning or drying) must be provided at accessible places; and also an adequate supply of wholesome drinking water.
7. Accommodation must be provided for clothing which is not in use.
8. For each sedentary worker there must be provided a seat of a design, construction and dimensions suitable for that worker.
9. Where persons employed to work in shop premises eat meals there, suitable and sufficient facilities for eating them must be provided.
10. All floors, stairs and passages must be of sound construction and properly maintained.
11. Every dangerous part of any machinery must be securely fenced, unless it is in such a position or of such construction as to be as safe as if it were fenced. No person under 18 can clean machinery if he is thereby exposed to risk of injury from a moving part.
12. No person can be required to lift or carry a load so heavy as to be likely to injure him.
13. A first-aid box or cupboard must be provided.
14. Means of escape in case of fire must be provided, as must appropriate fire-fighting equipment.
15. Where an accident occurs which causes death to an employee or disables him from working for more than 3 days, the occupier of the premises must at once send notice of the accident to the appropriate authority.

FAMILY LAW

ADOPTION OF CHILDREN

In England and Wales the adoption of children is regulated mainly by the Adoption of Children Acts, 1926 to 1949, and the Adoption Act, 1958. Further changes are contained in the Children Act 1975 though these are not yet fully in force. An order of court is necessary to legalize the adoption. Adoption puts the child adopted practically on the same footing as a child born to the adopter in lawful wedlock, in all matters of custody, education and maintenance; further, it is provided by the Act of 1958 that an adopted child shall be treated as the child of the adopter (and not the child of its natural parents) for the purpose of the devolution of property on an intestacy occurring, or under any disposition made, after the date of the adoption order. Applications are made to the High Court (Family Division), County Court, or Magistrates Court. Orders will not usually be made for a man to be *sole* adopter of a girl, and the applicant must be either:—

(a) Twenty-five years of age or over; or
(b) Twenty-one years of age or over and a relative (as defined in the Act of 1958) of the infant; or
(c) the mother or father of the infant.

Two spouses may jointly adopt an infant, but unless one of them is the mother or father of the infant, condition (a) or (b) above must be satisfied in respect of one of the applicants *and* the other spouse must have attained the age of twenty-one.

Except in relation to an infant who is not a United Kingdom national (where special provisions apply), the consent of the child's parents or guardian is required before an adoption order will be made, but in certain circumstances (e.g., where the parent or guardian has ill-treated or neglected the child) the Court may dispense with this consent. Since the 1949 Act, marriage between the adopter and the adoptee is prohibited, but marriages of that kind, solemnized before the passing of the Act, are not thereby invalidated.

The 1958 Act places restrictions on societies which make arrangements for the adoption of children; when the 1975 Act takes effect only Local Authorities and ministry approved societies will be able to arrange adoptions.

The Adoption Act, 1964, provides for effect to be given to adoption orders made in Northern Ireland, the Isle of Man and the Channel Islands.

The Adoption Act 1968 (which applies to Scotland) enables an adoption order to be made on the application of a person who is either habitually resident in Great Britain or possesses British nationality. The Act also provides for the recognition of certain overseas adoptions.

Scotland.—The Adoption of Children (Scotland) Acts, 1930 to 1949, and the Adoption Act, 1958, cover the law relating to the adoption of children in Scotland, where an Adopted Children Register is maintained. The Children Act 1975 also applies to Scotland. Applications are made to the Court of Session or the Sheriff Court within whose jurisdiction either the applicant or the child resides at the date of application. The Adoption Act, 1958, which is a consolidating Act, also applies, with modifications to Scotland, and reference is also made to the Adoption Act, 1960, which amends the law with respect to revocation of adoption orders and to the Adoption Act, 1968 (*see* above). The Succession (Scotland) Act, 1964, gives the adopted child the same rights of succession as a child born to the adopter in wedlock, but deprives him of any such rights in the estates of his natural parents.

All adoptions in Great Britain are registered in the Registers of Adopted Children kept by the Registrars General in London and Edinburgh respectively. Certificates from these registers including short certificates which contain no reference to adoptions, can be obtained on conditions similar to those relating to birth certificates, (See below.)

BIRTHS (REGISTRATION)

When a birth takes place, personal information of it must be given to the Registrar of Births and Deaths for the sub-district in which the birth occurred, and the register signed in his presence, by one of the following persons:—
1. The father or mother of the child. If they fail; 2. the occupier of the house in which the birth happened; 3. a person present at the birth; or, 4. the person having charge of the child. The duty of attending to the registration therefore rests firstly on the parents. The mother is responsible for the registration of the birth of an illegitimate child. The registration is required to be made within 42 days of the birth. Failure to do this, without reasonable cause, involves liability to a penalty of twenty pounds. The registration of a birth is free. In England or Wales, the informant, instead of attending before the registrar of the sub-district where the birth occurred, may make a declaration of the particulars required to be registered in the presence of any registrar. Under the Public Health Act, 1936, notice of every birth must be given by the father, or person in attendance on the mother, to the district medical officer of health by post within 36 hours of the birth. *This is in addition to the registration already mentioned.*

A " Stillbirth " must be registered and a certificate signed by the doctor or midwife who was present at the birth or has examined the body of the child must be produced to the registrar. The certificate must, where possible, state the cause of death and the estimated duration of the pregnancy. A stillbirth may only be registered within 3 months of the birth.

The re-registration of the birth of a person legitimated by the subsequent marriage of the parents is provided for in the Births and Deaths Registration Act, 1953. When the Children Act 1975 takes effect special provisions will apply to the registration and re-registration of births of abandoned children, and the re-registration of births of illegitimate children showing the father's name; the mother must be party to the latter application and if the child is under 16 must show the father's formal admission or a court's finding of paternity.

Birth at Sea: The master of a British ship must record any birth on board and send particulars to the Registrar General of Shipping.

Birth Abroad: Consular Officers are authorized to register births of British subjects occurring abroad. Certificates are procurable in due course at Registrar General's Office, London.

The registration of births occurring out of the United Kingdom among members of the armed forces, or occurring on board H.M. ships and aircraft, is provided for by the Registration of Births, Deaths and Marriages (Special Provisions) Act, 1957, applicable also to Scotland.

SCOTLAND

New provisions are included in the Registration of Births, Deaths and Marriages (Scotland) Act, 1965, which amends and re-enacts provisions in former Acts. Personal notification within 21 days of any birth, must be given to the registrar of (a) the registration district in which the birth took place, or (b) any registration district in which the mother of the child was ordinarily resident at the time of

the birth and (c) in the case of a foundling child, dead or alive, when the place of birth is not known, the registration district in which the child, or the body was found. When a child is born (in or out of Scotland) in a ship, aircraft or land vehicle during a journey and the child is conveyed therein to any place in Scotland, the birth shall, unless the Registrar General otherwise directs, be deemed to have occurred at that place.

The register must be signed in the presence of the registrar by the father or mother of the child, and if they fail, by one of the following: (a) any relative of either parent who has knowledge of the birth; (b) the occupier of the premises in which the child was, to the knowledge of that occupier, born; (c) any person present at the birth; (d) any person having charge of the child. Failure without reasonable cause involves a penalty not exceeding £20.

The name of the father of an illegitimate child may be entered in the register of births at the time of registration if jointly requested by the mother and father, and the latter's name may also be recorded at a later date on declaration by both parents. A free abbreviated certificate of birth will be issued to the informant at the time of registration. Provision is made for the re-registration of the birth of a person made legitimate by the subsequent marriage of the parents or whose birth entry is affected by any matter respecting status or paternity, or has been so made as to imply that he is a foundling.

A still-birth must be registered and a certificate, signed by the doctor or certified midwife present at the birth or who has examined the body of the child, must be produced.

CERTIFICATES
OF BIRTHS, MARRIAGES, OR DEATHS

England and Wales.—Certificates of Births, Deaths, or Marriages can be obtained at the Office of Population Censuses and Surveys, St. Catherine's House, 10, Kingsway, W.C.2 or from the Superintendent Registrar having the legal custody of the register containing the entry of which a certificate is required. Certificates of marriage can also be obtained from the incumbent of the church in which the marriage took place; or from the Nonconformist minister (or other " authorized person ") where the marriage takes place in a registered building (*see*, *post*, under Marriage).

Where the certificate is issued by the Local Register Office the fee payable for standard Death and Birth certificates is £1.25 at the time of registration, or until the completed register is handed over to the Superintendent Registrar. Thereafter the fee is £2.50. Where the certificate is issued by the General Register Office the fee is also £2.50, if applied for in person or £4.50 if applied for by post. Certificates at lower rates may be issued under certain statutes, and in particular (under the Births and Deaths Registration Act 1953) a short form of birth certificate showing name, sex and date of birth, but not parentage, may be obtained on payment of a fee of £1.25 from the Registrar General (when £2.75 handling charge is also payable) or from the Superintendent Registrar or Registrar.

It is considered desirable when a certificate is required to consult the nearest Register Office who, if told the exact or approximate date and place of registration, will be able to advise on the best way of obtaining it.

English Registers.—Records of births, deaths and marriages registered in England and Wales since 1837 are kept at the Office of Population Censuses and Surveys, St. Catherine's House, 10, Kingsway, W.C.2. *The Society of Genealogists* 37 Harrington Gardens, S.W.7, possess many records of Baptisms,

Marriages and Deaths prior to 1837, including copies, in whole or in part of about 4,000 Parish Registers.

Scottish Registers of Births, Deaths and Marriages.—Certificates of births, deaths or marriages registered from 1855 when compulsory registration commenced in Scotland can be obtained personally at the General Register Office, New Register House, Edinburgh, or from the appropriate local Registrar, on payment of the fee of £1 for a full extract entry of birth, death, or marriage, and 50p for a short certificate of birth. When the period searched is over 20 years additional fees are payable. A short certificate of registration of deaths is issued free of charge for National Insurance purposes in certain cases.

There are also available at the General Register Office old parish registers of the date prior to 1855, which were formally kept under the administration of the Established Church of Scotland. An extract of an entry in these registers may be obtained at the fee of £1. A fee of £1.50 per day is payable for a general search of all the Scottish registers.

DIVORCE, SEPARATION AND ANCILLARY MATTERS

Preliminary.—Matrimonial Suits may be conveniently divided into two classes, viz. (1) those in which it is sought to annul the marriage because of some defect; and (2) those in which, the marriage being admitted, it is sought to end the marriage or the duties arising from it. By virtue of the Matrimonial Causes Act, 1967, all matrimonial causes are now commenced in one of the divorce county courts designated by the Lord Chancellor. If they remain undefended, they are tried by a county court judge in one of these courts which has also been designated as a court of trial, or in the Royal Courts of Justice in London. If the suit becomes defended, it must be transferred to the High Court.

(1) *Nullity of Marriage.*—This is now mainly governed as to England and Wales by the Matrimonial Causes Act 1973. A marriage is void *ab initio* if the parties were within the prohibited degrees of affinity, or were not male and female, or if it was bigamous or if one of the parties was under the age of consent, i.e. 16, or in the case of a polygamous marriage entered into outside England and Wales, that either party was at the time of the marriage domiciled in England and Wales. Where the *formalities* of the marriage were defective, the marriage is generally void if *both* parties knew of the defect (*e.g.*, where marriage took place otherwise than in an authorized building). But absence of the consent of parents or guardians (or of the Court or other authority, in lieu thereof) in the case of minors does not invalidate the marriage.

A marriage is voidable (i.e. a decree of nullity may be obtained but until such time the marriage remains valid) on the following grounds—(a) incapacity of either party to consummate; (b) respondent's wilful refusal to consummate; (c) that either party did not validly consent to the marriage, whether in consequence of duress, mistake, unsoundness of mind or otherwise, (d) that either party at the time of marriage was a mentally disordered person; (e) that at the time of marriage the respondent was suffering from communicable venereal disease: (f) that at the time of the marriage the respondent was pregnant by another man. In cases (e) and (f) the petitioner must have been ignorant of the grounds at the date of the marriage and in (c), (d), (e) and (f) proceedings must be instituted within 3 years of the marriage. In all cases the court shall not grant a decree where the petitioner has led the respondent to believe that he

would not seek a decree and it would be unjust for it to be granted.

The 1973 Act provides that a decree of nullity in a voidable marriage only annuls the marriage from the date of the decree. The marriage remains valid until the decree, and any children of the marriage are legitimate. Children of a void marriage are illegitimate unless the father was domiciled in England and Wales at the child's birth (or father's death, if earlier) and at the time of conception (or marriage if later) both or either of the parents reasonably believed the marriage was valid.

A spouse's insistence upon the use of contraceptives will not constitute wilful refusal to consummate within (*b*) above, even though there has been no normal intercourse, but it may in certain circumstances constitute unreasonable behaviour for the purpose of divorce (as to which *see* below). Further it has been allowed as a *defence* to a charge of desertion against the aggrieved party.

(2) *Judicial Separation and Divorce.*—The second class of suit includes a suit for judicial separation (which does not dissolve a marriage) and a suit for divorce (which, if successful, dissolves the marriage altogether and leaves the parties at liberty to marry again). Either spouse may petition for judicial separation. It is not necessary to prove that the marriage has broken down irretrievably and the five facts listed (*a*) to (*e*) under divorce (below) are grounds for judicial separation.

Divorce.—The sole ground on which a divorce is obtainable by either husband or wife is the irretrievable breakdown of the marriage. However, the court is precluded from holding that a marriage has irretrievably broken down unless it is satisfied of one or more of the following facts: (a) that the respondent has committed adultery since the marriage and the petitioner finds it intolerable to live with the respondent; (b) such behaviour by the respondent that the petitioner cannot reasonably be expected to continue co-habitation; (c) desertion by the respondent for 2 years immediately before the petition; (d) 5 years separation immediately before the petition (but only 2 years where the respondent consents to the decree). Matrimonial Causes Act 1973.

The foregoing is subject to a clause prohibiting any petition for divorce (but not for judicial separation) before the lapse of three years from the date of marriage, except in the case of exceptional hardship (upon petitioner) or of exceptional depravity of respondent.

Desertion may be defined as a voluntary withdrawal from cohabitation by one spouse without just cause and against the wishes of the other. Where one spouse is guilty of conduct of a serious nature which forces the other to leave, the party at fault is said to be guilty of constructive desertion.

Provisions designed to encourage reconciliation.—The 1973 Act requires the solicitor for the petitioner to certify whether he has or has not discussed the possibility of a reconciliation and whether or not he has given the petitioner the names and addresses of persons qualified to help effect a reconciliation.

A total period of less than six months during which the parties have resumed living together is to be disregarded in determining whether the prescribed period of desertion or separation has been continuous. Similar provision for effecting a reconciliation exists in relation to the other proofs of break-down, but a petitioner cannot claim that it is intolerable to live with the other party if they have lived together for more than six months after discovery of the respondent's adultery.

Hearing the Petition.—Except in cases based on the respondent's behaviour (fact (b) above) the Court may, where there are no relevant children and the suit is undefended pronounce a decree nisi of divorce or judicial separation without either party attending Court; the petitioner's evidence is in the form of a sworn statement filed with the Court.

Intervention by Queen's Proctor.—At any time during the progress of a suit, and before the decree *nisi* is made absolute, the Queen's Proctor may intervene.

Decree Absolute.—Every decree of dissolution or nullity is in the first instance a decree *nisi*. The marriage subsists until the decree is made absolute, usually six weeks after decree *nisi*. After that date either spouse may marry again; but as to marriage within "Prohibited Degrees" *see* Marriage—Miscellaneous Notes, p. 1175. Under the 1973 Act, a decree *nisi* cannot normally be made absolute until the court is satisfied that arrangements have been made for the welfare of every child of the family who has not attained the age of sixteen which are satisfactory or the best which can be devised in the circumstances or that it is impracticable for the parties before the court to make any such arrangements.

Maintenance, etc.—The court has wide powers to order either party to the marriage to make financial provision (e.g. periodical payments, a lump sum, the transfer of property) for the other party or any child of the family, having regard to the party's means, the recipient's needs and all the important aspects of the case. The husband can be ordered to pay his wife's costs, even if she is unsuccessful in her suit or defence. A guilty co-respondent may be ordered to pay costs.

The court may, where the husband has wilfully neglected to provide reasonable maintenance for the wife or children, order the husband to make provision for them, *even though* no matrimonial suit is pending between the parties to the marriage, and while such an order is in force the court may also deal with custody of and access to the children.

CUSTODY OF CHILDREN ETC.

The Court may make orders in respect of access to and the custody, maintenance and education of children in connection with a suit for divorce, nullity or judicial separation (above) or with an application to the Magistrates (below) whether the suit succeeds or not. In addition, if there is no other matrimonial suit involved a parent may apply for custody under the Guardianship of Minors Acts 1971 and 1973, and any person may apply to the High Court for the child to be made a ward of court.

In all cases the welfare of the child is the first and paramount consideration. The categories of child who may be covered by any particular type of proceedings differ according to the nature of those proceedings and to the nature of the particular relief sought, but it should be borne in mind that in connection with divorce, nullity and judicial separation a child which has been *treated* by the spouses as a child of the family may be included as well as the children of the spouses themselves. In the case of a Magistrates' order the child must be that of at least one of the spouses which has been *accepted* by the other as a child of the family.

When the Children Act 1975 comes into effect a new procedure called "Custodianship" will be introduced, basically allowing long term foster parents to apply for custody of the foster child.

Any dispute relating to the above matters should be placed in the hands of a Solicitor without delay (see Legal Aid, etc. below) and in particular it should be borne in mind that where there is finan-

cial need (because of, e.g. continuing education or disability) maintenance may be ordered for children even beyond the age of majority.

SEPARATION BY AGREEMENT

Husband and wife may agree, with or without consideration, to separate and live apart, but the agreement, to be valid, must be followed by an immediate separation. It is most desirable to consult a solicitor in every such case.

MAGISTRATES' SEPARATION AND MAINTENANCE ORDERS

When a husband has been guilty of adultery or has been convicted of certain assaults or has deserted his wife, or has been guilty of persistent cruelty to her or to an infant child of the family, or of wilful neglect to maintain her or such a child, or where he is an habitual drunkard or drug addict, or insists on having intercourse while suffering from a venereal disease, or compels her to submit herself to prostitution, the wife may obtain relief from the local magistrates' court. A husband may apply on similar grounds, so far as they are applicable to him. In particular a wife can sometimes be guilty of the offence of wilful neglect to provide reasonable maintenance for her husband or children and an order can be made against her. The court may declare that the complainant is no longer bound to cohabit with the defendant. It may order the husband to pay a weekly sum in its discretion to the wife and may order her to make a similar payment to him if his earning capacity is impaired by age or illness. Provision may be made for legal custody of and access to any child of the family who is under the age of 16 years and for payment by either or both of the spouses of a weekly sum to the person entrusted with legal custody in respect of each child of the family up to the age of 16. If the court thinks the child would still be a dependent although over that age, similar payments may be ordered for support of the child up to the age of 21. The court cannot make an order that the parties need no longer cohabit or that either spouse shall support the other where the complainant has committed adultery during the marriage, unless the defendant has condoned or connived at, or by wilful neglect or misconduct conduced to, that act of adultery. The court has wide powers of revocation, revival and variation of orders already made. The order must be revoked if the parties have resumed cohabitation, and must be revoked, except so far as the order relates to the children, if the complainant is subsequently proved to have committed adultery since the marriage and the defendant has not condoned or connived at or by wilful neglect or misconduct conduced to that act of adultery. Complaints based on desertion or failure to maintain can be made whilst the offence continues. Complaints based on adultery must usually be made within 6 months of the complainant discovering it, all other complaints within 6 months of the offence itself. The Magistrates' Courts Act, 1952, separates the hearing of matrimonial disputes from ordinary court business; specifies the persons allowed to be present; limits newspaper reports, etc., etc.

SCOTLAND
DIVORCE

Actions of divorce can only be raised in the Court of Session which has jurisdiction to entertain such actions only if either of the parties to the marriage in question (a) is domiciled in Scotland on the date when the action is begun; or (b) was habitually resident in Scotland throughout the period of one year ending with that date.

The Scots Law of Divorce is now governed by the Divorce (Scotland) Act 1976, which for the purposes of divorce comes into force on January 1, 1977. As from that date the sole ground of divorce will be irretrievable breakdown of the marriage. This can only be established in one of the following ways:

(a) The defending spouse has committed adultery since the date of the marriage. Here it is not necessary for the pursuing spouse to prove that the fact of adultery made it intolerable to live with the defending spouse.

(b) The defending spouse has behaved in such a way that the pursuing spouse cannot reasonably be expected to cohabit with him or her. It is immaterial whether or not the conduct founded upon is active or passive.

(c) The defending spouse has deserted the pursuing spouse for a continuous period of two years. There must be no question of the pursuing spouse having refused a genuine and reasonable offer to adhere. Nor is irretrievable breakdown established if cohabitation is resumed for a period of more than three months, after the two year period has expired.

(d) There has been no cohabitation at any time during a continuous period of two years immediately preceding the action between the parties to the action, and the defending spouse consents to the divorce being granted.

(e) There has been no cohabitation at any time during a continuous period of five years, as in (d) *supra*, except that on the expiry of the five year period, the consent of the defending spouse is not required.

The facts of desertion and separation are not interrupted by the parties cohabiting for a period or periods not exceeding six months. However such a period or periods of cohabitation would not be included in the calculation of the two-year or five-year periods.

Encouragement of Reconciliation: The burden of promoting a reconciliation between spouses in a divorce action in Scotland falls upon the Court by virtue of the 1976 Act. Where an action of divorce has been raised, it may be postponed by the Court to enable the parties to seek to effect a reconciliation, if the Court feels that there may be a reasonable prospect of such reconciliation. If the parties do cohabit during such postponement, no account shall be taken of such cohabitation if the action later proceeds.

Maintenance, etc.: The 1976 Act also provides that either party to a marriage can apply to the Court at any time prior to decree being granted for (a) an order for a periodical allowance (b) an order for a capital sum or (c) a variation of a marriage settlement. The Court in granting or refusing such an order takes into account the respective means of the parties, and also all the circumstances of the case.

Nullity of Marriage.—A declaration of nullity of marriage may be obtained on the ground of any impediment, viz., consanguinity and affinity, subsistence of a previous marriage, non-age of one of the parties, incapacity or insanity of one of the parties, or by the absence of genuine consent.

SEPARATION

Under the Divorce (Scotland) Act 1976 *supra*, a decree of Judicial Separation can be obtained by proof of the same facts necessary to obtain decree of divorce—except that for the principle of irretrievable breakdown there is substituted that of grounds justifying separation.

CUSTODY OF CHILDREN

In actions for divorce and separation, the Court has a discretion in awarding the custody of the children of the parties. The welfare of the children is the paramount consideration, and the mere fact that a spouse is the guilty party in the action does not of itself deprive him or her of the right to claim custody. The Children Act 1975 (*supra*) also applies to Scotland.

ILLEGITIMACY AND LEGITIMATION
ENGLAND AND WALES

A man may be summoned to petty sessions on the application of the mother of an illegitimate child, or by the Supplementary Benefits Commission where benefit has been paid for the requirements of the child, and the Justices, on his being proved to be the father of the child, may make an order requiring him to pay for its maintenance and education a sum in their discretion. The woman is not bound to give evidence in every case but if she does so it must be *corroborated* in some material particular. The mother has the custody of her illegitimate children. *Prima facie* every child born of a married woman during a marriage is legitimate; and this presumption can only be rebutted by strong, distinct, satisfactory and conclusive evidence. However, under the Family Reform Act, 1969, any presumption of law as to the legitimacy (or illegitimacy) of any person may in civil proceedings be rebutted by evidence showing that it is more probable than not that the person is illegitimate (or legitimate) and in any proceedings where paternity is in question, blood tests may be ordered. If however the husband and wife are separated under an Order of the Court, a child conceived by the wife during such separation is presumed not to be the husband's child.

LEGITIMATION.—By the *Legitimacy Act*, 1926, which came into force on Jan. 1, 1927, where the parents of an illegitimate person marry, or have married, whether before or after that date, the marriage, if the father is at the date thereof domiciled in England or Wales, renders that person, if living, legitimate as from Jan. 1, 1927, or from the date of the marriage, whichever last happens. Under the Act of 1959, marriage legitimates a person even though the father or mother was married to a third person at the time when the illegitimate person was born. It is the duty of the parents to supply to the Registrar-General information for re-registration of the birth of a legitimated child.

Declarations of Legitimacy.—A person claiming that he, his parents, or any remoter ancestor has become legitimated, may petition the High Court or the County Court for the necessary declaration.

Rights and Duties of Legitimated Persons.—A legitimated person, his spouse or issue may take property under an intestacy occurring after the date of legitimation, or under any disposition (*e.g.*, a will) coming into operation after such date, as if he had been legitimate.

He must maintain all persons whom he would be bound to maintain had he been born legitimate, and he is entitled to the benefit of any Act of Parliament which confers rights on legitimate persons to recover damages or compensation. The Act specially provides that nothing therein contained is to render any person capable of succeeding to or transmitting a right to any dignity or title.

Property Rights of Illegitimate Children.—By the Family Law Reform Act, 1969, the rights of an illegitimate child on an intestacy are now broadly equated with those of a legitimate child. Also, in any deposition made after January 1, 1970, any reference to children and other relatives shall, unless the contrary intension appears, be construed as including references to, and to persons related through, illegitimate children.

SCOTLAND

Illegitimate Children (Scotland) Act, 1930.—The mother of an illegitimate child may raise an action of affiliation and aliment against the father, either in the Court of Session or, more usually, in the Sheriff Court. Where in any such action the Court finds that the defender is the father of the child, the Court shall, in awarding inlying expenses, or ailment, have regard to the means of the parties, and the whole circumstances of the case. The Court may, upon application by the mother or by the father of any illegitimate child, or in any action for aliment for an illegitimate child, make such order as it may think fit regarding the custody of such child and the right of access thereto of either parent, having regard to the welfare of the child and to the conduct of the parents and to the wishes as well of the mother as of the father and may on the application of either parent recall or vary such order. The obligation of the mother and of the father of an illegitimate child to provide aliment for such child shall (without prejudice to any obligation attaching at common law) endure until the child attains the age of sixteen.

By Scots Law an illegitimate child is legitimated by and on the date of the subsequent marriage of its parents and there is no objection to there having been an impediment to the marriage of the parents at the time of the child's conception—*see* the Legitimation (Scotland) Act, 1968, which came into operation on June 8, 1968, on which date thousands of existing illegitimate children were regarded as legitimated. By the Registration of Births, Deaths and Marriages (Scotland) Act, 1965, a child so legitimated, who has already been registered as illegitimate, may be re-registered as legitimate. The consent of the father of an illegitimate child to its adoption is not required.

The Law Reform (Miscellaneous Provisions) (Scotland) Act, 1968, gives an illegitimate child full rights of succession (including legitim) in the estate of both parents, while the father and mother share equally in the estate of their illegitimate child, Unless expressly excluded, a reference in a deed executed on or after 25th November, 1968, to a relationship, *e.g.*, "issue" or "children" is presumed to include illegitimate children.

MARRIAGE
A.—MARRIAGE ACCORDING TO RITES OF THE CHURCH OF ENGLAND

1. MARRIAGE BY BANNS.—The Marriage Act, 1949, prescribes audible publication according to the rubric, on three Sundays preceding the ceremony during morning service or, if there is no morning service on a Sunday on which the banns are to be published, during evening service. Where the parties reside in different parishes, the banns must be published in both. Under the Act, banns may be published and the marriage solemnized in the parish church, *which is the usual place of worship* of the persons to be married or either of them, although neither of such persons dwells in such parish; but this publication of banns is *in addition* to any other publication required by law and does not apply if the church or the residence of either party is in Wales. The Act provides specially for the case where one of the parties resides in Scotland and the other in England, the publication being then in the parish in England in which one party resides, and, according to the law and custom in Scotland, in the place where the other party resides. After the lapse of three months from the last time of publication, the banns become useless, and the

parties must either obtain a licence (*see below*), or submit to the republication of banns.

2. MARRIAGE BY LICENCE.—Marriage licences are of two kinds:—

(i) *A Common Licence*, dispensing with the necessity for banns, granted by the Archbishops and Bishops through their Surrogates, for marriages in any church or chapel duly licensed for marriages. A Common Licence can be obtained in London by application at the Faculty Office (1 The Sanctuary, Westminster, S.W.1) and (for marriages in London) at the Bishop of London's Diocesan Registry (1 The Sanctuary, S.W.1), by one of the parties about to be married. In the country they may be obtained at the offices of the Bishops' Registrars, but licences obtained at the Bishop's Diocesan Registry only enable the parties to be married in the diocese in which they are issued; those procured at the Faculty Office are available for *all* England and Wales. No instructions, either verbal or in writing, can be received, except from one of the parties. Affidavits are prepared from the personal instructions of one of the parties about to be married, and the licence is delivered to the party upon payment of fees amounting to six pounds. *No previous notice is required and the licence is available as soon as it is issued.* Before a licence can be granted one of the parties must make an affidavit that there is no legal impediment to the intended marriage; and also that one of such parties has had his or her usual place of abode for the space of fifteen days immediately preceding the issuing of the licence within the parish or ecclesiastical district of the church in which the marriage is to be solemnized, *or* the church in which the marriage is to be solemnized is the usual place of worship of the parties or one of them. In the country there may generally be found a parochial clergyman (Surrogate) before whom the affidavit may be taken, and whose office it is to deliver the licence personally to the applicant. (In some dioceses it is necessary for the Surrogate to procure the licence from the Bishop's Registry.) The licence continues in force for three months from its date.

(ii) *A Special Licence* granted by the Archbishop of Canterbury, under special circumstances, for marriage at any place with or without previous residence in the district, or at any time, etc.; but the reasons assigned must meet with his Grace's approval. Application must be made to the Faculty Office. Fees for licence, etc., £25.

3. MARRIAGE UNDER SUPERINTENDENT REGISTRAR'S CERTIFICATE.—A marriage may be performed in church on the Superintendent Registrar's Certificate (as to which see below) without banns, provided that the incumbent's consent is obtained. One of the parties must be resident within the ecclesiastical parish of the church in which the marriage is to take place unless the church is the usual place of worship of the parties or one of them.

MARRIAGE FEES.—The Church Commissioners settle tables of fees for all parishes. The usual fees are paid although a stranger-clergyman may be invited to perform the service.

B.—MARRIAGE UNDER SUPERINTENDENT REGISTRAR'S CERTIFICATE

The following marriages may be solemnized on the authority of a Superintendent Registrar's Certificate (either with or without a licence):—

(a) A marriage in a registered building (*e.g.*, a nonconformist church registered for the solemnization of marriages therein).

(b) A marriage in a register office.

(c) A marriage according to the usages of the Society of Friends (commonly called Quakers).

(d) A marriage between two persons professing the Jewish religion according to the usages of the Jews.

(e) A marriage according to the rites of the Church of England (*see above*—in this case the marriage can only be *without* licence).

NOTICE.—Notice of the intended marriage must be given as follows:—

(i) Marriage by certificate (*without* licence)—if both parties reside in the same regisration district, they must both have resided there for seven days before the notice can be given. It may then be given by either party. If the parties reside in different registration districts, notice must be given by each to the Superintendent Registrar of the district in which he or she resides, and the preliminary residential qualification of seven days must be fulfilled by each before either notice can be given.

(ii) Marriage by certificate (*with* licence)—one notice only is necessary, whether the parties live in the same or in different registration districts. Either party may give the notice, which must be given to the Superintendent Registrar of any registration district in which one of the parties has resided for the period of fifteen days immediately preceding the giving of notice, but both parties must be resident in England or Wales on the day notice is given.

The notice (in either case) must be in the prescribed form and must contain particulars as to names, marital status, occupation, residence, length of residence, and the building in which the marriage is to take place. The notice must also contain or have added at the foot thereof a solemn declaration that there is no legal impediment to the marriage, and, in the case of minors, that the consent of the person whose consent to the marriage is required by law (*see below*) has been duly given, and that the residential qualifications (mentioned above) have been complied with. A person making a false declaration renders himself or herself liable to prosecution for perjury. The notice is entered in the marriage notice book.

ISSUE OF CERTIFICATE:

(i) *Without licence.*—The notice (or an exact copy thereof) is affixed in some conspicuous place in the Superintendent Registrar's office for 21 days next after the notice was entered in the marriage notice book. After the lapse of this period the Superintendent Registrar may, provided no impediment is shown, issue his certificate for the marriage which can then take place at any time within three months from the date of the entry of the notice.

(ii) *With licence.*—The notice in this case is not affixed in the office of the Superintendent Registrar. After the lapse of one whole day (other than a Sunday, Christmas Day or Good Friday) from the date of entry of

the notice, the Superintendent Registrar may, provided no impediment is shown, issue his certificate and licence for the marriage, which can then take place on any day within three months from the date of entry of the notice.

SOLEMNIZATION OF THE MARRIAGE:

(i) *In a Registered Building.*—The marriage must generally take place at a building within the district of residence of one of the parties, but if the usual place of worship of either is outside the district of his or her residence, it may take place in such usual place of worship. Further, if there is not within the district of residence of one of the parties a registered building within which marriages are solemnized according to the rites and ceremonies which the parties desire to adopt in solemnizing their marriage, it may take place in an appropriate registered building in the nearest district.

The presence of a Registrar of Marriages is not necessary at marriages at registered buildings which have adopted the provisions of section 43 of the Marriage Act, 1949. This section provides for the appointment of an " authorized person " (a person, usually the minister or an official of the building, certified by the trustees or governing body as having been duly authorized for the purpose) who must be present and must register the marriage.

The marriage must be solemnized between the hours of 8 a.m. and 6 p.m. with open doors in the presence of two or more witnesses. The parties must at some time during the ceremony make the following declaration—" I do solemnly declare that I know not of any lawful impediment why I, A. B., may not be joined in matrimony to C. D." Also each of the parties must say to the other: " I call upon these persons here present to witness that I, A. B., do take thee, C. D., to be my lawful wedded wife [or husband]," *or*, if the marriage is solemnized in the presence of an authorized person without the presence of a Registrar, each party may say in lieu thereof: " I, A. B., do take thee, C. D., to be my wedded wife [or husband]."

(ii) *In a Register Office.*—The marriage may be solemnized in the office of the Superintendent Registrar to whom notice of the marriage has been given. The marriage must be solemnized between the hours of 8 a.m. and 6 p.m., with open doors in the presence of the Superintendent Registrar or a Registrar of the registration district of that Superintendent Registrar, and in the presence of two witnesses. The parties must make the following declaration: " I do solemnly declare that I know not of any lawful impediment why I, A. B., may not be joined in matrimony to C. D.," and each party must say to the other: " I call upon these persons here present to witness that I, A. B., do take thee, C. D., to be my lawful wedded wife [or husband]." No religious ceremony may take place in the Register Office, though the parties may, on production of their marriage certificate, go through a subsequent religious ceremony in any church or persuasion of which they are members.

(iii) *Other Cases.*—If both parties are members of the Society of Friends (Quakers), or if, not being in membership, they have been authorized by the Society of Friends to solemnize their marriage in accordance with its usages, they may be married in a Friends' meeting-house. The marriage must be registered by the registering officer of the Society appointed to act for the district in which the meeting house is situated. The presence of a Registrar of Marriages is not necessary.

If both parties are Jews they may marry according to their usages in a synagogue, which has certificate marriage secretary, or private dwelling-house at any hour; the building may be situated within or without the district of residence. The marriage must be registered by the secretary of the synagogue of which the man is a member. The presence of a Registrar of Marriages is not necessary.

FEES OF SUPERINTENDING REGISTRARS

For entering notice of a marriage by certificate (with or without licence) in the marriage notice book.................... £2
For a licence for marriage.................. £8
For a marriage by certificate (with or without licence) in the presence of a Registrar (including cost of certificate).... £3

C.—MARRIAGE UNDER REGISTRAR GENERAL'S LICENCE

The main purpose of the Marriage (Registrar General's Licence) Act, 1970, which came into force on January 1, 1971, is to enable non-Anglicans to be married in unregistered premises where one of the persons to be married is seriously ill, is not expected to recover and cannot be moved to registered premises. A fee of £15 is payable to the Registrar General for the licence, though he has power to remit this in whole or in part to avoid hardship.

MISCELLANEOUS NOTES

Consanguinity and Affinity.—A marriage between persons within the prohibited degrees of consanguinity or affinity is void. Relaxations have, however, been made by various statutes which have now been replaced by the Marriage Act, 1949 (see the 1st Schedule to the Act) and the Marriage (Enabling) Act, 1960. It is now permitted to contract a marriage with:—

Sister, aunt or niece of a former wife (whether living or not). Former wife of brother, uncle or nephew (whether living or not).

No clergyman can be compelled to solemnize any of the foregoing marriages, but he may allow his church to be used for the purpose by another minister.

Minors.—Persons under 18 years of age are generally required to obtain the consent of certain persons (see Marriage Act, 1949, section 3 and 2nd Schedule as amended by the Family Law Reform Act, 1969). Where both parents are living, both must consent, where one is dead, the survivor, or, if there is a guardian appointed by the deceased parent, the guardian and the survivor. No consent is required in the case of an infant's second marriage. In certain exceptional cases consent may be dispensed with, *e.g.*, the insanity of a parent. If consent is refused the Court may, on application being made, consent to the marriage; application can be made for this purpose to the High Court, the County Court, or a Court of Summary Jurisdiction. The Act *prohibits* any marriage where either party is under 16 years of age.

D.—MARRIAGE IN ENGLAND OR WALES WHEN ONE PARTY LIVES IN SCOTLAND OR NORTHERN IRELAND

Notice for a marriage by a Superintendent Registrar's certificate in a register office or registered building may be given in the usual way by the party resident in England. As regards Scotland, the party there, after a residence of fifteen days should either apply to the session clerk to publish banns or give notice of marriage to the registrar; as regards Northern Ireland, the party there, after a residence of seven days, must give notice to the District Registrar of Marriages. Notice cannot be given for such marriages to take place by Certificate *with* licence of the Superintendent Registrar.

Marriage of such parties may take place in a church of the Church of England after the publication of banns, or by Ecclesiastical licence.

MARRIAGES IN SCOTLAND

According to the law of Scotland, marriage is a contract which is completed by the mutual consent of parties.

Impediments to marriage: These render the marriage null and void. (*a*) Age: If either party is under the age of 16. (*b*) Forbidden Degrees: If the parties are within certain degrees of relationship. (*c*) Subsisting previous marriage. (*d*) Impotency of either party. (*e*) Non-residence, *i.e.*, if the legal requirement of prior residence of one or other of the parties in Scotland have not been complied with. (*f*) Insanity of either party.

No consent of parents or guardians is necessary. Marriages may be regular or " irregular."

Regular Marriages

A regular marriage is one which is celebrated by a Minister of religion or authorized Registrar after due notice by the proclamation of banns or publication by the Registrar, or by a Sheriff's licence. Any Minister of any denomination (including a person officiating at a Quaker wedding) who performs the ceremony is reckoned to be a minister of religion. It must be performed before two witnesses and one of the parties must either have his or her usual residence in the Registration District, or have resided there for at least 15 days before the ceremony or have a parent so residing there. No form, place or hours are prescribed by law. There are no canonical hours as in England. Public proclamation is made by (*a*) banns, or (*b*) notice by the Registrar. Banns must be proclaimed in a parish church situated within the registration district of the qualifying address of each party. It is ordered that the proclamation of banns should be made twice, but by immemorial practice proclamation on one Sunday is sufficient. The Clerk of the Kirk Session of the Parish takes in notices of banns and issues certificates of proclamation. The fee for proclamation may not exceed 75p. A certificate of proclamation of banns is only valid for three months.

Under the Marriage Notices (Scotland) Act, 1878, amended by the Marriage (Scotland) Act, 1956, a notice posted up in a conspicuous or accessible place on the board or outer wall of the Registrar's office is equivalent to the proclamation of banns, but a minister of the Church of Scotland is not bound, although he is entitled, to celebrate a marriage not preceded by banns. The statute is limited to persons with qualifying residence in Scotland or having parents so residing. Exhibition is made for 7 consecutive days, during which time any person may appear personally and lodge an objection in writing subscribed by him. If no objections are lodged the Registrar issues a certificate. Such certificate of publication is only valid for three months. Regulation made under the

Births, Deaths and Marriages (Scotland) Act, 1965 provide that the cost of publication is 75p, which includes the issue of a certificate by the Registrar (any subsequent extract costs £1). The Naval Marriages Act, 1908, regulates the publication of banns or of notice on board H.M. ships and the granting of certificates by the Officer-Commanding.

Marriage before Registrar: After obtaining a certificate of due publication as above it is competent for the parties to contract the marriage in the office of the authorized Registrar in his presence and in the presence of two witnesses. The fee for the ceremony is £2. Such a marriage is regular and valid in all respects.

Marriage by Licence: In unforeseen and exceptional circumstances—*see* Section 2 of the Marriage (Scotland) Act, 1939—where normal method of publication cannot be carried through, the Sheriff, on application by the parties may grant a licence (valid for ten days) which is otherwise deemed in all respects to be equivalent to a certificate of publication.

Irregular Marriages

Since the passing of the Marriage (Scotland) Act, 1939, only one form of irregular marriage is recognized, *viz.* marriage by co-habitation and habit and repute. If parties live together constantly as husband and wife, and if they are held to be such by the general repute of the neighbourhood, then there may arise a presumption from which marriage can be inferred. Before such marriage can be registered, however, a decree of declarator of marriage must be obtained from the Court of Session.

JURY SERVICE

Every local or parliamentary elector between the ages of eighteen and sixty-five who has resided in the United Kingdom, Channel Islands or Isle of Man for at least five years since he attained the age of thirteen will be qualified to serve on a jury unless he is " ineligible " or " disqualified ".

Ineligible persons include those who have at any time been judges, magistrates and certain senior court officials, those who within the previous ten years have been concerned with the law (such as barristers and solicitors and their clerks, court officers, coroners, police, prison and probation officers); priests of any religion and vowed members of religious communities; and certain sufferers from mental illness.

Disqualified persons are those who have at any time been sentenced by a Court in the United Kingdom, Channel Islands or Isle of Man, to a term of imprisonment exceeding five years, or who have in the previous ten years served any part of a sentence exceeding three months or been sentenced to Borstal.

Some others are excusable as of right. These include members and officers of the Houses of Parliament, full-time serving members of the forces (including Women's forces) and registered and practising members of the medical, dental, nursing, veterinary and pharmaceutical professions and any person who has served on a jury in the two years before he is summoned. In other cases the court may excuse a juror at its discretion (*e.g.*, where the service would be a hardship to the juror).

If a person serves on a jury knowing himself to be disqualified or inelegible he is liable to be fined up to £400 or £100 respectively.

A juror is entitled to subsistence and travelling expenses, compensation for other expenses incurred in consequence of attendance for jury service, loss of earnings and loss of national insurance benefits but certain maximum figures (which are revised from time to time) are laid down.

A verdict of a jury must normally be unanimous but after two hours consideration (or such longer period as the Court thinks reasonable), a majority verdict is acceptable if ten jurors agree to it (or nine if the size of the jury has been reduced to ten, *e.g.*, by illness during the trial).

Jury trial is now very unusual in civil cases but a person charged with any but the least serious crimes is entitled to be tried by a jury. The defendant may object to any juror if he can show that that juror ought not be on the jury (*e.g.*, because he is ineligible or is biased against him) and may object to seven jurors without giving any reason.

JURY SERVICE IN SCOTLAND

It is the duty of the sheriff principal of each sheriffdom, in respect of each sheriff court district in his sheriffdom, to maintain a book, known as the " general jury book ", containing the names and designations of persons within the district who are qualified and liable to serve as jurors. The book, which is compiled from information which every householder is required to provide, is kept open for the inspection by any person, upon payment of a nominal fee, at the sheriff clerk's office for the district. Part II of the Juries Act 1949 (amended by the Juries Act 1954 with regulations following thereon) applies only to Scotland and provides, *inter alia*, for the payment of travelling expenses and subsistence allowances to jurors and for loss of earnings.

The number of a jury in a civil cause in the Court of Session is twelve and in the Sheriff Court seven. In a criminal trial the number is fifteen, and in inquiries by Sheriff and jury under the Fatal Accidents Inquiry (Scotland) Act 1895 or the Fatal Accidents and Sudden Deaths Inquiry (Scotland) Act 1906 the number is seven. In Scotland there is no Coroner's Inquest.

QUALIFICATIONS

Every man or woman between the ages of 21 and 60 who is possessed of heritable property of the yearly value of at least £5, or of moveable property of the value of at least £200 Sterling, is qualified to serve on a jury.

Exemptions.—The following persons are exempt from serving on juries: peers, judges of the supreme courts, sheriffs, ministers of religion, parochial schoolmasters, practising lawyers, clerks and other officers of any court of justice, prison offices, university professors, practising physicians, surgeons, registered veterinary surgeons or midwives, registered dentists (if they wish to be exempt), officers in the Army, Navy or Air Force on full pay, officers of the Customs and Excise, messengers at arms, police and other officers of law, commissioners and other officers and employees of the Inland Revenue, lighthouse keepers and their assistants, soldiers of the regular Army or Air Force, officers and men of the Territorial Army and Royal Auxiliary Air Force, factory inspectors and airport police. Officers of the Post Office will not be compelled to serve.

Jurors failing to attend without good cause are liable to a penalty.

LANDLORD AND TENANT
ENGLAND AND WALES

Although basically the relationship between the parties to the lease is governed by the lease itself, the position is complicated by numerous statutory provisions. The few points dealt with may show the desirability of seeking professional assistance in these matters. Important provisions include:—

(1) As to agricultural holdings—the Agricultural Holdings Act, 1948. Among other things, this Act regulates the length of notice necessary to determine an agricultural tenancy, the tenant's right to remove fixtures on the land, his right to compensation for damage done by game, for improvements and for disturbance, and his right to require the consent of the Agricultural Land Tribunal to the operation of a notice to quit.

(2) As to business premises—the Landlord and Tenant Acts, 1927 and 1954, and the Law of Property Act 1969, Pt. I. Part II of the 1954 Act gives security of tenure to the tenant of most business premises, and in effect he can only be ousted on one or more of the seven grounds set out in the Act. In some cases, where the landlord can resume possession, the tenant is entitled to compensation.

(3) As to dwelling houses. The complicated mass of legislation is now mainly embodied in the Rent Acts 1968 and 1974, which does not extend to Scotland or Northern Ireland. If the house is within the Act, a tenant has a personal right to reside there, and he may only be ousted on certain grounds.

Such tenancies may be either controlled or regulated. A controlled tenancy is one which has been in existence since July 6, 1957; had at that time the protection of the Rent Acts and is of a house or part of a house the rateable value of which did not exceed £40 in London or £30 elsewhere on November 7, 1956. A regulated tenancy is one which is not controlled, and which falls within the following limits:—

(a) Rateable value on March 23, 1965 (or when first rated, if later)—not in excess of £400 in Greater London or £200 elsewhere OR
(b) Rateable value on March 22, 1973 (or when first rated, if later)—not in excess of £600 in Greater London or £300 elsewhere OR
(c) Rateable value on April 1, 1973 (or when first rated, if later)—not in excess of £1500 in Greater London or £750 elsewhere.

The essential difference between controlled tenancies and regulated tenancies is in the maximum rent recoverable. Under controlled tenancies, the maximum rent is ascertained by taking an appropriate multiple of the gross value for rating purposes of the property on November 7, 1956, whereas the maximum rent under a regulated tenancy is the rent agreed between the landlord and tenant, unless a fair rent has been registered, in which case that is the maximum rent recoverable. Application for the registration of a fair rent may be made by either the landlord or tenant, to the Local Rent Officer, and appeal against his decision lies to the Rent Assessment Committee.

S27 of the Housing Finance Act 1972 provides for the conversion of a controlled tenancy into a regulated tenancy on the issue of a certificate by the Local Authority that the house is provided with all standard amenities. The Housing Rents and Subsidies Act 1975 has repealed the former provision for conversion by reference to rateable value on a specific date. This Act also provides for the phasing of rent increases in the private sector.

(4) As to dwelling houses with resident landlords. The Rent Act 1974 gives tenants of furnished dwellings the same security of tenure as those of unfurnished dwellings unless the landlord lives in part of the house. In the latter case, and in the case of a tenancy of an unfurnished dwelling granted by a resident landlord after 13th August 1974, the tenancy may fall within Part VI of the Rent Act 1968, and the tenant may be granted relief from eviction by application to the Rent Tribunal after a notice to quit has been served, but before it has expired. The Rent Tribunal is empowered to delay

the operation of the notice to quit by 6 months, and by the end of that period, the tenant may apply for a further delay of 6 months. The landlord or the tenant may also apply to the Rent Tribunal for a reasonable rent to be registered, and once registered, this is the maximum rent recoverable.

(5) The Rent Act 1965 Act also provides that if any person with intent to cause the residential occupier of any premises to give up the occupation thereof does any act calculated to interfere with the peace or comfort of the residential occupier or members of his household, he shall be guilty of an offence. A further provision prevents a landlord enforcing a right to possession against a tenant (who is not already protected by any security of tenure legislation) without a court order, and there are special rules in such cases relating to agricultural employees.

(6) A notice to quit *any* dwellinghouse must be given at least four weeks before it is to take effect, and must be in writing and in the prescribed statutory form.

(7) Part I of the Landlord and Tenant Act, 1954, applies to most tenancies of houses for over twenty-one years at a ground rent. Where it applies, the contractual tenancy is continued until brought to an end in the manner prescribed by the Act, and in effect the landlord can only get possession on limited grounds.

Further, under the Leasehold Reform Act, 1967, tenants of houses under leases for over twenty-one years at rent less than two-thirds of the rateable value of the house are in most cases given a right to purchase the freehold or to take an extended lease for a term of fifty years, provided the tenant at the time when he seeks to exercise the right has been occupying the house as his residence for the last five years or for periods amounting to five years in the last ten years.

(8) Under the Housing Act, 1961 (which does not extend to Scotland), in a lease of a dwellinghouse granted after October 24, 1961, for a term of less than 7 years, there is implied a covenant by the landlord (a) to keep in repair the structure and exterior of the house and (b) to keep in repair and proper working order the installations in the house (i) for the supply of water, gas and electricity, and for sanitation, and (ii) for space heating or heating water.

SCOTLAND

A Lease is a Contract, the relationship of the parties being governed by the terms thereof. As is also the case in England (see the foregoing Section) legislation has played an important part in regulating that relationship. Thus, what at Common Law was an Agreement binding only the parties to the deed, becomes in virtue of Statute 1449 c. 17, a contract binding the landlord's successors, as purchasers or creditors, provided the following four conditions are observed; (1) the lease, if for more than one year, must be in writing, (2) there must be a rent, (3) there must be a term of expiry, and (4) the tenant must have entered into possession.

It would be impracticable in a brief section of these Notes to enter upon a general discussion of this branch of the law and, accordingly, the plan adopted in the preceding Section of quoting a few important Statutes is followed here.

The Agricultural Holdings (Scotland) Act, 1949 (amended by the Agriculture Act, 1958), which is a consolidating Act applicable to Scotland, contains provisions similar to those in the English Act,

alluded to in the preceding Section. It cannot here be analysed in detail.

It is of interest to note that the Small Landholders Act, 1911, provided for the setting up of the Land Court which has jurisdiction over a large proportion of agricultural and pastoral land in Scotland.

In Scotland business premises are not controlled by Statute to so great an extent as in England, but the Tenancy of Shops (Scotland) Acts, 1949 and 1964 give a measure of security to tenants of shops. These Acts enable the tenant of a shop who is threatened with eviction to apply to the Sheriff for a renewal of the tenancy. If the landlord has offered to sell the subjects to the tenant at an agreed price the application for a renewal of the tenancy may be dismissed. Reference should be made to Section 1 (3) of the 1949 Act for particulars of other circumstances under which the Sheriff has a discretion to dismiss an application. The Acts apply to premises held by the Crown or Government Departments, either as landlord or tenant.

The Housing (Scotland) Act 1969 and the Rent (Scotland) Act 1971, as amended by the Rent Act 1974, define controlled tenancies and regulated tenancies, both furnished and unfurnished, and lay down the system by which a landlord or tenant may obtain from the Rent Officer registration of a fair rent. The Acts also give to the tenants either of furnished or unfurnished lets a substantial degree of security of tenure. There are, however, certain exceptions; thus, they do not apply to tenancies where the interest belongs to the Crown, or to a local authority, a development corporation or the Housing Corporation of new towns. There must be a true tenancy for the Acts to apply. They do not apply to licensees such as lodgers or persons allowed to occupy houses on a grace and favour basis or to service occupiers. The Acts define the circumstances under which a landlord may apply for increased rent as a consequence of having carried out improvements to his property and also lay down the system of phasing of such rent increases. On the death of a statutory successor to a tenancy the tenancy may pass for a second time to a member of the family or a relative who has been in residence in the house for a period of at least six months The Acts also lay down the duties and functions of Rent Officers and Rent Assessment Committees with regard to unfurnished accommodation and of Rent Tribunals for furnished accommodation.

LEGAL AID

LEGAL AID IN CIVIL PROCEEDINGS

The Legal Aid Act 1974, is designed to make legal aid and advice more readily available for persons of small and moderate means. The main structure of the service is contained in the Act itself and the Regulations made thereunder, administered by the Law Society.

Legal aid is available for proceedings (including matrimonial causes) in the House of Lords, Court of Appeal, High Court, County Courts, Lands Tribunal, Restrictive Practices Court, before the Commons Commissioners, and civil proceedings in Magistrates' Courts. In any event, an application for legal aid will not be approved if it appears that the applicant would gain only a trivial advantage from the proceedings. Further, proceedings wholly or partly in respect of defamation are excepted from the scheme, as are also relator actions and election petitions.

Where a person is concerned in proceedings only in a representative, fiduciary or official capacity, his personal resources are not to be taken into account in considering eligibility for legal aid. Apart from this, eligibility in civil proceedings depends upon

an applicant's "disposable income" and "disposable capital". Legal aid cannot be granted if the former exceeds £1,790 per annum, and a person may be refused assistance if he has a disposable capital of more than £1,200 and it appears that he can afford to proceed without legal aid. Even so, the applicant *may* be required to contribute up to one third the excess of his disposable income above £570, together with the whole excess of his disposable capital above £250. Disposable income is calculated by making deductions from gross income in respect of certain matters such as dependants, interest on loans, income tax, rates, rent and other matters for which the applicant must or reasonably may provide. Disposable capital is calculated by excluding from gross capital part of the value of the house in which the applicant resides, of furniture and household possessions; allowances are made in respect of dependants. Except in cases where the spouses are living apart, or have a contrary interest, any resources of a person's wife or husband are to be treated as that person's resources. These figures will be assessed by the Department of Health and Social Security, and will be certified to a Local Committee, who will determine whether reasonable grounds exist for the grant of a civil aid certificate. Appeal from refusal of a certificate lies to an Area Committee. A person resident in England or Wales desiring legal aid may apply for a certificate to any Local Committee; if resident elsewhere application should be made to a Local Committee for London. However, if the application is made in respect of proceedings in an *appellate* court and the applicant is resident in England or Wales, application should generally be made to any *Area* Committee—if resident elsewhere, to an *Area* Committee for London. If a certificate is granted, the applicant may select his solicitor, and, if necessary, counsel from a panel. The costs of the assisted person's solicitor and counsel will be paid out of the legal aid fund. The court may order that the costs of a successful unassisted party shall be paid out of the legal aid fund.

LEGAL ADVICE AND ASSISTANCE

The Scheme is governed by the Legal Aid Act 1974.

Under this legal advice and assistance scheme a client may obtain such advice or assistance as is normally provided by a solicitor and if necessary the advice of a barrister may be obtained, but the scheme does not extend to taking any step in any proceedings before any court or tribunal. Where legal aid is available for civil proceedings (see above) or in criminal cases (see below) the scheme covers work done in making application for such legal aid.

A person is eligible for advice or assistance under the scheme provided his disposable capital does not exceed £250 and his disposable income does not exceed £30·00 per week or if he receives Supplementary Benefit or Family Income Supplement. For a married man or person with children or other dependants deductions will be made from gross income and capital and allowances are made in respect of income tax, National Insurance contributions, etc. It is intended that the financial limits shall approximate to those applying for legal aid in civil proceedings (see above). Except when they are separated or have conficting interests the means of husband and wife will be aggregated for the purpose of determining financial eligibility. If a person's disposable income exceeds £15·00 per week he will be required to pay a contribution as follows:—

Disposable income over—					
£16·00 but not over £17·00	contribution	£1·50
£17·00 „ „ „ £18·00	„	£3·00
£18·00 „ „ „ £20·00	„	£6·50
£20·00 „ „ „ £22·00	„	£9·00
£22·00 „ „ „ £24·00	„	£12·00
£24·00 „ „ „ £26·00	„	£15·00
£26·00 „ „ „ £28·00	„	£18·00
£28·00 „ „ „ £30·00	„	£21·00

Solicitor's costs and expenses, which should not together exceed £25 (V.A.T. exclusive) without leave of the Area Legal Aid Committee, will be paid out of the client's contribution and any monies recovered in respect of costs or damages from another party and the balance will be paid by the Legal Aid Fund.

The Act also extends the scheme to cover the costs of a solicitor who is present within the precincts of a magistrates' court or county court and is requested by the court to advise or represent a person who is in need of help.

LEGAL AID IN CRIMINAL CASES

The Legal Aid Act 1974 Part II provides for legal aid in criminal proceedings. A criminal court (*e.g.*, magistrates' court, Crown Court) has power to order legal aid to be granted where it appears desirable to do so in the interests of justice. The court shall make an order in certain cases, *e.g.*, where a person is committed for trial on a charge of murder. However, the court may not make an order unless it appears to the court that the person's means are such that he requires assistance in meeting the costs of the particular proceedings in question. Application should be made to the appropriate court where proceedings are to take place.

An applicant may be required to make a contribution towards the costs of the action. In order to ascertain the amount of this contribution he will have to produce written evidence of his means. Any assessment of means will be carried out by the Supplementary Benefits Commission, which will report to the court. No contribution will be required from a person who has insufficient means.

Any practising barrister or solicitor may act for a legally aided person in criminal proceedings unless excluded by reason of misconduct. In general where legal aid is given it will normally include representation by both counsel and solicitor. However, in connection with magistrates' courts, representation will be by solicitor alone unless it is a serious offence.

Where any doubt arises about the grant of a legal aid order that doubt is to be resolved in favour of the applicant. The court also has power to amend or revoke a legal aid order. Legal aid may also be granted in connection with appellate proceedings, *e.g.*, on appeal to the Criminal Division of the Court of Appeal under the Criminal Appeal Act, 1968.

SCOTLAND
Civil Proceedings

The Legal Aid (Scotland) Act, 1967 and the Legal Advice and Assistance Act, 1972 form the basis of a scheme to provide legal advice in most civil actions in the House of Lords on appeals from the Court of Session, in the Court of Session, the Lands Valuation Appeal Court, the Scottish Land Court, the Sheriff Court, the Restrictive Practices Court and Lands Tribunals for Scotland.

As to those to whom legal aid is available, the same considerations as to income and capital apply in Scotland as in England. (*See* the preceding paragraph.) A person believing himself to be eligible may instruct any solicitor of his own choice who

is on the official lists, or he may apply for a solicitor to one of the various Legal Aid Committees which are set up to administer the scheme. In a case where litigation is not immediately necessary, the client can seek advice under the Legal Advice and Assistance Act 1972 which is similar to the legal advice and assistance provisions of the Legal Aid Act 1974 (see above). In an instance where litigation is expected, application for a certificate granting legal aid is thereafter made to the appropriate Committee by the applicant's solicitor, who is required to prepare, for the signature of the applicant, a memorandum setting forth the grounds of the proposed action. Investigation into the applicant's financial means is carried out by the Supplementary Benefits Commission after the Committee has considered the memorandum and, on a suitable contribution, if any, by the applicant being approved, a Certificate is granted enabling the applicant to proceed with his action. The Legal Aid (Scotland) Act, 1967 provides for the payment (to a limited extent) out of the legal aid funds of expenses incurred by successful opponents of legally aided litigants.

LEGAL ADVICE

Legal advice, as distinct from legal aid in proceedings, is available to anyone in Scotland on terms similar to those stated in a preceding paragraph dealing with legal advice in England—the Scottish scheme being administered under the Legal Advice and Assistance Act 1972.

Criminal Proceedings

Legal Aid (Scotland) (Criminal Proceedings) Regulations, 1964, which came into operation in October 1964, provide for the administration of criminal legal aid.

TOWN AND COUNTRY PLANNING

The Town and Country Planning Act 1971 (consolidating earlier Acts) contains very far-reaching provisions affecting the liberty of an owner of land to develop and use it as he will. A person has generally to get planning permission before carrying out any development on his land from the Local Planning Authority. Development charge is not payable in respect of operations begun or uses of land instituted on or after November 18, 1952. By the Land Commission (Dissolution) Act 1971, betterment levy, which was formerly payable on the realization of the development value of land, is not chargeable on any transactions carried out after July 23, 1970. This Act extends to Scotland. A Development Land Tax is proposed which will be charged from August 1, 1976, in respect of the realization of development value of land in the U.K.

What is Development:—
(a) Carrying out of building, engineering, mining or other operations.
(b) Making a material change in use.
It is expressly provided that if one dwelling-house is converted into two or more dwelling-houses, this involves a material change in use.
Examples of what is not deemed Development:—
(a) Maintaining, improving or altering the interior of a building (except works for making good war damage), provided there is no material change to the exterior, with the exception that since January 1, 1969, any expansion of a building below ground level constitutes development.
(b) Change of use of property within the curtilage of a dwelling-house for a purpose incidental to the use of the dwelling-house as such. (It will,

however, be development if building operations are carried out.)
Application can be made to the Local Planning Authority to determine whether or not an operation or change of use constitutes development.
Planning Permission.—Application for such permission is not always necessary, as the Secretary of State may make Development Orders giving general permission for a specified type of development. Thus a General Development Order of 1973 specifies a number of types of development for which no permission is required, *e.g.*, enlargement of a dwelling-house (including erection of a garage), so long as the cubic content of the original dwelling (external measurement) is not exceeded by more than 50 cubic metres or one-tenth, whichever is greater, subject to a maximum of 115 cubic metres.
Appeal against refusal of permission lies to the Secretary of State and from his decision, in limited circumstances, to the High Court. If the result of the appeal is unsatisfactory, an applicant may in certain circumstances require the Council to purchase the land.
Enforcement Notice.—If development is carried out without permission, or in defiance of conditions attached to such permission, the Local Planning Authority may serve an enforcement notice on the owner of the land calling upon him to demolish or alter any building, or to discontinue the use of land, or to comply with the said conditions. If the notice is not complied with, the Local Planning Authority may take appropriate steps to enforce it, recovering their expenses from the owner for the time being of the land. Appeal against an enforcement notice lies to the Secretary of State.

VOTERS' QUALIFICATIONS

The franchise is governed by the Representation of the People Acts, the most important of which are the Act of 1949 (as amended) and the Act of 1969. Those entitled to vote as electors at a parliamentary election in any constituency are all persons resident there on the qualifying date who, at that date are British subjects or citizens of the Republic of Ireland of at least 18 years of age and not subject to any legal incapacity to vote. In addition, a person who is of voting age on the date of the poll at a parliamentary or local government election is entitled to vote, whether or not he is of voting age on the qualifying date. Accordingly, a qualified person will be entitled to be registered in a register of parliamentary electors or a register of local government electors if he will attain voting age within twelve months from the date on which the register is required to be published. Since the Electoral Registers Act of 1949, the registers are prepared once in each year only. Under the Electoral Registers Act, 1953, the Register (of parliamentary and local government electors or, in Northern Ireland, of parliamentary electors) is published not later than February 15 in each year and is for use in the period of 12 months commencing on February 16. The qualifying date referred to is, in England, Wales and Scotland the preceding October 10, and in Northern Ireland the preceding September 15.
The Register is prepared by the Registration Officer in each constituency in Great Britain. It is the registration officer's duty to have a house to house or other official inquiry made as to the persons entitled to be registered and to publish preliminary electors lists showing the persons appearing to him to be entitled to be registered. Any person whose name is omitted may claim registration, and any person on the list may object to the inclusion therein of other persons' names: the registration

officer determines the claims and objections which must generally be lodged by December 16 in each year. The procedure is slightly different for Northern Ireland.

Special provision is made for " Service voters " (and persons employed by the British Council in posts outside the United Kingdom), who include wives of Service voters resident with their husbands outside the United Kingdom. Such persons may make a Service declaration in a prescribed form and are then treated as resident at the address specified in the declaration. Service voters may vote by post or by proxy, on making the necessary application to the registration officer.

Certain other persons (*e.g.*, those unable to go in person to the polling station owing to the general nature of their occupation, blindness or other physical incapacity, etc.) may vote by post or in some cases, by proxy as " absent voters ". Section 5 of the 1969 Act extends to certain married persons the right to vote by proxy or by post.

The local government franchise now depends solely upon residence in the area, the previous non-resident qualification for owners of property having been abolished by the Representation of the People Act, 1969, with effect from February 16, 1970. There are provisions, similar to those relating to the parliamentary franchise, for the preparation of registers, etc., and in fact the same register is used, as far as possible, with a mark indicating those persons entitled to vote for local government purposes only. The Acts apply generally to Scotland where certain matters relating to local government and parliamentary elections are further regulated by Representation of the People (Scotland) Regulations, 1949.

INCOME TAX 1976–77

Income Tax is chargeable on the income of all individuals and persons other than bodies corporate.

Income Tax is a tax on annual income, represented by money or money's worth. In general, the charge to tax is on the full amount of income arising for the year of assessment, the fiscal year which runs from April 6 in one year to April 5 in the next, subject to the deductions authorized in the Income Tax Acts. Under Schedule D, however, the assessment is made on the profits or gains of a continuing trade or profession for the year preceding the year of assessment, which is called the " basis year ". The profits are arrived at on ordinary accountancy principles and then adjusted for tax purposes. The profits for the accounting year of the trade or profession which ends in the fiscal year preceding the year of assessment are the profits of the " basis year ".

Broadly, the charge to tax is on income arising in the United Kingdom, or on income derived from home or abroad by residents in the United Kingdom. An individual is resident and ordinarily resident in the United Kingdom if he is living here in the ordinary course of his life or for an extended period; also, though normally he lives here, if he is abroad for occasional residence only; or if he visits the United Kingdom year by year and, over a period of four years he spends an average of three months or more in this country, even though his main home is abroad.

The income of a married woman living with her husband is aggregated with his income although, with effect from the year of assessment 1976/77, this does not apply for the year of assessment in which the marriage occurs. Where the income falls to be aggregated, separate assessment (which divides the liability between husband and wife) may be claimed but the total tax due remains the same. The earned income of a married woman may be assessed as if she were not married provided that on the balance of their joint income the husband is assessed as a single man.

Income Tax is imposed at the rates specified by the annual Finance Acts. From April 1973 a single graduated tax replaced the separate income tax and surtax which operated in earlier years. After deducting personal allowances and reliefs the balance of income is now taxed at a basic rate of 35 per cent. Where the balance of income exceeds £5,000 the excess is charged at higher rates which start at 40 per cent. and reach a maximum of 83 per cent.

Where investment income exceeds £1,000 an investment income surcharge at 10 per cent. is payable on the first £1,000 of the excess and at 15 per cent. on the balance of the excess so that where income is sufficiently large to attract the maximum rate of 83 per cent. the top slice of investment income will be charged at 98 per cent. However, if the taxpayer or his wife living with him is sixty-five years of age the 10 per cent. surcharge is not payable on the first £500 of the excess over £1,000.

The enactments relating to Income Tax were consolidated in the Income and Corporation Tax Act 1970 as amended by subsequent Finance Acts.

The tables which follow show the tax payable for 1976/7 by an individual on the amount of income specified, after deduction of the personal allowance and children's allowance (where appropriate). The taxpayer may, however, be entitled to further reliefs which would reduce the tax payable below the amounts shown in the tables.

The income and profits of bodies corporate are subject to Corporation Tax which is outside the scope of this article. Some important changes in the system of Corporation Tax which came into effect in 1973/74 are, however, dealt with in a special article (*see* Index).

Assessment.—The Income Tax Acts provide for tax to be assessed and collected under a number of Schedules which deal with separate sources of income:

Schedule A.—Under this schedule are assessed those receipts previously dealt with under Case VIII of Schedule D, viz.: ground rents, certain other receipts from land (other than mineral rents and royalties), rents (less expenditure on maintenance, insurance and repairs) and premiums on leases for less than fifty years. Such premiums are assessed on the amount received less 2 per cent. for every year after the first year. " Lease " includes any tenancy. Furnished letting income is normally assessed under Case VI, Schedule D without distinguishing the receipts as between the space let and the furniture hire, but rent for the space can be distinguished and assessed under Schedule A, the profit on the hire of furniture being assessed under Case VI, Schedule D.

Under Schedule B.—Assessment under this Schedule is now restricted to woodlands in the United Kingdom managed on a commercial basis with a view to the realization of profits. The assessment of woodlands will be based on one third of the annual value of the land arrived at on the normal rating basis on the assumption that the lands were let and occupied in their natural and unimproved state. The taxpayer has the option to be assessed under Case I, Schedule D on the results shown by the accounts instead.

(1) Single Persons (under 65 years of age)

Income		Income all Earned		All Investment Income	
Ann.	(Wkly.)	Income Tax	Average Rate per cent.	Income Tax and Investment Income Surcharge	Average Rate per cent.
£728	(£14)	*Nil*	*Nil*	*Nil*	*Nil*
780	(£15)	£15·75	2·0	£15·75	2·0
832	(£16)	33·95	4·1	33·95	4·1
884	(£17)	52·15	5·9	52·75	5·9
936	(£18)	70·35	7·5	70·35	7·5
1,000		92·75	9·3	92·75	9·3
1,040	(£20)	106·75	10·3	110·75	10·7
1,250		180·25	14·4	205·25	16·4
1,500		267·75	17·8	317·75	21·2
1,750		355·25	20·3	430·25	24·6
2,000		442·75	22·1	542·75	27·1
2,250		530 25	23·6	667·75	29·7
2,500		617·75	24·7	792·75	31·7
2,750		705·25	25·6	917·75	33·4
3,000		792·75	26·4	1,042·75	34·8
3,500		967·75	27·6	1,292·75	36·9
4,000		1,142·75	28·6	1,542·75	38·6
4,500		1,317·75	29·3	1,792·75	39·8
5,000		1,492·75	29·9	2,042·75	40·9
6,000		1,856·00	30·9	2,556·00	42·6
7,000		2,294·25	32·8	3,144·25	44·9
8,000		2,782·50	34·8	3,782·50	47·3
9,000		3,320·75	36·9	4,470·75	49·7
10,000		3,909·00	39·1	5,209·00	52·1
12,000		5,172·25	43·1	6,772·25	56·4
15,000		7,235·50	48·2	9,285·50	61·7
20,000		10,948·75	54·7	13,748·75	68·7
25,000		15,039·95	60·2	18,589·95	74·4
30,000		19,189·95	64·0	23,489·95	78·3
40,000		27,489·95	68·7	33,289·95	83·2
50,000		35,789·95	71·6	43,089·95	86·2
100,000		77,289·95	77·3	92,009·95	92·0

Under Schedule C.—Assessed on the paying agent. Not of concern to the individual taxpayer.

Under Schedule D.—This schedule is divided into six cases as follows: Cases I and II—Profits of trades, business, commercial activities on land including farming, professions or vocations.

Case III.—Interest on Government Stocks not taxed at source (*e.g.*, War Loan, British Savings Bonds), bank deposit interest, discounts, etc. Interest on ordinary National Savings Bank and Trustee Savings Bank up to £40 is exempt from Income Tax. This exemption applies to both husband and wife separately. Interest on National Savings Bank and Trustee Savings Bank Special Investment Accounts is not exempt.

Cases IV and V.—Interest from foreign or Commonwealth securities, rents, dividends and all other unearned income; assessed on full amount arising, whether remitted or not, where person domiciled and ordinarily resident in the U.K. but on amount remitted only where person not domiciled in the U.K. or a British subject not ordinarily resident. Prior to April 1974 overseas pensions and profits from trades, business and professions exercised abroad were subject to tax if remitted to the U.K. by a person resident in the U.K. From April 6, 1974, persons who are resident and domiciled in the U.K. will be subject to U.K. tax on overseas pensions whether remitted to the U.K. or not, subject to a deduction of one tenth. Residents who are domiciled and ordinarily resident in the U.K. will be subject to U.K. tax assessment on profits from trades, businesses or professions exercised abroad whether remitted or not, subject to a deduction of one quarter.

Case VI.—Sundry profits and annual receipts not assessed under any other case, *e.g.*, insurance commission, post cessation receipts, certain premiums paid to persons other than landlords and numerous other receipts treated as income and specifically charged hereunder. As to furnished lettings, see under Schedule A.

Losses.—Under Cases I, II, V and VI losses can in general be carried forward against corresponding income or profits of subsequent fiscal years without time limits. Losses under Cases I and II (and from overseas activities to the extent that a profit would be assessable under Case V) may alternatively be set off against other income of the same year or the year next following.

Capital Gains.—A separate long-term gains tax was introduced in the Finance Act 1965 and this applies to gains realized on chargeable assets disposed of after April 6, 1965. In the case of assets owned on April 6, 1965 and disposed subsequently only the proportion of the gain attributable to the period after that date is chargeable. The detailed rules of this tax are outside the scope of this article.

From 1970/71 to 1975/76, both inclusive, where the combined sales of husband and wife do not produce more than £500, such sales will not attract capital gains tax. With effect from the year 1976/77 the limit is increased to £1000.

The calculation of gains and losses on quoted securities held at April 6, 1965, which are disposed of after March 19, 1968, may be made solely by

(2) Married Couple Without Children

Income		Income all Earned		All Investment Income	
Ann.	(Wkly.)	Income Tax	Average Rate per cent.	Income Tax and Investment Income Surcharge	Average Rate per cent.
£1,040	(£20)	*Nil*	*Nil*	*Nil*	*Nil*
1,200		£40·25	3·3	£51·75	4·3
1,300		75·25	5·8	96·75	7·4
1,400		110·25	7·9	141·75	10·1
1,500		145·25	9·7	186·75	12·4
1,750		232·75	13·3	299·25	17·1
2,000		320·25	16·0	411·75	20·6
2,250		407·75	18·1	605·25	26·9
2,500		495·25	19·8	657·50	26·3
2,750		582·75	21·2	782·50	28·5
3,000		670·25	22·3	907·50	30·2
3,500		845·25	24·1	1,157·50	33·1
4,000		1,020·25	25·5	1,407·50	35·2
4,500		1,195·25	26·6	1,657·50	36·8
5,000		1,370·25	27·4	1,907·50	38·1
6,000		1,720·25	28·7	2,407·50	40·1
7,000		2,136·75	30·5	2,974·00	42·5
8,000		2,607·50	32·6	3,594·75	44·9
9,000		3,128·25	34·8	4,265·50	47·4
10,000		3,699·00	37·0	4,986·25	49·9
12,000		4,944·75	41·2	6,532·00	54·4
15,000		6,990·50	46·6	9,027·75	60·2
20,000		10,686·25	53·4	13,473·50	67·4
25,000		14,749·45	59·0	18,286·70	73·1
30,000		18,899·45	63·0	23,186·70	77·3
40,000		27,199·45	68·0	32,986·70	82·5
50,000		35,499·45	71·0	42,786·70	85·6
100,000		76,999·45	77·0	91,786·70	91·8

reference to the market value at April 6, 1965, if the taxpayer elects to deal with all holdings in this way. Separate elections may, however, be made in relation to fixed interest stocks and preference shares and/or other quoted shares.

To the extent that capital gains from disposals after December 1973 of interests in land in the United Kingdom were development gains, computed under complicated provisions found in the 1974 Finance Act, they were chargeable to income tax under Case VI of Schedule D, only the balance of the gain being charged to capital gains tax. Development gains accruing from disposals on or after August 1st 1976 are not subject to income tax but may be chargeable to development land tax under the Development Land Tax Act 1976.

The rate of Capital Gains Tax payable by an individual is 30 per cent. but if the total of an individual's chargeable gains in any year of assessment does not exceed £5,000, one half the net gains may be charged at the taxpayer's marginal rate of tax, treating one half the gain as ordinary investment income. The effect of this is that the 30 per cent. rate is only used where the taxpayer's income is such as to attract a top rate (including where appropriate, investment income surcharge) in excess of 60 per cent. On sales of holdings in authorized unit trusts and approved investment trusts the capital gains tax payable is reduced by a credit equal to whichever is least of—

(i) the amount of the capital gains tax;
(ii) 17·5 per cent. of the chargeable gains on disposal of the units;
(iii) 17·5 per cent. of all chargeable gains accruing to the individual in the year.

From April 15, 1960, gains on the disposal of securities issued or guaranteed by the British Government are not subject to Capital Gains Tax. This exemption does not apply, however, where such stocks are sold within twelve months after being acquired.

Under Schedule E.—Income from all offices, employments and pensions, including salaries, wages, emoluments, director's fees, etc. Assessed on the actual earnings for the year of assessment. Foreign earnings of this type which prior to April 1974 would have been subject to the " remittance " basis of assessment are now assessable on the amount arising but subject to a deduction of 25 or 100 per cent., depending on the circumstances, viz: where the taxpayer is resident, ordinarily resident and domiciled in the U.K. and the employment is carried on wholly outside the U.K. for 365 days or more continuously the deduction will be 100 per cent. Similar earnings where the taxpayer is absent for a period less than 365 days will attract a deduction of 25 per cent.

There are special more complex rules to cover the emoluments received by persons resident but not domiciled in the U.K. from foreign employers. In general, where the duties are performed in the U.K. such earnings will be assessable subject to a deduction of 50 per cent. for and from 1974/75 but from 1976/77 the deduction will be reduced to 25 per cent. where the taxpayer has been resident in the U.K. for at least nine out of the last ten preceding tax years.

In arriving at the amount to be assessed under Schedule E all expenses incurred wholly, exclusively and necessarily in the performance of the duties of the office or employment may be deducted, including fees and subscriptions to certain professional bodies and learned societies and, within strict limits, depreciation allowances.

(3) Married Couples with One Child

Income	All Earned Income					
	One Child not over 11		One Child over 11 but not over 16		One Child over 16	
	Income Tax	Average Rate %	Income Tax	Average Rate %	Income Tax	Average Rate %
£1,385	*Nil*	*Nil*	*Nil*	*Nil*	*Nil*	*Nil*
1,400	£5·25	·4	*Nil*	*Nil*	*Nil*	*Nil*
1,500	40·25	2·7	£28·00	1·9	£17·50	1·1
1,750	127·75	7·3	115·50	6·6	105·00	6·0
2,000	215·25	10·8	203·00	10·1	192·50	9·6
2,250	302·75	13·5	290·50	12·9	280·00	12·4
2,500	390·25	15·6	378·00	15·1	367·50	14·7
2,750	477·75	17·4	465·50	17·0	455·00	16·5
3,000	565·25	18·8	553·00	18·4	542·50	18·1
3,500	740·25	21·1	728·00	20·8	717·50	20·5
4,000	915·25	22·9	903·00	22·6	892·50	22·3
4,500	1,090·25	24·2	1,078·00	24·0	1,067·50	23·8
5,000	1,265·25	25·3	1,253·00	25·1	1,232·50	24·8
6,000	1,615·25	26·9	1,603·00	26·7	1,592·50	26·5
7,000	2,001·75	28·6	1,986·00	28·4	1,972·50	28·2
8,000	2,457·50	30·7	2,440·00	30·5	2,425·00	30·3
9,000	2,963·25	32·9	2,944·00	32·7	2,927·50	32·5
10,000	3,519·00	35·2	3,498·00	35·0	3,480·00	34·8
12,000	4,749·75	39·6	4,727·00	39·4	4,707·50	39·2
15,000	6,780·50	45·2	6,756·00	45·0	6,735·00	44·7
20,000	10,461·25	52·3	10,435·00	52·2	10,412·50	52·1
25,000	14,500·45	58·0	14,471·40	57·9	14,446·50	57·8
30,000	18,650·45	62·2	18,621·40	62·1	18,596·50	62·0
40,000	26,950·45	67·4	26,921·40	67·3	26,896·50	67·2
50,000	35,250·45	70·5	35,221·40	70·4	35,196·50	70·4
100,000	76,750·45	76·7	76,721·40	76·7	76,696·50	76·7

Expenses allowances and payments in kind (less expenses incurred in performance of duties) to directors and employees enjoying emoluments of £5,000 (£2,000 before 1975/76) or more are assessable. From 1965/6 onwards expenses incurred in providing business entertainment (including hospitality of any kind and gifts) are not allowable except when provided for an overseas customer. Where any person has premises available for his use by reason of his employment and either pays no rent or pays less than the annual value he will be charged to tax on the annual value less any rent paid. Provision is also made for charging directors and employees to tax on the value of benefits obtained from the issue or transfer of shares on advantageous terms and from subsidized medical insurance schemes. Certain payments made on retirement or removal from a person's office or employment (in excess of £5,000) are assessable to tax on him.

Exemptions.—Unemployment, sickness and maternity benefit and grant, and death grant payable under the National Insurance Acts are not assessable to income tax, but (retirement, widows, etc.) pensions and child benefits (family allowances) are included in the charge under this schedule. Under Finance Act 1966 statutory redundancy payments are exempt from tax.

Where the emoluments are paid by an employer in the U.K., deduction of income tax is made by the employee's code number. As to P.A.Y.E. (pay as you earn) see further below.

Under Schedule F.—From April 6, 1966, onwards income tax was charged on all dividends and distributions made by a U.K. resident company. From April 1973 a U.K. resident company paying a dividend must account to the Revenue for advance corporation tax on the amount of the dividend paid. A shareholder who is resident in the U.K. and who receives such a dividend is taxable under Schedule F on the amount of the dividend plus the advance corporation tax appropriate to it, but is entitled to a credit against tax liability equal to the amount of the advanced corporation tax.

ALLOWANCES.—The following allowances and deductions are given in calculating the income tax payable; this serves to give relief thereon at the highest rate of tax paid but in general the allowances do not affect the investment income surcharge payable.

Personal Allowance.—To single person £735
To married man living with or normally maintaining his wife (but in year of marriage allowance is reduced by 1/12 of £350 for each fiscal month (i.e. ending May 5, June 5, etc.) which ended before the date of marriage) £1,085

When either husband or wife is absent from United Kingdom throughout a complete fiscal year they are treated as separate entities for tax purposes, each entitled to Single Personal Allowance. A married woman permanently separated from her husband is treated as a single woman.

Children.—For each child under 16 (or over that age at the beginning of the fiscal year and receiving full time instruction at a recognized educational establishment, or who is articled or apprenticed) and who does not have income in that year exceeding £350 in his own or her own right, the allowances are:

(a) Child over 16 at commencement of fiscal year £365
(b) Child over 11 at commencement of fiscal year £335
(c) Other children (each) £300

(4) Married Couples with Two Children

Income	All Earned Income					
	Two Children not over 11		Two Children over 11 but not over 16		Two Children over 16	
	Income Tax	Average Rate %	Income Tax	Average Rate %	Income Tax	Average Rate %
£1,633	*Nil*	*Nil*	*Nil*	*Nil*	*Nil*	*Nil*
1,650	£5·95	·4	*Nil*	*Nil*	*Nil*	*Nil*
1,750	40·95	2·3	£16·45	·9	*Nil*	*Nil*
2,000	128·45	6·4	103·95	5·2	£64·75	3·2
2,250	215·95	9·6	191·45	8·5	152·25	6·8
2,500	303·45	12·1	278·95	11·2	239·75	9·6
2,750	390·90	14·2	366·45	13·3	327·25	11·9
3,000	478·45	16·0	453·95	15·1	414·75	13·8
3,500	653·45	18·7	628·95	18·0	589·75	16·8
4,000	828·45	20·7	803·95	20·1	764·75	19·1
4,500	1,003·45	22·3	978·95	21·8	939·75	20·9
5,000	1,178·45	23·6	1,153·95	23·1	1,114·75	22·3
6,000	1,528·45	25·6	1,503·95	25·1	1,464·75	24·6
7,000	1,896·80	27·1	1,868·80	26·7	1,824·00	26·1
8,000	2,340·15	29·3	2,308·65	28·4	22,258·25	28·2
9,000	2,833·50	31·4	2,798·50	31·1	2,742·50	30·5
10,000	3,376·85	33·8	3,338·35	33·4	3,276·75	32·8
12,000	4,588·55	38·2	4,543·05	37·9	4,470·25	37·3
15,000	6,606·90	44·0	6,557·90	43·7	6,479·50	43·2
20,000	10,275·25	51·4	10,222·75	51·1	10,138·75	50·7
25,000	14,294·61	57·2	14,236·51	56·9	14,143·55	56·6
30,000	18,444·61	61·5	18,386·51	61·3	18,293·55	61·0
40,000	26,744·61	66·9	26,686·51	66·7	26,593·55	66·5
50,000	35,044·61	70·1	34,986·51	70·0	34,893·55	69·8
100,000	76,544·61	76·5	76,486·51	76·5	76,393·55	76·4

If a child who is under the age of eighteen years and is unmarried at the end of the year of assessment has earned income not exceeding £235, the full allowance will only be given if his investment income does not exceed £115. Scholarship or bursary does not count as income for this purpose. Marginal relief is given where a child's income exceeds £350 or, when appropriate, the investment income exceeds £115. The child relief will then be reduced by £1 for each £1 by which the child's income exceeds the relevant limit. " Child " includes step-child and adopted child. Child allowance is due to the person who has the custody of and maintains the child. If more than one person could claim the allowance, e.g., if a husband and wife are divorced or separated, the allowance will be apportioned between them as necessary. These allowances are reduced by £52 for each child for whom Child Benefit (Family Allowance) is due for the whole year 1976/7 and by an appropriately smaller amount where the allowance is received for only part of the year.

Dependent Relatives.—The maximum deduction for each dependent relative is normally £100 but an increased allowance of £145 may be claimed where the claimant is a woman (other than a married woman living with her husband). These allowances are reduced by £1 for every £1 by which the relative's own income (excluding voluntary allowances) exceeds the basic National Insurance Retirement Pension. Claimant must maintain relative who must be incapacitated by old age or infirmity from maintaining himself or herself, except in the case of his or his wife's widowed mother (which includes any woman living apart from her husband whose marriage has been dissolved or annulled). If more than one person gives support to the dependent relative then allowance is divided *pro rata*.

Daughter.—A person who by reason of his or his wife's old age or infirmity has to retain the services of a daughter resident with him or her is entitled to an allowance of £55.

Housekeeper or Person looking after children.— An allowance to:

(a) Widows and Widowers: Housekeeper allowance of £100 in respect of a housekeeper employed as such or a female relative of his or hers or of the deceased spouse acting as housekeeper. These females must be resident.

(b) Unmarried man: Housekeeper allowance of £100 in respect of a female relative living with and maintained by him to look after brothers or sisters for whom he is entitled to child allowance.

(c) If widow or widower entitled to the child allowance is also entitled to an allowance of £350. The relief is also available to a married man whose wife is totally incapacitated by physical or mental infirmity throughout the year. This relief cannot be claimed in addition to the housekeeper allowance of £100.

Blind Persons.—An allowance of £180 less the amount of any tax-free disability payment receivable may be claimed by a registered blind person provided that the Daughter's Allowance of £55 is not also claimed. Where both spouses are blind the maximum allowance is £360 less any tax-free disability receipts. The reliefs quoted are for a full year and must be scaled down where a person is registered as blind for only part of the year.

OTHER TAXES AND STAMP DUTIES

The Commissioners as a general rule allow deeds, etc., to be stamped after execution:—

WITHOUT PENALTY, ON PAYMENT OF DUTY ONLY. Deeds and instruments not otherwise excepted, within 30 days of *first* execution.

NOTE.—Where wholly executed *abroad*, the period begins to run from the date of arrival here.

PENALTIES ENFORCEABLE ON STAMPING, IN ADDITION TO DUTY:—

Instruments presented after the proper time (subject to special provisions in some cases and subject to the commissioner's power to mitigate) a penalty equal to the duty.............................. £10

AGREEMENT for Lease, *see* LEASES.

AGREEMENT FOR SALE OF PROPERTY—charged with *ad val.* duty as if an actual conveyance on sale with certain exceptions, *e.g.* agreements for the sale of land, stocks and shares, goods, wares or merchandise, or a ship (*see* s. 59 (1), Stamp Act 1891). If *ad val.* duty is paid on an agreement in accordance with this provision, the subsequent conveyance or transfer is not chargeable with any *ad val.* duty and the Commissioners will upon application either place a denoting stamp on such conveyance or transfer or will transfer the *ad val.* duty thereto. Further, if such an agreement is rescinded, not performed, etc., the Commissioners will return the *ad val.* duty paid.

AGREEMENT under seal subject to exemptions 50p

APPOINTMENT of a new trustee or in exercise of a power over property, not being by a will; also on retirement of trustee, although no new trustee be appointed............. 50p

ASSIGNMENT:

By way of sale—*see* Conveyance.

By way of gift—*see* Voluntary Disposition.

ASSURANCE—*see* Insurance Policies.

BEARER INSTRUMENT:

Inland bearer instrument, *i.e.* share warrant, stock certificate to bearer or any other instrument to bearer by which stock can be transferred, issued by a company or body formed or established in U.K. Duty of an amount equal to three times the transfer duty (usually £6% of the market value).

Overseas bearer instrument, *i.e.*, such an instrument issued in G.B. by a company formed out of the U.K. Duty equal to twice the transfer duty (usually £4% of the market value). Even if issued out of G.B. the instrument must be stamped before transfer in G.B. The issue or transfer of a bearer instrument relating to stock expressed in the currency of a territory outside the Scheduled territories is exempt from duty.

BILL OF SALE, Absolute, *see* CONVEYANCE ON SALE.

CAPITAL DUTY.—Where a *chargeable transaction* of a *capital company* takes place after July 31, 1973, duty of £1 is payable on every £100 or fraction of £100 of the actual value of the assets contributed by the members (as opposed to the previous duty of 50p per £100 of the nominal capital), provided the place of effective management of the company is in G.B. or its registered office is in G.B. but the place

of its effective management is outside the E.E.C. (Finance Act 1973).

A statement containing prescribed particulars must be delivered to the Commissioners within one month of the transaction unless there is an obligation under the Companies Act 1948 (*e.g.*, on the formation of a limited liability company) or the Limited Partnerships Act 1907 (*e.g.*, on the registration of a limited partnership) to send a statement to the registrar of companies as a result of the transaction.

Capital company includes a company incorporated with limited liability under U.K. law, a limited partnership under the Limited Partnerships Act 1907, a company incorporated according to the law of any other member of the E.E.C. and any other corporation or body of persons whose members have the right freely to dispose of their shares and whose liability for debts is limited.

Chargeable transaction includes the formation of a capital company, an increase in its capital by the contribution of assets of any kind, the transfer to G.B. of its place of effective management from a country outside the E.E.C. if its registered office is in such a country, and the transfer to G.B. of its registered office from a country outside the E.E.C. if its place of effective management is in such a country.

CAPITAL TRANSFER TAX

A new tax on the transmission of wealth, made by way of gift during a person's lifetime and on death, has been introduced by the Finance Act 1975. It applies retrospectively to March 27, 1974, unless the donor dies before March 13, 1975 (when Estate Duty or modified Estate Duty will apply).

Tax is charged at progressive rates on the cumulative totals of chargeable gifts made during a person's lifetime, with a final cumulation of the value of a person's estate on his death. The rates of tax for lifetime transfers are those shown in Table 1. For transfers on death, or within 3 years of death, the rates applicable are those in Table 2.

In calculating the value transferred on lifetime

TABLE 1

Value transferred		Rate of tax
Lower limit £	Upper limit £	Per cent.
0	15,000	*Nil*
15,000	20,000	5
20,000	25,000	7½
25,000	30,000	10
30,000	40,000	12½
40,000	50,000	15
50,000	60,000	17½
60,000	80,000	20
80,000	100,000	22½
100,000	120,000	27½
120,000	150,000	35
150,000	200,000	42½
200,000	250,000	50
250,000	300,000	55
300,000	500,000	60
500,000	1,000,000	65
1,000,000	2,000,000	70
2,000,000	—	75

TABLE 2

Value transferred		Rate of tax
Lower limit £	Upper limit £	Per cent.
0	15,000	Nil
15,000	20,000	10
20,000	25,000	15
25,000	30,000	20
30,000	40,000	25
40,000	50,000	30
50,000	60,000	35
60,000	80,000	40
80,000	100,000	45
100,000	120,000	50
120,000	150,000	55
150,000	500,000	60
500,000	1,000,000	65
1,000,000	2,000,000	70
2,000,000	—	75

gifts, the amount of tax paid by the donor on the gift must be taken into account. The value transferred on death is the value of the person's estate at his death.

Certain exemptions and reliefs are given, including:

(a) *For lifetime transfers only:*
 (i) The first £2,000 of gifts made in each tax year (April 6 to the following April 5) are exempt. Only the balance over £2,000 is taxable. There is provision for the carry forward of this relief for one year only, in so far as it has not been used in the previous year.
 (ii) Gifts not exceeding £100 to any one donee in the tax year are exempt. The excess only is taxable. This relief is in addition to the £2,000 relief.
 (iii) Gifts which are normal expenditure out of income are exempt, provided the donor is left with sufficient income to maintain his standard of living.
 (iv) Gifts in consideration of marriage are exempt up to £5,000 if made by a parent; £2,500 if made by a grandparent or some other lineal ancestor, or by one party to another; and £1,000 in any other case.
 (v) Gifts of certain types of property, including works of art, are exempt if made to a body not established or conducted for profit.

(b) *For lifetime transfers and on death:*
 (i) Transfers between spouses are exempt to the extent that the gift increases the value of the donee spouse's estate.
 (ii) Lifetime gifts to Charities and certain Political Parties are exempt without limit. If made on death or within one year of death, gifts are exempt up to £100,000 only.
 (iii) Gifts to listed heritage bodies, including National Gallery, British Museum, and Government Departments, are exempt.
 (iv) Agricultural relief:
 Provided certain conditions are satisfied, on a transfer of Agricultural land, the value is reduced to half the actual value. To satisfy the conditions, *inter alia*, the transferor must be a working farmer (as defined) and must have occupied the land for the purposes of Agriculture for two years up to the time of the transfer.

(c) *For transfers on death only:*
 Conditional exemptions exist for works of art, timber and for death on active service.

Tax must be paid within 6 months of the end of the month in which the chargeable event occurs unless the event is a lifetime transfer, made between April 5 and October 1 in any year, when tax is due at the end of the next following April. In certain circumstances, tax may be payable by instalments.

Interest on unpaid tax runs from the date the tax is due, at 6% p.a. on death and 9% p.a. otherwise.

The transition from Estate Duty
 The normal rules for Estate Duty apply for deaths up to November 12, 1974 (*see post*, p. 1189). For deaths after that date and before March 13, 1975, Estate Duty is levied, but at the rates given in Table 2 above, and, *inter alia*, transfers between spouses are totally exempt (and not limited to £15,000). No Capital Transfer Tax is payable on lifetime gifts where death occurs before March 13, 1975.

For deaths after March 12, 1975, Capital Transfer Tax only, applies.

CONTRACT, *see* AGREEMENT.

CONTRACT NOTE for the sale or purchase of any stock or marketable security; where the value of the stock or marketable security—

Exceeds £100 and does not exceed £500...	10p
,, £500 ,, ,, ,, ,, £1,500..	30p
,, £1,500...........................	60p
(Special adhesive stamps)	

Option Contract Notes are chargeable with half the above rates only, unless the option is a double one.

Contract Note following a duly stamped option contract note chargeable with half the above rates only.

CONTRACT OR GRANT FOR PAYMENT OF A SUPERANNUATION ANNUITY: for every £10 or fractional part of £10............... 5p

CONVEYANCE OR TRANSFER ON SALE (in the case of a Voluntary Disposition, *see* below, p. 1194) of any property (*except* stock or marketable securities for which, *see* above), where the Conveyance or Transfer contains a certificate of value certifying that the transaction does not form part of a larger transaction or a series of transactions in respect of which the aggregate amount or value of the consideration exceeds £15,000. nil
 Exceeds £20,000 (for every £50 or fraction of £50)........................... 25p
 Exceeds £25,000 (for every £50 or fraction of £50)........................... 50p
 Exceeds £30,000 (for every £50 or fraction of £50)........................... 75p
 If the Conveyance or Transfer on Sale does not contain the appropriate statement duty at the full rate of £1 for every £50 or fraction of £50 will be payable whatever the amount of the consideration.
 However, if the consideration does not exceed £300, and the instrument does not contain a certificate of value, then:
 Where the consideration:
 Does not exceed £5................... 10p
 Exceeds £5 but does not exceed £100, 20p per £10 or part.
 Exceeds £100 but does not exceed £300, 40p per £20 or part.

If in such a case the instrument is certified at £20,000 it is stamped at 25% of the above rates with a minimum of 5p; if certified at £25,000 it is stamped at 50% of the above rates; if certified at £30,000 it is stamped at 75% of the above rates with a minimum of 10p.

CONVEYANCE OR TRANSFER of any other kind
...........................fixed duty   50p
Included under this head are Transfers for nominal consideration within any of the following categories:

(a) Transfers vesting the property in trustees on the appointment of a new trustee of a pre-existing trust, or on the retirement of a trustee.

(b) Transfers, where no beneficial interest in the property passes, (i) to a mere nominee of the transferor; (ii) from a mere nominee of the transferee; (iii) from one nominee to another nominee of the same beneficial owner.

(c) Transfer to a residuary legatee of stock, etc., forming part of the residue divisible under a will.

(d) Transfers to a beneficiary under a will of a specific legacy of stock, etc. (*Note.*—Transfers by executors in discharge, or partial discharge, of a pecuniary legacy (unless made under an express power of appropriation) are chargeable with *ad valorem* duty on the amount of the legacy so discharged.)

(e) Transfers of stock, etc., forming part of an intestate's estate to the person entitled to it.

(f) Transfers to a beneficiary under settlement on a distribution of the trust funds of stock, etc., forming the share or part of the share of those funds to which the beneficiary is entitled in accordance with the terms of the settlement.

(g) Transfers on the occasion of a marriage to trustees of stocks, etc., to be held on the terms of a settlement made in consideration of marriage.

(h) Transfers by the liquidator of a company of stocks, etc., forming part of the assets of the company to the persons who were shareholders, in satisfaction of their rights on a winding-up.

The evidence necessary to establish that a transfer is liable to the fixed duty of 50p should take the form of a certificate setting forth the facts of the transaction. In cases falling within (b) such a certificate should be signed by (1) both transferor and transferee or (2) a member of a Stock Exchange or a solicitor acting for one or other of the parties or (3) an accredited representative of a bank; in the last case when the bank or its official nominee is a party to the transfer, the certificate, instead of setting out the facts, may be to the effect that " the transfer is excepted from Section 74 of the Finance (1909–10) Act 1910." A certificate in other cases should be signed by a solicitor or other person (*e.g.*, a bank acting as trustee or executor) having a full knowledge of the facts.

Registering Officers will in any case in which a Marketing Officer's certificate has not been given require such evidence in order to satisfy themselves that a transfer stamped with the 50p fixed duty is duly stamped.

COVENANT—For original creation and sale of any annuity, *see* CONVEYANCE.
Separate Deed of, made on occasion of sale, but not being an instrument chargeable with *ad valorem* duty as a Conveyance: same duty as a Conveyance on sale, but not to exceed......................   50p

DEATH DUTIES, *see* ESTATE DUTY.

DECLARATION OF TRUST, not being a Will or Settlement............................   50p

DEED of any kind not charged under some special head............................   50p

DEMISE, *see* LEASE.

DUPLICATE OR COUNTERPART
Same duty as original, but not to exceed..   50p

GIFT (*see* VOLUNTARY DISPOSITION, p. 1194).
GUARANTEE:
If under seal.........................   50p
HIRE-PURCHASE AGREEMENTS:
Under seal...........................   50p
(Finance Act 1907, s. 7)
N.B.—If the agreement amounts to a " credit-sale " the position is the same.
INSURANCE POLICIES:
Life:—
Exc. £50 and not exc. £1,000, for every £100 or part of £100................   5p
Exc. £1,000, for every £1,000 or any fractional part of £1,000.............   50p
Made after 1 August 1966 for period not exceeding 2 years....................   5p

LEASES:—Lease or tack for any definite term less than a year of any furnished dwelling-house or apartments where the rent for such term exceeds £250, £1; of any lands, tenements, etc., in consideration of any rent, according to the following table:—

Annual rent not exceeding	*Term not exceeding			Term exceeding 100 years
	7 years	35 years	100 years	
£	£ p	£ p	£ p	£ p
5	Nil	0·10	0·60	1·20
10	Nil	0·20	1·20	2·40
15	Nil	0·30	1·80	3·60
20	Nil	0·40	2·40	4·80
25	Nil	0·50	3·00	6·00
50	Nil	1·00	6·00	12·00
75	Nil	1·50	9·00	18·00
100	Nil	2·00	12·00	24·00
150	Nil	3·00	18·00	36·00
200	Nil	4·00	24·00	48·00
250	Nil	5·00	30·00	60·00
Exceeding £250 for every £50 or fraction of £50	0·05	1·00	6·00	12·00

*If the term is indefinite the same duty is payable as if the term did not exceed 7 years.

Agreement for lease not exceeding 35 years, same as actual lease.

Where a consideration other than rent is payable and duty is charged on that consideration at conveyance rates, the same graduation applies where the consideration does not exceed £30,000 as under Conveyance or Transfer on Sale (except stock or marketable securities), provided that any rent payable does not exceed £150 a year.

MORTGAGES are exempt.

POWER OF ATTORNEY, etc., for receiving certain prize-money or wages 5p

For the receipt of any money, or bill, or note, not exceeding £20, or of any periodical payments not exceeding £10 annually. 25p

For the receipt of dividends or interest of any stock, if for one payment only. 5p
Ditto in any other case 25p
Power of attorney of any other kind 50p

PROCURATION, Deed, etc., of. 50p

RECEIPTS FOR SALARIES, Wages and Superannuation, and other like allowances are exempt.

REVOCATION of any TRUST of Property not being a Will 50p

TRANSFER OF STOCK AND SHARES by way of gift or sale—for each £50 or part of £50 £1

UNIT TRUST INSTRUMENT—Any trust instrument of a unit trust scheme—For every

£100, and also for any fractional part of £100, of the amount or value of the property subject to the trusts created or recorded by the instrument. 25p

VOLUNTARY DISPOSITION *inter vivos*:—
On any instrument being a voluntary disposition (*inter vivos*) of any property (except stock or marketable securities, *see ante,* under Conveyance or Transfer) where the value of the property conveyed or transferred does not exceed £15,000 . . . . nil

Exceeds £15,000 but does not exceed £20,000 for every £50 and fraction of £50 25p

Exceeds £20,000 but does not exceed £25,000, for every £50 and fraction of £50 . . . . 50p

Exceeds £25,000 but does not exceed £30,000 for every £50 and fraction of £50 . . . . . . 75p

Exceeds £30,000, for every £50 and fraction of £50. . . . . £1

The instrument must contain similar certificates of value as a Conveyance or Transfer on Sale (*see* p. 1192), with the substitution of the words " property conveyed or transferred " for the word " consideration."

If the value of the property does not exceed £300 the same graduated rates apply as under Conveyance or Transfer on Sale (except Stock or marketable securities).

DISTRIBUTION OF PERSONAL INCOMES BEFORE AND AFTER TAX
Number of Incomes (Thousands)

Range of Income	1959–60	1964–65	1967–68	1968–69	1969–70	1970–71	1971–72	1972–73
£								
Income before tax								
180	1,965	..	..	..	..	..	..	..
275	540	408	263	263	..	..	..	..
300 / 330	2,233	1,814	1,295	1,181	730	..	..	..
400 / 420	2,307	1,878	1,492	1,387	1,222	883	699	..
500 / 595	6,403	4,537	3,869	3,668	3,355	3,021	2,436	1,385
750	3,986	4,501	3,912	3,613	3,291	2,943	2,698	2,314
1,000	1,658	3,498	3,600	3,484	3,243	3,627	2,982	2,325
1,250	614	2,028	2,875	3,001	2,959	2,093	1,979	2,243
1,500	283	956	1,862	2,212	2,487	2,315	2,343	2,323
1,750	165	455	979	1,361	1,729	1,981	2,149	2,196
2,000	187	399	727	949	1,356	3,453	2,772	3,284
2,500	100	193	301	355	508	888	1,334	1,969
3,000	106	180	245	308	387	608	896	1,379
4,000	50	84	121	129	161	228	291	436
5,000	27	50	65	72	86	116	136	160
6,000	26	48	59	70	83	106	134	143
8,000	12	22	28	31	36	47	53	68
10,000	6	12	15	16	19	24	26	39
12,000	5	9	12	12	14	16	20	26
15,000	3	6·5	7·2	8·7	9·4	10·8	12·4	17
20,000	2·6	5·2	5·5	6·3	7·1	7·3	9·0	11·8
50,000	0·2	0·5	0·4	0·5	0·6	0·6	0·9	0·8
100,000 and over	0·1	0·1	0·1	0·1	0·2	0·1	0·1	0·2
Total	20,678	21,074	21,732	22,128	21,683	21,368	20,970	20,319
Income after tax								
180	2,120	..	..	..	..	..	..	..
275	644	447	300	294	..	..	..	..
300 / 330	2,442	2,102	1,454	1,349	913	..	..	..
400 / 420	2,637	2,172	1,956	1,802	1,592	1,197	883	..
500 / 595	6,727	4,145	4,574	4,480	4,165	3,967	3,219	1,808
750	3,785	4,776	4,481	4,215	4,002	3,839	3,301	3,004
1,000	1,292	3,355	3,777	3,873	3,713	3,336	3,018	2,875
1,250	416	1,610	2,608	2,903	3,143	2,878	2,822	2,743
1,500	197	604	1,247	1,597	2,005	2,415	2,470	2,635
1,750	120	270	502	632	871	1,625	1,874	2,103
2,000	136	255	385	471	659	1,207	1,917	2,909
2,500	70	118	164	198	244	394	662	1,138
3,000	61	115	157	171	208	291	428	719
4,000	20	54	66	76	91	121	158	183
5,000	7·7	25·8	32·2	35·2	41·1	54	76	95
6,000	2·5	20·6	26·0	28·5	32·4	39	51	79
8,000	0·4	3·4	2·6	2·8	3·2	5	14	20
10,000 and over	0·2	0·9	0·5	0·5	0·8	0·6	4·6	9
Total	20,678	21,074	21,732	22,128	21,683	21,368	20,970	20,319

NATIONAL HEALTH SERVICE
(and Local Authority Personal Social Services)

The National Health Service came into being on July 5, 1948, as a result of the *National Health Service Act* 1946. The Act placed a duty on the Secretary of State for Social Services to promote the establishment in England of a comprehensive Health Service designed to secure improvement in the mental and physical health of the people and the prevention, diagnosis and treatment of illness. The Secretary of State for Wales administers the National Health Service in Wales. There are separate Acts for Scotland and Northern Ireland, where the Health Services are run on very similar lines. The Secretaries of State are responsible to Parliament for seeing that Health Services of all kinds of the highest possible quality are available to all who need them. They are advised by the Personal Social Services Council and the Central Health Services Council (and certain Standing Advisory Committees), appointed after consultation with the various interested bodies.

The National Health Service covers a comprehensive range of hospital, specialist, general practitioner (medical, dental, ophthalmic and pharmaceutical), artificial limb and appliance, ambulance, and community health service. Everyone normally resident in this country is entitled to use any of these services, there are no contribution conditions and the charges made (except those for amenity beds) are reduced or waived in cases of hardship. In addition the Secretary of State for Social Services is responsible under the Local Authority Social Services Act 1970 for the provision by local authorities of social services for the elderly, the handicapped, the disabled and also for families and children. Most of the cost of running the service is met from the Consolidated Fund—that is, from taxes. Other sources of finance are: (1) the weekly National Health Service contributions (since September 1957), which are estimated to produce about £225 million. (For convenience these are collected with the National Insurance contribution in a single combined weekly contribution); (2) local taxation, excluding Consolidated Fund grant to local authorities personal social services; (3) partial charges to patients for drugs and dressings, spectacles, dentures and dental treatment and amenity beds in hospital. The cost of the Health and Personal Social Services in England and Wales rose from £860 million in 1960–61 to an estimated total of £4,262 million in 1974–75. In Scotland the National Health Service vote totalled £535 million (estimate) in 1974–75 compared with a revised estimate of £390 million in 1973–74.

The NHS Reorganization Act 1973 placed a duty on the Secretary of State to provide an ambulance service to meet all reasonable requirements. As from April 1974 the ambulance service, which was formerly provided by the local authorities in England and Wales, was transferred to the control of the new Health Authorities and organized in England as 6 Metropolitan Services administered direct by Regional Health Authorities, whose areas were co-terminous with those of the Metropolitan Counties; 38 Area Services administered by Area Health Authorities and the London Ambulance Service. The NHS Ambulance Service operates approximately 6,000 vehicles, employs about 16,000, mainly uniformed, staff and carries over 20 million passengers annually.

THE HEALTH SERVICES

Family Doctor Service

In England and Wales the Family Doctor Service is organized by 98 Family Practitioner Committees which also organize the General Dental, Pharmaceutical and Ophthalmic Services for their areas. There is a Family Practitioner Committee for each Area Health Authority; members, who serve voluntarily, are appointed by local doctors, dentists, pharmacists and opticians (15), the Local Authority (4) and the Area Health Authority (11). Any doctor may take part in the Family Doctor Scheme, provided the area in which he wishes to practise has not already an adequate number of doctors, and about 23,000 general practitioners do so. They may at the same time have private fee-paying patients. Family doctors are paid for their Health Service work in accordance with a scheme of remuneration which includes *inter alia* a basic practice allowance, capitation fees, reimbursement of certain practice expenses and payments for " out of hours " work.

Everyone aged 16 or over can choose his doctor (parents or guardians choose for children under 16) and the doctor is also free to accept a person or not as he chooses. A person may change his doctor if he wishes, either at once if he has changed his address or obtained permission of the doctor on whose list he is, or by informing the Family Practitioners Committee (in which case 14 days must elapse before the other doctor can accept him). When people are away from home they can still use the Family Doctor Service if they ask to be treated as " temporary residents ", and in an emergency, if a person's own doctor is not available, any doctor in the service will give treatment and advice.

Patients are treated either in the Doctor's surgery or, when necessary, at home. Doctors may prescribe for their patients all drugs and medicines which are medically necessary for their treatment and also a certain number of surgical appliances (the more elaborate being provided through the hospitals).

Dental Service

Dentists, like doctors, may take part in the Service and may also have private patients. About 11,000 of the dentists available for general practice in England have joined the National Health Service. They are responsible to the Family Practitioners Committee in whose areas they provide services.

Patients are free to go to any dentist taking part in the Service and willing to accept them, and cannot register with any particular dentist. Dentists receive payment for items of treatment for individual patients, instead of the capitation fee received by doctors. There is no need for the patient to obtain a recommendation before seeking dental treatment. The dentist is able to carry out at once all normal conservative treatment (*e.g.* fillings), provision of dentures in some cases, emergency treatment and ordinary denture repairs; he seeks prior approval from the Dental Estimates Board before undertaking treatment when it involves the extraction of teeth and the provision of dentures (in some cases); extensive and prolonged treatment of the gums; inlays and crowns (in some cases); special appliances and oral surgery and certain other items.

A dentist may, with the approval of the Dental Estimates Board, charge his patients a prescribed sum for such types of treatment as crowns, inlays or metal dentures where these are not clinically necessary, if the patient wishes to have them. Where a denture supplied under the Service has to be replaced because of loss or damage the whole or part of the cost may be charged to the patient if he has been careless. In May, 1951, charges were introduced for dentures; these were increased in May, 1961, to £2 5s.–£2 15s. for the supply of one

denture or up to £5 for a set. In June, 1952, a charge of £1, or the full cost of any treatment if less than £1, was introduced. This charge was increased to £1 10s. from May 1, 1968. From Aug. 11, 1969, the charge for a set of dentures was increased to £6 5s., with proportionate increases for partial dentures. From April 1, 1971, the system of charges was changed so that patients became liable for a proportion of the cost of treatment, including the supply of dentures, if required, up to a maximum charge of £10 for one course of treatment, unless they were exempt from charges or entitled to remission on income grounds. A revised system of charges was introduced on January 1, 1976, so that the patient pays the full cost of each item of treatment (excluding dentures) up to a maximum charge of £3.50 for one course of treatment. In addition, the charges for the supply of a denture are as follows:—

for a denture bearing 1, 2 or 3 teeth	—£5.40
for a denture bearing 4 to 8 teeth	—£6.00
for a denture bearing more than 8 teeth	—£6.60
Maximum charge for course of treatment for more than one denture	—£12.00

Where a course of treatment includes both treatment and the supply of a denture(s) the overall charge is the total of the cost of treatment (subject to the £3.50 maximum) and the appropriate fixed charge for the denture(s) but subject to an overall maximum of £12.

No charge is made for clinical examination of a patient's mouth. Expectant mothers or mothers who have had a child during the preceding twelve months, children under 16, or 16 or over, but still in full-time attendance at school, do not pay charges. Other patients between 16 and 21 years of age pay the statutory charge for dentures and for alterations and additions to them.

Pharmaceutical Service

Patients may obtain drugs, medicines, appliances and oral contraceptives prescribed under the NHS from any pharmacy whose owner has entered into arrangements with the Family Practitioner Committee to provide this service. Almost all pharmacy owners have done so and display notices that they dispense under the NHS: the number of these pharmacies in England and Wales at the end of 1975 was about 10,000. There are also some appliance suppliers who only provide special appliances. In country areas where access to a pharmacy may be difficult patients may be able to obtain drugs etc. from their doctor.

Except for contraceptives (for which there is no charge), a charge of 20p is payable for each item supplied (25p or 50p for each piece of elastic hosiery) unless the patient is exempt and the declaration on the back of the prescription form is completed. Exemptions cover children under 16, people of pension age, expectant mothers and mothers of a child under one year of age, people suffering from certain medical conditions, people on low income, and war pensioners for their accepted disablements.

General Ophthalmic Service

General Ophthalmic Services, which are administered by Family Practitioner Committees, form part of the ophthalmic services available under the National Health Service and provide for the testing of sight and supply of glasses to meet more normal needs only. Diagnosis and specialist treatment of eye conditions is available through the Hospital Eye Service as well as the provision of glasses of a special type. Testing of sight may be carried out by any ophthalmic medical practitioner or ophthalmic optician, and glasses supplied by any ophthalmic optician or dispensing optician taking part in the Services. On the first occasion a person wishes to use the Services he must obtain a medical recommendation from his doctor that his sight needs testing. No further recommendation is required subsequently and the Services may be used direct.

Sight testing is free. The charges for lenses are on a flat rate basis and are £2.25 for each single-vision lens and £4.25 or £5 for each bifocal lens, according to type. The cost of the frame must also be paid. Children up to the age of 16 or older children attending school full-time may be supplied free of charge with standard lenses in children's standard frames. Additionally, school-children aged 10 years or over may be supplied with standard lenses without charge if any other type of NHS frame is used. The charge for the frame must then be paid.

Hospitals and Other Services

On July 5, 1948, ownership of 2,688 out of 3,040 voluntary and municipal hospitals in England and Wales was vested in the Minister of Health (now Secretary of State for Social Services). The Secretary of State has a duty to provide, to such extent as he/she considers necessary to meet all reasonable requirements, hospital and other accommodation; medical, dental, nursing and ambulance services; other facilities for the care of expectant and nursing mothers and young children, facilities for the prevention of illness, and the care and after-care of persons suffering from illness and such other services as are required for the diagnosis and treatment of illness. Convalescent treatment may also be provided for those who need it and surgical and medical appliances are supplied in appropriate cases.

Specialists and consultants who take part in the Service (and most of them do so) hold hospital appointments on a whole or part-time basis. Those who have part-time appointments can engage in private practice, including the treatment of their private patients in N.H.S. hospitals.

In a number of hospitals accommodation is available for the treatment of private in-patients who undertake to pay full hospital maintenance costs and (usually) separate medical fees to a specialist as well. The amount of these fees is a matter for agreement between doctor and patient.

Hospital charges for private resident patients are determined annually, on a national basis for classes of hospitals, by the Secretary of State in accordance with the Health Services and Public Health Act 1968. These charges are revised annually from April 1 each year to reflect the average cost for each class of hospital, which it is estimated will be incurred during the current financial year in the treatment of in-patients. They may also include a contribution towards capital costs.

For in-patients paying specialists' fees separately, the hospital daily charges from April 1, 1975 for accommodation and services in each class of hospital are as follows:

Class A. Long stay hospitals (other than hospitals in classes D and E).

Single Room	Other Accommodation
£14·80	£13·40

Class B. Psychiatric hospitals (other than hospitals in classes D and E)

Single Room	Other Accommodation
£9·30	£8·50

Class C. Acute and other hospitals (other than hospitals in Classes D and E)

Single Room	Other Accommodation
£26·28	£24·30

Class D. London Teaching hospitals as at 31/3/75.

Single Room	Other Accommodation
£37·10	£33·70

Class E. Provincial teaching hospitals and University hospitals as at 31/3/75.

Single Room	Other Accommodation
£31·20	£28·30

Certain hospitals have accommodation in single rooms or small wards which, if not required for patients who need privacy for medical reasons, may be made available to patients who desire it as an amenity. Amenity bed charges are at present £3 per day in single rooms and £1·50 per day in small wards. In such cases the patients are treated in every other respect as National Health patients. There is no charge for drugs supplied to National Health hospital in-patients but out-patients pay 20p per item unless they are exempt.

With certain exceptions, hospital out-patients have to pay fixed charges for dentures and glasses. The charge for glasses will be related to the type of lens prescribed; and for dentures will be up to £6.60 per denture, subject to an overall maximum charge of £12.00.

Local Authority Personal Social Services

Local authorities are responsible for the organization, management and administration of the personal social services and each authority has a Director of Social Services and a Social Services Committee responsible for the social services functions placed upon them by the Local Authority Social Services Act 1970. The "personal social services" are broadly speaking as follows: The services for children, including the care of children and young persons received into care, the provision of treatment for young offenders and adoption; family services, including the day care of pre-school children in day nurseries and by child minders, the care of unsupported mothers both in the community and in mother and baby homes, and the home help and meals on wheels services; services for the elderly and physically handicapped, including day centres, luncheon clubs and residential accommodation; services for the mentally ill and mentally handicapped, including day centres, clubs, adult training centres, workshops and residential accommodation.

CAR PRODUCTION IN MAIN PRODUCING COUNTRIES (thousands)

	1966	1967	1968	1969	1970	1971	1972	1973	1974	1975
United Kingdom...	1,604	1,552	1,816	1,717	1,641	1,742	1,921	1,747	1,534	1,268
France............	1,786	1,777	1,833	2,168	2,458	2,694	2,993	3,202	3,045	2,546
W. Germany......	2,830	2,296	2,862	3,313	3,528	3,697	3,521	3,650	2,840	2,908
Italy..............	1,282	1,439	1,545	1,477	1,720	1,701	1,732	1,823	1,631	1,349
Sweden...........	173	194	223	243	279	287	318	342	327	316
Japan.............	878	1,376	2,056	2,611	3,179	3,718	4,022	4,471	3,932	4,568
USA (Factory sales).	8,598	7,437	8,849	8,224	6,550	8,584	8,828	9,668	7,325	388
Canada...........	702	721	901	1,035	937	1,095	1,147	1,235	1,185	6,717
Total.............	17,853	16,792	20,085	20,788	20,292	23,308	24,482	26,138	21,819	20,060
UK % of total.....	9	9	9	8	8	9	9	8	7	6

BRITISH MOTOR VEHICLE PRODUCTION AND EXPORTS

Year	Weeks	Passenger Cars (including taxis)			Commercial Road Vehicles		
		For Export	Total	Weekly average	For Export	Total	Weekly average
1971.........52...		714,479	1,741,940	33,499	187,927	450,206	8,773
1972.........52...		613,430	1,921,311	36,948	135,470	408,019	7,848
1973.........52...		605,105	1,747,316	33,602	159,049	416,626	8,012
1974.........52...		596,199	1,534,119	29,502	170,194	402,566	7,742
1975.........52...		532,164	1,267,695	24,379	186,386	380,704	7,321

POSTAL REGULATIONS

For full conditions, exceptions, etc., *see* Post Office Guide. Associated volumes are London Post Offices and Streets, Postal Address and Index to Postcode Directions, and Post Offices in the United Kingdom.

CHIEF POSTAL SERVICES
LETTERS AND CARDS

Inland (U.K., Channel Islands and Irish Republic):—

Not over	First Class	Second Class
60 g.	8½p	6½p
100 g.	11½p	9p
150 g.	15p	11p
200 g.	18½p	14p
250 g.	22p	17p
300 g.	25½p	20p
350 g.	29p	23p
400 g.	32½p	26p
450 g.	36p	29p
500 g.	39½p	32p
750 g.	57p	47p
1 kg.	74½p	Not admissible over 750 g

Each extra 250 g or part thereof 17½p

Overseas:

(*a*) Surface mail. Not over 20 g. 10p; 50 g. 18p; 100 g. 24p; 250 g. 48p; 500 g. 92p; 1 kg. 160p; 2 kg. 260p.

WEIGHT LIMITS:—Inland, First Class, none. Second Class 750 g. Elsewhere, 2 kg. SIZE LIMITS: (A) If in roll form:—Inland and elsewhere (900 mm. for the greatest dimension); length + twice diameter, 1040 mm. (B) not in roll form:—(i) United Kingdom, Irish Republic; 610 mm × 460 mm × 460 mm. (ii) Overseas, length 600 mm. length + width + depth, 900 mm. Envelopes weighing under 60 g. should be oblong in shape, with the longer side at least 1·414 times the shorter side—minimum size 90 mm × 140 mm, maximum 120 mm × 235 mm. Envelopes outside these sizes and weighing under 60 g. will eventually be charged extra. Within the Inland Service envelopes or cards less than 100 mm × 70 mm must not be used. The standard of thickness for cards is 250 micrometres (0·01 in.) with a tolerance to an absolute limit of 230 micrometres (0·009 in.). To all overseas destinations the minimum limits for letters in the form of a roll are 170 mm for the length and twice the diameter combined (at least 100 mm for the greatest dimension), unless provided with a strong address label at least 100 mm in length and 70 mm in width. For letters other than in the form of a roll the minimum limits are one surface 140 mm in length, 90 mm in width, unless provided with a strong address label of 100 mm × 70 mm.

POST CARDS

To all destinations overseas:—7p.

Limit of size for destinations abroad: maximum, 148 mm in length, 105 mm in width; minimum, 140 mm in length, 90 mm in width.

PRINTED PAPERS, BOOKS

Overseas:—
Single packets

Not over 20 g, 6p; not over 50 g, 10p; not over 100 g, 13p; not over 250 g, 24p; not over 500 g, 43p; not over 1000 g, 72p; not over 2000 g, 101p. Normal weight limit 2000 g; but consignments of books or booklets weighing up to 5000 g may be sent as Printed Papers, as follows: not over 3000 g, 151p; not over 4000 g, 202p; not over 5000 g, 252p.

Posted in bulk as Direct Agents Bags.
Direct Agents Bags:—
Full rate: 50p per kg.
    Max rate (bags 30 kg max.) £15.
    Min rate bags(up to 23 kg) £11.50.

Reduced rate: 32p per kg.
    Max. rate (bags up to 30 kg max.) £9·60.
    Min. rate (bags up to 23 kg) £7·36.
Exceptionally, newspapers, periodicals, books, pamphlets, maps and musical scores which comply with the conditions shown in the Post Office Guide under Printed Papers at Reduced Rates may be sent abroad by surface mail only at the postage rate of:
Single packets

Not over 100 g, 13p; not over 250 g, 24p; not over 500 g, 43p; not over 1000 g, 72p.
Posted in bulk as Direct Agents Bags.

NEWSPAPERS

Inland (Newspapers " Registered at P.O."):—

Not over: 60 g, 6½p; 100 g, 9p; 150 g, 11p; 200 g, 14p; 250 g, 17p; 300 g, 20p; 350 g, 23p; 400 g, 26p; 450 g, 28p; 500 g, 32p; 750 g, 47p.

Publications registered at the P.O. as newspapers will be given First Class service at the newspapers postage rate, but *only* if posted by publishers or their agents, and prominently marked *Newspaper Post*. All other newspapers are transmitted as first or second class letters. Limit of weight 750 g. Limit of size as Letters.

Overseas: See printed papers.

SMALL PACKETS (*See also* p. 1201).

Overseas:

Not exceeding 100 g, 13p; 250 g, 24p; 500 g, 43p; 1 kg, 72p.

LIMITS: Maximum size, as for letters A and B ii. Minimum limits of size as for letters; Weight 1 kg in general but some countries only accept Small Packets weighing up to 500 g.

PARCELS

Should be marked " Parcel Post," and must be handed over the counter; postage must be prepaid by stamps, affixed by the sender.

Posters of over 2,500 parcels *per annum* may sign contracts to which special conditions apply.

The name and address of sender should be inside and (not too prominent) on the outside of every parcel and preferably be to the left of and at right angles to the name and address of the addressee.

A rural postman will accept any packets he can conveniently carry, except overseas letters intended for insurance or any parcels for abroad; but if on foot or cycle not more, without notice, than 10 kg from one person. Maildrivers need not accept between regular stopping points.

Parcels to or from Irish Republic, Channel Is, or I, of Man are liable to customs duty: except in last case, the sender must declare contents when posting. Addressee must pay a clearance fee if any duty be payable. Senders can undertake to pay customs charges of Irish Republic, Channel Islands and some *overseas countries* (a deposit is required).

Inland:—(Limit of size: length, 1·070 m.; length and girth combined, 2 m.):—

U.K. and Irish Republic:—

Not over	Ordinary	Local	
1 kg	55p	45p	Note: The Local Parcel Delivery Area comprises all places which have in their postal address the same post town name as that of the office of posting. For further details consult your local post office. Local parcel rates are not available in London Postal Districts.
2 kg	70p	60p	
3 kg	85p	75p	
4 kg	100p	90p	
5 kg	110p	99p	
6 kg	120p	109p	
7 kg	130p	119p	
8 kg	140p	129p	
9 kg	150p	139p	
10 kg	160p	149p	

Air Mail Services
For mode of packing, prohibitions, limits of size, &c., see Post Office Guide

Normal regulations as to make-up and acceptance of various categories of postal packets and parcels apply equally to air mail items. A blue air-mail label, obtainable free from post offices, must be affixed to each air mail item except letters, letter packets and postcards for Europe, for which no special air mail marking is required. Special air-mail rates apply to correspondence for members of H.M. Forces overseas (*see* leaflet PL(B)3116).

AIR LETTER FORMS, postage 10½p and 11p, may be sent to all countries. Enclosures are not permitted. You may get the special forms at post offices or use privately-manufactured forms which bear a statement that they have been approved by the Post Office, with the approval number. Unapproved forms will be treated as ordinary air mail letters.

PRINTED PAPERS. Small Packets and Newspapers may be sent by air to countries outside Europe at the rates shown in col. 3 below. NEWSPAPERS: Publications registered at the P.O. as newspapers may be sent at the reduced rates indicated in col. 4

below. There is no air mail service to Europe for these items. If the quickest transmission is desired the letter post rate should be paid.

European Countries (and *The Azores*)

Letters, letter packets and postcards for all European countries, prepaid at the ordinary international postage rates, are in general despatched daily by air or surface transport, whichever offer; earlier delivery. The rates are:—

Letters—Not over 20 g. 10p; 50 g. 10p; 100 g. 13p; 250 g. 24p; 500 g. 43p; 1000 g. 72p; 2000 g. 101p.
Postcards, 7p.

Air mail labels are not necessary.
Air Parcel Post to Europe. Rates are included in the Overseas Parcel Post tables, see pp. 1205–8.

Countries Outside Europe

Rates for letters, postcards and printed papers etc. appear below; for air parcel rates *see* pp. 1205–8.

COUNTRIES OUTSIDE EUROPE
For air mail services to Europe, see above; Air Parcel Rates, pp. 1205–8.

Destination	Rates of Postage									
	Letters				Printed Papers, Small Packets, Insured Boxes			Newspapers periodicals (on the PO Register)		
	Not over 15g	Not over 30g	Each add. 10g	Post cards	Not over 15g	Not over 30g	Each add. 10g	Not over 15g	Not over 30g	Each add. 10g
	p	p	p	p	p	p	p	p	p	p
Abu Dhabi..............	10½	21	6	8	6½	13	3	5	10	1½
Afghanistan..............	11	22	7½	9	7	14	3½	5	10	2
Ajman†..................	10½	21	6	8	6½	13	3	5	10	1½
Algeria..................	10½	21	6	8	6½	13	3	5	10	1½
Antigua.................	11	22	7½	9	7	14	3½	5	10	2
Argentina...............	11	22	7½	9	7	14	3½	5	11	2
Ascension†‡.............	11	22	7½	9	7	14	3½	5	11	2
Australia†‡.............	13	26	8	10	8	16	4½	6	12	2½
Bahamas†	11	22	7½	9	7	14	3½	5	10	2
Bahrain (State of)†......	10½	21	6	8	6½	13	3	5	10	1½
Bangladesh†.............	11	22	7½	9	7	14	3½	5	10	2
Barbados†...............	11	22	7½	9	7	14	3½	5	10	2
Belize†..................	11	22	7½	9	7	14	3½	5	10	2
Bermuda................	11	22	7½	9	7	14	3½	5	10	2
Bhutan†.................	11	22	7½	9	7	14	3½	5	10	2
Bolivia†‡...............	11	22	7½	9	7	14	3½	5	10	2
Botswana†..............	11	22	7½	9	7	14	3½	5	10	2
Brazil†..................	11	22	7½	9	7	14	3½	5	10	2
British Honduras	See Belize									
British Ind. Oc. Territory	No service									
Brunei†.................	11	22	7½	9	7	14	3½	5	10	2
Burma‡.................	11	22	7½	9	7	14	3½	5	10	2
Burundi†................	11	22	7½	9	7	14	3½	5	10	2
Cameroon†..............	11	22	7½	9	7	14	3½	5	10	2
Canada†‡...............	11	22	7½	9	7	14	3½	5	10	2
Caroline Islands†.........	13	26	8	10	8	16	4½	6	12	2½
Cayman Islands†.........	11	22	7½	9	7	14	3½	5	10	2
Central African Republic†..	11	22	7½	9	7	14	3½	5	10	2
Chad†..................	11	22	7½	9	7	14	3½	5	10	2

† No insured box service available for air mail.   ‡ Maximum weight limit for Small Packets: 1 lb.

Destination	Letters			Post cards	Printed Papers, Small Packets, Insured Boxes			Newspapers periodicals (on the PO Register)		
	Not over 15g	Not over 30g	Each add. 10g		Not over 15g	Not over 30g	Each add. 10g	Not over 15g	Not over 30g	Each add. 10g
	p	p	p	p	p	p	p	p	p	p
Chile‡	11	22	7½	9	7	14	3½	5	10	2
China†	13	26	8	10	8	16	4½	6	12	2½
Christmas Island (Indian Ocean)†	11	22	7½	9	7	14	3½	5	10	2
Cocos (Keeling) Islands	11	22	7½	9	7	14	3½	5	10	2
Colombia†‡	11	22	7½	9	7	14	3½	5	10	2
Comoro Islands†	11	22	7½	9	7	14	3½	5	10	2
Congo (People's Republic)†	11	22	7½	9	7	14	5½	5	10	2
Costa Rica†	11	22	7½	9	7	14	3½	5	10	2
Cuba†‡	11	22	7½	9	7	14	3½	5	10	2
Dahomey†	11	22	7½	9	7	14	3½	5	10	2
Dominica†	11	22	7½	9	7	14	3½	5	10	2
Dominican Republic†	11	22	7½	9	7	14	3½	5	10	2
Dubai†	10½	21	6	8	6½	13	3	5	10	1½
Ecuador†	11	22	7½	9	7	14	3½	5	10	2
Egypt (Arab Republic of)..	10½	21	6	8	6½	13	3	5	10	1½
El Salvador†	11	22	7½	9	7	14	3½	5	10	2
Equatorial Guinea†	11	22	7½	9	7	14	3½	5	10	2
Ethiopia†	10½	21	6	8	6½	13	3	5	10	1½
Falkland Islands and Dependencies	11	22	7½	9	7	14	3½	5	10	2
Fiji	13	26	8	10	8	16	4½	6	12	2½
French Guiana†	11	22	7½	9	7	14	3½	5	10	2
French Polynesia†	13	26	8	10	8	16	4½	6	12	2½
French Territory of the Afars and Issas	10½	21	6	8	6½	13	3	5	10	1½
French West Indies†	11	22	7½	9	7	14	3½	5	10	2
Fujairah†	10½	21	6	8	6½	13	3	5	10	1½
Gabon†	11	22	7½	9	7	14	3½	5	10	2
Gambia, The†	11	22	7½	9	7	14	3½	5	10	2
Gaza and Khan Yunis†	10½	21	6	8	6½	13	3	5	10	1½
Ghana	11	22	7½	9	7	14	3½	5	10	2
Gilbert and Ellice Islands†	13	26	8	10	8	16	4½	6	12	2½
Grenada†	11	22	7½	9	7	14	3½	5	10	2
Guatemala†	11	22	7½	9	7	14	3½	5	10	2
Guinea†	11	22	7½	9	7	14	3½	5	10	2
Guinea—Bissau† (Formerly Port. Gna)	11	22	7½	9	7	14	3½	5	10	2
Guyana	11	22	7½	9	7	14	3½	5	10	2
Haiti††	11	22	7½	9	7	14	3½	5	10	2
Honduras (Republic of)†	11	22	7½	9	7	14	3½	5	10	2
Hong Kong	11	22	7½	9	7	14	3½	5	10	2
India	11	22	7½	9	7	14	3½	5	10	2
Indonesia†	11	22	7½	9	7	14	3½	5	10	2
Iran	10½	21	6	8	6½	13	3	5	10	1½
Iraq†	10½	21	6	8	6½	13	3	5	10	1½
Israel†	10½	21	6	8	6½	13	3	5	10	1½
Ivory Coast†	11	22	7½	9	7	14	3½	5	10	2
Japan	13	26	8	10	8	16	4½	6	12	2½
Jordan†	10½	21	6	8	6½	13	3	5	10	1½
Kenya	11	22	7½	9	7	14	3½	5	10	2
Khmer Republic†	11	22	7½	9	7	14	3½	5	10	2
Korea†	13	26	8	10	8	16	4½	6	12	2½
Kuwait	10½	21	6	8	6½	13	3	5	10	1½
Laos†	11	22	7½	9	7	14	3½	5	10	2
Lebanon†	10½	21	6	8	6½	13	3	5	10	1½
Lesotho†	11	22	7½	9	7	14	3½	5	10	2
Liberia†	11	22	7½	9	7	14	3½	5	10	2

† No insured box service available for air mail.

Destination	Letters Not over 15g	Letters Not over 30g	Letters Each add. 10g	Post cards	Printed Papers, Small Packets, Insured Boxes Not over 15g	Printed Papers, Small Packets, Insured Boxes Not over 30g	Printed Papers, Small Packets, Insured Boxes Each add. 10g	Newspapers periodicals (on the PO Register) Not over 15g	Newspapers periodicals (on the PO Register) Not over 30g	Newspapers periodicals (on the PO Register) Each add. 10g
	p	p	p	p	p	p	p	p	p	p
Libyan Arab Republic†....	10½	21	6	8	6½	13	3	5	10	1½
Macao.................	11	22	7½	9	7	14	3½	5	10	2
Malagasy Republic†.......	11	22	7½	9	7	14	3½	5	10	2
Malawi.................	11	22	7½	9	7	14	3½	5	10	2
Malaya.................	11	22	7½	9	7	14	3½	5	10	2
Maldives (Republic of)†....	11	22	7½	9	7	14	3½	5	10	2
Mali†.................	11	22	7½	9	7	14	3½	5	10	2
Mariana Islands†.........	13	26	8	10	8	16	4½	6	12	2½
Marshall Islands†.........	13	26	8	10	8	16	4½	6	12	2½
Mauritania†.............	11	22	7½	9	7	14	3½	5	10	2
Mauritius...............	11	22	7½	9	7	14	3½	5	10	2
Mexico†...............	11	22	7½	9	7	14	3½	5	10	2
Mongolia (People's Republic)†....	13	26	8	10	8	16	4½	6	12	2½
Montserrat†.............	11	22	7½	9	7	14	3½	5	10	2
Morocco†...............	10½	21	6	8	6½	13	3	5	10	1½
Nauru Island†...........	13	26	8	10	8	16	4½	6	12	2½
Nepal..................	11	22	7½	9	7	14	3½	5	10	2
Netherlands Antilles......	11	22	7½	9	7	14	3½	5	10	2
New Caledonia...........	13	26	8	10	8	16	4½	6	12	2½
New Hebrides†..........	13	26	8	10	8	16	4½	6	12	2½
New Zealand............	13	26	8	10	8	16	4½	6	12	2½
New Zealand Territories†..	13	26	8	10	8	16	4½	6	12	2½
Nicaragua†.............	11	22	7½	9	7	14	3½	5	10	2
Nigeria.................	11	22	7½	9	7	14	3½	5	10	2
Niger Republic†..........	11	22	7½	9	7	14	3½	5	10	2
Norfolk Island†..........	13	26	8	10	8	16	4½	6	12	2½
Oman (Sultanate of)†.....	10½	21	6	8	6½	13	3	5	10	1½
Pakistan................	11	22	7½	9	7	14	3½	5	10	2
Panama (Republic of)†....	11	22	7½	9	7	14	3½	5	10	2
Panama Canal Zone†......	11	22	7½	9	7	14	3½	5	10	2
Papua New Guinea†......	13	26	8	10	8	16	4½	6	12	2½
Paraguay†..............	11	22	7½	9	7	14	3½	5	10	2
Peru†..................	11	22	7½	9	7	14	3½	5	10	2
Philippines†.............	13	26	8	10	8	16	4½	6	10	2½
Pitcairn Island†..........	13	26	8	10	8	16	4½	6	12	2½
Portuguese East Africa†...	11	22	7½	9	7	14	3½	5	10	2
Portuguese Timor†.......	13	26	8	10	8	16	4½	6	12	2½
Portuguese West Africa....	11	22	7½	9	7	14	3½	5	10	2
Puerto Rico†............	11	22	7½	9	7	14	3½	5	10	2
Qatar (State of)†.........	10½	21	6	8	6½	13	3	5	10	1½
Ras Al Khaimah†........	10½	21	6	8	6½	13	3	5	10	1½
Reunion†...............	11	22	7½	9	7	14	3½	5	10	2
Rhodesia†..............	11	22	7½	9	7	14	3½	5	10	2
Rwanda†...............	11	22	7½	9	7	14	3½	5	10	2
Sabah†................	11	22	7½	9	7	14	3½	5	10	2
St. Helena†.............	11	22	7½	9	7	14	3½	5	10	2
St. Kitts—Nevis—Anguilla†..	11	22	7½	9	7	14	3½	5	10	2
St. Lucia†..............	11	22	7½	9	7	14	3½	5	10	2
St. Pierre and Miquelon†...	11	22	7½	9	7	14	3½	5	10	2
St. Vincent†............	11	22	7½	9	7	14	3½	5	10	2
Samoa (U.S.A. Territory)†.	13	26	8	10	8	16	4½	6	12	2½
Sarawak†..............	11	22	7½	9	7	14	3½	5	10	2
Saudi Arabia†...........	10½	21	6	8	6½	13	3	5	10	1½
Senegal†...............	11	22	7½	9	7	14	3½	5	10	2
Seychelles†.............	11	22	7½	9	7	14	3½	5	10	2
Sharjah†...............	10½	21	6	8	6½	13	3	5	10	1½

† No insured box service available for air mail.

Destination	Letters			Post cards	Printed Papers, Small Packets, Insured Boxes			Newspapers periodicals (on the PO Register)		
	Not over 15g	Not over 30g	Each add. 10g		Not over 15g	Not over 30g	Each add. 10g	Not over 15g	Not over 30g	Each add. 10g
	p	p	p	p	p	p	p	p	p	p
Sierra Leone†	11	22	7½	9	7	14	3½	5	10	2
Singapore (Republic of)....	11	22	7½	9	7	14	3½	5	10	2
Solomon Islands†	13	26	8	10	8	16	4½	6	12	2½
Somali Democratic Republic..............	11	22	7½	9	7	14	3½	5	10	2
South Africa (Republic of)†	11	22	7½	9	7	14	3½	5	10	2
Spanish Territories of North Africa†	10½	21	6	8	6½	13	3	5	10	1½
Spanish West Africa†	10½	21	6	8	6½	13	3	5	10	1½
Sri Lanka (Republic of)...	11	22	7½	9	7	14	3½	5	10	2
Sudan (Democratic Republic of)†	10½	21	6	8	6½	13	3	5	10	1½
Surinam..................	11	22	7½	9	7	14	3½	5	10	2
Swaziland†	11	22	7½	9	7	14	3½	5	10	2
Syrian Arab Republic.....	10½	21	6	8	6½	13	3	5	10	1½
Taiwan (Formosa)........	13	26	8	10	8	16	4½	6	12	2½
Tanzania.................	11	22	7½	9	7	14	3½	5	10	2
Thailand†	11	22	7½	9	7	14	3½	5	10	2
Tibet†	11	22	7½	9	7	14	3½	5	10	2
Togo†	11	22	7½	9	7	14	3½	5	10	2
Tonga (Friendly Islands)†..	13	26	8	10	8	16	4½	6	12	2½
Tortola (British Virgin Islands)†	11	22	7½	9	7	14	3½	5	10	2
Trinidad and Tobago†	11	22	7½	9	7	14	3½	5	10	2
Tristan da Cunha†	11	22	7½	9	7	14	3½	5	10	2
Tunisia†	10½	21	6	8	6½	13	3	5	10	1½
Turks and Caicos Islands†.	11	22	7½	9	7	14	3½	5	10	2
Uganda..................	11	22	7½	9	7	14	3½	5	10	2
Umm al Qaiwain†	10½	21	6	8	6½	13	3	5	10	1½
U.S.A.†	11	22	7½	9	7	14	3½	5	10	2
Upper Volta†	11	22	7½	9	7	14	3½	5	10	2
Uruguay†	11	22	7½	9	7	14	3½	5	10	2
Venezuela†	11	22	7½	9	7	14	3½	5	10	2
Vietnam†	11	22	7½	9	7	14	3½	5	10	2
Virgin Islands of U.S.A.† ..	11	22	7½	9	7	14	3½	5	10	2
Wake Island†	12	26	8	10	8	16	4½	6	12	2½
Western Samoa†	13	26	8	10	8	16	4½	6	12	2½
Yemen Arab Republic†	10½	21	6	8	6½	13	3	5	10	1½
Yemen (People's Democratic Republic of).	10½	21	6	8	6½	13	3	5	10	1½
Zaire (Republic of)†	11	22	7½	9	7	14	3½	5	10	2
Zambia†	11	22	7½	9	7	14	3½	5	10	2

† No insured box service avaialbe for air mail.

GENERAL REGULATIONS

EXPORT RESTRICTIONS.—Under Department of Trade and Industry regulations the exportation of some goods by post is prohibited except under Department of Trade and Industry licence. Enquiries in the matter should be addressed to the Export Data Branch, Export Services and Promotions Division, Department of Trade and Industry, Export House, 50 Ludgate Hill, London, EC4M 7HU.

PROHIBITED ARTICLES.—Among prohibitions are offensive or dangerous things, packets likely to impede the P.O. sorters, and certain kinds of advertisement.

CERTIFICATE OF POSTING.—For non C.F. parcels the fee is 1p each (maximum 10p). May also be obtained for unregistered letters and unregistered postal packets (fee 1p).

RECORDED DELIVERY (inland, *not to Irish Republic*). Charge: 8p.—This service provides for a record of posting and delivery. Advice of delivery, a further 10p at time of posting, 20p after time of posting. Money and jewellery are not allowed. The service does not apply to parcels, railex or railway letters. Ask at the post office for full details.

UNPAID PACKETS, are charged *double postage* on delivery; UNDERPAID PACKETS, *double the deficiency*.

UNDELIVERED POSTAL PACKETS.—Undelivered postal packets are returned to the sender without charge provided the return address is indicated either on the outside of the envelope or inside. If the sender's address is not available, items not containing property are destroyed; however, if the packet contains something of intrinsic value, it is retained for up to three months pending reclaim before being disposed of. Perishable items within this category are dealt with as requisite. Exceptionally, items in the minimum weight step on which a rebate of postage has been allowed are destroyed unopened unless there is a return address shown on the outside of the cover. In addition, undeliverable second class mail in the minimum weight step, which, upon opening, is found to consist only of newspapers, magazines or commercial advertising material is also destroyed. (These rules are currently under revision: for the up-to-date position, consult the nearest post office.) *British packets undelivered abroad*; instructions for disposal are required if parcel is undeliverable and must be given at the time of posting.

REPLY COUPONS, for the purpose of prepaying replies to letters, are exchangeable abroad for stamps representing the minimum surface mail letter rate from the country concerned to the U.K. International Reply Coupons (valid in most countries) 20p. Sold at chief offices.

POSTE RESTANTE (solely for the convenience of travellers, and for three months only in any one town).—A packet may be addressed as a rule to any Post Office except Town Sub-Offices, and should have the words " Poste Restante " or " to be called for " in the address. If addressed to initials, fictitious names, or Christian name only, it is treated as undeliverable. Applicants must furnish sufficient particulars to ensure delivery to the proper person. Redirection from a Poste Restante is not undertaken for more than 1 month unless longer (up to 3 months) is applied for. Letters at a seaport for an expected ship are kept 2 months; otherwise letters are kept for 2 weeks—or for 1 month if originating from abroad—at the end of which time they are treated as undeliverable, unless bearing a request for return at or before the end of the period.

REDIRECTION.—(1) By agent of addressee: *Packets other than parcels, business reply and Freepost items* may be reposted free not later than the day after delivery (not counting Sundays and public holidays) if unopened and not tampered with, and if original addressee's name is unobscured. *Parcels* may be redirected free of charge within the same time limits, only if the original and the substituted address are both within the same local parcel delivery area (or within the London Postal Area). *Registered packets*, which must be taken to a Post Office, are *re-registered* free only up to day after delivery. (2) By the Post Office: Requests for redirection of *letters*, etc., should be on printed forms, obtainable from any post office, and must be signed by the person to whom the letters are to be addressed. The fees for redirection are as follows:—Redirection for a period not exceeding one month £1; redirection or renewal for a period not exceeding three months £2·50; redirection or renewal for a period not exceeding twelve months £6. A fee is payable for each different surname on the application form. Additional postage is generally due on redirected parcels (*see* above). Separate forms must be filled in for the forwarding of *telegrams*.

REGISTRATION, INLAND (First Class letters only).—All packets intended for registration should be marked " Registered " in bottom left-hand corner, and *must be handed to an officer of the Post Office, and a receipt taken*. The packets must be made up in a reasonably strong cover appropriate to their contents. Packets and letters must be fastened with adhesive (if tape is used it must be transparent and each piece must be signed or distinctively marked), or sealed with wax, lead, etc. Minimum fee: 45p, exclusive of postage. Advice of delivery, a further 10p at time of posting, 20p after time of posting. The latest time for registering is usually half an hour before the latest time for posting ordinary packets. Compulsory registration is applied to (a) any letter packet apparently meant for registration and wrongly posted (minimum fee less any prepaid excess postage); (b) letter packets found open (or undeliverable) and containing any bank or currency note, coin, jewellery, stamps, uncrossed bearer cheques, uncrossed postal orders without payee's name, etc., in each case £2 or more in value. Ask at the post office for full details.

COMPENSATION, INLAND.—Subject to certain prescribed regulations which are set out in the Post Office Guide, the Post Office pays compensation for (i) loss of or damage to registered letters, (ii) though not as a legal right, for loss of or damage to recorded delivery packets, parcels on which a compensation fee has been paid and for unregistered packets conveyed by Express Messenger all the way. The onus of making up properly any packet sent by post and of packing adequately any article or articles enclosed therein lies on the sender, and the Post Office does not accept any responsibility for loss arising from faulty or inadequate packing. No compensation is paid for consequential injury or damage arising in respect of anything sent by post. *Registered letters (including items sent to the Irish Republic and the Channel Islands):* The fees for registration are : 45p covering compensation up to £200; 50p, £400; 55p, £600 (maximum). (No legal right to compensation exists in respect of registered letters sent to and from Irish Republic or the Channel Islands.) Compensation Fee (C.F.) parcels, fees: 7p for compensation up to £10; 12p up to £50; 20p up to £100. *Recorded delivery packets:* maximum compensation £2 provided no

contents inadmissible. *Unregistered packets* conveyed by Express Messenger all the way: Maximum compensation £5.

Compensation in respect of money of any kind (coin, notes, orders, cheques, stamps, etc.) is only given if the money is sent by *registered letter* post in one of the special envelopes sold officially and, in the case of paper money, if particulars (for identification) are kept; the maximum compensation for coin, which must be packed so as not to move about, will not exceed £5 except in a case where the value of each coin exceeds its face value, *i.e.* numismatic coins. Compensation cannot be paid for loss or damage in the case of any packet containing anything not legally transmissible by post; and for fragile articles only if they have been adequately packed and the cover is conspicuously marked " Fragile, with care ". No compensation is paid for deterioration due to delay of perishable articles or for damage to exceptionally fragile articles, liquids or semi-liquids sent by letter or parcel post to or from Irish Republic, whether registered or not.

REGISTRATION, OVERSEAS (except for parcels and printed paper items posted in bulk), is in force to all countries with the exception of Chagos Islands, British Indian Ocean Territory, Republic of Maldives or North Vietnam. No compensation is payable for the loss of or damage to valuable articles or other items sent in an unregistered letter. Fee 45p. If claimed within a year compensation is paid to the sender for entire loss of registered packets while in the custody of a country in the Universal Postal Union, subject to certain conditions. Compensation is also payable for the partial or complete loss of or damage to the contents of registered items in the service with certain countries (*see* Post Office Guide for list).

INSURANCE, OVERSEAS, may be effected on packets to many countries at the following rates:—50p for up to £72 cover; 5p for each additional £35 up to £1·15 for £500. *For H.M. Ships abroad and also members of H.M. Army and Air Force overseas using closed Forces addresses* (*e.g.,* British Forces Post Office followed by a number) only parcels are insurable, up to £100. Packets containing valuable papers, (bank-notes, etc.), documents (press, etc.) and, in some cases, valuable articles such as jewellery, can be insured as letters, or as parcels if the country of origin does not accept durable goods in the letter post.

INSURED BOX POST.—Jewellery and precious articles (*not* letters or paper valuables) may be sent in insured boxes to certain countries. Customs declarations must be filled in.

The Post Office Guide should be consulted for details of the conditions of Insurance.

COMPENSATION up to a maximum of £8·20 may be given for loss or damage in the U.K. to *uninsured* parcels to or from most overseas countries, if certificate of posting is produced.

No compensation will be paid for any loss or damage due to the act of the Queen's Enemies.

CASH ON DELIVERY SERVICE, INLAND (*not* to or from Irish Republic, nor to H.M. Ships).—A sum (Trade Charge) up to £50 can, under certain conditions, be collected from addressee and remitted to sender of a parcel or registered letter posted at a Money Order Office. Fee (extra to normal postage and registration charges): 40p.

CASH ON DELIVERY, OVERSEAS.—Applicable to parcels only, but not all countries, nor to H.M. Naval and Military Forces and R.A.F. serving overseas. A fee of £1 per parcel must be prepaid in addition to the postage. The Trade Charge (amount to be collected) may not exceed £50, but to some countries the limit is lower. Addressee

has also to pay on delivery, besides Customs, if any a further fee (20p in U.K.) not prepayable. If Trade Charge cannot be collected, special rules for undeliverable C.O.D. parcels apply.

EXPRESS and SPECIAL SERVICES (INLAND).—In general the express service are limited to the hours of telegraph business, but the times vary according to the service used and local conditions. (1) *All the way*, by P.O. messenger, of packets, conspicuously marked " Express " above the address, handed over the counter. Inclusive charge, 50p per mile, or part of a mile, with 3p on each *separate* packet after the first. Live animals, liquids, and money may be delivered by this service. (2) *After transmission by post*, on *addressee's* application (50p per mile, or part of a mile, and 2½p for every ten or less additional packets). (3) *After transmission by post*, at *sender's* request " Special Delivery " from the ordinary delivery office, if messengers are available (60p.+ postage). This service is restricted to First Class letters and to parcels. Packets must be marked " Special Delivery," and letters bear a broad blue or black vertical line back and front. A similar line must be drawn completely round a packet or parcel. (4) *Special delivery on Sunday of postal packets* (*except parcels*) *handed in on Saturdays.* Limited inter-city services, for London, Belfast, and certain provincial cities (except that the service is not in operation from Southampton to Belfast) are available *only:* (1) Sundays: reciprocally between certain towns as shown in the Post Office Guide; (2) Good Friday: *to* London only *from* towns in (1). Delivery is made from offices only during periods when they are open for telegraphic business. The handing-in offices in London are:—The London Chief Office, King Edward St., London EC1A 1AA, W. and S.W. District Offices, and Camberwell Green, Clapham Common, Hammersmith, Holloway, Trafalgar Sq., Stratford, and Swiss Cottage (Branch Offices). Packets marked "Express: Sunday Delivery," must be handed in in time to catch *preceding* night mails (in London 12.45 p.m.–5.0 p.m. for provincial towns). The latest time of posting to Belfast should be ascertained at selected office of posting. Fee is £1·50 in addition to postage. Not available for parcels. (5) (*Railex.*) Postal packets which cannot be registered are despatched by rail, met, and specially delivered in Great Britain, Northern Ireland (Belfast, Larne and Londonderry only). Inclusive charges irrespective of weight but not exceeding 450 g. £4, but packets handed in in Northern Ireland for destinations in Great Britain or Northern Ireland may not exceed 60 g. (6) *A Railway Parcel* is similarly accelerated at the cost of a telegram, of railway charges, and of Service (1) at both ends of its journey. It should be marked " Railway Parcel, to be handed to Post Office messenger at .... Station."

RAILWAY LETTERS, &C.—A First Class letter, not liable to registration, may be handed in at the parcel or passenger booking office of a railway station of British Rail and certain other minor railway companies, at any time when the station is open to the public, for conveyance by the next available train. A railway letter may either be addressed to the called for at a station, or to the residence of the addressee in which case it is posted at the station named in the address. The service is available between any two stations in Great Britain and Northern Ireland and from Great Britain and Northern Ireland to the Irish Republic. It is not available at or to stations of the London Transport Executive. Fees (besides postage) are charged by British Rail or the minor railway companies on which railway letters travel. Enquiries about these fees should be made at the station at which railway letters are handed in. For

other combinations of rail and express, *see* preceding paragraph, Services (5) and (6).

AIRWAY LETTERS.—On certain internal air routes operated by the British Airways Corporation, First Class letters may be handed in at the airport or town terminal for conveyance by the next available direct air service to be transferred to the post at the distant airport or town terminal or to be called for at the airport or town terminal. Fee (besides postage) 55p, maximum weight 450 g. The conditions on which this service operates are, in general, similar to those applying to the Railway Letter Service. This service is not available to the Irish Republic, Isle of Man or to any country overseas. Full information can be obtained from any office of British Airways (European Division).

INTERNATIONAL EXPRESS SERVICE.—From the office of delivery by special messenger is available to or from certain countries. In some countries the service is restricted to certain towns. 60p is paid by the sender, the rest, if any, by addressee, according to the local regulations. (*See* P.O. Guide.)

DATAPOST.—This service offers a door-to-door overnight service to most parts of the country on a contract basis. Charges are negotiated with individual customers and reflect the services performed. Head Postmasters will provide full information on request.

This service is also available to the U.S.A., Brazil, Belgium, France, Japan, the Netherlands and Hong Kong.

BUSINESS REPLY AND FREEPOST (Inland, excluding Irish Republic).—These services enable a person or firm to receive replies to advertisements, letters from clients, etc. without prepayment of postage, the addressee paying the postage together with a handling charge of ½p per item delivered. A licence costing £15 p.a. must be obtained to use either service and these are available from Head Postmasters who will also provide any further information required.

POSTAGE FORWARD PARCEL SERVICE.—This service enables a person or firm to receive parcels from clients without prepayment of postage. A special label is used for this service. A licence costing £15 p.a., to use the service must first be obtained from the local Head Postmaster.

ARTICLES FOR THE BLIND (Inland, including Irish Republic). Books, papers, literature and specified articles specially adapted for the use of the blind are admissible subject to certain conditions. A packet should bear on the outside the indication " Articles for the Blind " and the name and address of the sender. Packets must be capable of easy examination in the post. Postage free.

BLIND LITERATURE, OVERSEAS (in other respects treated as Printed Papers):—Papers, periodicals and books, if printed in special type (also plates for embossing blind literature, and voice recordings and special paper intended solely for the use of the blind) subject to certain conditions of posting, marked outside " Literature for the Blind (Cécogrammes) ", with name and address of sender. Packets must be capable of easy examination in the post. They may be sent post free by surface route to all parts.

SMALL PACKETS POST (OVERSEAS).—For the transmission of goods (including trade samples) in the same mails as Printed Papers up to 1 kg. Registration is allowed; not insurance. Available to all countries, but to some countries there is a limit of 500 g. A customs declaration is required.

NEWSPAPER POST (INLAND).—For newspapers " registered at the P.O." (p. 1195).

Copies of registered newspapers may be posted by the publishers or their agents in wrappers open at both ends,

in unsealed envelopes approved by the Post Office for the purpose or without covers and tied with string which can be removed without cutting. Wrappers and envelopes must be prominently marked NEWSPAPER POST in the top left-hand corner and be easily removable for the purpose of examination. No writing or additional printing is permitted, other than the words " with compliments ", name and address of sender, request for return if undeliverable and a reference to a page.

Newspapers posted by the public or supplements to registered newspapers despatched apart from their ordinary publications are transmitted under the conditions governing the First or Second Class Letter Services.

STAMPS, ENVELOPES, POSTCARDS, &c.

£sd stamps are no longer valid for postage.

POSTAGE STAMPS (used also for receipts, telegrams and certain Inland Revenue duties) are sold for the respective values of ½p, 1p, 1½p, 2p, 2½p, 3p, 4p, 5p, 6p, 6½p, 7p, 7½p, 8p, 8½p, 9p, 9½p, 10p, 10½p, 11p, 20p, 50p, £1. Books containing 2 at ½p, 3 at 1p, 1 at 6p, 10p; 10 at 6½p, 65p; 10 at 8½p, 85p. Rolls of 6½p and 8½p stamps are sold. There are also mixed value rolls made up of strips of 2p, ½p, ½p, 1p, 1p (5p) and 6p, 2p, 1p, ½p, ½p (10p).

REGISTERED LETTER ENVELOPES printed with a 53½p stamp (45p for registration and 8½p for postage) are of three sizes: G, 156 mm × 95 mm, 56½p each; H, 203 mm × 120 mm, 57p each; K, 292 mm × 152 mm, 60½p each.

FORCES AIR LETTER FORMS issued against purchase of 6½p stamp.

LETTER CARDS printed with 6½p stamp, 8½p each; 8½p stamp, 10½p each.

POSTCARDS printed with 8½p stamp, 9½p each.

ENVELOPES printed with 8½p stamp: Size 1 (146 mm × 95 mm) 8p each; Size 2 (235 mm × 120 mm) 8½p each. With 8½p stamp; Size 1 (146 mm × 95 mm) 10p each; Size 2 (235 mm × 120 mm) 10½p each.

AIR LETTER FORMS printed with 10½p or 11p stamp, 10½p and 11p each.

Printed postage stamps cut out of envelopes, postcards, lettercards, air letter forms or newspaperwrappers may be used as adhesive stamps in payment of postage or telegrams provided they are not imperfect, mutilated or defaced in any way.

MONEY ORDERS

There is no Inland Ordinary Money Order Service. *Overseas Service.* Advice of Payment: 7½p (to certain countries). Payment may be stopped (fee 7½p).

Inland Telegraph Money Orders (and to Irish Republic, Channel Islands and Isle of Man).

Money may be transmitted by this means from most offices which despatch telegrams, and paid at most of those which also deliver telegrams, and at some other offices. On Sundays, Christmas Day, Boxing Day and Good Friday special arrangements apply (*see* Post Office Guide).

The fee is £2 per order (maximum value £100) plus cost of official Telegram of Advice, £1·40 minimum for Inland Orders (including orders to Channel Islands and Isle of Man) and £1·50 minimum for Irish Republic Orders and where applicable the charge for any private message sent with the order, 7p per word. (All charges for telegrams are subject to Value Added Tax in addition to the charges shown above).

Ordinary Money Orders for Abroad

The fee is £3 per order. Limits of amount of each order vary according to destination but in any case may not exceed £50; validity varies between one and twelve months (*see* Post Office Guide).

Telegraph Money Orders for Abroad

The fee is £3 per order, *plus* cost of official

Telegram of Advice (at Letter Telegram rate, if desired, to certain countries).

Application to remit money orders to countries outside the Scheduled Territories (formerly known as the Sterling Area) must be made on a special declaration form upon which the purpose of the remittance must be stated. This form is obtainable at any money order office, where it may be ascertained whether any particular country with which a money order service is in operation is outside the Scheduled Territories.

POSTAL ORDERS

Postal Orders (British pattern) are issued and paid at nearly all post offices in the United Kingdom during the ordinary hours of business on weekdays. They are also issued and/or paid in many countries within the Commonwealth and in a few other countries. Transmission of postal orders to overseas countries is restricted under Exchange Control Regulations and is prohibited to any country outside the British Postal Order Area, except to members of H.M. Forces under special arrangements (particulars of Exchange Control restrictions may be obtained at any post office transacting Postal Order business). British postal orders are paid and issued in the Channel Islands and the Isle of Man, and paid in the Irish Republic. They are printed with a counterfoil, for 10p and every multiple of 2½p up to 25p, then 30p and every multiple of 5p up to £1, then in £1 steps to £10. Adhesive unmarked current British Postage Stamps not exceeding two in number, if affixed in the two spaces provided, may increase the value of the order by not more than 4½p. Fees 10p up to £1, 7p; £2, £3, £4, £5, £6, £7, £8, £9, or £10, 9p. The name of the payee must be inserted. If not presented within six months of the last day of the month of issue, Orders must be sent to the local Head Postmaster, or in London to the District Postmaster to ascertain whether the order may still be paid.

INLAND TELEGRAMS

Telegrams are accepted during counter business hours at any post office at which telegraph business is transacted. They may also be handed with the necessary payment to messengers delivering telegrams or express letters. Telegrams may be tendered by telephone or telex at all times. All charges for telegrams are subject to Value Added Tax in addition to the charges shown below. Rate, 70p per telegram, plus 7p for each word. (To Irish Republic 80p per telegram plus 7p for each word.) Greetings telegrams on appropriately designed forms in decorative envelopes cost the rate of an ordinary telegram plus a surcharge of 40p. Greetings telegrams may be tendered by telephone or handed in in advance for delivery on a specified day. On Mondays to Fridays, if the Greetings telegram is handed in at any time before noon of the day before delivery is required, the surcharge is reduced to 20p. (Greetings service not available to and from Irish Republic.)

Overnight Telegram

An Overnight telegram may be tendered between 8 a.m. and 10.30 p.m. for delivery, normally by first post, the following morning. On days when there is no postal delivery, Overnight telegrams are held until the next postal delivery. The charge is 50p per telegram plus 4p for each word. The Overnight service is not available to the Irish Republic. A redirection charge of 50p per telegram is made if the original and new addresses are in the same delivery area or London Postal District. Overnight telegrams are normally redirected by post free of charge. In all other cases

the redirection charge is at the ordinary inland rate. In England, Wales and Northern Ireland a telegram tendered on Sundays, Good Friday and Christmas Day is charged 45p extra; in Scotland this surcharge applies to a telegram tendered on Sundays and on New Year's Day. Replies may be prepaid within the limits of 70p (minimum) and £3·50 (maximum), Irish Republic 70p (minimum) and £3·60 (maximum); the reply vouchers may be used in payment or part payment of any Post Office telegram or any telegraph, telex or telephone account rendered by the Post Office, or its value refunded to sender, the addressee or person applying on behalf of the sender of the original telegram, on completion of the declaration on the back of the voucher. Receipt for charges on telegrams accepted at post office counters free on request. Certified copy 45p; application to the local Head Postmaster must be within 3 months of the date of sending. There is no charge for delivery in the United Kingdom. In the Irish Republic delivery is free to addresses within 1 mile of the delivery office; beyond that any necessary charge will be collected on delivery.

TELEGRAPH OFFICE ALWAYS OPEN IN LONDON: — Trafalgar Sq., 24–28 William IV Street, WC2N 4DL.

INTERNATIONAL TELEGRAMS

The per word charges for ordinary or Full Rate telegrams from the United Kingdom to places abroad are shown on pp. 1205–8. Urgent Telegrams may be sent to many countries at double the ordinary per word rates.

For telegrams of a social character the GLT (Commonwealth Social Telegram) service at half the ordinary per word rates is available to Commonwealth countries. The service indicator GLT will be counted as a chargeable word.

Letter telegrams to certain countries are admitted at half the ordinary per word rates for messages in plain language of a lengthy though less urgent character for which the minimum charge is as for 22 words including the indicator LT. Full particulars as to which countries this facility is available can be obtained from any Post Office or International Telegraph Office.

In addition to these per word charges, the following fixed charges per telegram apply, irrespective of destination.

Ordinary	70p
Urgent	£1·40
GLT	70p
LT	70p

Phototelegrams, i.e. pictures, photographs, drawings, plans, printed, typed or written documents may be telegraphed in facsimile to many places in the world. Full particulars of all telegraph charges and services available to any country will be given on enquiry at any Post Office or International Telegraph Office.

RADIOTELEGRAMS

Radiotelegrams for transmission to ships at sea in any part of the world may be handed in at any Postal Telegraph Office or dictated over the telephone. The charge for radiotelegrams is 15p per word (standard rate). Radiotelegrams at the standard rate should be addressed Portishead Radio unless the sender nominates another coast station. The address should contain (1) the name or rank of the addressee, (2) the name of the ship and (3) the name of the coast station in the British Isles if the sender knows that the ship is within range of that station.

The charge for messages to H.M. Ships is 10p a word. The address should contain (1) the name

of the addressee and his rank or rating, (2) the word " Warship " (or " Submarine "), (3) the name of the ship (or identifying letters and number) and (4) the word " Admiraltyradio ".

In addition to the per word charges quoted a fixed charge of 70p per radiotelegram applies. There is a surcharge of 45p for radiotelegrams tendered on Sundays, Good Friday and Christmas Day. In Scotland, this surcharge is applied to radiotelegrams tendered on Sundays and New Year's Day.

Radiotelegrams may also be sent to R.A.F. vessels. Such radiotelegrams should be addressed in the same way as for commercial vessels and in addition should include the words " R.A.F. Vessel " before the name of the ship.

RADIOTELEPHONE SERVICE

Radiotelephone services are available between telephone subscribers (but not from coin-box telephones or call offices unless the caller is a holder of a telephone credit card) in Great Britain, Northern Ireland, the Channel Islands and the Isle of Man and suitably equipped ships. The service is generally available at all hours of the day and night, but the periods of communication with a particular ship vary with the ship's position and are dependent on radio conditions.

Calls are normally made through the coast stations, listed below, and callers should ask the local exchange telephone operator for SHIPS' TELEPHONE SERVICE adding, if known, the telephone number and name of the coast station through which the call should be made. If the name of the coast station is not known, the caller will be connected to Portishead Radio. When connected to the coast station operator, the caller should ask for SHIPS' RADIO TELEPHONE CALL giving the name of the ship and the name (or designation) of the person required.

Anglesey Radio.........	0407 83 0541
Bacton Radio (restricted short range VHF services)	Mablethorpe 3447
Clyde Radio (restricted short range VHF services)	Portpatrick 311
Cullercoats Radio........	089 44 31318
Humber Radio..........	Mablethorpe 3447
Ilfracombe Radio........	Ilfracombe 3453
Land's End Radio........	0736 77 493
Niton Radio.............	0983 730495
North Foreland Radio.....	0843 20592
Oban Radio.............	0631 2059
Portishead Radio.........	027 878 3291
Portpatrick Radio........	0776 81 311
Stonehaven Radio........	0569 2 2917
Thames Radio (restricted short range VHF services)	0843 20592
Wick Radio.............	Wick 2271
Shetland Radio (restricted short range VHF services)	Wick 2271

Charges vary according to the position of the ship. The rates are (for minimum of 3 minutes) Short range (within 50 miles of VHF station) 81p for 3 minutes. 27p for each additional minute.

Medium range (within 250 miles of U.K.). £1·35 for 3 minutes. 45p for each additional minute.

Long range (dependent on position of ship). £3·15 for 3 minutes, 90p or £1·05 respectively for each additional minute.

The service is available, for calls to and from H.M. Ships, subject to the approval of the Duty Commander M.O.D. Navy, through whom all calls to H.M. Ships should be booked. The charges are the same as those for merchant ships but as H.M. Ships do not normally keep watch for private radiotelephone calls from the shore, no attempt should be made to book a call to one of H.M. Ships unless prior arrangements have been made with the person concerned on the ship. The caller must be able to give the name of the coast station through which the call is to be made, or the approximate position of the ship at the time the call is required.

The holder of a telephone credit card issued in Great Britain, Northern Ireland, the Channel Islands or the Isle of Man may use it to make radiotelephone calls to ships at sea from any telephone in this country (including coin-box telephones and call offices) and have the charges debited to his own account.

INLAND TELEPHONES

The quarterly rental for an exclusive business exchange line is £9·75 and £8·25 for any other exclusive exchange line. For shared service, in which two subscribers share one line but have practically the same facilities as those provided by individual lines, each customer pays £4 per annum less than for exclusive line service. A condition of telephone service is that all new and removing residential customers since January, 1948, are liable to share their lines if called upon to do so. Subscriber trunk dialling (STD) facilities are provided at an increasing number of exchanges. Local and dialled trunk calls from these exchanges are charged in 3p units, 2p units from pay on answer coin-box lines. Charges from coin-box lines are Value Added Tax included whereas from ordinary lines Value Added Tax is not included on individual call charges but an 8 per cent. charge is made on customer's total bill to cover Value Added Tax. The length of time per unit depends on the distance of the call, from two minutes for a local call to ten seconds for distances over 56 kilometres. Additional time is allowed during the cheaper rates period.

From other exchanges local calls are charged 3p from ordinary lines and 2p from a call office or coin-box line. All trunk calls are obtained via the operator. Operator-controlled trunk calls from any exchange have a three minute minimum charge which varies with the distance but does not exceed 60p (75p to Irish Republic from non-coin-box telephones). Operator-controlled calls made from coin-box lines are charged in 3 minute periods at the coin-box tariff. All trunk calls are cheaper if made after 6 p.m. or at weekends. Personal calls (to specified person) 24p extra, if the person cannot be found nothing further is charged. For fuller information *see* Preface to Telephone Directory, Dialling Instruction Booklet (where appropriate) and Post Office Guide.

TELEX SERVICE

Annual rental of teleprinter, associated equipment and line to Telex exchange is from £380 per annum (depending upon the equipment required). The minimum call charge for International calls via the operator is three minutes. For subscriber-dialled calls to some Inter-Continental countries, the minimum call charge is one minute, and subscriber-dialled calls to the Continent are charged in 2½p units (*see* Post Office Guide for rates). Automatic equipment allowing messages to be sent at the maximum speed of 400 characters (60–70 words) per minute can be rented in addition. Descriptive leaflet available from all Telephone Area Offices; for local address *see* Telephone Directory.

DATA COMMUNICATIONS SERVICES

Data communications services provide for data transmission at speeds ranging from 50–50,000 bits per second (bit/s) over telegraph, speech and wideband circuits. They accommodate a number of additional facilities such as automatic calling and

answering, Dataplex and midnight line service. The services can be described briefly as follows:
Data over telegraph equipment. Data transmission over telegraph type circuits either on the public switched telex network or privately rented circuits at speeds up to 110 bit/s. PO terminals at 50 bit/s are provided on telex. On telegraph circuits either PO or privately supplied terminals which have been granted permission for connection may be used.

Datel 200 provides for duplex data transmission over speech type circuits either privately rented or on the public switched telephone network (PSTN) at up to 300 bit/s using PO modems and privately supplied terminal equipment which has been permitted for connection to the network.

Datel 600 provides for duplex data transmission over speech type circuits either privately rented or on the PSTN at up to 1200 bit/s using PO modems or privately supplied terminal equipment which has been permitted for connection to private circuits.

Datel 2400 provides for synchronous duplex data transmission over speech type private circuits at up to 2400 bit/s using PO modems or privately supplied terminal equipment which has been permitted for connection to private circuits.

Datel 2400 Dial-Up provides for synchronous duplex data transmission over the PSTN at up to 2400 bit/s using PO modems.

Datel 48K provides for data transmission at 40·8K, 48K or 50K bit/s over specially engineered wideband circuits using PO modems or privately supplied terminal equipment which has been permitted for connection to the network.

Data Control Equipment enables terminal to automatically originate and answer calls over the switched network.

Dataplex allows the data from a number of low speed terminals to be sent over a single high speed link, resulting in reduced user costs.

Midnight Line Service provides for unlimited subscriber dialled inland calls between midnight and 6 a.m. for a fixed annual rental.

INTERNATIONAL DATA TRANSMISSION SERVICES

(i) *Datel Services*
In the International context the term Datel has been adopted to refer to data transmission over the public switched telephone (or telex) networks.

Datel 100
This service provides for serial transmission of data at 50 bits per second using the telex network and is available to most European countries.

Datel 200
This service provides full duplex (simultaneous both way) serial transmission of data at speeds up to 200 bits per second using the public telephone network. Service is available to most of Europe, Bahrain, Dubai and the U.S.A. Note: Non European traffic is connected on a manual basis via the international exchange.

Datel 600
This service provides half duplex (bothway, but not simultaneous) serial transmission of data within the speed range of 600 to 1200 bits per second. Telephone networks, although designed for speech transmission are usually capable of carrying data transmissions at 600 bits per second and on some connections, 1200 bits per second should be obtainable. Service is available to most European countries and Australia, Bahrain and Dubai,

Canada, Hong Kong, New Zealand, Singapore and the U.S.A. (Note: Non-European traffic is connected on a manual basis via the international exchange.)

Datel 2400 (expected to be available the latter half of 1976). This service will allow serial transmission of digital data at 2400 bits per second using the public telephone network. A new Post Office modem, which will be obligatory in this service, is expected to be available in the latter half of 1976. Until that time the Post Office is prepared to allow the use of permitted non-Post Office modems by customers with a need for 2400 bits per second data transmission facilities over the international public telephone network subject to the agreement of the foreign administration(s) concerned.

The Post Office can give no guarantee of the rate or quality of data transmission in the case of facilities using non-Post Office modems.

Customers wishing to use non-Post Office modems to establish a facility must obtain permission to proceed from the Post Office.

(ii) *Leased Circuits*
International leased circuits are available for data transmission and are provided in accordance with the Recommendations of the International Telephone & Telegraph Consultative Committee (CCITT). Depending on the modulation method used, higher transmission rates than those offered by the Datel services are usually obtainable over voice bandwidth circuits.

In addition, high speed data transmission, e.g. 48K bits per second, may be achieved over wideband leases (telephone circuits grouped together to give 48KHz bandwidth) or by using special facilities provided via the INTELSAT satellite.

INTERNATIONAL TELEPHONES

The same charges apply for calls originating in any part of Great Britain, Northern Ireland and the Isle of Man. Callers with STD in many parts of this country can dial direct to numbers on many exchanges on the continent and in some other countries. Access to this facility (International Subscriber Dialling—ISD) is progressively being made available to more places in this country, and the number of places abroad to which calls may be dialled is also increasing, callers should consult their dialling codes booklet for information on how to make calls.

Directly dialled calls are charged in units of time costing 3p. Cheap rates apply from 8 p.m. to 6 a.m. nightly, and at any time on Saturdays and Sundays. Where access to ISD is not yet available, callers should ask the local operator for the International Exchange, specifying the country required.

The charges for calls via an operator are based on a three minute minimum. Transferred charge (collect) calls are available with some countries, and British Post Office telephone credit cards can be used in many countries for calls to the U.K.; charges for such calls incoming to this country may be higher than those for outgoing calls. A personal call service is available. (In many cases with an additional surcharge.)

Calls to Ships
For calls to ships at sea, *see* p. 1202.

SUNDAY ARRANGEMENTS

(For Express Services see p. 1199).
On SUNDAY *THROUGHOUT THE U.K.* there is no general delivery of letters and parcels.

Place	Charge Code —(see below)	Place	Charge Code —(see below)	Place	Charge Code —(see below)	Place	Charge Code —(see below)
Afghanistan	K	Faroe Is.	C	Madeira	F	Samoa (U.S.A. Territory)	K
Alaska	I	Fiji	J	Malagasy Rep.	K	Samoa (Western)	K
Albania	F	Finland	B	Malawi	K	San Marino	B
Algeria	F	France	A	Malaysia	J	Sao Tome	K
Andorra	A	French Guiana	K	Maldive Is.	J	Saudi Arabia	N
Angola	K	French Polynesia	K	Mali	K	Senegal	K
Antigua	I	French Territory of the		Malta	F	Seychelles	K
Antilles	I	Afars and Issas	K	Mariana Is.	K	Sierra Leone	K
Argentina	J	Gabon	K	Martinique	I	Singapore	L
Ascension	K	Gambia	K	Mauritania	K	Solomon Is.	K
Australia	L	Germany (Dem. Rep.)	C	Mauritius	K	Somali Dem. Rep.	K
Austria	C	Germany (Federal Rep.)	B	Mexico	K	South Africa	M
Azores	F	Ghana	K	Midway Island	K	South Vietnam	K
Bahamas	I	Gibraltar	C	Monaco	A	Spain	B
Bahrain	K	Gilbert and Ellice Is.	K	Montserrat	I	Spanish Territories of	
Barbados	H	Greece	D	Morocco	F	North Africa	C
Belgium	A	Greenland	J	Mozambique	K	Sri Lanka	K
Belize	I	Grenada	I	Nauru Island	K	Sudan	K
Bermuda	I	Guadeloupe	I	Netherlands	A	Surinam	I
Bolivia	K	Guatemala	K	New Caledonia	K	Swaziland	K
Botswana	J	Guinea	K	New Hebrides	K	Sweden	B
Brazil	K	Guinea Bissau	K	New Zealand	K	Switzerland	A
Brunei	F	Guyana	I	Nicaragua	K	Syria	K
Bulgaria	F	Haiti	I	Niger	K	Taiwan	J
Burma	K	Hawaii	H	Nigeria	J	Tanzania	J
Burundi	K	Honduras	K	Niue Island	K	Thailand	K
Cameroon	K	Hong Kong	L	Norfolk Island	K	Tobago	I
Canada	G	Hungary	E	Norway	B	Togo	K
Cape Verde Islands	K	Iceland	E	Oman (except Masirah)	N	Tonga	K
Carriacou	I	India	J	(Masirah only)	J	Tortola	I
Cayman Islands	H	Indonesia	K	Pakistan	K	Trinidad	I
Central African Rep	K	Iran	N	Panama	J	Trucial States	K
Chad	K	Iraq	K	Panama Canal Zone	J	Tunisia	E
Chile	J	Israel	M	Papua New Guinea	K	Turkey	F
Christmas Island	K	Italy	B	Paraguay	J	Turks Island	J
Colombia	J	Ivory Coast	K	Peru	J	Uganda	J
Congo	K	Jamaica	I	Philippines	C	United Arab Emirates	N
Cook (or Hervey) Is.	K	Japan	K	Poland	C	Upper Volta	K
Costa Rica	K	Jordan	K	Portugal	F	Uruguay	G
Cuba	I	Kenya	J	Portuguese Timor	K	U.S.A. (Except Alaska	
Cyprus	D	Khmer Rep.	K	Principe	K	and Hawaii)	G
Czechoslovakia	C	Korea (North)	K	Puerto Rico	H	U.S.S.R.	E
Dahomey	K	Korea (South)	K	Qatar	K	Vatican City	B
Denmark	B	Kuwait	M	Reunion	K	Venezuela	J
Dominica	I	Laos	K	Rhodesia	K	Virgin Is. of U.S.A.	H
Dominion Rep.	I	Lebanon	J	Rodriguez Island	K	Wake Island	K
Ecuador	K	Lesotho	J	Rumania	K	Yemen (Arab Rep.)	K
Egypt	K	Liberia	K	Rwanda	K	Yemen (People's Dem.	
El Salvador	K	Libya	E	St. Helena	K	Rep.)	K
Equatorial Guinea	K	Liechtenstein	B	St. Kitts-Nevis-Anguilla	I	Yugoslavia	C
Ethiopia	K	Luxembourg	A	St. Lucia	I	Zaire	K
Falkland Is.	J	Macao	K	St. Pierre and Miquelon	I	Zambia	J
				St. Vincent	I		

CHARGE CODES

	Calls Dialled Direct		Calls connected by the Operator		
	Full Rate	Cheap Rate	Minimum Charge	Per Additional Minute	Personal Call Surcharge
Charge Code	Seconds for 3p	Seconds for 3p			
			£	£	£
A	7·20	9·60	1·11	0·37	1·50
B	5·14	8·00	1·41	0·47	1·50
C	—	—	1·41	0·47	1·50
D	4·00	6·00	1·71	0·57	1·50
E	—	—	1·71	0·57	1·50
F	—	—	2·40	0·80	1·50
G	2·40	3·20	2·70	0·90	3·00
H	—	—	2·70	0·90	3·00
I	—	—	5·70	0·90	—
J	—	—	3·60	1·20	3·00
K	—	—	6·60	1·20	—
L	1·71	1·71	3·60	1·20	3·00
M	1·71	2·40	3·60	1·20	3·00
N	1·71	2·40	6·60	1·20	—

For mode of packing, prohibitions, etc., *see* Post Office Guide.

Telegrams	DESTINATION	AIR MAIL Weight limit 10kg Blue Air Mail labels essential		SURFACE MAIL			
		Not over ½kg	Each ½kg after or part thereof	Not over 1kg	Not over 3kg	Not over 5kg	Not over 10kg
p		£ p	£ p	£ p	£ p	£ p	£ p
16	Abu Dhabi.............................	2·50	55	2·25	3·25	4·60	7·15
16	Afghanistan...........................	3·30	65	3·05	4·50	6·15	9·00
16	Ajman★................................	No Service		2·40	3·25	4·55	7·15
11	Albania★.................. ....⋅..⋅	3·00	45	2·75	3·85	5·10	7·25
11	Algeria...............................	2·65	40	2·40	3·35	4·40	6·10
11	Andorra (via France).................	3·30	35	2·50	3·05	3·75	5·00
	Andorra (via Spain)..................	3·30	40	2·60	3·40	4·20	5·45
	Angola...............................	2·70	90	2·45	3·15	4·20	6·70
	Anguilla..............................	2·10	60	1·85	2·65	3·50	5·40
11	Antigua...............................	2·45	70	2·20	3·10	4·20	5·85
16	Argentina.............................	3·35	1·15	2·60	3·85	5·25	8·70
16	Ascension★............................	No Service		1·85	2·30	3·00	4·40
16	Australia★............................	3·35	1·65	2·25	3·70	5·20	8·45
11	Austria★..............................	2·55	30	2·30	3·05	3·90	5·20
11	Azores................................	2·80	40	2·55	3·50	4·75	6·25
11	Bahamas★..............................	2·75	70	2·30	2·85	3·65	5·70
16	Bahrain (State of)★...................	2·65	55	2·40	3·45	4·85	7·15
11	Balearic Isles★.......................	2·90	35	2·65	3·40	4·20	5·45
16	Bangladesh★...........................	2·80	80	2·30	3·35	4·40	6·95
11	Barbados..............................	2·80	60	2·35	2·90	3·75	5·85
11	Belgium...............................	2·80	30	2·25	2·80	3·50	4·75
11	Belize................................	2·80	70	2·30	2·85	3·45	5·40
16	Benin (formerly Dahomey)..............	2·80	90	2·55	3·40	4·35	6·20
11	Bermuda...............................	2·45	50	2·10	2·60	3·60	5·40
16	Bhutan★...............................	3·00	90	2·70	3·45	4·75	7·75
16	Bolivia★..............................	3·10	1·15	2·85	4·10	5·20	8·35
16	Botswana★.............................	2·70	90	2·45	3·40	4·40	5·85
	Botswana (Kasane and Kazungula)........			2·45	3·40	4·50	6·50
16	Brazil★...............................	3·59	95	3·00	4·15	5·60	8·90
	British Indian Ocean Territory★.......	No Service		1·95	2·60	3·65	5·60
	British Virgin Islands................	2·75	70	2·10	2·95	4·15	6·10
16	Brunei................................	3·65	95	2·60	3·90	5·50	8·60
11	Bulgaria..............................	3·15	45	2·90	4·00	5·25	7·30
16	Burma.................................	3·00	90	2·45	3·20	4·40	6·95
16	Burundi...............................	2·80	90	2·55	3·35	4·60	7·15
	Cambodia..............................						
16	Cameroon..............................	2·60	80	2·35	3·15	4·25	6·60
11	Canada★...............................	2·30	80	2·05	3·20	4·40	6·70
11	Canary Isles★.........................	2·30	40	2·05	2·85	3·65	5·15
16	Cape Verde Isles......................	2·40	75	2·15	3·15	4·15	6·15
16	Caroline Islands★.....................	3·30	1·05	2·25	3·70	5·75	10·50
11	Cayman Islands★.......................	2·40	70	2·15	3·60	5·15	8·50
16	Central African Republic..............	2·65	80	2·40	3·45	4·60	6·90
16	Chad..................................	2·85	80	2·60	3·65	4·95	7·05
16	Chile.................................	3·60	1·15	2·90	3·60	5·00	8·25
16	China (People's Republic of)★.........	3·15	1·30	2·90	4·75	6·70	10·15
16	Christmas Island (Indian Ocean)★......	3·00	1·00	2·75	3·85	5·50	9·00
16	Cocos (Keeling Islands)★..............	3·35	1·60	2·25	3·70	5·20	8·45
16	Colombia★.............................	3·00	95	2·30	3·45	4·70	7·70
16	Comoro Islands........................	3·00	1·00	2·75	3·85	5·10	7·45
16	Congo (People's Republic of)..........	2·50	90	2·25	3·30	4·40	6·35
11	Corsica...............................	2·75	35	2·50	3·25	4·20	5·90
16	Costa Rica★...........................	2·95	75	2·15	3·15	4·40	7·00
11	Cuba (Direct)★........................	3·05	95	2·40	2·95	3·60	5·50
	Cuba (Guantanamo Bay via U.S.A.).......			2·10	3·50	5·45	9·15
11	Cyprus................................	3·20	45	2·90	4·05	5·35	7·25
11	Czechoslovakia★.......................	2·70	35	2·45	3·25	4·20	5·65
16	Dahomey (see Benin)...................						
11	Denmark...............................	2·20	30	1·95	2·65	3·30	4·60
11	Dominica..............................	2·30	65	1·95	2·50	3·45	5·40
11	Dominican Republic★...................	2·40	75	2·05	2·60	3·50	5·35
16	Dubai★................................	2·50	60	2·25	3·25	4·60	7·15
16	Ecuador★..............................	3·35	90	2·50	3·60	4·95	8·15
11	Egypt (Arab Republic of)..............	3·40	35	3·15	3·85	4·50	6·10
16	El Salvador★..........................	3·35	75	2·80	3·40	4·50	7·00
16	Equatorial Guinea★....................	2·35	80	2·10	3·10	4·20	6·05
16	Ethiopia★.............................	2·80	75	2·55	3·65	5·10	8·40
16	Falkland Islands and Dependencies......	2·70	95	2·20	3·15	4·45	7·40
16	Faroe Isles...........................	2·40	25	1·95	2·65	3·30	4·60
16	Fiji..................................	3·10	1·55	2·20	3·25	4·50	7·25
11	Finland★..............................	2·70	45	2·45	3·40	4·25	5·60
11	France................................	3·30	25	2·50	3·05	3·75	5·00
16	French Guiana.........................	2·70	1·20	2·45	3·40	4·50	6·35
16	French Polynesia......................	4·15	1·60	2·75	3·65	4·80	6·90
16	French Territory of the Afars and Issas....	2·70	70	2·45	3·65	4·95	8·00
11	French West Indies....................	2·65	95	2·40	3·40	4·45	6·30

★ No insured box service available.

For mode of packing, prohibitions, etc., *see* Post Office Guide.

Telegrams	DESTINATION	AIR MAIL Weight limit 10kg Blue Air Mail labels essential		SURFACE MAIL			
		Not over ½kg	Each ½kg after or part thereof	Not over 1kg	Not over 3kg	Not over 5kg	Not over 10kg
		£ p	£ p	£ p	£ p	£ p	£ p
p 16	Fujairah★	No Service		2·40	3·25	4·55	7·15
16	Gabon	2·55	90	2·30	3·30	4·45	6·10
16	Gambia The	2·50	50	2·20	3·25	4·25	6·35
16	Gaza and Khan Yunis★	2·30	50	2·05	2·95	4·15	6·40
11	Germany, Democratic Republic of	3·00	35	2·75	3·65	4·55	5·90
11	Germany, Federal Republic of	3·00	35	2·20	2·80	3·55	5·00
16	Ghana	2·80	55	2·55	3·25	4·40	6·85
11	Gibraltar	2·30	30	2·05	2·85	3·65	4·90
16	Gilbert Islands (for Ellice Islands see Tuvalu)	3·55	1·40	2·35	3·65	5·25	8·75
11	Greece (*Direct*)	3·30	45	2·95	3·85	4·80	6·50
	Greece (*via* Belgium)			3·05	4·15	5·40	7·40
11	Greenland	2·60	75	1·95	2·65	3·30	4·60
11	Grenada	2·60	70	2·35	3·00	3·95	5·85
16	Guatemala★	2·90	75	2·40	2·95	4·00	6·35
16	Guinea★	2·60	80	2·35	3·20	4·00	5·90
	Guinea-Bissau	2·55	65	2·30	3·15	4·20	6·70
11	Guyana	2·85	65	2·35	2·95	4·00	6·10
11	Haiti★	2·75	75	2·20	2·80	3·50	4·95
16	Honduras (Republic of)	3·35	80	2·80	3·35	4·00	5·65
16	Hong Kong	2·55	85	2·10	3·15	4·35	6·75
11	Hungary	2·70	30	2·40	3·20	4·15	5·65
11	Iceland★	2·70	40	2·45	3·20	4·10	5·35
16	India	2·60	70	2·35	3·45	4·60	7·15
16	Indonesia★	3·50	1·10	2·70	3·25	3·95	6·35
16	Iran★	2·85	50	2·60	3·80	5·15	7·60
16	Iraq★	2·55	60	2·30	3·40	4·60	7·40
11	Israel★	2·40	45	2·15	3·15	4·40	6·75
11	Italy★	2·55	40	2·40	3·20	4·00	5·25
16	Ivory Coast	2·70	80	2·45	3·25	4·15	5·75
11	Jamaica★	2·75	70	2·50	3·10	4·10	5·95
16	Japan★	3·40	85	3·00	3·85	4·50	6·85
16	Jordan★	2·40	40	2·15	2·95	3·90	6·15
16	Kenya	2·30	60	2·05	3·20	4·45	6·85
	Khmer Republic: see Cambodia						
16	Korea (South only)★	3·40	1·00	2·55	3·25	4·35	6·95
16	Kuwait	2·50	50	2·25	3·00	4·20	6·75
16	Lao People's Democratic Republic	3·00	1·25	2·75	3·70	4·70	6·75
	Lebanon	2·70	45	2·40	3·20	4·45	7·15
16	Lesotho★	2·90	95	2·65	3·60	4·60	6·35
16	Liberia★	2·50	95	2·25	2·95	3·95	6·20
11	Libyan Arab Republic★	2·55	45	2·30	3·10	4·25	6·75
11	Luxembourg	2·30	30	2·05	2·80	3·55	4·65
16	Macao	2·75	95	2·35	3·10	4·25	6·95
16	Madeira	2·80	40	2·55	3·50	4·65	6·25
16	Malagasy Republic	2·95	1·15	2·70	3·90	5·50	7·25
16	Malawi	3·70	70	3·45	4·70	6·20	8·55
16	Malaya	2·80	90	2·10	2·95	4·15	6·65
	Maldives (Republic of)★	2·65	90	2·40	3·30	4·65	7·40
16	Mali	2·75	70	2·50	3·40	4·30	6·90
11	Malta	2·75	40	2·50	3·30	4·20	5·70
16	Mariana Islands★	2·60	1·80	2·25	3·70	5·75	10·50
16	Marshall Islands★	3·30	1·70	2·25	3·70	5·40	9·75
16	Mauritania	2·55	90	2·30	3·20	4·45	7·25
16	Mauritius	2·50	1·05	2·25	2·90	3·90	6·20
16	Mexico (*except* Chetumal)★	2·80	95	2·40	2·95	3·60	5·75
	Mexico (Chetumal *only*)★			2·55	3·15	3·85	5·75
	Mongolia (People's Republic)★	No Service		No Service			
11	Montserrat	2·40	65	2·15	3·00	3·70	5·50
11	Morocco	2·30	35	2·05	2·95	3·95	5·60
	Mozambique	2·90	90	2·30	3·20	4·50	6·95
16	Nauru Island★	3·60	1·55	2·15	3·50	4·95	8·25
16	Nepal	2·90	70	2·65	3·50	4·35	7·00
11	Netherlands	2·70	25	2·45	3·00	3·70	4·70
11	Netherlands Antilles	2·70	75	2·10	2·60	3·45	5·45
	Nevis	2·10	60	1·85	2·50	3·50	5·40
16	New Caledonia	3·60	1·45	2·70	3·85	5·40	9·15
16	New Hebrides★	3·60	1·30	2·70	3·85	5·40	9·15
16	New Zealand	3·75	1·55	2·30	3·50	4·90	7·95
	New Zealand Island Territory	3·15	2·15	2·20	3·50	4·90	7·95
16	Nicaragua★	2·90	85	2·30	2·95	4·10	6·35
16	Nigeria	2·65	50	2·40	3·25	4·45	6·70
16	Niger Republic	2·75	80	2·50	3·45	4·55	7·25
16	Norfolk Island★	3·00	1·75	2·65	3·70	5·20	8·50
11	Norway★	2·80	35	2·55	3·20	3·90	5·05
16	Oman (Sultanate of)	2·50	50	2·25	3·25	4·60	7·15
16	Pakistan	2·60	85	2·35	3·35	4·40	6·95
16	Panama (Republic of)	3·25	90	2·60	3·15	3·85	5·95

★ No insured box service available.

For mode of packing, prohibitions, etc., *see* Post Office Guide.

Telegrams	DESTINATION	AIR MAIL Weight limit 10kg Blue Air Mail labels essential		SURFACE MAIL			
		Not over ½kg	Each ½kg after or part thereof	Not over 1kg	Not over 3kg	Not over 5kg	Not over 10kg
p		£ p	£ p	£ p	£ p	£ p	£ p
16	Panama Canal Zone....................	2·40	90	1·95	3·00	4·40	7·20
16	Papua New Guinea....................	3·35	2·10	2·10	3·10	4·25	6·90
16	Paraguay★...........................	2·85	95	2·60	3·50	5·00	8·35
16	Peru★...............................	3·65	90	3·00	3·70	5·10	8·10
16	Philippines★.........................	2·70	1·00	2·10	2·60	3·45	5·10
16	Pitcairn Island★.....................	2·75	1·75	1·85	3·15	4·60	7·60
11	Poland★.............................	2·75	35	2·50	3·35	4·10	5·30
11	Portugal.............................	2·70	35	2·45	3·30	4·15	5·60
16	Portuguese East Africa: *see* Mozambique.....						
16	Portuguese Timor★...................						
16	Portuguese West Africa: *see* Angola; Guinea-Bissau; São Tomé and Principe..........						
	Principe: *see* São Tomé and Principe........						
11	Puerto Rico★.........................	2·50	90	2·10	3·30	4·60	7·10
16	Qatar (State of)★.....................	2·50	50	2·25	3·10	4·35	6·85
	Ras Al Khaimah★....................	No Service		2·40	3·25	4·55	7·15
16	Reunion.............................	2·85	1·15	2·60	3·55	4·55	6·40
16	Rhodesia★...........................	2·75	90	2·50	3·55	4·75	6·95
11	Romania★............................	2·80	40	2·55	3·50	4·55	6·35
16	Rwanda★.............................	2·55	95	2·30	3·20	4·45	6·95
16	Sabah...............................	2·75	95	2·10	2·95	4·15	6·65
16	St. Helena...........................	No Service		2·30	2·85	3·50	5·15
16	St. Kitts.............................	2·25	70	1·85	2·45	3·50	5·40
11	St. Lucia★...........................	2·60	65	2·10	2·65	3·60	5·20
11	St. Pierre and Miquelon...............	2·80	70	2·55	3·65	4·90	7·35
11	St. Vincent..........................	2·55	65	2·10	2·75	3·75	5·50
16	Samoa (U.S.A. Territory)★............	3·20	1·35	2·25	3·70	5·45	10·00
	São Tomé and Principe (Republic of)........	2·55	90	2·30	3·15	4·20	6·70
16	Sarawak.............................	2·75	95	2·10	2·95	4·15	6·65
16	Saudi Arabia.........................	2·55	70	2·30	3·20	4·45	7·20
16	Senegal..............................	2·55	65	2·30	3·10	3·90	6·20
16	Seychelles...........................	2·45	70	2·05	2·60	3·65	5·60
16	Sharjah★............................	3·15	50	2·40	3·25	4·60	7·15
16	Sierra Leone★........................	2·60	55	2·20	3·10	4·25	6·45
16	Singapore (Republic of)...............	2·70	90	2·10	2·95	4·15	6·65
16	Solomon Islands★....................	3·00	1·75	2·35	3·75	5·40	8·65
16	Somali Democratic Republic...........	2·75	65	2·50	3·75	5·25	8·60
16	South Africa (Republic of)★...........	2·65	90	1·90	2·70	3·70	5·45
11	Spain★..............................	2·90	35	2·65	3·40	4·20	5·45
11	Spanish Territories of North Africa★........	2·90	30	2·65	3·40	4·20	5·45
	Spanish West Africa..................	2·35	50	2·10	3·15	4·25	6·25
	Spitzbergen★........................	No Service		2·65	3·20	3·90	5·05
16	Sri Lanka (Republic of)...............	3·20	50	2·95	3·65	4·30	6·40
16	Sudan (Democratic Republic of)★........	3·00	55	2·75	3·80	5·00	7·40
16	Surinam.............................	2·80	90	2·30	2·85	3·50	5·45
16	Swaziland★...........................	2·40	95	2·15	3·05	4·40	6·75
11	Sweden..............................	2·55	30	2·30	3·05	3·75	5·10
11	Switzerland..........................	2·60	25	2·30	2·95	3·75	5·00
	Syrian Arab Republic.................	2·35	40	2·10	2·85	3·85	6·00
16	Taiwan..............................	2·90	1·00	2·40	3·10	4·10	6·60
16	Tanzania............................	2·65	70	2·05	3·20	4·45	6·85
16	Thailand★............................	3·10	90	2·85	3·65	4·45	6·40
	Tibet★..............................	No Service		No Service			
16	Togo................................	2·80	85	2·55	3·55	4·55	6·40
16	Tonga...............................	3·95	1·35	2·55	3·70	5·25	8·50
11	Tortola: *see* British Virgin Islands..........						
11	Trinidad and Tobago★.................	2·55	65	2·15	2·85	3·70	5·40
16	Tristan da Cunha★...................	2·80	90	2·20	2·95	4·35	6·70
11	Tunisia..............................	2·70	35	2·45	3·35	4·30	5·70
11	Turkey (*Direct*).....................	2·95	50	2·45	3·35	4·35	6·00
11	Turkey (*via* Belgium)................			2·70	3·90	5·30	7·65
11	Turks and Caicos Islands★.............	2·55	75	2·30	3·80	5·25	8·20
	Tuvalu (formerly Ellice Island)........	3·55	1·40	2·35	3·65	5·25	8·75
16	Uganda.............................	2·50	70	2·05	3·20	4·45	6·85
16	Umm Al Qaiwain★....................	No Service		2·40	3·25	4·55	7·15
16	Upper Volta.........................	2·90	75	2·65	3·70	4·85	7·00
16	Uruguay★............................	2·90	95	2·25	3·75	5·35	9·00
11★	U.S.A.★.............................	2·20	80	2·00	3·30	4·60	7·10
11	U.S.S.R. in Europe★..................	2·65	65	2·40	3·25	4·20	5·90
	U.S.S.R. in Asia★....................	3·10	70	2·85	3·95	5·10	7·75
11	Vatican City State★..................	2·50	45	2·25	2·95	3·80	5·10
16	Venezuela★...........................	3·20	80	2·70	3·25	4·15	6·15
	Vietnam (North).....................	No Service		No Service			
16	Vietnam (South)★....................						
16	Virgin Islands (U.S.A.)★..............	2·20	90	1·95	3·30	4·60	7·25
11	Wake Island★........................	2·70	1·45	2·25	3·70	5·40	9·75
16	Western Samoa.......................	3·20	1·35	2·20	2·95	4·15	6·85

★ No insured box service avaiable.

For mode of packing, prohibitions, etc., *see* Post Office Guide.

Telegrams	DESTINATION	AIR MAIL Weight limit 10kg Blue Air Mail labels essential		SURFACE MAIL			
		Not over ½kg	Each ½kg after or part thereof	Not over 1kg	Not over 3kg	Not over 5kg	Not over 10kg
		£ p	£ p	£ p	£ p	£ p	£ p
16	Yemen Arab Republic★...	2·70	75	2·25	3·45	4·85	7·90
16	Yemen People's Democratic Republic...	2·80	55	2·50	3·70	5·15	7·75
11	Yugoslavia...	2·75	40	2·50	3·45	4·50	6·10
16	Zaire (Republic of)★...	2·55	75	2·30	3·05	4·15	6·75
16	Zambia★...	2·95	75	2·70	3·95	5·70	8·85

★ No insured box service available.

POST OFFICE FINANCIAL RESULTS
(£ million)

	1974–75				1975–76				Total (1975–76)
	Telecom-munications	Posts	GRS★	DPS†	Telecom-munications	Posts	GRS★	DPS†	
INCOME									
Main services...	1349·6	708·8	26·6	27·2	2118·6	1013·7	38·9	34·7	3205·9
Other...	38·5	62·0	12·1	—	48·2	74·9	15·6	—	138·7
TOTAL...	1388·1	770·8	38·7	27·2	2166·8	1088·6	54·5	34·7	3344·6
EXPENDITURE									
Operating and Administration...	318·2	710·5	12·0	19·3	388·0	874·9	14·6	25·2	1302·7
Plant Maintenance...	167·6	11·5	—	—	223·7	14·7	—	—	238·4
Accommodation...	95·7	30·5	0·6	2·6	124·0	36·4	0·8	3·2	164·4
Motor Transport...	29·0	21·0	—	—	34·9	26·0	—	—	60·9
Net Interest Payable...	286·3	21·5	2·4	1·5	329·8	21·1	0·5	1·3	352·7
Depreciation...	367·9	16·4	0·5	3·1	480·6	21·5	0·3	3·4	505·8
Others‡...	317·9	68·6	26·5	0·3	431·1	103·2	37·2	0·3	571·8
TOTAL...	1582·6	880·0	42·0	26·8	2012·1	1097·8	53·4	33·4	3196·7
Profit/(Loss) for Year	(194·5)	(109·2)	(3·3)	0·4	154·7	(9·2)	1·1	1·3	147·9

NOTE: These figures include inter-business charges of £138·9m for 1975–76 and £107·9m for 1974–75.
★ Giro and Remittance Service—the results for 1975–76 are before charging taxation and dividend.
† Data Processing Service.
‡ Includes pension deficiency, purchasing and supply services, research and development, and payment in respect of external traffic.

THE PERIODS OF ENGLISH ARCHITECTURE

Date	Style
I. Before 55 B.C....	Ancient British.
II. 55 B.C. to A.D. 420...	Roman Period.
III. A.D. 449 to Norman Conquest (1066)...	Anglo-Saxon.
IV. 1066–1189 (*i.e.* to end 12th cent.)...	Norman.
V. 1189–1307 (*i.e.* 13th cent.)...	Early English (Lancet, or Geometrical).
VI. 1307–1377 (*i.e.* 14th cent.)...	Decorated (or Curvilinear).
VII. 1377–1485 (*i.e.* 15th cent.)...	Perpendicular (or Rectilinear).
VIII. 1485–1558 (*i.e.* first half 16th cent.)...	Tudor
IX. A.D. 1558–1625. Early Renaissance...	{ Elizabeth (A.D. 1558–1603). { Jacobean (A.D. 1603–1625).
X. A.D. 1625–1830. Late Renaissance...	{ Stuart (A.D. 1625–1702). { Queen Anne and Georgian (A.D. 1702–1830).
XI. Modern Architecture (The Age of Revivals) { 19th cent...	{ William IV. (A.D. 1830–1837). { Victoria (A.D. 1837–1901).
XII. Recent Architecture. 20th cent...	{ Edward VII. (A.D. 1901–1910). { George V. (A.D. 1910–1935). { Edward VIII. (A.D. 1936). { George VI. (A.D. 1936–1952).

EXPECTATION OF LIFE

(English Life Table No. 12, 1960–62)
Expectation of life at under 1 year of age is: Males, 68·09 years; Females, 74·00 years.

Age	Male	Female	Age	Male	Female	Age	Male	Female	Age	Male	Female
1	68·80	74·43	26	44·89	50·11	51	21·84	26·69	76	6·66	8·27
2	67·90	73·52	27	43·93	49·14	52	21·02	25·81	77	6·28	7·77
3	66·97	72·58	28	42·98	48·17	53	20·21	24·95	78	5·92	7·28
4	66·02	71·62	29	42·02	47·20	54	19·42	24·09	79	5·57	6·83
5	65·06	70·66	30	41·06	46·23	55	18·65	23·24	80	5·25	6·39
6	64·09	69·69	31	40·11	45·26	56	17·89	22·39	81	4·94	5·98
7	63·13	68·71	32	39·16	44·30	57	17·16	21·56	82	4·66	5·60
8	62·16	67·73	33	38·21	43·34	58	16·44	20·73	83	4·39	5·24
9	61·18	66·75	34	37·26	42·38	59	15·74	19·91	84	4·14	4·90
10	60·21	65·77	35	36·31	41·42	60	15·06	19·11	85	3·90	4·58
11	59·23	64·79	36	35·37	40·47	61	14·40	18·31	86	3·68	4·29
12	58·25	63·80	37	34·43	39·52	62	13·76	17·53	87	3·48	4·01
13	57·28	62·82	38	33·49	38·57	63	13·14	16·76	88	3·30	3·76
14	56·30	61·83	39	32·55	37·63	64	12·54	16·00	89	3·13	3·53
15	55·33	60·85	40	31·62	36·69	65	11·95	15·26	90	2·97	3·32
16	54·36	59·87	41	30·70	35·75	66	11·39	14·53	91	2·83	3·12
17	53·40	58·89	42	29·77	34·82	67	10·84	13·81	92	2·70	2·94
18	52·45	57·91	43	28·86	33·90	68	10·31	13·12	93	2·58	2·78
19	51·51	56·93	44	27·95	32·98	69	9·79	12·44	94	2·47	2·63
20	50·57	55·95	45	27·05	32·06	70	9·29	11·78	95	2·38	2·49
21	49·63	54·98	46	26·15	31·15	71	8·81	11·14	96	2·29	2·37
22	48·69	54·00	47	25·27	30·25	72	8·35	10·52	97	2·21	2·26
23	47·74	53·03	48	24·40	29·35	73	7·90	9·93	98	2·14	2·16
24	46·80	52·06	49	23·53	28·46	74	7·47	9·35	99	2·07	2·07
25	45·84	51·08	50	22·68	27·57	75	7·05	8·80	100	2·00	1·99

Comparative Table

	Males				Females			
Age	England and Wales	England	Wales	Greater London	England and Wales	England	Wales	Greater London
0	68·1	68·2	66·8	68·7	74·0	74·1	73·2	75·0
10	60·2	60·3	59·2	60·6	65·8	65·9	65·1	66·6
20	50·6	50·7	49·6	51·0	56·0	56·0	55·3	56·7
30	41·1	41·2	40·2	41·4	46·2	46·3	45·6	47·0
40	31·6	31·7	30·8	32·0	36·7	36·8	36·1	37·5
50	22·7	22·7	21·9	23·0	27·6	27·6	27·1	28·3
60	15·1	15·1	14·5	15·2	19·1	19·2	18·7	19·8
70	9·3	9·3	8·9	9·4	11·8	11·8	11·4	12·3
80	5·2	5·3	5·1	5·4	6·4	6·4	6·2	6·8

EXPECTATION OF LIFE IN YEARS: VARIOUS COUNTRIES

	ENGLAND AND WALES 1965–67		SCOTLAND 1968		NORTHERN IRELAND 1966–68		UNITED STATES 1967		AUSTRIA 1968	
Age	Male	Female	Male	Female	Male	Female	Male	Female	Male	Female
0	68·7	74·9	66·9	73·0	68·1	73·4	67·0	74·2	66·7	73·5
1	69·1	75·1	67·5	73·3	69·0	74·1	67·7	74·6	67·6	74·1
5	65·4	71·3	63·8	69·5	65·2	70·3	63·9	70·9	63·9	70·4
10	60·5	66·4	58·9	64·7	60·4	65·4	59·1	66·0	59·1	65·5
15	55·6	61·5	54·1	59·7	55·5	60·5	54·2	61·1	54·2	60·7
20	50·9	56·6	49·3	54·8	50·7	55·6	49·6	56·3	49·6	55·8
30	41·4	46·9	39·8	45·0	41·2	45·8	40·5	46·7	40·3	46·1
40	31·9	37·3	30·5	35·6	31·8	36·3	31·4	37·3	31·2	36·6
50	23·0	28·2	21·8	26·6	22·9	27·2	23·1	28·4	22·6	27·4
60	15·3	19·8	14·5	18·5	15·3	18·8	16·0	20·2	14·9	18·9
70	9·5	12·4	9·0	11·4	9·5	11·6	10·4	13·0	9·2	11·5
75	7·3	9·4	6·9	8·5	7·3	8·8	8·3	10·0	6·9	8·5
80	5·5	6·9	5·3	6·2	5·3	6·5	6·4	7·3	5·2	6·1
85	4·0	5·0	3·8	4·2	3·9	4·6	4·7	5·0	3·9	4·4

BRITISH PASSPORT REGULATIONS

Applications for United Kingdom passports must be made on the forms obtainable at any of the Passport Offices (addresses given below) or at any Main Post Office.

London.—Clive House, 70–78 Petty France, S.W.1.

Liverpool.—India Buildings, Water Street, Liverpool, 2.

Newport, Gwent.—Olympia House, Upper Dock Street.

Peterborough.—Passport Office, 55 Westfield Road, Peterborough.

Glasgow.—1st Floor, Empire House, 131 West Nile Street, Glasgow, C.1.

Hours. The above offices are open Mon.-Fri. 9 a.m. to 4.30 p.m. The Passport Offices are also open for cases of special emergency (*e.g.* death or serious illness) arising outside normal office hours between 4.30 p.m. and 5.30 p.m. (6.00 p.m. in London); and in *London* on Saturdays between 10 a.m. and noon.

Completed forms of application should be sent to one of the five Passport Offices, with photographs, supporting documents and the fee of £8, in the form of a Cheque or Postal Order which should be crossed and made payable to the Passport Office.

Persons resident in *Northern Ireland* may apply *in person* to the Foreign and Commonwealth Office Passport Agency, 1st Flr., Marlborough House, 30 Victoria Street, Belfast, or *by post* to the Passport Office, Glasgow.

A Passport cannot be issued or renewed by the Foreign and Commonwealth Office on behalf of *a person already abroad*; such person should apply, in a foreign country, to the nearest British Mission or Consulate, or, within the British Commonwealth outside the United Kingdom of Great Britain and N. Ireland, to the nearest British Passport issuing authority.

United Kingdom Passports are granted:—

(i) To citizens of the United Kingdom and Colonies.

(ii) To British subjects without citizenship.

(iii) To British Protected Persons.

A passport granted to a child under 16 will normally be valid for an initial period of five years, after which it may be extended for a further five years with no extra charge. A passport granted to a person over 16 will normally be valid for 10 years and will not be renewable. Thereafter, or if at any time the Passport contains no further space for visas, a new Passport must be obtained.

A Passport including particulars of the *holder's spouse* is not available for his/her use when he/she is travelling alone. A spouse's particulars may *only* be added at the time of issue of a passport.

Children who have reached the age of sixteen years require separate Passports. Their applications must be signed by one of their parents.

Passport applications must be countersigned by a Member of Parliament, Justice of the Peace, Minister of Religion, Doctor, Lawyer, Bank Officer, Police Officer or any person of similar standing who has been personally acquainted with the applicant for at least two years. The applicant's birth certificate and other evidence in support of the statements made in the application must be produced.

In the case of children under the age of 16 requiring a separate passport, an application should be made by one of the parents on form (B).

If the applicant for a Passport is a citizen of the United Kingdom and Colonies by naturalization or registration, the Certificate of Naturalization or registration must be produced with the application. British Passports are generally available for travel *to all countries.* The possession of a Passport does not, however, exempt the holder from compliance with any *Immigration Regulations* in force in British or foreign countries, or from the necessity of obtaining a *visa* where required.

PHOTOGRAPHS

Duplicate unmounted photographs of applicant (and his wife, if to be included in the Passport) must be sent. These photographs should be printed on *thin* paper and must not be glazed on the reverse side. A coloured photograph should not be submitted unless the supplier advises that the type is " passport approved ". They should measure not more than 2½ in. by 2 in. (63 mm. by 50 mm.), or less than 2 in. by 1½ in. (50 mm. by 38 mm.), and should be taken full face without a hat.

RENEWAL OF PASSPORTS

Applications for the renewal of United Kingdom passports must be made on Form D.

94-PAGE PASSPORTS

On May 1, 1973, a new type of passport became available. Intended to meet the needs of frequent travellers who fill standard passports well before the ten-year validity has expired, it contains 94 pages, is valid for ten years and costs £16.

British Visitors' Passports

A simplified form of travel document is available for British subjects (Citizens of the United Kingdom and Colonies) wishing to pay short visits (not exceeding three months) to certain foreign countries, *viz.*

ANDORA; AUSTRIA; BELGIUM; DENMARK; FINLAND; FRANCE (incl. CORSICA); GREECE (& THE GREEK ISLANDS); W. GERMANY (incl. West Berlin by air only); ICELAND; ITALY; LIECHTENSTEIN; LUXEMBURG; MONACO; NETHERLANDS; NORWAY; PORTUGAL (incl. MADEIRA & AZORES); SAN MARINO; SPAIN (incl. BALEARIC & CANARY ISLANDS); SWEDEN; SWITZERLAND; TURKEY.

A fee of £4·00 is charged for the issue of a British Visitors' Passport, which is valid for 12 months, cannot be amended and is not renewable; on expiry application should be made for a new passport if required. Particulars of an applicant's spouse and/or children under 16 years can be included at *the time of issue only* at no extra cost. A child of 8 years of age and over is eligible to hold a British Visitors' Passport. Applications for, or including, a person under 18 years of age (unless married or serving in H.M. Forces) must be countersigned by the legal guardian.

British Visitors' Passports are obtainable by application on Form VP (from any Main Post Office). Applicants in England, Scotland and Wales should take the completed form in person to any Main Post Office which will normally issue the passport without further delay; applicants in Northern Ireland to Foreign and Commonwealth Office Passport Agency, Belfast. *British Visitors' Passports are not obtainable from the Passport Offices.* Two recent passport photographs will be required of the applicant and three of his/her spouse, if to be included; photographs of children are not required. Size of photographs must be 2 in. × 1½ in. (50 mm. by 38 mm.) (*see also* PHOTOGRAPHS above). No visas are required on British Visitors' Passports.

Applicants must also produce for the purpose of identification a N.H.S. Medical Card, birth certificate or retirement pension book.

HALL-MARKS ON GOLD AND SILVER WARES
London (Goldsmiths' Hall) Date Marks
From 1478 to 1976.

𝕯	Lombardic, double cusps	1478–9 to 1497–8	𝖆	Roman letter, small	1736–7 to 1755–6
	Black letter, small......	1498–9 „ 1517–8		Old English, capitals	1756–7 „ 1775–6
	Lombardic	1518–9 „ 1537–8		Roman letter, small...	1776–7 „ 1795–6
	Roman and other capitals..................	1538–9 „ 1557–8		Roman letter, capitals	1796–7 „ 1815–6
	Black letter, small ...	1558–9 „ 1577–8		Roman letter, small...	1816–7 „ 1835–6
	Roman letter, capitals	1578–9 „ 1597–8		Old English, capitals	1836–7 „ 1855–6
	Lombardic, external cusps	1598–9 „ 1617–8		Old English, small ...	1856–7 „ 1875–6
	Italic letter, small ...	1618–9 „ 1637–8		Roman letter, capitals [A to M *square* shield N to Z as shown.]	1876–7 „ 1895–6
	Court hand	1638–9 „ 1657–8		Roman letter, small...	1896–7 „ 1915–6
	Black letter, capitals	1658–9 „ 1677–8		Black letter, small ...	1916–7 „ 1935–6
	Black letter, small ...	1678–9 „ 1696–7		Roman letter, capital	1936–7 „ 1955–6
	Court hand	1697 „ 1715–6 (From March 1697 only.)		Italic letter, small ...	1956–7 „ 1975–6
	Roman letter, capitals	1716–7 „ 1735–6			

Hall-marks are the symbols stamped on gold or silver articles to indicate that they have been chemically tested and that they conform to one of the legal standards. With certain exceptions, all gold or silver articles are required by law to be hall-marked before they are offered for sale. Hall-marking was instituted in 1300 under a statute of Edward I.

Normally a complete modern hall-mark consists of four symbols—the maker's mark, assay office mark, standard mark and date letter. Additional marks have been authorized from time to time.

Maker's Mark.—Instituted in 1363, the maker's mark was originally a device such as a bird or *fleur-de-lys* and now consists invariably of the initials of the Christian and surnames of the maker or of the firm.

Assay Office Mark.—The existing assay offices and their distinguishing marks are:—

LONDON (Goldsmiths' Hall).

A leopard's head (uncrowned from 1300 to 1478–9, when it became crowned until 1821, since when it has been uncrowned). From

1697–1720 this mark was used in London for gold only and not for silver.

BIRMINGHAM...................An anchor
SHEFFIELD.............A crown for silver and a York rose for gold
EDINBURGH.........................A castle
Offices formerly existed in other towns, e.g. Chester, Glasgow, Newcastle, Exeter, York and Norwich, each having its own distinguishing mark.

Standard Mark.—Instituted in 1544. The current legal standards and their marks are as follows:—

SILVER.—Sterling silver (92·5 per cent. silver) is marked by English assay offices with a *lion passant* and by the Edinburgh Assay Office with a *thistle*. A full-length figure of *Britannia* was impressed on

silver of a higher standard (95·84 per cent. silver) between 1697 and 1720 and this mark is still used occasionally by all British assay offices.

GOLD.—22 carat articles (91·6 per cent. gold) are marked by English offices with a crown followed by the figure 22; by the Edinburgh office with the figure 22 following the standard mark as for sterling silver (*see* above).

18 carat articles (75 per cent. gold) are marked by English assay offices with a crown followed by the figure 18.

All British assay offices mark 14 carat gold (58·5 per cent. gold) with the figures 14·585 and 9 carat gold (37·5 per cent. gold) with the figures 9·375.

Date Letter.—Instituted in 15th Century. The date letter denotes the year in which an article was assayed or hall-marked. Each alphabetical cycle

has a distinctive style of lettering or shape of shield. The date letters are different at the various assay offices and the particular office must be established from the assay office mark before reference is made to tables of date letters. The date letter is changed at the London Office in May each year and at Birmingham and Sheffield in July. Specimen shields and letters used by the London Office in each period from 1438 to date are shown on p. 1212.

OTHER MARKS

Duty Mark.—In 1784 an additional mark of the reigning sovereign's head was introduced to signify that the excise duty had been paid. The mark became obsolete on the abolition of the duty in 1890.

Silver Jubilee and Coronation Marks.—Voluntary marks were authorized to be used at manufacturers' request to commemorate the silver jubilee of King George V and Queen Mary and the

 Coronation of Her Majesty Queen Elizabeth II. The Jubilee Mark was used on silver made in 1933, 1934 and 1935 and the Coronation Mark on gold and
silver with date letter 1952/3 or 1953/4.

Foreign Wares.—Since 1842 foreign wares imported into Great Britain have been required to be hall-marked before sale. The marks consist of the importer's mark, a special assay office mark (*see* below), the decimal figures denoting fineness (together with the carat figure in the case of gold) and the annual date letter. The current assay office marks for foreign wares are as follows:—

LONDON.—The sign of the Constellation Leo.
BIRMINGHAM.—Equilateral triangle.
SHEFFIELD.—The sign of the Constellation Libra.
EDINBURGH.—St. Andrew's Cross.

CLOSE TIMES

Wild Birds.—The *Protection of Wild Birds Act, 1954*, lays down a close season for wild birds (other than Game Birds) from February 1 to August 31 inclusive, each year. Exceptions to these dates are made for—

Capercaillie and (except Scotland) *Woodcock*. Feb. 1—Sept. 30.

Snipe, Feb. 1—Aug. 11.

Wild Duck and Wild Goose (in or over water areas), Feb. 21—Aug. 31.

Birds which may be killed or taken outside the close season (except in Scotland on Sundays, on Christmas Day or in a prescribed area) are the above and coot, curlew (other than stone curlew), bar-tailed godwit, moorhen, plover (golden or grey), common red-shank, certain wild duck (common pochard, gadwall, mallard, pintail, shoveller, teal, tufted duck, wigeon) and certain wild geese (bean, Canada, pink-footed and white-fronted).

Certain wild birds may be killed or taken at any time by authorized persons—cormorant, crow, gull (black-backed or herring), jackdaw, jay, magpie, rook, shag, sparrow, starling, stockdove and wood pigeon; and, in Scotland only, goosander, red-breasted merganser and rock-dove. The sale of Wild Birds' Eggs is prohibited, except that gulls' eggs may be sold at any time and those of the lapwing (green or black plover) from Jan. 1—

April 14 inclusive.

Game Birds—In each case the dates are inclusive:—

Black Game—Dec. 11 to Aug. 19 (Aug. 31 in Somerset, Devon, and New Forest).

★*Grouse*—Dec. 11 to Aug. 11.

★*Partridge*—Feb. 2 to Aug. 31.

★*Pheasant*—Feb. 2 to Sept. 30.

★*Ptarmigan*—(Scotland only) Dec. 11 to Aug. 11.

It is also unlawful (in *England* and *Wales*) to kill the game marked ★ on a Sunday or Christmas Day.

Hunting and Ground Game.—There is no statutory close-time for fox-hunting or rabbit-shooting, nor for hares: but by an Act passed in 1892 the *sale* of hares or leverets in Great Britain is prohibited from March 1 to July 31 inclusive under a penalty of a pound. The First of November is the recognized date for the opening of the *fox-hunting* season, which continues till the following April. *Otter-hunting* lasts from mid-April to mid-September.

Deer.—The Deer Act, 1963, effective from Nov. 1, 1963, imposed the following close times. *Red Deer and Sika Deer*: Stags, May 1–July 31; Hinds, March 1–Oct. 31. *Fallow Deer and Roe Deer*: Buck, May 1–July 31; Doe, March 1–Oct. 31. Under the Act it is an offence to take or wilfully kill deer of any species from one hour after sunset to one hour before sunrise.

WEIGHTS AND MEASURES

The Weights and Measures Act of 1963 enacts the legal measures for Great Britain, basing them upon "United Kingdom primary standards" in the custody of the Standards Department of the Dept. of Trade. The primary standards are the yard, pound, metre and kilogramme. The GALLON, the capacity standard, wet or dry, is based upon the Pound. The Act of 1963 defines the GALLON as the space occupied by 10 pounds weight of distilled water of density 0·998 859 gramme per millilitre weighed in air of density 0·001 217 gramme per millilitre against weights of density 8·136 grammes per millilitre. The METRE and the LITRE have the meanings assigned by order of the Dept. of Trade to reproduce in English the international definition of these measures in force at the time of making of the orders.

New definitions for an *international yard* and *pound* were adopted on Jan. 1, 1959, by the standards laboratories of the United Kingdom, Canada, Australia, New Zealand, South Africa and the United States:
international yard = 0·914 4 metre.   *international pound* = 0·453 592 37 kilogramme.

The following list shows the definitions of measures set out in the Weights and Measures Act, 1963 and some useful conversions. *See also* Conversion Tables, p. 1218.

Measurement of Length

Imperial Units

Mile = 1,760 yards.	1 mil = 1/1000 inch.
Furlong = 220 yards.	12 inches (*in.*) = 1 foot (*ft.*).
Chain = 22 yards.	3 feet = 1 yard (*yd.*).
YARD = 0·914 4 metre.	6 feet = 1 fathom.
Foot′ = ⅓ yard.	22 yards = 1 chain = 100 links.
Inch″ = 1/36 yard.	10 chains = 1 furlong.
	8 furlongs = 1 mile = 1,760 yards.

Metric Units

Kilometre = 1,000 metres.	10 millimetres (*mm.*) = 1 centimetre (*cm.*) = 0·393 701 inch.
METRE (*see* above) = 1·094 yards.	10 centimetres = 1 decimetre (*dm.*) = 3·937 011 inches.
Decimetre = 1/10 metre.	10 decimetres = 1 METRE (*m.*) = 1·093 614 yards.
Centimetre = 1/000 metre.	10 metres = 1 dekametre (*dam.*) = 10·936 143 yards.
Millimetre = 1/1000 metre.	10 dekametres = 1 hectometre (*hm.*) = 109·361 43 yards.
	10 hectometres = 1 kilometre (*km.*) = 0·621 371 mile.

A kilometre is approximately *five-eighths* of a mile, so that 8 kilometres may be regarded as 5 miles.

Measurement of Area

Imperial Units

Square mile = 640 acres.	144 sq. inches = 1 sq. foot.
Acre = 4,840 square yards.	9 sq. feet = 1 sq. yard.
Rood = 1,210 square yards.	4 roods = 1 acre.
SQUARE YARD = a superficial area equal to that of a square each side of which measures one yard.	10 square chains = 1 acre = 4,840 sq. yards.
Square foot = 1/9 square yard.	640 acres = 1 square mile.
Square inch = 1/144 square foot.	

Metric Units

Hectare = 100 ares.	1 sq. centimetre = 0·155 sq. inch.
Dekare = 10 ares.	1 sq. METRE = 10·763 9 sq. feet = 1·195 99 sq. yds.
Are = 100 square metres.	1 are (*a.*) = 0·098 8 rood.
SQUARE METRE = a superficial area equal to that of a square each side of which measures one metre.	1 hectare (10,000 sq. metres) (*ha.*) = 2·471 05 acres.
Square decimetre = 1/100 square metre.	1 sq. kilometre = 0·386 102 sq. mile.
Square centimetre = 1/100 square decimetre.	
Square millimetre = 1/100 square centimetre.	

Measurement of Volume

Imperial Units

CUBIC YARD = a volume equal to that of a cube each edge of which measures one yard.	1,728 cubic inches = 1 cubic foot.
Cubic foot = 1/27 cubic yard.	27 cubic feet = 1 cubic yard.
Cubic inch = 1/1728 cubic foot.	

Metric Units

CUBIC METRE = a volume equal to that of a cube each edge of which measures one metre.	1 cubic metre (*cbm.* or *m³.*) = 35·314 7 cu. ft. = 1·307 95 cu. yds.
Cubic decimetre = 1/1000 cubic metre.	(1 stere (= 1 cu. metre) is used as a unit of measurement of timber.)
Cubic centimetre = 1/1000 cubic decimetre.	1 cubic cm. (water) = 1 gram; 1,000 cubic cm. (water) or 1 litre = 1 kilogram; 1 cubic metre (1,000 litres, 1,000 kilograms) = 1 metric ton.

Measurement of Capacity

Imperial Units

GALLON (*see* above).	4 gills = 1 pint.
Quart = ¼ gallon.	2 pints = 1 quart.
Pint = ½ quart.	4 quarts = 1 GALLON.
Gill = ¼ pint.	1 gallon = 160 fluid ounces.
Fluid ounce = 1/20 pint.	= 277·274 cubic inches.

Bushel = 8 gallons.	2 gallons = 1 peck.	1 hectolitre = 2·749 69 bushels.
Peck = 2 gallons.	4 pecks = 1 bushel.	1 hectolitre per hectare = 1·11 bushels per acre.
	8 bushels = 1 quarter.	1 quintal = 3·674 3 bushels.
	A chaldron is 36 bushels = 4½ quarters.	1 quintal per hectare = 1·49 bushels per acre.

Measurement of Capacity—*continued*

Fluid drachm=⅛ fluid ounce. | See Apothecaries' Weight (*below*).
Minim= 1/60 fluid drachm. |

Metric Units

Hectolitre= 100 litres.
LITRE= The volume occupied by the mass of 1 kilogramme of pure water at its temperature of maximum density and under a pressure of one standard atmosphere (14·696 lb. per sq. inch).
Decilitre= 1/10 litre.
Centilitre= 1/100 litre.
Millilitre= 1/1000 litre.

1 centilitre (*cl.*)=0·070 4 gill.
1 LITRE* (1/1,000 cubic metre) (*lit.*)= 1·759 8 pints
  =0·88 Imp. quart=0·22 Imp. gallon=61·025 5 cu. inch=0·035 315 7 cu. ft.
1 hectolitre (*hl.*)= 21·997 5 Imp. gallons= 26·417 1 U.S. gallons= 2·749 Imp. bushels= 2·837 7 U.S. bushels.

Measurement of Mass or Weight

Imperial Units

Ton= 2,240 pounds.
Hundredweight= 112 pounds.
Cental= 100 pounds.
Quarter= 28 pounds.
Stone= 14 pounds.
POUND= 0·453 592 37 kilogram.
Ounce= 1/16 pound.
Dram= 1/16 ounce.
Grain= 1/7,000 pound.

7,000 grains (*gr.*)= 1 pound (*lb.*).
16 drams (*dr.*)= 1 ounce (*oz.*).
16 ounces= 1 POUND (*lb.*).
14 pounds= 1 stone.
28 pounds= 1 quarter (of a *cwt.*).
4 quarters (112 *lb.*)= 1 hundredweight (*cwt.*).
20 hundredweight (2,240 *lb.*)= 1 ton.

20 pennyweights (*dwt.*)= 1 Troy ounce.

Ounce Troy= 480 grains
Pennyweight= 24 grains

For gold and silver the ounce, divided decimally, and *not* into grains, is the sole unit of weight. The Troy ounce is the same as the Apothecaries' ounce= 480 Avoirdupois grains (31·1035 *Grammes*) in weight. A Troy POUND (= 5,760 grains) is legalized in the United States.

Ounce apothecaries'= 480 grains. | See Apothecaries' Weight (*below*)
Drachm= ⅛ ounce apothecaries. |
Scruple= ⅓ drachm. |

Metric Units

Metric ton= 1,000 kilograms.
Quintal= 100 kilograms.

1 centigram (*cg.*)= 0·154 32 grains.
1 decigram (*dg.*)= 1·543 2 grains.
1 gramme (*grm.*)= 15·432 4 grains.
1 dekagram (*dag.*)= 5·643 8 drams.
1 hectogram (*hg.*)= 3·527 4 oz.
1 KILOGRAM (*kg.*)= 32·150 7 oz. Troy= 35·273 4 oz. Avoirdupois = 2·204 62 lb. Avoirdupois.
1 myriagram= 22·046 2 lb. Avoirdupois.
1 quintal (*q.*)= 100 kg.= 220·5 lb. Avoirdupois= 1·968 4 cwt.
1 tonne (*t.*)= 0·984 207 U.K. or long ton= 1·102 31 U.S. or short ton

Measurement of Electricity

Units of measurement of electricity, the AMPERE (unit of electrical current), the OHM (unit of electrical resistance), the VOLT (unit of difference of electrical potential) and the WATT (unit of electrical power) have the meanings assigned to them respectively by order of the Dept. of Trade, to reproduce in English the international definitions in force at the date of the making of the order.

Kilowatt= 1,000 watts. | Megawatt= 1,000,000 watts.

Apothecaries' Weight
Measures of Weight.

20 grains   = 1 scruple (℈1).
3 scruples = 1 drachm (ʒ1).
8 drachms= 1 ounce.

Measures of Capacity.

60 minims (*min.*) = 1 fluid drachm.
8 fluid drachms = 1 fluid ounce.
5 fluid ounces = 1 gill.
4 gills   = 1 pint.
8 pints   = 1 GALLON.

The Apothecaries' grain is the Avoirdupois grain, and the Apothecaries' ounce is the Troy ounce, of 480 grains. The Apothecaries' *drachm* is not the same as the Avoirdupois *dram*, and is spelled differently. A fluid ounce of distilled water at a temperature of 62° Fahrenheit is equal in weight to the Avoirdupois ounce (437·5 grains). A fluid *drachm* (54·6875 grains) is equal in weight to TWO Avoirdupois *drams*.

Angular or Circular Measure

60 seconds (″)= 1 minute (′).
60 minutes= 1 degree (°).

90 degrees= 1 right angle or quadrant.
Diameter of circle× 3·141 6= circumference.
Diameter squared× ·7854= area of circle.
Diameter squared× 3·141 6= surface of sphere.
Diameter cubed× ·523= solidity of sphere.
One degree of circumference× 57·3= radius.*
Diameter of cylinder× 3·141 6; product by length or height, gives the surface.
Diameter squared× ·7854; product by length or height, gives solid content.

* Or, one radian (the angle subtended at the centre of a circle by an arc of the circumference equal in length to the radius)= 57·3 degrees, nearly.
Note.—A circle of 7 yards diameter has, in practice, a circumference of 22 yards= 1 chain.

Water Measures

Cubic inch..............= 252·458 grains.
Gallon (277·274 cu. in.)....= 10 lb. (distilled).
Cubic foot..............= 62·321 lb.
35·943 cubic ft. (224 gals.).. = 1 ton.
Water for Ships: Tun, 210 gals., Butt 110, Puncheon 72, Barrel 36, Kilderkin 18 gals.

THERMOMETER COMPARISONS

Comparison between Scales of Fahrenheit, Réaumur and Centigrade.

CONVERSION: Let F = Fahr., C = Cent., R = Réaum.

$\star F = \frac{9C}{5} + 32$ $C = 5\frac{(F-32)}{9}$

$F = \frac{9R}{4} + 32$

$F = C + R + 32$ $R = \frac{4(F-32)}{9}$

★ Below 32° F. *subtract* 32.

CENT.	FAH'T.	RMR.	CENT.	FAH'T.	RMR.
°	°	°	°	°	°
100B.	212B.	80B.	25	77	20
99	210·2	79·2	24	75·2	19·2
98	208·4	78·4	23	73·4	18·4
97	206·6	77·6	22	71·6	17·6
96	204·8	76·8	21	69·8	16·8
95	203	76	20	68	16
94	201·2	75·2	19	66·2	15·2
93	199·4	74·4	18	64·4	14·4
92	197·6	73·6	17	62·6	13·6
91	195·8	72·8	16	60·8	12·8
90	194	72	15	59	12
89	192·2	71·2	14	57·2	11·2
88	190·4	70·4	13	55·4	10·4
87	188·6	69·6	12	53·6	9·6
86	186·8	68·8	11	51·8	8·8
85	185	68	10	50	8
84	183·2	67·2	9	48·2	7·2
83	181·4	66·4	8	46·4	6·4
82	179·6	65·6	7	44·6	5·6
81	177·8	64·8	6	42·8	4·8
80	176	64	5	41	4
79	174·2	63	4	39·2	3·2
78	172·4	62·4	3	37·4	2·4
77	170·6	61·6	2	35·6	1·6
76	168·8	60·8	1	33·8	0·8
75	167	60	*zero*	32	*zero*
74	165·2	59·2	1	30·2	0·8
73	163·4	58·4	2	28·4	1·6
72	161·6	57·6	3	26·6	2·4
71	159·8	56·8	4	24·8	3·2
70	158	56	5	23	4
69	156·2	55·2	6	21·2	4·8
68	154·4	54·4	7	19·4	5·6
67	152·6	53·6	8	17·6	6·4
66	150·8	52·8	9	15·8	7·2
65	149	52	10	14	8
64	147·2	51·2	11	12·2	8·8
63	145·4	50·4	12	10·4	9·6
62	143·6	49·6	13	8·6	10·4
61	141·8	48·8	14	6·8	11·2
60	140	48	15	5	12
59	138·2	47·2	16	3·2	12·8
58	136·4	46·4	17	1·4	13·6
57	134·6	45·6	18	*0·4*	14·4
56	132·8	44·8	19	2·2	15·2
55	131	44	20	4	16
54	129·2	43·2	21	5·8	16·8
53	127·4	42·4	22	7·6	17·6
52	125·6	41·6	23	9·3	18·4
51	123·8	40·8	24	11·2	19·2
50	122	40	25	13	20
49	120·2	39·2	26	14·8	20·8
48	118·4	38·4	27	16·6	21·6
47	116·6	37·6	28	18·4	22·4
46	114·8	36·8	29	20·2	23·2
45	113	36	30	22	24
44	111·2	35·2	31	23·8	24·8
43	109·4	34·4	32	25·6	25·6
42	107·6	33·6	33	27·4	26·4
41	105·8	32·8	34	29·2	27·2
40	104	32	35	31	28
39	102·2	31·2	36	32·8	28·8
38	100·4	30·4	37	34·6	29·6
37	98·6	29·6	38	36·4	30·4
36	96·8	28·8	39	38·2	31·2
35	95	28	40	40	32
34	93·2	27·2	41	41·8	32·8
33	91·4	26·4	42	43·6	33·6
32	89·6	25·6	43	45·4	34·4
31	87·8	24·8	44	47·2	35·2
30	86	24	45	49	36
29	84·2	23·2	46	50·8	36·8
28	82·4	22·4	47	52·6	37·6
27	80·6	21·6	48	54·4	38·4
26	78·8	20·8	49	56·2	39·2

NOTE.—The *normal* temperature of the *human body* is 98·4° F., or 37° (36·9°) C., or 29·5° R. *Freezing* point = 32° F. = 0° C. = 0° R.; *Boiling* point = 212° F. = 100° C. = 80° R. "*Absolute*" *Temperature* is Temperature reckoned from "*Absolute Zero*," which is at 273° C. below 0° C., 459·4° below 0° F., and 218·4° below 0° R. and is denoted by the letter "K."

An *Inch of Rain* on the surface of an acre (43,560 sq. feet) = 3,630 cubic feet = 100.992 tons.

Cisterns: A cistern 4 feet by 2½ and 3 deep will hold brimful 186·963 gallons, weighing 16 cwt. 2 qrs. 21·6 lbs. in addition to its own weight.

Million, Billion, etc.

Value in the United Kingdom

Million............... thousand × thousand (10^6)
Billion............... million × million (10^{12})
Trillion.............. million × billion (10^{18})
Quadrillion........... million × trillion (10^{24})

Value in U.S.A.

Million............... thousand × thousand (10^6)
Billion............... thousand × million (10^9)
Trillion.............. million × million (10^{12})
Quadrillion........... million × billion U.S. (10^{15})

United Kingdom (and other European) usage above follows the decision of the 9th Gen. Conference on Weights and Measures, 1948.

PAPER AND BOOK MEASURES

Writing Paper	*Printing Paper*
480 sheets = 1 ream	516 sheets = 1 ream
24 sheets = 1 quire	2 reams = 1 bundle
20 quires = 1 ream	5 bundles = 1 bale

Sizes of Writing and Drawing Papers

Emperor................	=	72 × 48	inches
Antiquarian..............	=	53 × 31	,,
Double Elephant..........	=	40 × 26¾	,,
Grand Eagle..............	=	42 × 28¾	,,
Atlas....................	=	34 × 26	,,
Colombier................	=	34½ × 23½	,,
Imperial.................	=	30 × 22	,,
Elephant.................	=	28 × 23	,,
Cartridge................	=	26 × 21	,,
Super Royal..............	=	27 × 19	,,
Royal....................	=	24 × 19	,,
Medium...................	=	22 × 17½	,,
Large Post...............	=	21 × 16½	,,
Copy or Draft............	=	20 × 16	,,
Demy.....................	=	20 × 15½	,,
Post.....................	=	19 × 15¼	,,
Pinched Post.............	=	18½ × 14¾	,,
Foolscap.................	=	17 × 13½	,,
Sheet and ⅓ Foolscap......	=	22 × 13½	,,
Sheet and ½ Foolscap......	=	24½ × 13½	,,
Double Foolscap..........	=	26½ × 16½	,,
Double Post..............	=	30½ × 19	,,
Double Large Post........	=	33 × 21	,,
Double Demy..............	=	31 × 20	,,
Brief....................	=	16½ × 13¼	,,
Pott.....................	=	15 × 12½	,,

Sizes of Printing Papers

Foolscap.................	=	17 × 13½	inches
Double Foolscap..........	=	27 × 17	,,
Crown....................	=	20 × 15	,,
Double Crown.............	=	30 × 20	,,
Quad Crown...............	=	40 × 30	,,
Double Quad Crown........	=	60 × 40	,,
Post.....................	=	19½ × 15½	,,
Double Post..............	=	31½ × 19½	,,
Double Large Post........	=	33 × 21	,,
Sheet and ½ Post.........	=	23½ × 19½	,,
Demy.....................	=	22½ × 17½	,,
Double Demy..............	=	35 × 22½	,,
Quad Demy................	=	45 × 35	,,
Music Demy...............	=	20 × 15½	,,
Medium...................	=	23 × 18	,,
Royal....................	=	25 × 20	,,
Super Royal..............	=	27½ × 20½	,,
Elephant.................	=	28 × 23	,,
Imperial.................	=	30 × 22	,,

Sizes of Brown Papers

Casing	=	46 × 36	inches
Double Imperial	=	45 × 29	,,
Elephant	=	34 × 24	,,
Double Four Pound	=	31 × 21	,,
Imperial Cap	=	29 × 22	,,
Haven Cap	=	26 × 21	,,
Bag Cap	=	$24 \times 19\frac{1}{2}$	,,
Kent Cap	=	21 × 18	,,

Sizes of Bound Books

Demy 16mo	=	$5\frac{5}{8} \times 4\frac{3}{8}$	inches
Demy 18mo	=	$5\frac{3}{4} \times 3\frac{3}{4}$	,,
Foolscap Octavo (8vo)	=	$6\frac{3}{4} \times 4\frac{1}{4}$	,,
Crown 8vo	=	$7\frac{1}{2} \times 5$	,,
Large Crown 8vo	=	$8 \times 5\frac{1}{4}$	,,
Demy 8vo	=	$8\frac{3}{8} \times 5\frac{5}{8}$	,,
Medium 8vo	=	$9\frac{1}{2} \times 6$	,,
Royal 8vo	=	$10 \times 6\frac{1}{4}$	,,
Super Royal 8vo	=	$10\frac{1}{4} \times 6\frac{7}{8}$	,,
Imperial 8vo	=	$11 \times 7\frac{1}{2}$	,,
Foolscap Quarto (4to)	=	$8\frac{1}{2} \times 6\frac{3}{4}$	,,
Crown 4to	=	$10 \times 7\frac{1}{2}$	,,
Demy 4to	=	$11\frac{1}{4} \times 8\frac{3}{4}$	,,
Royal 4to	=	$12\frac{1}{2} \times 10$	,,
Imperial 4to	=	15 × 11	,,
Crown Folio	=	15 × 10	,,
Demy Folio	=	$17\frac{1}{2} \times 11\frac{1}{4}$	,,
Royal Folio	=	$20 \times 12\frac{1}{2}$	,,
Music	=	$14 \times 10\frac{1}{4}$	,,

NOTE.—*Folio* means a sheet folded in half, *quarto* folded into four, and so on; thus, a crown 8vo page is one-eighth the size of a crown sheet. Books are usually bound up in sheets of 16 or 32 pages. *Octavo* books are generally printed 64 pages at a time (32 pages on each side of a sheet of quad); a crown octavo book of 320 pages will therefore require 5 sheets of quad crown, or 10 reams per 1,000 copies, the odd 16 sheets in each ream being allowed as waste. Newspapers (and some books in editions of 50,000 or over) are printed on rotary presses, for which the paper is supplied in continuous reels.

INTERNATIONAL PAPER SIZES

Simplification of the large number of stock paper sizes in use in the United Kingdom has been proceeding since publication of British Standard 730 in 1937. Recommendations made by the International Organization for Standardization were accepted by the United Kingdom in 1959 and it is considered that general adoption of the international or A size will bring great economies to users of paper.

The basis of the international series of paper sizes is a rectangle having an area of one square metre, the sides of which are in the proportion of $1:\sqrt{2}$. In other words, taking one side as X and the other as Y, the basic size provides the equation—$X:Y = 1:\sqrt{2}$; and $X \times Y = 1$. It may be noted that the proportions $1:\sqrt{2}$ have a geometrical relationship, the side and diagonal of any square being in this proportion. As the basic size is one square metre in area, this means that X=841 millimetres and Y=1,189 millimetres. The effect of this arrangement is that if the short side is doubled or the longer side is halved, *i.e.*, if the area of the sheet is doubled or halved, the shorter side and the longer side of the new sheet are still in the same proportion $1:\sqrt{2}$. This feature is particularly useful where photographic enlargement or reduction is used, as the proportions remain the same.

Description of the A series is by capital A followed by a figure. The basic size has the description A0 and the higher the figure following the letter, the greater is the number of sub-divisions and therefore the smaller the sheet. Half A0 is A1 and half A1 is A2. Where larger dimensions are required the A is *preceded* by a figure. Thus 2A means twice the size A0; 4A is four times the size of A0.

It is an essential feature of these series that the dimensions are of the trimmed or finished size.

'A' SERIES OF TRIMMED SIZES

Designation	SIZE	
	mm	inches
A 0	841 × 1189	33·11 × 46·81
A 1	594 × 841	23·39 × 33·11
A 2	420 × 594	16·54 × 23·39
A 3	297 × 420	11·69 × 16·54
A 4	210 × 297	8·27 × 11·69
A 5	148 × 210	5·83 × 8·27
A 6	105 × 148	4·13 × 5·83
A 7	74 × 105	2·91 × 4·13
A 8	52 × 74	2·05 × 2·91
A 9	37 × 52	1·46 × 2·05
A 10	26 × 37	1·02 × 1·46

Subsidiary Series.—A series of B sizes has been devised for use in exceptional circumstances when sizes intermediate between any two adjacent sizes of the A series are needed.

'B' SERIES OF TRIMMED SIZES

Designation	SIZE	
	mm	inches
B 0	1000 × 1414	39·37 × 55·67
B 1	707 × 1000	27·83 × 39·37
B 2	500 × 707	19·68 × 27·83
B 3	353 × 500	13·90 × 19·68
B 4	250 × 353	9·84 × 13·90
B 5	176 × 250	6·93 × 9·84
B 6	125 × 176	4·92 × 6·93
B 7	88 × 125	3·46 × 4·92
B 8	62 × 88	2·44 × 3·46
B 9	44 × 62	1·73 × 2·44
B 10	31 × 44	1·22 × 1·73

In addition there is a series of C sizes which is used much less. A is for magazines and books, B for posters, wall charts and other large items, C for envelopes particularly where it is necessary for an envelope (in C series) to fit into another envelope. The size recommended for business correspondence is A4.

Long Sizes.—Long sizes are obtainable by dividing any appropriate sizes from the two series above into three, four or eight equal parts parallel with the shorter side in such a manner that the proportions mentioned in paragraph 2 (above) are not maintained, the ratio between the longer and the shorter sides being greater than $\sqrt{2}:1$. In practice long sizes should be produced from the A series only.

CONVERSION TABLES FOR WEIGHTS AND MEASURES

NOTE.—The central figures in heavy type represent either of the two columns beside them, as the case may be. *Examples:*—1 centimetre = 0·394 inch and 1 inch = 2·540 centimetres. 1 metre = 1·094 yards and 1 yard = 0·914 metre. 1 kilometre = 0·621 mile and 1 mile = 1·609 kilometres.

Length | Area | Volume | Weight (Mass.)

Centimetres		Inches	Square Centimetres		Square Inches	Cubic Centimetres		Cubic Inches	Long Tons		Short Tons	Metric Tonnes		Short Tons
2·540	1	0·394	6·452	1	0·155	16·387	1	0·061	0·893	1	1·120	0·907	1	1·102
5·080	2	0·787	12·903	2	0·310	32·774	2	0·122	1·786	2	2·240	1·814	2	2·205
7·620	3	1·181	19·355	3	0·465	49·161	3	0·183	2·679	3	3·360	2·722	3	3·305
10·160	4	1·575	25·806	4	0·620	65·548	4	0·244	3·571	4	4·480	3·629	4	4·409
12·700	5	1·969	32·258	5	0·775	81·936	5	0·305	4·464	5	5·600	4·536	5	5·512
15·240	6	2·362	38·710	6	0·930	98·323	6	0·366	5·357	6	6·720	5·443	6	6·614
17·780	7	2·756	45·161	7	1·085	114·710	7	0·427	6·250	7	7·840	6·350	7	7·716
20·320	8	3·150	51·613	8	1·240	131·097	8	0·488	7·143	8	8·960	7·257	8	8·818
22·860	9	3·543	58·064	9	1·395	147·484	9	0·549	8·036	9	10·080	8·165	9	9·921
25·400	10	3·937	64·516	10	1·550	163·871	10	0·610	8·929	10	11·200	9·072	10	11·023
50·800	20	7·874	129·032	20	3·100	327·742	20	1·220	17·857	20	22·400	18·144	20	22·046
76·200	30	11·811	193·548	30	4·650	491·613	30	1·831	26·786	30	33·600	27·216	30	33·069
101·600	40	15·748	258·064	40	6·200	655·484	40	2·441	35·714	40	44·800	36·287	40	44·092
127·000	50	19·685	322·580	50	7·750	819·355	50	3·051	44·643	50	56·000	45·359	50	55·116
152·400	60	23·622	387·096	60	9·300	983·226	60	3·661	53·571	60	67·200	54·431	60	66·139
177·800	70	27·559	451·612	70	10·850	1147·097	70	4·272	62·500	70	78·400	63·503	70	77·162
203·200	80	31·496	516·128	80	12·400	1310·968	80	4·882	71·429	80	89·600	72·575	80	88·185
228·600	90	35·433	580·644	90	13·950	1474·839	90	5·492	80·357	90	100·800	81·647	90	99·208
254·000	100	39·370	645·160	100	15·500	1638·710	100	6·102	89·286	100	112·000	90·719	100	110·231

Metres		Yards	Square Metres		Square Yards	Cubic Metres		Cubic Yards	Metric Tonnes		Long Tons	Kilograms		Av. Pounds
0·914	1	1·094	0·836	1	1·196	0·765	1	1·308	1·016	1	0·984	0·454	1	2·205
1·829	2	2·187	1·672	2	2·392	1·529	2	2·616	2·032	2	1·968	0·907	2	4·409
2·743	3	3·281	2·508	3	3·588	2·294	3	3·924	3·048	3	2·953	1·361	3	6·614
3·658	4	4·374	3·345	4	4·784	3·058	4	5·232	4·064	4	3·937	1·814	4	8·819
4·572	5	5·468	4·181	5	5·980	3·823	5	6·540	5·080	5	4·921	2·268	5	11·023
5·486	6	6·562	5·017	6	7·176	4·587	6	7·848	6·096	6	5·905	2·722	6	13·228
6·401	7	7·655	5·853	7	8·372	5·352	7	9·156	7·112	7	6·889	3·175	7	15·432
7·315	8	8·749	6·689	8	9·568	6·116	8	10·464	8·128	8	7·874	3·629	8	17·637
8·230	9	9·843	7·525	9	10·764	6·881	9	11·772	9·144	9	8·858	4·082	9	19·842
9·144	10	10·936	8·361	10	11·960	7·646	10	13·080	10·161	10	9·842	4·536	10	22·046
18·288	20	21·872	16·723	20	23·920	15·291	20	26·159	20·321	20	19·684	9·072	20	44·092
27·432	30	32·808	25·084	30	35·880	22·937	30	39·239	30·481	30	29·526	13·608	30	66·139
36·576	40	43·745	33·445	40	47·840	30·582	40	52·318	40·642	40	39·368	18·144	40	88·185
45·720	50	54·681	41·806	50	59·799	38·228	50	65·398	50·802	50	49·210	22·680	50	110·231
54·864	60	65·617	50·168	60	71·759	45·873	60	78·477	60·963	60	59·052	27·216	60	132·277
64·008	70	76·553	58·529	70	83·719	53·519	70	91·557	71·123	70	68·894	31·752	70	154·324
73·152	80	87·489	66·890	80	95·679	61·164	80	104·636	81·284	80	78·737	36·287	80	176·370
82·296	90	98·425	75·251	90	107·639	68·810	90	117·716	91·444	90	88·579	40·823	90	198·416
91·440	100	109·361	83·613	100	119·599	76·455	100	130·795	101·605	100	98·421	45·359	100	220·464

Kilometres		Miles	Square Kilometres		Square Miles	Litres		Gallons	Bushels U.S.		Bushels U.K.	Hectares		Acres
1·609	1	0·621	2·590	1	0·386	4·546	1	0·220	1·032	1	0·969	0·405	1	2·471
3·219	2	1·243	5·180	2	0·772	9·092	2	0·440	2·064	2	1·938	0·809	2	4·942
4·828	3	1·864	7·770	3	1·158	13·638	3	0·660	3·096	3	2·907	1·214	3	7·413
6·437	4	2·485	10·360	4	1·544	18·184	4	0·880	4·128	4	3·876	1·619	4	9·884
8·047	5	3·107	12·950	5	1·931	22·730	5	1·100	5·160	5	4·845	2·023	5	12·355
9·656	6	3·728	15·540	6	2·317	27·276	6	1·320	6·192	6	5·814	2·428	6	14·826
11·265	7	4·350	18·130	7	2·703	31·822	7	1·540	7·224	7	6·783	2·833	7	17·297
12·875	8	4·971	20·720	8	3·089	36·368	8	1·760	8·256	8	7·752	3·237	8	19·769
14·484	9	5·592	23·310	9	3·475	40·914	9	1·980	9·288	9	8·721	3·642	9	22·240
16·093	10	6·214	25·900	10	3·861	45·460	10	2·200	10·321	10	9·689	4·047	10	24·711
32·187	20	12·427	51·800	20	7·722	90·919	20	4·400	20·641	20	19·379	8·094	20	49·421
48·280	30	18·641	77·700	30	11·583	136·379	30	6·599	30·962	30	29·068	12·140	30	74·132
64·374	40	24·855	103·600	40	15·444	181·839	40	8·799	41·282	40	38·758	16·187	40	98·842
80·467	50	31·069	129·499	50	19·305	227·298	50	10·999	51·603	50	48·447	20·234	50	123·555
96·561	60	37·282	153·399	60	23·166	272·758	60	13·199	61·923	60	58·137	24·281	60	148·263
112·654	70	43·496	181·299	70	27·027	318·217	70	15·398	72·244	70	67·826	28·328	70	172·974
128·748	80	49·710	207·199	80	30·888	363·677	80	17·598	82·564	80	77·516	32·375	80	197·684
144·841	90	55·923	233·099	90	34·749	409·137	90	19·798	92·885	90	87·205	36·422	90	222·395
160·934	100	62·137	258·999	100	38·610	454·596	100	21·998	103·205	100	96·695	40·469	100	247·105

SYMBOLS FOR CORRECTING PROOFS

Supplied by WILLIAM CLOWES & SONS LTD, Beccles, Suffolk, Printers of "WHITAKER"

Letter(s) or word(s) requiring alteration should be struck through IN INK in the text and the substitution should be written in the nearest margin followed by / (the symbol used to denote that the marginal mark is concluded). Insertions should be indicated by ∨ or ∧ at the conclusion of the marginal mark *and* at the desired place in the text.

Alteration required	Mark in margin	Mark in text	Alteration required	Mark in margin	Mark in text
Delete (take out)	ꝺ or ꝺ⫟	/ or ⸻ Vertical stroke to delete one or two letters; horizontal line to delete more	Take letter(s) or word(s) from beginning of one line to end of preceding line	*back* or *take back*	
Delete and close up	ꝺ̃ or ꝺ̃⫟	Strike out letter(s) not required and add "close up" mark above and below	Begin a new paragraph	n.p.	⌐ before first word of new paragraph
Close up: delete space between letters	◡	linking letters or words	No new para. here or run on with later matter	run on	between paras. or other matter
Use ligature (fi, fl, ffl, etc.) or diphthong (æ, œ)	◡ enclosing ligature or diphthong required	◡ enclosing letters to be altered	Spell out in full the abbreviation, contraction, or figure	spell out	Encircle words, etc., or figures concerned
Insert space between letters or words	#∧	∧	Insert omitted portion of copy	out – see copy	∧ Attach the relevant copy to the proof, indicating omitted portion
Leave as printed (i.e. a cancellation of previous marking)	stet	.... under letter(s) or word(s) crossed out but to be retained	Inserted or substituted letter(s), figure(s), or sign(s) under which this is placed to be superscript (i.e. high alignment) [1]	⌐ *(see footnote)*	∧ for insertions For substitutions encircle letter(s), figure(s), or sign(s) to be altered
Invert type (of letter(s) upside down)	↺	Encircle letter(s) to be altered	Inserted or substituted letter(s), figure(s), or sign(s) over which this is placed to be subscript (low alignment) [2]	⌐ *(see footnote)*	∧ for insertions For substitutions encircle letter(s), figure(s), etc., to be altered
"Battered" letter(s) to be replaced by similar but undamaged characters	✕	Encircle letter(s) or word(s) to be replaced and write the correct letter(s) in the margin	Change to lower case	l.c.	Encircle letter(s) to be altered
Push down space or "high" letter(s) or word(s)	⊥	Encircle space, letter(s), or word(s) affected	Replace "wrong fount" by letter(s) of correct fount	w.f.	Encircle letter(s) or word(s) to be altered
Transpose	tr. or trs.	⌐⌐ between letters or words, numbered when necessary	Change to capital letters	caps.	≡ under letter(s) or word(s) to be altered
Take letter(s) or word(s) from end of one line to beginning of next line	take over or over	⌐	Change to small capitals	s.c.	═ under letter(s) or word(s) to be altered

⌐ indicates a superior (superscript) figure one   ⌐ indicates an inferior (subscript) figure two

Alteration required	Mark in margin	Mark in text	Alteration required	Mark in margin	Mark in text
Use capital letters for initial letter(s) (as desired) and small capitals for rest of word(s)	*caps* & *s.c.*	≡ under initial letter(s) and = under the remainder of the word(s)	Move lines to the left	⌐	at right side of group of lines to be moved (indicating approx. position)
Change to bold type	*bold*	Draw wavy line under letter(s) or word(s) to be altered	Move portion of matter so that it is positioned as indicated	[ ]	at limits of required position
Change to roman type	*rom.*	Encircle letter(s) or word(s) to be altered	Raise lines	*raise*	over lines to be raised
Change to italic type	*italic*	Draw this straight line under letter(s) or word(s) to be altered	Lower lines	*lower*	under lines to be lowered
Letter(s) or word(s) to be underlined	*underline*	under letter(s), word(s), etc., to be underlined	Correct the vertical alignment	‖	‖
Equalize space between words	*eq.* #	⌐ between words	Straighten lines	=	through lines to be straightened
Reduce space	*less* #	⌐ between words	Insert parentheses (round-shaped brackets)	(/) or (/)/	ʌ or ʌ ʌ
Space to be inserted between lines or paragraphs	# >	Amount of space should be indicated	Insert [square] brackets	[/] or [/]/	ʌ or ʌ ʌ
To be placed in centre of line, etc.	*centre*	Position to be indicated by	Insert hyphen	/-/	ʌ
Indent one en (approx. space occupied by n of type in use)	*en* □ʌ	⌐ indicating approximate position	Insert en (=half-em) rule (*see above*)	*en* /	ʌ
Indent one em (approx. space occupied by M of type in use)	*em* □ʌ	⌐ Ditto	Insert one-em rule (*see above*)	*em* /	ʌ
Indent two ems (approx. space occupied by MM of type in use)	□□ʌ	⌐ Ditto	Insert two-em rule (*see above*)	*2-em* /	ʌ
Move to the left	⌐	Ditto	Insert apostrophe	ᶾ	ʌ
Move to the right	⌐	Ditto	Insert single quotation marks	ᶜ ᶾ	ʌ ʌ
Move lines to the right	⌐	at left side of group of lines to be moved (indicating approx. position)	Insert double quotation marks	ᶜᶜ ᶾᶾ	ʌ ʌ
			Insert ellipsis	...	ʌ
			Insert leader (visual guide to alignment in contents pages, etc.)	⊙⊙⊙	ʌ (*three, two, or one dot*)
			Insert shilling stroke (oblique)	(/)	ʌ

Punctuation   ᵔ ʌ   ᶾ /   ᶾ ʌ   ᶾ /   ⊙   ⊙   ?ʌ   ?/   !ʌ   !/

THE WORLD